The
EUROPA WORLD
OF LEARNING
2013

The

EUROPA WORLD
OF LEARNING
2013

63rd Edition

VOLUME II

NAMIBIA–ZIMBABWE
INDEX

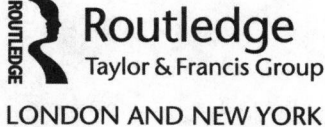

Routledge
Taylor & Francis Group

LONDON AND NEW YORK

Sixty-third edition published 2012
by Routledge
2 Park Square, Milton Park, Abingdon, Oxfordshire, OX14 4RN, United Kingdom

Simultaneously published in the USA and Canada
by Routledge
711 Third Avenue, New York, NY 10017

www.worldoflearning.com

Routledge is an imprint of the Taylor & Francis Group, an Informa business

© 2012 Routledge

First published 1947

Library of Congress Catalog Card Number 47-30172

ISBN: 978-1-85743-654-9 (The Set)
ISBN: 978-1-85743-668-6 (Vol. II)
ISSN: 0084-2117

Typeset in New Century Schoolbook
by Data Standards Limited, Frome, Somerset

Senior Editor: Anthony Gladman

Editorial Researchers: Joan Rita O'Brien (*Team Manager*), Sabiya Ashraf (*Senior Editorial Researcher*), Neha Attre, Nilanjana Bose, Sandeep Kaur, Shveta Sharma.

Editorial Assistant: Amy Welmers

Editorial Director: Paul Kelly

FSC
www.fsc.org
MIX
Paper from
responsible sources
FSC® C006021

FOREWORD

It gives us great pleasure to introduce the 2013 edition of THE EUROPA WORLD OF LEARNING. First published in 1947, it has since become established as an authoritative reference work on academic institutions all over the world.

THE EUROPA WORLD OF LEARNING is unique in offering information over the entire spectrum of academic activity. Our listings cover not just universities and colleges, but also research institutes, libraries and archives, museums and galleries and learned societies. Further to this, regulatory and representative bodies are covered in a section which also has details of relevant ministries, accrediting bodies and funding organizations. Each chapter has an introductory survey outlining the country's higher education system.

Each year we invite entrants to review and update their entries. Entrants may do so online at updates.worldoflearning.com, or by email to wol@routledge.co.uk. We are, as ever, grateful to those who help bring our information up to date with their prompt replies. Continuous research on the internet and in the world's press, as well as contact with official sources worldwide, supplements this method of revision.

In addition to the regular updating of our entries, this edition has expanded coverage of institutions in a number of areas. Special projects to update and expand our listings were undertaken in chapters covering the United States of America (including Guam, Puerto Rico and the United States Virgin Islands), and Australasia and the Pacific Islands (Australia, Fiji, French Polynesia, Kiribati, the Marshall Islands, Micronesia, Nauru, New Caledonia, New Zealand, Papua New Guinea, Samoa, the Solomon Islands, Tonga, Tuvalu and Vanuatu). There are also new chapters for Bonaire, Curaçao, Saba, Sint Eustatius, Sint Maarten and South Sudan.

THE EUROPA WORLD OF LEARNING also contains a collection of essays on themes pertinent to international higher education. In this edition all five essays relate to the theme of university rankings. Topics covered include the globalization of university rankings; the methodologies of ranking systems in China; the state of university rankings in Africa; how rankings might be reshaping higher education; and a view on how much faith we should (or should not) put in rankings. For details of the authors contributing to this edition please see page ix in Vol. I.

In the sections on Universities and Colleges, our classification follows the practice of the country concerned. This in no way implies any official evaluation on our part. Readers who are interested in the matter of the equivalence of institutions, degrees or diplomas should correspond directly with the institutions concerned, or with the national or international bodies set up for this purpose. Further information on these can be found in the Regulatory and Representative Bodies section of each chapter under the subheading Accreditation.

The online version of THE EUROPA WORLD OF LEARNING offers regular updates of content and an unprecedented level of access to institutions of higher education and learning worldwide, and to the people who work within them. See page vi or visit www.worldoflearning.com for further details.

August 2012

CONTENTS

ABBREVIATIONS

AB — Alberta
Abog. — Abogado (lawyer)
Acad. — Academician; Academy
ACT — Australian Capital Territory
Admin. — Administration; Administrative
AIDS — acquired immunodeficiency syndrome
AK — Alaska
AL — Alabama
Apdo — Apartado (Post Box)
approx. — approximately
AR — Arkansas
Arq. — Arquitecto (Spanish); Arquiteto (Portuguese)
Asscn — Association
Assoc. — Associate
Asst — Assistant
Atty — Attorney
Avda — Avenida
Ave — Avenue
Avv. — Avvocato (Advocate)
AZ — Arizona

BA — Bachelor of Arts
BC — British Columbia
Bd — Boulevard
Bdul — Bulevardul
BEng — Bachelor of Engineering
Bld — Boulevard
Bldg — Building
Blv — Boulevard
Blvd — Boulevard
Blvr — Bulevar
BP — Boîte postale
Br. — Branch
BRGM — Bureau de Recherches Géologiques et Minières
Brig. — Brigadier
Bro. — Brother
Brs — Branches
BSc — Bachelor of Science
Bul. — Bulvar (boulevard)
bulv. — bulvarỹs (boulevard)

c. — circa (approximately)
c/o — care of
CA — California
CAR — Central African Republic
Ccl — Council
CD-ROM — compact disc read-only memory
CEA — Commissariat à l'Energie Atomique
CEO — Chief Executive Officer
Chair. — Chairman; Chairperson; Chairwoman
CIRAD — Centre de Coopération Internationale en Recherche Agronomique pour le Développement
Cmdr — Commander
CNR — Consiglio Nazionale delle Ricerche
cnr — corner
CNRS — Centre National de la Recherche Scientifique
CO — Colorado
Co — Company; County
Col — Colonel
Col. — Colonia (District)
colln — Collection
Comm. — Commission
Commr — Commissioner
Conf. — Conference

Corpn — Corporation
Corresp. — Correspondent; Corresponding
CP — Caixa postal; Case postale; Casella postale (Post Box)
Cr — Contador
CRC — Cooperative Research Centre
CT — Connecticut
Cttee — Committee
cu — cubic

DC — District of Colombia
DE — Delaware
Del. — Delegate; Delegation
Dept — Department
Deptl — Departmental
devt — development
DF — Distrito Federal
Dipl. — Diploma
Dir — Director
Dist. — District
Div. — Division
Divs — Divisions
Doc. — Docent
Dott. — Dottore
Dott.ssa — Dottoressa
Doz. — Dozent (lecturer)
Dr — Doctor
Dr Hab. — Doktor Habilitowany (Assistant Professor)
Dr. — Drive
Dra — Doctora
Drs — Doctorandus (Dutch or Indonesian higher degree)
DVD — digital versatile disc

E — East; Eastern
e.g. — exempli gratia
Edif. — Edificio (Building)
edn — edition
Eng. — Engineer
EngD — Doctor of Engineering
esp. — especially
Est. — Established
etc. — et cetera
EU — European Union
Exec. — Executive

f. — founded
F.t.e. — Full-time equivalent
FAO — Food and Agriculture Organization
Fed. — Federal; Federation
FL — Florida
fmr — former
fmrly — formerly
Fr — Father
ft — feet

GA — Georgia
Gdns — Gardens
Gen. — General
Gov. — Governor
Govt — Government
GPOB — Government Post Office Box

HE — His (Her) Excellency; His Eminence
HEI — Higher Education Institution
HI — Hawaii
HIV — human immunodeficiency virus
HM — His (Her) Majesty
HND — Higher National Diploma
Hon. — Honorary; Honourable

HQ — Headquarters
HRH — His (Her) Royal Highness

IA — Iowa
ID — Idaho
IL — Illinois
ILO — International Labour Organization
IN — Indiana
Inc. — Incorporated
incl. — include; includes; including
Ind. — Independent
Ing. — Ingénieur (Engineer)
Instn — Institution
Int. — International
Ir — Insinyur (Engineer)
irreg. — irregular

Jl — Jalan (street)
Jr — Junior
JSC — Joint Stock Company
jt — joint
jtly — jointly

küç. — küçasi (street)
km — kilometre(s)
KS — Kansas
kv. — kvartal (apartment block); kvartira (apartment)
KY — Kentucky

LA — Louisiana
Lic. — Licenciado
Licda — Licenciada
Lt — Lieutenant
Ltd — Limited

m — metre(s)
m. — million
MA — Massachusetts; Master of Arts
Mag. — Magister (Masters degree)
Man. — Manager; Managing
MB — Manitoba
MBA — Master of Business Administration
MD — Maryland
ME — Maine
Mem. — Member
Mems — Members
MEng — Master of Engineering
Mgr — Monseigneur; Monsignor
MI — Michigan
Min. — Minister; Ministry
misc. — miscellaneous
mm — millimetre(s)
MN — Minnesota
MO — Missouri
MRC — Medical Research Council
MS — Mississippi
MSc — Master of Science
MSS — Manuscripts
MT — Montana

N — North; Northern
nám — náměstí (square)
NASA — National Aeronautics and Space Administration
Nat. — National
NB — New Brunswick
NC — North Carolina
ND — North Dakota
NE — Nebraska; Northeast; Northeastern

viii

PART FOUR
Namibia–Zimbabwe

NAMIBIA

The Higher Education System

From 1925 Namibia was under South African control, first as a League of Nations protectorate and then as a de facto province. Independence was finally achieved in 1990. The University of Namibia was founded in 1992, based on the former Windhoek Academy of Education, following a report by a presidential commission into the state of higher education in Namibia. The International University of Management (IUM—formerly the Institute of Higher Education, founded in 1994) was accorded university status in 2002. Higher education is also provided by the Polytechnic of Namibia (founded in 1980), six vocational colleges and four teacher-training colleges. The Ministry of Basic Education, Sport and Culture and the Ministry of Higher Education, Training and Employment Creation were combined in 2005 to form the Ministry of Education, which is responsible for higher education and vocational training. In 2007/08 19,970 students were enrolled in tertiary education.

The National Council of Higher Education (NCHE), established by the Higher Education Act No. 26/2003, advises the Minister of Education on coordination, accreditation and quality assurance in higher education; however, the Council's advice is non-binding, with the Minister retaining the right to ignore any suggestions. Proposed legislative amendments put forward in late 2010 would, if approved, clarify the role of the council and enable it to build capacity. Some observers noted that the NCHE would eventually need to become a fully independent body in order to strengthen its authority and effectiveness.

Undergraduate admission is based upon results in the International General Certificate of Secondary Education examinations; however, Higher International General Certificate of Secondary Education passes are given more weight when applicants are being evaluated. Non-degree university-level qualifications include two- or three-year Certificate courses and three- or four-year Diploma courses. Undergraduate Bachelors degree programmes last four years and are offered in most subject fields. The two foremost postgraduate degrees offered by the University of Namibia are the Masters and the Doctorate; the former is a one-year (full-time) or three-year (part-time) course, and the latter requires a minimum of two years of study following the Masters (or, in the case of administration and nursing science, a minimum of four years' part-time study). A joint cooperation agreement signed between the University of Namibia and the IUM in October 2010 aimed to enhance and expand collaboration between the two institutions, particularly within the fields of in areas of research, teaching, community service, and the exchange of students, staff and information materials.

Post-secondary technical and vocational education is offered by the Polytechnic of Namibia, and qualifications include Certificate (one year), Diploma (three years) and Bachelor of Technology. There are also a number of agricultural colleges, which offer Certificate and Diploma courses.

The Ministry of Education has developed the Education and Training Sector Improvement Programme (ETSIP), a 15-year strategic plan for 2006–20, the aim of which is comprehensively to reform the education and training sectors. The total cost of the first phase of the project (2006–11) was estimated at N $2,400m., which was to be jointly financed by the Namibian Government and a consortium of international development partners.

Regulatory Bodies

GOVERNMENT

Ministry of Education: Troskie House, Uhland St, PMB 13186, Windhoek; tel. (61) 2933111; fax (61) 224277; Minister NANGOLO MBUMBA.

Ministry of Youth, National Service, Sport and Culture: Windhoek; Minister JOHN MUTORWA.

Learned Societies

GENERAL

Namibia Scientific Society: POB 67, Windhoek 9000; tel. (61) 225372; fax (61) 226846; e-mail nwg@iafrica.com.na; f. 1925; ornithology, speleology, botany, archaeology, herpetology, astronomy, ethnology; 1,100 mems (900 ordinary, 200 exchange); library of 8,000 vols; Pres. B. GUHRING; publs *Journal* (1 a year), *Mitteilungen / Newsletter / Nuusbrief, Mitteilungen der Ornithologischen Arbeitsgruppe*.

UNESCO Office Windhoek: Windhoek 9000, POB 24519, Windhoek; located at: Oppenheimer House, 5 Brahms St, Windhoek West, Windhoek; tel. (61) 2917220; fax (61) 2917000; e-mail windhoek@unesco.org; designated Cluster Office for Angola, Lesotho, Namibia, South Africa and Swaziland; Dir JOHNNY McCLAIN.

ARCHITECTURE AND TOWN PLANNING

Namibia Institute of Architects: Love St, POB 1478, Windhoek; tel. (61) 231559; fax (61) 232007; e-mail nia@mweb.com.na; f. 1952; 98 mems; Pres. DEON PRETORIUS.

LANGUAGE AND LITERATURE

British Council: 1–5 Fidel Castro St, Windhoek; tel. (61) 226776; fax (61) 227530; e-mail general.enquiries@britishcouncil.org.na; internet www.britishcouncil.org/namibia; the office in Pretoria, South Africa, is responsible for all British Council work in Namibia (see chapter on South Africa); Officer in Charge PATIENCE MAHLALELA.

Goethe-Zentrum/Namibisch-Deutsche Stiftung für kulturelle Zusammenarbeit (Goethe-Centre/Namibian-German Institute for Cultural Cooperation): 1–5 Fidel Castro St, POB 1208, 9000 Windhoek; tel. (61) 225700; fax (61) 221256; e-mail il@nads.org.na; internet www.goethe.de/af/win/deindex.htm; f. 1988; affiliated to Goethe-Institut (see chapter on Germany); promotes use of the German language in Namibia and cultural exchange between Namibia and Germany; Dir SABINE ERLENWEIN.

Research Institutes

NATURAL SCIENCES

Biological Sciences

Gobabeb Training and Research Centre: POB 953, Walvis Bay; tel. (64) 694199; fax (64) 205197; e-mail gobabeb@gobabeb.org; internet www.gobabeb.org; f. 1963; research in Namib Desert and semi-arid Namibia, emphasizing basic and applied research, conservation biology, community applications, training and environmental education; library of 18,700 off-print colln, 13,000 bibliographic entries, 25 journals; Exec. Dir JOHN R. HENSCHEL; Librarian INGE A. HENSCHEL.

National Botanical Research Institute: c/o Ministry of Agriculture, Water and Forestry, Private Bag 13184, Windhoek; tel. (61) 2029111; fax (61) 258153; e-mail info@nbri.org.na; f. 1953; herbarium colln of 74,000 plant specimens; gene bank colln of 2,500 seed accessions; botanical reference library; incorporates National Botanic Garden; library of 3,053 books, 320 periodicals; Head Dr GILLIAN L. MAGGS-KÖLLING.

Libraries and Archives

Swakopmund

Sam Cohen Library: POB 361, Swakopmund; tel. (64) 402695; fax (64) 400763; e-mail office@swakopmund-museum.de; internet www.swakopmund-museum.de; f. 1977; attached to Museum Swakopmund; 10,000 vols on SW Africa and Africana, 20,000 historical pics, old Namibian maps; Chair. Prof. E. FOERTSCH; Man. P. BRÜGGEMANN; publs *Der Wahrheit eine Gasse, Precolonial times in South West Africa, Swakopmund—eine kleine Chronik*.

NEPAL

The Higher Education System

There are six state universities in Nepal, all of which are autonomous, and the oldest of which is Tribhuvan University (founded in 1959). University-level programmes are also offered by the B. P. Koirala Institute of Health Sciences and the National Academy of Medical Sciences. In 2008/09 there were 289,300 students enrolled in tertiary education. While the Ministry of Education administers the education system at the primary and secondary levels, Tribhuvan University is responsible for developing curriculums at college and Bachelors degree level.

Plans were mooted in the late 2000s for the creation of an open university, which would require parliamentary approval of the Higher Education Bill. This legislation was drafted in 2010 but still awaiting approval. Assuming enactment of the necessary legislation, a limited number of courses—in distance education, information technology and rural information management—was initially to be offered by the open university, with a significant expansion envisaged subsequently.

Admission to higher education is on the basis of successful completion of the School Leaving Certificate or the Higher Secondary Certificate. Students with the Higher Secondary Certificate may directly enter Bachelors degree courses (although, owing to the limited number of places and the high number of applicants, some students may also be required to pass an entrance examination in their chosen discipline), whereas students with the School Leaving Certificate must obtain the Proficiency Certificate, a university-level course lasting two years, which is regarded as the first cycle of university education. The second cycle of university-level education is the Bachelors degree, which lasts four years in most disciplines but slightly longer (five-and-a-half years) in disciplines such as medicine, veterinary medicine and animal husbandry. Following the Bachelors degree students may undertake a Postgraduate Diploma, which lasts for one year and enables students to submit a dissertation or complete a further year of study prior to enrolling in a Masters degree course. The latter is a two-year course, and requires the submission of a dissertation in all subjects. Subsequent to a Masters degree, a Master of Philosophy course, lasting between 18 months and three years, is offered in commerce, education, humanities and science disciplines. The highest university-level degree is the Doctor of Philosophy, awarded after a minimum of a further two years of study following the Masters.

The Council for Technical Education and Vocational Training, chaired by the Minister of Education, is responsible for the provision of technical and vocational education, which is offered at various secondary and post-secondary levels.

Regulatory and Representative Bodies

GOVERNMENT

Ministry of Education: Kaiser Mahal, Kathmandu; tel. (1) 4412804; fax (1) 4423252; e-mail infomoe@moe.gov.np; internet moe.gov.np; Min. DINA NATH SHARMA.

Ministry of Tourism and Civil Aviation: Singha Durbar, Kathmandu; tel. (1) 4211870; fax (1) 4211758; e-mail info@tourism.gov.np; internet www.tourism.gov.np; Min. LOKENDRA BISTA MAGAR.

Ministry of Youth and Sports: Kamalpokhari, Kathmandu; tel. (1) 4416788; fax (1) 4416489; e-mail info@moys.gov.np; internet www.moys.gov.np; Min. KAMALA ROKKA.

FUNDING

University Grants Commission: Sanothimi, Bhaktapur, POB 10796, Kathmandu; tel. (1) 6638548; fax (1) 6638552; e-mail ugc@ugcnepal.edu.np; internet www.ugcnepal.edu.np; f. 1994; advises govt of Nepal on establishment of new universities; formulates policy for allocation of govt grants to univs and higher education instns; maintains standard and quality of higher education; 11 mems; Chair. Prof. Dr GANESH MAN GURUNG.

Learned Societies

GENERAL

Nepal Academy/Nepal Pragya Pratisthan: GPOB 23058, Kamaladi, Kathmandu; tel. (1) 4221283; fax (1) 4221175; e-mail office@nepalacademy.org.np; internet www.nepalacademy.org.np; f. 1957 as Nepal Sahitya Kala Academy, present name 2007; promotes language, literature, culture, philosophy, social science of Nepal; awards prizes annually; 178 mems; library of 10,562 vols, 4,697 periodicals; Chancellor BAIRAGI KAINLA; Vice-Chancellor GANGA PRASAD UPRETY; publs Angan (1 a year, in Maithili), Journal of Nepalese Literature, Art and Culture (2 a year), Kavita (on Nepalese poetry, 4 a year), Pragyā (2 a year), Samakalin Sahitya (4 a year), Sayapatri (2 a year), Thayabhu (1 a year, in Newari).

Nepal Academy of Science and Technology: GPOB 3323, Khumaltar, Lalitpur; tel. (1) 5547715; fax (1) 5547713; e-mail info@nast.org.np; internet www.nast.org.np; f. 1982 as Royal Nepal Academy of Science and Technology; promotes science and technology; preserves and furthers modernisation of indigenous technologies; promotes research; facilitates technology transfer; 157 mems; library of 13,000 vols, 150 periodicals; Chancellor Rt Hon. PRIME MIN. OF NEPAL; Vice-Chancellor Prof. Dr SURENDRA RAJ KAFLE; Sec. Prof. Dr PRAKASH CHANDRA ADHIKARI; publs Nepal Journal of Science and Technology (1 a year), Vigyan Lekhmala (1 a year).

UNESCO Office Kathmandu: POB 14391, Sanepa-2, Lalitpur; Ring Rd, Bansbari, Kathmandu; tel. (1) 5554396; fax (1) 5554450; e-mail kathmandu@unesco.org; internet www.unesco.org/kathmandu; f. 1998; promotes peace; fosters sustainable devt and intercultural dialogue in Nepal through education, science, culture, communication, information; library of 4,500 vols, periodicals, reports, audiovisual materials; Head of Office and UNESCO Rep. AXEL PLATHE.

FINE AND PERFORMING ARTS

Indigenous Film Archive: POB 10487, Anamnagar, Kathmandu; tel. (1) 4102577; e-mail ifanepal@yahoo.com; internet ifanepal .org.np; f. 2006; provides a forum for film makers, film journalists, artists, actors, sociologists, activists; promotes and screens nat. and int. films, film related information on indigenous issues and topics; Chair. NABIN CHANDRA LIMBU; Vice-Chair. DIPENDRA LAMA.

LANGUAGE AND LITERATURE

Alliance Française de Katmandou (Alliance française in Kathmandu): Tripureshwor, Ganeshman Singh Path, POB 452 Kathmandu; tel. (1) 4241163; fax (1) 4242621; internet www.alliancefrancaise.org .np; offers courses and exams in French language and culture and promotes cultural exchange with France; Dir ANNE-LISE HEYNEN; Deputy Dir PRABIN BIKRAM RANA; Course Dir BENOÎT GILLET.

British Council: POB 640, Lainchaur, Kathmandu; tel. (1) 4410798; fax (1) 4410545; e-mail general.enquiry@ britishcouncil.org.np; internet www .britishcouncil.org/nepal; f. 1959; teaching centre; offers courses and exams in English language and British culture and promotes cultural exchange with the UK; 6,774 mems; library of 15,036 vols, 30 periodicals, 54 video cassettes, 219 audio items, DVDs and CD-ROMs; Dir Dr ROBERT MONRO.

RELIGION, SOCIOLOGY AND ANTHROPOLOGY

Nepal Institute of Peace: Kathmandu; tel. (1) 5526680; e-mail nageshbadu@gmail.com; internet www.idps-nepal.org; f. 2002; promotes peace through discussion, training, workshop, seminar, research work; Pres. SHIVA KUMAR DHUNGANA.

TECHNOLOGY

Biotechnology Society of Nepal: POB 8973, Kathmandu; Second Fl., 16 Gurju Marg, Dillibazar Height, Ward 32, Kathmandu; e-mail info@bsn.org.np; internet www.bsn.org.np; acts as focal point for dissipating information about Biotechnology in Nepal; initiates, promotes and propagates use of biotechnology; Pres. SAROJ RAJ GHIMIRE; Vice-Pres. RAVI BHANDARI.

Research Institutes

GENERAL

International Centre for Integrated Mountain Development (ICIMOD): GPOB 3226, Khumaltar, Kathmandu, Lalitpur; tel. (1) 5003222; fax (1) 5003277; e-mail info@icimod.org; internet www.icimod.org; f. 1983; autonomous org. sponsored by govts of the regional mem. countries, Austria, Denmark, Germany, the Netherlands, Norway and Switzerland, to help promote an economically and environmentally sound ecosystem, and to improve the living standards of the mountain people in the Hindu Kush–Himalayan region; aims to serve as a focal point for multi-disciplinary documentation, training and applied research, and as a consultative centre in scientific and practical matters pertaining to mountain devt; mem. countries: Afghanistan, Bangladesh, Bhutan, People's Republic of China, India, Myanmar, Nepal, Pakistan; Dir-Gen. DAVID JAMES MOLDEN; Deputy Dir-Gen. MADHAV KARKI.

Nepal Development Research Institute: GPOB 8975, EPC 2201, Kathmandu; Shree Durbar Tole, Pulchowk, Lalitpur; tel. (1) 5554975; fax (1) 5537362; e-mail info@ndri.org.np; internet www.ndri.org.np; f. 2004; provides analytical inputs for policy making on contemporary issues through research and dissemination of findings; research areas incl. policy analysis on nat. economy, infrastructure policy and planning, poverty reduction and sustainable livelihoods, climate change, agriculture and natural resources; Pres. Dr BASU DEV PANDEY; Exec. Dir and Vice-Pres. Dr DIVAS BAHADUR BASNYAT.

Nepal Institute of Development Studies: House 23, Madhur Marg, Chun Devi, Maharajgunj, POB 7647, Kathmandu; House 23, Madhur Marg, Chun Devi, Maharajgunj POB 7647, Kathmandu; tel. (1) 4721277; fax (1) 4721982; e-mail nids@mail.com.np; internet www.nids.org.np; f. 1998; focuses on issues which are associated to devt of Nepal; Exec. Dir Dr JAGANNATH ADHIKARI.

AGRICULTURE, FISHERIES AND VETERINARY SCIENCE

Nepal Agricultural Research Council: POB 5459, Kathmandu; Singhadurbar Pl., Kathmandu; tel. (1) 4256837; fax (1) 4262500; e-mail ednarc@ntc.net.np; internet narc.gov.np; f. 1991; conducts qualitative studies and researches on different aspects of agriculture; Exec. Dir Dr DIL BAHADUR GURUNG; publ. *Nepal Agriculture Research Journal* (1 a year).

ECONOMICS, LAW AND POLITICS

Institute for Policy Research and Development: GPOB 8975, Kathmandu; Kalimati, Kathmandu; tel. (1) 6212276; e-mail iprad@ntc.net.np; internet www.iprad.org.np; f. 1995; research on economic, social, management, institutional, legal, environmental issues; Chair. Dr PUSHPA RAJ RAJKARNIKAR; Vice-Chair. Dr BHIM PRASAD NEUPANE.

Institute of Integrated Development Studies: POB 2254, Mandikhatar, Kathmandu; tel. (1) 4371006; fax (1) 4378809; e-mail info@iids.org.np; internet www.iids.org.np; f. 1990; conducts policy-oriented research on Nepal's economic, social devt in

nat., regional, int. contexts; Chair. Dr MOHAN MAN SAINJU; Exec. Dir Dr BISHNU DEV PANT.

Nepal Institute for Policy Studies: POB 14352, Kathmandu; 90 Mahadevsthan Marga, Baneshwor, Kathmandu; tel. (1) 4482530; fax (1) 4462811; e-mail nips@nipsnepal.org; internet www.nipsnepal.org; f. 2008; conducts research on policy issues particularly on int. relations, security, democracy; library of 300 vols; Chair. RAJAN BHATTARAI.

RELIGION, SOCIOLOGY AND ANTHROPOLOGY

Center for Nepal and Asian Studies: POB 3757, Kathmandu; tel. (1) 4332078; fax (1) 4331184; e-mail info@cnastu.org.np; internet www.cnastu.org.np; f. 1969 as Institute of Nepal Studies, fmrly Institute of Nepal and Asian Studies, present name and status 1977; attached to Tribhuvan Univ.; research on issues and studies in social sciences incl. ethnic diversity, tradition and change in political values, cultural studies within Nepal and across other Asian countries; Exec. Dir Prof. Dr YAGYA PRASAD ADHIKARI; Deputy Dir NANI RAM KHATRI.

Institute for Social and Environmental Research—Nepal: POB 57, Bharatpur, Chitwan; Fulbari 1, Chitwan; tel. (56) 591054; fax (56) 592407; e-mail iser@wlink.com.np; internet isernepal.org.np; f. 2001; research areas incl. population dynamics, population and environmental dynamics, education and empowerment; br. in Kathmandu; Dir Dr DIRGHA JIBI GHIMIRE.

Lotus Research Centre: Khwayabahil, POB 59, Lalitpur; tel. (1) 5549343; e-mail info@lrcnepal.org; internet www.lrcnepal.org; f. 1988; research on cultural heritage and Buddhism of Nepal Mandala; Chair. Dr BHADRA RATNA BAJRACHARYA; Vice-Chair. INDRASIDDHI BAJRACHARYA; publ. *Paleswan*.

Lumbini International Research Institute: POB 39, Bhairahawa, Rupandehi; tel. and fax (71) 580175; e-mail liri@mos.com.np; internet www.lumbiniresearch.com; f. 1995; conducts research in Buddhism and other religions; library of 35,000 vols.

Libraries and Archives

Banke

Mahendra Library: Tribhuwan Chowk, Nepalgunj, Banke; tel. (81) 525492; e-mail info@nnl.org.np; f. 1947; attached to Nepal Nat. Library; 10,000 vols.

Kailali

Kailali Public Library: Dhangadi, Kailali; tel. (91) 521535; e-mail info@nnl.org.np; f. 1957; attached to Nepal Nat. Library; 7,000 vols, 82 journals; organises monthly discussions, talks with a literary theme.

Kathmandu

Dilliraman—Kalyani Regmi Memorial Library: Ward 2, Lazimpat, Kathmandu; GPOB 20865, Kathmandu; tel. (1) 4417835; fax (1) 4411090; e-mail dkrmlibrary@htp.com.np; internet www.drkrmlibrary.org; f. 1980; 30,000 vols; museum colln incl. archeological objects made of stone and other metals; Chief Librarian PASHUPATI NATH ADHIKARI.

Indian Cultural Centre: POB 6967, Bal Mandir, Naxal, Kathmandu; tel. (1) 4412715; internet www.indianembassy.org.np/indian-culture-center.php; f. 2007; promotes cultural ties between India and Nepal; Dir Dr GEETI SEN.

Kathmandu University Central Library: POB 6250, Kathmandu; Dhulikhel; e-mail

librarian@ku.edu.np; internet www.ku.edu.np/library; 45,000 vols, 1,100 CD-ROMs, 160 journals; Library Officer DEV RAJ ADHIKARY.

Kaiser Library: Kaiser Mahal, Kathmandu; tel. (1) 4411318; fax (1) 442010; e-mail klib.gov.np; internet www.klib.gov.np; f. 1969; 50,000 vols, 43 journals; Chief Librarian JANAKI KARMACHARYA.

National Archives: Ramshahpath, Kathmandu; tel. (1) 4264353; e-mail mail@nationalarchives.gov.np; internet www.nationalarchives.gov.np; f. 1967; collects and preserves archives; functions as public records management office for govt of Nepal; 12,000 vols, 30,000 MSS, 151,000 microfilm copies of MSS in private colln, 20,000 historical documents; Chief Archivist UTTAM KHANAL; publ. *Abhilekh* (1 a year).

Nepal Bharat Library: Nepal Airlines Bldg, New Rd Gate, Kathmandu; tel. (1) 4243497; fax (1) 4255414; e-mail librarian@eoiktm.org; internet www.indianembassy.org.np/nepal-bharat-library.php; f. 1956; colln on Indian culture, economy, engineering, entertainment, history, int. relations, literature, mass communication, medicine, politics, science and technology, society; 62,000 vols; Sr Librarian K. C. MEENA.

Tribhuvan University Central Library: Kirtipur, Kathmandu; tel. (1) 4330834; fax (1) 4226964; e-mail tucl@tucl.org.np; internet www.tucl.org.np; f. 1959; 350,000 vols, 450 periodicals; depository for the UN; Chief Librarian KRISHNA MANI BHANDARY (acting); publs *Education Quarterly*, *Journal of Tribhuvan University*, *Nepalese National Bibliography*.

Lalitpur

Madan Puraskar Pustakalaya: POB 42, Patan Dhoka, Lalitpur; tel. (1) 5005515; fax (1) 5536390; e-mail info@mpp.org.np; internet www.mpp.org.np; f. 1955; collects and preserves resources in Nepali language; manages Nepal's literary prizes: Madan Puraskar, Jagadamba Shree; 23,700 vols, 5,247 periodical titles, 28, 765 monographs, 13,000 ephemera in Nepali language, 710 MSS; Chair. KAMAL MANI DIXIT.

Nepal National Library: Harihar Bhawan, Pulchowk, POB 182, Lalitpur; tel. (1) 5521132; fax (1) 5010061; e-mail nnl@nnl.wlink.com.np; internet www.nnl.gov.np; f. 1957; 90,000 vols, 96 periodicals, 1,000 rare books and MSS, 7,000 children's books, 400 other items; Chief Librarian DASHARATH THAPA.

Pokhara

Pokhara Public Library: Mahendrapool, Pokhara; tel. (61) 521855; e-mail info@nnl.org.np; attached to Nepal Nat. Library; 4,000 vols.

Sunsari

Sarbajanik Vidyabhawan Library: Dharan, Sunsari; tel. (25) 526115; e-mail info@nnl.org.np; f. 1947; attached to Nepal Nat. Library.

Museums and Art Galleries

Kathmandu

Music Museum of Nepal: Tripureshwor, Kathmandu; tel. (1) 4242741; e-mail info@musicmuseumnepal.org; internet www.musicmuseumnepal.org; f. 2002 as Nepali Folk Musical Instrument Museum; displays musical instruments of Nepal; organises concerts; Dir RAM PRASAD KADEL.

National Museum of Nepal: Museum Rd, Chhauni, Kathmandu; tel. (1) 4211504; f. 1928; art, history, culture, ethnology, philately, natural history; library of 10,000 vols; Chief SANU NANI KANSAKAR; publ. *Nepal Museum.*

Natural History Museum: Manjushree Bajaar, Swayambhu, Kathmandu; tel. (1) 4271899; e-mail info@nhmnepal.org; internet nhmnepal.org; attached to Tribhuvan Univ.; collects and preserves floral, fauna, geological and other natural specimens of Nepal; publ. *Journal of Natural History Museum.*

Nepal Olympic Museum: c/o Nat. Sports Ccl, Tripureshwor, Kathmandu; tel. and fax (1) 4256560; e-mail info@sportsnepal.org; internet www.sportsnepal.org; f. 1999; preserves and collects sport related material of historic value; promotes sports; organises symposium, workshop, contests on sport; Pres. CHHITIJ ARUN SHRESTHA.

Patan Museum: Patan Darbar, Kathmandu; tel. and fax (1) 5521492; e-mail ptmuseum@mos.com.np; internet www .patanmuseum.gov.np; f. 1997; 18th century fmr royal palace housing Hindu and Buddhist sacred art of Nepal, Nepalese metalwork, photographs of Nepal taken in 1899, and a Hindu Tantric MS; Dir BHIM PRASAD NEPAL.

Pokhara

Gurkha Memorial Museum: Pokhara; tel. (61) 441762; e-mail gmtmuseum@wlink.com .np; internet www.gurkhamuseum.org.np; f. 1994; displays knives, medals, photographs, uniforms, items used by Gurkha soldiers; Chair. YAMBAHADUR GURUNG.

Universities

KATHMANDU UNIVERSITY

POB 6250, Dhulikhel
Telephone: (11) 661399
Fax: (11) 661443
E-mail: admission@ku.edu.np
Internet: www.ku.edu.np
Founded 1991
State control
Academic year: August to June
Language of instruction: English
Chancellor: Rt Hon. PRIME MIN. OF NEPAL
Pro-Chancellor: Hon. MIN. OF EDUCATION
Vice-Chancellor: Prof. Dr SURESH RAJ SHARMA
Registrar: Prof. Dr BHADRA MAN TULADHAR
Library Officer: Dr DEV RAJ ADHIKARY
Library: see Libraries and Archives
Number of teachers: 344
Number of students: 8,266 (incl. 4,897 enrolled in affiliated colleges)

DEANS

School of Arts: Dr MAHESH BANSKOTA
School of Education: Prof. Dr MANA PRASAD WAGLEY
School of Engineering: Prof. Dr BHOLA THAPA
School of Management: Prof. SUBAS K. C.
School of Medical Sciences: Dr NARENDRA BAHADUR RANA
School of Science: Prof. Dr PANNA THAPA

LUMBINI BUDDHIST UNIVERSITY

Bhrikuti Mandap, Exhibition Rd, Kathmandu
Siddharthanagar, Municipality-8, Rupandehi, Lumbini
Telephone: (1) 4246032

E-mail: info@lbu.edu.np
Internet: www.lbu.edu.np
Founded 2004
State control
Origin and development of Buddhism, religion and philosophy, Pali and Sanskrit Buddhist literature
Chancellor: Rt Hon. PRIME MIN. OF NEPAL
Pro-Chancellor: Hon. MIN. OF EDUCATION
Vice-Chancellor: Prof. TRI RATNA MANANDHAR
Registrar: Prof. KHADGA MAN SHRESTHA
Dean: Prof. SHANKER THAPA.

NEPAL SANSKRIT UNIVERSITY

POB 5003, Kathmandu
Beljhundi, Dang
Telephone and fax (1) 4221510
Internet: www.nsu.edu.np
Founded 1986, fmrly Mahendra Sanskrit Univ.
State control
Languages of instruction: English, Nepali, Sanskrit
Academic year: July to May

Depts of ayurveda, Buddhist philosophy and tantra, darshna, dernashast, economics, English, Hindi and Maithali, itihasa purana, karmakanda, mathematics, Nepali, nyaya, political science, purva mamamsa, veda, vedanta, vyakarana, yoga
Chancellor: Rt Hon. PRIME MIN. OF NEPAL
Pro-Chancellor: Hon. MIN. OF EDUCATION
Vice-Chancellor: Prof. SHIVA HARI MARAHAT-THA
Rector: Prof. NARAYAN KUMAR ACHARYA
Registrar: Dr JAGAT PRASAD UPADHYAYA
Librarian: KHEM RAJ GYNAWALI

Number of teachers: 315
Number of students: 2,400
Publications: *Maryada* (1 a year), *Ritumbara* (4 a year).

POKHARA UNIVERSITY

POB 427, Dhungepatan, Lekhnath Municipality, Kaski
Telephone: (61) 561046
Fax: (61) 560392
E-mail: vice-chancellor@pu.edu.np
Internet: www.pu.edu.np
Founded 1997
State control
Languages of instruction: English, Nepali
Academic year: August to June
Chancellor: Rt Hon. PRIME MIN. OF NEPAL
Pro-Chancellor: Hon. MIN. OF EDUCATION
Vice-Chancellor: Prof. KHAGENDRA PRASAD BHATTARAI
Registrar: Dr MAN BAHADUR K. C.

Library of 4,000 vols
Number of teachers: 1,550
Number of students: 20,229

DEANS

Faculty of Humanities and Social Science: Prof. Dr GEETA PRADHAN
Faculty of Science and Technology: ESHWOR CHANDRA BANIYA

PURBANCHAL UNIVERSITY

POB 142, Biratnagar, Morang
Telephone: (21) 22165
Fax: (21) 21204
E-mail: info@puniv.edu.np
Internet: www.purbuniv.edu.np
Founded 1995
State control
Academic year: August to June

Languages of instruction: English, Nepali
Faculties of arts, education, management, science and technology; 65 affiliated colleges
Chancellor: Rt Hon. PRIME MIN. OF NEPAL
Pro-Chancellor: Hon. MIN. OF EDUCATION
Vice-Chancellor: Prof. Dr MAHESHWOR MAN SHRESTHA

Publications: *Business Horizon, Expressions.*

TRIBHUVAN UNIVERSITY

POB 8212, Kirtipur, Kathmandu
Telephone: (1) 4330433
Fax: (1) 4331964
E-mail: vcoffice@tribhuvan-university.edu .np
Internet: www.tribhuvan-university.edu.np
Founded 1959
State control
Languages of instruction: English, Nepali
Academic year: July to June
Chancellor: Rt Hon. PRIME MIN. OF NEPAL
Pro-Chancellor: DINA NATH SHARMA
Vice-Chancellor: Prof. Dr HIRA BAHADUR MAHARJAN
Rector: Prof. GUNA NIDHI NYAUPANE
Registrar: Dr CHANDRA MANI PAUDEL
Chief Librarian: JANARDAN DHUNGANA
Library: see under Libraries and Archives
Number of teachers: 7,841
Number of students: 389,460 (incl. 2,30,066 enrolled in affiliated colleges)
Publications: *Contributions to Nepalese Studies, Economic Journal of Development Issues* (2 a year), *Education and Development* (CERID, 1 a year), *Journal of Development and Administrative Studies* (CEDA, 1 a year), *Nepalese Journal of Development and Rural Studies* (Central Department of Rural Development (Kirtipur), 2 a year), *Tribhuvan University Today* (1 a year), *TU Journal* (Research Division, 2 a year)

DEANS

Faculty of Education: Prof. Dr PRAKASH MAN SHRESTHA (acting)
Faculty of Humanities and Social Sciences: Dr TARA KANT PANDEY (acting)
Faculty of Law: Prof. Dr VIDYA KISHOR ROY
Faculty of Management: Prof. Dr PURUSOTTAM SHARMA (acting)
Institute of Agriculture and Animal Science: Prof. Dr SUNDAR MAN SHRESTHA
Institute of Engineering: Dr BHARAT RAJ PAHARI (acting)
Institute of Forestry: Prof. CHIRANJIBI PRASAD UPADHYAYA (acting)
Institute of Medicine: Prof. Dr ARUN SAYAMI
Institute of Science and Technology: Prof. Dr SUMAN LAL SHRESTHA (acting)

Deemed Universities

B. P. Koirala Institute of Health Science: POB 7053, Dharan, Kathmandu; tel. (25) 525555; fax (25) 520251; e-mail registrar@ bpkihs.edu; internet www.bpkihs.edu; f. 1993, present status 1998; colleges of dental surgery, nursing; medical college; school of public health and community medicine; Vice-Chancellor Prof. Dr BALBHADRA PRASAD DAS; Rector Prof. Dr RUPA RAJBHANDARI SINGH; Registrar NAND KUMAR THAPA; publ. *Parikrama.*

National Academy of Medical Sciences: Bir Hospital, POB 13606, Kathmandu; tel. and fax (1) 4247032; internet www.nams.org .np; Chancellor Rt Hon. PRIME MIN. OF NEPAL.

NETHERLANDS

The Higher Education System

Universiteit Leiden (Leiden University—founded in 1575, when the Low Countries or Netherlands were under Spanish rule) is the oldest existing university in the Netherlands. The seven northernmost provinces of the Netherlands formed the Treaty of Utrecht in 1579, declared their independence from Spain in 1581 and in 1648 were recognized as the independent United Provinces or Dutch Republic under the terms of the Treaty of Westphalia. Institutions established during 1579–1648 include Rijksuniversiteit Groningen (the University of Groningen—founded in 1614), Universiteit van Amsterdam (the University of Amsterdam—founded in 1632) and Universiteit Utrecht (Utrecht University—founded in 1636).

The modern higher education system is subject to a number of different legislative acts, including the Higher Professional Education Act, the University Education Act (both 1986) and the Higher Education and Research Act (1993). The last of these granted greater autonomy to institutions and introduced a 'credit'-based system for the award of degrees. The Netherlands participates in the Bologna Process to establish a European Higher Education Area, the first phase of which was to adopt a credit-based system of comparable degrees with two main cycles (undergraduate and graduate). Higher education institutions are either Universiteiten (universities) or Hogescholen (universities of professional education). The Minister of Education, Culture and Science, advised by an Education Council, is responsible for educational legislation and its enforcement. A system of accreditation was introduced in 2002, responsibility for which was accorded to the newly created Accreditation Organization of The Netherlands and Flanders. According to provisional estimates, in 2010/11 241,700 students were enrolled at the Netherlands' 13 universities, while some 416,900 students were enrolled at the 50 institutes of higher vocational education. In addition, in 2003 some 21,004 students were registered with the Open University (founded in 1984), which offers degree and diploma qualifications. Plans mooted in 2011 to bolster co-operation among, and perhaps ultimately to merge, three of the country's universities—Universiteit Leiden, Technische Universiteit Delft and Erasmus Universiteit Rotterdam—provoked vociferous opposition in 2011; critics of a possible merger argued that such a move would inevitably lead to a marked decline in standards at each of the constituent institutions.

Traditionally, the Netherlands has maintained subsidized fees for all students. However, from 2008 the Government ended subsidies for students from non-European Union (EU) countries. Moreover, new legislation enacted in April 2010 granted universities the right to set their own tuition fees for all students taking a second Bachelors or Masters degree, with effect from the beginning of the 2011/12 academic year.

Admission to degree-level education requires students to hold the Voorbereidend Wetenschappelijk Onderwijs (VWO—Preparatory Scientific Education), the Hoger Algemeen Voortgezet Onderwijs (HAVO—Higher General Continued Education) or the Hoger Beroepsonderwijs (HBO—Higher Applied Education). The two-tier system of undergraduate Bachelors and postgraduate Masters degrees was first introduced in 2002 and was to have been adopted by all university-level institutions by 2010. The undergraduate Bachelors degree is a three-year programme of study, starting with one year of general studies. The first postgraduate degree is the Masters, a one- to three-year course of study involving research, a written thesis or final test. A Masters in medicine lasts three years and students are required to study for a further three to six years to qualify for independent practice. Following completion of the Masters, the Doctorate is awarded after a minimum of four years of research and public defence of a thesis.

Other than the universities, undergraduate Bachelors degrees are also offered by the Hogescholen, which have mostly been founded since 1986. The main focus of the Hogescholen is on professional degrees and titles in several subject areas, including economics and management, engineering and technology, health care, behavioural science and social studies, agriculture and the environment, fine arts, performing arts and education. Since 2002 Hogescholen have also offered Masters degrees. A short cycle programme within the first cycle was introduced as a pilot programme from 2006 and was implemented as a permanent part of the education system in 2011. This short-cycle degree is called an Associate degree and comprises a minimum of 120 ECTS points. The Association of Hogescholen is responsible for quality assurance and accreditation.

Post-secondary technical and vocational education (Middelbaar Beroepsonderwijs—MBO) is administered according to the Adult and Vocational Education Act (1996). The MBO is divided into four levels of qualifications (in ascending order): assistant training (six months to one year), basic vocational training (two to three years), vocational training (two to four years) and management training (three to four years). Alternatively, school-leavers with 10 years of primary and secondary education may undertake apprenticeships based in the workplace.

Regulatory and Representative Bodies

GOVERNMENT

Ministry of Education, Culture and Science: POB 16375, 2500 BJ The Hague; Rijnstraat 50, 2515 XP The Hague; tel. (70) 4123456; fax (70) 4123450; internet www.rijksoverheid.nl/ministeries/ocw; Min. MARJA VAN BIJSTERVELDT-VLIEGENTHART; Sec. HALBE ZIJLSTRA.

ACCREDITATION

ENIC/NARIC Netherlands: Int. Recognition Dept, POB 29777, 2502 LT The Hague; Kortenaerkade 11, 2518 AX The Hague; tel. (70) 4260260; fax (70) 4260399; e-mail info@nuffic.nl; internet www.nuffic.nl; f. 1952; provides information on postgraduate int. courses; advises various educational and govt bodies on matters of academic equivalence and the recognition of professional credentials; promotes int. cooperation in several European and nat. exchange programmes; offers educational and scientific help to developing countries; Dir-Gen. Drs SANDER VAN DEN EIJNDEN; publs *Nieuwsbrief* (4 a year), *Study in the Netherlands: Your Gateway to Europe* (1 a year).

Nederlands-Vlaamse Accreditatieorganisatie (Accreditation Organisation of the Netherlands and Flanders): POB 85498, 2508 CD The Hague; Parkstraat 28, 2514 JK The Hague; tel. (70) 3122300; fax (70) 3122301; e-mail info@nvao.net; internet www.nvao.net; independently ensures the quality of higher education in the Netherlands and Flanders by assessing and accrediting programmes; Chair. K. L. L. M. (KARL) DITTRICH; Vice-Chair. GUIDO LANGOUCHE; Man. Dir RUDY DERDELINCKX.

NATIONAL BODIES

HBO-raad (Netherlands Association of Universities of Applied Sciences): POB 123, 2501 CC The Hague; Prinsessegracht 21, 2514 AP The Hague; tel. (70) 3122121; fax (70) 3122100; e-mail post@hbo-raad.nl; internet www.hbo-raad.nl; works to strengthen the social position of the univs of applied sciences; Pres. (vacant); Sec. Drs A. DE GRAAF.

Nederlandse Vereniging van Pedagogen en Onderwijskundigen (NVO) (Dutch Society of Educational Psychologists): St Jacobsstraat 331, 3511 BP Utrecht; tel. (30) 2322407; fax (30) 2369749; e-mail secretariaat@nvo.nl; internet www.nvo.nl; f. 1962; maintenance of standards in univ. education; Chair. Dr XAVIER MOONEN; Vice-

Chair. Drs MARJOLIJN WILSCHUT; Treas. Drs ROBBERT VAN KAMPEN; Dir Drs HANS BOSMAN; publs *Nederlands Tijdschrift voor Opvoeding, Vorming en Onderwijs* (6 a year).

Rectoren College (Rectors' Conference of the Netherlands): POB 19270, 3501 DG Utrecht; tel. (71) 5273130; fax (71) 5273052; e-mail hj.graafland@bb.leidenuniv.nl; Chair. D. F. J. BOSSCHER; Sec. F. VAN STEIJN.

Vereniging van Universiteiten (VSNU) (Association of Universities in the Netherlands): POB 13739, 2501 ES The Hague; Lange Houtstraat 2, 2511 CW The Hague; tel. (70) 3021400; fax (70) 3021495; e-mail post@vsnu.nl; internet www.vsnu.nl; f. 1985; promotes common interests of univs vis-à-vis Dutch and European politicians, govt and civil society orgs to create a forum for discussion; Pres. Dr SIJBOLT NOORDA; Dir JOSEPHINE SCHOLTEN.

Learned Societies
GENERAL

Koninklijke Hollandsche Maatschappij der Wetenschappen (Royal Holland Society of Sciences and Humanities): POB 9698, 2003 LR Haarlem; Spaarne 17, 2011 CD Haarlem; tel. (23) 5321773; fax (23) 5362713; e-mail hollmij@wxs.nl; internet www.hollmij .nl; f. 1752, present bldg 1841; furthers contact between scientists and laymen by arranging lectures, confs, symposia on scientific subjects; awards annual prizes and subsidies for research and publ. of scientific work; 350 mems, 350 dirs, 30 foreign mems; Chair. Dr A. H. G. RINNOOY KAN; Vice-Chair. M. E. BIERMAN-BEUKEMA TOE WATER; Treas. R. E. ROGAAR; publ. *Haarlem Presentations* (1 a year).

Koninklijke Nederlandse Akademie van Wetenschappen (Royal Netherlands Academy of Arts and Sciences): POB 19121, 1000 GC Amsterdam; Kloveniersburgwal 29, 1011 JV Amsterdam; tel. (20) 5510700; fax (20) 6204941; e-mail knaw@bureau.knaw.nl; internet www.knaw.nl; f. 1808, present name 1938; advises govt on matters related to scientific research; assesses the quality of scientific research (peer review); provides a forum for the scientific world and promotes int. scientific cooperation; acts as an umbrella org. for the institutes primarily engaged in basic and strategic scientific research and disseminates information; 300 mems (200 ordinary, 40 corresp., 60 foreign); Pres. Prof. Dr ROBBERT H. DIJKGRAAF; Vice-Pres. Prof. J. W. M. VAN DER MEER; Vice-Pres. Prof. D. G. YNTEMA; Sec.-Gen. Prof. Dr J. J. A. THOMASSEN; Dir for Gen. Affairs, Finance and Operations Dr K. HANS CHANG; Dir for Research Prof. Dr THEO W. MULDER; publs *Akademienieuws, Mededelingen der Afdeling Letterkunde, Verhandelingen der Afdeling Letterkunde, Verhandelingen Eerste en Tweede Reeks der Afdeling Natuurkunde, Verslag van de Gewone Vergaderingen der Afdeling Natuurkunde.*

Zuid-Afrikahuis (South Africa House): Keizersgracht 141, 1015 CK Amsterdam; tel. (20) 6249318; fax (20) 6382596; e-mail info@ zuidafrikahuis.nl; internet www .zuidafrikahuis.nl; f. 1939; study of Afrikaans language and literature, history and culture of South Africa; attached institutes: Netherlands-South African Soc., South African Institute; library of 46,000 vols; Librarian CORINE DE MAIJER; publ. *Maandblad Zuid-Afrika* (10 a year).

AGRICULTURE, FISHERIES AND VETERINARY SCIENCE

Groei & Bloei (Growth and Bloom): POB 485, 2700 AL Zoetermeer; Louis Pasteurlaan 6, 2719 EE Zoetermeer; tel. (79) 3681215; fax (79) 3681245; e-mail info@groei.nl; internet www.groei.nl; f. 1873 as Royal Soc. of Horticulture and Botany; 146 brs; 60,000 mems; Gen. Sec. J. P. VAN LEEUWEN; publ. *Groei & Bloei* (11 a year).

KLV Wageningen Alumni Netwerk (KLV Wageningen Alumni Network): POB 79, 6700 AB Wageningen; Gen. Foulkesweg 1A, 6703 BG Wageningen; tel. (317) 485191; fax (317) 483976; e-mail secretariaat.klv@wur.nl; internet www.klv.nl; f. 1886, present name 2009; network for Wageningen Univ. graduates and for other professionals with links to Wageningen; organizes workshops, debates, lectures related to entrepreneurship, career and networking in life sciences; 8,000 mems; Pres. TINY VAN BOEKEL; Vice-Pres. MARGRIET TIEMSTRA; Sec. ELMAR THEUNE; Treas. CAREL JASPERS; Dir PAUL DEN BESTEN; Vice-Dir ELVIRE SCHLÖSSER.

Koninklijke Nederlandse Bosbouw Vereniging (Royal Dutch Forestry Association): Parkweg 27, 2585 JH The Hague; tel. (70) 3688222; fax (70) 4162959; e-mail secretaris@ knbv.nl; internet www.knbv.nl; f. 1910; promotes forestry, landscape management, nature conservation; advocates functions and values of forests, such as carbon sequestration, historical monuments, nature, recreation, timber production, water, etc.; organises thematic meetings, symposia, excursions and study tours abroad; 600 mems; Chair. Dr Ir HANK H. BARTELINK; Vice-Chair. Ir ERWIN J. AL; Sec. Ing. MARLEEN VAN DEN HAM; publ. *Vakblad Natuur Bos Landschap* (10 a year).

Nederlandse Tuinbouwraad (Netherlands Horticultural Council): POB 1000, 1430 BA Aalsmeer; Legmeerdijk 313, 1431 GB Aalsmeer; tel. (29) 7395005; fax (29) 7395012; e-mail informatie@tuinbouwraad .nl; internet www.tuinbouwraad.nl; f. 1908; represents the common technical and economic interests of the mem. orgs; organizes int. horticultural exhibition 'Floriade'; 14 mem. nat. orgs of cooperatives and producers of edible and non-edible horticultural products; Chair. Dr NICO KOOMEN; Sec. Dr GEORGE TH. FRANKE.

ARCHITECTURE AND TOWN PLANNING

Erfgoedvereniging Heemschut: Nieuwezijds Kolk 28, 1012 PV Amsterdam; tel. (20) 6225292; fax (20) 6240571; e-mail info@ heemschut.nl; internet www.heemschut.nl; f. 1911; asscn for safeguarding the architectural heritage of the Netherlands; 12 provincial sub-cttees; 6,500 mems; Chair. P. BREUKINK; Dir KAREL LOEFF; Sec. K. LOEFF; publ. *Heemschut* (6 a year).

Genootschap Architectura et Amicitia: Duke Ellingtonstraat 34, 2324 LA Leiden; e-mail info@aeta.nl; internet www.aeta.nl; f. 1855; asscn of architects and individuals from related disciplines; 380 mems; Chair. RENS SCHULZE; Sec. FRANCISCA BENTHEM; publ. *FORUM* (1 a year).

Koninklijke Maatschappij tot Bevordering der Bouwkunst Bond van Nederlandse Architekten (BNA) (Royal Institute of Dutch Architects): POB 19606, 1000 GP Amsterdam; Jollemanhof 14, 1019 GW Amsterdam; tel. (20) 5553666; fax (20) 5553699; e-mail bna@bna.nl; internet www .bna.nl; f. 1919 by merger of Soc. for the Advancement of Architecture (f. 1842) and Asscn of Dutch Architects (f. 1908), present status 1957; promotes cultural, economic, skills, social profile of architect and architec-

ture; 3,000 mems; Chair. BJARNE MASTENBROEK; Vice-Chair. FREERK HOEKSTRA; Exec. Sec MARIJKE ZANDHUIS; publ. *BNABlad* (12 a year).

Nederlands Architectuur Instituut (Netherlands Architecture Institute): POB 237, 3000 AE Rotterdam; Museum Park 25, 3015 CB Rotterdam; tel. (10) 4401358; fax (10) 4366975; e-mail info@nai.nl; internet www.nai.nl; f. 1988, present location 1993; museum, archives, collns; 100 mems; library of 35,000 vols; Dir OLE BOUMAN; Man. Dir PETER HAASBROEK; publs *Delft Architectural Studies on Housing Design (DASH)* (2 a year), *Hunch* (2 a year), *OASE* (3 a year), *Open* (2 a year), *Positions* (irregular).

Raad voor Cultuur (Council for Culture): POB 61243, 2506 AE The Hague; RJ Schimmelpennincklaan 3, 2517 JN The Hague; tel. (70) 3106686; fax (70) 3614727; e-mail info@ cultuur.nl; internet www.cultuur.nl; f. 1995; statutory advisory body to the govt and both Chambers of Parliament for cultural and media policy; 9 mems; Chair. ELS H. SWAAB; Gen. Sec. KEES WEEDA.

Rijksdienst voor het Cultureel Erfgoed (National Heritage Board): POB 1600, 3800 BP Amersfoort; Smallepad 5, 3811 MG Amersfoort; tel. (33) 4217421; fax (33) 4217799; e-mail info@cultureelerfgoed.nl; internet www.cultureelerfgoed.nl; f. 1918, present name and status 2009; attached to Min. of Education, Culture and Science; conservation of nat. heritage; Dir Drs CEES VAN 'T VEEN; publ. *Tijdschrift van de Rijksdienst voor het Cultureel Erfgoed* (4 a year).

BIBLIOGRAPHY, LIBRARY SCIENCE AND MUSEOLOGY

FOBID Netherlands Library Forum: POB 90407, 2509 LK The Hague; tel. (70) 3140511; fax (70) 3140651; e-mail info@fobid .nl; internet www.fobid.nl; f. 1974; library umbrella org. for advocacy and devt in the field of legal matters, professional education, classification standards, int. affairs; promotion of cooperation and integration among public, research and spec. libraries in the Netherlands; mems: Netherlands Public Library Asscn (VOB), Netherlands Asscn for Library, Information and Knowledge Professionals (NVB), Nat. Library of the Netherlands (KB) and UKB, the cooperative Asscn of 13 univ. libraries, the Nat. Library and the Library of the Royal Dutch Acad. of Science; serves as int. office for library matters; Dir and Sec. Dr MARIAN KOREN.

Nederlandse Museumvereniging (Netherlands Museums Association): POB 2975, 1000 CZ Amsterdam; Rapenburgerstraat 123, 1011 VL Amsterdam; tel. (20) 5512900; fax (20) 5512901; e-mail info@ museumvereniging.nl; internet www .museumvereniging.nl; f. 1926; devt of museums in terms of professionalism and quality; 450 mems; Chair. ERIC FISCHER; Vice-Chair. and Sec. WILLEM BIJLEVELD; Treas. PETER VERHOEVEN; publ. *Museumvisie* (Museum Vision, 4 a year).

Nederlandse Vereniging voor Beroepsbeoefenaren in de bibliotheek-, informatie- en kennissector (NVB) (Netherlands Association for Library, Information and Knowledge Professionals): Mariaplaats 3, 3511 LH Utrecht; tel. (30) 2330050; fax (30) 2380030; e-mail info@nvbonline.nl; internet www.nvbonline.nl; f. 1912; maintenance of lawful regulation of library system; arrangement of meetings and int. cooperation; professional education; 1,300 individual and 500 institutional mems; Pres. Drs BART VAN DER MEIJ; Chair. M. G. WESSELING; Man. Dir Drs JAN VAN DER BURG; Sec. C. KORLVINKE; Treas.

HUIB VERHOEFF; publs *NVB—Nieuwsbrief, Informatie Professional*.

Vereniging Openbare Bibliotheken (Netherlands Public Library Association): POB 16146, 2500 BC The Hague; Grote Marktstraat 43, 2511 BH The Hague; tel. (70) 3090500; fax (70) 3090599; e-mail vereniging@debibliotheken.nl; internet www .debibliotheken.nl; f. 1908; defends common interests of the public library sector; 170 mem. instns; Chair. KARS VELING; Vice-Chair. and Treas. CHARLES NOORDAM; Sec. MARION MERTENS; publ. *Bibliotheekblad* (26 a year).

ECONOMICS, LAW AND POLITICS

Internationaal Juridisch Instituut (International Legal Institute): Spui 186, 2511 BW The Hague; tel. (70) 3460974; fax (70) 3625235; e-mail info@iji.nl; internet www.iji.nl; f. 1918; supplies legal opinions regarding private int. law and foreign (also mostly private) law to the Netherlands judiciary, the Netherlands bar and to other mems of the legal profession, such as civil law notaries; also gives information to judges and lawyers outside the Netherlands; Chair. Prof. A. V. M. STRUYCKEN; Vice-Chair. L. STRIKWERDA; Dir Prof. W. G. HUIJGEN; Deputy Dir E. N. FROHN; Sec. A .C. OLLAND; Treas. G. J. C. VAN ENGELEN.

Koninklijke Vereniging voor de Staathuishoudkunde (Royal Netherlands Economic Association): c/o De Nederlandsche Bank NV, POB 98, 1000 AB Amsterdam; tel. (20) 5242280; fax (20) 5242500; e-mail info@ kvsweb.nl; internet www.kvsweb.nl; f. 1849; promotes economic knowledge; 1,500 mems; Chair. Prof. Dr A. W. A. BOOT; Sec. and Treas. Prof. Dr J. SWANK; publs *Jaarboek* (4 a year), *Preadviezen* (1 a year).

Nederlandse Vereniging voor Internationaal Recht (Netherlands Branch of International Law Association): POB 9520, 2300 RA Leiden; Steenschuur 25, 2311 ES Leiden; tel. (71) 5277748; fax (71) 5277383; e-mail info@nvir.org; internet www.nvir.org; f. 1910; practices and promotes int. public and private law; 475 mems; Pres. Prof. W. J. M. VAN GENUGTEN; Hon. Sec. Prof. Dr M. M. T. A. BRUS; publ. *Mededelingen* (1 a year).

Vereniging voor Agrarisch Recht (Agrarian Law Society): Maliesingel 20, 3581 BE Utrecht; tel. (30) 2320826; fax (30) 2341644; e-mail hvanbasten@ verenigingagrarischrecht.nl; internet www .verenigingagrarischrecht.nl; f. 1959; promotes scientific and practical practice of agricultural law; 300 mems; Chair. Prof. G. M. F. SNIJDERS; Sec. and Treas. H. A. VAN BASTEN; publ. *Agrarisch Recht* (Agrarian Law).

Vereniging voor Arbeidsrecht (Labour Law Society): De Eem 15, 3448 DS Woerden; fax (348) 422635; e-mail info@ verenigingvoorarbeidsrecht.nl; internet www .verenigingvoorarbeidsrecht.nl; f. 1946; acts as a forum for those who practice labour law; 940 mems; Chair. Prof. WILLEM H. A. C. M. BOUWENS; Sec. P. DE CASPARIS; Treas. R. J. KOOIJ.

FINE AND PERFORMING ARTS

Arti et Amicitiae: Rokin 112, 1012 LB Amsterdam; tel. (20) 6245134; fax (20) 6225206; e-mail arti@arti.nl; internet www .arti.nl; f. 1839; a nat. soc. of painters, sculptors and graphic artists; exhibition gallery; 1,550 mems (incl. 550 artist mems); Chair. ARIE VAN DEN BERG; Vice-Chair. ROBERT SAMKALDEN; Sec DIRK JAN JAGER; publ. *De Nieuwe* (6 a year).

Koninklijke Nederlandse Toonkunstenaars Vereniging (Royal Dutch Musician's Union): Grote Bickersstraat 50A, 1013 KS Amsterdam; tel. (20) 5221020; fax (20) 6200229; e-mail office@kntv.nl; internet www.kntv.nl; f. 1875; promotes the interests of professional musicians working in the field of performing arts and education; 3,400 mems; Dir GUSTA KORTEWEG; publ. *KNTV-Magazine* (6 a year).

Rijksbureau voor Kunsthistorische Documentatie (Netherlands Institute for Art History): POB 90418, 2509 LK The Hague; Prins Willem-Alexanderhof 5, 2595 BE The Hague; tel. (70) 3339777; fax (70) 3339789; e-mail info@rkd.nl; internet www.rkd.nl; f. 1932, present status 1995; art-historical information centre; administers colln of documentary, library and archive material on Western art from late Middle Ages to present; library of 450,000 vols, periodicals and catalogues, and press-cuttings, archives, 7m. photos and reproductions; Chair. Prof. P. SCHNABEL; Dir Prof. Dr RUDI E.O. EKKART; publs *Oud-Holland* (4 a year), *RKD Bulletin* (2 a year).

Theater Instituut Nederland (Netherlands Theatre Institute): POB 10783, 1001 ET Amsterdam; Sarphatistraat 53, 1018 EW Amsterdam; tel. (20) 5513300; fax (20) 5513303; e-mail info@tin.nl; internet www .theaterinstituut.nl; f. 1924 as Theatre Museum, present name and status 1992; service org. and research institute for the professional theatre; theatre library; supports and promotes Dutch theatre and theatre persons nationally and internationally; organizes debates and exhibitions; library of 100,000 vols and sound archives and 6,000 video cassettes of the Dutch theatre; Chair. HANS ANDERSSON; Dir HENK SCHOLTEN; publs *Bulletin* (2 a year), *Carnet* (in French and English), *Nederlands Theaterjaarboek* (1 a year).

Vereniging Toonkunst Nederland (Society for the Advancement of Music): Atlantisplein 1, Room 2.04, 1093 NE Amsterdam; tel. (20) 6713091; e-mail info@ toonkunstnederland.nl; internet www .toonkunstnederland.nl; f. 1829, present status 2007; asscn of amateur choirs and orchestras; 5,000 mems; Chair. GERARD BROEKMANS; Sec. RIA ROELANDS.

Wagnergenootschap Nederland (Wagner Society Netherlands): De Helling 79, 1502 GE, Zaandam; tel. (75) 6157793; e-mail bestuur@wagnergenootschap.nl; internet www.wagnergenootschap.nl; f. 1961; promotes and studies works and life of composer Richard Wagner; 300 mems; Chair. TON HOGENES; Sec. JACK VAN DONGEN; Treas. JAN BURGER; publ. *Wagner After All* (5 a year).

HISTORY, GEOGRAPHY AND ARCHAEOLOGY

Centraal Bureau voor Genealogie (Central Bureau for Genealogy): POB 11755, 2502 AT The Hague; Prins Willem-Alexanderhof 22, 2595 BE The Hague; tel. (70) 3150570; fax (70) 3478394; internet www.cbg.nl; f. 1945; large genealogical and heraldic collns; 14,350 mems; library of 100,000 vols; Chair. Dr PIETER WINSEMIUS; Deputy Chair. Dr ELS M. KLOEK; Dir Dr A. J. LEVER; publs *Genealogie* (4 a year), *Jaarboek* (yearbook).

Internationaal Instituut voor Sociale Geschiedenis (International Institute of Social History): POB 2169, 1000 CD Amsterdam; Cruquiusweg 31, 1019 AT Amsterdam; tel. (20) 6685866; fax (20) 6654181; e-mail info@iisg.nl; internet www.iisg.nl; f. 1935; attached to Royal Netherlands Acad. of Arts and Sciences; documentation and research centre in the field of social history; colln,

preservation and availability of heritage of social movements worldwide; library of 1,000,000 vols, archives, especially on the labour movement, 60,000 periodicals; Gen. Dir Prof. Dr ERIK-JAN ZÜRCHER; Dir for Collns and Digital Infrastructure TITIA VAN DER WERF-DAVELAAR; Dir for Research MARCEL VAN DER LINDEN; Exec. Sec. MONIQUE KRUITHOF; publ. *International Review of Social History* (3 a year, plus supplement).

Koninklijk Fries Genootschap voor Geschiedenis en Cultuur/Keninklik Frysk Genoatskip foar Skiednis en Kultuer (Royal Frisian Society for History and Culture): Turfmarkt 11, 8911 KS Leeuwarden; tel. (58) 2555500; e-mail fries .genootschap@friesmuseum.nl; internet www .friesgenootschap.nl; f. 1827, present name 2003; promotes history and culture of Friesland; supports research in that field; 1,800 mems; Chair. Dr PIET HEMMINGA; Sec. LOURENS OLDERSMA; Treas. Drs DIRK VAN DER BIJ; publs *De Vrije Fries* (yearbook), *Fryslân* (4 a year).

Koninklijk Nederlands Aardrijkskundig Genootschap (Royal Dutch Geographical Society): POB 805, 3500 AV Utrecht; Ganzenmarkt 6, 3512 GD Utrecht; tel. (30) 2361202; fax (30) 2621290; e-mail info@ knag.nl; internet www.knag.nl; f. 1873; promotes geography as subject and profession; organizes confs, workshops, lectures, seminars; publishes scientific journals and books; 3,500 mems; Dir Drs EELKO POSTMA; Chair. HENK OTTENS; Treas. LEON BUSSCHOPS; publs *Geografie* (9 a year), *Tijdschrift voor Economische en Sociale Geografie (TESG)* (Journal of Economic and Social Geography, 5 a year).

Koninklijk Nederlands Historisch Genootschap (Royal Netherlands Historical Society): POB 90406, 2509 LK The Hague; Prins Willem-Alexanderhof 5, 2595 BE The Hague; tel. (70) 3140363; fax (70) 3140637; e-mail info@knhg.nl; internet www.knhg.nl; f. 1845; promotes historical studies and dissemination of historical research with spec. regard to history of low countries; 1,600 mems; Chair. Prof. Dr A. F. (LEX) HEERMA VAN VOSS; Dir Dr L. M. L. M. DE GOEI; Treas. Prof. Dr JORIS VAN EIJNATTEN; publs *Bijdragen en Mededelingen betreffende de Geschiedenis der Nederlanden* (The Low Countries' Historical Review, 4 a year), *HG-Nieuws* (4 a year, digital).

Koninklijk Oudheidkundig Genootschap (Royal Dutch Antiquarian Society): POB 74888, 1070 DN Amsterdam; Frans van Mierisstraat 92, 1071 RZ Amsterdam; tel. (20) 6747380; e-mail kog@ rijksmuseum.nl; internet www.kog.nu; f. 1858; colln of applied art (furniture, silver, sculpture, etc.), paintings, objects of historical value, prints and drawings concerning the topography of Amsterdam, manners and customs of the Netherlands; coins, medals, books; 540 mems; library of 6,100 vols; Pres. Drs NORBERT P. VAN DEN BERG; Sec. HESTER H. MANGER CATS-VAN DEN BERG; Treas. Dr J. KAMP.

Nederlandsch Economisch-Historisch Archief (NEHA) (Netherlands Economic-Historical Archives Society): Cruquiusweg 31, 1019 AT Amsterdam; tel. (20) 6685866; fax (20) 6654111; e-mail info@neha.nl; internet www.neha.nl; f. 1914; attached to Royal Netherlands Acad. of Arts and Sciences; specializes in economic history and business studies; 400 mems; library: see Libraries and Archives; Pres. Prof. Dr J. L. VAN ZANDEN; Sec. Dr E. A. G. VAN DEN BENT; Archivist JACK HOFMAN; Treas. Drs J. A. DE JONGH; publ. *Tijdschrift voor Sociale en Economische Geschiedenis* (4 a year).

Vereniging Gelre: Markt 1, 6811 CG Arnhem; tel. (26) 3521600; fax (26) 3521699; e-mail info@geldersarchief.nl; internet www .geldersarchief.nl; f. 1897; promotes practice of archeology, history and law of Gelderland; organizes seminars and symposia; Pres. Dr J. A. H. Bots; Sec. Dr F. J. W. van Kan; Treas. De Heer M. Gras; publs *Bijdragen en Mededelingen* (1 a year), *Werken*.

LANGUAGE AND LITERATURE

Alliance Française: POB 75736, 1070 AS Amsterdam; tel. (35) 6237667; e-mail info@ alliance-francaise.nl; internet www .alliance-francaise.nl; f. 1888; offers courses and exams in French language and culture and promotes cultural exchange with France; attached offices in Alkmaar, Amersfoort, Apeldoorn, Arnhem, Baarland, Bergen-op-Zoom, Betuwe, Boskoop, Brakel, Breda, Den Haag, Den Helder, Deventer, Dordrecht, Eindhoven, Enschede, Friesland, Hart van Zeeland, Hoorn, Kennemerland, Maastricht, Meppel, Nijmegen, Ommen, Roermond, Roosendaal, Rotterdam, Twente, Utrecht, Vorden, Walcheren, Zutphen and Zwolle; Pres. E. J. A. van Tinteren-America; publs *En France* (4 a year), *En Route* (1 a year).

British Council: Weteringschans 85A, 1017 RZ Amsterdam; tel. (20) 5506060; fax (20) 6207389; e-mail exams@britishcouncil.nl; internet www.britishcouncil.org/ netherlands; offers exams in English language and British culture and promotes cultural exchange with the UK; not open to gen. public; Dir Martin Hope.

Goethe-Institut: Herengracht 470, 1017 CA Amsterdam; tel. (20) 5312900; fax (20) 6384631; e-mail info@amsterdam.goethe .org; internet www.goethe.de/ins/nl/ams/ deindex.htm; offers courses and exams in German language and culture; promotes cultural exchange with Germany; attached centre in Rotterdam; Dir Dr Barbara Honrath.

Instituto Cervantes: Domplein 3, 3512 JC Utrecht; tel. (30) 2428477; fax (30) 2332970; e-mail cenutr@cervantes.es; internet utrecht .cervantes.es; f. 1992; offers courses and exams in Spanish language and culture and promotes cultural exchange with Spain and Spanish-speaking Latin and Central America; library of 14,000 vols; Dir Patricia Izquierdo Iranzo.

Maatschappij der Nederlandse Letterkunde (Society of Netherlands Literature): POB 9501, 2300 RA Leiden; Witte Singel 27, 2300 RA Leiden; tel. (71) 5272109; fax (71) 5272836; e-mail mnl@library.leidenuniv.nl; internet www .maatschappijdernederlandseletterkunde.nl; f. 1766; library administered by the library of Leiden Univ.; 1,700 mems; Chair. Peter Sigmond; Vice-Chair. Kris Humbeeck; Sec. Berry Dongelmans; Treas. Aad Groos; publs *Jaarboek der Maatschappij* (1 a year), *Nieuw Letterkundig Magazijn* (2 a year), *Tijdschrift voor Nederlandse Taal- en Letterkunde* (4 a year).

Netherlands Centre of the International PEN: Emmalaan 29, 3051 JC Rotterdam; tel. (10) 4229805; e-mail secretariaat@ pencentrum.nl; f. 1923; 350 mems; Pres. Hester Knibbe; Sec. René Appel; publ. *PEN Nieuwsbrief* (2 a year).

MEDICINE

Genootschap ter bevordering van Natuur-, Genees- en Heelkunde (Association for Advancement of Natural, Medical and Surgical Sciences): POB 94248, 1090 GE Amsterdam; tel. (20) 5255055; e-mail b.e .fabius@uva.nl; internet www.science.uva.nl/ ngh; f. 1790; encourages physics, medicine, surgery; awards individuals who contribute original research of great interest; Pres. Prof. Dr C. J. F. van Noorden; Sec. Prof. Dr J. J. O. O. Wiegerinck; Treas. Prof. Dr D. Roos.

Koninklijke Nederlandsche Maatschappij tot bevordering der Geneeskunst (Royal Dutch Medical Association): POB 20051, 3502 LB Utrecht; Domus Medica, Mercatorlaan 1200, 3528 BL Utrecht; tel. (30) 2823800; fax (30) 2823326; e-mail info@ fed.knmg.nl; internet knmg.artsennet.nl; f. 1849; professional org. for physicians of The Netherlands; improves quality of medical care and healthcare; library on history of medicine in the Netherlands; 49,000 mems; Chair. Prof. Dr Arie C. Nieuwenhuijzen Kruseman; publs *Arts in Spe* (4 a year), *Medisch Contact* (52 a year).

Koninklijke Nederlandse Maatschappij ter Bevordering der Pharmacie (Royal Dutch Association for the Advancement of Pharmacy): POB 30460, 2500 GL The Hague; Alexanderstraat 11, 2514 JL The Hague; tel. (70) 3737373; fax (70) 3106530; e-mail communicatie@knmp.nl; internet www .knmp.nl; f. 1842; promotes the interests of professional and industrial pharmacists; c. 3,500 mems; Pres. Jan Smits; Vice-Pres. Maayke Fluitman; Dir-Gen. Léon Tinke; Sec. Jard Baljet; Treas. Bart Smals; publ. *Pharmaceutisch Weekblad*.

Koninklijke Nederlandse Vereniging voor Microbiologie (KNVM) (Royal Netherlands Society for Microbiology): POB 214, 2600 AE Delft; tel. (10) 7509766; fax (62) 2607479; e-mail secretariaat@nvvm-online .nl; internet www.knvm.org; f. 1911; attached to Fed. of European Microbiological Socs; promotes microbiology in the Netherlands and Flanders; organizes symposia; 1,350 mems; Chair. Prof. Dr. H. A. B. Wösten; Vice-Chair. Prof. Dr J. A. G. van Strijp; Sec. Dr B. Duim; Sec. J. J. E. Bijlsma; Treas. Dr J. W. Sanders.

Nederlandse Vereniging voor Heelkunde (Association of Surgeons of the Netherlands): POB 20061, 3502 LB Utrecht; Domus Medica, Mercatorlaan 1200, 3528 BL Utrecht; tel. (30) 2823327; fax (30) 2823329; e-mail nvvh@nvvh.knmg.nl; internet www .heelkunde.nl; f. 1902; promotes surgery and interests of gen. surgeons; 1,330 mems (incl. 15 hon. mems, 200 assoc. mems, 490 asst mems); Chair. Dr P. J. van den Akker; Dir Drs B. X. Oude Elberink; Vice-Chair. Prof. Dr R. A. E. M. Tollenaar; Sec.-Gen. Dr G. A. P. Nieuwenhuijzen; Treas. Dr M. H. A. Bemelmans; publ. *Nederlands Tijdschrift voor Heelkunde* (12 a year); publ. *The European Journal of Surgery* (English, 12 a year).

Nederlandse Vereniging voor Neurologie (Netherlands Society for Neurology): POB 20050, 3502 LB Utrecht; Mercatorlaan 1200, 3528 BL Utrecht; tel. (30) 2823343; e-mail bureau@neurologie.nl; internet www .neurologie.nl; f. 1871, reorganized 1974; monitors, promotes and optimizes professional quality of care for people with diseases of the nervous system or muscles; 800 mems; Pres. Prof. Dr M. de Visser; Sec. Prof. Dr C. H. Polman; publ. *Clinical Neurology and Neurosurgery*.

Nederlandse Vereniging voor Orthodontische Studie (Netherlands Orthodontics Society): Mahatma Gandhistraat 10, 3066 VA Rotterdam; tel. (10) 2020006; e-mail info@nvos.info; internet www.nvos.info; f. 1946; offers guidance, training and information on changing insight and new methods; 700 mems; Chair. Herman van Beek; Vice-Chair. Carine Carels; Sec. Manfred Leunisse; publ. *Chain Nieuwsbrief* (2 a year).

Nederlandse Vereniging voor Psychiatrie (Netherlands Psychiatric Association): POB 20062, 3502 LB, Utrecht; Mercatorlaan 1200, 3528 BL, Utrecht; tel. (30) 2823303; fax (30) 2888400; e-mail info@nvvp.net; internet www.nvvp.net; f. 1871, reorganized 1973; 3,468 mems; Pres. Prof. Dr R. J. van der Gaag; Vice-Pres. Dr T. J. Heeren; Dir Peter Niesink; Treas. J. A. van Waarde; publ. *Tijdschrift voor Psychiatrie*.

Nederlandse Vereniging voor Tropische Geneeskunde en Internationale Gezondheidszorg (Netherlands Society for Tropical Medicine and International Health): POB 5032, 1200 MA Hilversum; tel. (63) 4306672; e-mail nvtg@xs4all.nl; internet www.nvtg.org; f. 1907; supports research; provides education; promotes exchange of expertise and knowledge in the field of tropical medicine and int. health for improvement of health care in low- and middle-income countries; 1,000 mems; Chair. Dr Pieter van den Hombergh; Sec. Dr J. F. Wendte; Treas. Drs J. H. M. Visschedijk; publ. *MT Bulletin of the Netherlands Society of Tropical Medicine and International Health* (4 a year).

Vereniging van Orthodontisten (Association of Orthodontists): Simon Vestdijkstraat 67, 3842 LK Harderwijk; tel. (65) 3264175; e-mail info@orthodontist.nl; internet www .orthodontist.nl; f. 1962; Chair. Drs N. E. P. Bennitt; Vice-Chair. Dr C. M. Korstjens; Sec. Drs G. P. Steenvoorden; Treas. Drs P. C. M. Zuurbier.

Vereniging voor Volksgezondheid en Wetenschap (Netherlands Society of Public Health and Science): Lindelaan 4, 2282 EX Rijswijk; tel. (70) 3030045; fax (70) 7168270; e-mail secretariaat@verenigingvenw.nl; internet www.verenigingvenw.nl; f. 1985, fmrly Algemene Nederlandse Vereniging voor Sociale Gezondheidszorg; scientific approach to health and health care questions; 800 mems; Pres. Prof. Dr J. Schuit; Sec. Ir I. Thien; Treas. Ir J. Jansen; publs *European Journal of Public Health* (4 a year), *Tijdschrift voor Gezondheidswetenschappen* (8 a year).

NATURAL SCIENCES

General

Koninklijke Nederlandse Natuurhistorische Vereniging (Royal Dutch Society for Natural History): POB 310, 3700 AH Zeist; Blvd 12, 3707 BM Zeist; tel. (30) 2314797; fax (30) 2368907; e-mail bureau@knnv.nl; internet www.knnv.nl; f. 1901; field biology; supports active participation in and with nature through natural history studies, by enjoying nature and through nature conservation; 8,300 mems; Chair. K. D. Waterreus; Sec. H. W. Zolf; Treas. H. ten Grotenhuis; publ. *Natura* (6 a year).

Natuurmonumenten: POB 9955, 1243 ZS 's-Graveland; Schaep en Burgh, Noordereinde 60, 1243 JJ 's-Graveland; tel. (35) 6559933; fax (35) 6563174; internet www .natuurmonumenten.nl; f. 1905; preserves nature, landscape and cultural history; controls 355 nature reserves; 830,000 mems; Pres. Prof. Dr Cees Veerman; Vice-Pres. and Sec. Prof. Dr Martin Wassen; Dir-Gen. Ir Jan Jaap de Graeff; Dir for Finance and Operations Drs Fedde Koster; Treas. Jan van den Belt; publ. *Natuurbehoud* (4 a year).

Stichting Natuur en Milieu (Society for Nature and Environment): POB 1578, 3500 BN Utrecht; Hamburgerstraat 28A, 3512 NS Utrecht; tel. (30) 2331328; fax (30) 2331311; internet www2.natuurenmilieu.nl; f. 1972, present location 2007; nature conservation and environmental protection; Chair. M. van Lier Lels; Dir Tjerk Wagenaar; publ. *Natuur en milieu* (12 a year).

Thijmgenootschap (Society of Christian Scholars in the Netherlands): Groesbeekseweg 125, 6524 CT Nijmegen; e-mail contact@thijmgenootschap.nl; internet www.thijmgenootschap.nl; f. 1904 as Vereeniging tot het Bevorderen van de Beoefening der Wetenschap onder de Katholieken in Nederland, present name 1947; promotes scientific reflection from a Christian perspective on devts in culture and soc.; 1,500 mems; Pres. Prof. Dr WIM B. H. J. VAN DE DONK; Sec. Prof. Drs J. S. L. A. W. B. ROES; Treas. ROLAND E. C. VAN DER PLUYM; publ. *Annalen van het Thijmgenootschap* (4 a year).

Biological Sciences

Koninklijke Nederlandse Botanische Vereniging (Royal Botanical Society of the Netherlands): c/o Dr. Ir. N. Smits, Alterra WUR, POB 47, 6700 AA Wageningen; e-mail nina.smits@wur.nl; internet www.knbv.eu; f. 1845; promotes knowledge of plants through education and research in areas such as plant ecology, plant molecular biology, plant physiology, plant taxonomy, vegetation science; 350 mems; Chair. Prof. Dr JOOP H. J. SCHAMINÉE; Vice-Chair. Prof. Dr THEO ELZENGA; First Sec. Dr TON PEETERS; Second Sec. Dr NINA SMITS; Treas. Dr TIJS KETELAAR; publ. *Plant Biology*.

Koninklijke Nederlandse Dierkundige Vereniging (Royal Dutch Zoological Society): c/o Dr P. H. M. Klaren, Radboud Univ. Nijmegen, Faculty of Science, Dept of Animal Physiology, Heyendaalseweg 135, POB 30, 6525 AJ Nijmegen; tel. (24) 3653245; fax (24) 3653229; e-mail p.klaren@science.ru.nl; internet www.kndv.nl; f. 1872; promotes zoological research; organizes symposia; 210 mems; Pres. Prof. Dr NICO M. VAN STRAALEN; Sec. Dr PETER H. M. KLAREN; Treas. Dr KATJA J. TEERDS; publs *Animal Biology* (4 a year, online (www.brill.nl/ab)), *Bionieuws* (24 a year).

Natura Artis Magistra (Royal Zoological Society): POB 20164, 1000 HD Amsterdam; Plantage Kerklaan 38–40, Amsterdam; tel. (900) 2784796; fax (20) 5233637; e-mail info@artis.nl; internet www.artis.nl; f. 1838; promotes humans connection with nature, relationship between nature and culture and degree of human interaction in this position; 8,000 mems; Dir Dr HAIG BALIAN; publs *Artis* (5 a year), *Contributions to Zoology*, *Artis Library* (4 a year), *Tijdschrift van Natura Artis Magistra* (4 a year).

Nederlandse Entomologische Vereniging (Netherlands Entomological Society): Sj. Tiemersma, Vlasakker 2, 8091 MP Wezep; tel. (38) 3758275; e-mail secretaris@nev.nl; internet www.nev.nl; f. 1845; promotes entomology; 5 regional brs; library of 21,000 vols, 4,400 journals, 100,000 reprints; 700 mems; Pres. Dr MATTY P. BERG; Vice-Pres. Prof. Dr MARCEL DICKE; Sec. SJ. TIEMERSMA; Treas. Dr P. OOSTERBROEK; publs *Entomologia Experimentalis et Applicata* (12 a year), *Entomologische Berichten* (6 a year), *Tijdschrift voor Entomologie* (4 a year).

Nederlandse Mycologische Vereniging (Dutch Mycological Society): Centraalbureau voor Schimmelcultures, POB 85167, 3508 AD Utrecht; Uppsalalaan 8, 3584 CT Utrecht; tel. (30) 2122600; e-mail nmv@mycologen.nl; internet www.mycologen.nl; f. 1908; studies fungi; 800 mems; Chair. ROB CHRISPIJN; Sec. JAC N. J. GELDERBLOM; Treas. AAD J. TERMORSHUIZEN; publ. *Coolia* (4 a year).

Nederlandse Ornithologische Unie (Dutch Ornithological Union): Sloet Marke 41, 8016 CJ Zwolle; e-mail nou.ledenadmin@gmail.com; internet nou.natuurinfo.nl; f. 1901; study of ornithology; 1,067 mems; library: c. 120 periodicals; Pres. Prof. Dr J.

M. TINBERGEN; Sec. PETER MILDERS; publs *Ardea* (2 a year), *Limosa* (4 a year).

Nederlandse Vereniging voor Parasitologie (Netherlands Society for Parasitology): c/o Dr J.J. Verweij, Laboratorium voor Parasitologie, L4-Q, LUMC, POB 9600, 2300 RC Leiden; e-mail j.j.verweij@lumc.nl; internet www.parasitologie.nl; f. 1961; promotes and exchanges scientific knowledge of infectious diseases caused by parasites; 250 mems; Pres. Prof. Dr ROBERT SAUERWEIN; Sec. Dr JACO. VERWEIJ; Treas. Dr CLEMENS KOCKEN.

Nederlandse Zoötechnische Vereniging (Netherlands Association for Animal Husbandry): POB 79, 6700 AB Wageningen; tel. (317) 483487; fax (317) 483976; e-mail info@nzvnet.nl; internet www.nzvnet.nl; f. 1930; platform for issues in the field of animals, people and environment; 530 mems; Pres. Ir GERT HEMKE; Sec. Ir G. H. JANSEN.

Mathematical Sciences

Koninklijk Wiskundig Genootschap (Royal Dutch Mathematical Society): CWI, POB 94079, 1090 GB Amsterdam; tel. (20) 5924226; fax (20) 5924199; e-mail wiskgenoot@wiskgenoot.nl; internet www.wiskgenoot.nl; f. 1778; organizes confs and symposia; 1,400 mems; library of 16,400 vols and journals of mathematics and its applications; Pres. Prof. Dr GERT VEGTER; Sec. Prof. Dr ROB D. VAN DER MEI; Treas. Dr SANDJAI BHULAI; publs *Nieuw Archief voor Wiskunde* (4 a year), *Pythagoras* (6 a year).

Vereniging voor Statistiek en Operationele Research (Netherlands Society for Statistics and Operations Research): POB 2095, 2990 DB Barendrecht; tel. (180) 623796; fax (180) 623670; e-mail admin@vvs-or.nl; internet www.vvs-or.nl; f. 1945; promotes study and application of statistics, operations research, relevant devts in mathematics in service of science and soc.; 800 mems; Chair. Prof. Dr R. D. GILL; Sec. Dr C. G. H. DIKS; Treas. Prof. Dr C. A. G. M. VAN MONTFORT; publs *Statistica Neerlandica* (4 a year), *Stator* (4 a year).

Physical Sciences

Koninklijk Nederlands Geologisch Mijnbouwkundig Genootschap (Royal Geological and Mining Society of the Netherlands): POB 30424, 2500 GK The Hague; Prinsessegracht 23, 2514 AP The Hague; tel. (70) 3919892; fax (70) 3919840; e-mail kngmg@mac.com; internet web.mac.com/kngmg; f. 1912; promotes the interests of earth sciences in the Netherlands; awards Van Waterschoot van der Gracht medal (an award for outstanding scientific achievement) and organizes the annual Staring lecture; sections for petroleum geology, paleobiolology, palynology, mineralogy, sedimentology, engineering geology and geochemistry; section for female professional earth scientists (GAIA) and various regional earth science asscns; 800 mems; Pres. MENNO DE RUIG; Sec. BARTHOLD SCHROOT; Treas. ARIAN STEENBRUGGEN; publs *Geo.brief* (8 a year), *Geologie en Mijnbouw* (Netherlands Journal of Geosciences, 4 a year).

Koninklijk Nederlands Meteorologisch Instituut (Royal Netherlands Meteorological Institute): POB 201, 3730 AE De Bilt; Wilhelminalaan 10, 3732 GK De Bilt; tel. (30) 2206911; fax (30) 2210407; e-mail prv@knmi.nl; internet www.knmi.nl; f. 1854, present location 1897; attached to Min. of Infrastructure and the Environment; meteorology, climatology, oceanography, seismology; conducts research on climate change; library of 140,000 vols, spec. collns incl. Polar expeditions; Dir-Gen. Dr Ir FRITS J. J. BROUWER; Exec. Dir. Drs D. R. VAN HATTEM; publs *Maandover zicht van het weer*, *Seismo-*

logical Bulletin, scientific reports and technical reports, daily weather maps, rain observations.

Koninklijke Nederlandse Chemische Vereniging (Royal Netherlands Chemical Society): POB 249, 2260 AE Leidschendam; Synthesium, Castellum C, Loire 150, 2491 AK The Hague; tel. (70) 3378790; fax (70) 3378799; e-mail kncv@kncv.nl; internet www.kncv.nl; f. 1903, present location 2006; promotes molecular sciences; 8,500 mems; Pres. Dr MARTIN POST; Vice-Pres. Drs JAN APOTHEKER; Sec. and Dir for Bureau Dr GABRIËLLE DONNÉ; Treas. Dr LENE HVIID; publs *Chemisch 2 Weekblad* (26 a year), *European Journal of Inorganic Chemistry* (12 a year), *European Journal of Organic Chemistry* (12 a year).

Koninklijke Nederlandse Vereniging voor Weer- en Sterrenkunde (Royal Dutch Society for Meteorology and Astronomy): Stichting De Koepel, Sterrenwacht 'Sonnenborgh', Zonnenburg 2, 3512 GB Utrecht; tel. (30) 2311360; fax (30) 2342852; e-mail info@dekoepel.nl; internet www.dekoepel.nl; f. 1901; public lectures, meetings, confs, observing sessions; 5,000 mems; Dir EDWIN MATHLENER; publs *Sterren & Planeten* (11 a year), *Sterrengids* (1 a year), *Zenit* (12 a year).

Nederlandse Natuurkundige Vereniging (Netherlands Physical Society): POB 41882, 1009 DB Amsterdam; Science Park 105, Kamer N227, 1098 XG Amsterdam; tel. (20) 5922211; fax (20) 5925155; e-mail bureau@nnv.nl; internet www.nnv.nl; f. 1921; improves study of physics and safeguards interests of physicists; 3,800 mems; Chair. Prof. Dr G. VAN DER STEENHOVEN; Sec. Prof. Dr P. J. G. MULDERS; Treas. Dr J. A. M. M. VAN HAAREN; publ. *Nederlands Tijdschrift voor Natuurkunde* (12 a year).

PHILOSOPHY AND PSYCHOLOGY

Algemene Nederlandse Vereniging voor Wijsbegeerte (General Netherlands Philosophical Society): c/o Erasmus Universiteit, Faculty of Philosophy, POB 1738, 3000 DR Rotterdam; Faculty of Philosophy, Campus Woudestein, H-Bldg, 5th Ffl., Burgemeester Oudlaan 50, 3062 PA Rotterdam; e-mail anvw@fwb.eur.nl; internet www.eur.nl/fw; f. 1933; 150 mems; Pres. Dr J. A. VAN RULER; Sec. Dr H. A. KROP; publ. *Algemeen Tijdschrift voor Wijsbegeerte*.

Affiliated Societies:

Internationale School voor Wijsbegeerte (International School of Philosophy): Dodeweg 8, 3832 RD Leusden; tel. (33) 4650700; fax (33) 4650541; e-mail info@isvw.nl; internet www.isvw.nl; f. 1916; courses and confs in philosophy; 3,000 mems; library of 3,000 vols; Man. Dir RENÉ GUDE; Dir for Operations CHANTAL ORTH.

KIVI Afdeling Filosofie en Techniek: 23 Prinsessegracht, POB 30424, 2500 GK The Hague; f. 1847; Chair. R. E. C. H. TIEPEL; Sec. J. GROENHOEF.

Nederlands Genootschap voor Esthetica (Dutch Association for Aesthetics): Grevingaheerd 181, 9737 SL Groningen; internet www.nge.nl; f. 1997; asscn for theoretical, philosophical, critical reflection on the arts and aesthetic dimensions of contemporary culture; Chair. SANDER VAN MAAS; Vice-Chair. HANS MAES; Sec. RII DALITZ; publ. *Esthetica: Tijdschrift voor Kunst en Filosofie* (online).

Nederlandse Vereniging voor Godsdienstwijsbegeerte: Ring 34, 3227 AS Oudenhoorn; f. 1995.

Nederlandse Vereniging voor Logica en Wijsbegeerte der Exacte Wetenschappen: POB 407, 9700 AK Groningen; tel. (50) 3636334; e-mail rineke@ai.rug.nl; internet www .verenigingvoorlogica.nl; f. 1947; organizes scientific symposia; 150 mems; Chair. Prof. Dr RINEKE VERBRUGGE; Sec. Dr FEMKE VAN RAAMSDONK.

Nederlandse Vereniging voor Wetenschapsfilosofie (Dutch Society for Philosophy of Science): Faculty of Philosophy, Univ. of Groningen, Oude Boteringestr. 52 Groningen; tel. (50) 3636148; fax (50) 3636160; e-mail info@nvwf.nl; internet www.nvwf.nl; f. 1979; org. of confs, workshops and lectures; 80 mems; Pres. F. A. MULLER; Sec. Dr JAN-WILLEM ROMEIJN.

Stichting voor Christelijke Filosofie (Association for Reformational Philosophy): POB 2220, 3800 CE Amersfoort; tel. (33) 4328288; fax (33) 4481940; e-mail directie@christelijkefilosofie.nl; internet www.christelijkefilosofie.nl; f. 1935; asscn for Christian philosophy, based on thinking of philosophers such as Dutch Dooyeweerd, Schuurman, Van Riessen, Vollenhoven, foreign philosophers such as Chaplin (UK), Clouser (USA), Strauss (South Africa); 535 mems; Pres. Drs A. BERGER; Vice-Pres. Drs D. A. MEINEMA; Sec. Drs W. VOLLBEHR; Dir HILLIE VD STREEK; publs *Philosophia Reformata* (in English, 2 a year), *Sophie* (in Dutch, 6 a year).

Vereniging voor Filosofie en Geneeskunde: p/a VUmc (MF) Afdeling Metamedica, Kamer D-322, t.a.v. E.J. Ettema Van der Boechorststraat 7, 1081 BT Amsterdam; tel. (6) 27490195; e-mail m.vanzwol@vumc.nl; internet www .filosofieengeneeskunde.nl; f. 1981; Pres. Prof. Dr TSJALLING SWIERSTRA; Sec. Drs MARJANNE VAN ZWOL.

Vereniging 'Het Spinozahuis': Paganinidreef 66, 2253 SK Voorschoten; tel. and fax (71) 5612759; e-mail info@spinozahuis .nl; internet www.spinozahuis.nl; f. 1897; promotes life and works of philosopher Benedictus de Spinoza; cultural monument, library, museum; library of 4,000 vols; 1,100 mems; Pres. L. VAN BUNGE; Sec. THEO VAN DER WERF; publ. *Mededelingen vanwege het Spinozahuis* (3 a year).

Vereniging voor Wijsbegeerte van het Recht: Faculty of Law, Kamerlingh Onnes Bldg, Steenschuur 25, Lorentzzaal, 2311 ES Leiden; e-mail penningmeester@ verenigingrechtsfilosofie.nl; internet www .verenigingrechtsfilosofie.nl; f. 1919; promotes practice of legal philosophy and legal theory; Pres. SANNE TAEKEMA; Sec. GERARD DROSTERIJ; publ. *Nederlands Tijdschrift voor Rechtsfilosofie & Rechtstheorie* (3 a year).

Vereniging voor Wijsbegeerte te 's-Gravenhage: Nassau Dillenburgstraat 33, 2596 AC 's-Gravenhage; tel. (20) 6322644; e-mail frankwitzen@restricted .nl; internet www .verenigingvoorwijsbegeerte.nl; f. 1907; 100 mems; Pres. Ir J. M. ALBERS; Sec. F. WITZEN R. A.

Wijsgerige Vereniging Thomas van Aquino: POB 37, 5260 AA Vught; Aloysiuslaan 2, 5262 AH Vught; tel. (73) 6579017; f. 1933; philosophical confs; 160 mems; Pres. Prof. Dr A. LEIJEN; Sec. Prof. Dr R. A. TE VELDE.

Bataafsch Genootschap der Proefondervindelijke Wijsbegeerte (Experimental Natural Philosophy Society): POB 597, 3000 AN Rotterdam; tel. (10) 4117947; e-mail secretariaat@bataafschgenootschap.nl; internet www.bataafschgenootschap.nl; f. 1769; organizes 6 lectures for mems each year; awards biannual prizes and an int. Steven Hoogendijk Award every 2 years; 400 mems; Pres. Prof. Ir L. VAN DER SLUIS; Dir Prof. Dr Ir J. K. VRIJLING; Dir Prof. Dr F. B. DE WAARDVAN DER SPEK; Dir Prof. Dr HUUG W. TILANUS; Sec. Ir G. H. G. LAGERS; Sec. Drs A. S. SIJSMA.

Nederlands Psychoanalytisch Genootschap (Netherlands Psychoanalytical Association): Maliestraat 1A, 3581 SH Utrecht; tel. (30) 2307080; fax (30) 2343883; e-mail npg@npsai-utrecht.nl; internet www .npg-utrecht.nl; f. 1947; organizes scientific meetings, lectures and symposia; 136 mems; library of 60,000 vols; Sec. RIA HAENTJENS DEKKER.

RELIGION, SOCIOLOGY AND ANTHROPOLOGY

Fryske Akademy: POB 54, 8900 AB Ljouwert; Doelestraat 8, 8911 DX Ljouwert; tel. (58) 2131414; fax (58) 2131409; e-mail fa@ fryske-akademy.nl; internet www .fryske-akademy.nl; f. 1938; attached to Royal Netherlands Acad. of Arts and Science; devoted to the scientific study of Friesland, the Frisians and their language, history and culture; 450 mems; library of 20,000 vols; Dir Prof. Dr R. SALVERDA; publs *De Vrije Fries* (history, 1 a year), *It Beaken* (scientific, 4 a year), *Ut de Smidte fan de Fryske Akademy* (information, 4 a year).

TECHNOLOGY

Economisch Instituut voor de Bouw (Economic Institute for the Building): POB 58248, 1040 HE Amsterdam; Basisweg, 10 1043 AP Amsterdam; tel. (20) 5831900; fax (20) 5831999; e-mail eib@eib.nl; internet www.eib.nl; f. 1956 as Economic Institute for the Bldg Industry; promotes applied research in org. bldg and economic analysis; Chair. CAREL A. ADRIAANSENS; Dir Drs T. H. VAN HOEK; Deputy Dir Drs O. M. VRIES; Sec. DEBBIE VAN AMERONGEN; Sec. G. KRAMER; publs *Algemene kosten in het bouwbedrijf* (1 a year), *Bedrijfseconomische kencijfers* (1 a year), *Bedrijfseconomische kencijfers in de gww-sector* (1 a year), *Verwachtingen bouwproductie en werkgelegenheid* (1 a year).

Koninklijk Instituut van Ingenieurs (KIVI NIRIA) (Royal Institute of Engineers (KIVI NIRIA)): POB 30424, 2500 GK The Hague; Prinsessegracht 23, 2514 AP The Hague; tel. (70) 3919900; fax (70) 3919840; e-mail info@kiviniria.nl; internet www .kiviniria.net; f. 2004, by merger of Dutch NIRIA Engineers Asscn and Royal Institute of Engineers; asscn for engineers and engineering students; promotes technology; 25,000 mems; Pres. MARTIN C. J. VAN PERNIS; Vice-Pres. JOOST J. WENTINK; Dir Ir P. L. M. GILISSEN; Sec. JACKY C. GERSIE; publ. *De Ingenieur Technologiemagazine* (26 a year); publs *Kivi-nieuws* (26 a year), *Technisch Weekblad* (52 a year), *Techno!*.

Technologiestichting STW (Technology Foundation): POB 3021, 3502 GA Utrecht; Van Vollenhovenlaan 661, 3527 JP Utrecht; tel. (30) 6001211; fax (30) 6014408; e-mail info@stw.nl; internet www.stw.nl; f. 1981; improves and stimulates applied sciences and engineering by sponsoring research at (technical) univs in the Netherlands and promotes cooperation between those institutes and industry; also assists in implementing spec. governmental research programmes; Dir Dr EPPO E. W. BRUINS; Deputy Dir Dr CHRIS A. M. MOMBERS; publ. *!nterval*.

Research Institutes
GENERAL

Adhesion Institute: Kluyverweg 1, 2629 HS Delft; tel. (15) 2785353; fax (15) 2787151; e-mail info@hechtingsinstituut.nl; internet www.adhesioninstitute.com; attached to Faculty of Aerospace Engineering, Delft Univ. of Technology; research focuses on latest devts on surface pre-treatment of metals and plastics, durability of adhesive bonds, the application of adhesive(s) and adhesive bond design, as well as (FEM)-calculations on structural adhesive bonding technology; Dir Dr J. A. POULIS.

Amsterdam Business School (ABS): Plantage Muidergracht, Room M2.42, 1018 WB Amsterdam; tel. (20) 5257384; fax (20) 5255092; e-mail abs-ri@uva.nl; internet www.abs.uva.nl; f. 2002; attached to Univ. of Amsterdam; research concerning accounting, business, finance, management; Dir Prof. Dr ALLAN HODGSON.

Amsterdam Center for Career Research (ACCR): De Boelelaan 1105, 1081 HV Amsterdam; tel. (20) 5986000; e-mail loopbanen@feweb.vu.nl; internet www.feweb .vu.nl/en/departments-and-institutes/accr; f. 2006; attached to VU Univ. Amsterdam; researches into factors contributing to growth of careers, in terms of devt and job level, within orgs.

Amsterdam Center for Entrepreneurship at VU: De Boelelaan 1085, 1081 Amsterdam; tel. (20) 5989906; fax (20) 5989904; e-mail infoacevu@feweb.vu.nl; internet www.feweb.vu.nl/acevu; research focuses on entrepreneurship as new venture creation, wealth creation as dominant motive to create new ventures, and entrepreneur as instigator of entrepreneurship; Dir Prof. ENNO MASUREL.

Amsterdam Institute for International Development (AIID): Trinity Bldg C, 3rd Fl., Room XT-3.17, Pietersbergweg 17, 1105 BM Amsterdam; tel. (20) 5661596; fax (20) 5665997; e-mail info@aiid.org; internet www .aiid.org; f. 2000; attached to Univ. of Amsterdam, Vrije Univ. Amsterdam; links the two univ. experts in int. devt and engages in policy debates; research on causes and consequences of poverty, human devt, governance and poverty, environment and devt, globalization and devt assistance.

Brabant Centre of Entrepreneurship: POB 513, 5600 MB Eindhoven; Multimedia-Paviljoen, Room 0.21, Horsten 1, 5612 AX Eindhoven; tel. (40) 4663320; e-mail info@ bc-e.nl; internet www.bc-e.nl; attached to Tilburg Univ.; Academic Dir Dr GEERT DUYSTERS; Business Dir KEES KOKKE.

Centre for Innovation Research: Faculty of Social and Behavioural Sciences, POB 90153, 5000 LE Eindhoven; Prisma Bldg, Warandelaan 2, 5037 AB Eindhoven; tel. (13) 4663057; fax (13) 4663002; e-mail cir@uvt.nl; internet www.tilburguniversity.nl/cir; attached to Tilburg Univ.; fundamental research on innovation; research themes incl. innovation strategy, org. of innovation, organizational learning; Dir Prof. Dr X. Y. F. MARTIN; Dir Prof. Dr M. T. H. MEEUS.

Centre for Development Studies (CDS): POB 800, Landleven 1, 9747 AD Groningen; tel. (50) 3637224; fax (50) 3633720; e-mail cds@rug.nl; internet www.rug.nl/cds/index; attached to Univ. of Groningen; fosters public debate on a wide range of topics varying from globalization, North–South relations and sustainable devt; Dir PIETER VAN HENSBROEK.

Centrum voor Justitiepastoraat (Interuniversity Centre for Prison Pastoral Studies): POB 90153, 5000 LE Tilburg; Prof.

Cobbenhagelaan 225, 5037 DB Tilburg; tel. (13) 4662609; e-mail info@centrumvoorjustitiepastoraat.nl; internet www.centrumvoorjustitiepastoraat.nl; f. 2009; attached to Tilburg Univ.; research and education on issues relevant for the work of prison chaplains, like restorative justice, reconciliation, humane detention, punishment; Dir Prof. Dr THEO W. A. DE WIT; Sec.-Gen. Drs RYAN A. T. VAN EIJK; publs *Twee heren dienen: Geestelijk verzorgers en hun beroepseer, Van kwaad verhalen.*

Competence Centre for Pension Research: POB 90153, 5000 LE Tilburg; Montesquieu Bldg, Warandelaan 2, Room M612, 5037 AB Tilburg; tel. (13) 4662412; fax (13) 4663073; e-mail frw.ccp@uvt.nl; internet www.tilburguniversity.nl/ccp; attached to Faculty of Law, Tilburg Univ.; research in the fields of tax and civil law aspects of pensions and other retirement provisions; Chair. Prof. Dr GERRY DIETVORST; Sec. TONIA NELEN.

European Banking Centre: Tilburg Univ., POB 90153, 5000 LE Tilburg; Koopmans Bldg, Room 3 16, Warandelaan 2, 5037 AB Tilburg; tel. (13) 4662468; e-mail ebc@uvt.nl; internet www.tilburguniversity.nl/ebc; attached to Tilburg Univ.; stimulates and disseminates banking research, with three essential areas of expertise: central banking and financial supervision, European banking and regulation, and int. banking and finance; Chair. Prof. Dr THORSTEN BECK.

European Institute of Retailing and Services Studies (EIRASS): POB 513, Vertigo 8.18, 5600 MB Eindhoven; tel. (40) 2472594; fax (40) 2438488; e-mail eirass@bwk.tue.nl; internet w3.bwk.tue.nl/nl/onderzoek/urban_planning/eirass; attached to Eindhoven Univ. of Technology; organizes confs; progress in retailing and consumer services (tourism, recreation, banking, aspects of transportation, etc.); Dir Prof. HARRY TIMMERMANS; Sec. LINDA VAN DE VEN.

European Research Institute in Service Science (ERISS): Room K 731, POB 90153, 5000 LE Tilburg; Warandelaan 2, 5037 AB Tilburg; tel. (13) 4663020; fax (13) 4663069; e-mail eriss@uvt.nl; internet www.tilburguniversity.nl/eriss; attached to Tilburg Univ.; research in innovation, service science with a focus on critical business process areas that span several knowledge-intensive business services within vertical industries; Chair. of Advisory Board Prof. Dr PIET RIBBERS; Scientific Dir Prof. Dr Ir M. P. PAPAZOGLOU; Man. Dir Prof. Dr W. J. A. M. VAN DEN HEUVEL; Sec. ALICE KLOOSTERHUIS.

European Values Study (EVS): Dept of Sociology, Tilburg Univ., POB 90153, 5000 LE Tilburg; School of Social and Behavioural Sciences, Tilburg Univ., Prisma Bldg, Warandelaan 2, 5037 AB Tilburg; tel. (13) 4662554; fax (13) 4663002; e-mail evs@uvt.nl; internet www.europeanvaluesstudy.eu; f. 1981; attached to Tilburg Univ.; research on basic human values; provides insights into the ideas, beliefs, preferences, attitudes, values and opinions of citizens all over Europe; how Europeans think about life, family, work, religion, politics and society; Chair. Prof. Dr PAUL DE GRAAF; Sec. Dr LOEK HALMAN.

EXPres: Van der Boechorststraat 9, 1081 Amsterdam; e-mail expres@fbw.vu.nl; internet www.expertisecentrum-expres.nl; f. 1989; attached to Vrije Univ. Amsterdam; research on rehabilitation, ergonomics and sports.

Groningen Research Institute for the Study of Culture (ICOG): POB 716, 9700 AS Groningen; Oude Kijk in 't Jatstraat 26, 9712 EK Groningen; tel. (50) 3635918; fax (50) 3635821; e-mail icog@rug.nl; internet www.rug.nl/let/onderzoek/onderzoekinstituten/icog; attached to Faculty of Arts, Univ. of Groningen; research on study of cultural processes, their manifestations and discussion of these subjects in Europe, Americas, E Mediterranean, Asian regions; Dir Prof. Dr GOFFE JENSMA.

Het Zijlstra Center: De Boelelaan 1105, 1081 HV Amsterdam; tel. (20) 5989865; e-mail info@hetzijlstracenter.nl; internet www.feweb.vu.nl/nl/afdelingen-en-instituten/het-zijlstra-center; f. 2009; attached to Univ. of Amsterdam; research focuses on management and operations of non-profits and govts that focus on solving social problems; contributes results to improvement of management of govts and civil society orgs; Dir Prof. Dr G. D. MINDERMAN; Sec. ANJA VAN EIJK.

iCRiSP—Centre for Conflict, Risk and Safety Perception: Citadel H 444, POB 217, 7500 AE Enschede; Citadel Bldg, H 444, Drienerlolaan 5, 7522 NB Enschede; tel. (53) 4896052; fax (53) 4892388; e-mail icrisp@utwente.nl; internet www.utwente.nl/ibr/icrisp; f. 2009; attached to Univ. of Twente; focuses on the implementation of knowledge from social and behavioural sciences regarding issues of conflict, risk, safety in public and private sectors of society; Dir Prof. Dr ELLEN GIEBELS; Dir Dr JAN GUTTELING.

Institute for Sport & Leisure: Univ. of Twente, bld. CTW - Z-115, Drienerlolaan 5, 7522 NB Enschede; tel. (53) 4893606; e-mail info@sportandleisure.nl; internet www.sportandleisure.nl; attached to Univ. of Twente; innovation, devt, prototyping, engineering for products within the field of sport and leisure.

Instituut voor Bedrijfs- en Industriële Statistiek (IBIS) (Institute for Business and Industrial Statistics): Plantage Muidergracht 12, 1018 TV Amsterdam; tel. (20) 5255203; e-mail info@ibisuva.nl; internet www.ibisuva.nl; f. 1994; attached to Univ. of Amsterdam; statistical methodology, business economic context of quality and efficiency improvement; Man. Dir Prof. Dr RONALD J. M. M. DOES.

International Victimology Institute Tilburg (INTERVICT): Room M734, POB 90153, 5000 LE Tilburg; Montesquieu Bldg, 7th Fl., Warandelaan 2, 5037 AB Tilburg; tel. (13) 4663526; fax (13) 4663546; e-mail intervict@uvt.nl; internet www.tilburguniversity.nl/intervict; attached to Tilburg Univ.; research areas incl. victims of abuse of power, crime and disaster; rights of victims; psychological effects of victimization; help provided to victims; social reactions to victims; Dir Prof. MARC S. GROENHUIJSEN; Deputy Dir Assoc. Prof. RIANNE M. LETSCHERT; Gen. Man. BARBARA M. VAN GORP.

IPIT Instituut voor Maatschappelijke Veiligheidsvraagstukken: Universiteit Twente, POB 217, 7500 AE Enschede; Capitool 15, Room C-201, Enschede; tel. (53) 4893280; fax (53) 4892159; e-mail ipit@bbt.utwente.nl; internet www.ipit.nl; attached to Univ. of Twente; law, public safety studies, law, risk analysis, risk management; research incl. functioning of insecurity and society, public safety maintenance system; Dir Prof. Dr M. JUNGER; Sec. J.L.M. (ANNETTE) VAN DER TUUK.

IVA Beleidsonderzoek en Advies: POB 90153, 5000 LE Tilburg; Campus Tilburg Univ., Bldg T, Warandelaan 2, 5037 AB Tilburg; tel. (13) 4668466; fax (13) 4668477; e-mail iva@uvt.nl; internet www.iva.nl; f. 1957; attached to Tilburg Univ.; applied scientific research, consultancy, implementation concerning current social devts, particularly in the domains of education, care and welfare, security, art, media and culture, labour and organizational issues; Pres. Prof. Dr MARC VERMEULEN; Man. Dir and Vice-Pres. MYLÈNE ZWAANS; Exec. Sec. ANNELIES VAN LEEUWEN.

IVO—Instituut voor Ontwikkelingsvraagstukken/Instituto de Estudios Para El Desarrollo (Development Research Institute): POB 90153, 5000 LE Tilburg; Tias Bldg, Office T-231, Warandelaan 2, 5037 AB Tilburg; tel. (13) 4662264; fax (13) 4663015; e-mail secr.ivo@uvt.nl; internet www.uvt.nl/ivo; f. 1963; attached to Tilburg Univ.; applied socio-economic research, training and capacity building in support of poverty alleviation in developing countries; Dir GERARD DE GROOT; Man. MARIA JOSÉ RODIL.

Kohnstamm Instituut (Kohnstamm Institute): POB 94208, 1090 GE Amsterdam; Plantage Muidergracht 24, 1018 TV Amsterdam; tel. (20) 5251226; fax (20) 5254029; e-mail secr@kohnstamm.uva.nl; internet www.kohnstamminstituut.uva.nl; f. fmrly as SCO-Kohnstamm Institute, present status 2009; attached to Univ. of Amsterdam; research areas incl. child rearing, child welfare, education; Man. Dir Drs J. E. KRAMER; Scientific Dir Drs G. LEDOUX; Deputy Dir Drs M. VAN ERP.

Kosmopolis Institute: POB 797, 3500 AT Utrecht; Univ. for Humanistics, Kromme Nieuwegracht 29, 3512 HD Utrecht; tel. (30) 2390100; e-mail kosmopolis@uvh.nl; internet www.uvh.nl; f. 2004; attached to Univ. for Humanistics; focuses on interdisciplinary teaching; training, research, networking on cosmopolitan dimensions of humanism in the world; Gen. Dir Prof. Dr HENK MANSCHOT; Deputy Dir Dr CAROLINE SURANSKY; Exec. Sec. DOROTHÉ VAN DRIEL.

Netspar, Network for Studies on Pensions, Ageing and Retirement: POB 90153, 5000 MB Tilburg; Tilburg Univ. Campus, Tias Bldg, Warandelaan 2, 5037 AB Tilburg; tel. (13) 4662109; fax (13) 4663066; e-mail secretariaat@netspar.nl; internet www.netspar.nl; f. 2005; attached to Tilburg Univ.; research areas incl. ageing, pensions, retirement; Chair. Prof. Dr FRANK VAN DER DUYN SCHOUTEN; Scientific Dir THEO NIJMAN; Man. Dir DOMINIQUE DE VET; publ. *Netspar Magazine* (2 a year).

Nexus Instituut (Nexus Institute): POB 90153, 5000 LE Tilburg; Tilburg Univ., Room T203-209, Warandelaan 2, 5037 AB Tilburg; tel. (13) 4663450; fax (13) 4663434; e-mail info@nexus-instituut.nl; internet www.nexus-instituut.nl; f. 1994; attached to Tilburg Univ.; centre for intellectual reflection; organizes confs and lectures; Chair. of Supervisory Board Dr WIM VAN DEN GOORBERGH; Pres. and CEO ROB RIEMEN; Vice-Pres. KIRSTEN WALGREEN; publ. *Nexus* (3 a year).

Nikos—Dutch Institute for Knowledge Intensive Entrepreneurship: Univ. of Twente, POB 217, 7500 AE Enschede; Drienerlolaan 5, 7522 NB Enschede; tel. (53) 4894512; fax (53) 4893919; e-mail nikos@mb.utwente.nl; internet www.utwente.nl/mb/nikos; attached to Univ. of Twente; innovative entrepreneurship, int. management, marketing, strategic management; Scientific Dir Prof. Dr AARD J. GROEN; Sec. GLORIA ROSSINI.

Onderzoekscentrum Preventie Overgewicht Zwolle (Research Centre for the Prevention of Overweight Zwolle): VU-Windesheim, Campus 2–6, POB 10090, 8000 GB Zwolle; tel. (88) 4699096; e-mail preventieovergewicht@windesheim.nl; research on designing, implementing, evaluating and disseminating knowledge related to prevention of obesity in 0–19-year-old children; Man. Dir Dr SASKIA VAN HELDEN.

Rathenau Instituut (Rathenau Institute): POB 95366, 2509 CJ The Hague; Anna van Saksenlaan 51, 2593 HW The Hague; tel. (70) 3421542; fax (70) 3633488; e-mail info@rathenau.nl; internet www.rathenau.nl; f. 1986 as Netherlands Org. for Technology Assessment, present name 1994; attached to Royal Netherlands Acad. of Arts and Sciences; supports social and political opinion-forming on issues arising from scientific and technological devt; Chair. Drs SANDER DEKKER; Sec. Drs JAN STAMAN.

Research Center voor Examinering en Certificering (RCEC) (Research Center for Examinations and Certification (RCEC)): POB 217, 7500 AE Enschede; tel. (53) 4893555; fax (53) 4894239; e-mail rcec@gw.utwente.nl; internet www.rcec.nl; f. 2007; attached to Univ. of Twente; stimulates and facilitates ind. research into examinations and certification; conducts research projects for public and private orgs; gives training in educational measurement; disseminates information by organizing confs on issues in examinations; Dir BERNARD P. VELDKAMP; Dir Dr PIET F. SANDERS.

Research Institute for Flexicurity, Labour Market Dynamics and Social Cohesion (ReflecT): Tilburg Univ., S 424, POB 90153, 5000 LE Tilburg; Simon Bldg (entrance at Prof. Verbernelaan), 4th Fl., Room S 424, 5000 LE Tilburg; tel. (13) 4662181; e-mail reflect@uvt.nl; internet www.tilburguniversity.nl/reflect; attached to Tilburg Univ.; combines legal, economic, sociological and psychological approaches and adopts a multi-level perspective in studying the interplay between various regulatory and institutional levels in society: the European/int., nat., sector and company/individual level; Dir Prof. A. C. J. M. (TON) WILTHAGEN; Sec. A. I. (ANNET) VAN HUIJKELOM.

Tilburg Centre of Finance: Loes de Groot, K 916, POB 90153, 5000 LE Tilburg; tel. (13) 4663041; fax (13) 4662875; e-mail tcf@uvt.nl; internet www.tilburguniversity.edu/research/institutes-and-research-groups/tcf; attached to Tilburg Univ.; research areas incl. actuarial profession, finance, governance and supervision; Mem. of Board Prof. Dr BAS WERKER; Mem. of Board Prof. Dr FRANK DE JONG; Mem. of Board Prof. Dr FRANS DE ROON.

Tilburg Sustainability Center (TSC): Tilburg Univ., POB 90153, 5000 LE Tilburg; Tilburg Univ., Koopmans Bldg, K405, Warandelaan 2, 5037 AB Tilburg; tel. (13) 4664148; e-mail tsc@uvt.nl; internet www.tilburguniversity.nl/tsc; f. 2009; attached to Tilburg Univ.; collaborative research between economists, legal scientists, sociologists and related disciplines on fundamental and applied problems in relation to sustainability; Scientific Dir Prof. Dr AART DE ZEEUW; Man. Dir Drs Ir HILDE BAERT.

Transport Infrastructure and Logistics (TRAIL) Research School: POB 5017, 2600 GA Delft; Delft Transport Centre, Kluyverweg 4, 2629 HT Delft; tel. (15) 2786046; fax (15) 2784333; e-mail info@rstrail.nl; internet www.rstrail.nl; f. 1997; collaboration of five Dutch univ.; research in mobility, transport, logistics, traffic, infrastructure and transport systems; Scientific Dir H. L. BEN IMMERS; Managing Dir and Deputy Scientific Dir VINCENT A. W. J. MARCHAU.

Tranzo—Scientific Centre for Care and Welfare: Tilburg School of Social and Behavioural Sciences, Tilburg Univ., POB 90153, 5000 LE Tilburg; Room T 515, Tias Bldg, Warandelaan 2, 5037 AB Tilburg; tel. (13) 4662969; fax (13) 4663637; e-mail tranzo@uvt.nl; internet www.tilburguniversity.edu/tranzo; attached to Tilburg Univ.; fundamental and applied research in care and services; Chair. Prof. Dr HENK GARRETSEN.

AGRICULTURE, FISHERIES AND VETERINARY SCIENCE

Alterra: POB 47, 6700 AA Wageningen; Droevendaalsesteeg 3, Bldg 101, 6708 PB Wageningen; tel. (317) 480700; fax (317) 419000; e-mail info.alterra@wur.nl; internet www.alterra.wur.nl; f. 2000 by merger of DLO Winand Staring Centre for Integrated Land, Soil and Water Research, Institut voor Bos- en Natuuronderzoek and part of DLO-Instituut voor Agrobiologisch Onderzoek; attached to Wageningen Univ. and Research Centre; practical and scientific research in disciplines related to the green world and the sustainable use of our living environment: knowledge of water, nature, biodiversity, climate, landscape, forest, ecology, environment, soil, landscape and spatial planning, geo-information, remote sensing, flora and fauna, urban green, man and soc. etc.; Man. Dir Ir C. T. (KEES) SLINGERLAND; Dir for Operations Ir AUKE H. DE BRUIN; publ. *Alterra Scientific Contributions*.

Centre for Development Innovation: POB 88, 6700 AB Wageningen; Lawickse Allee 11, Bldg 425, 6711 AN Wageningen; tel. (317) 486800; fax (317) 486801; e-mail info.cdi@wur.nl; internet www.cdi.wur.nl; attached to Wageningen Univ. and Research Centre; works on processes of innovation and change in areas of secure and healthy food, adaptive agriculture, sustainable markets and ecosystem governance; Dir Dr JIM WOODHILL; Deputy Dir WOUTER LEEN HIJWEEGE; Sec. ANNETTE VAN 'T HULL.

Food & Biobased Research: POB 17, 6700 AA Wageningen; Wageningen Campus, Bornse Weilanden 9, Bldg 118, 6708 WG Wageningen; tel. (317) 480084; fax (317) 483011; e-mail info.fbr@wur.nl; internet www.fbr.wur.nl; attached to Wageningen Univ. and Research Centre; research and devt org. for sustainable innovation in areas of healthy food, sustainable fresh food chains and biobased products; Man. Dir Prof. Dr RAOUL J. BINO; Dir for Operations Drs INGE T. J. GRIMM.

IMARES: POB 68, 1970 AB IJmuiden; Haringkade 1, 1976 CP IJmuiden; tel. (317) 480900; fax (317) 487326; e-mail imares@wur.nl; internet www.imares.wur.nl; f. 1912; attached to Wageningen Univ. and Research Centre; concentrates on research into strategic and applied marine ecology in areas covering aquaculture, coastal zone management, ecology, ecosystem based economy, environmental conservation and protection, fisheries, marine governance; Dir DICK POUWELS; Dir MARTIN SCHOLTEN.

International Institute for Land Reclamation and Improvement (Alterra–ILRI): POB 47, 6700 AA Wageningen; Droevendaalsesteeg 3, Wageningen; tel. (317) 495584; fax (317) 419000; e-mail ilri@ilri.nl; f. 1955; collects and disseminates information on land reclamation and improvement and undertakes supplementary research work; postgraduate courses; 30 staff; Dir Ir C. B. DE ZEEUW.

LEI: POB 29703, 2502 LS The Hague; Alexanderveld 5, 2585 DB The Hague; tel. (70) 3358330; fax (70) 3615624; e-mail informatie.lei@wur.nl; internet www.lei.wur.nl; f. 1940; attached to Wageningen Univ. and Research Centre; develops economic expertise for govt and industry in the field of food, agriculture and natural environment; offers a solid basis for socially and strategically justifiable policy choices; library of 20,000 vols; Dir-Gen. Prof. Dr Ir RUUD B. M. HUIRNE; Dir for Operations Ir LAAN C. VAN STAALDUINEN; Sec. R. VAN DEN BERG; Sec. S. FONTIJN; publ. *Leidraad* (6 a year).

Livestock Research: POB 65, 8200 AB Lelystad; Edelhertweg 15, 8219 PK Lelystad; tel. (320) 238238; fax (320) 238050; e-mail info.livestockresearch@wur.nl; internet www.livestockresearch.wur.nl; f. 1970, present status 2008, present name 2009; attached to Wageningen Univ. and Research Centre; 9 experimental farms in the Netherlands; develops knowledge, solutions for contemporary issues in the livestock sector; areas incl. animal nutrition, animal behaviour and welfare, genetics and genomics, innovation processes, livestock and environment; 140 mems; library of 20,000 vols; Gen. Dir Ir PAUL W. J. VRIESEKOOP; Man. for Operations JAN DIJK; publs *Rapporten* (6 a year), *Publikaties* (10 a year), *Jaarverslag* (1 a year), *Periodiek* (6 a year).

Nederlands Agronomisch-Historisch Instituut (Dutch Institute of Agricultural History): Oude Kijk in 't Jatstraat 26, 9712 EK Groningen; POB 716, 9700 AS Groningen; tel. (50) 3637672; e-mail nahi@rug.nl; internet www.rug.nl/let/nahi; f. 1949, present status 1998; advances study of and facilitates scientific research in agricultural history by maintaining institute at Groningen Univ. and Wageningen Univ. and Research Centre; library of 12,000 vols; Dir Prof. Dr PIM KOOIJ; Man. Dir Dr ERWIN H. KAREL; publ. *Historia Agriculturae* (1 or 2 a year).

Plant Research International: POB 16, 6700 AA Wageningen; Droevendaalsesteeg 1, Radix (Bldg 107), 6708 PB Wageningen; tel. (317) 486001; fax (317) 418094; e-mail info.plant@wur.nl; internet www.pri.wur.nl; f. 1991; attached to Wageningen Univ. and Research Centre; strategic and applied research in agrosystems, bioinformatics, crop ecology, crop protection, genetics and reproduction, genomics, metabolomics, proteomics; offers unique new perspectives for govts and private cos, for agriculture and horticulture, and for rural and environmental devt; library of 50,000 vols; Dir-Gen. Dr ERNST VAN DEN ENDE; Dir for Management Ir TON VAN SCHEPPINGEN; publs *Descriptive List of Fruit Varieties* (every 5 years), *Descriptive List of Ornamental Crops* (every 2 years), *Descriptive List of Trees* (every 5 years), *Descriptive List of Varieties of Field Crops*, *Descriptive List of Varieties of Vegetable Crops* (1 a year).

Plantenziektenkundige Dienst (Plant Protection Service): Geertjesweg 15, POB 9102, 6700 HC Wageningen; tel. (317) 496911; fax (317) 421701; f. 1899; activities incl. phytosanitary inspection of plants, issue of plant health certificates and design of laws for disease and pest prevention and control, integrated plant protection, diagnostics of diseases and pests; location offices, 3 per district; Dir Prof. Dr. L. VAN VLOTEN-DOTING; publs *Newsletter* (in Dutch, 8 a year), *Verslagen en Mededelingen Plantenziektenkundige Dienst* (Reports and Communications of the Plant Protection Service).

ARCHITECTURE AND TOWN PLANNING

Netherlands Graduate School of Urban and Regional Research: POB 80115, 3508 TC Utrecht; Willem C. van Unnikgebouw, Room 725A, Heidelberglaan 2, 3584 CS Utrecht; tel. (30) 2532250; fax (30) 2532037; e-mail nethur.geo@uu.nl; internet www.nethur.nl; urban, regional, housing research; jt initiative of 6 univs; Scientific

Dir Prof. Dr PIETER HOOIMEIJER; Dir for Education Dr BAS SPIERINGS.

Onderzoeksinstituut OTB (OTB Research Institute for the Built Environment): POB 5030, 2600 GA Delft; Jaffalaan 9, Bldg 30, 2628 BX Delft; tel. (15) 2783005; fax (15) 2784422; e-mail mailbox@otb.tudelft.nl; internet www.otb2.tudelft.nl; attached to Delft Univ. of Technology; research in the field of housing, construction, built environment; Academic Dir Prof. Dr PETER J. BOELHOUWER; Dir Prof. WILLEM KORTHALS ALTES; publ. *European Journal of Spatial Development*.

ECONOMICS, LAW AND POLITICS

Amsterdam Center for Entrepreneurship: Univ. of Amsterdam, Roetersstraat 11, Room E 2.28, 1018 WB Amsterdam; tel. (20) 5254110; fax (20) 5255652; e-mail ace-feb@uva.nl; internet www.ace-uva.nl; attached to Univ. of Amsterdam; research focuses on understanding the determinants of successful entrepreneurship; Scientific Dir CELINE MIRJAM VAN PRAAG; Exec. Dir ERIK BOER.

Amsterdam Center for Finance and Insurance: Finance Group, UvA Business School, Faculty of Economics and Business, Univ. of Amsterdam, Roetersstraat 11, 1018 WB Amsterdam; tel. (20) 5254256; fax (20) 5255285; e-mail acfi@uva.nl; internet www.feb.uva.nl/acfi; attached to Univ. of Amsterdam; researches in areas of quantitative finance and insurance and stimulates interaction between practitioners and academic researchers; Dir ANTOON PELSSER.

Amsterdam Center for Law & Economics (ACLE): Universiteit van Amsterdam, Roetersstraat 11, 1018 WB Amsterdam; tel. (20) 5254162; fax (20) 5255318; e-mail acle@uva.nl; internet www.acle.nl; attached to Univ. of Amsterdam; research areas incl. foundations of law and economics, competition and regulation, corporate governance and law; Dir Prof. Dr ARNOUD BOOT.

Amsterdam Centre for Corporate Finance (ACCF): Chandra Doest, Roetersstraat 11, 1018 WB Amsterdam; tel. (20) 5254162; fax (20) 5255318; e-mail office@accf.nl; internet www.accf.nl; promotes research on the interface between financial theory and corporate policy; provides a forum for dialogue between academics and practitioners; Dir Prof. Dr ARNOUD BOOT; Dir Prof. Dr JOSEPH MCCAHERY.

Amsterdam Centre for Environmental Law and Sustainability (ACELS): POB 1030, 1000 BA Amsterdam; Oudemanhuispoort 4–6, 1000 BA Amsterdam; tel. (20) 5253075; fax (20) 5254742; e-mail milieurecht-fdr@uva.nl; internet www.jur.uva.nl/cvm; f. 1988, fmrly Centre for Environmental Law, present name 2010; attached to Faculty of Law, Univ. of Amsterdam; research focuses on environmental law as a means of orienting market processes towards sustainable devt, especially problem of climate change; Dir Prof. ROSA UYLENBURG.

Amsterdam Centre for International Law (ACIL): Faculty of Law, Univ. of Amsterdam, POB 1030, 1000 BA Amsterdam; Faculty of Law, Univ. of Amsterdam, Oudemanhuispoort 4, 1012 CN Amsterdam; tel. (20) 5253361; fax (20) 5253495; e-mail acil-fdr@uva.nl; internet www.jur.uva.nl/aciluk/home.cfm; attached to Faculty of Law, Univ. of Amsterdam; research on int. constitutional law (incl. human rights law), int. responsibility, int. criminal justice, reception of int. law in domestic legal order; Exec. Dir Dr YVONNE DONDERS; publ. *Legal Issues of Economic Integration*.

Amsterdam Centre for Research in International Finance (CIFRA): Univ. of Amsterdam, Business Studies, Finance Group, Room E4.26, Roetersstraat 11, 1018 WB Amsterdam; tel. (20) 5254256; fax (20) 5255285; e-mail j.a.p.gompel@uva.nl; internet www1.fee.uva.nl/fm/cifra/cifra.htm; f. 1998; research areas incl. int. capital market integration and corporate finance and banking; Dir Prof. Dr ENRICO PEROTTI; Dir Prof. Dr STIJN CLAESSENS; Sec. JOLINDA GOMPEL.

Amsterdam Centre for Service Innovation (AMSI): Amsterdam Business School, Faculty of Economics and Business, Univ. of Amsterdam, Roetersstraat 11, 1018 WB Amsterdam; tel. (20) 5258620; fax (20) 5254177; e-mail w.vanderaa@uva.nl; internet www.abs.uva.nl/amsi/home.cfm; f. 2008; attached to Univ. of Amsterdam; research focuses on management of innovation in service firms and service orgs; Dir Dr WIETZE VAN DER AA; Chair. Prof. Dr M. W. DE JONG.

Amsterdam Institute for Business and Economic Research Foundation (AMBER): Main Bldg, VU Univ., 5th Fl., Room 5A-38, De Boelelaan 1105, 1081 HV Amsterdam; tel. (20) 5986080; fax (20) 5986127; e-mail amber@feweb.vu.nl; internet www.feweb.vu.nl/amber; attached to Faculty of Economics and Business Admin., VU Univ. Amsterdam; facilitates research for faculty of economics and business admin.; supports application for nat. and int. grants for research; Man. Dir Dr A. M. GROENENDIJK; Chair. Prof. Dr E. J. BARTELSMAN.

Amsterdams Instituut voor ArbeidsStudies (AIAS) (Amsterdam Institute for Advanced Labour Studies): Univ. of Amsterdam, Plantage Muidergracht 12, 1018 TV Amsterdam; tel. (20) 5254199; fax (20) 5254301; e-mail aias@uva.nl; internet www.uva-aias.net; f. 1998; attached to Univ. of Amsterdam; combines law, economics, sociology, psychology, occupational health studies for labour studies; Dir Dr WIEMER SALVERDA.

CentER Applied Research: Tilburg Univ., POB 90153, 5000 LE Tilburg; tel. (13) 4662347; fax (13) 4668780; internet www.tilburguniversity.nl/center-ar; f. 1931; attached to Tilburg Univ.; applied economic research; Dir Prof. Dr H. FLEUREN; Dir Drs J. DE RANITZ.

Center for Company Law: Tilburg Univ., Tilburg Law School, Dept of Business Law, POB 90153, 5000 LE Tilburg; Montesquieu Bldg, Warandelaan 2, 5037 AB Tilburg; tel. (13) 4662672; fax (13) 4662182; e-mail a.huijben@tilburguniversity.edu; internet www.tilburguniversity.edu/ccl; attached to Tilburg Univ.; research in the fields of corporate, property, securities, tax, insolvency law; also focuses on doing research in nat., int. and European aspects of the 'firm', its various legal forms, financing, governance, reorganization and accounting; Dir Assoc. Prof. GER J. H. VAN DER SANGEN; Dir Prof. Dr P. H. J. ESSERS; Dir Prof. M. J. G. C. RAAIMAKERS; Management Asst ANJA M. H. J. HUIJBEN-VAN DER ZANDEN.

Center for e-Government Studies (CFES): Univ. of Twente, Cubicus Bldg, POB 217, 7500 AE Enschede; Univ. of Twente, Cubicus Bldg, Drienerlolaan 5, 7522 NB Enschede; tel. (53) 4893299; fax (53) 4894259; e-mail an.vandijk@utwente.nl; internet www.utwente.nl/ibr/cfes; f. 2009; attached to Univ. of Twente; research on the electronic govt; advises governmental agencies, policy makers, politicians, stakeholders; Dir Prof. Dr JAN VAN DIJK.

CentER for Economic Research: POB 90153, 5000 LE Tilburg; tel. (13) 4663050; fax (13) 4663066; e-mail center@uvt.nl; internet center.uvt.nl; f. 1988, present status 1992; attached to Tilburg Univ.; academic research into economics, econometrics, finance and accounting, information management, marketing, operations research, organization; Dir Prof. Dr F. A. DE ROON.

Center for Nonlinear Dynamics in Economics and Finance (CeNDEF): Faculty of Economics and Econometrics, Univ. of Amsterdam, Roetersstraat 11, 1018 WB Amsterdam; tel. (20) 5254217; fax (20) 5254349; e-mail kesec-feb@uva.nl; internet www1.fee.uva.nl/cendef; f. 1998; research areas incl. non-linear dynamics in economics and finance; Dir Prof. Dr CARS HOMMES.

Center for Research in Experimental Economics and Political Decision-Making (CREED): Faculty of Economics and Econometrics, Univ. of Amsterdam, Bldg E2, 6th Fl., Roetersstraat 11, Amsterdam; tel. (20) 5254126; fax (20) 5255283; e-mail creed-fee@uva.nl; internet www1.fee.uva.nl/creed; attached to Univ. of Amsterdam; research programmes incl. economics of political decision making, bounded rationality and institutions, experimental economics; Dir ARTHUR SCHRAM.

Centre for Transboundary Legal Development: Tilburg Univ., POB 90153, 5000 LE Tilburg; Tilburg Univ., Montesquieu Bldg, 5th Fl., Warandelaan 2, 5037 AB Tilburg; tel. (13) 4668033; fax (13) 4668047; e-mail frw.eip.secretariaat@uvt.nl; internet www.tilburguniversity.nl/ctld; f. 2000; attached to Tilburg Univ.; ethics and jurisprudence, history of law, int. and European law, philosophy of law, social law; Dir Prof WILLEM VAN GENUGTEN; Coordinator Asst Prof. ANNA MEIJKNECHT.

Centraal Bureau voor de Statistiek (Central Bureau of Statistics): POB 24500, 2490 HA The Hague; Henri Faasdreef 312, 2492 JP The Hague; tel. (70) 3373800; fax (70) 3877429; e-mail infoserv@cbs.nl; internet www.cbs.nl; f. 1899, present status 2004; economic and social statistical research; br office in Heerlen; library not accessible to public; library of 410,000 vols, 100,000 microfiche; Dir-Gen. G. VAN DER VEEN; Deputy Dir G. BRUINOOGE; publs *Historical Statistics of the Netherlands*, *Statistical Yearbook of the Netherlands*, *Statistisch Bulletin* (52 a year).

Center for International Cooperation (CIS): De Boelelaan 1105, 1081 HV Amsterdam; Metropolitan Bldg, 4th Fl., Buitenveldertselaan 3–7, 1082 VA Amsterdam; tel. (20) 5989090; fax (20) 5989095; e-mail cis@vu.nl; internet www.cis.vu.nl; attached to VU Univ. Amsterdam; int. devt cooperation with partners in Asia, Africa and Latin America; contributes to capacity bldg efforts in developing countries; Dir KEES KOUWENAAR.

Centre for the Study of Democracy (CSD): Univ. of Twente, POB 217, 7500 AE Enschede; tel. (53) 4893270; fax (53) 4892590; e-mail j.k.vanderwoude@utwente.nl; internet www.utwente.nl/mb/csd; attached to Univ. of Twente; research on functioning of contemporary democracies; provides insight on innovation of democratic institutions; Dir Prof. Dr J. J. A. THOMASSEN; Exec. Dir Dr A. K. WARNTJEN; Exec. Dir Dr M. ROSEMA; Sec. JANINE VAN DER WOUDE.

Centrum van Procesrecht (Centre for Legal Procedure and Litigation): Tilburg Univ., POB 90153, 5000 LE Tilburg; Tilburg Univ., Montesquieu Bldg, Warandelaan 2, 5037 AB Tilburg; tel. (13) 4662254; fax (13) 4668102; e-mail m.j.w.dejong@uvt.nl; internet www.uvt.nl/cvp; attached to Tilburg Univ.; research in criminal law; Dir Prof. Dr

C. J. C. F. FIJNAUT; Dir Prof. M. S. GROEN-HUIJSEN.

Centrum voor Recht, Bestuur en Samen-leving (CRBS) (Centre for Law, Administration and Society): POB 716, 9700 AS Groningen; Harmonie, bldg 11, Oude Kijk in't Jatstraat 26, 9712 EK Groningen; tel. (50) 3636145; fax (50) 3636735; e-mail b.m.e .hallebeek@rug.nl; internet www.rug.nl/crbs/ index; f. 1990; attached to Faculty of Law, Univ. of Groningen; 3 legal areas transcending, interdisciplinary and internationally orientated research lines are brought together in 3 research centres; Admin. Dir Dr JOOP HOUTMAN; Academic Dir Prof. Dr O. COUWENBERG.

Economics Network for Competition and Regulation (ENCORE): Faculty of Economics, Univ. of Amsterdam, Roeters-straat 11, 1018 WB Amsterdam; tel. (20) 5257162; fax (20) 5255318; e-mail info@ encore.nl; internet www.encore.nl; f. 2003; attached to Faculty of Economics, Univ. of Amsterdam; int. research network; researches on available scientific knowledge on competition and regulation to benefit and improve policy making; Dir Prof. Dr MAAR-TEN PIETER SCHINKEL.

ECORYS: POB 4175, 3006 AD Rotterdam; Watermanweg 44, 3067 GG Rotterdam; tel. (10) 4538800; fax (10) 4530768; e-mail netherlands@ecorys.com; internet www .ecorys.nl; f. 1929 as Netherlands Economic Institute (NEI), present name and status 2000; economic research and policy advice; consulting and training; programme management and implementation; monitoring and evaluation; areas covered incl. economics and competitiveness, regions, cities and real estate, transport, mobility and infrastructure, social policy and govt; Man. Dir WIM SPIT.

Fiscaal Instituut Tilburg (FIT) (Tilburg Institute of Fiscal Law): POB 90153, 5000 LE Tilburg; Warandelaan 2, Montesquieu Bldg, Room M612, 5037 AB Tilburg; tel. (13) 4662412; fax (13) 4663073; e-mail fit@uvt .nl; internet www.uvt.nl/fit; f. 1968; attached to Tilburg Univ.; research in the field of Dutch and int. taxation, tax law system.

Groningen Centre for Law and Govern-ance: Attn. Eleonora Goljan, POB 716, 9700 AS Groningen; Harmonie bldg, Oude Kijk in 't Jatstraat 26, 9712 EK Groningen; tel. (50) 3635685; e-mail gcl@rug.nl; internet www .rug.nl/gcl; f. 2008; attached to Faculty of Law, Univ. of Groningen; contributes to legal research into the relationship between public and private interests; focuses on the interaction between public and private law and the function of law in the regulatory state; Academic Dir Prof. Dr AURELIA COLOMBI CIACCHI; Academic Dir Prof. Dr LEON VER-STAPPEN; Sec. ELEONORA GOLJAN.

Groningen Centre of Energy Law: POB 716, 9700 AS Groningen; tel. (50) 3635736; e-mail m.m.roggenkamp@rug.nl; internet www.rug.nl/rechten/onderzoek/gcel/index; f. 2007; attached to Faculty of Law, Univ. of Groningen; research covers the entire energy chain ('from well to burner tip') and incl. all legislation and regulation applying to the production, transmission and supply of energy, promotion of renewable energy sources, need to secure energy supply as well as issues concerning climate change and environmental protection; Dir Prof. MARTHA ROGGENKAMP.

Hugo Sinzheimer Instituut (HSUIK) (Hugo Sinzheimer Institute): Law Faculty, Univ. of Amsterdam, Oudemanhuispoort 4–6, 1012 CN Amsterdam; tel. (20) 5253400; fax (20) 5253648; e-mail hsi-fdr@uva.nl; internet www.jur.uva.nl/hsuik; f. 1993; attached to

Law Faculty, Univ. of Amsterdam; coordinates, implements and stimulates interdisciplinary research in labour law and social security law; Scientific Dir Dr ROBERT KNEGT.

Institute for Innovation and Govern-ance Studies (IGS): Univ. of Twente, POB 217, 7500 AE Enschede; Univ. of Twente, Bldg Ravelijn, 7522 NH Enschede; tel. (53) 4893423; fax (53) 4892159; e-mail info@igs .utwente.nl; internet www.utwente.nl/igs; attached to Univ. of Twente; faculty of behavioural sciences, engineering technology, geo-information science and earth observation; multi-disciplinary research, postgraduate research training in the field of governance and management of technological and social innovation; Scientific Dir Prof. Dr KEES AARTS; Exec. Dir SJOERD VAN TONGEREN; Sec. MARCIA CLIFFORD.

Institute for Management Research: POB 9108, 6500 HK Nijmegen; Thomas van Aquinostraat 5.0.39, 6525 GD Nijmegen; tel. (24) 3615995; fax (24) 3611568; e-mail imr@ fm.ru.nl; internet www.ru.nl/imr; attached to Radbound Univ. Nijmegen; conducts fundamental and applied research on devt, design and effectiveness of the public and private structures that regulate, govern, manage human interaction.

Institute of Social Studies: see under Colleges.

Instituut voor Informatierecht (Institute for Information Law): Kloveniersburgwal 48, 1012 CX Amsterdam; Korte Spinhuissteeg 3, 1012 CG Amsterdam; tel. (20) 5253406; fax (20) 5253033; e-mail ivir@ivir.nl; internet www.ivir.nl; f. 1989; attached to Faculty of Law, Univ. of Amsterdam; information society related to legal areas such as advertising law, commercial speech, digital consumer issues, domain names, freedom of expression, intellectual property law, internet regulation, media law, privacy, patents, telecommunications and broadcasting regulation, etc.

International Institute for Asian Stud-ies: POB 9500, 2300 RA Leiden; Rapenburg 59, 2311 GJ Leiden; tel. (71) 5272227; fax (71) 5274162; e-mail iias@iias.nl; internet www.iias.nl; f. 1993 by Royal Netherlands Acad. of Arts and Sciences and 3 Dutch univs; postdoctoral research in humanities and social sciences; promotes interdisciplinary and comparative study of Asia and nat. and int. cooperation; Chair. Prof. H. SCHULTE NORDHOLT; Dir PHILIPPE PEYCAM; Deputy Dir MANON OSSEWEIJER; Sec. AMPARO DE VOGEL.

Nederlands Instituut voor Internation-ale Betrekkingen 'Clingendael' (Netherlands Institute of International Relations 'Clingendael'): POB 93080, 2509 AB The Hague; Clingendael 7, 2597 VH The Hague; tel. (70) 3245384; fax (70) 3282002; e-mail info@clingendael.nl; internet www .clingendael.nl; f. 1983; research and training on int. relations especially int. diplomacy, Europe, int. security and conflict management and int. energy; debates, courses and publs; library of 26,000 vols, 300 periodicals, 150 current journals; Pres. Dr BERNARD R. BOT; Vice-Pres. Lt. Gen. M. L. M. URLINGS; Gen. Dir Prof. Dr KO COLIJN; Treas. H. D. A. HAKS; publ. *Internationale Spectator* (12 a year).

Nederlands Interdisciplinair Demogra-fisch Instituut (NIDI-KNAW) (Netherlands Interdisciplinary Demographic Institute): POB 11650, 2502 AR The Hague; Lange Houtstraat 19, 2511 CV The Hague; tel. (70) 3565200; fax (70) 3647187; e-mail info@nidi.nl; internet www.nidi.nl; f. 1970, present status 2003; attached to Royal Netherlands Acad. of Arts; research, train-

ing, information and documentation in the field of population studies; library of 6,000 vols, 2,500 reprints, 15,000 articles; Dir Prof. Dr LEO J. G. VAN WISSEN; Deputy Dir Drs NICO VAN NIMWEGEN; Sec. JACQUELINE VAN DER HELM; publs *Bevolking en Gezin* (3 a year), *Demos* (10 a year, online).

Nederlands Studiecentrum Criminali-teit en Rechtshandhaving (NCSR) (Netherlands Institute for the Study of Crime and Law Enforcement): POB 71304, 1008 BH Amsterdam; Room 0D-07, De Boelelaan 1105, 1081 HV Amsterdam; tel. (20) 5985239; fax (20) 5983975; e-mail nscr@nscr .nl; internet www.nscr.nl; f. 1992, reorganized 1999; attached to Netherlands Org. for Scientific Research; fundamental research, dissemination of knowledge in the field of crime and law enforcement; Chair. Prof. Y. BURUMA; Scientific Dir Prof. Dr G. J. N. BRUINSMA; Sec. ARIENA H. VAN POPPEL-VAN DIJK.

Research Amsterdam School of Econom-ics: Universiteit van Amsterdam, Roeters-straat 11, Room E5.31, 1018 WB Amsterdam; tel. (20) 5254276; fax (20) 5254254; e-mail resam-ase@uva.nl; internet www.ase.uva.nl/ aseresearch; f. fmrly as Research in Economics & Econometrics Amsterdam (RESAM); attached to Univ. of Amsterdam; research focuses to improve understanding of the operation of economic systems, behaviour of agents in the economy and the effects of economic policies; Dir Prof. Dr PETER BOS-WIJK.

Research Group for Methodology of Law and Legal Research: Faculty of Law, Tilburg Univ., Room M225, Montes-quieu Bldg, POB 90153, 5000 LE Tilburg; Montesquieu Bldg, Warandelaan 2, Room M225, 5037 AB Tilburg; tel. (13) 4662745; fax (13) 4662537; e-mail frw.methodology@ uvt.nl; internet www.tilburguniversity.nl/ legalmethodology; f. 2007; attached to Faculty of Law, Tilburg Univ.; research in methodology of judicial lawmaking and legal research; Dir Dr H. E. B. TIJSSEN; Sec. AUDREY WEISMANN.

SEO Economisch Onderzoek (SEO Economic Research): Univ. of Amsterdam, Gijs-bert van Tienhoven Bldg, Roetersstraat 29, 1018 WB Amsterdam; tel. (20) 5251630; e-mail secretariaat@seo.nl; internet www .seo.nl; f. 1949; attached to Univ. of Amsterdam; ind. applied economic research for govt and industry; Chair. JACQUES SCHRAVEN; Dir Prof. Dr B. E. BAARSMA; Treas. WALTER ETTY.

SOM Research Institute: POB 800, 9700 AV Groningen; Nettelbosje 2, Duisenberg Bldg, 9747 AE Groningen; tel. (50) 3633749; fax (50) 3633720; e-mail a.c.koning@rug.nl; internet www.rug.nl/som/index; attached to Faculty of Economics and Business, Univ. of Groningen; coordinating institute of 6 research programmes: human resource management and organisational behaviour; int. economics, business and management; economics, econometrics and finance; innovation and org.; marketing; operations management and operations research; Chair. Prof. ELMER STERKEN; Scientific Dir Prof. Dr TAMMO BIJMOLT.

Tilburg Graduate Law School: Tilburg Univ., POB 90153, 5000 LE Tilburg; Montesquieu Bldg, Warandelaan 2, 5037 AB, Tilburg; tel. (13) 4662694; fax (13) 4662537; e-mail law.tgls@uvt.nl; internet www .tilburguniversity.nl/law/graduateschool; f. fmrly as Schoordijk Institute; attached to Tilburg Univ.; interdisciplinary study of law, legal methodology; Dir Prof. J. HAN SOMSEN.

Tilburg Institute for Behavioral Eco-nomics Research (TIBER): Tilburg Univ., POB 90153, 5000 LE Tilburg; tel. (13)

4668394; fax (13) 4662067; e-mail d.a.stapel@uvt.nl; internet www.tilburguniversity.nl/tiber; attached to Tilburg Univ.; interdisciplinary research in psychological processes underlying individual choice and economic decision; Dir Prof. DIEDERIK A. STAPEL; Man. Dir Dr TON HEINEN.

Tilburg Institute for Interdisciplinary Studies of Civil Law and Conflict Resolution Systems (TISCO): Faculty of Law, Tilburg Univ., Montesquieu Bldg, Room M 928, POB 90153, 5000 LE Tilburg; Montesquieu Bldg, Warandelaan 2, Room M 928, 5037 AB Tilburg; tel. (13) 4662281; fax (13) 4662323; e-mail law.tisco@uvt.nl; internet www.tilburguniversity.nl/tisco; attached to Faculty of Law, Tilburg Univ.; interdisciplinary, empirical-based research in civil law; develops, integrates, and applies insight from negotiation theory, conflict research, dispute system design, (comparative) legal research, network theory, behavioural law, and law and economics; Academic Dir Prof. J. M. (MAURITS) BARENDRECHT; Man. Dir C. M. C. (CORRY) VAN ZEELAND.

Tilburg School of Politics and Public Administration: Tilburg School of Politics and Public Admin., Tilburg Univ., POB 90153, 5000 LE Tilburg; Montesquieu Bldg, Warandelaan 2, 5037 AB Tilburg; tel. (13) 4662128; fax (13) 4668149; e-mail frw.tspb .secretariaat@tilburguniversity.edu; internet www.tilburguniversity.nl/tspb; attached to Tilburg School of Politics and Public Admin., Tilburg Univ.; researches into legitimacy, multiplicity, vitality of public sector; Dept Chair. Prof. Dr G. J. M. (GABRIËL) VAN DEN BRINK; Dir Prof. Dr P. H. A. FRISSEN.

TILEC—Tilburg Law and Economics Centre: Tilburg Univ., POB 90153, 5000 LE Tilburg; Prof. Cobbenhagenlaan 221, Montesquieu Bldg, Room M512A, 5037 DE, Tilburg; tel. (13) 4668789; e-mail tilec@uvt .nl; internet www.tilburguniversity.nl/tilec; attached to Tilburg Univ.; research on economic regulation of markets; Dir Prof. Dr ERIC VAN DAMME; Dir Prof. Dr PIERRE LAROUCHE; Man. NICOLA HEEREN.

Tinbergen Institute: Gustav Mahlerplein 117, 1082 MS Amsterdam; tel. (20) 5251600; e-mail tinbergen@tinbergen.nl; internet www.tinbergen.nl; f. 1987; also located in Rotterdam; research areas incl. institutions and decision analysis, financial and international markets, labour, region and the environment, econometrics; Gen. Dir Prof. BAUKE VISSER.

EDUCATION

Centre for European Studies (CES): POB 217, 7500 AE Enschede; tel. (53) 4894106; fax (53) 4892159; e-mail n.s.groenendijk@utwente.nl; internet www.utwente.nl/mb/ces; f. 1998; attached to School of Management and Governance, Univ. of Twente; Dir Prof. Dr NICO GROENENDIJK.

Centre for Higher Education Policy Studies (CHEPS): POB 217, 7500 AE Enschede; tel. (53) 4893263; fax (53) 4340392; e-mail cheps@mb.utwente.nl; internet www.utwente.nl/mb/cheps; f. 1986; attached to Univ. of Twente; research focuses on dynamics of the transformation of higher education and research in the knowledge society; Dir Prof. Dr JÜRGEN ENDERS; Sec. KARIN VAN DER TUIN.

Centre for International Cooperation: De Boelelaan 1105, 1081 HV Amsterdam; Metropolitan Bldg, 4th Fl., Buitenveldertselaan 3–7, 1082 VA Amsterdam; tel. (20) 5989090; fax (20) 5989095; e-mail cis@vu.nl; internet www.cis.vu.nl; attached to Vrije Univ.; education and devt in higher education; ICT in teaching and research; manage-

ment and org. in higher education; natural resource management; Chair. Prof. Dr H. A. VERHOEF; Dir KEES KOUWENAAR; Sec. HENNY KEPPEL.

Groningen Institute for Educational Research: Grote Rozenstraat 3, 9712 TG Groningen; tel. (50) 3636631; fax (50) 3636670; internet www.rug.nl/gion/index; attached to Faculty of Behavioural and Social Studies, Univ. of Groningen; fundamental and contract research in teaching and education; Scientific Dir Prof. Dr ROEL BOSKER.

ICT in het Onderwijs (ICTO) (ICT in Education): Kanaalweg 2B, 2628 EB Delft; tel. (15) 2784686; e-mail icto@tudelft.nl; internet www.icto.tudelft.nl; attached to Delft Univ. of Technology.

Instituut voor Internationale Studien (Institute for International Studies): POB 9555, 2333 AK Leiden; tel. 5273411; fax 5273619; f. 1970; attached to Leiden Univ.; promotes cooperation in teaching between univ. depts; research on contemporary int. affairs; Dir Dr PH. P. EVERTS.

Top Institute for Evidence Based Education Research (TIER): Roetersstraat 11, 1018 WB Amsterdam; tel. (20) 5254311; fax (20) 5254310; e-mail s.m.postma@uva.nl; internet www.tierweb.nl; conducts and promotes research in the field of evidence based education; Scientific Coordinator Prof. Dr HENRIËTTE MAASSEN VAN DEN BRINK.

Twente Centre for Career Research (TCCR): Univ. of Twente, Bldg Cubicus, POB 217, 7500 AE Enschede; Univ. of Twente, Bldg Cubicus, Drienerlolaan 5, 7522 NB Enschede; tel. (53) 4893580; fax (53) 4892255; e-mail k.sanders@utwente.nl; internet www.utwente.nl/ibr/tccr; attached to Univ. of Twente; research programmes in the field of professional devt of teachers within education and health care; Dir Prof. Dr KARIN SANDERS.

FINE AND PERFORMING ARTS

Piet Zwart Institute: POB 1272, 3000 BG Rotterdam; Mauritsstraat 36, 3012 CJ Rotterdam; tel. (10) 7947405; internet pzwart .wdka.nl; attached to Willem de Kooning Acad. Rotterdam Univ.; offers int. Masters study and research programmes into professional practice of art, design, media and education.

HISTORY, GEOGRAPHY AND ARCHAEOLOGY

Centrum voor Technische Geowetenschappen (Centre for Technical Geoscience): Stevinweg 1, 2628 CN Delft; tel. (15) 2789511; fax (15) 2781189; e-mail ctg@tudelft.nl; internet www.citg.tudelft.nl; attached to Delft Univ. of Technology; integration of applied geosciences.

Groningen Institute of Archaeology: Poststraat 6, 9712 ER Groningen; tel. (50) 3636712; fax (50) 3636992; e-mail gia@rug.nl; internet www.rug.nl/let/onderzoek/onderzoekinstituten/gia/index; f. 1995; attached to Faculty of Arts, Univ. of Groningen; fundamental archaeological research with strong ecological component in Eurasia, Mediterranean and Arctic; stimulates and integrates fundamental research on past human societies and their environments, from the level of Palaeolithic hunter-gatherers to that of historical complex urban societies; library of 20,000 e-journals; Dir Prof. D. C. M. RAEMAEKERS; publs Paleo-aktueel (Dutch, 1 a year), Palaeohistoria (English, 1 a year), Tijdschrift voor Mediterrane Archeologie (Dutch, 1 a year).

Instituut voor Milieuvraagstukken (IVM) (Institute for Environmental Studies): De Boelelaan 1087, 1081 HV Amsterdam; De Boelelaan 1085, 1081 HV Amsterdam; tel. (20) 4449555; fax (20) 4449553; e-mail info@ivm.falw.vu.nl; internet www.ivm.vu.nl; f. 1971; attached to Vrije Univ.; multidisciplinary research in chemistry and biology, environmental economics, environmental policy and governance, spatial analysis and decision support; Dir Prof. Dr FRANS G. H. BERKHOUT.

Koninklijk Instituut voor Taal-, Land- en Volkenkunde (Royal Netherlands Institute of Southeast Asian and Caribbean Studies): POB 9515, 2300 RA Leiden; Reuvensplaats 2, 2311 BE Leiden; tel. (71) 5272295; fax (71) 5272638; e-mail kitlv@kitlv .nl; internet www.kitlv.nl; f. 1851; attached to Royal Netherlands Acad. of Arts and Sciences; advances the study of the social sciences and humanities of SE Asia and the Caribbean, particularly the fmr Dutch colonies of Indonesia and Suriname, and the fmr Netherlands Antilles and Aruba; library of 750,000 vols; spec. collns incl. Indonesia; Chair. Prof. Dr S. LEGÊNE; Vice-Chair. M. PLOMP; Dir Prof. Dr G. J. OOSTINDIE; publs Bijdragen tot Taal-, Land- en Volkenkunde (3 a year, in English), Nieuwe West-Indische Gids (New West Indian Guide, 2 a year, in English), Journal of Indonesian Social Sciences and Humanities (2 a year, in Dutch).

NIOD Instituut voor Oorlogs-, Holocaust- en Genocide Studies (NIOD Institute for War, Holocaust and Genocide Studies): Herengracht 380, 1016 CJ Amsterdam; tel. (20) 5233800; fax (20) 5233888; e-mail info@niod.knaw.nl; internet www.niod .knaw.nl; f. 1945, merger of Center for Holocaust and Genocide Studies and Netherlands Institute for War Documentation in 2010; attached to Royal Netherlands Acad. of Arts and Sciences; Dutch, German and Allied collns on the history of Second World War; conducts research on war, large-scale violence in the 20th century; library of 60,000 vols; Dir Prof. Dr MARJAN SCHWEGMAN.

Roosevelt Study Center: POB 6001, 4330 LA Middelburg; Abdij 8, 4331 BK Middelburg; tel. (118) 631590; fax (118) 631593; e-mail rsc@zeeland.nl; internet www .roosevelt.nl; f. 1986; attached to Royal Netherlands Acad. of Arts and Sciences; research institute, conf. centre and library on modern US history and Dutch–US relations; Pres. GEORGE R. J. VAN HEUKELOM; Sec. REIN JAN HOEKSTRA; Treas. JAN G. F. VELDHUIS; Dir Prof. Dr CORNELIS A. VAN MINNEN; Asst Dir Dr HANS KRABBENDAM; publ. The Roosevelt Review (1 a year).

Spatial Information Laboratory (SPINlab): De Boelelaan 1087, 1081 HV Amsterdam; tel. (20) 5989569; fax (20) 5989553; e-mail spinlab@ivm.vu.nl; internet www .feweb.vu.nl/gis/spinlab_website; attached to Vrije Univ.; research on spatial, geo-information with enphasis on their added value to environmental protection, health care, emergency and risk management, field work, transport, distribution, logistics, and marketing; Scientific Dir HENK SCHOLTEN; Sec. JESSICA ENDENDIJK.

Vening Meinesz Research School of Geodynamics: c/o Institute of Earth Sciences, Budapestlaan 4, 3584 CD Utrecht; tel. (30) 2535031; fax (30) 2535030; e-mail vmsg@geo.uu.nl; internet vmsg.geo.uu.nl; promotes and carries out geodynamic research, with spec. attention for the integration of geophysical, geological and Earth-oriented space research; Scientific Dir Prof. Dr RINUS WORTEL; Exec. Sec. Drs. JAN-WILLEM DE BLOK.

LANGUAGE AND LITERATURE

Amsterdam Centre for Language and Communication (ACLC): Spuistraat 210–212, Room 1.11, 1012 VT Amsterdam; tel. (20) 5252543; fax (20) 5253052; e-mail aclc-fgw@uva.nl; internet www.hum.uva.nl/aclc; attached to Faculty of Humanities, Univ. of Amsterdam; focuses on study of both functionally and formally oriented linguistic research; Academic Dir Prof. Dr KEES HENGEVELD; Man. Dir Dr ELS VERHEUGD-DAATZELAAR; Vice-Dir Dr ROB SCHOONEN; publ. *Linguistics in Amsterdam series.*

Center for Language and Cognition Groningen (CLCG): POB 716, 9700 AS Groningen; e-mail clcg@let.rug.nl; internet www.rug.nl/let/onderzoek/onderzoekinstituten/clcg/index; f. 1994; attached to Faculty of Arts, Univ. of Groningen; linguistic research; interaction between other linguistic research groups; Dir Prof. Dr Ir JOHN NERBONNE.

Centre for Language Studies: POB 9103, 6500 HD Nijmegen; Erasmusplein 1, 6525 HT Nijmegen; tel. (24) 3611807; fax (24) 3615481; e-mail cls@let.ru.nl; internet www.ru.nl/cls; attached to Faculty of Arts, Radboud Univ. Nijmegen; research in linguistics, language and speech technology and communication studies; Dir Prof. PAULA FIKKERT.

Max Planck Institute for Psycholinguistics: POB 310, 6500 AH Nijmegen; Wundtlaan 1, 6525 XD Nijmegen; tel. (24) 3521911; fax (24) 3521213; e-mail info@mpi.nl; internet www.mpi.nl; f. 1980; attached to German Max Planck Soc.; basic research on psychological, social and biological foundations of language; library of 30,000 vols, 20,000 bound journals, 30,000 online journals; Dir Prof. Dr PETER HAGOORT.

MEDICINE

Academic Centre for Dentistry Amsterdam: Gustav Mahler Laan 3004, 1081 LA Amsterdam; tel. (20) 5980380; e-mail info@acta.nl; internet www.acta.nl; br. at Almere; conducts scientific research, provides educational programmes, and delivers patient care in field of dentistry; research focuses on physiology and pathology of tissues in and around oral cavity; Dean Prof. Dr A. J. FEILZER; Dir for Research Prof. Dr V. EVERTS.

Academisch Medisch Centrum (AMC): POB 22660, 1100 DD Amsterdam; Meibergdreef 9, 1105 AZ Amsterdam; tel. (20) 5669111; fax (20) 5664440; internet www.amc.uva.nl; f. 1983; attached to Universiteit van Amsterdam; clinical and translational research; works as medical centre; Pres. and Dean Prof. Dr M. M LEVI; Vice-Pres. Dr R. J. M. HOPSTAKEN; publ. *AMC Magazine* (10 a year).

Centre for Healthcare Operations Improvement & Research (CHOIR): POB 217, 7500 AE Enschede; tel. (53) 4893447; fax (53) 4894858; e-mail e.w.hans@utwente.nl; internet www.utwente.nl/choir; attached to Univ. of Twente; research on healthcare; research areas incl. decision theory, logistics and operations management, information technology and management, operations research, purchase management, quality and safety management.

Centre of Research on Psychology in Somatic Diseases (CoRPS): POB 90153, 5000 LE Tilburg; Warandelaan 2, 5037 AB Tilburg; tel. (13) 4668720; fax (13) 4662067; e-mail corps@uvt.nl; internet www.tilburguniversity.nl/corps; attached to Tilburg Univ.; research on issues in the interface between medical and behavioural sciences; Academic Dir Prof. Dr JOHAN DENOLLET; Man. Dir J. H. (HANS) DIETEREN.

Centrum voor Ouderenonderzoek (CVO) (Center for Research on Aging): De Boelelaan 1081, 1081 HV Amsterdam; Metropolitan, Room Z-427, Buitenveldertselaan 3, 1081 HV Amsterdam; tel. (20) 5986891; fax (20) 5986810; internet www.cvo.vu.nl; f. 1996; attached to Vrije Univ. Amsterdam; research and education in gerontology and geriatrics; Head Dr F. J. M. MEILAND.

EMGO+ Institute for Health and Care Research: van der Boechorststraat 7, 1081 BT Amsterdam; tel. (20) 4448180; fax (20) 4448181; e-mail secretariaat.emgo@vumc.nl; internet www.emgo.nl; attached to Vrije Univ.; research in public and occupational health, primary care, rehabilitation, longterm care; Dir Prof. JOHANNES BRUG; Vice-Dir Prof. Dr PIM CUIJPERS; Vice-Dir Prof. Dr WILLEM VAN MECHELEN.

Graduate School of Neurosciences Amsterdam, Rotterdam: tel. (20) 4449641; e-mail els.borghols@cncr.vu.nl; internet www.onwar.nl; research in the field of neurosciences; Chair. of Advisory Board Prof. Dr F. H. LOPES DA SILVA; Dir Prof. Dr A. B. SMIT; Chair. of Teaching Cttee Dr C. N. LEVELT.

GUIDE—Research Institute for Chronic Diseases and Drug Innovation: POB 196, 9700 AD Groningen; Ant. Deusinglaan 1, Bldg 3217 'De Brug', Room 7.31, 9713 AV Groningen; tel. (50) 3633163; fax (50) 3632612; e-mail guideoffice@med.umcg.nl; internet www.graduateschoolguide.nl; attached to Univ. of Groningen; integrates clinical, biomedical and pharmaceutical research, which promotes education of researchers with a keen eye on the complete spectrum of biomedical research in a unique research and teaching environment: from bed to bench to drugs; Scientific Dir Prof. Dr HAN MOSHAGE.

Het Nederlands Kanker Instituut—Antoni van Leeuwenhoek Ziekenhuis (Netherlands Cancer Institute—Antoni van Leeuwenhoek Hospital): POB 90203, 1006 BE Amsterdam; Plesmanlaan 121, 1066 CX Amsterdam; tel. (20) 5129111; fax (20) 6172625; e-mail nkilib@nki.nl; internet www.nki.nl; f. 1916, present bldg 1959; library of 15,000 vols; basic and translational cancer research, clinical cancer research, diagnostic, surgical and medical oncology, radiotherapy; Patron HKH QUEEN BEATRIX; Chair. and Scientific Dir Prof. Dr A. J. M. BERNS; Sec. P. BELTMAN; Library Dir SUZANNE BAKKER; publ. *Scientific Report* (1 a year).

Institute for Cardiovascular Research: POB 7057, 1007 MB Amsterdam; Van der Boechorststraat 7, 1081 BT Amsterdam; tel. (20) 4448111; fax (20) 4448255; e-mail icar@vumc.nl; internet www.vumc.nl/afdelingen/icar-vu; f. 1992; attached to Vrije Univ.; research into aspects of cardiovascular diseases, cardiovascular function; Dir Prof. Dr V. W. M. VAN HINSBERGH.

Institute for Genetic and Metabolic Disease: Radboud Univ. Nijmegen Medical Centre, Geert Grooteplein Zuid 10, POB 9101, 6500 HB Nijmegen; Radboud Univ. Nijmegen Medical Centre, Geert Grooteplein 10, 6525 GA Nijmegen; tel. (24) 3619118; fax (24) 3668532; internet www.igmd.nl; attached to Radboud Univ. Nijmegen Medical Centre; clinical, applied and fundamental research on genetic and metabolic diseases; Dir Prof. Dr JAN SMEITINK.

Institute of Technical Medicine: Noordhorst, POB 217, 7500 AE Enschede; tel. (53) 4893300; fax (53) 4893288; e-mail j.a.dutrieux-schuit@utwente.nl; internet www.utwente.nl/tnw/itm; attached to Univ. of Twente; basic science and technology with clinical practice in medicine.

Instituut Beleid & Management Gezondheidszorg (iBMG) (Institute of Health Policy & Management): POB 1738, 3000 DR Rotterdam; J-Bldg, Campus Woudestein, Burgemeester Oudlaan 50, 3062 PA Rotterdam; tel. (10) 4081169; e-mail research@remove-this.bmg.eur.nl; internet www.bmg.eur.nl; f. 1982; attached to Erasmus Univ.; research school and educational programmes of Netherlands Institute for Health Sciences (Nihes) and Netherlands School of Public Health (NSPH); researches on competition and regulation in health care, quality and efficiency in health care, adaptation of orgs to competitive environment; Assoc. Dean Prof. Dr W. R. F. NOTTEN; Man. Dir Dr M. S. VEENSTRA; Dir for Research Prof. Dr W. B. F. (WERNER) BROUWER.

Instituut voor Fundamentele en Klinische Bewegingswetenschappen (Institute for Fundamental and Clinical Human Movement Sciences): van der Boechorststraat 9, 1081 BT Amsterdam; tel. (20) 5982000; e-mail ifkb@fbw.vu.nl; internet www.ifkb.nl; f. 1995; attached to Vrije Univ.; research into nature and significance of human movement; research themes incl. control, mechanics, metabolism; Chair. of Board Prof. Dr P. J. BEEK; Dir Dr Ir L. BLANKEVOORT; Dir Prof. Dr ARNOLD DE HAAN; Dir Prof. Dr Ir D. F. STEGEMAN.

Interuniversitair Cardiologisch Instituut Nederland (Interuniversity Cardiology Institute of the Netherlands): POB 19258, 3501 DG Utrecht; Catharijnesingel 52, 3511 GC Utrecht; tel. (30) 2333600; fax (30) 2315940; e-mail info@icin.knaw.nl; internet www.icin.nl; attached to Royal Netherlands Acad. of Arts and Sciences; scientific research in the field of cardiovascular diseases; alliance of 8 univ. cardiology depts; Dir Prof. Dr WIEK H. VAN GILST; Dir Prof. Dr ERNST E. VAN DER WALL; Gen. Man. JAN WEIJERS.

Koninklijk Instituut voor de Tropen (KIT) (Royal Tropical Institute): POB 95001, 1090 HA Amsterdam; Mauritskade 63, 1092 AD Amsterdam; tel. (20) 5688711; fax (20) 6684579; e-mail ils@kit.nl; internet www.kit.nl; f. 1910 as Colonial Institute, present bldg 1926, present name 1950; health policy and tropical medicine; int. research and training org. that focuses on improving communication between the W and non-Western world; collects and disseminates information on the developing world; library: see Libraries and Archives; Tropical Museum: see Museums and Art Galleries; Chair. Prof. Dr RUDY RABBINGE; Vice-Chair. PETER J. GROENENBOOM; Pres. Dr JAN DONNER.

Nederlands Instituut voor Neurowetenschappen (Netherlands Institute for Neuroscience): AMC, Meibergdreef 47, 1105 BA Amsterdam; tel. (20) 5665500; fax (20) 5666121; e-mail secretariaat@nin.knaw.nl; internet www.nin.knaw.nl; f. 2005; attached to Royal Netherlands Acad. of Arts and Sciences; carries out fundamental neuroscience research with spec. emphasis on the brain and the visual system; 18 research groups; Scientific Dir Dr PIETER R. ROELFSEMA; Man. Dir Dr RONALD VAN DER NEUT; Vice-Dir Dr CHRIS I. ZEEUW.

Nijmegen Centre for Evidence Based Practice (NCEBP): Radboud Univ. Nijmegen Medical Centre, Post 148, NCEBP, POB 9101, 6500 HB Nijmegen; Radboud Univ. Nijmegen Medical Centre, NCEBP, Geert Grooteplein 21, 6525 EZ Nijmegen; tel. (24) 3614639; e-mail info@ncebp.umcn.nl; internet www.ncebp.eu; attached to Radboud Univ.; conducts research that is aimed at individual patients and patient population,

and in a preventative sense also at healthy population; Scientific Dir Prof. Dr PAUL SMITS; Asst Scientific Dir Dr. GERDI EGBERINK.

Nijmegen Intitute for Infection, Inflammation and Immunity: POB 9101, Route 463, 6500 HB Nijmegen; tel. (24) 3668015; e-mail a.peters@aig.umcn.nl; internet www .n4i.nl; attached to Radboud Univ. Nijmegen Medical Centre; performs clinical translational and basic research on the interaction between microorganisms and the host, the inflammatory response and immune mechanisms as occur in autoimmune disorders and transplantation; Scientific Dir Prof. Dr JOS VAN DER MEER; Sec. GONNY PETERS.

Onderzoekschool Oncologie Amsterdam (Oncology Graduate School): c/o Dr. Esther M. Ruhé-Hoogervorst, De Boelelaan 1117, 1081 HV Amsterdam; tel. (20) 4443113; fax (20) 4442964; e-mail e.ruhe@vumc.nl; internet www.ooa-graduateschool.org; attached to Vrije Univ.; research in basic and clinical oncology; Chair. of Board Prof. Dr ANTON BERNS; Chair. Prof. Dr GERRIT A. MEIJER.

TNO Gezond Leven (TNO Healthy Living): POB 2215, 2301 CE Leiden; Wassenaarseweg 56, 2333 AL Leiden; tel. (88) 8669000; e-mail info-zorg@tno.nl; internet www.tno.nl; f. 1932; scientific research in the fields of public health and prevention of illness; postgraduate courses in occupational health; library of 20,000 vols; Chair. Ir JAN H. J. MENGELERS; Chair for Defence Research Board JAN WILLEM KELDER; Chair for Supervisory Board Dr C. A. LINSE; Exec. Sec. MARIAN NIEUWENHOUT; publ. *TNO Magazine* (4 a year).

VU Medisch Centrum (VU University Medical Center): POB 7057, 1007 MB Amsterdam; De Boelelaan 1117, 1081 HV Amsterdam; tel. (20) 4444444; fax (20) 4444645; e-mail uhp@vumc.nl; internet www.vumc.nl/meg; f. 2001 by merger of medical school and VU hospital; attached to Vrije Universiteit Medical Centre; research into magnetoencephalography; Chair. Drs E. B. MULDER; Vice-Chair. Prof. Dr T. J. F. SAVELKOUL; Dean Prof. Dr W. A. B. STALMAN.

W. Kahn Institute of Theoretical Psychiatry and Neuroscience: Het Nateland 1, 3911 XZ Rhenen Utrecht; tel. and fax (317) 618708; e-mail wimkahn1@hotmail.com; internet kahn-institute.tripod.com; f. 1997; 25 mems; develops theoretical models in the fields of psychiatry, psychology, neuroscience and philosophy, for the diagnosis and treatment of mental health disorders; 10 depts; Chair. Dr WILLEM H. J. MARTENS; Pres. Prof. Dr W. KAHN; Sec. W. A. TUIJTEN; publ. *WKITPN–Publication* (4 a year).

W. J. Kolff Institute for Biomedical Engineering and Materials Science: Antonius Deusinglaan 1, FB41, 9713 AV Groningen; tel. (50) 3633140; fax (50) 3633159; e-mail h.j.busscher@med.umcg.nl; internet www.rug.nl/umcg/onderzoek/ interfacultaireinstituten/bmsa/index; f. 1997; establishes a centre of expertise for the entire stage of biomedical materials science and its application involving basic materials science, medical product devt and clinical evaluation that contributes to the long-lasting well-being of patients in need of biomaterials implants and extra-corporal support systems; Scientific Dir Prof. Dr H. J. BUSSCHER.

NATURAL SCIENCES
General

CEDLA—Centrum voor Studie en Documentatie van Latijns-Amerika (CEDLA—Centre for Latin American Research and Documentation): Keizersgracht 395–397, 1016 EK Amsterdam; tel. (20) 5253498; fax (20) 6255127; e-mail secretariat@cedla.nl; internet www.cedla .uva.nl; f. 1964, present status 1971; social science research on Latin America; library: see Libraries and Archives; Dir Prof. Dr MICHIEL BAUD; publ. *ERLACS: European Review of Latin American and Caribbean Studies* (Revista Europea de Estudios Latinoamericanos y del Caribe, 2 a year, in English and Spanish).

CentERdata—Instituut voor Dataverzameling en Onderzoek (CentERdata—Institute for Data Collection and Research): POB 90153, 5000 LE Tilburg; Tias Bldg, Warandelaan 2, 5037 AB Tilburg; tel. (13) 4668325; fax (13) 4662764; e-mail centerdata@uvt.nl; internet www.centerdata.nl; attached to Tilburg Univ.; data colln, methodological and applied research; Dir Prof. Dr MARCEL DAS.

Groningen Research Institute of Pharmacy (GRIP): Dept of Pharmacy, Antonius Deusinglaan 1, 9713 AV Groningen; tel. (50) 3633275; fax (50) 3637943; internet www.rug .nl/farmacie/index; attached to Faculty of Mathematics and Natural Sciences, Univ. of Groningen; organises research in 11 pharmacy research groups; Scientific Dir Prof. Dr W. J. QUAX.

Kapteyn Astronomical Institute: POB 800, 9700 AV Groningen; Landleven 12, Zernike Bldg, 9747 AD Groningen; tel. (50) 3634073; fax (50) 3636100; internet www.rug .nl/sterrenkunde/onderzoek/index; f. 1896 as an astronomical laboratory; astronomical research; Scientific Dir Prof. Dr J. M. VAN DER HULST.

Nederlandse Organisatie voor Toegepast—Natuurwetenschappelijk Onderzoek (TNO) (Netherlands Organization for Applied Scientific Research): POB 6050, 2600 JA Delft; Schoemakerstraat 97, 2628 VK Delft; tel. (88) 8660000; fax (15) 2612403; e-mail wegwijzer@tno.nl; internet www.tno .nl; f. 1932; strategic policy and innovation consultancy; bldg, materials and information technology, mechanical and production engineering, product design and development, telecommunications, quality control, health and safety, nutrition, environment and energy; library of 16,000 vols; Chair. JAN MENGELERS; Sec. Drs S. J. VLAAR; publs *TNO Magazine* (in English), *Toegepaste Wetenschap* (in Dutch).

Nederlandse Organisatie voor Wetenschappelijk Onderzoek (NWO) (Netherlands Organization for Scientific Research): POB 93138, 2509 AC The Hague; Laan van Nieuw Oost-Indië 300, 2593 CE The Hague; tel. (70) 3440640; fax (70) 3850971; e-mail nwo@nwo.nl; internet www .nwo.nl; f. 1988; stimulates and coordinates pure and applied research in all fields of learning; funds researchers; Chair. Dr JOS ENGELEN; Dir-Gen.and Sec. Dr CEES DE VISSER; publ. *Jaarboek*.

Netherlands Graduate Research School of Science, Technology and Modern Culture (WTMC): Univ. Maastricht, Faculteit der Cultuur-en Maatschappijwetenschappen, WTMC, POB 616, 6200 MD Maastricht; e-mail wtmc@maastrichtuniversity.nl; internet www.wtmc.net; science and technology studies; study of devt of science, technology and modern culture; Scientific Dir Prof. Dr SALLY WYATT.

Netherlands Research School in Process Technology: OSPT Secretariat, Faculty of Engineering Technology, Bldg 'De Meander', POB 217, 7500 AE Enschede; OSPT office, Univ. of Twente, Bldg 'De Meander', Room ME-116, 7500 AE Enschede; tel. (53) 4894626; fax (53) 4894233; e-mail ospt@ tudelft.nl; internet ospt.tnw.utwente.nl; research in chemical engineering and process technology; five participant univ.; Scientific Dir Prof. Dr H. E. A. VAN DEN AKKER.

Oldendorff Research Institute: POB 90153, 5000 LE Tilburg; Prisma Bldg, Warandelaan 2, 5037 AB, Tilburg; tel. (13) 4663140; fax (13) 4668183; e-mail e.j .simons@uvt.nl; f. 2001; attached to Tilburg Univ.; int., multi-disciplinary, multi-level research in social sciences; Dir Prof. Dr KLAAS SIJTSMA; Man. A. G. J. J. (TON) HEINEN.

Radionuclide Centre (RNC): De Boelelaan 1085C, 1081 HV Amsterdam; tel. (20) 4449101; fax (20) 4449121; internet www .rnc.vu.nl; attached to Vrije Univ. Amsterdam; research on chemical, biological and medical research with Radionuclides at Type-2-level; facilitation and cooperation in processing and transport of radioactive waste and first aid with radioactive accidents; laundering of radioactive working clothes.

Stichting voor Wetenschappelijk Onderzoek van de Tropen (WOTRO) (WOTRO Science for Global Development): POB 93120, 2509 AC The Hague; Laan van Nieuw Oost Indië 300, 2593 CE The Hague; tel. (70) 3440763; fax (70) 3819874; e-mail wotro@nwo .nl; internet www.nwo.nl; f. 1964; attached to Netherlands Organisation for Scientific Research (NWO); research granting org.; focuses on programming, funding and monitoring research on global issues; supports scientific research on devt issues; Chair. Prof. WILLEM J. M. VAN GENUGTEN.

Stratingh Institute for Chemistry: Nijenborgh 4, 9747 AG Groningen; tel. (50) 3634233; fax (50) 3634296; e-mail stratingh@rug.nl; internet www.rug.nl/ stratingh; f. 1997; attached to Faculty of Mathematics and Natural Sciences, Univ. of Groningen; research in molecular chemistry; Scientific Dir Prof. Dr J. C. HUMMELEN.

Tilburg Centre for Logic and Philosophy of Science (TILPS): POB 90153, 5000 LE Tilburg; Dante Bldg, Warandelaan 2, 5037 AB Tilburg; e-mail tilps@ tilburguniversity.nl; internet www .tilburguniversity.nl/tilps; f. 2007; attached to Tilburg Univ.; Dir Prof. STEPHAN HARTMANN.

Van der Waals-Zeeman Institute: POB 94485, 1090 GL Amsterdam; Science Park 904, 1098 XH Amsterdam; tel. (20) 5255663; fax (20) 5255788; e-mail secr-wzi-science@ uva.nl; internet www.science.uva.nl/ research/wzi; attached to Univ. of Amsterdam; research areas incl. atomic physics, hard condensed matter, materials science, quantum optics, soft condensed matter; Dir Prof. Dr M. S. GOLDEN; Man. L. LUSINK.

Biological Sciences

Center for Behaviour and Neurosciences: Kerklaan 30, 9751 NN Haren; tel. (50) 3632053; e-mail d.g.m.beersma@rug.nl; internet www.rug.nl/fwn/onderzoek/ programmas/cbn; attached to Faculty of Mathematics and Natural Sciences, Univ. of Groningen; integral part of the Research School for Behavioural and Cognitive Neurosciences (BCN) of Univ. of Groningen; Dir Prof. Dr DOMIEN BEERSMA.

Centraalbureau voor Schimmelcultures (CBS—KNAW Fungal Biodiversity Centre): POB 85167, 3508 AD Utrecht; Uppsalalaan 8, 3584 CT Utrecht; tel. (30) 2122600; fax (30) 2512097; e-mail info@cbs.knaw.nl; internet www.cbs.knaw.nl; f. 1904, present location 2000; attached to Royal Netherlands Acad. of Arts and Sciences; researches on biosystematics of the fungal kingdom; maintains a world-renowned colln of filamentous fungi, yeasts and bacteria; research focus on the

taxonomy and evolution of fungi, functional aspects of fungal biology and ecology, using molecular and genomics approaches; Dir Prof. Dr PEDRO W. CROUS; publs *CBS Biodiversity Series* (2–3 a year), *IMA Fungus* (2 a year), *Persoonia* (2 a year), *Studies in Mycology* (3 a year).

Centre for Synthetic Biology: Nijenborgh 4, 9747 AG Groningen; tel. (50) 3633941; fax (50) 3634165; e-mail syntheticbiology@rug .nl; internet www.rug.nl/fwn/onderzoek/ instituten/csb/index; f. 2008; attached to Faculty of Mathematics and Natural Sciences, Univ. of Groningen; design, construction of cellular and biohybrid systems; founded by three leading research institutes of the faculty; Scientific Dir Prof. Dr BERT POOLMAN.

Donders Institute for Brain, Cognition and Behaviour: POB 9101, 6500 HB Nijmegen; Kapittelweg 29, 6525 EN Nijmegen; tel. (24) 3610750; fax (24) 3610989; e-mail info@ donders.ru.nl; internet www.ru.nl/donders/; attached to Radbound Univ. Nijmegen; consists of the Centre of Cognition, the Centre for Cognitive Neuroimaging and the Centre for Neuroscience; Administrative Dir ARTHUR WILLEMSEN.

Groningen Biomolecular Science and Biotechnology Institute: Nijenborgh 7, 9747 AG Groningen; tel. (50) 3634203; fax (50) 3632154; e-mail t.hummel@rug.nl; internet www.rug.nl/gbb/organisation/index; f. 1993; attached to Faculty of Mathematics and Natural Sciences, Univ. of Groningen; originates from collaboration between dept of biology and chemistry; composed of 13 research groups; Dir Prof. Dr A. J. M. DRIESSEN.

Hortus Botanicus: POB 9516, 2300 RA Leiden; Rapenburg 73, 2311 GJ Leiden; tel. (71) 5277249; fax (71) 5275199; e-mail hortus@hortus.leidenuniv.nl; internet www .hortusleiden.nl; f. 1590; attached to Universiteit Leiden; research in the field of botany; Scientific Dir Prof. Dr E. F. SMETS.

Hortus Haren Holland: POB 179, 9750 AD Haren; Kerklaan 34, 9751 NN Haren; tel. (50) 5370053; fax (50) 5371223; e-mail info@ hortusharen.nl; internet www.hortusharen .nl; f. 1642, renewed 1929; 8,000 species; CEO Drs J. C. KAPPENBURG.

Hubrecht Institute: POB 85164, 3508 AD Utrecht; Uppsalalaan 8, 3584 CT Utrecht; tel. (30) 2121800; fax (30) 2516464; e-mail nimwegen@niob.knaw.nl; internet www .hubrecht.eu; f. 1916 as Hubrecht Laboratory, present location 2000, present name 2007; attached to Royal Netherlands Acad. of Arts and Sciences; research on developmental and stem cell biology of animals; 17 research groups; Dir Prof. HANS CLEVERS; Business Dir Dr JOS KOELMAN; Deputy Dir Prof. JEROEN DEN HERTOG.

Instituut voor Plantenziektenkundig Onderzoek (IPO–DLO) (DLO–Research Institute for Plant Protection): POB 9060, 6700 WG Wageningen; tel. (317) 476000; fax (317) 410113; e-mail info@ipo.dlo.nl; f. 1949; prevention, management and control of plant diseases and pests; library of 24,000 vols; Dir Dr Ir N. G. HOGENBOOM.

Nederlands Instituut voor Onderzoek in de Katalyse (Netherlands Institute for Catalysis Research): 51 Anna v. Saksenlaan, POB 93223, 2509 AE Hague; tel. (70) 3440523; e-mail office@niok.nl; internet www.niok.nl; f. 1991; virtual institute consists of major catalysis groups of 7 Dutch univs; Scientific Dir Prof. BERT WECKHUYSEN.

Nationaal Herbarium Nederland (National Herbarium of the Netherlands): POB 9514, 2300 RA Leiden; Van Steenis Bldg, Einsteinweg 2, 2333 CC Leiden; tel. (71) 5273515; fax (71) 5273511; e-mail dewolf@nhn.leidenuniv.nl; internet www .nhn.leidenuniv.nl; f. 1999 by merger of Herbarium Vadense, Rijksherbarium Leiden and Utrecht Univ. Herbarium; attached to Universiteit Leiden; investigation of flora (taxonomy, geography), particularly of the Netherlands and the Tropics; br and research centre in Wageningen; library of 45,000 vols, 100,000 journal vols, 100,000 reprints, 90,000 microfiches, 40,000 plant illustrations; Chair. Prof. Dr S. B. MENKEN; Dir Prof. Dr E. F. SMETS; Sec. Dr J. B. MOLS; publs *Blumea* (in English), *Flora Malesiana* (Phanerog., ferns), *Flora Malesiana Bulletin*, *Gorteria* (Netherlands flora), *IAWA Journal* (4 a year), *Persoonia* (Mycology).

Nijmegen Centre for Molecular Life Sciences (NCMLS): 259 NCMLS, POB 9101, 6500 HB Nijmegen; Geert Grooteplein 28, 6525 GA Nijmegen; tel. (24) 3610707; fax (24) 3610909; e-mail info@ncmls.ru.nl; internet www.ncmls.edu; attached to Radbound Univ. Nijmegen Medical Centre; multidisciplinary research within molecular mechanisms of disease and molecular medicine, cell biology, translational research; Dir Prof. Dr RENÉ BINDELS.

Research School of Behavioural and Cognitive Neurosciences: POB 196, 9700 AD Groningen; Ant. Deusinglaan One, HPC FA33, Bldg 3217, Room 731, 9713 AV Groningen; tel. (50) 3634734; fax (50) 3638875; e-mail e.t.kuiper-drenth@umcg.nl; internet www.rug.nl/bcn; f. 1987; attached to Univ. of Groningen; integrates fundamental research and education; addresses neurobiological basis of behavioural and cognitive events; studies the physiological and pathological processes of the nervous system; 5 faculties of the Univ. of Groningen participate with a number of research institutes; focuses on bringing together clinical and preclinical researchers from different research institutes; offers Masters and doctorate programmes; Scientific Dir Prof. Dr H. W. G. M. BODDEKE.

Swammerdam Institute for Life Sciences: POB 94216, 1090 GE Amsterdam; Science Park 904, 1098 XH Amsterdam; tel. (20) 5257678; fax (20) 5257675; e-mail info-science@uva.nl; internet www.science .uva.nl/sils; attached to Univ. of Amsterdam; research related to cellular processes and interactions; multidisciplinary research in biology, (bio)chemistry, (bio)physics, data analysis technology, information technology, medicine; Dir Prof. Dr WILLEM. J. STIEKEMA.

Mathematical Sciences

Casimir Onderzoekschool (Casimir Research School): Management Office, Casimir Research School, Maddy Lansbergen, Lorentzweg 1, 2628 CJ Delft; tel. (15) 2787213; fax (15) 2781413; e-mail info@ casimir.researchschool.nl; internet casimir .researchschool.nl; f. 2004 by Leiden Institute of Physics and Kavli Institute of Nanoscience; graduate school for interdisciplinary physics and strong focus on nanoscience; Dir Prof. Dr Ir TEUN KLAPWIJK.

Centre for Theoretical Physics: Chemistry-Physics Bldg, Nijenborgh 4, 5111.0153, 9747 AG Groningen; tel. (50) 3634950; fax (50) 3634947; e-mail secrctn@rug.nl; internet www.rug.nl/natuurkunde/onderzoek/instituten/ctn/index; consists of four research groups: computational physics, theory of condensed matter, high energy physics, statistical physics.

Centrum Wiskunde & Informatica (CWI) (Centre for Mathematics and Computer Science): POB 94079, 1090 GB Amsterdam; Science Park 123, 1098 XG Amsterdam; tel. (20) 5929333; fax (20) 5924199; e-mail info@ cwi.nl; internet www.cwi.nl; f. 1946; fundamental scientific research in mathematics and computer science; library: see Libraries and Archives; Gen. Dir Prof. Dr JOS C. M. BAETEN; Dir Prof. PETER VAN LAARHOVEN.

Euler Institute for Discrete Mathematics and its Applications: c/o Dept of Mathematics and Computing Science, Eindhoven Univ. of Technology, POB 513, 5600 MB Eindhoven; tel. (40) 2472254; fax (40) 2475366; e-mail eidma@tue.nl; internet www .win.tue.nl/wsk/eidma; f. 1994; attached to Eindhoven Univ. of Technology; coding theory, combinatorial optimization and algorithms, discrete algebra and geometry, graph theory, information theory and cryptology; Chair. Prof. Dr A. M. COHEN; Scientific Dir Prof. Dr Ir HENK C. A. VAN TILBORG.

Eurandom: POB 513, 5600 MB Eindhoven; Den Dolech 2, 5612 AZ Eindhoven; tel. (40) 2478100; fax (40) 2478190; e-mail office@ eurandom.tue.nl; internet www.eurandom .tue.nl; attached to Eindhoven Univ. of Technology; probability theory, statistics, stochastic operations research; Chair. Prof. Dr FRANK VAN DER DUYN SCHOUTEN; Scientific Dir Prof. Dr Ir ONNO J. BOXMA; Man. Dir Drs CONNIE M. M. CANTRIJN.

Institute for Mathematics, Astrophysics and Particle Physics: POB 9010, 6500 GL Nijmegen; Huygens Bldg, Room HG03.830, Heyendaalseweg 135, 6525 AJ Nijmegen; tel. (24) 3652099; fax (24) 3652191; e-mail secr@ hef.ru.nl; internet www.ru.nl/imapp; f. 2005; attached to Faculty of Science, Radbound Univ. Nijmegen; research in mathematics, astrophysics and elementary particle physics; Dir Prof. Dr SIJBRAND DE JONG.

Instituut voor Hoge Energie Fysica (IHEF) (Institute for High Energy Physics): POB 41882, 1009 DB Amsterdram; Science Park 105, 1098 XG Amsterdam; tel. (20) 5925169; fax (20) 5925054; e-mail j.berger@ nikhef.nl; internet www.nikhef.nl/onderwijs/ universitaire-partners/uva-ihef; attached to Univ. of Amsterdam; high energy particle physics, subatomic physics, instrumentation; Dir Prof. Dr S. C. M. BENTVELSEN.

Instituut voor Programmatuurkunde en Algoritmiek (Institute for Programming Research and Algorithmics): Eindhoven Univ. of Technology, Dept of Mathematics and Computing Science, IPA Secretariat, POB 513, 5600 MB Eindhoven; Den Dolech 2, Room HG 7.22, 5600 MB Eindhoven; tel. (40) 2474124; fax (40) 2436685; e-mail ipa@ tue.nl; internet www.win.tue.nl/ipa; attached to Eindhoven Univ. of Technology; research areas incl. algorithms and complexity, formal methods, software technology and engineering; Scientific Dir Prof. Dr J. C. M. BAETEN.

Instituut voor Theoretische Fysica (Institute for Theoretical Physics): POB 94485, 1090 GL Amsterdam; Science Park 904, Amsterdam; tel. (20) 5255773; fax (20) 5255778; e-mail itf@science.uva.nl; internet www.science.uva.nl/research/itf; f. 1949; attached to Univ. of Amsterdam; Dir Prof. Dr KARELJAN SCHOUTENS.

Johann Bernoulli Institute of Mathematics and Computing Science (JBI): POB 407, 9700 AK Groningen; Nijenborgh 9, 9747 AG Groningen; tel. (50) 3633973; fax (50) 3633800; e-mail research@math.rug.nl; internet www.rug.nl/informatica/onderzoek/ bernoulli; attached to Faculty of Mathematics and Natural Science, Univ. of Groningen; 6 mathematics, 6 computer research programmes.

Kernfysisch Versneller Instituut (KVI) (Nuclear Physics Accelerator Institute): Zernikelaan 25, 9747 AA Groningen; tel. (50)

3633600; fax (50) 3634003; e-mail info@kvi .nl; internet www.rug.nl/kvi/index; f. 1971; attached to Univ. of Groningen; int. institute in fundamental and applied atomic and subatomic physics; Dir Prof. Dr KLAUS JUNG-MANN.

Korteweg—de Vries Instituut voor Wiskunde (Korteweg-de Vries Institute for Mathematics): POB 94248, 1090 GE Amsterdam; Fl. 4C, Science Park 904, 1098 XH Amsterdam; tel. (20) 5255217; fax (20) 5257820; internet www.science.uva.nl/ research/math; f. 1997, present location 2009; attached to Univ. of Amsterdam; research in mathematics; Dir Prof. Dr JAN J. O. O. WIEGERINCK; Man. Dr M. KRANEN-BURG; Man. L. STOLTE; Sec. EVELIEN WALLET.

Sterrenkundig Instituut Anton Pannekoek (Anton Pannekoek Astronomical Institute): POB 94249, 1090 GE Amsterdam; Science Park 904, 1098 XH Amsterdam; tel. (20) 5257491; fax (20) 5257484; e-mail secr-astro-science@uva.nl; internet www .astro.uva.nl; attached to Univ. of Amsterdam; research in high-energy astrophysics; Dir Prof. Dr MICHIEL VAN DER KLIS.

Physical Sciences

Centre for Ecological and Evolutionary Studies (CEES): POB 14, 9750 AA Haren; Biological Centre, Kerklaan 30, 9750 AA Haren; tel. (50) 3638357; fax (50) 3632295; e-mail cees-office@rug.nl; internet www.rug .nl/biologie/onderzoek/onderzoekinstituten/ cees/index; attached to Faculty of Mathematics and Natural Sciences, Univ. of Groningen; 7 research groups; coordinates the local research school ecology and evolution; Dir Prof. Dr LEONARDUS BEUKEBOOM.

Green Energy Initiative: Meander Bldg, POB 217, 7500 AE Enschede; Meander Bldg, Drienerlolaan 5, 7500 AE Enschede; tel. (53) 4892489; fax (53) 4894233; e-mail m.h .steenbergen@utwente.nl; internet www .utwente.nl/greenenergy; f. 2012; attached to Univ. of Twente; works to strengthen collaboration between the various scientific disciplines in renewable energy research at the Univ. of Twente; promotes successful implementation of innovations; enables a better contact for external parties; Scientific Dir Prof. Dr Ir L. LEFFERTS; Programme Director Ir J. P. EMMERZAAL; Sec. M. H. STEENBERGEN.

Institute for Molecules and Materials (IMM): POB 9010, 6500 GL Nijmegen; Huygens Bldg, Heyendaalseweg 135, 6525 AJ Nijmegen; tel. (24) 3653189; fax (24) 3652190; e-mail imm@science.ru.nl; internet www.ru.nl/imm; f. 2005; attached to Faculty of Science, Radbound Univ. Nijmegen; research in functional molecular structures and materials; Dir Prof. Dr ELIAS VLIEG; Man. Dir Dr IWAN HOLLEMAN; Sec. ERNA GOUWENS.

Institute for Wetland and Water Research (IWWR): POB 9010, 6500 GL Nijmegen; Heijendaalseweg 135, 6525 AJ Nijmegen; tel. (24) 3652294; fax (24) 3652830; e-mail m.frieling@science.ru.nl; internet www.ru.nl/iwwr; attached to Faculty of Science, Radbound Univ. of Nijmegen; joint research in microbiology, ecology, plant and environmental sciences; Dir Prof. Dr HANS DE KROON.

Instituut voor Biodiversiteit en Ecosysteem Dynamica (Institute for Biodiversity and Ecosystem Dynamics): POB 94248, 1090 GE Amsterdam; Science Park 904, 1098 XH Amsterdam; tel. (20) 5256635; fax (20) 5257832; e-mail ibed-dir-science@uva.nl; internet www.science.uva.nl/ibed; attached to Univ. of Amsterdam; research on biodiversity and evolution, geo-ecology and com-

munity dynamics; Dir Prof. Dr PETER TIENDEREN.

Nationaal Instituut voor Subatomaire Fysica (NIKHEF) (National Institute for Subatomic Physics): POB 41882, 1009 DB Amsterdam; Science Park 105, 1098 XG Amsterdam; tel. (20) 5922000; fax (20) 5925155; e-mail info@nikhef.nl; internet www.nikhef.nl; f. fmrly Nat. Institute for Nuclear Physics and High-Energy Physics, present name 1998; has a 900 MeV pulse stretcher and storage ring (AmPs) and auxiliary instrumentation for basic research in (astro) particle physics; Dir F. LINDE.

Nederlands Instituut voor Ecologie (Netherlands Institute of Ecology): POB 1299, 3600 BG Maarssen; Rijksstraatweg 6, 3631 AC Nieuwersluis; tel. (294) 239300; fax (294) 232224; e-mail m.albers@nioo.knaw.nl; internet www.nioo.knaw.nl; f. 1992 as Netherlands Institute for Ecological Research, present name 2002; attached to Royal Netherlands Acad. of Arts and Sciences; studies animal ecology, plant ecology, microbial ecology in terrestrial, freshwater and marine environments; incorporates Centre for Estuarine and Coastal Ecology (in Yerseke), Centre for Limnology (in Nieuwersluis) and Centre for Terrestrial Ecology (in Heteren); Dir Prof. Dr L. E. M. VET.

Netherlands Institute of Applied Geoscience TNO—National Geological Survey: POB 80015, 3508 TA Utrecht; Princetonlaan 6, 3584 CB Utrecht; tel. (30) 2564256; fax (30) 2564475; e-mail info@nitg .tno.nl; f. 1903; Dir Prof. Dr M. J. VAN BRACHT; publs *Geological Maps*, *Netherlands Journal of Geosciences* (4 a year).

NIOZ Koninklijk Nederlands Instituut voor Zeeonderzoek (NIOZ Royal Netherlands Institute for Sea Research): POB 59, 1790 AB Den Burg, Texel; Landsdiep 4, 1797 SZ 't Horntje, Texel; tel. (222) 369300; fax (222) 319674; e-mail cpr@nioz.nl; internet www.nioz.nl; f. 1876, present bldg 1976; attached to Netherlands Org. for Scientific Research; scientific marine research; ships; Chair. Prof. Dr PIER VELLINGA; Gen. Dir Prof. Dr HENK BRINKHUIS; Deputy Dir Prof. Dr Ir HERMAN RIDDERINKHOF; Sec. Prof. Dr E. A. KOSTER; Treas. GUUS F. C. VAN DER KAMP; publ. *Journal of Sea Research* (4 a year).

SRON Netherlands Institute for Space Research: Sorbonnelaan 2, 3584 CA Utrecht; tel. (88) 7775600; fax (88) 7775601; e-mail info@sron.nl; internet www.sron.nl; f. 1983 as Space Research Org. Netherlands, present name 2005; attached to Netherlands Org. for Scientific Research; develops and exploits equipment for space research and for terrestrial research from space; br. in Groningen; Chair. Ir P. A. O. G. KORTING; Vice-Chair. Prof. Dr W. J. VAN DER ZANDE; Scientific Dir and Gen. Dir Prof. Dr RENS WATERS; Man. Dir and Deputy Gen. Dir Dr ROEL GATHIER.

Stichting voor Fundamenteel Onderzoek der Materie (FOM) (Foundation for Fundamental Research on Matter): POB 3021, 3502 GA Utrecht; Van Vollenhoven-laan 659, 3527 JP Utrecht; tel. (30) 6001211; fax (30) 6014406; e-mail info@fom.nl; internet www.fom.nl; f. 1946; promotes, coordinates and finances fundamental physics research in the Netherlands through 200 univ. teams in 2 institutes of its own, and 1 used jtly with univs; Chair. Prof. Dr N. J. LOPES CARDOZO; Vice-Chair. Prof. Dr C. W. J. BEENAKKER; Dir Dr Ir WIM VAN SAARLOOS; Sec. PETRA VAN LULING.

Attached Institutes:

FOM—Dutch Institute for Fundamental Energy Research (DIFFER): POB 1207, 3430 BE Nieuwegein; Edisonbaan

14, 3439 MN Nieuwegein; tel. (30) 6096999; fax (30) 6031204; e-mail info@ differ.nl; internet www.differ.nl; f. 1959; research in plasma physics, plasma containment, heating, plasma surface interaction, EUV mirrors, solar fuels; library of 7,000 vols, 13,000 reports; Dir Dr M. C. M. VAN DE SANDEN.

FOM—Instituut voor Atoom- en Mole-cuulfysica (FOM Institute of Atomic and Molecular Physics (AMOLF)): POB 41883, 1009 DB Amsterdam; Science Park 104, 1098 XG Amsterdam; tel. (20) 7547100; fax (20) 7547290; e-mail info@amolf.nl; internet www.amolf.nl; f. 1949 as FOM Laboratory for Mass Spectrography, present name 1966; facilities incl. mass-spectrometers, spectrographs, molecular beam apparatus, microwave interferometers, laser equipment, beam plasma experiments, a PDP 11 computer and a nanocentre; library of 2,200 vols; Gen. Dir Dr ALBERT POLMAN; Man. BART VAN LEIJEN.

KVI (Nuclear-Physics Accelerator Institute): Zernikelaan 25, 9747 AA Groningen; tel. (50) 3633600; fax (50) 3634003; e-mail info@kvi.nl; internet www.kvi.nl; f. 1968; fundamental and applied atomic and subatomic physics; AVF cyclotron, ion sources, traps for short-living isotopes; Chair. Prof. K. DUPPEN; Dir Prof. KLAUS JUNGMANN; Exec. Sec. Dr MARJAN KOOPMANS.

Twente Water Centre: Horst Bldg, W 114, POB 217, 7500 AE Enschede; Horst Bldg, Drienerlolaan 5, 7522 NB Enschede; tel. (53) 4894320; fax (53) 4895377; e-mail water@ utwente.nl; internet www.utwente.nl/water; attached to Univ. of Twente; water systems and governance; Chair. for Scientific Programme Council Prof. Dr Ir ARJEN Y. HOEK-STRA; Sec. JOKE MEIJER-LENTELINK.

Van't Hoff Institute for Molecular Sciences: POB 94157, 1090 GD Amsterdam; Science Park 904, 1098 XH Amsterdam; tel. (20) 5255265; fax (20) 5255604; e-mail r.b .hippert@uva.nl; internet www.science.uva .nl/hims; research themes incl. bio-molecular synthesis, catalysis, computational chemistry, macromolecular and biosystems analysis, molecular photonics; Scientific Dir Prof. Dr AART W. KLEIJN.

Zernike Institute for Advanced Materials: POB 221, 9700 AE Groningen; Nijenborgh 4, 9747 AG Groningen; tel. (50) 3634843; fax (50) 3637732; e-mail t.t.m .palstra@rug.nl; internet www.rug.nl/ zernike/index; f. 2007 by merger of Materials Science Centre and Materials Science Centre plus; attached to Faculty of Mathematics and Natural Sciences, Univ. of Groningen; symbiotic studies of functional materials involving researchers from different disciplines; Scientific Dir Prof. Dr T. T. M. PALSTRA.

PHILOSOPHY AND PSYCHOLOGY

Amsterdam Centre for Child Studies: c/o Dr Dorien Graas, Van der Boechorststraat 1, 1081 BT Amsterdam; tel. (20) 5988785; e-mail info@ack.vu.nl; internet www.ack.vu .nl; f. 2002; attached to Vrije Univ. Amsterdam; research on insights in disturbed processes of child rearing and devt, and application and implementation of findings for policies and programmes concerning parents and children.

Behavioural Science Institute: POB 9104, 6500 HE Nijmegen; Montessorilaan 3, A.08.29, 6525 HR Nijmegen; tel. (24) 3610082; fax (24) 3615937; e-mail secr@bsi .ru.nl; internet www.ru.nl/bsi; attached to Faculty of Social Sciences, Radboud Univ. Nijmegen; research on principles and processes of human behaviour; Dir Prof. Dr MICHIEL KOMPIER.

Centre for Philosophy of Technology and Engineering Science: POB 217, 7500 AE Enschede; tel. (53) 4893297; e-mail p .bruulsema@utwente.nl; internet www .utwente.nl/gw/ceptes; attached to Univ. of Twente; research in philosophy of engineering science, technology; Dir PHILIP BREY; Sec. PETRA BRUULSEMA.

Heymans Institute for Psychological Research: Grote Kruisstraat 2/1, 9712 TS Groningen; tel. (50) 3638210; fax (50) 3636304; e-mail secr-onderzoekpsych@rug .nl; internet www.rug.nl/psy/onderzoek; attached to Dept. of Psychology, Univ. of Groningen; psychological research conducted within seven research programmes, participates in six research schools; Scientific Dir RITSKE DE JONG.

Psychology Research Institute: Diamantbeurs, Weesperplein 4, 1018 XA Amsterdam; tel. (20) 5256739; fax (20) 5256710; e-mail ozipsychologie-fmg@uva.nl; internet www .psychologie.uva.nl/psy_research; attached to Univ. of Amsterdam; research, bachelors and masters courses in psychology; Scientific Dir Prof. Dr G. A. KERKHOF; Sec. Drs J. J. W. VAN DER MEER.

Research Institute for Philosophy: POB 9103, 6500 HD Nijmegen; Erasmusplein 1, 6525 HT Nijmegen; tel. (24) 3612474; fax (24) 3615564; e-mail secretariaat@unie.ru.nl; internet www.ru.nl/english/research/ research_institutes/vm/research_institute_0; research programmes-rationality and cognition, hermeneutic philosophy, natural philosophy to science; includes centre for ethics.

RELIGION, SOCIOLOGY AND ANTHROPOLOGY

Amsterdam Institute for Social Science Research: Kloveniersburgwal 48, 1012 CX Amsterdam; Nieuwe Prinsengracht 130, 1018 VZ Amsterdam; tel. (20) 5252262; fax (20) 5252446; e-mail aissr@uva.nl; internet www.aissr.uva.nl; f. 2010 by merger of Amsterdam Institute for Metropolitan and Int. Devt, Amsterdam School for Social science Research, Institute for Migration and Ethnic Studies; attached to Univ. of Amsterdam; research in social sciences incl. anthropology, int. devt studies, geography and planning, political science, sociology, urban studies; Academic Dir Prof. Dr ANITA HARDON; Exec. Dir JOSÉ KOMEN.

Amsterdam School for Cultural Analysis: Spuistraat 210, Room 113, 1012 VT Amsterdam; tel. (20) 5253874; fax (20) 5254773; e-mail asca-fgw@uva.nl; internet www.hum.uva.nl/asca; attached to Univ. of Amsterdam; interdisciplinary, comparative studies across cultural and linguistic areas; Academic Dir CHRISTOPH LINDNER; Man. Dir ELOE KINGMA; Vice-Dir Dr WANDA STRAUVEN.

Babylon, Centre for Studies of Multicultural Society: POB 90153, 5000 LE Tilburg; Tilburg Univ., Warandelaan 2, Dante Bldg, 2nd Fl., 5037 AB Tilburg; tel. (13) 4662668; fax (13) 4662892; e-mail babylon@uvt.nl; internet www.tilburguniversity.nl/babylon; f. 2002; attached to Tilburg Univ.; research on characteristics and management of cultural, linguistic, religious diversity in multicultural society, taken from an int. comparative perspective; Dir Prof. Dr JAN BLOMMAERT; Assoc. Dir Prof. Dr FONS VAN DE VIJVER; Sec. KARIN BERKHOUT.

Centrum voor Patristisch Onderzoek (Centre for Patristic Research): POB 80101, 3508 TC Utrecht; tel. (30) 2532928; e-mail info@patristiek.eu; internet www.patristiek .eu; attached to Tilburg Univ.; research themes incl. early devt of Christian thinking

about man, society, creation, the triune God; Dir Prof. Dr PAUL VAN GEEST.

Globus Competence Centre for Globalization and Sustainable Development: POB 90153, 5000 LE Tilburg; Warandelaan 2, 5037 AB Tilburg; tel. (13) 4668010; fax (13) 4668699; e-mail viv.mestdagh@tiasnimbas .edu; internet www.tiasnimbas.edu/globus; f. 1998; attached to TiasNimbas Business School, Tilbug Univ.; globalization, sustainable devt; Chair. Prof. Dr K. ZOETEMAN; Exec. Dir Prof. Dr PAUL VAN SETERS.

DELETE Groningen Research Institute for the Study of Culture (ICOG): POB 716, NL-9700 AS Groningen; Oude Kijk in 't Jatstraat 26, 9712 EK Groningen; tel. (50) 3635918; fax (50) 3635821; e-mail icog@rug .nl; internet www.rug.nl/let/onderzoek/ onderzoekinstituten/icog; attached to Faculty of Arts, Univ. of Groningen; research on study of cultural processes, their manifestations and discussion of these subjects in Europe, Americas, E Mediterranean, Asian regions; Dir Prof. Dr GOFFE JENSMA.

Institute for Historical, Literary and Cultural Studies: POB 9103, 6500 HD Nijmegen; Erasmusplein 1, 6525 HT Nijmegen; tel. (24) 3612336; fax (24) 3615481; e-mail hlcs@let.ru.nl; internet www.ru.nl/ facultyofarts/research/research_institute_0; f. 1998; attached to Faculty of Arts, Radboud Univ. Nijmegen; research programmes on ancient world, memory, cultural and religious identities; history of politics and human life courses; literary criticism.

Institute for Migration and Ethnic Studies: Oudezijds Achterburgwal 185, 1012 DK Amsterdam; tel. (20) 5252504; fax (20) 5253628; e-mail imes@uva.nl; internet www .imes.uva.nl; attached to Univ. of Amsterdam; debates on migration as a social science issue; fosters dialogue across academic disciplines; promotes intellectual reflexivity; Co-Dir BARAK KALIR; Co-Dir OLGA SEZNEVA; Co-Dir FLORIS VERMEULEN.

Instituut voor Liturgische en Rituele Studies (ILRS) (Institute for Liturgical and Ritual Studies): POB 90153, 5000 LE Tilburg; Dante Bldg, Room 132, Warandelaan 2, 5037 AB, Tilburg; tel. (13) 4662056; fax (13) 4662892; e-mail ilrs@uvt.nl; internet www.tilburguniversity.nl/ilrs; attached to Tilburg Univ.; research areas incl. rituals, Christian liturgy, sacred places, sacraments, folk religious rites; Chair. Prof. Dr G. ROUWHORST; Sec. Dr PETRA VERSNEL; publs *Jaarboek voor liturgieonderzoek*, *Liturgia condenda*, *Meander*, *Netherlands Studies in Ritual and Liturgy*.

Interuniversity Centre for Social Science Theory and Methodology (ICS): ICS, Department of Sociology, Grote Rozenstraat 31, 9712 TG Groningen; tel. (50) 3636469; fax (50) 3636226; e-mail s.simon@ rug.nl; internet www.ics-graduateschool.nl; f. 1986; jt project of Univ. of Groningen, Utrecht Univ. and Radboud Univ. Nijmegen; located in sociology dept. of all three univs; Scientific Dir Prof. RAFAEL WITTEK.

LUCE—Centrum voor Religieuze Communicatie (LUCE—Centre for Religious Communication): POB 80101, 3508 TC Utrecht; Heidelberglaan 2, Utrecht; tel. (30) 2531882; fax (30) 2533665; e-mail luce-crc@ uvt.nl; f. 2007; attached to Tilburg Univ.; Dir HENK VAN HOUT.

Meertens Instituut: POB 94264, 1090 GG Amsterdam; Joan Muyskenweg 25, 1096 CJ Amsterdam; tel. (20) 4628500; fax (20) 4628555; e-mail info@meertens.knaw.nl; internet www.meertens.knaw.nl; f. 1926, present status 1952; attached to Royal Netherlands Acad. of Arts and Sciences; research into diversity and documentation

of Dutch language and culture; incl. ethnological studies, structural, dialectological and sociolinguistic study of language variation; organizes workshops, symposiums and confs; library of 70,000 vols, 4,000 journals; Dir Prof. Dr H. J. BENNIS.

Nederlandse Onderzoekschool voor Theologie en Religiewetenschap (NOSTER) (Netherlands School for Advanced Studies in Theology and Religion): POB 80.105, 3508 TC Utrecht; Trans 14, 3512 JK Utrecht; tel. (30) 2533105; fax (30) 2533241; e-mail noster@uu.nl; internet www.noster .org; attached to Utrecht Univ.; research in theology, religious studies; Pres. Dr PETER J. A. NISSEN; Exec. Sec. Dr CHARLOTTE VAN DER LEEST; Dir Prof. Dr A. J. A. C. M. (ANNE-MARIE) KORTE; Sec. ANJA H. HAVINGA; 200 teachers; 50 students; publ. *Studies in Theology and Religion (STAR)*.

Netherlands Institute for Advanced Study in the Humanities and Social Sciences (NIAS): Meijboomlaan 1, 2242 PR Wassenaar; tel. (70) 5122700; fax (70) 5117162; e-mail nias@nias.knaw.nl; internet www.nias.knaw.nl; f. 1970, present status 1998; attached to Royal Netherlands Acad. of Arts and Sciences; encourages research in the humanities and social sciences; fellowships awarded annually (25 to foreign scholars, 25 to Dutch scholars); Rector Prof. AAFKE C. J. HULK; publs *Jelle Zijlstra Lecture* (1 a year), *KB Lecture* (1 a year), *Ortelius Lecture* (every 2 years), *Uhlenbeck Lecture* (1 a year), *Willem F. Duisenberg Lecture* (1 a year).

Nijmeegs Instituut voor Sociaal en Cultureel Onderzoek (NISCO) (Nijmegen Institute for Social and Cultural Research): POB 9104, 6500 HE Nijmegen; Thomas van Aquinostraat 4, 6525 GD Nijmegen; tel. (24) 3615568; fax (24) 3612351; e-mail e.vanwijk@ maw.ru.nl; internet www.ru.nl/english/ research/research_institutes/vm/nijmegen_- institute; f. 2003; attached to Faculty of Social Sciences, Radbound Univ. Nijmegen; comparative questions on cohesion, inequality, rationalization within and between societies; Dir PAUL HOEBINK.

Research Institute for Theology and Religious Studies: POB 9103, 6500 HD Nijmegen; Erasmusplein 1, 6525 HT Nijmegen; tel. (24) 3612474; e-mail secretariaat@ unie.ru.nl; internet www.ru.nl/english/ research/research_institutes/vm/research_- institute; attached to Radboud Univ. Nijmegen; study of religious identities in multireligious societies.

SISWO—Instituut voor Maatschappijwetenschappen (SISWO—Institute for the Social Sciences): Plantage Muidergracht 4, 1018 TV Amsterdam; tel. (20) 5270600; fax (20) 6229430; e-mail siswo@siswo.uva.nl; internet www.siswo.uva.nl/angloam; f. 1960; initiates and coordinates policy-relevant social science research; Dir Prof. Dr H. G. DE GIER; publs *FACTA*, *KWALON*, *Tijdschrift voor Criminologie*.

Telos Brabants Centrum voor Duurzame Ontwikkeling (TELOS—Brabant Centre for Sustainable Development): POB 90153, 5000 LE Tilburg; Warandelaan 2, 5037 AB, Tilburg; tel. (13) 4668712; fax (13) 4663499; e-mail telos@uvt.nl; internet www .telos.nl; f. 1999; attached to Tilburg Univ.; research into sustainable system innovations, transitions in Brabant; Chair Prof. Dr Ir J. T. MOMMAAS.

Thomas Instituut te Utrecht: Heidelberglaan 2, 3584 CS Utrecht; tel. (73) 6135665; fax (73) 5482049; e-mail info@ instituut-thomas.nl; internet www .thomasinstituut.org; f. 1990, present status 2006; attached to Tilburg Univ.; study of work of St Thomas Aquinas; Dir Prof. Dr H. J. M. SCHOOT; Sec. for Studies Dr C. M. PUMPLUN.

TECHNOLOGY

3TU Centre for Ethics and Technology: POB 5015, 2600 GA Delft; tel. (15) 2787210; fax (15) 2786439; e-mail info@ ethicsandtechnology.eu; internet www .ethicsandtechnology.eu; studies ethical issues in devt, use and regulation of technology; Man. Dir Dr SABINE ROESER.

Advanced School for Computing and Imaging: TU Delft, EWI, Mekelweg 4, 2628 CD Delft; tel. (15) 2788032; fax (15) 2786632; e-mail asci@ewi.tudelft.nl; internet www.asci .tudelft.nl; research in computer systems; Scientific Dir Prof. Dr Ir A. W. M. SMEULDERS.

BatchKennisCentrum (Batch Knowledge Centre): POB 5015, 2600 GA Delft; Jaffalaan 5, 2628 GX Delft; tel. (15) 2781147; fax (15) 2783422; e-mail bkc@batchcentre.tudelft.nl; internet www.batchcentre.tudelft.nl; attached to Delft Univ. of Technology; provides information on batch literature, batch research, batch software, batch tutorials; Project Leader Dr Z. VERWATER-LUKSO.

Beta Research School for Operations Management and Logistics: Paviljoen C 07, POB 513, 5600 MB Eindhoven; tel. (40) 2474733; fax (40) 2472607; e-mail beta@tue .nl; internet beta.ieis.tue.nl; f. 1995, present status 1998; attached to Eindhoven Univ. of Technology; operational processes, computer science, labour psychology, mathematics, organizational behaviour; Scientific Dir Prof. Dr Ir G. J. VAN HOUTUM.

CIM Centrum Delft (CIM Centre Delft): Mekelweg 2, 2628 CD Delft; tel. (15) 2786876; fax (15) 2783910; e-mail b.r .meijer@tudelft.nl; f. 1985; attached to Delft Univ. of Technology; training and knowledge centre in the fields of computer integrated manufacturing (CID), automated production systems, robotics in corporate economic and organizational context.

Centre for Plasma Physics and Radiation Technology: Dept of Applied Physics, POB 513, 5600 MB Eindhoven; tel. (40) 2472779; fax (40) 2438060; e-mail office .cps@tue.nl; internet www.phys.tue.nl/cps; attached to Eindhoven Univ. of Technology; research in the field of astrophysical plasmas, cold etching and deposition plasmas, hot thermonuclear plasmas, micro-discharges, physics; devt, applications of radiation sources; Scientific Dir Prof. Dr M. C. M. VAN DE SANDEN; Sec. A. M. M. LOONEN.

Centre for Telematics and Information Technology: POB 217, 7500 AE Enschede; Zilverling Bldg, Drienerlolaan 5, 7522 NB Enschede; tel. (53) 4898031; fax (53) 4891070; e-mail office@ctit.utwente.nl; internet www.ctit.utwente.nl; attached to Univ. of Twente; research on design of advanced ICT systems and their application in a variety of application domains; Chair. of Supervisory Board Prof. Dr E. H. L. AARTS; Scientific Dir PETER M. G. APERS; Man. Dir IDDO BANTE.

Centrum voor Schone Technologie en Milieubeleid (Twente Centre for Studies in Technology and Sustainable Development): POB 217, 7500 AE Enschede; Ravelijn Bldg, Drienerlolaan 5, 7522 NB Enschede; tel. (53) 4893203; fax (53) 4894850; e-mail secr@cstm .utwente.nl; internet www.utwente.nl/mb/ cstm; f. 1988; attached to Univ. of Twente; environmental quality, governance, sustainable devt, technological innovation; Scientific Dir Prof. Dr HANS TH. A. BRESSERS; Man. Dir Dr MAARTEN J. ARENTSEN.

Communication Technology Basic Research and its Applications (COBRA): Bldg Potentiaal, Room PT 11.28, POB 513, 5600 MB Eindhoven; Bldg Potentiaal, Room PT 11.28, Den Dolech 2, 5612 AZ Eindhoven; tel. (40) 2473880; fax (40) 2455197; e-mail cobra@tue.nl; internet www.cobra.tue.nl; f. 1994; attached to Eindhoven Univ. of Technology; communication technologies basic research and applications; Scientific Dir Prof. Dr H. J. S. DORREN.

Delft Centre for Engineering Design: Mekelweg 2, 2628 CD Delft; tel. (15) 278 6794; fax (15) 2784717; e-mail j.w.m .tournoij@tudelft.nl; internet www.tudelft.nl; attached to Delft Univ. of Technology; Advanced Masters in Engineering Design; industry research; Dir Prof. Dr T. TOMIYAMA.

Delft Centre for Aviation: Jaffalaan 5, 2628 BX Delft; tel. (12) 2787553; e-mail a.r.c .dehaan@tudelft.nl; internet www.tudelft.nl; aviation research centre of Delft Univ. of Technology; researches air traffic systems, aviation processes, airport systems, landslide accessibility, sustainability analysis; Managing Dir Dr ALEXANDER DE HAAN.

Delft Institute for Earth-Oriented Space Research: POB 5058, Delft; Kluyverweg 1, 2600 GB Delft; tel. (15) 2782558; fax (15) 2782348; e-mail teunissen@deos.tudelft.nl; attached to Delft Univ. of Technology; incorporates field of spacecraft system integration and design that is essential for the devt of earth observation systems; Scientific Dir Prof. Dr Ir P. J. G. TEUNISSEN.

Delft Institute for Information Technology in Service Engineering: Stevinweg 1, 2628 CN Delft; tel. (15) 2785170; fax (15) 2785347; e-mail info@duwind.tudelft.nl; attached to Delft Univ. of Technology; Dir Prof. Dr H. G. SOL.

Delft Institute of Microsystems and Nanoelectronics (Dimes): Feldmannweg 17, 2628 CT Delft; tel. (15) 2786234; fax (15) 2787369; e-mail info@dimes.tudelft.nl; internet www.dimes.tudelft.nl; attached to Delft Univ. of Technology; research and education in microsystems and nanoelectronics through PhD programme; Scientific Dir Prof. Dr KEES BEENAKKER.

Delft University Wind Energy Research Institute: Kluyverweg 1, 2629 HS Delft; tel. (15) 2785170; fax (15) 2785347; e-mail duwind@tudelft.nl; internet www.duwind .tudelft.nl; f. 1999; attached to Delft Univ. of Technology; research on modern wind turbine technology.

Delft University Research Centre of Intelligent Sensor Microsystems: POB 5031, 2600 GA Delft; Mekelweg 4, EWI Bldg, 2628 CD Delft; tel. (15) 2785745; fax (15) 2785755; e-mail disens@tudelft.nl; internet www.disens.tudelft.nl; attached to Delft Univ. of Technology; research on sensors and actuators in microsystem technology; Dir Prof. Dr P. M. SARRO; Man. Dir Prof. Dr Ir J. H. HUIJSING; Sec. G. HOUWELING.

Dutch Institute of Systems and Control: Delft Centre for Systems and Control, Delft Univ. of Technology, DISC, Mekelweg 2, 2628 CD Delft; tel. (15) 2785172; fax (15) 2786679; e-mail s.m.vandermeer@tudelft.nl; internet www.disc.tudelft.nl; f. 1995 by Delft and Eindhoven Univ. of Technology and Univ. of Twente; interuniv. research institute, graduate school unites all academic research active in systems and control theory and engineering; Dir Prof. Dr Ir PAUL VAN DEN HOF.

Dutch National Research School Combination Catalysis Controlled by Chemical Design (NRSC-Catalysis): POB 513, 5600 MB Eindhoven; Den Dolech 2, Helix W 3.23, Eindhoven; tel. (40) 2473071; fax (40) 2475054; e-mail m.j.m.j.jong@tue.nl; internet www.nrsc-catalysis.nl; f. 1999; attached to Eindhoven Univ. of Technology; Dir Prof. Dr RUTGER A. VAN SANTEN; Man. Dr GABRIELA E. DIMA.

Energieonderzoek Centrum Nederland (ECN) (Energy Research Centre of the Netherlands (ECN)): POB 1, 1755 ZG Petten; Westerduinweg 3, 1755 LE Petten; tel. (22) 4564949; fax (22) 4568486; e-mail info@ecn .nl; internet www.ecn.nl; f. 1955 as Reactor Centrum Nederland—RCN; carries out energy research; under contract from the govt, nat. and int. orgs and industry; Man. Dir Ir PAUL A. O. G. KORTING; Dir Dr C. A. M. (KEES) VAN DER KLEIN; Dir PEDRO J. SAYERS.

Graduate School on Engineering Mechanics: c/o Dr Ir J. A. W. van Dommelen, Dept of Mechanical Engineering, Eindhoven Univ. of Technology, POB 513, W-hoog 4.133, 5600 MB Eindhoven; tel. (40) 2474060; fax (40) 2447355; e-mail engineering.mechanics@tue .nl; internet www.em.tue.nl; f. 1996; attached to Eindhoven Univ. of Technology; description, analysis, optimization of static and dynamic behaviour of materials, products, processes in variety of engineering applications; Scientific Dir Prof. MARC G. D. GEERS.

Hechtingsinstituut (The Adhesion Institute): Kluyverweg 1, 2629 HS Delft; tel. (15) 2785353; e-mail info@hechtinginstituut.nl; internet www.adhesioninstitute.com; f. 1990; attached to Delft Univ. of Technology; research in the field of structural adhesive bonds; part of the Faculty of Aerospace Engineering; Dir Dr J. A. POULIS.

IBR Centre for eHealth Research and Disease Management: Citadel H 411, POB 217, 7500 AE Enschede; Citadel Bldg H 411, Drienerlolaan 5, 7522 NB Enschede; tel. (53) 4892398; fax (53) 4892388; e-mail j .vangemert-pijnen@utwente.nl; internet www.utwente.nl/ibr/ehealth; attached to Univ. of Twente; examines technology's contribution to healthy lifestyle.

IBR Research Institute for Social Sciences and Technology: Citadel Bldg H 411, POB 217, 7500 AE Enschede; tel. (53) 4892398; fax (53) 4894259; e-mail ibr@ utwente.nl; internet www.utwente.nl/ibr; attached to Univ. of Twente; research on human behaviour; research themes incl. health assessment and promotion, learning, organization and communication, product design, safety and security, technical cognition; Scientific Dir Prof. Dr E. R. SEYDEL; Man. Dir Dr O. PETERS; Sec. M. G. STEGEHUIS-DE VEGTE.

Institute for Biomedical Technology and Technical Medicine: Zuidhorst Bldg, POB 217, 7500 AE Enschede; Zuidhorst Bldg, Drienerlolaan 5, 7522 NB Enschede; tel. (53) 4893367; fax (53) 4892319; e-mail mira@utwente.nl; internet www.utwente.nl/ mira; attached to Univ. of Twente; Scientific Dir Prof. Dr CLEMENS A. VAN BLITTERSWIJK; Man. Dir Dr Ir MARTIJN KUIT; Medical Dir Prof. Dr G. P. (PETER) VOOIJS; Dir for Education Drs HELEEN A. T. MIEDEMA.

Institute for Computing and Information Sciences: POB 9010, 6500 GL Nijmegen; Heyendaalseweg 135, 6525 AJ Nijmegen; tel. (24) 3652643; fax (24) 3652728; e-mail info@cs.ru.nl; internet www .ru.nl/icis; attached to Faculty of Science, Radboud Univ. Nijmegen; research on computer systems through model based system development, digital security and intelligent systems; Research Dir Prof. Dr T. M. HESKES.

Institute for Logic, Language and Computation: POB 94242, 1090 GE Amsterdam; Science Park 904, 1098 XH Amsterdam; tel.

(20) 5256051; fax (20) 5255206; e-mail illc@ uva.nl; internet www.illc.uva.nl; f. 1986 as Institute for Language, Logic and Information, present status 1991; attached to Univ. of Amsterdam; research in fundamental principles of encoding, transmission and comprehension of information; Dir Prof. Dr YDE VENEMA; Man. Drs JENNY BATSON; publ. *ILLC magazine* (1 a year).

Institute for Medical Technology Assessment (iMTA): POB 1738, 3000 DR Rotterdam; Burgemeester Oudlaan 50, 3062 PA Rotterdam; tel. (10) 4088571; fax (10) 4089081; e-mail vanoorschot@bmg.eur.nl; internet www.bmg.eur.nl/imta; f. 1988; attached to Erasmus Univ.; medical technology assessment, incl. health economics and health outcomes research; provides teaching and training in economic evaluation and MTA research; Vice-Dir Prof. Dr MAUREEN RUTTEN-VAN MÖLKEN; Sec. KARIN VAN OORSCHOT-LÖWENTHAL.

Institute for Science, Innovation and Society (ISIS): POB 9010, 6500 GL Nijmegen; Huygens Bldg, Room 02.832, Heijendaalseweg 135, 6525 AJ Nijmegen; tel. (24) 3653155; fax (24) 3553450; e-mail h.zwart@ science.ru.nl; internet www.ru.nl/science/ isis; f. 2005; attached to Faculty of Science, Radbound Univ. Nijmegen; analyses, assesses and improves societal embedding of science and technology; Dir Prof. Dr HUB ZWART.

Instituut voor Milieu en Agritechniek (IMAG-DLO) (Institute of Agricultural and Environmental Engineering): POB 43, 6700 AA Wageningen; Mansholtlaan 10–12, 6708 PA Wageningen; tel. (317) 476300; fax (317) 425670; e-mail postkamer@imag.dlo.nl; f. 1974; Dir Dr Ir AAD A. JONGEBREUR.

International Research Centre for Telecommunications and Radar: c/o Delft Univ. of Technology, POB 5031, 2600 GA Delft; Mekelweg 4, EWI Bldg, 2628 CD Delft; tel. (15) 2781034; fax (15) 2784046; e-mail d.a .u.meijer@tudelft.nl; f. 1994; attached to Delft Univ. of Technology; Dir Prof. Dr Ir LEO P. LIGTHART; Sec. DOMINIQUE A. U. MEIJER.

International Research Institute for Simulation, Motion and Navigation: POB 5058, 2600 GB Delft; Anthony Fokkerweg 1, 2629 HC Delft; tel. (15) 2782094; fax (15) 2786480; e-mail info@simona.tudelft.nl; attached to Delft Univ. of Technology; research institute in the field of simulation and transport; Man. Dir Ir MEINE P. OOSTEN; Management Asst VERA M. VAN BRAGT.

J. F. Schouten School for User–System Interaction Research: POB 513, 5600 MB Eindhoven; Paviljoen, R. 1.40, ingang Het Eeuwsel, Eindhoven; tel. (40) 2475938; fax (40) 2472607; e-mail jfs@tue.nl; internet www.industrialdesign.tue.nl/jfschouten; f. 1993; attached to Eindhoven Univ. of Technology; Scientific Dir Prof. Dr DON G. BOUWHUIS.

J. M. Burgerscentrum—Onderzoekschool voor Stromingsleer (JMBC) (J. M. Burgerscentrum—Research School for Fluid Mechanics): c/o TU Delft, Mekelweg 2, 2628 CD Delft; tel. (15) 2783216; e-mail jmburgerscentrum@tudelft.nl; internet www .jmburgerscentrum.nl; 60 research groups, 250 PhD students; Dir Prof. Dr Ir G. OOMS.

Kavli Institute of Nanoscience: Postbus 5046, 2600 GA Delft; Lorentzweg 1, 2628 CJ Delft; tel. (15) 2783163; fax (15) 2786600; e-mail nanoscience@tnw.tudelft.nl; internet www.tnw.tudelft.nl; f. 2004; attached to Delft Univ. of Technology; 6 research units, one nanofacility cleanroom; founded on grant by Kavli foundation; Dir Prof. Dr HANS MOOIJ.

Koiter Institute Delft: Kluyverweg 1, 2629 HS Delft; tel. (15) 2785460; fax (15) 2611465; e-mail r.deborst@lr.tudelft.nl; internet www .kid.tudelft.nl; attached to Delft Univ. of Technology; promotes mono-disciplinary activity in engineering mechanics.

Materials Analysis, Testing, Technology and Research: POB 513, 5600 MB Eindhoven; tel. (40) 2474950; fax (40) 2445619; e-mail i.m.j.j.v.d.ven-lucassen@tue.nl; attached to Eindhoven Univ. of Technology; Sec. Dr Ir I. M. M. J. VAN DE VEN-LUCASSEN.

Materials Innovation Institute (M2i): POB 5008, 2600 GA Delft; Mekelweg 2, 2628 CD Delft; tel. (15) 2782535; fax (15) 2782591; e-mail info@m2i.nl; internet www .m2i.nl; devt of new materials for sustainable economic growth; partnership between industy, govt, academia.

MESA+ Institute for Nanotechnology: POB 217, 7500 AE Enschede; NanoLab Bldg, Hallenweg 15, 7522 NB Enschede; tel. (53) 4892715; fax (53) 4892575; e-mail info@ mesaplus.utwente.nl; internet www.utwente .nl/mesaplus; attached to Univ. of Twente; research in nanotechnology; Scientific Dir Prof. Dr Ing DAVE BLANK.

Nationaal Lucht- en Ruimtevaartlaboratorium (NLR) (National Aerospace Laboratory): POB 90502, 1006 BM Amsterdam; Anthony Fokkerweg 2, 1059 CM Amsterdam; tel. (20) 5113113; fax (20) 5113210; e-mail info@nlr.nl; internet www .nlr.nl/public; f. 1919; fluid dynamics, flight mechanics, flight testing and operations, structures and materials, space technology, remote sensing, information technology, electronics and instrumentation; br. in Flevoland; library of 7,000 vols, 4,800 conf. proceedings, 2,500 theses, 112,000 reports, etc.; Chair. Drs ARIE KRAAIJEVELD; Gen. Dir Ir MICHEL PETERS; Gen. Sec. ERNST FOLKERS.

National Dutch Graduate Research School of Polymer Science and Technology (PTN): POB 6284, 5600 HG Eindhoven; tel. (40) 2475262; fax (40) 2475430; e-mail info@ptn.nu; internet www.ptn.nu; cooperation foundation stage for polymer research in univ. and industry.

National Dutch Graduate School of Polymer Science and Technology (PTN): POB 6284, 5600 HG Eindhoven; tel. (40) 2475262; fax (40) 2475430; e-mail info@ ptn.nu; internet www.ptn.nu; Chair. Ir DICK MEDEMA.

Onderzoekschool Engineering Mechanics (Graduate School on Engineering Mechanics): c/o Dr Ir J. A. W. van Dommelen, POB 513, WH 4.125, 5600 MB Eindhoven; tel. (40) 2474521; e-mail engineering.mechanics@tue .nl; internet www.em.tue.nl; f. 1996; research and education in engineering mechanics; works with Eindhoven Univ. of Technology, Delft Univ. of technology and Univ. of Twente; Scientific Dir Prof. Dr Ir M. G. D. (MARC) GEERS.

OnderzoekSchool ProcesTechnologie (Research School in Process Technology): Groen van Prinstererlaan 37, 3818 JN Amersfoort; tel. (53) 7009791; fax (53) 4891199; e-mail ospt@ispt.eu; internet ispt .eu; chemical engineering, process technology; Chair. of the Board Prof. Dr G. VAN DER STEENHOVEN; Scientific Dir Prof. Dr Ir H. E. A. VAN DEN AKKER; Exec. Sec. ELLIS WENNMACHER.

Onderzoekschool voor Integrale Product Vernieuwing (Graduate School of Integrated Product Innovation): Universiteit Twente, Faculteit der Werktuigbouwkunde, Centrum voor Integrale, Productie Vernieuwing, POB 217, 7500 AE Enschede; tel. (53) 4892520; research programme for

research groups in product innovation; Dir Prof. Dr Ir F. J. A. M. VAN HOUTEN.

Reactor Institute Delft: Mekelweg 15, 2629 JB Delft; tel. (15) 2785052; fax (15) 2786422; e-mail secretary-rid@tudelft.nl; attached to Delft Univ. of Technology; fundamental and applied scientific research in various fields, both nationally and internationally; houses Hoger Onderwijs Reactor (HOR); Dir Prof. Dr Ir TIM H. J. J. VAN DER HAGEN; Gen. Man Drs Ir RIK J. LINSSEN; Sec. LINDA HOOGENDONK-DEN OTTER.

Research School Integral Design of Structures: POB 5048, 2600 GA Delft; Faculty of Civil Engineering and Geosciences, Delft Univ. of Technology, Stevinweg 1, 2628 CN Delft; tel. (15) 2784578; fax (15) 2787438; e-mail info@osbouw.nl; internet www.osbouw .nl; f. 1994; inter-univ. research institute for structural design, structural engineering and building processes; Dir Prof. Dr Ir J. C. WALRAVEN.

School for Information and Knowledge Systems: Utrecht Univ., Dept of Information and Computing Sciences, Corine Jolles, Buys Ballot Laboratory, Princetonplein 5, Office 574, 3584 CC Utrecht; tel. (30) 2534083; fax (30) 2513791; e-mail office@siks.nl; internet www.siks.nl; f. 1996; research school for information and communication technology; network institute with 11 collaborating univs; Man. Dir Dr R. J. C. M. STARMANS.

ThermoPlastic Composite Research Centre: Palatijn 15, 7521 PN Enschede; tel. (88) 8773877; fax (88) 8773899; e-mail info@ tprc.nl; internet www.tprc.nl; f. 2009; attached to Univ. of Twente; research and devt of thermoplastic composites materials and technologies for mems; Gen. Man. HARALD HEERINK.

TICER—Tilburg Innovation Centre for Electronic Resources: POB 90153, 5000 LE Tilburg; tel. (13) 4662620; fax (13) 4668383; e-mail m.a.schuurman@uvt.nl; internet www.tilburguniversity.nl/ticer; f. 1995; attached to Tilburg Univ.; digital libraries and IT infrastructure; Man. JOLA PRINSEN; Logistics Man. MERRILEE SCHUURMAN.

Tilburg Centre for Cognition and Communication (TICC): POB 90153, 5000 LE Tilburg; Dante Bldg, Warandelaan 2, 5037 AB Tilburg; tel. (13) 4668118; e-mail ticc@uvt .nl; internet www.tilburguniversity.nl/ticc; attached to Tilburg Univ.; artificial intelligence, cognitive modelling, gaming, human–computer interaction; Dir Prof. Dr H. J. VAN DEN HERIK.

Tilburg Institute for Law, Technology and Society (TILT): POB 90153, 5000 LE Tilburg; Montesquieu Bldg, Warandelaan 2, 5037 AB Tilburg; tel. (13) 4668199; fax (13) 4663750; e-mail v.carter@uvt.nl; internet www.tilburguniversity.nl/tilt; attached to Tilburg Univ.; transnational study of law, society, technology; research areas incl. devts in ICT, biotechnology, other technologies; Gen. Dir Prof. Dr HAN SOMSEN; Dir for Research and Deputy Dir Prof. Dr RONALD E. LEENES; Dir for Studies Dr ANTON H. VEDDER; Dir for Human Resources Dr SIMONE VAN DER HOF; Sec. VIVIAN CARTER.

Twente Embedded Systems Initiative: POB 217, 7500 AE Enschede; tel. (53) 4894173; fax (53) 4893770; e-mail t.krol@cs .utwente.nl; internet www.tesi.utwente.nl; attached to Univ. of Twente; research activities in the field of embedded systems, embedded systems design; Head Prof. Dr Ir THIJS KROL.

Vakgroep Verkeer, Vervoer & Ruimte (Centre for Transport Studies): POB 217, 7500 AE Enschede; Bldg Horst, Drienerlolaan 5, 7522 NB Enschede; tel. (53) 4894322; fax (53) 4894040; e-mail d.alink-olthof@ utwente.nl; internet www.vvr.ctw.utwente .nl; attached to Univ. of Twente; provides traffic engineering courses in Bachelors programme; civil engineering and track traffic engineering and management within the Masters programme; Head Prof. Dr ERIC VAN BERKUM; Sec. DORETTE ALINK-OLTHOF.

Vermogenselektronica en Elektromagnetisch Conversie Centrum (Power Electronics and Electromagnetic Power Conversion Centre): Mekelweg 4, 2628 CD Delft; tel. (15) 2786259; fax (15) 2782968; attached to Delft Univ. of Technology.

Virtual Reality Initiative Twente: c/o Dr Ir H. van der Kooij, POB 217, 7500 AE Enschede; tel. (53) 4894779; internet vrint .ctit.utwente.nl; attached to Univ. of Twente; platform for all research groups involved with the devt and application of virtual reality tools.

Libraries and Archives

Alkmaar

Regionaal Archief Alkmaar (Regional Record Office Alkmaar): POB 9232, 1800 GE Alkmaar; Bergerweg 1, 1815 AC Alkmaar; tel. (72) 8508200; fax (72) 8508252; e-mail regionaal@archiefalkmaar .nl; internet www.archiefalkmaar.nl; f. 1990; municipal archives, books about Alkmaar and N Holland, etc.; also regional archives for the area; pictures, prints, maps, relating to Alkmaar and surroundings; 50,000 vols; Librarian M. JOUSTRA.

Amersfoort

Bibliotheek van het Oud-Katholiek Seminarie (Library of the Old Catholic Seminary): Koningin Wilhelminalaan 3, 3818 HN Amersfoort; tel. (33) 4617569; fax (33) 4619340; e-mail l.nieuwenhuiz@hetnet .nl; internet seminarie.okkn.nl; f. 1725; attached to Dept of Theology, Utrecht Univ.; Old Catholicism, Jansenism, Port-Royal, Church history of the Netherlands and Old-Catholic churches, ecumenism, titles edited before 1900 have been moved to the Library of Utrecht Univ.; 11,000 vols; Librarian L. NIEUWENHUIZEN.

Openbare Leeszaal en Bibliotheek (Public Library): Zonnehof 12, 3811 ND Amersfoort; tel. (33) 631914; f. 1913; 190,000 vols; Librarian E. A. MURRIS.

Amsterdam

Bibliotheca Philosophica Hermetica (Library of Hermetic Philosophy in Amsterdam): Bloemgracht 13–19, 1016 KC Amsterdam; tel. (20) 6258079; fax (20) 6200973; e-mail bph@ritmanlibrary.nl; internet www .ritmanlibrary.nl; f. 1984; private library, open to researchers by appt; 22,000 vols, incl 5,000 vols printed before 1800, 600 MSS, 17,000 modern titles; specialises in early printed books and MSS in the field of the Christian-hermetic tradition (alchemy, hermetism, mysticism and rosicrucianism); also modern biographical and bibliographical reference works, text-editions, scholarly works, books on the modern esoteric tradition; Man. Dir and Librarian ESTHER OOSTERWIJK-RITMAN; Curator Dr CIS VAN HEERTUM; Curator Drs JOSÉ BOUMAN.

Bibliotheek Centrum Wiskunde & Informatica (Library of the Centre for Mathematics and Computer Science): POB 94079, 1090 GB Amsterdam; Science Park 123, 1098 XG Amsterdam; tel. (20) 5924027; e-mail bibl@cwi.nl; internet www.cwi.nl/library; f. 1946; spec. scientific library on non-elemen-

tary mathematics and its applications and computer science; 45,700 vols, 1,000 current periodicals, 10,000 e-books, 158,000 reports; Library Man. AY-LING ONG.

Bibliotheek van het Koninklijk Instituut voor de Tropen (Library of the Royal Tropical Institute): POB 95001, 1090 HA Amsterdam; Mauritskade 63, 1092 AD Amsterdam; tel. (20) 5688462; fax (20) 6654423; e-mail library@kit.nl; internet www.kit.nl; f. 1910; 450,000 vols, 12,000 periodicals, 27,000 maps; Head of Information, Library and Documentation Drs J. H. W. VAN HARTEVELT.

Boekmanstichting Bibliotheek (Library of the Boekman Foundation): Herengracht 415, 1017 BP Amsterdam; tel. (20) 6243739; fax (20) 6385239; e-mail library@boekman.nl; internet www.boekman.nl; f. 1963; all fields of art and culture and related policy; 65,000 vols, 150 current periodicals; Head of Library MARJOLEIN VAN DER STEEN; publ. *Boekman*.

Centre for Latin American Research and Documentation: Keizersgracht 395–397, 1016 EK Amsterdam; tel. (20) 5253248; fax (20) 6255127; e-mail library@cedla.nl; internet www.cedla.uva.nl/60_library/ library_index.html; attached to Univ. of Amsterdam; social sciences, economy and history of Latin America; 1,222 journals, spec. collns incl. 20,000 microfiches, 3,500 microfilms.

Economisch-Historische Bibliotheek Amsterdam (Economic-History Library Amsterdam): Cruquiusweg 31, 1019 AT Amsterdam; tel. (20) 6685866; fax (20) 6654181; e-mail cse@iisg.nl; internet www .neha.nl; f. 1914; attached to Netherlands Economic-Historical Archives Foundation; 120,000 vols, spec. colln of 16th–18th-century books on commerce and book-keeping, and on Dutch business history and companies, 3,000 periodicals; Librarian J. J. SEEGERS; publ. *Tijdschrift voor Sociale en Economische Geschiedenis*.

Historical Documentation Centre for Dutch Protestantism: De Boelelaan 1105, 1081 HV Amsterdam; tel. (20) 5985270; e-mail hdc@vu.nl; internet www.hdc.vu.nl; f. 1971; attached to Vrije Univ. Amsterdam; collects and manages archives of persons and instns in protestant circles; promotes historical research, organizes symposia and workshops and publs; provides information and advice, and collaborates in educational and academic projects; Dir Prof. Dr G. HARINCK; Archivist J. F. SEIJLHOUWER.

KIT Library—Royal Tropical Institute: POB 95001, 1090 HA Amsterdam; Mauritskade 63, 1092 AD Amsterdam; tel. (20) 5688298; fax (20) 6654423; e-mail ils@kit.nl; internet www.kit.nl/smartsite .shtml?id=27569; information on international cooperation, sustainable social and economic development, poverty alleviation, health, cultural exchange and heritage, capacity building, and on the history of the former Dutch colonies; 260,000 vols, 4,500 journals, 30,000 articles, 25,000 maps, 800 atlases; Dir HANS VAN HARTEVELT.

Openbare Bibliotheek Amsterdam (Amsterdam Public Library): Oosterdoksstraat 110, 1011 DK Amsterdam; Oosterdokskade 143, 1011 DL Amsterdam; tel. (20) 5230701; fax (20) 5230955; e-mail dir@oba.nl; internet www.oba.nl; f. 1919; central library, 27 br libraries; 1.7m. vols and pieces of sheet music, spec. collns incl. AdamNet libraries, Hella Haasse, children's books in Spanish and home language, Europe Direct centres, international gay and lesbian information centre and archives, music collns; Dir HANS VAN VELZEN.

Rijksakademie van Beeldende Kunsten Bibliotheek (Library of the State Academy of Fine Arts): Sarphatistraat 470, 1018 GW Amsterdam; tel. (20) 5270303; fax (20) 5270301; e-mail infodesk@rijksakademie.nl; internet www.rijksakademie.nl; f. 1870, present status 1999; 33,000 vols, 85 magazines, 1,400 video cassettes and DVDs; art historic library; large colln of monographs, catalogues of exhibitions and books on visual arts, photography, video, applied art and architecture; Head MARIETTA DIRKER.

The Academy Library: POB 2169, 1000 CD Amsterdam; Cruquiusweg 31, 1019 AT Amsterdam; tel. (20) 6685866; fax (20) 6654181; e-mail ask@iisg.nl; internet www .iisg.nl/collections/akademiebibliotheek; f. 1808; attached to International Institute of Social History; formerly part of Library KNAW; contains library collns of Royal Netherlands Academy of Arts and Sciences collected in 19th century; 200,000 vols; spec. collns incl. collns of Willem Bilderdijk, Jacob van Lennep, Johannes Wertheim Salomonson; 15th, 16th century printings; western, eastern MSS; travel accounts and expedition reports; numismatics; Head CO SEEGERS.

Universiteitsbibliotheek Amsterdam (University of Amsterdam Library): POB 19185, 1000 GD Amsterdam; Singel 425, 1012 WP Amsterdam; tel. (20) 5252301; fax (20) 5252311; e-mail secr-uba@uva.nl; internet cf.uba.uva.nl/nl; f. 1578; incl. Bibliotheca Rosenthaliana (f. 1880, 100,000 vols, 850 MSS), Réveil-Archives, Vondel, Frederik van Eeden and Albert Verwey collns; Tetterode colln; several historical Church collns; libraries of Royal Dutch Book Trade Asscn, Royal Geographical Soc., Royal Netherlands Soc. of Medicine; 4m. vols, 145,000 maps, 160 medieval and 70,000 modern MSS, 500,000 letters; Head of Information Services A. DOEK; Dir Drs A. J. H. A. VERHAGEN; Man. for Spec. Collns Drs S. C. G. T. SCHOLTEN.

Universiteitsbibliotheek Vrije Universiteit (Free University Amsterdam University Library): De Boelelaan 1103, 1081 HV Amsterdam; De Boelelaan 1105, 1081 HV Amsterdam; tel. (20) 5985200; fax (20) 5985259; e-mail info@ubvu.vu.nl; internet www.ubvu.vu.nl; f. 1880; 1m. book titles in print; 2,560,991 e-books, 15,681 electronic journals, 70,000 documents produced prior to 1901, 36,000 maps; Chief Librarian JOSÉ H. M. FRIJNS; Deputy Librarian Prof. Dr AUGUST DEN HOLLANDER.

Arnhem

Gelders Archief (Gelders Archives): Markt 1, 6811 CG Arnhem; tel. (26) 3521600; fax (26) 3521699; e-mail info@geldersarchief.nl; internet www.geldersarchief.nl; f. 1877; contains archives of the Dukes of Gelders and succeeding provincial admins, and of other regional and local authorities; of private persons, families, enterprises, religious bodies, etc. (since 12th century); archive material for northern Limburg before 1580; Dir-Gen. Dr FRED J. W. VAN KAN.

Stichting Arnhemse Openbare en Gelderse Wetenschappelijke Bibliotheek (Arnhem Public and Learned Library): POB 1168, 6801 ML Arnhem; Koningstraat 26, 6811 DG Arnhem; tel. (26) 3543111; fax (26) 4458616; e-mail secretariaat@ bibliotheekarnhem.nl; internet www .biblioarnhem.nl; f. 1856; dist. libraries in Kronenburg, Presikhaaf; 14 regional libraries; 750,000 vols, 130 MSS; Library Dir RIA OUDEGA.

Assen

Drents Archief (Drenthe Archive): POB 595, 9400 AN Assen; Brink 4, 9401 HS Assen; tel. (59) 2313523; e-mail info@

drentsarchief.nl; internet www.drentsarchief .nl; f. 1879, present status 2005; public records of the Province of Drenthe; archives of private persons, institutions and enterprises; 7,500 vols; Dir DOUWE HUIZING.

Breda

De Bibliotheek Breda (Breda Public Library): POB 90192, 4800 RN Breda; Molenstraat 6, 4811 GS Breda; tel. (76) 5299500; fax (76) 5299502; e-mail aam .weterings@breda.nl; internet www .bibliotheekbreda.nl.

Sifria—van de Joodse Gemeente Breda (Sifria—library of the Jewish Congregation of Breda): NIG Breda, POB 1934, 4801 BX Breda; tel. (13) 5086008; e-mail info@ joodsbreda.nl; internet www.joodsbreda.nl/ bibliotheek.html; f. 1997; books on Jewish religion, tradition, history, philosophy; collns on holocaust, anti-Semitism, contemporary history of Israel; nonfiction science books, reference dept; works by Jewish writers.

Breukelen

Nyenrode Business Universiteit Library: Straatweg 25, POB 130, 3620 AC Breukelen; tel. (346) 291310; fax (346) 291230; e-mail library@nyenrode.nl; internet www.nyenrode.nl/library; attached to Nyenrode Business Univ.; library colln covers relevant areas of management studies; 25,000 vols; 350 printed journals; Library Head ONNO MASTENBROEK.

Bussum

Bibliotheek Narden-Bussum (Nard-Bussum Library): Wilhelminaplantsoen 18, 1404 JB Bussum; tel. (35)-6973000; fax (35)-6916772; e-mail info@ bibliotheeknaardenbussum.nl; internet www .bibliotheeknaardenbussum.nl.

Brunssum

Parkstad Limburg Bibliotheken: Rumpenerstraat 147, 6443 CC Brunssum; tel. (45) 4007560; e-mail info@ parkstadlimburgbibliotheken.nl; internet www.obparkstad.nl; consortium of 23 brs in Bocholtz, Brunssum, Heerlen, Hoensbroek, Hulsberg, Kerkrade, Klimmen, Landgraaf, Merkelbeek, Nuth, Ransdaal, Schimmert, Schinveld, Simpelveld and Voerendaal.

De Bilt

Bibliotheek van het Koninklijk Nederlands Meteorologisch Instituut (Library of the Royal Netherlands Meteorological Institute): POB 201, 3730 AE De Bilt; Wilhelminalaan 10, 3732 GK De Bilt; tel. (30) 2206855; fax (30) 2210407; e-mail bibliotheek@knmi.nl; internet www.knmi.nl/ bibliotheek; f. 1854; holds the nat. meteorological colln; 180,000 vols on meteorology, physical oceanography and geophysics (esp. seismology, ionosphere and geomagnetism); Librarian W. J. JANSEN.

Delft

Erfgoed Delft en Omstreken (Heritage of Delft and Surroundings): POB 78, 2600 ME Delft; Schoolstraat 7, 2611 HS Delft; tel. (15) 2602358; fax (15) 2138744; e-mail erfgoeddelft@delft.nl; internet www .erfgoed-delft.nl; f. 1859; protects cultural heritage of Delft and its surroundings; consists of Archaeology of Delft, Archives of Delft, Museum Lambert van Meerten, Museum Nusantara, Museum Het Prinsenhof, Kouwenhoven's little shop; 40,000 vols mainly on history of Delft, genealogy and heraldry; spec. collns: Delft early printed books, House of Orange-Nassau, Naundorff, 17th-century Dutch art, vols about Indonesia, contemporary art, archeology; Dir J. A.

METER; Head Librarian M. P. SCHOEMAKER-VAN WEEZENBERG.

TU Delft Library (Library of the Delft University of Technology): POB 98, 2600 MG Delft; Prometheusplein 1, 2628 ZC Delft; tel. (15) 2785678; fax (15) 2785706; e-mail library@tudelft.nl; internet www.library .tudelft.nl; f. 1842; technical and scientific library; 635,000 vols, 30,900 e-books, 37, 000 books published before 1900, 1,500 journals subscriptions, 13,500 e-journal subscriptions, 27,000 TU Delft Open Access publs, 14,000 online photos and videos, 4,000 data sets; Librarian Ir WILMA VAN WEZENBEEK.

Deventer

Stadsarchief en Athenaeumbibliotheek Deventer (City Archives and Deventer Municipal Library): POB 351, 7400 AJ Deventer; Klooster 12, 7411 NH Deventer; tel. (570) 693713; e-mail info.sab@saxion.nl; internet www.sabinfo.nl; f. 1560; library for town of Deventer and province of Overijssel and Saxion Univ. of applied sciences; 250,000 vols, 550 MSS, 380 incunabula, 400 post-incunabula; municipal archives 1241–1950, judicial archives 1423–1811, archives of chapter 1123–1591, church registers 1542–1811, notarial archives 1811–1905; Dir G. E. TULP.

Dordrecht

Erfgoedcentrum DiEP (Municipal Archives of Dordrecht): Stek 13, POB 8, 3300 AA Dordrecht; tel. (78) 6492311; fax (78) 6492388; e-mail erfgoedcentrumdiep@ dordrecht.nl; internet www .erfgoedcentrumdiep.nl; f. 1885, present name 2007; archives of the City of Dordrecht and of nearby towns; books and prints of Dordrecht and its environs; 40,000 vols, 800 periodicals; Archivist Drs TEUN DE BRUIJN; Librarian JAN ALLEBLAS.

Eindhoven

Informatie Expertise Centrum/Bibliotheek Technische Universiteit Eindhoven (Information Expertise Centre/ Library of the Eindhoven University of Technology): POB 513, 5600 MB Eindhoven; MetaForum Bbldg, Den Dolech 2, 5612 AZ Eindhoven; tel. (40) 2472381; fax (40) 2447015; e-mail helpdesk.bib@tue.nl; internet w3.tue.nl/nl/diensten/bib; f. 1956; 415,000 vols, 550 current print journals, 14,700 e-journals, 3,200 full-text TU/e dissertations, 1,500 microfiches and 66,000 other items; Head Librarian Drs JEANNE C. M. FIGDOR; Sec. CAROLA M. J. L. TAK.

Openbare Bibliotheek Eindhoven (Eindhoven Public Library): POB 488, 5600 AL Eindhoven; Gebouw de Witte Dame, Emmasingel 22, 5611 AZ Eindhoven; tel. (40) 2604260; fax (40) 2461225; e-mail info@ bibliotheekeindhoven.nl; internet www .bibliotheekeindhoven.nl; f. 1916; 9 brs; 800,000 vols; Man. and Dir Drs THIJS TORREMAN.

Enschede

ITC Library (Faculty of Geo-Information Science and Earth Organization Library): POB 217, 7500 AE Enschede; Hengelosestraat 99, Third Fl., Room 3-036, 7514 AE Enschede; tel. (53) 4874202; fax (53) 4874396; e-mail library@itc.nl; internet www.itc.nl/pub/home/library; attached to Univ. of Twente; specialized scientific library on remote sensing and geographical information sciences; Archivist HOMME MARTINUS; Librarian C. M. GERRITSEN.

University of Twente Library and Archive: POB 217, 7500 AE Enschede; Drienerlolaan 5, 7522 NB AE Enschede; tel. (53) 4892777; fax (53) 4893599; e-mail infoub@

utwente.nl; internet www.utwente.nl/ub; f. 1964; 375,000 vols, 2,700 periodicals, 250 printed journals, 14,000 e-journals; Librarian Drs P. G. G. M. DAALMANS; Sec. J. VROOM-VAN GORCUM.

Gouda

De Bibliotheek Gouda (Gouda Library): Spieringstraat 1, 2801 ZH Gouda; tel. (82) 590101; internet www.bibliotheekgouda.nl; central library and 3 br. libraries; 119,892 materials incl. 300,000 CDs, 10,000 music DVDs; Dir NAN VAN SCHENDEL.

Groningen

Bibliotheek der Rijksuniversiteit te Groningen (Library of the State University): POB 559, 9700 AN Groningen; Broerstraat 4, 9712 CP Groningen; tel. (50) 3635020; fax (50) 3634996; e-mail bibliotheek@rug.nl; internet www.rug.nl/ bibliotheek; f. 1615; 3m. vols, 1,100 MSS, 210 incunabula; Librarian MARJOLEIN NIEBOER.

Regionaal Historisch Centrum Groninger Archieven (RHC Groninger Archives): POB 30040, 9700 RM Groningen; Cascadeplein 4, 9726 AD Groningen; tel. (50) 5992000; fax (50) 5992050; e-mail info@ groningerarchieven.nl; internet www .groningerarchieven.nl; f. 2002 by merger of Nat. Archives Groningen and Municipal Archive Groningen; information centre for history of city and province of Groningen; about 12.5 miles of documents, maps, prints, books, newspapers, photos, film- and video cassettes from governmental bodies and private individuals; 35,000 vols; Chair. Drs J. A. J. STAM; Dir EDDY DE JONGE; Deputy Dir HARRY ROMIJN.

Haarlem

Bibliotheek van Teylers Museum (Teyler Museum Library): Spaarne 16, 2011 CH Haarlem; tel. (23) 5160960; fax (23) 5342004; e-mail info@teylersmuseum.nl; internet www.teylersmuseum.nl; f. 1784; 125,000 vols (natural sciences); Head Librarian Drs M. A. M. VAN HOORN.

Hbo-opleidingen Hogeschool Inholland Bibliotheek (Inholland University of Applied Sciences Library): Inholland University Haarlem, attn Library, POB 558, 2003 RN Harleem; Bijdorplaan 15, 2015 CE Harleem; tel. (23) 5412700; e-mail bibliotheek@inholland.nl; internet www .inholland.nl/bibliotheek; Head of Library RIA PAULIDES.

Noord-Hollands Archief (North Holland Archives): POB 3006, 2001 DA Haarlem; Jansstraat 40, 2011 RX Haarlem; tel. (23) 5172700; fax (23) 5172720; e-mail info@ noord-hollandsarchief.nl; internet www .noord-hollandsarchief.nl; f. 2005 by merger of Archives of Kennemerland and State Archives in North Holland; documentary heritage of province of North Holland, Kennemerland region (in particular the municipalities of Aalsmeer, Beverwijk, Bloemendaal, Haarlemmerliede and Spaarnwoude, Haarlemmermeer, Heemskerk, Heemstede, Uitgeest, Uithoorn, Velsen and Zandvoort) and of provincial capital Haarlem; Chair. B. B. SCHNEIDERS; Dir Drs L. ZOODSMA.

De Bibliotheek Haarlem en Omstreken: POB 204, 2000 AE Haarlem; Gasthuisstraat 32, 2011 XP Haarlem; tel. (23) 5115300; fax (23) 5115390; e-mail stadsbibliotheek@ haarlem.nl; internet www.sbhaarlem.nl; f. 1596, present status 2008; 452,000 vols, 280 MSS, 192 incunabula; Dir L. SLUYSER.

Kampen

Gemeentearchief Kampen (Record Office Kampen): Molenstraat 28, 8261 JW Kampen;

tel. (38) 3370770; fax (38) 3370779; e-mail gemeentearchief@kampen.nl; internet www .gemeentearchiefkampen.nl; archives of the town 1251–1955; Dir Drs H. DIJK; Archivist M. VINK-BOS; publ. *De Archieven der gemeente Kampen, I, II, III.*

Leeuwarden

Historisch Centrum Leeuwarden (Leeuwarden History Centre): Groeneweg 1, 8911 EH Leeuwarden; tel. (58) 2338399; fax (58) 2332315; e-mail historischcentrum@ leeuwarden.nl; internet www .historischcentrumleeuwarden.nl; f. 1838, fmrly Leeuwarden Municipal Archives; archives, publs, MSS about Leeuwarden; topographical colln, mainly historical; 18,000 vols; Man. Drs G. DE VRIES; Librarian W. VAN RIJNSOEVER.

TRESOAR Fries Historisch en Letterkundig Centrum (TRESOAR Frisian Historical and Literary Centre): POB 2637, 8901 AC Leeuwarden; Boterhoek 1, 8911 DH Leeuwarden; tel. (58) 7890789; fax (58) 7890777; e-mail info@tresoar.nl; internet www.tresoar.nl; f. 2002 by merger of the Frysk Letterkundich Museum en Dokumintaasjesintrum (FLMD), the Provincial and Buma library (PBF) and the Public Records Office in Friesland (RAF); collns mainly relating to Frisian literature and history; Chair. Drs J. A. DE VRIES; Dir Drs B. LOOPER; publ. *Letterhoeke.*

Leiden

Bibliotheek van de Maatschappij der Nederlandse Letterkunde (Library of the Society of Dutch Literature): POB 9501, 2300 RA Leiden; tel. (71) 5272814; fax (71) 5272836; e-mail mnl@library.leidenuniv.nl; internet www .maatschappijdernederlandseletterkunde.nl/ bibliotheek.php; f. 1766, managed by Leiden Univ. Library since 1876; awards prizes for literary debuts, cultural and historical works; organizes meetings and lectures; 110,000 vols, 3,300 MSS; Librarian Dr KURT DE BELDER; publs *Nieuwe Letterkundig Magazijn* (2 a year), *Tijdschrift voor Nederlandse Taal-en Letterkunde* (4 a year).

NCB Naturalis Library: POB 9517, 2300 RA Leiden; Darwinweg 2, 2333 CR Leiden; tel. (71) 5687668; fax (71) 5687666; e-mail library@ncbnaturalis.nl; internet science .naturalis.nl/library; research library of the Nat. Center for Biodiversity Naturalis; collns incl. biodiversity literature (flora and fauna), geology, mineralogy and palaeontogy; focus on the Netherlands, Europe and Southeast Asia; 100,000 vols, 8,000 journals, 200,000 zoology and geology papers; Head CAROLINE PEPERMANS; publs *Blumea: Biodiversity, evolution and biogeography of plants* (online (www.ingentaconnect.com/content/nhn/blumea)), *Contributions to Zoology* (online (www.ctoz.nl)), *Gorteria: Tijdschrift voor onderzoek aan de wilde flora, Persoonia: Molecular phylogeny and evolution of fungi* (online (www.persoonia.org)), *Scripta Geologica* (online (www.scriptageologica.nl)), *Zoologische mededelingen* (online (www.zoologischemededelingen.nl)).

Universitaire Bibliotheken Leiden (Leiden University Libraries): POB 9501, 2300 RA Leiden; Witte Singel 27, 2311 BG Leiden; tel. (71) 5272814; fax (71) 5272836; e-mail helpdesk@library.leidenuniv.nl; internet library.leiden.edu; f. 1575; 3.5m. vols, 1m. e-books, 30,000 e-journals, 50,000 MSS, 70,000 maps, 500 databases; Librarian KURT DE BELDER; Deputy Dir JOSJE CALFF.

Maastricht

Regionaal Historisch Centrum Limburg (Regional Historic Centre Limburg): St Pie-terstraat 7, 6211 JM Maastricht; tel. (43) 3285500; fax (43) 3255640; e-mail info@rhcl .nl; internet www.rhcl.nl; f. 2004 by merger of State Archives in Limburg and Municipal Archives; 60,000 vols; Dir Drs LITA WIGGERS.

Stadsbibliotheek Maastricht, Centre Céramique (Municipal Library): POB 1992, 6201 BZ Maastricht; Ave Céramique 50, 6221 KV Maastricht; tel. (43) 3505600; fax (43) 3505599; e-mail mail@sbm.nl; internet www.centreceramique.nl; f. 1662; 774,000 vols, incl. 107 incunabula, 297 post-incunabula, 1,600 periodicals, spec. collns and documentation relating to the Province of Limburg, devotional material and chess literature; Dir Dr ERIC P. G. WETZELS; publ. *Limburgensia.*

Universiteitsbibliotheek Maastricht (Maastricht University Library): POB 616, 6200 MD Maastricht; Inner City Library, Grote Looiersstraat 17, 6211 JH Maastricht; Randwyck Library, Universiteitssingel 50, 6229 ER Maastricht; tel. (43) 3885000; fax (43) 3884888; e-mail i.wijk@ maastrichtuniversity.nl; internet www .maastrichtuniversity.nl/web/library/home .htm; attached to Maastricht Univ.; includes digital library; 11,703 e-journals, 11,279 digital univ. publs; spec. collns incl. Jesuit colln of 265,000 vols; Univ. Librarian I. WIJK.

Middelburg

Zeeuws Archief (Zeeland Archives): POB 70, 4330 AB Middelburg; Hofplein 16, 4331 CK Middelburg; tel. (118) 678800; fax (118) 628094; e-mail info@zeeuwsarchief.nl; internet www.zeeuwsarchief.nl; f. 2000 by merger of State Archives in the province of Zeeland, Middelburg Municipal Archives and Veere Municipal Archives; contains documents on the history of Zeeland in gen.; Man. Dir Dr J. L. KOOL-BLOKLAND.

Zeeuwse Bibliotheek (Zeeland Library): POB 8004, 4330 EA Middelburg; Kousteensedijk 7, 4331 JE Middelburg; tel. (118) 654000; fax (118) 654001; e-mail info@ zeeuwsebibliotheek.nl; internet www .zeeuwsebibliotheek.nl; f. 1985; 880,000 vols, 7,500 MSS, 2,900 periodicals; Pres. Ir P. G. BOERMA; Vice-Pres. Drs G. A. EGAS REPÁRAZ; Dir Dr J. A. BRANDENBARG.

Nijkerk

Bibliotheek Nijkerk (Nijkerk Library): POB 198, 3860 AD Nijkerk; Frieswijkstraat 99, 3861 BK Nijkerk; tel. (33) 2451756; fax (33) 2460985; e-mail info@bibliotheeknijkerk .nl; internet www.bibliotheeknijkerk.nl.

Nijmegen

Universiteitsbibliotheek, Radboud Universiteit Nijmegen (Library of Radboud University Nijmegen): POB 9100, 6500 HA Nijmegen; Erasmuslaan 36, Nijmegen; tel. (24) 3612428; fax (24) 3615944; e-mail secretariaat@ubn.ru.nl; internet www.ru.nl/ ubn; f. 1923; 6 library brs; 2m. vols; Librarian Drs H. P. A. SMIT.

Oss

Bibliothek Oss (Oss Library): POB 815, 5340 AV Oss; Raadhuislaan 10, 5341 GM Oss; tel. (12) 622618; fax (12) 646950; e-mail contact@oboss.nl; internet www.oboss.nl; brs in Berghem, Heesch, Heeswijk-Dinther, Nistelrode, Lith, Ravenstein, Schaijk and Zeeland.

Rotterdam

Bibliotheek Gemeente Rotterdam (Rotterdam Library): Hoogstraat 110, 3011 PV Rotterdam; tel. (10) 2816100; fax (10) 2816181; e-mail communicatie@bibliotheek .rotterdam.nl; internet www.bibliotheek .rotterdam.nl; f. 1604; 23 dist. brs; 1,550,000 vols, 200 MSS, Erasmus colln 5,000 vols, 1,500 journals, 300,000 CDs; Dir Ir F. H. MEIJER.

Gemeentearchief Rotterdam (Municipal Archives of Rotterdam): POB 71, 3000 AB Rotterdam; Hofdijk 651, 3032 CG Rotterdam; tel. (10) 2675555; fax (10) 2675556; e-mail infogar@rotterdam.nl; internet www .gemeentearchief.rotterdam.nl; f. 1857; city archives, church records, notariate archives, Chamber of Commerce records 1797–1922, family archives, business archives, topographical collns, sound archives, historical library; 17 linear km of archives; Archivist and Man. Dir Drs JANTJE STEENHUIS.

Rotterdamsch Leeskabinet (Rotterdam Reading Cabinet): POB 1738, 3000 DR Rotterdam; Burgemeester Oudlaan 50, 3062 PA Rotterdam; tel. (10) 4081195; e-mail kabinet@ubib.eur.nl; internet www.eur.nl/ rlk; f. 1859; attached to Erasmus Univ.; history, art, art history, language and literature, biography, theology, philosophy, social sciences, geography; 250,000 vols; Chair. A. DUPAIN; Deputy Chair. Prof. Dr W. M. LAMMERTS VAN BUEREN; Sec. and Treas. J. DE MUINCK KEIZER; Librarian Drs PIERRE N. G. PESCH; publ. *Kwartaalbericht.*

Universiteitsbibliotheek Erasmus Universiteit Rotterdam (Library of the Erasmus University of Rotterdam): POB 1738, 3000 DR Rotterdam; Burgemeester Oudlaan 50, 3062 PA Rotterdam; tel. (10) 4081223; fax (10) 4089052; e-mail documentverwerking@ ubib.eur.nl; internet www.eur.nl/ub; f. 1913; economics and management, medicine and health, law, culture and soc.; 1m. vols, 5,400 current journals; Univ. Librarian Dr PAUL E. L. J. SOETAERT; Deputy Librarian Drs G. GORIS; Deputy Librarian Drs J. L. DE VRIES.

's-Hertogenbosch

Brabants Historisch Informatie Centrum (Brabant Historical Information Centre): POB 81, 5201 AB 's-Hertogenbosch; Zuid-Willemsvaart 2, 5211 NW 's-Hertogenbosch; tel. (73) 6818500; fax (73) 6146439; e-mail info@bhic.nl; internet www.bhic.nl; f. 1860 as Rijksarchief in de Provincie Noord Brabant; records since 13th century; record office contains approx. 200,000 vols; 40,000 vols, 8,000 charters; Dir Drs R. BASTIAANSE; Librarian F. VAN DE POL; publ. *Inventarisreeks.*

Openbare Bibliotheek 's-Hertogenbosch: POB 1253, 5200 BH 's-Hertogenbosch; Hinthamerstraat 72, 5211 MR 's-Hertogenbosch; tel. (73) 6802900; fax (73) 6144925; e-mail stadsbibliotheek@ bibliotheekdenbosch.nl; internet www .sbdenbosch.nl; f. 1915; 270,000 vols, 18,000 CDs; Dir J. J. T. E. (HANS) DERKS; Deputy Dir P. C. J. M. (ELLY) HUFF-MEULENBROEKS.

The Hague

Bibliotheek Den Haag (The Hague Public Library): POB 12653, 2500 DP The Hague; Spui 68, 2511 BT The Hague; tel. (70) 3534455; fax (70) 3534504; e-mail secr@ dobdenhaag.nl; internet www.dobdenhaag .nl; f. 1906; 980,000 vols, 190,000 children's books, music library of 55,000 vols and 60,000 CDs, 21,000 audio-visual items; 16 br., 2 mobile libraries; Dir CHARLES NOORDAM.

Bibliotheek van het Centraal Bureau voor de Statistiek (Library of Statistics Netherlands): POB 24500, 2490 HA The Hague; Henri Faasdreef 312, 2492 JP The Hague; tel. (70) 3375151; fax (70) 3375984; e-mail acquisitiev@cbs.nl; internet www.cbs .nl; f. 1899; not accessible to public from 2005; available for scientific research with prior appointment; 380,000 vols; Librarian D. L. M. WEIJERS.

Bibliotheek van het Vredespaleis (Peace Palace Library): Carnegieplein 2, 2517 KJ The Hague; tel. (70) 3024242; fax (70) 3024166; e-mail peacelib@ppl.nl; internet www.ppl.nl; f. 1913; int. public and municipal law, diplomatic history, int. relations; Grotius Colln; 700,000 vols; Dir JEROEN VERVLIET.

Koninklijke Bibliotheek (National Library of the Netherlands): POB 90407, 2509 LK The Hague; Prins Willem-Alexanderhof 5, 2595 BE The Hague; tel. (70) 3140310; fax (70) 3140450; e-mail info@kb.nl; internet www.kb.nl; f. 1798, present status 1993; responsible for the devt, documentation and management of the nat. cultural heritage; depository for all Dutch publs and the nat. bibliography; research library for the humanities and social sciences; centre of expertise in preservation and restoration; focal point of inter-library cooperation; 2.2m. books, 15,000 current periodicals, newspapers, MSS, spec. collns incl. chess, cookery, children's books; Chair. Drs L. C. BRINKMAN; Dir-Gen. Drs J. S. M. (BAS) SAVENIJE; publ. *Nederlandse Bibliografie.*

Nationaal Archief (National Archives): POB 90520, 2509 LM The Hague; Prins Willem Alexanderhof 20, 2595 BE The Hague; tel. (70) 3315400; fax (70) 3315540; e-mail info@nationaalarchief.nl; internet www.nationaalarchief.nl; f. 1802; 93 km of archives; 80,000 vols, 700 journals; Gen State Archivist MARTIN BERENDSE; publ. *Inventories of Archives.*

Tweede Kamer der Staten-Generaal; Dienst Bibliotheek en Dienst Documentatie (Dutch House of Representatives; Library Department and Documentation Department): Plein 2, POB 20018, 2500 EA The Hague; tel. (70) 3183040; fax (70) 3182307; internet www .houseofrepresentatives.nl; f. 1815; 100,000 vols; Librarian J. C. KEUKENS; Head of Documentation P. VAN RIJN.

Tilburg

Universiteit van Tilburg Bibliotheek (Tilburg University Library): POB 90153, 5000 LE Tilburg; Warandelaan 2, 5037 AB Tilburg; tel. (13) 662124; fax (13) 662996; e-mail library@uvt.nl; internet www.uvt.nl/ bibliotheek; f. 1927; economics, applied computer sciences, social sciences, law, history, philosophy, linguistics; 900,000 vols; Dir Ir M. J. VAN DEN BERG.

Utrecht

Bibliotheek Utrecht (Public Library): POB 80, 3500 AB Utrecht; Oude Gracht 167, Utrecht; tel. (30) 2861800; fax (30) 2861801; e-mail klantenservice@bibliotheek-utrecht .nl; internet www.bibliotheek-utrecht.nl; f. 1892; 14 br libraries and art library; 795,000 vols, music library; Dir A. G. J. VAN VLIMMEREN.

Het Utrechts Archief (Utrecht Archives): POB 131, 3500 AC Utrecht; Hamburgerstraat 28, 3512 NS Utrecht; tel. (30) 2866611; fax (30) 2866600; e-mail inlichtingen@hetutrechtsarchief.nl; internet www.hetutrechtsarchief.nl; f. 1805; records of the City and Province of Utrecht, church history, political pamphlets, regional newspapers, nat. railway history; 70,000 vols, 500,000 maps, drawings, prints and photographs, 18 km archival documents; Chair. ALEID WOLFSEN; Deputy Chair. VINCENT VAN DER BURG; Dir Drs SASKIA VAN DOCKUM; Head Archivist Dr K. VAN VLIET; Librarian Dr J. J. MEMMEN.

Universiteitsbibliotheek Utrecht (Library of Utrecht University): POB 80124, 3508 TC Utrecht; Heidelberglaan 3, 3584 CS Utrecht; tel. (30) 2536601; fax (30) 2538398; e-mail info@library.uu.nl; internet www.uu .nl/university/library; f. 1584; 4.5m. vols, 2,500 MSS, 900 incunabula, 110,000 vols printed before 1800, MSS and printed books of the medieval libraries of the Utrecht churches and religious houses, 2 16th-century private libraries; special collns in the fields of literature, theology, history, botany, medicine, 18th and 19th-century science libraries, and on the province and city of Utrecht; Univ. Librarian Drs H. P. A. SMIT.

Vlaardingen

Vlaardingen City Archives: Plein Emaus 5, 3135 JN Vlaardingen; tel. (10) 2484999; fax (10) 2484980; e-mail stadsarchief@ vlaardingen.nl; internet www.vlaardingen .nl/stadsarchief; f. 1948; 500 archives and collns related to city; oldest document from 1276.

Wageningen

Bibliotheek Wageningen UR (Wageningen UR Library): POB 9100, 6700 HA Wageningen; Droevendaalsesteeg 2, Wageningen; tel. (31) 7484440; fax (31) 7484761; e-mail servicedesk.library@wur.nl; internet library.wur.nl; f. 1873; colln of scientific literature esp. in fields of agrotechnology, food sciences, plant and animal sciences, soil science, geo-information, landscape and spatial planning, water and climate, ecosystem studies; 1.5m. vols, 15,000 current periodicals; Chief Librarian D. VAN ZAANE; publ. *Wageningen Agricultural University Papers.*

Zwolle

Historisch Centrum Overijssel (Historic Centre of Overijssel): POB 1510, 8001 BM Zwolle; Eikenstraat 20, 8021 WX Zwolle; tel. (38) 4266300; fax (38) 4266333; e-mail infohco@historischcentrumoverijssel.nl; internet www.historischcentrumoverijssel .nl; f. 2000; 60,000 vols; 18 km archive, 15,000 charters; 15,000 maps, prints, posters and drawings; 150,000 photographs; collns incl. provincial archives 1528–1948, judicial archives 1333–1979, notarial archives 1811–1915, old church registers and civil registers 1592–1942, archives of monasteries 1225–1811, industrial archives 1850–1980, Zwolle municipal archives 1265–1970, notarial archives 1811–1925, cadastral archives 1811–1980, family archives since 13th century; Chair. C. G. A. A. BREKELMANS; Dir Drs A. G. DE VRIES.

Museums and Art Galleries

Alkmaar

Stedelijk Museum Alkmaar: Canadaplein 1, 1811 KE Alkmaar; tel. (72) 5489789; e-mail museum@alkmaar.nl; internet stedelijkmuseumalkmaar.nl; f. c. 1550; municipal museum; antiquarian and art colln from Alkmaar and its environs, paintings by van Heemskerck, van de Velde the Elder, Allart and Caesar B. van Everdingen, Honthorst; objects incl. old silver, glass, pottery, porcelain, tiles and modern art; colln of antique toys and dolls; Dir LIDEWIJ DE KOEKKOEK; Curator CHRISTI KLINKERT.

Amstelveen

Cobra Museum voor Moderne Kunst (Cobra Museum of Modern Art): POB 2028, 1180 EA Amstelveen; Sandbergplein 1, 1181 ZX Amstelveen; tel. (20) 5475050; fax (20)

5475025; e-mail info@cobra-museum.nl; internet www.cobra-museum.nl; works by artists of CoBrA group (1948–51) and Dutch artists, incl. artists of Vrij Beelden (1945) and Creatie (1950–55) movements; Artistic Dir Dr K. WEITERING; Exec. Dir E. OTTENHOF.

Museum Jan van der Togt: Dorpsstraat 50, 1182 JE Amstelveen; tel. and fax (20) 6415754; e-mail info@jvdtogt.nl; internet www.jvdtogt.nl; f. 1991; colln of paintings, sculpture and glass; incl. architectural museum designs; temporary exhibitions; Curator TOMAS HILLEBRAND.

Amsterdam

Allard Pierson Museum: POB 94057, 1090 GB Amsterdam; Oude Turfmarkt 127, 1012 GC Amsterdam; tel. (20) 5252556; fax (20) 5252561; e-mail allard.pierson.museum@uva .nl; internet www.allardpiersonmuseum.nl; f. 1934, present location 1994; attached to Univ. of Amsterdam; archaeological museum; scientific research centre for students of archaeology and history of art, and public museum; archaeology of ancient Egypt, Near East, Greece, Etruria, Roman Empire; Dir-Gen. Prof. Dr W. HUPPERETZ; Scientific Dir Prof. Dr H. A. G. BRIJDER; publ. *Mededelingenblad van de Vereniging van Vrienden.*

Amsterdams Historisch Museum (Amsterdam Historical Museum): POB 3302, 1001 AC Amsterdam; Nieuwezijds Voorburgwal 357, Kalverstraat 92, Amsterdam; tel. (20) 5231822; fax (20) 6207789; e-mail info@ahm.nl; internet www.ahm.nl; f. 1926; exhibits of the city's history over 700 years incl. archaeological finds, artefacts, paintings, prints and models; spec. colln: Jan and Casper Luyken colln; library of 18,000 vols on history of Amsterdam, Dutch art history and applied industrial arts; Chair. HENK J. BROUWER; Vice-Chair. BEN VAN DER VEER; Dir RUTGER J. GRAAF SCHIMMELPENNINCK; Curator LAURA VAN HASSELT.

Anne Frank Museum: POB 730, 1000 AS Amsterdam; Prinsengracht 267, 1000 AS Amsterdam; tel. (20) 5567100; fax (20) 6207999; internet www.annefrank.org; f. 1960; Anne's hiding place, secret annexe; original MSS of diaries and samples of other writings Anne produced during her time in hiding; film exhibition; Exec. Dir HANS WESTRA; Man. Dir KLEIS BROEKHUIZEN.

Hermitage Amsterdam: POB 11675, 1001 GR Amsterdam; Amstel 51, 1001 GR Amsterdam; tel. (20) 5307488; e-mail mail@ hermitage.nl; internet www.hermitage.nl; exhibition devoted to Alexander the Great; has archive; Dir Prof. Dr MIKHAIL PIOTROVSKI.

Hortus Botanicus Amsterdam: Plantage Middenlaan 2A, 1081 DD Amsterdam; tel. (20) 6259021; fax (20) 6257006; e-mail info@ dehortus.nl; internet en.dehortus.nl; f. 1638, present status 1987; colln of species of plants from different countries; greenhouse; historic herb garden; Dir LENA EUWENS; publs *Het Hortusbericht, Hortuskrant* (4 a year).

Joods Historisch Museum (Jewish Historical Museum): POB 16737, 1001 RE Amsterdam; Nieuwe Amstelstraat 1, 1001 RE Amsterdam; tel. (20) 5310310; fax (20) 5310311; e-mail info@jhm.nl; internet www .jhm.nl; f. 1930; colln of 13,000 works of art, ceremonial items and historical objects related to Jewish history and culture; library of 43,000 vols; Dir JOËL CAHEN.

Museum Van Loon: Keizersgracht 672, 1017 ET Amsterdam; tel. (20) 6245255; e-mail info@museumvanloon.nl; internet www.museumvanloon.nl; f. 1672; colln of paintings, furniture, precious silver and porcelain from different centuries; canal house, coach house and garden; Chair. PHILIPPA VAN LOON.

Nederlands Scheepvaartmuseum Amsterdam (Netherlands Maritime Museum Amsterdam): POB 15443, 1001 MK Amsterdam; Kattenburgerstraat 7, Amsterdam; tel. (20) 5232222; fax (20) 5232213; e-mail info@scheepvaartmuseum .nl; internet www.scheepvaartmuseum.nl; f. 1916; closed until mid-2011 for reconstruction; models, paintings, charts, globes, technical drawings, nautical instruments, arms and relics, full-size replica East-Indiaman; library of 60,000 vols, spec. collns: early navigation textbooks, voyages and travel, navigation, Dutch sea atlases; Dir Dr WILLEM BIJLEVELD; Business Dir KARIN BRANDT; Dir for Collns Drs HENK DESSENS; publ. *Zee Magazijn* (4 a year).

NEMO: POB 421, 1000 AK Amsterdam; Oosterdok 2, 1011 VX Amsterdam; tel. (20) 5313233; fax (20) 5313535; e-mail info@ e-nemo.nl; internet www.e-nemo.nl; f. 1997; science centre; organizes exhibitions, theatre performances, films, workshops and demonstrations related to science and technology; Gen. Dir MICHIEL BUCHEL; Dir R. V. M VAN HATTUM.

Ons' Lieve Heer op Solder Museum (Our Lord in the Attic Museum): Oudezijds Voorburgwal 40, 1012 GE Amsterdam; tel. (20) 6246604; fax (20) 6381822; e-mail info@ opsolder.nl; internet www.opsolder.nl; f. 1888; merchant's house of 1661 with a clandestine Catholic church in the attic; exhibits of ecclesiastical art since 16th century; library of 1,500 vols; Chair. Drs M. A. M. ELSENBURG; Dir Drs J. KIERS; Exec. Sec. M. AARDEWIJN; Curator Drs T. BOERS.

Persmuseum: Zeeburgerkade 10, 1019 HA Amsterdam; tel. (20) 6928810; fax (20) 4680505; e-mail info@persmuseum.nl; internet www.persmuseum.nl; colln of newspapers and magazines from 1600, posters and other advertisements in press, political cartoons and press graphics, archives, photos of journalists, editors and publishers and library; Dir ANGELIE SENS; publ. *Jaarverslag*.

Rembrandthuis Museum (Rembrand House Museum): Jodenbreestr. 4, 1011 NK Amsterdam; tel. (20) 5200400; fax (20) 5200401; e-mail museum@rembrandthuis .nl; internet www.rembrandthuis.nl; f. 1907; Rembrandt's etchings and drawings, and paintings by his teacher and pupils; the artist lived here 1639–58; Dir JANRENSE BOONSTRA; Deputy Dir MICHIEL KERSTEN; Curator BOB VAN DEN BOOGERT; publ. *Kroniek van het Rembrandthuis* (Rembrandt House Chronicle, 2 a year).

Rijksmuseum (State Museum): POB 74888, 1070 DN Amsterdam; Stadhouderskade 42, 1071 ZD Amsterdam; tel. (20) 6747000; fax (20) 6747001; e-mail info@rijksmuseum.nl; internet www.rijksmuseum.nl; f. 1800; colln incl. major works by Rembrandt, Vermeer, Jan Steen, Frans Hals and other artists; paintings, sculpture, drawings, history, porcelain, glass, costumes, silver, furniture, Asiatic art (main museum closed till 2013 while major renovation work is undertaken; masterpieces colln of 400 of the most important works on display in the Philips Wing during this period); library of 80,000 vols; Chair. A. RUYS; Gen. Dir Prof. Drs W. M. J. PIJBES; Man. Dir J. W. SIEBURGH; Dir for Collns Drs T. D. W. DIBBITS; Curator for Paintings Dr J. P. FILEDT KOK; Curator for Sculpture and Applied Art Dr R. J. BAARSEN; Curator for Nat. Historical Colln Dr C. J. ZANDVLIET; Curator for Prints Drs G. LUIJTEN; Curator for Asiatic Art Drs P. C. M.

LUNSINGH SCHEURLEER; Librarian Drs G. J. M. KOOT; publ. *Bulletin* (4 a year).

Stedelijk Museum: POB 75082, 1070 AB Amsterdam; Paulus Potterstraat 13, 1071 CX Amsterdam; tel. (20) 5732911; fax (20) 6752716; e-mail info@stedelijk.nl; internet www.stedelijkmuseum.nl; f. 1895; modern paintings and sculpture, esp. American and European trends since 1950; graphics and drawings; applied arts and industrial design; temporary exhibitions on contemporary art; library of 170,000 vols, 210 periodicals; Dir ANN GOLDSTEIN (acting); publ. *Bulletin* (in Dutch and English).

Tropenmuseum (Museum of the Royal Tropical Institute): POB 95001, 1090 HA Amsterdam; Linnaeusstraat 2, 1092 CK Amsterdam; tel. (20) 5688200; fax (20) 5688548; e-mail info@tropenmuseum.nl; internet www.tropenmuseum.nl; f. 1916, present location 1926; attached to Royal Tropical Institute; 175,000 objects, 155,000 photographs and 10,000 drawings, paintings, documents etc; presents a picture of life and work in the tropics and sub-tropics; children's museum; library of 18,000 vols; Dir LEJO SCHENK.

Van Gogh Museum: POB 75366, 1070 AJ Amsterdam; Stadhouderskade 55, 1072 AB Amsterdam; tel. (20) 5705200; fax (20) 5705222; e-mail info@vangoghmuseum.nl; internet www.vangoghmuseum.nl; f. 1973; collns of the Vincent van Gogh Foundation; paintings and drawings by van Gogh and his contemporaries; van Gogh's personal colln incl. English and French prints and graphics, Japanese woodcuts, documents and personal correspondence with his brother, Theo van Gogh; Theo's personal colln; Western paintings, sculptures, drawings and prints from the period 1840 to 1920; archives of the art historian M. E. TRALBAUT; spec. colln: 19th century literature (mainly French) read by van Gogh; library of 24,000 vols; Chair. TRUDE MAAS-DE BROUWER; Dir AXEL RÜGER; Treas. PETER TIELEMAN; publs *Cahier Vincent* (scientific research, 1 a year), *Van Gogh Bulletin* (4 a year).

Verzetsmuseum Amsterdam: Plantage Kerklaan 61, 1018 CX Amsterdam; tel. (20) 6202535; fax (20) 6202960; e-mail info@ verzetsmuseum.org; internet www .verzetsmuseum.org/museum; f. 1985; colln of objects, photos and documents, film and sound fragments related to Second World War; temporary exhibitions on historical or contemporary themes; Pres. HANS BLOM; Sec. CARLA BASTIAANSEN; Treas. HANS HOEK; Dir LIESBETH VAN DER HORST.

Apeldoorn

CODA Museum: Vosselmanstraat 299, 7311 CL Apeldoorn; tel. (55) 5268400; fax (55) 5268499; e-mail mail@coda-apeldoorn.nl; internet www.coda-apeldoorn.nl; f. 1978; colln exhibits contemporary art and regional history, esp. jewellery and paper art; image bank; Dir Dr CARIN E. M. REINDERS.

Paleis Het Loo (Loo Palace): Koninklijk Park 1, 7315 JA Apeldoorn; tel. (55) 5772400; fax (55) 5772408; e-mail info@paleishetloo.nl; internet www.paleishetloo.nl; f. 1984; colln of portraits, furniture, documents, etc., relating to the Dutch royal family, the House of Orange-Nassau; library of 20,000 vols; Dir Prof. Dr J. R. TER MOLEN.

Arnhem

Historisch Museum Arnhem (Arnhem Historical Museum): Bovenbeekstraat 21, 6811 CV Arnhem; tel. (26) 3775300; fax (26) 3775398; e-mail hma@arnhem.nl; internet www.hmarnhem.nl; f. 1995; pre-1900 applied art, history, archaeology, glass and silver,

Delftware, topographic colln of Gelderland; closed till the end of 2013 due to re-location; Head of Public Affairs PETER DE KOK; publ. *Museumkrant* (2 a year).

Museum voor Moderne Kunst (Museum for Modern Art): Utrechtseweg 87, 6812 AA Arnhem; tel. (26) 3775300; fax (26) 3775353; e-mail mmka@arnhem.nl; internet www .mmkarnhem.nl; f. 1920; post-1900 sculpture, Dutch realist paintings, design, jewellery, contemporary art; Dir M. MEYER; Head of Public Affairs PETER DE KOK.

Nederlands Openluchtmuseum (Netherlands Open Air Museum): POB 649, 6800 AP Arnhem; Schelmseweg 89, 6816 SJ Arnhem; tel. (26) 3576111; fax (26) 3576147; e-mail info@openluchtmuseum.nl; internet www .openluchtmuseum.nl; f. 1912, present status 1991; history of daily life; information retrieval; library of 26,000 vols, 146 periodicals; Chair. Ir Drs JEROEN VAN DER VEER; Dir-Gen. Drs PIETER-MATTHIJS GIJSBERS; Man. Dir ADELHEID M. C. J. PONSIOEN.

Assen

Drents Museum: POB 134, 9400 AC Assen; Brink 8, 9401 HS Assen; tel. (592) 377773; internet www.drentsmuseum.nl; f. 1854, present status 1999; temporarily closed until autumn 2011; exhibits bog bodies, Pesse dugout canoe, Terracotta army of Xi'an; colln art nouveau, art deco and figurative art; photo archive; Dir MICHEL VAN MAARSEVEEN.

Brill

Historisch Museum Den Briel: Markt 1, 3231 AH Brill; tel. (181) 475475; fax (181) 475476; e-mail info@ historischmuseumdenbriel.nl; internet www .historischmuseumdenbriel.nl; f. 1912, present status 1998; colln of art historical prints by patron Alexander Verhuell; Curator Dr MARIJKE HOLTROP.

Delft

Leger Museum (Army Museum): POB 90004, 3509 AA Delft; Korte Geer 1, 2611 CA Delft; tel. (15) 2150500; fax (15) 2150544; e-mail info@legermuseum.nl; internet www .legermuseum.nl; f. 1913, present location 1984; contains more than 500,000 objects, incl. personal books, handwritten documents, prints and photographs, vehicles; exhibition covering 2,000 years of Netherlands' military history; weapons from prehistory to the present; uniforms, equipment, medals, paintings; library of 225,000 vols and colln of prints; Dir-Gen. CHRIS RONTELTAP; Dir for Collns DIRK STAAT; publ. *Armamentaria* (1 a year).

Museum Het Prinsenhof: POB 78, 2600 ME Delft; St Agathaplein 1, 2611 HR Delft; tel. (15) 2602358; fax (15) 2138744; e-mail gemeentemusea@delft.nl; internet www .prinsenhof-delft.nl; f. 1948; historical colln of City of Delft, paintings of the Delft School, Eighty Years' War, William the Silent; Dir ERIK DE GROOT.

Museum Lambert van Meerten: POB 78, 2600 ME Delft; Oude Delft 199, 2611 HD Delft; tel. (15) 2602358; fax (15) 2138744; e-mail gemeentemusea@delft.nl; internet www.lambertvanmeerten-delft.nl; f. 1909; 19th-century art collector's house; 16th–19th-century Dutch tiles, Delft faience, paintings, furniture; Dir ERIK DE GROOT; Curator Drs RONALD E. BROUWER.

Museum Nusantara: POB 78, 2600 ME Delft; Sint Agathaplein 4, 2611 HR, Delft; tel. (15) 2602358; fax (15) 2138744; e-mail erfgoeddelft@delft.nl; internet www .nusantara-delft.nl; f. as Ethnographic Museum of Delft; history and culture of the Indonesian archipelago; colln incl. exhibitions of Dutch involvement in Indonesia since the 17th century, incl. the Dutch East India Co. (1602–1799) and the Colonial Period (1800–1949); Indonesian art, culture, religion, musical instruments, puppets, jewellery, wooden carvings, masks, textiles; maquettes of 19th century, Indonesian houses and ships; Dir ERIK DE GROOT.

Den Helder

Marinemuseum (Dutch Naval Museum): Hoofdgracht 3, 1781 AA Den Helder; tel. (223) 657534; fax (223) 657282; e-mail info@ marinemuseum.nl; internet www .marinemuseum.nl; f. 1962; attached to Min. of Defence; history of the Royal Netherlands Navy since 1813, collns of models, navigational instruments, paintings, photographs, etc.; three-cylinder submarine 'Tonijn' (1966), minesweeper 'Abraham Crynssen' (1937), ironclad ram ship 'Schorpioen' (1868), and other craft; Dir Cmdr HARRY DE BLES.

Deventer

Gemeentemusea Deventer (Municipal Museums of Deventer): POB 5000, 7400 GC Deventer; tel. (570) 693783; fax (570) 693788; e-mail info@deventermusea.nl; internet www .deventermusea.nl; f. 1963; Dir C. F. C. G. BOISSEVAIN.

Associated Museums:

Historisch Museum Deventer (Historical Museum Deventer): POB 5000, 7400 GC Deventer; Brink 56, 7411 BV Deventer; tel. (570) 693780; fax (570) 693788; e-mail info@deventermusea.nl; internet www .historischmuseumdeventer.nl; f. 1913; local history, paintings, drawings, applied arts, bicycles; Dir C. F. C. G. BOISSEVAIN; publ. *Deventer jaarboek* (yearbook).

Speelgoedmuseum Deventer (Deventer Toy Museum): POB 5000, 7400 GC Deventer; Brink 47, 7411 BV Deventer; tel. (570) 693786; fax (570) 693788; e-mail info@ deventermusea.nl; internet www .speelgoedmuseumdeventer.nl; f. 1982; dolls, mechanical toys, toys, trains; Dir C. F. C. G. BOISSEVAIN.

Dordrecht

Dordrechts Museum: POB 1170, 3300 BD Dordrecht; Museumstraat 40, 3311 XP Dordrecht; tel. (78) 7708708; internet www .dordrechtsmuseum.nl; f. 1842; colln of paintings, drawings, prints, photos, sculptures and ceramics; conducts research and restoration work; Man. Dir P. J. SCHOON.

Drechterland

Museum Mohlmann for Representational Art: Westersingel 102–104, 9901 GK Appingedam; tel. (596) 682856; e-mail info@ museummohlmann.nl; internet www .robmohlmann.nl; f. 1995; 3 permanent collns: Canto-colln (124 works), Møhlmann-colln-I (250 present-day realistic and figurative works), Møhlmann-colln-II (40 works of painter), Mankes-colln (graphic works, letters and documents about the life of Jan Mankes); 3 exhibitions per year; Dir ROB MØHLMANN.

Eindhoven

Museum Kempenland: St. Antoniusstraat 7, 5616 RT Eindhoven; tel. (40) 2529093; fax (40) 2522344; e-mail secretariaat@ museumkempenland.nl; internet www .museumkempenland.nl; f. 1932; closed until mid-2011; colln of material culture of Eindhoven and region, Brabant painting, drawing and graphic arts and photography, Dutch small sculpture from 19th and 20th centuries; organizes lectures, choir performances,

publ., courses, tours; has library; Man. JAN VAN LAARHOVEN.

Van Abbemuseum: POB 235, 5600 AE Eindhoven; Bilderdijklaan 10, 5611 NH Eindhoven; tel. (40) 2381000; fax (40) 2460680; e-mail info@vanabbemuseum.nl; internet www.vanabbemuseum.nl; f. 1936; large colln of modern and contemporary art incl. works and archives by Lissitzky, Picasso, Kokoschka, Chagall, Beuys, McCarthy, Daniëls and Körmeling; library of 130,000 vols; Dir CHARLES ESCHE; Deputy Dir ULRIKE ERBSLÖH.

Enschede

Rijksmuseum Twenthe, Enschede (Twenthe Estate Museum, Enschede): Lasondersingel 129–131, 7514 BP Enschede; tel. (53) 4358675; fax (53) 4359002; e-mail info@ rijksmuseumtwenthe.nl; internet www .rijksmuseumtwenthe.nl; f. 1930; present status 1994; 8,000 art objects from the 13th century up to the present day; library of 15,000 vols; Dir LISETTE PELSERS; Curator for Fine Arts PAUL KNOLLE; Curator for Modern Art TON GEERTS; publs *Bulletin* (4 a year), *MUSE Rijksmuseum Twenthe* (2 a year).

Gouda

museumgoudA 'Het Catharina Gasthuis' (St Catherine Hospital, Municipal Museum): Achter de Kerk 14, 2801 JX Gouda; tel. (182) 331000; fax (182) 331019; e-mail info@ museumgouda.nl; internet www .museumgouda.nl; f. 1874; 18th-century town dispensary; antique toys, surgeons' Guild Room, decorative art since late 16th century, Gasthuis kitchen and chapel, important colln of art since 15th century; Dir GERARD DE KLEIJN.

Nationaal Farmaceutisch Museum (National Pharmaceutical Museum): Westhaven 29, 2801 PJ Gouda; tel. (182) 687142; fax (182) 331019; e-mail info@ farmaceutischmuseum.nl; internet www .farmaceutischmuseum.nl; f. 1938 reopened in 2008; exhibiting the history of Dutch apothecaries and the devt of the pharmaceutical profession; fmrly the 'The Blackmoor' Stedelijk Museum containing and managing authentic 18th-century tobacco shop, colln of Dutch clay pipes and Gouda pottery now transferred to Het Catharina Gasthuis en De Moriaan; Chair. Prof. Dr A. H. L. M. PIETERS; Deputy Chair. Dr R. H. A. SOREL; Dir Drs P. H. VREE; Treas. Drs C. B. M. HEERKENS.

Groningen

Groninger Museum: POB 90, 9700 ME Groningen; Museumeiland 1, 9711 ME Groningen; tel. (50) 3666555; fax (50) 3120815; e-mail info@groningermuseum.nl; internet www.groningermuseum.nl; f. 1894; prehistory and history; paintings of local school; Dutch and Flemish of 16th and 17th centuries: Fabritius, Jordaens, Rubens, Sweerts, Teniers; drawings: Rembrandt, Averkamp, Van Goyen, Cuyp, Lievens; painting since 19th century; extensive colln of Far-Eastern ceramics; colln of applied art; photography, design and fashion collns; library of 38,000 vols incl. book colln on modern art and artists and colln of modern art since 1979; Man. Dir KEES VAN TWIST; Dir PATTY WAGEMAN.

Noordelijk Scheepvaartmuseum (Northern Maritime Museum): Brugstraat 24, 9711 HZ Groningen; tel. (50) 3122202; fax (50) 3183751; e-mail info@ noordelijkscheepvaartmuseum.nl; internet www.noordelijkscheepvaartmuseum.nl; f. 1932; colln related to N Dutch shipping and shipbuilding history from Middle Ages to present, archives, library, photographs; Dir

J. W. VAN VEEN; Curator and Deputy Dir W. KERKMEIJER.

Haarlem

Frans Hals Museum (Frans Hals Museum): POB 3365, 2001 DJ Haarlem; Groot Heiligland 62, 2011 ES Haarlem; tel. (23) 5115775; fax (23) 5115776; e-mail office@ franshalsmuseum.nl; internet franshalsmuseum.nl; f. 1913; pictures since 15th century, focusing on the Haarlem school and Frans Hals; applied arts; Dir KAREL SCHAMPERS; Sec. JUDITH HARREN.

Teylers Museum: Spaarne 16, 2011 CH Haarlem; tel. (23) 5160960; fax (23) 5342004; e-mail info@teylersmuseum.nl; internet www .teylersmuseum.nl; f. 1784; paintings, drawings, palaeontology, geology, mineralogy, natural history, physics, numismatics; library of 125,000 vols (natural science); Dir Drs M. SCHARLOO; publs *Archives du Musée Teyler, Verhandelingen van Teylers Godgeleerd Genootschap, Verhandelingen van Teylers Tweede Genootschap*.

Heerlen

Thermenmuseum Heerlen: POB 1, 6400 AA Heerlen; Coriovallumstraat 9, 6411 CA Heerlen; tel. (45) 5605100; fax (45) 5603915; e-mail info@thermenmuseum.nl; internet www.thermenmuseum.nl; f. 1977; colln incl. Roman bath house excavated in 1940–41 and other objects from Roman period; Curator Dr KAREN JENESON.

Helmond

Gemeentemuseum Helmond: Kasteelplein 1, 5701 PP Helmond; tel. (492) 587716; fax (492) 587717; e-mail info@ gemeentemuseumhelmond.nl; internet www .gemeentemuseumhelmond.nl; colln of int. modern and contemporary art incl. works from 1970 to present; exhibits popular visual culture, incl. film and advertising; works of Alma, Burtynsky, Heijenbrock, Isaac Israels, Kollwitz, Meunier, Jan en Chartley Toorope and Van der Leck; Curator ANNEMIEKE HOGERVORST.

Hoorn

Westfries Museum: Achterom 2–4, 1621 KV Hoorn; Roode Steen 1, 1621 CV Hoorn; tel. (229) 280028; fax (229) 280029; e-mail info@wfm.nl; internet www.wfm.nl; f. 1879, baroque bldg dates from 1632; 17th- and 18th-century painting, prints, oak panelling, glass, pottery, silver, furniture, costumes, interiors, objects of trade, navigation and business, folk art, historical objects from Hoorn and West Friesland, prehistoric finds; Dir AD GEERDINK.

Leerdam

Nationaal Glasmuseum—De Glasblazerij (National Glass Museum—The Glass Factory): POB 78, 4140 AB Leerdam; Lingedijk 28–30, 4142 LD Leerdam; tel. (345) 614960; e-mail info@stichtingglas.nl; internet www.nationaalglasmuseum.nl; f. 1953, present status 2007; art glass, industrial glass and bottles, contemporary Dutch colln and works from other European countries and America; small library; Chair. AUBERT VAN ENGELEN; Dir ARNOUD ODDING; Curator HÉLÈNE BESANÇON.

Leeuwarden

Fries Museum: POB 1239, 8900 CE Leeuwarden; Turfmarkt 11, 8911 KS Leeuwarden; tel. (58) 2555500; fax (58) 2132271; e-mail info@friesmuseum.nl; internet www .friesmuseum.nl; f. 1827; painting, local history, archaeology, decorative arts, prints and drawings, Second World War, Mata Hari gallery, modern art; Chair. Prof. Dr L.

KOOPMANS; Dir-Gen. Drs SASKIA BAK; Man. Dir Ir ROEL WOERING; publ. *Visitor's Guide* (in English, French and German).

Keramiekmuseum Princessehof (Princessehof National Museum of Ceramics): Grote Kerkstraat 11, POB 1239, 8900 CE Leeuwarden; tel. (58) 2948958; fax (58) 2948968; e-mail info@princessehof.nl; internet www .princessehof.nl; f. 1917; Asian and European ceramics and tiles, contemporary ceramics; library of 20,000 vols; Dir-Gen. Drs SASKIA BAK; Man. Dir Ir ROEL WOERING; publ. *Keramika* (3 a year).

Leiden

Museum Boerhaave/Rijksmuseum voor de Geschiedenis van de Natuurwetenschappen en van de Geneeskunde (Museum Boerhaave/National Museum of the History of Science and Medicine): POB 11280, 2301 EG Leiden; Lange St Agnietenstraat 10, 2312 WC Leiden; tel. (71) 5214224; fax (71) 5120344; e-mail informatie@ museumboerhaave.nl; internet www .museumboerhaave.nl; f. 1907; historical scientific and medical instruments and documents, anatomical preparations, portraits; library of 25,000 vols, 75 periodicals, MSS; Dir Prof. Dr DIRK VAN DELFT; Exec. Sec. FRANCISCA PARMENTIER.

Museum Volkenkunde (National Museum of Ethnology): POB 212, 2300 AE Leiden; Steenstraat 1, 2312 BS Leiden; tel. (71) 5168800; fax (71) 5128437; e-mail pr@ volkenkunde.nl; internet www.volkenkunde .nl; f. 1837 as Ethnographic Museum in Leiden; collns from Africa, the Middle E, the Islamic and Indian cultural areas, the Far E, Pacific, SE Asia, the Americas and the circumpolar regions; library of 60,000 vols; Dir Dr STEVEN B. ENGELSMAN; Business Dir MIEP HUIVENAAR; Dir for Public Programmes and Devt JOHN SIJMONSBERGEN; publ. *Mededelingen*.

NCB Naturalis (Netherlands Centre for Biodiversity Naturalis): POB 9517, 2300 RA Leiden; Darwinweg 2, 2333 CR Leiden; tel. (71) 5687600; fax (71) 5687666; e-mail contact@ncbnaturalis.nl; internet www .ncbnaturalis.nl; f. 1820, merger of Zoological Museum Amsterdam, Nat. Museum of Natural History Naturalis and brs of Nat. Herbarium of the Netherlands; colln incl. more than 11m. objects related to fossils, insects, invertebrates, vertebrates; library of 108,000 vols, 8,000 periodical (zoology library 78,000 vols, 5,000 periodicals; geology library 30,000 vols, 3,000 periodicals), palaeontology; Gen. Dir Dr Ir BERT M. GEERKEN; Scientific Dir Prof. Dr ERIK F. SMETS; publs *Entomologische tabellen, Nederlandse Faunistische Mededelingen, Scripta Geologica, Technical Bulletin NNM, Zoölogische Bijdragen, Zoölogische Mededelingen, Zoölogische Verhandelingen*.

Rijksmuseum van Oudheden (National Museum of Antiquities): POB 11114, 2301 EC Leiden; Rapenburg 28, 2311 EW Leiden; tel. (71) 5163163; fax (71) 5149941; e-mail info@rmo.nl; internet www.rmo.nl; f. 1818; prehistoric, Roman and Medieval periods in the Netherlands; Egyptian, Mesopotamian, Greco-Roman and ancient European collns; library of 30,000 vols, 25 periodicals; Dir Drs WIM WEIJLAND.

Stedelijk Museum de Lakenhal Leiden (Cotton Hall Museum, Leiden): POB 2044, 2301 CA Leiden; Oude Singel 28–32, 2312 RA Leiden; tel. (71) 5165360; fax (71) 5134489; e-mail postbus@lakenhal.nl; internet www .lakenhal.nl; f. 1874; pictures of Leiden school; memorial table (triptych) and altar pieces by Lucas van Leyden and C. Engebrechtsz; Rembrandt, Jan Steen, Jan van

Goyen, van Mieris, Dou, modern Leiden school: Verster, Kamerlingh Onnes and contemporary Dutch art; furniture, silver, glass, tapestry, etc.; period rooms; history of the town; library of 4,604 vols, 10,500 catalogues; Dir META KNOL.

Limburg

Museum Het Domein Sittard: POB 230, 6130 AE Sittard; Kapittelstraat 6, 6131 ER Sittard; tel. (46) 4513460; fax (46) 4529111; e-mail info@hetdomein.nl; internet www .hetdomein.nl; colln of archaeological and historical artefacts, int. avant-garde, with emphasis on photography, video and crossover art; Dir PETER FRANSMAN.

Maastricht

Bonnefantenmuseum (Provincial Museum): POB 1735, 6201 BS Maastricht; Ave Céramique 250, 6221 KX Maastricht; tel. (43) 3290190; fax (43) 3290199; e-mail info@ bonnefanten.nl; internet www.bonnefanten .nl; f. 1863, refounded 1968; early Italian paintings (1300–1550); Neutelings colln (medieval sculpture and applied arts; Maasland sculpture (incl. works by Jan van Steffeswert); contemporary art (incl. works by René Daniëls, Peter Duig, Gary Hume, Sol LeWitt and Roman Signer); Chair. Drs J. H. H. MANS; Vice-Chair. Prof. Dr K. OTTENHEYM; Artistic Dir ALEXANDER M. U. VAN GREVENSTEIN; Man. Dir HARRIE DRAGSTRA; Treas. L. J. J. RULKENS; Sec. Drs J. VAN DEN BELT.

Natuurhistorisch Museum Maastricht (Maastricht Natural History Museum): De Bosquetplein 6–7, 6211 KJ Maastricht; De Bosquetplein 7, 6211 KJ Maastricht; tel. (43) 3505490; fax (43) 3505475; e-mail museum@ maastricht.nl; internet www.nhmmaastricht .nl; f. 1912; colln of 550,000 objects; flora, fauna and soils of the Limburg area, late Cretaceous fossils; library of 30,000 vols; Dir-Gen. Drs ERIC P. G. WETZELS; Man. CORRIEN DERKSEN; publ. *Natuurhistorisch Maandblad* (12 a year).

Muiden

Muiderslot: Stichting Rijksmuseum Muiderslot, Herengracht 1, 1398 AA Muiden; tel. (294) 256262; fax (294) 261056; e-mail info@muiderslot.nl; internet www .muiderslot.nl; 13th-century castle furnished in early 17th-century style: paintings, tapestries, furniture and armoury; Dir TIES HILGERS-MICHIELS VAN KESSENICH; Chair. H. J. E. BRUINS SLOT.

Naarden

Comenius Museum: Kloosterstraat 33, 1411 RS Naarden; tel. (35) 6943045; fax (35) 6941949; e-mail info@comeniusmuseum .nl; internet www.comeniusmuseum.nl; f. 1924; J. A. Comenius mausoleum and museum; library of 2,500 vols; Chair. H. VAN OOSTVEEN; Dir HANS VAN DER LINDE; Sec. H. VERHOEF; Treas. A. OVERDIEP.

Nijmegen

Museum Het Valkhof: POB 1474, 6501 BL Nijmegen; Kelfkensbos 59, 6511 TB Nijmegen; tel. (24) 3608805; fax (24) 3608656; e-mail mhv@museumhetvalkhof.nl; internet www.museumhetvalkhof.nl; f. 1999; archaeology, cultural history and fine art, mainly related to Nijmegen and the province of Gelderland; modern art, mainly related to the Netherlands; library of 22,400 vols in art library and 11,000 titles in archaeological library; Dir Drs MARIJKE BROUWER; Chair. R. MIGO.

Opmeer

Scheringa Museum voor Realisme (Scheringa Museum of Realist Art): Span-

broekerweg 162, 1715 GV Spanbroek; tel. (226) 351111; fax (226) 351859; e-mail info@ scheringamuseum.nl; internet www .scheringamuseum.nl; f. 1997; colln of paintings and drawings by Carel Willink, paper, sculptures, fashion creations, photographs, objects, and contemporary works of Realism; Dir BELIA VAN DER GIESSEN.

Oss

Museum Jan Cunen: Molenstraat 65, 5341 GC Oss; tel. (412) 629328; fax (412) 629335; e-mail museumjancunen@oss.nl; internet www.museumjancunen.nl; f. 1935; exhibits contemporary art focused on local history, archeology and industrial history; Dir NICOLETTE BARTELINK.

Otterlo

Kröller-Müller Museum: POB 1, 6730 AA Otterlo; Houtkampweg 6, 6731 AW Otterlo; tel. (318) 591241; fax (318) 591515; e-mail info@kmm.nl; internet www.kmm.nl; f. 1938; large colln of paintings by van Gogh, paintings and sculpture since 19th century, old masters, open-air modern sculpture colln (Moore, Serra, Volten), ceramics, drawings, graphic art; library of 40,000 vols; Dir Dr LISETTE PELSERS; Exec. Sec. Drs WANDA VERMEULEN.

Nederlands Tegelmuseum (Dutch Tile Museum): Eikenzoom 12, 6731 BH Otterlo; tel. (318) 591519; fax (318) 592000; e-mail info@nederlandstegelmuseum.nl; internet www.nederlandstegelmuseum.nl; f. 1963; extensive colln of Netherlands tiles since 1500; library of 930 vols; Dir M. H. VAN MEURS.

Roermond

Het Cuypershuis (The House of Cuypers): POB 900, 6040 AX Roermond; Pieter Cuyperssstraat 1, 6041 XG Roermond; tel. (475) 359584; fax (475) 336299; e-mail museum@ roermond.nl; internet museum.roermond.nl; f. 1932; archaeology, historical and contemporary art and design, architecture and art of Dr P. J. H. Cuypers (1827–1921); museum closed for renovation until spring 2011; Head Dr HANS VAN DE MORTEL.

Rotterdam

Chabotmuseum Rotterdam: Museumpark 11, 3015 CB Rotterdam; tel. (10) 4363713; fax (10) 4360355; e-mail mail@chabotmuseum .nl; internet www.chabotmuseum.nl; f. 1993, present status 2000; private Grootveld colln incl. paintings, sculptures, drawings and graphics by Chabot; Schortemeijer colln; enthnographic objects; artists' works, notes, letter, photographs and original sketches.

Historisch Museum Rotterdam (Rotterdam Historical Museum): Korte Hoogstraat 31, 3011 GK Rotterdam Centrum; tel. (10) 2176767; fax (10) 4782376; e-mail info@hmr .rotterdam.nl; internet www.hmr.rotterdam .nl; more than 100,000 objects; archaeology, art, domestic life, history, technology; Dir HANS WALGENBACH; publ. *Historisch Nu*.

Kunsthal Rotterdam: POB 23077, 3015 AA Rotterdam; Westzeedijk 341, 3015 AA Rotterdam; tel. (10) 4400301; e-mail communicatie@kunsthal.nl; internet www .kunsthal.nl; works of impressionism, Leonardo da Vinci, Blackfoot Indians, jewels of the orient, pop-art; 2 annual exhibitions: for children and on historico-cultural theme; Dir EMILY ANSENK; Curator JANNET DE GOEDE; Curator CHARLOTTE VAN LINGEN.

Maritiem Museum Rotterdam (Rotterdam Maritime Museum): POB 988, 3000 AZ Rotterdam; Leuvehaven 1, 3011 EA Rotterdam; tel. (10) 4132680; fax (10) 4137342; e-mail info@maritiemmuseum.nl; internet www.maritiemmuseum.nl; f. 1874, new bldg

1986; models of ships since 15th century, globes, atlases, 20,000 books; ironclad warship 'Buffel'; spec. children's exhibition; library of 35,000 vols, 25,000 journals; Chair. Ir P. O. VERMEULEN; Dir-Gen. FRITS LOOMEIJER; Man. Dir FRANS VAN HAMBURG; publ. *MM Journaal* (2 a year).

Museum Boijmans Van Beuningen: POB 2277, 3000 CG Rotterdam; Museumpark 18–20, 3015 CX Rotterdam; tel. (10) 4419400; fax (10) 4360500; e-mail info@boijmans.nl; internet www.boijmans.nl; f. 1849; approx. 140,000 objects; Dutch School incl. paintings by van Eyck, Bosch, Pieter Brueghel, Hals, Rembrandt, van Ruysdael, Hobbema, Jan Steen; Baroque School, French School, Impressionists; old, modern and contemporary paintings and sculpture; drawings since 15th century from Dutch, Flemish, French, German, Italian and Spanish schools, old and modern prints; glass, Dutch silver, old pewter, laces and ceramics, among which an important colln of Persian, Spanish, Italian and Dutch pottery and tiles; furniture, industrial design; sculpture garden; library of 125,000 vols and catalogues, 200 periodical titles; Chair. H. R. OKKENS; Gen. Man. SJAREL EX.

Nederlands Architectuurinstituut: POB 237, 3000 AE Rotterdam; Museumpark 25, 3015 CB Rotterdam; tel. (10) 4401358; fax (10) 4366975; e-mail collection@nai.nl; internet www.nai.nl; f. 1988, by merger of Stichting Architectuurmuseum, Nederlands Documentatiecentrum voor de Bouwkunst, and Stichting Wonen; Sonneveld house museum; maintains archive; library of 42,000 vols, 1,000 periodicals; Chair. WILLEM HEIN SCHENK; Vice-Chair. SANDER MIRCK.

Nederlands Fotomuseum: POB 23383, 3001 KJ Rotterdam; Wilhelminakade 332, 3072 AR Rotterdam; tel. (10) 2030405; fax (10) 2030406; e-mail info@nederlandsfotomuseum.nl; internet www.nederlandsfotomuseum.nl; 3m. negatives and colln of slides, prints and documents about life and work of Dutch photographers, amateur photography exhibition; archives of Katharina Eleonore Behrend and Hein Wertheimer; conserves and restores photographic material and provides advice about archival storage material; library of 11,000 vols; Dir RUUD VISSCHEDIJK.

Stedelijk Museum Schiedam: POB 208, 3100 AE Schiedam; Hoogstraat 112–114, 3111 HL Schiedam; tel. (10) 2463666; fax (10) 2463664; e-mail info@stedelijkmuseumschiedam.nl; internet www.stedelijkmuseumschiedam.nl; f. 1899; Major Gerrit Visser Bastiaansz's private colln of modern and contemporary art and historical artefacts; Dir DIANA A. WIND.

Wereldmuseum Rotterdam (World Museum Rotterdam): POB 361, 3000 AJ Rotterdam; Willemskade 25, 3016 DM Rotterdam; tel. (10) 2707172; fax (10) 2707182; e-mail info@wereldmuseum.nl; internet www.wereldmuseum.nl; f. 1885; exhibitions on regional collns, festivities, music, arts and crafts, modern non-western art; ethnological and archaeological collns from Indonesia, realm of Islam, Asia, Africa, America and Oceania; 100,000 objects and 100,000 photographs dating from 1860; Dir STANLEY BREMER.

Witte de With Centre for Contemporary Art: Witte de Withstraat 50, 3012 BR Rotterdam; tel. (10) 4110144; fax (10) 4117924; e-mail info@wdw.nl; internet www.wdw.nl; f. 1990; contemporary art and theory in context of Rotterdam and Netherlands; explores devts in contemporary art worldwide through exhibitions, theoretical and educational programmes, public events and publs; Dir DEFNE AYAS; Curator ZOË GRAY; Assoc. Curator AMIRA GAD.

's-Hertogenbosch

Noordbrabants Museum (North Brabant Museum): POB 1004, 5200 BA 's-Hertogenbosch; Verwersstraat 41, 5211 HT 's-Hertogenbosch; tel. (73) 6877877; fax (73) 6877899; e-mail info@noordbrabantsmuseum.nl; internet www.noordbrabantsmuseum.nl; f. 1981; North Brabant prehistorical, historical and folklore collns, paintings, sculpture, metalwork, prints, coins, etc.; Chair. W. M. VAN DEN GOORBERGH; Dir CHARLES DE MOOIJ; Gen. Man. LEO VAN ROZENDAAL; publ. *Noordbrabants Museum Nieuws* (4 a year).

The Hague

Escher in Het Paleis (Escher in The Palace): Lange Voorhout 74, 2514 EH The Hague; tel. (70) 4277730; fax (70) 4277731; e-mail info@escherinhetpaleis.nl; internet www.escherinhetpaleis.nl; f. 2002; works of Escher; exhibits works of art with biographical material incl. slide show, photographs, letters, studies of divisions of plane and preliminary sketches.

Fotomuseum Den Haag (The Hague Museum of Photography): POB 72, 2501 CB The Hague; Stadhouderslaan 43, 2517 HV The Hague; tel. (70) 3381144; fax (70) 3381155; e-mail info@fmdh.nl; internet www.fotomuseumdenhaag.nl; f. 2002; attached to Stichting Gemeentemuseum Den Haag; contemporary photography as well as photographs from the colln of the Gemeentemuseum; Dir BENNO TEMPEL; Deputy Dir HANS BUURMAN; Curator WIM VAN SINDEREN.

Gemeentemuseum Den Haag: POB 72, 2501 CB The Hague; Stadhouderslaan 41, 2517 HV The Hague; tel. (70) 3381111; fax (70) 3381112; e-mail info@gemeentemuseum.nl; internet www.gemeentemuseum.nl; f. 1862, present status 1999; Modern Art (since 19th century); Decorative Arts (ceramics, glass, silver, furniture) and design since early 20th century; costumes and fashion from 1750 to the present; musical instruments from 15th century to the present; art and music library; Chair. JOOP N. A. VAN CALDENBORGH; Dir BENNO TEMPEL; Deputy Dir HANS BUURMAN.

Mauritshuis, Het Koninklijk Kabinet van Schilderijen Mauritshuis (Mauritshuis, Royal Picture Gallery): POB 536, 2501 CM The Hague; Korte Vijverberg 8, 2513 AB The Hague; tel. (70) 3023456; fax (70) 3653819; e-mail communicatie@mauritshuis.nl; internet www.mauritshuis.nl; f. 1822, present status 1995; 15th-, 16th- and 17th-century Dutch and Flemish masters (Rembrandt, Vermeer, Hals, Rubens, Ruisdael, Ter Borch, van Dyck, Holbein, R. v.d. Weyden); Chair. A. BURGMANS; Sec. J. W. WINTER; Dir E. E. S. GORDENKER; Deputy Dir V. J. E. MOUSSAULT.

Museon: POB 30313, 2500 GH The Hague; Stadhouderslaan 37, 2517 HV The Hague; tel. (70) 3381338; fax (70) 3381339; e-mail info@museon.nl; internet www.museon.nl; f. 1904 as Museum for Education, present name and status 1985; astronomy and geology, biology and ecology, history and archaeology, geography and ethnology, science and technology; Dir MARIE-CHRISTINE VAN DER SMAN.

Museum Bredius: Lange Vijverberg 14, 2513 AC The Hague; tel. (70) 3620729; fax (70) 3639978; e-mail info@museumbredius.nl; internet www.museumbredius.nl; f. 1895; colln of paintings, drawings, German and Chinese ceramics, Dutch and English silver; Chair. Prof. Dr P. SCHNABEL; Man. R.

R. D. SWART; Sec. A. H. VERMEULEN; Treas. F. CH. M. TILMAN; Curator Dr J. HOOGSTEDER.

Museum Meermanno—Huis van het Boek: Prinsessegracht 30, 2514 AP The Hague; tel. (70) 3462700; fax (70) 3630350; e-mail info@meermanno.nl; internet www.meermanno.nl; f. 1848; medieval MSS, incunabula; modern typography, book plates, private press books; Dir MAARTJE DE HAAN; publ. *Leeslint* (2 a year).

Museum Mesdag: Laan van Meerdervoort 7F, 2517 AB The Hague; tel. (70) 3621434; fax (70) 3614026; e-mail uildriks@vangoghmuseum.nl; internet www.museummesdag.nl; f. 1903; attached to Van Gogh Museum, Amsterdam; Dutch pictures 1860–1920; French pictures of the Barbizon school; Oriental objects; Dir AXEL RÜGER; publs *Catalogue de l'école française XIX siècle, Museum Mesdag Nederlandse 19e eeuwse Schilderijen.*

Museum Rijswijk: Herenstraat 67, 2282 BR Rijswijk; tel. (70) 3903617; fax (70) 3368880; e-mail musryszh@xs4all.nl; internet www.museumryswyk.nl; temporary exhibitions; colln of excavated artefacts, mementos of the poet Hendrik Tollens, engravings, medals and treaty documents commemorating event that took place in 1697; Curator ARJAN KWAKERNAAK.

Museum voor Communicatie (Museum of Communication): Zeestraat 82, 2518 AD The Hague; tel. (70) 3307500; fax (70) 3608926; e-mail info@muscom.nl; internet www.muscom.nl; f. 1929, present name 1999; objects and documents, etc., concerning the history and working of the services of posts, telegraphs and telephones in the Netherlands; int. stamp gallery; library of 20,000 vols; Dir TITUS YOCARINI.

Utrecht

Cavaleriemuseum: Barchman Wuytierslaan 198, Amersfoort; tel. (33) 4661996; fax (33) 4661493; internet www.cavaleriemuseum.nl; colln of uniforms, small arms, silver, paintings, miniatures, scale, cavalry vehicles, tanks and armoured cars.

Centraal Museum Utrecht: POB 2106, 3500 GC Utrecht; Nicolaaskerkhof 10, 3512 XC Utrecht; tel. (30) 2362362; fax (30) 2332006; e-mail info@centraalmuseum.nl; internet www.centraalmuseum.nl; f. 1838; oldest municipal museum in the Netherlands; colln divided into 5 depts: old masters, modern art, design, fashion and local history; paintings and sculpture incl. old masters works by Saenredam, van Scorel and the Utrecht Caravaggists, incl. Ter Brugghen and van Honthorst; modern art colln from 20th century incl. works by van Doesburg, van der Leck and the Magic Realists Koch, Willink and Moesman; doll's house, 11th-century Utrecht ship, applied art and design; Rietveld colln, Dick Bruna colln; Dir EDWIN JACOBS; Deputy Dir MARCO GROB.

Geld Museum (Money Museum): POB 2407, 3500 GK Utrecht; Leidseweg 90, 3531 BG Utrecht; tel. (30) 2910492; fax (30) 2910467; e-mail info@geldmuseum.nl; internet www.geldmuseum.nl; f. 1816 as Rijksmuseum Het Koninklijk Penningkabinet, merged with Nederlands Muntmuseum 2004; coins from Greek and Roman times to the present, medals, paper money, engraved gems: serves as nat. and int. monetary institute for the main Dutch numismatics; library of 12,000 vols on numismatics and glyptics; Chair. Drs CEES MAAS; Dir HELEEN BUIJS; Curator Drs A. POL; Man. Div. Collns and Research CHRITSEL SCHOLLAARDT; Librarian ANS TER WOERDS; publs *De Beeldenaar* (6 a year), *Jaarboek voor Munt- en Penningkunde.*

Mondriaanhuis: POB 699, 3800 SR Amersfoort; Kortegracht 11, 3811 KG Amersfoort; tel. (33) 4600170; fax (33) 4614087; e-mail info@mondriaanhuis.nl; internet www .mondriaanhuis.nl; f. 1992; works of art from early figurative period of Piet Mondrian; exhibition of works by contemporary artists; colln of geometric abstract art and structural concrete art.

Veere

Museum 'De Schotse Huizen' (Museum of Scottish Homes): Kaai 25–27, 4351 AA Veere; tel. (118) 501744; e-mail info@deltacultureel .nl; internet www.schotsehuizen.nl; f. 1950; Chinese and Japanese ceramics; prints, nat. costumes, furniture, statues, exhibitions of paintings; sited in 16th-century merchants' houses; Dir JAN VAN DEN BROEKE.

Polderhuis Westkapelle Dijk- en Oorlogsmuseum: Zuidstraat 154–156, 4631 AK Westkapelle; tel. (118) 570700; e-mail info@ polderhuiswestkapelle.nl; internet www .polderhuiswestkapelle.nl/wie-zijn-we; f. 1999; presentation of history of dam village and its inhabitants; history of dike village: Second World War with bombing of dikes in Walcheren in 1944, flooding, closing dike and reconstruction of dike village; liberty bridge; temporary exhibitions in art and cultural and historical heritage; publ. *Polderhuisblad*.

Stadhuismuseum De Vierschaar (Town Hall Museum Vierschaar): Markt 5, 4351 AA Veere; tel. (118) 506064; e-mail info@ deltacultureel.nl; internet www .schotsehuizen.nl/devierschaar; f. 1881; tribunal, council-chamber and exhibition rooms; old standards and flags; pictures; golden cup of Maximilian from Burgundy (1546); memorabilia from the house of Oranje-Nassau; Dir PETER BLOM.

Venlo

Limburgs Museum: POB 1203, 5900 BE Venlo; Keulsepoort 5, 5911 BX Venlo; tel. (77) 3522112; fax (77) 3548396; e-mail info@ limburgsmuseum.nl; internet www .limburgsmuseum.nl; f. 2000; prehistory, Roman and medieval colln, history of Limburg, art and applied art; coins and medals; Chair. W. AERTS; Vice-Chair. M. DE LOO; Sec. and Treas. S. S. HUIJS; Dir Drs JOS SCHATORJÉ.

Vlissingen

Zeeuws Maritiem Muzeeum Vlissingen (Maritime Museum of Zeeland in Vlissingen): Nieuwendijk 15, 4381 BV Vlissingen; Nieuwendijk 11, 4381 BV Vlissingen; tel. (118) 412498; fax (118) 430307; e-mail info@ muzeeum.nl; internet www.muzeeum.nl; f. 2002, originally Stedelijk Museum Vlissingen (f. 1890); maritime colln (pilotage, lighthouses, marine archaeology, fishery); local history (souvenirs of Admiral de Ruyter, paintings, ceramics, wood carvings, engravings, tiles, coins and medals); library of 700 vols; Dir Drs WILBERT WEBER; Gen. Man. LEO DINGEMANSE.

Universities

DE HAAGSE HOGESCHOOL
(The Hague University of Applied Sciences)

Johanna Westerdijkplein 75, 2521 EN The Hague
Telephone: (70) 4458888
Fax: (70) 4458825
Internet: www.dehaagsehogeschool.nl
Chair.: ROB K. BRONS

Number of teachers: 1,700
Number of students: 20,000

ERASMUS UNIVERSITEIT ROTTERDAM
(Erasmus University)

POB 1738, 3000 DR Rotterdam
Burgemeester Oudlaan 50, 3062 PA Rotterdam
Telephone: (10) 4081111
E-mail: info@smc.eur.nl
Internet: www.eur.nl
Founded 1973 by merger of Nederlandse Economische Hogeschool (f. 1913) and Medische Faculteit Rotterdam (f. 1966)
Academic year: September to July
Chair. of Supervisory Board: Drs A. VAN ROSSUM
Chair. of Exec. Board: P. F. M. VAN DER MEER MOHR
Rector Magnificus: Prof. HENK SCHMIDT
Sec. of Supervisory Board: J. T. A. VAN MAURIK
Librarian: Dr P. E. L. J. SOETAERT
Library: see Libraries and Archives
Number of students: 23,867

DEANS
Erasmus MC (Medical Center): Prof. Dr HUIB POLS
Erasmus School of Economics: Prof. PHILIP HANS FRANSES
Erasmus School of Law: Prof. MAARTEN KROEZE
Faculty of History and Arts: Prof. Dr DICK DOUWES
Faculty of Philosophy: Prof. L. (WIEP) VAN BUNGE
Faculty of Social Sciences: Prof. Dr H. T. VAN DER MOLEN
Rotterdam School of Management: Prof. Dr GEORGE S. YIP

FONTYS HOGESCHOLEN
(Fontys University of Applied Sciences)

POB 347, 5600 AH Eindhoven
Telephone: (877) 877877
Fax: (877) 876233
E-mail: info@fontys.nl
Internet: www.fontys.nl
Pres.: MARCEL J. G. WINTELS
Sec.: H. J. M. (LENY) SCHEEPERS
Sec.: PIETER G. JANSSEN
Number of teachers: 3,111 (f.t.e.)
Number of students: 38,313

HOGESCHOOL LEIDEN

POB 382, 2300 AJ Leiden
Zernikedreef 11, 2333 CK Leiden
Telephone: (71) 5188800
Fax: (71) 5188801
E-mail: infohl@hsleiden.nl
Internet: www.hsleiden.nl
Br. in Rotterdam
Chair.: PAUL VAN MAANEN
Sec.: LISETTE VAN DE WEIJER
Number of teachers: 700
Number of students: 7,300

HOGESCHOOL ZEELAND
(HZ University of Applied Sciences)

Edisonweg 4, 4382 NW Vlissingen
Telephone: (118) 489155
E-mail: study@hz.nl
Internet: hz.nl
State control
Chair.: Drs H. J. SIMONS
Pres.: Drs PETER C. A. VAN DONGEN
Sec.: M. (RIEN) DE KLERK

Number of students: 4,000

HOGESCHOOL ZUYD
(Zuyd University)

POB 550, 6400 AN Heerlen
Nieuw Eyckholt, Heerlen
Telephone: (45) 4006060
E-mail: info@hszuyd.nl
Internet: www.hszuyd.nl
Campuses in Maastricht, Sittard-Geleen
Chair.: J. J. FRANSEN VAN DE PUTTE
Sec.: BERT NELISSEN
Number of teachers: 1,099
Number of students: 13,955

HOTELSCHOOL THE HAGUE—INTERNATIONAL UNIVERSITY OF HOSPITALITY MANAGEMENT

Brusselselaan 2, 2587 AH The Hague
Telephone: (70) 3512481
Fax: (70) 3512155
E-mail: info@hdh.nl
Internet: www.hotelschool.nl
Founded 1929
Campus in Amsterdam
Private control
Pres.: WIM DOOGE
Number of teachers: 180
Number of students: 1,900

NYENRODE BUSINESS UNIVERSITEIT
(Nyenrode Business University)

POB 130, 3620 AC Breukelen
Straatweg 25, 3621 BG Breukelen
Telephone: (346) 291211
Fax: (346) 264204
E-mail: info@nyenrode.nl
Internet: www.nyenrode.nl
Founded 1946
Private control
Languages of instruction: Dutch, English
Academic year: September to July
Rector: Prof. Dr MAURITS VAN ROOIJEN
Dean: Prof. Dr LEEN PAAPE
Registrar: R. GUIJT
Librarian: Dr ONNO MASTENBROEK
Library of 25,000 vols, 350 printed journals
Number of teachers: 68
Number of students: 350

OPEN UNIVERSITEIT
(Open University)

POB 2960, 6401 DL Heerlen
Valkenburgerweg 177, 6419 AT Heerlen
Telephone: (45) 5762888
Fax: (45) 5711486
E-mail: info@ou.nl
Internet: www.ou.nl
Founded 1984
State control
Language of instruction: Dutch
Chair.: Drs T. J. F. M. BOVENS
Chair. of Supervisory Board: A. H. BROUWER-KORF
Rector: Prof. Dr Ir F. MULDER
Pro-Rector: Prof. Dr W. M. G. JOCHEMS
Registrar: Y. SMEETS-BERKERS
Librarian: Y. SMEETS-BERKERS
Library of 30,000 vols
Number of teachers: 751
Number of students: 26,182
Publications: *Modulair*, *OnderwijsInnovatie* (4 a year)

DEANS
Educational Technology Expertise Centre: Prof. Dr W. M. G. JOCHEMS

School of Cultural Studies: Prof. Dr JAAP VAN MARLE
School of Education: Prof. Dr ELS BOSHUIZEN
School of Informatics: Prof. Dr A. (LEX) BIJLSMA
School of Law: Prof. EVERT STAMHUIS
School of Management: Prof. Dr HERMAN VAN DEN BOSCH
School of Natural Science: Prof. Dr PAQUITA PÉREZ SALGADO
School of Psychology: Prof. Dr R. VAN HEZE-WIJK

PROFESSORS

Educational Technology Expertise Centre:
JOCHEMS, W. M. G.
KIRSCHNER, P. A.
KOPER, E. J. R.
VAN MERRIENBOER, J. J. G.

Rude de Moor Centre:
COONEN, H. W. A. M.
STIJNEN, P. J. J.
VERMEULEN, M. J. M.
ZWANEVELD, G.

School of Cultural Studies:
MARLE, J. VAN
WESSEL, L. H. M.
VAN DER DUSSEN, W. J.

School of Education:
BOSHUIZEN, H. P. A.

School of Informatics:
BAKKER, R. R.
JEURING, J. T.
JOOSTEN, S. M. M.
UDINK TEN CATE, A.
VAN DE CRAATS, J.

School of Law:
BOON, P. J.
RINKES, J. G. J.
SLOOT, B. P.
SPOORMANS, H. C. G.

School of Management:
HEEMSTRA, F. J.
HERST, A. C. C.
HOMAN, T.
JEPMA, C. J.
KORSTEN, A. F. A.
KUSTERS, R. J.
PEER, H. W. G. M.
SEMEIJN, J. J. S.
STORM, P. M.
VAN DEN AARDEMA, H. M. J.
VAN DEN BOSCH, H. M. J.
VAN DEN HEIJDEN, B. I. J. M.
VERSTEGEN, B. H. J.

School of Psychology:
CLAESSEN, J. F. M.
VAN DER MOLEN, H. T.
VON GRUMBKOW, J.
VAN HEZEWIJK, R. W. J.
VAN KEMENADE, J. A.

School of Science:
GLASBERGEN, P.
MARTENS, P.
PEREZ SALGADO, F.
REIJNDERS, L.
VAN DAM-MIERAS, M. C. E.

RADBOUD UNIVERSITEIT NIJMEGEN
(Radboud University, Nijmegen)

POB 9102, 6500 HC Nijmegen
Comeniuslaan 4, 6525 HP Nijmegen

Telephone: (24) 3616161
Fax: (24) 3564606
E-mail: info@communicatie.ru.nl
Internet: www.ru.nl

Founded 1923 as Katholieke Universiteit Nijmegen, present name 2004
Private control
Languages of instruction: Dutch, English

Academic year: September to July
Trustees: STICHTING KATHOLIEKE UNIV.
Pres. of the Univ. Board: Ir R. J. DE WIJKERSLOOTH DE WEERDESTEYN
Vice-Pres. of the Univ. Board: A. A. J. M. FRANKEN
Rector Magnificus: Prof. Dr S. C. J. J. KORTMANN
Sec.-Gen.: Drs J. J. A. VAN DE RIET
Librarian: Dr N. J. GRYGIERCZYK

Number of teachers: 2,352
Number of students: 19,137

Publications: *Radboud Magazine* (4 a year), *Vox* (6 a year)

DEANS

Faculty of Arts: Prof. Dr P. L. SARS
Faculty of Law: Prof. Dr P. P. T. BOVEN-D'EERT
Faculty of Medical Sciences: Prof. Dr A. B. M. SMIT
Faculty of Philosophy, Theology and Religious Studies: Prof. Dr J. THIJSSEN
Faculty of Science: Prof. C. C. A. M. GIELEN
Faculty of Social Sciences: Prof. H. P. J. M. DEKKERS
Nijmegen School of Management: Prof. Dr Ir R. E. C. M. VAN DER HEIJDEN

RIJKSUNIVERSITEIT GRONINGEN
(University Of Groningen)

POB 72, 9700 AB Groningen
Broerstraat 5, 9700 AB Groningen

Telephone: (50) 3639111
Fax: (50) 3635380
E-mail: communicatie@rug.nl
Internet: www.rug.nl

Founded 1614
State control
Languages of instruction: Dutch, English
Academic year: September to September

Chair.: Prof. Dr SIBRAND POPPEMA
Chair. of Supervisory Board: R. J. HOEKSTRA
Rector Magnificus: Prof. Dr ELMER STERKEN
Registrar: BERT VERVELD
Librarian: MARJOLEIN NIEBOER

Number of teachers: 413
Number of students: 27,699

Publication: *Broerstraat 5* (4 a year)

DEANS

Faculty of Arts: Prof. Dr GERRY C. WAKKER
Faculty of Behavioural and Social Sciences: Prof. Dr HENK A. L. KIERS
Faculty of Economics and Business: Prof. Dr J. H. GARRETSEN
Faculty of Law: Prof. Dr JAN BEREND WEZE-MAN
Faculty of Mathematics and Natural Sciences: Prof. Dr JASPER S. KNOESTER
Faculty of Medical Science: Prof. Dr FOLKERT KUIPERS
Faculty of Philosophy: Prof. Dr MARTIN V. B. P. M. VAN HEES
Faculty of Spatial Sciences: Prof. Dr INGE HUTTER
Faculty of Theology: Prof. Dr GEURT HENK VAN KOOTEN

TECHNISCHE UNIVERSITEIT DELFT
(Delft University of Technology)

POB 5, 2600 AA Delft
Mekelweg 5, 2628 CC Delft

Telephone: (15) 2789111
Fax: (15) 2786522
E-mail: info@tudelft.nl
Internet: www.tudelft.nl

Founded 1842, present name 1986
State control
Language of instruction: Dutch
Academic year: September to July

Pres.: Drs D. J. VAN DEN BERG
Vice-Pres. and Rector Magnificus: Prof. Ir K. CH. A. M. LUYBEN
Vice-Pres. for Education: Drs P. M. M. RULLMANN
Sec. Gen.: Drs J. L. MULDER
Librarian: Ir W. J. S. M. VAN WEEZENBEEK
Library: see Libraries and Archives
Number of teachers: 2,683
Number of students: 16,427

Publications: *Delft Integraal, Delft Outlook, Delta, Jaarverslag, Quarterly Progress Report, Statistisch Jaarboek, Studiegids, Wetenschappelijk Verslag*

DEANS

Faculty of Aerospace Engineering: Prof. Dr Ir JACCO M. HOEKSTRA
Faculty of Applied Sciences: Prof. Dr Ir TIM VAN DER HAGEN (acting)
Faculty of Architecture: Prof. Ir KARIN LAGLAS
Faculty of Civil Engineering and Geosciences: Prof. Dr Ir BERT M. GEERKEN
Faculty of Electrical Engineering, Mathematics and Computer Science: Prof. Dr Ir ROB H. J. FASTENAU
Faculty of Industrial Design Engineering: (vacant)
Faculty of Mechanical, Maritime and Materials Engineering: (vacant)
Faculty of Technology, Policy and Management: Prof. Dr THEO A. J. TOONEN

TECHNISCHE UNIVERSITEIT EINDHOVEN
(Eindhoven University of Technology)

POB 513, 5600 MB Eindhoven
Den Dolech 2, 5612 AZ Eindhoven

Telephone: (40) 2479111
Fax: (40) 2463120
E-mail: cec@tue.nl
Internet: www.tue.nl

Founded 1956
State control
Languages of instruction: Dutch, English
Academic year: September to August

Chair. of Supervisory Board: Ir R. L. VAN IPEREN
Pres. of Exec. Board: Dr Ir A. J. H. M. PEELS
Sec. of Univ.: Dr M. M. N. UMMELEN
Rector Magnificus: Prof. Dr Ir C. J. VAN DUIJN
Chair. of the Univ. Council: J. P. VAN HAM
Librarian: Drs J. C. M. FIGDOR
Library: see under Libraries and Archives
Number of teachers: 2,032
Number of students: 7,700

Publication: *Slash* (3 a year)

DEANS

Dept of Applied Physics: Prof. Dr Ir K. KOPINGA
Dept of Architecture, Building and Planning: Prof. Ir E. S. M. NELISSEN
Dept of Biomedical Engineering: Prof. Dr P. A. J. HILBERS
Dept of Chemical Engineering and Chemistry: Prof. Dr J. C. SCHOUTEN
Dept of Electrical Engineering: Prof. Dr Ir A. C. P. M. BACKX
Dept of Industrial Design: Prof. Dr Ir A. C. BROMBACHER
Dept of Industrial Engineering and Innovation Sciences: Prof. Dr A. G. L. ROMME
Dept of Mathematics and Computer Science: Prof. Dr A. M. COHEN
Dept of Mechanical Engineering: Prof. Dr Ir L. P. H. DE GOEY

UNIVERSITEIT LEIDEN
(Leiden University)

POB 9500, 2300 RA Leiden
Rapenburg 70, 2311 EZ Leiden
Telephone: (71) 5272727
Fax: (71) 5273118
E-mail: info@leidenuniv.nl
Internet: www.leidenuniv.nl

Founded 1575
State control
Language of instruction: Dutch
Academic year: September to July

Rector Magnificus and Pres.: Prof. Dr P. F. VAN DER HEIJDEN
Vice-Rector: Prof. Dr M. C. E. VAN DAM-MIERAS
Vice-Pres.: Drs H. W. TE BEEST
Librarian: KURT DE BELDER
Library: see Libraries and Archives
Number of teachers: 1,125 (f.t.e.)
Number of students: 18,778

DEANS

Faculty of Archaeology: Prof. Dr WILLEM J. H. WILLEMS
Faculty of Humanities: Prof. Dr H. W. VAN DEN DOEL
Faculty of Science: Prof. SJOERD M. VERDUYN LUNEL
Faculty of Social Science: Prof. Dr P. SPINHOVEN
Leiden Law School: Prof. C. J. J. M. STOLKER
Leiden University Medical Center: Prof. Dr E. C. KLASEN (Chair. of Exec. Bd)

UNIVERSITEIT MAASTRICHT
(University of Maastricht)

POB 616, 6200 MD Maastricht
Minderbroedersberg 4–6, 6211 LK Maastricht
Telephone: (43) 3882222
Fax: (43) 3885247
E-mail: communicatie@maastrichtuniversity.nl
Internet: www.maastrichtuniversity.nl

Founded 1976 as State Univ. of Limburg, present name 2008, Univ. of Limburg (www.tul.edu) was est. in 2001, in partnership with Hasselt Universiteit (see chapter on Belgium)
State control
Languages of instruction: Dutch, English
Academic year: September to June

Chair. of Supervisory Board: Drs A. H. A. VEENHOF
Pres. of Exec. Board: Dr Ir J. M. M. RITZEN
Rector: Prof. Dr G. P. M. F. MOLS
Vice-Pres. of Exec. Board: Drs A. POSTEMA
Librarian: Dr I. M. WIJK
Publication: Doc UM ent (research and devts in problem-based learning, 2 a year)
Library of 410,000 vols, 2,400 current periodicals
Number of teachers: 3,500
Number of students: 14,500

DEANS

Faculty of Arts and Social Sciences: Prof. Dr. REIN DE WILDE
Faculty of Cultural Studies: Prof. Dr Ir W. E. BIJKER, Prof. Dr P. TUMMEC
Faculty of Health, Medicine and Life Sciences: Prof. Dr MARTIN PAUL
Faculty of Humanities and Sciences: Prof. Dr LOUIS BOON
Faculty of Law: Prof. Dr A. W. HERINGA
Faculty of Psychology and Neurosciences: Prof. Dr BERNADETTE JANSMA
School of Business and Economics: Prof. Dr JOS LEMMINK

UNIVERSITEIT TWENTE
(University of Twente)

POB 217, 7500 AE Enschede
Drienerlolaan 5, 7522 NB Enschede
Telephone: (53) 4899111
Fax: (53) 4892000
E-mail: info@utwente.nl
Internet: www.utwente.nl

Founded 1961

Chair. of Supervisory Board: Drs H. J. VAN ESSEN
Pres.: Dr A. H. FLIERMAN
Rector Magnificus: Prof. Dr H. BRINKSMA
Vice-Pres.: Ir K. J. VAN AST
Sec. of the Univ.: ERIK VAN KEULEN
Librarian: Drs P. G. G. M. DAALMANS
Library: see Libraries and Archives
Number of students: 9,000

DEANS

Faculty of Behavioural Sciences: Prof. Dr KAREN VAN OUDENHOVEN-VAN DER ZEE
Faculty of Electrical Engineering, Mathematics and Computer Science: Prof. Dr Ir TON MOUTHAAN
Faculty of Engineering Technology: Prof. Dr RIKUS EISING
Faculty of Geo-Information Science and Earth Observation: Prof. Dr Ir TOM VELDKAMP (Man. Dir)
Faculty of Science and Technology: Prof. Dr GERARD VAN DER STEENHOVEN
School of Management and Governance: Prof. Dr RAMSES WESSELS

UNIVERSITEIT UTRECHT
(Utrecht University)

POB 80125, 3508 TC Utrecht
Heidelberglaan 8, 3584 CS Utrecht
Telephone: (30) 2539111
Fax: (30) 2533388
E-mail: studievoorlichting@uu.nl
Internet: www.uu.nl

Founded 1636
Languages of instruction: Dutch, English
Academic year: September to July

Pres.: YVONNE C. M. T. VAN ROOY
Chair. of Supervisory Board: M. H. (RIEN) MEIJERINK
Rector Magnificus and Vice-Pres.: Prof. HANS STOOF
Sec.-Gen.: Dr JOOP J. M. KESSELS
Library: see Libraries and Archives
Number of teachers: 3,000
Number of students: 29,927
Publication: Ublad (univ. magazine, 52 a year)

DEANS

Faculty of Geosciences: Prof. Dr BERT VAN DER ZWAAN
Faculty of Humanities: Prof. Dr WILJAN VAN DEN AKKER
Faculty of Law, Economics and Governance: Prof. H. R. B. M. (HENK) KUMMELING
Faculty of Science: Prof. Dr JAN VAN REE
Faculty of Social and Behavioural Sciences: Prof. Dr WILLEM KOOPS
Faculty of Veterinary Medicine: Prof. Dr A. PIJPERS
University Medical Centre: Prof. Dr F. MIEDEMA

PROFESSORS

Faculty of Arts (Kromme Nieuwegracht 46, 3512 HJ Utrecht):

BRAIDOTTI, R., Comparative Women's Studies
DE GROOT, R., Music of the Low Countries after 1600
DE JONG, F., Islamic Languages and Cultures

EDEL, D. R., Celtic Languages
GERRITSEN, W. P., Dutch Medieval Literature
HART, P., Utrecht Studies
HECHT, P. A., History of Visual Arts in Renaissance and Modern Times
HERRLITZ, W., German Language
JANSSEN, H. L., Studies of Medieval Castles
JONG, M. B., Medieval History
KLAMT, J. C. J. A., History of Medieval Art
KLOEK, J. J., Social History of Literature
LANDSBERGEN, S. P. J., Language and Speech Automation
LASARTE, F. J., Latin-American Studies
MEYER, B. W., Visual Arts during the Renaissance in Italy and the Netherlands and their Underlying Relationship
MIJNHARDT, W. W., Post-Middle Ages History
MOORTGAT, J., Linguistics, Language Informatics
NOOTEBOOM, S. G., Linguistics, in particular Phonetics
OP DE COUL, P. M., History of Music after 1600
ORBÁN, A. P., Vulgar and Medieval Latin
OTTENHEYM, K. A., History of Architecture
POLLMANN, M. M. W., Social Functions of Language Disciplines
PRAK, M. R., Post-Medieval History (Social Relationships)
REULAND, E. J., Linguistics, specifically Syntax
RIGHART, J. A., Post-Medieval History, in particular Internal Political Relations
SANCISI-WEERDENBURG, H. W. A. M., Ancient History and Culture
SCHENKEVELD VAN DER DUSSEN, M. A., Dutch Renaissance Literature
SCHOENMAKERS, H., Theatre Science
SCHWEGMAN, M. J., Women's History
SICCAMA, J. G., History of Security Issues
STUMPEL, J. F. H. J., Iconology and Art Theory
URICCHIO, W., History of Film and Television
VAN BUUREN, M. B., Modern Literature (French)
VAN DEN HOVEN, P. J., Linguistics
VAN DER VOORT, C. M. M.
VAN EIJCK, D. J. N., Logical Aspects of Computational Linguistics
VAN ZANDEN, J. L., Post-Medieval History (Social Relationships)
VELLEKOOP, C., History of Music before 1600
VERKUIJL, H. J., Dutch Language
VOOGD, P. J. DE, Modern Literature
WESTHOFF, G. J., Didactics of Modern Languages
ZONNEVELD, W., Linguistics, in particular Phonology, English Linguistics

Faculty of Biology (Sorbonnelaan 16, 3584 CA Utrecht; tel. (30) 2532276):

BOERSMA, K. TH., Didactics of Biology
DURSTON, A. J., Organismal Embryology
GOOS, H. J. TH., Comparative Endocrinology
HOEKSTRA, W. P. M., Microbiology
HOGEWEG, P., Theoretical Biology
KOLLÖFFEL, CHR., Botany
LAAT, S. W. DE, Developmental Biology
LAMBERS, J. T., Ecophysiology
SAYER, J. A., International Aspects of Nature Protection
SEINEN, W., Biological Toxicology
VAN DAMME, J. M. M., Ecological Population Genetics
VAN DE GRIND, W. A. P. F. L., Comparative Physiology
VAN DEN BIGGELAAR, J. A. M., Experimental Embryology
VAN DER HORST, D. J., Metabolic Physiology
VAN DER MAAS, P. J. M., Plant Taxonomy

VAN HOOFF, J. A. R. A. M., Comparative Physiology

VAN LEEUWEN, C. J., Biological Toxicology (Ecological Risk Assessment)

VAN LOON, L. C., Phytopathology

VAN NOORDWIJK, A. J., Population Ecology of Animals

VERKLEIJ, A. J., Electromicroscopy

VERRIPS, C. T., Applied Molecular Biology

VISSCHER, H., Palaeobotany

VOORMA, H. O., Molecular Biology

WEISBEEK, P. J., Molecular Genetics

WERGER, M. J. A., Botanical Ecology

Faculty of Chemistry (Sorbonnelaan 16, 3584 CA Utrecht; tel. (30) 2533791; fax (30) 2533072):

BRANDSMA, L., Organic Chemistry

DE HAAS, G. H., Biophysics

DE KRUIJF, H. A. M., Toxicology and Society

DE KRUIJFF, B., Molecular Biology of Biomembranes

EGMOND, M. R., Applied Enzymology

FRENKEL, D., Physical Computer Simulation

GEUS, J. W., Inorganic Chemistry

HAVERKAMP, J., Analytical Chemistry

HOLLANDER, J. A., In vivo NMR Spectroscopy

JENNESKENS, L. W., Physical Organic Chemistry

KAMERLING, J. P., Organic Chemistry of Natural Substances

KAPTEIN, R., NMR Spectroscopy

KELLY, J. J., Electrochemistry

KONINGSBERGER, D. C., Inorganic Chemistry

KROON, J., Chemistry

LEKKERKERKER, H. N. W., Physical Chemistry

MEIJERINK, A., Chemistry of Solids

PHILIPSE, A. P., Physical Chemistry

TURKENBURG, W. C., Science and Society

VAN DE VEN, J., Materials Science

VAN DEN BOSCH, H., Biochemistry

VAN DER MAAS, J. H., Spectrochemical Analysis

VAN DUIJNEVELDT, F. B., Theoretical Chemistry

VAN EERDEN, J. P. J. M., Macroscopic Physical Chemistry

VAN EIJNDHOVEN, J. C. M., Technological Research of Aspect

VAN KOTEN, G., Organic Chemistry

VELDINK, G. A., Organic Aspects of Bio-Catalysis

VERHEIJ, H. M., Biochemistry

VLIEGENTHART, J. F. G., Bio-Organic Chemistry

WIRTZ, K. W. A., Biochemistry

Faculty of Earth Sciences (Budapestlaan 4, 3584 CD Utrecht; tel. (30) 2535050; fax (30) 2535030):

DAS, H. A., Radioanalysis in Geochemistry

EISMA, D., Marine Sedimentology

JONG, B. M. W. S. DE, Petrology and Experimental Petrology

LEEUW, J. W. DE, Organic Geochemistry

MEULENKAMP, J. E., Stratigraphy and Palaeontology

MONDT, J. C., Exploratory Geophysics

OONK, H. A. J., Thermodynamics

PRIEM, H. N. A., Isotope Geology

SNIEDER, R. K., Seismology

SPIERS, CH. J., Experimental Rock-Deformation

VAN DER WEIJDEN, C. H., Marine Geochemistry and Hydrochemistry

WHITE, S. H., Structural Geology and Tectonics

WONG, TH. E., Sedimentary Geology of Subsoils in the Netherlands

WORTEL, M. J. R., Tectonophysics

Faculty of Geosciences (Heidelberglaan 2, 3584 CS Utrecht; tel. (30) 2532044; fax (30) 2540604):

BURROUGH, P. A., Physical Geography of Landscapes

DIELEMAN, F. M. J., Human Geography of Urban Industrialized Countries

GLASBERGEN, P., Environmental Policies

GROENEWEGEN, P. P., Environmental and Social Aspects of Health and Health Care

HAUER, J., Methods and Techniques in Geographical Research

HOEKVELD, G. A., Education and Regional Geography

HOOIMEIJER, P., Regional Aspects of Population Issues

KOSTER, E. A., Landscape Architecture

KREUKELS, A. M. J., Urban and Regional Planning

LAMBOOY, J. G., Geographical Economics

LUNING, H. A., Town and Country Planning in Developing Countries

NIEUWENHUIS, J. D., Soil Mechanics of Natural Systems

ORMELING, F. J., Cartography

OTTENS, H. F. L., Human Geography

SCHILDER, G. G., History of Cartography

TERWINDT, J. H. J., Physiogeographical Processes

VAN DEN AKKER, C., Ground and Surface Water Quality

VAN DEN BERG, M., Urban and Regional Planning

VAN GINKEL, J. A., Human Geography

VAN RIJN, L. C., Mechanics of Fluids (Geographical Modelling)

VAN WEESEP, J., Human Geography

VELLINGA, M. L., Human Geography (Developing Countries)

VONKEMAN, G. H., Environmental Studies

WEVER, E., Human Geography (Economic Geography and International Economics)

Faculty of Law (Janskerhof 3, 3512 BK Utrecht; tel. (30) 2537017; fax (30) 2537300):

ANDRIESSEN, F. H. J. J., European Integration

BACKES, CH. W., Environmental Law

BAEHR, P. R., Human Rights

BAHLMAN, J. P., Business Economics

BOELE-WOELKI, K. S. R. D., International and Comparative Private Law

BOON, D., Animals and Law

BOVENKERK, F., Criminology

BOVENS, M. A. P., Philosophy of Law

BRANTS, C. H., Penal Law and Law of Criminal Procedure

BRINKHOFF, J. J., Industrial Property

BRUINSMA, J. F., Sociology of Law

CURTIN, D. M., Law of International Organizations

DALHUISEN, J. H., International Commercial Law

GROSHEIDE, F. W., Private Law

HARTKAMP, A. S., Private Law, particularly Civil Law

HEYMAN, H. W., Notarial Law

HOL, A. M., Theory of Law

HONDIUS, E. H., Civil Law

IDENBURG, PH. A., Management Sciences

IN 'T VELD, R. I., Management of Public Government

JASPERS, A. PH. C. M., Social Law

KABEL, J. J. C., Mass Media Law

KELK, C., Penitentiary Law

KOERS, A. W., International Law

KUMMELING, H. R. B. M., Constitutional and Administrative Law

KWIATKOWSKA, B., International Maritime Law

MEIJKNECHT, P. A. M., Civil Law

MOOIJ, A. W. M., Forensic Psychiatry

MORTELMANS, K. J. M., Social Economic Law

NIEUWENBURG, C. K. F., Political Economy

ROSCAM ABBING, H. D. C., Health Law

SCHILFGAARDE, P., Business Law

SIEGERS, J. J., Economics

SOONS, A. H. A., International Law

SPRUIT, J. E., History of Roman Law

STILLE, A. L. G. A., Notarial Law

SWART, A. H. J., Penitentiary Law

TEN BERGE, J. B. J. M., Administrative Law

VAN BUUREN, P. J. J., Governmental Law

VAN DEN BERGH, R., Economics of Law

VAN HALL, A., Law of Public Water and Water Boards

VAN HOOF, G. J. H., Social Economic Law

VAN HUIZEN, P. H. J. G., Commercial Traffic Law

VAN MENS, K. L. H., Fiscal Law

VAN REENEN, P., Causes of Violations of Human Rights

VERVAELE, J. A. E., Maintenance of Law and Order

VREE, J. K. DE, International and Political Relations

Faculty of Mathematics and Informatics (Budapestlaan 6, 3584 CD Utrecht; tel. (30) 2531515; fax (30) 2518394):

DE LANGE, J., Didactics of Teaching Mathematics and Computer Science

DIEKMANN, O., Applied Mathematics

DUISTERMAAT, J. J., Pure and Applied Mathematics

GILL, R. D., Stochastics

HAZEWINKEL, M., Algebraic Chemistry

LOOIJENGA, E. J. N., Pure Mathematics

MARS, J. G. M., Mathematics

MEERTENS, L. T. G., Programming Technology

MEIJER, J. J. CH., Informatics

OORT, F., Mathematics

OVERMARS, M. H., Computer Science

SIERSMA, D., Mathematics

SWIERSTRA, S. D., Informatics

TREFFERS, A., Field-Specific Education

VAN DALEN, D., Logic and Philosophy of Mathematics

VAN DER VORST, H. A., Mathematics

VAN LEEUWEN, J., Informatics

VERHULST, F., Quantitative Analysis of Dynamic Systems

ZAGIER, D. B., Pure Mathematics

Faculty of Medicine (Universiteitsweg 100, 3584 CG Utrecht; tel. (30) 2538888; fax (30) 2539025):

AKKERMANS, L. M. A., Gastrointestinal Physiology

BÄR, P. R., Experimental Neurology

BATTERMAN, J. J., Radiotherapy

BAX, N. M. A., Paediatric Surgery

BEEMER, F. A., Clinical Genetics

BERGER, R., Chemistry of Hereditary Metabolic Diseases

BERNARDS, R. A., Molecular Carcinogenesis

BIJLSMA, J. W. J., Rheumatology

BLIJHAM, G. H., Clinical Medicine

BORST, C., Experimental Cardiology

BOS, J. L., Physiological Chemistry

BOSMAN, F., Dental Physics

BOUMA, B. N., Biochemistry of Haemostasis

BREDEE, J. J., Cardio-Pulmonic Surgery

BRUYNZEEL-KOOMEN, C. A. F. M., Dermatology-Allergology

BUITELAAR, I. K., Biopsychosocial Determinants in Human Behaviour

BURBACH, J. P. H., Molecular Biology of Neuropeptides

CAPEL, P. J. A., Experimental Immunology

CLEVERS, J. C., Clinical Immunology

COHEN-KETTENIS, P. T., Gender Development and Child and Youth Psychopathology

DEJONCKERE, P. H., Speech Therapy and Phoniatrics

DE PUTTER, C., Special Dental Surgery

DE WILDT, D. J., Medical Pharmacology

DUIJNSTEE, M. S. H., Innovations in Home Care
DUURSMA, S. A., Clinical Medicine
EIKELBOOM, B. C., Vascular and Transplant Surgery
ERKELENS, D. W., Clinical Medicine
FELDBERG, M. A. M., Radiodiagnostics
GAST, G. C. DE, Haematology
GEUZE, J. J., Cytology
GISPEN, W. H., Molecular Pharmacology and Neuro-Pharmacology
GOOSZEN, H. G., Surgery
GROBBEE, D. E., Clinical Epidemiology
GRYPDONCLE, M. H. F., Nursing Science
HAUER, R. N. W., Clinical Electrophysiology
HEEREN, TH. J., Psychogeriatrics
HEINTZ, A. P. M., Oncological Gynaecology
HELDERS, P. J. M., Physiotherapy
HENGEVELD, M. W., Sexology
HILLEN, B., Functional Anatomy
HORDIJK, G. J., Oto-rhino-laryngology
TEN HORN, G. H. M. M., Psychiatric Care-Management
HUIZING, E. H., Oto-rhino-laryngology
JONGSMA, H. J., Medical Physiology
KAHN, R. S., Clinical and Biological Psychiatry
KATER, L., Clinical Immunopathology
KNAPE, J. TH. A., Anaesthesiology
KOERSELMAN, G. F., Psychotherapy
KON, M., Plastic and Reconstructive Surgery
KOOMANS, H. A., Nephrology
LAMMERS, J. W. J., Pulmonary Diseases
MALI, W. P. TH. M., Radiodiagnostics
MARX, J. J. M., General Internal Medicine
MOSTERD, W. L., Clinical Sports Medicine
OKKEN, A., Paediatrics
PEARSON, P. L., Medical Molecular Genetics
PETERS, A. C. B., Paediatric Neurology
PETERS, P. W. J., Teratology
POLL-THE, B. E., Clinical Congenital Metabolic Diseases
ROBLES DE MEDINA, E. O., Clinical Cardiology
SANGSTER, B., Health Protection
SAVELKOUL, T. J. F., Toxicology
SCHRIJVERS, A. J. P., General Health Care
SCHULPEN, T. W. J., Social Paediatrics
SITSEN, J. M. A., Clinical Pharmacology
SIXMA, J. J., Haematology
SLOOTWEG, P. J., Oral Pathology
SMOORENBURG, G. F., Experimental Audiology
SMOUT, A. J. P. M., Pathophysiology
STAAL, G. E. J., Enzymology
STILMA, J. S., Ophthalmology
STROUS, G. J. A. M., Cellular Biology
SUSSENBACH, J. S., Molecular Biology
TE VELDE, E. R., Desirable Fertility
THIJSSEN, J. J. H., Clinical Chemistry
TREFFERS, W. F., Ophthalmology
TULLEKEN, C. A. F., Neurosurgery
VAN BEL, F., Neonatology
VAN BERGE HENEGOUWEN, G. P., Gastroenterology
VAN BRONSWIJK, J. E. M. H., Biological Agents in Domestic Hygiene
VAN DE WAL, H. J. C. M., Cardiopulmonic Surgery of Infants and Children
VAN DEN TWEEL, J. G., Pathology
VAN DER DONK, J. A. W. M., Cell Biology
VAN DER VLIET, P. C., Physical Chemistry
VAN DER WERKEN, CHR., Acute Surgery
VAN DER WINKEL, J. G. J., Immunotherapy
VAN ENGELAND, H., Psychiatry of Children
VAN GIJN, J., Neurology
VAN HUFFELEN, A. C., Clinical Neurophysiology
VAN LONDEN, J., General Health Care
VAN NIEUWENHUIZEN, O., Paediatric Neurology in relation to Functional Morphology
VAN NORREN, D., Ophthalmological Physics
VAN REE, J. M., Psychopharmacology

VAN VEELEN, C. W. M., Functional Neuro-surgery
VAN VLOTEN, W. A., Dermatology
VAN VROONHOVEN, TH. J. M. V., General Surgery
VAN WAES, P. F. G. M., Röntgen Diagnostics
VAN WIMERSMA GREIDANUS, TJ. B., Neuroendocrinology
VELDMAN, J. E., Experimental Otology and Otoimmunology
VERBOUT, A. J., Orthopaedic Aspects of Spinal and Neuromuscular Disorders
VERHEIJ, T. J. M., Family Medicine
VERHOEF, J., Clinical Microbiology
VERSTEEG, D. H. G., Medical Pharmacology
VIERGEVER, M. A., Image-processing in Medicine
VISSER, G. H. A., Obstetrics
VOORN, TH. B., General Practice
WESTENBERG, H. G. M., Neurochemical Aspects of Psychiatry
WINNUBST, J. A. M., Psychology of Health and Illness
WOKKE, J. H. J., Neurology focusing on Neuromuscular Diseases
WOLTERS, W. H. G., Paediatric Psychology
ZEGERS, B. J. M., Paediatric Immunology
ZONNEVELD, F. W., Medical Representation Techniques

Faculty of Pharmacy (Sorbonnelaan 16, 3584 CA Utrecht; tel. (30) 2532525; fax (30) 2533953):

BAKKER, A., Pharmaceutical Practice
BEIJNEN, J. H., Bio-Analysis (Research in Clinical Medicine)
BULT, A., Pharmaceutical Analysis
CLERCK, F. F. P., Applied Pulmonary and Cardiovascular Pharmacology
CROMMELIN, D. J. A., Biopharmacy
DE JONG, J. G. A. M., Management Aspects of Pharmaceutical Practice
GLERUM, J. H., Clinical Pharmacy
HENNINK, W. E., Pharmaceutical Technology
JANSSEN, L. H. M., Pharmaceutical Chemistry
LABADIE, R. P., Pharmacognosy
LISKAMP, R. M. J., Molecular Medicinal Chemistry
MAES, R. A. A., Toxicology
NIJKAMP, F. P., Molecular Pharmacology
OLIVIER, B., Applied Pharmacology of the Central Nervous System
PORSIUS, A. J., Pharmacotherapy
RUITER, A., Food Chemistry and Bromatology
THIJSSEN, J. H. H., Clinical Chemistry
TOLLENAERE, J. P. A. E., Computational Medicinal Chemistry
VAN DIJK, H., Immunology of Phytochemicals
VERBATEN, M. N., Human Psychophysiology and Psychopharmacology

Faculty of Philosophy (Heidelberglaan 8, 3584 CS Utrecht; tel. (30) 2531831; fax (30) 2532816):

BERGSTRA, J. A., Applied Logic
GEERTSEMA, H. P., Calvinist Philosophy
MANSFELD, J., History of Philosophy in the Ancient World and the Middle Ages
MIDDELBURG, C. A., Applied Logic
RUNIA, D. T., The Tradition of Platonism in Relation to Early Christianity
SCHUHMANN, K. J., History of Modern and Renaissance Philosophy
VAN DALEN, D., Logic and Philosophy
VAN REIJEN, W. L., Political and Social Philosophy
VERBEEK, TH. H. M., 17th-Century Ideology from the Dutch Perspective

Faculty of Physics and Astronomy (Princetonplein 5, 3584 CC Utrecht; tel. (30) 2533284; fax (30) 2539282):

ANDRIESSE, C. D., Electricity Supplies
BEIJERINCK, H. C. W., Atomic and Interface Physics
BLEEKER, J. A. M., Space Research
BUIJS, A., Experimental Physics
BUILTJES, P. J. H., Chemistry of the Atmosphere
CROWE, A., Medical and Physiological Physics
DE RUIJTER, W. P. M., Physical Oceanography
DE WIJN, H. W., Solid State Physics
DE WIT, B. Q. P. J., Theoretical Physics
DE WITT HUBERTS, P. K. A., Reactor Physics
DIEKS, D. G. B. J., Foundations and Philosophy of the Natural Sciences
DIJKHUIS, J. I., Semiconductor Laser Optics
DRONKERS, J., Physics of Coastal Systems
ERKELENS, C. J., Human Physics
ERNÉ, F. C., Current Issues in Physics
ERNST, M. H. J. J., Theoretical Physics
FEINER, L. F., Theory of Condensed Materials
HABRAKEN, F. H. P. M., Physics Education
HEARN, A. G., Astrophysics
HEIDEMAN, H. G. M., Experimental Physics
HOLTSLAG, A. A. M., Meteorology (Forecasting) Techniques
HOOFT, T. W. J. M., Theory of Solids
KAMERMANS, R., Experimental Physics and Experimental Nuclear Physics
KOENDERINK, J. J., Human Physics
KUPERUS, M., Astrophysics
LAMERS, H. J. G. L. M., Astronomy
LELIEVELD, J., Atmospheric Chemistry
LEVINE, Y. K., Biophysics
LIJNSE, P. L., Development of Physics Concepts and Methods in Education
LOURENS, W., Physics Informatics
NIEHAUS, A., Experimental Physics
OERLEMANS, J., Dynamics of the Climate
POLMAN, A., Advancement of Atomic and Interface Physics
RUIJGROK, TH. W., Theoretical Physics and Mechanics
SARIS, F. W., Atomic and Molecular Physics
SCHÜLLER, F. C., Plasma Physics
SCHUURMANS, C. J. E., Meteorology
SINKE, W. C., Physical and Chemical Properties of Thin Layers
SMIT, J., Theoretical High-Energy Physics
T. JANSSEN, G., Theoretical Physics
TJON, J. A., Theoretical Physics
VAN BEIJEREN, H., Theoretical Physics
VAN DER WEG, W. F., Technical Physics
VAN HIMBERGEN, J. E. J. M., Theoretical Physics
VERBUNT, F. W. M., High-Energy Astrophysics
VERLINDE, E. P., Theoretical Physics
ZIMMERMAN, J. TH. F., Physical Oceanography

Faculty of Social Sciences (Heidelberglaan 1, 3584 CS Utrecht):

ADRIAANSENS, H. P. M., Social Sciences and Social Processes and Structures
BANCK, G. A., Anthropology of Brazil
BECKER, H. A., Sociology
BENSING, J. M., Clinical Psychology and Health Psychology
BIERMAN, D. J., Parapsychology
BRINKGEVE, C. D. A., Primary Forms of Cohabitation, Life-Course and Identity
Dr COENEN, H. M. H., Labour Issues
DEEN, N., Theory and Practice of Pupil Accompaniment
DERCKSEN, W. J., Social Sciences (Socio-Economic Policy)
DUBBELDAM, L. F. B., Education in Developing Countries
ELBERS, E. P. J. M., Communication, Thought and Culture Issues
ENGBERSEN, G. B. M., Welfare State System

ENTZINGER, H. B., Studies of Multi-Ethnic Societies

GRIENSVEN, G. J. P., Social Epidemiology with respect to HIV/AIDS

GROEBEL, F. J., Social Sciences (Psychology of Mass Communication)

HAAN, E. H. F. DE, Applied Experimental Psychology

HAGENDOORN, A. J. M. W., Social Sciences

HART, H. 'T, Statistics and Methodology of Pedagogical Research

HEIJMANS, P. G., Life Psychology

HOKSBERGEN, R. A. C., Adoption

HOX, J. J., Survey Research

IDENBURG, PH. A., Management Sciences

IMELMAN, J. D., Principles of Pedagogics

INGLEBY, J. D., Life Psychology

KANSELAAR, G., Educational Sciences, in particular Educational Psychology

KNULST, W. P., Education in Arts and Cultural Participation

KRUIJT, D. A. N. M., Development Issues

LAGERWEIJ, N. A. J., Pedagogics and Innovation in Teaching

LEEUW, F. L., Empirical Theoretical Analysis of the Social Effects of Government Policy

MANTE MEIJEE, E. A., Management and Renewal Processes in Large Organizations

OOSTINDIE, G. J., Anthropology of Comparative Sociology (Caribbean)

PILOT, A., Didactics

RAUB, W., Theoretical Sociology

RISPENS, J., Education of Problem Children

ROBBEN, A. C. G. M., Anthropology of Comparative Sociology (Latin America)

RUIJTER, A. DE, Social Anthropology

SCHAUFELI, W. B., Organizational Psychology

SCHETTKAT, R., Social and Institutional Economics

SCHNABEL, P., Mental Health Care

SCHOFFELEERS, J. H., Socio-Economic Changes and Forms of Meaning-Making

SEVENHUYSEN, S. L., Comparative Women's Studies

STEVENS, L. M., Orthopedagogics

STROEBE, W., Social and Organizational Psychology

TAZELAAR, F., Sociology

THIJSSEN, J. G. L., Business and Professional Education

TIELMAN, R. A. P., Social and Cultural Aspects of Humanism

TREFFERS, A., Field-Specific Education

VAN DEN BOUT, J., Bereavement Acceptance Process

VAN DER HEIJDEN, P. G. M., Statistics for Social Sciences

VAN DER LAAN, G., Foundations of Social Work

VAN DER ZWAN, A., Development of Views on the Adjustment of the Welfare State

VAN SON, M. J. M., Clinical and Health Care Psychology

VAN WAARDEN, B. F., Intervention, Organization and Policy Issues in Social Sciences

VAN WIJNGAARDEN, P. J., Sociological Aspects of Social Security Issues

VAN WYNGAARDEN, P. J., Social Security Issues

VAN ZANTWIJK, R. A. M., Anthropology and Ethno-History of the Indian Peoples of Latin America

VEENHOVEN, R., Humanism

VERMEER, A., Remedial Education

VRIENS, L. J. A., Peace Studies

VROON, P., Theoretical Psychology

WERTHEIM, A. H., Cognitive Ergonomics

WILTERDINK, N. A., Study of Long-term Processes in Social Sciences

WINTER, M. DE, Innovations in Primary Parent and Child Care

WUBBELS, TH., Teacher Behaviour as a Factor in the Learning Environment

Faculty of Theology (Heidelberglaan 2, 3584 CS Utrecht; tel. (30) 2531853; fax (30) 2533241):

ANDREE, T. G. I. M., Ideological Upbringing and Formation in a Multi-Religious Context

BECKING, B. E. H. J., Old Testament

BRÜMMER, V., Philosophy of Religion

DE REUVER, A., Education in Calvinist Theology

DEN BOEFT, J., Religious History of Hellenism

HEEGER, F. R., Ethics

HOUTEPEN, A. W. P., Ecumenics

IMMINK, F. G., Practical Theology

JONGENEEL, J. A. B., Missiology

KLOPPENBORG, M. A. G. T., History of Religions and Comparative Religious Studies

MAAS, T. A., Relationships between Christianity and Modern Culture

MUIS, J., Dogmatics

OTTEN, W., Church History

SCHROTEN, E., Christian Ethics

TIELEMAN, H. J., Sociology of Religions

VAN BELZEN, J. A., Psychology of Religion

VAN DER HORST, P. W., New Testament

VAN LEEUWEN, TH. M., Science of the Old Testament and History of Israelite Religion

VRIES, O. H. DE, History and Dogmas of the Baptism

Faculty of Veterinary Medicine (Yalelaan 1, 3584 CL Utrecht; tel. (30) 2534851; fax (30) 2537727):

BARNEVELD, A., General Surgery and Surgery of Large Domestic Animals

BEYNEN, A. C., Experimental Animals

BREUKINK, H. J., Clinical Veterinary Medicine

COLENBRANDER, B., Fertility

CORNELISSEN, A. W. C. A., Parasitology

DE VRIES, H. W., Medicine of Small Domestic Animals

DEN OTTER, W., Cell Biology and Histology

DIK, K. J., Radiology

EVERTS, M. F., Veterinary Physiology

FERON, V. J., Biological Toxicology

FINK-GREMMELS-GEHRMANN, J., Pharmacology of Domestic Animals

GIELKENS, A. J. L., Veterinary Medicine for Poultry Farms

GROMMERS, F. J., Relationship between Man and Animal

GRUYS, E., Pathology of Domestic Animals

HELLEBREKERS, L. J., Anaesthesiology of Laboratory Animals

HORZINEK, M. C., Virology

HUIS IN 'T VELD, J. H. J., Microbiology of Food Products of Animal Origin

JANSSEN, J., Knowledge of Veterinary Law

KROES, R., Biological Toxicology

MELOEN, R. H., Biomedical Identification

MOUWEN, J. M. V. M., Pathology

OSTERHAUS, A. D. M. E., Environmental Virology

PIJPERS, A., Veterinary Medicine for Poultry Farms

ROTTIER, P. J. M., Molecular Virology

RUITENBERG, E. J., Veterinary Immunology

RIJNBERK, A., Medicine of Small Domestic Animals

SCHALKEN, J. A., Veterinary Oncology

SLUYS, F. J., Medicine of Domestic Animals, Reproduction and Surgery

SPRUIJT, B. M., Good Health of Animals

TIELEN, M. J. M., Lodging and Provision of Animals

VAN DER WEYDEN, G. C., Obstetrics

VAN DER ZEIJST, B. A. M., Veterinary Bacteriology

VAN DER ZUTPHEN, L. F. M., Animals and Experimental Application

VAN DIJK, J. E., Pathology of Rare Animals/ Spontaneous Laboratory Animal Pathology

VAN EDEN, W., Veterinary Immunology

VAN GOLDE, L. M. G., Veterinary Biochemistry

VAN KNAPEN, F., Hygiene of Food of Animal Origin

VAN MIERT, A. S. J. P. A. M., Veterinary Pharmacology

VAN OIRSCHOT, J. T., Veterinarian Vaccinology

VAN OOST, B. A., Clinical and Molecular Genetics of Domestic Animals

VERHEIJDEN, J. H. M., Medicine of Pigs

VOS, J. G., Toxicological Pathology

WEIJS, W. A., Veterinary Anatomy and Embryology

UNIVERSITEIT VAN AMSTERDAM (University of Amsterdam)

POB 19268, 1000 GG Amsterdam
Spui 21, 1012 WX Amsterdam

Telephone: (20) 5259111
Fax: (20) 5252136
E-mail: info@uva.nl
Internet: www.uva.nl

Founded 1632 as Athenaeum Illustre, present name and status 1877

State control

Languages of instruction: Dutch, English

Academic year: September to July

Pres.: Dr LOUISE GUNNING-SCHEPERS

Rector Magnificus: Prof. DYMPH VAN DEN BOOM

Vice-Pres.: PAUL DOOP

Sec.-Gen.: MIEKE ZAANEN

Library Dir: Drs NOL VERHAGEN

Library: see Libraries and Archives

Number of teachers: 2,626 (f.t.e)

Number of students: 32,165

Publications: *Athenaeum Illustre* (4 a year), *Gids van de Universiteit van Amsterdam* (1 a year)

DEANS

Faculty of Dentistry: Prof. A. J. FEILZER

Faculty of Economics and Business: Prof. H. G. VAN DISSEL

Faculty of Humanities: Prof. F. P. I. M. VAN VREE

Faculty of Law: Prof. C. E. DU PERRON

Faculty of Medicine: Prof. M. M. LEVI

Faculty of Science: Prof. L. D. NOORDAM

Faculty of Social and Behavioural Sciences: Prof. E. H. F. DE HAAN

TILBURG UNIVERSITY

POB 90153, 5000 LE Tilburg
Warandelaan 2, 5037 AB Tilburg

Telephone: (13) 4669111
Fax: (13) 4663019
E-mail: info@tilburguniversity.edu
Internet: www.tilburguniversity.nl

Founded 1927 as Roomsch Katholieke Handelshoogeschool, present status 2006

State control

Languages of instruction: Dutch, English

Academic year: September to August

Chair.: R. F. M. LUBBERS

Pres. of Exec. Board: H. M. C. M. VAN OORSCHOT

Rector: Prof. Dr PHILIP EIJLANDER

Chief Admin. Officer: Drs M. H. VAN IEPEREN

Chief Information Officer: Ir M. VAN DEN BERG

Sec.-Gen.: Drs HUUB DEKKERS

Library of 800,000 vols, 11,000 periodical vols

Number of teachers: 992 (f.t.e.)

Number of students: 13,000

Publications: *Tilburg Research* (irregular), *UNIVERS* (online), *Until* (irregular)

DEANS

Law School: Prof. Dr RANDALL LESAFFER
School of Economics and Management: Prof. Dr KEES KOEDIJK
School of Humanities: Prof. Dr ARIE DE RUIJTER
School of Social and Behavioural Sciences: Prof. Dr KLAAS SIJTSMA
School of Theology: Prof. Dr ADELBERT DENAUX
TiasNimbas Business School: Prof. Dr Ir RAMON O'CALLAGHAN

UNIVERSITEIT VOOR HUMANISTIEK
(University for Humanistics)

POB 797, 3500 AT Utrecht
Kromme Nieuwegracht 29, 3512 HD Utrecht
Telephone: (30) 2390100
Fax: (30) 2340738
E-mail: info@uvh.nl
Internet: www.uvh.nl
Founded 1989
State control
Academic year: September to June
Chair.: Prof. Dr ARIE DE RUIJTER
Rector: Prof. Dr HANS A. ALMA
Librarian: M. A. M. BOERBOOM
Library of 22,000 vols
Number of teachers: 100
Number of students: 350

PROFESSORS

COENEN, H. L. M., Sciences of Man, Society and Culture
ELDERS, A. D. M., Theories of World Views
HOUTEN, D. J. VAN, Social Policy, Planning and Organization
KUNNEMAN, H. P., Practical Humanist Studies
MANSCHOT, H. A. M., Philosophy and Ethics
MASO, I., Philosophy of Science, Methodology and the Theory of Research
VRIES, T. DE, Regional Health Care

VRIJE UNIVERSITEIT, AMSTERDAM
(Free University, Amsterdam)

De Boelelaan 1105, 1081 HV Amsterdam
Telephone: (20) 5989898
Fax: (20) 5989899
E-mail: international@dienst.vu.nl
Internet: www.vu.nl
Founded 1880
Languages of instruction: Dutch, English
Academic year: September to September
Chair. of Supervisory Board: P. BOUW
Chair. of Exec. Board: R. M. SMIT
Rector: LEX BOUTER
Mem. of Exec. Board: H. J. RUTTEN
Library: see under Libraries and Archives
Number of teachers: 2,000
Number of students: 25,000
Publication: *VU Magazine*

DEANS

Faculty of Arts: Prof. Dr DOUWE G. YNTERNA
Faculty of Dentistry: Prof. A. FEILZER
Faculty of Earth and Life Sciences: Prof. BAUKE OUDEGA
Faculty of Economics and Business Administration: Prof. H. VERBRUGGEN
Faculty of Human Movement Sciences: Prof. P. J. BEEK
Faculty of Law: Prof. Dr E. SLIEDREGT
Faculty of Medicine: Prof. W. STALMAN
Faculty of Philosophy: Prof. R. VAN WOUDENBERG

Faculty of Psychology and Education: Prof. J. PASSCHIER
Faculty of Sciences: Prof. Dr H. IRTH
Faculty of Social Sciences: Prof. ANTON C. HEMERIJCK
Faculty of Theology: Prof. Dr WIM JANSE

WAGENINGEN UNIVERSITEIT
(Wageningen University)

POB 9101, 6700 HB Wageningen
Bldg no. 400, Costerweg 50, 6701 BH Wageningen
Telephone: (317) 480100
Fax: (317) 484884
E-mail: info@wur.nl
Internet: www.wageningenuniversity.nl
Founded 1876, present status 1918; attached to Wageningen Univ. and Research Centre
State control
Languages of instruction: Dutch, English
Academic year: September to August
Chair.: Dr A. A. DIJKHUIZEN
Rector Magnificus and Vice-Pres.: Prof. Dr M. J. KROPFF
Mem. of Exec. Board: Dr IJ. J. H. (TIJS) BREUKINK
Chair. of Supervisory Board: M. DE BOER
Chief Librarian: D. VAN ZAANE
Information Officer: S. VINK
Library: see under Libraries and Archives
Number of teachers: 500
Number of students: 6,427
Publication: *Wb*

PROFESSORS

ANTONIDES, G., Economics of Consumers and Households
BAKKER, J., Nematology, Physiology and Molecular Ecology of Nematodes
BEERS, G., Supply Chain Management
BERENDSE, F., Nature Conservation and Plant Ecology
BEULENS, A. J. M., Information Technology
BIGMAN, D., Global Food Security and Int. Trade
BINDELS, J., Nutrition during Growth and Devt
BINO, R. J., Metabolomica of Plants
BISSELING, A. H. J., Molecular Biology, Devt Biology of Plants
BLANS, G. H. T., Philosophy
BONGERS, F., Forest Ecology and Forest Management Group
BOOM, R. M., Food Process Engineering
BOT, G. P. A., Technical Physics
BOEKEL, M. A. J. S. VAN, Product Design and Quality Management
BREEMEN, N. VAN, Soil Formation and Ecopedology
BRINK, A. VAN DEN, Policy and Management in Land Use Planning
BREGT, A. K., Geo-Information Science, Geographical Information Systems
BRUGGEN, A. H. C. VAN, Biological Farming Systems
BRUSSAARD, L., Soil Biology and Biological Soil Quality
CAPELLE, A., Agrification
CLEEF, A. M., Tropical Nature Conservation and Vertebrate Ecology
COHEN STUART, M. A., Physical Chemistry and Colloid Chemistry
CROUS, P. W., Evolutionary Phytopathology
DENNY, P., Aquatic Ecology
DICKE, M., Entomology
DIJK, G. VAN, Theory and Practice of Agricultural Cooperative Organizations
DONS, H. J. M., Entrepreneurship in Life Sciences
ELFRING, T., Innovative Entrepreneurship
EMONS, A. M. C., Plant Cell Biology
FEDDES, R. A., Soil Physics, Ecohydrology and Groundwater Management

FLEER, G. J., Physical and Colloid Chemistry
FOLMER, H., General Economics
FOLSTAR, P., Knowledge Management of Innovation Processes in Food Production
FRERKS, G. E., Disaster Management
FREWER, L. J., Food Safety and Consumer Behaviour
GIJZEN, H. J., Environmental Biotechnology
GILLER, K. E., Plant Production Systems
GOEWIE, E. A., Social Aspects of Biological Farming
GOLDBACH, R. W., Virology
GORRIS, L. G. M., Food Safety Microbiology
GOVERDE, H. J. M., Political Science in Agriculture and Environment
GRASMAN, J., Mathematical and Statistical Methods
GROENEN, M. A. M., Animal Breeding and Genetics
HAMER, R. J., Technology of Cereal Proteins
HARTOG, L. A. DEN, Developments in Animal Production
HEIDE, D. VAN DER, Human and Animal Physiology
HEIJMAN, W. J. M., Rural Economics, Spatial Aspects of Rural Devt and Transformation
HEYTING, C., Molecular Cell Genetics
HIDDINK, G. J., Nutritional Extension by Intermediary
HOEKSTRA, R. F., Genetics, Populations and Quantitative Genetics
HOLTSLAG, B., Meteorology and Air Quality
HOOG, C. DE, Sociology of the Family
HOWARD-BORJAS, P. L., Gender Studies in Agriculture
HUIRNE, R. B. M., Economics of Animal Health and Food Safety
IERLAND, E. C. VAN, Environmental Economics and Natural Resources
JACOBSEN, E., Plant Breeding
JONGEN, W. M. F., Product Design and Quality Management
KATAN, M. B., Nutrition and Epidemiology
KEMP, B., Adaptation Physiology
KOK, F. J., Nutrition and Health
KOOIJ, D. VAN DER, Environmental Microbiology, Drinking Water Supply
KOOIJ, P., Agricultural History
KOORNNEEF, M., Genetics
KOOTEN, O. VAN, Horticultural Production Chains
KORTHALS, M. J. J. A. A., Applied Philosophy
KROEZE, J. H. A., Psychological and Sensorial Aspects of Food and Nutrition
KROMHOUT, D., Public Health Research
KROPFF, M. J., Crop and Weed Ecology
LANKVELD, J. M. G., Dairy Science
LEEMANS, R., Analysis of Environmental Systems
LEENTVAAR, J., Integrated Water Management
LEEUWEN, J. L. VAN, Experimental Zoology
LEEUWIS, C., Communication and Innovation Studies
LEIJNSE, A., Groundwater Quality
LENGKEEK, J., Socio-Spatial Analysis of Land Use (Recreation and Tourism)
LEUNISSEN, J. A. M., Bio-informatics
LENTEREN, J. C. VAN, Entomology
LINDEN, E. VAN DER, Food Physics
MAESEN, L. J. G. VAN DER, Plant Taxonomy and Geography
METZ, J. H. M., Technical Design of Farm Systems in Animal Husbandry
MEULEN, B. M. J. VAN DER, Law and Governance
MILITZ, H., Wood Science
MOHREN, G. M. J., Forest Ecology and Forest Management Group
MOL, A. P. J., Environmental Policy
MUISWINKEL, W. B. VAN, Cell Biology and Immunology
MULDER, B. M., Theoretical Cell Physics
MULDER, M., Agricultural Education
MÜLLER, J., Farm Technology

MÜLLER, M., Nutrition, Metabolism and Genomics

NIEHOF, A., Sociology of Consumers and Households

OENEMA, O., Management of Nutrient Fluxes and Soil Fertility

OMTA, S. W. F., Management Studies

OOYEN, A. J. J. VAN, Genetics in Food Technology

OPDAM, P. F. M., Landscape Ecology, Spatial Population Ecology

OSKAM, A. J., Agricultural Economics and Rural Policy

OUDE LANSINK, A. G. J. M., Business Economics

PENNINGS, J. M. E., Future Markets

PERDOK, U. D., Soil Technology

PLAS, L. H. W. VAN DER, Plant Physiology

PLOEG, J. D. VAN DER, Rural Sociology

PRINS, H. H. T., Resource Ecology

PUTTEN, W. H. VAN DER, Functional Biodiversity

RAATS, P. A. C., Continuum Mechanics

RABBINGE, R., Sustainable Devt and System Innovation

RICHARDS, P., Technology and Agrarian Devt

RIEMSDIJK, W. H. VAN, Soil Chemistry and Chemical Soil Quality

RIETJENS, I. M. C. M., Toxicology

RULKENS, W. H., Environmental Technology

SANDERS, J. P. M., Valorisation of Plant Production Chains

SAVELKOUL, H. F. J., Cell Biology and Immunology

SCHAAFSMA, G. J., Nutrition and Food

SCHAEPMAN, M. E., Geo-information Science, Remote Sensing

SCHANZ, H., Forest Policy and Forest Management

SCHEFFER, J. J. C., Medicinal and Aromatic Plant Science

SCHEFFER, M., Aquatic Ecology and Water Quality

SCHIPPERS, J. C., Water Supply Technology (IHE)

SCHOUTEN, M. G. C., Ecology of Nature Conservation

SCHULTZ, E., Land and Water Devt (IHE)

SCHUURMAN, E., Reformational Philosophy

SKIDMORE, A. K., Vegetation and Agricultural Land Use Survey

SLANINA, J., Measuring Methods in Atmospheric Research

SMIT, G., Molecular Flavour Science

SMITS, M. A., Animal Breeding and Genetics

SNOO, G. R. DE, Agri-Environment Schemes

SOSEF, M., Biosystematics

SPIERTZ, J. H. J., Crop Ecology, Nutrient and Metabolic Flows

SPRUIJT, B. M., Ethology and Animal Welfare

STAM, P., Plant Breeding, Selection Methods and Sustainable Resistance

STAMS, A. J. M., Microbiology

STAVEREN, W. A. VAN, Nutrition and Gerontology

STEIN, A., Spatial Statistics

STIEKEMA, W. J., Genome Informatics

STRATEN, G. VAN, Systems and Control

STROOSNIJDER, L., Erosion and Soil and Water Conservation

STRUIK, P. C., Crop Physiology

SUDHÖLTER, E. J. R., Organic Chemistry

SYKORA, K. V., Ecological Organisation and Management of Infrastructure

TAMMINGA, S., Animal Nutrition, Ruminants

TERPSTRA, M. J., Consumer Technology and Product Use

TRAMPER, J., Bioprocess Engineering

TRIJP, J. C. M. VAN, Marketing and Consumer Behaviour

TROCH, P. A., Hydrology and Quantitative Water Management

VALK, A. J. J. VAN DER, Land Use Planning

VAN ARENDONK, J. A. M, Animal Genetics and Breeding

VAN DEN BERG, J. A., Genomics

VAN BLADEREN, P. J., Toxico-Kinetics and Biotransformation

VEER, P. VAN 'T, Human Nutrition and Epidemiology

VELDKAMP, A., Soil and Land Evaluation

VERRETH, J. A. J., Fish Culture and Fisheries

VERSTEGEN, M. W. A., Animal Nutrition, Monogastrics

VERVLOET, J. A. J., Historical Geography of Landscaping in the Netherlands

VET, L. E. M., Evolutionary Ecology

VIERSSEN, W. VAN, Aquatic Ecology

VINCENT, L. F., Irrigation and Water Engineering

VISSER, L. E., Rural Development Sociology

VISSER, R. G. F., Plant Breeding

VLAK, J. M., Virology

VORAGEN, A. G. J., Food Chemistry

VOS, W. M. DE, Microbiology

VRIES, S. C. DE, Biochemistry

WAGENBERG, A. F. VAN, Facility Management

WIT, P. J. G. M. DE, Phytopathology, Plant-Pathogen Interactions

WOERKUM, C. M. J. VAN, Communication Management

ZACHARIASSE, L. C., Strategic Economics in Agribusiness

ZEE, S. E. A. T. M. VAN DER, Soil Chemistry and Chemical Soil Quality

ZIJPP, A. J. VAN DER, Animal Production Systems

ZWIETERING, M. H., Food Microbiology

Institutes of University Standing

ABC HOGESCHOOL

POB 8118, 3301 CC Dordrecht

Telephone: (78) 6186662

Fax: (78) 6181904

E-mail: info@abc-opleidingen.nl

Internet: www.abc-opleidingen.nl; attached to ABC Opleidingen.

ACADEMIE VERLOSKUNDE MAASTRICHT
(University of Midwifery Education and Studies Maastricht)

POB 1256, 6201 BG Maastricht
Universiteitssingel 60, 6229 ER Maastricht

Telephone: (43) 3885410

Fax: (43) 3885451

E-mail: info@av-m.nl

Internet: www.av-m.nl

Founded 1913

Man. Dir: R. W. A. A. VAN CRIMPEN

Sec.: S. NORDHAUSEN.

ACADEMIE VOOR OVERHEIDSJURISTEN
(Academy for Government Lawyers)

Lange Voorhout 62, 2514 EH The Hague

Telephone: (70) 3129850

Fax: (70) 3129849

E-mail: academie@acjur.nl

Internet: www.academievooroverheidsjuristen.nl

Founded 2009

Chair.: R. J. HOEKSTRA

Dean: Drs PETER VAN LOCHEM.

ACADEMIE VOOR WETGEVING
(Academy for Legislation)

Lange Voorhout 62, 2514 EH The Hague

Telephone: (70) 3129830

Fax: (70) 3129849

E-mail: academie@acwet.nl

Internet: www.academievoorwetgeving.nl

Founded 2001

Chair.: R. J. HOEKSTRA

Dean: Drs PETER VAN LOCHEM.

AMSTERDAM SCHOOL OF REAL ESTATE

POB 140, 1000 AC Amsterdam
Huys Azië, Jollemanhof 5, 1019 GW Amsterdam

Telephone: (20) 6681129

Fax: (20) 6680361

E-mail: info@asre.nl

Internet: www.asre.nl

Founded 1987

Chair.: Ir J. D. DOETS

Dir and Sec of the Board: Drs L. B. UITTENBOGAARD.

BUSINESS SCHOOL NETHERLANDS

POB 709, 4116 ZJ Buren
De Raadskamer, Herenstraat 25, 4116 BK Buren

Telephone: (344) 579030

Fax: (344) 579050

E-mail: international@bsn.eu

Internet: www.bsn.eu

Founded 1988

Dean: FRANCIS BLUM.

BUSINESS SCHOOL NOTENBOOM— INSTITUTE FOR BUSINESS, HOTEL AND LEISURE MANAGEMENT

POB 307, 5600 AH Eindhoven

Telephone: (40) 2520620

E-mail: hogeschool@notenboom.nl

Internet: www.notenboom.nl

Brs in Hilversum, Maastricht

Man: JAN THEO MELLEMA

Number of teachers: 120

CHRISTELIJKE AGRARISCHE HOGESCHOOL DRONTEN

De Drieslag 1, 8251 JZ Dronten

Telephone: (321) 386100

Fax: (321) 313040

E-mail: info@cah.nl

Internet: www.cah.nl

Br. in Almere

Dir: Ir W. VAN DE WEG

Exec. Sec.: DAALMEIJER VAN VUUREN.

CHRISTELIJKE HOGESCHOOL EDE

POB 80, 6710 BB Ede
Oude Kerkweg 100, 6717 JS Ede

Telephone: (318) 696300

Fax: (318) 696396

E-mail: info@che.nl

Internet: www.che.nl

Founded 1950, present status 1994, present name 1997

State control

Chair. of Supervisory Board: R. C. ROBBERTSEN

Head: Dr C. P. (KEES) BOELE

Number of teachers: 400

Number of students: 4,000

CHRISTELIJKE HOGESCHOOL WINDESHEIM

POB 10090, 8000 GB Zwolle
Campus 2–6, 8017 CA Zwolle

Telephone: (88) 4699777

Fax: (88) 4688822

E-mail: info@windesheim.nl

Internet: www.windesheim.nl

State control

Chair.: Prof. Dr A. W. C. A. CORNELISSEN
Sec.: Drs W. A. HOBBELEN
Number of teachers: 1,700
Number of students: 20,000

DRIESTAR HOGESCHOOL
(University for Teacher Education)

POB 368, 2800 AJ Gouda
Burg. Jamessingel 2, 2803 PD Gouda
Telephone: (182) 540333
Fax: (182) 538449
E-mail: internationaloffice@driestar-educatief.nl
Internet: www.driestar-hogeschool.nl
Founded 1944, present status 2005; attached to Driestar Educatief
Chair.: Drs L. N. (RENS) ROTTIER
Number of teachers: 275
Number of students: 1,400

EUROPORT BUSINESS SCHOOL

POB 21510, 3001 AM Rotterdam
Complex Weenahof, Schaatsbaan 61–91, Rotterdam
Telephone: (10) 2012320
Fax: (10) 2012321
E-mail: info@epbs.nl
Internet: www.epbs.nl
Chair.: JELLE MARCHAND.

FACULTEIT KATHOLIEKE THEOLOGIE TE UTRECHT
(School of Catholic Theology, Tilburg University)

POB 80101, 3508 TC Utrecht
Heidelberglaan 2, 3584 TC Utrecht
Telephone: (13) 4663800
Fax: (30) 2533665
E-mail: bureaufkt@uvt.nl
Internet: www.tilburguniversity.edu/nl/over-tilburg-university/schools/theologie
Founded 2007 by merger of Catholic Theological Univ. in Utrecht and Tilburg Faculty of Theology; attached to Tilburg Univ.
Academic year: September to September
Chair. of the Board: H. M. C. M. VAN OORSCHOT
Dean: Prof. Dr. A. J. DENAUX
Vice-Dean for Research: Prof. Dr P. H. A. I. JONKERS
Vice-Dean for Education: Dr. H. J. M. SCHOOT
Registrar: Drs G. A. VAN DER VELDEN-WESTERVELT
Number of teachers: 45
Number of students: 140

PROFESSORS

BEENTJES, P. C., Old Testament
FRISHMAN, J., Rabbinic Literature and Judaism
HELLEMANS, G. A. F., Social Sciences
JONKERS, P. H. A. I., Philosophy and History of Philosophy
MENKEN, M. J. J., New Testament
MÜLLER, D., Church History
POORTHUIS, M. J. H. M., Inter-Religious Dialogue
RIKHOF, H. W. M., Systematic Theology and History of Theology
ROUWHORST, G. A. M., History of Liturgy
SAROT, M., Fundamental Theology
VAN GEEST, P. C., Church History and History of Theology
VOSMAN, F. J. H., Moral Theology
WISSINK, J. B. M., Practical Theology

FEDERATIE BELASTINGACADEMIE BV

Brenkmanweg 6, 4105 DH Culemborg
Telephone: (345) 547024
Fax: (345) 547024
E-mail: fba@rb.nl
Internet: www.fbacademie.nl.

FONTYS BESTUURSACADEMIE— INSTITUUT VOOR BESTUURLIJKE INNOVATIE

POB 90903, 5000 GD Tilburg
Professor Gimbrerelaan 16, 5037 EK Tilburg
Telephone: (13) 4651351
Fax: (13) 4651379
E-mail: bestuursacademie@fontys.nl
Internet: www.bazn.nl
Founded 2002 as BAZN de bestuursacademie, present name and status 2011
Br in Amsterdam
Dir: PIETER BON.

GEREFORMEERDE HOGESCHOOL

POB 10030, 8000 GA Zwolle
Grasdorpstraat 2, 8012 EN Zwolle
Telephone: (38) 4255542
Fax: (38) 4230785
E-mail: info@gh-gpc.nl
Internet: www.gh.nl
Chair.: A. VAN DER VEER
Vice-Chair.: B. WESSELING
Sec.: D. DE JONGE
Number of teachers: 125
Number of students: 1,450

GERRIT RIETVELD ACADEMIE

Frederik Roeskestraat 96, 1076 ED Amsterdam
Telephone: (20) 5711600
Fax: (20) 5711654
E-mail: secretariaatcvb@grac.nl
Internet: www.gerritrietveldacademie.nl
Founded 1924, present status 1968, present name 1965
Private control
Chair.: TIJMEN VAN GROOTHEEST
Dir of Sandberg Institute: JURGEN BEY
Dir of Education: BEN ZEGERS
Dir of Operations: ANNELIES VAN EENNENNAAM
Sec.: STEVEN JONGEJAN
Dean of Fine Arts and Design: BEN ZEGERS
Library of 8,000 vols
Number of students: 1,000

HANZEHOGESCHOOL GRONINGEN, UNIVERSITY OF APPLIED SCIENCES
(Hanze University Groningen, University of Applied Sciences)

POB 30030, 9700 RM Groningen
Zernikeplein 7, 9747 AS Groningen
Telephone: (50) 5955555
Fax: (50) 5710634
E-mail: info@org.hanze.nl
Internet: www.hanze.nl
Founded 1798, present status 1993
Brs in offices in Amsterdam, Assen, Leeuwarden; 21 attached institutes
Chair.: Drs H. J. PIJLMAN
Number of teachers: 24,000
Number of students: 2,700

HBO NEDERLAND

Kortestraat 1, 6811 EN Arnhem
Telephone: (26) 3516379
Fax: (26) 4451023

E-mail: info@hbonederland.com
Internet: www.hbonederland.com
Founded 1987
Private control
Language of instruction: Dutch
Number of students: 3,000

HOGESCHOOL DIRKSEN ARNHEM

POB 3090, 6802 DB Amsterdam
Parkstraat 27, 6828 JC Arnhem
Telephone: (26) 3544644
Fax: (26) 3544698
E-mail: info@dirksen.nl
Internet: www.dirksen.nl.

HOGESCHOOL E3 ICT

Oranjeplein 97, 6224 KV Maastricht
Telephone: (43) 3638333
E-mail: info@e3.nl
Internet: www.e3.nl
Private control
Dir: MARCEL SNEL.

HOGESCHOOL EDITH STEIN— ONDERWIJSCENTRUM TWENTE

POB 568, 7550 AN Hengelo
M.A. de Ruyterstraat 3, 7556 CW Hengelo
Telephone: (74) 8516100
Fax: (74) 8516161
E-mail: info@edith.nl
Internet: www.edith.nl
Founded 1984, by merger of Pedagogische Academie Hoogveld and KLOS (Kleuter-Leidster Opleidingsschool), present name 1986
Private control
Language of instruction: Dutch
Dir: MANON KETZ
Chair.: HENK MULDERS
Number of teachers: 110
Number of students: 1,100

HOGESCHOOL HAS DEN BOSCH

POB 90108, 5223 DE 's-Hertogenbosch
Onderwijsboulevard 221, 5223 DE 's-Hertogenbosch
Telephone: (73) 6923600
Fax: (73) 6923699
E-mail: hasdb@hasdb.nl
Internet: www.hasdenbosch.nl
Languages of instruction: Dutch, English
Chair.: STEF VALK (acting)
Number of teachers: 300
Number of students: 1,700
Publication: HAS Beats Hogeschoolgeluiden (10 a year).

HOGESCHOOL HELICON

Socrateslaan 22A, 3707 GL Zeist
Telephone: (30) 6937900
Fax: (30) 6911440
E-mail: info@hhelicon.nl
Internet: www.hhelicon.nl
Founded 1995, by merger of Vrije Pedagogische Akademie te Zeist and Akademie voor Eurythmie te Den Haag, 1998 Vrije Muziek-Akademie te Zeist merged
Chair.: B. HOLVAST.

HOGESCHOOL INHOLLAND

POB 93043, 2509 AA The Hague
Theresiastraat 8, 2593 AN The Hague
Telephone: (70) 3120100
E-mail: info@inholland.nl
Internet: www.inholland.nl
Private control

Chair.: D. TERPSTRA
Pres.: GEERT DALES
Number of teachers: 2,900
Number of students: 37,500

HOGESCHOOL IPABO

POB 90506, 1006 BM Amsterdam
Jan Tooropstraat 136, 1061 AD Amsterdam
Telephone: (20) 6137079
Fax: (20) 6134645
E-mail: receptie@hs-ipabo.edu
Internet: www.hs-ipabo.edu
Private control
Language of instruction: Dutch
Chair.: Dr Ing. JAN W. M. A. HOUBEN
Number of teachers: 120
Number of students: 1,000

HOGESCHOOL ISBW

POB 266, 5300 AG Zaltbommel
Internet: www.isbw.nl
Founded 1931
Private control
Language of instruction: Dutch.

HOGESCHOOL IVA DRIEBERGEN

POB 33, 3970 AA Driebergen
Hogesteeg 2A, 3972 JT Driebergen
Telephone: (343) 512780
Fax: (343) 532187
E-mail: info@iva-driebergen.nl
Internet: www.iva-driebergen.nl
Founded 1930
Private control
Publication: LIVA Post.

HOGESCHOOL NOVI

POB 2068, 3500 GB Utrecht
Kobaltweg 44, 3542 CE Utrecht
Telephone: (30) 7115615
Fax: (30) 7115614
E-mail: info@novi.nl
Internet: www.novi.nl
Founded 1958, present status 1997
Dir: KEES LOUWMAN.

HOGESCHOOL NTI

POB 2222, 2301 CE Leiden
Schipholweg 101, 2301 XC Leiden
Telephone: (71) 7501040
Fax: (71) 5612550
E-mail: vragen@nti.nl
Internet: www.nti.nl
Founded 1997, present status 2000
Head: MARIANNE VAN WESTRIENEN
Number of teachers: 125
Number of students: 70,000

HOGESCHOOL PBNA

POB 68, 3330 AB Zwijndrecht
H.A. Lorentzstraat 1A, 3331 EE Zwijndrecht
Telephone: (78) 6253889
Fax: (78) 6253827
E-mail: examens@pbna.com
Internet: www.pbna.com
Founded 1912, present status 1999
Private control
Languages of instruction: Dutch, English, French, German, Polish, Portuguese
Number of students: 50,000

HOGESCHOOL THIM VAN DER LAAN

Newtonbaan 6, 3439 NK Nieuwegein
Telephone: (30) 2886670
Fax: (30) 2898811

E-mail: info@thimvanderlaan.nl
Internet: www.thim.nl
Founded 1974, as Thim van der Laan Hogeschool voor Fysiotherapie
Private control
Languages of instruction: Dutch, German
Dir of Education Affairs: R. M. VAN ECK
Number of students: 650

HOGESCHOOL TIO

Oudenoord 2, 3513 ER Utrecht
Telephone: (30) 6668836
Fax: (30) 6668397
Internet: www.tio.nl
Private control
Languages of instruction: Dutch, English
Dir: Ir M. W. DÜTHLER
Number of teachers: 250

HOGESCHOOL UTRECHT (HU)

Oudenoord 330, 3513 EX Utrecht
Telephone: (88) 4818181
E-mail: info@hu.nl
Internet: www.hu.nl
Founded 1995, present name 2005
Private control
Chair.: GERI BONHOF
Number of teachers: 3,500
Number of students: 30,000
Publication: magazine van Hogeschool Utrecht.

HOGESCHOOL VAN AMSTERDAM

POB 1025, 1000 BA Amsterdam
Spui, 21 1021 WX Amsterdam
Telephone: (20) 5953200
E-mail: voorzittercvb@uva.nl
Internet: www.hva.nl
Chair.: Dr LOUISE GUNNING-SCHEPERS
Exec. Sec.: J. M. KERSBERGEN
Sec.: ARJAN P. TROMMEL
Number of teachers: 3,101
Number of students: 41,770

HOGESCHOOL VAN ARNHEM EN NIJMEGEN

POB 5375, 6802 EJ Arnhem
Ruitenberglaan 31, 6826 CC Arnhem
Telephone: (26) 3691555
Fax: (26) 3691514
E-mail: info@han.nl
Internet: www.han.nl
Founded 1996, by merger of 3 instns
Chair.: Drs RON BORMANS
Number of teachers: 2,900
Number of students: 28,000

HOGESCHOOL VAN HALL LARENSTEIN
(Van Hall Larenstein University of Applied Sciences)

POB 9001, 6880 GB Velp
Larensteinselaan 26A, 6882 CT Velp
Telephone: (58) 3695749
Fax: (58) 3695727
E-mail: info@vanhall-larenstein.nl
Internet: www.vanhall-larenstein.nl
Founded 2003; attached to Wageningen UR
Languages of instruction: English, Dutch
Campuses in Velp, Wageningen
Man. Dir: ELLEN MARKS
Man Dir: RIEN KOMEN
Dir of Education: GEARTSJE OOSTERHOF
Dir of Education: GERRIT JEURING
Dir of Education: HANS HARDUS
Dir of Education: HANS VAN HAEREN

Dir of Education: HANS VAN ROOIJEN
Dir of Education: JAN VAN DER VALK
Dir of Education: JOS WINTERMANS
Dir of Education: WENDY ZUIDEMA
Number of teachers: 450
Number of students: 4,500

HOGESCHOOL WEST-NEDERLAND VOOR VERTALER EN TOLK

Chr. Scholengemeenschap Zandvliet, Bezuidenhoutseweg, 40, 2594 AW The Hague
Internet: www.west-nederland.nl
Founded 1994
Gen. Man.: A. MINKMAN.

HOGESCHOOL WITTENBORG

Laan van de Mensenrechten 500, 7331 VZ Apeldoorn
Telephone: (88) 6672688
Fax: (88) 6672699
Internet: www.wittenborg.nl
Founded 1987
State control
Language of instruction: English
Chair.: PETER BIRDSALL
Gen. Man.: KAREN PENNINGA
Number of teachers: 22
Number of students: 220

INHOLLAND SELECT STUDIES

POB 23145, 3001 KC Rotterdam
Posthumalaan 90, 3072 AG Rotterdam
Telephone: (10) 4399491
E-mail: selectstudies@inholland.nl
Internet: www.inholland.nl/select+studies.

INSTITUUT VOOR PSYCHOSYNTHESE

Biltstraat 200, 3572 BS Utrecht
Telephone: (30) 2714634
Fax: (30) 2762979
E-mail: info@psychosynthese.nl
Internet: www.psychosynthese.nl
Founded 1985, present status 1999
Dir-Gen.: DIEDERIK VAN ROSSUM
Dean of Student Affairs: INGRID VAN BEEK-VELDKAMP.

INTERCOLLEGE BUSINESS SCHOOL

Zeestraat 62, 2518 AC The Hague
Telephone: (70) 3451110
E-mail: denhaag@intercollege.nl
Internet: www.intercollege.nl
Founded 1979
Campuses in Amsterdam, Rotterdam, Utrecht
Private control.

ITV HOGESCHOOL VOOR TOLKEN & VERTALEN
(ITV School of Interpretation and Translation)

POB 14007, 3508 SB Utrecht
Padualaan 97, 3508 SB Utrecht
Telephone: (30) 2730818
Fax: (30) 2721497
E-mail: admin@itv-hogeschool.nl
Internet: www.itv-h.nl
Founded 1983
Private control
College of translation; uses premises, facilities of Utrecht univ.
Dir: SJOKEAN OOSTERBAAN
Number of teachers: 70
Number of students: 750

LANDELIJK EXPERTISECENTRUM SOCIALE INTERVENTIE

c/o Utrecht Univ., FSW/ASW, POB 80140, 3508 TC Utrecht
Van Unnikgebouw, Heidelberglaan 2, 3584 CS Utrecht
Telephone: (30) 2534920
E-mail: nfo@lesi.nl
Internet: www.lesi.nl
Founded 2004; attached to Utrecht Univ.
Dir: Prof. Dr ROELOF HORTULANUS
Publication: *Tijdschrift voor Sociale Interventies*.

MARKUS VERBEEK BUSINESS ACADEMY

POB 6546, 4802 HM Breda
Telephone: (76) 5499998
Fax: (76) 5425074
E-mail: info@mvba.nl
Internet: www.mvba.nl
Private control
Masters courses in business, management and finance
Dir: W. HAIR.

MARKUS VERBEEK PRAEHEP

Paasheuvelweg 35, 1105 BG Amsterdam Zuidoost
Telephone: (20) 5677800
Fax: (20) 5677810
E-mail: amsterdam@mvp.nl
Internet: www.markusverbeek.nl/
Founded 1896
Private control
Brs in Amsterdam, Rotterdam, Rijswijk, Zwolle, Eindhoven, Utrecht; provides Bachelors Masters and training in finance-related courses.

NHL HOGESCHOOL
(NHL University)

POB 1080, 8900 CB Leeuwarden
Rengerslaan 10, 8917 DD Leeuwarden
Telephone: (58) 2511888
Fax: (58) 2511899
E-mail: infocentrum@nhl.nl
Internet: www.nhl.nl
Private control
Language of instruction: Dutch
Academic year: September to September
Number of students: 10,500

NHTV INTERNATIONAAL HOGER ONDERWIJS BREDA
(NHTV Breda University of Applied Sciences)

POB 3917, 4800 DX Breda
Telephone: (76) 5332203
Fax: (76) 5332205
E-mail: communicatie@nhtv.nl
Internet: www.nhtv.nl
Founded 1966 as the Dutch Scientific Institute for Tourism
Private control
Specialist disciplines of games and media, hotel and facility, leisure, tourism, urban devt, logistics and mobility
Rector Magnificus: Prof. Dr JAAP LENGKEEK
Number of students: 7,000

PRO EDUCATION

POB 22799, 1100 DG Amsterdam
Atlas Complex, Gebouw Azië, Hoogoorddreef 5, 1101 BA Amsterdam
Telephone: (20) 5677999
Fax: (20) 5677901
E-mail: info@proeducation.nl
Internet: www.proeducation.nl
Founded 2002 by Univ. of Amsterdam; independent in 2004
Private control.

PROTESTANTSE THEOLOGISCHE UNIVERSITEIT
(Protestant Theological University)

POB 5021, 8260 GA Kampen
Koornmarkt 1, Kampen
Telephone: (38) 3371600
Fax: (38) 3371613
E-mail: bureau@mail.thuk.nl
Internet: www.thuk.nl
Founded 2007 by merger of Theological University Kampen (ThUK), Theological Research Institute (ThWI), Utrecht and Leiden, Evangelical Lutheran Seminary (ELS), Utrecht, Theological Seminary, Doorn; attached to Protestant Church in The Netherlands
Languages of instruction: Dutch, English
Academic year: September to August
Pres.: Dr HENK C. VAN DER SAR
Rector: Prof. Dr F. G. IMMINK
Dean of Students: Drs T. A. STRUIK
Head Librarian: J. W. PUTTENSTEIN
Library of 187,500 vols
Number of teachers: 30
Number of students: 172
Publications: *Documentatieblad voor de Geschiedenis van de Nederlandse zending en overzeese kerken* (2 a year, in Dutch), *Zeitschrift für Dialektische Theologie* (2 a year, in German)

PROFESSORS
DE LANGE, F., Ethics
HOLTROP, P. N., Missiology
HOUTMAN, C., Old Testament
JONKER, E. R., Pastoral Theology
KIRN, H.-M., Church History
KOFFEMAN, L. J., Church Polity
NEVEN, G. W., Dogmatics
ROUKEMA, R., New Testament

SAXION HOGESCHOLEN
(Saxion University of Applied Sciences)

POB 501, 7400 AM Deventer
Handelskade 75, 7417 DH Deventer
Telephone: (70) 603663
Fax: (70) 603123
E-mail: info@saxion.nl
Internet: www.saxion.nl
Founded 1998 by merger of Hogeschool Enschede and Hogeschool IJselland
State control
Campuses in Deventer, Enschede and Apeldoorn
Chair.: WIM BOOMKAMP
Number of teachers: 1,200
Number of students: 22,000
Publication: *Sax* (11 a year, online (sax.nu)).

SCHOEVERS

Papiermolen 10, 3994 DK Houten
Telephone: (30) 2808770
Fax: (30) 2808775
E-mail: info@schoevers.nl
Internet: www.schoevers.nl
Founded 1913
Dir: RIA VAN 'T KLOOSTER.

SOD-OPLEIDINGEN

POB 544, 3440 AM Woerden
De Bleek 6, 3447 GV Woerden
Telephone: (348) 485151
Fax: (348) 485148
E-mail: info@sod-opleidingen.nl
Internet: www.sod-opleidingen.nl
Private control
Languages of instruction: Dutch, English
Pres.: Drs J. C. M. COX
Sec.: R. DE NIEUWE
Dir: CASPER MOLMANS.

STENDEN HOGESCHOOL

POB 1298, 8900 CG Leeuwarden
Rengerslaan 8, 8917 DD Leeuwarden
Telephone: (58) 2441441
Fax: (58) 2441401
E-mail: info@stenden.com
Internet: www.stenden.com
Founded 2008 by merger of Christelijke Hogeschool Nederland with Hogeschool Drenthe
Private control
Pres.: PIM BREEBAART
Number of students: 11,000

STICHTING OPLEIDINGEN MUSCULOSKELETALE THERAPIE
(Musculoskeletal Therapy Foundation Training)

POB 585, 3800 AN Amersfoort
Softwareweg 5, 3821 BN Amersfoort
Telephone: (33) 4560737
Fax: (33) 4511769
E-mail: info@somt.nl
Internet: www.somt.nl
Education, research and clinic; offers Masters in manual therapy, basin physiotherapy, sports physiotherapy, physiotherapy in geriatrics and ultrasound
Dir: WILY SMEETS.

STOAS HOGESCHOOL

POB 245, 6710 BE Ede
Bovenbuurtweg 27, 6710 BE Ede
Telephone: (318) 675611
Fax: (318) 640420
E-mail: info@aeres.nl
Internet: www.stoashogeschool.nl
Founded 1981
Number of teachers: 71
Number of students: 774

THEOLOGISCHE UNIVERSITEIT APELDOORN
(The Theological University of Apeldoorn)

Wilhelminapark 4, 7316 BT Apeldoorn
Telephone: (55) 5775700
Fax: (55) 5226339
E-mail: info@tua.nl
Internet: www.tua.nl
Founded 1894, present name 1992
Pres.: Ir J. J. EBERWIJN
Rector: Prof. Dr G. C. DEN HERTOG
Vice-Rector: Prof. H. G. L. PEELS
Librarian: Prof. Dr N. VAN DER MIJDEN-GROENENDIJK
Library of 45,000 vols
Number of teachers: 11 (6 full-time, 10 part-time)
Number of students: 98 full-time
Publications: *Apeldoornse Studies* (2 a year), *Oikodomē* (4 a year), *TUA Conned* (3 a year).

THEOLOGISCHE UNIVERSITEIT VAN DE GEREFORMEERDE KERKEN
(Theological University of the Reformed Churches)

POB 5026, 8260 GA Kampen
Broederweg 15, 8261 GS Kampen
Telephone: (38) 4471710
Fax: (38) 4471711
E-mail: secretariaat@tukampen.nl
Internet: www.tukampen.nl
Founded 1854
Pres.: Prof. Dr M. TE VELDE
Man. Dir: N. VERSTEEG
Rector: Prof. Dr C. J. DE RUIJTER
Librarian: Drs G. D. HARMANNY
Library of 150,000 vols
Number of teachers: 16
Number of students: 80

PROFESSORS

DE BRUIJNE, A. L. TH., Ethics and Spirituality
DE RUIJTER, C. J., Pastoral Theology
KAMPHUIS, B., Dogmatics
KWAKKEL, G., Old Testament Exegesis
TE VELDE, M., Church History and Polity
VAN DER POL, F., Church History and History of Dogma
VAN HOUWELINGEN, P. H. R., New Testament Exegesis

TIASNIMBAS BUSINESS SCHOOL

POB 90153, 5000 LE Tilburg
Tias Bldg, Warandelaan 2, 5037 AB Tilburg
Telephone: (13) 4668600
Fax: (13) 4668699
E-mail: information@tiasnimbas.edu
Internet: www.tiasnimbas.edu
Founded 1982 as Tilburg Institute for Advanced Studies; attached to Tilburg Univ.
Br in Bonn, Eindhoven, Taipei, Utrecht
Private control
Chair.: Prof. Dr Ir R. O'CALLAGHAN
Chair. of Supervisory Board: RICK HARWIG
Deputy Chair. of Supervisory Board: PHILIP EIJLANDER
Dean: Prof. Dr Ir RAMON O'CALLAGHAN
Man. Dir: JAN HENK VAN DER WERFF
Academic Dean: PHILIP JOOS.

TRANSFERGROEP ROTTERDAM
(Transfer Group Rotterdam)

POB 420, 3000 AK Rotterdam
Hogeschool Rotterdam, locatie Museumpark, Burgemeester s'Jacobplein 1, 3015 CA Rotterdam
Telephone: (10) 7946800
Fax: (10) 7946801
E-mail: transfergroep@hro.nl
Internet: www.transfergroep.nl
Founded 1996; attached to Hogeschool Rotterdam
Private control
Undergraduate and postgraduate courses in business and management, coaching skills, health, education and training, welfare; specialist in organizational consulting and individual counselling programmes.

UNIVERSITY COLLEGE UTRECHT

POB 80145, 3508 TC Utrecht
Campusplein 1, 3584 ED Utrecht
Telephone: (30) 2539900
Fax: (30) 2539905
E-mail: ucu.info@uu.nl
Internet: www.uu.nl/university/college
Founded 1997; attached to Utrecht Univ.
State control
Dean: ROB VAN DER VAART

Number of teachers: 165
Number of students: 723

WEBSTER UNIVERSITY LEIDEN

Boommarkt 1, 2311 EA Leiden
Telephone: (71) 5168000
E-mail: info@webster.nl
Internet: www.webster.nl
Founded 1983
Private control
Dir: Prof. Dr JEAN MARISSING
Library of 19,000 e-books, 23,000 academic journals
Number of students: 400

Institutes of International Education

EUROPEAN INSTITUTE OF PUBLIC ADMINISTRATION

POB 1229, 6201 BE Maastricht
Telephone: (43) 3296222
Fax: (43) 3296296
E-mail: info@eipa.eu
Internet: www.eipa.eu
Founded 1981
Languages of instruction: English, French, German
Centres in Luxembourg, Barcelona; supported by mem. states of the European Union and the Commission of the EU; personal and organizational devts and policy support in European policy-making and implementation, EU institutions and political integration, European public management, community policies and internal markets, legal systems of the EU
Chair.: HENNING CHRISTOPHERSEN
Dir-Gen.: Prof. Dr MARGA PRÖHL
Dir for Finance and Org.: WIM VAN HELDEN
Library of 30,000 vols, 350 periodicals; European documentation centre; depositing library of the Council of Europe
Number of teachers: 60
Number of students: 15,000
Publications: *Conference Proceedings, Current European Issues.*

HOGESCHOOL ROTTERDAM
(Rotterdam University, University of Applied Sciences)

POB 25035, 3001 HA Rotterdam
Kralingse Zoom 91, 3063 ND Rotterdam
Telephone: (10) 7949494
Fax: (10) 7944211
E-mail: tudievoorlichting@hr.nl
Internet: www.hro.nl
Founded 1988, present status 2002
State control
Languages of instruction: English, Dutch
Academic year: September to July
Pres.: Drs J. A. C. F. TUYTEL
Asst Dir: MARJOLEIN BAKKER
Dir for Gen. and Admin. Affairs: HERMAN A. VEENEMA
Dir for Communications and External Relations: Drs J. E. (ANS) HUURMAN-VAN BUREN
Number of teachers: 3,000
Number of students: 28,500
Publication: *Profielen* (College Profiles magazine).

INTERNATIONAL INSTITUTE OF SOCIAL STUDIES

POB 29776, 2502 LT The Hague
Kortenaerkade 12, 2518 AX The Hague
Telephone: (70) 4260460
Fax: (70) 4260799
E-mail: info@iss.nl
Internet: www.iss.nl
Founded 1952, present status 2009; attached to Erasmus Univ. Rotterdam
Language of instruction: English
Rector: Prof. LEO DE HAAN
Chair. of Advisory Board: Prof. J. A. VAN GINKEL
Deputy Rector for Teaching: Dr JOS MOOIJ
Deputy Rector for Research: Prof. MOHAMED SALIH
Exec. Sec.: LINDA JOHNSON
Library of 100,000 vols, 400 print journals, 20,000 e-journals
Number of teachers: 60
Number of students: 300
Publication: *Development and Change* (5 a year)

PROFESSORS

BJÖRKMAN, J. W., Public Policy and Administration
DE LA RIVE BOX, L., International Cooperation
DIJK, M. P. VAN, Urban Management
ELSON, D., Feminist Development Economics
FITZGERALD, V., Development Economics
GRIMM, M., Development Economics
HAAR, G. TER, Religion and Development
HELMSING, B., Local and Regional Development
MURSHED, M., Economics of Conflict and Peace
OPSCHOOR, H., Economics of Environment and Development
PRONK, J., Theory and Practice of International Development
SAITH, A., Rural Economics
SALIH, M., Politics of Development
SCHRIJVER, N., International Law
WHITE, B., Rural Sociology
WUYTS, M., Applied Quantitative Economics

MAASTRICHT SCHOOL OF MANAGEMENT (MSM)

POB 1203, 6201 BE Maastricht
Endepolsdomein 150, 6229 EP Maastricht
Telephone: (43) 3870808
Fax: (43) 3870800
E-mail: info@msm.nl
Internet: www.msm.nl
Founded 1952
Private control
Language of instruction: English
Academic year: September to September
Chair. of the Board: Prof. P. R. H. M. VAN DER LINDEN
Vice-Chair. of the Board: F. J. M. TUMMERS
Dir and Dean: Prof. Dr PETER P. DE GIJSEL
Library of 10,000 vols
Number of teachers: 140 (40 resident, 100 visiting)
Number of students: 2,500
Publication: *MSM Research Papers: Management & Development* (2 a year)

PROFESSORS

ANKOLEKAR, SURESH, e-Business
DE GIJSEL, PETER P., Economics
ENGEL, PAUL G. H., Public Policy and Innovations
HELING, GEERT W. J., Organizational Behavior
JONES, MARC T., Strategic Management
NAUDÉ, WIM A., Development Economics and Entrepreneurship

NIKOLIK, DRAGAN A., Management Information Systems

RWEGASIRA, KAMI S. P., Financial Management and Accounting

SANDER, HARALD, Economics

SYBRANDY, ARTHUR, Marketing

VAN DIJK, MEINE PIETER, Entrepreneurship in Emerging Countries

VAN MOURIK, AAD, Economics

TRANSNATIONALE UNIVERSITEIT LIMBURG

c/o Maastricht Univ., POB 616, 6200 MD Maastricht

Telephone: (43) 3882222
E-mail: info@unimaas.nl
Internet: www.tul.edu

Founded 2001.

UNESCO–IHE, INSTITUTE FOR WATER EDUCATION

POB 3015, 2601 DA Delft
Westvest 7, 2611 AX Delft

Telephone: (15) 2151715
Fax: (15) 2122921
E-mail: info@unesco-ihe.org
Internet: www.unesco-ihe.org

Founded 1957 as IHE, present name and status 2003

State control

Language of instruction: English

Academic year: October to September

Postgraduate and PhD programmes; short courses; online courses in environmental science and technology, environmental planning and management, limnology and wetland ecosystems, water quality management, sanitary engineering, urban water engineering and management, water supply engineering, water quality management, water services management, water resources management, water conflict management, hydrology and water resources, hydraulic engineering and river basin devt, hydraulic engineering—coastal engineering and port devt, hydraulic engineering—land and water devt, hydroinformatics—modelling and information systems for water management

Rector: Prof. ANDRÁS SZÖLLÖSI-NAGY

Vice-Rector for Academic Affairs: Prof. STEFAN UHLENBROOK

Library of 25,000 vols
Number of teachers: 100
Number of students: 500

Schools of Art, Architecture and Music

Academie van Bouwkunst (Academy of Architecture): Waterlooplein 211, 1011 PG Amsterdam; tel. (20) 5318218; fax (20) 5318240; e-mail info@bwk.ahk.nl; internet www.ahk.nl/bouwkunst; f. 1908, present status 1987; attached to Amsterdam School of the Arts; offers courses in architecture, urban design and landscape architecture; library: 10,000 vols; 150 teachers; 200 students; Dir Drs AART OXENAAR.

Academie van Bouwkunst Maastricht (Maastricht Academy of Architecture): Brusselsestraat 75, 6211 PC Maastricht; tel. (43) 3219645; e-mail abm@hszuyd.nl; internet www.academievanbouwkunst.com; f. 1947, present status 2002; attached to Zuyd Univ.; offers Masters degree in architecture and related fields; 43 teachers; 55 students; Dir NIEK BISSCHEROUX.

Academie voor Architectuur en Stedebouw (School of Architecture and Urban Design): POB 90907, 5000 GJ Tilburg; Bisschop Zwijsenstraat 5, 5038 VA Tilburg; tel. (877) 874922; fax (877) 873522; e-mail aas@fontys.nl; internet www.fontyshogeschoolvoordekunsten.nl/architectuur_stedenbouw.aspx; f. 1936; attached to Fontys Univ. of Arts; architecture and town planning/design; library: 8,000 vols; 50 teachers; 80 students; Dir MARC K. T. M. GLAUDEMANS.

AKV – St Joost Breda: POB 90116, 4800 RA Breda; Beukenlaan 1, 4834 CR Breda; tel. (76) 5250302; fax (76) 5250305; e-mail info.akvstjoost@avans.nl; internet www.akvstjoost.nl; f. 1945; attached to Avans Univ.; br. in 's-Hertogenbosch; offers Bachelors and Masters courses in fine art, design; publ. *Leporello*.

Amsterdamse Hogeschool voor de Kunsten (Amsterdam School of the Arts): POB 15079, 1001 MB Amsterdam; Jodenbreestraat 3, Amsterdam; tel. (20) 5277710; fax (20) 5277712; e-mail info@ahk.nl; internet www.ahk.nl; f. 1987 by merger of Academy of Fine Art in Education, Amsterdam Academy of Architecture, Conservatorium van Amsterdam, Netherlands Film and Television Academy, Reinwardt Academy, Theatre School; offers Bachelors and Masters degrees in architecture, dance, film and television, fine art and design, music, theatre, museum studies; Chair. OLCHERT BROUWER; 750 teachers; 3,000 students.

ArtEZ Academie voor Art & Design (ArtEZ Academy of Art & Design): POB 1440, 7500 BK Enschede; Campus Univ. of Twente, Hallenweg 5, 7522 NH Enschede; tel. (53) 4824400; fax (53) 4824463; e-mail artdesign.enschede@artez.nl; internet www.artez.nl; f. 1949; attached to ArtEZ Institute of the Arts; fine arts, design, fashion, architecture; library: 8,000 vols; Chair. DINGEMAN KUILMAN; Dir S. HUISMANS.

ArtEZ Hogeschool voor de Kunsten (ArtEZ Institute of the Arts): POB 49, 6812 CE Arnhem; Onderlangs 9, 6812 CE Arnhem; tel. (26) 3535600; fax (26) 3535677; e-mail communicatie@artez.nl; internet www.artez.nl; f. 2002; architecture, design, dance, drama, fine arts, fashion, music; institutes in Arnhem, Enschede, Zwolle; Chair. DINGEMAN KUILMAN; Sec. LAURIEN TIMMERMANS; 600 teachers (420 f.t.e.); 3,059 students.

Avans Hogeschool (Avans University of Applied Sciences): POB 732, 5201 AS 's-Hertogenbosch; Onderwijsboulevard 215, 5223 DE 's-Hertogenbosch; tel. (73) 6295295; fax (73) 6214725; e-mail internationaloffice@avans.nl; internet www.studyatavans.com; f. 2004 by merger of Hogeschool Brabant and Hogeschool 's-Hertogenbosch; offers courses in painting, sculpture, graphic art, ceramics, environmental art, illustration, graphic design; brs in Breda, Tilburg; 19 attached schools, 4 support units, 1 learning and innovation centre; library: 10,000 vols; 2,000 teachers; 23,000 students; Chair. Drs PAUL L. A. RÜPP; Vice-Chair. Drs FRENCH J. M. VAN KALMTHOUT.

Codarts, Hogeschool voor de Kunsten (Codarts University for the Arts): Kruisplein 26, 3012 CC Rotterdam; tel. (10) 2171100; fax (10) 2171101; e-mail codarts@codarts.nl; internet www.codarts.nl; consists of the Rotterdams' Conservatorium and the Rotterdamse Dansacademie; library: 15,000 copies of sheet music; 300 teachers; 1,100 students; Pres. CAREL VAN EYKELENBURG; Dir JIKKIE VAN DER GIESSEN; publ. *Codarts Magazine* (4 a year).

Conservatorium Maastricht (Hogeschool Zuyd): Bonnefantenstraat 15, 6211 KL Maastricht; tel. (43) 3466680; fax (43) 3466689; e-mail info.conservatorium@hszuyd.nl; internet www.hszuyd.nl; f. 1956; Bachelors and Masters degrees; library: 30,000 vols; 110 teachers; 450 students; Dir HARRY CUSTERS (acting).

Attached Institutes:

Conservatorium Gent: Hoogpoort 64, 9000 Ghent, Belgium; Dir JAN RISPENS.

Fontys Conservatorium: Postbus 90907, 5000 GJ Tilburg; Dir JAN WIRKEN.

Conservatorium van Amsterdam: POB 78022, 1070 LP Amsterdam; Oosterdokskade 151, 1011 DL Amsterdam; tel. (20) 5277550; fax (20) 6761506; e-mail cva-info@ahk.nl; internet www.ahk.nl/conservatorium; f. 1884, present bldg 2008; attached to Amsterdam School of the Arts; offers courses in classical music, early music, jazz, opera, latin and popular music; library: 30,000 vols; 200 teachers; 800 students; Dir HANS VAN BEERS; Vice-Dir MICHEL DISPA; Vice-Dir RUUD VAN DIJK; publ. *Gebouwd voor Muziek*.

Design Academy Eindhoven: POB 2125, 5600 CC Eindhoven; Emmasingel 14, 3rd Fl., 5611 AZ Eindhoven; tel. (40) 2393939; fax (40) 2393940; e-mail info@designacademy.nl; internet www.designacademy.nl; f. 1950; offers Bachelors and Masters courses in contextual design, information design, social design; 200 teachers; 700 students; Chair. ANNE MIEKE EGGENKAMP.

Hogeschool Dansacademie Lucia Marthas (Dance Academy Lucia Marthas): Rustenburgerstraat 436, 1072 HK Amsterdam; tel. (20) 6761370; fax (20) 6707698; e-mail info@luciamarthas.nl; internet www.luciamarthas.nl; f. 1983; offers accredited HBO (higher vocational education) degrees and MBO degrees (intermediate vocational education); Man. C. VAN DER LOOP-MEESTERMAN; Man. LUCIA MARTHAS; Man. RUUD VAN DER KOOIJ.

Hogeschool der Kunsten (University of the Arts): Juliana van Stolberglaan 1, 2595 CA The Hague; tel. (70) 3151515; fax (70) 3151518; e-mail info@koncon.nl; internet www.koncon.nl; f. 1826 by merger of Royal Conservatory and the Royal Acad. of Fine Arts 1990, present name 2010; faculties of fine arts and design, music and dance; interfaculty of art and science; school for young talent; library: 50,000 vols; 265 teachers; 1,023 students; Chair. JACK VERDUYN LUNEL; Dir HENK VAN DER MEULEN.

Hogeschool voor de Kunsten Utrecht (Utrecht School of the Arts): POB 1520, 3500 BM Utrecht; Lange Viestraat 2B, Utrecht; tel. (30) 2349440; fax (30) 2349484; e-mail info@ssc.hku.nl; internet www.hku.nl; f. 1987 by merger of Utrechts Conservatorium, Academie voor Beeldende Kunsten Utrecht and Academie voor Expressie en door Woord en Gebaar; faculties of art and economics; art, media and technology; music; theatre; visual arts and design; interfaculty of art and economics; library: 36,000 vols; 350 teachers; 3,800 students; Chair. of Supervisory Board Drs P. C. KLAVER; Deputy Chair. of Supervisory Board Drs W. KARDUX; Pres. AD WISMAN; Dir CÉCILE DE VOS; publ. *Mahkuzine* (2 a year).

IHS—Institute for Housing and Urban Development Studies: Burgemeester Oudlaan 50, Bldg T, 14th Fl., 3062 PA Rotterdam; POB 1935, 3000 BX Rotterdam; tel. (10) 4089825; fax (10) 4089826; e-mail admission@ihs.nl; internet www.ihs.nl; f. 1948, present name 1991, present status 2003; attached to Erasmus Univ.; library: 15,000 vols; 53 teachers; 120 students; Dir KEES VAN ROOIJEN; Deputy Dir JAN FRANSEN.

Rijksakademie van Beeldende Kunsten (State Academy of Fine Arts): Sarphatistraat 470, 1018 GW Amsterdam; tel. (20) 5270300;

fax (20) 5270301; e-mail info@rijksakademie .nl; internet www.rijksakademie.nl; f. 1870, present location 1992, present status 1999; 1 and 2 year courses; organizes the Prix de Rome, the Netherlands; library: 33,000 vols, 85 magazines, 1,400 video cassettes and DVDs, large colln of monographs, catalogues of exhibitions and art theory books on visual arts, photography, video, applied art and architecture; Chair. of Board of Supervisors Prof. Dr L. J. GUNNING-SCHEPERS; Dir ELS VAN ODIJK; Librarian MARIETTA DIRKER.

Rotterdamse Academie van Bouwkunst (Rotterdam Academy of Architecture): POB 25035, 3001 HA Rotterdam; Heijplaatstraat 23, 3089 JB Rotterdam; tel. (10) 7944855; e-mail info@ravb.nl; internet www.ravb.nl; f. 1965; attached to Rotterdam Univ.; architecture and urban design; library: 10,000 vols; 225 students; Dir CHRIS VAN LANGEN; Business Dir BERT HOOIJER.

Sandberg Instituut: Fred. Roeskestraat 98, 1076 ED Amsterdam; tel. (20) 5882400; fax (20) 5882401; e-mail contact@sandberg.nl; internet www.sandberg.nl; f. 1990; attached to Gerrit Rietveld Acad.; Masters pro-grammes in fine arts, applied arts and design; courses validated by accreditation cttee NVAO; 41 students; Dir JURGEN BEY.

Willem de Kooning Academie (Willem de Kooning Academy): POB 1272, 3000 BG Rotterdam; Blaak 10 and Wijnhaven 61, Rotterdam; tel. (10) 7904750; fax (10) 7944766; e-mail wdka.communicatie@hro.nl; internet abk.hro.nl; f. 1773, present name 1998; attached to Rotterdam Univ.; 120 staff; library: 6,000 vols; Pres. RICHARD E. OUWER-KERK.

NETHERLANDS SPECIAL MUNICIPALITIES

BONAIRE

Learned Society

NATURAL SCIENCES

Biological Sciences

Stichting Nationale Parken Bonaire (STINAPA Bonaire): POB 368, Bonaire; tel. 7178444; fax 7177318; e-mail info@ stinapa.org; internet www.stinapa.org; 2 protected areas: Bonaire Nat. Marine Park (BNMP) and Washington Slagbaai Nat. Park (WSNP); protects Bonaire's natural and historical heritage; Dir ELSMARIE BEU-KENBOOM.

Research Intitutes

NATURAL SCIENCES

Biological Sciences

Bonaire National Marine Park: POB 368, Bonaire; tel. 7178444; fax 7177318; e-mail marinepark@stinapa.org; internet www.bmp .org; f. 1979; attached to STINAPA Bonaire; marine and ecological research; spec. in reef surveys; protects and manages natural, cultural and historical resources; Man. RAMON DE LEON.

CIEE Research Station Bonaire: Kaya gobernador n. Debrot 26, Kralendijk, Bonaire; tel. 7174140; internet www .cieebonaire.org; research on marine ecology and conservation; provides scientific data, analysis and support to Bonaire's environmental, educational and governmental bodies; Dir Dr RITA PEACHEY; publ. *Physis*.

SABA

Regulatory Body

GOVERNMENT

Department of Education: Power Street One, The Bottom, Saba; tel. 4163365; fax 4163362; Commr CHRIS JOHNSON.

Learned Society

NATURAL SCIENCES

Biological Sciences

Saba Conservation Foundation: POB 18, The Bottom, Saba; tel. 4163295; fax 4163435; e-mail info@sabapark.org; internet www .sabapark.org; f. 1987; preserves and enhances marine and terrestrial environment through education, scientific research and monitoring; 10 mems.

College

Saba University School of Medicine: POB 1000, Church St, The Bottom, Saba; tel. 4163456; fax 4163458; e-mail admissions@saba.edu; internet www.saba .edu; f. 1986; offers programmes in basic and clinical sciences; library: 8,600 books, 155 periodicals; 79 teachers; 585 students (postgraduate); Chair. of the Board of Trustees Dr PAUL L. DALBEC; Pres. JOSEPH CHU; Exec. Dean Dr HUGH K. DUCKWORTH; Assoc. Dean for Basic Sciences JAMES G. LEWIS; Assoc. Dean for Clinical Sciences MICHAEL ELIASTAM; Dir of Admissions Dr ALAN L. BERNSTEIN; Registrar BERNICE M. OUELLET; Library Dir SAMUEL JOHNSON.

SINT EUSTATIUS

Regulatory Body
GOVERNMENT

Department of Education, Culture and Sports: Govt Bldg, Oranjestad, Sint Eustatius; tel. 3182373; fax 3182324; Commr CLYDE VAN PUTTEN.

Learned Societies
HISTORY, GEOGRAPHY AND ARCHAEOLOGY

St Eustatius Centre for Archaeological Research (SECAR): Oranjestad, Sint Eustatius; internet www.secar.org; f. 2000; protects and develops historical resources; educates children, locals and visitors; Dir R. GRANT GILMORE, III.

NATURAL SCIENCES
Biological Sciences

St Eustatius National Parks Foundation (STENAPA): Gallows Bay, Sint Eustatius; tel. and fax 3182884; e-mail info@statiapark .org; internet www.statiapark.org; f. 1988; 3 nat. parks: St Eustatius Nat. Marine Park, Quill/Boven Nat. Park and Miriam Schmidt Botanical Gdn; protects biodiversity and tropical ecosystems; Pres. IRVING BROWN; Dir KATE WALKER; Sec. INGRID WALTHER; Treas. RUTH PANDT.

Museum
Oranjestad

Simon Doncker Museum: Simon Doncker House, Oranjestad, Sint Eustatius; tel. 3182693; fax 3182693; e-mail secar@hotmail .com; internet www.statiatourism.com/ museum; 2 galleries: colonial history and pre-Columbian history; spec. Granny Statia room.

University

UNIVERSITY OF SINT EUSTATIUS SCHOOL OF MEDICINE

POB 73, Goldenrock, Sint Eustatius

Telephone: 3182600
Fax: 3182088
E-mail: info@eustatiusmed.edu
Internet: www.eustatiusmed.edu

Founded 1999

Medical degree programme, incl. training in basic sciences and clinical education

Public control

Language of instruction: English

Academic year: September to August

Chair.: Dr CLYDE B. JENSEN
Pres.: LEONARD A. WISNESKI
Provost: Dr EZZELDIN NASSER
CEO: MICHAEL KNOPF
Vice-Pres. for Academic Devt: MARC POULIN
Vice-Pres. for Finance: JOHN BLUETHGEN
Dean of Int. Affairs: THAM NIMAL-RAJ.

ARUBA

The Higher Education System

There is one public university in the Dutch Dependency of Aruba, the Universiteit van Aruba (founded in 1988), which comprises four faculties—the Faculty of Arts and Science, the Faculty of Economics and Finance, the Faculty of Law, and the Faculty of Hospitality and Tourism Management Studies. There is also the Instituto Pedagogico Arubano (Aruban Teacher Training College), as well as a number of private institutions, including two medical schools—the Aureus University School of Medicine (formerly the All Saints University of Medicine, founded in 2004) and the Xavier University School of Medicine at Aruba (founded in 2004) . However, the majority of Aruban students who pursue higher education choose to do so abroad, generally in the Netherlands, although a significant number attend institutions in North America, South America or mainland Europe. In September 2008 there were 136 students enrolled at the Universiteit van Aruba, with a further 2,013 students enrolled at technical and vocational institutions. The main language of instruction is Dutch, but Papiamento is used in the lower levels of technical and vocational education.

Supervision of higher education is the responsibility of the Education Inspectorate, which assesses, monitors and promotes quality in education. Institutions are responsible for their own internal quality assurance and are encouraged to organize and access their activities from this perspective. There is currently no national qualifications framework in place in Aruba.

Admission to degree programmes at the Universiteit van Aruba requires students to hold the Voorbereidend Wetenschappelijk Onderwijs (VWO—Preparatory Scientific Education), the Hoger Algemeen Voortgezet Onderwijs (HAVO—Higher General Continued Education) or the Middelbaar Beroepsonderwijs (MBO—Middle Applied Education). Undergraduate Bachelors degree programmes last between three and four years, and grant access to postgraduate Masters programmes, which generally last between one and two years.

The Instituto Pedagogico Arubano offers the qualification of Graad van Volledig Bevoegd Leerkracht (Fully Qualified Teacher Qualification), which is comparable to a Bachelors degree in primary education in the Netherlands, or the Akte van Bekwaamheid van de tweede graad tot het geven van voortgezet onderwij (Teaching Certificate in Secondary Teaching, Level Two), which is comparable to a Bachelors degree in secondary education in the Netherlands. Both teacher training qualifications require a period of four years' study.

Regulatory Bodies
GOVERNMENT

Ministry of Economic Affairs, Social Affairs and Culture: L. G. Smith Blvd 76, Oranjestad; tel. 5885455; fax 5827526; e-mail minszi@setarnet.aw; Minister Drs MICHELLE JANICE HOOYBOER-WINKLAAR.

Ministry of Justice and Education: L. G. Smith Blvd 76, Oranjestad; tel. 5830004; fax 5827518; e-mail macs@setarnet.aw; Minister ARTHUR LAWRENCE DOWERS.

Libraries and Archives
Oranjestad

Archivo Nacional Aruba (National Archives of Aruba): Sabana Banco 60, Oranjestad; tel. 5834880; fax 5839275; e-mail ana@aruba.gov.aw; f. 1994; preservation and conservation of nat. and cultural heritage of Aruba; manages transferred govt and private records; supervises and inspects governmental archives; makes archival information accessible for public use; supplies information about records to public; conducts historical research and publishes result; promotes historical interest of the public by organizing exhibitions, presentations regarding history and culture; Dir Drs RAYMOND R. HERNANDEZ.

Biblioteca Nacional Aruba (National Library of Aruba): George Madurostr. 13, Oranjestad; tel. 5821580; fax 5825493; e-mail info@bibliotecanacional.aw; internet www.bibliotecanacional.aw; f. 1908 as first Public Library of Aruba 1949, mobile library 1968, present bldg 1982, present name and status 1986; 100,000 books; nat. library, with functions of public library and nat. information centre; br. in San Nicolas; 2 bookmobiles; Dir ASTRID J. T. BRITTEN.

Museums and Art Galleries
Oranjestad

Museo Arquelogico Aruba (Archaeological Museum of Aruba): J. E. Irausquinplein 2A, Oranjestad; tel. 5828979; fax 5838267; e-mail archeo@setarnet.aw; internet www.institutodicultura-aruba.com; attached to Instituto di Cultura Aruba; permanent colln of ceramic artefacts, shell and stone tools, ornaments from the first cultures of Aruba;

research, documentation, preservation of heritage and indigenous culture of Aruba.

Museo Historico Arubano (Aruban Historical Museum): Fort Zoutman z/n, Oranjestad; tel. and fax 5885199; e-mail museohistoricoarubano@hotmail.com; internet www.institutodicultura-aruba.com; f. fort built in 1798, est. as museum by Cultureel Centrum van Aruba 1983, admin. by Fundacion Museo Arubano since 1992; attached to Instituto di Cultura Aruba; archaeology, architecture, history.

Museo Numismatico Aruba (Aruba Numismatic Museum): Timbalstr. 11, Tarabana, Oranjestad; tel. 5828831; fax 5838246; e-mail numisaruba@hotmail.com; internet www.museumaruba.org; f. 1981; attached to Instituto di Cultura Aruba; holds private colln of Juan Mario Odor; colln of 35,000 items from 400 countries; Pres., J. M. Odor colln RAQUEL MADURO-ODOR; Dir, J. M. Odor colln DESIREE CROES.

San Nicolas

Aruban Model Trains Museum: Koolbaaibergstr. 12, San Nicolas; tel. and fax 5847321; internet www.institutodicultura-aruba.com; f. 2001; attached to Instituto di Cultura Aruba; colln of miniature trains; Dir J. DE VRIES.

Universities and Colleges
AUREUS UNIVERSITY SCHOOL OF MEDICINE

Wayaca 31C, Oranjestad

Telephone: 5832126
Fax: 5832127
E-mail: info@aureusuniversity.com
Internet: www.aureusuniversity.com

Founded 2004, fmrly All Saints Univ. of Medicine
Private control
Language of instruction: English
Academic year: January to December

Exec. Dean: Dr GURMIT CHILANA
Dean for Academic Affairs: Dr FRANK NAVARRETE
Dean for Clinical Affairs: Dr RICHARD SCOTT
Number of teachers: 17
Number of students: 190 medical, 77 premedical

Arubaanse Muziekschool (Aruban School of Music): Vondellaan 2, Oranjestad; tel. 5822888; fax 5836529; e-mail arumuziekschool@setarnet.aw; f. 1953; Gov-

ernment support; educational and recreational activities; centre for information and archive of musical pieces; Dir FELIX RAIMOND HOEK.

UNIVERSIDAD DI ARUBA
(University of Aruba)

Dr Schaepmanstr. z/n, San Nicholas

Telephone: 5845287
Fax: 5847274

Founded 1970
Private control
Language of instruction: English
Academic year: September to June

Pres.: Dr CARLIN I. BROWNE
Registrar: HILTONIA PETER
Librarian: LISA WEBB

Library of 6,000 vols
Number of teachers: 20
Number of students: 300

DEANS

College of Business Administration: Dr CARLIN I. BROWNE
College of Education: Dr RACHEL JONES
College of Languages: Dr JOSSY MANSUR
College of Liberal Arts: Rev. Fr WILLIAM LAKE

UNIVERSITEIT VAN ARUBA
(University of Aruba)

J. Irausquinplein 4, POB 5, Oranjestad

Telephone: 5823901
Fax: 5831770
E-mail: info@ua.aw
Internet: www.ua.aw

Founded 1988
State control
Languages of instruction: Dutch, English
Academic year: September to June

Pres.: FREDERIC GIBBS
Rector: GLENN THODÉ
Librarian: LEONIE BOERKAMP

Library of 20,000 vols
Number of teachers: 40
Number of students: 500

Publication: *Aruba Iuridica* (2 a year)

DEANS

Faculty of Arts and Sciences: PAULA KIBBELAAR
Faculty of Financial and Economic Studies: JOOST JACOBS
Faculty of Hospitality and Tourism Management: JOHN WARDLAW
Faculty of Law: CARLOS BOLLEN

CURAÇAO

The Higher Education System

Following the dissolution of the Netherlands Antilles and Curaçao's establishment as an autonomous constituent country within the Netherlands in October 2010, the provision of higher education on the island has been the responsibility of the newly created Ministry of Education, Science, Culture and Sports. There is one public university on Curaçao—the University of Curaçao Mr Dr Moises Frumencio da Costa Gomez (founded in 1970 as the Law College of the Netherlands Antilles; name changed to University of Netherlands Antilles and university status adopted in 1979; current name since 2011). In 2010/11

enrolment at the University totalled 2,096 students. Degree programmes are also available at the Inter-Continental University of the Caribbean (formerly the Curaçao Institute for Social and Economic Studies, which was a constituent division of the University of Netherlands Antilles prior to becoming an independent institution in 2009; current name adopted 2010) and at two private institutions—the University of the Dutch Caribbean and the Caribbean International University. In 2002/03 some 6,088 students were enrolled in vocational education.

Regulatory Body

GOVERNMENT

Ministry of Education, Science, Culture and Sports: Scharlooweg 102, Willemstad; tel. (9) 4615133; fax (9) 4624471; Minister LIONEL JANSEN.

Learned Societies

HISTORY, GEOGRAPHY AND ARCHAEOLOGY

National Archaeological and Anthropological Memory Management (NAAM): Johan van Walbeeckplein 13, Pietermaai, Willemstad; tel. (9) 4621933; fax (9) 4621936; e-mail info@naam.an; internet www.naam.an; f. 1998 fmrly Archaeological–Anthropological Institute of the Netherlands Antilles; present name 2008; promotes nat. and int. cooperation; knowledge acquisition; understanding of Caribbean heritage issues; incl. 10,000 artefacts of the Afro-Caribbean culture; archeological colln incl maritime artefacts; heritage management; library of 2,000 vols; Chair. LIONEL JANGA; Dir R. ANSANO; Sec. ALCA SINT JAGO; Treas. FLORENTINO OVERMAN.

NATURAL SCIENCES

Biological Sciences

CARMABI Foundation: Piscaderabaai z/n, POB 2090, Willemstad; tel. (9) 4624242; fax (9) 4627680; e-mail info@carmabi.org; internet www.carmabi.org; f. 1955 as a marine biological research station, merged with STINAPA 1996; terrestrial and marine ecology; Christoffel Park, Curaçao Marine Park, Savonet Museum, Research Station Carmabi, Carmabi Education (environmental education programmes); library of 3,000 vols; Chair. DITO ABBAD; Dir Ir. PAUL STOKKERMANS; Sec. JEFFREY SYBESMA; Treas. PETER BONGERS.

Physical Sciences

Meteorological Department Curaçao: Seru Mahuma, Willemstad; tel. (9) 8393366; fax (9) 8683999; e-mail admin-cur@meteo.an; internet www.weather.an; f. 1953, fmrly Meteorological Service of the Netherlands Antilles and Aruba, present location 1976, present name and status 2010; attached to Min. of Traffic, Transport and Urban Planning; provides weather forecasts and warnings for Curaçao and Caribbean islands;

offers services to sustain social-economic devt; Dir Dr A. A. E. MARTIS.

Libraries and Archives

Willmestad

Nationaal Archief (National Archives): Scharlooweg 75–79, Willemstad; tel. (9) 4614866; fax (9) 4616794; e-mail na@nationalarchives.an; internet www.nationalarchives.an; f. 1969; repository for all non-current govt records; collns of originals and microfilm copies of archives from 1713; 15,000 vols, 400,000 photographs and negatives and audiovisual materials; Dir Drs N. C. ROMER-KENEPA; publ. Lantèrnu.

Biblioteka Públiko Kòrsou/Openbare Bibliotheek Curaçao/Biblioteca Pública Curazao (Public Library Curaçao): Abraham. M. Chumaceiro Blvr 17, Willemstad; tel. (9) 4345200; fax (9) 4656247; e-mail publiclibrary@onenet.an; internet www.curaaopubliclibrary.an; f. 1922 as part of Govt Service of Culture and Education, present location 1988, present status 1997; Antillean and Caribbean colln; adult, children's, mobile and schools' library services, 1 br. library, 2 mobile libraries; 180,000 vols and small colln of audiovisual material; Chair. SHIK-TONG CHAN; Librarian R. M. DE PAULA; Sec. M. ROJER; Treas. D. PIMENTEL.

Mongui Maduro Library: POB 480, Landhuis Rooi Catootje, Willemstad; tel. (9) 7375119; fax (9) 7376875; e-mail info@madurolibrary.org; internet www.madurolibrary.org; Antilliana and Judaica collns; 3,000 vols.

Museums

Willmestad

Curaçao Museum: Van Leeuwenhoekstr z/n, Willemstad; tel. (9) 4623873; fax (9) 4623777; e-mail curmuseum@gmail.com; f. 1946 as The Curaçao Museum Foundation, present name and status 1948; housed in an old hospital for Dutch soldiers with yellow fever, built 1853; colln of antique furniture, local and int. art; traditional Curaçaoan kitchen; paintings by early 20th-century Dutch masters and contemporary Curaçao artists; carillon with 47 bells; botanical and sculpture garden and music pavilion; cockpit of first KLM airplane that crossed the Atlantic Ocean in 1934; Pres. C. WEEBER; publ. De Museumbode (4 a year).

Jewish Historical Cultural Museum: POB 322, Willemstad; tel. (9) 4611067; fax (9) 4654141; e-mail museum@snoa.com; internet www.snoa.com/snoa.html; f. 1970; cultural objects collected over 350 years of Jewish life in Curaçao.

Maritiem Museum Curaçao (Curaçao Maritime Museum): Van der Brandhofstraat One, Willemstad; tel. (9) 4652327; fax (9) 4652448; e-mail info@curaçaomaritime.com; internet www.curacaomaritime.com; f. 1998; exhibits 500 years of maritime history of Curaçao; authentic nautical charts, ship models and navigation equipment; Dir LEO HELMS.

Numismatic Museum: Centrale Bank van Curaçao en Sint Maarten, Simon Bolivar Plein One, Willemstad; tel. 4345500; fax 4615004; e-mail info@centralbank.an; internet www.centralbank.an/museum/museum.php; attached to Centrale Bank van Curaçao en Sint Maarten; displays Antillean currency from barter deals; use of coins from different countries; incl. commemorative coins.

Tele Musuem: Wilhelminaplein Four, Punda, Willemstad; tel. (9) 4652844; fax (9) 8890760; attached to UTS; history of telephone from the 1880s to the late 20th-century inventions, incl. fibre optic cables, computerization and teleconferencing.

Universities

AVALON UNIVERSITY SCHOOL OF MEDICINE (AUSOM)

Scharlooweg 25, Willemstad
Telephone: (9) 7173967
Fax: (9) 7173970
E-mail: admissions@avalonu.org
Internet: www.avalonu.org
Offers programmes in premedicine, doctor of medicine and clinical sciences
Academic year: January to December
Chancellor: Dr SHOKAT FATTEH
Pres.: Dr SAMIR FATTEH
Vice-Pres.: DILU DINANI
Dean of Academic Affairs: Dr SIREESHA BALA ARJA
Dean of Admissions: Dr SALEEM UMAR
Dean of Basic Sciences: Dr SATEESH BABU ARJA
Dean of Clinical Sciences: Dr NAZIM JAFFER
Registrar: MICHELLE RICHARDS.

CARIBBEAN INTERNATIONAL UNIVERSITY

World Trade Center Curaçao, Piscadera Bay
Telephone: (9) 4636192
Fax: (9) 463-6573
E-mail: info@ciucuracao.info
Internet: www.ciucuracao.org

Offers Bachelors and Masters degrees in banking, economy and finance and management; doctoral programmes in social sciences, education sciences and legal sciences; language courses in English and Spanish
Private control
Language of instruction: Dutch.

INTER-CONTINENTAL UNIVERSITY OF THE CARIBBEAN (ICUC)

Plaza Brion One, Otrobanda
Telephone: (9) 7666300
Fax: (9) 4656791
E-mail: info@icuc.org
Internet: www.icuc.org

Founded 1994, present status 2009, present name 2010

Offers Bachelors and Masters degrees through school of financial management, school of hospitality and tourism management, school of management and leadership, school of int. business and school of language studies
Private control.

ST. MARTINUS UNIVERSITY— FACULTY OF MEDICINE

Brionplein One, POB 2050, Otrobanda
E-mail: info@martinus.edu
Internet: www.martinus.edu

Founded 1842 as St. Martinus College

Offers Bachelors programme in medicine; provides undergraduate and graduate research opportunities
Private control
Academic year: January to May, July to November (2 semesters)
Dean of Academics: Dr THOMAS GEST
Dean of Basic Sciences: Dr KALICHARAN MISRA
Dean of Clinical Sciences: Dr REBECCA K. KARTJE
Vice-Pres. for Academic and Admin. Affairs: J. M. PARBHOO.

UNIVERSITY OF CURAÇAO MR DR MOISES FRUMENCIO DA COSTA GOMEZ

Jan Noorduynweg 111, Curaçao
Telephone: (9) 8442222
Fax: (9) 8448442
E-mail: una@una.an
Internet: www.una.an

Founded 1970 as The Law College of the Netherlands Antilles, univ. status 1979 as Univ. of the Netherlands Antilles, present name 2011
State control
Languages of instruction: Dutch, English
Academic year: September to June
Pres.: Ir H. J. BEHR
Rector: Dr F. DE LANOY (acting)
Gen. Dir: H. DE FRANÇA
Chief Admin. Officer: R. RAVENSTEIN
Library and Research Head: Drs M. GROENEWOUD
Library of 100,000 vols
Number of teachers: 235
Number of students: 2,096

DEANS

Faculty of Engineering: R. BULBAAI
Faculty of General Arts: Dr E. ECHTELD
Faculty of Law: Dr P. KLICK
Faculty of Social and Behavioural Sciences: (vacant)
Faculty of Social Sciences and Economics: R. SOPHIA (acting)

UNIVERSITY OF THE DUTCH CARIBBEAN

Landhuis Groot Davelaar, Willemstad
Telephone: (9) 7383300
Fax: (9) 7383320
E-mail: info@udc.an
Internet: www.udc.an

Offers business economics, commercial economics, higher legal education, higher tourism and recreational education, int. business and management studies
Private control
Language of instruction: Dutch.

College

Akademia di Músika 'Edgar Palm' (Edgar Palm Music Academy): Koninginnelaan z/n, Emmastad, Curaçao; tel. (9) 7373682; fax (9) 7378882; e-mail info@sentrokultural-korsou .org; internet www.sentrokultural-korsou .org; f. 1960; attached to Sentro Kultural Kòrsou (Cultureel Centrum Curaçao); instrumental, voice and gen. music education, theatre and visual art; 550 students; Dir ETZEL PROVENCE.

SINT MAARTEN

The Higher Education System

Following the dissolution of the Netherlands Antilles and Sint Maarten's establishment as an autonomous constituent country within the Netherlands in October 2010, the Sint Maarten Department of Education was reorganized as the Ministry of Education, Culture, Youth and Sports Affairs; the Ministry is the national agency responsible for the provision of higher education. The Government maintains a comprehensive bursary programme for university students, at both local and foreign institutions. A significant number of students who choose to pursue higher education do so at institutions based in North America, South America or the European mainland. The University of St Martin, based in Sint Maarten, caters for students both in Sint Maarten and in the French Overseas Collectivity of Saint-Martin, and offers programmes in conjunction with universities in other Caribbean islands, including degree courses in business, liberal arts, applied science, education, and hospitality. Medical education is available at the American University of the Caribbean School of Medicine (founded in 1978), which follows curricula equivalent to that taught in US medical colleges and is accredited by the Accreditation Commission of Colleges of Medicine. Graduates from the institution are able to obtain residency and licensure throughout the USA.

Regulatory Body

GOVERNMENT

Ministry of Education, Culture, Youth and Sports Affairs: Philipsburg; tel. 5429344; fax 5429342; Minister RHODA ARRINDELL.

Learned Societies

HISTORY, GEOGRAPHY AND ARCHAEOLOGY

St Maarten National Heritage Foundation and Museum: POB 631, Front St Seven, Philipsburg; tel. and fax 5424917; e-mail heritage@caribserve.net; internet www.museumsintmaarten.org; f. 1993, by merger of St Maarten Nat. Park Foundation and St Maarten Museum Foundation; promotes, protects and studies history, culture and natural environment of St Maarten; incl. reference library.

MEDICINE

Mental Health Foundation: Leopard Rd One, Cay Hill; tel. 5421677; fax 5421687; e-mail admin@mhf-sxm.com; internet www .mhf-sxm.com; f. 2006; psychiatric clinical care, prevention of mental health diseases; psychiatric home health care; Dir EILEEN HEALY; Pres. Dr FELIX HOLIDAY; Sec. FENNA ARNELL; Treas. ERIC VAN DER HOEK.

St Maarten AIDS Foundation: c/o Gerard van Osch, Union Rd, 144A, Cole Bay; tel. 5445374; e-mail info@sxmaidsfoundation .org; internet www.sxmaidsfoundation.org; f. 1991; promotes awareness about AIDS and sexually transmittable disease; prevention and reduction of AIDS epidemic.

NATURAL SCIENCES

Biological Sciences

Nature Foundation St Maarten: POB 863, Philipsburg; Wellsberg St 1A, Unit 25–26 Fisherman's Wharf Complex, Cole Bay; tel. 5444267; fax 5444268; internet www .naturefoundationsxm.org; f. 1987; promotes conservation of St Maarten's environment; Chair. JAN BEAUJON; Sec. FRANK BOEKHOUT; Treas. MALOU CARTY.

Library

Philipsburg

Philipsburg Jubilee Library: Ch. E. W. Vogestreet 12, Philipsburg; tel. 5422970; fax 5425805; e-mail info@stmaartenlibrary.org; internet www.stmaartenlibrary.org; f. 1923; books on biography, health and computers; bookmobile outreach programme; Chair. CHANTAL SCHAMINEE; Dir MONIQUE ALBERTS; Sec. MONIQUE HOFMAN; Treas. CLAYTON HOLIDAY.

Universities

AMERICAN UNIVERSITY OF THE CARIBBEAN SCHOOL OF MEDICINE

Medical Science Campus, One Univ. Dr., Jordan Rd, Cupecoy

Telephone: 5452298

Fax: 5452440

E-mail: registrar@aucmed.edu

Internet: www.aucmed.edu

Founded 1978, present location 1995

Academic year: January to April,May to August,August to December (3 semesters)

Medical sciences at St Maarten campus and clinical sciences in affiliated hospitals in the USA and UK

Chancellor: Dr PAUL S. TIEN

Chief Academic Officer: BRUCE KAPLAN

Chief Financial Officer: PAUL R. SUID

Dean of Medical Sciences: Dr RONALD J. TESTA

Dir of Admissions: MINDY GREENE

Librarian: CHRIS WILLIAMS

Registrar: DIMPLE AMARNANI

Library of 5,000 vols incl. books, videos, DVDs, CDs and 75 journals

Number of teachers: 500

Publication: *AUC Connections*.

UNIVERSITY OF ST MARTIN

One Soualiga Rd, POB 836, Philipsburg

Telephone: 5425171

E-mail: president@usmonline.net

Internet: www.usmonline.net

Founded 1989

Academic year: August to December,January to May,June to August (3 semesters)

Offers Bachelors degrees in arts in education, hospitality, tourism management

Pres.: ANNELIES VAN DEN ASSEM

Dean of Academic Affairs: GLEN YEUNG (acting)

Dir of Admissions: ANGELIQUE HAZEL

Librarian: MARK PAUL

Registrar: GLENDA BRAZIER.

NEW ZEALAND

The Higher Education System

New Zealand became a dominion, under the British Crown, in 1907 and achieved full independence in 1947, when it accepted the 1931 Statute of Westminster. Most of the major institutions of higher education were founded during the second half of the 19th century, notably the University of Otago (founded in 1869), the University of Canterbury (founded in 1873), Lincoln University (founded in 1878; current name and status since 1990) and the University of Auckland (founded in 1883; current status since 1962). Higher education consists of universities, polytechnic institutions, colleges of education (all of which had merged with universities by 2007) and schools of art and music. In 2003 there were eight state universities and 20 polytechnics. In 2009 there were 154,866 students enrolled at the universities and 180,709 students in the polytechnic system. There is a parallel education system for the indigenous Maori population, who account for 20% of school enrolment. Three Maori institutions (wānanga) in the tertiary sector provide higher learning in ahuatanga Māori (Maori tradition) according to tikanga Māori (Maori custom). In 2009 42,566 students were enrolled in the wānanga. Students from the Dependent Territory of Tokelau and the Associated States of the Cook Islands and Niue may receive higher education either through branches and campuses of the University of the South Pacific or through scholarships to study in New Zealand, Australia, Fiji and other Pacific countries.

Under the Education Act (1989) the Ministry of Education is the supreme body for the provision of education at all levels. The Tertiary Education Commission determines public higher education policy and administers funding, and the New Zealand Qualifications Authority (NZQA) oversees private education providers and government training establishments. The NZQA has established a New Zealand Register of Quality Assured Qualifications ('The Register'), which lists all quality-assured programmes of study and their international equivalency. It accredits and audits tertiary education providers, excluding universities, and other registered learning establishments that offer approved courses and award credits for registered qualifications. The universities are autonomous institutions, each governed by a Council, consisting of elected, appointed or co-opted members, and headed by a Vice-Chancellor. The Senate is an academic board with responsibility for academic affairs. Some 80% of the universities' funds are state-provided. In addition to government funding dispersed by the Tertiary Education Commission, the universities are also financed by tuition fees, which are subsidized by the State. Universities in New Zealand are not self-accrediting and must apply to offer new qualifications or new subjects to the Committee on University Academic Programmes of the New Zealand Vice-Chancellors' Committee, which acts under statutory authority in lieu of NZQA in the university sector. Following the Education Amendment Act (1990), the polytechnics, colleges of education and wānanga became autonomous institutions and award their own degrees.

Admission to higher education is on the basis of the National Certificate of Educational Achievement. The standard university-level degree system consists of Bachelors, Masters and Doctorate degrees but aspects such as period of study and criteria for award vary among the institutions owing to their autonomy. The Bachelors is often a three-year degree (although some disciplines such as medicine require upwards of five years) and is awarded on the basis of 'credits' accrued. An 'Honours' Bachelors degree is a four-year programme of study. The Masters is the first postgraduate degree, and varies in length from one to three years of full-time (or equivalent part-time) study. The PhD or DPhil is the highest university-level degree, awarded after a minimum of two years of research-based study leading to submission of a thesis. There are also 'higher' doctorates such as the DSc or DLitt awarded after publication of a corpus of work. Institutions of higher education operate a credit-transfer system, which allows students to complete their degree in an institution other than the one in which they started.

Post-secondary technical and vocational education is offered by the universities, institutes of technology, polytechnics, colleges of education, professional institutes and wānanga. The main qualifications are the National Certificate (four levels) and National Diploma.

During 2009 the Government strengthened the performance of institutes of technology and polytechnics by reshaping the nature of their governing councils and introducing a new investment-based approach to quality assurance. However, it was feared that austerity measures introduced as part of the 2012 budget, announced in May 2011, which included freezing the level of government subsidies for all but degree and postgraduate enrolment, as well as a reduction in the level of assistance offered by the student loan scheme, would impact negatively on higher education.

Regulatory and Representative Bodies

GOVERNMENT

Ministry for Culture and Heritage: POB 5364, Wellington 6145; Level 5, Radio New Zealand House, 155 The Terrace, Wellington 6011; tel. (4) 499-4229; fax (4) 499-4490; e-mail info@mch.govt.nz; internet www.mch .govt.nz; Minister for Arts, Culture and Heritage CHRISTOPHER FINLAYSON; Librarian FRAN McGOWAN.

Ministry of Education: POB 1666, Thorndon, Wellington 6140; 45–47 Pipitea St, Wellington 6140; tel. (4) 463-8000; fax (4) 463-8001; e-mail info@minedu.govt.nz; internet www.minedu.govt.nz; Min. ANNE TOLLEY.

Ministry of Research, Science and Technology: POB 5336, Wellington 6145; Level 10, 2 The Terrace, Wellington; tel. (4) 917-2900; fax (4) 471-1284; e-mail info@morst .govt.nz; internet www.morst.govt.nz; f. 1992; Min. Hon. Dr WAYNE MAPP.

ACCREDITATION

ENIC/NARIC New Zealand: PO Box 160, Wellington 6140; Level 13, 125 The Terrace, Wellington 6011; tel. (4) 463-3000; fax (4) 463-3112; e-mail pamela.hulston@nzqa.govt .nz; internet www.nzqa.govt.nz; f. 1990; secondary school examinations and qualifications; quality assurance of tertiary instns; Man. PAMELA HULSTON.

New Zealand Qualifications Authority: POB 160, Wellington 6140; Level 13, 125 The Terrace, Wellington 6011; tel. (4) 463-3000; fax (4) 463-3112; e-mail helpdesk@nzqa.govt .nz; internet www.nzqa.govt.nz; coordinates the admin. and quality assurance of nat. qualifications in NZ; responsible for quality assurance services to Institutes of Technology and Polytechnics; Board Chair. SUE SUCKLING; Chief Exec. Dr KAREN POUTASI.

NATIONAL BODIES

Distance Education Association of New Zealand: 78C White Rd, RD2, Otane, Central Hawkes Bay 4277; tel. and fax (6) 856-8022; e-mail admin@deanz.org.nz; internet www.deanz.org.nz; promotes growth, devt, research and good practice in distance education; Pres. Dr BILL ANDERSON; Sec. ANNA WEATHERSTONE; publ. *Journal of Open, Flexible and Distance Learning* (1 a year).

New Zealand Educational Institute/ NZEI Te Riu Roa: 178–182 Willis St, POB 466, Wellington 6140; tel. (4) 3822736; internet www.nzei.org.nz; f. 1883; New Zealand's largest education union; teachers and support staff working in primary, area and secondary schools and early childhood centres, special education and school advisory services; Nat. Pres. IAN LECKIE; Nat. Vice-Pres. FRANCIE GUY; Nat. Sec PAUL GOULTER.

Tertiary Education Commission: Level 10, 44 The Terrace, POB 27-048, Wellington 6141; 1 Ash Rd, Wiri Private Bag 76928, Manukau City 2241; tel. (4) 462-5200; fax (4) 462-5400; e-mail servicecentre@tec.govt.nz; internet www.tec.govt.nz; f. 2003; leads the govt's relationship with the tertiary sector and makes investments in tertiary education and training on the govt's behalf; Chair. WIRA GARDINER; Chief Exec. BELINDA CLARK.

Universities New Zealand/Te Pōkai Tara: POB 11915, Manners St, Wellington 6142; Level 9, 142 Lambton Quay, Wellington; tel. (4) 381-8500; fax (4) 381-8501; e-mail jackie.bailey@universitiesnz.ac.nz; internet www.universitiesnz.ac.nz; f. 1961; responsible for the quality of univ. programmes; administers a range of scholarships and represents the univs in the public interest, both nationally and internationally; Chair. Prof. PAT WALSH; Exec. Dir PENNY FENWICK.

Learned Societies
GENERAL

Royal Society of New Zealand: POB 598, Wellington 6140; 4 Halswell St, Thorndon, Wellington 6011; tel. (4) 472-7421; fax (4) 473-1841; internet www.royalsociety.org.nz; f. 1867; nat. academy of scholars representing the applied, biological, earth, engineering, information, medical, physical and social sciences; mathematics, technology, and humanities; 1,167 mems, 373 fellows, 65 constituent socs; Pres. Prof. Sir DAVID SKEGG; CEO Dr DIANNE MCCARTHY; publs *Journal of the Royal Society of New Zealand* (4 a year), *Kotuitui: New Zealand Journal of Social Sciences Online* (2 a year), *New Zealand Journal of Agricultural Research* (4 a year), *New Zealand Journal of Botany* (4 a year), *New Zealand Journal of Crop and Horticultural Science* (4 a year), *New Zealand Journal of Geology and Geophysics* (4 a year), *New Zealand Journal of Marine and Freshwater Research* (4 a year), *New Zealand Journal of Zoology* (4 a year).

AGRICULTURE, FISHERIES AND VETERINARY SCIENCE

Agronomy Society of New Zealand: 610 Rakaia Selwyn Rd, RD 2, Leeston 7682; e-mail c.r.mcgill@massey.ac.nz; internet agronomy.science.org.nz; f. 1970; promotes the advancement of scientific research and the practice of agronomy in New Zealand; encourages the flow of agronomic information; 150 mems; Pres. Dr BRUCE SEARLE; Sec. PAUL JOHNSTONE; Treas. JO TOWNSHEND; publ. *Agronomy New Zealand* (1 a year).

New Zealand Institute of Agricultural and Horticultural Science: POB 121-063, Henderson, Auckland; tel. (9) 812-8506; fax (9) 812-8503; e-mail secretariat@agscience .org.nz; internet www.agscience.org.nz; f. 1954; 800 mems; Sec. JENNY TAYLOR; publ. *AgScience* (6 a year).

New Zealand Institute of Forestry/Te Putahi Ngaherehere o Aotearoa Inc.: POB 10-513, Level 9, 93 The Terrace, Wellington 6143; tel. (4) 974-8421; fax (4) 473-9330; e-mail admin@nzif.org.nz; internet www.nzif.org.nz; f. 1927; promotes the best use of NZ's resources and encourages wise use of forest lands; 824 mems; Pres. ANDREW MCEWEN; Sec. JAMES TREADWELL; Treas. CHAYNE ZINSLI; publs *New Zealand Journal of Forestry* (4 a year), *NZIF Handbook* (1 a year).

New Zealand Society of Animal Production Inc.: c/o Dr Jane Kay, DairyNZ, Private Bag 3221, Hamilton; tel. and fax (7) 824-0916; e-mail nzsap.animal@xtra.co.nz; internet nzsap.org.nz; f. 1940; fosters research in all areas of animal production incl. production systems, nutrition, meat science, animal welfare, wool science, animal breeding and genetics; 530 mems; Pres. ANDREW GREER; Exec. Sec. Dr JANE KAY; Sec. DAVID PACHECO; publ. *Proceedings* (1 a year).

New Zealand Society of Soil Science Inc.: c/o Dr Trish Fraser, Crop and Food Research, Private Bag 4704, Christchurch; tel. (3) 325-6400; fax (3) 325-2074; e-mail trish.fraser@plantandfood.co.nz; internet nzsss.science.org.nz; f. 1952; encourages the advancement of soil science; organizes annual conf.; promotes knowledge of soil science; lobbies govt on science funding and scientific issues; 400 mems; Pres. Dr ALLAN HEWITT; Sec. Dr TRISH FRASER.

New Zealand Veterinary Association (Inc.): POB 11-212, Wellington 6142; Level 2, 44 Victoria St, Wellington 6011; tel. (4) 471-0484; fax (4) 471-0494; e-mail nzva@vets .org.nz; internet www.nzva.org.nz; f. 1923; represents and provides services and promotes standards for and on behalf of veterinarians; 1,750 mems; CEO JULIE HOOD; Pres. Dr GAVIN SINCLAIR; Sec. TRISH THORPE; publs *New Zealand Veterinary Journal* (6 a year, also online), *Vetscript* (11 a year).

Royal Agricultural Society of New Zealand (Inc.): POB 54, Woodend 7641; tel. (3) 313-1004; fax (3) 313-1003; e-mail debbie@ ras.org.nz; internet www.ras.org.nz; f. 1924; promotes the devt of agricultural, pastoral, horticultural, stock-raising and forestry resources in NZ; 1,000 individual mems, 170 institutional mems; library of 1,000 vols; Pres. BRUCE ORR; Exec. Officer DEBBIE CAMERON; publ. *On Show* (2 a year).

ARCHITECTURE AND TOWN PLANNING

New Zealand Institute of Architects: POB 2516 Shortland St, Auckland 1140; Suite 1.5, 72 Dominion Rd, Mt Eden, Auckland 1024; tel. (9) 623-6080; fax (9) 623-6081; internet www.nzia.co.nz; f. 1905; supports the needs of its mem. architects, and promotes architecture and the living environment of all New Zealanders; 2,800 mems; Chief Exec. BEVERLEY MCRAE; Pres. PATRICK CLIFFORD.

New Zealand Institute of Surveyors: 5th Fl., St John House, 114 The Terrace, Wellington; tel. (4) 471-1774; fax (4) 471-1907; e-mail nzis@surveyors.org.nz; internet www .surveyors.org.nz; f. 1888; concerned with the professional and ethical conduct of surveyors; monitors and maintain the professional and ethical conduct of surveyors in New Zealand; 1,300 mems; Pres. ANDREW STIRLING; publs *NZ Surveyor* (1 a year), *Survey Quarterly* (4 a year).

BIBLIOGRAPHY, LIBRARY SCIENCE AND MUSEOLOGY

Museums Aotearoa Te Tari o Nga whare Taonga o Te Motu/The Museums of New Zealand (Inc.): POB 10-928, Wellington 6143; Level 8, 104 The Terrace, Wellington 6011; tel. (4) 499-1313; fax (4) 499-6313; e-mail mail@museums-aotearoa.org.nz; internet www.museums-aotearoa.org.nz; f. 1947; ind. professional body; represents museums and museum employees in NZ; 327 mems; Exec. Dir PHILLIPA TOCKER; publs *Museums Aotearoa Quarterly*, *New Zealand Directory of Museums* (1 a year), *Te Ara—Journal of Museums Aotearoa* (2 a year, print and online).

New Zealand Book Council: Stephenson and Turner House, 156–158 Victoria St, Te Aro, Wellington 6011; tel. (4) 801-5546; fax (4) 801-5547; e-mail admin@bookcouncil.org .nz; internet www.bookcouncil.org.nz; f. 1972; promotes love for books and reading through a wide range of programmes; 2,500 mems (individuals, schools, libraries, booksellers, publishers); Chair. PETER BIGGS; Chief Exec. NOEL MURPHY; publ. *Booknotes* (4 a year).

New Zealand Library Association (Inc.): POB 12-212, Thorndon, Wellington 6144; Level 4, 156–158 Victoria St, Wellington 6011; tel. (4) 801-5543; fax (4) 801-5542; e-mail admin@lianza.org.nz; internet www .lianza.org.nz; f. 1910; also known as Library and Information Association of New Zealand Aotearoa (LIANZA); professional organisation for the NZ library and information management profession; 2,281 (1,884 individual mems, 397 institutional mems); Pres. JANE HILL; Exec. Dir ALLI SMITH; publs *Library Life* (26 a year), *The NZ Library & Information Management Journal* (2 a year, online).

ECONOMICS, LAW AND POLITICS

New Zealand Institute of International Affairs: c/o Victoria Univ. of Wellington, Rm 507, Level 5, W Wing Railways, Pipitea Campus, POB 600, Wellington 6140; tel. (4) 463-5356; e-mail admin@vuw.ac.nz; internet www.victoria.ac.nz/nziia; f. 1934; promotes understanding of int. questions and problems, particularly those relating to New Zealand, the Pacific, Asia, and the Commonwealth; Pres. Hon. DOUGLAS KIDD; Dir BRIAN LYNCH; Exec. Officer NGAIRE FLYNN; publ. *New Zealand International Review* (6 a year).

New Zealand Law Society: POB 5041, Wellington 6145; 26 Waring Taylor St, Wellington 6011; tel. (4) 472-7837; fax (4) 473-7909; e-mail inquiries@lawsociety.org.nz; internet www.lawsociety.org.nz; f. 1869; has statutory responsibility for regulating the legal profession (barristers and solicitors) in New Zealand; offers membership services to those lawyers who also choose to be mems; 11,100 mems; Pres. JONATHAN TEMM; Sec. CHRISTINE GRICE; Exec. Dir CHRISTINE GRICE (acting); publ. *LawTalk* (24 a year).

Population Association of New Zealand: POB 225, Wellington; tel. (9) 484 6247; fax (4) 471-4412; e-mail alison.reid@ aucklandcouncil.govt.nz; internet panz.rsnz .org; f. 1974; promotes population research, understanding and policy devt; 122 mems; Pres. ALISON REID; Sec. ADELE QUINN; Treas. JAMES NEWELL; publs *Monographs* (irregular), *New Zealand Population Review* (1 a year), *Technical Papers*.

FINE AND PERFORMING ARTS

Creative New Zealand (Arts Council of New Zealand Toi Aotearoa): Old Public Trust Bldg, Level 2, 131–135 Lambton Quay, POB 3806, Wellington 6011; tel. (4) 473-0880; fax (4) 471-2865; e-mail info@creativenz.govt .nz; internet www.creativenz.govt.nz; f. 1994; statutory body formed to encourage and promote the practice and appreciation of the arts; invests in a wide variety of artists and artistic orgs involved with all areas of the arts; brs in Auckland, Christchurch and Wellington; 7 mems; Chair. ALAN SORRELL; Chief Exec. STEPHEN WAINWRIGHT.

New Zealand Maori Arts and Crafts Institute: Te Puia, Hemo Rd, Rotorua; tel. (7) 348-9047; fax (7) 348-9045; e-mail reservations@tepuia.com; internet www .tepuia.com; f. 1963; works towards the promotion, preservation and perpetuation of

Maori arts, crafts and culture; 70 mems; Chief Exec. ANDREW TE WHAITI.

HISTORY, GEOGRAPHY AND ARCHAEOLOGY

New Zealand Archaeological Association (Inc.): POB 6337, Dunedin 9059; tel. (3) 474-7474; fax (3) 477-5993; e-mail publications@nzarchaeology.org; internet www.nzarchaeology.org; f. 1954; supports the archaeological community via its mems, officers and its publs and a regular electronic newsletter; 350 mems; Pres. R. WALTER; Sec. LYNDA WALTER; publs *Archaeology in New Zealand* (4 a year), *Journal of Pacific Archaeology* (2 a year), *Monograph series* (irregular).

New Zealand Cartographic Society (Inc.): ENV, Univ. of Auckland, PMB 92019, Auckland; tel. (9) 373-7599; fax (9) 373-7434; e-mail info@cartography.org.nz; internet www.cartography.org.nz; f. 1971; promotes devt of cartography; Pres. GEOFF AITKEN; Sec. ANTONI MOORE.

New Zealand Geographical Society Inc.: c/o School of Environment, Univ. of Auckland, PMB 92019, Auckland 1142; tel. (9) 373-7599; fax (9) 373-7434; e-mail nzgs@auckland.ac.nz; internet www.nzgs.co.nz; f. 1944; promotes and encourages the study of geography; brs in Auckland, Christchurch, Dunedin, Hamilton, Palmerston N and Wellington; biennial conf.; mem. of the Int. Geographical Union via its membership of The Royal Society of New Zealand; 400 mems. (375 in NZ, 25 overseas); Pres. Prof. JOHN OVERTON; Vice-Pres. ANN POMEROY; Sec. Dr MARIA BOROVNIK; Treas. Dr DAVID HAYWARD; publ. *New Zealand Geographer* (3 a year).

New Zealand Historic Places Trust/Pouhere Taonga: Antrim House, 63 Boulcott St, POB 2629, Wellington 6140; tel. (4) 472-4341; fax (4) 499-0669; e-mail information@historic.org.nz; internet www.historic.org.nz; f. 1955; ind. trust with statutory responsibilities; identifies, investigates, registers and preserves historic places, incl. archaeological sites, traditional sites and old European and Maori heritage; 25,000 nat. mems; Chair. SHONAGH KENDERDINE; Chief Exec. BRUCE CHAPMAN; publ. *Heritage New Zealand* (4 a year).

New Zealand Historical Association: c/o Dept of History, Univ. of Auckland, Private Bag 92019, Auckland; internet www.nzha.org.nz; f. 1979; works with the NZ History Teachers' Asscn; promotes historical study, teaching and research; holds regular nat. and regional conferences; gives financial or other assistance to the publication of historical research in NZ; expresses opinions on issues of public policy which concern historical study, teaching or research; 300 mems; Pres. Dr. CATHARINE COLEBORNE; Sec. Dr JAMES BEATTIE.

LANGUAGE AND LITERATURE

Alliance Française: POB 11141 Manners St, Wellington 6142; The Dominion Bldg Level 3, 78 Victoria St, Wellington 6142; tel. (4) 472-1272; fax (4) 472-2936; e-mail alliance@paradise.net.nz; internet www.french.co.nz; offers courses and exams in French language and culture and promotes cultural exchange with France; centres in Auckland, Christchurch, Dunedin, Hamilton, Nelson, N Shore, Palmerston N, Rotorua, Timaru and Whangerei; library of 7,000 vols, 1,500 books for children, 150 audio books, 880 CDs, 750 DVDs, 15 magazines; Pres. DAN TAIT-JAMIESON; Sec. CHRISTINE REARDON STONYER; Treas. KAREN MORRIS; Administration Man. PETER CRISP.

British Council: POB 91488 AMC, Auckland 1142; 5E Endeans Bldg, 2 Queen St, Auckland; tel. (9) 302-3560; fax (9) 307-3670; e-mail enquiries@britishcouncil.org.nz; internet www.britishcouncil.org.nz; offers courses and exams in English language and British culture and promotes cultural exchange with the UK; attached office in Auckland; Dir INGRID LEARY.

New Zealand Society of Authors (PEN NZ Inc.): POB 7701 Wellesley St, Auckland 1141; Level 4 Duthie Whyte Bldg, 120 Mayoral Dr., Auckland; tel. and fax (9) 356-8332; e-mail nzsa@clear.net.nz; internet www.authors.org.nz; f. 1934; promotes cooperation and support amongst writers; encourages writing in New Zealand and works to protect the interests of writers; awards annual and biannual prizes; has representatives on major literary bodies; 1,450 mems; Pres. TONY SIMPSON; Chief Exec. MAGGIE TARVER; Exec. Dir LIZ ALLEN; publ. *The New Zealand Author* (6 a year).

MEDICINE

Dietitians NZ: POB 5065, Wellington 6145; Level 2 Mibar Bldg, 85 Victoria St, Wellington 6011; tel. (4) 473-3061; e-mail admin@dietitians.org.nz; internet www.dietitians.org.nz; f. 1943; professional asscn of registered dietitians and assoc. nutrition professionals; aims to ensure that mems are recognized as the most credible source of food and nutrition knowledge within New Zealand, and to promote good health through appropriate food and nutrition, using evidence-based scientific research; 550 mems; Pres. CHRISTINE STEWART; CEO PETRINA TURNER-BENNY; publ. *Nutrition & Dietetics* (published jtly with Dietitians Asscn of Australia).

New Zealand Medical Association: POB 156, Wellington 6140; 26 The Terrace, Wellington; tel. (4) 472-4741; fax (4) 471-0838; e-mail nzma@nzma.org.nz; internet www.nzma.org.nz; f. 1886; provides advocacy on behalf of doctors and their patients and provides support and services to mems and their practices; 5,000 mems; Chair. Dr PAUL OCKELFORD; Pres. Dr AINE MCCOY; Chief Exec. CAMERON MCIVER; publ. *New Zealand Medical Journal* (20 a year).

Physiological Society of New Zealand (Inc.): c/o Dept of Physiology, Otago School of Medical Sciences, Univ. of Otago, Private Bag 913, Dunedin; tel. (3) 479-7252; internet www.physoc.org.nz; f. 1972; aims to enhance the quality of physiological and related research, and to establish links with similar research socs throughout the world; 180 mems; Pres. Prof. PETER HUNTER; Sec. Dr KIRK L. HAMILTON; Treas. Assoc. Prof. IAN LEGRICE; publ. *Proceedings* (1 a year).

NATURAL SCIENCES

General

New Zealand Association of Scientists: POB 1874, Wellington 6140; e-mail contact@scientists.org.nz; internet www.scientists.org.nz; f. 1940; promotes and increases public awareness of science; debates scientific issues and influences govt science policy; improves working conditions for scientists and promotes the free exchange of knowledge and int. cooperation; Pres. Dr JAMES RENWICK; Sec. Dr FIONA MCDONALD; publ. *New Zealand Science Review* (4 a year).

Biological Sciences

Entomological Society of New Zealand (Inc.): Bioprotection and Ecology Div., POB 84, Lincoln Univ., Canterbury 7647; tel. (3) 384-0163; e-mail secretary@ento.org.nz; internet ento.org.nz; f. 1951; 250 mems;

Pres. Dr PHIL LESTER; Vice-Pres. Dr LISA BERNDT; Sec. PAULINE SYRETT; Treas. Dr RUDI SCHNITZLER; publ. *New Zealand Entomologist* (1 a year).

New Zealand Ecological Society (Inc.): POB 5075, Christchurch 8542; tel. (3) 318-1056; fax (3) 318-1061; e-mail nzecosoc@paradise.net.nz; internet nzes.org.nz; f. 1951; promotes the study of ecology and the application of ecological knowledge; membership open to any person interested in ecology; holds annual conf.; 600 mems; Pres. MEL GALBRAITH; Vice-Pres. FLEUR MASEYK; Sec. SHONA MYERS; Treas. CLAYSON HOWELL; publ. *New Zealand Journal of Ecology* (2 a year).

New Zealand Freshwater Sciences Society (Inc.): c/o Janine Wech, NIWA, Private Bag 8602, Christchurch; tel. (3) 348-8987; fax (3) 348-5548; internet freshwater.science.org.nz; f. 1968 as New Zealand Limnological Soc., present name 2005; promotes interest in all aspects of fresh and brackish water research in New Zealand; 420 mems; Pres. Prof. DAVID HAMILTON; Sec. and Treas. Dr BRIAN SORRELL; publ. *New Zealand Journal of Marine and Freshwater Research*.

New Zealand Marine Sciences Society: Private Bag 2, Nelson 7042; fax (3) 546-9464; e-mail conference@nzmss.org; internet nzmss.org; f. 1960; concerned with all aspects of marine science in New Zealand; 400 mems, 47 inst. mems; Pres. COLIN MCLAY; Vice-Pres. MARY LIVINGSTON; Sec. HELEN KETTLES; Treas. CHRIS CORNELISEN; publ. *Marine Sciences Review* (1 a year).

New Zealand Microbiological Society (Inc.): Dept of Oral Sciences, Univ. of Otago, POB 647, Dunedin 9001; tel. (3) 479-5471; fax (3) 479-7078; e-mail geoffrey.tompkins@stonebow.otago.ac.nz; internet www.nzms.org.nz; f. 1956; fosters and disseminates knowledge of microbiology in NZ; non-profit org. run by volunteers from all microbiological professions; 422 mems; Pres. Dr ADRIAN COOKSON; Sec. Dr RALPH JACK; Treas. Dr RICHARD MUIRHEAD; publ. *New Zealand Microbiology* (3 a year).

New Zealand Society for Parasitology Inc.: c/o Caroline Costall, Private Bag 11008, Palmerston N 4442; tel. (6) 351-8685; fax (6) 353-7853; e-mail caroline.costall@agresearch.co.nz; internet nzsp.science.org.nz; f. 1972; study of parasites of plants and animals; encourages the dissemination of information and new devt in Parasitology for education and betterment of society; 100 mems; Pres. Dr COLIN MCKAY; Sec. Dr CAROLINE COSTALL; Treas. Dr DEAN REYNECKE; publ. *Proceedings* (1 a year).

New Zealand Society of Plant Biologists: Private Bag 11 600, Palmerston N; tel. (6) 356-8300; fax (7) 573-3871; e-mail secretary@plantbiology.science.org.nz; internet plantbiology.science.org.nz; f. 1974 as New Zealand Society of Plant Physiologists; present name 2006; promotes the teaching and research of plant biology in NZ; encourages exchange of information amongst professional scientists, academics and research students with interests in plant biology; 160 mems; Pres. Dr MIKE CLEARWATER; Vice-Pres. Prof. BRIAN JORDAN; Sec. Dr MARIAN MCKENZIE; Treas. Dr TINA SUMMERFIELD.

Ornithological Society of New Zealand (Inc.): c/o POB 834, Nelson 7040; e-mail secretary@osnz.org.nz; internet www.osnz.org.nz; f. 1939; encourages, organizes and promotes the study of birds and their habitat; 1,000 mems; Pres. DAVID LAWRIE; Exec. Officer INGRID HUTZLER; Sec. PETER GAZE; Treas. PAUL GARNER-RICHARDS; publ. *Notornis* (4 a year).

Mathematical Sciences

New Zealand Mathematical Society: c/o Dept of Maths and Stats, Univ. of Canterbury, Private Bag 4800, Christchurch 8140; e-mail a.james@math.canterbury.ac.nz; internet nzmathsoc.org.nz; f. 1974; 226 mems; Pres. Dr GRAHAM WEIR; Sec. Dr ALEX JAMES; Treas. Dr PETER DONELAN; publ. *NZ Journal of Mathematics* (2 a year).

New Zealand Statistical Association (Inc.): POB 1731, Wellington; internet www.stats.org.nz; f. 1948; works towards making intelligent use of statistical thinking and good statistical practice; 400 mems; Pres. JAMES CURRAN; Sec. BEATRIX JONES; publ. *Australian and New Zealand Journal of Statistics* (published jtly with Statistical Soc. of Australia (Inc.), 4 a year).

Physical Sciences

Geoscience Society of New Zealand: POB 38951, Wellington, Mail Centre 5045; e-mail admin@gsnz.org.nz; internet www.gsnz.org.nz; f. 1955 by merger of New Zealand Geophysical Soc.; encourages the advancement of geological sciences in NZ; confs, lecture series, field trips, br. meetings; 8 brs; 900 mems; Pres. Dr SCOTT NODDER; Vice-Pres. ANDREW GORMAN; Vice-Pres. KATE CLARK; Sec. KAT HOLT; Treas. DAVID SKINNER.

Meteorological Society of New Zealand: POB 6523, Te Aro, Wellington; e-mail info@metsoc.rsnz.org; internet metsoc.rsnz.org; f. 1979; 300 mems; Pres. MIKE REVELL; Sec. SIMON KJELLBERG; publ. *Weather and Climate* (1 a year).

New Zealand Institute of Chemistry (Inc.): c/o Richard Rendle, POB 39-112, Harewood, Christchurch; tel. (3) 359-7275; fax (3) 359-7248; e-mail nzic.office@nzic.org.nz; internet www.nzic.org.nz; f. 1931; promotes the study, practice, teaching and management of chemistry; 6 brs; 1,000 mems; Pres. GORDON REWCASTLE; Hon. Gen. Sec. RICHARD RENDLE; Treas. COLIN FREEMAN; publ. *Chemistry in New Zealand* (4 a year).

New Zealand Institute of Physics: c/o Geoff Willmott, Industrial Research Ltd, POB 31-310, Lower Hutt 5040; tel. (4) 931-3220; fax (4) 931-3117; e-mail secretary@nzip.org.nz; internet www.nzip.org.nz; promotes the study, practice and teaching of physics; 6 brs; 310 mems; Pres. Dr BEN RUCK; Sec. Dr GEOFF WILLMOTT; Treas. Prof. MICHELE GOVERNALE.

New Zealand Society for Biochemistry and Molecular Biology (Inc.): Animal and Food Sciences Div., Lincoln Univ., POB 84, Canterbury; internet nzsbmb.science.org.nz; f. 1972; 400 mems (230 full mems, 170 student mems); Pres. MATT TEMPLETON; Sec. KERRY LOOMES; Treas. WAYNE PATRICK; publ. *NZ BioScience* (4 a year).

Royal Astronomical Society of New Zealand (Inc.): POB 3181, Wellington 6140; e-mail secretary@rasnz.org.nz; internet www.rasnz.org.nz; f. 1920 as New Zealand Astronomical Society, Royal Charter 1946; promotion and extension of knowledge of astronomy and related brs of science; 180 mems; Pres. G. ROWE; Exec. Sec. RORY O'KEEFFE; publ. *Southern Stars* (4 a year).

PHILOSOPHY AND PSYCHOLOGY

New Zealand Psychological Society (Inc.): Level 4 AMP Chambers, 187 Featherston St, POB 4092, Wellington 6140; tel. (4) 473-4884; fax (4) 473-4889; e-mail office@psychology.org.nz; internet www.psychology.org.nz; f. 1967; promotes the discipline of psychology as a science, high standards of ethical and professional practice, and provides professional support and devt to mems; 1,000 full mems, 200 student and subscriber mems; Pres. FRANK O'CONNOR; Exec. Dir Dr PAMELA HYDE; publs *NZ Journal of Psychology* (3 a year, online), *Professional Practice of Psychology in Aotearoa New Zealand*, *Psychology Aotearoa* (2 a year).

RELIGION, SOCIOLOGY AND ANTHROPOLOGY

Polynesian Society: tel. (9) 373-7599; fax (9) 373-5409; e-mail jps@auckland.ac.nz; internet www.arts.auckland.ac.nz/ant/jps/polysoc.html; f. 1892; promotes studies and publs about the Polynesians and other Pacific peoples past and present; library deposited in the Alexander Turnbull Library; 1,000 mems; Pres. JOAN METGE; Sec. and Treas. RANGIMARIE RAWIRI; publs *Journal* (4 a year), *Memoirs* (irregular).

TECHNOLOGY

Institution of Professional Engineers New Zealand: POB 12241, 101 Molesworth St, Wellington 6144; 158 The Terrace, Wellington 6011; tel. (4) 473-9444; fax (4) 474-8933; e-mail ipenz@ipenz.org.nz; internet www.ipenz.org.nz; f. 1914; 12,000 mems; represents professional engineers from all disciplines in NZ; 15 brs; Pres. Dr STEVE REINDLER; Vice-Pres. DERRICK ADAMS; Chief Exec. Dr ANDREW CLELAND; publ. *e.nz* (6 a year).

New Zealand Computer Society (Inc.): POB 10044, Wellington 6143; L24, Grand Plimmer Tower 2, Gilmer Terrace, Wellington 6011; tel. (4) 473-1043; fax (4) 473-1025; e-mail info@nzcs.org.nz; internet www.nzcs.org.nz; f. 1960; develops the professional skills of its mems and promotes excellence in information and communication technology; 5 brs; 1,650 mems; Pres. RAY DELANY; Chief Exec. PAUL MATTHEWS.

New Zealand Hydrological Society: POB 12300, Thorndon, Wellington 6144; tel. (6) 357-1605; e-mail admin@hydrologynz.org.nz; internet www.hydrologynz.org.nz; f. 1961; publishes books; organizes annual conf.; 570 mems.; Pres. JOSEPH THOMAS; Sec. GIL ZEMANSKY; Treas. MIKE EDE; publ. *Journal of Hydrology (New Zealand)* (2 a year).

New Zealand Society for Earthquake Engineering: POB 2193, Wellington 6140; tel. and fax (4) 565-3650; e-mail exec@nzsee.org.nz; internet www.nzsee.org.nz; f. 1968; promotes the advancement of the science and practice of earthquake engineering, and cooperation among scientists, engineers and other professionals in the field; 700 mems; Pres. PETER WOOD; Exec. Officer WIN CLARK.

Operational Research Society of New Zealand (Inc.): POB 6544, Wellesley St, Auckland 1141; internet www.orsnz.org.nz; f. 1964; promotes operational research and management science in New Zealand in both academic and industrial aspects; 150 mems; Pres. ANDREW MASON; Sec. GEOFFREY PRITCHARD; Treas. ANDREA RAITH.

Research Institutes

AGRICULTURE, FISHERIES AND VETERINARY SCIENCE

AgResearch: 5th Fl., Tower Block, Ruakura Research Centre, East St, Private Bag 3123, Hamilton 3240; tel. (7) 834-6600; fax (7) 834-6640; internet www.agresearch.co.nz; f. 1992 as New Zealand Pastoral Agriculture Research Institute Ltd; groups for Agriculture and Environment, Applied Biotechnologies and for Food and Health; Chair. SAM ROBINSON; Chief Exec. Dr TOM RICHARDSON; publs *AgResearch Now* (2 a year), *Science Review*.

New Zealand Institute of Food Science and Technology (Inc.): POB 5574, Terrace End, Palmerston North 4441; Shop 9, Rossmont Shopping Centre, 57 Vogel St, Palmerston North 4414; tel. (6) 356-1686; fax (6) 356-1687; e-mail rosemary@nzifst.org.nz; internet www.nzifst.org.nz; f. 1965; professional body for the food science and technology industry in NZ; divs of dairy, food marketing, food safety, nutrition and sensory evaluation; regular branch meetings, technical sessions and an annual conference; education and vocational guidance for young people; 9 brs; 1,000 student, standard and professional mems; Pres. CATHY MCARDLE; Exec. Man. ROSEMARY HANCOCK; Hon. Treas. DAVID ILLINGWORTH; publ. *Food New Zealand* (6 a year).

Plant & Food Research—New Zealand Institute for Plant & Food Research, Ltd: Private Bag 92169, Auckland Mail Centre, Auckland 1142; 120 Mt Albert Rd, Sandringham, Auckland 1025; tel. (9) 925-7000; fax (9) 925-7001; internet www.plantandfood.co.nz; f. 2008 by merger of HortResearch—Horticulture and Food Research Institute of New Zealand, Ltd (f. 1992) and New Zealand Institute for Crop and Food Research Ltd (f. 1992); integrated fruit research using resources in fruit, plants and sustainable production systems to develop technologies and innovative fruit and food products; library of 16,000 monograph titles, 5,500 periodical titles; Chair. MICHAEL AHIE; Chief Exec. Officer PETER LANDON-LANE.

Scion Research: 9 Sala St, Private Bag 3020, Rotorua 3046; tel. (7) 343-5899; fax (7) 358-0952; e-mail info@scionresearch.com; internet www.scionresearch.com; f. 1947; govt-owned Crown Research Institute providing research and technology devt for the forestry and wood product industries; focuses on the devt of biomaterials from plants; library of 300,000 vols (incl. monographs and periodicals); Chief Exec. Officer Dr WARREN PARKER; Librarian CLAIRE MILLER; publ. *NZ Journal of Forestry Science* (1 a year).

ECONOMICS, LAW AND POLITICS

New Zealand Institute of Economic Research: POB 3479, Wellington 6140; 8 Halswell St, Thorndon, Wellington; tel. (4) 472-1880; fax (4) 472-1211; e-mail econ@nzier.org.nz; internet www.nzier.org.nz; f. 1958; non-profit incorporated soc.; provides economic consultation, forecasting and research in NZ and overseas; Chair. MICHAEL WALLS; Chief Exec. JEAN-PIERRE DE RAAD; Sec. J. MATTHEWSON; Dir BRENT LAYTON; publs *New Zealand Industry and Regions* (1 a year), *Quarterly Predictions* (4 a year), *Quarterly Survey of Business Opinion* (4 a year), *Update* (12 a year).

EDUCATION

New Zealand Council for Educational Research: POB 3237, Wellington 6140; 10th Fl., W Block, Education House, 178–182 Willis St, Wellington; tel. (4) 384-7939; fax (4) 384-7933; internet www.nzcer.org.nz; f. 1934; fosters the study of, and research into, educational matters; prepares and publishes reports for teachers and others in the profession; library of 7,900 vols; Chair. Assoc. Prof. ALISON GILMORE; Board Sec. JOANNE EDGECOMBE; Treas. PETER COOLBEAR; Dir ROBYN BAKER; publs *Curriculum Matters* (1 a year), *New Zealand Annual Review of Education* (2 a year), *New Zealand Journal of Educational Studies* (2 a year), *Set—Research Information for Teachers* (2 a year).

MEDICINE

Auckland Medical Research Foundation: POB 110139, Auckland Hospital, Auckland 1148; Ground Fl., 89 Grafton Rd, Auckland 1010; tel. (9) 923-1701; fax (9) 362-0458; e-mail amrf@medicalresearch.co.nz; internet www.medicalresearch.co.nz; f. 1955; financed by public subscription to sponsor and encourage medical research; Chair. Prof PETER BROWETT; Exec. Dir KIM MCWILLIAMS.

Canterbury Medical Research Foundation: Level 1/230 Antigua St, Christchurch 8011; tel. (3) 353-1240; fax (3) 374-2176; e-mail health@cmrf.org.nz; internet www.cmrf.org.nz; f. 1960; promotion and support of all aspects of medical research; privately financed; Pres. ROBERT STEWART; Treas. GEOFF BOLDERSTON; Exec. Dir GUY JOHNSON.

Hawke's Bay Medical Research Foundation (Inc.): POB 596, Napier; tel. and fax (6) 879-9199; e-mail secretary@hbmrf.org.nz; internet hbmrf.org.nz; f. 1961; works to foster and support medical research and health education in and outside Hawke's Bay; Pres. ANDREW WARES; Sec. J. M. BAXTER.

Health Research Council of New Zealand: POB 5541, Wellesley St, Auckland 1141; Level 3, ProCARE Bldg, 110 Stanley St, Auckland 1010; tel. (9) 303-5200; fax (9) 377-9988; e-mail info@hrc.govt.nz; internet www.hrc.govt.nz; f. 1990; initiates, funds and supports health research; advises the govt on issues of health research ethics; Chair. ROBERT STEWART; Chief. Exec. Dr ROBIN OLDS.

Palmerston North Medical Research Foundation: c/o POB 949, Palmerston North 4440; tel. (6) 357-0640; fax (6) 358-9105; e-mail sb@naylorlawrence.co.nz; internet www.pnmrf.org.nz; f. 1959; privately financed; gen. medical research; Pres. JOHN CHRISP; Vice-Pres. Prof. H. BLAIR; Sec. MICHAEL LAWRENCE.

Wellington Medical Research Foundation: c/o The Secretary, POB 51-211, Wellington; tel. (4) 232-5475; fax (4) 232-5494; e-mail info@wmrf.co.nz; internet www.wmrf.co.nz; f. 1960; privately financed; supports all forms of medical research; Pres. of the Foundation and Chair. of Council I. R. SMALL; Sec. and Treas. K. ROSS MACDONALD.

NATURAL SCIENCES

Biological Sciences

Cawthron Institute: 98 Halifax St E, Private Bag 2, Nelson 7042; tel. (3) 548-2319; fax (3) 546-9464; e-mail info@cawthron.org.nz; internet www.cawthron.org.nz; f. 1919; scientific and technological research into the management and devt of NZ's coastal and freshwater systems; library of 4,500 vols; Chair. IAN KEARNEY; Chief Exec. GILLIAN WRATT; publ. *Cawthron Lectures* (1 a year).

Institute of Environmental Science and Research Ltd (ESR): Kenepuru Science Centre, 34 Kenepuru Dr., POB 50-348, Porirua 5240; tel. (4) 914-0700; fax (4) 914-0770; e-mail enquiries@esr.cri.nz; internet www.esr.cri.nz; f. 1992; provides scientific research and consulting services related to public health, environmental health and forensic science to public and private sectors in New Zealand and the Asia-Pacific region; research centres in Auckland, Wellington and Christchurch; 325 mems; library of 34,000 vols; Chief Exec. GRAHAM SMITH.

Landcare Research New Zealand Ltd: Canterbury Agriculture and Science Centre, Gerald St, POB 40, Lincoln; tel. (3) 325-6700; fax (3) 325-2127; internet www.landcareresearch.co.nz; f. 1992 as a Crown Research Institute; research, consultancy

services and technology devt focused on enhancing natural, productive and urban environments to ensure the future economic prosperity of NZ; other activities incl. environmental sciences, informatics, biosystematics, nationally significant databases and collns, remote-sensing and GIS; specialist library; Chief Exec. Dr RICHARD GORDON.

Physical Sciences

Carter Observatory: POB 2909, Wellington 6140; tel. (4) 910-3140; fax (4) 472-8230; e-mail info@carterobservatory.org; internet www.carterobservatory.org; f. 1941; the nat. observatory; astronomical research and planetarium; nat. centre for receipt and distribution of astronomical information; cooperation with schools, colleges and universities for education in astronomy; library of 20,000 vols, 434 journals; Chair. RICHARD J. BENTLEY; Dir Dr SARAH RUSHOLME; Senior Astronomer BRIAN CARTER.

GNS Science: POB 30-368, Lower Hutt 5040; One Fairway Dr., Avalon, Lower Hutt 5010; tel. (4) 570-1444; fax (4) 570-4600; e-mail webmaster@gns.cri.nz; internet www.gns.cri.nz; f. 1865 as New Zealand Geological Survey; DSIR Geology & Geophysics 1990; Institute of Geological and Nuclear Sciences Ltd 1992; GNS Science 1995; Crown Research Institute; earth and isotope research and consultancy; maintains collns of rocks, minerals and fossils of NZ and other countries, including Suter colln of NZ Mollusca; responsible for nat. geological mapping, geophysics and hazard studies, and all applied geology incl. petroleum exploration, geothermal energy, and groundwater; library of 40,000 vols, 15,000 photos; Chair. TOM CAMPBELL; Chief Exec. Dr ALEX MALAHOFF; Dir IAN GRAHAM; publs *Globe Magazine* (1 a year), *NZ Volcanological Record* (1 a year).

Mount John University Observatory: POB 56, Lake Tekapo 7945; tel. (3) 680-6000; fax (3) 680-6005; e-mail hod-secretary@phys.canterbury.ac.nz; internet www.phys.canterbury.ac.nz/research/mt_john/index.shtml; f. 1963; operated by Univ. of Canterbury; research esp. into variable stars, stellar spectroscopy and gravitational microlensing; 4 research telescopes in total with apertures of 1.8 m, 1.0 m and 2 of 0.6 m; Dir Prof. K. R. POLLARD.

National Institute of Water and Atmospheric Research Ltd–NIWA: Private Bag 99940, 41 Market Pl., Viaduct Harbour, Auckland 1149; tel. (9) 375-2050; fax (9) 375-2051; e-mail enquiries@niwa.co.nz; internet www.niwa.co.nz; f. 1992; manages and makes use of the natural environment in a sustainable manner; Nat. Climate Centre; Nat. Centre for Fisheries and Aquaculture; Nat. Centre for Climate–Energy Solutions; Nat. Centre for Water Resources; Nat. Centre for Aquatic Biodiversity and Biosecurity; Nat. Centre for Coasts and Oceans; Natural Hazards Centre; Chair. CHRIS MACE; Chief Exec. JOHN MORGAN.

New Plymouth Astronomical Society: POB 818, New Plymouth; e-mail nickandviv@gmail.com; f. 1920; Pres. NICK GLADSTONE; Sec. ROBYN CADE; Treas. MICHAEL KRUSE.

TECHNOLOGY

New Zealand Institute for Industrial Research and Development (Industrial Research Ltd): Gracefield Research Centre, 69 Gracefield Rd, POB 31-310, Lower Hutt 5040; tel. (4) 931-3000; fax (4) 566-6004; e-mail info@irl.cri.nz; internet www.irl.cri.nz; f. 1992; Crown Research Institute; conducts research and devt into science and technology, and advises on implementing its

results commercially; Chair. MICHAEL LUDBROOK; Chief Exec. SHAUN COFFEY; Dir JAN EVANS-FREEMAN.

Libraries and Archives

Auckland

Auckland Libraries: POB 92300, Auckland 1142; tel. (9) 301-0101; fax (9) 307-7741; e-mail allison.dobbie@aucklandcouncil.govt.nz; internet www.aucklandlibraries.govt.nz; f. 1880, merger of local authorities in Auckland region 2010; 55 community libraries, 4 mobile libraries, central library; libraries of Auckland, Franklin, Manukau, North Shore, Papakura, Rodney, Waitakere; 3,487,691 vols (incl. books, lending magazines, reference serials, UN and FAO depository colln, music sound recordings, DVD and video cassettes), 133 online databases; spec. collns incl. founding donation from Sir George Grey, medieval MSS, incunabula, early printed books, maps, sheet music, photographs, early Maori MSS and printed works; Man. ALLISON DOBBIE.

University of Auckland Library: Private Bag 92019, Auckland Mail Centre, Auckland 1142; tel. (9) 373-7599; fax (9) 373-7565; e-mail lending.library@auckland.ac.nz; internet www.library.auckland.ac.nz; f. 1884; 2m. print vols; consists of a General Library, 9 divisional libraries and 12 subject specialist libraries, 3 Information Commons facilities; Univ. Librarian JANET COPSEY.

Christchurch

Christchurch City Libraries: POB 1466, Christchurch 8140; tel. (3) 941-7923; fax (3) 941-7075; e-mail library@ccc.govt.nz; internet christchurchcitylibraries.com; f. 1859; 19 libraries, one mobile library and a digital library; 1,105,903 vols, incl. 360,000 vols; Library Man. CAROLYN ROBERTSON; Librarian for Serials and Preservation COLLEEN FINNERTY.

Library, Teaching and Learning George Forbes Memorial Library Lincoln University: POB 64, Lincoln Univ., Lincoln, Canterbury 7647; tel. (3) 321-8530; fax (3) 325-2944; e-mail libser@lincoln.ac.nz; internet library.lincoln.ac.nz; f. 1960; specializes in agriculture, commerce and management, primary production, science and engineering, social sciences incl. landscape architecture, and tourism, environment and natural resource management; 229,657 vols, 114,504 books, 1,357 current print periodicals, 53,336 electronic periodicals; Univ. Librarian Prof. PENNY CARNABY; publ. *Lincoln University Research Archive*.

University of Canterbury Library: Private Bag 4800, Christchurch; Warehouse, 20 Kirkwood Ave, Ilam, Christchurch 8041; tel. (3) 366-7001; fax (3) 364-2055; e-mail helpdesk@libr.canterbury.ac.nz; internet library.canterbury.ac.nz; f. 1879; colln. distributed across 5 libraries; 1,800,000 items; spec. collns incl. Macmillan Brown Colln of New Zealand and Pacific Materials; 1,831,995 vols; Assoc. Univ. Librarian H. JENKS.

Dunedin

Dunedin Public Libraries: 230 Moray Pl., Dunedin 9016, POB 5542, Dunedin 9058; tel. (3) 474-3690; fax (3) 474-3660; e-mail library@dcc.govt.nz; internet www.dunedinlibraries.govt.nz; f. 1908; network of five libraries and two bookbuses; 709,992 vols, 30,000 books and 15,000 magazines; heritage collns incl. McNab New Zealand colln (90,509 vols) and numerous spec. collns, incl. illuminated MSS and Bibles, Samuel

Johnson, Sir Walter Scott, Charles Dickens, Walt Whitman, Farjeon, hymn books, autographed letters; Library Services Man. BERNIE HAWKE.

New Zealand Law Society Library, Otago Branch: Level 2 Mooney's Bldg, 28 Lower Stuart St, Private Bag 1901, Dunedin; tel. (3) 477-0596; fax (3) 474-1886; e-mail otago@nzlslibrary.org.nz; internet www .lawsociety.org.nz/home/for_lawyers/law_library; f. 1859; private library for use by mems and assoc. mems of the New Zealand Law Soc., the Judiciary and the Ministry of Justice Court staff; 13,500 vols, consisting of statutes, regulations, law reports, unreported judgments, treaties; and a rep. selection of New Zealand secondary sources (textbooks, law journals, dictionaries and encyclopedias); Library Asst NICOLA STEDMAN.

University of Otago Library: POB 56, Dunedin 9054; tel. (3) 479-8910; fax (3) 479-8947; e-mail ask.library@otago.ac.nz; internet www.library.otago.ac.nz; f. 1869; consists of several libraries: Central (arts, commerce, humanities, social sciences,), Dental, Education, Hocken, Law, Medical, Science (major NZ and Pacific research collns incl. archives, pictorial collns, exhibition gallery); special collns incl. early European imprints, de Beer Exhibition Gallery and Otakou Press; 1,109,344 vols, 536,242 serials, 6,030 titles, 229,336 e-titles; Univ. Librarian HOWARD AMOS.

Hamilton

University of Waikato Library: Private Bag 3105, Hamilton 3240; The Univ. of Waikato, 21 Ruakura Rd, Hamilton 3240; tel. (7) 838-4111; fax (7) 838-4017; e-mail library@waikato.ac.nz; internet www .waikato.ac.nz/library; f. 1964; incorporates Central, Education, Law libraries and New Zealand colln; 1,065,957 vols, 2,092 print serial titles and 187,870 electronic resources; Univ. Librarian ROSS HALLETT.

Palmerston North

Palmerston North City Library: Private Bag 1948, Palmerston North 4440; tel. (6) 351-4100; fax (6) 351-4102; e-mail pncl@pncc .govt.nz; internet citylibrary.pncc.govt.nz; f. 1876; lending, reference, children's, audiovisual, archives sections; 4 brs; 1 mobile library; 250,000 vols; Library Man. ANTHONY LEWIS.

Tauranga

Tauranga City Libraries: Private Bag 12022, Tauranga 3110; Library Arcade, Cnr Wharf and Willow St, Tauranga; tel. (7) 577-7177; fax (7) 578-6787; e-mail library@ tauranga.govt.nz; internet library.tauranga .govt.nz; f. 1906 from Mechanics Institute (f. 1871); information, New Zealand and local history collns; 4 brs and 1 mobile; 325,000 vols; Man. for Libraries JILL BEST.

Wellington

Archives New Zealand: POB 12-050, Wellington; 10 Mulgrave St, Thorndon, Wellington 6011; tel. (4) 499-5595; fax (4) 495-6210; e-mail written.reference@dia.govt.nz; internet www.archives.govt.nz; f. 1926; attached to Dept of Internal Affairs; gathers, stores and protects a wide range of materials; Nat. War Art Colln; Treaty of Waitangi; public reference services in Wellington and at regional offices in Auckland, Christchurch and Dunedin; gateway at Wellington office; 102,000 linear m of archives, 1,579,000 photographs, 42,603 films and video cassettes, 540,000 maps and plans; 6,000,000 legislative, exec. and judicial records of New Zealand govt incl. provincial govts; minister-

ial papers; public reference services in Wellington and at regional offices in Auckland, Christchurch and Dunedin; Chief Archivist and Gen. Man. GREG GOULDING.

Museum of New Zealand, Te Papa Tongarewa, Te Aka Matua Research Library: Cable St, Wellington; tel. (4) 381-7000; fax (4) 381-7370; e-mail library@tepapa .govt.nz; internet www.tepapa.govt.nz/ researchattepapa/libraryandinfocentre/; f. 1867; 150,000 vols; Knowledge Man. SHARMAN BUCKLE.

National Library of New Zealand/Te Puna Matauranga o Aotearoa: POB 1467, Wellington 6140; tel. (4) 474-3000; fax (4) 474-3035; e-mail information@dia.govt .nz; internet www.natlib.govt.nz; f. 1965; Wellington bldg closed for redevelopment due to 2010 earthquakes; selected collns relocated at 77 Thorndon Quay, Wellington and at Archives New Zealand; other collns closed until the Wellington bldg reopens in 2012; receives all New Zealand publs (conventional and electronic) on legal deposit; collns of New Zealand MSS, sound recordings, music, prints, paintings, drawings and ephemera; oral history and the works of John Milton; 940,863 vols, 10,466 current print periodical titles, 12 main microform collns, 16,812 audio titles in the gen. collns, 778 e-books, 35 databases, 33,418 e-journals, 593,249 items in the schools collns; Nat. Librarian BILL MACNAUGHT.

Constituent Library:

Alexander Turnbull Library: POB 12-349, Wellington 6144; tel. (4) 474-3120; fax (4) 474-3063; e-mail alexander .turnbull-library@dia.govt.nz; internet www.natlib.govt.nz/atl; f. 1920; spec. collns incl. New Zealand and the Pacific, Milton, Katherine Mansfield; 30,000 oral history audio cassettes; 10,000 linear m of MSS; 105,000 drawings, paintings, prints and cartoons; 4,964,446 photographic prints, negatives and albums; 60,000 maps; 50,000 sound recordings; 7,000 video cassettes; 1,100 computer files; 195,000 items of ephemera (incl. 19,500 posters); 458,000 newspaper issues; 1,216,000 vols of periodicals; 3,740 music scores; 30,000 online publs; 3,500 websites; 387,500 vols, incl. 32,000 rare books, chiefly in English literature; Chief Librarian CHRIS SZEKELY; publs *Off the Record* (1 a year), *Turnbull Library Record* (1 a year).

Parliamentary Library: PMB 18041, Parliament Bldgs, Wellington 6160; tel. (4) 817-9999; fax (4) 471-2551; e-mail parlinfo@ parliament.govt.nz; internet www .parliament.nz; f. 1858; research, reference and information services for mems of parliament and parliamentary staff; services to the public incl. Parliamentary Information Service and Int. Documents Service; 500,000 vols, spec. collns: New Zealand, incl. official publs, overseas official and parliamentary publs; Parliamentary Librarian and Group Man., Information and Knowledge BARBARA MCPHEE (acting); publs *Bills Digests* (irregular, online), *Electorate Profiles* (online), *Research Papers* (irregular, online), *Monthly Economic Review* (12 a year, online).

Victoria University of Wellington Library: POB 3438, Wellington; tel. (4) 463-5249; fax (4) 471-2070; e-mail library@ vuw.ac.nz; internet library.victoria.ac.nz/ library; f. 1899; 5 libraries serving all of the university's campuses; Architecture and Design Library, Central Library, Commerce Library, Law Library, W. J. Scott Education Library; 1.3m. vols and 70,000 print and electronic periodical titles; Univ. Librarian SUE ROBERTS.

Wellington City Libraries: POB 1992, Wellington 6140; 65 Victoria St, Wellington 6011; tel. (4) 801-4040; fax (4) 801-4047; e-mail enquiries@wcl.govt.nz; internet www .wcl.govt.nz; f. 1893; 11 br. libraries, 1 central library; 625,000 vols, 200,000 magazines, 96,000 audiovisual items; Man. for Libraries JANE HILL.

Museums and Art Galleries

Auckland

Auckland Art Gallery Toi o Tāmaki: POB 5449, Wellesley St, Auckland 1141; Corner of Kitchener and Wellesley St, Auckland 1010; tel. (9) 379-1349; fax (9) 302-1096; internet www.aucklandartgallery.com; f. 1888; 15,000 works; European paintings since 12th century, sculpture, prints and drawings, Frances Hodgkins colln, Colin McCahon colln, Fuseli drawings, New Zealand painting since 19th century, sculpture and prints; photographs and artists' books, audio- and video-tapes; John Weeks archive; library: research library of 33,000 vols; Dir CHRIS SAINES.

Auckland War Memorial Museum: Private Bag 92018, Victoria St W, Auckland 1142; The Auckland Domain Parnell, Auckland; tel. (9) 306-7076; fax (9) 379-9956; e-mail info@aucklandmuseum.com; internet www.aucklandmuseum.com; f. 1852; natural history, ethnology (especially NZ Maori and Oceanic), applied arts (especially Asian, European and NZ ceramics, English furniture, textiles), soc. and war history; conservation laboratory; war memorial for the province; library of 100,000 vols; Dir ROY CLARE; Library Services Man. BRUCE RALSTON; publ. *Records* (1 a year).

Museum of Transport and Technology (MOTAT): POB 44-114, Point Chevalier, Auckland 1246; Great North Rd and Meola Rd, Western Springs, Auckland 1022; tel. (9) 815-5800; fax (9) 846-4242; e-mail enquiries@ motat.org.nz; internet www.motat.org.nz; f. 1964; operates on 2 sites, exhibiting vehicles, aircraft, machinery and equipment of historical and technical interest, incl. an extensive aircraft colln, vintage agricultural and military vehicles, steam and diesel engines, a working tram line and travelling exhibitions; library: Walsh Memorial Library 12,000 vols, 1,500 serial titles, technical manuals, photographs, maps, plans, archives, Whites Aviation Photographic prints, archives relating to pioneer aviators Jean Batten and Richard Pearse, Les Downey rail photograph colln, Air New Zealand, TEAL, Nat. Airways Corpn and New Zealand Flying School Archives; Dir JEREMY HUBBARD.

Christchurch

Canterbury Museum: Rolleston Ave, Christchurch 8013; tel. (3) 366-5000; fax (3) 366-5622; e-mail info@canterburymuseum .com; internet www.canterburymuseum .com; f. 1867; cultural and natural history of the Canterbury region, in NZ and global contexts; Antarctic age of discovery and exploration; archaeology, ethnology, geology, zoology, extinct bird studies; Asian and European arts; Canterbury archives; pictorial history; research library; spec. research library on the Antarctic; Dir ANTHONY E. WRIGHT; publ. *Records of the Canterbury Museum* (1 a year).

Christchurch Art Gallery/Te Puna o Waiwhetu: Worcester Blvd, Christchurch 8001; tel. (3) 941-7300; fax (3) 941-7301; e-mail info@christchurchartgallery.org.nz;

internet christchurchartgallery.org.nz; f. 1932, as Robert McDougall Art Gallery and McDougall Contemporary Art Annex, present name and location 2003; one of the largest art collns in New Zealand; nat. and int. touring exhibitions; works by local artists; Dir JENNY HARPER; publ. *Bulletin* (4 a year).

Dunedin

Dunedin Public Art Gallery: 30 The Octagon, POB 566, Dunedin; tel. (3) 477-4000; fax (3) 474-3250; e-mail dpagmail@dcc.govt.nz; internet www.dunedin.art.museum; f. 1884; maintains a conservation laboratory; holdings incl.: 14th–19th century European paintings, NZ paintings from 1870, Australian paintings 1900–70, British watercolours, portraits and landscapes; Japanese prints since the 18th century, NZ prints since the 19th century; old and modern masters, incl. oils by Claude Lorrain and Monet; decorative arts collns of furniture, ceramics, glass, oriental rugs, gallery dedicated to works of painter Frances Hodgkins; Dir PRISCILLA PITTS.

Otago Museum: POB 6202, Dunedin 9059; 419 Great King St, Dunedin; tel. (3) 474-7474; fax (3) 477-5993; e-mail mail@otagomuseum.govt.nz; internet www.otagomuseum.govt.nz; f. 1868; colln of over 2m. natural science specimens and human history artefacts; NZ and Pacific anthropology, classical archaeology, European and Asian ceramics, 'Discovery World' Science Centre, NZ crafts, southern geology and fossils; Chief Exec. SHIMRATH PAUL.

Theomin Gallery, Dunedin: 'Olveston', 42 Royal Terrace, Dunedin; tel. (3) 477-3320; fax (3) 479-2094; e-mail olveston@xtra.co.nz; internet www.olveston.co.nz; built 1904–06; Jacobean-style house designed by British architect Sir Ernest George for David Edward Theomin; bequeathed to the city by his daughter, Dorothy, 1966; opened to the public 1967; antique furniture, ceramics, crystal, bronzes, Persian rugs, silver, early English, European and NZ oils and watercolours; Man. GRANT BARRON.

Gisborne

Tairawhiti Museum: POB 716, Gisborne; Kelvin Rise, Stout St, Gisborne; tel. (6) 867-3832; fax (6) 867-2728; e-mail info@tairawhitimuseum.org.nz; internet www.tairawhitimuseum.org.nz; f. 1954; soc. history, Maori treasures (taonga Maori), fine arts, photography, surfboards, 'Star of Canada' wreck colln, natural history, oral history archive, textiles; local archives, cards and postcards, maps, plans, theatrical programmes; temporary exhibitions of fine arts and crafts, C-Co 12th Maori Battalion; Board Chair. API MAHUIKA; Treas. ALLAN DE LAUTOUR; Dir Dr DAVID BUTTS.

Gore

Eastern Southland Gallery (Inc.): Cnr Main and Norfolk St, POB 305, Gore; tel. (3) 208-9907; fax (3) 208-1210; e-mail jgeddes@goredc.govt.nz; f. 1983; exhibitions: art works, craft work, historical displays; cultural centre for presentation of films, lectures, music, poetry, etc.; Dir JIM GEDDES.

Hokitika

West Coast Historical Museum: 17 Hamilton St, POB 171, Hokitika 7842; tel. (3) 755-6898; fax (3) 755-5011; e-mail enquiries@hokitikamuseum.co.nz; internet www.hokitikamuseum.co.nz; soc. exhibits, working models; audiovisual programme on 19th-century W Coast goldmining industry and colonial settlement; Poutini Maori and 19th-century immigrant histories; pounamu (NZ greenstone), gold; maintains research centre with local history archives and large photograph colln; Curator JULIA BRADSHAW.

Invercargill

Anderson Park Art Gallery (Inc.): POB 5095, Invercargill 9843; tel. (3) 215-7432; fax (3) 215-7472; e-mail andersonparkgallery@xtra.co.nz; f. 1951; mainly New Zealand works; Dir JOHN HUSBAND; Deputy Dir HELEN NICOLL.

Southland Museum and Art Gallery: POB 1012, Invercargill; Queens Park, 108 Gala St, Invercargill; tel. (3) 219-9069; fax (3) 218-3872; e-mail office@southlandmuseum.co.nz; internet www.southlandmuseum.com; f. 1915; natural history; Maori and colonial history; 'Victoriana'; 4 art galleries; astronomical observatory; Tuatara breeding colony; sub-Antarctic centre; education programmes; Man. GAEL RAMSAY.

Napier

Hawke's Bay Cultural Trust: POB 248, Napier; tel. (6) 835-7781; fax (6) 835-9249; e-mail info@hbmag.co.nz; f. 1989; Man. DOUGLAS LLOYD JENKINS.

Institutions Under the Trust's Control:

Faraday Centre: POB 7021, Napier; 1 Faraday St, Napier; tel. (6) 835-2338; fax (6) 835-9249; e-mail faraday@hbct.co.nz; internet www.faraday.hbmag.co.nz; f. 1979; science and technology education (stationary, hot-air and steam engines; steam traction engines, horse-drawn phaeton and hearse, bath-chairs; audio recording and broadcasting equipment; printing presses; early hospital and surgical equipment; high voltage displays, Wimshurst machine, Tesla coil); workshops for young people; Man. DAVID PREBENSEN.

Hawke's Bay Museum and Art Gallery: 65 Marine Parade, 9 Herschell St, POB 248, Napier; tel. (6) 835-7781; fax (6) 835-9249; e-mail info@hbmag.co.nz; internet www.hbmag.co.nz; f. 1936; Hawke's Bay Museum and Art Gallery is now closed in order to undertake a redevt project; Maori and NZ art and material culture, painting, pottery and sculpture, decorative arts, 1931 earthquake and dinosaur exhibitions; regional archives; library; Dir DOUGLAS LLOYD JENKINS.

Nelson

Nelson Provincial Museum: Town Acre 445, POB 853, Nelson; tel. (3) 548-9588; fax (3) 548-9589; e-mail enquiries@museumnp.org.nz; internet www.nelsonmuseum.org.nz; f. 1841; Maori and European history; reference library, 1,200,000 photographs (since 1860s), archives (since 1840s).

The Suter Art Gallery/Te Aratoi o Whakatu: 208 Bridge St, POB 751, Nelson 7040; tel. (3) 548-4699; fax (3) 548-1236; e-mail info@thesuter.org.nz; internet www.thesuter.org.nz; f. 1895; not-for-profit community org.; local and int. art works; early New Zealand watercolours; programme of exhibitions, events, performances and films; Dir JULIE CATCHPOLE (acting); publ. *The Suter Programme* (4 a year).

Oamaru

Forrester Gallery: Waitaki Dist. Council, Private Bag 50058, Oamaru 9444; Nine Thames St, Oamaru; tel. (3) 433-0853; fax (3) 434-1654; e-mail info@forrestergallery.com; internet www.forrestergallery.com; f. 1983; housed in a neo-classical bldg constructed in 1884; works of art and architectural drawings related to North Otago and New Zealand; programme of exhibitions and cultural events; Dir WARWICK SMITH; Curator ALICE LAKE-HAMMOND.

Paihia

Waitangi Treaty Grounds: Waitangi Nat. Trust, POB 48, Paihia 0247; 26 Tau Henare Dr., Paihia 0200; tel. (9) 402-7437; fax (9) 402-8303; e-mail waitangiestate@waitangi.net.nz; internet www.waitangi.net.nz; f. 1932; historic Treaty House; carved Maori meeting house and war canoe; exhibits of NZ historical interest up to 1840; visitor centre complex and audiovisual programme on signing of Treaty of Waitangi between Maori Chiefs and British Crown on 6 February 1840; live Maori theatre and spec. education programmes; Deputy Chief Exec. ANDY LARSEN.

Timaru

Aigantighe Art Gallery: 49 Wai-iti Rd, Timaru 7910; tel. (3) 688-4424; internet www.timaru.govt.nz/art-gallery; f. 1956; New Zealand and European paintings, prints, sculpture and ceramics; Dir FIONA CIARAN.

Wanganui

Sarjeant Gallery: Queen's Park, POB 998, Wanganui 4540; tel. (6) 349-0506; fax (6) 349-0507; e-mail info@sarjeant.org.nz; internet www.sarjeant.org.nz; f. 1919; 5,500 art-works; 16th-century European art through to 21st-century NZ Art; collns incl. works in all media; historic and modern works on paper; NZ and int. sculptures, pottery, ceramics and glass; bronze works; video art and paintings by contemporary artists and old masters; photography exhibitions; Curator and Public Programmes Man. GREG DONSON.

Whanganui Regional Museum: POB 352, Watt St, Wanganui; tel. (6) 349-1110; fax (6) 347-6512; e-mail info@museum.queenspark.org.nz; f. 1895; Taonga Maori, natural history, local social history; archives; Dir S. E. DELL.

Wellington

New Zealand Academy of Fine Arts: 1 Queens Wharf, Wellington; tel. (4) 499-8807; fax (4) 499-2612; e-mail info@nzafa.com; internet www.nzafa.com; f. 1882; art gallery promoting NZ artists and the visual arts in NZ through 8 annual exhibitions; Pres. IAN HAMLIN; Sec. CARLA WILD; Treas. KELVIN WONG; Dir JUSTIN MORGAN.

Te Papa: Cable St, POB 467, Wellington 6011; tel. (4) 381-7000; fax (4) 381-7070; e-mail mail@tepapa.govt.nz; internet www.tepapa.govt.nz; f. 1992 as the Museum of New Zealand Te Papa Tongarewa Act; museum opened 1998; art, history, Maori culture, natural environment; colln of Maori taonga, incl. Te Hau-ki-Turanga (oldest extant Maori building in NZ); Polynesian, Micronesian and Melanesian art and culture; paintings, drawings, graphic art, photography and sculpture by NZ and foreign artists; collns of works by Natalia Gontcharova, Frances Hodgkins, Raymond McIntyre and Colin McCahon; maintains Hector Library (systematic biology, ethnology, early European South Pacific exploration and art reference material); Chief Exec. MICHAEL HOULIHAN.

Universities

AUCKLAND UNIVERSITY OF TECHNOLOGY

Private Bag, 92006, Auckland 1142
Telephone: (9) 921-9999

Fax: (9) 921-9812
Internet: www.aut.ac.nz
Founded 1895 as Auckland Technical School,
became Seddon Memorial Technical Col-
lege 1913, Auckland Technical Institute
1960, Auckland Institute of Technology
1989, present name 2000
State control
Language of instruction: English
Academic year: January to December
Chancellor: (vacant)
Vice-Chancellor: Dr DEREK MCCORMACK
Deputy Vice-Chancellor: Dr ROBERT ALLEN
Pro-Vice-Chancellor for Int. Relations: Prof
NIGEL HEMMINGTON
Pro-Vice-Chancellor for Research: Prof.
RICHARD BEDFORD
Pro-Vice-Chancellor for Learning and Teach-
ing and Pro-Vice-Chancellor for Maori
Advancement: Prof. PARE KEIHA
Pro-Vice-Chancellor for North Shore: Prof.
MAX ABBOTT
Pro-Vice-Chancellor: Prof. PHILIP SALLIS
Pro-Vice-Chancellor: Prof. IAN SHIRLEY
Gen. Counsel: Dr ANDREA VUJNOVICH
Univ. Librarian: Dr LARRAINE SHEPHERD
Library of 234,125 vols
Number of teachers: 1,001 f.t.e.
Number of students: 26,243

DEANS

Faculty of Applied Humanities: Prof. NIGEL
HEMMINGTON
Faculty of Business and Law: Dr GEOFF
PERRY
Faculty of Culture and Society: Prof. NIGEL
HEMMINGTON
Faculty of Design and Creative Technologies:
DESNA JURY
Faculty of Health and Environmental Sci-
ences: Prof. MAX ABBOTT
Faculty of Science and Engineering: Prof.
ROY GEDDES
Te Ara Poutama (Faculty of Maori Develop-
ment: Assoc. Prof. PARE KEIHA

LINCOLN UNIVERSITY

POB 84, Lincoln Univ., Christchurch 7647
Ellesmere Junction Rd, Springs Rd, Lincoln,
Canterbury
Telephone: (3) 325-2811
Fax: (3) 325 3850
E-mail: info@lincoln.ac.nz
Internet: www.lincoln.ac.nz
Founded 1878, fmrly the Canterbury Agri-
cultural College and from 1961 to 1989
Lincoln College, a constituent college of the
Univ. of Canterbury, from 1990 an autono-
mous univ.
State control
Academic year: February to October
Chancellor: THOMAS LAMBIC
Vice-Chancellor: Prof. ROGER FIELD
Deputy Vice-Chancellor: Dr CHRIS KIRK
Librarian: PENNY CARNABY
Library: see under Libraries and Archives
Number of teachers: 219
Number of students: 3,323
Publications: Infolinc (12 a year), Landforms
(1 a year)

DEANS

Faculty of Agriculture and Life Sciences:
Prof. BRUCE MCKENZIE
Faculty of Commerce: Dr PATRICK ALDWELL
Faculty of Environment, Society and Design:
Dr GREG RYAN

PROFESSORS

BOND, S., Property Studies
CONDRON, L., Biochemistry
CULLEN, R., Resource Economics
DI, H., Soil And Environmental Science

EASON, C., Wildlife Management
EDWARDS, G., Dairy Production
FALLOON, R., Plant And Food
HUGHLEY, K., Environmental Management
LIYANARACHICHI, G., Accounting
MATEAR, S., Marketing
MATUNGA, H., Maori Studies
MCKENZIE, B., Agronomy
MOOT, J., Crop And Pasture Physiology
PALMER, D., Biochemical Pathology
PERKINS, H., Human Geography
SAUNDERS, C., Economics
SMALLMAN, C., Business Management

MASSEY UNIVERSITY

Private Bag 11-222, Palmerston North 4442
Tennent Dr., Palmerston North 4474
Telephone: (6) 356-9099
Fax: (6) 350-2263
E-mail: contact@massey.ac.nz
Internet: www.massey.ac.nz
Founded 1926 as Massey Agricultural Col-
lege and merged with the Palmerston N
Branch of the Victoria Univ. of Wellington
1963; full autonomy granted 1964;
absorbed Wellington Polytechnic 1998
State control
Academic year: February to November
Chancellor: Dr RUSSELL BALLARD
Pro-Chancellor: Dr ALISON PATERSON
Vice-Chancellor: Prof. STEVE MAHAREY
Deputy Vice-Chancellor for Academic
Affairs: Prof. MASON DURIE
Deputy Vice-Chancellor for Research and
External Relations: Prof. NIGEL LONG
Univ. Registrar: S. D. MORRISS
Librarian: JOHN REDMAYNE
Number of teachers: 1,255
Number of students: 39,657

PROFESSORS

ANDERSON, R. D., Sciences
BAILEY, W. C., Food Nutrition and Human
Health
BARRY, T., Veterinary, Animal and Biomedi-
cal Sciences
BIRKBECK, J., Food Nutrition and Human
Health
BLAIR, H. T., Veterinary, Animal and Biome-
dical Sciences
BODDY, J., Health Sciences
BRIGHT, G., Mechatronics
BRODIE, A. M., Fundamental Sciences
BROWN, I., History
CAHAN, S. F., Accountancy
CARRYER, J. B., Health Sciences
CHAMBERLAIN, K. P., Psychology
CHAPMAN, J. W., Learning and Teaching
CHATTERJEE, S., Applied and International
Economics
CHETTY, S., Commerce
CHISTI, Y., Biotechnology
CLELAND, D. J., Technology and Engineering
CODD, J. A., Social and Policy Studies in
Education
CORBALLIS, R. P., English and Media Studies
CRESSWELL, M. J., History, Philosophy and
Politics
CROPP, G. M., Language Studies
CULLEN, J. L., Learning and Teaching
DAVIES, C., Particle Technology
DE BRUIN, A., Commerce
DEVLIN, M., Management
DURIE, M. H., Maori Studies
ENGELBRECHT, H.-J., Applied and Inter-
national Economics
EVANS, I., Psychology
FIRTH, E. C., Veterinary, Animal and Biome-
dical Sciences
FLENLEY, J. R., People, Environment and
Planning
FREYBURG, C., Information Systems
GARRICK, D. J., Veterinary, Animal and
Biomedical Sciences

GENDALL, P. J., Marketing
GILL, H. S., Food, Nutrition and Animal
Health
GUILFORD, W. G., Veterinary, Animal and
Biomedical Sciences
HARGREAVES, R. V., Finance, Banking and
Property Studies
HARKER, R. K., Education
HAWICK, K., Computer Science
HENDY, M. D., Mathematics
HERMANSSON, G. L., Health and Human
Development
HEWETT, E. W., Food, Nutrition and Human
Health
HODGSON, J., Natural Resources
HODGSON, R. M., Information Sciences and
Technology
HOLMES, C. W., Veterinary, Animal and
Biomedical Sciences
HOWE, K. R., History, Philosophy and Politics
HUNT, G. J., Aviation
HUNTER, J. J., Information and Mathematical
Sciences
INKSON, J. H., Management and Inter-
national Business
INKSON, K., Management and International
Business
JAMESON, P., Plant Biology
LAGROW, S. J., Health Sciences
LAMBERT, D. M., Molecular Biosciences
LASWAD, F., Accountancy
LEATHERN, J., Neuropsychology
LOCK, A. J., Psychology
LONG, N., Psychology
MACDONALD, B. K., Humanities and Social
Sciences
MCKIBBIN, R., Information and Mathematical
Sciences
MCLACHLAN, R., Mathematics
MADDOX, I., Industrial Bioscience
MALLON, M., Human Resource Management
MEISTER, A. D., Applied and International
Economics
MELLOR, D. J., Food, Nutrition and Human
Health
MERRICK, P. L., Psychology
MILNE, K. S., Sciences
MOORE, C. I., Finance, Banking and Property
Studies
MORGAN, S., Fine Arts
MORRIS, R. S., Veterinary, Animal and Bio-
medical Sciences
MOUGHAN, P. J., Food, Nutrition and Human
Health
MUNFORD, R. E., Sociology, Social Policy and
Social Work
MURPHY, B., Commerce
NASH, R., Social and Policy Studies in Edu-
cation
OFFICER, D., Chemistry
ONO, K., Language Studies
OPENSHAW, R., Social and Policy Studies in
Education
OVERTON, J. D., People, Environment and
Planning
PARRY, D. A., Fundamental Sciences
PEARCE, N. E., Public Health Research
PENNY, E. D., Molecular Biosciences
PERERA, H. M. B., Accountancy
RAE, A. N., Applied and International Eco-
nomics
REEVES, R., Chemistry
ROCHE, M., Health Sciences
ROSE, L. C., Commerce
SCHEWE, K.-D., Information Systems
SCOTT, D. B., Molecular Biosciences
SHOUKSMITH, G., Psychology
SIGNAL, A., Physics
SINGH, H., Food, Nutrition and Human
Health
SISSONS, J. D., People, Environment and
Planning
SPOONLEY, P., Social and Cultural Studies
SPRINGETT, B. P., Natural Resources
STABLEIN, R., Management
SULLIVAN, P. A., Molecular Biosciences

TENNANT, M., Health Sciences
THOMSON, D. W., History, Philosophy and Politics
TILLMAN, R. W., Natural Resources
TRAWICK, M. J., People, Environment and Planning
TUNMER, W. E., Learning and Teaching
VAN DER WALT, N. T., Management and International Business
VITALIS, T., Management
WATERS, J., Chemistry
WILLIAMSON, N. B., Veterinary, Animal and Biomedical Sciences
WINGER, R. J., Food, Nutrition and Human Health

UNIVERSITY OF AUCKLAND

PMB 92019, Auckland 1142

Telephone: (9) 373-7999
Fax: (9) 373-7400
E-mail: studentinfo@auckland.ac.nz
Internet: www.auckland.ac.nz

Founded 1883 as Auckland Univ. College; univ. status 1962
Academic year: January to November

Chancellor: ROGER FRANCE
Pro-Chancellor for Equal Opportunities: TRUDIE MCNAUGHTON
Pro-Vice-Chancellor for Māori: JIM PETERS
Vice-Chancellor: Prof. STUART MCCUTCHEON
Deputy Vice-Chancellor for Academic Affairs: Prof. JOHN MORROW
Deputy Vice-Chancellor for Research: Prof. JANE HARDING
Deputy Vice-Chancellor for Strategic Engagement: Prof. IAIN MARTIN
Registrar: TIM GREVILLE
Dir of Admin.: ADRIENNE CLELAND
Library: see under Libraries and Archives
Number of teachers: 1,981 (full-time)
Number of students: 38,551

Publication: *University of Auckland Research Report* (1 a year)

DEANS

Business School: Prof. GREG WHITTRED
Faculty of Arts: Assoc. Prof. JAN CROSTHWAITE
Faculty of Education: Assoc. Prof. GRAEME AITKEN
Faculty of Engineering: Prof. MICHAEL DAVIES
Faculty of Law: Dr ANDREW STOCKLEY
Faculty of Medical and Health Sciences: Prof. JOHN FRASER
Faculty of Science: Prof. GRANT GUILFORD
Nat. Institute of Creative Arts and Industries: Prof. JENNY DIXON

PROFESSORS

ADAMS, P., Applied Behavioural Science
ANAE, M., Pacific Studies
ANDERSON, C. A., Medicine
ASHER, I., Paediatrics
AUSTIN, G. L., Physics
BAKER, E. N., Biological Sciences, Chemistry
BAKER, M., Sociology
BELICH, J. C., History
BELLAMY, A. R., Biological Sciences
BHATTACHARYYA, D., Mechanical Engineering
BISHOP, J. C., Philosophy
BLACK, P. M., Geology
BOOTH, G., Creative and Performing Arts
BOOTH, R., Molecular Medicine and Pathology
BOWMAKER, G., Chemistry
BOWMAN, R. G., Accounting and Finance
BOXALL, P., Management and Employment Relations
BOYS, J. T., Electrical and Electronic Engineering
BRIMBLE, M. A., Chemistry
BRODIE, R. J., Marketing

BROWETT, P., Pathology
BROWNE, P., Geology
BYBLEW, W., Sport and Exercise Science
CALUDE, C. S., Computer Science
CANNELL, M., Physiology
CARMICHAEL, H., Physics
CARTER, I. R., Sociology
CARTWRIGHT, R. W., International Business
CHEN, J. J. J., Chemical and Materials Engineering
CHEN, X. D., Chemical and Materials Engineering
CLARK, G., Chemistry
CLARK, P. J. A., Chinese
CLARK, R. G., Molecular Medicine
COLLINS, I. F., Engineering Science
COOPER, G. J. S., Biological Sciences and Medicine
CORBALLIS, M. C., Psychology
CORRADO, C., Accounting and Finance
COSTER, G. D., General Practice
COVIELLO, N., Marketing
CRAIG, J. L., Geography and Environmental Science
CROSIER, K. E., Molecular Medicine and Pathology
CROSTHWAITE, J., European Languages and Literatures
DANAHER, P. J., Marketing
DAVISON, M. C., Psychology
DENNY, W., Auckland Cancer Society Research Centre
DIXON, J., Planning
DRAGUNOW, M., Pharmacology and Clinical Pharmacology
DUFFY, G. G., Chemical and Materials Engineering
DUNN, M. R., Fine Arts
DUNN, W., Business
DURING, M. J., Molecular Medicine
EAGLES, I. G., Commercial Law
ELLIS, R., Applied Language Studies and Linguistics
EMANUEL, D. M., Accounting and Finance
EVANS, P. J., Law
FAULL, R. L. M., Anatomy
FERGUSON, L., Auckland Cancer Society Research Centre
FERGUSON, W. G., Chemical and Materials Engineering
FLAY, R., Mechanical Engineering
FORER, P. C., Geography and Environmental Science
FRASER, J., Molecular Medicine
GAO, W., Chemicals and Materials Engineering
GARDNER, R. C., Biological Sciences
GAULD, D. B., Mathematics
GEERTSHUIS, S., Continuing Education
GILMOUR, R. S., Liggins Institute
GLUCKMAN, P. D., Liggins Institute
GONZALEZ-CASANOVAS, R., Spanish
GORMAN, D., Medicine
GRANTHAM, R., Commercial Law
GRAY, V. J., Classics and Ancient History
GRUNDY, J., Computer Science
GUSTAFSON, B. S., Political Studies
HAARHOF, E. J., Architecture
HARDING, J. E., Obstetrics and Gynaecology
HARRIS, B. V., Law
HARVEY, J. D., Physics
HATCHER, S., Psychiatry
HATTIE, J. A., Education
HAWORTH, N. A. F., International Business
HAZLEDINE, T. J., Economics
HOLLIS, S., English
HOOL, R. B., Economics
HORROCKS, R., Film, Television and Media Studies
HOSKING, J., Computer Science
HOUSLEY, G., Physiology
HUNT, J. G., Architecture
HUNTER, P. J., Bioengineering Institute
HURSTHOUSE, R., Philosophy
IRWIN, G. J., Anthropology
JACKSON, M. P., English

JACKSON, P. S., Mechanical Engineering
JACKSON, R., Community Health
JACOBS, R., Optometry and Vision Science
JENSEN, C., Anatomy with Radiology
KALLONIATIS, M., Optometry
KELSEY, J., Law
KILPATRICK, J., Nursing
KIRKNESS, A. C., Applied Language Studies and Linguistics
KISTLER, J., Biological Sciences
KLETTE, R., Computer Science
KYDD, R. R., Psychiatry
LARSEN, K., English
LEES, H., Music
LE HERON, R. B., Geography and Environmental Science
LENNON, D. R., Paediatrics
LIPSKI, J., Physiology
LORRIGAN, G., Business
LUCIANO, B., Italian
MCCARTHY, D. C., Psychology
MCCORMICK, R., Goodfellow Unit
MCGHEE, C., Ophthalmology
MCKECHNIE, P., Classics and Ancient History
MCNAUGHTON, S., Education
MACPHERSON, C., Sociology
MANTELL, C. D., Maori and Pacific Health
MARTIN, G. J., Mathematics
MARTIN, I., Surgery
MAXTON, J. K., Law
MELLSOP, G., South Auckland Clinical School
MELVILLE, B., Civil and Resource Engineering
MERRY, A., Anaesthesiology
MITCHELL, E. A., Paediatrics
MITCHELL, M. D., Pharmacology and Clinical Pharmacology
MOLLOY, M. A., Women's Studies
MONTGOMERY, J. C., Biological Sciences
MORIARTY, S., Accounting and Finance
MORROW, J., Political Studies
MUTU, M., Maori Studies
MYERS, M., Management Science and Information Systems
NEICH, R., Anthropology
NEILL, M. A. F., English
NEVILLE, R., Property
NICHOLSON, T., Education
O'CONNOR, C. J., Chemistry
O'SULLIVAN, M., Engineering Science
OWENS, R. G., Psychology
PARRY, B. R., Surgery
PAVLOV, B., Mathematics
PAXTON, J., Pharmacology and Clinical Pharmacology
PENDER, M. J., Civil and Resource Engineering
PERRY, N., Film, Television and Media Studies
PETERS, M., Education
PETRIE, K., Health Psychology
PHILPOTT, A., Engineering Science
POWELL, M. J., Management and Employment Relations
RAMSAY, R. L., French
RANKIN, E. A., Art History
REA, H. H., Medicine
REAY, B. G., History
REID, I. R., Medicine
REILLY, I. L., Mathematics
ROBINSON, V., Education
RUSSELL, D. K., Chemistry
RYAN, D. M., Engineering Science
SALCIC, Z., Electrical and Electronic Engineering
Dame SALMOND, M. A., Anthropology, Maori Studies
SCHWERDTFEGER, P., Chemistry
SCOTT, A. J., Statistics
SCOTT, D., Statistics
SCRIVEN, M., Education
SHARP, R. A., Political Studies
SHAW, J., Pharmacy
SHEPHEARD, C., Fine Arts
SIMPSON, I. J., Medicine
SLEIGH, J., Anaesthesia

SMALL, J., Economics
SMITH, G., Education
SMITH, L., Education
SMITH, W., Geography and Environmental Science
SPALINGER, A., Classics and Ancient History
SPICER, B. H., Accounting and Finance
SRINIVASAN, A., Management Science and Information Systems
STONE, P., Obstetrics and Gynaecology
STURM, T. L., English
SUTTON, D. G., Anthropology
TAGGART, M. B., Law
THOMAS, D. R., Community Health
THOMBORSON, C. D., Computer Science
THORNE, P., Audiology
TIBBLES, J., Music
TINDLE, C., Physics
VALE, B. A., Architecture
VOIT, F., German Languages and Literature
VOWLES, J., Political Studies
WAINWRIGHT, E., Theology
WATTS, P., Law
WELLS, R. M. G., Biological Sciences
WENDT, A., English
WILD, C., Statistics
WILLIAMS, P. W., Geography and Environmental Science
WILLIAMSON, A. G., Electrical and Electronic Engineering
WILSON, M. G., Management and Employment Relations
WILSON, M. J., Classics and Ancient History
WILSON, W., Auckland Cancer Society Research Centre
WILTON, R., Accounting and Finance
WONG, J., Accounting and Finance
ZHANG, Y., Asian Studies

UNIVERSITY OF CANTERBURY

Private Bag 4800, Christchurch 8140
Warehouse 20 Kirkwood Ave, Ilam, Christchurch 8041
Telephone: (3) 366-7001
Fax: (3) 364-2999
E-mail: info@canterbury.ac.nz
Internet: www.canterbury.ac.nz
Founded 1873
State control
Academic year: February to November
Chancellor: Dr REX WILLIAMS
Vice-Chancellor: Dr ROD CARR
Deputy Vice-Chancellor: Prof. IAN TOWN
Asst Vice-Chancellor for Māori Affairs: Sir TIPENE O'REGAN
Registrar: JEFF FIELD
Chief Financial Officer: Dr YVONNE SHANAHAN
Dir of Human Resources: PAUL O'FLAHERTY
Pro-Vice-Chancellor for Arts: Prof. ED ADELSON
Pro-Vice-Chancellor for Business and Economics: Assoc. Prof. RICHARD SCRAGG (acting)
Pro-Vice-Chancellor for Education: Prof. GAIL GILLON
Pro-Vice-Chancellor for Engineering: Prof. PETER JACKSON
Pro-Vice-Chancellor for Law: Prof. JAN EVANS-FREEMAN
Pro-Vice-Chancellor for Science: Prof. PAUL FLEMING
Pro-Vice-Chancellor for Int. and Student Services: Dr NELLO ANGERILLI
Pro-Vice-Chancellor for Learning Resources: Prof. SUE MCKNIGHT
Librarian: (vacant)
Library: see under Libraries and Archives
Number of teachers: 605 (f.t.e.)
Number of students: 22,001

DEANS

College of Business and Economics: Prof. ADRIAN SAWYER (acting)

College of Engineering: Dr SHAYNE GOOCH
College of Science: Assoc. Prof. WENDY LAWSON
College of Education: Prof. GAIL GILLON
Faculty of Creative Arts Faculty of Humanities and Social Sciences: KATE VAN HEUGTEN
Postgraduate Studies: Prof. STEVE WEAVER
School of Law: Assoc. Prof. RICHARD SCRAGG

PROFESSORS

College of Arts:
BERCOVITCH, J., Political Science
CARSTAIRS-MCCARTHY, A. D., Linguistics
COPELAND, B. J., Philosophy and Religious Studies
FRANCIS, M., Political Science
HEMPENSTALL, P. J. A., History
KUIPER, K., Linguistics
MACDONALD, G. F., Philosophy
MCNAUGHTON, H. D., English
MAJOR, M., Music
MONDRY, H., Russian
ROCHFORT, A. D., Fine Arts
THORNS, D. C., Sociology and Anthropology
WILLIAMS, M., Culture, Literature and Society
ZANKER, G., Classics
College of Business and Economics:
BALL, A., Accountancy
CLARKE, B. J., Accountancy, Finance and Information Systems
CRAGG, P., Accountancy
HALL, C. M., Management
HAMILTON, R. T., Management
MILNE, M., Accountancy
OXLEY, L., Economics
College of Engineering and Forestry:
BLAKIE, R. J., Electrical and Computer Engineering
BODGER, P., Electrical and Computer Engineering
BRIDGES, D. S., Mathematics and Statistics
BUCHANAN, A. H., Civil Engineering
CARR, A. J., Civil and Natural Resources
DAVID, T., Mechanical Engineering
FEE, C. J., Chemical and Process Engineering
GOUGH, P. T., Electrical and Computer Engineering
MILLANE, R. P., Electrical and Computer Engineering
PAWLIKOWSKI, K., Computer Science and Software Engineering
SIRISENA, H. R., Electrical and Computer Engineering
STEEL, M., Mathematics and Statistics
TAKOAKA, T., Computer Science and Software Engineering
TAYLOR, D. P., Electrical and Electronic Engineering
WALKER, J. C., Forestry
WALL, D., Mathematics and Statistics
College of Science:
BAGGALEY, W. J., Physics and Astronomy
BLUNT, J. W., Chemistry
BUTLER, P. H., Physics and Astronomy
COLE, J. W., Geological Sciences
COXON, J. M., Chemistry
DAVIDSON, W., Biological Sciences
FLETCHER, G., Psychology
GERRARD, J., Biological Sciences
HARLAND, P. W., Chemistry
HEARNSHAW, J., Physics and Astronomy
HUGHES, R., Psychology
JACKSON, R. R., Biological Sciences
JAMESON, P. E., Biological Sciences
KELLY, D., Biological Sciences
KEMP, S., Psychology
MCEWAN, M., Chemistry
MUNROE, M. H., Chemistry
PAWSON, E. J., Geography
PHILLIPS, L. F., Chemistry
ROBB, M. P., Communication Disorders

SCHIEL, D. R, Biological Sciences
STEEL, P., Chemistry
STURMAN, A. P., Geography
TAYLOR, R. P., Physics and Astronomy
WEAVER, S. D., Geology
WILLIAMSON, B., Chemistry
School of Law:
FINN, J., Law
JOSEPH, P. A., Law
TODD, S. M. D., Law
WEBB, D., Law

UNIVERSITY OF OTAGO

POB 56, Dunedin 9054
Telephone: (3) 479-1100
Fax: (3) 474-8692
E-mail: university@otago.ac.nz
Internet: www.otago.ac.nz
Founded 1869
State control
Language of instruction: English
Academic year: February to November
Chancellor: J. F. WARD
Pro-Chancellor: S. J. MCLAUCHLAN
Vice-Chancellor: Prof. HARLENE HAYNE
Deputy Vice-Chancellor for Research and Enterprise: Prof. R. J. BLAIKIE
Deputy Vice-Chancellor for Academic and Int. Affairs: Prof. V. A. SQUIRE
Pro-Vice-Chancellor for Commerce: Prof. G. L. BENWELL
Pro-Vice-Chancellor for Health Sciences: Prof. P. R. CRAMPTON
Pro-Vice-Chancellor for Humanities: B. D. MOLOUGHNEY
Pro-Vice-Chancellor for Sciences: Prof. K. A. HUNTER
Pro-Vice-Chancellor Int. Affairs: Prof. S. J. TODD
Registrar and Sec. to the Council: Prof. J. A. FLOOD
Librarian: H. B. AMOS
Library: see under Libraries and Archives
Number of teachers: 1,469
Number of students: 21,728

DEANS

College of Education: L. F. SMITH
Dunedin School of Medicine: J. B. ADAMS
Faculty of Law: R. M. HENAGHAN
Faculty of Medicine: P. R. CRAMPTON
Otago School of Medical Sciences: H. D. NICHOLSON
School of Dentistry: G. J. SEYMOUR
School of Maori, Pacific and Indigenous Studies: M. P. J. REILLY
School of Pharmacy: S. B. DUFFULL
School of Physical Education: D. G. BOOTH
School of Physiotherapy: G. D. BAXTER
School of Surveying: (vacant)
Univ. of Otago, Christchurch: P. R. JOYCE
Univ. of Otago, Wellington: C. D. COLLINGS

PROFESSORS

ABRAHAM, W. C., Psychology
ACKERLEY, C., English
ADLER, R. W., Accountancy and Business Law
AHDAR, R., Law
AN HUEF, A., Mathematics
ANDERSON, J. S., Law
ANDERSON, T. J., Medicine
ANSTEY, P., Philosophy
ARDAGH, M. W., Surgery
ATKINSON, M. D., Computer Science
BALLAGH, R. J., Physics
BARKER, R., Mathematics and Statistics
BARTLETT, R., Physical Education
BARUSCH, A., Social Work
BAXTER, G. D., Physiotherapy
BEAUTRAIS, A., Psychological Medicine
BEGG, E., Medicine
BENNETT, J., History

BENWELL, G., Information Science
BHATIA, M., Pathology
BILKEY, D., Psychology
BINNS, J. A., Geography
BLAKELY, A., Public Health
BOOTH, D., Physical Education
BRADSTOCK, A., Theology and Public Issues
BRAITHWAITE, A. W., Pathology
BREMER, P., Science
BROOKER, S., Chemistry
BROOKES, B., History
BROOKING, T. W. H., History
BURGESS, C. D., Medicine
BURNS, C. W., Zoology
CAMPBELL, A. J., Medicine
CAMPBELL-HUNT, C., Management
CANNON, R., Oral Sciences
CHAMBERS, S. T., Pathology
CLEMENTS, K., Peace and Conflict Studies
COLOMBO, M., Psychology
COOK, G., Microbiology and Immunology
COOPER, A. F., Geology
CRACK, T. F., Finance and Quantitative Analysis
CRAMPTON, P., Public Health
CRANE, J., Medicine
CRAW, D., Geology
CROOKS, T. J., Education
DARLOW, B. A., Paediatrics
DAVIS, D. K., Communication Studies
DAWKINS, K., Law
DAWSON, J. B., Law
DELAHUNT, B., Pathology
DENNIS, J., Music
DICKINSON, K., Botany
DOMINIK, W. J., Classics
DOWELL, A. C., General Practice
DOYLE, T. C. A., Medicine
DRUMMOND, J. D., Music
DUFFULL, S., Pharmacy
ECCLES, R., Pathology
ECONOMIDES, K., Law
EDWARDS, P., Public Health
ELLIS, P. M., Psychological Medicine
ENDRE, Z. H., Medicine
EVANS, D. M., Biomedical Ethics
FARELLA, M., Oral Sciences
FERGUSON, M. M., Stomatology
FERGUSSON, D. M., Psychological Medicine
FIELDING, D. J., Economics
FLEMING, J., Zoology
FOX, A. G., English
FRASER, R., Pathology
FRAUENDIENER, J., Mathematics and Statistics
FRIZELLE, F. A., Surgery
GARDINER, C., Physics
GEARE, A. J., Economics
GEMMELL, N., Anatomy and Structural Biology
GIBSON, R. S., Human Nutrition
GILLETT, G. R., Neurosurgery and Biomedical Ethics
GLUE, P., Psychological Medicine
GORDON, K., Chemistry
GRATTAN, D., Anatomy and Structural Biology
GRAY, B., Marketing
GREEN, D. P. L., Anatomy and Structural Biology
GRIFFIN, J. F. T., Microbiology
GROVER, S., Management
HALL, C. M., Tourism
HALL, G., Law
HANNAH, J., Surveying
HANNAH, R., Classics
HANTON, L., Chemistry
HAROLD, G., Childhood Studies
HARRIS, W., Politics
HAUG, A., Economics
HAYNE, H., Psychology
HENAGHAN, R. M., Law
HERBISON, A. E., Physiology
HERBISON, G., Preventive and Social Medicine
HIGHAM, J., Tourism

HIGHTON, J., Medical and Surgical Sciences
HILL, P., Preventive and Social Medicine
HOEK, J., Marketing
HOWDEN-CHAPMAN, P., Public Health
HUNTER, K. A., Chemistry
HUTTON, J. D., Obstetrics and Gynaecology
JACKSON, S., Physical Education
JOHANNESSON, A., Paediatrics and Child Health
JOHNSON, H., Music
JONES, D., Bioethics
JOYCE, P. R., Psychological Medicine
KARDOS, T. B., Oral Studies and Orthodontics
KEARSLEY, G. W., Social Science
KENNEDY, M., Pathology
KETTLE, A., Pathology
KIESER, J. A., Oral Sciences and Orthodontics
KNIGHT, R. G., Psychology
KRAUSE, K., Biochemistry
KÜCH, P., Irish Studies
LAI, K., Education
LAING, R. M., Clothing and Textile Science
LAMONT, I., Biochemistry
LANGLEY, J. D., Preventive and Social Medicine
LAWSON, R. W., Marketing
LOVER, M., Oral Diagnostic and Surgical Sciences
MCCALL, J., Medical and Surgical Sciences
MCCARTHY, A., History
MCGEE, R., Preventive and Social Medicine
MCILVANNEY, L., Scottish Studies
MCNAUGHTON, N., Psychology
MCQUILLAN, A., Chemistry
MAHONEY, R., Law
MANN, J., Human Nutrition
MATISOO-SMITH, E., Anatomy and Structural Biology
MAY, H., Education
MEHIGAN, T., Languages and Cultures
MERCER, A., Microbiology and Immunology
MERCER, A., Zoology
MILLER, J., Psychology
MOLLER, H., Agriculture, Food and Environment
MOLOUGHNEY, B., Humanities
MOLTENO, A., Medical and Surgical Sciences
MORGAN, R., Geography
MORISON, I., Pathology
MULDER, R., Psychological Medicine
MURDOCH, D., Pathology
MUSGRAVE, A., Philosophy
NACEY, J., Surgery and Anaesthesia
NEL, P., Politics
NICHOLLS, M., Medicine
NICHOLSON, H., Anatomy and Structural Biology
NORRIS, P., Pharmacy
NORRIS, R., Geology
OEY, I., Food Science
OWEN, P., Economics
PATMAN, R., Politics
PAUL, C., Preventive and Social Medicine
PEART, N., Law
PORTER, R., Psychological Medicine
POULIN, R., Zoology
POULTON, R., Preventive and Social Medicine
PRINGLE, K., Obstetrics and Gynaecology
PURVIS, M., Information Science
RADES, T., Pharmacy
RADNER, H., Media, Film and Communication
RAEBURN, I., Mathematics and Statistics
REEVE, A., Biochemistry
REILLY, M., Maori, Pacific and Indigenous Studies
RICHARDS, A., Medicine
ROAKE, J., Surgery
ROBERTON, D., Medicine
ROBERTSON, S., Paediatrics and Child Health
ROBINSON, B., Chemistry
RONSON, C., Microbiology and Immunology
ROTH, P., Law
SELLMAN, J., Psychological Medicine
SEYMOUR, G., Higher Education Development Centre and Dentistry

SHEPHARD, K., Higher Education Development Centre
SHIPTON, E., Anaesthesia
SIMPSON, J., Chemistry
SKEAFF, C., Human Nutrition
SKEGG, P., Law
SMILLIE, J., Law
SMITH, J., Education
SMITH, L., Education
SMITH, P., Pharmacology and Toxicology
SMITH, R., Chemistry
SPENCER, H., Zoology
SQUIRE, V., Mathematics and Statistics
STRINGER, M., Anatomy and Structural Biology
SULLIVAN, S., Physiotherapy
SUMMERHAYES, G., Anthropology
SWAIN, M., Oral Rehabilitation
TAGG, J., Microbiology and Immunology
TANNOCK, G., Microbiology and Immunology
TAPSELL, P., Maori, Pacific and Indigenous Studies
TATE, W., Biochemistry
TAYLOR, B., Women's and Children's Health
TAYLOR, D., Medical and Surgical Sciences
THOMSON, C., Human Nutrition
THOMSON, W., Oral Sciences
TILYARD, M., General Practice
TODD, S., Marketing
TOOP, L., Public Health and General Practice
TOWNSEND, C., Zoology
TREBILCO, P., Theology and Religion
TRIBBLE, E., English
TUCKER, I., Pharmacy
VAN RIJ, A., Medical and Surgical Sciences
WALKER, R., Medical and Surgical Sciences
WALLIS, G., Zoology
WEISS, H., Preventive and Social Medicine
WHITE, K., Psychology
WICKENS, J., Anatomy and Structural Biology
WILKINSON, T., Medicine
WILSON, G., Marine Science
WILSON, J., Botany
WILSON, P., Women's and Children's Health
WINTERBOURN, C., Pathology
WYVILL, G., Computer Science
YOON, H., Pathology

UNIVERSITY OF WAIKATO

Te Whare Wānanga o Waikato gate one, Knighton Rd, Private Bag 3105, Hamilton 3240

Telephone: (7) 856-2889
Fax: (7) 838-4300
E-mail: info@waikato.ac.nz
Internet: www.waikato.ac.nz

Founded 1964
Academic year: February to November

Chancellor: JIM BOLGER
Vice-Chancellor: Dr ROY CRAWFORD
Deputy Vice-Chancellor: Dr Prof. ALISTER JONES
Univ. Librarian: ROSS HALLETT
Library: see under Libraries and Archives
Number of teachers: 654
Number of students: 12,642

DEANS

Faculty of Arts and Social Sciences: Dr Prof. DAVID LUMSDEN (acting)
Faculty of Computing and Mathematical Sciences: Prof. GEOFF HOLMES
Faculty of Education: Dr Prof. ROGER MOLTZEN
Faculty of Science and Engineering: Dr Prof. BRUCE CLARKSON
School of Maori and Pacific Development: Prof. LINDA SMITH
Te Piringa—Faculty of Law: Prof. BRADFORD W. MORSE
Waikato Management School: Dr Prof. FRANK SCRIMGEOUR

PROFESSORS

APPERLEY, M. D., Computing and Mathematical Sciences
BARRATT, A. A. T., English
BARTON, B., Law
BEARDON, C., Computer Sciences
BEDFORD, R. D., Geography
BING, D., Political Science and Public Policy
BISHOP, R., Maori Education
BOOTH, D., Sport and Leisure Studies
CARY, C., Biological Sciences
CLARK, D., Management
CLEARY, J. G., Computer Sciences
CORNER, J., Management Systems
CRAIG, I., Mathematics
CUBITT, S., Screen and Media Studies
DANIEL, R. M., Biological Sciences
EGGLETON, I., Accounting
ERICKSEN, N., International Global Change Institute
FARRAR, J. H., Law
FARRELL, R. L., Biological Sciences
FOULDS, L. R., Management Systems
GILLESPIE, A. M., Law
GILSON, C. H. J., Strategic Management and Leadership
GLYNN, E. L., Human Development and Counselling
GRANT, B., Sport and Leisure Studies
GREEN, T. G. A., Biological Sciences
HAMILTON, D., Biological Sciences
HARCOURT, M., Strategic Management and Leadership
HEALY, T. R., Earth Sciences
HOLMES, M. J., Economics
JOHN, N., Statistics
JONES, A. T., Wilf Malcolm Institute of Educational Research
KALNINS, E. G., Mathematics
KAMP, P. J. J., Earth Sciences
KOOPMAN-BOYDEN, P. G., Arts and Social Sciences
LAWRENCE, S., Accounting
LEITCH, S., Public Relations and Marketing
LOWE, A., Accounting
McGEE, C., Wilf Malcolm Institute of Educational Research
McKIE, D., Management Communication
McQUEEN, B., Management Systems
MAY, S., Arts and Language Education
MIDDLETON, S. C., Policy, Cultural and Social Studies in Education
MOLAN, P. C., Biological Sciences
MORGAN, H. W., Biological Sciences
MOTION, J., Management Communication
NELSON, C. S., Earth Sciences
NICHOLSON, B. K., Chemistry
O'DRISCOLL, M., Psychology
POOL, D. I., Population Studies
POOT, J., Population Studies
PRATT, M. J., Management Studies
PRICE, R., Science and Engineering
QUICK, S. P., Biological Sciences
REEDY, T., Maori Sustainable Enterprise
REEVES, S., Computer Science
RICHARDSON, N. A., Management
RITCHIE, J., Psychology
ROA, T. C., Maori and Pacific Development
RYAN, C. A., Tourism Management
SCARPA, R., Economics
SCRIMGEOUR, F. G., Economics
SILVESTER, W. B., Biological Sciences
SMYTH, J., Wilf Malcolm Institute of Educational Research
SNEYD, A. D., Mathematics
SPILLER, P. R., Law
STOKES, E. M., Geography, Tourism and Environmental Planning
TE AWEKOTUKWU, N. A., Maori and Pacific Development
VAREY, R. J., Marketing and International Management
VOS, E. A. J., Finance
WALKER, G. M., English
WILKINS, A. L., Chemistry

WILKINS, R. J., Biological Sciences
WITTEN, I. H., Computer Science
YATES-SMITH, G. R. A., Maori and Pacific Development
ZIRKER, D., Arts and Social Sciences
ZORN, T. E., Management Communication

VICTORIA UNIVERSITY OF WELLINGTON

POB 600, Wellington 6140
Telephone: (4) 472-1000
Fax: (4) 499-4601
E-mail: info-desk@vuw.ac.nz
Internet: www.victoria.ac.nz
Founded 1897
Languages of instruction: English, Maori
Academic year: March to February (3 trimesters)

Chancellor: Emeritus Prof. IAN MCKINNON
Pro-Chancellor for Univ. Council: HELEN SUTCH
Vice-Chancellor: Prof. PAT WALSH
Deputy Vice-Chancellor for Academics: Prof. PENNY BOUMELHA
Deputy Vice-Chancellor for Research: Prof. NEIL QUIGLEY
Pro-Vice-Chancellor for Commerce and Admin.: Prof. BOB BUCKLE
Pro-Vice-Chancellor for Education: Prof. DUGALD SCOTT
Pro-Vice-Chancellor for Govt Relations: Prof. TONY SMITH
Pro-Vice-Chancellor for Humanities and Social Sciences: Prof. DEBORAH WILLIS
Pro Vice-Chancellor Int.: Prof. ROB RABEL
Pro-Vice-Chancellor for Maori: Prof. PIRI SCIASCIA
Pro-Vice-Chancellor for Science; Architecture and Design; Engineering Professor: Prof. DAVID BIBBY
Asst Vice-Chancellor for Academic Affairs: Assoc. Prof. DAVID CRABBE
Chief Financial Officer: WAYNE MORGAN
Chief Operating Officer: ANDREW SIMPSON
Dir for Campus Services: JENNY BENTLEY
Dir for Human Resources: ANNEMARIE DE CASTRO

Library: see under Libraries and Archives
Number of teachers: 1,871 full-time
Number of students: 22,310

Publications: *Staff and Student Research* (1 a year), *Victorious* (3 a year)

DEANS

Faculty of Architecture and Design: Prof. DAVID MACKAY (acting)
Faculty of Commerce and Admin.: Prof. BOB BUCKLE
Faculty of Education: Prof. DUGALD SCOTT
Faculty of Engineering: Prof. JOHN HINE
Faculty of Graduate Research: Prof. LAURIE BAUER
Faculty of Humanities and Social Sciences: Prof. DEBORAH WILLIS
Faculty of Law: Prof. TONY SMITH
Faculty of Maori: Prof. PIRI SCIASCIA
Faculty of Science: Prof. DAVID BIBBY

PROFESSORS

Faculty of Architecture and Design (tel. (4) 463-6200; fax (4) 463-6204; e-mail architecture@vuw.ac.nz; internet www.victoria.ac.nz/architecture):

BRAND, D., Architecture
FRASER, S., Design

Faculty of Commerce and Administration (tel. (4) 463-5376; fax (4) 463-5360; e-mail fca-sao@vuw.ac.nz; internet www.victoria.ac.nz/fca):

BOSTON, J., Govt
BROCKLESBY, J., Management
CORBETT, L., Management
CUMMINGS, S., Management

DAVIES, J., Management
EVANS, L. T., Economics and Finance
GORMAN, G., Information Management
HALL, V. B., Economics and Finance
HUFF, S., Information Management
LOVE, N., Management
PEARCE, D., Tourism Management
SCOTT, C. D., Govt
STOKES, T., Govt
VAN ZIJL, T., FCA

Faculty of Education (tel. (4) 463-9500; fax (4) 463-9649; e-mail teaching@vuw.ac.nz; internet www.victoria.ac.nz/education):

HALL, C. G. W.
MEYER, L.
SIGAFOOS, J.

Faculty of Humanities and Social Sciences (tel. (4) 463-5208; fax (4) 463-5209; e-mail hum-socsci-office@vuw.ac.nz; internet www.victoria.ac.nz/fhss):

BAUER, L., Linguistics and Applied Language Studies
CLARK, M., History, Philosophy, Political Science and Int. Relations
DAVIDSON, J. F., Art History, Classics and Religious Studies
HOLMES, J., Linguistics and Applied Language Studies
LEVINE, S., History, Philosophy, Political Science and Int. Relations
MORRIS, P., Art History, Classics and Religious Studies
NATION, P., Linguistics and Applied Languages
PRATT, J., Social and Cultural Studies
STERELNY, K., History, Philosophy, Political Science and Int. Relations

Faculty of Law (tel. (4) 463-6366; fax (4) 463-6365; e-mail law-enquiries@vuw.ac.nz; internet www.victoria.ac.nz/law):

ANDERSON, G.
ANGELO, A. H.
ATKIN, B.
McLACHLAN, C.
McLAUCHLAN, D. W.
PREBBLE, J.
SMITH, T.

Faculty of Science (tel. (4) 463-5101; fax (4) 463-5122; e-mail science-faculty@vuw.ac.nz; internet www.victoria.ac.nz/science):

BARRETT, P. J., Earth Sciences
CALLAGHAN, P., Chemical and Physical Sciences
DOWNEY, R., Mathematics, Statistics and Operations Research
GARNOCK-JONES, P., Biological Sciences
GOLDBLATT, R. I., Engineering and Computer Science
HINE, J., Mathematics, Statistics and Computer Science
JOHNSTON, J., Chemical and Physical Sciences
KAISER, A., Chemical and Physical Sciences
KHMALADZE, E., Mathematics, Statistics and Operations Research
LEKNER, J., Chemical and Physical Sciences
SCHENK, S., Psychology
SMITH, E., Earth Sciences
TALLON, J., Chemical and Physical Sciences
WARD, C., Psychology
WARD, T., Psychology
WHITTLE, G., Mathematics, Statistics and Operations Research

Polytechnic Institutions

Bay of Plenty Polytechnic: Private Bag 12001, Tauranga 3143; tel. (7) 571-0190; e-mail info@boppoly.ac.nz; internet www.boppoly.ac.nz; offers professional courses at degree, certificate and diploma levels; 9,443 students (3,374 full-time); Chair. IAN TURNER; Deputy Chair. Dr NEIL BARNS; publ. *Prospectus* (1 a year).

Central Institute of Technology: Private Box 40740, Upper Hutt; tel. (4) 527-6398; fax (4) 527-6359; f. 1960; full-time technician and professional education; 330 staff; 5,000 enrolments; library: 29,000 vols, 800 periodicals (570 current); CEO T. BOYLE.

Christchurch Polytechnic Institute of Technology: POB 540, Christchurch Mail Centre, Christchurch 8140; tel. (3) 379-8150; fax (3) 366-6544; e-mail info@cpit.ac.nz; internet www.cpit.ac.nz; f. 1965; courses at trade technician, professional and degree levels, recreational and community courses; specializes in information technology, with pathways to Monash Univ. (Australia) Masters programmes; library: 48,000 items; 1,180 teachers (350 full-time, 830 part-time); 17,600 students; Chief Exec. KAY GILES; Dir JOHN W. SCOTT; publ. *Prospectus* (1 a year).

Hutt Valley Polytechnic: Private Bag 39803, Te Puni Mail Centre, Petone, nr Wellington; tel. (4) 568-3419; fax (4) 568-6849; f. 1976; courses in trades, commercial and technical subjects; 180 staff, 10,000 enrolments; library of 20,000 items; Chief Exec. W. J. MATTHEW.

Manukau Institute of Technology: Private Bag 94006, Manukau City 2241; Corner of E Tamaki Rd and Newbury St, Otara, Manukau City 2023; tel. (9) 968-8000; fax (9) 968-8701; e-mail info@manukau.ac.nz; internet www.manukau.ac.nz; f. 1970; courses in trade, technical and professional subjects; library: 55,000 vols; 409 teachers; 32,674 students; Chief Exec. Dr PETER BROTHERS; Chief Financial Officer JOHN STRIBRNY; Dir for Academic Operations PETER QUIGG; Dir for Student Affairs JULIE WOODS; Dir for External Relations STUART MIDDLETON.

Nelson Marlborough Institute of Technology: POB 643, Blenheim 7240; tel. (3) 578-0215; fax (3) 578-0216; e-mail info@nmit .ac.nz; internet www.nmit.ac.nz; offers certificate-, diploma- and degree-level courses; campus in Nelson; Chair. ROSS BUTLER; Dep-

uty Chair. ANDREW ROWE; Chief Exec. TONY GRAY.

Open Polytechnic of New Zealand: Private Bag 31914, Lower Hutt 5040; 3 Cleary St, Lower Hutt 5011; tel. (4) 913-5300; fax (4) 913-5308; e-mail brochurecentre@ openpolytechnic.ac.nz; internet www .openpolytechnic.ac.nz; f. 1946 as Technical Correspondence School; present name 1990; certificate- to degree-level courses by distance and open learning methods in business, social science, professional, technical, agriculture, horticulture, trades and self-improvement subjects; 37,000 students; Chief Exec. CAROLINE SEELIG.

Otago Polytechnic: The Geoff Mason Admin. Centre, F Block Forth St, Private Bag 1910, Dunedin 9054; tel. (3) 477-3014; fax (3) 471-6870; e-mail info@op.ac.nz; internet www.otagopolytechnic.ac.nz; f. 1966; degrees, diplomas and certificates in fine arts, business, engineering, architectural technology, health sciences, tourism and sports; 236 teachers; 9,000 students; library: 30,000 vols; Chief Exec. PHIL KER; Chief Exec. Officer JEANETTE CORSON.

Southern Institute of Technology: Private Bag 90114, 133 Tay St, Invercargill 9840; tel. (3) 211-2699; fax (3) 214-4977; e-mail info@sit.ac.nz; internet www.sit.ac.nz.

UNITEC Institute of Technology: Private Bag 92025, Victoria St W, Auckland 1142; tel. (9) 849-4180; fax (9) 815-2901; e-mail study@unitec.ac.nz; internet www.unitec.ac .nz; f. 1976; faculties of Architecture and Design, Arts and Social Sciences, Business, Health and Environmental Sciences; Applied Technology Institute; library: 88,834 vols; 1,100 teachers; 23,000 students; Chief Exec. Dr RICK EDE; Dir Dr JOHN A. WEBSTER; Exec. Dean for Academic Devt RAY MELDRUM; Registrar REBECCA EWERT.

Waikato Institute of Technology: Private Bag 3036, Waikato Mail Centre, Hamilton 3240; tel. (7) 834-8888; fax (7) 858-7513; e-mail info@wintec.ac.nz; internet www .wintec.ac.nz; f. 1968; courses at Masters degree, diploma, certificate, professional technician and trades levels; community education; library: 62,800 vols; 365 teachers; 13,100 students (4,500 full-time, 8,600 part-time); Chief Exec. Officer MARK FLOWERS.

Wellington Institute of Technology: Private Bag 39803, Wellington Mail Centre, Lower Hutt 5045; 11 Kensington Ave, Petone, Wellington; tel. (4) 920-2400; fax (4) 920-2401; e-mail information@weltec.ac.nz; internet www.weltec.ac.nz; academic year February to December; provides diplomas and degrees for various professional spheres; 11,000 students; Chief Exec. Dr LINDA SISSONS; Electronic Services and Reference Librarian ANNE GRANT.

Schools of Art and Music

Elam School of Fine Arts: Faculty of Fine Arts, Univ. of Auckland, Private Bag 92019, Auckland; Main Fine Arts Bldg 431, Level 4, 20 Whitaker Pl., Auckland; tel. (9) 373-7599; fax (9) 308-2302; e-mail info-creative@ auckland.ac.nz; internet www.creative .auckland.ac.nz; f. 1950; fine arts instn; art and design activities in a interdisciplinary studio environment; library: 35,000 vols; 35 teachers; 450 students; Head of School Prof. JONATHAN MANE-WHEOKI.

SAE Institute: 12 Heather St, Parnell, Auckland; tel. (9) 373-4712; fax (9) 373-4713; e-mail auckland@sae.edu; internet auckland.sae.edu; f. 1976; 50 institutes around the world; offers courses in media studies, audio engineering, film making, electronic music production, multimedia and web design, games programming, animation and music business; CEO Dr THOMAS MISNER; Institute Prin. and Company Dir JOSEPH CAMPUS.

School of Fine Arts: Univ. of Canterbury, Private Bag 4800, Christchurch 8140; tel. (3) 364-2159; fax (3) 364-2858; e-mail jan .saville@canterbury.ac.nz; internet www.fina .canterbury.ac.nz; f. 1882; BA, BA (Hons), BFA, BFA (Hons), MA, MFA and PhD degrees; courses in art history, art theory, film, graphic design, painting, photography, printmaking and sculpture; library: 10,000 vols, including index of NZ historic buildings, 100,000 slides, 4,985 works in the art colln and 100,000 architectural drawings; 20 teachers; 785 students; Centre Dir HUBERT KLAASSENS; Head Prof. DESMOND ROCHFORT.

NICARAGUA

The Higher Education System

The oldest institution of higher education in Nicaragua is the Universidad Nacional Autónoma de Nicaragua (founded in 1812), which dates from the Spanish colonial period. Nicaragua became part of the Central American Federation in 1821 and declared its independence in 1838. There are nine universities recognized by the Consejo Nacional de Universidades (National Council of Universities), of which four are state-run, and a large number of commercial schools. There are also many unrecognized universities. In October 2011 the Institute of Intercultural Communication, part of the Universidad de las Regiones Autónomas de las Costa Caribe Nicaragüense, was destroyed after being set alight by students protesting against the university's leadership for allegedly undermining the autonomy of the student body. The action followed a four-day hunger strike earlier in the month, which had forced the cancellation of classes and left two students in need of hospital treatment. In 2003/04 a total of 103,577 students attended universities and other higher education institutes.

The Consejo Nacional de Universidades is the body responsible for all strategic planning. The principal officer of each university is a Rector, who is assisted by a number of Vice-Rectors; individual Faculties are headed by Deans.

Admission to higher education is on the basis of the Bachillerato, the leading secondary school qualification, and an entrance examination. The Licenciado, the main undergraduate degree, is a four- or five-year course of study; a professional title may also be awarded depending on the subject. Following the Licenciado, the first postgraduate degree is the Maestría, which lasts two years and culminates with the submission of a thesis.

Institutions of higher education also offer two- or three-year courses in technical and vocational education. The main qualification studied for is the Técnico Superior.

Regulatory and Representative Bodies

GOVERNMENT

Ministry of Education: Complejo Cívico Camilo Ortega Saavedra, Managua; tel. 265-1451; e-mail rivash@mecd.gob.ni; internet www.mined.gob.ni; Min. Dr MIRIAM RÁUDEZ.

NATIONAL BODY

Consejo Nacional de Universidades (National Council of Universities): De donde fue el Sandy, Carretera a Masaya, 2 cuadras arriba y 1 cuadra al lago, Managua; tel. 278-1053; fax 278-3385; e-mail cnuni@ibw.com .ni; internet www.cnu.edu.ni; f. 1990; 14 mems; Pres. Ing. TELÉMACO TALAVERA SILES; Sec. Ing. ARTURO COLLADO MALDONADO; publ. *Universidad y Sociedad*.

Learned Societies

BIBLIOGRAPHY, LIBRARY SCIENCE AND MUSEOLOGY

Asociación Nicaragüense de Bibliotecarios y Profesionales afines: Apdo postal 3257, Calle F. Guzman Bolanos, Altamira del Est, Casa 120, Managua; e-mail anibipa@ yahoo.com; f. 1983.

LANGUAGE AND LITERATURE

Academia Nicaragüense de la Lengua (Nicaraguan Academy of Letters): Apdo 2711, Managua; located at: Avda del Campo 42, Las Colinas, Managua; fax 249-5389; e-mail pavsa@munditel.com.ni; internet www.anl.edu.ni; f. 1928; corresp. of the Real Academia Española (Madrid); 13 mems; Dir JORGE EDUARDO ARELLANO SANDINO; Sec. FRANCISCO ARELLANO OVIEDO.

Alliance Française: Apdo 2370, Managua; Planes de Altamira, De la Embajada de México ½ Cuadra al Norte, Managua; tel. 2267-2811; fax 2267-8287; e-mail culturalafmga@gmail.com; internet www .alianzafrancesa.org.ni; f. 1951; offers courses and examinations in French language and culture and promotes cultural exchange with France; attached teaching centre in León and Granada; Dir NICOLAS BLASQUEZ; Sub Dir MARIE-PIERRE BAYLOCQ; Culture Coordinator SARA BOLT KALFON.

MEDICINE

Sociedad de Oftalmología Nicaragüense: Clínica Especializada, Managua; f. 1949; Pres R. LACAYO G.

Sociedad Nicaragüense de Psiquiatría y Psicología: Centro Médico, Managua; f. 1962; Pres. Dr R. GUTIÉRREZ.

Research Institutes

ECONOMICS, LAW AND POLITICS

Instituto Nicaragüense de Investigaciones Económicas y Sociales (INIES): Apdo postal C-16, Managua; Avda Bolívar, Antojitos 2 cuadra al sur Managua; tel. 266-2485; fax 266-8503; e-mail inies@sdnnic.apc .org; f. 1981 to inform and conduct research on developing alternatives for the more vulnerable sectors of the national population; documentation centre of 8,000 items, 250 periodicals; Dir BLADIMIR VARELA HIDALGO; publs *Boletín Socioeconómico* (4 a year), *Cuadernos de Investigación* (irregular).

NATURAL SCIENCES

Physical Sciences

Observatorio Geofísico: Apdo postal 1761, Managua; tel. 225-1023; f. 1980; geophysics, geology, seismology, vulcanology; publ. *Boletín Sismológico* (1 a year).

Libraries and Archives

Bluefields

Biblioteca Raiti: Alcaldía Municipal, Bluefields, Zelaya; tel. 822-2502; Librarian JANICE TAYLOR.

Chinandega

Biblioteca 'Eduardo Montealegre': Parque Las Rosas 2 cuadras al sur, Chinandega; tel. 341-2950; Librarian ANA LUISA PANIAGUA GONZÁLEZ.

León

Biblioteca Rubén Dario de la Universidad Nacional Autónoma de Nicaragua: Frente a la panadería León Dorado, León; tel. 311-3508; f. 1816; 36,000 vols; Dir NORMA FLORES.

Managua

Archivo Nacional de Nicaragua: Del Cine Cabrera 2½ Cuadras al Lago, Managua; tel. 222-6290; fax 222-2722; e-mail binanic@tmx .com.ni; internet http://manfut.org/museos/ archivonacional.html; f. 1882; 40,356 vols; Dir ALFREDO GONZÁLEZ VILCHEZ; publs *Boletín Técnico Informativo*, *Gaceta Oficial*.

Biblioteca del INCAE Business School: Apdo 2485, Managua; tel. 2265-8141 ext. 228; fax 2265-8617; e-mail antonio.acevedo@incae .edu; internet conocimiento.incae.edu/es/ biblioteca; f. 1968 as Depositary Library Food and Agricultural Organization of the United Nations and the World Bank; academic business library of 34,417 vols and 111 periodical titles on business admin., economic devt and Central American social and economic conditions; colln of 16,000 case materials for teaching of management; Dir Lic. ANTONIO ACEVEDO; publs *Bibliografía de Casos* (1 a year), *Gerencia—Artículos Nuevos* (irregular), *INCAE Business Review* (4 a year), *Mini-Bibliografía* (12 a year), *Nuevas Adquisiciones* (12 a year), *Revistas—Números Temáticos* (irregular).

Biblioteca Nacional 'Rubén Dario': Apdo Postal 3514, Managua; Palacio Nacional de la Cultura, Antigua Catedral, Managua; tel. and fax 222-2722; e-mail dibinacr@racsa.co .cr; internet www.abinia.org/nicaragua; f. 1880; 80,000 vols; Dir JIMMY ALVARADO MORENO.

Masaya

Biblioteca 'El Ateneo': Masaya; f. 1941; new collection of literature on philately and numismatics; Dir Dr SANTIAGO FAJARDO F.

Nagarote

Biblioteca Municipal: Costado sur Parque Central, Nagarote, León; tel. 313-2244; Dir Prof. JOSÉ ÁNGEL PALACIOS.

Museums and Art Galleries

Managua

Museo Nacional de Nicaragua: Apdo 416, Colonia Dambach, Managua; tel. 222-5291; internet manfut.org/museos/nacional.html; f. 1896; archaeology, ceramics, zoology, botany and geology; library of 500 vols; Dir LEONOR MARTÍNEZ DE ROCHA.

Masaya

Museo 'Tenderí': Villa Nindirí, Masaya; archaeological remains from the Chorotega Indian culture; coins and medals from the Spanish colonial era.

Universities

ESCUELA INTERNACIONAL DE AGRICULTURA Y GANADERÍA

Apdo postal 5, Rivas
Telephone: 453-3551
Fax: 453-3957
E-mail: eiag@tmx.com.ni
Dir: Fr GREGORIO BARREALES

Academic programmes in agriculture, management, veterinary science and zootechnology.

UNIVERSIDAD CENTROAMERICANA

Pista de la Resistencia, Apdo 69, Managua
Telephone: 277-3026
Fax: 267-0106
E-mail: asrector@ns.uca.edu.ni
Internet: www.uca.edu.ni
Founded 1961
Private control
Academic year: February to December
Rector: Dra MAYRA LUZ PÉREZ DÍAZ
Vice-Rector for Gen. Affairs: P. JESÚS MANUEL SARIEGO
Vice-Rector for Academic Affairs: RENATA RODRIGUEZ
Vice-Rector for Research and Postgraduates: SANDRA RUIZ
Sec.-Gen.: P. MIGUEL ÁNGEL RUIZ
Dir of Admin.: Lic. RÓGER URIARTE GÓMEZ
Librarian: Lic. GLORIA MARÍA MORALES
Number of teachers: 324 (72 full-time, 252 part-time)
Number of students: 6,401
Publications: *Cuadernos de Sociología*, *Diakonía*, *Encuentro* (24 a year), *Envío* (12 a year), *WANI* (4 a year)

DEANS

Faculty of Administration: GUILLERMO BORNEMANN
Faculty of Agriculture and Stockbreeding: VERA AMANDA SOLÍS REYES
Faculty of Communications: Dr GUILLERMO ROTHSCHUH
Faculty of Foreign Languages: RAMÓN BERMÚDEZ
Faculty of Humanities: DONALD MÉNDEZ QUINTANA
Faculty of Law: MANUEL ARKUZ ULLOA

UNIVERSIDAD NACIONAL AGRARIA

Km 12½ Carretera Norte, Managua
Telephone: 233-1619
Fax: 233-1950

Internet: www.una.edu.ni
Founded 1929, present name and status 1990
Rector: Ing. FRANCISCO TELÉMACO TALAVERA SILES
Vice-Rector Gen.: Ing. ALBERTO SEDILES JAEN
Dir for Camoapa Campus: Ing. LUIS HERNÁNDEZ MALUEÑO
Dir for Juigalpa Campus: Ing. ARISTIDES TABLADA CALERO
Registrar: Lic. RONALD QUIROZ OCAMPO
Library of 12,000 vols, 500 periodicals
Number of students: 2,217
Publications: *Boletín Informativo* (12 a year), *La Calera* (2 a year)

DEANS

Faculty of Agronomy: Dr DENNIS SALAZAR CENTENO
Faculty of Animal Sciences: Ing. ELMER GUILLEN CORRALES
Faculty of Natural Resources and the Environment: Lic. ESTHER CARBALLO MADRIGAL
Faculty of Rural Development: Dr ELGIN VIVAS VILLACHICA

UNIVERSIDAD NACIONAL AUTÓNOMA DE NICARAGUA

Apdo Postal 663, Managua
De Enel Central 2½ km al sur, Villa Fontana, Managua
Telephone: 278-6769
Fax: 278-2990
E-mail: unan@unan.edu.ni
Internet: www.unan.edu.ni
Founded 1812
Academic year: June to March
State control
Rector: FRANCISCO GUZMÁN PASOS
Vice-Rector: ELMER CISNEROS MOREIRA
Vice-Rector for Academic Affairs: Dr GUSTAVO SILES GONZÁLEZ
Vice-Rector for Admin. Affairs: Lic. JAIME LÓPEZ LOWERY
Registrar: Dra NÍVEA GONZÁLEZ ROJAS
Library Dir: SIDAR RIVERA MARÍN
Library: see Libraries and Archives
Number of teachers: 709
Number of students: 24,629
Publications: *Cuadernos Universitarios* (4 a year), *Gaceta Universitaria* (6 a year), *Revista Médica* (2 a year)

DEANS

Faculty of Economics: ABEL MEMBREÑO GALEANO
Faculty of Education and Humanities: Lic. ALEJANDRO GENET CRUZ
Faculty of Medicine: Dr FRANCISCO CORTÉZ HERNÁNDEZ
Faculty of Sciences: Lic. HUGO GUTIÉRREZ OCÓN

UNIVERSIDAD NACIONAL DE INGENIERÍA

Avda Universitaria Frente Escuela de Danza, Apdo Postal 5595, Managua
Telephone: 277-1650
Fax: 267-3709
Internet: www.uni.edu.ni
Founded 1983
State control
Academic year: March to December
Rector: Ing. ALDO URBINA VILLALTA
Vice-Rector: Ing. SERGIO ENRIQUE ALVAREZ GARCÍA

Vice-Rector for Academic Affairs: Arq. ANA ULMOS VADO
Vice-Rector for Administrative Affairs: Ing. NÉSTOR GALLO ZELEDÓN
Vice-Rector for Research and Development: Lic. SERGIO MARTÍNEZ TRAÑA
Registrar: Ing. DIEGO ALFONSO MUÑOZ LATINO
Librarian: Lic. VIOLETA BONICHE SOMARRIBA
Number of teachers: 409
Number of students: 7,518
Publications: *Campus* (6 a year), *Nexo* (4 a year, scientific review), *Teckno* (6 a year)

DEANS

Faculty of Architecture: Arq. VÍCTOR ARCIA GÓMEZ
Faculty of Chemical Engineering: SILVIO ROJAS ZAMBRANA
Faculty of Construction Technology: Ing. JULIO MALTEZ MONTIEL
Faculty of Electrotechnology and Computer Science: Ing. ARIEL ROLDÁN PAREDES
Faculty of Industrial Technology: Ing. DANIEL CUADRA HORNEY
Faculty of Sciences and Systems: RONALD TORRES MERCADO

UNIVERSIDAD POLITÉCNICA DE NICARAGUA

Apdo 3595, Managua
Costado Sur Colonia Rubén Darío, Managua
Telephone: 289-7740
Fax: 249-9232
E-mail: rectoria@upoli.edu.ni
Internet: www.upoli.edu.ni/default.html
Founded 1967 as institute, university status 1977
Private control
Academic year: March to December
Rector: Ing. EMERSON PÉREZ SANDOVAL
Vice-Rector: Dra LIDIA RUTH ZAMORA
Vice-Rector for Academic Affairs: Dra MIRNA CUEVAS RUIZ
Vice-Rector for Students: Lic. BLANCA ROSA GALARZA
Registrar: TOMÁS HANDELL TÉLLEZ RUIZ
Librarian: Licda AURA CELA CORTEZ SILVA
Number of teachers: 101
Number of students: 1,475

DEANS

School of Administration, Commerce and Finance: MIGUEL MURILLO
School of Design: D. I. EDUARDO VANEGAS
School of Economics: EYRA REYES
School of Engineering: Licda GLADYS AGUILAR
School of Law: Dr OSCAR CASTILLO GUIDO
School of Nursing: MARGARITA GUEVARA
School of Tourism: AMPARO MENDOZA

College

Instituto Centroamericano de Administración de Empresas (INCAE): Apdo 2485, Managua; Campus Francisco de Sola Montefresco, Km 15½ Carretera Sur, Managua; tel. 265-8141; fax 265-8617; e-mail incaenic@ mail.incae.edu.ni; internet www.incae.ac.cr; f. 1964 with technical assistance from Harvard Business School; 16-month degree programme in business administration; executive training programmes; management research and consulting; 53 teachers; library: see Libraries and Archives; Rector Dr ROBERTO ARTAVIA.

NIGER

The Higher Education System

The Republic of Niger was formerly part of French West Africa and obtained independence from France in 1960. The Ecole Nationale d'Administration du Niger (founded in 1963) is the oldest current institution of higher education and the Université Abdou Moumouni (founded in 1971; formerly Université de Niamey) was the first university-level institution. The other leading institution is the Université Islamique du Niger (founded in 1986). In 2008/09 there were 9,882 students enrolled in the two universities.

The principal officer of a university is the President or Rector, elected by the faculty to serve three-year, renewable terms of office. A Vice-President is also elected to assist the President. Deans of Faculty and Heads of Department are also elected to their posts and serve for three years and two years, respectively. The Ministry for Secondary and Higher Education, Research and Technology is responsible for all tertiary education.

The entry requirement for higher education courses is the Baccalauréat; however, students who do not hold the Baccalauréat can gain admission by taking an entrance examination. In 2009 the Government introduced the LMD (Licence–Master–Doctorat) reforms, in order to bring the university degree

system closer into line with the European model under the Bologna Process in a bid to harmonize degree structures, credit systems and quality assurance procedures in all higher education programmes and institutions in Niger, as well as in the other seven member states of the West African Economic and Monetary Union, all of which have implemented, or have pledged to implement by 2013, the LMD degree system. Under the new simplified structure, there is a three-year first cycle of study leading to the award of the Licence, followed by a second-cycle, two-year Master degree (merging the previous Maîtrise and Diplôma qualifications) and a third-cycle, three-year Doctorat course. The new structure also introduced a credit-transfer system, enabling students to complete their degree in a department or institution other than the one in which they started, or to leave university and complete their studies at a later date.

Specialist non-university education is offered by institutes attached to the relevant Ministries, including schools and centres for administration, public health, civil aviation and information technology. The Brevet de Technicien Supérieur is awarded to those completing between two and three years of vocational post-secondary education.

Regulatory Bodies
GOVERNMENT

Ministry of Culture, the Arts and Communication: BP 452, Niamey; tel. 20-72-28-74; fax 20-73-36-85; Minister OUMAROU HADARY.

Ministry of Secondary and Higher Education, Research and Technology: BP 628, Niamey; tel. 20-72-26-20; fax 20-72-40-40; e-mail mesnt@intnet.ne; Minister Prof. SIDIKOU OUMAROU.

Learned Society
LANGUAGE AND LITERATURE

Alliance Française: BP 126, Agadez; tel. 20-44-05-82; offers courses and examinations in French language and culture and promotes cultural exchange with France; attached teaching centre in Maradi.

Research Institutes
GENERAL

Institut de Recherche pour le Développement (IRD): Ave de Maradi BP 11416, Niamey; tel. 20-75-38-27; fax 20-75-20-54; e-mail irdniger@ird.ne; internet www.ird.ne; medical entomology, hydrology, genetics, ecology, soil sciences, botany, agronomy, economics, linguistics, sociology; in co-operation with Org. for Co-ordination and Cooperation in the Fight against Endemic Diseases; library: documentation centre of 2,500 vols; Dir FRANCIS KAHN; see main entry under France.

Institut de Recherches en Sciences Humaines (IRSH) de l'Université Abdou Moumouni: BP 318, Niamey; tel. 20-73-51-41; f. 1975 as successor to Institut Français

d'Afrique Noire and Centre Nigérien de Recherches en Sciences Humaines; 6 sections: art and archaeology, history and popular traditions, linguistics and nat. languages, Arabic MSS, geography and environmental devt, sociology of devt, devt economics; library of 30,000 vols; Dir ABDOULAYE MAGA; publs *Etudes Nigériennes* (irregular), *Mu Kara Sani* (2 a year).

AGRICULTURE, FISHERIES AND VETERINARY SCIENCE

Institut de Recherches sur les Fruits et Agrumes (IRFA): BP 886, Niamey; Dir C. LENORMAND; see main entry under France.

Institut National de Recherches Agronomiques au Niger (INRAN): BP 149, Niamey; e-mail inran@intnet.ne; soil science; stations at Tarna and Kolo; Dir J. NABOS.

Laboratoire Vétérinaire de Niamey: Niamey.

Station Avicole et Centre d'Elevage Caprin: Maradi; f. 1961; Dir HASSANE BAZA.

Station Sahélienne Expérimentale de Toukounous: Service d'Elevage du Niger, Toukounous/Filingué; f. 1931; selection and breeding of Zebu Azaouak cattle and distribution of selected bulls to improve the local heterogeneous breed; Dir Dr MANFRED LINDAU; publ. *Berlin Münchner Tierärztliche Wochenschrift*.

HISTORY, GEOGRAPHY AND ARCHAEOLOGY

Centre d'Etudes Linguistiques et Historiques par Tradition Orale: BP 878, Niamey; tel. 20-73-54-14; fax 20-73-36-54; f. 1974; 25 mems; library of 1,250 vols; oral tradition, African languages and cultures; publishes works in African languages, French and English; publ. *Les Cahiers du CELHTO*.

TECHNOLOGY

Bureau de Recherches Géologiques et Minières (BRGM): BP 11458, Niamey; tel. 20-72-23-25; Dir G. BERNERT; see main entry under France.

Office National de l'Energie Solaire: BP 621, Niamey; tel. 20-73-45-05; f. 1965; 40 staff; research, post-univ. and technical courses; Dir Eng. ALBERT WRIGHT.

Libraries and Archives
Niamey

Archives de la République du Niger: BP 550, Niamey; tel. 20-72-26-82; fax 20-72-36-54; f. 1913; documents to the end of the 19th century; Dir IDRISSA YANSAMBOU.

Centre d'Information et de Documentation Economique et Sociale (CIDES): Ministère des Finances et du Plan, BP 862, Niamey; tel. 20-72-33-11; fax 20-73-59-83; f. 1988; attached to Min. of Economy, Finance and Planning; 10,500 vols; Dir MALIKI ABDOULAYE; publ. *CIDES-Flash* (6 a year).

Museum
Niamey

Musée National du Niger: BP 248, Niamey; tel. and fax 20-73-43-21; f. 1959; representative colln of tribal costumes, crafts, tribal houses; incl. park and zoo, geological and mineral exhibition, ethnographic museum, palaeontology and pre-history museums; also Handicrafts Centre and Cultural Activities Centre; Curator NÉINO CHAÏBOU.

Universities

UNIVERSITÉ ABDOU MOUMOUNI DE NIAMEY

BP 237, 10896 Niamey
Telephone: 20-31-57-13
Fax: 20-31-58-62

Founded 1971, univ. status as Univ. de Niamey 1973, present name 1999
State control
Language of instruction: French
Academic year: October to June

Rector: Prof. HABIBOU ABARCHI
Sec.-Gen.: Dr SALIFOU MAÎMOUNA
Librarian: SAIDOU HAROUNA
Library of 62,000
Number of teachers: 304
Number of students: 13,000
Publications: *Annales de l'Université Abdou Moumouni* (1 a year), *Etudes Nigériennes*, *Mu Kara Sani* (2 a year)

DEANS

Faculty of Agronomy, Arts and Humanities: ADAM TOUDOU
Faculty of Arts and Humanities: TANDINA OUSMANE
Faculty of Economics and Law: ALOU MAHAMANE TIDJANI
Faculty of Health Sciences: SAIDOU MAMADOU
Faculty of Science: ABDOULAYE ALHASSANE

UNIVERSITÉ ISLAMIQUE DU NIGER
(Islamic University in Niger)

BP 11507, Niamey, Say
Telephone: 20-72-39-03
Fax: 20-73-37-96
E-mail: unislam@intnet.ne
Internet: www.universite.say.ne

Founded 1986 by the Islamic Conf. Org.
Language of instruction: Arabic
Number of teachers: 20
Number of students: 350

Rector: Prof. ABDEL JAOUAD SEKKAT
Faculties of Arabic Language and Islamic Studies.

College

Ecole Nationale d'Administration du Niger: Rue Martin Luther King Jr, BP 542, Niamey; tel. 20-72-31-83; fax 20-72-43-83; e-mail enaniger@intnet.ne; f. 1963 to train civil servants and other officials; library: 27,000 vols; 116 teachers (56 full-time, 60 part-time); 431 students; Dir DJIBO ISSAKA; publ. *Revue* (2 a year).

NIGERIA

The Higher Education System

The oldest institution of higher education in Nigeria is the Federal College of Agriculture, Ibadan (founded in 1921), while the oldest university is the University of Ibadan (founded in 1948; formerly University College, Ibadan), originally founded in conjunction with the University of London (United Kingdom). Expansion of the university system began following Nigeria's independence in 1963, and the universities established during 1960–70 are referred to as the 'first generation' universities, among them the University of Nigeria (founded in 1960), Obafemi Awolowo University (founded in 1961; present name since 1987), Ahmadu Bello University (founded in 1962), the University of Lagos (founded in 1962) and the University of Benin (founded in 1970). Education is partly the responsibility of the state governments, although the Federal Government has played an increasingly important role since 1970, and universities may be federally, state or privately administered. In 2005 there were 724,856 students enrolled in 80 universities and 237,708 in 178 poly/monotechnics. By 2008 the number of universities had increased to 95. There are three kinds of university: federal universities, the majority of which were formed during the 15 years immediately following independence; state universities, which were established from 1979 in each of Nigeria's 36 states; and private universities, the establishment of which was enabled by legislation approved by the Government in 1993. Degrees from the federal universities are generally more highly regarded than those from state or private universities.

The Governing Board or Council is the governing body of the federal universities, and its members are government appointees. The chief executive role is taken by the Vice-Chancellor in universities, the Rector in polytechnics and the Provost in colleges of education. Funding for public universities is channelled through different parastatal agencies for different types of institution, namely the National Universities Commission (NUC—universities), the National Board for Technical Education (NBTE—polytechnics) and the National Commission for Colleges of Education (colleges). The NUC is also responsible for accreditation and quality assurance for all institutions with degree-awarding powers, which takes place on a six-yearly cycle.

Admission to higher education is made on the basis of sufficient passes in the Senior School Certificate (SSC) and the University Matriculation Examination (UME), administered by the Joint Admissions and Matriculation Board. However, students with acceptable GCE A Level qualifications may enter directly into the second year of a four-year undergraduate course, negating the need for the UME, although GCEs have now been replaced by the SSC in all but a few private schools. Most undergraduate Bachelors degrees last four years, but programmes leading to the award of professional titles last five years and degrees in medicine and dentistry take six years to complete. A student awarded a first- or second-class Bachelors degree with Honours may be admitted to the first postgraduate degree, the Masters, study for which lasts for one to two years. Following the Masters, the Doctorate is the highest university-level degree, and consists of a two- or three-year period of research, submission of a thesis and an oral examination (viva).

Polytechnics and colleges offer post-secondary technical and vocational education. The most popular qualifications offered by these institutions are the two-year Ordinary National Diploma, the two-year Higher National Diploma, entry to which requires the Ordinary National Diploma and one year of relevant work experience, and the Full Professional Diploma, which is open only to holders of the Higher National Diploma and lasts for a minimum of 18 months. Programmes are accredited by the NBTE, which sets standards for non-university further and higher education. Additionally, the Ministry of Health offers professional courses in a number of related fields, including community health, environmental health, food hygiene and public health nursing, completion of which leads to professional registration either with the Ministry or with the West Africa Health Examinations Board.

A number of universities were severely afflicted by a six-month strike in 2010–11; the industrial action was provoked by a memorandum of understanding (MOU), signed in 2009, which sought to increase wages and improve working and living conditions on university campuses. Federal and private universities moved to implement the MOU in 2010, but many state universities, particularly in southern Nigeria, declared themselves unable to do so owing to financial constraints. Following protracted negotiations with staff unions, the administration of President Goodluck Jonathan was reported to have agreed to increase central government funding to help the universities to implement the MOU. Academic activities were subsequently resumed at the affected universities from early 2011. However, the universities in question were prohibited from admitting students for the 2011/12 academic year, having failed to complete the previous year's academic schedule.

Regulatory and Representative Bodies

GOVERNMENT

Ministry of Culture and Tourism: Phase II Federal Secretariat, Block A, 1st Floor, Shehu Shagari Way, Abuja; tel. (9) 2348311; fax (9) 23408297; e-mail akayode@nigeria.gov.ng; internet www.visit-nigeria.gov.ng; Minister ADETOKUNBO KAYODE.

Ministry of Education: New Federal Secretariat Complex, Shehu Shagari Way, Central Area District, PMB 146, Abuja; tel. (9) 5237838; e-mail enquires@fme.gov.ng; internet www.fme.gov.ng; Minister IGWE AJA-NWACHUKWU.

ACCREDITATION

National Universities Commission: Aja Nwachukwu House, Plot 430, Aguiyi Ironsi St, Maitama District, PMB 237, Garki GPO, Abuja; tel. (9) 4133176; fax (9) 4133520; e-mail webmaster@nuc.edu.ng; internet www.nuc.edu.ng; f. 1962; Exec. Sec. Prof. JULIUS OKOJIE.

Learned Societies

GENERAL

UNESCO Office Abuja: PMB 424, Garki, Abuja; located at: Plot 777, Bouake St (off Herbert Macauley Way), Wuse Zone 6, Abuja; tel. (9) 4618502; fax (9) 5238094; e-mail abuja@unesco.org; Dir HUBERT CHARLES.

AGRICULTURE, FISHERIES AND VETERINARY SCIENCE

Fisheries Society of Nigeria: PMB 12529, Lagos; f. 1976; 500 mems; Pres. OLATUNDE OLANIYI; Gen. Sec. B. B. ADEKOYA; publs *Fishery Bulletin*, *Fish Network* (4 a year), *Proceedings*.

Forestry Association of Nigeria: POB 4185, Ibadan, Oyo State; tel. (64) 626535; internet www.forestrynigeria.org; f. 1970 to further interest in forests and forest resources management and utilization; 61 life mems; 1,000 ordinary mems; 17 corporate mems; Pres. BELLOI ABBA YAKASA; Sec. P. C. OBIAGA; publs *FAN Newsletter*, *Nigerian Journal of Forestry*, *Proceedings of Annual Conference*.

Nigerian Veterinary Medical Association: c/o Nigerian Veterinary Medical Institute, POB 38, Vom, Plateau State; f. 1963 to advance the science and art of veterinary medicine, including its relationship to public health and agriculture; 891 mems; Pres. Dr L. H. LOMBIN; Sec. Dr L. Y. NYAM; publs *Nigerian Veterinary Journal* (2 a year), *Tropical Veterinarian* (2 a year), *Zariya Veterinarian* (2 a year).

West African Association of Agricultural Economics: c/o Dept of Agricultural Economics, University of Ibadan, Ibadan, Oyo State; fax (8) 87222872; f. 1972; 250 mems from Benin Republic, Burkina Faso, Cameroon, Côte d'Ivoire, Ghana, Liberia, Mali, Nigeria, Senegal, Sierra Leone and Togo; Pres. Prof. Dr ANTHONY E. IKPI; Sec. Dr THOMAS EPONOU; publ. *West African Journal of Agricultural Economics*.

ARCHITECTURE AND TOWN PLANNING

Nigerian Institute of Architects: 2 Kukawa Close, Garki II, Abuja; tel. (9) 4802518; e-mail info@niarchitects.org; internet www.niarchitects.org; f. 1960; 87 Fellows, 1,370 full mems; 874 graduate mems; Pres. Arc. ERIC CHUKWUKA; publs *NIA Journals, NIA Newsletter, NIA Yearbook and Diary, Shelter for Nigerians*.

BIBLIOGRAPHY, LIBRARY SCIENCE AND MUSEOLOGY

Nigerian Library Association: c/o National Library of Nigeria, Sanusi Dantata House, Business Central District, PMB 1, Garki GPO 900001, Abuja; tel. (9) 2346773; e-mail info@nla-ng.org; internet www.nla-ng.org; f. 1962; 5,000 mems; established to safeguard and promote the professional interests of librarians; to promote the establishment and development of libraries; to assist in the promotion of legislation considered necessary for the establishment, regulation and management of libraries in Nigeria; to encourage bibliographical study, research and library co-operation; Pres. VICTORIA OKOJIE; publs *Nigerian Libraries* (2 a year), *NLA Newsletter* (2 a year), occasional papers.

ECONOMICS, LAW AND POLITICS

Nigerian Bar Association: Plot 1261, Adeola Hopewell St, Victoria Island, Lagos; tel. and fax (1) 4618287; internet www.nigerianbar.com; f. 1962; Pres. Chief BAYO OJO; Gen. Sec. NIMI WALSON-JACK.

Nigerian Economic Society: Dept of Econ., Univ. of Ibadan, Ibadan; tel. (2) 7800395; e-mail adminofficer@nigerianeconomicsociety.org; internet www.nigerianeconomicsociety.org; f. 1957; advances the study and promotes investigation of economic and social problems, with spec. reference to Nigeria; 3,581 mems (incl. 2,000 full mems, 500 assoc. mems, 1,000 life mems, 24 corporate mems, 44 institutional mems and 13 life corporate mems); library of 51 vols; Pres. Prof. K. S. ADEYEMI; Sec. Dr OMO AREGBEYEN; publs *Nigerian Journal of Economic and Social Studies (NJESS)* (3 a year), *Proceedings of Annual Conferences*.

Nigerian Institute of International Affairs: 13 Kofo Abayomi Rd, Victoria Island, POB 1727, Lagos; tel. (1) 9500983; fax (1) 2611360; e-mail dgeneral@niianet.org; internet www.niianet.org; f. 1961; a non-political and non-profit-making org. for the study of int. affairs, to disseminate and maintain information on int. issues through confs, lectures and discussions; 2,344 mems; library of 69,324 vols, 1,707 periodicals, 20,509 pamphlets, 333,085 press clippings; Dir-Gen. Prof. BOLA A. AKINTERINWA (acting); publs *Nigeria: Bulletin on Foreign Affairs* (4 a year), *Nigerian Forum* (12 a year), *Nigerian Journal of International Affairs* (4 a year).

Nigerian Institute of Management: Plot 22, Idowu Taylor St, POB 2557, Victoria Island, Lagos; tel. (1) 2615105; fax (1) 614116; e-mail registrar@managementnigeria.org; internet www.managementnigeria.org; f. 1961; a professional body for the management profession; aims to determine standards of knowledge and skills to be attained by persons seeking to become management professionals; and to regulate and control the profession of management; academic programmes offered include the Professional Diploma in Management and Postgraduate Diploma in Management (with Obafemi Owalowo University, Ile-Ife—see Federal Universities); 20,000 mems; library of 2,300 vols; Dir-Gen. Chief L. E. A. AIMIUWU; publ. *Management in Nigeria* (4 a year).

Nigerian Political Science Association (NPSA): c/o The Secretariat, School of Social Sciences, University of Port Harcourt, PMB 5323, Port Harcourt; f. 1973 to research in politics and government in Nigeria; 200 mems; Pres. Prof. L. ADELE JINADU; Vice-Pres. Dr Y. R. BARONGO; National Sec. Dr CLIFF EDOGUN; publ. *Newsletter*.

EDUCATION

Committee of Vice-Chancellors of Nigerian Federal Universities: 4 Parakou St, Wuse II, Abuja; tel. (9) 5237655; f. 1962; acts as a coordinating body for Federal Univs; offers advice to govt and univ. governing councils on educational matters; 24 fed. univ. mems; Sec.-Gen. Prof. MUSA ABDULLAHI.

HISTORY, GEOGRAPHY AND ARCHAEOLOGY

Historical Society of Nigeria: c/o Dept. of History, University of Lagos, Lagos; internet www.hsnonline.org; f. 1955 to encourage interest and work in connection with the study of history, especially Nigerian history; Pres. Prof. MONDAY B. ABASIATTAI; Sec. Dr I. R. AMADI; publs *Bulletin of News* (4 a year), *Journal, Tarikh* (2 a year).

Nigerian Geographical Association: c/o Dept of Geography, University of Ibadan, Ibadan; tel. (22) 400550; f. 1955; to further interest in geography and its methods of teaching with special reference to Nigeria; 500 mems; Pres. Prof. ADETOYE FANIRAN; publ. *Nigerian Geographical Journal*.

LANGUAGE AND LITERATURE

Alliance Française: c/o French Consulate, Maison de France 2, Aromire Rd (on Kingsway Rd, opp. Ikoyi Hotel), Ikoyi, Lagos; tel. (1) 2692365; fax (1) 2694181; internet www.maisondefrance-ng.com; offers courses and exams in French language and culture and promotes cultural exchange with France; attached teaching centres in Enugu, Ibadan, Ikoyi, Ikoyi-Yaba, Ilorin, Jos, Kaduna, Kano, Lagos, Lagos-Yaba, Maiduguri, Owerri and Port Harcourt.

British Council: Plot 2935, IBB Way, Maitama, PMB 550, Garki, Abuja; tel. (9) 41378707; fax (9) 4130902; e-mail infonigeria@ng.britishcouncil.org; internet www.britishcouncil.org/nigeria; offers courses and exams in English language and British culture and promotes cultural exchange with the UK; attached offices in Lagos and Kano; Dir, Nigeria and Regional Dir, West Africa Dr JOHN RICHARDS.

Goethe-Institut: 10, Ozumba Mbadiwe Ave, opp. 1004 Flats, Victoria Island, Lagos State; tel. (1) 2610717; fax (1) 2617916; e-mail verw@lagos.goethe.org; internet www.goethe.de/af/lag/deindex.htm; offers courses and exams in German language and culture and promotes cultural exchange with Germany; library of 6,000 vols; Dir MICHAEL MÜLLER-VERWEYEN.

MEDICINE

Nigerian Dental Association: c/o Dept of Oral Pathology and Biology, School of Dental Sciences, University of Lagos, PMB 12003, Lagos; fax (1) 5849582; e-mail ndass1966@yahoo.co.uk; Pres. Dr KOFO WINFUNKE SAVAGE; Sec.-Gen. Dr O. A. OREBANJO.

Nigerian Medical Association: POB 1108, Adeniyi Jones Ave, Ikeja, Marina, Lagos; tel. (1) 4801569; fax (1) 4936854; e-mail info@nigeriannma.org; internet www.nigeriannma.org; f. 1951; 35,000 mems; Chair. (vacant); Pres. Dr WOLE ATOYEBI; Sec.-Gen. Dr WAPADA INUWA BALAMI.

Nigerian Society for Microbiology: c/o Prof. Nduka Okafor, Anambra State University of Technology, PMB 1660 Enugu State; f. 1973 to promote the advancement of medical, veterinary, agricultural and industrial microbiology; holds annual conferences in the Nigerian universities; 130 mems; Pres. Dr A. O. EIIOFOR; publ. *Nigerian Journal for Microbiology* (2 a year).

Nutrition Society of Nigeria: c/o Dept of Human Nutrition, Faculty of Public Health, College of Medicine, University of Ibadan, Ibadan, Oyo State; e-mail nutrisocng@yahoo.com; f. 1963; 350 mems; Pres. Prof. ISAAC O. AKINYELE; publ. *Nigerian Nutrition Newsletter*.

NATURAL SCIENCES

General

Nigerian Academy of Science: NSPRI House, 32–36 Barikisu Iyede St, PMB 1004, University of Lagos Post Office, Akoko, Yaba, Lagos; tel. (1) 7916130; e-mail info@nas.org.ng; internet www.nas.org.ng; f. 1977; 120 fellows; Pres. Prof. D. U. U. OKALI; Academic Sec. (Physical Sciences) Prof. A. O. ESOGBUE; Academic Sec. (Biological Sciences) Prof. N. M. GADAZAMA; publs *Discourses* (2 a year), *Newsletter* (2 a year), *Nigerian Journal of Agricultural Sciences* (1 a year), *Nigerian Journal of Medical Sciences* (1 a year), *Nigerian Journal of Natural Sciences* (1 a year), *Proceedings of the Nigerian Academy of Science* (4 a year).

Biological Sciences

Ecological Society of Nigeria: c/o Department of Biological Sciences, University of Lagos, Lagos; f. 1973; 373 mems; Pres. Prof. J. K. EGUNJOBI; Sec. C. CHIKE OKAFO; publs *Newsletter, Proceedings*.

Entomological Society of Nigeria: c/o Department of Crop Protection, Ahmadu Bello University, PMB 1044, Samaru, Zaria, Kaduna State; f. 1965 to further the study of insects in Nigeria; 250 mems; Pres. Prof. S. N. OKIWELU; Sec. O. O. ADU; publs *Nigerian Entomologists' Magazine* (1 a year), *Nigerian Journal of Entomology* (1 a year).

Genetics Society of Nigeria: c/o International Institute of Tropical Agriculture, Oyo Rd, PMB 5320, Ibadan, Oyo State; f. 1972 to further interest in genetics for the benefit of mankind and in the various areas of crops, livestock and medicine; 75 mems; Pres. Dr O. A. OJOMO; Sec. Dr A. O. ABIFARIN; publ. *Proceedings*.

Physical Sciences

Geological Survey of Nigeria: PMB 2007, Kaduna South; tel. (62) 212003; f. 1919; geological mapping; mineral exploration; geophysical and geochemical surveys and consultation on geological problems; library of 34,000 vols; Chief Officer J. I. NEHIKHARE.

OKUNEYE, P. A., Agricultural Economics and Farm Management
OLADOKUN, M. A. O., Horticulture
OLAGOKE, S. T. O., Crop Protection
OLASANTAN, F. O., Horticulture
ONWUKA, C. F., Animal Nutrition
PHILLIP, D., Agricultural Economics and Farm Management
TAYO, T. O., Plant Physiology and Crop Production

UNIVERSITY OF AGRICULTURE, MAKURDI

PMB 2373, Makurdi, Benue State
Telephone: (44) 533204
Founded 1988, previously campus of the University of Jos, now a fully independent university
Federal control
Language of instruction: English
Academic year: October to September
Chancellor: HRH, Igwe (Barr) I. U. NNAJI (Eze Odezurigbo III of Nike, Enugu)
Vice-Chancellor: Prof. D.V. UZA
Registrar: Dr S. A. EDE
Librarian: SUGH LOHO
Number of teachers: 446
Number of students: 7,654
Publication: *Journal of Agriculture, Science and Technology* (2 a year)

DEANS

College of Agricultural Economics and Mgt: Prof. O.J. OKWO
College of Agricultural Engineering and Engineering Technology: Dr I. O. AGBEDE
College of Agricultural Science Education: Prof. A. A. EKOJA
College of Agronomy: Dr M. O. ADEYEMO
College of Animal Science: Prof. O.I.A. OLUREMI
College of Food Science and Technology: Prof. C.C. ARIAHU
College of Forestry and Fisheries: Dr L.O. TIAMIYU
College of Veterinary Medicine: Prof. P.A. ONYEYILI
School of Postgraduate Studies: Prof. E.I. KUCHA

AHMADU BELLO UNIVERSITY

Zaria
Telephone: (69) 550581
Fax: (69) 550022
E-mail: registrar@abu.edu.ng
Founded 1962
Federal control
Language of instruction: English
Academic year: November to August
Vice-Chancellor: Prof. ABDULLAHI MUSTAPHA
Deputy Vice-Chancellor for Academic Affairs: Prof. ALI MOSES ADAMU
Deputy Vice-Chancellor for Admin.: Prof. IDRIS ISA FUNTUA
Registrar: Dr ISAH MOHAMMED ABBASS
Librarian: Prof. ZAKARI MOHAMMAD
Number of teachers: 2,064
Number of students: 35,783
Publications: *Inaugural Lectures* (4 a year), *University Bulletin* (26 a year), *University Gazette, University Public Lectures* (12 a year), *University Research Report*

DEANS

Faculty of Administration: Dr B. SABO
Faculty of Agriculture: Prof. M. C. DIKE
Faculty of Arts: Dr M. L. AMIN
Faculty of Education: Prof J. GWANI
Faculty of Engineering: Prof. O. J. MUDIARE
Faculty of Environmental Design: Prof. M. B. YUNUSA

Faculty of Law: Prof. N. M. JAMO
Faculty of Medicine: Dr S. SHEHU
Faculty of Pharmaceutical Sciences: Dr M. I. SLE
Faculty of Science: Prof. A. J. NOK
Faculty of Social Sciences: Prof. R. A. DUNMOYE
Faculty of Veterinary Medicine: Prof. N. D. G. IBRAHIM
School of Postgraduate Studies: Prof. J. ADEBAYO

PROFESSORS

Faculty of Administration (Kongo Campus, Zaria):

ABDULLAHI, S., Business Administration
ABDULSALAMI, I., Public Administration

Faculty of Agriculture (Agricultural Complex, A. B. U. Main Campus, Zaria):

ATALA, T. K., Rural Sociology
DIKE, M. C., Crop Protection
OGUNLELA, V. B., Agronomy
OLAREWAJU, J. D., Plant Science
OLUFAJO, O. O., Agronomy
OLUKOSI, J. O., Agricultural Economics
VOH, J. P., Rural Sociology

Faculty of Arts (tel. (69) 551540):

ABAH, O. S., English
MAHADI, A., History
MOHAMMED, A., English
NASIDI, Y. A., English

Faculty of Education (e-mail deaneduc@yahoo.com):

ADEYANJU, F. B., Physical and Health Education
CHADO, M. A., Physical and Health Education
KOLO, F. D., Education
LADAN, B. A., Physical and Health Education
OLAOFE, I. A., Education
VENKATESWARLU, K., Physical and Health Education
ZAKARI, M., Library Science

Faculty of Engineering (e-mail deaneng@abu.edu.ng):

ADEFILA, S. S., Chemical Engineering
AKU, S. Y., Mechanical Engineering
FOLAYAN, C. O., Mechanical Engineering
OKUOFU, C. A., Water Resources and Environmental Engineering
OYINOLA, A. K., Metallurgical Engineering

Faculty of Environmental Design (e-mail deanen@abu.edu.ng):

OGUNTONA, T., Industrial Design
SA'AD, H. T., Architecture

Faculty of Law:

CHUKKOL, K., Public Law

Faculty of Medicine:

ADEKEYE, E. A., Dental Surgery
AHMED, M. H., Psychiatry
AIKHIONBARE, H. A., Paediatrics
ALI, M. A., Human Physiology
OGALA, W. N., Paediatrics
ONYEMELUKWE, G. C., Medicine
YAKUBU, A. M., Paediatrics

Faculty of Pharmaceutical Sciences (tel. (69) 951209; e-mail emabdu@abu.edu.ng):

AGUYE, I. A., Pharmacy and Clinical Pharmacy
HUSSEIN, I., Pharmacology and Clinical Pharmacy
ILYAS, M., Pharmacy and Medicinal Chemistry
MUSTAPHA, A., Pharmaceutical and Medicinal Chemistry
ONAOLAPO, J. A., Pharmaceutical Science and Microbiology

Faculty of Science (tel. (69) 551886; e-mail science@abu.edu.ng):

AHMAD, A., Microbiology

AMUPITAN, J. O., Chemistry
ARIYO, J. A., Geography
AWODI, S., Biological Sciences
BELLO, K. O., Textile Science and Technology
IKE, E. C., Geology
IYUN, J. F., Chemistry
KOLAWOLE, E. G., Textile Science and Technology
NKEONYE, P. O., Textile Science and Technology
OSAZUWA, I. B., Physics

Faculty of Social Sciences (tel. (69) 551540; fax (69) 550022):

DUNMOYE, A., Political Science
KWANASHIE, M., Economics
NKOM, S., Sociology

Faculty of Veterinary Medicine (tel. (69) 551358; e-mail deanvet@abu.edu.ng):

ABDULLAHI, U., Veterinary Surgery and Medicine
AGBEDE, R. I. S., Parasitology and Entomology
ESIEVO, K. A. N., Veterinary Pathology and Medicine
GHAJI, A., Veterinary Anatomy
HAMBOLU, J. O., Anatomy
KWAGA, J. P. K., Veterinary Public Health and Preventive Medicine
OGWU, D., Veterinary Surgery and Medicine
OJO, S. A., Veterinary Anatomy
UMOH, J. U., Veterinary Public Health and Preventive Medicine
ZARIA, L. T., Veterinary Pathology and Microbiology

Centres:

ABUBAKAR, S., National Agricultural Research and Liaison Services
ADAMU, A. M., National Animal Production Research Institute
ADEGBEHIN, J. D., National Agricultural Research and Liaison Services
ALIYU, J. S., Institute of Education
BAIKIE, A., Institute of Education
EDUVIE, L. V., National Animal Production Research Institute
GEFU, J. O., National Animal Production Research Institute
OTCHERE, E. O., National Animal Production Research Institute
VOH, A., National Animal Production Research Institute

BAYERO UNIVERSITY

PMB 3011, Kano
Telephone: (64) 666023
Fax: (64) 665904
E-mail: registrar@buk.edu.ng
Founded 1977
Federal control
Language of instruction: English
Academic year: October to July (2 semesters)
Chancellor: HRH OBA SIJUWADE OKUNADE OLUBUSE, II (Ooni of Ife)
Chair. of Council: MUHD ADAMU JUMBA
Vice-Chancellor: Prof. ABUBAKAR ADAMU RASHID
Deputy Vice-Chancellor for Academic Affairs: Prof. MUHD YAHUZA BELLO
Deputy Vice-Chancellor for Admin.: Prof. ABDULRASHID GARBA
Registrar: SANI IBRAHIM AMIN
Librarian: Prof. IBRAHIM LUKMAN DISO
Library of 170,000 vols, 2,200 periodicals
Number of teachers: 793
Number of students: 28,941
Publications: *Bayero University Quarterly News, University Public Lectures* (1 a year)

DEANS

Faculty of Agriculture: Prof. AUWALU MANSUR BINDAWA
Faculty of Arts and Islamic Studies: Prof. SAIDU A. BABURA
Faculty of Education: Dr IBRAHIM M. YAKASAI
Faculty of Law: Dr A. B. AHMAD
Faculty of Medicine: Dr ABDU LAWAN
Faculty of Science: M. S. SULE
Faculty of Social and Management Sciences: Prof. SULEIMAN ALIYU KANTUDU
Faculty of Technology: Dr A. U. ALHAJI
General Studies Unit: Dr LAWAN S. TAURA (Dir)
Postgraduate School: Prof. SADIQ ISA RADDA

PROFESSORS

ABBA, I. A., History
ABDULKADIR, D., Centre for the Study of Nigerian Languages
ABDULKADIR, M. S., History
ABDULLAHI, M., Sociology
ABUBAKAR, M. A., Arabic
ABUBAKAR, M. M.
ADAMU, U. A., Education
AHMED, K., Geography
AJIBERO, M., Library Science
AYODELE, J. T., Chemistry
AZARE, G. D., Education
BICHI, A. Y., Centre for the Study of Nigerian Languages
BICHI, M. Y., Education
DAMBATTA, B. B., Chemistry
DANGAMBO, A., Nigerian Languages
DISO, S. I., Mechanical Engineering
DUZE, M. C., Sociology
EGBON, M., Mass Communication
ESSIET, E. U., Geography
FAGBEMI, A. O., Education
FALOLA, J. A., Geography
FATOPE, M. O., Physics
GUSAU, S. M., Nigerian Languages
HASHIM, I., Political Science
IBRAHIM, M., Paediatrics
JEGA, A. M., Political Science
JIBRIL, M. M., English Language
JOWITT, D. R., English and European Languages
KATANDE, J., Electrical Engineering
MAIWAQDA, D. A., Education
MUHAMMAD, A. R., History
OCHOGWU, M., Library Science
OLOFIN, E. A., Geography
PEDRO, I. A., Economics
RUJBANI, S. M., Mathematics
SALIHI, A., Mechanical Engineering
SALIM, B. A., Nigerian Languages
SANI, M. A. Z., Nigerian Languages
SHEA, P. J., History
SULEIMAN, M. D., History
TABI'U, M., Islamic Law
UMAR, I. H., Physics
YADUDU, A. H., Law
YAHAYA, D., History
ZAHRADEEN, M. S., Islamic Studies
ZAHRADEEN, U., Management Science

UNIVERSITY OF BENIN

Ugbowo-Lagos Rd, Ugbowo, PMB 1154, Benin City
Telephone: (52) 600443
Fax: (52) 241156
E-mail: registrar@uniben.edu
Internet: www.uniben.edu
Founded 1970
Federal control
Language of instruction: English
Academic year: October to June
Chancellor: HRH Alhaji Dr MUHAMMADU BARKINDO ALIYU MUSDAFA
Pro-Chancellor: Sir GABRIEL TOBY
Vice-Chancellor: Prof. O. G. OSHODIN
Deputy Vice-Chancellor for Academic Affairs: Prof. E. A. ONIBERE

Deputy Vice-Chancellor for Admin.: Prof. J. A. OKHUOYA
Registrar: G. O. OGBOGHODO
Librarian: S. A. OGUNROMBI (acting)
Library of 265,144 vols
Number of teachers: 1,182
Number of students: 31,247
Publications: *Benin Journal of Educational Studies, Faculty of Arts Journal* (4 a year), *Faculty of Education Journal* (2 a year), *Journal of the Humanities, Physical Health Education and Recreational Journal, University of Benin Law Journal* (1 a year)

DEANS

Faculty of Agriculture: Prof. U. J. IKHATUA
Faculty of Arts: Prof. A. O. ASAGBA
Faculty of Education: Prof. MON NWADIANI
Faculty of Engineering: Prof. F. O. EDEKO
Faculty of Law: Prof. A. ATSEGBUA
Faculty of Life Sciences: Prof. C. C. OSUBOR
Faculty of Management Sciences: Prof. B. A. AGBONIFOH
Faculty of Pharmacy: Prof. E. O. OSAZUWA
Faculty of Physical Sciences: Prof. S. M. OGBONNWAN
Faculty of Social Sciences: Prof. C. O. OKOLOCHA
School of Dentistry: Prof. B. D. O. SAHEED
School of Medicine: Prof. D. E. OVIASU
School of Postgraduate Studies: Prof. R. O. ELAIHO

PROFESSORS

ABIODUN, P. O., Child Health
ADEMOROTI, C. M. A., Chemistry
AFE, J. O., Educational Psychology and Curriculum Studies
AGBADUDU, A. B., Business Administration
AGBAKWURU, E. O. P., Pharmaceutical Chemistry
AGHENTA, J. A., Educational Administration and Foundations
AHONKHAI, S. I., Chemistry
AJISAFE, M. O., Physical and Health Education
AKERELE, A., Business Administration
ALAKIJA, W., Community Health
ANAO, A. R., Accounting
ASALOR, J. O., Mechanical Engineering
AUDU, T. O. K., Chemical Engineering
AWANBOR, D., Educational Psychology and Curriculum Studies
AWARITEFE, A. A., Mental Health
AYANRU, D. K. G., Microbiology
AYANRU, J. O., Ophthalmology
BADMUS, G. A., Educational Psychology and Curriculum Studies
BAFOR, B. E., Geology
EBEIGBE, A. B., Physiology
EBEWELE, R. O., Chemical Engineering
ECHENIM, K., Modern Languages
EGHAFONA, N. O., Microbiology
EGUDU, R. N., English and Literature
EHIAMETALOR, E. T., Educational Administration and Foundations
EKUNDAYO, J. A., Microbiology
GRILLO, B. O., Anatomy
HUGBO, P. G., Pharmaceutical Microbiology
IGBAFE, A. I., History
IGENE, J. O., Animal Science
IKEDIUGWU, F. E. O., Microbiology
IKENEBOMEH, M. J., Microbiology
IKHATUA, J. U., Animal Science
ILOHA, M. A., Economics and Statistics
IMEOKPARIA, G. E., Geology
IMOGIE, A. I., Educational Psychology and Curriculum Studies
IREMIREN, G. O., Crop Science
IWU, G. O., Chemistry
KUALE, P. A., Civil Engineering
NDIOKWERE, C. L., Chemistry
NWAGWU, N. A., Educational Administration and Foundations

NWANZE, E. C., Biochemistry
NWOKOYE, D. N., Civil Engineering
OBADAN, M. I., Economics and Statistics
OBASEIKI-EBOR, E. E., Pharmaceutical Microbiology
OBASOHAN, A. O., Medicine
OBIANWU, H. O., Pharmacology and Toxicology
OBIKA, L. F., Physiology
OBUEKWE, C. O., Microbiology
ODEBUNMI, A., Educational Psychology and Curriculum Studies
ODIME, O., Surgery
OFOEGBU, R. O., Surgery
OFUANI, O. A., English and Literature
OGBEIDE, N. O., Chemistry
OGBEIDE, O., Community Health
OGBIMI, A. O., General Studies
OGONOR, J. I., Pharmaceutical Chemistry
OGUDE, S. E., English and Literature
OHWOVORIOLE, E. N., Mechanical Engineering
OJOGWU, L. I., Medicine
OKAFOR, F. C., Geography and Regional Planning
OKEH, P. I., Modern Languages
OKEKE, E. O., Mathematics
OKHAMAFE, A. O., Pharmaceutics and Pharmaceutical Technology
OKHUOYA, J. A., Botany
OKIEIMEN, F. E., Chemistry
OKOH, S. E. N., Economics and Statistics
OKOJIE, C. E., Economics and Statistics
OKOLO, A. A., Child Health
OKOLOKO, G., Botany
OKONOFUA, F. E., Obstetrics and Gynaecology
OKOR, R. S., Pharmaceutics and Pharmaceutical Technology
OLA, R. F., Physics
OLOMU, J. M., Animal Science
OMIUNU, F. G. I., Geography and Regional Planning
OMU, F. I. A., History
OMUTA, G. E. D., Geography and Regional Planning
ONOKERHORAYE, A. G., Geography and Regional Planning
OPUTE, F. I., Botany
OROBATOR, S. E., Physics
ORONSAYE, A. U., Obstetrics and Gynaecology
OSAGIE, A. U., Biochemistry
OSAZE, R. E., Business Administration
OSHODIN, O. G., Physical and Health Education
OWIE, I., Physical and Health Education
OYAIDE, W. J., Agricultural Economics and Extension Services
SADA, P. O., Geography and Regional Planning
SALAMI, L. A., Mechanical Engineering
SANNI, B. S., Chemistry
UCHE, C., Sociology and Anthropology
UFOMATA, D., Restorative Dentistry
URAIH, N., Microbiology
WEMAMBU, S. N. C., Medical Microbiology

UNIVERSITY OF CALABAR

PMB 1115, Calabar, Cross River State
Telephone: (87) 232790
Fax: (87) 231766
E-mail: webadmin@unicaledu.org
Internet: www.unicaledu.org
Founded 1975, previously a campus of the University of Nigeria
Federal control
Language of instruction: English
Academic year: October to July
Chancellor: HRH IGWE KINGSLEY CHIME (Eze of Abia)
Vice-Chancellor: Prof. IVARA EJEMOT ESU
Deputy Vice-Chancellor for Academic Affairs: Prof. A. I. ESSIEN
Deputy Vice-Chancellor for Admin.: Prof. JOHN O. OFEM

Registrar: E. E. EFFIOM
Librarian: Dr OLU OLAT LAWAL
Number of teachers: 707
Number of students: 22,678 (full-time)

DEANS

Faculty of Agriculture: Prof. A. I. ESSIEN
Faculty of Arts: Prof. CHRIS NWAMUO
Faculty of Basic Medical Sciences: Prof. I. B. UMOH
Faculty of Clinical Sciences: Dr C. E. ANTIA-OBONG (acting)
Faculty of Education: Prof. S. C. UCHE (acting)
Faculty of Laboratory and Allied Health Sciences: Prof. A. E. UDOH (acting)
Faculty of Law: N. O. ITA (acting)
Faculty of Science: Prof. JOHN O. OFFEM
Faculty of Social Sciences: Prof. JOHN E. NDEBBIO
College of Medical Sciences: Prof. SPENCER EFEM
Graduate School: Prof. EBONG W. MBIPOM

PROFESSORS

Faculty of Agriculture:
  AMALU, U. C., Soil Science
  ASUQUO, B. O., Animal Science
  ESSIEN, A. I., Animal Science
  ESU, I., Soil Science
Faculty of Arts:
  ABASIATTAI, M. B., History
  EKO, E. O., English and Literary Studies
  ERIM, E. O, History
  ESSIEN, O. E. A., Languages and Linguistics
  IKONNE, C. U. E., English and Literary Studies
  IWE, N. S. S., Religious Studies and Philosophy
  JOHN, E. E., Languages and Linguistics
  NOAH, M. E., History
  NWAMUO, C. I., Theatre Arts
  ORISAWAYI, D., English and Literary Studies
  UKA, K., Theatre Arts
  UYA, O. E., History
Faculty of Education:
  ABODERIN, A. O., Curriculum and Teaching
  AMADI, L. E., Curriculum and Teaching
  DENGA, D. I., Educational Foundations and Administration
  ENUKOHA, O. I.
  ESU, A. E.
  IKPAYA, B. O.
  NWACHUKWU, D. N., Guidance and Counselling
  OMOJUWA, J. O.
  UCHE, S. C.
College of Medical Sciences:
  AKPAN, J. O., Pharmacology
  ANDY, J. J., Medicine
  ATTAH, E. B., Pathology
  BASSEY, O. O., Surgery
  BOLARIN, D. M., Chemical Pathology
  BRAIDE, V. B., Pharmacology
  EFEM, S., Surgery
  EJEZIE, G. C., Medical Microbiology and Parasitology
  EKA, O. U., Biochemistry
  ESSIEN, E. U., Biochemistry
  ONUBA, O. O., Surgery
  OSIM, E. E., Physiology
  OTU, A. A., Surgery
  UMOH, I. B., Biochemistry
  UTSALO, S. J., Medical Microbiology, Parasitology
Faculty of Science:
  AKPAN, E. B., Geology
  BRAIDE, E. I., Parasitology
  EKPA, O. D., Chemistry
  EKPE, U. J., Chemistry
  EKWERE, S. J., Geology

EKWUEME, B. N., Geology
IBOK, U. J., Chemistry
LIPCSY, Z.
MBIPOM, E. W., Physics
MENKITI, A. I., Physics
OFFEM, J. O., Chemistry
OKUWEZE, E. E., Physics
PETERS, S. W., Geology
USUA, E. J., Biological Sciences
UWAH, E. J., Physics
Faculty of Social Sciences:
  BASSEY, C. O., Political Science
  EBONG, M. O., Geography, Regional Planning
  ETUK, E. J., Management Studies
  NDEBBIO, J. E. U., Economics
  OBOT, J. U., Geography, Regional Planning
  OTTONG, J. G., Sociology
  SULE, R. A. O., Geography, Regional Planning
Institute of Oceanography:
  ANTAI, E. E.
  HOLZLONER, S.
  OBIEKEZIE, A. I.
Institute of Public Policy and Administration:
  UYA, O. E.

FEDERAL UNIVERSITY OF TECHNOLOGY, AKURE

PMB 704, Akure, Ondo State
Telephone: (34) 243744
Fax: (34) 230450
Internet: futa-edu.ng
Founded 1981
State control
Language of instruction: English
Academic year: October to September
Chancellor: Emir of Lafia ISA MUSTAPHA AGWAI II
Vice-Chancellor: Prof. PETER O. ADENIYI
Deputy Vice-Chancellor for Academic: Prof. O. C. ADEMOSUN
Deputy Vice-Chancellor for Devt: Prof. A. M. BALOGUN
Registrar: Dr E. F. OYEBADE
Librarian: O. A. OKE (acting)
Number of teachers: 442
Number of students: 13,432
Publications: *Journal of Applied Tropical Agriculture* (4 a year), *Journal of Urban and Environmental Research* (every 2 years), *Nigerian Journal of Pure and Applied Physics* (4 a year)

DEANS

School of Agriculture and Agricultural Technology: Prof. J. A. FUWAPE
School of Engineering and Engineering Technology: Prof. C. O. ADEGOKE
School of Environmental Technology: Prof. D. O. OLANREWAJU
School of Mines and Earth Sciences: Prof. J. S. OJO
School of Sciences: Prof. K. O. IPINMOROTI
School of Postgraduate Studies: Prof. V. A. ALETOR

FEDERAL UNIVERSITY OF TECHNOLOGY, MINNA

PMB 65, Minna, Niger State
Telephone and fax (66) 222422
E-mail: futmx@skannet.com
Internet: www.futminna.net
Founded 1983
Fed. control
Language of instruction: English
Academic year: October to September (2 semesters)

Chancellor: The Olu of Warri, HRH OGIAME ATUWASE II
Pro-Chancellor: Prof. RUFA'I AHMED ALKALI
Vice-Chancellor: Prof. MUHAMMED SALIHU AUDU
Deputy Vice-Chancellor: Dr AKIM O. OSUNDE
Registrar: MALLAM M. D. USMAN
Bursar: M. A. BELLO
Librarian: MUHAMMAD IBN MUHAMMAD
Number of teachers: 698
Number of students: 13,589
Publications: *Journal of Agricultural Technology* (2 a year), *Journal of Science, Technology and Mathematics Education* (2 a year), *Nigeria Journal of Technological Research* (2 a year), *Proceedings of the National Engineering Conference* (1 a year)

DEANS

School of Agriculture and Agricultural Technology: Prof. K. M. BABA
School of Engineering and Engineering Technology: Prof. J. O. ODIGUORE
School of Environmental Technology: Prof. O. O. MORENKEJI
School of Science and Science Education: Prof. MUSA GALADIMA
Postgraduate School: Prof. SAMUEL L. LAMAI

FEDERAL UNIVERSITY OF TECHNOLOGY, OWERRI

PMB 1526, Owerri, Imo State
Telephone: (83) 233228
E-mail: vc@futo.edu.ng
Founded 1980
Federal control
Language of instruction: English
Academic year: October to July
Chancellor: HRH Dr SHEKARAU ANGYU MASSA-IBI
Pro-Chancellor: VITA O. ABBA
Vice-Chancellor: Prof. CELESTINE O. E. ONWULIRI (acting)
Deputy Vice-Chancellor for Academic Affairs: Prof. E. T. ESHETT
Deputy Vice-Chancellor for Admin.: Prof. M. I. NWUFO
Registrar: C. O. OMEIRE
Bursar: R.-U. AKUJOBI
Librarian: J. E. NWOGU
Library of 68,345 vols
Number of teachers: 699
Number of students: 21,307
Publications: *Annual Review, Centre for Industrial Studies, Erosion News* (4 a year)

DEANS

School of Agriculture and Agricultural Technology: Prof. C. C. ASIABAKA
School of Engineering and Engineering Technology: Prof. O. N. OGUOMA
School of Management Technology: Prof. G. E. NWORUH
School of Science: Dr F. C. EZE (acting)
Postgraduate School: Prof. C. D. OKEREKE

PROFESSORS

ACHI, P., Mechanical Engineering
AGBOGU, A., Political Science
AGWU, E., Transport Management Technology
AKPAN, E., Engineering
AKUJOR, C., Astrophysics and Space Physics
ALAEZI, O., Curriculum and Vocational Education
ANANABA, S., Geophysics
ANEKE, L., Chemical Engineering
ANUNUSO, C., Analytical Chemistry
ANYANWU, B., Microbiology
ANYANWU, E., Mechanical Engineering
ARIRIATU, L., Industrial Microbiology
ASIABAKA, C., Agricultural Extension

ASIEGBU, L., Ethical Philosophy
DURU, J., Water Resources Engineering
EHEDURU, G., Information Management Technology
EJIKE, E., Chemistry
EMEHAROLE, P., Public Health Technology
ENYIEGBULAM, M., Polymer Science and Technology
ESHETT, E., Pedology
ESONU, B., Animal Nutrition
EZE, F., Physics
IBE, K., Geology
IHEONYE, A., Polymer and Textile Engineering
ILOEJE, M., Animal Genetics
IWUAGWU, C., Geology
IWUALA, M., Biology
IWUOHA, C., Food Science and Technology
MBAKWE, R., Forestry and Wildlife Management
NDUKA, A., Theoretical Physics and Applied Mathematics
NJOKU, J., Agricultural Economics
NJOKU, O., Biology
NJIRIBEAKO, I., Chemical Engineering
NTAMERE, C., Economics
NWABUEZE, R., Microbiology
NWACHUKWU, B., Civil Engineering
NWACHUKWU, E., Computer Science
NWADIARO, C., Fisheries and Aquaculture
NWAFOR, O., Mechanical Engineering
NWANKITI, A., Crop Science and Technology
NWANKWOR, G., Geology
NWIGWE, H., Biotechnology
NWORUH, G., Statistics
NWUFO, M., Plant Pathology
OBAH, B., Petroleum Engineering
OBIEFUNA, J., Horticulture
OFOH, M., Crop Science Technology
OGBOBE, O., Polymer and Textile Engineering
OGBOGU, S., Electrical/Electronic Engineering
OGBULIE, J., Microbiology
OGUOMA, O., Mechanical Engineering
OGWEUEGBU, M., Industrial Chemistry
OGWUDE, I., Transport Management
OGWUDE, S., English Literature
OKEREKE, C., Environmental Engineering
OKPALA, K., Chemical Engineering
OKORAFOR, O., Metallurgical Engineering
ONONIWU, J., Solid State Physics
ONU, N., Geophysics
ONUOHA, G., Chemistry
ONWUAGBA, B., Physics
ONWULIRI, C., Zoology/Parasitology/Biotechnology
ONWULIRI, V., Biochemistry
ONYEAGORO, E., Mechanical Engineering
ONYEJEKWE, D., Mechanical Engineering
ONYEJIEKWE, E., Public Health Technology
ONYEMAOBI, O., Material and Metallurgical Engineering
ONYEZE, G., Industrial Biochemistry
ONYIRIUKA, S., Organic Chemistry
OREBIYI, J., Agricultural Economics
OSONDU, K., Pure Mathematics
OSUALA, F., Biotechnology
OSUAGWU, O., Information Management Technology
OSUJI, G., Soil Science
OWUAMA, O., Environmental Technology
OZOH, P., Environmental Management and Toxicology
UBBAONU, C., Food Processing and Product Development
UDEDIBIE, A., Animal Nutrition
UFODIKE, E., Fisheries and Aquaculture
UKOHA, A., Biochemistry

FEDERAL UNIVERSITY OF TECHNOLOGY, YOLA

PMB 2076, Yola, Adamawa State
Telephone and fax (75) 624416

E-mail: vcfuty@yahoo.com
Internet: www.futy.edu.ng

Founded 1981, present status 1988
Federal control
Language of instruction: English
Academic year: October to September
Chancellor: HH Oba GABRIEL ADEKUNLE AROMOLARAN II
Vice-Chancellor: Prof. ABDULLAHI YUSUFU RIBADU
Registrar: Alh. AHMED USMAN W/CHEKKE
Librarian: Prof. B. S. H. WOMBOH
Library of 29,000 vols
Number of teachers: 345
Number of students: 9,701

Publication: *Technology and Development* (1 a year)

DEANS

School of Agriculture and Agricultural Technology: Prof. A. KADAMS
School of Engineering and Engineering Technology: Prof. P. B. OMAJI
School of Environmental Sciences: Dr F. ILLESANMI
School of Management and Information Technology: Prof. S. O. ANYANWU
School of Pure and Applied Sciences: Dr A. OKOLO
School of Technology and Science Education: Dr L. C. EZUGU
School of Postgraduate Studies: Prof. G. FAKUADE

UNIVERSITY OF IBADAN

Ibadan
Telephone: (2) 7511988
E-mail: vc@mail.ui.edu.ng
Internet: www.ui.edu.ng

Founded 1948 as University College, Ibadan, a constituent College of the University of London, UK, present name and status 1962
Federal control
Language of instruction: English
Academic year: September to July
Chancellor: HH ALHAJI ADO BAYERO
Vice-Chancellor: Prof. OLUFEMI A. BAMIRO
Deputy Vice-Chancellor for Academics: Prof. A. A. B. AGBAJE
Deputy Vice-Chancellor for Admin.: Prof. ELIJAH A. BAMGBOYE
Registrar: OMOTAYO O. IKOTUN
Librarian: Dr B. A. OLADELE
Library: see under Libraries and Archives
Number of teachers: 1,214
Number of students: 19,521

Publications: *Digest of Statistics, Ivory Tower, Official Bulletin, Official Gazette, Order of Proceedings, Pocket Statistics, Research Bulletin of the Centre for Arabic Documentation* (2 a year), *Student Information Handbook, University Calendar*

DEANS

Faculty of Agriculture and Forestry: Prof. F. K. EWETE
Faculty of Arts: Prof. P. A. OGUNDEJI
Faculty of Basic Medical Sciences: Prof. O. D. OLALEYE
Faculty of Clinical Sciences: Prof. O. M. OLUWATOSIN
Faculty of Dentistry: Prof. GHEMISOLA A. OKE
Faculty of Education: Prof. J. B. BABALOLA
Faculty of Law: Prof. OLUYEMISI A. BAMGBOSE
Faculty of Pharmacy: Prof. J. O. MOODY
Faculty of Science: Prof. K. O. ADEBOWALE
Faculty of Social Sciences: Prof. KASSEY GARBA
Faculty of Technology: Prof. A. E. OLULEYE
Faculty of Veterinary Medicine: Prof. V. O. TAIWO

Postgraduate School: Prof. L. POPOOLA
Student Affairs: Prof. A. E. FALAYE

PROFESSORS

Faculty of Agriculture and Forestry:
ADEJUMO, O., Animal Science
ADEOYE, G., Agronomy
AIYELARI, E., Agronomy
AKEN'OVA, M., Agronomy
AKINSOYINU, A., Animal Science
AKORODA, M., Agronomy
ATIRI, G., Crop Protection and Environmental Biology
AYODELE, A., Wildlife and Fisheries
BADA, S., Forest Resources Management
EKPO, E., Crop Protection and Enviromental Biology
EWETE, F., Crop Protection and Enviromental Biology
FALAYE, A., Wildlife and Fisheries
FALUSI, A., Agricultural Economics
FATUROTI, E., Wildlife and Fisheries
FAWOLE, B., Crop Protection and Enviromental Biology
IKOTUN, B., Crop Protection and Enviromental Biology
IKPI, A., Agricultural Economics
IYAYI, E., Animal Science
LADELE, A., Agricultural Extension and Rural Development
LONGE, O., Animal Science
LUCAS, E., Agronomy
OGUNKUNLE, A., Agronomy
OGUNYEMI, S., Crop Protection and Enviromental Biology
OLAWOYE, J., Agricultural Extension and Rural Development
OLOGHOBO, A., Animal Science
OMUETI, J., Agronomy
OSHO, J., Forest Resources Management
POPOOLA, L., Forest Resources Management
TEWE, O., Animal Science
TIJANI-ENIOLA, H., Agronomy
TOGUN, A., Crop Protection and Enviromental Biology

Faculty of Arts:
ABDULRAHMON, M., Arabic and Islamic Studies
ADEBAYO, A., European Studies
ADEKOYA, O., English
ADESANOYE, F., Communication and Language Arts
AKINYEYE, O., History
DASYLVA, A., English
DRURGBA, A., Religious Studies
EGBOKHARE, F., Linguistics and African Languages
ELUGBE, B., Linguistics and African Languages
IRELE, J., Philosophy
LAWAL, O., History
ODEJIDE, I., Communication and Language Arts
OGUNDEJI, P., Linguistics and African Languages
OLADIPO, O., Philosophy
OMAMOR, P., Linguistics and African Languages
OMOSINI, O., History
OSOFISAN, B., Theatre Arts
OWOLABI, D., Linguistics and African Languages
OYELEYE, A., English
OYETADE, S., Linguistics and African Languages

Faculty of Basic Medical Sciences:
ADENIYI, F., Chemical Pathology
AGBEDANA, E., Chemical Pathology
AKANG, E., Pathology
AKEN'OVA, Y., Haematology
BAKARE, R., Medical Microbiology and Parasitology
BOLARINWA, A., Physiology

FAROMBI, E., Biochemistry
MADUAGWU, E., Biochemistry
OGUNBIYI, J., Pathology
OLALEYE, D., Virology
OLORUNSOGO, O., Biochemistry
OSOTIMEHIN, B., Chemical Pathology
OYEBOLA, D., Physiology
SHOKUNBI, W., Haematology
SHOKUNBI, M., Anatomy
SOWUNMI, A., Pharmacy and Therapeutics

Faculty of Clinical Sciences:
ADEBAMOWO, C., Surgery
ADEGBOYE, V., Surgery
ADEKUNLE, A., Obstetrics and Gynaecology
ADEWOLE, I., Obstetrics and Gynaecology
AJAIYEOBA, A., Ophthalmology
AKINYINKA, O., Paediatrics
AMANOR-BOADU, S., Anaesthesia
ARIJE, A., Medicine
AROWOJOLU, A., Obstetrics and Gynaecology
ASUZU, M., Community Medicine
BAIYEROJU, A., Ophthalmology
BAIYEWU, O., Psychiatry
CAMPBELL, O., Radiotherapy
FALADE, A., Paediatrics
GEORGE, A., Medicine
GUREJE, O., Psychiatry
IJADUOLA, G., Otorhinolaryngology
ILESANMI, A., Obstetrics and Gynaecology
KADIRI, S., Medicine
NWAORGU, O., Otorhinolaryngology
OGUNNIYI, A., Medicine
OGUNSEYINDE, A., Radiology
OJENGBEDE, O., Obstetrics and Gynaecology
OLUWATOSIN, O., Surgery
OMIGBODUN, A., Obstetrics and Gynaecology
OMOKHODION, S., Paediatrics
OMOKHODION, F., Community Medicine
OSINUSI, K., Paediatrics
SALAKO, B., Medicine
SANYA, A., Physiotherapy
SHITTU, O., Surgery
SOYANNWO, O., Anaesthesia

Faculty of Dentistry:
AROWOJOLU, M. O., Preventive Dentistry
LAWOYIN, J. O., Oral Pathology
OBIECHINA, A. E., Oral & Maxillofacial Surgery
OKE, G. A., Preventive Dentistry

Faculty of Education:
AJAYI, E., Educational Management
AKINTAYO, M., Adult Education
ALEGBELEYE, G., Library, Archival and Information Studies
ATINMO, M., Library, Archival and Information Studies
AYODELE-BAMISAIYE, O., Teacher Education
BABALOLA, J., Educational Management
MABAWONKU, I., Library, Archival and Information Studies
NWAZUOKE, A., Special Education
OGUNDELE, B., Human Kinetics and Health Education
OGUNSANYA, M., Educational Management
UWAKWE, C., Guidance and Counselling

Faculty of Law:
AGBEDE, I., Private and Business Law
ANIFALAJE, J., Private and Business Law
BAMGBOSE, O., Private and Business Law
OMOROGBE, O., Public and International Law
OWOADE, M., Public and International Law

Faculty of Pharmacy:
AJAIYEOBA, E. O., Pharmacognosy
BABALOLA, C. P., Pharmaceutical Chemistry
ERHUN, W. O., Clinical Pharmacy and Pharmacy Administration
ITIOLA, O. A., Pharmaceutical and Industrial Pharmacy

JAIYEOBA, K. T., Pharmaceutical and Industrial Pharmacy
MOODY, J. O., Pharmacognosy

Faculty of Public Health:
AKINYELE, I. O., Human Nutrition and Dietetics
ATINMO, T., Human Nutrition and Dietetics
AYENI, O., Epidemiology, Medical Statistics and Environmental Health
BAMGBOYE, E. A., Epidemiology, Medical Statistics and Environmental Health
OLADEPO, O., Health Promotion and Education

Faculty of Science:
ADEBOWALE, K., Chemistry
ADELEKE, B., Chemistry
ADESOMOJU, A., Chemistry
BAMIRO, F., Chemistry
EKHAGUERE, G., Mathematics
EKUNDAYO, O., Chemistry
ELUEZE, A., Geology
FARAI, I., Physics
FOLORUNSO, C., Archaeology and Anthropology
HASSAN, A., Zoology
HUSSAIN, L., Physics
ILORI, S., Mathematics
LAWUYI, O., Archaeology and Anthropology
ODAIBO, A., Zoology
ODERINDE, R., Chemistry
ODIAKA, T., Chemistry
ODUNFA, S., Botany and Microbiology
OKUNADE, A., Physics
OLADIRAN, E., Physics
OLAYINKA, A., Geology
ONIANWA, P., Chemistry
OSIBANJO, O., Chemistry
OSOFISAN, A., Computer Science
OSONUBI, O., Botany and Microbiology
OYELARAN, P., Archaeology and Anthropology
SANNI, A., Botany and Microbiology
UGWUMBA, O., Zoology
WOODS, J., Chemistry

Faculty of Social Sciences:
ADENIKINJU, A., Economics
AFOLAYAN, A., Geography
AGBAJE, A., Political Science
AGBOLA, S., Urban and Regional Planning
ARIYO, A., Economics
AWETO, A., Geography
AYENI, M., Geography
BALOGUN, S., Psychology
EGWAIKHIDE, F., Economics
EHIGIE, B., Psychology
GARBA, A., Economics
GARBA, P., Economics
GBADEGESIN, A., Geography
GBOYEGA, E., Political Science
IKPORUKPO, C., Geography
ISIUGO-ABANIHE, U., Sociology
IWAYEMI, A., Economics
OGUNKOLA, E., Economics
OKAFOR, S., Geography
OKE, E., Sociology
OKUNADE, A., Political Science
OLOFIN, S., Economics
OSINOWO, H., Psychology
OYEJIDE, T., Economics
SOYIBO, A., Economics
SUBERU, R., Political Science
SUNMOLA, A., Psychology

Faculty of Technology:
ADEGOKE, G., Food Technology
ADEKOYA, L., Mechanical Engineering
AGBEDE, O., Civil Engineering
ALABI, B., Mechanical Engineering
AWORH, O., Food Technology
BAMIRO, O., Mechanical Engineering
CHARLES-OWABA, O., Industrial and Production Engineering
OLORUNSOLA, A., Agricultural Engineering

OLULEYE, A., Industrial & Production Engineering
ONILUDE, M., Agricultural Engineering
SANGODOYIN, A., Agricultural Engineering

Faculty of Veterinary Medicine:
ABATAN, M., Veterinary Physiology and Pharmacy
ADEYEFA, C., Veterinary Medicine
AGBEDE, S., Veterinary Public Health
AKINBOADE, O., Veterinary Microbiology and Parasitology
AKPAVIE, S., Veterinary Pathology
ANOSA, V., Veterinary Pathology
AROWOLO, R., Veterinary Physiology and Pharmacy
FAGBEMI, B., Veterinary Microbiology and Parasitology
FAYEMI, O., Veterinary Surgery and Reproduction
NOTTIDGE, H., Veterinary Medicine
OBI, T., Veterinary Medicine
OGUNDIPE, G., Veterinary Public Health
OKE, B., Veterinary Anatomy
OLADOSU, L., Veterinary Medicine
OLUFEMI, B., Veterinary Medicine
ONWUKA, S., Veterinary Anatomy
OYEWALE, J., Veterinary Physiology and Pharmacy
TAIWO, V., Veterinary Pathology

UNIVERSITY OF ILORIN

PMB 1515, Ilorin, Kwara State
Telephone: (31) 221691
Fax: (31) 221937
E-mail: registra@unilorin.edu.ng
Internet: www.unilorin.edu.ng

Founded 1975
Federal control
Language of instruction: English
Academic year: September to June

Chancellor: HRH AMBROSE ALLAGOA
Vice-Chancellor: Prof. SHAMSUDEEN ONYI-LOKWU ONCHE AMALI
Deputy Vice-Chancellor for Academic Affairs: Prof. ISHAQ OLANREWAJU OLOYEDE
Deputy Vice-Chancellor for Admin.: Prof. LUKE DAYO EDUNGBOLA
Registrar: O. O. OYEYEMI
Librarian: Prof. M. I. AJIBERO

Library of 155,000 vols, 2,800 periodicals
Number of teachers: 644
Number of students: 18,488

Publications: *News Bulletin* (52 a year), *University Calendar*

DEANS

Faculty of Agriculture: Prof. J. O. ATTEH
Faculty of Arts: Prof. R. D. ABUBAKRE
Faculty of Business and Social Sciences: Prof. I. O. TAIWO
Faculty of Education: Prof. E. A. OGUNSAKIN
Faculty of Engineering and Technology: Prof. O. A. ADETIFA
Faculty of Health Sciences: Prof. M. A. ARAOYE
Faculty of Law: Prof. Z. O. AJE
Faculty of Science: Prof. T. O. OPOOLA
Post-Graduate School: Prof. J. A. MORAKINYO

UNIVERSITY OF JOS

PMB 2084, Jos, Plateau State
Telephone: (73) 610514
Fax: (73) 610514
Internet: www.uiowa.edu/intlinet/unijos

Founded 1975
Federal control
Language of instruction: English
Academic year: September to June (2 semesters)

Chancellor: HRH Oba Dr FESTUS IBIDAPO
  ADEDINSEWO ADESANOYE OSEMAWE OF ONDO-
  LAND
Pro-Chancellor: Prof. MUSA ABDULLAHI
Vice-Chancellor: Prof. MONDAY MANGYWAT
Deputy Vice-Chancellor for Academic
  Affairs: Prof. A. O. MALU
Deputy Vice-Chancellor for Admin.: Prof. J.
  O. A. ONYEKA
Registrar: Z. D. GALAM
Librarian: Dr A. OCHAI
Number of teachers: 745
Number of students: 14,378

DEANS AND DIRECTORS

Faculty of Arts: Prof. E. B. AJULO
Faculty of Education: Prof. I. J. IHENACHO
Faculty of Environmental Sciences: Prof. A.
  A. ADEPETU
Faculty of Law: Dr J. M. NASIR
Faculty of Medical Sciences: Prof. J. O.
  OGUNRANTI
Faculty of Natural Sciences: Prof. M. S. AUDU
Faculty of Pharmaceutical Sciences: Prof. F.
  OKWUASABA
Faculty of Social Sciences: Prof. S. G. TYODEN
School of Postgraduate Studies: Prof. G. A.
  UBOM
Institute of Education: Dr A. Y. MALLUM
Centre for Continuing Education: Dr E. A.
  ABAMA
Centre for Development Studies: Dr J. S.
  ILLAH

PROFESSORS

Faculty of Arts:
  AIRE, Y. O., Languages and Linguistics
  AJE, A. O., Languages and Linguistics
  AJULO, E. B., English
  AMALI, S. O. O., Theatre Studies
  BASHIR, I. L., History
  CYRIL, I. O., Religious Studies
  JAMES, I., History
  JEMKUR, J. F., History
  MANGVWAT, M. Y., History
  YAHYA, M. T., Religious Studies

Faculty of Education:
  ABANG, T., Special Education
  ADEWOLE, M. A., Philosophy of Education
  AKINNADE, C. T. O., Science and Technical
    Education
  AKPAN, E. U. U., Science and Technology
    Education
  AWOTUNDE, P. O., Science Education
  IHENACHO, I. J., Special Education
  LASSA, P. N., Mathematics Education
  MALLUM, M. P., Guidance and Counselling
  OZOJI, E., Special Education
  UDOH, S. U., Social Science Education

Faculty of Environmental Sciences:
  ADEPETU, A. A., Geography and Planning
  KOLAWOLE, J. O., Building

Faculty of Law:
  ADUBA, J. N., Public and Law

Faculty of Medical Sciences:
  ADOGA, G. I., Biochemistry
  ANAKWE, G. E., Biochemistry
  IDOKO, J. A., Medicine
  IHEZUE, C. H., Surgery
  ISICHEI, H. U., Psychiatry
  MALU, A. O., Medicinal Radiology
  OKOYE, Z. S. C., Biochemistry
  UBOM, G. A., Enzymology and Molecular
    Biology

Faculty of Natural Sciences:
  AGINA, S. E., Botany
  AJAYI, J., Zoology
  AKUESHI, C. O., Plant Pathology
  AUDU, M. S., Mathematics
  DUHLINSKA, D. D., Protozoology, Insect
    Pathology
  EGILA, J. N., Chemistry
  EKPENYONG, K. I., Chemistry

EKWENCHI, M. M., Chemistry
HUSAINI, S. W. H., Plant Taxonomy and
  Cytogenetics
IFENKWE, O. P., Botany
LIVERPOOL, L. S. O., Mathematics
NWUFO, B. T., Chemistry
OGBONNA, C. I., Botany
OGEZI, I. E., Geology and Mining
OJOJEKWU, P. C., Zoology
ONUMANYI, P., Mathematics
ONWULIRI, C. O. E., Zoology
ONYEKA, J. O. A., Zoology
POPOV, T. V., Zoology
SHAMBE, T. S., Chemistry
UFODIKE, E. B. C., Zoology
UTAH, E. U., Physics

Faculty of Pharmaceutical Sciences:
  IRANLOYE, T. A., Pharmacology and
    Pharmaceutical Technology
  OKWUASABA, F., Pharmacology and Clinical
    Pharmacy
  SOKOMBA, E. N., Pharmacology

Faculty of Social Sciences:
  ALLI, W. O., International Relations
  ALUBO, S. O., Sociology
  ETANNIBI, E. O., Sociology
  IBANGA, U. A., Sociology
  NWEZE, A., Psychology
  TYODEN, G. S., Political Economy

Centre for Development Studies:
  OJOWU, O., Economics

UNIVERSITY OF LAGOS

Lagos
Telephone: (1) 4932660
Fax: (1) 4932667
E-mail: vc@unilag.edu
Internet: www.unilag.edu
Founded 1962
Fed. control
Language of instruction: English
Academic year: October to June

Chancellor: HRH Alhaji Dr ALIYU O. OBAJE
  (the Attah Igala)
Pro-Chancellor: Chief AFE BABALOLA
Vice-Chancellor: Prof. OYE IBIDAPO-OBE
Deputy Vice-Chancellor for Academic Affairs
  and Research: Prof. OLUSOGA A. SOFOLA
Deputy Vice-Chancellor for Management:
  (vacant)
Registrar: C. F. A. OLUMIDE
Librarian: S. O. OLANLOKUN
Library: see under Libraries and Archives
Number of teachers: 969
Number of students: 39,783
Publications: Imodoye, A Journal of Africa
  Philosophy (1 a year), Journal of Econom-
  ics and Policy Analysis (1 a year), Journal
  of Engineering Research (1 a year), Jour-
  nal of Private and Property Law (1 a year),
  Journal of Society, Development and Pub-
  lic Health (1 a year), LAANGBASA (Jona
  Ise Akadani Ede Yoruba) (African Studies,
  1 a year), Lagos Historical Review (1 a
  year), Lagos Journal of Environmental
  Studies (1 a year), Lagos Review of English
  Studies (1 a year), Nigerian Journal of
  Business and Social Science (1 a year),
  Nigerian Journal of Health and Biomedical Sciences (2 a year), Nigerian Journal of
  Industrial Relations (1 a year), Nigerian
  Journal of Management Studies (1 a year),
  Nigerian Journal of Philosophy (1 a year),
  UNILAG Communication Review (1 a
  year), UNILAG Journal of Business (1 a
  year), UNILAG Journal of Politics (1 a
  year), UNILAG Sociological Review (1 a
  year)

DEANS

College of Medicine: Prof. S. O. ELEHSA
  (Provost)

Faculty of Arts: Prof. C. S. MOMOH
Faculty of Business Administration: Prof. W.
  ADEWUNMI
Faculty of Education: Prof. DURO ADENAYO
  AJEYALEMI
Faculty of Engineering: Prof. O. O. AKINDELE
Faculty of Environmental Sciences: Prof. R.
  O. IYAGBA
Faculty of Law: Prof. CHIOMA AGOMO
Faculty of Pharmacy: Prof. H. A. B. COKER
Faculty of Science: Prof. O. O. AMUND
Faculty of Social Sciences: Prof. L. OLURODE
School of Basic Medical Sciences: Prof. S. A.
  ADIGUN
School of Clinical Sciences: Prof. A. O.
  GRANGE
School of Dental Sciences: Prof. J. A. AKIN-
  WANDE
School of Postgraduate Studies: Prof. F. O.
  OLATUNJI

PROFESSORS

ABAELU, A. M., Biochemistry
ABASS, O., Computer Science
ABIDOYE, R. O., Community Health
ABUDU, O. O., Obstetrics and Gynaecology
ADEBAYO, N., Sociology
ADEDIMILA, A. S., Civil Engineering
ADEGBENRO, O., Electrical and Electronics
  Engineering
ADEGBOLA, O., Geography
ADEGOKE, K. A., Curriculum Studies (Educa-
  tion)
ADEJUGBE, M. O. A., Economics
ADEKOLA, S. A., Electrical and Electronics
  Engineering
ADELEMO, I. A., Geography
ADENIYI, P. O., Geography
ADEOGUN, A. A., Commercial and Industrial
  Law
ADE-OJO, S., European Languages
ADEPOJU, J. A., Mathematics
ADEROGBA, K., Mathematics
ADEWALE, A. O., Adult Education
ADEWUNMI, W., Banking and Finance
ADEYEMI, A. A., Public Law
ADEYEMI, J. D., Psychiatry
ADEYEMI, S. D., Surgery
ADEYEMI-DORO, H. O., Surgery
ADIGUN, S. A., Physiology
ADU, D. I., Mathematics
AGOMO, C. K., Commercial and Industrial
  Law
AJAYI, O., Mathematics
AJEYALEMI, S. D., Curriculum Studies (Edu-
  cation)
AKEJU, T. A., Civil Engineering
AKERE, J. F., English
AKINDELE, O. O., Mechanical Engineering
AKINFELEYE, R. A., Mass Communication
AKINGBADE, J. F., Business Administration
AKINOLA, M. O., European Languages
  (French)
AKINSETE, I., Haematology and Blood Trans-
  fusion
AKINTOLA-ARIKAWE, J. O., Geography
AKINTONWA, A., Pharmacology
AKINWADE, J. A., Oral and Maxillofacial
  Surgery
AKINWANDE, A. I., Biochemistry
AKO, C. T., Chemical Engineering
AKPATA, T. V. I., Botany and Microbiology
ALABA, I. O., African Languages and Litera-
  ture (Yoruba)
ALABA OGUNSANWO, Political Science
ALO, B. I., Chemistry
AMUND, O. O., Botany and Microbiology
ARIGBABU, S. O., Surgery
ASIKA, M. N., Business Administration
AWONUSI, V. O., English
AWOSOPE, C. O., Electrical and Electronics
  Engineering
AYENI, J. O., Computer Science
AYENI, O. O., Surveying
BALOGUN, O. Y., Geography
BALOGUN, S. A., Metallurgical Engineering

BANDELE, E. O., Medicine
BELLO, R. A., Chemical Engineering
COKER, A. O., Medical Microbiology and Parasitology
COKER, H. A. B., Pharmaceutical Chemistry
DANESI, M. A., Medicine
DENLOYE, A. O., Chemical Engineering
DON-PEDRO, K., Zoology, Marine Biology and Fisheries
DUROSIMI-ETTI, F. A., Radiation Biology, Radiotherapy and Radiodiagnosis
EDEBIRI, U., European Languages (French)
EGBERONGBE, F. O. A., Surveying and Geoinformatics
EJIOGU, A. M., Educational Administration
ELESHA, S. O., Morbid Anatomy
ERUVBETINE, A. E., English
EZE, L. N., Psychology
EZEIGBO, C. U., Surveying and Geoinformatics
EZEIGBO, T. A., English
FAGBAMIYE, E. O., Educational Administration
FAGBENRO-BEYIOKU, A. F., Microbiology and Parasitology
FAJEMIROKUN, F. A., Surveying and Geoinformatics
FAMUYIWA, O. O., Psychiatry
FOGAM, P. K., Commercial and Industrial Law
FOLARIN, B. A., Psychology
FOLAWIYO, A. F. A., Physical and Health Education
GBADAMOSI, T. G. O., History
GIWA-OSAGIE, O. O. F., Obstetrics and Gynaecology
GRANGE, A. O., Clinical Pathology
IBIDAPO-OBE, O., Systems Engineering
IFUDU, N. D., Pharmacy and Pharmaceutical Technology
IGWILO, C. I., Pharmacy and Pharmaceutical Technology
IJAOLA, O. O., Electrical and Electronics Engineering
IKULAYO, P. B., Physical and Health Education
ISIEKWE, M. C., Dental Sciences
IYAGBA, R. O., Building
IYIEGBUNIWE, W. C., Finance
JEBODA, S. O., Preventive Dentistry
JOHNSON, M. A., European Languages (French)
JOHNSON, T. O., Medicine
KAMMA, C. M., Mechanical Engineering
KAZEEM, A. A., Clinical Pathology
KENKU, M. A., Mathematics
KUKOYI, A. A., European Languages (French)
KUSEMIJU, K., Marine Science
KWOFIE, E. N., European Languages (French)
LAWAL, A., History
LAWAL, O. O., Education
MAJEKODUNMI, A. A., Surgery
MAKANJU, O. A., Psychology
MAKANJUOLA, W. A., Zoology
MALAKA, S. L. O., European Languages (French)
MOMOH, C. S., Philosophy
MOREGBE, J. I., Philosophy
NINALOWO, A., Sociology
NWANKO, D. I., Zoology, Marine Biology and Fisheries
OBEBE, B. J., Curriculum Studies
ODEIGAH, P. G. C., Zoology, Marine Biology and Fisheries
ODIETE, W. O., Zoology, Marine Biology and Fisheries
ODUGBEMI, T., Medical Microbiology and Parasitology
ODUKOYA, O. O., Oral Pathology
ODUTOLA, T. A., Medicine
OGBOJA, O., Chemical Engineering
OGEDENGBE, O. K., Obstetrics and Gynaecology
OGUNDOWOLE, E. K., Philosophy
OGUNLESI, M. M., Chemistry
OGUNSANWO, A. C. A., Political Science

OGUNTOYE, A. O., Educational Administration
OHWOVORIOLE, A. E., Medicine
OJO, S. A., European Languages (French)
OJO, S. O., Geography
OKENIMKPE, M. N., Adult Education
OKEOWO, P. A., Surgery
OKORO, C. C., Electrical and Electronics Engineering
OKOTORE, R. O., Biochemistry
OLATUNJI, F. O., Chemical Engineering
OLOWOKUDEJO, J. O., Botany and Microbiology
OLUKOJU, A. O., History
OLUMIDE, Y. M., Medicine
OLUNLOYO, V. O. S., Mechanical Engineering
OLURODE, O., Sociology
OLUSANYA, O., Architecture
OLUWAFEMI, C. O., Physics
OMOLUABI, P. F., Psychology
OMO-MALAKA, S. L., Zoology, Marine Biology and Fisheries
OMOREGBE, J., Philosophy
OMOTOLA, J. A., Private and Property Law
OSEGBE, D. N., Surgery
OSIBOGUN, A. O., Community Health
OSINBAJO, Y., Public Law
OSIPITAN, T. A. I., Public Law
OSUNTOKUN, J. O., History
OTOBO, D., Industrial Relations and Personnel Management
OWHOTU, V. B., Curriculum Studies
OWOEYE, I. O., Physiotherapy
OYEBANDE, L., Geography
OYEBODE, A., Jurisprudence and International Law
OYEDIRAN, M. A., Child Health and Primary Care
OYEKANMI, F. A. D., Sociology
OYELELE, D. A., Geography
DA ROCHA-AFODU, J. T., Surgery
SOFOLA, O. A., Physiology
SOFOLUWE, A. B., Computer Science
SOTE, E. O., Child Dental Health
SOTE, G. A., Psychology
SOWEMIMO, G. O. A., Surgery
SUSU, A. A., Chemical Engineering
TALABI, S. O., Mechanical Engineering
TAYO, F., Clinical Pharmacy
TOMORI, S., Economics
UCHE, L. U., Mass Communication
UCHEGBU, A., Jurisprudence and International Law
UNAH, J. I., Philosophy
UTUAMA, A. A., Private and Property Law
UZOCHUKWU, S., African Languages and Literature (Igbo)
UZODIKE, E. N. U., Private and Property Law
VINCENT, T., English
WILLIAMS, G. O., Zoology, Marine Biology and Fisheries

UNIVERSITY OF MAIDUGURI

PMB 1069, Maiduguri, Borno State
Telephone: (76) 232949
E-mail: root@unimaid.edu.ng
Internet: www.unimaid.edu.ng
Founded 1975
Fed. control
Language of instruction: English
Academic year: October to June
Chancellor: His Royal Majesty Dr EKPENYONG OKONKO UDOUTUN
Pro-Chancellor and Chairman of Council: Dr BOLANLE OLAWALE BABALAKIN
Vice-Chancellor: Prof. MOHAMMED MALA DAURA
Deputy Vice-Chancellor for Academic Services: (vacant)
Deputy Vice-Chancellor for Central Admin.: (vacant)
Registrar: Dr LAWAN BUKAR ALHAJI
Librarian: JAMES ABAYOMI AGAJA (acting)
Number of teachers: 700

Number of students: 30,000
Publications: *Annals of Borno, Inaugural Lecture and Convocation Speeches*

DEANS

College of Medical Sciences: Prof. A. A. TAHIR
Faculty of Agriculture: Prof. J. D. KWARI
Faculty of Arts: Prof. YAKUBU MUKHTAR
Faculty of Education: Prof. IBRAHIM NJODI
Faculty of Engineering: Prof. M. I. BUGAJE
Faculty of Law: Dr YUSUF M. YUSUF (acting)
Faculty of Management Sciences: Prof. AMINU AYUBA (acting)
Faculty of Science: Prof. M. Y. BALLA (acting)
Faculty of Social Sciences: Prof. S. S. IFAH (acting)
Faculty of Veterinary Medicine: Prof. A. G. AMBALI

PROFESSORS

ABAH, J. O., English
ABUBAKAR, A., Languages and Linguistics
ABUBAKAR, S., History
ADENIJI, F. A., Agricultural Engineering
AGUOLU, C. C., Library Science
AL-AMIN, J.D.
ALKALI, M. NUR, History
AMALI, I. O. O., English
AMBALI, A. G., Veterinary Medicine
ANASO, A. B., Crop Science
AYUBA, A., Management Science
AZEKE, T. O., Education
BABU, S. S., Veterinary Medicine, Microbiology and Parasitology
BADEJO, B. R., Languages and Linguistics
BRANN, C. M. B., Language and Linguistics
BWALA, S. A., Medicine
CAREW, P. F. C., Education
CHHANGANI, R. C., Common Law
CHIBUZO, G. A., Veterinary Anatomy
DAWHA, E. M. K., Library Science
DLAKWA, H., Social Science
EGWU, G. O., Veterinary Anatomy
ENYIKWOLA, O., Human Physiology
GADZAMA, M. N., Science
GOPAL, B. V., Biological Sciences
GUKAS, G. H., Industrial Design
HARRY, T. O., Microbiology
HASSAN, A. W., Surgery
HUSSAINI, I. M., Pharmacy
IDOKO, E. F., Theatre Arts
IGBOKWE, I. O., Veterinary Pathology
IGUN, U. A., Sociology and Anthropology
JACKS, J. W., Medicine
JIBOYEWA, D. A., Education
KAGU, B., Education
KALU, A. U., Veterinary, Public Health and Preventive Medicine
KOROMA, D. S. M., History
MALGWI, D., Physics
MBAHI, A. A., Creative Arts
MOHAMMED, I., Medicine
MSHELIA, B., P. H. E.
MSHELIA, E. D., Physics
ODO, P. E., Crop Science
OGUNBAMERU, B. O.
OHU, J. O., Agricultural Engineering
OMOTARA, B., Community Medicine
ONI, A., Continuing Education
PATE, U., Mass Communication
PINDIGA, H. U., Medicine
RICHARDS, W. S., Biological Sciences
SHEHU, U., Community Medicine
SODIPO, W., Biochemistry
TIJANI, K., Political Science and Administration
UBOSI, C. O., Animal Science
WAZIRI, I., History
ZARIA, L. T., Veterinary Microbiology and Parasitology

MICHAEL OKPARA UNIVERSITY OF AGRICULTURE, UMUDIKE

PMB 7267, Umuahia, Umuahia, Abia State
Telephone: (82) 440555
Fax: (82) 440555

Founded 1992 as Federal University of Agriculture, Umudike; present name and status 2000

Vice-Chancellor: Prof. OGBINNAYA C. ONWUDIKE
Deputy Vice-Chancellor: Prof. HILARY O. EDEOGA
Registrar: JULIA N. UCHE
Librarian: ALOYSIUS ONONOGBO
Library of 8,500 vols
Number of teachers: 158
Number of students: 1,248

DEANS

College of Agricultural Economics, Rural Sociology and Extension: Prof. ALOYSIUS NWOSU
College of Animal Science and Animal Health: Prof. JOHN IBEAWUCHI
College of Biological and Physical Sciences: Dr OBIOHA EZEREONYE
College of Crop and Soil Sciences: Dr CHIDA AMADIOHA
College of Food Processing and Storage Technology: Prof. ENOCH AKOBUNDU
College of Natural Resources and Environmental Management: Prof. EME AKACHUKU
School of Postgraduate Studies: Prof. SYLVESTER IBE

PROFESSORS

AKACHUKU, E. A., Natural Resources and Environmental Management
AKOBUNDU, E. N. T., Food Processing and Storage Technology
ALUKO, P., Natural Resources and Environmental Management
ANASO, H. U., Crop and Soil Sciences
ASIEGBU, J. C., Crop and Soil Sciences
CHIBOKA, V. O., Biological and Physical Sciences
EDEOGA, H. O., Biological and Physical Sciences
EKWUEME, B. N., Biological and Physical Sciences
ELUWA, M. C., Biological and Physical Sciences
IBE, S. N., Animal Science and Animal Health
IBEAWUCHI, J. A., Animal Science and Animal Health
MENKITI, A. I., Biological and Physical Sciences
NJOKU, P. C., Animal Science and Animal Health
NWAGBO, E. C., Agricultural Economics, Rural Sociology and Extension
NWOKE, B. E. B., Biological and Physical Sciences
NWOSU, A. C., Agricultural Economics, Rural Sociology and Extension
OBIZOBA, I. C., Food Processing and Storage Technology
OKERE, L. C., Agricultural Economics, Rural Sociology and Extension
OKOH, P. N., Biological and Physical Sciences
ONWUDIKE, O. C., Animal Science and Animal Health
ONYENWEAKU, C. E., Agricultural Economics, Rural Sociology and Extension
UWAEGBUTE, A. C., Food Processing and Storage Technology
UWAKAH, C. T., Agricultural Economics, Rural Sociology and Extension

NATIONAL OPEN UNIVERSITY OF NIGERIA

14–16 Ahmadu Bello Way, PMB 80067, Victoria Island, Lagos
Telephone: (1) 8188849
Fax: (1) 2712665
Kaduna Campus Fmr NETC Campus, Kaduna-Zaria Rd, Rigachikun Kaduna
E-mail: centralinfo@nou.ed.ng
Internet: www.nou.edu.ng

Founded 1983; suspended by government 1984; re-opened 2001

Vice-Chancellor: Prof. OLUGBEMIRO JEGEDE
Registrar: JOSEPHINE O. AKINYEMI
Number of students: 78,935

Courses for adults by correspondence and distance teaching at 40 study centres serving each state and local government area of Nigeria; Schools of Arts and Social Sciences, Business and Human Resource Management, Education and Science and Technology; Centre for Continuing Education; Regional Training and Research Institute for Open and Distance Learning (RETRIDAL).

UNIVERSITY OF NIGERIA

Nsukka, Enugu State
Telephone: (42) 771911
Internet: www.unn.edu.org

Founded 1960
Fed. control
Language of instruction: English
Academic year: September to June

Chancellor: Emir of Zazzau Alhaji Dr SHEHU IDRIS
Pro-Chancellor: Prof. BOLANLE AWE
Vice-Chancellor: Prof. BARTO N. OKOLO
Deputy Vice-Chancellor for Academic Affairs: Prof. I. U. ASUZU
Deputy Vice-Chancellor for Admin.: Prof. EGBEKE AJA
Deputy Vice-Chancellor (Enugu Campus): Prof. R. E. UMEH
Registrar: A. I. OKONTA (acting)
Librarian: Dr CHARLES O. OMEKWU

Library: see Libraries and Archives
Number of teachers: 1,122
Number of students: 29,482

DEANS

College of Medicine: Prof. B. J. C. ONWUBERE
Faculty of Agriculture: Prof. K. P. BAIYERI
Faculty of Arts: Prof. I. U. NWADIKE
Faculty of Biological Sciences: Prof. C. E. A. OKEZIE
Faculty of Business Administration: Prof. IKE E. NWOSU
Faculty of Dentistry: Prof. E. NDIOKWELU
Faculty of Education: Prof. S. A. EZEUDU
Faculty of Engineering: Prof. J. C. AGUWAMBA
Faculty of Environmental Studies: Prof. J. U. OGBUEFI
Faculty of Health Sciences and Technology: Prof. G. C. OKOYE
Faculty of Law: Prof. F. N. MONYE
Faculty of Medical Sciences: Prof. F. U. EZEPUE
Faculty of Pharmaceutical Sciences: Prof. P. O. OSADEBE
Faculty of Physical Sciences: Prof. M. O. OYESANYA
Faculty of Social Sciences: Prof. E. O. EZEANI
Faculty of Veterinary Medicine: Prof. C. N. UCHENDU
School of General Studies: Prof. E. OGBONNA
School of Postgraduate Studies: Prof. A. N. AKWANYA

PROFESSORS

ADEILUYI, J. O., Civil Engineering
AGAJELU, S. I., Geoinformatics and Surveying

AGHAJI, M. A. C., Medical Sciences and Dentistry
AGU, C. C., Economics
AGUWA, C. N., Clinical Pharmacy and Pharmacy Management
AKAH, P. A., Pharmacology and Toxicology
AKAMIGBO, F. O. R., Soil Science
AKUBUE, A. U., Educational Foundations
ALI, A., Institute of Education
AMAZIGO, J. C., Mathematics
AMUCHEAZI, E. C., Political Science
AMUCHIE, F. A., Health and Physical Education
ANATSUI, E. K., Fine and Applied Arts
ANIAKOR, C. C., Fine and Applied Arts
ANIKA, S. M., Veterinary Physiology and Pharmacology
ANYADIKE, R. N. C., Geography
ANYANWU, S. U., Health and Physical Education
ARUA, E. O., Agricultural Economics
ASIEGBU, J. E., Crop Science
ASUZU, I. U., Veterinary Physiology and Pharmacology
ATTAH, C. A., Surgery
AZUBUIKE, J. C., Paediatrics
CHIDEBELU, S. A. N. D., Agricultural Economics
CHIDUME, C. E., Mathematics
CHIEJINA, S. N., Veterinary Parasitology and Entomology
CHIKWENDU, V. E., Archaeology
CHUKWU, C. C., Veterinary Medicine
EBIGBO, P. O., Psychological Medicine
EDOKA, B. E., Library and Information Science
EGBUNIWE, N., Civil Engineering
EGONU, I. T. K., Foreign Languages and Literature
EGWIM, P. O., Medical Biochemistry
EJIOFOR, L. J. C., Political Science
EKE, E. I., Educational Foundations
EKECHUKWU, O. V., Mechanical Engineering
ENEKWE, O., English
ESEDEBE, P. O., History
EYO, I. E., Psychology
EZEASOR, D. N., Veterinary Anatomy
EZEILO, B. N., Psychology
EZEJI, S. C. O. A., Vocational Teacher Education
EZEKWE, C. I., Mechanical Engineering
EZEOKE, A. C. J., Chemical Pathology
EZEPUE, M. C., Geology
EZE-UZOMAKA, O. J., Civil Engineering
HARBOR-PETERS, V. F., Science Education
IBEMESSI, J. A., Pure and Industrial Chemistry
IGBOELI, G., Animal Science
IGWILO, B. N., Fine and Applied Arts
IHEKORONYE, A. I., Food Science and Technology
IHEZUE, U. H., Psychological Medicine
IJOMA, J. O., History
IKEJIANI-CLARK, M. I. O., Public Administration and Local Government
IKENE, A. I., Home Science and Technology
IKPEZE, E. I., Economics
ILOABACHIE, G. C., Obstetrics and Gynaecology
ILOBA, C., Crop Science
ILOEJE, O. C., Mechanical Engineering
IMAGA, E. U. L., Management
KENE, R. O. C., Veterinary Surgery and Obstetrics
MADUBUNYI, L. C., Veterinary Parasitology and Entomology
MADUEWESI, E. J., Educational Foundations
MBAGWU, J. S. C., Soil Science
MODUM, E. P., Languages
MODUM, U., Accountancy
NGODDY, P. O., Food Science and Technology
NJOKO, O. N., History
NWABUEZE, E. P., Dramatic Arts
NWACHUKWU, P A., Linguistics and Nigerian Languages
NWACHUKWU, T. A., Educational Foundations

NWAFOR, J. C., Geography
NWAGBO, E. C., Agricultural Economics
NWAKOBY, B. A. N., Community Medicine
NWALA, T. U., Philosophy
NWANKITI, O. C., Botany
NWOSU, I. E., Marketing
NZE, C. B., Philosophy
NZEAKO, A. N., Electronic Engineering
OBANU, Z. A., Food Science and Technology
OBI, I. U., Crop Science
OBI, M .E., Soil Science
OBI, S. K. C., Microbiology
OBIANYO, N. E. N., Surgery
OBIDOA, O., Biochemistry
OBIKEZE, D. S., Sociology and Anthropology
OBIZOBA, I. C., Home Science and Nutrition
OBOEGBULAM, S. I., Veterinary Pathology and
  Microbiology
ODIGBOH, E. U., Agricultural Engineering
ODUKWE, A. O., Mechanical Engineering
OGBAZI, J. N., Vocational Teacher Education
OGBUJI, R. O., Crop Science
OHAEGBU, A. U., Languages
OKAFOR, B. C., Otolaryngology
OKAFOR, C. O., Pure and Industrial Chemistry
OKAFOR, E. C., Pure and Industrial Chemistry
OKAFOR, F. C., Zoology
OKAFOR, F. O., Banking and Finance
OKAFOR, F. U., Philosophy
OKEKE, C. E., Physics and Astronomy
OKEKE, E. A. C., Education
OKEKE, H. N., Physics and Astronomy
OKEKE, P. N., Physics and Astronomy
OKOGBUE, C. O., Geology
OKOLI, F. C., Public Administration and
  Local Government
OKONKWO, P. O., Pharmacology and Thera-
  peutics
OKORAFOR, A. E., Economics
OKORE, A. O., Economics
OKORIE, J. U., Vocational Teacher Education
OKORJI, E. C., Agricultural Economics
OKORO, B. A., Paediatrics
OKORO, O. M., Vocational Teacher Education
OKOYE, J. O. A., Veterinary Pathology and
  Microbiology
OKPALA, J. I. N., Education
OKPARA, E., Psychology
OKPOKO, A. I., Archaeology
OLAITAN, S. O., Vocational Teacher Educa-
  tion
OLI, J. M., Medicine
OLOIDI, O., Fine and Applied Arts
ONAH, J. O., Marketing
ONONOGBU, I. C., Biochemistry
ONUKOGU, I. B., Statistics
ONUOHA, K. M., Geology
ONWU, N., Religion
ONYEGEGBU, S. O., Mechanical Engineering
ONYEJEKWE, D. C., Mechanical Engineering
ORANU, R. N., Vocational Teacher Education
OSUAGWU, C. C., Electronic Engineering
OSUALA, E. C., Vocational Teacher Education
OSUALA, J. D. C., Adult Education and
  Extramural Studies
OYEOKU, O. K., Fine and Applied Arts
OZIOKO, J. O. C., Psychology
OZUMBA, B. C., Obstetrics and Gynaecology
PAL, S., Physics and Astronomy
SOLUDO, C. C., Economics
UCHE, P. I., Statistics
UKAEJIOFO, E. O., Medical Laboratory Sci-
  ence
UME, J. A., Estate Management
UMEH, L. C., Urban and Regional Planning
UMEH, T. A., Adult Education and Extra-
  mural Studies

ATTACHED INSTITUTES
**Centre for Energy Research and Devel-
opment:** Nsukka; Dir Prof. E. C. OKORJI
(acting).

**Centre for Equipment Maintenance and
Development:** Nsukka; Dir Prof. I. C.
OBIZOBA.
Institute of African Studies: Nsukka; Dir
Prof. O. O. ENEKWE.
Institute for Development Studies: Uni-
versity of Nigeria, Enugu Campus, Enugu;
Dir Prof. E. U. L. IMAGA.
Institute of Education: Nsukka; Dir Prof.
E. A. C. OKEKE.
Veterinary Teaching Hospital: Nsukka;
Dir Dr L. J. E. ORAJAKA (acting).

NNAMDI AZIKIWE UNIVERSITY
PMB 5025, Awka, Anambra State
Telephone: (80) 60492273
E-mail: info@unizik.edu.ng
Founded 1992
Federal govt control
Languages of instruction: English, French,
  Hausa, Igbo, Yoruba
Academic year: October to June
Chancellor: Emir of Ilorin Alhaji SULU GAM-
  BARI
Pro-Chancellor: SENAS UKPANAH
Vice-Chancellor: Prof. B. C. E. EGBOKA
Deputy Vice-Chancellor for Academic
  Affairs: Prof. J. E. AHANEKU
Deputy Vice-Chancellor for Admin.: Prof.
  BEN C. OKEKE
Registrar: C. C. OKEKE (acting)
Librarian: EMMA ONWUKA (acting)
Provost, College of Health Sciences: Prof.
  OKEY IKPEZE
Bursar: U. J. AGU (acting)
Library of 65,000 vols
Number of teachers: 842
Number of students: 36,000
Publications: *Journal of Arts and Human-
  ities, Journal of Economic Studies, Journal
  of Education Management, Journal of
  Management Studies, Journal of Voca-
  tional and Adult Education, Tropical Jour-
  nal of Medical Research, UNIZIK Law
  Journal*

DEANS
Faculty of Agriculture: Prof. NONSO NNA-
  BUIFE
Faculty of Arts: Prof. DAN AGU
Faculty of Basic Medical Sciences: Prof. ED
  NWOBODO
Faculty of Education: Prof. SAM OKEKE
Faculty of Engineering and Technology: Prof.
  D. O. ONUKWULI
Faculty of Environmental Sciences: Prof. C.
  C. EGOLUM
Faculty of Health Sciences and Technology:
  Dr C. C. ONYENEKWE (acting)
Faculty of Law: Prof. KEN NWOGU
Faculty of Management Sciences: Prof. C. I.
  ONWUCHEKWA
Faculty of Medicine: Prof. A. M. E. NWOFOR
Faculty of Natural Sciences: Prof. P. A. C.
  OKOYE
Faculty of Pharmaceutical Sciences: Prof. C.
  O. ESIMONE
Faculty of Physical Sciences: Prof. F. C.
  ODIBO
Faculty of Social Sciences: Prof. E. A. EGBOH
Postgraduate School: Prof. LUKE ANIKE

PROFESSORS
Confucius Institute:
  NENGWEN, J.
Faculty of Arts:
  AGBODIKE, C.
  AGU, D.
  ANAGBOGU, P.
  ANIZOBA, O.
  DUKOR, E.
  EKPUNOBI, D.

EYISI, J.
MADU, J.
MBANUGO, C.
NDUKA, D.
NZOMIWU, J.
OKEKE, D.
ONYEKAONWU, G.
UMEASIEGBU, R.
UMEH, O.
Faculty of Education:
  ABONE, O.
  AKUDOLU, L.
  AKUEZUILO, E.
  ANAGBOGU, M.
  EBENEBE, R.
  EZE, T.
  IKE, A.
  NDINECHI, G.
  NDU, A.
  NNADOZIE, J.
  OGBALU, A.
  OKAFOR, J.
  OKONKWO, O.
  ORAEMESI, J.
  UMEDUM, S.
  UMEASIEGBU, G.
  UNACHUKWU, G.
Faculty of Engineering and Technology:
  IGBOKWE, P.
  IJOMAH, M.
  INYIAMA, H.
  KATCHY, E.
  NNUKA, E.
  NWOBU, R.
  OFODILE, E.
  OGBUAGU, J.
  OKEKE, S.
  ONUKWULI, O.
  UBA NWUBA, E.
Faculty of Law:
  OKAFOR, I.
Faculty of Management Sciences:
  IKEZUE, C.
  MBACHU, A.
  NZE, F.
  OKAFOR, F.
  ONWUCHEKWA, C.
  OSISIOMA, B.
  UMEBALI
Faculty of Medicine:
  ADINMA, J.
  AGBATA, A.
  AHANEKU, J.
  ANYANWU, S.
  EGBUONU, I.
  EKEJINDU, G.
  EMELE, F.
  EZECHUKWU, C.
  IKPEZE, O.
  MBONU, O.
  MELUDU, S.
  NWOFOR, A.
  NWOFOR, A.
  NWOSU, S.
  OFIAELI, R.
  OKAFOR, P.
  OKONKWO, J.
  ORAKWE, J.
  OSUIGWE, A.
  UMEH, B.
  UWAKWE, R.
Faculty of Natural Sciences:
  AJIWE, V.
  AKPUAKA, M.
  ANASO, H.
  ANENE, G.
  ANIZOBA, M.
  ANYAKOHA, M.
  CHUKWURAH, E.
  EBOATU, A.
  EKEJIUBA, I.
  EKPUNOBI, A.
  ENEANYA, C.

EZEKWE, N.
EZEONU, E.
MBANUGO, J.
MOORE, C.
NWAORGU, O.
ODIBO, F.
OGUM, G.
OKAKA, A.
OKEREKE, G.
OKOYE, P.
ONOCHIE, C.
ONYALI, O.
ONYEAGU, S.
ORAJAKA, I.
OYEKA, C.
OYEKA, I.
UMEGO, M.
UMEH, C.

Faculty of Pharmaceutical Sciences:
ESIMONE, C. O.

Faculty of Social Sciences:
DIKE, M.
EYIUCHE, A.
NWANUNOBI, C.
NWUNELI, O.
OBI, A.
OKUNNA, C.

OBAFEMI AWOLOWO UNIVERSITY

Ile-Ife
Telephone: (36) 230290
Fax: (36) 232401
E-mail: registra@oauife.edu.ng
Internet: www.oauife.edu.ng
Founded 1961 as University of Ife, present
name 1987
Federal control
Language of instruction: English
Academic year: September to July
Chancellor: Alhaji KABIR USMAN
Pro-Chancellor: Alhaji SHETIMA A. M. LIB-
ERTY
Vice-Chancellor: Prof. ROGER MAKANJUOLA
Deputy Vice-Chancellor for Academic
Affairs: Prof. A. A. ADEDIRAN
Deputy Vice-Chancellor for Admin.: Prof. L.
O. KEHINDE
Registrar: B. O. ILUYOMADE
University Bursar: O. ODEYEMI
University Librarian: M. O. AFOLABI

Library: see under Libraries and Archives
Number of teachers: 1,343
Number of students: 22,742

Publications: *Calendar, Gazette, Handbook,
Ife Studies in English Language, Odu: A
Journal of West African Studies* (2 a year),
*Quarterly Journal of Administration, Sec-
ond Order* (2 a year), *University Bulletin*

DEANS

Faculty of Administration: O. OJO
Faculty of Agriculture: R. ADEYEMO
Faculty of Arts: O. T. AKINRINADE
Faculty of Basic Medical Sciences: M. A.
DUROSINMI
Faculty of Clinical Sciences: J. A. OWA
Faculty of Dentistry: O. D. OTUYEMI (acting)
Faculty of Education: D. K. AKANBI
Faculty of Environmental Design and Man-
agement: C. A. AJAYI
Faculty of Law: M. O. ADEDIRAN
Faculty of Pharmacy: A. O. OGUNDAINI
Faculty of Science: M. A. BADEJO
Faculty of Social Sciences: J. A. FABAYO
Faculty of Technology: M. O. FABORODE

PROFESSORS

Faculty of Administration:
ERERO, E. J., Public Administration
OJO, O., International Relations
OMOPARIOLA, O., Management and
Accounting

ORIBABOR, P. E., Management and
Accounting
SESAY, A., International Relations
SOREMEKUN, O., International Relations

Faculty of Agriculture:
ADEBAYO, A. A., Soil Science
ADEPETU, J. A., Soil Science
ADERIBIGBE, A. O., Animal Science
ADEYEMO, R., Agricultural Economics
ADUAYI, E. A., Soil Science
AINA, P. O., Soil Science
AJOBO, O., Agricultural Economics
AKINGBOHUNGBE, A. E., Plant Science
AKINYEMIJU, O. A., Plant Science
ALOFE, C. O., Plant Science
FAKOREDE, M. A., Plant Science
ILORI, J. O., Animal Science
JIBOWO, A. A., Agricultural Extension and
Rural Sociology
LADIPO, J. L., Plant Science
LAOGUN, E. A., Agricultural Extension and
Rural Sociology
MATANMI, B. A., Plant Science
OBISESAN, I. O., Plant Science
OKUSAMI, T. A., Soil Science
OLAYINKA, A., Soil Science
SONAIYA, E. B., Animal Science

Faculty of Arts:
ADEDIRAN, A. A., History
ADEWOLE, L. O., African Languages and
Literature
AJUWON, B., African Languages and Lit-
erature
AKINRINADE, O. T., History
IBITOKUN, B. M., English
ILESANMI, T. M., Religious Studies
KOLAWOLE, M. E. M., English
MAKINDE, M. A., Philosophy
MANUS, C. U., Modern European Lan-
guages
NWEZEH, E. C., Foreign Languages
OLANIYAN, R. A., History
OLAYIWOLA, D. O., Religious Studies
OLOMOLA, G. O. I., History
OLORUNFEMI, A., History
OMOSINI, O., History
ONIBERE, S. G. A., Religious Studies
VIDAL, A. O., Music

Faculties of Basic Medical Sciences, Clinical
Sciences and Dentistry:
ADEJUYIGBE, O., Surgery
ADELEKAN, D. A., Community Health
ADEYEMO, A. O., Surgery
AKINOLA, D. O., Surgery
AKINSOLA, A., Medicine
ARIGBABU, O., Surgery
BALOGUN, M. O., Medicine
CAXTON-MARTINS, A. E., Anatomy and Cell
Biology
DARE, F. O., Obstetrics and Gynaecology
DUROSINMI, M. A., Haematology and
Immunology
ELEGBE, R. A., Physiological Sciences
FAJEWONYOMI, B. A., Community Health
FAKUNLE, J. B., Chemical Pathology
JINADU, M. I., Nursing
MAKANJUOLA, R. O. A., Mental Health
ODESANMI, W. O., Morbid Anatomy and
Forensic Medicine
OGUNBODEDE, E. O., Preventive Dentistry
OGUNNIYI, S. O., Obstetrics and Gynaecol-
ogy
OJO, O. S., Morbid Anatomy and Forensic
Medicine
OJOFEITIMI, E. O., Community Health and
Nutrition
ONWUDIEGWU, U., Obstetrics and Gynaecol-
ogy
OTUYEMI, O. D., Child Dental Health
OWA, J. A., Paediatrics and Child Health
OYEDEJI, G. A., Paediatrics and Child
Health

Faculty of Education:
ADEYANJU, S. A., Physical and Health
Education
AKANBI, D. K., Educational Technology
EHINDERO, O. J., Institute of Education
FASOKUN, T. O., Continuing Education
FAWOLE, J. O., Physical Education
OBIDI, S. S., Education, Foundation and
Counselling
OGUNDARI, J. T., Physical and Health Edu-
cation
OKUNROTIFA, E. B., Physical and Health
Education

Faculty of Environmental Design and Man-
agement:
AJAYI, C. A., Estate Management
AMOLE, S. A., Architecture
AREMU, P. S. O., Fine Arts
FADARE, S. O., Urban and Regional Plan-
ning
IGHALO, J. I., Estate Management
OGUNJUMO, A., Urban and Regional Plan-
ning
OLAJUYIN, L. O., Urban and Regional Plan-
ning

Faculty of Law:
ADEDIRAN, M. O., Public Law
FABUNMI, J. O., Business Law
OKORODUDU-FUBARA, M. T., International
Law

Faculty of Pharmacy:
ADESANYA, S. A., Pharmacognosy
ADESINA, S. K., Drug Research
ADEWUNMI, C. O., Drug Research
ALADESANMI, J. A., Pharmacognosy
ELUJOBA, A. A., Pharmacognosy
LAMIKANRA, A., Pharmaceutics
OGUNBONA, F. A., Pharmaceutical Chemis-
try
OGUNDAINI, A. O., Pharmaceutical Chem-
istry
OGUNDARI, O., Pharmaceutical Chemistry
OLUGBADE, T. O., Pharmaceutical Chemis-
try
ONAWUNMI, G. O., Pharmaceutics
ONYEJI, O. C., Pharmaceutical Chemistry
ORAFIDIYA, O. O., Pharmaceutics
SOFOWORA, E. A., Pharmacognosy

Faculty of Science:
ADEDOKUN, J. A., Physics
ADEGOKE, J. A., Zoology
ADESULU, E. A., Zoology
ADEWUSI, S. R. A., Chemistry
AFOLAYAN, A., Biochemistry
AFUWAPE, M. A., Mathematics
AJAYI, E. O. B., Physics
AJAYI, T. R., Geology
AKANNI, M. S., Chemistry
AKINRELERE, E. A., Mathematics
AKO, B. D., Geology
AKO-NAI, K. A., Microbiology
ALADEKOMO, J. B., Physics
AMIRE, O. A., Chemistry
AMUSA, A., Physics
ARAWOMO, G. A. O., Zoology
ASAOLU, S. O., Zoology
AUBICJO, F. O. I., Chemistry
BALOGUN, E. E., Physics
BALOGUN, R. A., Zoology
FAKUNLE, C. O., Chemistry
IGE, W. J., Chemistry
IMORU, C. O., Mathematics
ISAWUMI, M. A. (Natural History Museum)
ISICHEI, A. O., Botany
KOLAWOLE, D. O., Microbiology
NWACHUKWU, J. I., Geology
OBAFEMI, C. A., Chemistry
ODEYEMI, O., Microbiology
ODU, E. A., Botany
OGUNKOYA, L. O., Chemistry
OJO, J. F., Chemistry
OKON, E. E., Zoology
OLANIYI, H. B., Physics

OLAREWAJU, V. O., Geology
OLOMO, J. B., Physics
OLORODE, O., Botany
OLORUNFEMI, M. O., Geology
OLUTIOLA, P. O., Microbiology
ONAJOBI, F. D., Biochemistry
OSADEBE, F. A. N., Physics
OSHOBI, E. O., Mathematics
RAHAMAN, M. A., Geology
SALAMI, M. B., Geology
SALAU, A. A. M., Physics
SHONUKAN, O. O., Microbiology

Faculty of Social Sciences:

ADESINA, F. A., Geography
ADEWUYI, A. A., Demography and Social Statistics
AFONJA, S., Sociology and Anthropology
EBIGBOLA, J. A., Demography and Social Statistics
EKANADE, O., Geography
FABAYO, J. A., Economics
JEJE, L. K., Geography
ODEBIYI, A. I., Sociology and Anthropology
OGUNBADEJO, F. O., Political Science
OGUNKOYA, O. O., Geography
OLORUNTIMEHIN, O., Sociology and Anthropology
OLOWU, A. A., Psychology
TOGONU-BICKESTETH, T., Psychology

Faculty of Technology:

ADEGBOYEGA, G. A., Electronic and Electrical Engineering
ADEKOYA, L. O., Mechanical Engineering
AFONJA, A. A., Metallurgical and Materials Engineering
AJAYI, G. O., Electronic and Electrical Engineering
AJIBOLA, O. A., Agricultural Engineering
BURAIMAH-IGBO, L. A., Electronic and Electrical Engineering
FABORODE, M. O., Agricultural Engineering
FAPOHUNDA, M. O., Agricultural Engineering
FASHAKIN, J. B., Food Science and Technology
IGE, M. T., Agricultural Engineering
ILLORI, M. O., Technology, Planning and Development Unit
KEHINDE, L. O., Electronic and Electrical Engineering
KUKU, T. A., Electronic and Electrical Engineering
LASISI, F., Agricultural Engineering
LAYOKUN, S. K., Chemical Engineering
MAKANJUOLA, G. A., Agricultural Engineering
MOJOLA, O. O., Mechanical Engineering
OGEDENGBE, M. O., Civil Engineering
OGUNSUA, A. O., Food Science and Technology
SANNI, S. A., Chemical Engineering
SOLOMON, B. O., Chemical Engineering
TAIWO, O., Chemical Engineering

AFFILIATED INSTITUTES

Institute of Agricultural Research and Training (IART), Ibadan: see under Research Institutes.

Institute of Education: Ile-Ife; f. 1962; sponsored by the University, the Oyo State Ministry of Education and the Association of Principals of Teacher Training Colleges and Secondary Schools in the State; a mobile library equipped with books, audiovisual aids and film aids for demonstration among colleges and secondary schools; Dir O. J. EHINDERO.

UNIVERSITY OF PORT HARCOURT

PMB 5323, Port Harcourt, Rivers State
Telephone: (84) 335218
Fax: (84) 230903
E-mail: registrar@uniport.edu.ng

Internet: www.uniport.edu.ng
Founded 1975
Federal control
Language of instruction: English
Academic year: October to July
Chancellor: HRH Alhaji MUSTAPHA UMAR EL-KANEMI (Shehu of Borno)
Pro-Chancellor: Prof. (Emer.) ALHAJI L. A. K. JIMOH
Vice-Chancellor: Prof. NIMI DIMPKA BRIGGS
Deputy Vice-Chancellor for Academic Affairs: Prof. J. D. OKOH
Deputy Vice-Chancellor for Admin.: Prof. M. O. C. ANIKPO
Registrar: Dr CHRIS ALAFONYEKA TAMUNO
Librarian: Prof. E. O. AYALOGU
Library of 90,000 vols, 220 foreign current journals, depository rights for UN publications
Number of teachers: 560
Number of students: 26,672
Publications: *Biologia Africana* (2 a year), *Journal of Education in Developing Areas—JEDA* (1 a year), *Kiabara* (2 a year), *Library Waves* (2 a year)

DEANS

Faculty of Basic Medical Sciences: Prof. O. O. EBONG
Faculty of Clinical Sciences: Prof. K. E. O. NKANGINIEME
Faculty of Dentistry: Prof. F. OKOISOR
Faculty of Engineering: Prof. C. UMEZURIKE
Faculty of Humanities: Prof. S. I. UDOIDEM
Faculty of Management Sciences: Prof. D. P. S. ASECHEMIE
Faculty of Pharmacy: Prof. O. K. UDEALA
Faculty of Science: Prof. C. M. OJINNAKA
Faculty of Social Sciences: Prof. W. J. OKOWA
School of Graduate Studies: Prof. W. I. BELL-GAM

PROFESSORS

College of Health Sciences:

ANAH, C. O., Cardiology
ASOGWA, S. E., Preventative and Social Medicine
BRAMBAIFA, N., Pharmacology
BRIGGS, N. D., Obstetrics and Gynaecology
DATUBO-BROWN, D. D., Surgery
EBONG, O. O., Pharmacology
EKE, F., Paediatrics
EKE, N., Surgery
ELECHI, E. N., Surgery
ESSIEN, E. N., Haematology
JOHN, T., Obstetrics and Gynaecology
NKANGINIEME, K. E. O., Paediatrics
NWANKWOALA, R. N. P., Pharmacology
ODIA, O. J., Medicine
OKOISOR, F., Dentistry
ORUAMABO, R. S., Paediatrics
UDEALA, O. K., Pharmacy
WAKWE, V. C., Chemical Pathology

Faculty of Education:

AWOTUA-EFEBO, E. B., Educational Technology
BARIKOR, C. N., Adult Education
DIENYE, N. E., Science Education
DIKE, H. I., Curriculum and Educational Technology
EHEAZU, B. A., Adult and Non-Formal Education
ENAOWHO, J. O., Educational Management and Planning
GBAMANJA, S. P. T., Curriculum and Educational Technology
JOE, A. I., Psychology, Guidance and Counselling
OKEKE, B. S., Education Administration
OKOH, J. D., History and Philosophy of Education
UKWUJE, R. P. I., Educational Psychology, Guidance and Counselling

Faculty of Engineering:

AJIENKA, J. A., Petroleum Engineering
EBONG, M. B., Civil Engineering
KUYE, A. O., Chemical Engineering
NWAOGAZIE, I. L., Civil Engineering
ONYEKONWU, M. A., Petroleum Engineering
UMEZURIKE, C., Mechanical Engineering

Faculty of Humanities:

BESTMAN, M. T., French
CHUKWUMA, H. O., Oral Literature
EJITUWU, N. C., History
EJIZU, C. I., Religious Studies
EKWELIE, S. A., Linguistics
EMENANJO, E. N., Linguistics
IKONNE, C., English
ILEGA, D., Religious Studies
MADUKA, C. T., Comparative Literature
NNOLIM, C. E., Literature
NWODO, C. S., Philosophy
UDOIDEM, S. I., Philosophy

Faculty of Management Sciences:

ASECHEMIE, D. P. S., Accounting
BARIDAM DON, O. M., Management
NWACHUKWU, C. C., Management

Faculty of Science:

ABBEY, B. W., Biochemistry
AKPOKODJE, E. A., Geology
AMAJOR, L. C., Geology
ANOSIKE, E. O., Enzymology and Protein Chemistry
ANUSIEM, A. C. I., Thermochemistry and Biophysical Chemistry
ARENE, F. O. I., Animal and Environmental Biology
ARINZE, A. E., Plant Science and Biotechnology
AYALOGU, E. O., Biochemistry
EBENIRO, J. O., Physics
EFIU-VWEVWERE, B. J. O., Biodegradation and Environmental Toxicology
EKEKE, G. I., Biochemistry
ETU-EFEOTOR, J. O., Sedimentology, Sedimentary Geochemistry
KINAKO, P. D. S., Botany
LALE, N. E. S., Crop Science
NYANANYO, B. L., Plant Science and Biotechnology
OJINNAKA, C. M., Organic and Natural Products Chemistry
OKIWELU, S. N., Entomology
OKOLI, B. S., Genetics
OKPOKWASILI, G. S. C., Microbiology
OTI, M. N., Geology

Faculty of Social Sciences:

AGIOBENEBO, T. J., Economics
ANIKPO, M. O. C., Sociology
BELL-GAM, W. I., Geography
EKPENYONG, S., Sociology
ETENG, I. A., Sociology
GBOSI, A. A., Economics
IBODJE, S. W. E., Political and Administrative Studies
OKOKO, K. A. B., Political and Administrative Studies
OJO, O. J. B., Political and Administrative Studies
OKOWA, W. J., Economics

USMANU DANFODIYO UNIVERSITY

Dundaye Village, PMB 234, Sokoto
Telephone: (60) 234042
Fax: (60) 235519
E-mail: registrar@udusok.edu.ng
Internet: www.udusok.edu.ng
Founded 1975
Federal control
Language of instruction: English
Academic year: November to July
Chancellor: (vacant)
Vice-Chancellor: Prof. A.S. MIKAILA

Deputy Vice-Chancellor for Academic Affairs: Dr A. A. ZURU
Registrar: A. S. USMAN
Librarian: AHMED ABDU BALARABE (acting)
Number of teachers: 371
Number of students: 11,617

Publications: *Calendar, Convocation Speeches, News Bulletin* (12 a year), *Student Handbook* (1 a year), *University Lecture Series*

DEANS

Faculty of Agriculture: Dr H. M. TUKUR (acting)
Faculty of Arts and Islamic Studies: Dr M. M. DANGANA (acting)
Faculty of Education and Extension Services: Dr F. A. KALGO (acting)
Faculty of Law: Mal. M. I. SAID
Faculty of Management and Administration: Prof. S. A. DIYO
Faculty of Science: Dr U. ABUBAKAR
Faculty of Social Sciences: (vacant)
Faculty of Veterinary Medicine: Dr A. I. DANEJI
College of Health Sciences: Dr W. E. K. OPARA
Postgraduate School: Dr R. A. SHEHU

PROFESSORS

ABDULKAREEM, A., Health Sciences
ABDULRAHMAN, D. A., Sociology
ABDULRAHMAN, F. W., Chemistry
ABUBAKAR, M. K., Biochemistry
ADAMU, M., History
ADEYANJU, J. B., Veterinary Medicine
AGALEA, A. S., Arabic
AUDU, M. S., Mathematics
BADEJO, O. A., Health Sciences
BANDE, T. M., Political Science
BASHAR, M. L. A., Economics
BASHIR, A. M., Accounting
BILBIS, L. S., Biochemistry
BIRNIWA, H. A., Nigerian Languages
DANIEL, S. O., Community Health
DORA, J. S., Geography
ILIYA, M. A., Geography
IPINJOLU, J. K., Forestry and Fisheries
JUNAID, M. I., Education
KALGO, F. A., Education
KAURA, J. M., Islamic Studies
KYIOGWON, U. B., Agricultural Economics and Extension
MAGAJI, M. D., Crop Science
MAJEED, Q., Biological Sciences
MAMMAN, A. B., Geography
MIKAILU, A. S., Business Administration
MUKOSHY, I. A., Nigerian Languages
OBEMBE, A. Y. O., Medicine
OPARA, W. E., Surgery
SALAWU, A. A., Education
SHEHU, B., Surgery
SHEIDU, A. D., Accounting
YAQUB, N. O., Political Science
ZURU, A. A., Chemistry

UNIVERSITY OF UYO

1 Ikpa Rd, PMB 1017, Uyo, Akwa Ibom State
Telephone: (85) 200303
Fax: (85) 202694
E-mail: vc@uniuyo.edu.ng
Internet: www.uniuyo.edu.ng

Founded 1983 as University of Cross River State, then renamed University of Akwa Ibom State; present name 1991
Fed. govt control
Language of instruction: English
Academic year: October to July

Chancellor: The Emir of Fika, Haj. Dr MUHAMMADU ABALI MUHAMMADU IBN IDRISSA
Vice-Chancellor: Prof. COMFORT MEMFIN EKPO

Deputy Vice-Chancellor for Academic Affairs: Prof. ANTHONY AKPAN
Deputy Vice-Chancellor for Admin.: Prof. CHARLES UKO
Dean of Student Affairs: ENO IBANGA
Registrar: Prof. EDAK UMONDAK
Librarian: Prof. FELICIA ETIM
Library of 84,628 vols, 271 periodicals
Number of teachers: 800
Number of students: 18,082

Publications: *Journal of Humanities, Journal of Research in Education and the Humanities, Uyo Social Science Journal*

DEANS

Faculty of Agriculture: Prof. ENEFIOK UDO
Faculty of Arts: Prof. DESMOND WILSON
Faculty of Basic Medical Sciences: Prof. ENOMFON AKPAN
Faculty of Business Administration: Dr ENEFIOK ESSIEN
Faculty of Clinical Sciences: Dr TIMOTHY NOTTIDGE
Faculty of Education: Prof. QUEENDOLEEN OBINAJU
Faculty of Engineering: Dr LINUS ASUQUO
Faculty of Environmental Studies: Prof. GODFREY UDO
Faculty of Law: Prof. NSONGURUA UDOMBANA
Faculty of Pharmacy: Prof. SABINA OFUEFULE
Faculty of Science: Prof. ALFRED ITAH
Faculty of Social Sciences: Prof. INNOCENT MODO
Post-Graduate Studies: Prof. JOSEPH OBINAJU
School of Continuing Education: Prof. TRENCHARD IBIA

PROFESSORS

ABASIATTAI, M. B., History
ABASIEKONG, E. M., Sociology
ABODERIN, A., Chemistry
ACHALU, O. E., Health Education
AFOLABI, M., Library Science
ANWANA, U. I., Guidance and Counselling
EKA, D., English
EKONG, E. E., Sociology
EKPENYONG, S., Sociology and Anthropology
EKPO, A. H., Economics
EKPO, N. M., Physics
EKPO, O. E., Curriculum Studies
ENOH, C. O. E., Geography
ESHIET, I. T., Chemistry and Education
ESSIEN, E. E., Pharmaceutical Chemistry
ETTE, S. I., Biochemistry
ETUK, U. A., Philosophy
EZE, O. C., Law
IBE-BASSEY, G. S., Educational Technology
IKKIDEH, I. S., English
IWOK, E. R., Accounting
NWA, E. U., Engineering
OKON, E. D., Zoology
UDO, E. J., Soil Science
UDOFOT, M. A., Curriculum Studies
UKPONG, I. I., Economics
UMOH, J. E., Animal Science
UMOH, P. U., Law
USORO, E., Geography

STATE UNIVERSITIES

ABIA STATE UNIVERSITY

PMB 2000, Uturu, Abia State
Telephone: (88) 220785
Internet: www.abia-state-uni.net
Founded 1981 as Imo State University; present name c. 1993
State control
Language of instruction: English
Academic year: October to August

Chancellor: Ambassador Dr Chief M. T. MBU
Vice-Chancellor: Prof. OGWO E. OGWO
Deputy Vice-Chancellor: Prof. STELLA OGBUAGU
Pro-Chancellor: EMEKA NWANKPA

Registrar: O. E. ONUOHA
Librarian: HERBERT I. IWUJI
Library of 27,000 vols
Number of teachers: 640
Number of students: 7,050

DEANS

College of Agriculture and Veterinary Medicine: Dr V. O. IMOH
College of Biological and Physical Sciences: Dr C. I. OGBONNAYA
College of Business Administration: Dr I. AJA-NWACHUKU
College of Education: Prof. V. C. NWACHUKU
College of Engineering and Environmental Studies: Dr M. A. IJIOMA (acting)
College of Humanities and Social Sciences: Prof. J. O. J. NWACHUKWU-ABADA
College of Legal Studies: M. O. UNEGBU (acting)
College of Medicine and Health Sciences: A. U. MBANASO (Provost)

PROFESSORS

AKPUAKA, F. C., Medicine and Health Sciences
ALEZI, O., Education
EBEOGU, A. N., Humanities and Social Sciences
EKE, F., Medicine and Health Sciences
MADUABUM, M. A., Education
MBATA, G. N., Biological and Physical Sciences
MKPA, M. A., Education
NWACHUKU, V. C., Education
NWACHUKWU-AGBADA, J. O. J., Humanities and Social Sciences
OGBONNAYA, C. I., Biological and Physical Sciences
OGBUAGU, S. C., Humanities and Social Sciences
OGWO, E. O., Marketing
ONOFEGHARA, N., Education
ONOH, J. K., Finance
ONUIGBO, W. I., Medicine and Health Sciences
OPARA-NADI, O. I., Agriculture and Veterinary Medicine
UWAKAH, C. T., Agriculture and Veterinary Medicine

ADAMAWA STATE UNIVERSITY

PMB 25, Mubi, Adamawa State
Telephone: (805) 8421126
Fax: (803)6131590
E-mail: info@adsu.edu.ng
Internet: www.adsu.edu.ng
Founded 2002
State control
Language of instruction: English
Academic year: October to August (2 semesters)

Vice-Chancellor: Dr ALKASUM ABBA
Deputy Vice-Chancellor: Dr SAIDU IBRAHIM
Registrar: J. M. GARNVWA
Bursar: KUMTHI EZRA ANJILI
Univ. Librarian: BELLO Y. DAHIRU
Dir for Academic Planning: S. M. MORUPPA

Library of 35,089 vols, 60 journals, 5,000 vols of e-books, 2,000 e-journals
Number of teachers: 461
Number of students: 5,719

Publications: *Adamawa Business Journal* (2 a year), *Adamawa Journal of Management and Decision Analysis* (2 a year), *ADSU Journal of Social and Development Studies* (2 a year)

DEANS

Faculty of Agriculture: Dr NEILS SHELLENG
Faculty of Science: Dr MOSES ZIRA ZARUWA
Faculty of Social and Management Sciences: Dr ABDULSALAM JIBRIL

Postgraduate School: Prof. MERCY OGUNSOLA-
BANDELE
School of Remedial and Basic Studies: ELI
TARTIYUS (Dir)

UNIVERSITY OF ADO-EKITI
PMB 5363, Ado-Ekiti, Ekiti State
Telephone: (30) 250026
E-mail: registrar@unad.edu.ng
Internet: www.unadportal.com
Founded 1982
Vice-Chancellor: Prof. DIPO KOLAWOLE
Deputy Vice-Chancellor for Academics: Prof.
O. OLAOFE
Deputy Vice-Chancellor for Devt: Prof. J. A.
ADEGUN
Dir for Directorate of Distance Learning:
Prof. R. O SEWEJE
Dir for General Studies Unit: Prof. K. AJAYI
Dir for Pre-Degree Programmes: Prof. E. O.
OLANIPEKUN
Registrar: OMOJOLA AWOSUSI
Bursar: F. M. FAPOHUNDA
Librarian: G. O. OGUNLEYE
Library of 110,000 vols
Number of teachers: 445
Number of students: 20,352 (1,4652 full-
time, 5,700 part-time)
Publication: *Nigerian Journal of Banking
and Financial Issues* (2 a year)

DEANS
College of Medicine: Prof. D. D. OYEBOLA
Faculty of Agricultural Sciences: Prof. A. S.
FASINA
Faculty of Arts: Dr T. F. JEMIRIYE (acting)
Faculty of Education: Prof. G. A. AKINLEYE
Faculty of Engineering: Dr S. B. ADEYEMO
(acting)
Faculty of Law: T. I. AKOMOLEDE
Faculty of Management Sciences: Prof. J. A.
OLOYEDE
Faculty of Science: Prof. S. S. ASAOLU
Faculty of Social Sciences: Prof. A. L. ADE-
SINA (acting)
School of Postgraduate Studies: Prof. J. O.
ARIBISALA

PROFESSORS
ADEBAYO, W., Social Sciences
ADELOWO, E., Arts
ADERIBIGBE, E., Science
ADERIBIGBE, F., Science
ADERIYE, J., Science
ADETIFA, O., Engineering
ADEYOJU, K., Agricultural Sciences
AFOLABI, F., Social Sciences
AGAGU, A., Political Science
AJAJA, O., Engineering
AKINDUTIRE, I., Education
AKINLEYE, G., Education
AKINTAYO, E., Science
ALONGE, M., Education
BANDELE, S., Education
ESAN, G., Medicine
FAKUNLE, J., Science
FALUYI, M., Science
FAMUREWA, O., Science
IBIJOLA, E., Mathematical Sciences
KAYODE, J., Science
KOLAWOLE, D., Social Sciences
LUCAS, E., Agricultural Sciences
MUKOLU, I., Physics
OGUNLADE, A., Education
OGUNSINA, J., Arts
OJO, S., Faculty of Engineering
OKE, G., Faculty of Law
OLOMOLA, G., History and International
Studies
OLORUNSOLA, S., Science
OMOSINI, O., Arts
OWOLABI, I., Elect/Elect. Engineering
OWUAMANAM, D., Education

OWUAMANAM, T., Education
OYINLOYE, A., Science
UKOYEN, J., Arts

AMBROSE ALLI UNIVERSITY
PMB 14, Ekpoma, Edo State
Telephone: (55) 98448
Founded 1981
State control
Language of instruction: English
Academic year: September to August
Chancellor: HRH Alhaji Dr UMARU FARUQ
BAHAGO (Emir of Minna)
Vice-Chancellor and Chief Executive: Prof.
D. O. AIGBOMIAN
Deputy Vice-Chancellor for Academic
Affairs: Dr G. B. EFOGHE
Deputy Vice-Chancellor for Admin.: (vacant)
Provost, College of Medicine: Prof. G. O.
AKPEDE
Registrar: G. T. OLAWOLE
Librarian: M. E. OJO-IGBINOBA
Library of 94,000 vols
Number of teachers: 500
Number of students: 18,000
Publications: *AAU* (journal of the Faculty of
Education, 1 a year), *Iroro* (journal of the
Faculty of Arts and Social Sciences, 1 a
year)

DEANS
Faculty of Agriculture: Dr P. O. ONOLEMHEM-
HEN (acting)
Faculty of Arts: Prof. F. I. EMORDI
Faculty of Clinical Sciences: F. ALUFOHAI
Faculty of Education: Prof. M. O. OMO-OJUGO
Faculty of Engineering and Technology: Prof.
C. A. AJUWA
Faculty of Environmental Studies: Dr Ing. S.
O. IZOMOH (acting)
Faculty of Law: Prof. A. D. BADAIKI
Faculty of Medicine: Dr C. P. ALOAMAKA
Faculty of Natural Sciences: Prof. F. EGHAR-
EVBA (acting)
Faculty of Social Sciences: Prof. B. E.
AIGBOKHAN

PROFESSORS
AGBONLAHOR, D. E., Microbiology
AIGBOKHAN, B. E., Economics
AIGBODION, D. O., Educational Foundations
AKINBODE, A., Geography and Regional Plan-
ning
ALOAMAKA, C. P., Physiology
DIME, C. A., Religious and Cultural Manage-
ment
ECHEKWUBE, A. O., Philosophy
EFOGHE, G. B., Psychology
EGUAVOEN, O. I., Chemistry
EMIOLA, A., Law
EMORDI, F. I., Modern Languages
IJOMAH, B. I. C., Sociology
IMOBIGHE, T. A., Political Science
KURNOW, K., History
LONGE, J. B., Economics
OAIKHINAN, E. P., Engineering, Technology
and Development
OKECHA, S. A., Chemistry
OMO-OYUGO, M. O., Curriculum and Instruc-
tion
OSEMEIKHIAN, J. E. A., Physics
REMISON, S. U., Crop Science
SEGYNOLA, A. A., Geography and Regional
Planning
UNOMAH, A. C., History
YESUFU, A. K., Electrical and Electronic
Engineering

BENUE STATE UNIVERSITY
PMB 102119, Makurdi, Benue State
Telephone: (44) 533811
Fax: (44) 534040

E-mail: root@bensu.edu.ng
Founded 1992
Language of instruction: English
Accredited by National Universities Commis-
sion, Abuja
Vice-Chancellor: Prof. AKASE P. SORKA
Deputy Vice-Chancellors: Prof. TONY EDOH
(Admin), Prof. TYOHDZUAH P. AKOSU (Aca-
demic)
Registrar: TIMOTHY I. UTILE
Librarian: JOHNATHAN A. OCHEIBI
Library of 67,000 vols
Number of teachers: 558
Number of students: 13,649 (12,070 full-
time, 1,579 part-time)
Publications: *Faculty of Arts Journal, Fac-
ulty of Education Journal*

DEANS
Faculty of Allied Sciences: EMMANUEL O.
NWOKEDI
Faculty of Arts: Dr JOSEPH T. KERKER
Faculty of Clinical Sciences: MARGARET M.
ARAOYE
Faculty of Education: Dr NANCY AGBE
Faculty of Law: AKAA T. IMBWASEH
Faculty of Management Science: SYLVESTER
ORSAAH
Faculty of Science: Prof. EMMANUEL AGBA
Faculty of Social Science: Prof. ADAGBA
OKPAGA
Postgraduate School: Prof. JOSEPH FIASE

PROFESSORS
ACHUA, J., Accounting
ADEJIR, T., Languages and Linguistics
AGBA, E. H., Physics
ANGYA, C. A., Theatre Arts
ANYANDE, G., Economics
APAM, J., Political Science
CHIAWA, M., Maths and Computer Science
GAFFA, T., Biological Science
GYUSE, T., Geography
KEGHKU, T., Mass Communication
KPELAI, T., Business Management
MOTI, J. S., Religion and Philosophy
NEVKAA, J. N., Educational Foundations
NYITSE, L. M., English
ODEY, M. O., History
SAMBA, J. N., Commercial and Property Law
SHINDI, J. A., Psychology
UTULU, R. E., Curriculum and Teaching
WEGH, F. S., Sociology
YIASE, S. G., Chemistry

EBONYI STATE UNIVERSITY
PMB 053, Abakaliki, Ebonyi State
Telephone: (43) 221093
E-mail: vc@ebsu-edu.net
Internet: www.ebsu-edu.net
Founded 1999
Language of instruction: English
Vice-Chancellor: Eng. Prof. FRANK I IDIKE
Deputy Vice-Chancellor: Prof. EGWU U. EGWU
Registrar: SAM NTE EGWU
Librarian: FRIDAY U. IBIAM
Library of 27,000 vols
Number of teachers: 792
Number of students: 22,029 (11,441 full-
time; 10,588 part-time)

DEANS
Faculty of Agriculture and Natural
Resources Management: Prof. EKUMA O.
EKUMANKAMA
Faculty of Applied and Natural Sciences:
Prof. JAMES C. OGBONNA
Faculty of Arts: Dr CLEMENT MGBADA
Faculty of Basic Medical Sciences: Prof.
SUNDAY O. ELOM
Faculty of Biological Sciences: Dr IBIAM UDU

Faculty of Clinical Medicine: Prof. ESTHER U. AJULUCHUKWU
Faculty of Education: Prof. BERNARD ALUMODE
Faculty of Health Science and Technology: Asst Prof. C. O. EDEOGU
Faculty of Law: M. AJA NWACHUKWU
Faculty of Management Sciences: Dr FIDELIS OKPATA
Faculty of Physical Sciences: Prof. OBINI EKPE
Faculty of Social Sciences: Dr EUGENE NWEKE
School of Postgraduate Studies: Prof. SUNDAY N. AGWU

PROFESSORS

AKUBILO, C. J. C., Agricultural Economics, Management and Extension
ALAKU, S. O., Animal Production and Fisheries Management
ALI, A., Computer Science Education
AMUCHIE, F. A., Human Kinetics and Health Education
ANEZI-ONWU, O. N., Medicine
ATTAH, C. A., Surgery
AZUBUIKE, M. M., Computer Science Education
DIRIBE, C. O., Medical Biochemistry
EGWU, E. U., Management and Marketing
EGWUATU, V. E., Obstetrics and Gynaecology
EKUMANKAMA, E. O., Food Science
EZEIFEKA, G. O., Applied Microbiology
EZEILO, J. O., Industrial Mathematics and Applied Statistics
IBE, S., Animal Production and Fisheries Management
IBEMISI, J. A., Industrial Chemistry
IHEME, B. A., Law
INYIAMA, H. C., Computer Science
MARIRE, B. N., Animal Production and Fisheries Management
MGBODILE, M. U. K., Chemical Pathology
NDU, U., Applied Biology
NNOKE, F. N., Soil and Environmental Management
OBI, I. U., Crop Production and Landscape Management
OBIAKO, M. N., Surgery
OBIDOA, O., Medical Biochemistry
OBINNA, O. E., Economics
OBIONU, C. N., Community Medicine
OGAH, F., Crop Production and Landscape Management
OGBONNA, J. C., Biochemistry and Biotechnology
OJI, C., Surgery
OKAGBUE, R. N., Applied Microbiology
OKAKA, A. N. C., Biochemistry and Biotechnology
OKAKA, J. C., Food Science
OKANY, M. C., Law
OKOGBUE, C. O., Geology and Exploration Geophysics
OKOLI, E. C., Food Science
OKOLI, F. C., Political Science and Public Administration
OKORJI, E. C., Agricultural Economics, Management and Extension
OLUIKPE, B. O., English
ONUAGULUCHI, G., Pharmacology and Therapeutics
ONYENEKE, C. E., Biochemistry and Biotechnology
OSISIOMA, B. C., Accountancy
UBAH, C. N., History and International Relations
UCHE, C. U., Banking and Finance
UKPABI, S. C., History and International Relations
UKWU, U. I., Economics
UMEH, E. D., Crop Production and Landscape Management
UMEJI, A. C., Geology and Exploration Geophysics
UMEZUIKE, I. A., Law
UMOH, S. M., Management and Marketing

ENUGU STATE UNIVERSITY OF SCIENCE AND TECHNOLOGY

PMB 01660, Enugu
Telephone: (42) 451244
Fax: (42) 335705
E-mail: esut@compuserve.com
Internet: www.esut.edu.ng
Founded 1980
Campuses at Enugu and Nsukka
State control
Academic year: January to October (two semesters)
Language of instruction: English
Chancellor: Dr Chief ERNEST ADEGUNLE OLADEINDE SHONEKAN
Pro-Chancellor: Igwe Dr C. A. ABANGWU
Vice-Chancellor: Prof. SAMUEL CHUKWU
Deputy Vice-Chancellor: Prof. Rev. Canon CHINEDU NEBO
Registrar: B. N. UZOIGWE
Librarian: Dr N. ENE
Number of teachers: 472
Number of students: 29,827
Publication: *Journal of Science and Technology* (2 a year)

DEANS

Faculty of Agriculture: Prof. B. N. MARIRE
Faculty of Applied Natural Sciences: Prof. A. C. OKONKWO
Faculty of Basic Medical Sciences: Prof. S. E. ASOGWA
Faculty of Education: Prof. O. O. ONOWOR
Faculty of Law: Dr OBI S. OGENE
Faculty of Management Sciences: P. E. EMEKEKWUE
Faculty of Social Sciences: Dr D. N. NWATU
School of Engineering: Prof. G. N. ONOH
School of Environmental Sciences: Prof. A. N. AGU
School of Postgraduate Studies: Prof. R. C. OKAFOR

PROFESSORS

ADIBE, E. C., Geography and Meteorology
AGAJELU, S. I., Surveying and Photography
AGU, N., Geography and Meteorology
AKUBUILO, C. J. C., Agriculture
ALAKU, S. O., Animal Science
ANEKE, L. E., Chemical Engineering
ANOWOR, O. O., Foundations of Education
ASOGWA, S. E., Community Medicine
CHIDOBEM, I. J., Animal Science
CHUKWU, S. C., Cooperatives
ENE, J. C., Applied Natural Sciences
MADUEWESI, J. N. C., Applied Natural Sciences
MARIRE, B. N., Animal Science
MOGBO, J. O., Foundations of Education
NEBO, C. O., Mechanical and Materials Engineering
NWORGY, O. C., Applied Biology
OCHO, L. O., Foundations of Education
OHUCHE, R. O., Industrial Mathematics and Statistics
OKAFOR, N., Applied Microbiology and Brewing
OKAFOR, R. C., Foundations of Education
OKAKA, J. C., Agriculture
OKONKWO, C. A. C., Applied Biology
OKORIE, B. A., Mechanical and Materials Engineering
ONOH, G. N., Electrical and Electronic Engineering
ONYEHALU, A. S., Foundations of Education
UGWU, I. C., Urban and Regional Planning
UMEH, E. D., Applied Biology

IMO STATE UNIVERSITY

PMB 2000, Owerri, Imo State
Telephone: (83) 221687
Fax: (83) 232716

Founded 1981
Vice-Chancellor: Prof. TONY G. ANWUKAH
Registrar: FRANCIS E. NWANKWO
Number of teachers: 230
Number of students: 15,991

DEANS

Faculty of Agriculture and Veterinary Medicine: A. ONWEAGBA
Faculty of Business Administration: INNOCENT OKONKWO
Faculty of Education: D. A. ONYEJEMEZI
Faculty of Engineering and Environmental Sciences: U. O. NKWOGU
Faculty of Humanities: ROSE ACHOLONU
Faculty of Law: U. S. F. NNABUE
Faculty of Science: E. N. MGBENU
Faculty of Social Sciences: C. B. NWACHUKWU
College of Medical and Health Sciences: B. C. JIBURUM
Postgraduate School: F. N. MADUBUIKE

KANO STATE UNIVERSITY OF TECHNOLOGY, WUDIL

PMB 3244, Kano, Kano State
Telephone: (64) 241149
Fax: (64) 241175
Founded 2001
Chancellor: ALHAJI ALIKO DANGOTE
Vice-Chancellor: SHAWKI A. A. SEOUD
Registrar: A. U. ABDURAHIM.

LADOKE AKINTOLA UNIVERSITY OF TECHNOLOGY

PMB 4000, Ogbomoso, Oyo State
Telephone: (38) 720285
Fax: (38) 720750
Founded 1990 as Oyo State University of Technology; present name 1991
Vice-Chancellor: Prof. AKINOLA M. SALAU
Registrar: Y. O. GBADAMOSI
Library of 19,604 vols
Number of teachers: 439
Number of students: 12,245

DEANS

Faculty of Agriculture: J. I. OLAIFA
Faculty of Engineering and Technology: J. O. OJEDIRAN (acting)
Faculty of Environmental Sciences: R. O. R. KALILU
Faculty of Medical Sciences: P. O. AKINWISU (acting)
Faculty of Pure and Applied Sciences: R. O. AYENI

LAGOS STATE UNIVERSITY

PMB 1087, Apapa, Lagos State
Telephone: (1) 5884048
Fax: (1) 5884048
E-mail: veecee@lasu.org
Founded 1983
State control
Language of instruction: English
Academic year: October to July
Vice-Chancellor: Prof. ABISOGUN OLUBODE LEIGH
Registrar: OLUWATOYIN GLADSTONE OSHUN
Librarian: T. A. B. SERIKI
Library of 63,000 vols
Number of teachers: 513
Number of students: 35,544 (16,422 full-time, 19,122 part-time)
Publications: *ECOFLASH, Educational Perspectives, Enhancing Quality Education in Nigeria, Journal of Humanities* (2 a year), *Journal of Prospects in Science, LASU Jurist, LASU Law Journal, LASU Social*

Science Journal, Nigerian Journal of Research & Review in Science

DEANS

Faculty of Arts: Dr KUMLE LAWAL
Faculty of Education: Prof. ADEMOLA ONIFADE
Faculty of Engineering: Prof. P. A. O. ADEGBUYI
Faculty of Law: Prof. B. A. SUSU
Faculty of Management Science: Prof. O. J. FAPOHUNDA
Faculty of Sciences: Prof. MARTIN A. ANATEKHAI
Faculty of Social Sciences: Prof. TAYO ODUMOSU
College of Medicine: Prof. WOLE ALAKIJA
Postgraduate School: Prof. C. O. OSHUN

PROFESSORS

ABDUL-KUREEM, H., Medical Biochemistry
ADARAMOLA, F., International Law and Jurisprudence
AJAJA, O., Mechanical Engineering
AJOSE, S. O., Electronics and Computer Engineering
AKINRIMISI, E. O., Haematology and Blood Transfusion
ALAKIJA, W., Community and Primary Healthcare
ANETEKHAI, M. A., Fisheries Science
ASHIRU, O. A., Anatomy
BAMGBOYE, O. A., Chemistry
DADA, O. A., Chemical Pathology
FAPOHUNDA, O. J., Business Administration
HUNPONU-WUSU, O. O., Community and Primary Healthcare
IKHARIALE, M. A., Public Law
MATANMI, S. O., Industrial Relations and Personnel Management
OBAFUNWA, J. O., Pathology
ODERINDE, B. B., Curriculum Studies
ODUBUNMI, E. O., Curriculum Studies
ODUMOSU, A. O., Geography and Planning
ODUMOSU, T., Communications
OKANLAWON, A., Anatomy
OKEBUKOLA, P. A. O., Curriculum Studies
OLUKOYE, A. O., Chemical Pathology
ONABANJO, A. O., Medical Microbiology
ONIFADE, A., Public Law
OSINBAJO, O. O., Public Law
OYERINDE, J. P. O., Medical Biochemistry
SAGOE, A. O., Haematology and Blood Transfusion
TUNDE, S., Communications and Educational Management
YEROKUN, O. A., Business Law

NIGER DELTA STATE UNIVERSITY

PMB 1, Abraka, Delta State
Telephone: (54) 66027
Founded 1992

Vice-Chancellor: Prof. F. M. A. UKOLI
Registrar: E. E. AVBIOROKOMA
Librarian: LAWRENCE OGBENI.

OLABISI ONABANJO UNIVERISTY

PMB 2002, Ago-Iwoye, Ogun State
Telephone: (37) 432384
Fax: (37) 432384
Internet: www.oou-ng.com
Founded 1982
State Government control
Academic year: October to July
Chancellor: Dr AYOOLA OBA OTUDEKO
Pro-Chancellor: Prof. BIYI AFONJA
Vice-Chancellor: Prof. AFOLABI SOYODE
Deputy Vice-Chancellors: Prof. E. O. A. AJAYI, Prof. ODUTOLA OSILESI
Registrar: APOSTLE SAMUEL O. AJAYI
Librarian: O. K. ODUSANYA
Library of 106,709 vols
Number of teachers: 699

Number of students: 43,382 (28,221 full-time, 15,161 part-time)
Publications: *Ago-Iwoye Journal of Social and Behavioural Sciences* (2 a year), *GEGE Journal of the English Department* (1 a year), *International Journal of Accountancy, Finance and Management Sciences* (2 a year), *Journals of History and Diplomatic Studies* (1 a year), *Journal of Philosophy and Development.* (1 a year), *Journal of Public Law and Practice* (1 a year), *Journal of Social and Management Sciences* (1 a year), *Nigerian Journal of Private and Commercial Law* (1 a year), *OSU Journal of Educational Studies* (1 a year), *OYE Journal of Arts* (1 a year), *Private and Commercial Law Additional Information* (1 a year), *Studies in Curriculum* (4 a year)

DEANS

Faculty of Agricultural Management and Rural Development: Dr AIHONSU JOHN (Provost)
Faculty of Agricultural Production and Renewable Resources: Prof. S. O. OSUNLAJA
Faculty of Arts: Prof. KAMALDEEN BALOGUN
Faculty of Basic Medical Sciences: Prof. JIDE OLOWOOKERE
Faculty of Clinical Sciences: Prof. FEMI ADELOWO
Faculty of Education: Prof. OLATUNJI ODEDEYI
Faculty of Engineering: Prof. J. AKINYEMI
Faculty of Environmental Technology: Prof. TOYIN OGUNTONA
Faculty of Law: Prof. JUSTUS SOKEFUN
Faculty of Management Sciences: Dr S. A. TELLA (acting)
Faculty of Pharmacy: Prof. M. N. FEMIOYEWO
Faculty of Science: Prof. AFOLABI ADEBANJO
Faculty of Social Sciences: Dr WALE OLAITAN
College of Agricultural Sciences: Prof. S. F. ADEDOYIN (Provost)
College of Engineering and Technology: Prof. R. O. FAGBENLE (Provost)
Obafemi Awolowo College of Health Sciences: Prof. M. A. OLANREWAJU (Provost)
Postgraduate School: Prof. O. O. KEHINDE PHILLIPS (Provost)

PROFESSORS

ADEBANJO, A., Chemical Sciences
ADEDIPE, V. O., Educational Foundations and Management
ADEDOYIN, S. F., Agricultural Extension and Rural Sociology
ADEJONWO, K. O., Crop Production
ADESEMOWO, P. O., Educational Foundations and Management
ADESIMI, A. A., Agribusiness and Farm Management
ADETORO, O. O., Obstetrics and Gynaecology
AFEJUKU, D. H., Private and Commercial Law
AJAYI, E. O. A., Educational Foundations and Management
AJIBADE, E. S., Educational Foundations and Management
ALAUSA, O. K., Community Medicine and Primary Care
AWODERU, V. A., Biological Sciences
AYANLAJA, S. A., Soil Science and Farm Mechanisation
BALOGUN, K A., Religious Studies
BENEDICT, J. N., Curriculum Studies and Instructional Technology
DADA, O. A., Haematology and Blood Transfusion
DADA, S. S., Earth Sciences
EJIWUNMI, A. B., Anatomy
ERINOSHO, O. A., Sociology
FEMI, O. M. N., Pharmaceutics and Pharmaceutical Technology

HASSAN, T., Educational Foundations and Management
IYANIWURA, J. O., Mathematical Sciences
JAYESIMI, A. E. A., Medicine
KEHINDE-PHILLIPS, O. O., Earth Sciences
ODEDEYI, TUNJI, Sports Science and Health Education
ODUGBEMI, O. O., Geography and Regional Planning
ODUMUYIWA, E. A., Religious Studies
OGUNBA, OYIN, English
OGUNDERO, V. W., Biological Sciences
OGUNYEMI, E. O., Chemical Pathology and Haematology
OLAGUNJU, O. P., Educational Foundations and Management
OLANREWAJU, D. M., Paediatrics
OLOWOOKERE, J. O., Biochemistry
OLOWU, A. O., Paediatrics
OLUDIMU, O. L., Agricultural Economics
OSILESI, O., Biochemistry
OSONUBI, O., Biological Sciences
OSUNLAJA, S. O., Crop Production
OWORU, O. O., Crop Production
OYEDEJI, O. A., Curriculum Studies and Instructional Technology
OYEGUNLE, O. A., Anaesthesia
OYESIKU, O. O., Geography and Regional Planning
SANWO, J. O., Crop Production
SOSANWO, O. A., Mathematical Sciences
SULE-ODU, A. O., Obstetrics and Gynaecology
TAIWO, A., Educational Foundations and Management

RIVERS STATE UNIVERSITY OF SCIENCE AND TECHNOLOGY

PMB 5080, Port Harcourt, Rivers State
Telephone: (84) 233288
Fax: (84) 230720
E-mail: info@ust.edu.ng
Founded 1971, univ. status 1980
State control
Language of instruction: English
Academic year: October to July

Chancellor: (vacant)
Pro-Chancellor: Hon. Justice (rtd) ADOLPHUS KARIBI-WHYTE
Vice-Chancellor: Prof. B. B. FAKAE
Deputy Vice-Chancellor: Prof. H. I. HART
Registrar: DABA C. ODIMABO
Librarian: Dr B. E. AHIAUZU

Library of 2,000 vols
Number of teachers: 496
Number of students: 20,060

Publication: *News Bulletin* (4 a year)

DEANS

Faculty of Agriculture: Prof. J. P. ALAWA
Faculty of Engineering: Prof. ALEX J. AKOR
Faculty of Environmental Sciences: VICTOR A. AKUJURU (acting)
Faculty of Law: F. O. AKAAKAR (acting)
Faculty of Management Sciences: Prof. SETH ACCRA-JAJA (acting)
Faculty of Science: Prof. FRIDAY B. SIGALO
Faculty of Technical and Science Education: Prof. W. AMAEWHULE (acting)
Postgraduate School: Prof. EMMANUEL N. AMADI

PROFESSORS

Faculty of Agriculture:

ACHINEWHU, S. C., Food Science
AMAKIRI, M. A., Soil Science
AMAKIRI, S. F., Animal Science
GIAMI, S., Food Science
IGBEN, M. S., Agricultural Economics/Extension
ISIRIMAH, N. O., Crop/Soil Science
MONSI, A., Animal Science
OGBURIA, M. N., Food Science
ONUEGBU, B. A., Crop/Soil Science

OPUWARIBO, E. E., Crop/Soil Science
ORUWARI, B. M., Animal Science
WAHUA, T. A. T., Crop/Soil Science
WEKHE, S. N, Animal Science

Faculty of Engineering:
ABOWEI, M. F. N.
CHINWAH, J. G.
HART, H. I., Mechanical Engineering
IDERIAH, F. J. K., Mechanical Engineering
IDONIBOYE-OBU, K. I., Chemical/Petro-
chemical Engineering
JOHNARRY, T., Civil Engineering
ODI-OWEI, S., Mechanical Engineering
WAMI, E. N.

Faculty of Environmental Sciences:
FUBARA, D. M. J., Geodesy
TEME, S. C., Geology

Faculty of Management Sciences:
ACCRA-JAJA, S., Business Administration
AHIAUZU, A. I., Business Administration
FUBARA, B. A., Business Administration
GBOSI, A. N., Management Science
JOHNNIE, P. B., Business Administration
ONOH, J. K., Banking & Finance

Faculty of Science:
ABBEY, S. D., Medical Laboratory
AMADI, E. N., Biology
EKWEOZOR, I. K. E., Biology
NWANKWO, S. I., Chemistry
OKWAKPAM, B. A., Biology
OMUARU, V. O. T., Chemistry

Faculty of Technical and Science Education:
AHIAKWO, M. J., Science and Technical
Education
AMAEHULE, W. A., Business Education
KOKO, M. N., Business Education
WOKOCHA, A. M., Educational Foundations

PRIVATE UNIVERSITIES

ABTI AMERICAN UNIVERSITY OF NIGERIA

2 Ahmed Onibudo St, POB 73688, Victoria
Island, Lagos

Telephone: (1) 3200695
E-mail: abtiuniversity@yahoo.com
Internet: www.abti-american.edu.ng

Founded 2005 in partnership with the
American University, Washington, DC,
USA

Number of students: 200

President: Dr DAVID HUWILER
Dean of Students and Registrar: Dr BARRY
MORRIS.

BABCOCK UNIVERSITY

Ilishan-Remo, Ogun

Telephone: (1) 7613797
E-mail: registrar@babcockuni.edu.ng
Internet: www.babcockuni.edu.ng

Founded 1999, fmrly Adventist Seminary of
West Africa
Seventh-Day Adventist Church control
Language of instruction: English

Pres. and Vice-Chancellor: Prof. JAMES
KAYODE MAKINDE

Number of teachers: 233
Number of students: 5,600
Library of 58,000 vols, 664 periodicals

DEANS

School of Education and Humanities: Prof.
JOSHUA M. A. OYINLOYE
School of Law and Security Studies: ZAC O.
OLOMOJOBI
School of Management and Social Sciences:
(vacant)
School of Science and Technology: Prof.
GRACE OLUWATOYIN TAYO

PROFESSORS

School of Education and Humanities
Department of History and International
Studies:
ADEWOYE, O., Legal History
NENGEL, J. G., Intergroup Relations
Department of Languages and Literary
Studies:
AKPOROBARO, I. A., Literary Studies, Afri-
can and European Literature
OSISANWO, I. A., English Language, Phon-
etics and Grammar
Department of Mass Communication:
AKANBI, D. K., Instructional Media and
Communication
ALAO, D., Journalism and International
Communication
KIO, J., Speech Communication and
Human Relations

School of Law and Security Studies:
AGEDE, I. S., Alternative Dispute Reso-
lution, Arbitration, Conflict of Law and
Jurisprudence
OLIYIDE, S., Banking, Commercial Law and
Law of International Trade
OLOMOJOBO, Z. O., Military and Constitu-
tional Law

School of Management and Social Sciences:
AINA, A., Political Science, Political Strat-
egies
AJAYI, F., Political Science
AKINOLA, J., Educational Management
ASIKA, N., Business Management,
Research Methods
MAKINDE, J., Political Science, Political
History
OGUNDAIRO, M., Economics
OLALOKU, F., Economics

School of Science and Technology
Department of Agriculture:
DARAMOLA, D. S., Soil Science
TAYO, G. O., Animal Nutrition
Department of Biosciences and
Biotechnology:
FAPOHUNDA, S. O., Industrial Microbiology
KOLAWOLE, D. O., Medical Microbiology

Department of Chemical and Environmental
Sciences:
ESAN, E. B., Botany and Biotechnology
OGUNWENMO, K. O., Biosystematics and
Cytogenetics
ONAJOBI, F. D., Lipids and Membrane
Biochemistry

Department of Computer and Mathematics:
ADELODUN, J. F., Mathematics
OMOTOSHO, O. J., Computer Engineering
and Instrumentation
Department of Nursing Sciences:
FASHINA, E. M., Clinical Psychology and
Nursing

Department of Public and Allied Health:
AKINBOYE, D. O., Medical Parasitology
FAJEWONYOMI, B. A., Community Health
and Epidemiology

BENSON IDAHOSA UNIVERSITY

PMB 1100, University Way, Off Upper
Adesuwa Grammar School Rd, Benin City

Telephone: (52) 253764
E-mail: president@biu.edu.ng
Internet: www.biu.edu.ng

Founded 2002
Private control
Language of instruction: English

Vice-Chancellor: Prof. MACDONALD IDU
Chief Financial Officer: ANDY AKEN'OVA
Librarian: W. MOKOGWU (acting)

Library of 48,000 vols, 450 periodicals

Number of teachers: 211
Number of students: 2,821 (F. t. e.)

DEANS

Faculty of Agriculture and Agricultural
Technology: Prof. J. O. OYEDEJI
Faculty of Basic Sciences: Dr C. L. IGELEKE
Faculty of Law: Prof. C. C. OHURUOGU

COVENANT UNIVERSITY

10 km Idiroko Rd,, Canaan Land, Ota, Ogun
State

Telephone: (1) 7900724
E-mail: contact@covenantuniversity.com
Internet: www.covenantuniversity.com

Founded 2002

Chancellor: Dr DAVID OYEDEPO
Vice-Chancellor: Prof. AIZE OLOHIGBE IMOUO-
KHOME OBAYAN

Colleges of Business and Social Sciences,
Human Development and Science and Technology.

IGBINEDION UNIVERSITY

PMB 0006, Okada, Benin-City

Telephone and fax (52) 260005
E-mail: pefs@skannet.com
Internet: www.igbinedionuniversity.edu.ng

Founded 1999

Vice-Chancellor: Prof. EGHOSA EMMANUEL
OSAGHAE
Deputy Vice-Chancellor: Prof. L. C. CHIEDOZI
Dean of Student Affairs: Prof. GILBERT O.
NWOBU
Registrar: Dr SALLY AKWUGO ASAGWARA
Librarian: Dr R. OLORUNSOLA (acting)

DEANS AND PROVOSTS

College of Agriculture: Prof. ADETOKUNBO
ADEOLA (Dean)
College of Arts and Social Sciences: Dr
ANGELU M. ONWUEJEOGU (Dean)
College of Business and Management Stud-
ies: Prof. A. E. OKOYE (Dean)
College of Engineering: Dr T. S. WARA (act-
ing) (Dean)
College of Health Sciences: Prof. TUNDE
DARAMOLA (Provost)
College of Law: Prof. M. O. OGUNGBE (Dean)
College of Natural and Applied Sciences:
Prof. ALEXANDER E. ODAIBO (Dean)
College of Pharmacy: Prof. SAMSON ESEZOBOR
(Dean)
School of Basic Medical Sciences: Prof. A. A.
ODUTOGA (Dean)
School of Clinical Medicine: Prof. L. C.
CHIEDOZIE (Dean)
School of Postgraduate Studies: Prof.
ABAYOMI ONI (Dean)

PROFESSORS

ADELUSI, Pharmacy
ADEOLA, A., Wildlife and Forestry
AGBA, M., Microbiology
AGBONLAHOR, D., Microbiology and Medical
Laboratory Sciences
AIBONI, S., Law
AWOGUN, I., Medical Microbiology
BAXTER-GRILLO, D., Anatomy
CHIEDOZIE, L., Surgery
DARAMOLA, T., Community Health
EKEH, J., Electrical and Electronic Engineer-
ing
EKUNDARE, R., Economics
ESEZOBOR, S., Pharmacy
NAREBO, D., Law
NWOBU, G., Medical Laboratory Sciences
ODAIBO, A., Biological Sciences: Zoology
ODUTUGA, A., Biochemistry
OFUOROFO, I., Chemical Pathology
OGUNBIYI, J., Morbid Anatomy
OGUNGBE, M., Law

OKOYE, A., Accountancy
OLUOHA, U., Chemical Pathology
ONI, A., Mechanical Engineering
ONWUJEOGWU, A., Sociology and Anthropology
OSAGHAE, Political Science
OSENI, T., Agronomy
OSIFO, N., Pharmacology
PADONU, M., Community Health
YESUFU, English

PAN-AFRICAN UNIVERSITY

2 Ahmed Onibudo St, POB 73688, Victoria Island, Lagos
Telephone: (1) 3200695
Founded 2002
Vice-Chancellor: Prof. ALBERT J. ALOS
Postgraduate degree programmes in business administration and economics.

Polytechnics and Colleges

FEDERAL POLYTECHNIC, ADO-EKITI

PMB 5351, Ado-Ekiti, Ekiti State
Telephone: (30) 250523
E-mail: fedpolyado@fedpolyado.org
Internet: www.fedpolyado.org
Founded 1977
Academic year: February to November
Rector: Prof. O. AJAJA
Registrar: A. I. AJAYI
Librarian: M. O. OLASEHINDE
Library of 15,706 vols, 845 periodicals
Number of teachers: 290
Number of students: 6,161
Publications: *Expertus* (sustainable development, 2 a year), *Research Journal* (1 a year)

HEADS OF SCHOOLS

Business Studies: A. O. AKINYEMI
Engineering: D. A. T. ADEGBOYEGA
Environmental Studies: G. S. OLORUNOJE
Science and Computer Studies: D. O. ORIMAYE

AKANU IBIAM FEDERAL POLYTECHNIC, UNWANA

PMB 1007, Afikpo, Ebonyi State
Telephone: (90) 500180
Founded 1981
Rector: F. O. OTUNTA
Deputy Rector for Academic Affairs: E. I. IGWEONU
Deputy Rector for Admin.: M. I. ANUNA
Dir for Academic Planning and Devt: T. N. ISINEYI
Dir for Information and Communication Technology: E. U. EZEROAH (acting)
Registrar: A. D. OKONO
Librarian: UGWUOGU O. UGWUOGU (acting)
Library of 36,200 vols, 350,000 e-books
Number of teachers: 290
Number of students: 5,200
Publication: *Information Bulletin* (4 a year)

DEANS

School of Business: J. K. J. OKONKWO
School of Engineering Technology: E. C. ARIHILAM (acting)
School of Environmental Studies: R. I. J. ONYENSO
School of Industrial Technology: A. A. OSAI
School of Science and General Studies: F. U. ATTAH

FEDERAL POLYTECHNIC, AUCHI

PMB 13, Auchi, Edo State
Telephone: (57) 200148
Fax: (57) 200148
Founded 1973
Rector: Sir O. F. EBOREIME
Registrar: F. O. OGUNBOR
Librarian: J. O. AGHOJA
Library of 38,250 vols
Number of teachers: 305
Number of students: 9,500

DIRECTORS OF SCHOOLS

Applied Sciences and Technology: P. AWERIALE
Art and Design: Prince OSAGIE-ERESE
Business Studies: J. EDEMODE
Engineering: S. OHIMAI
Environmental Studies: C. V. AJOKU

FEDERAL POLYTECHNIC, BAUCHI

PMB 0231, Bauchi
Telephone: (77) 543630
Fax: (77) 540465
E-mail: registrar@bauchipoly.edu.ng
Internet: www.bauchipoly.edu.ng
Founded 1979
Academic year: October to July
Rector: Surv. I. S. JAHUN
Registrar: Alhaji LABARAN IBRAHIM
Librarian: Mallam N. O. TOYYO
Library of 35,900 vols
Number of teachers: 257
Number of students: 8,667

DEANS

School of Business Studies: C. P. EJIKEME
School of Engineering Technology: Eng. J. D. KONNI
School of Environmental Technology: J. A. ALEREGE
School of General Studies: Mal. M. L. GARBA
School of Technology: S. M. KUMO

BENUE STATE POLYTECHNIC, UGBOKOLO

PMB 2215, Otukpo, Benue State
Founded 1976
State control
Language of instruction: English
Academic year: October to September
Rector: Dr Y. W. AWODI
Deputy Rector: A. T. IKEREVE
Registrar: D. O. ONA
Librarian: M. A. SHINYI
Number of teachers: 115
Number of students: 1,505
Publication: *New Bulletin* (12 a year)

DEANS

School of Art and Design: B. Y. EBUTE (acting)
School of Business and Administrative Studies: E. A. ADEGBE
School of Engineering: P. E. AGBESE
School of Technology: P. U. ANYOGO

FEDERAL POLYTECHNIC, BIDA

PMB 55, Bida, Niger State
Telephone: (66) 461707
Founded 1977
Academic year: October to July
Rector: Eng. UMARU SANI-ANGO
Registrar: S. F. IKO
Librarian: S. A. KASIMU
Library of 26,105 vols
Number of teachers: 377
Number of students: 9,097

Publication: *Polymath Journal*

DIRECTORS

School of Applied Arts and Science: Dr S. O. ADEYEMO
School of Business and Management: P. KARICKSON
School of Engineering: Engr A. SULE
School of Environmental Studies: S. M. OB'LAMA
School of Preliminary Studies: ABDULLAHI MANN

POLYTECHNIC, BIRNIN KEBBI

PMB 1034, Birnin Kebbi, Kebbi State
Telephone: (68) 320597
Fax: (68) 320597
E-mail: kbpoly@skannet.com.ng
Founded 1976
Academic year: October to July
Rector: Arc. MUHAMMAD KABIR NABADE
Registrar: BELLO BAGUDU ABUBAKAR
Librarian: YUSUF ABUBAKAR ARGUNGU
Library of 13,761 vols
Number of teachers: 350
Number of students: 3,678
ND and HND courses; postgraduate diplomas in management and public administration

DEANS

School of Accounting and Finance: UMARU SULE
School of Business and Public Administration: UMAR M. S. RAHA
School of Environmental Design: TIMOTHY O. IBIRONKE
School of Industrial Engineering: ISHAYA H. JOSHUA
School of Natural Resources Engineering: ABUBAKAR MIKAIL
School of Sciences: ABUBAKAR UMAR BASHAR
School of Surveying and Land Administration: (vacant)
School of Vocational and Technical Education: UMAR A. RUFAI

POLYTECHNIC, CALABAR

PMB 1110, Calabar, Cross River State
Telephone: (87) 222303
Founded 1973
State control
Language of instruction: English
Academic year: October to June
Rector: Engr R. E. EKANEM
Deputy Rector: Dr R. A. ITAM
Registrar: G. F. A. ONUGBA
Librarian: J. S. UMOH
Library of 25,000 vols
Number of teachers: 213
Number of students: 5,000

DIRECTORS OF SCHOOLS AND CENTRES

School of Agriculture: Dr E. J. OROK
School of Applied Science: U. U. ASUQUO
School of Business and Management: P. O. N. ABANG
School of Communication Arts: Dr M. E. EKERE
School of Education: Dr JOE IBANGA
School of Engineering: Dr E. U. UYE
School of Environmental Studies: A. DIAWUO
Computer Centre: T. O. EYO (acting)
Continuing Education Centre: N. U. UMOH
Centre for General and Preliminary Studies: L. O. I. OGUEZE
Industrial Coordination and Public Relations Unit: M. J. MBONG (acting)
Polytechnic Industrial Consultancy Services Unit: Dr I. U. UGOT

FEDERAL POLYTECHNIC, EDE

PMB 231, Ede, Osun State
Telephone: (35) 360096
Fax: (35) 360640
E-mail: edepoly@pinet.net
Vice-Chancellor: Deacon JOSEPH S. OKE.

POLYTECHNIC, IBADAN

PMB 022, U.I. Post Office, Ibadan
Telephone: (22) 8133356769
Fax: (22) 8101122
E-mail: rector@polyibadan.edu.ng
Founded 1961, polytechnic status 1971
State control
Language of instruction: English
Rector: Prof. O. A. ODUNOLA
Deputy Rector: N. A. ADEBAYO
Registrar: TOSHO AYANWALE
Bursar: G. O. D. OLOJEDE
Chief Librarian: O. A. OBIKOYA
Library of 68,000 vols
Number of teachers: 576
Number of students: 9,250
Publications: *Calendar/Prospectus* (1 a year), *PolyNews*

DEANS

Faculty of Business and Communication Studies: FEMI ARAMIDE
Faculty of Engineering: Eng. T. I. OYEDEMI
Faculty of Environmental Studies: T. A. OLURIN
Faculty of Financial and Management Studies: S. B. BABARINDE
Faculty of Science: O. A. OLUBAMIWA

FEDERAL POLYTECHNIC, IDAH

PMB 1037, Idah, Kogi State
Telephone: (58) 800128
Founded 1977
Rector: Dr JOSEPH EGILA
Deputy Rector: Dr D. O. BELLO
Registrar: S. A. OGUNLEYE
Librarian: J. I. ITANYI
Library of 19,489 vols
Number of teachers: 136
Number of students: 3,200
Publication: *News Bulletin* (12 a year)

DIRECTORS OF SCHOOLS

School of Business Studies: M. A. OKPANACHI
School of Engineering: Surv. P. IYAJI
School of Technology: E. O. NDA-SULEIMAN

FEDERAL POLYTECHNIC, ILARO

PMB 50, Ilaro, Ogun State
Telephone: (39) 440005
Founded 1979
Rector: Dr Prince S. A. OLATERU-OLAGBEGI
Vice-Rector: Dr K. O. JIBODU
Registrar: R. O. EGBEYEMI
Librarian: R. OLA BELLO
Library of 16,000 vols
Number of students: 3,000

DIRECTORS

School of Applied Science: Dr J. O. A. OMOLE
School of Business Studies: J. O. ABIBU
School of Engineering: F. O. AREGBE

INSTITUTE OF MANAGEMENT AND TECHNOLOGY

PMB 01079, Enugu, Enugu State
Telephone: (42) 250416
Founded 1973
Academic year: October to August
Rector: Prof. E. C. ONYENEJE

Deputy Rector: Dr JOHN ORJIH
Registrar: BARTH O. EZEA
Librarian: DONALD M. OZOALOR
Library of 50,000 vols
Number of teachers: 360
Number of students: 20,000
Publications: *IMT News* (4 a year), *Journal of Financial Studies* (1 a year), *Journal of Technology Education* (1 a year)

DIRECTORS OF SCHOOLS

Business Studies: Rev. Canon SAM EZUGWU
Communication Arts: HENRY U. ANIUGBO
Distance Learning and Continuing Education: NICK A. OBODO
Engineering: Dr CHARLES N. UDE
Financial Studies: Dr WILSON ANI
General Studies: UMEAYO S. MADUKWE
Technology: EMEKA G. ANI

KADUNA POLYTECHNIC

PMB 2021, Kaduna
Telephone: (62) 211551
Internet: kadpoly.edu.ng
Founded 1968
Rector: Eng. Dr D. I. ISAH
Deputy Rector for Academics: MAL MUHAMMADU LAWAL JIBBIN
Deputy Rector for Admin.: JENNY YOHANNA MIVANYI
Registrar: ABDULLAHI AHMAN
Librarian: ALIYU IDRIS GURAGI
Library on three campuses of 56,000 vols
Number of teachers: 1,123
Number of students: 17,320

DIRECTORS

College of Administration Studies and Social Sciences: Dr HAJIYA ASMAU SANI MAIKUDI
College of Business and Management Studies: Dr ALIYU MAMMAN
College of Engineering: Eng. ABU BAKAR SALIHU OVAJIMOH
College of Environmental Studies: KEFAS JERICHO
College of Science and Technology: MOSES OBAFUNMI (acting)

KANO STATE POLYTECHNIC

PMB 3401, B. U. K. Rd, Kano
Telephone: (64) 666058
Founded 1976
Rector: Arch. HAMZA SAID
Registrar: SULAIMAN ABDULLAHI
Chief Librarian: Alhaji WADA TAFIDA KURAWA
Library of 30,276 vols
Number of teachers: 510
Number of students: 12,826
Publication: *News Bulletin* (12 a year)

DIRECTORS

School of Management Studies: HAJIYA ASABE B. BORODO
School of Social and Rural Development: SULAIMAN HASHIM
School of Technology: YUSUFU SULE GAYA

HASSAN USMAN KATSINA POLYTECHNIC

PMB 2052, Katsina
Telephone: (65) 32816
Founded 1983
Rector: KABIR IBRAHIM MATAZU
Registrar: ABDU HALLIRU ABDULLAHI
Director, Library Services: MANNIR ISA BATAGARAWA
Library of 18,000 vols
Number of teachers: 501
Number of students: 3,506

DIRECTORS OF COLLEGES

College of Administration and Management Studies: Alhaji ABDULLAHI BAWA
College of Legal and General Studies: Alhaji MUSA SULE
College of Science and Technology: ALIYU ABUBAKAR BAKORI

FEDERAL POLYTECHNIC, KAURA NAMODA

PMB 1012, Kaura-Namoda, Zamfara State
Telephone: (63) 60452
E-mail: namodapoly@plet.net
Founded 1983
Academic year: October to July
Rector: Eng. NA'INNA MOHAMMAD AUDI
Vice-Rector: C. APRAKU
Registrar: A. DANBOYI
Librarian: Alhaji SANUSI UMAR KSAURI
Library of 11,450 vols
Number of teachers: 152
Number of students: 3,268
Publications: *Kanajoge* (2 a year), *Namoda Telescope* (2 a year), *Polytechnic News Bulletin* (12 a year)

DIRECTORS

School of Business Management: AMOS OYEYIOLA
School of Engineering: Eng. ABUBAKAR LUGARD
School of Environmental Studies: TAJUDEEN YUSUF
School of General Studies: Alhaji IBRAHIM KAMBA
School of Science and Technology: Isa MOHAMMAD KUTIGI

KWARA STATE POLYTECHNIC

PMB 1375, Ilorin
Telephone: (31) 221441
Internet: www.kwarapolytechnic.com
Founded 1972
Language of instruction: English
Academic year: October to July
Rector: ALHAJI MAS'UD ELELU
Deputy Rector for Academics: M. O. OLASEHINDE
Deputy Rector for Admin.: Dr F. A. J. BELLO
Registrar: M. O. SALAMI
Librarian: ADESEKO
Library of 50,155 vols
Number of teachers: 650
Number of students: 17,000
Publication: *Techforum* (2 a year).

LAGOS STATE POLYTECHNIC

PMB 21606, Ikeja, Lagos State
Telephone: (1) 523528
Founded 1977
Rector: B. OLORO
Deputy Rector: J. B. AGUNBIADE
Registrar: OLUWOLE O. OJIKUTU
Chief Librarian: E. O. SOYINKA
Library of 29,558 vols, 1,880 in spec. colln
Number of teachers: 222
Number of students: 4,287
Publications: *Laspotech News* (4 a year), *Poly Handbook* (1 a year).

MOSHOOD ABIOLA POLYTECHNIC, ABEOKUTA

PMB 2210, Abeokuta, Ogun State
Telephone: (80) 33230941
E-mail: mapolylib2002@yahoo.com
Internet: www.mapoly.educ.ng
Founded 1979

Rector: Alhaji WAHEED A. KADIRI
Deputy Rector: Arch. OLATOKUNBO FOWODE
Registrar: Maj. (retd) A. B. BADMOS
Librarian: BOLA ADEOSUN
Library of 22,097 vols
Number of teachers: 165
Number of students: 15,000
Publications: *Liberal Forum* (1 a year), *Polymath* (1 a year), *Social Philosophy* (1 a year)

DIRECTORS

School of Business and Management Studies:
O. A. SOBANDE
School of Communication and General Studies: S. O. FAMUYIWA
School of Engineering: Dr M. O. ABDUL
School of Environmental Studies: A. A. JEGEDE
School of Pure and Applied Science: A. S. AROWOLO
Centre for Part-time Studies: O. A. SOILE

FEDERAL POLYTECHNIC, MUBI

PMB 35, Mubi, Adamawa State
Telephone: (75) 882771
Founded 1979
Academic year: October to July
Rector: Alhaji M. A. ABBA
Deputy Rector: E. E. ETUK
Registrar: B. BELLO
Librarian: T. S. TARFA
Library of 23,601 vols
Number of teachers: 184
Number of students: 3,338
Publications: *Applied Science and Management* (1 a year), *Sabon Dale* (1 a year)

DIRECTORS

School of Business Studies and General Studies: A. S. YAHAYA
School of Engineering: I. DAGWA
School of Science and Technology: A. BAWA

FEDERAL POLYTECHNIC, NASARAWA

PMB 001, Nasarawa, Nasarawa State
Telephone: (47) 66707
E-mail: fpnas@yahoo.com
Founded 1983
Rector: Dr IDRIS BUGAJE.

FEDERAL POLYTECHNIC, NEKEDE

PMB 1036, Owerri, Imo State
Telephone: (83) 231516
Founded 1978
Rector: Eng. O. I. NWANKWO
Registrar: C. D. ONUKOGU
Librarian: J. U. OBASI
Library of 24,837 vols
Number of teachers: 257
Number of students: 30,000

DEANS

School of Business and Public Administration: S. C. NSOFOR
School of Engineering Technology: J. N. AMADI
School of Environmental Design: G. O. C. NWACHUKWU
School of General Studies: Dr N. C. ANUMIHE
School of Industrial Sciences: C. A. OMENKA

FEDERAL POLYTECHNIC, OFFA

PMB 420, Offa, Kwara State
Telephone: (31) 800160

Founded 1979
Rector: Dr ABDUL-RAZAQ BELLO.

FEDERAL POLYTECHNIC, OKO

PMB 21, Aguata, Anambra State
Telephone: (48) 911144
Founded 1979
Rector: Dr U. C. NZEWI
Registrar: Sir O. C. A. OFOCHEBE
Librarian: Dr OBIORA NWOSU
Library of 150,000 vols
Number of students: 9,298
Publications: *Federal Polytechnic Library* (4 a year), *Journal of Accountancy* (Nigerian edition, 2 a year), *The Polytechnic Accountant* (1 a year)
Courses in accountancy, architecture, banking and finance, business administration and management, business studies, environmental design, estate management and building technology, information technology, library science, marketing, mass communication, secretarial studies, technology.

ONDO STATE POLYTECHNIC

POB 1019, Owo, Ondo State
Telephone: (51) 241045
Founded 1980
Rector: Prof. A. S. ADEDIMILA
Deputy Rector: KEHINDE ALAO
Registrar: R. F. AKERELE
Librarian: M. O. POPOOLA
Library of 25,000 vols
Number of teachers: 173
Number of students: 9,710

DEANS

Business Studies: Chief A. O. OLALEYE
Engineering: Rev. S. A. ADEGBEMIRO
Environmental Studies: E. A. ARIGBEDE
Food Technology: J. K. AJAYI

PETROLEUM TRAINING INSTITUTE

PMB 20, Effurun, Delta State
Telephone: (53) 250774
Fax: (53) 250774
Internet: pti.nigeria.org
Founded 1972
Federal control
Language of instruction: English
Academic year: October to July
Principal and Chief Exec.: N. C. DENNAR
Director of Finance and Supplies: A. O. IKIMI
Director of Studies: G. I. ORAKA
Registrar: A. S. EWERE
Chief Librarian: E. M. A. DUDU
Library of 54,013 vols
Number of teachers: 189
Number of students: 2,520
Publication: *PTI News* (4 a year).

PLATEAU STATE POLYTECHNIC, BARKIN LADI

PMB 02023, Bukuru, Plateau State
Founded 1978, present status 1980
Rector: Eng. ALEXANDER A. T. KEBANG
Registrar: TIMOTHY A. ANJIDE
Director of Administration: LAMI A. ENATTO
Librarian: J. E. KOTSO
Library of 11,393 vols
Number of teachers: 121
Number of students: 2,260
Publication: news bulletins and student's handbook

DEANS

School of Administration and General Studies: L. A. ENATTO
School of Engineering and Environmental Studies: Dr R. JATAU
School of Management Studies: ELIZABETH PAM
School of Science and Technology: K. D. DABER

DIRECTORS

Centre for Continuing Education: ELIZABETH K. PAM
Consultancy and Applied Research Division: Eng. O. O. OLUSANYA

YABA COLLEGE OF TECHNOLOGY

PMB 2011, Yaba, Lagos State 234
Telephone: (1) 7742155
Fax: (1) 7917565
Internet: www.yabatech.edu.ng
Founded 1948
Federal control
Academic year: October to July
Rector: O. OWOSO
Registrar: F. F. TAIWO (acting)
Deputy Rector for Academic Affairs: A. O. AGBAJE-WILLIAMS
Deputy Rector for Admin.: Eng. A. I. ABIODUN
Polytechnic Librarian: R. I. OLOGBONSAIYE
Library of 70,000 vols
Number of teachers: 800
Number of students: 14,000
Publications: *Newsletter*, *Prospectus* (1 a year), *Yabatech News* (4 a year), *YCT Academic Journal* (published by various departments, each semester)

DIRECTORS

School of Art, Design and Printing: MAO OMOIGHE
School of Engineering: Eng. P. K. ADEGBOYEGA
School of Environmental Studies: Arch. A. A. ADENIJI
School of Management: IFY MAFINZE
School of Science: I. A. ABIODUN
School of Technology: O. AKINJAIYEJU

Federal College of Agriculture, Akure: Ado-Ekiti Rd, Akure, Ondo State; tel. and fax (34) 240891; f. 1957; library: 10,000 vols; 30 teachers; 1,000 students; Principal Dr A. O. AYODELE.

Federal College of Agriculture, Ibadan: Institute of Agricultural Research and Training, PMB 5029, Moor Plantation, Ibadan; tel. (2) 2312070; f. 1921; 33 teachers; 319 students; Provost Dr D. S. DARAMOLA.

Federal College of Forestry: Forestry Research Institute of Nigeria, PMB 5054, Ibadan; tel. (22) 411035; f. 1941; technical forestry training, National and Higher National Diploma courses; vocational courses; library: 4,800 vols; 20 teachers; 520 students; Dir Dr ISAAC I. ERO.

Federal School of Dental Hygiene: 1 Broad St, PMB 12562, Lagos; f. 1957; Principal Dr S. JOHNSON.

National Eye Centre: Off Nnamdi Azikiwe Way, PMB 2267, Kaduna; tel. and fax (62) 313956; e-mail neckad@yahoo.com; f. 1979; provides postgraduate ophthalmic training (medical and surgical), TOT IOL microsurgical course, ophthalmic nursing training, clinical services; 9 teachers; 16 students; Chief Medical Dir Dr C. P. OZEMELA; publs *Newsletter* (4 a year), *Pharmacy News* (12 a year).

NORWAY

The Higher Education System

The oldest current institutions of higher education were founded before Norway declared its independence from Swedish rule in 1905. The state Universitetet i Oslo (founded in 1811) is the oldest university; the next oldest university is the state Universitetet for Miljø- og Biovitenskap (Norwegian University of Life Sciences—founded in 1859). The first institution founded in the independent period was the private Teologiske Menighetsfakultet (Norwegian Lutheran School of Theology—founded in 1907). In 2008/09 there were 77 institutes of higher education (including universities). In 2009 247,021 students were enrolled in higher education, of which 91,782 were enrolled at universities and their equivalent.

Higher education is administered according to the Universities and Colleges Act (1995). Norway participates in the Bologna Process to establish a European Higher Education Area, the first phase of which is to adopt a credit-based system of comparable degrees with two main cycles (undergraduate and graduate). The Norwegian Agency for Quality Assurance in Education (NOKUT) is an independent government body established in 2003 to monitor and develop the quality of higher education in Norway through evaluation, accreditation and recognition of quality assurance systems, institutions and study programmes. The primary responsibility for quality assurance rests with the individual higher education institution, but internal quality assurance systems must adhere to nationally set standards and are externally evaluated by NOKUT. Institutions and programmes are not accredited for a defined period; accreditation is valid until revoked. NOKUT makes its decisions independently of the Ministry of Education and Research. Norway is the only country in Europe that still adheres to the policy of free higher education for all students regardless of country of origin. As a result, Norwegian institutions have reported significant increases in the number of applications received from foreign students in recent years. There have been increasingly vocal calls for universities to be afforded greater economic autonomy, with the right to determine how best to divest funding from the Government.

Admission to higher education is on the basis of successful completion of secondary education; however, since 2000 applicants have also been admitted with non-formal qualifications. In 2003 a two-tier Bachelorgrad and Mastergrad degree system was implemented in accordance with the principles of the Bologna Process. Norwegian institutions award degrees on the basis of the European Credit Transfers System, with each year equivalent to 60 'credits'. The standard undergraduate degree is the Bachelorgrad, which lasts three years, and the first postgraduate degree is the Mastergrad, a course lasting one-and-a-half to two years. The final postgraduate and highest university degree is the Doktorgrad, awarded after three to four years of study; the title of the degree awarded may vary depending on the subject area.

Post-secondary vocational and technical education is available at technical colleges (Teckniske Fagskoler), university colleges and state colleges. Programmes at these institutions last for two to three years.

Regulatory and Representative Bodies

GOVERNMENT

Ministry of Culture: POB 8030 Dep., 0030 Oslo; Akersgt. 59, Oslo; tel. 22-24-90-90; fax 22-24-95-50; e-mail postmottak@kud.dep.no; internet www.regjeringen.no/kud; Minister ANNIKEN HUITFELDT.

Ministry of Education and Research: POB 8119 Dep., 0032 Oslo; Akersgt. 44, Oslo; tel. 22-24-90-90; fax 22-24-27-64; e-mail postmottak@kd.dep.no; internet www.regjeringen.no/kd; Minister of Education KRISTIN HALVORSEN; Minister of Research and Higher Education TORA AASLAND; Sec.-Gen. TROND FEVOLDEN.

ACCREDITATION

ENIC/NARIC Norway: NOKUT—Norwegian Agency for Quality Assurance in Education, POB 1708 Vika, 0121 Oslo; tel. 21-02-18-60; fax 21-02-18-01; e-mail postmottak@nokut.no; internet www.nokut.no; Dir-Gen. TERJE MØRLAND.

Nasjonalt Organ for Kvalitet i Utdanningen (Norwegian Agency for Quality Assurance in Education): POB 1708 Vika, 0121 Oslo; Kronprinsensgt. 9, Oslo; tel. 21-02-18-00; fax 21-02-18-01; e-mail postmottak@nokut.no; internet www.nokut.no; f. 2002; ind. governmental agency; controls and develops the quality of Norwegian higher education instns through the evaluation, accreditation and recognition of quality assurance systems, instns and education programmes; Chair. Prof. PETTER AASLESTAD; CEO PER ARNE SYRRIST.

NATIONAL BODIES

Norges Forskningsråd (The Research Council of Norway): POB 2700, St Hanshaugen, 0131 Oslo; Stensberggt 26, Oslo; tel. 22-03-70-00; fax 22-03-70-01; e-mail post@forskningsradet.no; internet www.forskningsradet.no; attached to Ministry of Education and Research; promotes and supports basic and applied research in all areas of science, technology, medicine and the humanities; awards research grants and fellowships and runs its own research establishments (see elsewhere under Research Institutes); Chair. GEIR STENE-LARSEN; publ. Forskning (4 a year).

Norsk Forbund for Fjernundervisning og Fleksibel Utdanning (NFF) (Norwegian Association for Distance Education and Flexible Education): Lilleakerveien 23, 0283 Oslo; tel. 22-51-04-80; fax 22-51-04-81; e-mail nade@nade-nff.no; internet www.nade-nff.no; f. 1968; 37 mems; Chair. SVEIN QVIST-ERIKSEN; Exec. Dir TORHILD SLÅTTO; publ. Synkron (magazine).

Riksantikvaren (Directorate for Cultural Heritage): Dronningensgt. 13, POB 8196 Dep., 0034 Oslo; tel. 22-94-04-00; fax 22-94-04-04; e-mail postmottak@ra.no; internet www.riksantikvaren.no; f. 1912; directorate responsible for nat. monuments and sites, medieval bldgs; archives; library of 60,000 vols, 700,000 photographs; special collns incl. Norwegian churches, restoration and conservation of paintings and sculptures; Dir-Gen. JØRN HOLME; publs La stå! (Let Stand!, 2 a year), Årringer (Tree Rings, 1 a year).

Senter for Internasjonalisering av Høgre Utdanning (SIU) (Norwegian Centre for International Cooperation in Higher Education): POB 1093, 5809 Bergen; Vaskerelven 39, 5014 Bergen; tel. 55-30-38-00; fax 55-30-38-01; e-mail siu@siu.no; internet siu.no; f. 2004; promotes int. cooperation in education and research; Chair. Prof. SONNI OLSEN; Dir ALF RASMUSSEN (acting); publ. Global Knowledge (magazine on politics and global implication in research and higher education).

Universitets- og Høgskolerådet (Norwegian Association of Higher Education Institutes): Pilestredet 46B, 0167 Oslo; tel. 22-45-39-50; e-mail uhr@uhr.no; internet www.uhr.no; f. 2000 by merger of the Norwegian Ccl of State Colleges and the Norwegian Ccl of Univs; 46 mem. institutions; Chair. JAN I. HAALAND; Gen. Sec. JOHN SPELL.

Learned Societies

GENERAL

Det Kongelige Norske Videnskabers Selskab (Royal Norwegian Society of Sciences and Letters): Erling Skakkesgt. 47C, Postuttak, 7491 Trondheim; tel. 73-59-21-57; fax 73-59-58-95; e-mail post@dknvs.no; internet www.dknvs.no; f. 1760; 689 mems (528 Norwegian, 142 foreign, 1 hon., 18 assoc.); Pres. Prof. KRISTIAN FOSSHEIM; Gen. Sec. KRISTIAN OVERSKAUG; publ. Skrifter.

Norske Videnskaps-Akademi (Norwegian Academy of Science): Drammensveien 78, 0271 Oslo; tel. 22-12-10-90; fax 22-12-10-99; e-mail dnva@online.no; internet www.dnva.no; f. 1857; sections: Mathematics and Natural Sciences, Historical and Philosophical Sciences; 885 mems (476 Norwegian, 409 foreign); Pres. Prof. NILS CHRISTIAN STENSETH; Sec.-Gen. Prof. ØIVIND ANDERSEN; publs

Årbok, *Avhandlinger*, *Physica Scripta* (12 a year), *Zoologica Scripta* (6 a year).

ARCHITECTURE AND TOWN PLANNING

Norske Arkitekters Landsforbund (NAL) (Norwegian Architects' Association): Josefines gt. 34, 0351 Oslo; tel. 23-33-25-00; fax 23-33-25-01; e-mail nal@arkitektur.no; internet www.arkitektur.no; f. 1911; 4,300 mems; Pres. KJERSTI NERSETH; publs *Arkitektnytt* (20 a year), *Byggekunst* (8 a year), *Norske Arkitektkonkurranser*.

BIBLIOGRAPHY, LIBRARY SCIENCE AND MUSEOLOGY

Norsk Bibliotekforening (Norwegian Library Association): POB 6540, Etterstad, 0606 Oslo; tel. 23-24-34-30; fax 23-24-34-30; fax 22-67-23-68; e-mail nbf@norskbibliotekforening.no; internet www.norskbibliotekforening.no; f. 1913; 3,200 mems; Pres. INGEBORG RYGH HJORTHEN; Sec.-Gen. HEGE NEWTH NOURI; publ. *Bibliotekforum* (8 a year).

ECONOMICS, LAW AND POLITICS

Norsk Forening for Internasjonal Rett (International Law Association, Norwegian Branch): c/o Wiersholm Mellbye and Bech, POB 1400 Vika, 0115 Oslo; Ruseløkkveien 26, 0115 Oslo; tel. 21-02-10-00; fax 21-02-10-01; e-mail veem@wiersholm.no; internet www.nfir.no; f. 1925; 77 mems; Pres. ROLF EINAR FIFE; Sec. VEGARD EMAUS.

Statsøkonomisk Forening (Economic Association of Norway): Ullern Alle 59, 0381 Oslo; tel. and fax 63-90-05-76; f. 1883; approx. 300 mems; Pres. Prof. KJELL STORVIK; Sec. BJÖRN STENSETH.

FINE AND PERFORMING ARTS

Arts Council Norway: POB 101 Sentrum, 0102 Oslo; tel. 22-47-83-30; fax 22-33-40-42; e-mail post@kulturrad.no; internet www.kulturrad.no; f. 1965, merged with ABM-utvikling—Statens Senter for Arkiv, Bibliotek og Museum 2011; aims, in connection with the Cultural Fund, to encourage artistic life and cultural activities in Norway and to distribute the resources of the Fund in grants and subsidies; 9 mems appointed by the Statsraid (Council of State) and 4 by the Storting (parliament) all for a period of 4 years; Chair. BENTEIN BAARDSON; Dir GURI SKJELDAL; publs *Notatserien* (irregular), *Rapportserien* (irregular).

MIC Norsk Musikkinformasjon (Music Information Centre Norway): POB 2674 Solli, 0203 Oslo; Henrik Ibsensgt. 110, Solli Pl., Oslo; tel. 23-27-63-00; fax 23-27-63-01; e-mail info@mic.no; internet www.mic.no; f. 1979; promotes and offers information on Norwegian music of all genres, composers, music instns, performing groups and artists; aims to build up a representative colln of contemporary Norwegian music; mem. of the Int. Asscn of Music Information Centres; comprises a MSS library, orchestral materials, reference library, copying service; library: MSS colln of more than 7,000 Norwegian musical works; Dir MARTIN REVHEIM; publ. *Ballade* (in Norwegian, online).

Norske Billedkunstnere (Association of Norwegian Visual Arts): Grubbegt. 14, 0179 Oslo; tel. 23-25-60-30; fax 23-25-60-49; e-mail nbk@billedkunst.no; internet www.billedkunst.no; f. 1889, reorganized 1979 and 1988; a nat. asscn of professional artists' orgs; the Norwegian Govt's Advisory Bd on questions relating to graphic arts; mem. of UNESCO's Int. Artists Ascn (IAA); 2,700 mems; Chair. HILDE ROGNSKOG; Sec. GJERT GJERTSEN; publ. *Billedkunstneren* (7 a year).

HISTORY, GEOGRAPHY AND ARCHAEOLOGY

Fortidsminneforeningen (Foreningen til norske Fortidsminnesmerkers Bevaring) (Society for the Preservation of Ancient Monuments in Norway): Dronningensgt. 11, 0152 Oslo; tel. 23-31-70-70; fax 23-31-70-50; e-mail post@ fortidsminneforeningen.no; internet www .fortidsminneforeningen.no; f. 1844; works towards protecting Norwegian cultural heritage sites and creating a common understanding of their value; owns and cares for 40 properties, among those 8 stave churches incl. the World Heritage site at Urnes; 7,500 mems; Sec.-Gen. ELISABETH SEIP; Head of Org. FREDRIC MONCLAIR; publs *Årbok* (1 a year), *Fortidsvern* (4 a year), *Gode Råd serien* (irregular).

Kirkehistorisk Samfunn (Church History Society): Markalléen 7, 1368 Stabekk; e-mail peder.eidberg@baptist.no; f. 1956; 43 mems; Pres. Prof. JAN SCHUMACHER; Sec. Prof. Dr PEDER A. EIDBERG.

Landslaget for Lokalhistorie (National Association of Local History): Institutt for Historie og Klassiske Fag, NTNU, 7491 Trondheim; tel. 73-59-63-95; fax 73-59-64-41; e-mail post@historielag.org; internet www.historielag.org; f. 1920; 415 mem. historical socs; Pres. KURT TVERLI; Man. JOSTEIN MOLDE; publs *Heimen* (4 a year), *Lokalhistorisk* (4 a year).

Norsk Arkeologisk Selskap (Norwegian Archaeological Society): Huk Aveny 35, 0287 Oslo; tel. 22-43-87-92; fax 22-13-52-86; e-mail nas@arkeologi.no; internet www.arkeologi .no; f. 1936; 800 mems; Pres. CHRISTEN AASS; Sec.-Gen. EGIL MIKKELSEN; publ. *Viking* (1 a year).

Norsk Lokalhistorisk Institutt: POB 8045 Dep, 0031 Oslo; Observatoriegt. 1B, 0254 Oslo; tel. 22-92-51-30; fax 22-92-51-31; e-mail nli@lokalhistorie.no; internet www .lokalhistorie.no; f. 1955; guidance for local historians, research in local history incl. publication of sources, etc., valuable for research; library of 20,000 vols; Dir KNUT SPRAUTEN.

Norsk Slektshistorisk Forening (Norwegian Genealogical Society): Øvre Slottsgt. 2B, 0157 Oslo; tel. 22-33-30-30; e-mail kontor@ genealogi.no; internet www.genealogi.no; f. 1926; 2,100 mems; Chair. RUNE NEDRUD; Sec. JAN I. KRISTIANSEN; publs *Genealogen* (2 a year), *Norsk Slektshistorisk Tidsskrift* (2 a year).

Norske Historiske Forening (Norwegian Historical Society): Avdeling for historie, POB 7805, 5020 Bergen; tel. 22-85-67-59; fax 22-85-52-78; e-mail hifo@sv.uit.no; internet hifo.b.uib.no; f. 1869; 1,000 mems; Pres. DAY HUNDSTAD; Sec. ELISE NICOLAISEN; publ. *Historisk Tidsskrift* (4 a year).

LANGUAGE AND LITERATURE

Alliance Française: POB 34, Sentrum, 5803 Bergen; Vågsallmenningen 12, Gamle Norges Bank, 3. etasje, Bergen; e-mail alliance.francaise@uib.no; internet www .france-bergen.no; offers courses and examinations in French language and culture and promotes cultural exchange with France; 100 mems.

British Council: Storgaten 10B, 0155 Oslo; tel. 22-39-61-90; fax 22-42-40-39; e-mail british.council@britishcouncil.no; internet www.britishcouncil.org/norway; offers courses and examinations in English language and British culture and promotes cultural exchange with the UK; Country Man. KAROLINE TELLUM-DJARRAYA.

Den Norske Forfatterforening (Norwegian Authors' Union): POB 327 Sentrum, 0103 Oslo; tel. 23-35-76-20; fax 22-42-11-07; e-mail post@forfatterforeningen.no; internet www.forfatterforeningen.no; f. 1893; 583 mems; Chair. SIGMUND LØVÅSEN; Gen. Sec. METTE MØLLER.

Det Norske Akademi for Sprog og Litteratur (Norwegian Academy for Language and Literature): Rosenborggaten 3, 0356 Oslo; tel. 91-10-45-19; fax 22-60-03-74; e-mail akademiet@riksmalsforbundet.no; internet www.riksmalsforbundet.no; f. 1953; protects and authorizes dictionaries of the traditional 'Riksmaal'; 50 mems; Chair. Mag. NILS HEYERDAHL; Sec. Prof. KARIN GUNDERSEN.

Goethe-Institut: Grønland 16, 0188 Oslo; tel. 22-05-78-80; fax 22-17-20-04; e-mail info@oslo.goethe.org; internet www.goethe .de/oslo; offers courses and examinations in German language and culture and promotes cultural exchange with Germany; library of 6,000 vols, 30 periodicals; Dir Dr KRISTIAN ZAPPEL.

Norsk PEN (Norwegian Centre of International PEN): Wergelandsveien 29, 0167 Oslo; tel. 22-60-74-50; fax 22-60-74-51; e-mail pen@norskpen.no; internet www.norskpen .no; f. 1922; contact for Norwegian writers with the rest of the writing world; defends freedom of expression worldwide, with a spec. focus on Afghanistan, Belarus, People's Republic of China, Tunisia, Turkey and the Middle East; 370 mems; Pres. ANDERS HEGER; Sec.-Gen. CARL MORTEN IVERSEN.

MEDICINE

Norsk Farmasøytisk Selskap (Norwegian Pharmaceutical Society): POB 5070, Majorstuen, 0301 Oslo; tel. 21-62-02-23; fax 22-60-81-73; e-mail farm-sel@online.no; internet www.nfs.no; f. 1924; furthers scientific and practical devt of pharmacy; 550 mems; Chair. BRITT WOLDEN; Sec. RØNNAUG LARSEN.

Norsk Kirurgisk Forening (Norwegian College of Surgeons): POB 1152 Sentrum, 0107 Oslo; Legenes hus, Akersgt. 2, Oslo; tel. 23-10-90-00; fax 22-10-91-80; e-mail trazumo@legeforeningen.no; internet www .legeforeningen.no/nkf; f. 1911; 1,135 mems; Chair. OLAUG VILLANGER; Sec. TATJANA RAZUMOVA; publ. *Vitenskapelige forhandlinger* (1 a year).

Norske Laegeforening (Norwegian Medical Association): POB 1152 Sentrum, 0107 Oslo; tel. 23-10-90-00; fax 23-10-90-10; e-mail informasjon@legeforeningen.no; internet www.legeforeningen.no; f. 1886; 27,164 mems; Pres. Dr TORUNN JANBU; Sec.-Gen. Dr GEIR RIISE; publ. *Tidsskrift for den norske lægeforening* (24 a year).

Det Norske Medicinske Selskab (Norwegian Medical Society): POB 1130 Blindern, 0318 Oslo; tel. 22-85-06-73; e-mail oivind .larsen@medisin.uio.no; internet www.dnms .no; f. 1833 as continuation of a medical reading soc.; open medical lectures; medical and cultural programmes; 250 mems; Chair. Prof. Dr ØIVIND LARSEN; Sec. ASTRID NYLENNA; publ. *Michael Quarterly* (4 a year).

Norske Tannlegeforening (NTF) (Norwegian Dental Association): POB 3063 Elisenberg, 0207 Oslo; Frederik Stangsgt. 20, 0264 Oslo; tel. 22-54-74-00; fax 22-55-11-09; e-mail tannlegeforeningen@tannlegeforeningen.no; internet www.tannlegeforeningen.no; f. 1884; 4,500 mems, 21 local asscns; Pres. LYNGSTAD GUNNAR; Sec.-Gen. DAG E. REITE (acting); publ. *Den norske tannlegeforenings Tidende* (12 a year).

NATURAL SCIENCES

General

Polytekniske Forening (Polytechnical Society): Rosenkrantzgt. 7, 0159 Oslo; tel. 22-42-68-70; fax 22-42-58-87; e-mail polyteknisk@polyteknisk.no; internet www.polyteknisk.no; f. 1852; 7,000 mems; Chair. J. R. WAALER; Sec.-Gen. FREDRIK EVJEN; publ. *Teknisk Ukeblad* (52 a year).

Selskapet til Vitenskapenes Fremme (Society for the Advancement of Science): Noreidstraumen 31, c/o Guldborg, 5251 Søreidgrend; e-mail guldborg.sovik@biomed.uib.no; internet www.vitenskap-bergen.no; f. 1927; promotes and encourages intellectual activities generally by regular series of lectures, excursions; 200 mems; Pres. Prof. DAG E. HELLAND; Gen. Sec. Prof. GULDBORG SØVIK.

Biological Sciences

Norsk Botanisk Forening (Norwegian Botanical Association): Naturhistorisk Museum, POB 1172 Blindern, 0318 Oslo; tel. 22-85-17-01; fax 22-85-18-35; e-mail post@botaniskforening.no; internet www.botaniskforening.no; f. 1935; 1,500 mems; Pres. MARIT ERIKSEN; Sec. MARIANNE KARLSEN; publ. *Blyttia* (4 a year).

Physical Sciences

Norsk Geologisk Forening (Geological Society of Norway): NGU, POB 6315 Sluppen, 7491 Trondheim; tel. 73-90-40-00; fax 73-92-16-20; e-mail ngf@geologi.no; internet www.geologi.no; f. 1905; 1,400 mems; Pres. ARVID NØTTVEDT; Sec.-Gen. GUNN KRISTIN HAUKDAL; publ. *Norsk Geologisk Tidsskrift* (4 a year).

Norsk Kjemisk Selskap (Norwegian Chemical Society): POB 1107 Blindern, 0317 Oslo; tel. 22-85-55-56; fax 22-85-54-41; internet www.kjemi.no; f. 1893; 2,000 mems; Pres. KENNETH RUUD; Gen. Sec. HARALD WALDERHAUG; publ. *Kjemi*.

TECHNOLOGY

Norges Tekniske Vitenskapsakademi (Norwegian Academy of Technological Sciences): Lerchendal Gård, 7491 Trondheim; tel. 73-59-54-63; fax 73-59-08-30; e-mail ntvamail@ntva.ntnu.no; internet www.ntva.no; f. 1955; 500 mems; Pres. Dr KJELL ARNE INGEBRIGTSEN; Sec.-Gen. HEIN JOHNSON.

Teknisk-Naturvitenskapelig Forening (Tekna) (Norwegian Society of Chartered Technical and Scientific Professionals (Tekna)): POB 2312 Solli, 0201 Oslo; Dronning Mauds gate 15, Oslo; tel. 22-94-75-00; fax 22-94-75-01; e-mail post@tekna.no; internet www.tekna.no; f. 1874; professional society; promotes research and development; represents engineering profession in its relations with other organizations and countries; 53,104 mems; Pres. MARIANNE HARG; Sec.-Gen. KENNETH STIEN; publs *Magasinet Tekna* (10 a year), *Sivilingeniøren* (10 a year), *Teknisk Ukeblad* (52 a year), *Våre veger* (10 a year).

Research Institutes

GENERAL

Chr. Michelsens Institutt: POB 6033 Bedriftssenteret, 5892 Bergen; Jektevikksbakken 31, Bergen; tel. 47-93-80-00; fax 47-93-80-01; e-mail cmi@cmi.no; internet www.cmi.no; f. 1930; independent, non-profit research institution with a focus on Sub-Saharan Africa, South and Central Asia, the Middle East, Balkans and South America; library of 70,000 vols; Dir OTTAR MÆSTAD.

Nordlandsforskning (Nordland Research Institute): POB 1490, 8049 Bodø; tel. 75-51-76-00; fax 75-51-72-34; e-mail nf@nforsk.no; internet www.nordlandsforskning.no; f. 1979; inter-disciplinary research across a wide range of fields, with a particular focus on social sciences and business management; Admin. Dir AGNETE ALSOS; Man. Dir HANNE OESTERDAL.

Norsk Samfunnsvitenskapelig Datatjeneste (NSD) (Norwegian Social Science Data Services): Harald Hårfagres gt. 29, 5007 Bergen; tel. 55-58-21-17; fax 55-58-96-50; e-mail nsd@nsd.uib.no; internet www.nsd.uib.no; f. 1971; attached to Universitetet i Bergen; Dir BJØRN HENRICHSEN.

Stein Rokkan Senter for Flerfaglige Samfunnsstudier (Stein Rokkan Centre for Professional Social Studies): Nygårdsgt. 5, 5015 Bergen; tel. 55-58-97-10; fax 55-58-97-11; e-mail rokkansenteret@uni.no; internet rokkan.uni.no; f. 2002 by merger of Senter for Samfunnsforskning (Centre for Social Research) and Norsk Senter for Forskning i Ledelse, Organisasjon og Styring (Norwegian Centre for Research in Organization and Management); attached to Universitetet i Bergen; multi-disciplinary research centre for social and cultural studies; Dir JAN ERIK ASKILDSEN; publ. *Tidsskrift for Velferdsforskning* (Journal of Social Research, 4 a year).

ECONOMICS, LAW AND POLITICS

Centre for Peace Studies: Faculty of Humanities, Social Sciences and Education, Universitetet i Tromsø, 9037 Tromsø; tel. 77-64-43-00; fax 77-64-59-19; e-mail mail@peace.uit.no; internet www.peace.uit.no; f. 2002; attached to Universitetet i Tromsø; examines, promotes and facilitates dialogue pertaining to non-violent conflict resolution and the creation of peace; Dir TONE BLEIE.

Norsk Utenrikspolitisk Institutt (Norwegian Institute of International Affairs): POB 8159 Dep., 0033 Oslo; C. J. Hambros pl. 2D, Oslo; tel. 22-99-40-00; fax 22-36-21-82; e-mail internett@nupi.no; internet www.nupi.no; f. 1959; int. economics, devt studies, European integration, collective security, Russian studies, UN, peacekeeping; library of 20,000 vols; Dir JAN EGELAND; publs *Forum for Development Studies* (3 a year), *Hvor Hender Det?* (24 a year), *Internasjonal Politikk* (4 a year), *Nordisk Østforum* (4 a year).

Norske Nobelinstitutt (Norwegian Nobel Institute): Henrik Ibsens gt. 51, 0255 Oslo; tel. 22-12-93-00; fax 22-12-93-17; e-mail postmaster@nobel.no; internet www.nobel.no; f. 1903; follows devt of int. relations (especially work for the pacific settlement of them) in order to advise the Nobel Peace Prize Cttee; research dept; library of 200,000 vols, 200 periodicals; Dir GEIR LUNDESTAD.

Peace Research Institute Oslo (PRIO): POB 9229 Grønland, 0134 Oslo; Hausmanns gt. 7, 0186, Oslo; tel. 22-54-77-00; fax 22-54-77-01; e-mail info@prio.no; internet www.prio.no; f. 1959; multi-disciplinary research on peace- and conflict-related topics; library of 22,000 vols, 340 journals; Chair. BERNT AARDAL; Dir KRISTIAN BERG HARPVIKEN; publs *Journal of Peace Research* (6 a year), *Security Dialogue* (6 a year).

Statistisk Sentralbyrå (Statistics Norway): POB 8131 Dep., 0033 Oslo; Kongens gt. 6, Oslo; tel. 21-09-00-00; fax 21-09-49-73; e-mail ssb@ssb.no; internet www.ssb.no; f. 1876; library of 160,000 vols; Dir-Gen. HANS HENRIK SCHEEL; publs *Norges offisielle statistikk* (series, Official Statistics of Norway, irregular), *Økonomiske analyser* (Economic Survey), *Sosiale og Økonomiske studier* (Social and Economic Studies), *Statistiske analyser* (Statistical Survey), *Statistisk årbok* (Statistical Yearbook).

EDUCATION

Centre for Flexible Education (U-vett): Teorifagsbygget hus 1, Universitetet i Tromsø, 9037 Tromsø; tel. 77-64-65-58; fax 77-64-55-50; e-mail postmottak@uvett.uit.no; internet uit.no/uvett; attached to Universitetet i Tromsø; Asst Dir INGER ANN HANSSEN.

HISTORY, GEOGRAPHY AND ARCHAEOLOGY

Roald Amundsen Centre for Arctic Research: 9037 Tromsø; tel. 77-64-52-41; e-mail arctic.info@arctic.uit.no; internet uit.no/amundsen/438; f. 1989; attached to Universitetet i Tromsø; aims to encourage inter-disciplinary cooperation in Arctic research and teaching; Head of Admin. GEIR GOTAAS.

LANGUAGE AND LITERATURE

Center for Advanced Study in Theoretical Linguistics (CASTL): Faculty of Humanities, Social Sciences and Education, Universitetet i Tromsø, 9037 Tromsø; tel. 77-64-47-51; fax 77-64-42-39; e-mail tore.bentz@uit.no; internet castl.uit.no; f. 2002; attached to Universitetet i Tromsø; aims to foster a greater understanding of the nature of syntactic, morphological and phonological variation, in order to be able to determine along which grammatical parameters any two languages vary; Dir MARIT WESTERGAARD.

MEDICINE

Helseøkonomi Bergen (HEB) (Health Economics Bergen): Herman Fossgt. 6, 5007 Bergen; tel. 55-58-92-00; fax 55-58-92-10; e-mail oddvar.kaarboe@econ.uib.no; internet heb.rokkan.uib.no; attached to Universitetet i Bergen; economic analysis of health; assessment of profitability and distributional effects of health care and treatment; Dir ODDVAR KAARBØ.

Nasjonalt Forskningssenter innen Komplementær og Alternativ Medisin (NaFKAM) (National Research Centre in Complementary and Alternative Medicine): Forskningsparken I, Sykehusveien 23, 9037 Tromsø; tel. 77-64-66-50; fax 77-64-68-66; e-mail nafkam@helsefak.uit.no; internet uit.no/nafkam; f. 2000; conducts inter-disciplinary research into a wide range of fields, incl. clinical studies and patients' use of alternative treatments; Dir VINJAR MAGNE FØNNEBØ; publ. *NAFKAM skriftserie* (irregular).

Nasjonalt Senter for Distriktsmedisin (NSDM) (National Centre of Rural Medicine): Institutt for Samfunnsmedisin, Universitetet i Tromsø, 9037 Tromsø; tel. 77-64-48-16; fax 77-64-48-31; e-mail ivar.aaraas@uit.no; internet www.nsdm.no; f. 2007; attached to Universitetet i Tromsø; promotes research, professional devt projects, education and networking among physicians and health personnel in rural and remote areas to bridge the gap between academia and practice and contributes to quality, recruitment and stability in rural health services; Gen. Man. Prof. IVAR J. AARAAS.

Research Centre for Health Promotion: Faculty of Psychology, Christies gt. 13, 5020 Bergen; tel. 55-58-28-08; e-mail adm-hemil@psych.uib.no; internet www.uib.no/rg/hemil; f. 1988; attached to Universitetet i Bergen; Head of Institute MAURICE B. MITTELMARK.

Senter for Samisk Helseforskning (Centre for Sami Health Research): POB 71, Storgt. 39, 9735 Karasjo; tel. 78-46-89-00; fax 78-46-89-10; e-mail ragnhild.kalstad@ism.uit.no; internet uit.no/medsamisk; f. 1999; attached to Universitetet i Tromsø; aims to promote inter-disciplinary and multi-disciplinary research and development on the health and living conditions among the Sami population in Norway; Dir RAGNHILD V. KALSTAD.

NATURAL SCIENCES

Biological Sciences

Havforskningsinstituttet (Institute of Marine Research): POB 1870 Nordnes, 5817 Bergen; Nordnesgt. 50, 5005 Bergen; tel. 55-23-85-00; fax 55-23-85-31; e-mail post@imr.no; internet www.imr.no; f. 1900; attached to Min. of Fisheries and Coastal Affairs; applied research related to fisheries; divisions: marine environment, marine living research, aquaculture (with two experimental stations), coastal zone; library of 80,000 vols; Man. Dir TORE NEPSTAD; publs *Facts and Figures* (every 2 years), *Fisken og Havet*.

Marine Biological Station: Espelamdsveien 232, 5258 Blomsterdalen; attached to Universitetet i Bergen; open to research workers from all countries; equipped for large-scale experimental work on primary and secondary production; Man. AGNES AADNESEN.

Norwegian Structural Biology Centre (NorStruct): Faculty of Sciences, University of Tromsø, 9037 Tromsø; tel. 77-64-40-70; e-mail norstruct@chem.uit.no; internet uit.no/norstruct; attached to Universitetet i Tromsø; Dir ARNE O. SMALÅS.

Physical Sciences

Centre for Theoretical and Computational Chemistry: Universitetet i Oslo, Department of Chemistry, POB 1033 Blindern, 0315 Oslo; Universitetet i Tromsø, Department of Chemistry, 9037 Tromsø; tel. 77-62-31-00; e-mail post@ctcc.no; internet www.ctcc.no; f. 2007; collaborative project between Universitetet i Oslo and the Universitetet i Tromsø; aims to be an internationally renowned contributor to the devt and application of quantum-mechanical modelling in chemistry and materials science; Head of Admin. STIG EIDE.

Meteorologiske Institutt (Norwegian Meteorological Institute): POB 43 Blindern, 0313 Oslo; Niels Henrik Abels vei 40, Oslo; tel. 22-96-30-00; fax 22-96-30-50; e-mail post@met.no; internet www.met.no; f. 1866; library of 30,000 vols; Dir ANTON ELIASSEN; publs *Klimatologisk månedsoversikt* (12 a year), *Technical Report* (irregular).

Nansen Environmental and Remote Sensing Center: Thormøhlensgt. 47, 5006 Bergen; tel. 55-20-58-00; fax 55-20-58-01; e-mail admin@nersc.no; internet www.nersc.no; attached to Universitetet i Bergen; aims to make significant contribution to the understanding, monitoring and forecasting of the environment and climate on regional and global scales through coordination and participation in nat. and int. research programmes; Dir STEIN SANDVEN.

Norges Geologiske Undersøkelse (Geological Survey of Norway): POB 6315 Sluppen, 7491 Trondheim; Leiv Eirikssons vei 39, 7040 Trondheim; tel. 73-90-40-00; fax 73-92-16-20; e-mail ngu@ngu.no; internet www.ngu.no; f. 1858; library of 120,000 vols and 950 periodicals; Man. Dir MORTEN SMELROR; publs *Bulletin* (irregular, in English, online only), *Gråsteinen* (irregular, in Norwegian).

Norsk Polarinstitutt (Norwegian Polar Institute): Fram Centre, 9296 Tromsø; Hjalmar Johansens gt. 14, Tromsø; tel. 77-75-05-00; fax 77-75-05-01; e-mail post@npolar.no; internet www.npolar.no; f. 1928; research, monitoring and topographic mapping of Norwegian polar regions; advises Norwegian

authorities on matters concerning polar environmental management; scientific investigations in the fields of geology, geophysics and biology; topographical mapping, responsible for Norwegian Antarctic Research expeditions; scientific logistical support; admin. and maintenance of all-year scientific stations in Ny-Ålesund, Svalbard (Sverdrup Station) and Dronning Maud Land, Antarctica (Troll Station); library of 13,000 vols and 12,000 pamphlets and authors' MSS; Dir Dr JAN-GUNNAR WINTHER; publ. *Polar Research* (irregular).

RELIGION, SOCIOLOGY AND ANTHROPOLOGY

Instituttet for Sammenlignende Kulturforskning (Institute for Comparative Research in Human Culture): POB 2832 Solli, 0204 Oslo; Drammensveien 78, Oslo; tel. and fax 22-55-42-07; e-mail kulturfo@online.no; internet kulturfo.webhotell.no; f. 1922; comparative study of languages, religions, folklore, law, ethnology, archaeology, and sociology, sponsoring research programmes and publishing; Chair. Prof. ARNE BUGGE AMUNDSEN; Vice-Chair. AUD TALLE; Sec. IDA SLETTA; publ. *Institute for Comparative Research in Human Culture. Series B* (irregular).

Senter for Aldersforskning (Centre for Research on the Elderly): Institutt for Klinisk Medisin, Medisinske Fakultet, Universitetet i Tromsø, 9037 Tromsø; tel. 77-62-08-94; e-mail sat@fagmed.uit.no; internet uit.no/172; f. 2000; attached to Universitetet i Tromsø; multi-disciplinary research into the medical, health and social concerns of the elderly; Dir MAGNHILD NICOLAISEN (acting).

Senter for Kvinne og Kjønnsforskning (Kvinnforsk): Universitetet i Tromsø, 9037 Tromsø; tel. 77-64-52-40; fax 77-64-64-20; e-mail kvinnforsk@skk.uit.no; internet uit.no/kvinnforsk; f. 1995; attached to Universitetet i Tromsø; Dir LISE NORDBRØND; publ. *Kvinnforsk Skritserie* (irregular).

Senter for Kvinne og Kjønnsforskning (SKOK) (Centre for Women's and Gender Research): POB 7805, 5020 Bergen; Ida Bloms hus, Allégt. 34, 5007 Bergen; tel. 55-58-24-71; fax 55-58-96-64; e-mail post@skok.uib.no; internet www.uib.no/skok; attached to Universitetet i Bergen; research fields incl. feminist theory, gender theory, women's studies, philosophy, sociology, anthropology, cultural studies, psychoanalysis, sexuality, development studies, migration studies and family history; Dir Prof. ELLEN MORTENSEN.

TECHNOLOGY

Institutt for Energiteknikk (Institute for Energy Technology): POB 40, 2027 Kjeller; Instituttveien 18, 2007 Kjeller; tel. 63-80-60-00; fax 63-81-63-56; e-mail firmapost@ife.no; internet www.ife.no; f. 1948; int. research institute for energy and nuclear technology; undertakes research and devt within the energy and petroleum sectors, carries out assignments in nuclear technology, safety and environmental research; Man. Dir EVA S. DUGSTAD.

NIVA—Norsk Institutt for Vannforskning (NIVA—Norwegian Institute for Water Research): Gaustadalléen 21, 0349 Oslo; tel. 22-18-51-00; fax 22-18-52-00; e-mail niva@niva.no; internet www.niva.no; f. 1958; research and contract projects on technical, economical and sanitary problems in connection with water supply, waste water and pollution in rivers and lakes/fjords; library of 5,000 vols, 25 periodicals in print, 3,900 online periodicals; Admin. Dir GRETA BENTZEN; publ. *Arbok*.

Norges Geotekniske Institutt (NGI) (Norwegian Geotechnical Institute): POB 3930 Ullevaal Stadion, 0806 Oslo; Sognsveien 72, Oslo; tel. 22-02-30-00; fax 22-23-04-48; e-mail ngi@ngi.no; internet www.ngi.no; f. 1953; soil, rock and snow mechanics, foundation engineering, dams, offshore structures, instrumentation, rock engineering, geoenvironmental engineering; library of 20,000 vols, 300 periodicals, Terzaghi Library, Peck Library; Admin. Dir SUZANNE LACASSE.

NORSAR: POB 53, 2027 Kjeller; Gunnar Randers vei 15, 2007 Kjeller; tel. 63-80-59-00; fax 63-81-87-19; internet www.norsar.no; f. 1968; research on a wide range of topics within the field of seismology and seismic exploration; Dir ANDERS DAHLE; publ. *Technical Summary* (2 a year).

Norsk Institutt for By- Og Regionforskning (Norwegian Institute for Urban and Regional Research): Gaustadalléen 21, 0349 Oslo; tel. 22-95-88-00; fax 22-60-77-74; e-mail nibr@nibr.no; internet www.nibr.no; f. 1967; 90 mems; library of 23,000 vols, 200 periodicals; Dir HILDE LORENTZEN; publ. *Regionale Trender* (irregular).

Norsk Institutt for Luftforskning (Norwegian Institute for Air Research): POB 100, 2027 Kjeller; Instituttveien 18, 2007 Kjeller; tel. 63-89-80-00; fax 63-89-80-50; e-mail nilu@nilu.no; internet www.nilu.no; f. 1969; nat. and int. research and consultation in air pollution, atmospheric dispersion and measurements, meteorological measurements and analysis, instrumentation and chemical analysis; library of 9,000 vols, 130 periodicals; Dir KARI NYGAARD.

Norsk Regnesentral (Norwegian Computing Centre): POB 114 Blindern, 0314 Oslo; Gaustadalléen 23 A-B, 0373 Oslo; tel. 22-85-25-00; fax 22-69-76-60; e-mail nr@nr.no; internet www.nr.no; f. 1952; contract research and devt projects in information and communication technology and applied statistical modelling; library of 4,000 vols, 250 periodicals; Man. Dir LARS HOLDEN.

Norwegian Marine Technology Research Institute (MARINTEK): POB 4125 Valentinlyst, 7450 Trondheim; Otto Nielsens veg 10, 7052 Trondheim; tel. 73-59-55-00; fax 73-59-57-76; e-mail marintek@marintek.sintef.no; internet www.sintef.no/home/marintek; f. 1984; mem. of the SINTEF Group; research, devt and technical consultancy in the maritime sector for industry and the public sector; develops and verifies technological solutions for the shipping and maritime equipment industries and offshore petroleum production; HQ and laboratories in Trondheim, Norway and subsidiaries in Houston, Texas and Rio de Janeiro, Brazil; library of 11,000 vols, 365 periodicals; Pres. ODDVAR EIDE; publ. *Marintek Review* (irregular).

NUTEC—Norsk Undervannsteknologisk Senter A/S (FALCK NUTEC—Norwegian Underwater Technology Centre): Gravdalsveien 255, POB 6, Ytre Laksevåg, 5848 Bergen; tel. 55-94-20-00; fax 55-94-20-01; e-mail companymail@falcknutec.no; internet www.nutec.no; f. 1976, present name adopted 1981; test and research centre for underwater technology, full-scale testing, diving, hyperbaric medicine and physiology, safety analysis, education and training; consulting services; library of 5,000 vols, 170 periodicals; Man. Dir ELI MOEN SÆTER.

Papirindustriens Forskningsinstitutt (PFI) (Paper and Fibre Research Institute): Høgskoleringen 6B, 7491 Trondheim; tel. 73-60-50-65; fax 73-55-09-99; e-mail firmapost@pfi.no; internet www.pfi.no; f. 1923; Pres. Dr PHILIP ANDRÉ REME.

Senter for Internasjonal Økonomi og Skipsfart (SIØS) (Centre for International Economics and Shipping): Norwegian School of Economics and Business Administration, Helleveien 30, 5035 Bergen; tel. 55-95-92-62; fax 55-95-93-50; e-mail sasamndm@debetmhs.no; f. 1958; aims to provide a centre for research fellows in sea transport, shipping economics and int. economics from Norway and abroad, and to promote cooperation with similar institutions; library of 3,500 vols, 1,600 periodicals, reports, etc.; Dir Prof. GUTTORM SCHJELDERUP; Sec. ANNE LIV SCRASE.

SINTEF: POB 4760 Sloop, 7465 Trondheim; Strindveien 4, Trondheim; tel. 73-59-30-00; fax 73-59-33-50; e-mail info@sintef.no; internet www.sintef.no; f. 1950 as Stiftelsen for Industriell og Teknisk Forskning ved Norges Tekniske Høgskole (Foundation for Scientific and Industrial Research at the Norwegian Institute of Technology); present name adopted 2007; undertakes contracts in science and technology research for industry and others; 7 affiliated research institutes; Pres. UNNI M. STEINSMO.

SINTEF Byggforsk (SINTEF Building and Infrastructure): POB 124 Blindern, 0314 Oslo; Forskningsveien 3B, Oslo; tel. 22-96-55-55; fax 22-69-94-38; e-mail byggforsk@sintef.no; internet www.sintef.no; f. 1953, reorganized 1985 as an ind. institute; merged with Norges byggforskningsinstitutt (NBI) 2007; library of 25,000 vols, 250 periodicals; Exec. Dir HANNE RØNNEBERG.

SINTEF Energi (SINTEF Energy): 7034 Trondheim; tel. 73-59-72-00; fax 73-59-72-50; e-mail energy.research@sintef.no; internet www.sintef.no; f. 1958 as Elektrisitetsforsyningens Forskningsinstitutt; renamed SINTEF Energiforskning 1998; present name adopted 2010; research and devt in the field of energy, esp. electricity generation, transmission, distribution and consumption; Man. Dir SVERRE AAM.

Transportøkonomisk Institutt (Institute of Transport Economics): Gaustadalléen 21, 0349 Oslo; tel. 22-57-38-00; fax 22-60-92-00; e-mail toi@toi.no; internet www.toi.no; f. 1958 as a govt dept; reorganized as ind. institute 1964; library of 30,000 vols, 200 periodicals; Chair. SIGURD LARSEN; publ. *Samferdsel* (Communication, 10 a year).

VilVite, Bergen Vitensenter (VilVite, Bergen Science Centre): HIB, Thormøhlensgt. 51, 5006 Bergen; tel. 55-59-45-00; e-mail post@vilvite.no; f. 2005; attached to Universitetet i Bergen; research and learning centre of technology, natural sciences and mathematics; Dir SVEIN ANDERS DAHL.

Libraries and Archives
Arendal
Arendal Bibliotek (Arendal Library): Torvet 6, POB 786 Stoa, 4809 Arendal; tel. 37-01-39-13; fax 37-01-30-80; e-mail arendal@arendal.folkebibl.no; internet www.arendal.folkebibl.no; f. 1832, inc. *Aust-Agder Fylkesbibliotek* (East Agder County Library) 1972; 200,000 vols; Head Librarian OLA EIKSUND.

Ås
Universitetet for Miljø- og Biovitenskap, Biblioteket (Norwegian University of Life Sciences, Library): POB 5003, 1432 Ås; Chr. M. Falsens vei 18, Tårnbygningen, Ås; tel. 64-96-50-00; fax 64-96-55-01; e-mail biblioteket@umb.no; internet www.umb.no/biblioteket; f. 1859; literature concerning all branches of agricultural science and forestry, conservation of natural resources, biology, etc.; 500,000 vols; Head Librarian DAG GUTTORMSEN (acting).

Bergen
Bergen offentlige Bibliotek (Municipal and County Library): Strømgt. 6, 5015 Bergen; tel. 55-56-85-00; fax 55-56-85-55; e-mail post@bergenbibliotek.no; internet bergenbibliotek.no; f. 1872; 600,000 vols; Grieg colln of 135 MSS and 5,700 letters; 6 brs and 1 mobile library; City Librarian TRINE KOLDERUP FLATEN.

Universitetsbiblioteket i Bergen (University of Bergen Library): POB 7808, 5020 Bergen; Stein Rokkans hus, Nygårdsgt. 5, 5015 Bergen; tel. 55-58-25-32; fax 55-58-46-20; e-mail post@ub.uib.no; internet www.uib.no/ub; f. 1825 as Bergens Museums Bibliotek; 1,780,000 books and journals, 240,000 photographs, 110,600 microforms, 42,800 maps and atlases, 6,400 audio recordings, 3,600 MSS; Library Dir RANDI E. TAXT.

Drammen
Drammensbiblioteket (Drammen Library): POB 3554, 3007 Drammen; Grønland 58B, 3045 Drammen; tel. 32-04-54-00; fax 32-80-64-53; e-mail bibliotek@drmk.no; internet www.dbib.no; f. 1916 as Drammen Bibliotek; present name adopted 2007 following merger with Buskerud fylkesbibliotek (Buskerud County Library) and the library at Høgskolen i Buskerud (Buskerud University College); 300,000 vols; Faculty Librarian HUGO HØYMO.

Hamar
Statsarkivet i Hamar (Regional State Archives): Lille Strandgate 3, 2317 Hamar; tel. 62-55-54-40; fax 62-52-94-48; e-mail sahamar@arkivverket.no; internet www.arkivverket.no/arkivverket/hamar; f. 1917; public record office, archives; public reading room open on weekdays; 23,000 vols; Chief Archivist VIGDIS STENSBY.

Kristiansand
Kristiansand Folkebibliotek (Kristiansand Public Library): POB 476, 4665 Kristiansand; Rådhusgt. 11, 4611 Kristiansand; tel. 38-12-49-10; fax 38-12-49-49; e-mail post.folkebibliotek@kristiansand.kommune.no; internet www.kristiansand.folkebibl.no; f. 1909; 3 brs; 300,000 vols; Chief Librarian ANNE KRISTIN UNDLIEN.

Oslo
Deichmanske Bibliotek (Oslo Public Library): Arne Garborgs pl. 4, 0179 Oslo; tel. 23-43-29-00; fax 22-11-33-89; e-mail postmottak.deichman@kul.oslo.kommune.no; internet www.deichmanske-bibliotek.oslo.kommune.no; f. 1785; 1,378,109 vols, incl. 1,118,274 books, 22,231 audio books, 31,438 music recordings, 19,239 video cassettes and DVDs; Chief Librarian LIV SÆTEREN.

Patentstyret (Norwegian Industrial Property Office): POB 8160 Dep., 0033 Oslo; Sandakerveien 64, 0484 Oslo; tel. 22-38-73-00; fax 22-38-73-01; e-mail mail@patentstyret.no; internet www.patentstyret.no; f. 1911; 25,000 vols of scientific and technical books and periodicals of reference for patent research; Head of Dept OTTO SCHARFF; publs *Designtidende* (Design Gazette), *Norsk Varemerketidende*, *Patenttidende* (Patent Gazette, 52 a year), *Varemerketidende* (Trademark Gazette, 52 a year).

Riksarkivet (National Archives of Norway): Sognsveien 221, POB 4013, Ullevål Stadion, 0806 Oslo; tel. 22-02-26-00; fax 22-23-74-89; e-mail riksarkivet@arkivverket.no; internet www.arkivverket.no; f. 1817; takes charge of the archives of the mins and other brs of the central admin.; collns incl. medieval documents, maps and drawings, MSS and transcripts; 60,000 vols; Nat. Archivist IVAR FONNES; Head Librarian TURID ASKJEM; publ. *Arkivmagasinet* (3 a year).

Statistisk Sentralbyrås Bibliotek og Informasjonssenter (Statistics Norway, Library and Information Centre): POB 8131 Dep., 0033 Oslo; Kongensgt. 6, Oslo; tel. 21-09-46-42; fax 21-09-45-04; e-mail biblioteket@ssb.no; internet www.ssb.no/biblioteket; f. 1917; open to the public; OECD deposit library; European Statistical Data Support; 80,000 vols: mainly economic, demographic and statistical literature (incl. official and int. statistics); Librarian BJØRG GLESNE; publ. *Biblioteksnytt* (12 a year, online only).

Universitetsbiblioteket i Oslo (University of Oslo Library): POB 1085, Blindern, 0317 Oslo; tel. 22-85-40-50; fax 22-84-41-50; e-mail postmottak@ub.uio.no; internet www.ub.uio.no; f. 1811; academic library; depositary library; spec. collns of papyri and orientalia; 3,538,004 vols; Library Dir BENTE R. ANDREASSEN.

Utenriksdepartementets Dokumentasjonssenter (Documentation Centre of the Ministry of Foreign Affairs): POB 8114 Dep., 0032 Oslo; 7 Juni-Plassen 1, Oslo; tel. 22-24-36-00; fax 22-24-95-80; e-mail post@mfa.no; internet www.ud.dep.no; f. 1900; literature on foreign affairs, int. law and int. relations; not open to the public; Head Librarian RITA AARS-NICOLAYSEN.

Rjukan
Rjukan Bibliotek (Public Library of Rjukan): POB 93, 3661 Rjukan; Torget 1, 3660 Rjukan; tel. 35-08-25-60; fax 35-08-25-65; e-mail bibliotek@tinn.kommune.no; internet www.tinn.kommune.no; f. 1914; 3 brs; 110,000 vols; colln on history, philosophy and sociology of the working class; colln on local and regional history; Chief Librarian TINE KAAE ANDERSEN.

Stavanger
Stavanger Bibliotek (Stavanger Library): POB 310, 4002 Stavanger; Sølvberggt. 2, Stavanger; tel. 51-50-74-65; fax 51-50-70-25; e-mail biblioteket@stavanger-kulturhus.no; internet www.stavanger-kulturhus.no/stavanger_bibliotek; f. 1885; municipal library for the town of Stavanger, central library for the county of Rogaland; 500,000 vols; music and picture colln; Librarian KURT KRISTENSEN.

Tønsberg
Tønsberg og Nøtterøy Bibliotek (Tønsberg and Nøtterøy Public Library): Storgt. 16, 3126 Tønsberg; tel. 33-35-49-00; fax 33-35-49-69; e-mail tbg@tnb.no; internet www.tnb.no; f. 1909; 220,000 vols; Chief Librarian VIGDIS G. JAKOBSEN.

Trondheim
Universitetsbiblioteket i Trondheim (NTNU library): Høgskoleringen 1, 7491 Trondheim; tel. 73-59-51-10; fax 73-59-51-03; e-mail ubit@ub.ntnu.no; internet www.ntnu.no/ub; f. 1768; attached to Norges Teknisk-Naturvitenskapelige Universitet (NTNU); receives deposit copies of all Norwegian books; comprises 10 faculty libraries, incl. arts, social sciences, science, technology, architecture, medicine; nat. resource library for architecture and technology; 2,878,000 books and periodicals, 421,500 photographs, 84,500 electronic books, 32,500 maps, 19,500 MSS, 12,000 electronic journals; Dir LISBETH TANGEN.

Ulefoss

Telemark Fylkesbibliotek/Nome Folke-bibliotek (Telemark/Nome County Library): Ringsevja 2, 3830 Ulefoss; tel. 35-94-89-20; fax 35-94-89-40; e-mail telfy@t-fk.no; internet www.tm.fylkesbibl.no; f. 1942; 150,000 vols, 200 periodicals; Librarian LILLIAN NILSSEN.

Museums and Art Galleries

Bergen

Bergen Museum, Universitetet i Bergen: POB 7800, 5020 Bergen; H. Hårfagresgt. 1, 5007 Bergen; tel. 55-58-93-60; fax 55-58-93-64; e-mail publikum@bm.uib.no; internet www.uib.no/bergenmuseum; f. 1825, part of University 1948; comprises two units, Cultural History Collns (Norwegian culture and folk art) and Natural History Collns (anthropology, archaeology, botany, geology and zoology); Dir SIRI JANSEN; publ. *Arbok for Bergen Museum* (Bergen Museum Yearbook).

Vestlandske Kunstindustrimuseum (West Norway Museum of Decorative Art): Nordahl Brungt. 9, 5014 Bergen; tel. 55-33-66-33; fax 55-33-66-30; e-mail permanenten@kunstmuseene.no; internet www.vk.museum .no; f. 1887; 20,000 objects incl. Norwegian and European furniture, glass, porcelain, silver and textiles from the Renaissance to modern times; Gen. Munthe's colln of Chinese art; library of 20,000 vols; Dir JORUNN HAAKESTAD; Curators ANNE BRITT YLVISÅKER, TROND INDAHL.

Bodø

Norsk Luftfartsmuseum (National Norwegian Aviation Museum): POB 1124, 8001 Bodø; Olav V gt., Bodø; tel. 75-50-78-50; fax 75-50-78-51; e-mail flymuseum@luftfart .museum.no; internet www.luftfart.museum .no; f. 1998; depicts cultural and technical background of Norway's civil and military aviation history; Dir SVEN SCHEIDERBAUER.

Salten Museum: Prinsensgt. 116, 8005 Bodø; tel. 75-50-35-00; fax 75-52-58-05; e-mail post@saltenmuseum.no; internet www.saltenmuseum.no; f. 1888; covers most aspects of life in the county of Nordland; 80,000 items, specialities: fisheries, boats, etc.; 9 br. museums; library of 6,000 vols; Dir HARRY ELLINGSEN.

Drammen

Drammens Museum–Fylkesmuseum for Buskerud: Konnerudgt. 7, 3045 Drammen; tel. 32-20-09-30; e-mail post@drammens .museum.no; internet www.drammens .museum.no; f. 1908; merged with Drammen Art Society 1996; 50,000 artefacts of art and cultural history, incl. paintings, furniture, glass, ceramics; library of 16,000 vols; Dir ÅSMUND THORKILDSEN; publ. *Årbok* (Yearbook).

Fredrikstad

Fredrikstad Museum: Tøihusgt. 41, 1632 Fredrikstad; tel. 69-30-40-30; fax 69-95-85-01; e-mail fredrikstadmuseum@ ostfoldmuseene.no; internet www .fredrikstad.kommune.no/museet/; f. 1903; cultural and military history of the town and district; Curator TOVE M. THØGERSEN.

Hamar

Hedmarksmuseet: Strandvegen 100, 2315 Hamar; tel. 62-54-27-00; fax 62-54-27-13; e-mail post@domkirkeodden.no; internet www.hedmarksmuseet.no; f. 1906 as Opplandenes Folkemuseum; renamed Hedmarks-museet og Domkirkeodden 1945, and subsequently as above; comprises 50,000 artefacts; colln of 2m. photographs; open-air museum and medieval colln; ruins of the medieval cathedral, bishop's palace (now housing a modern exhibition), and other medieval ruins; excavations in progress; farm buildings depicting local history and domestic life; library of 14,000 vols; Dir STEINAR BJERKESTRAND; Chief Curator BJØRN SVERRE HOL HAUGEN; publ. *Årbok Fra Kaupang og bygd.*

Attached Museums:

Kirsten Flagstad Museum: POB 1053, 2305 Hamar; Kirkegt. 11, 2305 Hamar; tel. 62-54-27-00; fax 62-54-27-13; e-mail post@ kirsten-flagstad.no; internet www .kirsten-flagstad.no; f. 1985; dedicated to the life and work of opera singer Kirsten Flagstad (1895–1962), born in Hamar; Chair. RAGNHILD NYHUS.

Norsk Utvandrermuseum (Norwegian Emigrant Museum): Åkershagan, 2312 Ottestad; tel. 62-57-48-50; fax 62-57-48-51; e-mail admin@emigrantmuseum.no; internet www.emigrantmuseum.no; f. 1955; Chair. GEORG A. BROCH.

Lillehammer

Lillehammer Kunstmuseum (Lillehammer Art Museum): Stortorget 2, POB 264, 2602 Lillehammer; tel. 61-05-44-60; fax 61-25-19-44; e-mail post@ lillehammerartmuseum.com; internet www .lillehammerartmuseum.com; f. 1927 as Lillehammer City Colln of Paintings; present name adopted 1994; contains collns of Norwegian paintings, sculpture and graphic art, historical and contemporary art exhibitions; Chair. GUNNAR K. HAGEN.

Maihaugen (Maihaugen Open Air Museum): Maihauvegen 1, 2609 Lillehammer; tel. 61-28-89-00; fax 61-26-95-93; e-mail post@maihaugen.no; internet www .maihaugen.no/maihaugen; f. 1887; open-air museum with 200 bldgs of historical interest from 1200 till 2001; 30 old workshops in a new exhibition hall; exhibitions of Norwegian history and folk culture; library of 20,000 vols; Dir GAUTE JACOBSEN.

Oslo

Astrup Fearnley Museet for Moderne Kunst (Astrup Fearnley Museum of Modern Art): POB 1158 Sentrum, 0107 Oslo; Dronningensgt. 4, Oslo; tel. 22-93-60-60; fax 22-93-60-65; e-mail info@fearnleys.no; internet afmuseet.no; f. 1993; Norwegian and int. contemporary art; Dir GUNNAR B. KVARAN.

Forsvarsmuseet (Armed Forces Museum): Oslo mil Akershus, 0015 Oslo; tel. 23-09-35-82; fax 23-09-31-90; e-mail fmu.kontakt@mil .no; internet www.fmu.mil.no; f. 1978; depicts technical and historical progress of the Norwegian military from Viking era to cold war years; library of 175,000 vols; Dir RUNAR GJERALD; Curator NINI FRITZNER; publs *Fosvarsmuseets Årbok, Forsvarsmuseets skrifter* (irregular).

Kon-Tiki Museet (Kon-Tiki Museum): Bygdøynesveien 36, 0286 Oslo; tel. 23-08-67-67; fax 23-08-67-60; e-mail kon-tiki@ kon-tiki.no; internet www.kon-tiki.no; archaeology of Easter Island, eastern Polynesia, the Galapagos Islands and Peru; boats and artefacts from Thor Heyerdahl's expeditions; library of 12,000 vols; Dir MAJA BAUGE.

Kulturhistorisk Museum (Museum of Cultural Heritage): POB 6762 St Olavs plass, 0130 Oslo; Frederiksgt. 2, 0164 Oslo (Historical Museum); Huk Aveny 35, 0287 Oslo (Viking Ship Museum); tel. 22-85-19-00; fax 22-85-19-38; e-mail postmottak@khm.uio.no; internet www.khm.uio.no; f. 1999; attached to Universitetet i Oslo; exhibits from prehistoric and Viking times, incl. Viking ships (at Bygdøy), and the Middle Ages, Norwegian coins, collns from Africa, South America, North America, East Asia and the Arctic; collns incl. 1,647,592 artefacts pertaining to cultural history, 4,504 art history works, 558,000 photographs; library of 70,000 vols; Dir Prof. Dr EGIL MIKKELSEN; publs *KHM skrifter* (1 a year), *Norske Oldfunn* (Norwegian Archaeological Finds, irregular), *Nytt om runer* (Rune News, 1 a year), *Varia* (irregular).

Munch Museum: POB 2823 Tøyen, 0608 Olso; Tøyengt. 53, 0578 Oslo; tel. 23-49-35-00; fax 23-49-35-01; e-mail info.munch@ munch.museum.no; internet www.munch .museum.no; f. 1963; colln of 1,100 paintings, 4,700 drawings and 15,500 prints, bequeathed to the city of Oslo by Edvard Munch; library of 22,000 vols, incl. colln of Munch's private letters, notes and diaries, and Munch's private book colln; Dir STEIN OLAV HENRICHSEN.

Nasjonalmuseet for Kunst, Arkitektur og Design (National Museum of Art, Architecture and Design): POB 7014, St. Olavs plass, 0130 Oslo; Kristian Augusts gt. 23, Oslo; tel. 21-98-20-00; fax 21-98-20-93; e-mail info@nasjonalmuseet.no; internet www .nasjonalmuseet.no; f. 2003 by merger of the Norwegian Museum of Architecture, the Museum of Decorative Arts and Design, the Museum of Contemporary Art and the Nat. Gallery; library of 30,000 vols; Dir AUDUN ECKHOFF.

Naturhistorisk museum, Universitetet i Oslo (Natural History Museum, University of Oslo): POB 1172 Blindern, 0318 Oslo; tel. 22-85-16-30; fax 22-85-17-09; e-mail informasjon@nhm.uio.no; internet www.nhm .uio.no; houses 7.4m. artefacts (c. 65% of the total natural history collns nationwide); Dir Prof. ARNE BJØRLYKKE.

Constituent Museums:

Botanisk hage og Botanisk museum (Botanical Garden and Botanical Museum): POB 1172 Blindern, 0318 Oslo; Sarsgt. 1, 0562 Oslo; tel. 22-85-16-30; fax 22-85-18-35; e-mail informasjon@nhm.uio .no; internet www.nhm.uio.no/om-museet/museets-bygninger/botanisk-museum; f. 1814 (garden), 1863 (museum); attached to Universitetet i Oslo; taxonomy and plant ecology; museum not open to the general public; library of 45,000 vols; Dir Prof. ARNE BJØRLYKKE; publ. *Sommerfeltia* (irregular).

Geologisk museum (Geological Museum): POB 1172 Blindern, 0318 Oslo; Sarsgt. 1, 0562 Oslo; tel. 22-85-16-30; fax 22-85-17-09; e-mail informasjon@nhm.uio .no; internet www.nhm.uio.no/om-museet/museets-bygninger/geologisk-museum; f. 1920; attached to Universitetet i Oslo; rocks, minerals and fossils; research laboratories in mineralogy, petrology, geochemistry and palaeontology, dinosaurs, meteorites and Ida; library of 75,000 vols; Dir Prof. ARNE BJØRLYKKE.

Zoologisk museum (Zoological Museum): POB 1172 Blindern, 0318 Oslo; Sarsgt. 1, 0562 Oslo; tel. 22-85-16-30; fax 22-85-18-37; e-mail informasjon@nhm.uio.no; internet www.nhm.uio.no/om-museet/museets-bygninger/zoologisk-museum; f. 1910; attached to Universitetet i Oslo; public exhibitions of Norwegian and world fauna; Norwegian vertebrates and invertebrates, Arctic, Antarctic and exotic, particularly Australian, research collns; library of 28,000 vols, 53,000 pamphlets; Dir Prof. ARNE BJØRLYKKE.

Norsk Folkemuseum (Norwegian Museum of Cultural History): POB 720 Skøyen, 0214 Oslo; Museumsveien 10, Bygdøy, Oslo; tel. 22-12-37-00; fax 22-12-37-77; e-mail post@norskfolkemuseum.no; internet www.norskfolkemuseum.no; f. 1894; consists of indoor and open-air sections comprising 230,000 objects; spec. exhibits in the indoor section incl. rural culture (incl. display of folk dresses and folk art), church history, toys, Sámi (Lapp) colln; open-air museum consists of: 159 old bldgs (incl. 13th-century Gol stave church and four other medieval bldgs), examples of different farms from most of Norway, urban structures arranged as an old town quarter, museum shop, artisans; library of 45,000 vols; Dir OLAV AARAAS; Librarian TONE ODDEN.

Norsk Maritimt Museum (Norwegian Maritime Museum): Bygdøynesvn. 37, 0286 Oslo; tel. 24-11-41-50; fax 24-11-41-51; e-mail fellespost@marmuseum.no; internet www.marmuseum.no; f. 1914; museum opened 1974; Norwegian maritime history and coastal culture; colln of ship portraits, maritime paintings, models, instruments, historic ships and traditional small craft, full-size original ship interiors; library of 30,000 vols, archives of photographs and plans, MSS, maps, occasional papers, research reports; Dir ESPEN WÆHLE; Asst Dir EYVIND BAGLE; Asst Dir FRODE KVALØ; publs *Norsk Maritimt Museum. Arbok* (Yearbook), *Norsk Maritimt Museum. Rapport* (irregular), *Norsk Maritimt Museum. Skrifter* (series, irregular).

Norsk Teknisk Museum (Norwegian Museum of Science and Technology): Kjelsåsveien 143, 0491 Oslo; tel. 22-79-60-00; internet www.tekniskmuseum.no; f. 1914; library of 40,000 vols; Man. Dir HANS WEINBERGER; publ. *Yearbook*.

Vigeland-museet: Nobelsgt. 32, 0268 Oslo; tel. 23-49-37-00; fax 23-49-37-01; e-mail postmottak.vigeland@vigeland.museum.no; internet www.vigeland.museum.no; f. 1947; life and work of sculptor Gustav Vigeland; colln comprises 1,600 sculptures, 12,000 drawings and 400 woodcarvings; museum closed to public between Aug. 2010 and May 2011 owing to major renovation work; Dir JARLE STRØMODDEN; Curator GURI SKUGGEN; Curator TRINE OTTE BAK NIELSEN.

Sandefjord

Kommandør Chr. Christensens Hvalfangstmuseum (Commdr Chr. Christensen's Whaling Museum): POB 396, 3201 Sandefjord; Museumsgt. 39, 3210 Sandefjord; tel. 94-79-33-41; fax 33-46-37-84; e-mail hvalfangstmuseet@vestfoldmuseene.no; internet www.hvalfangstmuseet.no; f. 1917; shows the devt of whaling from primitive to modern times; geography, ethnology, zoology, maritime history, etc.; incl. photograph colln comprising some 150,000 images; Dir SIDSEL HANSEN.

Skien

Telemark Museum: Øvregt. 41, 3715 Skien; tel. 35-54-45-00; fax 35-52-01-59; e-mail post@telemark.museum.no; internet telemarkmuseum.no; f. 1909 as Fylkesmuseet for Telemark og Grenland (County Museum of Telemark and Grenland); present name adopted 1998; conservation and research on items of historical interest from the Telemark region; situated in Brekkeparken, with open-air museum (log houses dating from the Middle Ages) and a manor house furnished in 17th-, 18th- and 19th-century styles; collns on folk art, handicrafts, navigation, church art, Ibsen Colln and Ibsen's childhood home, Venstøp Farm; library of 6,000 vols; Dir LENE E. WALLE.

Stavanger

Arkeologisk Museum i Stavanger (Museum of Archaeology, Stavanger): POB 478, 4002 Stavanger; Peder Klowsgt 30A, Stavanger; tel. 51-84-60-00; fax 51-84-61-99; e-mail ams@ark.museum.no; internet www.ark.museum.no; f. 1975; own library, scientific archive; Dir ARNE JOHAN NERØY (acting); publ. *Frá haug ok heiðni* (scientific magazine, 4 a year).

Museum Stavanger (MUST): Muségt. 16, 4010 Stavanger; tel. 51-84-27-00; fax 51-84-27-01; e-mail post@stavanger.museum.no; internet www.stavanger.museum.no; f. 1877 as Stavanger Museum; present name adopted 2010, following merger with Rogaland Art Museum; urban and rural culture, zoology, ornithology; a maritime museum, a canning museum, a medical museum, a children's museum, a printing museum and the mansions of Ledaal and Breidablikk are in the museum's care; library of 65,000 vols; Man. Dir GRO PERSSON.

Tromsø

Tromsø Museum (Universitetetsmuseet): Lars Thøringsvei 10, 9037 Tromsø; tel. 77-64-50-00; fax 77-64-55-20; e-mail museumspost@uit.no; internet uit.no/tmu; f. 1872; attached to Universitetet i Tromsø; 6 sections: Archaeology, Botany, Cultural History, Geology, Sami Ethnography, Zoology; library of 180,000 vols; Dir MARIT ANNE HAUAN; publs *Ottar* (5 a year, in Norwegian), *Skrifter* (irregular, in Norwegian), *Tromura* (scientific reports, irregular, in Norwegian), *Way North* (irregular, in English).

Trondheim

Nordenfjeldske Kunstindustrimuseum (National Museum of Decorative Arts): Munkegt. 5, 7013 Trondheim; tel. 73-80-89-50; fax 73-80-89-51; e-mail post@nkim.museum.no; internet www.nkim.no; f. 1893; depts of furniture, textiles, glass, ceramics, metalwork from the 14th century onwards; special colln of Japanese art and textiles; Dir JAN-LAURITZ OPSTAD.

NTNU Vitenskapsmuseet (Museum of Natural History and Archaeology, of the Norwegian University of Science and Technology): 7491 Trondheim; Erling Skakkes gt. 47A, Trondheim; tel. 73-59-21-45; fax 73-59-22-23; e-mail post@vm.ntnu.no; internet www.ntnu.no/vitenskapsmuseet; f. 1760; graduate and research instn of the univ.; archaeological, botanical and zoological depts; mineralogical and numismatic collns; marine station; schools service; Dir Prof. AXEL CHRISTOPHERSEN; publs *Fauna norvegica* (peer-reviewed journal, 1 a year, in English), *Gunneria* (original works in archaeology, cultural history, botany and zoology, irregular, in English and Norwegian), *Vitark—Acta Archaelogica Nidrosiensi* (Norwegian and Nordic research and insight into archaeological problems, irregular, in English and Norwegian).

Universities

NORGES TEKNISK-NATURVITENSKAPELIGE UNIVERSITET (NTNU)
(Norwegian University of Science and Technology)

7491 Trondheim
Telephone: 73-59-50-00
Fax: 73-59-53-10
E-mail: postmottak@adm.ntnu.no
Internet: www.ntnu.no

Founded 1996 to replace the Univ. of Trondheim (which included the Norwegian Institute of Technology, the College of Arts and Science and the Museum of Natural History and Archaeology)

Academic year: August to June

Chair.: MARIT ARNSTAD
Rector: TORBJØRN DIGERNES
Pro-Rector for Education and Quality of Learning: BERIT KJELDSTAD
Pro-Rector for Research: KARI MELBY
Pro-Rector for External Relations and Innovation: JOHAN E. HUSTAD
Dir for Finance and Property: FRANK ARNTSEN
Dir for Organization and Information: TROND SINGSAAS

Number of teachers: 2,800
Number of students: 20,000

Publications: *Gemini* (irregular), *Spor* (2 a year)

DEANS

Faculty of Architecture and Fine Art: TORE I. HAUGEN
Faculty of Engineering Science and Technology: INGVALD STRØMMEN
Faculty of Humanities: KATHRINE SKRETTING
Faculty of Information Technology, Mathematics and Electrical Engineering: GEIR ØIEN
Faculty of Medicine: STIG A. SLØRDAHL
Faculty of Natural Sciences and Technology: BJØRN HAFSKJOLD
Faculty of Social Sciences and Technology Management: JAN MORTEN DYRSTAD

PROFESSORS

Faculty of Architecture and Fine Art (tel. 73-55-02-75; e-mail fak-adm@ab.ntnu.no; internet www.ntnu.no/ab):

BERGAUST, K., Fine Art
BJØNNESS, H. C., Urban Design and Planning
BLEIKLIE, S., Architectural Design and Management
BOOKER, C. A., Architectural Design, Form and Colour Studies
BRAND, P., Architectural Design, Form and Colour Studies
FISKAA, H., Urban Design and Planning
FURUNES, A.-K., Fine Art
GAMDRUP, M., Fine Art
GRYTLI, E. R., Architectural Design, History and Technology
GUSTAVSEN, A., Architectural Design, History and Technology
HESTNES, A. G., Architectural Design, History and Technology
HØYEM, H., Architectural Design, History and Technology
JAUKKURI, M. H., Fine Art
LARSEN, K., Architectural Design and Management
LARSEN, K. E., Architectural Design, History and Technology
LUND, F., Architectural Design, Form and Colour Studies
MATUSIAK, B., Architectural Design, Form and Colour Studies
MEDALEN, T., Urban Design and Planning
RØE, B., Urban Design and Planning
SAMBOLEC, D., Fine Art
SHETELIG, C. F. L., Architectural Design and Management
SIEM, J. H., Architectural Design, History and Technology
STEEN, O., Architectural Design and Management
STØA, E., Architectural Design and Management
SVENDSEN, S. E., Architectural Design and Management

Faculty of Engineering Science and Technology (tel. 73-59-45-01; fax 73-59-47-90; e-mail postmottak@ivt.ntnu.no; internet www.ivt.ntnu.no):

AMDAHL, J., Marine Structures
ANDERSEN, B., Production and Quality Engineering
ANDERSSON, H. I., Fluids Engineering
ASHEIM, H. A., Petroleum Engineering, Production
BAKKEN, L. E., Thermal Engineering
BARDAL, E., Machine Design and Materials Technology
BELL, K., Structural Engineering, Structural Mechanics
BERGE, S., Marine Structures
BOLLAND, O., Thermal Engineering
BRATTEBØ, H., Environmental Engineering
BRATTELAND, E., Marine Technology
BRATTLI, B., Engineering Geology
BREDESEN, A. M., Refrigeration Engineering
BREVIK, I. H., Fluids Engineering
BROCH, E., Engineering Geology
BRULAND, A., Project Management and Construction Engineering
DIGERNES, T., Marine Systems Design
EIKEVIK, T. M., Food Engineering in the Marine Sector
ENDAL, A., Marine Systems Design
ERTESVÅG, I. S., Thermal Energy
FALTINSEN, O. M., Marine Hydrodynamics
FIKSDAL, L., Urban Water Systems
FJELDAAS, S., Machine Design
GJØRV, O. E., Structural Engineering, Concrete
GOLAN, M., Petroleum Engineering, Production
GRANDE, L. O., Marine Geotechnical Engineering
GUDMUNDSSON, J. S., Petroleum Engineering Production
GUNDERSEN, T., Process, Energy and Systems Engineering
GUSTAFSON, C.-G., Materials and Processes, Materials Technology
HAAGENSEN, P. J., Structural Engineering, Steel and Light Metal
HAAVALDSEN, T., Bldg Technologies
HALMØY, E., Materials and Processes, Materials Technology
HANSSEN, S. O., Heating, Ventilation and Sanitary Engineering
HÅRKEGÅRD, G., Machine Design and Materials Technology
HERTWICH, E., Thermal Energy
HØISETH, K. V., Structural Engineering, Concrete
HOLM, K. R., Geomatics
HOLT, R. M., Petroleum Engineering, Drilling Technology
HOLTHE, K. H., Structural Engineering, Structural Mechanics
HOPPERSTAD, O. S., Structural Engineering, Steel and Light Metal
HORVLI, I., Highway Engineering
HOVD, A., Highway Engineering
HOVDE, P. J., Bldg Technologies
HUSTAD, J. E., Thermal Energy
IRGENS, F., Structural Engineering, Structural Mechanics
JELMERT, T. A., Petroleum Engineering, Reservoir Technology
JOHANNESSEN, S., Transport Engineering
JOHNSEN, R., Corrosion and Surface Technology
KANSTAD, T., Structural Engineering, Concrete
KILLINGTVEIT, Å., Engineering Hydrology
KLEPPE, J., Petroleum Engineering, Reservoir Technology
KOCH, W. H., Production and Quality Engineering
KRAMMER, G., Environmental Engineering
KRILL, A., Geology

KRISTIANSEN, S., Marine Systems Design
KROGSTAD, P.-Å., Fluids Engineering
LANDRØ, M., Applied Geophysics
LANGSETH, M., Structural Engineering, Sheet and Light Metal
LARSEN, C. M., Marine Structures
LARSEN, P. K., Structural Engineering, Sheet and Light Metal
LEIRA, B. J., Marine Structures
LI, C., Mining Engineering
LIEN, T. K., Production and Quality Engineering
LILE, O. B., Petroleum Engineering, Applied Geophysics
LIPPARD, S. J., Petroleum Geology
LØSET, S., Arctic Technology
MAGNUSSEN, O. M., Industrial Fish Processing
MALO, K. A., Structural Engineering, Sheet and Light Metal
MALVIK, T., Resources Geology
MATHISEN, K. M., Structural Engineering, Structural Mechanics
MIDTBØ, T., Geomatics
MINSAAS, K. J., Marine Hydrodynamics
MOAN, T., Marine Structures
MOE, G., Port and Ocean Engineering
MYRAN, T., Engineering Geology
MYRHAUG, D., Marine Hydrodynamics
NÆSS, A., Marine Technology
NIELSEN, K. O., Mining Engineering
NIELSEN, T. K., Fluids Engineering
NILSEN, B., Engineering Geology
NORDAL, S., Geotechnical Engineering
NOREM, H. A., Transport Engineering
NØRSTRUD, H., Fluids Engineering
NOVAKOVIC, V., Heating, Ventilation and Sanitary Engineering
NYDAL, O. J., Indoor Environmental Engineering
ØDEGAARD, H., Environmental Engineering, Urban Water Systems
OKSMAN, K., Materials and Processes
PETTERSEN, B., Marine Hydrodynamics
PRESTVIK, T., Geology, Petrology
RASCH, F. O., Production and Quality Engineering
RASMUSSEN, M., Marine Engineering
RAUSAND, M., Production and Quality Engineering
REMSETH, S. N., Structural Engineering, Structural Mechanics
ROALD, S., Project Management and Construction Engineering
RØDLAND, A., Petroleum Engineering (Drilling Technology)
ROKOENGEN, K., Engineering Geology
ROLSTADÅS, A., Production and Quality Engineering
RØLVÅG, T., Computer-Aided Engineering
SÆTRAN, L. R., Fluids Engineering
SAGER, T. Ø., Transport Engineering
SAMSET, K. F., Project Management and Construction Engineering
SANDVIK, K. L., Mineral Dressing
SANGESLAND, S., Petroleum Engineering (Drilling Technology)
SCHILLING, W., Urban Water Systems
SELLEVOLD, E. J., Structural Engineering, Concrete
SINDING-LARSEN, R., Resources Geology
SIVERTSEN, O. I., Machine Design
SKALLERUD, B. H., Structural Engineering, Structural Mechanics
SØNJU, O. K., Thermal Energy
SØRENSEN, A. J., Marine Hydrodynamics
SØRENSEN, S. I., Structural Engineering, Concrete
STEEN, S., Marine Technology and Experience Hydrodynamics
STRØMMEN, E. N., Structural Engineering, Structural Mechanics
STRØMMEN, I., Refrigeration Engineering
STØLE, H., Hydro Power Devt
STØREN, S., Materials and Processes, Materials Technology

SYVERTSEN, T. G., Structural Engineering, Structural Mechanics
THAULOW, C., Materials Processes, Materials Technology
THUE, J. V., Building Technology
TJELFLAAT, P. O., Indoor Environmental Engineering
TORSÆTER, O., Petroleum Engineering, Reservoir Technology
TØNDER, K., Machine Design, Materials Technology
URSIN, B., Petroleum Engineering, Seismatics
VALBERG, H. S., Materials and Processes, Materials Technology
VALLAND, H., Marine Engineering
VATN, J., Production and Quality Engineering
VENNESLAND, Ø., Structural Engineering, Concrete
WANG, K., Production and Quality Engineering
WESTBY, O., Marine System Design
WHITE, M. F., Marine Engineering
WHITSON, C. H., Petroleum Engineering, Reservoir Technology
YTREHUS, T., Fluids Engineering
ZHANG, Z., Solid State Mechanics

Faculty of Humanities (tel. 73-59-65-95; fax 73-59-10-30; e-mail postmottak@hf.ntnu.no; internet www.ntnu.no/hf):

AARSET, H. E., Literature
AASLESTAD, P., Scandinavian Studies and Comparative Literature
ÅFARLI, T. A., Scandinavian Studies and Comparative Literature
ALTERHAUG, B., Musicology
ANDERSEN, H. W., History
BAKKA, E., Musicology
BENDER JØRGENSEN, L., Archaeology
BERGMANN, S., Religious Studies
BORGERSEN, T., Media Studies
BULL, I, History
DAHL, S. L., History
DOMMELEN, W. A. van, Linguistics
DYBVIG, M., Philosophy
ELIASSEN, K. O., Literature
EVENSEN, L. S., Applied Linguistics
FAUSKEVÅG, S. E., Romance Literature
FEIGS, W. G., Germanic Languages
FINDAL, W., History of Art
FINKE, S., Philosophy
FISKUM, B., Musicology
FOSS, G., General Literature
FRETHEIM, T., Literature
GIMNES, S., Scandinavian Literature
HAGLAND, J. R., Scandinavian Literature and Comparative Literature
HALVORSEN, A., Romance Studies
HANKELN, R., Medieval Music
HAUG, A., Medieval Studies
HAWTHORN, J., English Literature
HELLAN, L., Applied Linguistics
HERNÆS, P. O., History
HETLAND, J., Germanic Languages
IMSEN, S., History
IVERSEN, G., Film Studies
JASINSKI, M. E., Maritime Architecture
JONSSON, L. S., Musicology
KALDAL, I., History
KNOWLES, J., Philosophy
LEDANG, O. K., Musicology
LIE, M., Social Anthropology
LIE, S., Literature
MÆHLUM, B. K., Norwegian Language
MELBY, K., History, Women's Research
MITCHELL, D., English Literature
MOLANDER, B., Philosophy
NEUMANN, B. O., German Literature
NILSEN, H. N., Literature
NORDGÅRD, T., Linguistics
NYLANDER, L., Literature
ØFSTI, A., Philosophy
ØSTBY, P., History of Technology
ØSTERUD, E., Literature

PETERI, G. G., History
RASMUSSEN, B., Drama and Theatre
RISE, H., Church Music
SAWYER, B., History
SHERRY, R. G., English
SIMENSEN, J., History
SKRETTING, K., Media Studies
SØRENSEN, K. H., History of Technology
SØRENSSEN, B., Film Studies
STUGU, O. S., History
SUPPHELLEN, S., History
TVINNEREIM, H. S., History of Art
ULRICHSEN, J. H., Religious Studies
VIDEN, G., History
VULCHANOVA, M. D., English Language
WYLLER, T., Philosophy

Faculty of Information Technology, Mathematics and Electrical Engineering (tel. 73-59-42-02; fax 73-59-36-28; e-mail postmottak@ime.ntnu.no; internet www.ime.ntnu.no):

AAGESEN, F. A., Telematics
AAMODT, A., Artificial Intelligence
AARNES, J. F., Mathematics
AAS, E. J., Physical Electronics
ANDRESEN, S. H., Telematics
BAAS, N. A., Mathematics
BLAKE, R., Image Processing
BRATSBERG, S. E., Database Systems
BRATBERGSENGEN, K., Database Systems
BRÆK, R., Telematics
CONRADI, R., Software Engineering
DIGERNES, T., Mathematics
DIVITINI, M., Software Engineering
DO, V. T., Telematics
DONG, H., Telecommunications
DOWNING, K., Artificial Intelligence
EGELAND, O., Engineering Cybernetics
EMSTAD, P. J., Telematics
ENGAN, H. E., Physical Electronics
ENGEN, S., Mathematical Statistics
FAANES, H. H., Electrical Power Engineering
FIMLAND, B.-O., Physical Electronics
FJELDLY, T. A., Physical Electronics
FORSSELL, B., Telecommunications
FOSS, B. A., Engineering Cybernetics
FOSSEN, T. I., Engineering Cybernetics
FOSSO, O. B., Electrical Power Engineering
GREPSTAD, J., Physical Electronics
GULLA, F. A., Database Systems
GUTTEBERG, O., Satellite Communications
HAG, K., Mathematics
HALAAS, A., Algorithm Theory and Construction
HELVIK, B. E., Telematics
HENRIKSEN, R., Engineering Cybernetics
HOLDEN, H., Mathematics
HOLEN, A. T., Electrical Power Engineering
HOLTE, N., Telecommunications
HOVD, M., Engineering Cybernetics
HOVEM, J. M., Telecommunications
HUGHES, P., Database Systems
HVASSHOVD, S.-O., Database Systems
ILSTAD, E., Electric Power Engineering
JACCHERI, M. L., Software Engineering
JOHANSEN, T. A., Engineering Cybernetics
KNAPSKOG, S. J., Telematics
KRISTIANSEN, L., Telematics
KRISTIANSEN, U. R., Telecommunications
KROGSTAD, H. E., Mathematics
KURE, Ø., Telematics
LANDSTAD, M. B., Mathematics
LINDQVIST, B. H., Mathematical Statistics
LINDQVIST, L. P., Mathematics
LORENTZEN, L., Mathematics
LYUBARSKII, Y., Mathematics
MALVIG, K. E., Engineering Cybernetics
MJØLSNES, S. F., Telematics
MONTEIRO, E., Human–Computer Interaction
MÜLLER, R. R., Wireless Networks
NÆSS, A., Mathematical Statistics
NATVIG, L., Computer Architecture and Design

NILSEN, R., Electrical Power Engineering
NØRSETT, S. P., Mathematics
NORUM, L. E., Electrical Power Engineering
NYGÅRD, M., Database Systems
NYSVEEN, A., Electrical Power Engineering
ØIEN, G. E., Telecommunications
OMRE, K. H., Mathematical Statistics
ONSHUS, T. E., Engineering Cybernetics
OWREN, B., Mathematics
PERKIS, A., Digital Image Processing
PETTERSEN, K. Y., Engineering Cybernetics
PETTERSEN, O., Engineering Cybernetics
RAMSTAD, T. A., Telecommunications
REITEN, I., Mathematics
RØNNEKLEIV, A., Physical Electronics
RØNNINGEN, L. A., Telematics
RØNQVIST, E., Mathematics
ROUDAKOV, A., Mathematics
RUE, H., Mathematical Statistics
SÆTHER, T., Physical Electronics
SEIP, K., Mathematics
SINDRE, G., Information Systems
SKAAR, J., Photonics
SKAU, C. F., Mathematics
SKRAMSTAD, T., Human–Computer Interaction
SMALØ, S. O., Mathematics
SOLBERG, Ø., Mathematics
SØLVBERG, A., Information Systems
SØLVBERG, I., Information Management
STRAUME, E., Mathematics
STÅLHANE, T., Software Engineering
SVENDSEN, T., Telecommunications
SVENSSON, P., Telecommunications
SVAASAND, L. O., Physical Electronics
UNDELAND, T. M., Electrical Power Engineering
WANGENSTEEN, I., Electrical Power Engineering
YTTERDAL, T., Physical Communications

Faculty of Medicine (tel. 73-59-88-59; fax 73-59-88-65; e-mail dmf-post@medisin.ntnu.no; internet www.medisin.ntnu.no):

AADAHL, P., Anaesthesiology
ANGELSEN, B. A. J., Biomedical Engineering
AUSTGULEN, R., Cancer Research and Molecular Medicine
BACKE, B., Laboratory Medicine, Children's and Women's Health
BASSØE, C. F., Neuroscience
BENTZEN, N., Public Health and General Practice
BERGH, K., Laboratory Medicine, Children's and Women's Health
BOVIM, G., Neurology
BRATLID, D., Laboratory Medicine, Children's and Women's Health
BRUBAKK, A.-M., Laboratory Medicine, Children's and Women's Health
BRUBAKK, A. O., Physiology
CHEN, D., Cancer Research and Molecular Medicine
CLIFFORD, G., Child Psychiatry
DALE, O., Anaesthesiological Pharmacology
DRABLØS, F., Cancer Research and Molecular Medicine
ELLINGSEN, Ø., Physiology
ESPEVIK, T., Cancer Research and Molecular Medicine
FARUP, P. G., Applied Clinical Research
FINSEN, V., Neuroscience
GØTESTAM, K. G., Neuroscience
GRILL, V., Cancer Research and Molecular Medicine
GRIMSMO, A., Public Health and General Practice
GRØNBECK, J. E., Surgery and Gastroenterology
HARALDSETH, O., MR/Radiology
HAUGEN, O. A., Morphology
HELGERUD, J., Sports Physiology
HOLMEN, J., Nord-Trøndelag Health Study

IVERSEN, O.-J., Laboratory Medicine, Children's and Women's Health
JACOBSEN, G., Public Health and General Practice
JOHNSEN, R., Public Health and General Practice
JYNGE, P., Physiology
KAASA, S., Cancer Research and Molecular Medicine
KLEPP, O., Oncology
KLUNGLAND, H., Laboratory Medicine, Children's and Women's Health
KROKAN, H. E., Cancer Research and Molecular Medicine
LÆGREID, A., Microarray
LAMVIK, J., Cancer Research and Molecular Medicine
LARSSON, B. S., Child Psychiatry
LEIVSETH, G., Neuroscience
LØVIK, M., Public Health
LYDERSEN, S., Cancer Research and Molecular Medicine
MIDELFART, A., Neuroscience
MOSER, M.-B., Neuroscience
NILSEN, O. G., Cancer Research and Molecular Medicine
OTTERLEI, M., Cancer Research and Molecular Medicine
PETERSEN, H., Public Health and General Practice
RØNNINGEN, H., Neuroscience
RYGNESTAD, T., Laboratory Medicine
SAND, T., Neurology
SANDVIK, A. K., Cancer Research and Molecular Medicine
SCHEI, B., Public Health and General Practice
SKORPEN, F., Nord-Trøndelag Health Study
SLØRDAHL, S. A., Physiology
SLØRDAL, L., Laboratory Medicine, Children's and Women's Health
SLUPPHAUG, G., Cancer Research and Molecular Medicine
SONNEWALD, U., Neuroscience
STOVNER, L. J., Neuroscience
SUNDAN, A., Cancer Research and Molecular Medicine
SVEBAK, S., Neuroscience
SYVERSEN, T., Neuroscience
SYVERSEN, U., Cancer Research and Molecular Medicine
TORP, H., Biomedical Engineering
VATTEN, L. J., Public Health and General Practice
VIDEM, V., Laboratory Medicine, Children's and Women's Health
VIK, T., Public Health and General Practice
WAAGE, A., Haematology
WALDUM, H., Cancer Research and Molecular Medicine
WESTIN, S., Public Health and General Practice
WIBE, A., Cancer Research and Molecular Medicine
WIDERØE, T.-E., Nephrology
WITTER, M., Neuroscience

Faculty of Natural Sciences and Technology (tel. 73-59-41-97; fax 73-59-14-10; e-mail postmottak@nt.ntnu.no; internet www.ntnu.no/nt):

ALSBERG, B. K., Physical Chemistry
AMUNDSEN, T., Etology
ANDERSEN, R., Terrestrial Ecology
ANDERSEN, R., Zoo Physiology
ANTHONSEN, T., Organic Chemistry
ARMBRUSTER, W. S., Evolution, Ecology
ARNBERG, L., Process Metallurgy
ÅSTRAND, P. O., Physical Chemistry
BAKKE, J. M., Organic Chemistry
BAKKEN, J. A., Process Metallurgy
BECH, C., Zoology
BERG, O. K., Freshwater Ecology
BLEKKAN, E. A., Chemical Engineering, Catalysis and Petrochemistry

BONES, A., Cell and Molecular Biology
BORG, A., Surface Physics
BRATAAS, A., Theoretical Physics
CARLSEN, P. H., Organic Chemistry
CHEN, D., Chemical Engineering, Catalysis and Petrochemistry
CHRISTENSEN, B. E., Biopolymer Chemistry
DAVIES, C., Biophysics and Medical Technology
EINARSRUD, M.-A., Inorganic Chemistry
ELGSÆTER, A., Biological Physics
ENGH, T. A., Metallurgy
FIKSDAHL, A., Organic Chemistry
FOOSNÆS, T., Inorganic Chemistry
FOSSHEIM, K., Material Physics
FOSSUM, J. O., Condensed-Matter Physics
GRANDE, T., Inorganic Chemistry
GREGERSEN, Ø. W., Chemical Engineering, Pulp and Paper Technology
GRONG, Ø., Process Metallurgy
HAARBERG, G. M., Electrochemistry
HÆGG, M.-B., Chemical Engineering, Separation Technology
HAFSKJOLD, B., Physical Chemistry
HAGEN, K., Physical Chemistry
HANSEN, A., Theoretical Physics
HERTZBERG, T., Chemical Engineering, Process Systems Engineering
HOGSTAD, O., Zoology
HOLMEN, A., Chemical Engineering, Catalysis and Petrochemistry
HOLMESTAD, R., Material Physics
HØYE, J. S., Theoretical Physics
HUNDERI, O., Surface Physics
HYTTERBORN, H., Plant Ecology
IVERSEN, T.-H., Cell Biology
JAKOBSEN, H. A., Chemical Engineering, Reactor Technology
JENSSEN, B. M., Ecotoxicology
JOHANSEN, B., Cell and Molecular Biology
JOHNSSON, A., Biophysics and Medical Technology
KJELSTAD, B. J., Ultraviolet Radiation
KJELSTRUP, S., Physical Chemistry, Thermodynamics
KOCH, H., Physical Chemistry
KOLBEINSEN, L., Process Metallurgy
KOLBENSTVEDT, H., Theoretical Physics
LANGELAND, A. L., Freshwater Ecology
LEVINE, D. W., Biochemical Engineering
LINDGREN, M., Experimental Optics
LINDMO, T., Biophysics and Medical Technology
LJONES, T., Biophysical Chemistry
LOHNE, O., Physical Metallurgy
LØKBERG, O. J., Applied Optics
MARTHINSEN, K., Physical Metallurgy
MELØ, T. B., Biophysics and Medical Technology
MIKKELSEN, A., Biophysics and Medical Technology
MO, F., Crystallography
MOKSNES, A., Terrestrial Ecology
MORK, K. J., Theoretical Physics
MØRK, P., Chemical Engineering, Polymer and Colloid Chemistry
MUSTAPARTA, H., Neurophysiology
MYRHEIM, J., Anyons
NAQVI, K. R., Biophysics and Medical Technology
NES, E.-A., Physical Metallurgy
NESSE, N., Chemical Engineering, Separation Technology
NICHOLSON, D. G., Materials Science
NILSSEN, K. J., Zoophysiology, Aquaculture
NISANCIOGLU, K., Electrochemistry
OLAUSSEN, K., Anyons
OLSEN, Y., Marine Biology
ØSTGAARD, K., Environmental Biotechnology
ØSTVOLD, T., Inorganic Chemistry
ØYE, H. A., Inorganic Chemistry
PREISIG, H., Chemical Engineering, Process Systems Engineering
RAAEN, S., Experimental Condensed Matter Physics

REINERTSEN, H., Aquaculture, Marine Biology
ROSENQVIST, G., Etology
RØSKRAFT, E., Evolutionary Biology
ROVEN, H. J., Physical Metallurgy
RYUM, N., Physical Metallurgy
SÆTHER, B.-E., Terrestrial Ecology
SAKSHAUG, E., Marine Biology
SAMUELSEN, E. J., Material Physics
SCHRØDER, K. H., Analytical Chemistry
SJØBLOM, J., Chemical Engineering, Polymer and Colloid Chemistry
SKAGERSTAM, B.-S., Theoretical Physics
SKJÅK-BRÆK, G., Biotechnology, Biopolymer Chemistry
SKOGESTAD, S., Chemical Engineering, Process Systems Engineering
SKULLERUD, H., Electron and Ion Physics
SMIDSRØD, O., Biotechnology, Biopolymer Chemistry
SOLBERG, J. K., Physical Metallurgy
STEINNES, E., Environmental Technology
STOKKE, B. T., Biophysics and Medical Technology
STØLEVIK, R. E., Physical Chemistry
STRØM, A. R., Biotechnology, Molecular Genetics
SUDBØ, A., Theoretical Physics
SUNDE, S., Hydrogen Technology
SVENDSEN, H. F., Chemical Engineering, Reactor Technology
TANGSTAD, M., Process Metallurgy
TUNOLD, R., Electrochemistry
VADSTEIN, O., Biotechnology
VALBERG, A., Biophysics and Medical Technology
VALLA, S., Biotechnology, Molecular Genetics
VÅRUM, K., Marine Biochemistry
WRIGHT, J., Marine Biochemistry
YSTENES, M., Inorganic Chemistry
ZACHARIASSEN, K. E., Zoophysiology

Faculty of Social Sciences and Technology Management (tel. 73-59-19-00; fax 73-59-19-01; e-mail postmottak@svt.ntnu.no; internet www.ntnu.no/svt):

ALMÅS, R., Sociology
BERG, N. G., Human Geography
BERGE, E., Sociology
BJØRGEN, I. A., Psychology
BORGE, L.-E., Economics
BRANDTH, B., Sociology
BRØGGER, J. C., Social Anthropology
CHRISTIANSEN, M., Industrial Economics
DAHL-JØRGENSEN, C., Social Anthropology
DALE, B. E., Geography
DYRSTAD, J. M., Economics
ERRING, B. B., Social Anthropology
ESPNES, G. A., Programme for Social Work
ETTERMA, G., Sports Sciences
FET, A. M., Organizational Studies
GAIVORONSKI, A. A., Industrial Economics
HAAVELSRUD, M., Education
HESTAD, K., Psychology
HOEL, T. L., Education
HOPMANN, S., Education
HOVDEN, J., Organizational Studies
HVINDEN, B., Sociology
IMSEN, G. M., Education
INGVALDSEN, R. P., Sports Sciences
JACOBSEN, K. H., Psychology
JENSEN, A.-M., Sociology
JENSSEN, A. T., Political Science
JONES, M. R. H., Geography
KARLSEN, A., Economic Geography
KAUL, H., Psychology
KNUTSEN, T., Political Science
KOLSTAD, A., Psychology
KREKLING, S., Psychology
KVANDE, E., Sociology
LEIULFSRUD, H., Sociology
LEVIN, M., Organizational Studies
LISTHAUG, O., Political Science
LORENTZEN, S., Education
LUND, R., Geography

LUNHEIM, R., Organizational Studies
MARTINUSSEN, W. M., Sociology
MEER, A. L. VAN DER, Psychology
MOSER, E., Neuroscience
MOSER, M.-B., Neuroscience
MOSES, J., Political Science
MOXNES, K., Sociology
NORDAHL, H. M., Psychology
NORDVIK, H., Psychology
NYGREEN, B., Industrial Economics
QVORTRUP, J., Sociology
RAMET, S., Political Science
RASMUSSEN, B., Sociology
RASMUSSEN, K., Psychology
RATTSØ, J. G., Economics
RINGDAHL, G. I., Health Psychology
RINGDAL, K., Sociology
RUNDMO, T., Psychology
SÆTNAN, A. R., Sociology
SAKSVIK, P. Ø., Psychology
SCHIEFLOE, P.-M., Sociology
SIGMUNDSSON, H., Sociology
SIMKUS, A., Sociology
SJØBERG, B.-M. D., Psychology
SKAALVIK, E. M., Education
SKONHOFT, A., Economics
SOLEM, K. E., Political Science
SOLEM, O., Organizational Studies
STEINSHOLT, K., Education
STILES, T. C., Psychology
TORVIK, R., Economics
TØSSEBRO, J., Programme for Social Work
VEREIJKEN, E., Sports Sciences
VIKAN, A., Psychology
WAAGØ, S., Organizational Studies
WEEL, F. VAN DER, Psychology
WESTGAARD, R. H., Organizational Studies
WICHSTRØM, L., Psychology
WIJST, D. VAN DER, Industrial Economics

Museum of Natural History and Archaeology (tel. 73-59-21-45; fax 73-59-22-23; e-mail post@vm.ntnu.no; internet www.ntnu.no/vitenskapsmuseet):

CHRISTOPHERSEN, A., Archaeology
FLATBERG, K. I., Botany
HOGSTAD, O., Zoology
JASINKSI, M. E., Maritime Archaeology
JOHANSEN, A. B., Archaeology
MOEN, A., Botany
MORK, J., Population Genetics
OLSEN, Y., Marine Physiology
SAKSHAUG, E., Marine Botany
SOGNES, K., Archaeology
SOLEM, J. O., Zoology

UNIVERSITETET FOR MILJØ—OG BIOVITENSKAP (UMB)
(Norwegian University of Life Sciences)

POB 5003, 1432 Ås
Telephone: 64-96-50-00
Fax: 64-96-50-01
E-mail: postmottak@umb.no
Internet: www.umb.no

Founded 1859 as State College, present name and status 2005, plans mooted for merger with Norges Veterinærhøgskole (Norwegian School of Veterinary Science)
Language of instruction: English, Norwegian
Academic year: August to August

Rector: Prof. HANS FREDRIK HOEN
Vice-Rectors: Prof. RUTH HAUG, Asst Prof. MARI SUNDLI TVEIT
Univ. Dir: SIRI MARGRETHE LÖKSA
Dir of Human Resources: PER ANDERS AUTHEN
Dir of Research: RAGNHILD SOLHEIM
Dir of Studies: OLE-JØRGEN TORP
Library Dir: DAG GUTTORMSEN

Number of teachers: 640 , incl. 80 full profs
Number of students: 4,200 , plus 460 postgraduates

UNIVERSITETET I AGDER
(University of Agder)

POB 422 Kristiansand, 4604 Grimstad
Telephone: 38-14-10-00
Fax: 38-14-10-01
E-mail: post@uia.no
Internet: www.uia.no

Founded 1994 as Høgskolen i Agder (Agder
University College) by merger of 6 regional
colleges; univ. status acquired and present
name adopted 2007

Rector: TORUNN LAUVDAL
Vice-Rector for Education: MARIT AAMODT
NIELSEN
Vice-Rector for Research, Devt and Innovation: DAG G. AASLAND
Man. Dir: TOR A. AAGEDAL
Chief Librarian: ELSE-MAGRETHE BREDLAND

Library of 200,000 vols, 1,500 periodicals
Number of teachers: 600
Number of students: 8,000

UNIVERSITETET I BERGEN
(University of Bergen)

POB 7800, 5020 Bergen
Telephone: 55-58-00-00
Fax: 55-58-96-43
E-mail: post@uib.no
Internet: www.uib.no

Founded 1946
State control
Academic year: August to June

Rector: Prof. SIGMUND GRØNMO
Deputy Rector: Prof. BERIT ROKNE
Vice-Rector for Education: Prof. KUVVET
ATAKAN
Vice-Rector for Int. Relations: Prof. ASTRI
ANDRESEN
University Dir: KARI TOVE ELVBAKKEN
Library Dir: JAN S. VAAGEN

Library: see under Libraries and Archives
Number of teachers: 1,900
Number of students: 14,500

Publications: *Ilicifolia* (irregular), *Naturen* (6
a year, popular scientific review), *Sarsia* (6
a year)

DEANS

Faculty of Humanities: Prof. GJERT KRISTOF-
FERSEN
Faculty of Law: Prof. ASBJØRN STRANDBAKKEN
Faculty of Mathematics and Natural Sciences: Prof. DAG RUNE OLSEN
Faculty of Medicine and Dentistry: Prof.
NINA LANGELAND
Faculty of Psychology: Prof. GERD KVALE
Faculty of Social Sciences: Prof. KNUT HEL-
LAND

PROFESSORS

Faculty of Humanities (tel. 55-58-93-80; fax
55-58-93-83; e-mail post@hf.uib.no; internet
www.uib.no/hf):

ÅDLAND, E., General Literature
AKSELBERG, G., Nordic Language
ALVER, B. G., Folklore
ANGVIK, B., Spanish
ARMSTRONG, C. I., British Literature
ÅRSETH, A., Nordic Language
BAGGE, S. H., History
BELL, J. N., Arabic
BERGGREEN, B., Ethnology
BJØRGO, N., Archaeology
BJØRKELO, A., History
BONDEVIK, J., Nordic Language
BØRTNES, J., Russian Literature
BREIVIK, L. E., English Philology
BROWN, E., Philosophy
BUVIK, P., General Literature
CHRISTENSEN, K. K., General Linguistics
DANBOLT, G., History of Art
DE CUZZANI, P. M., Philosophy

DYRVIK, S., History
DYVIK, H. J., General Linguistics
ENDSJØ, D., Religious Studies
FJELL, T. I., Cultural Studies and History of
Art
FLØTTUM, K., French Language
FORSBERG, L. L., Archaeology
GILHUS, A. I. S., Religion
GRØNLIE, T., History
GULLVEIG, B. A., Folklore
HAAVERT, I. E., History
HÄGG, T., Classical Philology
HÅLAND, R., African Archaeology
HALMØY, O., French Language
HALVERSEN, S., Philology
HAUG, E., History
HAUGEN, O. E., Nordic Language
HELLE, L. J., Russian Language
HENSHILWOOD, C., Archaeology
HESTVIK, A., General Linguistics
HOLGERNES, B., Philosophy
HOLM, H. V., Philology
HOVLAND, E., History
HUBBARD, W. H., History
JANICKI, K., English Philology
JOHANNESSEN, H., Philosophy
JOHANNESSEN, K. S., Philosophy
JOHNSEN, K. O., Philosophy
KIILERICH, B. K., History of Art
KITTANG, A., General Literature
KOLLER, W., German Language
KRISTOFFERSEN, G., Nordic Language
KROEPELIEN, B., History of Art
LIE, R. K., Philosophy
LINNEBERG, A., General Literature
LUNDE, I., Russian Language and Literature
MCCAFFERTY, K., British Literature
MELVE, L., History
MEYER, J. C., History of Art
MEYER, S., European Culture
MIKAELSSON, L., Religion
MORTENSEN, E., General Literature
MUNDAL, E., Nordic Languages
NAGEL, A.-H., History
NORDENSTAM, T., Philosophy
O'FAHEY, R. S., History
ØSTBY, E., Archaeology
ØVERLAND, O., American Literature
ØYE, I., Archaeology
PIERCE, R., Egyptology
QUESEDA-PACHECO, M. A., Spanish
ROKSTAD, K., Philosophy
RYDVING, L. O. H., Religion
SÄÄTELÄ, S. T. S., Philosophy
SÆTRE, L., General Literature
SANAKER, J. K., French Language
SANDBERG, B., German Literature
SANDØY, H., Nordic Language
SCHRØTER, H. G., History
SELBERG, T., Folklore
SILLARS, S. J., English Philology
SKÅNLAND, M. H., Linguistics
SKARSTEN, R., Humanistic Informatics
SKILLEÅS, O. M., Philosophy
SKIRBEKK, G., Philosophy
SKULSTAD, A. S., English Philology
STEGANE, I., Nordic Language
STRAUSBERG, M., Religion
SVENDSEN, L. F., Philosophy
THOMASSEN, E., Religion
UTAKER, A., Philosophy
VELAND, R. M., French Language
VENNESLAN, K., Philosophy
VIKØR, K. S., History
WINTHER, T., French Language
WÆRNESS, K. E., Sociology

Faculty of Law (tel. 55-58-95-00; fax 55-58-
95-71; e-mail post@jurfa.uib.no; internet
www.uib.no/jur):

ÅLL, J.
ÅSEN, H. S.
ASKELAND, B.
BERNT, J. F.
FRANTZEN, T.

GIERTSEN, J.
HOLGERSEN, G.
HUSABØ, E. J.
KONOW, B.-E.
KRÜGER, K.
LUNDE, T.
MÆLAND, H. J.
MONSEN, E.
NORDTVEIT, E.
NYGAARD, N.
RASMUSSEN, Ø.
SÆBO, R.
SØVIG, K. H.
SUNDE, J.
TRUYEN, F.

Faculty of Mathematics and Natural Sciences (tel. 55-58-20-62; fax 55-58-96-66;
e-mail post@mnfa.uib.no; internet www.uib
.no/matnat):

AKSNES, D., Chemistry
AKSNES, D. L., Fisheries Biology
ANDERSEN, Ø. M., Chemistry
BÅMSTEDT, U., Fisheries Biology
BERG, C. C., Botany
BERGE, G., Mathematics
BERNTSEN, J., Mathematics
BEZEM, M. A., Computer Science
BIRKELAND, N.-K., Microbiology
BIRKS, H. J. B., Botany
BJØRSTAD, P. E., Computer Science
BRATBAK, G., Microbiology
BRIX, O., Zoology
CSERNAI, L., Physics
DAHLE, H. K., Mathematics
DYSTHE, K., Mathematics
ECKHOFF, K. S., Mathematics
ECKHOFF, R. K., Physics
EIGEN, G., Physics
ENDRESEN, C., Fisheries Biology
ENGEVIK, L. E., Mathematics
ESPEDAL, M., Mathematics
ESPELID, T. O., Computer Science
FERNØ, A., Fisheries Biology
FJOSE, A., Molecular Biology
FOSSEN, F., Geology
FRANCIS, G. W., Organic Chemistry
FRODESEN, A. G., Physics
FURNES, H., Petroleum Geology
FYHN, H. J., Milieu Physiology
GABRIELSEN, R., Petroleum Geology
GADE, H. G., Physical Oceanography
GAMMELSRØD, T., Physical Oceanography
GISKE, J., Fisheries Biology
GRAHL-NIELSEN, O., Chemistry
GRAUE, A., Physics
GRØNÅS, S., Meteorology
GUDMUNDSSON, A., Geology
HAMMER, E. A., Physics
HANSEN, J. P., Physics
HANYGA, A., Applied Geophysics
HAUGAN, P. M., Geophysics
HAVSKOV, J., Applied Geophysics
HELLAND, D. E., Molecular Biology
HELLAND-HANSEN, W., Geology
HELLESETH, T., Computer Science
HEUCH, I., Mathematics
HOBÆK, H., Physics
HOFFMAN, A. C., Physics
HØGSTEDT, G., Zoology
HØILAND, H., Physical Chemistry
HOLME, A., Mathematics
HUSEBYE, E., Applied Geophysics
HUSEBYE, S., Chemistry
JAKOBSEN, P. J., Zoology
JANSEN, E., Geology
JENSEN, H. B., Molecular Biology
JOHANNESEN, O. M., Physical Oceanography
JOHNSEN, T., Mathematics
JØRGENSEN, P. M., Botany
KALAND, P. E., Botany
KLØVE, T., Computer Science
KNUDSEN, L. R., Computer Science
KNUTSEN, G., Microbiology
KOCBACH, L., Physics

KOLLTVEIT, K., Physics
KRISTOFFERSEN, Y., Seismology
KRYVI, H., Zoology
KVALHEIM, O. M., Chemistry
KVAMME, B., Physics
LARSSON, P., Zoology
LAURITZEN, S.-E., Geology
LIEN, T., Microbiology
LILLEHAUG, J., Molecular Biology
LILLESTØL, E., Physics
LØVLIE, R., Geomagnetism
MAALØE, S. B., Geology
MÆLAND, E., Applied Geophysics
MALYSHEV, A., Computer Science
MANGERUD, J., Quaternary Geology
MANNE, R. E., Chemistry
MJELDE, R., Applied Geophysics
MOE, D., Botany
MUNTHE-KAAS, H., Computer Science
MYKLEBOST, K., Physics
NÆVDAL, G., Fisheries Biology
NEMEC, W., Geology
NESJE, A., Geology
NYLUND, A., Fisheries Biology
ØIEN, A. H., Mathematics
OSLAND, P., Physics
PAULSEN, J., Mathematics
PEDERSEN, R.-B., Geology
RAAE, A. J., Molecular Biology
ROBINS, B., Geology
RØDSETH, Ø. J., Mathematics
RØHRICH, D., Physics
RYE, N. M., Geology
SÆTHER, O. A., Zoology
SÆTHRE, L. J., Chemistry
SALVANES, A. G. V.
SCHRADER, H., Geology
SEJRUP, H. P., Geology
SKARTVEIT, A., Physical Oceanography
SKOGEN, A., Botany
SKORPING, A., Zoology
SLETTEN, E., Physical Chemistry
SLETTEN, J., Inorganic Chemistry
SONGSTAD, J., Inorganic Chemistry
SØRÅS, F., Physics
SØREVIK, T., Computer Science
STAMNES, J. J., Physics
STEFANSSON, S., Fisheries Biology
STEIHAUG, T., Informatics
STORETVEDT, K. M., Geomagnetism
STORØY, S., Computer Science
STRAY, A., Mathematics
STRØMME, S. A., Mathematics
STUGU, B., Physics
SUNDVOR, E., Seismology
SVENDSEN, H., Physical Oceanography
SVENDSEN, J.-I., Physics
SYDNES, L. K., Chemistry
TAI, X.-C., Mathematics
TALBOT, M. R., Petroleum Geology
TELLE, J. A., Computer Science
THINGSTAD, T. F., Microbiology
TJØSTHEIM, D. B., Statistics
TØNSBERG, T., Botany
TORSVIK, V. L., Microbiology
TOTLAND, G. K., Zoology
TVERBERG, H., Mathematics
ULLTANG, Ø., Fisheries Biology
VÅGEN, J. S., Physics
WALTHER, B. T., Molecular Biology
WILLASSEN, E., Zoology
YTREHUS, Ø., Computer Science

Faculty of Medicine and Dentistry (tel. 55-58-20-86; fax 55-58-96-82; e-mail post@mofa.uib.no; internet www.uib.no/mofa):

AKSNES, L., Clinical Medicine
ÅRLI, J. A., Clinical Medicine
ÅRSTAD, H. J., Surgical Sciences
ARVIDSON, K. F., Dentistry
ÅSTROM, A. N., Dentistry
BÆRHEIM, A., General Practice
BAKKE, M., Biomedicine
BAKKEN, V., Oral Microbiology
BERG, E., Prosthesis
BERGE, M. E., Prosthodontics

BERGE, T. I., Dentistry
BERGGREEN, E., Biomedicine
BINDOFF, L., Clinical Medicine
BJERKNES, R., Clinical Medicine
BJERKVIG, R., Biomedicine
BJØRGE, T., Epidemiology
BJØRVATN, B., General Practice
BLYSTAD, A., Nursing Science
BØ, L., Clinical Medicine
BOLSTAD, A. I., Dental Research
BOMAN, H., Clinical Medicine
BRAMHAM, C. R. E., Biomedicine
BRÅTVEIT, M., Physiology
BRUDVIK, P., Dentistry
DALTVEIT, A. K., Epidemiology
DØSKELAND, S. E., Biomedicine
EIDE, R., Dental Materials
ENGESÆTER, L. B., Surgical Sciences
ESPELID, I., Paedodontics
FASMER, O. B., Clinical Medicine
GERDES, H.-H., Biomedicine
GJENGEDAL, E., Praxeology
GJERDET, N. R., Dental Materials
GJESDAL, S., Public Health
GREVE, G., Clinical Medicine
GRONG, K., Surgical Sciences
GULLBERG, D., Biomedicine
HAAVIK, R., Biomedicine
HALSE, A., Oral Radiology
HARTVEIT, E., Biomedicine
HAUG, K., General Practice
HAUKAAS, S. A., Surgical Sciences
HAVER, B., Clinical Medicine
HELLE, K. B., Biomedicine
HELLEM, S., Oral Surgery
HOLSTEN, F., Clinical Medicine
HØVDING, G., Clinical Medicine
HUSBY, P., Surgical Sciences
IVERSEN, O.-E., Clinical Medicine
JOHANNESSEN, A. C., Oral Pathology
JONUNG, J. A. T., Surgical Sciences
JØRGENSEN, H., Clinical Medicine
KETTUNEN, P., Biomedicine
KISERUD, T., Clinical Medicine
KLOCK, K., Dentistry
KROHN, J., Clinical Medicine
KRÜGER, P. G., Biomedicine
KUSCHE-GULLBERG, M., Biomedicine
LARSEN, T., Biomedicine
LEKNES, K., Dentistry
LEKVEN, J., Surgical Sciences
LORENS, J., Biomedicine
LUND, A., Clinical Medicine
LUNDERVOLD, A., Biomedicine
LUND-JOHANSEN, M., Surgical Sciences
LUUKKO, K. A., Biomedicine
MÆLAND, J., Social Medicine
MARTINEZ, A., Biomedicine
MELAND, E., General Practice
MOE-NILSSEN, R., Physiotherapy
MOEN, B. E., Occupational and Environmental Medicine
MØLLER, P., Surgical Sciences
MUSTAFA, K., Dentistry
MYKLEBUST, R., Biomedicine
NATVIG, G., Nursing Science
NJØLSTAD, P. R., Clinical Medicine
NORGÅRD, G., Clinical Medicine
NORHEIM, O. F., Medical Ethics
NYLAND, H. I., Clinical Medicine
OLOFSSON, J., Surgical Sciences
ØYMAR, K., Clinical Medicine
PETERSEN, K. A., Praxeology
PRYME, I. F., Biomedicine
RÅDAL, M. J., Odontophobia and Paedodontics
RASMUSSEN, S., Clinical Medicine
RØDAHL, E, Clinical Medicine
RØRVIK, J., Surgical Sciences
ROSLAND, J. H., Surgical Sciences
SALVESEN, H. B., Clinical Medicine
SARASTE, J., Biomedicine
SØNDENAA, K., Surgical Sciences
STEEN, V. M., Clinical Medicine
STRAND, G., Dentistry
TANG, T., Clinical Medicine

TAXT, T., Biomedicine
TENSTAD, O., Biomedicine
TJØLSEN, A., Biomedicine
VASSTRAND, E., Dentistry
VEDELER, A., Biomedicine
VISTE, A., Surgical Sciences
WESTER, K., Surgical Sciences
WIIG, H., Biomedicine
WIK, G., Clinical Medicine
WISTH, P. J., Orthodontics

Faculty of Psychology (tel. 55-58-27-10; fax 55-58-98-71; e-mail post@psyfa.uib.no; internet www.uib.no/psyfa):

AARØ, L. E., Social Psychology
ANDERSSEN, N., Social Psychology
ASBJØRNSEN, A E., Biological and Medical Psychology
BØHM, G., Social Psychology
DALLAND, T., Social Psychology
EID, J., Social Psychology
EINARSEN, S., Social Psychology
HAVIK, O. E., Clinical Psychology
HELLAND, T., Biological and Medical Psychology
HUGDAHL, K., Somatic Psychology
JOHNSEN, B. H., Social Psychology
KVALE, G, Clinical Psychology
LABERG, J. C., Clinical Psychology
LÆNG, B., Biological and Medical Psychology
LINSTRØM, T. C., Social Psychology
LUNDERVOLD, A., Biological and Medical Psychology
MANGER, T., Social Psychology
MATTHIESEN, S., Social Psychology
MURISON, R., Physiological Psychology
NIELSEN, G. H., Clinical Psychology
NORDHUS, I. H., Clinical Psychology
PALLESEN, S., Social Psychology
REBER, R., Biological and Medical Psychology
SAM, D. L., Personal Psychology
SANDAL, G. M., Social Psychology
SKOGSTAD, A., Social Psychology
STORMARK, K. M., Child Psychology
SUNDBERG, H., Physiological Psychology
VOLLMER, F., Personal Psychology
WICKLUND, R. A., Social Psychology

Faculty of Social Sciences (tel. 55-58-90-50; fax 55-58-90-52; e-mail post@svfa.uib.no; internet www.uib.no/svf):

AMUNDSEN, E. S., Economics
ÅRRESTAD, J., Economics
ÅSE, T. H., Geography
BAKKE, M., Media Studies
BJELLAND, A. K., Social Anthropology
BLEIKLIE, I., Administration and Organization Theory
DAVIDSEN, P., Geography
EIDE, M., Media Studies
FIMREITE, A., Administration and Organization Theory
FLÅM, S. D., Economics
FLØYSAND, A., Geography
GOODNOW, K. J., Media Studies
GRAN, T., Administration and Organization Theory
GRIPSRUD, J., Media Studies
GRØNHAUG, R., Social Anthropology
GRØNMO, S., Sociology
GULBRANDSEN, Ø., Social Anthropology
HENRIKSEN, G., Social Anthropology
HOLT-JENSEN, A., Geography
HVIDING, E., Social Anthropology
HÅLAND, G., Social Anthropology
JOHANSEN, A., Media Studies
KAPFERER, B., Social Anthropology
KAPFERER, J., Sociology
KJELDSEN, J. E., Media Studies
KNUDSEN, J. C., Social Anthropology
KORSNES, O., Sociology
KUHNLE, S., Comparative Politics
LÆGREID, P., Administration and Organization Theory
LARSEN, P. L., Media Studies

LILLEHAUG, B. W., Media Studies
LINDSTRØM, U. A., Comparative Politics
LINDKVIST, K. B., Geography
LITHMAN, Y., Sociology
LOMMERUD, K. E., Economics
LUNDBERG, A., Geography
MANGER, L. O., Social Anthropology
MIDTBØ, T., Comparative Politics
MOXNES, E., Geography
NILSEN, A., Sociology
OPDAHL, A. L., Information Science
ØSTBYE, H., Media Studies
RISA, A. E., Economics
RONESS, P. G., Administration and Organization Theory
RUSTEN, G., Geography
SÆTREN, H., Administration and Organization Theory
STRAND, T., Administration and Organization Theory
SVÅSAND, L. G., Comparative Politics
STRAND, T., Administration and Organization Theory
TESSEM, B., Information Science
TJØTTA, S., Economics
TORSVIK, G., Economics
TVEDT, T., Geography
UHDE, A., Economics
ØYEN, E., Sociology

Bergen Museum (tel. 55-58-93-60; fax 55-58-93-64; e-mail publikum@bm.uib.no; internet www.uib.no/bergenmuseum):

ACHEN, H. VON, Art History
BERG, C. C., Botany
FOSSEN, H., Geology
INDRELID, S., Archaeology
JØRGENSEN, P. O., Botany
MOE, D., Botany
ØVSTEDAL, D. O., Botany
SÆTHER, O. A., Zoology
TØNSBERG, T., Botany
WILLASSEN, E., Zoology

UNIVERSITETET I OSLO
(University of Oslo)

POB 1072, Blindern, 0316 Oslo
Telephone: 22-85-50-50
Fax: 22-85-44-42
E-mail: informasjon@uio.no
Internet: www.uio.no
Founded 1811
State control
Academic year: August to June (two semesters)
Rector: Prof. OLE-PETTER OTTERSEN
Pro-Rector: Dr INGA BOSTAD
Dir: Dr GUNN-ELIN AA. BJØRNEBOE
Vice-Rectors: Prof. RAGNHILD HENNUM, Prof. DORIS JORDE
Library Dir: BENTE R. ANDREASSEN
Library: see under Libraries and Archives
Number of teachers: 2,400
Number of students: 27,700

Publications: *Apollon* (4 a year, in Norwegian; 1 a year, in English), *Uniforum* (16 a year)

DEANS

Faculty of Dentistry: Prof. PÅL BRODIN
Faculty of Education: Prof. VIBEKE GRØVER AUKRUST
Faculty of Humanities: Prof. TRINE SYVERTSEN
Faculty of Law: Prof. HANS PETTER GRAVER
Faculty of Mathematics and Natural Sciences: Prof. KNUT FÆGRI
Faculty of Medicine: Prof. FINN G. B. WISLØFF
Faculty of Social Sciences: Prof. KNUT HEIDAR
Faculty of Theology: Prof. TRYGVE E. WYLLER

PROFESSORS

Faculty of Dentistry (POB 1142 Blindern, 0317 Oslo

Geitmyrsvn. 69-71, 0455 Oslo; tel. 22-85-20-00; fax 22-85-23-32; e-mail infoskranke@odont.uio.no):

BARKVOLL, P., Dental Surgery
BJØRNLAND, T., Oral Surgery and Medicine
BRODIN, P., Physiology
BRYNE, M., Oral Biology
DEMBIK, Z., Dentistry
ELLINGSEN, J. E., Prosthetic Dentistry
ERIKSEN, H. M., Cariology
ESPELAND, L. V., Dentistry
ESPELID, L., Dentistry
GRYTTEN, J. I., Community Dentistry, Health Economics
HALTENSEN, T. S., Oral Biology
HANSEN, B., Periodontology
HOLST, D. J., Social Dentistry
HAANÆS, H. R., Dental Surgery
HAAPASALO, M., Endodontics
JACOBSEN, I., Pedodontics
JOKSTAD, A., Dentistry
KLINGE, R. F., General and Oral Anatomy
KOPPANG, H. S., General and Oral Pathology
KOPPANG, R., Material Sciences
LARHEIM, T. A., Dentistry
LYNGSTADAAS, S. P., Dentistry
ØGAARD, B., Orthodontics
OLSEN, I., Microbiology
OSMUNDSEN, H., Biochemistry
PREUS, H. R., Periodontology
RISNES, S., General and Oral Anatomy
RYKKE, M., Dentistry
RØED, A., Physiology
SCHEIE, A. AA, Microbiology
SCHENCK, K., Immunology
SKOGLUND, L. A., Dental Pharmacology
SOLHEIM, T., Oral Pathology
STENVIK, A., Orthodontics
THRANE, P. S., Oral Pathology
TRONSTAD, L., Endodontics
TVEIT, A. B., Dentistry
VASSEND, O., Behavioural Science
WÅLER, S. M., Dentistry

Faculty of Education (Helga Engs hus, Sem Sælands vei 7, POB 1161 Blindern, 0318 Oslo; tel. 22-85-82-76; fax 22-85-82-41; e-mail postmottak@uv.uio.no):

BEFRING, E., Special Education
BIRKEMO, A., Pedagogy
BRÅTEN, I., Pedagogy
BROCK-UTNE, B., Pedagogy
DALE, E. L., Pedagogy
DALEN, M., Special Education
ENGELSEN, B. U., General Didactics
GJESME, T., Pedagogy
GJONE, G., Teacher Education and School Development
HAGTVET, B. E., Education, Dyslexia
HANDAL, G., Pedagogy
HAUGE, T. E., Pedagogy
HERTZBERG, F., Teacher Education
JENSEN, R., Pedagogy
JORDE, D., Teacher Education
JORDELL, K. Ø., Pedagogy
LAHN, L. C., Pedagogy
LIE, S., Pedagogy
LIEBERG, S., Pedagogy
LUND, T., Special Education
LYCKE, K. H., Pedagogy
LØVLIE, L., Pedagogy
MARTINSEN, H., Psychology
NIELSEN, H. B., Pedagogy
OSTAD, S., Pedagogy
ØSTERUD, S., Pedagogy
ØZERK, K., Pedagogy
RUDBERG, M., Pedagogy
RYE, H., Special Education
SIMENSEN, A. M., Teacher Education
SJØBERG, S., Pedagogy (Natural Science)
SKOGEN, K., Special Education
STAFSENG, O., Pedagogy
TELLEVIK, J. M., Special Education
TJELDVOLL, A., Pedagogy
TVEIT, K., Pedagogy

ULVUND, S. E., Pedagogy
VONEN, A. M., Pedagogy, Linguistics
WIGGEN, G., Pedagogy

Faculty of Humanities (Administrasjonsbygn., 8 et., POB 1079 Blindern, 0316 Oslo; tel. 22-85-62-93; fax 22-85-45-50):

AKSNES, H., Musical Theory
ALLERN, S., Media and Communication Research
AMUNDSEN, A. B., Folklore
ANDERSEN, Ø., Classical Philology (Greek)
ANDERSEN, P. T., Nordic Literature
ASHEIM, O., Philosophy
ASKEDAL, J. O., German Language
ASZTALOS, M. M., Classical Philology (Latin)
AUESTAD, R. A., Japanese Language
AÚKRÚST, K. H., History of Religions
BACHE-WIIG, H., Nordic Literature
BAUNE, Ø., Philosophy
BENSKIN, M., English Language
BERGE, K. L., Nordic Language
BJERKE, Ø. L. S., Fine Art History
BJØRDAL, F., Philosophy
BJØRGUM, J., History
BJØRKVOLD, J. R., Musicology
BJØRNFLATEN, J. J., Slavonic Languages
BJORVAND, H., German Linguistics
BLIKSRUD, L., Nordic Literature
BØ, G., Norwegian Literature
BØ-RYGG, A., General Aesthetics
BRAAVIG, J., History of Religion
BRANDT, J. R., Classical Archaeology
BRENDEMOEN, B., Turkish Language
BRULAND, K., History
BRYNHILDSVOLL, K., Research on Ibsen
COLLETT, F. P., History
DAHL, H. F., Media and Communication Research
DIMAS, P., Philosophy
EDZARD, L. E., Hebrew and Semitic Languages
EGGE, Å., History
EIFRING, H., Modern Chinese Languages
ELSNESS, J., English Language
EMILSSON, E. K., Ancient Philosophy
ENGER, H.-O., Scandinavian Languages and Linguistics
ERIKSEN, A., Folklore
ERIKSEN, T. B., History of Ideas
FAARLUND, J. T., Nordic Language and Literature
FARNER, G., Dutch
FEHR, D., Literature
FJELD, R. E. V., Lexicography
FØRLAND, T. E., History
FREIIN VON VILLIEZ, C., Philosophy
FRELLESVIG, B., Japanese Language and Culture
FRICKE, C., Philosophy
FRIEDMAN, R. M., History
FUGLESTAD, F., History
GAMMELGAARD, K., Central and Eastern European Languages
GJELSVIK, O., Philosophy
GLAMBEK, I., Art History
GODØY, R. I., Musical Theory
GULDBRANDSEN, E. E., Music History
GUNDERSEN, K., French Literature
GUSTAVSSON, A., Ethnology
GUTH, S., Arabic and Middle Eastern Studies
HAARBERG, F., Nordic Literature
HAGEMANN, G., History
HANSEN, C. F., German Language
HANSEN, J. E. E., History of Ideas
HARBSMEIER, C. H., East Asian Languages
HAREIDE, J., Nordic Literature
HAREIDE, S., Philosophy
HASSELGÅRD, H., English Language
HAWKINS, S., Music
HEDEAGER, L., Nordic Archaeology
HELLAND, H. P., French
HEYERDAHL, G. B., History of Ideas
HJELDE, S., History of Religions

HOBÆK HAFF, M., French Language
HODNE, B., Folklore
HOEL, K., Fine Art History
IMENES, O., Philosophy
IVERSEN, I., General Literary Science
JERVELL, H. R., Computer Science
JOHANNESSEN, F. E., History
JOHANNESSEN, J. B., Linguistics
JOHANSEN, K. E., Philosophy
JOHANSSON, A., Modern Economic History
JØRGENSEN, J. G., Nordic Literature
KAARE, B. H., Folklore
KELLER, J. C., Nordic Archaeology
KJELDSTADLI, K., Modern History
KJETSAA, G., Russian Literature
KOLSTØ, P., Russian and East European Studies
KRISTOFFERSEN, K. E., Linguistics, Philology
KROGH, T., History of Ideas
KROGSETH, O., History of Christianity
KVÆRNE, P., History of Religions
KVIFTE, T., Folk Music
LANGE, E., History
LANGHOLM, T., Computer Science
LANZA, E., Linguistics
LAÚK, E., Media and Communication
LIE, S., Norwegian Language
LIEPE, L., Art History
LØDRUP, H., Linguistics
LØNNING, J. T., Computer Science
LOTHE, J., British Literature
LYCHE, C., French, Phonetics
MELBERG, B. A. E., Literature
MOEN, I., Linguistics
MØNNESLAND, S., Slavonic Languages
MORGAN, N., Fine Art History
MYHRE, J., History
NAGUIB, S. N., Cultural History, Cultural Analysis
NEDKVITNE, A., History
NYGAARD, J., Theatre Science
OTTOSSON, K., Icelandic
PEDERSEN, A., Philosophy
PETTERSON, E. R., Fine Art History
PHARO, H., History
PRELL, H.-P., German Language
PRICE, P. G., History
QUILLER, B., History of Ideas
RAMBERG, B., Philosophy
RAND, K. A., English Language
RASMUSSEN, T., Media and Communication
REINTON, R., Literary Theory
REM, T., English Literature
RIAN, Ø., History
RINDAL, M., Nordic Onomastics
ROGAN, B., Ethnology
RØNNING, H., Media and Communication Research
RUUD, E., Musicology
SÆBØ, K. J., German Language
SAGMO, I., German Literature
SALBERG, T. K., French
SANDE, S., Classical Archaeology
SAÚGSTAD, F., Philosophy
SCHAANNING, E., History of Ideas
SCHMIDT, T., Nordic Literature
SERCK-HANSSEN, C., Philosophy
SIMONSEN, H. G., Linguistics
SIRGES, T., German Language
SKATTURN, I., Francophone Studies
SKAUG, E., Art Conservation
SKEI, H. H., Literary Theory
SKOGERBØ, E., Media and Communication Research
SKRE, D., Archaeology
SLETSJØE, A., Portuguese Language
SØRENSEN, Ø., Modern History
STEINFELD, T., Nordic Language and Literature
STEINSLAND, G. S., History of Religions
STENE-JOHANSEN, K., Literary Theory
STENGAARD, B., Ibero-Romance Philology
STENSVOLD, A., History of Religions
SYVERTSEN, T., Media and Communication
TEEUWEN, M. J., Japanese

THEIL, R., English Literature
THORSEN, L. E., Ethnology
TORP, A., Nordic Languages
URSTAD, T. S., British Literature
VETLESEN, A. J., Philosophy
VIKØR, L. S., Nordic Linguistics
VOLLSNES, A., Music
WALDAHL, R., Media and Communication Research
WERENSKIOLD, M., Fine Art History
WICHSTRØM, A., Fine Art History
WIKSHÅLAND, S., Musicology
WORREN, D., Nordic Linguistics
YSTAD, V., Nordic Literature
YTREBERG, E., Media and Communication
ZOLLER, C. P., South Asian Studies
ZWARTJES, O., Spanish Language

Faculty of Law (POB 6706 St Olavs plass 5, 0130 Oslo)
Karl Johans gt. 47, 0162 Oslo; tel. 22-85-93-00; fax 22-85-01-80; e-mail postmottak@jus.uio.no; internet www.jus.uio.no):

ANDENÆS, K., Sociology of Law
ANDENÆS, M., European Law
ANDREASSEN, B., Human Rights and Governance
ARNESEN, F., European Law
BAILLIET, C. M., International Law
BING, J., Law
BOE, E., Law
BUGGE, H. CHR., Law
BULL, H. J., Law
BULL, K. S., Law
CORDERO-MOSS, G., International Law
EIDE, E., Economics and Statistics
ENG, S., Law
ERICSSON, K., Criminology
ESKELAND, S., Criminal Law
EVJU, S., Civil Law
FAUCHALD, O. K., International Law
FINSTAD, L., Criminology
FØLLESDAL, A., Human Rights Law
GIERTSEN, H., Criminology
GJEMS-ONSTAD, O., Tax Law
GRAVER, H. P., Sociology of Law
HAGSTRØM, V., Civil Law
HELLUM, A., Women's Law
HJELMENG, E. J., Tort Law
HØIGÅRD, I. C., Criminology
HOV, J., Civil Law
JOHANSEN, P. O., Criminology
JOHNSEN, J. T., Law
KAASEN, K., Law
KJØNSTAD, A., Law
LARSEN, A., Criminology
LILLEHOLT, K., Civil Law
MESTAD, O., European Law
MICHALSEN, D., Law History
PRIEUR, A. I., Criminology
ROBBERSTAD, A., European Law
ROGNSTAD, O.-A., Private Law
RØSÆG, E., Transportation Law
SAND, I. J., Public Law
SANDBERG, K., Children's and Women's Law
SCHARTUM, D. W., Administrative Informatics
SEJERSTED, F., European Law
SIMONSEN, L., Private Law
SMITH, E., Constitutional Law
STENVIK, A., Private Law
STRIDBECK, U., Criminology
SVERDRUP, T., Family Law
TORVUND, O., Private Law
TRONVOLL, K., Law
ULFBECK, V., Law
ULFSTEIN, G., International Law
WILHELMSEN, T. L., Insurance Law
WOXHOLTH, G., Civil Law
ZIMMER, F., Tax Law

Faculty of Mathematics and Natural Sciences (Fysikkbygn., POB 1032 Blindern, 0315 Oslo; tel. 22-85-52-00; fax 22-85-43-67; e-mail postmottak@matnat.uio.no; internet www.matnat.uio.no):

AAGAARD, P., Geology
AALEN, R., Biology
AARNES, H., Biology
AASEN, A. J., Pharmacy
AASHAMAR, K., Physics
AKSNES, K., Astrophysics
ALBREGTSEN, F., Computer Science
ALVE, E., Geology
ANDERSEN, T. B., Geology
ANDERSSON, K. K., Biochemistry
ANDRESEN, A., Geology
AUSTRHEIM, H., Geology
BAKKE, O., Biology
BEDOS, E. CHR., Mathematics
BENNECHE, T., Chemistry
BERG, T., Cell Biology
BERG, Y., Informatics
BERTELSEN, A., Mechanics
BEUTH, F. E., Mathematics
BJØRLYKKE, K. O., Geology
BØLVIKEN, E., Statistics
BORGAN, Ø., Statistics
BRATTELI, O., Mathematics
BRAVINA, L., Physics
BRODERSEN, H., Mathematics
BUGGE, L., Physics
BURAN, T., Physics
BYE, R., Chemistry
CARLSSON, M., Astrophysics
CHRISTOPHERSEN, N., Informatics
CORFU, F., Geology
DÆHLEN, M., Mathematical Modelling
DAHL, G., Informatics
DAHLBACK, A., Physics
DALE, B., Geology
DØVING, K., Zoophysiology
EEG, J. O., Physics
ELIASSEN, F., Computer Science
ELLINGSRUD, G., Mathematics
ELVERHØI, A., Quaternary Geology
ENGVOLD, O., Astrophysics
ESKILD, W., Biochemistry
FÆGRI, K., Chemistry
FALEIDE, J. I., Geology
FEDER, J. G., Physics
FINSTAD, T., Physics
FJELLVÅG, H., Chemistry
FLEKKØY, E. G., Physics
FLOATER, M. S., Informatics
FURUSETH, S., Chemistry
GABRIELSEN, O. S., Biochemistry
GALPERINE, I., Physics
GELIUS, L.-J., Geophysics
GJESSING, S., Computer Science
GJEVIK, B., Hydrodynamics
GOEBEL, V. H., Informatics
GØRBITZ, C. H., Chemistry
GOTTSCHALK, L., Geophysics
GRAY, J. S., Marine Zoology
GREIBROKK, T., Analytical Chemistry
GRUE, J., Mechanics
GUNDERSEN, G., Chemistry
GUNDERSEN, K., Biology (Physiology)
GUNDERSEN, L.-L., Chemistry
GUTTORMSEN, M., Physics
HAALAND, A., Chemistry
HAGELBERG, E., Zoology
HAGEN, J. O. M., Geography
HANSEN, E. W., Chemistry
HANSEN, F. K., Chemistry
HANSETH, O., Informatics
HANSTEEN, V., Astrophysics
HELGAKER, T., Chemistry
HELLAND, I., Statistics
HELLESLAND, J., Mechanics
HESSEN, D., Zoology
HESTMARK, G., Biology
HJORT, N. L., Statistics
HJORTH-JENSEN, M., Nuclear Physics
HØEG, K., Geology
HOFF, P., Chemistry
HØGÅSEN, H., Theoretical Physics
HØILAND, K., Biology
HOLE, E. O., Physics
HOLM, P., Mathematics
HOLM, S., Signal Processing

HOLTET, J. A., Physics
HUMLUM, O., Geography
INGEBRETSEN, F., Physics
ISAKSEN, I., Meteorology
IVERSEN, T., Geophysics
JAHREN, B., Mathematics
JAKOBSEN, K. S., Biology
JAMTVEIT, B., Geology
JOHANSEN, H. T., Pharmacy
JOHANSEN, T. H., Physics
JØRGENSEN, M., Informatics
KAARTVEDT, S., Marine Biology
KAASBØLL, F. F., Informatics
KAREN, P., Chemistry
KARLSEN, J., Pharmacy
KJELDSETH-MOE, O., Astrophysics
KLAVENESS, D., Biology
KLAVENESS, J., Pharmacy
KOLSTØ, A. B., Microbiology
KOOMEY, J. M., Pharmacology
KRISTENSEN, T. A., Biochemistry
KRISTJANSSON, F. E., Geophysics
KROGDAHL, S., Computer Science
LAANE, C. M., Botany
LAMBERTSSON, A., Genetics
LAMPE, H. M., Biology
LANDE, T. S., Computer Science
LANGTANGEN, H. P., Informatics
LEER, E., Astrophysics
LEINAAS, H. P., Zoology
LEINAAS, J. M., Physics
LIESTØL, K., Mathematical Modelling
LILJE, P. V., Astrophysics
LILLERUD, K. P., Chemistry
LINDQVIST, B. H., Zoology
LINDSTRØM, T., Mathematics
LØVHØIDEN, G., Physics
LØW, E., Mathematics
LUND, W., Chemistry
LUNDANES, E., Chemistry
LUTKEN, C. A., Physics
LYCHE, T. J. W., Mathematical Modelling
LYSNE, O., Communication Systems
MÅLØY, K. J., Physics
MALTERUD, K. E., Pharmacognosy
MARTINSEN, Ø. G., Physics
MAUPIN, V., Geophysics
MOEN, J. I., Physics
MØLLENDAL, H., Chemistry
MØLLER-PEDERSEN, B., Informatics
MØRKEN, K., Numerical Analysis
MYHRE, A. M., Geology
NAGY, J., Geology
NATVIG, B., Mathematical Statistics
NEUMANN, E. R., Geology
NIELSEN, C. J., Chemistry
NILSSON, G. E., Biology (Physiology)
NISSEN-MEYER, J., Biochemistry
NORBY, P. Æ., Chemistry
NORBY, T. E., Chemistry
NORDAL, I., Botany
NORMANN, D., Mathematical Logic
NYSTRØM, B., Organic Chemistry
ØKSENDAL, B., Mathematics
OLSBYE, U., Chemistry
OLSEN, A., Physics
OMTVEDT, F. P., Chemistry
OSNES, E., Physics
OWE, O., Computer Science
PAULSEN, B. S., Pharmacognosy
PAULSEN, R. E., Pharmacy (Microbiology)
PECSELI, H., Physics
PEDERSEN, G. K., Mathematics
PEDERSEN-BJERGAARD, S., Pharmacy
PETTERSEN, E. O., Physics
PIENE, R., Mathematics
PLAGEMANN, T. P., Informatics
PODLADTCHIKOV, Y., Geology
PRYDZ, K., Biochemistry
RANESTAD, K., Mathematics
RASMUSSEN, K. E., Pharmaceutical Analysis
RAVNDAL, F., Theoretical Physics
READ, A. L., Physics
REKSTAD, J. B., Physics
RISE, F., Chemistry

RISEBRO, N. H., Mathematics
ROGNES, J., Mathematics
ROOS, N., Cell Biology
ROOTS, J., Chemistry
RUENESS, J., Marine Biology
RUSTAN, A., Pharmacy
SAATCIOGLU, F., Biology
SÆTRE, G.-P., Biology
SAGSTUEN, E., Physics
SAHAY, S., Informatics
SAMDAL, S., Chemistry
SAND, O., Zoophysiology
SANDE, S. A., Pharmacy
SANDHOLT, P. E., Physics
SANDLIE, I., Biology
SCHUMACHER, T., Botany
SEIP, H. M., Chemistry
SIREVÅG, R., Microbiology
SJØBERG, D., Informatics
SKAALI, T. B., Physics
SKRAMSTAD, J., Chemistry
SLAGSVOLD, T., Zoology
SMISTAD, G., Pharmacy
SØRÅSEN, O., Microelectronics
SPILLING, P., Telematics and Telecommunications
STABELL, B., Geology
STABELL, R., Astrophysics
STAPNES, S., Physics
STEEN, H., Biology
STENERSEN, J. H. V., Biology
STENSETH, N. C., Zoology
STØLEN, S., Chemistry
STORDAL, F., Meteorology
STØRMER, E., Mathematics
SUDBØ, AA., Optoelectronics
SVENSSON, B. G., Physics
SWENSEN, A. R., Mathematics (Statistics)
TAFTØ, J., Physics
THRONDSEN, J., Marine Biology
TILSET, M., Chemistry
TOMTER, P., Mathematics
TØNNESEN, H. H., Clinical Pharmacy
TOVERUD, E., Pharmacy
TRULSEN, J., Astrophysics
TVEITO, A., Informatics
TVETER, T. S., Physics
UGGERUD, E., Chemistry
VESETH, L., Physics
VØLLESTAD, A. L., Biology (Zoology)
WEBER, J. E., Geophysics
WINTHER, R., Mathematical Modelling

Faculty of Medicine (POB 1018 Blindern, 0315 Oslo
Domus Medica, Sognsvannsvn.9, Oslo; tel. 22-85-05-00; fax 22-85-05-01; e-mail delarkiv-sekretariatet@medisin.uio.no; internet www.med.uio.no):

AALEN, O. O., Statistics
AASEN, A., Surgery
AGARTZ, I., Psychiatry
AURSNES, I. A., Pharmacology
BENESTAD, H. B., Physiology
BERG, O. T., Health Administration
BERG, T., Physiology
BJERTNESS, E., Epidemiology
BJUNE, G. A., International Health
BJÅLIE, E. G., Anatomy
BLOMHOFF, H. K., Medical Biochemistry
BLOMHOFF, R., Nutrition Research
BOE, J., Respiratory Medicine
BOGEN, B., Immunology
BOTTEN, G. S., Health Administration
BRANTZAEG, P., Immunology
BREIVIK, H., Anaesthesiology
BRODAL, P., Anatomy
BROSSTAD, F. R., Internal Medicine Research
BRUUSGAARD, D., Social Security Medicine
BUKHOLM, G., Bacteriology
CARLSEN, K.-H., Paediatrics
CHRISTOFFERSEN, T., Pharmacology
CLAUSEN, O. P. F., Pathology
COLLAS, P., Biochemistry
COLLINS, A. R., Nutrition Research

DANBOLT, N. C., Physiology
DREVON, C., Nutrition Research
DUTTAVOY, A. K., Nutrition Research
EVENSEN, S. A., Haematology
FINSET, A., Medical Behavioural Research
FOSSUM, S., Anatomy
FRIGESSI, A., Medical Statistics
FRØLAND, S. S., Clinical Medicine
FUGELLI, P., Social Medicine
FYRAND, O. L., Dermatology
GEIRAN, O., Cardiovascular Surgery
GIESDAL, K., Cardiology
GLOVER, J., Physiology
GORDELADZE, J. O., Medical Biochemistry
GRØHOLT, B., Psychiatry
GRØTTUM, P., Medical Computer Science
HAGEN, T. P., Health Administration
HANSSON, V., Medical Biochemistry
HAUG, F. M., Anatomy
HEGGELUND, P., Neurophysiology
HEIBERG, A. N., Psychiatry
HJORTDAHL, P., Medicine
HØGLEND, P. A., Psychiatry
HOLCK, P., Anatomy
HORN, R., Medical Biochemistry
HØSTMARK, T. A., Preventive Medicine
HUITFELDT, H., Pathology
HUSBY, G., Rheumatology
ILEBEKK, A. B., Experimental Medicine
INGSTAD, B., Social Medicine
IVERSEN, I. G. H., Physiology
IVERSEN, P. O., Nutrition Research
IVERSEN, T., Health Economics
JAHNSEN, T., Biochemistry
JELLUM, E., Clinical Biochemistry
KASE, B. F., Paediatrics
KIERULF, P., Clinical Chemistry
KIRKEVOLD, M., Medicine
KJEKSHUS, J., Cardiology
KLEPP, K. I., Nutrition Research
KOLBENSTVEDT, A. N., Radiology
KOLSET, S. O., Nutrition Research
KVITTINGEN, E. A., Clinical Biochemistry
LAAKE, P., Medical Statistics
LÆRUM, F., Clinical Medicine
LARSEN, Ø., Medical History
LEVY, F. O., Pharmacology
LIE, S. O., Paediatrics
LINDEGAARD, K., Neurosurgery
LOGE, F. H., Medical Behavioural Research
LORENSEN, M., Nursing Science
LØVSTAD, R., Medical Biochemistry
MADSHUS, I. H., Molecular Biology
MENGSHOEL, A. M., Health Science
MEYER, H. E., Social Medicine
MOUM, T., Medical Behavioural Research
MULLER, F., Pharmacology
NAFSTAD, P., Social Medicine
NATVIG, J. B., Immunology
NICOLAYSEN, G., Physiology
NJÅ, A., Neurophysiology
NYBERG-HANSEN, R., Neurology
NÆSS, O., Pathology
ORMSTAD, K., Forensic Medicine
OS, I., Pharmacology
OSNES, J. B., Pharmacology
ØSTVOLD, A. C., Neurochemistry
OTTERSEN, O. P., Anatomy
PEDERSEN, J. I., Nutrition Research
REIBERÅS, O., Orthopaedics
REIKVAM, Å., Pharmacotherapy
REINHOLT, F. P., Pathology
RINVIK, E., Anatomy
ROGDE, S., Forensic Medicine
ROGNUM, T. O., Forensic Medicine
ROLLAG, H., Bacteriology
ROLSTAD, B., Anatomy
SAGVOLDEN, T., Neurophysiology
SANDANGER, B., Medical Behavioural Research
SANDNES, D. L., Pharmacology
SAUGSTAD, O. D., Paediatrics
SEJERSTED, O. M., Experimental Research
SKOMEDAL, T., Pharmacology
SOLBAKK, J. H., Medical Ethics

SOLLID, L. M., Transplantation Immunology
STEEN, P. A., Anaesthesiology
STOKKE, O., Clinical Biochemistry
STORM, J., Physiology
STORM-MATHISEN, J., Anatomy
STRAAND, F., Social Medicine
STRAY-PEDERSEN, B., Obstetrics and Gynaecology
SØRENSEN, T., Psychiatry
TASKÉN, K., Medical Biochemistry
TELLNES, G., Social Security Medicine
TØNJUM, T., Microbiology
UNDLIEN, D. E., Medical Genetics
URSIN, G., Nutrition Research
VAAGE, I. F., Traumatology
VAGLUM, P., Psychiatry
VATN, M. H., Clinical Epidemiology
VØLLESTAD, N. K., Health Science
WAAL, H., Psychiatry
WALAAS, S. I., Biochemistry
WALLØE, L., Physiology
WANDEL, M., Nutrition Research

Faculty of Social Sciences (Eilert Sundts hus, 3. et., POB 1084 Blindern, 0317 Oslo; tel. 22-85-62-64; fax 22-85-48-25; e-mail sv-info@sv .uio.no; internet www.sv.uio.no):

ALBUM, D., Sociology
ANDRESEN, S. E., Political Science
ARCHETTI, E. P., Social Anthropology
ASHEIM, G. B., Economics
BALDERSHEIM, H., Political Science
BERKAAK, O. A., Social Anthropology
BIRKELUND, G. E., Sociology
BIØRN, E., Economics
BJERKHOLT, O., Economics
BJØRKLÚND, R., Psychology
BJØRKLÚND, T., Political Science
BLAKAR, R. M., Social Psychology
BORGE, A. I. H., Psychology
BREKKE, K. A., Economics
BRENNEN, T., Psychology
BROCH, H. B., Social Anthropology
BROCHMANN, G., Sociology
CHECKEL, F. T., Political Science
CHRISTENSEN, T., Political Science
CHRISTIANSEN, V., Economics
DUCKERT, J., Psychology
EGEBERG, M., Political Science
ENGELSTAD, F., Sociology
ERIKSEN, G. T. H., Social Anthropology
FEHR, N. H., Economics
FJELL, A., Psychology
FØRSUND, F., Economics
FRØNES, I., Sociology
FURST, E. L., Social Anthropology
GULLESTAD, S. E., Psychology
HAAVIND, H., Psychology
HAGTVET, B., Political Science
HAGTVET, K. A., Psychology
HANSEN, M. N., Sociology
HANSEN, T., Political Science
HARTMANN, E. F., Psychology
HEIDAR, K., Political Science
HELLEVIK, O., Political Science
HESSELBERG, J., Social Geography
HOEL, M. O., Economics
HOLDEN, S., Economics
HOVI, J., Political Science
HOWELL, S. L., Social Anthropology
HVEEM, H., Political Science
HYLLAND, AA., Economics
KALLAND, A., Social Anthropology
KALLENBERG, R., Sociology
KEILMAN, N. W., Demography
KIRKEBØEN, G., Psychology
KNUTSEN, O., Political Science
KRAVDAL, Ø., Demographics
KROGSTAD, A., Sociology
LANDRØ, N. I., Psychology
LEIRA, A., Sociology
LUND, D., Economics
LUND, S. E., Social Anthropology
MAGNUSSEN, S. J., Psychology
MALNES, R. S., Political Science

MASTEKAASA, A., Sociology
MATLARY, F. H., Political Science
MEHLUM, H., Economics
MELHUS, M., Social Anthropology
MJØSET, L., Sociology
MOENE, K. O., Economics and Statistics
MONSEN, J., Psychology
MYDSKE, P. K., Political Science
NARUD, H. M., Political Science
NIELSEN, T. H., Social Sciences and Humanities
NILSSEN, T., Economics
NORDBY, T., Political History
NYBORG, K., Economics
NYMOEN, R., Economics
OMMUNDSEN, R., Psychology
ØSTERUD, Ø., Conflict and Peace Research
OTNES, P., Sociology
PEDERSEN, W., Social Geography
PONS, F., Psychology
RASCH, B. E., Political Science
REINVANG, I., Psychology
RØDSETH, A., Economics
RØNNESTAD, H., Psychology
ROSE, L. E., Political Science
RØYSAMB, E., Psychology
SCHWEDER, T., Statistics
SKJEIE, H., Political Science
SKOE, E. E. A., Psychology
SKOG, O., Sociology
STEEN, A., Political Science
STOKKE, K., Social Geography
STORESLETTEN, K., Economics
STRAND, J., Economics
SUNDET, J. M., Psychology
SUNDET, K. S., Psychology
SYDSÆTER, K., Mathematics
SØRENSEN, T., Sociology
SØRUM, A., Social Anthropology
TALLE, A., Social Anthropology
TEIGEN, K. H., Psychology
TETZCHNER, S. V., Psychology
TJERSLAND, O. A., Psychology
TORGERSEN, S. O., Psychology
TØRNQUIST, O., Political Science
ULLTVEIT-MOE, K. H., Economics
UNDERDAL, A., Political Science
VASSEND, O., Psychology
VISLIE, J., Economics
VOLLRATH, M., Psychology
WALHOVD, K., Psychology
WESSEL, T., Social Geography
WIDERBERG, K., Sociology
WIKAN, U., Social Anthropology
WILLASSEN, Y., Economics
WOLD, A. H., Psychology

Faculty of Theology (POB 1023 Blindern, 0315 Oslo
Domus Theologica, Blindernvn. 9, 0371 Oslo; tel. 22-85-03-00; fax 22-85-03-01; e-mail postmottak@teologi.uio.no; internet www.tf .uio.no):

CHRISTOFFERSEN, S. A., Systematic Theology
DOKKA, T. S., New Testament and Systematic Theology
ELSTAD, H., Church History and Religious Sociology
FRØYSHOV, S. R., Liturgy and Ancient Christianity
HAFSTAD, K., Systematic Theology
KVANVIG, H. S., Old Testament
LEIRVIK, O. B., Inter-Religious Studies
MOXNES, H., New Testament
NODERVAL, Ø., Ancient Christianity
RASMUSSEN, T., History of the Church
RUYTER, K., Religious Ethics
SALOMONSEN, J., Religious Anthropology
STORDALEN, T., Old Testament
THORKILDSEN, D., Church History
TØNNESEN, A. V., Church History
WYLLER, T. E., Systematic Theology

Biotechnology Centre of Oslo (EMBIO) (POB 1125 Blindern, 0317 Oslo

Forskringsparken, Gaustadalleen 21, 0349 Oslo; tel. 22-84-05-00; fax 22-84-05-01; e-mail postmottak@biotek.uio.no; internet www .biotek.uio.no):

TASKÉN, K. (Dir)

Natural History Museum and Botanical Gardens (POB 1172 Blindern, 0318 Oslo
Sars' gt. 1, Monradgt., 0562 Oslo; tel. 22-85-16-30; fax 22-85-17-09; e-mail informasjon@ nhm.uio.no; internet www.nhm.uio.no):

ANDERSEN, K. I., Zoology
BACHMANN, L., Zoology
BAKKE, T. A., Zoology
BJORKLUND, K. R., Palaeontology
BORGEN, L., Botany
BROCHMANN, C., Botany
BRUTON, D. L., Palaeontology
ELVEN, R., Botany
GULDEN, G., Botany
HALVORSEN, O., Zoology
LIFJELD, J. T., Zoology
ØKLAND, R. H., Botany
SUNDING, P., Botany
VAN BERGEN, I. J., Mineralogy
WIIG, Ø., Zoology and Mammalogy

Kulturhistorisk Museum (POB 6762 St Olavs plass, 0130 Oslo; tel. 22-85-19-00; fax 22-85-19-38; e-mail postmottak@khm.uio.no; internet www.khm.uio.no):

CHRISTENSEN, A. E., Scandinavian Archaeology
KNIRK, J. E., Medieval History
MIKKELSEN, E., Nordic Archaeology
ØSTMO, E., Stone Age and Bronze Age
PLATHER, U., Art Conservation Chemistry
RESI, H. G., Iron Age
SVENSSON, T. G., Social Anthropology

UNIVERSITET I STAVANGER
(University of Stavanger)

4036 Stavanger
Arne Rettedal hus, Kjell Arholmsgt. 41, Stavanger
Telephone: 51-83-10-00
Fax: 51-83-30-50
E-mail: post@uis.no
Internet: www.uis.no
Founded 1994 as Høgskolen i Stavanger; univ. status acquired and present name adopted 2005
State control
Languages of instruction: Norwegian, English

Rector: ASLAUG MIKKELSEN
Vice-Rector: EGIL GABRIELSEN
University Dir: PER RAMVI
Strategy and Communication Dir: ANNE SELNES
Librarian: ESPEN SKJOLDAL

Number of teachers: 1,200
Number of students: 8,300
Library of 250,000 vols, 3,000 periodicals

DEANS

Faculty of Humanities: TOR HAUKEN
Faculty of Natural Science and Technology: ARNE BJØRKUM
Faculty of Social Sciences: MARIT BOYESEN

UNIVERSITETET I TROMSØ
(University of Tromsø)

9037 Tromsø
Telephone: 77-64-40-00
Fax: 77-64-49-00
E-mail: postmottak@uit.no
Internet: uit.no
Founded 1968, merged with Høgskolen i Tromsø (Tromsø Univ. College) 2009
State control
Academic year: August to June (2 semesters)
Rector: Prof. JARLE AARBAKKE

Pro-Rector for Education: Prof. BRITT VIGDIS EKELI

Pro-Rector for Research and Devt: CURT RICE

Univ. Dir: LASSE LØNNUM

Library Dir: HELGE SALVESEN

Number of teachers: 1,900

Number of students: 6,700

Publications: *Journal of Department of Community Medicine*, *Journal of Faculty of Law*, *Nordlit* (literature), *Ottar* (popular science), *Poljarnyj Vestnik* (Russian language and literature), *Ravnetrykk* (univ. library journal), *Speculum Boreale* (history), *Troll* (literature), *Uvett* (education)

DEANS

Faculty of the Arts: KJELL MAGNE MÆLEN

Faculty of Health Sciences: ARNFINN SUNDSF-JORD

Faculty of Humanities, Social Sciences and Education: PETTER NAFSTAD

Faculty of Law: HEGE BRÆKHUS

Faculty of Life Sciences, Fisheries and Economics: EDEL ELVEVOLL

Faculty of Science and Technology: MORTEN HALD

PROFESSORS

Faculty of the Arts (tel. 77-66-03-04; fax 77-61-88-99; e-mail postmottak@kunstfak.uit .no):

LUNDBERG, L., Creative Writing
SIEPEN, N., Contemporary Art
SONJASDOTTER, A., Contemporary Art

Faculty of Health Sciences (tel. 77-64-46-01; fax 77-64-53-00; e-mail postmottak@helsefak .uit.no):

ANDERSEN, T., Community Medicine
ARNESEN, E., Community Medicine
BJØRKLID, E., Medical Biology
BLIX, A. S., Medical Biology
BRANDL, M., Pharmacy
DAHL, S. G., Medical Biology
EL-GEWELY, M. R., Medical Biology
FOLKOW, L., Medical Biology
FØNNEBØ, V., Community Medicine
FØRDE, O. H., Community Medicine
GRAM, I. T., Community Medicine
GREINER-TOLLERSRUD, O. K., Medical Biology
HASVOLD, T., Community Medicine
HOLTEDAHL, K., Community Medicine
HUSEBEKK, A., Medical Biology
HUSEBY, N.-E., Medical Biology
HØYER, G., Community Medicine
JACOBSEN, B. K., Community Medicine
JENSEN, E., Pharmacy
JOHANSEN, S., Medical Biology
JOHANSEN, T., Medical Biology
LARSEN, T., Medical Biology
LOENNECHEN, T., Pharmacy
NIELSEN, K. M., Pharmacy
LUND, E., Community Medicine
MERCER, J., Medical Biology
MELBYE, H., Community Medicine
MJØS, O. D., Medical Biology
MOENS, U., Medical Biology
NIELSEN, K. M., Pharmacy
NJØLSTAD, I., Community Medicine
NORDØY, E., Medical Biology
OLSEN, J. A., Community Medicine
OLSVIK, Ø., Medical Biology
ØRBO, A., Medical Biology
REKVIG, O.-P., Medical Biology
RINNE, A., Medical Biology
SAGER, G., Medical Biology
SMEDSRØD, B., Medical Biology
STOKKAN, K.-A., Medical Biology
SUNDSFJORD, A., Medical Biology
SYLTE, I., Medical Biology
WILLASSEN, N. P., Medical Biology
WINBERG, J.-O., Medical Biology
YTREHUS, K., Medical Biology

Faculty of Humanities, Social Sciences and Education (tel. 77-64-43-00; e-mail postmottak@hsl.uit.no):

AARSÆTHER, N.
ANDERSSON, D. T.
ALHAUG, G.
BARSTAD, G.
BERTELSEN, R.
BLANKHOLM, P.
BOUVRIE, S. DES
BULL, T.
DAMM, C.
DRIVENES, E.-A.
EGEBERG, E. H.
ENGELSTAD, E.
GAASLAND, R.
HOFSTEN, H. W. VON
KARLSEN, O.
KONSTANTINOV, Y.
LIEPE, L.
LINDGREN, A.-R.
LUND, N. W.
LÖNNGREN, L.
MØRCK, E.
MYRSTAD, A.
NESSET, T.
OLSEN, B.
RAMCHAND, G.
RICE, C.
SCHMIDT, M.
STARKE, M.
SVENONIUS, P.
SVONNI, M.
SWAN, T.
TARALDSEN, K. T.
VALESTRAND, H.
WESTVIK, O. M. J.
WÆRP, H. H.

Faculty of Law (tel. 77-64-41-97; fax 77-64-47-75; e-mail postmottak@jus.uit.no):

CHRISTIANSEN, P.
HAUGLI, T.

Faculty of Life Sciences, Fisheries and Economics (tel. 77-64-60-00; e-mail eksped@nfh .uit.no):

AMUNDSEN, P.-A., Aquatic Biology
BØGWALD, J., Marine Biotechnology
CLARK, D., Economics and Management
EILERTSEN, H. C., Aquatic Biology
ELVEVOLL, E. O., Marine Biotechnology
FALK-PETERSEN, I. B., Aquatic Biology
FEVOLDEN, S.-E., Aquatic Biology
FLÅTEN, O., Economics and Management
GULLIKSEN, B., Aquatic Biology
HERSOUG, B., Economics and Management
HOLM, P., Economics and Management
JENTOFT, S., Economics and Management
JOBLING, M., Aquatic Biology
JOHNSEN, H. K., Aquatic Biology
JØRGENSEN, E., Aquatic Biology
JØRGENSEN, J. B., Marine Biotechnology
JØRGENSEN, T. ø., Marine Biotechnology
KLEMETSEN, J., Aquatic Biology
KRISTIANSEN, S., Aquatic Biology
OLAFSEN, J. A., Marine Biotechnology
OLSEN, K. K., Aquatic Biology
OLSEN, R. L., Marine Biotechnology
OLSEN, S. O., Economics and Management
ROBERTSON, B., Marine Biotechnology
SCHULZ, C.-E., Economics and Management
TANDE, K., Aquatic Biology
TRONDSEN, T., Social and Marketing Studies
VASSDAL, T., Economics and Management
WASSMANN, P., Aquatic Biology

Faculty of Science and Technology (tel. 77-64-40-01; fax 77-64-47-65; e-mail postmottak@nt.uit.no):

ANDERSEN, J., Biology
ANSHUS, O. J., Computer Science
ASLAKSEN, T., Physics
BERGH, S., Geology
BHUVANESWARI, T. V., Biology

CARLSON, R., Chemistry
DAHL, D., Chemistry
ELTOFT, T., Physics
ESSER, R., Physics
FLÅ, T., Mathematics and Statistics
FOLSTAD, I., Biology
GHOSH, A., Chemistry
GODTLIBSEN, F., Mathematics and Statistics
HALD, M., Geology
HANSEN, L. K., Chemistry
HANSSEN, A., Physics
HARTVIGSEN, G., Computer Science
HAVNES, O., Physics
HOUGH, E., Chemistry
IMS, R. A., Biology
JACOBSEN, S., Physics
JOHANSEN, D., Computer Science
JOHNSEN, B., Mathematics and Statistics
JUNTILLA, O., Biology
KRUGLIKOV, B., Mathematics and Statistics
LA HOZ, C., Physics
LYCHAGIN, V., Mathematics and Statistics
MELANDSØ, F., Physics
MIENERT, J., Geology
MJØLHUS, E., Mathematics and Statistics
OLSON, L., Mathematics and Statistics
PRASOLOV, A., Mathematics and Statistics
RAVNA, E. K., Geology
RUUD, K., Chemistry
RYPDAL, K., Physics
RØEGGEN, I., Physics
SMALÅS, A., Chemistry
SVENDSEN, J. S., Chemistry
SVENNING, M., Biology
VORREN, K.-D., Biology
VORREN, T., Geology
YOCCOZ, N., Biology

Colleges of University Standing

ARKITEKTHØGSKOLEN I OSLO
(Oslo School of Architecture)

POB 6768 St Olavs plass, 0130 Oslo
Maridalsveien 29, 0175 Oslo

Telephone: 22-99-70-00
Fax: 22-99-71-90
E-mail: postmottak@aho.no
Internet: www.aho.no

Founded 1945
State control
Academic year: September to June

Rector: KARL OTTO ELLEFSEN
Vice-Rector: BIRGER SEVALDSON
Dir: EINAR FAGERÅ
Library Dir: SISSEL MOUM

Library of 40,000 vols
Number of teachers: 120
Number of students: 700

Publication: *Research Magazine* (1 a year)

PROFESSORS

DAHL, K. E., Urbanism and Landscape
DAHLE, E., Architectural Design
DOBLOUG, M., Architectural Design
DUNIN-WOYSETH, H., Form, Theory and History
EDEHOLT, H., Design
FJELD, P. O., Architectural Design
GERSTLAUER, R., Architectural Design
HERMANSEN, C., Architectural Design
HJELTNES, K., Architectural Design
HØLMEBAKK, B., Form, Theory and History
HVATTUM, M., Form, Theory and History
JENSEN, J., Architectural Design
KLEVEN, B., Architectural Design
LØKSE, O., Form and Design
MICHL, J., Industrial Design
MORRISON, A., Design
ROBBINS, E., Urbanism and Landscape

SANDAKER, B., Building Technology
SEVALDSON, B., Design
SKJØNSBERG, T., Form and Design
THIIS-EVENSEN, T., Architectural Theory and History
TOSTRUP, E., Form, Theory and History
TVILDE, D., Urbanism and Landscape

BERGEN ARKITEKTHØGSKOLE
(Bergen School of Architecture)

POB 39, 5841 Bergen
Sandviksboder 59–61A, 5035 Bergen
Telephone: 55-36-38-80
Fax: 55-36-38-81
E-mail: adm@bas.org
Internet: www.bergenarkitektskole.no
Founded 1986, fully recognized 1990
Private control
Languages of instruction: English, Norwegian
Academic year: September to June

Deputy Rector: SIXTEN RAHLFF
Head of Student Affairs: SIV GJERDE AARDAL
Head of Library: LINE FRØYLAND

Library of 3,000 vols, 20 int. magazines, spec. focus on architecture, soc., art, landscape, architecture, history and bldgs in northern climate, bldg history of Norway's W coast, foreign culture and disaster risk migration
Number of teachers: 50 (incl. part-time)
Number of students: 150

HANDELSHØYSKOLEN BI
(BI Norwegian School of Management)

0442 Oslo
Nydalsveien 37, 0484 Oslo
Telephone: 46-41-00-00
Fax: 21-04-80-00
E-mail: info@bi.no
Internet: www.bi.no
Founded 1943
Private control
Languages of instruction: Norwegian, English
Academic year: September to June

Rector: TOM COLBJØRNSEN
Deputy-Rector: DAG MORTEN DALEN
Vice-Rector: ULF HENNING OLSSON
Exec. Dir: JENS PETTER TØNDEL
Library Dir: DAGMAR LANGEGGEN

Number of teachers: 370
Number of students: 19,931 (incl. part-time)

HØGSKOLEN I BODØ
(Bodø University College)

POB 1490, 8049 Bodø
Mørkvedtråkket 30, 8049 Bodø
Telephone: 75-51-72-00
Fax: 75-51-74-57
E-mail: postmottak@hibo.no
Internet: www.hibo.no
Founded 1994 by merger of 3 univ. colleges in Bodø
State control
Languages of instruction: English, Norwegian
Academic year: August to June

Rector: PÅL A. PEDERSEN
Dir: STIG FOSSUM
Registrar and Dir for Marketing and Communications: HEGE NERDAL RASCH
Exec. Librarian: GITTE KOLSTRUP

Number of teachers: 305
Number of students: 5,000

DEANS

Bodø Graduate School of Business: SVEN-ARE JENSSEN
Faculty of Biosciences and Aquaculture: REID HOLE

Faculty of Social Sciences: HANNE THOMMASEN
School of Professional Studies: ARNE FJALSTAD

HØGSKOLEN I NARVIK
(Narvik University College)

POB 385, 8505 Narvik
Lodve Langesgt. 2, Narvik
Alta campus: Follumsvei 33, 9510 Alta
Telephone: 76-96-60-00 (Narvik)
Fax: 76-96-68-10 (Narvik)
E-mail: postmottak@hin.no
Internet: www.hin.no
Founded 1955
Vice-Chancellor: ARNE ERIK HOLDØ
Admin. Dir: KNUT RAVLO (acting)
Library Dir: ELLEN JULIN
Library of 20,000 items
Number of teachers: 170
Number of students: 1,300

DEANS

Faculty of Health and Society: ÅSE BERIT VRENNE
Faculty of Technology: ARNE LAKSÅ

NORGES HANDELSHØYSKOLE
(Norwegian School of Economics and Business Administration)

Helleveien 30, 5045 Bergen
Telephone: 55-95-90-00
Fax: 55-95-91-00
E-mail: nhh.postmottak@nhh.no
Internet: www.nhh.no
Founded 1936
State control
Academic year: September to June

Rector: JAN I. HAALAND
Vice-Rector: GUNNAR E. CHRISTENSEN
Dir: OLE HOPE
Library Dir: SISSEL HAFSTAD
Library of 280,000 vols, 1,600 periodicals
Number of teachers: 210
Number of students: 3,000

DEANS

Faculty of Accounting, Auditing and Law: KATARINA ÖSTERGREN
Faculty of Economics: ØYSTEIN THØGERSEN
Faculty of Finance and Management Science: FRODE SÆTTEM
Faculty of Professional and Intercultural Communication: SUNNIVA WHITTAKER
Faculty of Strategy and Management: TOR FREDRIKSEN

PROFESSORS

Faculty of Accounting, Auditing and Law:
BJØRNENAK, T., Management Accounting
EILIFSEN, A., Financial Accounting and Auditing
GJESDAL, F., Management and Financial Accounting
JOHNSEN, A., N., Financial Accounting
MONSEN, N., Governmental Accounting
ÖSTERGREN, K., Cost Accounting and Project Management
STUART, I., Auditing
Faculty of Economics:
BASBERG, B., Economic History
BIVAND, R., Economic and Quantitative Geography
BJORVATN, K., Economic Development and Geography
BREKKE, K., Health Economics
BRUNSTAD, R., Macroeconomics
BRUNT, L., Economic History
CAPPELEN, A., Experimental Economics
GRYTTEN, O., Macroeconomic History
HAGEN, K. P., Public Economics

HANNESSON, R., Fisheries Economics
HÅLAND, J. I., International Economics
KIND, H. J., Industrial Organization and International Economics
KLOVLAND, J. T., Macroeconomics and Economic History
KRISTIANSEN, E. G., Microeconomics
MATHIESEN, L., General Equilibrium Modelling
NILSEN, O. A., Labour Economics and Investment
NORMAN, V. D., International Economics
SALVANES, K. G., Labour Economics and Industrial Organization
SCHROTYEN, F., Public Economics
SØRGARD, L., Industrial Organization
STEEN, F., Econometrics and Industrial Organization
STRANDENES, S. P., International and Shipping Economics
THØGERSEN, O., Macroeconomics and Social Security
TUNGODDEN, B., Social Choice Theory and Development Economics
VATNE, E., Economic Geography

Faculty of Finance and Management Science:
ÅSE, K. K. P., Finance and Insurance Mathematics
BJERKSUND, P., Investment and Risk Management
BJØRNDAL, M. H., C., Operations Research and Management
EKERN, S., Finance
ESKELAND, G. S., Environmental Economics and Public Finance
FOROS, O., Industrial Organization and Management Science
GJERDE, O., Finance and Operations Management
HANSEN, T., Personal Finance and Management Control Systems
JOHNSEN, T., Finance
JÖRNSTEN, K., Finance
JÖRNSTEN, K., Production Planning and Control
LEITE, T., Financial Markets and Intermediation
LENSBERG, T., Decision Theory
LILLESTØL, J., Statistics and Probability
MØEN, J., Microeconometrics and Productivity Analysis
OLSEN, T. E., Financial Contracting
PERSSON, S.-A., Finance and Economics of Insurance
RÖNNQVIST, M., Operations Research and Logistics
SÆTTEM, F., Finance
SANDAL, L. K., Applied Mathematics and Management Science
SCHJELDERUP, G., Microeconomics
STENSLAND, G., Investment and Risk Management
UBØE, J., Mathematics and Statistics

Faculty of Professional and Intercultural Communication:
DAHL, T., English
MARTÍNEZ, J. A., Spanish
SIMONNÆS, I., German
WHITTAKER, S., French

Faculty of Strategy and Management:
BREIVIK, E., Brand Management and Consumer Trends
BROCHS-HAUKEDAL, W., Management and Organizational Behaviour
ESPEDAL, B., Organizational Learning and Adaptation
FOSS, K., Competitive Strategy
FUGLSETH, A.-M., System Development
GOODERHAM, P., International and Knowledge Management
GREVE, A., Organization Theory
HAUGLAND, S., Strategic Management and Organization Theory

HEM, L., Brand Management and Consumer Trends
IMS, K., Business Ethics and Management
LINES, R., Market Research and Strategy
MEYER, C., Strategy, Merger and Acquisitions
NORDHAUG, O., Organization Theory and Management
NYSVEEN, H., Interactive Marketing and Product Development
PEDERSON, P. E., Innovation and Information Management
ROGNES, J. K., Negotiation
SELART, M., Organizational Behaviour and Human Resources Management
SUPPHELLEN, M., Brand Management and Consumer Trends
THORBJØRNSEN, H., Consumer Psychology and Trends
TROYE, S., Market Research and Consumption Patterns

NORGES IDRETTSHØGSKOLE
(Norwegian School of Sport Sciences)

POB 4014 Ullevål Stadion, 0806 Oslo
Sognsveien 220, Oslo

Telephone: 23-26-20-00
Fax: 22-23-42-20
E-mail: postmottak@nih.no
Internet: www.nih.no

Founded 1968
State control
Academic year: August to June

Rector: SIGMUND LOLAND
Vice-Rector: INGER-ASHILD BY
Dir: BAARD WIST
Library Dir: HEGE UNDERTHUN

Library of 70,000 vols
Number of teachers: 100
Number of students: 1,500

Publication: *Moving Bodies* (2 a year)

HEADS OF DIVISION

Division of Coaching and Psychology: NICOLAS LEMYRE
Division of Culture and Society: DAG VIDAR HANSTAD
Division of Physical Education and Paedagogy: GUNN ENGELSRUD
Division of Physical Performance: JAN CABRI
Division of Sports Medicine: ROALD BAHR

NORGES VETERINÆRHØGSKOLE
(Norwegian School of Veterinary Science)

POB 8146 Dep, 0033 Oslo
Telephone: 22-96-45-00
Fax: 22-59-73-09
E-mail: post@nvh.no
Internet: www.nvh.no

Founded 1935, plans mooted for merger with Universitetet for Miljø- og Biovitenskap (Norwegian University of Life Sciences)
Academic year: August to June

Rector: YNGVILD WASTESON
Vice-Rector: HALVOR HEKTOEN
Admin. Dir: BIRGER KRUSE
Head of Secretariat: HANS GRAN
Head Librarian: ANNE CATHRINE MUNTHE

Library of 77,000 vols
Number of teachers: 114
Number of students: 470 , incl. 80 postgraduate

PROFESSORS

ALESTRØM, P., Biochemistry
ANDRESEN, Ø., Reproduction
ANSOK, S. B., Anatomy and Pathology

AULIE, A., Physiology
BERG, K. A., Reproduction
BJERKÅS, I., Anatomy
DOLVIK, N. I., Large Animal Clinical Sciences
ELIASSEN, K., Biochemistry and Physiology
EVENSEN, Ø., I., Aquatic Medicine and Nutrition
FARSTAD, W., Reproduction
FRØSLIE, A., Forensic Medicine
GJERDE, B., Parasitology
GODFROID, J., Arctic Veterinary Medicine
GRANUM, P. E., Food Hygiene
GRAVE, K., Pharmacology and Toxicology
GRØNDALEN, J., Small Animal Clinical Sciences
GRØNSTØL, H., Large Animal Clinical Sciences
HARBITZ, I., Biochemistry
HORSBERG, T. E., Pharmacology
KARLBERG, K., Reproduction
KROGDAHL, A., Nutrition
LANDSVERK, T., Pathology
LARSEN, J. J., Microbiology
LINGAAS, F., Animal Genetics
LØKEN, T., Large Animal Clinical Sciences
MOE, L., Small Animal Clinical Sciences
NESBAKKEN, T., Food Hygiene
ØDEGAARD, S., Reproduction
PAULSON, J. E., Food Hygiene
POPPE, T., Anatomy and Pathology
REIMERS, E., Anatomy and Pathology
REITE, O. B., Aquaculture and Fish Diseases
RIMSTAD, E., Virology
RØED, K. H., Animal Genetics
RØNNINGEN, K., Animal Genetics
ROPSTAD, E., Reproduction
SIMENSEN, E., Research Farm
SJAASTAD, Ø., Physiology
SKJERVE, E., Food Hygiene
SMITH, A., Laboratory Animals
SØLI, N., Pharmacology and Toxicology
SØRUM, H., Microbiology
TEIGE, J., Pathology
TRANULIS, M., Biochemistry and Physiology
TRYLAND, M., Arctic Veterinary Medicine
TVERDAL, A., Animal Genetics
ULVUND, M., Sheep and Goat Research
WALDELAND, H., Sheep and Goat Research
WASTESON, Y., Food Hygiene
YNDESTAD, M., Food Hygiene

TEOLOGISKE MENIGHETSFAKULTET
(MF Norwegian School of Theology)

POB 5144 Majorstuen, 0302 Oslo
Gydasvei 4, 0302 Oslo

Telephone: 22-59-05-00
Fax: 22-59-05-05
E-mail: post@mf.no
Internet: www.mf.no

Founded 1907
Private control
Languages of instruction: English, Norwegian
Academic year: August to June

Rector: Prof. Dr VIDAR L. HAANES
Dir: BEATE PETTERSEN
Dean of Research: Prof. KARL OLAV SANDNES
Dean of Studies: Dr ØYSTEIN LUND
Librarian: ELNA OLINE STRANDHEIM

Library of 73,000 vols and 500 periodicals
Number of teachers: 75
Number of students: 1,100

Publications: *Studia Theologica* (2 a year), *Nordic Journal for Religion and Society* (2 a year)

PROFESSORS

AFDAL, G., Philosophy of Religious Education
ENGEDAL, L. G., Psychology of Religion

ENGELSVIKEN, T., Missiology
GRAVEM, P., Systematic Theology
HEGSTAD, H., Systematic Theology
HEIENE, G., Systematic Theology
HENRIKSEN, J.-O., Systematic Theology
HVALVIK, R., The New Testament
KÖRTING, C., The Old Testament
KVALBEIN, H., The New Testament
MOGSTAD, S. D., Philosophy of Religious Education
OFTESTAD, B. T., Church History
SANNES, K. O., Systematic Theology
SKARSAUNE, O., Church History
THORBJØRNSEN, S. O., Systematic Theology
WEYDE, K. W., The Old Testament

Schools of Art and Music

Griegakademiet (Grieg Academy): Humanistiske fakultet, POB 7805, 5020 Bergen; Lars Hillesgt. 3, 5015 Bergen; tel. 55-58-69-50; fax 55-58-69-60; e-mail post@grieg.uib.no; internet www.uib.no/grieg; f. 1905; education of musicians, music teachers and organists; offers teacher-training and Bachelors and Masters degree courses; 120 students; Head of Institute FRODE THORSEN.

Kunstakademiet i Trondheim, Norges Teknisk-Naturvitenskaplige Universitet (Trondheim Academy of Fine Art, Norwegian University of Science and Technology): NTNU, 7491 Trondheim; Innherredsveien 7, Trondheim; tel. 73-59-79-00; fax 73-59-79-20; e-mail adm@kit.ntnu.no; internet www.kit.ntnu.no; f. 1946; offers Bachelors and Masters degree courses in fine art; 11 staff; 58 students; library: 5,000 vols; Pres. IVAR SMEDSTAD; publ. *Kitsch* (4 a year).

Kunsthøgskolen i Bergen (KHIB) (Bergen National Academy of the Arts): Strømgt. 1, 5015 Bergen; tel. 55-58-73-00; fax 55-58-73-10; e-mail khib@khib.no; internet www.khib.no; offers Bachelors and Masters degree courses in ceramics, fine arts, interior and furniture design, photography, textiles and printmaking, visual communication; library: 15,000 vols, 200 periodicals; 45 teachers; 300 students; Pres. KETIL SCHREINER EVJEN.

Kunsthøgskolen i Oslo (KHiO) (National Academy of Oslo): POB 6853 St Olavs plass, 0130 Oslo; Fossveien 24, 0551 Oslo; tel. 22-99-55-80; fax 22-99-55-85; e-mail khio@khio.no; f. 1996 by merger of Statens Håndverks og Kunstindustriskole (Nat. College of Art and Design), Statens Kunstakademi (Nat. Academy of Fine Arts), Statens Balletthøgskole (Nat. College of Ballet), Statens Teaterhøgskole (State University of Theatre) and Statens Operahøgskole (State Opera Academy); offers Bachelors and Masters degree courses; comprises faculties of design, visual arts and performing arts; library: 80,000 vols; 138 teachers; 496 students; Pres. GYRID GARSHOL.

Norges Musikkhøgskole (Norwegian Academy of Music): POB 5190 Majorstua, 0302 Oslo; Slemdalsveien 11, 0369 Oslo; tel. 23-36-70-00; fax 23-36-70-01; e-mail mh@nmh.no; internet www.nmh.no; f. 1973, merged with Eastern Norway Conservatory of Music 1996; offers Bachelors, Masters and PhD degree courses; library: 75,000 books and items of sheet music, 31,000 audio recordings, 750 video cassettes and DVDs; 130 teachers; 541 students; Dir INGEBORG HARSTEN.

OMAN

The Higher Education System

Until independence was confirmed in 1951, Oman had a special relationship with the United Kingdom. The first institutions of higher education were founded in the 1980s, notably Sultan Qaboos University (founded 1986). In 2009/10 there were 15,357 students enrolled at the university. In 2004/05 there were 23,286 students enrolled in 34 other institutions of higher education (six teacher-training colleges, the College of Shari'a and Law, five technical colleges, the Oman Tourism College, the College of Banking and Financial Studies, 16 institutes of health and four vocational training centres).

The Ministry of Education has supreme authority over general education, but the Ministry of Higher Education is responsible for tertiary education, the Ministry of Manpower oversees most vocational and technical training and the Ministry of Health coordinates health sciences, nursing and pharmaceutical education. The Ministries sponsor an estimated 6,000 students per year to attend higher education.

Success in the secondary thanawiya amma (school leaving certificate) examinations is the main basis for admission to higher education. Prior to commencing the undergraduate Bachelors degree, students are required to take a one-year Foundation course; this consists of English language, information technology (IT) and study skills training. The Bachelors degree is usually a four-year course and students must accrue at least 120 'credits' in order to graduate. Medical students must first complete a four-year Bachelor of Health Sciences degree before proceeding to a three-year postgraduate programme in Clinical Medicine. The first postgraduate degree is the Diploma, which is approximately equivalent to half a Masters degree. Following completion of the Masters, the PhD is the highest university degree. In 2009 there were 15 doctoral programmes on offer at Sultan Qaboos University.

Technical and vocational education at the post-secondary level is offered by technical industrial colleges, vocational training centres, professional institutes and seven higher colleges of technology. The technical industrial colleges award National Diplomas after upwards of two years of study and workplace training; admission is on the basis of the thanawiya amma. However, the National Diploma system is gradually to be phased out in favour of a system of vocational and occupational training. The vocational training centres offer one- or two-year programmes of training for skilled and semi-skilled workers, and qualifications are equivalent to the United Kingdom National Vocational Qualification (NVQ). The Ministry of Health administers 16 institutes to train nursing and medical science professionals; these include 12 nursing institutes, as well as the Institute of Health Sciences, the Oman Assistant Pharmacy Institute, the Oman Institute of Public Health and the Oman Medical Records Institute. The Nursing and Midwifery Council of Oman, established by the Ministry of Health in 2001, is charged with regulating the nursing profession and the education of its members. The higher colleges of technology, the principal of which is the Higher College of Technology in Muscat, offer a one-year Certificate, a two-year Diploma and a three-year Higher Diploma, all of which require a foundation year (covering English, Mathematics and IT) following successful completion of the thanawiya amma. The Higher College of Technology in Muscat also offers a four-year Bachelor of Technology degree.

In 2009 there were 25 private tertiary education providers under licence from the Ministry of Higher Education. These institutions are classified into private universities, private university colleges and private colleges. Most of these were established by foreign providers to meet the demand of school leavers entering higher education as the existing provision for higher education in the public sector is insufficient. The three private university colleges—Caledonian College of Engineering, Majan College and Sur University College—are affiliated to recognized overseas degree providers. Caledonian College of Engineering offers an undergraduate Diploma, a Bachelors (Ordinary) and a Bachelors (Honours) degree in Engineering validated by Glasgow Caledonian University. The awards align to levels within the Scottish Credit and Qualifications Framework. Majan University College offers Bachelors (Honours) degrees in IT, Business and Marketing and Finance, which are validated by the University of Bedfordshire. Sur University College offers Australian Bachelors (Honours) degrees in IT and Commerce, which are validated by Bond University in Queensland. There are 20 private colleges in Oman, some of which have ties with overseas institutions. They do not offer Bachelors degrees but two-year Diploma and three-year Advanced Diploma programmes, the majority of which are in Business, IT and Engineering.

Established in 2001, the Oman Accreditation Council (OAM) is responsible for the external quality assurance and quality enhancement of higher education institutions and programmes. The OAM created a National Qualifications Framework in 2005 to standardize qualifications offered by tertiary education providers in terms of level, learning outcomes and volume of study.

Regulatory and Representative Bodies

GOVERNMENT

Ministry of Education: POB 3, Muscat 113; tel. 24775209; fax 24704465; e-mail moe@moe.gov.om; internet www.moe.gov.om; Minister MADINA BINT AHMED BIN NASIR AL-SHIBANIYAH.

Ministry of Heritage and Culture: POB 668, Muscat 113; tel. 24641300; fax 24641331; e-mail info@mhc.gov.om; internet www.mhc.gov.om; Minister SAYYID HAITHM BIN TARIQ AL-SAID.

Ministry of Higher Education: POB 82, Ruwi 112; tel. 24340999; fax 24340172; e-mail info_dept@mohe.gov.om; internet www.mohe.gov.om; Minister Dr RAWYA BINT SAUD BIN AHMAD L-BUSAIDIYAH.

ACCREDITATION

Oman Accreditation Council: POB 1255, Al Khuwair 133; tel. 24475170; fax 24475168; e-mail enquiries@oac.gov.om; internet www.oac.gov.om; accredits public institutes, and public and private colleges and univs; 11 mems; Chair. Dr HAMED AL-DHAHAB.

Learned Societies

HISTORY, GEOGRAPHY AND ARCHAEOLOGY

Historical Association of Oman: POB 3941, Ruwi 112; tel. 24141674; fax 24143212; e-mail artsdean@hotmail.com; internet www.hao.org.om; f. 1971; study of history, monuments and natural history of Oman; organizes lectures and field trips to places of interest; library of 400 vols; 200 mems; Pres. Dr ISAM BIN ALI BIN AHMED AL-RAWAS; publs *Geology of Oman*, *The Journal of Oman Studies*, *The Sambuq*, *Traditional Spinning and Weaving in the Sultanate of Oman*, *Turtles in the Sultanate of Oman*.

LANGUAGE AND LITERATURE

British Council: Road One, Madinat al Sultan, Qaboos West, POB 73, Muscat 115; tel. 24681000; fax 24681090; e-mail bc.muscat@om.britishcouncil.org; internet www.britishcouncil.org/me-oman.htm; teaching centre; offers courses and exams in English language and British culture and promotes cultural exchange with the UK; attached office in Seeb; Dir JIM SCARTH; Dir, Teaching and Examination Services MARY STANSFIELD.

Research Institutes

AGRICULTURE, FISHERIES AND VETERINARY SCIENCE

Directorate of Water Resources Research: c/o Min. of Regional Municipalities and Water Resources, POB 323, Muscat; activities include hydrological surveys, water conservation, etc.

Marine Sciences and Fisheries Centre: c/o Ministry of Agriculture and Fisheries, POB 467, Muscat; tel. 24740062; fax 24740159; f. 1987; biological research, conservation, ecology, food technology, oceanography; includes a library and aquarium.

Libraries and Archives

Bowshar

Central Medical Library: Min. of Health-Royal Hospital, POB 1331, Seeb, Bowshar 111; tel. 24595971 ext. 454; fax 24594247; f. 1970; 7,000 vols, 122 periodicals; spec. collns: Min. of Health reports, health reports, WHO collns; Head of Medical Library AFFRA SAID AL SHAMSI; Librarian IMAN MAHFOODH AL HARTHY.

Muscat

Archives of the Directorate General of Heritage: Min. of Heritage and Culture, POB 668, Muscat 113; f. 1976; 5,000 MSS, 50,000 archives; Dir-Gen. MOHAMMED SAID AL-WOHAIBI.

Museums and Art Galleries

Muscat

Oman Natural History Museum (ONHM): Ministry of Heritage and Culture, Al Khuwair, Muscat; tel. 24641510; f. 1983; incl. the Nat. Herbarium of Oman and the Nat. Shell and Coral Colln, and the Insect and Osteological Collns.

Qurm

Oman Museum, Qurm: c/o Min. of Heritage and Culture, POB 668, Muscat 113; Al Alam St, behind Ministry of Information, Madinat Sultan Qaboos, Muscat; tel. 24600946; attached to Min. of Heritage and Culture; Oman's 5,000-year history with displays on shipbuilding, Islam and fort architecture.

Ruwi

National Museum at Ruwi: Way 3123, off Al'Noor St, near Al Fallaj Hotel, Ruwi, Muscat; tel. 24701289; f. 1978; formerly the Museum of Bait Assayed, Nadir bin Faisal bin Turki; exhibits incl. silver ornaments, copper crafts and samples from Omani ships; holy relics incl. a letter sent by The Prophet to the rulers of Oman A'bd and Jaiifer, sons of Al Julanda, dated 8th century Hijri; belongings of the Al Busaidi dynasty, rulers of Zanzibar; attached to Ministry of Heritage and Culture.

Universities

DHOFAR UNIVERSITY

POB 2509, Salalah 211
Telephone: 23225061
Fax: 23225064
E-mail: du@du.edu.om
Internet: www.du.edu.om

Founded 2004
Vice-Chancellor: MUHAMMAD FAOUR

DEANS

College of Arts and Applied Sciences: HUSSEIN YAGHI
College of Commerce and Business Administration: NIMR EID
College of Engineering: FARID CHAABAN

GERMAN UNIVERSITY OF TECHNOLOGY IN OMAN

POB 1816, Athaibah 130
Telephone: 24493051
Fax: 24495568
E-mail: info@gutech.edu.om
Internet: www.gutech.edu.om; attached to RWTH Aachen University, Germany

Founded 2006
Private control

Faculties of economics and planning, information technology and mathematics, sciences.

UNIVERSITY OF NIZWA

POB 33, Birkat Al Mouz PC 616
Telephone: 25446234
Fax: 25443400
E-mail: rose@unizwa.edu.om
Internet: www.unizwa.edu.om

Founded 2004
Private control
Languages of instruction: Arabic, English
Academic year: September to July
Chancellor: Prof. AHMED KHALFAN AL RAWAHI
Vice-Chancellor for Academic Affairs: Prof. ABDULAZIZ YAHYA AL KINDI
Vice-Chancellor for Graduate Studies and Research: Dr ABDALLAH MOHAMMED OMEZZINE

DEANS

College of Arts and Sciences: Dr ABDULLAH SAIF AL TOBI
College of Economics, Management and Information Systems: Dr AHMED MASOUD AL KINDI
College of Engineering and Architecture: Prof WALEED A. THANOON
College of Pharmacy and Nursing: Prof NAFSIAH BINTI SHAMSUDIN

SOHAR UNIVERSITY

POB 44, Sohar 311
Telephone: 26720101
Fax: 26720102
E-mail: soharuni@omantel.net.om
Internet: www.soharuni.edu.om

Founded 1998 as Sohar College of Applied Sciences; univ. status 2001
Private control

Affiliated to Queensland University, Australia

Vice-Chancellor: Dr ABOOD HAMAD AL SAWAFI

DEANS

Faculty of Business: Dr MOHIT KUMAR KOLAY
Faculty of Computing and Information Technology: Dr WAIL M. OMAR
Faculty of Engineering: (vacant)
Faculty of Humanities and Social Sciences: (vacant)

SULTAN QABOOS UNIVERSITY

POB 50, 123, Al-Khod, Muscat
Telephone: 24141111
Fax: 24413391
E-mail: webmaster@squ.edu.om
Internet: www.squ.edu.om

Founded 1986
State control
Academic year: September to May
Vice-Chancellor: Dr ALI AL-BEMANI
Dean of Admissions and Registration: Dr. HAIDER ALI RAMADAN
Library Dir: Dr MOOSA NASSER AL-MUFARAJI
Library of 120,698 vols
Number of teachers: 964
Number of students: 12,591

Publications: *Journal of Scientific Research: Agricultural Marine Sciences* (2 a year), *Journal of Scientific Research: Medical Sciences* (2 a year), *Journal of Scientific Research: Science and Technology* (2 a year)

DEANS

College of Agriculture and Marine Sciences: Dr SANMUGAM A. PRATHAPAR
College of Arts and Social Sciences: Dr ISSAM ALI AL-RAWAS
College of Commerce and Economics: Dr DARWISH AL-MOHARBY
College of Education: Dr THUWAYBA AHMED AL-BARWANI
College of Engineering: Dr ALI AL-HARETHI
College of Law: Dr MOHAMED SAMI GAMALELDIN
College of Medicine and Health Sciences: Dr BAZDAWI AL-RIYAMI
College of Nursing: Prof. BAZDAWI M. S. AL-RIYAMI (acting)
College of Science: Dr ADEL YOUSSEF

DIRECTORS

Centre for Environmental Studies and Research: Prof. REGINALD VICTOR
Centre for Human Resources and Staff Development: ABDUL BASIT TALIB RAJAB AL-HAMMADI
Centre of Educational Technology: KHALID KHAMIS AL-SAADI
Centre of Information Systems: ALI OBAID AL-MAJEENI
Language Centre: Dr WILLIAM HARSBARGER
Remote Sensing Centre: Dr ANDY KWARTENG
Student Counselling Centre: SAUD MOHAMMAD ALI SULAIMAN
Water Research Centre: Dr SANMUGAM A. PRATHAPAR

Colleges

Al Buraimi University College: tel. 25641866; fax 25641855; e-mail info@buc.edu.om; internet www.buc.edu.om; private control; diploma, advanced diploma and Bachelor degree levels; depts of business administration and accounting, English language and literature, information technology; Dir YAQOOB M. FAKEER.

College of Banking and Financial Studies: POB 3122, Ruwi 112; tel. 24505796; fax 24502525; e-mail info@cbfs.edu.om; internet www.cbfs.edu.om; f. 1998 as Institute of Banking and Financial Studies; present name and status 2004; state control; courses in accounting, banking, business, computing, English, insurance; Chair. IQBAL ALI KHAMIS AL LAWATI; Dean Dr ASHRAF NABHAN AL NABHANI.

Higher College of Technology: POB 74, Al Khuwair 133; tel. 24473600; fax 24473611; internet www.hct.edu.om; f. 1984 as Oman Technical Industrial College; present name and status 2001; under control of the Ministry of Manpower; Bachelors degree; depts of applied sciences, business studies, engineering, fashion design, information technology, pharmacy, photography; 600 teachers; 7,300 students; Dean Dr OBAID AL SAEEDI.

Institute of Health Sciences: POB 3720, 112 Ruwi, Muscat; tel. 24560085; fax 24560384; f. 1982; under the Ministry of Health; library: 5,000 vols; 36 teachers; 244 students; Dean ALYA MOHAMMED MUSALLEM AL-RAWAHY; publ. *Quarterly Medical News Journal.*

Institute of Public Administration: POB 1994, Ruwi 112; tel. 24600205; fax 24602066; e-mail ipa@ipa.gov.om; internet www.ipa.gov .om; f. 1977; training, research and consultancy; library of 12,000 Arabic vols, 3,800 foreign; 70 Arabic periodicals, 5 foreign; 1,000 students per year attend courses; 57 staff; Dir-Gen. SULEIMAN BIN HILAL AL-ALAWI; publ. *Al-Edari* (4 a year).

Mazoon University College: POB 101, Muscat 133; tel. 24513301; e-mail mazoonco@omantel.net.om; internet www .mazooncollege.edu.om; private control; f. 1999; affiliated to Missouri University of Science and technology, USA in partnership with Banasthali Vidyapith, Jaipur, India; Masters Degree, Bachelors Degree and Associate Diploma in Accounting, Business Administration, Computer Science, Economics, English, Information Science and Technology, Management Information Systems and Psychology; Man. Dir Dr JUMA S. AL GHAILANI; Dir of Student Affairs and Registration JIHAD IBRAHIM JABARIN.

Middle East College of Information Technology: POB 79, al Rusayl 124; tel. 24446698; fax 24446028; e-mail info@mecit .edu.om; internet www.mecit.edu.om; Private control; f. 2000; affiliated to Coventry Univ., UK; depts of business studies, computing, cultural studies, design technology, electronics and communication, mathematics and applied sciences.

Modern College of Business and Science: POB 100, al Khuwair 133; tel. 24482802; fax 24482729; e-mail info@mcbs .edu.om; internet www.mcbs.edu.om; f. 1996; private control; Assoc. of Science in business admin., computer science, information communication technology; BA in arts; BSc in business admin., computer science; Dean BADR EL DIN A. IBRAHIM.

Muscat College: POB 2910, Ruwi 112; tel. 24503821; fax 24504954; e-mail info@ mctcollege.com; internet www.mctcollege .com; f. 1996; private control; affiliated to University of Stirling, UK and Scottish Qualifications Authority; Bachelor degrees in accountancy and finance, business studies, computing science; Chair. Dr AHMED BIN ABDULLA AL-GHAZALI.

Oman Dental College: POB 835, Muscat 116; tel. 24696171; fax 24696174; e-mail info@omandentalcollege.org; internet www .omandentalcollege.org; private control; affiliated to AB Shetty Memorial Institute of Dental Sciences, India.

Oman Medical College: POB 620, Azaiba 130; tel. 24504608; fax 24504820; e-mail admissions@omc.edu.om; internet www.omc .edu.om; f. 2000; private control; affiliated to West Virginia Univ., USA; degrees in Doctor of Medicine and Bachelor of Pharmacy; Dean of Boshwar Campus Dr DIANA BEATTIE; Dean of Sohar Campus Dr SALEH MOHAMMED AL KHUSAIBY.

Oman Tourism and Hospitality Academy: POB 822, al Khoud 132; tel. 521105; fax 522283; e-mail office@otha.edu.om; internet www.otha.edu.om; f. 2001; affiliated to the International Institute of Tourism and Management, Krems and the International Management Centre, University of Applied Sciences, Krems, Austria.

Salalah College of Technology: Thumrait Rd, Salalah, Dhofar 211; e-mail webmaster@ sct.edu.om; internet www.sct.edu.om; state control; f. 1979 as a Vocational Training Centre; 1993 became Technical Industrial College; present name 2001; attached to Ministry of Manpower; depts of business, engineering, information technology; 197 teachers; 2,132 students; Dean Dr HASSAN KASHOOB.

Sur University College: POB 400, Sur 411; tel. 25542888; fax 25540737; internet www .suc.edu.om; private control; affiliated to Bond Univ., Australia; depts of business administration and commerce, information systems and technology; Chair. MUBARAK JUMA BAHWAN; Dean Dr AHMAD ABDEL-AZIZ SHARIEH.

Waljat Colleges of Applied Sciences: POB 197, Muscat 124; tel. 24446660; fax 24449196; e-mail info@waljatcolleges.edu .om; internet www.waljatcolleges.edu.om; in partnership with Birla Institute of Technology; Dean Dr A. M. AGRAWAL.

PAKISTAN

The Higher Education System

In 1947 Pakistan declared its independence from the former British Indian Empire. The oldest current institutions of higher education were established during the period of British rule, among them the Government College University (founded in 1897), Liaquat University of Medical and Health Sciences (founded in 1881; present name and status since 2001) and the University of the Punjab (founded in 1882). Consequently, the university system is closely based on the late 19th-century British model (particularly the University of London) of federal institutions, consisting of a centralized administration and affiliated colleges. Universities and degree-awarding institutions are broadly divided into 'general' and 'professional' categories. In 2009/10 there were 132 universities and degree-awarding institutions. In 2010/11 there were 1,105,307 students enrolled at such institutions. In 2009/10 there were also 3,399 arts and science colleges and 1,275 professional colleges (including educational colleges); enrolment totalled 1,147,800 and 458,835, respectively. The Allama Iqbal Open University has been established with the technical support of the British Open University. With the assistance of the Asian Development Bank, 11 polytechnic institutes and a national teacher-training college have been established by the Government. Training is provided for teachers at polytechnic, commercial and vocational institutes. In 2009 the Government announced an initiative calling for an increase in the percentage of the 17–23-year-old age group with access to higher education, from the existing level of 5% to 10% by 2015. If the objective were to be achieved, significant government funding and other support would be required.

In late 2002 the Higher Education Commission (HEC) replaced the University Grants Commission as the national controlling body of higher education. The HEC is responsible for, inter alia, dispersal of government funding, formation of higher education policy, evaluation, accreditation and quality assurance. Government proposals, announced in mid-2011, to disband the HEC and transfer its functions to various ministries, so as to ensure that budgetary and other higher education matters go through proper parliamentary channels for approval, received a mixed response, with some arguing that it would be detrimental to the higher education sector, while others contended that the Government should go further and create a new government ministry devoted exclusively to higher education. In the mean time, however, the HEC still has authority over both public and private institutions, although universities are still autonomous institutions. The chairman of the university is the Chancellor, while the chief executive and academic officer is the Vice-Chancellor, aided by Pro-Vice-Chancellors. Bodies of institutional and academic control include the Senate, Syndicate, Academic Council, Boards of Faculty and Study, Selection Board, Advanced Studies and Research Board, Finance and Planning Committee, Affiliation Committee and Disciplinary Committee.

Admission to higher education is based on the secondary school leaving certificate. From the mid-2000s the Bachelors degree programme was reformed from two- or three-year programmes—Bachelors (Pass) and Bachelors (Honours), respectively—to a four-year course of study. Specialist degrees leading to professional titles in architecture and medicine are five-year programmes of study. Bachelors degrees in law, education and library science are postgraduate degrees, admission to which are based upon completion of an undergraduate Bachelors degree. Postgraduate diplomas are one-year courses taken following a relevant first degree. The Masters is a postgraduate degree requiring two years of study following the Bachelors; it consists of coursework and final examinations. The Master of Philosophy (MPhil) lasts two years, and is a research-based degree taken after a Masters in arts, commerce or science. The highest university degree is the PhD, requiring a minimum of three years of study after award of the Masters.

Technical and vocational education at the post-secondary level is available at polytechnics and colleges of technology, which are the responsibility of the National Institute of Science and Technical Education. At a provincial level Boards of Technical Education are the responsible bodies. Polytechnics specialize in three-year Diploma courses and colleges of technology offer degree courses to holders of the Polytechnic Diplomas (in addition to the Diploma). Several professional bodies are authorized to issue Diplomas and certificates, among them the College of Physicians and Surgeons Pakistan, the Institute of Chartered Accountants of Pakistan, the Institute of Cost and Management Accountants of Pakistan and the Pakistan Nursing Council.

Regulatory and Representative Bodies

GOVERNMENT

Ministry of Education: Block D, Pakistan Secretariat, Islamabad; tel. (51) 9201392; fax (51) 9202851; e-mail minister@moe.gov.pk; internet www.moe.gov.pk; Minister Prof. MIR HAZAR KHAN BIJARANI; Federal Sec. ABDUR RAUF CHAUDHRY.

Attached Departments:

Department of Libraries.

Federal Directorate of Education: Rohtas Rd, Muave Ave, Sector G-9/4, Islamabad; tel. (51) 9260230; fax (51) 9260569; e-mail info@fde.gov.pk; internet www.fde.gov.pk; f. 1967; Dir-Gen. ATIF MEHMOOD KAYANI.

Ministry of Science and Technology: Aga Khan Rd, F-5/1, Islamabad; tel. (51) 9202790; fax (51) 9204541; e-mail minister@most.gov.pk; internet www.most.gov.pk; Min. MIR CHANGEZ KHAN JAMALI.

ACCREDITATION

Higher Education Commission: Sector H-9, E Service Rd, Islamabad; tel. (51) 9040000; e-mail info@hec.gov.pk; internet www.hec.gov.pk; f. 2002; evaluates, improves and promotes Pakistan's higher education and research sector; est. accreditation ccls in areas of computing, agricultural education, teachers education and business education; est. quality assurance agency to develop policies and guidelines to ensure improvement in the quality of higher education throughout the country; 17 mems; library of 41,000 vols, 232 periodicals; Chair. Dr JAVAID R. LAGHARI; Exec. Dir Prof. Dr SYED SOHAIL H. NAQVI; publs *Guide to the Equivalence of Qualifications in Pakistan* (irregular), *Handbook of Centres of Excellence and Advanced Studies*, *Handbook of Colleges*, *Handbook of Universities of Pakistan* (every 2 years), *Higher Education News* (4 a year), *Statistics on Higher Education in Pakistan*.

Pakistan Engineering Council: Attaturk Ave (E), G-5/2, POB 1296, Islamabad; tel. (51) 2829348; fax (51) 2276224; e-mail chairman@pec.org.pk; internet www.pec.org.pk; f. 1976; statutory functions incl. registration of engineers, consulting engineers, constructors/operators; accreditation of engineering programmes run by univs/instns; ensures and manages continuing professional devt; assists the Fed. govt as think tank; establishes standards for engineering products and services; safeguarding the interest of its mems; Chair. SYED ABDUL QADIR SHAH.

Learned Societies

GENERAL

Quaid-i-Azam Academy: 297 M. A. Jinnah Rd, Karachi 74800, Sindh; tel. (21) 99215238; fax (21) 99215236; e-mail qaak@quaidiazamacademy.com; internet www.quaidiazamacademy.com; f. 1976; Min. of Inter Provincial Coordination; research on Quaid-i-Azam Mohammad Ali Jinnah, on the historical background (incl. cultural, religious, literary, linguistic, social, economic and political aspects) of the Pakistan Movement, and various aspects of Pakistan; gives scholarships and professorships; awards Quaid-i-Azam Academic and Literary Prizes for scholarly works; holds seminars and lectures; photostat vols of Archives of Freedom Movement; photostat files of Quaid-i-Azam Papers; 52 photostat vols of Shamsul Hasan collns, Sadar Abdur Rab Nishtar collns, 2,000 microfilms of various pre-partition newspapers and other collns; publishes bibliographies, research studies, biographies, monographs and documents (in English, Urdu and dialects); library of 30,000 vols; Exec. Head MUHAMMAD ARIF AZIM; Dir Dr SHEHLA KAZMI (acting).

UNESCO Office Islamabad: St 8 House 17 Sector F 7/3, Islamabad 2034; tel. (51) 2611170; fax (51) 2600250; e-mail islamabad@unesco.org; internet unesco.org .pk; f. 1945; education, basic sciences, culture, communication and information, natural sciences, social and human sciences; Dir Dr KOZUE KAY NAGATA; Deputy Dir Dr ROSHAN CHITRAKAR.

ARCHITECTURE AND TOWN PLANNING

Pakistan Council of Architects and Town Planners: Suite 111, First Fl., R. S. M. Sq., E-1 Shaheed-e-Millat Rd, Karachi 75350, Sindh; tel. (21) 4523129; fax (21) 4541099; internet www.pcatp.org.pk; f. 1983 as a statutory body by the Govt of Pakistan; regulates professions of architecture and town planning; 797 mems; Chair. SHAMA USMAN.

BIBLIOGRAPHY, LIBRARY SCIENCE AND MUSEOLOGY

Library Promotion Bureau: 1239/9 Dastgir Soc., Fed. B Area, Karachi 75270, Sindh; tel. and fax (21) 6321959; f. 1965; promotes librarianship in Pakistan; coordinates with all orgs engaged in promotional activities; publs reference books, books on library and information science, text books on library science, bibliographies, directories, etc.; Pres. M. ADIL USMANI; Sec.-Gen. Dr NASIM FATIMA; publ. *Pakistan Library and Information Science Journal* (4 a year).

National Book Foundation: 6 Mauve Area, G-8/4, Taleemi Chowk, POB 1169, Islamabad; tel. (51) 2255572; fax (51) 9261534; e-mail books@nbf.org.pk; internet www.nbf.org.pk; f. 1972; attached to Min. of Education; promotes writing, research and publ; promotes literacy, organizes book festivals and exhibitions, operates book promotion schemes, publishes Braille books; 128 mems; Man. Dir MAZHAR-UL-ISLAM; Sec. MUHAMMAD ASLAM RAO; publ. *Kitab* (in English and Urdu).

Pakistan Library Association: c/o Office of Executive Committee, PLA Headquarters, Quetta Balochistan; tel. (51) 9214041; fax (51) 9210006; e-mail info@pla.org.pk; f. 1957; represents librarians in Pakistan; develops and improves libraries; office of Exec. council rotates every 2 years between PLA brs in Balochistan, Sindh, Punjab, Khyber Pakhtunkhwa; 1,329 mems; Pres. Prof. MALAHAT KALEEM SHERWANI; Vice-Pres. NUZHAT YASMEEN; Sec. RIAZ ALI KHASKHELI; publs *Conference Proceedings* (1 a year), *PLA Journal* (4 a year).

Regional Branches:

Balochistan Branch: Quetta, Balochistan; e-mail bb@pla.org.pk; Pres. ABDUR RAHMAN QAISARANI.

Federal Branch: Islamabad; e-mail fb@ pla.org.pk; Pres. MUSHAHID HUSSAIN.

Khyber Pakhtunkhwa Branch: Peshawar, Khyber Pakhtunkhwa; e-mail nwfp@ pla.org.pk; Pres. MUHAMMAD KHAN MARAWAT.

Punjab Branch: Punjab Univ. Library, Quaid-e-Azam Campus, Lahore 54000, Punjab; tel. (42) 99230863; e-mail info@ plapunjab.org; internet plapunjab.org; Pres. CHAUDHRY MUHAMMAD HANIF.

Sindh Branch: Liaquat Memorial Library Bldg, Stadium Rd, Ground Fl., Karachi, Sindh; tel. (333) 2658156; e-mail plasindh@ gmail.com; internet pla-sindhbranch .weebly.com; Pres. Prof. SHEREEN GUL SOOMRO.

ECONOMICS, LAW AND POLITICS

Institute of Cost and Management Accountants of Pakistan: St 18/C, Block-6, Gulshan-e-Iqbal, POB 17642, Karachi 75300, Sindh; tel. (21) 99243900; fax (21) 99243342; e-mail ed@icmap.com.pk; internet www.icmap.com.pk; f. 1951; regulates cost and management accountancy profession in Pakistan; arranges professional devt programmes; 4,620 mems; library of 32,000 vols; Pres. ZIA UL MUSTAFA AWAN; Vice-Pres. GHULAM MUSTAFA QAZI; Exec. Dir MUSHTAQ AHMED MADRASWALA; publs *Cost Audit Handbook*, *Glossary of Management Accounting*, *History of Management Accounting Profession in Pakistan*, *Students' Handbook* (1 a year).

Pakistan Institute of International Affairs: Aiwan-e-Sadar Rd, POB 1447, Karachi 74200, Sindh; tel. (21) 35682891; fax (21) 35686069; e-mail info@piia.org.pk; internet www.piia.org.pk; f. 1947; 650 mems; library: see Libraries and Archives; studies int. affairs and promotes scientific study of int. politics, Pakistan foreign policy, economics, jurisprudence; conducts research and surveys; maintains clipping files of chronology of events; organizes lectures, round-table discussions, and seminars on relevant subjects; Chair. Dr MASUMA HASAN; Hon. Sec. SYED ABDUL MINAM JAFRI; publ. *Pakistan Horizon* (4 a year).

EDUCATION

Punjab Bureau of Education: Punjab Public Service Commission, 2 Agha Khan (Davis Rd), Lahore, Punjab; tel. (42) 9202762; fax (42) 9202766; e-mail info@ppsc .gop.pk; internet www.ppsc.gop.pk; f. 1958; clearing house for information on education of all aspects and levels, within Pakistan and abroad; Documentation Section, Statistical Section, Publication Section and Research Section; library of 10,000 vols and periodicals; Dir SAJJAD HUSSAIN NAQVI; publ. *Educational Statistics* (1 a year).

FINE AND PERFORMING ARTS

Arts Council of Pakistan: M. R. Kayani Rd, Karachi 74200, Sindh; tel. (21) 99213090; fax (21) 99213074; e-mail art_council_khi@ yahoo.com; f. 1956; promotes and develops fine arts and crafts, drama, music; 6,597 mems; Chair. ROSHAN ALI SHAIKH; Pres. MUHAMMAD AHMED SHAH; Exec. Dir FEROZE AHMED; publ. *Khabar Nama*.

Lok Virsa/National Institute of Folk and Traditional Heritage: Garden Ave, Shakarparian, POB 1184, Islamabad; tel. (51) 9252106; fax (51) 9252096; e-mail info@ lokvirsa.org.pk; internet lokvirsa.org.pk; f. 1974; preserves and promotes traditional culture, folk arts and folklore of Pakistan; museum, publishing house, media centre, sound archive; library of 10,000 vols; Exec. Dir KHALID JAVAID; publs *Lok Punjab*, *Mai Ni Main Kinno Akhan*, *Rag Swaroop*.

Pakistan National Council of the Arts: Plot 5, F-5/1, Islamabad; tel. (51) 9205273; fax (51) 9208810; e-mail pncoaisb@gmail .com; internet www.pnca.org.pk; f. 1973; promotes visual and performing arts, nat. heritage; offices in Karachi, Lahore; library of 3,000 vols; Dir-Gen. TAUQEER AHMED NASIR.

HISTORY, GEOGRAPHY AND ARCHAEOLOGY

Department of Archaeology and Museums: First Fl., Block 4, Sitara Market, G-7 Markaz, , Islamabad; tel. (51) 9206236; fax (51) 2201592; e-mail doam@cyber.net.pk; f. 1947; explores, excavates and scientifically conserves archaeological, historical and cultural heritage of Pakistan; develops a documentary and published record; exhibits material in the museums for educational research and amusement; Dir-Gen. Dr FAZAL DAD KAKAR; publ. *Pakistan Archaeology* (1 a year).

Pakistan Historical Society: Bait al-Hikmah, Hamdard Univ. campus, Madinat al-Hikmah, Karachi 74600, Sindh; tel. (21) 36616001; fax (21) 36611755; e-mail phs@ hamdard.edu.pk; f. 1950; historical studies and research, particularly history of Islam and the sub-continent; library of 10,000 vols, 80 MSS; Pres. SADIA RASHID; Gen. Sec. Dr ANSAR ZAHID KHAN; publ. *Journal of the Pakistan Historical Society (Historicus)* (4 a year).

LANGUAGE AND LITERATURE

Alliance Française d'Islamabad: House 9, St 49, F 6/4, Islamabad; tel. (51) 2825218; fax (51) 9213730; e-mail contact@afislamabad .org; internet www.afislamabad.org; offers courses and exams in French language and culture and promotes cultural exchange with France; attached teaching centres in Karachi, Lahore and Peshawar; library of 1,500 vols; Dir MATTHIEU DECLERCQ; Asst Dir NAUMAN AHMED.

Anjuman Taraqqi-e-Urdu Pakistan: D-159, Block 7, Gulshan-e-Iqbal, Karachi 75300, Sindh; tel. (21) 34973296; e-mail anjumantarraqieurdu@hotmail.com; f. 1903 in pre-partition India, 1948 in Pakistan; promotes Urdu language and literature; prepares a 6-volume bibliography of Urdu books in collaboration with UNESCO; library of 30,000 vols, research library of 48,000 vols and 4,000 MSS; Pres. AFTAB AHMED KHAN; Hon. Sec. JAMILUDDIN AALI; publs *Qaumi Zaban* (12 a year), *Urdu* (4 a year).

Balochi Academy: Adalat Rd, Quetta, Balochistan; tel. (81) 2829566; e-mail academy@balochiacademy.org; internet www .balochiacademy.org; f. 1958; promotes Balochi language and literature, publishes books on Balochi history, poetry, culture, folk stories, and a Balochi–Urdu dictionary and encyclopaedia; 48 mems; library of 40,000 vols; Chair. MUHAMMAD SIDDIQ BALOCH; Gen. Sec. ABDUL QADIR SHAHWANI ASEER.

British Council: POB 1135, Islamabad; tel. (21) 35839932; fax (51) 111425425; e-mail info@britishcouncil.org.pk; internet www .britishcouncil.org/pakistan; offers courses and exams in English language and British culture and promotes cultural exchange with the UK; attached offices in Faisalabad, Karachi, Lahore, Multan, Peshawar and Quetta; Dir DAVID MARTIN.

Goethe-Institut: 2 Brunton Rd, Civil Lines, Karachi; tel. (21) 35661633; fax (21) 35661632; e-mail info@karachi.goethe.org; internet www.goethe.de/karachi; f. 1956; offers courses and exams in German language; cultural activities incl. lectures, seminars, workshops and concerts from

Germany; library of 3,715 vols, 20 periodicals; Dir Dr MARKUS LITZ; Admin. Man. S. A. FAROOQ.

Institute of Islamic Culture: 2 Club Rd, Lahore, Punjab; tel. (42) 36363127; e-mail iic-lhr@hotmail.com; f. 1950; publishes books on Islamic subjects in English and Urdu; Dir KAZI JAVED; publ. *Al-Ma'arif* (in Urdu, 4 a year).

Iqbal Academy: POB 1308, 6th Fl., Academy Block, Aiwan-e-Iqbal Complex, off Egerton Rd, Lahore, Punjab; tel. (42) 6314510; fax (42) 6314496; e-mail info@iap.gov.pk; internet www.allamaiqbal.com; f. 1951; promotes, disseminates study and understanding of works and teachings of Allama Iqbal; publishes books and pamphlets on Dr Allama Iqbal; library of 30,000 vols; Dir MUHAMMED SUHEYL UMAR; publs *Iqbaliyat* (2 a year, in Urdu; 1 a year, in Arabic, Farsi and Turkish), *Iqbalnama, Iqbal Quarterly, Iqbal Review* (2 a year, in English).

National Language Authority: Pitras Bukhari Rd, H-8/4, Islamabad; tel. (51) 9250311; fax (51) 9250310; e-mail secretary@nla.gov.pk; internet www.nla.gov .pk; f. 1979; promotes Urdu as the nat., official, judicial and instructional language of Pakistan; organizes seminars and conferences; offers courses; develops Urdu terminology in various disciplines; compiles dictionaries; library of 25,000 vols; Chair. Dr ANWAR AHMED; Sec. SARFARAZ TARIQ; publ. *Akhbar-e-Urdu* (12 a year).

Attached Centre:

Centre of Excellence for Urdu Informatics: tel. (51) 9250317; e-mail nlauit@ apollo.net.pk; Urdu IT Wing of the NLA; develops Urdu keyboard layouts for computers and computer codes (Standardized Urdu Code Plate), and localization of Microsoft Urdu Office and Windows XP; mem of UNICODE, Inc.; Project Dir Dr ATTASH DURRANI; Project Man. AGHA ABID HUSSAIN MEMON.

Pakistan Academy of Letters: H 8/1, Islamabad; tel. (51) 9250570; fax (51) 9250590; e-mail pakistanacademyoflettersisb@gmail.com; internet www.pal.gov.pk; f. 1976; promotes literary works; determines research priorities in literature; evaluates the performance of literary bodies; sets up Bureau of Translation; introduces Pakistani literature to foreign readers; organizes seminars on literary and academic issues; advises the Govt on int. literary gatherings; nominates recipients for various literary awards and distinctions; provides financial assistance to scholars; library of 20,000 vols; Chair. ABDUL HAMEED; Dir-Gen. (vacant); publs *Adbiyat* (4 a year, in Urdu), *Bibliography of Pakistani Literature, Pakistani Literature* (2 a year), *Selection of Pakistani Literature* (12 a year).

Regional Offices:

Balochistan Office: Espeni Rd, Quetta; tel. (81) 2823473; Resident Asst Dir AFZAL MURAAD.

Khyber Pakhtunkhwa Office: Attached Dept Complex, Block 15, Khyber Rd, Peshawar; tel. (91) 9211139; Resident Asst Dir Dr MUHAMMAD AZAM AZAM.

Punjab Office: House 74/A3-1, Abu Bakar Block, New Garden Town, Lahore, Punjab; tel. (42) 35852974; Resident Asst Dir ALTAF AHMAD QURESHI.

Sindh Office: 80A, Block 2, P. E. C. H. S., Khalid Bin Waleed Rd, Karachi; tel. (21) 4531588; Resident Asst Dir AGHA NOOR MUHAMMAD PATHAN.

Pakistan American Cultural Centre: 11 Fatima Jinnah Rd, Karachi, Sindh; tel. (21) 35215305; fax (21) 35653837; e-mail info@

pacc.edu.pk; internet www.pacc.edu.pk; f. 1959; promotes relation between people of Pakistan and America; offers language services, cultural activities; Exec. Dir MUHAMMAD SIKANDER IQBAL.

Pakistan Writers Guild: Guild House, 1 Montgomery Rd, Lahore, Punjab; tel. (42) 6367124; e-mail info@pakwritersguild.org; internet www.pakwritersguild.org; f. 1959; 4 regional offices; promotes authorship, dispenses literary prizes, concerned with welfare of writers; Sec. AHMED OMAR SHARIF; publs *Ham Qalam* (12 a year), *Khaber Namay* (12 a year).

Pashto Academy: Univ. of Peshawar, Peshawar, Khyber Pakhtunkhwa; tel. (91) 9216486; fax (91) 5704272; e-mail pashtoacademy@yahoo.com; internet pashto .upesh.edu.pk; f. 1955; research into Pashto language and literature, history, art and culture; research cell for study of life and works of Khushal Khan Khattak and his contemporaries; research library; Dir Prof. Dr SALMA SHAHEEN; Librarian SARFERAZ KHAN MARWAT; publ. *Pukhto* (12 a year).

Sindhi Adabi Board: POB 12, Jamshorro 76070, Sindh; tel. (22) 9213421; fax (22) 9213422; e-mail bookinfo@sindhiadabiboard .org; internet www.sindhiadabiboard.org; f. 1951; autonomous literary and cultural instn; fosters the language, literature and culture of the Sindh region; publishes books in English, Sindhi, Urdu, Persian and Arabic; library of 10,000 vols, 450 MSS; Chair. MAKHDOOM JAMEELUZZAMAN; publs *Gul Phul* (children's, 12 a year), *Mehran* (4 a year), *Sartyoon* (women's, 12 a year).

Urdu Academy: 33C Model Town 'A', Bahawalpur, Punjab; f. 1959; develops Urdu literature and language; publishes books in English and Urdu; Sec. MASUD HASSAN SHIHAB; publ. *Az-Zubair* (4 a year, in Urdu).

Urdu Dictionary Board: ST-18/A, Block 5, Gulshan-e-Iqbal, Off University Rd, Karachi 75300, Sindh; tel. (21) 34988887; internet www.udb.gov.pk; f. 1958 as Urdu Devt Board, present name 1982; publishes books and dictionaries in Urdu; projects incl. a comprehensive, 23-vol. Urdu Dictionary; library of 15,638 vols; Chair. FED. MIN. OF EDUCATION; Pres. Dr FARMAN FATEH PURI; Chief Editor FAHMID RIAZ.

Urdu Science Board: 299 Upper Mall, Lahore 54000, Punjab; tel. (42) 5758475; fax (42) 5789215; e-mail ubfi@urduscienceboard .com; f. 1962; aims to remove deficiencies in Urdu language, particularly in the fields of technology, natural and social sciences; coordinates work of other orgs engaged in related fields; prepares standard dictionaries of scientific and technical terms; library of 10,000 vols; Dir-Gen. KHALID IQBAL YASIR; publ. *Urdu Science Magazine* (4 a year).

MEDICINE

College of Physicians and Surgeons Pakistan: Seventh Central St, Defence Housing Authority Phase II, Karachi 75500, Sindh; tel. (21) 99207100; fax (21) 99207120; e-mail administration@cpsp.edu.pk; internet www.cpsp.edu.pk; f. 1962; promotes specialist practice of medicine, surgery and gynaecology and allied disciplines by means of improvement in hospital teaching and methods; arranges postgraduate medical, surgical and other specialist training; provides for medical research and organizes scientific confs for Pakistani and foreign medical experts; awards diplomas of MCPS and FCPS; 9,366 mems (MCPS), 6,900 fellows (FCPS); short course on research methodology, biostatistics, medical writing and computer learning, CME for medical and allied health teachers, CME in RH primary

care providers (medical), computer training workshop for medical librarians in Pakistan, diploma in health system management; 12 regional centres; library of 10,000 books, 10,000 journals, 7,000 periodicals, 7,500 dissertations, 375 CD-ROMs, 1,300 audio journals, 1,322 video cassettes, 600 WHO books and monagrams, 171 slides, 1,835 x-rays, medical databases and journals; 18,390 mems; Pres. Prof. ZAFARULLAH CHAUDHRY; Vice-Pres. Prof. TARIQ MAHMOOD KHAN; Vice-Pres. Prof. KHALID MASOOD GONDAL; Sec. Capt. Dr QAZI JALALUDDIN AHMED; Registrar Prof. GHULAM ASGHAR CHANNA; Chief Librarian BAIBA AWAN; publ. *Journal of the College of Physicians and Surgeons Pakistan* (12 a year).

Pakistan Academy of Medical Sciences: 238 Jinnah Colony, Faisalabad, Punjab; tel. (411) 31795; f. 1975; promotes medical sciences and arts; awards annual Gold Medal; holds annual PAMS Lecture; 56 Fellows; Pres. Prof. KHALID J. AWAN; Sec.-Gen. IFTIKHAR A. MALIK; publ. *Pakistan Journal of Ophthalmology* (4 a year).

Pakistan Medical Association: PMA House, Garden Rd, POB 7267, Karachi 74400; tel. and fax (21) 2226443; e-mail jpma_jpma@hotmail.com; f. 1948; Pres. Dr TIPU SULTAN; Sec.-Gen. Dr MIRZA ALI AZHAR; publ. *Journal of Pakistan Medical Association* (12 a year).

NATURAL SCIENCES

General

Pakistan Academy of Sciences: 3 Constitution Ave, G-5/2, Islamabad; tel. (51) 9225159; fax (51) 9225159; e-mail pas .editor@gmail.com; internet www.paspk.org; f. 1953; promotes research in pure and applied sciences; establishes and maintains libraries; awards grants, fellowships and gold medals; 117 mems (87 fellows, 22 foreign fellows, 8 gen.); Pres. Prof. Dr ATTA-UR-RAHMAN; Vice-Pres. Prof. Dr KHALID MAHMOOD KHAN; Vice-Pres. Prof. Dr M. QASIM JAN; Sec.-Gen. Prof. Dr G. A. MIANA; publs *Proceedings of Symposia, Monographs* (irregular), *Proceedings of the Pakistan Academy of Sciences* (4 a year), *Yearbook.*

Pakistan Association for the Advancement of Science: First Fl., 67 Shadman Plaza, Shadman Market, Lahore, Punjab; tel. (42) 37578770; fax (42) 37503893; e-mail cmsaleem@wol.net.pk; internet www.paas .com.pk; f. 1947; promotes science in all its brs, incl. its application to practical problems and research; organizes nat. conferences; publishes journals; 1,500 mems; Pres. Prof. Dr MUHAMMAD ARSHAD; Vice-Pres. Prof. Dr MUHAMMAD AMJAD; Gen. Sec. Prof. Dr MUHAMMAD SALEEM CHAUDHRY; publs *Pakistan Journal of Science* (4 a year), *Pakistan Journal of Scientific Research* (4 a year), *Proceedings of the All Pakistan Science Conference* (every 3 years), *Proceedings of the National Seminars* (every 3 years).

Scientific Society of Pakistan: Univ. of Karachi Campus, Karachi, Sindh; tel. (21) 4463144; f. 1954; promotes science through the nat. language (Urdu); 3,500 mems; Pres. Dr SYED IRTIFAQ ALI; Sec. AFTAB HASAN; publs *Jadeed Science* (6 a year, in Urdu), *Proceedings of Annual Science Conferences* (in Urdu), *Science Bachchon Key Liye* (12 a year, in Urdu), *Science Nama* (26 a year, in Urdu).

Mathematical Sciences

Centre for Advanced Studies in Mathematics: Opposite Sector U, D. H. A., Lahore Cantt, Lahore 54792, Punjab; tel. (42) 35608013; fax (42) 35722591; e-mail casm@ lums.edu.pk; internet casm.lums.edu.pk;

attached to Lahore Univ. of Management Sciences; promotes interaction between mathematicians and experts of other disciplines; holds workshops, conferences; 16 mems, 10 Assoc. mems; Dir Dr FAQIR M. BHATTI; Sec. NOREEN IRSHAD.

PHILOSOPHY AND PSYCHOLOGY

Pakistan Philosophical Congress: Dept of Philosophy, Univ. of the Punjab, New Campus, Lahore, Punjab; tel. (42) 5863984; f. 1954; promotes philosophical studies; Pres. Dr ABDUL KHALIQ; Sec. Dr NAEEM AHMAD; publ. *Pakistan Philosophical Journal* (1 a year).

RELIGION, SOCIOLOGY AND ANTHROPOLOGY

Hamdard Foundation Pakistan: Al Majeed, Hamdard Centre, Nazimabad 3, Karachi 74600, Sindh; tel. (21) 36616001; fax (21) 36611755; e-mail hfp@ hamdardfoundation.org; internet www .hamdardfoundation.org; f. 1964; administers and controls charitable and philanthropic work from the voluntary contribution of Hamdard Laboratories (WAQF) Pakistan; oversees the establishment of academic and educational institutes; 7 mems; library: see Libraries and Archives; Pres. SADIA RASHID; Vice-Pres. Dr NAVAID UL ZAFAR; Dir of Admin. SYED SHAMIM AKHTER RIZVI; publs *Hamdard-i-Sehat* (12 a year), *Hamdard Islamicus* (4 a year), *Hamdard Medicus* (4 a year), *Hamdard Naunehal* (12 a year), *Historicus* (4 a year).

Heritage Foundation: E-6 Fourth Gizri St, DHA 4, Karachi 75500, Sindh; tel. (21) 5834215; fax (21) 5863474; e-mail info@ heritagefoundationpak.org; internet www .heritagefoundationpak.org; f. 1980; engages in research, publication and conservation of Pakistan's cultural heritage; outreach programme KaravanPakistan, est. 2000, involves youth and communities in safeguarding heritage; attached research institute; Chair. and CEO YASMEEN LARI.

Jamiyat-ul-Falah: Akbar Rd, Saddar, POB 7141, Karachi 74400, Sindh; f. 1950; Tamizuddin Khan Memorial Library (8,000 vols), Quran, Tafseer, Hadees, and Seerat collection; Falah Islamic Centre, Falah Social Service Centre, Falah Majlis-e-Adab (literary society), Falah Pakistan Studies Centre, Falah Muslim World Studies Centre, Falah Science Studies Centre; Sec.-Gen. SHAMSUD-DIN KHALID AHMED; publ. *Voice of Islam* (12 a year, in English).

Karachi Theosophical Society: Jamshed Memorial Hall, M. A. Jinnah Rd, Karachi 74200; tel. (21) 2721275; e-mail secretary@ tospakistan.com; f. 1896; 150 mems; activities incl. study of comparative religion, philosophy and science; investigation of unexplained laws of nature; library of 20,000 vols; Pres. AMANULLAH AMIR; Vice-Pres. JAMIL AHMAD; Hon. Sec. KAIKOBAD J. DINSHAW; publs *The Karachi Theosophist* (6 a year), *Theosophy in Karachi* (6 a year).

Shariah Academy: Sector H-10, Islamabad; tel. (51) 9258060; e-mail director.dawah@iiu .edu.pk; f. 1981, present status 1985; attached to Int. Islamic Univ.; promotes Islamic legal philosophy and orientation in Islamic Law; Dir-Gen. Dr SAHIBZADA SAJID-UR-REHMAN.

TECHNOLOGY

Institution of Electrical and Electronics Engineers Pakistan (IEEEP): C-2, Mezzanine Fl., 15th Commercial St, Phase II DHA, Karachi, Sindh; tel. (21) 35392965; fax (21) 5313968; e-mail ieeepkhi@yahoo.co.uk;

internet www.ieeepkhi.org; f. 1979; head office in Lahore; promotes dissemination of knowledge and improves professional standard; lectures, seminars and publns on electrical and electronic telecommunication engineering; 4,450 (2,300 corporate mems, 2,150 individual mems); library of 2,050 vols, 6,000 periodicals; Chair TAHIR SALEEM; Vice-Chair. OBAID UR REHMAN; Vice-Pres. S. S. A. JAFRI; publs *Quarterly Electrical Journal*, *The Electrical Engineer* (12 a year).

Institution of Engineers (Pakistan): IEP Bldg, Ground Fl., Gulberg III, Lahore 54660, Punjab; tel. (42) 35754043; fax (42) 5759449; e-mail iephqr@gmail.com; internet www.iep .com.pk; f. 1948; promotes and advances science, practice and business of engineering in all its brs; regional offices in Faisalabad, Hyderabad, Islamabad, Karachi, Peshawar, Quetta; Sub centres in Bahrain, Jeddah, Riyadh; 50,000 mems (corporate and individual); Pres. ZAFFARUDDIN A. ZUBERI; Dir RAJA MUHAMMAD RAFIQUE KHAN; publ. *The Pakistan Engineers* (12 a year).

Research Institutes

GENERAL

Area Study Centre: Peshawar, Khyber Pakhtunkhwa; tel. (91) 9216764; fax (91) 9216661; e-mail ascpesh@gmail.com; internet asc.upesh.edu.pk; f. 1978; attached to Univ. of Peshawar; research on Central Asia; Dir Prof. Dr SARFARAZ KHAN; library of 18,880 vols; publ. *Central Asia* (2 a year).

Pakistan Study Centre: Main Univ. Rd, Karachi 75270, Sindh; tel. (21) 9261300; fax (21) 9261632; e-mail psc@uok.edu.pk; f. 1983; attached to Univ. of Karachi; research in social sciences; Dir Prof. Dr SYED JAFFAR AHMED; publ. *Pakistan Perspectives*.

AGRICULTURE, FISHERIES AND VETERINARY SCIENCE

Central Cotton Research Institute: Pakistan Central Cotton Committee, 47-A Hussain Centre, Darul Aman Housing Soc., Main Shahrah-e-Faisal, Karachi, Sindh; tel. (61) 9201128; e-mail pccc@super.net.pk; f. 1970; divs: agronomy, breeding and genetics, cytogenetics, entomology, pathology, physiology, fibre technology, statistics, transfer of technology; processing of cotton varieties and their release for cultivation in the local environment; library of 1,530 vols; Dir Dr M. ARSHAD; publ. *The Pakistan Cottons*.

Pakistan Agricultural Research Council: Plot 20 Sector G-5/1, Islamabad; tel. (51) 9203966; fax (51) 9202968; e-mail chair@ comsats.net.pk; internet www.parc.gov.pk; f. 1978; aims to undertake, aid, promote and coordinate agricultural research; sets up research ests; arranges training of high-level scientists in agricultural sciences; generates, acquires and disseminates information relating to agriculture; library of 21,000 vols, 1,166 periodicals; Chair. Dr IFTIKHAR AHMAD; publs *Pakistan Journal of Agricultural Research* (4 a year), *Pakistan Journal of Agricultural Social Sciences* (2 a year), *PARC News* (12 a year), *Progressive Farming* (6 a year).

Pakistan Forest Institute: Univ. of Peshawar Campus, Peshawar 25000, Khyber Pakhtunkhwa; tel. (91) 49580; tel. (91) 71260; f. 1947; library: see Libraries and Archives; Forestry Museum; training courses leading to BSc and MSc in Forestry; Dir-Gen. Dr K. M. SIDDIQUI; publ. *Pakistan Journal of Forestry* (2 a year).

Punjab Veterinary Research Institute: Ghazi Rd, Lahore Cantonment, Punjab; tel.

(42) 9220140; fax (42) 9220142; f. 1963; promotes and improves devt of the livestock industry and control diseases; production of vaccines, research on animal health problems; disease diagnosis and investigation; development of improved laboratory techniques; part of the Punjab Livestock and Dairy Devt Dept.

Rice Research Institute Dokri: Dokri, Larkana 77080, Sindh; tel. (74) 4080328; fax (74) 4080283; f. 1938; research on various aspects of rice incl. varietal improvement, control of insect pests, diseases and weeds, grain quality; library of 4,426 vols, 1,523 periodicals.

Veterinary Research Institute: Bacha Khan Chowk, Charsadda Rd, POB 367, Peshawar 25000, Khyber Pakhtunkhwa; tel. (91) 9210218; fax (91) 9210220; e-mail directorvri@hotmail.com; f. 1949; research on livestock and poultry diseases, production of veterinary biologics and diagnostic agents; 45 mems; library of 1,000 vols; Dir Dr SAADULLAH JAN; publ. *Journal of Animal Health and Production* (4 a year).

ECONOMICS, LAW AND POLITICS

Applied Economics Research Centre: Univ. of Karachi, POB 8403, Karachi 75270, Sindh; tel. (21) 99261541; fax (21) 99261545; e-mail aerc@cyber.net.pk; internet www.aerc .edu.pk; f. 1973; policy-orientated quantitative research on problems in applied economics; courses leading to MPhil and PhD in Economics; library of 40,000 vols; 250 periodicals; Dir Prof. Dr NUZHAT AHMAD; publ. *Pakistan Journal of Applied Economics* (2 a year).

Centre for South Asian Studies: Univ. of the Punjab, Quaid-i-Azam Campus, Lahore 54590, Punjab; tel. (42) 99231143; fax (42) 99232039; e-mail director.csas@pu.edu.pk; f. 1973, present 1975; interdisciplinary research on South Asia, incl. economics, politics, sociology, foreign affairs, and other social devts of the area; programme incl. data collection and analysis; sponsors seminars; library of 12,000 vols; Dir Dr UMBREEN JAVAID; publ. *South Asian Studies* (2 a year, in English).

Federal Bureau of Statistics: Statistics Div., Govt of Pakistan, 5-SLIC Bldg, F-6/4, Blue Area, Islamabad; tel. (51) 9208489; fax (51) 9203233; e-mail statpak@statpak.gov .pk; internet www.statpak.gov.pk; f. 1950; library of 4,600 vols, 41,200 periodicals; Dir-Gen. Dr NOOR MUHAMMAD LARIK; publs *Census of Manufacturing Industries* (1 a year), *Foreign Trade Statistics of Pakistan* (separate series for imports and exports, each 1 a year), *Macro Economic Indicators of Pakistan* (4 a year), *Monthly Statistical Bulletin*, *National Accounts* (1 a year), *Pakistan Statistical Yearbook* (1 a year), *Reviews of Foreign Trade* (12 a year), *Statistical Pocket Book of Pakistan* (1 a year).

Institute of Strategic Studies: Sector F-5/ 2, Islamabad; tel. (51) 9204423; fax (51) 9204658; e-mail strategy@issi.org.pk; internet www.issi.org.pk; f. 1973; provides a broad-based and informed public understanding of vital strategic and allied issues affecting Pakistan and the int. community at large; library of 14,000 vols and 70 journals; Chair. GUL HANEEF; Dir-Gen. ASHRAF JEHAN-GIR QAZI; Dir of Americas NAJAM RAFIQUE; Dir of East Asia FAZAL-UR-RAHMAN; Dir of Russia and Central Asia SIMBAL KHAN (acting); Dir of South Asia FAHMIDA ASHRAF; publ. *Strategic Studies* (4 a year).

National Institute of Public Administration: 78 Shahrah-e-Quaid-e-Azam, Lahore; tel. (42) 9200921; fax (42) 9200926; internet www.niplahore.gov.pk; f. 1961; training in public admin. for officers of fed. and provincial govt; research in public admin.; consultancy services to the govt; library of 30,000 vols; Dir-Gen. SIKANDAR SHAMI; publ. *Public Administration Review* (4 a year).

Pakistan Institute of Development Economics: Quaid-i-Azam Univ. campus, POB 1091, Islamabad 44000; tel. (51) 9248051; fax (51) 9248065; e-mail pide@pide.org.pk; internet www.pide.org.pk; f. 1957; theoretical and empirical research in devt economics; provides in-service training in economic analysis, research methods, and project planning, preparation, appraisal, implementation and evaluation techniques; PhD programme in economics; library of 33,750 vols, 220 current periodicals, 6,200 microfiches, 22,700 research papers and reports; Vice-Chancellor Dr RASHID AMJAD; Jt Dir Dr MUSLEH-UD DIN; Jt Dir Dr REHANA SIDDIQUI; Chief Librarian TARIQ MAHMOOD; publ. *Pakistan Development Review* (4 a year).

Pakistan Institute of Human Rights: Centre 177, St 68, F-10/3, Islamabad 46000; tel. (51) 2294601; fax (51) 2294602; e-mail info@pihr.org.pk; internet www.pihr.org.pk; f. 1998; non-profit, non-aligned research-based academic instn promoting human rights; Chair. and Founder Dr SYED MOHAMMED ANWER; Dir ABDUR REHMAN, FAZAL I RABBI; Dir FAZAL I RABBI; Dir HINA BASHARAT; Dir MUHAMMAD RAUF CHAUDHRY; Dir NIAZ. A. ABASSI; Dir SYED TANVER HAIDER.

Punjab Economic Research Institute (PERI): 24 Mianmir Rd, Upper Mall Scheme, Lahore, Punjab; f. 1955; attached to Planning and Development Dept, Govt of Punjab; undertakes socioeconomic investigations and coordinates research in economic problems of Pakistan; collects, compiles and interprets statistical data; publishes the results and findings of investigations; Dir AZIZ A. ANWAR; Sec. A. R. ARSHAD.

HISTORY, GEOGRAPHY AND ARCHAEOLOGY

National Centre of Excellence in Geology: Peshawar 25120, Khyber Pakhtunkhwa; tel. (91) 9216427; fax (91) 9218183; e-mail masifk@upesh.edu.pk; internet nceg.upesh.edu.pk; f. 1974; attached to Univ. of Peshawar; research in earth sciences; library of 9,192 vols; Dir Prof. Dr MUHAMMAD ASIF KHAN; publ. *Journal of Himalayan Earth Sciences* (1 a year).

National Institute of Historical and Cultural Research: Quaid-e-Azam Univ., New Campus, Shadara Rd, Islamabad; tel. (51) 2896153; fax (51) 2896152; e-mail nihcr@yahoo.com; internet www.nihcr.edu.pk; f. 1973 as Nat. Commission on Historical and Cultural Research, present name and status 1983; promotes studies on the history and culture of South Asian Muslims, genesis and growth of Muslim freedom movement; publishes research studies in history and culture, bibliographies, indices etc.; library of 50,000 vols, a colln of historical records, old newspapers, journals, photocopies of rare material, microfilms, microfiches; Dir SYED UMAR HAYAT (acting); Librarian HAZOOR BAKHSH CHANNA; publs *Majallah-i-Tarikh wa Thaqafat* (2 a year, in Urdu), *Pakistan Journal of History and Culture* (2 a year, in English).

Research Society of Pakistan: c/o the Vice Chancellor, Univ. of the Punjab, Lahore, Punjab; tel. (42) 9211631; f. 1963; research on cultural, political, literary, linguistic, economic, historical, topographical and archaeological features of Pakistan; library of 12,000 vols; Pres. Prof. Dr MUJAHID KAMRAN; Vice-Pres. IRSHAD AHMAD HAQQANI; Dir AFZAL HAQ; publ. *Journal of the Research Society of Pakistan* (2 a year).

MEDICINE

Cancer Research Institute: Dept and Institute of Radiotherapy, Jinnah Postgraduate Medical Centre, Rafiqui (H.J.) Shaheed Rd, Karachi 75510, Sindh; tel. (21) 9201300; e-mail edojpmc@jpmc.com.pk; f. 1954.

Pakistan Medical Research Council: Shahrah-e-Jamhuriat, G-5/2, Islamabad; tel. (51) 9216793; fax (51) 9216774; e-mail pmrc@comsats.net.pk; internet www.pmrc.org.pk; f. 1962; promotes research in fields of medicine and public health; disseminates and arranges utilization of this research; establishes liaison with nat. and int. orgs; research centres in medical colleges in Lahore, Karachi, Peshawar, Islamabad, Multan and Quetta; library of 4,800 vols; Pres. MIR AIJAZ HUSSAIN JAKHRANI; Exec. Dir Dr HUMA QURESHI; Librarian FAYYAZ AHMAD PIRZADO; publ. *Pakistan Journal of Medical Research* (4 a year).

NATURAL SCIENCES

General

Fazl-i-Omar Research Institute: Rabwah, Chenabnagar, Jhang 35460, Punjab; tel. (4524) 211082; fax (4524) 212296; f. 1946; promotes study of science and the devt of industries in Pakistan; library of 10,000 vols; Dir MUBARAK MUSLEH-UD-DIN AHMAD.

Pakistan Council for Science and Technology: Shahrah-e-Jamhuriat, off Constitution Ave, , Sector G-5/2, Islamabad; tel. (51) 9205157; fax (51) 9205171; e-mail info@pcst.org.pk; internet www.pcst.org.pk; f. 1961; advises the govt on science and technology policy; devises measures for promotion, devt and application of science and technology in Pakistan; library of 1,200 vols; Chair. Dr TARIQ-UR-RAHMAN; Librarian SHAGUFTA SHAHEEN; publs *Science, Science and Technology in the Islamic World* (4 a year), *Science, Technology and Development* (6 a year).

Pakistan Council of Scientific and Industrial Research (PCSIR): Constitution Ave, Sector G-5/2, Islamabad 74200; tel. (51) 9225395; fax (51) 9225372; e-mail chairman@pcsir.gov.pk; internet www.pcsir.gov.pk; f. 1953; attached to Min. of Science and Technology; promotes scientific and industrial research and its applications to the devt of the nat. industries and the utilization of the natural resources of the country; laboratories in Islamabad, Karachi, Lahore, Peshawar, Quetta, Skardu; Scientific and Technical Information Centre; library: see Libraries and Archives; Chair. Dr SHOUKAT PARVEZ; Sec. AHMAD SAGHIR; publ. *Pakistan Journal of Scientific and Industrial Research* (6 a year).

Biological Sciences

Centre for Molecular Genetics: Main Univ. Rd, Karachi 75270, Sindh; tel. and fax (21) 4966045; e-mail cmg@uok.edu.pk; attached to Univ. of Karachi; advanced research in genetic engineering, microbial genetics, molecular genetics; Dir Dr NUZHAT AHMED.

Centre of Biotechnology and Microbiology: Peshawar, Khyber Pakhtunkhwa; tel. (91) 9216485; fax (91) 5843767; e-mail biotech@upesh.edu.pk; internet biotech.upesh.edu.pk; f. 2001; attached to Univ. of Peshawar; research areas incl. genetics, physiology, medicinal plants and biotechnology, microbiology; Dir Prof. Dr BASHIR AHMAD.

Centre of Excellence in Marine Biology: Univ. of Karachi, Karachi 75270, Sindh; tel. (21) 9261300; e-mail info@cemb-pk.edu.pk; internet www.cemb-ku.edu.pk; f. 1969, present status 1975; research in marine biology; library of 5,210 vols, 1, 670 journals; Chair. Prof. Dr PIRZADA QASIM RAZA SIDDIQUI; Dir Prof. Dr JAVED MUSTAQUIM; publs *CEMB News* (2 a year), *Pakistan Journal of Marine Biology* (2 a year).

Department of Plant Protection: Jinnah Ave, Malir Halt, Karachi, Sindh; tel. (21) 9248612; fax (21) 9248673; e-mail info@plantprotection.gov.pk; internet www.plantprotection.gov.pk; f. 1947; attached to Min. of Food, Agriculture and Livestock; survey and control of desert locust population, control of crop pests by air; executes Plant Quarantine Act 1976 and Pakistan Agriculture Pesticide Ordinance 1971 and its rules 1973; advises Fed. and Provincial govts on plant protection matters; library of 22,085 vols, 13 current periodicals; Dir-Gen. Dr TASNEEM AHMAD.

Institute of Industrial Biotechnology: GC Univ., Lahore, Punjab; tel. (42) 99211634; e-mail ikmhaq@yahoo.com; f. 1990 as Biotechnology Research Centre, Dept of Botany, present status in 2005; attached to GC Univ.; research in microbiology and biotechnology; library of 10,000 vols; Dir Prof. Dr IKRAM UL HAQ.

Institute of Sustainable Halophyte Utilization: Main Univ. Rd, Karachi 75270, Sindh; tel. (21) 34820253; fax (21) 34820258; e-mail majmalk@uok.edu.pk; internet www.halophyte.org; attached to Univ. of Karachi; research areas incl. biochemistry and molecular biology, ecology, ecophysiology, halophyte utilization; Dir Dr M. AJMAL KHAN.

National Nematological Research Centre: Main Univ. Rd, Karachi 75270, Sindh; tel. and fax (21) 99261387; e-mail nnrc@uok.edu.pk; attached to Univ. of Karachi; research areas incl. molecular taxonomy, biology, pathogenicity, population dynamics, control of plant parasitic nematodes, use of marine nematodes as pollution indicators, entomopathogenic nematodes, nematodes in biological control of insect pests, human nematology; library of 800 vols; Dir Prof. Dr SHAHINA FAYYAZ; publ. *Pakistan Journal of Nematology (PJN)* (2 a year).

Zoological Survey Department: Govt of Pakistan, Kalma Chowk, Bhara Kahu, Islamabad 44000; tel. (51) 2233121; fax (51) 2233511; e-mail zoology@isb.comsats.net.pk; internet www.zsd.gov.pk; f. 1948; research in ecology, biodiversity, marine biology, and wildlife of Pakistan; library of 10,810 vols, 125 periodicals, 1,600 reprints; Dir ABDUL WAHAB; publ. *Records/Zoological Survey of Pakistan* (1 a year).

Research Laboratory:

Marine Biological Research Laboratory: Block 67, Pakistan Secretariat, Shahrah-e-Iraq, Saddar, Karachi 74200; tel. (21) 9203334; e-mail zsd6167@imulti.net.pk; f. 1962.

Mathematical Sciences

Abdus Salam School of Mathematical Sciences (ASSMS): GC Univ., 68-B, New Muslim Town, Lahore 54600, Punjab; tel. (42) 99231859; fax (42) 35864946; e-mail info@sms.edu.pk; internet www.sms.edu.pk; f. 2003; attached to GC Univ.; fundamental research in mathematical and allied sciences; library of 2,000 vols; Dir-Gen. Dr A. D. RAZA CHOUDHARY; publs *Journal of Prime Research in Mathematics (JPRM)* (Mathematics Magazine), *Math Track* (Mathematics Magazine).

Physical Sciences

Astronomical Observatory of the University of the Punjab: c/o Dept of Space Science, Quaid-i-Azam Campus, Univ. of the Punjab, Lahore 54590, Punjab; tel. (42) 99239294; e-mail chairman.spsc@pu.edu.pk; f. 1920, reorganized in 1986 within the Univ. Dept of Space Science; teaching and research in astronomy, remote sensing, GIS, telecommunication and atmospheric science; courses at undergraduate and graduate level; works in cooperation with nat. and int. institutes; Chair. Dr MUHAMMAD ALI.

Centre for Advanced Studies in Physics (CASP): 1 Church Road, GC Univ., Lahore, Punjab; tel. (42) 99211589; e-mail ahriaz@gcu.edu.pk; f. 1954; attached to GC Univ.; research in Atomic and Nuclear Physics; Dir Prof. Dr RIAZ AHMAD.

H. E. J. Research Institute of Chemistry: c/o Int. Centre for Chemical and Biological Sciences, Main Univ. Rd, Karachi 75270, Sindh; tel. (21) 99261701; fax (21) 99261713; e-mail hej@cyber.net.pk; internet www.iccs.edu/hej; attached to Univ. of Karachi; research areas incl. biosynthesis, cancer, computational chemistry, genetic engineering, plant biotechnology, textile and food chemistry, tropical disease, spectroscopy; library of 7,000 vols, 177 journals; Dir Prof. Dr ATTA-UR-RAHMAN.

Institute of Chemical Sciences: Peshawar 25120, Khyber Pakhtunkhwa; tel. (91) 9216652; e-mail chemistry@upesh.edu.pk; f. 1955; attached to Univ. of Peshawar; research in analytical chemistry, biochemistry, fuel and applied chemistry, inorganic chemistry, physical chemistry, organic chemistry; Dir Prof. Dr IMDAD ULLAH.

Institute of Environmental Studies: Main Univ. Rd, Karachi 75270, Sindh; tel. and fax (21) 9261386; e-mail ies@uok.edu.pk; f. 1982; attached to Univ. of Karachi; research on environment and related fields; library of 5,000 vols; Dir Dr MOAZZAM ALI KHAN.

Institute of Marine Science: Main Univ. Rd, Karachi 75270, Sindh; tel. (21) 99261300; e-mail ims@uok.edu.pk; f. 1981; attached to Univ. of Karachi; research in ecological, biological and geological aspect of marine environment; Dir Dr RASHIDA QARI.

National Centre of Excellence in Physical Chemistry: Peshawar 25120, Khyber Pakhtunkhwa; tel. (91) 9216766; fax (91) 9216671; e-mail ncepc@upesh.edu.pk; internet ncepc.upesh.edu.pk; f. 1978; attached to Univ. of Peshawar; research areas incl. advance oxidation technology for water treatment, coal and biomass as alternate fuel, electrochemistry, fine particles science, hetrogeneous catalysis, macromolecular chemistry, radiation and photochemistry, solution and gas phases kinetics, surface chemistry, polymer chemistry, tribology; Dir Prof. Dr HASAN M KHAN; publ. *Physical Chemistry*.

Pakistan Atomic Energy Commission (PAEC): POB 1114, Islamabad; tel. (51) 9204276; fax (51) 9204908; e-mail sipr@paec.gov.pk; internet www.paec.gov.pk; f. 1956; responsible for the devt of nuclear technology as part of Pakistan's nuclear power programme; operates nuclear power plants in Karachi and Chashma; promotes peaceful use of atomic energy in agriculture, medicine, industry and hydrology; searches for indigenous mineral deposits suitable for the production of atomic energy; trains project personnel; Chair. Dr ANSAR PARVEZ; Sec. JAVED IQBAL KHWAJA; publ. *The Nucleus* (4 a year).

Pakistan Meteorological Department: POB 1214, Sector H-8/2, Islamabad; tel. (51) 9250367; fax (51) 9250368; e-mail pakmet_islamabad@yahoo.com; internet www.pakmet.com.pk; f. 1947; provides hydrometeorological and geophysical services for protection of life, property and the environment, increased safety on land, at sea and in the air, sustainable economic growth; issues of different types of weather and flood forecasts, warnings and advisories; investigates the behaviour of the atmosphere and exploits this knowledge for short- and long-term weather predictions; undertakes research and devt activities in various disciplines such as weather modifications and the wind potential of coastal and northern areas of Pakistan; Dir-Gen. ARIF MAHMOOD; publ. *Pakistan Journal of Meteorology* (2 a year).

PHILOSOPHY AND PSYCHOLOGY

Institute of Clinical Psychology: Main Univ. Rd, Karachi 75270, Sindh; tel. (21) 34613584; fax (21) 34615369; e-mail icp@uok.edu.pk; f. 1983; attached to Univ. of Karachi; research and professional training in clinical psychology, psychotherapy, psychological assessment, diagnostic testing, speech therapy, occupational therapy, rehabilitation and other related areas; Dir Dr RIYAZ AHMAD; publs *Pakistan Journal of Clinical Psychology (PJCP)* (2 a year), *Pakistan Journal of Psychology (PJP)* (official journal).

RELIGION, SOCIOLOGY AND ANTHROPOLOGY

Centre of Excellence for Women's Studies: Main Univ. Rd, Karachi 75270, Sindh; tel. (21) 99261300; e-mail cews@uok.edu.pk; f. 1989; attached to Univ. of Karachi; library of 4,000 vols; Dir Dr NASREEN ASLAM SHAH; publ. *Pakistan Journal of Gender Studies*.

Dawah Academy: Shah Faisal Complex, Islamabad; tel. (51) 9258060; e-mail director.dawah@iiu.edu.pk; internet dawah.iiu.edu.pk; f. 1985; attached to Int. Islamic Univ.; research in Islamic studies, Dawah; library of 25,000 vols, 166 journals; Dir-Gen. Dr SAHIBZADA SAJID-UR-REHMAN.

Institute of Sindhology: Allama I. I. Kazi Campus, University of Sindh, Jamshoro 76070, Sindh; tel. (22) 2771386; fax (22) 2772494; e-mail director@sindhology.usindh.edu.pk; internet www.sindhology.com.pk; f. 1962 as Sindhi Academy, present name 1964; publishes research material in foreign languages; develops working tools (dictionaries, historical surveys, etc.) for scholars; research in history, culture, literature and fine arts; incl. bureau of production, publn and translation, documentation, information and research cell, research library, dept of preservation of documents and rare material, anthropological research centre with Sindh Art Gallery and Museum, dept of performing arts, sound and film with ethnomusical gallery; photographic and microform sections; library: see Libraries; Dir SHOUKAT HUSSAIN SHORO; publs *Sindhi Adab* (1 a year, in Sindhi), *Sindhological Studies* (2 a year, in English).

Islamic Research Institute: POB 1035, Islamabad 44000; Sector H-10, Islamabad; tel. (51) 2281289; fax (51) 2250821; e-mail dgiri@iiu.edu.pk; internet iri.iiu.edu.pk; f. 1960, present status 1980; attached to Int. Islamic Univ.; develops and disseminates methodology for research in various fields of Islamic learning; interprets teachings of Islam; studies contemporary problems of Islam; contributes to the revival of Islamic heritage; organizes study groups, seminars, conferences, etc.; serves as a clearing house

on various aspects of Islam; library of 55,000 vols and periodicals, 550 microfilms, 140 MSS, 760 photostats, 150 cassettes; Chair. Dr ANWAR HUSSAIN SIDDIQI; Dir-Gen. Dr MUHAMMAD KHALID MASUD; publs *Al-Dirasat al-Islamiyyah* (4 a year), *Fikr-o-Nazar* (4 a year), *Islamic Studies* (4 a year, in English).

Shaykh Zayed Islamic Centre: Peshawar 25120, Khyber Pakhtunkhwa; tel. (91) 9216746; fax (91) 9216746; e-mail szic@upesh.edu.pk; internet www.szic.pk; f. 1985; attached to Univ. of Peshawar; research in Arabic language, Islamic studies; library of 15,000 vols; Dir Prof. Dr DOST MUHAMMAD KHAN.

Sheikh Zayed Islamic Centre: Main Univ. Rd, Karachi 75270, Sindh; tel. (21) 99261081; fax (21) 99261082; e-mail szic@uok.edu.pk; internet szic.edu.pk; attached to Univ. of Karachi; research in Islamic studies; Dir Dr NOOR AHMED SHAHTAAZ; publ. *As–Saqafat–ul Islamia* (4 a year, in Arabic, English, Urdu).

Sustainable Development Study Centre: Science Blk Bldg, GC Univ., Lahore; tel. (42) 9213357; e-mail dr.aminulhaq@gcu.edu.pk; f. 2003; attached to GC Univ.; research areas incl. sustainable livelihoods, environmental management, community devt; library of 400 vols; Dir Prof. Dr AMIN-UL-HAQ KHAN.

TECHNOLOGY

Hydrocarbon Development Institute of Pakistan: Plot 18, St 6, Sector H-9/1, POB 1308, Islamabad; tel. (51) 9258301; fax (51) 9258310; e-mail info@hdip.com.pk; internet www.hdip.com.pk; f. 1975; attached to Min. of Petroleum and Natural Resources; research and services in petroleum geology and geochemistry, resource estimation, enhanced oil recovery, petroleum products testing and evaluation, petroleum processing technology, coal utilization technology, inter-fuel substitution, energy conservation, environmental control, compressed natural gas, energy database, oil and gas advisory and training services; laboratories in Islamabad, Karachi; library of 1,500 vols, 44 periodicals; Dir-Gen. IRSHAD ALI KHOKHAR; Sec. SHAHID ALI KHAN; publs *Pakistan Energy Yearbook* (1 a year), *Pakistan Journal of Hydrocarbon Research* (every 2 years).

Institute of Industrial Electronics Engineering: ST-22/C, Block-6, Gulshan-e-Iqbal, Karachi 75300, Sindh; tel. (21) 99244218; fax (21) 4982353; e-mail info@iiee.edu.pk; internet iiee.edu.pk; f. 1989; research in field of industrial electronics engineering; library of 2,500 vols; Prin. Dr RIAZUDDIN ABRO.

Irrigation Research Institute: Shahrah-e-Quaid-e-Azam, Lahore, Punjab; f. 1925; deals with irrigation and allied engineering problems in Pakistan; 2 field model stations, 2 substations and subsidiary laboratories for soils, foundation engineering, tube well experiments, etc.; library of 20,000 vols; Admin. SAAD HARROON.

Pakistan Council of Research in Water Resources: Khyaben-e-Johar Rd, Sector H 8/1, Islamabad; tel. (51) 9101282; fax (51) 9101280; e-mail pcrwr_ibd@yahoo.com; internet www.pcrwr.gov.pk; f. 2007; attached to Min. of Science and Technology; promotes research in fields of water and environment, hydraulics, irrigation, drainage, reclamation, tube wells and flood control; regional centres in Bahawalpur, Lahore, Peshawar, Quetta, Tando Jam; library of 10,000 vols; Chair. Dr MUHAMMAD ASLAM TAHIR; Dir-Gen. CH. MUHAMMAD AKRAM; Dir LUBNA NAHEED BUKHARI; publs *Fresh Arrivals and Periodicals Content Service* (4 a year), *Journal of Drainage and Water Management* (2 a year),

Pakistan Journal of Water Resources (2 a year).

Pakistan Institute of Cotton Research and Technology: Moulvi Tamizuddin Khan Rd, Karachi 74200, Sindh; tel. (21) 9202558; fax (21) 9205941; e-mail pccc@super.net.pk; f. 1956; fundamental and applied research on cotton fibres, yarns and fabrics; provides testing facilities and training to agriculture, trade and industry; library of 30,000 vols, 350 periodicals; Dir I. H. RESHAMWALA; publ. *The Pakistan Cottons* (4 a year).

Pakistan Institute of Management: Management House, Shahrah-e-Iran, Clifton, Karachi 75600, Sindh; tel. (21) 9251711; fax (21) 9251715; e-mail registration@pim.com.pk; internet www.pim.com.pk; f. 1954; offers 140 short courses in functional and integrated aspects of management each year; research on management issues; br. in Lahore; library of 6,000 vols, 60 films, 60 periodicals; Dir ZARRAR R. ZUBAIR; publ. *Pakistan Management Review* (4 a year).

Pakistan Standards and Quality Control Authority: St 7/A, Block 3, Scheme 36, Gulistan-e-Juhar, Karachi, Sindh; tel. (21) 34023842; fax (21) 34021420; e-mail dgeneral@psqca.com.pk; internet www.psqca.com.pk; f. 1996; attached to Min. of Science and Technology; mem. of ISO, International Electrotechnical Commission (IEC), Organisation Internationale de Métrologie Légale (OIML); fosters and promotes standards and conformity assessment; recommends nat. standards for the measurement of length, weight, volume and energy, prepares and promotes general adoption of standards on nat. and int. basis relating to materials and commodities, simplification in industry and commerce, enforcement of standards, etc.; library of 1,852 vols, 148,955 nat. and int. standards; Dir-Gen. PIR BAKHSH KHAN JAMALI; publs *Pakistan Standards Specification*, *PSI Yearbook*, *Test Methods and Code of Practice*.

Libraries and Archives

Bahawalpur

Central Library: Bahawalpur, Punjab; tel. (621) 80658; f. 1948; mobile library; audiovisual and microfiche secs; language laboratory; collections: books, newspapers and periodicals since 1948; some 19th-century newspapers and periodicals; map gallery; children's library; braille library; 105,960 vols (36,070 Urdu, 61,730 English, 8,160 other languages), 175 MSS (120 Arabic, 55 Persian and Urdu); 34 microfilms, 70 films; Chief Librarian MUHAMMAD ASHRAF JALAL.

Sir Sadiq Muhammad Khan Library: Bahawalpur, Punjab; tel. (62) 9255483; e-mail chief.librarian@iub.edu.pk; internet library.iub.edu.pk; f. 1975; attached to Islamia Univ. of Bahawalpur; 225,000 vols, 40,000 e-books; Chief Librarian MUHAMMAD RAFIQ AWAN; publs *Journal of Educational Research*, *Journal of Social Sciences and Humanities* (2 a year), *Ulum-e-Islamia Research Journal*.

Dera Ismail Khan

Gomal University Central Library: Dera Ismail Khan, Khyber Pakhtunkhwa; tel. (966) 750424; f. 1974; 60,000 vols; Librarian MUHAMMAD SADIQ JAVAID.

Faisalabad

University of Agriculture Library: Faisalabad 38040, Punjab; tel. (41) 9200161; e-mail luaf98@yahoo.com; internet www.uaf.edu.pk/library/lib_overview.html; f. 1961;

internet access, audiovisual section, Global Information Centre (GIC), Information Resource Centre (IRC), access to HEC Digital Library; depository library for FAO and World Bank publs; 255,475 vols, 22,925 MSS; Head Library Dept Prof. ZAHID ATA.

Hyderabad

Pakistan National Central Library and Culture Centre: Hyderabad, Sindh; f. 1958; 19,000 vols; Dir M. R. SIDDIQI.

Shamsul Ulema Daudpota Sindh Government Library: Hyderabad; f. 1951; attached to Culture and Tourism Dept, Sindh; 59,000 vols; Librarian (vacant).

Islamabad

Allama Iqbal Open University Central Library: Sector H-8, Islamabad; tel. (51) 9250040; e-mail reacmsf@gmail.com; internet www.aiou.edu.pk; f. 1974; 1m. vols; colln of theses, monographs and term papers; archives and govt papers colln; Librarian Dr SHAH FARRUKH (acting); publs *Ilm Ki Roshni* (2 a year, in Urdu), *Journal of Social Sciences and Humanities* (2 a year), *Maarif-e-Islami* (2 a year, in Urdu), *Pakistan Journal of Education* (2 a year).

Dr Raziuddin Siddiqi Memorial Library: Islamabad 45320; tel. (51) 2872563; fax (51) 2821397; e-mail librarian@qau.edu.pk; internet www.qau.edu.pk/lib; f. 1966; attached to Quaid-i-Azam Univ.; 195,000 vols, 223 current periodicals, 11,200 online journals; special collection of 29,000 vols on Indo–Pakistani history and Oriental literature; 269 MSS; 20,000 abstracts provided by Higher Education Commission of Pakistan; Librarian MEHBOOB HUSSAIN KHAN.

International Islamic University Central Library: POB 1243, H-10 Campus, Islamabad; tel. (51) 9257955; fax (51) 9258054; e-mail library@iiu.edu.pk; internet www.iiu.edu.pk; f. 1980; teaching, research facilities; 350,000 vols, 108 periodicals and journals; Chief Librarian SHER NOWROOZ KHAN; Prin. Librarian for Periodicals MUHAMMAD ZULQARNAIN AKHTAR (acting); Librarian for Reader Services QARI MAQBOOL SIDDIQUI.

Islamabad Public Library: Block 12-A, G-8 Markaz, Islamabad; tel. (51) 9260795; e-mail nlpiba@isb.paknet.com.pk; f. 1950; 34,000 vols; spec. collns incl. central and provincial govt publs; Deputy Dir HAFIZ KHUBAIB; Sr Librarian MUHAMMAD TARIQ.

Ministry of Agriculture and Works Library: Min. of Agriculture, Food and Underdeveloped Areas Library, Govt of Pakistan, Islamabad; f. 1947; 26,000 vols, 159 periodicals; Librarian S. S. FATIMI; publs *Economic Survey of the Muslim Countries*, *Food and Forestry*.

National Archives of Pakistan: Admin. Block Area, Block N, Pakistan Secretariat, Islamabad; tel. (51) 9202044; fax (51) 9246398; e-mail info@nap.gov.pk; internet www.nap.gov.pk; f. 1951; acquisition, classification and preservation of public and private records of permanent and historical value; provides reference service and assistance to accredited scholars; promotes ideology of Pakistan by projecting the Muslim efforts in acquiring independence; 35,000 vols, 1,859 MSS, 450 oral archives (300 audio cassettes, 150 video cassettes), 1,614 titles of newspapers and periodicals, gazetteers of 109 dists, 31,000 govt publs, Quaid-i-Azam Papers, All India Muslim League Records; Dir-Gen. HABIB AHMED KHAN; Deputy Dir IRSHAD AHMED; Deputy Dir TAHIRA TANVEER; Deputy Dir ZAHIR GUL; publs *Archival Sources in South Asia*, *The Pakistan Archives* (2 a year).

National Assembly Library: Islamabad; tel. (51) 9205626; fax (51) 9206220; e-mail haji.hattar@yahoo.com; internet www.na.gov.pk/en/library.php; f. 1947; 80,000 vols, 160 current periodicals, UN publs; Librarian Haji HATTAR.

National Library of Pakistan: Constitution Ave, POB 1982, Islamabad 44000; Nat. Library Bldg, Sharah-e-Jamhoriat, G-5, Islamabad; tel. (51) 9214523; fax (51) 9221375; e-mail nlpiba@isb.paknet.com.pk; internet www.nlp.gov.pk; f. 1993; depository library for all Pakistani publs, ISBN agency for Pakistani publs; 180,000 vols, 600 MSS, 80,000 microfiches, 500,000 pages on microfilm; Dir-Gen. CH. MUHAMMAD NAZIR; publs *Directory of Periodicals and Newspapers* (irregular), *Pakistan National Bibliography* (1 a year).

Pakistan Scientific and Technological Information Centre (PASTIC): PASTIC Nat.Centre, Quaid-i-Azam Univ. Campus, POB 1217 Islamabad 44000; tel. (51) 9248103; fax (51) 9248113; e-mail dg@pastic.gov.pk; internet www.pastic.gov.pk; f. 1956 as PANSDOC under Pakistan Council of Scientific and Industrial Research, reorganized 1974 under Pakistan Science Foundation; sub-centres at Faisalabad, Karachi, Lahore, Peshawar, Quetta, Muzaffarabad; facilities incl. documentation services, scientific and technical information services, scientific and technical publs and compilation of scientific bibliographies, patent services, environmental information service, reprographic services; 8,000 vols, 900 journals, 300 current periodicals, 300,000 patents, 1,340 NTIS reports; Dir-Gen. Dr KHALIL AHMAD IBUPOTO; Dir NAGEEN AINUDDIN; Sr Librarian SYED HABIB AKHTAR JAFRI; publ. *Pakistan Science Abstracts* (agriculture (1 a year), animal sciences (1 a year), biology and biotechnology (1 a year), chemistry (1 a year), earth sciences (1 a year), information (1 a year), communication and space sciences (1 a year), mathematics and statistics (1 a year), medicine (1 a year), pharmaceutics (1 a year), plant sciences (1 a year)).

Jamshoro

Allama I. I. Kazi Central Library: Allama I. I. Kazi Campus, Jamshoro 76080, Sindh; tel. (22) 2771681; fax (22) 9213181; e-mail info@library.usindh.edu.pk; internet www.library.usindh.edu.pk; f. 1947 as Sindh Univ. Library; attached to Univ. of Sindh; 356,843 vols, 23 current periodicals, 700 MSS; Librarian MUHAMMAD AZAM ROONJHO; Asst Librarian ASGHAR ALI.

Institute of Sindhology Library: Allama I. I. Kazi Campus, Univ. of Sindh, Jamshoro 76070; tel. (22) 2771386; fax (22) 2772494; e-mail director@sindhology.usindh.edu.pk; internet www.sindhology.com.pk; f. 1962; 109,000 vols (Arabic, Balochi, English, Pashito, Persian, Sindhi, Urdu and other languages), 14,500 periodical bound vols, 32,000 rare books, 500 microfilms; 2,200 audio tapes, 3,500 slides, 1,700 MSS, 700 bound vols; 3,800 bound vols of newspapers; Librarian GUL MUHAMMED N. MUGHAL; publs *Sindhi Adab* (2 a year, in Sindhi), *Sindhological Studies* (2 a year, in English).

Mehran University of Engineering & Technology Library: Jamshoro, Sindh; tel. (22) 2771169; fax (22) 2772250; e-mail librarian@admin.muet.edu.pk; internet www.muet.edu.pk/academics/library; f. 1977; attached to Mehran Univ. of Engineering & Technology; 125,000 vols, incl. journals; Librarian AZAM ALI HALEPOTA.

Karachi

All Pakistan Educational Conference Library: 1-5-45/100 Altaf Brelvi Rd, Karachi

74600, Sindh; tel. (21) 621195; f. 1886; 35,000 vols on Aligarh and Pakistan Movement; Sec. SAYED MUSTAFA ALI BRELVI.

Bait al-Hikmah Library: Madinat al-Hikmah, Muhammad bin Qasim Ave., off Sharae Madinat al-Hikmah, Karachi 74700, Sindh; tel. (21) 36440055; e-mail baitalhikmah@hotmail.com; internet www.baitalhikmah.com; f. 1989; attached to Hamdard Foundation; specializes in education, herbal science, history, Indo–Pakistani history, information technology, Islamic studies, literature, medical science, management, social sciences, traditional medicine; 468,983 vols, 29,525 periodicals, 1,208 current periodicals, 1,738 MSS, 1,911 rare books, 690 microfilms, 2,821 audio cassettes, 40,125 photographs, 16,357 stamps, maps and charts; 3,680,000 newspaper clippings covering 1,300 subjects; Dir-Gen FURQAN AHMAD SHAMSI; Chief Librarian SYED AKHTAR ALI.

Dr Mahmud Husain Library: Karachi 75270, Sindh; tel. (21) 9261300; e-mail librarian@uok.edu.pk; internet www.uok.edu.pk/library; f. 1952; attached to Univ. of Karachi; depository of personal book colln of Muhammad Ali Jinnah; UN colln; 360,000 vols, 110,000 journals, 22,000 vols in seminar libraries, 8,000 theses and reports; Head Librarian Prof. MALAHAT KALEEM SHERWANI; Chief Librarian RASHIDA AMAN.

Islamic Documentation and Information Centre (IDIC): SS College of Liberal Arts and Social Sciences, Univ. Rd, Karachi 75000, Sindh; tel. (21) 4978274; fax (21) 4976181; f. 1983; 5,250 vols in English and Urdu, 60 current periodicals; Dir-Gen. Dr MANZOOR AHMAD.

Khalikdina Hall Library Association: M. A. Jinnah Rd, Karachi, Sindh; tel. (21) 7732228; fax (21) 2638000; f. 1856; language classes, social and cultural events; 50,218 vols; Pres. TARIQ RAHMANI; Chief Librarian QARI HILAL AHMED RABBANI.

Liaquat Hall Library: Bagh-e-Jinnah, Abdullah Haroon Rd, Karachi, Sindh; f. 1852 as Frere Hall Library; 52,000 vols; Asst Dir SYEDA SHAHANA ALVI.

Liaquat Memorial Library: c/o Tourism and Cultural Dept, Govt. of Sindh, Stadium Rd, Karachi, Sindh; tel. (21) 9230116; f. 1950; 150,000 vols; Dir SHAHZOR TABANI.

National Bank of Pakistan, Head Office Library: Central Directorate of State Bank of Pakistan, I. I. Chundrigar Rd, Karachi, Sindh; tel. (21) 2414783; f. 1949; colln of books, technical reports, govt documents, periodicals and magazines relating mainly to the subjects of economics, banking, finance, management and commerce; 60,000 vols (45,000 English, 15,000 Oriental); Librarian SALIHA MOIN; publs *Index of Economic Literature* (12 a year), *List of Acquisitions* (4 a year).

NED University of Engineering and Technology Central Library: University Rd, Karachi 75270, Sindh; tel. (21) 9243261; fax (21) 9243255; e-mail libadmin@neduet.edu.pk; internet www.neduet.edu.pk/library; f. 1977; 160,305 vols, 121 current periodicals; Chief Librarian MEHER YASMEEN KHAN.

Pakistan Institute of International Affairs Library: Aiwan-e-Sadar Rd, POB 1447, Karachi 74200, Sindh; tel. (21) 35682891; fax (21) 35686069; e-mail info@piia.org.pk; internet www.piia.org.pk; f. 1947; newspaper clippings on int. politics, econ. and jurisprudence; 34,900 vols, 100 journals, 44 microfilms, 210 audio tapes; Information Resource Librarian MUNAWAR SULTANA RAZIUDDIN; Chief Librarian ISHRA-TULLAH SIDDIQUI; publ. *Pakistan Horizon*

(scholarly articles, chronology of events and other documents relating to Pakistan, 4 a year).

Scientific Information Centre: PCSIR Laboratories Campus, Shahrah-e-Dr Salimuzzaman Siddiqui, Karachi 75280, Sindh; tel. (21) 34651739; fax (21) 34651738; e-mail info@pjsir.org; f. 1958; attached to Pakistan Ccl of Scientific and Industrial Research; Dir Dr GHULAM QADIR SHAIIKH; publs *Pakistan Journal of Scientific and Industrial Research* (6 a year), *PCSIR Research and Development Programme* (1 a year).

State Bank of Pakistan Library: I. I. Chundrigar Rd, Karachi 74000, Sindh; tel. (21) 99212460; fax (21) 99211009; e-mail bashir.zia@sbp.org.pk; internet www.sbp.org.pk/library; f. 1949; 85,000 books, 40,000 bound periodicals; Chief Librarian BASHIR AHMAD ZIA.

Lahore

Atomic Energy Minerals Centre Library: POB 658, Lahore, Punjab; tel. (42) 5758661; fax (42) 5757903; f. 1961; Dir MUHAMMAD MANSOOR.

Dyal Singh Trust Library: 25 Nisbet Rd, Lahore, Punjab; tel. (42) 7229483; fax (42) 7233631; e-mail info@dyalsingh.org.pk; internet www.dyalsingh.org.pk; f. 1908; 146,000 vols; Sr Librarian NUSRAT ALI ATH-EER; publ. *Minhaj* (4 a year).

Ewing Memorial Library: Forman Christian College, Ferozepur Rd, Lahore 54600, Punjab; tel. (42) 9231581; fax (42) 9230703; e-mail contact@fccollege.edu.pk; f. 1943; attached to Forman Christian College; 100,000 vols; Chief Librarian BUSHRA ALMAS JASWAL.

Gad & Birgit Rausing Library: Opposite Sector U, D. H. A, Lahore, Punjab; tel. (42) 35608169; fax (42) 35898307; e-mail library@lums.edu.pk; internet library.lums.edu.pk; attached to Lahore Univ. of Management Sciences; 200,000 vols, 35,000 journals; Library Dir Dr MUHAMMAD RAMZAN.

GC University Library: GC Univ. Library, Katchery Rd, Lahore 54000, Punjab; tel. (42) 99213348; fax (42) 99213349; e-mail library@gcu.edu.pk; internet www.gcu.edu.pk/library; f. 1872 as Fazal-i-Hussain Library; 310,717 vols, 236 journals; Chief Librarian ABDUL WAHEED; publ. *GCU Lahore Newspapers Index.*

Government Punjab Public Library: Library Rd, Shahrah-e-Quaid-e-Azam (Mall Rd), Lahore, Punjab; tel. (42) 99211649; fax (42) 99211651; e-mail info@gppl.org.pk; internet gppl.org.pk; f. 1884; Bait-ul-Quran Section with Quranic MSS, rare material on the Quran, audio visual units; ladies and children section; arranges seminars and lectures for the promotion of library activities; 350,000 vols, 5,100 bound vols of periodicals, 1,800 MSS, 75 English and 100 Oriental language periodicals; Chief Librarian AZRA USMAN (acting).

Islamia College Library: Civil Lines, Lahore 54000, Punjab; f. 1958; 50,061 vols, 53 current periodicals; Librarian MUNIR AHMAD NAEEM; publ. *Faran* (1 a year).

National Library of Engineering Sciences: Univ. of Engineering and Technology, Grand Trunk Rd, Lahore 54890, Punjab; tel. (42) 9029243; fax (42) 9230222; e-mail lib@uet.edu.pk; internet www.uet.edu.pk; f. 1961; attached to Univ. of Engineering and Technology; 125,000 vols, 60,000 bound copies of scientific and technical periodicals; Librarian MANZOOR A. K. ANJUM.

Quaid-e-Azam Library: Bagh-e-Jinnah, Shahra-e-Quaid-e-Azam, Lahore, Punjab; tel. (42) 99201007; fax (42) 99201006; e-mail

qallahore@gmail.com; internet www.qal.org.pk; f. 1984; research and reference facilities; spec. colln: dissertations on Pakistan and Islam; 110,000 vols, 350 current periodicals; Dir-Gen. of Punjab Libraries SAEED AHMAD NAWAZ; Chief Librarian ABID ALI GILL; publs *Informit* (4 a year), *Makhzan* (2 a year).

University of the Punjab Library: Quaid-e-Azam Campus, Lahore 54590, Punjab; tel. (42) 99231126; fax (42) 99230892; e-mail chieflibrarian@pu.edu.pk; internet www.pulibrary.edu.pk; f. 1873 as Punjab Univ. College Library, present name 1882; attached to Univ. of the Punjab; 525,000 vols, incl. 24,000 MSS; Chief Librarian CH. MUHAMMAD HANIF.

Multan

Bahauddin Zakariya University Library: Bosan Rd, Multan; e-mail librarysc@bzu.edu.pk; f. 1975; attached to Bahauddin Zakariya Univ.; 109,000 vols, 20 current periodicals, 20 slides; Librarian MAQBOOL AHMAD CHAUDHRY; publs *Journal of Research* (humanities), *Journal of Research* (sciences), *Law Research Journal.*

Muzaffarabad

University of Azad Jammu and Kashmir Central Library: Muzaffarabad, Azad Jammu and Kashmir; tel. (300) 5228090; fax (51) 9259152; e-mail chief.librarian@ajku.edu.pk; f. 1980; attached to Univ. of Azad Jammu and Kashmir; 120,000 vols; Chief Librarian SARDAR MUHAMMAD SALEEM.

Peshawar

Archival Museum: Directorate of Archives, Govt of NWFP, Peshawar, Khyber Pakhtunkhwa; tel. (521) 274831; f. 1950; 71,000 vols; Dir TARIQ MANSOOR JALALI.

Central Forest Library: Pakistan Forest Institute, Peshawar, Khyber Pakhtunkhwa; tel. (91) 9216196; fax (91) 9216203; e-mail dg_pfi@yahoo.com; f. 1947; 25,000 vols, 20,000 periodicals; Librarian YOUSAF KHAN; publ. *Pakistan Journal of Forestry* (2 a year).

Central Library—University of Peshawar: Peshawar, Khyber Pakhtunkhwa; tel. (91) 9216701; fax (91) 9216470; f. 1951; also houses Oriental colln of valuable and rare books, MSS; 2,000,000 vols, 10,400 periodicals, 693 Persian, Arabic and Pashto MSS; Librarian IBRAR MOHAMMAD.

Quetta

University of Balochistan Library: Sariab Rd, Quetta, Balochistan; tel. (81) 9211247; fax (81) 9211277; internet www.uob.edu.pk/library.htm; f. 1971; 120,000 vols, 1,000 rare books, 4,000 microfiche cards, periodicals, depository library of World Bank, UNESCO and UNICEF; Librarian ABDUL JALIL KHAN.

Taxila

Archaeological Library: Taxila Museum, Taxila, Rawalpindi, Punjab; f. 1960; 1,450 vols on history and arts, especially the ancient history and archaeology of Pakistan; Custodian GULZAR MOHAMMAD KHAN.

Museums and Art Galleries

Harappa

Archaeological Museum: Dist. Sahiwal, Harappa, Punjab; f. 1926, re-established 1967; antiquities from site of the pre-historic and proto-historic site (3500–1500 BC); Curator MUHAMMAD HASSAN KHOKHAR.

Karachi

National Museum of Pakistan: e-mail zubairam@hamdard.net.pk Burns Garden, Dr Ziauddin Ahmed Rd, Karachi 74200, Sindh; tel. (21) 9212839; fax (21) 9212798; f. 1950; Pakistan's cultural heritage from Stone Age to the birth of Pakistan; Superintendent Qasim Ali Qasim; publs *Museum Journal, Pakistan Archaeology*.

Quaid-i-Azam Birthplace, Reading Room, Museum and Library: Wazir Mansion, Chagla St, Kharadar, Karachi, Sindh; tel. (21) 2434904; f. 1953; library of 5,000 vols (incl. spec. colln on Indo-Pakistani history); Custodian Tahir Saee.

Lahore

Directorate of Archives and Archival Museum: Punjab Civil Secretariat, Lahore, Punjab; tel. (42) 7322381; fax (42) 212693; f. 1924; consists of Historical Record Office, Central Record Office and Museum; library of 150,000 vols; Dir Syed Ishrat Ali Shah; publ. *Urdu Nama* (12 a year).

Industrial and Commercial Museum: Poonch House, Multan Rd, Lahore, Punjab; f. 1950; permanent colln of raw material resources, handicrafts, art-ware and manufactured products of Pakistan; industrial library, reading-room, auditorium attached; provides free economic intelligence to trade and industry; Curator Mushtaq Ahmad.

Lahore Fort Museum: Lahore 54000, Punjab; Mughal Gallery: Mughal paintings, coins, calligraphy, MSS, carving; Sikh Gallery: arms and armour, paintings of Sikh period; Sikh Painting Gallery: oil paintings from the Princess Bamba colln; Curator Anjum Javed; Asst Curator Sha-Bano.

Lahore Museum: Opp. old Univ. Hall, Shahrah-e-Quaid-i-Azam, Lahore, Punjab; tel. (42) 7322835; internet www .lahoremuseum.org; f. 1864; collns of Graeco-Buddhist sculpture, Indo-Pakistani coins and miniature paintings of the Mughal, Rajput, Kangra and Pahari schools; Hindu, Buddhist and Jaina sculpture, local arts, Chinese porcelain, armoury, fabrics, Pakistani postage stamps, modern paintings, Oriental MSS, Islamic calligraphy, archives and photographs on Pakistan Movement; library of 35,000 vols; Dir Dr Saifur Rahman Dar; publs *Catalogue of Coins, Catalogue of Miniatures, Guide Book, Guide to Gandhara Gallery, Guide to Manuscripts*.

Lahore Zoo: 92 Shahrah-e-Quaid-i-Azam, Mall Rd, Lahore, Punjab; tel. (42) 36314684; fax (42) 36304683; e-mail info@lahorezoo.com .pk; internet www.lahorezoo.com.pk; f. 1872; houses animals of 136 species incl. 82 species of birds, 8 species of reptiles and 45 species of mammals; Dir Shafqat Ali.

Larkana

Archaeological Museum: Mohenjodaro, Larkana, Sindh; tel. (741) 459051; f. 1924; variety of antiquities unearthed from the prehistoric site of Mohenjodaro, dating from 3,000 BC; Curator Saeed Jatoi.

Peshawar

Peshawar Museum: Near Old Deans Hotel, Peshawar, Khyber Pakhtunkhwa; f. 1907; collns incl. sculptures of the Gandhara School; colln of images of the Buddha, the Bodhisattvas, Buddhist deities, reliefs illustrating the life of the Buddha and Jataka stories, architectural pieces and minor antiquities excavated at Charsadda, Sahri-Bahlol, Shahji-ki-Dheri, Takht-i-Bahi and Jamal Garhi; Muslim gallery of Quranic MSS and MSS in Arabic and Persian languages; ethnological section; Curator Nidaul-lah Sehrai.

Taxila

Archaeological Museum: Taxila, Rawalpindi, Punjab; tel. and fax (596) 9314270; e-mail nasiraladand2003@yahoo.com; f. 1928; Gandhara sculptures in stone and stucco; gold and silver ornaments; household utensils, pottery; antiquities of every description from the sites of Taxila and monastic area from 6th century BC to 5th century AD; library: see Libraries and Archives; Curator Abdul Nasir Khan.

Universities

ABASYN UNIVERSITY

Ring Rd (Charsadda Link), Peshawar
Telephone: (91) 2247264
Fax: (91) 2248675
E-mail: vc@abasyn.edu.pk
Internet: www.abasynuniv.edu.pk
Founded 2007
Private control
Academic year: January to May, June to September, August to December (3 semesters)
Offers Masters degree in computer sciences, management studies
Chancellor: Imran Ullah
Vice-Chancellor: Prof. Dr Fida Muhammad Khan
Registrar: Muhammad Iqbal
Controller of Examinations: Muhammad Iftikhar
Publication: *Journal of Social Sciences*.

AGA KHAN UNIVERSITY

Stadium Rd, POB 3500, Karachi 74800
Telephone: (21) 34930051
Fax: (21) 34934294
E-mail: aku@aku.edu
Internet: www.aku.edu
Founded 1983
Private control
Language of instruction: English
Academic year: January to August
Chancellor: HE Aga Khan
Pres.: Firoz Rasul
Provost and Chief Academic Officer: Dr Greg Moran
Vice-Pres. for Health and Operational Services: Allaudin Merali
Vice-Pres. for Human Resources: Carol Joan Ariano
Dir-Gen. of Resource Devt: Zahir Janmohamed (acting)
Dir-Gen. and Chief Financial Officer: Al-Karim Haji
Registrar: Louis R. Ariano
Librarian: Normand Demers
Library of 137,000 vols 265 print journal titles, 70,500 online books, 27,000 online periodicals
Number of teachers: 650
Number of students: 2,256

DEANS
Faculty of Arts and Sciences, East Africa: Dr Rafique Keshavjee
Institute for Educational Development, East Africa: Prof. Pauline Rea-Dickins
Institute for Educational Development, Karachi: Dr Muhammad Memon
Institute for the Study of Muslim Civilisations: Dr Farouk Topan (Dir)
Medical College: Dr Farhat Abbas
Medical College, East Africa: Robert Armstrong
Nursing and Midwifery, East Africa: Dr Yasmin Amarsi

Research and Graduate Studies: Dr El-Nasir Ma Lalani
School of Nursing, Karachi: Dr Rozina Karmaliani

PROFESSORS
Amarsi, Y., Nursing
Badruddin, S. H., Community Health Sciences
Baig, S. M., Medicine
Bhutta, A. B., Paediatrics
Billoo, A. G., Paediatrics
Chohan, U., Anaesthesia
Connor, J. D., Pharmacology
Farah, I., Education
Filali-Ansary, A., Education (London)
Frossard, P., Biochemistry
Gilani, A. H., Pharmacology
Hamid, S., Medicine
Harleeh-Jones, B. A., Education
Hasan, R., Microbiology
Hasan, S. H., Pathology
Hussain, R., Microbiology
Iqbal, M. P., Biochemistry
Jabbar, A., Medicine
Jafri, S. M. W., Medicine
Kamal, A., Anaesthesia
Karim, M. S., Community Health Sciences
Kayani, N., Pathology
Khan, F. A., Anaesthesia
Khan, F. H., Anaesthesia
Khan, I. A., Paediatrics
Khan, J. A., Medicine
Khan, K. M., Anatomy
Khan, M. A., Medicine
Khan, M. M., Psychiatry
Khan, S. M., Surgery
Khurshid, M., Pathology
King, L., Nursing (Kenya)
MacLeod, G., Education
Memon, M., Education
Nizami, S. Q., Paediatrics
Pardhan, S., Education
Pervez, S., Pathology
Qureshi, R. H., Family Medicine
Raja, A. J., Surgery (Kenya)
Rees, J., Radiology (Kenya)
Rizvi, J. H., Obstetrics and Gynaecology
Siddiqui, A. A., Biochemistry
Talati, J., Surgery
Vellani, C. W., Medicine
Zuberi, R. W., Family Medicine

ATTACHED RESEARCH INSTITUTES
Institute for Educational Development: IED-PDC, 1-5/B-VII, F.B. Area, POB 13688, Karimabad, Karachi 75950; tel. (21) 6347611; fax (21) 6347616; e-mail ied@aku.edu; f. 1993; Dir Prof. Muhammad Memon; publ. *Research and Policy Studies*.

Institute for the Study of Muslim Civilisations: 4–5 Bedford Sq., London WC1B 3RA, United Kingdom; tel. (20) 7907-1020; fax (20) 7907-1030; e-mail ismc@aku.edu; Dir Prof. Abdou Filali-Ansary; Librarian Waseem Farooq.

AIR UNIVERSITY

Sector E–9, PAF Complex, Islamabad 44000
Telephone: (51) 9262557
Fax: (51) 9260158
E-mail: admissions@mail.au.edu.pk
Internet: www.au.edu.pk
Founded 2002
State control
Academic year: September to August (3 semesters)
Vice-Chancellor: Dr Ijaz Ahmad Malik
Registrar: Zafar Ahmed
Dir of Academic Affairs: Dr Q. Isa Daudpota
Librarian: Mamoona Kousar
Library of 13,000 vols, 22 journals
Number of teachers: 120

Number of students: 2,103

DEANS

Faculty of Admin. Sciences: Dr Ikramullah Shad
Faculty of Basic and Applied Sciences: Dr Abdullah Sadiq
Faculty of Engineering: Dr Zafar-Ullah Koreshi
Faculty of Social Sciences and Humanities: Abida Hassan (acting)

AL-KHAIR UNIVERSITY

Gujrat Rd, Bhimber, Azad Jammu and Kashmir
Telephone: (5828) 201611
Internet: www.alkhair.edu.pk
Founded 1994
Private control
Chancellor: Pres. of Azad Jammu and Kashmir
Pro-Chancellor: Dr Muhammad Bashir Goraya
Rector and Vice-Chancellor: Prof. Dr A. Q. Ansari
Pro-Vice-Chancellor: Imtiaz Aqdas
Registrar: Manzoor Hussain Sheikh
Controller of Examinations: Ch. Muhammad Bashir

DEANS

Faculty of Computer Sciences: Dr Ishtiaq Ahmed Gondal
Faculty of Education: Prof. Dr M. Mahmood Hussain Awan

ALHAMD ISLAMIC UNIVERSITY

Zarghoon Rd, Quetta
Telephone: (81) 2451342
Fax: (81) 2451439
E-mail: president@aiu.edu.pk
Internet: www.aiu.edu.pk
Founded 2005
Private control
Pres.: Prof. Shakeel Ahmed Roshan
Dean: Prof. Mehru Nisa Khan
Registrar: Urwa Jawed
Controller of Examinations: Mohsin Javed

Faculties of arts, education, engineering, Islam, law, science, technology.

ALLAMA IQBAL OPEN UNIVERSITY

Sector H–8, Islamabad 44000
Telephone: (51) 9057816
Fax: (51) 9250026
E-mail: director_sac@aiou.edu.pk
Internet: www.aiou.edu.pk
Founded 1974 as People's Open Univ., present name 1977
State control
Languages of instruction: English, Urdu
Academic year: April to March
Chancellor: Pres. of Islamic Republic of Pakistan
Pro-Chancellor: Min. of Education
Vice-Chancellor: Prof. Dr Nazir Ahmed Sangi
Registrar: Hafeez Ullah
Librarian: Prof. Dr Shah Farrukh (acting)
Library: see Libraries and Archives
Number of teachers: 166
Number of students: 512,635

Publications: *Ilm Ki Roshni* (2 a year), *Jamia Nama* (12 a year, in English and Urdu), *Journal of Social Sciences and Humanities* (2 a year), *Marif-I-Islami* (2 a year), *Pakistan Journal of Education* (2 a year), *Sehen Ujala* (2 a year)

DEANS

Faculty of Arabic and Islamic Studies: Prof. Dr Ali Asghar Chishti
Faculty of Education: Prof. Dr Rehana Masrur
Faculty of Sciences: Prof. Dr Nowshad Khan
Faculty of Social Sciences and Humanities: Prof. Dr Abdul Hafeez

BAHAUDDIN ZAKARIYA UNIVERSITY

Univ. Campus, Bosan Rd, Multan 60800
Telephone: (61) 9210097
Fax: (61) 9210098
E-mail: regbzu@brain.net.pk
Internet: www.bzu.edu.pk
Founded 1975 as Univ. of Multan; present name 1979
State control
Languages of instruction: English, Urdu
Academic year: October to September
Chancellor: Gov. of Punjab
Vice-Chancellor: Prof. Dr Syed Khawaja Alqama
Registrar: Prof. Dr Syed Muhammad Ali
Controller of Examination: Malik Munir Hussain
Librarian: Abdul Majeed
Library: see under Libraries and Archives
Number of teachers: 500
Number of students: 20,000

Publications: *Journal of Research (Humanities), Journal of Research (Science), Journal of Research of Business Management, Journal of Research of the Faculty of Islamic Studies and Languages*

DEANS

Faculty of Arts and Social Science: Prof. Dr S. Khawaja Alqama
Faculty of Commerce, Law and Business Administration: Prof. Dr Hayat M. Awan
Faculty of Engineering and Technology: Prof. Dr Abdul Aziz Mazhar
Faculty of Islamic Studies and Languages: Prof. Dr Zafar Iqbal
Faculty of Medicine and Dentistry: Prof. Dr Shabbir Ahmad Nasir
Faculty of Pharmacy: Prof. Dr Khalid Hussain Janbaz
Faculty of Science and Agriculture: Prof. Dr Humayun Pervez
Faculty of Veterinary Sciences: Prof. Dr Ch. Sikandar Hayat

BAHRIA UNIVERSITY

Main Campus: Shangrila Rd, Sector E-8, Islamabad 44000
Telephone: (51) 9260271
Fax: (51) 9260885
Karachi Campus: 13 Nat. Stadium Rd, Karachi
Telephone: (21) 9240002
Fax: (21) 9240351
E-mail: info@bahria.edu.pk
Internet: www.bahria.edu.pk
Founded 2000
State control
Language of instruction: English
Academic year: January to June
Pro-Chancellor: Mohammad Asif Sandila
Rector: Shahid Iqbal
Pro-Rector: Muhammad Ehsan Saeed
Registrar: Dr Mohammad Javed Khan
Head of Libraries: Sher Afzal Khan
Library of 45,000 vols
Number of students: 9,500

Publications: *Bahria Journal of Professional Psychology, Bahria University Journal of Information & Communication Technology, Journal of Bahria University Medical & Dental College (BUMDC)*

DEANS

Islamabad Campus:
Internet: www.bci.edu.pk
Faculty of Engineering: Prof. Dr Muhammad Altaf Mukati
Faculty of Sciences: Dr Muhammad Riaz
Karachi Campus:
E-mail: src@bimcs.edu.pk
Internet: www.bimcs.edu.pk
Computer Science and Engineering: Prof. Naeem Janjua
Management Sciences: Naveed Mohammad Khan

BALOCHISTAN UNIVERSITY OF ENGINEERING AND TECHNOLOGY

Khuzdar, Balochistan
Telephone: (848) 412524
Fax: (848) 413197
E-mail: registrar@buetk.edu.pk
Internet: www.buetk.edu.pk
Founded 1987 as Balochistan Engineering College; present name and status 1994
State control
Vice-Chancellor: Brig. Mukhtar Ahmad Khan
Registrar: Mohammad Alam Baloch
Controller of Examinations: Muhammad Yousaf Bangulzai
Librarian: Mohammad Anwar

DEANS

Faculty of Engineering: Dr Zahor Ahmed

BALOCHISTAN UNIVERSITY OF INFORMATION TECHNOLOGY, ENGINEERING AND MANAGEMENT SCIENCES

Sumungli Rd, Jinnah Town, Quetta, Balochistan
Telephone: (81) 9201051
Fax: (81) 9201064
E-mail: vc@buitms.edu.pk
Internet: www.buitms.edu.pk
State control
Vice-Chancellor: Eng. Ahmed Farooq Bazai
Pro-Vice-Chancellor: Prof. Dr M. A. K. Malghani
Registrar: Mohammad Afzal Kasi
Librarian: Gulam Murtaza Shahwani
Publication: *Research Journal*

DEANS

Faculty of Arts and Basic Sciences: Dr Mohammad Nawaz
Faculty of Engineering: Prof. Dr Syed Abid Hussain
Faculty of Information and Communication Technology: Prof. Dr Abdul Hussain Shah Bukhari
Faculty of Life Sciences and Informatics: Prof. Dr Dost M. Baloch
Faculty of Management Sciences: Prof. Barkat Ali

BAQAI MEDICAL UNIVERSITY

51 Deh Tor, Gadap Rd, Super Highway, POB 2407, Karachi 74600
Telephone: (21) 34410293
E-mail: info@baqai.edu.pk
Internet: www.baqai.edu.pk
Founded 1988 as Baqai Medical College, present name and status 1996
Private control

Institutes of cardiovascular diseases, clinical nutrition, diabetology and endocrinology, health sciences, health management sciences, haematology, pharmaceutical sciences, , reproduction and devt, information technology, medical technology, oncology,

physical therapy rehabilitation, pathology;
Baqai Medical College; Baqai Dental College

Chancellor: Prof. Dr FAREED UDDIN BAQAI
Vice-Chancellor: Prof. Dr SYED AZHAR AHMED
Pro-Vice-Chancellor: Prof. Dr ZAHIDA BAQAI
Registrar: Prof. KHURSHEED ALI KHAN.

BEACONHOUSE NATIONAL UNIVERSITY

3-C Zafar Ali Rd, Gulberg V, Lahore
Telephone: (42) 35718260
Fax: (42) 35760254
E-mail: info@bnu.edu.pk
Internet: www.bnu.edu.pk

Founded 2003
Private control

Vice-Chancellor: SARTAJ AZIZ
Librarian: NIGHAT SALEEMI
Number of teachers: 80

DEANS

School of Architecture: Prof. Dr GULZAR
HAIDER
School of Computer and Information Tech-
nology: Prof. Dr KHAVER ZIA
School of Education: Dr TARIQ RAHMAN
School of Liberal Arts: Dr HAFIZ A. PASHA
School of Media and Mass Communication:
Prof. Dr MEHDI HASAN
School of Social Science: Dr HAFIZ A. PASHA
School of Visual Arts and Design: Prof.
SALIMA HASHMI

CECOS UNIVERSITY

Hayatabad, Peshawar, Khyber Pakh-
tunkhwa
Telephone: (91) 5860291
Fax: (91) 5860294
Internet: www.cecos.edu.pk

Founded 1986, present status 2001
Private control

Pres.: MUHAMMAD TANVEER JAVED
Vice-Chancellor: Prof. Dr RIAZ A. KHATTAK

College of Engineering and Information
Technology; Institute of Management and
Information Sciences; CECOS Data Insti-
tute; CECOS-Frontier College of Business
Education; CECOS London College

Number of teachers: 150
Number of students: 1,800

CITY UNIVERSITY OF SCIENCE & INFORMATION TECHNOLOGY

Dalazak Rd, Peshawar, Khyber Pakh-
tunkhwa
Telephone: (91) 2584161
Fax: (91) 2584170
E-mail: info@cusit.edu.pk
Internet: www.cityuniversity.edu.pk

Founded 2001
Private control

Pres.: MUHAMMAD SABUR SETHI
Vice-Pres.: Prof. Dr MUHAMMAD ASRAR KHAT-
TAK
Vice-Chancellor: Prof. Dr ANWAR F. CHISTHI
Registrar: ZAFAR AHMED
Controller of Examinations: AMJAD ALI
Librarian: ABDUL HAMEED

Depts of chemistry, computer science, education, electrical engineering, English,
Islamic studies, management science, mathematics, Urdu
Number of students: 21,000

COMSATS INSTITUTE OF INFORMATION TECHNOLOGY

Park Rd, Chak Shahzad, Islamabad
Telephone: (51) 9247000

Fax: (51) 9247006
E-mail: registrar@comsats.edu.pk
Internet: www.ciit.edu.pk

Founded 1998, present status 2000
State control

Rector: Dr SYED MUHAMMAD JUNAID ZAIDI
Registrar: Dr ARSHAD S. MALIK
Controller of Examinations: MUHAMMAD
SOHAIL GHANI WARAICH
Number of teachers: 1,745
Number of students: 18,000

DEANS

Faculty of Architecture and Design: Dr S. M.
JUNAID ZAIDI
Faculty of Business Administration: Prof. Dr
SYED AMJAD FARID HASNU
Faculty of Engineering: Prof. Dr SHAHID
AHMED KHAN
Faculty of Information Science and Technol-
ogy: Dr SAJJAD MOHSIN
Faculty of Sciences: Prof. Dr ARSHAD SALEEM
BHATTI

DADABHOY INSTITUTE OF HIGHER EDUCATION

SNPA-17/B, Block 3, KCHSU Ltd, off Sha-
heed-e-Millat Rd, Karachi
Telephone: (21) 34389102
Fax: (21) 34389147
E-mail: admission@dadabhoy.edu.pk
Internet: www.dadabhoy.edu.pk

Founded 2000, present status 2003
Private control

Rector: Prof. Dr S. ALTAF HUSSAIN

DEANS

Faculty of Computer and Mathematical Sci-
ences: Dr JAWAID QUAMAR
Faculty of Management, Media and Social
Sciences: Dr M. M. H. SIDDIQUI

DAWOOD COLLEGE OF ENGINEERING AND TECHNOLOGY

M. A. Jinnah Rd, Karachi 74800, Sindh
Telephone: (21) 99231195
Fax: (21) 99230710
E-mail: registrar@dcet.edu.pk
Internet: www.dcet.edu.pk

Founded 1962, present status 2007
State control

Faculties of architecture and planning, basic
sciences, mathematics and humanities,
chemical engineering, computer system
engineering, electronic engineering, energy
and environment engineering, industrial
engineering and management, metallurgy
and materials engineering, petroleum and
gas engineering, telecommunication engineering

Prin.: Dr MUHAMMAD ALI SHEIKH
Dean of Dawood College of Electronic Engin-
eering: Prof. RASHID BAIG
Registrar: GHULAM SHABBIR BHOGIO
Controller of Examinations: GUL MUHAMMAD
BHAYO

Library of 30,269 vols
Number of teachers: 70
Number of students: 1,451

DOW UNIVERSITY OF HEALTH SCIENCES

Baba-E-Urdu Rd, Karachi 74200
Telephone: (21) 99215754
Internet: www.duhs.edu.pk

Founded 2003
State control

Offers Bachelors degree in dental technology,
medical technology, nursing, physical medi-

cine; Masters courses incl. biostatistics and
epidemiology, diabetes and endocrinology,
dental surgery, health profession education,
jurisprudence, nursing, physiotheraphy.

FATIMA JINNAH WOMEN UNIVERSITY

Old Presidency, The Mall, Rawalpindi 4600,
Punjab
Telephone: (51) 9270050
Fax: (51) 9271168
E-mail: registrar@fjwu.edu.pk
Internet: www.fjwu.edu.pk

Founded 1998
State control

Vice-Chancellor: Prof. Dr SAMINA AMIN QADIR
Registrar: Dr MARYAM RAB
Controller of Examinations: Dr MUSSARET
ANWAR SHEIKH
Librarian: ZAFAR JAVED NAQVI

Library of 23,000 vols

DEANS

Faculty of Arts and Social Sciences: Prof. Dr
SAMINA AMIN QADIR
Faculties of Law, Commerce, Management
and Admin. Sciences, Science and Technology: Prof. Dr NAHEED ZIA KHAN

FEDERAL URDU UNIVERSITY OF ARTS, SCIENCE AND TECHNOLOGY

MSC Block, Block 9, University Rd, Gulshan-
e-Iqbal, Karachi 75300
Telephone: (21) 99244141
E-mail: info@fuuast.edu.pk
Internet: www.fuuast.edu.pk

Founded 2002
State control

Vice-Chancellor: Prof. Dr MUHAMMAD QAISER
Registrar: Prof. Dr QAMR-UL-HAQ
Controller of Examinations: WAQAR-UL-HAQ
Librarian: MUKHTAR ASHRAF

Number of teachers: 450
Number of students: 12,000

DEANS

Faculty of Arts: FAROOQ PERVAIZ MUGAL
(acting)
Faculty of Business Admin., Commerce and
Economics: Dr SULAMAN D. MUHAMMAD
(acting)
Faculty of Law: Dr JUSTIS
Faculty of Pharmacy: Dr ALI AKBAR SIAL
(acting)
Faculty of Science and Technology: Prof. Dr
JAMAL HAIDER

FORMAN CHRISTIAN COLLEGE

Ferozepur Rd, Lahore 54600
Telephone: (42) 99231581
Fax: (42) 99230703
E-mail: contact@fccollege.edu.pk
Internet: www.fccollege.edu.pk

Founded 1864 as Lahore Mission College,
present name 1894, present status 2004
Private control

Depts of biological sciences, chemistry, computer science, economics, education, English, geography, health and physical
education, history, mass communication,
mathematics, philosophy, physics, political
science, psychology, religious studies, sociology, statistics, Urdu

Rector: Dr PETER H. ARMACOST
Exec. Vice-Rector: Dr C. J. DUBASH
Exec. Vice-Rector: Dr JIM TEBBE
Prin.: Dr CHRISTY MUNIR
Registrar: Dr HAMID SAEED
Dean of Students: CHERYL BURKE

Controller of Examinations: Dr MIAN WAJA-
HAT HUSSAIN
Librarian: BUSHRA ALMAS JASWAL
Library: see under Libraries and Archives
Number of students: 4,664

FOUNDATION UNIVERSITY ISLAMABAD

Defense Ave, Phase-I, DHA, Islamabad
Telephone: (51) 5788446
Fax: (51) 5788633
E-mail: registrar@fui.edu.pk
Internet: www.fui.edu.pk
Founded 2002
Private control
Chancellor: NAEEM KHALID LODHI
Pres.: MUHAMMAD MUSTAFA KHAN
Rector: Prof. Dr BELAL A. KHAN
Registrar: TANWIR-UL-ISLAM
Dir: ZAHID PARVEZ (acting)
Library of 6,000 vols

DEANS

Faculty of Education: Prof. Dr MAQSUD ALAM
BUKHARI

FRONTIER WOMEN UNIVERSITY

Asamia Rd, Peshawar, Khyber Pakh-
tunkhwa
Telephone: (91) 9212422
E-mail: info@fwu.edu.pk
Internet: www.fwu.edu.pk
Founded 2005
State control
Academic year: December to June
Faculties of Arabic, bioinformatics, computer
science, economics, English language and
literature, Islamiyat, mathematics, micro-
biology, statistics
Vice-Chancellor: Prof. Dr SYEDA FARHANA
JAHANGIR.

GANDHARA UNIVERSITY

Canal Rd, Univ. Town, Peshawar, Khyber
Pakhtunkhwa
Telephone: (91) 5844429
Fax: (91) 5844428
E-mail: info@gandhara.edu.pk
Internet: www.gandhara.edu.pk
Founded 2002
Private control
Offers Bachelors and Masters degree in
medicine, dentistry
Chair.: ROEEDA KABIR
Vice-Chancellor: Dr R. A .K. TAHIRKHAILI.

GC UNIVERSITY

Katchery Rd, Lahore 54000, Punjab
Telephone: (42) 99213340
Fax: (42) 99213341
E-mail: registrar@gcu.edu.pk
Internet: www.gcu.edu.pk
Founded 1864, present status 2002
State control
Vice-Chancellor: Prof. Dr MUHAMMAD KHA-
LEEQ-UR-RAHMAN
Registrar: SYED ANJUM NISAR
Controller of Examinations: ASHRAF SHABBIR
BOKHARI
Chief Librarian: ABDUL WAHEED
Library: see Libraries and Archives
Number of teachers: 436
Number of students: 7,382

DEANS

Faculty of Arts and Social Sciences: Prof. Dr
M. KHALID PERVAIZ

Faculty of Languages, Islamic and Oriental
Learning: Prof. Dr SOHAIL AHMAD KHAN
Faculty of Science and Technology: Prof. Dr
IKRAM UL HAQ

GHULAM ISHAQ KHAN INSTITUTE OF ENGINEERING SCIENCES AND TECHNOLOGY

Topi 23640, Khyber Pakhtunkhwa
Telephone: (938) 271858
Fax: (938) 271865
E-mail: rector@giki.edu.pk
Internet: www.giki.edu.pk
Founded 1993
Private control
Language of instruction: English
Academic year: August to December,January
to May,June to July (3 semesters)
Bachelors degree courses incl. engineering
sciences, management sciences and human-
ities
Pres.: SHAMS-UL-MULK
Rector: JEHANGIR BASHAR
Pro-Rector for Academics: Prof. Dr F. AHMAD
KHALID
Dean of Student Affairs: Dr JUNAID MUGHAL
Controller of Examinations and Registrar:
MUHAMMAD FAHEEM AKHTAR
Library of 17,000 vols
Number of teachers: 34

GIFT UNIVERSITY

GIFT Univ. Chowk, Gujranwala 52250
Telephone: (55) 3892989
Fax: (55) 3890266
E-mail: president@gift.edu.pk
Internet: www.gift.edu.pk
Founded 2002
Private control
Pres.: MUHAMMAD ANWAR DAR
Rector: Prof. Dr MOHAMMAD IQBAL TAHIR
Registrar: NAVEED AHMAD MUGHAL
Dean: Dr SURRAYA SHAFI MIR
Librarian: SAJIDA BASHIR
Faculties of accounting and finance, art,
design and architecture, arts and social
sciences, business and commerce, computer
sciences, management sciences
Library of 10,500 vols.

GOMAL UNIVERSITY

Dera Ismail Khan, Khyber Pakhtunkhwa
Telephone: (966) 750424
Fax: (966) 750255
E-mail: vc@gu.edu.pk
Internet: www.gu.edu.pk
Founded 1974
State control
Languages of instruction: English, Urdu
Academic year: September to June
Chancellor: GOV. OF KHYBER PAKHTUNKHWA
Vice-Chancellor: Prof. Dr MANSOOR AKBAR
KUNDI
Registrar: MUHAMMAD JAN KHAN
Controller of Examinations: MUSHATQUREH-
MAN
Dir of Academics: FARIDULLAH KHAN
Librarian: MUHAMMAD SADIQ JAVAID
Library: see Libraries and Archives
Number of teachers: 335
Number of students: 6,720
Publication: *Gomal University Journal of
Research* (2 a year)

DEANS

Faculty of Agriculture: Dr SAID MIR KHAN
Faculty of Arts: Dr UMER ALI KHAN
Faculty of Pharmacy: Dr GUL MAJID KHAN

Faculty of Sciences: Dr MUSA KALEEM
BALOCH

PROFESSORS

AHMAD, H. K., Agriculture
BALOCH, J. J., Physics
KHAN, A. G., Agriculture
KHAN, A. S., Pharmacy
KHAN, I. U., Pharmacy
KHAN, K. Z., Economics
KHAN, L. U., Agriculture
KHAN, M. A., Physics
KHAN, M. F., Pharmacy
KHAN, M. K., Chemistry
KHAN, M. Q., Agriculture
KHAN, Z. A., Chemistry
QAZI, N. S., Pharmacy
SAEED, A., Biological Sciences

GOVERNMENT COLLEGE UNIVERSITY, FAISALABAD

Allama Iqbal Rd, Faisalabad
Telephone: (41) 9200886
Fax: (41) 9201419
E-mail: info@gcuf.edu.pk
Internet: www.gcuf.edu.pk
Founded 1897, present status 2002
State control
Vice-Chancellor: Dr ZAKIR HUSSAIN
Registrar: MUHAMMAD AKRAM
Controller of Examinations: JAVED ASLAM
BAJWA
Librarian: MUHAMMAD ASHFAQ
Library of 80,400 vols
Number of teachers: 461
Number of students: 13,571

DEANS

Faculty of Arts and Social Science: Dr
PARVAIZ AZEEM
Faculty of Islamic and Oriental Learning:
Prof. Dr HAFEEZ-UR-REHMAN
Faculty of Management and Admin. Sci-
ences: Dr MUHAMMAD SHAHBAZ ARIF
Faculty of Science and Technology: Prof. Dr
NAUREEN AZIZ QURESHI

GREENWICH UNIVERSITY

Greenwich House, DK-10, 38th St, Darak-
shan, Phase VI Defence Housing Author-
ity, Karachi 75500
Telephone: (21) 35840397
Fax: (21) 35851910
E-mail: gu@greenwichuniversity.edu.pk
Internet: www.greenwichuniversity.edu.pk
Private control
Vice-Chancellor: SEEMA MOGHUL

DEANS

Faculty of Management Sciences and Infor-
mation Studies: Prof. Dr MUNIR ALI SHAH
RIZVI
Faculty of Social Sciences and Humanities:
Prof. Dr MUNIR WASTI

HAJVERY UNIVERSITY

43–52 Industrial Area, Gulberg III, Lahore,
Pakistan
Telephone: (42) 35717130
Fax: (42) 35755564
E-mail: registrar@hup.edu.pk
Internet: www.hup.edu.pk
Founded 2002
Private control
Chair.: ATIF MUSHTAQ
Dir of Admin.: MUHAMMAD LATIF
Number of teachers: 235
Number of students: 5,000

DEANS

HU Business School: Prof. Dr MUHAMMAD ASLAM

HU School of Commerce and Banking: Prof. Dr MUHAMMAD ASLAM

HU School of Engineering and Computer Sciences: Prof. Dr NAEEM AKHTER KHAN AFRIDI

HAMDARD UNIVERSITY

Sharae Madinat Al-Hikmah, Muhammad bin Qasim Ave, Karachi 74600

Telephone: (21) 36440017
E-mail: huvc@hamdard.edu.pk
Internet: www.hamdard.edu.pk

Founded 1991
Private control

Chancellor: S. M. ZAFAR
Vice-Chancellor: Prof. Dr NASIM A. KHAN
Registrar: Col (retd) RAFIQ AHMED
Library of 500,000 vols, 1,629 MSS
Number of students: 5,000

DEANS

Faculty of Eastern Medicine: Prof. Dr HK. ABDUL HANNAN

Faculty of Engineering Sciences and Technology: Prof. Dr ABDUL REHMAN MEMON

Faculty of Health and Medical Sciences: Prof. Dr ALEY HASAN ZAIDI

Faculty of Humanities and Social Sciences: Dr SYED ABDUL AZIZ

Faculty of Legal Studies: NASIR ASLAM ZAHID

Faculty of Management Sciences: Prof. Dr MATIN A. KHAN

Faculty of Pharmacy: Prof. Dr JAVEID IQBAL

HAZARA UNIVERSITY

Mansehra, Khyber Pakhtunkhwa

Telephone: (997) 530732
Fax: (997) 530046
E-mail: registrar@hu.edu.pk
Internet: www.hu.edu.pk

Founded 2002
State control
Language of instruction: English
Academic year: January to December (2 semesters)

Vice-Chancellor: Prof. Dr SYED SAKHAWAT SHAH
Registrar: Prof. Dr MUQARRAB SHAH

DEANS

Faculty of Arts: Prof. Dr SAEED ANWAR
Faculty of Health Sciences: Prof. Dr MUQARRAB SHAH
Faculty of Law and Admin. Sciences: Prof. Dr SOHAIL SHAHZAD
Faculty of Science: Prof. Dr BAKHTIAR MUHAMMAD

HITEC UNIVERSITY

Taxila Cantt

Telephone: (51) 4542714
E-mail: registrar@hitecuni.edu.pk
Internet: www.hitecuni.edu.pk

Founded 2007, present status 2009
Private control

Vice-Chancellor: QAMAR ZAMAN
Registrar: M. REHMAN AWAN
Controller of Examinations: MAHMOOD AHMED SIDDIQUI
Dir of Admin.: ASIM UL HAQ
Dir of Student Affairs: ZAHOOR SULTAN

Depts of electrical engineering, humanities and basic sciences, Islamic studies, management science, mathematics, mechanical engineering.

IMPERIAL COLLEGE OF BUSINESS STUDIES

C Block, Izmir Society, Canal Rd, Lahore 53800

Telephone: (42) 37499301
Fax: (42) 37499085
E-mail: registrar@imperial.edu.pk
Internet: www.imperial.edu.pk

Founded 1991, present status 2002
Private control

Chair.: MUNAWAR AHMAD
Pro-Rector: ASIM N. AHMAD

DEANS

Department of Management and Business Studies: Dr NISAR AHMAD
Faculty of Computing and Information Sciences: Prof. Dr M. A. PASHA

INDUS INSTITUTE OF HIGHER EDUCATION

ST-2D, Block-17, Karachi, Sindh

Telephone: (21) 4801430
Fax: (21) 4985320
E-mail: indus@indus.edu.pk
Internet: www.indus.edu.pk
Private control

Chair.: KHALID AMIN
Rector: Prof. Dr MUNEER QURESHI
Registrar: AYUB SHEIKH
Dir: WAHID FAROOQUI
Librarian: FARHANA MAQSOOD

DEANS

Faculty of Business Admin.: Prof. Dr HANIF MUHAMMAD
Faculty of Engineering: Dr SYED FAISAL AHMED BUKHARI
Faculty of Fashion and Textile Design: Dr AHMED NIAZ

INDUS VALLEY SCHOOL OF ART AND ARCHITECTURE

ST-33, Block 2, Scheme 5, Clifton, Karachi, Sindh

Fax: (21) 35861048
E-mail: info@indusvalley.edu.pk
Internet: www.indusvalley.edu.pk

Founded 1989, present status 1994
Private control

Architecture, communication design, fine art, interior design, liberal arts; postgraduate degree offered in apparel design, photography, textile design

Exec. Dir: SAMINA RAEES KHAN
Registrar: RASHID RAZA
Librarian: ABID KHAN

Library of 9,500 vols
Number of students: 440

INSTITUTE OF BUSINESS ADMINISTRATION

University Rd, Karachi 75270, Sindh

Telephone: (21) 38104700
Fax: (21) 99261508
E-mail: info@iba.edu.pk
Internet: www.iba.edu.pk

Founded 1955, present status 1994
State control

Patron: GOV. OF SINDH
Dean and Dir: Dr ISHRAT HUSAIN
Registrar: AHMED ZAHEER
Librarian: MUHAMMAD ANWAR

Faculties of business admin., computer science,

Library of 40,000 vols, 50 journals
Number of teachers: 165
Number of students: 1,600

INSTITUTE OF BUSINESS AND TECHNOLOGY (BIZTEK)

Main Ibrahim Hydri Rd, Korangi Creek, Karachi, Sindh

Telephone: (21) 35120461
Fax: (21) 35092384
E-mail: info@biztek.edu.pk
Internet: www.biztek.edu.pk

Founded 2001
Private control
Academic year: June to April (3 semesters)

Chancellor: NOMAN ABID LAKHANI
Rector: Dr SYED KASHIF RAFI (acting)
Librarian: SYEDA ZAREEN NAZ

DEANS

Faculty of Computer Sciences and Information Technology: Dr MANSOOR UZ ZAFAR DAWOOD
Faculty of Management Sciences and Social Sciences: Dr MUHAMMAD ALI SIDDIQUI

INSTITUTE OF BUSINESS MANAGEMENT

Korangi Creek, Karachi 75190, Sindh

Telephone: (21) 35090961
Fax: (21) 35090968
E-mail: iobm@iobm.edu.pk
Internet: www.iobm.edu.pk

Founded 1995
Private control

Chancellor: AFTAB AHMED KHAN
Pres.: SHAHJEHAN S. KARIM
Rector: TALIB SYED KARIM
Exec Dir of Admissions and Finance: SABINA MOHSIN
Controller of Examinations: NAZ SOOMRO
Librarian: MUNOVER AZMATULLAH

Library of 25,000 vols

DEANS

College of Business Management: Prof. Dr JAVED A. ANSARI

INSTITUTE OF MANAGEMENT SCIENCES

23 E-III, Gulberg-III, Lahore 54600, Punjab

Telephone: (42) 35751115
Fax: (42) 35758665
E-mail: info@pakaims.edu.pk
Internet: www.pakaims.edu.pk

Founded 1986 as Canadian School of Management-Lahore Learning Centre, present name and status 2002
Private control

Rector: Dr KHALID RANJHA
Pro-Rector: Prof. Dr ZAFAR ALTAF
Dean: Prof. Dr M. AFZAL BEG

Depts of business admin., computer science.

INSTITUTE OF MANAGEMENT SCIENCES

1-A, Sector E-5, Phase VII, Hayatabad, Peshawar, Khyber Pakhtunkhwa

Telephone: (91) 5861024
Fax: (91) 5861026
E-mail: info@imsciences.edu.pk
Internet: www.imsciences.edu.pk

Founded 1995, present status 2005
State control

Dir: Dr NASSER ALI KHAN
Jt Dir: Dr MUHAMMAD MOHSIN KHAN
Deputy Dir: FAYAZ AHMAD
Controller of Examinations: SYED MABOOD GUL KAKA KHEL

Centres of computer sciences, information technology, management sciences; school of liberal arts.

INSTITUTE OF SPACE TECHNOLOGY

POB 2750, Islamabad 44000
Telephone: (51) 9075401
Fax: (51) 9273310
E-mail: info@ist.edu.pk
Internet: www.ist.edu.pk
Founded 2002
State control

Vice-Chancellor: IMRAN RAHMAN
Dean: Dr ABDUL AZIZ MAZHAR
Registrar: FAROUQUE KHOKHAR

Faculties of aeronautics and astronautics, communication systems engineering, humanities and sciences, materials science and engineering, research and devt; campus in Karachi

Library of 6,300 vols, 59 periodicals.

INTERNATIONAL ISLAMIC UNIVERSITY

POB 1243, Islamabad
Sector H-10, Islamabad
Telephone: (51) 9258067
Fax: (51) 9257915
E-mail: rector@iiu.edu.pk
Internet: www.iiu.edu.pk
Founded 1980 as Islamic Univ., present name 1985
State control
Academic year: September to August

Chancellor: PRES. OF PAKISTAN
Pro-Chancellor: (vacant)
Rector: Prof. FATEH MUHAMMAD MALIK
Pres.: Dr MUMTAZ AHMAD
Vice-Pres. for Admin., Finance and Planning: Dr SAHIBZADA SAJID-UR-REHMAN
Dir of Academics: SHAGUFTA HAROON
Chief Librarian: SHER NOWROZ KHAN

Library: see Libraries and Archives
Number of teachers: 97
Number of students: 17,000

Publications: *Al-Dirasat Al-Islamiya* (4 a year, in English), *Fikr-O-Nazar* (4 a year, in Urdu), *Insights* (4 a year), *Islamic Studies* (4 a year, in English), *Journal of Business and Management Sciences* (2 a year), *Mayar* (in Urdu)

DEANS

Faculty of Arabic Language: Dr MUHAMMAD MAKHLOF
Faculty of Basic and Applied Sciences: Prof. Dr MUHAMMAD IRFAN KHAN
Faculty of Engineering and Technology: Prof. Dr GHULAM YASIN CHOHAN
Faculty of Languages, Literature and Humanities: Dr RASHEED AMJAD
Faculty of Management Sciences: Prof. Dr M. BASHIR KHAN
Faculty of Shariah and Law: Prof. Dr MUHAMMAD ZIA-UL-HAQ
Faculty of Social Sciences: Prof. Dr N. B. JUMANI
Faculty of Usuluddin: Dr ZAFAR ULLAH BAIG

IQRA UNIVERSITY

Defence View, Shaheed-e-Millat Rd, Karachi 75500, Sindh
Fax: (21) 35894806
E-mail: info@iqra.edu.pk
Internet: www.iqra.edu.pk
Founded 1998
Private control

Chancellor: HUNAID H. LAKHANI
Vice-Chancellor: Dr U. A. G. ISANI
Exec. Sec.: ANWER ALI
Registrar: Dr S. AKIF HASAN
Controller of Admin.: M. KAMRAN KHAN
Controller of Examinations: NAJEEB US SAQ-LAIN

Librarian: MAHWISH KHAN
Number of teachers: 125

DEANS

Faculty of Engineering Sciences and Technology: KAMRAN RAZA (acting)
Faculty of Management Sciences: Dr M. A. K. CHISHTY

ISLAMIA COLLEGE, PESHAWAR

Univ. Campus, Jamrod Rd, Peshawar 25120, Khyber Pakhtunkhwa
Telephone: (91) 5850235
Fax: (91) 9216432
E-mail: registrar@icp.edu.pk
Internet: www.icp.edu.pk
Founded 1913
State control

Vice-Chancellor: AJMAL KHAN
Registrar: Dr GOHAR ZAMAN
Controller of Examinations: JAVED KHAN
Librarian: SAJJAD HUSSAIN
Library of 90,000 vols, 1,261 MSS

DEANS

Faculty of Social and Behavioural Sciences: Prof. Dr NAUSHAD KHAN

ISLAMIA UNIVERSITY OF BAHAWALPUR

Bahawalpur
Telephone: (62) 9250235
Fax: (62) 9250335
E-mail: vc@iub.edu.pk
Internet: www.iub.edu.pk
Founded 1925 as Jamia Abbasia, present name and status 1975
State control
Languages of instruction: English, Urdu
Academic year: September to August

Chancellor: GOV. OF PUNJAB
Vice-Chancellor: Prof. Dr MUHAMMAD MUKH-TAR
Registrar: MUHAMMAD MUNIR REHMANI
Chief Librarian: (vacant)
Library: see under Libraries and Archives
Number of teachers: 585
Number of students: 14,500

Publications: *Journal of Educational Research* (2 a year), *Journal of Social Sciences and Humanities* (2 a year), *Ulum–e–Islamia* (2 a year, in English, Persian and Urdu)

DEANS

Faculty of Arts: Prof. Dr RAZIA MUSARRAT
Faculty of Education: Prof. Dr KARAMAT MEHMOOD (acting)
Faculty of Islamic Learning: Prof. Dr SALEEM TARIQ KHAN
Faculty of Management Sciences: Prof. Dr MUHAMMAD MUKHTAR
Faculty of Pharmacy and Alternative Medicine: Prof. Dr MAHMOOD AHMED
Faculty of Science: Prof. Dr AFTAB AHMAD

ISRA UNIVERSITY

Hala Rd, Hyderabad, Sindh
Telephone: (22) 2030181
Fax: (22) 2030180
E-mail: admissions@isra.edu.pk
Internet: www.isra.edu.pk
Founded 1997
Private control

Chancellor: Prof. Dr ASADULLAH KAZI
Vice-Chancellor: Prof. Dr GHULAMQADIR KAZI
Pro-Vice-Chancellor of Engineering and Management Studies: Dr HAMEEDULLAH KAZI

Pro-Vice-Chancellor of Health Sciences: Dr ABDUL GHANI KAZI
Pro-Vice-Chancellor of Islamabad Campus: Prof. Dr ALTAF ALI G. SHAIKH
Pro-Vice-Chancellor of Karachi Campus: Prof. Dr GHULAM HUSAIN SIDDIQI
Library of 10,000 vols
Number of students: 1,500

DEANS

Faculty of Commerce, Economics and Management Sciences: Prof. Dr MOHAMMAD IQBAL BHATTI
Faculty of Dentistry: Prof. Dr RAFIQUE AHMED MEMON
Faculty of Engineering, Science and Technology: Prof. Dr MOHAMMAD IQBAL BHATTI
Faculty of Medicine and Allied Medical Sciences: Prof. Dr NAZIR ASHRAF LAGHARI

JINNAH UNIVERSITY FOR WOMEN

5 C Nazimabad, Karachi 74600, Sindh
Telephone: (21) 36620857
Fax: (21) 36620614
E-mail: info@juw.edu.pk
Internet: www.juw.edu.pk
Founded 1998
Private control
Academic year: January to May, July to November (2 semesters)

Chancellor: Prof. NOOR-US-SABAH CHUGHTAI
Vice-Chancellor: Prof. Dr NAEEM FAROOQUI
Registrar: Dr QAZI NAWAB MANZAR
Controller of Examinations: SHAHID ALI KHAN

Library of 30,000 vols
Number of teachers: 150
Number of students: 3,000

DEANS

Faculty of Arts: JAMILA KHANUM
Faculty of Pharmacy: Prof. Dr GHULAM SARWAR
Faculty of Science: Dr NEELOFAR SHAUKAT

KARACHI INSTITUTE OF ECONOMICS AND TECHNOLOGY

Korangi Creek, Karachi 75190, Sindh
Telephone: (21) 35091114
Fax: (21) 35091118
E-mail: info@pafkiet.edu.pk
Internet: www.pafkiet.edu.pk
Founded 2000
Private control

Chancellor: Dr MOHAMMAD IZHAR-UL-HASAN
Pres.: M. KHALID HUSAIN
Vice-Pres. and Dean of Academics: Prof. Dr SYED IRFAN HYDER
Dir of Admin.: UBAID M. ABBASI
Librarian: SYED MUHAMMAD IDREES

Colleges of computing and information sciences, engineering, English and communication skills, humanities and sciences, management sciences, media and arts.

KARAKORAM INTERNATIONAL UNIVERSITY

Univ. Rd, Gilgit 15100, Khyber Pakhtunkhwa
Telephone: (5811) 960440
Fax: (5811) 960039
E-mail: vcoffice@kiu.edu.pk
Internet: www.kiu.edu.pk
Founded 2002
State control

Chancellor: PRES. OF ISLAMIC REPUBLIC OF PAKISTAN
Vice-Chancellor: Prof. Dr NAJMA NAJAM
Number of teachers: 186
Number of students: 1,171

DEANS

Sciences: Prof. Dr AQUILA ISLAM
Social Sciences and Humanities: Prof. Dr
SHAFIQ JULLUNDHRY

KHADIM ALI SHAH BUKHARI INSTITUTE OF TECHNOLOGY (KASBIT)

Bldg 1, 84-B S. M. C. H. S., off Shahrah-e-Faisal, Karachi 74400, Sindh

Telephone: (21) 4314970
Fax: (21) 4525525
E-mail: info@kasbit.edu.pk
Internet: www.kasbit.edu.pk

Founded 1999
Private control

Chancellor: ARIF ALI SHAH BUKHARI
Vice-Chancellor: SYED ALI ABBAS ABIDI

Publications: *Journal of Economics and Business Research* (1 a year), *KASBIT Business Journal*

DEANS

Faculty of Management Sciences: Prof. Dr
MUHAMMAD MAHMUD

KHYBER MEDICAL UNIVERSITY

PDA Bldg, Block IV, Phase 5, Hayatabad, Peshawar, Khyber Pakhtunkhwa

Telephone: (91) 9217703
Fax: (91) 9217704
Internet: www.kmu.edu.pk

Founded 2006
State control
Academic year: September to January,February to June (2 semesters)

Institutes of basic medical science, health professional education, physical medicine and rehabilitation, public health and social science; postgraduate college of nursing

Vice-Chancellor: Prof. Dr MOHAMMAD HAFIZULLAH
Registrar: FAZAL MAHMOOD KHAN
Dir of Academics, Admissions and Quality Assurance: Prof. Dr SHAD MOHAMMAD
Controller of Examinations: Prof. Dr SHAHNAZ AKHTAR.

KHYBER PAKHTUNKHWA AGRICULTURAL UNIVERSITY

Peshawar, Khyber-Pakhtunkhwa

Telephone: (91) 9216518
Fax: (91) 9216520
E-mail: registraraup@yahoo.com
Internet: www.aup.edu.pk

Founded 1981
State control
Language of instruction: English
Academic year: January to December

Chancellor: GOV. OF KHYBER PAKHTUNKHWA
Vice-Chancellor: Prof. Dr KHAN BAHADAR MARWAT
Registrar: Dr MOHAMMAD ZULFIQAR
Librarian: ATTAULLAH
Library of 113,600 vols
Number of teachers: 202 full-time, 77 part-time
Number of students: 8,000

Publications: *Journal of Development Studies* (irregular), *Pakistan Journal of Weed Science Research* (4 a year), *Sarhad Journal of Agriculture* (4 a year)

DEANS

Faculty of Animal Husbandry and Veterinary Sciences: Prof. Dr M. SUBHAN QURESHI
Faculty of Crop Production Sciences: Prof. Dr ZAHOOR A. SWATI

Faculty of Crop Protection Sciences: Prof. Dr MIAN INAYATULLAH
Faculty of Nutrition Sciences: Prof. Dr ALAM ZEB
Faculty of Rural Social Sciences: ZAHID HUSSAIN

KING EDWARD MEDICAL UNIVERSITY

Nelagumbad, Anarkali, Lahore 54000, Punjab

Telephone: (42) 9211145
E-mail: kemcol@brain.net.pk
Internet: www.kemu.edu.pk

Founded 1860, fmrly King Edward Medical College, present name and status 2005
State control

Chancellor: GOV. OF PUNJAB
First Vice-Chancellor: Prof. MUMTAZ HASAN
Vice-Chancellor and Pro-Vice-Chancellor: Prof. ASAD ASLAM KHAN
Library of 50,279 vols

DEANS

Faculty of Public Health and Preventive Medicine: Prof. Dr MAAZ AHMAD

KOHAT UNIVERSITY OF SCIENCE & TECHNOLOGY

Bannu Rd, off Jerma, Kohat 26000, Khyber Pakhtunkhwa

Telephone: (922) 554565
Fax: (922) 554556
Internet: www.kust.edu.pk

Founded 2001
State control
Academic year: November to March,April to August (2 semesters)

Vice-Chancellor: Dr NASIR JAMAL KHATTAK
Registrar: Prof. Dr IHSAN ELLAHI
Dir for Works: ALTAF HUSSAIN
Dir for Finance: MUHAMMAD ZAFAR KHAN
Librarian: MURAD ALI
Library of 25,000 vols

DEANS

Faculty of Biological Sciences: Prof. Dr SHAFIQ UR REHMAN
Faculty of Physical Sciences: Prof. FIDA YOUNUS KHATTAK

LAHORE COLLEGE FOR WOMEN UNIVERSITY

Jail Rd, Lahore 54000, Punjab

Telephone: (42) 99201950
Fax: (42) 99203077
E-mail: registrar@lcwu.edu.pk
Internet: www.lcwu.edu.pk

Founded 1922, present name and status 2002
State control

Vice-Chancellor: Prof. Dr SABIHA MANSOOR
Registrar: RIFFAT SAQLAIN
Librarian: HINA AZIZ
Number of teachers: 513 (455 full-time, 58 part-time)
Number of students: 6,457 (5,534 full-time, 923 part-time)

DEANS

Faculty of Engineering, Technology and Management Sciences: Prof. Dr FARHAT SALEEMI
Faculty of Humanities, Islamic and Oriental Learning: NAUSHABA FAROOQ (acting)
Faculty of Natural Sciences: Prof. Dr KAUSER JAMAL CHEEMA
Faculty of Social Sciences: Prof. RIFFAT SAQLAIN

PROFESSORS

ALI, Y., Physics
CHEEMA, K. J., Environmental Sciences
CHEEMA, K. J., Zoology
GOHAR, K., Economics
MAHMOOD, A. S., Mathematics
MATEEN, B., Environmental Sciences
NAVQI, R. F., Fine Arts
NAWAZ, R., Islamic Studies

LAHORE SCHOOL OF ECONOMICS

Intersection Main Blvd, Phase VI DHA, Burki Rd, Lahore 53200, Punjab

Telephone: (42) 36560938
Internet: www.lahoreschoolofeconomics.edu.pk

Founded 1993, present status 1997
Private control

Rector: SHAHID AMJAD CHAUDHRY
Registrar: VIQAR AHMED
Controller of Examinations: ROMANA NOOR
Librarian: QAISAR SULTANA

Publication: *Lahore Journal of Economics* (2 a year)

DEANS

Faculty of Business Admin.: Prof. SOHAIL ZAFAR
Faculty of Economics: AZAM CHAUDHRY

LAHORE UNIVERSITY OF MANAGEMENT SCIENCES

Opposite Sector U, D. H. A., Lahore Cantt, Lahore 54792, Punjab

Telephone: (42) 5722670
Fax: (42) 5722591
E-mail: admissions@lums.edu.pk
Internet: www.lums.edu.pk

Founded 1985
Private control
Language of instruction: English
Academic year: September to June

Chancellor: PRES. OF ISLAMIC REPUBLIC OF PAKISTAN
Pro-Chancellor: SYED BABAR ALI
Vice-Chancellor: ADIL NAJAM
Pro-Vice-Chancellor: Dr AHMAD J. DURRANI
Rector: ABDUL RAZAK DAWOOD
Chief Librarian: MUHAMMAD RAMZAN
Library: see Libraries and Archives
Number of teachers: 123
Number of students: 1,750

Publications: *Asian Journal of Management Cases* (2 a year), *LUMS Business Recorder* (1 a year), *PLUMS* (1 a year)

DEANS

School of Humanities, Social Sciences and Law: Dr ANJUM ALTAF
School of Science and Engineering: ASAD A. ABIDI
Suleman Dawood School of Business: ARIF NAZIR BUTT

PROFESSORS

ALI, I., Business History and Business Policy
BABRI, H. A., Computer Science
BEG, I., Mathematics
GHANI, J. A., Strategy and Marketing
HASSAN, S. Z., Management Information Systems and Management of Technology
IQBAL, M. A., Computer Science and Mathematics
KHURSHID, A., Technology and Organizational Management
MAUD, M. A., Computer Science
NASIM, A., Business–Government Relations
SARWAR, S. M., Computer Science
SIPRA, N., Finance
ZAMAN, A., Econometrics
ZAMAN, A., Mathematics

LASBELA UNIVERSITY OF AGRICULTURE, WATER AND MARINE SCIENCES

Uthal, Lasbela 90150, Balochistan
Telephone: (853) 610847
Fax: (853) 610903
E-mail: info@luawms.edu.pk
Internet: www.luawms.edu.pk

Founded 2005
State control

Chancellor: Gov. OF BALOCHISTAN
Vice-Chancellor: Dr ABDUL HAMEED BAJOI
Registrar: SHER AHMED QAMBRANI
Dir of Student Affairs: TAIMOOR KHAN
Librarian: YAHYA HABIB

DEANS

Faculty of Agriculture: Prof. Dr ABDUL JABBAR MALIK
Faculty of Marine Sciences: Dr JAVED MUSTAQUIM
Faculty of Veterinary and Animal Sciences: Prof. Dr M. SHARIF PHULLAN
Faculty of Water Resources Management: Prof. Dr MUHAMMAD ISHAQ GHAZNAVI

LIAQUAT UNIVERSITY OF MEDICAL & HEALTH SCIENCES

Jamshoro, Sindh
Telephone: (22) 9213305
Fax: (22) 9213306
E-mail: registrar@lumhs.edu.pk
Internet: www.lumhs.edu.pk

Founded 1881, present name and status 2001
State control

Vice-Chancellor: Prof. Dr NOSHAD A. SHAIKH
Registrar: MOHAMMAD SALEH RAJAR

Publication: *Journal of Liaquat University of Medical and Health Sciences (JLUMHS)*

DEANS

Faculty of Basic Medical Sciences: Prof. SHAHEEN SHAH
Faculty of Community Medicine and Public Health Sciences: Prof. RAFIQUE AHMED SOOMRO
Faculty of Dentistry: Prof. RAFQUE AHMED MEMON
Faculty of Medicine and Allied Sciences: Prof. ALLAH BACHAYO MEMON
Faculty of Surgery and Allied Sciences: Prof. GHULAM ALI MEMON

MEHRAN UNIVERSITY OF ENGINEERING & TECHNOLOGY

Jamshoro, 76062 Sindh
Telephone: (22) 2772250
Fax: (221) 2771382
E-mail: vc@admin.muet.edu.pk
Internet: www.muet.edu.pk

Founded 1963 as constituent college of Univ. of Sindh; present status 1977
State control
Language of instruction: English
Academic year: October to August

Chancellor: Gov. OF SINDH
Pro-Vice-Chancellor: Prof. Dr MUHAMMAD ASLAM UQAILI
Vice-Chancellor: Dr ABDUL QADEER KHAN RAJPUT
Registrar: Prof. Dr TAUHA HUSSAIN ALI
Librarian: AZAM ALI HALEPOTA

Library: see Libraries and Archives
Number of teachers: 270
Number of students: 3,702

Publication: *Research Journal of Engineering and Technology* (4 a year)

DEANS

Faculty of Architecture and Civil Engineering: Prof. Dr GHOS BUX KHASKELI
Faculty of Electrical, Electronics and Computer Engineering: Prof. Dr BHAWANI SHANKAR CHOWDHRY
Faculty of Engineering: Prof. Dr ABDUL GHANI PATHAN
Faculty of Science, Technology and Humanities: Prof. Dr MOHAMMAD IBRAHIM PANHWAR

MINHAJ UNIVERSITY, LAHORE

Near Hamdard Chowk, Township, Lahore, Punjab
Telephone: (42) 35145621
Fax: (42) 35116779
E-mail: info@mul.edu.pk
Internet: www.mul.edu.pk

Founded 2005
Private control

Chancellor: Gov. OF PUNJAB
Vice-Chancellor: Prof. Dr ALI MUHAMMAD
Registrar: MUHAMMAD AHMAD
Controller of Examinations: MUHAMMAD YAQUB
Librarian: SHAHID MEHMOOD

Library of 50,000 vols

DEANS

Faculty of Basic Sciences and Mathematics: Prof. Dr ALI MUHAMMAD
Faculty of Commerce and Management Sciences: Prof. Dr MUHAMMAD ASLAM GHOURI
Faculty of Computer Science and Information Technology: Prof. Dr ALI MUHAMMAD
Faculty of Islamic Studies: Prof. Dr OBED ULLAH
Faculty of Languages: Prof. Dr ZAHOOR AHMAD AZHAR
Faculty of Social Sciences: Prof. Dr SYED RAZA UL HAQ

MIRPUR UNIVERSITY OF SCIENCE & TECHNOLOGY

Allama Iqbal Rd, Mirpur 10250, Azad Jammu and Kashmir
Telephone: (5827) 961037
Fax: (5827) 961039
E-mail: info@must.edu.pk
Internet: www.must.edu.pk

Founded 1980 as Ali Ahmed Shah Univ. College of Engineering and Technology, present name and status 2008
State control

Chancellor: PRES. OF AZAD JAMMU AND KASHMIR
Vice Chancellor: Prof. NAIB HUSSAIN CH.
Registrar: MUHAMMAD SHABIR MIRZA
Controller of Examinations: MUHAMMAD KHALID
Chief Librarian: MUHAMMAD WARIS

Faculties of arts, engineering, sciences; campuses in Mirpur, Bhimber.

MOHAMMAD ALI JINNAH UNIVERSITY

Islamabad Expressway, Kahuta Rd, Zone-V, Islamabad
Telephone: (51) 2512800
E-mail: info@jinnah.edu.pk
Internet: www.jinnah.edu.pk

Founded 1998
Private control

Chancellor: MIAN AMER MAHMOOD
Pres.: Prof. Dr ABDUL WAHAB
Exec. Vice-Pres.: Prof. Dr M. MANSOOR AHMED
Registrar: G. A. NAQI SYED
Controller of Examinations: SAQIB NAVEED

Library of 90,000 vols

DEANS

Faculty of Engineering and Applied Sciences: Dr ABDUL QADIR
Faculty of Management and Social Sciences: Dr ANWAR FAZIL CHISHTI

MOHI-UD-DIN ISLAMIC UNIVERSITY, NERIAN SHARIF

Plot 2A, I-9 Markaz, Islamabad
Telephone: (51) 4859658
Fax: (51) 4859657
E-mail: miuuniversity@hotmail.com
Internet: www.miu.edu.pk
Private control
Academic year: September to March (2 semesters)

Faculties of education and social sciences, health and medical sciences, management sciences and information technology

Chancellor: ALLA-UD-DIN SIDDIQUI
Vice-Chancellor: MUHAMMAD KHURSHID

Library of 17,400 vols.

NATIONAL COLLEGE OF ARTS

4 Shahrah-e-Quaid-Azam, Lahore, Punjab
Telephone: (42) 99210599
Fax: (42) 99210500
E-mail: info@nca.edu.pk
Internet: www.nca.edu.pk

Founded present name 1958, present status 1985
State control

Bachelor degrees in fine arts, design and architecture; Masters degree in interior design

Prin.: Prof. SAJJAD KAUSAR (acting)
Registrar: NADEEM HASAN KHAN
Librarian: RUBINA IMTIAZ

Publication: *Journal of Contemporary Arts and Culture.*

NATIONAL COLLEGE OF BUSINESS ADMINISTRATION & ECONOMICS

40 E/I Gulberg-III, Lahore, Punjab
Telephone: (42) 35752716
Fax: (42) 35752547
E-mail: info@ncbae.edu.pk
Internet: www.ncbae.edu.pk

Founded 1994, present status 2002
Private control

Chair.: MIAN SHAMIM HAIDER
Rector: Dr MUNIR AHMAD

Faculties of applied economics, applied mathematics, applied statistics, business admin., computer science, environmental management, fine arts.

NATIONAL DEFENCE UNIVERSITY

E-9, Islamabad
Telephone: (51) 9260651
Fax: (51) 9260663
E-mail: presidentndu@ndu.edu.pk
Internet: ndu.edu.pk
State control

Chancellor: PRES. OF ISLAMIC REPUBLIC OF PAKISTAN
Pres.: AGHA MUHAMMAD UMER FAROOQ
Registrar: Dr M. F. K. LODHI
Controller of Examinations: Dr S. Q. M. ZAIDI

Depts of govt and public policy, int. relations, leadership studies, peace and conflict studies, strategic and nuclear studies

Library of 70,000 vols

Publication: *NDU Journal* (2 a year).

NATIONAL TEXTILE UNIVERSITY

Sheikhupura Rd, Faisalabad 37610, Punjab
Telephone: (41) 9230081
Fax: (41) 9230098
E-mail: info@ntu.edu.pk
Internet: www.ntu.edu.pk

Founded 1959 as Institute of Textile Technology, renamed Nat. College of Textile Engineering 1976, present name and status 2002
State control

Rector: Dr NIAZ AHMAD
Registrar: Prof. JAVAID IQBAL (acting)
Sr Librarian: MUSHTAQ AHMAD SIDDIQUI
Library of 16,000 vols, 33 journals
Number of teachers: 35
Number of students: 600

DEANS

Faculty of Engineering and Technology: Dr TANVEER HUSSAIN
Faculty of Sciences: Prof. JAVAID IQBAL

NATIONAL UNIVERSITY OF COMPUTER AND EMERGING SCIENCES

A. K. Brohi Rd, H-11/4, Islamabad
Telephone: (51) 8314100
Fax: (51) 4100619
E-mail: info@nu.edu.pk
Internet: www.nu.edu.pk

Founded 2000
Private control
Academic year: January to June,August to December (2 semesters)

Campuses in Karachi, Lahore, Peshawar
Chancellor: WASIM SAJJAD
Rector: Dr AMIR MUHAMMED
Pro-Rector: SYED REFAQAT
Dean: Dr M. AYUB ALVI
Registrar: Dr M. LATIF VIRK
Number of students: 4,000

NATIONAL UNIVERSITY OF MODERN LANGUAGES

Main Campus, Sector H–9, Islamabad 44000
Telephone: (51) 9257646
Fax: (51) 9257679
E-mail: info@numl.edu.pk
Internet: www.numl.edu.pk

Founded 1970, present name and status 2000
State control
Academic year: January to December (2 semesters)

Chancellor: PRES. OF ISLAMIC REPUBLIC OF PAKISTAN
Rector: MASOOD HASAN
Dir-Gen.: AZAM JAMAL
Dir of Academic Affairs: RIASAT HUSSAIN
Dir of Admin.: MUHAMMAD YASIN
Library Dir: MUHAMMAD ABBAS
Dir of Int. Relations: KAMRAN JAHANGIR
Dir of Student Affairs: TAJ MUHAMMAD
Registrar: SAJIDA TAHIR
Library of 115,000 vols
Number of teachers: 315
Number of students: 12,422

Publications: *Daryaft* (1 a year), *Research Magazine* (2 a year), *Takhleeqi Adab* (1 a year)

DEANS

Faculty of Advance Integrated Studies and Research: Dr SHAZRA MUNNAWER
Faculty of Engineering and Information Technology: Dr MUHAMMAD AKBAR
Faculty of English Language, Literature and Applied Linguistics: Dr RUBINA KAMRAN
Faculty of Management Sciences: Prof. Dr RASHID AHMAD KHAN

Faculty of Near Eastern Language and Culture: Dr SYED ALI ANWAR
Quality Enhancement Cell: Dr SOHAILA JAVED

NATIONAL UNIVERSITY OF SCIENCES AND TECHNOLOGY

H–12, Islamabad
Telephone: (51) 90851001
Fax: (51) 90851007
E-mail: info@nust.edu.pk
Internet: www.nust.edu.pk
State control

Rector: MUHAMMAD ASGHAR
Pro-Rector for Academics: Dr ASIF RAZA
Registrar: SALIM DAUD
Dir of Admin.: NASIR HUSSAIN
Dir of Research: SALMAN ABSAR
Dir of Student Affairs: MAHMUD BASHIR BAJWA

Campuses in Rawalpindi, Karachi and Risalpur; colleges of aeronautical engineering (Risalpur), civil engineering (Risalpur), electrical and mechanical engineering (Rawalpindi), marine engineering (Karachi), medical sciences (Rawalpindi), telecommunication engineering (Rawalpindi).

NED UNIVERSITY OF ENGINEERING AND TECHNOLOGY

Main University Rd, Karachi 75270
Telephone: (21) 99261261
Fax: (21) 99261255
E-mail: vc@neduet.edu.pk
Internet: www.neduet.edu.pk

Founded 1922 as NED Govt Engineering College, univ. status 1977
State control
Language of instruction: English
Academic year: February to December

Chancellor: GOV. OF SINDH
Pro-Chancellor: EDUCATION MIN. OF SINDH
Vice-Chancellor: Eng. ABUL KALAM
Pro-Vice-Chancellor: Prof. Dr MUZZAFFAR MAHMOOD
Pro-Vice-Chancellor: Dr SAHIBZADA FAROOQ AHMAD RAFEEQI
Registrar: Eng. JAVED AZIZ KHAN
Chief Librarian: MEHER YASMEEN KHAN
Library: see under Libraries and Archives
Number of teachers: 460
Number of students: 8,000

Publications: *NED University of Engineering and Research* (2 a year), *Research Journal* (4 a year), *Versity News* (12 a year)

DEANS

Faculty of Bio-Medical Engineering: Prof. NEELOFUR MASTER (acting)
Faculty of Chemical and Process Engineering: Prof. Dr MUHAMMAD TUFAIL
Faculty of Civil Engineering and Architecture: Prof. Dr SAROSH HASHMAT LODI
Faculty of Electrical and Computer Engineering: Prof. Dr MUZZAFFAR MAHMOOD
Faculty of Information Sciences and Humanities: Prof. Dr MAHMOOD KHAN PATHAN
Faculty of Mechanical and Manufacturing Engineering: Prof. Dr NAZIMUDDIN QURESHI

PROFESSORS

AHMED, N., Architecture and Planning
ALI, A., Materials Engineering
ALI, M., Urban and Infrastructure Engineering
ALI, S., Polymer and Petrochemical Engineering
ALTAF, T., Electrical Engineering
ANJUM, S., Physics
BAIG, M., Mathematics
FAROOQUI, R., Civil Engineering

HAQUE, S., Computer Science and Information Technology
HASHMI, S., Automotive and Marine Engineering
IQBAL, S., Industrial and Manufacturing Engineering
JAFRI, A., Bio-Medical Engineering
KHALID, A., Mechanical Engineering
KHAN, A., Civil Engineering
KHAN, R., Earthquake Engineering
KHATOON, H., Computer and Info. Systems Engineering
MAHMOOD, K., Materials Engineering
MEMON, I., Chemical Engineering
MURTAZA, A., Petroleum Engineering
NAEEM, A., Architecture and Planning
PASHA, K., Textile Engineering
QADIR, A., Urban and Infrastructure Engineering
QAZI, S., Electrical Engineering
RAFI, M., Earthquake Engineering
SATTAAR, S., Computer Science and Information Technology
SHAIKH, A., Environmental Engineering
SIDDIQUI, M., Mechanical Engineering
SYED, K., Polymer and Petrochemical Engineering
TARIQ, Q., Computer and Info. Systems Engineering
WAHAB, Q., Electronic Engineering
YASMIN, F., Bio-Medical Engineering
ZAIDI, S., Electronic Engineering

NEWPORTS INSTITUTE OF COMMUNICATIONS AND ECONOMICS

159/O, Block-3, Kashmir Rd, PECHS, Karachi, Sindh
Telephone: (21) 34541067
E-mail: info@newports.edu.pk
Internet: www.newports.edu.pk

Founded 1993 as Karachi Campus of Newport Univ. of California, present status 2002
Private control

Chair.: SADIQ JAMAL
Rector: HUMA BUKHARI
Registrar: SALMAN JAMAL

DEANS

Faculty of Business and Admin.: Prof. Dr M. WASIM
Faculty of Computer Science: SAJJAD HUSSAIN MAHESRI

NORTHERN UNIVERSITY

3-The Mall, Nowshera Cantonment, Khyber Pakhtunkhwa, Nowshera
Telephone: (923) 613485
Internet: www.northern.edu.pk

Founded 2002
Private control

Pres.: SAWAR KHAN
Rector: Dr DOST MOHAMMAD KHAN
Registrar: MUHAMMAD ASHRAF
Controller of Examinations: ZAFAR IQBAL

DEANS

Faculty of Admin. Sciences: Prof. SALMA S. ASHRAF
Faculty of Arts and Social Sciences: Prof. Dr R. A. FAROOQ
Faculty of Engineering and Information Technology: Prof. Dr SULEMAN ASHRAF
Faculty of Sciences: Prof. Dr MUHAMMAD ULLAH

NWFP UNIVERSITY OF ENGINEERING AND TECHNOLOGY

POB 814, Univ. Campus, Peshawar 25120, Khyber Pakhtunkhwa
Telephone: (91) 9216796

Fax: (91) 9216663
E-mail: registrar@nwfpuet.edu.pk
Internet: www.nwfpuet.edu.pk
Founded 1980
State control
Language of instruction: English
Academic year: November to September

Chancellor: GOV. OF KHYBER PAKHTUNKHWA
Vice-Chancellor: SYED IMTIAZ HUSSAIN GILANI
Registrar: IMTIAZ AHMAD KHAN
Dean: Prof. AZZAM UL ASSAR
Librarian: ABDUR RASHID

Campuses at Abbottabad, Bannu and Mardan

Library of 14,000 vols
Number of teachers: 347
Number of students: 3,365

Publication: *Journal of Engineering and Applied Sciences* (2 a year)

PROFESSORS

AKBAR SHAH, S. R., Mechatronics Engineering
GUL JADOON, K., Mining Engineering
HUSSAIN, I., Industrial Engineering
INAYATULLAH KHAN BABAR, M., Computer Science and Information Technology (Non Engineering)
JADOON, K. G., Chemical Engineering
MAHMOOD, Z., Agricultural Engineering
NAEEM KHAN, A., Civil Engineering
TAJIK, S. J., Mechanical Engineering
UR REHMAN, S., Basic Science and Islamiat
YAHYA, K. M., Computer System Engineering
ZAHIR KHAN, M., Electrical and Electronics Engineering

PIMSAT UNIVERSITY

177/2, IEP Bldg, Shahrah-e-Faisal, Karachi, Sindh
Telephone: (21) 2789888
Fax: (21) 2789891
E-mail: info@pimsat-khi.edu.pk
Internet: www.pimsat-khi.edu.pk
Private control

Chair. and Rector: MUNAWAR AHMAD
Exec. Dir and Registrar: ASIM N. AHMAD
Controller of Examinations: SYED MASOOD RAZA
Librarian: SAADIA TAYYABA

DEANS

Dept of Applied Technologies: Dr S. N. IQBAL
Dept of Management of Science: Dr Z. A. KHAN

PIR MEHR ALI SHAH ARID AGRICULTURE RAWALPINDI

Shamsabad, Muree Rd, Rawalpindi
Telephone: (51) 9290466
Fax: (51) 9290459
E-mail: registrar@uaar.edu.pk
Internet: www.uaar.edu.pk
Founded 1979; present name and status 1994
State control

Vice-Chancellor: Prof. Dr KHALID MEHMOOD KHAN
Registrar: MALIK MAQBOOL HUSSAIN AWAN

Controller of Examinations: MUHAMMAD NISAR
Librarian: ZAMMURAD AHMAD IQBAL

DEANS

Faculty of Crop and Food Sciences: Dr ABDUL KHALIQ
Faculty of Forestry Range Management and Wildlife: Prof. Dr SARWAT NAZ MIRZA
Faculty of Sciences: Dr AZRA KHANUM
Faculty of Veterinary and Animal Sciences: Prof. Dr NEMAT ULLAH

PRESTON UNIVERSITY

15 Banglore Town, Shahrah-e-Faisal, Karachi, Sindh
Telephone: (21) 4534663
Fax: (21) 4525881
E-mail: karachi@preston.edu.pk
Internet: www.preston.edu.pk
Founded 1984 as School of Business and Commerce, present status 2004
Private control
Academic year: September to January, February to June, July to August (3 semesters)

Campuses at Faisalabad, Islamabad, Kohat, Lahore, Peshawar

Chancellor: Dr ABDUL BASIT
Pro-Chancellor: SYED DEEDAR HUSSAIN SHAH
Vice-Chancellor: Dr NAZIR A. MUGHAL
Library of 8,000 vols
Number of teachers: 52

DEANS

Faculty of Business Administration: Dr IBRAHIM SHAH BUKHARI
Faculty of Education: Dr FATIMA RAZI
Faculty of Engineering and Technology: Prof. Dr ABDUL RAZZAQUE MEMON
Faculty of Social Sciences: Dr IBRAHIM SHAH BUKHARI

QUAID-E-AWAM UNIVERSITY OF ENGINEERING, SCIENCES AND TECHNOLOGY

Nawabshah 67480, Sindh
Telephone: (244) 9370387
Fax: (241) 9370367
E-mail: info@quest.edu.pk
Internet: www.quest.edu.pk
Founded 1963 as constituent college of Univ. of Sindh, present name and status 1996
State control
Language of instruction: English
Academic year: January to December

Vice-Chancellor: Prof. Dr ALI BUX SOOMRO
Registrar: MUSHTAQ SOHAIL SOOMRO
Controller of Examinations: NAZIR AHMED DURANI
Librarian: GHULAM FAROOQUE CHANNAR
Library of 52,234 vols; 25,000 online research journals
Number of teachers: 173
Number of students: 2,753

Publication: *Quaid-e-Awam University Research Journal of Engineering, Science and Technology* (2 a year)

DEANS

Faculty of Engineering: Prof. Dr SALEEM RAZA SAMO
Faculty of Technology: Prof. Dr GHULAM HUSSAIN WAGAN

QUAID-I-AZAM UNIVERSITY

Islamabad 45320
Telephone: (51) 90644050
E-mail: vco@qau.edu.pk
Internet: www.qau.edu.pk
Founded 1967 as Univ. of Islamabad, present name 1976
State control
Language of instruction: English
Chancellor: PRES. OF ISLAMIC REPUBLIC OF PAKISTAN
Vice-Chancellor: Prof. Dr MASOOM YASINZAI
Registrar: Dr SHAFEEQ UR REHMAN
Controller of Examination: MUHAMMAD AQEEL GILLANI
Librarian: MEHBOOB HUSSAIN KHAN
Library: see under Libraries and Archives
Number of teachers: 195
Number of students: 3,995

Publications: *Journal of Science* (2 a year), *Journal of Social Science, Scrutiny* (2 a year)

DEANS

Faculty of Biological Sciences: Dr ABDUL HAMEED
Faculty of Medicine: Dr SYED FAZLE HADI
Faculty of Natural Sciences: Dr QAISER MUSHTAQ
Faculty of Social Sciences: Dr EATZAZ AHMED

ATTACHED INSTITUTES

Area Study Centre for Africa, North & South America: c/o Quaid-i-Azam Univ., Islamabad 45320; tel. (51) 2896006; fax (51) 2896007; e-mail ascqau@yahoo.com; attached to Quaid-i-Azam Univ.; conducts research in fields of American, Latin American, Canadian and African Studies; publ. *Pakistan Journal of American Studies* (2 a year).

National Institute of Pakistan Studies: c/o Quaid-i-Azam Univ., Islamabad 45320; tel. (51) 90644010; e-mail trahman@nips.qau.edu.pk; internet www.qau.edu.pk/nips; f. 1983; attached to Quaid-i-Azam Univ.; Dir Prof. Dr TARIQ RAHMAN.

National Institute of Psychology: c/o Quaid-i-Azam Univ., Shahdra Rd, Islamabad; tel. (51) 90644031; fax (51) 2896012; e-mail nip@nip.edu.pk; internet www.nip.edu.pk; f. 1976; attached to Quaid-i-Azam Univ.; research in psychology; library of 9,500 vols; Dir Prof. Dr ANILA KAMAL; publ. *Pakistan Journal of Psychological Research* (2 a year).

QURTUBA UNIVERSITY OF SCIENCE AND INFORMATION TECHNOLOGY

K-1, Phase III, Hayatabad, Peshawar, Khyber Pakhtunkhwa
Telephone: (91) 5812117
Fax: (91) 5825837
E-mail: query@qurtuba.edu.pk
Internet: www.qurtuba.edu.pk
Founded 2001
Private control

Pres.: Dr MUHAMMAD ZULFIQAR KHAN NIAZI
Vice-Chancellor: Prof. Dr HAMEEDULLAH KHAN ALIZAI
Registrar: SHER BAHADUR

Depts of botany, education, English, management sciences and information technology, pharmacy, political science and int. relations, Urdu; campus at Dera Ismail Khan

Publications: *Journal of Managerial Sciences* (2 a year), *The Dialogue* (4 a year).

RIPHAH INTERNATIONAL UNIVERSITY

Sector I-14, Hajj Complex, Peshawar Rd, Islamabad
Telephone: (51) 8446000
Fax: (51) 5469636
Internet: www.riphah.edu.pk
Founded 2002
Private control
Chancellor: MUHAMMAD ZULFIQAR KHAN
Pro-Chancellor: M. HASSAN KHAN
Vice-Chancellor: Prof. Dr ANIS AHMAD
Library of 80,000 vols, 20,000 journals

DEANS

Faculty of Computing: SAAD NAEEM ZAFAR
Faculty of Engineering and Applied Sciences: Prof. Dr MIRZA MUHAMMAD JAVED
Faculty of Management Sciences: Prof. M. AMANULLAH KHAN
Faculty of Pharmaceutical Sciences: Dr INA-MUL HAQ

SARDAR BAHADUR KHAN WOMEN'S UNIVERSITY

Brewery Rd, Quetta, Balochistan
Telephone: (81) 9213304
Fax: (81) 9213308
E-mail: vc_secretariat@sbkwu.edu.pk
Internet: www.sbkwu.edu.pk
Founded 2004
State control
Chancellor: GOV. OF BALOCHISTAN
Vice-Chancellor: SULTANA BALOCH
Registrar: Prof. JAMILA QAZI
Faculties of management and computer sciences, natural sciences, social sciences
Number of students: 3,000

SARHAD UNIVERSITY OF SCIENCE & INFORMATION TECHNOLOGY

36B Chinar Rd, Univ. Town, Peshawar, Khyber Pakhtunkhwa
Telephone: (91) 5846508
E-mail: vc@suit.edu.pk
Internet: suit.edu.pk
Founded 2001, present status 2008
Private control
Vice-Chancellor: Prof. Dr SALIM-UR-REHMAN
Registrar: MUHAMMAD NASIR
Controller of Examinations: SALMAN FAIZ
Library of 30,000 vols

DEANS

Faculty of Arts, Social Sciences and Education: Prof. Dr ATHAR KHAN KOTI
Faculty of Engineering: Prof. GHULAM RUHULLAH
Faculty of Life Sciences: Prof. Dr KAMRAN AHMAD CHISTI
Faculty of Sciences: Prof. Dr NAZIR SHAH KHATTAK

SHAH ABDUL LATIF UNIVERSITY

Khairpur, Sindh
Telephone: (243) 9280051
Fax: (243) 9280060
E-mail: info@salu.edu.pk
Internet: www.salu.edu.pk
Founded 1975, present status 1987
State control
Languages of instruction: English, Sindhi, Urdu
Academic year: September to June
Chancellor: GOV. OF SINDH
Vice-Chancellor: Prof. Dr NILOFER SHAIKH
Pro-Vice-Chancellor: Prof. Dr ABDULLAH PHULPOTO
Registrar: Prof. SYED AHMED HUSSAIN SHAH
Librarian: MUHAMMAD SALEH BHATTI
Library of 40,311 vols
Number of teachers: 186
Number of students: 5,000
Publications: *Aashikar* (1 a year, in Sindhi, research), *Almas* (online), *Ancient Sindh* (1 a year, research), *Bhittai* (1 a year, in Sindhi, research), *ELF Annual Research Journal* (in English), *Indus Journal of Mathematical Sciences*, *International Journal of Chemical & Biological Science*, *Scientific Sindh* (1 a year, research), *The Commerce and Economic Review* (1 a year, research), *The Diplomat* (2 a year)

DEANS

Faculty of Arts and Social Sciences: Prof. SYED AHMED HUSSAIN SHAH
Faculty of Commerce and Business Admin.: Prof. SHAH MUHAMMAD LUHRANI
Faculty of Law: Prof. QALANDAR BUX PHUL-POTO
Faculty of Natural Sciences: Prof. MIANDAD ZARDARI

SHAHEED BENAZIR BHUTTO UNIVERSITY

Sheringal, Dir (Upper), Khyber Pakhtunkhwa
Telephone: (944) 885529
Fax: (944) 885805
Internet: www.sbbu.edu.pk
Founded 2009
State control
Vice-Chancellor: Prof. Dr JEHANDAR SHAH
Registrar: BADSHAH HUSSAIN
Controller of Examinations: MUHAMMAD ROZ KHAN

Depts of botany, biotechnology, computer science, English, environmental science, forestry, management studies, pharmacy, sociology, zoology.

SHAHEED MOHTARMA BENAZIR BHUTTO MEDICAL UNIVERSITY

Larkana, Sindh
Telephone: (74) 9410724
E-mail: info@smbbmu.edu.pk
Internet: www.smbbmu.edu.pk
Founded 2009
State control
Vice-Chancellor: Prof. AKBAR HAIDER SOOMRO
Registrar: Prof. AMANULLAH JOKHIO
Controller of Examinations: Prof. SAIFULLAH JAMRO
Publication: *Journal of SMBBMU*

DEANS

Faculty of Basic Medical Sciences: Prof. MUHAMMAD ASHRAF MEMON
Faculty of Medicine and Allied Sciences: Prof. ABRAR SHAIKH
Faculty of Surgery and Allied Sciences: Prof. SYED IMTIAZ ALI SHAH

SHAHEED ZULFIKAR ALI BHUTTO INSTITUTE OF SCIENCE AND TECHNOLOGY

90 and 100 Clifton, Karachi 75600, Sindh
Fax: (21) 35830446
E-mail: info@szabist.edu.pk
Internet: www.szabist.edu.pk
Founded 1995
Private control
Pres.: Dr SAQIB RIZAVI
Vice-Pres. for Academics: Dr AMANAT ALI JALBANI
Controller of Examinations: ALIYA SALEEM
Dir of Admin.: SHAFQAT MUHAMMEDALLY
Librarian: MUHAMMAD ARIF
Campuses at Hyderabad, Islamabad, Larkana, Dubai
Number of students: 2,200
Publication: *Journal of Independent Studies and Research*

DEANS

Faculty of Management Sciences: Prof. Dr AMANAT ALI JALBANI
Faculty of Social and Media Sciences: Dr FOUZIA NAEEM KHAN

SINDH AGRICULTURE UNIVERSITY, TANDOJAM

Tandojam Dist., Hyderabad, Sindh
Telephone: (22) 2765870
Fax: (22) 2765300
E-mail: info@sau.edu.pk
Internet: www.sau.edu.pk
Founded 1977
State control
Language of instruction: English
Academic year: October to March
Chancellor: GOV. OF SINDH
Vice-Chancellor: Dr A. Q. MUGHAL
Registrar: HAFIZULLAH MEMON
Controller of Examinations: AHMED KHAN NAGRAJ
Librarian: ABDUL LATIF ANSARI
Library of 75,000 vols, 10,500 foreign journals, 6,500 Pakistani journals
Number of teachers: 222
Number of students: 3,930
Publications: *Pakistan Journal of Agriculture, Agricultural Engineering and Veterinary Sciences* (2 a year, in English), *SARANG Magazine* (1 a year, in English, Sindhi and Urdu), *SAUNI News* (4 a year, in English, Sindhi and Urdu), *Seerat Supplement* (1 a year, in English, Sindhi and Urdu), *Zarat Sindh* (4 a year)

DEANS

Faculty of Agricultural Engineering: Prof. Dr MUHAMMAD SAFFAR
Faculty of Agricultural Social Science: KHALID AHMED MAHAR
Faculty of Animal Husbandry and Veterinary Sciences: Dr AMIR BUX KALHORO
Faculty of Crop Production: Prof. Dr SHAMSUDDIN TUNIO
Faculty of Crop Protection: Dr MAQSOOD ANWAR RUSTAMANI

PROFESSORS

ABRO, G. H., Entomology
ABRO, H. K., Plant Breeding and Genetics
ANSARI, N. N., Poultry Husbandry
ARAIN, M. H., Plant Pathology
BALOCH, A. F., Horticulture
BALOCH, G. M., Animal Nutrition
BHUTTO, H. B., Irrigation and Drainage
BURIRO, U. A., Agronomy
CHANDIO, B. A., Land and Water Management
CHANG, M. A., Plant Breeding and Genetics
CHANNA, A. N., Plant Physiology and Biochemistry
DEHO, N. A., Horticulture
DEVERAJANI, B. T., Land and Water Management
JAKHARO, A. A., Soil Science
KADRI, A. A., English
KALHORO, A. B., Surgery and Obstetrics
KHAN, M. M., Entomology
KUMBAHAR, M. I., Animal Breeding and Genetics

KUMBHAR, M. B., Plant Breeding and Genetics
LARIK, A. S., Plant Breeding and Genetics
LEGHARI, N. H., Farm Power and Machinery
LOHAR, M. K., Entomology
MAHAR, S., Farm Power and Machinery
MEMON, K. S., Soil Science
MEMON, M. A., Animal Physiology and Biochemistry
MEMON, N. A., Land and Water Management
MEMON, R. A., Agricultural Education Extension and Short Courses
MIRBAHAR, K. B., Animal Reproduction
MIRBAHAR, R. B., Plant Physiology and Biochemistry
MIRJAT, M. S., Irrigation and Drainage
MUGHAL, A. Q., Farm Power and Machinery
NENWANI, K. L., Soil Science
NIZAMANI, S. M., Plant Protection
PARDEHI, M., Anatomy and Histology
PATHAN, M. A., Plant Pathology
PHULLAN, M. S., Parasitology
PHULPOTO, P. B., Agricultural Economics
PUNO, H. K., Soil Science
QAYYUN KHAN, S. M., Agronomy
RAHU, G. M., Entomology
RAJPER, M. M., Biotechnology
RIZVI, N.-UL-H., Entomology
SAIF, M. S., Soil Science
SHAH, A. J., Plant Breeding and Genetics
SHAIKH, B. A., Animal Physiology and Biochemistry
SIDDIQUI, L. A., Veterinary Microbiology
SIYAL, N. B., Soil Science
SOOMRO, A. L., Soil Science
SOOMRO, M. S., Energy and Environment
TNIO, K., Agronomy
WAGGAN, M. R., Soil Science

SIR SYED UNIVERSITY OF ENGINEERING & TECHNOLOGY

University Rd, Karachi 75300, Sindh
Telephone: (21) 34988000
Fax: (21) 4982393
E-mail: registrar@sssuet.edu.pk
Internet: www.ssuet.edu.pk
Founded 1993
Private control
Chancellor: Z. A. NIZAMI
Vice-Chancellor: Prof. Dr SAIYID NAZIR AHMAD
Registrar: SHAH MAHMOOD H. SYED
Librarian: MAQSOOD ALAM SIDDIQUI
Library of 56,000 vols
Number of teachers: 210
Number of students: 4,500

DEANS

Faculty of Basic and Applied Sciences: Prof. Dr S. JAWAID HASAN RIZVI
Faculty of Engineering: Prof. Dr S. M. MAKHDUMI

SUKKUR INSTITUTE OF BUSINESS ADMINISTRATION

Air Port Rd, Sukkur, Sindh
Telephone: (71) 5630272
Fax: (71) 5632465
E-mail: info@iba-suk.edu.pk
Internet: www.iba-suk.edu.pk
Founded 1994
State control
Faculties of computer science, engineering, management science
Chancellor: GOV. OF SINDH
Dir: Dr NISAR AHMED SIDDIQUI
Registrar: ZAHID HUSSAIN KHAND
Controller of Examinations: IMRAN KHAN
Librarian: IMDAD HUSSAIN ABRO
Library of 15,000 vols.

SUPERIOR GROUP OF COLLEGES

Main Raiwind Rd,
Telephone: (42) 35330361
E-mail: admissions@superior.edu.pk
Internet: www.superior.edu.pk
Founded 2004
Private control
Chair. and Rector: Prof. Dr CH. ABDUL REHMAN
Pro-Rector for Academics: Prof. Dr ZAFAR IQBAL
Pro-Rector for Research: Prof. Dr SIKANDAR KHAN
Registrar: PIRZADA SAMI ULLAH SABRI
Controller of Examinations: ASIM MASOOD
Librarian: MUHAMMAD RAFIQ KHAN

Faculties of business and management sciences, economics and commerce, engineering and technology, information technology and computer sciences, law, medical and health sciences, pharmacy
Library of 18,000 vols.

TEXTILE INSTITUTE OF PAKISTAN

EZ/1/P-8, Eastern Zone, Bin Qasim, Karachi, Sindh
Telephone: (21) 38109641
Fax: (21) 38109658
E-mail: info@tip.edu.pk
Internet: www.tip.edu.pk
Founded 1994, present status 2001
Private control
Chancellor: ARIF HASAN
Pres.: Dr ANBAHAN ARIADURAI

Undergraduate degree courses in business, design, science; programmes incl. textile science, textile design technology, textile management and marketing, textile technology
Library of 20,000 vols.

UNIVERSITY OF AGRICULTURE, FAISALABAD

Faisalabad
Telephone and fax (41) 9200161
E-mail: vc@uaf.edu.pk
Internet: www.uaf.edu.pk
Founded 1909 as Punjab Agricultural College, present name 1973
State control
Language of instruction: English
Academic year: October to September
Chancellor: GOV. OF PUNJAB
Vice-Chancellor: Prof. Dr IQRAR AHMAD KHAN
Registrar: CH. MUHAMMAD HUSSAIN
Controller of Examinations: Prof. Dr TANWIR AHMAD MALIK
Librarian: Prof. Dr ASGHAR ALI
Library: see under Libraries and Archives
Number of teachers: 598
Number of students: 11,745
Publications: *Journal of Agricultural Sciences* (4 a year), *Journal of Veterinary Science*, *Pakistan Entomologist*, *Research Studies*

DEANS

Faculty of Agricultural Economics and Rural Sociology: Prof. Dr MUHAMMAD IQBAL ZAFAR
Faculty of Agricultural Engineering and Technology: Prof. Dr RAI NIAZ AHMAD
Faculty of Agriculture: Prof. Dr MUHAMMAD ASHFAQ
Faculty of Animal Husbandry: Prof. Dr MUHAMMAD SARWAR
Faculty of Sciences: Prof. Dr MUHAMMAD ASHRAF
Faculty of Veterinary Science: Prof. Dr LAEEQ AKBAR LODHI

PROFESSORS

Division of Education and Extension (tel. (41) 9200186):
Department of Rural Home Economics:
ALMAS, K.
Faculty of Agricultural Economics and Rural Sociology (tel. (41) 9200196):
Department of Agricultural Economics:
HUSSAIN, Z.
Faculty of Agricultural Engineering and Technology (tel. (41) 9200194; e-mail mssabir_uaf@yahoo.com):
Department of Farm Machinery and Power:
SABIR, M. S.
Department of Food Technology:
ANJUM, F. M.
Department of Irrigation and Drainage:
CHAUDHRY, M. R.
Department of Structural and Environmental Engineering:
ALI, M. A.
SIAL, J. K.
Faculty of Agriculture (tel. (41) 9200193; fax (41) 614335; e-mail deanagri@fsd.paknet.com.pk):
Department of Agricultural Entomology:
RANA, M. A.
Department of Agronomy:
AKHTAR, M.
ALI, A.
ATTA, Z
HUSSAIN, A.
MALIK, M. A.
Department of Horticulture:
IBRAHIM, M.
KHAN, I. A.
KHAN, M. A.
Department of Plant Breeding and Genetics:
AZHAR, F. M.
ASLAM, M.
KHAN, I. A.
MEHDI, S.
SALEEM, A.
SALEEM, M.
Department of Plant Pathology:
CHOHAN, R. A.
KHAN, S. M.
Department of Soil Science:
ARSHAD, M.
GHAFOOR, A.
GILL, M. A.
HASSAN, A. U.
RANJHA, A. M.
Faculty of Animal Husbandry (tel. (41) 9200195):
Department of Animal Nutrition:
SARWAR, M.
Department of Livestock Management:
GONDAL, K. Z.
YOUNAS, M.
Department of Poultry Husbandry:
HAQ, A.
Faculty of Sciences (tel. (41) 9200197):
Department of Botany:
ASHRAF, M.
Department of Chemistry:
NAWAZ, R.
SHEIKH, M. A.
Department of Mathematics and Statistics:
KHAN, M. I.
Department of Physics:
CHAUDHRY, M. A.
Department of Zoology and Fisheries:
QURESHI, J. I.

Faculty of Veterinary Science (tel. (41) 9200725; e-mail drmsakhter@hotmail.com):

Department of Animal Reproduction:

LODHI, L. A.
SAMAD, H. A.

Department of Physiology and Pharmacology:

AKHTAR, M. S.
NAWAZ, M.

Department of Veterinary Microbiology:

SIDDIQU, M.

Department of Veterinary Pathology:

ANJUM, A. D.

UNIVERSITY OF AZAD JAMMU AND KASHMIR

City Campus, CMH Rd, Muzaffarabad 13100
Telephone: (5822) 960418
Fax: (5822) 960437
E-mail: registrar@ajku.edu.pk
Internet: www.ajku.edu.pk

Founded 1980
State control
Languages of instruction: English, Urdu
Academic year: September to October

Vice-Chancellor: Prof. Dr HABIB-UR-REHMAN
Registrar: Prof. Dr MUHAMMAD QAYYUM KHAN
Controller of Examinations: Prof. Dr MUHAM-MAD RUSTAM KHAN
Chief Librarian: SARDAR MUHAMMAD SALEEM

Library: see Libraries and Archives
Number of teachers: 256
Number of students: 1,800

Publications: *Al-Muhaqqiq* (1 a year), *Kashmir Economics Review* (1 a year), *Kashmir Journal of Geology* (1 a year), *Kashmir Journal of Language Research* (1 a year), *Kashmir Research Journal of Natural Sciences* (1 a year)

DEANS

Muzaffarabad Campus (Main Campus):

Faculty of Arts: Prof. Dr RAJA NASIM AKHTAR
Faculty of Sciences: Prof. Dr MUHAMMAD HALEEM KHAN

Kotli Campus:

Faculty of Admin. Sciences: Prof. Dr MUSH-TAQ AHMED MALIK

Mirpur Campus:

Faculty of Engineering and Technology: Prof. CH. NAIB HUSSAIN
Faculty of Home Economics: RAFIA KHANAM

Rawalakot Campus:

Faculty of Agriculture: Dr DILNAWAZ AHMED GARDAZI

UNIVERSITY OF BALOCHISTAN

Sariab Rd, Quetta
Telephone: (81) 9211268
Fax: (81) 9211277
E-mail: netadmin@uob.edu.pk
Internet: www.uob.edu.pk

Founded 1970
State control
Languages of instruction: English, Urdu
Academic year: March to December

Chancellor: NAWAB ZULFIQAR ALI MAGSSI
Vice-Chancellor: Prof. MUHAMMAD MASOOM YASINZAI
Registrar: HAJI ABDUL WASAY ABID (acting)
Librarian: ABDUL JALIL KHAN BAZAI

Number of teachers: 255
Number of students: 3,650

Publications: *Acta Mineralogica Pakistanica* (2 a year), *Middle East Journal of Area Studies Centre*

DEANS

Faculty of Arts: Prof. GHULAM NABI ACHAKZAI

UNIVERSITY OF CENTRAL PUNJAB

1 Khayaban-e-Jinnah Rd, Johar Town, Lahore, Punjab
Telephone: (42) 35880007
Fax: (42) 35954892
E-mail: info@ucp.edu.pk
Internet: www.ucp.edu.pk

Founded 1999, present status 2002
Private control

Chair.: MIAN AMER MAHMOOD
Pro-Rector: Prof. Dr MUHAMMAD ZAFARULLAH

Library of 20,000 vols
Number of students: 8,000

DEANS

Faculty of Arts and Social Sciences: Dr KHALID ZAHEER
Faculty of Commerce: MUHAMMAD AZHAR IKRAM AHMAD
Faculty of Engineering: Dr TABREZ A. SHAMI
Faculty of Information Technology: Dr ABDUL AZIZ
Faculty of Law: Dr HADIA AWAN
Faculty of Pharmacy: Dr MUHAMMAD JAM-SHAID

UNIVERSITY OF EAST

Latifabad, Hyderabad, Sindh
Telephone: (22) 3868612
Fax: (22) 3868634
E-mail: info@uoe.edu.pk
Internet: www.uoe.edu.pk

Founded 1999
Private control
Academic year: July to January,December to June,May to August (3 semesters)

Depts of business administration, civil technology, computer science and information technology, education, electrical technology, mechanical technology, Urdu

Chancellor: Dr KHALIDA MANDHRO
Pres.: ZAFAR UL ISLAM
Vice-Chancellor: Prof. ABDUL QADEER
Registrar: Prof. Dr M. A. CHANG
Controller of Examinations: MIR MUHAMMAD

Library of 10,000 vols.

UNIVERSITY OF EDUCATION

Township Campus, College Rd, Township, Lahore 5400, Punjab
Telephone: (42) 5216530
Fax: (42) 5216524
Internet: www.ue.edu.pk

Founded 2002
State control

Vice-Chancellor: Prof. Dr FAIZ-UL-HASAN
Registrar: MUHAMMAD SAEED AKHTAR (acting)
Librarian: NAEEM SARWAR

3 Campuses in Lahore; further campuses in Attock, Faisalabad, Jauharabad, Multan, Okara and Vehari; 33 affiliated colleges

Publication: *Journal of Research and Reflections in Education* (2 a year)

DIRECTORS

Arts and Social Sciences: Prof. Dr MUZAFFAR ABBAS
Education: Dr KHALID MEHMOOD
Islamic and Oriental Learning: (vacant)
Management and Admin. Sciences: (vacant)
Science and Technology: Dr ABRAR HUSSAIN (acting)

UNIVERSITY OF ENGINEERING AND TECHNOLOGY, LAHORE

Grand Trunk Rd, Lahore 54890, Punjab
Telephone: (42) 99029227
Fax: (42) 99029205
E-mail: registrar@uet.edu.pk
Internet: www.uet.edu.pk

Founded 1921 as Mughalpura Technical College
State control
Language of instruction: English
Academic year: January to December

Chancellor: GOV. OF PUNJAB
Pro-Chancellor: MIN. OF EDUCATION
Vice-Chancellor: Lt-Gen. (retd) MUHAMMAD AKRAM KHAN
Registrar: Lt-Col (retd) ABDUL RAUF
Controller of Examinations: M. ASIF
Librarian: MANZOOR AHMAD KHAN ANJUM

Library: see Libraries and Archives
Number of teachers: 913
Number of students: 9,694

Publications: *ECHO* (1 a year), *Varsity News* (26 a year)

DEANS

Faculty of Architecture and Planning: Prof. Dr EHSAN ULLAH BAJWA
Faculty of Chemical, Mineral And Material Science: Prof. Dr A. R. SALEEMI
Faculty of Civil Engineering: Prof. Dr ABDUL SATTAR SHAKIR
Faculty of Electrical Engineering: Prof. Dr ZUBAIR KHAN
Faculty of Mechanical Engineering: Prof. Dr SALIM ABID TABASSUM
Faculty of Natural Sciences, Humanities and Islamic Studies: Prof. Dr FAZEELAT TAHIRA

PROFESSORS

Department of Architecture (tel. (42) 99029223; e-mail sakbar@gmail.com):

AKBAR, S.
AWAN, M. Y.
GELANI, I. A. S.
HUSSAIN, M.
MALIK, R. A.
REHMAN, A.

Department of Chemical Engineering (tel. (42) 99029488; e-mail pd_govsect@yahoo .com):

AHMAD, M. M.
KHAN, J. R.
MAMOOR, G. M.
NAVEED, S.
SALARYA, A. K.
SALEEMI, A. R.

Department of Chemistry (tel. (42) 99029200; e-mail saeed_a786@hotmail.com):

AMJAD, M.
HAQ, I. U.
TAHIRA, F.

Department of City and Regional Planning (tel. (42) 99029203):

ANJUM, G. A.
BAJWA, E. U.
ISLAM, Q. U.
MALIK, T. H.
ZAIDI, S.-UL-H.

Department of Civil Engineering (tel. (42) 99029202; e-mail ilyas@uet.edu.pk):

ASHRAF, M.
CHAUDHRY, M. Y.
CHISHTY, F. A.
ILYAS, M.
MIAN, Z.
RIZWAN, S. A.
SHAKIR, A. S.
SHEIKH, A. S.
TAHIR, M. A.

Department of Computer Science and Engineering (tel. (42) 99029260; e-mail mamaud@uet.edu.pk):

ASIM, M. R.
MALIK, A. A.

Department of Electrical Engineering (tel. (42) 99029229; fax (42) 99227507; e-mail mna@uet.edu.pk):

BUKHARI, S. H.
CHUGHTAI, M. A.
KHAN, Z. A.
QURESHI, S. A.
SALEEM, M. M.
SHAH, A. H.
SHAMI, T. A.
SHEIKH, N. M.

Department of Humanities and Social Sciences (tel. (42) 99029493; e-mail chairmanhmss@uet.edu.pk):

ZAIDI, M. H.

Department of Islamic Studies (tel. (42) 99029246; e-mail misraeel@yahoo.com):

YAHYA, M. A.

Department of Mathematics (tel. (42) 99029210; e-mail ffffz_khan@hotmail.com):

AHMAD, M. O.
CH., N. M.
SHAH, N. A.

Department of Mechanical Engineering (tel. (42) 99029467; e-mail chairmanmech@uet.edu.pk):

ALI, S.
CHAUDHRY, I. A.
HUSSAIN, I.
KHAN, M. I.
MIRZA, M. R.
PIRACHA, J. L.
QURESHI, A. H.
SHAH, F. H.
TABASSUM, S. A.

Department of Metallurgical and Materials Engineering (tel. (42) 99029207; e-mail mohammad_ajmal@hotmail.com):

AJMAL, M.
HASSAN, F.
IQBAL, J.
ZAIDI, S. Q. H.

Department of Mining and Geological Engineering (tel. (42) 99029212; e-mail akram@uet.edu.pk):

AKRAM, M.
CHATTAH, N. H.
HUSSAIN, S. A.
KIRMANI, F. A.
RANA, M. T.

Department of Petroleum and Gas Engineering (tel. (42) 99029471; e-mail chairmanpetroleum@uet.edu.pk):

KHAN, A. S.

Department of Physics (tel. (42) 99029204; e-mail chairmanphy@uet.edu.pk):

REHMAN, M. K. (Chair)

Institute of Environmental Engineering and Research (tel. (42) 99029248; e-mail ajbari57@hotmail.com):

AHMAD, K.
ALI, W.
AZIZ, J. A.
BARI, A. J.
HYAT, S.
ZIAI, K. H.

UNIVERSITY OF ENGINEERING AND TECHNOLOGY, TAXILA

Taxila 47050, Punjab
Telephone: (596) 9314216
Fax: (596) 9047420
E-mail: registrar@uettaxila.edu.pk
Internet: web.uettaxila.edu.pk/uet

State control
Vice-Chancellor: Prof. Dr MUHAMMAD ABBAS CHOUDHARY
Registrar: AZIZ UR REHMAN
Controller of Examinations: MAHMOOD AKHTAR
Librarian: MUHAMMAD ANWAAR
Library of 25,000 vols
Publication: *Taxila Engineering Journal*

DEANS

Faculty of Basic Sciences and Humanities: Prof. Dr MUMTAZ AHMAD KAMAL
Faculty of Civil and Environmental Engineering: Prof. Dr MUMTAZ AHMAD
Faculty of Electronics and Electrical Engineering: Prof. Dr AHMAD KHALIL KHAN
Industrial Engineering and Management Sciences: Prof. Dr SHAHAB KHUSHNOOD
Faculty of Mechanical and Aeronautical Engineering: Prof. Dr SHAHAB KHUSHNOOD
Faculty of Telecommunications and Information Engineering: Prof. Dr ADEEL AKRAM

PROFESSORS

AHMAD, S., Mechanical Engineering
AHMED, S., Civil Engineering
AMIN, M., Electrical Engineering
CHOWDHRY, M. A., Electrical Engineering
FAROOQ, U., Electrical Engineering
GHUMMAN, A. R., Civil Engineering
IQBAL ALVI, M. S., Mechanical Engineering
JAMAL, H., Electrical Engineering
JAVAID, M. A., Basic Sciences
KAMAL, M. A., Civil Engineering
KHAN, A. K., Electrical Engineering
KHAN, M. A., Mechanical Engineering
KHAN, S. A., Civil Engineering
KHUSHNOOD, S., Mechanical Engineering
NISAR, H., Civil Engineering
SAHIR, M. H., Mechanical Engineering
ZAFRULLAH, Electrical Engineering

UNIVERSITY OF FAISALABAD

4 km Sargodha Rd, Faisalabad 38850, Punjab
Telephone: (41) 8868326
Fax: (41) 8868220
E-mail: info@tuf.edu.pk
Internet: www.tuf.edu.pk
Founded 2002
Private control
Chair.: MIAN MUHAMMAD HANIF
Vice-Chair.: MIAN MUHAMMAD RASHEED
Pro-Rector: Prof. Dr ABDUL KARIM BALOCH
Registrar: IZHAR UL AHSAN
Controller of Examinations: HAMID NAWAZ SHIEKH

DEANS

Faculty of Arts and Social Sciences: Prof Dr ZAHOOR AHMED AZHAR
Faculty of Engineering and Technology: Prof. Dr A. D. CHAUDARY
Faculty of Health Sciences: Prof. Dr A. G. REHAN
Faculty of Management Studies: Prof. Dr M. ASLAM CHAUDHRY

UNIVERSITY OF GUJRAT

Hafiz Hayat Campus, Jalalpur Jattan Rd, Gujrat, Punjab
Telephone: (53) 3643112
Fax: (53) 3642167
E-mail: info@uog.edu.pk
Internet: uog.edu.pk
Founded 2003
State control
Chancellor: GOV. OF PUNJAB
Vice-Chancellor: Prof. Dr MOHAMMAD NIZAMMUDDIN
Registrar: MUHAMMAD AKRAM BHATTI

Dir of Admin. and Coordination: AZRA ZULFIQAR GHANI
Controller of Examinations: Prof. MAQSOOD AKHTER

Faculties of basic sciences, computer science and information technology, engineering and technology, Oriental and Islamic Studies, social sciences; schools of art and design, business and management sciences, law.

UNIVERSITY OF HEALTH SCIENCES

Shaikh Zayed Hospital Medical Complex, Khayaban-e-Jamia, Lahore 54600, Punjab
Telephone: (42) 99231304
Fax: (42) 99230870
E-mail: info@uhs.edu.pk
Internet: www.uhs.edu.pk
Founded 2002
State control
Chancellor: GOV. OF PUNJAB
Vice-Chancellor: Prof. MALIK HUSSAIN MUBASHAR
Registrar: Prof. MUHAMMAD ZAFAR IQBAL
Librarian: ABID ALI GILL
Offers medical, dental, nursing, biomedical engineering, paramedic education
Number of students: 39,000

UNIVERSITY OF KARACHI

Main Univ. Rd, Karachi 75270, Sindh
Telephone: (21) 99261300
Fax: (21) 99261340
E-mail: info@uok.edu.pk
Internet: www.uok.edu.pk
Founded 1951
State control
Language of instruction: English, Urdu
Academic year: September to August
Chancellor: GOV. OF SINDH
Vice-Chancellor: Prof. Dr PIRZADA QASIM RAZA SIDDIQUI
Pro-Vice-Chancellor: Prof. Dr NASIRUDDIN KHAN
Pro-Vice-Chancellor for Academic Affairs: Prof. Dr SHAHANA UROOJ KAZMI
Registrar: Prof. M. KALEEM RAZA KHAN
Head Librarian: Prof. MALAHAT KALEEM SHERWANI
Library: see under Libraries and Archives
Number of teachers: 800
Number of students: 24,000
Publications: *Jareeda* (Journal of the Bureau of Composition, Compilation and Translation, 1 a year), *Journal of Science* (2 a year), *Pakistan Journal of Botany* (2 a year), *Pakistan Journal of Nematology* (2 a year), *Pakistan Journal of Psychology* (4 a year)

DEANS

Faculty of Arts: Prof. Dr ZAFAR IQBAL
Faculty of Education: Prof. Dr M. ISMAIL BROHI
Faculty of Engineering: Prof. Dr DARAKHSHAN J. HALEEM
Faculty of Islamic Studies: Prof. Dr REHANA FIRDOUS
Faculty of Law: Prof. KHURSHEED A. HASHMI
Faculty of Management and Administration Sciences: Prof. Dr M. ABUZAR WAJIDI
Faculty of Medicine: Prof. Dr S. M. ABBAS HUSSAIN
Faculty of Pharmacy: Prof. Dr GHAZALA H. RIZWANI
Faculty of Science: Prof. Dr DARAKHSHAN J. HALEEM

PROFESSORS

Faculty of Arts:
AHMED, N., Islamic History
ANSARI, A. M. S., Urdu

ARAB, A. K., Arabic
FATIMA, N., Library and Information Science
HAQ, I., Arabic
HUMAYUN, S., Public Administration
HUSAIN, F., Sindhi
HUSAIN, S. M. A., Economics
HUSSAIN, J., General History
MEHDI, S. S., International Relations
MEMON, S., Sindhi
MIRZA, S. Q., Mass Communication
MURTAZA, M. R., Mass Communication
REHMAN, K., Sociology
SAJDIN, M., Commerce
SHAHEED, M. A., Arabic
SHAMSUDDIN, M., Mass Communication
SHERWANI, M. K., Library and Information Science
TAFHIMI, S., Persian
WAJIDI, M. A., Public Administration
WAZARAT, T. A., International Relations

Faculty of Islamic Studies:
RASHID, A., Islamic Studies
SIDDIQUI, M. A. S., Islamic Learning

Faculty of Pharmacy:
AHMED, M., Pharmacognosy
AHMED, M. A., Pharmaceutics
AHMED, S. P., Pharmacology
AHMED, T., Pharmaceutics
ALI, S. A., Pharmaceutics
BAIG, A. E., Pharmaceutics
HUSSAIN, W., Pharmaceutical Chemistry
MANZAR, K. N., Pharmaceutical Chemistry
REHMAN, S. B., Pharmacology
SAIFY, S. Z., Pharmaceutical Chemistry
SHAIKH, D., Pharmaceutics
SULTANA, N., Pharmaceutical Chemistry

Faculty of Science:
AFTAB, N., Biochemistry
AHMED, A., Applied Chemistry
AHMED, E., Statistics
AHMED, F., Physics
AHMED, I., Zoology
AHMED, I. K., Physics
AHMED, N., Genetics
AHMED, S., Botany
AKHTAR, S. K., Physics
AKHTAR, W., Physics
ALI, S. I., Applied Chemistry
ANIS, K., Physics
ANSARI, A. A., Applied Physics
ARAYN, M. S., Chemistry
ARSHAD, R., Physiology
ATHAR, H. S. A., Biochemistry
AZEEM, A., Physiology
AZHAR, A., Biochemistry
AZIZ, K., Botany
AZMATULLAH, M., Geology
BARKATI, S., Zoology
BURNI, S. M. A., Computer Science
FAHIMUDDIN, Chemistry
FARID, A., Philosophy
HALEEM, M. A., Biochemistry
HAMEED, S., Applied Chemistry
HASAN, H., Zoology
HASNAIN, S. N., Biochemistry
HASNI, S., Biochemistry
HUSAIN, V., Geology
HUSSAIN, M. R., Physics
IQBAL, M., Zoology
IQBAL, Z., Botany
JABEEN, D., Biochemistry
JAHANGIR, S., Biochemistry
JAVED, W., Zoology
KAZMI, M. A., Zoology
KAZMI, Q. B., Zoology
KAZMI, S. A., Chemistry
KAZMI, S. U., Microbiology
KHAN, A. F., Microbiology
KHAN, F., Applied Chemistry
KHAN, K. R., Physiology
KHAN, M. A., Botany
KHAN, M. ALTAF, Microbiology
KHAN, M. I., Botany

KHAN, N., Mathematics
KHANUM, A., Biochemistry
KHATOON, H., Microbiology
KHATOON, K., Botany
MAHMOOD, Z., Statistics
MALIK, A., Research Institute of Chemistry
MALIK, S. A., Chemistry
MAQSOOD, Z. T., Chemistry
MEHDI, F., Botany
MOHSIN, S. I., Geology
MUHAMMAD, I., Biochemistry
NAEEM, R. K., Mathematics
NAQVI, I. I., Chemistry
NAQVI, S. M. M. R., Physics
NAQVI, S. R. R., Chemistry
NAZAMI, S. S., Chemistry
NOOR, F., Chemistry
NUSRAT, J., Microbiology
QADEER, A., Applied Physics
QADRI, M. U., Geology
QAISER, M., Botany
QAMAR, J., Mathematics
QASIM, R., Biochemistry
QIDWAI, A. A., Physics
QIDWAI, I. M., Biochemistry
QURESHI, M. A., Physiology
QURESHI, N. M., Physiology
RAFI, F., Physiology
RAOOF, M. A., Physics
RASOOL, S. A., Microbiology
RAZZAQI, T. F., Biotechnology
REHMAN, A. U., Research Institute of Chemistry
RIZVI, N., Zoology
SAIFULLAH, S. M., Botany
SHAIKH, S. A., Geology
SHAHEEN, B., Research Institute of Chemistry
SHAMEEL, M. M., Botany
SHAMS, N., Applied Chemistry
SHAUKAT, S. S., Botany
SIDDIQI, J. S., Statistics
SIDDIQI, N. S., Biochemistry
SIDDIQI, P. A., Zoology
SIDDIQI, P. Q. R., Physiology
SIDDIQI, R., Microbiology
SIDDIQI, S. A., Chemistry
SIDDIQI, Z., Chemistry
SIDDIQUI, A. J., Statistics
SIDDIQUI, K. A., Physics
ULLAH, N., Geology
USMAN, M., Botany
USMANI, A. A., Chemistry
VAHIDY, A. A., Genetics
VAHIDY, R., Microbiology
YASMEN, N., Zoology
ZAIDGHAM, N. A., Geology
ZAIDI, S. A. H., Applied Chemistry
ZAIDI, S. S. H., Applied Physics
ZEENAT, I., Psychology

UNIVERSITY OF LAHORE

1 km Raiwind Rd, Lahore, Punjab
Telephone: (42) 35963421
Fax: (42) 7515519
E-mail: info@uol.edu.pk
Internet: uol.edu.pk
Private control

Rector: Dr SALEEM SHUJA

Faculties of civil engineering, computer science and information technology, electrical engineering, electronics, health sciences, law, mechanical engineering, nursing, pharmacy; institute of molecular biology and biotechnology; Lahore business school; school of creative arts.

UNIVERSITY OF MALAKAND

Chakdara, Malakand, Khyber Pakhtunkhwa
Telephone: (936) 763441
Fax: (936) 763491
E-mail: vicechancellor@uom.edu.pk
Internet: www.uom.edu.pk

Founded 2001
State control

Vice-Chancellor: Prof. Dr M. RASUL JAN
Registrar: Dr MIR AZAM KHAN (acting)
Dean of Studies: Prof. Dr RAHMAT ALI KHAN

Depts of biotechnology, botany, chemistry, computer science and information technology, economics, education, English, Islamic studies, law, management studies, mathematics, political science, pharmacy, physics, sociology and social work, software engineering, statistics, tourism and hotel management, zoology

Library of 9,655 vols
Number of students: 2,029

UNIVERSITY OF MANAGEMENT AND TECHNOLOGY

C-II, Johar Town, Lahore, Punjab
Telephone: (42) 35212801
Fax: (42) 35184789
E-mail: info@umt.edu.pk
Internet: umt.edu.pk

Founded 1990 as Institute of Leadership and Management, present status 2002, present name 2004
Private control

Rector: Dr HASAN SOHAIB MURAD
Pro-Rector: Dr A. R. KAUSAR
Registrar: SALMAN SAEED QURESHI
Controller of Examinations: ASIF SAEED HAIDER
Librarian: SOHAIL ASLAM

Library of 50,000
Number of teachers: 200
Number of students: 4,500

DEANS

School of Business and Economics: FAHEEM UL ISLAM
School of Science and Technology: Dr ABDUL AZIZ BHATTI
School of Social Sciences and Humanities: Prof. Dr ABDUL HAMEED

UNIVERSITY OF PESHAWAR

Peshawar, Khyber Pakhtunkhwa
Telephone: (91) 9216701
Fax: (91) 9216470
E-mail: vice_chancellor@upesh.edu.pk
Internet: www.upesh.edu.pk

Founded 1950
State control
Language of instruction: Arabic, English, Pashto, Persian, Urdu
Academic year: September to June

Chancellor: GOV. OF KHYBER PAKHTUNKHWA
Vice-Chancellor: Prof. Dr AZMAT HAYAT KHAN
Registrar and Dir of Admissions: Dr S. FAZL-I-HADI (acting)
Provost: Dr FAZLUR REHMAN
Controller of Examination: IFTIKHAR HUSSAIN KHAN
Dir of Admin.: ISHTIAQULLAH KHAN
Librarian: IBRAR MOHAMMAD

Library: see Libraries and Archives
Number of teachers: 599
Number of students: 14,060

Publications: *Geological Bulletin* (1 a year), *Journal of Humanities and Social Sciences* (1 a year), *Journal of Law and Society* (1 a year), *Peshawar University Review* (1 a year)

DEANS

Faculty of Arts and Humanities: Prof. Dr M. FAROOQ SWATI
Faculty of Islamic and Oriental Studies: Prof. Dr QIBLA AYAZ
Faculty of Life and Environmental Sciences: Prof. Dr FARRUKH HUSSAIN

Faculty of Management and Information Sciences: Prof. Dr ABDUL QAIYUM
Faculty of Numerical and Physical Sciences: Prof. Dr MUHAMMAD RIAZ KHAN
Faculty of Social Sciences: Prof. Dr NAEEM-UR-REHMAN

PROFESSORS

ABBASI, J. A., Geology
ADEEL, M. A., Institute of Education and Research
ALI, A., Law
ALI, T., Archaeology
AYAZ, Q., Islamic Studies
BANGASH, G. T., History
GILANI, S. Z., Education (Psychology)
HANIF, M., Islamic Studies
HUSSAIN, F., Biotechnology
IQBAL, M., Statistics
JAN, A.-H., Zoology
JAN, M. Q., Geology
KHAN, A., Geography
KHAN, M., Chemistry
KHAN, M. A., Chemistry
KHAN, M. J., Geology
KHAN, Z. A., Mathematics
KHATTAK, N. S., Electronics
MAJID, M., Geology
MIAN, I., Geology
NAWAZ, A., Geography
NASIR, G., Persian
NOOR, I., Mathematics
QAZI, S., Islamic Studies
RAFIQ, M., Geology
RAHMAN, C., English
RAHMAN, F., Physics
RAHMAN, M., English
RASHID, H., Chemistry
REHANA, N., Chemistry
REHMAN, S. S., Environmental Sciences
RIAZ, M., Physics
RIAZ, M. N., Psychology
SHAH, R., Pashto
SULAIMAN, M., Zoology

UNIVERSITY OF SARGODHA

Sargodha, Punjab
Telephone: (451) 9230811
Fax: (451) 9230837
E-mail: info@uos.edu.pk
Internet: www.uos.edu.pk
Founded 2002
State control
Vice-Chancellor: Prof. Dr MOHAMMAD AKRAM CHAUDHARY
Acting Registrar and Dir of Academics: Prof. Dr SHAUKAT ALI
Dir of Student Affairs: IJAZ ASGHAR BHATTI
Controller of Examinations: MUHAMMAD IQBAL QURESHI
Number of teachers: 700
Number of students: 16,000

DEANS

Faculty of Agriculture: Prof. Dr MUHAMMAD AFZAL
Faculty of Arts, Social Sciences and Law: Prof. Dr RASHID AHMED KHAN
Faculty of Islamic and Oriental Learning: Prof. Dr MAQBOOL HUSSAIN SIAL
Faculty of Management and Admin. Sciences: Prof. Dr MAQBOOL HUSSAIN SIAL
Faculty of Medical and Health Sciences: Prof. Dr MUHAMMAD ZAHOOR UL HASSAN DOGAR

PROFESSORS

AHMED, I., Arts and Social Sciences
ALI, M., Chemistry
ARIF, S., English
BUKHARI, A., Islamic and Oriental Learning
HAQ, F., Chemistry
IQBAL, M., Science and Technology
SULTANA, N., Mathematics
TAHIR, M., Chemistry

UNIVERSITY OF SCIENCE AND TECHNOLOGY, BANNU

Bannu, Khyber Pakhtunkhwa
Telephone: (928) 633825
Fax: (928) 633821
Internet: www.ustb.edu.pk
State control
Vice-Chancellor: Prof. Dr ASMATULLAH KHAN

Depts of botany, biotechnology, chemistry, English, physics, Islamic studies and research.

UNIVERSITY OF SINDH

Allama I. I. Kazi Campus, Dadu Dist., Jamshoro 76080, Sindh
Telephone: (22) 9213150
Fax: (22) 9213152
E-mail: vc@usindh.edu.pk
Internet: www.usindh.edu.pk
Founded 1947 in Karachi
State control
Languages of instruction: English, Sindhi, Urdu
Chancellor: GOV. OF SINDH
Vice-Chancellor: Prof. Dr NAZIR A. MUGHAL
Pro-Vice-Chancellor: Prof. Dr PARVEEN SHAH
Registrar: AKHTAR AHMED MEMON
Controller of Examinations: MUHAMMAD ALI PATHAN
Librarian: MUHAMMAD AZAM ROONJHO
Library: see under Libraries and Archives
Number of teachers: 644
Number of students: 19,000
Publications: *Ariel* (1 a year, in English), *Grassroot* (2 a year, English), *Kinjhar* (1 a year, in Sindhi), *Sindhi Arab* (1 a year, in Sindhi), *Sindhological Studies* (1 a year, in English), *Sindh University Journal of Education* (1 a year, in English), *Sindh University Research Journal (Science)*, *Sindh University Research Journal (Social Sciences)* (1 a year, in English), *Tahqiq* (1 a year, in Urdu), *University of Sindh Arts Research Journal* (1 a year, in English)

DEANS

Faculty of Arts: Prof. Dr KHUWAJA NOOR AFROZE
Faculty of Commerce and Business Admin.: Prof. Dr NOOR MUHAMMAD JAMALI (acting)
Faculty of Education: Prof. Dr MUNSHI PARVEEN (acting)
Faculty of Islamic Studies: Prof. Dr SANAUL-LAH BHUTTO
Faculty of Law: JHAMAT
Faculty of Natural Sciences: Prof. Dr RAJPUT MUHAMMAD TAHIR
Faculty of Pharmacy: Prof. Dr DAYO ABDUL-LAH
Faculty of Social Sciences: Prof. Dr IQBAL AHMED PANHWAR

PROFESSORS

Department of Botany:

ABRO, H.
AHMED, B.
HASSANI, S. S.
MEMON, A. H.
RAJPUT, M. T.
SAHITO, M. A.
SHAIKH, W.
TIRMIZI, S. A.
YASMIN, S.

Department of Comparative Religion and Islamic Culture:

BHUTTO, S.

Department of Fine Arts:

BHATTI, M. A.

Department of Muslim History:

ANSARI, A. S.
BHUTTO, M.

BUGHIO, M. M.

Department of Sindhi:

BUGHIO, M. Q.
HUSSAIN, K. K.
IMDAD, S.
KHUWAJA, N. A.

UNIVERSITY OF SOUTH ASIA

47 Tufail Rd, Lahore Cantonment, Punjab
Telephone: (42) 36672942
Fax: (42) 36650983
E-mail: info@usa.edu.pk
Internet: www.usa.edu.pk
Founded 2004
Private control
Chancellor: GOV. OF PUNJAB

Faculties of art and fashion design, computer sciences, engineering and technology, health sciences, humanities and social sciences, law, management sciences; depts of intermediate studies, teaching.

UNIVERSITY OF THE PUNJAB

Quaid-e-Azam Campus, POB 54590, Lahore, Punjab
Telephone: (42) 99231102
Fax: (42) 99231103
E-mail: registrar@pu.edu.pk
Internet: pu.edu.pk
Founded 1882
State control
Languages of instruction: English, Urdu
Chancellor: GOV. OF PUNJAB
Vice-Chancellor: Prof. Dr MUJAHID KAMRAN
Pro-Vice-Chancellor: (vacant)
Registrar: Prof. Dr MUHAMMAD AKHTAR
Controller of Examinations: Prof. Dr LIAQAT ALI
Chief Librarian: CH. MUHAMMAD HANIF
Library: see under Libraries and Archives
Number of teachers: 739
Number of students: 30,608

DEANS

Faculty of Arts and Humanities: Prof. Dr S. QALB-I-ABID
Faculty of Behavioural and Social Sciences: Prof. Dr MUHAMMAD HAFEEZ
Faculty of Commerce: Prof. Dr MUHAMMAD EHSAN MALIK
Faculty of Economics and Management Sciences: Prof. Dr MUHAMMAD EHSAN MALIK
Faculty of Education: Prof. Dr HAFIZ MUHAMMAD IQBAL
Faculty of Engineering and Technology: Prof. Dr JAVAID AHMAD
Faculty of Islamic Studies: Prof. Dr HAFIZ MAHMOOD AKHTAR
Faculty of Law: Prof. Dr MUHAMMAD EHSAN MALIK
Faculty of Life Sciences: Prof. Dr MUHAMMAD EHSAN MALIK
Faculty of Medicine and Dentistry: (vacant)
Faculty of Oriental Learning: Prof. Dr HAFIZ MAHMOOD AKHTAR
Faculty of Pharmacy: Prof. Dr S. QALB-I-ABID
Faculty of Science: Prof. Dr HARIS RASHID

PROFESSORS

Faculty of Arts and Humanities (Quaid-e-Azam Campus, Lahore, Punjab; tel. (42) 9231167; e-mail dean.ahs@pu.edu.pk):

ABID, M., Pakistan Studies Centre
ABID, Q., History
AHMAD, A., Philosophy
AHMAD, N., Philosophy
AHSAN, A. S., Research Society of Pakistan
BUTT, A. R., Economics
CHAUDHRY, M. A., Economics
GILL, S. A., History
HAFEEZ, M., Philosophy

HASNAT, S. F., Political Science
JABEEN, N., Administrative Sciences
JADOON, M. Z. I., Administrative Sciences
JAVED, M. A., Sports Sciences and Physical
Education
JULLANDHRY, M. S., Mass Communication
MALIK, M. E., Business Administration
MALIK, M. H., Social Sciences
MIRZA, M. S., Women Studies
SHEIKH, M. D., Mass Communication
SIRAJUDDIN, S. S., English Language and
Literature
ZAKAR, M. Z., Sociology

Faculty of Commerce (Quaid-e-Azam Campus, Lahore, Punjab; tel. (42) 9231154; fax
(42) 9231259; e-mail dean.commerce@pu.edu
.pk):

ALI, L.
BUTT, Z. A.
CHAUDHARY, N. A.
SAEED, K. A.

Faculty of Education (Quaid-e-Azam Campus, Lahore, Punjab; tel. (42) 9231264; fax
(42) 9231156; e-mail dean.education@pu.edu
.pk):

HAMEED, A.
IQBAL, M. Z.
KHALID, M. I.
KHAN, Z. A.
MIRZA, M. S.
ZAIDI, S. N. R.

Faculty of Engineering and Technology
(Quaid-e-Azam Campus, Lahore, Punjab;
tel. (42) 9230343; fax (42) 9231159; e-mail
dean.engg@pu.edu.pk):

AHMAD, J.
AKHTAR, N. A.
BUTT, M. A.
BUTT, M. T. Q.
DILAWARI, A. H.
NAWAZ, S.
RIZVI, S. Z. H.

Faculty of Islamic Studies (Allama Iqbal
Campus, Lahore, Punjab; tel. (42) 9210837;
fax (42) 9210837; e-mail dean.is@pu.edu.pk):

AKHTAR, H. M., Islamic Studies
CHAUDHARY, M. A., Arabic
FATIMA, S., Islamic Studies
HASAN, M., Urdu
HASHMI, R., Urdu
KHAN, S. A., Urdu
MOEEN, M., Arabic
SHAH, M. A., Iqbal Studies
SHAUKAT, J., Islamic Studies

Faculty of Law (Quaid-e-Azam Campus,
Lahore, Punjab; tel. (42) 9231276; fax (42)
9231278; e-mail dean.ems@ pu.edu.pk):

MALIK, D. M.
NAEEM, M.

Faculty of Pharmacy (Allama Iqbal Campus,
Lahore, Punjab; tel. (42) 9211617; e-mail
dean.pharmacy@pu.edu.pk):

RIAZ, M.

Faculty of Science (Quaid-e-Azam Campus,
Lahore, Punjab; tel. (42) 9231162; fax (42)
9230242; e-mail dean.science@pu.edu.pk):

ABBASI, G. Q., Mathematics
ABDULLAH, T., Solid-State Physics
AHMAD, Z., Geology
AKHTAR, M. W., Biochemistry and Biotechnology
AKHTER, A. S., Statistics
ALEEM, F., High-Energy Physics
ANWAR, C. J., Chemistry
ASGHAR, R., Business and Information
Technology
AZHAR, S., Business and Information Technology
BHATTI, S. A., Mathematics
BUTT, A. R., Business and Information
Technology

DIN, S., Business and Information Technology
DIN, S., Mathematics
FAROOQ, U., Geology
GHAZANFAR, M., Geology
GULZAR, F., Geography
HAFEEZ, M., Business and Information
Technology
HASNAIN, S., Botany
IDREES, M., Business and Information
Technology
IKRAM, N., Solid-State Physics
IQBAL, J., Chemistry
JAMAL, K., Business and Information Technology
KAMRAN, M., Physics
KHAN, Z. A., Business and Information
Technology
LATIF, S., Business and Information Technology
MANSOOR, G. D., Business and Information
Technology
NAZAR, F. M., Solid-State Physics
RAO, A. A., Business and Information
Technology
RASHID, K. H., High-Energy Physics
RAZA, A., Business and Information Technology
RIAZUDDIN, S., Advanced Molecular Biology
SHAKOORI, A. R., Microbiology and Molecular Genetics
SIDDIQI, S. A., Solid-State Physics
SOHAIL, M., Business and Information
Technology
SOHAIL, S., Business and Information Technology
ZAIDI, N. R., Business and Information
Technology

UNIVERSITY OF VETERINARY AND ANIMAL SCIENCES

Syed Abdul Qadir Jillani Rd, Lahore 54600,
Punjab

Telephone: (42) 99211374
Fax: (42) 99211461
E-mail: webmaster@uvas.edu.pk
Internet: www.uvas.edu.pk

Founded 1882; present name and status 2002
State control

Chancellor: GOV. OF PUNJAB
Vice-Chancellor: Prof. Dr TALAT NASEER
PASHA
Registrar: Dr MUHAMMAD AFZAL
Controller of Examinations: SAJJAD HYDER
Librarian: MIAN MUHAMMAD ILYAS

DEANS

Faculty of Animal Production and Technology: Prof. Dr MUHAMMAD ABDULLAH
Faculty of Biosciences: Prof. Dr IJAZ AHMAD
Faculty of Fisheries and Wildlife: Prof. Dr
MUHAMMAD AKRAM
Faculty of Life Sciences Business Management: Prof. Dr HABIB-UR-REHMAN
Faculty of Veterinary Science: Prof. Dr NASIM
AHMAD

UNIVERSITY OF WAH

The Mall, Quiad Ave, Wah Cantonment,
Punjab

Telephone: (51) 905522255
Fax: (51) 9314311
E-mail: info@uow.edu.pk
Internet: uow.edu.pk

Founded 2005, present status 2009
Private control

Chancellor: GOV. OF PUNJAB
Vice-Chancellor: Prof. Dr M. MAQBOOL
AHMAD
Controller of Examinations: Dr SIKANDAR
AZAM

Library of 51,000 vols

DEANS

Faculty of Basic Sciences: Prof. Dr M.
MAQBOOL AHMAD

VIRTUAL UNIVERSITY OF PAKISTAN

M. A. Jinnah Campus, Defence Rd, Off
Raiwind Rd, Lahore, Punjab
Fax: (42) 99200604
E-mail: registrar@vu.edu.pk
Internet: www.vu.edu.pk

Founded 2002
State control

Chancellor: PRES. OF ISLAMIC REPUBLIC OF
PAKISTAN
Rector: Dr NAVEED A. MALIK

Depts of computer science, economics, English, Islamic studies, management sciences,
mass communication, mathematics, Pakistan studies, physics, psychology, sociology,
statistics; uses free-to-air satellite television
broadcasts, internet to provide education.

ZIAUDDIN UNIVERSITY

4/B, Shahrah-e-Ghalib, Block 6, Clifton,
Karachi 75600, Sindh

Telephone: (21) 35862937
Fax: (21) 35862940
E-mail: info@zu.edu.pk
Internet: www.zu.edu.pk

Founded 2005
Private control

Chancellor: Dr ASIM HUSSAIN
Rector: YUSUF HAROON
Vice-Chancellor: Dr ANWER EJAZ BEG (acting)
Registrar: MUHAMMAD YOUSUF
Librarian: SYED AHMED NAQVI

DEANS

Postgraduate Clinical: Dr EJAZ AHMED VOHRA
Ziauddin College of Nursing: SEEMA REHAN
AFGHANI
Ziauddin College of Pharmacy: Dr KHWAJA
ZAFAR AHMED
Ziauddin Medical College: Dr KAMRAN
HAMEED

Colleges

Bolan Medical College: Quetta, Balochistan; e-mail principal@bmc.edu.pk; internet
www.bmc.edu.pk; f. 1972; offers graduate
courses in medical and dental sciences;
Prin. Prof Dr SHANAZ NASEER BALOCH; Vice-Prin. Prof. SHAH MUHAMMAD MARRI.

Government College of Technology:
Mandi Bahauddin, Rasul, Punjab; tel. (546)
553216; fax (546) 553110; e-mail gctrasul@
yahoo.com; internet www.gctrasul.edu.pk; f.
1873, present status 1972; diploma and
degree courses in technology and civil engineering; library: 25,076 vols; 90 teachers;
4,062 students; Prin. MAZHAR ABBAS NAQVI.

Government Polytechnic Institute: Paris
Rd, Sialkot, Punjab; tel. (52) 9250199; 3-year
diploma courses in electrical, mechanical,
civil engineering, auto and diesel technologies; library: 12,999 vols.

Islamabad Medical and Dental College:
Main Muree Rd, Bhara Kahu, Islamabad; tel.
(51) 2807201; fax (51) 2807200; e-mail info@
imdcollege.com; internet www.imdcollege
.com; f. 2007; offers courses in dental and
medical sciences; library: 10,000 vols, 27
periodical titles; 100 teachers; Dean Prof.
Dr M. NASEEMULLAH; Man. Dir YASIR NIAZI.

Jinnah Postgraduate Medical Centre:
Rafiqui (H. J.) Shaheed Rd, Karachi 75510,
Sindh; tel. (21) 9201300; e-mail edojpmc@
jpmc.com.pk; internet www.jpmc.com.pk; f.

1958; provides postgraduate training and education (incl. doctorate) in basic medical subjects; also degrees in medical technology, occupational therapy and physiotherapy, diplomas in general and postgraduate nursing, other full-time certificate courses; library: 19,000 books, 21,000 bound periodicals, 500,000 loose periodicals; Exec. Dir Dr TASNEEM AHSAN; Dir SIMI JAMALI; publ. *Annals* (4 a year).

Kinnaird College for Women: 93 Jail Rd, Lahore, Punjab; tel. (42) 9203781; fax (42) 9203788; e-mail info@kinnaird.edu.pk; internet www.kinnaird.edu.pk; f. 1913; offers intermediate, undergraduate, Masters programmes; depts of accounting and finance, Arabic, biochemistry, biotechnology, botany, business studies, chemistry, computer sciences, economics, English, environmental sciences, fine arts, food sciences and nutrition, French, geography, int. relations and Pakistan studies, Islamic studies, mathematics, media studies, music, philosophy, physical education, physics, political science, psychology, social work, statistics, Urdu, zoology; library: 28,000 vols; 3,300 students; Prin. Dr RUKHSANA DAVID.

National School of Public Policy: Shahrah-i-Quaid-i-Azam, Upper Mall, Lahore 54000, Punjab; tel. (42) 99202943; fax (42) 9204521; e-mail info@nspp.gov.pk; internet www.nspp.gov.pk; f. 1960 as Pakistan Admin. Staff College; present name and status 2002; training in admin. management for sr execs from govt and public enterprises, private sector, Commonwealth and third world countries; also research and publs on the subject; consultancy and advisory service in public admin.; campuses in Islamabad, Karachi, Lahore, Peshawar, Quetta; Rector. MUHAMMED ISMAIL QURESHI; publ. *Pakistan Administration* (2 a year).

Pakistani Swedish Institute of Technology: Landhi, GPOB 186, Karachi, Sindh; f. 1957; training in electrical, mechanical, woodworking, welding and clothing technology; library: 20,000 vols; 35 teachers; 2,000 students; Dir IMAM ALI SOOMRO.

Rawalpindi Government College of Technology: Shahrah-e-Shershah, Rawalpindi, Punjab; f. 1958; 3-year diploma courses in various subjects, degree courses in electrical power technology, electronics and communication technology; library: 22,000 vols; 1,700 students; Prin. MUHAMMAD AFSAR; publ. *Technician* (1 a year).

Swedish–Pakistani Institute of Technology: Rehman Shaheed Rd, Near Service More, Gujrat 50700, Punjab; tel. (53) 3524819; fax (53) 3524819; e-mail contact@spitgujrat.com; internet www.spitgujrat.com; f. 1966; 3-year diploma courses in electrical engineering, mechanical engineering, electronics, instrumentation, foundry, pattern making, metallurgy and welding technology, auto and diesel technology, automation and control technology; 1-year post-diploma course in biomedical technology; library: 15,000 vols; 46 teachers; 593 students; Prin. MUHAMMAD IQBAL DUGAL.

PALAU

The Higher Education System

The Republic of Palau's independence in 1994, under a Compact of Free Association with the USA, marked the end of the US-administered Trust Territory of the Pacific Islands that had been established in 1947. The Ministry of Education is the responsible body of higher education. The Palau National Scholarship Board offers assistance to selected students who wish to pursue their post-secondary education abroad but intend to return to Palau. The Palau Community College (formerly the Micronesian Occupational College) is the sole institution of higher education and is accredited by the Western Association of Schools and Colleges (USA). Its current name and status were adopted following implementation of the Palau Higher Education Act of 1993, which established it as an independent college with its own governing board. The College offers associate degrees (approximately equivalent to the first two years of a four-year degree in the USA) and certificates in a number of fields including agricultural science, business, criminal justice, liberal arts and nursing. According to the results of the 2005 census, there were 545 students in tertiary education that year. The Bureau of Curriculum and Programme Development, a division of the Ministry of Education, is responsible for the provision of adult and community education.

Regulatory Bodies

GOVERNMENT

Ministry of Community and Cultural Affairs: POB 100, Koror 96940; tel. 488-1126; fax 488-3354; e-mail mcca@palaunet .com; internet www.palaugov.net/palaugov/executive/ministries/mcca/mcca.htm; Minister FAUSTINA K. REHUHER-MARUGG.

Ministry of Education: POB 189, Koror 96940; tel. 767-1464; fax 767-1465; e-mail moe@palaumoe.net; internet www.palaugov .net/palaugov/executive/ministries/moe/moe .htm; Minister MASA-AKI EMESIOCHEL.

Learned Societies

BIBLIOGRAPHY, LIBRARY SCIENCE AND MUSEOLOGY

Palau Association of Libraries (PAL): Koror; e-mail palau.libraries@gmail.com; internet palaulibraries.weebly.com; dedicated to improvement and devt of Palau libraries; Pres. SANDY FERNANDEZ; Vice-Pres. MARGA B. ATEN; Sec. MEGAN K. BEARD; Treas. LORI ISAO.

NATURAL SCIENCES

Biological Sciences

Palau Conservation Society: POB 1811, Bai Ra Maibrel, Koror 96940; tel. 488-3993; fax 488-3990; e-mail pcs@palaunet.com; internet www.palauconservation.org; f. 1994; works with the community to preserve the nation's unique natural environment and perpetuate its conservation ethic for the economic and social benefit of present and future generations of Palauans and for the enjoyment and education of all; Chair. Dr CALEB OTTO; Exec. Dir ELBUCHEL SADANG; Sec. SANDRA S. PIERANTOZZI; Treas. KEOBEL SAKUMA.

Research Institutes

NATURAL SCIENCES

Biological Sciences

Coral Reef Research Foundation (CRRF): POB 1765, Koror 96940; tel. 488-5255; fax 488-5513; e-mail crrf@palaunet .com; internet www .coralreefresearchfoundation.org; f. 1991; special emphasis on species diversity work, colln for biomedical screening, environmental monitoring, reef fish spawning biology and devt of new techniques for marine research work; focus on increasing knowledge of coral reefs and other tropical marine environments to allow intelligent conservation and management decisions; Dir and Pres. Dr PATRICK L. COLIN.

Palau International Coral Reef Center: POB 7086, Koror 96940; tel. 488-6950; fax 488-6951; e-mail picrc@palaunet.com; internet www.picrc.org; f. 1999; aims to protect and conserve marine biodiversity; educates public about ecological, economic and cultural importance of coral reefs; provides facilities for research, professional training, workshops and conferences on marine research and management; centre for marine research, training and educational activities; indoor gallery displays several closed-system aquariums exhibiting marine organisms; outdoor marine park features open-system aquariums that exhibit different plant and animal dwellers of these habitats; Chair. Dr PATRICK TELLEI; CEO SANDRA S. PIERANTOZZI; Sec. and Treas. LOLITA K. GIBBONS-DECHERONG.

Libraries and Archives

Koror

Palau Congress Library: POB 8, Koror 96940; tel. 488-2507; fax 488-5653; f. 1981; 5,000 vols of committee reports, journals and legislative history on all public laws enacted by the Palau Nat. Congress; Librarian HARRY BESEBES.

Palau National Archives: POB 100, Koror 96940; tel. 488-4720; fax 488-4502; e-mail archives@palaunet.com; internet www .palaugov.net/palaugov/executive/ministries/ mcca/archive.htm; f. 1988; 2,200 16-mm and 110 35-mm cartridges/rolls of microfilms processed during the Trust Territory era; Chief Archivist NAOMI NGIRAKAMERANG.

Palau Public Library: POB 189, Koror 96940; tel. 488-2973; fax 488-2830; e-mail library@palaumoe.net; internet www .palaumoe.net/publib/about.html.xhtml; 11,000 vols; spec. collns: Pacific area, legislative records of Palau House of Delegates, nuclear topics; Librarian BEDEBII SADANG.

Singichi Ikesakes Law Library: POB 248, Koror 96940; tel. 488-4979; fax 488-1597; e-mail palaujudiciary@palaunet.com; internet www.palaugov.net/judiciary/ judiciary_llibrary.html; 16,000 vols incl. sources of Palauan and int. law; houses legal vols, treatises and reference books; Law Librarian LORI ISAO.

Museums

Koror

Belau National Museum: POB 666, Koror 96940; Ngerbeched Hamlet, Koror; tel. 488-2265; fax 488-3183; e-mail bnm@palaunet .com; internet www.belaunationalmuseum .org; f. 1955; preserves, promotes nat. heritage; exhibits natural, cultural, social and historical values; develops arts at all levels; 4,500 cultural objects relating to anthropology, traditional and contemporary art, history and natural history, media colln of 25,000 photographic slides, 6,000 prints, negatives, films, video cassettes and sound recordings, traditional men's meeting hall, botanical garden; library of 5,000 vols, and periodicals, maps, posters, research papers and articles; Dir and Curator OLYMPIA ESEL MOREI.

Etpison Museum: POB 7049, Koror 96940; tel. 488-6730; fax 488-4718; e-mail info@ etpisonmuseum.org; internet www .etpisonmuseum.org; f. 1999; colln incl. tools, artefacts, heirlooms, traditional Pacific and Palauan currency, childbirth ceremony of Palau, archaeological sites, rare shells and antique maps; Curator and Dir MANDY THIJSSEN ETPISON.

PALESTINIAN AUTONOMOUS AREAS

The Higher Education System

Palestinian education has been severely disrupted since 1987, when the university sector in the Gaza Strip and the West Bank was closed by military order. The universities were not re-opened until 1992. Since late 2000 the al-Aqsa intifada (uprising) has led to further strain on relations between the Palestinian Authority (PA) and Israel. All aspects of political, social and economic life in the occupied territories have been affected by the deteriorating security situation, including the higher education sector. In 2010 the Government announced a drive intended to modernize the sector; plans included expanding access to higher education, which was to involve the provision of additional funding to institutions and students alike, the development of five international programmes with foreign universities, and the improvement of quality control across the higher education system. The oldest university is Hebron University, which was founded in 1971. In 2010 there were 11 universities (including Al-Quds Open University), nine university colleges and 20 community colleges in the Palestinian Autonomous Areas. In 2008/09 there were a total of 182,453 students enrolled in tertiary education.

In May 1994 the PA assumed responsibility for education in Gaza and parts of the West Bank. Higher education is regulated by the Ministry of Education and Higher Education, while the Ministry of Labour is responsible for vocational training centres. The specific requirements for the completion of undergraduate and postgraduate degrees are set out in Article 20 of Law No. 11 of 1998 for Higher Education. The Accreditation and Quality Assurance Commission (AQAC) was established in 2002 as an autonomous body functioning under the Ministry of Education and Higher Education. Its main duties include the licensing and accreditation of new higher education institutions, the accreditation of undergraduate and postgraduate programmes and the promoting of quality assurance within the higher education sector. Programme accreditation is not yet compulsory at all institutions.

Admission to higher education requires students to pass the Tawijihi (secondary school certificate) examinations. Arts and science undergraduate degree programmes require a score of at least 65% in the Tawijihi for entry, while engineering, medical technology, pharmacy and veterinary degrees require at least 80%, and medicine and dental programmes require at least 90%. Some programmes, e.g. medicine and dentistry, also require the applicant to pass an English proficiency test as well as an interview for entry.

Undergraduates may study for a Diploma, which lasts between a few months and three years. Some Diplomas represent roughly half the content of a Bachelors degree in the same subject. Others are more vocational in their nature and are regarded as post-secondary non-tertiary qualifications. The main undergraduate qualification is the Bachelors degree, which is generally awarded after four years of study, and requires the completion of at least 120 credit hours following the Tawijihi. Students are required to select three categories of subjects: those specific to a degree programme (offered by the appropriate departments), those relevant to a degree programme (offered by faculties) and those of a more general nature (offered centrally by the university). Examples of the latter include Islamic studies and the History of Jerusalem. With the exception of dentistry, only two degree titles are awarded on completion of a Bachelor degree—Bachelor of Arts and Bachelor of Science. Degrees in dentistry, engineering, pharmacy and veterinary medicine require five years' study, and degrees in medicine six years'. Degree programmes in these subjects are only available at selected universities.

The first postgraduate qualification is the Higher Diploma, which is awarded after the completion of at least 30 credit hours (one year) of study following the Bachelors degree. Higher Diplomas are offered only by the Birzeit University and are available only in selected subjects (development, gender studies, law, medical laboratory technology, primary health care supervision and training).

Study for a Masters degree is generally one to two years in length following the award of the Bachelors degree, and may include the submission of a thesis. For most Masters programmes, taught courses constitute the majority of the required credit hours. At some universities where a thesis is required, candidates may be awarded a Higher Diploma should their thesis not meet the required standard, or if the comprehensive examination is failed.

Doctoral studies are typically three years in duration, and require the completion of a minimum of 45 credit hours following the completion of a Masters degree (with a minimum grade of 'very good'). Doctoral degrees are only offered by the Faculty of Graduate Studies at An-Najah National University, and currently the only doctorate available is in the field of chemistry .This doctorate is divided evenly between taught courses and a research project. Candidates must obtain a grade of at least 75% in the taught courses in order to proceed to the research component. A submitted dissertation must be defended by the candidate in front of a panel of specialists from the department.

Regulatory Bodies

GOVERNMENT

Ministry of Culture: POB 147, Ramallah; tel. (2) 2986205; fax (2) 2986204; e-mail moc@moc.pna.ps; Minister SIHAM AL-BARGHOUTHI.

Ministry of Education and Higher Education: POB 576, Al-Masioun, Ramallah; tel. (2) 2983200; fax (2) 2983222; e-mail moehe.p@gmail.com; internet www.moehe.gov.ps; Minister of Education LAMIS AL-ALAMI; Minister of Higher Education Dr ALI AL-JARBAWI.

ACCREDITATION

Accreditation and Quality Assurance Commission: Ministry of Education and Higher Education, POB 1932, Ramallah; tel. (2) 2980140; fax (2) 2954518; e-mail aqac@p-ol.com; internet www.aqac.mohe.gov.ps; f. 2002; autonomous body attached to the Min.; board of 12 mems; Dir Prof. MOHAMMED M. A ALSUBU; Sec. GHADEER A'LI ZA'AL AHMAD.

Learned Societies

GENERAL

UNESCO Office Ramallah: POB 2154, Ramallah, West Bank; 17 Ahliyya College St, Ramallah, West Bank; tel. (2) 2959740; fax (2) 2959741; e-mail ramallah@unesco.org; Dir BECHIR LAMINE.

LANGUAGE AND LITERATURE

Alliance Française: Peace Centre, POB 1166, Bethlehem; e-mail afbeth@p-ol.com; tel. (2) 2750777; offers courses and exams in French language and culture and promotes cultural exchange with France; Pres. PAULINE ANASTAS.

British Council: 31 Nablus Rd, POB 19136, 97200 Jerusalem; tel. (2) 6267111; fax (2) 6283021; e-mail information@ps.britishcouncil.org; internet www.britishcouncil.org/ps.htm; offers courses and exams in English language and British culture and promotes cultural exchange with the UK; attached offices in Gaza (building destroyed during civil unrest in March 2006), Hebron, Khan Yunis, Nablus and Ramallah; Dir-Gen. KEN CHURCHILL.

Research Institutes
GENERAL

Applied Research Institute, Jerusalem: Caritas St., Bethlehem; tel. (2) 2741889; fax (2) 2776966; e-mail pmaster@arij.org; internet www.arij.org; f. 1990; dedicated to promoting applied research, technology transfers, sustainable devt and the self-reliance of the Palestinian people through greater control over their natural resources; Pres. Eng. DAOUD ISTANBULI; Vice-Pres. SALIM ZUGBI; Treas. Dr NASRI QUMSIYEH; Sec. Dr NABEEL 'EDEILY; publ. *Report* (12 a year).

Health, Development, Information and Policy Institute: POB 1351, Ramallah; tel. (2) 2985372; fax (2) 2985917; e-mail hdip@hdip.org; internet www.hdip.org; f. 1989; policy research and planning regarding the Palestinian health care and development system in the West Bank and Gaza Strip.

Muwatin/The Palestinian Institute for the Study of Democracy: POB 1845, Ramallah; tel. (2) 2951108; fax (2) 2960285; e-mail muwatin@muwatin.org; internet www.muwatin.org; f. 1992 to promote the study and development of democracy in Palestine; Dir Dr GEORGE GIACAMAN.

Palestinian Academic Society for the Study of International Affairs: POB 19545, Jerusalem; 18 Hatem Al-Ta'i St., Wadi Al-Joz; tel. 2-6264426; fax 2-6282819; e-mail passia@passia.org; internet www.passia.org; f. 1987; deals with nat., Arab and int. aspects of the Palestinian Question through academic research, dialogue and publs; library of 2,000 vols; Chair. Dr MAHDI ABDUL HADI.

ECONOMICS, LAW AND POLITICS

Institute of Law: POB 14, Birzeit, West Bank; tel. (2) 2982009; fax (2) 2982137; e-mail iol.programs@birzeit.edu; internet lawcenter.birzeit.edu; research areas incl. comparative law, law and society, constitutional law and legislative support; Dir Dr GHASSAN FARAMAND.

MEDICINE

Institute of Community and Public Health: POB 143, Birzeit; tel. (2) 2982019; fax (2) 2982079; e-mail icph@birzeit.edu; internet icph.birzeit.edu; f. 1982; attached to Birzeit Univ.; research for devt of health related issues and health system; 5 units: child health, epidemiology, mental health, women's health and health systems management; Dir Dr ABDULLATIF HUSSEINI.

NATURAL SCIENCES

Institute of Environmental and Water Studies: POB 14, Birzeit; tel. and fax (2) 2982120; e-mail wsi@birzeit.edu; internet iews.birzeit.edu; f. 2001 as Water Studies Institute, present name 2007; attached to Birzeit Univ.; research for developing technologies on water resources management, distribution and wastewater treatment; Dir Dr NIDAL MAHMOUD.

RELIGION, SOCIOLOGY AND ANTHROPOLOGY

Institute of Women's Studies: POB 14, Birzeit, West Bank; tel. (2) 2982013; fax (2) 2982958; e-mail swadi@birzeit.edu; internet home.birzeit.edu/wsi; f. 1994; research on women's rights, gender relations and social policy in the local and regional context; library of 6,262 vols; Dir Dr ISLAH JAD; publ. *Institute of Women Studies*.

Libraries
Nablus

Nablus Municipality Public Library: Shwetreh St, Nablus, West Bank; tel. (9) 2383356; fax (9) 2374690; e-mail nab_lib@nablus.org; internet www.nablus.org; f. 1969; 70,000 vols, mainly in Arabic and English; Librarian ALI TOUQAN.

Ramallah

Public Library: Ramallah, West Bank; f. 1962; 3,500 vols; Librarian ADEL UWAIS.

Museums
Bethlehem

Baituna al-Talhami Museum/Bethlehem Folklore Museum: c/o Arab Women's Society, POB 19, Star St, Bethlehem; tel. (2) 2742431; fax (2) 2742589; f. 1948 as centre for Palestinian refugees, museum established 1979; 2 houses of typical Palestinian architecture, furnished with colln of traditional Palestinian household items and colln of photographs, furniture, and works of art illustrating life of Bethlehem residents in 1900–1932; open daily except Thursdays and Sundays.

Gaza

Al-Math'af/Recreational Cultural House: Sodaniya, Rasheed St, Gaza; tel. (8) 2858444; fax (8) 2858440; e-mail info@almathaf.ps; internet www.almathaf.ps; f. 2008; archaeology and antiquities; Dir JAWDAT AL-KHOUDARY.

Universities
AL-AQSA UNIVERSITY

POB 4051 Gaza
Telephone: (8) 282826809
Fax: (8) 2082826819
E-mail: it_affairs@alaqsa.edu.ps
Internet: www.alaqsa.edu.ps
Founded 1991
State control
Academic year: July to January
Faculties of admin. sciences, arts, education, fine arts, media, physical education, sciences; (Educational Studies Campus destroyed by Israeli military in March 2004)
Pres.: SALAM ALAGHA
Number of teachers: 350
Number of students: 21,000
Library of 113,200 vols.

AL-AZHAR UNIVERSITY

POB 1277, Jamal Abdl Naser St, Gaza
Telephone: (8) 2824020
Fax: (8) 2823180
E-mail: alazhar@alazhar-gaza.edu
Internet: www.alazhar-gaza.edu
Founded 1991
State control
Languages of instruction: Arabic, English
Pres.: Prof. Dr ABED AL KHALEQ AL FARAH
Vice-Pres. for Academic Affairs: Prof. Dr SAMI MUSLEH
Vice-Pres. for Admin. and Financial Affairs: Prof. Dr ALI AL NAJAR
Vice-Pres. for Planning and Quality Assurance: Dr NABEEL ABU SHAABAN
Number of teachers: 396
Number of students: 18,156

DEANS

Faculty of Agriculture: Prof. Dr NSER ABU FOUL
Faculty of Applied Sciences: Prof. Dr OMAR ABU TIAM
Faculty of Arts and Human Sciences: Dr MOHAMMED SALAH ABU HAMAIDA
Faculty of Economics and Administrative Sciences: Dr SAMIR ABU MUDALALAH
Faculty of Dentistry: Dr ABDEL NASSER ABU SHAHLA
Faculty of Education: Dr SOHAIB EL-AGHA
Faculty of Engineering and Information Technology: Prof. Dr SAMY ABU NASSER
Faculty of Intermediate Studies: Dr MOHAMMAD AJOUR
Faculty of Law: Dr ABED AL RAHMAN ABU AL NSIR
Faculty of Medicine: Dr SAMIR ISMAIL
Faculty of Pharmacy: Dr SULIMAN AL JBUR
Faculty of Science: Dr OMAR MILAD
Faculty of Shari'a: Dr NAEIM EL MASRY

ATTACHED CENTRES

Centre for Continuing Education: Dir Dr WAEL THABET.
Centre for Drug Analysis and Research: Dir Dr SULAIMAN AL JOBOUR.
Centre for Food Analysis: Dir Dr ABED EL-RAZEQ SALAMA.
Centre for Information Technology: Dir Dr MONTASER EL HALABI.
Institute of Water and Environment: Dir Dr YOUSIF ABU MAYLA.

AL-QUDS OPEN UNIVERSITY

POB 51800, Sheikh Jarrah, Musa Feidi St, East Jerusalem
Telephone: (2) 5816239
Fax: (2) 5816734
E-mail: administrative@qou.edu
Internet: www.qou.edu
Founded 1991
State control
Pres.: Prof. YOUNIS AMIR
Vice-Pres. for Academic Affairs: Prof. SUFIAN KAMAL
Vice-Pres. for Admin.: Dr SAMIR NAJDI
Library of 20,800 vols (16,000 in Arabic, 4,800 in English), 80 periodicals
Number of teachers: 356 academic supervisors apart from part-time instructors
Number of students: 60,699
Programmes in agriculture, education, management and entrepreneurship, social and family devt and technology and applied science; campus in Riyadh, Saudi Arabia, open to Palestinian nationals or people of Palestinian origin; 22 educational regions and study centres in the West Bank and Gaza Strip, in addition to a br. in Saudi Arabia; also has 5 centres that deal with IT, media production and education.

AL-QUDS UNIVERSITY

POB 51000, Jerusalem
Telephone: (2) 5838652
Fax: (2) 5838653
E-mail: president@alquds.edu
Internet: www.alquds.edu
Founded 1979
Private control
Language of instruction: English
Academic year: October to August
Pres.: Prof. SARI NUSSEIBEH
Vice-Pres.: Prof. HASAN DWEIK
Asst to the Pres. for Academic Affairs: Dr SAED ZEEDANI
Asst to the Pres. for Planning and Devt: Dr BADIE SARTAWI

Dean of Scientific Research: Dr SAMIRA
  BARGHOUTHI
Librarian: HAKIM BESHAWI
Library of 100,000 vols
Number of teachers: 431
Number of students: 11,631

DEANS

Faculty of Admin. and Economics Sciences:
  Dr MAHMOOD ALJAFARE
Faculty of Arts: Dr MUNTHER DAJANI
Faculty of Dentistry: Dr MUSA BAJALI
Faculty of Engineering: Dr HUSSEIN JADDU
Faculty of Health Professions: Dr VARSEEN
  SHAHEEN
Faculty of Islamic Studies: Dr SAID AL-QEEQ
Faculty of Law: Prof. ALI KHASHAN
Faculty of Medicine: Prof. HANI ABDEEN
Faculty of Pharmacy: Dr RAFIK KARAMAN
Faculty of Public Health: Dr SHAHEEN
  MOHAMMAD
Faculty of Science and Technology: Dr AMIN
  AHMAD LEGHROUZ

ATTACHED RESEARCH INSTITUTES

Abu-Jihad Centre for Political Prisoners' Affairs: tel. and fax (2) 2792515; e-mail info@aj-museum.alquds.edu; internet www.aj-museum.alquds.edu.

Al-Quds Human Rights Clinic: tel. (2) 2790417; fax (2) 2799717; e-mail info@aqhrclinic.alquds.edu; f. 2006; Dir MUNIR NUSEIBAH.

Al-Quds Nutrition and Health Research Institute: tel. (2) 6289798; fax (2) 6289849; e-mail enquire@anahri.alquds.edu; internet anahri.alquds.edu; Dir Dr ZIAD ABDEEN.

American Studies Institute: tel. (2) 2989184; fax (2) 2957072; e-mail info@americanstudiespalestine.org; internet asi.arts.alquds.edu; Dir Prof. MOHAMMED S. DAJANI DAOUDI.

Centre for Chemical and Biological Analysis: tel. (2) 2796961; f. 1999; Dir Dr MUSTAFA KHAMIS.

Centre for Development in Primary Health Care: tel. (2) 2952767; fax (2) 2981526; e-mail cdphc@palnet.com; internet cdphc.alquds.edu.

Centre for Human Rights and Humanitarian Law: f. 2006; Dir Dr MOHAMMAD SHALALDEH.

Centre for Jerusalem Studies: tel. (2) 6287517; fax (2) 6284920; e-mail huda@planet.edu; internet www.jerusalem-studies.alquds.edu; Dir HUDA IMAM.

Centre for Radiation Science and Technology: e-mail lahham@crst.alquds.edu; internet www.crst.alquds.edu; Dir Dr A. LAHHAM.

Child Institute: tel. (2) 5859955; fax (2) 6569182; e-mail pci@admin.alquds.edu; Dir Dr KHULOUD KHAYYAT DAJANI.

Community Action Centre: internet www.cac-alquds.org.

Ethnomusicology Research and Studies Centre: e-mail adileh@art.alquds.edu; Dir Prof. MUTASEM ADILEH.

INSAN Centre for Gender and Women's Studies: tel. (2)2791344; e-mail fadwal@arts.alquds.edu; Dir Dr FADWA ALLABADI.

Institute of Archaeology: tel. (2) 2959276; Dir Dr MARWAN ABU KHALAF.

Institute of Area Studies: Dir Dr AZIZ HEIDER.

Institute of Business and Economic Studies: tel. and fax (2) 2799497; e-mail mjafari@admin.alquds.edu; Dir MAHMOUD K. EL-JAFARI.

Institute of Modern Media: tel. (2) 2964213; fax (2) 2959275; e-mail info@imm.ps; internet www.imm.ps.

Islamic Research Centre: tel. (2) 6275228; f. 1987; Dir Dr MOSTAFA ABU SWAI.

Issam Sartawi Centre: tel. (2) 5859955; fax (2) 5853918; e-mail msdajani@art.alquds.edu; f. 1998; Dir Prof. MUNTHER S. DAJANI.

Jericho Local Urban Observatory Centre: tel. (2) 2799753; fax (2) 2796960; e-mail juoc@admin.alquds.edu; internet www.jluo.alquds.edu; Dir Dr FAYEZ FREIJAT.

Language Resource Centre: tel. (2) 6275228; f. 1995; Dir Dr OMAR ABU HOMOS.

Medical Research Centre: Dir Dr MYSA EL-AZZEH.

Said Khoury IT Centre of Excellence: tel. (2) 2790852; fax (2) 2791508; internet www.itce.alquds.edu.

Science and Technology Centre: tel. (2) 2799234; f. 1998; Dir Dr HASAN DWEIK.

Science Discovery Centre: e-mail info@sep.alquds.edu; internet www.sep.alquds.edu.

AN-NAJAH NATIONAL UNIVERSITY

Omar Ibn Khattab St, POB 7, Nablus, West Bank
Telephone: (9) 2345113
Fax: (9) 2345982
E-mail: info@najah.edu
Internet: www.najah.edu
Founded 1977
State control
Academic year: September to June
Languages of instruction: Arabic, English(for science faculties)
Academic year: September to June
Chair., Board of Trustees: SABIH AL-MASRI
Pres.: Prof. RAMI HAMDALLAH
Vice-Pres. for Academic Affairs: Prof. MAHER NATSHEH
Vice-Pres. for Administrative Affairs: Dr SA'ED AL-KONI
Vice-Pres. for Community Affairs: Dr MOHAMAD HANOON
Deputy Pres. for Strategic and Int. Affairs: Dr KHERIEH RASSAS
Deputy Pres. for Graduate Affairs: Prof. JAWAD FATAYER
Deputy Pres. for Planning, Devt and Quality Assurance: Dr ALLAM MOUSA
Dean of Admission and Registration: ABDULLAH ALNASSER
Dean of Student Affairs: MUSA ABU DIYEH
Librarian: HANI JABER
Library of 300,000 vols, 27,000 periodicals
Number of teachers: 1,340 (820 full-time, 520 part-time)
Number of students: 20,000
Publications: *An-Najah 'A base of Science and Technology'* (in Arabic and English), *An-Najah Journal of Research* (separate series for natural sciences and humanities)

DEANS

Faculty of Agriculture: Dr MUNQEZ SHTAYA
Faculty of Arts: Prof. MAHER ABU ZANT
Faculty of Economics and Administrative Sciences: Dr NAFEZ ABU BAKER
Faculty of Educational Sciences: Dr SAMI AL-KAILANI
Faculty of Engineering: Dr ABED RAHIM ABU SAFA
Faculty of Fine Arts: Dr HASAN M. N'ERAT
Faculty of Graduate Studies: Dr MOHAMMAD ABU JAFAR
Faculty of Information Technology: Dr BAKER ABDALHAQ
Faculty of Islamic Law (Shari'a): Dr JAMAL AL-KILANI

Faculty of Law: Dr AKRAM DAOUD
Faculty of Media: Dr ATEF SALAMEH
Faculty of Medicine and Health Sciences: Prof. ANWAR DUDIN
Faculty of Science: Prof. SULAIMAN KHALIL
Faculty of Veterinary Medicine: Dr HATEM ATALLA
Hisham Hijjawi College of Technology: Dr SHAKER BITAR

ATTACHED RESEARCH INSTITUTES

Academic Programme for the Study of Involuntary Migration: e-mail frc@najah.edu; Dir SAMER AQROUQ.

Central Medical Laboratory: e-mail cml@najah.edu; Dir Dr SULAIMAN KHALIL.

Centre for Continuing Education: e-mail cec@najah.edu; Dir Dr MUSADDAQ ALMASRI.

Centre for Urban and Regional Planning: e-mail abhamid@najah.edu; Dir Dr ALI ABDUL HAMEED.

Chemical, Biological and Drugs Analysis Centre: e-mail nidalzatar@najah.edu; Dir Dr NIDAL ZATAR.

Community Service Centre: Dir BILAL SALAMEH.

Computer Research Centre: e-mail cc@najah.edu; Dir NAJEH ABU SAFYYEH.

Construction and Transport Research Centre: e-mail alsahili@yahoo.com; Dir Dr KHALED AL-SAHILI.

Earth Sciences and Seismic Engineering Centre: e-mail seiscen@najah.edu; Dir Dr JALAL ALDABEEK.

Energy Research Centre: Dir Dr EMAD BRAIK.

Korean Palestinian IT Institute of Excellence (KPITIE): e-mail kaitie@najah.edu; Dir KHALID BARHAM.

Measurement and Evaluation Centre: e-mail mec2006@najah.edu; Dir Dr ABDEL-NASSER ALQADDOUMI.

Opinion Polls and Survey Studies Centre: e-mail polls@najah.edu; Dir Dr HUSSEIN AHMAD.

Poison Control and Drug Information Centre (PCDIC): e-mail poison@najah.edu; Dir Dr ANSAM SAWALHA.

UNESCO Chair on Human Rights and Democracy: e-mail uchrdn@najah.edu; Dir SAMER AQROUQ.

Water and Environmental Studies Institute: e-mail wesi@najah.edu; Dir Dr MARWAN HADDAD.

ARAB AMERICAN UNIVERSITY—JENIN

Jenin
E-mail: asaleh@aauj.edu
Internet: www.aauj.edu
Founded 2000
Private control
Faculties of admin. and financial sciences, allied medical sciences, arts and sciences, dentistry, engineering and information technology, law
Pres.: Dr ADLI SALEH
Vice-Pres. for Academic Affairs: Dr NASER HAMAD
Vice-Pres. for Planning and Devt: Dr ZAKI M. SALEH
Library of 60,000 vols.

BETHLEHEM UNIVERSITY

POB 9, Bethlehem, West Bank
Rue des Frères, Bethlehem, West Bank
Telephone: (2) 2741241
Fax: (2) 2744440
E-mail: info@bethlehem.edu

Internet: www.bethlehem.edu
Founded 1973
Private control (Roman Catholic)
Languages of instruction: Arabic, English
Academic year: September to June
Chancellor: Archbishop ANTONIO FRANCO
Vice-Chancellor: Br DANIEL CASEY
Pres.: Archbishop FOUD TWAL
CEO: Br PETER BRAY
Vice-Pres. for Academic Affairs: Br ROBERT SMITH
Vice-Pres. for Devt: Br JACK CURRAN
Vice-Pres. for Finance and Planning: SAMI EL-YOUSEF
Dean of Students: MAHMOUD HAMMAD
Registrar: MARY JUHA
Librarian: Dr MELLIE BRODRETH
Library of 90,000 vols
Number of teachers: 184 (132 full-time, 52 part-time)
Number of students: 3,000

DEANS

College of Arts: JAMAL DAIBES
College of Business Administration: Dr FADI KATTAN
College of Education: RIZEK SLEIBI
College of Nursing and Health Sciences: AMAL ABU NIJMEH
College of Sciences: Dr HAIFA KONKAR

ATTACHED RESEARCH INSTITUTES

Hereditary Research Laboratory: tel. (2) 2744233; fax (2) 2744440; e-mail mkanaan@bethlehem.edu; internet hrl.bethlehem.edu; f. 1993; Dir Dr MOIEN KANAAN.

Institute for Community Partnership: tel. (2) 2770936; fax (2) 2745559; e-mail icp@bethlehem.edu; internet icp.bethlehem.edu; f. 1989; Dir MOUSSA RABADI.

UNESCO Biotechnology Educational and Training Centre: tel. (2) 2765404; fax (2) 2765404; e-mail niraki@bethlehem.edu; f. 1995; Dir Dr NAIM IRAKI.

Water and Soil Environmental Research Unit: e-mail wseru@bethlehem.edu; internet wseru.bethlehem.edu; f. 1988; Dir Dr ALFRED ABED RABBO.

BIRZEIT UNIVERSITY

POB 14, Birzeit, West Bank
Telephone: (2) 2982000
Fax: (2) 2810656Also Birzeit Univ. Liaison Office, POB 950666, Amman, Jordan
Telephone: (6) 5527181
Fax: (6) 5527202
E-mail: pr@birzeit.edu
Internet: www.birzeit.edu
Founded 1924 as school, 1951 college, present status 1975
Private control
Languages of instruction: Arabic, English
Academic year: September to June (2 semesters), 2 summer sessions
Pres.: Prof. KHALIL HINDI
Pres.: Dr ADNAN AL-YEHYA
Vice-Pres. for Academic Affairs: Dr ADEL ZAGHA
Vice-Pres. for Admin. and Financial Affairs: DIANA SAYEJ
Vice-Pres. for Community Outreach: Dr MUNIR QAZZAZ
Head Librarian: DIANA SAYEJ
Library of 210,982 vols, 13,540 e-books, 12,856 e-journals
Number of teachers: 495 (375 full time, 120 part-time)
Number of students: 9,913

DEANS

Faculty of Arts: Dr MAHER AL-HASHWEH

Faculty of Commerce and Economics: Dr NIDAL SABRI
Faculty of Education: Dr MAHER HASHWEH
Faculty of Engineering: Dr FAISAL AWADAL-LAH
Faculty of Graduate Studies: Dr LIZA TARAKI
Faculty of Information Technology: Dr ADNAN AL-YEHYA
Faculty of Law and Public Admin.: Dr SALEH ABDEL-JAWWAD
Faculty of Nursing and Allied Health Professions: Dr TAMER ESSAWI
Faculty of Science: Dr SIMON KUTTAB

HEBRON UNIVERSITY

POB 40, Hebron, West Bank
Telephone: (2) 2220995
Fax: (2) 2229303
E-mail: info@hebron.edu
Internet: www.hebron.edu
Founded 1971
Ind. nat. univ.
Languages of instruction: Arabic, English
Academic year: September to June
Chair., Board of Trustees: Dr NABIL AL-JABARI
Pres.: Dr SAMIR A. ABUZNAID
Vice-Pres. for Academic Affairs: Prof. RADWAN BARAKAT
Vice-Pres. for Admin. Affairs: ZIAD AL JABARI
Vice-Pres. for External Affairs: Dr NIMER ABUZAHRA
Vice-Pres. for Quality Assurance: Dr HASAN IFLAIFEL
Registrar: AMAL AL-NATSHEH
Librarian: SALAH ABU SNANEH
Library of 65,000 vols
Number of teachers: 350
Number of students: 7,800

DEANS

Faculty of Agriculture: Dr SABRI SAGHIR
Faculty of Arts: Dr SALAH ALSHROUF
Faculty of Education: Dr JAMAL ABU MARAQ
Faculty of Finance and Management: Dr MUHAMMED AL-JABARI
Faculty of Graduate Studies: Prof. FAKHRI HASAN
Faculty of Islamic Studies: Prof. HUSSEIN AL-TARTORI
Faculty of Nursing: Dr HUSSEIN JABAREEN
Faculty of Pharmacy: Dr TAWFEQ KAIMARI
Faculty of Science and Technology: Dr NABIL HASASNEH

ISLAMIC UNIVERSITY OF GAZA

POB 108, Gaza
Telephone: (8) 2860700
Fax: (8) 2860800
E-mail: pres@iugaza.edu.ps
Internet: www.iugaza.edu.ps
Founded 1978
Academic year: September to June
Pres.: Dr KAMALAIN SHAATH
Vice-Pres. for Academic Affairs: Prof. MOHAMMED SHABAT
Vice-Pres. for Admin. Affairs: Prof. SALEM HELLES
Vice-Pres. for External Relations: Prof. RIFAT RUSTOM
Dean of Library: Dr WALEED AL-AMOUDY
Dean of Planning and Devt: Dr ABDELMAJEED NASSAR
Dean of Student Affairs: Dr KAMAL GHNAIM
Library of 100,300 vols in central library
Number of students: 20,888
Publication: *Journal* (2 a year)

DEANS

College of Arts: Prof. MAHMOUD EL-AMOUDI
College of Business: Prof. MAJED EL-FARRA
College of Education: Prof. ELYAN AL-HOLY

College of Engineering: Prof. SHAFIQ JENDYA
College of Foundations of Religion: Dr SALEM SALAMEH
College of Information Technology: Prof. NABEEL HEWAIHY
College of Islamic Law: Dr MAHER AL-HOLY
College of Medicine: Dr MOFEED MOKHALLATI
College of Nursing: Dr ASHRAF EL-JEDI
College of Religion Foundation: Dr MOHAMMED BKHAIT
College of Science: Dr NIZAM AL-ASHQAR

PROFESSORS

College of Arts:
  ABO ALI, N. KH.
  AMOUDI, M. A.
  OLWAN, M. SH.
  OLWAN, N. S.
College of Business:
  EDWAN, A. I.
College of Education:
  ASQOUL, M.
  EL-HELOU, M. W.
College of Engineering:
  AWAD, M.
  ENSHASSI, A.
  KUHAIL, Z. S.
College of Religion Foundation:
  HALABIYA, A. A.
  HAMMAD, N. H.
College of Science:
  ABDEL-LATIF, M.
  ASHOUR, M. M.
  EL-ATRASH, M. S.
  EL-AZIZ, E. E. A.
  EL-NAKHAL, H. A.
  HABIL, E.
  SARSOUR, M. E.
  SHABAT, M. M.
  SHUBAIR, M. E.

PALESTINE POLYTECHNIC UNIVERSITY

Hebron, West Bank
Telephone: (2) 2229812
Fax: (2) 2217248
E-mail: info@ppu.edu
Internet: www.ppu.edu
Founded 1978
State control
Pres.: DAWOD AL-ZATARY

Colleges of admin. sciences and informatics, applied professions, applied sciences, engineering and technology
Number of students: 5,000

Colleges

Bethlehem Bible College: POB 17166, 91190 Jerusalem; tel. (2) 2741190; fax (2) 2743278; e-mail info@bethlehembiblecollege.edu; internet www.bethlehembiblecollege.edu; f. 1979; Private control; Christian Bible College; accredited by Ministry of Education and Higher Education and Middle East Association of Theological Education; Pres. Prof. BISHARA AWAD.

Community College of Applied Sciences: POB 1415, Gaza; tel. (8) 2868999; fax (8) 2847404; e-mail info@ccast.edu.ps; internet www.ccast.edu.ps; f. 1998; State control; accredited by Ministry of Education and Higher Education; Dean YEHIA ROSHDI SIRAJ.

Ibrahimieh Community College: POB 19014, 91190 Jerusalem; tel. (8) 6286361; fax (8) 6262984; e-mail icc@ibrahimieh.edu; internet www.ibrahimieh.edu; f. 1998; State control; accredited by Ministry of Education and Higher Education.

National Institute for Administration: Al-Bireh; f. 2004; Palestinian Economic Council for Development and Construction; public admin. training for Palestinian Ministries, public orgs, private sector; Dir Dr MOHAMMED DAJANI.

National Institute for Technology: Ramallah; f. 2001; Palestinian Economic

Council for Development and Construction; higher education courses in software engineering, web and e-commerce solutions devt, system engineering, database devt and network engineering; English language courses; Dir ADEL LAFI.

Palestine Technical College, Deir al-Balah: POB 6037, Deir al-Balah; tel. (8) 2531171; fax (8) 2538101; e-mail eng_ptc@ptcdb.edu.ps; internet www.ptcdb.edu.ps;

State control; accredited by Ministry of Education and Higher Education.

Tulkarm Community College: West Bank; f. 1931; library: 30,000 vols; 27 teachers; 400 students; teacher training college preparing teachers of agriculture, science, mathematics, computer science, Arabic, Islamic and social studies, English and physical education; Dean Dr M. Z. GHAZALEH.

PANAMA

The Higher Education System

In 1821 Panama became independent from Spain as part of Gran Colombia, declaring its separate independence in 1903. The Universidad de Panamá (founded in 1935) is the oldest university. There are four public universities, with regional centres in the provinces, and 12 private universities, including one specializing in distance learning. In 2007/08 there were 134,290 students enrolled in tertiary education.

Higher education is centralized under the authority of the Ministry of Education. In late 2010 the National Council for the Evaluation and Accreditation of University Education launched the first nation-wide initiative to evaluate and accredit tertiary institutions in Panama, in an attempt to identify those institutions failing to meet standards set by the Ministry of Education.

Admission to higher education is made on the basis of a Bachillerato (specialized secondary school certificate) relevant to the intended field of study. Applicants must also pass an entrance examination. Undergraduates study for four or five years for the Licenciado (Bachelors) degree or a professional title. Following the Licenciado a further two years of study is required for the postgraduate Maestría (Masters) degree.

Technical and vocational education is offered by institutions of higher education; the leading programme of study is the Técnico, which requires two to three years of study. Adult education is administered by the Institute for Training and Utilization of Human Resources.

Regulatory and Representative Bodies

GOVERNMENT

Ministry of Education: Edif. Poli y Los Rios, Avda Justo Arosemena, Calles 26 y 27, Apdo 0816-04049, Panamá 3; tel. 511-4400; fax 262-9087; e-mail meduca@meduca.gob .pa; internet www.meduca.gob.pa; Minister LUCINDA MOLINAR.

NATIONAL BODY

Consejo de Rectores de Panamá (Panama Rectors' Council): Albrook, Ancón, Edificio Nº 868, Panamá; tel. 315-0959; fax 315-1601; e-mail rectores@cwpanama.net; internet www.pa/consejo; f. 1995; Pres. Dra NOEMÍ LUCILA CASTILLO JAÉN; Exec. Sec. NURIA ARAGUAS SAMBRANO.

Learned Societies

HISTORY, GEOGRAPHY AND ARCHAEOLOGY

Academia Panameña de la Historia (Panama Academy of History): Apdo 973, Zona 1, Panamá; f. 1921; Pres. MIGUEL A. MARTÍN; Sec. ROGELIO ALFARO; publ. Boletín.

LANGUAGE AND LITERATURE

Academia Panameña de la Lengua (Panama Academy of Language): Apdo 0816-06740, Panamá; Calle Manuel María Icaza, esquina con Calle 50, Panamá; tel. 223-0717; fax 263-3910; e-mail aplengua@cwpanama .net; corresp. of the Real Academia Española (Madrid); 4 mems, 14 elected mems; Dir BERNA PÉREZ AYALA DE BURRELL; Sec. MARGARITA J. VÁSQUEZ Q.; publ. Boletín.

Alliance Française: Apdo Postal 4305, Zona 5, Panamá; Calle 49, por la Avda Federico Boyd, entrando por la bolsa de valores, Bella Vista, Panamá; tel. 223-7376; fax 264-1931; e-mail alliance@cableonda.net; internet www.afpanama.org; offers courses and exams in French language and culture and promotes cultural exchange with France; attached teaching centres in David.

Research Institutes

AGRICULTURE, FISHERIES AND VETERINARY SCIENCE

Instituto de Investigación Agropecuaria de Panamá (Institute of Agricultural Research): Ciudad del Saber, Clayton, Panamá 6-4391; tel. 317-0519; fax 317-0510; f. 1975; to increase the yields and productivity of agricultural producers; establishes rules for agricultural research carried out in the public sector; advises the govt on the formulation and application of scientific policies and on agricultural technology; promotes technical training at all levels in the agricultural sector; Dir Dr REYNALDO PÉREZ-GUARDIA.

EDUCATION

Instituto para la Formación y Aprovechamiento de los Recursos Humanos (Institute for the Training and Development of Human Resources): Apdo 6337, Zona 5, Panamá; Via España, al lado de la agencia Thrifti Car Rental, Panamá; tel. 269-6666; fax 263-6101; internet www.ifarhu.gob.pa; f. 1965 for the devt of technical training and the rational use of the country's human resources in order to improve its economic and social devt; 9 regional agencies, 8 student centres and an Information and Documentation Centre (see below); Dir-Gen. Licda GLORIA ROVIRA; publs Cidinforma (12 a year), Mujer al Cambio (1 a year), Orientifarhu (4 a year).

MEDICINE

Instituto Conmemorativo Gorgas de Estudios de la Salud (Gorgas Commemorative Institute of Health Research): Apdo 6991, Zona 5, Panamá; Avda Justo Arosemena entre Calle 35 y 36, Panamá; tel. 227-4111; fax 225-4366; e-mail igorgas@gorgas .gob.pa; internet www.gorgas.gob.pa; f. 1921; library of 50,000 vols; Dir Dr JORGE MOTTA; publ. Boletín Informativo (4 a year, online).

NATURAL SCIENCES

Biological Sciences

Smithsonian Tropical Research Institute: Apdo Postal 0843-03092, Balboa, Ancón; Roosevelt Ave, Building 401, Tupper, Balboa, Ancón; tel. 212-8000; fax 212-8148; internet www.stri.org; f. 1923; administered by the Smithsonian Institution; researches and promotes tropical biology, education and conservation; the institute has extensive marine and terrestrial research facilities; library of 66,000 vols, 850 periodicals; Dir Dr IRA RUBINOFF.

Libraries and Archives

Panamá

Archivo Nacional: Apdo 6618, Zona 5, Panamá; Avda Perú entre Calle 31 y 32, Zona 5, 6618 Panamá; tel. 225-0944; fax 225-1937; e-mail arnapa@cwpanama.net; internet www.registro-publico.gob.pa; f. 1912; 3,400 vols; Dir FLORENCIO R. MUNOZ B.; publ. Boletín Informativo (2 a year).

Biblioteca del Instituto Nacional de Estadística y Censo: Apdo 0816–01521, Panamá; tel. 510-4829; fax 510-4801; e-mail elsid@contraloria.gob.pa; internet www .contraloria.gob.pa/inec; f. 1949; compiles and publishes statistical information about Panama and its provinces incl. details of the Nat. Census; 60,000 vols; Dir DANIS P. CEDEÑO H.; Librarian ELSI P. DE MEJÍA; publs Censo Nacional Agropecuario (every 10 years, also on CD-ROM), Censos Nacionales de Población y Vivienda (every 10 years, also on CD-ROM), Censos Nacionales Económicos (every 10 years), Compendios Estadísticas Provinciales (every 2 years), Estadística Panameña (32 series, each 1 a year), Informe del Contralor (1 a year, also on CD-ROM), Panamá en Cifras (1 a year, also on CD-ROM).

Biblioteca Interamericana Simón Bolívar: Estafeta Universitaria, Panamá; tel. 223-8786; fax 223-3734; e-mail biblis1@ ancon.up.ac.pa; f. 1935 as Biblioteca de la Universidad de Panamá, name changed 1978; 285,855 vols incl. 9,000 vols in medical library; maintains interchange with 200 institutions; Dir Prof. DAYSI DE JEAN FRANÇOISE; publ. Boletín Bibliográfico (2 a year).

Biblioteca Nacional (National Library): Apdo 7906, Zona 9, Panamá; Parque Recreativo y Cultural Omar, Vía Porras, San Francisco, Panamá; tel. 224-9466; fax 224-9988; internet www.binal.ac.pa; f. 1892 as Biblioteca Colón, reorganized as Biblioteca Nacional 1942; a branch of the Ministry of Education's Public Libraries system, its special function is to provide a Government information service; 200,000 vols (incl. bound

PRIVATE UNIVERSITIES

PANAMA

reviews and periodicals); Admin. Dir MARÍA MAJELA BRENES; publ. *LOTERIA.*

Centro de Información y Documentación Institucional: Apdo 6337, Zona 5, Panamá; tel. 262-2109; fax 262-1179; e-mail cidi@ifarhu.gob.pa; internet www.ifarhu.gob .pa; f. 1980; 5,000 vols; Dir Lic. INES PERALTA DE VARGAS; publs *Orientifarhu, Cidinforma* (bibliographical information), *Alertas* (specialized bibliographical information), *Mujer al Cambio* (women's psychological and social issues, 1 a year).

Museums and Art Galleries
Panamá

Dirección Nacional del Patrimonio Histórico: Apdo 0816-07812, Zona 5, Panamá; tel. 232-7485; fax 232-7644; internet www .inac.gob.pa; f. 1974; conservation and admin. of Panama's historical heritage; library of 8,000 vols; Dir Lic. LINETTE MONTENEGRO.

Instituto Panameño de Arte/Museo de Arte Contemporáneo: Apdo 4211, Zona 5, Panamá; tel. 262-8012; fax 262-3376; e-mail info@macpanama.org; internet www .macpanama.org; f. 1962; museum; library of 3,000 vols; Dir REINIER RODRÍGUEZ FERGUSON.

Museo de Arte Religioso Colonial: Apdo 662, Zona 1, Panamá; Avda A y Calle 3ra., San Felipe, Panamá; tel. and fax 228-2897; f. 1974; sited in restored 17th-century Dominican chapel; varied collection of objects of religious art of the Colonial period; cultural programmes and lectures; Dir Prof. NORIS NÚÑEZ DE ALVAREZ.

Museo de Ciencias Naturales: Apdo 662, Zona 1, Panamá; Avda Cuba, Calle 29 y 30, Calidonia, Panamá; tel. 225-0645; fax 225-0646; e-mail museocienciasnaturales@yahoo .com; internet www.pa/cultura/museos/ ciencias; f. 1975; natural history, geology and palaeontology; fauna of Panama and other countries; library of 300 vols; Dir Profa NURIA ESQUIVEL DE BARILLAS.

Museo de Historia de Panamá: Apdo 662, Zona 1, Panamá; Palacio Municipal, Avda Central, entre Calles 6 y 7 Oeste, Panamá; tel. and fax 228-6231; f. 1977; Dir Licda NILKA FUENTES; publ. guide books.

Public Universities
UNIVERSIDAD AUTÓNOMA DE CHIRIQUÍ

El Cabrero, David, Chiriquí
Telephone: 775-1114
Fax: 774-4050
E-mail: rectoria@unachi.ac.pa
Internet: www.unachi.ac.pa
Founded 1994; present name and status 1995
State control
Rector: VIRGILIO A. OLMOS APARICIO
Vice-Rector for Academic Affairs: DANIEL CARRILLO
Vice-Rector for Admin.: ETELVINA DE BONAGAS
Vice-Rector for Research and Postgraduate Affairs: Dra JUANA RAMOS CHUE
Sec.-Gen.: BLANCA RÍOS
Number of teachers: 560
Number of students: 8,500
Publications: *Bitacora* (society, culture and science, 4 a year), *Econometrín* (economics), *El Observator* (social communication),

Revista, Senda Universitaria (12 a year), *Supra* (Spanish language)
Faculties of business administration and accountancy, economics, education sciences, humanities, law, medicine, natural sciences, nursing, public administration, social communication; School of Chemistry; campuses in Boquete, Oriente and Barú.

UNIVERSIDAD ESPECIALIZADA DE LAS AMERICAS
(Specialized University of the Americas)

Albrook Edificio 808, Apdo 0843-01041, Panamá
Telephone: 501-1000
Fax: 501-1041
E-mail: rectoria@udelas.ac.pa
Internet: www.udelas.ac.pa
Founded 1997
State control
Language of instruction: Spanish
Rector: Dra BERTA TORRIJOS DE AROSEMENA
Vice-Rector: Dr JUAN BOSCO BERNAL
Gen. Sec.: ERIC GARCÍA
Librarian: YISELA ARROCHA
Library of 10,000 vols
Number of teachers: 873
Number of students: 6,222

DEANS

Faculty of Integrated Health and Rehabilitation: GRACIELA AMBULO
Faculty of Social and Special Education: ELIZABETH DE TAM

UNIVERSIDAD DE PANAMÁ

Ciudad Universitaria 'Dr Octavio Méndez Pereira', El Cangrejo, Apdo Estafeta Universitaria, Panamá
Telephone: 263-6133
Fax: 264-3733
Internet: www.up.ac.pa
Founded 1935
State control
Language of instruction: Spanish
Academic year: March to December
Rector: Dr GUSTAVO GARCÍA DE PAREDES
Vice-Rector for Academic Affairs: Dr JUSTO MEDRANO
Vice-Rector for Admin.: Dr CARLOS BRANDARIZ ZÚÑIGA
Vice-Rector for Extension: Dr ARIOSTO E. ARDILLA MARTÍNEZ
Vice-Rector for Research and Graduate Studies: Dra BETTY ANN ROWE DE CATSAMBANIS
Vice-Rector for Student Affairs: Dr NELSON NOVARRO
Registrar: ONFALA LÓPEZ DE BELLO
Librarian: Prof. DAYSI DE JEAN FRANÇOISE
Number of teachers: 3,662
Number of students: 65,225
Publications: *Boletines Estadísticos, Campus, ECO, EDU, Hacia La Luz, Memoria, Revistas Jurídicas Panameñas, Revista Universidad, Scientia*

DEANS

Faculty of Agriculture: Dr JUAN MIGUEL MIGUEL OSORIO
Faculty of Architecture: Arq. MARÍA T. DE BENAVIDES
Faculty of Business Administration and Accountancy: RUTH E. MATA
Faculty of Computer Science, Electronics and Communication: Dra DIANA CHEN
Faculty of Economics: Prof. GABRIEL VELÁSQUEZ
Faculty of Education: Prof. TOMÁS GARIBALDI
Faculty of Fine Arts: Prof. EFRAIN CASTRO

Faculty of Humanities: Dr MIGUEL ÁNGEL CANDANEDO ORTEGA
Faculty of Law and Political Sciences: Dr ROLANDO MURGAS TORRAZZA
Faculty of Medicine: Dr SERGIO FUENTES
Faculty of Natural and Exact Sciences and Technology: Prof. RAMIRO GÓMEZ
Faculty of Nursing: ELBA E. DE ISAZA
Faculty of Odontology: Dra OMAR LÓPEZ
Faculty of Pharmacy: Dra ANGELA DE AGUILAR
Faculty of Public Administration: NICOLÁS JEROME
Faculty of Social Communication: Prof. HARRY IGLESIAS
Faculty of Veterinary Medicine: Dr CARLOS G. MORÁN R.

UNIVERSIDAD TECNOLOGICA DE PANAMÁ

Campus 'Víctor Levi Sasso', Apdo Postal 0819-07289, El Dorado, Panamá
Telephone: 560-3178
Fax: 560-3181
E-mail: utp@utp.ac.pa
Internet: www.utp.ac.pa
Founded 1981
State control
Academic year: March to December
Pres.: Ing. MARCELA PAREDES DE VÁSQUEZ
Vice-Pres. for Academic Affairs: Ing. LUIS BARAHONA
Vice-Pres. for Admin. Affairs: Ing. MYRIAM GONZÁLEZ BOUTET
Vice-Pres. for Research and Graduate Studies: Dr MARTÍN CANDANEDO
Dir of External Affairs: Ing. JAIME JAEN
Librarian: Lic. EDILDA F. DE MORALES
Number of teachers: 1,428
Number of students: 17,000
Publications: *Boletín Informativo* (12 a year), *El Tecnológico* (bulletin, 12 a year), *I+D Tecnológico* (1 a year), *International Affairs Bulletin* (12 a year), *Memorias* (1 a year)

DEANS

Faculty of Civil Engineering: Ing. MARINA SAVAL DE GUERRA
Faculty of Computer Science Engineering: Ing. RAUL BARAHONA
Faculty of Electrical Engineering: Ing. CELSO SPENCER
Faculty of Mechanical Engineering: Dr VÍCTOR SÁNCHEZ
Faculty of Science and Technology: Dr ELEICER CHING

Private Universities
UNIVERSIDAD ABIERTA Y A DISTANCIA DE PANAMÁ
(Open and Distance Learning University of Panama)

Apdo 87-2526, Panamá 7
Calle 39 Este, Bella Vista Edif. 5–57 entre Ave Cuba y Ave Perú, Panamá
Telephone: 227-7242
Fax: 227-7243
E-mail: generalunadp@cwpanama.net
Internet: www.unadp.ac.pa
Founded 1994
Private control
Language of instruction: Spanish.

UNIVERSIDAD CATÓLICA SANTA MARÍA LA ANTIGUA

Apdo 0819-08550, Panamá
Telephone: 230-8200

1669

Fax: 230-3433
E-mail: rectoria@usma.ac.pa
Internet: www.usmapanama.com
Founded 1965, reorganized 1973
Private control
Language of instruction: Spanish (except the Hotel and Restaurant Management programme)
Academic year: January to December (three semesters)
Chancellor: Mgr José Domingo Ulloa Mendieta
Rector: Mgr Carlos Alberto Voloj Pereira
Vice-Rector for Academic Affairs: Mgr. Dimas Quiel Reyes
Vice-Rector for Admin. Affairs: Prof. Luis Pabón Ordoñes
Vice-Rector for Research and Postgraduate Affairs: Mgr. María Eugenia Pérez de Alemán
Registrar: Mgr. Ingrid Miroslava Chang Valdés
Librarian: Lic. Irene de Carvajal
USMA Colon Br. Dir: Prof. Nedelka Nuñez
USMA Chiriquí Br. Dir: Prof. Fatima Pitti
USMA Los Santos Br. Dir: Prof. Fulvia Ocaña
Library of 65,000 vols
Number of teachers: 400
Number of students: 4,500
Publications: *Boletín Informativo* (1 a year), *Iustitia et Pulchritudo* (1 a year), *Revista La Antigua* (2 a year)

DEANS

Administrative Sciences: Prof. Lía Cordoba
Humanities and Religious Studies: Prof. Francisco Blanco
Law and Political Science: Prof. Victor Delgado

Natural Sciences and Technology: Prof. Humberto Mena
Social Sciences: Prof. Melva Palacios de Mon

UNIVERSIDAD DEL ISTMO

Av. Justo Arosemena, Calle 40 y 41, Panamá
Telephone: 227-8822
Fax: 227-8831
E-mail: informacion@udi.edu
Internet: www.udi.edu
Founded 1963
Private control
Rector: Pablo Michelsen
Campuses in Chiriquí, David and La Chorrera.

UNIVERSIDAD INTERAMERICANA DE PANAMÁ

Avda Manuel Espinosa Batista, Panamá
Telephone: 208-4444
Internet: www.uip.edu.pa
Founded 1992
Private control
Language of instruction: Spanish
Academic year: January to December
Pres.: William J. Salom
Rector: Noemí Castillo Jaén
Number of teachers: 500
Number of students: 5,800

UNIVERSIDAD LATINA DE PANAMÁ

Apdo 87-0887, Via Ricardo J. Alfaro, Calle Aragón, Catilla, Panamá 7
Telephone: 230-8600
Fax: 230-8686

E-mail: web@ulat.ac.pa
Internet: www.ulat.ac.pa
Founded 1989, present status 1991
Private control
Rector: Dr Modaldo Tuñon
Registrar: Claudia Marín
Library Dir: Aura Arosemena
Number of teachers: 600
Number of students: 7,000
Campuses in Chitré, David and Santiago

DEANS

Faculty of Administrative and Economic Sciences: Augusto A. Corro
Faculty of Communication Sciences: Nedelka Galvez
Faculty of Computer Sciences and Telecommunications: Lujan Gonzales
Faculty of Education Sciences: Gladys de Jaén
Faculty of Health Sciences: Dr Jorge Medrano
Faculty of Law and Political Sciences: Octavio Del Moral
Faculty of Social Sciences: (vacant)

Schools of Arts and Music

Escuela Nacional de Danzas: Apdo 662, Zona 1, Panamá; f. 1948.

Escuela Nacional de Teatro: Apdo 662, Zona 1, Panamá; f. 1974; 10 teachers; 40 students; Dir Prof. Iván R. García.

PAPUA NEW GUINEA

The Higher Education System

In 1906 the Territory of Papua came under Australian control, and in 1914 the former German possession of New Guinea became a Trust Territory, also under Australian control. A joint administration for the two territories was established by Australia in July 1949, and the name Papua New Guinea was adopted in 1971. Independence was achieved in 1975. Major institutions of higher education were first established in the 1960s, including the Papua New Guinea Institute of Public Administration—founded in 1963—and the University of Papua New Guinea, the University of Vudal—renamed the Papua New Guinea University of Natural Resources and Environment in 2005—and the Papua New Guinea University of Technology (all founded in 1965). There are now four state universities and two private universities. In addition to the universities there are nine teacher-training colleges, as well as higher education institutions that cater for specific professional training, such as a medical school, which had a total enrolment of 656 students in early 2005. In 1998/99 there were 13,761 students enrolled in tertiary education. The Office of Higher Education, which was established by the Higher Education Act of 1983, is the administrative and executive agency for higher education in Papua New Guinea.

Admission to higher education is on the basis of the Grade 12 Higher School Certificate. However, students with the Grade 10 Secondary School Certificate may enter a degree course after completing a foundation year. In addition to the standard undergraduate Bachelors degree, which is a four-year programme of study, universities offer two- to four-year diploma and certificate-level courses. Degree courses in medicine and law are five years in duration. Following the Bachelors, the Masters is the first postgraduate degree and lasts between one and three years. Finally, the PhD is the highest university-level degree and requires students to undertake a period of relevant training prior to starting the course. The PhD itself requires a minimum of three years' study and research for the preparation and submission of a thesis.

Most technical and vocational education starts at the secondary Grade 10-level, and consists of one- to two-year certificate and three-year diploma programmes at technical colleges and specialized professional institutes.

Regulatory Body

GOVERNMENT

Department of Education: Fin Corp Haus, POB 446, Waigani, NCD; tel. 3013555; fax 3254648; internet www.education.gov.pg; Min. for Education THEO ZURENOUC (acting); Min. for Higher Education, Research, Science and Technology DAVID ARORE; Sec. MUSAWE SINEBARE.

ACCREDITATION

Office of Higher Education: Level Two, Mutual Rumana Waigani Dr., POB 5117, Boroko, 111 NCD; tel. 3012051; fax 3258386; internet www.ohe.gov.pg; Dir-Gen. Dr WILLIAM TAGIS.

Learned Societies

BIBLIOGRAPHY, LIBRARY SCIENCE AND MUSEOLOGY

Papua New Guinea Library Association: c/o National Library Service, POB 734, Waigani, NCD; f. 1973; 200 mems; Pres. MARGARET J. OBI; Sec. JENNY WAL; publs *Directory of Libraries in Papua New Guinea*, *PNGLA Nius* (2 a year), *Toktok bilong haus buk* (Journal, 4 a year).

ECONOMICS, LAW AND POLITICS

Papua New Guinea Institute of Banking and Business Management: ToRobert Centre, Vanama Crescent, POB 1721, Lawes Rd, Port Moresby NCD; tel. 3212088; fax 3212960; e-mail customerservice@ibbm.com.pg; internet www.ibbm.com.pg; f. 1965; training in admin., finance, banking, commerce, supervisory and management skills; Exec. Dir. SWETA SUD.

LANGUAGE AND LITERATURE

Alliance Française: UPNG Campus, Kuri Dom Bldg, Port Moresby; tel. and fax 3267120; e-mail info@afportmoresby.org; internet www.afportmoresby.org; offers courses and exams in French language and culture and promotes cultural exchange with France; library of 1,500 vols.

NATURAL SCIENCES

General

Papua New Guinea Scientific Society: c/o National Museum and Art Gallery, POB 5560, Boroko; tel. 3252422; fax 3251779; e-mail pngmuseum@global.net.pg; f. 1949; promotes sciences, exchange scientific information, preserve scientific collns and establish museums; 203 mems; Pres. H. SAKULAS; publ. *Proceedings*.

Research Institutes

GENERAL

National Research Institute: POB 5854, Boroko, NCD; tel. 3260300; fax 3260213; e-mail nri@nri.org.pg; internet www.nri.org.pg; f. 1961 as New Guinea Research Unit, present name 1989; research insocial, political, economic, educational and cultural issues in Papua New Guinea; research focus on wealth creation, universal basic education, governance and public sector and environment and people; library of 10,000 vols; Dir Dr THOMAS WEBSTER; publ. *TaimLain: A Journal of Contemporary Melanesian Studies*.

AGRICULTURE, FISHERIES AND VETERINARY SCIENCE

Lowlands Agricultural Experiment Station: Kerevat, POB 204, Kokopo, East New Britain Province; tel. 9839145; fax 9839129; f. 1928; food crops, spices, soil and land management, entomology and plant pathology.

ECONOMICS, LAW AND POLITICS

Institute of National Affairs: POB 1530, Port Moresby NCD; tel. 3211045; fax 3217223; e-mail inapng@daltron.com.pg; internet www.inapng.com; f. 1979; conducts research in economy, taxation, land, trade, coastal shipping, industrialization, law and order, agriculture, mining, small business, govt expenditure, fisheries, forestry, human capital formation and labour; publishes smaller research papers and speech series papers; Pres. DAVID PEATE; Exec. Dir and Treas. and Sec. PAUL BARKER.

MEDICINE

Papua New Guinea Institute of Medical Research: POB 60, Goroka, 411 EHP; tel. 5322800; fax 5321998; e-mail info@pngimr.org.pg; internet www.pngimr.org.pg; f. 1968; brs: Goroka, Madang, Maprik and Wewak; research in matters relating to research into human health and disease within Papua New Guinea incl. medical, human biological, nutritional and sociological research; library of 5,000 vols; Dir Prof. PETER SIBA.

Libraries and Archives

Boroko

National Archives and Public Records Service: POB 1089, Boroko; tel. 3256200; fax 3254251; f. 1957; br. of Nat. Library Service, Division of the Dept of Education; repository for the public archives and records of Papua New Guinea; Reference Service and Microfilm Unit, Records Management Service and Records Centre Service for govt offices and statutory bodies; br. repository in Lae: 10,000 linear m and 1,000 maps and plans, and photographic archives; Chief Archivist JACOB HELEVAWA; publs *Guides to Groups of Records in the National Archives* (irregular), *Patrol Reports* (microfiche, irregular).

Lae

Matheson Library, Papua New Guinea University of Technology: PMB, Lae, 411; tel. 4734351; fax 4734363; e-mail ikisikel@lib

.unitech.ac.pg; f. 1965; 600 serial titles, 4,000 audiovisual items; spec. colln: Papua New Guinea; microfilm unit produces microfiche edns of all major PNG serial publications; 99,250 vols (Taraka campus); Univ. Librarian ISMAEL ISIKEL KAVANAMUR (acting).

Waigani

National Library Service: POB 734, Waigani; tel. 3256200; fax 3251331; f. 1975; nat. reference library; legal deposit library; ISBN agency for Papua New Guinea; advisory services, lending and educational services; important holdings of New Guineana, particularly govt publs; Papua New Guinea colln; films and videos of Papua New Guinea; mobile school library service; 50,000 vols, 4,000 films and video recordings; Dir-Gen. DANIEL PARAIDE; publs *Directory of Libraries in Papua New Guinea* (irregular), *OLA Nius* (6 a year), *Papua New Guinea Directory of Information Sources in Science and Technology* (irregular), *Papua New Guinea National Bibliography* (1 a year), *Selective Times Index to PNG* (1 a year).

University of Papua New Guinea 'Michael Somare Library': c/o Univ. of Papua New Guinea, POB 320, University Post Office, Waigani; tel. 3260900; fax 3267187; f. 1965; 500,000 vols, 2,000 current journals, 25,000 vols in law section; Librarian IVARATURE KIVIA; publs *New Guinea Archives: A Listing* (microfiche), *New Guinea Photographic Index* (microfiche).

Subordinate library:

Medical Library: POB 5623, Boroko; f. 1976; 65,000 vols; Librarian L. WANGATAU; publ. *Papua New Guinea Medical Journal*.

Museum and Art Gallery
Boroko

Papua New Guinea National Museum and Art Gallery: POB 5560, Boroko; tel. 3252422; fax 3251779; e-mail pngmuseum@global.net.pg; f. 1954; field research in archaeology, cultural anthropology, natural history; educational tours, public programmes, broadcasts, etc.; aims to implement the National Cultural Property (Preservation) Act to protect Papua New Guinea's cultural heritage, and establish museums; library of 4,500 vols; Dir SIMON PAUL PORAITUK.

Universities

DIVINE WORD UNIVERSITY

POB 483, Madang
Telephone: 4222907
Fax: 4222812
E-mail: info@dwu.ac.pg
Internet: www.dwu.ac.pg

Founded 1979 as Divine Word Institute, present status 1996
Campuses in Modilon, Port Moresby, St Benedict and Mt Hagen; academic programmes incl. faculty of theology
Private control
Language of instruction: English
Academic year: February to October (2 semesters)
Pres.: JAN CZUBA
Vice-Pres.: Dr CECILIA NEMBOU
Vice-Pres. for Academic Affairs: Prof. PAMELA NORMAN
Vice-Pres. for Admin.: BENJAMIN NAING
Vice-Pres. for Corporate Services, Devt and Self-Reliance: NEIL HERMES

Vice-Pres. for Research and Postgraduate Studies: Dr MARETTA KULA SEMOS
Vice-Pres. for Student Affairs: ANDREW SIMPSON
Dean of Students: ANDREW POHON
Dean of Studies: PAMELA NORMAN
Registrar: CECILIA N'DROWER
Dir of Library: DAVID LLOYD
Library of 43,320 vols, 1,350 e-books and 1659 e-journals
Publication: *DWU Research Journal* (2 a year)

DEANS

Faculty of Arts: Dr LINDA SUE CROWL
Faculty of Business and Management: Dr ROMULO LINDIO
Faculty of Education: Dr CATHERINE NONGKAS
Faculty of Flexible Learning: Dr LYNUS YAMUNA
Faculty of Health Sciences: Dr PASCAL MICHON

PACIFIC ADVENTIST UNIVERSITY

PMB, Boroko, 111 NCD
Telephone: 3280200
Fax: 3281257
E-mail: administration@pau.ac.gp
Internet: www.pau.ac.pg

Founded 1984 as Pacific Adventist College, present status 1997
Campuses in Koiari Park and Boroko; affiliated campuses: Fiji and Sonoma
Private control
Language of instruction: English
Academic year: February to August
Chancellor: Dr BARRY OLIVER
Vice-Chancellor: Dr BEN THOMAS
Deputy Vice-Chancellor: TRACIE MAFILE'O
Dir of Research and Postgraduate Studies: Dr LALEN SIMEON
Dir of Student Services: THOMAS DAVAI (acting)
Registrar: PELE ALU
Number of teachers: 41
Number of students: 379
Publication: *Davaria*

DEANS

School of Arts and Humanities: Dr JENNIFER LITAU
School of Business: Dr KHIN MAUNG KYI
School of Education: Dr KURESA TAGA'I
School of Health Science: NINA PANGIAU
School of Science and Technology: ELISAPESI MANSON (acting)
School of Theology: Dr DAVID THIELE

PAPUA NEW GUINEA UNIVERSITY OF NATURAL RESOURCES AND ENVIRONMENT

PMB, Rabaul, E New Britain Province
Telephone: 9839144
Fax: 9839166
Internet: www.unre.ac.pg

Founded 1965 as Vudal Agricultural College, present status 1997, present name 2005
Campuses in Vudal, Popondetta, Sepik Central and Kavieng
Language of instruction: English
Academic year: February to November
State control
Language of instruction: English
Depts of management studies, agriculture, fisheries, forestry
Chancellor and Chair.: (vacant)
Pro-Chancellor: MARGARET ELIAS
Pro-Vice-Chancellor for Academic and Planning: (vacant)

Pro-Vice-Chancellor for Admin. and Devt: (vacant)
Vice-Chancellor: Prof. Dr PHILIP SIAGURU
Registrar: HENRY GIOVEN
Bursar: JACKSON RODGERS
Librarian: BRUCE NINGAKUN
Library of 25,000
Number of teachers: 20
Number of students: 380

DEANS

School of Natural Resources: Dr ALAN QUARTERMAN

PAPUA NEW GUINEA UNIVERSITY OF TECHNOLOGY

PMB, Lae
Telephone: 4734206
Fax: 4757776
E-mail: lfugre@admin.unitech.ac.pg
Internet: www.unitech.ac.pg

Founded 1965 as Papua New Guinea Institute of Higher Technical Education, present name and status 1973
Depts of agriculture, applied physics, applied science, architecture and bldg, business studies, communications and devt studies, civil engineering, electrical and communication engineering, forestry, mathematics and computer science, mechanical engineering, mining engineering and surveying and lands
Language of instruction: English
State control
Academic year: February to November (2 semesters)
Chancellor: A. TOLOLO
Pro-Chancellor: R. KEKEDO
Vice-Chancellor and Pro-Vice Chancellor for Admin.: Dr MISTY BALOILOI
Pro-Vice Chancellor for Academic: Dr MUHAMMED A. SATTER
Registrar: ALLAN J. Q. SAKO
Univ. Librarian: ISMAEL ISIKEL KAVANAMUR (acting)
Library: see under Libraries and Archives
Number of teachers: 92
Number of students: 2,600
Publications: *UniTech Reporter* (12 a year), *Research Report*, *Vice-Chancellor's Report*.

UNIVERSITY OF GOROKA

POB 1078, Goroka, EHP
Telephone: 5311727
Fax: 5311742
Internet: www.uog.ac.pg

Founded 1997 by merger of two faculties of Univ. of Papua New Guinea (UPNG) and Goroka Teacher's College (GTC)
State control
Language of instruction: English
Academic year: January to December
Chancellor: PETER BAKI
Vice-Chancellor: Dr GAIRO ONAGI (acting)
Pro-Vice-Chancellor for Academic Affairs and Devt: Dr MICHAEL MEL (acting)
Pro-Vice-Chancellor for Admin.: Dr JAMES YOKO (acting)
Dir of Student Services: MONICA PUSAL
Dir of Student Admin.: E. MAKARAI
Librarian and Head of Dept: LEAH KALAMOROH
Library of 100,000 vols of monographs, 110 periodicals, 400 serials and 1000 visual items
Number of teachers: 80
Number of students: 1,800
Publication: *Papua New Guinea Journal of Teacher Education* (1 a year)

DEANS

Faculty of Education: Dr KAPA DARIUS KELEP-
MALPO
Faculty of Humanities: DAVID AWAY HOSEA
Faculty of Science: Dr POORANALINGHAM
JEYARATHAN
School of Graduate Studies: Dr SAM NAJIKE

UNIVERSITY OF PAPUA NEW GUINEA

Box 320, University Post Office, Waigani
Telephone: 3260900
Fax: 3267187
E-mail: pr&m@upng.ac.pg
Internet: www.upng.ac.pg
Founded 1965

Campuses: Waigani (HQ) and Taurama
Language of instruction: English
State control
Academic year: February to September (2
semesters)
Chancellor: Sir ALKAN TOLOLO
Pro-Chancellor: Dr ROSEMARY KEKEDO
Vice-Chancellor: Prof. ROSS HYNES
Deputy Vice-Chancellor: N. R. KUMAN
Registrar: VINCENT MALAIBE
Library: see under Libraries and Archives
Number of teachers: 700
Number of students: 4,416
Publications: *Melanesian Law Journal* (2 a
year), *PNG Law, Research in Melanesia* (2
a year), *Science in New Guinea* (4 a year),

South Pacific Journal of Psychology (1 a
year), *Yagl-Ambu*

DEANS

Centre for Research and Postgraduate Stud-
ies: Dr Prof. SIMON SAULEI
School of Business Admin.: Prof. Dr ALBERT
MELLAM
School of Humanities and Social Science:
Prof. Dr KENNETH SUMBUK
School of Law: S. KAIPU (acting)
School of Medicine and Health Sciences: Prof.
Dr ISI KEVAU
School of Natural and Physical Sciences:
Prof. Dr L. HILL (acting)

PARAGUAY

The Higher Education System

Paraguay, ruled by Spain from the 16th century, achieved independence in 1811. The oldest institution of higher education is the Universidad Nacional de Asunción (founded in 1889). The next oldest university was not opened until the 1960s. Following the end of military rule in 1989, several universities were established in the 1990s. The governing law of higher education is Law 136/93 (1993), which led to the creation of the Consejo de Universidades (Council of Universities). In 2006/07 there were 180,367 students enrolled in university-level education. In 2001 there were a total of 111 university-level institutions.

Applicants must have the Bachillerato in order to gain admission to higher education, and universities may set individual entry requirements. The Título de Licenciatura is the main undergraduate degree, and is awarded after four years of study. Under Law 136/93 the Título de Licenciatura is both an academic and a professional title. Undergraduate degrees in professional fields of study, such as economics, engineering, law and medicine, last upwards of four years. There is no uniform system of postgraduate degrees, which were not available in Paraguay before 1991. However, the Universidad Nacional de Asunción has established a system that is being considered by the Consejo de Universidades, consisting of: Diplomado (Diploma), a postgraduate short course in a professional field of study; Especialización (Specialization), undertaken as part of the undergraduate degree; Maestría (Masters), which lasts two years; and Título de Doctorado (Doctorate) or Doctor en Ciencias (Doctor of Sciences), which were available at nine universities (four public and five private) in 2005.

Post-secondary technical and vocational education is available mainly at instituciones técnicas superiores (higher technical institutions) under the authority of the Dirección de Institutos Técnicos Superiores (Directorate of Higher Technical Institutes). The Título de Técnico Superior is awarded after completion of two years or 1,500 classroom hours of study.

The Agencia Nacional de Evaluación y Acreditación de la Educación Superior (ANEAES—National Agency for Evaluation and Accreditation of Higher Education) was founded in 2003 following the enactment of Law 2072/03. ANEAES is the national body for quality assurance and accreditation of higher education at undergraduate and postgraduate levels. Paraguay also participates in the Mecanismo Experimental de Acreditación de Carreras del MERCOSUR.

Regulatory and Representative Bodies

GOVERNMENT

Consejo Nacional de Educación y Cultura (CONEC) (National Council for Education and Culture): Tte. Aponte 609 y Juan de Salazar, Asunción; tel. (21) 226-341; e-mail secret_conec@webmail.com.py; internet www.mec.gov.py/conec; autonomous org. working with the Min. of Education and Culture on the formulation and implementation of nat. policy on education and culture; proposes ways to develop and improve the educational system; mems are appointed by the Pres. of the Republic and serve a term of 3 years; 12 mems; Pres. THE MINISTER OF EDUCATION AND CULTURE; Admin. Dir Lic. MIRTA ELIZABETH ARMOA.

Dirección General de Educación Superior (Directorate of Higher Education): O'Leary 615 esq. Gral. Díaz, Edif. Lider II, Piso 4, Asunción; tel. (21) 498-716; e-mail info@educacionsuperior.mec.gov.py; internet educacionsuperior.mec.gov.py; Dir-Gen. Dr DOMINGO PEDROZO.

Ministry of Education and Culture: Chile, Humaitá y Piribebuy, Asunción; tel. (21) 44-3078; fax (21) 44-3919; internet www.paraguaygobierno.gov.py/mec; Minister MARÍA ESTER JIMÉNEZ.

ACCREDITATION

Agencia Nacional de Evaluación y Acreditación de la Educación Superior (ANEAES) (National Agency for Evaluation and Accreditation of Higher Education): 25 de Mayo 640 esq. Antequera Edificio 'Garantía', Piso 2 ofic. 203, Asunción; tel. (21) 444-644; e-mail info@aneaes.gov.py; internet www.aneaes.gov.py; f. 2003; Pres. Dra CARMEN QUINTANA-HORÁK.

Learned Societies

GENERAL

Academia de la Lengua y Cultura Guaraní (Academy of the Guaraní Language and Culture): Calle España y Mompox, Asunción; f. 1975; Pres. Dr RUFINO AREVALO PARIS; Sec. ANTONIO E. GONZÁLEZ; publ. *Revista*.

LANGUAGE AND LITERATURE

Academia Paraguaya de la Lengua Española (Paraguayan Academy of the Spanish Language): Avda España 1098, Asunción; tel. (21) 206-048; fax (21) 224-106; e-mail acapales@sce.cnc.una.py; internet www.aparle.org; f. 1927; corresp. of the Real Academia Española (Madrid); 26 mems; Pres. JOSÉ ANTONIO MORENO RUFFINELLI; Gen. Sec. Dra RENÉE FERRER DE ARRÉLLAGA; publ. *Anales*.

Alliance Française: Estigarribia 1039, Calle Estados Unidos, Casilla de Correo 2076, Asunción; tel. (21) 210-503; fax (21) 212-697; e-mail info@alianzafrancesa.edu.py; internet www.alianzafrancesa.edu.py; offers courses and exams in French language and culture and promotes cultural exchange with France; Dir FERNAND DEFOURNIER.

MEDICINE

Sociedad Paraguaya de Pediatría (Paediatrics Society): Mcal Estigarribia 1764 c/ Rca Francesa, Asunción; tel. (21) 447-493; fax (21) 226-795; e-mail sppsecre@spp.org.py; internet www.spp.org.py; f. 1938; Pres. Dr RAÚL ALBERTO OLMEDO SISUL; Gen. Sec. Dra MARÍA DEL ROCÍO BOGADO.

RELIGION, SOCIOLOGY AND ANTHROPOLOGY

Asociación Indigenista del Paraguay: Mompox y Manuel Gondra, CC 1838, 1209 Asunción; tel. (21) 448-592; fax (21) 448-592; e-mail aindigenistadelpy@tigo.com.py; internet www.aip.org.py; f. 1942; anthropology, devt of indigenous communities; 170 mems; library of 1,640 vols; Pres. Dr RICARDO AZORERO MORENO; Sec. MARIA JOSÉ MORENO.

Research Institutes

ECONOMICS, LAW AND POLITICS

Centro Interdisciplinario de Derecho Social y Economía Política (CIDSEP): Alberdi 855 casi Piribebuy, Asunción; tel. (21) 445-429; e-mail cidsep@conexion.com.py; internet www.cidsep.org; f. 1986; attached to Universidad Católica 'Nuestra Señora de la Asunción'; Dir Dr CARLOS ALBERTO GONZÁLEZ.

Centro Paraguayo de Estudios de Desarrollo Económico y Social: Mariscal Estigarribia, 1050 Asunción.

HISTORY, GEOGRAPHY AND ARCHAEOLOGY

Instituto Geográfico Militar: Av. Artigas 920 casi Saltos del Guaira, Asunción; tel. (21) 222-443; fax (21) 204-959; e-mail disergemil@highway.com.py; Dir Coronel ÓSCAR ANTONIO NÚÑEZ; Sec. E. LÓPEZ MOREIRA.

MEDICINE

Instituto Nacional de Parasitología (National Institute of Parasitology): Instituto de Microbiología, Facultad de Medicina, Casilla Correo 1102, Asunción; f. 1963; 5 mems; library; Dir Dr ARQUIMEDES CANESE; publ. *Revista Paraguaya de Microbiología* (1 a year).

RELIGION, SOCIOLOGY AND ANTHROPOLOGY

Centro de Estudios Antropológicos de la Universidad Católica: Casilla de Correo 1718, Asunción; fax (21) 441-044; e-mail ceaduc@uca.edu.py; internet www.ceaduc.uca.edu.py; f. 1950, affiliated to Universidad Católica 'Nuestra Señora de la Asuncion' 1971; 25 mems; Dir JOSÉ ZANARDINI; Sec. MYRIAN AURORA GAONA MARTÍNEZ; publs *Estudios Paraguayos, Suplemento Antropológico, Universidad Católica* (2 a year).

Centro Paraguayo de Estudios Socio-lógicos: Eligio Ayala 973 e/ Brasil y EE.UU., Asunción; tel. (21) 443-734; fax (21) 446-617; e-mail cpi@supernet.com .py; f. 1964; research and development in social sciences: migra-tion, bi-lingualism, population structure, rural development, role of women in the work force, education, etc.; library: specia-lized library of 5,000 vols, 4,000 documents; Dir MARÍA MAGDALENA RIVAROLA; publ. *Revista Paraguaya de Sociología* (3 a year).

TECHNOLOGY

Centro Paraguayo de Ingenieros: Avda España 959, Casilla 336, Asunción; tel. 202-424; fax 205-019; e-mail cpi@supernet.com .py; internet www.cpi.org.py; f. 1939; Pres. Ing. NICANOR FLEITAS BAREIRO; Sec. Ing. CÉSAR MANUEL LÓPEZ BOSIO; publ. *Ingeniería 2000* (1 a year).

Instituto Nacional de Tecnología, Nor-malización y Metrología (INTN): Avda Artigas 3973 y Gral Roa, Asunción; tel. (21) 290-160; fax (21) 290-873; e-mail intn@intn .gov.py; internet www.intn.gov.py; f. 1965; carries out research and technological stud-ies, and lays down technical norms; Dir Ing. OSCAR SALAZAR YARYES; publ. *Normas Técni-cas Paraguayas*.

Libraries and Archives

Asunción

Archivo del Ministerio de Relaciones Exteriores (Archive of the Ministry of For-eign Affairs): Calle Juan E. Oleary 222 esq. Pdte Franco, Asunción; tel. (21) 493-928; fax (21) 493-210; e-mail smareski@mre.gov.py; internet www.mre.gov.py; contains 200 lin-ear m of documents incl. Colecciones de los Documentos Diplomáticos from 1870 and the Archivo General de las Indias from 1545.

Archivo Nacional de Asunción: Mcal. Estigarribia esq. Iturbe, Asunción; tel. and fax (21) 447-311; e-mail info@ archivonacionaldeasuncion.org; internet archivonacionaldeasuncion.org; f. 1544; attached to Dirección General de Archivos, Bibliotecas y Museos de la Secretaría de Cultura; c. 7,000 vols of documents and 2.5m. records dating from 1534; Dir NORMA IBÁÑEZ DE YEGROS.

Biblioteca Americana (American Library): Mariscal Estigarribia e Iturbe, Asunción; attached to the Museo Nacional de Bellas Artes (*q.v.*).

Biblioteca de la Sociedad Científica del Paraguay (Library of the Paraguayan Sci-entific Society): Andrés Barbero 230 esq. Artigas, Asunción; tel. (21) 205-438; f. 1921; 29,300 vols on science.

Biblioteca Nacional: De la Residenta 820 casi Perú, Asunción; tel. (21) 204-670; e-mail info@bibliotecanacional.org; internet www .bibliotecanacional.org; f. 1887; 44,000 vols; Dir Lic. RAMÓN ROLANDI TORRES.

Biblioteca Pública del Ministerio de Defensa Nacional (Public Library of the Ministry of Defence): Avda Mariscal López y Vicepresidente Sánchez, Planta baja, Asun-ción; tel. (21) 223-965; fax (21) 210-052; e-mail mendozah@cu.com.py; internet www .mdn.gov.py; 2,000 vols, 7,000 photographs; Dir Col HUGO RAMÓN MENDOZA MARTÍNEZ.

Museums and Art Galleries

Asunción

Casa de la Independencia: 14 de Mayo esq. Pdte Franco, Asunción; tel. (21) 493-918; e-mail info@casadelaindependencia.org.py;

internet www.casadelaindependencia.org .py; f. 1965; historical museum of the colonial period; Pres. Dr GERARDO FOGEL; Dir Prof. CARLOS ALBERTO PUSINERI SCALA.

Colección Carlos Alberto Pusineri Scala: Lugano 1153 e/ Hernandarias y Lugano, Asunción; tel. (21) 420370; e-mail museocarlospusineri@gmail.com; internet www.museopusineri.org; f. 1950; collns of Guaraní archaeology, trophies of Paraguayan wars, colonial objects; small library of Para-guayan history, numismatics and anthropol-ogy; Dir CARLOS ALBERTO PUSINERI SCALA.

Jardín Botánico y Museo de Historia Natural (Botanical Gardens and Natural History Museum): Artigas y Av. Primer Presidente, Asunción; tel. (21) 290-269; fax (21) 291-255; f. 1914; herbarium, zoological garden and museum, bacteriological labora-tory, agricultural experimental station; Dir Ing. GILDO INSFRÁN GUERROS; publ. *Revista*.

Museo Etnográfico 'Andrés Barbero': España 217, Asunción; tel. and fax (21) 441696; e-mail museobarbero@ museobarbero.org.py; internet www .museobarbero.org.py; f. 1929; archaeology, ethnography, ethnology, history, archives, MSS, photographs, world music; library of 30,000 vols; Dir Lic. ADELINA PUSINERI; Vice-Dir Lic. RAQUEL ZALAZAR.

Museo Histórico Militar (Museum of Mili-tary History): Avda Mariscal López 140 y Vicepresidente Sánchez, Planta baja del edificio del Ministerio de Defensa Nacional, Asunción; tel. (21) 223-965; fax (21) 210-052; e-mail mendozah@cu.com.py; internet www .mdn.gov.py; f. 1942; recent war collns; Dir Col HUGO RAMÓN MENDOZA MARTÍNEZ.

Museo Nacional de Bellas Artes: Mariscal Estigarribia esq. Iturbe, Asunción; tel. (21) 447-716; f. 1887; the paintings and sculpture of Juan Silvano Godoy form the basis of the collection; Dir JOSÉ LATERZA PARODI.

Yaguarón

Museo Doctor Francia: Yaguarón; f. 1968; relics of Paraguay's first dictator, 'El Supremo'; Pres. Dr FABIO RIVAS; Dir Dr JULIO CÉSAR CHAVES.

Universities

UNIVERSIDAD AMERICANA

Avda Brasilia 1100, Asunción

Telephone and fax (21) 295-710
E-mail: universidad@uamericana.edu.py
Internet: www.uamericana.edu.py

Founded 1994

School of administration and economics

Pres.: Dr ANDRÉS BENKÖ KAPUVÁRY
Rector: Dr BENJAMÍN FERNÁNDEZ BOGADO
Vice-Rector for Academic Affairs: Ing. EDMUNDO DURÁN
Vice-Rector for Administration and Finance: Ing. RODOLFO CORTHORN
Vice-Rector for International Relations: Lic. SERGIO SOMERVILLE

Library of 5,000 vols, 100 periodicals
Number of teachers: 200
Number of students: 4,000

UNIVERSIDAD AUTÓNOMA DE ASUNCIÓN

Jejuí 667, entre O'Leary y 15 de Agosto, Asunción

Telephone: (21) 440-980
Fax: (21) 497-299
E-mail: info@uaa.edu.py
Internet: www.uaa.edu.py

Founded 1978 as Escuela Superior de Admin-istración de Empresas; present name and status 1991

Private control
Languages of instruction: English, Portu-guese, Spanish
Academic year: March to February

Rector: Dr JOSÉ DE JESÚS RÍOS TORRES
Vice-Rector: JUAN DE DIOS GARBETT SCHAERER
Secretary-General: Lic. MARÍA LUISA PUERTAS LÓPEZ

Library of 17,500 vols
Number of teachers: 400
Number of students: 6,000

Publication: *Revista Internacional de Inves-tigación en Ciencias Sociales*

DEANS

Faculty of Economics and Business Admin-istration: Dr SALVIO GÓMEZ ZORRILLA
Faculty of Health Sciences: Dr FRANCISCA ROMERO DE FLORES
Faculty of Humanities and Communication Sciences: MARIEN PEGGY MARTÍNEZ
Faculty of Law, Politics and Social Science: Dr ANTONIO SOLJANCIC
Faculty of Science and Technology: Lic. HUGO CORREA EDWARDS

UNIVERSIDAD AUTÓNOMA DEL PARAGUAY

Gen. Díaz 1053, Colón 568, Asunción

Telephone: (21) 441-924
Fax: (21) 447-579
E-mail: rectorado@uap.edu.py
Internet: www.uap.edu.py

Founded 1991

Rector: Dr CARLOS LAHAYE AGUIAR
Vice-Rector: Dr ARNALDO LATAZA MIGONE

DEANS

Faculty of Behavioural Sciences: Prof. Dr JOSÉ ANTONIO ARIAS
Faculty of Obstetrics: Prof. Dr REINALDO BARRETO M.
Faculty of Optics: Lic. LEONARDO GARCÍA
Pierre Fauchard Faculty of Dentistry: Prof. Dr ARMANDO MERCADO B.

UNIVERSIDAD CATÓLICA 'NUESTRA SEÑORA DE LA ASUNCIÓN'

Cantaluppi y G. Molinas, Asunción

Telephone: (21) 441-044
Fax: (21) 445-245
E-mail: relinter@uc.edu.py
Internet: www.uc.edu.py

Founded 1960
Private control
Language of instruction: Spanish
Academic year: March to December

Chancellor: Mgr IGNACIO GORGOZA (Bishop of Encarnación)
Rector: Mgr Dr MICHEL MARCEL GIBAUD WESTERMANS
Vice-Rector for Academic Affairs: Prof. Dra CARMEN QUINTANA DE HORAK
Vice-Rector for Administrative Affairs: Prof. Lic. CARLOS L. AYALA VERA
Secretary-General: (vacant)
Director of the Office of Institutional Rela-tions: Abog. MINERVA IZQUIERDO
Librarian: Licda MARGARITA KALLSEN

Number of teachers: 1,922
Number of students: 18,000

Publications: *Anuario* (university), *Anuario* (Faculty of Law and Diplomatic Science), *Anuario* (Faculty of Philosophy and Human Sciences), *Cuadernos de Discusión* (Faculty of Philosophy and Human Sci-ences), *Estudios Antropológicos* (Anthropo-logical Studies), *La Quincena* (Faculty of Philosophy and Human Sciences), *Lila*, *Revista Jurídica* (Juridical Review), *Uni-versitas* (Tomás Moro Institute of the Fac-ulty of Law and Diplomatic Science),

Ventana Abierta (Faculty of Philosophy and Human Sciences)

DEANS

Admissions Courses (Asunción): Prof. Lic. XENIA JERMOLIEF DE CATTONI (Dir)
Conservatoire (Asunción): Prof. Abog. GLORIA MAZÓ (Dir)
Department of Theology and Pastoral Action (Asunción): Pbro SILVIO SUÁREZ (Dir)
Faculty of Accounting (Alto Paraná): Lic. ARMÍN NICOLÁS VILLAGRA
Faculty of Accounting, Administration and Economics (Asunción): Prof. Lic. HÉCTOR ENRIQUE ALMIRÓN FIGUEREDO
Faculty of Accounting, Administration and Economics (Concepción): Lic. MARÍA VICTORIA COELHO DE SOUZA DE PÉREZ
Faculty of Accounting and Administration (Guairá): Lic. DAXI SILVANA DUARTE DE GARCÍA
Faculty of Agriculture (Caaguazú): Ing. Agr. PAULINO INVERNIZZI
Faculty of Chemistry (Guairá): Quim. NILSA BATTAGLIA DE MARECOS
Faculty of Economics (Itapúa): Lic. FRANCISCO SOLANO MACIEL
Faculty of Education (Guairá): Lic. RICARDA AIDEÉ JIMÉNEZ DE CABRERA
Faculty of Education (Itapúa): Lic. MARÍA ISABEL MADRAZZO DE GARAY
Faculty of Education, Law and Early Education (Concepción): Lic. JOSEFINA OVELAR DE BENÍTEZ
Faculty of Health Sciences (Alto Paraná): Dra PETRONA VÁZQUEZ DE CARDOZO
Faculty of Health Sciences (Asunción): Prof. Dr JOSÉ CORVALÁN
Faculty of Law (Alto Paraná): Dr PORFIRIO ZACARÍAS LEÓN
Faculty of Law (Caaguazú): Abog. SILVIO MARTÍNEZ JIMÉNEZ
Faculty of Law (Guairá): Abog. ESTHER LISBOA VDA. DE BOGADO
Faculty of Law (Itapúa): Abog. SERGIO MARTYNIUK
Faculty of Law and Diplomatic Science (Asunción): Prof. Abog. JOSÉ MARÍA CABRAL ALCARAZ
Faculty of Medicine (Guairá): Dr FRANCISCO DUARTE LEGAL
Faculty of Philosophy and Human Sciences (Asunción): Prof. Lic. ILDE SILVERO ÁLVAREZ
Faculty of Science and Technology (Asunción): Prof. Ing. JUAN ALBERTO GONZÁLEZ MEYER
Faculty of Science and Technology (Itapúa): Arq. MARIO ZAPUTOVICH RUOSH
Faculty of Technology (Alto Paraná): Ing. MANUEL CHAMORRO ALDERETE
Higher Institute of Theology (Asunción): Pbro JOAQUÍN MEDINA (Dir)

CAMPUSES

Alto Paraná: Pro-Rector Lic. HUGO EUGENIO RIVAROLA GODOY.
Asunción: Pro-Rector Ing. GERÓNIMO BELLASSAI BAUDO.
Caaguazú: Pro-Rector Abog. ALBERTO GODOY VERA.
Carapeguá: Pro-Rector (vacant).
Concepción: Pro-Rector Lic. MARGARITA MARÍA PÁEZ DE COMELLI.
Guairá: Pro-Rector Lic. RUFINO FERNÁNDEZ RAMOS.
Itapúa: Pro-Rector Dr JESÚS RENÉ HAURÓN.

UNIVERSIDAD COLUMBIA DEL PARAGUAY

25 de Mayo 658 y Antequera, Asunción
Telephone: (21) 206-526
Fax: (21) 490-811

Internet: www.columbia.edu.py
Founded 1991
Rector: ROBERTO ELÍAS CANESE
Courses offered in accountancy and business studies, computer engineering, hotel management and tourism, law, marketing, organizational psychology, social engineering.

UNIVERSIDAD COMUNERA

San José 630 y Artigas, Asunción
Telephone: (21) 223-892
Founded 1992
Rector: ADRIANO IRALA BURGOS
Faculties of agricultural administration, tourism.

UNIVERSIDAD DEL CONO SUR DE LAS AMÉRICAS

Avda España 372 Calle Brasil, Asunción
Telephone: (21) 213-872
Fax: (21) 212-658
E-mail: ucsa@ucsa.py
Internet: www.ucsa.edu.py
Founded 1996
Rector: Ing. LUIS ALBERTO LIMA
Academic Director: Lic. ANDRÉS ANTONIO VILLALBA COLMÁN
Vice-Rector for Administration: Lic. HELGA MARÍA DE SARUBBI
Vice-Rector for Postgraduate Studies: Lic. JUDITH FARIAS DA FONSECA
Vice-Rector for Research and Development: Lic. JOSÉ BLÁS VILLALBA

SUBJECT COORDINATORS

Business: Lic. CLARISSA MELINA RODRÍGUEZ CAÑETE
Engineering: Ing. JOSÉ JUAN RICART BOSSI
Social Studies: Lic. NANCY MIRIAN CAÑETE DE GINZO

UNIVERSIDAD DEL NORTE

Avda España 676, entre Rosa Peña y Boquerón, Asunción
Telephone: (21) 229-450
Fax: (21) 228-217
E-mail: info@uninorte.edu.py
Internet: www.uninorte.edu.py
Founded 1991
Academic year: March to December
Rector: JUAN MANUEL MARCOS
Library of 20,000 vols

DEANS

Faculty of Business Administration: CÉSAR CRUZ ROA
Faculty of Chemistry: ANA KALENIUSKA
Faculty of Education and Humanities: SERGIO MARCOS GUSTAFSON
Faculty of Engineering: LUIS FERNANDO MEYER CANILLAS
Faculty of Health Sciences: CARLOS MICHELETTO
Faculty of Law and Politics: CARMEN GUBETICH DE CATTONI
Faculty of Medicine: JUAN CARLOS CHAPARRO
Faculty of Technology: CARLOS CABALLERO
Postgraduate Faculty: JUAN MANUEL MARCOS

UNIVERSIDAD DEL PACÍFICO

México 775, Asunción
Telephone: (21) 450-287.

UNIVERSIDAD EVANGÉLICA DEL PARAGUAY

José Berges 459, Asunción
Telephone: (21) 223-496
Fax: (21) 223-496

E-mail: unievangelica@rieder.net.py
Internet: www.uep.edu.py
Founded 1994
Academic year: February to December
Faculties of accounting, administration and economics, health sciences, humanities and educational sciences, modern languages, music, nursing, psychology and human development, theology
Rector: DIONISIO ÓRTIZ MUTTI
Vice-Rector: MELITA WALL
Sec.-Gen.: ESTEBAN MISSENA DEL CASTILLO
Number of teachers: 193
Number of students: 1,374

UNIVERSIDAD NACIONAL DE ASUNCIÓN

Avda España, Nº 1098, Asunción 910
Telephone: (21) 227-682
Fax: (21) 224-106
E-mail: sgeneral@rec.una.py
Internet: www.una.py
Founded 1889
State control
Language of instruction: Spanish
Academic year: March to December
Rector: Prof. Ing. Agr. PEDRO GERARDO GONZÁLEZ
Vice-Rector: Prof. Arq. AMADO FRANCO NAVONI
Gen. Sec.: Prof. Ing. Agr. JULIO RENÁN PANIAGUA ALCARAZ
Librarian: Lic. JULIA ROMÁN RODRÍGUEZ
Library of 184,810 vols, 54,260 periodicals, 3,010 audiovisual materials
Number of teachers: 6,200
Number of students: 41,138
Publications: *Researches and UNA studies* (2 a year), *UNA Revista* (2 a year, electronic)

DEANS

Faculty of Agricultural Engineering: Prof. Ing. Agr. LORENZO MEZA LÓPEZ
Faculty of Architecture, Design and Art: Prof. Arq. RICARDO MANUEL MEYER CANILLAS
Faculty of Chemistry: Prof. Dr ANDRÉS AMARILLA
Faculty of Dentistry: Prof. Dr RUBÉN DI TORE AQUINO
Faculty of Economics: Prof. Dr ANTONIO RAMÓN RODRÍGUEZ ROJAS
Faculty of Engineering: Prof. Ing. ISACIO EUSEBIO VALLEJOS AQUINO
Faculty of Exact and Natural Sciences: Prof. CONSTANTINO NICOLÁS GUEFOS KAPSALIS
Faculty of Law and Social Sciences: Prof. Dr ANTONIO FRETES
Faculty of Medicine: Prof. Dr ANÍBAL HERIBERTO PERIS MANCHINI
Faculty of Philosophy: Prof. Lic. MARÍA ANGÉLICA GONZÁLEZ DE LEZCANO
Faculty of Veterinary Sciences: Prof. Dr FROILÁN ENRIQUE PERALTA TORRES
Polytechnic Faculty: Prof. ABEL CONCEPCIÓN BERNAL CASTILLO

UNIVERSIDAD NACIONAL DEL ESTE

POB 389, Calle 3 y Los Palmitos, Ciudad del Este, Alto Paraná
Telephone: (61) 63804
Fax: (61) 68664
Internet: www.une.edu.py
Founded 1993
Rector: Dr GLIBERTO RUIZ CARVALLO
Vice-Rector: Lic. VÍCTOR ALFREDO BRÍTEZ CHAMORRO
Faculties of agricultural engineering, economics, health sciences, law and social sciences, philosophy.

PERU

The Higher Education System

From the 16th century Peru was under Spanish control until independence was declared in 1821 and achieved in 1824. The oldest universities date from the period of Spanish rule, notably the Universidad Nacional Mayor de San Marcos de Lima (founded in 1551) and the Universidad Nacional de San Cristóbal de Huamanga (founded in 1677). The Universidad Nacional de la Libertad (founded in 1824) was the first university established in the independent period; its founder was Simón Bolívar. The Universidad Nacional de San Agustín de Arequipa (founded in 1828) followed shortly after. Higher education consists of pre-university and university levels. The Constitution of 1993 abolished the right to free university education. In 2000 there were 435,637 students in university-level education, and in 2008 there were 343,321 students enrolled at other institutions of higher education. In the same year 286,677 students were enrolled in vocational institutions and 20,472 attended specialist institutions. In 2007 there were 25 national and 10 private universities, 150 teacher training institutes and 250 higher technological institutes.

The Ministry of Education is responsible for certain higher education institutions, but universities are largely autonomous. However, the Asamblea Nacional de Rectores (National Assembly of Rectors) is responsible for the coordination of universities at a national level and for ensuring that national standards are met. Technical and vocational education is provided under the supervision of the Dirección General de Educación Superior y Técnico Profesional (General Directorate of Higher and Technical and Professional Education).

Students must hold the Certificado de Educación Secundaria Común Completa (certificate of completion of secondary educa-

tion) in order to sit the university entrance examination. The first undergraduate degree is the Bachiller (Bachelors), awarded after a three- to five-year period of specialization. Upon completion of a thesis, the Licenciado or professional title is then awarded. Some of the larger public universities offer postgraduate degrees, which are primarily the Maestría (Masters) and the Doctorado (Doctorate—the highest academic qualification in the education system); both degrees require completion of two years of study.

Post-secondary technical and vocational education is provided by Institutos Superiores Pedagógicos (Teacher Training Institutes) and Institutos Superiores Tecnológicos (ISTs—Higher Technological Institutes). The Especialista Profesional and Título de Bachiller Profesional are the main qualifications offered by the ISTs. There is no assessment scheme to demonstrate the quality of training provided by either, although some initial steps towards more rigorous standards have been taken by the Ministry of Education. Traditional areas such as farming, commerce and technical have been overtaken by new subjects, such as business administration, accounting, electronics and information technologies. Public ISTs have economic difficulties keeping up with innovations and, with a few exceptions, are seen to have weak links with employers. The private sector has adapted to the changing needs of employers, but standards are variable. A definite link can be seen between the price of a private IST course and the quality of training given. A few private universities in Lima offer three-year technical diplomas of similar standing to those of the private ISTs. Training for industrial work is offered by the National Service for Industrial Training. This has over 35 training centres in Lima and major cities throughout Peru.

Regulatory and Representative Bodies

GOVERNMENT

Ministry of Education: Avda Van De Velde 160, cuadra 33, Avda Javier Prado Este, San Borja, Lima 41; tel. (1) 435-3900; fax (1) 437-0471; e-mail postmaster@minedu.gob.pe; internet www.minedu.gob.pe; Minister José Antonio Chang Escobedo; Permanent Sec. José Enrique Cabrera García.

NATIONAL BODY

Asamblea Nacional de Rectores (Rectors' National Assembly): Calle Aldabas 337, Urb. Las Gardenias, Surco, Lima 33; tel. (1) 275-4608; e-mail webmaster@anr.edu.pe; internet www.anr.edu.pe; f. 1983; 34 mems; library of 30,000 vols; Pres. Dr Iván Rodríguez Chávez; Exec. Dir Ing. José Torres Vásquez; publs *Universidad, Escuelas y/o Carreras Profesionales, Grados y Títulos* (statistical bulletin), *Desarrollo Universitario* (bulletin).

Learned Societies

GENERAL

Academia Peruana de la Lengua (Peruvian Academy of Language): Palacio de Osambela, Conde de Superunda 298, Lima 1; fax (1) 427-7987; internet academiaperuanadelalengua.org; f. 1887;

corresp. of the Real Academia Española (Madrid); 30 mems; Dir Dr Luis Jaime Cisneros; Sec. Dr Martha Hildebrandt; publ. *Boletín* (1 a year).

UNESCO Office Lima: Avda Javier Prado Este 2465, San Borja, Lima 41; tel. (1) 224-2526; fax (1) 476-9872; e-mail unescope@amauta.rcp.net.pe; internet www.unesco.org/lima; Rep. Patricia Uribe Arango.

ARCHITECTURE AND TOWN PLANNING

Colegio de Arquitectos del Perú: Avda San Felipe 999, Jesús María, Lima 11; tel. (1) 265-4098; fax (1) 471-5058; internet www.cap.org.pe; f. 1962; 3,717 mems; library of 3,500 vols; Dean Javier Sota Nadal.

BIBLIOGRAPHY, LIBRARY SCIENCE AND MUSEOLOGY

Asociación Peruana de Archiveros (Peruvian Association of Archivists): Archivo General de la Nación, Calle Manuel Cuadros s/n, Palacio de Justicia, Apdo 3124, Lima.

Colegio de Bibliotecólogos del Perú: Avda 2 de Mayo 1545, Oficina 218, Lima 27; fax (1) 442-7513; e-mail informes@bibliotecologos.pe; internet bibliotecologos.pe; f. 1990; 320 mems; Dean Norma Altamirano de Hurtado.

EDUCATION

Asociación Nacional de Educadoras Sampedranas: Máximo Abril 695, Jesús María, Lima 11; tel. (1) 310562; f. 1910; aims to contribute to the development and improvement of national education; educa-

tional research, 'Education for Peace', educational innovation, institutional development; 6,200 mems; library of 1,000 vols with special collection: 'Education for Peace'; Pres. Peregrina Morgan de Goñi; Sec. Nanete Pérez de Pilco.

FINE AND PERFORMING ARTS

Asociación de Artistas Aficionados: Jr. Ica 323, Centro Histórico, Lima Cercado; tel. (1) 428-0432; e-mail aaasociacion@yahoo.com; internet aaasociacion.iespana.es; f. 1938; 254 mems; presentation of plays, classical ballet and varied music programmes.

Instituto de Arte Peruano 'José Sabogal' (José Sabogal Institute of Peruvian Art): Avda Alfonso Ugarte 650, Apdo. 3048, Lima 1; tel. (1) 423-5892; fax (1) 423-5892; e-mail mncp@inictel.gob.pe; internet museodelacultura.perucultural.org.pe; f. 1946; under the auspices of the Museo Nacional de la Cultura Peruana; publ. *Revista del Museo Nacional* (1 a year).

Instituto Nacional de Cultura: Avda Javier Prado este 2465, Lima 41; tel. (1) 476-9933; fax (1) 476-9888; e-mail comunicaciones@inc.gob.pe; internet www.inc.gob.pe; f. 1971; official cultural institute; 24 brs; Dir Dr Luis Guillermo Lumbreras; publs *Revista Arqueológicas, Revista Gaceta Cultural, Revista de Historia y Cultura, Revista del Museo Nacional.*

Instituto Peruano de Cultura Hispánica (Peruvian Institute of Hispanic Culture): Calle de la Riva 426, Lima; f. 1947; 280 mems; publ. *Boletín.*

HISTORY, GEOGRAPHY AND ARCHAEOLOGY

Centro de Estudios Histórico-Militares del Perú (Centre of Historico-Military Studies of Peru): Paseo Colón 150, Lima 1; tel. (1) 230415; f. 1944; 1,098 mems; library of 13,800 vols; publ. *Revista*.

Centro de Investigación y Restauración de Bienes Monumentales del Instituto Nacional de Cultura: Casilla 5247, Jr. Ancash 769, Lima.

Instituto Geográfico Nacional (National Geographic Institute): Ave A. Aramburú 1190–1198, Surquillo, Lima 34; tel. (1) 475-3030; fax (1) 475-9960; e-mail jefatura@ign.gob.pe; internet www.ign.gob.pe; f. 1921; 300 mems; library of 3,200 vols; Man. Gral Div CARLOS ALFONSO TAFUR GANOZA; publ. topographical, physical and political maps of Peru, *Boletín Informativo*.

Instituto Vizcardo de Estudios Históricos (Vizcardan Institute of Historical Studies): Porta 540, Miraflores, Lima; f. 1954; study of revolutionary movements for Spanish-American independence (1781–1820); publ. *Revista*.

Sociedad Geográfica de Lima (Lima Geographical Society): Jirón Puno 450, Apdo 1176, Lima 100; tel. (1) 427-3723; fax (1) 426-9930; e-mail antunez@socgeolima.org; f. 1888; library of 13,400 vols, also archives, maps and museum; 750 mems, including corresp. and hon.; Pres. Dr SANTIAGO ANTÚNEZ DE MAYOLO RYNNING; Vice-Pres. Ing. ZANIEL NOVOA GOICOCHEA; publs *Anuario Geográfico del Perú*, *Boletín* (1 a year), *Diccionario Geográfico del Perú*, *Forjando los Genios del Mañana* (1 a year).

LANGUAGE AND LITERATURE

Alliance Française de Lima: Avda Arequipa 4595, Casilla 18, 1667 Lima; tel. (1) 610-8000; fax (1) 610-8020; e-mail informes@alianzafrancesa.org.pe; internet www.alianzafrancesa.org.pe; offers courses and exams in French language and culture and promotes cultural exchange with France; attached teaching centres in Arequipa, Chiclayo, Cusco, Huancayo, Iquitos, Piura and Trujillo; Dir of Operations, Peru PAUL-ÉLIE LÉVY.

British Council: 22nd Fl., Torre Parque Mar, Avda Jose Larco 1301, Miraflores, Lima 18; tel. (1) 617-3060; fax (1) 617-3065; internet www.britishcouncil.org/peru; offers courses and examinations in English language and British culture and promotes cultural exchange with the UK; Dir FRANK FITZPATRICK.

Goethe-Institut: Jr. Nazca 722, Jesús María, Lima 100; tel. (1) 433-3180; fax (1) 431-0494; e-mail info@lima.goethe.org; internet www.goethe.de/ins/pe/lim/esindex.htm; f. 1966; offers courses and exams in German language and promotes cultural exchange with Germany; library of 7,500 vols, 24 periodicals; Dir PETRA BEHLKE-CAMPOS; Dir for Admin. FRANK MEYER.

MEDICINE

Academia de Estomatología del Perú (Peruvian Academy of Stomatology): Calle Los Próceres 261, 2do Piso, Urb. Sta Constanza, Lima 33; tel. (1) 435-1623; fax (1) 435-1623; e-mail academiadeestomatologia@terra.com.pe; internet www.academiadeestomatologiadelperu.com; f. 1929; 165 mems; library of 600 vols; Pres. Dra ESTHER FLORES MUBARAK; Sec. PATRICIA FRY OROPEZA; publ. *Estomatología Integrada* (2 a year).

Academia Nacional de Medicina (National Academy of Medicine): Avda Belén 331, San Isidro, Lima; tel. (1) 441-3938; e-mail academia.nac@speedy.com.pe; internet www.acadnacmedicina.org.pe; f. 1884; 40 mems; 40 associate mems; 40 corresp. and hon. mems; Pres. Dr GINO COSTA ELICE; Perm. Sec. Dr JAVIER MARIATEGUI; publ. *Boletín de la Academia Nacional de Medicina*.

Academia Peruana de Cirugía: Malecón Armendáriz 791, Miraflores; f. 1940; activities relate to the development of surgery in Peru; national and foreign membership; 100 titular mems and unlimited number of associates; Pres. Dr LUIS GURMENDI; publ. *Revista*.

Asociación Médica Peruana (Peruvian Medical Association): Jirón Camaná 381, of. 207, Lima 1; tel. (1) 427-4590; fax (1) 321-0037; e-mail amp@amp.pe; internet www.amp.pe; f. 1920; 1,499 mems; Pres. Dr HERBERTH CUBA GARCÍA; Gen. Sec. Dr JULIO CÉSAR SÁNCHEZ TONOHUYE; publ. *Revista Médica Peruana*.

Federación Médica Peruana (Peruvian Medical Federation): Jr. Almirante Guisse 2165, Lince, Lima; tel. (1) 470-5036; fax (1) 265-2890; e-mail federacion_medica_peruana@yahoo.es; internet www.federacionmedicaperuana.org; f. 1942; 1,230 mems; Pres. Dr LEONCIO DIAZ DIAZ; Gen. Sec. Dr MANUEL ALVAREZ LARRAONDO; publ. *Boletín de la Federación Médica Peruana*.

Sociedad Peruana de Neumología (Peruvian Society of Respiratory Medicine): Avda Guardia Civil 236, San Isidro, Lima 27; tel. (1) 226-2867; internet www.spneumologia.org.pe; f. 1935; 280 mems; Pres. Dr ALBERTO MATSUNO FUCHIGAMI; Gen. Sec. Dr ANTONIO TOKUMOTO KISHABA; publs *Boletín Informativo*, *Revista SPN*.

NATURAL SCIENCES

Biological Sciences

Sociedad Entomológica del Perú: Apartado Postal 14-0413, Lima; Universidad Nacional Agraria La Molina, Avda La Universidad s/n, Museo de Entomología, Lima 14; tel. (1) 349-5647 ext. 330; e-mail sepperu@sepperu.net; internet www.sepperu.net; f. 1956; 700 mems; library of 9,500 vols; Pres. ELIZABETH YOLANDA NÚÑEZ SACARÍAS DE DIOSES; Sec. MÓNICA NARREA CANGO; publ. *Revista Peruana de Entomología* (1 a year).

Mathematical Sciences

Instituto Nacional de Estadística (National Institute of Statistics): Avda Gral Garzón 662, Jesús María, Lima 11; tel. (1) 433-3104; fax (1) 433-3159; e-mail infoinei@inei.gob.pe; internet www.inei.gob.pe; f. 1975; involved in population, housing, socio-economic and agricultural censuses and surveys; plans statistical policy of country; library of 9,000 vols; Dir FARID MATUK CASTRO; publs *Compendio Económico* (1 a year), *Cuentas Nacionales—PBI Nacional* (1 a year), *Indice de precios al consumidor* (12 a year), *Informe Económico Mensual* (12 a year).

Physical Sciences

Asociación Peruana de Astronomía: Morro Solar s/n, Chorrillos, Lima 9; fax (1) 431-3084; e-mail wcentauri@apa.com.pe; internet www.apa.com.pe; f. 1946; 550 mems; library of 1,000 vols, 1,000 periodicals; Pres. Ing. VÍCTOR ESTREMADOYRO; Sec. Dr JOSÉ DOMINGO GÓMEZ SÁNCHEZ; publ. *Boletín* (3 a year).

Sociedad Geológica del Perú (Peruvian Geological Society): Arnaldo Marquez 2277, Distrito de Jesús María, Lima 11; tel. (1) 461-2362; fax (1) 461-5272; e-mail sgp@sgp.org.pe; internet www.sgp.org.pe; f. 1924; 800 mems; library of 40,000 vols; Pres. Ing. CARLOS MORALES BERMÚDEZ LÁMPARO; publs *Boletín* (1 a year), *Resumenes Extendidos* (conference proceedings, every 3 years).

Sociedad Peruana de Espeleología y Carstología (Peruvian Speleological and Karstological Society): Casilla 18-1209, Lima 18; La Mariscala 115, Lima 27; fax (1) 261-5305; e-mail peru.spec@gmail.com; f. 1965; Pres. Ing. CARLOS MORALES-BERMÚDEZ LÁMPARO; publ. *Cavernas Peruanas*.

Sociedad Química del Perú (Peruvian Chemistry Society): Avda Nicolas de Araníbar 696, Sta. Beatriz, Lima; tel. (1) 472-3925; internet www.sqperu.com; f. 1933; 1,200 mems; library of 5,600 vols; Pres. Dr JUAN JOSÉ LEÓN CAM; Gen. Sec. Dr JORGE REINALDO ANGULO CORNEJO; publ. *Revista* (4 a year).

RELIGION, SOCIOLOGY AND ANTHROPOLOGY

Centro Amazónico de Antropología y Aplicación Práctica (CAAAP): Apdo 14-0166, Lima 14; Avda González Prada 626, Magdalena del Mar, Lima; tel. (1) 460-0763; fax (1) 463-8846; e-mail caaapdirec@caaap.org.pe; internet www.caaap.org.pe; f. 1974; defends the cultural identity and the way of life of marginalized Amazonian people and seeks to protect natural resources in the Amazonian region; library of 5,000 vols; Dir FABIOLA LUNA; publs *Amazonía Peruana* (2 a year), *El Trueno* (4 a year), *Nuestra Tierra—Nuestra Vida* (4 a year).

Instituto de Estudios Etnológicos (Institute of Ethnological Studies): Avda Alfonso Ugarte 650, Apdo. 3048, Lima 1; tel. (1) 423-5892; fax (1) 423-5892; e-mail mncp@inictel.gob.pe; internet museodelacultura.perucultural.org.pe; f. 1946; under auspices of Museo Nacional de la Cultura Peruana; publ. *Revista del Museo Nacional* (1 a year).

Instituto de Estudios Islámicos: Calle Rey de Bahamonde 121, Vista Alegre, Surco, Lima 33; tel. (1) 489720; f. 1959; sound archives, numismatic collection, etc.; interests include economics, sociology and politics of contemporary Muslim world, the Palestinian problem, the Iranian Islamic revolution, the al-Fateh (Jamahiriya) revolution, and the diffusion of Islamic religious values in South America; special interest in Islamic-America relations in 16th and 17th centuries and nowadays; Pres. Dr RAFAEL GUEVARA BAZÁN; Chief Officer Prof. ELVA ZEGARRA TORREBLANCA.

Instituto Indigenista Peruano (Peruvian Institute of Indian Affairs): c/o Ministerio de Agricultura, Avda Salaverry s/n, Jesús María, Lima 11; f. 1946; studies the specific problems of indigenous groups; library of 1,500 vols, 1,046 periodicals; Dir Ing. CARLOS EDUARDO MENDOZA SALDIVAR; publ. *Perú-Indígena* (1 a year).

TECHNOLOGY

Asociación de Ingenieros Civiles del Perú: Nicolás de Piérola 788, 4° piso, Casilla 1314, Lima.

Asociación Electrotécnica Peruana: Av. República de Chile 284, Oficina 201, Jesús María, Lima; tel. (1) 330-4635; fax (1) 433-6543; e-mail informes@aep-peru.org; internet www.aep-peru.org; f. 1943; Pres. Ing. ALEX SALAZAR MARZAL; Sec. Ing. JORGE FLORES MARCHENA.

Instituto Peruano de Ingenieros Mecánicos: Avda República de Chile 284, Of. 201, Lima; Dir ROBERTO HEREDIA ZAVADA.

Sociedad de Ingenieros del Perú (Society of Peruvian Engineers): Avda Nicolás Piérola

788, Casilla 20085, Lima Cercado; tel. (1) 423-3804; fax (1) 424-6514; e-mail soc_ing_peru@terra.com.pe; library of 15,000 vols; Pres. Ing. RAUL GUERRA PÉREZ; Exec. Sec. Arq. CÉSAR SILVA HURTADO; publ. *Ingenería* (3 a year).

Research Institutes
GENERAL

Institut de Recherche pour le Développement (IRD): Casilla 18-1209, Lima 18; Calle Teruel 357, Mirafolores, Lima 18; tel. (1) 441-3223; fax (1) 441-3223; e-mail perou@ird.fr; internet www.peru.ird.fr; f. 1967; research in geology, agronomy, botany, ecology, economy, archaeology, geography; 15 staff; library of 950 vols; natural history museum; Rep. GÉRARD HÉRAIL; publ. *Boletín Sistemas Agrarios*; see main entry under France.

AGRICULTURE, FISHERIES AND VETERINARY SCIENCE

Estación Experimental Vista Florida: km 8 Carretera a Ferreñafe, Chiclayo; tel. (74) 238753; fax (74) 272950; e-mail vflorida@inia.gob.pe; f. 1970; crops research (plant protection, rice, corn, beans, sorghum); 26 staff; library of 5,000 vols; Dir Ing. SEGUNDO FERNÁNDEZ ROMERO.

Instituto Nacional de Investigación y Promoción Agropecuaria (National Agricultural Research Institute): Avda Guzmán Blanco 390, Lima 5; tel. (1) 317159; f. 1929; library of 50,000 vols; technical staff 350; Exec. Dir Dr JAVIER GAZZO FERNÁNDEZ DÁVILA; publs *Revista de Investigación Avances en Investigación, Serie de Boletín Investigación, Avances en Investigación, Serie de Boletín Técnico, Informes Especiales, Divulgaciones, Boletín Bibliográfico*.

ECONOMICS, LAW AND POLITICS

Instituto Peruano para la Investigación de la Estadística: Avda Benavides 190, Lima 18; tel. (1) 464064; f. 1974; study of statistics in general, and especially in relation to economics; library of 5,000 vols; organizes symposia, seminars, courses, etc.

EDUCATION

Instituto Experimental de Educación Primaria No. 1: Barranco, Avda Miraflores 200, Lima; f. 1940; studies systems and methods for the development of learning and the means to evaluate and control the results; library of scholastic texts; Dir Prof. NARCISO GONZÁLEZ CH.; publ. *Boletín*.

MEDICINE

Instituto de Cultura Alimentaria Birchner-Benner: Diez Canseco 487, Miraflores, Lima; fax (1) 444-4250; f. 1979; research into diet, especially of meat-substitutes and high-nutrition and low-cost food mixtures; warns about inadequate diet; promotes agriculture by biological methods; film and sound archives; Pres. CÉSAR MORALES GARCÍA; Sec. MARCELA CÁRDENAS.

Instituto de Investigaciones Alérgicas 'Dr Luis E. Betetta' ('Dr Luis E. Betetta' Allergy Research Institute): Avda La Marina 2501, San Miguel, Lima; tel. and fax (1) 578-1083; e-mail www.alergia.betetta@speedy.com.pe; f. 1965.

Instituto Nacional de Salud (National Institute of Health): Cápac Yupanqui No. 1400, Jesús Maria, Lima 11; tel. (1) 471-3254; fax (1) 471-7443; internet www.ins.gob.pe; f. 1936; communicable diseases, occupational

diseases, nutritional disorders, food and drug quality control, research, production of vaccines and reagents, traditional medicine; library of 5,000 books, 30,000 journals, 1,000 theses; Head Dr CÉSAR NÁQUIRA VELARDE; publs *Boletín* (52 a year), *Revista Peruana de Medicina Experimental y Salud Pública* (4 a year).

NATURAL SCIENCES
General

Instituto del Mar del Perú (IMARPE) (Peruvian Marine Institute): Esq. Gral. Valle y Gamarra, Apdo 22, Callao; tel. (51) 420-2000; internet www.imarpe.gob.pe; f. 1964; oceanography, marine biology, fisheries, aquaculture, aquatic ecotoxicology, hydroacoustics, biodiversity; library of 75,000 vols; Pres. Contra-Almirante HUGO ARÉVALO ESCARÓ; Exec. Dir Econ. GODOFREDO CAÑOTE SANTAMARINA; Scientific Dir Biol. RENATO GUEVARA-CARRASCO; publs *Boletín* (scientific papers, 1 or 2 a year), *Informe* (research results, 6 a year), *Informe Progresivo* (current research activities, 12 a year).

Biological Sciences

Instituto de Biología Andina (Institute of Andean Biology): Facultad de Medicina de San Fernando, Universidad Nacional Mayor de San Marcos, Avda Grau 755, Lima 1; tel. (1) 619-7000; e-mail ofinfmed@unmsm.edu.pe; f. 1930; affiliated to the Faculty of Medicine, San Marcos Univ.; laboratories in Lima, Morococha and Puno; mobile laboratory research on physiology of inhabitants of the Andes and their resistance to high altitudes, acclimatization and fertility of animals taken to high altitudes with a view to industrial use, methods of hygiene, adaptive faculties of humans at great heights, chronic mountain sickness and remedies, ecology and sociological problems; library of 1,091 vols, 400 periodicals; Dir Dr TULIO VELÁSQUEZ; publ. *Archivos del Instituto de Biología Andina* (4 a year).

Physical Sciences

Dirección General de Meteorología del Perú (National Meteorological Service): Jr. Cahuide 785, Jesús María, Lima 11; tel. (1) 614-1414; e-mail webmaster@senamhi.gob.pe; internet www.senamhi.gob.pe; f. 1928; 79 primary stations; publ. *Boletín* (1 a year).

Instituto Geofísico del Perú (Geophysical Institute): Calle Badajoz 169, Mayorazgo IV Etapa, Lima; tel. (1) 317-2300; e-mail web@geo.igp.gob.pe; internet www.igp.gob.pe; f. 1919 as Huancayo Magnetic Observatory of the Carnegie Institution of Washington, transferred to the Peruvian Government 1947; education sector; observatories in Huancayo, Jicamarca, Ancón, Arequipa and Lima; basic and mission-oriented research; international programmes in geomagnetism, seismology, atmospheric sciences, solar activity and natural hazards; Pres. Dr MANUEL CHANG.

TECHNOLOGY

Instituto Geológico, Minero y Metalúrgico (Institute of Geology, Mining and Metallurgy): Apdo 889, Avda Canadá 1470, San Borja, Lima; tel. (1) 224-2965; fax (1) 225-4540; e-mail info@ingemmet.gob.pe; internet www.ingemmet.gob.pe; f. 1978; carries out and coordinates geological mapping at regional scale and evaluates mineral resources; environmental assessment and ecological zonification; provides mining and metallurgical information; library of 33,098 vols; Pres. ROMULO MUCHO MAMANI; Dir HUGO RIVERA MANTILLA; publs *Boletín Serie A: Carta Geológica Nacional* (irregular),

Boletín Serie B: Geología Económica (irregular), *Boletín Serie C: Geodinámica e Ingeniería Geológica* (irregular), *Boletín Serie D: Estudios Regionales* (irregular), *Informes Técnicos* (irregular), *Newsletter* (electronic, 12 a year).

Instituto Peruano de Energía Nuclear (Peruvian Nuclear Energy Institute): Av. Canadá 1470, San Borja, Lima 41; tel. (1) 226-0030; fax (1) 226-0026; e-mail sege@ipen.gob.pe; internet www.ipen.gob.pe; f. 1975; researches into peaceful uses of nuclear energy in medicine, biology, agriculture and industry, prospecting, mining and processing of uranium ores; management of nuclear reactor and operation of a radioisotope production plant; nucleo-electricity planning; training and research; library: information and documentation centre of 75,000 vols, periodicals, monographs; Pres. JORGE DU BOIS GERVASI; Exec. Dir Dr CONRADO SEMINARIO ARCE; publs *Boletín de Informaciones* (4 a year), *Informes*.

Affiliated Institute:

Centro Superior de Estudios Nucleares: Avda Canadá 1470, San Borja, Lima 41; tel. (1) 226-0030; fax (1) 224-8991; e-mail csen@ipen.gob.pe; f. 1972; information and training centre on nuclear energy and its applications; Dir Prof. EDGARD MEDINA FLORES.

Libraries and Archives
Arequipa

Biblioteca de la Universidad Nacional de San Agustín: Calle Santa Catalina 117, Arequipa; f. 1900; 430,000 vols, 1,204 pamphlets and 535 periodicals; in addition the University has 12 specialized libraries; Dir Dr JORGE DÍAZ ENCINAS; publ. *Revista de Investigación de la Universidad*.

Biblioteca Pública Municipal de Arequipa: Portal de la Municipalidad 110, Arequipa; f. 1879; 51,500 vols; Librarian WALTER ALVAREZ THOMAS; also houses *Casa de la Cultura*.

Callao

Biblioteca de la Escuela Naval del Perú (Naval School Library): La Punta, Callao; f. 1914; Librarian ABEL ULLOA FERNÁNDEZ-PRADA; specialized library of 6,500 vols.

Biblioteca Pública Municipal Piloto: Esq. Ruiz y Colón, Apdo 270, Callao; tel. (14) 290558; f. 1936, reorganized 1957; 48,312 vols; 42 mems; Dir ROSA SÁNCHEZ DE WU.

Lima

Archivo General de la Nación (National Archives): Jr. Camaná 125 con Pasaje Piura, Lima; tel. (1) 427-5930; fax (1) 426-7221; e-mail agn.peru@mail.pol.com.pe; internet archivogeneral.gob.pe; f. 1861; 2 sections, Administrative and Historical; Dir Dr LIZARDO PASQUEL COBOS; publs *Legislación Archivística Peruana, Revista del AGN*.

Archivo Histórico Municipal: Jr. Conde de Superunda 141, 2do piso, Palacio Municipal, Lima; tel. (1) 315-1540; e-mail biblioteca@munlima.gob.pe; internet www.munlima.gob.pe/biblioteca/archivo_municipal; f. 1963; documents, certificates from the 19th century; Librarian LUIS E. WUFFARDEN.

Biblioteca Central de la Universidad Nacional de Ingeniería: Avda Tupac Amaru 210, El Rimac, Lima 25; tel. (1) 481-1070; e-mail webmaster@uni.edu.pe; internet www.lisnet.uni.edu.pe; 29,000 vols; Librarian JUANA PAREJA MARMANILLO.

Biblioteca Central de la Universidad Nacional Mayor de San Marcos (San Marcos National University General Library): Avda Germán Amézaga s/n, Lima 1; tel. (1) 619-7000 ext. 7618; e-mail achoquem@unmsm.edu.pe; internet sisbib .unmsm.edu.pe; f. 1551; the colln corresponding to the colonial period was incorporated in the *Biblioteca Pública*—now the *Biblioteca Nacional*—when the latter was founded in 1821; the Peruvian Section has valuable material on history, law, and literature; Head of Library System Lic. ALEJANDRO SALOMÓN CHOQUE MARTÍNEZ; 450,000 vols; publ. *Boletín Bibliográfico* (1 a year).

Biblioteca de la Municipalidad de Lima: Jr. Conde de Superunda 141, 2do piso, Palacio Municipal, Lima; tel. (1) 315-1540; e-mail biblioteca@munlima.gob.pe; f. 1935; gen. reference about Lima and its municipal govt; 22,000 vols; Librarian LUZMILA TELLO.

Biblioteca del Ministerio de Relaciones Exteriores (Library of the Ministry of Foreign Affairs): Palacio Torre-Tagle, Jirón Ucayali 363, Lima; tel. (1) 311-2952; f. 1921; 30,000 vols; Dir MANUEL G. GALDO; publ. *Maris Aestus*.

Biblioteca Nacional del Perú (National Library): Avda Abancay 4ta Cdra s/n, Lima 01; tel. (1) 428-7690; fax (1) 427-7331; internet www.binape.gob.pe; f. 1821 by José de San Martín; possesses copies of the first printed works in Peru and the Americas; 736,465 vols, 32,500 MSS, 12,499 maps, 11,000 photographs, 2,164,413 periodicals; Dir Dr SINESIO LÓPEZ JIMÉNEZ; publs *Bibliografía Peruana* (1 a year), *Bibliografías de intelectuales Peruanos* (irregular), *Boletín de la Biblioteca Nacional* (irregular), *Gaceta Bibliotecaria del Perú* (irregular), *Fénix* (1 a year), *Revista Libros y Artes* (4 a year).

Sistema de Bibliotecas de la Pontificia Universidad Católica del Perú: Apdo 1761, Lima; tel. (1) 626-2000 ext. 3400; fax (1) 626-2861; e-mail biblio@pucp.edu.pe; internet biblioteca.pucp.edu.pe; f. 1917; 800,000 vols, 26,049 audiovisual items, 2,260 electronic items; Dir CARMELA VILLA-NUEVA; System Librarian RAUL SIFUENTES.

Museums and Art Galleries

Arequipa

Museo Arqueológico (Archaeological Museum): Avda Independencia s/n, Ciudad Universitaria, Arequipa; tel. (54) 229719; f. 1933; ceramics, mummies; Dir Dr E. LINARES MÁLAGA.

Ayacucho

Museo Histórico Regional de Ayacucho (Regional Historical Museum of Ayacucho): Jirón, Calle 28 de Julio Noi 106, Ayacucho; tel. (66) 912056; f. 1946; archaeology, anthropology, history and popular crafts; library of 4,724 vols (incl. bound periodicals); Dir FREDY LAGOS ARRIARÁN; publ. *Anuario*.

Callao

Museo del Ejército del Perú (Army Museum of Peru): Fortaleza del Real Felipe, Plaza de la Independencia s/n, Callao; tel. (14) 429-0532; f. 1984; Dir LUIS LOAYZA MORALES.

Museo Naval del Perú (Naval History Museum): Avda Jorge Chávez 123, Plaza Grau, Callao; tel. (14) 613-6868 ext. 6794; fax (14) 429-4793; e-mail informes@ museonaval.com.pe; internet www .museonaval.com.pe; f. 1958; library: special-ist library of 7,948 vols; Dir Contralmirante FERNANDO CASARETTO ALVARADO; publ. *Fuentes para la Historia Naval*.

Cuzco

Museo Arqueológico: Cuesta del Almir-ante 103 esq. Calle Ataúd, Cusco; tel. (84) 237380; remains from the Inca period incl. stone objects, funerary metalwork, ceramics, textiles, vessels, evidence of trepanning, embalming, gold, silver, copper and tur-quoise idols, ceremonial objects, jugs; 17th-century portraits of Incas and Indian chiefs; Dir Dr LUIS A. PARDO.

Museo Histórico Regional del Cusco: Calle Heladeros s/n, Cusco; tel. (84) 223-245; fax (84) 223-831; f. 1946; Peruvian colonial art, Cusco schools of painting affiliated to Inst. Nacional de Cultura; Dir ANTONIA VEGA CENTENO B.; publ. *Revista del Museo Histórico Regional*.

Huancayo

Museo Arqueológico 'Federico Gálvez Durand' de la Gran Unidad Escolar 'Santa Isabel': Jr. Santa Isabel 567, San Carlos, Huancayo; tel. (64) 231061; f. 1952; 1,654 archaeological specimens from Nazca and other Peruvian cultures; examples of weaving, gold and bronze ornaments, fossils.

Huánuco

Museo Regional 'Leoncio Prado': Calle 2 de Mayo 680, Huánuco; f. 1945; natural history; Curator RICARDO E. FLORES.

Huaráz

Museo Arqueologico de Ancash: Avda Luzuriaga 762, Plaza de Armes, Huaráz, Ancash; tel. (43) 42-1551; fax (43) 42-4849; e-mail museoarqueologicodeancash@hotmail .com; internet www.mcultura.gop.pe; f. 1935; pre-Hispanic history of the Ancash region; exhibits incl. ceramics, metalwork, textiles, human remains; collns from the Chavín, Recuay, Moche, Wari, Chimu and Inca cultures; largest Lithic Park in South America, incl. stone carvings and megalithic statues from the Recuay culture; Dir Arq. RAFAEL PALOMINO PRADO; publ. *Cuadernillo de Difusión*.

Ica

Museo Cabrera: Plaza de Armas, Calle Bolívar 174, Ica; tel. (56) 231933; f. 1966; collection of ancient engraved stones and pottery; library of 100,000 vols; Dir (vacant).

Lambayeque

Museo Regional Arqueológico 'Bruning' de Lambayeque (Bruning Archaeological Museum): Avda Huamachuco s/n, Lambaye-que; tel. (74) 232-110; fax (74) 233-440; f. 1924; nearly 8,000 exhibits, of which 1,366 gold, 110 silver; textile, ceramic, wooden and stone pieces; 2 unique blue and black granite mortars incised with mythological figures in 'Chavin' style; Dir WALTER ALVA.

Lima

Museo de Arte de Lima (Museum of Art): Paseo Colón 125, Lima; tel. (1) 423-6332; fax (1) 331-0126; e-mail prensa@museodearte .org.pe; internet www.museodearte.org.pe; inaugurated in its present form in 1961; exhibits of Peruvian art from its origins to the present day; Pre-Columbian Dept: ceramics, carvings, Paracas woven material dating from 400BC; Colonial Dept: furniture, sculpture, paintings, religious art, silver; Modern Dept: furniture and paintings since 19th century; an important film archive; studio art courses; library of 4,000 items; restoration and conservation laboratory; Dir NATALIA MAJLUF BRAHIM; publ. *Bulletin* (6 a year).

Museo de Arte Italiano: Paseo de la República 250, Lima 1; tel. (1) 423-9932; fax (1) 423-9932; f. 1923; 1920s Italian art donated by the Italian colony in Peru; organizes courses and conferences; library of 500 vols; Dir IRENE VELAOCHAGA REY.

Museo de Historia Natural de la Universidad Nacional Mayor de San Marcos (Natural History Museum of the National University of San Marcos): Apartado 14-0434, Lima 14; Avda Arenales 1256, Jesús María, Lima; tel. (1) 471-0117; fax (1) 265-6819; e-mail museohn@unmsm.edu.pe; internet museohn.unmsm.edu.pe; f. 1918; incl. Herbario San Marcos (USM), with 300,000 specimens largely of Peruvian flora and units of zoology, botany, ecology, and geosciences; zoological collns; library of 8,000 vols; Dir Prof. Dr GERARDO LAMAS MÜLLER; publs *Boletín del Museo de Historia Natural UNMSM, Nueva Serie* (irregular), *Memorias, Serie 'A' Zoología, Serie 'B' Botánica, Serie 'C' Geología, Serie de Divulgación* (irregular).

Museo del Virreinato (Museum of the Viceroys): Quinta de Presa, Jirón Chira 344, Rímac, Lima; tel. (1) 481-3867; f. 1935; sited in an 18th-century mansion; exhibits relating to the period of the Spanish Viceroys; Dir JOSÉ FLORES ARAOS; publ. *Revista*.

Museo Geológico de la Universidad Nacional de Ingeniería del Perú (Geological Museum of the National University of Engineering): Campus Universitario, Av. Túpac Amaru km 4.5, Rimac, Lima; tel. (1) 481-1070 ext. 364; fax (1) 382-2174; e-mail cpinto@uni.edu.pe; f. 1891 as Museo de Yacimentos Minerales y Metalíferos de la Escuela Nacional de Ingenieros, name changed 1955; incorporates the Raymondi collections; Chief of Dept. of Geology JULIO DAVILA V.

Museo Larco (Larco Museum): Avda Bolívar 1515, Pueblo Libre, Lima 21; tel. (1) 461-1312; fax (1) 461-5640; e-mail webmaster@museolarco.org; internet museolarco.org; f. 1926; Peruvian pre-Colum-bian history; colln of gold, silver, erotica; 45,000 classified archaeological objects; library of 10,000 vols; Exec. Dir ANDRÉS ALVAREZ CALDERÓN; Curator ULLA HOLM-QUIST.

Branch Museum:

Museo de Arte Precolombino: Plaza de Las Nazarenas 231, Cusco; tel. (84) 233-210; fax (84) 233-210; e-mail amap@ infonegocio.net.pe; internet map .perucultural.org.pe; f. 2003; arts of ancient Peruvian cultures; 450 objects from 1250BC to AD 1532; Dir ANDRÉS ALVAREZ CALDERÓN; Exec. Dir EDGAR CASA-VERDE.

Museo Nacional de Arqueología, Antropología e Historia del Perú (National Museum of Archaeology, Anthropology and History): Plaza Bolívar s/n, Pueblo Libre, Lima 21; tel. (1) 463-5070; fax (1) 463-2009; f. 1945; library of 30,000 vols; colln contains pre-Inca and Inca remains, and artefacts from the colonial and republican periods; Dir FERNANDO ROSAS MOSCOSO; publs *Boletines, Arqueológicas, Historia y Cultura, Cuadernos de Investigaciones*.

Museo Nacional de la Cultura Peruana: Avda Alfonso Ugarte 650, Apdo 3048, Lima 1; tel. (1) 423-5892; fax (1) 423-5892; e-mail mncp@inc.gob.pe; internet museodelacultura .perucultural.org.pe; f. 1946; responsible for Instituto de Estudios Etnológicos and the Instituto de Arte Peruano 'José Sabogal'; popular art and ethnography; ethno-histor-ical library and a photographic archive; Dir

GLADYS ROQUEZ DIAZ; publs *Revista del Museo Nacional* (1 a year), *Boletín* (4 a year).

Museo Postal y Filatélico del Perú (Postal and Philatelic Museum): Pasaje Piura, Lima 1; tel. (1) 428-0400; f. 1931; library of 100 vols; Dir DORA IBERICO CASTRO.

Trujillo

Museo de Arqueología e Historia de la Universidad Nacional de Trujillo: Jr. Junín 682, Trujillo; tel. (44) 249322; f. 1946; Dir Dr JORGE ZEVALLOS QUIÑONES; publ. *Chimor*.

National Universities

UNIVERSIDAD NACIONAL AGRARIA LA MOLINA

Avda La Molina s/n, La Molina, Lima 12

Telephone: (1) 349-5647
E-mail: orgi@lamolina.edu.pe
Internet: www.lamolina.edu.pe

Founded 1902, fmrly Escuela Nacional de Agricultura
Language of instruction: Spanish
Academic year: April to December (2 semesters)

Rector: Ing. FRANCISCO DELGADO DE LA FLOR BADARACCO
Dir for Postgraduate School: Dr SALOMÓN HELFGOTT
Dir for Int. Office: Ing. ROBERTO UGAS
Number of teachers: 495
Number of students: 4,100

Publication: *Anales Científicos* (3 a year)

DEANS

Agricultural Engineering: Dr ABEL MEJIA MARCACUZCO
Agronomy: Dr LEONOR MATTOS CALDERÓN
Economics and Planning: Ing. LUÍS JÍMENEZ DÍAZ
Fisheries: Ing. RAÚL PORTURAS OLAECHEA
Food Science and Technology: Dr AUGUSTO MONTEZ GUTIÉRREZ
Forestry: Ing. JOSÉ DANCE CABALLERO
Postgraduate School: Dr SALOMÓN HELFGOTT
Sciences: Dr EDUARDO GÓMEZ-CORNEJO BELGRANO
Zootechnics: Dr MAÑUEL ROSEMBERG BARRON

UNIVERSIDAD NACIONAL AGRARIA DE LA SELVA

Avda Universitaria s/n km 1.5, Tingo María Huánuco

Telephone: (62) 562342
Fax: (62) 561156
E-mail: unas@unas.edu.pe
Internet: www.unas.edu.pe

Founded 1964
State control
Language of instruction: Spanish
Academic year: April to December

Rector: Dr MILTHON MUÑOZ BERROCAL
Vice-Rector for Academic Affairs: Dr JOSÉ WILFREDO ZAVALA SOLORZANO
Vice-Rector for Admin. Affairs: Ing. JYTAVCLERH VARGAS CLEMENTE
Sec.-Gen.: TITO F. GONZÁLEZ MANRIQUE DE LARA
Central Library Dir: KARINA DEL AGUILA VELA
Number of teachers: 190
Number of students: 1,533

Publication: *Tropicultura*

DEANS

Agronomy: Ing. SEGUNDO RODRIGUEZ DELGADO
Animal Breeding: Ing. MIGUELPEREZ OLANO

Economics and Administration: Lic. VICTOR CHACON LOPEZ
Food Industries: Ing. RAUL NATIVIDAD FERRER
Information Systems: Dr MAXIMO DIONISIO GARMA
Renewable Natural Resources: Ing. LUCIO MANRIQUE DE LARA SUÁREZ

UNIVERSIDAD NACIONAL DEL ALTIPLANO

Av. Floral 1153, Puno

Telephone: (51) 352-206
E-mail: webmaster@unap.edu.pe
Internet: www.unap.edu.pe

Founded 1856
Academic year: March to December
Rector: Dr VICTOR TORRES ESTEVES
Admin. Vice-Rector for Econ.: FRANCISCO GUTIERREZ GUTIERREZ
Vice-Rector: Prof. VICTOR GALLEGOS MONROY
Head of Personnel and Gen. Services: HERMOGENES MENDOZA ANCCO
Librarian: Prof. SERAFÍN CALSIN MAMANI

Number of teachers: 623
Number of students: 10,202

Publications: *Revistas problemáticas, Revista Universitaria, Revista Visión Agraria*

DEANS

Accounting and Administration: E. PINEDA QUISPE
Agricultural Engineering: W. SALAS PALMA
Agriculture: R. SERRUTO COLQUE
Biological Sciences: S. ATENCIO LIMACHI
Chemical Engineering: N. VILLAFUERTE PRUDENCIO
Civil Engineering, Architecture and Systems: P. ARROYO GONZALES
Economic Engineering: L. AVILA ROJAS
Education: J. L. CACERES MONROY
Health Sciences: R. LÓPEZ VELÁSQUEZ
Law and Political Science: J. VALDEZ PEÑARANDA
Metallurgy and Geological Engineering: H. MANRIQUE MEZA
Mining Engineering: V. NAVARRO TORRES
Nursing: N. CALSIN CHIRINOS
Postgraduate School: F. CÁCEDA DÍAZ
Social Sciences: M. CANO OJEDA
Social Work: G. PINTO SOTELO
Statistics for Engineering: E. CALMET URIA
Veterinary Medicine and Stockbreeding: Prof. C. SÁNCHEZ VIVEROS

UNIVERSIDAD NACIONAL DE LA AMAZONÍA PERUANA

Apdo 496, Iquitos
Sargento Lores 385, Iquitos, Loreto

Telephone: (65) 234140
E-mail: infounap@unapiquitos.edu.pe
Internet: www.unapiquitos.edu.pe

Founded 1962
State control
Language of instruction: Spanish
Academic year: April to February (2 terms)

Rector: Dr ANTONIO PASQUEL RUIZ
Vice-Rector for Academic Affairs: Econ. CARLOS HERNÁN ZUMAETA VÁSQUEZ
Gen. Sec.: Ing. MARÍA ISABEL MAURY LAURA
Librarian: MARGARITA FASANANDO VÁSQUEZ

Number of teachers: 400
Number of students: 3,200

Publication: *Conocimiento*

DEANS

Faculty of Administration and Accountancy: Prof. HEDMER PASQUEL CHONG
Faculty of Agronomy Science: Ing. JULIO VÁSQUEZ RAMÍREZ
Faculty of Biology: ANDRÉS URTEAGA CAVERO

Faculty of Chemistry: Ing. JESÚS LÓPEZ SANGAMA
Faculty of Education and Humanities: Prof. JOSÉ ZUMAETA TORRES
Faculty of Food Sciences: Ing. JORGE TORRES LUPERDI
Faculty of Forestry: Ing. JOSÉ TORRES VÁSQUEZ
Faculty of Human Medicine: Dr MARIO THEMME RUNCIMAN
Faculty of Nursing: Enf. PABLO CASTRO TRELLES
Faculty of Zootechnics: Ing. FERNANDO ARAUJO PAREDES

UNIVERSIDAD NACIONAL DE ANCASH 'SANTIAGO ANTÚNEZ DE MAYOLO'

Apdo 70, Huáraz, Ancash

Telephone: (43) 422-085
Fax: (43) 421-393
E-mail: jnunez00@yahoo.com
Internet: www.unasam.edu.pe

Founded 1977
State control
Language of instruction: Spanish
Academic year: April to December

Rector: Dr FERNANDO CASTILLO PICON
Vice-Rector for Academic Affairs: Mag. ROOSWELT VILLALOBOS
Vice-Rector for Admin.: Mag. CARLOS REYES PAREJA
Sec.: Econ. WILMER SICCHA CUSTODIO
Librarian: Ing. OSCAR RUIZ CASIMIRO

Number of teachers: 400
Number of students: 6,500

Publications: *Avance Santiaguino* (12 a year), *Informativo UNASAM, Revista de Investigacion de la UNASAM* (3 a year)

DEANS

Faculty of Agricultural Sciences: Ing. PEDRO COLONIA CERNA
Faculty of Civil Engineering: Ing. FELISMERO SALINAS FERNÁNDEZ
Faculty of Economic and Administrative Sciences: Econ. DARIO VAREAS ARCE
Faculty of Education: Lic. VICTOR PAREDES ESTEÍA
Faculty of Environmental Sciences: Ing. CESAR DAVILA PAREDES
Faculty of Food Industry Engineering: Ing. DANIEL REEVES ITA
Faculty of Law and Political Science: Abog. FABIAN ANICETO LUCERO
Faculty of Medicine: Lic. RIBIANA LEÓN HUERTA
Faculty of Mining, Geological and Metallurgical Engineering: Ing. JACINTO ISIDRO GIRALDO
Faculty of Science: Lic. ESMELIN NIGUIN ALAYO

UNIVERSIDAD NACIONAL DE CAJAMARCA

Avda Atahualpa 1050, Cajamarca

Telephone: (76) 363263
Fax: (76) 362796
E-mail: webmaster@unc.edu.pe
Internet: www.unc.edu.pe

Founded 1962
State control
Language of instruction: Spanish
Academic year: March to December (2 semesters)

Rector: Prof. CÉSAR A. PAREDES CANTO
Vice-Rectors: Dr HOMERO BAZÁN ZURITA, Ing. AURELIO MARTOS DÍAZ
Librarian: LUIS RONCAL

Number of teachers: 387
Number of students: 5,700

DEANS

Agriculture: Dr ISIDORO SÁNCHEZ VEGA
Animal Husbandry: Ing. TULIO MONDRAGÓN RONCAL
Economics, Administration and Accountancy: Prof. SEGUNDO CIEZA YAÑEZ
Education: Dr JOSUÉ TEJADA ATALAYA
Engineering: Ing. JULIO GUZMÁN PERALTA
Health: Dr JORGE CÉSPEDES ABANTO
Social Sciences: Prof. ALIDOR LUNA TELLO
Veterinary Medicine: Dr ROBERTO ACOSTA GÁLVEZ

UNIVERSIDAD NACIONAL DEL CALLAO

Saenz Peña 1060, Apdo 138, Callao

Telephone: (14) 296-608
Fax: (14) 296-607
E-mail: rector@redunac.unac.edu.pe
Internet: www.unac.edu.pe

Founded 1966
State control
Language of instruction: Spanish
Academic year: April to December (2 terms)

Rector: ALBERTO ARROYO VIALE
Vice-Rector: VICTOR MEREA LLANOS
Vice-Rector: GLORIA SAENZ ORREGO
Registrar: PABLO ARELLANO UBILLUZ
Librarian: LUIS CARRASCO VEREGAS

Number of teachers: 550
Number of students: 12,000

Publications: *Catálogo de Informes de Investigación* (1 a year), *Ciencia y Tecnología* (1 a year)

DEANS

Accounting: CARLOS HÚRTADO CRIADO
Administration: CÉSAR ANGULO RODRÍGUEZ
Chemical Engineering: PABLO DIAZ BRAVO
Economics: JUAN NUNURA CHULLY
Electrical and Electronic Engineering: FRANCO VELIZ LIZÁRRAGA
Environmental Engineering: MARIA TERESA VALDERRAMA ROJAS
Fish and Food Engineering: JUVENCIO VRIOS AVENDOÑO
Health Sciences: ARCELIA ROJAS SALAZAR
Industrial and Systems Engineering: MANUEL MORI PAREDES
Mathematics and Physics: ROEL MARIA VIDAL GUZMÁN
Mechanical Engineering: FELIX GUERRERO ROLDAN
Postgraduate School: LIDA SANÉZ FALCÓN

UNIVERSIDAD NACIONAL DEL CENTRO DEL PERÚ

Ciudad Universitaria, Avda Mariscal Castilla s/n km. 5, El Tambo Huancayo

Telephone: (64) 481062
E-mail: rrpp@uncp.edu.pe
Internet: www.uncp.edu.pe

Founded 1959
State control
Language of instruction: Spanish
Academic year: April to December (2 terms)

Rector: Ing. ESAÚ TIBERIO CARO MEZA
Vice-Rector for Academic Affairs: Ing. HUGO AYALA SÍNCHEZ
Chief Admin. Officer: Prof. KRÚGER SARAPURA YUPANQUI
Librarian: Dr FERNANDO ARAUCO VILLAR

Number of teachers: 705
Number of students: 8,395

Publications: *Boletín Informativo* (12 a year), *Ciencias Agrarias, Proceso* (irregular)

DEANS

Accountancy: CPC HERNANDO PAYANO ROJAS
Administration: Lic. ANDRÉS ILDEFONSO SUÁREZ

Agronomy: Ing. GLICERIO LÓPEZ ORIHUELA
Anthropology: Ing. JULIO BARRERA YUPANQUI
Architecture: Arq. FELIPE ARIAS MATOS
Chemical Engineering: Ing. ANTONIO COCHACHI GUADALUPE
Economics: Econ. MANUEL LARRAURI ROJAS
Education and Humanities: Lic. CARLOS GAMBOA DEL CARPIO
Electrical, Electronic and Systems Engineering: Ing. HÉCTOR TORRES MARAVÍ
Food Engineering: Ing. LIBIA GUTIÉRREZ GONZALES
Forestry: Ing. PEDRO ARIZAPANA ANCCASI
Mechanical Engineering: Ing. RAÚL MAYCO CHÁVEZ
Medicine: Dr RIGOBERTO ZÚNIGA MERA
Metallurgical Engineering: Ing. EUGENIO MUCHA BENITO
Mining Engineering: Ing. ÓRISON DELZO SALOMÉ
Nursing: Lic. HÉCTOR ZAPATA RIVERA
Social Work: Lic. LIDIA LAGONES MIRANDA
Stockbreeding: Ing. HUMBERTO RODRÍGUEZ LANDEO
Postgraduate School: Dr PABLO MOSOMBITE PINEDO

UNIVERSIDAD NACIONAL DANIEL ALCIDES CARRIÓN

Edificio Estatal No. 4, San Juan Pampa, Cerro de Pasco, Pasco

Telephone and fax (63) 422197
E-mail: webmaster@undac.edu.pe
Internet: www.undac.edu.pe

Founded 1965

Rector: Prof. NORBERTO GONZALES PERALTA

Number of teachers: 90
Number of students: 1,000

Faculties of economics, education, mining, metallurgy.

UNIVERSIDAD NACIONAL DE EDUCACIÓN 'ENRIQUE GUZMÁN Y VALLE'

Avda Enrique Guzmán y Valle s/n, La Cantuta, Chosica, Lima 15

Telephone: (1) 313-3700
Internet: www.une.edu.pe

Founded 1967
State control
Language of instruction: Spanish
Pres.: Dra DORALIZA TOVAR TORRES
First Vice-Pres. for Academic Affairs: Dra LUZ DORIS SÁNCHEZ PINEDO
Second Vice-Pres. for Admin.: VIDAL BAUTISTA CARRASCO
Gen. Sec.: Dra GLADYS RAMÍREZ ADRIANZÉN
Registrar: Prof. MIREIA SOLÉ ALABART
Librarian: MARGARITA LÓPEZ M.

Library of 16,500 vols
Number of teachers: 190
Number of students: 9,744

Publication: *Cantuta*

DEANS

Faculty of Humanities: HUMBERTO VARGAS SALGADO
Faculty of Sciences: LILIANA SUMARRIVA BUSTINZA
Faculty of Technology: JOSÉ ASTOLAZA DE LA CRUZ
Postgraduate School: Dr JORGE JHONCON KOOYIP (Dir)

UNIVERSIDAD NACIONAL FEDERICO VILLARREAL

Jr. Carlos Gonzáles 285, Maranga, San Miguel, Lima

Telephone: (14) 720-9720
E-mail: rector@unfv.edu.pe

Internet: www.unfv.edu.pe

Founded 1963
State control
Language of instruction: Spanish
Academic year: April to December

Rector: Dr JOSÉ MARÍA VIAÑA PÉREZ
Vice-Rector for Academic Affairs: Dr NANCY OLIVERO PACHECO
Vice-Rector for Research: Dr FELICIANO TIMOTEO ONCEVAY ESPINOZA
Gen. Sec.: Dr ECKERMAN PANDURO ANGULO
Dir-Gen. for Administration: Dr JUAN OSWALDO ALFARO BERNEDO

Number of teachers: 2,354
Number of students: 22,449

Publications: *Gaceta El Villarrealino, Hipótesis, Villarreal en el tercer milenio, Síntesis Academica, Villarreal al Futuro, Wiñay Yachay, Yachaywasi*

DEANS

Architecture and Urbanism: Dr LUIS ALBERTO LEÓN ESPINOZA
Administration: Dr GUDELIA DOMITILA VIGO SÁNCHEZ
Civil Engineering: Dr ROQUE ALBERTO SÁNCHEZ CRISTOBÁL
Economics Sciences: Dr ÓSCAR PONGO ÁGUILA
Education: Dra MANUEL JESÚS ASMAT ASMAD
Electronic Engineering and Computing: Dr JUSTO PASTOR SOLÍS FONSECA
Financial and Accounting Sciences: Dra PEDRO JUAN ANTON DE LOS SANTOS
Geographical Engineering, Environmental and Ecotourism: Dr ELÍAS ALFONSO VALVERDE TORRES
Humanities: LORGIO ADALBERTO GUIBOVICH DEL CARPIO
Industrial and Systems Engineering: Dr CRISTINA ASUNCIÓN ALZAMORA RIVERO
Law and Political Science: Dr VÍCTOR TAQUÍA VILA
Medicine: Dr LUIS ALBERTO HUARACHI QUINTANILLA
Medical Technology: Dr REGINA MEDINA ESPINOZA
Natural Sciences and Mathematics: Mag. CARLOS MARCO SANTA CRUZ CARPIO
Oceanography, Fisheries and Food Sciences: Dr LUIS ALBERTO DÁVILA SOLAR
Odontology: Mag. ALEJANDRO SALAZAR FUERTES
Psychology: Lic. FLORITA PINTO HERRERA
Social Sciences: Dr ISAAC ROBERTO ÁNGELES LAZO

UNIVERSIDAD NACIONAL DE HUANCAVÉLICA

Ciudad Universitaria Paturpampa, Huancavelica

Telephone: (67) 751-380
Fax: (67) 751-551
E-mail: secretaria@unh.edu.pe
Internet: www.unh.edu.pe

Founded 1990

Rector: MANUEL J. BASTO SÁEZ
Vice-Rector for Academic Affairs: Dr ALFONSO CORDERO FERNÁNDEZ
Vice-Rector for Admin.: ADOLFO R. CORTAVARRIA
Sec.-Gen.: Lic. ALEJANDRO RODRIGO QUILCA

DEANS

Faculty of Business Administration: RAÚL RUA SULCA
Faculty of Education: ZEIDA P. HOCES LA ROSA
Faculty of Engineering: Dr OMAR BURGA MOSTACERO
Faculty of Nursing: Lic. BENJAMINA ORTIZ ESPINAR

UNIVERSIDAD NACIONAL HERMILIO VALDIZÁN

Av. Universitaria 601, Cayhuayna, Huánuco

Telephone: (62) 512-341

Fax: (62) 513-360

Internet: www.unheval.edu.pe

Founded 1964

State control

Language of instruction: Spanish

Academic year: April to July;August to December (2 semesters)

Rector: Dr Víctor Pedro Cuadros Ojeda

Vice-Rector for Academic Affairs: Dr Pedro Getulio Villavicencio Guardia

Vice-Rector for Admin.: Erasmo Fernández Sixto

Head of Admin.: Lic. Esteban Medina Avila

Dir of Post Degree: Dr Lorenzo Pasquel Loarte

Librarian: Lic. Aurora Ampudia Dávila

Library of 25,967 vols

Number of teachers: 568

Number of students: 9,606

DEANS

Accountancy and Financial Sciences: Guillermo Arevalo Ríos

Administrative Sciences and Tourism: Dr Roger Wilfredo Céspedes Revelo

Agrarian Sciences: David Alcides Maquera Lupaca

Business Management: CPC Arturo Rivera y Caldas

Civil Engineering and Architecture: Ing. Clifton Paucary Montenegro

Economic Sciences: Emigidio Ramos Cornelio

Health Sciences: Edilberto Enrique Suero Rojas

Industrial Engineering: Dr Guillermo Augusto Bocangel Weydert

Law and Political Science: Dr Armando Pizarro Alejandro

Nursing: Nancy Guillermina Veramendi Villavicencio

Obstetrics: Víctor Quispe Sulca

Sciences of Education and Humanities: Arturo Lucas Cabello

Social Sciences: Ortzy Fortunato Lovón Rondón

Veterinary Medicine and Zootechnics: Augusto Bazan Garcìa

UNIVERSIDAD NACIONAL DE INGENIERÍA

Avda Túpac Amaru 210, Rimac, Lima 25

Telephone: (1) 481-1070

E-mail: webmaster@uni.edu.pe

Internet: www.uni.edu.pe

Founded 1896 as Escuela Nacional de Ingenieros del Perú, present name 1955

State control

Language of instruction: Spanish

Academic year: April to December

Rector: Dr José Ignacio López Soria

Vice-Rectors: Ing. Miguel Angel Saenz Lizarzaburu, Dr Casio Ore Ore

Sec.-Gen.: Dr Abelardo Ludeña Luque

Library: see Libraries and Archives

Number of teachers: 996

Number of students: 12,241

Publications: Boletín 'Quilca', Revista Técnica 'Tecnia', Revista Artes y Ciencias 'Amaru'

DEANS

Faculty of Architecture, Town Planning and Fine Arts: Arq. Javier Sota Nadal

Faculty of Chemical and Manufacturing Engineering: Ing. Lucio Ramos Benavente

Faculty of Civil Engineering: Ing. Genaro Humala Aybar

Faculty of Economics and Social Sciences: Lic. Jorge Abadie Linares

Faculty of Electrical and Electronic Engineering: Ing. Jubert Chávez Serrano

Faculty of Environmental Engineering: Ing. Jorge Pflucker

Faculty of Geology, Mining and Metallurgical Engineering: Ing. Pedro Máximo Angeles Beteta

Faculty of Industrial and Systems Engineering: Ing. Luis Flores Fonseca

Faculty of Mechanical Engineering: Ing. Juan Hori Asano

Faculty of Petroleum Engineering: Ing. Arturo Burga Acosta

Faculty of Science: Dr Jaime Avalos Sánchez

UNIVERSIDAD NACIONAL JORGE BASADRE GROHMANN

Calle Alto Bolivia 1594, Tacna

Telephone: (52) 583000

E-mail: sredo@unjbg.edu.pe

Internet: www.unjbg.edu.pe

Founded 1971 as Universidad Nacional de Tacna

State control

Language of instruction: Spanish

Academic year: April to December

Chancellor: Dr Carlos Valente Rossi

Rector: Dr hab Vicente M. Castañeda Chávez

Vice-Rectors: Mgr Dante Manzanares Cáceres, Dr Elí Espinoza Atencia

Sec.-Gen.: Lic. Carlos Polo Bravo

Librarian: Ing. Alberto Pacheco Pacheco

Library of 29,000 vols

Number of teachers: 457

Number of students: 4,903

Publications: Ciencia y Tecnología (1 a year), Memoria de Gestión (1 a year), Revista Materno Infantil (1 a year)

DEANS

Accounting: CPC Betty Cohaila Calderón

Administration: Ing. Eco. Jesús Olivera Cáceres

Agriculture: Ing. Eloy Casilla García

Education: Prof. Oliver Ballón Montesinos

Fishing Engineering: Dr Elí Espinoza Atencia

Food Industry Engineering: Dr Miguel Larrea Céspedes

Law and Arts: Psic. Carlos Pauca Lazo

Medicine: Dr Jorge López Claros

Metallurgical Engineering: Ing. Raúl Del Pozo Tello

Mining Engineering: Ing. Dante Morales Cabrera

Nursing: Mgr. Dalila Salas Romero

Obstetrics: Obst. Miriam Ríos Moreno

Science: Lic. Ramón Vera Roalcaba

Postgraduate School: Mgr Pelayo Delgado Tello

UNIVERSIDAD NACIONAL JOSÉ FAUSTINO SÁNCHEZ CARRIÓN

Ciudad Universitaria, Avda Mercedes Indacochea s/n, Huacho, Lima

Telephone: (1) 232-6097

Internet: www.unjfsc.edu.pe

Founded 1968

Rector: Lic. Severo Llanos Bayona

Library of 5,000 vols

Number of teachers: 100

Number of students: 3,000

Depts of administration, engineering, fisheries, nutrition, sociology.

UNIVERSIDAD NACIONAL MAYOR DE SAN MARCOS

Edificio Jorge Basadre, Ciudad Universitaria, Lima 1

Telephone: (1) 619-7000

E-mail: cooperacion.unmsm@gmail.com

Internet: www.unmsm.edu.pe

Founded 1551

Public control

Language of instruction: Spanish

Academic year: March to December

Rector: Dr Luis Fernando Izquierdo Vásquez

Vice-Rector for Academic Affairs: Dr Víctor Peña Rodríguez

Vice-Rector for Research: Dr Aurora Marrou Roldán

Library of 470,448 vols

Number of teachers: 3,059

Number of students: 28,041

Publications: Boletín, Compendios, Revista de San Marcos.

UNIVERSIDAD NACIONAL MICAELA BASTIDAS DE APURIMAC

Avda Arenas 121, Abancay

Telephone: (83) 322-577

Internet: www.unamba.edu.pe

Founded 2000

State control

Pres.: Dr Carroll Dale Salinas

Vice-Pres. for Academic Affairs: Dalin Omar Encomenderos

Vice-Pres. for Admin.: Alfonso Víctor Bustinza Choque

Sec.-Gen.: Abog. Corina Velásquez Sánchez

Number of teachers: 104

Number of students: 1,500

COORDINATORS OF ACADEMIC PROGRAMMES

Agricultural Engineering: Ing. Fulgencio Vilcanqui Pérez

Business Administration: Lic. Yudberto Vilca Colque

Education: Ing. Jesús Manuel Ibarra Cabrera

Mining: Ing. Nelson Palemon Meza Peña

UNIVERSIDAD NACIONAL PEDRO RUIZ GALLO

Avda Juan XXIII 339, Lambayeque

Telephone: (74) 590-393

E-mail: webmaster@unprg.edu.pe

Internet: www.unprg.edu.pe

Founded 1970

State control

Language of instruction: Spanish

Rector: Ing. Angel Diaz Celis

Vice-Rector: Ing. Pedro Casanova Chirinos

Librarian: Dr Guillermo Baca Aguinaga

Number of teachers: 261

Number of students: 5,460

Publications: Boletín Informativo (12 a year), Universidad (1 a year).

UNIVERSIDAD NACIONAL DE PIURA

Esquina Apurimac-Tacna 719–743, Apdo 295, Piura

Telephone: (74) 324603

Fax: (74) 321931

E-mail: postmast@tallan.unp.edu.pe

Internet: www.unp.edu.pe

Founded 1961

State control

Language of instruction: Spanish

Academic year: March to December

Rector: Ing. Freddy Aponte Guerrero

Vice-Rector for Academic Affairs: Ing. LUÍS GUZMÁN FARFÁN
Vice-Rector for Admin.: Ing. ORLANDO ZAPATA COLOMA
Admin. Dir: Lic. JORGE RODRÍGUEZ RIVERA
Librarian: Dr LUÍS VEGA FARFÁN
Number of teachers: 481
Number of students: 8,503
Publications: *Boletines*, *Universalia* (scientific journal, 2 a year)

DEANS

Faculty of Accounting and Finance: MÁXIMO MÁRQUEZ TACURA
Faculty of Administrative Sciences: Lic. VICENTE SÁNCHEZ JUÁREZ
Faculty of Agronomy: Dr CÉSAR DELGADILLO FUKUSAKI
Faculty of Animal Husbandry: ADRIÁN GUZMÁN ZAGARRO
Faculty of Architecture: MIGUEL ADRIANZÁN HUANCAS
Faculty of Civil Engineering: Ing. RICARDO CARRASCO SOTOMAYOR
Faculty of Economics: Econ. JOSÉ ORDINOLA BOYER
Faculty of Fisheries Engineering: MANUEL MOGOLLÓN LÓPEZ
Faculty of Human Medicine: Dr RAÚL CASTILLO ZÚÑIGA
Faculty of Industrial Engineering: Lic. MARK SADOWSKY SMITH
Faculty of Law and Political Sciences: Dr CARLOS CORNEJO GUERRERO
Faculty of Mining Engineering: Ing. RICARDO DILLON LONG
Faculty of Sciences: SAUL CÉSPEDES LOMPARTE
Faculty of Social Sciences and Education: Econ. LORENZO ALVILES VALEZMORO

UNIVERSIDAD NACIONAL DE SAN AGUSTÍN DE AREQUIPA

Calle Santa Catalina 117, Arequipa
Telephone: (54) 237808
Fax: (54) 237808
Internet: www.unsa.edu.pe
Founded 1828
State control
Language of instruction: Spanish
Academic year: April to December
Rector: Dr ROLANDO CORNEJO CUERVO
Vice-Rector for Academic Affairs: Dr VALDEMAR MEDINA HOYOS
Vice-Rector for Admin.: Dr MILTON TALAVERA SOTO
Gen. Sec.: LUIS ALBERTO VALDIVIA RODRÍGUEZ
Library: see Libraries
Number of teachers: 1,453
Number of students: 22,899
Publications: *Boletín Bibliográfico*, *Boletín Estadístico* (1 a year)

DEANS

Accounting and Administration: EDGAR RÍOS VILLENA
Architecture and Town Planning: CÉSAR MÁRQUEZ MARES
Biological and Agricultural Sciences: VALDEMAR MEDINA HOYOS
Civil Engineering: ENRIQUE CAMPOS MATTOS
Economics: EDGAR ACOSTA Y GUTIÉRREZ
Education: VÍCTOR HUGO LINARES HUACO
Geology and Geophysics: MELECIO LAZO ANGULO
History and Social Sciences: VÍCTOR RAÚL SACCA ABUSABAL
Law: RAYMUNDO NÚÑEZ LOZADA
Medicine: BENJAMÍN PAZ ALIAGA
Natural and Formal Sciences: ANDRÉS REYNOSO ORTIZ
Nursing: ESPERANZA VALDIVIA AMPUERO

Philosophy and Humanities: TERESA ARRIETA TRONCOSO DE GUZMÁN
Process Engineering: MARIO LOZADA REYNOSO
Production and Services Engineering: JOSÉ HERNÁNDEZ VALLEJOS
Psychology and Industrial and Public Relations: CÉSAR SALAS MORALES

UNIVERSIDAD NACIONAL DE SAN ANTONIO ABAD DEL CUSCO

Apdo 921, Cusco
Avda de la Cultura 733, Cusco
Telephone: (84) 604-100
Fax: (84) 238-156
E-mail: webmaster@unsaac.edu.pe
Internet: www.unsaac.edu.pe
Founded 1962, reorganized 1969
Depts of accountancy, animal husbandry, economics, education, geology and mining, technology
Rector: Ing. CARLOS CHACON GALINDO
Number of teachers: 450
Number of students: *c.* 16,000
Publication: *Revista Universitaria* (1 a year).

UNIVERSIDAD NACIONAL DE SAN CRISTÓBAL DE HUAMANGA

Portal Independencia No. 57, Ayacucho
Telephone: (66) 312-230
Fax: (66) 312-510
E-mail: postmaster@unsch.edu.pe
Internet: www.unsch.edu.pe
Founded 1677, reopened 1959
State control
Language of instruction: Spanish
Academic year: March to July,August to December
Rector: MV JORGE DEL CAMPO CAVERO
Vice-Rector for Academic Affairs: Dr RAMIRO PALOMINO MALPARTIDA
Vice-Rector for Admin.: MSc JORGE SOTERO GARCÍA BLÁSQUEZ MOROTE
Gen. Sec.: Ing. MAURO VARGAS CAMARENA
Librarian: MARIA ISABEL MATTA DURAN
Number of teachers: 450
Number of students: 6,000
Publications: *Boletín UNSCH*, *Guamangengis*, *Signos y Obras*

DEANS

Agronomy: Ing. CÉSAR ROLANDO RUIZ CANALES
Biological Sciences: VICTOR ALEGRIA VALERIANO
Chemical and Metallurgical Engineering: Ing. CLEMENTE LIMAYLLA AGUIRRE
Economics and Administration: AURELIO ELORRIETA ESPINOZA
Education: Prof. HECTOR ELIAS VEGA LEON
Law and Political Sciences: Dr DANIEL QUISPE PÉREZ
Mining and Civil Engineering: Ing. CARLOS AUBERTO PRADO PRADO
Nursing: Prof. VICENTE VALVERDE BALTAZAR
Obstetrics: Dr SADOT TORRES RAMOS
Social Sciences: TULA RUTH ALARCON ALARCON

UNIVERSIDAD NACIONAL SAN LUIS GONZAGA DE ICA

Prolongación Ayabaca C-9, Urb. San José, Ica
Telephone: (56) 228-406
E-mail: webmaster@unica.edu.pe
Internet: www.unica.edu.pe
Founded 1961
Academic programmes in agronomy, arts and education, civil engineering, dentistry, economic and social sciences, fisheries and biological sciences, law, mechanical engineering

and electricity, medicine, pharmacy and biochemistry, veterinary medicine
Rector: Dr CESAR ANGELES CABALLERO
Sec.-Gen.: Dr MIGUEL CALDERÓN REINA
Number of teachers: 459
Number of students: 6,295
Publications: *Educación Dental*, *Letras y Educación*.

UNIVERSIDAD NACIONAL DE SAN MARTÍN

Jr. Maynas 177, Tarapoto
Telephone: (42) 524253
E-mail: informes@unsm.edu.pe
Internet: www.unsm.edu.pe
Founded 1979
Rector: Ing. M. Sc. ALFREDO QUINTEROS GARCÍA
Sec.-Gen.: Ing. JAIME RAMÍREZ NAVARRO
Librarian: JORGE YUNGBLUTH ZEGARRA
Number of teachers: 41
Number of students: 410

UNIVERSIDAD NACIONAL DEL SANTA

Avda Pacífico 508, Urb. Buenos Aires Apdo 10, Nuevo Chimbote
Telephone: (44) 311249
Fax: (44) 311556
Internet: www.uns.edu.pe
Founded 1984; present status 1998
Rector: ESTEBAN HORNA BANCES
Vice-Rector for Academic Affairs: PEDRO MONCADA BECERRA
Vice-Rector for Admin.: Ing. PEDRO GAMARRA LEIVA
Number of teachers: 160
Number of students: 3,100

DEANS

Faculty of Education and Humanities: Lic. BETTY RISCO RODRÍGUEZ
Faculty of Engineering: Ing. VICTOR CASTRO ZAVALETA
Faculty of Science: Lic. AMÉRICA ODAR ROSARIO

UNIVERSIDAD NACIONAL DE TRUJILLO

Jr. Independencia 389, Trujillo
Telephone: (44) 205-513
Fax: (44) 256-629
E-mail: rectorado@unitru.edu.pe
Internet: www.unitru.edu.pe
Founded 1824
State control
Language of instruction: Spanish
Academic year: April to December
Rector: Dr VÍCTOR CARLOS SABANA GAMARRA
Vice-Rector for Academic Affairs: Dr JUAN CÉSAR MURO MOREY
Vice-Rector for Admin.: Dr ORLANDO VELÁSQUEZ BENITES
Librarian: Dr CESAR GAMARRA SÁNCHEZ
Library of 28,000 vols
Number of teachers: 980
Number of students: 15,000
Publications: *Amauta—Archivos de Oftalmología del Norte del Perú*, *Lenguaje y Ciencia*, *Memoria Rectoral*, *Revista de Derecho*, *Revista del Museo de Arqueología y Antropología*

DEANS

Agricultural Sciences: NELSON RÍOS CAMPOS
Biological Sciences: Dr JOSÉ MOSTACERO LEÓN
Chemical Engineering: Dr JUAN GUERRERO LLUNCOR

Economic Sciences: Dr ENRIQUE RODRÍGUEZ RODRÍGUEZ

Education and Communication Sciences: Dr JULIO ALDAMA FLORES

Engineering: Ing. JUAN SÁNCHEZ BUSTAMANTE

Law and Political Sciences: Dr TEÓDULO SANTOS CRUZ

Medical Sciences: Dra LOURDES ARMAS FAVA

Nursing: Dra FLOR LUNA VICTORIA MORI

Pharmacy and Biochemistry: Dr SEGUNDO RONCAL SALDAÑA

Physical and Mathematical Sciences: Dr MARCIAL VÁSQUEZ ARTEAGA

Social Sciences: Dr GUILLERMO GUTIÉRREZ CHACÓN

UNIVERSIDAD NACIONAL DE TUMBES

Centro Cívico, 3er Piso, Tumbes

Telephone: (72) 522810

E-mail: oginf@untumbes.edu.pe

Internet: www.untumbes.edu.pe

Founded 1984

Rector: Dr ADÁN ALVARADO BERNUY

Vice-Rector for Academic Affairs: Dr CÉSAR MANTILLA AVALOS

Vice-Rector for Admin.: AUBERTO HIDALGO MOGOLLÓN

DEANS

Faculty of Agrarian Sciences: FRANCISCO ALBURQUEQUE VIERA

Faculty of Economics: MANUEL PAZ LÓPEZ

Faculty of Fishery: CÉSAR ESTUARDO POMA SÁNCHEZ

Faculty of Health Sciences: GINO ANTONIO MORETTI OTOYA

Faculty of Law and Social Sciences: RICARDO NOBLECILLA MORÁN

UNIVERSIDAD NACIONAL DE UCAYALI

Avda Centenario km. 6, Pucallpa

Telephone: (61) 579962

Fax: (61) 592236

E-mail: imagen@unu.edu.pe

Internet: www.unu.edu.pe

Founded 1979

State control

Language of instruction: Spanish

Rector: Dr VICTOR CHÁVEZ VÁSQUEZ

Vice-Rector for Academic Affairs: Ing. DANIEL BALAREZO INFANTE

Vice-Rector for Admin.: Dr MIGUEL NOLTE MANZANARES

Registrar: Ing. Admin. ROMEL PINEDO RÍOS

Librarian: RAUL JAVIER GUTIÉRREZ PINEDA

Number of teachers: 178

Number of students: 1,400

DEANS

Administration and Accountancy: Lic. Admin. PEDRO ORMEÑO CARMONA

Agronomy: OSCAR LLAPAPASCA PAUCAR

Forest Sciences: Ing. CARLOS FACHIN MATOS

Health: ISABEL ESTEBAN ROBLADILLO

Private Universities

PONTIFICIA UNIVERSIDAD CATÓLICA DEL PERÚ

Avda Universitaria 1801, San Miguel, Lima 32

Telephone: (1) 626-2000

Fax: (1) 626-2170

E-mail: secgen@pucp.edu.pe

Internet: www.pucp.edu.pe

Founded 1917

Private control

Language of instruction: Spanish

Academic year: March to December (2 terms)

Rector: Dr MARCIAL RUBIO CORREA

Vice-Rector for Academic Affairs: Dr EFRAÍN GONZALES DE OLARTE

Vice-Rector for Admin.: CARLOS FOSCA PASTOR

Sec.-Gen.: Dr RENÉ ORTIZ CABALLERO

Registrar: IVAN CALDAS

Dir for Institutional Affairs: ROCÍO VILLANUEVA

Librarian: Dra CARMEN VILLANUEVA

Library: see under Libraries and Archives

Number of teachers: 2,500

Number of students: 19,000

Publications: *Agenda Internacional* (2 a year), *Análisis Económico de Coyuntura* (12 a year), *Anthropológica* (1 a year), *Areté* (2 a year, philosophy), *Boletín de Arqueología* (1 a year, archaeology), *Boletín del Instituto Riva-Agüero* (1 a year), *Debates en Sociología* (2 a year, sociology), *Derecho* (1 a year, law), *Economía* (1 a year, economics), *Educación* (2 a year, education), *Electro Electrónica* (2 a year), *Espacio y Desarrollo* (1 a year), *Histórica* (2 a year), *Lexis* (2 a year, linguistic and literary review), *Pensamiento Constitucional* (1 a year), *Pro Matemática* (2 a year), *Revista de Psicología* (2 a year, psychology), *Revista de Química* (2 a year, chemistry), *Synergies Pérou* (1 a year, didactology of languages and cultures), *Tren de Sombras* (4 a year, cinema)

DEANS

Arts (General Studies Programme): Prof. PABLO QUINTANILLA PÉREZ-WICHT

Faculty of Administration and Accounting: OSCAR DÍAZ BECERRA

Faculty of Architecture and Planning: FREDERICK COOPER LLOSA

Faculty of Communication Arts and Sciences: Prof. JUAN GARGUREVICH REGAL

Faculty of Education: CARMEN COLOMA MANRIQUE

Faculty of Fine Arts: ALBERTO AGAPITO ABURTO

Faculty of Humanities: Prof. SUSANA REISZ CANDREVA

Faculty of Law: Prof. VILLAVICENCIO

Faculty of Science and Engineering: DANIEL TORREALVA

Faculty of Social Sciences: ALAN FAIRLIE

Graduate School: Prof. PATRICIA MARTÍNEZ URIBE

Science (General Studies Programme): Prof. CARLOS PIZARRO ORTIZ

UNIVERSIDAD FEMENINA DEL SAGRADO CORAZÓN

Avda Los Frutales 954, Urb. Santa Magdalena Sofía, La Molina, Apdo 0005, Lima 41

Telephone: (1) 436-4641

Fax: (1) 436-3247

E-mail: postmast@unife.edu.pe

Internet: www.unife.edu.pe

Founded 1962

Private control

Language of instruction: Spanish

Academic year: April to December (2 semesters)

Rector: Dra R. M. ELGA GARCÍA ASTE

Vice-Rector for Admin.: Dra GRACIELA RUIZ DURÁN

Vice-Rector for Academic Affairs: Dra ROSA MARÍA REUSCHE LARI

Librarian: Lic. MARÍA LA SERNA DE MÁS

Library of 67,340 vols

Number of teachers: 321

Number of students: 2,292

Publications: *Revista de Educación, Cuaderno de Psicología, Revista de Psicología, Puente, Consensus, Avances en Psicología, Comunifé*

DEANS

Architecture: Arq. CARMEN ÁNGELA SALVADOR WADSWORTH

Education: Dr AGUSTÍN CAMPOS ARENAS

Engineering: Mg. JUAN MANUEL FERNÁNDEZ CHAVESTA

Law and Political Sciences: Dr LUIS FELIPE ALMENARA BRYSON

Psychology and Humanities: Dra. VICTORIA GARCÍA GARCÍA

Translation, Interpreting and Communications: Lic. ROSSANA SORLANO VERGARA

Postgraduate School: Dra GLORIA BENAVIDES VÍA

UNIVERSIDAD DE HUÁNUCO

Jr. Hermilio Valdizán 871, 2° Piso, Huánuco

Telephone and fax (62) 513-154

E-mail: info@udh.edu.pe

Internet: www.udh.edu.pe

Founded 1984

Rector: RAUL ISRAEL OLIVERA

Vice-Rector: RAFAEL ISRAEL OLIVERA

Admin. Officer: MANUEL MANRIQUE MARCOS

Librarian: MARY DIAZ PAIVA

Number of teachers: 55

Number of students: 1,700

DEANS

Faculty of Forestry Engineering: NILO LÓPEZ TELLO

Faculty of Law and Politics: EMERICO ISRAEL OLIVERA

Faculty of Obstetrics: MANUEL ISRAEL OLIVERA

UNIVERSIDAD INCA GARCILASO DE LA VEGA

Avda San Felipe 890, Jesús María, Lima

Telephone: (1) 471-1784

E-mail: vrac@uigv.edu.pe

Internet: www.uigv.edu.pe

Founded 1964

Private control

Rector: Dr LUIS CERVANTES LINAN

Sec.-Gen.: Dr ALFONSO CARRIZALES ULLOA

Librarian: NANCY HARMAN DE ALVARADO

Number of teachers: 240

Number of students: 7,000

Publication: *Garcilaso*

DIRECTORS

Accountancy: T. MOYA DE ROJAS

Administration: G. SUXE MONTERO

Economics: M. DELGADO ULLOQUE

Education: A. CASTRO URBINA

Industrial Engineering: L. TITO ATAURIMA

Law: R. CASTRO NESTAREZ

Social Sciences: A. CASTRO URBINA

Social Work: B. CORDOVA SUÁREZ

UNIVERSIDAD DE LIMA

Apdo 852, Lima 100

Telephone: (1) 437-6767

Fax: (1) 437-8066

E-mail: postmaster@ulima.edu.pe

Internet: www.ulima.edu.pe

Founded 1962

Private control

Language of instruction: Spanish

Academic year: April to December

Rector: Dra ILSE WISOTZKI LOLI

Vice-Rector: Mag. CÉSAR VIALARDI SACÍN

Admin. and Gen. Services: Ing. JOSÉ ANTONIO LIZÁRRAGA

Librarian: NELLY CASAS PASTOR

Number of teachers: 900

Number of students: 14,000

Publications: *Ciencia Económica* (2 a year), *Contratexto* (1 a year), *Ingeniería Industrial, Ius et Praxis* (2 a year), *Lienzo* (1 a year), *Noticias* (12 a year), *Persona* (1 a year)

DEANS

Administration: CARLOS BRESANI
Communication Sciences: ÓSCAR QUÉZADA
Economics: ALBERTO TOKESHI
General Studies: CÉSAR VIALARDI
Industrial Engineering: JAIME LEÓN
Law: OSWALDO HUNDSKOPF
Psychology: EDWIN SALAS
Systems Engineering: JORGE CHUE

UNIVERSIDAD DEL PACÍFICO

Avda Salaverry 2020, Jesús María, Apdo 4683, Lima 11

Telephone: (1) 219-0100
Fax: (1) 219-0140
E-mail: ori@up.edu.pe
Internet: www.up.edu.pe

Founded 1962
Private control
Language of instruction: Spanish
Academic year: March to December

Rector: Prof. FELIPE PORTOCARRERO
Vice-Rector: Prof. MATILDE SCHWALB
Gen. Sec.: Prof. CARLOS LUIS AGUSTI
Dir of Institutional Relations: CECILIA MONTES
Registrar: Prof. MIGUEL CHANG
Librarian: ROSA DORIVAL

Library of 50,000 vols, 1,500 periodicals, 500 multimedia titles, thesis and entrepreneurial projects
Number of teachers: 900
Number of students: 3,400 (2,800 full-time undergraduate, 600 part-time graduate)

Publications: *Apuntes, Punto de Equilibrio*

DEANS

Business: Prof. EDUARDO MINDREAU
Business Engineering: Prof. OSCAR DE AZAMBUJA
Economics: Prof. ARLETTE BELTRAN
Graduate School: Prof. ELSA DEL CASTILLO
Law: Prof. FERNANDO CANTUARIAS

UNIVERSIDAD PERUANA CAYETANO HEREDIA

Av. Honorio Delgado 430, Urb. Ingeniería, Lima

Telephone: (1) 319-0000
E-mail: postmaster@upch.edu.pe
Internet: www.upch.edu.pe

Founded 1961
Private control
Language of instruction: Spanish
Academic year: April to March

Rector: Dr OSWALDO ZEGARRA ROJAS
Vice-Rector for Academic Affairs: Dr DAVID LOZA FERNÁNDEZ
Vice-Rector for Research: Dr ALBERTO RAMÍREZ RAMOS
Vice-Rector for Admin. Affairs: Dr RODOLFO ZAVALA ULFFE
Sec.-Gen.: JUAN JIMÉNEZ BENDEZU

Number of teachers: 450
Number of students: 4,264

Publications: *Acta Herediana, Boletín UPCH, Revista Acta Andina, Revista Estomatológica, Revista Médica Herediana*

DEANS

Faculty of Education: Dr MAÑUEL BELLO DOMINGUEZ
Faculty of Medicine: Dr LUIS CARAVEDO REYES

Faculty of Nursing: Dr MARGOT ZARATE LEÓN
Faculty of Public Health and Administration: Dr ALEJANDRO LLANOS CUENTAS
Faculty of Sciences and Philosophy: Dr ABRAHAM VAISBERG WOLACH
Faculty of Stomatology: Dr FERNANDO DONAYRE GONZALES
School of Postgraduate Studies: Dr ENRIQUE MACHICADO ZAVALA

UNIVERSIDAD DE PIURA

Avda Ramón Mugica 131, Urbanización San Eduardo, POB 353, Piura

Telephone: (73) 284-500
Fax: (73) 284-510
E-mail: info@udep.pe
Internet: www.udep.edu.pe

Founded 1969
Private control
Language of instruction: Spanish
Academic year: March to December

Pres.: Dr ANTONIO ABRUÑA PUYOL
Vice-Pres.: ANTONIO MABRES TORELLÓ
Vice-Pres.: DANTE GUERRERO CHANDUVÍ
Vice-Pres.: JESÚS CHIYÓN DE MARES
Vice-Pres.: SERGIO BALAREZO SALDAÑA
Gen. Sec.: WILLIAM ZAPATA JIMÉNEZ
Librarian: Dr MARÍA JOSÉ ANDRADE DE HAKANSSON

Number of teachers: 233
Number of students: 5,400

Publications: *Boletín electrónico DesdelCampus, Libro de Humanidades, Mercurio Peruano, Periódico Campus, Revista Amigos, Revista de Investigacion de Derecho, Revista de Investigacion de Comunicacion*

DEANS

Faculty of Communications: MELA SALAZAR VELARDE
Faculty of Economics and Business Administration: MARIELA GARCÍA ROJAS
Faculty of Education: FLOR HAU YON PALOMINO
Faculty of Engineering: Dra. SUSANA VEGAS CHIYÓN
Faculty Of Humanities: Arq. ERNESTO MAVILA UGARTE
Faculty of Law: Dr CARLOS HAKANSSON NIETO
Faculty of Sciences and Humanities: Arq. ERNESTO MAVILA UGARTE

UNIVERSIDAD RICARDO PALMA

Avda Benavides 5440, Urb. Las Gardenias, Santiago de Surco, Apdo 18-0131, Lima

Telephone: (1) 275-0450
Fax: (1) 275-0468
E-mail: webmaster@urp.edu.pe
Internet: www.urp.edu.pe

Founded 1969
Private control
Language of instruction: Spanish
Academic year: April to December

Rector: Dr IVÁN RODRÍGUEZ CHÁVEZ
Vice-Rectors: Dr HUGO SÁNCHEZ CARLESSI, Arq. ROBERTO CHANG CHAO
Sec.-Gen.: Lic. GERARDO CHOQUE MARTINEZ
Librarian: Mg. ROSARIO VALDIVIA PAZ SOLDÁN

Number of teachers: 650
Number of students: 9,000

Publications: *Revista, Revista Arquitextos, Revista Biotempus, Revista de la Facultad de Ciencias Económicas, Revista de la Faculdad de Lenguas Modernas, Revista de la Facultad de Psicología, Revista Perfiles de Ingeniería, Tradición*

DEANS

Faculty of Architecture and Town Planning: Arq. OSWALDO VELÁSQUEZ HIDALGO

Faculty of Biological Sciences: Dra REINA ZUÑIGA DE ACLETO
Faculty of Economics: Dr RONALD FIGUEROA AVILA
Faculty of Engineering: Mg. LEONARDO ALCAYHUAMAN ACCOSTUPA
Faculty of Medicine: Dr MANUEL HUAMÁN GUERRERO
Faculty of Modern Languages: Dra DORA BAZÁN DE DEVOTO
Faculty of Psychology: Dr RAÚL YAÑEZ CANNON

UNIVERSIDAD DE SAN MARTÍN DE PORRES

Ciuadad Universitaria, Avda Las Calandrias s/n, Santa Anita, Lima

Telephone: (1) 362-0064
Fax: (1) 317-2365
E-mail: rectorado@usmp.edu.pe
Internet: www.usmp.edu.pe

Founded 1962
Private control
Language of instruction: Spanish
Academic year: March to December

Rector: Dr JOSE ANTONIO CHANG ESCOBEDO
Vice-Rector: Dr RAÚL EDUARDO BAO GARCÍA
Chief Planning Officer: OSCAR BECERRA
Gen. Dir of Admin.: Ing. JORGE UREÑA SCHRACK

Library of 160,000 vols
Number of teachers: 4,100
Number of students: 34,000

Publications: *Gobernabilidad, Horizonte Medico, Kiru, Martín, Revista Peruana de Obstetricia y Enfermería, Vox Juris*

DEANS

Faculty of Accounting, Economy and Finance: Dr DOMINGO SÁENZ YAYA
Faculty of Administration and Human Resources: Dr DANIEL HERNÁN VALERA LOZA
Faculty of Communication, Tourism and Psychology: Dr JOHAN LEURIDAN HUYS
Faculty of Dentistry: Dr CARLOS ENRIQUE CAVA VERGIU
Faculty of Engineering and Architecture: Dr GUSTAVO TATAJE SALAS
Faculty of Human Medicine: Dr FRANK LIZARASO CAPARÓ
Faculty of Law: Dr RUBÉN DARÍO SANABRIA ORTIZ
Faculty of Obstetrics and Nursing: Mag. HILDA BACA NEGLIA

College

UNIVERSIDAD ESAN

Apdo 1846, Lima 100

Telephone: (1) 317-7200
Fax: (1) 345-1328
E-mail: cendoc@esan.edu.pe
Internet: www.esan.edu.pe

Founded 1963, as a jt venture between the Peruvian Govt and the US Dept of State Agency for Int. Devt to promote the socio-economic devt of the region; training in management at graduate level and for executives

Dir: JORGE TALAVERA TRAVERSO

Library of 50,000 vols
Number of teachers: 37
Number of students: 3,000

Publications: *Cuadernos de Difusión* (2 a year), *Documentos de Trabajo, INFORME-SAN* (institutional bulletin, 26 a year).

Schools of Art and Music

Conservatorio Nacional de Música (National Conservatory of Music): Jr. Carabaya 429, Lima; tel. (1) 426-9677; fax (1) 426-5658; e-mail cnmdg@terra.com.pe; f. 1908 as Academia Nacional de Música 'Alcedo', autonomous since 1966; performance, musicology, education, composition; choir and orchestra; library: 14,000 books and musical scores, and record library; 87 teachers; 400 students; Dir Gen. ENRIQUE ITURRIAGA ROMERO; Acad. Dir CARMEN ESCOBEDE REVOREDO; publ. *Conservatorio* (1 a year).

Affiliated Institutes:

Conservatorio Regional de Música del Norte 'Carlos Valderrama': Independencia 572 (2° piso), Trujillo; tel. (44) 235392; fax (44) 235392; e-mail crmncv@ qnet.com.pe; f. 1946; 42 teachers; 450 students; Dir CARLOS E. PAREDES ABAD.

Escuela Regional de Música de Huánuco: Dir JAIME DÍAZ.

Escuela Superior de Formación Artística 'Mario Urteaga': km. 3.5 Carretera Baños del Inca, Cajamarca; tel. (44) 826010; fax (44) 821209; e-mail esfamusica@yahoo.com; f. 1984; 9 teachers; 89 students; Dir RAMÓN BAZÁN FIGUEROA.

Escuela Superior de Música 'Condorcunca': Jirón 28 de Julio No 122, Ayacuche; tel. (64) 812598; e-mail esma@ goalsnet.com.pe; f. 1957; 33 teachers; 152 students; Dir PEDRO RAMÓN CASTILLA HUAYHUA.

Escuela Superior de Música 'José María Valle Riestra': Avda Bolognesi No 890, Piura; tel. (74) 322632; e-mail esmjmvr@lanet.com.pe; f. 1951; 23 teachers; 203 students; Dir REYNALDO E. BURGO PÉREZ.

Escuela Superior de Música 'Luis Duncker Lavalle': Calle 4 s/n, Coop. Labramara J. L. Bustamante y Rivero, Arequipa; tel. (54) 424510; fax (54) 425723; e-mail esma@terra.com.pe; f. 1945; 33 teachers; 251 students; Dir ELÍAS ADOLFO CHÁVEZ.

Escuela Superior Pública de Formación Artística 'Francisco Lase': Avda 2 de Mayo No 412, Tacna; tel. (54) 711601; fax (54) 711601; e-mail esfafl@correoweb .com; internet www.geocities.com/esfafl; f. 1989; 45 teachers; 315 students; Dir DAVID ORTIZ OVIEDO.

Instituto Superior de Música 'Leandre Alviña Miranda': Tocuyeres 526, San Blas, Cusco; tel. (84) 231621; fax (84) 231621; e-mail ismlam.cusco@latinmail .com.pe; f. 1950; 36 teachers; 192 students; Dir ESTEBAN ITUPA LLAVINA.

Escuela Nacional Superior Autónoma de Bellas Artes del Perú (Autonomous National School of Fine Arts): Jirón Ancash 681, Lima; tel. (1) 427-2200; internet www .ensabap.edu.pe; f. 1918; to train artists and teachers; library: 5,000 vols; Dir PEDRO BENITO ROTTA BISSO; publ. *Anuario Académico*.

Escuela Regional de Bellas Artes 'Diego Quispe Tito': Calle Márquez 271, Cusco; tel. (84) 231-491.

Escuela Superior Pública de Arte Carlos Baca Flor: Calle Sucre 111, Cercado, Arequipa; tel. (54) 281-291; f. 1951.

PHILIPPINES

The Higher Education System

From the 16th century until 1898 the Philippines were under Spanish control. They were ceded to the USA under the terms of the Treaty of Paris (1898) and remained under US control until independence was achieved in 1946. The Philippines' colonial inheritance is reflected in its higher education system. The two oldest institutions, the University of San Carlos (founded in 1595; current status since 1948) and the University of Santo Tomás (founded in 1611), are both private Catholic universities, while universities founded during or after the period of US control are modelled on US institutions. In 2009/10 there were 2,770,965 students enrolled in 2,180 higher education institutions (607 public, 1,573 private).

More than 80% of higher education institutions in the Philippines are privately run. The Commission on Higher Education (CHED), established by the Higher Education Act of 1994 as part of a broad reform programme of the education system, is the supreme national body for public and private universities. It is responsible, inter alia, for quality assurance, accreditation (which is mandatory), and policy formulation and planning. Higher education institutions (both public and private) that are deemed by the CHED to have reached the highest standard of teaching and research in specific subject areas are designated as Centres of Excellence and receive additional funding from the Government. Additional accreditation and quality assurance may be sought from one of four agencies, namely: Philippine Accrediting Association of Schools, Colleges and Universities; Philippine Association of Colleges and Universities, Commission on Accreditation; Association of Christian Schools and Colleges—Accrediting Agency, Inc.; and Accrediting Agency of Chartered Colleges and Universities in the Philippines. All four bodies are members of the Federation of Accreditating Agencies of the Philippines.

Admission to higher education is on the basis of satisfactory performance in the High School Diploma and the university entrance examination. For most Filipino degrees, students are expected to accrue a specified number of credits each semester throughout the duration of the degree in order to graduate. Associate degrees are offered by community colleges and universities and are two-year programmes of study in the arts and sciences. The first full undergraduate degree is the Bachelors, usually a four-year course, but certain subjects may require longer periods of study, such as law and medicine (both eight years). The postgraduate degrees are the Masters and PhD. The Masters lasts for two years and consists of full-time study and the submission of a thesis. For a PhD, students are required to undertake at least three years of study and research, and to complete a dissertation.

The Technical Education and Skills Development Authority (TESDA) is the controlling body of post-secondary technical and vocational education, which is offered by public and private technical/vocational institutes and specialist institutions. The duration of programmes varies from one to three years; in some instances programmes are geared towards a Certificate system of four levels. All technical and vocational education providers must be accredited by the TESDA.

Regulatory and Representative Bodies

GOVERNMENT

Department of Education: DepED Complex, Meralco Ave, Pasig City, 1600 Metro Manila; tel. (2) 632-13-61; fax (2) 638-86-34; internet www.deped.gov.ph; Sec. of Education ARMIN A. LUISTRO.

ACCREDITATION

Accrediting Agency of Chartered Colleges and Universities in the Philippines, Inc. (AACCUP): 812 Future Point Plaza 1, 112 Panay Ave, South Triangle, Quezon City; tel. (2) 415-9016; fax (2) 415-8995; e-mail aaccup@axti.com; internet www.aaccupqa.org.ph; f. 1987; accredits curricular programmes in the Philippines, particularly for state univs and colleges; 107 mems (104 state univs and colleges, 3 local colleges); Pres. and Chair. of Board of Trustees Dr RUPERTO S. SANGALANG; Exec. Dir Dr MANUEL T. CORPUS.

Federation of Accrediting Agencies of the Philippines (FAAP): Unit 302 Puno Building, 47 Kalayaan Ave, Diliman, Quezon City; tel. (2) 927-9645; f. 1976; NGO founded to improve the quality of education by means of voluntary accreditation for private higher education instns; Pres. Dr FELICIANA A. REYES.

Philippine Accrediting Association of Schools, Colleges and Universities (PAASCU): Unit 107, The Tower at Emerald Sq., J. P. Rizal corner P. Tuazon Sts, 1109 Quezon City; tel. (2) 911-2845; fax (2) 911-0807; e-mail info@paascu.org.ph; internet www.paascu.org.ph; f. 1957; private org. accrediting academic programmes that meet commonly accepted standards of quality education; has accredited programmes in 229 instns; Chair. of Board of Dirs Dr RAMON C. REYES; Exec. Dir CONCEPCION V. PIJANO.

Philippine Association of Colleges and Universities, Commission on Accreditation (PACUCOA): Suite 7M Eagle Star Condominium, Dela Rosa St, Loyola Heights, Katipunan Ave, Quezon City; tel. (2) 426-0089; e-mail pacucoa@yahoo.com; f. 1967; accredits private colleges and univs; 125 mem. schools with 799 programmes; Chair. Dr ROSITA L. NAVARRO; Exec. Dir Dr ADLAI C. CASTIGADOR.

FUNDING

Fund Assistance to Private Education (FAPE): 7th Floor, Concorde Condominium, Salcedo cnr Benavides Sts, Legaspi Village, Makati City; tel. (2) 816-4136; fax (2) 818-0013; f. 1968; perpetual trust fund set up by the Philippines govt with help from the US govt; funds are provided by interest earned on the initial capital augmented by donations and grants; Exec. Dir CAROLINA PORIO.

NATIONAL BODIES

Association of Catholic Universities of the Philippines, Inc.: University of Santo Tomás (Room 111, Main Bldg), España, Manila; tel. (2) 731-35-44; fax (2) 740-97-27; f. 1973 to serve the interests of the 21 Catholic univs in the Philippines; Pres. Fr TAMERLANE R. LANA; Sec. Gen. Prof. GIOVANNA V. FONTANILLA; publ. ACUP Newsletter (1 a year).

Catholic Educational Association of the Philippines (CEAP): 7 Road 16, Bagong Pag-asa, 1105 Quezon City; tel. (2) 426-2679; fax (2) 426-2670; e-mail ceap@edsamail.com.ph; internet www.eccceonline.org/ceap; f. 1941; Pres. Fr RODERICK SALAZAR, Jr.

Commission on Higher Education: Higher Education Development Center (HEDC) Bldg, C. P. Garcia St, U. P. Diliman, Quezon City; tel. (2) 351-7413; fax (2) 441-1177; e-mail info@ched.gov.ph; internet www.ched.gov.ph; f. 1994; governing body covering public and private higher education instns as well as degree-granting programmes in all tertiary educational insts in the Philippines; Chair. Dr PATRICIA B. LICUANAN; Exec. Dir Dr WILLIAM C. MEDRANO.

Coordinating Council for Private Educational Association (COCOPEA): 89-C 9th Ave, Cubao, Quezon City; tel. (2) 913-2932; fax (2) 911-5888; promotes excellence in private higher education instns; Pres. JUANITO M. ACANTO.

Philippine Association of Colleges and Universities (PACU): Unit 601 Richmonde Plaza, Ortigas Centre, San Miguel Ave, Pasig City; tel. (2) 638-5635; fax (2) 637-6795; e-mail pacuinc@yahoo.com; internet www.pacu.org.ph; f. 1932; Pres. Dr VICENTE K. FABELLA; Sec. Dr PATRICIA B. LAGUNDA.

Philippine Association of Private Schools, Colleges and Universities (PAPSCU): 10th Fl., Bldg 7, Emilio Aguinaldo College, 113 Gonzales cnr San Marcelino Sts, UN Ave, Ermita, Manila; tel. (2) 522-0097; fax (2) 523-3117; e-mail papscu2005@yahoo.com.ph; internet www.papscu.org.ph; f. 1956; Pres. Dr JOSE PAULO E. CAMPOS.

Philippine Association of State Universities and Colleges: 2nd Fl., ITC Bldg, EARIST Compound, Valencia St, Sta Mesa, Manila; tel. (2) 716-0944; fax (2) 716-0430; f. 1967; ind. but attached to Dept of Education; aims to foster excellence in higher education, to promote communication among its mem. institutions, to encourage studies on higher education, to secure adequate government support for education, to encourage inter-institutional assistance through fellowships, grants, teacher exchange, accreditation; 75 mem. institutions; library with special collections on education; Pres. ELDIGARIO D. GONZALES; Exec. Dir Dr FREDERICK S. PADA; publ. *Baliham* (4 a year).

Learned Societies

GENERAL

Academia Filipina (Philippine Academy): 47 Juan Luna St, San Lorenzo Village, 1200 Makati, Metro Manila; tel. (2) 817-1128; fax (2) 817-1135; f. 1924; corresp. of the Real Academia Española (Madrid); 15 mems; Dir ALEJANDRO ROCES; Sec. SALVADOR B. MALIG.

AGRICULTURE, FISHERIES AND VETERINARY SCIENCE

Crop Science Society of the Philippines: c/o Phil Rice, Los Baños, Pili Drive, College, Laguna; tel. (49) 536-3635; e-mail asian@laguna.net; internet www.cssp.org.ph; f. 1970; 3,000 mems; Pres. NORVIE L. MANIGBAS; Vice-Pres. RENATO A. REANO; publ. *Philippine Journal of Crop Science* (3 a year).

Philippine Society of Agricultural Engineers: ATI Bldg Elliptical Rd, Diliman, Quezon City; tel. and fax (2) 920-4071; e-mail contact@psae.net; internet psae.net; f. 1950; 5,800 mems; Pres. Dr TERESITO G. AGUINALDO.

Philippine Veterinary Medical Association: Unit 233, Union Square Condominium, 15th Ave, Cubao, Quezon City; tel. (2) 911-3159; internet www.pvma.com.ph; f. 1907; 5,274 mems; Pres. Dr TOMAS C. LAZARO, II.

ARCHITECTURE AND TOWN PLANNING

United Architects of the Philippines (UAP): 53 Scout Rallos St, Diliman, Quezon City 1103; tel. (2) 412-6374; fax (2) 372-1796; e-mail uap@united-architects.org; internet www.united-architects.org; f. 1974 following merger of Philippine Institute of Architects, League of Philippine Architects and Association of Philippine Government Architects; Pres. EDRIC MARCO C. FLORENTINO; Sec.-Gen. GIL C. EVASCO.

BIBLIOGRAPHY, LIBRARY SCIENCE AND MUSEOLOGY

Association of Special Libraries of the Philippines (ASLP): Room 301, National Library Bldg, Kalaw St, Ermita, Manila; tel. (2) 524-4611; e-mail ladladj@dlsu.edu.ph; internet www.aczafra.com; f. 1954; 556 mems; Pres. JOCELYN L. LADAD; Sec. ARLENE Y. GONZALES; publs *ASLP Bulletin* (4 a year), *ASLP Newsletter* (4 a year), *Directory of Special Libraries*.

HISTORY, GEOGRAPHY AND ARCHAEOLOGY

Philippine Historical Association: c/o Office of External Affairs, St Mary's College, 37 M. Ignacia Ave, 1103 Quezon City; tel. 413-4076 ext. 222; fax 374-3073; e-mail glo.santos@yahoo.com; f. 1955; 500 mems; Pres. Prof. AMBETH OCAMPO; Exec. Dir Dr GLORIA M. SANTOS; publs *PHA Balita* (2 a year), *Philippine Historical Bulletin* (1 a year).

LANGUAGE AND LITERATURE

Alliance Française: POB 2899, 128 Manila; located at: 209 Nicanor Garcia St, Bel Air II, 1209 Makati City; tel. (2) 895-75-85; fax (2) 899-36-54; e-mail info@alliance.ph; internet www.alliance.ph; offers courses and examinations in French language and culture and promotes cultural exchange with France; Dir PHILIPPE NORMAND.

British Council: 10th Fl., Taipan Pl., F. Ortigas Jr Ave, Ortigas Centre, Pasig City 1605, Manila; tel. (2) 914-1011; fax (2) 914-1020; e-mail britishcouncil@britishcouncil.org.ph; internet www.britishcouncil.org/philippines; teaching centre; offers courses and examinations in English language and British culture and promotes cultural exchange with the UK; library; Dir GILL WESTAWAY.

Goethe-Institut: POB 1744, Makati Central Post Office, 1257 Makati City; 4-5/F Adamson Centre, 121 Leviste St, Salcedo Village, 1227 Makati City; tel. (2) 817-0978; fax (2) 817-0979; e-mail goetheinfo@manila.goethe.org; internet www.goethe.de/manila; f. 1961; offers courses and examinations in German language and culture and promotes cultural exchange with Germany; library of 3,000 vols; Dir RICHARD KÜNZEL.

Instituto Cervantes: 855 T. M. Kalaw St, Ermita, 1000 Manila; tel. (2) 526-14-82; fax (2) 526-14-49; e-mail cenmni@cervantes.es; internet manila.cervantes.es; f. 1991; offers courses and examinations in Spanish language and culture and promotes cultural exchange with Spain and Spanish-speaking countries; library of 23,000 vols, 1,500 CDs and audio cassettes, 2,000 video cassettes and 500 DVDs; Dir EDUARDO CALVO; Sec. KATERINA VENERACIÓN.

Komisyon sa Wikang Filipino: Watson Bldg, 1610 J. P. Laurel St, San Miguel, Manila; tel. (2) 734-55-46; fax (2) 736-03-15; internet www.komfil.gov.ph; f. 1991 (fmrly Institute of Philippine Languages); develops, promotes and standardizes Filipino and other Philippine languages; library of 5,000 vols; Chair. Dr PONCIANO B. P. PINEDA.

MEDICINE

Manila Medical Society: 800 Taft Ave, Manila; tel. (2) 524-9944; fax (2) 525-6771; e-mail mmsi@yahoo.com; internet www.geocities.com/mmsi1902; f. 1902; 1,249 mems; Pres. Dr ASCENSION F. BAUTISTA; Sec. Dr FELICISIMA B. BACON.

Philippine Medical Association: PMA Bldg, North Ave, Quezon City; tel. (2) 929-6366; fax (2) 929-6951; e-mail medical@pma.com.ph; internet www.pma.com.ph; f. 1903; 107 component societies, 60 affiliated speciality societies; Pres. Dr MODESTO O. LLAMAS; Sec.-Gen. Dr REY MELCHOR SANTOS; publ. *Journal*.

Philippine Paediatric Society, Inc.: POB 3527, Manila; f. 1947; 620 mems; Pres. Dr JOEL S. ELISES; Sec. Dr VICTOR S. DOCTOR; publ. *Philippine Journal of Paediatrics* (6 a year).

Philippine Pharmaceutical Association: 815 R. Papa St. Sampaloc, 1008 Manila; tel. (2) 50-9006; fax (2) 522-3230; f. and incorporated 1920; 8,000 mems; Pres. Dr LOURDES TALAG ECHAUZ; Exec. Sec. Dr NORMA V. LERMA.

NATURAL SCIENCES

General

National Academy of Science and Technology: 2nd Fl., Philippine Science Heritage Centre, DOST Complex, Gen. Santos Ave, Bicutan, Taguig City, 1631 Metro Manila; tel. (2) 837-2071; fax (2) 837-3170; e-mail secretariat@nast.ph; internet www.nast.dost.gov.ph; f. 1976; advises the Pres. and Cabinet on policies concerning science and technology nationally; Pres. Dr EMIL Q. JAVIER; Sec. Dr EVELYN MAE TECSON-MENDOZA.

Physical Sciences

Philippine Council of Chemists: 2227 Severino Reyes St, Sta Cruz, POB 1202, Manila 2805; f. 1958; 200 mems; Nat. Pres. MIGUEL G. AMPIL; Gen. Sec. P. B. CARBONELL; publ. *Bulletin*.

TECHNOLOGY

Philippine Institute of Mining, Metallurgical and Geological Engineers: POB 1595, Manila; f. 1940; 117 mems; Pres. JONES R. CASTRO; Sec.-Treas. LEOPOLDO F. ABAD.

Philippine Society of Civil Engineers: c/o Bureau of Public Works, Bonifacio Drive, Manila; f. 1918; assumed present title 1933; Pres. FLORENCIO MORENO; Sec.-Treas. TOMAS DE GUZMÁN; publ. *The Philippine Engineering Record* (4 a year).

Philippine Society of Mechanical Engineers: 19 Scout Bayoran St, South Triangle, Quezon City; tel. (2) 371-1819; fax (2) 372-4341; e-mail info@psme.org; internet www.psme.org; f. 1952; Pres. Eng EDIMAR V. SALCEDO.

Research Institutes

GENERAL

Advanced Science and Technology Institute: ASTI Bldg., C. P. Garcia Ave., Technology Park Complex, U.P. Campus, Diliman, Quezon City, 1101; tel. (2) 426-9755; fax (2) 925-8598; e-mail info@asti.dost.gov.ph; internet www.asti.dost.gov.ph; conducts research and devt in information and communications technology and microelectronics; Dir DENIS F. VILLORENTE.

Institute of Philippine Culture, Ateneo de Manila University: Frank Lynch Hall, Social Devt Complex, Loyola Heights, Quezon City 1108; tel. and fax 426-6067; e-mail ipc@admu.edu.ph; internet www.ipc-ateneo.org; f. 1960 as a univ. research org.; undertakes studies directed towards solving devt problems, particularly in the areas of upland devt, local governance, agrarian reform, community health, resources management, irrigation, forestry, women and sustainable agriculture; assists devt agencies; trains agency personnel and local communities in the use of research methodologies; library of 7,000 vols, 3,000 reprints and 104 multimedia vols; Dir Dr WILFREDO F. ARCE; publs *Culture and Development Series, IPC Discussion Papers, IPC Final Reports, IPC Monograph Series, IPC Papers, IPC Social Explorations Series*.

National Research Council of the Philippines: General Santos Ave, Bicutan, Taguig City; tel. (2) 837-6141; fax (2) 837-6143; e-mail nrcpinfo@dost.gov.ph; internet mis.dost.gov.ph/nrcp; f. 1933; supports basic research in a wide variety of fields; 12 scientific divisions; 2,250 mems; library of 1,300 vols; Pres. Prof. FORTUNATO T. DELA PEÑA; Exec. Dir Dr PACIENTE A. CORDERO, Jr; publs *Newsletter* (4 a year), *NRCP Research*

Journal (4 a year), *Technical Bulletin* (irregular).

AGRICULTURE, FISHERIES AND VETERINARY SCIENCE

Bureau of Plant Industry: 692 San Andres St, Malate, Manila; tel. (2) 525-7857; fax (2) 521-7650; e-mail cu.bpi@da.gov.ph; internet bpi.da.gov.ph; f. 1930; conserves and develops Philippine plant genetic resources and ensures the protection and devt of the plant industry; library of 10,000 vols; Dir Dr CLARITO M. BARRON.

Forest Products Research and Development Institute (FPRDI): Narra St, Forestry Campus, UP College, Los Baños, Laguna 4031; tel. (49) 536-2360; fax (49) 536-3630; e-mail fprdi@dost.gov.ph; internet www.fprdi.dost.gov.ph; f. 1957; conducts basic and applied research on forestry, forest products and other related areas; undertakes the transfer of completed research; provides technical services and industrial manpower training; library of 17,000 vols, 8,042 books, 3,431 reports, 4,500 vols of periodicals; Dir IV Dr ROMULO T. AGGANGAN; Sec. Dr MARIO G. MONTEJO; publs *Forest Products Technoflow*, *FPRDI Journal* (1 a year), *Lexicon of Philippine Trees*.

Philippine Rice Research Institute: Central Experiment Station Maligaya, Science City of Muñoz, Nueva Ecija; tel. (44) 456-0277; e-mail prri@philrice.gov.ph; internet www.philrice.gov.ph; f. 1960; aims to sustain the country's self-sufficiency in rice; undertakes and funds a national research and development programme for rice and rice-based farming systems; trains scientists, farmer leaders and agribusiness managers; Exec. Dir Dr LEOCADIO S. SEBASTIAN.

EDUCATION

Science Education Institute: c/o Department of Science and Technology, 3rd PTRI Bldg, Bicutan, Taguig, 1604, Metro Manila; tel. (2) 837-1359; fax (2) 837-1924; e-mail webmaster@sei.dost.gov.ph; internet www.sei.dost.gov.ph; Dir Dr ESTER B. OGENA.

Southeast Asian Ministers of Education Organization Regional Center for Educational Innovation and Technology (SEAMEO INNOTECH): Commonwealth Ave, Diliman, Quezon City 1101; tel. (2) 924-7681; fax (2) 921-0224; e-mail info@seameo-innotech.org; internet www.seameo-innotech.org; f. 1970; identifies basic educational problems common to the SE Asian region and assists the SE Asian Mins of Education Org. mem. countries in the solution of these problems; conducts training, devt, research, evaluation, information and communications technology and other spec. programmes; library of 18,000 vols; Dir Dr ERLINDA C. PEFIANCO; publs *INNOTECH Journal* (2 a year), *INNOTECH Newsletter* (2 a year).

MEDICINE

Food and Nutrition Research Institute: c/o Department of Science and Technology, Gen. Santos Ave, Bicutan, Taguig 1604, Metro Manila; tel. (2) 837-2934; fax (2) 837-3164; e-mail mvc@fnri.dost.gov.ph; internet www.fnri.dost.gov.ph; f. 1987; Dir Dr MARIO V. CAPANZANA.

NATURAL SCIENCES

Physical Sciences

Philippine Institute of Volcanology and Seismology: PHIVOLCS Bldg, C. P. Garcia Ave, U.P. Campus, Diliman, Quezon City; tel. (2) 426-14-68; fax (2) 929-83-66; e-mail phivolcs@x5.phivolcs.dost.gov.ph; internet www.phivolcs.dost.gov.ph; f. 1952; library of 3,000 vols; Dir RENATO U. SOLIDUM, Jr.

TECHNOLOGY

Industrial Technology Development Institute: DOST Compound, Gen. Santos Ave, Bicutan, Taguig 1631, Metro Manila; tel. (2) 837-2071; fax (2) 837-6156; e-mail nea@dost.gov.ph; internet www.mis.dost.gov.ph/itdi; f. 1951; carries out research and development in the areas of food processing, materials science, chemicals and minerals, electronics and process control, fuels and energy, microbiology and genetics, and the environment; Dir Dr NUNA E. ALMANZOR.

Metals Industry Research and Development Centre: MIRDC Compound, Gen. Santos Ave, Bicutan, Taguig 1604, Metro Manila; tel. (2) 837-0431; fax (2) 837-0430; e-mail adcruz@dost.gov.ph; internet www.mirdc.dost.gov.ph; f. 1972; research and devt, quality control, and testing of metal products; Exec. Dir ARTHUR LUCAS D. CRUZ; publ. *Metals Industry Trends and Events* (newsletter, 3 a year).

Mines and Geosciences Bureau: North Ave, Diliman, Quezon City, 1100, Metro Manila; tel. (2) 920-91-20; fax (2) 920-16-35; e-mail central@mgb.gov.ph; internet www.mgb.gov.ph; f. 1898; administers the utilization and management of the country's mineral wealth; conducts geological, mining, metallurgical, chemical and other research; undertakes geological and mineral exploration surveys; library of 4,200 vols; Dir JEREMIAS DOLINO; publs *Mineral Gazette* (2 a year), *Mineral Industry Indicators* (2 a year), *National Directory of Producing Mines and Quarries in the Philippines* (1 a year), *Philippine Mineral Industry Review* (4 a year), *Philippine Mineral Statistics* (1 a year).

Philippine Nuclear Research Institute: Commonwealth Ave, Diliman, Quezon City 1101; tel. (2) 920-8787; fax (2) 920-1646; e-mail nrlsd@pnri.dost.gov.ph; internet www.pnri.dost.gov.ph; f. 1958; peaceful applications of nuclear energy; library of 19,069 vols; Dir Dr ALUMANDA M. DELA ROSA (acting); publ. *Philippines Nuclear Journal* (1 a year).

Philippine Textile Research Institute: Gen. Santos Ave, Bicutan, Taguig City, Metro Manila; tel. and fax (2) 837-1325; e-mail ptri@dost.gov.ph; internet www.ptri.dost.gov.ph; f. 1967; conducts applied research and devt for textile industry; undertakes transfer of completed researches to end-users or via linkage units of other govt agencies; provides technical services and training programmes; Dir Dr CARLOS C. TOMBOC.

Libraries and Archives

Bacalod City

Bacalod City Library: Bacalod City, Negros Occidental; e-mail mcorpuz@bacolodcity.gov.ph; 50,000 vols.

Cagayan de Oro City

Cagayan de Oro City Public Library: Apolinar Velez St, Cagayan de Oro City; tel. (8822) 72-55-60; Librarian MYRNA F. ACEDERA.

Xavier University Library: Ateneo de Cagayan, Corrales Ave, Cagayan de Oro City 9000; tel. (8822) 72-31-16 ext. 2302; fax (8822) 72-71-63; e-mail librarytech@xu.edu.ph; internet library.xu.edu.ph; f. 1933; 121,500 vols, 376 periodicals; Dir, Univ.

Libraries ANNABELLE P. ACEDERA; publ. *Kinaadman.*

Cebu City

Cebu City Public Library: Osmeña Blvd., Cebu City; tel. (32) 253-1526; Librarian CIRILA A. DELOS REYES.

University of San Carlos Library: P. del Rosario St, 6000 Cebu City; tel. (32) 253-1000 ext. 133; fax (32) 254-04-32; e-mail direklib@usc.edu.ph; internet www.usc.edu.ph; f. 1947; 269,705 vols incl. 21,320 vols of Filipiniana, 3,360 titles of periodicals (44,992 vols total); 3,502 audiovisual items; spec. colln for local studies held in Cebuano Studies Centre at above address; Dir of Libraries Dr MARILOU P. TADLIP.

Davao City

Davao City Library: 3rd Fl., SP Building, San Pedro St, Davao City; tel. (82) 227-3137; fax (82) 226-8913; e-mail citylib@davaocity.gov.ph; Librarian NORA FE ALAJAR.

Dumaguete

Silliman University Library: 6200 Dumaguete City, Negros Oriental; tel. and fax (35) 422-7208; e-mail sulib@su.edu.ph; internet su.edu.ph; f. 1906; 200,000 items; Librarian LORNA YSO; publs *Convergence* (arts and sciences, irregular), *Silliman Journal* (humanities, social sciences and sciences, 2 a year).

Makati City

Asian Institute of Management, Knowledge Resource Centre Library: 123 Paseo de Roxas, POB 2095, Makati City 1260; tel. (2) 892-4011; fax (2) 817-2663; e-mail vong@aim.edu; internet www.aim.edu; f. 1968; 20,000 vols; Chief Librarian VIRGINIA ONG.

Filipinas Heritage Library: Nielson Tower, Ayala Triangle Makati Ave, Makati City, 1224; tel. (2) 892-1801; fax (2) 892-1810; e-mail asklibrarian@filipinaslibrary.org.ph; internet www.filipinaslibrary.org.ph; f. 1996; research library specializing in Philippine art and culture; Himig colln of vintage Philippine music; Elpidio Quirino presidential papers; spec. collns: Roderick Hall colln on Second World War in the Philippines; Memorare colln on the Liberation of Manila; Armengol colln; photography; museology; migration; 13,000 vols; Dir MA. ANTONIA ORTIGAS; Librarian MARIA CECILIA AYSON.

Manila

Adamson University Library: 900 San Marcelino St, Ermita, 1000 Manila; tel. (2) 524-2011 ext. 131; fax (2) 524-8038; e-mail hdecastro@adamson.edu.ph; internet www.adamson.edu.ph; f. 1933; Dir of Libraries HELEN C. DE CASTRO.

Ateneo de Manila University Rizal Library: Katipunan Ave, Loyola Heights, Quezon City 1108; tel. (2) 426-6001; fax (2) 426-5961; e-mail ltdavid@ateneo.edu; internet rizal.lib.admu.edu.ph; f. 1967; 240,000 vols, 36,000 bound periodicals, 325,000 microforms; preservation of spec. collns, incl. Filipiniana colln, Rizaliana, American Historical colln, Pardo de Tavera colln and the Ateneo Library of Women's Writings; Dir Prof. LOURDES T. DAVID; publs *Asian Perspectives in the Humanities and the Arts, Journal of Philippine Studies*.

Far Eastern University Library: POB 609, Quezon Blvd, Manila 1008; 3rd Fl., NRH Bldg, Nicanor Reyes Sr St, Sampaloc, Manila 1008; tel. (2) 735-5649; e-mail evelyn_sf@hotmail.com; f. 1928; 82,243 vols; Librarian Dr EVELYN S. FABITO.

Manila City Library: 2nd Fl., Sining Kayumanggi Bldg, Mehan Garden, Malate, Manila; tel. (2) 523-8688; Chief Librarian FILEMON L. GECOLEA.

National Library of the Philippines: POB 2926, T. M. Kalaw St, 1000 Ermita, Manila; tel. (2) 310-5032; fax (2) 524-2329; e-mail antonio.santos@nlp.gov.ph; internet web.nlp.gov.ph; f. 1887; 1,691,030 vols, 6,250 periodicals, 813,095 MSS, 51,680 vols of theses and dissertations, 10,332 audio cassettes, 6,004 microfilms, 2,190 sheet maps, 388 CD-ROMs; also 762,459 vols in public libraries and 8,579 vols in bookmobiles; Dir ANTONIO M. SANTOS; publ. *Philippine National Bibliography* (1 a year).

Philippine Women's University Library: 1743 Taft Ave, Manila 1004; tel. 526-8421; fax 526-6935; e-mail library@pwu.edu.ph; internet www.pwu.edu.ph; f. 1919; 4 br. libraries; social sciences, pure sciences, applied sciences, music, arts, literature, history, Filipiniana, women's colln, Asian colln, archive colln; 80,056 vols; Chief Librarian DIONISIA M. ANGELES; publs *PWU Research Journal, The Philippine Educational Forum.*

Science and Technology Information Institute, Department of Science and Technology: DOST Complex, Gen. Santos Ave, Upper Bicutan, Taguig City, Metro Manila; tel. (2) 837-2191; fax (2) 837-7518; e-mail litanobleza@yahoo.com; internet www .stii.dost.gov.ph; f. 1988; acquisition of science and technology information materials, technical information processing, library and reference services, science information services, databanking, training in science and technology information and computer applications; training on ScINET Integrated Library Management System (SILMS); provides communication and publication services, prepares audiovisual materials on science and technology, press releases, documentary films/video, coordinates and facilitates radio and television interviews of scientists and science managers; 10,534 vols, 2,549 periodicals, 1,903 theses and dissertations, 1,661 nonprints, 32,708 analytics and 251 investigative projects, 411 technical reports; Dir RAYMUND E. LIBORO; publs *Philippine Journal of Science* (2 a year), *Philippine Men of Science* (1 a year), *Philippine Science and Technology Abstracts* (2 a year), *S&T Post* (4 a year), *Specialized Bibliographies.*

Technological University of the Philippines Library: Ayala Blvd, Ermita, Manila 1000; tel. (2) 302-7750 ext. 601; internet www .tup.edu.ph; 34,170 items; Dir Dr WILHELMINA G. BORJAL.

University of the East Library: 2219 Claro M. Recto Ave, Manila 2806; internet online.ue.edu.ph/manila/library; 183,000 vols; Dir of Libraries NORMA I. JHOCSON.

University of Manila Central Library: 546 Dr M. V. de los Santos St, Sampaloc, Manila; e-mail library@dlsu.edu.ph; internet www.dlsu.edu.ph/library; f. 1913; 28,600 vols; other libraries; 23,000 vols; Assistant Chief Librarian JUAN MARTIN GUASCH.

University of the Philippines Manila, University Library: 650 Pedro Gil St, Ermita, Manila 1000; tel. (2) 526-4253; fax (2) 526-5847; e-mail tdugenia@mail.upm.edu .ph; internet lib.upm.edu.ph; main library and 9 br. libraries; Librarian THERESA P. DUGENIA.

University of Santo Tomás Library: España St, Manila 1015; tel. (2) 731-30-34; fax (2) 740-97-09; e-mail library@mnl.ust.edu .ph; internet library.ust.edu.ph; 391,120 vols; collections of Filipiniana and rare and ancient books; special libraries of Ecclesiastical Faculties, Medicine, Music, Engineer-ing, Fine Arts and Commerce; High School and Elementary School libraries; Prefect of Libraries Fr ANGEL APARICIO; Chief Librarian Prof. ERLINDA F. FLORES.

Quezon City

Loyola School of Theology Library: POB 240, U.P. Quezon City; tel. (2) 426-5966; e-mail lwakefield@admu.edu.ph; internet www.lst.edu/library.asp; f. 1965; 69,000 vols, 18,000 vols of periodicals; Librarian CRISANTA C. ROSALES; publ. *Landas (The Way)* (2 a year).

University of the Philippines Diliman University Library: Gonzalez Hall, Diliman, Quezon City 1101; tel. (2) 926-1877; fax (2) 926-1876; e-mail salvacion.arlante@up .edu.ph; internet www.mainlib.upd.edu.ph; f. 1922; 1,055,048 vols, 32,671 periodical titles; 26 brs; Dir SALVACION M. ARLANTE; publ. *Index to Philippine Periodicals* (4 a year).

Museums and Art Galleries

Cebu City

CAP Art Centre and President Osmeña Memorabilia: 60 Osmeña Blvd, Cebu City; tel. (32) 217-519; fax (32) 218-102; f. 1986; work by artists from all parts of the Philippines; memorabilia concerning the late President Osmeña; Curator MARY F. ABAD.

Casa Gorordo Museum: 35 Lopez Jaena St., Cebu City; tel. (32) 255-5645; fax (32) 253-2380; fmr home of the first Filipino Bishop of Cebu, now restored as a typical 19th-century residence; furniture, paintings, religious relics, pottery and ceramics; Exec. Dir CHARLES MUERTEGUI.

Southwestern University Museum: Urgello Rd, Cebu City 6000; tel. and fax (32) 253-6500; internet www.cebu-online .com/swum; prehistoric, archaeological, ethnographic, ecclesiastical and art objects; Dir TONETTE S. PAÑARES.

University of San Carlos Museum: P. del Rosario St, Cebu City 6000; tel. (32) 253-1000 loc 191; fax (32) 253-1000; e-mail museum@ usc.edu.ph; internet www.usc.edu.ph; f. 1967; Spanish colonial, ethnographic, archaeological and natural science objects; Curator MARLENE SOCORRO SAMSON.

Davao City

Davao Museum: Zonta Bldg, Insular Village Phase I, Lanang, Davao City; f. 1977; tribal art, local costumes, jewellery, textiles, handicrafts, musical instruments; Curator Dr HEIDI K. GLORIA.

Makati City

Ayala Museum: Makati Avenue, Greenbelt Park, Ayala Center, Makati City 1224; tel. (2) 757-7117; fax (2) 757-3588; e-mail museum_inquiry@ayalamuseum.org; internet www.ayalamuseum.org; f. 1967; archaeological, ethnographic and fine arts collections; paintings by Philippine artists Juan Luna, Fernando Amorsolo and Fernando Zobel; 60 dioramas illustrating Philippine history; models of ships and watercraft; Dir Dr FLORINA H. CAPISTRANO-BAKER.

Makati Museum: J. P. Rizal St, Población, Makati City; tel. (2) 896-0277; native arts and crafts, paintings by contemporary Filipino artists; Curator LINGLING CERVANTES.

Manila

Lopez Memorial Museum: Benpres Bldg, Ground Floor, Exchange Rd, cnr Meralco Ave, Ortigas Centre, Pasig City, Manila; tel. (2) 631-24-17; e-mail pezseum@skyinet.net; internet www.lopezmuseum.org.ph; f. 1960; paintings by the Filipino painters Juan Luna, Felix Resurreccion Hidalgo and others; letters and MSS of Jose Rizal; library of 16,000 vols, including rare Filipiniana; Dir MERCEDES LOPEZ VARGAS.

Malacañang Palace Presidential Museum: J. P. Laurel St, San Miguel, Manila; tel. 521-2301; internet www.op.gov .ph/museum; f. 1993; memorabilia of all former Philippine presidents; Dir MA. EDNA S. GAFFUD.

Metropolitan Museum of Manila: Bangko Sentral ng Pilipinas Complex, Roxas Blvd, Manila 1004; tel. (2) 536-1566; fax (2) 523-0613; e-mail info@metmuseum.ph; internet metmuseum.ph; f. 1976; fine arts museum: painting, sculpture, graphic arts, decorative arts, prehistoric gold, pottery; Museum Dir ERIC ZERRUDO; Exhibition and Education Programme Man. CRUZ MAY LYN.

Museo ng Arkidiyosesis ng Maynila (MANA): POB 132, 1099 Manila;; tel. (2) 527-7631; fax (2) 527-3956; e-mail rcam@ pldtdsl.net; internet www.rcam.org; f. 1987, fmrly Archdiocesan Museum of Manila; history of the Catholic Church in the Philippines; Dir Fr ALBERT C. A. FLORES.

National Museum of the Philippines: P. Burgos Ave, Padre Burgos St, Manila 1000; tel. (2) 527-1215; fax (2) 527-0306; e-mail directornatmuse@yahoo.com; internet www .nationalmuseum.gov.ph; f. 1901; divs of anthropology, archaeology, botany, geology, zoology, museum education, restoration and engineering, arts, cultural properties, planetarium; 19 br. museums and sites; museology training, workshops, outreach activities, lectures; library of 5,442 vols; Dir JEREMY R. BARNS; Dir CECILIO G. SALCEDO; Dir MAHARLIKA A. CUEVAS; Chief Admin. Officer DIONISIO O. PANGILINAN; publ. *National Museum Papers* (scientific journal, 1 a year).

Attached Sites:

Angono Petroglyphs Site Museum: National Museum, Binangonan Branch, Binangonan, Rizal, (Region IV) Luzon; tel. (2) 527-4192; the most ancient Filipino work of art, dating from c. 1000BC; 127 drawings of human and animal figures; declared a nat. cultural treasure.

Balanghai Shrine: National Museum, Butuan Branch, Libertad, Butuan City, Mindanao (Region XIII); remains of the earliest known watercraft in the country, dating from AD 320.

Bolinao Branch Museum: National Museum, Bolinao Branch, Bolinao, Pangasinan, (Region I) Luzon; archaeological and general museum; Head GINA DE VERA.

Butuan Branch Museum: National Museum Butuan Branch, Doongan, Butuan City, Mindanao (Region XIII); tel. 527-4192; archaeological artefacts from Agusan del Norte and ethnographic materials from several local ethnic communities; Head MARGARITA CEMBRANO.

Cagsawa Branch: Albay, Luzon; geological materials from the Mayon volcano, archaeological and ethnographic collns; Head ALICE ALAURIN.

Cotabato City Branch: Cotabato City, Mindanao; ethnographic colln of local tribal materials; Head DANIEL LACERNA.

Fort Pilar Branch Museum: National Museum, Fort Pilar Branch, Fort Pilar, Zamboanga City, Mindanao (Region IX); tel. (2) 527-4192; f. 1985; material culture of 3 ethnic groups, traditional boats; dioramas depicting 400 species of marine life; Head EUFEMIA CATOLIN.

Fort San Pedro Branch: Cebu City, Cebu; ceramics, archaeological artefacts depicting the history of a sunken 16th-century Spanish galleon; Head VICENTE SECUYA.

Jolo Branch Museum: National Museum, Jolo Branch, Jolo, Sulu, Mindanao; tel. (2) 527-4192; material culture of Sulu; Head BELEN UDDIN.

Kabayan Branch: National Museum, Kabayan Branch, Kabayan, Benguet, (Region I) Luzon; tel. (2) 527-4192; material culture of the Ibalois and the Kankanaey; Head JULIET IGLOSO.

Kiangan Branch: National Museum, Kiangan Bran, Kiangan, Ifugao, Luzon; tel. (2) 527-4192; anthropological materials, Ifugao house.

Lubuagan Branch: Lubuagan, Kalinga, Luzon; ethnographic colln on culture of the Kalinga.

Magsingal Branch: National Museum, Magsingal Branch, Vigan City, Ilocos Sur, (Region I) Luzon; tel. (2) 527-4129; ethnographic colln on the Ilocano people and liturgical arts; Head REMEDIOS PALACPAC.

Peñablanca Branch: Peñablanca, Cagayan, Luzon; finds from the cave sites of Peñablanca.

Puerto Galera Branch: Puerto Galera, Oriental Mindoro, Luzon; archaeological history of Puerto Galera; Head MAMERTO CONTRERAS.

Tabon Cave Complex: National Museum, Quezon Branch, Tawa-tawa, Quezon, Palawan (Region IV); tel. (2) 527-4192; natural heritage of the region; ethnographic materials from 3 local ethnic groups; archaeological artefacts from the Tabon Caves; Head VIVIAN BROWN.

Tuguegarao Branch: Tuguegarao City, Cagayan, Luzon; prehistory of the Cagayan Valley; ethnographic exhibits; Head AIREEN MELAD.

Vigan Branch: National Museum, Vigan Branch, Vigan City, Ilocos Sur, Luzon (Region I); tel. (75) 554-2065; culture of the Ilocano people through archaeological and ethnographic materials; Head REMEDIOS PALACPAC.

San Agustín Museum: POB 3366, General Luna St, Intramuros, Manila 1002; tel. and fax (2) 527-4060; f. 1972; located in 400-year-old San Agustín monastery; Hispano-Philippine religious art (paintings, sculptures, etc.); library of 3,000 vols; Dir Dr PEDRO G. GALENDE.

University of Santo Tomas Museum(UST Museum): 3rd Fl., Main Bldg, Univ. of Santo Tomás, España Blvd, Sampaloc Manila 1015; tel. (2) 781-1815; fax (2) 740-9718; e-mail museum@mnl.ust.edu.ph; internet www.ustmuseum.ust.edu.ph; f. 1871; sections on natural history, Philippine ethnography, Philippine religious images, coins, medals and memorabilia, visual arts, and archeology; Dir Fr ISIDRO C. ABAÑO; publ. *UST Museum Newsletter* (2 a year).

Marikina City

Philippine Science Centrum: E-Com Bldg, Riverbanks Centre, 84 Andres Bonifacio Ave, Barangka, Marikina City, 1803 Metro Manila; tel. (2) 942-5136; fax (2) 942-5091; e-mail pfst@science-centrum.ph; internet www.science-centrum.ph; f. 1990; attached to Philippine Foundation for Science and Technology; promotes science education; interactive museum with sections on lights, bodyworks, mathematics, electricity and magnetism, water, vision and perception, bioethics and biotechnology, earth science, space; Exec. Dir MAY PAGSINOHIN; Head

of Operations EDICEL HERRERA; publs *DISCOVER!* (4 a year), *PSC Manual of Exhibits* (4 a year).

Pasay City

Cultural Centre of the Philippines Museum/Museo ng Kalinangang Pilipino: CCP Complex, Roxas Blvd, Pasay City, Metro Manila; tel. (2) 832-5094; fax (2) 832-3683; e-mail museo@culturalcenter.gov.ph; internet www.culturalcenter.gov.ph; f. 1988; traditional Filipino art and traditional Asian musical instruments; exhibitions of modern art; tableaux and artefacts of Philippine traditional and folk cultural practices; lectures by artists and curators; Officer-in-Charge VICTORIA T. HERRERA.

Quezon City

Ateneo Art Gallery: Level 2 Rizal Library Spec. Collns Bldg, Ateneo de Manila Univ., Katipunan Ave, Loyola Heights, Quezon City 1108; tel. (2) 426-6001 ext. 4160; fax (2) 426-6488; e-mail ijaucian@ateneo.edu; internet www.ateneoartgallery.org; f. 1960; works by Filipino artists since 1945; Dir and Chief Curator RAMON E. S. LERMA.

Jorge B. Vargas Museum and Filipiniana Research Centre: Roxas Ave, Univ. of the Philippines, Diliman, Quezon City 1101; tel. (2) 928-1927; fax (2) 928-1925; e-mail vargasmuseum@gmail.com; internet vargasmuseum.upd.edu.ph; f. 1987; Philippine oil paintings, watercolours, pastels, drawings and sculpture from the 1880s to the 1960s, incl. work by the artists Lorenzo Guerrero, Simon Flores, Juan Luna, Felix Resurrecion Hidalgo, Fabian de la Rosa, Fernando Amorsolo, Jorge Pineda, Vicente Rivera y Mir, Victorio Edades, Juan Aralleno and Diosdado Lorenzo, and by the sculptors Guillermo Tolentino and Graciano Nepomuceno; archives, newspaper cuttings, photographs; colln also incl. Vargas archives and philatelic and numismatic memorabilia; library of 3,193 vols, 1,542 vols of periodicals; Curator Dr PATRICK FLORES.

Universities

ADAMSON UNIVERSITY

900 San Marcelino St, Ermita, 1000 Manila
Telephone: (2) 524-20-11
Fax: (2) 524-73-23
E-mail: glbanaga@adamson.edu.ph
Internet: www.adamson.edu.ph

Founded 1932
Private (Roman Catholic)
Languages of instruction: English, Filipino
Academic year: June to March

Pres.: Fr GREGORIO L. BAÑAGA
Vice-Pres. for Finance: Fr MAXIMINO RENDON
Vice-Pres. for Academic Affairs: Fr FRANCISCO NICOLAS MAGNAYE, JR
Vice-Pres. for Student Affairs: Fr ANDREW BAYAL
Registrar: Sr NILDA IBAÑEZ
Librarian: HELEN DE CASTRO

Library: See Libraries and Archives
Number of teachers: 460
Number of students: 28,390

Publications: *Adamson Chronicle* (12 a year), *Adamson News* (12 a year), *Touchstone* (4 a year)

DEANS

College of Architecture: Arch PETER VILLANUEVA
College of Business Administration: Dr VIRGINIA CALABRIA
College of Education: Dr SERVILLANO MARQUEZ

College of Engineering: JESUS MANALASTAS
College of Law: ANTONIO ABAD
College of Liberal Arts: Dr SERVILLANO MARQUEZ
College of Nursing: Prof. NARESSIA BALLENA
College of Pharmacy: RYAN PEKSON
College of Sciences: Dr GLADIOLA SANTOS
Graduate School: JOSE GENARO YAP-AYSON

AKLAN STATE UNIVERSITY

Banga, Aklan 5601, Western Visayas
Telephone: (36) 267-6567
Fax: (36) 267-5801
E-mail: webmaster@asu.edu.ph
Internet: www.asu.edu.ph

Founded 1918 as Capiz Farm School, present name and status 2001
State control
Academic year: June to March

Pres.: Dr BENNY A. PALMA
Vice-Pres. for Academic Affairs: Dr ERSYL T. BIRAY
Vice-Pres. for Admin.: Eng. MERLINE I. MARCELINO
Vice-Pres. for Research, Extension, Training and ICT: ROBERTO L. SALADAR
Univ. Sec.: MICHELLE M. TAN
Dir for Library and Information Technology: EDELINA L. MATEO
Dir. for Student Affairs: EDILBERTO L. SOLIDUM

DEANS

College of Agriculture, Forestry and Environmental Sciences: Dr MARILYN E. ROMAQUIN (acting)
College of Fisheries and Marine Sciences: Prof. EDUARDO B. PASTRANA (acting)
College of Hospitality and Rural Resource Management: Prof. MARIVEL S. VILLORENTE (acting)
College of Industrial Technology: Eng. LESLIE S. CABANEZ (acting)
College of Teacher Education: Dr EDNA I. GONZALES
School of Arts and Sciences: Dr MARY EDEN M. TERUEL (acting)
School of Management Sciences: Dr CECILE O. LEGASPI
School of Veterinary Medicine: Dr CECILIA T. REYES (acting)

ANGELES UNIVERSITY FOUNDATION

Angeles City
Telephone and fax (632) 246-8383
Internet: www.auf.edu.ph

Founded 1962
Private control
Languages of instruction: English, Filipino
Academic year: June to March

Chancellor: Dr EMMANUEL Y. ANGELES
Pres.: JOSEPH EMMANUEL L. ANGELES
Vice-Pres. for Academic Affairs: Dr ARCHIMEDES T. DAVID
Vice-Pres. for Admin.: Prof. SYLVIA M. SORIANO
Vice-Pres. for Finance: Dr LORETO A. CANLAS
Registrar: Prof. MELLANY M. PUNU
Librarian: AMOR MARTIN

Library of 100,000 vols
Number of teachers: 400
Number of students: 8,000

Publications: *Alumnews, AUF Journal, AUF News, Datalink, MPA Perspective, Nurscene, The Pioneer*

DEANS

College of Allied Medical Professions: CONSUELO P. MACALALAD
College of Arts and Sciences: Dr NUNILON G. AYUYAO

College of Business Administration: LEONIDA F. CAYANAN
College of Computer Science: CAESAR R. MAÑALAC
College of Criminology: LUCIA M. HIPOLITO
College of Education: LUCENA P. SAMSON
College of Engineering and Technology: Eng. JOSÉ L. MACAPAGAL, JR
College of Medicine: Dr REYNALDO V. LOPEZ
College of Nursing: ZENAIDA S. FERNANDEZ
Graduate School: Dr CONCESA MILAN BADUEL
Law: JOSE C. VITUG

AQUINAS UNIVERSITY OF LEGAZPI

Rawis, Legazpi City 4500
Telephone and fax (52) 482-0540
E-mail: secgen@aq.edu.ph
Internet: www.aq.edu.ph
Founded 1948, present status 1968
Private (Roman Catholic) control
Languages of instruction: Bikol, English, Filipino
Academic year: June to May
Pres.: Very Rev. Dr RAMONCLARO G. MENDEZ
Vice-Pres.: Fr ROBERTO G. REYES
Sec.-Gen.: VIRGILIO S. PERDIGON, Jr
Registrar: LETICIA R. ROQUE
Librarian: JANE L. BEBENG
Library of 54,992 vols
Number of teachers: 237
Number of students: 4,137
Publications: *Aquinas University Research Journal, Balintataw* (Mind; student ccl newsletter), *Gimata* (New Moon; Awakening; admin. newsletter), *Tagba* (Harvest; research journal), *Phoenix* (college student organ), *The Prism* (high school student organ)

DEANS

College of Arts, Sciences and Education: Dr SUSAN G. BOBADILLA
College of Business Administration: Dr JEAN C. DELA TORRE
College of Law: Atty EMERSON B. AQUENDE
College of Nursing and Health Sciences: VICENTE B. PERALTA
Graduate School: Dr ROSALINDA B. BARQUEZ
Polytechnic Institute (Engineering, Architecture, Computer Science): MARIA TERESA P. BONDAD

ARELLANO UNIVERSITY

2600 Legarda St, Sampaloc, Manila
Telephone: 60-74-41
Internet: www.arellano.edu.ph
Founded 1938
Language of instruction: English
Private control
Chair., Board of Trustees: Atty FLORENTINE CAYCE, Jr
Pres.: JOSE T. ENRIQUEZ
Exec. Vice-Pres.: PAULINO F. CAYCO
Registrar: JOSEFA V. LEBRON
Librarian: ALFREDO C. VALDEZ
Number of teachers: 335
Number of students: 10,326
Publications: *Arellano Standard, Philippine Education Quarterly*

DEANS

Arellano Law College: Atty MARIANO M. MAGSALIN
College of Arts and Sciences: Dr SERGIA G. ESGUERRA
College of Commerce: FRANCISCO P. CAYCO
College of Education and Normal College: Dr AMPARO S. LARDIZABAL
College of Nursing: Dr PRAXEDES S. M. DELA ROSA
Graduate School: Dr AMPARO S. LARDIZABAL

ATENEO DE DAVAO UNIVERSITY

E. Jacinto St, 8016 Davao City
Telephone: (82) 221-2411
Fax: (82) 226-4116
E-mail: admissions@addu.edu.ph
Internet: www.addu.edu.ph
Founded 1948
Private control
Language of instruction: English
Academic year: June to March
Pres.: Fr JOEL E. TABORA
Registrar: EDGAR PASCUA II
Dir of Libraries: LEONISA P. SALES
Library of 104,857 vols
Number of teachers: 512 (372 full-time, 140 part-time)
Number of students: 7,925
Publications: *Journal of Business and Governance* (4 a year), *Tambara* (1 a year)

DEANS

College of Engineering and Architecture: Dr RANDELL ESPINA
College of Law: MANUEL P. QUIBOD
College of Nursing: Dr PATRIA MANALAYSAY
School of Arts and Sciences: Fr Dr. DANIEL MCNAMARA
School of Business and Governance: ARLENE COSAPE

ATENEO DE MANILA UNIVERSITY

POB 154, Manila
Telephone: 426-6001
Internet: www.ateneo.edu
Founded 1859, present status 1959
Languages of instruction: English, Filipino
Private control
Academic year: June to March (2 semesters and a summer term)
Pres.: Rev. JOSE RAMON T. VILLARIN
Vice-Pres. for Admin. and Planning: Dr EDNA P. FRANCO
Vice-Pres. for Finance and Treas.: JOSE SANTOS
Vice-Pres. for Loyola Schools: Dr JOHN PAUL C. VERGARA
Vice-Pres. for Professional Schools: Dr ALFREDO R. A. BENGZON
Dir. of Library: LOURDES T. DAVID
Library of 219,562 vols, 309,659 vols of non-print resources, 37 databases, 45,000 e-books, 25,000 e-journals, 22,801 vols of microforms, 3,872 vols of audiovisual materials
Number of teachers: 1,026, 609 f.t.e.
Number of students: 8,000
Publications: *Asian Perspectives on the Arts and Humanities, Budhi, Kritika Kultura, Landas—Journal of Loyola School of Theology, Loyola Schools Review, Philippine Studies*

DEANS

Ateneo Graduate School of Business: ALBERT BUENVIAJE
Ateneo Law School: Atty CESAR VILLANUEVA
Ateneo School of Medicine and Public Health: Dr ALFREDO R. A. BENGZON
John Gokongwei School of Management: RODOLFO P. ANG
School of Government: Dr ANTONIO G. LA VINA
School of Humanities: Dr MARIA LUZ C. VILCHES
School of Science and Engineering: Dr FABIAN C. DAYRIT
School of Social Sciences: Fr JOSE M. CRUZ

BATANGAS STATE UNIVERSITY

Rizal Ave, Batangas City 4200
Telephone: (43) 778-2170
Fax: (43) 778-2170
E-mail: webmaster@batstate-u.edu.ph
Internet: www.batstate-u.edu.ph
Founded 1903 as Manual Training School; present name and status 2001
State control
Academic year: June to March
Pres.: Dr ERNESTO M. DE CHAVEZ
Sr Exec. Vice-Pres.: Dr ROLANDO L. LONTOC, Sr
Exec. Vice-Pres.: Dr PORFIRIO C. LIGAYA
Vice-Pres.: Dr MARITESS D. MANLOÑGAT (Academic Affairs), LUZVIMINDA ROSALES (Admin. and Finance), Dr FELIX M. PANOPIO (Extension Campus Operation), Dr JESSIE A. MONTALBO (ICT, Infrastructure Devt and External Affairs), Dr ROLANDO M. LONTOK, Jr (Research, Public Relations, Planning and Devt, and Univ. Sec.)
Dir (Library Services): Prof. ARACELI H. LUNA
Central campuses in Batangas City (Don Pablo Borbon Campuses 1 and 2) and extension campuses in Balayan, Calaca, Lipa City (Don Claro M. Recto Campus), Lobo, Malvar (Jose P. Laurel Polytechnic College Campus), Nasugbu (ARASOF Campus), Padre Garcia, Rosario, San Juan and Taysan

DEANS

College of Accountancy (Don Pablo Borbon Campus 1 and Lipa City): Prof. MARIA CARMEN L. VIDAL
College of Arts and Science: Prof. RACHEL EVANGELIO
College of Engineering (Lipa City): Eng. ERMA QUINAY
College of Engineering, Architecture and Fine Arts (Don Pablo Borbon Campus 2): Prof. ROGELIO A. ANTENOR
College of Industrial Technology (Don Pablo Borbon Campuses 1 and 2): Dr ROLANDO M. LONTOK, Jr
College of Industrial Technology (Balayan, Calaca, and Lipa City Campuses): Prof. MAXIMO PANGANIBAN
College of Liberal Arts: Dr GLORIA G. MENDOZA
College of Physical Education and Human Kinetics: Prof. EDUARDO EVANGELIO
Graduate School: Dr ROLANDO L. LONTOC
School of Business and Economics: Prof. MARITESS D. MANLOÑGAT
School of Developmental Communication: Prof. CYNTHIA Q. MANALO
School of Energy, Earth and Transportation Engineering: Dr JESSIE A. MONTALBO
School of Food and International Hospitality Management: Prof. TERESA KALALO
School of Governance, Peace and Development Studies: Prof. RACHEL EVANGELIO
School of Informatics and Computing Sciences: Dr JESSIE A. MONTALBO

ATTACHED RESEARCH CENTRE

Batangas Centre for Research and Special Studies: Dir Prof. JOCELYN R. CASTILLO.

BENGUET STATE UNIVERSITY

La Trinidad, Benguet 2601
Telephone: (74) 422-24-01
Fax: (74) 442-22-81
E-mail: cip@bsu.edu.ph
Internet: www.bsu.edu.ph
Founded 1916, univ. status 1985
Language of instruction: English
Academic year: June to May
Pres.: Dr CIPRIANO C. CONSOLACION
Vice-Pres.: Dr FRANCO T. BAWANG
Designated Vice-Pres.: Dr MARCOS A. BULIYAT (Academic Affairs), Dr ROGELIO D. COLTING (Research and Extension), Dr TESSIE M. MERESTELA (Planning and Devt)
Dir of Admissions: VIRGINIA R. DUGAT

Dir of Student Affairs: Prof. WILFREDO B. MINA
Registrar: (vacant)
Librarian: Dr NORA J. CLARAVALL
Library of 34,000 vols
Number of teachers: 290
Number of students: 6,598 on degree courses
Publications: *BSU Extension*, *BSU Research Journal*, *Highland Express*, *college publications*

DEANS

College of Agriculture: Dr DANILO P. PADUA
College of Arts and Sciences: Dr EDNA A. CHUA
College of Engineering and Applied Technology: GENARO W. MACASIEB, Jr
College of Forestry: MELECIO A. BALANGEN
College of Home Economics and Technology: Dr JANE K. AVILA
College of Nursing: Dr FLORENCE C. CAWAON
College of Teacher Education: Dr PERCYVERANDA A. LUBRICA
College of Veterinary Medicine: Dr RUTH C. DIEGO
Graduate School: Dr DOMINADOR S. GARIN

BICOL UNIVERSITY

Rizal St, Legazpi City 4500
Telephone: (5221) 449-13
Internet: www.bicol-u.edu.ph
Founded 1970
State control
Languages of instruction: English, Filipino
Academic year: June to May (2semesters and a summer term)
Pres.: LYLIA CORPORAL-SENA
Vice-Pres.: EMILIANO A. ABERIN
Vice-Pres. for Academic Affairs: NELIA S. CIOCSON
Registrar: CARMELINA O. BALLARES
Librarian: EXALTACION R. RESONTOC
Library of 35,380 vols
Number of teachers: 568
Number of students: 12,572
Publications: *BU Bulletin* (6 a year), *Graduate Forum* (2 a year), *Outreach* (4 a year), *R & D Journal*, *Research Monitor* (2 a year), *The Bicol Universitarian* (4 a year), *The Cassette*, *The Gearcast*, *The Mentor*, *The Net*

DEANS

Agriculture: JUSTINO R. ARBOLEDA
Arts and Sciences: SUSANA C. CABREDO
Education: OSCAR L. LANDAGAN
Engineering: EDUARDO M. LORIA
Fisheries: OFELIA S. VEGA
Nursing: PAZ G. MUÑOZ
Graduate School: NELIA S. CIOCSON
Institute of Communication and Cultural Studies: RAMONA B. RAÑESES
School of Arts and Trades: EDGAR R. CAMBA

BULACAN STATE UNIVERSITY

Malolos, Bulacan 3000
Telephone and fax (44) 791-0153
E-mail: bsu-ice@bulsu.edu.ph
Internet: www.bulsu.edu.ph
Founded 1904 as Bulacan Trade School, present name and status 1993
Regional campuses in Bustos, Hagonoy, Meneses and Sarmiento
State control
Academic year: June to March
Pres.: Dr MARIANO C. DE JESUS
Vice-Pres. for Academic Affairs: Dr DANILO S. HILARIO
Vice-Pres. for Planning, Research and Extension: Dr ANTONIO L. DEL ROSARIO

Vice-Pres. for Admin. and Finance: EVANGELINA G. CUSTODIO
Dean for Student Affairs: NICANOR DE LA RAMA
Registrar: LEILANI M. LIZARDO
Librarian: VIRGINIA C. MIRANDA
Number of teachers: 973 (391 full-time, 582 part-time)
Number of students: 30,873

DEANS

College of Architecture and Fine Arts: SATURNINA PARUNGAO
College of Arts and Letters: VICTOR RAMOS
College of Business Administration: HELEN BAESA
College of Criminal Justice Education: AMANDO VICENTE
College of Education: Dr LUZVIMINDA TANTOCO
College of Engineering: Dr NICANOR DE LA RAMA
College of Home Economics: CECILIA PASCUAL
College of Industrial Technology: Dr ALEXANDER DELA PAZ
College of Information and Communications Technology: FAUSTO HILARIO
College of Law: PASCUAL LACAS
College of Nursing: LOIDA CRESPO
College of Physical Education, Recreation and Sports: RAQUEL MENDOZA
College of Science: NORA TAN
College of Social Sciences and Philosophy: REYNALDO NAGUIT
Graduate School: Dr VICTORIA P. VALENZUELA

CAGAYAN STATE UNIVERSITY

Carig, Tuguegarao City 3500
Telephone: (78) 844-01-07
Fax: (78) 844-41-19
E-mail: abcortes@scan.com.ph
Founded 1978 by merger of Northern Luzon State College of Agriculture and Cagayan Valley College of Arts and Trades
Academic year: June to March
Pres.: Dr ARMANDO B. CORTES
Vice-Pres. for Academic Affairs: Dr ELEUTERIO C. DE LEON
Dir for Research: ROMILLO N. TRINIDAD
Number of teachers: 500
Number of students: 10,300
Publications: *CSU Research Journal* (2 a year), *Faculty Journal* (1 a year), *Research Journal of the Graduate School*

Colleges of agriculture, arts and sciences, engineering, fisheries, industrial technology, medicine, teacher training, and graduate school.

CAVITE STATE UNIVERSITY

Bancod, Indang, Cavite 4122
Telephone: (46) 4150-010
Fax: (46) 4150-013
E-mail: cvsu_rc@cavite.net
Founded 1906; fmrly Don Severino Agricultural College; present name and status 1998
Pres.: Dr RUPERTO S. SANGALANG

Colleges of arts, trades, fisheries; courses in agriculture, business administration, development studies, economics, education, engineering, environmental studies, food technology, hotel and restaurant management, mass communication, mathematics and computer science, natural sciences and technology.

CEBU NORMAL UNIVERSITY

Osmeña Blvd, Cebu City, Cebu 6000
Telephone and fax (32) 253-9611

E-mail: info@cnu.vis.ph
Internet: www.cnu.edu.ph
Founded 1902, as Cebu Normal Secondary School; present name and status 1998
State control
Academic year: June to March
Pres.: Dr MARCELO T. LOPEZ
Vice-Pres. for Academic Affairs: Dr MERLEA A. CABALQUINTO
Vice-Pres. for Admin.: Dr BIBIANA T. ISOK
Registrar: ALFREDO V. ALBARICO
Dean for Student Affairs: GWENDELINA A. VILLARANTE
Univ. Librarian: MARILYN LASPIÑAS
Number of students: 6,910

DEANS

College of Arts and Sciences: Dr FLORIZA N. LAPLAP
College of Nursing: Dr DAISY R. PALOMPON (acting)
College of Teacher Education: Dr FILOMENA T. DAYAGBIL
Graduate School: Dr BERNADITA M. SOLEDAD

CENTRAL LUZON STATE UNIVERSITY

Muñoz, Nueva Ecija 3120
Telephone: (6344) 456-0107
Fax: (6344) 456-5187
Internet: www.clsu.edu.ph
Founded 1907, attained univ. status 1964
State control
Languages of instruction: English, Filipino
Academic year: June to March
Pres.: Dr RODOLFO C. UNDAN
Vice-Pres.: Dr RUBEN C. SEVILLEJA (Academic Affairs), Prof. REYNALDO S. GUTIERREZ (Admin.), Prof. ONOFRE F. RINGOR (Business Affairs), Dr HONORATO L. ANGELES (Research, Extension and Training)
Dean of Students: Dr ZENAIDA M. SERNA
Dir of Admissions: Dr MELISSA E. AGULTO
Librarian: Prof. CELIA D. DE LA CRUZ
Number of teachers: 373
Number of students: 6,489
Publications: *CLSU Collegian* (2 a year), *CLSU Newsletter* (12 a year), *CLSU Research Digest* (2 a year), *CLSU Scientific Journal* (2 a year)

DEANS

College of Agriculture: Dr FEDERICO O. PEREZ
College of Arts and Sciences: Dr MARILOU G. ABON
College of Business Administration and Accountancy: Dr DANILO S. CASTRO
College of Education: Dr DANILO G. TAN
College of Engineering: Dr IRENEO C. AGULTO
College of Fisheries: Dr ARSENIA G. CAGAUAN
College of Home Science and Industry: Dr HILARIA T. CUARESMA
College of Veterinary Science and Medicine: Dr JESUS S. DE LA ROSA
Institute of Graduate Studies: Dr CYNTHIA C. DIVINA

CENTRAL MINDANAO UNIVERSITY

University Town, Musuan, Bukidnon 8710
Telephone: (88) 3561910
Fax: (88) 8442520
E-mail: cmu.musuan@eudora.com
Internet: www.cmu.edu.ph
Founded 1952 as the Mindanao Agricultural College; Univ. 1965
State control
Languages of instruction: English, Filipino
Academic year: June to March (2 semesters and a summer school)
Pres.: Dr MARDONIO M. LAO

Vice-Pres.: Dr EMMANUEL A. LARIOSA (Academic Affairs), Dr PORFERIO M. BALANAY (Admin.), Dr HERMINIO M. PAUA (Research and Extension)
Registrar: Prof. NELLIE C. LASTIMOSA
Librarian: Prof. ESTHER E. DINAMPO

Library of 23,000 vols
Number of teachers: 311
Number of students: 5,371
Publications: *CMU Journal of Food, Agriculture and Nutrition* (4 a year), *Barangay Balita* (4 a year), *Newsletter* (4 a year)

DEANS

College of Agriculture: Dr CELSO C. TAUTHO
College of Arts and Sciences: Dr CECILIA B. AMOROSO
College of Education: Dr MARINA I. LIZARDO
College of Engineering: Prof. REYNALDO G. JUAN
College of Forestry: Dr JAMES O. LACANDULA
College of Home Economics: Dr NERISSA A. MACARAYAN
College of Veterinary Medicine: Dr JOSE ALEXANDER C. ABELLA
Graduate School: Dr EVELYN L. BARRIDO

CENTRAL PHILIPPINE UNIVERSITY

POB 231, Iloilo City 5000
Telephone: (33) 7-34-71
Fax: (33) 20-36-85
Internet: www.cpu.edu.ph
Founded 1905
Language of instruction: English
Private control
Academic year: June to March (2 terms)
Pres.: AGUSTIN A. PULIDO
Treas.: ROSALENE J. MADERO
Vice-Pres. for Academic Affairs: ELMA S. HERRADURA
Registrar: ESTHER S. BASIAO
Librarian: VICTORY D. GABAWA

Number of teachers: 280
Number of students: 9,280

Publications: *Centralite* (student annual), *Link* (Alumni organ), *Southeast Asia Journal*, *The Central Echo* (student paper)

DEANS

College of Agriculture: ENRIQUE S. ALTIS
College of Arts and Sciences: LYNN J. PAREJA
College of Commerce: MILAGROS V. DIGNADICE
College of Education: LORNA D. GELLADA
College of Engineering: WALDEN S. RIO
College of Law: JUANITO M. ACANTO
College of Nursing: BETTY T. POLIDO
College of Theology: JOHNNY V. GUMBAN
School of Graduate Studies: MIRIAM M. TRAVIÑA

CENTRO ESCOLAR UNIVERSITY

9 Mendiola St, San Miguel, Manila
Telephone: (2) 735-59-91
Fax: (2) 735-59-91
E-mail: ceu1@galileo.fapenet.org
Internet: www.ceu.edu.ph
Founded 1907
Languages of instruction: English, Filipino
Private control
Academic year: June to March
Pres.: Dr ROSITA L. NAVARRO
Vice-Pres.: Dr ROSITA L. NAVARRO (Academic Affairs, concurrent with Univ. Presidency), LUCILA C. TIONGCO (Alumni Affairs), CARMELITA E. LA O' (Business Affairs), Dr MARIA L. AYUYAO (Exec.), JOSEPHINE E. MAPE (Finance)
Registrar: LUCIA D. GONZALES
Librarian: Dr TERESITA G. HERNANDEZ

Number of teachers: 800
Number of students: 22,691

Publications: *Academe, Ciencia y Virtud* (4 a year), *Graduate and Faculty Studies* (1 a year), *Rose and the Leaf* (1 a year), *The Clarion* (4 a year)

DEANS

College of Dentistry: Dr RENATO M. SISON
College of Medical Technology: Dr PRISCILLA A. PANLASIGUI
College of Nursing: MERLINA V. LOCQUIAO
College of Optometry: Dr JESSICA L. FLOR
College of Science: Dr ZENAIDA M. AUSTRIA
Graduate School: Dr ROSITA L. NAVARRO
School of Accountancy, Business, Secretarial and Public Administration: Dr CONRADO E. IÑIGO, Jr
School of Arts and Humanities: Dr CECILIA G. VALMONTE
School of Education, Music and Social Work: Dr PAZ I. LUCIDO
School of Pharmacy: Dr OLIVIA M. LIMUACO
School of Tourism, Family Economics and Nutrition: Dr CARMINA P. CATAPANG

DE LA SALLE UNIVERSITY

2401 Taft Ave, Malate, Manila 1004
Telephone: (2) 523-4148
Fax: (2) 521-9094
E-mail: quebengcoc@dlsu.edu.ph
Internet: www.dlsu.edu.ph
Founded 1911
Private control
Languages of instruction: English, Filipino
Academic year: May to April
Pres.: Bro. ARMIN A. LUISTRO
Chancellor: Dr CARMELITA I. QUEBENGCO
Vice-Chancellor for Academics: Dr JULIUS B. MARIDABLE
Vice-Chancellor for Research: Dr WYONA C. PATALINGHUG
Vice-Chancellor for Admin.: Dr CARMELITA I. QUEBENGCO
Asst Vice-Chancellor for Academic Services: AGNES G. YUHICO
Asst Vice-Chancellor for Campus Services: ENRICO J. CORDERO
Asst Vice-Chancellor for Campus Devt: AURELLANO O. DE LA CRUZ, Jr
Registrar: EDWIN P. SANTIAGO
Dir of Library: ANA MARIA B. FRESNIDO

Library of 258,591
Number of teachers: 950
Number of students: 14,400 (12,000 undergraduate, 2,400 postgraduate)

Publications: *Asia–Pacific Education Researcher* (2 a year), *Asia-Pacific Social Science Review* (2 a year), *DLSU Business and Economics Review* (2 a year), *Ideya* (2 a year), *Journal of Research in Science, Computing and Engineering* (3 a year), *Malay* (2 a year), *URCO Digest* (3 a year)

DEANS

College of Business and Economics: Dr MYRNA S. AUSTRIA
College of Computer Studies: Dr CASLON L. CHUA
College of Education: Dr ROSE MARIE SALAZAR-CLEMEÑA
College of Engineering: Dr PAG-ASA D. GASPILLO
College of Liberal Arts: Dr ANTONIO P. CONTRERAS
College of Science: Dr GERARDO C. JANAIRO

PROFESSORS

ABELLA, L. C., Chemical Engineering
AUSTRIA, M. S., Economics
AZCARRAGA, A. P., Software Technology
BERNARDO, A. B. I., Counselling and Educational Psychology
CABRERA, E. C., Biology
CARANDANG, J. S. R. V., Biology
CLAVERIA, F. G., Biology
CONTRERAS, A. P., Political Science
CORPUZ, C. C., History
CRUZ, I. R., Literature
CULABA, A. B., Mechanical Engineering
DADIOS, E. P., Manufacturing Engineering Management
DEL MUNDO, C. A., Jr, Communication
DIESTO, S. D., Mathematics
EDRALIN, D. M., Business Management
ESTAÑERO, R. A., Civil Engineering
EVASCO-PERNIA, M., Literature
GALLARDO, S. M., Chemical Engineering
GARCIA, L. R., Jr, Marketing Management
GASPILLO, P. D., Chemical Engineering
GERVACIO, S. V., Mathematics
GRIPALDO, R. M., Philosophy
HILA, A. C., History
INTAL, P. S., Jr, Economics
JANAIRO, G. C., Chemistry
LAMBERTE, E. E., Behavioural Sciences
LICUANAN, W. R. Y., Biology
MAGLAYA, A. B., Mechanical Engineering
ORETA, A. W. C., Civil Engineering
PALISOC, S. T., Physics
PASCASIO, A. A., Mathematics
PATALINGHUG, W. C., Chemistry
PRUDENTE, M. S., Science Education
RAGASA, C. Y., Chemistry
ROBLES, A. C., JR, International Studies
ROCES, S. A., Chemical Engineering
SALAZAR-CLEMEÑA, R. M., Counselling and Educational Psychology
SANTOS, P. V. M., Literature
SISON, R. C., Software Technology
TULLAO, T. S., Jr, Economics
UNITE, A. A., Economics

DON MARIANO MARCOS MEMORIAL STATE UNIVERSITY

Bacnotan, La Union 2515
Telephone: (72) 888-5677
Fax: (72) 888-3191
Internet: www.dmmmsu.edu.ph
Founded 1960 as La Union Agricultural School; present name and status 1980
State control
Academic year: June to March
Pres.: Dr ERNESTO R. GAPASIN
Vice-Pres. (Academic Affairs): Dr AMELIA O. BACUNGAN
Vice-Pres. (Admin.): (vacant)
Vice-Pres. (Planning and Devt): Dr ELVI C. BUGAOAN
Vice-Pres. (Research and Public Relations): Dr FLORENTINA S. DUMLAO

HEADS OF OPERATING UNITS

Apiculture Training and Development Center: Dr APOLONIO S. SITO (Dir)
Graduate College: Dr NORMA B. NATINO (Dean)
Mid La Union Campus: Dr RODOLFO R. APIGO (Chancellor)
North La Union Campus: Dr ORLANDO O. ALMOITE (Chancellor)
Open University System: Dr CONCEPCION L. BEDERIO (Dir)
Sericulture Research Development Institute: Dr RICARDO C. BRIONES (Dir)
South La Union Campus: Dr INOCENCIO I. MANGAOANG, Jr

FAR EASTERN UNIVERSITY

POB 609, Manila
Telephone: (2) 735-56-21
Fax: (2) 735-02-32
Internet: www.feu.edu.ph
Founded 1928 as Institute of Accountancy, incorporated in 1934 as Far Eastern Univ.
Private control
Language of instruction: English
Academic year: June to March

Pres.: EDILBERTO C. DE JESUS
Vice-Pres. on Academic Affairs: LYDIA A. PALAYPAY
Registrar: JOHN J. MACASIO (acting)
Chief Librarian: ZENAIDA M. GALANG
Library: see Libraries and Archives
Number of teachers: 1,320
Number of students: 25,106

Publications: *Ambon* (1 a year), *Arts and Science Review* (2 a year), *Cultural Forum* (irregular), *Far Eastern University Journal* (2 a year), *FEU Newsletter* (4 a year), *Papers Etcetera* (2 a year), *Transition* (1 a year)

DEANS

Institute of Accounts, Business and Finance: DANNY A. CABULAY
Institute of Architecture and Fine Arts: VICTORIANO O. AVIGUETERO, Jr
Institute of Arts and Sciences: ANGEL O. ABAYA
Institute of Education: JOVITO B. CASTILLO
Institute of Graduate Studies: JOVITO B. CASTILLO (Co-ordinator)
Institute of Law: ANDRES D. BAUTISTA
Institute of Nursing: NORMA M. DUMADAG

FOUNDATION UNIVERSITY

Dumaguete City 6200
Telephone: (35) 422-9167
Fax: (35) 225-0167
E-mail: op@foundationu.com
Internet: www.foundationu.com

Founded 1949
Language of instruction: English
Private control
Academic year: June to March (2 semesters)

Pres.: Dr MIRA D. SINCO (acting)
Vice-Pres. for Academic Affairs: Dr EVA C. MELON
Vice-Pres. for Finance and Admin.: VICTOR VICENTE G. SINCO
Vice-Pres. for Student Life and External Affairs: DINNO WILLIE D. DEPOSITARIO
Registrar: GLENE MAY D. LUSARES
Librarian: LILIBETH D. BUSLON

Library of 55,023 vols
Number of teachers: 169
Number of students: 4,000

Publications: *Foundation Time* (12 a year), *FU Recorder* (12 a year), *Graduate Journal* (2 a year), *Greyhound* (Magazine), *Law Forum* (2 a year), *Pillar* (1 a year), *University Recorder* (2 a year)

DEANS

College of Agriculture: LILIAN P. SUMAGAYSAY
College of Arts and Sciences: Dr MIRA D. SINCO
College of Business and Economics: Dr EVA C. MELON
College of Education: Dr THELMA E. FLORENDO
College of Law and Jurisprudence: ELEUTERIO E. CHIU (RETD)
College of Nursing: NENITA P. TAYKO
Graduate School: Dr APARICIO H. MEQUI
Habalo School of Hospitality Management: CHARLOTTE V.
School of Computer Studies: DAE P.
School of Industrial Engineering: Eng. MARLON A. TANILON

GREGORIO ARANETA UNIVERSITY FOUNDATION

Araneta University Post Office, Malabon, Metro Manila 1404
Telephone: 366-90-53
Fax: 361-90-54
E-mail: gauf@gauf.curricula.net
Internet: www.gauf.curricula.net

Founded 1946; reorganized as a foundation 1965
Private control
Languages of instruction: English, Filpino
Academic year: June to March

Pres.: Dr MANUEL D. PUNZAL
Exec. Vice-Pres.: Dr ROSENDA A. DE GRACIA
Dir for Academic Affairs: Dr MA. CORAZON V. TADENA
Registrar: Prof. TERESITA R. GUTIERREZ
Librarian: Prof. FELISA W. DADOR
Number of teachers: 156 (69 full-time, 87 part-time)
Number of students: 3,012

Publications: *Araneta Research Journal* (4 a year), *Compendium of Veterinary Research* (1 a year), *Harvest* (1 a year), *The Philippine Veterinarian* (4 a year), *Tinig* (12 a year)

DEANS

College of Agriculture and Forestry: Dr ANASTACIO T. MERCADO
College of Arts and Sciences: Dr LILLIAN L. PENA
College of Business and Accountancy: Dr NELLIE A. ASUNCION
College of Education: Dr LYDIA S. JUSAY
College of Engineering and Technology: Dr LEOVIGILDO A. MANALO
College of Veterinary Medicine: Dr DANIEL C. VENTURA, Jr
Graduate School: Dr MA. CORAZON V. TADENA

ISABELA STATE UNIVERSITY

San Fabian, Echague, Isabela 1318
Telephone: 22013

Founded 1978
State control
Language of instruction: English
Academic year: June to May

Pres.: Dr RODOLFO C. NAYGA
Vice-Pres.: Dr MARIANO P. BALUAG
Registrar: THELMA T. LANUZA
Librarian: ROMULA P. ROMERO

Library of 11,818 vols
Number of teachers: 477
Number of students: 4,340

Publications: *CVIARS Monitor*, *Forum*, *Geyser*, *Hexachord*, *Mediator*, *Research Journal*

DEANS

College of Agriculture: Dr FRANCISCO M. BASUEL
College of Arts and Sciences: Dr JESUS B. GOLLAYAN
College of Forestry: Dr ROBERTO R. ARAÑO
Graduate Studies: Dr NELSON T. BINAG
Polytechnic College: Dr ESPERANZA BUENO
School of Business Administration: Prof. RELLI C. PABLEO
School of Development Communication: Prof. LOLITA G. SARANGAY
School of Engineering: JOSE J. LORENZANA
Teachers' College: Dr SACRIFICIA T. CATABUI

LEYTE NORMAL UNIVERSITY

Paterno St, Tacloban City, Leyte 6500
Telephone: (53) 321-2176
Fax: (53) 325-6122
Internet: lnu.evis.net.ph

Founded 1921 as Leyte Normal School; present name and status 1995
State control
Academic year: June to March

Pres.: Dr CRESCENCIA V. CHAN-GONZAGA

Publication: *LNU Research Journal* (1 a year)

Colleges of arts and sciences, commerce, education, engineering and management, development and entrepreneurship.

MANILA CENTRAL UNIVERSITY

Edsa, 1400 Caloocan
Telephone: 364-10-71
Internet: www.mcu.edu.ph

Founded 1904
Private control
Language of instruction: English
Academic year: June to March

Pres.: Dr ARISTOTLE T. MALABANAN
Vice-Pres. for Academic Affairs: Dr LYDIA L. TAGANGUIN
Vice-Pres. for Admin. Affairs: Dr RENATO C. TANCHOCO, Jr
Dir for Finance: MILA PEREZ
Registrar: AINI SALVADORA
Librarian: OPHELIA ENRIQUEZ
Number of teachers: 240
Number of students: 5,500

Publications: *Gold and Purple*, *Research Journal*, *The Pharos*, *The Pulse*

DEANS

College of Arts and Sciences: Dr EVA JAVIER
College of Business Administration: Dr DENNIS SANDOVAL
College of Dentistry: Dr JEROME ALCAZAREN
College of Medical Technology: PETRONA BENITEZ
College of Medicine: Dr DIVINA BEATO
College of Nursing: Dr LINA SALARDA
College of Optometry: Dr FRANCISCO BAETIONG, Jr
College of Pharmacy: MARICON BOIE
College of Physical Therapy: EDUARDO PEREGRINO
Graduate School: Dr JOSE MALLARI
School of Midwifery: Dr LINA SALARDA

MANUEL L. QUEZON UNIVERSITY

916 R. Hidalgo, Quiapo, Manila
Telephone: (2) 734-0121
Fax: (2) 733-7976
E-mail: mlq@mlqu.edu.ph
Internet: www.mlqu.edu.ph

Founded 1947

Pres.: AMADO C. DIZON
Vice-Pres. for Academic Affairs: MARTHA A. MOGOL
Exec. Officer, Regent: MA. VICTORIA O. CHAN
Registrar: Prof. GREGORIO A. DEL VALLE, Jr
Treas., Regent: AMADOR D. ALVENDIA
Chief Librarian: Prof. FLORDELIZA M. TORRES
Number of teachers: 291
Number of students: 8,355

Publications: *Junior Quezonian*, *MLQU Graduate Journal*, *MLQU Law Quarterly*, *MLQU Newsletter*

DEANS

Faculty of Accountancy and Business: ENRIQUE A. B. GABRIEL
Faculty of Architecture: CARLOS B. BANAAG
Faculty of Arts and Science: LETICIA L. LAVA
Faculty of Criminology: CLETO B. SENOREN
Faculty of Education: VIRGINIA P. GANIR
Faculty of Engineering: ANTERO P. MANGUNDAYAO
Faculty of Graduate Studies: MARTHA A. MOGOL
Faculty of Law: NORBERTO S. GONZALES
Faculty of Secretarial Education and Technology: PILAR E. SOTO
Faculty of the Institute of Computer Education: JUANITA M. UMAGAT

MARIANO MARCOS STATE UNIVERSITY

Batac, Ilocos Norte
Telephone: 792-31-91
Fax: (77) 792-31-31
Internet: www.mmsu.edu.ph
Founded 1978
State control
Language of instruction: English
Academic year: June to March
Pres.: Dr ELIAS L. CALACAL
Vice-Pres. for Academic Affairs: Dr NANCY B. BALANTAC
Vice-Pres. for Admin.: Dr HERALDO L. LAYAOEM
Vice-Pres. for Research and Extension: Dr RODOLFO A. NATIVIDAD
Registrar: Dr NENITA P. BLANCO
Admin. Officer: MANUEL B. CORPUZ
Librarian: Prof. BUCALEN C. SABOY
Library of 55,511 vols
Number of teachers: 485
Number of students: 11,761

DEANS

College of Agriculture and Forestry: Dr SALUD F. BARROGA
College of Aquatic Sciences and Technology: Prof. RODOLFE V. LADDARAN
College of Arts and Sciences: Dr ANABELLE C. FELIPE
College of Business, Economics and Accountancy: Dr MARIETTA M. BONOAN
College of Education: Dr VICENTE A. BONDAN
College of Engineering and Technology: Engr CARLOS F. UNGSON
College of Technology: Prof. NESTOR M. AGNGARAYNGAY
Graduate School: Dr LORENZA S. MATIAS
Institute of Health Sciences: Prof. VIOLETA M. GLOVA

ATTACHED CENTRES

Business Resource Development Centre: Head Prof. LORNA FERNANDEZ.
Centre for Applied Research and Technology Transfer: Dir Prof. FELIPE R. ESTA.
Fulbright American Studies Resource Centre: Dir Prof. BUCALEN C. SABOY.
Iloko Research and Information Centre: Dir Dr ERNESTO MA. CADIZ.
Regional Science Teaching Centre: Dir Prof. LEO VER DOMINGO.

MINDANAO STATE UNIVERSITY

MSU Campus, Marawi City 9700
Telephone: (63) 3521002
E-mail: op@msumain.edu.ph
Internet: www.msumain.edu.ph
Founded 1961
Language of instruction: English
Academic year: June to May
Pres.: Dr CAMAR A. UMPA
Exec. Vice-Pres. and Chancellor: Dr DATUMANONG A. SARANGANI
Vice-Pres. for Academic Affairs: Prof. YUSOPH LATIP
Vice-Pres. for Admin. and Finance: Dr DATUMANONG SARANGANI (acting)
Vice-Pres. for Planning and Devt: Prof. SAIDALE MOHAMAD
Registrar: JESSIE SILANG
Librarian: LAWANSAN MANGORAC
Number of teachers: 1,220
Number of students: 12,000
Publications: *Alumni Monitor, CSSH Graduate Research Journal, Darangen, Mindanao Arts and Culture Professional Papers Publication, Mindanao Journal, Mindanao Varsitarian* (12 a year), *Ongangen,*

OVCRE Bulletin, Pagsibol, Piglas, Unirescent

DEANS

College of Agriculture: Dr CAMAR MIKUNUG
College of Business Administration: Dr MERLYN TAN
College of Education: Dr PENDILILANG GUNTING
College of Engineering: Prof. RODRIGO BAID (acting)
College of Fisheries: Dr JULIETA LAGMAY
College of Forestry and Environmental Sciences: Dr GERARDO GAVINE
College of Health Sciences: Dr MINDAMORA MUTIN
College of Hotel and Restaurant Management: Dr CECILLE MAMBUAY
College of Law: BASARI D. MAPUPUNO
College of Medicine: Dr ANGELO MANALO
College of Natural Sciences and Mathematics: Prof. RAMBE RAMEL
College of Public Affairs: Dr NASRODEN GURO
College of Social Sciences and Humanities: Prof. BONIFACIO R. TACATA
College of Sports and Physical Recreation: Prof. HASAN MARANDA
Graduate School: Dr COSAIN DERICO
Institute of Science Education: Dr EMERITA MOTI
King Faisal Centre for Islamic and Arabic Studies: Prof. TALIB BENITO
Regional Science Training Centre: Dr DOLORES PATTUINAN
School of Information Technology: Dr PEPE L. MADRID

ATTACHED INSTITUTE OF TECHNOLOGY

Iligan Institute of Technology of the Mindanao State University

Andres Bonifacio Ave, Tibanga, Iligan City 9200
Telephone: (63) 2214056
Fax: (63) 2214056
E-mail: mpsalazar50@gmail.com
Internet: www.msuiit.edu.ph
Founded 1968
State control
Languages of instruction: English, Filipino
Academic year: June to April
Chancellor: Prof. MARCELO P. SALAZAR
Vice-Chancellor for Academic Affairs: Dr ARNULFO P. SUPE
Vice-Chancellor for Admin. and Finance: Dr POLAUS M. BARI
Vice-Chancellor for Research and Extension: Dr OLGA M. NUÑEZA
Registrar: Dr LYDIE D. PADERANGA
Librarian: MELES F. CASTILLANO
Library of 58,975 vols
Number of teachers: 490
Number of students: 7,778
Publications: *Gazette* (4 a year), *Mindanao Forum* (1 a year)

DEANS

College of Arts and Social Sciences: Prof. NORA A. CLAR
College of Business Admin.: Dr JULITA W. BOKINGO
College of Education: Prof. ESMAR N. SEDURIFA
College of Engineering: Dr FELICIANO B. ALAGAO
College of Science and Mathematics: Dr JINKY B. BORNALES
Integrated Development School: Dr MANUEL B. BARQUILLA
School of Engineering Technology: Prof. SANTIAGO R. EVASCO
School of Graduate Studies: Dr JERSON N. OREJUDOS

NATIONAL UNIVERSITY

551 Mariano F. Jhocson St, Sampaloc, Manila
Telephone: 61-34-31
Internet: www.nu.edu.ph
Founded 1900
Language of instruction: English
Private control
Academic year: June to March
Pres.: JESUS M. JHOCSON
Registrar: LETICIA J. PAGUIA
Head of Graduate Studies: ZENAIDA N. MAGIBA
Librarian: CONSUELO J. MIGUEL

DEANS

College of Architecture: FERNANDO ABAD
College of Civil, Chemical and Sanitary Engineering: ROMULO D. COLOMA
College of Commerce: LETICIA J. PAGUIA (acting)
College of Dentistry: Dr GREGORIO D. GABRIEL
College of Education: DOMINGO L. DIAZ
College of Electrical, Industrial and Mechanical Engineering: ROMULO D. COLOMA
College of Liberal Arts: ZENAIDA N. MAGIBA
College of Pharmacy: CELIA V. LANSANG

NUEVA ECIJA UNIVERSITY OF SCIENCE AND TECHNOLOGY

Gen. Tinio St, Cabanatuan City 3100, Central Luzon
Telephone: (44) 463-1201
Fax: (44) 463-0226
E-mail: president@nuest.edu.ph
Internet: www.nuest.edu.ph
Founded 1929 as Nueva Ecija Trade School; present name and status 1998
State control
Academic year: June to March
Pres.: Dr GEMILIANO C. CALLING
Campuses at Fort Magsaysay, Gabaldon, San Isidro and Sumacab; Colleges of arts and science, business and management technology, computer studies, education, engineering and industrial technology; Graduate School.

PALAWAN STATE UNIVERSITY

Tiniguiban Heights, Puerto Princesa City 5300
Telephone: (48) 433-2379
Fax: (48) 433-5303
E-mail: psu@pal-onl.com
Internet: www.psu.itgo.com
Founded 1972 as Palawan Teacher's College; present name and status 1994
State control
Academic year: June to March
Pres.: Dr TERESITA L. SALVA
Exec. Vice-Pres.: Dr CARLOS A. ALCANTARA
Vice-Pres. for Academic Affairs: Dr ELIZABETH J. MAGAY
Vice-Pres. for Admin.: MARILYN GONZALES PABLICO
Vice-Pres. for Finance: DESTIDCHADO S. VILLASARIO
Registrar: VENERANDA L. LAGROSA
Univ. Librarian: LOURDES C. SALVADOR.

PAMANTASAN NG LUNGSOD NG MAYNILA
(University of the City of Manila)

Intramuros, Manila 1002
Telephone: (2) 527-79-41
E-mail: info@plm.edu.ph
Internet: www.plm.edu.ph
Founded 1965
City government control
Languages of instruction: English, Filipino

Academic year: June to March (2 semesters); summer term for graduate schools; trimestral for graduate programmes in management and engineering

Pres. (CEO): Atty RAFAELITO M. GARAYBLAS (acting)

Exec. Vice-Pres. (COO): Atty GLADYS FRANCE J. PALARCA

Vice-Pres. for Academic Affairs: Dr VIRGINIA N. SANTOS

Vice-Pres. for Admin.: DANILO A. BALUYOT

Univ. and Board Sec.: Dr ANCHELA BIAG

Vice-Pres. for Finance and Planning: ANGELITA G. SOLIS

Registrar: Dr ESTER D. JIMENEZ

Librarian: REBECCA JOCSON

Univ. Treasurer: ANGELES RAMOS

Library of 52,000 vols, 3,400 periodicals

Number of teachers: 822 incl. 301 full-time, 521 part-time

Number of students: 9,283

Publications: *Ang Pamantasan*, *PLM Review*, *PLM Star Post*

DEANS

College of Accountancy and Economics: Prof. NONALYN V. GESALAN

College of Architecture and Urban Planning: GIL C. EVASCO

College of Arts and Sciences: Dr DOLORES B. LIWAG

College of Business and Public Administration: NILO D. BULADACO

College of Education: MYRNA G. GIL

College of Engineering and Technology: Prof. RICHARD C. REGALA, Jr

College of Human Devt: Dr DAISY P. HICARTE

College of Law: Atty ERNESTO P. MACEDA, Jr.

College of Liberal Arts: Prof. EVELYN L. SEBASTIAN

College of Management and Entrepreneurship: Prof. NEIL B. GAMUS

College of Mass Communication: Prof. LUDMILA R. LABAGNOY

College of Medicine: Dr EUGENIO A. PICAZO

College of Nursing: Prof. MARILYN R. NILO A. CAPANGPANGAN

College of Physical Education, Recreation and Sports: Prof. SUSAN C. MERCADO

College of Physical Therapy: Prof. PRIME ROSE TEODULICE M. LANETE

College of Science: Prof. PROCULA B. AMARILLO

College of Tourism, Hotel and Travel Industry Management: Prof. MA. CRISTINA A. MAPUYAN

Emeritus College: Prof. ESPERANZA B. BAUTISTA

Graduate School of Arts, Sciences, Education and Nursing: Dr TERESITA P. SALVADOR

Graduate School of Business and Government: Dr ROBERT G. ONG

Graduate School of Engineering: Engr. FELIX F. ASPIRAS

Graduate School of Law: ANGELINA SANDOVAL-GUTIERREZ

Graduate School of Management: Dr NERI S. PESCADERA

PANGASINAN STATE UNIVERSITY

Lingayen, Pangasinan

Telephone: (75) 542-6103

Fax: (75) 542-8694

Internet: www.psu.edu.ph

Founded 1979

State control

Languages of instruction: English, Filipino

Academic year: June to May

Pres.: Dr RUFINO O. ESLAO

Vice-Pres. for Academic Affairs: Dr REYNALDO P. SEGUI

Vice-Pres. for Research and Extension: Dr PORFERIO L. BASILIO

Vice-Pres. for Admin.: Dr ALFREDO F. AQUINO

Admin. Officer: EMERITO J. URBANO

Librarian (Lingayen): ARACELI P. UNTALAN

Library of 50,000 vols

Number of teachers: 308

Number of students: 5,830

Publications: *Banyuhay* (2 a year), *PSU Chronicle*, *PSU Graduate School Journal*, *Research and Extension Bulletin* (4 a year), *The Aqua Sounds*, *The Farm Breeze*, *The Golden Harvest*, *The Green Hills*, *The Ocean View*, *The Reflections*, *The Technologist*, *The Technotrends*

DEANS

College of Agriculture, PSU-Infanta: Prof. ARTEMIO M. REBUGIO

College of Agriculture: PSU-San Carlos City: Dr LEONARDO E. MONGE

College of Agriculture, PSU-Santa Maria: Dr LYDIO E. CALONGE

College of Arts, Sciences and Technology, PSU-Lingayen: Dr VICTORIANO C. ESTIRA

College of Arts, Trades and Technology, PSU-Asingan: Prof. ESTER E. LOMBOY

College of Education, PSU-Bayambang: Dr APOLINARIO G. BAUTISTA

College of Engineering and Technology, PSU-Urdaneta: Dr EUSEBIO E. MICLAT

College of Fisheries, PSU-Binmaley: Dr PORFERIO L. BASILIO

Graduate School (Urdaneta Centre, Bayambang Center, Lingayen Centre): Dr RODOLFO C. ASANION

PARTIDO STATE UNIVERSITY

San Juan Bautista, Goa, Camarines Sur 4422

Telephone: (54) 453-0235

Fax: (54) 453-1301

E-mail: psu-goa@asia.com

Internet: ecommunity.ncc.gov/psu

Founded 1941 as Partido High School; present name and status 2001

State control

Academic year: June to March

Pres.: Dr MODESTO D. DETERA

Vice-Pres. for Academic Affairs: Dr MINDA P. FORMALEJO

Vice-Pres. for Admin.: LEONCIO P. OBIAS

Campuses in Caramoan, Lagonoy, Sagñay, Salogon, San Jose and Tinambac; Depts of business education, engineering, graduate studies, teacher education and technology.

PHILIPPINE NORMAL UNIVERSITY

Taft Ave, Cnr Ayala Blvd, Manila 1000

Telephone: (2) 527-0374

Fax: (2) 536-6471

Internet: www.pnumanila.com.ph

Founded 1901; present name and status 1991

State control

Academic year: June to March

Pres.: Dr NILO L. ROSAS.

PHILIPPINE WOMEN'S UNIVERSITY

Taft Ave, 1004 Manila

Telephone: (2) 526-69-34

Fax: (2) 536-81-69

Internet: www.pwu.edu.ph

Founded 1919

Private control

Language of instruction: English

Academic year: June to March

Chair. of the Board of Trustees: Hon. HELENA Z. BENITEZ

Pres.: Dr JOSE CONRADO BENITEZ

Chancellor, Cavite Campus: Dr AMELIA REYES

Chancellor, Manila Campus, and Vice-Pres. for Academic Affairs: Dr DOLORES LASAN

Chancellor, Quezon City Campus: Dr SYLVIA MONTES

Vice-Pres.: JULITA DADO (Admin. and Finance), ENCARNACION RARALIO (Planning, Devt and External Affairs)

Registrar: LILIA ROBOSA

Librarian: DIONISIA ANGELES

Library: see Libraries and Archives

Number of teachers: 479

Number of students: 10,675

Publications: *Journal on the Environment and Habitat*, *Journal on Women's Health*, *Philippine Educational Forum* (2 a year), *PWU Bulletin* (4 a year), *PWU Research Journal* (2 a year), *The Maroon and White* (1 a year), *The Philwomenian* (12 a year)

DEANS

College of Arts and Sciences: Dr ELIZABETH DELA CRUZ

College of Distance Education: LUMEN LARGOZA

College of Education: Dr CECILIO DUKA

College of Music: MERCEDES DUGAN (Head)

College of Nursing: CONSTANCIA P. PITPITAN

College of Pharmacy: ZENAIDA SADIWA

Conrado Benitez Institute of Business Education: Dr CONSUELO ANG

Institute of Fine Arts and Design: LORNA SALUTAL (Head)

Institute of Medical Sciences and Technology: Dr NINI FESTIN LIM

Philippine Institute of Nutrition, Food Science and Technology: ROMUALDA GUIRRIEC

Philippine School of Social Work: Dr NENITA M. CURA (Dir)

POLYTECHNIC UNIVERSITY OF THE PHILIPPINES

Anonas St, Santa Mesa, Manila

Telephone: (2) 716-26-44

Fax: (2) 716-11-43

E-mail: omcarague@edsamail.com.ph

Internet: www.pup.edu.ph

Founded 1904

State control

Languages of instruction: English, Filipino

Academic year: June to March

Pres.: Dr OFELIA M. CARAGUE

Vice-Pres. for Academic Affairs: Dr SAMUEL M. SALVADOR

Vice-Pres. for Admin.: Dr DANTE G. GUEVARRA

Vice-Pres. for Student Services: Dr MOISES S. GARCIA

Vice-Pres. for Finance: Dr CARMELA S. PEREZ

Vice-Pres. for Research and Devt: Dr NORMITA A. VILLA

Registrar: Prof. MELBA D. ABALETA

Library Officer: Dr IRENE D. AMORES

Library of 205,365 vols

Number of teachers: 1,381

Number of students: 42,988

Publications: *BISIG* (Journal of Labour and Industrial Relations), *Campus Circular*, *CLMC Update*, *Graduate Forum*, *Journal of Economics and Politics* (4 a year), *Journal of Open and Distance Education*, *PUP Monograph* (1 a year), *PUP Open University Newsletter* (12 a year), *PUP Studies*, *Statistical Bulletin*, *The Catalyst* (12 a year), *Trends* (4 a year)

DEANS

College of Accountancy and Law: Dr GLORIA T. BAYSA

College of Architecture and Fine Arts: Arch. GLORIA T. BAYSA

College of Arts: Dr AMALIA C. ROSALES

College of Business: Dr ERLINDA C. GARCIA

College of Computer Management and Information Technology: Prof. GISELA MAY A. ALBANO

College of Economics, Finance and Politics: Dr ROMAN R. DANNUG

College of Engineering and Architecture: VICKY S. CRUZ

College of Languages and Mass Communication: Prof. WILHELMINA N. CAYANAN

College of Office Administration and Business Teacher Education: Prof. AVELINA C. BUCAO

College of Physical Education and Sports: Prof. MARIPRES P. PASCUA

College of Science: ADELA JAMORABO-RUIZ

College of Tourism, Hotel and Restaurant Management: MA. TERESA C. VILLAR

Commonwealth: DORIS B. GATAN

Graduate School: Dr VICTORIA C. NAVAL

Institute of Cooperatives: ELENITA S. MANTALABA

Open University: Dr CARMENCITA L. CASTOLO

Taguig Campus: AMELITA A. LAURENTE

Technical School: JOSEFINA R. TAN

RAMON MAGSAYSAY TECHNOLOGICAL UNIVERSITY

Iba, Zambales 2201, Central Luzon

Telephone: (47) 811-1683
Fax: (47) 811-1683

Founded 1910; present name and status 2001
State control

Courses in biology, education, engineering, hotel and restaurant management, mathematics and computer science, psychology, public administration, technology

Academic year: June to March

Pres.: Dr FELICIANO S. ROSETE.

RIZAL TECHNOLOGICAL UNIVERSITY

Boni Ave, Mandaluyong City 1550

Telephone: (2) 533-6041
Fax: (2) 532-0665
E-mail: riztech@mnl.cyberspace.com.ph

Founded 1969
State control
Academic year: June to March

Pres.: Dr JOSÉ Q. MACABALLUG

Courses in architecture, business administration, education, engineering, english, industrial and organizational psychology, mathematics, natural sciences, political science, statistics, technology.

SAINT LOUIS UNIVERSITY

POB 71, 2600 Baguio City

Telephone: (74) 442-2793
Fax: (74) 442-2842
E-mail: picrodir@slu.edu.ph
Internet: www.slu.edu.ph

Founded 1911
Private control (Roman Catholic)
Languages of instruction: English, Filipino
Academic year: June to March (2 semesters)

Pres.: Fr PAUL VAN PARIJS

Vice-Pres. for Academic Affairs: Engr JOSE MARIA PANGILINAN

Vice-Pres. for Finance: EVANGELINE O. TRINIDAD

Vice-Pres. for Admin.: ARNULFO SORIANO

Registrar: VIOLETA GARCIA

Dean, Student Affairs: GIL ESPIRITU

Dir of Libraries (College-Level): VIRGILIO C. FUERTE

Library of 107,214 vols
Number of teachers: 669
Number of students: 23,584

Publications: *Buhay SLU* (12 a year), *Cordillera Researches and Studies* (1 a year),

SLU Chronicle (4 a year), *SLU Research Journal* (2 a year)

DEANS

College of Accountancy and Commerce: NOEL B. DE LEON

College of Education: ROQUE Q. BERNARDEZ

College of Engineering and Architecture: JOSELITO BUHANGIN

College of Human Sciences: TERESITA AZARCON

College of Information and Computing Sciences: RANDY FLORES

College of Law: CEAZAR ORACION

College of Medicine: ROBERTO LEGASPI

College of Natural Science: GAUDELIA A. REYES

College of Nursing: MARY GRACE LACANARIA

SILLIMAN UNIVERSITY

6200 Dumaguete City, Negros Oriental

Telephone: (35) 4227195
Fax: (35) 2254768
E-mail: pres@su.edu.ph
Internet: www.su.edu.ph

Founded 1901
Private control
Language of instruction: English
Academic year: June to May

Pres.: Dr AGUSTIN A. PULIDO

Vice-Pres. for Academic Affairs: Dr BETTY C. ABREGANA

Vice-Pres. for Finance: JEAN G. ESPINO

Registrar: ANNABELLE E. PAA

Librarian: LORNA TUMULAK-YSO

Library: see Libraries and Archives
Number of teachers: 253
Number of students: 6,500

Publications: *Convergence* (1 a year), *Educator* (every 5 years), *Infoline* (12 a year), *Ingenium* (2 a year), *Insights* (2 a year), *Nurse* (2 a year), *Sands and Corals* (literary magazine, 1 a year), *Scoop* (1 a year), *Silliman Journal* (humanities, social sciences and sciences, 2 a year), *Sillimanian Magazine* (1 a year), *Stones and Pebbles* (1 a year), *SUCN Abstracts* (irregular)

DEANS

College of Agriculture: Prof. EDNA DUMANCAS

College of Arts and Sciences: Prof. CARLOS MAGTOLIS

College of Business Administration: TABITHA TINAGAN

College of Education: Dr JESUSA CORAZON GONZALES

College of Engineering: Dr BENJAMIN TOBIAS

College of Law: MYLES BEJAR

College of Nursing and Allied Medical Sciences: Dr MARIA TERESITA S. SINDA

College of Performing Arts: Prof. JOSEPH BASA

Divinity School: Dr NORIEL CAPULONG

School of Basic Education: Prof. LETICIA ALCALA

School of Communication: CELIA ACEDO

SOUTHWESTERN UNIVERSITY

Villa Aznar, Urgello St, Cebu City 6000

Telephone: (32) 256-27-43
Fax: (32) 253-75-01
E-mail: president@swu.edu.ph
Internet: www.swu.edu.ph

Founded 1946
Private control
Languages of instruction: English, Filipino
Academic year: June to March

Pres.: Dr ALICIA P. CABATINGAN

Vice-Pres. for Academic Affairs: Dr FRANCES F. LUMAIN

Vice-Pres. for Admin.: THELMA G. GARCIA

Vice-Pres. for Finance: LASSI MATTI A. HOLOPAINEN

Registrar: FRANCISCO B. BACALLA

Librarian: VIRGINIA P. MOLLANEDA

Number of teachers: 540
Number of students: 10,768

Publications: *SWU Graduate School Journal* (1 a year), *SWU Research Digest* (2 a year)

DEANS

College of Arts and Sciences: CATALINO C. ABOS

College of Commerce: FLORDELIS R. RIVERA

College of Dentistry: Dr CORNELIA R. NOVAL

College of Engineering: CARLOS S. SATIEMBRE

College of Law: Atty JONAH S. VILLAGONZALO

College of Medical Technology: ALMA A. HOLOPAINEN

College of Medicine: Dr MARILYN T. ZARRAGA

College of Nursing: Dr CARMEN V. N. SAN LORENZO

College of Optometry: Dr ARLEN O. DORIO

College of Pharmacy: Dr ALTHEA R. ARENAJO

College of Physical Therapy: DAVID M. MATHEU

College of Veterinary Medicine: Dr JOCELYN A. TINGSON

Graduate School: Dr ALICIA P. CABATINGAN

Institute of Computer Science: Eng. AL BENJIE C. LOZADA

Institute of Physical Education and Sports: MELQUIADES B. GONZALEZ

Maritime College: Comm. CARMELO T. SIMOLDE

Teachers' College: Dr FRANCES F. LUMAIN

TARLAC STATE UNIVERSITY

Romulo Blvd, Tarlac City, Tarlac 2300

Telephone: (45) 982-0110
Fax: (45) 982-3317
E-mail: tsu@mozcom.com.ph

Founded 1906 as Tarlac Trade School; present name and status 1989
State control
Academic year: June to March

Pres.: Dr DOLORES G. MATIAS

Courses in architecture, business administration, education, engineering, fine arts, journalism, mathematics and computer science, natural sciences, nutrition, social sciences, technology, theatre.

TECHNOLOGICAL UNIVERSITY OF THE PHILIPPINES

POB 3171, Ayala Blvd, Ermita, Metro Manila

Telephone: (2) 523-22-93
Fax: (2) 523-22-93
Internet: www.tup.edu.ph

Founded 1901
State control
Languages of instruction: English, Filipino
Academic year: June to March

Pres.: Dr FEDESERIO C. CAMARAO

Vice-Pres. for Academic Affairs: Prof. JOSEFINO P. GASCON

Vice-Pres. for Admin. and Finance: Prof. RADAMES M. DOCTOR

Vice-Pres. for Planning and Devt: Prof. PERLA S. ROXAS

Vice-Pres. for Research and Extension: Dr EMILIANA V. R. TADEO

Dir, TUP Cavite: Prof. ENRICO R. HILARIO

Dir, TUP Taguig: Dr FEDERICO RAMOS

Dir, TUP Visayas: Dr LEONCIO JAMERA

Registrar: Dr MILAGROS I. CACHOLA

Library Dir: Dr WILHELMINA G. BORJAL

Library: see Libraries and Archives
Number of teachers: 573
Number of students: 18,915

Publications: *Philippine Journal of Industrial Education and Technology* (2 a year), *TUP.com* (4 a year), *TUP Graduate Journal* (1 a year)

DEANS

College of Architecture and Fine Arts: Dr DIONISIO A. ESPRESSION, Jr
College of Engineering: Prof. FLORENCIO G. BALANAY, Jr
College of Industrial Education: Dr OLYMPIO V. CAPARAS
College of Industrial Technology: Prof. BUENAVENTURA V. SABATER
College of Liberal Arts: Dr MARCELO B. APAR
College of Sciences: Dr ADORA S. PILI

PROFESSORS

AGBAYANI, J., Economics
ALTO, R., Education
APAR, M., Filipino
ARRIETA II, C., Tool and Die Technology
BALUYUT, F., Education
BELEN, V., English
BELGICA, A., Career Education
BUAQUIÑA, V., Mathematics
CACHOLA, M., Foods
CALO, R., Physical Education
CAMARO, G., Research, Life Sciences, Ecology
CAPARAS, O., Industrial Arts
DE LEON, L., Education
DELOS REYES, V., Education
DIMAYUGA, Z., Education
DOMANTAY, D., Education
GABRIEL, P., English
GALANG, E., Family and Community Education
GARINO, N., Electrical Technology, Technology Management
GATMAYTAN, R., Chemistry
GOLLAYAN, R., Chemistry
GRAZA, N., Mechanical Engineering
HILARIO, E., Education
HUANG, A., Mathematics
IGNACIO, M., Mathematics
IMLAN, J., Public Administration
JANIER, J., Mathematics
JOAQUIN, A., Drafting Technology
LABUGUEN, F., Foods
LEJANO, B., Civil Engineering
MACAM, Jr, V., Civil Engineering
MANALASTAS, J., Civil Engineering
MANALASTAS, S., Chemistry Education
MANGAO, F., Mathematics
MATIC, V., Chemistry
MENDOZA, M., Social Studies
OBNAMIA, C., English, Journalism, Education
PACIO, A., Mathematics Education
PANGAN, M., Mathematics
PANGILINAN, M., Social Studies
PEREDA, P., Education
PEREZ, J., Sociology
PILI, A., Chemistry
RIVERA, A., Education
ROLLUQUI, G., Electronic Engineering Technology, Computer Technology
SALTIVAN, L., Physics
TABANERA, M. D., Physics
TRACENA, M., English
VALDERRAMA, L., Public Administration
VELAS, F., Cultural Affairs
VERAYO, E., Education
VILLAMEJOR, S., English
ZARATAN, L., Education Research

UNIVERSITY OF BAGUIO

General Luna Rd, Baguio City 2600
Telephone: (74) 4423071
Fax: (74) 4423071
E-mail: ub@ubaguio.edu
Internet: www.ubaguio.edu
Founded 1948 as a Technical School

Private control; granted deregulated status by the Philippine Comm. on Higher Education
Languages of instruction: English, Filipino
Academic year: June to March
Pres.: HERMINIO C. BAUTISTA
Vice-Pres. for Academic Affairs: Dr PERFECTO M. LOPEZ
Vice-Pres. for Admin.: Dr REBECCA C. CAJILOG
Registrar: Eng. MELBA E. BALIWAN
Librarian: BIRGIT S. SANTIAGO
Library of 75,223 vols
Number of teachers: 415
Number of students: 18,085
Publications: *The Leaven* (4 a year), *University of Baguio Journal* (2 a year)

DEANS

College of Commerce: MARY HAYDEE AGNES E. DABUCOL
College of Dentistry: Dr VERONICA S. GARCIA
College of Education: Dr AGNES T. BAUTISTA
College of Engineering: Eng. RENATO D. TANDOC
College of Hotel and Restaurant Management: JANE P. LIU
College of Information and Communications Technology: Eng. LAKAN-ASA R. BAUTISTA
College of Law: DANIEL T. FARIÑAS
College of Liberal Arts: Dr TERESITA DE GUZMAN
College of Medical Technology: CONSTANTINO WI
College of Nursing: CATALINA B. ALINDUZA
College of Physical Therapy and Optometry: ESMERELDA M. GATCHALLAN
Graduate School: Dr AGNES T. BAUTISTA
Law Enforcement Academy: Dr MILLER F. PECKLEY

UNIVERSITY OF EASTERN PHILIPPINES

University Town, Northern Samar, 6400
Telephone and fax (55) 251-86-11
E-mail: admin@uep.edu.ph
Internet: www.uep.edu.ph
Founded 1918
State control
Languages of instruction: English, Filipino
Academic year: June to March
Pres.: Dr MAR P. DE ASIS
Vice-Pres.: Dr ROLANDO A. DELORINO
Vice-Pres. for Academic Affairs: Dr FELISA L. SANICO
Vice-Pres. for Admin. Affairs: Dr BALTAZAR MARTIRES
Vice-Pres. for External Affairs: Dr MINDANILLA B. BROTO
Registrar: Dr ROGELIO BANAGBANAG
Librarian: FE G. BAOY
Library of 22,823 vols
Number of teachers: 496
Number of students: 9,492
Publications: *The Pacific Journal of Science and Technology, The Pillar, UEP Graduate Journal*

DEANS

College of Agriculture: Dr LEON A. GUEVARA
College of Arts and Communication: Dr ESTRELLITA PINCA
College of Business Administration: Dr AURORA CALADES
College of Education: Dr RONATO BALLADO
College of Engineering: ROMEO D. ATENCIO
College of Law: Atty MARLON FRITZ BROTO
College of Nursing: Prof. MA. LINDA S. AGUS
College of Science: Dr ABRAHAM HERIALES
College of Veterinary Medicine: Dr GERRY CAMER
Graduate School: Dr VIRGINIA BALANON

UNIVERSITY OF MANILA

546 Dr M. V. de los Santos St, Sampaloc, Manila 1008
Telephone: 7413637
Fax: 7413640
Founded 1913
Private, non-sectarian instn
Language of instruction: English
Academic year: June to May (three terms)
Pres.: Dr VIRGILIO DE LOS SANTOS
Exec. Vice-Pres.: Atty ERNESTO LL. DE LOS SANTOS
Vice-Pres. for Academic Affairs: Dr EMILY D. DE LEON
Registrar: Dr VIRGILIO DE LOS SANTOS
Chief Librarian: CORAZON G. PAYTE
Number of teachers: 250
Number of students: 7,500
Publications: *The Gold Leaf, The UM Law Gazette, The University of Manila Graduate School Journal*

DEANS

College of Business Administration and Accountancy: NELSON S. ABELEDA
College of Criminology: FORTUNATO S. RIVERA
College of Education: EMILY D. DE LEON
College of Engineering: ARSENIO A. RONQUILLO
College of Foreign Service: BENJAMIN D. QUINERI
College of Law: MICHAEL P. MORALDE
College of Liberal Arts: ROSALIA V. MOLINA
Graduate Studies: EMILY D. DE LEON

UNIVERSITY OF MINDANAO

Bolton St, Davao City, Mindanao
Telephone: (82) 227-54-56
Fax: (82) 221-73-35
E-mail: um@mozcom.com
Internet: www.umindanao.edu.ph
Founded 1946
Private control
Language of instruction: English
Academic year: June to March
Pres.: GUILLERMO P. TORRES, JR.
Exec. Vice-Pres. for Academic Affairs: Dr PEDRO B. SAN JOSE
Exec. Vice-Pres. for Operations: GLORIA E. DETOYA
Sr Vice-Pres. for Academic Planning and Services: Dr EUGENIO S. GUHAO, JR.
Sr Vice-Pres. for Treasury: SANDRA G. ANGELES
Vice-Pres. for ICT: EDGARDO O. CASTILLO
Vice-Pres. for Institutional Affairs: MARIA JULIETA R. TORRES
Vice-Pres. for Student Personnel Services/ Registrar: Dr CARMENCITA E. VIDAMO
Vice Pres.-for Physical Plant: FELICISIMO RAMOS
Number of teachers: 620
Number of students: 19,720
Publications: *Communique, Journal of Arts and Sciences, The Frontier, Journal of the Graduate School, UM Research and Publication Journal*

DEANS

Arts and Sciences: GERLIETA S. RUIZ
College of Architecture: ILUMINADO C. QUINTO
College of Business Administration: VICENTE SALVADOR E. MONTAÑO
College of Criminology: Dr CARMELITA B. CHAVEZ
College of Education: Dr MARILOU T. LOZARITA (Asst Dean)
College of Engineering: LEO LARGO
College of Law: MELCHOR QUITAIN
College of Nursing: OFELIA B. LARIEGO
Graduate School: EUGENIO S. GUHAO
Technical School: GERARDO SALAS

UNIVERSITY OF NEGROS OCCIDENTAL-RECOLETOS

Lizares Ave, POB 214, 6100 Bacolod City
Telephone: 433-2449
Fax: 433-1709
E-mail: unorpro@yahoo.com
Internet: www.uno-r.edu.ph
Founded 1941
Private control
Language of instruction: English
Academic year: June to March
Pres.: Fr DIONISIO CACHERO
Comptroller: Fr EDUARDO CELIZ
Registrar: Dr CARMENDA LEONORAS
Librarian: ARABELLA M. ANANORIA
Number of teachers: 330
Number of students: 7,879
Publications: *The Tolentine Star* (2 a semester), *UNO-R Journal of the Graduate School (Raison d'Etre)* (4 a year)

DEANS

Graduate School: JOEL A. ALVE
College of Arts and Sciences: NIEVES HIBALER-PEPITO
College of Business and Accountancy: Dr JOHN CLIFFORD SALUGSUGAN
College of Criminal Justice Education: JASMIN PARRENO
College of Education: Dr OFELIA POSECION
College of Engineering: Eng. CHRISTOPHER G. TACLOBOS
Elementary Dept: SUNYA PHI SUMALDE
High School Dept: SOL ABELLAR
School of Agriculture: Dr EVANGELINE O. ABOYO
School of Law: Atty JOHN PAOLO VILLASOR

UNIVERSITY OF NORTHERN PHILIPPINES

Vigan, Ilocos Sur
Telephone: 28-10
Internet: www.unp.edu.ph
Founded 1965
State control
Languages of instruction: English, Filipino
Academic year of 2 semesters
Pres.: Dr DOROTEA C. FILART
Exec. Vice-Pres.: Prof. LEO OANDASAN
Vice-Pres. for Academic Affairs: Dr PACITA B. ANTIPORDA
Univ. Sec.: Prof. RAMONA VEGA
Dir of Admissions: ELEUTERIA REMUCAL
Dir of Research: Prof. NORMA I. CACHOLA
Librarian: PEROMA L. PACIS
Library of 28,369 vols
Number of teachers: 392
Number of students: 7,017
Publications: *New Vision* (4 a year), *Tandem* (6 a year)

DEANS

Faculty of Arts and Sciences: Dr FRANCISCO C. MACANAS
Faculty of Business Administration: Dr LUMEN ALMACHAR
Faculty of Teacher Education: Dr CIRILO PARRA
Faculty of the Graduate School: SALVADOR S. EDER
Institute of Criminology: Prof. PLACIDO UNCIANO
Institute of Engineering: Eng. ROGELIO ANINAG
Institute of Fine Arts: Prof. FLORO PERLAS
Institute of Nursing and Paramedical Services: Prof. LILIA SALVADOR
Institute of Social Work and Community Development: DANIEL COLCOL
Institute of Technical Education and Cottage Industries Development: Prof. WILHELMINA VERGARA

UNIVERSITY OF NUEVA CACERES

Jaime Henandez Ave, Naga City 4400
Telephone: 21-21-84
Internet: www.unc.edu.ph
Founded 1948
Private control
Languages of instruction: English, Filipino
Academic year: June to March (two semesters)
Pres.: Dr DOLORES H. SISON
Exec. Vice-Pres.: PERFECTO O. PALMA
Vice-Pres. for Admin.: JAIME HERNÁNDEZ, Jr
Registrar: NELIA E. SAN JOSE
Librarian: Dr PERPETUA S. PORCALLA
Number of teachers: 327
Number of students: 8,061
Publications: *Nueva Caceres Bulletin* (6 a year), *Nueva Caceres Review, Red and Gray* (1 a year), *The Trailblazer* (12 a year)

DEANS

College of Arts and Sciences and Education: LOURDES S. ANONAS
College of Engineering: MAXIMINO O. PANELO, Jr
College of Law and Commerce: PERFECTO O. PALMA
School of Graduate Studies and Research: MILAGROS Z. REYES

PROFESSORS

ALMOITE, G. E. O., Public Administration
ANONAS, L. S., Methods of Research
BARIAS, A. M.
CADAG, D., Engineering Management, Highway Engineering, Water Resources Engineering, Hydrology
CONDA, A., Development of the Novel
ENOJADO, V. F., Human Relations, Principles of Guidance
EVORA, M., Electrical Engineering, Refrigeration Engineering
FORTUNO, R. Z., Production, Planning Control
GROYON, S., Psychology
PALMA, M. B., Civil Procedure, Special Proceedings
PORCALLA, P., Library Science
REYES, M., Educational Planning, Personnel Administration, Inferential Statistics
SEPTIMO, C., Power Plant Design, Steam Power Engineering, Industrial Plant Design

UNIVERSITY OF PANGASINAN

Arellano St, Dagupan City
Telephone: (75) 522-5635
Fax: (75) 522-2496
E-mail: registrar@upang.edu.ph
Internet: www.upang.edu.ph
Founded 1925; Univ. status 1968
Private control
Languages of instruction: English, Filipino
Academic year: June to March
Pres.: CESAR T. DUQUE
Registrar: TERESITA R. VISTRO
Librarian: IDA F. ROSARIO
Library of 20,500 vols
Number of teachers: 218
Number of students: 10,340
Publication: *The Researcher* (2 a year)

DEANS

College of Accountancy, Commerce, Secretarial Administration and Management Accounting: MARIETTA B. SORIO
College of Architecture: FREDDIE O. ARCALAS
College of Computer Science and Technology: MARIETTA B. SORIO
College of Education: Dr TITO G. ROCABERTE
College of Engineering: Dr LUIS M. ORTEGA
College of Law: HERMOGENES S. DECANO
College of Liberal Arts: Dr OFELIA C. RAYOS

College of Medical Technology: MARIA D. AVELINO
College of Nursing: Dr VIRTUD P. OLOAN
College of Physical Therapy: Dr MELECIO M. PENA III
School of Graduate Studies: Dr ALELI N. CORNISTA
University Elementary Laboratory School: NENITA Y. VICTORIO
University High School: NENITA T. RAYOS (Principal)

UNIVERSITY OF RIZAL SYSTEM

URS Tanay Main Campus, J. P. Rizal St, Sampaloc, Tanay, Rizal 1980
Telephone: (2) 401-4900
Fax: (2) 674-2543URS Morong Campus, Sumulong St, Morong, Rizal 1960
Telephone: (2) 653-1735
E-mail: urstanay_main@yahoo.com
Internet: www.urs.edu.ph
Founded 1959 as Rizal Agricultural School; present name and status 2001
State control
Academic year: June to May (2 semesters)
Number of teachers: 15,407
Number of students: 582
Pres.: Dr OLIVIA F. DE LEON
Vice-Pres. for Academic Affairs: Dr ARACELI M. BOBADILLA
Vice-Pres. for Admin. and Finance: Dr DEMETRIA A. SAN JUAN
Vice-Pres. for Research, Devt, Extension and Production: Dr HERMY D. ESTRABO
Chancellor for Cluster 1 (Tanay, Cardona, Rodriguez): Dr ALLEN U. BAUTISTA
Chancellor for Cluster 2 (Morong, Cainta, Taytay): Dr RENEECILIA B. PAZ DE LEON
Chancellor for Cluster 3 (Angono, Antipolo, Binangonan, Pililla): Dr GLORIA P. SARABIA

CAMPUS DIRECTORS

URS Main Campus (Tanay): Dr FLORIE B. GAPIDO
URS Angono: Dr ROWENA A. LAROZA
URS Antipolo: Prof. ALLEN U. BAUTISTA
URS Binangonan: Dr DEMETRIA A. SAN JUAN
URS Cainta: Dr MANUEL S. ORDONEZ
URS Morong: Dr HERMY D. ESTRABO
URS Pililla: Dr GLORIA P. SARABIA
URS Rodriguez: Dr TERESITA BUENVIAJE

UNIVERSITY OF SAN AGUSTÍN

General Luna St, 5000 Iloilo City
Telephone: (33) 337-4841
Fax: (33) 337-4403
E-mail: info@usa.edu.ph
Internet: www.usa.edu.ph
Founded 1904, Univ. status 1953
Private control
Languages of instruction: English, Filipino
Academic year: June to March
Pres.: Fr RAUL M. MARCHAN
Vice-Pres. for Academic Affairs: Fr GENEROUS P. GONESTO
Vice-Pres. for Admin.: Fr EDGARDO L. LAZO
Vice-Pres. for Student Affairs: Fr PEDERITO A. APARECE
Registrar: GEMMA B. HALILI
Librarian: EPIFANIA A. PACLIBAR
Number of teachers: 524
Number of students: 10,250
Publications: *Augustinian Interdisciplinary Journal* (2 a year), *Augustinian Legacy* (1 a year), *Augustinian Research Journal* (1 a year), *Communitas* (2 a year), *The Augustinian* (6 a year), *The Augustinian Mirror* (2 a year)

WORLD OF LEARNING

DEANS

College of Arts and Sciences: Dr ISIDORO CRUZ
College of Business Admin. and Accountancy: Dr LUCIO ENCIO
College of Commerce: NEOMISIA GONZALES
College of Education: Dr ALEX FACINABAO
College of Engineering and Architecture: Ing. REYNALDO ASUNCION
College of Law: JUANA JUDITA P. NAFARRETE
College of Nursing: SOFIA COSETTE MONTE-BLANCO
College of Pharmacy and Medical Technology: VICTORIA SUSTENTO
Conservatory of Music: Fr JONAS MEJARES
Graduate School: Dr RUBY CATALAN

UNIVERSITY OF SAN CARLOS

Cebu City, 6000
Telephone: (32) 253-1000
Fax: (32) 255-4341
E-mail: president@usc.edu.ph
Internet: www.usc.edu.ph
Founded 1595, present status 1948
Private control
Language of instruction: English
Academic year: June to March (2 terms)

Pres.: Fr DIONISIO M. MIRANDA
Vice-Pres. for Academic Affairs: Fr ANTHONY SALAS
Vice-Pres. for Admin.: Fr ELENO BUCIA
Vice-Pres. for Finance: Fr GENEROSO RICARDO Jr REBAYLA
Registrar: ROMEO E. YAP
Dir of Library System: MAXIE DOREEN L. CABARRON
Library of 309,446 vols, 42,024 periodicals
Number of teachers: 1,051 (810 full-time, 241 part-time)
Number of students: 18,824

Publications: Journal of Business Studies (2 a year), Philippine Quarterly of Culture and Society (4 a year), Philippine Scientist (1 a year), The University Bulletin (26 a year), USC Graduate Journal (2 a year)

DEANS

College of Architecture and Fine Arts: JOSEPH MICHAEL P. ESPINA
College of Arts and Sciences: Dr RAMON S. DEL FIERRO
College of Education: Dr ANTONIO E. BATOMALAQUE
College of Engineering: ANDRESA S. ALLERA
School of Business and Economics: Dr CHALLONER MATERO
School of Health Care Professions: ANTONIA F. PASCUAL
School of Law and Governance: Atty ALEX L. MONTECLAR

UNIVERSITY OF SAN JOSE-RECOLETOS

Corner Magallanes and P. Lopez Sts, 6000 Cebu City
Telephone: (32) 253-7900
Fax: (32) 254-1720
E-mail: usjr@usjr.edu.ph
Internet: www.usjr.edu.ph
Founded 1947, univ. status 1984
Private (Roman Catholic) control
Language of instruction: English
Academic year: June to March

Pres.: Rev. Fr CONSTANTINO B. REAL
Vice-Pres. for Admin.: Rev. Fr CORNELIO E. MORAL
Vice-Pres. for Academics: Rev. Fr SIXTO M. BITANGJOL
Vice-Pres. for Business and Finance: Rev. Fr LEONARDO P. PAULIGUE
Vice-Pres. for Student Welfare: Rev. Fr ANTHONY A. MORILLO

Dir of Basak Campus: Rev. Fr RAUL M. BUHAY
Registrar: DEMETRIO QUIRANTE
Librarian: EVELYN A. LIM
Library of 190,000 vols
Number of teachers: 500
Number of students: 13,000

Publications: Faculty Research Journal (1 a year), Forward (1 a year), Josenian (1 a year), Precedent (2 a year), USJ-R Journal of Research (Graduate School publication, 2 a year), USJ-R Updates (newsletter, 4 a year)

DEANS

College of Arts and Sciences: Dr CORAZON A. TAN
College of Commerce: Dr SUSAN CHUNG
College of Education: Dr ALMA ANG
College of Engineering: Dr EVANGELINE EVANGELISTA
College of Law: ALICIA E. BATHAN
College of Nursing: RAOUL
Graduate School: (vacant)
Grade School Department: PURA S. WAGAS
High School Department: SONIA F. PAGLINAWAN
Religious Education Centre: Fr CORNELIO E. MORAL

UNIVERSITY OF SANTO TOMÁS

España St, Manila
Telephone: 731-31-01
Fax: 732-74-86
Internet: www.ust.edu.ph
Founded 1611
Private (Roman Catholic) control
Academic year: June to March

Grand Chancellor: Very Rev. TIMOTHY RADCLIFFE
Vice-Chancellor: Very Rev. QUIRICO PEDREGOSA
Rector: Fr TAMERLANE R. LANA
Vice-Rector: Fr ERNESTO M. ARCEO
Sec.-Gen.: Fr RODEL ALIGAN
Registrar: Prof. RODOLFO N. CLAVIO
Prefect of Libraries: Fr ANGEL APARICO
Chief Librarian: Prof. ERLINDA FLORES
Number of teachers: 1,438
Number of students: 32,061

Publications: Academia, Acta Manilana, Boletín Eclesiástico, Commerce Journal, Education Journal, Journal of Graduate Research, Journal of Medicine, Law Review, Nursing Journal, Philippiniana Sacra, Science Journal, Thomasian, Unitas, Varsitarian

DEANS

College of Architecture and Fine Arts: LUIS FERRER
College of Commerce and Business Administration: Prof. AMELIA HALILI
College of Education: Dr CLOTILDE ARCANGEL
College of Nursing: Prof. GLENDA VARGAS
College of Science: Dr GLORIA BERNAS
Conservatory of Music: Prof. ERLINDA FULE
Faculty of Arts and Letters: Dr ARMANDO DE JESUS
Faculty of Canon Law: Fr JAVIER GONZALES
Faculty of Civil Law: Dr AMADO DIMAYUGA
Faculty of Engineering: Dr MARILYN MABINI
Faculty of Medicine and Surgery: Dr ANGELES TAN-ALORA
Faculty of Pharmacy: Dr ROSALINDA SOLEVILLA
Faculty of Philosophy: Fr ERNESTO ARCEO
Faculty of Sacred Theology: Fr FAUSTO GOMEZ
Graduate School: Fr JOSE ANTONIO AUREADA
Institute of Religion: Fr RODEL ALIGAN

UNIVERSITY OF SOUTHEASTERN PHILIPPINES

Bo. Obrero, Davao City 8000
Telephone: (82) 225-4696
Fax: (82) 221-7737
E-mail: pio@usep.edu.ph
Internet: www.usep.edu.ph
Founded 1978
State control
Language of instruction: English
Academic year: June to March

Pres.: Dr PERFECTO A. ALIBIN
Vice-Pres. for Academic Affairs: Dr MARCELO M. ANGELIA
Vice-Pres. for Admin.: Dr RODULFO C. SUMUGAT
Univ./Board Sec.: MARNIE GRACE I. SONICO
Chancellor (Tagum-Mabini Campus): Prof. CEFERINO T. BASTIAN
Vice-Pres. for Research, Devt and Extension: Dr SOPHREMIANO B ANTIPOLO
Registrar: VIC JEAN A. SOLLER
Librarian: Prof. RESTITUTA D. MACARAYO
Number of teachers: 592
Number of students: 13,000

Publications: Headlight (2 a year), Newsletter

DEANS

College of Arts and Sciences: Dr EVEYTH DELIGERO
College of Education: Dr BONIFACIO GABALES
College of Engineering: Dr LYNDON ROBLE
College of Governance Business and Economics: Dr SHERLITO SABLE
College of Technology: Dr ANNWEDA C. MINA
Institute of Computing: VAL A. QUIMNO (acting)
School of Applied Economics: Dr AGUSTINA TAN-CRUZ

UNIVERSITY OF SOUTHERN MINDANAO

Kabacan 9407, North Cotabato
Telephone: (64) 248-21-38
Fax: (64) 248-21-38
Internet: www.usm.edu.ph
Founded 1954 as Institute of Technology, present name 1980
State control
Languages of instruction: English, Filipino
Academic year: June to December (2 semesters)

Colleges of agriculture, engineering, home and ecological sciences, education, arts and sciences, trade and industry; institutes of veterinary science, Middle Eastern and Asian studies, development economics management, animal science and aquaculture, nursing

Pres.: Dr JESUS ANTONIO GAMIDO DERIJE
Vice-Pres.: Dr NAOMI G TANGONAN
Vice-Pres.: ABRAHAM G CASTILLO
Vice-Pres.: Dr PALASIG U AMPANG
Vice-Pres.: ANTONIO N TACARDON
Registrar: Dr PRISCILLA P COSTES
Librarian: ANITA SORNITO
Number of teachers: 434
Number of students: 9,152

Publications: CA Research Journal, USMARC Monitor, USM Research and Development Journal (2 a year).

UNIVERSITY OF SOUTHERN PHILIPPINES

Mabini St, Cebu City
Telephone: (32) 232-5939
Fax: (32) 231-0178
Internet: www.usp.ph
Founded 1927; Univ. status 1949
Private control

Pres.: OSCAR JEREZA
Registrar: ERLINDA M. CAMPOS
Number of teachers: 197
Number of students: 7,439

DEANS

College of Arts and Sciences: INOCENTA GO
College of Commerce: GERONIMO S. ANA
College of Education: ISABELITA CONALES (acting)
College of Engineering: ROMULO JEREZA
Graduate School: Dr ROSETTA MANTE
Graduate School of Law: RONALD DUTERTE
School of Social Work: INOCENTA GO

UNIVERSITY OF THE EAST

Main Campus, 2219 Claro M. Recto Ave, Manila 1008

Telephone: (2) 735-5471
Fax: (2) 735-6972
E-mail: admission@ue.edu.ph
Internet: www.ue.edu.ph

Caloocan Campus, 105 Samson Rd, Caloocan City, Metro Manila 1400

Telephone: (2) 367-4572
Fax: (2) 364-2659
E-mail: admissions_cal@ue.edu.ph
Internet: www.ue.edu.ph/caloocan
Academic year: June to April
Founded 1946 as the Philippine College of Commerce and Business Admin., present name 1951
Private control
Chair. of the Board and Chief Exec. Officer: LUCIO C. TAN
Pres. and Chief Academic Officer: Dr ESTER A. GARCIA
Exec. Vice-Pres. and Chief Admin. Officer: CARMELITA G. MATEO
Chancellor of UE Caloocan: Dr ZOSIMO M. BATTAD
Chancellor of UE Manila: Dr LINDA P. SANTIAGO
Dir for Student Affairs of Caloocan: CLEMENTE A. DIWAS
Dir for Student Affairs of Manila: MERCY L. CANDELARIA
Registrar: ERWIN B. BERMILLO
Dir of Libraries: LORETO GARCIA
Library: see under Libraries and Archives
Number of teachers: 725
Number of students: 19,000
Publications: *Graduate School Research Journal, Law Update, Research Bulletin, UE Panorama Yearbook, UE Today*

DEANS

Caloocan Campus:

College of Arts and Sciences: JULIAN E. ABUSO
College of Business Administration: Dr ROGELIO V. PAGLOMUTAN
College of Engineering: Dr VICTOR R. MACAM Jr
College of Fine Arts: CELINO B. SANTIAGO
Elementary and Secondary Laboratory Schools: BENILDA L. SANTOS (Principal)
Physical Education Department: FERNANDO Z. OLONA (acting)

Manila Campus:

College of Arts and Sciences: JUSTINA M. EVANGELISTA
College of Business Administration: Dr VERONICA N. ELIZALDE (acting)
College of Computer Studies and Systems: RODANY A. MERIDA
College of Dentistry: Dr RHODORA H. LUCIANO
College of Education: Dr EVELINA M. VICENCIO
College of Engineering: Dr DOMINADOR S. PAGBILAO

College of Fine Arts: GERARDO M. TAN
College of Law: Justice AMADO D. VALDEZ
Elementary and Secondary Laboratory Schools: NIEVA J. DISCIPULO (Principal)
Graduate School: Dr AVELINA A. DE LA REA
Physical Education Department: RODRIGO M. ROQUE (acting) (Asst Dir)

AFFILIATED MEDICAL CENTRE

University of the East Ramon Magsaysay Memorial Medical Centre

64–68 Aurora Blvd, Barangay Doña Imelda, Quezon City 1113

Telephone: (2) 715-0861
E-mail: registrar@uerm.edu.ph
Internet: www.uerm.edu.ph
Founded 1957
Affiliated to Univ. of the East
Chief Librarian: JULIANA M. NOCES-GASMEN
Library of 31,150 vols, 342 periodicals

DEANS

Graduate School: Dr TERESA S. LUDOVICE-YAP
College of Medicine: Dr ALFARETTA LUISA T. REYES
College of Nursing: Dr CARMELITA C. DIVINA-GRACIA
College of Physical Therapy: Dr RAQUEL S. CABAZOR

UNIVERSITY OF THE PHILIPPINES SYSTEM

UP Diliman, Quezon City
Telephone and fax (2) 926-15-72
E-mail: op@up.edu.ph
Internet: www.up.edu.ph
Founded 1908
Public control
Languages of instruction: English, Filipino
Academic year: June to May (2 terms, 1 summer session)
Pres.: Dr ALFREDO PASCUAL
Vice-Pres. for Academic Affairs: Prof. GISELA CONCEPCION
Vice-Pres. for Admin.: Prof. ARLENE A. SAMANIEGO
Vice-Pres. for Devt: Prof. ARMIN B. SARTHOU Jr
Vice-Pres. for Planning and Finance: Prof. EDGARDO G. ATANACIO
Vice-Pres. for Public Affairs: Prof. ISABELITA O. REYES
Vice-Pres. for Legal Affairs: Prof. MARAGTAS AMANTE
Sec.: Prof. LILIAN DE LAS LLAGAS
Library: see under Libraries and Archives
Number of teachers: 3,952
Number of students: 50,668
Publications: *The Carillon* (online), *UP Forum* (28 a year), *UP Newsletter* (12 a year), *UP Statistics* (1 a year).

CONSTITUENT CAMPUSES

UP at Baguio

Baguio
Telephone: (74) 442-38-88
E-mail: opa@upb.edu.ph
Internet: www.upb.edu.ph
State control
Language of instruction: English
Academic year: June to March
Chancellor: Prof. RAYMUNDO ROVILLOS
Vice-Chancellor for Academic Affairs: Prof. WILFREDO ALANGUI
Vice-Chancellor for Admin.: Prof. JESSICA CARIÑO
Registrar: Prof. JOCELYN RAFANAN
Librarian: BRENDA MARIE DOGUP
Library of 81,964 vols

Number of teachers: 140
Number of students: 2,528

DEANS

College of Arts and Communication: Prof. PURIFICACION DELIMA
College of Science: Prof. WILFREDO ALANGUI
College of Social Sciences: Prof. RAYMUNDO ROVILLOS
Institute of Management: Prof. CORAZON ABANSI

University of the Philippines, Cebu

Gorordo Ave, Lahug, Cebu City
Telephone: (2) 231-30-86
Fax: (2) 232-81-04
E-mail: dean.upcebu@gmail.com
Internet: www.upcebu.edu.ph
Language of instruction: English
Academic year: June to May
Officer-in-Charge: Prof. TERESITA RODRIGUEZ
College Sec. and Registrar: PATRICIA ANNE NAZARENO
College Librarian: MYLAH PEDRANO
Library of 28,009
Number of teachers: 123
Number of students: 1,289

UP at Diliman

Internet: www.upd.edu.ph
Chancellor: SERGIO S. CAO
Vice Chancellor for Academic Affairs: Prof. LORNA I. PAREDES
Vice Chancellor for Admin.: Prof. MARY DELIA G. TOMACRUZ
Vice Chancellor for Community Affairs: Prof. CYNTHIA GRACE C. GREGORIO
Vice Chancellor for Research and Devt: Prof. LUIS G. SISON
Vice Chancellor for Student Affairs: Prof. ELIZABETH L. ENRIQUEZ
Registrar: Prof. PAMELA C. CONSTANTINO
Librarian: SALVACION M. ARLANTE

DEANS

Archaeological Studies Program: Prof. VICTOR J. PAZ
Asian Centre: Prof. MARIO I. MICLAT
Asian Institute of Tourism: Prof. CORAZON P. RODRIGUEZ
College of Architecture: Prof. DANILO A. SILVESTRE
College of Arts and Letters: Prof. FLORA ELENA R. MIRANO
College of Business Administration: Prof. ERLINDA S. ECHANIS
College of Education: Prof. VIVIEN M. TALISAYON
College of Engineering: Prof. ROWENA CRISTINA L. GUEVARA
College of Fine Arts: Prof. ROWENA CRISTINA L. GUEVARA
College of Home Economics: Prof. ADELAIDA V. MAYO
College of Human Kinetics: Prof. LEILANI L. GONZALO
College of Law: Prof. MARVIC MARIO VICTOR F. LEONEN
College of Mass Communication: Prof. ROLAND B. TOLENTINO
College of Music: Prof. RAMÓN Ma. G. ACOYMO
College of Science: Prof. CAESAR A. SALOMA
College of Social Science and Philosophy: ZOSIMO E. LEE
College of Social Work and Community Development: Prof. AMERYLLIS TORRES
Institute of Islamic Studies: Prof. MASHUR BIN-GHALIB JUNDAM
National College of Public Administration and Governance: Prof. ALEX B. BRILLANTES Jr
School of Economics: EMMANUEL S. DE DIOS

School of Labour and Industrial Relations: Prof. JORGE V. SIBAL
School of Library and Information Science: Prof. VYVA AGUIRRE
School of Statistics: Prof. ERNIEL BARRIOS
School of Urban and Regional Planning: Prof. CANDIDO A. CABRIDO Jr
UP Extension Programme in Pampanga: Prof. JULIETA C. MALLARI

UP at Los Baños

Internet: www.uplb.edu.ph
Chancellor: Prof. LUIS REY I. VELASCO
Vice Chancellor for Admin.: Prof. ROBERTO F. RAÑOLA Jr
Vice Chancellor for Community Affairs: Prof. VIRGINIA R. CARDENAS
Vice Chancellor for Instruction: Prof. RITA P. LAUDE
Vice Chancellor for Planning and Devt: Prof. RUBEN D. TANQUECO
Vice Chancellor for Research and Extension: Prof. ENRICO P. SUPANGCO
Registrar: Prof. MYRNA G. CARANDANG
Librarian: CONCEPCION DL. SAUL

DEANS

College of Agriculture: Prof. DOMINGO E. ANGELES
College of Arts and Sciences: Prof. ASUNCION K. RAYMUNDO
College of Development Communication: Prof. CLEOFE S. TORRES
College of Economics and Management: Prof. LIBORIO S. CABANILLA
College of Engineering and Agro-Industrial Technology: Prof. VICTOR B. CRUZ
College of Forestry and Natural Resources: Prof. REX VICTOR O. CRUZ
College of Human Ecology: Prof. SUE LIZA C. SAGUIGUIT
College of Public Affairs: Prof. AGNES C. ROLA
College of Veterinary Medicine: Prof. CONRADO A. VALDEZ
Graduate School: Prof. OSCAR B. ZAMORA
School of Environmental Science and Management: Prof. MARIA VICTORIA O. ESPALDON

UP at Manila

Internet: www.upm.edu.ph
Chancellor: Prof. Dr RAMON L. ARCADIO
Vice Chancellor for Academic Affairs: Prof. JOSEFINA G. TAYAG
Vice Chancellor for Admin.: Prof. ORLINO O. TALENS
Vice Chancellor for Planning and Devt: Prof. ZORAYDA E. LEOPANDO
Vice Chancellor for Research: Prof. LULU C. BRAVO
Registrar: SUSAN B. VILLEGAS
Librarian: THERESA P. DUGENIA
Library: see Libraries and Archives

DEANS

College of Allied Medical Professions: Prof. CONCEPCION C. CABATAN
College of Arts and Sciences: Prof. REYNALDO H. IMPERIAL
College of Dentistry: Prof. VICENTE O. MEDINA
College of Medicine: Prof. ALBERTO B. ROXAS
College of Nursing: Prof. JOSEFINA A. TUAZON
College of Pharmacy: Prof. JOCELYN S. BAUTISTA-PALACPAC
College of Public Health: Prof. NINA G. GLORIANI
Graduate School: LILIA A. REYES
National Institutes of Health: Prof. LULU C. BRAVO
National Teacher-Training Centre for the Health Professions: Prof. ERLYN A. SANA

School of Health Sciences: Prof. JUSIE LYDIA J. SIEGA-SUR

UP on Mindanao

Internet: www.upmin.edu.ph
Chancellor: Prof. GILDA C. RIVERO
Vice Chancellor for Academic Affairs: Prof. EMMA RUTH V. BAYOGAN
Vice Chancellor for Admin.: Prof. MIGUEL D. SOLEDAD
Registrar: Prof. KAREN JOYCE G. CAYAMANDA
Librarian: BRICCIO M. MERCED

DEANS

College of Humanities and Social Sciences: Prof. MA. ARACELI DANS-LEE
College of Science and Mathematics: Prof. REYNALDO G. ABAD
School of Management: Prof. SYLVIA B. CONCEPCION

UP in the Visayas

Internet: www.upv.edu.ph
Chancellor: Prof. MINDA J. FORMACION
Vice Chancellor for Academic Affairs: Prof. LEONOR M. SANTOS
Vice Chancellor for Admin.: Prof. LOUISE ANNETTE B. ESCOTO
Vice Chancellor for Planning and Devt: Prof. ALICE JOAN G. FERRER
Vice Chancellor for Research and Extension: Prof. JANE S. GEDUSPAN
Registrar: Prof. MARILYN Z. ALCARDE
Librarian: ANA T. MONES

DEANS

College of Arts and Sciences: Prof. ROMMEL A. ESPINOSA
College of Fisheries and Ocean Sciences: Prof. CARLOS C. BAYLON
College of Management: Prof. JOY C. LIZADA
School of Technology: Prof. LUZETTE T. TERUEL
UPV Cebu College: Prof. ENRIQUE M. AVILA
UPV Tacloban College: Prof. MARGARITA DELA CRUZ

UP Open University

Internet: www.upou.org
Chancellor: Prof. GRACE JAVIER ALFONSO
Vice Chancellor for Academic Affairs: Prof. MARIA FE V. MENDOZA
Vice Chancellor for Finance and Admin.: Prof. MELINDA F. LUMANTA
Registrar: Prof. RICARDO T. BAGARINAO
Librarian: AUDREY ANDAY

DEANS

Faculty of Education: Prof. MA. THERESA DE VILLA
Faculty of Information and Communication Studies: Prof. MELINDA D.P. BANDALARIA
Faculty of Management and Development Studies: Prof. INOCENCIO E. BUOT, Jr

UNIVERSITY OF THE VISAYAS

6000 Cebu City
Telephone: (32) 253-28-85
Internet: www.uv.edu
Founded 1919
Private control
Languages of instruction: English, Filipino
Academic year: June to May
Pres.: EDUARDO R. GULLAS
Exec. Vice-Pres.: JOSE R. GULLAS
Registrar: JOSEFINA T. ARREZA
Librarian: EDNA CAGA
Number of teachers: 600

Number of students: 18,214
Publications: *Spectrum* (Graduate Research Journal), *Statistical Bulletin*, *Strategies* (Education Journal), *The Visayanian*, etc

DEANS

College of Arts and Sciences: ERLINDA L. PEPITO
College of Commerce: SOLEDAD CUMBRA
College of Criminology: EMMANUEL PEPITO
College of Engineering and Architecture: MARCIALITO VALENZONA
College of Law: AMADEO SENO
College of Medicine: RENATO ESPINOSA
College of Nursing: LOURDES FERNAN
College of Pharmacy: CARMEN YAP
Graduate School: FE NECESARIO
Nautical School: GODOFREDO COSIDO
Teachers' College: AURORA A. ECONG

VISAYAS STATE UNIVERSITY

Visca, Baybay, Leyte 6521
Telephone: (53) 335-2601
Fax: (53) 335-2601
Internet: www.vsu.edu.ph
Founded 1924 as Baybay Agricultural School, present name and status 2001
State control
Languages of instruction: English, Filipino
Academic year: June to March
Colleges of agriculture, arts and science, education, engineering and agri-industries, forestry and veterinary medicine, management and economics, nursing; Graduate School; Open Univ. system
Pres.: Dr JOSE L. BACUSMO
Number of teachers: 400

WEST VISAYAS STATE UNIVERSITY

Luna St, La Paz, Iloilo City, Iloilo 5000
Telephone: (33) 320-0870
Fax: (33) 320-0879
Internet: www.wvsu.edu.ph
Founded 1924 as Iloilo Normal School; present name and status 1986
State control
Academic year: June to March
Pres.: Dr LOURDES C. ARAÑADOR
Colleges of arts and sciences, education, mass communications, medicine and nursing; Institute of information and communications technology.

WESTERN MINDANAO STATE UNIVERSITY

Normal Rd, Baliwasan, 7000 Zamboanga City
Telephone: 991-1040
Fax: 991-3065
Internet: www.wmsu.edu.ph
Founded 1918
State control
Languages of instruction: English, Filipino
Academic year: June to March (2 semesters)
Pres.: Dr ELDIGARIO D. GONZALES
Vice-Pres. for Academic Affairs: Dr MARLENE C. TILLAH
Vice-Pres. for Admin. and Finance: Dr CLEMENCIO M. BASCAR
Vice-Pres. for Research Extension and Training: (vacant)
Registrar: JULIETA A. DEL ROSARIO
Librarian: SALUD C. LAQUIO
Library of 50,000 vols
Number of teachers: 436
Number of students: 12,397
Publication: *Bulletin*

DEANS

Admissions: Prof. RUTH N. JUNIO
College of Agriculture: ERIBERTO D. SALANG
College of Arts and Sciences: Dr RAIMUNDA J. BANICO
College of Criminology: Prof. EFFRENDY ESTIPONA
College of Education: Prof. FELICITAS F. FALCATAN
College of Engineering and Technology: Eng. MOHAMMAD NUR MOHAMMAD
College of Forestry: Prof. DINO A. SABELLINA
College of Home Economics: Prof. NOEMI S. ENRIQUEZ
College of Law: Atty EDUARDO F. SANSON
College of Nursing: Prof. TERESITA C. MARBELLA
College of Science and Mathematics: Dr ELBIA P. AQUINO
College of Social Work: Prof. BAGIAN ABDULKARIM
Extension Services: Dr ABDULAJID A. IBBA
Graduate School: Prof. OFELIO R. MENDOZA
Institute of Asian and Islamic Studies: Prof. NURUDDIN I. UNGGANG
Institute of Physical Education, Sports and Cultural Affairs: Prof. ALICIA LOURDES SORIANO
Research Center: Dr ALFREDO DUCANES
Student Affairs: Eng. ARMANDO ARQUIZA

XAVIER UNIVERSITY—ATENEO DE CAGAYAN

Corrales Ave, 9000 Cagayan de Oro City
Telephone: (8822) 72-31-16
Fax: (8822) 857-31-19
E-mail: pres@xu.edu.ph
Internet: www.xu.edu.ph
Founded 1933
Private control
Language of instruction: English
Academic year: June to March (2 terms)

Pres.: Rev. Fr ROBERTO C. YAP
Registrar: VERNA A. LAGO
Univ. Librarian: ESTRELLA CALDAMO CABUDOY

Library of 148,307 vols
Number of teachers: 608
Number of students: 10,921

Publications: *Kinaadman (Wisdom)* (1 a year), *XU Graduate School Journal* (2 a year)

DEANS

Faculty of Arts and Sciences: Dr DULCE. DAWANG
Faculty of College of Agriculture: ROEL RAVANERA
Faculty of Commerce: Dr VIRGINIA YACAPIN
Faculty of Education: Dr LOURDES TOLOD
Faculty of Engineering: Ing. ELISEO B. LINOG, JR
Faculty of Law: RAUL R. VILLANUEVA
Faculty of Medicine: Dr RUTH S. BELTRAN
Faculty of Nursing: Dr RAMONA HEIDI C. PALAD
Graduate School: Dr ISAIAS S. SEALZA

Colleges
GENERAL

San Beda College: Mendiola St, Manila; tel. 735-60-11; fax 735-59-94; e-mail sbc@dns.sbc.edu.ph; f. 1901; private control; constituent grade and high schools and colleges of law, arts and sciences; library: 120,464 vols; 276 teachers; 6,006 students; Rector Rev. BERNARDO M. PEREZ; Librarian MARLO CHAVEZ.

St Paul College of Manila: 680 Pedro Gil St, Malate, Manila, POB 3062; tel. (2) 524-56-87; fax (2) 525-66-20; e-mail spcm@spcm.edu.ph; internet www.spcm.edu.ph; f. 1912; private control; first degree courses in computer science, hotel and restaurant management, psychology, education, commerce, secretarial administration, nursing, communication arts, music; library: 47,898 vols; 148 teachers; 2,800 students; Pres. Sis. NATIVIDAD DE JESUS FERAREN.

St Scholastica's College: 2560 Leon Guinto St, Malate, Metro Manila 1004, POB 3153; tel. (2) 524-7686; fax (2) 521-2593; e-mail maryjohn@ssc.edu.ph; internet www.ssc.edu.ph; f. 1906; private control (sectarian); schools of accountancy, arts and sciences, commerce, music, music education; 516 teachers; 6,601 students; Pres. Sis. MARY JOHN MANANZAN.

State Polytechnic College of Palawan: Aborlan, 5302 Palawan; tel. 433-4480; f. 1910; courses in agriculture, forestry, fisheries, environmental management, engineering and technology, education, arts, science, rural development; library: 22,500 vols; Pres. Dr CONCEPTO B. MAGAY; publs *SPCP-IMS Research Journal* (2 a year), *SPCP Research Journal* (irregular).

ECONOMICS

Asian Institute of Management: Eugenio Lopez Foundation Bildg, Joseph R. McMicking Campus, 123 Paseo de Roxas, Makati City, 1260; tel. (632) 8924011; fax (632) 8179240; e-mail admissions@aim.edu.ph; internet www.aim.edu.ph; f. 1968 by Ateneo de Manila Univ., De La Salle University, the Harvard Business School and the Ford Foundation; academic units and degree programmes: Washington SyCip Graduate School of Business (MBA, Master in Management), Centre for Development Management (Master in Development Management), Asian Centre for Entrepreneurship (Master in Entrepreneurship), Executive Education and Life Long Learning Centre (Executive MBA, Certificate Programmes); library: more than 25,000 books and periodicals, more than 30,000 learning material items; 61 teachers; Pres. ROBERTO F. DE OCAMPO; Dean VICTORIA S. LICUANAN.

MEDICINE

Bicol Christian College of Medicine: AMEC-BCCM Postal Station, Rizal St, Legazpi City 4901; tel. (5221) 44433; fax (5221) 455058; f. 1980; 4-year undergraduate courses; library: 30,052 vols; Pres. EMMANUEL F. AGO; Dean, College of Medicine Dr ANGELITA F. AGO.

Cebu Doctors' University College of Medicine: CDU Administrative Offices Bldg, Gov. M. Roa St, Cebu City 6000; tel. and fax (32) 253-4919; e-mail cdu-cm@cebudoctorsuniversity.edu; internet www.cebudoctorsuniversity.edu/medicine; f. 1977; library: 11,800 vols; 160 staff; 360 students; Pres. POTENCIANO V. LARRAZABAL; Sec. POTENCIANO S. D. LARRAZABAL, III; Treas. PHILIP ANTHONY S. D. LARRAZABAL; Dean ENRICO B. GRUET; publ. *Proceedings* (2 a year).

TECHNOLOGY

Leyte Institute of Technology: Salazar St, Tacloban City; f. 1965; courses in engineering, science, industrial technology, education and vocational training; postgraduate courses; 309 staff; library: 17,000 vols; Pres. GREGORIO T. DE LA ROSA; Registrar FRANKLIN A. COLASITO; publs *College Journal, Graduate School Bulletin, Industrial Wheel*.

Lyceum of the Philippines: Real and Muralla Sts, Intramuros, POB 1264, Manila; tel. (2) 527-55-48; fax (2) 527-17-61; internet www.lyceumphil.edu.ph; f. 1952; private control; Faculties of law, graduate studies, mechanical engineering, mass communication, journalism, arts and sciences, foreign service, economics, business administration, office management, technical vocational, hotel and restaurant management, secretarial science, computer engineering, electronics and communication engineering, political science, legal studies, Filipino, literature, history, humanities, mathematics, psychology, biology, tourism, accountancy, legal secretarial administration, computer science, secondary education, banking and finance, management, marketing, computer data management and processing, tax and customs administration, cruise line management, nursing and medical transcription; library: 45,000 vols; 300 teachers; 10,000 students; Pres. ROBERTO P. LAUREL.

Mapùa Institute of Technology: Muralla St, Intramuros, Manila; tel. (832) 527-7916; fax (832) 527-5161; f. 1925; private control; Faculties of architecture and planning, industrial design, industrial engineering, mining and metallurgical engineering, civil engineering, electrical engineering, electronics and communications engineering, mechanical engineering, geology, environmental and sanitary engineering, chemical engineering and chemistry, computer engineering; 13,000 students; Pres. OSCAR B. MAPÙA, Sr.

Namei Polytechnic Institute: 123 A Mabini St, Mandaluyong, Metro Manila; tel. 531-73-28; fax 815-63-37; f. 1947; private control; courses in naval architecture and marine engineering, B. S. marine transportation, marine engineering, mechanical engineering, electrical engineering; Pres. MARIA VICTORIA P. ESTRELLA; Registrar PERLA G. CRUZ.

Naval Institute of Technology: Naval, Biliran 6543; f. 1972; library: 10,000 vols; 83 teachers; 2,500 students; Pres. Dr JUANITO S. SISON.

Palompon Institute of Technology: Palompon, Leyte; tel. (53) 5559841; fax (53) 3382501; e-mail pit@glinesnx.com.ph; internet foo.ncc.gov.ph/ecommunity/pit; f. 1972; courses in marine transportation and engineering; engineering technology; technical and vocational education; customs administration; radio communication; domestic science; industrial technology, shipping management, teacher education, information technology, industrial engineering, Doctor and Master programmes; library: 10,434 vols; 114 teachers; 2,776 students; Pres. Dr JUANITO S. SISON.

POLAND

The Higher Education System

Higher education in Poland dates from the 14th century, with the establishment of Uniwersytet Jagielloński (Jagiellonian University—founded in 1364), the country's oldest university. Several institutions of higher education were founded in the 18th and 19th centuries, including Uniwersytet Wrocławski (the University of Wrocław—founded in 1702), Akademia Muzyczna im. Fryderyka Chopina w Warszawie (the Frederick Chopin Academy of Music in Warsaw—founded in 1810) and Uniwersytet Warszawki (the University of Warsaw—founded in 1816). Many institutions of higher education were founded during the period of Communist rule (1948–89) and still more have been created since the fall of Communism; by 2004/05 there were 400 higher education establishments in Poland (including 17 universities and 22 technical universities), which by 2007/08 had a total of 2,166,000 students.

The Ministry of Science and Higher Education is the state authority responsible for higher education, which is administered according to the Higher Education Act (1990) and Act of Academic Title and Degrees (1990). Higher education is provided by universities (uniwersytet), technical universities (politechnika) and non-university level institutions (wyzsze szkoly zawodowe). The senate of each higher education institution sets admission rules and procedures, including the total number of students to be enrolled each year, as well as programmes of study. Public universities are funded from the state budget, with allocations determined by the Minister of National Education, while private universities are mainly funded by the student tuition fees. Poland has one of the highest rates globally of private sector higher education, with around one-third of all students enrolled in private institutions. However, in recent years the private sector has appeared to be in decline; at the beginning of the 2011/12 academic year, the number of students enrolled in private institutions had fallen by 80,000 compared with 2007, and 17 private institutions were in various stages of liquidation. As a result, there has been a series of mergers, as well as concerted efforts to attract greater numbers of foreign students. Poland participates in the Bologna Process to establish a European Higher Education Area, the first phase of which is to adopt a credit-based system of comparable degrees with two main cycles (undergraduate and graduate).

The main criterion for admission to higher education is the Świadectwo dojrzałości (secondary school 'maturity' certificate) and some institutions may set entrance examinations. Poland has implemented a two-tier Bachelors and Masters degree system, in accordance with the principles of the Bologna Process, but some old-style degree programmes are still offered, mostly by institutions of professional education. The primary examples of these types of degree are the Licencjat (Bachelors) and Inzynier, which are awarded after three- to four-year courses of higher professional education. The undergraduate Bachelors degree is a three- or four-year course of study equivalent to the initial stages of the old-style Magister (Masters). The new Masters is now a separate postgraduate degree lasting one to two years; however, students in mainly professional fields of study continue to work towards integrated Masters programmes. Admission to the highest level of university degree, the Doktor (Doctorate), requires the Masters. The Doctorate is awarded following the submission and defence of a thesis and success in doctoral examinations.

Technical and vocational education at the post-secondary level is offered by post-secondary schools (szkoly policealne or, in the case of nursing and midwifery institutes, szkoly pomaturalne) and schools of higher professional education (wyzsze szkoly zawodowe); the latter were established following the Act on Schools of Higher Vocational Education (1997) and offer Licencjat and Inzynier qualifications. Admission to post-secondary schools requires students to hold the Swiadectwo ukończenia liceum ogólnokształcącego (certificate of completion of lyceum); some courses may also require the Świadectwo dojrzałości.

The Act on Schools of Higher Vocational Education of 1997 established the Accreditation Commission for Higher Vocational Education, and the State Accreditation Committee (created on the basis of the amended Higher Education Act of 1990) has been in operation since 2002.

Regulatory and Representative Bodies

GOVERNMENT

Ministry of Culture and National Heritage: ul. Krakowskie Przedmieście 15/17, 00-071 Warsaw; tel. (22) 4210100; fax (22) 8260726; e-mail rzecznik@mkidn.gov.pl; internet www.mkidn.gov.pl; Minister BOGDAN ZDROJEWSKI; Gen. Dir GRAŻYNA OŻAREK.

Ministry of National Education: Al. Szucha 25, 00-918 Warsaw; tel. (22) 3474100; fax (22) 5224100; e-mail informacja@men.gov.pl; internet www.men.gov.pl; Minister KATARZYNA HALL; Gen. Dir ROBERT BARTOLD.

Ministry of Science and Higher Education: ul. Wspólna 1/3, 00-529 Warsaw; tel. (22) 5292718; fax (22) 6280922; e-mail sekretariat.bm@nauka.gov.pl; internet www.nauka.gov.pl; Min. Prof. BARBARA KUDRYCKA; Gen. Dir MAREK KUCIŃSKI.

ACCREDITATION

Centralna Komisja do Spraw Stopni i Tytułów (Central Commission for Degrees and Titles): pl. Defilad 1 (PKiN), 00-091 Warsaw; tel. (22) 826-82-38; fax (22) 620-33-24; e-mail kancelaria@ck.gov.pl; internet www.ck.gov.pl; defines fields and disciplines within sciences and the arts in which academic and professional titles and degrees are awarded; grants relevant instns the right to award such titles and degrees; ratifies awards of Dr hab. degrees; Pres. Prof. Dr hab. TADEUSZ KACZOREK; Sec. Prof. OSMAN ACHMATOWICZ.

ENIC/NARIC Poland: Dept of Higher Education Org. and Supervision, Min. of Science and Higher Education, ul. Wspólna 1/3 00-529 Warsaw; tel. (22) 628-67-76; fax (22) 628-35-34; e-mail enic-naric@nauka.gov.pl; internet www.enic-naric.net/index.aspx?c=poland; responsible for the recognition of foreign credentials for both academic and professional purposes; gives opinions and information on documents of higher education obtained abroad; provides information on the recognition procedures of foreign education in Poland, assists those who wish to seek recognition of Polish educational credentials abroad; Head HANNA RECZULSKA.

Państwowa Komisja Akredytacyjna (State Accreditation Committee): ul. Żurawia 32/34, 00-515 Warsaw; tel. (22) 622-07-18; fax (22) 621-15-84; internet www.pka.edu.pl; f. 2001; supports Polish public and non-public higher education instns in the devt of educational standards matching the best models adopted in Europe and the world; conducts obligatory assessments of the quality of education and gives opinions on applications submitted by higher education instns to provide degree programmes; Pres. Dr hab. ZBIGNIEW MARCINIAK; Sec. Dr hab. MIECZYSŁAW WACŁAW SOCHA.

Uniwersytecka Komisja Akredytacyjna (University Accreditation Commission): Uniwersytet im. A. Mickiewicza, ul. Wieniawskiego 1, 61-712 Poznań; tel. (61) 829-25-02; fax (61) 829-24-92; e-mail pkaz@amu.edu.pl; internet www.uka.amu.edu.pl; f. 1998; matches the quality of univ. education in Poland with that in the EU; promotes high quality courses of study and the univs offering them; harmonizes the standards of educational quality at univs; 21 mems; Chair. Prof. Dr hab. MAREK WĄSOWICZ; Sec. Prof. Dr hab. ZBIGNIEW PALKA.

FUNDING

Komitet Badań Naukowych (State Committee for Scientific Research): ul. Wspólna 1/3, 00-529 Warsaw; tel. (22) 529-27-18; fax (22) 628-09-22; e-mail dip@kbn.gov.pl; internet kbn.icm.edu.pl; f. 1991; draws up guidelines on scientific policy, submits plans for budgetary expenditure in the area of science and technology, distributes funds among instns and research teams and controls spending, and signs int. agreements on co-operation in science and technology; Chair. MICHAŁ KLEIBER; Gen. Dir KRYSTYN WEREMOWICZ.

NATIONAL BODIES

Konferencja Rektorów Akademickich Szkół Polskich (Conference of Rectors of Academic Schools in Poland): ul. Wybrzeze Wyspianskiego 27, 50-370 Wrocław; tel. (71) 320-29-60; fax (71) 320-32-22; e-mail krasp@pwr.wroc.pl; internet www.krasp.org.pl; f. 1997; voluntary asscn of rectors representing those instns of higher education awarding doctorates (or equivalent) in at least 1 scientific discipline; 105 mems, 3 assoc. instns; Pres. Prof. TADEUSZ LUTY; Sec. Gen. Prof. ANDRZEJ KRASNIEWSKI.

Rada Główna Szkolnictwa Wyższego (Central Council for Higher Education): ul. Wspólna 1/3, 00-529 Warsaw; tel. (22) 529-25-64; fax (22) 529-27-68; e-mail radaglowna@mnisw.gov.pl; internet www.rgsw.edu.pl; formulates opinions on how higher education should be developed and on all proposed legislation concerning higher education; Pres. Prof. Dr hab. JERZY BŁAŻEJOWSKI.

Learned Societies

GENERAL

Bydgoskie Towarzystwo Naukowe (Bydgoszcz Scientific Society): ul. Jezuicka 4, 85-102 Bydgoszcz; tel. and fax (52) 322-22-68; e-mail btn@um.bydgoszcz.pl; f. 1959; 553 mems; library of 17,500 vols; Pres. Prof. Dr hab. HENRYK Z. WREMBEL; Sec.-Gen. Dr GRZEGORZ DOMINIAK; publs *Bydgostiana Kolokwium Wiedzy o Ziemi* (irregular), *Ekologia i Technika* (6 a year), *Prace Wydziału Nauk Humanistycznych* (1 a year), *Prace Wydziału Nauk Przyrodniczych* (1 a year), *Prace Wydziału Nauk Technicznych* (1 a year), *Przegląd Bydgoski* (1 a year).

Gdańskie Towarzystwo Naukowe (Gdańsk Scientific Society): ul. Grodzka 12, 80-841 Gdańsk; tel. (58) 301-21-24; fax (58) 305-81-31; e-mail gtn@3net.pl; f. 1922 as Gdańsk Society of Friends of Science and Art; sections of social sciences and humanities, biological and medical sciences, mathematical, physical and chemical sciences, technical sciences, earth sciences; 572 mems; Pres. Prof. JAN DRWAL; Sec. Prof. JERZY BŁAŻEJOWSKI; publ. *Acta Biologica et Medica*.

Kieleckie Towarzystwo Naukowe (Kielce Scientific Society): ul. Zamkowa 5, 25-009 Kielce; tel. (41) 344-54-53; fax (41) 344-54-53; e-mail ktn@pu.kielce.pl; internet www.pu.kielce.pl/ktn; f. 1958; regional scientific research in history, philology, medicine, geology, geography and nature conservation, psychology, sociology and education, physics, mathematics, engineering; 464 mems; library of 4,620 vols; Pres. Prof. Dr hab. ADAM MASSALSKI; Sec. Prof. Dr hab. MAREK JÓŹWIAK; publs *Rocznik Świętokrzyski* (Yearbook), *Studia Kieleckie* (irregular).

Łomżyńskie Towarzystwo Naukowe im. Wagów (The Brothers Waga Łomża Scientific Society): ul. Długa 13, 18-400 Łomża; tel. and fax (86) 216-32-56; e-mail zegalska@poczta.onet.pl; internet www.ltn.lomza.pl; f. 1975; agriculture, economics, environmental protection, ethnology, geography, history, linguistics, natural history, veterinary science, settlement of NE Poland, sociology; 250 mems; library of 20,000 vols; Pres. Prof. Dr hab. HALINA KARAŚ; Dir Mgr inż ELŻBIETA ŻEGALSKA; publs *Archiwalia badauia regianalne* (1 a year), *Pogranicze w Jezyku i Kulturze* (1 a year), *Polszczyzna Mazowsza i Podlasia* (1 a year), *Studia Gwolrozneweze* (1 a year), *Studia Łomżyńskie* (1 a year).

Lubelskie Towarzystwo Naukowe (Lublin Scientific Society): Pl. Litewski 2, 20-080 Lublin; tel. and fax (81) 532-13-00; e-mail biuro@ltn.lublin.pl; f. 1957; 722 mems; 5 sections: humanities, biology, mathematics-physics-chemistry, technical science, mining and geography; Pres. Prof. Dr hab. EDMUND K. PROST; Sec.-Gen. Prof. Dr JAN MALARCZYK.

Polska Akademia Nauk (PAN) (Polish Academy of Sciences): Pałac Kultury i Nauki, Plac Defilad 1, POB 24, 00-901 Warsaw; tel. (22) 620-49-70; fax (22) 620-49-10; e-mail akademia@pan.pl; internet www.pan.pl; f. 1952; divs: biological and agricultural sciences, engineering sciences, humanities and social sciences, mathematics, physics, chemistry and earth sciences, medical sciences; attached research institutes: see under Research Institutes; colln: science and technology, future studies, praxiology, library and information science, bibliography; 515 mems (171 ordinary, 145 corresp., 199 foreign); library of 413,697 vols; Pres. Prof. MICHAL KLEIBER; Vice-Pres Prof. ANDRZEJ GORSKI; Vice-Pres Prof. MAREK C. CHMIELEWSKI; Vice-Pres Prof. MIROSLAWA MARODY; Vice-Pres Prof. RYSZARD GORECKI; publs *Academia. The Magazine of the Polish Academy of Sciences* (4 a year, in English and Polish), *Acta Arithmetica* (4 a year), *Acta Biochimica Polonica* (4 a year), *Acta Geologica Polonica* (4 a year), *Acta Neurobiologicale Experimentalis* (4 a year), *Acta Physica Polonica* (4 a year), *Acta Poloniae Historica* (2 a year), *Acta Protozoologica* (4 a year), *Acta Physiologiae Plantarum* (4 a year), *Archeologia* (1 a year), *Archives of Metallurgy and Materials* (4 a year), *Archivum Immunologiae et Therapiae Experimentalis* (6 a year), *Bulletin of the Polish Academy of Sciences:* Series: *Technical Sciences* (4 a year), *Chemia Analityczna* (4 a year), *Chemical and Process Engineering* (4 a year), *Ethnologia Polonia* (1 a year), *Etudes et Travaux* (1 a year), *Folia Neuropathologica* (4 a year), *Fundamenta Mathematicae* (4 a year), *Journal of Animal and Feed Sciences* (4 a year), *Nauka* (4 a year), *Oceanologia* (4 a year), *Onomastica* (1 a year), *Pamiętnik Literacki* (4 a year), *Polish Journal of Food and Nutrition Sciences* (4 a year), *Polish Journal of Pharmacology* (6 a year), *Polish Journal of Veterinary Sciences* (4 a year), *Studia Logica* (4 a year), *Studia Mathematica* (4 a year).

Poznańskie Towarzystwo Przyjaciół Nauk (Poznań Society of Friends of Arts and Sciences): ul. Sew. Mielżyńskiego 27/29, 61-725 Poznań; tel. (61) 852-74-41; fax (61) 852-22-05; e-mail sekretariat@ptpn.poznan.pl; internet www.ptpn.poznan.pl; f. 1857; 1,070 mems; library of 197,176 books, 5,024 periodical titles, 1,432 MSS, 15,157 old books incl. incunabula, 1,839 maps and atlases, 711 microfilms; Pres. Prof. Dr hab. JACEK WIESIOŁOWSKI; Sec.-Gen. Dr LECH TORLIŃSKI; publs *Badania Fizjograficzne nad Polską Zachodnią* (Series A (Geography) Series B (Botany) Series C (Zoology)), *Bulletin de la Société des Amis des Sciences et des Lettres de Poznań—Série D: Sciences Biologiques*, *Lingua Posnaniensis, Roczniki Dziejów Spolecznych i Gospodarczych, Slavia Antiqua, Slavia Occidentalis, Sprawozdania Poznańskiego Towarzystwa Przyjaciół Nauk*.

Towarzystwo Naukowe Płockie (Płock Scientific Society): plac Narutowicza 8, 09-402 Płock; tel. (24) 366-99-50; fax (24) 262-26-04; e-mail aktnp@interia.pl; internet www.tnp.org.pl; f. 1820; 416 mems; library of 328,149 vols; Pres. Dr hab. Inż. ZBIGNIEW KRUSZEWSKI; Sec.-Gen. Dr WIESŁAW KOŃSKI; publs *Notatki Płockie* (4 a year), *Sprawozdanie z działalności* (Yearbook).

Towarzystwo Naukowe w Toruniu (Scientific Society of Toruń): ul. Wysoka 16, 87-100 Toruń; tel. (56) 622-39-41; fax (56) 622-39-41; e-mail tnt.biuro@wp.pl; internet www.tnt.torun.pl; f. 1875; concerned with historical, legal and social studies, philology, philosophy and natural sciences; 490 mems; library of 112,340 vols; Pres. Prof. MARIAN BISKUP; Gen. Sec. Prof. MARIAN KALLAS; publs include *Roczniki, Fontes* (irregular), *Prace Archaeologiczne* (irregular), *Prace Popularnonaukowe* (irregular), *Prace Wydziału Filologiczno-Filozoficznego* (irregular), *Sprawozdania* (1 a year), *Studia Iuridica* (irregular), *Studia Societatis Scientiarum Toruniensis* (various series: geography and geology, botany, zoology, astronomy, physiology, medicine, all irregular), *Zapiski Historyczne* (4 a year, concerned chiefly with Pomeranian problems).

Towarzystwo Naukowe Warszawskie (Warsaw Scientific Society): ul. Nowy Świat 72, 00-330 Warsaw; tel. (22) 657-27-18; fax (22) 657-28-26; e-mail sekretariat@tnw.waw.pl; internet www.tnw.waw.pl; f. 1907; 430 mems; Pres. Prof. JANUSZ LIPKOWSKI; Sec.-Gen. Prof. EWA WOLNICZ-PAWŁOWSKA; publ. *Rocznik TNW* (1 a year).

Towarzystwo Przyjaciół Nauk w Przemyślu (Society of Science and Letters of Przemyśl): ul. Kościuszki 7, 37-700 Przemyśl; tel. (16) 678-56-01; e-mail tpntpn@wp.pl; internet www.tpn.vt.pl; f. 1909; 266 mems; library of 60,000 vols; Pres. Prof. Dr hab. ZDZISŁAW BUDZYŃSKI; Sec.-Gen. Dr MACIEJ DALECKI; publs *Acta Medica Premisliensia, Biblioteka Przemyska, Polska południowo-wschodnia w epoce nowożytnej Źródła dziejowe, Rocznik Przemyski*.

Towarzystwo Wiedzy Powszechnej (Universal Education Society): Pałac Kultury i Nauki, Plac Defilad 1, VI flor, Room 602, 00-901 Warsaw; tel. (22) 826-56-30; fax 620-33-06; e-mail twp@twp.pl; internet www.twp.pl; f. 1950; general adult education; runs private schools providing vocational, secondary and post-secondary education; founded 5 schools of higher education of which 2 award Masters qualifications; organizes discussions, lectures, seminars, confs, popular science and training sessions; 6,000 mems; library of 2,000 vols; Pres. EDWARD BALAWEJDER; Gen. Dir ZENON GAWORCZUK; publ. *Edukacja Dorosłych* (12 a year).

Towarzystwo Wolnej Wszechnicy Polskiej (Society of the Polish Free University): ul. Górnośląska 20, 00-484 Warsaw; tel. (22) 621-73-55; fax (22) 625-38-34; e-mail mlipowski@mercury.ci.uw.cdu.pl; f. 1882; permanent education, research and application services, specialized interests clubs; 1,000 mems; library of 10,000 vols; Pres. Dr Inż. MIKOŁAJ Ł. LIPOWSKI; Sec.-Gen. (vacant); publs *Człowiek w Społeczeństwie* (irregular), *Kalendarz Samorządowy* (1 a year), *Zeszyty Naukowe* (irregular).

Wrocławskie Towarzystwo Naukowe (Wrocław Scientific Society): ul. Parkowa 13, 51-616 Wrocław; tel. (71) 348-40-61; e-mail wtn@wtn.wroc.pl; internet www.wtn.wroc.pl; f. 1946; studies social and exact sciences; 482 mems; Pres. Prof. Dr ANDRZEJ MULAK; Sec.-Gen. Prof. Dr JAN ZARZYCKI; publs *Annales Silesiae, Litteraria, Prace Wrocławskiego Towarzystwa Naukowego, Rozprawy Komisji Historii Sztuki, Rozprawy Komisji Językowej, Sląskie Prace Bibliologiczne i Bibliotekoznawcze, Seminaria Naukowe WTN.*

AGRICULTURE, FISHERIES AND VETERINARY SCIENCE

Polskie Towarzystwo Gleboznawcze (Polish Society of Soil Science): ul. Wiśniowa 61, 02-520 Warsaw; tel. (22) 849-48-16; f. 1937; 750 mems; Pres. Prof. Dr hab. PIOTR SKŁODOWSKI; Sec. Prof. Dr hab. JÓZEF CHOJNICKI; publ. *Roczniki Gleboznawcze* (4 a year).

Polskie Towarzystwo Leśne (Polish Forest Society): ul. Bitwy Warszawskiej 1920r. nr 3, 02-362 Warszawa; tel. (22) 822-14-70; e-mail sylwan@ibel.waw.pl; f. 1882; 4,314 mems; library of 2,023 vols; Pres. Prof. Dr ANDRZEJ GRZYWACZ; Sec. Dr JAN ŁUKASZEWICZ; publ. *Sylwan* (12 a year).

Polskie Towarzystwo Nauk Weterynaryjnych (Polish Society of Veterinary Sciences): Zarząd Główny PTNW, ul. Nowoursynowska 159C, 03-776 Warsaw; tel. (22) 59-31-606; fax (22) 59-31-606; e-mail ptnw@sggw.pl; internet www.ptnw.pl; f. 1952; lectures and seminars in 12 divs throughout Poland; congress every 4 years; 1,360 mems; library of 2,500 vols; Pres. Prof. Dr ZYQMUNT PEJSAK; Sec. Dr JWONA MARKOWSKA-DANIEL; publ. *Medycyna Weterynaryjna* (12 a year).

Polskie Towarzystwo Zootechniczne (Polish Society of Animal Production): Kaliska 9, 02-316 Warsaw; tel. (22) 822-17-23; e-mail ptz_redakcja@alpha.sggw.waw.pl; f. 1922; 1,200 mems; library of 2,630 vols; Pres. Prof. ZYGMUNT REKLEWSKI; Dir Inż. ANNA ZABŁOCKA-IDCZAK; publs *Animal Production Review* (12 a year), *Animal Production Review Applied Science Reports* (1 a year).

ARCHITECTURE AND TOWN PLANNING

Stowarzyszenie Architektów Polskich (Association of Polish Architects): ul. Foksal 2, 00-950 Warsaw; tel. (22) 827-87-12; fax (22) 827-87-13; e-mail sarp@sarp.org.pl; internet sarp.org.pl; f. 1934; 5,100 mems; Sec.-Gen. DARIUSZ MIECHOWSKI; publ. *Komunikat SARP* (12 a year).

Towarzystwo Urbanistów Polskich (Society of Polish Town Planners): ul. Lwowska 5, lokal 100, 00-660 Warsaw; tel. (22) 875-97-56; fax (22) 875-97-56; e-mail zg@tup.org.pl; internet www.tup.org.pl; f. 1923; conducts and supports activity serving spatial management of Poland; realizes principles of sustainable devt and ensures spatial order; advertises new research and design methods; 1,300 mems; Pres. Prof. Dr hab. TADEUSZ MARKOWSKI; Sec.-Gen. Dr Ing. TOMASZ MAJDA; publs *Biblioteka Urbanisty, Przeglad Urbanistyczny* (4 a year).

BIBLIOGRAPHY, LIBRARY SCIENCE AND MUSEOLOGY

Stowarzyszenie Archiwistów Polskich (Polish Archivists Association): ul. Bonifraterska 6 lok. 21, 00-213 Warsaw; tel. (22) 831-83-63; fax (22) 831-31-71; e-mail sap@sap .waw.pl; internet www.sap.waw.pl; Pres. Dr WŁADYSŁAW STĘPNIAK; Sec.-Gen. (vacant); publ. *Archiwista* (4 a year).

Stowarzyszenie Bibliotekarzy Polskich (Polish Librarians Association): National Library, al. Niepodleglosci 213, 02-086 Warsaw; tel. (22) 608-28-25; fax (22) 825-53-49;

e-mail biuro@sbp.pl; internet www.sbp.pl; f. 1917; 7,800 mems in 16 regional divs; Pres. ELŻBIETA STEFAŃCZYK; Sec.-Gen. MARZENA PRZYBYSZ; publs *Bibliotekarz* (12 a year), *Poradnik Bibliotekarza* (12 a year), *Przegląd Biblioteczny* (4 a year), *Zagadnienia Informacji Naukowej* (4 a year).

ECONOMICS, LAW AND POLITICS

Polskie Towarzystwo Demograficzne (Polish Demographic Society): al. Niepodległości 164, room 3, 02-554 Warsaw; tel. 48-22-3379273; e-mail ewaf@sgh.waw.pl; f. 1982; 250 mems; Pres. ZBIGNIEW STRZELECKI; Sec. LUCYNA NOWAK; publ. *Polish Population Review* (2 a year).

Polskie Towarzystwo Ekonomiczne (Polish Economic Society): Nowy Swiat 49, 00-042 Warsaw; tel. (22) 827-99-04; fax (22) 827-99-04; e-mail zk@pte.pl; internet www.pte.pl; f. 1945; 6,220 mems; Pres. Prof. Dr hab. ZDZISŁAW SADOWSKI; Gen. Sec. Prof. Dr hab. URSZULA PŁOWIEC; publ. *Ekonomista* (6 a year).

Polskie Towarzystwo Towaroznawcze (Polish Society for Commodity Science): ul. Sienkiewicza 4, 30-033 Cracow; tel. (12) 633-08-21; e-mail adamczyw@ae.krakow.pl; internet www.ae.krakow.pl; f. 1963; 500 mems; Pres. Prof. WACŁAW ADAMCZYK; Sec. Dr STANISŁAW POPEK; publ. *Towaroznawstwo—Problemy Jakości* (1 a year).

EDUCATION

Polskie Towarzystwo Pedagogiczne (Polish Educational Research Association): ul. Smulikowskiego 6/8, 00-389 Warsaw; tel. (22) 826-10-11, ext. 249; e-mail biuro@ptp-pl .org; internet www.ptp-pl.org; f. 1981; 300 mems; Pres. Prof. Dr hab. ZBIGNIEW KWIECIŃSKI; Vice-Pres. Prof. Dr hab. HENRYKA KWIATKOWSKA; Vice-Pres. Prof. Dr hab. JOANNA MICHALAK; Sec.-Gen. Prof. Dr hab. MARIAN WALCZAK; publs *Forum Oświatowe* (Educational Forum, 4 a year), *Problemy Wczesnej Edukacji* (Problems of Early Education, 2 a year), *Przegląd Historyczno-Oświatowy* (Historical-Educational Review, 2 a year), *Studia Pedagogiczne* (Pedagogic Studies, 1 a year).

FINE AND PERFORMING ARTS

Polskie Stowarzyszenie Filmu Naukowego (Polish Association of Scientific Film): ul. Mokotowska 58 pok. 1, 00-534 Warsaw; tel. (22) 629-08-32; internet galaxy.uci.agh .edu.pl/~kpfn; Pres. GRZEGORZ KOWALEWSKI; Sec.-Gen. STANISŁAW ŚLEDŹ; publ. *Film Naukowy* (2 a year).

Stowarzyszenie Historyków Sztuki (Art Historians Association): Rynek Starego Miasta 27, 00-272 Warsaw; tel. (22) 635-96-99; fax (22) 635-90-74; e-mail shs@shs.pl; internet www.shs.pl; f. 1934; search and publication, popularization of art history; 1,406 mems; library of 28,492 vols; Pres. Prof. Dr hab. MARIA POPRZĘCKA; Sec.-Gen. Dr KATARZYNA NOWAKOWSKA-SITO; publs *Materiały do Dziejów Rezydencji w Polsce, Materiały Seminariów Metodologicznych, Materiały Sesji SHS, Materiały Sesji Oddziałowych*.

Towarzystwo im. Fryderyka Chopina (Fryderyk Chopin Society): Pl. Pilsudskiego 9, 00-078 Warsaw; tel. (22) 826-65-49; tel. (22) 826-65-49; e-mail info@chopin.pl; internet www.tifc.chopin.pl; f. 1934; 600 mems; permanent Secretariat of the Int. Chopin Record Competitions 'Grand Prix du Disque-Frédéric Chopin'; central Chopin museum, library, phototheque and phonotheque for study of Chopin's life and preparation of complete edition of his works; organization

of concerts; Gen. Dir ANTONI GRUDZIŃSKI; publs *Annales Chopin, Chopin Studies*.

Warszawskie Towarzystwo Muzyczne (Music Society in Warsaw): ul. Morskie Oko 2, 02-511 Warsaw; tel. (22) 849-68-56; e-mail wtm@wtm.org.pl; internet www.wtm.org.pl; f. 1871; 300 mems; Pres. ANNA MALEWICZ-MADEY; Sec. ZOFIA KOSTROWSKA-STAŃCZYKOWSKA.

HISTORY, GEOGRAPHY AND ARCHAEOLOGY

Polskie Towarzystwo Geograficzne (Polish Geographical Society): Krakowskie Przedmieście 30, 00-927 Warsaw; tel. (22) 826-17-94; fax (22) 826-17-94; e-mail ptg@uw .edu.pl; internet www.ptg.pan.pl/mainen .htm; f. 1918; 1,500 mems; library of 17,000 vols; Pres. Prof. Dr JERZY BAŃSKI; Sec. Dr TOMASZ WITES; Treas. Dr KONRAD CZAPIEWSKI; publs *Czasopismo Geograficzne* (Geographical Journal, 4 a year), *Polski Przegląd Kartograficzny* (Polish Cartographical Review, 4 a year), *Prace Komisji Geografii Komunikacji* (1 a year), *Studia Obszarów Wiejskich* (Rural Studies, 1 a year), *Teledetekcja Srodowiska* (1 a year).

Polskie Towarzystwo Historyczne (Polish Historical Society): Rynek Starego Miasta 29/31, 00-272 Warsaw; tel. (22) 831-63-41; e-mail pth@ihpan.edu.pl; internet historicus .umk.pl/pth; f. 1886; 4,137 mems; 53 local brs, 4 research centres; Pres. Prof. Dr KRZYSTOF MIKULSKI; Sec. Prof. Dr hab. ZOFIA T. KOZŁOWSKA; publs *Komunikaty Mazursko-Warmińskie* (4 a year), *Przegląd Historyczny* (4 a year), *Sobótka-Sląski Kwartalnik Historyczny* (4 a year), *Studia i Materiały do dziejów Wielkopolski i Pomorza* (series), and several annuals.

Polskie Towarzystwo Numizmatyczne (Polish Numismatic Society): tel. and fax (22) 831-39-28; e-mail ptn@ptn.pl; internet www.ptn.pl; f. 1991; 2,500 mems; library of 3,645 vols; Pres. Prof. Dr hab. MARIUSZ MIELCZAREK; Sec. ADAM ZAJĄC; publ. *Biuletyn Numizmatyczny* (4 a year).

Stowarzyszenie Miłośników Dawnej Broni i Barwy (Historic Arms and Uniforms Association): al. 3 Maja 1, 30-062 Cracow; tel. (12) 295-55-77; fax (12) 295-55-55; e-mail kontakt@bronibarwa.org.pl; internet www.bronibarwa.org.pl; f. 1957; 270 mems; Pres. Prof. Dr hab. ALEKSANDER GUTERCH; Sec. MICHAL DZIEWULSKI; publ. *Studia do dziejów dawnego uzbrojenia i ubioru wojskowego*.

Towarzystwo Miłośników Historii i Zabytków Krakowa (Society of Friends of the History and Monuments of Cracow): ul. Sw. Jana 12, 31-018 Cracow; tel. (12) 421-27-83; fax (12) 423-10-74; e-mail tmhzk@tmhzk .krakow.pl; internet www.tmhzk.krakow.pl; f. 1896; 650 mems; Pres. Prof. Dr hab. JERZY WYROZUMSKI; Sec. OLGA DYBA; publs *Biblioteka Krakowska, Kraków Dawniej i Dziś, Rocznik Krakowski, Rola Krakowa w dziejach narodu*.

LANGUAGE AND LITERATURE

Alliance Française: AF, BUW, ul. Dobra 56/66, 00-312 Warsaw; tel. (22) 552-71-65; fax (22) 552-71-67; e-mail alliance.francaise@ neostrada.pl; internet www.af-enpologne.pl; offers courses and exams in French language and culture and promotes cultural exchange with France; attached offices in Białystok, Cieszyn, Gdańsk, Gorzow, Katowice, Łódź, Lublin, Opole, Poznań, Rybnik, Rzeszów, Szczecin, Toruń, Wałbrzych and Wrocław; Dir PATRICK RENARD.

British Council: 00-697 Warsaw, Al Jerozolimskie 59; tel. (22) 695-59-00; fax (22)

621-99-55; e-mail bc.warsaw@britishcouncil
.pl; internet www.britishcouncil.pl; teaching
centre and library; offers courses and exams
in English language and British culture and
promotes cultural exchange with the UK;
attached teaching centre in Kraków; Dir
SUSAN MAINGAY.

Goethe-Institut: ul. Chmielna 13A, 00-021
Warsaw; tel. (22) 505-90-00; fax (22) 505-90-
10; e-mail sekretariat@warschau.goethe.org;
internet www.goethe.de/warschau; f. 1990;
offers courses and exams in German language and culture and promotes cultural
exchange with Germany; attached centre in
Cracow; library of 15,000 vols, 30 periodicals;
Dir Dr MARTIN WÄLDE.

Instituto Cervantes: ul. Myśliwiecka 4, 00-
459 Warsaw; tel. (22) 622-54-22; fax (12) 622-
54-13; e-mail cenvar@cervantes.es; internet
varsovia.cervantes.es; offers courses and
exams in Spanish language and culture and
promotes cultural exchange with Spain and
Spanish-speaking Latin and Central America; library of 16,000 vols; Dir JOSEP MARIA DE
SAGARRA ANGEL.

Polskie Towarzystwo Filologiczne (Polish Philological Society): Al Mickiewicza 9/11,
VI p., 31-120 Kraków; tel. (12) 633-63-77 ext.
2324; f. 1893; promotes classical studies; 500
mems; library of 2,500 vols; Pres. Prof. Dr
hab. KAZIMIERZ KORUS; Sec. Dr HUBERT
WOLANIN; publ. *EOS* (1 a year).

Polskie Towarzystwo Fonetyczne (Polish
Phonetic Association): Instytut Lingwistyki
UAM, ul. Międzychodzka 5, 60-371 Poznań;
tel. (61) 829-27-06; fax (61) 829-27-00; e-mail
fonetyka@amu.edu.pl; internet www.staff
.amu.edu.pl/~fonetyka; f. 1980; linguistic
phonetics, phonetics in medicine and technology; 112 mems; Pres. GRAŻYNA DEMENKO;
Sec. MARIUSZ OWSIANNY.

Polskie Towarzystwo Językoznawcze
(Polish Linguistic Society): al. A. Mickiewicza
31, 31-120 Cracow; e-mail ptj@civ.pl; internet
www.ptj.civ.pl; f. 1925; 585 mems; organizes
meetings for mems and annual scientific
confs; Pres. Prof. RENATA PRZYBYLSKA; Sec.
Dr RENATA BURA; publ. *Biuletyn* (1 a year).

Polskie Towarzystwo Neofilologiczne
(Modern Language Association of Poland):
UAM, Collegium Novum, al. Niepodległości
4, pok. 014, 61-874 Poznań; tel. (61) 853-37-
64; e-mail poltowneo@gmail.com; internet
www.poltowneo.org; f. 1929; 184 mems; Pres.
WERONIKA WILCZYŃSKA; Sec. ANNA BARBARA
CIEŚLICKA; publ. *Neofilolog* (2 a year).

**Towarzystwo Literackie im. Adama
Mickiewicza** (Mickiewicz Literary Society):
Nowy Świat 72, 00-330 Warsaw; tel. 22 65-
72-879; e-mail towarzystwo_literackie@wp
.pl; internet www.towarzystwo_literackie
.webpark.pl; f. 1886; 1,600 mems; arranges
lectures on literature mainly in the provinces; Pres. Prof. Dr hab. GRAŻYNA BOR-
KOWSKA; Vice-Pres. Dr JACEK WÓJCICKI; Sec.
Dr IRENA SZYPOWSKA.

Związek Literatów Polskich (Union of
Polish Writers): Krakowskie Przedmieście
87/89, 00-079 Warsaw; tel. (22) 826-57-85;
e-mail owzlp@o2.pl; internet literatura.waw
.pl; f. 1920; 700 mems; library of 40,000 vols
and cuttings; Pres. MAREK WAWRZKIEWICZ;
Gen. Sec. GRZEGORZ WIŚNIEWSKI.

MEDICINE

**Polskie Lekarskie Towarzystwo Radi-
ologiczne** (Polish Medical Society of Radiology): c/o Assoc. Prof. Jan Baron,
Nuklearnej Śląskiej Akademii Medycznej –
SP CSK AM, ul. Medyków 14, 40-752
Katowice; tel. and fax (32) 252-55-66; e-mail
gwawrzonek@csk.katowice.pl; internet www
.polradiologia.org; f. 1925; 1,700 mems; Pres.

Asst Prof. JAN BARON; Vice-Pres. Prof. MAREK
SĄSIADEK; Vice-Pres. ANDRZEJ URBANIK;
Treas. Dr JOANNA GIBIŃSKA; Sec. Dr MAGDA-
LENA MACHNIKOWSKA-SOKOŁOWSKA; publ.
Polski Przegląd Radiologiczny (4 a year).

Polskie Towarzystwo Anatomiczne (Polish Anatomical Society): ul. Chałubińskiego
5, 02-004 Warsaw; tel. (22) 629-52-82; fax
(22) 629-52-82; e-mail mbruska@ump.edu.pl;
internet www.pta.info.pl; f. 1923; 400 mems;
Pres. MAŁGORZATA BRUSKA; Sec. Dr
AGNIESZKA PRZYSTAŃSKA; publs *Folia Morpho-
logica*, *Postępy Biologii Komórki* (Advances
in Cell Biology).

**Polskie Towarzystwo Anestezjologii i
Intensywnej Terapii** (Polish Society of
Anaesthesiology and Intensive Therapy):
Katedra i Klinika Anestezjologii i Intensyw-
nej Terapii AM SPSK Nr 4, ul. Jaczewskiego
8, 20-954 Lublin; tel. (81) 724-43-32; fax (81)
742-52-56; internet www.anestezjologia.org
.pl; f. 1959; Pres. Prof. Dr hab. n. med.
ANDRZEJ NESTOROWICZ; Sec.-Gen. Dr n. med.
ANNA FIJAŁKOWSKA; publ. *Anestezjologia
Intensywna Terapia* (6 a year).

**Polskie Towarzystwo Badań Radiacyj-
nych im. Marii Skłodowskiej-Curie** (M.
Skłodowska-Curie Polish Society for Radiation Research): ul. Chocimska 24, 00-791
Warsaw; tel. (22) 849-77-74; fax (22) 849-29-
64; e-mail ptbr@pzh.gov.pl; internet www
.ptbr.pzh.gov.pl; f. 1967; 229 mems; Pres.
Prof. Dr hab. ANTONI GAJEWSKI; Sec. Dr
MAŁGORZATA ROCHALSKA.

**Polskie Towarzystwo Chirurgów Dzie-
cięcych** (Polish Association of Paediatric
Surgeons): Dept of Pediatric Surgery, Medical Univ. of Białystok, L. Zamenhof Children's Univ. Hospital, ul. Waszyngtona 17,
15-274 Białystok; tel. (48)857-45-09-21; fax
(48)857-45-09-20; e-mail ptchdsek@gmail
.com; internet www.ptchd.pl; f. 1965; 500
mems; Pres. Assoc. Prof. Dr WOJCIECH
DEBEK; Sec.-Gen. Dr DZIENIS-KORONKIEWICZ
EWA; publs *Standardy Medyczne-Problemy
Chirurgii Dziecięcej* (4 a year), *Surgery in
Childhood International* (4 a year).

Polskie Towarzystwo Chorób Płuc (Polish Phthisiopneumonological Society): ul.
Płocka 26, 01-138 Warsaw; tel. (32) 271-56-
08; fax (32) 274-56-64; internet www.ptchp
.org; f. 1934; research into tuberculosis and
chest diseases; Pres. Prof. Dr hab. med.
WŁADYSŁAW PIERZCHAŁA; publ. *Pneumonolo-
gia i Alergologia Polska* (12 a year).

**Polskie Towarzystwo Diagnostyki
Laboratoryjnej** (Polish Laboratory Diagnostics Society): c/o Dr n. med. Andrzej
Marszałek, Zakład Diagnostyki Laboratoryjnej 10 WSK z Polikliniką SPZOZ, ul. Powstańców Warszawy 5, 85-680 Bydgoszcz; tel.
(52) 378-48-87; fax (52) 377-33-10; internet
www.diagnostykalab.pl/diagnost/ptdl/teren
.htm; f. 1963; 3,500 mems; Pres. Prof. Dr n.
med. MAREK PARADOWSKI; Sec. Dr n. med.
ANDRZEJ MARSZAŁEK; publ. *Diagnostyka
Laboratoryjna* (4 a year).

**Polskie Towarzystwo Epidemiologów i
Lekarzy Chorób Zakaźnych** (Polish Society of Epidemiology and Infectious Diseases):
ul. Sw. Floriana 12, 85-030 Bydgoszcz; tel.
(52) 322-48-70; fax (52) 345-71-95; e-mail
kikchzak@amb.bydgoszcz.pl; f. 1958; 1,200
mems; Pres. Prof. WALDEMAR HALOTA; Sec. Dr
EWA TOPCZEWSKA-STAUBACH; publ. *Przegląd
Epidemiologiczny* (4 a year).

Polskie Towarzystwo Farmaceutyczne
(Polish Pharmaceutical Society): ul. Długa
16, 00-238 Warsaw; tel. and fax (22) 831-15-
42; e-mail zarzad@ptfarm.pl; internet www
.ptfarm.pl; f. 1947; 7,000 mems; Pres. Prof.
Dr hab. JANUSZ PLUTA; publs *Acta Poloniae
Pharmaceutica* (6 a year), *Bromatologia i*

Chemia Toksykologiczna (4 a year), *Farm-
acja Polska* (12 a year).

Polskie Towarzystwo Farmakologiczne
(Polish Pharmacological Society): Katedra i
Zakład Patofizjologii, Uniwersytet
Medyczny, Jaczewskiego 8, 00-927 Wars-
zawa; tel. (12) 662-32-58; fax (22) 826-21-16;
e-mail lason@if-pan.krakow.pl; internet
pharmacology.slam.katowice.pl; f. 1965; 341
mems; Pres. Prof. Dr WŁADYSŁAW LASON; Sec.
Prof. Dr BOGUSŁAWA BUDZISZEWSKA; publ.
Pharmacological Reports (abstracts of the
Int. Congresses of the Polish Pharmaco-
logical Soc.).

Polskie Towarzystwo Fizjologiczne (Polish Physiological Society): 16 Grzegórzecka
St, 31-531 Cracow; tel. (12) 421-10-06; fax
(12) 421-15-78; e-mail agata.ptak-belowska@
uj.edu.pl; internet www.ptf.ifzz.pl; f. 1936;
promotes scientific activity in all fields of
physiology incl. most gastrointestinal, endocrine, cardiovascular, neural, respiratory
and kidney physiology; 300 mems; Pres.
Prof. Dr WIESLAW W. PAWLIK; Sec. Dr AGATA
PTAK-BELOWSKA; publ. *Journal of Physiology
and Pharmacology*.

Polskie Towarzystwo Fizyki Medycznej
(Polish Society of Medical Physics): c/o Dr
Ewa Zalewska, Instytut Biocybernetyki i
Inżynierii Biomedycznej PAN, ul. Ks. Troj-
dena 4, 02-109 Warsaw; e-mail k.zaremba@
ire.pw.edu.pl; internet ptfm.ire.pw.edu.pl; f.
1965; 150 mems; Pres. Prof. GRZEGORZ PAW-
LICKI; Sec. Dr EWA ZALEWSKA; publ. *Polish
Journal of Medical Physics and Engineering*.

Polskie Towarzystwo Gerontologiczne
(Polish Society of Gerontology): Wisniowa St
41/66D, 02-520 Warsaw; tel. and fax (50) 101-
63-65; fax (22) 812-11-89; e-mail
gerontologia@gerontologia.org.pl; internet
www.borgis.pl/ptg; f. 1973; 320 mems; Pres.
Pres. PIOTR BTEDOWSKI; Vice-Pres. for Medical Cttee Prof. BARBARABIEN; Vice-Pres. for
Social Cttee Prof. MAEGORZATA HALICKA;
publ. *Gerontologia Polska* (4 a year).

Polskie Towarzystwo Ginekologiczne
(Polish Gynaecological Society): Klinika
Onkologii Ginekologicznej Małgorzata Skow-
rońska, ul. Polna 33, 60-535 Poznań; tel. (61)
841-92-65; fax (61) 841-94-65; e-mail ptgzg@
gpsk.am.poznan.pl; internet www.gpsk.am
.poznan.pl/ptg; br. in Wrocław; Pres. Prof. Dr
hab. MAREK SPACZYŃSKI; Sec. Prof. Dr hab.
LESZEK PAWELCZYK; publ. *Ginekologia Polska*
(12 a year).

Polskie Towarzystwo Higieniczne (Pol-
ish Hygiene Society): ul. Karowa 31, 00-324
Warsaw; tel. (22) 826-63-20; fax (22) 826-82-
36; internet www.pth.pl; f. 1898; Pres. Assoc.
Prof. CEZARY W. KORCZAK; Sec. Dr PAWEŁ
GORYŃSKI; publs *Druk Bibliofilski 'Hygeia'*,
Problemy Higieny, *Problemy Higieny Pracy*.

**Polskie Towarzystwo Higieny Psychicz-
nej** (Polish Mental Health Society): Targowa
59/16, 03-729 Warsaw; tel. (22) 818-65-99;
e-mail pthp@poczta.onet.pl; safeguarding the
mental and moral health of the individual; f.
1935; 1,250 mems; library of 2,500 vols; Pres.
ANDRZEJ BAŁANDYNOWICZ; publ. *Zdrowie Psy-
chiczne* (4 a year).

**Polskie Towarzystwo Immunologii Dos-
wiadczalnej i Klinicznej** (Polish Society
for Experimental and Clinical Immunology):
ul. Garbary 15, 61-866 Poznań; tel. (61) 854-
06-65; fax (61) 852-85-02; internet www
.immuno.pl; f. 1969; 500 mems; Pres. Prof. Dr
hab. ANDRZEJ MACKIEWICZ; Scientific Sec. Dr
hab. DARIUSZ KOWALCZYK; Technical Sec. Dr
hab. PIOTR WYSOCKI; publs *Central European
Journal of Immunology* (4 a year, in English), *Integryna—Biuletyn PTI* (4 a year, in
Polish).

Polskie Towarzystwo Kardiologiczne (Polish Cardiological Society): ul. Stawki 3A/1, 00-193 Warsaw; tel. (22) 887-18-56; fax (22) 887-18-58; e-mail zarzad.glowny@ptkardio.pl; internet www.ptkardio.pl; Pres. Prof. Dr hab. ADAM TORBICKI; Sec. Prof. Dr hab. TOMASZ PASIERSKI; publs *Folia Cardiologica* (12 a year), *Kardiologia Polska* (12 a year).

Polskie Towarzystwo Lekarskie (Polish Medical Association): Al. Ujazdowskie 24, 00-478 Warsaw; tel. and fax (22) 628-86-99; e-mail ptl@interia.pl; internet www.ptl.org .pl; f. 1951; 25,000 mems; Pres. Prof. Dr hab. med. JERZY WOY-WOJCIECHOWSKI; Secs Dr FELICJA ŁAPKIEWICZ, Dr ZBIGNIEW MILLER; publs *Polski Tygodnik Lekarski* (52 a year), *Przegląd Lekarski* (12 a year), *Wiadomości Lekarskie* (26 a year).

Polskie Towarzystwo Medycyny Pracy (Polish Society of Occupational Medicine): ul. Teresy 8, 90-950 Łódź; tel. (42) 631-47-75; fax (42) 631-47-19; e-mail jolantaw@imp.lodz.pl; internet www.imp.lodz.pl/ptmp/ptmp.htm; f. 1969; Pres. Prof. Dr hab. RYSZARD ANDRJEZAK; Sec. Dr JOLANTA WALUSIAK; publs *International Journal of Occupational Medicine and Environmental Health* (4 a year, in English), *Medycyna Pracy* (6 a year).

Polskie Towarzystwo Medycyny Sądowej i Kryminologii (Polish Society of Forensic Medicine and Criminology): ul. Sędziowska 18A, 91-304 Łódź; tel. (42) 654-45-36; fax (42) 654-42-93; e-mail ptmsik@ptmsik.pl; internet www.ptmsik.pl; f. 1938; forensic medicine, toxicology, genetics, other forensic science; 200 mems; Chair. Prof. JAROSŁAW BERENT; Vice-Chair. Doc. MARIA KAŁA; Vice-Chair. Prof. PAWEŁ KRAJEWSKI; publ. *Archiwum Medycyny Sądowej i Kryminologii* (4 a year).

Polskie Towarzystwo Medycyny Społecznej i Zdrowia Publicznego (Polish Society of Social Medicine and Public Health): ul. Chodźki 1, 20-093 Lublin; tel. (81) 740-57-53; fax (81) 740-57-52; e-mail mchbt@eskulap.am.lublin.pl; f. 1916; 1,800 mems; Pres. Prof. Dr hab. n. med. LESZEK WDOWIAK; publ. *Problemy Medycyny Społecznej* (Problems in Social Medicine, 2 or 3 a year).

Polskie Towarzystwo Medycyny Sportowej Zarząd Główny (Polish Society of Sports Medicine): Plac Hallere 1 90-647 Łódź; tel. (42) 639-32-15; fax (42) 639-32-18; e-mail sekretariat@ptms.org.pl; internet www.ptms.org.pl; f. 1937; Pres. Prof. ARTUR DZIAK; Sec. WOJCIECH DRYGAS; publ. *Medycyna Sportowa* (4 a year).

Polskie Towarzystwo Nauk Żywieniowych (Polish Society of Nutritional Sciences): ul. Nowoursynowska 159C, 02-776 Warsaw; tel. (22) 59-37-110; fax (22) 59-37-117; e-mail ptnz@sggw.pl; internet ptnz.sggw .pl; f. 1980; 300 mems; Pres. Prof. Dr hab. ANNA BRZOZOWSKA; Sec. Prof. Dr hab. JULIUSZ PRZYSLAWSKI; publ. *Polish Journal of Food and Nutrition Sciences* (4 a year).

Polskie Towarzystwo Neurochirurgów (Polish Society of Neurosurgeons): ul. Żeromskiego 113, 90-549 Łódź; tel. (42) 639-35-51; f. 1964; 279 mems; Pres. Prof. Dr hab. ANDRZEJ RADEK; publ. *Neurologia i Neurochirurgia Polska* (6 a year).

Polskie Towarzystwo Neurologiczne (Polish Neurological Society): ul. Jaczewskiego 8, 20-950 Warsaw; tel. (81) 742-54-20; fax (81) 742-54-20; e-mail neurolog@asklepios.am.lublin.pl; internet www .neurologiapolska.pl; f. 1934; Pres. Prof. ZBIGNIEW STELMASIAK; Sec. ANNA SZCZPAŃSKA-SZEREJ; publ. *Neurologia i Neurochirurgia Polska* (6 a year).

Polskie Towarzystwo Onkologiczne (Polish Oncological Society): ul. Garncarska 11, 31-115 Cracow; tel. and fax (12) 422-87-60; internet www.pto.io.gliwice.pl; f. 1921; 720 mems; Pres. Prof. Dr hab. MARIAN REINFUSS; Sec. Prof. Dr hab. JAN KULPA; publ. *Nowotwory* (4 a year).

Polskie Towarzystwo Ortopedyczne i Traumatologiczne (Polish Orthopaedic and Traumatological Society): ul. Konarskiego 13, 05-400 Otwock; tel. and fax (22) 779 54 18; internet www.ptoitr.pl; f. 1928; Pres. Prof. Dr hab. TADEUSZ SZYMON GAŹDZIK; Sec. Dr MAREK BOŻEK; publs *Chirurgia Narządów Ruchu i Ortopedia Polska* (6 a year), *Kwartalnik Ortopedyczny* (4 a year).

Polskie Towarzystwo Patologów (Polish Society of Pathologists): ul. Unii Lubelskiej 1, 71-252 Szczecin; tel. and fax (91) 487-00-32; e-mail polpat@ams.edu.pl; internet www .pol-pat.pl; f. 1958; 581 mems; Pres. Prof. Dr hab. WENANCJUSZ DOMAGAŁA; Sec. Dr ELŻBIETA URASIŃSKA; publ. *Patologia Polska* (4 a year, in English).

Polskie Towarzystwo Pediatryczne (Polish Paediatric Society): ul. Sporna 36/50, 91-738 Łódź; tel. (42) 617-29-29; fax (42) 617-28-82; e-mail ptpzg@csk.am.lodz.pl; internet csk .am.lodz.pl/ptpzg; f. 1908; 4,500 mems; Pres. Prof. Dr hab. KRYSTYNA WĄSOWSKA-KRÓLIKOWSKA; Sec. Prof. Dr hab. JERZY STAŃCZYK; publs *Pediatria Polska* (12 a year), *Przegląd Pediatryczny* (4 a year).

Polskie Towarzystwo Pielęgniarskie (Polish Nurses Association): Reymonta 8/12, 01-842 Warsaw; tel. (22) 663-63-45; fax (22) 388-18-51; internet www.ptp.na1.pl; f. 1924, revived 1954; 3,500 mems; library of 3,000 vols; Pres. DOROTA KILANSKA; Sec. GRAZYNA WYSIADECKA; publs *Biuletyn Polskiego Towarzystwa Pielęgniarskiego* (4 a year), *Problemy Pielęgniarstwa* (Nursing Topics).

Polskie Towarzystwo Psychiatryczne (Polish Psychiatric Association): Al. Sobieskiego 1/9, 02-957 Warsaw; tel. and fax (22) 842-40-87; e-mail wciorka@ipin.edu.pl; internet www.psychiatria.org.pl; f. 1920; 1,400 mems; Pres. Prof. Dr JACEK WCIORKA; publs *Archives of Psychiatry and Psychotherapy* (4 a year), *Psychiatria Polska* (6 a year), *Psychoterapia* (4 a year).

Polskie Towarzystwo Stomatologiczne (Polish Dental Association): ul. Montelupich 4, 30-155 Kraków; tel. (12) 424-54-42; fax (12) 424-54-94; e-mail biurozgpts@gmail.com; internet www.pts.net.pl; f. 1951; 6,000 mems; Pres. Assoc. Prof. Dr hab. BARTLOMIEJ W. LOSTER; Vice-Pres. Prof. Dr hab. HONORATA SHAW; Vice-Pres. Prof. Dr hab. ELZBIETA MIERZWINSKA-NASTALSKA; Vice-Pres. Prof. Dr hab. MAREK ZIETEK; Sec. Dr MAŁGORZATA RADWAN-OCZKO; publs *Czasopismo Stomatologiczne* (12 a year), *Dental and Medical Problems* (4 a year), *Dental Forum* (2 a year), *Implantoprotetyka* (4 a year), *Protetyka Stomatologiczna* (6 a year).

Polskie Towarzystwo Toksykologiczne (Polish Toxicological Society): POB 199, 90-950 Łódź; ul. Św. Teresy od Dzieciątka Jezus 8, 90-950 Łódź; tel. (42) 631-45-02; fax (42) 656-83-31; e-mail impx@imp.lodz.pl; internet www.imp.lodz.pl/nowy_pttox; f. 1978; 305 mems; Pres. Prof. Dr hab. KONRAD RYDZYŃSKI; Sec. Dr JOLANTA GROMADZIŃSKA; publ. *Acta Poloniae Toxicologica* (2 a year).

Polskie Towarzystwo Urologiczne (Polish Urological Society): ul. Bursznowa 2, 04-749 Warsaw; tel. and fax (22) 815-68-61; e-mail info@pturol.org.pl; internet www .pturol.org.pl; f. 1949; 800 mems; Pres. Prof. Dr hab. ANDRZEJ BORÓWKA; Sec. Prof. ROMUALD ZDROJOWY; publs *Przegląd Urologiczny* (6 a year), *Urologia Polska* (4 a year).

Polskie Towarzystwo Walki z Kalectwem (Polish Society for Rehabilitation of the Disabled): ul. Oleandrów 4 m. 10, 00-629 Warsaw; tel. and fax (22) 825-70-50; e-mail twk@idn.org.pl; internet twk.idn.org.pl; f. 1960; popularizing progressive ideas in prophylaxis and changing social attitudes towards the disabled; Pres. Dr PIOTR JANASZEK; Sec. Dr ZBIGNIEW KAŹMIERAK; publ. *Life of the Polish Society for Rehabilitation of the Disabled Information Bulletin*.

Stowarzyszenie Neuropatologów Polskich (Association of Polish Neuropathologists): ul. Pawińskiego 5, 02-106 Warsaw; tel. (61) 661-92-34; fax (61) 661-98-12; e-mail jszymas@ampat.amu.edu.pl; internet snp .amu.edu.pl; f. 1964; 51 mems; Pres. Prof. Dr JANUSZ SZYMAŚ; Sec. Dr HALINA WEINRAUDER; publ. *Folia Neuropathologica* (4 a year).

Towarzystwo Chirurgów Polskich (Society of Polish Surgeons): ul. Banacha 1A, 02-097 Warsaw; tel. and fax (22) 658-36-62; e-mail tchp@mp.pl; internet tchp.org.pl; f. 1889; 3,150 mems; Pres. Prof. ZBIGNIEW PUCHALSKI; Sec.-Gen. Prof. MAREK KRAWCZYK; publ. *Polski Przegląd Chirurgiczny* (12 a year).

Towarzystwo Internistów Polskich (Polish Society of Internal Medicine): Skawińska 8, 31-066 Cracow; tel. (12) 430-54-15; fax (12) 293-42-28; e-mail tip@mp.pl; internet tip.org .pl; f. 1906; advances knowledge of internal medicine, represents Polish internal medical physicians; organizes Congress (every 4 years), annual Nat. Educational Conf. on Internal Medicine and Polish–Slovak Conf. on Internal Medicine; 3,000 mems; Pres. Prof. TOMASZ GUZIK; Sec. Dr PIOTR GAJEWSKI; publ. *Polskie Archiwum Medycyny Wewnętrznej* (Polish Archives of Internal Medicine, 12 a year, in English).

NATURAL SCIENCES

Biological Sciences

Polskie Towarzystwo Biochemiczne (Polish Biochemical Society): ul. Pasteura 3, 02-093 Warsaw; tel. (22) 589-23-52; fax (22) 589-24-99; e-mail ptbioch@nencki.gov.pl; internet www.ptbioch.edu.pl; f. 1958; 1,200 mems; Pres. Prof. ANDRZEJ DZUGAJ; Sec. Prof. MARIA JOLANTA REDOWICZ; publs *Acta Biochimica Polonica* (online, 4 a year), *Postępy Biochemii* (Advances in Biochemistry, 4 a year).

Polskie Towarzystwo Biofizyczne (Polish Biophysical Society): ul. Chałubińskiego 10, 50-368 Wrocław; tel. (71) 784-14-15; fax (71) 784-00-88; e-mail hendrich@biofiz.am.wroc .pl; internet www.ptbf.am.wroc.pl; f. 1972; 250 mems; Pres. Prof. Dr hab. MARIA KOTER-MICHALAK; Sec. Dr ANETA KOCEVA-CHYLA; publ. *Current Topics in Biophysics* (2 a year, in English, supplement in Polish).

Polskie Towarzystwo Biometryczne (Polish Biometric Society): Poznań Univ. of Life Sciences, Wojska Polskiego 28, 60-637 Poznań; tel. and fax (61) 848-71-40; e-mail smejza@up.poznan.pl; internet www.polbiom .up.poznan.pl; f. 1961; biometry, applied mathematical statistics in medicine, agriculture, biology, genetics, ecology; 230 mems; Pres. Prof. Dr hab. STANISLAW MEJZA; Sec Dr JOLANTA KRZYSZKOWSKA; Sec Dr KATARZYNA AMBROZY; publs *Biometrical Letters* (2 a year, online (www.au.poznan.pl/biometrical.letters)), *Colloquium Biometricum* (1 a year).

Polskie Towarzystwo Botaniczne (Polish Botanical Society): Al. Ujazdowskie 4, 00-478 Warsaw; f. 1922; 1,320 mems; library of 24,651 vols; Pres. Prof. Dr JAN J. RYBAZYŃSKI; publs *Acta Agrobotanica, Acta Mycologica, Acta Societatis Botanicorum Poloniae, Biuletyn Ogrodów Botanicznych Muzeów i*

Zbiorów, Monographiae Botanicae, Rocznik Sekcji Dendrologicznej Pol. Tow. Bot., Wiadomości Botaniczne.

Polskie Towarzystwo Entomologiczne (Polish Entomological Society): Dabrowskiego 159, 60-594 Poznań; tel. (61) 848-79-19; e-mail bunalski@up.poznan.pl; internet pte.up.poznan.pl; f. 1923; theoretical and applied entomology; 500 mems; library of 11,000 vols; Pres. Dr hab. MAREK BUNALSKI; Vice-Pres. Prof. Dr hab. JAROSŁAW BUSZKO; Vice-Pres. Prof. Dr hab. RYSZARD SZADZIEWSKI; Sec. Dr PAWEŁ SIENKIEWICZ; publs *Klucze do Oznaczania Owadów Polski* (Keys for Identification of Polish Insects, irregular), *Polish Entomological Monographs* (irregular), *Polskie Pismo Entomologiczne* (Polish Journal of Entomology, 4 a year), *Wiadomości Entomologiczne* (Entomological News, 4 a year).

Polskie Towarzystwo Fitopatologiczne (Polish Phytopathological Society): ul. Wojska Polskiego 71c, 60-625 Poznań; tel. (61) 848-77-08; fax (61) 848-77-11; e-mail mmanka@up.poznan.pl; internet www.up.poznan.pl/ptfit; f. 1971; scientific meetings, field days, confs and symposia of sections incl. nomenclature and teaching, biological control of plant diseases, plant virology, seed pathology, mycology and mycotoxins, biochemistry and genetics of plant pathogens, woody plant diseases, bacteriology, new pathogens and diseases; 300 mems; Pres. Prof. Dr hab. MAŁGORZATA MAŃKA; Sec. Dr Ing. DOROTA SZOPIŃSKA; publ. *Phytopathologia* (4 a year, in English).

Polskie Towarzystwo Genetyczne (Polish Genetics Society): ul. Ciszewskiego 8 , 02-786 Warsaw; tel. and fax (22) 853-09-31; fax (22) 853-09-31; e-mail k_charon@hotmail.com; internet jay.au.poznan.pl/ptg; f. 1963; 762 mems; Pres. Prof. Dr hab. MAREK ŚWITONSKI; Sec. Prof. Dr hab. KRYSTYNA MAŁGORZATA CHARON; publ. *Genetica Polonica* (4 a year).

Polskie Towarzystwo Hydrobiologiczne (Polish Hydrobiological Society): ul. Banacha 2, 02-097 Warsaw; tel. (22) 554-64-43; fax (22) 554-64-26; internet www.pth.home.pl; f. 1959; 12 brs nationally; 400 mems; Pres. Prof. Dr hab. MARCIN PLIŃSKI; Sec. Dr JAN IGOR RYBAK; publs *Fauna Słodkowodna Polski*, *Wiadomości Hydrobiologiczne* (online).

Polskie Towarzystwo Mikrobiologów (Polish Society of Microbiologists): ul. Chocimska 24, 00-791 Warsaw; tel. (22) 542-12-38; fax (22) 542-13-07; internet www .microbiology.pl; f. 1927; 800 mems; Pres. Prof. DANUTA DZIERŻANOWSKA; Sec. Dr JOLANTA SZYCH; publs *Journal of Polish Microbiology* (English, 4 a year), *Medycyna Doświadczalna i Mikrobiologia* (Experimental Medicine and Microbiology, Polish, 4 a year), *Postępy Mikrobiologii* (Advances in Microbiology, Polish, 4 a year).

Polskie Towarzystwo Parazytologiczne (Polish Parasitological Society): Twarda 51–55, 00-818 Warsaw; tel. (22) 697-89-95; fax (22) 620-62-27; internet www.ptparasit.org .pl; f. 1948; 390 mems; Pres. Prof. PIOTR KURNATOWSKI; publs *Katalog Fauny Pasozytniczej Polski* (irregular), *Monografie Parazytologiczne* (irregular), *Wiadomości Parazytologiczne* (4 a year).

Polskie Towarzystwo Zoologiczne (Polish Zoological Society): Sienkiewicza 21, 50-335 Wrocław; tel. (71) 375-40-49; fax (71) 322-50-44; e-mail ptzol@biol.uni.wroc.pl; f. 1935; 750 mems; library of 55,000 vols; Pres. Dr hab. Prof. MARTA BOROWIEC; Sec. ANDRZEJ JABŁOŃSKI; publs *Notatki Ornitologiczne*, *Przegląd Zoologiczny*, *The Ring* (4 a year), *Zoologica Poloniae.*

Mathematical Sciences

Polskie Towarzystwo Matematyczne (Polish Mathematical Society): ul. Sniadeckich 8, 00-956 Warsaw; tel. (22) 522-81-46; e-mail zgptm@ptm.org.pl; internet www.ptm .org.pl; f. 1919; 1,300 mems; Pres. Prof. STEFAN JACKOWSKI; publs *Annales Societatis Mathematicae Polonae: Series I Commentationes Mathematicae, Popularny Miesięcznik Matematyczno-Fizyczno-Astronomiczny DELTA* (Mathematical and Physical Popular, 12 a year), *Series II Wiadomości Matematyczne* (Mathematical News), *Series III Matematyka Stosowana* (Applied Mathematics), *Series IV Fundamenta Informaticae, Series V Didactica Mathematicae* (Didactics of Mathematics), *Series VI Antiquitates Mathematicae* (History of Mathematics).

Polskie Towarzystwo Statystyczne (Polish Statistical Association): Al. Niepodległości 208, 00-925 Warsaw; tel. (22) 625-42-89; f. 1912; statistics, informatics, economics and econometrics; c. 1,000 mems; Pres. Prof. CZESŁAW DOMAŃSKI; Sec. JÓZEF GWOZDOWSKI; publs *Biuletyn Informacyjny* (Bulletin of Information, 4 a year), *Wiadomości Statystyczne* (Statistics in Transition, 4 a year).

Physical Sciences

Polskie Towarzystwo Astronomiczne (Polish Astronomical Society): ul. Bartycka 18, 00-716 Warsaw; tel. (22) 841-00-41 ext. 146; fax (22) 841-00-46; e-mail pta@pta.edu .pl; internet www.pta.edu.pl/pta; f. 1923; 219 mems; Pres. Prof. Dr hab. ANDRZEJ WOSZCZYK; Sec. Dr ADAM MICHALEC; publs *Delta, Urania – Postępy Astronomii* (Progress in Astronomy).

Polskie Towarzystwo Chemiczne (Polish Chemical Society): ul. Freta 16, 00-227 Warsaw; tel. (22) 831-13-04; fax (22) 831-13-04; e-mail zgptchem@chemix.ch.pw.edu.pl; internet www.ptchem.lodz.pl; f. 1919; 2,350 mems; library of 2,400 vols; Pres. Prof. JERZY KONARSKI; Sec. Prof. ROMAN MIERZECKI; publs *Chemical Analysis* (6 a year), *Orbital* (Society News, 6 a year), *Polish Journal of Chemistry, Wiadomości Chemiczne* (Chemical News).

Polskie Towarzystwo Fizyczne (Polish Physical Society): ul. Hoża 69, 00-681 Warsaw; tel. and fax (22) 621-26-68; e-mail ptf@ fuw.edu.pl; internet ptf.fuw.edu.pl; f. 1920; 1,800 mems; library of 1,300 vols; Pres. Prof. Dr hab. WIESLAW A. KAMINSKI; Gen. Sec. Prof. BOHDAN GRZADKOWSKI; publs *Acta Physica Polonica A and B* (12 a year, in English, French, German and Russian), *Delta* (12 a year, in Polish), *Postępy Fizyki* (Advances in Physics, 6 a year), *Reports on Mathematical Physics* (6 a year, in English).

Polskie Towarzystwo Geofizyczne (Polish Geophysical Society): ul. Podleśna 61, 01-673 Warsaw; tel. (22) 569-45-62; f. 1947; devt of geophysical sciences and their popularization; 450 mems; library of 5,000 vols; Pres. Dr ALFRED DUBICKI; Sec.-Gen. Dr JERZY SZKUTNICKI; publ. *Przegląd Geofizyczny* (Geophysical Review, 4 a year).

Polskie Towarzystwo Geologiczne (Polish Geological Society): Oleandry 2A, 30-063 Cracow; tel. (12) 633-20-41; fax (12) 633-22-70; e-mail ptg@uj.edu.pl; internet www .ptgeol.pl; f. 1921; 875 mems; library of 9,397 vols, 25,883 journals; Pres. Dr hab. MARIAN ADAM GASINSK; Sec. Dr Inż. JOZEF CHOWANIEC; publ. *Annales Societatis Geologorum Poloniae/Rocznik Polskiego Towarzystwa Geologicznego/Annals of the Polish Geological Society* (3 a year).

Polskie Towarzystwo Milośników Astronomii (Polish Amateur Astronomical Society): ul. św. Tomasza 30/8, 31-027 Cracow; tel. (12) 422-38-92; internet ptma-zg .astronomia.pl; f. 1919; 3,000 mems; amateur observations, instrument-making, popularization of astronomy; Pres. Prof. ZBIGNIEW KOWALSKI; Sec. Dr HENRYK BRANCEWICZ; publ. *Urania* (12 a year) and reports.

Polskie Towarzystwo Mineralogiczne (Mineralogical Society of Poland): Al. Mickiewicza 30, 30-059 Cracow; tel. (12) 617-24-36; fax (12) 633-43-30; e-mail szydlak@uci .agh.edu.pl; internet uranos.cto.us.edu.pl/ ~ptmin; f. 1969; 195 mems; Pres. Prof. PIOTR WYSZOMIRSKI; Sec. Dr TADEUSZ SZYDŁAK; publ. *Mineralogia Polonica* (2 a year).

Polskie Towarzystwo Nautologiczne (Polish Nautological Society): ul. 3 Maja 12a m 7, 81-357 Gdynia; tel. and fax (58) 620-49-75; internet www.ptn-nautologia.pl; f. 1958; history of human involvement with the sea; 150 mems; library of 2,800 vols; Pres. Prof. Dr DANIEL DUDA; Sec. Dr ELŻBIETA SKUPIŃSKA-DYBEK; publ. *Nautologia* (4 a year).

PHILOSOPHY AND PSYCHOLOGY

Polskie Towarzystwo Filozoficzne (Polish Philosophical Society): Pałac Staszica, ul. Nowy Świat 72, p.160, 00-330 Warsaw; tel. (22) 826-52-31, ext. 759; fax (22) 657-27-59; internet www.ptfilozofia.pl; f. 1904; study of all traditional philosophical disciplines; 826 mems; library of 7,200 vols; Pres. Prof. Dr hab. WŁADYSŁAW STRÓŻEWSKI; Sec. Dr WANDA KAMIŃSKA; publ. *Ruch Filozoficzny* (Philosophical Movement, 4 a year).

Polskie Towarzystwo Psychologiczne (Polish Psychological Association): Stawki 5/7, 00-183 Warsaw; tel. and fax (22) 831-13-68; e-mail ptp@engram.psych.uw.edu.pl; internet www.ptp.org.pl; f. 1948; 2,000 mems; Pres. Prof. ADAM NIEMCZYNSKI; Gen. Sec. Dr TERESA PANAS; publs *Nowiny Psychologiczne* (Psychological Newsletter, 4 a year), *Przegląd Psychologiczny* (Psychological Review, 4 a year).

Polskie Towarzystwo Semiotyczne (Polish Semiotic Society): c/o Institute of Philosophy, Warsaw Univ., ul. Krakowskie Przedmieście 3, 00-927 Warsaw; tel. (22) 826-57-34; fax (22) 826-57-34; e-mail pts1@ pts.edu.pl; internet www.pts.edu.pl; f. 1968; all aspects of semiotics: signs, sign systems, information, communication, indirect cognition; applied semiotics; philosophy of language, linguistics, logic; 150 mems; library of 1,700 vols; Pres. Prof. JERZY PELC; Sec.-Gen. Dr TADEUSZ CIECIERSKI; publ. *Studia Semiotyczne* (irregular).

RELIGION, SOCIOLOGY AND ANTHROPOLOGY

Polskie Towarzystwo Antropologiczne (Polish Anthropological Society): Umultowska 89, 61-614 Poznań; tel. (61) 829-57-13; e-mail pta@antropo.uni.wroc.pl; internet www.pta.uni.maszt.pl; f. 1925; 317 mems; library of 10,000 vols; Chair. MARIA KACZMAREK; Sec. Dr ANITA SZWED; publ. *Przegląd Antropologiczny* (Anthropological Review, 1 a year).

Polskie Towarzystwo Kryminalistyczne (Polish Society of Criminologists): ul. Zgoda 11 lok. 300, 00-018 Warsaw; tel. (22) 692-43-85; fax (22) 692-83-81; e-mail biuro@ kryminalistyka.pl; internet www .kryminalistyka.pl; f. 1973; forensic science; 350 mems; Pres. Prof. Dr hab. MARIUSZ KULICKI; Sec. Mgr inż. TOMASZ BEDNAREK; publ. *Z Zagadnień Współczesnej Kryminalistyki* (irregular).

Polskie Towarzystwo Ludoznawcze (Polish Ethnological Society): Szczytnicka 11, 50-382 Wrocław; tel. (71) 321-16-10; fax (71) 321-16-14; e-mail ptl@ptl.info.pl; internet www.ptl.info.pl; f. 1895; cultural anthropol-

ogy, folklore; 735 mems; library of 43,869 vols; Pres. MICHAL BUCHOWSKI; Sec. JERZY ADAMCZEWSKI; Librarian ALEKSANDRA MICHALOWSKA; publs *Archiwum Etnograficzne, Atlas Polskich Strojów Ludowych, Biblioteka Literatury Ludowej, Biblioteka Popularna, Biblioteka Zesłańca, Dziedzictwo Kulturowe, Dzieła Wszystkie O. Kolberga, Komentarze do Polskiego Atlasu Etnograficznego, Literatura Ludowa* (6 a year), *Łódzkie Studia Etnograficzne* (1 a year), *Lud* (1 a year), *Prace Etnologiczne, Prace i Materiały Etnograficzne*.

Polskie Towarzystwo Orientalistyczne (Polish Oriental Society): c/o Wydział Orientalistyczny UW, ul. Krakowskie Przedmieście 26/28, 00-927 Warsaw; tel. (22) 552-03-53; e-mail pto.orient@uw.edu.pl; internet www .orient.uw.edu.pl/pto; f. 1922; 146 mems; Pres. MAREK MEJOR; Sec.-Gen. MARIA KOZLOWSKA; publ. *Przegląd Orientalistyczny* (4 a year).

Polskie Towarzystwo Religioznawcze (Polish Society for the Science of Religions): skr. poczt. 151, 00-959 Warsaw; tel. (22) 625-26-42; e-mail estachowska@ptr.edu.pl; internet www.ptr.edu.pl; f. 1958; history, theory, methodology, sociology, psychology of religions; 165 mems; Pres. Prof. Dr hab. ZBIGNIEW STACHOWSKI; Scientific Sec. Dr EWA STACHOWSKA; publ. *Przegląd Religioznawczy* (4 a year).

Polskie Towarzystwo Socjologiczne (Polish Sociological Association): ul. Nowy Świat 72, 00-330 Warsaw; tel. and fax (22) 826-77-37; e-mail pts@ifispan.waw.pl; internet www .pts.org.pl; f. 1957; the main professional org. of sociologists in Poland; 1,040 mems; Pres. Prof. GRAŻYNA SKĄPSKA; Exec.-Sec. Prof. ZBIGNIEW RYKOWSKI; publs *Informacja Bieżąca* (Current Bibliographical Information, 2 a year), *Polish Sociological Review* (4 a year).

Polskie Towarzystwo Teologiczne (Polish Theological Society): ul. Kanonicza 3, 31-002 Cracow; tel. (12) 394-56-76; fax (12) 422-56-90; e-mail zarzad@ptt.net.pl; internet www.ptt.net.pl; f. 1924; Pres. Rev. Prof. KAZIMIERZ PANUŚ; Sec. Rev. KAZIMIERZ MOSKALA; publ. *Ruch Biblijny i Liturgiczny* (4 a year).

Towarzystwo Naukowe Organizacji i Kierownictwa (Scientific Society for Organization and Management): ul. Górska 6/10 lok. 71 00-740 Warsaw; tel. (22) 625-44-85; fax (22) 629-21-27; e-mail bzg@tnoik.org; internet www.tnoik.org; f. 1925; 32,000 individual mems, 5,000 collective mems; library of 15,000 vols; Pres. Prof. Dr hab. RYSZARD BOROWIECKI; Gen. Sec. Mgr WŁODZIMIERZ HAUSNER; publ. *Przegląd Organizacji* (12 a year).

TECHNOLOGY

Akademia Inżynierska w Polsce (Academy of Engineering in Poland): ul. Czackiego 3/5, 00-950 Warsaw; tel. (22) 828-64-45; fax (22) 827-29-49; e-mail aip@aip.medianet.pl; internet www.aip.medianet.pl; f. 1992; Pres. Prof. Dr hab. BOGDAN JERZY NEY; Gen. Sec. Prof. Dr JANUSZ DYDUCH.

Federacja Stowarzyszeń Naukowo-Technicznych–Naczelna Organizacja Techniczna (FSNT-NOT) (Polish Federation of Engineering Associations): ul. Czackiego 3/5, 00-950 Warsaw; tel. (22) 826-74-61; fax (22) 827-29-49; e-mail notdgz@not.org.pl; internet not.org.pl; 230,000 mems; Pres. Dr WOJCIECH RATYNSKI; Sec.-Gen. KAZIMIERZ WAWRZYNIAK; publ. *Przegląd Techniczny* (52 a year).

Polskie Towarzystwo Akustyczne (Polish Acoustical Society): Umultowska 85, 61-614 Poznań; tel. (58) 626-28-72; fax (58) 625-48-46; e-mail kozaczka@pg.gda.pl; internet www .ippt.gov.pl/akustyka; Pres. Prof. Dr hab. Inż. EUGENIUSZ KOZACZKA; Sec.-Gen. Dr Inż. GRAŻYNA GRELOWSKA; publ. *Archives of Acoustics* (continuous).

Polskie Towarzystwo Astronautyczne (Polish Astronautical Society): Bartycka 18a, 00-716 Warsaw; tel. (22) 840-37-66; fax (22) 840-31-31; e-mail poczta@ptastronaut .org.pl; internet www.ptastronaut.org.pl; f. 1954; scientific, educational, and popular astronautics, planetology, bio-astronautics, space physics, CETI, and space law; 40 mems; Pres. MACIEJ MROCZKOWSKI; Vice-Pres. ANDRZEJ KOTARSKI; Vice-Pres. Prof. RUDOLF KLEMENS; publ. *Postępy Astronautyki* (Progress in Astronautics, irregular).

Polskie Towarzystwo Elektrotechniki Teoretycznej i Stosowanej (Polish Society for Theoretical and Applied Electrical Engineering): ul. Koszykowa 75, Politechnika Warszawska, Wydz. Elektryczny, Gmach Electrotechniki p. 310, 00-662 Warsaw; tel. and fax (22) 625-67-25; e-mail ptetis@ien.pw .edu.pl; internet www.ee.pw.edu.pl/ptetis; f. 1961; brs in 13 major towns; 750 mems; Pres. Prof. Dr hab. Inż. KRZYSZTOF KLUSZCZYŃSKI; Gen. Sec. Dr Inż. WŁODZIMIERZ KAŁAT.

Polskie Towarzystwo Ergonomiczne (Polish Ergonomics Society): ul. Narbutta 85 p. 103, 02-524 Warsaw; tel. and fax (22) 234-82-09; e-mail sekretariat@ ergonomia-polska.com; internet www .ergonomia-polska.com; f. 1977; Pres. Prof. EWA GÓRSLUZ; Gen. Sec. MACIEJ MAJEWSKI; publ. *Ergonomia* (2 a year).

Polskie Towarzystwo Mechaniki Teoretycznej i Stosowanej (Polish Society of Theoretical and Applied Mechanics): Dept of Civil Engineering, Warsaw University of Technology, Al. Armii Ludowej 16, p. 650, 00-637 Warsaw; tel. (22) 825-71-80; fax (22) 825-71-80; e-mail biuro@ptmts.org.pl; internet www.ptmts.org.pl; f. 1958; 976 mems; brs in 17 other towns; Pres. Prof. JÓZEF KUBIK; Gen. Sec. Dr WIESŁAW NAGÓRKO; publ. *Journal of Theoretical and Applied Mechanics* (4 a year).

Research Institutes
GENERAL

Instytut Kultury (Institute of Culture): e-mail info@instytutkultury.pl; internet instytutkultury.pl; f. 1974; library of 35,000 vols; Dir JAN STANISLAW WOJCLECHOWSKI; publ. *Prace Instytutu Kultury*.

Instytut Podstaw Inżynierii Środowiska PAN (Institute of Environmental Engineering): ul. M. Skłodowskiej-Curie 34, 41-819 Zabrze; tel. (32) 271-64-81; fax (32) 271-74-70; e-mail ipis@ipis.zabrze.pl; internet www .ipis.zabrze.pl; f. 1961; attached to Polish Acad. of Sciences; air and water pollution control, land reclamation, energy conservation, influence of pollutants on plants; library of 14,000 vols; Dir Prof. Dr hab. Inż. CZESŁAWA-ROSIK DULEWSKA (acting); Dir Doc. Dr hab. Inż. JOANNA KYZIOŁ (acting); publs *Archiwum Ochrony Srodowiska* (Archives of Environmental Protection, 4 a year, with summaries in English and Russian), *Prace i Studia* (irregular).

Instytut Slawistyki PAN (Institute of Slavic Studies): ul. Bartoszewicza 1b m. 17, 00-337 Warsaw; tel. and fax (22) 826-76-88; e-mail sekretariat@ispan.waw.pl; internet www.ispan.waw.pl; f. 1954; attached to Polish Acad. of Sciences; library of 124,000 vols; Dir Dr ANNA ZIELIŃSKA; Vice-Dir ANNA ENGELKING; publs *Acta Baltico-Slavica, Cognitive Studies/Etudes Cognitives, Colloquia Humanistica, Studia z Filologii Polskiej i Słowiańskiej, Slavia Meridionalis, Sprawy Narodowościowe*.

Instytut Sportu (Institute of Sport): ul. Trylogii 2/16, 01-982 Warsaw; tel. (22) 834-08-12; fax (22) 835-09-77; e-mail insp@insp .waw.pl; internet www.insp.pl/default.htm; f. 1978; library of 6,130 vols; Dir Prof. Dr hab. RYSZARD GRUCZA; publ. *Biology of Sport* (4 a year).

Zakład Badań Narodowościowych PAN (Centre for the Study of Nationalities): Stary Rynek 78/79, 61-772 Poznań; tel. and fax (61) 852-09-50; e-mail zbnpan@man.poznan.pl; f. 1973; attached to Polish Acad. of Sciences; library of 1,800 vols; Dir Prof. Dr hab. WOJCIECH J. BURSZTA; publ. *Sprawy Narodowościowe* (Issues of Nationality, 2 a year).

Zakład Krajów Pozaeuropejskich PAN (Centre for Studies on Non-European Countries): Nowy Swiat 72, 00-330 Warsaw; tel. (22) 826-63-56; fax (22) 826-63-56; e-mail csnec@zkppan.waw.pl; f. 1978; attached to Polish Acad. of Sciences; library of 16,000 vols; Dir Dr JERZY ZDANOWSKI; publs *Acta Asiatica Varsoviensia* (in English and French, 1 a year), *Hemispheres* (in English and French, 1 a year).

AGRICULTURE, FISHERIES AND VETERINARY SCIENCE

Instytut Agrofizyki im. Bohdana Dobrzańskiego PAN (Institute of Agrophysics): ul. Doświaczalna 4, 20-290 Lublin; tel. (81) 744-50-61; fax (81) 744-50-67; internet www .ipan.lublin.pl; f. 1968; attached to Polish Acad. of Sciences; library of 3,000 vols; Dir Prof. Dr hab. JÓZEF HORABIK; publs *Acta Agrophysica* (2 a year), *International Agrophysics* (4 a year), *Polish Journal of Soil Science* (2 a year).

Instytut Badawczy Leśnictwa (Forestry Research Institute): ul. Bitwy Warszawskiej 1920 r. 3, 00-973 Warsaw; tel. (22) 823-45-65; fax (22) 822-49-35; e-mail ibl@ibles.waw.pl; internet www.ibles.waw.pl; f. 1930; comprises 14 scientific sections covering all aspects of forestry, especially factors of environment, silviculture and selection, tree-planting, forest economics, management, forest work organization, protection, forest plant pathology, game management, water economy, logging mechanization and transport; main documentation and information centre of forestry; brs at Cracow, Białowieża and Katowice; library of 69,000 vols; Dir Prof. Dr hab. eng. A. KLOCEK; publs *Folia Forestalia Polonica* (Series A—Forestry, in English, irregular), *Leśne Prace Badawcze* (Forest Research Papers, 4 a year), *Notatnik Naukowy, Nowości Piśmiennictwa Leśnego* (12 a year).

Instytut Biotechnologii Przemysłu Rolno-Spożywczego (Institute of Agricultural and Food Biotechnology): ul. Rakowiecka 36, 02-532 Warsaw; tel. (22) 849-02-24; fax (22) 849-04-26; e-mail ibprs@ibprs.pl; internet www.ibprs.pl; f. 1949; biotechnology: improvement of microbial strains, fermentation processes (beer, wine, spirits, organic acids), malt, yeasts, enzymatic preparations, microbial preparations; technology of fruit and vegetable products, food analysis, food concentration, storage and processing of grain, bread and pastry baking; culture collection of industrial micro-organisms; library of 22,000 vols; Dir Prof. ROMAN GRZYBOWSKI; publ. *Prace Instytutów i Laboratoriów Badawczych Przemysłu Spożywczego* (in Polish with summaries in English, 1 a year).

Instytut Budownictwa, Mechanizacji i Elektryfikacji Rolnictwa (Institute for Building, Mechanization and Electrification

in Agriculture): ul. Rakowiecka 32, 02-532 Warsaw; tel. (22) 49-32-31; fax (22) 49-17-37; e-mail selian@ibmer.waw.pl; f. 1950; research into the mechanization of farming, economics and management, land reclamation, farm building and energy sources; library of 47,783 vols; Dir ALEKSANDER SZEPTYCKI; publs *Inżynieria Rolnicza* (irregular), *Prace NaukowoBadawcze IBMER* (1 a year), *Problemy Inżynierü Rolniczej* (4 a year), *Przegląd Dokumentacyjny—Technika Rolnicza* (6 a year).

Instytut Ekonomiki Rolnictwa i Gospodarki Żywnościowej (Institute of Agricultural and Food Economics): ul. Świętokrzyska 20, 00-002 Warsaw; tel. (22) 505-44-44; fax (22) 827-19-60; e-mail ierigz@ierigz.waw.pl; internet www.ierigz.waw.pl; f. 1983, fmrly Inst. of Agricultural Economics; library of 41,000 vols; scientific and research work, focused on issues of economic production and social situation of rural areas in Poland, agriculture and broadly conceived food economy; Dir Prof. Dr ANDRZEJ KOWALSKI; publs *Analizy Rynkowe* (Market Analyses, 2 a year for main commodities), *Rynek Rolny* (Agricultural Market, 12 a year), *Zagadnienia Ekonomiki Rolnej* (Problems of Agricultural Economics, 6 a year).

Instytut Fizjologii i Żywienia Zwierząt im. Jana Kielanowskiego PAN (Kielanowski Institute of Animal Physiology and Nutrition): ul. Instytucka 3, 05-110 Jabłonna; tel. (22) 782-41-75; fax (22) 774-20-38; f. 1955; attached to Polish Acad. of Sciences; study of nutrition of ruminants, pigs and poultry, digestive processes, neuroendocrinology, endocrinology of reproduction; library of 5,000 vols; Dir Dr JACEK SKOMIAT.

Instytut Fizjologii Roślin im. Franciszka Górskiego PAN (Institute of Plant Physiology): ul. Niezapominajek 21, 30-239 Cracow; tel. (12) 425-18-33; fax (12) 425-18-44; e-mail ifr@ifr-pan.krakow.pl; internet www.ifr-pan.krakow.pl; f. 1956; attached to Polish Acad. of Sciences; laboratories; plant growth and development, photosynthesis, biology of stress, metabolism of fungi; myxomycetes; Dir Prof. Dr hab. FRANCISZEK DUBERT; publ. *Acta Physiologiae Plantarum* (4 a year).

Instytut Genetyki i Hodowli Zwierząt PAN (Institute of Genetics and Animal Breeding): Jastrzębiec ul. Postępu 1, 05-552 Wólka Kosowska; tel. (22) 756-17-11; fax (22) 756-16-99; e-mail e.dymnicki@ighz.pl; internet www.ighz.edu.pl/index.htm; f. 1955; attached to Polish Acad. of Sciences; research work in animal genetics with special reference to farm animals; 130 mems; library of 6,000 vols, 5,640 journals; Dir Prof. EDWARD DYMNICKI; publs *Animal Science Papers and Reports* (4 a year), *Prace i Materiały Zootechniczne* (irregular).

Instytut Genetyki Roślin PAN (Institute of Plant Genetics): ul. Strzeszyńska 34, 60-479 Poznań; tel. (61) 823-35-11; fax (61) 823-36-71; e-mail office@igr.poznan.pl; internet www.igr.poznan.pl; f. 1961; attached to Polish Acad. of Sciences; basic genetic research on cultivated plants, genomics, biometrics, molecular biology, plant stresses; Dir Prof. WOJCIECH K. ŚWIĘCICKI; publ. *Journal of Applied Genetics* (4 a year).

Instytut Meteorologii i Gospodarki Wodnej (Institute of Meteorology and Water Management): ul. Podleśna 61, 01-673 Warsaw; tel. (22) 569-42-99; fax (22) 569-43-01; e-mail sekretariat@imgw.pl; internet www.imgw.pl; f. 1973 from fmr State Institute of Hydrology and Meteorology and the Institute of Water Management; collections of data from 61 meteorological stations, 149 meteoro-logical posts, 893 hydrological posts, 1,027 pluviometric posts and 100 groundwater posts; library of 98,500 vols; Dir Prof. Dr eng. JAN ZIELIŃSKI; publ. *Wiadomości Instytutu Meteorologii i Gospodarki Wodnej* (Reports, 4 a year).

Instytut Nawozów Sztucznych (Fertilizers Research Institute): 24-110 Puławy; tel. (81) 473-14-00; fax (81) 473-14-10; e-mail ins@ins.pulawy.pl; internet www.ins.pulawy.pl; f. 1948; research and devt work in synthesis gases and hydrogen, carbon dioxide, nitrogen oxides, nitric acid and its salts, mineral fertilizers, catalysts and sorbents, derivatives of methanol and urea, supercritical carbon dioxide extraction; environmental protection; unit operations; new processes and products; library of 36,990 vols; Gen. Dir Dr CEZARY MOZEŃSKI; publ. *Przemysł Nawozowy* (4 a year).

Instytut Ogrodnictwa (Research Institute of Horticulture): ul. Konstytucji 3 Maja 1/3, 96-100 Skierniewice; tel. (46) 833-34-34; fax (46) 833-31-86; e-mail io@inhort.pl; internet www.inhort.pl; f. 1951; 4 divs: beekeeping, floriculture, pomology, vegetable crops; 6 field stations; 3 accredited laboratories; library of 37,578 vols; Dir Prof. Dr FRANCISZEK ADAMICKI; publs *Journal of Fruit and Ornamental Plant Research* (2 a year), *Nowości Warzywnicze* (2 a year), *Pszczelnicze Zeszyty Naukowe* (Journal of Apiculture Science, 2 a year), *Zeszyty Naukowe Instytutu Sadownictwa i Kwiaciarstwa* (1 a year).

Instytut Przemysłu Cukrowniczego (Institute of the Sugar Industry): ul. Inzynierskiej 4, 05-084 Leszno k Blonia, Warsaw; tel. (22) 725-90-88; tel. and fax (22) 725-66-61; e-mail dyrektor@inspcukr.pl; internet www.inspcukr.bip.waw.pl; f. 1898; research into all brs of the sugar industry; raw product, sugar beet, technological, analytical, mechanical, environmental protection depts; library of 1,500 vols; Dir ANTONI LAUDAŃSKI; publs *Burak cukrowy—gazeta dla plantatorów* (irregular), *Informacja dekadowa z przebiegu Kampanii* (9 a year), *Informacja o wynikach produkcyjnych i danych techniczo-technologicznych przemysłu cukrowniczego* (1 a year).

Instytut Roślin i Przetworów Zielarskich (Research Institute of Medicinal Plants): ul. Libelta 27, 61-707 Poznań; tel. (61) 665-95-40; fax (61) 665-95-51; e-mail iripz@iripz.pl; internet www.iripz.pl; f. 1947; botany, plant breeding, agrotechnology, pest control, phytochemistry, pharmaceutical analysis, technology of plant drugs, pharmacology; library of 13,000 vols; Dir PRZEMYSŁAW MROZIKIEWICZ; publ. *Herba Polonica* (4 a year).

Instytut Rozwoju Wsi i Rolnictwa PAN (Institute of Rural and Agricultural Development PAS): Nowy Świat 72, 00-330 Warsaw; tel. (22) 826-63-71; fax (22) 657-27-50; e-mail irwir@irwirpan.waw.pl; internet www.irwirpan.waw.pl; f. 1971; attached to Polish Acad. of Sciences; researches into the process of developing agriculture and rural soc.; 42 mems; library of 7,000 vols; Dir Prof. ANDRZEJ ROSNER; publs *Problems of Rural and Agricultural Development* (4 or 5 a year in Polish, summaries in English), *Village and Agriculture* (4 a year in Polish, 1 a year supplement of selected papers in English), studies and monographs (research series).

Instytut Rybactwa Śródlądowego im. Stanisława Sakowicza (Inland Fisheries Institute): ul. Oczapowskiego 10, 10-719 Olsztyn; tel. (89) 524-01-71; fax (89) 524-05-05; e-mail irs@infish.com.pl; internet www.infish.com.pl; f. 1951; Dir Prof. Dr hab. BOGUSŁAW ŻDANOWSKI; publs *Archives of Pol-ish Fisheries* (2 a year), *Komunikaty Rybackie* (6 a year).

Instytut Środowiska Rolniczego i Leśnego PAN (Institute for Agricultural and Forest Environment): ul. Bukowska 19, 60-809 Poznań; tel. (61) 847-5603; fax (61) 847-3668; e-mail kedan@man.poznan.pl; internet www.isrl.poznan.pl; f. 1979; attached to Polish Acad. of Sciences; study of energy flow and cycling of matter, evaluation of ecological guidelines for landscape management, and strategy for nature conservancy; library of 35,000 vols; Vice-Dir Prof. Dr hab. ANDRZEJ KĘDZIORA.

Instytut Technologiczno-Przyrodniczy (Institute of Technology and Life Sciences): Falenty, Al. Hrabska 3, 05-090 Raszyn; tel. (22) 720-05-31; fax (22) 628-37-63; e-mail itep@itep.edu.pl; internet www.itep.edu.pl; f. 2010; advocacy, devt, education, research, training and innovation in agriculture; flood and drought management, grassland farming, land devt, sustainable devt of rural areas, rural sanitation, water management in agriculture; library of 47,200 vols and 8,900 vols in spec. collns; Dir Prof Dr hab. Inż. EDMUND KACA; publs *Journal of Water and Land Development* (1 a year), *Problemy Inżynierii Rolniczej* (4 a year), *Water – Environment – Rural Areas* (2 a year).

Instytut Technologii Drewna (Wood Technology Institute): Winiarska St 1, 60-654 Poznań; tel. (61) 849-24-00; fax (61) 822-43-72; e-mail office@itd.poznan.pl; internet www.itd.poznan.pl; f. 1952; responsible for solving problems of the wood processing industry and for developing new technical processes; library of 27,381 vols; Dir Dr WLADYSLAW STRYKOWSKI; publ. *Drewno (Wood)* (2 a year).

Instytut Uprawy, Nawożenia i Gleboznawstwa—Państwowy Instytut Badawczy (Institute of Soil Science and Plant Cultivation—State Research Institute): Czartoryskich 8, 24-100 Puławy; tel. (81) 886-34-21; fax (81) 886-45-47; e-mail iung@iung.pulawy.pl; internet www.iung.pulawy.pl; f. 1917; pedology; utilization and protection of agricultural land; soil chemistry, plant physiology, biochemistry, microbiology, soil and crop management, production technology of cereals, forage crops, tobacco and hops, etc.; Dir Prof. Dr hab. SEWERYN KUKUŁA; publs *Monografie i Rozprawy Naukowe* (in Polish and summaries in English), *Pamiętnik Puławski* (2 or 3 a year), *Polish Journal of Agronomy* (2–4 a year), *Studia i Raporty IUNG-PIB* (in Polish), *Zalecenia Agrotechniczne* (every 5 years).

Instytut Warzywnictwa (Research Institute of Vegetable Crops): ul. Konstytucji 3 Maja 1/3, 96-100 Skierniewice; tel. (46) 833-22-11; fax (46) 833-31-86; e-mail iwarz@iwarz.pl; internet www.iwarz.pl; f. 1964; research into the devt of practical guidelines for the rational and economic devt of vegetable production; Dir Prof. Dr hab. FRANCISZEK ADAMICKI; publs *Biuletyn Warzywniczy* (Vegetable Research Bulletin, 2 a year), *Nowości Warzywnicze* (Vegetable Crops News, 2 a year).

Instytut Zootechniki (Institute of Animal Husbandry): k. Krakowa, 32-083 Balice; tel. (12) 258-81-11; fax (12) 285-67-33; e-mail izooinfo@izoo.krakow.pl; internet www.izoo.krakow.pl; f. 1950; 5 scientific depts, 11 experimental stations; library of 125,000 vols; Dir Prof. J. KRUPIŃSKI; publs *Annals of Animal Science* (4 a year), *Reports on Animal Performance Testing* (1 a year), *Wiadomosci Zootechniczne* (4 a year).

Morski Instytut Rybacki w Gdyni (Sea Fisheries Institute in Gdyni): ul. Kołłątaja 1,

81-332 Gdynia; tel. (58) 735-61-00; fax (58) 735-61-10; e-mail sekrdn@mir.gdynia.pl; internet www.mir.gdynia.pl; f. 1923; departments of ichthyology, oceanography, fishing technique, technology of fish processing, seafishery economics, scientific information; 2 brs at Szczecin and Swinoujście; library of 24,000 vols; Dir Doc. Dr hab. TOMASZ LINKOWSKI; publ. *Bulletin of the Sea Fisheries Institute*.

Państwowy Instytut Weterynaryjny—Państwowy Instytut Badawczy (National Veterinary Research Institute): ul. Partyzantów 57, 24-100 Pulawy; tel. (81) 889-32-63; fax (81) 886-25-95; e-mail sekretariat@piwet .pulawy.pl; internet www.piwet.pulawy.pl; f. 1945; veterinary microbiology, immunology, parasitology, toxicology, etc.; 16 scientific departments including those at Bydgoszcz and Zduńska Wola; library of 21,771 vols; Dir Gen. Dr KRZYSZTOF NIEMCZUK.

ARCHITECTURE AND TOWN PLANNING

Instytut Gospodarki Mieszkaniowej (Housing Research Institute): ul. Filtrowa 1, 00-925 Warsaw; tel. (22) 825-09-53; fax (22) 825-06-83; e-mail igmuchm@polbox.com; internet www.orgmasz.waw.pl/w/jbr/k7.htm; f. 1952; research and development in housing problems: dwelling construction and stock, investment process, construction market; library of 8,770 vols, 76 periodicals; Dir Dr RYSZARD UCHMAN; publs *Problemy Rozwoju Budownictwa* (4 a year), *Sprawy Mieszkaniowe* (4 a year).

Instytut Gospodarki Przestrzennej i Mieszkalictwa (Institute of Spatial Management and Housing): ul. Targowa 45, 03-728 Warsaw; tel. (22) 619-13-50; fax (22) 619-24-84; e-mail igpik@igpik.waw.pl; internet www.igpik.waw.pl; f. 1986; physical planning, architecture, municipal economy; library of 70,000 vols, including several special collns; Dir WŁODZIMIERZ BUCHALSKI; publ. *Geospatial information–key asset of spatial planning* (2 a year).

Instytut Techniki Budowlanej (Building Research Institute): ul. Filtrowa 1, 00-611 Warsaw; tel. (22) 825-04-71; fax (22) 825-52-86; e-mail itb@itb.pl; internet www.itb.pl; f. 1945; research in the use of building materials and methods of construction; library of 104,000 vols; Dir MAREK KAPROŃ; publ. *Prace Instytutu Techniki Budowlanej* (4 a year).

ECONOMICS, LAW AND POLITICS

Instytut Badań Rynku, Konsumpcji i Koniunktur (Institute for Market, Consumption and Business Cycles Research): Al. Jerozolimskie 87, 02-001 Warsaw; tel. (22) 628-55-85; fax (22) 628-24-79; e-mail sekretariat@ibrkk.pl; internet ibrkk.pl; f. 1950; 135 mems; library of 40,000 vols; Dir Dr hab. RYSZARD MICHALSKI; publs *Bieżąca informacja o publikacjach z zakresu rynku w kraju i na świecie* (12 a year), *Biuletyn Informacyjny COINTE* (6 a year), *Materiały Informacyjno-Szkolebiowe* (series), *Przedsiębiorstwo i Rynek* (4 a year), *Przegląd Dokumentacyjny* (4 a year), *Rocznik IRWIK* (series).

Instytut Ekspertyz Sądowych (Institute of Forensic Research): ul. Westerplatte 9, 31-033 Cracow; tel. (12) 422-87-55; fax (12) 422-38-50; e-mail ies@ies.krakow.pl; internet www.ies.krakow.pl; f. 1929; depts of criminalistics, traffic accident investigation, forensic toxicology, forensic psychology, forensic haemogenetics; library of 5,092 vols; Dir Assoc. Prof. MARIA KAŁA; Librarian KINGA TECHMAŃSKA; publs *Paragraf na Drodze* (12 a year), *Z Zagadnień Nauk Sądowych* (Problems of Forensic Sciences, 4 a year).

Instytut Nauk Ekonomicznych PAN (Institute of Economics of the Polish Academy of Sciences): Pałac Staszica, ul. Nowy Swiat 72, 00-330 Warsaw; tel. (22) 657-27-07; fax (22) 826-72-54; e-mail inepan@inepan .waw.pl; internet www.inepan.waw.pl; f. 1981; attached to Polish Acad. of Sciences; researches contemporary economic theory, economic policy, analysis, forecasts and strategic studies concerning the Polish economy; analyzes world economy and European integration and their influence on the devt of the Polish economy; library of 15,000 vols; Scientific Ccl Chair. Prof. JERZY OSIATYŃSKI; Dir Prof. LESZEK JASIŃSKI; publs *Gospodarka Polski – Prognozy i Opinie* (Polish Economy – Forecasts and Opinions, 2 a year), *Monografie* (irregular), *Opera Minora* (irregular), *Raport o innowacyjności gospodarki* (Report on Innovation in the Polish Economy, 1 a year), *Studia Ekonomiczne* (4 a year), *Working Papers* (irregular).

Instytut Nauk Prawnych PAN (Institute of Legal Studies): Pałac Staszica, ul. Nowy Swiat 72, 00-330 Warsaw; tel. (22) 826-75-71; fax (22) 826-78-53; e-mail inp@inp.pan.pl; internet www.inp.pan.pl; f. 1956; attached to Polish Acad. of Sciences; legal research; 66 mems; library of 44,000 vols; Dir Prof. Dr hab. WŁADYSŁAW CZAPLIŃSKI; publs *Archiwum Kryminologii* (irregular), *Droit Polonais Contemporain* (4 a year, in French and English), *Orzecznictwo sądów polskich* (12 a year), *Polish Yearbook of International Law* (in English), *Polska Bibliografia Prawnicza* (yearbook), *Studia Prawnicze* (4 a year).

Instytut Organizacji i Zarządzania w Przemyśle 'ORGMASZ' (Institute of Organization and Management in Industry): ul. Żelazna 87, 00-879 Warsaw; tel. (22) 654-60-61; fax (22) 620-43-60; e-mail instytut@ orgmasz.waw.pl; internet www.orgmasz .waw.pl; f. 1953; library of 11,200 vols, spec. colln; Dir Inż RYSZARD WIECZORKOWSKI; publ. *Ekonomika i Organizacja Przedsiębiorstwa* (Business Economics and Organization, 12 a year).

Instytut Pracy i Spraw Socjalnych (Institute of Labour and Social Studies): Bellottiego 3B, 01-022 Warsaw; tel. (22) 636-72-00; fax (22) 636-72-00; e-mail instprac@ipiss.com .pl; internet www.ipiss.com.pl; f. 1963; research into labour, wages, income distribution, living standards, social security and social insurance, labour law, human resources management, collective labour relations, family problems and family policy; Dir BOŻENNA BALCERZAK-PARADOWSKA; publs *Materiały z Zagranicy* (irregular), *Opracowania PCZ* (irregular), *Polityka Społeczna* (Social Policy, 12 a year), *Raport IPiSS* (irregular), *Zarządzanie Zasobami Ludzkimi* (Human Resources Management, 6 a year).

Instytut Przedsiębiorstwa (Institute of Entreprise): ul. Madalińskiego 6/8, pok.106, 02-554 Warsaw; tel. 848-59-28; fax 564-86-71; e-mail rstach@sgh.waw.pl; internet www.sgh.waw.pl; f. 2006; research on enterprise devt and competitiveness of enterprises and regions; organizes lectures for general audience, doctoral seminars, and confs; Dir Prof. Dr hab. IRENA LICHNIAK; Sec. RENATA STACHOWICZ; publs *Mongrafie i Opracowania* (2 a year), *Studia i Analizy* (3 or 4 a year), *Szara Seria* (3 or 4 a year).

Instytut Studiow Politycznych PAN (Institute of Political Studies): ul. Polna 18/ 20, 00-625 Warsaw; tel. (22) 825-52-21; fax (22) 825-21-46; e-mail politic@isppan.waw.pl; internet www.isppan.waw.pl; f. 1990; attached to Polish Acad. of Sciences; develops theoretical work and empirical studies of post-communist socs; library of 19,885 vols; Dir Prof. EUGENIUSZ C. KRÓL; publs *Civitas* (1

a year), *Europa Środkowo-Wschodnia* (Central-Eastern Europe Yearbook), *Kultura i Społeczeństwo* (Culture and Society, 4 a year), *Rocznik Polsko-Niemiecki* (Polish-German Yearbook), *Studia Polityczne* (Political Studies, 2 a year).

Instytut Turystyki (Institute of Tourism): ul. Merliniego 9a, 02-511 Warsaw; tel. (22) 844-63-47; fax (22) 844-12-63; e-mail it@intur .com.pl; internet www.intur.com.pl; f. 1972; social, economic and spatial aspects of tourism, professional training and provision of information; library of 12,609 vols, 3,304 periodicals, special collns of 3,280 vols; Dir Dr KRZYSZTOF ŁOPACIŃSKI; publ. *Problemy Turystyki* (4 a year).

Instytut Wymiaru Sprawiedliwości (Institute of Justice): ul. Krakowskie Przedmieście 25, 00-950 Warsaw; tel. (22) 826-03-63; fax (22) 826-24-01; e-mail iws@iws.org.pl; internet www.iws.org.pl; f. 1992; financed and supervised by the Min. of Justice but operates independently; sections of civil law, criminal law and criminology, and statistical analysis and methodology; library of 5,500 vols; Dir Prof. Dr hab. ANDRZEJ SIEMASZKO.

Instytut Zachodni im. Zygmunta Wojciechowskiego (Institute for Western Affairs): Mostowa 27, 61-854 Poznań; tel. (61) 852-76-91; fax (61) 852-49-05; e-mail izpozpl@rose .man.poznan.pl; internet www.iz.poznan.pl; f. 1945; for the study of Polish–German relations up to the acquisition of Polish western territories, and since 1945, and of Western European economic, political, historical, juridical, social and cultural matters; library of 100,000 vols; Dir Prof. Dr hab. ANDRZEJ SAKSON; publ. *Przegląd Zachodni* (4 a year).

Państwowy Instytut Naukowy–Instytut Śląski w Opolu (Government Research Institute–Silesian Institute in Opole): ul. Piastowska 17, 45-081 Opole; tel. and fax (77) 453-60-32; e-mail instytutslaski@wp.pl; internet www.instytutslaski.opole.pl; f. 1957; departments: historical and German–Polish relationships research, regional research; library of 72,000 vols (history since 19th century, contemporary history, social economics, Silesiana); Dir Prof. Dr hab. STANISŁAW SENFT; publs *Region and Regionalism* (in English, irregular), *Śląsk Opolski* (4 a year), *Studia Śląskie* (1 a year), *Zeszyty Odrzańskie* (1 a year).

Polski Instytut Spraw Międzynarodowych (Polish Institute of International Affairs): POB 1010, ul. Warecka 1A, 00-950 Warsaw; tel. (22) 556-80-00; fax (22) 556-80-99; e-mail pism@pism.pl; internet www.pism.pl; f. 1996; research in int. affairs; courses for civil servants, confs; library of 156,000 vols; Dir Dr MARCIN ZABOROWSKI; Head of Library ANDRZEJ KAMINSKI; publs *Polish Quarterly of International Affairs* (4 a year, in English), *Polski Przegląd Dyplomatyczny* (4 a year, in Polish), *Rocznik Polskiej Polityki Zagranicznej* (1 a year, in Polish), *Sprawy Międzynarodowe* (4 a year, in Polish).

EDUCATION

Centrum Badań Polityki Naukowej i Szkolnictwa Wyższego (Centre for Science Policy and Higher Education): ul. Nowy Swiat 69, 00-046 Warsaw; tel. and fax (22) 826-07-46; e-mail crphe@plearn.pl; f. 1973; planning and forecasting development of higher education; modernization of instruction and organization of higher education; Dir Prof. IRENEUSZ BIAŁECKI; publ. *Nauka i Szkolnictwo Wyższe* (Science and Higher Education, 2 a year).

Instytut Badań Edukacyjnych (Institute for Educational Research): ul. Górczewska 8,

01-180 Warsaw; tel. (22) 241-71-00; fax (22) 241-71-11; e-mail ibe@ibe.edu.pl; internet ibe .edu.pl; f. 1952; conducts research and devt work for education; prepares analyses, expert opinions, reports and forecasts for the Min. of Nat. Education; library of 100,000 vols; Dir Prof. MICHAL FEDEROWICZ; publ. *Edukacja* (4 a year).

Instytut Kształcenia Zawodowego (Institute of Vocational Education): ul. Jana Pawła II 14, 47-220 Kędzierzyn-Koźle; tel. (77) 483-40-53; fax (77) 483-40-53; f. 1972; 113 staff; library of 18,000 vols; Dir STANISŁAW KACZOR; publs *Biblioteka Kształcenia Zawodowego*, *Pedagogika Pracy* (1 a year), *Szkoła-Zawód-Praca* (1 a year).

FINE AND PERFORMING ARTS

Instytut Sztuki PAN (Institute of Art): ul. Długa 26/28, 00-950 Warsaw; tel. (22) 504-82-18; fax (22) 831-31-49; e-mail ispan@ispan.pl; internet www.ispan.pl; f. 1949; attached to Polish Acad. of Sciences; fine arts, architecture, music, theatre, film, cultural anthropology; 125 mems; library of 140,000 vols; photographic archive of 450,000 negatives; phonographic library of 80,000 items; 16,000 audio cassettes; Dir Dr hab. LECH SOKÓŁ; publs *Almanach Sceny Polskiej* (Almanack of the Polish Stage, 1 a year), *Biuletyn Historii Sztuki* (4 a year), *Dagerotyp* (Daguerrotype, 1 a year), *Konteksty. Polska Sztuka Ludowa* (4 a year), *Kwartalnik Filmowy* (4 a year), *Muzyka* (4 a year), *Pamiętnik Teatralny* (4 a year), *Rzeczy Teatralne* (Theatre Miscellaneous, 1 a year).

HISTORY, GEOGRAPHY AND ARCHAEOLOGY

Instytut Archeologii i Etnologii PAN (Institute of Archaeology and Ethnology of the Polish Academy of Sciences): Al. Solidarności 105, 00-140 Warsaw; tel. (22) 620-28-81; fax (22) 624-01-00; e-mail director@iaepan.edu.pl; internet www.iaepan.edu.pl; f. 1953; attached to Polish Acad. of Sciences; prehistoric, classical, early medieval and industrial archaeology, medieval and modern history of material culture, ethnography, ethnology; library of 185,000 vols; Dir Prof. ANDRZEJ BUKO; publs *Archaeologia Polona*, *Archaeologia Urbium*, *Archaeological Reports*, *Archaeological Review*, *Archaeology*, *Archaeology of Poland*, *Bibliotheca Antiqua*, *Culture of Early Medieval Europe*, *Ethnologia Polona*, *Inventaria Archaeologica*, *Library of Polish Ethnography*, *Polish Archaeological Abstracts*, *Polish Archaeological Researches*, *Polish Ethnographic Atlas*, *Polish Ethnography*, *Quarterly Journal of the History of Material Culture*, *Studia Ethnica*, *Studies and Materials of the History of Material Culture*.

Instytut Geodezji i Kartografii (Institute of Geodesy and Cartography): ul. Modzelewskiego 27, 02-679 Warsaw; tel. (22) 329-19-00; fax (22) 329-19-50; e-mail igik@igik.edu.pl; internet www.igik.edu.pl; f. 1945; cartography, geodesy, photogrammetry, remote sensing, GIS; library of 16,200 vols; Dir Dr MAREK BARANOWSKI; Chief of Library BARBARA SMYL; publs *Geoinformation Issues*, *Informacja Bibliograficzna Geodezji i Kartografii* (12 a year), *Monographic Series* (1–3 a year), *Prace IGIK* (2–3 a year), *Proceedings of Institute of Geodesy and Cartography* (1–3 a year), *Rocznik Astronomiczny* (1 a year), *Technicznej i Ekonomicznej Geodezji i Kartografii* (4 a year).

Instytut Geografii i Przestrzennego Zagospodarowania im. S. Leszczyckiego PAN (Stanisław Leszczycki Institute of Geography and Spatial Organization): ul. Twarda 51/55, 00-818 Warsaw; tel. (22) 697-

88-41; fax (22) 620-62-21; e-mail igipzpan@twarda.pan.pl; internet www.igipz.pan.pl; f. 1953; attached to Polish Acad. of Sciences; geomorphology, hydrology, climatology, geoecology, economic geography, urban and population studies, geography of agriculture and rural areas, global development, political geography, regional planning, environmental management, ecodevelopment, European studies, cartography, geographic information systems; library of 132,113 vols, 50,804 vols of periodicals, 4,483 atlases, 80,180 maps, 1,149 antique; Dir Prof. Dr PIOTR KORCELLI; publs *Atlas Warszawy* (irregular), *Bibliografia Geografii Polskiej* (1 a year), *Dokumentacja Geograficzna* (irregular), *Europa XXI* (irregular), *Geographia Polonica* (2 a year), *Geopolitical Studies* (irregular), *Monografie* (irregular), *Prace Geograficzne* (irregular), *Przegląd Geograficzny* (4 a year).

Instytut Historii im. Tadeusza Manteuffla PAN (Institute of History): Rynek Starego Miasta 29/31, 00-272 Warsaw; tel. and fax (22) 831-36-42; e-mail ihpan@ihpan.edu .pl; internet www.ihpan.edu.pl; f. 1953; attached to Polish Acad. of Sciences; studies political and social history from the Middle Ages to the modern era; specific fields of research: Poland and Central-Eastern Europe, origins and history of modern Poland, history of Polish culture, social changes in post-Second World War Poland, history of mass migrations in 19th and 20th centuries, history of totalitarian systems and the Second World War; library of 65,000 vols; Dir Prof. WOJCIECH KRIEGSEISEN; Chief of Research Org. Dept HANNA KORDOWICZ; publs *Acta Poloniae Historica* (2 a year, in English), *Czasopismo Prawno-Historyczne* (2 a year), *Dzieje Najnowsze* (4 a year), *Kwartalnik Historyczny* (4 a year), *Odrodzenie i Reformacja w Polsce* (1 a year), *Roczniki Dziejów Społecznych i Gospodarczych* (1 a year), *Roczniki Historyczne* (1 a year), *Studia z Dziejów Rosji i Europy Środkowo-Wschodniej* (1 a year), *Studia Źródłoznawcze. Commentationes* (1 a year).

Zakład Archeologii Śródziemnomorskiej PAN (Research Centre for Mediterranean Archaeology): Nowy Świat 72, Pałac Staszica (pok. 33), 00-330 Warsaw; tel. and fax (22) 826-65-60; e-mail zaspan@zaspan.waw.pl; internet zaspan.waw.pl; f. 1956; attached to Polish Acad. of Sciences; study, documentation and publ. of results of Polish and foreign excavations in the Middle East, Nubian studies, incl. surveys and excavations; publs of ancient objects in Polish museums; library of 13,600 books, 6,900 vols of periodicals; Dir Prof. KAROL MYŚLIWIEC; Vice-Dir Prof. ZSOLT KISS; publs *Alexandrie* (irregular), *Deir el-Bahari* (irregular), *Etudes et Travaux*, *Nea Paphos* (irregular), *Nubia* (irregular), *Saqqara* (irregular), *Tell Atrib* (irregular), *Travaux du Centre d'Archéologie Méditerranéenne*.

LANGUAGE AND LITERATURE

Instytut Badań Literackich PAN (Institute of Literary Research): Nowy Świat 72, Pałac Staszica, 00-330 Warsaw; tel. and fax (22) 826-99-45; e-mail ibadlit@ibl.waw.pl; internet www.ibl.waw.pl; f. 1948; attached to Polish Acad. of Sciences; 20 scientific departments, and sections in Poznań, Toruń and Wrocław; research in the theory of literature, history of Polish literature, and sociology of literature; library of 450,000 vols, spec. colln: 85,000 vols; Dir Prof. ELŻBIETA SARNOWSKA-TEMERIUSZ; publs *Pamiętnik Literacki* (Literary Journal, 4 a year), *Teksty Drugie* (Texts, 6 a year).

Instytut Języka Polskiego PAN (Polish Language Institute): al. Mickiewicza 31, 31-120 Cracow; tel. and fax (12) 632-87-13; internet www.ijp-pan.krakow.pl; f. 1973; attached to Polish Acad. of Sciences; library of 20,000 vols; Dir Prof. Dr hab. PIOTR ŻMIGRODZKI; publs *Antroponimia Polski od XVI do końca XVIII w.*, *Nazwy miejscowe Polski*, *Nazwy wodne Polski* (electronic version), *Onomastica* (1 a year), *Polonica* (1 a year), *Prace* (series), *Prace Instytutu Języka Polskiego PAN* (series), *Słownik gwar polskich* (1 a year), *Słownik gwar Ostródzkiego*, *Słownik języka polskiego XVII i I polowy XVIII wieku*, *Słownik laciny średniowiecznej w Polsce*, *Słownik polskich leksemów potocznych*, *Słownik polszczyzny Jana Kochanowskiego*, *Socjolingwistyka* (1 a year), *Studies in Polish Linguistics* (1 a year), *Wielki słownik języka polskiego* (electronic version).

MEDICINE

Centrum Onkologii, Instytut im. Marii Skłodowskiej-Curie (Marie Sklodowska-Curie Memorial Cancer Centre and Institute of Oncology): ul. Roentgena 5, 02-781 Warsaw; tel. (22) 546-20-00; internet www.coi .waw.pl; f. 1932; brs at Cracow and Gliwice; fundamental cancer research, clinical research, diagnosis and treatment, epidemiology; co-ordinates Nat. Cancer Programme; 247 scientific staff; library of 23,458 vols; Dir Prof. Dr hab. MAREK P. NOWACKI; publs *Journal of Oncology* (6 a year), *Nowotwory* (4 a year).

Instytut Biocybernetyki i Inżynierii Biomedycznej PAN (Institute of Biocybernetics and Biomedical Engineering): ul. Trojdena 4, 02-109 Warsaw; tel. (22) 659-91-43; fax (22) 659-70-30; e-mail ibib@ibib.waw.pl; internet www.ibib.waw.pl; f. 1975; attached to Polish Acad. of Sciences; collaborates with WHO; mem. of UNESCO Global Network for Molecular and Cell Biology; field of activities: biomeasurements, artificial internal organs, mathematical and physical modelling of physiological systems and processes, computerized image analysis, computer-aided medical diagnosis; library of 23,800 vols; Dir Prof. ANDRZEJ WERYŃSKI; publs *Biocybernetics and Biomedical Engineering* (4 a year), *Prace IBIB PAN* (IBIB PAN Reports, irregular).

Attached Centre:

Miedzynarodowe Centrum Biocybernetyki (International Centre for Biocybernetics): 02-109 Warsaw, ul. Trojdena 4; tel. (22) 659-91-43; fax (22) 658-28-72; e-mail maciej.nalecz@ibib.waw.pl; internet www .ibib.waw.pl/icb.html; f. 1988; attached to Polish Acad. of Sciences; int. centre for research and training in biocybernetics and biomedical engineering; organizes 5 seminars a year; Dir Prof. MACIEJ NAŁECZ; publ. *Lecture Notes of the ICB Seminars*.

Instytut Farmaceutyczny (Pharmaceutical Research Institute): ul. Rydygiera 8, 01-793 Warsaw; tel. (22) 456-39-00; fax (22) 456-38-38; e-mail kontakt@ifarm.waw.pl; internet www.ifarm.waw.pl; f. 1952; organic synthesis of pharmaceutically active substances, process development, pharmaceutical finished forms, bioequivalence and bioavailability of drug products; library of 12,200 vols, 350 periodical titles; Dir Dr WIESŁAW SZELEJEWSKI.

Instytut Farmakologii PAN (Institute of Pharmacology): ul. Smętna 12, 31-343 Cracow; tel. (12) 637-40-22; fax (12) 637-45-00; e-mail ifpan@if-pan.krakow.pl; internet www .if-pan.krakow.pl; f. 1954; attached to Polish Acad. of Sciences; behavioural, biochemical, molecular, electrophysiological, pharmacokinetic and histochemical aspects of psychopharmacology and neuropsychopharmacology; modelling and synthesis of potential, centrally acting agents; acclimatization of medicinal plants and their phytochemical investigation; library of 11,322 vols, 15,055 periodicals; Dir Prof. Dr hab. KRZYSZTOF WEDZONY; publ. *Pharmacological Reviews* (6 a year).

Instytut Genetyki Człowieka PAN (Institute of Human Genetics): ul. Strzeszyńska 32, 60-479 Poznań; tel. (61) 823-30-11; fax (61) 823-32-35; e-mail igcz@man.poznan.pl; internet www.igcz.poznan.pl; f. 1974; attached to Polish Acad. of Sciences; Dir Prof. Dr JERZY NOWAK.

Instytut Hematologii i Transfuzjologii (Institute of Haematology and Blood Transfusion): ul. Chocimska 5, 00-957 Warsaw; tel. (22) 849-85-07; fax (22) 848-89-70; e-mail hematol@ihit.waw.pl; internet www.ihit .waw.pl; f. 1951; Dir Prof. KRZYSZTOF WARZOCHA; publs *Acta Haematologica Polonica* (4 a year), *Sprawozdania Roczne z Działalności Instytutu* (1 a year).

Instytut Immunologii i Terapii Doświadczalnej im. Ludwika Hirszfelda PAN (L. Hirszfeld Institute of Immunology and Experimental Therapy): ul. Rudolfa Weigla 12, 53-114 Wrocław; tel. (71) 337-11-72; fax (71) 337-13-82; e-mail bednorz@iitd .pan.wroc.pl; internet www.iitd.pan.wroc.pl; f. 1952; attached to Polish Acad. of Sciences; research work in basic and clinical immunology, microbiology, immunochemistry, immunogenetics, experimental and bacteriophage therapy; library of 24,000 vols; Dir Prof. Dr ANDRZEJ GÓRSKI; publs *Archivum Immunologiae et Therapiae Experimentalis* (English, 6 a year), *Postępy Higieny i Medycyny Doświadczalnej* (Polish, 6 a year).

Instytut Kardiologii im. Prymasa Tysiąclecia Stefana Kardynała Wyszyńskiego (Cardinal Stefan Wyszyński Institute of Cardiology): ul. Alpejska 42, 04-628 Warsaw; tel. (22) 343-46-00; fax (22) 343-45-00; e-mail bn@ ikard.pl; internet www.ikard.pl; f. 1980; library of 4,344 vols; Dir-Gen. Prof. WITOLD RUŻYŁŁO; publ. *Biblioteka Kardiologiczna* (Cardiological Library, irregular).

Instytut Matki i Dziecka (Mother and Child Research Institute): ul. Kasprzaka 17A, 01-211 Warsaw; tel. (22) 327-70-00; fax (22) 327-70-01; internet www.imid.med.pl; f. 1948; research into the physiology and medicine of reproduction; Dir Prof. Dr hab. WOJCIECH WOŹNIAK; publ. *Development Period Medicine* (4 a year).

Instytut Medycyny Doświadczalnej i Klinicznej im. M. J. Mossakowskiego PAN (Medical Research Centre): ul. Pawińskiego 5, 02-106 Warsaw; tel. (22) 608-64-93; fax (22) 668-55-32; e-mail sekretariat@cmdik.pan.pl; internet www .cmdik.pan.pl; f. 1967; attached to Polish Acad. of Sciences; depts of physiology and neurophysiology, neuroimmunology, neurochemistry, neuropathology, neurology, neurosurgery, experimental transplantology, endocrinology and cellular biology at the ultrastructural (immunocytochemical and histochemical) level located at the Ochota campus, attached to the Bielanski Hospital; 1 unit (Dept of Endocrinology) located at the Warsaw Medical Univ.; library of 10,000 vols, 164 periodicals; Dir Prof. Dr hab. ZBIGNIEW CZERNICKI; publ. *Folia Neuropathologica* (4 a year).

Instytut Medycyny Morskiej i Tropikalnej (Institute of Maritime and Tropical Medicine): ul. Powstania Styczniowego 9B, 81-519 Gdynia; tel. and fax (58) 622-33-54; e-mail poczta@immt.gdynia.pl; f. 1939; attached to Medical University of Gdańsk; research in maritime occupational health, tropical medicine and epidemiology, toxicol-

ogy, microbiology, travel medicine; clinic; postgraduate courses; 340 staff; WHO Inter-Regional Collaborating Centre on Maritime Occupational Health; Dir Dr W. NAHORSKI; publ. *International Maritime Health* (4 a year).

Instytut Medycyny Pracy i Zdrowia Środowiskowego (Institute of Occupational Medicine and Environmental Health): ul. Kościelna 13, 41-200 Sosnowiec; tel. (32) 266-08-85; fax (32) 266-11-24; internet www .imp.sosnowiec.pl; f. 1950; occupational toxicology; Dir Prof. Dr hab. JERZY A. SOKAL.

Instytut Medycyny Pracy im. prof. dra med. Jerzego Nofera (Nofer Institute of Occupational Medicine): ul. Sw. Teresy 8, 91-348 Łódź; tel. (42) 631-45-02; fax (42) 656-83-31; e-mail impx@imp.lodz.pl; internet www .imp.lodz.pl; f. 1954; research in occupational medicine and hygiene, physiology, psychology, toxicology, neurotoxicology, carcinogenesis, pathology and epidemiology, management of occupational health service, radiation protection and the diagnosis and treatment of occupational diseases and acute poisonings, scientific information; Dir Prof. KONRAD RYDZYŃSKI; publs *Informacja Expresowa–Ostre Zatrucia* (Express Information–Acute Poisoning, 4 a year), *International Journal of Occupational Medicine and Environmental Health* (in English, 4 a year), *Medycyna Pracy* (Occupational Medicine, 6 a year).

Instytut Medycyny Wsi im. Witolda Chodźki (W. Chodźko Institute of Agricultural Medicine): POB 185, ul. Jaczewskiego 2, 20-950 Lublin; tel. (81) 747-80-27; fax (81) 747-86-46; e-mail imw@galen.imw.lublin.pl; internet www.imw.lublin.pl; f. 1951; environmental and agricultural medicine, family doctor training, health service organization in rural areas; library of 14,000 vols; Dir Prof. Dr hab. JERZY ZAGÓRSKI; publs *Annals of Agricultural and Environmental Medicine* (electronic and 2 a year), *Medycyna Ogólna* (electronic and 4 a year), *Sprawozdania z działalności Instytutu* (1 a year), *Zdrowie Publiczne* (electronic and 4 a year).

Instytut Psychiatrii i Neurologii (Institute of Psychiatry and Neurology): ul. Sobieskiego /9, 02-957 Warsaw; tel. (22) 458-28-00; e-mail ipin@ipin.edu.pl; internet www.ipin .edu.pl; f. 1951; library of 26,300 vols; Dir Prof. STANISŁAW PUŻYŃSKI; publs *Alkoholizm i Narkomania* (4 a year), *Farmakoterapia w Psychiatrii i Neurologii* (4 a year), *Postępy Psychiatrii i Neurologii* (4 a year).

Instytut Zdrowia Publicznego (Institute for Public Health): ul. Chełmska 30/34, 00-725 Warsaw; tel. (22) 851-43-69; fax (22) 841-06-52; e-mail sekretariat@il.waw.pl; internet www.il.waw.pl; pharmaceutical microbiology and laboratory accreditation; library of 7,000 vols; Dir Prof. Dr hab. ZBIGNIEW E. FIJAŁEK; publs *Biuletyn Informacyjny Instytutu Leków* (irregular), *Biuletyn Leków* (4 a year).

Instytut Żywności i Żywienia (National Food and Nutrition Institute): ul. Powsińska 61/63, 02-903 Warsaw; tel. (22) 842-21-71; fax (22) 842-11-03; e-mail jarosz@izz.waw.pl; internet www.izz.waw.pl; f. 1963; multidisciplinary scientific research in the field of human nutrition; library of 15,000 vols; Dir MIROSŁAW JAROSZ; publs *Żywienie Człowieka i Metabolizm* (4 a year), *Żywność, Żywienie a Zdrowie* (4 a year).

Państwowy Zakład Higieny (National Institute of Hygiene): ul. Chocimska 24, 00-791 Warsaw; tel. (22) 849-76-12; fax (22) 849-74-84; internet www.pzh.gov.pl; f. 1918; 15 departments covering all aspects of epidemiology, bacteriology, virology, parasitology, vaccines and sera control, medical statistics, radiologic control and radiobiology, immuno-

pathology, communal hygiene, foodstuffs, environmental toxicology, school hygiene, health education, biological contamination control; courses in public health; library of 45,000 vols; Dir-Gen. Prof. JAN K. LUDWICKI; publs *Medycyna Doświadczalna i Mikrobiologia* (4 a year), *Przegląd Epidemiologiczny* (4 a year), *Roczniki Państwowego Zakładu Higieny* (4 a year).

NATURAL SCIENCES

General

Instytut Historii Nauki PAN (Institute for the History of Science): Pałac Staszica, Nowy Swiat 72, pok. 9, 00-330 Warsaw; tel. (22) 657-27-46; fax (22) 826-61-37; e-mail ihn@ ihnpan.waw.pl; internet www.ihnpan.waw .pl; f. 1954; attached to Polish Acad. of Sciences; library of 20,000 vols; Dir Prof. Dr hab. KALINA BARTNICKA; publs *Analecta* (2 a year), *Archiwum Dziejów Oświaty* (1 a year), *Kwartalnik Historii Nauki i Techniki* (4 a year), *Medycyna Nowożytna* (2 a year), *Organon* (in French, English and Russian, 1 a year), *Rozprawy z Dziejów Nauki i Techniki* (1 a year).

Instytut Oceanologii PAN (Institute of Oceanology): ul. Powstańców Warszawy 55, POB 68, 81-712 Sopot; tel. (58) 551-72-81; fax (58) 551-21-30; e-mail office@iopan.gda.pl; internet www.iopan.gda.pl; f. 1953; attached to Polish Acad. of Sciences; marine physics, hydrodynamics, marine chemistry, marine ecology, genetics of marine organisms; library of 7,000 vols, 240 periodicals; Dir Prof. STANISLAW MASSEL; publ. *Oceanologia* (4 a year, in English).

Biological Sciences

Centrum Badań Ekologicznych PAN (Centre for Ecological Research): Dziekanów Leśny, Ul. M. Konopnickiej 1, 05-092 Łomianki; tel. (22) 751-30-46; fax (22) 751-31-00; e-mail cbe@cbe-pan.pl; internet www .cbe-pan.pl; f. 2002; attached to Polish Acad. of Sciences; population and community studies, landscape ecology, ecological bioenergetics, biogeochemistry, agroecology, polar research, hydrobiology, plant ecology, soil ecology, vertebrate ecology, modelling of ecological processes; library of 75,000 vols; Dir Prof. JANUSZ UCHMAŃSKI; publs *Polish Journal of Ecology* (original papers in English, 4 a year), *Wiadomości Ekologiczne* (with English summary).

Instytut Biochemii i Biofizyki PAN (Institute of Biochemistry and Biophysics): ul. Pawińskiego 5A, 02-106 Warsaw; tel. (22) 659-70-72; fax (22) 592-21-90; e-mail secretariate@ibb.waw.pl; internet www.ibb .waw.pl; f. 1957; attached to Polish Acad. of Sciences; research work in the fields of molecular genetics, biotechnology, biochemistry, biophysics, bioinformatics; library of 16,000 vols, 140 periodicals, 1,000 online periodicals; Dir Prof. WŁODZIMIERZ ZAGÓRSKI-OSTOJA.

Instytut Biologii Doświadczalnej im M. Nenckiego (M. Nencki Institute of Experimental Biology): ul. Pasteura 3, 02-093 Warsaw; tel. (22) 822-28-31; fax (22) 822-53-42; internet www.nencki.gov.pl; f. 1918; attached to Polish Acad. of Sciences; scientific research work in the fields of biochemistry, cell biology, molecular biology, neurophysiology and experimental psychology; library of 68,000 vols; Dir Prof. JERZY DUSZYŃSKI; publs *Acta Neurobiologiae Experimentalis* (4 a year), *Acta Protozoologica* (4 a year).

Instytut Botaniki im. Władysława Szafera PAN (W. Szafer Institute of Botany): Lubicz 46, 31-512 Cracow; tel. (12) 421-51-44; fax (12) 421-97-90; internet bobas.ib-pan

.krakow.pl; f. 1954; attached to Polish Acad. of Sciences; library of 164,533 vols; Dir Prof. Dr ZBIGNIEW MIREK; publs *Acta Palaeobotanica* (International Journal of Palaeobotany), *Fragmenta Floristica et Geobotanica Polonica* (Material on the Flora and Vegetation of Poland, in Polish), *Polish Botanical Journal*.

Instytut Chemii Bioorganicznej PAN (Institute of Bio-organic Chemistry): ul. Noskowskiego 12/14, 61-704 Poznań; tel. and fax (61) 852-85-03; e-mail ibch@ibch .poznan.pl; internet www.ibch.poznan.pl; f. 1980; attached to Polish Acad. of Sciences; bio-organic chemistry, crystallochemistry of nucleic acids, proteins and their components; molecular biology, genetics and genetic engineering of plants, applied phytochemistry, biochemistry, bioinformatics; library of 3,300 vols; Dir Prof. Dr WOJCIECH T. MARKIEWICZ.

Instytut Dendrologii PAN (Institute of Dendrology): ul. Parkowa 5, 62-035 Kórnik; tel. (61) 817-00-33; fax (61) 817-01-66; e-mail idkornik@man.poznan.pl; internet www .idpan.poznan.pl; f. 1952; attached to Polish Acad. of Sciences; dendrology, acclimatization, systematics and geography of woody plants, tree genetics, tree physiology, seed physiology, tree resistance to pathogens, frost and pollution; 40 scientists; library of 40,000 vols; Dir Prof. JACEK OLEKSYN; publ. *Dendrobiology* (2 a year).

Instytut Ochrony Przyrody PAN (Institute of Nature Conservation): ul. A. Mickiewicza 33, 31-120 Cracow; tel. (12) 632-22-21; fax (12) 632-24-32; e-mail sekretariat@iop .krakow.pl; internet www.iop.krakow.pl; f. 1920; attached to Polish Acad. of Sciences; research work on all problems relating to nature conservation, biological conservation, landscape ecology, interaction between human activity and the biosphere; field stations in Wrocław and Zakopane; library of 21,000 vols, 19,000 periodicals, 19,000 maps and photographs; Dir Prof. HENRYK OKARMA; publs *Chrońmy Przyrodę Ojczystą* (Let Us Protect the Nature of our Homeland, 6 a year), *Nature Conservation* (in English, 1 a year), *Studia Naturae* (irregular).

Instytut Paleobiologii im. Romana Kozłowskiego PAN (Institute of Paleobiology): ul. Twarda 51/55, 00-818 Warsaw; tel. (22) 697-88-50; fax (22) 620-62-25; e-mail paleo@twarda.pan.pl; internet www.paleo .pan.pl; f. 1952; attached to Polish Acad. of Sciences; library of 12,000 vols, 24,000 vols of periodicals; Dir Prof. JERZY DZIK; publs *Acta Palaeontologica Polonica* (4 a year), *Palaeontologia Polonica* (irregular).

Instytut Parazytologii im Witolda Stefańskiego PAN (W. Stefański Institute of Parasitology): ul. Twarda 51/55, 00-818 Warsaw; tel. (22) 620-62-26; fax (22) 620-62-27; e-mail iparpas@twarda.pan.pl; f. 1952; attached to Polish Acad. of Sciences; scientific research work in parasitology, including animal parasitism, its origin, prevalence, manifestations and effects in natural and experimental parasite-host systems; departments of biodiversity, molecular biology, epizootiology and pathology, and deer farming; library: documentation centre and library of 25,666 vols (e-mail: libripar@twarda.pan.pl); Dir Prof. ANDRZEJ MALCZEWSKI; Librarian Dr hab. WŁADYSŁAW CABAJ; publ. *Acta Parasitologica* (4 a year).

Instytut Systematyki i Ewolucji Zwierząt PAN (Institute of Systematics and Evolution of Animals): ul. Sławkowska 17, 31-016 Cracow; tel. (12) 422-19-01; fax (12) 422-42-94; e-mail office@isez.pan.krakow.pl; internet www.isez.pan.krakow.pl; f. 1865; attached to Polish Acad. of Sciences; library of 85,000 vols; Dir Prof. ADAM NADACHOWSKI;

publs *Acta Zoologica Cracoviensia* (4 a year), *Folia Biologica* (4 a year).

Zakład Badania Ssaków PAN (Mammal Research Institute): ul. Gen. Waszkiewicza 1C, 17-230 Białowieża; tel. (85) 682-77-50; fax (85) 682-77-52; e-mail mripas@zbs.bialowieza .pl; internet www.zbs.bialowieza.pl; f. 1954; attached to Polish Acad. of Sciences; scientific research in biomorphology, ecology, ecophysiology, genetics, taxonomy and fauna of mammals; colln of 180,000 specimens; library of 34,000 vols; Dir Prof. Dr hab. JAN M. WÓJCIK; publ. *Acta Theriologica* (4 a year).

Zakład Biologii Wód im. Karola Starmacha PAN (Institute of Freshwater Biology): ul. Sławkowska 17, 31-016 Cracow; tel. (12) 421-50-82; fax (12) 422-21-15; f. 1952; attached to Polish Acad. of Sciences; study of the plant and animal communities in ponds, rivers and dam reservoirs and productivity of these ecosystems, hydrochemistry and fisheries; hydrobiological station at Goczałkowice; biological fisheries station at Brzączowice; library of 29,000 vols and 1,520 periodicals; Dir Dr GRAŻYNA MAZURKIEWICZ-BOROŃ; publs *Ecohydrology and Hydrobiology*, *Supplementa ad Acta Hydrobiologica*.

Mathematical Sciences

Instytut Matematyczny PAN (Institute of Mathematics): ul. Sniadeckich 8, POB 21, 00-956 Warsaw; tel. (22) 522-81-00; fax (22) 629-39-97; e-mail im@impan.gov.pl; internet www.impan.gov.pl; f. 1948; attached to Polish Acad. of Sciences; scientific research work in mathematics and applications; local brs in Cracow, Gdańsk, Katowice, Łódź, Poznań, Toruń and Wrocław; 100 mems; library of 134,000 vols; Dir Prof. Dr hab. STANISŁAW JANECZKO; publs *Acta Arithmetica* (online), *Annales Polonici Mathematici* (online), *Applicationes Mathematicae* (online), *Bulletin* (online), *Colloquium Mathematicum* (online), *Dissertationes Mathematicae* (online), *Fundamenta Mathematicae* (online), *Studia Mathematica* (online).

Attached Centre:

Międzynarodowe Centrum Matematyczne im. Stefana Banacha (Stefan Banach International Mathematical Centre): ul. Sniadeckich 8, POB 21, 00-956 Warsaw; tel. (22) 522-82-32; fax (22) 622-57-50; e-mail office@impan.pl; internet www.impan.pl/bc; f. 1972 by an agreement of Academies of East European countries; br. of the Institute of Mathematics; promotion of int. cooperation in mathematics through organizing research and training semesters, workshops, confs and symposia in different fields of mathematics; no permanent staff; Dir Prof. Dr hab. STANISŁAW JANECZKO.

Physical Sciences

Centrum Astronomiczne im. Mikołaja Kopernika PAN (Copernicus Astronomical Centre): ul. Bartycka 18, 00-716 Warsaw; tel. (22) 841-10-86; fax (22) 841-00-46; e-mail camk@camk.edu.pl; internet www.camk.edu .pl; f. 1957; attached to Polish Acad. of Sciences; astronomy and astrophysics; library of 20,000 vols; Dir Prof. Dr hab. MAREK SARNA.

Centrum Badań Kosmicznych PAN (Space Research Centre): ul. Bartycka 18A, 00-716 Warsaw; tel. (22) 840-37-66; fax (22) 840-31-31; e-mail cbk@cbk.waw.pl; internet www.cbk.waw.pl; f. 1977; attached to Polish Acad. of Sciences; space physics, planetary geodesy, remote sensing; library of 9,000 vols; Dir Dr hab. MAREK BANASZKIEWICZ;

publ. *Artificial Satellites—Journal of Planetary Geodesy* (4 a year).

Centrum Fizyki Teoretycznej PAN (Centre for Theoretical Physics): Al. Lotników 32/46, 02-668 Warsaw; tel. (22) 847-09-20; fax (22) 843-13-69; e-mail cft@cft.edu.pl; internet www.cft.edu.pl; f. 1980; attached to Polish Acad. of Sciences; classical and quantum field theory, gen. relativity, statistical physics, quantum and atom optics, particle astrophysics; Dir Prof. LECH MANKIEWICZ.

Centrum Materiałów Polimerowych i Węglowych PAN (Centre of Polymer and Carbon Materials PAS): Marii Curie-Skłodowskiej 34, POB 20, 41-819 Zabrze; tel. (32) 271-60-77; fax (32) 271-29-69; e-mail sekretariat@cmpw-pan.edu.pl; internet www .cmpw-pan.edu.pl; f. 1968; attached to Polish Acad. of Sciences; research to develop novel polymers, carbon-polymer materials, carbon materials and catalysts, and to examine their properties so as to utilize them in biotechnology, microtechnology, optoelectronics, protection of the environment and healthcare; library of 14,608 vols; Dir Prof. Dr hab. ANDRZEJ DWORAK; Dir for Scientific Affairs ANDRZEJ F. BOROWSKI; publ. *Polish Journal of Applied Chemistry* (4 a year).

Institute of High Pressure Physics: POB 65, 01-142 Warsaw; located at: ul. Sokołowska 29/37, 01-142 Warsaw; tel. (22) 632-50-10; fax (22) 632-42-18; e-mail sylvek@ unipress.waw.pl; internet www.unipress .waw.pl; f. 1972; attached to Polish Acad. of Sciences; effects of high pressure on metals and semiconductors, high pressure metal formation and crystal growth, cold isostatic pressing, hot isostatic pressing and sintering; manufacture of high pressure laboratory equipment; Dir Prof. Dr hab. SYLWESTER POROWSKI.

Instytut-Centrum Badań Molekularnych i Makromolekularnych PAN (Centre of Molecular and Macromolecular Studies): ul. Sienkiewicza 112, 90-363 Łódź; tel. (42) 684-71-13; fax (42) 684-71-26; e-mail cbmm@bilbo.cbmm.lodz.pl; internet www .cbmm.lodz.pl; f. 1972; attached to Polish Acad. of Sciences; hetero-organic chemistry, organic chemistry of sulphur, bio-organic chemistry, polymer physics, polymer chemistry, hetero-organic polymers, instrumental and elemental analysis; library: over 15,000 vols; Dir Prof. MARIAN MIKOŁAJCZYK.

Instytut Chemii Fizycznej PAN (Institute of Physical Chemistry): Kasprzaka 44/52, 01-224 Warsaw; tel. (22) 343-31-08; fax (22) 343-33-33; e-mail ichf@ichf.edu.pl; internet ichf .edu.pl; f. 1955; attached to Polish Acad. of Sciences; research work in physico-chemical fundamentals incl. chemical engineering and chemical technology as follows: physical chemistry of metal-hydrogen systems including surface science and heterogeneous catalysis, analytical physical chemistry and instrumentation, experimental thermodynamics of organic mixtures, spectroscopy, including special-purpose apparatus, calorimetry including special-purpose apparatus and instrumentation, theory of chemical kinetics, electrochemistry and corrosion, fuel cells, molten salts, process kinetics, statistical mechanics and thermodynamics of irreversible phenomena; library of 99,147 vols; Dir Prof. ALEKSANDER JABLONSKI.

Instytut Chemii Organicznej PAN (Institute of Organic Chemistry PAS): Kasprzaka 44/52, 01-224 Warsaw; tel. (22) 631-87-88; fax (22) 632-66-81; e-mail icho-s@icho.edu.pl; internet www.icho.edu.pl; f. 1954; attached to Polish Acad. of Sciences; research in synthetic organic chemistry and natural products chemistry; library of 28,648 vols; Dir Prof. SŁAWOMIR JAROSZ; Research Dir

Prof. WITOLD DANIKIEWICZ; Deputy Dir Dr PIOTR LIPKOWSKI.

Instytut Fizyki PAN (Institute of Physics): Al. Lotników 32/46, 02-668 Warsaw; tel. (22) 843-70-01; fax (22) 843-09-26; e-mail director@ifpan.edu.pl; internet www.ifpan .edu.pl; f. 1953; attached to Polish Acad. of Sciences; research in condensed matter physics: semiconductors, magnetics, superconductors, atomic and molecular physics, quantum optics, spectroscopy, X-ray crystallography, crystal growth; 350 mems; library of 28,000 vols; Dir Prof. Dr hab. JACEK KOSSUT; publs *Acta Physica Polonica* (12 a year), *Monographs in Physics* (irregular), *Proceedings of Conferences in Physics* (irregular).

Instytut Fizyki Plazmy i Laserowej Mikrosyntezy im. Sylwestra Kaliskiego (S. Kaliski Institute of Plasma Physics and Laser Microfusion): ul. Hery 23, 01-497 Warsaw; tel. (22) 638-14-60; fax (22) 666-83-72; e-mail office@ifpilm.pl; internet www .ifpilm.pl; f. 1976; library of 1,000 vols; Dir Prof. ANDRZEJ GALKOWSKI.

Instytut Fizyki Jądrowej im. Henryka Niewodniczańskiego Polskiej Akademii Nauk (Henryk Niewodniczański Institute of Nuclear Physics of Polish Academy of Sciences (IFJ PAN)): ul. Radzikowskiego 152, 31-342 Cracow; tel. (12) 662-80-00; fax (12) 662-84-58; e-mail dyrektor@ifj.edu.pl; internet www.ifj.edu.pl; f. 1955; attached to Polish Acad. of Sciences; particle physics and astrophysics, nuclear physics and strong interactions physics, condensed matter physics, interdisciplinary research, physics methods in radiation and environmental biology, environmental physics, medical physics, dosimetry, nuclear geophysics, econophysics, radiochemistry and engineering of nano-materials; library of 19,000 vols; 8,000 journals; Dir-Gen. Prof. MAREK JEŻABEK.

Instytut Fizyki Molekularnej PAN (Institute of Molecular Physics): ul. Mariana Smoluchowskiego 17, 60-179 Poznań; tel. (61) 869-51-00; fax (61) 868-45-24; e-mail office@ifmpan.poznan.pl; internet www .ifmpan.poznan.pl; f. 1975; attached to Polish Acad. of Sciences; physics of magnetics, ferroelectrics and liquid crystals; molecular interactions in liquids; molecular electronics; nanostructures; radiospectroscopy (EPR, NMR, NQR); superconductivity and low-temperature physics; library of 23,500 vols; Dir Prof. Dr hab. ANDRZEJ JEZIERSKI; publ. *Molecular Physics Reports* (4 a year).

Instytut Geofizyki PAN (Institute of Geophysics): ul. Księcia Janusza 64, 01-452 Warsaw; tel. (22) 691-59-54; fax (22) 691-59-15; e-mail sn@igf.edu.pl; internet www.igf .edu.pl; f. 1952; attached to Polish Acad. of Sciences; seismology and physics of the Earth's interior, geomagnetism, palaeomagnetism, physics of the atmosphere, hydrology and polar research; library of 44,000 vols; Dir Prof. Dr hab. PAWEŁ ROWIŃSKI; publs *Acta Geophysica Polonica* (4 a year), *Publications* (irregular).

Instytut Katalizy i Fizykochemii Powierzchni PAN (Institute of Catalysis and Surface Chemistry): ul. Niezapominajek 8, 30-239 Cracow; tel. (12) 639-51-01; fax (12) 425-19-23; e-mail ncikifp@cyf-kr.edu.pl; internet www.ik-pan.krakow.pl; f. 1968; attached to Polish Acad. of Sciences; kinetics and mechanism of heterogeneous, homogeneous and enzymatic catalytic reactions, solid state chemistry, properties and dynamics of colloids, inter-facial phenomena, electrochemistry of interfaces; library of 9,000 vols; Dir Prof. MAŁGORZATA WITKO.

Instytut Mechaniki Górotworu PAN (Strata Mechanics Research Institute): ul.

Reymonta 27, 30-059 Cracow; tel. (12) 637-62-00; fax (12) 637-28-84; e-mail dziurzyn@ img-pan.krakow.pl; internet www.img-pan .krakow.pl; f. 1954; attached to Polish Acad. of Sciences; mechanics of granular media, rock deformation, gas and rock-mass outbursts, low-speed flow of fluids, dynamics of air flow, flow through porous media, micromeritics; library of 23,000 vols; Dir Prof. WACŁAW DZIURZYŃSKI; publ. *Archives of Mining Sciences* (4 a year).

Instytut Nauk Geologicznych PAN (Institute of Geological Sciences): Twarda 51/55, 00-818 Warsaw; tel. (22) 697-87-01; fax (22) 620-62-23; e-mail ingpan@twarda.pan.pl; internet www.ing.pan.pl; f. 1956; attached to Polish Acad. of Sciences; stratigraphy, sedimentology, tectonics, petrography, mineralogy and isotope geochemistry, quaternary geology, hydrogeology, micropalaeontology; runs undergraduate and PhD courses; library: (in Warsaw and Cracow) 42,700 books, 100,700 periodicals, 11,030 maps; Dir Prof. TERESA MADEYSKA; publs *Archiwum Mineralogiczne* (irregular), *Geologia Sudetica* (1 a year), *Studia Geologica Polonica* (irregular), *Studia Quaternaria* (1 a year).

Instytut Niskich Temperatur i Badań Strukturalnych PAN (Institute of Low Temperature and Structure Research PAS): POB 1410, 50-950 Wrocław 2; ul. Okólna 2, 50-422 Wrocław; tel. (71) 343-50-21; fax (71) 344-10-29; e-mail intibs@int.pan.wroc.pl; internet www.int.pan.wroc.pl; f. 1966; attached to Polish Acad. of Sciences; physics and chemistry of solids: electronic and crystallographic structure, low temperature phenomena, magnetism, superconductivity; library of 22,000 vols; Dir Prof. Dr hab. ANDRZEJ JEŻOWSKI; Scientific Sec. ANDRZEJ KOCZARSKI.

Instytut Problemów Jądrowych im. Andrzeja Sołtana (A. Sołtan Institute for Nuclear Studies): 05-400 Świerk/Otwock; tel. (22) 718-05-83; fax (22) 779-34-81; e-mail sins@ipj.gov.pl; internet www.ipj.gov.pl; f. 1983, fmrly part of Institute of Nuclear Research; library of 27,000 vols; nuclear physics, elementary particle physics, plasma physics, accelerator physics and technology, material research using nuclear technology, spectrometric technology and nuclear electronics; Dir Prof. ZIEMOWID SUJKOWSKI.

Państwowy Instytut Geologiczny (Polish Geological Institute): ul. Rakowiecka 4, 00-975 Warsaw; tel. (22) 849-53-51; fax (22) 849-53-42; e-mail sekretariat@pgi.gov.pl; internet www.pgi.gov.pl; f. 1919, name changed 1987; geological, hydrogeological and geo-environmental mapping; geological and hydrogeological national survey; central chemical laboratory; 8 brs; geological museum; library of 160,000 vols, 32,000 bound periodicals, 520,000 maps and atlases, 326,000 geological documents; Dir Prof. TADEUSZ PERYT; publs *Bibliografia Geologiczna Polski* (Geological Bibliography of Poland, 1 a year), *Biuletyn* (irregular), *Geological Quarterly*, *Prace* (Memoirs, irregular).

PHILOSOPHY AND PSYCHOLOGY

Instytut Filozofii i Socjologii PAN (Institute of Philosophy and Sociology): Nowy Świat 72, 00-330 Warsaw; tel. (22) 826-71-81; fax (22) 826-78-23; internet www.ifispan .waw.pl; f. 1956; attached to Polish Acad. of Sciences; library of 173,258 vols; Dir Prof. HENRYK DOMAŃSKI; publs *Archiwum Historii Filozofii i Myśli Społecznej* (irregular), *ASK—Społeczeństwo—Badania—Metody* (irregular), *Etyka* (irregular), *Mediaevalia Philosophica Polonorum* (irregular), *Prakseologia* (irregular), *Studia Logica* (in English, 4

a year), *Studia Mediewistyczne* (irregular), *Studia Socjologiczne* (4 a year).

Instytut Psychologii PAN (Institute of Psychology): ul. Chodakowska 19/31, 03-815 Warsaw; tel. (22) 517-99-16; fax (22) 517-99-17; e-mail sekretariat@psychpan.waw.pl; f. 1980; attached to Polish Acad. of Sciences; social psychology, personality, general psychology, psycholinguistics, cognitive and decision processes, political psychology, ecological psychology, cross-cultural psychology; library of 8,000 vols; Dir Prof. BOGDAN WOJCISZKE; publ. *Studia Psychologiczne* (4 a year).

RELIGION, SOCIOLOGY AND ANTHROPOLOGY

Polska Akademia Nauk Zakład Antropologii (Polish Academy Of Sciences Institute of Anthropology): ul. Kuźnicza 35, 50-951 Wrocław 56; tel. (71) 343-86-75; fax (71) 343-81-50; e-mail sekretariat@antro.pan .wroc.pl; internet www.antro.pan.wroc.pl; f. 1952; attached to Polish Acad. of Sciences; biological aspects of social stratification, human growth and development, indicators of individual biological conditions, biological basis of human behaviour and reproduction; library of 18,500 vols; Dir Assoc. Prof. SŁAWOMIR KOZIEŁ.

Żydowski Instytut Historyczny im. Emanuela Ringelbluma (Emanuel Ringelblum Jewish Historical Institute): ul. Tłomackie 3/5, 00-090 Warsaw; tel. (22) 827-92-21; fax (22) 827-83-72; e-mail secretary@jhi.pl; internet www.jhi.pl; f. 1947; research on Jewish history, educational activities, public lectures, film shows, seminars, workshops and exhibitions; incl. a museum of Jewish art and martyrology, archives and library; library of 60,000 vols, 600 MSS; Dir Prof. Dr PAWEŁ SPIEWAK; publs *Jewish History Quarterly* (4 a year, summary in English), *Kwartalnik Historii Zydow*.

TECHNOLOGY

Centralny Instytut Ochrony Pracy–Państwowy Instytut Badawczy (CIOP-PIB) (Central Institute for Labour Protection—National Research Institute): ul. Czerniakowska 16, 00-701 Warsaw; tel. (22) 623-36-78; fax (22) 623-36-93; e-mail oinip@ciop .pl; internet www.ciop.pl; f. 1950; research and devt on occupational health and safety; determination of exposure limits; standardization; testing and certification of machinery and manufacturing devices as well as personal and collective protective equipment; implementation and certification of occupational health and safety management systems; certification of the competence of personnel and educational bodies active in occupational health and safety; education and training; consultations; promotion; information and publishing; library of 31,000 vols; Dir Prof. DANUTA KORADECKA; publs *Bezpieczeństwo Pracy—Nauka i Praktyka* (Occupational Safety—Science and Practice, 12 a year), *International Journal of Occupational Safety and Health* (4 a year, in English), *Podstawy i Metody Oceny Srodowiska Pracy* (Principles and Methods of Assessing the Working Environment, 4 a year).

Główny Instytut Górnictwa (Central Mining Institute): Plac Gwarków 1, 40-166 Katowice; tel. (32) 258-16-31; fax (32) 259-65-33; e-mail gig@gig.katowice.pl; internet www.gig.katowice.pl; f. 1945; research work in rock mechanics, mining systems, blasting technique, gas, dust, water and rock burst hazards, clean coal technologies utilization and recovery of waste water, material engineering, noise and vibration control, environmental protection; 608 mems; library of

390,000 vols; Gen. Dir Prof. JÓZEF DUBIŃSKI; publs *Prace Naukowe* (Transactions, irregular, about 20 papers a year), *Prace Naukowe—Górnictwo i Srodowisko* (4 a year).

Instytut Automatyki Systemów Energetycznych (Institute of Power Systems Automation): ul. Wystawowa 1, 51-618 Wrocław; tel. (71) 348-42-21; fax (71) 348-21-83; e-mail bujko@iase.wroc.pl; internet www.iase.wroc .pl; f. 1949; automatic control systems, computer systems and networks, database systems, data communication for electric power system operation, expert systems, exploitation and management; library of 21,000 vols, 5,400 vols of reports; Dir Prof. Dr Ing. JAN BUJKO; publs *Biuletyn IASE* (2 a year in 12 a year *Energetyka* journal), *Informator Patentowy Energetyki* (4 a year), *Prace IASE* (1 a year).

Instytut Badań Systemowych PAN (Systems Research Institute): ul. Newelska 6, 01-447 Warsaw; tel. (22) 381-02-75; fax (22) 381-01-05; e-mail ibapan@ibspan.waw.pl; internet www.ibspan.waw.pl; f. 1977; attached to Polish Acad. of Sciences; control and optimization theory and applications, methods of systems analysis, information technology; library of 45,000 vols; Dir Prof. Dr hab. ZBIGNIEW NAHORSKI; Deputy Dir for Scientific Research Prof. Dr hab. SLAWOMIR ZADROZNY; publs *Badania Systemowe* (series of monographs), *Control and Cybernetics* (4 a year), *Working Papers IBS PAN* (continuous).

Instytut Badawczy Dróg i Mostów (Road and Bridge Research Institute): ul. Jagiellońska 80, 03-301 Warsaw; tel. (22) 811-32-31; fax (22) 811-17-92; e-mail ibdim@ibdim .edu.pl; internet ibdim.edu.pl; Dir Prof. Dr hab. Inż. LESZEK RAFALSKI; publs *Drogi i Mosty* (Roads and Bridges, 4 a year), *Nowości Zagranicznej Techniki Drogowej* (3–4 a year), *Prace Instytutu Badawczego Dróg i Mostów* (4 a year), *Studia i Materiały* (irregular).

Instytut Biopolimerów i Włókien Chemicznych (Institute of Biopolymers and Chemical Fibres): ul. M. Skłodowskiej-Curie 19/27, 90-570 Łódź; tel. (42) 637-67-44; fax (42) 637-62-14; e-mail ibwch@ibwch.lodz.pl; internet www.ibwch.lodz.pl; f. 1952; chemistry, technology, application of chemical fibres, environmental protection, natural polymers, their modification, applied biotechnology, medical and agricultural applications of polymers and fibres; library of 9,548 vols; Man. Dr DANUTA CIECHAŃSKA; publ. *Fibres and Textiles in Eastern Europe.*

Instytut Budownictwa Wodnego PAN (Institute of Hydroengineering): ul. Kościerska 7, 80-328 Gdańsk; tel. (58) 522-29-00; fax (58) 552-42-11; e-mail sekr@ibwpan .gda.pl; internet www.ibwpan.gda.pl; f. 1953; attached to Polish Acad. of Sciences; river, estuary and reservoir hydraulics, maritime hydraulics, soil mechanics and foundation engineering, environmental engineering; library of 24,000 vols; Dir Prof. ANDRZEJ SAWICKI; publs *Archives of Hydroengineering and Environmental Mechanics* (4 a year), *Proceedings* (irregular).

Instytut Chemii Nieorganicznej (Institute of Inorganic Chemistry): ul. Sowińskiego 11, 44-100 Gliwice; tel. (32) 231-30-51; fax (32) 231-75-23; e-mail sekret@ichn.gliwice.pl; internet www.ichn.gliwice.pl; f. 1948; library of 18,000 vols; Dir Dr Inż. BOŻENNA PISARSKA; publ. *Bieżąca Informacja Chemiczna seria— NIEORGANIKA* (Bibliography selected from current papers, 12 a year).

Instytut Chemii Przemysłowej (Industrial Chemistry Research Institute): Rydygiera 8, 01-793 Warsaw; tel. (22) 633-97-98; fax (22) 633-82-95; e-mail ichp@ichp.pl; internet www.ichp.pl; f. 1922; research into

carbo- and petrochemistry, organic synthesis, polymer and plastics technology, industrial catalysis, household chemistry products and disinfectants, environmental impact technology, process safety, chemical process engineering, instrumental analysis, medical diagnostic tests, biotechnology; Bureau for Ozone Layer Protection; Nat. Centre for Ecological Management in the Chemical Industry; library of 49,600 vols, 55,540 periodicals; Dir Prof. JOZEF MENES; publ. *Polimery* (12 a year).

Instytut Chemii i Techniki Jądrowej (Institute of Nuclear Chemistry and Technology): ul. Dorodna 16, 03-195 Warsaw; tel. (22) 504-12-05; fax (22) 811-15-32; e-mail sekdyrn@ichtj.waw.pl; internet www.ichtj .waw.pl; f. 1955; library of 41,000 vols; Dir Prof. ANDRZEJ G. CHMIELEWSKI; publs *INCT Reports* (Series A and B, irregular), *Nukleonika* (4 a year, with 2 or 3 supplements), *Postepy Techniki Jadrowej* (4 a year, in Polish).

Instytut Elektrotechniki (Electrotechnical Institute): ul. Pożaryskiego 28, 04-703 Warsaw; tel. (22) 812-20-00; fax (22) 615-75-35; e-mail iel@iel.waw.pl; internet www.iel.waw .pl; f. 1946; research and manufacture of electric machines, apparatus and appliances; library of 45,000 vols, 500 periodicals; Gen. Dir Assoc. Prof. Dr WIESLAW WILCZYŃSKI; publ. *Prace Instytutu Elektrotechniki* (Proceedings of the Electrotechnical Institute).

Instytut Energetyki (Institute of Power Engineering): ul. Mory 8, 01-330 Warsaw; tel. (27) 211-02-00; fax (22) 836-63-63; e-mail instytut.energetyki@ien.com.pl; internet www.ien.com.pl; f. 1953; library of 53,000 vols; Man. Dr JACEK WAŃKOWICZ; publs *Biuletyn Instytutu Energetyki* (6 a year), *Prace Instytutu Energetyki* (irregular).

Instytut Energii Atomowej (Institute of Atomic Energy): 05-400 Otwock-Swierk; tel. (22) 718-00-01; fax (22) 779-38-88; e-mail iea@cyf.gov.pl; internet www.iea.cyf.gov.pl; f. 1983; fmrly Inst. of Nuclear Research; reactor technology, radiation protection and dosimetry, quality standards for nuclear reactors, condensed matter physics, nuclear power plants, radioactive waste management; library of 16,000 vols, 685 periodicals; Dir Prof. Dr hab. KRZYSZTOF WIETESKA.

Instytut Informatyki Teoretycznej i Stosowanej PAN (Institute of Theoretical and Applied Informatics): ul. Bałtycka 5, 44-100 Gliwice; tel. (32) 231-73-19; fax (32) 231-70-26; e-mail office@iitis.gliwice.pl; internet www/iitis.gliwice.pl; f. 1969; attached to Polish Acad. of Sciences; 35 staff; research areas: performance evaluation of computer networks, computer vision, quantum informatics; library of 6,000 vols; Dir Prof. Dr TADEUSZ CZACHORSKI; publ. *Archiwum Informatyki Teoretycznej i Stosowanej* (4 a year).

Instytut Inżynierii Chemicznej PAN (Institute of Chemical Engineering PAS): ul. Bałtycka 5, 44-100 Gliwice; tel. (32) 234-69-15; fax (32) 231-03-18; e-mail secret@iich .gliwice.pl; internet www.iich.gliwice.pl; f. 1958; attached to Polish Acad. of Sciences; chemical and process engineering: chemical reaction engineering, adsorption, membrane separation, mass and heat transfer, environmental and bioprocess engineering, renewable energy sources; library of 6,677 vols; Dir Prof. Dr hab. Inż. KRZYSZTOF WARMUZINSKI; publs *Chemical and Process Engineering-Inzynieria Chemiczna i Procesowa* (4 a year), *Prace Naukowe Instytutu Inzynierii Chemicznej PAN.*

Instytut Łączności (National Institute of Telecommunications): ul. Szachowa 1, 04-894 Warsaw; tel. (22) 512-81-00; fax (22) 512-86-25; e-mail info@itl.waw.pl; internet www.itl

.waw.pl; f. 1951; telecommunications, data transmission, satellite telecommunications, optical transmission, information technology, radiocommunications, EMC; library of 56,405 vols; Dir WOJCIECH HALKA; publs *Journal of Telecommunications and Information Technology* (4 a year), *Telekomunikacja i Techniki Informacyjne* (4 a year).

Instytut Lotnictwa (Institute of Aviation): Al. Krakowska 110/114, 02-256 Warsaw; tel. (22) 846-00-11; fax (22) 846-44-32; e-mail ilot@ilot.edu.pl; internet www.ilot.edu.pl; f. 1926; library of 92,000 vols; Dir Dr WITOLD WIŚNIOWSKI; publs *Biblioteka Historyczna* (1 a year), *Biblioteka Naukowa* (Scientific Library, 2 a year), *Prace Instytutu Lotnictwa* (Transactions of the Institute of Aviation, 6 a year), *Przegląd Dokumentacyjny* (12 a year), *Tematy Prac Wykonawczych w Instytucie Lotnictwa* (1 a year).

Instytut Maszyn Matematycznych (Institute of Mathematical Machines): ul. Ludwika Krzywickiego 34, 02-078 Warsaw; tel. (22) 621-84-41; fax (22) 629-92-70; e-mail imasmat@imm.org.pl; internet bi.imm.org.pl; f. 1957; computer science and technology, training and education; library of 28,000 vols; Dir ROMAN CZAJKOWSKI; publ. *Techniki Komputerowe—Biuletyn Informacyjny* (irregular).

Instytut Maszyn Przepływowych im. R. Szewalskiego PAN (R. Szewalskiego Institute of Fluid Flow Machinery): ul. Gen. J. Fiszera 14, 80-952 Gdańsk; tel. (58) 341-12-71; fax (58) 341-61-44; e-mail imp@imp.gda .pl; internet www.imp.gda.pl; f. 1956; attached to Polish Acad. of Sciences; fundamental research, design methods, construction and development of machines and equipment for energy conversion in flow, measuring techniques and instrumentation in connection with fluid-flow machines, solid-state mechanics, machinery diagnostics, plasma physics; library of 23,000 vols; Dir Prof. Dr hab. JAROSŁAW MIKIELEWICZ; publs *Archives of Energetics* (2 a year), *Archives of Thermodynamics* (4 a year), *Transactions* (2 a year), *Zeszyty Naukowe* (bulletin, irreg.).

Instytut Maszyn Spożywczych (Institute of Food Processing Machinery): ul. Otwocka 1B, 03-759 Warsaw; tel. (22) 619-12-61; fax (22) 619-87-94; e-mail ims@orgmasz.waw.pl; internet www.orgmasz.waw.pl/w/ims/ims_a .htm; f. 1954; research and application in all fields of food processing, marketing and catering machinery and equipment; automation; energy-saving techniques; library of 4,984 vols, 141 periodicals, 20,066 leaflets; Dir Assoc. Prof. WALDEMAR P. RACZKO; publ. *Postępy Techniki* (Developments in Food Processing Technology, 3 a year).

Instytut Mechanizacji Budownictwa i Górnictwa Skalnego (Institute for Mechanized Construction and Rock Mining): ul. Racjonalizacji 6/8, 02-673 Warsaw; tel. (22) 843-02-01; fax (22) 843-21-80; e-mail imb@imbigs.org.pl; internet www.imbigs.org .pl; f. 1951; mechanized construction, industry of construction material machinery, construction and road-building machinery; rock mining machinery; waste management and recycling; normalization, using systems and techniques of machines and equipment; quality systems and product certification; protection of man and environment in construction; construction materials, rock mining and road-building industry; training of building machinery operators; library of 6,997 vols, 49 periodicals; Dir STEFAN GORALCZYK; publs *Działalność Instytutu Mechanizacji Budownictwa* (1 a year), *Przegląd Mechaniczny*, *Wiadomości IMB* (4 a year).

Instytut Metali Niezelaznych (Institute of Non-ferrous Metals): ul. Sowińskiego 5, 44-

100 Gliwice; tel. (32) 238-02-00; fax (32) 231-69-33; e-mail imn@imn.gliwice.pl; internet www.imn.gliwice.pl; f. 1952; processing of non-ferrous ores and other mineral materials; pyro- and hydrometallurgical processes of metals recovery from ores and concentrates, and recovery of accompaning metals; waste treatment and utilization; new alloys and composites; processing of metals and alloys; environmental protection; analytical chemistry of metals; 422 mems; library of 35,000 vols, 270 current periodicals, 15,000 reports; Dir Prof. Dr ZBIGNIEW ŚMIESZEK; publ. *Biuletyn Instytutu Metali Nieżelaznych* (12 a year).

Instytut Metalurgii i Inżynierii Materiałowej im. Aleksandra Krupkowskiego PAN (A. Krupkowski Institute of Metallurgy and Materials Science): ul. W. Reymonta 25, 30-059 Cracow; tel. (12) 295-28-00; fax (12) 295-28-04; e-mail office@imim-pan.krakow.pl; internet www.imim.pl; f. 1952; attached to Polish Acad. of Sciences; metallurgical thermodynamics, physical metallurgy, metal working; library of 25,000 vols; Dir Prof. Dr PAWEŁ ZIĘBA; Deputy Dir Prof. Dr JAN BONARSKI; Research Dir Prof. Dr WŁADYSŁAW GĄSIOR; publ. *Archives of Metallurgy and Materials* (4 a year).

Instytut Metalurgii Żelaza im. Stanisława Staszica (Stanislaw Staszic Institute of Ferrous Metallurgy): ul. K. Miarki 12–14, 44-100 Gliwice; tel. (32) 234-52-05; fax (32) 234-53-00; e-mail imz@imz.pl; internet www.imz.pl; f. 1945; library: 34,800 books, 21,850 vols of periodicals; Dir Dr ADAM SCHWEDLER; publ. *Prace Instytutu Metalurgii Żelaza* (transactions, 4 a year).

Instytut Mineralnych Materiałow Budowlanych (Institute of Mineral Building Materials): ul. Oświęcimska 21, 45-641 Opole; tel. (77) 456-3201; fax (77) 456-2661; e-mail immb@immb.opole.pl; internet www.immb.opole.pl; f. 1954; basic and applied research in mineral building materials technology, thermal engineering and environmental protection; br. in Cracow; library of 11,800 vols, 4,000 vols of reports; Dir Assoc. Prof. JERZY DUDA; publ. *Prace IMMB* (2 a year).

Instytut Morski (Maritime Institute): ul. Długi Targ 41/42, 80-830 Gdańsk; tel. (58) 301-16-41; fax (58) 301-35-13; internet www.im.gda.pl; f. 1950; economic and technical research in shipping, harbour and coastal engineering, corrosion, maritime law; 120 staff; library of 80,000 vols; Dir Asst Prof. Dr Eng. JAN CURZYTEK; Scientific Dir Prof. zw. Dr hab. Inż. BOLESŁAW MAZURKIEWICZ; publs *Informacja ekspresowa*, *Materiały Instytutu Morskiego*, *Prace Instytutu Morskiego*, *Przegląd Informacji*, *Zeszyty Problemowe Gospodarki Morskiej*.

Instytut Nafty i Gazu (Oil and Gas Institute): ul. Lubicz 25A, 31-503 Cracow; tel. (12) 421-00-33; fax (12) 421-00-50; e-mail office@inig.pl; internet www.igng.krakow.pl; f. 1945; oil and gas recovery industry, gas transport and storage, gas use, and related topics; library of 110,000 vols; Dir Prof. Dr hab Inż. MARIA CIECHANOWSKA; publs *Nafta-Gaz* (12 a year), *Prace*, *Przegląd Bibliograficzno-Faktograficzny 'Nafta-Gaz'* (4 a year).

Instytut Obróbki Plastycznej (Metal Forming Institute): ul. Jana Pawła 14, 61-139 Poznań; tel. (61) 657-05-55; fax (61) 657-07-21; e-mail inop@inop.poznan.pl; internet www.inop.poznan.pl; f. 1948; research and devt works on non-metallurgical metal forming; library of 24,500 vols; Dir HANNA WISNIEWSKA-WEINERT; publ. *Obróbka Plastyczna Metali* (4 a year).

Instytut Odlewnictwa (Foundry Research Institute): ul. Zakopiańska 73, 30-418 Cracow; tel. (12) 266-26-19; fax (12) 266-08-70; e-mail iod@iod.krakow.pl; internet czapla.iod.krakow.pl/infocast/inst_odl.html; f. 1946; research into foundry materials, technological processes, alloys and additives; library of 10,000 vols, 45 periodicals; Pres. Dr JERZY TYBULCZUK; publ. *Odlewnictwo – Nauka i Praktyka* (6 a year).

Instytut Podstaw Informatyki Polskiej Akademii Nauk (Institute of Computer Science Polish Academy of Sciences): ul. J. K. Ordona 21, 01-237 Warsaw; tel. (22) 836-28-41; fax (22) 837-65-64; e-mail ipi@ipipan.waw.pl; internet www.ipipan.waw.pl; f. 1976; attached to Polish Acad. of Sciences; library of 16,400 vols, 250 periodicals; research depts of Theoretical Foundations of Computer Science and Artificial Intelligence; Dir-Gen. Prof. JACEK KORONACKI; Dir (Scientific Affairs) BEATA KONIKOWSKA; Dir (Economic Affairs) BOGUSLAW MARTYNIAK; Sec. MICHAL CIESIOLKA; publs *Machine Graphics and Vision* (4 a year), *Prace IPI PAN* (ICS PAS Reports, irregular).

Instytut Podstawowych Problemów Techniki PAN (Institute of Fundamental Technological Research): ul. Pawińskiego 5B, 02-106 Warsaw; tel. (22) 826-12-81; fax (22) 826-98-15; e-mail director@ippt.gov.pl; internet www.ippt.gov.pl; f. 1953; attached to Polish Acad. of Sciences; applied mechanics, vibrations, ultrasonics, ultrasound in medicine, acoustics, electromagnetic fields, mechanical systems, energy problems, automatics and robotics, building structures, computational science and engineering; library of 80,000 vols; Dir Prof. ANDRZEJ NOWICKI; Scientific Ccl Chair. Prof. KAZIMIERZ SOBCZYK; publs *Archives of Acoustics* (4 a year), *Archives of Civil Engineering* (4 a year), *Archives of Mechanics* (6 a year), *Biblioteka Akustyki i Ultradźwięków* (Acoustics and Ultrasound Series), *Biblioteka Mechaniki Stosowanej* (Applied Mechanics Series), *CAMES–Computer Assisted Mechanics and Engineering Sciences* (4 a year), *Engineering Transactions* (4 a year), *Prace IPPT* (IFTR Reports).

Instytut Przemysłu Gumowego 'Stomil' ('Stomil' Rubber Research Institute): ul. Harcerska 30, 05-820 Piastów; tel. (22) 723-60-25; fax (22) 723-71-96; internet www.ipgum.pl; f. 1953; research in all brs of rubber technology and its development; library of 6,000 vols; Dir Dr JACEK MAGRYTA; Scientific Board Chair. Prof. Dr hab. ZBIGNIEW FLORJAŃCZYK; publs *Elastomery* (6 a year), *Guma–Elastomery–Przetwórstwo Informacje bieżace* (12 a year), *Rubber–Elastomers–Processing Technology* (in English, 12 a year).

Instytut Przemysłu Organicznego (Institute of Industrial Organic Chemistry): ul. Annopol 6, 03-236 Warsaw; tel. (22) 811-12-31; fax (22) 811-07-99; e-mail ipo@ipo.waw.pl; internet www.ipo.waw.pl; f. 1947; research on plant pesticides and biocides, auxiliary chemical products, organic intermediate products, blasting materials, chemical safety, toxicology and ecotoxicology; 235 mems; library of 36,700 vols, 171 periodicals; Dir Dr KAROL BUCHALIK; publs *Central European Journal of Energetic Materials* (4 a year), *Organika—Prace Naukowe Instytutu Przemysłu Organicznego* (1 a year), *Pestycydy* (4 a year).

Instytut Spawalnictwa (Institute of Welding): ul. Bł. Czesława 16–18, 44-100 Gliwice; tel. (32) 231-00-11; fax (32) 231-46-52; e-mail is@is.gliwice.pl; internet www.is.gliwice.pl; f. 1945; fundamental and developmental research, acceptance tests, certification, consulting, training, safety of welders, standardization, manufacture; library of 12,000 vols, 36 periodicals; Dir Prof. JAN PILARCZYK; publ. *Biuletyn Instytutu Spawalnictwa* (6 a year).

Instytut Systemów Sterowania (Institute of Control Systems): ul. Długa 1-3, 41-506 Chorzów; tel. (32) 247-28-20; fax (32) 246-25-91; e-mail office@iss.pl; internet www.iss.pl; f. 1977; Dir LESZEK E. ŻYCHOŃ; publs *Komunikaty Naukowe ISS*, *Prace Naukowe Instytutu Systemów Sterowania* (irregular).

Instytut Szkła, Ceramiki, Materiałów Ogniotrwałych i Budowlanych w Warszawie (Institute of Glass, Ceramics, Refractory and Construction Materials in Warsaw): ul. Postępu 9, 02-676 Warsaw; tel. (22) 843-74-21; fax (22) 843-17-89; e-mail info@isic.waw.pl; internet www.isic.waw.pl; f. 1952; basic research on all aspects of glass and ceramics technology; library of 15,000 vols and spec. colln of 5,000 vols; Dir ZDZISŁAW STACHURA; publ. *Szkło i Ceramika* (6 a year).

Instytut Technologii Elektronowej (Institute of Electron Technology): Al. Lotników 32/46, 02-668 Warsaw; tel. (22) 548-77-00; fax (22) 847-06-31; e-mail cambroz@ite.waw.pl; internet www.ite.waw.pl; f. 1966; research and devt in physics and technology of low dimensional semiconductor structures for photonics, silicon semiconductor nanostructures and microsystems, sensors; designing of integrated schemes and systems; hybrid microelectronics; characterization of nanostructures; library of 11,000 vols; Dir Prof. Dr hab. Inż. CEZARY A. AMBROZIAK; publs *Biblioteka Elektroniki* (irregular), *Electron Technology Internet Journal* (online).

Instytut Technologii Materiałów Elektronicznych (Institute of Electronic Materials Technology): ul. Wólczyńska 133, 01-919 Warsaw; tel. (22) 835-30-41; fax (22) 864-54-96; e-mail itme@itme.edu.pl; internet www.itme.edu.pl; f. 1979; library of 20,000 vols; Gen. Man. Dr ZYGMUNT ŁUCZYŃSKI; Scientific Dir Prof. ANDRZEJ JELEŃSKI; publs *Materiały Elektroniczne* (4 a year), *MST News – Poland* (4 a year).

Instytut Technologii Nafty im. Prof. Stanisława Pilata (Institute of Petroleum Processing): ul. Łukasiewicza 1, 31-429 Cracow; tel. (12) 617-75-28; fax (12) 617-75-22; e-mail itn@itn.com.pl; internet www.itn.com.pl; f. 1958; petroleum refining and petrochemistry, standardization of products and testing methods, new methods of analysis and production, fuel and oil additives; library of 20,000 vols; Man. Dir Dr LESZEK ZIEMIAŃSKI; publ. *Nafta Gaz* (12 a year).

Instytut Transportu Samochodowego (Motor Transport Institute): ul. Jagiellońska 80, 03-301 Warsaw; tel. (22) 811-09-44; fax (22) 811-09-06; e-mail awojciech@its.waw.pl; internet www.its.home.pl; f. 1952; focuses on operation of motor transport in the market economy, road traffic organization, and environmental protection; library of 22,000 vols, 50 periodicals; Dir Dr ANDRZEJ WOJCIECHOWSKI; Scientific Cttee Chair. Prof. Dr hab. Inż. JERZY MERKISZ; publs *Bezpieczeństwo Ruchu Drogowego* (4 a year), *Transport Samochodowy* (4 a year).

Instytut Włókien Naturalnych (Institute of Natural Fibres): ul. Wojska Polskiego 71B, 60-630 Poznań; tel. (61) 845-58-00; fax (61) 841-78-30; e-mail sekretar@inf.poznan.pl; internet www.inf.poznan.pl; f. 1930; complex research on production and processing of natural fibres (flax, hemp, kenaf, jute, silk), environmental protection, processing of waste products, plant biotechnology, properties of fibre, yarn, fabrics and textiles, composites, flame retardants, plant protection; cultivation and harvesting of fibrous plants and natural dyestuffs; library of 20,278 vols, 7,800 in special collns; Gen. Dir Prof. Dr RYSZARD KOZŁOWSKI; Scientific Board Chair.

Prof. Dr Bogumił Laszkiewicz; publs *Euroflax* (2 a year), *Journal of Natural Fibers* (4 a year), *Natural Fibres, Włókna Naturalne* (1 a year).

Instytut Włókiennictwa (Textile Research Institute): ul. Brzezińska 5/15, 92-103 Łódź; tel. (42) 616-31-95; fax (42) 679-26-38; e-mail info@mail.iw.lodz.pl; internet www.iw.lodz .pl; f. 1945; textile raw materials, technology of yarn manufacturing, non-woven fabrics, textile chemical processing; library of 17,559 vols and 12,879 in spec. colln; Dir Jolanta Mamenas; Scientific Council Chair. Prof. Dr hab. Kazimierz Kopias; publ. *Prace Instytutu Włókiennictwa* (1 a year).

Instytut Wzornictwa Przemysłowego (Institute of Industrial Design): ul. Świętojerska 5/7, 00-236 Warsaw; tel. (22) 860-00-66; fax (22) 831-64-78; e-mail iwp@ iwp.com.pl; internet www.iwp.com.pl; f. 1950; research into design and ergonomics of industrial products; ergonomic research and data selection; design for the disabled; standardization; technical information service; organization of national and foreign exhibitions, seminars, conferences etc.; library of 42,000 vols, 270 titles of periodicals, collection of special editions, etc.; Dir Prof. Halina Walter; Scientific Council Pres. Prof. Jerzy Wuttke; publs *Design Library Series*, *Express News*, *Studies and Materials*.

Polski Komitet Normalizacyjny (Polish Committee for Standardization): Świętokrzyska 14, 00-050 Warsaw; tel. (22) 556-76-00; fax (22) 556-77-80; e-mail prezeskr@pkn.pl; internet www.pkn.pl; f. 1924; library has collections of Polish National Standards, ISO, IEC, EN and foreign standards; Pres. Janusz Szymański; publ. *Normalizacja* (12 a year).

Przemysłowy Instytut Automatyki i Pomiarów (Industrial Research Institute of Automation and Measurements): Al. Jerozolimskie 202, 02-486 Warsaw; tel. (22) 874-00-00; fax (22) 874-02-20; e-mail piap@piap .pl; internet www.piap.pl; f. 1965; development of automation equipment, measuring instruments and industrial robots; library of 24,000 vols; Dir Prof. Stanisław Kaczanowski; publ. *Pomiary Automatyka Robotyka* (12 a year).

Przemysłowy Instytut Elektroniki (Industrial Institute of Electronics): ul. Długa 44/50, 00-241 Warsaw; tel. (22) 831-52-21; fax (22) 831-30-14; e-mail pie@pie.edu .pl; academic year pie.edu.pl; automatic production lines and technical equipment, equipment for thermal and chemical processes, test and measuring systems; Dir Dr Inż. Józef Wiechowski; Scientific Board Chair. Prof. Dr hab. Inż. Mieczysław Hering; publ. *Prace PIE* (4 a year).

Przemysłowy Instytut Maszyn Budowlanych (Construction Equipment Research Institute): ul. Napoleona 2, 05-230 Kobyłka; tel. (22) 786-23-26; fax (22) 786-18-30; e-mail pimb@pimb.com.pl; internet www.pimb.com .pl; f. 1952; library of 14,000 vols; Dir Dr Andrzej Machniewski; publ. *Prace PIMB* (irregular).

Przemysłowy Instytut Maszyn Rolniczych (Industrial Institute of Agricultural Machinery): ul. Starołęcka 31, 60-963 Poznań; tel. (61) 871-22-00; fax (61) 879-32-62; e-mail office@pimr.poznan.pl; internet www .pimr.poznan.pl; f. 1946; design and testing of agricultural machines and equipment; library of 11,000 vols; Man. Dir Dr Inż. Tadeusz Pawłowski; Scientific Council Chair. Prof. zZw. Dr Inż. Zdzisław Kośmicki; publs *Ciągniki i maszyny rolnicze. Budowa, przeznaczenie* (every 2 years), *Journal of Research and Applications in Agricultural*

Engineering (4 a year), *Katalog—cennik ciągników i maszyn rolniczych* (2 a year).

Przemysłowy Instytut Motoryzacji (Automotive Industry Institute): ul. Jagiellońska 55, 03-301 Warsaw; tel. (22) 811-14-21; fax (22) 811-60-28; e-mail info@pimot.org .pl; internet www.pimot.org.pl; f. 1972; Dir Dr Inż Lech Sokalski; Scientific Council Chair. Prof. Dr hab. Inż. Jerzy Barzykowski.

Przemysłowy Instytut Telekomunikacji (Telecommunications Research Institute): ul. Poligonowa 30, 04-051 Warsaw; tel. and fax (22) 810-23-81; e-mail office@pit.edu.pl; internet www.pit.edu.pl; f. 1934; radar technology, microwave technology and antennas, command control communication, intelligent systems (C3I); library of 22,000 vols; Dir Dr Roman Dufrene; Scientific Ccl Chair. Prof. Dr Stanisław Sławiński; publs *Postępy Radiotechniki* (2 a year), *Prace Przemysłowego Instytutu Telekomunikacji* (2 a year).

Libraries and Archives

Białystok
Biblioteka Politechniki Białostockiej (Library of Białystok University of Technology): ul. Wiejska 45C, 15-351 Białystok; tel. (85) 746-93-30; fax (85) 746-93-32; e-mail biblioteka@pb.edu.pl; internet biblioteka.pb .edu.pl; f. 1951; 242,519 vols, 605 periodicals (print), 89,001 spec. collns; Dir Joanna Putko; Deputy Dir Grażyna Bożek.

Bydgoszcz
Wojewódzka i Miejska Biblioteka Publiczna im. dr. Witolda Bełzy w Bydgoszczy (Bydgoszcz Dr W. Bełza Voivodship and Public Municipal Library): ul. Długa 39, 85-034 Bydgoszcz; tel. (52) 323-80-08; fax (52) 328-73-90; e-mail sekretariat@ wimbp.bydgoszcz.pl; internet www.wimbp .bydgoszcz.pl; f. 1903; 1,027,234 vols, incl. 8,228 old books, 6,550 maps and atlases, 1,201 MSS; Dir Ewa Stelmachowska; publ. *Bibliotekarz Kujawsko-Pomorski* (2 a year).

Cracow
Biblioteka Główna Akademii Pedagogicznej im. KEN (Main Library of the Pedagogical University of Cracow): ul. Podchorążych 2, 30-084 Cracow; tel. (12) 662-63-61; fax (12) 637-22-43; e-mail info@tessa.wsp .krakow.pl; internet www.ap.krakow.pl/ biblio/; f. 1946; 654,504 vols, 48,526 periodicals, 1,857 sound recordings; also audiovisual materials, CD-ROMs and microforms; Dir Teresa Wildhardt.

Biblioteka Jagiellońska (Jagiellonian Library): al. Mickiewicza 22, 30-059 Cracow; tel. (12) 663-35-55; fax (12) 633-09-03; e-mail ujbj@uj.edu.pl; internet www.bj.uj.edu.pl; f. 1364; colln: nat. library for books before 1800, central library of general scientific, Polish affairs, humanities, Polish writing of the 15th–18th centuries; 4,851,214 vols, 2,288,469 books, 862,664 periodicals, 35,266 online journals, 106,036 old prints (3,666 incunabula), 32,216 MSS, 38,588 music prints, 58,295 drawings and items of graphic art, 50,097 maps and atlases, and also flysheets and microforms; 44 univ. institute libraries; 1,961,321 units; Dir Prof. Dr Zdzisław Pietrzyk; publs *Bibliotheca Iagellonica, Fontes et Studia* (irregular), *Bulletin of the Jagiellonian Library* (1 a year).

Biblioteka Naukowa PAU i PAN w Krakowie (Scientific Library of the Polish Academy of Arts and Sciences and the Polish Academy of Sciences in Cracow): ul. Sławkowska 17, 31-016 Cracow; tel. (12) 431-00-21; fax (12) 422-29-15; e-mail biblioteka@pau .krakow.pl; f. 1856; 339,570 annual vols of

periodicals relating to the social and biological sciences, 147,066 MSS, old prints, cartography, graphic arts; 715,024 vols, 153,549 MSS, 345,069 periodicals; Dir Karolina Grodziska; publ. *Rocznik Biblioteki Naukowej PAU i PAN w Krakowie* (Yearbook).

Wojewódzka Biblioteka Publiczna w Krakowie (Cracow Voivode Public Library): ul. Rajska 1, 31-124 Cracow; tel. (12) 632-59-07; fax (12) 633-22-10; e-mail biblioteka@wbp .krakow.pl; internet www.wbp.krakow.pl; f. 1945; 550,000 vols; 771 regional brs; Dir Dr Artur Paszko; publ. *Notes Biblioteczny* (2 a year).

Częstochowa
Biblioteka Główna Politechniki Częstochowskiej (Main Library of Częstochowa University of Technology): Al. Armii Krajowej 36, 42-201 Częstochowa; tel. (34) 361-44-73; fax (34) 365-15-07; e-mail biblioteka@adm .pcz.czest.pl; internet www.bg.pcz.czest.pl; f. 1950; 495,519 vols, incl. 157,742 books, 76,559 periodicals, 261,218 standards, patents; Dir Dr Dagmara Bubel.

Gdańsk
Biblioteka Główna Politechniki Gdańskiej (Central Library of Gdańsk Technical University): ul. G. Narutowicza 11/12, 80-952 Gdańsk; tel. 47-25-75; fax 47-27-58; e-mail library@sunrise.pg.gda.pl; 1,096,000 vols incl. 494,000 books, 113,000 periodicals, 491,000 standards, patents; Librarian Mgr Janina Ligman; publs *Bibliografia Publikacji Pracowników Naukowych Politechniki Gdańskiej* (Bibliography of Publications of Scientific Workers of the Technical University of Gdańsk, irregular), *Raport Politechniki Gdańskiej* (Report of the Technical University of Gdansk, 1 a year), *Wykaz Nabytków* (List of Acquisitions, 12 a year).

Polska Akademia Nauk Biblioteka Gdańska (Polish Academy of Sciences Gdańsk Library): Wałowa 15, 80–858 Gdańsk; tel. (58) 301-22-51; fax (58) 301-55-23; e-mail bgpan@bgpan.gda.pl; internet www.bgpan.gda.pl; f. 1596; Research and Public Library; colln: humanities, social sciences, maritime, Pomeranian and Gdańsk affairs; 579,657 vols, incl. 60,446 old books, 664 incunabula, 96,631 periodicals, 9,779 MSS, 10,765 maps, 8,119 graphics; Dir Dr Zofia Tylewska-Ostrowska; publ. *Libri Gedanenses* (1 a year).

Gliwice
Biblioteka Główna Politechniki Śląskiej (Central Library of Silesian University of Technology): ul. Kaszubska 23, 44-100 Gliwice; tel. (32) 237-12-69; fax (32) 237-15-51; e-mail bg.sekr@polsl.pl; internet www.bg .polsl.pl; f. 1945; 589,063 vols in main library and 201,198 vols in departmental libraries, 92,223 journals and periodicals, 198,704 spec. collns; collns incl. technical and technology sciences, mathematics, physics, chemistry, materials technology, metallurgy, chemistry, building, architecture, mineral and mining, geology, traffic, sanitary, environmental, civil, power, electrical and electronics, informatics, telecommunications and mechanical engineering, bioengineering; Dir Dr Inż. Krzysztof Ziolo; Vice-Dir Mgr Maria Rychlewska; publ. *Biuletyn Biblioteki Głównej Politechniki Śląskiej*.

Katowice
Biblioteka Główna Śląskiego Uniwersytetu Medycznego w Katowicach (Main Library of the Medical University of Silesia): ul. Poniatowskiego 15, 40-055 Katowice; tel. (32) 208-35-37; fax (32) 208-35-87; e-mail biblio@sum.edu.pl; internet www.sum.edu

.pl; f. 1948; 172,075 vols; Head of Library
 EWA NOWAK; Librarian JUSTYNA SEIFFERT;
publ. *Biuletyn Informacyjny SUM* (irregular).

Biblioteka Śląska (Silesian Library): Plac
Rady Europy 1, 40-021 Katowice; tel. (32)
208-37-40; fax (32) 208-37-20; e-mail bsl@bs
.katowice.pl; internet www.bs.katowice.pl; f.
1922; colln: social science, economics, literature relating to Silesia; 1,425,459 books (incl.
28,701 old vols), 200,416 vols of periodicals,
13,400 MSS, 17,758 maps and atlases, 8,047
drawings and prints, 26,842 postcards,
15,442 photographs, 242,645 documents of
social life; Dir Prof. Dr hab. JAN MALICKI;
publs *Bibliografia Bieżąca Województwa
Śląskiego* (4 a year), *Bibliografia Śląska* (1
a year), *Bibliografia Województwa Śląskiego*
(1 a year), *Książnica Śląska* (irregular).

Kielce

**Biblioteka Główna Politechniki
Świętokrzyskiej** (Central Library of
Świętokrzyska Technical University): Al.
Tysiąclecia Państwa Polskiego 7, 25-314
Kielce; tel. (41) 342-44-83; fax (41) 344-76-
35; e-mail library@eden.tu.kielce.pl; internet
lib.tu.kielce.pl; f. 1966; 115,425 books, 34,468
vols of periodicals, 50,881 standards; Dir
DANUTA KAPINOS.

Łódź

Biblioteka Uniwersytetu Łódzkiego
(Library of Łódź University): ul. Matejki 32/
38, 90-237 Łódź; tel. (42) 635-60-02; fax (42)
665-57-42; e-mail bulinf@lib.uni.lodz.pl;
internet www.lib.uni.lodz.pl; f. 1945;
1,326,079 vols, 510,140 vols of periodicals,
3,971 MSS, 24,127 maps and atlases, 42,386
vols of music, 19,991 music records, 53, 725
iconographic items, 28,619 old prints,
126,526 public relations documents, 3,600
microfilms, 307,806 microfiches, 4,586 CDs;
Dir MARIA WROCIAWSKA.

Wojewódzka i Miejska Biblioteka Publiczna im. Marszałka Józefa Piłsudskiego w Łodzi (The Jozef Pilsudski
Regional and Municipal Public Library in
Lodz): ul. Gdańska 100/102, 90-508 Łódź; tel.
(42) 636-68-35; fax (42) 637-21-02; e-mail
sekretariat@hiacynt2.wimbp.lodz.pl; internet www.wimbp.lodz.pl; f. 1917; general;
special subjects socio-economic science and
the arts; 755,000 vols, 545,000 periodicals,
129,000 vols in special collns; Dir BARBARA
CZAJKA; publ. *Sprawozdanie z działalności
WiMBP* (1 a year).

Lublin

**Biblioteka Główna Uniwersytetu Marii
Curie-Skłodowskiej w Lublinie** (Central
Library of the M. Curie-Skłodowska University): ul. I. Radziszewskiego 11, 20-950
Lublin; tel. and fax (81) 537-58-35; e-mail
kasbo@eos.umcs.lublin.pl; internet www.bg
.umcs.lublin.pl; f. 1944; general scientific
colln of 2,527,251 vols, including 494,867
vols of periodicals, 16,000 online journals,
803 MSS, 369,207 patents, 40,272 maps and
atlases, 33,707 drawings and illustrations,
14,954 music scores, 19,215 ancient books, 4
incunabula, 2,814 dissertations, 4,900 audio
cassettes and records; Dir Dr BOGUSŁAW
KASPEREK.

Wojewódzka i Miejska Biblioteka Publiczna im. Hieronima Łopacińskiego
(Hieronim Łopacinski Voivodship Public
Library): ul. Narutowicza 4, 20-950 Lublin;
tel. (81) 528-74-00; fax (81) 528-74-06; e-mail
info@hieronim.wbp.lublin.pl; internet www
.wbp.lublin.pl; f. 1907; regional, humanistic,
scientific and educational colln; 480,240 vols,
11,898 old vols, 43,620 periodicals, 2,897
MSS, 4,245 maps and atlases, 97,944 ephemera, 40,501 drawings and illustrations, 3,861

microfilms; Dir ZOFIA CIURUŚ; Deputy Dir
JOANNA CHAPSKA; publs *Bibliotekarz Lubelski*
(1 a year), *Dostrzegacz Biblioteczny* (4 a
year).

Poznań

Biblioteka Kórnicka PAN (Library of the
Polish Academy of Sciences, Kórnik): 62-035
Kórnik, near Poznań; tel. (61) 817-00-81; fax
(61) 817-19-30; e-mail bkpan@amu.edu.pl;
internet www.bkpan.poznan.pl; f. 1828;
191,784 books, 79,680 periodicals, 15,222
MSS, 30,055 old prints, 14,000 graphics;
collections on history, history of Polish literature, history of art, history of culture;
attached literary museum; Dir Prof. Dr hab.
STANISŁAW SIERPOWSKI; publ. *Pamiętnik Biblioteki Kórnickiej.*

Biblioteka Raczyńskich (Raczyńsky
Library): Plac Wolności 19, 61-739 Poznań;
tel. (61) 852-94-42; fax (61) 852-98-68; e-mail
sekret@bracz.edu.pl; internet www.bracz
.edu.pl; f. 1829; scientific and educational
collection; 1,592,654 vols, 17,854 old books,
44,851 periodicals, 10,038 MSS, 11,596 maps
and atlases, 37,083 ex-libris, 21,374 photos,
1,514 drawings and illustrations, 164 microfilms, 84,517 audio and video items; Dir
WOJCIECH SPALENIAK.

Biblioteka Uniwersytecka (Library of
Adam Mickiewicz University): Skr. Poczt.
526, ul. Ratajczaka 38/40, 61-816 Poznań;
tel. (61) 829-38-20; fax (61) 829-38-24; e-mail
library@amu.edu.pl; internet lib.amu.edu.pl;
f. 1919; supports the academic programmes
of the University and the University's curriculum in natural sciences, the humanities,
mathematics, chemistry, physics, social science, law and languages; supports research
activity of the academic community; acquisition, organization and dissemination of information; provides training in computer
literacy and web-based searches; 2,731,000
vols in central library, incl. 100,240 ancient
vols, 5,600 MSS, 30,000 maps and atlases,
2,059,000 vols in departmental libraries; Dir
Dr ARTUR JAZDON; publ. *Biblioteka* (1 a year).

Rzeszów

Biblioteka Główna Politechniki Rzeszowskiej (Central Library of Rzeszów University of Technology): ul. Pola 2, 35-959
Rzeszów; tel. (17) 854-25-33; fax (17) 854-25-
33; e-mail bgprz@prz.rzeszow.pl; internet
www.prz.rzeszow.pl/biblio/biblio.htm; f.
1951; 143,500 books, 33,600 vols of periodicals, 139,000 items in spec. colln; Dir Mgr
ELŻBIETA KAŁUŻA.

Sopot

Biblioteka Uniwersytetu Gdańskiego
(Library of the University of Gdańsk): ul.
Wita Stwosza 53, 80-308 Gdańsk; tel. (58)
523-32-10; fax (58) 523-32-09; e-mail bib@bg
.ug.edu.pl; internet www.bg.ug.edu.pl; f.
1970; 989,157 vols, 315,187 periodicals,
58,887 e-journals; spec. collns: 167,936 items;
Dir GRAŻYNA JAŚKOWIAK.

Szczecin

Biblioteka Główna Uniwersytetu Szczecińskiego (Library of University of Szczecin): ul. A. Mickiewicza 16, 70-384 Szczecin;
tel. (91) 444-23-60; fax (91) 444-23-62;
internet bg.univ.szczecin.pl; f. 1985;
1,300,000 vols; Dir JOLANTA GOC; publs
*Bibliografia publikacji pracowników Uniwersytetu Szczecińskiego, Wykaz ważniejszych
nabytków* (irregular).

**Książnica Pomorska im. Stanisława
Staszica** (Stanisław Staszic Pomeranian
Library): ul. Podgórna 15, 70-205 Szczecin;
tel. (91) 481-91-10; fax (91) 481-91-15; e-mail
ksiaznica@ksiaznica.szczecin.pl; internet
www.ksiaznica.szczecin.pl; f. 1905; 848,087

vols, 157,930 vols of periodicals, 3,243 MSS,
30,410 early books, 250,010 govt documents,
38,287 standards, 9,036 maps and atlases,
19,032 records, 4,755 audio cassettes, 2,407
CDs, 3,986 microforms; Dir LUCJAN BĄBOLEWSKI; publs *Bibliografia Pomorza Zachodniego. Piśmiennictwo polskie i Piśmiennictwo
zagraniczne* (Bibliography of Western
Pomerania. Polish Literature and Foreign
Literature), *Bibliotekarz Zachodniopomorski*
(The West Pomeranian Librarian, 4 a year).

Toruń

**Wojewódzka Biblioteka Publiczna –
Książnica Kopernikańska w Toruniu**
(Copernicus Library of Toruń): ul. Słowackiego 8, 87-100 Toruń; tel. (56) 622-66-42; fax
(56) 622-55-13; e-mail ksiaznica@ksiaznica
.torun.pl; internet www.ksiaznica.torun.pl; f.
1923; international exchange of information,
bibliographic enquiries, archival research,
research on cultural and political history of
Pomerania; 769,419 books, incl. 26,300 old
books, 92,926 vols of periodicals, 700 MSS,
3,807 cartographic units; Dir Mgr TERESA E.
SZYMOROWSKA; publs *Folia Toruniensia*
(irregular), *Regional Bibliography of
Kujawy-Pomerania* (on CD-ROM, 1 a year).

Warsaw

Archiwum Akt Nowych (Central Archive
of Modern Records): ul. Hankiewicza 1, 02-
103 Warsaw; tel. (22) 589-31-18; fax (22) 589-
30-01; e-mail sekretariat@aan.gov.pl;
internet www.aan.gov.pl; f. 1919; Dir
TADEUSZ KRAWCZAK.

Archiwum Główne Akt Dawnych (Central Archives of Historical Records): ul.
Długa 7, 00-263 Warsaw; tel. (22) 831-54-
19; fax (22) 831-16-08; e-mail archagad@
poczta.onet.pl; internet www.archiwa.gov.pl/
agad; f. 1808; archives from 13th century to
1918; 22,946 vols, 412,704 records; Dir Dr
HUBERT WAJS.

Archiwum Polskiej Akademii Nauk
(Archives of the Polish Academy of Sciences):
ul. Nowy Swiat 72, 00-330 Warsaw; tel. (22)
657-28-48; fax (22) 826-81-30; e-mail
archiwum@apan.waw.pl; internet www.apan
.waw.pl; f. 1953; 26,000 vols; brs in Cracow,
Poznań, Katowice; Dir Dr HANNA KRAJEWSKA;
publ. *Biuletyn Archiwum PAN* (1 a year).

Biblioteka Narodowa (National Library):
al. Niepodległości 213, 02-086 Warsaw; tel.
(22) 608-29-99; fax (22) 825-52-51; e-mail
biblnar@bn.org.pl; internet www.bn.org.pl; f.
1928; State central library; colln of writings
in Polish and relating to Poland; basic foreign
publications in the social sciences and
humanities; library science literature; houses
the Bibliographic Institute, the Institute of
the Book and Reading; 2,609,188 books,
930,642 vols of periodicals, 27,366 MSS,
161,994 old books, 122,480 maps and atlases,
489,412 drawings, photographs, illustrations, leaflets and posters, 121,049 music
scores, 2,311,044 items of social ephemera,
268,676 reels of microfilm; Dir Dr TOMASZ
MAKOWSKI; publs *Biuletyn Informacyjny Biblioteki Narodowej* (Information Bulletin, 4 a
year), *Polish Libraries Today* (in English,
irregular), *Rocznik Biblioteki Narodowej*
(National Library Yearbook, scientific library
science periodical, electronic, with English
summaries).

**Biblioteka Publiczna m. st. Warszawy-
Biblioteka Główna Województwa Mazowieckiego** (Warsaw Public Library—Central Library of Masovia Province): ul.
Koszykowa 26–28, POB 365, 00-950 Warsaw;
tel. (22) 621-78-52; fax (22) 621-19-68; e-mail
biblioteka@biblpubl.waw.pl; internet www
.biblpubl.waw.pl; f. 1907; gen. colln;
1,249,083 vols, 13,000 old prints, 4,000
MSS, 18,400 maps and atlases, 39,600 stand-

ards, 3,933 drawings, 5,900 records; Dir MICHAŁ STRĄK; publ. *Bibliotekarz* (The Librarian, 12 a year).

Biblioteka Sejmowa (Sejm Library): ul. Wiejska 4, 00-902 Warsaw; tel. (22) 694-24-29; fax (22) 694-17-78; e-mail parlib@sejm .gov.pl; internet parlib.sejm.gov.pl; f. 1919; law, political and social sciences, modern history, economics; 507,000 vols, 291,000 books, 113,000 vols of periodicals, 97,000 parliamentary, official and int. publs, 1,067m. archival documents, 61,000 sound and video recordings of Sejm meetings; Dir Dr WOJCIECH KULISIEWICZ.

Biblioteka Szkoły Głównej Handlowej (Library of Warsaw School of Economics): ul. Rakowiecka 22B, 02-521 Warsaw; tel. (22) 564-95-05; fax (22) 564-86-90; e-mail infnauk@sgh.waw.pl; internet www.sgh.waw .pl/biblioteka; f. 1906; colln: economics, sociology, social policy, geography, economic history, politics, statistics and demography, accounting, finance, cooperative movement, law, labour problems, foreign trade, marketing, industry, agriculture, transport, business and management; 1,033,343 vols; Dir Dr MARIA REKOWSKA; Librarian MONIKA KOWALIK; publs *Bibliografia Opublikowanego Dorobku Pracowników Naukowo-Dydaktycznych SGH, Przegląd Bibliograficzny Czasopiśmiennictwa Ekonomicznego* (4 a year).

Biblioteka Uniwersytecka w Warszawie (Warsaw University Library): Dobra 56–66, 00-312 Warsaw; tel. (22) 552-56-60; fax (22) 552-56-59; e-mail buw@uw.edu.pl; internet www.buw.uw.edu.pl; f. 1816; 2,937,104 vols, incl. 130,342 early imprints, 676,477 periodicals, 6,990 MSS, 12,052 maps, 35,475 maps and prints, 17,839 microforms, 72,797 vols of printed music, 112,137 vols ephemera; Dir EWA KOBIERSKA-MACIUSZKO; publ. *Prace Biblioteki Uniwersyteckiej w Warszawie* (irregular).

Centralna Biblioteka Rolnicza 'Michała Oczapowskiego' (Central Agricultural Library of Michał Oczapowski): POB 360, 00-950 Warsaw; ul. Krakowskie Przedmieście 66, 00-950 Warsaw; tel. (22) 826-60-41; fax (22) 826-01-57; e-mail listy@cbr.net.pl; internet www.cbr.edu.pl; f. 1955; br. at Puławy; mem. of Agris-FAO, IAALD; centre for information and documentation in agriculture and for exchange with scientific instns abroad; 311,100 vols and 605 current periodical titles on agriculture and related sciences; Dir Dr RYSZARD MIAZEK; publs *Bibliography of Polish Agricultural and Food Economy Literature* (12 a year), *Current Information on Agriculture in the World* (52 a year).

Centralna Biblioteka Statystyczna (Central Statistical Library): al. Niepodległości 208, 00-925 Warsaw; tel. (22) 608-31-43; fax (22) 608-31-88; e-mail b.lazowska@stat.gov .pl; internet statlibr.stat.gov.pl; f. 1918; colln: scientific and specialized (economic and social subjects, with emphasis on statistics); 480,000 books, 1,500 periodical titles, 5,000 maps and atlases; Dir Mgr BOŻENA ŁAZOWSKA; publs *Bibliografie Piśmiennictwa Demograficznego, Bibliografia Polskiego Piśmiennictwa Statystycznego* (irregular), *Bibliografia Wydawnictw Głównego Urzędu Statystycznego* (irregular), *Biuletyn Nabytków, Roczniki zagraniczne w zbiorach Centralnej Biblioteki Statystycznej*.

Centralna Biblioteka Wojskowa im. Marszałka Józefa Piłsudskiego (Marshal Joseph Pilsudski Central Military Library): ul. Ostrobramska 109, 04-041 Warsaw; tel. (22) 681-79-52; fax (22) 681-69-40; e-mail informacja@cbw.pl; internet www.cbw.pl; f. 1919; 610,482 vols, 143,313 periodicals; special collection: 162,942 vols; Dir Col. Dr

ALEKSANDRA SKRABACZ; publs *Informator Naukowy Centralnej Biblioteki Wojskowej* (irregular), *Polska Bibliografia Wojskowa* (Polish Military Bibliography, 4 a year).

Główna Biblioteka Lekarska (Central Medical Library): ul. Chocimska 22, 00-791 Warsaw; tel. (22) 849-78-51; fax (22) 849-78-02; e-mail gbl@gbl.waw.pl; internet www.gbl .waw.pl; f. 1945; collection of medical items, drawings and illustrations; 422,279 vols, 4,000 old vols, 1,156 MSS and 154,442 periodicals, 44,246 microforms; Dir Dr ALEKSANDER TULCZYŃSKI; publs *Biuletyn Głównej Biblioteki Lekarskiej* (2 a year), *Polska Bibliografia Lekarska* (yearbook).

Główna Biblioteka Pracy i Zabezpieczenia Społecznego (Central Library of Labour and Social Security): ul. Limanowskiego 23, 02-943 Warsaw; tel. (22) 642-04-73; fax (22) 642-19-27; e-mail gbpizs@gbpizs.gov .pl; internet www.gbpizs.gov.pl; f. 1974; attached to Min. of Labour and Social Policy; colln: labour, wages, social affairs and related matters; 57,000 vols, 16,927 periodicals, c. 1,000 titles; Dir ANNA PASZEK; publs *Bibliography of economic and social problems of labour* (1 a year), *Documentation Review* (12 a year), *Special Bibliographies* (irregular).

Naczelna Dyrekcja Archiwów Państwowych (Head Office of State Archives): ul. Rakowiecka 2D, 02-517 Warsaw; tel. (22) 565-46-00; fax (22) 565-46-14; e-mail ndap@ archiwa.gov.pl; internet www.archiwa.gov .pl; f. 1951; 21,433 vols; Gen. Dir Prof. WŁADYSŁAW STĘPNIAK; publs *Archeion* (2 a year), *Miscellanea Historico-Archivistica* (1 a year), *Nowe Miscellanea Historyczne* (1 a year).

Ośrodek Informacji Naukowej Polskiej Akademii Nauk (Centre for Information Science of the Polish Academy of Sciences): Pałac Staszica, ul. Nowy Świat 72, 00-330 Warsaw; f. 1953; 23,000 vols, 900 scientific periodicals from all over the world on social science and other scientific disciplines; Dir Dr ANDRZEJ GROMEK; publs *Przegląd Informacji o Naukoznawstwie* (Review of Information on Science of Science, 4 a year), *Przegląd Literatury Metodologicznej* (Review of Methodological Literature, 2 a year), *Zagadnienia Informacji Naukowej* (Problems of Information Science, 2 a year).

Ośrodek Przetwarzania Informacji (Information Processing Centre): ul. Niepodległości 188B, 00-950 Warsaw; tel. (22) 825-12-40; fax (22) 825-33-19; e-mail opi@opi.org .pl; internet www.opi.org.pl; f. 1990; international co-operation, technology transfer, information services on research and development; database management; Dir Dr OLAF GAJL; publ. *Informator Nauki Polskiej* (Polish Research Directory, every 2 years).

Wrocław

Biblioteka Uniwersytecka we Wrocławiu (Wrocław University Library): Karola Szajnochy, 10 St, 50-076 Wrocław; tel. (71) 346-31-20; fax (71) 346-31-66; e-mail sekretariat1@bu.uni.wroc.pl; internet www .bu.uni.wroc.pl; f. 1945; Silesiaca and Lusatica; bibliography, int. relations between Poland and other Slavonic countries and Germany; 3,895,727 vols, 1,230,628 books, 369,488 journals, 42,363 microfilms, 475,777 spec. collns; Dir GRAŻYNA PIOTROWICZ; publs *Bibliografia Piśmiennictwa o Uniwersytecie Wrocławskim* (irregular), *Bibliografia Publikacji Pracowników Uniwersytetu Wrocławskiego* (1 a year), *Bibliothecalia Wratislaviensia* (irregular).

Dolnośląska Biblioteka Publiczna im. Tadeusza Mikulskiego we Wrocławiu (T. Mikulski Dolnoslaska Public Library):

Rynek 58, 50-116 Wrocław; tel. (71) 344-39-03; fax (71) 344-18-08; e-mail wbp@wbp.wroc .pl; internet wbp.wroc.pl; 253,000 vols, 128,000 spec. colln; Dir ANDRZEJ TYWS; publ. *Książka i Czytelnik* (2 a year).

Zakład Narodowy im. Ossolińskich (Ossoliński National Institute): ul. Szewska 37, 50-139 Wrocław; tel. (71) 344-44-71; fax (71) 344-85-61; e-mail znio@znio.pl; internet www.oss.wroc.pl; f. 1817; colln incl. MSS, old prints, graphics, drawings, bookplates, postcards, numismatic material, decorative items, badges, social documents, microforms, digitalized objects; 1,800,000 vols; Dir Dr ADOLF JUZWENKO; Sr Librarian JOANNA GRZESKOWIAK-STEPOWICZ; publs *Czasopismo Zakładu Narodowego im. Ossolińskich* (1 a year), *Rocznik Wrocławski* (1 a year).

Museums and Art Galleries

Bydgoszcz

Muzeum Okręgowe im. Leona Wyczółkowskiego (L. Wyczółkowski Museum): Gdańska 4, 85-006 Bydgoszcz; tel. and fax (52) 585-98-16; e-mail muzeum@muzeum .bydgoszcz.pl; internet www.muzeum .bydgoszcz.pl; f. 1880; Polish art since 19th century; paintings and graphic art of Leon Wyczółkowski and gallery of contemporary Polish paintings; Archaeological and Local History brs and Coin Room; library of 46,000 vols; Dir Dr MICHAL WOŹNIAK.

Bytom

Muzeum Górnośląskie w Bytomiu (Upper Silesian Museum): Pl. Jana III Sobieskiego 2, 41-902 Bytom; tel. (32) 281-82-94; fax (32) 281-34-01; e-mail mgbytom@us.edu.pl; internet www.muzeum.bytom.pl; f. 1927 in Katowice, transferred in 1945; history, archaeology, ethnography, natural history, Polish and foreign art; branch museum (ul. W. Korfantego 34, Bytom); library of 51,300 vols; Dir MIECZYSŁAW DOBKOWSKI; publ. *Rocznik Muzeum Górnośląskiego w Bytomiu* (annals).

Cracow

Muzeum Archeologiczne w Krakowie (Archaeological Museum in Cracow): ul. Senacka 3, 31-002 Cracow; tel. (12) 422-75-60; fax (12) 422-77-61; e-mail mak@ma .krakow.pl; internet www.ma.krakow.pl; f. 1850; library of 11,753 vols, 16,726 periodicals; Dir Dr JACEK RYDZEWSKI; publs *Materiały Archeologiczne* (1 a year), *Materiały Archeologiczne Nowej Huty* (1 a year).

Muzeum Etnograficzne im. S. Udzieli w Krakowie (Ethnographic Museum in Cracow): ul. Krakowska 46, 31-066 Cracow; tel. (12) 430-60-23; fax (12) 430-63-30; internet www.mek.krakow.pl; f. 1910; folk art and folk culture of Poland; also foreign collections from Europe, Asia, Africa, S. America; archives; library of 30,000 vols; Dir MARIA ZACHOROWSKA; publ. *Rocznik Muzeum Etnograficznego w Krakowie* (1 a year).

Muzeum Historyczne m. Krakowa (Historical Museum of the City of Crakow): Krzysztofory, Rynek Główny 35, 31-011 Crakow; tel. and fax (12) 422-32-64; e-mail promocja@mhk.pl; internet www.mhk.pl; f. 1899; traditions, history and culture of the city of Crakow, model houses, arms and clocks, history of the theatre in Crakow, history and culture of the Jews in Crakow, history of the Crakow Fowler Brotherhood, upheaval and martyrdom of the Polish people in the period 1936–1956; special collection of 1,171 items; library of 23,810 vols; Dir

MICHAŁ NIEZABITOWSKI; publ. *Krzysztofory-Zeszyty Naukowe* (1 a year).

Muzeum Narodowe w Krakowie (National Museum in Cracow): 3 Maja ave 1, 30-062 Cracow; tel. (12) 295-56-20; fax (12) 295-55-55; e-mail dyrekcja@muz-nar.krakow .pl; internet www.muzeum.krakow.pl; f. 1879; history, fine art, costume and textiles, arms and armour, numismatics, house-museums of Matejko, Wyspiański, Mehoffer and Szymanowski, Japanese art and technology; library of 300,000 vols and Czartoryski Library; Dir ZOFIA GOŁUBIEW; publs *Notae Numismaticae Zapiski Numizmatyczne* (Numismatic Notes, 1 a year), *Rozprawy i Sprawozdania Muzeum Narodowego w Krakowie* (yearbook).

Zamek Królewski na Wawelu (Wawel Royal Castle): Wawel 5, 31-001 Cracow; tel. (12) 422-51-55; fax (12) 422-19-50; e-mail zamek@wawel.krakow.pl; internet www .wawel.krakow.pl; f. 1930; collns of art in the Royal Castle: Italian Renaissance furniture, King Sigismund August's 16th-century colln of Flemish tapestries, Italian and Dutch painting, Polish carpets; Royal treasury: crown jewels, historical relics, banners, gold objects; armoury: Polish and West European weapons; objects of Oriental art: Persian and Turkish weaponry and tents; oriental rugs, Chinese and Japanese pottery; colln relating to the history of Wawel Hill, other archaeological materials, Polish stove tiles from 15th to 18th centuries; 18th-century Meissen porcelain; library of 15,000 vols, 390 periodicals; Dir Prof. Dr hab. JAN OSTROWSKI; publs *Acta Archaeologica Waweliana*, *Biblioteka Wawelska*, *Studia Waweliana* (1 a year).

Frombork

Muzeum Mikołaja Kopernika (Nicholas Kopernik Museum): ul. Katedralna 8, 14-530 Frombork; tel. (55) 244-00-71; fax (55) 244-00-72; e-mail frombork@frombork.art.pl; internet www.frombork.art.pl; f. 1948; biographical exhibits; history of astronomy; astronomical observatory; example of Foucault's pendulum; planetarium; modern art gallery; history of medicine; herb garden; library of 20,500 vols; Dir Mgr HENRYK SZKOP; publ. *Komentarze Fromborskie* (1 a year).

Gdańsk

Centralne Muzeum Morskie (Polish Maritime Museum): ul. Olowianka 9–13, 80-751 Gdańsk; tel. (58) 301-86-11; fax (58) 301-84-53; e-mail info@cmm.pl; internet www.cmm .pl; f. 1960; depts of ports development, history of shipbuilding, history of maritime shipping and trade, marine fine arts, history of yachting, underwater archaeology, educational services; special vessel for underwater archaeological investigations; laboratory for conservation of artefacts recovered from sea; Lighthouse Museum in Rozewie; also br. in Hel (history of Polish fishery; open-air exhibition of types of fishing boats); br. in Tczew (history of Polish inland navigation); 4 historic ships (incl. sailing ship 'Dar Pomorza', fmr Polish school-ship); library of 42,000 vols, archives: plans, drawings, photos, documents; Dir Dr Inż. JERZY LITWIN.

Muzeum Archeologiczne w Gdańsku (Archaeological Museum in Gdańsk): ul. Mariacka 25/26, 80-958 Gdańsk; tel. (58) 301-50-31; fax (58) 301-52-28; e-mail mag@ archeologia.pl; internet www.archeologia.pl; f. 1953; library of 23,000 vols; Dir HENRYK PANER; publs *Gdańsk Archaeological Museum African Reports*, *Pomorania Antiqua*.

Muzeum Historyczne Miasta Gdańska (History Museum of the City of Gdańsk): ul. Długa 46/47, 80-831 Gdańsk; tel. (58) 767-91-

00; e-mail kancelaria@mhmg.pl; internet www.mhmg.gda.pl; f. 1970; Dir ADAM KOPERKIEWICZ.

Muzeum Narodowe w Gdańsku (National Museum in Gdańsk): ul. Toruńska 1, 80-822 Gdańsk; tel. (58) 301-70-61; fax (58) 301-11-25; e-mail info@muzeum.narodowe.gda.pl; internet www.muzeum.narodowe.gda.pl; f. 1872; art since 12th century, craftwork since 15th century, photography, ethnography (collns held at various locations); library of 19,224 vols, 3,506 periodicals; Dir TADEUSZ PIASKOWSKI.

Kielce

Muzeum Narodowe w Kielcach (National Museum in Kielce): Pl. Zamkowy 1, 25-010 Kielce; tel. (41) 344-40-14; fax (41) 344-82-61; e-mail poczta@mnki.pl; internet www.mnki .pl; f. 1908; brs: Museum of Stefan Żeromski's early years, Henryk Sienkiewicz Museum in Oblęgorek; library of 40,000 vols; Dir Dr ROBERT KOTOWSKI; publ. *Rocznik Muzeum Świętokrzyskiego* (1 a year) from vol 10 *Rocznik Muzeum Narodowego w Kielcach*.

Łódź

Centralne Muzeum Włókiennictwa (Central Museum of Textiles): ul. Piotrkowska 282, 93-034 Łódź; tel. (42) 683-26-84; fax (42) 684-33-55; e-mail sekretariat@ muzeumwlokiennictwa.pl; internet www .muzeumwlokiennictwa.pl; f. 1960; collections of textile tools and machines, documents of history of textile industry, Polish and foreign artistic textiles, industrial textiles, ancient and modern clothes, folk textiles; Łódź Wooden Architecture Open-Air Museum; library of 12,500 vols; Dir NORBERT ZAWISZA.

Muzeum Archeologiczne i Etnograficzne: Pl. Wolności 14, 91-415 Łódź; tel. (42) 632-84-40; fax (42) 632-97-14; f. 1956; archaeology, ethnography, numismatics; radio-chemical laboratory; library of 47,000 vols; Dir Dr hab. RYSZARD GRYGIEL; publ. *Prace i Materiały Muzeum Archeologicznego i Etnograficznego* (archaeology, ethnography, numismatics and conservation series).

Muzeum Sztuki w Łodzi (Art Museum): ul. Więckowskiego 36, 90-743 Łódź; tel. (42) 633-97-90; fax (42) 632-99-41; e-mail muzeum@ muzeumsztuki.lodz.pl; internet www .muzeumsztuki.lodz.pl; f. 1929; departments: Gothic art; foreign painting of the 15th to 19th centuries; Polish painting since 17th century; international modern and contemporary art; Księży Młyn house with late 19th-century interior décor; library of 36,000 vols; Dir MIROSŁAW BORUSIEWICZ.

Lublin

Muzeum Lubelskie w Lublinie (Lublin Provincial Museum): The Castle (Zamek), ul. Zamekowa 9, 20-117 Lublin; tel. and fax (81) 532-17-43; e-mail kancelaria@zamek-lublin .pl; internet www.zamek-lublin.pl; f. 1906; regional archaeological, historical and ethnographic collection, Polish and foreign paintings and decorative art; armoury; numismatics; conservation dept; 14th-century Holy Trinity Chapel, with 15th-century paintings; 13th-century dungeon; library of 20,000 vols; Dir ZYGMUNT NASALSKI; publ. *Studia i Materiały Lubelskie*.

Państwowe Muzeum na Majdanku (State Museum at Majdanek): ul. Droga Męczenników Majdanka 67, 20-325 Lublin; tel. (81) 710-28-21; fax (81) 710-28-65; e-mail sekretariat@majdanek.eu; internet www .majdanek.eu; f. 1944; fmr Nazi concentration camp; Dir TOMASZ KRANZ; publ. *Zeszyty Majdanka* (irregular).

Olsztynek

Muzeum Budownictwa Ludowego — Park Etnograficzny w Olsztynku (The Folk Architecture Museum and Ethnographic Park in Olsztynku): ul. Leśna 23, 11-015 Olsztynek; tel. and fax (89) 519-21-64; e-mail mbl@muzeumolsztynek.com.pl; internet www.muzeumolsztynek.com.pl; f. 1962; protection of folk culture; 9,885 exhibits; library of 10,768 vols; Dir MARIAN JUSZCZYŃSKI.

Oświęcim

Państwowe Muzeum Auschwitz-Birkenau w Oświęcimiu/Auschwitz-Birkenau Memorial and Museum in Oświęcim: ul. Więźniów Oświęcimia 20, 32-603 Oświęcim; tel. (33) 844-81-02; fax (33) 843-19-34; e-mail muzeum@auschwitz.org.pl; internet www .auschwitz.org.pl; f. 1947; former Nazi concentration camp at Auschwitz-Birkenau, illustrating system of mass extermination; colln incl. concentration camp documents and objects; library of 30,000 vols, 2,500 periodicals and archives; Dir Mgr JERZY WRÓBLEWSKI; publs *Pro Memoria* (in Polish and English), *Zeszyty Oświęcimskie* (in Polish and German).

Poznań

Muzeum Archeologiczne w Poznaniu (Poznań Archaeological Museum): ul. Wodna 27, 61–781 Poznań; tel. (61) 852-82-51; fax (61) 852-82-51; e-mail muzarp@man.poznan .pl; internet www.muzarp.poznan.pl; f. 1857; archaeology of Greater Poland and the Nile basin; library of 54,087 vols; Dir Prof. Dr MARZENA SZMYT; publs *Biblioteka Fontes Archaeologici Posnanienses* (irregular), *Fontes Archaeologici Posnanienses* (1 a year), *Studies in African Archaeology* (irregular).

Muzeum Narodowe (National Museum): Al. Marcinkowskiego 9, 61-745 Poznań; tel. (61) 856-80-00; fax (61) 851-58-98; e-mail mnp@mnp.art.pl; internet www.mnp.art.pl; f. 1857; medieval art, European paintings 14th–19th centuries, Polish paintings since 15th century, prints and drawings, sculpture, numismatics, modern art; br. museums specializing in ethnography, Poznań history, military history, musical instruments, applied arts; library of 89,000 vols; Dir Prof. Dr hab. WOJCIECH SUCHOCKI; publs *Monographs*, *Studia Muzealne* (1 a year).

Sanok

Muzeum Budownictwa Ludowego w Sanoku (Museum of Folk Architecture in Sanok): ul. Traugutta 3, 38-500 Sanok; tel. (13) 463-09-04; fax (13) 463-53-81; e-mail skansen.sanok@pro.onet.pl; f. 1958; traditional architecture, interiors, folk arts and crafts, icons; library of 18,900 vols on the Orthodox church and ethnography; Dir Mgr JERZY GINALSKI; publs *Acta Scansenologica* (every 2 years), *Materiały Muzeum Budownictwa Ludowego w Sanoku* (every 2 years).

Szczecin

Muzeum Narodowe w Szczecinie (National Museum in Szczecin): ul. Staromłyńska 27, 70-561 Szczecin; tel. (91) 431-52-00; fax (91) 431-52-04; e-mail biuro@muzeum .szczecin.pl; internet www.muzeum.szczecin .pl; f. 1945; Pomeranian art and archaeology, Polish art since 19th century, African and Asian art, maritime and ethnological collections; library of 77,831 vols; Dir LECH KARWOWSKI; publs *Mare Articum—The Baltic Art Magazine* (2 a year), *Materiały Zachodniopomorskie* (1 a year).

Sztutowo

Państwowe Muzeum Stutthof w Sztutowie (State Museum in Sztutowo): ul. Muzealna 6, 82-110 Sztutowo; tel. (55) 247-83-53; fax (55) 247-83-58; e-mail stutthof@stutthof.pl; internet www.stutthof.pl/en/main.htm; former Nazi concentration camp of Stutthof; f. 1962; Dir ROMUALD DRYNKO; publ. *Zeszyty Muzeum Stutthof* (1 a year).

Toruń

Muzeum Etnograficzne w Toruniu (Ethnographical Museum in Toruń): Wały gen. Sikorskiego 19, 87-100 Toruń; tel. (56) 622-80-91; fax (56) 622-89-44; internet www.zabytki.pl/sources/muzea/t/torun-etnograf.html; f. 1959; folk culture of northern Poland; library of 18,142 vols; Dir Dr HUBERT CZACHOWSKI; publ. *Rocznik Muzeum Etnograficznego w Toruniu* (1 a year).

Muzeum Okręgowe w Toruniu (District Museum in Toruń): Rynek Staromiejski 1, Ratusz, 87-100 Toruń; tel. (56) 622-36-84; fax (56) 622-40-29; e-mail muzeum@muzeum.torun.pl; internet www.muzeum.torun.pl; f. 1861; 14th- to 20th-century art (painting, graphics, sculpture, handicrafts), Far-Eastern art, history, archaeology, militaria, numismatics, Copernicus museum; library of 25,000 vols; Dir Dr ANNA KOSICKA; publ. *Rocznik Muzeum w Toruniu* (Toruń Museum Yearbook).

Warsaw

Muzeum Historyczne m. st. Warszawy (History Museum of the City of Warsaw): Rynek Starego Miasta 28, 00-272 Warsaw; tel. (22) 635-16-25; fax (22) 831-94-91; f. 1948; exhibits relating to the history of Warsaw from the 10th century; library of 42,000 vols; Dir Prof. JANUSZ DURKO; publ. *Almanach Muzealny* (every 2 years).

Muzeum i Instytut Zoologii PAN (Institute of Zoology): ul. Wilcza 64, 00-679 Warsaw; tel. (22) 629-32-21; fax (22) 629-63-02; e-mail sekretariat@miiz.waw.pl; internet www.miiz.waw.pl; f. 1819; attached to Polish Acad. of Sciences; research in various fields of zoology; molecular and 3-dimensional morphometrics laboratory; research station at Łomna near Warsaw; zoological collections of 8,178,000 specimens; archives and documents; library of 117,696 vols, 696 current periodicals, 4,953 maps; Dir Prof. WIESŁAW BOGDANOWICZ; publs *Acta Chiropterologica* (2 a year), *Acta Ornithologica* (2 a year), *Annales Zoologici* (4 a year), *Fragmenta Faunistica* (2 a year).

Muzeum Literatury im. Adama Mickiewicza (Adam Mickiewicz Museum of Literature): Rynek Starego Miasta 20, 00-272 Warsaw; tel. (22) 831-40-61; fax (22) 831-76-92; e-mail sekretariat@muzeumliteratury.pl; internet www.muzeumliteratury.pl; f. 1951; museum of literary history of Poland especially 19th and 20th centuries; library of 110,000 vols; Dir JANUSZ ODROWĄŻ-PIENIĄŻEK; publ. *Blok-Notes Muzeum Literatury*.

Muzeum Narodowe w Warsawie (National Museum in Warsaw): ul. Jerozolimskie 3, 00-495 Warsaw; tel. (22) 621-10-31; fax (22) 622-85-59; e-mail muzeum@mnw.art.pl; internet www.mnw.art.pl; f. 1862; paintings and sculpture; prints and drawings; numismatics; decorative arts and crafts; photography; Egyptian, Greek, Roman and Byzantine (Nubian) art; medieval and modern Polish art since 12th century; 14th- to 19th-century foreign painting; also administers the Poster Museum at Wilanów, Królikarnia Palace in Warsaw and, outside Warsaw, Nieborów Palace; Otwock Palace; library of 130,000 vols; Dir FERDYNAND RUSZCZYC; Dir for Colln, Research and Education Dr DOROTA FOLGA JANUSZEWSKA; publ. *Bulletin du Musée National de Varsovie* (4 a year).

Muzeum Niepodległości (Museum of Independence): ul. Solidarności 62, 00-240 Warsaw; tel. (22) 827-37-70; fax (22) 827-03-23; e-mail promocja@muzeumniepodleglosci.art.pl; internet www.muzeumniepodleglosci.art.pl; f. 1990; history of Polish independence movements; library of 29,230 vols, 3,960 periodicals; Dir Dr ANDRZEJ STAWARZ.

Muzeum Techniki w Warszawie (Warsaw Museum of Technology): Pałac Kultury i Nauki, 00-901 Warsaw; tel. (22) 656-67-59; fax (22) 620-47-10; f. 1875; popularization of science and technology and their history, preservation of monuments of technology; planetarium; cinema; local branches: Museum of Ancient Metallurgy in Nowa Słupia, Museum of the old Polish Basin in Sielpia, water-powered forges in Stara Kuźnica and Gdańsk, 19th-century blast furnace in Chlewiska, Museum of Industry in Old Rolling Mill, Warsaw; library of 17,160 vols; Dir JERZY JASIUK.

Muzeum Wojska Polskiego (Polish Military Museum): ul. Jerozolimskie 3, 00-495 Warsaw; tel. (22) 629-52-71; fax (22) 629-58-43; e-mail muzeumwp@muzeumwp.pl; internet www.muzeumwp.pl; f. 1920; colln of 79,000 weapons, uniforms, banners, decorations, etc; permanent exhibition showing Polish military history since 10th century; militaria from Asia, Africa, Australia; colln of modern paintings, sculptures and graphics; iconographic colln; conservation workshops for metal, textile, wooden, leather and paper exhibits; library of 40,000 vols; Dir Prof. JANUSZ CISEK; publ. *Muzealnictwo Wojskowe* (Military Museology, irregular).

Ogród Botaniczny—Centrum Zachowania Różnorodności Biologicznej PAN (Botanical Garden—Centre for the Conservation of Biological Diversity): 76, ul. Prawdziwa 2, POB 45, 02-973 Warsaw; tel. (22) 648-38-56; fax (22) 757-66-45; e-mail obpan@ikp.atm.com.pl; internet www.obpanwar.pl; f. 1974; attached to Polish Acad. of Sciences; conservation and evaluation of genetic resources of plants; library of 8,000 vols; Dir JERZY PUCHALSKI; publs *Biuletyn* (1 a year), *Prace* (reports, irregular).

Państwowe Muzeum Archeologiczne (State Archaeological Museum): ul. Długa 40, 00-950 Warsaw; tel. (22) 831-32-21; fax (22) 831-51-95; e-mail pma@pma.pl; internet www.pma.pl/main.html; f. 1923; prehistoric and proto-historic exhibits; organizes regional and field exhibitions, and carries out archaeological excavations throughout Poland; archaeological stores at Rybno; library of 55,000 vols; Dir Dr WOJCIECH BRZEZINSKI; publ. *Wiadomości Archeologiczne* (irregular).

Państwowe Muzeum Etnograficzne w Warszawie (State Ethnographic Museum in Warsaw): ul. Kredytowa 1, 00-056 Warsaw; tel. (22) 827-76-41; fax (22) 827-66-69; e-mail pme@pme.art.pl; internet www.pme.art.pl; f. 1888; Polish and non-European ethnographical collection; library of 23,000 vols; Dir Dr JAN WITOLD SULIGA; publ. *Zeszyty Państwowego Muzeum Etnograficznego w Warszawie* (Reports, 1 a year).

Polska Akademia Nauk Muzeum Ziemi w Warszawie (Museum of the Earth): ul. Na Skarpie 20–26, 00-488 Warsaw; tel. (22) 629-80-63; fax (22) 629-74-97; e-mail sekretariat@mz-pan.pl; internet www.mz-pan.pl; f. 1932; attached to Polish Acad. of Sciences; collns: Polish minerals, rocks, meteorites, fossil flora and fauna, Baltic amber; Dir Dr RYSZARD SZCZĘSNY; publ. *Prace Muzeum Ziemi PAN*.

Zamek Królewski w Warszawie—Pomnik Historii i Kultury Narodowej (Royal Castle in Warsaw, National History and Culture Memorial): Pl. Zamkowy 4, 00-277 Warsaw; tel. (22) 657-21-70; fax (22) 657-21-27; e-mail zamek@zamek-krolewski.art.pl; internet www.zamek-krolewski.art.pl; f. 1980; furniture, carpets and rugs, paintings, sculpture, applied arts, drawings, numismatics; library of 25,000 vols; Dir ANDRZEJ ROTTERMUND; publ. *Kronika Zamkowa* (2 a year).

Wieliczka

Muzeum Żup Krakowskich Wieliczka (Cracow Saltworks Museum in Wieliczka): Zamkowa 8, 32-020 Wieliczka; tel. (12) 422-19-47; fax (12) 278-30-28; e-mail promocja@muzeum.wieliczka.pl; internet www.muzeum.wieliczka.pl; f. 1951; history, archaeology, geology, history of art and ethnography, archives, metal conservation laboratory; library of 18,000 vols, spec. collns: photographs, mining maps; Dir Prof. ANTONI JODŁOWSKI; publ. *Studia i Materiały do Dziejów Żup Solnych w Polsce* (1 a year).

Wrocław

Muzeum Architektury (Museum of Architecture): ul. Bernardyńska 5, 50-156 Wrocław; tel. (71) 343-36-75; fax (71) 344-65-77; e-mail muzeum@ma.wroc.pl; internet www.ma.wroc.pl; f. 1965; Polish and other architecture; modern art; library of 7,000 vols; Dir Dr JERZY ILKOSZ.

Muzeum Historyczne we Wrocławiu (Historical Museum in Wrocław): ul. Sukiennice 14/15, 50-107 Wrocław; tel. (71) 44-57-30; fax (71) 44-47-85; f. 1970; Dir MACIEJ ŁAGIEWSKI.

Muzeum Narodowe we Wrocławiu (National Museum in Wrocław): Pl. Powstańców Warszawy 5, 50-153 Wrocław; tel. (71) 372-51-50; fax (71) 343-56-43; e-mail muzeumnarodowe@wr.onet.pl; internet www.mnwr.art.pl; f. 1948; collection of medieval art, Polish painting since 17th century, European painting since 16th century, decorative arts, prints, photographs, ethnography and history relating to Silesia, panoramic painting 'Battle of Racławice'; numismatics; library of 92,889 vols; Dir MARIUSZ HERMANSDORFER; publ. *Roczniki Sztuki Śląskiej* (1 a year).

Zakopane

Muzeum Tatrzańskie im. Tytusa Chałubińskiego (T. Chałubiński Tatra Museum): ul. Krupówki 10, 34-500 Zakopane; tel. (18) 201-52-05; fax (18) 206-38-72; e-mail biuro@muzeumtatrzanskie.pl; internet www.muzeumtatrzanskie.pl; f. 1888; main museum: geology, regional flora, fauna, history and ethnography; glass paintings, pottery, sculpture, wooden, metal and leather ware, costumes, musical instruments, etc.; museum of the Zakopane style—inspirations (local culture sources of the style); museum of the Zakopane style (architecture, furniture, textiles, ceramics and jewellery plus pastels by St Ignacy Witkiewicz); Wł. Hasior Art Gallery; Kornel Makuszyński Museum; art gallery in Koziniec (temporary exhibitions) and 4 brs outside Podhale and Spisz regions; library of 50,000 vols; Dir Mgr TERESA JABŁOŃSKA; publ. *Rocznik Podhalański*.

Universities

KATOLICKI UNIWERSYTET LUBELSKI JANA PAWŁA II
(John Paul II Catholic University of Lublin)

ul. Racławickie 14, 20-950 Lublin

Telephone: (81) 445-41-05
Fax: (81) 445-41-91
E-mail: dwz@kul.lublin.pl
Internet: www.kul.lublin.pl

Founded 1918
Private control
Academic year: October to June

Chancellor: Archbp Prof. Dr hab. JÓZEF ŻYCIŃSKI
Rector: Rev. Prof. Dr hab. STANISŁAW WILK
Vice-Rector for Admin. and Finances: Prof. Dr hab. STANISŁAW ZIĘBA
Vice-Rector for Research, and Int. and Public Relations: Rev. Prof. Dr hab. SŁAWOMIR NOWOSAD
Vice-Rector for Didactics and Education: Prof. Dr hab. JÓZEF FERT
Librarian: Rev. Dr TADEUSZ STOLZ

Library of 1,800,000 vols (incl. dept libraries) of which 1,000,000 books, 50,000 old books, 35,000 vols of periodicals, 5,000 MSS, 3,000 maps and atlases, 10,000 music scores, 10,000 audio cassettes and records, 15,000 graphic items

Number of teachers: 1,185
Number of students: 18,672

Publications: *Acta Mediaevalia*, *Człowiek i Przyroda* (2 a year), *Ethos* (4 a year), *KERYGS* (2 a year), *Law–Administration–Church* (4 a year), *Przegląd Uniwersytecki* (6 a year), *Roczniki Filozoficzne* (1 a year), *Roczniki Humanistyczne* (1 a year), *Roczniki Nauk Prawnych* (1 a year), *Roczniki Nauk Społecznych* (1 a year), *Roczniki Psychologiczne* (1 a year), *Roczniki Teologiczne* (1 a year), *Studia Norwidiana* (1 a year), *Studia Polonijne* (1 a year), *Summarium*, *Zeszyty Naukowe KUL* (4 a year), *Vox Patrum* (2 a year)

DEANS

Faculty of Humanities: Prof. Dr hab. KRZYSZTOF NARECKI
Faculty of Law, Canon Law and Administration: Rev. Prof. Dr hab. ANTONI DĘBIŃSKI
Faculty of Mathematics and Natural Sciences: Rev. Prof. Dr hab. RYSZARD SMARZEWSKI
Faculty of Philosophy: Prof. Dr hab. STANISŁAW JANECZEK
Faculty of Social Sciences: Prof. Dr hab. ANDRZEJ SĘKOWSKI
Faculty of Theology: Rev. Prof. Dr hab. MIROSŁAW KALINOWSKI
Off-Campus Faculty of Legal and Economic Sciences: Rev. Prof. Dr hab. JAN ZIMNY (Stalowa Wola): Rev. Prof. Dr hab. TADEUSZ GUZ (Tomaszów Lubelski)
Satellite Faculty of Social Sciences: Rev. Prof. Dr hab. MARIAN WOLICKI

PROFESSORS

Faculty of Humanities (tel. (81) 445-41-45; fax (81) 445-41-90):

ANDRUSIW, S., Ukrainian Literature
CHODKOWSKI, R., Classical Linguistics, Greek Literature
DEPTUA, C., History of Medieval Culture
ECKMANN, A., Classical Linguistics, Ancient Christian Literature
KACZMAREK, W., Drama and Theatre
KNAPIŃSKI, R., Art History
KONEFAŁ, J., 19th–20th Centuries History of Social and Political Movements
KUCZYŃSKA, J., Medieval Polish Art
LAMEŃSKI, L., Modern Art History

MAZURCZAK, M., General Medieval Art History
MAKARSKI, W., Linguistics
OŁDAKOWSK, M., Contemporary Literature
PODBIELSKI, H., Classical Greek Philology
WOŹNIAK, A., Russian Literature

Faculty of Law, Canon Law and Administration (tel. (81) 445-37-31; fax (81) 445-37-26; e-mail prawa@kul.lublin.pl):

CIOCH, H., Civil Law
DĘBIŃSKI, A., Roman Law
HRYSZCZUK, W., Medical Law and Forensic Medicine
KOŚĆ, A., Philosophy of Law
KRUKOWSKI, J., Canon Law
ŁĄCZKOWSKI, W., Financial Law, Administrative Law
MISZTAL, H., Canon Law, Law and Religion
SZAJKOWSKI, A., Commercial Law
TYSZCZYK, B., History of State and Law
WITCZAK, W., Forensic Medicine
ZUBERT, B., Canon Law

Faculty of Mathematics and Natural Sciences (tel. (81) 445-45-52; fax (81) 445-35-36):

CICHOCKA, E., Agriculture
FISCHER-MALANOWSKA, Z., Ecology
GOSZCZYŃSKI, W., Horticulture
HOŁUBIEC, J., Numerical Analysis and Programming
JANICKI, A., Information Technology
MATUS, P., Mathematics
RZYMOWSKI, W., Mathematics Application
SKOWRONSKI, T., Toxicology
STĘPNIEWSKA, Z., Agricultural Engineering
SZESZKO, M., Mathematics and Computer Science
SZYSZKA, R., Molecular Biology
URBANOWICZ, P., Computer Science
WOJCIECHOWSKA, W., Ecology, Hydrobiology
ZIĘBA, S., Humanistic Ecology

Faculty of Philosophy (tel. (81) 445-42-51; fax (81) 445-41-90; e-mail filozofia@kul.lublin.pl):

BRONK, A., Philosophy of Science
GAŁKOWSKI, J., Ethics, Political Philosophy
KICZUK, S., Logic
MARYNIARCZYK, A., Metaphysics
SZOSTEK, A., Ethics
WIELGUS, S., History of Philosophy, Medieval Philosophy
ZIELIŃSKI, E., History of Ancient and Medieval Philosophy
ŻYCIŃSKI, J., Philosophy of Nature, Philosophy of Science

Faculty of Social Sciences (tel. (81) 445-35-48; fax (81) 445-42-93; e-mail wns@kul.lublin.pl):

BIELA, A., Experimental Psychology, Industrial Psychology, Environmental Psychology
BRAUN-GAŁKOWSKA, M., Educational Psychology, Family Psychology
DYCZEWSKI, L., Sociology of Culture, Sociology of Family
GILOWSKA, Z., Economics, Local Finance
MARIAŃSKI, J., Sociology of Religion, Sociology of Morals
SĘKOWSKI, A., Rehabilitative Psychology
WÓJCIK, S., Sociology, Local Policy
ZALESKI, Z., Experimental Psychology

Faculty of Theology (tel. (81) 445-38-41; fax (81) 445-38-45; e-mail teolog@kul.lublin.pl):

DRĄCZKOWSKI, F., Patristics
GŁOWA, W., Pastoral Theology, Liturgy
KAMIŃSKI, R., Pastoral Theology, Organization of Pastoral Care
PACIOREK, A., Biblical Studies
RUBINKIEWICZ, R., Biblical Studies
RUSECKI, M., Fundamental Theology
TRONINA, A., Biblical Studies
WITCZYK, H., Biblical Studies
WILK, S., History of Monasteries

ZASĘPA, T., Contemporary Forms of Communication of the Faith
ZIMOŃ, H., Religious Studies

Off-Campus Faculty of Legal and Economic Sciences (ul. Lwowska 68, 22-600 Tomaszow Lubelski; tel. and fax (84) 664-45-74):

ANTONOWICZ, L., International Public Law
CZEREWKO, G., Theory of Economics
KOSSAK, W., Civil Law
KRUKOWSKI, J., Theory of Law
MISZTAL, H., Canon Law
SRUTWA, J., Church History of Law
WOJCIECHOWSKI, W., Econometrics and Statistics

Satellite Faculty of Social Sciences (ul. Ofiar Katynia 6, 37-450 Stalowa Wola; tel. (15) 642-25-35):

NYCZKAŁO, N., Education
WOLICKI, M., Education

SZKOŁA GŁÓWNA GOSPODARSTWA WIEJSKIEGO W WARSZAWIE
(Warsaw University of Life Sciences–SGGW(WULS-SGGW))

ul. Nowoursynowska 166, 02-787 Warsaw

Telephone: (22) 593-10-00
Fax: (22) 593-10-87
E-mail: rektor@sggw.pl
Internet: www.sggw.pl

Founded 1816
Languages of instruction: English, Polish
Academic year: October to June

Chancellor: Dr WŁADYSŁAW SKARŻYŃSKI
Rector: Prof. Dr. hab. ALOJZY SZYMAŃSKI
Pro-Rector for Devt: Prof. Dr hab. WIESŁAW SKARŻYŃSKI
Pro-Rector for Didactics: Prof. Dr hab. KRYSTYNA GUTKOWSKA
Pro-Rector for Science: Prof. Dr hab. JAN NIEMIEC
Librarian: Mgr JERZY LEWANDOWSKI

Library of 249,151 books, 149,597 vols of periodicals
Number of teachers: 1,266
Number of students: 27,108

Publication: *Annals* (in 8 series)

DEANS

Faculty of Agriculture and Biology: Prof. Dr hab. GRAŻYNA GARBACZEWSKA
Faculty of Animal Science: Prof. Dr hab. PIOTR BRZOZOWSKI
Faculty of Applied Informatics and Mathematics: Prof. Dr hab. BOLESŁAW BORKOWSKI
Faculty of Economic Sciences: Prof. Dr hab. BOGDAN KLEPACKI
Faculty of Engineering and Environmental Science: Prof. Dr hab. JERZY JEZNACH
Faculty of Food Sciences: Prof. Dr hab. DOROTA WITROWA-RAJCHERT
Faculty of Forestry: Prof. Dr hab. MICHAŁ ZASADA
Faculty of Horticulture and Landscape Architecture: Dr hab. MAREK SZYNDEL
Faculty of Humanities: Dr hab. FRANCISZEK KAMPKA
Faculty of Human Nutrition and Consumer Sciences: Prof. Dr hab. JOANNA GROMADZKA
Faculty of Production Engineering: Prof. Dr hab. ANDRZEJ CHOCHOWSKI
Faculty of Veterinary Medicine: Prof. Dr hab. MARIAN BINEK
Faculty of Wood Technology: Dr hab. ADAM KRAJEWSKI

PROFESSORS

Faculty of Agriculture and Biology (02-776 Warsaw, ul. Nowoursynowska 159; tel. (22) 593-25-19; fax (22) 593-25-06; e-mail dwrb@sggw.pl):

BIELAWSKI, W., Biochemistry

BLASZCZYK, M., Biochemistry
BOGATEK – LESZCZYNSKA, R., Plant Physiology
CHOJNICKI, J., Soil Science
CZEPINSKA – KAMINSKA, D., Soil Science
GARBACZEWSKA, G., Botany
GOLINOWSKI, W., Botany
GWOREK, B., Soil Science
KOZANECKA, T., Soil Science
KUSINSKA, A., Soil Science
LABETOWICZ, J., Agrochemistry
LENART, S., Soil and Land Management
LOBOCKA, M., Biochemistry
MADRY, W., Mathematical Statistics And Experimentation
PIETKIEWICZ, S., Plant Physiology
PODLASKI, S., Plant Physiology
PRACZ, J., Soil Science
RADECKI, A., Soil and Land Management
ROZBICKI, J., Crop Production
RUSSEL, S., Biochemistry
RUTKOWSKA, B., Agrochemistry
STYPINSKI, P., Agronomy
WYSZYNSKI, Z., Crop Production
ZAGDANSKA, B., Biochemistry
ZAGORSKI, Z., Soil Science

Faculty of Animal Science (02-786 Warsaw, ul. Ciszewskiego 8; tel. (22) 593-65-06; fax (22) 593-65-10; e-mail dwnz@sggw.pl):

BRZOZOWSKI, M., Fur Animal Breeding
BRZOZOWSKI, P., Cattle Breeding
CHARON, K., Animal Genetics
CHRZANOWSKI, S., Horse Breeding
DYMNICKA, M., Animal Nutrition
GRODZKI, H., Cattle Breeding
KALETA, T., Animal Genetics
KAMIONEK, M., Zoology
KOSLA, T., Animal Hygiene
KULISIEWICZ, J., Swine Breeding
MICHALSKA, E., Animal Genetics
NALECZ-TARWACKA, T., Cattle Breeding
NIEMIEC, J., Poultry Breeding
NIZNIKOWSKI, R., Sheep and Goats Breeding
OLECH-PIASECKA, W., Animal Genetics
OSTASZEWSKA, T., Ichthyobiology and Fisheries
PEZOWICZ, E., Zoology
RADZIK-RANT, A., Sheep and Goats Breeding
REKIEL, A., Animal Breeding
SAWOSZ-CHWALIBOG, E., Animal Nutrition, Biotechnology
SCIESINSKI, K., Animal Breeding
SKOMIAL, J., Animal Nutrition
SOKOL, J., Economics, Animal Nutrition
ZARSKI, T., Animal Hygiene

Faculty of Applied Informatics and Mathematics (02-776 Warsaw, ul. Nowoursynowska 159; tel. (22) 593-72-10; fax (22) 593-72-11; e-mail wzim@sggw.pl):

BINDERMAN, Z., Mathematics
BORKOWSKI, B., Econometrics
CHMIELEWSKI, L., Informatics
CIARKOWSKI, A., Computer Applications
JANOWICZ, M., Physics
JEZIERSKI, J., Mathematics
LAUDANSKI, Z., Biometrics
ORLOWSKI, A., Physics
RUSEK, M., Physics
SMOLIK, S., Econometrics
STRASBURGER, A., Mathematics
SZCZESNY, W., Informatics
TWARDOWSKA, K., Mathematics
WIERZBICKI, E., Technical Applications
WITKOWSKA, D., Econometrics, Financial Engineering
ZAWISTOWSKI, Z., Computer Applications
ZIELINSKI, W., Statistics and Biometrics
ZUBEREK, W., Informatics

Faculty of Economic Sciences (02-787 Warsaw, ul. Nowoursynowska 166; tel. and fax (22) 593-40-10; e-mail dwne@sggw.pl):

BAGIENSKI, S., Organization and Management
JEDRZEJCZYK, I., Law and Finances
JUSZCZYK, S., Banking
KLEPACKI, B., Economics of Production and Logistics
KRZYZANOWSKA, K., Communication
KRZYZANOWSKI, J., International Economic Relations
MAJEWSKI, E., Organization and Management
MANTEUFFEL, H., International Economic Relations
PODSTAWKA, M., Law and Finances
PUDELKIEWICZ, E., Marketing
RUNOWSKI, H., Organization and Management
SAWICKA, J., Agrarian Policy and Law
SIKORSKA-WOLAK, I., Rural Development
STANKO, S., Agricultural Economics
SZWACKA-MOKRZYCKA, J., Marketing
WASILEWSKI, M., Accountancy, Banking
WOJCICKI, W., Economic Policies
WOLOSZYN, J., Organization
ZIETARA, W., Organization and Management

Faculty of Engineering and Environmental Science (02-776 Warsaw, ul. Nowoursynowska 159; tel. (22) 593-50-10; fax (22) 593-50-15; e-mail dwiks@sggw.pl):

BANASIK, K., Hydrology, Erosion and Sedimentation
BUCZKOWSKI, W., Civil Engineering
GARBULEWSKI, K., Environmental Geotechnics
HEWELKE, P., Environmental Improvement
IGNAR, S., Hydrology, Water Management
JEZNACH, J., Environmental Improvement, Drainage and Irrigation
KERNYTSKYY, I., Descriptive Geometry
KUBRAK, J., Hydraulics
LECHOWICZ, Z., Environmental Geotechnics
MOSIEJ, J., Environmental Improvement
NAGORKO, W., Civil Engineering
OKRUSZKO, T., Hydrology
PIEKUT, K., Natural Bases of Environmental Engineering
PIERZGALSKI, E., Environmental Improvement, Drainage and Irrigation
POLONSKI, M., Engineering Management
POPEK, Z., Water Engineering
SZYMANSKI, A., Geotechnical Engineering
WAGROWSKA, M., Civil Engineering
WYSOCKI, J., Geodesy
ZELAZO, J., Water Engineering
ZOLTOWSKI, W., Civil Engineering

Faculty of Food Sciences (02-776 Warsaw, ul. Nowoursynowska 159C; tel. (22) 593-75-07; fax (22) 593-75-05; e-mail dwnoz@sggw.pl):

BIALECKA-FLORJANCZYK, E., Organic Chemistry
BLAZEJAK, S., Biotechnology, Microbiology
CEGLINSKA, A., Crop Technology
GNIEWOSZ, M., Biotechnology, Microbiology
KAZIMIERCZUK, Z., Food Chemistry
KOWALCZYK, R., Food Engineering
KOWALSKI, B., Food Chemistry
KRYGIER, K., Fats and Oils Technology
LENART, A., Food Engineering
MITEK, M., Fruit and Vegetables Technology
MROCZEK, J., Meat Technology
OBIEDZINSKI, M., Food Quality
ORZESZKO, A., Organic Chemistry
PALACHA, Z., Food Engineering
PISULA, A., Meat Technology
RACZYNSKA, E., Organic Chemistry
SLOWINSKI, M., Meat Technology
WITROWA-RAJCHERT, D., Food Engineering

Faculty of Forestry (02-776 Warsaw, ul. Nowoursynowska 159; tel. (22) 593-80-10; fax (22) 593-80-08; e-mail dwl@sggw.pl):

ALEKSANDROWICZ – TRZCINSKA, M., Mycology and Forest Pathology

ANDRZEJCZYK, T., Silviculture
BEDKOWSKI, K., GIS in Forestry
BORECKI, T., Forest Management
BOROWSKI, J., Forest Entomology
BRZEZIECKI, B., Silviculture, Forest Management
DUDEK, A., Dendrometry
GOSZCZYNSKI, J., Forest Zoology
GRZYWACZ, A., Mycology and Forest Pathology
KLAPEC, B., Forestry Economics
MAZUR, S., Entomology and Forest Protection
MISCICKI, S., Forest Management
MOSKALIK, T., Forest Resources Utilisation
MOZGAWA, J., GIS in Forestry
OLENDEREK, H., GIS in Forestry
PASCHALIS-JAKUBOWICZ, P., Forest Resources Utilisation
PLOTKOWSKI, L., Forestry Economics
PORTER, B., Forest Resources Utilisation
SKLODOWSKI, J., Entomology and Forest Protection
STEPIEN, E., Forest Management
TARASIUK, S., Silviculture, Forest Management
TRACZ, H., Forest Entomology and Ecology
WASILEWSKI, M., Forest Zoology
WERKA, J., Forest Zoology
ZAJACZKOWSKI, S., Botany, Tree Physiology
ZAKRZEWSKI, J., Botany
ZYBURA, H., Silviculture, Forest Management

Faculty of Horticulture and Landscape Architecture (02-776 Warsaw, ul. Nowoursynowska 159; tel. (22) 593-20-10; fax (22) 593-20-11; e-mail dwoa@sggw.pl):

BURZA, W., Plant Genetics, Breeding and Biotechnology
DABROWSKI, Z., Applied Entomology
GAJC-WOLSKA, J., Vegetable and Medicinal Plants
GAJEWSKI, M., Vegetable and Medicinal Plants
GAWRONSKA, H., Natural Sciences in Horticulture
GAWRONSKI, W., Natural Sciences in Horticulture
IGNATOWICZ, S., Applied Entomology
JABLONSKA, L., Horticultural Economics
JADCZUK-TOBJASZ, E., Pomology
KARPINSKI, S., Plant Genetics, Breeding and Biotechnology
KIELKIEWICZ, M., Applied Entomology
KOBRYN, J., Vegetable and Medicinal Plants
KOSMALA, M., Landscape Art
KOZLOWSKI, M., Applied Entomology
KROLIKOWSKI, J., Landscape Art
LUKASZEWSKA, A., Ornamental Plants
MALESZY, S., Plant Genetics, Breeding and Biotechnology
NIEMIROWICZ-SZCZYTT, K., Plant Genetics, Breeding and Biotechnology
OSINSKA, E., Vegetable and Medicinal Plants
PADUCH-CICHAL, E., Plant Pathology
PLANDER, W., Plant Genetics, Breeding and Biotechnology
PRZYBECKI, Z., Plant Genetics, Breeding and Biotechnology
PRZYBYLA, A., Pomology
RAKOCZY-TROJANOWSKA, M., Plant Genetics, Breeding and Biotechnology
RYLKE, J., Landscape Art
SZULCZEWSKA, B., Landscape Architecture
SZYNDEL, M., Plant Pathology
SZYSZKO, J., Evaluation and Assessment of Natural Resources
TOMALA, K., Pomology
TOMCZYK, A., Applied Entomology
WAKULINSKI, W., Plant Pathology
WEGLARZ, Z., Vegetable and Medicinal Plants
WYSOCKI, C., Environmental Protection

ZARSKA, B., Environmental Protection

Faculty of Humanities (02-787 Warsaw, ul. Nowoursynowska 166; tel. (22) 593-47-10; fax (22) 593-47-01; e-mail dwnh@sggw.pl):

BLESZYNSKA, K., Pedagogy
BOBRYK, J., Psychology
CZAPLIGO-SIKORSKA, J., Sociology
GRYKO, C., Sociology
JEDRZEJKO, M., Pedagogy
KAMPKA, F., Sociology, Political Science
KORAB, K., Rural Sociology, Social Communication
LASTAWSKI, K., Political Science
PODEDWORNA, H., Sociology
PRZYCHODZEN, Z., Pedagogy, Sociology
SNIHUR, S., Philosophy
STEPKA, S., Political Science, History
WALKIEWICZ, W., Political Science
WOJTOWICZ, A., Sociology
ZANIEWSKA, T., Pedagogy, Sociology of Culture

Faculty of Human Nutrition and Consumer Sciences (02-776 Warsaw, ul. Nowoursynowska 159C; tel. (22) 593-70-10; fax (22) 593-70-15; e-mail dwnzk@sggw.pl):

BRZOZOWSKA, A., Human Nutrition
FILIP, R., Gastroenterology, Dietetics
GROMADZKA-OSTROWSKA, J., Nutritional Physiology, Dietetics, Reproductive Regulation
GRONOWSKA-SENGER, A., Human Nutrition
GUTKOWSKA, K., Consumer Behaviour, Marketing Research
KAWECKA, W., Human Immunology, Medical Mycology
KOLOZYN-KRAJEWSKA, D., Food Technology, Food Hygiene and Microbiology
KOWRYGO, B., Food Policy and Management
LASKOWSKI, W., Consumption Research
OZIMEK, I., Consumer Protection, Consumer Behaviour
PRZYBYLSKI, W., Catering Technology, Meat Science
REMBIALKOWSKA, M., Organic Agriculture, Food Quality
ROSOLOWSKA-HUSZCZ, D., Dietetics, Nutritional Physiology
SWIDERSKI, F., Functional Food and Commodities
WASZKIEWICZ-ROBAK, B., Functional Food and Commodities
WIERZBICKA, A., Food Engineering; Food Quality

Faculty of Production Engineering (02-787 Warsaw, ul. Nowoursynowska 164; tel. and fax (22) 593-45-01; e-mail dwip@sggw.pl):

BULINSKI, J., Agricultural and Forest Machinery
CHOCHOWSKI, A., Energy Management
FABIRKIEWICZ, A., Production Engineering
GACH, S., Farm Machinery
JAROS, M., Agricultural Engineering
KALETA, A., Technical Sciences
KLIMKIEWICZ, M., Technical Infrastructure
KRAWIEC, F., Production Organization and Management
KUPCZYK, F., Production Organization and Management
LISOWSKI, A., Agricultural and Forest Machinery
MAJEWSKI, Z., Production Engineering
SKROBACKI, A., Production Engineering
SZTYBER, J., Forestry Mechanization
TRAJER, J., Technical Sciences
WASCINSKI, T., Production Organization and Management
WASZKIEWICZ, C., Farm Machinery
WOJDALSKI, J., Technical Infrastructure

Faculty of Veterinary Medicine (02-776 Warsaw, ul. Nowoursynowska 159; tel. and fax (22) 593-60-15; e-mail dwmw@sggw.pl):

BINEK, M., Bacteriology, Molecular Biology

BORYCZKO, Z., Animal Gynaecology, Animal Reproduction
DEBSKI, B., Biochemistry
FRYMUS, T., Veterinary Epidemiology
GRALAK, M., Animal Physiology
KANIA, B., Animal Physiology
KATKIEWICZ, M., Animal Gynaecology, Animal Reproduction
KLECZKOWSKI, M., Clinical Diagnosis, Internal Medicine
KLUCINSKI, W., Clinical Diagnosis, Internal Medicine
KOBRYN, H., Anatomy
LECHOWSKI, R., Internal Medicine
LEONTOWICZ, H., Animal Dietetics
MALINOWSKI, E., Livestock Disease, Internal Medicine
MOTYL, T., Animal Physiology
NIEMIALTOWSKI, M., Preclinical Science, Animal Immunology
ORZECHOWSKI, A., Animal Physiology
OSTASZEWSKI, P., Animal Dietetics
SYSA, P., Histology and Embryology
SZCZAWINSKI, J., Hygiene of Food of Animal Origin
WEDRYCHOWICZ, H., Parasitology
WIECHETEK, M., Pharmacology, Toxicology
ZABIELSKI, R., Animal Physiology

Faculty of Wood Technology (02-776 Warsaw, ul. Nowoursynowska 159; tel. (22) 593-85-10; fax (22) 593-85-15; e-mail dwtd@sggw.pl):

BAJKOWSKI, B., Mechanical Processing of Wood
BEER, P., Furniture Quality and Technology
DOLOWY, K., Physics
DZBENSKI, W., Wood Science
GORSKI, J., Mechanical Processing of Wood
KRAJEWSKI, A., Wood Protection
KRAJEWSKI, J., Wood Protection
KRUTUL, D., Wood Science
NICEWICZ, D., Composite Wood Products
OSIPIUK, J., Mechanization and Automatization
SWACZYNA, I., Construction and Technology of Final Wood Products
ZIELONKA, P., Economics

UNIWERSYTET GDAŃSKI
(University of Gdańsk)

Ul. Bażyńskiego 1A, 80-952 Gdańsk
Telephone: (58) 523-24-00
Fax: (58) 552-03-11
E-mail: rekug@ug.gda.pl
Internet: www.ug.edu.pl

Founded 1970
State control
Academic year: October to June

Rector: Prof. Dr hab. BERNARD LAMMEK
Pro-Rectors: Prof. Dr hab. MARIA MENDEL, Prof. Dr hab. GRZEGORZ WĘGRZYN, Prof. Dr hab. MIROSŁAW KRAJEWSKI, Prof. Dr hab. JÓZEF WŁODARSKI
Admin. Dir: Dr JERZY GWIZDAŁA
Librarian: Mgr URSZULA SAWICKA
Library: see Libraries and Archives
Number of teachers: 1,700
Number of students: 32,000

Publications: *Prace Habilitacyjne*, *Skrypty*, *Zeszyty Naukowe*

DEANS
Faculty of Biology: Prof. Dr hab. DARIUSZ SZLACHETKO
Faculty of Chemistry: Prof. Dr hab. Inż. ANDRZEJ WIŚNIEWSKI
Faculty of Economics: Prof. Dr hab. KRZYSZTOF DOBROWOLSKI
Faculty of History: Prof. Dr hab. ZBIGNIEW OPACKI
Faculty of Languages: Prof. Dr hab. ANDRZEJ CEYNOWA

Faculty of Law and Administration: Prof. Dr hab. JAROSŁAW WARYLEWSKI
Faculty of Management: Prof. Dr hab. JERZY BIELIŃSKI
Faculty of Mathematics, Physics and Informatics: Prof. Dr hab. WŁADYSŁAW ADAM MAJEWSKI
Faculty of Oceanography and Geography: Prof. Dr hab. ADAM KRĘŻEL
Faculty of Social Sciences: Prof. Dr hab. BEATA PASTWA-WOJCIECHOWSKA
Intercollegiate Faculty of Biotechnology of University of Gdańsk and Medical University of Gdańsk: Prof. Dr hab. EWA ŁOJKOWSKA

UNIWERSYTET ŁÓDZKI
(University of Łódź)

Narutowicza 65, 90-131 Łódź
Telephone: (42) 365-40-00
Fax: (42) 678-39-58
E-mail: rektorat@uni.lodz.pl
Internet: www.uni.lodz.pl

Founded 1945
State control
Language of instruction: Polish
Academic year: October to September

Rector: Prof. Dr hab. WLODZIMIERZ NYKIEL
Pro-Rector for Economic Relations: Prof. Dr hab. BOGDAN GREGOR
Pro-Rector for Int. Relations: Prof. Dr hab. ZOFIA WYSOKINSKA
Pro-Rector for Research: Prof. Dr hab. JOANNA JABLKOWSKA
Pro-Rector for Students: Prof. Dr hab. PAWEL MASLANKA
Pro-Rector for Teaching: Prof. Dr hab. ANTONII ROZALSKI
Admin. Dir: Dr JAROSLAW GRABARCZYK
Librarian: Dr JAN JANIAK
Library: see Libraries and Archives
Number of teachers: 2,355
Number of students: 43,000

Publications: *Acta Universitatis Lodziensis* (Research Bulletin), *Kronika Uniwersitetu Łódzkiego*

DEANS
Faculty of Biology and Environmental Protection: Prof. Dr hab. ELZBIETA ZADZINSKA
Faculty of Chemistry: Prof. Dr hab. BOGUSLAW KRYCZKA
Faculty of Economics and Sociology: Prof. Dr hab. JAN GAJDA
Faculty of Educational Sciences: Prof. Dr hab. GRZEGORZ MICHALSKI
Faculty of Geographical Sciences: Prof. Dr hab. TADEUSZ MARSZAL
Faculty of International and Political Studies: Prof. Dr hab. TOMASZ DOMANSKI
Faculty of Law and Administration: Prof. Dr hab. AGNIESZKA LISZEWSKA
Faculty of Management: Prof. Dr hab. EWA WALINSKA
Faculty of Mathematics: Prof. Dr hab. RYSZARD PAWLAK
Faculty of Philology: Prof. Dr hab. PIOTR STALMASZCZYK
Faculty of Philosophy and History: Prof. Dr hab. ZBIGNIEW ANUSIK
Faculty of Physics and Applied Informatics: Prof. Dr ANNA URBANIAK-KUCHARCZYK

PROFESSORS
Faculty of Biology and Environmental Protection (ul. Pilarskiego 14, 90-231 Łódź; tel. (42) 635-40-16; fax (42) 635-45-06; e-mail dziekan@biol.uni.lodz.pl):

BAŃBURA, J., Biology, Ecology
BARTOSZ, G., Biophysics
BŁASIAK, J., Molecular Genetics
BRYSZEWSKA, M., Biophysics
DŁUGOŃSKI, J., Microbiology

DUDA, W., Biochemistry
GABARA, B., Cytology and Cytochemistry
GALICKA, W., Ecology and Zoology of Vertebrates
GAŹDZICKI, A., Geology
GRZYBKOWSKA, M., Zoology, Ecology
GWOŹDZIŃSKI, K., Molecular Biology
HEREŹNIAK, J., Biology
JAKUBOWSKA-GABARA, J., Geobotany
JANAS, K., Plant Physiology
JAWORSKI, A., Microbiology
JAŻDŻEWSKI, K., Zoology
JÓŹWIAK, Z., Biochemistry
KACA, W., Microbiology
KILIAŃSKA, Z., Biochemistry
KONOPACKI, J., Neurophysiology
KRAJEWSKA, W., Biochemistry
KUKULSKA-GOŚCICKA, T., Immunology
KWIATKOWSKA, M., Plant Cytology and Cytochemistry
ŁAWRYNOWICZ, M., Botany, Mycology
LIGOWSKI, R., Biology, Oceanography
LIPIŃSKA, A., Biochemistry
LISZEWSKI, S., Economic Geography
MARKOWSKI, J., Biology, Theriology
MASZEWSKI, J., Cell Biology
OLACZEK, R., Plant Systems and Geography
PENCZAK, T., Zoology, Fish Ecology
PIECHOCKI, A., Zoology
ROMANIUK, A., Animal Physiology and Neurophysiology
RÓŻALSKA, B., Infectious Biology
RÓŻALSKI, A., Microbiology
RUDNICKA, W., Immunology
SIDORCZYK, Z., Microbiology
SZWEDA-LEWANDOWSKA, Z., Molecular Biophysics
URBANEK, H., Biochemistry
WACHOWICZ, B., Biochemistry
ZALEWSKI, M., Biology

Faculty of Economics and Sociology (ul. Polskiej Organizacji Wojskowej 3/5, 90-255 Łódź; tel. (42) 635-51-12; fax (42) 635-50-32; e-mail dziekes@uni.lodz.pl):

BOKSZAŃSKI, Z., Cultural Sociology
BORKOWSKA, S., Business Administration
BUCHNER-JEZIORSKA, A., Sociology
DĘBSKI, W., Commerce and International Finance
DOKTÓR, K., Industrial Sociology
DOMAŃSKI, C., Statistics
DURAJ, J., Economics and Organization of Industry
GAJDA, J., Economics
JÓZEFIAK, C., Economics
KOCIK, L., Sociology
KRYŃSKA, E., Economics, Economic Policy
KUCHARSKA-STASIAK, E., Economics of Urban Development
KULPIŃSKA, J., Industrial Sociology
KWIATKOWSKI, E., Theory of Economy
LEWANDOWSKA, L., Economics, Industrial Economics
MARSZAŁEK, A., Economics
MILO, W., Econometrics, Statistics
MORTIMER-SZYMCZAK, H., Planning and Economic Policy
PIĄTKOWSKI, W., History of Economic Theory
PIOTROWSKA-MARCZAK, K., Finance
RUDOLF, S., Political Economy of Capitalism
SKODLARSKI, J., International Economic Relations
SUCHECKA, J., Economics
SUŁKOWSKI, B., Cultural Sociology
TOMASZEWICZ, Ł., Econometrics
TRZASKALIK, T., Economics
WARZYWODA-KRUSZYŃSKA, W., Sociology
WELFE, A., Econometrics
WELFE, W., Econometrics and Statistics
WOJCIECHOWSKI, E., Economics of Urban Development

Faculty of Educational Sciences (ul. Kopernika 55, 90-553 Łódź; tel. (42) 639-07-76; fax (42) 639-07-77):

BŁASZCZYK, J., Physical Education
BŁASZCZYK, T., Science of Art
BUCZYŃSKI, A., Physical Education
DOWLASZ, B., Music Education
FLORKOWSKI, A., Psychology
JAŁMUŻNA, T., Pedagogy
KACZOROWSKI, S., Science of Art
KĘDZIORA, J., Biochemistry
KOCUR, J., Psychiatry
MARYNOWICZ-HETKA, E., Social Pedagogy
ORKISZ, S., Physical Education and Health
PAŃCZYK, J., Pedagogy
ŚLIWERSKI, B., Pedagogy
WIERZBIŃSKI, A., Music Education
WÓDKA, B., Science of Art

Faculty of Geographical Sciences (ul. Pilarskiego 14/16, 90-231 Łódź; tel. (42) 635-45-09; e-mail dziekan@geo.uni.lodz.pl):

BACHVAROV, M., Urban Geography and Tourism
HEFFNER, K., Political Geography and Regional Studies
JELONEK, A., Social and Economic Geography
KŁYSIK, C., Climatology and Meteorology
KOTER, M., Environmental Biophysics
KOWALCZYK, A., Urban Geography and Tourism
KOŻUCHOWSKI, K., Physical Geography
LASKOWSKI, S., Pedology
LISZEWSKI, S., Economic Geography
MARSZAŁ, T., Social and Economic Geography
MATCZAK, A., Urban Geography
WERWICKI, A., Economic Geography

Faculty of International and Political Studies (ul. Składowa 41/43, 90-127 Łódź; tel. (42) 675-42-74; fax (42) 678-49-16; e-mail interul@uni.lodz.pl):

DE LAZARI, A., Eastern Studies
DOMAŃSKI, T., Euromarketing
DUBICKI, T., History
DZIEKAN, M., History of Arabic Literature
KMIECIŃSKI, J., Archaeology
KUCZYŃSKI, K. A., German Literature
MICHOWICZ, W., History of International Relations (Dir)
OLEKSY, E., American Literature
PRZEBINDA, G., Russian Philology

Faculty of Law and Administration (ul. Składowa 43, 90-127 Łódź; tel. (42) 635-40-21; fax (42) 678-45-33; e-mail dziekanat@wpia.uni.lodz.pl):

BIŃCZYCKA-MAJEWSKA, T., Labour Law
BORKOWSKI, J., Administrative Law
BRONIEWICZ, W., Civil Procedure
CHRÓŚCIELEWSKI, W., Administrative Procedure
DĘBOWSKA-ROMANOWSKA, T., Financial Law
GRZEGORCZYK, T., Penal Procedure
HOŁYST, B., Criminology
JANKOWSKI, J., Civil Law
KATNER, W., Civil Law
KMIECIAK, Z., Administrative Procedure
LELENTAL, S., Penal Law
LEWANDOWSKI, H., Labour Law
LEWASZKIEWICZ-PETRYKOWSKA, B., Civil Law
MARCINIAK, A., Civil Procedure
MATUSZEWSKI, J., History of State and Law
MATUSZEWSKI, J., Medieval History, History of Law
NYKIEL, W., Financial Law
PYZIAK-SZAFNICKA, M., Civil Law
RYMASZEWSKI, Z., History of State and the Law
SEWERYŃSKI, M., Labour Law
SZYMCZAK, T., Constitutional Law
TYLMAN, J., Penal Procedure
WŁODARCZYK, W., Social Insurance and Social Policy Law

ZIRK-SADOWSKI, M., Theory of State and Law

Faculty of Management (ul. Matejki 22/26, 90-237 Łódź; tel. (42) 635-50-50; fax (42) 635-53-06; e-mail wzdziek@uni.lodz.pl):

DIETL, J., Commercial Economics
GREGOR, W., Organization and Management, Marketing
GREGORCZYK, B., Organization and Management, Banking
JANOWSKA, Z., Human Resources, Management Accountancy
JARUGA, A., Cost Accounting, Management Accountancy
KOBYLIŃSKI, W., Quality Management
ŁAŃCUCKI, J., Management
MARKOWSKI, T., Economics of Urban Development
MIKOŁAJCZYK, Z., Theory of Organization and Management
PIASECKI, B., Economics and Organization of Industry
SIKORSKI, C., Organization and Management
SZYMCZAK, J., Management
ZIELIŃSKI, J. S., Computer Science

Faculty of Mathematics (ul. Banacha 22, 90-238 Łódź; tel. (42) 635-59-49; fax (42) 635-42-66; e-mail facmath@imul.uni.lodz.pl):

BALCERZAK, M., Real Analysis
CHĄDZYŃSKI, J., Complex Variables
GOLDSTEIN, S., Functional Analysis
JAJTE, R., Probability Theory
JAKUBOWSKI, Z., Analytical Functions
MIKOŁAJCZYK, L., Analytical Functions
NOWAKOWSKI, A., Optimization Theory
PASZKIEWICZ, A., Functional Analysis
PAWLAK, R., Functional Analysis
WALCZAK, P., Geometry
WALCZAK, S., Analytical Functions
WALISZEWSKI, W., Geometry
WILCZYŃSKI, W., Real Analysis
WŁODARCZYK, K., Functional Analysis, Complex Analysis

Faculty of Philology (ul. Kósciuszki 65, 90-514 Łódź; tel. (42) 639-02-53; fax (42) 639-02-54; e-mail filolog@uni.lodz.pl):

BIEŃKOWSKA, D., Polish Language
BOLECKI, W., Romance Literature and Contemporary Literature
CYBULSKI, M., Polish and Slavonic Languages
CZYŻEWSKI, S., Theory of Literature
DEJNA, K., Polish and Slavonic Languages
DUNIN-HORKAWICZ, J., Research on Books
GALA, A., Polish Language
GAZDA, G., Theory of Literature
HELMAN, A., Film
JABŁKOWSKA, J., German Philology
JANICKA-ŚWIDERSKA, I., English Philology
JANISZEWSKA-ZEIDLER, A., Theory of Literature, Theatre and Film
KAMIŃSKA, M., Polish and Slavonic Languages
KORYTKOWSKA, M., Slavonic Studies
KULIGOWSKA-KORZENIEWSKA, A., History of Theatre
LEWANDOWSKA-TOMASZCZYK, B., English Language
MAŁEK, E., Russian Literature
MUCHA, B., Russian Literature
NOWIKOW, W., Spanish Philology
NURCZYŃSKA-FIDELSKA, E., Theory of Literature
OKOŃ, J., Old Polish Literature
POKLEWSKA, K., Polish Literature
PUSZ, W., History of Polish Literature
RATAJCZAK, D., Theory of Literature
SADZIŃSKI, R., German Philology
STARNAWSKI, J., Old Polish Literature
SYPNICKI, J., French Language
TADEUSIEWICZ, H., Research on Books
TARANTOWICZ, A., German Philology
UMIŃSKA-TYTOŃ, E., Polish Language

WIŚNIEWSKI, B., Classical Philology
WOLSKA, B., History of 18th- and 19th-century Polish Literature
WRÓBLEWSKI, W., Classical Philology and Philosophy

Faculty of Philosophy and History (ul. Lindleya 3/5, 90-131 Łódź; tel. (42) 635-43-50; fax (42) 678-39-58):

BRZEZIŃSKI, A., Archaeology
CERAN, W., Prehistory and Medieval History
GAJDA-KRYNICKA, J., Philosophy
GŁOSEK, M., Prehistory
GROMCZYŃSKI, W., History of 19th- and 20th-century Philosophy
HASSAN ALI JAMSHEER, Near East Studies
HUNGER, R., History of Art
KAJZER, L., Medieval History, Archaeology
KRAWCZYK-WASILEWSKA, V., Cultural Anthropology, Ethnography
LIPIŃSKA, J., History of Art
MĄCZYŃSKA, M., Archaeology
MALINOWSKI, G., Logic
MATERSKI, W., Recent World History
NOWACZYK, A., Logic
PANASIUK, R., History of 19th-century Philosophy
PIÓRCZYŃSKI, J., Philosophy
PUŚ, P., 19th- and 20th-century Economic History of Poland
SAMUŚ, W., Recent Polish History
STYCZYŃSKI, M., History of Russian Philosophy
SZCZYGIELSKI, W., Modern Polish History
SZTABIŃSKI, G., Aesthetics
SZYNKIEWICZ, S., Ethnology
TUCHAŃSKA, B., Philosophy of Science
WIERUSZEWSKA-ADAMCZYK, M., Ethnography
WIŚNIEWSKI, E., Russian History
ZAJĄCZKOWSKI, S. M., Medieval Polish History

UNIWERSYTET IM. ADAMA MICKIEWICZA W POZNANIU
(Adam Mickiewicz University in Poznań)

ul. H. Wieniawskiego 1, 61-712 Poznań
Telephone: (61) 852-64-25
Fax: (61) 829-41-11
E-mail: rectorof@amu.edu.pl
Internet: www.amu.edu.pl
Founded 1919

Rector: Prof. Dr hab. STANISŁAW LORENC
Pro-Rectors: Prof. Dr hab. BRONISŁAW MARCINIAK, Prof. Dr hab. BOGUSŁAW MRÓZ, Prof. Dr hab. KAZIMIERZ PRZYSZCZYPKOWSKI, Prof. Dr hab. BOGDAN WALCZAK, Prof. Dr hab. JANUSZ WIŚNIEWSKI
Registrar: Mgr STANISŁAW WACHOWIAK
Librarian: Dr ARTUR JAZDON

Library: see Libraries and Archives
Number of teachers: 2,634
Number of students: 51,677

DEANS

Faculty of Biology: Prof. Dr hab. ANDRZEJ LESICKI
Faculty of Chemistry: Prof. Dr hab. GRZEGORZ SCHROEDER
Faculty of Education and Fine Arts in Kalisz: Prof. JERZY RUBIŃSKI
Faculty of Educational Studies: Prof. Dr hab. WIESŁAW AMBROZIK
Faculty of Geography and Geology: Prof. Dr hab. JANUSZ CHOIŃSKI
Faculty of History: DANUTA MINTA-TWORZOWSKA
Faculty of Law and Administration: ANDRZEJ SZWARC
Faculty of Mathematics and Computer Science: Prof. Dr hab. ZBIGNIEW PALKA

Faculty of Modern Languages and Literature: Prof. Dr hab. JÓSEF DARSKI
Faculty of Physics: Prof. Dr hab. ANDRZEJ DOBEK
Faculty of Polish and Classical Philologies: Prof. Dr hab. ANTONI SMUSZKIEWICZ
Faculty of Social Sciences: Prof. Dr hab. JAN GRAD
Faculty of Theology: Prof. Dr hab. PAWEŁ BORTKIEWICZ

PROFESSORS

Faculty of Biology (ul. Umultowska 89, 61-614 Poznań; tel. (61) 829-55-52; fax (61) 829-55-50; e-mail dziekan@amu.edu.pl):

AUGUSTYNIAK, H., Biochemistry
BALCERKIEWICZ, S., Plant Ecology
BEDNORZ, J., Animal Ecology
BIELAWSKI, J., Animal Cytology
BŁASZAK, Cz., Animal Ecology
BOBOWICZ, M., Plant Genetics
BUJAKIEWICZ, A., Mycology
BURCHARDT, L., Hydrobiology
CIEŚLIK, J., Anthropology
GOŹDZICKA-JÓZEFIAK, A., Biochemistry
GWÓŹDŹ, E., Plant Ecophysiology
HRYNIEWIECKA, L., Biochemistry
JACKOWIAK, B., Botany
KRASKA, M., Hydrobiology
KRZAK, M., Plant Genetics
LATOWSKI, K., Plant Taxonomy
LISIEWSKA, M., Mycology
NIEDBAŁA, W., Animal Ecology
PIONTEK, J., Anthropology
PRUS-GŁOWACKI, W., Plant Genetics
RATAJCZAK, L., Plant Physiology
RATAJCZAK, W., Plant Physiology
STĘPCZAK, K., Zoology
STRZAŁKO, J., Anthropology
SZWEYKOWSKA-KULIŃSKA, Z., Biochemistry
WOJTASZEK, P., Biochemistry
WOŹNY, A., Plant Cytology
ŻUKOWSKI, W., Plant Taxonomy

Faculty of Chemistry (ul. Grunwaldzka 6, 60-780 Poznań; tel. (61) 829-13-35; fax (61) 865-80-08; e-mail depchem@amu.edu.pl):

BRZEZIŃSKI, B., Bio-organic Physical Chemistry
BUREWICZ, A., Teaching of Chemistry
DEGA-SZAFRAN, Z., Physical Organic Chemistry
FIEDOROW, R., Catalysis
GAWROŃSKI, J., Organic Chemistry, Stereochemistry
JARCZEWSKI, A., Physical Organic Chemistry
JASKÓLSKI, M., Crystallography and Biological Chemistry
KATRUSIAK, A., Crystallography
KONARSKI, J., Theoretical Chemistry
KOPUT, J., Physical Chemistry
KORONIAK, H., Synthesis and Structure of Organic Compounds
KOWALAK, S., Catalysis
LIS, S., Rare Earths
ŁOMOZIK, L., Coordination Chemistry, Bioinorganic Chemistry
MARCINIAK, B., Photochemistry
MARCINIEC, B., Organometallic Chemistry, Molecular Catalysis
NAWROCKI, J., Water Treatment Technology
PARYZEK, Z., Organic and Natural Products Chemistry
RADECKA-PARYZEK, W., Coordination and Macrocyclic Chemistry, Bioinorganic Chemistry
ROZWADOWSKA, M., Asymmetric Synthesis, Alkaloid Chemistry
RYCHLEWSKA, U., Crystallography
SARBAK, Z., Adsorption and Catalysis, Environmental Protection
SCHROEDER, G., Organic Chemistry
SIEPAK, J., Water and Soil Analysis
SZAFRAN, M., Physical Organic Chemistry

WACHOWSKA, H., Chemistry of Coal
WASIAK, W., Instrumental Analysis
WOJCIECHOWSKA, M., Heterogeneous Catalysis
WOLSKA, E., Solid-state Chemistry and Magnetochemistry
WYRZYKIEWICZ, E., Mass Spectrometry of Organic Compounds
WYSOCKA, W., Natural Products Chemistry
ZIOŁEK, M., Heterogeneous Catalysis

Faculty of Education and Fine Arts in Kalisz (62-800 Kalisz; tel. (62) 767-07-30; fax (62) 764-57-21; e-mail wpa@amu.edu.pl):

JANKOWSKI, D., Education
NAWROT, A., Fine Arts
NIEKRASZ, A., Methodology of Art
WERNER, B., Music Arts

Faculty of Educational Studies (ul. Szamarzewskiego 89, 60-569 Poznań; tel. (61) 847-49-00; fax (61) 847-49-00):

DUDZIKOWA, M., School Education
FRĄCKOWIAK, T., Social Education
GNITECKI, J., Methodology of Education
MELOSIK, Z., Comparative Education
POTULICKA, E., Comparative Education
PRZYSZCZYPKOWSKI, K., Adult Education
SKRZYPCZAK, J., Adult Education
STRYKOWSKI, W., Educational Technology
ZANDECKI, A., Youth Educational Problems
ŻOŁĄDŹ-STRZELCZYK, D., Pedagogy, History of Education

Faculty of Geography and Geology (ul. Fredry 10, 61-701 Poznań; tel. (61) 852-02-98; fax (61) 853-02-10; e-mail dziego@amu.edu.pl):

CHOIŃSKI, J. A., Hydrology
CIERNIEWSKI, J., Remote Sensing
FEDOROWSKI, J., Palaeozoology
GŁAZEK, J., Dynamic and Regional Geology
GŁĘBOCKI, B., Economic Geography
GÓRSKI, J., Hydrogeology
KANIECKI, A., Hydrology
KOSTRZEWSKI, A., Dynamic Geomorphology, Geoecology
KOZACKI, L., Integrated Physical Geography
LORENC, S., Geology, Petrography
MUSZYŃSKI, A., Mineralogy, Petrography
NOWACZYK, B., Geomorphology
PARYSEK, J., Socioeconomic Geography
ROGACKI, H., Spatial Management
SKOCZYLAS, J., Petroarchaeology, Archometry
TOBOLSKI, K., Palaeobotany
WOŚ, A., Climatology, Meteorology

Faculty of History (ul. Sw. Marcin 78, 61-809 Poznań; tel. (61) 852-87-79; fax (61) 852-47-82; e-mail dhist@amu.edu.pl):

BŁASZCZYK, G., East European History
BUCHOWSKI, M., European Ethnology, Theory of Anthropology
FOGEL, J., Bronze and Early Iron Age Prehistory
HAUSER, P., Contemporary History
JASIEWICZ, Z., Ethnology of Poland and Central Asia
JASIŃSKI, T., Medieval History
KOŚKO, A., Prehistory of Poland
KOTŁOWSKI, T., Contemporary History
KOWAL, S., Economic History
LABUDA, A., History of Art
ŁAZUGA, W., Modern History
MOLIK, W., Modern Polish History
MROZEWICZ, L., Ancient History
OLEJNIK, K., Military History
OLSZEWSKI, W., Modern and Contemporary History
PIOTROWSKI, P., History of Contemporary Art
POSERN-ZIELIŃSKI, A., Ethnology of the Americas, Anthropology of Ethnicity
SCHRAMM, T., Modern History
SERWAŃSKI, M., Modern History
SIERPOWSKI, S., Contemporary History

SKIBIŃSKI, S., History of Medieval Art
STRZELCZYK, J., Medieval History
WYRWA, A., History
ZAWADZKI, S., Ancient History

Faculty of Law and Administration (ul. Św. Marcin 90, 61-809 Poznań; tel. (61) 853-68-43):

CHOBOT, A., Labour Law
GOMUŁOWICZ, A., Financial Law
GULCZ, M., Economics
KĘPIŃSKI, M., European Law
KIJOWSKI, A., Labour Law
KOŁECKI, H., Criminal Law
ŁĄCZKOWSKI, W., Financial Law
MAŁECKI, J., Financial Law
NIEDBAŁA, Z., Labour Law
OWOC, M., Criminal Law
PATRYAS, W., Theory of State and Law
SMYCZYŃSKI, T., Civil Law
SOŁTYSIŃSKI, S., Civil Law
STACHOWIAK, S., Criminal Procedure
SZWARC, A. J., Criminal Law
TYRANOWSKI, J., International Law
WRONKOWSKA-JAŚKIEWICZ, S., Theory of State and Law
ZEDLER, F., Civil Procedure

Faculty of Mathematics and Computer Science (ul. Umultowska 87, 61-614 Poznań; tel. (61) 829-53-11; fax (61) 829-53-15; e-mail wmiuam@math.amu.edu.pl):

BATÓG, T., Mathematical Logic, Mathematical Linguistics
BUSZKOWSKI, W., Logic, Linguistics, Computation Theory
DOMAŃSKI, P., Functional Analysis
DREWNOWSKI, L., Functional Analysis
HUDZIK, H., Functional Analysis
KACZOROWSKI, J., Number Theory
KĄKOL, J., Functional Analysis, Topology
KAROŃSKI, M., Discrete Mathematics and Probability
KRZYŚKO, M., Mathematical Statistics
KUBIACZYK, I., Mathematics
ŁUCZAK, T., Discrete Mathematics and Probability
MARZANTOWICZ, W., Mathematics
MASTYŁO, M., Functional Analysis
MURAWSKI, R., Mathematical Logic, Philosophy of Mathematics
PYCH-TABERSKA, P., Approximation Theory
RUCIŃSKI, A., Discrete Mathematics and Probability
SZUFLA, ST., Differential Equations
WASZAK, A., Functional Analysis

Faculty of Modern Languages and Literature (ul. Niepodległości 4, 61-874 Poznań; tel. (61) 852-22-03; fax (61) 853-69-33; e-mail spuppel@amu.edu.pl):

ANDRUSZKO, Cz., Russian Literature
BAŃCZEROWSKI, J., General Linguistics
DARSKI, J., German Linguistics
DZIUBALSKA-KOŁACZYK, K., English Linguistics
FISIAK, J., English Linguistics
GUSSMANN, E., English Linguistics
KALISZAN, J., Russian Linguistics
KAROLAK, Cz., German Literature
KASZYŃSKI, S., Austrian Literature and Culture
KOPCEWICZ, A., American Literature
KOPYTKO, R., English Linguistics
KRYSZTOFIAK-KASZYŃSKA, M., Danish Literature
ŁABĘDZKA, I., Romance Literature
LIPOŃSKI, W., Anglo-Saxon Studies
ŁOBACZ, P., General Linguistics
MAJEWICZ, A., Oriental Linguistics
MALINOWSKI, W., Romance Literature
MARKUNAS, A., Methodology of Russian Language Teaching
ORŁOWSKI, H., German Literature
PAPIÓR, J., German Literature and Culture
PFEIFFER, W., Applied Linguistics
PIOTROWSKI, B., History of Scandinavia

POGONOWSKI, J., Mathematical Linguistics
PUPPEL, S., English Linguistics
SCHATTE, CH., German Linguistics
SIEK-PISKOZUB, T., English Linguistics
SIKORSKA, L., English Literature
SOBKOWIAK, W., English Linguistics
STEFFEN-BATOGOWA, M., General Linguistics
SYPNICKI, J., Romance Linguistics
TOMASZKIEWICZ, T., Romance Linguistics
WĄSIK, Z., General Linguistics
WILCZYŃSKA, W., Applied Linguistics
WÓJTOWICZ, M., Russian Linguistics
ZGÓŁKA, T., General Linguistics

Faculty of Physics (ul. Umultowska 85, 61-614 Poznań; tel. (61) 829-51-56; fax (61) 829-51-55; e-mail dobek@amu.edu.pl):

BARNAS, J., Solid-state Physics
BŁASZAK, M., Mathematical Physics
BŁASZCZAK, Z., Molecular Optics
DOBEK, A., Biophysics
HOJAN, E., Electroacoustics
JACYNA-ONYSZKIEWICZ, Z., Quantum Physics
JURGA, K., Radiospectroscopy
JURGA, S., Radiospectroscopy and Molecular Physics
KAMIENIARZ, G., Computer Physics
KOZIEROWSKI, M., Nonlinear Optics
KURZYŃSKI, M., Statistical Physics
ŁABOWSKI, M., Molecular Acoustics
MAKAREWICZ, R., Environmental Acoustics
MICNAS, R., Solid-state Physics
MRÓZ, B., Ferroelectrics
NAWROCIK, W., Physics
OZIMEK, E., Psychoacoustics
PARZYŃSKI, R., Quantum Electronics
PATKOWSKI, A., Molecular Biophysics
PUSZKARSKI, H., Solid-state Physics
ROBASZKIEWICZ, S., Solid-state Physics
SCHWARZENBERG-CZERNY, A., Astronomy
ŚLIWIŃSKA-BARTKOWIAK, M., Physics
STANKOWSKA, J., Molecular Physics
TANAŚ, R., Nonlinear Optics
WĄSICKI, J., Physics
WNUK, E., Astronomy

Faculty of Polish and Classical Philologies (ul. Niepodległości 4, 67-874 Poznań; tel. (61) 852-71-27; fax (61) 852-71-27):

ABRAMOWSKA, J., Polish Literature, Historical Poetics
ADAMCZYK, M., Old Polish Literature
BĄBA, S., Idioms and Culture of Polish Language
BAKUŁA, B., 20th-century Literature
BALCERZAN, E., Polish Literature, Theory of Literature and 20th-century Literature
BARTOL, K., Classical Philology
BOREJSZO, M., Polish Linguistics
CHRZĄSTOWSKA, B., New Teaching Methods, History of Polish Literature
CZAPLIŃSKI, P., Theory of Literature, Literary Criticism
DANIELEWICZ, J., Hellenistic Philology
DWORACKI, S., Hellenistic Philology
HENDRYKOWSKA, M., Film History and Theory
KRĄŻYŃSKA, Z., Polish Linguistics
LEGEŻYŃSKA, A., Theory of Literature
LEWANDOWSKI, I., Latin Philology
LEWANDOWSKI, T., Polish Literature
NOWAK, H., Polish Dialectology
POKRZYWNIAK, J. T., Old Polish Literature
PRZYBYLSKI, R. K., Theory of Literature, History of Literature
RATAJCZAK, D., Polish Drama
RZEPKA, W., Polish Linguistics
SMUSZKIEWICZ, A., Teaching of Polish Language and Literature
TROJANOWICZ, Z., 19th-century Polish Literature
WALCZAK, B., Polish Linguistics
WIEGANDT, E., History of Contemporary Literature
WYDRA, W., Editorial and Bibliography

WYSŁOUCH, S., Polish Literature, Theory of Literature and 20th-century Literature
ZGÓŁKA, T., General Linguistics
ZGÓŁKOWA, H., Polish Linguistics

Faculty of Social Sciences (ul. Szamarzewskiego 89, 60-568 Poznań; tel. (61) 847-25-71; fax (61) 847-15-55; e-mail socuam@amu.edu.pl):

ANDRZEJEWSKI, B., History of German Philosophy
BRZEZIŃSKA, A., Development
BRZEZIŃSKI, J., Methodology of Psychology
BUKSIŃSKI, T., Social Philosophy, Philosophy of History
CHYŁA, W., Culture
DROZDOWICZ, Z., Philosophy of Religion
GOLKA, M., Sociology of Culture, Social Anthropology
JAMROZIAKOWA, A., Aesthetics
KOSMAN, M., History
KOSMANOWA, B., History of Science
KOSZEL, B., History and Political Science
MALENDOWSKI, W., Political Science
NOWAK, L., Philosophy of Science, Political Philosophy
NOWAKOWA, I., Philosophy of Science
ORCZYK, J., Economics and History
PAŁUBICKA, A., Theory of Culture
PUŚLECKI, Z., International Economic Relations
SAKSON, A., Sociology of Ethnic Minorities, Sociology of Youth
SĘK, H., Health and Clinical Psychology
SOBCZAK, J., Law
STACHOWSKI, R., History of Psychological Thought
TITTENBRUN, J., Theory and Practice of Privatization
WOŹNIAK, Z., Sociology of Medicine
ZAMIARA, T., Philosophy of Science
ZIÓŁKOWSKI, M., Sociological Theory

Faculty of Theology (ul. Wieżowa 2–4, 61-111 Poznań; tel. (61) 829-39-90; fax (61) 851-97-35; e-mail thfac@man.poznan.pl):

BRANIAK, J., Sociology
CZĘSZ, B., Theology, Patristic Theology
LEWEK, A., Theology, Religious Communication
NIPARKO, R., Christian Pedagogy
PONIŻY, B., Theology, Old Testament Exegisis
PYTEL, J., Theology, New Testament Exegisis
STEFAŃSKI, J., Theology
SZPET, J., Theology, Religious Education
TARNOWSKI, K., Philosophy
WĘCŁAWSKI, T., Theology, Fundamental Theology
WEJMAN, H., Theology of Spirituality

UNIWERSYTET JAGIELLOŃSKI (Jagiellonian University)

ul. Gołębia 24, 31-007 Cracow

Telephone: (12) 422-10-33
Fax: (12) 422-63-06
E-mail: rektor@adm.uj.edu.pl
Internet: www.uj.edu.pl

Founded 1364
Academic year: October to June

Rector: Prof. Dr hab. KAROL MUSIOŁ
Vice-Rector for Collegium Medicum: Prof. Dr hab. WIESŁAW PAWLIK
Vice-Rector for Devt: Prof. Dr hab. PIOTR TWORZEWSKI
Vice-Rector for Educational Affairs: Prof. Dr hab. MARIA SZEWCZYK
Vice-Rector for Personal and Financial Affairs: Prof. Dr hab. WŁADYSŁAW MIODUNKA
Vice-Rector for Research and Int. Relations: Prof. Dr hab. SZCZEPAN BILINSKI
Administrator: Dr TADEUSZ SKARBEK
Librarian: Prof. Dr hab. ZDZISŁAW PIETRZYK

Library: see Libraries and Archives
Number of teachers: 3,407
Number of students: 41,086

Publications: *Acta Physica Polonica B* (12 a year), *Ad Americam* (1 a year), *Alma Mater* (12 a year), *Biuletyn Biblioteki Jagiellońskiej* (1 a year), *Cracow Indological Studies* (irregular), *Estetyka i Krytyka* (4 a year), *Eurasian Prehistory* (2 a year), *Forum Europejskie* (4 a year), *Foton* (4 a year), *Kronika* (1 a year), *Kwartalnik Religioznawczy NOMOS* (4 a year), *Management in Culture* (2 a year), *Materiały Edukacyjne Bibliotekoznawstwa i Informacji Naukowej* (1 a year), *MODUS Prace z Historii Sztuki* (1 a year), *Nowy Filomata* (4 a year), *Peregrinus Cracoviensis* (irregular), *Politea* (1 a year), *Prace Archeologiczne* (irregular), *Prace Archeologiczne—Studies in Ancient Art and Civilization* (irregular), *Prace Geograficzne* (irregular), *Prace Historyczne* (1 a year), *Principia* (2 a year), *Przekładaniec* (literary translation, 2 a year), *Recherches Archéologiques* (irregular), *Reports on Mathematical Logic* (1 a year), *Reports on Philosophy* (1 a year), *Romanica Cracoviensia* (1 a year), *Schedae Informaticae*, *Studia z zakresu Prawa Pracy i Polityki Społecznej* (1 a year), *Universitatis Jegellonicae Acta Mathematica* (1 a year), *Zeszyty Naukowe Uniwersytetu Jagiellońskiego* (1 a year in 26 series), *Zeszyty Prasoznawcze* (4 a year), *Zmieniające się przedsiębiorstwo w zmieniającej się politycznie Europie* (1 a year)

DEANS

Faculty of Biology and Earth Sciences: Prof. Dr hab. KAZIMIERZ KRZEMIEŃ
Faculty of Biotechnology: Prof. Dr hab. KAZIMIERZ STRZAŁKA
Faculty of Chemistry: Prof. Dr hab. LEONARD M. PRONIEWICZ
Faculty of Health Care: Prof. Dr hab. JOLANTA JAWOREK
Faculty of History: Prof. Dr hab. ANDREZJ BANACH
Faculty of International and Political Studies: Prof. Dr hab. WIESŁAW KOZUB-CIEMBRONIEWICZ
Faculty of Law and Administration: Prof. Dr hab. TADEUSZ WŁUDYKA
Faculty of Management and Social Communication: Prof. Dr hab. MICHAŁ DU VALL
Faculty of Mathematics and Computer Science: Prof. Dr hab. MAREK JARNICKI
Faculty of Medicine: Prof. Dr hab. WOJCIECH NOWAK
Faculty of Pharmacy: Prof. Dr hab. JOANNA SZYMURA-OLEKSIAK
Faculty of Philology: Prof. Dr hab. MARCELA SEWIĄTKOWSKA
Faculty of Philosophy: Prof. Dr hab. MARIA FLIS
Faculty of Physics, Astronomy and Applied Computer Science: Prof. Dr hab. JERZY SZWED
Faculty of Polish Studies: Prof. Dr hab. JACEK POPIEL

PROFESSORS

Faculty of Biology and Earth Sciences (tel. (12) 422-63-48; fax (12) 430-14-73; e-mail binoz@adm.uj.edu.pl; internet www.uj.edu.pl/uj-guide/biol.en.html):

BILIŃSKA, B., Animal Physiology
BILIŃSKI, Sz., Cell Biology
BOBEK, B., Wildlife Research
CHEŁMICKI, W., Geography
DĄBROWSKI, Z., Animal Physiology
DOMANSKI, B., Geography
DZWONKO, Z., Plant Ecology
FALNIOWSKI, A., Malacology
GÓRECKI, A., Ecology
GREGORASZCZUK, E., Animal Physiology

GUZIK, Cz., Population and Agricultural Geography
JACKOWSKI, A., Geography of Religion
KACZANOWSKI, K., Anthropology
KOZŁOWSKI, J., Hydrobiology
KRZEMIEŃ, K., Geomorphology
KUTA, E., Cytology and Embryology of Plants
LASKOWSKI, R., Ecology
LITYŃSKA, A., Glycobiology
ŁOMNICKI, A., Population Ecology
MARCHLEWSKA-KOJ, A., Mammalian Reproduction
MORYCOWA, E., Palaeozoology
MYDEL, R., Geographical Studies on Japan
OBRĘBSKA-STARKEL, B., Climatology
OLECH, M., Plant Taxonomy
OSZCZYPKO, N., Geology
PETRYSZAK, B., Systematic Zoology and Zoological Geography
PŁYTYCZ, B., Evolutionary Immunology
PRZYWARA, L., Plant Cytology and Embryology
RADOMSKI, A., Geology
RAFIŃSKI, J., Evolutionary Biology
SAWICKA-KAPUSTA, K., Ecology, Environmental Protection
ŚKIBA, S., Soil Geography and Pedology
ŚLĄCZKA, A., Tectonics and Stratigraphy
SZOŁTYS, M., Zoology
SZYMURA, J. M., Zoology
TRZCIŃSKA-TACIK, H., Botany
TURNAU, K., Plant Taxonomy and Phytogeography
UCHMAN, A., Geology, Sedimentology, Ichnology
WEINER, J., Ecological Bioenergetics and Evolutionary Ecosystems
WIDACKI, W., Geography
WOJTUSIAK, J., Zoology
WOYCIECHOWSKI, M., Ecology and Evolution
ŻABIŃSKI, W., Geology
ZAJĄC, A., Plant Taxonomy and Phytogeography
ZAJĄC, M., Phytogeography
ZEMANEK, A., Botany
ZEMANEK, B., Phytogeography
ZUCHIEWICZ, W., Geology

Faculty of Biotechnology (ul. Gronostajowa 7, 30-387 Cracow; tel. (12) 252-60-02; fax (12) 252-69-02; e-mail sekretariat@mol.uj.edu.pl; internet www.mol.uj.edu.pl):

DUBIN, A., Biochemistry
FRONCISZ, W., Biophysics
GABRYŚ, H., Plant Physiology
KLEIN, A., Biochemistry
KOJ, A., Biochemistry
KOROHODA, Wł., Cell Biology
ŁUKIEWICZ, S., Biophysics
PASENKIEWICZ-GIERULA, M., Molecular Biophysics
POTEMPA, J., Biochemistry, Biotechnology
PRYJMA, J., Microbiology and Immunology
SARNA, T., Biophysics
STRZAŁKA, K., Biochemistry
WASYLEWSKI, Z., Physical Biochemistry
WIĘCKOWSKI, S., Plant Physiology
ŻAK, Z., Animal Biochemistry

Faculty of Chemistry (ul. Ingardena 3, 30-060 Cracow; tel. (12) 633-63-77 ext. 2215; fax (12) 634-05-15; e-mail sekretar@chemia.uj.edu.pl; internet www.ch.uj.edu.pl):

BARAŃSKI, A., Chemical Kinetics
BOGDANOWICZ-SZWED, K., Chemistry of Heterocyclic Compounds
DATKA, J., Inorganic Chemistry and Infrared Spectroscopy
DZIEMBAJ, R., Catalysis, Solid State Chemistry and Technology
HODOROWICZ, S. A., Crystallography and Solid State Chemistry
JUSZKIEWICZ, A., Physical and Environmental Chemistry

KOŚCIELNIAK, P., Analytical and Forensic Chemistry
NAJBAR, J., Physical Chemistry, Photophysics and Photochemistry
NAJBAR, M., Inorganic and Environmental Catalysis
NALEWAJSKI, R. F., Theoretical Chemistry, Quantum Chemistry
NOWAKOWSKA, M., Physical Chemistry, Photochemistry of Polymers
OLEKSYN, B., Crystallography and Crystal Chemistry
PALUCH, M., Physical Chemistry, Surface Chemistry
PARCZEWSKI, A., Chemometrics and Analytical Chemistry
PAWLIKOWSKI, M., Theoretical Chemistry, Molecular Spectroscopy
PETELENZ, P., Theoretical Chemistry
PRONIEWICZ, L.M., Chemical Physics, Molecular Spectroscopy
SILBERRING, J., Biochemistry and Neurochemistry
STASICKA, Z., Inorganic and Coordination Chemistry
STOCHEL, G., Inorganic and Bioinorganic Chemistry
WÓJCIK, M., Physical Chemistry, Molecular Spectroscopy

Faculty of Health Care (ul. Michałowskiego 12, 31-126 Cracow; tel. (12) 421-41-41; fax (12) 421-41-41; e-mail kbrzezns@cm-uj.krakow.pl; internet www.cm-uj.krakow.pl):

CZABAŁA, J., Psychology
GOLINOWSKA, S., Health Economics
HAŁUSZKA, J., Environmental Health
PILC, A., Pharmacology
SPODARYK, K., Physiotherapy
SZAFRAN, Z., Biochemistry
WŁODARCZYK, W., Health Policy

Faculty of History (tel. (12) 422-77-62; fax (12) 430-14-67; e-mail historia@adm.uj.edu.pl; internet www.uj.edu.pl/uj-guide/history.en.html):

BACZKOWSKI, K., General Medieval History
BAŁUS, K., History of Late Modern Art
BRZOZA, Cz., Modern Polish History
CENTAROWICZ, A., General Modern History
CHOCHOROWSKI, J., Archaeology
CHWALBA, A., Documentation of Polish Independence Movements
CIAŁOWICZ, K, Archaeology
DĄBROWA, E., Ancient History
DYBIEC, J., History of Science and Culture
DZIELSKA, M., Byzantine History
FABIAŃSKI, M., History of Modern Art
GĄSOWSKI, T., Polish Modern History
GEDL, M., Archaeology
GINTER, B., Archaeology
GRYGLEWICZ, T., History of Contemporary Art
JARZĘBSKA, A., 20th-century Polish History
KACZANOWSKI, P., Archaeology
KOZŁOWSKI, J., Archaeology
MAŁKIEWICZA, A., History of Modern Art
MICHALEWICZ, A., Economic and Social History
OSTROWSKI, JAN, History of Art
OSTROWSKI, JANUSZ, Classical Archaeology
PAJA-STACH, J., Contemporary Polish Music
PAPUCI-WŁADYKA, E., Archaeology
PARCZEWSKI, M., Polish and Modern Archaeology
PIROŻYŃSKI, J., General Modern History
QUIRINI-POPŁAWSKA, D., Medieval History
ROBOTYCKI, Cz., Polish Ethnography, Anthropology of Culture
ROJEK, W., General Modern History
ŚLIWA, J., Mediterranean Archaeology
ŚNIEŻYŃSKA-STOLOT, E., History of Ideas
SZCZUR, S., Medieval History

Faculty of International and Political Studies (tel. (12) 422-02-25; fax (12) 422-02-25; e-mail wsmip@adm.uj.edu.pl; internet www.uj.edu.pl/wydzmiedzpol):

BABIŃSKI, G., Sociology of Interethnic Relationships
CZIOMER, E., International Relations
FLORKOWSKA-FRANCIĆ, H., History of International Migration Movements
KAPISZEWSKI, A., Middle East Studies
KOZUB-CIEMBRONIEWICZ, M., Modern Political Movements and Political Thought
MACH, Z., Anthropology
MAJCHROWSKI, J. M., Recent Political History of Poland, History of Political and Legal Doctrines, Religious Policy
MANIA, A., World History of the 20th Century
MIODUNKA, W., Applied Linguistics in Polish Language Teaching
PURCHLA, J., Economic History and History of Art
RAŹNY, A., East Slavonic Philology
STAWOWY-KAWKA, I., History of Balkan Countries
SUCHANEK, L., Russian and Soviet Literature
WALASZEK, A., History of International Migration Movements
ZIĘBA, A., Constitutional Law
ZYBLIKIEWICZ, L., International Relations

Faculty of Law and Administration (tel. (12) 422-37-42; fax (12) 423-11-21; e-mail prawo@adm.uj.edu.pl; internet www.uj.edu.pl/uj-guide/law&adm.en.html):

BARAN, KA., General Legal History
BARAN, KRZ., Labour Law
BIERNAT, S., European Law
BŁACHUT, J., Criminology
BRZEZIŃSKI, B., Financial Law
CHOJNICKA, K., History of Political and Legal Thought
ĆWIĄKALSKI, K., Criminal Law
CZAJOWKI, J., Modern Political Systems
DROZD, E., Civil Law, Private International Law
GABERLE, A., Criminology
GAWLIK, B., Civil Law
GIZBERT-STUDNICKI, T., Theory and Philosophy of Law
GRZYBOWSKI, M., Modern Political Systems
HOFMAŃSKI, P., Criminal Procedure
HOŁDA, Z., Sentencing and Penal Procedure
JASKÓLSKI, M., History of Political and Legal Thought
KISIEL, W., Territorial Self-Government
KRAJEWSKLI, K., Criminology
KUBAS, A., Civil Law
LANKOSZ, K., International Public Law
LICHOROWICZ, A., Agricultural Law
MĄCZYŃSKI, A., Civil and International Private Law
MALEC, J., History of Administration
PAŁECKI, K., Theory and Sociology of Law
PŁESZKA, K., Theory and Philosophy of Law
PREUSSNER-ZAMORSKA, J., Civil Law
PYZIOŁ, W., Private Business Law
SARKOWICZ, R., Theory and Philosophy of Law
SARNECKI, P., Constitutional Law
SONDEL, J., Roman Law
STEC, M., Private Business Law
STELMACH, J., Theory and Philosophy of Law
ŚWIĄTKOWSKI, A., Labour Law
SZEWCZYK, M., Criminal Law
SZUMAŃSKI, A., International Business Law
TRAPLE, E., Civil Law
URUSZCZAK, W., History of Ecclesiastical Law
WAGNER, B., Labour Law
WALASZEK-PYZIOŁ, A., Public Business Law
WASILEWSKI, A., Environmental Protection Law

WŁUDYKA, T., Economics Policy
WOJCIKIEWICZ, J., Forensic and Police Science
WOŚ, T., Administration Law, Administration Procedures Law
ZAWADA, K., Civil Law and International Private Law
ZIMMERMAN, J., Administrative Procedures
ZOLL, A., Criminal Law

Faculty of Management and Social Communication (tel. (12) 422-10-33 ext. 1132; fax (12) 421-49-75; e-mail orzech@adm.uj.edu.pl; internet gemini.miks.uj.edu.pl):

BAŃKA, A., Organizational Psychology
BARTA, J., Copyright Law, Press Law and Information Law
BEDNARCZYK, M., Tourism Management
BOBROWSKI, J., Linguistics, Communication
GOBAN-KLAS, T., Theory of Mass Communication, Public Relations
GODZIC, W., Media and Film Studies
HELMAN, A., Film Studies
LASKOWSKI, R., Linguistics, Slavic Language and Social Communication
LIBERSKA, B., International Economics
LUBASZEWSKI, W., Electrical Transformation of Information
LUBELSKI, T., Film Studies
MAREK, T., Psychology of Work, Organization and Management
MARKIEWICZ, R., Copyright Law, Information Law and Industrial Property Law
MATCZEWSKI, A., Industrial Management
NĘCKI, Z., Social Psychology
OKOŃ-HORODYŃSKA, E., Economics, Management
ORZECHOWSKI, E., Arts Management, History of Theatre
PISAREK, W., Media Research, Social Linguistics
PLEŚNIAROWICZ, K., Arts Management, Performance Theory
PRZEWŁOCKI, R., Medical Science, Neuroscience, Pharmacology
SOWA, K., Management of Higher Education, Sociology
STACHÓWNA, G., Film Studies
STĘPNIEWSKI, J., Accounting, Auditing, Operational Management
SURDYKOWSKA, S., International Accounting and Corporate Finance, Management, Accounting, Comparative Economics Systems
SZUMPICH, S., Management, Accounting, Comparative Economics Systems
SZWAJA, J., Civil and Commercial Law, Industrial Property Law
WIDACKI, J., Criminal Law, Management of Public Security
WILK, E., Media and Film Studies
WITKOWSKI, L., Philosophy, Theory of Arts and Education
WOJCIECHOWSKI, J., Communication and Librarianship

Faculty of Mathematics and Computer Science (tel. (12) 422-10-33 ext. 1145; fax (12) 430-14-67; e-mail matinf@adm.uj.edu.pl; internet www.mat-inf.uj.edu.pl):

DENKOWSKI, Z., Optimization and Control Theory
DRUŻKOWSKI, L. M., Analytic and Algebraic Geology
FLASIŃSKI, M., Artificial Intelligence Systems
GANCARZEWICZ, J., Differential Geometry
IDZIAK, P. M, Foundations of Computer Science
JARNICKI, M., Complex Analysis
MROZEK, M., Numerical Methods
OMBACH, J., Dynamical Systems
OPOZDA, B., Differential Geometry
PAWŁUCKI, W., Singularity Theory
PELCZAR, A., Analysis, Differential Equations

PLEŚNIAK, W., Complex Analysis, Theory of Approximations
RUSEK, K., Algebraic Geometry
SĘDZIWY, S., Numerical Methods
SICIAK, J., Complex Analysis
SRZEDNICKI, R., Differential Equations
STOCHEL, J., Functional Analysis, Theory of Operators
SZAFIRSKI, B., Differential Equations, Theory of Turbulence
SZAFRANIEC, F. H., Functional Analysis, Theory of Operators
TWOREWSKI, P., Analytical and Algebraic Geometry
WINIARSKI, T., Analytic and Algebraic Geometry

Faculty of Medicine (ul. Św. Anny 6, 31-008 Cracow; tel. (12) 422-54-44; fax (12) 422-40-06; e-mail dziekwl@cm-uj.krakow.pl; internet www.cm-uj.krakow.pl/pliki/en_lekarski.html):

ADAMEK-GUZIK, T., Internal Medicine
ALEKSANDROWICZ, J., Psychotherapy, Psychiatry
ANDRES, J., Anaesthesiology
BASTA, A., Gynaecology and Oncology
BOGDAŁ, J., Gastroenterology, Internal Medicine
BOGDASZEWSKA-CZABANOWSKA, J., Dermatology
BOMBA, J., Psychiatry
BRZOZOWSKI, T., Physiology
CICHOCKI, T., Histology
DEMBIŃSKA-KIEĆ, A., Clinical Biochemistry
DEMBIŃSKI, A., Physiology
DOBROWOLSKI, Z., Urology
DUBIEL, J. S., Cardiology
GIEROWSKI, J., Psychiatry
GRODZIŃSKA, L., Pharmacology
HECZKO, P., Microbiology
KACIŃSKI, M., Neurology
KARCZ, D., Surgery
KAWECKA-JASZCZ, K., Cardiology
KLIMEK, R., Gynaecology, Obstetrics
KONIECZNY, L., Biochemistry
KORBUT, R., Pharmacology
KULIG, J., Surgery
LAUTERBACH, R., Paediatrics
LITWIN, J., Histology
MAJEWSKI, S., Dental Prosthetics
MALEC, E., Paediatric Cardiac Surgery
MARCINKIEWICZ, J., Immunology
MIODOŃSKI, A., Laryngology
MIRECKA, J., Histology
MUSIAŁ, J., Internal Medicine
NASKALSKI, J., Clinical Biochemistry
NIŻANKOWSKA-MOGILNICKA, E., Pulmonology
OBTUŁOWICZ, K., Internal Medicine
PACH, J., Toxicology
PAWLĘGA, J., Oncology
PAWLICKI, R., Histology
PAWLIK, W., Physiology
PIETRZYK, J., Paediatrics
PIWOWARSKA, W., Cardiology
POPIELA, T., Gastroenterological Surgery
RATAJCZAK, M., Transplantology
REROŃ, E., Laryngology
ROKITA, E., Medical Physics
RYN, Z., Psychiatry
SIERADZKI, J., Metabolic Diseases
SKŁADZIEŃ, J., Otolaryngology
SKOTNICKI, A., Haematology
SŁADEK, K., Internal Medicine
STACHURA, J., Pathomorphology
STARZYCKA, M., Ophthalmology
SUŁOWICZ, W., Nephrology
SZCZEKLIK, A., Internal Medicine
THOR, P., Physiopathology
TOBIASZ-ADAMCZYK, B., Epidemiology and Preventive Medicine
TRACZ, W., Cardiology
WYSOCKI, A., Surgery
ZARZYCKI, D., Orthopaedics
ZEMBALA, M., Microbiology, Immunology

ZIĘBA, A., Psychiatry

Faculty of Pharmacy (ul. Medyczna 9, 30-688 Cracow; tel. (12) 657-54-56; fax (12) 657-02-62; e-mail mfdmicha@cyf-kr.edu.pl; internet www.cm-uj.krakow.pl):

BOJARSKI, J., Organic Chemistry
BRANDYS, J., Toxicology
BUDAK, A., Pharmaceutical Microbiology
CZARNECKI, R., Pharmacodynamics
JAŚKIEWICZ, J., Biochemical Analysis
KIEĆ-KONOWICZ, K., Chemical Technology of Drugs
PAWŁOWSKI, M., Pharmaceutical Chemistry
RZESZUTKO, W., Inorganic Chemistry
STAREK, A., Biochemical Toxicology
SZYMURA-OLEKSIAK, J., Pharmacokinetics
ZACHWIEJA, Z., Food Chemistry, Nutrition
ZIEJA, A., Pharmaceutical Chemistry

Faculty of Philology (tel. (12) 422-11-03; fax (12) 422-11-03 ext. 1102; e-mail filolog@adm.uj.edu.pl; internet www.filg.uj.edu.pl):

BALBUS, S., Theory of Literature
BOCHENEK-FRANCZAKOWA, R., French Literature
BOROWSKI, A., Polish Philology
BORYŚ, W., Comparative and Historical Slavic Etymology, Serbo-Croatian Linguistics
BRZEZINA, M., Linguistics
BUJNICKI, T., History of Polish Literature
DUNAJ, B., Linguistics
FIUT, A., Polish Philology
GIBIŃSKA-MARZEC, M., English Literature
HOMBEK, D., Polish Philology
JARZĘBSKI, J., History of Polish Literature
JAWORSKI, S., History of Polish Literature
KAPUŚCIK, J., Russian Literature and History
KŁAŃSKA, M., German Philology
KORNHAUSER, J., Slavonic Philology
KORPANTY, J., Classical Philology
KORUS, K., Classical Philology
KORYTOWSKA, M., Comparative Literature
KOWALIKOWA, J., Methodology of Teaching Polish Literature
KULAWIK, A., Theory of Literature
KUREK, H., Polish Philology
LABOCHA, J., Polish Philology
LIPIŃSKI, K., German Philology, History of German Literature, Translation
MAŃCZAK-WOHLFELD, E., English Linguistics
MARKOWSKI, M., History of Polish Literature
MELANOWICZ, M., Japanese Literature
MICHALAK-PIKULSKA, B., Arabic Literature
MICHALIK, J., Theatre Studies
MIODOŃSKA-BROOKES, E., Polish Philology
MUSKAT-TABAKOWSKA, E., Cognitive Linguistics and Theory of Translation
NAUMOW, A., Slavonic Philology
NYCZ, R., Polish Philology
PISOWICZ, A., Iranian and Armenian Linguistics
PRZEBINDA, G., Russian Literature and History, Ukrainian Culture and History
SKARŻYŃSKI, M., Polish Philosophy
ŚLIWIŃSKI, W., Polish Philology
SMOCZYŃSKI, W., General and Indo-European Linguistics
STABRYŁA, S., Classical Philology
STACHOWSKI, M., Turkic and Altaic Linguistics
STALA, M., History of Polish Literature
STYKA, J., Classical Philology
ŞUGIERA, M., Theatre Studies
ŚWIĄTKOWSKA, M., Romance Philology
SZCZUKIN, W., Russian Literature, Culture and History, Theory of Literature
SZTURC, W., Comparative Literature
WALECKI, W., History of Polish Literature
WIDŁAK, S., Romance Philology
WŁODARSKI, M., History of Polish Literature
WRÓBEL, H., Polish and Czech Philology

WYKA, M., History of Polish Literature
ZABORSKI, A., Chamito-Semitic Linguistics
ZAJADA, A., Polish Philology
ZARĘBIANKA, Z., History of Polish Language
ZIEJKA, F., History of Polish Philology

Faculty of Philosophy (tel. (12) 422-11-36; fax (12) 430-14-75; e-mail filozof@adm.uj.edu.pl; internet www.phils.uj.edu.pl):

ALEKSANDER, T., Adult Education
DRABINA, J., History of Christianity
FLIS, A., Sociology of Culture
FLIS, M., Sociology of Culture, Anthropology
FRYSZTACKI, K., Sociology
GALEWICZ, W., Philosophy
GORLACH, K., Sociology
GROTT, B., Religious Studies
GRYZMAŁA-MOSZCZYŃSKA, H., Psychology of Religion
KOCIK, L., Sociology
KUBIAK, H., Sociology of Politics
LEGUTKO, R., Political Philosophy
LIPIEC, J., Philosophy
MIKLASZEWSKA, J., Philosophy
NĘCKA, E., Psychology
OCHMANN, J., Religious Studies
PACZKOWSKA-ŁAGOWSKA, E., Philosophy
PAŁKA, S., Methodological Elements of Education
PALUCH, A., Sociology
PERZANOWSKI, J., Philosophy and Logic
PIĄTEK, Z., Philosophy of Natural Sciences
PILECKA, W., Psychology
RODZIŃSKI, S., Pedagogy
SKOCZYŃSKI, J., Philosophy
SLANY, K., Sociology
STRÓŻEWSKI, W., Philosophy, Ontology
SUCHOŃ, W., Philosophy
SZTOMPKA, P., Sociological Theory
SZYMAŃSKA-ALEKSANDROWICZ, B., Philosophy
SZYMAŃSKI, M., Pedagogy, Sociology
URBAN, B., Pedagogy
WILKOSZEWSKA, K., Philosophy of Aesthetics
WOLEŃSKI, J., Philosophy, Epistemology
WROŃSKI, A., Logic and Philosophy

Faculty of Physics, Astronomy and Applied Computer Science (ul. Reymonta 4, 30-059 Cracow; tel. (12) 632-48-88 ext. 5703; fax (12) 433-70-86; e-mail fais@adm.uj.edu.pl; internet www.fais.uj.edu.pl):

ARODŹ, H., Field Theory
BAŁANDA, A., Nuclear Physics
BARA, J., Nuclear Physics
BIAŁAS, A., Theory of Elementary Particles, Astrophysics
BLICHARSKI, J. S., Radiospectroscopy, Biophysics
BODEK, K., Nuclear Physics
DOHNALIK, T., Atomic and Optical Physics
FIAŁKOWSKI, K., Theoretical Physics
FULIŃSKI, A., Statistical Physics
GAWLIK, W., Atomic and Optical Physics, Photonics
JURKIEWICZ, J., Theoretical Physics
KAMYS, B., Nuclear Physics
KOTAŃSKI, A., Computer Science, High Energy Physics
KRÓLAS, K., Nuclear Physics
KULESSA, R., Nuclear Physics
KUTSCHERA, M., Astrophysics
ŁATKA, K., Experimental Physics
LONGA, L., Statistical Physics
MACHALSKI, J., Radioastronomy and Extragalactic Astronomy
MAJKA, Z., Hot Matter
MALEC, E., Relativity, Astrophysics
MASŁOWSKI, J., Radioastronomy and Cosmic Physics
MICEK, S., Experimental Computer Physics
MOŚCICKI, J., Soft Matter Physics
MUSIOŁ, K., Atomic Physics
NOWAK, M., Theoretical Physics
OLEŚ, A. M., Theoretical Physics

OSTROWSKI, M., Astronomy
PĘDZIWIATR, A., Experimental Physics
RICHTER-WĄS, E., Applied Numerical Methods, High Energy Physics
ROKITA, E., Medical Physics, Environmental Physics
ROŚCISZEWSKI, K., Condensed Matter Theory
SPAŁEK, J., Condensed Matter Theory
STANEK, J., Solid State Physics
STARUSZKIEWICZ, A., General Relativity, Electrodynamics, Astrophysics
SZWED, J., Applied Numerical Methods, High Energy Physics
SZYMOŃSKI, M., Experimental Physics
SZYTUŁA, A., Solid State Physics, Magnetism
TOMALA, K., Radiospectroscopy
URBAN, S., Solid State Physics
WALUŚ, W., Nuclear Physics
WARCZAK, A., Experimental Physics
WITAŁA, H., Nuclear Physics
WOSIEK, J., Theoretical Computer Physics
WRÓBEL, S., Solid State Physics
ZAKRZEWSKI, J., Atomic and Optical Physics, Photonics
ZALEWSKI, K., Particle Theory

UNIWERSYTET KARDYNAŁA STEFANA WYSZYŃSKIEGO W WARSZAWIE
(Cardinal Stefan Wyszyński University in Warsaw)

ul. Dewajtis 5, 01-815 Warsaw

Telephone: (22) 839-52-21
Fax: (22) 839-52-45
E-mail: rektorat@uksw.edu.pl
Internet: www.uksw.edu.pl

Founded 1954 as Akademia Teologii Katolickiej; present name and status 1999
Academic year: October to June

Rector: Prof. Dr hab. HENRYK SKOROWSKI
Vice-Rector for Gen. Affairs and Scientific Research: Rev. Prof. Dr hab. RYSZARD RUMIANEK
Vice-Rector for Education and Int. Cooperation: Rev. Prof. Dr hab. JAN BIELECKI
Vice-Rector for Devt and Student Affairs: Prof. Dr hab. ZBIGNIEW CIEŚLAK
Admin. Dir: Mgr inż MAREK LEPA
Librarian: Mgr PIOTR LATAWIEC

Library of 200,000 vols
Number of teachers: 520
Number of students: 15,392

Publications: *Collectanea Theologica* (4 a year), *Jus Matrimoniale* (1 a year), *Kroniki UKSW* (4 a year), *Maqom* (2 a year), *Prawo Kanoniczne* (4 a year), *Saeculum Christianum* (2 a year), *Studia nad Rodziną* (2 a year), *Studia Philosophiae Christianae* (2 a year), *Studia Psychologica* (1 a year), *Studia Theologica Varsaviensia* (2 a year), *Wiadomości UKSW* (12 a year), *Zeszyty Prawnicze* (1 a year)

DEANS

Faculty of Canon Law: Rev. Prof. Dr hab. JULIAN KAŁOWSKI
Faculty of Christian Philosophy: Rev. Prof. Dr hab. JÓZEF DOŁĘGA
Faculty of History and Social Sciences: Rev. Prof. Dr hab. HENRYK SKOROWSKI
Faculty of Humanities: Dr TOMASZ CHACHULSKI
Faculty of Law: Prof. Dr hab. CEZARY MIK
Faculty of Mathematics and Science: Prof. Dr hab. MAREK KOWALSKI
Faculty of Theology: Rev. Prof. Dr hab. STANISŁAW URBAŃSKI

PROFESSORS

Faculty of Canon Law (tel. (22) 839-52-64; fax (22) 561-88-12; e-mail prawokan@uksw .edu.pl):

BŁESZYŃSKI, J., Civil Law
BRZOZOWSKI, A., Civil Law
DĘBIŃSKI, A., Roman Law
DYBOWSKI, T., Civil Law
GÓRALSKI, W., Ecclesiastical Matrimonial and Family Law
GRĘŹLIKOWSKI, J., History of Law
JEMIELITY, W., History of Ecclesiastical Polish Law
KAŁOWSKI, J., Law of Consecration Life Institutes and Apostolic Life Associations
KIWIOR, W., Procedural Law
KRUKOWSKI, J., Religion and Concordat Law
PASTUSZKO, M., Law of Sacraments
SOBAŃSKI, R., Theory of Ecclesiastical Law
STAWNIAK, H., Law of Teaching Services
SYRYJCZYK, J., Ecclesiastical Criminal Law
SZTYCHMILER, R., Ecclesiastical Procedural Law
WROCEŃSKI, J., Ecclesiastical Law of Persons

Faculty of Christian Philosophy (tel. (22) 561-88-53; fax (22) 561-88-53; e-mail wfch@ uksw.edu.pl):

ANDRZEJUK, A., Philosophy
ARANOWSKA, E., Methodology of Psychological Sciences
BIELECKI, J., Psychology of Religion
BOŁOZ, J., Bioethics
BOMBIK, M., Logic
DOŁĘGA, J., Philosophy of Nature
GAŁUSZKO, K., Preservation of Nature
GASIUL, H., Psychology of Personality
GERAS, G., Judicial and Penitentiary Psychology
HAŁACZEK, B., Anthropology, History and Philosophy of Science
JAKUBIK, A., Clinical Psychology
KLIMSKI, T., History of Philosophy
LATAWIEC, A., Philosophy of Nature
LEMAŃSKA, A., Philosophy of Nature
MACEWICZ, J., Genetics
MATCZAK, A., Developmental Psychology
MORAWIEC, E., Philosophy, Metaphysics
NIEZNAŃSKI, E., Logic, Methodology of Sciences
NOWICKA, G., Biochemistry
PODREZ, E., Ethics
PORĘBSKI, S., History of Polish Philosophy
RYŚ, M., Psychology of Marriage and Family
SAREŁO, Z., Ethics
SINIARSKA-WOLAŃSKA, A., Ecology
SOCHOŃ, J., History of Philosophy, Philosophy of Religion
STOJANOWSKA, E., Social Psychology
STRZAŁECKI, A., General Psychology, Psychodiagnosis
TERELAK, J., Psychology of Labour and Stress
TYLKA, J., Clinical Psychology
ZABŁOCKI, K., Pedagogy, Psychology of Revalidation and Rehabilitation

Faculty of History and Social Sciences (tel. (22) 561-88-10; fax (22) 561-88-10; e-mail wnhis@uksw.edu.pl):

BALICKI, J., Political Science
BANIA, Z., History of Medieval and Modern Architecture
CYWIŃSKI, B., Contemporary History
DĄBEK, S., Musicology
DĄBROWSKA, T., Archaeology
DADAK-KOZICKA, K., Musicology
DELUGA, W., History of Art
DROZD, J., International Relations
DYLUS, A., Philosophy and Ethics
GRONKIEWICZ-WALTZ, H., Administrative and Banking Law

GROSFELD, J., Political Economy
JANOCHA, M., History of Art
JUROS, H., Moral Theology, Ethics
KOBIELUS, S., History of Art
KOBYLIŃSKI, Z., Archaeology
KOŁOSOWSKI, T., History of Early Christian Literature
KORAL, J., Political Science
KOZŁOWSKI, S., Archaeology
KRASNODĘBSKI, Z., Philosophy and Sociology
MAJKOWSKI, W., Sociology of the Family
MANDZIUK, J., History of the Church
MAZURKIWEICZ, P., Political Science
MIŚKIEWICZ, M., Archaeology
MOISAN-JABLONSKI, CH., History of Art
NAUMOWICZ, J., History of Early Christian Literature
NAWROT, E., History
OCHOCKI, A., Demography
ODZIEMKOWSKI, J., History
POKORA, H., History of Art
POTOCKI, A., Sociology
REKŁAJTIS, E., Arabic Philology
SKOROWSKI, H., Political Science
SZYMONIK, K., Arts of Music
TRZECIAK, M., Sociology
UERTZ, R., Political Science
WILSKA, M., Archaeology
WÓJTOWICZ, A., Sociology
WYSOCKI, W., History
ZBUDNIEWEK, J., History of the Church
ZIEMER, K., Political Science
ŻYRO, T., Political Science

Faculty of Humanities (tel. (22) 839-77-63; e-mail polonistyka@uksw.edu.pl):

BIEŃKOWSKA, E., History of 19th- and 20th-century Literature, Comparative Literature, Literary Criticism
BOBROWSKA, B., History of Literature of the Second Half of the 19th Century
DOPART, B., Romantic Literature
DUMA, J., History of Language
DYBCIAK, K., History of 20th-century Literature, Literary Criticism
JANUS, E., History of Language
KOSTKIEWICZOWA, T., History of 18th-century Literature, Theory of Literature
KUCZYŃSKA-KWAPISZ, J., Education for Handicapped People
ŁUKASZUK-PIEKARA, M, 20th-century Literature
PAWŁOWSKI, K., Classical Philology, Theory of Literature
PISKUREWICZ, J., History of Child-rearing
PRUSSAK, M., Science of Theatre, History of Literature of the Second Half of the 19th Century, Science Publications
SMOLIŃSKA-THEISS, B., Education
SURZYSZKIEWICZ, J., Education
THEISS, W., Social Education
WARZECHA, J., Biblical Studies
WOLNICZ-PAWŁOWSKA, E., History of Language
ZIELIŃSKA, A., Linguistics

Faculty of Law (ul. Wóycickiego 1/3, 01-938 Warsaw; tel. (22) 569-96-50; fax (22) 569-97-45; e-mail prawo@uksw.edu.pl):

BORUTA, M., Labour Law
CIEŚLAK, Z., Administrative Law
GRANAT, M., Constitutional Law
JĘDRZEJEWSKA, M., Civil Proceedings
JURCEWICZ, A., Agrarian Law
KACZYŃSKI, L., Labour Law
KALLAS, M., History of the Political System and Law in Poland
LIPOWICZ, I., European Administrative Law
MAJEWSKI, J., Criminal Law
MIK, C., International and European Law
MORAWSKI, L., Theory and Philosophy of Law
NOWAK-FAR, A., Financial Law
OMYŁA, M., Logic and Methodology of Legal Sciences
PRUSAK, F., Criminal Procedure

STOJANOWSKA, W., Family Law
STRZYCZKOWSKI, K., Private Economic Law
SZAJKOWSKI, A., Private Economic Law
SZPOR, G., Informatics Law
ZABŁOCKI, J., Roman Law
ZIELIŃSKI, A., Civil Proceedings

Faculty of Mathematics and Natural Science (tel. (22) 561-89-29; e-mail matematyka@ uksw.edu.pl):

ALSTER, K., Mathematics
CHEŁMIŃSKI, K., Mathematics
CHOJNACKI, W., Mathematics
CYTOWSKI, J. W., Computer Science
GAJDA, M., Physics
GODLEWSKI, M., Physics
GÓRECKI, J., Chemistry
HERBICH, J., Chemistry
HOŁYST, R., Chemistry
JABŁOŃSKI, A., Chemistry
KARPIŃSKI, Z., Chemistry
KIJOWSKI, J., Physics
KORYBUT-DASZKIEWICZ, B., Chemistry
KOTLARSKI, H., Mathematics
KOWALSKI, M. A., Mathematics
KRYNICKI, M., Mathematics
KULPA, W., Mathematics
KUŚ, M., Physics
KUTNER, W., Chemistry
ŁUNARSKA-BOROWIECKA, E., Chemistry
MACEK, W., Physics
MAINARDI, S., Economy
MAZUR, T., Mathematics
MOSTOWSKI, J., Physics
NANIEWICZ, Z., Mathematics
NOWICKA-TARASZEWSKA, J., Chemistry
RUSINEK, J., Mathematics
RZĄŻEWSKI, K., Physics
SKOŚKIEWICZ, T., Physics
SKWARCZYŃSKI, M., Mathematics
SOCHA, L., Computer Science
TURSKI, L. A., Physics
TURZAŃSKI, M., Mathematics
WALUK, J., Chemistry
ZAGRODNY, D., Mathematics
ZAREMBA, L., Mathematics

Faculty of Theology (tel. (22) 839-92-82; e-mail wtdz@uksw.edu.pl):

BALTER, L., Dogmatic Theology
BARTNICKI, R., Biblical Studies
BEŁCH, K., Pastoral Theology
BOKWA, I., Dogmatic Theology
CHROSTOWSKI, W., Biblical Studies
CZAJKOWSKI, M., Biblical Studies
DECYK, J., Liturgy
DURAK, A., Liturgy
DZIUBA, A., Moral Theology
GACKA, B., Dogmatic Theology
GÓRALCZYK, P., Moral Theology
GRACZYK, M., Moral Theology
JABŁOŃSKI, S., Mariology
KARWACKI, R., Fundamental Theology
KULISZ, J., Fundamental Theology
LEWANDOWSKI, J., Dogmatic Theology
LEWEK, A., Theology of Mass Media
MATWIEJUK, K., Liturgics
MĘDALA, S., Biblical Studies
MIERZWIŃSKI, B., Pastoral Theology
MISIASZEK, K., Catechesis
MROCZKOWSKI, I., Moral Theology
MURAWSKI, R., Catechesis
NOWAK, J., Liturgy
OGÓREK, P., Theology of Spirituality
OZOROWSKI, E., Dogmatic Theology
PAZERA, W., Homiletics
PIETRZYK, Z., History of the Church
PIKUS, T., Fundamental Theology
PRZYBYŁOWSKI, J., Pastoral Theology
RUMIANEK, R., Biblical Studies
SAKOWICZ, E., Religion
SALIJ, J., Dogmatic Theology
SEWERYNIAK, H., Fundamental Theology
TYLKI-SZYMAŃSKA, A., Family Studies
URBAŃSKI, S., Theology of Spirituality
WARCHOŁ, E., History of the Church
WARZESZAK, J., Dogmatic Theology

ZABIELSKI, J., Moral Theology
ZAŁĘSKI, J., Biblical Studies

UNIWERSYTET MARII CURIE-SKŁODOWSKIEJ
(Marie Curie-Skłodowska University)

Plac Marii Curie-Skłodowskiej 5, 20-031 Lublin

Telephone: (81) 537-51-07
Fax: (81) 537-51-02
E-mail: rector@ramzes.umcs.lublin.pl
Internet: www.umcs.lublin.pl

Founded 1944
Academic year: October to June

Rector: Prof. Dr hab. WIESŁAW ANDRZEJ KAMIŃSKI
Pro-Rector for Devt: Prof. Dr hab. JERZY WĘCŁAWSKI
Pro-Rector for Gen. Affairs: Prof. Dr hab. TADEUSZ BOROWIECKI
Pro-Rector for Scientific Research, Int. Relations and Off-Campus Centres: Prof. Dr hab. ANNA TUKIENDORF
Pro-Rector for Students and Teaching: Prof. Dr hab. ANNA PAJDZIŃSKA
Chief Admin. Officer: Inż. MACIEJ GRUDZIŃSKI
Librarian: Dr BOGUSŁAW KASPEREK

Library: gen. scientific colln of 2,528,340 vols, including 338,853 vols of periodicals, 10,168 online journals, 803 MSS, 369,207 patents, 40,272 maps and atlases, 14,954 music scores, 19,215 ancient books, 2,814 dissertations, 4,822 audio cassettes and records
Number of teachers: 1,805
Number of students: 34,758
Publication: *Annales Universitatis Mariae Curie-Skłodowska*

DEANS

Faculty of Biology and Earth Sciences: Prof. Dr hab. RYSZARD DĘBICKI
Faculty of Chemistry: Prof. Dr hab. ANDRZEJ DĄBROWSKI
Faculty of Economics: Prof. Dr hab. ELŻBIETA SKRZYPEK
Faculty of Fine Arts: Prof. Dr hab. URSZULA BOBRYK
Faculty of Humanities: Prof. Dr hab. HENRYK GMITEREK
Faculty of Law and Administration: Prof. Dr hab. ANTONI PIENIĄŻEK
Faculty of Mathematics, Physics and Computer Science: Prof. Dr hab. KRZYSZTOF POMORSKI
Faculty of Philosophy and Sociology: Prof. Dr hab. JACEK PAŚNICZEK
Faculty of Political Science: Prof. Dr hab. STANISŁAW MICHAŁOWSKI
Faculty of Psychology and Pedagogy: Prof. Dr hab. ZDZISŁAW BARTKOWICZ

PROFESSORS

Faculty of Biology and Earth Sciences (ul. Akademicka 19, 20-030 Lublin; tel. (81) 537-52-16; fax (81) 537-52-14; internet binoz .umcs.lublin.pl):

BEDNARA, J., Anatomy and Plant Cytology
BYSTREK, J., Plant Systematics
DĘBICKI, A., Soil Science
DERNAŁOWICZ-MALARCZYK, E., Biochemistry
DROŻAŃSKI, W., Microbiology
FIEDERUK, J., Microbiology
GRANKOWSKI, N., Molecular Biology
HARASIMIUK, M., Geomorphology
JAKUBOWICZ, T., Biochemistry and Immunology
KAŁKOWSKA, K., Animal Physiology
KANDEFER-SZERSZEŃ, M., Microbiology
KRUPA, Z., Plant Physiology
KUREK, E., Environmental Microbiology
LEONOWICZ, A., Biochemistry
MICHALCZYK, Z., Hydrography

PĘKALA, K., Physical Geography and Geomorphology
ROGALSKI, J., Molecular Biology
RUSSA, R., Microbiology
SIRKO, M., Cartography
SKORUPSKA, A., Microbiology
ŚNIEZKO, R., Botany
SWIĘS, F., Botany
SZCZODRAK, J., Microbiology
TRĘBACZ, K., Biology and Biophysics
WOJCIECHOWSKI, K., Geography
WOJTANOWICZ, J., Physical Geography and Geomorphology
ZAWADZKI, T., Plant Physiology

Faculty of Chemistry (Plac Marii Curie-Skłodowskiej 3, 20-030 Lublin; tel. (81) 537-57-16; fax (81) 533-33-48; e-mail chemia@ hermes.umcs.lublin.pl; internet chemia.umcs .lublin.pl):

BOROWIECKI, T., Chemical Technology
BORÓWKO, M., Physical Chemistry
CHIBOWSKI, E., Physical Chemistry
CHIBOWSKI, S., Physical Chemistry
DAWIDOWICZ, A., Physical Chemistry
DĄBROWSKI, A., Theoretical Chemistry
FERENC, W., Inorganic Chemistry
GAWDZIK, B., Physical Chemistry
GOWOREK, J., Physical Chemistry
HUBICKA, H., Inorganic Chemistry
HUBICKI, Z., Inorganic Chemistry
JAŃCZUK, B., Physical Chemistry
KOZIOŁ, A., Chemistry, X-ray Crystallography
LEBODA, R., Physical Chemistry of Surfaces and Chromatography
MACHOKI, A., Heterogeneous Catalysis, C1 Chemistry
MATYNIA, T., Organic Chemistry
NARKIEWIEZ-MICHAŁCK, J., Theoretical Chemistry
NAZIMEK, D., Physical Chemistry
PATRYKIEJEW, A., Physical Chemistry
PIETRUSIEWICZ, K., Organic Chemistry
PIKUS, S., X-ray Crystallography-powder Diffraction
PODKOŚCIELNY, W., Organic Chemistry
RAYSS, J., Physical Chemistry
RÓŻYŁŁO, J., Physical Chemistry
RUDZINSKI, W., Theoretical Chemistry
SOKOŁOWSKI, S., Theoretical Chemistry
STASZCZUK, P., Physical Chemistry
WOLIŃSKI, K., Quantum Chemistry, Methods and Applications
WÓJCIK, W., Physical Chemistry

Faculty of Economics (tel. (81) 537-54-62; fax (81) 537-54-62; e-mail ekonomia@ramzes .umcs.lublin.pl; internet ekonomia.umcs .lublin.pl):

GRABOWIECKI, J., Political Economy
KARPUŚ, P., Economics
KOZŁOWSKI, S., Economics
MAMEARZ, M., Economics, Financial Markets
MUCHA-LESZKO, B., Political Economy, Economic Planning
POMORSKA, A., Finances
RONCK, H., Economics
RUDNICKI, M., Economics of Agriculture
SIKORSKI, C., Economics
SKOWRONEK, Cz., Industrial Economics
SKRZYPEK, E., Economics
SOBCZYK, G., Economics
SZYMAŃSKI, Z., Economics, History of Economic Thought
SZYNAL, J., Economics, Banking
WĘCŁAWSKI, J., Economics, Banking
WICH, U., Urban Planning
ZALEWA, J., Agricultural Economics
ZUKOWSKI, M., Economics

Faculty of Fine Arts (ul. Kraśnicka 2b, 20-718 Lublin; tel. (81) 523-53-91; fax (81) 523-53-91; e-mail warto@klio.umcs.lublin.pl):

BERNATOWICZ, M., Conducting
BOBRYK, U., Conducting

DĄBROWSKA, B., Conducting
GÓRSKI, K., Conducting
GRYKA, J., Graphics
HERMAN, M., Painting
JAWORSKA, A., Conducting
JAWORSKI, L., Conducting
KIERSKI, J., Sculpture
KOŁODZIEJ, R., Graphics
LECH, P., Graphics
MAZUREK, G., Graphics
MIELESZKO, S., Teaching of Sculpture
NALEPKA, J., Music Education
NAWROT-TRZCIŃSKA, I., Photographics
NIEDŹWIEDŹ, Z., Graphics
ORDYK-CZYZŻEWSKA, E., Conducting
POPEK, A., Graphics
PRZYCHODZIŃSKA-KACICZAK, M., Music Education
RZECHOWSKA-KLAUZA, G., Conducting
SMOCZYŃSKI, M., Painting
SNOCH, M., Graphics
STYKA, A., Painting
SWIECA, C., Music Education
WOJCIECHOWSKI, J., Painting
WRÓBLEWSKI, W., Painting
ZAWADZKI, T., Painting
ŻUKOWSKI, S., Painting

Faculty of Humanities (Plac Marii Curie-Skłodowskiej 4, 20-031 Lublin; tel. (81) 537-54-66; fax (81) 537-54-66; internet www.umcs .lublin.pl):

BARTMIŃSKI, J., History of Polish Literature
BLAIM, A., English Literature
BONIECKA, B., History of Polish Literature
GMITEREK, M., Modern History
GRABIAS, S., Applied and Sociolinguistics
KARDELA, H., English Philology
KĘSIK, M., French Linguistics
KOKOWSKI, A., Archaeology
KOLEK, L., English Literature
KOLODZIEJ, E., Archiving
KORDELA, H., English Philology
KOSYL, Cz., Polish Philology
KRAJKA, W., Theory of Literature, History of English Literature
KRUK, S., History of Polish Theatre
LEWANDOWSKI, J., Modern History
LEWICKI, R., Linguistics
MAZUR, J., Polish Linguistics
MIKULEC, B., Modern History
MISIEWICZ, J., Theory of Literature
MYRDZIK, B., History of Polish Literature
NIEZNANOWSKI, S., Old Polish Literature
ORŁOWSKI, J., History of Russian Literature
PLISIECKI, J., Film
POMORSKI, J., Methodology and History of Historiography
RADZIK, T., Contemporary History
SAWECKA, H., Theory of Romance Literature
ŚLADKOWSKI, W., Modern History
ŚWIĘCH, W., Modern Polish Literature
STĘPNIK, K., Polish Literature
SZCZYGIEŁ, R., Medieval History
SZYMAŃSKI, J., Auxiliary Sciences of History
TOKARSKI, R., Polish Language
TRELIŃSKA, B.
WIŚNIEWSKA, H., Polish Linguistics
WOŹNIAKIEWICZ-DZIADOSZ, M., Theory of Literature

Faculty of Law and Administration (tel. (81) 537-51-26; fax (81) 537-54-05; internet pia .umcs.lublin.pl):

BOJARSKI, T., Penal Law
CHORĄŻY, K., Administrative Law
GDULEWICZ, E., Constitutional Law
KIDYBA, A., Economic Law
KMIECIK, R., Penal Law
KOROBOWICZ, A., History of State and Law
KURYŁOWICZ, M., Roman Law
LESZCZYŃSKI, L., Theory of State and Law
OLESZKO, A., Civil Law

POŹNIAK-NIEDZIELSKA, M., Economic Law
SAWCZUK, M., Civil Procedure
SKRĘTOWICZ, E., Penal Law
SKUBISZ, R., European Community Law
SZRENIAWSKI, J., Administrative Law and Administrative Science
TOKARCZYK, R., History of Political Thought
WĄSEK, A., Penal Law and Criminology
WITKOWSKI, W., History of State and Law
WÓJTOWICZ, W., Financial Law
WRÓBEL, A., European Community Law
ZDYB, M., Administrative Law

Faculty of Mathematics, Physics and Computer Science (Plac Marii Curie-Skłodowskiej 2, 20-031 Lublin; tel. (81) 537-52-12; fax (81) 537-52-71; internet mfi.umcs.lublin.pl):

ADAMCZYK, B., Physics
BARAN, A., Computer Science
BUDZYŃSKI, M., Experimental Physics
GLADYSZEWSKI, L., Theoretical Physics
GOEBEL, K., Differential Equations
GOWOREK, T., Nuclear Physics
GÓŹDŹ, A., Theoretical Physics
GRUSZECKI, W., Biophysics
HAŁAS, ST., Experimental Physics
JAŁOCHOWSKI, M., Experimental Physics
KAMIŃSKI, W., Nuclear Physics
KOMOROWSKI, T., Differential Equations
KORCZAK, Z., Solid Body Physics
KOZICKI, J., Computer Science
KRAWCZYK, W., Biophysics
KRZYŻ, J., Analytic Functions
KUCZUMOW, T., Differential Equations
KUREK, J., Differential Geometry
MĄCZKA, D., Experimental Physics
MICHALAK, L., Experimental Physics
MIKOŁAJCZAK, P., Solid Body Physics
MURAWSKI, K., Computer Science
NOWAK, M., Analytic Functions
POMORSKA, B., Theoretical Physics
POMORSKI, K., Theoretical Physics
PRUS, S., Functional Analysis
RYCHLIK, Z., Probability Theory
RZYMOWSKI, W., Differential Equations
SIELANKO, J., Nuclear Physics
SIELEWIESIUK, J., Physics and Biophysics
SYZNAL, D., Probability Theory
SZEZERBA, J., Computer Science
TARANKO, E., Theoretical Physics
TARANKO, R., Theoretical Physics
WANIURSKI, J., Analytical Functions
WÓJCIK, L., Experimental Physics
WYSOKIŃSKI, K., Theoretical Physics
ZĄBEK, S., Numerical Methods
ZAŁUŻNY, M., Theoretical Physics
ZIĘBA, W., Probability Theory
ZŁOTKIEWICZ, E., Analytic Functions
ŻUK, J., Experimental Physics

Faculty of Philosophy and Sociology (Plac Marii Curie-Skłodowskiej 4, 20-030 Lublin; tel. (81) 537-54-79; fax (81) 537-54-81; e-mail dziekfis@ramzes.umcs.lublin.pl; internet bacon.umcs.lublin.pl):

CZARNECKI, Z., History of Philosophy
FILIPIAK, M., Sociology
JEDYNAK, S., Ethics
KOSIŃSKI, S., Sociology
LIBISZEWSKA-ZÓŁTKOWSKA, M., Sociology
MIZIŃSKA, J., Epistemology
OGRYZKO-WIEWIÓROWSKA, M., Sociology
PAŚNICZEK, J., Logic
STYK, J., Sociology
SYMOTIUK, S., Philosophy of Culture
TOKARSKI, S., Sociology of Medicine

Faculty of Political Science (Plac Litewski 3, 20-080 Lublin; tel. (81) 532-42-78; fax (81) 533-66-10; e-mail poldziek@sokrates.umcs.lublin.pl; internet www.politologia.pl):

CHAŁUPCZAK, H., International Relations
CZARNOCKI, A., International Relations
HOŁDA, Z., Human Rights
HUDZIK, J., Political Philosophy
JACHYMEK, J., Political Thought
JANUSZ, G., International Relations

JELENKOWSKI, M., Political Doctrines
KUCHARSKI, W., National Minorities
MAJ, Cz., International Relations
MAJ, F., Contemporary History
MICH, W., Contemporary History
MICHAŁOWSKI, S., Local Government
MIECZKOWSKI, A., Contemporary History
OLSZEWSKI, E., Political Movements
PIETRAŚ, M., International Relations
PIETRAŚ, Z. J., International Relations
STĘPICŃ, S., Contemporary History
SZELIGA, Z., Constitutional Law
WÓJCIK, A., Contemporary History
ŻMIGRODZKI, M., Political Systems

Faculty of Psychology and Pedagogy (ul. Narutowicza 12, 20-950 Lublin; tel. (81) 537-63-04; fax (81) 537-04-27; internet pip.umcs.lublin.pl):

BARTKOWICZ, Z., Pedagogy
CACKOWSKA, M., Didactics
CHODKOWSKA, M., Sociology
GAJDA, M., Pedagogy
GAŚ, Z., Psychopathology
GUZ, S., Pedagogy
HERZYK, A., Neuropsychology
KACZMAREK, B., Psychology
KĘPSKI, Cz., Pedagogy
KIRENKO, J., Pedagogy
KRASOWICZ-KUPIS, G., Psychology
KUCHA, R., History of Learning and Education
KWIATKOWSKA, G., Philosophy
OCHMAŃSKI, M., High School Pedagogy
PALAK, Z., Pedagogy
POPEK, S., Psychology
SARAN, J., Pedagogy
STACHYRA, J., Pedagogy
WĘGLIŃSKI, A., Pedagogy

UNIWERSYTET MEDYCZNY W ŁODZI
(Medical University of Łódź)

ul. Kościuszki 4, 90-419 Łódź

Telephone: (42) 632-51-00
Fax: (42) 630-07-07
E-mail: rektor@rkt.am.lodz.pl
Internet: www.umed.lodz.pl

Founded 2002 by the merger of Łódź Medical Acad. and Łódź Military Medical Acad.
State control

Rector: Prof. ANDRZEJ LEWIŃSKI

Number of teachers: 1,177
Number of students: 23,127

DEANS

Faculty of Medicine: Prof. KAZIMIERZ JĘDRZEJEWSKI
Faculty of Medicine and Dentistry: Prof. WIELISŁAW PAPIERZ
Faculty of Military Medicine: Prof. JAN BŁASZCZYK
Faculty of Pharmacy: Prof. JADWIGA SZYMAŃSKA
Faculty of Physiotherapy: Prof. JUREK OLSZEWSKI
Faculty of Public Health: Prof. ANNA JEGIER

UNIWERSYTET MEDYCZNY W BIAŁYMSTOKU
(Medical University of Białystok)

ul. Kilińskiego 1, 15-089 Białystok

Telephone: (85) 748-54-00
Internet: www.amb.edu.pl

Founded 1950

Faculties: medicine with divisions of dentistry and medical education, pharmacy with division of laboratory medicine, health sciences

Rector: Prof. Dr hab. JACEK NIKLIŃSKI

Library of 235,000 vols
Number of teachers: 660
Number of students: 1,762

Publication: *Annals*.

UNIWERSYTET MEDYCZNY W LUBLINIE
(Medical University in Lublin)

ul. Aleje Racławickie 1, 20-059 Lublin

Telephone: (81) 528-84-00
Internet: www.umlub.pl

Founded 1950

Rector: Prof. Dr hab. ANDRZEJ KSIĄŻEK

Library of 250,000 vols
Number of teachers: 1,180
Number of students: 3,535

Faculties: Medicine, Pharmacy and Nursing.

UNIWERSYTET MIKOŁAJA KOPERNIKA W TORUNIU
(Nicholas Copernicus University of Toruń)

ul. Gagarina 11, 87-100 Toruń

Telephone: (56) 654-29-51
Fax: (56) 654-29-44
E-mail: rektor@uni.torun.pl
Internet: www.uni.torun.pl

Founded 1945
State control
Language of instruction: Polish
Academic year: October to September (2 terms)

Rector: Prof. Dr hab. ANDRZEJ RADZIMIŃSKI
Vice-Rectors: Prof. Dr hab. ANDRZEJ TRETYN, Prof. Dr hab. DANUTA JANICKA, Prof. Dr hab. WŁODZIMIERZ KARASZEWSKI, Prof. Dr hab. WITOLD WOJDYŁO, Prof. Dr hab. MAŁGORZATA TAFIL-KLAWE
Registrar: Dr PAWEŁ MODRZYŃSKI
Librarian: Dr KRZYSZTOF NIERZWICKI

Library of 1,155,888 vols, 563,862 vols of periodicals, 54,912 old books, 82,117 manuscripts, 14,227 cartographic publications, 62,711 graphics and posters, 87,376 musical scores, 11,366 records; 754,086 vols in departmental libraries; special collns: Pomeranica, Copernicana, Baltica, Polish Emigration Archives
Number of teachers: 2,222
Number of students: 31,000

Publications: *Bulletin of Geography, Socioeconomic Series, Chaotic and Regular Dynamics, Comparative Law Review, Eastern European Countryside, Logic and Logical Philosophy, Medical and Biological Sciences, Open Systems and Information Dynamics, Prussia Sacra* (published jointly with Max-Planck-Institut, Göttingen), *Reports on Mathematical Physics, Topological Methods in Nonlinear Analysis, Theoria et Historia Scientiarum, Toruński Rocznik Praw Człowieka i Pokoju*

DEANS

Faculty of Biology and Earth Sciences: Prof. Dr hab. WIESAW KOZAK
Faculty of Chemistry: Prof. Dr hab. JERZY ŁUKASZEWICZ
Faculty of Economics and Management: Prof. Dr hab. JÓZEF STAWICKI
Faculty of Education Sciences: Prof. Dr hab ALEKSANDER NALASKOWSKI
Faculty of Fine Arts: Prof. Dr hab. PIOTR KLUGOWSKI
Faculty of Health Sciences: Prof. Dr hab ZBIGNIEW BARTUZI
Faculty of History: Prof. Dr hab. JACEK GZELLA
Faculty of Humanities: Prof. Dr hab. ANDRZEJ SZAHAJ
Faculty of Languages: Prof. Dr hab. ADAM BEDNAREK
Faculty of Law and Administration: Prof. Dr hab. ANDRZEJ SOKALA

Faculty of Mathematics and Computer Science: Prof. Dr hab. ANDRZEJ ROZKOSZ

Faculty of Medicine: Prof. Dr hab. HENRYK KAŹMIERCZAK

Faculty of Pharmacy: Prof. Dr hab BRONISŁAW GRZEGORZEWSKI

Faculty of Physics, Astronomy and Informatics: Prof. Dr hab. STANISŁAW CHWIROT

Faculty of Political Sciences and Int. Studies: Prof. Dr hab. ROMAN BÄCKER

Faculty of Theology: Rev. Prof. Dr hab. JAN PERSZON

PROFESSORS

Faculty of Biology and Earth Sciences (ul. Gagarina 9, 87-100 Toruń; tel. (56) 611-44-41; fax (56) 611-47-72; e-mail baranow@biol .uni.torun.pl; internet www.biol.uni.torun .pl):

BEDNAREK, R., Soil Science
BEDNARSKA, E., Plant Cytology
BUSZKO, J., Entomology, Zoogeography
CAPUTA, M., Animal Physiology
CEYNOWA-GIEŁDON, M., Plant Taxonomy, Geobotany
CHWIROT, B., Plant and Animal Cytology
DAHM, H., Microbiology
DONDERSKI, W., Microbiology, Biotechnology
FALKOWSKI, J., Economic Geography, Spatial Management
GIZIŃSKI, A., Hydrobiology
GNIOT-SZULŻYCKA, J., Biochemistry
GÓRSKA-BRYLASS, A., Plant Cytology
KOPCEWICZ, J., Plant Physiology
KRIESEL, G., Anthropology
MAIK, W., Social Geography
NIEWAROWSKI, W., Physical Geography, Palaeogeography
REJEWSKI, M., Plant Ecology
SADURSKI, A., Hydrobiology and Environmental Protection
SZUPRYCZYŃSKI, J., Geomorphology
TRETYN, A., Plant Physiology

Faculty of Chemistry (ul. Gagarina 7, 87-100 Toruń; tel. (56) 654-29-38; fax (56) 654-24-77; e-mail wydzial@chem.uni.torun.pl; internet www.chem.uni.torun.pl):

BUSZEWSKI, B., Analytical Chemistry
CHOSTENKO, A., Nuclear Chemistry
GRODZICKI, A., Inorganic Chemistry
KITA, P., Inorganic Chemistry
ROZWADOWSKI, M., Physical Chemistry
RYCHLICKI, G., Physical Chemistry
SADLEJ, A., Theoretical Chemistry
TRYPUĆ, M., Chemical Technology
ZAIDLEWICZ, M., Organic Chemistry

Faculty of Economics and Management (ul. Gagarina 13A, 87-100 Toruń; tel. (56) 611-46-08; fax (56) 654-24-50; e-mail krystyna@econ .uni.torun.pl; internet www.econ.uni.torun .pl):

BOGDANIENKO, J., Investment Economics
DREWIŃSKI, M., Management
GŁUCHOWSKI, J., Finance Management
JAWOROWSKI, P., Agricultural Economics
KACZMARCZYK, S., Marketing
MELLER, J., Human Resources Management
SMOLEŃSKI, S., Marketing
SOJAK, S., Accounting
STANKIEWICZ, M., Strategic Management and Planning
SUDOŁ, S., Industrial Management
SZULCE, H., Marketing
WIŚNIEWSKI, Z., Employment Policy
ZIELIŃSKI, Z., Econometrics

Faculty of Fine Arts (ul. Sienkiewicza 30/32, 87-100 Toruń; tel. (56) 622-70-51; fax (56) 622-59-71; internet www.uni.torun.pl/ wydzialy/wszp):

BEBARSKA, J., Sculpture
CANDER, K., Painting
CHMIELEWSKI, B., Drawing

CHMIELEWSKI, W., Drawing
FLIK, J., Painting
GUTTFELD, A., Painting
KILJAŃSKI, L., Graphics
KRUSZELNICKI, Z., History of Art
LIMONT, W., Art Education
MALINOWSKI, J., History of Art
PAWŁOWSKI, M., Graphics
PRĘGOWSKI, J., Painting
PRZYBYLIŃSKI, B., Graphics
ROUBA, B., Restoration of Painting
SKIBIŃSKI, S., Medieval Art and Architecture
SŁOBOSZ, J., Graphics
STRZELCZYK, A., Conservation on Painting and Leather
SZAŃKOWSKI, M., Sculpture
TAJCHMAN, J., Restoration of Architectural Monuments
WOLSKI, L., Painting
ZIOMEK, M., Painting

Faculty of History (Pl. Teatralny 2A, 87-100 Toruń; tel. (56) 622-62-03; fax (56) 622-28-44; e-mail atom@his.uni.torun.pl; internet www .his.uni.torun.pl):

CHUDZIAK, J., Archaeology of Buildings
DYGDAŁA, J., 16th- to 18th-century Polish History
KALEMBKA, S., Polish and General History
KOZŁOWSKI, R., Modern Polish History
KUTZNER, M., Polish and General Medieval History of Art
MALISZEWSKI, K., 16th- to 18th-century Polish and General History
MAŁŁEK, A., 16th- to 18th-century Polish and General History
MIELCZAREK, M., Classical Archaeology and Numismatics
NOWAKOWSKI, A., Medieval Archaeology and Military History
OLCZAK, J., Medieval Archaeology and History of Glass
POMIAN, K., Polish and General Modern History of Art and Culture
RADZIMIŃSKI, A., Medieval Church History
REZMER, W., Polish Army between the Two World Wars
STASZEWSKI, J., 16th- to 18th-century Polish and General History
SUDZIŃSKI, R., Modern Polish History
SYMONIDES, J., EU and International Law
TANDECKI, J., Polish-German Relationship
TONDEL, J., History of the Book
WAŹBIŃSKI, Z., History of Art
WENTA, J., Medieval History
WOJCIECHOWSKI, M., 19th- and 20th-century Polish and General History
WOŹNICZKA-PARUZEL, B., Bibliotherapy
ZAREMSKA, H., Cultural History

Faculty of Humanities (ul. Fosa Staromiejska 1A, 87-100 Toruń; tel. (56) 611-36-10; fax (56) 652-27-69; e-mail whminus@ped .uni.torun.pl; internet www.uni.torun.pl/ wydzialy/wh):

ADAMSKI, W., Social Structures and Transformations
BAŃKA, A., Psychology
BOROWICZ, R., Sociology of Education
BYBLUK, M., Teaching of Languages
HUBNER, P., History of Science, Sociology of Institutions
KALETA, A., Rural Sociology
KOWALIK, S., Special Education
KWIECIŃSKI, Z., Sociology of Education
ŁUKASZEWICZ, R., School Education
MELOSIK, Z., General Education
MUCHA, J., Social Anthropology and History of Sociology
NALASKOWSKI, A., General Education
PAWLAK, J., History of Philosophy and Social Thought
PERZANOWSKI, J., Logic and Philosophy
PÓŁTURZYCKI, J., General Education
SCHULZ, R., General Education
SIEMIENIECKI, B., Technology in Education

SZAHAJ, A., Political Philosophy, Philosophy of Culture
SZULAKIEWICZ, M., Political Culture
TEMPCZYK, M., Philosophy of Natural Science
TYBURSKI, W., Ethics
WINCŁAWSKI, W., History of Sociology
ZANDECKI, A., General Education
ZELAZNY, M., Aesthetics, History of Philosophy

Faculty of Languages (Coll. Maius, ul. Fosa Staromiejska 3, 87-100 Toruń; tel. (56) 611-35-10; fax (56) 622-66-59; internet www.uni .torun.pl/wydzialy/wf):

BEZWIŃSKI, A., Russian Literature
BRZOZA, H., Russian Literature
FRIEDEL, T., Slavonic and Polish Linguistics
GROCHOWSKI, M., General Linguistics, Semiotics
HARTMANN, H., German Literature
KALLAS, K., Contemporary Polish Syntax
KRYSZAK, J., Contemporary Polish Poetry
SAUERLAND, K., German Literature
SAWICKA, I., Slavonic Linguistics
SKUCZYŃSKI, J., History of Polish Literature and Theatre
SPEINA, J., 20th-century Polish Prose
SZARMACH, M., Greek Literature, Second Sophistry
SZUPRYCZYŃSKA, M., Contemporary Polish Syntax
WĄSIK, Z., English Linguistics
WISZNIOWSKA-MAJCHRZYK, M., English Drama
WRÓBLEWSKI, W., Classical Philology

Faculty of Law and Administration (ul. Gagarina 15, 87-100 Toruń; tel. (56) 611-41-10; fax (56) 611-40-05; e-mail kandydat_wpia@cc.uni.torun.pl; internet www.law.uni.torun.pl):

BORODO, A., Financial Law
BRZEZIŃSKI, B., Public Finance Law
BULSIEWICZ, A., Criminal Law
FILAR, M., Penal Law
JASUDOWICZ, T., Human Rights
JUSTYŃSKI, J., Political and Legal Doctrines
KALLAS, M., History of the Polish State
KOLASIŃSKI, K., Labour Law
KULICKI, M., Crime Detection
LANG, A., Theory of Law and State
ŁASZEWSKI, R., History of Law
LUBIŃSKI, K., Civil Law
MAREK, A., Criminal Law
MIK, C., European Law, Human Rights
MORAWSKI, L., Theory of Law and State
NESTEROWICZ, M., Civil Law
OCHENDOWSKI, E., Administrative Law

Faculty of Mathematics and Computer Science (ul. Chopina 12/18, 87-100 Toruń; tel. (56) 611-34-10; fax (56) 622-89-79; e-mail wmii@mat.uni.torun.pl; internet www.mat .uni.torun.pl):

GÓRNIEWICZ, L., Nonlinear Analysis
JAKUBOWSKI, A., Theory of Probability
KAMIŃSKI, B., Ergodic Theory
KWIATKOWSKI, J., Ergodic Theory
LEMAŃCZYK, M., Ergodic Theory
NAGAJEW, A., Theory of Probability, Statistics
SIMSON, D., Algebra
SKOWROŃSKI, A., Algebra
TYC, A., Algebra

Faculty of Physics, Astronomy and Informatics (ul. Grudziądzka 5/7, 87-100 Toruń; tel. (56) 611-33-10; fax (56) 611-53-97; e-mail lidia@phys.uni.torun.pl; internet www.phys .uni.torun.pl):

BĄCZYNSKI, A., Molecular Spectroscopy, Optoelectronics
BALTER, A., Molecular Spectroscopy, Photophysics, Molecular Biophysics
BIELSKI, A., Atomic and Molecular Physics, History of Physics

CHWIROT, S., Atomic and Optical Physics

DEMBIŃSKI, S., Quantum Optics, Chaos Theory

DUCH, W., Computational Intelligence, Cognitive Science and Theoretical Physics

JANKOWSKI, K., Atomic and Molecular Physics, Computational Methods in Physics

JASKÓLSKI, W., Atomic and Molecular Physics, Physics of Low-dimensional Structures

KARWOWSKI, J., Atomic and Molecular Physics

KOSSAKOWSKI, A., Theoretical Physics, Statistical Physics

KREŁOWSKI, J., Astrophysics

KUS, A., Radio Astronomy

MĘCZYŃSKA, H., Solid State Physics

RACZYŃSKI, A., Atomic and Molecular Physics

ROZPŁOCH, F., Condensed Matter Physics, Physics of Carbon

SZUDY, J., Atomic and Molecular Physics, Optical Collisions

WOJTOWICZ, A., Solid State Physics, Optoelectronics

WOLSZCZAN, A., Radio Astronomy, Pulsars

WOSZCZYK, A., Astrophysics, Physics of Comets

WYBOURNE, B., Atomic and Molecular Physics

ZAREMBA, J., Atomic and Molecular Physics

Faculty of Theology (ul. Mickiewicza 121, 87-100 Toruń; tel. (56) 611-49-90; fax (56) 611-49-91; internet www.uni.torun.pl/wydzialy/wt):

BAGROWICZ, J., Catechetic and Religious Education

GRABOWSKI, M., Christian Philosophy

RYCHLICKI, C., Dogmatic and Ecumenical Theology

UNIWERSYTET OPOLSKI
(Opole University)

pl. Kopernika 11a, 45-058 Opole

Telephone: (77) 454-58-71

Fax: (77) 454-51-22

E-mail: sekretariat@uni.opole.pl

Internet: www.uni.opole.pl

Founded 1994 by the merger of Opole Teacher Training College and the Theological-Pastoral Institute of Opole

State control

Chancellor: ANDRZEJ KIMLA

Deputy Chancellor: GRZEGORZ KŁOSIŃSKI

DEANS

Faculty of Economics: Prof. JANUSZ SŁODCZYK

Faculty of History and Education: Prof. STEFAN MAREK GROCHALSKI

Faculty of Mathematics, Physics and Chemistry: Prof. HUBERT WOJTASEK

Faculty of Natural Sciences and Technology: Prof. ANDRZEJ GAWDZIK

Faculty of Philology: Prof. IRENA JOKIEL

Faculty of Theology: Prof. TADEUSZ DOLA

UNIWERSYTET PRZYRODNICZY W LUBLINIE
(Lublin University of Life Sciences)

ul. Akademicka 13, 20-950 Lublin

Telephone: (81) 445-66-22

Fax: (81) 533-35-49

E-mail: poczta@up.lublin.pl

Internet: www.ar.lublin.pl

Founded 1955

Faculties: agricultural engineering, agriculture, animal husbandry, horticulture, veterinary science

Rector: Prof. Dr hab. MARIAN WESOŁOWSKI

Library of 336,000 vols

Number of teachers: 640

Number of students: 6,000

Publications: *Annales UMCS, Excerpta Veterinaria Lublin* (in English), *Sectio DD Medicina Veterinaria, Sectio E Agricultura, Sectio EE Zootechnica, Sectio EEE Horticulture.*

UNIWERSYTET PRZYRODNICZY W POZNANIU
(Poznań University of Life Sciences)

ul. Wojska Polskiego 28, 60-637 Poznań

Telephone: (61) 848-72-00

Fax: (61) 848-71-46

E-mail: rektorat@up.poznan.pl

Internet: www.au.poznan.pl

Founded 1951

Faculties: agronomy, animal breeding and biology, food science and nutrition, forestry, horticulture, land reclamation and environmental engineering, wood technology

Rector: Prof. GRZEGORZ SKRZYPCZAK

Library of 641,000 vols

Number of teachers: 782

Number of students: 9,016

UNIWERSYTET RZESZOWSKI
(Rzeszów University)

ul. Rejtana 16C, 35-959 Rzeszów

Telephone: (17) 872-10-00

Fax: (17) 852-20-44

E-mail: rektor@univ.rzeszow.pl

Internet: www.univ.rzeszow.pl

Founded 2001 through the merger of the Pedagogical Univ. of Rzeszów, the Marie Curie Skłodowska Univ., Lublin (Rzeszów branch) and the Economics Faculty of the Agricultural Acad. of Krakow

State control

Rector: Prof. WŁODZIMIERZ BONUSIAK

Pro-Rector for Education: Prof. STANISŁAW KRAWCZYK

Pro-Rector for Foreign Relations: Prof. STANISŁAW SAGAN

Pro-Rector for Scientific Research and Finances: Prof. JERZY KITOWSKI

Pro-Rector for Student Affairs and Accreditation: Prof. EWA ORLOF

DEANS

External Faculty of Biotechnology (Kolbuszowa): Prof. IGOR Z. ZUBRZYCKI

Faculty of Agriculture and Biology: Prof. CZESŁAW PUCHALSKI

Faculty of Arts and Education: Prof. MIECZYSŁAW RADOCHOŃSKI

Faculty of Economics: Prof. SYLWESTER MAKARSKI

Faculty of Health Sciences: Prof. RYSZARD CIEŚLIK

Faculty of History and Sociology: Prof. ALEKSANDER BOBKO

Faculty of Law: Prof. JAN ŁUKASIEWICZ

Faculty of Mathematics and Natural Sciences: Prof. JERZY TOCKI

Faculty of Philology: Prof. STANISŁAW ULIASZ

Faculty of Physical Education: Prof. KAZIMIERZ OBODYŃSKI

UNIWERSYTET ŚLĄSKI W KATOWICACH
(University of Silesia in Katowice)

Bankowa 12, 40-007 Katowice

Telephone: (32) 359-13-00

Fax: (32) 359-20-55

E-mail: rektor@us.edu.pl

Internet: www.us.edu.pl

Founded 1968

State control

Languages of instruction: English, Polish

Academic year: October to June

Chancellor: Dr AGNIESZKA SKOŁUCKA

Rector: Prof. WIESŁAW BANYŚ

Pro-Rector: MIROSŁAW NAKONIECZNY

Pro-Rector: Prof. STANISŁAW KUCHARSKI

Pro-Rector: RYSZARD KOZIOŁEK

Pro-Rector: Prof. ANDRZEJ KOWALCZYK

Dir of Library: Prof. DARIUSZ PAWELEC

Library of 1,453,658 vols, 15,300 periodicals

Number of teachers: 2,049

Number of students: 30,092

Publications: *Acta Chromotographica, Annales Mathematicae Silesianae, Chowanna, Folia Philosophica, Gazeta Uniwersytecka, Geographia. Studia et Dissertationes, Górnośląskie Studia Socjologiczne, Neophilologica, Postscriptum Polonistyczne, Problemy Prawa Prywatnego Międzynarodowego, Romanica Silesiana, Średniowiecze Polskie i Powszechne, Studia Politicae Universitatis Silesiensis, Wieki Stare i Nowe, Z Dziejów Prawa*

DEANS

Faculty of Biology and Environmental Protection: Prof. IWONA SZAREJKO

Faculty of Computer and Materials Sciences: Prof. DANUTA STRÓŻ

Faculty of Earth Sciences: Prof. ADAM IDZIAK

Faculty of Ethnology and Educational Science: Prof. ZENON GAJDZICA

Faculty of Fine Arts and Music: Prof. MAŁGORZATA ŁUSZCZAK

Faculty of Law and Administration: CZESŁAW MARTYSZ

Faculty of Mathematics, Physics and Chemistry: Prof. ALICJA RATUSZNA

Faculty of Pedagogy and Psychology: Prof. STANISŁAW JUSZCZYK

Faculty of Philology: Prof. RAFAL MOLENCKI

Faculty of Radio and Television: Prof. KRYSTYNA DOKTOROWICZ

Faculty of Social Sciences: Prof. WIESŁAW KACZANOWICZ

Faculty of Theology: Prof. ANTONI BARTOSZEK

PROFESSORS

Faculty of Biology and Environmental Protection (ul Jagielońska 28, 40-032 Katowice; tel. (32) 200-94-61; fax (32) 200-93-61; e-mail biologia@us.edu.pl; internet www.wbios.us.edu.pl):

BIELAŃSKA-GRAJNER, I., Hydrobiology

CIEPAŁ, R., Ecology

GAJ, M., Genetics

GORCZYCA, J., Zoology

HASTEROK, R., Plant Anatomy and Cytology

HERCZEK, A., Zoology

KARCZ, W., Histology and Animal Embryology

KLAG, J., Cell Biology

KURCZYŃSKA, E., Biophysics and Plant Morphogenesis

KWIATKOWSKA, D., Biochemistry

ŁABUŻEK, S., Plant Anatomy and Cytology

MAŁUSZYŃSKA, J., Genetics

MAŁUSZYŃSKI, M., Animal Physiology and Ecotoxicology

MIGULA, P., Ecology

PALOWSKI, B., Plant Physiology

PIETRUSZKA, M., Microbiology

PIOTROWSKA-SEGET, Z., Microbiology

RADZIEJEWSKA-LEBRECHT, J., Systematic Botany

ROSTAŃSKI, A., Ecology

SKUBAŁA, P., Hydrobiology

STRZELEC, M., Histology and Animal Embryology

ŚWIĄTEK, P., Genetics

SZAREJKO, I., Zoology

WĘGIEREK, P., Geobotany and Nature Protection

WIKA, S., Plant Physiology

Faculty of Computer and Materials Sciences (Żytnia 12, 41-205 Sosnowiec; tel. (32) 269-18-46; fax (32) 269-18-52; e-mail dwt@us.edu.pl; internet www.wiinom.us.edu.pl):

BOGDANOWICZ, W., Materials Science
BORYCZKA, M., Computer Science
BORYCZKA, U., Computer Science
CYBO, J., Materials Science
CZECH, Z., Computer Science
CZEKAJ, D., Materials Science
DEC, J., Materials Science
DENISZCZYK, J., Materials Science
GROBE, L., Materials Science
ILCZUK, J., Materials Science
KANSY, J., Materials Science
KOTARSKI, W., Computer Science
KUPKA, M., Materials Science
LELĄTKO, J., Materials Science
PORWIK, P., Computer Science
SKONIECZNY, W., Materials Science
SKULSKI, R., Materials Science
STRÓŻ, D., Materials Science
SUROWIEC, M., Materials Science
WAKULICZ-DEJA, A., Computer Science
WOKULSKA, K., Materials Science
WRÓBEL, Z., Computer Science

Faculty of Earth Sciences (ul. Będzińska 60, 41-200 Sosnowiec; tel. (32) 368-94-00; fax (32) 291-58-65; e-mail wnoz@us.edu.pl; internet www.wnoz.us.edu.pl):

ANDREJCZUK, W., Regional Geography and Tourism
CZAJA, S., Physical Geography
CZYLOK, A., Physical Geography
FABIAŃSKA, M., Geochemistry
GALUSKIN, E., Geochemistry
GŁUCHOWSKI, E., Stratigraphy and Palaeontology
IDZIAK, A., Applied Geology
JANECZEK, J., Geochemistry
JANIA, J., Geomorphology
JANKOWSKI, A., Physical Geography
KARWOWSKI, Ł., Geochemistry
KLIMEK, K., Quaternary Paleogeography and Paleoecology
KOWALCZYK, A., Hydrogeology and Engineering Geology
KRUSZEWSKA, K., Geochemistry
MALIK, I., Reconstruction of the Geographical Environment
NIEDŹWIEDŹ, T., Climatology
PULINA, M., Physical Geography
RACKI, G., Stratigraphy and Palaeontology
RAHMONOV, O., Physical Geography
RUNGE, J., Social Geography
RZĘTAŁA, M., Hydrology and Water Management
SZAJNOWSKA-WYSOCKA, A., Settlement Geography
SZCZYPEK, T., Physical Geography
TEPER, L., Applied Geology
TKOCZ, M., Spatial Economy
ZUBEREK, W., Applied Geology

Faculty of Ethnology and Educational Science (ul. Bielska 62, 43-400 Cieszyn; tel. (33) 854-61-35; fax (33) 854-61-01; e-mail dziekanat.weinoe@us.edu.pl; internet www.weinoe.us.edu.pl):

BUKOWSKA-FLOREŃSKA, I., Ethnology and Cultural Anthropology
GAJDZICA, Z., Pedagogy
KAJFOSZ, J., Ethnology and Cultural Anthropology
KIEDOS, J., Pedagogy
KŁODNICKI, Z., Ethnology and Cultural Anthropology
LEWOWICKI, T., Pedagogy
MRÓZEK, R., Pedagogy
MURZYN, A., Pedagogy
OGRODZKA-MAZUR, E., Pedagogy
OLBRYCHT, K., Cultural Education
REMIN, M., Pedagogy
RUSEK, H., Ethnology and Cultural Anthropology

SMYRNOVA-TRYBULSKA, Y., Pedagogy
SZCZUREK-BORUTA, A., Pedagogy
SZUŚCIK, U., Pedagogy
ZILINEK, M., Pedagogy

Faculty of Fine Arts and Music (62 Bielska St, 43-400 Cieszyn; tel. (33) 854-62-40; fax (33) 854-61-02; e-mail wart@wart.us.edu.pl; internet www.wart.us.edu.pl):

ADAMUS, J., Painting
CIENCIAŁA, W., Music
DANEL-BOBRZYK, H., Music
DELEKTA, E., Graphic Arts
FOBERT, J., Sculpture
GONIEWICZ-URBAŚ, H., Music Education
HOŁARD, J., Graphic Design
JACYKÓW, W., Interdisciplinary Artistic Creation
KNOPEK, J., Graphic Arts
KOŁODZIEJCZYK, L., Music
KORZISTKA, M., Art Theory
KOWALCZYK-KLUS, A., Interdisciplinary Artistic Creation
KULA, K., Painting
KURAJ, E., Music
LASOŃ, A., Painting
ŁUSZCZAK, M., Interdisciplinary Artistic Creation
MACIUSZKIEWICZ, R., Painting
MICHALAK, R., Music
OSTROWSKI, A., Graphic Design
PICHURA, J., Music
PIECH-KALARUS, J., Graphic Arts
PIELESZ, R., Graphic Design
RUS, T., Painting
ŚMIETANA, S., Music
SUTRYK, W., Sculpture
SZAREK, A., Music
TUREK, K., Music
UCHYŁA-ZROSKI, J., Music
WARCHOŁ-SOBIESIAK, M., Music

Faculty of Law and Administration (ul. Bankowa 11B, 40-007 Katowice; tel. (32) 359-16-55; fax (32) 359-20-65; e-mail wpia@us.edu.pl; internet www.wpia.us.edu.pl):

BIŃCZYCKA-MAJEWSKA, T., Law
BISZTYGA, A., Law
CIĄGWA, J., Law
DOLNICKI, B., Law
DUKIET-NAGÓRSKA, T., Law
FUCHS, B., Law
GLUMIŃSKA-PAWLIC, J., Law
GÓRECKI, J., Law
GRABOWSKA, G., Law
GRABOWSKI, J., Law
KALUS, S., Law
KOWALSKI, W., Law
ŁABNO, A., Law
ŁASZCZYCA, G., Administration
LIPIŃSKI, A., Law
LITYŃSKI, A., Law
MAŁAJNY, R., Law
MARSZAŁ, K., Law
MARTYSZ, C., Law and Administration
MIKOŁAJCZYK, B., Law
MIKOŁAJCZYK, M., Law
MIKOSZ, R., Law
OGIEGŁO, L., Law
PAZDAN, M., Law
PIKULSKA-RADOMSKA, A., Law
POPIOŁEK, W., Law
ROTT-PIETRZYK, E., Law
STRZĘPKA, J., Law
TOBOR, Z., Law
WIDŁA, T., Law
WILK, L., Law
WITOSZ, A., Law
ZACHARKO, L., Law and Administration
ZDEBEL, M., Law
ZGRYZEK, K., Law

Faculty of Mathematics, Physics and Chemistry (ul. Bankowa 14, 40-007 Katowice; tel. (32) 359-15-50; fax (32) 359-16-15; e-mail dziekanat@mfc.us.edu.pl; internet w3.mfc.us.edu.pl):

BARON, K., Mathematics
BEDNAREK, L., Astrophysics and Cosmology
BIESIADA, M., Astrophysics and Cosmology
BŁASZCZYK, A., Set Theory
BORGIEŁ, W., Theoretical Physics
BRÓDKA, A., Biophysics and Molecular Physics
BURIAN, A., Biophysics and Molecular Physics
CHEŁKOWSKA, G., Solid State Physics
CHOLEWA, J., Mathematics
CZYŻ, H., Field Theory and Particle Physics
DAJKA, J., Theoretical Physics
DASZYKOWSKI, M., Chemometrics
DŁOTKO, T., Mathematics
DRZAZGA, Z., Medical Physics
DUDA, H., Physics of Crystals
DZIK, W., Mathematical Logic
FLAKUS, H., Chemistry
FUGIEL, B., Biophysics and Molecular Physics
GBURSKI, Z., Computational Physics and Electronics
GER, R., Mathematics
GLUZA, J., Field Theory and Particle Physics
GROŃ, T., Physics of Crystals
JASTRZĘBSKA, M., Solid State Physics
JAWORSKA, M., Chemistry
KANIA, A., Ferroelectrics
KISIEL, J., Nuclear Physics
KOCOT, A., Biophysics and Molecular Physics
KOŁODZIEJ, K., Field Theory and Particle Physics
KOMINEK, Z., Mathematics
KOSTUR, M., Theoretical Physics
KOWALSKA, T., Chemistry
KROK-KOWALSKI, J., Physics of Crystals
KROMPIEC, S., Chemistry
KUCHARSKI, S., Chemistry
KUŚ, P., Organic Synthesis
KUSZ, J., Physics of Crystals
LIGĘZA, J., Mathematics
ŁUCZKA, J., Theoretical Physics
MACHURA, B., Crystallography
MARCZAK, W., Chemistry
MAŚKA, M., Theoretical Physics
MATLENGIEWICZ, M., Chemistry
MIERZEJEWSKI, M., Theoretical Physics
MUSIAŁ, M., Chemistry
NOWAK, A., Mathematics
PALUCH, M., Biophysics and Molecular Physics
PISARSKI, W., Chemistry
PLEWIK, S., Mathematics
POLAŃSKI, J., Chemistry
RATUSZNA, A., Solid State Physics
ROLEDER, K., Experimental Physics
RUDNICKI, R., Mathematics
RZOSKA, S., Biophysics and Molecular Physics
SABLIK, M., Mathematics
SCHAB-BALCERZAK, E., Chemistry
SITKO, R., Chemistry
SKRZYPEK, D., Solid State Physics
SŁADEK, A., Mathematics
SŁADKOWSKI, J., Astrophysics and Cosmology
ŚLEBARSKI, A., Solid State Physics
SOCHA, L., Physics
SUŁKOWSKI, W., Chemistry
SZADE, J., Solid State Physics
SZOPA, M., Theoretical Physics
SZOT, K., Experimental Physics
TALIK, E., Solid State Physics
UJMA, Z., Experimental Physics
WALCZAK, B., Chemistry
WESTWAŃSKI, B., Theoretical Physics
WRZALIK, R., Biophysics and Molecular Physics
ZAIONC, M., Mathematics
ZIOŁO, J., Biophysics and Molecular Physics
ZIPPER, E., Theoretical Physics

ZRAŁEK, M., Field Theory and Particle Physics

Faculty of Pedagogy and Psychology (ul. Grażyńskiego 53, 40-126 Katowice; tel. (32) 359-97-39; fax (32) 359-98-11; e-mail pips@us .edu.pl; internet www.wpips.us.edu.pl):

GÓRNIK-DUROSE, M., Psychology
JUSZCZYK, S., Pedagogy
KARANDASHEV, Y., Psychology
KNAPIK, M., Pedagogy
KOŻUSZNIK, B., Psychology
KRASOŃ, K., Pedagogy
KURINCOVA, V., Pedagogy
MANDAL, E., Psychology
NOWAK, A., Pedagogy
SACHER, W., Pedagogy
SEIDLER, P., Pedagogy
SENKO, T., Pedagogy
STANIK, J., Psychology
STANKOWSKI, A., Pedagogy
SYREK, E., Pedagogy
TOKARZ, M., Psychology

Faculty of Philology (plac Sejmu Śląskiego 1, 40-032 Katowice; tel. (32) 200-92-63; fax (32) 200-92-33; e-mail filologia@us.edu.pl; internet www.fil.us.edu.pl):

ALEKSANDROWICZ, T., Classical Philology
BANYŚ, W., French Philology
BEDNARSKI, M., Classical Philology
BIAŁAS, Z., English Philology
BORKOWSKA, E., English Philology
CICHOŃSKA, M., Slavonic Philology
CUDAK, R., Polish Philology
CZAPIK-LITYŃSKA, B., Slavonic Philology
CZERWIŃSKI, P., Russian Philology
DUTKA, E., Polish Philology
DZIADEK, A., Polish Philology
FEHR, H., German Philology
FONTAŃSKI, H., Russian Philology
GABRYŚ-BARKER, D., English Philology
GONDEK, E., Scientific Information and Library Science
GÓRSKA, E., English Philology
GUTKOWSKA, B., Polish Philology
GWÓŹDŹ, A., Film and Media Studies
HESKA-KWAŚNIEWICZ, K., Polish Philology
ILUK, J., German Philology
JAKÓBCZYK, J., Polish Philology
JANOWSKA, A., Polish Philology
JARCZYK, M., Polish Philology
JARZĄBEK, R., Slavonic Philology
JASKÓŁA, E., Polish Philology
JĘDRZEJKO, E., Polish Philology
KALAGA, W., English Philology
KISIEL, M., Polish Philology
KITA, M., Polish Philology
KLESZCZ, K., Polish Philology
KŁOSIŃSKA, K., Polish Philology
KOSOWSKA, E., Cultural Studies
KRASUSKI, K., Comparative Literature
KRYZIA, W., Slavonic Philology
KUNCE, A., Cultural Studies
ŁYDA, A., English Philology
MALICKI, J., Polish Philology
MALINOWSKA, E., Polish Philology
MARCINIAK, P., Classical Philology
MAZUREK, H., Russian Philology
MICZKA, T., Polish Philology
MIELCZAREK, Z., German Philology
NAWARECKI, A., Polish Philology
NIESPOREK-SZAMBURSKA, B., Polish Philology
OGIERMAN, L., Scientific Information and Library Science
OLEJNICZAK, J., Polish Philology
OPACKA-WALASEK, D., Polish Philology
OSTASZEWSKA, D., Polish Philology
PAWELEC, D., Polish Philology
PIECHOTA, M., Polish Philology
PIKALA-TOKARZ, B., Slavonic Philology
PYTASZ, M., Polish Philology
ROTT, D., Polish Philology
RÓŻYCKI, E., Scientific Information and Library Science
RYBA, J., Polish Philology

SIERADZKA, D., Scientific Information and Library Science
SKUDRZYK, A., Polish Philology
SŁAWEK, E., Polish Philology
SŁAWEK, T., Comparative Literature
SOBCZYK, J., Polish Philology
SOCHA, I., Scientific Information and Library Science
STAWNICKA, J., Slavonic Philology
SYNOWIEC, H., Polish Philology
SZEWCZYK, G., German Philology
TAMBOR, J., Polish Philology
TERMIŃSKA-KORZON, K., English Philology
UNIŁOWSKI, K., Polish Philology
WĄCHOCKA, E., Cultural Studies
WANDZIOCH, M., French Philology
WARCHALA, J., Polish Philology
WĘŻOWICZ-ZIÓŁKOWSKA, D., Cultural Studies
WIDŁA, H., Romance Philology
WILKOŃ, A., Polish Philology
WILKOŃ, T., Scientific Information and Library Science
WITOSZ, B., Polish Philology
WOŹNICZKA, Z., Cultural Studies
WYSOCKA, M., English Philology
ZABIEROWSKI, S., Cultural Studies
ZELER, B., Cultural Studies
ŻYDEK-BEDNARCZUK, U., Cultural Studies

Faculty of Radio and Television (1B Bytkowska St, 40-955 Katowice; tel. (32) 259-70-11; fax (32) 258-70-70; e-mail writv@ us.edu.pl; internet www.writv.us.edu.pl):

BAJON, F., Film and Television Directing
DOKTOROWICZ, K., Media Management and Production
FIDYK, A., Film and Television Directing
HUDON, W., Cinematography
ŁUKASZEWICZ, J., Cinematography
ŚLĘZAK, P., Media Management and Production
STUHR, J., Film and Television Directing
UHMA, M., Film and Television Production
ŻAKOWICZ, A., Cinematography
ZANUSSI, K., Film and Television Directing

Faculty of Social Sciences (ul. Bankowa 11, 40-007 Katowice; tel. (32) 359-12-63; fax (32) 359-21-25; e-mail dziekan@wns.us.edu.pl; internet www.wns.us.edu.pl):

BARAŃSKI, M., Political Science
BARCIAK, A., History
BARTOSZEK, A., Sociology
BUDZYŃSKA, E., Sociology
CZAKON, T., Philosophy
DEMBIŃSKI, B., Philosophy
FERTACZ, S., History
GIERULA, M., Political Science
GLIMOS-NADGÓRSKA, A., History
IWANEK, J., Political Science
JACHIMOWSKI, M., Political Science
KACZANOWICZ, W., History
KACZMAREK, R., History
KAUTE, W., Political Science
KIEPAS, A., Philosophy
KOLCZYŃSKI, M., Political Science
KUBOK, D., Philosophy
ŁACIAK, P., Philosophy
ŁOMIŃSKI, B., Political Science
MICHALCZYK, S., Political Science
MIKUŁOWSKI-POMORSKI, J., Political Science
MITRĘGA, M., Political Science
NAWROCKI, T., Sociology
NORAS, A., Philosophy
ONISZCZUK, Z., Political Science
PANIC, I., History
PAWELEC, T., History
SPERKA, J., History
STOLARCZYK, M., Political Science
SWADŹBA, U., Sociology
SZCZEPAŃSKI, M., Sociology
SZOTEK, B., Philosophy
ŚLĘCZEK-CZAKON, D., Philosophy
ŚWIĄTKIEWICZ, W., Sociology
WIECZOREK, K., Philosophy
WÓDZ, J., Sociology

WÓDZ, K., Sociology
WRÓBEL, S., Political Science

Faculty of Theology (ul. Wita Stwosza 17A, 40-042 Katowice; tel. (32) 356-90-56; fax (32) 356-90-55; e-mail sekretariat@wtl.us.edu.pl; internet www.wtl.us.edu.pl):

BUDNIAK, J., Theology
CELARY, I., Theology
DROŻDŻ, A., Theology
GÓRECKI, J., Theology
GÓRSKI, J., Theology
KOZYRA, J., Theology
KRĘTOSZ, J., Theology
KRZYSTECZKO, H., Theology
MALINA, A., Theology
MYSZOR, J., Theology
MYSZOR, W., Theology
PASTWA, A., Theology
REGINEK, A., Theology
SŁOMKA, J., Theology
SZYMIK, J., Theology
ŻĄDŁO, A., Theology

UNIWERSYTET SZCZECIŃSKI
(Szczecin University)

ul. Papieża Jana Pawła II 22A, 70-453 Szczecin

Telephone: (91) 444-11-72
Fax: (91) 444-11-74
E-mail: rektorat@univ.szczecin.pl
Internet: www.us.szc.pl
Founded 1985
State control
Language of instruction: Polish
Academic year: October to September

Rector: Prof. Dr hab. ZDZISŁAW CHMIELEWSKI
Vice-Rector for Academic Affairs: Prof. Dr hab. WALDEMAR TARCZYŃSKI
Vice-Rector for Devt and Org.: Prof. Dr hab. STANISŁAW CZEPITA
Vice-Rector for Education Affairs: Prof. Dr hab. HENRYK BABIS
Admin. Officer: EUGENIUSZ KISIEL

Library: see Libraries and Archives
Number of teachers: 1,008
Number of students: 26,793

Publication: *Przegląd Uniwersytecki* (The Univ. Review, 6 a year)

DEANS

Faculty of Arts: Prof. Dr hab. EDWARD WŁODARCZYK
Faculty of Economics and Management: Prof. Dr hab. TERESA LUBIŃSKA
Faculty of Law and Administration: Prof. Dr hab. ZBIGNIEW OFIARSKI
Faculty of Management and Economics of Services: Prof. Dr hab. JÓZEF PERENC
Faculty of Mathematics and Physics: Prof. Dr hab. RYSZARD LEŚNIEWICZ
Faculty of Natural Sciences: Prof. Dr hab. LUCJAN AGAPOW

PROFESSORS

ALEKSIEJENKO, M., Arts
BĄKOWSKI, W., Economics
BIAŁECKI, T., Arts
BRONK, H., Economics
CHMIELEWSKI, Z., Arts
CHWESIUK, K., Economics
CZAPLEWSKI, R., Economics
CZERNIATIN, W., Mathematics
DEPTUŁA, W., Natural Sciences
DOROZIK, L., Economics
DUDZIŃSKI, J., Economics
DZIEDZICZAK, I., Economics
FARYŚ, J., Arts
GIZA, A., Arts
GŁODEK, Z., Economics
GŁOWACKI, A., Arts
GÓRBIEL, A., Law
GRANOWSKI, J., Physics
GRZYWACZ, W., Economics

HADACZEK, B., Arts
HŁYŃCZAK, A. J., Natural Sciences
HOZER, J., Economics
JANASZ, W., Economics
JASKOT, K., Arts
JASZCZANIN, J., Natural Sciences
KARWOWSKI, J., Economics
KĘPCZYŃSKI, J., Natural Sciences
KIZIUKIEWICZ, T., Economics
KOPYCIŃSKA, D., Economics
KOROBOW, W., Mathematics
KOŹMIAN, D., Arts
KUCHARSKA, E., Arts
LUKS, K., Economics
MEJBAUM, W., Arts
MOŁCZANOWA, O., Arts
NOWAKOWSKI, A., Economics
PERENC, J., Economics
PRUSAK, F., Law
RADOMSKA-TOMCZUK, M., Fine Arts
ROGALSKA, S., Natural Sciences
ROGALSKI, M., Natural Sciences
RZEPA, T., Social Sciences
SIERGIEJEW, N., Physics
SŁAWIK, K., Law
ŚLIAŽAS, J., Natural Sciences
STANIELEWICZ, J., Arts
SULIKOWSKI, A., Arts
SUŁKOWSKI, Cz., Economics
SYGIT, M., Medical Sciences
SZAŁEK, B., Economics, Arts
SZLAUER, L., Natural Sciences
URBAŃCZYK, E., Economics
WAŚNIEWSKI, T., Economics
WIERZBICKI, T., Economics
WOŹNIAK, R., Arts
ZALEWSKI, P., Economics
ZAWADZKI, J., Economics

UNIWERSYTET TECHNOLOGICZNO-PRZYRODNICZY IM. J. J. ŚNIADECKICH W BYDGOSZCZY
(University of Technology and Agriculture in Bydgoszcz)

ul. Kordeckiego 20, 85-225 Bydgoszcz

Telephone: (52) 373-14-50
Fax: (52) 374-93-27
E-mail: rektor@utp.edu.pl
Internet: www.utp.edu.pl

Founded 1951

Faculties: agriculture, animal husbandry, chemical technology and engineering, civil engineering, electronics and telecommunication, environmental engineering, management and marketing, mechanics and machine construction, technical physics

Rector: Prof. Dr hab. Inż. ANTONI BUKALUK

Library of 239,706 vols, 51,243 periodicals
Number of teachers: 656
Number of students: 9,900

Publications: *Image Processing and Communications* (in English, 4 a year), *Zeszyty Naukowe* (in Polish, with Russian and English summaries, irregular).

UNIWERSYTET WARMIŃSKO-MAZURSKI W OLSZTYNIE
(University of Warmia and Mazury in Olsztyn)

ul. M. Oczapowskiego 2, 10-719 Olsztyn

Telephone: (89) 523-33-30
Fax: (89) 523-44-56
E-mail: rektor@uwm.edu.pl
Internet: www.uwm.edu.pl

Founded 1999 through merger of Olsztyn University of Agriculture and Technology, Higher School of Pedagogy, and Warmian Theological Institute
State control

Rector: Prof. Dr hab. JÓZEF GÓRNIEWICZ
Pro-Rector: Dr WOJCIECH JANCZUKOWICZ
Pro-Rector for Devt: Dr SZCZEPAN FIGIEL

Pro-Rector for Staff Affairs: Dr TADEUSZ RAWA
Pro-Rector for Research and Cooperation with Nat. Economy: Dr WŁADYSŁAW KORDAN
Pro-Rector for Student Affairs: Dr TADEUSZ RAWA
Dir of Admin.: Dr WOJCIECH CYMERMAN

Library of 823,374 vols, 1,811 periodicals
Number of teachers: 1,680
Number of students: 30,000

Publications: *Acta Neophoilologica* (1 or 2 a year), *Acta Polono-Ruthenica* (1 or 2 a year), *Economic Sciences* (1 or 2 a year), *Echa Przeszłości* (1 or 2 a year), *Forum Oświatowe* (1 or 2 a year), *Forum Teologiczne* (1 or 2 a year), *Humanistyka i Przyrodoznawstwo* (1 or 2 a year), *Natural Sciences* (1 or 2 a year), *Prace Językoznawcze* (1 or 2 a year), *Technical Sciences* (1 or 2 a year)

DEANS

Faculty of Agriculture and Environmental Management: Prof. JAN KUCHARSKI
Faculty of Animal Bioengineering: Prof. MANFRED LOREK
Faculty of Arts and Educational Sciences: Dr EUGENIUSZ ŁAPIŃSKI
Faculty of Biology: Prof. JADWIGA PRZAŁA
Faculty of Engineering and Technical Sciences: Prof. KAZIMIERZ WIERZBICKI
Faculty of Environmental Sciences and Fisheries: Dr IRENA WOJNOWSKA-BARYŁA
Faculty of Food Sciences: Prof. ZBIGNIEW ŚMIETANA
Faculty of Geodesy and Land Management: Dr RYSZARD ŻRÓBEK
Faculty of Humanities: Prof. ANDRZEJ STANISZEWSKI
Faculty of Management and Business Administration: Dr HENRYK LELUSZ
Faculty of Theology: Rev. Prof. ALOJZY SZORC
Faculty of Veterinary Medicine: Prof. TOMASZ JANOWSKI

UNIWERSYTET WARSZAWSKI
(University of Warsaw)

Krakowskie Przedmieście 26–28, 00-927 Warsaw

Telephone: (22) 552-00-00
Fax: (22) 826-32-62
Internet: www.uw.edu.pl

Founded 1816
Academic year: October to June

Rector: Prof. Dr hab. PIOTR WĘGLEŃSKI
Vice-Rectors: Prof. Dr hab. MAREK WĄSOWICZ, Prof. Dr hab. WŁODZIMIERZ BORODZIEJ, Prof. Dr hab. JAN MADEY, Prof. Dr hab. WOJCIECH MACIEJEWSKI
Administrative Director: JERZY PIESZCZURYKOW
Librarian: Dr HENRYK HOLLENDER

Library: see Libraries and Archives
Number of teachers: 2,602
Number of students: 55,790

Publications: *Acta Philologica* (irregular), *Africana Bulletin* (irregular), *American Studies* (irregular), *Barok* (2 a year), *Filozofia Nauki* (irregular), *Ikonotheka* (irregular), *Japonica* (irregular), *Journal of Juristic Papyrology* (irregular), *Kwartalnik Pedagogiczny* (4 a year), *Novensia* (irregular), *Orientalia Varsoviensia* (irregular), *Phytoocenosis* (irregular), *Polityka Wschodnia* (irregular), *Przegląd Glottodydaktyczny* (irregular), *Przegląd Historyczny* (4 a year), *Przegląd Humanistyczny* (4 a year), *Stosunki Międzynarodowe* (irregular), *Studia Europejskie* (4 a year), *Studia Palmyreńskie* (irregular), *Studia Politologiczne* (irregular)

DEANS

Faculty of Applied Linguistics and East Slavonic Languages: Prof. Dr hab. ANTONI SEMCZUK
Faculty of Applied Social Sciences and Social Rehabilitation: Prof. Dr hab. MARCIN KRÓL
Faculty of Biology: Prof. Dr hab. MICHAŁ KOZAKIEWICZ
Faculty of Chemistry: Prof. Dr hab. STANISŁAW GŁĄB
Faculty of Economic Science: Prof. Dr hab. MARIAN WIŚNIEWSKI
Faculty of Education: Prof. Dr hab. ALICJA SIEMAK-TYLIKOWSKA
Faculty of Geography and Regional Studies: Prof. Dr hab. MARIA SKOCZEK
Faculty of Geology: Prof. Dr hab. BRONISŁAW MATYJA
Faculty of History: Prof. Dr hab. PIOTR BIELIŃSKI
Faculty of Journalism and Political Science: Prof. Dr hab. GRAŻYNA ULICKA
Faculty of Law and Administration: Prof. Dr hab. MIROSŁAW WYRZYKOWSKI
Faculty of Management: Prof. Dr hab. KAZIMIERZ RYĆ
Faculty of Mathematics, Informatics and Mechanics: Prof. Dr hab. STEFAN JACKOWSKI
Faculty of Modern Languages and Oriental Studies: Prof. Dr EMMA HARRIS
Faculty of Philosophy and Sociology: (vacant)
Faculty of Physics: Prof. Dr hab. KATARZYNA CHAŁASIŃSKA-MACUKOW
Faculty of Polish Philology: Prof. Dr hab. STANISŁAW DUBISZ
Faculty of Psychology: Prof. Dr hab. DANUTA KĄDZIELAWA

PROFESSORS

Faculty of Applied Linguistics and East Slavonic Languages (Szturmowa 4, 02-678 Warsaw; tel. (22) 553-42-23; fax (22) 553-42-24; internet www.uw.edu.pl/wlsifw):

GRUCZA, F., Linguistics
KIELAR, B., Linguistics
KOZAK, S., Ukrainian Philology
KRZESZOWSKI, T., Linguistics
LUKSZYN, J., Russian Philology
NAMOWICZ, T., German Philology
SEMCZUK, A., Russian Philology
SLIWOWSKI, R., Russian Philology
SZYSZKO, T., Russian Philology
WAWRZYŃCZYK, J., Linguistics
ZMARZER, W., Linguistics

Faculty of Applied Social Sciences and Social Rehabilitation (Żurawia 4, 00-503 Warsaw; tel. (22) 621-91-22; fax (22) 625-40-86):

BAŁANDYNOWICZ, A., Resocialization, Prevention
BOKSZAŃSKI, Z., Sociology
JAWŁOWSKA, A., Sociology
KACZYŃSKA, E., History of Social Economics
KICIŃSKI, K., Sociology of Morals
KRÓL, M., History of Ideas
KULPIŃSKA, J., Sociology
KURCZEWSKI, J., Sociology, Sociology of Law
KWAŚNIEWSKI, J., Labour Law, Deviation Sociology
MISIAK, W., Sociology
PILCH, T., Education
PRZECŁAWSKI, K., Sociology
RZEPLIŃSKI, A., Law, Criminology
ŚWIDA-ZIEMBA, H., Sociology
SZYMANOWSKI, T., Penal Law
TYMOWSKI, A., Social Politics
WOJCIK, P., Political Science, Social Politics
ZABOROWSKI, Z., Psychology
ZIEMBA, Z., Philosophy

Faculty of Biology (Miecznikowa 1, 02-096 Warsaw; tel. (22) 554-11-03; fax (22) 554-11-06; internet www.biol.edu.pl):

BARTNIK, E., Molecular Biology, Genetics
BRYŁA, J., Biochemistry—Metabolism

CHARZYŃSKA, M., Embryology
CHRÓST, R., Microbiology
CYMBOROWSKI, B., Animal Physiology
DOBROWOLSKI, K., Zoology, Ecology
DOBRZAŃSKA-KACZANOWSKA, J., Zoology
FALIŃSKI, J., Botany, Ecology
GLIWICZ, M., Zoology, Hydrobiology
HREBENDA, J., Microbiology
JERZMANOWSKI, A., Biochemistry
KACPERSKA-LEWAK, A., Plant Physiology, Biochemistry
KACZANOWSKI, A., Zoology
KŁOSOWSKI, S., Ecology of Water Plants
KOZAKIEWICZ, M., Ecology
KURAŚ, M., Experimental Biology
MARKIEWICZ, Z., Microbiology
MORACZEWSKI, J., Zoology
MYCIELSKI, R., Microbiology
PIECZYŃSKA, E., Zoology, Hydrobiology
PIEKAROWICZ, A., Microbiology
POSKUTA, J., Plant Physiology
PREJS, A., Zoology, Hydrobiology
RYCHTER, A., Plant Physiology
SIŃSKI, E., Zoology
STAROŃ, K., Molecular Biology
STĘPIEŃ, P., Molecular Biology, Genetics
SYMONIDES, E., Botany, Ecology
TARKOWSKI, A., Embryology
TOMASZEWICZ, H., Botany
WĘGLEŃSKI, P., Molecular Biology, Genetics
WILKOMIRSKY, B., Botany
WŁODARCZYK, M., Microbiology
WOJCIECHOWSKI, Z., Biochemistry
ZIELENKIEWICZ, P., Experimental Biology

Faculty of Chemistry (Pasteura 1, 02-096 Warsaw; tel. (22) 822-02-11; fax (22) 822-59-96; e-mail dziekan@chem.uw.edu.pl; internet www.chem.uw.edu.pl):

BILEWICZ, R., Analytical Chemistry
BORUCKA-BUKOWSKA, J., Physical Chemistry and Molecular Spectroscopy
CHAŁASIŃSKI, G., Theoretical Chemistry
CZERWIŃSKI, A., Physical Chemistry
FIGASZEWSKI, Z., Physical Chemistry
GADOMSKI, W., Physical Chemistry, Optics
GALUS, Z., Mineral Chemistry
GŁĄB, B., Analytical Chemistry
GOLIMOWSKI, J., Analytical Chemistry
IZDEBSKI, J., Organic Chemistry
JAWORSKI, J., Chemistry and Food Technology
JEZIORSKI, B., Analytical Chemistry
JURCZAK, J., Organic Chemistry
KALINOWSKI, M., Physical Chemistry
KASPRZYCKA-GUTTMAN, T., Chemical Technology
KOCZOROWSKI, Z., Electrochemistry
KOLIŃSKI, A., Theoretical Chemistry
KRYGOWSKI, T., Physical Chemistry
KULESZA, P., Electrochemistry
LEŚ, A., Theoretical Chemistry
NIEDZIELSKI, J., Organic Chemistry
OSZCZAPOWICZ, J., Organic Chemistry
PIELA, L., Theoretical Chemistry
SADLEJ, J., Physical Chemistry
SAMOCHOCKA, K., Radiochemistry
STOJEK, Z., Electrochemistry
SZYDŁOWSKI, J., Radiochemistry
TEMERIUSZ, A., Organic Chemistry
TROJANOWICZ, M., Analytical Chemistry
WRONA, P., Analytical Chemistry
ŻYLICZ, M., Biochemistry

Faculty of Economic Science (Długa 44/50, 00-241 Warsaw; tel. (22) 554-91-44; fax (22) 831-28-46; internet www.wne.uw.edu.pl):

BAKA, W., Banking and Finance
DANILUK, M., Public Finance
DOBROCZYŃSKI, M., International Economics
GMYTRASIEWICZ, M., Economics, Business
GÓRECKI, B., Econometrics
JEZIERSKI, A., Economic History
KASPRZAK, T., Business, Informatics
KLEER, J., Economics

KOTOWICZ-JAWOR, J., Economics
KOZIŃSKI, W., Banking and Finance
LUBBE, A., International Economics
ŁUKASZEWICZ, A., Economic Policy
MACIEJEWSKI, W., Econometrics
MORECKA, Z., Political Economy
OKÓLSKI, M., Statistics, Demography
OPOLSKI, K., Banking and Finance
RUTKOWSKI, J., Political Economy
SADOWSKI, Z., Theory of Economic Development
SIWIŃSKI, W., International Economics
SZEWORSKI, A., Political Economy
SZTYBER, W., Political Economy, Public Finance
TIMOFIEJUK, I., Statistics
WIECZORKIEWICZ, A., Banking and Finance
WILKIN, J., Political Economy, Agricultural Economics

Faculty of Education (Mokotowska 16/20, 00-561 Warsaw; tel. (22) 553-08-18; fax (22) 629-89-79; e-mail pedagog@mail.uw.edu.pl; internet www.pedagog.uw.edu.pl):

BARTNICKA, K., Education History
FRĄCZEK, A., Psychology
KRUSZEWSKI, K., Education
KUPISIEWICZ, C., Didactics, Comparative Education
KWIATKOWSKA, H., Education
LEWOWICKI, T., Adult Education
MIESZALSKI, S., Didactics
POŁTURZYCKI, J., Education
PRZECŁAWSKA, A., Social Education
THEISS, W., Education
WILGOCKA-OKOŃ, B., Education
WOJNAR, I., Education
WOYNAROWSKA, B., Social Medicine
ZACZYŃSKI, W., Didactics

Faculty of Geography and Regional Studies (Krakowskie Przedmieście 30, 00-927 Warsaw; tel. (22) 552-06-31; fax (22) 552-15-21; e-mail globus@wgsr.uw.edu.pl; internet www.wgsr.uw.edu.pl):

CIOŁKOSZ, A., Cartography, GIS
DEMBICZ, A., Economic Geography, Socioeconomic Geography of Latin America
GRYGORENKO, W., Cartography
GUDOWSKI, J., Economic Geography
GUTRY-KORYCKA, M., Hydrogeology, Hydrology
KOSTROWICKA, A., Economic Geography, Geography of Tourism
KOWALCZYK, A., Economic Geography
MAKOWSKI, J., Regional Geography
MIKULSKI, Z., Hydrogeography, Hydrology
MYCIELSKA-DOWGIAŁŁO, E., Geomorphology
PLIT, F., Regional Geography of Africa
RICHLING, A., Physical Geography, Landscape Ecology
SOCZYŃSKA, U., Hydrology
STOPA-BORYCZKA, M., Climatology

Faculty of Geology (Żwirki i Wigury 93, 02-089 Warsaw; tel. (22) 822-58-84; fax (22) 554-00-01; e-mail dziekstu@geo.uw.edu.pl; internet www.geo.uw.edu.pl):

BAŁUK, W. A., Palaeontology
DRĄGOWSKI, A., Environmental Protection
GRABOWSKA-OLSZEWSKA, B., Engineering Geology
KACZYŃSKI, R., Engineering Geology
KOWALSKI, W., Geochemistry, Mineralogy
KRAJEWSKI, S., Hydrogeology
KUTEK, J., Tectonics, Stratigraphy
LINDNER, L., Quaternary Geology
MACIOSZCZYK, A., Hydrogeology
MACIOSZCZYK, T., Hydrogeology
MAŁECKA, D., Hydrogeology
MARCINOWSKI, R., Stratigraphy
MARKS, L., Quaternary Geology
MATYSIAK, S., Mechanics of Solids
MYŚLIŃSKA, E., Engineering Geology
ORŁOWSKI, S., Stratigraphy
PINIŃSKA, J., Engineering Geology, Geomechanics

RADWAŃSKI, A., Geology
RONIEWICZ, P., Sedimentology
SPECZIK, S., Geology of Ore Deposits
SZULCZEWSKI, M., Stratigraphy, Sedimentology
WIERZBOWSKI, A., Stratigraphy
WYRWICKI, R., Geology of Ore Deposits

Faculty of History (tel. (22) 552-05-45; fax (22) 826-21-30; internet www.his.uw.edu.pl/wh):

AUGUSTYNIAK, U., History of Culture
BANASZKIEWICZ, J., Modern History
BIEŃKOWSKA, B., History of Culture, Library Science
BRAVO, B., Ancient History
BUCHWALD-PELC, P., Library Science
BUKO, A., Archaeology
BUKOWSKI, Z., Archaeology
CHMIELEWSKI, W., Archaeology
CHRÓSCICKI, J., History of Art
CZEKANOWSKA-KUKLIŃSKA, A., Musicology
DASZEWSKI, W., Archaeology
FIAŁKOWSKI, K., Library Science
GARLICKI, A., History
GAWLIKOWSKI, M., Archaeology
GODLEWSKI, W., Archaeology
GOŁĄB, M., Musicology
HELMAN-BEDNARCZYK, Z., Musicology
JAŚKIEWICZ, D., History of the USSR
JUSZCZAK, W., History of Art
KARPOWICZ, M., History of Art
KIZWALTER, T., 19th-Century History
KOLENDO, J., Archaeology
KOŁODZIEJSKA, J., Library Science
KOZŁOWSKI, S., Archaeology
KULA, M., General History
LASOTA-MOSKALEWSKA, A., Biology, Archaeozoology
LENGAUER, W., History
ŁUKASIEWICZ, J., History
MACISZEWSKI, J., History
MĄCZAK, A., Modern History
MICHAŁEK, K., Modern History, History of the USA
MIKOCKI, T., History of Art
MIŁOBĘDZKI, J. A., History of Art
MODZELEWSKI, K., Medieval History
MURASZKIEWICZ, M., Library Science
MYŚLIWIEC, K., Archaeology
NIWIŃSKI, A. S., History, Egyptology
NOWAKOWSKI, W., Archaeology
OKULICZ-KOZARYN, J., Archaeology
PAPUZIŃSKA-BEKSIAK, J., Literature
PERZ, M., Musicology
POKROPEK, M., Ethnography
PONIATOWSKA, I., History of Music
POPPE, A., Medieval History
POPRZĘCKA, M., History of Art
POTKOWSKI, E., History
RAKOWSKI, A., Musical Acoustics
RUDNICKI, S., 19th- and 20th-century Polish History
RUSINOWA, J., Modern History
SAMSONOWICZ, H., Medieval History
SKUBISZEWSKI, P., Medieval History of Art
SOCHACKI, Z., Archaeology
SOKOLEWICZ, Z., Ethnography
SUCHODOLSKI, S., Archaeology
SWIDERKÓWNA, A., Papyrology
SZAFLIK, J., History
TANTY, M., History of Slavonic Countries
TOMASZEWSKI, J., Political Science
TYMOWSKI, M., Modern History
TYSZKIEWICZ, J., Medieval History
WASILEWSKI, T., Medieval History
WAWRYKOWA, M., Modern History
WIERCIŃSKI, A., Archaeology
WIPSZYCKA-BRAVO, E., Ancient History
WOJCIECHOWSKI, M., Modern History
WYROBISZ, A., Medieval History
ZADROŻYŃSKA-BARĄCZ, A., Ethnography
ŻARNOWSKA, A., Modern Polish History
ŻERAŃSKA-KOMINEK, S., Musicology

Faculty of Journalism and Political Science (Krakowskie Przedmieście 3, 00-047 Warsaw; tel. (22) 552-02-18; fax (22) 828-94-99; e-mail wdinp@mail.uw.edu.pl; internet www.wdnip.uw.edu.pl):

AULEYTNER, J., Economy
BASZKIEWICZ, J., Political Science
BRALCZYK, J., Journalism
DANECKI, J., Political Economy
DOBRZYCKI, W., Law and International Relations
FILIPIAK, T., Political Science
FILIPOWICZ, S., History of Social-Political Thought
GOŁĘBIOWSKI, B., Political Science
GOŁEMBSKI, F., Political Science
GOLKA, B., Journalism
HALIŻAK, M., Political Science
KASPRZYK, L., International Relations
KUKUŁKA, J., Political Science
KUŹNIAR, R., International Relations
ŁUKASZUK, L., International Law
MICHALSKI, B., Journalism
MROZEK, A. B., Political Science
PARZYMIES, S., International Relations
PIEKARA, A., Social Politics
PRZYBYSZ, K., Political Science
RAJKIEWICZ, A., Political Science
SATKIEWICZ, A. H., Theory of Style, Polish Language
SKRZYPEK, A., History
SOBCZAK, J., Law
SYMONIDES, J., International Relations
WŁADYKA, W., Political History
WOJTASZCZYK, K., Political Science
ZIELIŃSKI, E., Modern Political Systems

Faculty of Law and Administration (tel. (22) 552-03-95; fax (22) 826-99-25; internet www.uw.edu.pl/wpia):

BARDACH, J., History of Law
BŁESZYŃSKI, J., Civil Law
DYBOWSKI, T., Civil Law
ERECIŃSKI, T., Civil Law
FLOREK, L., Labour Law
GARDOCKI, L., Penal Law
GARLICKI, L., Constitutional Law
IZDEBSKI, H., History of Law
JĘDRASIK-JANKOWSKA, I., Labour Law
JĘDRZEJEWSKA, M., Civil Law
KRUSZYŃSKI, P., Penal Law
OKOLSKI, J., Civil Law
PIETRZAK, M., History of Law
PIETRZYKOWSKI, K., Civil Law
PIONTEK, E., International Law
RAJSKI, J., Civil Law
REJMAN, G., Penal Law
SAFJAN, M., Civil Law
SALWA, Z., Labour Law
SKOWROŃSKA-BOCIAN, E., Civil Law
SÓJKA-ZIELIŃSKA, K., History of Law
SZYSZKOWSKA, M., Philosophy of Law
TOMASZEWSKI, T., Penal Law
TRZCIŃSKI, J., Constitutional Law
TURSKA, A., Sociology of Law
WĄSOWICZ, M., History of Law
WIERZBOWSKI, M., Administrative Law
WINCZOREK, P., Theory of State and Law
ZABŁOCKA, M., Roman Law
ZIELIŃSKI, A., Civil Law

Faculty of Management (Szturmowa 3, 02-678 Warsaw; tel. (22) 553-40-00; fax (22) 553-40-01; internet www.wz.uw.edu.pl):

BOLESTA-KUKUŁKA, K., Sociology of Management
BUCZKOWSKI, L., Techniques of Management
GŁOWACKI, R., Marketing
JAROSZYŃSKI, A., Administrative Law
KISIELNICKI, J., Industrial Economy and Informatics
KRZYŻOWSKI, R., Social Economics
KWIATKOWSKI, S., Theory of Management
MAJCHRZYCKA-GUZOWSKA, A., Financial Law

MUSZALSKI, W., Employment
OBŁÓJ, K., Organization and Management
RYĆ, K., Economic Theory
ŚLIWA, J., Planning
SOBCZAK, K., Administrative Law
SOPOĆKO, A., Theory of Organization
SZPRINGER, W., Administrative Law
ZAWIŚLAK, A., Theory of Management

Faculty of Mathematics, Informatics and Mechanics (Banacka 2, 02-097 Warsaw; tel. (22) 554-42-14; fax (22) 554-42-00; e-mail mim@mimuw.edu.pl; internet www.mimuw.edu.pl):

BESSAGA, C., Mathematical Analysis
BIAŁYNICKI-BIRULA, A., Mathematics
BOJDECKI, T., Theory of Elasticity
BROWKIN, J., Mathematics
DRYJA, M., Informatics
ENGELKING, R., Mathematics
GRABOWSKI, J., Mathematics
JACKOWSKI, S., Mechanics
KREMPA, J., Mathematics
KWAPIEŃ, S., Mathematics
LIGOCKA, E., Mathematics
MOSZYŃSKA, M., Mathematics
PALCZEWSKI, A., Mathematics
PERADZYŃSKI, Z., Mathematics
POL, R., Mathematics
PUCZYŁOWSKI, E., Mathematics
RYTTER, W., Informatics
SEMADENI, Z., Mathematics
SIEKLUCKI, K., Mathematics
SKOWRON, A., Mathematics
SZAŁAS, A., Informatics
TARLECKI, A., Informatics
TIURYN, J., Mathematics
TORUŃCZYK, H., Mathematics
TURSKI, W., Informatics
WOJTASZCZYK, P., Mathematics
WOŹNIAKOWSKI, H., Informatics
ZBIERSKI, P., Mathematics
ŻOŁĄDEK, H., Mathematics

Faculty of Modern Languages and Oriental Studies (Browarna 8/10, 00-311 Warsaw; tel. (22) 552-09-50; fax (22) 826-75-28; e-mail dznfilol@mail.uw.edu.pl; internet www.neofilologia.uw.edu.pl):

ASZYK-BANGS, U., Linguistics
BOGACKI, B. K., Italian Philology
BOGUSŁAWSKI, A., Russian Philology
BOJAR, B., Formal Linguistics
BYRSKI, M. K., Oriental Philology
BYSTYDZIEŃSKA, G., English Studies
CZOCHRALSKI, J., German Philology
DANECKI, J., Oriental Philology
KAŁUŻYŃSKI, S., Oriental Philology
KOMOROWSKA-JANOWSKA, H., Linguistics
KOTAŃSKI, W., Oriental Philology
KÜNSTLER, M., Sinology
ŁYCZKOWSKA, K., Oriental Philology
MAJDA, T., Oriental Philology
MAŁCUŻYŃSKI, P., Literature
MANTEL-NIEĆKO, J., Ethiopian Philology
MELANOWICZ, M., Oriental Philology
PIŁASZEWICZ, S., African Philology
POPKO, M., Oriental Philology
RUBACH, J., English Philology
RUSIECKI, J., English Linguistics
SALWA, P., Italian Literature
SAUERLAND, K. K., German Philology
SEMENIUK-POLAKOWSKA, M., Linguistics
SKARŻYŃSKA-BOCHEŃSKA, K., Oriental Philology
SKŁADANEK, B., Iranian Philology
SKŁADANEK, M., Oriental Philology
SŁUPSKI, Z., Oriental Philology
TUBIELEWICZ, J., Oriental Philology
UGNIEWSKA-DOBRZAŃSKA, J., Italian Philology
WEŁNA, J. A., English Philology
WESELIŃSKI, A., English Literature
WIKTOROWICZ, J., German Philology
WIŚNIEWSKI, J., English Literature
ŻABOKLICKI, K., French Philology

Faculty of Philosophy and Sociology (00-046 Warsaw, Nowy Świat 69; tel. (22) 826-09-62; fax (22) 826-09-62; internet www.is.uw.edu.pl/wfis):

AUGUSTYNEK, Z., Philosophy
CIUPAK, E., Sociology
DEMBIŃSKA-SIURY, D., Philosophy
JADACKI, J., Philosophy
JANKOWSKI, H., Sociology
JASIŃSKA-KANIA, A., Sociology
KOŹMIŃSKI, A., Sociology
KUCZYŃSKA, A., Philosophy
KUCZYŃSKI, J., Philosophy
MARKIEWICZ, B., Philosophy
MARODY, M., Sociology
MORAWSKI, W., Sociology
NOWICKA-RUSEK, E., Sociology
OMYŁA, M., Logic Philosophy
PELC, J., Logic
ROSIŃSKA-ZIELIŃSKA, Z., Philosophy
SIEMEK, M. J., Philosophy
SIEMIEŃSKA-ŻOCHOWSKA, R., Sociology
SMOLICZ, J. J., Sociology
STANISZKIS, J., Sociology
WIATR, J., Sociology

Faculty of Physics (Hoża 69, 00-681 Warsaw; tel. (22) 553-21-23; fax (22) 625-23-36; e-mail dziekfiz@fuw.edu.pl; internet www.fuw.edu.pl):

BADEŁEK, B., Experimental Physics
BAJ, M., Solid Body Physics
BARANOWSKI, J., Experimental Physics
BAŻAŃSKI, S., Theoretical Physics
BIAŁYNICKI-BIRULA, I., Optics and Mechanics
BLINOWSKI, J., Solid Body Physics
CHAŁASIŃSKA-MACUKOW, K., Optics
CIBOROWSKI, J. A., Experimental Physics
CIEŚLAK-BLINOWSKA, K., Medical Physics
DEMIAŃSKI, M., Theoretical Physics
DOBACZEWSKI, J., Theoretical Physics
DZIEMBOWSKI, W., Astronomy
ERNST, K., Atomic Physics
GAJ, J., Solid Body Physics
GRAD, M., Geophysics
GRYNBERG, M., Solid Body Physics
HAMAN, K., Geophysics
KALINOWSKI, J., Molecule Elementary Physics
KAMIŃSKA, M., Solid Body Physics
KIJOWSKI, J., Theoretical Physics
KOPCZYŃSKI, W., High Energy Physics
KOWALCZYK, P., Experimental Physics
KRÓLIKOWSKI, J., High Energy Physics
KRÓLIKOWSKI, W., Atomic Physics
KRUSZEWSKI, A., Astronomy
KUBIAK, M., Astrophysics
KURCEWICZ, W., Nuclear Physics
LELIWA-KOPYSTYŃSKI, J., Geophysics
LESYNG, B., Biophysics
MAURIN, K., Mathematical Methods in Physics
MIELNIK, B., Theoretical Physics
NAMYSŁOWSKI, J., Theoretical Physics
NAPIÓRKOWSKI, M., Statistics Physics
NAZAREWICZ, W., Solid Body Physics
PIASECKI, J., Theoretical Physics
POKORSKI, S., Theoretical Physics
RADZEWICZ, C., Experimental Physics
ROHOZIŃSKI, St., Atomic Physics
RYKACZEWSKI, K., Experimental Physics
SHUGAR, D., Biophysics
SKRZYPCZAK, E., High Energy Physics
SOSNOWSKA, I., Experimental Physics
STĘPIEŃ, K., Astronomy
STĘPNIEWSKI, R., Solid Body Physics
SYM, A., Physics
SZOPLIK, T., Optics
SZYMACHA, A., Atomic Physics
TRAUTMAN, A., Electrodynamics and Theory of Relativity
TWARDOWSKI, A., Solid Body Physics
UDALSKI, A., Astrophysics
WILHELMI, Z., Atomic Physics
WÓDKIEWICZ, K., Optics

WORONOWICZ, S., Mathematical Methods in Physics
WRÓBLEWSKI, A., Experimental Physics
ZAKRZEWSKI, J., High Energy Physics
ŻYLICZ, J., Experimental Physics

Faculty of Polish Philology (Obożna 8, 00-927 Warsaw; tel. (22) 552-04-28; fax (22) 826-07-83; internet www.polon.uw.edu.pl):

BARTNICKA, B., Polish Philology, Linguistics
CZAPLEJEWICZ, E., Polish Literature
DOMAŃSKI, J., Classical Philology
DREWNOWSKI, T., History of Polish Literature
DUBISZ, S., Polish Philology
FRYBES, S., Polish Literature
GRZEGORCZYKOWA, R., Polish Philology
HANDKE, R., Theory of Literature
KARWACKA, H., Polish Literature
KOWALCZYK, A., History of Literature
KUPISZEWSKI, W. M., Polish Philology, Linguistics
LAM, A., Polish Philology, Literature
MACIEJEWSKI, J., History of Polish Literature
MAKOWSKI, S., History of Literature
MARKOWSKI, A., Polish Philology, Linguistics
MENCWEL, A., Science of Culture
MITOSEK, Z., Theory of Literature
NOWICKA-JEŻOWA, A., Literature, History of Polish Literature
OSIŃSKI, Z., Science of Culture
OWCZAREK, B., Theory of Literature
PELC, J., History of Literature
PUZYNINA, J., Polish Philology, Linguistics
SIATKOWSKA, E., Slavonic Philology, Linguistics
SIATKOWSKI, J., Slavonic Philology, Linguistics
SMOCZYŃSKI, W., Linguistics
SMUŁKOWA, E., Slavonic Philology, Linguistics
STAROWIEYSKI, M., Classical Philology
SUDOLSKI, Z., Polish Philology, Literature
SULIMA, R., Science of Culture
SWIDZIŃSKI, M., Polish Literature, Linguistics
TABORSKI, R., Polish Literature
WOJTCZAK-SZYSZKOWSKI, J., Classical Philology

Faculty of Psychology (Stawki 5/7, 00-183 Warsaw; tel. (22) 554-97-00; fax (22) 635-79-91; e-mail dean@sci.psych.uw.edu.pl; internet www.psych.uw.edu.pl):

GAŁKOWSKI, T., Educational Psychology
GRZELAK, J., Social Psychology
GRZESIUK, L., Psychopathology and Psychotherapy
JARYMOWICZ, M., Personality Psychology
KOFTA, M., Personality Psychology
KOŚCIELSKA, M., Clinical Psychology
KOZIELECKI, J., Cognitive Psychology
MATCZAK, A., Individual Differences
MATYSIAK, J., Biological Psychology
MIKA, S., Social Psychology
STRELAU, J., Individual Differences
WIECZORKOWSKA-NEJTARDT, G., Social Psychology
ZALEWSKA, M., Clinical Psychology

UNIWERSYTET W BIAłYMSTOKU (University of Białystok)

ul. Marii Sklodowskiej-Curie 14 15-097 Białystok

Telephone: (85) 745-70-01
Fax: (85) 744-77-49
E-mail: rektorat@uwb.edu
Internet: www.uwb.edu.pl
Founded 1997
State control
Academic year: October to June (2 semesters)
Rector: Prof. JERZY NIKITOROWICZ

Vice-Rector for Economic Affairs and Regional Contacts: Prof. Dr MAREK PRONIEWSKI
Vice-Rector for Research and International Relations: Prof. Dr BEATA GODLEWSKA-ŻYŁKIEWICZ
Vice-Rector for Students and Teaching Affairs: Prof. Dr ELŻBIETA AWRAMIUK
Vice-Rector for Univ. Organization and Development: Prof. Dr DARIUSZ KIJOWSKI
Librarian: HALINA BRZEZIŃSKA-STEC
Library of 559,575 vols, 74,784 periodicals
Number of teachers: 908
Number of students: 18,308

DEANS

Faculty of Administration in Siedlce: Prof. STANISŁAW BOŻYK
Faculty of Biology and Chemistry: Prof. ANATOL KOJŁO
Faculty of Economics and Informatics in Vilnius: Prof. JAROSLAV VOLKONOVSKI
Faculty of Economics and Management: Prof. Dr ROBERT CIBOROWSKI
Faculty of History and Sociology: Prof. ANDRZEJ SADOWSKI
Faculty of Law: Prof. LEONARD ETEL
Faculty of Mathematics and Informatics: Prof. ANATOL ODZIJEWICZ
Faculty of Pedagogy and Psychology: Prof. Dr ELWIRA JOLANTA KRYŃSKA
Faculty of Philology: Prof. BOGUSŁAW NOWOWIEJSKI
Faculty of Physics: Prof. EUGENIUSZ ŻUKOWSKI

UNIWERSYTET WROCŁAWSKI (University of Wrocław)

pl. Uniwersytecki 1, Wrocław
Telephone: (71) 343-68-47
Fax: (71) 3744-34-21
E-mail: rektorat@adm.uni.wroc.pl
Internet: www.uni.wroc.pl
Founded 1702, rebuilt 1945
State control
Language of instruction: Polish
Academic year: October to June (two terms)
Rector: Prof. Dr hab. ZDZISŁAW LATAJKA
Vice-Rector for Scientific Research and Foreign Relations: Prof. Dr hab. KRZYSZTOF WÓJTOWICZ
Vice-Rector for Gen. Affairs: (vacant)
Vice-Rector for Student Affairs: Prof. Dr hab. JERZY MARÓN (acting)
Vice-Rector for Teaching Affairs: Prof. Dr hab. KRYSTYNA GABRYJELSKA
Admin. Officer: Dr BEATA LENKIEWICZ
Librarian: Mgr Inż. GRAŻYNA PIOTROWICZ
Library: see Libraries and Archives
Number of teachers: 1,720
Number of students: 41,663

Publication: *Acta Universitatis Wratislaviensis*

DEANS

Faculty of Chemistry: Prof. Dr hab. JERZY PIOTR HAWRANEK
Faculty of Historical and Pedagogical Sciences: Prof. Dr hab. BOGDAN ROK
Faculty of Law and Administration: Prof. Dr hab. MAREK BOJARSKI
Faculty of Mathematics and Computer Science: Prof. Dr hab. RYSZARD SZEKLI
Faculty of Natural Sciences: Prof. Dr hab. ANDRZEJ WITKOWSKI
Faculty of Philology: Prof. Dr hab. WŁADYSŁAW DYNAK
Faculty of Physics and Astronomy: Prof. Dr hab. HENRYK CUGIER
Faculty of Social Sciences: Prof. Dr hab. BERNARD ALBIN

PROFESSORS

Faculty of Chemistry (ul. F. Joliot-Curie 14, 50-383 Wrocław; tel. (71) 375-72-90; fax (71) 375-74-20; e-mail dziekanat@wchuwr.chem.uni.wroc.pl; internet www.chem.uni.wroc.pl/indexpol.htm):

HAWRANEK, J., Electronic Data Processing
JAKUBAS, R., Physical Chemistry
JEZIERSKI, A., Inorganic Chemistry
KISZA, A., Physical Chemistry
KOLL, A., Physical Chemistry
KONOPIŃSKA, D., Organic Chemistry
KOZLOWSKI, H., Bioinorganic and Biomedicinal Chemistry
LATAJKA, Z., Theoretical Chemistry and Chemical Physics
LATOS-GRAŻYŃSKI, L., General Chemistry
LIS, T., Crystallography
MROZIŃSKI, J., Methodology of Chemistry
PRUCHNIK, F., Environmental Chemistry and Protection
RATAJCZAK, H., Theoretical Chemistry and Chemical Physics
SIEMION, I., Organic Chemistry
SKRZYPIEC-LEGENDZIEWICZ, J., Analytical Chemistry
SOBCZYK, L., Physical Chemistry
SOBOTA, P., Inorganic Chemistry for Natural Scientists
ZIÓŁKOWSKI, J., Inorganic Chemistry

Faculty of Historical and Pedagogical Sciences (ul. Szewska 48, 50-139 Wrocław; tel. (71) 375-22-23; fax (71) 343-28-55; e-mail dziekan@hist.uni.wroc.pl; internet www.wnhip.hist.uni.wroc.pl):

ADAMCZYK, M., Comparative Pedagogy
BANAŚ, P., Science of Art
CIESIELSKI, M., History of Eastern Europe
CZAPLIŃSKI, M., History of Silesia
DERWICH, M., Centre for Studies of Religious Orders and Church Congregations
KULAK, T., General and Polish History since 19th century
KUSIAK, F., Economic History, Demography and Statistics
MATWIJOWSKI, K., 16th–18th-century General and Polish History
OCHMAN-STANISZEWSKA, S., 16th–18th-century General and Polish History
PIETRZAK, J., 16th–18th-century General and Polish History
POTYRAŁA, B., General Pedagogy
ROK, B., 16th–18th-century General and Polish History
WACHOWSKI, K., Medieval Archaeology
WRZESIŃSKI, W., Contemporary History
ŻABSKI, E., Philosophical and Methodological Foundations of Psychology
ŻERELIK, R., Centre for Studies of Religious Orders and Church Congregations

Faculty of Law and Administration (ul. Uniwersytecka 22–26, 50-145 Wrocław; tel. (71) 343-71-64; fax (71) 375-27-84; internet www.prawo.uni.wroc.pl):

ADAMIAK, B., Administrative Proceedings and Judicial Control of Administrative Activity
BANASZEK, B., Constitutional Law
BEDNARSKI, T., Statistics and Operation Researches
BŁAS, A., Administrative Law
BOĆ, J., Administrative Law
BOGUNIA, L., Criminal Law Practice
BOJARSKI, M., Law of Petty Offences and Penal Fiscal Law
DZIAŁOCHA, K., Constitutional Law
FOJCIK-MASTALSKA, E., Financial Law
FRĄCKOWIAK, J., Economic and Commercial Law
GNIEWEK, E., Civil Law and International Private Law
JENDROŚKA, J., Administrative Proceedings and Judicial Control of Administrative Activity

JONCA, K., Political and Legal Doctrines
KACZMAREK, T., Substantive Penal Law
KAŹMIERCZYK, S., Theory and Philosophy of Law
KEGEL, Z., Crime Detection
KIERES, L., Administrative Economic Law
KOLASA, J., International Economic Relations
KONIECZNY, A., History of Administration
MACIEJEWSKI, M., Political and Legal Doctrine
MĄDRZAK, H., Civil Procedure
MASTALSKI, R., Financial Law
OLSZEWSKI, L., International Economic Relations
ORZECHOWSKI, K., History of Polish State and Law
POŁOMSKI, F., History of Polish State and Law
ŚWIDA, Z., Penal Proceedings
SZURGACZ, H., Labour Law
TRZCIŃSKI, J., Crime Detection

Faculty of Mathematics and Computer Science (pl. Grunwaldzki 2–4, 50-384 Wrocław; tel. and fax (71) 375-74-91; e-mail dziekan@math.uni.wroc.pl; internet www.math.uni.wroc.pl/wydzial/index.php):

BILER, P., Differential Equations
BOŻEJKO, M., Mathematical Analysis
DAMEK, E., Geometry
DUDA, R., History and Methodology of Mathematics
HULANICKI, A., Functional Analysis
KISIELEWICZ, A., Algebra and Theory of Numbers
KOPOCIŃSKI, B., Applied Mathematics
NARKIEWICZ, W., Algebra and Theory of Numbers
NEWELSKI, Algebra and Theory of Numbers
PACHOLSKI, L., Programming Languages
PYTLIK, T., Functional Analysis
ROLSKI, T., Stochastic Processes
SYSŁO, M., Programming Methods
SZCZOTKA, W., Applications of Mathematics
SZWARC, R., Mathematical Analysis
URBANIK, K., Theory of Probability

Faculty of Natural Sciences (ul. Kuźnicza 35, 50-138 Wrocław; tel. and fax (71) 343-57-28):

BOROWIEC, L., Animal Systematics
CEBRAT, S., Genome Studies
DŻUGAJ, A., Animal Physiology
KOZUBEK, A., Lipids and Liposomes
KUPRIŃSKI, T., Anthropology
ŁOBODA, J., Social and Economic Geography
OGORZAŁEK, A., Zoology
OTLEWSKI, J., Protein Engineering
POLANOWSKI, A., Biotechnology of Proteins
SACHANBIŃSKI, M., Museum of Mineralogy and Section of Gemmology
SADOWSKA, A., Geology (Palaeobotany)
SIKORSKI, A., Cell Biology
SZOPA-SKÓRKOWSKI, J., Genetic Biochemistry
TOMIAŁOJĆ, L., Natural Museum
WESOŁOWSKI, T., Bird Ecology
WILUSZ, T., Enzymology
WITKOWSKI, A., Avian Ecology
WYRZYKOWSKI, J., Regional Geography and Tourism

Faculty of Philology (pl. Biskupa Nankiera 15, 50-140 Wrocław; tel. and fax (71) 343-30-29; e-mail dziekanat.fil@uni.wroc.pl):

DĄBROWSKA, A., Applied Linguistics
DEGLER, J., Theory of Culture and Performing Arts
DYNAK, W., Methodology of Teaching Polish Language and Literature
JANIKOWSKI, K., Scandinavian Studies, German Language
JASTRZĘBSKI, J., Theory of Culture
KAMIŃSKA-SZMAJ, I., Contemporary Polish
KLIMOWICZ, T., Russian Literature and Culture

KOLBUSZEWSKI, J., History of Polish Literature before 1918
KUNICKI, W., German Literature before 1848
ŁAWIŃSKA-TYSZKOWSKA, J., New Latin Philology
ŁUGOWSKA, J., Theory of Culture and Performing Arts
MIGOŃ, A., Theory and History of Books
MIGOŃ, K., Theory and History of Books
MIODEK, J., History of Polish
PISAREK, L., Russian Studies
PRĘDOTA, S., Dutch Lexicology and Lexicography
PYSZNY, J., Polish Literature since 1918
SAWICKI, P., Italian Studies
SOKOLSKI, J., History of Early Polish Literature
SZASTYŃSKA-SIEMION, A., Greek Philology
TOMICZEK, E., Applied Linguistics
WIECZOREK, D., Ukrainian Studies
ŻABSKI, T., History of Polish Literature before 1918
ZAWADA, A., Polish Literature since 1918

Faculty of Physics and Astronomy (pl. M. Borna 9, 50-204 Wrocław; tel. (71) 375-94-04; fax (71) 321-76-82; e-mail dziekan@ift.uni.wroc.pl; internet www.wfa.uni.wroc.pl):

CISZEWSKI, A., Microstructure Surface Experimental Physics
CUGIER, H., Astrophysics and Classical Astronomy
CZAPLA, Z., Experimental Physics (Dielectrics Physics)
HABA, Z., Theoretical Physics (Field Theory)
KIEJNA, A., Absorption Experimental Physics
KOŁACZKIEWICZ, J., Experimental Physics (Spectroscopy of Field Emission)
ŁOPUSZAŃSKI, J., Theoretical Physics (Mathematical Methods in Physics)
LUKIERSKI, J., Theoretical Physics (High-Energy Physics and Theory of Fundamental Particles)
MRÓZ, S., Experimental Physics (Electron Spectroscopy)
PĘKALSKI, A., Theoretical Physics (Nonlinear Dynamics and Complex Systems)
POPOWICZ, Z., Theoretical Physics (Field Theory)
REDLICH, K., Theoretical Physics (High-Energy Physics and Theory of Fundamental Particles)

Faculty of Social Sciences (ul. Koszarowa 3, 51-149 Wrocław; tel. (71) 375-51-92; fax (71) 326-10-11; e-mail sekretariat@wns.uni.wroc.pl; internet www.wns.uni.wroc.pl):

ALBIN, B., International Studies (Eastern Europe Research)
ANTOSZEWSKI, A., Political Sciences (Political Systems)
BAL, K., Philosophy (German Philosophy)
BOKAJŁO, W., Contemporary Political Ideas
DĄBROWSKI, S., Political Sciences (Contemporary History and Social Movements)
GAJDA-KRYNICKA, J., Philosophy (History of Philosophy)
GELLES, R., International Studies
HULANICKA, B., Sociology of Political Relations
JABŁONSKI, A., Theory of Politics
KOSIAN, J., History of Philosophy in Silesia
ŁOS-NOWAK, T., International Relations
ŁUKASZEWICZ, R., Studies in Alternatives of Human Education
PISAREK, H., Epistemology and Ontology
SIEMIANOWSKI, A., Philosophy of Science and Culture
STANDTMUELLER, E., Studies on European Union
SURMACZYŃSKI, M., Sociology (Sociology of Political Relations)
WOLAŃSKI, M., Research in East European Studies

UNIWERSYTET ZIELONOGÓRSKI
(University of Zielona Góra)

ul. Licealna 9, 65-417 Zielona Góra

Telephone: (68) 328-20-00
Fax: (68) 324-55-97
E-mail: rektorat@uz.zgora.pl
Internet: www.uz.zgora.pl

Founded 2001 through merger of Politechnika Zielonogórska and Wyższa Szkoła Pedagogiczna im. Tadeusza Kotarbińskiego

State control

Rector: Prof. Dr hab. CZESŁAW OSĘKOWSKI
Pro-Rector for Scientific Research and Int. Cooperation: Prof. Dr hab. Inż TADEUSZ KUCZYŃSKI
Pro-Rector for Devt: Prof. Dr hab. KRZYSZTOF URBANOWSKI
Pro-Rector for Student Affairs: Prof. Dr hab. LONGIN RYBIŃSKI
Pro-Rector for Educational Quality: Prof. Dr hab. WIELISŁAWA OSMAŃSKA-FURMANEK

Library of 425,255 vols
Number of teachers: 1,177
Number of students: 23,127

Publications: *Applied Mathematics and Computer Science* (4 a year), *Applied Mechanics and Engineering* (4 a year), *Discussiones Mathematicae* (4 series, each 2 a year), *Management* (2 a year), *Studia Zachodnie* (1 a year), *Zeszyty Naukowe* (irregular)

DEANS

Faculty of Arts: Prof. Dr hab. ANDRZEJ TUCHOWSKI
Faculty of Education and Social Sciences: Prof. Dr Inż. WIELISŁAWA OSMAŃSKA-FURMANEK
Faculty of Electrotechnology, Informatics and Telecommunications: Prof. Dr hab. Inż. JERZY BOLIKOWSKI
Faculty of Exact Sciences: Prof. Dr hab. MIECZYSŁAW BOROWIECKI
Faculty of Humanities: Prof. Dr hab. ANDRZEJ KSENICZ
Faculty of Land and Environmental Engineering: Prof. Dr hab. Inż. HENRYK GREINERT
Faculty of Mechanical Engineering: Prof. Dr hab. Inż. RYSZARD ROHATYŃSKI
Faculty of Management: Prof. Dr hab. DANIEL FIC

WARSZAWSKI UNIWERSYTET MEDYCZNY
(Medical University of Warsaw)

ul. Żwirki i Wigury 61, 02-091 Warsaw

Telephone: (22) 572-09-13
Fax: (22) 572-01-54
Internet: www.wum.edu.pl

Founded 1789

Rector: Prof. Dr hab. MAREK KRAWCZYK

Library of 400,000 vols
Number of teachers: 1,185
Number of students: 3,200

Faculties: dentistry, health sciences, medicine, pharmacy, postgraduate education

Publication: *Medycyna-dydaktyka-wychowanie* (Medicine-Didactics-Education, 4 a year).

Technical Universities

AKADEMIA GÓRNICZO-HUTNICZA IM. STANISŁAWA STASZICA W KRAKOWIE
(AGH University of Science and Technology)

ul. Mickiewicza 30, 30-059 Cracow
Telephone: (12) 617-20-02
Fax: (12) 633-46-72
E-mail: rektorat@uci.agh.edu.pl
Internet: www.agh.edu.pl

Founded 1919
State control
Languages of instruction: Polish, English
Academic year: October to June

Rector: Prof. RYSZARD TADEUSIEWICZ
Vice-Rector for Gen. Affairs: Prof. ANTONI TAJDUŚ
Vice-Rector for Education: Prof. ANDRZEJ ŁĘDZKI
Vice-Rector for Int. Affairs: Prof. ANDRZEJ KORBEL
Vice-Rector for Science: Prof. JANUSZ KOWAL
Chief Admin. Officer: HENRYK ZIOŁO
Librarian: Mgr EWA DOBRZYŃSKA-LANKOSZ
Library of 407,247 vols, 138,287 vols periodicals, 769,333 items spec. collns
Number of teachers: 2,014
Number of students: 29,237

Publications: *Automatyka* (Automatics, 2 a year), *Computer Science* (1 a year), *Elektrotechnika i Elektronika* (Electrical Engineering, 2 a year), *Geodezja* (Mining Surveying, 2 a year), *Geologia* (Geology, 4 a year), *Górnictwo* (Mining, 4 a year), *Inżynieria Środowiska* (Environmental Engineering, 2 a year), *Kliertnictwo Nafta Gaz* (Drilling Oil and Gas, 1 a year), *Mechanika* (Mechanics, 4 a year), *Metallurgy and Foundry Engineering* (2 a year), *Opuscula Mathematica* (1 a year), *Telekomunikacja Cyfrowa* (1 a year)

DEANS

Faculty of Applied Mathematics: Prof. ADAM PAWEŁ WOJDA
Faculty of Applied Social Sciences: Dr ANNA SIWIK
Faculty of Drilling, Oil and Gas: Prof. STANISŁAW STRYCZEK
Faculty of Electrical Engineering, Automatics, Computer Science and Electronics: Prof. TADEUSZ ORZECHOWSKI
Faculty of Foundry Engineering: Prof. STANISŁAW RZADKOSZ
Faculty of Fuels and Energy: Prof. JANINA MILEWSKA-DUDA
Faculty of Geology, Geophysics and Environmental Protection: Prof. Dr TADEUSZ SŁOMKA
Faculty of Management: Prof. Dr WIESŁAW WASZKIELEWICZ
Faculty of Materials Science and Ceramics: Prof. JERZY LIS
Faculty of Mechanical Engineering and Robotics: Prof. WŁODZIMIERZ KOWALSKI
Faculty of Metallurgy and Materials Science: Prof. Dr ZBIGNIEW MALINOWSKI
Faculty of Mining and Geoengineering: Prof. JERZY KLICH
Faculty of Mining, Surveying and Environmental Engineering: Prof. JAN GOCAŁ
Faculty of Non-Ferrous Metals: Prof. WOJCIECH LIBURA
Faculty of Physics and Applied Computer Science: Prof. KAZIMIERZ JELEŃ

POLITECHNIKA BIAŁOSTOCKA
(Białystok Technical University)

ul. Wiejska 45A, 15-351 Białystok
Telephone: (85) 742-23-93
Fax: (85) 742-23-93

E-mail: rektorat@pb.bialystok.pl
Internet: www.pb.bialystok.pl

Founded 1949
State control
Languages of instruction: Polish, Russian, English
Academic year: October to June

Rector: Prof. Dr hab. Inż. MICHAŁ BOŁTRYK
Vice-Rectors: Prof. Dr hab. Inż. SŁAWOMIR ADAM SORKO, Prof. Dr hab. Inż. FRANCISZEK SIEMIENIAKO, Prof. Dr hab. Inż MIKOŁAJ BUSŁOWICZ
Registrar: Inż. MIROSŁAW MILEWSKI
Librarian: Mgr BARBARA KUBIAK
Library: see Libraries and Archives
Number of teachers: 773
Number of students: 16,500

Publications: *Zeszyty Naukowe* (irregular), *Matematyka, Fizyka, Chemia* (irregular), *Elektryka* (irregular), *Mechanika* (irregular), *Budownictwo* (irregular), *Inżynieria Środowiska* (irregular), *Budowa i Eksploatacja Maszyn* (irregular), *Architektura* (irregular), *Ekonomia i Zarządzanie* (irregular), *Informatyka* (irregular)

DEANS

Faculty of Architecture: Prof. Dr hab. Inż. arch. ANDRZEJ BASISTA
Faculty of Civil Engineering and Environmental Sciences: Prof. Dr hab. Inż. CZESŁAW MIEDZIAŁOWSKI
Faculty of Electrical Engineering: Prof. Dr hab. Inż. BRUNON LEJDY
Faculty of Mechanics: Prof. Dr hab. Inż. ANDRZEJ SEWERYN
Faculty of Computer Science: Prof. Dr hab. Inż. LEON BOBROWSKI
Faculty of Management: Prof. zw. Dr hab. Inż. JOANICJUSZ NAZARKO
Institute of Mathematics and Physics: Prof. Dr hab. TADEUSZ ŁUKASZEWICZ

PROFESSORS

Faculty of Architecture (ul. Krakowska 9, 15-875 Białystok; tel. (85) 742-29-29; fax (85) 742-29-29; e-mail arch@pb.bialystok.pl):

AGRANOWICZ-PONOMARIEWA, E., Interior Design
BASISTA, A., Architecture
BISSENIK, A., Interior Design
BORKOWSKA-LARYSZ, B., Interior Design
DEBIS, J., Painting
DURMANOW, W., Urban Design
DWORAKOWSKI, A., Architecture and Graphics
IODO, I., Town Planning
KALISZUK, H., Interior Design
KUKAWSKI, T., Architecture and Graphics
PINIŃSKI, Z., Architecture
RYCHTER, Z., Theory of Building
RYMASZEWSKI, B., Preservation of Monuments
SAWCZUK, H., History of Architecture
SZCZYKOWSKA-ZAŁESKA, J., Sculpture
WŁODARCZYK, J., Architecture

Faculty of Civil Engineering and Environmental Engineering (ul. Wiejska 45E, 15-351 Białystok; tel. (85) 742-04-18; fax (85) 742-24-13; e-mail malasz@pb.bialystok.pl):

BĄK, G., Building Engineering
BANASZUK, H., Environmental Protection
BOŁTRYK, M., Civil Engineering
BRYŁKA, J., Physical Chemistry
CZERWIŃSKI, A., Forest Botany, Phytosociology
DENCZEW, S., Water Supply and Sewer Systems
DZIENIS, L., Waterworks and Sewerage
GARNCAREK, R. J., Building Engineering, Mechanical Engineering
GRABOWSKI, R. J., Geodesy and Cartography
JEZIERSKI, W., Physics of Building

KRÓLIKOWSKI, A., Waterworks and Sewerage
LEWANDOWSKI, W., Inorganic Chemistry
ŁAPKO, A., Civil Engineering
MIEDZIAŁOWSKI, Cz., Building Construction
OWCZAREK, S., Bridge Construction
PIEŃKOWSKI, K., Fluid Mechanics, Thermal Mechanics
RADZISZEWSKI, P., Road Engineering
ROSOCHACKI, ST. J., General Chemistry
SORKO, S. A., Thermal Techniques
STACHURSKI, W., Building Construction
TRIBIŁŁO, R., Theory of Building Structures
WIATER, J., Agricultural Technology
WIERZBICKI, T., Environmental Engineering, Water and Waste Technology

Faculty of Electrical Engineering (ul. Wiejska 45D, 15-351 Białystok; tel. (85) 742-05-66; fax (85) 742-16-57; e-mail welpb@pb.bialystok.pl):

BADURSKI, J., Internal Medicine, Laboratory Diagnostics
BOLKOWSKI, ST., Electrotechnics and Metrology
BUSŁOWICZ, M., Control Theory, Automatics
CITKO, T., Electrical Engineering, Automatics
CYWIŃSKI, K., Electrotechnology
CZAWKA, G., Electronic Systems
DOROSZ, J., Chemical Technology
DYBCZYŃSKI, W., Lighting
GOŁĄBIOWSKI, J., Electrotechnology
GRISZYN, J., Radiation and Navigation Technology
JORDAN, A., Electrical Engineering, Electrical Metrology
KORNILUK, W., Safety in Electroenergetics
NIEBRZYDOWSKI, J., Electrical Engineering
RAFAŁOWSKI, M., Applied Optics
SIKORSKI, A., Power Electronics
SOWA, A., Electrotechnology
SWIERCZ, M., Biocybernetics, Biomedical Engineering
TWARDY, L., Electro-energetics
ZAJĄC, A., Optoelectronics

Faculty of Mechanics (ul. Wiejska 45C, 15-351 Białystok; tel. (85) 742-15-41; fax (85) 742-11-12; e-mail w.mechaniczny@pb.bialystok.pl):

CZECH, M., Mechanics, Materials Rheology
DĄBROWSKI, J. R., Chemical Engineering, Machine Construction
GAWRYSIAK, M., Mechanical Engineering, Mechatronics
HEJFT, R., Mechanics, Machine Construction
JAWOREK, K., Automatic Control and Robotics
KARPOWICZ, Ś., Automation Engineering
KOWALEWSKI, Z., Applied Mechanical Engineering
KURZYDŁOWSKI, K., Materials Technology
ŁACH, J., Mechanics, Machine Construction
LINDSTEDT, P., Automatic Control and Robotics
MATYSIAK, ST., Computer Techniques
MIATLUK, M., Machine Construction
OSIPIUK, W., Mechanics, Machine Construction
PIWNIK, J., Mechanics, Plastics
PUCIŁOWSKI, K., Mechanics
RAWSKI, F., Automobile Engineering
SEWERYN, A., Mechanics, Resistance of Materials
SIEMIENIAKO, F., Automatic Control and Robotics
SKIEPKO, T., Thermodynamics and Fluid Mechanics
SULYM, H., Applied Mechanical Engineering

Faculty of Computer Science (tel. (85) 742-82-06; fax (85) 742-34-23; e-mail sekretar@ii.pb.bialystok.pl):

BOBROWSKI, L., Biocybernetics
DAŃKO, W., Mathematical Logic
GRZESZCZUK, P., Mathematics
GUŁAKOW, I., Optoelectronics
JARMOLIK, W., Technical Informatics
OSTANIN, A., Computer Science
PIOTROWSKI, A., Technical Informatics
STEPANIUK, J., Mathematics
SZODA, Z., Mathematics
TRZĘSICKI, K., Logic
WIERZCHOŃ, S., Computer Science

Faculty of Management (ul.Ojca Tarasiuka 2, 06-001 Kleosin; tel. (85) 663-22-08; fax (85) 663-19-88; e-mail magda@pb.bialystok.pl):

BARSZCZAK, T., Agricultural Technology
CELMAROWSKI, Cz., Machine Construction
GARBACZEWSKA, G., Biology
IGNATIUK, S., Agricultural Engineering
JĘDRUSZCZAK, M., Agricultural Technology and Agribusiness
JUREWICZ, S., Economics, Mechanics
KLEMENTOWICZ, T., History of Political and Economic Doctrines
KORZUCH, A., Finance and Accountancy
KORZUCH, B., Management
KOWALCZEWSKI, W., Organization and Management, Economics
KUBICKA, H., Agricultural Technology
KURLISZYN-MOSKAL, A., Environment and Tourism Management
ŁAGOWSKA, B., Horticulture
ŁOBODA, T., Biology
MĄDRY, W., Mathematics
MICHAŁOWSKI, K., Environment and Tourism Management
MILASZEWSKI, P., Economics, Environmental Engineering and Environmental Protection
NARUSZEWICZ, S., Law, International Economics
NAZARKO, J., Electrical Power Engineering
NICZYPORUK, A., Agricultural Technology
POPŁAWSKI, W. T., Sociology
SADOWSKI, M., Environmental Protection
SASINOWSKI, H., Economics
SOKÓŁ, J., Animal Science
ŚLUSARCZYK, J., Humanities
TOMCZONEK, Z., Humanities, History
WASIAK, A., Chemistry, Materials Engineering, Mechanical Engineering

Institute of Mathematics and Physics (tel. (85) 742-82-00; fax (85) 742-23-93; e-mail wrobi@pb.bialystok.pl):

BARTOSIEWICZ, Z., Mathematical Theory and Control
ŁUKASZEWICZ, T., Physics
MARCZENKO, WŁ., Control Theory
REWIŃSKI, A., Physics

POLITECHNIKA CZĘSTOCHOWSKA
(Częstochowa University of Technology)

ul. Dąbrowskiego 69, 42-200 Częstochowa
Telephone: (34) 325-04-98
Fax: (34) 361-23-85
E-mail: rektor@adm.pcz.czest.pl
Internet: www.pcz.pl
Founded 1949
State control
Academic year: October to June
Rector: Prof. Dr hab. Inż. HENRYK DYJA
Pro-Rectors: Prof. Dr hab. Inż. ANDRZEJ RUSEK, Prof. Dr hab. Inż. MARIA NOWICKA-SKOWRON, Prof. Dr hab. Inż. JÓZEF KOSZKUL
Executive Director: Mgr MAREK REMBISZ
Librarian: Mgr MAŁGORZATA HANKIEWICZ
Library: see Libraries and Archives
Number of teachers: 878
Number of students: 20,975

Publication: *Turbulence* (1 a year)

DEANS

Faculty of Civil Engineering: Prof. Dr hab. Inż. SŁAWOMIR KOSIŃSKI
Faculty of Electrical Engineering: Prof. Dr hab. Inż. ANDRZEJ ROMAN
Faculty of Environmental Protection and Engineering: Prof. Dr hab. Inż. MARTA JANOSZ-RAJCZYK
Faculty of Management: Prof. Dr hab. JANUSZ SZOPA
Faculty of Materials Processing Technology and Applied Physics: Prof. Dr hab. Inż. JERZY SIWKA
Faculty of Mechanical Engineering and Computer Science: Prof. Dr hab. Inż. JERZY WŁODARSKI

PROFESSORS

Faculty of Civil Engineering (ul. Akademicka 3, 42-200 Częstochowa; tel. (34) 325-09-30):

BOBKO, T., Technology, Organization of Building
CZECH, L., Geometrical Construction, Civil Engineering
DREWNOWSKI, S., Materials Engineering, Structural Engineering
KLEIBER, M., Structural Engineering
KONIECZNY, S., Structural Mechanics
KOSIŃSKI, S., Structural Mechanics
KOZŁOWSKI, R., Civil Engineering
KWIATEK, J., Civil Engineering, Geotechnology
PRZYBYŁO, W., Structural Mechanics, Civil Engineering
PUSZKARIOWA, E., Building Materials
RAJCZYK, J., Civil Engineering
SŁUŻALEC, A., Mathematics, Mechanics
SYGUŁA, S., Bridge Construction, Civil Engineering

Faculty of Electrical Engineering (ul. Armii Krajowej 17, 42-200 Częstochowa; tel. (34) 325-08-22; fax (34) 325-08-23; e-mail dziekanat@el.pcz.czest.pl; internet www.el.pcz.czest.pl):

BIERNACKI, Z., Electrotechnics, Measurements, Design of Measuring Equipment
BRZOZOWSKI, W., Electrical Engineering, Power Stations
DOBRZAŃSKA, I., Electrical Engineering, Electrical Power Management
ISKIERKA, S., Electrotechnics
JANICZEK, R., Electrotechnology
KRAWCZYK, A., Electrotechnics
KRUCZININ, A. M., Electrotechnology
MINKINA, W., Electronics
POPOV, B., Informatics
ROJEK, R., Electronics, Automatics
ROLICZ, P., Electrotechnics
ROMAN, A., Electronics, Magnetic Materials
RUSEK, A., Electric Motors
SAWICKI, A., Electrotechnology
SOIŃSKI, M., Magnetic Materials, Material Engineering
SOKALSKI, K., Physics
SOWA, P., Electroenergetics
WYSOCKI, J., Electronics, Computer Engineering
ZĄBKOWSKA-WACŁAWEK, M., Electrotechnology

Faculty of Environmental Protection and Engineering (tel. (34) 325-04-62; fax (34) 325-04-63; e-mail wiis@adm.pcz.czest.pl):

BIEŃ, J., Geology, Hydrogeology
BIS, Z., Mechanics, Thermodynamics
BOHDZIEWICZ, J., Environmental Engineering
DEWIATOW, W., Mechanics, Structural Engineering
GIRCZYS, J., Sanitary Engineering
GODZIK, S., Environmental Engineering

GUMNITSKY, J., Biochemistry, Biotechnology
HŁAWICZKA, S., Environmental Engineering
JAGIEŁA, K., Electrotechnology
JANIKOWSKI, R., Environmental Engineering
JANOSZ-RAJCZYK, M., Environmental Engineering
KISIEL, A., Sanitary Engineering
KOSIŃSKI, W., Environmental Engineering
KUCHARSKI, R., Environmental Engineering
MALINA, G., Sanitary Engineering
NOWAK, W., Sanitary Engineering
PISAREK, J., Mechanics, Machine Building Technology
SANITSKY, M., Environmental Engineering

Faculty of Management (ul. Armii Krajowej 19B, 42-200 Częstochowa; tel. (34) 325-03-25; e-mail wz@zim.pcz.czest.pl; internet zim.pcz.czest.pl):

ANTOSZKIEWICZ, J., Organization and Management
BARTZ, B., Economics, Logistics
BORKOWSKI, S., Organization and Management, Metallurgy
BOROWIECKI, R., Organization and Management
BUKOWSKI, L., Machine-Building Technology, Management
BUKUVKA, O., Production Engineering
CHRZAN, P., Econometrics, Statistics
DURAJ, J., Organization and Management
DURLIK, I., Marketing
FIEDOROWICZ, K., Economics
GOŁUCHOWSKI, J., Informatics
GORCZYCKA, E., Economics, Organization and Management
GRZESZCZYK, T., Economics, Law
GUBARIENI, N., Informatics
GURGUL, E., Agrotechnology
JASTRZĘBOWSKI-HOFFMAN, Z., History, Politics
KATKOW, A., Informatics
KIEŁTYKA, L., Automatics in Management
KLIBER, J., Materials Engineering, Metallurgy
KLISIŃSKI, J., Economics, Marketing
KONODYBA-SZYMAŃSKI, B., Metallurgy
LEWANDOWSKI, J., Organization and Management, Machine Building Technology
MALISZEWSKI, J., Economics, Organization and Management
MILIAN, L., Sociology, Organization and Management
MOSZKIEWICZ, M., Economics
NOWAK, C., Agricultural Technology
NOWICKA-SKOWRON, M., Economics, Organization and Management
NOWICKI, A., Organization and Management, Informatics
PABIAN, A., Organization of Building
PARTYKA, M., Mathematics, Informatics
RUBACHOW, A., Organization and Management Economics
SITEK, E., Economics
SOBOLAK, L., Organization and Management
SUCHECKA, J., Economics
SZOPA, J., Theoretical and Applied Mechanics, Applied Mathematics, Computers
SZTUKA, J., Marketing
SZUWALSKI, K., Organization and Management
VARKOLY, L., Materials Engineering, Computer Engineering
WOŹNIAK-SOBCZAK, B., Economics, Organization and Management
ZACHOROWSKA, A., Economics
ZAWISŁAWSKA, D., Economics
ŻÓŁTOWSKI, B., Process Engineering and Organization

Faculty of Materials Processing Technology and Applied Physics (ul. Armii Krajowej 19, 42-200 Częstochowa; tel. (34) 325-07-13; fax (34) 361-38-88; e-mail dziekanat@mim.pcz .czest.pl; internet www.mim.pcz.czest.pl):

BALA, H., Corrosion of Metals
BOCHENEK, A., Metallurgy, Materials Science
BRASZCZYŃSKI, J., Metallurgy, Foundry Technology
BUDZIK, R., Metallurgy of Ferrous Metals
DYJA, H., Plastic Working of Metals
DZILIŃSKI, K., Physics
GOLIS, B., Plastic Working of Metals
HRABAŃSKI, R., Physics
JEZIORSKI, L., Metallurgy, Metals Science
JOWSA, J., Metallurgy
KNAP, F., Plastic Working of Metals
KONOPKA, Z., Metallurgy, Foundry Technology
ŁĘDZKI, A., Metallurgy, Steelmaking
LESIK, L., Metallurgy
LIS, A., Materials Engineering, Metallurgy
MIELCZAREK, E., Thermodynamics in Power Engineering, Heat Engineering
MOREL, S., Heat Engineering
NITKIEWICZ, Z., Metallurgy, Materials Engineering
PIETRZYK, M., Metallurgy
PILARCZYK, J., Metallurgy, Materials Science
PIŁKOWSKI, Z., Foundry, Steelmaking
SIWKA, J., Metallurgy, Steelmaking
SŁUPEK, S., Metallurgy, Heat Engineering
STACHURA, S., Metals Science
WASZKIELEWICZ, W., Organization and Management, Metallurgy
WIERZBICKA, B., Metallurgy, Casting of Non-ferrous Metals
WOLKENBERG, A., Metals Science
WYSŁOCKI, B., Physics of Magnetic Materials
WYSŁOCKI, J., Physics, Physics of Magnetic Materials
ZAPART, M., Physics
ZAPART, W., Physics of Magnetic Materials
ZBROSZCZYK, J., Physics

Faculty of Mechanical Engineering and Computer Science (ul. Armii Krajowej 21, 42-200 Częstochowa; tel. (34) 325-05-61; fax (34) 325-05-04; e-mail dziekanat@itm.pcz.czest .pl):

CUPIAŁ, K., Machines and Internal Combustion Engines
DOMAŃSKI, Z., Physics, Biophysics
DROBNIAK, S., Fluid Mechanics, Fluid Flow Machines
GAJEWSKI, W., Thermodynamics
GIERZYŃSKA-DOLNA, M., Mechanical Engineering, Plastics Processing Machines and Technology
JARŻA, A., Fluid Mechanics
KENSIK, R., Welding
KLAJNY, R., Fluid Mechanics
KOMPANEC, L., Informatics
KOSZKUL, J., Plastics Materials
KRIVOI, S., Mathematics
KUBARSKI, J., Mathematics
KUKLA, S., Mathematics, Mechanics
KUKURYK, B., Plastic Working of Metals
MAJCHRZAK, E., Mathematics
MAZANEK, E., Machine Design
MELECHOW, R., Machine-Building Technology
MENDERA, K., Machines and Internal Combustion Engines
MIRKOWSKI, J., Mechanics and Internal Combustion Engines
MOCHNACKI, B., Mathematics
NIESZPOREK, T., Machine-Building Technology
PARKITNY, R., Applied Mechanics and Foundry Technology
PIECH, H., Computer Engineering
POSIADAŁA, B., Applied Mechanics

RUTKOWSKA, D., Informatics
RUTKOWSKI, L., Informatics, Cybernetics
SCZYGIOL, N., Applied Mechanics
SEWASTJANOW, P., Mathematics
SUBERLAK, O., Plastics Materials
SZOPA, R., Mathematics
TOMSKI, L., Machine Design, Applied Mechanics
TUBIELEWICZ, K., Machine-Building Technology
WIERZBICKI, E., Applied Mathematics, Mechanics
WŁODARSKI, J., Plastics Processing Machines and Technology
WOLAŃSKI, R., Thermodynamics, Thermal Processes in Welding
WOŹNIAK, C., Mathematics, Mechanics
WYRZYKOWSKI, R., Informatics

POLITECHNIKA GDAŃSKA
(Gdańsk University of Technology)

ul. G. Narutowicza 11/12, 80-952 Gdańsk

Telephone: (58) 341-57-91
Fax: (58) 341-58-21
E-mail: rektor@pg.gda.pl
Internet: www.pg.gda.pl
Founded 1945
Academic year: October to July

Rector: Prof. JANUSZ RACHOŃ
Vice-Rectors: Prof. RYSZARD KATULSKI, Prof. ROMUALD SZYMKIEWICZ, Prof. WOJCIECH SADOWSKI, Prof. WŁADYSŁAW KOC
Chief Admin. Officer: EWA MAZUR
Librarian: BOŻENA HAKUĆ
Library: see Libraries and Archives
Number of teachers: 1,200
Number of students: 20,000

Publications: *Advances in Materials Sciences* (Journal, 4 a year), *Inżynieria Morska i Geotechnika* (Journal, 4 a year), *Pismo PG* (Journal, 12 a year), *Polish Maritime Research* (Journal, 4 a year), *Wykazy Nowych Nabytków Biblioteki* (Library Acquisitions Lists, 4 a year), *Zeszyty Naukowe Politechniki Gdańskiej* (Scientific Papers of the Technical Univ. of Gdańsk, irregular)

DEANS

Faculty of Applied Physics and Mathematics: JAN GODLEWSKI
Faculty of Architecture: ANDRZEJ. BARANOWSKI
Faculty of Chemistry: JACEK NAMIEŚNIK
Faculty of Civil and Environmental Engineering: KRZYSZTOF. WILDE
Faculty of Electrical and Control Engineering: KAZIMIERZ. JAKUBIUK
Faculty of Electronics, Telecommunications and Informatics: HENRYK. KRAWCZYK
Faculty of Management and Economics: PIOTR DOMINIAK
Faculty of Mechanical Engineering: ADAM BARYLSKI
Faculty of Ocean Engineering and Ship Technology: (vacant): MAREK DZIDA

PROFESSORS

Faculty of Applied Physics and Mathematics (Narutowicz 11/12, 80-952 Gdańsk; tel. (58) 347-13-10; fax (58) 347-28-21; internet www .mif.pg.gda.pl):

GŁAZUNOW, J., Mathematical Analysis, Applied Mathematics
GODLEWSKI, J., Physics
KALINOWSKI, J., Physics
KAMONT, Z., Differential Equations
LEBLE, S., Theoretical and Mathematical Physics
MURAWSKI, L., Physics, Solid State Physics
ROMANOWSKI, A., Algebra
SADOWSKI, W., Solid State Physics

SIENKIEWICZ, J., Physics, Applied Informatics
SZMYTKOWSKI, Cz., Atomic and Molecular Physics

Faculty of Architecture (Narutowicz 11/12, 80-952 Gdańsk; tel. and fax (58) 347-13-15; e-mail dziekanarch@pg.gda.pl; internet www .pg.gda.pl/architektura):

GÓRA, J., Painting
KITA, A., Painting
STAWICKA-WAŁKOVSKA, M., Healthy Housing (Urban and Building) and Environmental Assessment of Buildings (Sustainable Buildings)

Faculty of Civil and Environmental Engineering (Narutowicz 11/12, 80-952 Gdańsk; tel. (58) 347-22-05; fax (58) 347-20-44; e-mail biuruyd@pg.gda.pl; internet cenwil.bl.pg.gda .pl/wilis/):

BOGDANIUK, B., Traffic Engineering
GODYCKI CWINKO, T., Theory of Reinforced and Prestressed Concrete Structures
JUDYCKI, J., Road Construction
KOWALCZYK, Z., Technology and Management in Civil Engineering
KOWALIK, P., Geodesy
KRYSTEK, R., Traffic Engineering
OBARSKA-PEMPKOWIAK, H., Environmental Engineering
OLAŃCZUK-NEYMAN, K., Environmental Engineering
SIKORA, Z., Civil Engineering, Soil Mechanics and Geomechanical Computation
SZYMCZAK, Cz., Structural Mechanics
SZYMKIEWICZ, R., Hydrology
ZADROGA, B., Soil Mechanics and Foundation Engineering
ZIÓŁKO, J., Steel Structures

Faculty of Chemistry (Narutowicz 11/12, 80-952 Gdańsk; tel. (58) 347-13-45; fax (58) 347-26-94; e-mail dzknt@chem.pg.gda.pl; internet www.pg.gda.pl/chem):

BALAS, A., General Chemistry
BIERNAT, J., General Chemistry
BIZIUK, M., Environmental Analytical Chemistry, Elemental Analysis, Spectrophotometric Analysis
BOROWSKI, E., Biochemistry
DAROWICKI, K., Electrochemistry, Corrosion and Corrosion Protection
HĘDRZYCKA, K., Biochemistry
HUPKA, J., Chemical Engineering
KAMIŃSKI, M., Chemical Technology
KAWALEC-PIETRENKO, B., Chemical Engineering
KOŁODZIEJCZYK, A., Organic Chemistry
KONOPA, J., Organic Chemistry
KUR, J., Molecular Biology
LEWANDOWSKI, W., Heat Technology, Chemical Engineering
MAZERSKI, J., Molecular Modelling, Chemometrics, Biophysics
MILEWSKI, S., Biochemistry
NAMIEŚNIK, J., Analytical Chemistry
PACYNA, J., Environmental Chemistry, Environmental Engineering, Environmental Analysis and Monitoring
POŁOŃSKI, T., Organic Chemistry, Stereochemistry, Molecular Modelling, Chiroptical Spectroscopy
RACHOŃ, J., Organic Chemistry
SYNOVIEĆKI, J., Technical Science
WOJNOWSKI, W., Inorganic Chemistry

Faculty of Electrical and Control Engineering (Narutowicz 11/12, 80-952 Gdańsk; tel. (58) 347-12-58; fax (58) 347-18-02; e-mail dean@ely.pg.gda.pl; internet www.ely.pg.gda .pl):

BRDYŚ, M., Control Systems
JAKUBIUK, K., Principles of Electrotechnics, Electrical Apparatus
KOWALSKI, Z., Industrial Automation
KRAWCZUK, M., Mechanics

KRZEMIŃSKI, Z., Electrical Drives and Power Electronics
MARECKI, J., Electrical Power Engineering
PAZDRO, P., Electrical Apparatus and Traction
SZCZERBA, Z., Electrical Power Engineering
WOLNY, A., High-Voltage Current Switching
ZAJCZYK, R., Power Engineering
ZIMNY, P., Theoretical Electromagnetic Field

Faculty of Electronics, Telecommunications and Informatics (Narutowicz 11/12, 80-952 Gdańsk; tel. (58) 347-12-45; fax (58) 341-61-32; e-mail deans@eti.pg.gda.pl; internet www.eti.pg.gda.pl):

CZYŻEWSKI, A., Sound Engineering
GÓRSKI, J. K., Software Engineering, Informatics
KOWALCZUK, Z., Automatic Control and Robotics
KRAWCZYK, H., Computer Science, Parallel Architectures and Fault-Tolerance
KUBALE, M., Discrete Optimization
MALINA, W., Computer Science and Pattern Recognition
MAZUR, J., Microwave Techniques
MROZOWSKI, M., Electromagnetic Field Theory, Microwaves
NIEDŹWIECKI, MACIEJ, Automatic Control
NOWAKOWSKI, A., Electronics Technology
POLOWCZYK, M., Telecommunications Technology
RUTKOWSKI, D., Principles of Telecommunications
SOBCZAK, W., Cybernetics
SPIRALSKI, L., Electronic Equipment
STEPNOWSKI, A., Marine Acoustics, Telecommunications
WOŹNIAK, J., Telecommunications, Computer Communication Systems
ZIELONKO, R., Electronic Equipment Technology
ZIENTALSKI, M., Electronic Equipment Technology

Faculty of Management and Economics (Narutowicz 11/12, 80-952 Gdańsk; tel. (58) 347-18-99; fax (58) 347-18-61; e-mail dziekani@mech.pg.gda.pl; internet www.zie.pg.gda.pl):

ADAMKIEWICZ, A., Research and Development of Social, Economic and Technological Systems
DASZKOWSKA, M., Principles of Marketing, Services Marketing, the Service Economy

Faculty of Mechanical Engineering (Narutowicz 11/12, 80-952 Gdańsk; tel. (58) 347-20-32; fax (58) 347-10-25; e-mail dziekani@mech.pg.gda.pl; internet www.mech.pg.gda.pl):

BALCERSKI, A., Marine Diesel Engines and Ship Power Plants
EJSMONT, J., Machine Building and Maintenance
NEYMAN, A., Tribology
PRZYBYLSKI, W., Manufacturing Engineering
PUZYREWSKI, R., Fluid Mechanics
STĄSIEK, J., Thermodynamics and Heat Transfer
WALCZAK, W., Welding
WITTBRODT, E., Mechanics and Machine Dynamics, Applied Mechanics
ZIELIŃSKI, A., Materials Engineering

Faculty of Ocean Engineering and Ship Technology (Narutowicz 11/12, 80-952 Gdańsk; tel. (58) 347-16-62; fax (58) 341-47-12; e-mail sekoce@pg.gda.pl; internet www.oce.pg.gda.pl/wydziai):

BRANDOWSKI, A., Engineering Safety and Reliability, Ship Technology
DOMACHOWSKI, Z., Automatic Control of Power Engineering Plants

GIRTLER, J., Ship Power Plants and Diesel Engines
KOLENDA, J., Mechanics of Ship Structures
ROSOCHOWICZ, K., Ship Technology
SZANTYR, J., Mechanics, Ship Hydrodynamics

POLITECHNIKA KRAKOWSKA IM. TADEUSZA KOŚCIUSZKI
(Cracow University of Technology)

Warszawska 24, 31-155 Cracow
Telephone: (12) 628-20-00
Fax: (12) 628-20-71
E-mail: r-0@admin.pk.edu.pl
Internet: www.pk.edu.pl
Founded 1945
State control
Language of instruction: Polish
Academic year: October to June (2 semesters)
Rector: Prof. Dr hab. Inż. JÓZEF GAWLIK
Pro-Rectors: Dr hab. Inż. RAFEŁ PALEJ, Dr hab. Inż. Arch. WOJCIECH KOSIŃSKI, Prof. Dr hab. Inż. KAZIMIERZ FURTAK, Prof. Dr hab. Inż. JÓZEF GAWLIK, Dr hab. Inż. Arch. WACŁAW CELADYN
Chief Admin. Officer: Mgr Inż. ZBIGNIEW SKAWICKI
Librarian: Mgr MAREK GÓRSKI
Library of 234,600 vols, 81,221 periodicals, 422,127 standards, patents, etc.
Number of teachers: 1,167
Number of students: 17,357
Publications: *Czasopismo Techniczne* (Technical Bulletin, irregular; series on Architecture, Civil Engineering, Chemistry, Mechanics, Electrotechnics, Environmental Science), *Zeszyty Naukowe i Monografie Politechniki Krakowskiej* (Scientific Papers, irregular; series on Architecture, Civil Engineering, Environmental Engineering, Mechanics, Electrical and Computer Engineering, Chemical Engineering and Technology, Basic Technical Sciences, Human, Economic and Social Sciences)

DEANS

Faculty of Applied Physics and Computer Modelling: Dr hab. RYSZARD ZACH
Faculty of Architecture: Prof. Zw. Dr hab. Inż. arch. DARIUSZ KOZŁOWSKI
Faculty of Chemical Engineering and Technology: Prof. Zw. Dr hab. Inż. ZBIGNIEW ŻUREK
Faculty of Civil Engineering: Prof. Dr hab. Inż. JACEK ŚLIWIŃSKI
Faculty of Electrical and Computer Engineering: Dr hab. Inż. PIOTR DROZDOWSKI
Faculty of Environmental Engineering: Dr hab. Inż. KRZYSZTOF KNAPIK
Faculty of Mechanical Engineering: Dr hab. Inż. KRZYSZTOF SZUWALSKI

PROFESSORS

Faculty of Applied Physics and Computer Modelling (Podchorążych 1, 30-084 Cracow; tel. (12) 638-07-28; fax (12) 638-07-28; e-mail f-0@admin.pk.edu.pl; internet www.pk.edu.pl/wftimk):

ARTEMOWICZ, O., Algebra
CISOWSKI, J., Solid State Physics
GRAFIJCZUK, W., Mechanics
KOZARZEWSKI, B., Theoretical Physics, Quantum Computation
ŁAWRENIUK, S., Differential Equations
ŁOPUSZAŃSKI, O., Spectral Theory of Operators
OSTOJA-GAJEWSKI, A., Applied Mechanics
PLICZKO, A., Mathematics
Faculty of Architecture (tel. (12) 628-20-20; fax (12) 628-20-20; e-mail a-0@admin.pk.edu.pl; internet www.pk.edu.pl/arch):

BARTKOWICZ, B., Urban Design and Spatial Planning

BIEDA, K., Urban Design Theory and Practice
BÖHM, A., Architecture, Landscape Architecture
BULIŃSKI, W., Architectural Design
DOUSA, S., Sculpture
GOŁOGÓRSKA-KUCIA, E., Painting and Drawing
KADŁUCZKA, A., History of Architecture and Monument Preservation
KOZŁOWSKI, D., Architectural Design and Theory
KUŚNIERZ, K., History of Urban Design
LENARTOWICZ, J. K., Design of Industrial Architecture
MITKOWSKA, A., History of Architecture and Urban Design
SERUGA, W., Urban and Architectural Design
SIEWNIAK, M., Landscape Architecture
WYŻYKOWSKI, A., Urban and Architectural Design

Faculty of Chemical Engineering and Technology (tel. (12) 628-20-35; fax (12) 628-20-35; e-mail wiitch@indy.chemia.pk.edu.pl; internet www.chemia.pk.edu.pl):

BARAŃSKI, A., Organic Chemistry and Physical Organic Chemistry
KOWALSKI, Z., Inorganic Chemical Technology
PIELICHOWSKI, J., Chemistry and Technology of Polymers, Organic Synthesis
STOKŁOSA, A., Physical Chemistry, Solid State Physical Chemistry
TABIS, B., Chemical Engineering
ŻUREK, Z., Solid State Chemistry, Materials Science

Faculty of Civil Engineering (tel. (12) 628-20-23; fax (12) 628-20-23; e-mail l-0@admin.pk.edu.pl; internet www.pk.edu.pl/wil):

ADAMSKI, A., Transport Control Computer Systems, Management and Control Decision-making, Optimization Problems
CHRZANOWSKI, M., Fracture Mechanics and Rheology
CICHOŃ, C., Theory of Structure, Numerical Analysis
CZYCZUŁA, W., Rail and Air Transport Infrastructure, Transportation Systems
DYDUCH, K., Reinforced and Prestressed Concrete Structures, Industrial Buildings, Modernization
FLAGA, A., Structural Mechanics, Building Aerodynamics, Wind Engineering
FLAGA, K., Bridges, Tunnels, Concrete Structures, Technology of Concrete, Nondestructive Testing
FURTAK, K., Bridges, Tunnels, Concrete Structures
KAWECKI, J., Structural Mechanics
ORKISZ, J., Theory of Structure, Structural Mechanics
RUDNICKI, A., Traffic and Highway Engineering, Transportation Systems
ŚLIWIŃSKI, J., Concrete Technology, Building Materials
STACHOWICZ, A., Structural Mechanics, General and Industrial Building, Concrete Structures
SZEFER, G., Solid and Structural Mechanics
TRACZ, M., Traffic and Highway Engineering
WASZCZYSZYN, Z., Structural Mechanics, Strength of Materials, Artificial Intelligence, Neurocomputing and Microcomputing

Faculty of Electrical and Computer Engineering (tel. (12) 628-20-43; fax (12) 628-20-43; e-mail e-0@admin.pk.edu.pl; internet www.elektron.pk.edu.pl):

JAGIEŁŁO, A., Electrical Machines
LAYER, E., Electrical Metrology

MALECKI, P., Experimental Particle Physics, Online Computing, Detector Control Systems

MOŚCIŃSKI, J., Computer Systems, Large-scale Computing, Network Security, Wireless Networking

SAPIECHA, K., Computer Architecture and Programming

SIWCZYŃSKI, M., Electrotechnics, Circuit Theory and Signals

SOBCZYK, T., Electrical Machines

SZARANIEC, E., Mathematical Geophysics

Faculty of Environmental Engineering (tel. (12) 628-28-01; fax (12) 628-20-40; e-mail s-0@admin.pk.edu.pl; internet www.wis.pk.edu.pl):

BRYŚ, H., Surveying in Engineering

DĄBROWSKI, W., Water Supply, Waste Water Disposal, Sanitary Engineering

KANDEFER, S., Thermal Engineering, Combustion Processes, Use of Thermal Waste, Air Protection Systems

KOCWA-KALUCH, R., Environmental Biology, Microbiology of Water, Waste Water and Air

MACZEK, K., Refrigeration, Air Conditioning, Environmental Engineering

NACHLIK, E., Hydraulics and Water Management

PIASEK, Z., Geodesy and Cartography for Environmental Engineering, Numerical Geodesy

SŁOTA, H., Water Management

WYSOKIŃSKI, L., Geotechnics, Environmental and Geological Engineering, Civil Engineering

Faculty of Mechanical Engineering (Jana Pawła II 37, 31-864 Cracow; tel. (12) 648-14-32; fax (12) 648-14-32; e-mail m-0@admin.pk.edu.pl; internet www.mech.pk.edu.pl):

CYKLIS, J., Production Engineering

DYLĄG, M., Chemical Engineering, Chemical Industry Equipment, Environmental Engineering

GAWLIK, J., Machining, Design of Cutting Tools

GOLEC, K., Internal Combustion Engines, Engine Cold-starting, Feeding Systems, Turbocharging

KAMIEŃSKI, J., Industrial Equipment

KAZIOR, J., Machine Technology, Powder Metallurgy, Stainless Steels

KNAPCZYK, J., Motor Vehicles and Tractors, Robotics, Theory of Machines and Mechanisms

KOZŁOWSKI, R., Physical Metallurgy and Heat Treatment, Power Engineering Materials Science

MATRAS, Z., Fluid Mechanics, Rheology, Chemical Engineering, Power Engineering

MAZURKIEWICZ, S., Experimental Mechanics, Biomechanics

MICHAŁOWSKI, S., Machine Dynamics, Robotics

MUC, A., Plate and Shell Structures, Mechanics of Composite Materials

NIZIOŁ, J., Theoretical and Applied Mechanics, Machine Dynamics

OPRZĘDKIEWICZ, J., Reliability of Mechanical Devices

RUP, K., Fluid Mechanics, Heat and Mass Transfer

RYŚ, J., Machine Design, Gears, Pressure Vessels

SENDYKA, B., Internal Combustion Engines

SKRZYPEK, J., Theory of Plasticity, Rheology, Damage

TALER, J., Power Machines and Engineering, Heat Transfer, Thermodynamics

WANTUCH, E., Production Engineering

WOJNAR, L., Tribology

WOŁKOW, J., Hydraulic and Pneumatic Control and Drives

ZALEWSKI, W., Power Equipment and Systems, Refrigerating and Air-conditioning Systems

ZIELINSKI, A., Computer Methods of Structural Mechanics, Computer-aided Machine Design

POLITECHNIKA ŁÓDZKA
(Łódź University of Technology)

116 Żeromskiego St 90-924 Łódź

Telephone: (42) 631-20-01

Fax: (42) 631-85-22

E-mail: rector@adm.p.lodz.pl

Internet: www.p.lodz.pl

Founded 1945

State control

Languages of instruction: English, French, Polish

Academic year: October to June (2 semesters)

Chancellor: Dr STANISŁAW STARZAK

Rector: Prof. STANISŁAW BIELECKI

Vice-Rector: Prof. IRENEUSZ ZBICIŃSKI

Vice-Rector: Prof. KRZYSZTOF JÓŹWIK

Vice-Rector: Prof. PIOTR SZCZEPANIAK

Vice-Rector: Prof. WOJCIECH WOLF

Librarian: Mgr Inż. BŁAŻEJ FERET

Library of 258,530 vols, 707 current periodicals, 232,383 patents and standards

Number of teachers: 1,478

Number of students: 20,072

Publications: *Budownictwo* (in Polish), *Bulletin* (in Polish), *Chemia* (in Polish and English), *Chemia Spożywcza i Biotechnologia* (in Polish and English), *Cieplne Maszyny Przepływowe* (in Polish and English), *Elektryka* (in Polish and English), *Inżynieria Chemiczna i Procesowa* (in Polish and English), *Journal of Applied Computer Science* (in English), *Mechanics and Mechanical Engineering* (in English), *Organizacja i Zarządzanie* (in Polish), *Physics* (in English), *Rozprawy Naukowe* (in Polish and English), *Włókiennictwo* (in Polish), *Zeszyty Naukowe Politechniki Łódzkiej* (in Polish and English)

DEANS

Faculty of Biotechnology and Food Science: Prof. MARIA KOZIOŁKIEWICZ

Faculty of Chemistry: Prof. PIOTR PANETH

Faculty of Civil Engineering, Architecture and Environmental Engineering: Prof. DARIUSZ GAWIN

Faculty of Electrical, Electronic, Computer and Control Engineering: Prof. SŁAWOMIR WIAK

Faculty of Material Technologies and Textile Design: Prof. RYSZARD KORYCKI

Faculty of Mechanical Engineering: Prof. BOGDAN KRUSZYŃSKI

Faculty of Organization and Management: Prof. RYSZARD GRĄDZKI

Faculty of Process and Environmental Engineering: Prof. STANISŁAW LEDAKOWICZ

Faculty of Technical Physics, Information Technology and Applied Mathematics: Prof. GRZEGORZ BĄK

Institute of Papermaking and Printing: Prof. BARBARA SURMA-SLUSARSKA, Prof. NADZW

PROFESSORS

Faculty of Biotechnology and Food Science (Wólczańska 171/173, 90-924 Łódź; tel. (42) 631-34-01; fax (42) 631-34-02; e-mail deanbiof@adm.p.lodz.pl; internet www.snack.p.lodz.pl):

AMBROZIAK, W., Fermentation Technology

ANTCZAK, T., Technical Biochemistry

BIELECKI, S., Technical Biochemistry

BUJACZ, G., Protein Crystallography, Structural Biochemistry

CEDZYŃSKA, K., Organic Chemistry, Environmental Protection

GRABKA, J., Food Engineering, Sugar Technology

ICIEK, J., Chemical Food Technology, Food Engineering

KOZIOŁKIEWICZ, M., Biotechnology, Chemistry, Technical Biotechnology

KRÓL, B., Food Technology

KULA, J., Chemical Technology

LIBUDZISZ, Z., Technical Microbiology

NEBESNY, E., Food Technology

OKRUSZEK, A., Biotechnology, Organic Chemistry

SZOPA, J., Technical Microbiology

TURKIEWICZ, M., Biochemistry, Enzymology

TWARDOWSKI, T., Technical Biochemistry

WYSOCKI, S., Physical And Theoretical Chemistry

ŻAKOWSKA, Z., Technical Microbiology

Faculty of Chemistry (Zeromskiego 116, 90-924 Łódź; tel. (42) 631-31-00; fax (42) 631-31-03; e-mail deanchem@adm.p.lodz.pl; internet www.chemia.p.lodz.pl):

ABRAMCZYK, H., Molecular Spectroscopy, Laser Spectroscopy, Physical and Theoretical Chemistry

BEM, H., Physical and Nuclear Chemistry

CZAJKOWSKI, W., Dyes Chemistry and Technology, Organic Chemistry and Technology

GĘBICKI, J. M., Organic Physical Chemistry, Photochemistry, Spectroscopy, Radiation Chemistry, Biocrystallography

GŁÓWKA, M., Biocrystallography

HAWLICKA, E., Physical and Theoretical Chemistry, Computation Chemistry

JANECKI, T., Organic Chemistry

JÓŹWIAK, W., Chemical Catalysis, Environmental Protection

KAMIŃSKI, Z., Organic Chemistry

KAROLAK-WOJCIECHOWSKA, J., Physical and Theoretical Chemistry, Crystallography

MARCINEK, A., Physical Chemistry, Radiation Chemistry

PANETH, P., Physical and Theoretical Chemistry, Biochemistry

ROSIAK, J. M., Biomaterials Engineering, Polymer Chemistry, Radiation Technology

RYNKOWSKI, J., General Chemistry, Chemical Catalysis, Environmental Protection

RZYMSKI, W., Polymer Chemistry and Technology

SOKOŁOWSKA, J., Dyes Chemistry and Technology

ULAŃSKI, J., Physics and Physical Chemistry of Polymers

ZABORSKI, M., Rubber Chemistry and Technology

Faculty of Civil Engineering, Architecture and Environmental Engineering (Politechniki 6, 90-924 Łódź; tel. (42) 631-35-00; fax (42) 631-35-02; e-mail deanarch@p.lodz.pl; internet www.p.lodz.pl/bais):

CZKWIANIANC, A., Concrete Structures

JOCZ, J., Sculpture

JUZWA, J., Industrial Architecture, Planning of Industrial Areas

KAMIŃSKA, M., Concrete Structures

KLEMM, P., Building Physics, Building Materials, Acoustics of the Architectural and Urban Environment

PAWŁOWSKI, P., History of Town Planning, Planning for Urban Revitalization

PRZEWŁOCKI, S., Engineering Geodesy, Building Metrology, Cartography, Descriptive Geometry

ROGOWSKI, B., Fracture Mechanics, Contact and Inclusion Mechanics, Mechanics of Piezo-electro-magneto-elastic Materials, 'Smart' Materials and 'Intelligent' Structures, Coupled Fields

SABINIAK, H., Heating, Air Conditioning and Ventilation Engineering, Powerdriving and Exploitation of Machinery

Faculty of Electrical, Electronic, Computer and Control Engineering (B. Stefanowskiego 18/22, 93-924 Łódź; tel. (42) 631-25-02; fax (42) 636-47-02; e-mail deanelec@sir.p.lodz.pl; internet wee.p.lodz.pl):

ANDERS, G., Reliability Analysis, Power Cable Thermal Rating, Asset Management, Project Management

BARTOSZEWICZ, A., Control Engineering and Robotics, Control Theory

JEZIERSKI, E., Control of Robots

KACPRZAK, T., Telecommunications, Electronic Devices and Systems, Neural Networks

KOŁACIŃSKI, Z., Electrical Apparatus, Plasma Technologies

KOSZMIDER, A., Instrument Transformers, Applied Electrical Engineering

KUŚMIEREK, Z., Electrical Metrology

KUŹMIŃSKI, K., Control Theory, Automation

LISIK, Z., Semiconductor Devices, Microelectronic Technology, High Temperature Electronics, Optical and Electrical Integrated Systems

MATERKA, A., Telecommunications, Signals Processing, Medical Electronics

MIELCZARSKI, W., Power Engineering

MOSIŃSKI, F., Stochastic Processes, High Voltage Engineering

NAPIERALSKI, A., Microelectronics, Electronic Circuits, Power Electronics, Computer Engineering, Thermography

NOWACKI, Z., Electrical Drive Control, Power Electronics

NOWICZ, R., Electrical Engineering, Transformers

OSTALCZYK, P., Control Engineering and Robotics, Electric Drive Automation

PAWELSKI, W., Electronic Devices and Circuits, Power Electronics

PAWLIK, M., Thermal Power Plant Energy Economics

SANKOWSKI, D., Computerized Data Measurement, Identification and Control of Electrothermal Systems

STRZELCZYK, A., Electrical Engineering, Power Engineering

TADEUSIEWICZ, M., Circuit Theory, Theoretical Electrotechnology

WIAK, S., Computer-aided Design, Electrodynamics

ZAKRZEWSKI, K., Electric Machines and Transformers, Applied Electrodynamics

Faculty of Material Technologies and Textile Design (Zeromskiego 116, 90-924 Łódź; tel. (42) 631-33-00; fax (42) 636-48-23; e-mail dzw4@adm.p.lodz.pl):

CYGAN, W., Tapestry

DEMS, K., Structural Mechanics

FRYDRYCH, I., Mechanical Technology of Textiles, Clothing

GNIOTEK, K., Automation of Textile Processes, Measurement Science and Systems

JANTAS, R., Chemical Technology

KOWALSKI, K., Knitting Technology

KOPIAS, K., Knitting Technology

KRUCIŃSKA, I., Mechanical Technology of Textiles, Metrology

LIPP-SYMONOWICZ, B., Chemical Technology of Textiles

MASAJTIS, J., Mechanical Technology of Textiles

NAWROT, A., Tapestry

RYBICKI, F. E., Chemical Technology of Textiles

SNYCERSKI, M., Mechanical Technology of Textiles

WYSOKIŃSKA, Z., Economics

ZAJACZKOWSKI, J., Mechanics, Textiles

Faculty of Mechanical Engineering (B. Stefanowskiego 1/15, 90-924 Łódź; tel. (42) 631-22-00; fax (42) 631-22-03; e-mail deanmech@sir.p.lodz.pl; internet www.p.lodz.pl/mechaniczny):

AWREJCEWICZ, J., Dynamics, Control, Biomechanics

BURCAN, J., Precision Engineering, Medical Engineering

CZOLCZYNSKI, K., Mechanics, Machine Engineering

FODEMSKI, T., Thermodynamics, Heat Transfer

GAWROŃSKI, Z., Materials Engineering

GAZICKI-LIPMAN, M., Materials Engineering

GOŁĄBCZAK, A., Production Engineering

KAPITANIAK, T., Mechanics, Machine Dynamics

KOLAKOWSKI, Z., Applied Mechanics

KRÓLAK, M., Applied Mechanics

KRUSZYŃSKI, B., Machining, Manufacturing and Machine Tools Surface Technology

KRYSIŃSKI, J., Fluid-flow Machinery

KULA, P., Machine Design, Materials Engineering

MITURA, S., Materials Engineering

NIEZGODZINSKI, T., Mechanics, Applied Mechanics

ORYŃSKI, F., Machine Tools, Machine Dynamics

PAWELSKI, Z., Machine Design

PIETROWSKI, S., Materials Engineering, Foundry

TOMCZYK, I., Machine Design, Control

WALKOWIAK, B., Medical Engineering

WIŚNIEWSKI, M., Machine Design, Tribology

Faculty of Organization and Management (Piotrkowska 266, 90-924 Łódź; tel. (42) 631-37-68; fax (42) 684-79-93; e-mail dz-w9-4@adm.p.lodz.pl; internet www.oizet.p.lodz.pl):

BALENDRA, R., Management

BARANOWSKI, K., Humanities

LACHIEWICZ, S., Management

LECEWICZ-BARTOSZEWSKA, J., Ergonomics

LEWANDOWSKI, J., Management

MARTIN, C., Management

PENC, J., Strategy Management

POMYKALSKI, A., Economics

Faculty of Process and Environmental Engineering (Wólczańska 213, 90-924 Łódź; tel. (42) 631-37-00; fax (42) 636-56-63; e-mail deanev@wipos.p.lodz.pl; internet wipos.p.lodz.pl):

HEIM, A., Mechanical Engineering, Chemical Engineering

KAMIŃSKI, W., Environmental Engineering, Chemical Engineering

LEDAKOWICZ, S., Chemical Engineering and Bioprocess Engineering, Environmental Engineering, Chemical Technology

MUCHA, M., Chemical Engineering, Chemical Technology

PIDDUBNIAK, D., Mechanics

TYCZKOWSKI, J., Materials Science, Chemical Engineering, Chemistry

WODZIŃSKI, P., Chemical Engineering, Mechanical Engineering

ZARZYCKI, R., Environmental Engineering

ZBICIŃSKI, I., Chemical Engineering, Environmental Engineering

Faculty of Technical Physics, Information Technology and Applied Mathematics (Wólczańska 215, 90-924 Łódź; tel. (42) 631-36-01; fax (42) 631-36-02; e-mail dz-w7-7@adm.p.lodz.pl; internet www.ftims.p.lodz.pl; publ. *Intelligent Internet Exploration*):

BĄK, G., Solid State Physics, Dielectrics

BALCERZAK, M., Real Analysis

GAJEK, L., Statistics, Financial and Actuarial Mathematics

JACYMIRSKI, M., Signal Processing Methods and Fast Algorithms, Technical and Medical Diagnosis

JEMEĆ, W., Cytography, Asymptotic Methods, Integral Equations

KUCHARCZYK, W., Solid State Physics

MIŚKIEWICZ, L., Artistic Composition of Images and Virtual Spaces, Computer Graphics, Visualization

NAKWASKI, W., Semiconductor Laser Physics, Computer Physics

PRZANOWSKI, M., Theory of Relativity, Mathematical Physics

PRZERADZKI, B., Differential Equations, Dynamical Systems

STACHIW, P., Numerical Methods, Methods of Optimization, System Theory

SZCZEPANIAK, P. S., Computational Intelligence, Pattern Recognition, Knowledge Extraction, Technical and Medical Applications

Institute of Papermaking and Printing (Wólczańska 223, 90-924 Łódź; tel. (42) 636-88-22; fax (42) 631-38-01; e-mail inpapsek@p.lodz.pl; internet www.inpap.p.lodz.pl):

KAWKA, W., Processes and Equipment in the Paper Industry

PRZYBYSZ, K., Paper Technology

SURMA-SLUSARSKA, B., Chemistry of Wood, Pulp and Paper Technology

TOPOLNYTSKYY, P., Processes and Equipment in the Paper Industry

WANDELT, P., Pulp and Paper Technology

POLITECHNIKA LUBELSKA
(Technical University of Lublin)

ul. Nadbystrzycka 38D, 20-618 Lublin

Telephone: (81) 538-11-00

Fax: (81) 532-26-12

E-mail: politechnika@pollub.pl

Internet: www.pollub.pl

Founded 1953

State control

Language of instruction: Polish

Academic year: October to June (2 semesters)

Rector: Prof. JOZEF KUCMASZEWSKI

Vice-Rectors: Prof. WITOLD STEPNIEWSKI, Prof. MAREK OPIELAK, Prof. ANDRZEJ WACWLORDARCZYK

Chief Admin. Officer: MIECZYSLAW HASIAK

Library Dir: Mgr Inż. STEFAN WÓJTOWICZ

Library of 172,000 vols, 97,000 standards and technical catalogues

Number of teachers: 566

Number of students: 12,000

DEANS

Faculty of Civil and Sanitary Engineering: Prof. BOGUSLAV SZMYGIN

Faculty of Electrical Engineering and Computer Science: Prof. WOLDEMAR WOJCIK

Faculty of Environmental Engineering: Prof. LUCJAN PAWLOWSKI

Faculty of Management Sciences and Principles of Technology: Prof. JERZY LIPSKI

Faculty of Mechanical Engineering: Prof. HENRYK KOMSTA

PROFESSORS

Faculty of Civil and Sanitary Engineering:

BUREK, R., Heating, Ventilation and Automation

CIEŚLAK, W., Mathematics and Engineering Geometry

CIĘŻAK, T., Institute of Civil Engineering and Architecture

FLAGA, A., Structural Mechanics

HALICKA, A., Civil Engineering Structures

KRZOWSKI, Z., Geotechnics

KUKIEŁKA, J., Highway Engineering

OLSZTA, W., Water Supply and Waste Water Removal

POMORSKA, K., Chemical Engineering

SADOWSKI, T., Solid Mechanics

Faculty of Electrical Engineering and Computer Science:

BOBROWSKI, A., Mathematics
GRZEGÓRSKI, S., Informatics
JANOWSKI, T., Institute of Electrical Engineering and Electrotechnologies
KOLANO, J., Electrical Drive Systems
KOSMULSKI, M., Electrochemistry
LOZBIN, V., Automatics and Metrology
MAJKA, K., Power Plants and Energy Management
PIETRZYK, W., Computer and Electrical Engineering
RUTKA, Z., Power Networks and Protection
WOJCIK, W., Electronics
ZIELENSKI, W., Mechanics, Polymer Processing
ŻUKOWSKI, P., Electrical Devices and High-Technology Engineering

Faculty of Environmental Engineering:

KWIETNIEWSKI, M., Water Supply and Sewage Disposal
OLSZTA, W., Water Management
OZONEK, J., Indoor Environment Engineering
PAWLOWSKI, L., Institute of Environmental Production Engineering
PAWLOWSKI, L., Water, Waste Water and Waste Technology
SOBCZUK, H., Thermal Techniques
SOLDATOV, V., Sustainable Development
STEPNIEWSKI, W., Land Protection

Faculty of Management Sciences and Principles of Technology:

BANEK, T., Quantitative Methods
BAUM, T., Ergonomics
BOJAR, E., Economics
LENIK, K., Principles of Technology
LIPSKI, J., Enterprise Organization
OLCHOWIK, J., Institute of Physics
PAWLAK, M., Organization and Management
SITKO, W., Management
SKOWRON, S., Marketing
WANIURSKI, J., Applied Mathematics

Faculty of Mechanical Engineering:

JONAK, J., Machine Design
KOCZAN, L., Mathematics, Analytical Functions
KUCZMASZEWSKI, J., Production Engineering
NIEWCZAS, A., Internal Combustion Engines and Transportation
OPIELAK, M., Food Processing Engineering
SIKORA, R., Mechanics, Polymer Processing
SWIC, A., Institute of Technical Systems of Information
SZABELSKI, K., Applied Mechanics
TARKOWSKI, P., Tribology, Motor Vehicles and Internal Combustion Engines
WEROŃSKI, A., Physical Metallurgy, Heat Treatment
WEROŃSKI, W., Metal Forming

POLITECHNIKA POZNAŃSKA
(Poznań University of Technology)

Pl. Marii Skłodowskiej-Curie 5, 60-965 Poznań

Telephone: (61) 665-35-37
Fax: (61) 665-37-70
E-mail: rector@put.poznan.pl
Internet: www.put.poznan.pl

Founded 1919
State control
Academic year: October to September

Chancellor: Dr JANUSZ NAPIERAŁA
Rector: Prof. ADAM HAMROL
Vice-Rector for Educational Affairs: Prof. Dr hab. STEFAN TRZCIELIŃSKI
Vice-Rector for Gen. Affairs: Prof. Dr hab. KAROL NADOLNY

Vice-Rector for Scientific and Int. Affairs: Prof. Dr hab. ALEKSANDRA RAKOWSKA
Chief Admin. Officer: Dr MIROSŁAW STROIŃSKI
Registrar: Mgr KRYSTYNA DŁUGOSZ
Chair. of Library: Prof. Dr NADOLNY KAROL
Library of 237,680 vols, 74,668 vols of periodicals, 46,811 standards, 154,358 patents
Number of teachers: 1,200
Number of students: 20,000

Publications: *Fasciculi Mathematici* (in English), *Foundations of Computing and Decision Sciences* (4 a year, in English), *Zeszyty Naukowe Politechniki Poznańskiej* (Faculty Bulletins, in Polish and English)

DEANS

Faculty of Architecture: Prof. Dr JERZY SUCHANEK
Faculty of Chemical Technology: Prof. Dr ANDRZEJ OLSZANOWSKI
Faculty of Civil and Environmental Engineering: Prof. JANUSZ WOJTKOWIAK
Faculty of Computing: Prof. Dr JERZY NAWROCKI
Faculty of Electrical Engineering: Prof. Dr KONRAD SKOWRONEK
Faculty of Electronics and Telecommunications: Prof. Dr PAWEŁ SZULAKIEWICZ
Faculty of Engineering Management: Prof. Dr LESZEK PACHOLSKI
Faculty of Mechanical Engineering and Management: Prof. ADAM HAMROL
Faculty of Technical Physics: Prof. Dr MIROSŁAW DROZDOWSKI
Faculty of Machines and Transportation: Prof. Dr MAREK IDZIOR

POLITECHNIKA RZESZOWSKA
(Rzeszów University of Technology)

POB 85, Al. Powstańców Warszawy 12, 35-959 Rzeszów

Telephone: (17) 854-12-60
Fax: (17) 854-12-60
E-mail: rektor@prz.edu.pl
Internet: www.prz.edu.pl

Founded 1963 as High School of Engineering, present status 1974
State control
Academic year: October to September

Rector: Prof. MAREK ORKISZ
Vice-Rector for Devt: Prof. KAZIMIERZ BUCZEK
Vice-Rector for Education: ADAM MARCINIEC
Vice-Rector for Research: Prof. LEONARD ZIEMIAŃSKI
Admin. Dir: Mgr JANUSZ BURY
Library Dir: Dr MONIKA ZUB
Library: see under Libraries and Archives
Number of teachers: 730
Number of students: 15,000

Publications: *Folia Scientiarum Universitatis Technicae Resoviensis*, *Zeszyty Naukowe*

DEANS

Faculty of Chemistry: Prof. HENRYK GALINA
Faculty of Civil and Environmental Engineering: PIOTR KOSZELNIK
Faculty of Electrical and Computer Engineering: Assoc. Prof. GRZEGORZ MASŁOWSKI
Faculty of Management: Assoc. Prof. GRZEGORZ OSTASZ
Faculty of Mathematics and Applied Physics: IWONA WŁOCH
Faculty of Mechanical Engineering and Aeronautics: JAROSŁAW SĘP

POLITECHNIKA ŚLĄSKA
(Silesian University of Technology)

ul. Akademicka 2A, 44-100 Gliwice

Telephone: (32) 231-23-49
Fax: (32) 237-16-55
E-mail: rek.sekr@polsl.gliwice.pl

Internet: www.polsl.gliwice.pl

Founded 1945
State control
Academic year: October to June

Rector: Prof. Dr WOJCIECH ZIELIŃSKI
Vice-Rector for Education: Prof. Dr RYSZARD K. WILK
Vice-Rector for Org. and Devt: Prof. Dr WOJCIECH CHOLEWA
Vice-Rector for Research and Industrial Cooperation: Prof. Dr MARIAN DOLIPSKI
Chief Admin. Officer: WOJCIECH WYDRYCHIEWICZ

Library: see Libraries and Archives
Number of teachers: 1,707
Number of students: 30,042

Publication: *Zeszyty Naukowe Politechniki Śląskiej* (Research Review—various titles)

DEANS

Faculty of Architecture: Prof. NINA JUZWA
Faculty of Automatic Control, Electronics and Computer Science: Prof. JERZY RUTKOWSKI
Faculty of Chemistry: Prof. JERZY SUWIŃSKI
Faculty of Civil Engineering: Prof. STANISŁAW MAJEWSKI
Faculty of Electrical Engineering: Assoc. Prof. BOGUSŁAW GRZESIK
Faculty of Materials Science and Metallurgy: Dr LESZEK BLACHA
Faculty of Mathematics and Physics: Dr STANISŁAW KOCHOWSKI
Faculty of Mechanical Engineering: Prof. Dr LESZEK DOBRZAŃSKI
Faculty of Mining and Geology: Assoc. Prof. KRYSTIAN PROBIERZ
Faculty of Organization and Management: Prof. ANDRZEJ KARBOWNIK
Faculty of Power and Environmental Engineering: Prof. Dr MICHAŁ BODZEK
Faculty of Transport: Prof. ANDRZEJ WILK

POLITECHNIKA ŚWIĘTOKRZYSKA
(Kielce University of Technology)

ul. Tysiąclecia Państwa Polskiego 7, 25-314 Kielce

Telephone: (41) 342-41-00
Fax: (41) 344-29-97
E-mail: rek@tu.kielce.pl
Internet: www.tu.kielce.pl/en

Founded 1965
State control
Academic year: October to June

Rector: Prof. Dr hab. STANISŁAW ADAMCZAK
Vice-Rector for Int. Cooperation: Prof. Dr hab. ZBIGNIEW RUSIN
Vice-Rector for Research: Prof. Dr hab. LESZEK PŁONECKI
Vice-Rector for Research Personnel Devt: Prof. Dr hab. CZESŁAW KUNDERA
Vice-Rector for Student Affairs: Prof. Dr hab. MAŁGORZATA SUCHAŃSKA
Admin. Officer: Dr Eng. ANDRZEJ SĘK
Library: see Libraries and Archives
Number of teachers: 382
Number of students: 8,170

DEANS

Faculty of Civil and Environmental Engineering: Prof. Dr hab. JERZY ZBIGNIEW PIOTROWSKI
Faculty of Electrical and Computer Engineering: Prof. Dr hab. ANDRZEJ KAPŁON
Faculty of Management and Computer Modelling: Prof. Dr hab. DARIUSZ BOJCZUK
Faculty of Mechatronics and Machinery Building: Prof. Dr hab. LESZEK RADZISZEWSKI,

PROFESSORS

Faculty of Civil and Environmental Engineering (tel. (41) 342-45-41; fax (41) 344-37-84; e-mail wbldzie@tu.kielce.pl; internet www.tu.kielce.pl/en/wbiis):

BEZAK-MAZUR, E., Environmental Protection

BOROWICZ, T., Structural Mechanics, Computer Methods in Structural Mechanics

DĄBEK, L., Environmental Chemistry

DĄBKOWSKI, Sz., Water Engineering, Hydraulics

DACHOWSKI, R, Technology and Organization in Civil Engineering

FARYNIAK, L., Civil Engineering

GILEWSKI, W., Structural Mechanics

GOŁASKI, L., Strength of Materials

IWAŃSKI, M., Road Construction Technologies

KOWAL, Z., Metal Constructions and Theory of Structures

KOZŁOWSKI, T., Soil Mechanics, Foundation Engineering

KULICZKOWSKI, A., Environmental Engineering, Trenchless Technologies

ŁOMOTOWSKI, J., Water and Sewage Treatment

MIRSKI, J., Theory of Designing Coatings of Structures

NITA, P., Airfield Construction

ORZECHOWSKI, T., Heat Transfer, Heating and Ventilation

OWSIAK, Z., Concrete Technology

PIASTA, J., Concrete Technology and Prefabrication

PIASTA, W. G., Concrete Technology and Prefabrication

PIOTROWSKI, J. Z., Physics of Buildings, Heating and Ventilation

PURGAL, P., Heating and Ventilation

PROSKURIAKOW, V., Architecture

RUDZIŃSKI, L., Building Repair and Maintenance

RUSIN, Z., Building Materials

RYMASZEWSKI, B., History and Theory of Historical Monuments' Conservation

SERUGA, W., Architecture and Urban Planning

SIKORSKI, M., Land Amelioration

STROJ, A., Heating, Ventilation and Air Conditioning

SZCZEPAŃSKI, W., Art Science

TRĄMPCZYŃSKI, W., Strength of Materials, Mechanics

WAWRZEŃCZYK, J., Building Materials, Concrete Technology

WEHLE-STRZELECKA, S., Architecture and Urban Planning

ŻYGADŁO, M., Waste Management, Waste Disposal and Treatment

Faculty of Electrical and Computer Engineering (tel. (41) 342-41-29; fax (41) 344-77-58; e-mail weaii@tu.kielce.pl; internet www.tu.kielce.pl/en/faculties/weaii):

AUGUSTYN, J., Metrology

DENIZIAK, S., Computer Science

GAD, S., Power Electronics, Electrical Engineering

GORZAŁCZANY, M., Electronics and Intelligent Systems, Computer Engineering, Digital Systems

JASTRIEBOW, A., Computer Science

KACZMAREK, Z., Theoretical Electrical Engineering and Metrology

KAPŁON, A., Power Electronics and Electrical Drives, Electrical Engineering

KUŚMIERZ, J., Metrology

ŁASTOWIECKI, J., Power Electronics and Electric Drives

MARCINIAK, M., Telecommunications

NADOLSKI, R., Electrical Machines, Electrical Engineering

NOWICKI, T., Technical Science

RÓŻOWICZ, A., Lighting Technology

SAPIECHA, K., Computer Science

STACHULEC, K., Modern Solid Physics

STEFAŃSKI, T., Management and Control Systems, , Identifications and Control Systems

STĘPIEŃ, J., Power Engineering

SUCHAŃSKA, M., Telecommunications and Photonics

SZCZEŚNIAK, Z., Automatization of Technical Process; Components and Devices of Electronics and Control Systems

TUNIA, H., Power Electronics

WCIŚLIK, M., Automatic Control Devices and Systems, , Automatic Control, Electrical Engineering

WŁODARCZYK, M., Theoretical Electrical Engineering

WORWA, K., Informatics, Technical Science

Faculty of Management and Computer Modelling (tel. (41) 342-44-40; fax (41) 342-43-06; e-mail wzimk@tu.kielce.pl; internet www.tu.kielce.pl/en/wzimk):

BEDNARCZYK, J., Economics and Management

BOJCZUK, D., Production Engineering Optimisation Methods

CICHOŃ, C., Applied Computer Science

GIERULSKI, W., Production Engineering, Process Modelling

GRYSA, K., Mathematics

JASTRZĘBSKA-SMOLAGA, H., Economic Strategies

KOTOWSKA-JELONEK, M., Economics and Management

MATCZYŃSKI, M., Production Engineering, Process Modelling

MEDUCKI, S., Economic Strategies

OKNIŃSKI, A., Physics

OKSANYCH, A., Economics and Management

PIELORZ, A., Mathematics

PŁOSKI, A., Mathematics

STADNYTSKYY, Y., Economics and Management

Faculty of Mechatronics and Machinery Building (tel. (41) 342-44-20; fax (41) 344-86-98; e-mail wmibm@tu.kielce.pl; internet www.tu.kielce.pl/en/wmibm):

ADAMCZAK, S., Machine Design and Maintenance; Engineering Metrology; Quality Systems; Automated Measurement Systems

AMBROZIK, A., Machine Design and Maintenance; Motor and Tractor Vehicles; Combustion Piston Engines

ANTOSZEWSKI, B., Machine Design and Maintenance; Tribology; Sealing Technologies

CHAŁUPCZAK, J., Metallurgy; Metal Forming; Mechanical Engineering

DINDORF, R., Machine Design and Maintenance; Automation of Fluid Systems; Hydraulic and Pneumatic Automation Systems; Mechatronics; Hydraulic Drive and Control Systems

DZIADOŃ, A., Materials Engineering; Metal Science; Heat Treatment

FARANA, R., Industrial Process and Equipment Control

GAJEWSKI, M., Metallurgy; Foundry Engineering

JANECKI, D., Automation and Robotics, Computer Science; Surface Metrology; Control Theory; Modelling and Simulation

KORUBA, Z., Mechanical Engineering; Mechanical System Dynamics; Numerical Methods; Aerial Vehicle Control

KUNDERA, Cz., Machine Design and Maintenance; Machine Dynamics and Control; Mechanical Engineering; Tribology

LISCAK, S., Transport Technology

MIKO, E., Machine Design and Maintenance; Industrial Process Control

MUCHA, Z., Machine Design and Maintenance; Laser Process Control

MYCZUDA, Z., Automation and Robotics, Computational Methods and Control Systems

NEIMITZ, A., Mechanical Engineering; Mechanics of Solids

OZIMINA, D., Machine Design and Maintenance; Tribology

PŁONECKI, L., Machine Design and Maintenance; Hydraulic and Pneumatic Automation Systems; Machine Control; Laser System Control

RADOWICZ, A., Mechanical Engineering; Mechanics of Solids; Engineering Mechanics

RADZISZEWSKI, B., Theoretical Mechanics; Theory of Stability

RADZISZEWSKI, L., Mechanical Engineering; Vibroacoustics

ROKACH, I., Machine Design and Maintenance; Fracture Mechanics

SPADŁO, S., Machine Design and Maintenance; Industrial Process Control

STAMIROWSKI, J., Automation and Robotics; Computer Science; Information Technology for Business; Computer-aided Engineering

STAŃCZYK, T. L., Machine Design and Maintenance; Machine Dynamics

WESOŁOWSKI, Z., Mechanical Engineering; Dynamics of Continuous Media; Laser Processing of Metals

ZOWCZAK, W., Machine Design and Maintenance; Optimization of Mechanical Systems

POLITECHNIKA WARSZAWSKA (Warsaw University of Technology)

Pl. Politechniki 1, 00-661 Warsaw

Telephone: (22) 234-72-11

Fax: (22) 621-68-92

E-mail: soltyski@rekt.pw.edu.pl

Internet: www.pw.edu.pl

Founded 1826

State control

Languages of instruction: English, Polish

Academic year: October to September

Rector: Prof. WŁODZIMIERZ KURNIK

Vice-Rector for Academic Affairs: Prof. LECH CZARNECKI

Vice-Rector for Gen. Affairs: Prof. ROMAN GAWROŃSKI

Vice-Rector for Płock Campus: Prof. JACEK KIJEŃSKI

Vice-Rector for Scientific Affairs: Prof. TADEUSZ KULIK

Vice-Rector for Student Affairs: Prof. WŁADYSŁAW WIECZOREK

Chief Admin. Officer: Dr KRZYSZTOF DZIEDZIC

Librarian: Mgr JOLANTA STĘPNIAK

Library of 1,551,537 vols, 1,200 periodical titles, 7,500 electronic periodical titles, 220,000 special collns, incl. 34,000 Polish, European and int. standards

Number of teachers: 2,538

Number of students: 35,156

Publication: *Prace naukowe—Politechnika Warszawska* (Scientific Works—Warsaw University of Technology)

DEANS

Business School: Dr WITOLD ORŁOWSKI (Dir)

College of Economics and Social Sciences (Płock Campus): Dr JACEK KUBISSA (Dir)

College of Social Science and Administration: Prof. HELENA KISILOWSKA (Dir)

Faculty of Architecture: Prof. STEFAN WRONA

Faculty of Automobile and Construction Machinery Engineering: Prof. JERZY BAJKOWSKI

Faculty of Chemical and Process Engineering: Prof. JERZY BAŁDYGA

Faculty of Chemistry: Prof. ZBIGNIEW BRZÓZKA

Faculty of Civil Engineering: Prof. HENRYK ZOBEL

Faculty of Civil Engineering, Mechanics and Petrochemistry (Płock Campus): Prof. JACEK KIJEŃSKI

Faculty of Electrical Engineering: Prof. STANISŁAW WINCENCIAK

Faculty of Electronics and Information Technology: Prof. JAN SZMIDT

Faculty of Environmental Engineering: Prof. BERNARD ZAWADA

Faculty of Geodesy and Cartography: Prof. WITOLD PRÓSZYŃSKI

Faculty of Management: Prof. TADEUSZ KRUPA

Faculty of Materials Science and Engineering: Prof. JERZY SZAWŁOWSKI

Faculty of Mathematics and Information Science: Prof. IRMINA HERBURT

Faculty of Mechatronics: Prof. KRZYSZTOF LEWENSTEIN

Faculty of Physics: Prof. RAJMUND BACEWICZ

Faculty of Power and Aeronautical Engineering: Prof. JERZY BANASZEK

Faculty of Production Engineering: Prof. ANDRZEJ KOCAŃDA

Faculty of Transport: Prof. WOJCIECH WAWRZYŃSKI

PROFESSORS

College of Economics and Social Sciences (Płock Campus) (Łukasiewicza 17, 09-400 Płock; tel. (24) 367-21-26; fax (24) 262-90-08; e-mail knes@pw.plock.pl):

BIAŁOŃ-SOCZYŃSKA, L., Economics of Industry, Economics of Science, Marketing

GÓRALSKI, W., Domestic Relations Law, Canon Law

KRAJEWSKA, A., Economics, Fiscal Policy and Taxation Theory

KRAJEWSKI, S., Innovative and Structural Policies, Enterprise Operation and Privatization

MARCINIAK, S., Economics of Innovation, Macroeconomics

OBRĘBSKI, T., Labour Economics, Industrial Relations

PACHO, W., Financing Strategies of Public Limited Companies

SPYCHALSKI, G., History of Economics, Modern Economics

STAWICKI, J., Econometrics and Statistics

WĄSOWICZ, M., Economic Theory, Environmental Economics

WITKOWSKA, J., International Economics, European Integration

ZIELIŃSKI, R., Economic Theory, Defence Economics

College of Social Science and Administration (Noakowskiego 18/20, 00-668 Warsaw; tel. (22) 621-36-92; fax (22) 825-37-46; e-mail kolegium@kns.pw.edu.pl; internet www.kns.pw.edu.pl):

BIAŁOŃ-SOCZYŃSKA, L., Economics of Industry, Economics of Science, Marketing

MARCINIAK, S., Economics of Innovation, Macroeconomics

NIEWIADOMSKI, Z., Public Administration, Self-government, Physical Planning

OBRĘBSKI, T., Economics, Labour Economics, Industrial Relations

ZAWADZKA, Z., Economics, Finance, Banking

Faculty of Architecture (Koszykowa 55, 00-659 Warsaw; tel. (22) 628-28-87; fax (22) 628-32-36; e-mail dziekan@arch.pw.edu.pl; internet www.arch.pw.edu.pl):

BENEDEK, W., Housing Design and Public Utilities

BRYKOWSKA, M., History of Towns and Architecture

CHMIELEWSKI, J. M., Urban Design and Town Planning

GAWLIKOWSKI, A. Z., Urban Design and Town Planning

GZELL, S., Urban Design and Town Planning

HRYNIAK, Z., Urban Design and Town Planning

KŁOSIEWICZ, L., Contemporary Architecture

KUBICA, B., Fine Arts—Sculpture

KUCZA-KUCZYŃSKI, K., Housing Design and Public Utilities

PAWŁOWSKI, Z., Building Structures

ROGUSKA, J., History of Towns and Architecture

SZPARKOWSKI, Z., Industrial Buildings

SZULBORSKI, K., Building Structures

TOMASZEWSKI, A., Conservation of Monuments, History of Architecture

WERNER, W., Economics of Investment Processes and Management

WIŚNIEWSKA, M., Housing Design and Public Utilities

WRONA, S., Computer-Aided Architectural Design

Faculty of Automobile and Construction Machinery Engineering (Narbutta 84, 02-524 Warsaw; tel. (22) 849-03-01; fax (22) 849-03-06; e-mail dzk@simr.pw.edu.pl; internet www.simr.pw.edu.pl):

BIAŁAS, S., Geometrical Accuracy in Machinery Design, Tolerance Technology

BOGACZ, R., Dynamics of Means of Transport

DĄBROWSKI, Z., Machine Design, Vibroacoustics

GOŁOŚ, K., Fatigue in Materials

KURNIK, WŁ., Dynamics of Mechanical Systems, Mechatronics

MADEJ, J., Mechanics of Rail Vehicles

OSIŃSKI, J., Dynamics of Mechanical Systems

RADKOWSKI, ST., Safety in Technical Systems, Technical Diagnostics

STARCZEWSKI, Z., Dynamics of Mechanical Systems, Dynamics of Rotors and Journal Bearing System

SZLAGOWSKI, J., Plastics Design of Structures, Automation of Construction Machinery

SZUMANOWSKI, A., Electromechanical Propulsion Systems, Energy Storage, Hybrid and Electric Vehicles

TYLIKOWSKI, A., Dynamics of Mechanical Systems, Mechatronics

WICHER, J., Mechanics, Dynamics of Mechanical Systems

WRÓBEL, J., Theory of Machine Design

Faculty of Chemical and Process Engineering (Waryńskiego 1, 00-645 Warsaw; tel. and fax (22) 825-14-40; e-mail dziekan@ichip.pw.edu.pl; internet www.ichip.pw.edu.pl):

BAŁDYGA, J., Chemical Reactor Engineering

BIŃ, A. K., Process Kinetics, Environmental Protection Processes

CHMIELEWSKI, A. G., Environmental Engineering, Separation Processes

GAWROŃSKI, R., Membrane Processes

GRADOŃ, L., Chemical Engineering, Aerosol Mechanics

POHORECKI, R., Chemical Reactor Engineering, Bioprocess Engineering

SIENIUTYCZ, S., Process Thermodynamics, Non-equilibrium Thermodynamics

SZEWCZYK, K. W., Biochemical Technology, Bioprocess Engineering

SZWAST, Z., Process Optimization

WOLNY, A., Chemical Engineering

Faculty of Chemistry (Noakowskiego 3, 00-664 Warsaw; tel. and fax (22) 628-27-41; e-mail dziekan@ch.pw.edu.pl; internet www.ch.pw.edu.pl):

BRZÓZKA, Z., Analytical Chemistry

DOMAŃSKA-ŻELAZNA, U., Physical Chemistry

FLORJAŃCZYK, Z., Organic Chemistry, Polymer Science

GRYFF-KELLER, A., Organic Chemistry

GRZYWA, E., General Chemistry

JAROSZ, M., Analytical Chemistry

JOŃCZYK, A., Organic Chemistry and Technology

KASIURA, K., Inorganic and Analytical Chemistry

KIJEŃSKI, J., Organic Chemistry, Catalysis

KSIĄŻCZAK, A., Theory and Technology of Explosives

ŁOBIŃSKI, R., Analytical Chemistry

MĄKOSZA, M., Organic Chemistry and Technology

PLENKIEWICZ, J., Biotransformation in Organic Chemistry

PROŃ, A., Polymer Science, Solid State Technology

ROKICKI, G., Organic Chemistry, Polymer Science

SERWATOWSKI, J., Physical Organic Chemistry

WIECZOREK, W., Solid State Technology

Faculty of Civil Engineering (Armii Ludowej 16, 00-637 Warsaw; tel. (22) 825-59-37; fax (22) 825-88-99; e-mail dziekanat@il.pw.edu.pl; internet www.il.pw.edu.pl):

ABRAMOWICZ, M., Reinforced Concrete Structures

CHRABACZYŃSKI, G., Building Production and Prefabrication

CZARNECKI, L., Technology of Building Materials

GOMULIŃSKI, A., Structural Mechanics

JAWORSKI, K., Technology of Building Materials

KARCZEWSKI, J., Metal Constructions, Spatial Structures

KNAUFF, M., Building Construction

NAGÓRSKI, R., Structural Mechanics

OBRĘBSKI, J., Structural Mechanics

RADOMSKI, W., Bridge Engineering

RUNKIEWICZ, L., Building Construction

SUCHORZEWSKI, W., Construction of Roads, Streets and Bridges

SZCZEŚNIAK, W., Structural Mechanics

WITKOWSKI, M., Structural Mechanics, Computers in Civil Engineering

WOJEWÓDZKI, W., Theory of Elasticity and Plasticity

ŻÓŁTOWSKI, W., Metal Constructions

Faculty of Civil Engineering, Mechanics and Petrochemistry (Płock Campus) (Łukasiewicza 17, 09-400 Płock; tel. (24) 262-62-54; fax (24) 367-22-25; e-mail zielinski@pw.plock.pl; internet www.pw.plock.pl):

BOCHEŃSKI, C., Agricultural Engineering

BUKOWSKI, A., Technology of Plastics

CHOCHOWSKI, A., Solar Power Engineering

DWILIŃSKI, L., Construction and Reliability of Agricultural Machinery

FRĄCZEK, K., Carbon Derivatives Technology, Polymer Chemistry

KAJDAS, Cz., Technology and Processing of Petroleum and its Products, Tribopolymerization

KAMIŃSKI, E., Mechanical Appliances and Machinery

KOSIŃSKI, W., Cartography and Surveying

PONIEWSKI, M., Heat Engines and Thermal Equipment

POWIERŻA, L., Systems Engineering

PYSIAK, J., Physical Solid-State Chemistry

RÓŻYCKI, C., Trace Analysis, Chemometrics

ŚCIŚLEWSKI, Z., Durability

URBANIEC, K., Food Industry Machinery

WŁODARCZYK, W., Building Constructions

WOLSKI, L., Physics of Buildings, Sanitary Systems

ZIELIŃSKI, J., Technology of Petroleum and Plastics

ŻUK, D., Agricultural Engineering

Faculty of Electrical Engineering (pl. Politechniki 1, 00-661 Warsaw; tel. (22) 629-25-31; fax (22) 625-75-24; e-mail ura@dean.ee.pw.edu.pl; internet www.ee.pw.edu.pl):

BĄK, J., Lighting Technology
BARLIK, R., Industrial Electronics and Electrical Drives, Power Electronics
BOLKOWSKI, S., Circuit Theory and Electromagnetic Fields
CELIŃSKI, Z., Nuclear Technology
CICHOCKI, A., Circuit Theory
CIOK, Z., High-voltage Technology
DMOWSKI, A., Industrial Electronics
FLISOWSKI, Z., High-voltage Technology
HERING, M., Electro-heating Technology
KACZOREK, T., Linear Control Systems
KAŹMIERKOWSKI, M., Industrial Electronics and Intelligent Control
KOCZARA, N., Electrical Drives and Generation of Power
KRZEMIŃSKI, S., Circuit Theory
KUJSZCZYK, S., Power Systems and Electrical Networks
MACHOWSKI, J., Power Systems and Electrical Networks
MAKSYMIUK, J., Electrical Apparatus
MIKOŁAJUK, K., Circuit Theory and Electromagnetic Fields
OSOWSKI, S., Artificial Intelligence—Neural Networks
RAWA, H., Circuit Theory and Electromagnetic Fields
SIKORA, J., Circuit Theory and Electromagnetic Fields
SUPRONOWICZ, H., Industrial Electronics
TRZASKA, Z., Circuit Theory and Electromagnetic Fields
TUMAŃSKI, S., Electrical Measurements
WINCENCIAK, S., Circuit Theory and Electromagnetic Fields

Faculty of Electronics and Information Technology (Nowowiejska 15–19, 00-665 Warsaw; tel. (22) 825-37-58; fax (22) 825-19-84; e-mail dziekan@elka.pw.edu.pl; internet www.elka.pw.edu.pl):

DĄBROWSKI, M., Computer Networks and Switching
DOBROWOLSKI, J., Computer-aided Design of Microwave Circuits, Monolithic Microwave Integrated Circuits
EBERT, J., High-power Radiotechnology
GALWAS, B., Microwave Electronics and Photonics
GWAREK, P., Microwave Technology
HOLEJKO, K., Telecommunications and Opto-electronics
JACHOWICZ, R., Measurement Systems and Sensors
JAKUBOWSKI, A., Microelectronics, Metal-oxide-semiconductor Devices
KUDREWICZ, J., Theory of Electronic Systems
KUŹMICZ, W., Microelectronics
ŁUBA, T., Computer Engineering, Digital Systems Design
LUBACZ, J., Information and Communication Technologies
MAJKUSIAK, B., Microelectronics
MALINOWSKI, K., Information Engineering and Control Systems
MODELSKI, J., Microwaves, Satellite and Cable Television
MORAWSKI, R. Z., Measurement and Instrumentation
MORAWSKI, T., Microwave Technology
MULAWKA, J., Computer Science, Artificial Intelligence
MURASZKIEWICZ, M., Information and Knowledge Systems, Databases, Networking
PAWŁOWSKI, Z., Medical and Nuclear Electronics
PIÓRO, M., Information and Communication Technologies
ROSŁONIEC, S., Microwave Technology

RYBIŃSKI, H., Information Systems, Databases
SZCZEPAŃSKI, P., Optoelectronics, Laser Physics
TRACZYK, W., Knowledge-based Systems
WIERZBICKI, A., Optimization and Decision Theory
WOJCIECHOWSKI, J., Electronics, Telecommunication Networks, Signals and Systems
WOŹNICKI, J., Electronics, Optoelectronics
ZABRODZKI, J., Computer Science, Computer Graphics

Faculty of Environmental Engineering (Nowowiejska 20, 00-653 Warsaw; tel. (22) 621-45-60; fax (22) 625-73-77; e-mail dziekan@is.pw.edu.pl; internet www.is.pw.edu.pl):

BIEDUGNIS, S., Water Supply and Sewerage Systems, Sanitary and Environmental Engineering
JĘDRZEJEWSKA-ŚCIBAK, T., Indoor Air Quality, Ventilation and Air Conditioning
KINDLER, J., Water Resources Management and Environmental Systems
MAŃKOWSKI, S., Heat Engineering
MITOSEK, M., Hydraulics, Fluid Mechanics
MIZIELIŃSKI, B., Ventilation and Air Conditioning
NAWALANY, M., Environmental Engineering, Groundwater Protection
OSIADACZ, A., Gas Engineering
PISARCZYK, S., Building Engineering, Geotechnology
ROMAN, M., Water Supply and Sewerage Systems, Sanitary and Environmental Engineering

Faculty of Geodesy and Cartography (pl. Politechniki 1, 00-661 Warsaw; tel. (22) 660-72-23; fax (22) 621-36-80; e-mail dziekanat@gik.pw.edu.pl; internet www.gik.pw.edu.pl):

ADAMCZEWSKI, Z., Theory of Adjustment, Geodetic Computation
BARLIK, M., Geodesy, Gravimetry
BIAŁOUSZ, S., Soil Mapping and Remote Sensing, Geographical Information Systems
CZARNECKI, K., Geodesy
CZICHON, H., Technology of Printing
MACIEJEWSKA, A., Soil Conservation and Land Protection
MAKOWSKI, A., Cartography
MARTUSEWICZ, J., Surveying for Tunnelling
MERWIŃSKI, R., Printing Technology
PRÓSZYŃSKI, W., Engineering Surveying, Theory of Adjustment
ROGOWSKI, J., Geodetic Astronomy, Satellite Geodesy
SKŁODOWSKI, P., Soil Science, Soil Conservation
SKÓRCZYŃSKI, A., Surveying, Theory of Adjustment
ŚLEDZIŃSKI, J., Satellite Geodesy
WILKOWSKI, W., Rural Land Management

Faculty of Materials Science and Engineering (Wołoska 141, 02-507 Warsaw; tel. (22) 849-99-29; fax (22) 660-85-14; e-mail wim@inmat.pw.edu.pl; internet www.inmat.pw.edu.pl):

GRABSKI, M. W., Physics of Plastic Deformation
KURZYDŁOWSKI, K. J., Materials Characterization and Modelling
LEONOWICZ, M., Magnetic Materials
OLSZYNA, A., Ceramic Materials
MICHALSKI, A., Surface Engineering
SZUMMER, A., Functional Construction of Materials
WIERZCHOŃ, T., Surface Engineering

Faculty of Mathematics and Information Science (pl. Politechniki 1, 00-661 Warsaw; tel. (22) 621-93-12; fax (22) 625-74-60; e-mail sekretariat@mini.pw.edu.pl; internet www.mini.pw.edu.pl):

JANECZKO, S., Singularity Theory and Symplectic Geometry
KLEIBER, M., Computer Methods in Mechanics
LONC, Z., Discrete Mathematics
MACUKOW, B., Artificial Intelligence
MĄCZYŃSKI, M., Algebra, Mathematical Foundations of Quantum Theory
MARCINIAK, K., Computer Graphics and Geometry
MUSZYŃSKI, J., Differential Equations
PLUCIŃSKA, A., Probability and Stochastic Processes
ROMANOWSKA, A., Algebra
SPIEŻ, S., Topology

Faculty of Mechatronics (Św. A. Boboli 8, 02-525 Warsaw; tel. (22) 849-07-11; fax (22) 849-99-36; e-mail dean@mchtr.pw.edu.pl; internet www.mchtr.pw.edu.pl):

CIEŚLICKI, K., Fluid Mechanics
DUNAJSKI, Z., Biomedical Engineering
GAMBIN, W., Mechanics
JANISZOWSKI, K., Automatic Control and Robotics, System Identification
JÓŹWICKI, R., Design of Optical Instruments
KOŚCIELNY, J. M., Automatic Control, Fault Detection
KUJAWIŃSKA, M., Applied Optics, Machine Vision
KUREK, J., Automatic Control and Robotics, Control Theory
MRUGALSKI, Z., Design of Precision Devices
OLEKSIUK, T., Design of Precision Devices
PAŁKO, T., Biomedical Engineering
PATORSKI, K., Applied Optics, Design of Optical Instruments
PAWLICKI, W. G., Biomedical Engineering
RATAJCZYK, E., Measuring Apparatus

Faculty of Physics (Koszykowa 75, 00-662 Warsaw; tel. (22) 660-72-67; fax (22) 628-21-71; e-mail dziekan@if.pw.edu.pl; internet www.if.pw.edu.pl):

ADAMCZYK, A., Liquid Crystals
BACEWICZ, R., Solid State Physics
BOGUSZ, W., Solid State Physics
ĆWIOK, S., Nuclear Physics
HOŁYST, J., Physics of Complex Systems
KOSIŃSKI, R., Physics of Magnetism
KROK, F., Solid State Physics
SŁOWIŃSKI, B., Nuclear Physics
STRZAŁKOWSKI, I., Solid State Physics
SUKIENNICKI, A., Physics of Magnetism
WOLIŃSKI, T., Optoelectronics
ŻEBROWSKI, J., Physics of Complex Systems

Faculty of Power and Aeronautical Engineering (Nowowiejska 24, 00-665 Warsaw; tel. (22) 621-53-10; fax (22) 625-73-51; e-mail dziekan@meil.pw.edu.pl; internet www.meil.pw.edu.pl):

ARCZEWSKI, K., Analytical Mechanics, Multibody Systems
BANASZEK, J., Thermodynamics, Mathematical Methods of Heat Transfer
DIETRICH, M. (acting), Mechanical Engineering, Biomedical Engineering
DOMANSKI, R., Heat Transfer, Thermodynamics, Environmental Engineering
FURMAŃSKI, P., Heat Transfer, Thermodynamics, Thermal Properties of Materials
GORAJ, Z., Aerodynamics, Flight Dynamics, Aircraft Design
JEDRAL, W., Power Engineering, Pumping Machinery and Installations
KĘDZIOR, K., Modelling of Human Movement, Systems Dynamics, Robotics and Biomechanics
LEWANDOWSKI, J., Environmental Engineering, Power Engineering, Control of Power Plants
LEWITOWICZ, J., Aircraft Maintenance, Aerospace Engineering
MARYNIAK, J., Flight Mechanics

MILLER, A., Power Engineering, Gas and Steam Turbines

PORTACHA, J., Power Engineering, Power Plants

RYCHTER, T., Internal Combustion Engines, Combustion

SADO, J., Thermodynamics, Refrigeration, Plasma Physics

STUPNICKI, J., Fundamentals of Machine Construction

STYCZEK, A., Mathematical Methods of Fluid Mechanics

SZOPA, T., Safety Engineering

SZUMOWSKI, A., Fluid Mechanics, Gas Dynamics, Aerodynamic Noise Control

WOLAŃSKI, P., Combustion, Aero Engines

ŻOCHOWSKI, M., Strength of Materials

Faculty of Production Engineering (Narbutta 85, 02-524 Warsaw; tel. (22) 849-97-95; fax (22) 849-94-34; e-mail dean@wip.pw.edu.pl; internet www.wip.pw.edu.pl):

BOSSAK, M., Computational Mechanics, Computer-aided Design

GRUDZEWSKI, W., Organization and Management

HEJDUK, J., Organization and Management

JEMIELNIAK, K., Production Engineering

KACZOROWSKI, M., Materials Science and Engineering

KISIELNICKI, J., Organization and Management

KLASZTORNY, M., Applied Mechanics

KOCAŃDA, A., Metal-forming

KOZAK, J., Production Engineering

LEWANDOWSKI, J., Economics

MASŁOWSKI, A., Automation and Robotics

MASŁYK-MUSIAŁ, E., Organization and Management

MONKIEWICZ, J., Organization and Management

NOWICKI, B., Production Engineering

PERZYK, M., Casting Technology

SANTAREK, K., Organization and Management

SZAFARCZYK, M., Machine Tools Control and Drive

SZENAJCH, W., Mechanical Engineering, Automatic Control of Industrial Processes

TKACZYK, S., Organization and Management

WILCZYŃSKI, A., Mechanical Engineering

WŁOSIŃSKI, W., Materials Technology

Faculty of Transport (Koszykowa 75, 00-662 Warsaw; tel. (22) 660-73-11; fax (22) 621-56-87; e-mail dziekan@it.pw.edu.pl; internet www.it.pw.edu.pl):

BORGOŃ, J., Air Traffic Control

CHUDZIKIEWICZ, A., Dynamics and Diagnostics of Means of Transport

DĄBROWA-BAJON, M., Rail Traffic Control

DYDUCH, J., Control Systems

KISILOWSKI, J., Dynamics and Diagnostics of Mechanical Systems

LESZCZYŃSKI, J., Organization and Technology of Transport

MANEROWSKI, J., Flight Mechanics

NIEDZIELA, T., Image Processing

SMALKO, Z., Maintenance and Operation of Vehicles

POLITECHNIKA WROCŁAWSKA
(Wrocław University of Technology)

Wybrzeże Wyspiańskiego 27, 50-370 Wrocław

Telephone: (71) 320-26-00
Fax: (71) 322-36-64
E-mail: kancelaria.rektora@pwr.wroc.pl
Internet: www.pwr.wroc.pl
Founded 1945
State control
Languages of instruction: English, Polish
Academic year: October to June

Rector: Prof. TADEUSZ WIĘCKOWSKI

Vice-Rector for General Affairs: Prof. JERZY WALENDZIEWSKI

Vice-Rector: Prof. LUDWIK RUSIŃSKI

Vice-Rector: Dr LUDOMIR JANKOWSKI

Vice-Rector for Teaching: Prof. JERZY ŚWIĄTEK

Vice-Rector for Gen. Affairs: Prof. JERZY WALENDZIEWSKI

Vice-Rector for Research: Prof. EUGENIUSZ RUSIŃSKI

Vice-Rector for Education: Prof. ANDRZEJ KASPRZAK

Vice-Rector for Devt: Prof. CEZARY MADRYAS

Vice-Rector for Student Affairs: Dr ZBIGNIEW SROKA

Chief Admin. Officer: Mgr Inż. JAROSŁAW M. JANISZEWSKI

Librarian: Dr HENRYK SZARSKI

Library of 900,000 vols, incl. 4,500 periodical titles

Number of teachers: 2,000

Number of students: 33,000

Publications: *Acta – Bioengineering and Biomechanics* (2 a year), *Architectus Systems* (2 a year), *Badania Operacyjne i Decyzje* (4 a year), *Environmental Protection Engineering* (4 a year), *Fizykochem. Problemy Mineralurgii* (1 a year), *Geometria Wykreślna i Grafika Inżynierska* (1 a year), *Materials Science* (4 a year), *Optica Applicata* (4 a year), *Pryzmat* (12 a year), *Semestr* (12 a year), *Studia Geotechnica et Mechanica* (4 a year), *Systems – Journal of Transdisciplinary Systems Science* (2 a year), *Systems Science* (4 a year)

DEANS

Department of Fundamental Studies: Assist Prof. JANUSZ GÓRNIAK

Faculty of Architecture: Prof. STANISŁAW MEDEKSZA

Faculty of Chemistry: Prof. ANDRZEJ MATYNIA

Faculty of Civil Engineering: Prof. JERZY HOŁA

Faculty of Computer Science and Management: Prof. JERZY ŚWIĄTEK

Faculty of Electrical Engineering: Prof. MARIAN SOBIERAJSKI

Faculty of Electronics: Prof. JAN ZARZYCKI

Faculty of Environmental Engineering: Prof. JAN DANIELEWICZ

Faculty of Fundamental Problems of Technology: Prof. ZBIGNIEW OLSZAK

Faculty of Geoengineering, Mining and Geology: Prof. LECH GŁADYSIEWICZ

Faculty of Mechanical and Power Engineering: Prof. MACIEJ CHOROWSKI

Faculty of Mechanical Engineering: Prof. EDWARD CHLEBUS

Faculty of Microsystem Electronics and Photonics: Prof. ANDRZEJ DZIEDZIC

ZACHODNIOPOMORSKI UNIWERSYTET TECHNOLOGICZNY W SZCZECINIE
(West Pomeranian University of Technology, Szczecin)

ul. Piastów 17, 70-310 Szczecin

Telephone: (91) 434-67-51
Fax: (91) 449-40-15
E-mail: rektor@zut.edu.pl
Internet: www.zut.edu.pl
Founded 2009, by merger of Akademia Rolnicza w Szczecinie and Politechnika Szczecińska
Language of instruction: Polish
Academic year: October to September

Rector: Prof. Dr hab. Inż. WŁODZIMIERZ KIERNOŻYCKI

Pro-Rector for Organization and Academic Development: Prof. Dr hab. Inż. JAN B. DAWIDOWSKI

Pro-Rector for Science: Prof. Dr hab. Inż. RYSZARD KALEŃCZUK

Pro-Rector for Education: Prof. Dr hab. Inż. WITOLD BIEDUNKIEWICZ

Pro-Rector for Student Affairs: Prof. Dr hab. Inż. JACEK WRÓBEL

Chancellor: Inż. JAROSŁAW POTACZEK

Bursar: JAROSŁAW POTACZEK

Dir of Library: Mgr ANNA GRZELAK-ROZENBERG

Library of 556,525 vols of special colln, 446,341 books, 156,229 vols of periodicals

Number of teachers: 1,114

Number of students: 13,233

Publications: *Acta Ichthyologica et Piscatoria* (2 a year), *Acta Scientiarum Polonorum. Ser. Piscaria* (4 a year), *Acta Scientiarum Polonorum. Ser. Zootechnica* (4 a year), *Advances in Agricultural Sciences* (irregular), *Electronic Journal of Polish Agricultural Universities. Ser. Fisheries* (4 a year), *Folia Pomeranae Universitatis Technologiae Stetinensis* (4 a year), *Forum Uczelniane* (4 a year), *Polish Journal of Chemical Technology* (4 a year)

DEANS

Dept of Civil Engineering and Architecture: Prof. Dr hab. Inż. HALINA GARBALIŃSKA

Dept of Computer Science: Prof. Dr hab. Inż. ANTONI WILIŃSKI

Faculty of Biotechnology and Animal Husbandry: Dr hab. JAN UDAŁA

Faculty of Chemical Technology and Engineering: Prof. Dr hab. JACEK SOROKA

Faculty of Economics: Prof. Dr hab. GRAŻYNA KARMOWSKA

Faculty of Electrical Engineering: Prof. Dr hab. Inż. STEFAN DOMEK

Faculty of Environment Management and Agriculture: Prof. Dr hab. ALEKSANDER BRZÓSTOWICZ

Faculty of Food Sciences and Fisheries: Prof. Dr hab. Inż. WALDEMAR DĄBROWSKI

Faculty of Marine Technology: Dr hab. Inż. BOGUSŁAW ZAKRZEWSKI

Faculty of Mechanical Engineering and Mechatronics: Prof. Dr hab. Inż. STEFAN BERCZYŃSKI

Higher Institutes
AGRICULTURE

Akademia Rolnicza im. Hugona Kołłątaja w Krakowie (Agricultural University of Cracow): ul. Mickiewicza 21, 31-120 Cracow; tel. (12) 662-42-60; fax (12) 633-62-45; e-mail recint@ar.krakow.pl; internet www.ar.krakow.pl; f. 1890; State control; faculties of agriculture and economics, food technology, animal science, environmental engineering and land surveying, forestry, horticulture, agricultural engineering; language of instruction: Polish; library: 618,576 vols; 747 teachers; 12,646 students; Rector Prof. JANUSZ ŻMIJA; publs *Acta Scientiarum Polonorum* (irregular), *Zeszyty Naukowe* (in Polish or English).

Akademia Rolnicza we Wrocławiu (Agricultural University of Wrocław): Norwida 25, 50-375 Wrocław; tel. (71) 320-51-01; fax (71) 320-54-04; e-mail rektor@ozi.ar.wroc.pl; internet www.ar.wroc.pl; f. 1951; faculties of biology and animal science, environmental engineering and geodesy, veterinary medicine, food science, agriculture; library: 180,000 vols; 750 teachers; 11,500 students; Rector Prof. Dr hab. MICHAŁ MAZURKIEWICZ; publs *Acta Scientiarum Polonorum* (online), *Electronic Journal of Polish Agricultural Universities* (online), *Zeszyty Naukowe*.

ECONOMICS, SOCIAL SCIENCES

Akademia Ekonomiczna im. Karola Adamieckiego w Katowicach (Karol Adamiecki University of Economics in Katowice): ul. 1 Maja 50, 40-287 Katowice; tel. (32) 257-70-00; e-mail akademia@ae.katowice.pl; internet www.ae.katowice.pl; f. 1937; faculties of management and economics; library: 330,000 vols; 446 teachers; 9,784 students; Rector Prof. Dr hab. JAN PYKA; publ. *Studia Ekonomiczne* (Economic Studies, irregular).

Akademia Ekonomiczna im. Oskara Langego we Wrocławiu (Wrocław University of Economics): Komandorska 118/120, 53-345 Wrocław; tel. (71) 368-01-00; fax (71) 367-27-78; e-mail www@ae.wroc.pl; internet www.ae.wroc.pl; f. 1947; faculties: engineering and economics, national economy, computer science and management, regional economy and tourism; library: 350,000 vols; 683 teachers; 18,644 students (16,144 undergraduate, 2,500 postgraduate); Rector Prof. zw. Dr hab. MARIAN NOGA; publs *Argumenta Oeconomica* (4 a year), *Prace Naukowe Akademii Ekonomicznej im O. Langego we Wrocławiu*.

Akademia Ekonomiczna w Krakowie (Cracow University of Economics): Rakowicka 27, 31-510 Cracow; tel. (12) 293-57-00; fax (12) 293-50-17; e-mail akademia@ae.krakow.pl; f. 1925; faculties of economics, management and commodity science; library: 530,000 vols, 1,630 periodicals; 630 teachers; 20,000 students; Rector Prof. Dr hab. TADEUSZ GRABIŃSKI; publs *Argumenta Oeconomica Cracoviensia*, *Zeszyty Naukowe* (Scientific Papers).

Akademia Ekonomiczna w Poznaniu (University of Economics in Poznań): ul. Niepodległości 10, 60-967 Poznań; tel. (61) 856-90-00; fax (61) 866-89-24; internet www.ae.poznan.pl; f. 1926; faculties of management, economics and commodity science; library: 439,356 vols; 608 teachers; 16,860 students; Rector Prof. Dr WITOLD JUREK; publs *Debiuty Ekonomiczne*, *Podręczniki*, *Prace Doktorskie Obronione v Akademii Ekonomicznej w Poznaniu* (1 a year), *The Poznan University Review*, *Zeszyty Naukowe Seria I*, *Zeszyty Naukowe Seria II–Prace habilitacyjne*.

Akademia Leona Koźmińskiego (Kozminski University): ul. Jagiellońska 57–59, 03-301 Warsaw; tel. (22) 519-21-00; fax (22) 814-11-56; e-mail wspiz@wspiz.edu.pl; internet www.wspiz.edu.pl; f. 1993; MBA degree courses; library: 35,000 vols; 240 teachers; 5,170 students (3,400 undergraduate, 1,770 postgraduate); Rector Prof. ANDRZEJ K. KOŹMIŃSKI.

Szkoła Główna Handlowa (Warsaw School of Economics): ul. Niepodległości 162, 02-554 Warsaw; tel. (22) 337-90-00; fax (22) 849-53-12; e-mail information@sgh.waw.pl; internet www.sgh.waw.pl; f. 1906; economics, finance and banking, European studies, spatial economy, public administration, quantitative methods and information systems, finance and banking, international relations, management and marketing; library: see Libraries and Archives; 900 teachers; 16,451 students (6,544 full-time, 6,131 extra-mural, 2,626 postgraduate, 1,150 PhD); Rector Prof. MAREK ROCKI; Exec. Dir Dr PIOTR WACHOWIAK; publs *National Economy* (12 a year), *Poland: International Economic Report* (1 a year).

MEDICINE

Akademia Medyczna im. Karola Marcinkowskiego w Poznaniu (Karol Marcinkowski University of Medical Sciences in Poznań): ul. Fredry 10, 61-701 Poznań; tel. (61) 852-03-42; fax (61) 852-04-55; e-mail info@usoms.poznan.pl; internet www.usoms.poznan.pl; f. as Univ. faculty 1920; Univ. status 1950; faculties of medicine, pharmacy, health sciences (with nursing, physiotherapy, public health); sections of stomatology, clinical analysis; library: 328,773 vols; 1,013 teachers; 3,714 students; Rector Prof. Dr LEON DROBNIK; publs *Annual* (with supplements), *Annual Medical News*.

Akademia Medyczna im. Ludwika Rydygiera w Bydgoszczy (Ludwik Rydygier Medical University in Bydgoszcz): ul. Jagiellońska 13, 85-067 Bydgoszcz; tel. (52) 585-33-00; fax (52) 585-33-08; e-mail rektor@amb.bydgoszcz.pl; internet www.amb.bydgoszcz.pl; f. 1984; library: 64,000 vols, 16,000 periodicals; 545 teachers; 3,714 students; Rector Prof. Dr hab. DANUTA MIŚCICKA ŚLIWKA.

Akademia Medyczna we Wrocławiu (Wrocław Medical University): 50-367 Wrocław, ul. Pasteura 1; tel. (71) 784-10-01; fax (71) 784-01-09; e-mail rektor@am.wroc.pl; internet www.am.wroc.pl; f. 1950; faculties of medicine, dentistry, nursing and pharmacy, postgraduate training; library: 190,367 books, 76,322 papers; 884 teachers; 3,900 students; Rector Prof. Dr hab. LESZEK PARADOWSKI; publ. *Advances in Clinical and Experimental Medicine* (4 a year).

Akademia Medyczna w Gdańsku (Medical University of Gdańsk): ul. Marii Skłodowskiej-Curie 3a, 80-210 Gdańsk; tel. (58) 349-10-00; fax (58) 349-12-00; e-mail rektor@amg.gda.pl; internet www.amg.gda.pl; f. 1945; faculties of medicine (with sub-faculties of dentistry and nursing), health sciences, pharmacy and (jointly with Univ. of Gdańsk) biotechnology; library: 544,316 vols; 915 teachers; 2,700 students; Rector Prof. Dr WIESŁAW MAKAREWICZ; publ. *Annales Academiae Medicae Gedanensis* (1 a year).

Akademia Medyczna w Łodzi (Medical University of Łódź): ul. Kościuszki 4, 90-419 Łódź; tel. (42) 632-21-13; fax (42) 632-23-47; e-mail akmed@rkt2.rkt.am.lodz.pl; f. 1945; faculty of medicine (Dean Prof. ANDRZEJ JOSS) with sub-faculties of stomatology, public health, and nursing; faculty of pharmacy (Dean Prof DARIA ORSZULAK-MICHALAK) with sub-faculty of laboratory medicine and college of cosmetology; library: 291,309 vols; 935 teachers; 3,058 students; Rector Prof. HENRYK STĘPIEŃ; publ. *Annales Academiae Medicae Lodziensis* (irregular).

Centrum Medyczne Kształcenia Podyplomowego (Medical Centre for Postgraduate Education): ul. Marymoncka 99–103, 01-813 Warsaw; tel. (22) 569-37-00; e-mail dyrektor@cmkp.edu.pl; internet www.cmkp.edu.pl; f. 1970; faculties of basic sciences, clinical medicine, stomatology, pharmacy, family medicine; school of public health and social medicine; library: 46,000 vols; Dir Prof. Dr hab. med. JOANNA JĘDRZEJCZAK.

Collegium Medicum Uniwersytetu Jagiellońskiego (Jagiellonian University, Medical College): ul. Sw. Anny 12, 31-008 Cracow; tel. (12) 422-04-11; fax (12) 422-25-78; e-mail mabertma@cyf-kr.edu.pl; internet www.cm-uj.krakow.pl; f. 1364; faculties of medicine (with division of dentistry), pharmacy (with division of medical analysis), health care (with Institute of Nursing and Institute of Public Health); Vice-Rector Prof. MAREK ZEMBALA; Representatives of the Rector Prof. JACEK S. DUBIEL (Gen. Affairs), Prof. JANUSZ PACH (Clinical Affairs), Prof. WIESŁAW PAWLIK (Education and Foreign Cooperation), Prof. RYSZARD LAUTERBACH (Scientific Research and Postgraduate Training); library 210,000 vols; 1,200 staff, 100 full professors; 4,600 students; publs *Annales Collegii Medici Universitatis Jagiellonicae Cracoviensis* (1 a year), *The Methodical Review* (1 a year).

Pomorska Akademia Medyczna w Szczecinie (Pomeranian Academy of Medicine in Szczecin): ul. Rybacka 1, 70-204 Szczecin; tel. (91) 480-07-00; fax (91) 480-07-05; internet www.pam.szczecin.pl; f. 1948; faculties of dentistry, medicine, nursing; 1,094 teachers; 1,743 students; Rector Prof. Dr hab. n. med. PRZEMYSŁAW NOWACKI; publs *Annales Academiae Medicae Stetinensis*, *Biuletyn* (12 a year).

Śląska Akademia Medyczna w Katowicach (Medical University of Silesia in Katowice): ul. Warszawska 14, 40-006 Katowice; tel. (32) 251-49-64; fax (32) 208-35-61; e-mail rektor@slam.katowice.pl; internet www.slam.katowice.pl; f. 1948; medical, dental, pharmaceutical and nursing faculties; research in medicine and medical analysis, with special interest in cardiology, cardiac surgery, nephrology, gastroenterology, pulmonary diseases, environmental and occupational medicine; library: see Libraries; 1,517 teachers; 4,682 students; Rector Prof. Dr hab. TADEUSZ WILCZOK; publs *Annales Academiae Medicae Silesiensis* (1 a year), *Annales Societatis Doctrinae Studentium* (irregular), *Wiadomości Lekarskie* (12 a year).

Szkoła Wyższa Psychologii Społecznej (School of Social Psychology): Chodakowska 19/31, 03-815 Warsaw; tel. (22) 517-96-00; fax (22) 517-99-21; e-mail centrum.informacji@swps.edu.pl; internet www.swps.edu.pl; f. 1996; library: 12,000 vols; 243 teachers; 8,314 students; Pres. Prof. ANDRZEJ ELIASZ; publs *Charaktery* (jt publ., 12 a year), *Czasopismo Psychologiczne* (jt publ., 2 a year), *Kultura Popularna* (2 a year), *Psychologia Jakości Życia* (2 a year), *Studia Psychologiczne* (jt publ., 2 a year).

TECHNOLOGY AND ENGINEERING

Akademia Morska w Gdyni (Gdynia Maritime University): ul. Morska 83, 81-225 Gdynia; tel. (58) 620-75-12; fax (58) 620-67-01; e-mail rector@am.gdynia.pl; internet www.am.gdynia.pl; f. 1920; mechanics, navigation, management and marketing, electrical engineering; library: 84,000 vols, 7,000 in spec. colln; 370 teachers; 8,500 students; Rector Prof. JÓZEF LISOWSKI; publs *Joint Proceedings*, *Scientific Journal*, *Zeszyty Naukowe*.

Akademia Morska w Szczecinie (Maritime University of Szczecin): ul. Wały Chrobrego 1–2, 70-500 Szczecin; tel. (91) 480-94-00; e-mail rektor@am.szczecin.pl; internet www.wsm.szczecin.pl; f. 1969; faculties of marine engineering, navigation, transport engineering and economics; library: 93,000 vols; 1,871 students; Rector Prof. and Master Mariner STANISŁAW GUCMA; publ. *Zeszyty Naukowe* (4 a year).

Politechnika Koszalińska (Technical University of Koszalin): Sniadeckich 2, 75-453 Koszalin; tel. (94) 342-60-20; fax (94) 342-03-74; e-mail kupk@tu.koszalin.pl; internet www.tu.koszalin.pl; f. 1968; depts of mechanical engineering, civil and environmental engineering, electronics, and economics and management; Institute of Design; library: 99,800 vols; 512 teachers; 15,767 students; Rector Prof. Dr hab. KRZYSZTOF WAWRYN; publs *Koszalińskie Studia i Materiały* (2 a year), *Na Temat* (6 a year), *Zeszyty Naukowe* (Research Review, 4 a year).

Politechnika Opolska (Technical University of Opole): ul. Stanisława Mikołajczyka 5, 45-271 Opole; tel. (77) 400-60-00; fax (77) 400-60-50; e-mail rektor@po.opole.pl;

internet www.po.opole.pl; f. 1966; academic year October to September (first semester); Rector Prof. Dr PIOTR WACH; Pro-Rector for Science Prof. JERZY SKUBIS; Pro-Rector for Students Dr hab. STANISŁAW WITCZAK; Pro-Rector for Organizational Affairs Dr ZYGMUNT KASPERSKI; Dir of Admin. LEON PRUCNAL; library: 370,000 vols; 429 teachers; 12,224 students; publs *Skrypty* (1 a year), *Studies and Monographs* (1 a year), *Zeszyty Naukowe* (Scientific Papers, 1 a year).

Politechnika Radomska im. Kazimierza Pułaskiego (K. Pułaski Technical University in Radom): ul. Malczewskiego 29, 26-600 Radom; tel. (48) 361-70-10; fax (48) 361-70-12; e-mail rektor@kiux.man.radom.pl; internet www.man.radom.pl; f. 1950; faculties of mechanical engineering, transport, materials science and footwear production technology, economics, teacher training, labour, business and finance, banking, mathematics, physics, chemistry, plastics, cosmetic chemistry, art, food industry, fine art education, history, information technology, sociology, statistics, politics, geography, ecology, foodstuffs economy, law; library: 144,000 vols, 66,000 in spec. collns; 506 teachers; 12,500 students; Rector Prof. Dr hab. Inż. WINCENTY LOTKO; publs *Economics* (2 series), *Mechanics* (1 series), *Pedagogics* (2 series), *Prace Naukowe* (4 series, 1, 2, 3 or 4 of each a year), *Transport* (4 series).

THEOLOGY

Chrześcijańska Akademia Teologiczna (Christian Theological Academy): ul. Miodowa 21, 00-246 Warsaw; tel. (22) 831-95-97; fax (22) 635-95-44; e-mail chat@chat.edu.pl; internet www.chat.edu.pl; f. 1954; library: 55,000 vols; 76 teachers; 955 students; Rector Archbishop Prof. Dr hab. JEREMIASZ JAN ANCHIMIUK; publ. *Rocznik Teologiczny* (2 a year).

Schools of Art and Music

Akademia Muzyczna im. Feliksa Nowowiejskiego w Bydgoszczy (F. Nowowiejski Academy of Music in Bydgoszcz): ul. Słowackiego 7, 85-008 Bydgoszcz; tel. (52) 321-11-42; fax (52) 321-23-50; e-mail sekr@ amuz.bydgoszcz.pl; internet www.amuz .bydgoszcz.pl; f. 1979; 100 teachers; 402 students; Rector Prof. JERZY KASZUBA.

Akademia Muzyczna im. Fryderyka Chopina w Warszawie (Frederick Chopin Academy of Music in Warsaw): ul. Okólnik 2, 00-368 Warsaw; tel. (22) 827-72-41; fax (22) 827-83-10; e-mail info@chopin.edu.pl; internet www.chopin.edu.pl; f. 1810; 7 faculties: composition, conducting and theory of music, keyboard instruments, orchestral instruments, vocal performance, general music education, sound engineering; teacher training; library: 20,000 books and 71,000 scores; 330 teachers; 814 students; Rector Prof. RYSZARD ZIMAK; publs *Prace Biblioteki Głównej, Zeszyty Naukowe*.

Akademia Muzyczna im. Grażyny i Kiejstuta Bacewiczów w Łodzi (Academy of Music in Łódź): Gdańska 32, 90-716 Łódź; tel. (42) 662-16-01; fax (42) 662-16-60; e-mail rektorat@amuz.lodz.pl; internet www.amuz .lodz.pl; f. 1945; composition, theory, eurhythmics, music education; instrumental and vocal technique, performance; library: 32,000 scores, 8,000 vols, 6,000 records and CDs, 300 periodicals; 208 teachers; 574 students; Rector Prof. ANTONI WIERZBIŃSKI.

Akademia Muzyczna im. Ignacego Jana Paderewskiego w Poznaniu (Academy of Music in Poznań): ul. Sw. Marcin 87, 61-808 Poznań; tel. (61) 856-89-10; fax (61) 853-66-76; e-mail amuz@amuz.edu.pl; internet www .amuz.edu.pl; f. 1920; faculties of composition, theory, conducting, instrumental technique, vocal technique, music teaching; Rector Prof. BOGUMIŁ NOWICKI.

Akademia Muzyczna im. Karola Lipińskiego we Wrocławiu (Academy of Music in Wrocław): pl. 1-go Maja 2, 50-043 Wrocław; tel. (71) 355-55-53; fax (71) 355-91-05; e-mail info@amuz.wroc.pl; internet www .amuz.wroc.pl; f. 1948; depts of composition, conducting, music theory and music therapy, instrumental music, vocal music, music education; library: 113,015 vols; 185 teachers; 685 students; Rector Prof. GRZEGORZ KURZYŃSKI.

Akademia Muzyczna im. Karola Szymanowskiego w Katowicach (Academy of Music in Katowice): ul. Zacisze 3, 40-025 Katowice; tel. (32) 255-40-17; fax (32) 256-44-85; internet www.am.katowice.pl; f. 1929; faculties of composition, music theory and education, instrumental music, vocal music and theatrical art, jazz and popular music; library: 100,000 vols; spec. colln: music in Silesia; 170 teachers; 745 students; Rector Prof. JULIAN GEMBALSKI.

Akademia Muzyczna im. Stanisława Moniuszki w Gdańsku (Stanisław Moniuszko Academy of Music in Gdańsk): ul. Łakowa 1–2, 80-743 Gdańsk; tel. (58) 300-92-01; fax (58) 300-92-10; e-mail muzyczna@ amuz.gda.pl; internet www.amuz.gda.pl; f. 1947; faculties of composition and theory, music performance, music education; 165 teachers; 433 students; library: 92,000 vols; Rector Prof. BOGDAN KUŁAKOWSKI; publs *Bibliografia* (irregular), *Kultura Muzyczna Północnych Ziem Polski* (irregular), *Muzyka Pomorza* (irregular), *Prace Specjalne* (irregular), *Rocznik Informacyjny* (1 a year), *Skrypty i Podręczniki* (irregular), *Zeszyty Naukowe* (irregular).

Akademia Muzyczna w Krakowie (Academy of Music in Cracow): ul. Sw. Tomasza 43, 31-027 Cracow; tel. (12) 422-32-50; fax (12) 422-23-43; e-mail zbrektor@cyf-kr.edu.pl; internet www.amuz.krakow.pl; f. 1888; faculties of composition, theory and conducting; instrumental performance; vocal technique; teacher training and choir conducting; also postgraduate studies; library: 47,000 vols; 365 teachers; 644 students; Rector Prof. STANISLAW KRAWCZYNISKI.

Akademia Sztuk Pięknych im. Jana Matejki w Krakowie (Academy of Fine Arts in Cracow): pl. Matejki 13, 31-157 Cracow; tel. (12) 422-24-50; fax (12) 422-65-66; e-mail zerektor@cyf-kr.edu.pl; internet www.asp.krakow.pl; f. 1818; faculties of painting, sculpture, conservation and restoration of works of art, graphic arts, industrial design, interior design; postgraduate studies in theatre, film and television stage design; European poster colln up to 1939; library: 86,500 vols, 21,000 graphic items, 7,500 posters; 244 teachers; 845 students; Rector Prof. STANISŁAW RODZIŃSKI; Library Dir JADWIGA WIELGUT-WALCZAK; publ. *Studia i materiały konserwatorskie* (1 a year).

Akademia Sztuk Pięknych im. Władysława Strzemińskiego w Łodzi (Władysław Strzemiński Academy of Fine Arts in Łódź): Ul. Wojska Polskiego 121, 91-726 Łódź; tel. (42) 656-10-56; fax (42) 656-21-92; e-mail rektorat@asp.lodz.pl; internet www .asp.lodz.pl; f. 1945; textile faculty (depts of textile, fashion, painting, sculpture, drawing and composition); faculty of graphic art and painting (depts of graphic design, printmaking, painting, visual problems); faculty of visual education; faculty of industrial design; library: 30,000 vols; 240 teachers; 1,500 students; Rector Prof. GREG CHOJNACKI; Librarian KRYSTYNA LOREK.

Akademia Sztuk Pięknych w Gdańsku (Academy of Fine Arts in Gdańsk): Targ Węglowy 6, 80-836 Gdańsk; tel. (58) 301-44-40; fax (58) 301-22-00; e-mail office@asp.gda .pl; internet www.asp.gda.pl; f. 1945; faculties of painting, graphics, sculpture, architecture and industrial design; library: 10,450 vols; 130 teachers; 875 students; Rector Prof. TOMASZ BOGUSŁAWSKI.

Akademia Sztuk Pięknych w Poznaniu (Academy of Fine Arts in Poznań): ul. Marcinkowskiego 29, 60-967 Poznań; tel. (61) 855-25-21; fax (61) 852-80-91; e-mail office@asp.poznan.pl; internet www.asp .poznan.pl; f. 1919, state-controlled from 1921; faculties of painting, printmaking, sculpture, interior architecture and design, art education, multimedia communication; library: 60,000 vols; 189 full-time teachers; 1,264 full-time students; Rector Prof. WOJCIECH MÜLLER; Vice-Rectors Prof. ANDRZEJ WIELGOSZ, Prof. ASP MARCIN BERDYSZAK, Prof. PIOTR KURKA; Admin. Dir WIESŁAWA SZOKALEWICZ.

Akademia Sztuk Pięknych we Wrocławiu (Academy of Fine Arts in Wrocław): ul. Plac Polski 3/4, 50-156 Wrocław; tel. (71) 343-80-31; fax (71) 343-15-58; e-mail info@asp .wroc.pl; internet www.asp.wroc.pl; f. 1946; faculties of painting, sculpture, graphic arts, glass and ceramics design, interior architecture, industrial design; library: 14,000 vols; Rector Prof. JACEK SZEWCZYK.

Akademia Sztuk Pięknych w Warszawie (Academy of Fine Arts in Warsaw): Krakowskie Przedmieście 5, 00-068 Warsaw; tel. (22) 826-19-72; fax (22) 826-21-14; f. 1904 as Szkoła Sztuk Pięknych (School of Fine Arts), renamed 1927; depts of painting, sculpture, interior design, graphics, industrial design, conservation of works of art; spec. studies: tapestry, scenography; library: 24,500 books, 5,578 vols of periodicals; 296 teachers; 1,020 students; Rector Prof. ADAM MYJAK; Library Dir Mgr IRENA KURNICKA-KĘPA; publs *Rocznik* (1 a year, in English and Russian), *Zeszyty Naukowe ASP* (Scientific Copy Books ASP).

Akademia Teatralna im. Al. Zelwerowicza w Warszawie (A. Zelwerowicz Academy of Theatre in Warsaw): ul. Miodowa 22/24, 00-246 Warsaw; tel. (22) 831-69-25; fax (22) 831-91-01; e-mail rektorat@at.edu.pl; internet www.at.edu.pl; f. 1932; faculties of acting, directing, theatre studies, puppetry; library: 39,000 vols; 110 teachers; 360 students; Rector Prof. LECH ŚLIWONIK.

Państwowa Wyższa Szkoła Filmowa Telewizyjna i Teatralna im. Leona Schillera w Łodzi (National School of Film, Television and Theatre in Łódź): Targowa 61/63, 90-323 Łódź; tel. (42) 674-39-43; fax (42) 674-81-39; e-mail swzfilm@filmschool .lodz.pl; internet www.filmschool.lodz.pl; f. 1948; faculties of film and television direction, film and television camerawork, acting, production; courses in screen-writing, television production, photography; library: 40,000 vols; 118 teachers (96 full-time, 22 part-time); 825 students (incl. 600 extra-mural); Rector Prof. HENRYK KLUBA.

Państwowa Wyższa Szkoła Teatralna im. Ludwika Solskiego w Krakowie (State Theatre Academy in Cracow): ul. Strasewskiego 21–22, 31-109 Cracow; tel. (12) 422-18-55; fax (12) 422-02-09; e-mail rektor@pwst.krakow.pl; internet www.pwst .krakow.pl; f. 1945; faculties of acting and stage craft; puppet theatre section (Wrocław); Rector Prof. EWA KUTRYŚ.

PORTUGAL

The Higher Education System

Portugal was ruled by a monarchy from the 11th century until it was overthrown in 1910 and a republic was declared. The two oldest current universities, Universidade de Lisboa (founded 1288) and Universidade de Coimbra (founded 1290), date from the late 13th century and were the only such institutions until 1911, when Universidade do Porto was founded. Portugal was governed by a dictatorship during 1932–74, the later years of which saw the establishment of several prominent universities, but most institutions of higher education were founded after the restoration of civilian government in 1975. Higher education is divided into two strands, universities and other institutions (polytechnic institutes, higher schools, professional institutes and schools of art and music). In 2008/09 there were 373,002 students at 301 institutions of higher education.

Universities became autonomous institutions under the University Autonomy Law (1988), which granted them the power to devise curricula, award degrees and define the equivalency of foreign awards. The Ministry of Education oversees state universities, polytechnics and specialized tertiary education institutions, while the Ministry of the Economy and Employment is responsible for vocational education. The Statute of the Private Higher Education Institution is the legislation governing private institutions, which are not allowed to offer degree-level programmes but instead offer five-year diploma courses. The Ministry of Education is the accrediting body for private institutions, overseeing the programmes and curricula available. Portugal participates in the Bologna Process to establish a European Higher Education Area, the first phase of which is to adopt a credit-based system of comparable degrees with two main cycles (undergraduate and graduate).

Portuguese students are admitted to higher education on the basis of the Diploma de Ensino Secundário (secondary school diploma) and an entrance examination known as the Concurso nacional (for public institutions) or the Concurso local (for private institutions). Applicants over the age of 23 who do not hold the Diploma de Ensino Secundário may take a special entrance examination, the Exame Extraordinário de Avaliação de Capacidade para Acesso ao Ensino Superior. Following the passage of the Comprehensive Law on Higher Education in 2005, a two-tier degree system, comprising the Licenciado (Bachelors) and Mestre (Masters), was introduced in both universities and polytechnic institutes in accordance with the principles of the Bologna Process. The Licenciado is usually a three- or four-year programme of study, although courses in some subjects may last longer, such as medicine and dentistry (six years). Under the new system, some degrees are integrated courses of study culminating with award of the Mestre, which is otherwise a separate postgraduate degree lasting for one or two years. The Doutor (Doctorate) is the highest academic degree, and is offered only by universities. Students may spend up to five or six years in study and research. Beyond doctoral studies, students who have shown great ability as researchers and who have special teaching expertise in a certain area can take the examinations for the award of the Agregação.

The Decree Law 26/89 (1989) legislated the creation of Escolas Profissionais (professional schools) primarily aimed at upper secondary-level students. Courses are between one and three years in duration, and combine academic education and vocational training.

Regulatory and Representative Bodies

GOVERNMENT

Ministry of Culture: Palácio Nacional da Ajuda, 1349-021 Lisbon; tel. (21) 361-45-00; fax (21) 364-98-72; e-mail gmc@mc.gov.pt; internet www.portaldacultura.gov.pt; Min. MARIA GABRIELA CANAVILHAS.

Ministry of Education: Avda. 5 de Outubro 107, 1069-018 Lisbon; tel. (21) 781-18-00; fax (21) 781-18-35; e-mail gme@me.gov.pt; internet www.min-edu.pt; Min. ISABEL ALÇADA; Sec. of State ALEXANDRE VENTURA.

Ministry of Labour and Social Solidarity: Praça de Londres 2, 1049-056 Lisbon; tel. (21) 844-11-00; fax (21) 842-41-08; e-mail gmtss@mtss.gov.pt; internet www.mtss.gov .pt; f. 1916 as Min. of Labour and Social Welfare; Min. MARIA HELENA ANDRÉ; Head of the Office Dr ANA LUCIA REIS.

Ministry of Science, Technology and Higher Education: Palácio de Laranjeiras, Estrada de Laranjeiras 197–205, 1649-018 Lisbon; tel. (21) 723-10-00; fax (21) 727-14-57; e-mail mctes@mctes.gov.pt; internet www .mctes.pt; Min. Prof. JOSÉ MARIANO REBELO PIRES GAGO; Sec. of State MANUEL HEITOR.

ACCREDITATION

ENIC/NARIC Portugal: NARIC Centre, Direcção-Geral do Ensino Superior, Av. Duque de Ávila 137, 1069-016 Lisbon; tel. (21) 312-60-00; fax (21) 312-60-20; e-mail info .naric@dges.mctes.pt; internet www.dges .mctes.pt/dges/pt/reconhecimento/naricenic;

f. 1986; establishes and carries out nat. policy on higher education; Dir-Gen. Prof. ANTONIO MORÃO DIAS; Sub-Dir-Gen. Dr CRISTINA JACINTO.

NATIONAL BODIES

Associação Portuguesa do Ensino Superior Privado (Portuguese Association of Private Higher Education Institutions): Av. da República 47, 1° dto, 1050-188 Lisbon; tel. (21) 799-48-60; fax (21) 799-48-69; e-mail contactos@apesp.pt; internet www.apesp.pt; works towards the full integration of non-state higher education in the Portuguese educational system; Pres. Prof. JOÃO DUARTE REDONDO; Vice-Pres. Prof. Dr MIGUEL FARIA.

Conselho Coordenador do Ensino Particular e Cooperativo (Coordinating Council for Private and Cooperative Education): Av. 5 de Outubro 89, 2°, 1050-050 Lisbon; tel. (21) 797-29-10; fax (21) 795-67-93; e-mail ccepc@mail.telepac.pt; f. 1980; works for the integration of private and co-operative education into the nat. educational and training system; Pres. Dr ANTÓNIO DE ALMEIDA COSTA; Dir MARIA DE CONCEIÇÃO REIS.

Conselho Coordenador dos Institutos Superiores Politécnicos (Coordinating Council for Polytechnic Institutes): Av. 5 de Outubro 89, 3°, 1050-050 Lisbon; tel. (21) 792-83-60; fax (21) 792-83-69; e-mail ccisp@ ccisp.pt; internet www.ccisp.pt; f. 1979; representative body for public polytechnic instns with influence in all aspects of their operation; Pres. Dr. JOÃO SOBRINHO TEIXEIRA; Vice-Pres. Prof. RUI TEIXEIRA; Sec. CRISTINA ROCHA.

Conselho de Reitores das Universidades Portuguesas (Council of Rectors of the Portuguese Universities): Edifício O, Campus do Lumiar, Estrada do Paço do Lumiar, 1649-038 Lisbon; tel. (21) 360-29-50; fax (21) 364-00-11; e-mail crup@crup.pt; internet www.crup.pt; f. 1979; coordination and global representation of its mems; formulates nat. policies in education, science and culture; prepares legislatures and participates in debates; contributes to the devt of education, research and culture; networking; creation, integration, modification or termination of educational public univs; 16 (incl. public mem. univs and 1 Portuguese Catholic Univ.); Pres. Prof. Dr ANTÓNIO RENDAS; Sec.-Gen. Dr JOÃO MELO BORGES.

Conselho Nacional de Educação (National Council for Education): Rua Florbela Espanca, 1700-195 Lisbon; tel. (21) 793-52-45; fax (21) 797-90-93; e-mail cnedu@cne .min-edu.pt; internet www.cnedu.pt; f. 1982, present status 1987; ind. advisory body on all aspects of the Portuguese educational system; Pres. Prof. ANA MARIA DIAS BETTENCOURT; Sec.-Gen. MANUEL MIGUÉNS; publs Estudos e Relatórios (Studies and Reports), Pareceres e Recomendações (Statements and Recommendations, 1 a year).

Direcção-Geral de Inovação e de Desenvolvimento Curricular (DGIDC) (Department for Innovation and Curricular Development): Av. 24 de Julho 140, 1399-025 Lisbon; tel. (21) 393-45-00; fax (21) 393-46-95; e-mail dgidc@dgidc.min-edu.pt; internet www.dgidc.min-edu.pt; educational research, innovation in teaching practice, curriculum devt and evaluation, spec. education, and distance learning; library of 23,000 vols, 1,500 periodicals; Pres. Dra CRISTINA PAULO; Dir-Gen. Dr LUÍS CAPUCHA; publs *Inovação* (3 a year), *Noesis* (4 a year).

Learned Societies

GENERAL

Academia das Ciências de Lisboa (Lisbon Academy of Sciences): Rua da Academia das Ciências 19, 1249-122 Lisbon; tel. (21) 321-97-30; fax (21) 342-03-95; e-mail geral@acad-ciencias.pt; internet www.acad-ciencias.pt; f. 1779; attached to Min. of Science, Technology and Higher Education; establishes ongoing, valuable contacts with other academies to promote cultural exchanges, research fellowships and joint programmes to renew their ancestral tradition; weekly lectures on science and humanities topics; 189 nat. mems; library: see Libraries and Archives; Pres. Prof. ADRIANO MOREIRA; Sec.-Gen. Prof. Dr MARIA SALOMÉ PAIS; Librarian LEONOR PINTO; publs *Memórias da Classe de Ciências*, *Memórias da Classe de Letras*.

Sociedade Científica da Universidade Católica Portuguesa (Scientific Society of the Portuguese Catholic University): Edifício Biblioteca João Paulo II, 5° andar, Universidade Católica Portuguesa, Palma de Cima, 1649-023 Lisbon; tel. (21) 721-41-36; fax (21) 721-41-59; e-mail scientif@lisboa.ucp.pt; internet www.scucp.ucp.pt; f. 1980; attached to Universidade Católica Portuguesa; advances intellectual, artistic, moral and spiritual forms of a Christian-inspired culture as a means to the fulfilment of man, promotes research in a perspective of interdisciplinarity aiming at a synthesis of knowledge; 15 sections: arts, biology, philosophy, law, history, economics, environmental sciences, literature and linguistics, education, theology, exact and natural sciences, applied sciences and engineering, health sciences and technology, social sciences and politics, communication and information sciences; library of 500 vols; 400 mems; Chair. Prof. MÁRIO JÚLIO BRITO DE ALMEIDA COSTA; Vice-Pres. Prof. Dr ANTÓNIO PEDRO BARBAS HOMEM; Sec. Prof. Dr MARÍLIA PEREIRA LÚCIO DOS SANTOS LOPES HANENBERG; publs *Colecção Cadernos*, *Lumen Veritatis*.

BIBLIOGRAPHY, LIBRARY SCIENCE AND MUSEOLOGY

Associação Portuguesa de Bibliotecários, Arquivistas e Documentalistas (Portuguese Association of Librarians, Archivists and Documentalists): Rua Morais Soares, 43C, 1° dto e frte, 1900-341 Lisbon; tel. (21) 816-19-80; fax (21) 815-45-08; e-mail apbad@apbad.pt; internet www.apbad.pt; f. 1973; promotes better policy and practice of information management, improved scientific, technical and cultural devt of its mems; organizes training and refresher courses; 1,500 mems; Pres. ANTÓNIO JOSÉ DE PINA FALCÃO; Vice-Pres. CRISTINA MARIA REALINHO RIBEIRO; Sec. MARIA JOSÉ VITORINO GONÇALVES; Treas. LEONARDA DE JESUS RODRIGUES GALHANAS; publ. *Cadernos BAD* (2 a year).

ECONOMICS, LAW AND POLITICS

Ordem dos Economistas (Economists' Association): Rua da Estrela 8, 1200-669 Lisbon; tel. (21) 392-94-70; fax (21) 396-14-28; e-mail geral@ordemeconomistas.pt; internet www.ordemeconomistas.pt; f. 1976; brs in Azores, Madeira and Norte; 12,500 mems; Dir FRANCISCO MURTEIRA NABO; publs *Anuário do Economista* (1 a year), *Cadernos*

de Economia (4 a year), *Carta Informativa* (4 a year).

EDUCATION

Associação das Universidades de Língua Portuguesa (Association of Universities of Portuguese Language): Av. Santos Dumont, 67, 2°, 1050-203 Lisbon; tel. (21) 781-63-60; fax (21) 781-63-69; e-mail aulp@aulp.org; internet www.aulp.org; promotes cooperation between univs and educational and research institutions by facilitating exchange of researchers and students, encouraging reflection on the role of higher education and devt of joint scientific and technological research and the widespread exchange of information; Pres. Prof. Dr CLÉLIO CAMPOLINA DINIZ; Vice-Pres. JOÃO TETA; Vice-Pres. ANTÓNIO LEÃO CORREIA E SILVA; Vice-Pres. JOÃO PINTO GUERREIRO; Vice-Pres. RUI MARTINS.

Camões—Instituto da Cooperação e da Língua, I. P. (Camões - Institute of Cooperation and Language, I. P.): Rua Rodrigues Sampaio 113, 1150-279 Lisbon; Av. da Liberdade 270, 1250-149 Lisbon; tel. (21) 310-91-00; fax (21) 314-39-87; e-mail icgeral@instituto-camoes.pt; internet www .instituto-camoes.pt; f. 1929 as Junta de Educação Nacional, present name 2012; attached to the Min. of Foreign Affairs; promotes teaching of Portuguese language and culture abroad; awards grants to foreign students in Portugal; publishes works on Portuguese language and culture; 250 mems; library of 10,000 vols; Pres. ANA PAULA LABORINHO; Vice-Pres. MÁRIO JOSÉ FILIPE DA SILVA; Vice-Pres. MARIA DINAH BANDEIRA SANTOS SILVA AZEVEDO NEVES; publ. *Camões* (irregular).

Instituto Açoriano de Cultura (Azorean Institute of Culture): Apdo 67, 9700-220 Angra do Heroísmo; Alto das Covas, 9700-220 Angra do Heroísmo; tel. and fax (295) 21-44-42; e-mail iac@iac-azores.org; internet www.iac-azores.org; f. 1955; Pres. PAULO ALEXANDRE MARTINS RAIMUNDO; Sec. Dr FILIPA ALEXANDRA DE MOURA MAGALHÃES TAVARES; publs *Atlântida* (1 a year), *Insula* (1 a year).

FINE AND PERFORMING ARTS

Academia Nacional de Belas Artes (National Academy of Fine Arts): Largo da Academia Nacional de Belas Artes, 1200-005 Lisbon; tel. (21) 346-70-91; fax (21) 342-75-00; e-mail geral@academiabelasartes.pt; internet www.academiabelasartes.pt; f. 1932; library of 25,000 vols, incl. some 16th-century work; 20 mems; Pres. Prof. Arq. AUGUSTO PEREIRA BRANDÃO; Sec. Arq. ANTÓNIO MARQUES MIGUEL; publs *Inventário Artístico de Portugal*, *Revista-Boletim de Belas Artes*.

Instituto Gregoriano de Lisboa (Gregorian Institute of Lisbon): Av. 5 de Outubro 258, 1600-038 Lisbon; tel. (21) 793-37-37; fax (21) 795-04-15; e-mail secretaria@inst-gregoriano.rcts.pt; internet www .inst-gregoriano.rcts.pt; f. 1953 as Centro de Estudos Gregorianos (Gregorian Studies Centre), present name and status 1976; public school of music; courses on Gregorian chant, organ, piano, harpsichord, violin, cello and recorder; 49 mems; library of 1,361 vols, 1,641 scores, 665 CDs, c. 150 DVDs; Dir Dr MARIA LUÍSA OLIVEIRA; Deputy Dir Dr RICARDO MONTEIRO; publ. *Modus* (musicology, irregular).

Sociedade Nacional de Belas Artes (National Society of Fine Arts): Palacio das Belas Artes, Rua Barata Salgueiro 36, 1250-044 Lisbon; tel. (21) 313-85-10; fax (21) 313-85-19; e-mail geral@snba.pt; internet www

.snba.pt; f. 1901; exhibitions of painting, sculpture, drawing, etc.; organizes courses in design, painting, drawing, visual education, sociology, aesthetics and history of art; 1,350 assocs; 832 mems; library of 5,200 vols; Pres. EMÍLIA NADAL; Vice-Pres. JOSÉ JOÃO BRITO; Sec. Dr CRISTINA AZEVEDO TAVARES; Treas. AMÉRICO SILVA; publ. *Boletim Informativo* (2 a year).

HISTORY, GEOGRAPHY AND ARCHAEOLOGY

Academia Portuguesa da História (Portuguese Academy of History): Palácio dos Lilases, Alameda das Linhas de Torres 198–200, 1769-024 Lisbon; tel. (21) 754-90-60; fax (21) 759-13-82; e-mail acad.port.historia@sapo.pt; internet www .academiaportuguesadahistoria.gov.pt; f. 1720; research on historical topics; providing historical information; 40 mems, 190 corresp. mems; library of 180,000 vols; Pres. Prof. Dra MANUELA MENDONÇA; Sec.-Gen. Prof. Dr MIGUEL CORRÊA MONTEIRO; publs *Anais*, *Boletim*, *Documentos Medievais Portugueses*, *Fontes Narrativas da História Portuguesa*, *Itinerários Régios*, *Subsídios para a História Portuguesa*.

Associação dos Arqueólogos Portugueses (Association of Portuguese Archaeologists): Largo do Carmo 4, 1° dto, 1200-092 Lisbon; tel. and fax (21) 346-04-73; e-mail aap@mail.pt; internet www.museusportugal .org/aap; f. 1863 as Asscn of Portuguese Civil Architects; 640 mems; library of 10,500 vols; Pres. Dr JOSÉ MORAIS ARNAUD; Vice-Pres. Dr JOÃO JOSÉ FERNANDES GOMES; Sec. Dr PAULO DE ALMEIDA FERNANDES; Treas. Dr JOSÉ BAPTISTA DOMINGOS; publ. *Arqueologia e História* (irregular).

Instituto De Gestão Do Património Arquitectónico e Arqueológico (Institute for Management of Architectural and Archaeological Heritage): Palácio Nacional da Ajuda, 1349-021 Lisbon; tel. (21) 361-42-00; fax (21) 363-70-47; e-mail igespar@igespar .pt; internet www.igespar.pt; f. 2007 by merger of Portuguese Architectural Heritage Institute and Portuguese Archaeological Institute; attached to Min. of Culture; manages, safeguards, conserves and enhances those assets that, due to their historical, artistic, landscape, scientific, social and technical value, integrate Portugal's listed architectural and archaeological heritage; Dir GONÇALO COUCEIRO; Deputy Dir JOÃO PEDRO CUNHA RIBEIRO; Deputy Dir LUÍS FILIPE CAPAZ COELHO; publs *Estudos Património* (2 a year), *Portuguesa de Arqueologia*.

Instituto Geográfico Português (Portuguese Geographical Institute): Rua Artilharia Um 107, 1099-052 Lisbon; tel. (21) 381-96-00; fax (21) 381-96-99; e-mail igeo@igeo.pt; internet www.igeo.pt; f. 2002, by merger of Instituto Português de Cartografia e Cadastro and Centro Nacional de Informação Geográfica; attached to Min. of the Environment, Territorial Planning and Regional Devt; nat. cartographic authority, provides official geographical information, fosters training and research; main brs in Ponta Delgada, Beja, Faro, Castelo Branco, Santarém, Funchal and Mirandela; Gen. Dir. Lt-Gen. CARLOS MOURATO NUNES; Librarian MARIA DIAS.

Instituto Histórico da Ilha Terceira (IHIT) (Terceira Island Historical Institute): Convento de São Francisco, Ladeira de São Francisco, Angra do Heroísmo, Terceira, 9700 The Azores; tel. (29) 521-31-47; e-mail ihit@ihit.pt; internet www.ihit.pt; f. 1942, present location 1991; historical, cultural, anthropological, scientific and patrimonial studies and research; consultancy and educational activities; academic partnerships; residential instn for the UNESCO Azores Centre; 70 mems; library of 1,000 vols; Pres. Dr FRANCISCO DOS REIS MADURO-DIAS; Sec. Dr MIGUEL CORTE-REAL DA SILVEIRA MONJARDINO; Treas. Dr ANTÓNIO BENTO FRAGA BARCELOS; publ. *Boletim do Instituto Histórico da Ilha Terceira* (1 a year).

Real Instituto Arqueológico de Portugal (Royal Archaeological Institute of Portugal): Praça Rainha D. Filipa 4, 6° dto, 1600 Lisbon; tel. (21) 759-11-09; e-mail dphadb@sapo.pt; f. 1868; Pres. and Sec.-Gen. Dr JOSÉ ANTÓNIO FALCÃO; publs *Actas*, *Trabalhos*.

Real Sociedade Arqueológica Lusitana (Royal Lusitanian Archaeological Society): Hospital do Espírito Santo, Praça Conde do Bracial 3, 7540 Santiago do Cacém; tel. (269) 82-63-80; f. 1849; archaeological, historical and ethnological studies; has own museum, archives and library; 150 mems, 97 corresp. mems, 50 fellows; Pres. Dr JOSÉ ANTÓNIO FALCÃO; Gen.-Sec. Dr LÍLIA RIBEIRO DA SILVA TAVARES; publs *Anais*, *Boletim*, *Memórias*, *Repertorium Fontium Studium Artis Historiae Portugaliae Instaurandum*, *Trabalhos*.

Sociedade de Geografia de Lisboa (Lisbon Geographical Society): Rua das Portas de Santo Antão 100, 1150-269 Lisbon; tel. (21) 342-54-01; fax (21) 346-45-53; e-mail geral@socgeografialisboa.mail.pt; internet www.socgeografialisboa.pt; f. 1875; studies geography, history and ethnology of the Portuguese; organizes confs; library of 205,240 vols, 2,020 periodicals, 6,000 MSS, 155 theses/dissertations, 3 sheets printed music, 10,050 maps; 1,500 mems; Pres. Prof. LUÍS AIRES-BARROS; Sec.-Gen. Prof. Dr. JOÃO PEREIRA NETO; Sec.-Gen Prof. ANTÓNIO DIOGO PINTO; Treas. Prof. Dr. CARLOS LOPES BENTO; publs *Boletim* (scientific and literary journal, 1 a year), *Memórias* (irregular), *Relatório* (1 a year).

Sociedade Martins Sarmento (Martins Sarmento Society): Universidade do Minho, Rua Paio Galvão, 4814-509 Guimarães; tel. (253) 41-59-69; fax (253) 51-94-13; e-mail sms@msarmento.org; internet www.csarmento.uminho.pt; f. 1881; archaeology and culture; 600 mems; library of 100,000 vols; Pres. ANTÓNIO AMARO DAS NEVES; publs *Boletim* (4 a year), *Revista de Guimarães* (1 a year).

LANGUAGE AND LITERATURE

Alliance Française: Rua Pinheiro Chagas 60, Apdo 2049, 3000-333 Coimbra; tel. (239) 70-12-52; fax (239) 40-48-50; e-mail afcoimbra@gmail.com; internet www.alliancefr.pt; offers courses and exams in French language and culture and promotes cultural exchange with France; attached offices in the Algarve, Beja, Caldas da Rainha, Entroncamento, Évora, Guimarães, Leiria, Lisbon, Monção, Portalegre, Setúbal, Vila Real and Viseu; Dir of Operations ALAIN DIDIER.

Associação Portuguesa de Escritores (Portuguese Writers' Association): Rua de S. Domingos à Lapa 17, 1200-832 Lisbon; tel. (21) 397-18-99-7; fax (21) 397-23-41; e-mail a.p.escritores@mail.telepac.pt; f. 1973; protects the interests of Portuguese writers, promotes Portuguese literature abroad, supports cultural activities, conferences, debates, confers several literary prizes, etc.; over 600 mems; library of 7,500 vols; Pres. Dr JOSÉ MANUEL MENDES.

British Council: Rua Luís Fernandes 1–3, 1249-062 Lisbon; tel. (21) 321-45-00; fax (21) 347-61-51; e-mail lisbon.enquiries@pt.britishcouncil.org; internet www.britishcouncil.org/portugal; f. 1938; teaching centre; offers courses and exams in English language and British culture and promotes cultural exchange with the UK; attached teaching centres in Almada, Alverca, Cascais, Coimbra, Foz do Douro, Miraflores, Parede and Porto; Dir ROSEMARY HILHORST; publ. *In English*.

Goethe-Institut: Campo dos Mártires da Pátria 37, 1169-016 Lisbon; tel. (21) 882-45-10; fax (21) 885-00-03; e-mail info@lissabon.goethe.org; internet www.goethe.de/portugal; offers courses and exams in German language and culture and promotes cultural exchange with Germany; attached centre in Porto; library of 14,000 vols, 50 periodicals; Dir Dr JOACHIM BERNAUER.

Instituto Cervantes de Lisboa: Rua Santa Marta 43F, 1169-119 Lisbon; tel. (21) 310-50-20; fax (21) 315-22-99; e-mail cenlis@cervantes.es; internet lisboa.cervantes.es; f. 1991 as Spanish Cultural Centre, present name and status 1993; offers courses and exams in Spanish language and culture and promotes cultural exchange with Spain and Spanish-speaking Latin and Central America; library of 30,000 vols; Dir JOSÉ MARÍA MARTÍN VALENZUELA; Sec. PAULA DE SOUSA PRUDÊNCIO; Head Librarian CECILIA GÁNDARAS PÉREZ.

Sociedade Portuguesa de Autores (Portuguese Society of Authors): Av. Duque de Loulé 31, 1069-153 Lisbon; tel. (21) 359-44-00; fax (21) 353-02-57; e-mail geral@spautores.pt; internet www.spautores.pt; f. 1925 as Sociedade de Escritores e Compositores Teatrais Portugueses; copyright protection and authors' rights; cultural activities; 23,000 mems; library of 33,000 vols, 6,000 periodicals; Pres. MANUEL FREIRE; CEO JOSÉ JORGE LETRIA; publ. *Autores* (4 a year).

MEDICINE

Ordem dos Farmacêuticos (Pharmaceutical Society): Rua da Sociedade Farmacêutica 18, 1169-075 Lisbon; tel. (21) 319-13-80; fax (21) 319-13-99; e-mail direccao.nacional@ordemfarmaceuticos.pt; internet www.ordemfarmaceuticos.pt; f. 1835; famous colln of Portuguese pharmacopoeias; unique MS *Historia Pharmaceutica das Plantas Exóticas* by Frei João de Jesus Maria, with permit to print from the Holy Office; 9,950 mems; library of 5,040 vols; Chair. Prof. Dr CARLOS MAURÍCIO GONÇALVES BARBOSA; Pres. JOÃO GONÇALVES DA SILVEIRA; Sec. CARLOS ALBERTO LARANJEIRA HENRIQUES; Sec. MARGARIDA MENDES MARQUES GOMES CARNEIRO; publ. *Revista do Ordem dos Farmacêuticos* (6 a year).

Ordem dos Médicos (Portuguese Medical Association): Av. Almirante Gago Coutinho 151, 1749-084 Lisbon; tel. (21) 842-71-00; fax (21) 842-71-99; e-mail omcne@omcne.pt; internet www.ordemdosmedicos.pt; f. 1938; regulation of medical practice; independence of practitioners; 39,419 mems; Pres. Prof. JOSÉ MANUEL SILVA; publs *Acta Médica Portuguesa* (6 a year), *Revista* (12 a year).

Sociedade Anatómica Portuguesa (Portuguese Anatomical Society): Lab. de Anatomia Normal, Faculdade de Medicina de Coimbra, 3049 Coimbra; f. 1930; 184 mems; Pres. Prof. Dr ANTÓNIO CARLOS MIGUÉIS.

NATURAL SCIENCES

General

Serviço de Informação e Documentação (Information and Documentation Service): Av. D. Carlos I 126, 1249-074 Lisbon; tel. (21) 392-43-00; fax (21) 390-74-81; internet alfa.fct.mctes.pt; f. 1936; attached to Fundação para a Ciência e a Tecnologia; nat. centre of scientific and technical information; library of 3,000 Portuguese, 5,000 foreign books, 350 periodicals; Dir GABRIELA LOPES DA SILVA.

Biological Sciences

Sociedade Broteriana (Botanical Society): Instituto Botânico, Universidade de Coimbra, 3049 Coimbra; tel. (239) 82-28-97; fax (239) 82-07-80; e-mail socbrot@ci.uc.pt; f. 1880; 300 mems; library of 122,000 vols; Chair. Prof. JOSÉ F. M. MESQUITA; publs *Anuário*, *Boletim* (1 a year), *Memórias* (irregular).

Sociedade Portuguesa de Ciências Naturais (Portuguese Natural Science Society): Faculdade de Ciências, Campo Grande, 1749-016 Lisbon; tel. (21) 750-00-00; fax (21) 750-00-09; e-mail spcn@fc.ul.pt; f. 1907; 938 mems; library of 30,000 vols; Pres. HUMBERTO ROSA; publs *Boletim*, *Natura*, *Naturalia*.

Sociedade Portuguesa de Ecologia (Portuguese Society of Ecology): Faculdade de Ciências da Univ. de Lisboa, Edif. C4, 1° Piso, Sala 4.1.10, Campo Grande 1749-016 Lisbon; tel. and fax (21) 7500439; e-mail speco@fc.ul.pt; internet speco.fc.ul.pt; f. 1995; scientific soc. for environmentalists; Pres. HELENA FREITAS; Sec. PAULA SOBRAL; publs *Cadernos de ecologia* (1 a year), *Revista de biologia* (1 a year), *Revista Ecologi@* (3 a year).

Mathematical Sciences

Instituto Nacional de Estatística (National Statistical Institute): Av. António José de Almeida, 1000-043 Lisbon; tel. (21) 842-61-00; fax (21) 842-63-80; e-mail ine@ine.pt; internet www.ine.pt; f. 1935; production and dissemination of official statistical information; 750 mems; library of 12,000 vols, 2,500 periodicals; Pres. ALDA MARIA DAS NEVES CARNEIRO DE CAETANO CARVALHO; Vice-Pres. MARIA HELENA DE SOUSA CORDEIRO; Vice-Pres. PEDRO JORGE NUNES DA SILVA DIAS; publs *Statistical Review*, *Statistical Yearbook* (in English and Portuguese).

Physical Sciences

Sociedade Geológica de Portugal (Portugal Geological Society): Rua da Escola Politécnica, 58, 1269-102 Lisbon; tel. and fax (96) 458-20-09; e-mail webmaster@socgeol.org; internet socgeol.org; f. 1940; asscn of individuals and legal entities that promotes devt of knowledge concerning the geological sciences and cooperate with other stakeholders; 500 mems; library of 1,200 vols; Pres. ROGÉRIO BORDALO DA ROCHA; Vice-Pres. FILOMENA DINIZ; Sec. JOSÉ CARLOS KULLBERG; Sec. JOSÉ MANUEL ROMÃO; Treas. RUI TABORDA; publ. *Boletim da Sociedade Geológica de Portugal*.

Sociedade Portuguesa de Química (Portuguese Chemical Society): Av. da República 45–3, 1050-187 Lisbon; tel. (21) 793-46-37; fax (21) 795-23-49; e-mail sede@spq.pt; internet www.spq.pt; f. 1911; holds Chemistry Olympics; brs in Aveiro, Braga, Coimbra, Oporto, Vila Real, Coimbra, Faro, Covilhã and Braga Meetings; confs and symposiums; 2,000 mems; Pres. MÁRIO NUNO DE MATOS SEQUEIRA BERBERAN E SANTOS; Vice-Pres. MARIA JOSÉ DIOGO DA SILVA CALHORDA; Gen. Sec. JOAQUIM LUÍS BERNARDES MARTINS DE FARIA; Treas. MARIA MANUEL MARTINHO SEQUEIRA BARATA MARQUES; publ. *Química* (4 a year).

RELIGION, SOCIOLOGY AND ANTHROPOLOGY

Academia Internacional da Cultura Portuguesa (International Academy of Portuguese Culture): Rua das Portas de Santo Antão 100, 1150-269 Lisbon; tel. (21) 342-10-81; fax (21) 342-10-33; e-mail aicportuguesa@clix.pt; f. 1965; attached to Min. of Culture;

seeks to promote research into the culture of Portuguese communities living outside the nat. territory; 50 mems; Pres. Dr CARLOS MONJARDINO; Vice Pres. Prof. Dr JUSTINO MENDES DE ALMEIDA; Vice Pres. Prof. OSCAR BARATA; publ. *Boletim*.

Sociedade Portuguesa de Antropologia e Etnologia (Portuguese Anthropological and Ethnological Society): Faculdade de Ciências do Porto, Praça Gomes Teixeira, 4099-002 Porto; tel. (22) 208-71-49; fax (22) 202-69-03; e-mail vojsoj@sapo.pt; internet spae.no.sapo.pt; stimulates and develops the main anthropological research in its different areas and creates an interdisciplinary perspective; f. 1918; 100 mems; library of 10,000 vols; Pres. Prof. VÍTOR OLIVEIRA JORGE; Sec. PAULO CASTRO SEIXAS; publ. *Trabalhos de Antropologia e Etnologia* (2 a year).

TECHNOLOGY

Ordem dos Engenheiros (Portuguese Association of Engineers): Av. António Augusto de Aguiar 3D, 1069-030 Lisbon; tel. (21) 313-26-00; fax (21) 352-46-32; e-mail secretariageral@ordemdosengenheiros.pt; internet www.ordemengenheiros.pt; f. 1936; holds seminars, conf. etc. on topics useful to engineers; 28,000 mems; library of 23,000 vols, 500 periodical titles; Pres. Eng. CARLOS ALBERTO MATIAS RAMOS; Vice-Pres. JOSÉ MANUEL PEREIRA VIEIRA; Vice-Pres. VICTOR MANUEL GONÇALVES DE BRITO; publ. *Ingenium* (review, 12 a year).

Research Institutes
GENERAL

Centro de Estudos do Território, Cultura e Desenvolvimento (Territory, Culture and Development Research Centre): Universidade Lusófona de Humanidades e Tecnologias, Av. do Campo Grande 376, 1749-024 Lisbon; tel. (21) 751-55-00; fax (21) 751-55-09; e-mail zoran.roca@ulusofona .pt; internet tercud.ulusofona.pt; f. 2008, fmrly Applied Social Sciences Research Unit; attached to Faculty of Architecture, Urban Planning, Geography and Arts, Univ. Lusófona de Humanidades e Tecnologias; planning, management and evaluation of territorial devt in urban and rural settings; valorization of natural and cultural heritage and other components of territorial identities as devt recourses; Dir Dr ZORAN ROCA; publs *Arquitectura e Educação* (online), *Cadernos de Sociomuseologia* (online), *Malha Urbana* (online).

Centro de Estudos Transdisciplinares para o Desenvolvimento (CETRAD) (Transdisciplinary Studies Centre for Development): Av. Almeida Lucena 1, 5000-660 Vila Real; tel. (25) 930-22-00; fax (25) 930-22-49; e-mail cetrad@utad.pt; internet www .cetrad.info; f. 2002; attached to Univ. of Trás-os-Montes and Alto Douro; research incl. globalization and state policies; innovation, markets and orgs; society, territory and resources; Dir CHRISTOPHER GERRY; Deputy Dir FRANCISCO DINIZ; Deputy Dir ALBERTO BAPTISTA.

CERAP—Centre d'Étude et de Recherche Appliquée en Psychopédagogie Perceptive (Centre for Applied Research and Study in Perceptual Psychoeducation): Praça 9 de Abril 349, 4249-004 Porto; e-mail info@ cerap.org; internet www.cerap.org; f. 2004; attached to Univ. Fernando Pessoa; studies the particular relationship individuals have to the 'sensible' experience of the body and the place of the 'sensible' body in educational, formative and existential learning processes;

Dir Prof. Dr DANIS BOIS; publ. *Réciprocités* (2 a year).

Fundação para a Ciência e a Tecnologia (Science and Technology Foundation): Av. D. Carlos I 126, 1249-074 Lisbon; tel. (21) 392-43-00; fax (21) 390-74-81; e-mail presidencia@fct.mctes.pt; internet www.fct .mctes.pt; f. 1997, fmrly Nat. Board of Scientific and Technological Research; attached to Min. of Science, Technology and Higher Education; evaluates, finances and promotes institutions, programmes and projects in the fields of science and technology; also concerned with the education and qualifications in human resources; library of 15,500 vols; Pres. Prof. JOÃO JOSÉ DOS SANTOS SENTIEIRO.

Instituto de Altos Estudos (Institute for Advanced Studies): c/o Academia das Ciências de Lisboa, Rua Academia das Ciências 19, 1249-122 Lisbon; tel. (21) 321-97-30; fax (21) 342-03-95; e-mail geral@ acad-ciencias.pt; internet www.acad-ciencias .pt; f. 1931; attached to Lisbon Acad. of Sciences; Pres. Prof. ADRIANO MOREIRA.

Instituto de Investigação Científica Tropical (Tropical Science Research Institute): Rua da Junqueira 86–1, 1300-344 Lisbon; tel. (21) 361-63-40; fax (21) 363-14-60; e-mail iict@iict.pt; internet www2.iict.pt; f. 1883; develops scientific research in tropical areas of humanities and natural sciences; enhances scientific and technical capacity of countries with which it cooperates; promotes preservation of heritage; Pres. Prof. Dr JORGE BRAGA DE MACEDO; Vice-Pres. Dr ANTÓNIO JOSÉ LOPES DE MELO; Sec. JOÃO NOGUEIRA; publs *Boletim da Filmoteca Ultramarina Portuguesa, Comunicações do IICT* (series: Agrarian Sciences; Biological Sciences; Ethnological and Ethnomuseological Sciences; Geographical Sciences; Earth Sciences), *Estudos de Antropologia Cultural e Social, Estudos de Ciências Políticas e Sociais, Estudos de História e Cartografia Antiga—Memórias, Estudos e Ensaios e Documentos, Index Seminum, Leba* (quaternary, prehistory, archaeology), *Memórias, Revista Internacional de Estudos Africanos, Separatas do Centro de Estudos de História e Cartografia Antiga, Studia.*

Research Centres:

> **Centro de Ambiente e Ciências da Terra do Instituto de Investigação Científica Tropical** (Environment and Earth Sciences Centre): Aleja D. Afonso Henriques 41, 4° dto, 1000-123 Lisbon; tel. (21) 847-64-05; fax (21) 840-79-65; e-mail cgeol@iict.pt; internet www.iict.pt.

> **Centro de Antropobiologia do Instituto de Investigação Científica Tropical** (Anthropobiology Centre): Av. Óscar Monteiro Torres 34, 1° esq, 1000-219 Lisbon; tel. (21) 796-66-70; e-mail cantp@ iict.pt; internet www.iict.pt; f. 1954; Dir (vacant).

> **Centro de Antropologia Cultural e Social do Instituto de Investigação Científica Tropical** (Cultural and Social Anthropology Centre): Av. Ilha da Madeira, Edifício Museu, 1400-203 Lisbon; tel. (21) 301-52-64; fax (21) 301-19-45; e-mail cacst@iict.pt; internet www.iict.pt; f. 1962; Dir Dra CLARA SARAIVA.

> **Centro de Botânica do Instituto de Investigação Científica Tropical** (Botany Centre): Travessa Conde da Ribeira 9, 1300-142 Lisbon; tel. (21) 361-63-40; e-mail cbotn@iict.pt; internet www.iict.pt; f. 1948; Dir Dra MARIA ADÉLIA DINIZ.

> **Centro de Cartografia do Instituto de Investigação Científica Tropical** (Cartography Centre): Travessa Conde da

Ribeira 7–9, 1300-007 Lisbon; tel. (21) 361-63-40; fax (21) 363-14-60; e-mail ccart@iict.pt; internet www.iict.pt; f. 1946; Dir Prof. Eng. ARMANDO SEPÚLVEDA.

> **Centro de Cristalografia e Mineralogia do Instituto de Investigação Científica Tropical** (Crystallography and Mineralogy Centre): Alameda D. Afonso Henriques 41, 4° esq, 1000-123 Lisbon; tel. (21) 847-65-96; fax (21) 840-79-65; e-mail ccris@iict.pt; internet www.iict.pt; f. 1957; Dir Prof. Dra MARIA ONDINA FIGUEIREDO.

> **Centro de Desenvolvimento Global do Instituto de Investigação Científica Tropical** (Global Development Centre): Rua João de Barros 27, 1300-319 Lisbon; tel. (21) 364-27-32; e-mail des@iict.pt; internet www.iict.pt.

> **Centro de Detecção Remota para o Desenvolvimento do Instituto de Investigação Científica Tropical** (Remote Sensing for Development Centre): Travessa Conde da Ribeira 9, 1300-142 Lisbon; tel. (21) 361-63-40; fax (21) 364-00-46; e-mail ccart@iict.pt; internet www.iict .pt.

> **Centro de Ecofisiologia, Bioquímica e Biotecnologia Vegetal do Instituto de Investigação Científica Tropical** (Ecophysiology, Biochemistry and Vegetal Biotechnology Centre): Av. da República, Quinta do Marquês, 2784-505 Oeiras; tel. (21) 454-46-82; fax (21) 454-46-89; e-mail eco-bio@iict.pt; internet www.iict.pt; Dir. ANTÓNIO EDUARDO BAPTISTA LEITÃO.

> **Centro de Estudos Africanos e Asiáticos do Instituto de Investigação Científica Tropical** (African and Asian Studies Centre): Rua da Junqueira 30, 1°, 1349-007 Lisbon; tel. (21) 362-26-21; fax (21) 362-26-26; e-mail cestaa@iict.pt; internet www.iict.pt; f. 1983; Dir Prof. Dra JILL REANEY DIAS.

> **Centro de Estudos de Fitossanidade do Armazenamento do Instituto de Investigação Científica Tropical** (Research Centre on Plant Health during Storage): Travessa Conde da Ribeira 9, 1300-142 Lisbon; tel. (21) 361-63-40; e-mail cefa@iict.pt; internet www.iict.pt; f. 1955; Dir Prof. Dr ANTÓNIO MARQUES MEXIA.

> **Centro de Estudos de História e Cartografia Antiga do Instituto de Investigação Científica Tropical** (History and Early Cartography Research Centre): Rua da Junqueira 30, r/c, 1349-007 Lisbon; tel. (21) 360-05-82; e-mail cesth@iict.pt; internet www.iict.pt; f. 1961; history of Portuguese expansion overseas, African history; library of 9,200 vols, 430 periodicals; Dir Dra MARIA EMÍLIA MADEIRA SANTOS; publs *Boletim da Filmoteca Ultramarina Portuguesa* (irregular), *Studia* (2 a year).

> **Centro de Estudos de Pedologia do Instituto de Investigação Científica Tropical** (Pedology Studies Centre): Tapada da Ajuda, 1349-018 Lisbon; tel. (21) 365-31-00; e-mail cestp@iict.pt; internet www.iict.pt; f. 1960; Dir Prof. Eng. RUI PINTO RICARDO.

> **Centro de Estudos de Produção e Tecnologia Agrícolas do Instituto de Investigação Científica Tropical** (Agricultural Technology and Production Studies Centre): Tapada da Ajuda, Edifício das Agro-Indústria e Agronomia Tropical, 1349-018 Lisbon; tel. (21) 361-72-40; e-mail cestt@iict.pt; internet www.iict.pt; f. 1960; Dir (vacant).

> **Centro de Etnologia Ultramarina do Instituto de Investigação Científica Tropical** (Overseas Ethnology Centre):

Av. Ilha da Madeira, 1400-203 Lisbon; tel. (21) 301-21-18; fax (21) 301-19-45; e-mail cetno@iict.pt; internet www.iict.pt; f. 1962; Dir Dra MARGARIDA LIMA DE FARIA.

Centro de Fotogrametria do Instituto de Investigação Científica Tropical (Photogrammetry Centre): Rua João de Barros 27, 1300-319 Lisbon; tel. (21) 364-27-32; e-mail cfotg@iict.pt; internet www .iict.pt; f. 1983; Dir Prof. Dr ARMANDO SEPÚLVEDA.

Centro de Geodesia do Instituto de Investigação Científica Tropical (Geodesy Centre): Rua da Junqueira 534, 1300-341 Lisbon; tel. (21) 363-18-62; fax (21) 364-19-47; e-mail cgeod@iict.pt; internet www.iict.pt; f. 1983; Dir Eng. JOSÉ FRIAS DE BARROS.

Centro de Geografia do Instituto de Investigação Científica Tropical (Geography Centre): Rua Ricardo Espírito Santo 7, c/v esq, 1200-790 Lisbon; tel. and fax (21) 395-67-72; e-mail cgeog@iict.pt; internet www.iict.pt; f. 1983; Dir Prof. Dr ILÍDIO DO AMARAL.

Centro de Geologia do Instituto de Investigação Científica Tropical (Geology Centre): Alameda D. Afonso Henriques 41, 4° dto, 1000-123 Lisbon; tel. (21) 847-64-05; fax (21) 840-79-65; e-mail cgeol@iict .pt; internet www.iict.pt; f. 1958; Dir Prof. Dr RICARDO AUGUSTO QUADRADO.

Centro de Investigação das Ferrugens do Cafeeiro do Instituto de Investigação Científica Tropical (Coffee Rusts Research Centre): Quinta do Marquês, 2784-505 Oeiras; tel. (21) 454-46-80; fax (21) 454-46-89; e-mail cferc@iict.pt; internet www.iict.pt; f. 1955; Dir MARIA DO CÉU M. L. SILVA.

Centro de Pré-História e Arqueologia do Instituto de Investigação Científica Tropical (Prehistory and Archaeology Centre): Travessa Conde da Ribeira 7, 1300-142 Lisbon; tel. (21) 361-63-40; e-mail cphst@iict.pt; internet www.iict.pt; f. 1954; Dir Prof. Dr A. TEODORO DE MATOS.

Centro de Sociedades e Culturas Tropicais do Instituto de Investigação Científica Tropical (Societies and Tropical Cultures Centre): Rua da Junqueira 30, 1°, 1349-007 Lisbon; tel. (21) 360-05-81; fax (21) 360-05-87; e-mail cestaa@iict.pt; internet www.iict.pt.

Centro de Sócio-Economia do Instituto de Investigação Científica Tropical (Socio-Economics Centre): Travessa Conde da Ponte 9, 1°, 1300-141 Lisbon; tel. (21) 363-57-48; fax (21) 363-96-03; e-mail csoec@iict.pt; internet www.iict.pt; f. 1956; Dir Prof. Dr JORGE BRAGA DE MACEDO.

Centro de Veterinária e Zootecnia do Instituto de Investigação Científica Tropical (Veterinary and Zootechnics Centre): R. João de Barros, 27 1300-319 Lisbon; tel. (21) 364-27-29; fax (21) 363-42-38; e-mail dcn@iict.pt; internet www.iict .pt; f. 1983; Dir Dr LUÍS ALFARO CARDOSO.

Centro de Zoologia do Instituto de Investigação Científica Tropical (Zoology Centre): Rua da Junqueira 14, 1300-343 Lisbon; tel. (21) 363-70-55; e-mail czool@iict.pt; internet www.iict.pt; f. 1948; Dir Dr LUÍS F. MENDES.

Unidade de Investigação de Florestas e Produtos Florestais do Instituto de Investigação Científica Tropical (Forests and Forest Products Research Unit): Tapada da Ajuda, 1349-017 Lisbon; tel. (21) 363-46-62; fax (21) 365-33-38; e-mail jose.rodrigues@iict.pt; internet www.iict .pt; f. 1948; Dir JOSÉ RODRIGUES.

Instituto de Orientação Profissional (Institute of Professional Guidance): Rua José Carlos dos Santos 7, 1700-256 Lisbon; tel. (21) 346-33-57; fax (21) 346-33-58; e-mail geral@iop.ul.pt; internet www.iop.ul.pt; f. 1925, present status 1989; attached to Univ. of Lisbon; fundamental and applied research; develops educational tools and techniques; Dir Prof. Dr MARIA EDUARDA DUARTE.

AGRICULTURE, FISHERIES AND VETERINARY SCIENCE

Centro de Ciência Animal e Veterinária (CECAV) (Centre for Animal and Veterinary Sciences (CECAV)): Univ. of Tras-os-Montes and Alto Douro, Apdo 1013, 5001-801 Vila Real; tel. (25) 935-04-08; fax (25) 935-04-82; e-mail arnaldos@utad.pt; internet www .cecav.utad.pt; f. 2002; attached to Univ. of Trás-os-Montes and Alto Douro; fundamental and applied research in veterinary and animal science; disseminates knowledge in animal health and production with emphasis on increasing efficiency and sustainability of livestock production and safety of products of animal origin without compromising on the surrounding environment and economic conditions; main research areas incl. animal production, animal physiology and pathology and quality and food safety of animal products; Dir ARNALDO DIAS DA SILVA; Vice-Dir CRISTINA GUEDES; Vice-Dir JOSÉ MANUEL ALMEIDA.

Centro de Investigação e de Tecnologias Agro-Ambientais e Biológicas (Centre for the Research and Technology of Agro-Environmental and Biological Sciences): Univ. of Trás-os-Montes and Alto Douro, Quinta de Prados, Apdo 1013, 5001-801 Vila Real; tel. (23) 935-04-75; fax (25) 935-06-29; e-mail citab@utad.pt; internet www.citab.utad.pt; f. 2007 by merger of 3 instns; attached to Univ. of Trás-os-Montes and Alto Douro; ecointegrity, integrative biology and quality and biosystems engineering; research focuses on devt and upgrading of agriculture and forestry production chains; Dir EDUARDO AUGUSTO DOS SANTOS ROSA; Vice-Dir PEDRO JOSÉ DE MELO TEIXEIRA PINTO; Vice-Dir RUI MANUEL VÍTOR CORTES.

Estação Agronómica Nacional (National Agronomical Research Station): Av. República, Quinta do Marquês, Nova Oeiras, 2784-505 Oeiras; tel. (21) 440-35-00; fax (21) 441-60-11; e-mail dir.ean@iniap.min-agricultura .pt; f. 1937; comprises depts of agronomy, entomology, experimental statistics, genetics and plant breeding, pedology, phytopathology, plant physiology, microbiology, systematic botany and plant sociology; library of 172,000 vols; Dir MARIA CRISTINA LOPES; Librarian ROSÁRIO SÁ; publs Agronomia Lusitana, Index Seminum.

Instituto Nacional de Recursos Biológicos IP (National Institute of Biological Resources IP): R. Barata Salgueiro 37–4°, 1250-042 Lisbon; tel. (21) 313-17-41; fax (21) 313-17-83; e-mail presidencia@inrb.pt; internet www.inrb.pt; f. 2006; attached to Min. of Agriculture, Rural Devt and Fisheries; supports research of public policies for the valuation of biological resources in the defence of nat. interests and in the continuation and deepening of EU common policies; Pres. Dr MARIA ROSA TOBIAS SÁ.

Unidade de Silvicultura e Produtos Florestais (Forestry Research Unit of INRB): Quinta do Marquês, 2780-159 Oeiras; tel. (21) 446-37-00; fax (21) 446-37-01; e-mail uispf@inia.inrb.pt; f. 1979; forestry research unit of the Instituto Nacional de Recursos Biológicos; 4 research depts; library of 3,500 vols; Dir Dr EDMUNDO SOUSA; publ. Silva Lusitana.

ECONOMICS, LAW AND POLITICS

Centro de Estudos Sociais da Faculdade de Economia da Universidade de Coimbra (Centre for Social Studies): Colégio de São Jerónimo, Apdo 3087, 3001-401 Coimbra; tel. (23) 985-55-70; fax (23) 985-55-89; e-mail ces@ces.uc.pt; internet www.ces.uc.pt; f. 1978, present status 2002; attached to School of Economics, Univ. of Coimbra; research and advanced training in social sciences and humanities; library of 13,000 vols, 800 periodicals; Dir Prof. Dr BOAVENTURA SOUSA SANTOS; Pres. PEDRO HESPANHA; Vice-Pres. SILVIA PORTUGAL; Sec.-Gen. LASSALLE PAIVA; publ. Revista Crítica de Ciências Sociais (4 a year).

Centro de Investigação do Instituto de Estudos Políticos (Research Centre of the Institute for Political Studies): Univ. Católica Portuguesa, Palma de Cima, 1649-023 Lisbon; tel. (21) 721-41-29; fax (21) 727-18-36; internet www.iep.lisboa.ucp.pt; f. 2001; attached to Institute for Political Studies, Univ. Católica Portuguesa; supports scientific research in various brs of science policy, incl. int. relations, comparative politics, public policy, history of political thought and political theory; Scientific Dir Prof. Dr JOÃO CARLOS ESPADA; Scientific Coordinator Dr LÍVIA FRANCO.

EDUCATION

ILG—Instituto Leopoldo Guimarães (Leopoldo Guimarães Institute): Rua Fernando Miguel Cabanas, 2950-616 Palmela; e-mail geral@institutolg.com; internet www .institutolg.com; f. 2008; attached to Univ. Fernando Pessoa; promotes lifelong learning in Portugal, cooperating with such instns for higher education, with public and enterprise dedicated to scientific research; provides teacher training and Masters programmes; Dir Prof. LEOPOLDO GUIMARÃES.

Kie—Associação Conhecimento, Inovação e Educaçã (Kie—Association of Knowledge, Innovation and Education): Edif. Panoramic (Parque das Nações), Av. do Atlântico 1.19.02 A, Escritório 6.05, 1990-096 Lisbon; tel. (21) 894-33-05; fax (21) 214-13-32; e-mail terezaventura@ufp.edu.pt; internet www.kie.pt; f. 2009; attached to Univ. Fernando Pessoa; promotes research and training in continuing education and lifelong learning; provides Masters programmes; Pres. MARIA TEREZA ROMANO VENTURA; Chair. MARIA DE FÁTIMA PAIVA S. COELHO; Treas. HÉLIO JOÃO DA SILVA COELHO.

HISTORY, GEOGRAPHY AND ARCHAEOLOGY

Centro de Estudos do Baixo Alentejo (Centre for Lower Alentejo Studies): c/o Real Sociedade Arqueológica Lusitana, Hospital do Espírito Santo, Praça Conde do Bracial 3, 7540 Santiago do Cacém; tel. (269) 82-63-80; f. 1944; Dir The Pres. of the Royal Lusitanian Archaeological Soc. (q.v.); Sec.-Gen. The Gen.-Sec. of the Royal Lusitanian Archaeological Soc. (q.v.).

Centro de Estudos Geográficos da Universidade de Lisboa (Centre of Geographical Studies of the University of Lisbon): IGOT - Edif., Faculdade de Letras, Alameda da Universidade, 1600-214 Lisbon; tel. (21) 794-02-18; fax (21) 793-86-90; e-mail ceg@ campus.ul.pt; internet www.ceg.ul.pt; f. 1943; funded by the Fundação para a Ciência e a Tecnologia (q.v.), the European Commission and other nat. and int. orgs; research into human and regional geography, geoecology, physical and environmental geography and fluvial, coastal dynamics; supports teaching activities; library of 35,000 vols; Pres. CARLOS ALBERTO MEDEIROS; Scientific

Dir Prof. Dr DIOGO JOSÉ BROCHADO DE ABREU; Sec. LUÍS MANUEL COSTA MORENO; publ. *Finisterra* (2 a year).

Centro de Estudos Históricos e Etnológicos (Centre for Historical and Ethnological Studies): Serra do Balas, Areias, 2240 Ferreira do Zêzere; tel. (249) 39-14-08; f. 1983; Pres. Dr JORGE M. RODRIGUES FERREIRA; Sec. ANABELA BENTO; publ. *Série Arqueológica*.

Centro de Geologia da Universidade do Porto (Geology Centre of the University of Porto): Dept de Geologia da FCUP, Rua do Campo Alegre 687, 4169-007 Porto; tel. (22) 040-24-72; fax (22) 040-24-90; e-mail fmnoronh@fc.up.pt; internet www.cguporto .org; f. 1978; attached to Univ. of Porto; devt of research in earth sciences; Coordinator Prof. FERNANDO NORONHA.

Centro de Investigação em Ciência e Engenharia Geológica (Centre for Research in Science and Engineering Geology): Dept de Ciências da Terra, Faculdade de Ciências e Tecnologia, Quinta da Torre 2829-516 Caparica; tel. (21) 294-85-73; fax (21) 294-85-56; e-mail sec-dct@fct.unl.pt; internet www.cicege.fct.unl.pt; f. by merger of Centre for Geological Studies (CEG) and the Research Centre for Applied Geoscience (CIGA); attached to Univ. Nova de Lisboa; research in areas of sedimentary geology, stratigraphy, palaeontology, geological mapping, ornamental rocks, applied geology and engineering geology; publ. *Ciências da Terra*.

Centro de Investigação Marinha e Ambiental (Centre for Marine and Environmental Research): Univ. do Algarve, Faculdade de Ciências e Tecnologia, Edif. 7, Campus de Gambelas, 8005-139 Faro; tel. (28) 980-09-00; fax (28) 980-00-69; e-mail cima@ualg.pt; internet cima.ualg.pt; research areas incl. large-scale geological processes and their local record, marine morphosedimentary processes and impact of environmental changes; Gen. Coordinator TOMASZ BOSKI.

Centro de Petrologia e Geoquímica (Centre for Petrology and Geochemistry): Av. Rovisco Pais 1049-001 Lisbon; tel. and fax (21) 840-08-06; e-mail jose.marques@ist .utl.pt; internet cepgist.ist.utl.pt; research, teaching and consulting in hydrogeology, groundwater quality, isotope hydrology, monument stone decay and conservation, environmental geochemistry, applied mineralogy and petrology; Scientific Coordinator JOSÉ MANUEL MARQUES.

Centro de Vulcanologia e Avaliação de Riscos Geológicos (Centre for Volcanology and Geological Risk Assessment): c/o Univ. dos Açores, Edif. do Complexo Científico, 3º Piso, Ala Sul, 9501-801 Ponta Delgada; tel. (29) 665-01-47; fax (29) 665-01-42; e-mail patricia.ij.raposo@azores.gov.pt; internet www.cvarg.azores.gov.pt; f. 1997; attached to Univ. of Azores; supports research of devt of earth sciences and prediction of disasters, natural calamities; focuses on technical and scientific cooperation nationally and internationally in the field of volcanology and associated phenomena, incl. volcanic eruptions, earthquakes, explosions of steam, toxic gas release, mass movements and tsunamis; mem. of the World Org. of Volcano Observatories (WONO); Dir MARIA GABRIELA PEREIRA DA SILVA.

Evolução Litosférica e Meio Ambiente Superficial: Departamento de Geociências, Universidade de Aveiro, Campus de Santiago, 3810-193 Aveiro; tel. (23) 437-03-57; fax (23) 437-06-05; e-mail sec@geo.ua.pt; internet www.ua.pt/geo; f. 1998; attached to Geosciences Dept, Univ. of Aveiro; interdisciplinary studies in fundamental and applied

aspects of geology and biology; Dir JORGE MEDINA.

'Infante D. Luís' Geophysical Institute: Rua da Escola Politécnica 58, 1250-102 Lisbon; tel. (21) 392-18-63; fax (21) 390-81-87; e-mail presidente.igidl@fc.ul.pt; internet www.igidl.ul.pt; f. 1853; attached to Univ. of Lisbon; geophysics, seismology, meteorology, climatology, solar radiation; maintains Portugal's oldest meteorological series; library of 4,000 vols, 1,075 journals; Pres. JORGE MIGUEL DE MIRANDA; Sec. ANABELA MARTINS.

Instituto Geofísico (Geophysical Institute): Av. Dr Dias da Silva, 3000-134 Coimbra; tel. (23) 979-34-20; fax (23) 979-34-28; e-mail iguc@ci.uc.pt; internet www1.ci.uc.pt/iguc; f. 1864; attached to Univ. of Coimbra; meteorological, magnetic and seismological observatory; library of 16,000 vols; Dir Prof. Dr ANTÓNIO FERREIRA SOARES; publs *Magnéticas e Sismológicas* (1 a year), *Observações Meteorológicas*.

LANGUAGE AND LITERATURE

Centro de Estudos em Letras (Centre for Studies in Languages, Linguistics and Literature): tel. (25) 935-07-01; fax (25) 935-07-87; e-mail cel@utad.pt; internet www.utad .pt/pt/investigacao/cel/index.html; f. 2003; research in languages and linguistics, literature, culture and communication; Dir Prof. Dr JOSÉ MANUEL CARDOSO BELO; Dir Prof. Dr MANUEL GONÇALO SÁ FENANDES.

Instituto de Estudos Clássicos (Classical Studies Institute): Faculdade de Letras, Universidade de Coimbra, 3004-530 Coimbra; tel. (23) 985-99-81; fax (23) 983-67-33; e-mail classic@ci.uc.pt; internet www.uc.pt/ fluc/eclassicos/iec; f. 1944; attached to Faculty of Arts, Univ. of Coimbra; teaching, research, promotion of classics in Portugal; library of 15,000 vols, 500 periodicals; Dir Dr JOSÉ LUIS LOPES BRANDÃO; Sec. Dr LUÍSA DE NAZARÉ FERREIRA; Sec. Dr SUSANA MARQUES PEREIRA.

Instituto de Lexicologia e Lexicografia da Língua Portuguesa (Institute of Lexicology and Lexicography of the Portuguese Language): c/o Academia das Ciências de Lisboa, Rua da Academia das Ciências 19, 1249-122 Lisbon; tel. (21) 321-97-30; fax (21) 342-03-95; e-mail geral@acad-ciencias.pt; internet www.acad-ciencias.pt; f. 1987; attached to Lisbon Acad. of Sciences; Pres. Prof. Dr ARTUR ANSELMO; Sec. Dr SÉRGIO LOURENÇO.

Instituto Português da Sociedade Científica de Goerres (Portuguese Institute of the Goerres Research Society): Universidade Católica Portuguesa, Reitoria, Palma de Cima, 1649-023 Lisbon; tel. (21) 721-40-00; fax (21) 726-05-46; e-mail mrato@reitoria.ucp .pt; internet www.ucp.pt; f. 1962; research on history, legal history, language and Portuguese literature; also known as Institute Vieira; Office Sec. Dr MARIA EUGÉNIA RATO; library of 9,000 vols; publ. *Portugiesische Forschungen*.

MEDICINE

Association for Innovation and Biomedical Research on Light and Image: Azinhaga Sta. Comba, Celas, 3000-548 Coimbra; tel. (23) 948-01-00; fax (23) 948-01-17; e-mail aibili@aibili.pt; internet www.aibili .pt; f. 1989, present location 1994; develops new products for health imaging, pharmaceutical and biotechnology cos; CEO CECÍLIA MARTINHO; Pres. JOSÉ CUNHA-VAZ.

'Câmara Pestana' Bacteriological Institute: Rua do Instituto Bacteriológico, 1169-110 Lisbon; tel. (21) 882-32-90; fax (21) 885-14-37; e-mail reitoria@reitoria.ul.pt; internet

www.ul.pt; f. 1892, present status 1911; attached to Univ. of Lisbon; areas of research incl. several domains of public health, namely diphtheria, streptococci, clinical microbiology and analysis of biology products; nat. lab for anti-tuberculosis vaccine; responsible for Portugal's anti-rabies programme; Dir Prof. JOSÉ MELO CRISTINO.

Centro de Estudos de Vectores e Doenças Infecciosas Doutor Francisco Cambournac (Dr Francisco Cambournac Centre for the Study of Vectors and Infectious Diseases): c/o Instituto Nacional de Sáude Dr Ricardo Jorge, Av. da Liberdade 5, 2965-575 Águas de Moura; tel. (26) 593-82-90; fax (26) 591-22-22; e-mail cevdi@insa.min-saude .pt; internet www.insa.pt; f. 1938 as the Malaria Institute, present name since 1987; attached to Nat. Institute of Health Dr Ricardo Jorge; research and diagnostic activities on vectors and vector-borne diseases incl. hantavirus, arbovirus, phlebovirus, arenavirus, borrelia, francisella, rickettsia, ehrlichia, anaplasma, coxiella and bartonella; vector studies incl. the determination of species present in Portugal and surveillance to prevent or minimize risk of introduction of new species; library of 3,400 vols; Dir Dr MARIA SOFIA NUNCIO.

Centro de Investigação em Desporto, Saúde e Desenvolvimento Humano (Research Centre in Sports, Health and Human Development Science): CIFOP— Sports Dept, Rua Doutor Manuel Cardona, 5000-558 Vila Real; tel. (25) 933-01-05; fax (25) 933-01-68; e-mail cidesd.geral@utad.pt; internet cidesd.org; f. 2007 by merger of 6 research units from the Polytechnic Institute of Bragança; attached to Univ. of Trás-os-Montes and Alto Douro; cross-institutional technical and scientifically multi-disciplinary unity of applied and fundamental research; 3 main domains of sports performance, health, professional and pedagogical intervention; Dir Dr ANTÓNIO JOSÉ SILVA.

Centro de Neurociências e Biologia Celular (Centre for Neuroscience and Cell Biology): Dept of Zoology, Univ. of Coimbra, 3004-51 Coimbra; tel. (23) 985-57-60; fax (23) 985-34-09; e-mail info@cnc.uc.pt; internet www.cnbc.pt; attached to Univ. of Coimbra; translates basic knowledge into clinical applications to improve diagnostics and develop novel therapeutic approaches; Pres CATARINA RESENDE DE OLIVEIRA; Vice-Pres. EUCLIDES PIRES; Vice-Pres. CARLOS FARO; Vice-Pres. LEONOR ALMEIDA.

Instituto de Biologia Molecular e Celular (Institute of Molecular and Cell Biology): Rua do Campo Alegre 823, 4150-180 Porto; tel. (22) 607-49-00; fax (22) 609-91-57; e-mail info@ibmc.up.pt; internet www.ibmc.up.pt; f. 2000; attached to Univ. of Porto; research focuses on genetic diseases, infectious diseases and immunology, neuroscience, stress and structural biology; Dir CLAUDIO SUNKEL; Vice-Dir MARIA JOÃO SARAIVA; Vice-Dir MÓNICA SOUSA; Chair. CHRISTOPHER LEAVER.

Instituto de Ciências Biomédicas de Abel Salazar (Abel Salazar Biomedical Sciences Institute): Largo Prof. Abel Salazar, 2, 4099-003 Porto; tel. (22) 206-22-00; fax (22) 206-22-32; e-mail conped@icbas.up.pt; internet www.icbas.up.pt; f. 1975; attached to Univ. of Porto; fundamental and applied research in health and life sciences; Dir ANTÓNIO SOUSA PEREIRA.

Instituto de Medicina Molecular (Institute of Molecular Medicine): Faculdade de Medicina da Universidade de Lisboa, Av. Professor Egas Moniz, 1649-028 Lisbon; tel. (21) 799-94-11; fax (21) 799-94-12; e-mail imm@fm.ul.pt; internet www.imm.ul.pt; f. 2001; attached to Min. of Science, Technology and Higher Education; research into cell and devt biology, immunology and infectious diseases, neurosciences and oncology; Pres. J. LOBO ANTUNES; Vice-Pres. JOAQUIM ALEXANDRE RIBEIRO; Exec. Dir M. CARMO-FONSECA; Sec. PATRÍCIA DA CUNHA.

Instituto de Patalogia e Imunologia da Universidade do Porto (Institute of Molecular Pathology and Immunology of the University of Porto): Rua Dr Roberto Frias s/n, 4200-465 Porto; tel. (22) 557-07-00; fax (22) 557-07-99; e-mail ipatimup@ipatimup.pt; internet www.ipatimup.pt; f. 1989; attached to Univ. of Porto; associated laboratory of Min. of Science, Technology and Higher Education; research focuses on causes and evolution of human oncologic diseases; Dir MANUEL SOBRINHO SIMÕES.

Instituto Gulbenkian de Ciência (Gulbenkian Science Institute): Apdo 14, 2781-901 Oeiras; Rua da Quinta Grande, 6, 2780-156 Oeiras; tel. (21) 440-79-00; fax (21) 440-79-70; internet www.igc.gulbenkian.pt; attached to Fundação Calouste Gulbenkian; biomedical research and education in areas of genetic basis of devt and evolution of complex systems; privileged organism-centred approaches in experimental models that incl. plants, yeast, flies and mice, and on the genetics of complex human diseases; library of 16,868 vols; Chair. for Scientific Advisory Board SYDNEY BRENNER; Dir ANTONIO COUTINHO; Deputy Dir JOSÉ MÁRIO LEITE.

Instituto Nacional de Medicina Legal (National Institute of Legal Medicine): Largo da Sé Nova, 3000-213 Coimbra; tel. (23) 985-42-20; fax (23) 983-64-70; e-mail correio@inml.mj.pt; internet www.inml.mj.pt; f. 1919; attached to Faculty of Medicine, Univ. of Coimbra; nat. instn of reference in forensic science; library of 5,000 vols, 45 periodicals; Dir Prof. Dr DUARTE NUNO PESSOA VIEIRA.

Instituto Nacional de Saúde Dr. Ricardo Jorge (National Institute of Health Dr. Ricardo Jorge): Av. Padre Cruz, 1649-016 Lisbon; tel. (21) 751-92-00; fax (21) 752-64-00; e-mail info@insa.min-saude.pt; internet www.insa.pt; f. 1899 as Central Institute of Hygiene, present status 1971; attached to Min. of Health; research and technological devt; epidemiological and health services research; external quality assurance for laboratories; diffusion of scientific culture; fostering capacities, knowledge and skills and by providing specialized services, incl. prevention of genetic diseases; nat. reference laboratory and nat. health observatory; Pres. JOSÉ PEREIRA MIGUEL.

Observatório de Medicina Integrativa—Centro de Estudos Avançados em Ciências da Saúde (Centre for Integrative Medicine—Centre for Advanced Studies in Health Sciences): Rua Joaquim Bonifácio, 21–2 Andar, 1150-195 Lisbon; tel. (21) 315-11-43; fax (21) 317-44-48; e-mail cidalia.paradelo@omi.pt; internet www.omi.pt; attached to Univ. Fernando Pessoa; promotes creation and devt of an integrative medicine combining conventional and unconventional medicines through practical work and research of multidisciplinary teams; provides advanced modules, Masters courses in alternative forms of medicine; Pres. Prof. ANGELO LUCAS.

NATURAL SCIENCES
General

Centro de Matemática (CM) (Centre for Mathematics): e-mail egs@utad.pt; internet www.utad.pt/pt/investigacao/c_matematica/index.html; attached to Univ. of Trás-os-Montes and Alto Douro; Dir Prof. Dr EMILIA JOAQUINA GIRALDES SOARES.

Centro de Química—Vila Real (CQVR) (Chemistry Centre—Vila Real): Univ. of Trás-os-Montes and Alto Douro, Chemistry Dept, Edif. de Geociências, 2 stage, 5001-801 Vila Real; tel. (25) 935-02-27; e-mail ptavares@utad.pt; internet home.utad.pt/~cqvr; f. 2001; attached to Univ. of Trás-os-Montes and Alto Douro; develops fundamental and applied chemistry research in areas of organic chemistry, natural products and food chemistry, materials chemistry, environmental chemistry; Dir PEDRO MANUEL DE MELO BANDEIRA TAVARES; Vice-Dir JOSÉ ALCIDES SILVESTRE PERES; Vice-Dir MARIA CRISTINA FIALHO OLIVEIRA.

Centro de Recursos Naturais e Ambiente (Centre for Natural Resources and the Environment): Instituto Superior Técnico, Av. Rovisco Pais 1049-001 Lisbon; tel. (21) 841-74-25; fax (21) 841-73-89; e-mail juliar@ist.utl.pt; internet cerena.ist.utl.pt; f. 2006; attached to Instituto Superior Técnico; multi-disciplinary research and advanced activities in natural resources and environment for modelling and management of natural resources, the benefit of raw materials and solid residues, geoengineering, geotechnics, biomonitoring, environmental modelling and environmental remediation; Pres. AMÍLCAR SOARES.

Institution of Marine Research: 'Centro Interdisciplinar de Coimbra', c/o Dept of Zoology, Univ. of Coimbra, 3000 Coimbra; tel. (23) 983-63-86; fax (23) 982-36-03; e-mail imar@ci.uc.pt; internet www.imar.pt; f. 1991; contributes to the scientific basis of policy support; establishes and promotes key areas of scientific research on a multiyear scale; empowers the Portuguese marine sciences community, making it competitive on a European and int. level; Pres. R. SERRÃO SANTOS; Vice-Pres. Prof. J. C. MARQUES; Vice-Pres. Prof. MANUEL GRAÇA; Vice-Pres. Prof. O. FERREIRA.

Instituto Botânico 'Dr Júlio Henriques' (Botanical Institute): Arcos do Jardim, 3049 Coimbra; tel. (239) 82-28-97; f. 1775; attached to Univ. of Coimbra; botanical garden, study in botany; library of 114,000 vols; Dir Prof. Dr J. FIRMINO MOREIRA MESQUITA; publs *Boletim*, *Index Seminum*, *Memórias* and *Anuário* of Sociedade Broteriana.

Instituto da Conservação da Natureza e da Biodiversidade (Institute for Nature Conservation and Biodiversity): Rua de Santa Marta 55, 1169-230 Lisbon; tel. (21) 350-79-00; fax (21) 350-79-84; e-mail icnb@icnb.pt; internet www.icnb.pt; f. 1993 as Instituto da Conservação da Natureza (ICN); attached to Min. of Environment and Territorial Planning; sustainable management of wild animal and plant species; designation of land and marine protected areas; integrates the objectives of nature conservation and sustainable use of natural resources into planning policies and sectorial policies; implements nat. strategy for nature conservation and biodiversity and develops nat. programme for nature conservation; warrants compliance with both EU and int. law in matters related to nature conservation and biodiversity; Pres. TITO ROSA; Vice-Pres. FÁTIMA FERNANDES; Vice-Pres. CARLOS FIGUEIREDO.

Instituto de Investigação Científica 'Bento da Rocha Cabral' (Institute of Scientific Research): Calçada Bento Rocha Cabral 14, 1257-047 Lisbon; tel. and fax (21) 388-29-93; e-mail geral@ircabral.org; internet www.ircabral.org; f. 1922; biochemical research, histology and embryology, bacteriology, physiology, history and philosophy of science; Dir MANUEL DIAMANTINO PIRES

BICHO; publs *Relatórios*, *Travaux de Laboratoire*.

Sociedade Afonso Chaves (Afonso Chaves Society): Edifício do Museu Carlos Machado, Rua de Santo André, Apdo 258, Ponta Delgada Codex, 9500-903 The Azores; tel. (296) 28-38-14; f. 1932; ethnography, natural history, geophysics and geology of the Azores; Pres. Prof. ANTÓNIO MANUEL DE FRIAS MARTINS; Sec. Dr CARLOS MEDEIROS; publ. *Açoreana* (1 a year).

Biological Sciences

Centro de Genómica e Biotecnologia (CGB) (Centre for Genomics and Biotechnology): e-mail hgp@utad.pt; internet www.utad.pt/pt/investigacao/cgb/index.html; attached to Univ. of Tras-os-Montes and Alto Douro; Dir Prof. Dr HENRIQUE GUEDES PINTO.

Instituto de Investigação das Pescas e do Mar (INRB) (Institute of Fisheries and Maritime Research): Av. de Brasília, 1449-006 Lisbon; tel. (21) 302-70-00; fax (21) 301-59-48; e-mail ipimar@ipimar.pt; internet inrb.pt/ipimar; f. 1978; attached to Min. of Agriculture, Rural Devt and Fisheries; marine biology, fisheries, aquaculture, marine environment, aquatic products technology; library of 11,000 monographs, 2,000 periodicals; Dir LEONOR NUNES; publs *IPIMAR Divulgação*, *Notícias IPIMAR*, *Publicações Avulsas*, *Relatórios Científicos e Técnicos*.

Jardim Botânico (Botanical Gardens): Jardim Botânico da Universidade de Lisboa, Rua da Escola Politécnica 58, 1250-102 Lisbon; tel. (21) 392-18-00; fax (21) 397-08-82; e-mail jbactividades@museus.ul.pt; internet www.jb.ul.pt; f. 1878; attached to Univ. of Lisbon; taxonomy and systematics, biomonitoring, biodiversity and conservation; library of 18,000 vols; Dir Prof. Dr MARIA AMÉLIA LOUÇÃO; publs *Delectus Sporarum et Seminum* (1 a year), *Portugaliae Acta Biologica* (irregular), *Revista de Biologia* (irregular).

Physical Sciences

Instituto de Plasmas e Fusão Nuclear (Institute for Plasma and Nuclear Fusion): Av. Rovisco Pais, 1049-001 Lisbon; tel. (21) 841-76-96; fax (21) 841-78-19; e-mail ipfn@ipfn.ist.utl.pt; internet www.ipfn.ist.utl.pt; f. 2008, by merger of Centro de Fusão Nuclear (CFN) and Centro de Física de Plasmas (CFP); attached to Instituto Superior Técnico; carries out research projects and supports formation actions and scientific divulgation in its thematic areas; Pres. CARLOS VARANDAS.

Instituto de Meteorologia (Institute of Meteorology): Rua C do Aeroporto, 1749-077 Lisbon; tel. (21) 844-70-00; fax (21) 844-70-40; e-mail informacoes@meteo.pt; internet www.meteo.pt; f. 1946; provides information to the population, socio-economic activities and public entities adjusted to their needs pursuing nat. politics in meteorology, climate and geophysics; library of 34,000 vols; Pres. ADÉRITO VICENTE SERRÃO; publs *Açores* (1 a year), *Anuário Climatológico de Portugal*, *Anuário Sismológico de Portugal* (1 a year), *Boletim Climatológico Mensal dos Açores* (12 a year), *Boletim Meteorológico para a Agricultura* (36 a year), *Boletim Sismológico Preliminar do Continente e Madeira* (12 a year), *Projecto 12 do PIDDAC* (12 a year), *Resumos Meteorológicos para a Aeronáutica* (12 a year), *Revista do Instituto Nacional de Meteorologia e Geofísica* (4 a year).

Observatório Astronómico da Universidade de Coimbra (Coimbra Univ. Astronomical Observatory): Santa Clara, 3040-004 Coimbra; tel. (239) 80-23-70; fax (239) 80-23-79; e-mail obsastuc@mat.uc.pt; internet www

.mat.uc.pt/~obsv; f. 1772, present location 1951; library of 3,500 vols; education and research in astronomy and geophysics; Dir Asst Prof. JOÃO FERNANDES; publs *Anais do Observatorio Astronomico da Universidade de Coimbra* (12 a year), *Efemérides Astronómicas* (1 a year), *Publicações* (60' and 70').

Observatório Astronómico de Lisboa (Lisbon Astronomical Observatory): Tapada da Ajuda, 1349-018 Lisbon; tel. (21) 361-67-30; fax (21) 361-67-50; e-mail info@oal.ul.pt; internet www.oal.ul.pt; f. 1861; part of the Faculty of Sciences, Univ. of Lisbon, since 1995; the country's official timekeeper; carries out scientific research through its attached site; provides astronomical information to the public and civil soc.; promotes teaching of astronomy in schools; library of 13,500 vols; Dir Prof. RUI JORGE AGOSTINHO; Deputy Dir Prof. PAUL CRAWFORD; publs *Dados Astronómicos* (1 a year), *O Observatório* (12 a year).

Attached Site:

Centro de Astronomia e Astrofísica da Universidade de Lisboa (Astronomy and Astrophysics Centre of the University of Lisbon): Tapada da Ajuda, Edifício Leste, 2°, 1349-018 Lisbon; tel. (21) 361-67-39; fax (21) 361-67-52; e-mail caaul@oal.ul.pt; internet www.oal.ul.pt/caaul; f. 2000; research into extragalactic and galactic astrophysics, the Sun, planetary and space sciences, cosmology and gravitational physics; Scientific Coordinator Dr JOSE AFONSO.

RELIGION, SOCIOLOGY AND ANTHROPOLOGY

Centro de Investigação em Antropologia e Saude (Research Centre for Anthropology and Health): tel. (239) 85-41-00; fax (239) 82-34-91; e-mail cia@ci.uc.pt; internet www.uc.pt/cia; f. 1994; study of human health, disease and well-being in past and living populations from a biocultural perspective; operates through 4 sections: anthropology of past populations; genetics, population and disease; human biology, health and society; studies in material culture; library of 44,790 vols, 330 periodicals; Coordinator Prof. Dra CRISTINA PADEZ; publ. *Antropologia Portuguesa*.

Comissão Nacional de Arte Sacra e do Património Cultural da Igreja (National Committee for Sacred Art and the Cultural Heritage of the Church): Santuário de Fátima, Apdo 31, 2496 Fátima; tel. (249) 53-33-47; fax (249) 53-33-43; f. 1989; Pres. ANTÓNIO FRANCISCO MARQUES; Gen. Sec. Dr JOSÉ ANTÓNIO FALCÃO.

Instituto de Ciências Sociais (Institute of Social Sciences): Av. Prof. Aníbal de Bettencourt 9, 1600-189 Lisbon; tel. (21) 780-47-00; fax (21) 794-02-74; e-mail instituto.ciencias .sociais@ics.ul.pt; internet www.ics.ul.pt; f. 1962, present status 2002, present building 2003; attached to Univ. of Lisbon; studies contemporary socs with spec. emphasis on Portugal and socs and cultures with which Portugal has an historical relationship, either in Europe or in other regions of the world; library of 40,000 books, 313 periodicals; Dir Prof. JORGE VALA.

Instituto Português de Artes e Tradições Populares (Portuguese Institute of Folk Arts and Traditions): Travessa do Passadiço 1, 7540 Santiago do Cacém; tel. (269) 82-63-80; f. 1979; Dir Prof. Dr PERE FERRÉ; Gen. Sec. Dr JOSÉ ANTÓNIO FALCÃO; publs *Biblioteca de Artes e Tradições Populares*, *Novos Inquéritos*.

TECHNOLOGY

Centro Aquicola do Rio Ave (Inland Fisheries Station): 4481 Vila do Conde; tel. (252) 63-12-41; fax (252) 63-25-94; f. 1886; fresh water fisheries and aquaculture; 15 staff; library of 1,000 vols; Dir EUARDO LENCASTRE.

Instituto Hidrográfico (Hydrographic Institute): Rua das Trinas 49, 1249-093 Lisbon; tel. (21) 094-30-00; fax (21) 094-32-99; e-mail mail@hidrografico.pt; internet www.hidrografico.pt; f. 1960; hydrographic surveys, physical oceanography, magnetic compass adjustments, laboratory; library of 12,000 vols; Dir-Gen. Vice-Admiral AGOSTINHO RAMOS DA SILVA; publs *Anais*, *Hidrográfico* (1 a year), *Hidromar*.

Laboratório Nacional de Energia e Geologia (LNEG) (National Laboratory for Energy and Geology): Estrada do Paço do Lumiar 22, 1649-038 Lisbon; tel. (21) 092-46-00; fax (21) 716-09-01; e-mail info@lneg.pt; internet www.lneg.pt; f. 1977; attached to Min. of the Economy, Innovation and Devt; research and devt in technological innovation for application in the fields of energy, new systems, processes and products, environmental management and sustainability, geological resources and hazards, public health and safety, defence and space, laboratory support and testing; library of 38,000 vols; Pres. MARIA TERESA COSTA PEREIRA DA SILVA PONCE DE LEÃO.

Attached Centres:

Campus de Coimbra (Coimbra Branch): Rua Coronel Júlio Veiga Simão-Loreto, 3020 Coimbra; tel. (239) 82-37-97; fax (239) 82-90-00; e-mail info@lneg.pt; internet www.lneg.pt.

Centro de Dados Geológico-Mineiro Alfragide (Geological and Mining Data Centre, Alfragide): Estrada da Portela, Zambujal-Alfragide, Apdo 7586, 2611-901 Amadora; tel. (21) 092-46-00; fax (21) 471-90-18; e-mail atendimento@ineti.pt; internet www.ineti.pt/campus/campus_frameset.aspx.

Centro de Estudos Geológicos e Mineiros de Beja (Geological and Mining Studies Centre, Beja): Rua Frei Amador Arrais 39, r/c, Apdo 104, 7801-902 Beja; tel. (28) 431-13-10; fax (28) 432-59-74; e-mail inetibeja@ineti.pt; internet e-geo.ineti.pt/centros/centro_beja.htm; f. 1944.

Laboratório de S. Mamede de Infesta: Rua da Amieira, Apdo 1089, 4466-901 S. Mamede de Infesta; tel. (22) 040-00-00; fax (22) 951-40-40; e-mail atendimento@ineti .pt; internet www.ineti.pt; f. 1953; Dir MÁRIO RUI MACHADO LEITE.

Museu Geológico de Portugal (Geological Museum of Portugal): see under Museums and Art Galleries.

Laboratório Nacional de Engenharia Civil (National Civil Engineering Laboratory): Av. Brasil 101, 1700-066 Lisbon; tel. (21) 844-30-00; fax (21) 844-30-11; e-mail lnec@lnec.pt; internet www.lnec.pt; f. 1946; attached to Min. of Public Works, Transport and Communications; pursues public policies, which are under the responsibility of the various mins; provides expert support to public authorities in various public admin. sectors, particularly with regard to quality and safety of works, protection and re-qualification of natural and built patrimony, as well as technological upgrading and innovation in bldg construction sector; library of 142,000 vols; Pres. CARLOS ALBERTO DE BRITO PINA; publs *Especificações* (standards, regulations), *Memórias* (technical papers).

Libraries and Archives

Agualva-Cacém

Biblioteca Municipal de Agualva-Cacém (Agualva-Cacém Municipal Library): Praceta das Descobertas 20A, 2735-095 Caçem; tel. (21) 432-80-39; fax (21) 432-80-41; f. 1997; 11,452 vols, 21 periodicals.

Amadora

Bibliotecas Municipais da Amadora (Amadora Municipal Libraries): Rua Capitão Plácido de Abreu, Venteira, 2700 Amadora; tel. (21) 494-80-40; fax (21) 491-49-50; e-mail biblioteca.amadora@clix.pt; internet www .cm-amadora.pt/bibliotecas; f. 1960.

Angra do Heroísmo

Biblioteca Pública e Arquivo Regional de Angra do Heroísmo (Public Library and Archives of Angra do Heroísmo): Palácio Bettencourt, Rua da Rosa 49, 9700-171 Angra do Heroísmo, The Azores; tel. (295) 40-10-00; fax (295) 40-10-09; e-mail bpar .angra.info@azores.gov.pt; internet www .bparah.azores.gov.pt/html/bparah-biblioteca+documental+e+publica.html; f. 1956; 250,000 vols, 3.5m. MSS; Dir Dr MARCOLINO CANDEIAS COELHO LOPES; publs *Arquivo Distrital de Angra do Heroísmo*, *Boletim da Biblioteca Pública*.

Braga

Arquivo Distrital de Braga (Braga District Archives): Universidade do Minho, Largo do Paço, 4704-553 Braga; tel. (253) 60-11-77; fax (253) 60-11-80; e-mail sec@adb .uminho.pt; internet www.adb.uminho.pt; f. 1917, present status 1976; attached to Universidade do Minho; 1,498 linear m of documents since 6th century; Dir Dr ELÍSIO SILVA MAIA ARAÚJO.

Biblioteca Pública de Braga (Braga Public Library): Largo do Paço, 4704-553 Braga; tel. and fax (253) 60-11-35; e-mail bpb@bpb .uminho.pt; internet www.bpb.uminho.pt; f. 1841; attached to Universidade do Minho; 500,000 vols, 27,000 periodicals, 53 incunabula; Dir Dr ELÍSIO SILVA MAIA ARAÚJO.

Bragança

Arquivo Distrital de Bragança (Bragança District Archives): Rua Miguel Torga, 5300-037 Bragança; tel. (273) 30-02-70; fax (273) 30-02-79; e-mail mail@adbgc.dgarq.gov.pt; internet adbgc.dgarq.gov.pt; f. 1916; 2,072 linear m of documents; Dir Dr ALDA BERENGUEL.

Cascais

Biblioteca 'Condes de Castro Guimarães': Av. Rei Humberto II de Itália, Parque Marechal Carmona, 2750-327 Cascais; tel. (21) 481-53-26; fax (21) 482-53-81; f. 1930; 25,000 vols; history, art, philosophy, literature, archaeology, local history; Librarian ANTÓNIO MANUEL GONÇALVES DE CARVALHO; publ. *Arquivo de Cascais—Boletim Cultural do Município* (1 a year).

Coimbra

Arquivo da Universidade de Coimbra (Archives of Coimbra University): Universidade de Coimbra, Rua de S. Pedro 2, 3000-370 Coimbra; tel. (23) 985-98-55; fax (23) 982-09-87; e-mail auc-geral@auc.uc.pt; internet www.uc.pt/auc; f. 1901; Dir Prof. Dr JOSÉ PEDRO MATOS PAIVA; Deputy Dir JÚLIO DE SOUSA RAMOS; publ. *Boletim* (1 a year).

Biblioteca Geral Universidade de Coimbra (General Library University of Coimbra): Largo da Porta Férrea, 3000-447 Coimbra; tel. (23) 985-98-15; fax (23) 982-71-35; e-mail secretaria@bg.uc.pt; internet www.uc.pt/bguc; f. 1291; 800,000 vols, 27,300 periodicals; 7 faculty br. libraries; Dir Prof. Dr CARLOS MANUEL BAPTISTA FIOLHAIS; Deputy Dir ANTÓNIO EUGÉNIO MAIA DO AMARAL; publs *Acta Univ. Conimbrigensis*, *Boletim da Biblioteca Geral da Universidade de Coimbra* (1 a year), *Divulgação Bibliográfica*, *Revista da Universidade de Coimbra* (1 a year), *Sumários das Publicações Periódicas Portuguesas* (10 a year).

Attached Library:

Biblioteca Joanina: Largo da Porta Férrea, 3000-447 Coimbra; tel. (23) 985-98-41; fax (23) 982-71-35; e-mail joanina@bg.uc.pt; internet bibliotecajoanina.uc.pt; f. 1728; 55,935 vols; Dir Prof. Dr CARLOS FIOLHAIS.

Biblioteca Municipal de Coimbra (Coimbra Public Library): Rua Pedro Monteiro, 3000-329 Coimbra; tel. (23) 970-26-30; fax (23) 970-24-96; e-mail biblioteca@cm-coimbra.pt; internet www.cm-coimbra.pt/biblioteca; f. 1922; network of 8 small annexe libraries and a mobile library; 613,157 vols, 3,084 video cassettes and DVDs, 8,463 audio cassettes and CDs, 30,000 journals, 973 books in braille, 1,471 audiobooks; Chief Librarian MARIA-JOSÉ MIRANDA; publ. *Arquivo Coimbrão: boletim da Biblioteca Municipal de Coimbra* (irregular).

Évora

Biblioteca Pública de Évora (Évora Public Library): Largo Conde de Vila Flor, 7000-804 Évora; tel. (26) 676-93-30; fax (26) 676-93-31; e-mail bpevora@bpe.pt; f. 1805; 644,000 vols; Dir JOSÉ ANTÓNIO CALIXTO.

Funchal

Arquivo Regional da Madeira (Madeira Regional Archives): Caminho dos Álamos 35, Santo António, 9020-064 Funchal; tel. (29) 170-84-00; fax (29) 170-84-02; e-mail arm@arquivo-madeira.org; internet www.arquivo-madeira.org; f. 1931, present name 1980, present bldg 2005; 8,500 vols on specialized history, 300,000 MSS; memories of admin. of the islands of Madeira and Porto Santo from dawn of their settlement to rise of process of autonomy in 20th century; Dir MARIA FÁTIMA ARAÚJO DE BARROS FERREIRA; publ. *Arquivo Histórico da Madeira*.

Biblioteca Municipal do Funchal (Municipal Library): Palácio de São Pedro, Rua da Mouraria 31, 9000-047 Funchal; tel. (291) 22-28-49; fax (291) 22-77-30; e-mail bmfunchal@gmail.com; f. 1838; 150,000 vols; Librarian RICARDO ARAUJO.

Biblioteca Pública Regional da Madeira (Madeira Regional Public Library): Caminho dos Álamos 35, Santo António, 9020-064 Funchal, Madeira; tel. (291) 70-84-10; fax (291) 70-84-12; e-mail geral@bprmadeira.org; internet www.bprmadeira.org; f. 1979 as Library of Contemporary Documentation, present name 2003, present status 2007; legal deposit library; 200,000 vols; Dir MARIA DA PAZ DE AZEREDO PAIS.

Guimarães

Biblioteca Municipal Raul Brandão (Municipal Library): Largo Cónego José Maria Gomes, 4800-419 Guimarães; tel. (253) 51-57-10; e-mail biblioteca@cm-guimaraes.pt; internet www.bmrb.pt; f. 1992; 70,000 monographs, 6,600 audiovisual documents, about 1,000 electronic documents, 510 periodicals and a local fund with approx. 21,500 vols and postcards, posters, maps, etc.; incl. local studies library.

Horta

Biblioteca Pública e Arquivo Regional João José da Graça—Horta (João José da Graça—Horta Public Library and Regional Archive): Rua Walter Bensaúde 14, 9900-142 Horta, Faial, The Azores; tel. (292) 20-25-50; fax (292) 39-13-44; e-mail bpar.horta.info@azores.gov.pt; internet edt-gra.azores.gov.pt/portal/pt/entidades/pgra-drcultura-bpah; f. 1886, present location 2008; 60,000 vols; Librarian MANUEL PITA SÃO BENTO.

Leiria

Arquivo Distrital de Leiria (District Archives Leiria): Apdo 1145, 2401-801, Leiria; Rua Marcos Portugal 4, 2400-179 Leiria; tel. (244) 82-00-50; fax (244) 82-00-59; e-mail mail@adlra.dgarq.gov.pt; internet adleiria.pt; f. 1916, present bldg 1997; 30,000 books, 496 microfilms; Dir ACÁCIO FERNANDO DOS SANTOS LOPES DE SOUSA.

Lisbon

Arquivo Histórico Militar (Military Historical Archives): Largo dos Caminhos de Ferro 2, 1100-105 Lisbon; tel. (21) 884-25-63; fax (21) 884-25-14; f. 1921; Dir Tenente-Coronel ANICETO AFONSO; publs *Boletim*, *Noticias* (2 a year).

Arquivo Histórico Parlamentar (Parliamentary Historical Archives): Palácio de S. Bento, 1249-068 Lisbon; tel. (21) 391-90-00; fax (21) 391-74-70; e-mail manuela.magalhaes@ar.parlamento.pt; internet www.parlamento.pt; 180,000 vols; history, law, economics, statistics and texts from int. orgs; Dir MANUELA MAGALHÃES.

Arquivo Municipal de Lisboa (Municipal Archives of Lisbon):internet arquivomunicipal.cm-lisboa.pt; f. 12th century; publ. *Cadernos*.

Constituent Centres:

Arquivo do Arco do Cego: Rua Nunes Claro 8A, 1000-209 Lisbon; tel. (21) 841-11-70; fax (21) 848-46-38; e-mail arqmun.acego@cm-lisboa.pt; f. 1919; documents since 1834.

Arquivo Fotográfico: Rua da Palma 246, 1100-394 Lisbon; tel. (21) 884-40-60; fax (21) 886-16-14; e-mail arqmun.fotografico@cm-lisboa.pt; f. 1942; images since end of 19th century.

Arquivo Histórico: Rua B, Bairro da Liberdade, lote 3 a 6, piso 1, 1070-017 Lisbon; tel. (21) 380-71-00; fax (21) 380-71-12; e-mail dba.dga@cm-lisboa.pt; f. 1931; documents since 12th century.

Arquivo Intermédio: Rua B, Bairro da Liberdade, lote 3 a 6, piso 0, 1070-017 Lisbon; tel. (21) 380-71-00; fax (21) 380-71-99; e-mail arqmun.intermedio@cm-lisboa.pt; f. 1985; city admin. documents.

Biblioteca Central de Marinha (Naval Library): Praça do Império, 1400-206 Lisbon; tel. (21) 365-85-20; fax (21) 365-85-23; e-mail biblioteca.marinha@marinha.pt; internet www.marinha.pt/pt/amarinha/actividade/areacultural/biblioteca; f. 1835; valuable edns; 126,616 vols; Dir Alm. RUI VILAS BOAS TAVARES.

Biblioteca da Academia das Ciências de Lisboa (Library of the Academy of Sciences): Rua da Academia das Ciências 19, 1249-122 Lisbon; tel. (21) 321-97-30; fax (21) 342-03-95; e-mail biblioteca@acad-ciencias.pt; internet www.acad-ciencias.pt; f. 1779; Portuguese language and culture; 1,000,000 vols, 3,000 MSS, 100 incunabula; Dir Prof. Dr JUSTINO MENDES DE ALMEIDA; Librarian LEONOR PINTO.

Biblioteca da Assembleia da República (Library of the Assembly of the Republic): Palácio de S. Bento, 1249-068 Lisbon; tel. (21) 391-41-41; fax (21) 391-41-45; e-mail bib@ar.parlamento.pt; internet sisgerar.parlamento.pt/sitebib/site/homepage.htm; f. 1836, present name 1974; 200,000 vols; spec. collns:

nat. legislation and old books from the libraries of religious orders; offers its services to mems of parliament, admin., parliamentary bodies and officials, and staff of parliamentary groups; also open to gen. public; Dir JOSÉ LUÍS M. TOMÉ.

Biblioteca de Ajuda (Ajuda Library): Palácio Nacional da Ajuda, 1349-021 Lisbon; tel. and fax (21) 363-85-92; e-mail bib_ajuda@bnportugal.pt; f. 1756, present location 1880; 100,000 vols, 30,000 MSS, 5,000 music MSS, 213 incunabula; Dir Dr CRISTINA PINTO BASTO.

Biblioteca de Arte da Fundação Calouste Gulbenkian (Art Library of Calouste Gulbenkian Foundation): Av. de Berna 45A, 1067-001 Lisbon; tel. (21) 782-35-98; fax (21) 782-30-44; e-mail artlib@gulbenkian.pt; internet www.biblarte.gulbenkian.pt; f. 1968; reference library for research in the fields of fine arts and architecture; 353,200 vols specializing in art, monographs, periodicals, architectural drawings, photographs; Dir ANA PAULA GORDO.

Biblioteca do Exército (Army Library): Largo do Outeirinho da Amendoeira, 1100-386 Lisbon; tel. (21) 884-24-56; fax (21) 884-25-26; e-mail bibex.director@mail.exercito.pt; internet www.exercito.pt; f. 1884; 100,000 vols; Dir Col FRANCISCO DIAS COSTA.

Biblioteca e Arquivo Histórico do Ministério das Obras Públicas, Transportes e Comunicações (Library and Historical Archive of the Ministry of Public Works, Transport and Communications): Rua Vale de Pereiro 4, 1250-271 Lisbon; tel. (21) 319-42-00; fax (21) 319-42-18; e-mail biblioteca@sg.moptc.pt; internet www.bahop.moptc.pt; f. 1852; collects, treats and conserves cases completed and printed books and MSS belonging to the min.; 13,000 vols, documents since 16th century, 200,000 textual documents on industry, agriculture, forestry, trade, public works, etc., 1,100 periodicals; Dir Dra PAULA CRISTINA UCHA.

Biblioteca Francisco Pereira de Moura (Higher Institute of Economics and Management Library): Instituto Superior de Economia e Gestão, Rua do Quelhas 6, 1200-781 Lisbon; tel. (21) 392-28-88; fax (21) 397-26-84; e-mail biblio@iseg.utl.pt; internet www.iseg.utl.pt/biblioteca; f. 1911 as Higher Institute of Commerce; attached to Universidade Técnica de Lisboa; European documentation centre of Universidade Técnica de Lisboa and depository library of World Bank; Scientific Dir Prof. Dr JOSÉ PEREIRINHA.

Biblioteca Municipal Central (Central Municipal Library): Palácio Galveias, Largo do Campo Pequeno, 1049-046 Lisbon; tel. (21) 780-30-20; fax (21) 780-30-57; e-mail bib.galveias@cm-lisboa.pt; internet blx.cm-lisboa.pt; f. 1931; 332,673 vols; Dir Dra MANUELA RÊGO.

Biblioteca Nacional de Portugal (National Library of Portugal): Campo Grande 83, 1749-081 Lisbon; tel. (21) 798-20-00; fax (21) 798-21-38; e-mail bn@bnportugal.pt; internet www.bnportugal.pt; f. 1796; 3,000,000 vols, 50,000 newspapers and periodicals, 36,000 MSS; collects, processes and preserves nation's bibliographic heritage and makes it available to intellectual and scientific community; uses latest technologies to conduct online bibliographic research from anywhere in the world; Dir Dr JORGE COUTO; publ. *Leituras* (2 a year).

DGARQ—Direcção-Geral de Arquivos (Directorate General for the Portuguese Archives): Alameda da Universidade, Campo Grande, 1649-010 Lisbon; tel. (21) 781-15-00; fax (21) 793-72-30; e-mail secretariado@dgarq.gov.pt; internet www.dgarq.gov.pt; f. 2007; attached to Min. of Culture; colln dates from 9th century; Nat. Archives network, processing and preservation of conventional and digital records; Dir SILVESTRE LACERDA; publ. *DGARQ Boletim* (news and information, 4 a year).

Serviço de Biblioteca e Documentação Diplomática (Library and Diplomatic Documentation Service): Ministério dos Negócios Estrangeiros, Palácio das Necessidades Largo do Rilvas, 1399-030 Lisbon; tel. (21) 394-63-05; fax (21) 394-60-29; internet www .mne.gov.pt/mne/pt/ministerio/id/biblioteca; f. 1994, present status 2007; attached to Min. of Foreign Affairs; 80,000 vols; Dir MARIA HELENA LOPES DE NEVES PINTO.

Mafra

Biblioteca do Palácio Nacional de Mafra (Mafra National Palace Library): Terreiro de D. João V, 2640-492 Mafra; tel. (261) 81-75-50; fax (261) 81-19-47; e-mail pnmafra@ippar .pt; f. 18th century; 40,000 vols; notable colln of rare books, esp. incunabula and books from the 17th–18th centuries; Dir MARIA MARGARIDA MONTENEGRO.

Ponta Delgada

Biblioteca Pública e Arquivo Regional de Ponta Delgada (Ponta Delgada Public Library and Regional Archive): Largo do Colégio, 9500-054 Ponta Delgada, São Miguel, The Azores; tel. (29) 628-20-85; fax (29) 628-12-16; e-mail bpar.pdelgada.info@ azores.gov.pt; internet www.bparpd.azores .gov.pt/index.html; f. 1841; 120,000 vols in spec. collns, 40,000 monographs, 5,000 serials, 3,000 m of archive material; Dir CARLOS GUILHERME RILEY.

Porto

Arquivo Distrital do Porto (District Archives): Rua das Taipas 90, 4050-598 Porto; tel. (22) 339-51-70; fax (22) 339-51-79; e-mail info@adporto.org; internet www.adporto.pt; f. 1931, present location 1995; attached to Min. of Culture; 200,000 vols; Dir MARIA JOÃO PIRES DE LIMA; publ. *Boletim do Arquivo Distrital do Porto*.

Arquivo Histórico Municipal do Porto (Municipal Historical Archives): Rua da Alfândega 10, 4050-029 Porto; tel. (22) 206-04-00; fax (22) 206-04-01; e-mail dmarquivos@cm-porto.pt; internet www .cm-porto.pt; f. 1980; 5,000 vols; colln incl. numerous series handwritten scrolls, illuminated MSS, drawings, photographs, etc.; Head of Section MARIA HELENA DE PAIVA GIL BRAGA.

Biblioteca Pública Municipal do Porto (Municipal Library): Rua D. João IV (ao Jardim de São Lázaro), 4049-017 Porto; tel. (22) 519-34-80; fax (22) 519-34-88; e-mail bpmp@cm-porto.pt; internet www-porto .pt; f. 1833, present location 1842; 1,390,000 vols, 9,411 MSS, 246 incunabula; Dir CARLA FONSECA; publ. *Biblioteca Portucalensis* (1 a year).

Santarém

Biblioteca Municipal de Santarém (Municipal Library of Santarém): Rua Braamcamp Freire, 2000-094 Santarém; tel. (24) 333-02-40; fax (24) 330-44-79; e-mail biblioteca@cm-santarem.pt; internet www .cm-santarem.pt/cultura/biblioteca/paginas/ default.aspx; f. 1880; 100,000 vols; Librarian Dr LUIS NAZARÉ FERREIRA.

Setúbal

Arquivo Distrital de Setúbal (District Archives of Setúbal): Rua Prof. Borges de Macedo, Manteigadas Sul, 2910-001 Setúbal; tel. (26) 570-99-00; fax (26) 570-99-35; e-mail mail@adstb.dgarq.gov.pt; internet adstb .dgarq.gov.pt; f. 1965, present bldg 2001;

4,800 m of documents; documents since 16th century; Dir GLÓRIA SANTOS.

Sintra

Arquivo Municipal de Sintra/Arquivo Histórico (Sintra Municipal Archives/Historical Archives): Palácio Valenças, Rua Visconde de Monserrate 1, 2710-591 Sintra; tel. (21) 923-69-09; fax (21) 923-87-78; e-mail geral@cm-sintra.pt; internet www.cm-sintra .pt; f. 1939; 60,000 documents since 14th century.

Biblioteca Municipal de Sintra: Rua Gomes de Amorim 12/14, 2710-569 Sintra; tel. (21) 923-61-70; fax (21) 923-61-79; e-mail geral@cm-sintra.pt; internet www.cm-sintra .pt; f. 1939; 60,000 vols.

Torres Novas

Biblioteca Municipal Gustavo Pinto Lopes: Jardim das Rosas, 2350-444 Torres Novas; tel. (249) 81-03-10; fax (249) 81-03-19; e-mail biblioteca@cm-torresnovas.pt; internet biblioteca.cm-torresnovas.pt; f. 1937; 70,000 vols; Librarian and Dir Dr LUÍS FILIPE CORREIA DIAS.

Vila Nova de Gaia

Biblioteca Municipal de Vila Nova de Gaia (Municipal Library): Rua de Angola, 4430-014 Vila Nova de Gaia; tel. (22) 374-56-70; fax (22) 374-56-79; e-mail bmgaia@ gaianima.pt; internet www.bmgaia.gaianima .pt; f. 1933; 101,000 vols, 2,246 periodicals; Coordinator CRISTINA MARGARIDE.

Vila Real

Arquivo Distrital de Vila Real (Vila Real District Archives): Av. Almeida Lucena 5, 5000-660 Vila Real; tel. (25) 933-08-20; fax (25) 932-57-12; e-mail correio@advrl.org.pt; internet www.advrl.org.pt; f. 1965, present status 2007; 31,590 vols, 3,000 m of documents, 180 m of Portuguese legislation since 1715; Dir PAULO MESQUITA GUIMARÃES; publs *Arquivos de Trás-os-Montes e Alto Douro— Instrumentos de Descrição*, *Estudos Transmontanos e Durienses*, *Memórias de Vila Real*, *Memórias do Tempo*.

Viseu

Arquivo Distrital de Viseu (Viseu District Archives): Largo de Santa Cristina, 3504-515 Viseu; tel. (23) 243-03-80; fax (23) 242-18-00; e-mail mail@advis.dgarq.gov.pt; internet www.ad-viseu.com; f. 1932, present bldg 2003; 450,000 documents; collns of scrolls, books, music and books of liturgy; Dir MARIA DAS DORES ALMEIDA HENRIQUES.

Museums and Art Galleries

Alenquer

Museu Municipal 'Hipólito Cabaço' (Municipal Museum 'Hipólito Cabaço'): Rua Maria Milne e Carmo 2, 2580-319 Alenquer; tel. and fax (26) 373-33-04; e-mail museu@ cm-alenquer.pt; f. 1975; archaeological, historical and ethnographical collections; 4,000 exhibits; Dir JOÃO JOSÉ FERNANDES GOMES.

Alpiarça

Casa dos Patudos—Museu de Alpiarça (Alpiarça Museum): Rua José Relvas, 2090-102 Alpiarça; tel. (24) 355-83-21; fax (24) 355-64-44; e-mail museudospatudos@cm-alpiarca .pt; internet www.cm-alpiarca.pt; f. 1960; residence of José Relvas; art collns of José Relvas; furniture, porcelains, paintings, tapestries; library of 4,000 vols incl. historical archive; Dir Dr NUNO PRATES.

Amadora

Centro Ciência Viva de Amadora (Interactive Science Centre of Amadora): Rua Gonçalves Ramos 54B, 2700-036 Amadora; tel. (21) 491-13-13; fax (21) 493-09-00; e-mail info@amadora.cienciaviva.pt; internet amadora.cienciaviva.pt; f. 2003; interactive displays on scientific and technological topics, incl. town planning and electricity; Exec. Dir MARTA VELOSO.

Angra do Heroísmo

Museu de Angra do Heroísmo (Angra do Heroísmo Museum): Ladeira de São Francisco, 9701-875 Angra do Heroísmo, Ilha Terceira, The Azores; tel. (29) 524-08-00; fax (29) 524-08-17; e-mail museu.angra .info@azores.gov.pt; internet museu-angra .azores.gov.pt; f. 1949; historical museum; permanent exhibition on the history of the Azores Islands; paintings, ceramics, furniture, sculpture, ethnography, arms, guns, carriages; Dir MARIA HELENA DE MENESES ORMONDE.

Braga

'D. Diogo de Sousa' Museu Regional de Arqueologia ('D. Diogo de Sousa' Regional Archaeological Museum): Rua dos Bombeiros Voluntários, 4700-025 Braga; tel. (25) 327-37-06; fax (25) 361-23-66; e-mail mdds@ imc-ip.pt; internet mdds.imc-ip.pt; f. 1918 as D. Diogo de Sousa Museum of Archaeology and Arts; colln ranges from the Palaeolithic to the Middle Ages; visits to local archaeological sites; library of 8,000 vols; Dir Dra MARIA ISABEL CUNHA E SILVA.

Bragança

Museu do Abade de Baçal (Abbot of Baçal Museum): Rua Conselheiro Abílio Beça 27, 5300-011 Bragança; tel. (27) 333-15-95; fax (27) 332-32-42; e-mail mabadebacal@imc-ip .pt; internet www.ipmuseus.pt; f. 1915 as Regional Museum of Art Works, Parts and Archaeological Numismatics of Bragança, present name 1935; archaeology, epigraphy, sacred art, paintings, gold items, numismatics, furniture, ethnography; Dir ANA MARIA AFONSO.

Cascais

Museu 'Condes de Castro Guimarães': Av. Rei Humberto II de Itália, Parque Marechal Carmona, 2750 Cascais; tel. (21) 481-53-04; fax (21) 482-54-04; e-mail mccg@ cm-cascais.pt; internet www.cm-cascais.pt; f. 1931; *Crónica* about the kings of the first dynasty of Duarte Galvão, 16th-century illuminated *Codex* on parchment, 17th-century Indo-Portuguese counting frames, paintings, oriental porcelain; furniture, silverware; library of 2,826 vols; Curator MARIA JOSÉ REGO DE SOUSA.

Castelo Branco

Museu de Francisco Tavares Proença Júnior: Largo Dr José Dias Lopes, 6000-462 Castelo Branco; tel. (27) 234-42-77; fax (27) 234-78-80; e-mail mftpj@ipmuseus.pt; internet www.ipmuseus.pt; f. 1910, present bldg 1971; archaeological colln of objects found in megalithic tombs at Beira Baixa; Bronze-Age weapons and objects from a complete workshop found at Castelo Novo; illustrations of rupestral art in the Tagus sanctuary; Roman epigraphy; art gallery (16th-century Portuguese School and Brussels tapestries); Bishop's Gallery (18th- and 19th-century paintings); ethnographic collns; ceramic collns; regional embroidery workshop; textiles, incl. oriental and Indo-Portuguese embroidered bedcovers; Dir AIDA RECHENA.

Coimbra

Museu da Ciência da Universidade de Coimbra (Museum of Science, University of Coimbra): Laboratorio Chimico, Largo Marquês de Pombal, 3000-272 Coimbra; tel. (23) 985-43-50; fax (23) 985-43-59; e-mail geral@museudaciencia.org; internet www .museudaciencia.pt; f. 2006; attached to Univ. of Coimbra; 240,000 objects in categories of natural history, ethnography, scientific instruments and models.

Museu Nacional de Ciência e Técnica 'Dr Mário Silva' (National Museum of Science and Technology 'Dr Mário Silva'): Palacete Sacadura Botte, Rua dos Coutinhos 23, 3000 Coimbra; tel. (23) 985-19-40; fax (23) 985-19-49; e-mail mnct@mnct.mces.pt; internet www.museudaciencia.pt; f. 1971; attached to Min. of Science, Technology and Higher Education; information science, medicine, physics, graphic arts, photography, cinema, radio, industrial technology; Dir Prof. Dr PAULO GAMA MOTA.

Museu Nacional de 'Machado de Castro' ('Machado de Castro' National Museum): Largo Dr José Rodriguez 3000-236 Coimbra; tel. (239) 853070; fax (239) 853079; e-mail mnmachadodecastro@imc-ip.pt; internet mnmachadodecastro.imc-ip.pt; f. 1919; est. in the old Bishop's Palace built over Roman galleries, renewed in the 16th century and recently adapted; antiquities, sculpture, paintings, silver-work, priests' vestments, tapestries, ceramics, glass, furniture; Dir ANA ALCOFORADO.

Coruche

Coruche Museu Municipal (Municipal Museum Coruche): Rua Júlio Maria de Sousa, 2100-192 Coruche; tel. (24) 361-08-20; fax (24) 361-08-21; e-mail museu .municipal@cm-coruche.pt; internet www .museu-coruche.org; f. 2001; 230,398 pieces, mostly archaeological and ethnographic; library of 4,102 vols; Dir ANA SANTOS.

Évora

Museu de Évora: Largo do Conde de Vila Flor, 7000-804 Évora; tel. (26) 670-26-04; fax (26) 670-80-94; e-mail mevora@ipmuseus.pt; internet museudevora.imc-ip.pt; f. 1915; paintings: large collns of 16th-century Flemish and Portuguese works; 17th-century works; local prehistoric tools and Roman art and archaeology; sculpture from middle ages to the 19th century; 18th-century Portuguese furniture and silver; library of 4,000 vols; Dir ANTÓNIO CAMÕES GOUVEIA.

Faro

Museu Marítimo 'Almirante Ramalho Ortigão' (Maritime Museum): Rua da Comunidade Lusíada Capitania do Porto do Faro, 8000-253 Faro; tel. (28) 989-49-90; fax (28) 989-49-96; e-mail biblioteca.dms@clix.pt; f. 1931; regional methods of fishing, instruments, models of ships and equipment, paintings of marine fauna, sailors' handicrafts; Curator Capt. LUÍS FERNANDO TAVARES DOS BEIS ÁGOAS.

Museu Municipal de Faro (Faro Municipal Museum): Largo Afonso III, N.° 14 8000-167 Faro; tel. (28) 987-08-27; fax (28) 987-00-38; e-mail dmar.dc@cm-faro.pt; internet www .cm-faro.pt; f. 1894; history, archaeology, ethnography, art from 16th to 19th centuries, photography, toys; Dir Dr MARCO LOPES; publ. *Anais do Municipio do Faro* (1 a year).

Figueira da Foz

Museu Municipal 'Santos Rocha' (Municipal Museum 'Santos Rocha'): Rua Calouste Gulbenkian, 3080-084 Figueira da Foz; tel. (23) 340-28-40; fax (23) 340-28-48; e-mail museu@cm-figfoz.pt; f. 1894; art, archae-ology, ethnology, coins and medals, Indo-Portuguese furniture, weapons; library of 14,300 vols; Manager ANA PAULA CARDOSO; Manager MANUELA SILVA; Manager SÓNIA PINTO.

Funchal

Museu da Quinta das Cruzes: Calçada do Pico 1, 9000-206 Funchal, Madeira; tel. (29) 174-06-70; fax (29) 174-13-84; e-mail mqc .drac@madeira-edu.pt; internet www .museuquintadascruzes.com; f. 1946, present status 2004; decorative arts and small clusters of archaeological and ethnographic objects; Dir TERESA PAIS; publs *Porcelana da China—Colecção do Museu Quinta das Cruzes, Um Olhar do Porto.*

Museu de Arte Sacra (Museum of Sacred Art): Rua do Bispo 21, 9000-073 Funchal, Madeira; tel. (29) 122-89-00; fax (29) 123-13-41; e-mail masf@netmadeira.com; internet www.museuartesacrafunchal.org; f. 1955; diocesan museum; art of the 15th–18th centuries, Flemish art of the 15th and 16th centuries, sculpture, jewellery; Scientific Dir LUIZA CLODE.

Museu de Arte Contemporânea (Museum of Contemporary Art): Fortaleza de São Tiago, Rua do Portão de São Tiago, 9060-250 Funchal, Madeira; tel. (29) 121-33-40; fax (29) 121-33-48; e-mail mac.funchal.drac@ madeira-edu.pt; f. 1966, present location 1992; Portuguese art since the 1960s; Dir JOSÉ MANUEL DE FREITAS SAINZ-TRUEVA.

Musee de História Natural do Funchal (Museum of Natural History of Funchal): Rua da Mouraria 31, 9004-546 Funchal, Madeira; tel. (29) 122-97-61; fax (29) 122-51-80; e-mail mmf@cm-funchal.pt; f. 1929; natural history museum and marine aquarium; large colln of marine animals, esp. deep-sea fish and crustaceans; library on marine biology; garden of medicinal and aromatic plants; Dir RICARDO ARAÚJO; publs *Bocagiana* (irregular), *Boletim* (1 a year).

Guimarães

Museu da Sociedade Martins Sarmento (Museum of the Martins Sarmento Society): Rua Paio Galvão, 4814-509 Guimarães; tel. (25) 341-59-69; fax (25) 351-94-13; e-mail sms@msarmento.org; internet www .csarmento.uminho.pt; f. 1885; archaeology; numerous exhibits relating to Portuguese Celtic, Roman and Visigothic periods; ethnography, numismatics, contemporary art; Dir Dr J. SANTOS SIMÕES.

Museu de Alberto Sampaio (Alberto Sampaio Museum): Rua Alfredo Guimarães, 4800-407 Guimarães; tel. (25) 342-39-10; fax (25) 342-39-19; e-mail masampaio@imc-ip.pt; internet masampaio.imc-ip.pt; f. 1928; religious painting and sculpture, goldsmiths' and silversmiths' art, priestly garments, ceramics; research on industrial archaeology and anthropology; Dir Dr MANUEL SAMPAYO GRAÇA.

Paço dos Duques de Bragança (Palace of the Dukes of Braganza): Rua Conde D. Henrique, 4810-245 Guimarães; tel. (25) 341-22-73; fax (25) 351-72-01; e-mail pduques@imc-ip.pt; internet pduques.imc-ip .pt; f. 1910; attached to Portuguese Institute of Architectural Heritage; 15th-century palace and nat. monument; 17th- and 18th-century art, tapestries, ceramics, faience, furniture; Dir Dra ANTÓNIO PONTE.

Lamego

Museu de Lamego: Largo de Camões, 5100-147 Lamego; tel. (25) 460-02-30; fax (25) 465-52-64; e-mail mlamego@imc-ip.pt; internet www.ipmuseus.pt; f. 1917 as Museum of Works of Art, Archaeology and Numismatics; colln of 16th-century Brussels tapestries, Portuguese painting of 16th–18th centuries, sculpture, religious ornaments; Dir Dr AGOSTINHO PAIVA RIBEIRO.

Leiria

Museu da Imagem em Movimento (Museum of the Moving Image): Largo de São Pedro, Cerca do Castelo, 2400-235 Leiria; tel. (24) 483-96-75; e-mail mimo@cm-leiria .pt; internet mimo.cm-leiria.pt; f. 1996; commemorates the centenary of the creation of cinema; photographic archive, documentation centre.

Lisbon

Casa-Museu Dr. Anastácio Gonçalves: Avda 5 de Outubro 6–8, 1050-055 Lisbon; tel. (21) 354-08-23; fax (21) 354-87-54; e-mail cmag@ipmuseus.pt; internet www .cmag-ipmuseus.pt; f. 1980; 2,000 works of Portuguese paintings and foreign furniture; Dir JOSÉ RIBEIRO.

Centro de Arte Moderna—Fundação Calouste Gulbenkian (Centre for Modern Art—Calouste Gulbenkian Foundation): Rua Dr Nicolau de Bettencourt, 1050-078 Lisbon; tel. (21) 782-34-74; fax (21) 782-30-34; e-mail camjap@gulbenkian.pt; internet cam .gulbenkian.pt; f. 1983; Portuguese and foreign modern art; documentation and research depts, workshops, outdoor amphitheatre; Dir ISABEL CARLOS.

Jardim e Museu Agrícola Tropical do Instituto de Investigação Científica Tropical (Garden and Museum of Tropical Agriculture): Calçada do Galvão, Belém, 1400-171 Lisbon; tel. (21) 363-70-23; fax (21) 362-02-10; internet www.iict.pt/revista/ rev06/vrev0603.htm; e-mail jmat@iict.pt; f. 1906; Dir MARIA CÂNDIDA LIBERATO.

Museu Arqueológico do Carmo (Archaeological Museum): Largo do Carmo, 1200-092 Lisbon; tel. (21) 347-86-29; fax (21) 342-42-55; e-mail carlavf@mac.pt; internet www .museusportugal.org/aap; f. 1863; administered by Associação dos Arqueólogos Portugueses; prehistoric, Roman, Visigothic and medieval collns; sarcophagi, religious sculpture, coins, etc.

Museu Calouste Gulbenkian: Av. de Berna 45A, 1067-001 Lisbon; tel. (21) 782-30-00; fax (21) 782-30-32; e-mail info@ gulbenkian.pt; internet www.museu .gulbenkian.pt; f. 1969; Gulbenkian art colln containing works since 2800BC; antique classical and oriental art, Egyptian, Assyrian, Greek, Roman, Islamic and Far Eastern art; European painting, sculpture, illuminated MSS, tapestries and fabrics, furniture, silverware, jewellery, glass, medals, coins; Dir Dr JOÃO CASTEL-BRANCO PEREIRA.

Museu da Cidade (City Museum): Palácio Pimenta, Campo Grande 245, 1700-091 Lisbon; tel. (21) 751-32-00; fax (21) 757-18-58; e-mail museudacidade@cm-lisboa.pt; internet www.museudacidade.pt; f. 1942, present location 1979; history of devt of Lisbon shown by archaeological, historical, artistic and ethnological documents and exhibits; an 'ensemble' of the 18th-century period and a large model of Lisbon before the earthquake of 1755; Dir ANA CRISTINA LEITE.

Museu da Música (Music Museum): Estação do Metropolitano Alto dos Moinhos, Rua João de Freitas Branco, 1500-359 Lisbon; tel. (21) 771-09-90; fax (21) 771-09-99; e-mail mmusica@imc-ip.pt; internet www .museudamusica.imc-ip.pt; f. 1994; attached to Instituto dos Museus e da Conservação; more than 1,000 instruments of both classical and popular traditions, European wind, key and percussion instruments of the 16th–19th centuries, Portuguese clavichords, harpsichords and 19th-century string instruments, also African, Asian and Portuguese folk instruments; iconography; sound archive of 6,000 items; printed documents and MSS; Dir MARIA HELENA TRINDADE.

Museu de Arte Popular (Museum of Folk Art): Av. de Brasília, 1400-038 Lisbon; tel. (21) 301-12-82; fax (21) 301-11-28; e-mail museuartepopular@gmail.com; f. 1948; folk art, ethnology; 13,000 objects; Dir ANDREIA GALVAO.

Museu de Artes Decorativas (Museum of Decorative Arts): Fundação Ricardo do Espírito Santo Silva, Largo das Portas do Sol 2, 1100-411 Lisbon; tel. (21) 888-19-91; fax (21) 881-46-83; e-mail museu@fress.pt; internet www.fress.pt; f. 1953; incl. Ricardo do Espírito Santo Silva's private colln of Portuguese furniture, silver, china, paintings, rugs, tapestries, etc., and workshops in which craftsmen are trained in all aspects of traditional interior arts; Dir MARIA DA CONCEIÇÃO AMARAL.

Museu de Ciência da Universidade de Lisboa (Museum of Science, University of Lisbon): Rua da Escola Politécnica 56, 1250-102 Lisbon; tel. (21) 392-18-08; e-mail geral@museus.ul.pt; internet www.mc.ul.pt; f. 1985; 10,000 scientific instruments; conducts research and supports postgraduate studies in close collaboration with the Inter-Univ. Centre for the History of Science and Technology (CIUHCT) in the areas of history of science, history of the history of collns and scientific instruments; library of 30,000 vols; Dir ANA MARIA EIRÓ; Asst Dir LUÍS SARAIVA.

Museu de São Roque (Museum of São Roque): Igreja de São Roque, Largo Trindade Coelho (ao Bairro Alto), 1200-470 Lisbon; tel. (21) 323-50-65; fax (21) 323-54-01; e-mail info@museu-saoroque.com; internet www.museu-saoroque.com; f. 1905; collns of religious paintings, Church vessels in precious metals, embroidered vestments by Italian artists of the 18th century; works from the chapel of St John the Baptist in the adjacent museum of the 16th-century Church of St Roque; educational services and temporary exhibitions; Dir TERESA FREITAS MORNA.

Museu do Chiado (Chiado Museum): Rua Serpa Pinto 4, 1200-444 Lisbon; tel. (21) 343-21-48; fax (21) 343-21-51; e-mail mnac-museudochiado@imc-ip.pt; internet www.museudochiado-ipmuseus.pt; f. 1911; painting and sculpture since 1850; library of 6,000 vols; Dir PEDRO LAPA.

Museu Etnológico da Sociedade de Geografia de Lisboa (Ethnological Museum of Geographical Society of Lisbon): Rua das Portas de St Antão 100, 1150-269 Lisbon; tel. (21) 342-54-01; fax (21) 346-45-53; e-mail geral@socgeografialisboa.mail.pt; internet socgeografia-lisboa.planetaclix.pt; f. 1875; native arts, arms, clothing, musical instruments from Africa, India, China, Indonesia and Timor, statues of navigators and historians, relics of voyages of discovery, scientific instruments; Curator Dra MANUELA CANTINHO.

Museu Geológico de Portugal (Geological Museum of Portugal): Rua Academia das Ciências 19, 2, 1200-003 Lisbon; tel. (21) 346-39-15; fax (21) 342-46-09; e-mail museugeol@lneg.pt; internet www.lneg.pt; f. 1848; palaeontology, stratigraphy, archaeology and mineralogy; fossils from the Cambrian to the Tertiary period.

Museu Militar (Military Museum): Largo do Museu de Artilharia, 1100-468 Lisbon; tel. and fax (21) 884-25-69; e-mail museumilitar@portugalmail.pt; internet www.exercito.pt/sites/musmillisboa/paginas/default.aspx; f. 1851, present name 1926; exhibits of Portuguese military history, light arms, ancient artillery and other equipment, paintings since 18th century; Dir Col LUIS SODRE DE ALBUQUERQUE.

Museu Mineralógico e Geológico (Museum of Mineralogy and Geology): Rua da Escola Politécnica 58, 1250-102 Lisbon; tel. (21) 392-18-24; fax (21) 390-58-50; e-mail smineralogia@fc.ul.pt; internet www.mnhn.ul.pt/geologia/geologia.htm; f. 1837; attached to Museu Nacional de História Natural; geology, petrology, mineralogy, palaeontology and museology; Dir Prof. FERNANDO JOSÉ ARRAIANO DE SOUSA BARRIGA; Curator Dr CÉSAR LOPES; Curator Dra LILIANA PÓVOAS; publs *Gaia* (journal of geosciences), *Memórias de Geociencias* (irregular).

Museu Nacional de Arqueologia do Dr Leite de Vasconcelos (National Museum of Archaeology): Praça do Império, 1400-206 Lisbon; tel. (21) 362-00-00; fax (21) 362-00-16; e-mail mnarq.info@imc-ip.pt; internet www.mnarqueologia-ipmuseus.pt; f. 1893; attached to Secretaria Estado da Cultura; library of 25,000 vols; Dir Dr LUÍS RAPOSO; Archaeologist ADOLFO SILVEIRA MARTINS; publ. *O Arqueólogo Português*.

Museu Nacional de Arte Antiga (National Museum of Ancient Art): Rua das Janelas Verdes, 1249-017 Lisbon; tel. (21) 391-28-00; fax (21) 397-37-03; e-mail mnarteantiga@imc-ip.pt; internet www.mnarteantiga-ipmuseus.pt; f. 1884; Portuguese and foreign plastic and ornamental art from the 12th century to 19th century; library of 36,000 vols; Dir Prof. Dr ANTÓNIO FILIPE PIMENTEL; Deputy Dir Dr JOSÉ ALBERTO SEABRA CARVALHO.

Museu Nacional de Etnologia (National Ethnological Museum): Av. Ilha da Madeira, 1400-203 Lisbon; tel. (21) 304-11-60; fax (21) 301-39-94; e-mail mnetnologia@ipmuseus.pt; internet www.mnetnologia-ipmuseus.pt; f. 1965, present bldg 1976; Portuguese rural artefacts; collns representing the people and cultures of Lusophone Africa, Mali, Côte d'Ivoire, Ghana, Nigeria, Cameroon, Indonesia, Timor, Macau, and the Amazonian Indians; library: 20,000 books and periodicals; Dir Prof. Dr JOAQUIM PAIS DE BRITO.

Museu Nacional de História Natural (National Museum of Natural History): Universidade de Lisboa, Rua da Escola Politécnica 58, 1250-102 Lisbon; tel. (21) 392-18-90; fax (21) 392-18-41; internet www.mnhn.ul.pt; f. 1859; library of 27,000 vols; Dir for Botany Prof MARIA AMELIA MARTINS-LOUÇÃO; Dir for Mineralogy and Geology Prof. FERNANDO BARRIGA; Dir for Zoology and Anthropology Dra MARIA GRAÇA RAMALHINHO; publs *Arquivos do Museu Bocage*, *Gaia* (journal of geosciences), *Portugaliae Acta Biologica*, *Revista de Biologia (Lisboa)* (1 a year).

Museu Nacional do Azulejo (National Tile Museum): Rua da Madre de Deus 4, 1900-312 Lisbon; tel. (21) 810-03-40; fax (21) 810-03-69; e-mail mnazulejo@imc-ip.pt; internet mnazulejo.imc-ip.pt; f. 1965; colln of 7,271 tiles, 368 ceramics, 698 prints and engravings, 47 tools; library of 6,000 monographs.

Museu Nacional do Teatro (National Theatre Museum): Estrada do Lumiar 10, 1600-495 Lisbon; tel. (21) 756-74-10; fax (21) 757-57-14; e-mail mnteatro@ipmuseus.pt; internet museudoteatro.imc-ip.pt; f. 1982; 250,000 pieces of costumes, props, sets, posters, programmes, records, sheet music, 120,000 photographs; library of 35,000 vols; Dir JOSÉ ALVAREZ; Librarian SOFIA PATRÃO.

Museu Nacional do Traje (National Museum of Costume): Largo Júlio de Castilho-Lumiar, 1600-483 Lisbon; tel. (21) 756-76-20; fax (21) 759-12-24; e-mail mntraje@imc-ip.pt; internet museudotraje.imc-ip.pt; f. 1977; colln of garments and accessories of Portuguese people since 1882; Dir Dr CLARA PINTO.

Museu Nacional dos Coches (National Coach Museum): Praça Afonso de Albuquerque, Belém, 1300-044 Lisbon; tel. (21) 361-08-50; fax (21) 363-25-03; e-mail mncoches@imc-ip.pt; internet www.museudoscoches.pt; f. 1905 by Queen Amélia in the Riding School of the Royal Palace; comprehensive colln of carriages and coaches since 1619, many by famous craftsmen, incl. those of the Portuguese ex-Royal Family; sedan chairs, harness and equipment, royal liveries, etc., silver trumpets; section of portraits, paintings and engravings; Dir Dra SILVANA BESSONE.

Museu Numismático Português (Portuguese Numismatic Museum): Imprensa Nacional-Casa da Moeda, Av. António José de Almeida, 1000-042 Lisbon; tel. (21) 781-07-00; fax (21) 789-07-08; e-mail mramos@incm.pt; f. 1933; important collns of Portuguese and Colonial, Iberian, Roman and Visigothic coins; also Portuguese and foreign medals; temporarily closed to the public; library of 20,000 vols; consists of Documentation and Information Centre, and Historical Archives of the Nat. Press and the Lisbon Mint; Dir Dr MARGARIDA RAMOS; publ. *Diário da República*.

Museu Rafael Bordalo Pinheiro: Campo Grande 382, 1700-097 Lisbon; tel. (21) 817-06-67; fax (21) 757-18-58; e-mail museu.bordalopinheiro@cm-lisboa.pt; internet www.museubordalopinheiro.pt; f. 1916 as a biographical museum; originals and reproductions of famous caricatures, ceramics, satirical documents; library of 1,600 vols; Chief Man. ANA CRISTINA LEITE; Museum Coordinator PEDRO BEBIANO BRAGA; publs *António Maria* (52 a year), *Lanterna Mágica* (365 a year), *Pontos nos ii* (52 a year).

Odivelas

Núcleo Museológico do Posto de Comando do Movimento das Forças Armadas (Command Post of the Armed Forces Movement): Quartel do Regimento de Engenharia 1 Av. do Regimento de Engenharia 1, 1675-103 Pontinha; tel. (21) 932-08-00; e-mail cultura@cm-odivelas.pt; internet www.cm-odivelas.pt; f. 2001; commemorates the revolution of 25 April 1974, covering the main events during 24–26 April 1974.

Pêro Pinheiro

Museu do Ar (Air Museum): Granja do Marquês, 2715-021 Pêro Pinheiro; tel. (21) 967-89-84; fax (21) 967-89-38; e-mail museudoar@emfa.pt; internet www.emfa.pt/www/po/musar/index.php; f. 1969; Air Force museum, 10,000 pieces.

Porto

Museu de Arte Contemporânea de Serralves (Serralves Museum of Contemporary Art): Rua D. João de Castro 210, 4150-417 Porto; tel. (22) 615-65-00; fax (22) 615-65-33; e-mail serralves@serralves.pt; internet www.serralves.com; f. 1999; Portuguese and int. art since the late 1960s; library: reference art library; Dir JOÃO FERNANDES; Asst Dir ULRICH LOOCK.

Museu de Etnologia do Porto (Ethnological Museum of Porto): Largo de São João Novo 11, 4000 Porto; f. 1945 as Museum of Ethnography and History of Douro Litora; ethnology, archaeology and history; temporarily closed to the public; Dir (vacant).

Museu do Carro Eléctrico (Tram Museum): Alameda Basílio Teles 51, 4150-127 Porto; tel. (22) 615-81-85; fax (22) 507-11-50; e-mail dsgalmeida@stcp.pt; internet www.museudocarroelectrico.pt; f. 1992; colln of trams used in Portugal for public transport; Dir CRISTINA PIMENTEL.

Museu Nacional da Imprensa (National Printing Press Museum): Estrada Nacional 108, 206, 4300-316 Porto; tel. (22) 530-49-66; fax (22) 530-10-71; e-mail mni@ museudaimprensa.pt; internet www .museudaimprensa.pt; f. 1997; colln incl. materials of foundry, printing, binding and engraving; Dir LUIS HUMBERTO MARCOS; Asst Dir ISABEL GONÇALVES; Sec. JOANA MOTA.

Museu Nacional de Soares dos Reis (National Museum): Palacio dos Carrancas, Rua D. Manuel II, 4050-342 Porto; tel. (22) 339-37-70; fax (22) 208-28-51; e-mail mnsr .div@imc-ip.pt; internet mnsr.imc-ip.pt; f. 1833; paintings, sculpture, jewellery, furniture, pottery, glass, metalwork; Dir Dra TERESA VIANA.

Attached Museums:

Casa Museu Fernando de Castro: Rua de Costa Cabral 716, 4200-211 Porto; tel. (22) 339-37-70; f. 1952; colln of Fernando de Castro; ceramics, sculpture, painting.

Sacavém

Museu de Cerâmica de Sacavém (Museum of Ceramics Sacavém): Urbanização Real Forte, 2685 Sacavém; tel. (21) 940-98-00; fax (21) 949-98-98; e-mail museu_ceramica@cm-loures.pt; internet www.cm-loures.pt/aa_patrimonioredemuseussacavema.asp; f. 2000; colln of ceramics, fine arts and others.

Setúbal

Museu de Setúbal (Setúbal Museum): Rua do Balneário Dr Paulo Borba, 2900-261 Setúbal; tel. (26) 553-78-90; fax (26) 553-78-93; e-mail museu.setubal@mun-setubal.pt; internet www.ipmuseus.pt; f. 1961; 16th-century art, sacred sculpture, decorative arts, archaeology, numismatics; Dir FERNANDO ANTÓNIO BAPTISTA PEREIRA.

Museu do Trabalho Michel Giacometti (Museum of the Work—Michel Giacometti): Largo Defensores da República, 2910-470 Setúbal; tel. (26) 553-78-80; fax (26) 553-78-89; e-mail museu.trabalho@mun-setubal.pt; internet www.mun-setubal.pt/museutrabalho; f. 1995; ethnographic colln of Michel Giacometti; Dir ISABEL VICTOR.

Sintra

Museu Arqueológico de São Miguel de Odrinhas (São Miguel de Odrinhas Archaeological Museum): Av. Prof. Dr D. Fernando d'Almeida, Odrinhas, 2710 Sintra; tel. (21) 961-35-74; fax (21) 961-35-78; e-mail museudeodrinhas@sapo.pt; internet www .museudeodrinhas.pt; f. 1955; epigraphs from Etruscan times to the modern age, important colln of Roman inscriptions and carved stones; archaeological artefacts from the Middle Palaeolithic to the 18th century; publ. *Actividades Ludico-didacticas*.

Sintra Museu de Arte Moderna (Sintra Museum of Modern Art): Av. Heliodoro Salgado, 1270 Sintra; tel. (21) 924-81-70; fax (21) 924-81-77; e-mail info@ sintramodernart.com; internet www .berardomodern.com; f. 1987; art representing 14 movements; Curator PEDRO AGUILAR; Sec. JOANA DE ÁVILA.

Torres Novas

Museu Municipal Carlos Reis (Carlos Reis Municipal Museum): Rua do Salvador 10, 2350-415 Torres Novas; tel. (24) 981-25-35; fax (24) 983-90-99; e-mail museu .municipal@cm-torresnovas.pt; internet www.cm-torresnovas.pt/pt/conteudos/espacoequipamentos/museu; f. 1937; archaeological, historical, fine arts, ethnographical,

religious art, numismatics; library of 200 vols; Dir MARIA ELVIRA MARQUES TEIXEIRA.

Vila Nova de Gaia

Casa Museu Teixeira Lopes (Teixeira Lopes House and Museum): Rua Teixeira Lopes 32, 4400-320 Vila Nova de Gaia; tel. (22) 375-12-24; fax (22) 375-20-95; e-mail cmteixeiralopes@gaianima.pt; internet www .cm-gaia.pt; f. 1933; comprises the home of the sculptor António Teixeira Lopes (1866–1942) and the adjacent Galerias Diogo de Macedo; sculpture and paintings since 19th century, furniture, ceramics, tapestries, decorative arts; Dir DOLPHIN SOUSA.

Vila Viçosa

Museu-Biblioteca da Casa de Bragança (Museum and Library of the House of Bragança): Paço Ducal, Terreiro do Paço, 7160-251 Vila Viçosa; tel. (26) 898-06-59; fax (26) 898-98-08; e-mail palacio.vilavicosa@ mail.telepac.pt; internet www.fcbraganca.pt; f. 1933; tapestry, furniture, tiles, European and Chinese ceramics, portraits of the Royal Family, arms, photographs, coaches and carriages; rare 16th-century printed books, Italian 16th-century majolica, and 17th- and 18th-century musical archives; library of 40,000 vols; Curator Dra MARIA DE JESUS MONGE; Curator TIAGO SALGUEIRO; Librarian Dr JOÃO LUÍS DA COSTA RUAS.

Viseu

Museu Grão Vasco: Adro da Sé, 3500-195 Viseu; tel. (23) 242-20-49; fax (23) 242-12-41; e-mail mgv@imc-ip.pt; internet www .ipmuseus.pt; f. 1916; furniture, tapestry, plate, ceramics and glassware, prints and Portuguese paintings; Dir Dra ANA PAULA ABRANTES.

Universities
UNIVERSIDADE ABERTA

Palácio Ceia Rua da Escola Politécnica, 141–147, 1269-001 Lisbon

Telephone: (21) 391-63-00
Fax: (21) 391-65-17
E-mail: contas@univ-ab.pt
Internet: www.uab.pt

Founded 1988
State control
Language of instruction: Portuguese
Academic year: October to July

Number of teachers: 200
Number of students: 9,000

Rector: Dr CARLOS REIS
Vice-Rector: Dr CARLA MARIA BISPO PADREL DE OLIVEIRA
Vice-Rector: ALDA MARIA SIMÕES PEREIRA
Vice-Rector: Dr DOMINGOS JOSÉ ALVES CAEIRO
Pro-Rector: JOÃO CARLOS RELVÃO CAETANO

PROFESSORS
Department of Education and Distance Learning:
AMANTE, L.
BASTOS, G.
FRUTUOSO HENRIQUES, S.
GOULÃO, M. DE F.
GRAVE, L.
IVONE GASPAR, M.
LEBRES AIRES, M. L.
MALHEIRO DA SILVA, S.
MANUEL MARTINS MENDES, A.
MANUELA MALHEIRO FERREIRA, M.
MARGARIDA LOUREIRO CARDOSO, T.
MARIA SIMÕES PEREIRA, A.
MIRANDA, B.
MOREIRA, D.
MOREIRA MARTINS, A.

MORGADO, L.
OLIVEIRA, I.
PAULA MARTINS PEREIRA AFONSO, A.
PINTO MARTINS, A.
TINOCA, L.
Department of Humanities:
ALEXANDRE MAGALHÃES NUNES DA SILVA, P.
ANTÓNIO ALVES DOS REIS, C.
AURÉLIA RODRIGUES DE ALMEIDA, C.
BÄR, G.
BÁRBARA DE SOUSA MONTES RODRIGUES MARQUES DIAS, H.
BATORÉO, H.
CARLOS FERNANDES AVELAR, M.
CARLOS PIMENTA GONÇALVES, L.
CASTILHO PAIS, C.
CHENOLL MORA, A.
DE JESUS CRESPO CANDEIAS VELEZ RELVAS, M.
DO CÉU MARTINS MONTEIRO MARQUES, M.
DO ROSÁRIO DA CUNHA DUARTE, M.
DO ROSÁRIO SAMPAIO SOARES DE SOUSA LEITÃO LUPI BELLO, M.
FILIPA PALMA DOS REIS, M.
FONSECA CLAMOTE CARRETO, C.
GÖTTSCHE, K.
ISABEL PEREIRA TEIXEIRA VASCONCELOS, A.
JOAQUIM DE AZEVEDO TEIXEIRA, R.
JOSÉ FILIPE DA SILVA, M.
MALHEIRO, H.
MANUEL LOPES FIRMINO, J.
MARIA DA CONCEIÇÃO FERREIRA DA SILVA, E.
MARIA DE BARROS DIAS, I.
MARIA DE JESUS FERREIRA NOBRE, A.
MARIA DOS SANTOS FALÉ, I.
MARIA FERIN CUNHA DE ALBUQUERQUE VELOSO, M.
MARIA LOUREIRO DE ROBOREDO SEARA, I.
MARIA PONTES CAPITÃO PEDROSA, I.
MARIA SANTOS GRAÇA DE VASCONCELOS RODRIGUES, C.
MARIA SEQUEIRA, R.
MIGUEL GUERREIRO NOBRE, R.
NASCIMENTO PIEDADE, A.
PAULA DA SILVA MACHADO, A.
PAULA S. MENDES COELHO, M.
RITA DE SÁ SOVERAL PADEIRA, A.
SALOMÃO, R.
SCOTT CHILDS, J.
TERESA DE NORONHA CARDOSO ROCHA, M.
VILA MAIOR, D.
Department of Science and Technology:
AMADOR, F.
ARAÚJO, A.
ARAÚJO, J.
AZEITEIRO, U.
BACELAR NICOLAU, P.
BIDARRA DE ALMEIDA, J.
BORGES SEIXAS, S.
CAETANO, F.
CARAPETO, C.
CARDOSO, V.
CARVALHO, G.
CAVIQUE, L.
COELHO, J.
DO ROSÁRIO O. D. RAMOS, M.
FERNANDES MARCOS, A.
GONZAGA ALBUQUERQUE, L.
JOÃO OLIVEIRA, M.
JORGE EDMUNDO, M.
LUCINDA MATOS FERNANDES, M.
LUÍSA CORREIA, A.
MARTINHO MARTINS, C.
MIGUEL MARQUES DE SOUSA, N.
MORAIS, J.
OLIVEIRA, A.
OLIVEIRA, T.
PADREL DE OLIVEIRA, C.
PAULA FERNANDES, A.
PAULA MARTINHO, A.
PESTANA DA COSTA, F.
PINTO DE MOURA, A.
QUARESMA, J.
REMÉDIOS, J.
ROCIO, V.

São Mamede, J.
Sasportes, R.
Shirley, P.
Silva Pereira, P.
Sofia Ferreira da Silva Caeiro, S.

Department of Social Sciences and Management:

Albuquerque, R.
Alexandra Gago da Câmara, M.
Alexandra Gonçalves, C.
Alexandre Rodrigues Dias de Sousa, I.
Alves, F.
Alves Caeiro, D.
António Ferreira Porfírio, J.
Bäckström, B.
Caetano, J.
Carmo, H.
Carrilho Negas, M.
Carrilho Ribeiro Mendes, T.
Cristina Henriques Lopes dos Reis, F.
das Candeias Sales, J.
do Carmo Teixeira Pinto, M.
do Rosário Alves de Almeida, M.
do Rosário Bastos, M.
do Rosário de Abreu de Matos Bernardo, M.
Eduardo Martins, A.
Ferreira da Silva, L.
Filipe Mouta Lopes, M.
Filomena Andrade, M.
Flor, P.
Fontes, J.
Gronita, J.
Isabel da Conceição João, M.
João Branco, M.
Joaquim, T.
Joaquim Marques de Almeida, J.
Luis Cunha Cardoso, J.
Magano, O.
Manuel Costa, P.
Manuel Trindade, J.
Maria Millán Costa, A.
Marie Luc Philippe Jacquinet, M.
Miguel Custódio Ferrão Neto Simão, J.
Miranda, J.
Nunes, C.
Nunes, P.
Oliveira Ramos, P.
Paiva, A.
Paula Avelar, A.
Paula Beja Horta, A.
Paula Cordeiro, A.
Paulo Gomes da Silva, V.
Pedro Ramos dos Santos Pinho, C.
Rafael Santos Branco, C.
Ramos, N.
Ribeiro, J.
Sousa, L.
Sousa Nunes, T.
Teixeira Isaías, P.
Vidal, N.
Vieira, C.

UNIVERSIDADE ATLÂNTICA
(Atlantic University)

Fábrica da Pólvora de Barcarena, 2730-036 Barcarena
Telephone: (21) 439-82-00
Fax: (21) 430-25-73
E-mail: geral@uatlantica.pt
Internet: www.uatlantica.pt
Founded 1996
State control
Language of instruction: Portuguese
Academic year: October to December
Pres.: Prof. Dr Nelson Lourenço
Sec.-Gen.: Dr Natália do Espírito Santo

PROFESSORS
Department of Planning, Environment and Society:

Alexandre Coelho, J.
Almeida Pinto, G.

Augusto, R.
Barroso, P.
Canhoto da Silva, J.
Carneiro Martins, P.
Catarina Afonso, A.
Célia Gomes, A.
de Fátima Geada, M.
do Rosário Jorge, M.
Félix, S.
Fonseca Ferreira, A.
Lourenço, N.
Meirelles, I.
Monteiro da Cruz, P.
Pacheco, D.
Paulo Zbyszewski, J.
Pinto da Silva, P.
Piriquito Costa, J.
Rodrigues, L.
Russell, D.
Russo Machado, C.
Simão, J.
Taborda, F.
Teixeira d'Azevedo, R.
Tirone, L.
Valentim, A.
Vilhena, J.

Department of Science and Information Technology and Communication:

Aguiar, A.
Alexandre Coelho, J.
Augusto, R.
Barroso, P.
Cabecinha, F.
Caçador, D.
Caldas, A.
Canhoto, J.
Carneiro Martins, P.
Célia Gomes, A.
Chaves, M.
Cruz, P.
Dutschke, G.
Falcato, A.
Geada, F.
Meirelles, I.
Miguel Oliveira, L.
Pinto, G.
Piriquito Costa, J.
Taborda, F.
Valentim, A.
Valentim, J.

School of Health:

Afonso, A.
Almeida, C.
Almeida, L.
Almeida, L.
António Pessoa, J.
Antunes, V.
Baltar, C.
Bárcia, S.
Barreiros, P.
Barros, R.
Borrego, M.
Brandão, R.
Breda, J.
Caiado Gomes, J.
Calisto, C.
Cardoso, J.
Carmo, S.
Carvalhal, A.
Carvalho, M.
Carvalho Rodrigues, L.
Casasnovas, A.
Catarina Afonso, A.
Cláudia de Sousa, A.
Costa, M.
Couceiro, J.
da Lapa, M.
Duarte, D.
Durão, C.
Faustino, R.
Feliciano, E.
Félix, S.
Fernandes, R.
Fernandes, S.
Figueiredo, P.

Fragata, I.
Germano, A.
Godinho, J.
Isabel Ferreira, A.
Isabel Rito, A.
Jacobsohn, L.
João Fernandes, M.
João Santos, M.
Jorge, R.
Kopke, R.
Leão, J.
Lopes, J.
Lopes, N.
Lucas, L.
Lúcia Silva, A.
Lúcio, I.
Madeira, P.
Magalhães, Z.
Mamede, R.
Manuel Vidal, M.
Mareco, R.
Marques, R.
Martins, E.
Maurício, J.
Mendonça Lima, F.
Menezes, A.
Mercês, A.
Mesquita, A.
Morais, T.
Moura, J.
Nascimento, G.
Neto, T.
Oliveira, C.
Oliveira, I.
Paixão, P.
Passão, V.
Paula Vital, A.
Paz, S.
Perdigão, E.
Pereira Coutinho, A.
Pinho, M.
Pinto, E.
Pires, A.
Postolache, G.
Rainho, A.
Ramalho, M.
Ramos, C.
Ramos, J.
Rato, J.
Rato, J.
Ribeiro, H.
Sande Lemos, P.
Serra, S.
Serrano, M.
Silva Nunes, J.
Tecelão, S.
Tomás, A.
Valente, H.
Valentim, A.
Vanessa Antunes, A.
Vassalo, P.
Vitor, L.
Vitor, L.

UNIVERSIDADE AUTÓNOMA DE LISBOA
(Autonomous University of Lisbon)

Rua de Santa Marta 56, 1169-023 Lisbon
Telephone: (21) 317-76-46
Fax: (21) 317-76-03
E-mail: secgeral@universidade-autonoma.pt
Internet: www.universidade-autonoma.pt
Founded 1985
State control
Language of instruction: Portuguese
Rector: Prof. Dr Justino Mendes de Almeida
Registrar: Prof. Dr Jorge Tracana de Carvalho
Librarian: Prof. Dr Miguel Faria
Library of 20,000 vols
Number of teachers: 500
Number of students: 8,700

DIRECTORS

Department of Architecture: Prof. FLAVIO BARBINI
Department of Communication Science: Prof. Dr ANTÓNIO BERNARDO
Department of Documentation Sciences: Prof. Dr JOSÉ MANUEL SUBTIL
Department of Modern Languages and Literature: Prof. Dr ISABEL MARIA FERNANDES DA SILVA
Department of Psychology and Sociology: Prof. Dr JOÃO HIPÓLITO
Department of Science and Technology: Prof. Dr ALBERTO CARNEIRO
Department of Tourism: GABRIELA MOURA

UNIVERSIDADE CATÓLICA PORTUGUESA
(Catholic University of Portugal)

Palma de Cima, 1649-023 Lisbon
Telephone: (21) 721-40-00
Fax: (21) 727-02-56
E-mail: info@reitoria.ucp.pt
Internet: www.ucp.pt
Founded 1967
Private control
Language of instruction: Portuguese
Academic year: September to July
Chancellor: Patriarch JOSÉ POLICARPO
Rector: Prof. Dr MANUEL BRAGA DA CRUZ
Vice-Rector: Prof. MARIA LUÍSA HOMEM LEAL DE FARIA GERALDES BARBA
Vice-Rector: Prof. PETER DAMIEN STILWEL
Librarian: Prof. JOSÉ CÂNDIDO DE OLIVEIRA MARTINS

Number of teachers: 1,000
Number of students: 11,300

Publications: Didaskalia (2 a year), Direito e Justiça (3 a year), Economia (3 a year), Gestão e Desenvolvimento, Humanística e Teológica, Lusitania Sacra, Máthesis, Povos e Culturas, Revista Portuguesa de Filosofia (4 a year), Revista Portuguesa de Humanidades, Theologica (4 a year)

DIRECTORS

Faculty of Arts: Prof. AIRES DO COUTO
Faculty of Economics and Management (Lisbon): Prof. FÁTIMA BARROS
Faculty of Economics and Management (Porto): Prof. ÁLVARO DO NASCIMENTO
Faculty of Engineering: Prof. MANUEL BARATA MARQUES
Faculty of Human Sciences: Prof. ISABEL CAPELOA GIL
Faculty of Law: Prof. RUI MEDEIROS
Faculty of Philosophy: Prof. NUNO DA SILVA GONÇALVES
Faculty of Social Sciences: Prof. MARIA DA GRAÇA DIAS FERREIRA ALVES
Faculty of Theology: Prof. PETER STILWELL
Castro College of Biotechnology: FRANCISCO XAVIER MALCATA
Castro College of Science and Technology: C. PASSOS MORGADO
Education Institute: JOAQUIM AZEVEDO
European Studies Institute: ERNÁNI LOPES
Institute of Bioethics: ANA SOFIA CARVALHO
Institute for Canon Law: Prof. M. SATURNINO GOMES
Institute for Distance Learning: ROBERTO CARNEIRO
Institute of Health Sciences: Prof. A. CASTRO CALDAS
Oriental Studies Institute: LUIS FILIPE THOMAZ
Political Studies Institute: JOÃO CARLOS ESPADA
School of Fine Arts: Prof. JOAQUIM AZEVEDO
University Institute for Development and Social Progress: Prof. J. RIBEIRO GOMES

UNIVERSIDADE DA BEIRA INTERIOR
(University of Beira Interior)

Convento de Sto. António, 6201-001 Covilhã
Telephone: (27) 531-97-00
Fax: (27) 531-90-57
E-mail: geral@ubi.pt
Internet: www.ubi.pt
Founded 1986
State control
Language of instruction: Portuguese
Rector: JOÃO ANTÓNIO DE SAMPAIO RODRIGUES QUEIROZ
Admin. Officer: Dr JOÃO CARLOS CORREIA LEITÃO
Librarian: Dra JOANA LOPES DIAS
Library of 74,000 vols
Number of teachers: 460
Number of students: 6,000
Publication: Boletim Informativo 'Urbi@Orbi'.

UNIVERSIDADE DA MADEIRA
(University of Madeira)

Colégio dos Jesuitas, Rua dos Ferreiros, 9000-082 Funchal, Madeira
Telephone: (29) 120-94-00
Fax: (29) 120-94-10
E-mail: pinus@uma.pt
Internet: www.uma.pt
Founded 1988
State control
Academic year: September to August
Rector: Prof. Dr JOSÉ MANUEL NUNES CASTANHEIRA DA COSTA
Vice-Rector: Prof. Dr GONÇALO NUNO RAMOS FERREIRA DE GOUVEIA
Vice-Rector: Profa Dra SANDRA MARIA FREITAS MENDONÇA
Vice-Rector: Prof. Dr MIGUEL XAVIER JESUS JOSEFAT FERNANDES
Pro-Rector: Prof. Dr BERNARDO GUIDO DE VASCONCELOS
Pro-Rector: Prof. Dr JOAQUIM JOSÉ SANCHES PINHEIRO
Pro-Rector: Prof. Dr MORGADO DIAS
Administrator: Dra CARLA CRÓ ABREU
Librarian: Dra MARIA YOLANDA PEREIRA DA SILVA

Library of 129,000 vols
Number of teachers: 252
Number of students: 3,544

UNIVERSIDADE DE AVEIRO
(University of Aveiro)

Campus Universitário de Santiago, 3810-193 Aveiro
Telephone: (23) 437-02-00
Fax: (23) 437-09-85
E-mail: sre@ua.pt
Internet: www.ua.pt
Founded 1973
State control
Academic year: September to July
Rector: Prof. MANUEL ANTÓNIO ASSUNÇÃO
Vice-Rector: Prof. Dr JOAQUIM DA COSTA LEITE
Vice-Rector: Prof. Dr EDUARDO ANSELMO FERREIRA DA SILVA
Vice-Rector: Prof. Dr CARLOS DE PASCOAL NETO
Vice-Rector: Prof. JOSÉ FERNANDO FERREIRA MENDES
Vice-Rector: Prof. Dr. JOSÉ ALBERTO DOS SANTOS RAFAEL
Pro-Rector: Prof. Dr ARTUR DA ROSA PIRES
Pro-Rector: Prof. Dr JOSÉ CLAUDINO CARDOSO
Pro-Rector: Prof. Dr LILIANA XAVIER DE SOUSA
Pro-Rector: Prof. Dr OSVALDO ROCHA PACHECO
Pro-Rector: Prof. Dr GILLIAN OWEN MOREIRA
Chief Admin. Officer: Dr JOSÉ DA CRUZ COSTA

Librarian: Dra MARIA EMÍLIA M. FERREIRA ARAÚJO
Number of teachers: 952
Number of students: 13,000
Publication: Lineas (4 a year).

UNIVERSIDADE DE COIMBRA
(University of Coimbra)

Palácio dos Grilos Rua da Ilha, 3004-531 Coimbra
Telephone: (23) 985-99-00
Fax: (23) 982-79-94
E-mail: ucadmin@adm.uc.pt
Internet: www.uc.pt
Founded 1290 (in Lisbon)
State control
Language of instruction: Portuguese
Academic year: September to July
Rector: Prof. Dr FERNANDO JORGE RAMA SEABRA SANTOS
Vice-Rector: Prof. Dr HENRIQUE DO CARMO SANTOS MADEIRA
Vice-Rector: Prof. Dr ANTONIO MANUEL DE OLIVEIRA GOMES MARTINS
Vice-Rector: Prof. Dra CRISTINA MARIA SILVA ROBALO CORDEIRO
Pro-Rector: Prof. Dr JOSÉ ANTÓNIO OLIVEIRA BANDEIRINHA
Pro-Rector: Prof. Dr MARGARIDA ISABEL MANO TAVARES SIMÕES LOPES MARQUES DE ALMEIDA
Pro-Rector: Prof. Dr JOSÉ ANTÓNIO RAIMUNDO MENDES DA SILVA
Pro-Rector: Prof. Dr FERNANDO ALBERTO DEOMÉTRIO RODRIGUES ALVES GUERRA
Administrator: CÉLIA CRAVO
Registrar: Dr CARLOS JOSÉ LUZIO VAZ
Gen. Library Dir: Prof. Dr CARLOS MANUEL BAPTISTA FIOLHAIS
Dir of Univ. Archives: Prof. Dr MARIA JOSÉ AZEVEDO SANTOS

Library: see Libraries and Archives
Number of teachers: 1,472 , incl. 494 profs
Number of students: 21,165

Publications: Acta Universitatis Conimbrigensis, Anuário da Universidade, Biblos, Boletim da Biblioteca da Universidade de Coimbra, Boletim da Faculdade de Direito, Boletim das Ciências Económicas, Boletim do Arquivo da Universidade, Boletim do Centro de Estudos Geográficos, Boletim do Laboratório de Fonética Experimental, Brasilia, Conimbriga, Humanitas, Revista Ciência Biológica, Revista da Universidade, Revista de História Literária de Portugal, Revista Portuguesa de Filologia, Revista Portuguesa de História, Revista Portuguesa de Pedagogia

DEANS

Faculty of Arts: Prof. Dr CARLOS MANUEL BERNARDO ASCENSO ANDRÉ
Faculty of Economics: Prof. Dr JOSÉ JOAQUIM DINIS REIS
Faculty of Law: Prof. Dr ANTÓNIO DOS SANTOS JUSTO
Faculty of Medicine: Prof. Dr MANUEL AMARO DE MATOS SANTOS ROSA
Faculty of Pharmacy: Prof. Dr AMÍLCAR CELTA FALCÃO RAMOS FERREIRA
Faculty of Psychology and Education: Prof. Dr LUÍSA MARIA ALMEIDA MORGADO
Faculty of Science and Technology: Prof. Dr JOÃO GABRIEL MONTEIRO DE CARVALHO E SILVA
Faculty of Sports Science and Physical Education: Profa Dra JOSÉ PEDRO LEITÃO FERREIRA

UNIVERSIDADE DE ÉVORA
(University of Évora)

Largo dos Colegiais 2, 7004-516 Évora

Telephone: (26) 674-08-00
Fax: (26) 674-08-06
E-mail: uevora@uevora.pt
Internet: www.uevora.pt

Founded 1559, present status 1973
State control
Language of instruction: Portuguese
Academic year: September to September

Rector: Prof. CARLOS ALBERTO DOS SANTOS BRAUMANN
Vice-Rector: Prof. HERMÍNIA MARIA VASCONCELOS ALVES VILAR
Vice-Rector: Prof. JOSÉ MANUEL MARTINS CAETANO
Vice-Rector: Prof. MANUEL D'OREY CANCELA D'ABREU
Pro-Rector: Prof. JACINTO ANTÓNIO SETÚBAL VIDIGAL DA SILVA
Pro-Rector: Prof. MARTA DA CONCEIÇÃO SOARES SILVA DA CRUZ SILVÉRIO
Pro-Rector: Prof. JOSÉ MANUEL MADEIRA BELBUTE
Library Dir: Prof. SARA MARQUES PEREIRA
Library of 146,000 vols
Number of teachers: 577
Number of students: 7,625

Publication: *UELINE* (online (www.ueline.uevora.pt))

DIRECTORS

Institute for Research and Advanced Training: SOUMODIP SARKAR
School of Arts: CHRISTOPHER CONSITT BOCHMANN
School of Nursing: MANUEL JOSÉ LOPES
School of Science and Technology: PAULO QUARESMA
School of Social Sciences: JOSÉ MACHADO

PROFESSORS

BRAUMANN, C. A. S., Stochastic Processes
CARVALHO, M. J. G. P. R., Agricultural Sciences
CLARA, M. I. E. DA, Plant Pathology
CORTE-REAL, J. A. M., Physics
FERREIRA, A. A. C. G., Soil Conservation
LOPES, R. M. E. J., Natural Resource Economics
LOURENÇO, M. E. V., Plant Physiology
MACHADO, J. A. S. G., History of Art
MARQUES, C. A. F., Agricultural Economics
MORAIS, J. M. C., Toxicology
OLIVEIRA, M. R. G., Phytotechnics
PINHEIRO, A. C. A., Agricultural Economics
RAMOS, F. M., Social and Cultural Anthropology
ROSA, R. M. V. N., Energetics, Climatology and Materials
SANTOS, M. A. O. P., Physics
SERRALHEIRO, R. P., Soil and Water Engineering
ZORRINHO, J. C. D., Information Systems Analysis

UNIVERSIDADE DE LISBOA
(University of Lisbon)

Alameda da Universidade, Cidade Universitária, 1649-004 Lisbon

Telephone: (21) 796-76-24
Fax: (21) 793-36-24
E-mail: reitoria@reitoria.ul.pt
Internet: www.ul.pt

Founded 1288, restored 1911
State control
Academic year: September to July

Rector: Prof. ANTÓNIO SAMPAIO DA NÓVOA
Vice-Rector: Prof. MARIA AMÉLIA BOTELHO DE PAULO MARTINS CAMPOS

Vice-Rector: Prof. ANTÓNIO EMÍLIO PEIXOTO VASCONCELOS TAVARES
Vice-Rector: Prof. CARLOS BAPTISTA LOBO
Administrator: Dra LUÍS PEDRO GOMES COSTA PAULITOS
Librarian: Dra MARIA LEAL VIEIRA
Number of teachers: 1,797
Number of students: 22,245
Publications: *Agenda* (12 a year), *Boletim*

DIRECTORS

Faculty of Dental Medicine: Prof. Dr JOÃO MANUEL DE AQUINO MARQUES
Faculty of Fine Arts: Prof. LUÍS JORGE GONÇALVES
Faculty of Law: Prof. Dr EDUARDO VERA CRUZ PINTO
Faculty of Letters: Dr ANTÓNIO MARIA MACIEL DE CASTRO FEIJÓ
Faculty of Medicine: Prof. Dr JOSÉ FERNANDES E FERNANDES
Faculty of Pharmacy: Prof. Dr JOSÉ A. GUIMARÃES MORAIS
Faculty of Psychology: Prof. MARIA BARROS
Faculty of Science: Prof. Dr JOSÉ MANUEL PINTO PAIXÃO
Institute of Education: Prof. JOÃO PEDRO DA PONTE
Institute of Social Sciences: Prof. Dr JORGE VALA

UNIVERSIDADE DE TRÁS-OS-MONTES E ALTO DOURO
(University of Trás-os-Montes and Alto Douro)

Apdo 1013, 5000-801 Vila Real

Telephone: (25) 935-00-00
Fax: (25) 935-04-80
E-mail: reitoria@utad.pt
Internet: www.utad.pt

Founded 1973, present status 1986
State control
Language of instruction: Portuguese
Academic year: September to July

Rector: Prof. Dr CARLOS ALBERTO SEQUEIRA
Vice-Rector: Prof. Dr MARIA SOLINA DE JESUS CURADO QUINTAS DINIS POETA
Vice-Rector: Prof. Dr JORGE MANUEL TEIXEIRA DE AZEVEDO
Vice-Rector: Prof. Dr CARLOS DA COSTA ASSUNÇÃO
Pro-Rector: Prof. Dr ANTÓNIO AUGUSTO FONTAÍNHAS FERNANDES
Pro-Rector: Prof. Dr FERNANDO MANUEL COELHO FRANCO MARTINS
Pro-Rector: Prof. Dr ANTÓNIO JOSÉ ROCHA MARTINS DA SILVA
Pro-Rector: Prof. Dr JOÃO MANUEL PEREIRA BARROSO
Pro-Rector: Prof. Dr ISABEL ALEXANDRA FERREIRA DA SILVA VAZ NICOLAU
Pro-Rector: Prof. Dr ALEXANDRA SOFIA MIGUÉNS FIDALGO ESTEVES
Registrar: Dra ELSA JUSTINO
Administrator: RUI JORGE CORDEIRO DOS SANTOS
Librarian: Dra MARGARIDA CARVALHO
Number of teachers: 502
Number of students: 8,393

Publications: *A UTAD em Números, Annals of UTAD, Boletim Informativo da UTAD, Yearbook of UTAD*

DIRECTORS

School of Agriculture and Veterinary Sciences: Prof. Dr VICENTE DE SEIXAS E SOUSA
School of Humanities and Social Sciences: Prof. Dr CHRISTOPHER GERRY
School of Life Sciences and Environment: Prof. Dr ANTÓNIO FONTAÍNHAS FERNANDES
School of Science and Technology: Prof. Dr JOSÉ AFONSO MORENO BULAS CRUZ

UNIVERSIDADE DO ALGARVE
(University of Algarve)

Campus da Penha, 8005-139 Faro

Telephone: (289) 80-01-00
Fax: (289) 80-00-61
E-mail: info@ualg.pt
Internet: www.ualg.pt

Founded 1979
State control
Languages of instruction: English, Portuguese
Academic year: September to July

Rector: Prof. Dr JOÃO PINTO GUERREIRO
Administrator: Dr JOÃO MANUEL PAULO RODRIGUES
Dir of Library: Prof. Dr ANTÓNIO ROSA MENDES
Number of teachers: 820
Number of students: 10,000

Publications: *Jornal Algarve Académico* (1 a year), *Revista Encontros Científicos, UALGzine*

DEANS

Engineering Institute: Prof. ILÍDIO MESTRE
Faculty of Economics: Prof. Dr EFIGÉNIO REBELO
Faculty of Human and Social Sciences: Prof. Dr ANTÓNIO BRANCO
Faculty of Science and Technology: Prof. Dr RUI CABRAL E SILVA
Faro School of Health: Prof. ANA DE FREITAS
School of Education and Communication: Prof. CAROLINA DE SOUSA
School of Management, Hospitality and Tourism: Prof. Dr PAULO ÁGUAS

UNIVERSIDADE DO MINHO

Largo do Paço, 4704-553 Braga

Telephone: (25) 360-11-09
Fax: (25) 360-11-05
E-mail: gcii@reitoria.uminho.pt
Internet: www.uminho.pt

Founded 1973
State control
Language of instruction: Portuguese
Academic year: October to July

Rector: Prof. Dr ANTÓNIO M. DA CUNHA
Vice-Rector: Prof. RUI VIEIRA CASTRO
Vice-Rector: Prof. MARGARIDA PROENÇA
Vice-Rector: Prof. JOSÉ F. MENDES
Vice-Rector: Prof. GRACIETE DIAS
Pro-Rector: Prof. VASCO TEIXEIRA
Pro-Rector: Prof. PAULA CRISTINA MARTINS
Pro-Rector: Prof. FELISBELA LOPES
Pro-Rector: Prof. CLÁUDIA VIANA
Chief Admin. Officer: Eng. JOSÉ F. AGUILAR MONTEIRO
Librarian: Dr ELOY RODRIGUES
Number of teachers: 1,200
Number of students: 16,000

Publications: *Cadernos do Noroeste, Ciência Jurídica, Fórum, Revista Portuguesa de Educação, UM Boletim, UM Jornal*

DIRECTORS

Health Sciences School: Prof. MARIA CECÍLIA LEMOS PINTO ESTRELA LEÃO
Institute of Arts and Human Sciences: Prof. MARIA EDUARDA BICUDO AZEREDO KEATING
Institute of Education: Prof. LEANDRO SILVA ALMEIDA
Institute of Social Sciences: MIGUEL SOPAS MELO BANDEIRA
School of Architecture: Prof. PAULO JORGE SOUSA CRUZ
School of Economics and Management: Prof. JOSÉ ANTÓNIO OLIVEIRA ROCHA
School of Engineering: Prof. PAULO ANTÓNIO ALVES PEREIRA
School of Law: Prof. HEINRICH EWALD HORSTER

School of Nursing: Prof. MARIA ISABEL GOMES SOUSA LAGE
School of Psychology: ÓSCAR FILIPE COELHO NEVES GONÇALVES
School of Sciences: Prof. ESTELITA GRAÇA LOPES RODRIGUES VAZ

PROFESSORS

ALVES BERNARDO, C. A., Polymer Engineering
ALVES FERREIRA, J. F., Physics
ALVES PEREIRA, P. A., Civil Engineering
ARAÚJO, M. D., Textile Engineering
ASSUNÇÃO MONTENEGRO, M. I., Chemistry
BARBOSA FREITAS, V. L., Computer Science
BORGES ALMEIDA, J. M., Physics
CABEÇO SILVA, A. A., Textile Engineering
CADIMA RIBEIRO, J. A., Economics
CALADO FERREIRA, M. I., Physics
CARVALHO PROENÇA, A. J., Computer Science
COUTO TEIXEIRA, J. A., Biological Engineering
DUARTE POUSADA, A. S., Polymer Engineering
EIRAS CAPELA, J. V., History
ESGALHADO VALENÇA, J. M., Computer Science
ESTANQUEIRO ROCHA, A., Philosophy
ESTRELA LEÃO, M. C., Biology
FARHANGMEHR, M., Management and Public Administration
GOMES CORREIA, A., Civil Engineering
GOMES COVAS, J. A., Polymer Engineering
GOMES MENDES, J. F., Civil Engineering
GOMES MOTA, M. J., Biological Engineering
GUIMARÃES ALMEIDA, L. M., Textile Engineering
GUIMARÃES RODRIGUES, A. J., Industrial Engineering
LEMOS MARTINS, M., Communication Science
MACHADO SANTOS, S., Computer Science
MAGALHÃES CUNHA, A. A., Polymer Engineering
MONTEIRO COUTO, C. A., Electronics Engineering
OLIVEIRA CAMPOS, A. M., Chemistry
OLIVEIRA ROCHA, J. A., Management and Public Administration
PEREIRA CARMELO, J. M., Physics
PEREIRA VIEIRA, J. M., Civil Engineering
RAMOS MORGADO, R. J., Electronics Engineering
REGO PAIVA PROENÇA, M. F., Chemistry
ROCHA ARMADA, M. J., Management and Public Administration
ROCHA GOMES, J. I., Textile Engineering
RODRIGUES VAZ, E. G., Mathematics
SALVADOR PINHEIRO, J. D., Biological Engineering
SANCHES SIMÕES, J. M., Childhood Studies
SANTOS SOARES, L. J., Biological Engineering
SILVA FERRAZ, A. M., Economics
SILVA LIMA, N. M., Childhood Studies
SILVA MAIA, H. L., Chemistry
SIMÕES CARVALHO, M. G., Childhood Studies
TAVARES OLIVEIRA, D. R., Biological Engineering
VARELA FREITAS, C. M., Childhood Studies

UNIVERSIDADE DO PORTO
(University of Porto)

Praça Gomes Teixeira, 4099-002 Porto

Telephone: (22) 040-80-00
Fax: (22) 040-81-86
E-mail: up@up.pt
Internet: www.up.pt

Founded 1911
Public control
Academic year: September to July
Language of instruction: Portuguese

Rector: Prof. Dr JOSÉ CARLOS MARQUES DOS SANTOS
Vice-Rector: ANTÓNIO CARDOSO
Vice-Rector: ANTÓNIO MARQUES
Vice-Rector: JORGE GONÇALVES
Vice-Rector: MARIA DE LURDES CORREIA FERNANDES

Pro-Rector: EMÍDIO GOMES
Pro-Rector: JOSÉ SARSFIELD CABRAL
Pro-Rector: LÍGIA MARIA RIBEIRO
Pro-Rector: MANUEL JANEIRA
Pro-Rector: PATRÍCIA TEIXEIRA LOPES
Administrator: JOSÉ ANGELINO BRANCO

Number of teachers: 1,895
Number of students: 29,896 (12,205 undergraduate, 17,691 postgraduate)

Publications: *Arquivos de Medicina* (medicine), *Arquivos Portugueses de Cirurgia* (surgery), *Cadernos de Consulta Psicologica* (consultant psychology), *Cadernos de Literatura Comparada* (comparative literature), *Douro*, *Estudos CEJD* (sport), *Mediaevalia* (medieval studies), *Revista Africana Studia* (African studies), *Revista de Filosofia* (philosophy), *Revista de Geografia* (geography), *Revista de História* (history), *Revista de Línguas e Literaturas* (languages and literature), *Revista Educação Sociedade e Cultura* (education, society and culture), *Revista Estudos*, *Revista Patrimônio* (nat. heritage), *Revista População e Sociedade* (population and society), *Revista Portugália*, *Revista Portuguesa de Ciências do Desporto* (sports sciences), *Sociologia* (sociology), *Terceira Margem* (Brazilian studies)

DIRECTORS

Abel Salazar Institute of Biomedical Sciences: ANTÓNIO SOUSA PEREIRA
Faculty of Architecture: CARLOS ALBERTO ESTEVES GUIMARÃES
Faculty of Arts: Prof. Dr MARIA DE FÁTIMA MARINHO
Faculty of Dental Medicine: Prof. Dr AFONSO MANUEL PINHÃO FERREIRA
Faculty of Economics: JOÃO PROENÇA
Faculty of Engineering: SEBASTIÃO JOSÉ CABRAL FEYO DE AZEVEDO
Faculty of Fine Arts: FRANCISCO LARANJO
Faculty of Law: CÂNDIDO AGRA
Faculty of Medicine: Dr JOSÉ AGOSTINHO MARQUES LOPES
Faculty of Nutrition and Food Sciences: MARIA DANIEL VAZ DE ALMEIDA
Faculty of Pharmacy: JOSÉ COSTA LIMA
Faculty of Psychology and Education: JOSÉ ALBERTO DE AZEVEDO E VASCONCELOS CORREIA
Faculty of Science: ANTÓNIO FERNANDO SILVA
Faculty of Sport Science and Physical Education: JORGE OLÍMPIO BENTO
Porto Business School: BELMIRO MENDES DE AZEVEDO

UNIVERSIDADE DOS AÇORES
(University of the Azores)

Rua da Mãe de Deus s/n, Apdo 1422, 9501-801 Ponta Delgada The Azores

Telephone: (29) 665-00-00
Fax: (29) 665-00-05
E-mail: uacgeral@uac.pt
Internet: www.uac.pt

Founded 1976, present status 1980
State control
Language of instruction: Portuguese
Academic year: September to June

3 Campuses: Campus de Ponta Delgada, Campus da Horta, Campus de Angra do Heroísmo

Rector: Prof. Dr AVELINO DE FREITAS DE MENESES
Vice-Rector: Prof. Dr JORGE MANUEL ROSA DE MEDEIROS
Vice-Rector: Prof. Dr. JOSÉ LUÍS VASCONCELOS BRANDÃO DA LUZ
Pro-Rector for Mobility and Cooperation: Prof. Dr LUÍS MANUEL VIEIRA DE ANDRADE

Pro-Rector for Activities Coordination of Horta Campus: Dr RICARDO DA PIEDADE ABREU SERRÃO SANTOS
Pro-Rector for Activities Coordination of Angra do Heroísmo Campus: Prof. Dr ALFREDO EMILIO SILVEIRA DE BORBA
Pro-Rector for Area of Evaluation and Quality: Prof. Dr JORGE MANUEL ÁVILA DE LIMA
Pro-Rector for Coordination of Lifelong Learning: Prof. Dr MARIA TERESA PIRES DE MEDEIROS
Administrator: Dra ANA PAULA CARVALHO HOMEM DE GOUVEIA
Librarian: Dra MARIA JOÃO MOTA MELO

Library of 200,000 vols
Number of teachers: 470
Number of students: 6,068

Publication: *Archipélago* (series on human sciences, natural sciences).

UNIVERSIDADE FERNANDO PESSOA
(University Fernando Pessoa)

Praça 9 de Abril 349, 4249-004 Porto

Telephone: (22) 507-13-00
Fax: (22) 550-82-69
E-mail: gri@ufp.edu.pt
Internet: www.ufp.pt

Founded present status 1996
Private control
Languages of instruction: Portuguese, English
Academic year: September to June

Rector: Prof. Dr SALVATO TRIGO

Library of 71,502 vols
Number of teachers: 230
Number of students: 3,868

Publications: *A Obra Nasce* (Architecture), *Antropológicas* (Anthropology Journal), *Cadernos de Comunicação e Linguagem* (Communication and Language), *Cadernos de Estudos Latino-americanos* (Latin American Studies), *Cadernos de Estudos Mediáticos*, *Cibertextualidades* (Informatic Text and Cyber literature), *Consciências*, *Nuestra America* (Latin American Studies), *Revista da FCHS* (Journal of the Faculty of Human and Social Sciences), *Revista da FCS* (Journal of the Faculty of Health Sciences), *Revista da FCT* (Journal of the Faculty of Science and Technology)

DEANS

Health Sciences: Prof. Dr LUIS MARTINS
Human and Social Sciences: Prof. INÊS GOMES
Science and Technology: Prof. ALVARO MONTEIRO

UNIVERSIDADE LUSÍADA
(Lusíada University)

Rua da Junqueira 188–198, 1349-001 Lisbon

Telephone: (21) 361-15-00
Fax: (21) 363-83-07
E-mail: info@lis.ulusiada.pt
Internet: www.ulusiada.pt

Founded 1986 by Cooperativa de Ensino Univ. Lusíada
Private control
Academic year: October to June

Campuses in Lisbon, Oporto and Vila Nova de Famalição

Rector: Prof. Dr DIAMANTINO DURÃO
Vice-Rector: Prof. Dr JOSÉ J. GONÇALVES DE PROENÇA
Librarian: Dr MADALENA FERNANDES

Library of 15,000 vols
Number of teachers: 986
Number of students: 17,041

Publications: *Boletim Informativo*, *CDE Bulletin*, *Pólis* (legal-political studies), *Revista Lusíada de Ciência e Cultura*.

UNIVERSIDADE LUSÓFONA DE HUMANIDADES E TECNOLOGIAS
(Lusophone University of Humanities and Technology)

Campo Grande 376, 1749-021 Lisbon

Telephone: (21) 751-55-00
Fax: (21) 757-70-06
Internet: www.ulusofona.pt
State control
Language of instruction: Portuguese
Rector: Prof. Dr MÁRIO C. MOUTINHO
Vice-Rector: Prof. Dr ÁUREA DO CARMO ADÃO
Pro-Rector: Prof. Dr. AUGUSTO PEREIRA BRANDÃO

Library of 1,300 vols, 60,000 monographs.

UNIVERSIDADE NOVA DE LISBOA
(New University of Lisbon)

Campus de Campolide, 1099-085 Lisbon

Telephone: (21) 371-56-00
Fax: (21) 371-56-14
E-mail: unl@unl.pt
Internet: www.unl.pt
Founded 1973
State control
Academic year: October to July
Rector: Prof. Dr ANTÓNIO MANUEL BENSABAT RENDAS
Vice-Rector: JOSÉ PEREIRA
Vice-Rector: MARIA ARMÉNIA CARRONDO
Vice-Rector: MIGUEL DE OLIVEIRA CORREIAL
Vice-Rector: JOÃO PAULO CRESPO
Pro-Rector: LUÍS ESPINHA DA SILVEIRA
Pro-Rector: HENRIQUE TEIXEIRA
Pro-Rector: VÁLTER LÚCIO
Pro-Rector: PAULO JOSÉ JUBILADO SOARES DE PINHO
Administrator: Dra FERNANDA ANTÃO

Number of teachers: 1,449
Number of students: 18,233

Publications: *Faculdade de Ciências Médicas: Annual Report, Faculdade de Ciências Médicas: Nova Medicina* (4 a year), *Faculdade de Ciências Sociais e Humanas: Bulletin, Portuguese and Japanese Studies* (1 a year), *Faculdade de Ciências Sociais e Humanas: Cadernos de Cultura* (irregular), *Faculdade de Ciências Sociais e Humanas: Cadernos de Filosofia* (2 a year), *Faculdade de Ciências Sociais e Humanas: Ethnologia* (irregular), *Faculdade de Ciências Sociais e Humanas: Faces de Eva: estudos sobre a mulher* (2 a year), *Faculdade de Ciências Sociais e Humanas: Fórum Sociológico* (2 a year), *Faculdade de Ciências Sociais e Humanas: Geolnova* (2 a year), *Faculdade de Ciências Sociais e Humanas: Revista da FCSH* (1 a year), *Faculdade de Ciências Sociais e Humanas: Revista de Estudos Anglo-Portugueses* (1 a year), *Faculdade de Ciências Sociais e Humanas: Working Paper* (irregular), *Faculdade de Direito Cultura: Revista de História e Teoria das Ideias* (1 a year), *Frontal* (irregular), *Instituto de Tecnologia Química e Biológica: Revista Portuguesa de Saúde Pública* (2 a year, 1 annual themed journal), *Thémis* (2 a year).

UNIVERSIDADE PORTUCALENSE INFANTE D. HENRIQUE

Rua Dr António Bernardino de Almeida 541, 4200-072 Porto

Telephone: (22) 557-20-00
Fax: (22) 557-20-10
E-mail: up@upt.pt
Internet: www.upt.pt
Founded 1986
Private control
Language of instruction: Portuguese
Academic year: September to July

Rector: Prof. Dr FRANCISCO DA COSTA DURÃO
Vice-Rector: Prof. Dr AMÍLCAR DA COSTA PEREIRA MESQUITA
Gen.-Sec.: Prof. Dr JOSÉ MANUEL TEDIM
Chief Admin. Officer: ANTÓNIO ALVES MONTEIRO
Librarian: Profa Dra MANUELA BARRETO NUNES

Library of 46,150 vols
Number of teachers: 230
Number of students: 3,100

Publications: *Africana, Revista de Ciências da Educação, Revista de Ciências Históricas, Revista Jurídica*

DIRECTORS

Department of Economics and Business: Prof. Dr LUÍS MIGUEL PACHECO
Department of Education and Heritage: ISABEL VAZ DE FREITAS
Department of Innovation, Science and Technology: Prof. MARIA FILOMENA CASTRO LOPES
Department of Law: Prof. Dr MARIA MANUELA MAGALHÃES SILVA

UNIVERSIDADE TÉCNICA DE LISBOA
(Technical University of Lisbon)

Alameda de Santo António dos Capuchos 1, 1169-047 Lisbon

Telephone: (21) 881-19-01
Fax: (21) 881-19-90
E-mail: gre@reitoria.utl.pt
Internet: www.utl.pt
Founded 1930
State control
Language of instruction: Portuguese
Academic year: September to July
Rector: Prof. FERNANDO MANUEL RAMÔA CARDOSO RIBEIRO
Vice-Rector: Prof. LUÍS MANUEL DOS ANJOS FERREIRA
Vice-Rector: Prof. Dr VÍTOR FERNANDO DA CONCEIÇÃO GONÇALVES
Vice-Rector: Prof. HELENA MARGARIDA NUNES PEREIRA
Pro-Rector: Prof. Dr NUNO PAULO DE SOUSA ARROBAS CRATO
Pro-Rector: Prof. Dr MANUEL ALMEIDA RIBEIRO
Pro-Rector: Prof. Dr PAULO JORGE PIRES FERREIRA
Pro-Rector: Prof. Dr JOSÉ MANUEL FRAGOSO ALVES DINIZ
Administrator: Prof. EDUARDO LOPES RODRIGUES
Librarian: D. UMBELINA NASCIMENTO

Library of 500,000 vols, 2,8000 periodicals
Number of teachers: 1,822
Number of students: 22,503

Publications: *DAXIYANGGUO, Portuguese Review of Asiatic Studies, Episteme Review, European Review of Economics and Finance, ISCSP—Estudes Politicos e Sociais, ISEG—Estudes de Economia, Portuguese Economic Journal, Portuguese Review of International and Community Relations, Portuguese Review of Veterinary Sciences.*

Colleges

Escola Náutica Infante D. Henrique (Infante D. Henrique Nautical School): Av. Eng. Bonneville Franco, 2770-058 Paço d'Arcos; tel. (21) 446-00-10; fax (21) 442-95-46; e-mail info@enautica.pt; internet www.enautica.pt; f. 1972; provides training in merchant navy; Pres. ABEL AMORIM.

Escola Superior de Actividades Imobiliárias (School of Real Estate): Praça Eduardo Mondlane, 7C Edifício Coopemi, 1950-104 Lisbon; tel. (21) 836-70-10; fax (21) 836-70-19; e-mail esai@esai.pt; internet www.esai.pt; f. 1990; Dir Prof. Dr LEANDRO PEREIRA.

Escola Superior de Enfermagem da Cruz Vermelha Portuguesa de Oliveira de Azeméis (School of Nursing of the Portuguese Red Cross Oliveira de Azemeis): Rua da Cruz Vermelha, Cidacos, Apdo 1002, 3720-126 Oliveira de Azeméis; tel. (25) 666-14-30; fax (25) 666-14-32; e-mail secretaria@esenfcvpoa.eu; internet www.esenfcvpoa.eu; f. 2002; polytechnic instn of nursing and health sciences education; Pres. HENRIQUE PEREIRA; Vice-Pres. FERNANDA PRÍNCIPE.

Escola Superior de Enfermagem de Coimbra (Nursing School of Coimbra): *Campus A:* Avda Bissaya Barreto, Apdo 55, 3001-901 Coimbra; *Campus B:* Rua 5 de Outubro, Apdo 55, 3001-901 Coimbra; tel. (23) 980-28-50; fax (23) 944-26-48; internet www.esenfc.pt; f. 2004 by merger of Nursing School of Higher Education Dr. Ângelo da Fonseca (f. 1881) with Nursing School of Higher Education Bissaya Barreto (f. 1971); Pres. MARIA DA CONCEIÇÃO SARAIVA DA SILVA COSTA BENTO; Vice-Pres. FERNANDO MANUEL DIAS HENRIQUES; Vice-Pres. JOSÉ REIS DOS SANTOS ROXO; publ. *Revista Referência*.

Escola Superior de Enfermagem de Lisboa (Lisbon Nursing School): Pólo Maria Fernanda Resende, Parque da Saúde, na Av. do Brasil 53-B, 1700-063 Lisbon; tel. (21) 792-41-00; fax (21) 792-41-97; internet www.esel.pt; f. 2004 by merger of School of Nursing Artur Ravara, School of Nursing Calouste Gulbenkian, Lisbon, School of Nursing and Francisco Garcia College of Nursing Maria Fernanda Resende; library: 22,300 vols, 170 periodicals, 2,500 digital journals; Pres. Prof. Dr MARIA FILOMENA MENDES GASPAR; Vice-Pres. Prof. OLGA MARIA ORDAZ FERREIRA; Vice-Pres. Prof. JOÃO CARLOS BARREIROS DOS SANTOS; publ. *Pensar Enfermagem*.

Escola Superior de Hotelaria e Turismo do Estoril (School of Hospitality and Tourism, Estoril): Av. Condes de Barcelona, 2769-510 Estoril; tel. (21) 004-07-00; fax (21) 004-07-19; e-mail info@eshte.pt; internet www.eshte.pt; offers graduate and postgraduate courses in tourism, travel and hospitality; 110 teachers; Pres. Prof. Dr FERNANDO MOREIRA.

Escola Superior de Saúde Egas Moniz (Egas Moniz School of Health Sciences): Egas Moniz, Cooperativa de Ensino Superior, Crl Campus Universitário, Quinta da Granja, Monte de Caparica, 2829-511 Caparica; tel. (21) 294-68-07; fax (21) 294-68-32; e-mail essem@egasmoniz.edu.pt; internet www.egasmoniz.com.pt; f. 1999; offers Masters courses in health sciences; Dir Prof. Dr JOSÉ A. DE SALIS AMARAL.

Escola Superior de Tecnologia da Saúde de Coimbra (School of Health Technology of Coimbra): Rua 5 de Outubro, S Martinho do Bispo, Apdo 7006, 3046-854 Coimbra; tel. (23) 980-24-30; fax (23) 981-33-95; e-mail geral@estescoimbra.pt; internet www.estescoimbra.pt; f. 1993; clinical analyses, audiology, cardiology, dietetics and nutrition, pharmacy, physiotherapy, radiology and environmental health; library: 4,357 monographs, 6,150 periodicals; 1,000 students; Pres. JORGE CONDE.

Escola Superior de Tecnologia da Saúde do Porto (School of Health Technology Porto): R. Valente Perfeito 322, 4400-330 Vila Nova de Gaia; tel. (22) 206-10-00; fax (22) 206-10-01; e-mail geral@estsp.ipp.pt; internet www.estsp.ipp.pt; f. 1980, present status 2004; offers Masters courses in health technology; Pres. AGOSTINHO CRUZ.

Escola Superior Enfermagem S. José de Cluny (St Joseph of Cluny School of Nursing): Rampa de Quinta de Sant' Ana 22, 9050-282 Funchal, Madeira; tel. (29) 174-34-44; fax (29) 174-36-26; e-mail geral@esesjcluny.pt; internet www.esesjcluny.pt; f. 1940; offers graduate and postgraduate courses in nursing; Pres. IRMÃ SOARES; publ. *O Cluny* (4 a year).

Escola Superior Gallaecia: Largo das Oliveiras, 4920-275 Vila Nova de Cerveira; tel. (25) 179-40-54; fax (25) 179-40-55; e-mail esg@esg.pt; internet www.esg.pt; f. 1992; attached to Fundação Convento da Orada; studies and research in design, ecology and landscape, arts and multimedia; offers Masters degree in architecture and urbanism; Pres. Prof. Dr MARIANA CORREIA.

Escola Universitária Vasco da Gama (Vasco da Gama University School): Mosteiro S. Jorge de Miléu, Estrada da Conraria, Castelo Viegas, 3040-714 Coimbra; tel. (23) 944-44-44; fax (23) 943-76-27; e-mail geral@euvg.net; internet www.euvg.net; f. 2000; attached to Associação Cognitária S. Jorge de Miléu; architecture and veterinary medicine; Pres. Prof. Dr MACHADO FARIA.

Instituto Nacional de Administração (National Institute for Public Administration): Palácio dos Marqueses de Pombal, 2784-540 Oeiras; tel. (21) 446-53-00; fax (21) 446-54-44; e-mail ina@ina.pt; internet www.ina.pt; f. 1979; training and research in public admin., law, European affairs, management, computer science, human resources management; European Documentation Centre; 373 teachers; 11,473 students; library: 19,000 vols, 250 periodicals; Pres. Prof. ANTÓNIO CORREIA DE CAMPOS; publ. *Legislação: Cadernos de Ciência de Legislação* (3 a year).

Instituto Piaget: Quinta de Arreinela de Cima, 2800-305 Almada; tel. (21) 294-62-50; fax (21) 294-62-51; e-mail info@almada.ipiaget.org; internet www.ipiaget.org; f. 1979; offers courses in clinical analysis and public health, social sciences, communications science and intercultural development, chemical sciences and the environment, complementary studies, education, artistic and industrial design, design and management of teaching materials, economics and business, economics and management of health sciences, infant education, nursing, food engineering, civil engineering, contract engineering and maintenance management, electrical engineering, physiotherapy, music, human, social and school nutrition, basic education, psychology, environmental health, sociology.

National Campuses:

   Campus Académico de Almada: Quinta de Arreinela de Cima, 2800-305 Almada; tel. (21) 294-62-50; fax (21) 294-62-51; e-mail info@almada.ipiaget.org; internet www.ipiaget.org.

   Campus Universitário de Viseu: Estrada do Alto do Gaio, Galifonge, Lordosa, 3515-776 Viseu; tel. (23) 2 91-01-00; fax (23) 2 91-01-80; e-mail info@viseu.ipiaget.org; internet www.ipiaget.org.

   Complexo de Ensino Superior de Macedo de Cavaleiros: Rua Dr António Oliveira Cruz, 5340-257 Macedo de Cavaleiros; tel. (27) 842-00-40; fax (27) 842-54-30; e-mail info@macedo.ipiaget.org; internet www.ipiaget.org.

   Escola Superior de Saúde—Jean Piaget Silves: Enxerim, 8300-025 Silves; tel. (28) 244-01-70; fax (28) 244-01-71; e-mail info@silves.ipiaget.org; internet www.ipiaget.org.

   ESS Jean Piaget: Escola Superior de Saúde, Alameda Jean Piaget, Gulpilhares, 4405-678 Vila Nova de Gaia; tel. (22) 753-66-20; fax (22) 753-66-39; e-mail info@gaia.ipiaget.org; internet www.ipiaget.org.

   ISEIT Mirandela: Av. 25 de Abril, 5370-202 Mirandela; tel. (27) 820-01-50; fax (27) 826-52-03; e-mail info@mirandela.ipiaget.org; internet www.ipiaget.org.

   Santo André: Bairro das Flores, Apdo 38, 7500-999 Vila Nova de Santo André; tel. (26) 970-87-10; fax (26) 970-87-27; e-mail info@standre.ipiaget.org; internet www.ipiaget.org.

   Vila Nova de Gaia: Escola Superior de Educação, Rua António Sérgio, Apdo 551, 4410-269 Canelas, Vila Nova de Gaia; tel. (22) 753-76-00; fax (22) 753-76-81; e-mail info@gaia.ipiaget.org; internet www.ipiaget.org.

International Campuses:

   Universidade Jean Piaget de Angola: see separate entry in Angola chapter.

   Universidade Jean Piaget de Cabo Verde: see separate entry in Cape Verde chapter.

Instituto Politécnico da Guarda: Av. Dr Francisco Sá Carneiro 50, 6300-559 Guarda; tel. (27) 122-01-10; fax (27) 122-26-90; e-mail ipg@ipg.pt; internet twintwo.ipg.pt; f. 1980; courses in education, public relations, computer science, civil engineering, mechanical engineering and business management; 258 teachers; 3,700 students; Pres. Prof. Dr CONSTANTINO MENDES REI; Vice-Pres. Prof. Dr FERNANDO AUGUSTO SÁ NEVES SANTOS; Vice-Pres. Prof. Dr GONÇALO POETA FERNANDES; publs *Educação e Tecnologia* (2 a year), *Revista Egitania Sciencia* (2 a year).

Instituto Politécnico de Beja: Rua Pedro Soares, Campus do Instituto Politécnico de Beja, Apdo 6155, 7800-295 Beja; tel. (28) 431-44-00; fax (28) 431-44-01; e-mail geral@ipbeja.pt; internet www.ipbeja.pt; f. 1987; 231 teachers; 3,500 students; library: 35,000 vols; Dir Dr JOSÉ LUÍS RAMALHO.

Instituto Politécnico de Bragança: Campus de Santa Apolónia, Apdo 1101, 5301-856 Bragança; tel. (27) 333-06-90; fax (27) 331-36-84; e-mail ipb@ipb.pt; internet www.ipb.pt; f. 1983; agriculture, education, technology, management, communication and health; campus in Mirandela; 310 teachers; 7,000 students; Dir Prof. DIONÍSIO A. GONÇALVES.

Instituto Politécnico de Castelo Branco, Escola Superior Agrária: Quinta da Senhora de Mércules, Apdo 119, 6001-909 Castelo Branco; tel. (27) 233-99-00; fax (27) 233-99-01; e-mail esa@ipcb.pt; internet www.esa.ipcb.pt; f. 1983; higher courses in agriculture (vegetable production, animal production, forestry production, natural resources management, edible oil production); 70 teachers; 1,400 students; library: 22,000 vols; Dir CELESTINO ANTÓNIO MORAIS DE ALMEIDA; publs *AGROforum*, *Bibliografia Temática*, *Boletim Bibliográfico*, *Folha Bibliográfica Mensal*.

Instituto Politécnico de Lisboa: Estrada de Benfica 529, 1549-020 Lisbon; tel. (21) 710-12-00; fax (21) 710-12-35; e-mail academica@sc.ipl.pt; internet www.ipl.pt; f. 1985; 13,000 students; Pres. Dr ALBERTO A. ANTAS DE BARROS JÚNIOR; Administrator Dr ANTÓNIO JOSÉ CARVALHO MARQUES.

Constituent Institutes:

   Escola Superior de Communicação Social: Campus de Benfica do IPL, 1549-014 Lisbon; tel. (21) 711-90-00; fax (21) 716-25-40; e-mail servicos_academicos@escs.ipl.pt; internet www.escs.ipl.pt; f. 1987; academic year September to July;

library of 3,919 vols, 8,799 periodicals; 62 teachers; 866 students; Pres. Dr JOÃO PEDRO ABREU.

   Escola Superior de Dança: Rua da Academia das Ciências 5, 1200-003 Lisbon; tel. (21) 324-47-70; fax (21) 324-02-71; e-mail geral@esd.ipl.pt; internet www.esd.ipl.pt; f. 1983; academic year September to July; 17 teachers; 83 students; library of 1,270 vols; Pres. Prof. FERNANDO CRESPO; publ. *Dança*.

   Escola Superior de Educação: Campus de Benfica do IPL, 1549-003 Lisbon; tel. (21) 711-55-00; fax (21) 716-61-47; e-mail eselx@eselx.ipl.pt; internet www.eselx.ipt.pt; f. 1985; academic year September to July; library of 28,000 vols, 8,500 periodicals; 96 teachers; 1,065 students; Pres. Dra AMÁLIA GARRIDO BÁRRIOS.

   Escola Superior de Música: Campus de Benfica do IPL, 1500-651 Lisbon; tel. (21) 322-49-40; fax (21) 347-14-89; e-mail esml@esm.ipl.pt; internet www.esml.ipl.pt; f. 1983; academic year October to June; library of 1,500 vols and 5,000 music scores; 43 teachers; 140 students; Dir Prof. JOSÉ JOÃO GOMES DOS SANTOS.

   Escola Superior de Teatro e Cinema: Av. Marquês de Pombal 22B, 2700-571 Amadora; tel. (21) 498-94-00; fax (21) 498-94-01; e-mail estc@estc.ipl.pt; internet www.estc.ipl.pt; f. 1983; academic year September to July; library of 10,000 vols, 2,000 periodicals; 43 teachers; 208 students; Pres. Prof. FILIPE OLIVEIRA.

   Escola Superior de Tecnologia da Saúde de Lisboa (ESTeSL): Av. D João II, Lote 4.69.01, 1990-096 Lisbon; tel. (21) 898-04-00; fax (21) 898-04-60; e-mail estesl@estesl.ipl.pt; internet www.estesl.ipl.pt; f. 1981; Pres. Prof. MANUEL CORREIA; publ. *Saúde & Tecnologia*.

   Instituto Superior de Contabilidade e Administração de Lisboa (ISCAL): Av. Miguel Bombarda 20, 1069-035 Lisbon; tel. (21) 798-45-00; fax (21) 798-45-98; internet www.iscal.ipl.pt; f. 1754 as Aula de Comércio, present name 1976; academic year September to July; library of 6,566 vols, 211 periodicals; 202 teachers; 3,334 students; Dir of Services Dr GRACIETTE PINTO CORREIA.

   Instituto Superior de Engenharia de Lisboa (ISEL): Rua Conselheiro Emídio Navarro 1, 1959-007 Lisbon; tel. (21) 831-70-00; fax (21) 831-70-01; e-mail isel@isel.ipl.pt; internet www.isel.ipl.pt; f. 1852 as Instituto Industrial de Lisboa, present name 1974; academic year September to July; library of 9,388 vols, 312 periodicals; 551 teachers; 5,495 students; Pres. Dr JOSÉ CARLOS LOURENÇO QUADRADO.

Instituto Politécnico de Portalegre: Praça do Município Apdo 84, 7301-901 Portalegre; tel. (245) 30-15-00; fax (245) 33-03-53; e-mail geral@ipportalegre.pt; internet www.ipportalegre.pt; f. 1985; 250 teachers; 3,000 students; Pres. JOAQUIM MOURATO.

Constituent Schools:

   Escola Superior Agrária de Elvas (ESAE): Edifício do Trem Alto, Av. 14 de Janeiro, Apdo 254, 7350-903 Elvas; tel. (26) 862-85-28; fax (26) 862-85-29; e-mail esae@esaelvas.pt; internet www.esaelvas.pt; 5 teachers; 25 students; Dir Eng. GONÇALO J. P. ANTUNES BARRADAS.

   Escola Superior de Educação (ESE): Praça da República. Apdo 125, 7300-957 Portalegre; tel. (245) 33-94-00; fax (245) 20-46-19; e-mail esep@mail.esep.ipportalegre.pt; internet www.esep.pt; f. 1985; 72 teachers; 671 students; Pres. Dr CARLOS

BRANDÃO; Librarian Dr DOMINGOS BUCHO; publ. *Aprender*.

Escola Superior de Saúde de Portalegre: Av. de Santo António, Apdo 89, 7301-901 Portalegre; tel. (24) 530-04-30; fax (24) 530-04-39; e-mail geral@essp.pt; internet www.essp.pt; Pres. Prof. FRANCISCO ALBERTO MOURATO VIDINHA.

Escola Superior de Tecnologia e Gestão (ESTG): Lugar do Abadessa, Apdo 148, 7301-901 Portalegre; tel. (24) 530-02-00; fax (24) 530-02-30; e-mail estg@estgp.pt; internet baco.estgp.pt; 45 teachers; 695 students; Pres. ARTUR JORGE ROMÃO; Librarian Bac. CATARINA ELIAS BARRADAS.

Instituto Politécnico de Santarém: Complexo Andaluz, Apdo 279, 2001-904 Santarém; tel. (24) 330-95-20; fax (24) 330-95-38; e-mail relacoes.publicas@ipsantarem.pt; internet www.ipsantarem.pt; f. 1979; colleges of agriculture, education, management, sport, health; Social Services; library: 38,900 vols; 270 teachers; 3,936 students; Pres. Prof. J. A. GUERRA JUSTINO; Vice-Pres. MARIA TERESA PEREIRA SERRANO; Vice-Pres. HÉLDER ORLANDO CARDOSO PEREIRA.

Instituto Politécnico de Setúbal: Largo Defensores da República 1, 2910-470 Setúbal; tel. (26) 554-88-20; fax (26) 523-11-10; e-mail ips@spr.ips.pt; internet www.ips.pt; f. 1981; 5 colleges: Escola Superior de Tecnologia de Setúbal, Escola Superior de Educação, Escola Superior de Ciências Empresariais, Escola Superior de Tecnologia do Barreiro, Escola Superior de Saúde; courses in education, management and technology; Pres. Prof. Dr ARMANDO PIRES.

Instituto Politécnico de Viana do Castelo (Viana do Castelo Polytechnic Institute): Praça General Barbosa, 4900-347 Viana do Castelo; tel. (25) 880-96-10; fax (25) 882-90-65; e-mail dmoreira@ipvc.pt; internet www.ipvc.pt; f. 1980; 5 schools offering undergraduate and postgraduate degree courses; teacher-training college, agricultural college, schools of technology and management, nursing, business studies; Pres. Prof. RUI TEIXEIRA.

Instituto Politécnico de Viseu (Polytechnic Institute of Viseu): Av. José Maria Vale de Andrade, 3504-510 Viseu; tel. (23) 248-07-00; fax (23) 248-07-50; e-mail ipv@pres.ipv.pt; internet www.ipv.pt; f. 1979; Schools of education, technology, agrarian, technology and management, health, welfare services; higher training in teacher training, media studies, cultural studies, social service, sports, multimedia, engineering, management, marketing, tourism, agrarian sciences, nursing; 400 teachers; 7,000 students; Dir Eng. FERNANDO LOPES RODRIGUES SEBASTIÃO; publs *Forum Media* (2 a year), *Millenium* (4 a year).

Instituto Superior Bissaya Barreto: Campus do Conhecimento e da Cidadania, Apdo 7049, 3046-901 Coimbra; tel. (23) 980-04-50; fax (23) 980-04-95; e-mail isbb@isbb.pt; internet www.isbb.pt; f. 1927; law and public admin.; Dir Prof. Dr MARIA LUÍSA FERREIRA CABRAL DOS SANTOS VEIGA; Pres. Prof. Dr RUI NOGUEIRA LOBO ALARCÃO E SILVA.

Instituto Superior de Ciências da Saúde-Norte (Institute of Health Sciences-North): Coop. de Ensino Superior, Politécnico e Universitário, CRL R. Central de Gandra 1317, 4585-116 Gandra Prd; tel. (22) 415-71-00; fax (22) 415-71-02; e-mail info@cespu.pt; internet www.cespu.pt; f. 1984, present name 1993, present location 1995; attached to Cooperative Education, Polytechnic and University (CESPU); higher education in health related courses; 380 profs; Dir Prof. Dr JORGE PROENÇA.

Instituto Superior de Ciências do Trabalho e da Empresa (Higher Institute of Labour and Enterprise): Avda das Forças Armadas, 1649-026 Lisbon; tel. (21) 790-30-00; fax (21) 796-47-10; e-mail geral@iscte.pt; internet iscte.pt; f. 1972; offers Bachelors, Masters and Doctoral courses in management, social and technological sciences; library: 56,000 vols, 17,000 periodicals; 400 teachers; 6,000 students; Dir LUÍS ANTERO RETO; publ. *Portuguese Journal of Social Science*.

Instituto Superior de Línguas e Administração (ISLA): Quinta do Bom Nome, Estrada da Correia 53, 1500-210 Lisbon; tel. (21) 030-99-08; fax (21) 030-99-17; e-mail jose.inacio@lx.isla.pt; internet www.isla.pt; f. 1962; business management, marketing, human resources, computer science for management, applied mathematics, translation, tourism, secretarial studies; library: 20,000 vols; 260 teachers; 3,000 students; Dir Prof. Dr TAWFIQ RKIBI; publ. *Revista Portuguesa de Management*.

Instituto Superior Politécnico Portucalense: Rua do Paço 3, 4560 Penafiel; tel. (25) 571-10-54; fax (25) 571-10-53; f. 1990; courses in local govt admin., accounting, management, computer studies; library: 5,000 vols; 73 teachers; 620 students; Dir Dr JOAQUIM M. SILVA CUNHA.

Schools of Art

Escola Superior Artística do Porto (Art School of Porto): Largo de S. Domingos 80, 4050-545 Porto; tel. (22) 339-21-30; fax (22) 339-21-39; e-mail geral@esap.pt; internet www.esap.pt; f. 1982; 130 teachers; 780 students; Pres. ALEXANDRA TREVISAN DA SIVEIRA PACHECO.

Escola Superior de Belas-Artes (Higher School of Fine Arts): Av. Rodrigues de Freitas 265, 4049-021 Porto; tel. (22) 519-24-00; fax (22) 536-70-36; e-mail directivo@fba.up.pt; internet www.fba.up.pt; f. 1836, present name and status 1994; attached to Univ. of Porto; design, painting, sculpture, art sciences, drawing, geometry; library: 13,300 vols, 11,000 slides, 160 audiovisual titles, 50 electronic documents, antique book colln; Pres. Prof. JOSÉ VAZ; Vice-Pres. HEITOR ALVELOS.

Escola Universitária das Artes de Coimbra (Coimbra University School of Arts): Campus Universitário da ARCA, Lordemão, 3020-244 Coimbra; tel. (23) 949-74-00; fax (23) 983-85-33; e-mail info@arca.pt; internet www.arca.pt; f. 1989, present location 1996; offers Bachelors and Masters degrees in architecture, art and design; Sec. PAULA FONSECA.

QATAR

The Higher Education System

Qatar was part of the Ottoman Turkish Empire until 1916 when it came under British protection. British control was extended in 1934 and in 1971 independence was achieved. The traditional education system was based on Koranic and Shari'a (Islamic law) studies, but in 1973 the largely secular College of Education was founded and it became the University of Qatar in 1977. The University remains the sole national provider of higher education and consists of seven Colleges; degrees are approved by the United Kingdom's Quality Assurance Agency. In 2007/08 a total of 7,245 students were enrolled at the University. Education City Qatar, the Qatar Foundations' flagship project which opened in 2003, hosts branch campuses of six US universities and numerous other educational and research institutions. A Science and Technology Park, designed to establish Qatar as a regional hub for research and development, was officially opened at Education City in 2009.

Admission to undergraduate courses at the University of Qatar is based upon results achieved in Al-Thanawaya Al-Amah (general secondary certificate) examinations. Students are admitted to the University before their applications are considered by the individual Colleges, some of which require students to sit an entrance examination. Degrees are awarded on a 'credit' basis, and students are required to accumulate a specified number of credits before graduating, depending on the degree applied for. There are mandatory Foundation courses for students in engineering, science, economics and administration, consisting of English, mathematics and IT training. The foremost undergraduate degree is the Bachelors, which generally takes three years to complete, although degrees in some subjects take longer (e.g. the Bachelor of Science in pharmacy, which lasts five years). The main postgraduate courses are the Postgraduate Diplomas and Certificates, Masters and Doctorates. Postgraduate Certificate and Diploma courses are between two and five semesters in duration and are available in education, library science and architectural planning. Masters degree courses last one year and students are required to maintain a specified grade point average. Doctoral degrees (mainly PhD) are not yet widespread.

The main post-secondary qualification for technical and vocational education is the Diploma in Technology, available from Colleges of Technology.

Regulatory Bodies

GOVERNMENT

Ministry of Education and Higher Education: POB 80, al-Waqf Tower, al-Dafna, Doha; tel. 44941111; fax 44941445; e-mail e.alhorr@moe.edu.qa; internet www.moe.edu.qa; Minister SAAD BIN IBRAHIM AL-MAHMOUD.

NATIONAL BODY

Qatar Museums Authority: POB 2777, Doha; tel. 4525555; fax 4525556; e-mail info@qma.com.qa; internet www.qma.com.qa; coordinating body for nat. museums; incl. Qatar National Museum, Museum of Islamic Art; spec. collns of Orientalist art, Islamic coins, natural history, antique weapons; Chief Exec. Officer ABDULLAH AL-NAJJAR; Exec. Dir Dr ROGER MANDLE.

Learned Societies

GENERAL

UNESCO Office Doha: 66 Lusail St, West Bay, POB 3945, Doha; tel. 4113293; fax 4113015; e-mail doha@unesco.org; internet www.unesco.org/doha; designated Cluster Office for Bahrain, Kuwait, Oman, Qatar, Saudi Arabia and United Arab Emirates; Dir HAMED AL-HAMMAMI.

EDUCATION

Qatar Foundation: POB 5825, Doha; tel. 4540000; fax 4806117; e-mail info@qf.org.qa; internet www.qf.org.qa; education, scientific research and community development; responsible for Education City project; f. 1995; Pres. Dr MOHAMMAD FATHY SAOUD.

LANGUAGE AND LITERATURE

British Council: 93 Al-Sadd St, POB 2992 Doha; tel. 4251888; fax 4423315; e-mail general.enquiries@qa.britishcouncil.org; internet www.britishcouncil.org/me-qatar.htm; offers courses and examinations in English language and British culture and promotes cultural exchange with the UK.

Research Institutes

ECONOMICS, LAW AND POLITICS

Center for International and Regional Studies: POB 23689, Doha; tel. 4578400; fax 4578401; internet cirs.georgetown.edu; attached to School of Foreign Service in Qatar; research into regional and int. issues; Dir MEHRAN KAMRAVA.

RAND-Qatar Policy Institute: POB 23644, Doha; tel. 4927400; fax 4927410; e-mail rand-qatarpolicyinstitute@rand.org; internet www.rand.org/qatar; Private control; attached to RAND Corporation and Qatar Foundation; analysis into public policy; Dir RICHARD E. DARILEK.

HISTORY, GEOGRAPHY AND ARCHAEOLOGY

Gulf Cooperation Council Folklore Centre: POB 7996, Doha; tel. 4861999; fax 4867170; f. 1982 to collect, study, disseminate and protect indigenous local folklore mainly in the fields of literature, customs and traditions, music and dance, arts and crafts; mem. states: Bahrain, Kuwait, Oman, Qatar, Saudi Arabia, UAE; library of 4,853 vols, 110 journals, also video cassettes, cassette recordings and photographic material; Dir-Gen. ABDULRAHMAN AL-MANNAI; publ. *Al Ma'thurat Al Sha'biyyah* (4 a year).

MEDICINE

Doha International Institute for Family Studies and Development: POB 34080, Doha; tel. 4548200; fax 4548249; e-mail diifsd@qf.org.qa; internet www.fsd.org.qa; attached to Qatar Foundation; research and scholarship on the legal, sociological, and scientific basis of the family as the natural and fundamental group unit of society; f. 2004.

Libraries and Archives

Doha

College of the North Atlantic-Qatar Campus Library System: POB 24449, Doha; tel. 4952051; e-mail reference@cna-qatar.edu.qa; internet www.cna-qatar.com/library; incl. Al-Rayyan Library spec. colln of Pre-nursing, Health Sciences, English Language Learning; Dir PATRICIA SUTHERLAND.

Qatar National Library: POB 205, Doha; tel. 4429955; fax 4429976; e-mail qanaly@qatar.net.qa; f. 1962; 218,600 vols in Arabic, 33,800 vols in English, 1,300 Arabic MSS, 454 vols on microfilm, 1,288 periodicals on microfilm and 10,248 on microfiche, bibliographic services on subjects of local interest; 5 brs; Dir ABDULLA NASSER AL-ANSARI.

Qatar University Library: POB 2713, Doha; tel. 4852406; fax 4835092; e-mail library@qu.edu.qa; internet www.qu.edu.qa/library; f. 1973.

Research and Documents Division: POB 923, Amir's Office, Doha; tel. 4425497; fax 4310518; f. 2003; Dir Dr SULTAN JASIM AL-JABER.

Museums and Art Galleries

Doha

Museum of Islamic Art: POB 2777, Doha; tel. 4224444; e-mail infomia@qma.com.qa; internet www.mia.org.qa; attached to Qatar Museums Authority; Early Islamic Art, Iran and Central Asia (12th–19th century), Egypt and Syria (12th–15th century), Turkey (16th–18th century), India (16th–18th century).

Qatar National Museum: Doha; tel. 4442911; e-mail qnm2000@hotmail.com; internet www.qnm.8m.com; attached to Qatar Museums Authority; opened 1975; consists of 5 major sections: the old Amiri

Palace (9 19th-century buildings), the new palace, aquarium, lagoon, botanical garden; collns: ethnography, archaeo-history, geology, botany, zoology, jewellery, numismatics, perfumery; Dir IBRAHIM JABER AL-JABER.

Universities

CARNEGIE MELLON QATAR

POB 24866 Doha
Telephone: 4548400
Fax: 4548410
E-mail: ug-admission@qatar.cmu.edu
Internet: www.qatar.cmu.edu

Founded 2004; attached to Carnegie Mellon Univ., Pittsburgh, USA and the Qatar Foundation
Private control

Dean: Dr CHUCK THORPE
Librarian: NIKKI KRYSAK

Business and Computer Science.

NORTHWESTERN UNIVERSITY IN QATAR

POB 34102 Doha
Telephone: 4545100
E-mail: nu-qadmissions@northwestern.edu
Internet: www.qatar.northwestern.edu

Founded 2004; attached to Northwestern Univ., Illinois, USA and the Qatar Foundation
Private control

Dean: JOHN D. MARGOLIS

Schools of Communication and Journalism.

STENDEN UNIVERSITY QATAR

POB 36037 Doha
Telephone: 4888116
E-mail: info@chn.edu.qa
Internet: www.stenden.com/en/stenden/locations/qatar; attached to Stenden Univ., Netherlands

International Hospitality Management, Tourism Management, International Business and Management Studies.

TEXAS A&M UNIVERSITY AT QATAR

POB 23874, Doha
Telephone: 4230010
Fax: 4230011
E-mail: info@qatar.tamu.edu
Internet: www.qatar.tamu.edu

Founded 2003; attached to Texas A&M Univ., Texas, USA
Private control

Dean and Chief Exec. Officer: Dr MARK H. WEICHOLD
Librarian: CAROLE THOMPSON

Library of 3,900,000 vols, 90 periodicals
Number of students: 300

Chemical Engineering, Electrical and Computer Engineering, Mechanical Engineering, Petroleum Engineering.

UNIVERSITY OF QATAR

POB 2713, Doha
Telephone: 4852222
Fax: 4835043
E-mail: info@qu.edu.qa
Internet: www.qu.edu.qa

Founded 1973 as College of Education, Univ. status 1977
State control
Language of instruction: Arabic
Academic year: September to June

Chair.: HH Sheikh TAMIN BIN HAMAD AL THANI (Heir Apparent)
Pres.: Prof. Dr SHEIKHA ABDULLAH AL-MISNAD
Vice-Pres. and Chief Financial Officer: Dr HUMAID ABDULLAH AL-MIDFAA
Vice-Pres. and Chief Academic Officer: Dr SHEIKHA JABOR AL-THANI
Vice-Pres. for Student Affairs: Dr OMAR MOHAMED AL-ANSARI
Vice-Pres. for Research: Dr HASSAN AL-DERHAM
Vice-Pres. for Institutional Planning and Devt: Prof. SAIF SAID AL-SOWAIDI
Library Dir: TAG ELSIR IBRAHIM S. KARDAMAN

Library of 360,000 vols (Arabic and English), 1,040 periodicals
Number of teachers: 705
Number of students: 7,245
Publication: *Fruits of Knowledge* (1 a year)

DEANS

College of Arts and Science: Dr SIHAM AL-QARADAWI
College of Business and Economics: Prof. Dr MUHAMMAD K. NAJDAWI (acting)
College of Education: Prof. Dr HESSA AL-SADIQ
College of Engineering: Dr MAZEN HASNAH
College of Law: Dr HASSEN ABDULRAHIM AL-SAYED
College of Pharmacy: Prof. Dr PETER JEWESSON
College of Shari'a Law and Islamic Studies: Dr AISHA YOUSIF AL-MANNAI

ATTACHED INSTITUTES

Computer Centre: Dir Dr JIHAD MUHAMMAD AL-JAAM.

Documentation and Humanities Research Centre: colln, classification and preparation of documents pertaining to the field of humanities as a basic source of research, and the issuing of documented research papers; specialized research on the heritage of the Gulf area in all its aspects: social, cultural, linguistic and literary; Dir Dr SAIF AL-MEREIKHI.

Educational Research Centre: educational research and studies that contribute to the devt of education in the State of Qatar, oriented among other things toward improvement of the educational process, curricula and textbooks; Dir Dr NASRA REDA BAGHER.

Educational Technology Centre: Dir Dr JIHAD MOHAMMED AL-JAAM.

Gulf Studies Centre: Dir Dr HASSAN AL-ANSARI.

Scientific and Applied Research Centre: to develop experience in scientific, industrial and agricultural fields with spec. reference to industries, natural resources, agriculture and animal resources of Qatar; and to contribute to the transfer of technology and adapt it for application in Qatar; Dir Dr MOHSIN ABDULLAH AL-ANSI.

Sirra and Sunna Research Centre: research related to the *Sirra* of the Prophet Mohamed, i.e. his preaching, moral and spiritual values, and his life, and the *Sunna* of the Prophet Muhammad, i.e. his sayings and acts, which are the second source of guidance for the practice of Islam after the holy Koran; Dir Prof. YOUSUF AL-QARADAWI.

VIRGINIA COMMONWEALTH UNIVERSITY IN QATAR

Doha
Telephone: 4927200
E-mail: vcuqadmissions@qatar.vcu.edu
Internet: www.qatar.vcu.edu

Founded 2003; attached to Virginia Commonwealth Univ., USA and the Qatar Foundation
Private control

Dean: ALLYSON VANSTONE

Library of 16,000 vols

Bachelor of Fine Arts degree in Fashion Design, Graphic Design or Interior Design.

Colleges

Centre for GIS: POB 22088 Doha; tel. 4955112; fax 4955011; e-mail masoun@gisqatar.org.qa; internet www.gisqatar.org.qa; attached to Urban Planning and Devt Authority; Regional Training Centre for Geospatial Information Systems.

College of the North Atlantic-Qatar: 68 Al-Tarafa, Duhail North, POB 24449, Doha; tel. 4952222; fax 4952200; e-mail info@cna-qatar.edu.qa; internet www.cna-qatar.com; attached to College of the North Atlantic, Canada; f. 2002; 400 teachers; 2,300 students; Technical College offering 4 programmes in Business Studies, Engineering Technology, Health Sciences, Information Technology; Security Academy, Centre for Banking and Financial Studies; Pres. Dr HAROLD JORCH.

Language Teaching Institute: POB 3224, Doha; tel. 4657690; fax 4665465; f. 1972; part-time courses in Arabic, Persian, English, French, for mature students already in employment; library: 6,000 vols; 29 teachers; 504 students; Dir MUHAMMAD HASSAN AL-SIDDIQI.

Qatar Aeronautical College: POB 4050 Doha; tel. 4408888; fax 4357034; e-mail qacadmn@qatar.net.qa; internet www.qac.edu.qa; Dir-Gen. ALI IBRAHIM AL-MALKI; Dir for Academic Affairs Dr SAID ABDULLAH AL-SULEIMAN.

School of Foreign Service in Qatar: POB 23689 Doha; tel. 4578100; fax 4578241; e-mail sfsqadmissions@georgetown.edu; internet qatar.sfs.georgetown.edu; Private control; attached to Georgetown Univ., USA; Dean of Academic Affairs VICTORIA PEDRICK; Dir of Library FRIEDE WIEBE; Dir of Public Affairs CHARLES NAILEN.

Weill Cornell Medical College in Qatar: Doha; tel. 4928402; fax 4928422; e-mail jadmissions@qatar-med.cornell.edu; internet qatar-weill.cornell.edu; Private control; attached to Cornell Univ., Ithaca, NY, USA; Dir JAVAID I. DHEIKH.

ROMANIA

The Higher Education System

Formerly part of the Ottoman Turkish Empire, Romania became an independent kingdom in 1881. In 1947 King Michael was forced to abdicate and the Romanian People's Republic was proclaimed. Romania became a one-party state under the communist Romanian Workers' Party. Communist rule ended in 1989, when the regime of President Ceauşescu was overthrown in a revolution; multi-party democracy was established in 1991. The oldest current institutions of higher education are mostly specialist establishments dating from the first half of the 19th century, among them the Universitatea 'Politehnica' din Bucureşti (founded in 1818), the Academia de Muzică 'Georghe Dima' (founded in 1819), the Universitatea de Ştiinţe Agronomice şi Medicină Veterinara Bucureşti (founded in 1852) and the Universitatea de Medicină şi Farmacia 'Carol Davila' (founded in 1857; current name since 1990). There was an expansion of higher education during the period of reform (1859–66) initiated by Alexander Ioan Cuza, the first elected Domnitor of the United Principalities of Wallachia and Moldova (which later became independent Romania). Current institutions established during that period include the Unversitatea 'Alexandru Ioan Cuza' Iaşi (founded in 1860), the Universitatea de Arte 'George Enescu' (founded in 1860; current name since 1960), the Universitatea Naţională de Muzică din Bucureşti (founded in 1864) and the Universitatea din Bucureşti (founded in 1864). In 2007/08 there were 106 institutions of higher education. The number of students enrolled at such institutions in 2009/10 totalled 775,000.

The Ministry of Education, Research, Youth and Sport is responsible for higher education, which is governed by the Constitution (1991) and the Education Act (1995). Education at public institutions is free. Romania participates in the Bologna Process to establish a European Higher Education Area, the first phase of which is to adopt a credit-based system of comparable degrees with three main cycles (undergraduate, postgraduate and doctoral).

Admission to higher education is on the basis of the Bacalaureat (secondary school diploma) and success in the university entrance examination. Higher education is divided into short- and long-term courses. Short-term courses consist solely of the three-year Diploma de Absolvire and are offered by Colegii Universitare (university colleges). Long-term higher education consists of undergraduate and postgraduate degrees, principally the undergraduate Diploma de Licenta (Bachelors) and postgraduate Diploma de Master (Masters) degrees, in accordance with the principles of the Bologna Process. The Diploma de Licenta is a programme of study lasting four to six years, depending on the field of study. Following the Diploma de Licenta, graduates may study for one or two years for the award of, principally, the Diploma de Master or Diploma de Studii postuniversitare (Professional Postgraduate Diploma). Finally, the highest university-level degree is the Doktorat (Doctorate), a programme of study lasting three to seven years.

Post-secondary technical and vocational education (Şcoala Postliceală) consists of one- to three-year training courses at three levels of specialization. Courses are assessed by a practical examination, a written paper and preparation and presentation of a project.

Since 2006 the Agenţia Română de Asigurare a Calităţii în Învăţământul Superior (ARACIS—Romanian Agency for Quality Assurance in Higher Education) has been in charge of university accreditation. ARACIS is a full member of the European Association for Quality Assurance in Higher Education. Accreditation is a two-stage process. The first step is trust licensing, which gives institutions the right to organize admission examinations. The second step is accreditation, which gives institutions the right to administer degree examinations and issue diplomas (degrees) recognized by the Ministry of Education, Research, Youth and Sport.

Regulatory and Representative Bodies

GOVERNMENT

Ministry of Culture and National Heritage: Şos. Kiseleff 30, 011374 Bucharest 1; tel. (21) 224-46-65; fax (21) 222-83-20; e-mail ministru@cultura.ro; internet www.cultura.ro; Minister HUNOR KELEMEN; Sec.-Gen. MIRCEA CRISTIAN STAICU.

Ministry of Education, Research, Youth and Sport: Str. Gen. Berthelot 28–30, Sector 1, 010168 Bucharest; tel. (21) 405-62-00; fax (21) 312-47-19; internet www.edu.ro; Minister DANIEL FUNERIU; Sec.-Gen. GHEORGHE ASĂNICĂ.

ACCREDITATION

Agenţia Română de Asigurare a Calităţii în Învăţământul Superior (ARACIS) (Romanian Agency for Quality Assurance in Higher Education): Str. Spiru Haret 12, 010176 Bucharest; tel. (21) 206-76-00; fax (21) 312-71-35; e-mail mail@aracis.ro; internet www.aracis.ro; f. 2006; draws up procedures and sets accreditation standards for the assessment of different types of programmes and higher education providers, and submits them to the Ministry of Education, Research, Youth and Sport for approval; carries out assessments and submits accreditation reports to the Ministry; draws up and reviews the nat. reference standards and the performance indicators to assess and assure the quality of higher education; devises and promotes policies and strategies to improve the quality of education in Romania; 17 mems; Pres. Prof. Dr IOAN CURTU; Gen. Sec. Prof. Dr MIHAI ARISTOTEL UNGUREANU.

ENIC/NARIC Romania: Nat. Centre for Recognition and Equivalence of Diplomas Granted Abroad, Str. Gen. Berthelot 28–30, Sector 1, 010168 Bucharest; tel. (21) 405-63-22; fax (21) 313-10-13; e-mail cornelmun@yahoo.com; internet www.cnred.edu.ro; Dir CORNELIU MUNTEANU.

NATIONAL BODY

Romanian Council of Rectors: Splaiul Independenţei 313, 060042 Bucharest; tel. (21) 402-91-00; fax (21) 318-10-01; e-mail e_andronescu@rectorat.pub.ro; internet www.upb.ro; Rector Prof. ECATERINA ANDRONESCU.

Learned Societies

GENERAL

Academia Română (Romanian Academy): Calea Victoriei 125, 010071 Bucharest; tel. (21) 212-86-40; fax (21) 211-66-08; e-mail solunca@acad.ro; internet www.acad.ro; f. 1866; sections of Philology and Literature (Chair. EUGEN SIMION), Historical and Archaeology Sciences (Chair. ALEXANDRU ZUB), Mathematical Sciences (Chair. ROMULUS CRISTESCU), Physical Sciences (Chair. HORIA SCUTARU), Chemical Sciences (Chair. MARIUS ANDRUH), Biological Sciences (Chair. MAYA SIMIONESCU), Geonomical Sciences (Chair. MIRCEA SĂNDULESCU), Technical Sciences (Chair. GLEB DRĂGAN), Agricultural Sciences and Forestry (Chair. CRISTIAN HERA), Medical Sciences (Chair. LAURENŢIU POPESCU), Economics, Legal Sciences and Sociology (Chair. MUGUR ISĂRESCU), Philosophical, Theological, Psychological and Pedagogical Science (Chair. ALEXANDRU SURDU), Arts, Architecture and Audiovisual (Chair. MIHNEA GHEORGHIU), Information Science and Technology (Chair. MIHAI DRĂGĂNESCU); 181 mems; attached research institutes: see Research Institutes; library: see Libraries and Archives; Pres. IONEL HAIDUC; Vice Pres. DAN BERINDEI; Sec.-Gen. PĂUN ION OTIMAN; publs *Annuaire Roumain d'Anthropologie, Anuar de lingvistică şi istorie literară* (Yearbook of Linguistics and Literary History), *Buletinul Societăţii Numismatice Române* (1 a year), *Cahiers de linguistique théorique et appliquée, Calitatea vieţii* (Quality of Life), *Cellulose Chemistry and Technology, Cercetări de lingvistică* (Linguistic Researches), *Fonetică şi dialectologie* (Phonetics and Dialectology), *Functional and Architectural Electronics, Historia Urbana,*

Limba română (The Romanian Language), *Mathematica, Nyelv- és Irodalomtudományi Közlemények, Ocrotirea naturii şi a mediului înconjurător* (The Protection of Nature and of the Environment), *Revista de etnografie şi folclor* (Journal of Ethnography and Folklore), *Revista de psihologie* (Journal of Psychology), *Revista română de demografie* (Romanian Journal of Demography), *Revue d'analyse numérique et de théorie de l'approximation, Revue des études sud-est européennes, Revue Roumaine de biochimie, Revue Roumaine de biologie: Série de biologie animale, Revue Roumaine de biologie: Série de biologie végétale, Revue Roumaine de chimie, Revue Roumaine de géologie, géophysique et géographie* (3 series), *Revue Roumaine de Linguistique, Revue Roumaine de mathématiques pures et appliquées, Revue Roumaine de philosophie, Revue Roumaine de psychologie, Revue Roumaine des sciences économiques, Revue Roumaine des sciences juridiques, Revue Roumaine des sciences techniques: Série de mécanique appliquée, Revue Roumaine des sciences techniques: Série électrotechnique et énergétique, Romanian Astronomical Journal, Romanian Chemical Quarterly Review, Romanian Journal of Biophysics, Romanian Journal of Sociology, Romanian Neurosurgery, Romanian Reports of Physics, Studii şi cercetări de antropologie* (Studies and Research in Anthropology), *Studii şi cercetări de biochimie* (Studies and Research in Biochemistry), *Studii şi cercetări de biologie: Seria biologie animală* (Studies and Research in Biology: Series of Animal Biology), *Studii şi cercetări de biologie: Seria biologie vegetală* (Studies and Research in Biology: Series of Plant Biology), *Studii şi cercetări de geologie, geofizică şi geografie* (Studies and Research in Geology, Geophysics and Geography, 3 series), *Studii şi cercetări de mecanică aplicată* (Studies and Research in Applied Mechanics), *Studii şi cercetări lingvistice* (Studies and Research in Linguistics), *Studii şi cercetări matematice* (Studies and Research in Mathematics), *Synthesis–Bulletin du Comité National de Littérature comparée, Travaux de l'Institut de Spéléologie 'Émile Racovitza'*.

Asociaţia Culturală 'Pro Basarabia şi Bucovina' (Bessarabia and Bucovina Cultural Association): Str. Blănari 23, Sector 3, Bucharest; tel. and fax (21) 314-03-59; e-mail probasarabiasibucovina@yahoo.com; internet www.probasarabia.ro; f. 1990; 60,000 mems; Pres. ION RADU; publ. *Dor E Basarabia*.

Centrul European de Cultură, Bucureşti (European Cultural Centre, Bucharest): Sfinţii Voievozi St 49–51, 4th Fl., Apt. 16, Sector 1, 010968 Bucharest; tel. (21) 650-81-45; fax (21) 650-32-80; e-mail cti@clicknet.ro; internet www.studyabroad.ro; f. 1990; organizes int. postgraduate seminars on European issues; promotes Romania as an attractive cultural tourist destination, through research, publs and study tours; promotes colleges and univs in W Europe, the USA, Canada and Australia, which offer int. programmes related to undergraduate and postgraduate studies in Romania; 1,300 mems; library of 3,000 vols, 40 periodicals; Pres. Acad. DAN BERINDEI; Exec. Dir MARIA BURS-POPESCU.

Institutul Cultural Român (Romanian Cultural Institute): Aleea Alexandru 38, 011824 Bucharest; tel. (31) 710-06-06; fax (31) 710-06-07; e-mail icr@icr.ro; internet www.icr.ro; f. 2003; promotes Romanian culture abroad; publishes works by Romanian and foreign authors, dictionaries, history texts and other literature; institutes in Berlin, Brussels, Budapest (with a br. in Szeged), Istanbul, Kishinev, Lisbon, London, Madrid, New York, Paris, Prague, Rome, Stockholm, Tel Aviv, Venice, Vienna and Warsaw; 130 mems; Pres. HORIA-ROMAN PATAPIEVICI; publs *Curierul Românesc* (12 a year), *Destin Românesc* (4 a year), *Dilema* (48 a year), *Euresis* (2 a year), *Glasul Bucovinei* (4 a year), *Lettres internationales* (4 a year), *Plural* (2 a year), *România Culturală* (online), *Transylvanian Review* (4 a year).

Societatea Cultural-Ştiinţifică 'Getica' (Getica Cultural Scientific Society): POB 37-149, 70060 Bucharest 37; Str. Plantelor 8–10, 023974 Bucharest; tel. (21) 318-47-57; e-mail contact.gandirea@yahoo.com; internet www.gandirea.ro; f. 1990; 87 mems; library of 7,000 vols; Pres. GABRIEL GHEORGHE; publ. *Getica* (irregular).

AGRICULTURE, FISHERIES AND VETERINARY SCIENCE

Academia de Ştiinţe Agricole şi Silvice 'Gheorghe Ionescu-Şişeşti' (Academy of Agricultural and Forestry Sciences 'Gheorghe Ionescu-Şişeşti'): Bdul Mărăşti 61, 011464 Bucharest 1; tel. (21) 318-44-54; fax (21) 318-44-55; e-mail secretariat@asas.ro; internet www.asas.ro; f. 1969; sections of Soil Science, Land Reclamation and Environmental Protection in Agriculture, Field Crops, Horticulture, Animal Husbandry, Veterinary Medicine, Forestry Science, Agrarian Economics and Rural Development, Food Industry, Agricultural Mechanization; 211 mems (81 full and corresp., 40 hon., 90 assoc.); attached research institutes: see Research Institutes; library: see Libraries and Archives; Pres. Prof. Dr GHEORGHE SIN; Sec.-Gen. Prof. Dr MARIAN IANCULESCU; publs *Buletinul informativ al Academiei de Ştiinţe Agricole şi Silvice* (1 a year), *Bulletin de l'Académie des Sciences Agricoles et Forestières* (1 a year), *Bulletin of the Academy of Agricultural and Forestry Sciences* (1 a year), *Yearbook* (1 a year).

Asociaţia Economiştilor Agrarieni din România (Agrarian Economists Association of Romania): Bdul Mărăşti 61, 011464 Bucharest; tel. (21) 617-21-80; f. 1990; 42 mems; library of 4,000 vols; Pres. Prof. N. N. CONSTANTINESCU; Gen. Sec. RADU COTIANU.

Societatea Inginerilor Agronomi (Agronomists Society): Bdul Mărăşti 59, 011464 Bucharest; tel. (21) 618-22-30; f. 1990; 3,500 mems; Pres. Prof. Dr MIHAI VĂJIALĂ; Gen. Sec. Dr RUXANDRA CIOFU.

Societatea Naţională Română pentru Ştiinţa Solului (Romanian National Soil Science Society): Bdul Mărăşti 61, 011646 Bucharest; tel. (21) 318-43-49; fax (21) 318-43-48; e-mail mdumitru@icpa.ro; f. 1962; 494 mems; library of 3,592 vols; Pres. Dr MIHAIL DUMITRU; Gen. Sec. CONSTANTIN CRĂCIUN; publs *Bulletin Informativ* (1 a year), *Ştiinţa Solului* (2 a year).

Societatea Română de Zootehnie (Romanian Society of Animal Production): Bdul Mărăşti 59, 011464 Bucharest; tel. (21) 618-22-30; fax (21) 312-56-93; f. 1990; 4,500 mems; Pres. Prof. STEFAN POPESCU-VIFOR; Sr Sec. Dr AGATHA POPESCU.

ARCHITECTURE AND TOWN PLANNING

Uniunea Arhitecţilor din România (Union of Architects of Romania): Str. Dem Dobrescu 5, 010014 Bucharest; tel. and fax (21) 315-60-73; e-mail ma@com.pcnet.ro; internet www.uniuneaarhitectilor.ro; f. 1891; 2,010 mems; library of 13,000 vols; Pres. Arch. PETER DERER; publs *Architectura* (4 a year), *Buletin Informativ* (12 a year).

ECONOMICS, LAW AND POLITICS

Asociaţia de Drept Internaţional şi Relaţii Internaţionale (Association of International Law and International Relations): Şoseaua Kiseleff 47, 011314 Bucharest; tel. (21) 222-44-22; fax (21) 222-74-62; f. 1965; 500 mems; library of 8,000 vols; Pres. CORNELIU MĂNESCU; Sec.-Gen. MIRCEA MALIŢA.

Asociaţia Română de Drept Umanitar (Romanian Association of Humanitarian Law): Piaţa Haralambie Botescu 11–13, 050892 Bucharest; tel. and fax (21) 311-99-19; e-mail ardu.association@gmail.com; internet www.ardu.ro; f. 1990; 200 mems; library of 5,000 vols; Pres. Dr IONEL CLOŞCĂ; Gen. Sec. GHEORGHE BĂDESCU; publ. *Revista română de drept umanitar*.

FINE AND PERFORMING ARTS

Asociaţia Artiştilor Fotografi din Romania (Art Photographers Association): Piaţa Unirii, 2–4, Oradea; e-mail office@aafr.ro; internet www.aafr.ro; f. 1956; 1,615 mems; library of 12,000 photographic magazines; Pres. ŞTEFAN TÓTH; publs *Foto Magazin* (online), *Fotografia şi Video* (6 a year).

Asociaţia Artiştilor Plastici—Bucureşti (Artists Association of Bucharest): Str. Nicolae Balcescu 18, 021051 Bucharest; tel. (21) 613-38-60; f. 1973; 1,800 mems; Pres. Dr Eng. IOAN CEZAR CORĂCI; Gen. Sec. DAN SEGĂRCEANU.

Uniunea Artiştilor Plastici din România (Romanian Union of Fine Arts): Bdul Nicolae Balcescu, 1, 010433 Bucharest; tel. (21) 212-79-54; fax (21) 212-79-58; e-mail office@uappr.ro; internet www.uappr.ro; f. 1972; 4,170 mems; library of 12,000 vols; Pres. Prof. Dr DUMITRU SERBAN; publs *Arta* (art review, 4 a year), *Info* (12 a year).

Uniunea Cineaştilor din România (Romanian Film Makers Union): Str. Mendeleev 28–30, 010365 Bucharest; tel. (21) 316-80-84; fax (21) 311-12-46; e-mail czucin@ucin.ro; internet www.ucin.ro; f. 1963; 900 mems; Pres. MIHNEA GHEORGHIU; Vice Pres. CONSTANTIN PIVNICIERU; Sec. CARMEN ZAMFIRESCU.

Uniunea Compozitorilor şi Muzicologilor din România—Asociatia Pentru Drepturi De Autor (Composers and Musicologists Union of Romania): Calea Victoriei 141, 010071 Bucharest; tel. (21) 311-79-76; fax (21) 316-58-80; e-mail ada@ucmr-ada.ro; internet www.ucmr-ada.ro; f. 1920; 432 mems; library of 50,000 vols incl. spec. colln of Romanian music (printed scores and MSS); Dir Gen. ANA ACHIM; Sec. CARMEN RADULESCU; publs *Actualitatea Muzicală* (24 a year), *Muzica* (4 a year).

Uniunea Teatrală din România (Romanian Association of Theatre Artists): Str. George Enescu 2–4, 010306 Bucharest; tel. (21) 311-32-14; fax (21) 312-09-13; internet www.uniter.ro; f. 1990; 900 mems; Pres. ION CARAMITRU; publs *Anuarul teatrului românesc* (Romanian Theatre Yearbook), *Semnal teatral* (Theatre Signal, 4 a year).

HISTORY, GEOGRAPHY AND ARCHAEOLOGY

Comitetul Naţional al Istoricilor (National Committee for Historical Sciences): Calea Victoriei 125, 010071 Bucharest; tel. (21) 212-86-29; fax (21) 312-02-09; f. 1955; Pres DAN BERINDEI; Sec.-Gen. CONSTANTIN BUŞE; publ. *Nouvelles d'études d'histoire* (irregular).

Federaţia Filatelică Romana (Romanian Philatelic Federation): Str. Boteanu 6, POB 1-29, 010027 Bucharest; tel. (21) 313-89-21; fax (21) 310-40-04; e-mail federatia_filatelica@yahoo.com; internet www.federatia-filatelica.ro; f. 1891; 25,000 mems; library of 3,000 vols; Pres. LEONARD PASCANU; Sec.-Gen. SERGIU GABUREAC; publ. *Filatelia* (12 a year).

Societatea de Ştiinţe Geografice din România (Society of Geographical Sciences of Romania): Bdul Bălcescu 1, 010041 Bucharest; tel. (21) 614-93-50; f. 1875; 5,000 mems; library of 4,000 vols; Exec. Pres. POSEA GRIGORE; publs *Bulletin, Terra*.

Societatea de Ştiinţe Istorice din România (Society of Historical Sciences of Romania): Bd Regina Elisabeta 4–12, 030018 Bucharest; tel. (21) 313-13-29; fax (21) 321-05-35; e-mail ssi_r@yahoo.com; internet www .societateistorie.ro; f. 1949; 5,000 mems; Chair. Prof. Dr NICHITA ADĂNILOAIE; Pres. Prof. Dr IOAN SCURTU; Sec.-Gen Prof. Dr BOGDAN TEODORESCU; publ. *Studii şi articole de istorie* (1 a year).

Societatea Numismatică Română (Romanian Numismatic Society): Str. Popa Tatu 20, 010805 Bucharest; tel. (21) 642-26-02; f. 1903; 3,000 mems; library of 4,010 vols; Pres. Dr CONSTANTIN PREDA; Sec.-Gen. AURICĂ SMARANDA; publ. *Buletinul* (1 a year).

LANGUAGE AND LITERATURE

Alliance Française: Str. Emile Zola 6, 011847 Bucharest; tel. (21) 231-05-15; fax (21) 231-05-19; e-mail thierry.dumas@ diplomatie.fr; offers courses and examinations in French language and culture and promotes cultural exchange with France; attached offices in Braşov, Constanţa, Craiova, Medgidia, Piteşti and Ploieşti.

British Council: Calea Dorobantilor 14, 010572 Bucharest; tel. (21) 307-96-00; fax (21) 307-90-01; e-mail contact@britishcouncil .ro; internet www.britishcouncil.org/romania .htm; teaching centre; offers courses and examinations in English language and British culture and promotes cultural exchange with the UK; attached offices in Braşov, Cluj, Iaşi, and Timişoara; library of 16,000 vols; Dir LILIANA BIGLOU; Teaching Centre Man. DIANA BERLINSCHI.

Goethe-Institut: Str. Tudor Arghezi 8–10, 020945 Bucharest; tel. (21) 311-97-62; fax (21) 312-05-85; e-mail info@bukarest.goethe .org; internet www.goethe.de/ins/ro/buk/ deindex.htm; offers courses and examinations in German language and culture and promotes cultural exchange with Germany; also responsible for Goethe-Institut work in Moldova; library in Chisinau; library of 12,000 vols; Dir BEATE KÖHLER.

Instituto Cervantes: Str. Marin Serghiescu 12, 021016 Bucharest; tel. (21) 210-27-37; fax (21) 210-77-67; e-mail cenbuc@cervantes.es; internet bucarest.cervantes.es; offers courses and examinations in Spanish language and culture and promotes cultural exchange with Spain and Spanish-speaking Latin and Central America; library of 20,000 vols; Dir JUAN CARLOS VIDAL GARCÍA.

Institut Français: Bdul Dacia 77, 020051 Bucharest; tel. (21) 316-38-36; fax (21) 316-02-25; e-mail denis.soriot@culture-france.ro; internet www.institut-francais.ro; f. 1936; library of 35,000 vols; Dir DENIS SORIOT; Sec.-Gen. STÉPHANE BERGEOT.

PEN Club: Str. Transilvaniei 56, 010799 Bucharest; tel. (21) 312-58-54; fax (21) 311-11-12; f. 1924, re-f. 1990; 50 mems; Pres. ANA BLANDIANA; Sec. DENISA COMANESCU.

Societatea Română de Lingvistică (Romanian Society of Linguistics): Calea 13 Septembrie 13, 050711 Bucharest; tel. (21) 641-27-57; f. 1941; Pres. Prof. EMANUEL VASILIU; Sec. LAURENŢIU THEBAN.

Societatea Română de Lingvistică Romanică (Romanian Society of Romance Linguistics): Str. Edgar Quinet 7, 010017 Bucharest; f. 1962; 250 mems; library of 2,000 vols; Pres. Dr MARIUS SALA; Gen. Sec. SANDA REINHEIMER RÎPEANU; publ. *Bulletin* (irregular).

Uniunea Scriitorilor din România (Romanian Writers' Union): Calea Victoriei 115, 010071 Bucharest; tel. (21) 316-58-29; fax (21) 312-96-34; e-mail w_u_ro@yahoo .com; internet www.uniuneascriitorilor.ro; f. 1949; 2,400 mems; Pres. NICOLAE MANOLESCU; Dir. Gen. ALEXANDRU ISTRATE; publs *Apostrof, Caiete Critice, Contrapunct, Convorbiri literare* (1 a year), *Helikon, Lato, Luceafărul, Memoria, Orizont, Ramîuri, România Literară, Secolul 20, Vatra, Viaţa Românească.*

MEDICINE

Academia de Ştiinţe Medicale (Academy of Medical Sciences): Splaiul Independenţei 99–101, 061621 Bucharest; tel. (21) 311-53-80; fax (21) 311-53-81; e-mail adsm@adsm.ro; internet www.adsm.ro; f. 1935; sections of Fundamental Biomedical Sciences (Pres. Dr NICOLAE MANOLESCU), Internal Medicine (Pres. CONSTANTIN I. POPA), Surgery Clinic (Pres. Prof. Dr IRINEL POPESCU); attached research institutes: see Research Institutes; 82 mems, 14 corresp. mems; Pres. Prof. Dr LAURENTIU POPESCU; Sec.-Gen. Prof. Dr MIHAIL ZAMFIRESCU.

Asociaţia Medicală Română (Romanian Medical Association): Str. Ionel Perlea 10, 010209 Bucharest; tel. and fax (21) 314-10-71; e-mail amr@medica.ro; f. 1873; 38 affiliated socs; Pres. Prof. Dr VALERIU POPESCU; Sec.-Gen. Prof. Dr EMANOIL POPESCU; publs *Buletin A.M.R.* (4 a year), *Despre MÆDICA— a Journal of Clinical Medicine* (4 a year), *Practica Medicala* (4 a year), *Revista Medicala Romana* (4 a year), *Revista Romana de Boli Infectioase* (4 a year), *Revista Romana de Neurologie* (4 a year), *Revista Romana de Pediatrie* (4 a year), *Revista Romana de Reumatologie* (4 a year), *Revista Romana de Stomatologie* (4 a year).

Societatea de Medici şi Naturalişti Iaşi (Society of Physicians and Naturalists in Iaşi): Bdul Independenţei 16, POB 25, 700098 Iaşi; tel. (232) 14-29-80; f. 1830; medicine, pharmacy, dentistry; 1,640 mems; Chair. Prof. ION HĂULICĂ; publ. *Revista Medico-Chirurgicală* (multilingual, English abstracts, 4 a year).

Societatea Română de Stomatologie (Romanian Society of Stomatology): Str. Ionel Perlea 10, 70754 Bucharest; tel. (21) 314-20-80; fax (21) 312-13-57; f. 1923; Pres. Prof. Dr EMILIAN HUTU; Sec. Dr MARION VLADIMIR CONSTANTINESCU; publ. *Stomatologia* (4 a year).

NATURAL SCIENCES
General

Asociaţia Oamenilor de Ştiinţă din România (Academy of Romanian Scientists): Splaiul Independenţei 54, 050094 Bucharest; tel. (21) 314-74-91; fax (21) 314-75-39; e-mail aosromania@yahoo.com; internet www.aos.ro; f. 1956; Pres. Prof. Dr VASILE CÂNDEA; Scientific Sec.-Gen. Prof. Dr DORU-SABIN DELION.

Biological Sciences

Societatea de Ştiinţe Biologice din România (Society of Biological Sciences of Romania): Intrarea Portocalelor 1–3, 060101 Bucharest; f. 1949; 9,000 mems; library of 6,100 vols; Chair. Prof. Dr ION ANGHEL; Sec.-

Gen. Dr CONSTANTIN VOICA; publ. *Natura* (4 a year).

Mathematical Sciences

Societatea de Ştiinţe Matematice din România (Romanian Mathematical Society): Str. Academiei 14, 010014 Bucharest; tel. (21) 314-46-53; fax (21) 312-40-72; e-mail office@rms.unibuc.ro; internet www.rms .unibuc.ro; f. 1895; 5,000 mems; Pres. RADU GOLOGAN; Vice-Pres. DORU STEFANESCU; publs *Bulletin Mathématique de la Societe des Sciences Mathematiques de Roumanie* (4 a year), *Gazeta Matematică Seria A, Revista de cultura matematica* (4 a year), *Gazeta Matematică Seria B, Revista de cultura matematica pentru tineret* (12 a year).

Physical Sciences

Societatea Geologică a României (Geological Society of Romania): Str. Caransebeş, 012271 Bucharest; internet www.geosociety .ro; f. 1930; 500 mems; Pres. Dr ANTONETA SEGHEDI; Gen. Sec. TITUS BRUSTUR; publ. *Buletinul* (1 a year).

RELIGION, SOCIOLOGY AND ANTHROPOLOGY

Asociaţia Slaviştilor din România (Slav Studies Association of Romania): Str. Pitar Moş 7–13, 010451 Bucharest; tel. (21) 318-1579; fax (21) 211-9940; e-mail kgeambasu@ yahoo.com; internet www.unibuc.ro; f. 1956; promotes comparative Romanian-Slav studies at univ. level, in the fields of culture and civilization, of linguistics, literature, history, anthropology, ethnology, theory and practice of translation; promotes research in the Bulgarian, Croatian, Czech, Polish, Russian, Serbian, Slovakian, Slovenian, Ukrainian languages and literatures; library of 46 vols; 150 mems; Pres. Prof. Dr CONSTANTIN GEAMBAŞU; Vice-Pres. Dr MARIANA MANGIULEA; Vice-Pres. Prof. Dr ANTOANETA OLTEANU; Sec. Dr ANDREEA DUNAEVA; publ. *Romanoslavica* (1 a year).

Institutul Biblic şi de Misiune al Bisericii Ortodoxe Române (Biblical and Missionary Institute of the Romanian Orthodox Church): Intrarea Miron Cristea 6, 040162 Bucharest; tel. (21) 406-71-94; fax (21) 300-05-53; e-mail tipogr.inst.biblic@rdslink.ro; internet www.edituraparhiei.ro; f. 1925; publishes the synodal Romanian versions of the Holy Scripture, liturgical books, patristic texts, handbooks and treatises for Romanian theological schools, contemporary Orthodox literature; 14 mems; Dir. AURELIAN MARINESCU; Sec. Fr EUGEN MORARU; publs *Biserica Ortodoxa Româna* (4 a year), *Ortodoxia* (2 a year).

Societatea de Etnologie din România (Ethnology Society of Romania): Str. Zalomit 12, 010151 Bucharest; tel. and fax (21) 311-03-23; e-mail rica_org@yahoo.com; f. 1990; 200 mems; library; Pres. Dr. GEORGE ANCA; Sec. ION MOANŢA; publs *Etnologie românească* (4 a year), *Liber* (4 a year), *School of Indology* (4 a year), *Trivium* (4 a year).

TECHNOLOGY

Asociaţia Generală a Inginerilor din România (General Association of Engineers of Romania): Calea Victoriei 118, 70179 Bucharest; tel. (21) 316-89-94; fax (21) 312-55-31; e-mail office@agir.ro; internet www .agir.ro; f. 1881; 16,300 mems; library of 32,000 vols; Pres. Prof. Dr Ing. MIHAI MIHĂIŢĂ; publs *Anuarul AGIR* (1 a year), *Buletinul Tehnic AGIR* (4 a year), *Univers Inginersec* (24 a year).

Research Institutes

GENERAL

Anastasie Fătu Botanical Garden of Alexandru Ioan Cuza University of Iaşi: Str. Dumbrava Roşie 7–9, 700487 Iaşi; tel. (232) 20-13-73; fax (232) 20-13-85; e-mail gbot.is@uaic.ro; internet www.botanica.uaic.ro; f. 1856; attached to Universitatea 'Alexandru Ioan Cuza' Iaşi; organizes research; Dir Prof. CĂTĂLIN TĂNASE; Scientific Sec. Dr ADRIAN OPREA; publ. *Journal of Plant Development*.

The Astronomic Observatory: Aleea M. Sadoveanu 5, 700490 Iaşi; internet www.uaic.ro; f. 1913; attached to Universitatea 'Alexandru Ioan Cuza' Iaşi.

AGRICULTURE, FISHERIES AND VETERINARY SCIENCE

Aquaproiect, SA: Spl. Independenţei 294, 060031 Bucharest; tel. (21) 316-00-35; fax (21) 316-00-42; e-mail office@aquaproiect.ro; internet www.aquaproiect.ro; f. 1953; design and consulting in environmental engineering and water management; library of 10,000 vols; Technical Dir Dipl. Eng. GHEORGHE BRĂTIANU.

Centrul de Cercetare—Dezvoltare pentru Combaterea Eroziunii Solului Perieni (Research and Development Centre for Soil Erosion Control Perieni): Perieni, 737405 Judetul Vaslui; tel. and fax (235) 55-01-55; e-mail office@cesperieni.ro; internet cesperieni.ro; f. 1954; attached to Acad. of Agricultural and Forestry Sciences, Bucharest; study on soil erosion by means of standard runoff check plots, determinations of optimal doses of fertilizers, establishing species and mixtures of perennial herbs necessary to rehabilitate deteriorated pastures, experimental studies on forestal shelter belts, research on soil erosion control by agrotechnical methods (conservation agriculture), studies on types of crop rotation on sloping land, establishing crops range (sorts) on sloping land, chemical weed control, water balance on agricultural land deteriorated by gullies and/or landslides; Dir Dr DUMITRU NISTOR.

Centrul de Cercetăre-Dezvoltare pentru Cultura Plantelor pe Nisipuri (Central Research Station for Plant Cultivation on Sand): Jud. Dăbuleni, 207220 Dolj; tel. (251) 33-44-02; fax (251) 33-43-47; e-mail ccdcpndabuleni@yahoo.com; f. 1959; attached to Acad. of Agricultural and Forestry Sciences; 111 mems; library of 14,315 vols; Dir-Gen. Dr Eng. AURELIA DIACONU; publ. *Anales* (1 a year).

Centrul Naţional de Geodezie, Cartografie, Fotogrammetrie şi Teledecţie (National Centre of Geodesy, Cartography, Photogrammetry and Remote-Sensing): Bdul Expoziţiei 1A, 012101 Bucharest; tel. (21) 224-42-84; fax (21) 224-19-96; e-mail cngcft@ancpi.ro; internet www.cngcft.ro; f. 1958; library of 6,000 vols; Dir ILEANA SPIROU; publs *Analele CNGCFT* (1 a year), *Buletinul de Fotogrammetrie şi Teledetecţie*, *Revistei de Geodezie*.

Institutul de Cercetare-Dezvoltare pentru Apicultură (Research and Development Institute for Beekeeping): Bdul Ficusului 42, 013975 Bucharest; tel. (21) 232-50-60; fax (21) 232-02-87; e-mail secretariat@icdapicultura.ro; f. 1974; attached to Acad. of Agricultural and Forestry Sciences; researches on biology honeybees, beekeeping technologies, melliferous flora and pollination, honeybee pathologies, apitherapy; genetic fund conservation program; production of veterinary medicines for honeybees; production of food supplements and medicines based on bee products; library of 11,300 vols, 4,400 periodicals; Gen. Dir Dr CRISTINA MATEESCU; publ. *România apicolă* (12 a year).

Institutul de Cercetare-Dezvoltare pentru Cultura şi Industrializarea Sfeclei de Zahăr şi Substanţelor Dulci (Research and Development Institute for the Cultivation and Processing of Sugar Beet and Sweet Substances): Judeţul Călarasi, 915200 Fundulea; tel. and fax (242) 64-24-23; f. 1981; attached to Acad. of Agricultural and Forestry Sciences; Dir Dr Ing. AURELIAN POPA; publs *Scientific Works—Beet and Sugar* (1 a year), *Health of Plants* (1–3 a year), *Cereal and Technical Plants* (1–3 a year), *Agricultural Papers* (1–4 a year).

Institutul de Cercetare Dezvoltare pentru Ecologie Acvatica, Pescuit si Acvacultura (Research and Development Institute for Aquatic Ecology, Fishing and Aquaculture): Str. Portului 54, 800211 Galaţi; tel. (236) 41-69-14; fax (236) 41-42-70; e-mail icdeapa@gmail.com; internet www.icdeapa.ro; f. 1981; attached to Acad. of Agricultural and Forestry Sciences; fundamental and applied research, studies for environmental licences, evaluation in aquaculture and fishing, consulting, technical assistance; Dir Prof. NECULAI PATRICHE; Scientific Sec. Dr MARILENA TALPES.

Institutul de Cercetare—Dezvoltare pentru Pajisti (Grassland Research—Development Institute): Str. Cucului 5, 500128 Braşov; tel. (268) 47-27-81; fax (268) 47-52-95; f. 1969; attached to Acad. of Agricultural and Forestry Sciences; library of 7,000 vols; Gen. Man. Dr TEODOR MARUSCA; publ. *Lucrări ştiinţifice* (1 a year).

Institutul de Cercetare Dezvoltare pentru Pomicultura (Fruit-Growing Research Institute): Mărăcineni, Str. Mărului 402, 117450 Argeş; tel. (248) 27-80-66; fax (248) 27-84-77; e-mail office@icdp-pitesti.ro; internet www.icdp.ro; f. 1967; attached to Acad. of Agricultural and Forestry Sciences; 10 experimental fruit stations; research areas incl. breeding studies, biotechnology, pest control and virology; 33 mems; library of 25,000 vols; Dir Gen. COMAN MIHAIL; publ. *Lucrările Ştiinţifice ale Institutul de Cercetare Dezvoltare pentru Pomicultura* (1 a year).

Institutul de Cercetare—Dezvoltare pentru Protecţia Plantelor (Research and Development Institute for Plant Protection): Bdul Ion Ionescu de la Brad 8, Sector 1, 013813 Bucharest; tel. (21) 269-32-34; fax (21) 269-32-39; e-mail secretariat_stiintific@icdpp.ro; internet icdpp.ro; f. 1967; attached to Acad. of Agricultural and Forestry Science; draws up new technologies to increase food chain safety incl. means and methods of biological protection against pathogen attack to accomplish sustainable devt objectives in agriculture and to complete and carry out ecological agriculture systems; application of nat. and int. strategies for research activity in plant protection; devt and improvement of rapid diagnosis techniques for pathogens; eco-toxicology studies and research works necessary to register plant protection products in accordance with EU acquis; library of 9,000 vols; Dir and Gen. Man. Prof. Dr HORIA ILIESCU; publs *Anale ICDPP* (1 a year), *Romanian Journal for Plant Protection* (4 a year).

Institutul de Cercetare şi Dezvoltare pentru Bovine (Institute for Bovine Research and Development): Sect. Agricol Ilfov, 077015 Baloteşti; tel. (21) 266-12-02; fax (21) 266-12-06; e-mail icpcb@k.ro; f. 1970; attached to Acad. of Agricultural and Forestry Sciences; library of 11,000 vols; Dir Dr Ing. IOAN CUREU; publs *Presentation* (every 5 years), *Taurine—Scientific Works* (1 a year).

Institutul de Cercetare şi Dezvoltare pentru Valorificarea Produselor Horticole (Institute of Research and Development for Marketing Horticultural Products): Intrarea Binelui 1A, POB 1-93, 042146 Bucharest; tel. (21) 312-90-37; fax (21) 330-36-85; f. 1967; attached to Acad. of Agricultural and Forestry Sciences; library of 3,575 vols; Dir Dr Eng. ANDREI GHERGHI; publs *Lucrări ştiinţifice* (1 a year), *Horticultura* (12 a year).

Institutul de Cercetare şi Inginerie Tehnologică pentru Irigaţii şi Drenaje (Research and Technological Engineering Institute for Irrigation and Drainage): Judeţul Giurgiu, 087010 Băneasa; tel. (246) 28-50-23; fax (246) 28-50-24; e-mail scdid@easynet.ro; f. 1977; attached to Acad. of Agricultural and Forestry Sciences; library of 5,700 vols, 763 periodicals; Dir Dr Ing. GHEORGHE CRUTU; publ. *Scientific Papers on Irrigation and Drainage* (1 a year).

Institutul de Cercetare şi Producţie pentru Creşterea Ovinelor şi Caprinelor (Research and Production Institute for Sheep and Goat Breeding): Str. I. C. Brătianu 248, Judeţul Constanţa Palas, 900316 Constanţa; tel. and fax (241) 63-95-06; e-mail icdcoc@relsys.ro; f. 1897; attached to Acad. of Agricultural and Forestry Sciences; Dir Ing. RADU RĂDUCU.

Institutul de Cercetare şi Producţie pentru Creşterea Păsărilor şi Animalelor Mici (Research and Production Institute for Poultry and Small Animal Breeding): Sect. Agricol Ilfov, 077015 Baloteşti; fax (21) 795-10-23; f. 1970; attached to Acad. of Agricultural and Forestry Sciences; Dir Ing. GRIGORE MUSCALU.

Institutul de Cercetări Dezvoltare pentru Legumicultură şi Floricultură (Research and Development Institute for Vegetable and Flower Growing): Judeţul Ilfov, 077185 Vidra; tel. and fax (21) 361-20-94; e-mail inclf@mediasat.ro; internet www.icdlfvidra.ro; f. 1967; attached to Acad. of Agricultural and Forestry Sciences; research into plant breeding and seed production, soil science, plant protection and flower-growing; library of 500 vols; Dir Dr MARCEL COSTACHE; publ. *Annals*.

Institutul de Cercetări pentru Cereale şi Plante Tehnice (Research Institute for Cereals and Industrial Crops): Judeţul Fundulea, 915200 Călăraşi; tel. (242) 311-07-22; fax (242) 311-07-22; f. 1957; attached to Acad. of Agricultural and Forestry Sciences; library of 12,000 vols; Dir GHEORGHE SIN; publs *Analele* (1 a year), *Probleme de agrofitotehnie teoretică şi aplicată*, *Probleme de genetică teoretică şi aplicată*, *Probleme de protecţia plantelor* (4 a year), *Romanian Agricultural Research* (every 2 years).

Institutul de Cercetări pentru Viticultură şi Vinificaţie (Research Institute for Viticulture and Wine-Making): Str. Valea Mantei 1, Judeţul Valea Călugărească, 107620 Prahova; tel. (244) 23-66-90; fax (244) 23-63-89; e-mail icvv@xnet.ro; f. 1967; Man Dr Eng. NICOLAE VARGA; attached to Acad. of Agricultural and Forestry Sciences; library of 14,000 vols; publ. *Anale* (research papers).

Institutul de Cercetări şi Amenajări Silvice (Forest Research and Management Institute): Eroilor Blvd. 128, 077190 Voluntari/Ilfou; tel. (21) 350-32-38; fax (21) 350-32-45; e-mail icas@icas.ro; internet www.icas.ro; f. 1933; attached to Acad. of Agricultural and Forestry Sciences; library of 32,000 vols; Man. GHEORGHE DUMITRIU; Man. HEINRICH

FLORENTINA; Sec. VIOLETA TIRON; publs *Analele Ilas, Bucovina Forestiera.*

Institutul de Chimie Alimentară (Research Institute for Food Chemistry): Str. Gârlei 1, 013721 Bucharest; tel. (21) 230-50-90; fax (21) 230-03-11; e-mail ica@sunu.rnc.ro; f. 1950; attached to Acad. of Agricultural and Forestry Sciences; library of 25,000 vols; Dir Prof. Dr GHEORGHE MENCI-NICOPSCHI; publ. *Ştiinţe şi Tehnologii Alimentare* (Food Sciences and Technology, 4 a year).

Institutul Naţional de Cercetare—Dezvoltare Marină 'Grigore Antipa' (National Institute for Marine Research and Development 'Grigore Antipa'): Bdul Mamaia 300, POB 3, 900001 Constanţa; tel. (41) 54-32-88; fax (41) 83-12-74; e-mail office@alpha.rmri.ro; internet www.rmri.ro; f. 1970; attached to Min. of Environment and Forests; library of 38,000 vols and periodicals; Dir Dr Ing. SIMION NICOLAEV; Scientific Dir Dr TANIA ZAHARIA; publ. *Cercetări Marine* (1 a year).

Institutul Naţional de Cercetare-Dezvoltare pentru Biologie si Nutriţie Animala (National Research Development Institute for Animal Biology and Nutrition): Judet Ilfov, 077015 Baloteşti; tel. (21) 351-20-81; fax (21) 351-20-80; e-mail secretariat@ibna.ro; internet www.ibna.ro; f. 1970; attached to Acad. of Agricultural and Forestry Sciences; library of 5,000 vols; Gen. Man. Prof. Dr HORIA GROSU; Dir of Science Dr CATALIN DRAGOMIR; publs *Anale* (1 a year), *Archiva Zootechnica* (in English, 4 a year).

Institutul Naţional de Cercetare Dezvoltare pentru Cartof si Sfeclă de Zahar (Research and Development Institute for Potato and Sugar Beet): Str. Fundăturii 2, 500470 Braşov; tel. (268) 47-67-95; fax (268) 47-66-08; e-mail icpc@potato.ro; internet www.potato.ro; f. 1967; attached to Acad. of Agricultural and Forestry Sciences, Bucharest; 55 mems; library of 10,000 vols; Gen. Dir Dr SORIN CHIRU; Scientific Dir Dr VICTOR DONESCU; publs *Anale* (scientific papers, 1 a year), *Cartoful în România* (The Potato in Romania, 4 a year), *Tehnologie* (1 a year).

Institutul Naţional de Cercetare-Dezvoltare pentru Pedologie, Agrochimie şi Protecţia Mediului—ICPA Bucureşti (National Research and Development Institute for Soil Science, Agrochemistry and Environment Protection—ICPA Bucharest): Bdul Mărăşti 61, 71331 Bucharest; tel. (21) 318-44-63; fax (21) 318-43-48; e-mail office@icpa.ro; internet www.icpa.ro; f. 1970; attached to Acad. of Agricultural and Forestry Sciences; characterization and quantification of natural resources and environment; inventorying and monitoring natural resources and environment; plant nutrition and soil/plant fertilization; sustainable management of natural resources and environment, soil pollution, global change, rural devt; waste management; standards and methodologies on natural resources and environment; soil/land/environment data computing, agricultural/environment information services; library of 9,000 vols; Dir Dr Ing. MIHAIL DUMITRU; Scientific Dir Dr CATALIN SIMOTA; publ. *Anale* (1 a year).

Institutul Naţional de Cercetări-Dezvoltare pentru Protecţia Mediului (National Institute for Research and Development of Environmental Protection): Splaiul Independenţei 294, 060031 Bucharest; tel. (21) 318-20-57; fax (21) 318-20-01; e-mail icim@icim.ro; internet www.icim.ro; f. 1952; library of 5,000 vols; Dir Gen. Prof. Dr NECULAI MIHAILESCU.

Institutul Naţional de Medicină Veterinară Pasteur (Pasteur National Institute of Veterinary Medicine): Calea Giuleşti 333, 77826 Bucharest; tel. (21) 220-64-86; fax (21) 220-69-15; f. 1909; attached to Acad. of Agricultural and Forestry Sciences; library of 30,000 vols; Dir Dr C. ŞTIRBU; publ. *Studies and Research in Veterinary Medicine* (1 a year).

Societatea Comerciala Romsuintest Periş SA (Trade Society Romsuintest Periş SA): Judeţul Ilfov, 077150 Periş; tel. (21) 796-07-05; fax (21) 796-07-01; f. 1970; attached to Acad. of Agricultural and Forestry Sciences; research into pig-breeding; library of 8,000 vols; Dir Dr ŞTEFAN MANTEA; publ. *Lucrări ştiinţifice* (Scientific Work, 1 a year).

Staţiunea Centrală de Cercetări pentru Cultura şi Industrializarea Tutunului (Central Research Station for Tobacco Growing and Industrialization): Str. Gârlei 1, 013721 Bucharest; tel. (21) 230-45-75; fax (21) 230-51-58; f. 1929; attached to Acad. of Agricultural and Forestry Sciences; Dir MARIANA TIGĂU; publ. *Buletinul tutunului* (1 a year).

Staţiunea de Cercetăre-Dezvoltare Agricola Brăila (Brăila Agricultural Research and Development Station): Şoseaua Vizirului km. 9, Judeţul Brăila, 810008 Brăila; tel. (239) 68-46-95; fax (239) 68-47-44; f. 1954; attached to Acad. of Agricultural and Forestry Sciences; 12 mems; Dir Dr Ing. MARCEL BULARDA; Scientific Sec. Dr Ing. VISINESCU IOAN; publ. *Scientific Works* (1 a year).

ARCHITECTURE AND TOWN PLANNING

Centrul pentru Noi Arhitecturei Electronice (Centre for New Electronic Architecture): Bdul Armata Poporului 1–3, Bucharest; tel. (21) 631-78-00; attached to Romanian Acad.; Dir ŞTEFAN GHEORGHE.

Institutul Naţional de Cercetare-Dezvoltare în Construcţii, Urbanism şi Dezvoltare Teritorială Durabilă URBAN-INCERC (National Institute for Research and Development in Constructions, Urbanism and Sustainable Spatial Development URBAN-INCERC): Şoseaua Pantelimon 266, 021652 Bucharest; tel. (21) 255-02-70; fax (21) 255-00-62; e-mail urban-incerc@incd.ro; internet www.incd.ro; f. 1957; fundamental and applied research in urban and territorial planning, architecture, constructions and the economy of bldgs; library of 350,000 vols, 200 current periodicals; Gen. Dir Dr VASILE MEITA; publs *Buletin roman de agremente tehnice in constructii* (12 a year), *Constructii/Constructions* (2 a year), *Probleme de economia constructiilor* (12 a year), *Urbanism. Arhitectura. Constructii / Urbanism. Architecture. Constructions* (4 a year, online (uac.incerc.ro/EN/index.htm).

Prodomus SA—Institut de Studii şi Proiectare pentru Construcţii Civile (Institute of Research and Design for Civil Engineering Works): Str. Nicolae Filipescu 53–55, 020961 Bucharest; tel. (21) 211-78-40; f. 1949; housing, social bldgs; Dir Eng. CORNELIU VELICU; publs *'bdi'* (bulletin of documentation and information), *Prodomus—SA.*

Proed SA—Institut de Studii şi Proiectare pentru Lucrări Tehnico-Edilitare (Studies and Design Institute for Public Works): Str. Tudor Arghezi 21, 020943 Bucharest; tel. (21) 211-55-10; fax (21) 210-18-01; f. 1949; water, sewerage and other public facilities, traffic organization and public transport; Man. Dir Gen. CONSTANTIN HOTULETE; publ. *'bdi'* (bulletin of documentation and information, 4 a year).

ECONOMICS, LAW AND POLITICS

Institutul de Cercetări Juridice 'Acad. Andrei Rădulescu' (Institute of Judicial Research of the Academy Andrei Rădulescu): Calea 13 Septembrie 13, Sector 5, 050711 Bucharest; tel. (21) 318-81-30; fax (21) 318-24-53; e-mail icj_juridic@yahoo.com; internet www.icj.ro; f. 1954; attached to Romanian Acad.; research in all branches of law; library of 7,120 vols, 2,210 periodicals; Pres. Prof. EMIL GHEORGHE MOROIANU; Sec. Dr BOGDAN PĂTRAŞCU; publ. *Studii de Drept Românesc* (4 a year).

Institutul 'Gheorghe Zane' de Cercetări Economice şi Sociale (Gheorghe Zane Institute for Economic Research): Str. Theodor Codrescu 2, 700481 Iaşi; tel. and fax (332) 10-65-07; e-mail magdalena_lazar15@yahoo.com; internet www.ices.ro; f. 1992; attached to Romanian Acad.; library of 40,000 vols; Dir Prof. TEODOR DIMA; publs *Anuarul de Cercetări Economice, Anuarul Idei şi Valori Perene, Symposion.*

Institutul Naţional de Cercetări Economice 'Costin C. Kiritescu' (National Institute of Economic Research 'Costin C. Kiritescu'): Calea 13 Septembrie 13, 050711 Bucharest; tel. and fax (21) 318-81-06; e-mail ciumara@zappmobile.ro; internet www.ince.ro; f. 1990; attached to Romanian Acad.; Dir-Gen. Prof. Dr MIRCEA CIUMARA; Dirs-Gen. Adjunct Prof. Dr CONSTANTIN CIUTACU, Prof. Dr NAPOLEON POP, Prof. Dr VALERIU IOAN-FRANCE; Scientific Sec. Dr LUMINITA CHIVU; publs *Analele INCE* (4 a year), *Probleme economice* (47 a year), *Româna de Economie* (2 a year), *Romanian Economic Research Observer* (6 a year), *Romanian Economic Review* (2 a year), *Studii şi cercetări economice* (12 a year).

Attached Institutes:

Centrul de Cercetări Financiare şi Monetare 'Victor Slăvescu' (Centre of Financial and Monetary Research 'Victor Slăvescu'): tel. and fax (21) 318-24-19; e-mail icfm01@icfm.ro; internet www.icfm.ro; f. 1967 as Centrul de Finanţe, Preţuri şi Probleme Valutare 'Victor Slăvescu', present name and status 2001; attached to Romanian Acad.; library of 700 vols; Dir Dr NAPOLEON POP; publ. *Studii Financiare* (Financial Studies, 4 a year).

Centrul de Economia Industriei şi a Serviciilor (Centre for the Industrial and Service Economy): tel. and fax (21) 318-24-18; e-mail office@iei.ro; internet www.iei.ro; f. 1977; attached to Romanian Acad.; Dir Dr MIHAI-SABIN MUSCALU; Dir Adjunct Dr MARIUS BULEARCA; publs *Probleme economice* (Economic Problems, 47 a year), *Revista de Economie Industriala* (1 a year).

Centrul Român de Economie Comparată şi Consens: tel. (21) 411-60-75; fax (21) 411-54-86; internet www.ince.ro/ecc.htm; f. 1999; attached to Romanian Acad.; Dir TUDOREL POSTOLACHE.

Institutul de Economie Mondială 'Costin Murgescu' (Institute of World Economy 'Costin Murgescu'): tel. (21) 318-24-60; fax (21) 318-24-54; e-mail office@iem.ro; internet www.iem.ro; f. 1967; attached to Romanian Acad.; library of 21,500 vols, 320 periodicals, World Bank depository library; Dir Dr CONSTANTIN CIUPEGEA; Scientific Sec Dr VIRGINIA CÎMPEAN; publs *Buletin de preţuri şi cotaţii pe piaţa internaţională* (144 a year), *Conjunctura economiei mondiale* (1 a year), *Euroinfo* (2 a year), *Eurolex* (4 a year), *Evoluţia preţurilor internaţionale* (2 a year), *Piaţa internaţională* (96 a year).

Institutul de Economie Naţională (Institute of National Economy): tel. and fax (21) 318-24-67; e-mail office@ien.ro; internet www.ien.ro; f. 1953 as Institute for Economic Research of the Romanian Academy, present status 1990; attached to Romanian Acad.; Dir GHEORGHE ZAMAN; Dir Adjunct CONSTANTIN CIUTACU; publ. *Revista Româna de Economie* (Romanian Economic Review, in English, 2 a year).

Institutul de Prognoză Economică (Institute for Economic Forecasting): tel. and fax (21) 318-81-48; e-mail ipe@ipe.ro; internet www.ipe.ro; f. 1970 as Centre of Planning Studies and Research (attached to State Planning Cttee); reorg. as Institute for Planning and Forecasting (attached to State Planning Cttee and National Institute for Economic Research) 1977; present status 1990; attached to Romanian Acad.; Dir Prof. Dr LUCIAN-LIVIU ALBU; Dir Adjunct Dr MARIOARA IORDAN; publ. *Romanian Journal for Economic Forecasting* (4 a year).

EDUCATION

Institutul de Cercetări pentru Inteligenţă Artificială (Research Institute for Artificial Intelligence): Calea 13 Septembrie 13, 050711 Bucharest; tel. (21) 318-81-03; fax (21) 318-81-42; e-mail office@racai.ro; internet www.racai.ro; f. 1994 as Centrul de Cercetări Avansate în Învăţarea Automată, Prelucrarea Limbajului Natural şi Modelarea Conceptuală, present name 2002; attached to Romanian Acad.; researches in areas of natural language processing, machine learning, knowledge acquisition, computer-aided instruction, structural-phenomenological modelling; Dir Prof. Dr IOAN DAN TUFIS; Scientific Dir Dr ANGELA IONITA; Hon. Dir GHEORGHE TECUCI.

FINE AND PERFORMING ARTS

Institutul de Arheologie şi Istoria Artei al Academiei Române (Institute of Archaeology and History of Art of the Romanian Academy): Str. M. Kogălniceanu 12–14, 400084 Cluj-Napoca; tel. (264) 59-11-25; fax (264) 59-44-70; e-mail iaiacluj@yahoo.com; internet www .institutarheologie-istoriaarteicj.ro; f. 1990; attached to Romanian Acad.; library of 20,874 vols; Dir Dr MARIUS PORUMB; Asst Dir Dr CORIOLAN HORATIU OPREAN; publs *Ars Transsilvaniae* (1 a year), *Ephemeris Napocensis* (1 a year).

Institutul de Istoria Artei 'G. Oprescu' (G. Oprescu Institute of the History): 196 Calea Victoriei, Sector 1, 010098 Bucharest; tel. and fax (21) 314-40-70; e-mail istartro@ yahoo.com; internet www.istoria-artei.ro; f. 1949; attached to Romanian Acad.; Romanian medieval art, Byzantine art, modern art, architecture, theatre, music, cinema; library of 72,000 vols, 108,000 photographs, 21,000 film negatives, 12,593 glass negatives; Dir Dr ADRIAN-SILVIU IONESCU; Scientific Sec. Dr MARINA SABADOS; publs *Revue Roumaine d'Histoire de l'Art: Série Beaux-Arts* (1 a year), *Studii şi Cercetări de Istoria Artei: Artă Plastică* (1 a year), *Studii şi Cercetări de Istoria Artei: Teatru, Muzică, Cinematografie* (1 a year).

HISTORY, GEOGRAPHY AND ARCHAEOLOGY

Centrul de Istorie şi Civilizaţie Europeană (Centre for History and European Civilization): Aleea M. Sadoveanu 3, parter, 700490 Iaşi; tel. (232) 21-24-41; fax (232) 21-24-41; f. 1992; attached to Romanian Acad.; Dir GHEORGHE BUZATU; publ. *Europa XXI* (every 2 years).

Centrul pentru Studiul Istoriei Evreilor din România (Centre for the Study of the History of Jews in Romania): Str. Mămulari 4, 1st Fl., Apt. 1, 030772 Bucharest; tel. and fax (21) 315-10-45; e-mail csier_fcer@yahoo .com; f. 1977; attached to the Fed. of Jewish Communities in Romania; Dir Dr LIVIU ROTMAN; publ. *Buletinul* (bulletin, 2 a year).

Institutul de Arheologie (Institute of Archaeology): Str. Lascăr Catargi 18, 700107 Iaşi; e-mail arheoligieiasi@yahoo .com; internet www.arheo.ro; tel. and fax (332) 10-61-73; f. 1990; attached to Romanian Acad.; research in archaeology and ancient history; Dir Prof. Dr ALEXANDER RUBEL; Asst Dir Dr VIRGIL MIHAILESCU-BÎRLIBA; publs *Arheologia Moldovei* (1 a year), *Bibliotheca Archaeologica Iassiensis* (irregular), *Bibliotheca Archaeologica Moldaviae* (irregular), *Honoraria* (irregular), *Studia Et Acta Historiae Iudaeorum Romaniae.*

Institutul de Arheologie 'Vasile Pârvan' (Vasile Pârvan Institute of Archaeology): Str. Henri Coandă 11, 010667 Bucharest; tel. and fax (21) 212-88-62; e-mail ionmotzoichicideanu@archaeology.ro; internet www.instarhparvan.ro; f. 1956; attached to Romanian Acad.; library of 200,000 vols; Dir Prof. Dr ALEXANDRU VULPE; publs *Dacia—Revue d'Archéologie et d'Histoire Ancienne* (1 a year), *Materiale şi cercetări arheologice* (1 a year), *Studii şi cercetări de istorie veche* (4 a year), *Studii şi cercetări de numismatică* (every 2 years), *Thraco-Dacica.*

Institutul de Geografie (Institute of Geography): Str. Dimitrie Racoviţă 12, 023993 Bucharest; tel. (21) 313-59-90; fax (21) 311-12-42; e-mail geoinst@fx.ro; f. 1944; attached to Romanian Acad.; library of 50,000 vols, 200 periodicals, 1,900 atlases and maps; Dir Prof. Dr DAN BĂLTEANU; publ. *Revista Geografică* (1 a year).

Institutul de Istorie 'A. D. Xenopol' (A. D. Xenopol Institute of History): Str. Lascăr Catargi 15, 700107 Iaşi; tel. and fax (332) 10-61-72; e-mail institut@xenopol.iasi.astral.ro; internet www.academiaromana-is.ro/ adxenopol; f. 1941; attached to Romanian Acad.; Romanian and world history; library of 58,000 vols, 900 titles; Dir Prof. Dr GHEORGHE CLIVETI; Dir Adjunct Prof. Dr GHEORGHE CLIVETI; Sec. MIHAELA CAZACU; publs *Anuarul Institutului de Istorie A. D. Xenopol* (1 a year), *Studia et Acta Historiae Iudaeorum Romaniae* (1 a year), *Xenopoliana. Buletinul Fundaţiei Academice A. D. Xenopol* (4 a year).

Institutul de Istorie 'Nicolae Iorga' (Nicolae Iorga Institute of History): Bdul Aviatorilor 1, 011851 Bucharest; tel. (21) 212-53-37; fax (21) 311-03-71; e-mail institul.iorga@email.ro; internet www.iini .ro; f. 1937; attached to Romanian Acad.; historical research (middle ages to 20th century); library of 130,000 vols; Dir Dr OVIDIU CRISTEA; Scientific Sec. Dr ILEANA CAZAN; publs *Historical Yearbook* (1 a year), *Revista Istorică* (6 a year), *Revue Roumaine d'histoire* (4 a year), *Studii şi Materiale de Istorie Contemporana* (1 a year), *Studii şi Materiale de Istorie Medie* (1 a year), *Studii şi Materiale de Istorie Modernă* (1 a year).

University '1 December 1918' Alba Iulia Systemic Archaeology Institute: Str. Mihai Viteazul 12, 510010 Alba Iulia; tel. (258) 81-70-71; fax (258) 81-84-59; e-mail arhsis@uab.ro; internet www.bcum.uab.ro; f. 2001; attached to Universitatea '1 Decembrie 1918' din Alba Iulia; archaeology; preservation and restoration of archaeological sites; Dir Dr MIHAI GLIGOR.

LANGUAGE AND LITERATURE

Institutul de Filologie Română 'Al. Philippide' (Al. Philippide Institute of Romanian Philology): Str. Theodor Codrescu 2, 700481 Iaşi; tel. and fax (332) 10-65-08; e-mail secretariat_philippide@yahoo.com; internet www.academiaromana-is.ro/ philippide; f. 1927; attached to Romanian Acad.; depts of lexicology and lexicography, dialectology, toponymy, literature, ethnology; 41 mems; library of 60,000 vols; Dir Prof. Dr EUGEN MUNTEANU; publs *Anuar de Lingvistică şi Istorie Literară*, *Buletinul* (4 a year), *Philologica Jassyensia* (2 a year).

Institutul de Istorie şi Teorie Literară 'G. Călinescu' (G. Călinescu Institute of Literary History and Theory): Calea 13 Septembrie 13, 050711 Bucharest; tel. and fax (21) 318-81-06 ext. 2023; e-mail instcalinescu@yahoo.com; internet www .institutulcalinescu.ro; f. 1949; attached to Romanian Acad.; library of 15,000 vols; Dir Prof. Dr EUGEN SIMION; publs *Revista de Istorie şi Teorie Literară* (4 a year), *Synthesis* (1 a year).

Institutul de Lingvistica 'Iorgu Iordan–Al. Rosetti' (Iorgu Iordan–Al. Rosetti Institute of Linguistics): Calea 13 Septembrie 13, 050711 Bucharest; tel. and fax (21) 318-24-52; e-mail inst@lingv.ro; internet www.lingv .ro; f. 1949; attached to Romanian Acad.; Dir MARIUS SALA; publs *Fonetică şi Dialectologie* (1 a year), *Limba Română* (6 a year), *Revue Roumaine de Linguistique* (4 a year), *Studii şi Cercetări Lingvistice* (2 a year).

MEDICINE

Centre for Drug Research: 1 Mai Ave 66, 200638 Craiova; tel. (251) 523929; attached to Universitatea de Medicină şi Farmacie din Craiova.

Centrul de Sănătate Publică (Public Health Centre): Str. Gh. Marinescu 40, 540136 Târgu Mureş; tel. (265) 21-83-60; fax (265) 21-93-20; e-mail secretariat@ cspmures.ro; internet www.cspmures.ro; f. 1956 as Scientific Research Base, present name and status 2001; attached to Acad. of Medical Sciences; library of 12,000 vols; Dir Prof. Dr FRANCISC JESZENSZKY.

Centrul Metodologic de Parodontologie (Paradontology Methodological Centre): Str. 11 Iunie 10, 040172 Bucharest; tel. (21) 641-20-79; f. 1968; library of 326 vols; Dir Dr THEODORA GUȚU.

Centrul Regional de Sanatate Publica Iaşi (Regional Center of Public Health Iaşi): Str. Dr V. Babeş 14, 700465 Iaşi; tel. (232) 26-18-40; fax (232) 21-03-99; e-mail crsp.iasi@ insp.gov.ro; internet www.pub-health-iasi.ro; f. 1930; attached to Nat. Institute of Public Health, Min. of Health; library of 17,000 vols; Dir Prof. Dr LUMINIŢA SMARANDA IANCU; Dir Adjunct Dr OANA IACOB; publ. *Journal of Preventive Medicine* (4 a year).

Institutul Cantacuzino (Cantacuzino Institute): Spl. Independenţei 103, CP 1-525, 050096 Bucharest; tel. (21) 306-91-00; fax (21) 306-93-07; e-mail office@cantacuzino .ro; internet www.cantacuzino.ro; f. 1921; attached to Acad. of Medical Sciences; microbiology, immunology and epidemiology of communicable diseases, biotechnology; library of 119,714 vols; Gen. Dir Dr RADU IORDACHEL; Sec.-Gen. FELICIA MARDALE; publ. *Romanian Archives of Microbiology and Immunology* (4 a year).

Institutul de Endocrinologie 'C.I. Parhon' (C. I. Parhon Institute of Endocrinology): Bdul Aviatorilor 34–36, 011863 Bucharest; tel. (21) 317-20-41; fax (21) 317-06-07; e-mail contact@parhon.ro; internet www.instparhon.ro; f. 1946; attached to

Acad. of Medical Sciences; library of 65,800 vols; Man Dr PAUN DIANA LORETA; Dir Medical Dr GRIGORIE DANIEL; Dir Admin. Ing. SIMION MARIETA; publ. *Romanian Journal of Endocrinology* (4 a year).

Institutul de Fiziologie Normală și Patologică 'D. Danielopolu' (D. Danielopolu Institute of Normal and Pathological Physiology): Bdul Ion Mihalache 11A, 011171 Bucharest; tel. (21) 312-89-38; fax (21) 312-59-37; e-mail ifnp@cmb.ro; f. 1949; attached to Acad. of Medical Sciences; library of 49,000 vols; Dir Prof. Dr GR. BENETATO; publ. *Romanian Journal of Physiology* (4 a year).

Institutul de Fonoaudiologie și Chirurgie Funcțională ORL 'Prof. Dr. D. Hociotă' (Prof. Dr. D. Hociotă Institute of Phono-Audiology and ENT Surgery): Str. Mihai Cioranu 21, 050751 Bucharest; tel. (21) 410-21-70; fax (21) 410-02-78; e-mail secretariat@ifacforl.ro; internet ifacforl.ro; f. 1972 as Centrul Medical de Fonoaudiologie și Chirurgie Funcțională O.R.L.; attached to Acad. of Medical Sciences; library of 2,000 vols; Man. MARINESCU ANDREEA; Admin. Dir BANGIU MIHAIL-ADRIAN; Finance Dir SUE MIHAELA-CRISTINA; Medical Dir STANESCU RALUCA DANIELA.

Institutul de Medicină Internă 'Nicolae Gh. Lupu' (Nicolae Gh. Lupu Institute of Internal Medicine): Șoseaua Ștefan cel Mare 19–21, 020125 Bucharest; tel. (21) 611-13-70; e-mail cbaicus@clicknet.ro; f. 1949; attached to Acad. of Medical Sciences; library of 72,000 vols; Dir Prof. C. TANASESCU; publ. *Romanian Journal of Internal Medicine* (4 a year).

Institutul de Neurologie și Psihiatrie (Institute of Neurology and Psychiatry): Șoseaua Berceni 10–12, 041915 Bucharest; tel. (21) 683-78-31; f. 1950; attached to Acad. of Medical Sciences; library of 7,957 vols; Dir Prof. V. VOICULESCU; publ. *Neurologie et Psychiatrie* (series of *Revue Roumaine de Médecine*, 4 a year).

Institutul de Patologie și Genetică Medicală 'V. Babeș' (V. Babeș Institute of Pathology and Medical Genetics): Splaiul Independenței 99–101, 050096 Bucharest; tel. (21) 411-51-52; fax (21) 411-51-05; f. 1887; attached to Acad. of Medical Sciences; genetics, immunology, pathology and ultrastructure; library of 20,000 vols; Dir Prof. Dr L. M. POPESCU; publ. *Romanian Journal of Morphology and Embryology* (4 a year).

Institutul de Sănătate Publică, București (Institute of Public Health, Bucharest): Str. Dr Leonte 1–3, 050463 Bucharest; tel. (21) 318-36-20; fax (21) 312-34-26; e-mail directie@ispb.ro; internet ispb.ro; f. 1927; attached to Min. of Health; library of 36,000 vols; separate medical history library of 41,000 vols; Dir Gen. Dr MIHAI MARIUS DAN; publ. *Sănătate și Prevenție* (4 a year).

Institutul de Sănătate Publică 'Prof. Dr Iuliu Moldovan' (Prof. Dr Iuliu Moldovan Institute of Public Health): Str. Louis Pasteur 6, 400349 Cluj-Napoca; tel. (264) 59-42-52; fax (264) 59-98-91; e-mail inst@ispcj.ro; internet www.ispcj.ro; f. 1930; monitors public health in 11 Transylvanian counties, provides technical assistance, continuing education, field applied scientific research, public health services; library of 30,150 vols; Dir Prof. Dr IOAN STELIAN BOCȘAN.

Institutul de Sănătate Publică 'Prof. Dr Leonida Georgescu', Timișoara (Prof. Dr Leonida Georgescu Institute of Public Health, Timișoara): Bdul Dr Victor Babeș 16, 300226 Timișoara; tel. and fax (256) 49-21-01; e-mail rox_mol@yahoo.com; internet www.ispt.ro; f. 1946; attached to Acad. of Medical Sciences; library of 14,966 vols; Dir Prof. Dr ROXANA MOLDOVAN; publs *Annals of the Institute of Public Health, Timișoara* (1 a year), *Documentary Booklet* (1 a year).

Institutul de Virusologie 'Ștefan S. Nicolau' (IVN) (Ștefan S. Nicolau Institute of Virology): Șoseaua Mihai Bravu 285, 030304 Bucharest; tel. and fax (21) 324-25-90; e-mail ivngripa@b.astral.ro; internet www.virology .ro; f. 1949; attached to Romanian Acad.; WHO Virus Collaborating Centre; research on respiratory viral infections, arboviral infections, viral hepatitis, AIDS; 60 mems; library of 60,000 vols, 200 periodicals; Dir Dr MIHAI STOIAN; Hon. Dir Dr COSTIN CERNESCU; Scientific Sec. C.N. ZAHARIA; publs *Proceedings of the Romanian Academy, series B, Science and Life* (in English, 2 a year), *Studii și Cercetări de Virusologie* (in Romanian, 2 a year).

Institutul Național de Medicină Legală 'Mina Minovici' (Mina Minovici National Institute for Legal Medicine): Șoseaua Vitan-Bârzești 9, 042122 Bucharest; tel. (21) 332-11-56; fax (21) 334-62-60; e-mail danderme@ legmed.ro; internet www.legmed.ro; f. 1892; forensic genetics, forensic toxicology, forensic pathology, clinical forensic medicine, forensic psychiatry, forensic anthropology; library of 20,000 vols; Dir Prof. Dr DAN DERMENGIU; publ. *Romanian Journal of Legal Medicine* (4 a year, online (www.rjlm.ro)).

Institutul Oncologic 'Al. Trestioreanu' (Al. Trestioreanu Institute of Oncology): Șoseaua Fundeni 252, 022338 Bucharest; tel. (21) 227-1400; fax (21) 318-3262; e-mail secretariat@iob.ro; internet www.iob.ro; f. 1949; attached to Acad. of Medical Sciences; research; teaching; methodology; training of specialized personnel; library of 41,144 vols; Man. Prof. Dr RODICA ANGHEL; Medical Dir Dr ILEANA CONDREA; Admin. Dir ELENA ILIESCU; publ. *Oncologia* (4 a year).

Institutul pentru Controlul de Stat al Medicamentului și Cercetări Farmaceutice 'Petre Ionescu-Stoian' (Petre Ionescu-Stoian State Institute for Drug Control and Pharmaceutical Research): Str. Aviator Sănătescu 48, 011478 Bucharest; tel. (21) 224-10-79; fax (21) 230-50-83; e-mail dd@ns .icsmcf.ro; f. 1929; Dir Prof. Dr DUMITRU DOBRESCU; publ. *Farmaco-vigilenţa* (Drug Monitoring, 4 a year).

Research Centre for Microscopic Morphology and Immunology: Str. Petru Rareș 2, 200349 Craiova; tel. and fax (351) 46-14-58; e-mail cmi@umfcv.ro; internet www.umfcv.ro; attached to Universitatea de Medicină și Farmacie din Craiova.

Research Centre of Gastroenterology and Hepatology: 1 Mai Ave 66, 200638 Craiova; tel. (251) 310287; e-mail ccgh@ umfcv.ro; attached to Universitatea de Medicină și Farmacie din Craiova; Dir TUDOREL CIUREA.

NATURAL SCIENCES
Biological Sciences

Institutul de Biochimie (Institute of Biochemistry): Spl Independenței 296, 060031 Bucharest; tel. (21) 223-90-69; fax (21) 223-90-68; internet www.biochim.ro; f. 1990; attached to Romanian Acad.; research into protein science, particularly the biosynthesis and function of proteins and glycoproteins; 47 mems; Dir Dr STEFANA M. PETRESCU; publ. *Romanian Journal of Biochemistry* (2 a year).

Institutul de Biologie (Institute of Biology): Splaiul Independenței 296, 060031 Bucharest; tel. (21) 221-92-02; fax (21) 221-90-71; e-mail biologie@ibiol.ro; internet www .ibiol.ro; f. 1957 as Biological Research Centre, present name and status 1990; attached to Romanian Acad.; library of 200,000 vols; Dir Dr MADALIN ENACHE; Scientific Sec. Dr ZAMFIR MEDANA; publ. *Romanian Journal of Biology* (2 a year).

Institutul de Biologie și Patologie Celulară 'Nicolae Simionescu' (Institute of Cellular Biology and Pathology 'Nicolae Simionescu'): Bogdan Petriceicu Hașdeu 8, POB 35-14, 050568 Bucharest; tel. (21) 319-45-18; fax (21) 319-45-19; internet www.icbp .ro; f. 1979; attached to Romanian Acad.; Dir MAYA SIMIONESCU.

Institutul de Cercetări Biologice Cluj-Napoca (Biological Research Institute of Cluj-Napoca): Str. Republicii 48, 400015 Cluj-Napoca; tel. and fax (264) 19-12-38; e-mail icb@mail.dntcj.ro; internet www.icb .dntcj.ro; f. 1958; attached to Institutul Național de Cercetare-Dezvoltare pentru Științe Biologice; biology, biotechnology, plant and animal ecology, molecular taxonomy, physiology; library of 13,019 vols, 25,120 periodicals; Dir Dr GHEORGHE COLDEA; Scientific Dir Dr M. KEUL; Scientific Sec. Dr V. V. POP; publ. *Contribuții Botanice* (1 a year).

Institutul de Cercetări Biologice Iași (Iași Biological Research Institute): Bdul Carol I 20, 700505 Iași; tel. (232) 21-82-03; fax (232) 21-81-21; internet www.icb-iasi.ro; f. 1964 as Institute of General and Applied Biology, present name 1996; attached to Institutul Național de Cercetare-Dezvoltare pentru Științe Biologice; library of 35,000 vols; Dir Dr ALEXANDRU MANOLIU.

Institutul de Cercetări Eco-Muzeale Tulcea (Institute of Eco-Museal Research Tulcea): Str. 14 Noiembrie 1, 820009 Tulcea; tel. and fax (240) 51-32-31; e-mail icemtl@ icemtl.ro; internet www.icemtl.ro; f. 1950, present status 1993; attached to Tulcea County Council; archaeology, natural history, history, ethnography, art; library of 50,000 vols; Dir FLORIN GEORGE TOPOLEANU; publ. *Peuce* (1 a year).

Institutul Național de Cercetare-Dezvoltare pentru Științe Biologice (National Institute of Research and Development for Biological Sciences): Splaiul Independentei 296, sector 6, C.P. 17–16, 060031 Bucharest; tel. (21) 220-77-80; fax (21) 220-76-95; e-mail office@dbio.ro; internet www .dbioro.eu; f. 1996; research in the life sciences; devt of organisms in specific environmental conditions, biodiversity and preservation of the nat. geno-fund.

Mathematical Sciences

Institutul de Matematică 'Octav Mayer' (Octav Mayer Institute of Mathematics): Bdul Carol I 8, 700501 Iași; tel. and fax (232) 21-11-50; e-mail ivrabie@uaic.ro; f. 1948; attached to Romanian Acad.; library of 20,000 vols; Dir VIOREL BARBU; publ. *Studii și Cercetări Științifice*.

Institutul de Matematică 'Simion Stoilow' (Simion Stoilow Institute of Mathematics): POB 1-764, 014700 Bucharest; Str. Calea Grivitei 21, 010702 Bucharest; tel. (21) 319-65-06; fax (21) 319-65-05; e-mail vasile.brinzanescu@imar.ro; internet www .imar.ro; f. 1949, re-f. 1990; 128 mems; attached to Romanian Acad.; library of 35,000 vols, 121,000 journals; Dir Prof. Dr ȘERBAN A. BASARAB; publs *Mathematical Reports* (4 a year), *Revue Roumaine de Mathématiques Pures et Appliquées* (6 a year).

Institutul de Statistică Matematică și Matematică Aplicată 'Gheorghe Mihoc-Caius Iacob' (Gheorghe Mihoc-Caius Iacob Institute of Mathematical Statistics and Applied Mathematics): Calea 13 Septembrie 13, Casa Academiei Române, 050711 Bucharest; tel. (21) 318-24-33; fax (21) 318-24-39;

e-mail miosifes@acad.ro; internet www.csm
.ro; f. 1964; attached to Romanian Acad.;
Dir MARIUS IOSIFESCU; publs *Mathematical
Reports* (1 a year), *Revue Roumaine de
Mathématiques Pures et Appliquées* (Romanian Journal of Pure and Applied Mathematics, 1 a year).

Physical Sciences

Institutul Astronomic (Institute of Astron-
omy): Str. Cuțitul de Argint 5, 040557
Bucharest; tel. (21) 335-68-92; fax (21) 337-
33-89; e-mail vmioc@aira.astro.ro; internet
www.astro.ro; f. 1908, re-f. 1990; attached to
Romanian Acad.; library of 10,000 vols; Dir
Dr VASILE MIOC; Deputy Dir Dr NEDELIA
ANTONIA POPESCU; publs *Anuarul Astronomic*
(Astronomical Yearbook, 1 a year), *Roma-
nian Astronomical Journal* (2 a year).

Institutul de Cercetări Chimice (Institute of Chemical Research): Splaiul Independenței 202, 060021 Bucharest; tel. (21) 315-
32-99; fax (21) 312-34-93; f. 1950; natural and
bioactive products, technological engineering, chemical products and technologies;
Gen. Man. SEVER ȘERBAN.

**Institutul de Chimie Fizică 'Ilie Murgu-
lescu'** (Ilie Murgulescu Institute of Physical
Chemistry): Splaiul Independenței 202,
060021 Bucharest; tel. (21) 316-79-12; fax
(21) 312-11-47; e-mail mpopa@icf.ro; internet
www.icf.ro; f. 1963; attached to Romanian
Acad.; Dir MIHAI VASILE POPA; Deputy Dir Dr
VLAD T. POPA; Scientific Sec. Dr MIRCEA
OLTEANU; publs *Revue Roumaine de Chimie*
(12 a year), *Roumanian Chemical Quarterly
Review*.

**Institutul de Chimie Macromoleculară
'Petru Poni' al Academiei Romane**
('Petru Poni' Institute of Macromolecular
Chemistry of the Romanian Academy): Str.
Aleea Grigore Ghica Vodă 41A, 700487 Iași;
tel. (232) 21-74-54; fax (232) 21-12-99; e-mail
bcsimion@icmpp.ro; internet www.icmpp.ro;
f. 1949; attached to Romanian Acad.;
research in polymer chemistry, polymer
physics and material science; library of
100,000 vols; Dir Acad. Dr BOGDAN CRISTOFOR
SIMIONESCU; Deputy Dir Dr ANTON AIRINEI;
Deputy Dir Dr VALERIA HARABAGIU.

**Institutul de Chimie Organică 'Costin D.
Nenițescu'** (Costin D. Nenițescu Institute of
Organic Chemistry): Splaiul Independenței
202B, 060023 Bucharest; tel. (21) 316-79-00;
fax (21) 312-16-01; e-mail pfilip@cco.ro;
internet www.cco.ro; f. 1949; attached to
Romanian Acad.; basic research in organic
chemistry, fine organic synthesis and structural analysis of organic compounds; Dir Dr
Ing. PETRU IVAN FILIP.

Institutul de Chimie Timișoara (Timișoara Institute of Chemistry): Bdul Mihai
Viteazul 24, 300223 Timișoara; tel. (256) 49-
18-18; fax (256) 49-18-24; e-mail ocostisor@
acad-icht.tm.edu.ro; internet acad-icht.tm
.edu.ro; f. 1967; attached to Romanian Acad.;
library of 10,000 vols; Dir Dr OTILIA COSTI-
SOR; Hon. Dir ZENO SIMON; Dir Adjunct
Scientific Dr LUDOVIC SAYTI; Scientific Sec
Dr RAMONA TUDOSE; publ. *Annals of the West
University of Timișoara, Chemistry Series* (2
or 3 a year).

**Institutul de Geodinamică 'Sabba S.
Ștefănescu'** ('Sabba S. Ștefănescu' Institute
of Geodynamics): Str. Jean Louis Calderon
19–21, 020032 Bucharest; tel. (21) 317-21-26;
fax (21) 317-21-20; e-mail inst_geodin@
geodin.ro; internet www.geodin.ro; f. 1990;
attached to Romanian Acad.; geophysical
research; study of space-time variations;
monitoring of space-time variations of gravitational, geomagnetic, geoelectric fields of,
modelling of the thermo-mechanical evolution of the lithosphere, non-linear analysis of

geodynamic systems, studies of endogeneous
processes in the geodynamic evolution of the
Romanian territory, study of heliosphere/
geomagnetic field; organizes PhD programmes; Dir Dr CRISAN DEMETRESCU; Deputy Dir Dr Ing. DUMITRU STANICA; Hon. Dir
Dr Ing. DOREL ZUGRAVESCU; publs *Revue
Roumaine de Géophysique* (1 a year), *Studii
si Cercetari de Geofizica* (1 a year).

Institutul de Speologie 'Emil Racoviță'
(Emil Racoviță Institute of Speleology): Calea
13 Septembrie no. 13, Sector 5, 050711
Bucharest; tel. (21) 311-08-29; fax (21) 318-
81-32; e-mail iser_b@yahoo.com; internet
www.iser.ro; f. 1920; attached to Romanian
Acad.; biospeleology, phreatobiology, edapho-
biology, palaeobiology, sedimentology, geohy-
drochemistry, karstology, geospeleology,
palaeoclimatology, karst protection, arheo-
metry; Dept. in Cluj-Napoca; library of 5,800
vols, 770 periodicals; Dir IOAN POVARA; Deputy Dir CRISTIAN GORAN; Librarian CIUMASU
IOANA; publs *Theoretical and Applied Karstology* (1 a year), *Travaux de l'Institut de
Spéologie 'Emile Racovitza'* (1 a year).

Institutul Geologic al României (Romanian Geological Institute): Str. Caransebeș 1,
012271 Bucharest; tel. (21) 318-13-28; fax
(21) 318-13-26; e-mail geol@igr.ro; internet
igr.ro; f. 1906; library of 270,000 vols; conservation and recovery of drilling cores; colln
of minerals, rocks, flowers; monitoring of
mining areas; fundamental and applied
research; technological devt; studying and
forecasting; deciphering geological composition and evolution of the country; defining
areas of useful minerals; preparation and
editing of geological, hydrogeological, geophysical and geochemical maps; fundamental
and basic research in areas of mineralogy,
palaeontology, stratigraphy, geochemistry,
regional geology, hydrogeology, geotechnics,
magnetometry, gravimetry, geoelectricity,
seismics; studies on impact of human activities on groundwater pollution; studies on
devt of earth sciences according to int.
economic situation; expertise in mine
flowers, precious stones; research and analysis of geomagnetic field distribution; gravitational, geothermal, electromagnetic fields in
Romania; geoinformational system (GIS);
geoid; analysis of satellite images; Dir-Gen.
Dr STEFAN MARINCEA; publs Romanian journals of mineralogy, petrology, mineral
deposits and environmental geochemistry,
stratigraphy, palaeontology, tectonics and
regional geology, geophysics (1 a year),
Memorii (irregular).

**Institutul National de Cercetare-Dez-
voltare 'Delta Dunarii'** (Danube Delta
National Institute for Research and Development): Str. Babadag 165, 820112 Tulcea;
tel. (240) 53-15-20; fax (240) 53-35-47; e-mail
office@indd.tim.ro; internet www.indd.tim
.ro; f. 1970; attached to Min. of Environment;
promotes the conservation of biodiversity and
the sustainable devt of wetlands in Romania
and the Danube Delta area; library of 40,000
vols; Gen. Dir Eng. ROMULUS ȘTIUCĂ; Scientific Dir Dr MIRCEA STARAS; Technical Dir
Eng. DAN DAVID; Financial Dir ANA BULETE;
publs *Annals, Review of Ecological Restoration in the Danube Delta Biosphere Reserve*.

**Institutul Național de Cercetare Dezvol-
tare pentru Chimie si Petrochimie**
(National Institute of Research and Development for Chemistry and Petrochemistry):
Spl. Independentei 202, sector 6, O.P. 35,
060021 Bucharest; tel. (21) 316-30-72; fax
(21) 312-34-93; e-mail general.manager@
icechim.ro; internet www.icechim.ro; f. 2004;
scientific research and technological devt;
depts of biotechnology, chemical and petrochemical technology; Dir-Gen. Ing. SANDA
VELEA.

**Institutul Național de Cercetare-Dez-
voltare pentru Fizică Tehnică—IFT
Iași** (National Institute of Research and
Development for Technical Physics): 47
Mangeron Blvd, 700050 Iași; tel. (232) 43-
06-80; fax (232) 23-11-32; e-mail info@
phys-iasi.ro; internet www.phys-iasi.ro; f.
1955; fundamental and applied research
activities in field of magnetism and magnetic
materials; design and fabrication of new
sensors for biomedical applications, sensors
and actuators based on magnetoelastic phenomena, magnetic field sensors and spin-
valve devices; devt of medicine and biotechnology, design and fabrication of non-
destructive control sensors; library of 5,548
vols; Gen. Dir Dr NICOLETA LUPU; Dir of
Research Prof. Dr HORIA CHIRIAC; publ. *Proceedings* (every 2 years).

**Institutul Național de Meteorologie și
Hidrologie** (National Institute of Meteorology and Hydrology): Șoseaua București-
Ploiești 97, 013686 Bucharest; tel. (21) 318-
32-40; fax (21) 316-31-43; e-mail relatii@
meteo.inmh.ro; internet www.meteoromania
.ro; f. 1884 as Meteorological Service of
Romania, present name and status 1970;
climatology; physics of atmosphere; agrometeorology; meteorological methodology;
numeric modelling; long-range forecasting;
remote sensing and GIS laboratory; Dir Gen.
Dr ION SANDU; publs *Bibliografia hidrologică*
(1 a year), *Bibliografia meteorologică* (1 a
year), *Hydrology Journal* (2 a year), *Meteorology Journal* (2 a year), *Studii și Cercetări*
(in 2 parts: Meteorology, Hydrology; 1 vol. a
year).

Institutul Național de Metrologie
(National Institute of Metrology): Șoseaua
Vitan-Bîrzești 11, Sector 4, 042122 Bucharest; tel. (21) 334-55-20; fax (21) 334-55-33;
e-mail office@inm.ro; internet www.inm.ro; f.
1951; attached to Romanian Bureau of Legal
Metrology; devt, maintenance, utilization of
nat. measurement standards; providing tra-
ceability to the SI; dissemination of units of
measurement at nat. level; library of 15,000
vols; Dir Dr MIRELLA BUZOIANU; Scientific Dir
Eng. MIRELLA BUZOIANU; publ. *Metrologie* (4 a
year).

**Institutul Național pentru Fizică și
Inginerie Nucleară 'Horia Hulubei'**
(Horia Hulubei National Institute of Physics
and Nuclear Engineering): St. Reactorului
30, 077125 Bucharest-Măgurele; tel. (21)
404-23-00; fax (21) 404-44-40; e-mail
dirgen@ifin.nipne.ro; internet www.ifin.ro; f.
1949; research and devt in physical and
natural sciences; library of 385,000 vols;
Dir-Gen. Prof. Dr NICOLAE VICTOR ZAMFIR;
Scientific Sec Dr IOAN URSU; publs *Conference Proceedings, IFA-Preprints, Romanian
Journal of Physics* (12 a year), *Romanian
Reports in Physics* (12 a year).

PHILOSOPHY AND PSYCHOLOGY

**Institutul de Filosofie si Psihologie
'Constantin Rădulescu-Motru'** (Institute
of Philosophy and Psychology 'Constantin
Rădulescu-Motru'): Calea 13 Septembrie 13,
O.P. 5, POB 15–8, 050711 Bucharest; tel. (56)
318-81-06; fax (21) 318-24-42; e-mail
amarhan@ipsihologie.ro; internet ipsihologie
.ro; f. 2002 by merger of Institute of Philosophy (f. 1953) and Institute of Psychology (f.
1956); attached to Romanian Acad.; research
in philosophy, with focus on ethics, aesthetics, logic and ontology, epistemology;
research in psychology, with focus on social
and cross-cultural psychology, work and
organizational psychology, cognitive ergonomics, personality and devt; Dir ALEXANDRU
SURDU; Scientific Sec. Dr BOGDAN DANCIU;
publs *Revista de Filosofie* (4 a year), *Revista*

de Psihologie (4 a year), *Revue Roumaine de Psylosophy* (2 a year), *Romanian Journal of Psychology* (2 a year).

RELIGION, SOCIOLOGY AND ANTHROPOLOGY

Institutul de Antropologie Francisc I. Rainer (Francisc Rainer Institute of Anthropology): Bdul Eroilor Sanitari 8, POB 35-13, 050474 Bucharest; tel. (21) 317-50-71; fax (21) 317-50-72; e-mail franciscrainer@yahoo.com; internet www.antroplogia.ro; f. 1937; attached to Romanian Acad.; library of 7,000 vols, 25 periodicals; Dir Dr CRISTIANA GLAVCE; Scientific Sec. Dr MATEI STIRCEA-CRACIUN; publ. *Annuaire d'Etudes Anthropologiques* (1 a year).

Institutul de Cercetări Socio-Umane 'C. S. Nicolaescu-Plopsor' (C. S. Nicolaescu-Plopsor Institute for Research in Social and Human Sciences): Str. Unirii 68, 200345 Craiova; tel. (251) 52-33-30; fax (251) 52-57-02; e-mail avramcezar@yahoo.com; internet icsu.ro; f. 1965; attached to Romanian Acad.; library of 300,000 vols; Dir Prof. Dr CEZAR GABRIEL AVRAM; publs *Anuarul Institutului de Cercetari Socio-Umane* (1 a year), *Arhivele Olteniei* (1 a year).

Institutul de Cercetări Socio-Umane din Sibiu (Institute for Studies in Social Sciences and Humanities from Sibiu): B-dul Victoriei 40, 550024 Sibiu; tel. (269) 21-26-04; fax (269) 21-66-05; e-mail secretariat@icsusib.ro; internet www.icsusib.ro; f. 1956; attached to Romanian Acad.; history and culture of Transylvanian Saxons; their relationship to history and culture of Romanians in the immediate environment and in Transylvania; Transylvanian Saxon dialect; urban history; ethnology; library of 8,000 vols, 10,300 periodicals; Man. Dr PAUL NIEDERMAIER; publs *Anuarul (Yearbook)* (1 a year), *Forschungen zur Volks- und Landeskunde* (2 a year), *Historia Urbana* (2 a year), *Studii şi Comunicări de Etnologie* (1 a year).

Institutul de Cercetări Socio-Umane 'Gheorghe Şincai' al Academiei Române ('Gheorghe Şincai' Institute for Social Sciences and Humanities): Str. Al. Papiu Ilarian 10A, 540074 Târgu Mureş; tel. and fax (265) 26-02-38; e-mail icsu_ms@clicknet.ro; internet www.icsumures.acad-cluj.ro; f. 1957; attached to Romanian Acad.; history, comparative cultural studies, image and identity studies, social history, political and diplomatic history, history of literature, historical, cultural and confessional relations in Transylvania, Romanian-European cultural and political relations, perceptions of contemporary historical phenomena; library of 338,290 vols; Dir Dr CORNEL SIGMIREAN; publ. *Anuarul Institutului de Cercetari Socio-Umane 'Gheorghe Şincai'* (1 a year).

Institutul de Etnografie şi Folclor 'Constantin Brăiloiu' (Constantin Brăiloiu Institute of Ethnography and Folklore): Str. Tache Ionescu 25, 010353 Bucharest; tel. (21) 318-39-00; fax (21) 318-39-01; e-mail ief.brailoiu@gmail.com; internet www.acad.ro/ief; f. 1949; Nat. Folk Archives of sound, image and MSS; fundamental and advanced scientific research and related activities in the fields of folk literature, ethnomusicology, ethnocoreology, ethnography; library of 60,000 vols; Dir Dr SABINA ISPAS; Scientific Sec. Dr ION GHINOIU; publs *Anuarul Institutului de Etnografie si Folclor, Journal of Ethnography and Folklore* (2 a year).

Institutul de Sociologie 'Dimitrie Gusti' (Dimitrie Gusti Institute of Sociology): Calea 13 Septembrie 13, 050711 Bucharest; tel. (21) 411-85-32; e-mail insoc@insoc.ro; f. 1965; attached to Romanian Acad.; Man. Dir Prof. Dr ILIE BĂDESCU; publs *Revue Roumaine des Sciences Sociales—série de Sociologie* (4 a year, English edn 2 a year), *Sociologie Românească* (6 a year).

Institutul de Ştiinţe Politice şi Relaţii Internaţionale (Institute of Political Sciences and International Relations): Bdul Iuliu Maniu 1–3, Corp A, etaj 7, 061071 Bucharest; tel. and fax (21) 316-96-61; e-mail ispri@ispri.ro; internet www.ispri.ro; f. 1990, as Institute of Social Theory and Political Science; attached to Romanian Acad.; library of 1,000,000 vols; Dir Prof. Dr ION BULEI; publs *Revista de Ştiinţe Politice şi Relaţii Internaţionale* (4 a year), *Revista Romana de Teorie Socială* (4 a year), *Revue Roumaine de Teorie Sociale* (3 a year), *Romanian Journal of Political Science and International Relations* (2 a year).

Institutul de Ştiinţe Socio-Umane (Institute of Social and Human Sciences): Str. T. Codrescu 2, 700481 Iaşi; tel. (232) 11-59-87; f. 1969; attached to Romanian Acad.; library of 35,000 vols; Dir TUDOREL DIMA; publs *Anuar de Ştiinţe Socio-Umane, Revista Romana de Sociologie* (2 a year), *Romanian Journal of Sociology*.

Institutul de Studii Banatice 'Titu Maiorescu' (Titu Maiorescu Institute for Research): Str. Mihai Viteazul 24, 300223 Timişoara; tel. and fax (256) 49-18-23; e-mail icsutm@acad-tim.tm.edu.ro; f. 1970; attached to Romanian Acad.; library of 8,000 vols; Dir Prof. Dr CRISU DASCĂLU; publs *Caietul Cercului de Studii* (2 a year), *Dialectologie* (1 a year), *Limbăliterară* (1 a year), *Poetică* (1 a year), *Revista de studii banatice* (2 a year), *Studii de istorie a Banatului* (1 a year), *Toponimie* (1 a year).

International Association for South-East European Studies: Str. Nicolae Racota 12–14, Apt. 18, Bucharest 011393; tel. (21) 224-29-65; fax (21) 224-29-64; e-mail aiesee@rdslink.ro; f. 1963; attached to ICPHS, UNESCO; social sciences; promotes the study of the civilizations spread over the Balkans and South-East Europe; 29 mems; library of 40,000 vols; Pres. LUAN OMARI; Gen. Sec. RAZVAN THEODORESCU; publ. *Revue de l'AIESEE* (1 a year).

TECHNOLOGY

Institutul de Informatică Teoretică (Institute of Computer Science): Str. Gh. Asachi 2, 700481 Iaşi; tel. (332) 10-65-05; e-mail vapopei@iit.tuiasi.ro; internet www.iit.tuiasi.ro; f. 1984; attached to Romanian Acad.; Dir Prof. H. N. TEODORESCU; Scientific Sec. VASILE APOPEI.

Institutul de Mecanica Solidelor (Institute of Solids Mechanics): Str. Constantin Mille 15, 10141 Bucharest; tel. and fax (21) 312-67-36; e-mail siret@imsar.bu.edu.ro; internet www.imsar.ro; f. 1949 as Institute of Applied Mechanics 'Traian Vuia', present name 1990; attached to Romanian Acad.; control of dynamic systems, mechanics of deformable media, ultrasonics, tribology, mechatronics and robotics; control strategies based on artificial intelligence methods; wave propagation techniques for characterization of mechanical properties; dynamics of elastic structures; direct and inverse methods for biomechanic systems; ultrasonic methods for improvement of non-destructive testing; mechanical and tribological properties investigation for classical and unconventional materials; bio-tribology; methods, strategies for robotics and mechatronics; Dir Dr TUDOR SIRETEANU; Deputy Dir Dr Ing. LUCIAN CAPITANU; Scientific Sec. Dr ARON IAROVICI; publ. *Revue Roumaine des Sciences Techniques Série de Mécanique appliquée* (Romanian Journal of Technical Sciences—Applied Mechanics, 3 a year).

Institutul National de Cercetare Dezvoltare pentru Metale Neferoase Şi Rare (National Institute of Research And Development for Non-Ferrous and Rare Metals): Bdul Biruinţei 102, Pantaleon; tel. and fax (21) 352-20-48; e-mail imnr@imnr.ro; internet www.imnr.ro; f. 1966; research in nanostructured materials; ecotechnologies and environment protection; Dir Dr Ing. TEODOR VELEA; Scientific Dir Dr Ing. ROXANA PITICESCU.

Institutul Naţional de Cercetare-Dezvoltare pentru Protecţia Mediului (ICIM Bucureşti) (National Research and Development Institute for Environmental Protection (ICIM Bucharest)): Splaiul Independenţei 294, 060031 Bucharest; tel. (21) 318-20-57; fax (21) 318-20-01; e-mail icim@icim.ro; internet www.icim.ro; f. 1952; attached to Min. of Environment; management, control of water, land and air quality; integrated monitoring of environmental factors; control of water pollution; water technologies; technologies and equipment for cleaning sewage; sludge-processing; aquatic ecosystems; biodiversity; fluid mechanics; dispersion of pollutants; noise pollution and vibrations; solid waste management; environmental impact of construction; library of 20,000 vols and journals; Dir-Gen. Prof. Dr Ing. NECULAI MIHAILESCU; Scientific Dir Dr VASILICA DAESCU; publs *An Environment for the Future* (1 a year), *The Environment* (4 a year).

Institutul Naţional de Informare şi Documentare (National Institute for Information and Documentation): Str. I. D. Mendeleev 21–25, 010362 Bucharest; tel. (21) 315-87-65; fax (21) 312-67-34; e-mail inid@iniduw.inid.ro; internet www.inid.ro; f. 1949; promotes the use of modern equipment for automatic data processing in the area of documentary information; library: see Libraries and Archives; Dir-Gen. TIBERIUS IGNAT; publs *Asigurarea şi Promovarea Calităţii* (4 a year), *Informarea şi Documentarea Modernă* (4 a year), *Management şi Marketing Coentemporan* (4 a year).

Libraries and Archives
Alba Iulia

Biblioteca Judeţeană 'Lucian Blaga' Alba (Alba 'Lucian Blaga' District Library): Str. Dr Camil Velican 22, 510113 Alba Iulia; tel. (258) 81-14-43; fax (258) 81-72-04; e-mail bjalba@gmail.com; internet www.bjalba.ro; f. 1943; 250,000 vols; Dir MIOARA POP.

Biblioteca Naţională a României, Filiala Batthyaneum (National Library of Romania, Batthyaneum Branch): Str. Gabriel Bethlen 1, 510009 Alba Iulia; tel. and fax (258) 81-19-39; e-mail ileana.darja@bibnat.ro; internet www.bibnat.ro/filiala-batthyaneum-s75-ro.htm; f. 1798; attached to Biblioteca Naţională; 71,149 vols, 4,327 periodicals; spec. collns of 1,778 MSS since 9th century, 571 incunabula, documents, rare books, ex-libris; mineralogical and numismatic colln; scientific instruments, clocks; religious art; 18th-century astronomical observatory; Dir-Gen. Dr ELENA TÎRZIMAN.

Alexandria

Biblioteca Judeţeană 'Marin Preda' Teleorman (Teleorman 'Marin Preda' District Library): Str. Bucuresti Bl. T3, 140101 Alexandria; tel. and fax (247) 31-07-06; e-mail bjmarinpreda@yahoo.com; f. 1949; 148,718 vols; Man. VIOREL FOTA.

Arad

Biblioteca Judeţeană 'A. D. Xenopol' Arad (Arad 'A. D. Xenopol' District Library): Str. Gheorghe Popa de Teiuş 2–4, 310022 Arad; tel. and fax (257) 25-65-10; e-mail bja-director@aradlibrary.org; internet www .aradlibrary.org; f. 1913; 21,522 vols; Dir FLORIN DIDILESCU; Sec CRISTINA TEIUŞANU.

Bacău

Biblioteca Judeţeană 'Costache Sturdza' Bacău (Bacău 'Costache Sturdza' District Library): Str. Aleea Parcului 9, 688843 Bacău; tel. (234) 51-31-26; fax (334) 40-51-74; e-mail g.muraru@bjbc.ro; internet www.bjbc.ro:8080/bjbc; f. 1893; 430,000 vols and periodicals; Dir GABRIELA MURARU; Economic Dir MARIA TUDORACHE; publs *Bibliografia Judeţului Bacău, Cartea, Ex-Libris.*

Baia Mare

Biblioteca Judeţeană 'Petre Dulfu' Maramureş (Maramureş 'Petre Dulfu' District Library): Bdul Independenţei 4B, 430123 Baia Mare; tel. (262) 27-55-83; fax (262) 27-58-99; e-mail biblioteca@bibliotecamm.ro; internet www.bibliotecamm.ro; f. 1951; 433,828 vols; Dir-Gen. TEODOR ARDELEAN.

Bistriţa

Biblioteca Judeţeană Bistriţa-Năsăud (Bistriţa-Năsăud District Library): Str. Gării 2, 420041 Bistriţa; tel. and fax (263) 23-70-03; e-mail pia_olimpia@yahoo.com; internet www.bjbn.ro; f. 1951; 28 mems; 209,530 vols; Dir OLIMPIA POP; publs *Labirint, Specialty Journal* (1 a year).

Blaj

Biblioteca Documentară 'Timotei Cipariu' ('Timotei Cipariu' Documentary Library): Str. Petru Pavel Aron 2–4, 515400 Blaj; tel. (258) 71-01-10; f. 1754; attached to Cluj-Napoca br. library of Romanian Academy; 30,000 vols in humanities and sciences; spec. colln of rare and ancient books on history of the Romanian people.

Botoşani

Biblioteca Judeţeană 'Mihai Eminescu' Botoşani (Botoşani County Library): Str. Calea Naţională 64, 710028 Botoşani; tel. (231) 51-46-86; fax (231) 53-33-34; e-mail biblioteca@petar.ro; internet www .bibliotecabotosani.ro; f. 1882; 500,000 vols; Dir Prof. CORNELIA VIZITEU; publs *Catalogul Fondului Documentar, Catalogul Fondului Documentar 'Mihai Eminescu', Studii eminescologice/ Études sur Eminescu/ Eminescu Studies/ Eminescu Studien* (1 a year).

Brăila

Biblioteca Judeţeană 'Panait Istrati' Brăila (Brăila 'Panait Istrati' County Library): Calea Călăraşilor 52, 810010 Brăila; tel. (239) 61-12-92; fax (239) 61-95-90; e-mail bjpi@bjbraila.ro; internet www .bjbraila.ro; f. 1881; 388,968 vols, 4 brs; coordinates activity of 3 city libraries and 39 village libraries; Dir DRAGOS ADRIAN NEAGU; publ. *Ex-libris* (1 a year).

Braşov

Biblioteca Judeţeană 'George Bariţiu' Braşov ('George Bariţiu' County Library Braşov): Bdul Eroilor 33–35, 500036 Braşov; tel. (268) 41-93-38; fax (268) 41-50-79; e-mail biblgb@rdsbv.ro; internet www.bjbv.ro; f. 1835; 800,000 vols; reading and loan services; cultural and social activities, courses, lectures, conferences and workshops; Man. Dr DANIEL NAZARE.

Biblioteca Universităţii 'Transilvania' din Braşov (Transylvania University of Braşov Central Library): Str. Iuliu Maniu 41, 500091 Braşov; tel. (268) 47-60-50; fax (268) 47-60-51; e-mail biblioteca@unitbv.ro; internet www.unitbv.ro/biblio; f. 1948; 790,000 vols; Dir Prof. Dr Eng. ELENA HELEREA.

Bucharest

Arhivele Naţionale ale României (National Archives): Bdul Regina Elisabeta 49, 050013 Bucharest; tel. (21) 312-67-10; fax (21) 312-58-41; e-mail secretariat.an@mai .gov.ro; internet www.arhivelenationale.ro; f. 1831; 1,221,500 medieval documents, 22,000 seals, 12,820 MSS, 816,929 ft modern documents, 735,680 vols of plans and maps; documentary libraries; Dir Dr DORIN DOBRINCU; publ. *Revista Arhivelor* (1 a year).

Attached Library:

Biblioteca Documentară a Arhivelor Naţionale (Documentary Library of the National Archives): Bdul Regina Elisabeta 49, 050013 Bucharest; tel. (21) 303-70-80; fax (21) 312-58-41; e-mail publicatii.an@ mira.gov.ro; internet www .arhivelenationale.ro; f. 1862; 70,000 vols, 50,000 periodicals; Dir Dr DORIN DOBRINCU; Library Coordinator CAMELIA COJOCARU; Librarian VALENTINA DINU; publ. *Revista Arhivelor* (Archives Review).

Biblioteca Academiei Române (Library of the Romanian Academy): Calea Victoriei 125, 010071 Bucharest; tel. (21) 212-82-84; fax (21) 212-58-56; e-mail biblacad@biblacad.ro; internet www.biblacad.ro; f. 1867; legal nat. deposit for Romanian and UN publs; produces Romanian nat. bibliography of books and serials; 11,500,000 vols, 3.6m. monographs, 5.3m. serials, 500,000 historical documents, 350,000 photographs; spec. collns incl. Romanian, Greek, Slavonic, Oriental and Latin MSS; drawings, engravings, photographs, music MSS, maps; numismatic colln; Dir Gen. FLORIN FILIP; Dir Adjunct CORNEL LEPADATU; publs *Cărţi intrate în reţeaua bibliotecilor Academiei Române* (1 a year), *Periodice intrate în reţeaua bibliotecilor Academiei Române* (1 a year), *Publicaţii Periodice Româneşti.*

Biblioteca Centrală a Academiei de Ştiinţe Agricole şi Silvice 'Gheorghe Ionescu-Şişeşti' (Central Library of the Gheorghe Ionescu-Şişeşti Academy of Agricultural and Forestry Sciences): Bdul Mărăşti 61, 011464 Bucharest; f. 1928; 136,000 vols; Chief Librarian N. FLORESCU; publs *Bibliografia agricolă curentă română* (4 a year), *Cărţi străine intrate in bibliotecile din România—seria Agricultură* (12 a year), *Noutăţi documentare FAO* (12 a year).

Biblioteca Centrală Academiei de Studii Economice (Central Library of the Academy of Economic Studies): Piaţa Romană 6, 010374 Bucharest; tel. (21) 319-19-00; fax (21) 319-18-99; e-mail rectorat@ase.ro; internet www.biblioteca.ase.ro; f. 1913; 900,000 vols; Dir ALINA CROITORU; publ. *The Bibliographical Bulletin* (2 a year).

Biblioteca Centrală a Universităţii 'Politehnica' din Bucureşti (Central Library of Politehnica University of Bucharest): Calea Grivitei 132, 060042 Bucharest; tel. (21) 402-39-82; fax (21) 312-70-44; e-mail c_albu@library.pub.ro; internet www.library .pub.ro; f. 1868; 1,094,360 vols and periodicals; Dir Ing. CRISTINA ALBU; publ. *Scientific Bulletin* (4 series: mechanical engineering, electrical engineering, chemistry and materials science, applied mathematics and physics).

Biblioteca Centrală Universitară 'Carol I' (Central University Library 'Carol I'): Str. Boteanu 1, Sector 1, 010027 Bucharest; tel. and fax (21) 312-01-08; e-mail mireille.radoi@ bcub.ro; internet www.bcub.ro; f. 1891; 1,866,413 vols; Dir-Gen. Dr MIRELLE CARMEN RĂDOI; Librarian GETA COSTACHE; publs *Ghidul lucrărilor de referinţe în colecţiile Bibliotecii Centrale Universitare 'Carol I' din Bucureşti* (Guide to Reference Works in the Collns of the Library of Bucharest Univ., 2 a year), *Informaţie şi Formaţie* (12 a year), *UniBib* (online).

Biblioteca de Documentare Medicală 'Dr Dimitrie Nanu' (Dr Dimitrie Nanu Medical Documentation Library): Str. Pitar Moş 7–15, 010451 Bucharest; tel. (21) 211-04-30; fax (21) 211-11-45; f. 1951; attached to Centrul de Calcul, Statistică Sanitară şi Documentare Medicală; 310,556 vols; Dir FELICIA-IOANA DOBRESCU.

Biblioteca Documentară de Istorie a Medicinei (Documentary Library of the History of Medicine): Str. Dr Leonte 1–3, 050463 Bucharest; tel. (21) 638-40-10; fax (21) 312-34-26; f. 1953; 50,200 vols, 1,100 periodicals, 3,500 MSS and documents, 5,200 museum pieces; Dir Prof. MARIOARA GEORGESCU.

Biblioteca Institutului Naţional de Informare şi Documentare (Library of the National Institute for Information and Documentation): Str. I. D. Mendeleev 21–25, 010362 Bucharest; tel. (21) 313-40-10; fax (21) 312-67-34; e-mail inid_bucuresti@home .ro; internet www.inid.ro; f. 1949; 743,000 vols incl. 135,000 periodicals; Chief Librarian DACIA CRISTIANA STATIE.

Biblioteca Metropolitană Bucureşti (Bucharest Metropolitan Library): Str. Tache Ionescu 4, 010354 Bucharest; tel. (21) 316-83-00; fax (21) 316-36-25; e-mail biblioteca@ bmms.ro; internet www.bmms.ro; f. 1831; 1,337,078 vols, periodicals, newspapers, musical scores; Dir Gen. Dr FLORIN ROTARU; publs *Bibliografia oraşului Bucureşti* (1 a year), *Biblioteca Bucureştilor* (12 a year), *Buletinul Bibliotecilor din Franţa* (12 a year).

Biblioteca Naţională a României (National Library of Romania): Bdul Unirii nr. 22, 030833 Bucharest; tel. (21) 314-24-34; fax (21) 312-33-81; e-mail biblioteca@bibnat .ro; internet www.bibnat.ro; f. 1838; 9,000,000 vols; acts as copyright deposit library and nat. bibliographic agency; incorporates research centre for librarianship and book pathology and restoration; spec. collns of MSS, old and rare books, musical scores, photographs, maps, prints, old illustrated postcards and drawings; Dir-Gen. Dr ELENA TÎRZIMAN; publs *ABSI—Abstracte în bibliologie şi ştiinţa informării* (4 a year), *Aniversări culturale* (2 a year), *Bibliografia Naţională Română* (6 series), *Biblioteconomie—Culegere de traduceri prelucrate* (4 a year), *Catalogul colectiv al cărţilor străine intrate în bibliotecile din România* (4 a year), *Repertoriul periodicelor străine intrate în bibliotecile din România* (1 a year), *Revista Biblioteca* (12 a year), *Revista Bibliotecii Naţionale a României* (2 a year), *Revista Română de Conservare şi Restaurare* (1 a year), *Revista Română de Istorie a Cărţii* (1 a year).

Biblioteca Pedagogică Naţională 'I. C. Petrescu' ('I. C. Petrescu' National Education Library): Str. Zalomit 12, 010151 Bucharest; tel. and fax (40) 311-03-23; e-mail director@bpn.ro; internet www.bpn .ro; f. 1880; 480,000 educational vols and periodicals; methodological centre for the nat. network of school libraries; Dir-Gen. Dr GEORGE ANCA; Librarian MANUELA POPA; publs *Bibliografia pedagogică* (1 a year), *Éducation en Roumanie* (Education in Romania, 1 a year), *Informare tematică* (1 a year), *LIBER. Revistă pentru bibliotecile pedagogice şi şcolare* (4 a year), *Modernizarea* *învăţămîntului* (1 a year), *Studii de biblioteconomie şi informare documentară* (irregular).

Biblioteca Universităţii de Arte Bucureşti (Library of the Bucharest University of Fine Arts): Str. Gen. Budişteanu 19, 010773 Bucharest; tel. (21) 314-32-11; f. 1864; 60,000 vols, 261,262 slides and photographs; spec. colln: 19th- and 20th-century European fine-art periodicals; Dir GABRIELA BĂJENARU.

Biblioteca Universităţii de Ştiinţe Agronomice şi Medicină Veterinară (Library of the University of Agronomic Sciences and Veterinary Medicine): Bdul Mărăşti 59, 011464 Bucharest; tel. (21) 318-25-67; fax (21) 318-28-88; e-mail biblioteca_usamv@yahoo.com; f. 1868; 480,000 350,000 vols; Dir CARMEN CONSTANTIN; publs *Agronomy, Biotechnology, Horticulture, Land Reclamation, Veterinary Medicine, Zootechnics.*

Biblioteca Universităţii Naţionale de Muzică din Bucureşti (Library of the Bucharest University of Music): Str. Ştirbei Vodă 33, 010102 Bucharest; tel. (21) 314-26-10; e-mail biblioteca@unmb.ro; internet www.unmb.ro; f. 1864; 261,103 vols, 107,608 scores, 16,545 recordings, 7,200 audio cassettes, 19,526 periodicals, 3,083 theses, 521 MSS, 33,103 books; Head CIOPONEA MARIA.

Centrul de Informare şi Documentare Economică (Centre of Economic Information and Documentation): Casa Academiei Române, Calea 13 Septembrie 13, 050711 Bucharest; tel. (21) 318-24-38; fax (21) 318-24-32; e-mail cide@zappmobile.ro; internet www.ince.ro; f. 1990; attached to Romanian Acad.; Dir IOAN-FRANC VALERIU; publs *Analele INCE* (4 a year), *Caiete Critice* (12 a year), *Marketing Management* (6 a year), *Probleme Economice* (48 a year), *Revista Română de Economie* (2 a year), *Romanian Economic Research Observer* (12 a year), *Romanian Journal of Economic Forecasting* (4 a year), *Studii şi Cercetări Economice* (12 a year).

S. C. Biblioteca Chimiei SA (S. C. Chemistry Library SA): Calea Plevnei 139B, 060011 Bucharest; tel. and fax (21) 314-24-47; e-mail biblioteca_de_chimie@syscom18.com; internet www.bch.ro; f. 1956; provides access to nat. and foreign scientific and technical literature; 46,000 vols, 141,000 vols of periodicals; Gen. Man. Ing. ION ANDRONACHE; publs *Materiale Plastice* (4 a year), *Revista de Chimie* (12 a year).

Serviciul de Documentare al Ministerului Învăţământului: Str. Spiru Haret 12, 010716 Bucharest; tel. (21) 614-26-80; fax (21) 312-47-53; f. 1971; information and documentation on teaching and educational management abroad; Romanian legislation on education; Head EUGENIU TOMA; publs *Buletinul Ministerului Învăţământului* (4 a year), *Educaţie-Învăţământ* (2 a year).

Serviciul de Informare, Documentare şi Informatizare al Academiei de Ştiinţe Agricole şi Silvice 'Gheorghe Ionescu-Şişeşti' (Information, Documentation and Electronic Information Service of the Gheorghe Ionescu-Şişeşti Academy of Agricultural and Forestry Sciences): Bdul Mărăşti 61, 011464 Bucharest; tel. (21) 618-25-54; fax (21) 617-01-55; f. 1928; attached to Acad. of Agricultural and Forestry Sciences; 147,000 vols and CD-ROMs; Head Dr C. KEVORCHIAN; publ. *Curierul ASAS* (4 a year).

Buzău

Biblioteca Judeţeană 'V. Voiculescu' Buzău (Buzău 'V. Voiculescu' District Library): Bdul Unirii 140, 120360 Buzău; tel. (238) 72-15-09; fax (238) 71-72-83; e-mail sorin.burlacu@bjvvbuzau.ro; internet bjvvbuzau.ro; f. 1873; 290,000 vols; Dir SORIN BURLACU.

Călăraşi

Biblioteca Judeţeană 'Al. Odobescu' Călăraşi (Călăraşi 'Al. Odobescu' District Library): Str. Bucureşti 102, 910161 Călăraşi; tel. (242) 31-67-57; fax (242) 31-67-57; f. 1883; 265,254 vols; Dir GHIŢĂ DUMITRU.

Cluj-Napoca

Biblioteca Centrală Universitară 'Lucian Blaga' ('Lucian Blaga' Central University Library): Str. Clinicilor 2, 400006 Cluj-Napoca; tel. (264) 59-70-92; fax (264) 59-76-33; e-mail informatii@bcucluj.ro; internet www.bcucluj.ro; f. 1872; 3,665,271 vols; Gen.-Dir Prof. Dr DORU RADOSAV; Deputy Dir OLIMPIA CURTA; publs *BIBLIOREV, PHILOBIBLON* (online (www.philobiblon.eu)).

Biblioteca Centrală 'Valeriu Bologa' (Central Library): Victor Babes 8, 400012 Cluj-Napoca; tel. and fax (264) 59-72-56; e-mail irobu@umfcluj.ro; internet www.umfcluj.ro/lista.aspx?t=biblioteca-prezentare; f. 1949; attached to Univ. of Medicine and Pharmacy; 321,000 vols and periodicals, online collns; Dir IOANA ROBU; publ. *Clujul Medical* (4 a year).

Biblioteca Filialei Cluj-Napoca a Academiei Române (Library of the Cluj-Napoca Branch of the Romanian Academy): Str. M. Kogălniceanu 12–14, 400084 Cluj-Napoca; tel. (264) 59-50-27; e-mail biblacadcj@yahoo.com; internet www.bibacadcj.ro; f. 1950; 760,000 vols and periodicals on the humanities and science, 179 incunabula, 2m. documents; spec. collns incl. Romanian, Latin, Hungarian, Slavonic MSS; Dir Prof. Dr IOAN CHINDRIS; publ. *Biblioteca si Cercetarea.*

Biblioteca Judeţeană 'Octavian Goga' Cluj ('Octavian Goga' Cluj County Library): Calea Dorobanţilor 104, 400061 Cluj-Napoca; tel. (264) 43-03-23; fax (264) 59-54-28; e-mail bjc@bjc.ro; internet www.bjc.ro; f. 1921; 3 br. libraries; 97 mems; 765,700 vols; Dir SORINA STANCA; Deputy Dir FLOAREA ELENA MOŞOIU; publs *Anul editorial clujean, Buletin UE-INFO* (1 a year), *Calendarul evenimentelor şi manifestărilor culturale* (1 a year).

Biblioteca Universităţii Tehnică din Cluj-Napoca (Library of Cluj-Napoca Technical University): Str. Republicii 107, 400020 Cluj-Napoca; tel. (264) 40-19-99; fax (264) 43-04-08; e-mail calin.campean@biblio.utcluj.ro; internet www.utcluj.ro/biblioteca; f. 1884, reorganized in 1948; 700,000 vols and 3,000 periodicals; Dir Dipl. Eng. CĂLIN CÂMPEAN; publ. *Acta Technica Napocensis* (in English, 1 a year).

Constanţa

Biblioteca Judeţeană 'Ioan N. Roman' Constanţa ('Ioan N. Roman' Constanţa County Library): Str. Mircea cel Bătrân 104A, 900663 Constanţa; tel. and fax (241) 61-62-44; fax (241) 61-44-82; e-mail bjc@biblioteca.ct.ro; internet www.biblioteca.ct.ro; f. 1931; 650,000 vols; Dir Dr LILIANA LAZIA; publs *Bibliografia Dobrogei* (1 a year), *Biblion* (2 a year).

Craiova

Biblioteca Judeţeană 'Alexandru şi Aristia Aman' Dolj (Public Library 'Alexandru and Aristia Aman' County Dolj): Str. M. Kogălniceanu 9, 200390 Craiova; tel. (251) 53-22-67; fax (251) 52-31-77; e-mail lucian.dindirica@aman.ro; internet www.aman.ro; f. 1908; 466,000 vols; Dir LUCIAN DINDIRICĂ.

Biblioteca Universităţii din Craiova (University of Craiova Library): Str. A. I.

Cuza 13, 200585 Craiova; tel. and fax (251) 41-24-79; e-mail bib@central.ucv.ro; internet biblio.central.ucv.ro; f. 1966, by merger of Agronomic Institute Library (f. 1948) and Pedagogical Institute Library (f. 1959); 1,071,290 vols; Dir Dr MIHAI COŞOVEANU.

Deva

Biblioteca Judeţeană 'Ovid Densusianu' Hunedoara-Deva (Hunedoara-Deva 'Ovid Densusianu' District Library): Str. 1 Decembrie 26, 330025 Deva; tel. and fax (254) 21-64-57; e-mail bibliotecadeva@upcmail.ro; internet www.bibliotecadeva.ro; f. 1951; 330,000 vols, periodicals and audiovisual items; Dir GABRIELA MARCU; publ. *Vox Libri* (4 a year).

Drobeta-Turnu Severin

Biblioteca Judeţeană 'I. G. Bibicescu' Mehedinţi (Mehedinţi 'I. G. Bibicescu' District Library): Str. Traian 115, 220134 Drobeta-Turnu Severin; tel. and fax (252) 31-56-82; f. 1921; 450,000 vols; Dir RALUCA ŞTEFANIA GRAF.

Focşani

Biblioteca Judeţeană 'Duiliu Zamfirescu' Vrancea (Vrancea 'Duiliu Zamfirescu' District Library): Str. M. Kogălniceanu 12–13, 620036 Focşani; tel. and fax (237) 21-45-62; e-mail bjfocsani@vrancea.info; internet www.bjvrancea.ro; f. 1910; 198,000 vols; Dir TEODORA FÎNTÎNARU.

Galaţi

Biblioteca Judeţeană 'V. A. Urechia' Galaţi (Galaţi 'V. A. Urechia' County Library): Str. Mihai Bravu 16, 800208 Galaţi; tel. (236) 41-10-37; fax (236) 31-10-60; e-mail bvau@bvau.ro; internet www.bvau.ro; f. 1890; 709,434 vols; Man. Prof. ZANFIR ILIE; Dir Adjunct LETIŢIA BURUIANĂ; Dir Adjunct GETA EFTIMIE; publs *Asociaţia* (4 a year), *Buletinul Fundaţiei Urechia* (2 a year), *Revista trimestrială de Cultură: Axis Libri* (4 a year).

Biblioteca Universităţii 'Dunarea de Jos' din Galaţi (University of Galaţi 'Dunarea de Jos' Library): Str. Domnească 47, 800008 Galaţi; tel. (236) 41-41-12; fax (236) 46-13-53; e-mail biblioteca@ugal.ro; internet www.lib.ugal.ro; f. 1948; 480,000 vols mainly on science, technology and engineering, food industry, history, theology, languages and literature, economics; Dir MIOARA VONCILĂ.

Giurgiu

Biblioteca Judeţeană 'I. A. Bassarabescu' Giurgiu (Giurgiu District 'I. A. Bassarabescu' Library): Soseaua Bucuresti 53, 080033 Giurgiu; tel. and fax (246) 21-23-46; e-mail bibliotecagr@pscomp.ro; internet www.bjgiurgiu.info; f. 1951; 199,178 vols and periodicals; Dir Prof. ION GAGHII; publ. *Libris.*

Iaşi

Biblioteca Centrală a Universităţii de Medicină şi Farmacie 'Gr. T. Popa' Iaşi (Central Library of the Gr. T. Popa University of Medicine and Pharmacy in Iaşi): Str. Vasile Alecsandri 7, 700054 Iaşi; tel. (232) 21-37-01; fax (232) 21-82-24; e-mail vscutariu@biblio.umfiasi.ro; internet biblio.umfiasi.ro; f. 1882; central library with 90 brs; 264,243 vols; Dir Prof. VIORICA SCUTARIU.

Biblioteca Centrală Universitară 'Mihai Eminescu' Iaşi (University 'Mihai Eminescu' Central Library Iaşi): Str. Păcurari 4, 700511 Iaşi; tel. (232) 26-42-45; fax (232) 26-17-96; e-mail bcuis@bcu-iasi.ro; internet www.bcu-iasi.ro; f. 1835; 2,456,909 vols; Dir-Gen. Prof. Dr ALEXANDRU CĂLINESCU; Dir

Gen. Adjunct NICOLETA POPESCU; Economic Dir VLADIMIR PETREA.

Biblioteca Judeţeană 'Gh. Asachi' Iaşi (Iaşi 'Gh. Asachi' District Library): Str. Palat 1, 700019 Iaşi; tel. (232) 21-33-53; fax (232) 21-21-70; e-mail bibiasi@hotmail.com; internet www.bjiasi.ro; f. 1920; 600,000 vols, 12,000 records; Dir Prof. Dr CĂTĂLIN BORDEIANU; Dir Adjunct VALERIU STANCU; publ. *Bibliographical Annual of the Iaşi District.*

Biblioteca Universităţii Tehnice 'Gheorghe Asachi' Iaşi (Library of the Iaşi Gheorghe Asachi Technical University): Bdul Carol I 11, 700506 Iaşi; tel. and fax (232) 21-27-73; e-mail mstirbu@library.tuiasi .ro; internet www.library.tuiasi.ro; f. 1937; 1m. vols; Library Man. MIHAELA STIRBU; publ. *Iaşi Polytechnic Magazine* (1 a year).

Miercurea-Ciuc

Biblioteca Judeţeană Kájoni János: Piaţa Libertăţii 16, 530100 Miercurea-Ciuc; tel. (266) 37-17-90; fax (266) 37-19-88; e-mail info@bibliohr.topnet.ro; internet bibliohr .topnet.ro; f. 1950; 242,000 vols; Dir KATALIN-MARIA KOPACZ.

Năsăud

Biblioteca Documentară Năsăud (Năsăud Documentary Library): Str. Grănicerilor 41, 425200 Năsăud; tel. (263) 36-20-02; f. 1931; attached to Cluj-Napoca br. library of Romanian Academy; 53,323 vols; Dir MARIA ŞUTEU.

Oradea

Biblioteca Judeţeană 'Gheorghe Şincai' Bihor Oradea ('Gheorghe Şincai' Bihor Oradea District Library): Str. Armatei Române 1A, 410100 Oradea; tel. (359) 80-03-68; fax (259) 43-12-57; e-mail bibliobihor@ yahoo.com; internet www.bibliobihor.ro; f. 1911; public county library; 700,000 vols; Dir Man. Prof. LIGIA-ANTONIA MIRIŞAN.

Piatra-Neamţ

Biblioteca Judeţeană 'G. T. Kirileanu' Neamţ (Neamţ 'G. T. Kirileanu' District Library): Bdul Republicii 15, 610005 Piatra-Neamţ; tel. (233) 21-15-24; fax (233) 21-03-79; e-mail bib_gtk_neamt@yahoo.com; internet www.bibgtkneamt.ro; f. 1956; 286,424 vols and periodicals; Dir CONSTANTIN BOSTAN.

Piteşti

Biblioteca Judeţeană Argeş 'Dinicu Golescu' (Argeş District Library 'Dinicu Golescu'): Str. Victoriei 18, 110017 Piteşti; tel. (248) 22-30-30; fax (248) 22-34-16; e-mail bjdgarges@gmail.com; internet www.bjarges .ro; f. 1880; 404,849 vols and periodicals, 2,018 audiovisual items, 120 electronic documents; Dir Dr MIHAIL OCTAVIAN SACHELARIE.

Ploieşti

Biblioteca Centrală a Universităţii Petrol-Gaze din Ploieşti (Central Library of Petroleum-Gas University of Ploieşti): Bdul Bucureşti 39, 100680 Ploieşti; tel. (244) 57-31-71; fax (244) 57-58-47; e-mail biblioteca@ upg-ploiesti.ro; internet www.upg-ploiesti.ro; f. 1948; 284,947 vols; Man. STANCIU GILDA; Librarian NICOLAE MADALINA.

Biblioteca 'Nicolae Iorga' Prahova ('Nicolae Iorga' Library): Str. Sublocotenent Erou Călin Cătălin 1, 100066 Ploieşti; tel. (244) 12-19-00; fax (244) 51-83-43; e-mail bjprahova@yahoo.com; internet bni.asesoft .ro; f. 1921; 550,000 vols; Dir Prof. NICOLAE BOARU.

Râmnicu Vâlcea

Biblioteca Judeţeană 'Antim Ivireanul' Râmnicu Vâlcea (Vâlcea 'Antim Ivireanul' District Library): Str. Carol I 26, 240591 Râmnicu Vâlcea; tel. (350) 40-17-94; fax (250) 73-92-21; e-mail biblioteca_antim@bjai.ro; internet www.bjai.ro; f. 1950; 400,000 vols; Dir SANDA CONSTANTINESCU; publ. *Biblioteca Vâlceană—Revista de Cultură a Bibliotecii Judeţene 'Antim Ivireanul'.*

Reşiţa

Biblioteca Judeţeană 'Paul Iorgovici' Reşiţa (Reşiţa 'Paul Iorgovici' District Library): Str. Paul Iorgovici 50, 320026 Reşiţa; tel. (55) 21-25-35; fax (55) 21-16-87; e-mail bjpi_resita@yahoo.com; internet bjpiresita.blogspot.com; f. 1952; 287,000 vols; Dir NICOLAE SÂRBU; publ. *Revista Noastră.*

Satu Mare

Biblioteca Judeţeană Satu Mare (Satu Mare District Library): Str. Decebal 2, 440006 Satu Mare; tel. (261) 71-58-60; fax (261) 71-11-99; e-mail santa@p5net.ro; internet www.bibliotecasatumare.ro; f. 1951; 379,553 vols; Dir VOICU D. RUSU.

Sf. Gheorghe

Biblioteca Judeţeană 'Bod Péter' Megyei Könyvtár (Covasna County Public Library): Gábor Áron 14, 520008 Sfantu Gheorghe; tel. and fax (267) 35-16-09; e-mail biblio@kmkt.ro; internet www.kmkt .ro; f. 1880; 220,000 vols; Man. Dr SZABOLCS SZONDA.

Sibiu

Biblioteca Judeţeană 'Astra' Sibiu (Sibiu 'Astra' District Library): Str. Gh. Bariţiu 5–7, 550178 Sibiu; tel. (269) 21-05-51; fax (269) 21-57-75; e-mail bjastrasibiu@yahoo.com; internet www.bjastrasibiu.ro; f. 1861; 688,377 vols; 4 brs; Dir ONUC NEMEŞ-VINTILĂ; publs *DeLiriKoN* (4 a year), *Mlădite* (4 a year).

Biblioteca Muzeului Brukenthal (Library of Brukenthal Museum): Piaţa Mare 4, 550163 Sibiu; tel. (269) 21-16-99; fax (269) 21-15-45; e-mail info@brukenthalmuseum.ro; internet www.brukenthalmuseum.ro; f. 1817; 280,000 vols; Dir-Gen. Prof. Dr SABIN ADRIAN LUCA; Head of Library CONSTANTIN ITTU.

Slatina

Biblioteca Judeţeană 'Ion Minulescu' Olt (Olt 'Ion Minulescu' District Library): Bdul A.I. Cuza 3B, 230025 Slatina; tel. and fax (349) 40-75-17; e-mail bibljolt@yahoo .com; internet www.bibliotecaslatina.ro; f. 1931; 231,667 vols and periodicals; Dir Dr PAUL MATIU.

Slobozia

Biblioteca Judeţeană 'Ştefan Bănulescu' Ialomiţa (Ialomiţa 'Ştefan Bănulescu' District Library): Bdul Matei Basarab 26, 920031 Slobozia; tel. and fax (243) 23-00-55; e-mail biblioteca_ialomita@bji.ro; internet www.bji.ro; f. 1933; 132,242 vols and periodicals; Dir MIHAELA RACOVIŢEANU; publ. *Salonul Anual de Carte* (1 a year).

Suceava

Biblioteca Bucovinei 'I. G. Sbierea' ('I. G. Sbierea' Library of Bucovina): Str. Mitropoliei 4, 720035 Suceava; tel. (30) 21-31-90; fax (30) 53-07-98; internet www.biblioteca .suceava.ro; f. 1923; 342,509 vols and periodicals; Dir GHEORGHE-GABRIEL CĂRĂBUŞ.

Târgovişte

Biblioteca Judeţeană 'Ion Heliade Rădulescu' Dâmboviţa (Dâmboviţa 'Ion Heliade Rădulescu' District Library): Str. Stelea 2, 130018 Târgovişte; tel. (245) 61-23-16; fax (372) 87-04-42; e-mail office@bjdb .ro; internet www.bjdb.ro; f. 1944; 273,000 vols and periodicals; Dir Prof. VĂDAN CARMEN; publ. *Curier.*

Târgu Jiu

Biblioteca Judeţeană 'Christian Tell' Gorj (Gorj 'Christian Tell' District Library): Str. Calea Eroilor 23, 210135 Târgu Jiu; tel. and fax (253) 21-49-04; e-mail bjgorj@ bibliotell.ro; internet www.bibliotell.ro; f. 1934; 301,582 vols; Dir Dr OLIMPIA BRATU.

Târgu Mureş

Biblioteca Documentară 'Teleki-Bolyai' ('Teleki-Bolyai' Documentary Library): Str. Bolyai 17, 540067 Târgu Mureş; tel. (265) 16-18-57; f. 1962, by the merger of Teleki library (f. 1802) and Bolyai library (f. 1557); books in the natural and social sciences before 19th century; maps, incunabula and MSS; 200,000 vols; Dir DIMITRIE POPTĂMAŞ.

Biblioteca Judeţeană Mureş (Mureş County Library): Str. Georges Enescu 2, 540052 Târgu Mureş; tel. (265) 26-26-31; fax (265) 26-43-84; internet www.bjmures .ro; f. 1913; 900,000 vols; Dir MONICA AVRAM; publs *Biblitheca Marisiana, Libraria.*

Timişoara

Biblioteca Centrală Universitară 'Eugen Todoran' (Central University Library 'Eugen Todoran'): Bdul V. Pârvan 4A, 300223 Timişoara; tel. (256) 49-03-53; fax (256) 49-40-04; e-mail dostafe@bcut.ro; internet www.bcut.ro; f. 1948 as Biblioteca Universităţii Timişoara, present name 2000; 991,673 vols and periodicals; Gen. Man. Prof. Dr VASILE DOCEA; Deputy Gen. Man Ing. DELIA PÂRŞAN; Deputy Gen. Man. Dr Ing. DOINA OSTAFE.

Biblioteca Judeţeană Timiş (Timiş District Library): Piaţa Libertăţii 3, 300077 Timişoara; tel. (256) 43-07-46; fax (256) 43-39-98; e-mail secretariat@bjt.ro; internet www.bjt.ro; f. 1904; 750,000 vols; Dir PAUL EUGEN BANCIU.

Tulcea

Biblioteca Judeţeană 'Panait Cerna' Tulcea (Tulcea County Library 'Panait Cerna'): Str. Isaccei 20, 820241 Tulcea; tel. and fax (240) 51-38-33; e-mail bjt@ tulcealibrary.ro; internet www.tulcealibrary .ro; f. 1879; 303,795 vols, 7,472 audiovisual materials and 17,045 periodicals; Man. OVIDIU GHIONU.

Vaslui

Biblioteca Judeţeană 'Nicolae Milescu Spătarul' Vaslui (Vaslui 'Nicolae Milescu Spătarul' County Library): Str. Hagi Chiriac 2, 730129 Vaslui; tel. and fax (35) 31-37-67; e-mail office@bjvaslui.ro; internet www .bjvaslui.ro; f. 1951; organizes exhibitions and cultural events; 250,000 vols; Man. Prof. GELU VOICU BICHINEŢ.

Zalău

Biblioteca Judeţeană 'Ioniţă Scipione Bădescu' Sălaj (Sălaj 'Ioniţă Scipione Bădescu' District Library): Str. Iuliu Maniu 13, 450016 Zalău; tel. (360) 56-69-19; fax (260) 63-20-07; e-mail biblio@bjs.ro; internet www.bjs.ro; f. 1950; 196,894 vols; Dir Prof. FLORICA POP; publ. *Revista I.D.E.I.*

Museums and Art Galleries

Aiud

Muzeul de Istorie Aiud (Aiud Museum of History): Piaţa Consiliul Europei 24, Judeţul Alba, 515200 Aiud; tel. (258) 86-54-59; fax (258) 86-12-80; e-mail paulscrobota@gmail .com; internet muzeu-aiud.cimec.ro; f. 1796; 30,000 museum objects; archaeology of the primitive commune, the Dacian-Roman period and the pre-feudal period; library of 1,800 vols; Dir PAUL VASILE SCROBOTĂ.

Muzeul de Ştiinţele Naturii Aiud (Aiud Natural Sciences Museum): Str. Bethlen Gabor 1, 515200 Aiud; tel. (258) 86-25-69; e-mail paulscrobota@gmail.com; internet muzeu-aiud.cimec.ro; f. 1796; collns of geology, mineralogy, palaeontology, botany, zoology; library of 500 vols; Dir PAUL VASILE SCROBOTĂ.

Alba Iulia

Muzeul Naţional al Unirii (National Museum of Unification): Str. Mihai Viteazul 12–14, 510010 Alba Iulia; tel. (258) 81-33-00; fax (258) 81-18-53; e-mail muzeulalba_relatiipublice@yahoo.com; internet www.mnuai.ro; f. 1888; exhibits relating to prehistoric and Roman archaeology, medieval era, ecclesiastical history, ethnography and Romanian Union; library of 70,000 vols; Dir Dr GABRIEL TIBERIU RUSTOIU; publs *Apulum—Acta Musei Apulensis* (1 a year), *Bibliotheca Musei Apulensis* (1 a year).

Alexandria

Muzeul Judeţean Teleorman (Teleorman County Museum): Str. 1848 1, 140033 Alexandria; tel. and fax (247) 31-47-61; e-mail muzjudteleorman@yahoo.com; internet www .muzeulteleorman.ro; f. 1952 as Alexandria Museum of History; archaeology, art, ethnography, history, numismatics, palaeontology; Man. Dr PAVEL MIREA; publ. *Buletinul Muzeului Judetean Teleorman Seria Arheologie* (1 a year).

Arad

Complexul Muzeal Arad (Arad Museum Complex): Piaţa George Enescu 1, 310131 Arad; tel. (257) 28-18-47; fax (257) 28-01-14; e-mail office@museumarad.ro; internet www .museumarad.ro; f. 1893; archaeology, history, ethnology, natural sciences, fine and applied art; Man. Dr PETER HÜGEL; publs *Armonii Naturale* (natural history, every 2 years), *Studii şi Comunicări* (studies and communications of art and architecture, every 2 years), *Zarandul* (ethnology, every 2 years), *Ziridava* (archaeology and history, every 2 years).

Bacău

Complexul Muzeal de Ştiinţele Naturii 'Ion Borcea' Bacău ('Ion Borcea' Natural Sciences Museum Complex of Bacău): Str. Aleea Parcului 9, 600033 Bacău; tel. and fax (234) 51-20-06; e-mail muzstnatbc@yahoo .com; internet www.adslexpress.ro/ muzstnat/index.htm; f. 1964; botany, geology, mineralogy, palaeontology, zoology; incl. Natural Sciences Museum of Bacău, vivarium of Bacău, Astronomic Observatory and Ion Borcea Memorial House, Racova, Bacău county; education, research; library of 23,000 vols; Man. Dr GABRIELA GURĂU; Deputy Dir Dr ORTANSA JIGAU; publ. *Studii şi Comunicări* (1 a year).

Complexul Muzeul 'Iulian Antonescu' Bacău (Bacău 'Iulian Antonescu' Museum Complex): Str. 9 Mai 7, 600037 Bacău; tel. and fax (234) 51-24-44; e-mail muzeuistorie_bacau@yahoo.com; internet

www.cmiabc.ro; f. 1957; history, art, archaeology, ethnography, literature; library of 9,000 vols; Dir Prof. SILVIA IACOBESCU; publ. *Carpica* (1 a year).

Baia Mare

Muzeul Judeţean Maramureş (Maramureş District Museum): Str. Monetăriei 1–3, 430406 Baia Mare; tel. and fax (262) 21-19-27; e-mail muzeumm@rdslink.ro; internet www.muzeumm.baiamare.rdsnet.ro; f. 1899; archaeology, ethnography, history, planetary, Romanian art; library of 20,000 vols; Dir Gen. Prof. GRIGORE MAN; publ. *Marmaţia* (1 a year).

Associated Museum:

Muzeul de Mineralogie Baia Mare (Baia Mare Mineralogical Museum): Bdul Traian 8, 430212 Baia Mare; tel. and fax (262) 22-75-17; e-mail muzmin@rdslink.ro; internet www.muzeuminbm.ro; f. 1989; exhibition of rocks; minerals; mineralogical and crystallographic research; library of 900 vols; Man. IOAN BOB.

Bistriţa

Muzeul Judeţean Bistriţa (Bistriţa County Museum): Str. Gen. Grigore Bălan 19, 420016 Bistriţa; tel. and fax (263) 21-10-63; f. 1950; Dir Dr IOAN CHINTAUAN; publs *Revista Bistriţei* (history), *Studii şi Cercetări Etnoculturale*, *Studii şi Cercetări Ştiinţele Naturii*.

Botoşani

Muzeul Judeţean Botoşani (Botoşani District Museum): Str. Unirii 15, 710221 Botoşani; tel. (231) 51-34-46; fax (231) 53-69-89; e-mail istorie@muzeubt.ro; internet www .muzeubt.hhe.ro; f. 1955; history, archaeology, ethnography, fine arts; incl. 'Nicolae Iorga' and 'George Enescu' memorial houses; library of 10,000 vols; Man. Prof. LUCICA PÂRVAN.

Brad

Muzeul de Istorie şi Etnografie Brad (Brad History and Ethnography Museum): 335200 Brad; f. 1987; traditional arts and crafts, spec. colln of wooden objects; Curator MIHAI DAVID.

Brăila

Muzeul Brăilei (Brăila Museum): Piaţa Traian 3, 810153 Brăila; tel. (339) 40-10-02; fax (339) 40-10-03; e-mail sediu@ muzeulbrailei.ro; internet www .muzeulbrailei.ro; f. 1881; archaeology, history, fine arts, ethnography, natural sciences; library of 26,000 vols and periodicals; Dir Dr IONEL CÂNDEA; Dir Adjunct VALERIU SÎRBU; Dir Adjunct ZAMFIR BĂLAN; publs *Analele Brăilei* (every 2 years), *ISTROS* (every 2 years).

Bran

Muzeul Bran (Bran Museum): Str. Traian Mosoiu 495–498, 507025 Bran; tel. (268) 23-83-33; fax (268) 47-56-07; e-mail contact@ muzeul-bran.ro; internet www.muzeul-bran .ro; f. 1957; Bran castle, history, ethnography, feudal art; Dir NARCIS DORIN ION.

Braşov

Muzeul, Biblioteca şi Arhiva Istorică a Primei Şcoli Româneşti din Scheii Braşovului (Museum, Library and Historical Archive of First Romanian School of Braşov): Piaţa Unirii 1, 500123 Braşov; tel. (268) 14-38-79; f. 1933; historical museum in building of first Romanian school (15th century); Dir Dr VASILE OLTEANU.

Muzeul de Artă (Art Museum): Bdul Eroilor 21, 500030 Braşov; tel. (268) 47-72-86; fax (268) 47-51-72; e-mail contact@muzeulartabv

.ro; internet www.muzeulartabv.ro; f. 1949; decorative arts, Romanian fine arts; Dir BARTHA ÁRPÁD.

Muzeul de Etnografie (Ethnographical Museum): Bdul Eroilor 21A, 500030 Braşov; tel. (268) 47-62-43; fax (268) 47-55-62; e-mail muzeu@etnobrasov.ro; internet www .etnobrasov.ro; Dir Dr LIGIA FULGA.

Muzeul Judeţean de Istorie Braşov (Braşov District History Museum): Nicolae Bălcescu 67, 500019 Braşov; tel. and fax (268) 47-23-50; internet istoriebv.ro; f. 1908; library of 23,000 vols; Dir Dr RADU ŞTEFĂNESCU; publ. *Cumidava*.

Bucharest

Muzeul Căilor Ferate Române (Romanian Railway Museum): Calea Griviţei 193A, 010711 Bucharest; tel. (21) 223-06-60; f. 1939; attached to Min. of Transport; materials, parts, documentary illustrating the evolution of rail transport.

Muzeul de Istorie al Evreilor din România 'Sef Rabin Dr Moses Rosen' (History Museum of the Romanian Jews 'Chief—Rabbi Dr Mose Rosen'): Str. Mămulari 3, 030771 Bucharest; tel. (21) 311-08-70; e-mail jewishmuseum.bucharest@gmail.com; f. 1978; Pres. Dr Ing. JOSE BLUM; Dir Dr E. MAXIM.

Muzeul Literaturii Române (Museum of Romanian Literature): Bdul Dacia 12, 010412 Bucharest; tel. (21) 212-58-45; fax (21) 212-58-46; internet www.mlr.ro; f. 1957; library of 80,000 vols and periodicals and 46,000 MSS and photographs; historical documents; old and rare books; art objects; periodicals; photographs; audio/video colln; publ. *Manuscriptum* (4 a year).

Muzeul Militar Naţional (National Military Museum): Str. Mircea Vulcănescu 125–127, 77116 Bucharest; tel. (21) 319-59-04; fax (21) 319-59-03; e-mail director@ muzeulmilitar.ro; internet www.defense.ro/ muzeumilitar; f. 1923; library of 36,856 vols; Dir Col ILIE SCHIPOR; publ. *Buletinul Muzeului Militar Naţional*.

Muzeul Municipiului Bucureşti (Bucharest Municipality Museum): Bdul I. C. Brătianu 2, 030174 Bucharest; tel. (21) 315-68-58; fax (21) 310-25-62; e-mail mmb@ muzeulbucurestiului.ro; internet www .muzeulbucurestiului.ro; f. 1921; 10 affiliated museums; library of 53,700 vols; Dir Dr IONEL IONITA; publ. *Bucuresti: Materiale de Istorie si Muzeografie*.

Muzeul Naţional al Satului 'Dimitrie Gusti' (National Village Museum 'Dimitrie Gusti'): Şoseaua Kiseleff 28–30, 011347 Bucharest; tel. (21) 317-91-03; fax (21) 317-90-68; e-mail contact@muzeul-satului.ro; internet www.muzeul-satului.ro; f. 1936; open-air nat. museum of village life since 17th century; library of 30,000 vols, 130,000 photographs; Dir-Gen. Dr PAULA POPOIU.

Muzeul Naţional al Ţăranului Român (National Museum of the Romanian Peasant): Şoseaua Kiseleff 3, 011341 Bucharest; tel. (21) 317-96-61; fax (21) 317-96-60; e-mail info@muzeultaranuluiroman.ro; internet www.muzeultaranuluiroman.ro; f. 1906; colln of 100,000 items on peasant art and traditions; research in field of ethnology and anthropology; Dir Gen. Dr VIRGIL STEFAN NITULESCU; publ. *MARTOR* (review, in French and English, 1 a year).

Muzeul Naţional Cotroceni (Cotroceni National Museum): Bdul Geniului 1, 060116 Bucharest; tel. (21) 317-31-06; fax (21) 312-16-18; e-mail vizitare@aim.com; internet www.muzeulcotroceni.ro; f. 1991; Romanian art, medieval architecture, decorative art, history; museum pedagogy; tours and visits;

organizes confs, exhibits and workshops; Dir ADINA RENŢEA.

Muzeul Naţional de Artă al României (National Museum of Art of Romania): Calea Victoriei 49–53, 010063 Bucharest; tel. (21) 314-81-19; fax (21) 312-43-27; e-mail national .art@art.museum.ro; internet www.mnar .arts.ro; f. 1950; European art since 14th century, Romanian religious and secular works of art from 14th–18th centuries, Romanian modern art since 19th century; also administers Arts Collections Museum, Theodor Pallady Museum, K. H. Zambaccian Museum; library of 4,000 vols; Gen. Dir ROXANA THEODORESCU.

Muzeul Naţional de Istorie a României (National History Museum of Romania): Calea Victoriei 12, 030026 Bucharest; tel. (21) 315-82-07; fax (21) 311-33-56; e-mail direct@mnir.ro; internet www.mnir.ro; f. 1972; library of 45,000 vols; Dir Dr CRIŞAN MUŞEŢEANU; Gen. Man. Dr ERNEST OBERLAN-DER-TARNOVEANU; publs *Cercetări arheologice*, *Cercetări numismatice*, *Muzeul Naţional*.

Muzeul Naţional de Istorie Naturală 'Grigore Antipa' ('Grigore Antipa' National Natural History Museum): Şoseaua Kiseleff 1, 011341 Bucharest; tel. (21) 312-88-26; fax (21) 312-88-63; e-mail imatache@antipa.ro; internet www.antipa.ro; f. 1834; zoology, hydrobiology, anatomy, oceanography, ecology, zoogeography, ethnography, anthropology; library of 30,200 vols, 20,000 periodicals; Dir-Gen. Adjunct IOANA MATACHE; publ. *Travaux* (1 a year).

Muzeul Naţional Filatelic: Calea Victoriei 12, sector 3, Bucharest; tel. (12) 312-74-99; fax (21) 312-55-85; internet www .muzeulfilatelic.ro; f. 1990; history of stamps and post; exhibits.

Muzeul Naţional 'George Enescu' ('George Enescu' National Museum): Calea Victoriei 141, 010071 Bucharest; tel. (21) 318-14-50; fax (21) 312-91-82; e-mail office@ georgeenescu.ro; internet www.georgeenescu .ro; f. 1956; Dir ILINCA DUMITRESCU.

Muzeul Poliţiei Române: c/o Poliţia Română, Str. Mihai Voda 6, sector 5, Bucharest; tel. (21) 208-25-25; internet www.politiaromana.ro; f. 2000.

Muzeul Tehnic 'Prof. Ing. Dimitrie Leonida' (Prof. Eng. Dimitrie Leonida Museum of Technology): Str. Candiano Popescu 2, 040583 Bucharest; tel. and fax (21) 336-77-77; e-mail muztech@fdeb.rdsnet.ro; f. 1909; library of 25,000 vols; Dir Dipl. Eng. NICOLAE DIACONESCU; publ. *Anuar*.

Buzău

Muzeul Judeţean Buzău (Buzău County Museum): N. Balcescu 50, 120360 Buzău; tel. (238) 71-05-61; fax (238) 71-06-38; e-mail home@muzeubuzau.ro; internet www .muzeubuzau.ro; f. 1951; history, archaeology, folk art, contemporary and decorative arts; library of 20,875 vols; Man. Dr SEBASTIAN MATEI; publs *Analele Buzăului*, *Mousaios* (1 a year).

Călăraşi

Muzeul Dunării de Jos (Museum of the Lower Danube): Str. 1 December 1918 1, 910019 Călăraşi; tel. (242) 31-13-01; fax (242) 33-16-09; e-mail cjcalarasi@calarasi.ro; internet www.calarasi.ro; f. 1951; archaeology, numismatics, medieval history, modern arts, natural history, ethnography of the area; Dir Dr MARIAN NEAGU; Pres. GEORGE RADUCU FILIPESCU; Vice-Pres. DANIEL STEPHEN DRAGULIN; Sec. ALAN VIRTEJANU.

Câmpulung

Muzeul Zonal Câmpulung (Câmpulung Zonal Museum): Str. Negru Vodă 119, 115100 Câmpulung; tel. (248) 11737; f. 1880; history, arts, natural science, ethnography, folk art; Dir ŞTEFAN TRÂMBACIU; publs *Istoria Câmpulungului şi a zonei Muscel*, *Studii şi comunicări*.

Câmpulung Moldovenesc

Muzeul Artei Lemnului (Wooden Art Museum): Calea Transilvaniei 10, 725100 Câmpulung Moldovenesc; tel. (230) 31-13-78; f. 1936; ethnography, history, arts, folk art; Dir MARCEL ZAHANICIUC.

Caracal

Muzeul Romanaţiului Caracal (Caracal Museum of the Romanaţi): Str. Libertăţii 26, 235200 Caracal; tel. (249) 51-13-44; f. 1951; history, ethnography, art, lapidarium; Dir PAUL LICĂ.

Caransebeş

Muzeul Judeţean de Etnografie şi a Regimentului de Graniţă-Caransebeş (Caransebeş County Museum of Ethnography and Border Regiment): Piaţa Gen. Ion Dragalina 2, 325400 Caransebeş; tel. (255) 51-41-73; fax (255) 51-21-93; e-mail mjergcaransebes@yahoo.com; internet www .muzeul-caransebes.ro; f. 1963; history of the border regiment; Banat's history ethnography, folk art, archaeology; incl. Tibiscum, the Roman archaeological site; Dir Prof. Dr ADRIAN ARDEŢ; publs *Studii şi Comunicări de Etnografie şi Istorie*, *Tibiscum / Acta Musei Caransebesiensis - Serie Nouă*.

Cluj-Napoca

Grădina Botanică Alexandru Borza (The Alexandru Borza Botanical Garden): Republicii St 42, 400015 Cluj-Napoca; tel. and fax (264) 59-21-52; e-mail gradina.botanica@ ubbcluj.ro; internet www.ubbcluj.ro; f. 1920; attached to Babes-Bolyai Univ.; ornamental, phytogeographic, systematic, economic and medicinal sections; 51 mems; library of 25,000 vols; Dir Dr VASILE CRISTEA; publs *Contribuţii botanice* (1 a year), *Flora Romaniae Exsiccata*, *Delectus seminum* (1 a year), *The Seeds Catalogue and the Botanical Contributions review*.

Muzeul Etnografic al Transilvaniei (Transylvanian Museum of Ethnography): Memorandum St 21, 400114 Cluj-Napoca; tel. (264) 59-23-44; fax (264) 59-21-48; e-mail contact@muzeul-etnografic.ro; internet www .muzeul-etnografic.ro; f. 1922; incl. open-air nat. ethnographic park; Dir SIMONA MUNTEANU.

Muzeul Naţional de Artă Cluj: Piaţa Unirii 30, 400098 Cluj-Napoca; tel. (264) 59-69-52; e-mail macn@cluj.astral.ro; internet www.macluj.ro; f. 1951; Romanian and foreign art from 16th to 21st centuries; library of 9,000 vols; Dir Dr CALIN STEGEREAN.

Muzeul Naţional de Istorie a Transilvaniei (National History Museum of Transylvania): Str. Constantin Daicoviciu 2, 400020 Cluj-Napoca; tel. (264) 19-56-77; fax (264) 19-17-18; internet www.museum.utcluj.ro; f. 1859; library of 28,000 vols; Dir IOAN PISO; publ. *Acta Musei Napocensis* (1 a year).

Muzeul Zoologic al Universităţii 'Babeş Bolyai' Cluj-Napoca (Zoological Museum of the Cluj-Napoca 'Babeş Bolyai' University): Str. Clinicilor 5–7, 400006 Cluj-Napoca; tel. (264) 59-57-39; e-mail dceuca@hasdeu .ubbcluj.ro; internet www.ubbcluj.ro; f. 1859; integrated in the Faculty of Biology and Geology; incl. exhibits, scientific collns, museum reserve; Dir Dr IION COROIU; publ. *Studia* (1 a year).

Constanţa

Complexul Muzeal de Ştiinţe ale Naturii (Natural History Museum Complex): Bdul Mamaia 255, 900522 Constanţa; tel. (241) 54-70-55; fax (241) 48-12-36; e-mail office@ delfinariu.ro; internet www.delfinariu.ro; f. 1958; aquarium, dolphinarium, planetarium, astronomical observatory, micro-reservation; Dir GABRIELA PLOTOAGĂ; publ. *Pontus Euxinus*.

Muzeul de Artă (Art Museum): Bdul Tomis 84, 900657 Constanţa; tel. (241) 61-70-12; f. 1961; Romanian paintings and other works of art; Dir DOINA PAULEANU.

Muzeul de Artă Populară (Folk Art Museum): Bdul Tomis 32, 900742 Constanţa; tel. (241) 61-61-33; fax (241) 61-61-33; e-mail muzeuetno@yahoo.com; internet muzeuetno .blogspot.com; Dir Dr MARIA MAGIRU.

Muzeul de Istorie Naţională şi Arheologie Constanţa (Constanţa Museum for National History and Archaeology): Piaţa Ovidiu 12, 900745 Constanţa; tel. (241) 61-87-63; e-mail minaconstanta@gmail.com; internet www.minac.ro; f. 1879; educational, archaeological activities; affiliated archaeological museums of Histria, Tropaeum Traiani, Harsova and Cernavoda; library of 41,000 vols; Dir Dr GABRIEL CUSTUREA; publs *Analele Dobrogei* (modern and contemporary history; 1 a year), *Pontica* (archaeology, ancient and medieval history, numismatic; 1 a year).

Muzeul Marinei Române (Romanian Naval Museum): Str. Traian 53, 900725 Constanţa; tel. (241) 61-90-35; fax (241) 61-90-35; e-mail naval.museum@yahoo.com; internet www.navy.ro; f. 1969; history of Romanian navy and merchant fleet; Dir Cmdr Dr GLODARENCO OLIMPIU MANUEL.

Corabia

Muzeul de Arheologie şi Etnografie Corabia (Corabia Archaeological and Ethnographical Museum): Str. Cuza Vodă 65, 235300 Corabia; tel. (249) 56-13-64; Dir FLOREA BÂCIU.

Craiova

Muzeul Regional al Olteniei (Regional Museum of Oltenia): Madona Dudu St. 14, 200410 Craiova; tel. (251) 41-77-56; fax (251) 41-94-35; e-mail office@muzeulolteniei.ro; internet www.muzeuloltenei.ro; f. 1915; incorporates museums of art, ethnography, natural history, and archaeology and history; library of 12,000 vols; Gen. Man. Prof. Dr MIHAI VIOREL FIFOR; publ. *Oltenia—Studii şi cercetări*.

Curtea de Argeş

Muzeul de Istorie şi Etnografie (History and Ethnography Museum): Str. Negru Vodă 2, 115300 Curtea de Argeş; tel. (248) 1-14-46; Dir N. MOISESCU.

Deva

Muzeul Civilizaţiei Dacice şi Romane Deva (Deva Museum of Dacian and Roman Civilization): Bdul 1 Decembrie 1918 nr. 39, 2700 Deva, Hunedoara; tel. (254) 21-22-00; fax (254) 21-22-00; e-mail museum@ worldwidesam.net; internet museum .worldwidesam.net; f. 1882; archaeology, history, natural sciences, numismatics, art, ethnography; incorporates museum of Roman archaeology at Sarmizegetusa and the ethnographical museums at Orăştie and Brad; library of 30,980 vols; Dir ADRIANA RUSU-PESCARU; publ. *Sargetia. Acta Musei Devensis*.

Drobeta-Turnu Severin

Muzeul Regiunii 'Porţile de Fier' ('Iron Gates' Regional Museum): Str. Independenţei 2, 220171 Drobeta-Turnu Severin; tel. (52) 31-21-77; fax (52) 32-00-27; f. 1882; natural history, ethnography, archaeology and Roman ruins; aquarium; Dir Dr ION KNOWNGA; Deputy Dir Dr GABRIEL CRACIUNESCU; publ. *Drobeta* (1 a year).

Focşani

Muzeul Vrancei (Vrancea Museum): Bdul Gării 5, 620012 Focşani; tel. (237) 22-28-90; f. 1951; incorporates museums of ethnography (open-air), natural history, and history and archaeology; Dir HORIA DUMITRESCU.

Galaţi

Muzeul Judeţean de Istorie (District Museum of History): Str. Maior Iancu Fotea 2, 800017 Galaţi; tel. (236) 41-42-28; fax (236) 46-07-97; e-mail muzeuistoriegalati@yahoo.com; internet www.migl.ro; f. 1939; colln on Alexandru Ioan Cuza; presentation on Galaţ city; colln of antique coins and medals; archaeological and ethnographic collns; library of 10,000 vols; Dir Prof. CRISTIAN DRAGOS CALDARARU; publ. *Danubius* (online (www.revistadanubius.ro)).

Attached Museums:

Complexul Muzeal de Ştiinţele Naturii (Natural Science Museum Complex): Str. Regiment 11 Siret, 800340 Galaţi; tel. (236) 41-18-98; fax (236) 41-44-75; e-mail contact@cmsngl.ro; f. 1956; flora and fauna of the region, botanical and zoological gardens, aquarium; Dir Ing. CAMELIA GROSU.

Muzeul de Arta Vizuala (Visual Art Museum): Str. Domnească 141, 800163 Galaţi; tel. (236) 41-34-52; fax (236) 31-25-02; e-mail contact@mavgl.ro; internet www.mavgl.ro; f. 1956; Dir DAN BASARAB NANU.

Gherla

Muzeul de Istorie Gherla: Str. Mihai Viteazul 6, Judeţul Cluj, 405300 Gherla; tel. (264) 24-19-47; fax (264) 24-16-66; e-mail mihaimester@personal.ro; f. 1881; Daco-Roman archaeology, ethnography, local history; library of 4,221 vols; Dir RODICA PINTEA.

Giurgiu

Muzeul Judeţean 'Teohari Antonescu' (Giurgiu District Museum): Str. Constantin Dobrogeanu Gherea nr 3, 080024 Giurgiu; tel. (246) 21-68-01; e-mail muzeuljudeteangiurgiu@gmail.com; internet muzulgiurgiu.ro; f. 1934; history, ethnography; medieval archaeology, prehistoric archaeology, memorial history; Dir TRAIAN POPA; publ. *File de istorie*.

Goleşti

Muzeul Viticulturii şi Pomiculturii Goleşti (Viticulture and Tree Growing Museum from Goleşti): Ştefăneşti Commune, Judeţul Argeş, 117715 Goleşti; tel. and fax (248) 26-63-64; e-mail cmngolesti@yahoo.com; internet www.muzeulgolesti.ro; f. 1939; history of fruit- and vine-growing; library of 13,000 vols; Dir Dr FILOFTEIA PALLY.

Gura Humorului

Muzeul Obiceiurilor Populare din Bucovina (Museum of Bucovinean Folk Traditions): Piaţa Republicii 2, 725300 Gura Humorului; tel. (230) 23-11-08; fax (230) 23-50-51; e-mail muzeulhumor@gmail.com; f. 1958; ethnographic colln; colln of numismatics; colln of songs, historic and natural sciences; library of 2,415 vols; Dir ELVIRA ROMANIUC.

Iaşi

Complexul Naţional Muzeal 'Moldova' Iaşi ('Moldova' Iaşi National Museum Complex): Piaţa Ştefan cel Mare şi Sfânt 1, 700028 Iaşi; tel. and fax (232) 21-83-83; internet www.palatulculturii.ro; f. 1992; closed for renovation during 2011; Dir VAL CONDURACHE; publs *Anuarul Muzeului Etnografic al Moldovei* (1 a year), *Buletinul Centrului de Restaurare-Conservare* (2 a year), *Buletinul Ioan Neculce* (1 a year), *Cercetări istorice* (1 a year).

Selected Constituent Museums:

Muzeul de Artă din Iaşi (Iaşi Art Museum): Piaţa Ştefan cel Mare şi Sfânt 1, 700028 Iaşi; tel. (232) 31-41-36 ext. 124; fax (232) 21-83-83; internet www.palatulculturii.ro; f. 1860; Curator IVONA ARAMĂ.

Muzeul de Istorie a Moldovei (History Museum of Moldavia): Piaţa Ştefan cel Mare şi Sfânt 1, 700028 Iaşi; tel. (232) 31-41-36 ext. 135; fax (232) 21-83-83; internet www.palatulculturii.ro; f. 1916; incl. Al. I. Cuza Memorial Museum, in Ruginoasa, Mihail Kogalniceanu Memorial Museum in Iaşi, Museum of the Union in Iaşi (dedicated to the period of creating and maintaining the union of the Romanian lands), History Museums in Hârlău and Paşcani, and archaeological sites at Cucuteni and Cotnari; Curator SENICA TURCANU.

Muzeul Etnografic al Moldovei (Ethnographic Museum of Moldavia): Piaţa Ştefan cel Mare şi Sfânt 1, 700028 Iaşi; tel. (232) 31-41-36 ext. 144; fax (232) 21-83-83; internet www.palatulculturii.ro; f. 1943; Curator VASILE MUNTEANU.

Muzeul Ştiinţei şi Tehnicii 'Ştefan Procopiu' (Museum of Science and Technology 'Stefan Procopiu'): Piaţa Ştefan cel Mare şi Sfânt 1, 700028 Iaşi; tel. (232) 31-41-36 ext. 145; fax (232) 21-83-83; internet www.palatulculturii.ro; f. 1955; incl. Iaşi Memorial Museum 'Poni-Cernatescu'; Curator LENUŢA CHIRIŢĂ.

Muzeul de Istorie Naturală Iaşi (Iaşi Natural History Museum): Str. Română 40, 700312 Iaşi; f. 1834; attached to Alexandru Ioan Cuza Univ.; geology, palaeontology, zoology; Dir Dr ION COJOCARU.

Muzeul Literaturii Române Iaşi: Str. Vasile Pogor 4, Iaşi; tel. (232) 41-03-40; fax (232) 21-32-10; e-mail contact@muzeulliteraturiiiasi.ro; internet www.muzeulliteraturiiiasi.ro; f. 1918; organizes exhibits, confs; modern and contemporary Romanian literature; publ. *Dacia literară*.

Mangalia

Muzeul de Arheologie 'Callatis' Mangalia (Callatis Archaeological Museum of Mangalia): Şoseaua Constanţei 23, 905500 Mangalia; tel. (341) 14-67-63; e-mail sorinmarcelcolesniuc@yahoo.com; internet www.muzeulcallatis.ro; f. 1924; prehistory, Greek and Roman periods, ancient Greek colony of Callatis; library of 2,900 vols; Dir Dr SORIN MARCEL COLESNIUC; publ. *Studia Callatiana*.

Mediaş

Muzeul Municipal Mediaş (Mediaş Municipal Museum): Str. M. Viteazu 46, 551034 Mediaş; tel. (269) 84-12-99; fax (269) 84-12-29; f. 1950; history, natural history, ethnography, incl. classical and contemporary arts; Dir Dr PETER WEBER.

Miercurea Ciuc

Muzeul Secuiesc al Ciucului/Csíki Székely Múzeum (Szekler Museum of Ciuc): Piaţa Cetăţii 2, Judeţul Harghita, 530132 Miercurea Ciuc; tel. (266) 37-20-24; fax (266) 31-17-27; e-mail info@csikimuzeum.ro; internet www.csikimuzeum.ro; f. 1930; history, ethnography, archaeology, 20th-century art history, old books; library of 9,000 vols; Dir ZSOLT GYARMATI.

Mogoşoaia

Centrul Naţional de Cultura Mogoşoaia (Mogoşoaia National Cultural Centre): Brâncoveanu Palace, Ilfov, Str. Valea Parcului 1, Com., 077135 Mogoşoaia; tel. (21) 490-40-22; fax (21) 225-66-90; e-mail pbpb@xnet.ro; f. 1702; medieval Romanian art; Dir DOINA MANDRU.

Năsăud

Muzeul Năsăudean (Năsăud Museum): Str. Grănicerilor 19, 425200 Năsăud; tel. (263) 36-29-67; history, ethnography; Dir IOAN RADU NISTOR.

Negresti Oas

Muzeul Ţării Oaşului: Str. Victoriei 140, Negresti Oas, Satu Mare; tel. and fax (261) 85-48-39; internet www.oasmuseum.ro; colln of ethnography and folk art.

Oradea

Muzeul Ţării Crişurilor (Criş County Museum): Bdul Dacia 1–3, 410464 Oradea; tel. (259) 41-27-24; fax (259) 41-27-25; e-mail contact@mtariicrisurilor.ro; internet www.mtariicrisurilor.ro; f. 1971; history, art, ethnography and natural science; library of 30,000 vols; Gen. Man. Prof. Dr AUREL CHIRIAC; publs *Biharea* (ethnography and art, 1 a year), *Crisia* (history and archaeology, 1 a year), *Nymphaea* (natural sciences, 1 a year).

Orăştie

Sectia de Etnografie şi Artă Populară Orăştie (Dept of Ethnography and Folk Art Orăştie): Piata Aurel Vlaicu 1, 335700 Orăştie; tel. and fax (254) 24-73-00; f. 1952; Curator COSMA AURELIAN.

Petroşani

Muzeul Mineritului (Mining Museum): Str. N. Bălcescu 12, 332026 Petroşani; tel. (254) 54-17-44; f. 1961; history of mining in the Jiu Valley; Dir DUMITRU PELIGRAD.

Piatra-Neamţ

Complexul Muzeal Judeţean Neamţ (Neamţ District Museums Complex): Bdul Mihai Eminescu 10, 610029 Piatra-Neamţ; tel. (233) 21-74-96; e-mail muzeupn@yahoo.com; internet www.neamt.ro; f. 1978; archaeology, history, arts, memoirs, ethnography, natural sciences colln; Dir GHEORGHE DUMITROAIA.

Selected Affiliated Museums:

Muzeul de Artă Piatra-Neamţ (Piatra-Neamţ Art Museum): Piaţa Libertăţii 1, 610100 Piatra-Neamţ; tel. (233) 21-68-08; internet www.neamt.ro; f. 1980; Romanian art; Curator VIOLETA DINU.

Muzeul de Etnografie Piatra-Neamţ (Piatra-Neamţ Ethnography Museum): Piaţa Libertăţii 1, 610100 Piatra-Neamţ; tel. (233) 21-68-08; internet www.neamt.ro; Curator FLORENTINA BUZENSCHI.

Muzeul de Istorie şi Arheologie Piatra-Neamţ (Piatra-Neamţ History and Archaeology Museum): Bdul Mihai Eminescu 10, 610029 Piatra-Neamţ; tel. (233) 21-81-08; e-mail muzeupn@yahoo.com; internet www.neamt.ro; f. 1934; archaeological colln; Curator GHEORGHE DUMITROAIA; publ. *Memoria Antiquitatis* (1 a year).

Muzeul de Ştiinţele Naturii Piatra-Neamţ (Piatra-Neamţ Natural History

Museum): Str. Petru Rareş 26, 610119 Piatra-Neamţ; tel. (233) 22-42-11; internet www.neamt.ro; f. 1960; colln of fossil fish; Curator NICOLETA LĂCĂTUS; publ. *Studii şi comunicări* (1 a year).

Piteşti

Muzeul Judeţean Argeş (Argeş County Museum): Str. Armand Călinescu 44, 110047 Piteşti; tel. and fax (248) 21-25-61; e-mail muzeuarges@yahoo.com; internet www.muzeu-judetean-arges.ro; f. 1928; history, art, natural history, archaeology, numismatics, fine arts, planetarium, museum of sports, editorial house (Editura Ordessos); organizes nat. and int. exhibits; library of 22,000 vols; Gen. Dir Dr SPIRIDON CRISTOCEA; Dir Adjunct Dr DRAGOS MANDESCU; publs *Argessis—Studii şi comunicări* (Studies and Reports), *Argessis—Studii şi comunicări* (history series and natural science series, 1 a year), *Naturalia* (ecology, 1 a year).

Ploieşti

Muzeul Judeţean de Artă Prahova: Bdul Independenţei 1, 100028 Ploieşti; tel. (244) 52-22-64; fax (244) 51-13-75; e-mail office@artmuseum.ro; internet www.artmuseum.ro; f. 1931, present name 1955; Dir FLORIN SICOIE; Deputy Dir ALICE NECULEA.

Muzeul Judeţean de Istorie şi Arheologie Prahova (Prahova District Museum of History and Archaeology): Str. Toma Caragiu 10, 100042 Ploieşti; tel. and fax (244) 51-44-37; e-mail histmuseumph@yahoo.com; internet www.histmuseumph.ro; f. 1953; library of 60,247 vols; Dir-Gen. LIA MARIA VOICU; Deputy Dir EUGEN STANESCU; Deputy Dir MARINELA PENEŞ; Dir VALERIA ANGHEL; publs *Studii şi comunicări* (1 a year), *Yearbook Museum of History and Archaeology Prahova*.

Muzeul Judeţean de Stiintele Naturii Prahova (Prahova County Natural Sciences Museum): Erou Calin Catalin 1, 100066 Ploieşti; tel. (244) 59-78-96; fax (244) 51-19-70; e-mail office@muzbioph.ro; internet www.muzbioph.ro; f. 1956; Dir Gen. Prof. Dr EMILIA IANCU; Dir PETRESCU VICTOR; publ. *Comunicări şi referate*.

Muzeul Naţional al Petrolului (National Oil Museum): Str. Dr Bagdazar 8, 100575 Ploieşti; tel. (244) 59-75-85; fax (244) 51-95-42; e-mail muzeu.petrol@petrom.com; f. 1961; history of the Romanian oil industry; library of 3,000 vols; Dir GABRIELA TĂNĂSESCU.

Rădăuţi

Muzeul Etnografic Rădăuţi (Rădăuţi Ethnographic Museum): Piaţa Unirii 63, 725400 Rădăuţi; tel. (230) 46-25-65; internet www.muzeulradauti.ro; f. 1920; Dir TRAJAN POSTOLACHE.

Râmnicu Vâlcea

Muzeul Judeţean Vâlcea: Calea Traian 143, Râmnicu Vâlcea; tel. (250) 73-81-21; e-mail mjv@avansoft.ro; internet www.muzee-valcea.ro; f. 1955; cultural institution specialized in research, conservation, restoration and cultural heritage.

Attached Museums:

Casa Memoriala Anton Pann: Str. Stirbei Voda 4, Râmnicu Vâlcea; tel. and fax (250) 73-80-26.

Colectia de arta plastica Alexandru Balintescu: comuna Costesti, la aprox. 5 km de orasul Horezu, drumul spre m-rea Bistria, Judeţul Valcea; tel. and fax (250) 73-81-21; Colln of fine arts.

Complexul Muzeal Maldaresti: comuna Maldaresti, la aprox. 3 km de orasul Horezu; tel. and fax (250) 86-15-10.

Muzeul de arheologie si arta religioasa Gh. Petre-Govora: Baile Govora, Judeţul Valcea; tel. and fax (250) 73-81-21; archeological colln, incl. material, coins, works of art and rare books.

Muzeul de Arta Casa Simian: Strada Carol I 25, Râmnicu Vâlcea; tel. and fax (250) 73-81-21; painting and sculpture from 18th, 19th and 20th centuries.

Muzeul de Istorie a Judetului Valcea: Calea lui Traian 143, Râmnicu Vâlcea; tel. and fax (250) 73-81-21; e-mail mjv@avansoft.ro; collns of Palaeolithic, Neolithic and Bronze ages.

Muzeul Satului Valcean: Comuna Bujoreni, Judeţul Valcea; tel. (250) 74-68-69; images of traditional rural settlements.

Reghin

Muzeul Etnografic Reghin (Reghin Ethnographic Museum): Str. Vînătorilor 51, Judeţul Mureş, 545300 Reghin; tel. (265) 51-25-71; e-mail muzeureghin@yahoo.com; internet muzeureghin.xhost.ro; f. 1960; folk art, textiles, wood icons, costumes; library of 2,336 vols, 3,186 slides, 128 ethnological films; Dir MARIA BORZAN; Librarian ADRIAN BUGNAR.

Reşiţa

Muzeul Banatului Montan (Museum of the Mountainous Banat): Bdul Republicii 10, 320151 Reşiţa; tel. (355) 40-12-19; fax (355) 40-12-20; e-mail office@muzeulbanatuluimontan.ro; internet www.muzeulbanatuluimontan.ro; f. 1959; culture; research; museography; museology; archaeology; library of 27,000 vols; Dir Dr DUMITRU ŢEICU; publs *Arheologia Medievală, Banatica, Yearbook*.

Roman

Muzeul de Istorie Roman (Museum of Roman History): Str. Cuza Vodă 19, 611009 Roman; tel. (233) 72-77-26; fax (233) 72-77-26; f. 1957; Curator Dr VASILE URSACHI.

Satu Mare

Muzeul Judeţean Satu Mare (Satu Mare District Museum): Bdul Vasile Lucaciu 21, 440031 Satu Mare; tel. (261) 73-75-26; fax (261) 76-87-61; e-mail muzeusm@gmail.com; internet www.muzeusm.ro; f. 1891; history, ethnography, paintings by Aurel Popp; library of 60,000 vols; Man. VIOREL CIUBOTA; publs *Satu Mare, Studii şi Comunicări*.

Sf. Gheorghe

Székely Nemzeti Múzeum/Muzeul Naţional Secuiesc (National Szekler Museum): Kós Károly u. 10.sz, Kovászna megye/Str. Kós Károly 10, jud. Covasna, 520055 Sfântu Gheorghe; tel. (267) 31-24-42; fax (267) 31-24-43; e-mail office.sznm@gmail.com; internet www.sznm.ro; f. 1875; history, ethnography, archaeology, natural history, icons, classical and modern Hungarian art; library of 110,000 vols; Dir MIHÁLY VARGHA; Sec. TÜNDE TAMÁS; publs *Acta Margitensia* (1 a year), *Acta Siculica* (1 a year).

Sibiu

Complexul Naţional Muzeal 'ASTRA' (ASTRA National Museum Complex): Piaţa Mică 11, jud. Sibiu, 550182 Sibiu; tel. (269) 21-81-95; fax (269) 21-80-60; e-mail office@muzeulastra.ro; internet www.muzeulastra.ro; f. 1963; present name 2001; incl. Muzeul de Etnografie Universală 'Franz Binder'; Muzeul Civilizaţiei Populare Traditionale ASTRA; Muzeul Civilizaţiei Transilvane Astra; Muzeul de Etnografie şi Artă Populară

Săsească 'Emil Sigerus'; Proiectul unui Muzeu al Culturii şi Civilizaţiei Rromilor; library of 16,428 vols; Dir VALERIU ION OLARU; publ. *Cibinium* (Romanian museology and the history of traditional folk civilization, every 2 years).

Muzeul Naţional Brukenthal (Brukenthal National Museum): Piaţa Mare 4–5, Sibiu; tel. (269) 21-76-91; fax (269) 21-15-45; e-mail info@brukenthalmuseum.ro; internet www.brukenthalmuseum.ro; f. 1817; history, ethnography, 15th- to 18th-century European painting; library: see Libraries and Archives; Dir-Gen. SABIN ADRIAN LUCA; Scientific Dir GHEORGHE BAN; publs *Cibinium, Studii şi Communicări*.

Affiliated Museums:

Muzeul de Istorie a Farmaciei: Piaţa Mică 26, Sibiu; tel. (269) 21-81-91; f. 1972.

Muzeul de Istorie 'Casa Altemberger': Str. Mitropoliei 2, Sibiu; tel. (269) 21-81-43; e-mail dragos.diaconescu@brukenthalmuseum.ro; Dir Dr DRAGOŞ DIACONESCU.

Muzeul de Istorie Naturală din Sibiu (Sibiu Natural History Museum): Str. Cetăţii 1, 550160 Sibiu; tel. (369) 10-17-82; e-mail rodica.ciobanu@brukenthalmuseum.ro; f. 1849; library of 65,000 vols; Dir Dr RODICA CIOBANU; publ. *Studii şi Comunicări de Ştiinţe Naturale*.

Muzeul de Vânătoare 'August Von Spiess': Str. Şcoala de Înot 4, Sibiu; tel. (369) 10-17-84; f. 1966.

Sighetu Marmaţiei

Muzeul Maramureşului, Sighetul Marmaţiei (Sighetul Marmaţiei Maramures Museum): Str. Libertăţii 15, 435500 Sighetul Marmaţiei; tel. and fax (262) 31-15-21; e-mail muzeulmaramuresului@yahoo.com; internet www.muzeulmaramuresului.ro; f. 1873; history, ethnography, natural history, open-air museum, memorial houses (Elie Wiesel's memorial house, Dr Ioan Mihaly de Apşa's memorial house, etc., traditional houses preserved in situ); Dir Prof. GHEORGHE TODINCA; Curator BARZ MIRELA ANA; publ. *Acta Musei Maramorosiensis* (1 a year).

Sighişoara

Muzeul de Istorie Sighişoara (Sighişoara History Museum): Piaţa Muzeului 1, 545400 Sighişoara; tel. and fax (265) 77-11-08; e-mail info@muzeusighisoara.com; internet www.muzeusighisoara.com; f. 1899; weapon colln; Dir Dr NICOLAE TESCULA.

Slatina

Muzeul Judeţean Olt (Olt District Museum): Str. Ana Ipătescu 1, 230079 Slatina; tel. and fax (249) 41-52-79; e-mail muzeu_olt@yahoo.com; internet www.mjolt.ro; f. 1951; archaeology collns; Dir LAURENTIU GUTICA-FLORESCU.

Slobozia

Muzeul Judeţean Ialomiţa (Ialomiţa District Museum): Bdul Matei Basarab 30, 920055 Slobozia; tel. (243) 23-00-54; e-mail office@mjialomita.ro; internet www.cicnet.ro; history, ethnography, archaeology, and plastic art; painting, graphics, sculpture; Dir FLORIN VLAD.

Suceava

Muzeul Naţional al Bucovinei (Bucovina National Museum): Str. Ştefan cel Mare 33, 720003 Suceava; tel. (230) 71-64-39; f. 1900; folk art, history, natural history, astronomical observatory, planetarium, Romanian fine arts; library of 91,000 vols; Dir PAVEL BLAJ; publ. *Suceava—Anuarul Muzeului judeţean* (history and natural sciences sections).

Târgovişte

Complexul National Muzeal 'Curtea Domneasca' (The National Museum Complex 'The Royal Court'): Str. Justiţiei 7, 130014 Târgovişte, jud. Dambovita; tel. and fax (245) 61-28-77; e-mail contact@ muzee-dambovitene.ro; internet www .muzee-dambovitene.ro; f. 1940; archaeology, ethnography, fine arts, history of books and printing in Romania; Dir GH. BULEI; publ. *Vallachica*.

Târgu Jiu

Muzeul Judeţean Gorj (Gorj District Museum): c/o Muzeul de Istorie şi Arheologie, Str. Geneva 8, 210136 Târgu Jiu; tel. (253) 21-20-44; fax (253) 21-20-44; Dir Prof. VASILE MARINOIU.

Constituent Museums:

Muzeul Arhitecturii Populare din Gorj (Gorj Museum of Folk Architecture): open-air Curtişoara village, 215101 Bumbeşti-Jiu; f. 1968; Curator Prof. VASILE PETRE.

Muzeul de Artă (Art Museum): Parcul Central, 210132 Târgu Jiu; tel. (253) 21-85-50; f. 1982; Romanian contemporary art; sculptures by Brâncuşi; Curator CARMEN SILVIA ŞOCU.

Muzeul de Istorie şi Arheologie (History and Archaeology Museum): Str. Geneva 8, Jud. Gorj, 210136 Târgu Jiu; tel. (253) 21-20-44; f. 1894; library of 10,000 vols.

Târgu Mureş

Muzeul Judeţean Mureş (Mureş District Museum): Str. Horea 24, 540036 Târgu Mureş; tel. (265) 42-56-34; Dir VALER POP; publ. *Marisia* (1 a year).

Attached Museums:

Muzeul de Arheologie şi Istorie (Archaeology and History Museum): Str. George Enescu 2, 540052 Târgu Mureş; tel. (265) 43-25-12.

Muzeul de Artă (Art Museum): Str. George Enescu 2, 540052 Târgu Mureş; tel. (265) 43-21-79; f. 1913; art of the 19th and 20th centuries.

Timişoara

Muzeul Banatului Timişoara (Timiş Museum of the Banat): Piaţa Huniade nr. 1, în clădirea monument istoric, Castelul Huniazilor, 300002 Timişoara, Timiş; tel. (256) 49-13-39; fax (256) 20-13-21; e-mail muzeul.banatului@yahoo.com; internet www .muzeulbanatului.ro; f. 1872; archaeology, natural history, ethnography, art; Dir DAN LEOPOLD CIOBOTARU; publ. *Analele Banatului* (1 a year).

Vaslui

Muzeul Judeţean 'Ştefan cel Mare' Vaslui (Vaslui District 'Stephen the Great' Museum): Piaţa Independenţei 1, 730240 Vaslui; tel. (235) 31-16-26; e-mail museumvs@yahoo.com; f. 1975; ancient history and archaeology, ethnography and folk art, modern Romanian art; library of 5,000 vols; Dir IOAN MANCAŞ; publ. *Acta Moldaviae Meridionalis* (5–10 a year).

Zalău

Muzeul Judeţean de Istorie şi Artă Sălaj (Sălaj District Museum of History and Art): Str. Unirii 9, 450042 Zalău; tel. (260) 61-22-23; fax (260) 66-17-06; e-mail muzeu@zalau .astral.ro; f. 1951; library of 14,975 vols; Dir DUMITRU GHEORGHE TAMBA; publ. *Acta Musei Porolissensis* (1 a year).

Universities

UNIVERSITATEA '1 DECEMBRIE 1918' DIN ALBA IULIA
(1 December 1918 University, Alba Iulia)

Str. Gabriel Bethlen 5, 510009 Alba Iulia
Telephone: (258) 80-61-30
Fax: (258) 81-26-30
E-mail: cond@uab.ro
Internet: www.uab.ro

Founded 1991
State control
Languages of instruction: English, French, Romanian
Academic year: October to July

Rector: Prof. Dr Eng. VALER DANIEL BREAZ
Vice-Rector for Education and Institutional Strategy and Quality: Assoc. Prof. Dr LUCIA CABULEA
Vice-Rector for Financing, Human Resources and Investments: Prof. Dr NICOLAE TODEA
Vice-Rector for Scientific Research, Int. Relations, Financing and Investments: Prof. Dr. MOISE IOAN ACHIM
Deputy Gen. Man.: Eng. GAVRILA TRAXLER
Chief Accountant: TAMARA CONTOR
Sec.-in-Chief: CRISTINA HAVA
Library Dir: CORINA TATAR

Library of 111,859 vols, 17,000 periodicals
Number of teachers: 159
Number of students: 4,500

Publications: *Acta Universitatis Apulensis* (1 a year), *Pro Cont* (every 2 years), *RevCad* (1 a year), *Revista Annales Universitatis Apulensis*

DEANS

Faculty of History and Philology: Prof. Dr ILEANA VOICHITA GHEMES
Faculty of Law and Social Sciences: Assoc. Prof. Dr IOAN GANFALEAN
Faculty of Orthodox Theology: Prof. Dr EMIL JURCAN
Faculty of Sciences: Prof. Dr MARIA POPA

UNIVERSITATEA 'ALEXANDRU IOAN CUZA' IAŞI

Bdul Carol I 11, 700506 Iaşi
Telephone: (232) 20-10-00
Fax: (232) 20-11-21
E-mail: contact@uaic.ro
Internet: www.uaic.ro

Founded 1860
State control
Academic year: October to July

Rector: Prof. Dr VASILE IŞAN
Vice-Rector for Alumni and Graduate Affairs: Prof. Dr CARMEN CREŢU
Vice-Rector for Institutional Devt: Prof. Dr Rev. GHEORGHE POPA
Vice-Rector for Int. Relations: Prof. Dr HENRI LUCHIAN
Vice-Rector for MA and PhD Studies: Prof. Dr GHEORGHE IACOB
Vice-Rector for Research and Innovation: Prof. Dr GHEORGHE POPA
Vice-Rector for Undergraduate Studies: Prof. Dr CONSTANTIN SĂLĂVĂSTRU
Univ. Chancellor: Prof. Dr CĂTĂLIN TĂNASE
Univ. Chief Sec.: OANA CONSTANDACHE
Gen. Admin. Man.: BOGDAN-EDUARD PLEŞCAN
Int. Relations Officer: LIVIA VRĂNESCU
Dir of Central Univ. Library: Prof. Dr ALEXANDRU CĂLINESCU

Library: see Libraries and Archives
Number of teachers: 838
Number of students: 38,000

Publication: *Analele Universităţii*

DEANS

Faculty of Biology: Prof. Dr ION MOGLAN
Faculty of Chemistry: Prof. Dr DUMITRU GÂNJU
Faculty of Computer Science: Prof. Dr GHEORGHE GRIGORAŞ
Faculty of Economics: Prof. Dr DINU AIRINEI
Faculty of Geography and Geology: Prof. Dr OVIDIU GABRIEL IANCU
Faculty of History: Prof. Dr ALEXANDRU FLORIN PLATON
Faculty of Law: Prof. Dr TUDOREL TOADER
Faculty of Letters: Prof. Dr ŞTEFAN AVĂDANEI
Faculty of Mathematics: Prof. Dr OVIDIU CÂRJĂ
Faculty of Orthodox Theology: Rev. Prof. Dr VIOREL SAVA
Faculty of Philosophy: Prof. Dr NICU GAVRILUŢĂ
Faculty of Physical Education and Sport: Assoc. Prof. MARIN CHIRAZI
Faculty of Physics: Prof. Dr MIHAI TOMA
Faculty of Psychology and Education Sciences: Prof. Dr ION DAFINOIU
Faculty of Roman Catholic Theology: Rev. Assoc. Prof. EMIL DUMEA

PROFESSORS

Faculty of Biology (Bdul Carol I 20, A, 700505 Iaşi; tel. (232) 20-10-72; fax (232) 20-14-72; e-mail admbio@uaic.ro; internet www.bio .uaic.ro):

AILIESEI, O., Microbiology, Immunology
ARTENIE, V., Biochemistry
CHIFU, T., Environmental Protection and Nature Preservation, Environmental Biodiversity, Phylogenesis
COJOCARU, D., Enzymology, Biochemistry
ION, I., Vertebrate Zoology
MIRON, I., Aquaculture, Limnology
MISĂILĂ, C., Animal Physiology
MITITIUC, M., Phytopathology, Biogeography
MOGLAN, I., Invertebrate Zoology
MURARIU, A., Vegetal Physiology, Basis of Environment Protection
MUSTAŢĂ, GH., Evolutionary Biology
NEACŞU, I., Biophysics, Molecular Biology
ŞTEFAN, N., Vegetal Taxonomy, Phytosociology, Phytocenology
TĂNASE, C., Micology, Botany
TOMA, C., Plant Anatomy, Vegetal Cytology, Phylogenesis
TOMA, O., Structural Organization of Proteins and Nucleic Acids
ZAMFIRACHE, M. M., Vegetal Physiology

Faculty of Chemistry (Bdul Carol I 11, 700506 Iaşi; tel. (232) 20-13-63; fax (232) 20-13-13; e-mail infochem@uaic.ro; internet www.chem.uaic.ro):

BÎCU, E., Organic Chemistry
BOURCEANU, G., Physical Chemistry
CONSTANTINESCU, M., Physical Chemistry
DROCHIOIU, G., Biochemistry
DULMAN, V., Analytical Chemistry
IORDAN, A., Inorganic Chemistry
MANGALAGIU, I., Organic Chemistry
NEMŢOI, G., Electrochemistry
PALAMARU, M., Inorganic Chemistry
POPOVICI, E., Material Sciences
PUI, A., Inorganic Chemistry
VASILE, A., Chemical Technology

Faculty of Computer Science (Str. G. Berthelot 16, 700483 Iaşi; tel. (232) 20-10-90; fax (232) 20-14-90; e-mail secretariat@info.uaic .ro; internet www.infoiasi.ro):

CRISTEA, D., Artificial Intelligence, Natural Language Processing
CROITORU, C., Algorithms, Combinatorial Optimization
FELEA, V., Databases, Logic Programming
GRIGORAS, GH., Programming, Computer Construction
JUCAN, T., Formal Languages, Petri Nets
LUCANU, D., Formal Methods in Software Engineering, Semantic Web

LUCHIAN, H., Meta-heuristics
MASALAGIU, C., Logic in Computer Science
ȚIPLEA, F. L., Algebraic Foundations of Computer Science, Coding Theory and Cryptography, Computability, Decidability and Complexity, Security Protocols, Programme Analysis

Faculty of Economics (Bdul Carol I nr. 22, 700505 Iași; tel. (232) 20-10-70; fax (232) 21-70-00; e-mail feaa@uaic.ro; internet www.feaa.uaic.ro):

AIRINEI, D., Data Warehouses, Business Information Technologies, End-User Computing
ANDONE, I., Accounting Information Systems and Expert Systems in Accounting
ASANDULUI, L., Demography
BEDRULE-GRIGORUȚĂ, V., Public Services Management
BRĂILEAN, T., Economic Politics
BUCĂTARU, D., Business Finances
BUDUGAN, D., Managerial Accounting
CIOBANU, I., Management
COCRIȘ, V., Money and Credit, Risk Management in Banking
DUMITREAN, E., Financial Accounting
DUMITRIU, F., Information Systems Design
FĂTU, T., Business Information Technologies
FILIP, G., Public Finances
FILIP, M., Business Information Technologies, End-User Computing
FOTACHE, D., Groupware, Enterprise Resource Planning, Business Information Technologies
FOTACHE, M., Databases, Information and Knowledge Management
GEORGESCU, I., Fundamentals of Accounting, Managerial Accounting
GEORGESCU, M., Office Information Systems, Business Information Technologies
GRAMA, A., End-User Computing, Business Information Technologies
HOROMNEA, E., Fundamentals of Accounting
IGNAT, I., Macroeconomics
IȘAN, V., Economics
JABA, E., Statistics
JABA, O., Management
LUTAC, G., Political Economics
MAXIM, E., Management and Marketing
MEȘNIȚĂ, G., Project Management, Information Systems Analysis
MIHĂESCU, S., Finances, Finance and Banking Control
MIRONIUC, M., Financial and Accounting Management of the Company
MUNTEANU, A., Information Systems Audit
MUNTEANU, C., Marketing
NECHITA, V., Political Economy
NICA, P., Management
NIȚĂ, V., Merchandising, Hotel Management
ONOFREI, M., Financial Management, Decision in Public Administration
OPREA, D., Information Systems Design, Project Management
PASCARIU, G., European Economics
PEKAR, V., Agricultural Economics
PETRESCU, S., Economic Analysis, Evaluation Concepts and Theories in Business
PINTILESCU, C., Multivariate Statistics, Data Analysis
POHOAȚĂ, I., Economic Doctrines
PRALEA, S., International Economics
PRISACARIU, M., Capital Markets, Modern Management of the Portofolio
PRODAN, A., Human Resource Managements
PRUTIANU, S., Business Communication and Negotiations
SASU, C., Marketing
SCORȚESCU, GH., Public Accounting

STOICA, O., European Financial and Monetary Integration, European Financial Markets
STEFURA, G., Public Budgetary Process
TABĂRĂ, N., Fundamentals of Accounting, Compared Accounting Systems
ȚARCĂ, M., Economic Statistics
TOFAN, A., Management
ȚUGUI, A., End-User Computing, Expert Systems
VOINEA, G., International Foreign Exchange and Financial Relations, Local Finances
ZAIT, A., Direct Marketing, Public Relations
ZAIȚ, D., Intercultural Management

Faculty of Geography and Geology (Bdul Carol I nr. 20A, 700505 Iași; tel. (232) 20-10-74; fax (232) 20-14-74; e-mail geoiasi@uaic.ro; internet www.geo.uaic.ro):

APOSTOL, L., Human Geography
BRÂNZILĂ, M., Geology and Palaeontology
GROZA, O., Human Geography
IANCU, O. G., Geochemistry
IAȚU, C., Human Geography
IONIȚĂ, I., Geomorphology
LĂCĂTUȘU, R., Physical Geography
MUNTELE, I., Human Geography
ROMANESCU, GH., Physical Geography
RUSU, C., Physical Geography of Romania
RUSU, E., Human Geography

Faculty of History (tel. (232) 20-10-56; fax (232) 20-11-56; e-mail istorie@uaic.ro; internet www.history.uaic.ro):

BĂDĂRĂU, G., Modern History
BÎRLIBA, L., Ancient History
BOUNEGRU, O., Ancient History
CIUPERCĂ, I., Contemporary World History
CLIVETTI, G., Modern History
CRISTIAN, V., Modern World History
GOROVEI, S., Medieval History
IACOB, G., Contemporary History
LÁSZLÓ, A., Ancient History
PLATON, F., Medieval History
PUNGĂ, G., Medieval History
SOLCANU, I., Medieval History
SPINEI, V., Ancient History
SZEKELY, M., Medieval History
URSULESCU, N., Ancient History
ZAHARIUC, P., Medieval History
ZUGRAVU, N., Ancient History

Faculty of Law (Bdul Carol I nr. 11, 700506 Iași; tel. (232) 20-10-58; fax (232) 20-11-58; e-mail drept@uaic.ro; internet www.laws.uaic.ro):

CIUCĂ, V., Roman Law
DURAC, G., Civil Procedure
MACOVEI, I., International Trade Law
THEODORU, G., Criminal Procedure
TOADER, T., Criminal Law, Special Part

Faculty of Letters (Bdul Carol I nr. 11, 700506 Iași; tel. (232) 20-10-52; fax (232) 20-11-52; e-mail letters@uaic.ro; internet www.letters.uaic.ro):

ALBU, R., English Language
AVĂDANEI, ST., American Literature
BLUMENFELD, O., English Language and Literature
CĂLINESCU, A., French Literature
CĂRĂUȘU, M. L., Romanian Language
CERNĂUȚI GORODEȚCHI, M., Comparative Literature
CIUBOTARU, M., Romanian Language
COTORCEA, L., Russian Literature
CUȚITARU, L. C., English and American Literature
DIACONU, D., Spanish Literature
DIMITRIU, R., English Language
DOROBĂȚ, D., English Literature
GAFTON, A., Romanian Language
GOGÂLNICEANU, C. L., English Language
HOIȘIE, A., German Literature
JEANRENAUD, M., French Literature
LĂCĂTUȘU, T., English Language

MUNTEANU, E., Romanian Language
MUREȘANU, M., French Literature
PETRESCU, M., French Language
PIRVU, S., English Literature
POPESCU, I., French Literature
PORUCIUC, A., English Language
PRICOP, C., Romanian Literature
SECRIERU, M. L., Romanian Language

Faculty of Mathematics (Bd. Carol I nr. 11, 700506 Iași; tel. and fax (232) 20-10-60; e-mail admmath@uaic.ro; internet www.math.uaic.ro):

ANASTASIEI, M., Geometry
ANICULĂESEI, GH., Applied Mathematics
ANIȚA, S., Applied Mathematics
ARNĂUTU, V., Applied Mathematics
BARBU, V., Applied Mathematics
BRÂNZEI, D., Geometry
CÂRJĂ, O., Mathematical Analysis
CHIRIȚĂ, S., Applied Mathematics
FLORESCU, L., Mathematical Analysis
HÂVÂRNEANU, T. D., Applied Mathematics
IEȘAN, D., Applied Mathematics
ILIOI, C., Applied Mathematics
LEFTER, C. G., Applied Mathematics
MIRON, R., Applied Mathematics
OPROIU, V., Geometry
POP, I., Geometry
POPA, C. G., Applied Mathematics
POPA, E., Mathematical Analysis
PRECUPANU, A., Mathematical Analysis
PRECUPANU, T., Mathematical Analysis
RĂSCANU, A., Applied Mathematics
TOFAN, I., Algebra
TURINICI, M., Applied Mathematics
VRABIE, I., Applied Mathematics
ZĂLINESCU, C., Mathematical Analysis

Faculty of Orthodox Theology (Str. Closca 9, 700066 Iași; tel. (232) 25-84-30; e-mail contact@teo.uaic.ro; internet www.teologie.uaic.ro):

ACHIMESCU, N., History and Philosophy of Religions
PETRARU, GH., Missiology and Ecumenism
POPA, GH., Christian Morals and Orthodox Morals
SANDU, I., Branch Orthodox Theology, Cultural Inheritance
SAVA, V., Liturgical Theology and Practice
SEMEN, P., Study and Biblical Exegesis of the Old Testament
TEȘU, I. C., Orthodox Spirituality

Faculty of Philosophy (Bdul Carol I nr. 11, 700506 Iași; tel. (232) 20-10-54; fax (232) 20-11-54; e-mail alexandru.durnea@uaic.ro; internet philosophy.uaic.ro):

ADĂMUȚ, A., History of Philosophy
AFLOROAEI, ST., Ontology, Hermeneutics, Metaphysics
BACIU, M., Sociology
BALAHUR, D., Sociology
BEJAN, P., Hermeneutics
CARPINSCHI, A., Political Science
COZMA, C., Ethics
DIMA, T., Logic and Epistemology
DUMITRESCU, P., History of Philosophy
GAVRILUȚĂ, N., Sociology
GHIDEANU, T., History of Philosophy
IOAN, P., Logic
IONESCU, I., Sociology
MARIN, C., History of Philosophy
MIFTODE, V., Sociology, Social Anthropology
NISTOR, M., Aesthetics, History and Philosophy of Religions
POEDE, G., Political Sciences
RÂMBU, N., Philosophy of Culture and Hermeneutics
SĂLĂVĂSTRU, C., Logic and Semiology
STĂNCIULESCU, T. D., Semiotics and Philosophy of Creation
TEODORESCU, G., Sociology

Faculty of Physical Education and Sport (Str. Toma Cozma nr. 3, 700554 Iași; tel. (232) 20-

10-26; fax (232) 20-11-26; e-mail admefs@
uaic.ro; internet www.sport.uaic.ro):

BĂLTEANU, V., Massage
DROSESCU, P., Anatomy
IACOB, I., Sports Management

Faculty of Physics (tel. (232) 20-10-50; fax
(232) 20-11-50; e-mail admphys@uaic.ro;
internet www.physics.uaic.ro):

BIBOROSCH, L., Plasma Physics
CĂLŢUN, O. F., Electricity and Magnetism
CREANGĂ, D. E., Biophysics
DARIESCU, C., Quantum Mechanics
DARIESCU, M. A., Quantum Mechanics
DOROHOI, O. D., Optics and Spectroscopy
DUMITRAŞCU, N. V., Plasma Physics
GEORGESCU, V., Solid State Physics
IACOMI, F. D., Solid State Physics
IGNAT, E. M., Theoretical Physics
LOZNEANU, E., Plasma Physics
LUCA, D., Solid State Physics
LUCHIAN, T., Biophysics
MARDARE, D., Biophysics
MELNIG, V., Biophysics
MERCHEŞ, I., Theoretical Physics
MITOŞERIU, L., Electricity and Magnetism
POPA, G., Plasma Physics
RUSU, G., Solid State Physics
RUSU, M., Solid State Physics
SANDULOVICIU, M., Plasma Physics
SINGUREL, G., Spectroscopy and Quantum
Optics
STANCU, A., Electricity and Magnetism
STRAT, M., Optics and Spectroscopy
TOMA, M., Plasma Physics

Faculty of Psychology and Education (Str.
Toma Cozma 3, 700554 Iaşi; tel. (232) 20-10-
28; fax (232) 21-06-60; e-mail secretariat@
psih.uaic.ro; internet www.psychology.uaic
.ro):

ANTONESEI, L., Pedagogy
CONSTANTIN, A., Psychology
CONSTANTIN, T., Psychology
COZMA, T., General Education
CREŢU, C., Psycho-pedagogy of Excellence
and Creativity
CUCOŞ, C., Pedagogy
DAFINOIU, I., Medical Psychology
GHEORGHIU, M. D., Psychology
HAVARNEANU, E., Psychology
IACOB, L., Psychology
NECULAU, A., Social Psychology
ŞOITU, L., Pedagogy
TURLIUC, N., Medical Psychology and Spe-
cial Psycho-pedagogy

Faculty of Roman Catholic Theology (Bdul
Carol I 11, 700506 Iaşi; tel. (232) 20-11-15;
fax (232) 20-11-14; e-mail ftrc@uaic.ro;
internet www.ftrc.uaic.ro):

DUMEA, E., Church History

UNIVERSITATEA 'ANDREI ŞAGUNA' DIN CONSTANŢA
(Andrei Saguna University of Constanţa)

Bdul Alexandru Lapusneanu 13, 900196
Constanţa

Telephone and fax (241) 66-25-20
E-mail: contact@andreisaguna.ro
Internet: www.andreisaguna.ro
Founded 1992
Private Control

Rector: Prof. Dr AUREL PAPARI
Dir-Gen.: Dr ADRIAN PAPARI
Chancellor: Prof. Dr LEFTER CHIRICA

DEANS

Department of Shipping and Maritime and
Inland Waterway Transport: Prof. Dr
TĂNASE SUSANU
Faculty of Economics: Dr GEORGE PAPARI
Faculty of Law and Administrative Sciences:
Dr GABRIEL NAGHI

Faculty of Mass Communication and Polit-
ical Science: Dr IOAN DAMASCHIN
Faculty of Psychosociology: Dr LIVICA FRATI-
MAN

UNIVERSITATEA 'ATHENAEUM' DIN BUCUREŞTI
(Athenaeum University of Bucharest)

Str. Giuseppe Garibaldi 2A, Sector 2, Bucharest

Telephone: (21) 230-57-38
Fax: (21) 231-74-18
E-mail: secretariat@univath.ro
Internet: www.univath.ro
Founded 1990
Private control
Languages of instruction: English, Romanian
Academic year: October to June

Rector: Prof. Dr EMILIA VASILE

Library of 20,925
Number of teachers: 85
Number of students: 1,500

Publication: Internal Auditing & Risk Management

DEANS

Faculty of Economics: Dr ION NITU
Faculty of Public Administration: Dr ARON
LIVIU DEAC

UNIVERSITATEA 'AUREL VLAICU' DIN ARAD

Bdul Revoluţiei 7, POB 2/158, 310130 Arad

Telephone: (257) 28-30-10
Fax: (257) 28-00-70
E-mail: rectorat@uav.ro
Internet: www.uav.ro
State control
Academic year: October to July

Rector: Prof. Dr LIZICA MIHUT
Pres.: Prof. Dr ANTON ILICA
Vice-Rectors: Prof. Dr Ing. IOAN RADU, Prof.
Dr FLORENTINA MUNTEANU, Prof. Dr ALINA
ZAMFIR
Scientific Sec.: Dr Ing. GHEORGHE SIMA

Publications: Educatia Plus (2 a year),
Revista AGORA, Scientific and Technical
Bulletin

DEANS

Faculty of Design: Prof. Dr FLOREA LUCACI
Faculty of Educational Sciences, Psychology
and Social Sciences: Prof. Dr ANTHON ILICA
Faculty of Economic Sciences: Assoc. Prof. Dr
SPÎNU MARIAN-NICU
Faculty of Engineering: Dr Eng Prof. DOINA
MORTOIU
Faculty of Exact Sciences: Assoc. Prof. Dr
SORIN NĂDĂBAN
Faculty of Food Engineering, Tourism and
Environmental Protection: Prof. Dr Ing.
BUJOR PANCAN
Faculty of Humanities and Social Sciences:
Prof. Dr FLOREA LUCACI, Prof. Dr IONEL
FUNERIU
Faculty of Physical Education and Sport:
Assoc. Prof. DAN BANCIU
Faculty of Theology: Prof. Dr IOAN TULCAN

UNIVERSITATEA 'BABEŞ-BOLYAI' CLUJ-NAPOCA

Str. M. Kogălniceanu 1, 400084 Cluj-Napoca

Telephone: (264) 19-43-15
Fax: (264) 19-19-06
Internet: www.ubbcluj.ro
Founded 1919
Languages of instruction: German, Hungar-
ian, Romanian
Academic year: October to July (2 semesters)

Rector: Prof. Dr ANDREI MARGA

Vice-Rector for Devt: NICOLAE BOCŞAN
Vice-Rector for Economic Cooperation,
Financing and Admin.: Assoc. Prof. CRIS-
TINA CIUMAŞ
Vice-Rector for Human Resources and Staff
Securement; Alumni Cooperation: Prof.
POMPEI COCEAN
Vice-Rector for Int. Affirmation and
Cooperation: Prof. TOADER NICOARĂ
Sec.-Gen.: BATIZ ENIKŐ
Librarian: Prof. Dr DORU RADOSAV
Library: see Libraries and Archives
Number of teachers: 1,700
Number of students: 53,000

Publications: Botanical Contributions, Brain
and Cognition and Behaviour, Colloquia:
Journal of Central European History,
Judaic Library Collection, Papers of Transition, Studi Italo-Romeni, Studia Universitatis Babeş-Bolyai

DEANS

Department of Theatre and Television: LIVIU
MALITA
Faculty of Biology and Geology: V. CRISTEA
Faculty of Business: Assoc. Prof JOHN CHRIS-
TIAN CHIFU
Faculty of Chemistry and Chemical Engin-
eering: Assoc. Prof. MAJDIK CORNELIA
Faculty of Economics: D. RACOVIŢAN
Faculty of European Studies: Prof. Dr LADI-
SLAU GYÉMÁNT
Faculty of Geography: Prof. PETREA MAHO
Faculty of Greek Catholic Theology: A. GOŢIA
Faculty of History and Philosophy: Dr OVIDIU
GHITTA
Faculty of Law: Prof. Dr PAUL DOE
Faculty of Letters: I. POP
Faculty of Mathematics and Computer Sci-
ence: Prof. Dr LEON ŢÂMBULEA
Faculty of Orthodox Theology: Rev. JOHN
CHIRILA
Faculty of Physical Education and Sports: M.
ALEXEI
Faculty of Physics: Prof. Dr ONUC COZAR
Faculty of Political Science and Public
Administration: V. BOARI
Faculty of Protestant Theology: Z. GÁLFI
Faculty of Psychology and Education: Prof.
Dr CĂLIN FELEZEU
Faculty of Roman Catholic Theology: J.
MARTON
Faculty of Sociology and Social Work: DAN
CHIRIBUCĂ

PROFESSORS

Faculty of Biology and Geology:

BALINTONI, I. C., Geotectonics
BEDELEAN, I., Mineralogy
BUCUR, I., Palaeontology
COMAN, N., Genetics
CRISTEA, V., Botany
DRĂGAN BULARDA, M., Microbiology
MUREŞAN, I., Mineralogy
PÉTERFI, L. S., Botany
PETRESCU, I., Palaeobotany
POPESCU, O., Cell Biology
TARBA, C., Biophysics
TOMESCU, N., Zoology
TRIFU, M., Plant Physiology
TUDORANCEA, C., Ecology
VLAD, Ş. N., Petrology

Faculty of Business:

GIURGIU, A., Finance
VORZSÁK, M., Micro and Macroeconomics

Faculty of Chemistry and Chemical Engineering:

AGACHI, P. Ş., Chemical Engineering
BĂLDEA, I., Physical Chemistry
CORDOŞ, E., Analytical Chemistry
DIUDEA, M., Organic Chemistry
GROSU, I., Organic Chemistry
HOROVITZ, O., Physical Chemistry
MAGER, S., Organic Chemistry

POPESCU, C., Physical Chemistry
SILAGHI-DUMITRESCU, I., Inorganic Chemistry
SILBERG, I. A., Organic Chemistry
SILVESTRU, C., Inorganic Chemistry
VLASSA, M., Organic Chemistry

Faculty of Economics:

AVORNICULUI, C., Data Processing in Economics
AVRAM-NIȚCHI, R., Data Processing in Economics
BĂTRÎNCEA, I., Economic Analysis
BEJU, V., Finance
CĂINAP, I., Economic Analysis
CISTELECAN, L., Finance
DIȚU, G., Political Economy
DRĂGOESCU, A., Political Economy
DRĂGOESCU, E., Finance
DUMBRAVĂ, P., Accountancy
FLOREA, I., Statistics
FRĂȚILĂ, R., Manufacture and Marketing of Products
GHIȘOIU, N., Data Processing in Economics
GORON, S., Data Processing in Economics
ILIEȘ, L., Transport Management
IONESCU, T., Political Economy
LAZĂR, D., Marketing
LAZĂR, I., Agricultural Management
MIHUȚ, I., Management
NAGHI, M., Management
NISTOR, I., Finance
NISTOR, L. I., Macroeconomic Forecasting
NIȚCHI, I. Ș., Data Processing in Economics
OPREAN, D., Data Processing in Economics
OPREAN, I., Accountancy
OPREAN, V., Data Processing in Economics
PAINA, N., Marketing
PÂNTEA, P., Accountancy
PLĂIAS, I., Marketing
POP, S. I., Management
POPESCU, G., Political Economy
POSTELNICU, G., Political Economy
PURDEA, D., Management
RACOVIȚAN, D., Data Processing in Economics
ROȘCA, T., Finance
STĂNEANU, G., Finance
TEMEȘ, I., Accountancy
TULAI, C., Finance
VINCZE, M., Agricultural Economics
VORZSÁK, A., Marketing

Faculty of European Studies:

BÎRSAN, M., Management of European Institutions
GYEMANT, L., European Studies
MARGA, A., Philosophy
PĂUN, N., Management of European Institutions

Faculty of Geography:

CIANGĂ, N., Human Geography
COCEAN, P., Regional Geography
GÂRBACEA, V., Regional Geography
MAC, I., Physical Geography
POP, G., Human Geography
RABOCA, N., Economic Geography
SOROCOVSCHI, V. E., Hydrology
SURD, V., Rural Geography

Faculty of Greek Catholic Theology:

GOȚIA, A., Catechetical Theology
GUDEA, N., History of the Greek Catholic Church

Faculty of History and Philosophy:

BĂRBULESCU, M., Ancient History and Archaeology
BOCȘAN, N., Modern History
CIPĂIANU, G. A., Contemporary History
CODOBAN, A. T., Philosophy
CSUCSUJA, Ș., Contemporary History
EDROIU, N., Medieval History of Romania
GLODARIU, I., Ancient History
ILUȚ, P., Sociology
MAGYARI, A., Modern History
MUSCĂ, V., History of Philosophy

PAVEL, T., Modern History
PISO, I., Ancient History and Archaeology
POP, I. A., Medieval History
PUȘCAȘ, V., Contemporary History
ROTARIU, T., Sociology
TEODOR, P., Medieval History of Romania
ȚOCA, M., History of Art
VESE, V., Contemporary History

Faculty of Law:

COSTIN, M. N., Commercial Law
POP, L., Civil Law
URSA, V., Criminal Law
ZĂPÎRȚAN, L., Political Science

Faculty of Letters:

BACIU, I., French Language
BORCILĂ, M., General Linguistics
CĂPUȘAN, M., French Literature
CSEKE, E., Hungarian Literature and Society
DRAGOȘ, E., History of the Romanian Language
FANACHE, V., History of Romanian Literature
GRUIȚA, G., Contemporary Romanian Language
KOZMA, D., Hungarian Literature
MUTHU, M., Theory of Literature and Aesthetics
OLTEAN, Ș., History of the English Language
PAPAHAGI, M. D., Italian Literature
PÉNTEK, J., General Linguistics
PETRESCU, I., History of Romanian Literature
POP, I., History of Romanian Literature
POP, R., French Literature
ȘEULEAN, I., Folklore and Cultural Anthropology
STANCIU, V., English Literature
VARTIC, I., Comparative Literature and Theory of Drama
ZDRENGHEA, M., Contemporary English Literature

Faculty of Mathematics and Computer Science:

ANDRICA, D., Geometry
BLAGA, P., Numerical Analysis
BOIAN, F. M., Informatics
BOTH, N., Algebra
BRECKNER, W. W., Functional Analysis and Optimization
CĂLUGĂREANU, G., Algebra
COBZAȘ, Ș., Functional Analysis
COMAN, G., Numerical Analysis
DUCA, D., Mathematical Analysis
DUMITRESCU, D., Informatics
FRENȚIU, M., Informatics
KOLUMBÁN, I., Mathematical Analysis
MICULA, G., Differential Equations
MIHOC, I., Probability Theory
MOCANU, P., Mathematical Analysis
MOLDOVAN, G., Informatics
MUNTEAN, E., Informatics
MUREȘAN, A., Applied Mathematics
NÉMETH, A., Mathematical Analysis
PÂRV, B., Informatics
PETRILA, T., Fluid Mechanics
POP, M. I., Fluid Mechanics
POP, V., Astronomy
PURDEA, I., Algebra
RUS, A. I., Differential Equations
SĂLĂGEAN, G. Ș., Mathematical Analysis
SZILÁGYI, P., Differential Equations
TÂMBULEA, L., Informatics
TRIF, D., Differential Equations
URECHE, V., Astronomy
VASIU, A., Geometry

Faculty of Orthodox Theology:

ICĂ, I., Fundamental Theology
MORARU, A., History of the Orthodox Church

Faculty of Physical Education and Sports:

BENGEANU, C., Volleyball

BRĂTUCU, L. S., Anatomy and Physiology
MAROLICARU, M., Methodology of Scientific Research
NETA, G., Football

Faculty of Physics:

ARDELEAN, I., Materials Science
BARBUR, I., Solid State Physics
BURZO, E., Solid State Physics
COLDEA, M., Solid State Physics
COSMA, C., Physics of Radiation
COZAR, O., Atomic and Molecular Physics
CRIȘAN, M., Theoretical Physics
CRIȘAN, V., Solid State Physics
CRISTEA, G., Solid State Physics
ILIESCU, T., Optics and Spectroscopy
ILONCA, G., Solid State Physics
POP, I., Solid State Physics
ȘIMON, S., Solid State Physics
TATARU, E., Electronics
ZNAMIROVSCHI, V., Atomic and Nuclear Physics

Faculty of Political Science and Public Administration:

BOARI, V., Political Ideology
STEGĂROIU, D. C., Management of Human Resources

Faculty of Psychology and Education:

GOIA, V., Methodology
IONESCU, M., Education
LĂSCUȘ, V., Education
MICLEA, M., Psychology
PITARIU, H., Psychology
PREDA, V., Psychology for Teaching

Faculty of Roman Catholic Theology:

MARTON, J., Ecclesiastical History

UNIVERSITATEA BIOTERRA DIN BUCURESTI
(Bioterra University of Bucharest)

Str. Garlei 81, Sector 1, Bucharest
Telephone: (21) 269-34-47
Fax: (21) 269-34-38
E-mail: nicolaebio@yahoo.com
Internet: www.bioterra.ro

Founded 1994
Private control

Rector: Prof. Dr FLOAREA NICOLAE
Rector for Scientific Activity and International Relations: Prof. Dr STAN PETRESCU
Rector for Teaching: Prof. Dr ION CHIPAILA
Scientific Sec.: Dr DANIELA MIHAILA

Library of 20,547 vols, 3,196 titles

DEANS

Faculty of Agrotourism: Prof. Dr Ing. MIHAI MARES
Faculty of Food Engineering: Prof. Dr Ing. ATUDOSIEI NICOLE

UNIVERSITATEA 'BOGDAN-VODĂ' DIN CLUJ-NAPOCA
(Bogdan-Vodă University of Cluj-Napoca)

Str.Grigore Alexandrescu 26A, Cluj-Napoca
Telephone: (264) 59-87-87
Fax: (264) 59-18-30
E-mail: ubv@ubv.ro
Internet: www.ubv.ro

Founded 1992
Private control

Pres.: Prof. JARADAT MOHAMMAD
Rector: Prof. PURDEA DUMITRU
Vice-Rector: RACOVITAN DAN

DEANS

Faculty of Economics: Prof. Dr PAȘÔCA NICOLAE
Faculty of Law: Dr MOCUȚA GHEORGHE
Faculty of Physical Education and Sports: Prof. NEȚA GHEORGHE

UNIVERSITATEA 'CONSTANTIN BRANCOVEANU' DIN PITEŞTI
(Constantin Brancoveanu University of Piteşti)

Calea Bascovului 2A, Piteşti
Telephone: (248) 21-26-27
Fax: (248) 21-64-27
E-mail: pitesti@univcb.ro
Internet: www.univcb.ro

Founded 1991
Private control

Rector: Prof. Dr ALEXANDRU PUIU
Pro-Rector for Economic Activity: Prof. Dr OVIDIU PUIU
Pro-Rector for Didactic Activity: Prof. Dr MARIUS GUST
Pro-Rector for Scientific Activity: Prof. Dr ION SCURTU
Scientific Sec.: Dr MIHAELA DUTU

Publication: *Strategii manageriale* (magazine)

DEANS

Department of Administrative and Communication Sciences, Brăila: Dr DORIAN RAIS
Department of Finance and Accounting, Piteşti: Prof. Dr SILVIA DUGAN
Faculty of Legal, Administrative and Communication sciences, Piteşti: Dr MIHAELA ASANDEI
Faculty of Management Marketing in Business Economics, Brăila: Dr ELENA ENACHE
Faculty of Management Marketing in Business Economics, Piteşti: Prof. Dr RADU GABRIEL PARVU
Faculty of Management Marketing in Business Economics, Râmnicu Vâlcea: Prof. Dr IULIANA CIOCHINA

UNIVERSITATEA 'CONSTANTIN BRANCUSI' DIN TÂRGU JIU

Bdul Republicii 1, Târgu Jiu
Telephone: (253) 21-43-07
Fax: (253) 21-57-94
E-mail: univ@utgjiu.ro
Internet: www.utgjiu.ro
State control
Language of instruction: English
Academic year: October to June

Rector: Prof. Dr ADRIAN GORUN
Pro-Rector: Prof. Dr Ing STEFAN GHIMISI
Pro-Rector: Prof. Dr MIHAI CRUCERU
Pro-Rector: Dr LIVIU NEAMTU

Library of 120,000 vols
Number of teachers: 154
Number of students: 6,000

Publications: *Analele UCB, Revista de matematică, Revista de mecanică.*

UNIVERSITATEA CRESTINA 'DIMITRIE CANTEMIR'
('Dimitrie Cantemir' Christian University)

Splaiul Unirii 176, Sector 4, Bucharest
Telephone: (21) 330-79-00
Fax: (21) 330-87-74
E-mail: office@ucdc.ro
Internet: www.ucdc.ro
Founded 2002
Private control

Pres.: Prof. Dr MOMCILO LUBURICI
Rector: Prof. Dr CORINA DUMITRESCU ADRIANA
Pro-Rector: Prof. Dr CRISTIANA CRISTUREANU
Pro-Rector: Prof. Dr VELCEA ION
Scientific Sec.: Prof. Dr BIJI ELENA
Number of students: 20,000

DEANS

Faculty of Foreign Languages and Literatures: Assoc. Prof. GABRIELA LUPCHIAN

Faculty of International Business and Economics: Prof. Dr VIRGIL ADASCĂLIŢEI
Faculty of Juridical and Administrative Sciences: Assoc. Prof. PETRICA TRUSCA
Faculty of Tourism and Commercial Management: Prof. Dr CAPRARESCU GHEORGHITA

UNIVERSITATEA DANUBIUS DIN GALAŢI
(Danubius University of Galaţi)

Bdul Galaţi 3, 800654 Galaţi
Telephone: (372) 36-12-07
Fax: (372) 36-12-92
E-mail: rectorat@univ-danubius.ro
Internet: www.univ-danubius.ro
Founded 1992
Private control

Rector: Prof. Dr BENONE PUSCA
Pro-Rector for Scientific Research: Prof. Dr VIOREL ARITON
Pro-Rector for Teaching: Dr ANDY CORNELIU PUSCA
Dir-Gen.: Prof. Dr DRAGOMIR GEORGETA
Scientific Sec.: Prof. Dr DOINITA ARITON

Library of 30,000 vols, 2,000 periodicals

DEANS

Faculty of Communication Sciences: DUMITRU TIUTIUCA
Faculty of Economic Sciences: Dr RODICA PRIPOAIE
Faculty of Law: Prof. Dr VASILICA NEGRUŢ
Faculty of International Relations and European Studies: Dr ANIŞOARA POPA

UNIVERSITATEA DE ARTĂ ŞI DESIGN DIN CLUJ-NAPOCĂ

Pta. Unirii 31, 400098 Cluj-Napoca
Telephone and fax (264) 59-81-90
E-mail: secretarsef@uad.ro
Internet: www.uartdcluj.ro
Founded 1925

Pres.: Prof. Dr IOAN SBÂRCIU
Rector: Prof. Dr RADU SOLOVASTRU
Gen Sec.: ANAMARIA BOCEAN

DEANS

Faculty of Applied Arts and Design: Dr ALEXANDRU ALAMOREANU
Faculty of Fine Arts: Dr RADU SOLOVASTRU

DIRECTORS

Dept for Teacher Training: Prof. MARIOARA PETCU
Fine and Decorative Arts Colleges: Dr DOREL MOISE

UNIVERSITATEA DE ARTĂ TEATRALĂ ŞI CINEMATOGRAFICĂ 'I. L. CARAGIALE'
(I. L. Caragiale University of Drama and Cinematography)

Str. Matei Voievod 75–77, 021452 Bucharest
Telephone: (21) 252-74-57
Fax: (21) 252-58-81
E-mail: rector1@unatc.ro
Internet: www.unatc.ro
Founded 1950

Rector: Prof. Dr GELU COLCEAG
Scientific Sec.: Prof. Dr DAN VASILIU
Library of 95,000 vols (incl. English theatre library of 5,000 vols)
Number of teachers: 190
Number of students: 680

UNIVERSIŢATEA DE ARTĂ TEATRALĂ TÂRGU MUREŞ
(University of Dramatic Art of Târgu Mureş)

Str. Köteles Sámuel nr. 6, 540057 Târgu Mureş
Telephone and fax (265) 26-62-81
E-mail: uat@uat.ro
Internet: www.uat.ro
Founded 1954 as Institutul de Teatru 'Szentgyörgyi István'

Rector: Dr GÁSPÁRIK ATTILA
Chancellor: Dr OANA LEAHU
Chief Sec.: ALÍZ BORDI
Library of 40,000 vols
Number of teachers: 81
Number of students: 130
Faculties of arts, music, theatre.

UNIVERSITATEA DE ARTE 'GEORGE ENESCU'

Str. Horia 7–9, 700126 Iaşi
Telephone: (232) 21-25-49
Fax: (232) 21-25-51
E-mail: enescu@arteiasi.ro
Internet: www.arteiasi.ro
Founded 1860, renamed 1960
Academic year: October to May

Rector: Prof. Dr VIOREL MUNTEANU
Vice-Rector for Scientific Activities: Assoc. Prof. Dr FLORIN GRIGORAS
Vice-Rector for Teaching Activities: Assoc. Prof. Dr DORU ALBU
Chancellor: Assoc. Prof. Dr ANCO CIOBOTARU
Sec.: Eng. TANIA SCAFARU
Librarian: IOAN BĂDULEŢ
Library of 190,000 vols, incl. books and periodicals; 7,000 records, 1,500 audio cassettes
Number of teachers: 134
Number of students: 1,279

Publication: *Byzantion* (Byzantine studies)

DEANS

Faculty of Composition, Musicology and Musical and Theatrical Education: Dr LAURA OTILIA VASILIU
Faculty of Fine and Decorative Arts and Design: Prof. Dr ATENA ELENA SIMIONESCU
Faculty of Musical Interpretation: Dr TATIANA LAURA POCINOC

UNIVERSITATEA DE NORD, BAIA MARE
(North University of Baia Mare)

Str. Victor Babes 62A, 430083 Baia Mare, Maramureş
Telephone: (262) 21-89-22
Fax: (262) 27-61-53
E-mail: dan.calin.peter@ubm.ro
Internet: www.ubm.ro
Founded 1961, as Institute of Higher Education; univ. status 1990
State control
Academic year: October to June

Rector: Prof. Dr Ing DAN CALIN PETER
Vice-Rector: Prof. Dr VASILE VIMAN
Vice-Rector: GEORGETA CORNITA
Scientific Sec.: Prof. Dr Ing GHEORGHE DAMIAN
Chief Librarian: LAURA VARGA
Library of 2,000,000 vols
Number of teachers: 198
Number of students: 5,520

Publications: *Physics Journal, Proceedings of the Mathematical Creativity Seminar, Scientific Bulletin of Chemistry and Biology, Scientific Bulletin of Economics, Scientific Bulletin of Electrotechnology, Electronics, Automation, Scientific Bulletin of Foreign*

Languages, Scientific Bulletin of Mathematics and Informatics, Scientific Bulletin of Pedagogy, Psychology and Methodology, Scientific Bulletin of Philology, Scientific Bulletin of Philosophy and Theology, Scientific Bulletin of Tribology and Machine Construction Technology, The Maramureş Orthodoxy

DEANS

Faculty of Engineering: Prof. Dr RADU COTETIU
Faculty of Letters: Prof. Dr PETRU DUNCA
Faculty of Mineral Resources and Environment: Prof. Dr VASILE OROS
Faculty of Sciences: Assoc. Prof. Dr NICOLAE POP

PROFESSORS

Faculty of Engineering (Str. Dr V. Babeş 62A, 430083 Baia Mare; tel. (362) 40-12-65; fax (262) 27-61-53):

COTETIU, A.
COTETIU, R.
FILIP, D.
LOBONTIU, M.
NASUI, V.
OPREA, C.
PETER, D. C.
PEREAN, L.
TIPLEA, V.
TISAN, V.
TOADER, C.
UNGUREANU, N.

Faculty of Letters (Str. Victoriei 76, 430122 Baia Mare; tel. (262) 27-63-05; fax (262) 27-54-36):

CORNITA, C.
CORNITA, G.
DUNCA, P.
GLODEANU, G.
ISTRATE, A.
MUNTEANU, C.

Faculty of Mineral Resources and Environment (Str. Dr V. Babeş 62A, 430083 Baia Mare; tel. (362) 40-12-66; fax (262) 27-61-53):

BANCILA-AFRIM, N.
BUD, I.
DAMIAN, F.
OROS, V.

Faculty of Sciences (Str. Victoriei 76, 430122 Baia Mare; tel. (262) 27-60-59; fax (262) 27-53-68):

ARDELEAN, G.
BERINDE, V.
HUTIRA, T.
MICU, C.
MIHALY-COZMUTH, A.
MODORAN, D.
MORAR, G.
POP, I.
VIMAN, V.

UNIVERSITATEA DE VEST DIN TIMIŞOARA
(West University of Timişoara)

Bdul V. Pârvan 4, 300223 Timişoara, Timiş
Telephone: (256) 59-21-11
Fax: (256) 59-23-10
E-mail: secretariat@rectorat.uvt.ro
Internet: www.uvt.ro

Founded 1944
State control
Academic year: October to June

Rector: Prof. Dr IOAN TALPOS
Vice-Rector for International Relations: Prof. Dr FLORIN FOLTEAN
Vice-Rector for Administrative Affairs: Prof. Dr PETRU STEFEA
Vice-Rector for Research Affairs: Prof. Dr VASILE OSTAFE

Vice-Rector for Student Affairs: Prof. DOREL JULEAN
Chief Sec.: MIHAELA RĂDUŢĂ
Chancellor and Scientific Sec.: Prof. Dr DAN MOGA
Librarian: Prof. VASILE ŢARA
Number of teachers: 719
Number of students: 18,603
Publications: *Analele Universităţii de Vest din Timişoara, Seria Fizica, Analele Universităţii de Vest din Timişoara, Seria Drept, Analele Universităţii de Vest din Timişoara, Seria Geografie, Analele Universităţii de Vest din Timişoara, Seria Teologie, Analele Universităţii de Vest din Timişoara-Seria Sociologie, Psihologie, Pedagogie şi Asistenta Sociala, Analele Universităţii de Vest din Timişoara, Seria Matematica–Informatica, Analele Universităţii de Vest din Timişoara, Seria Stiinte Filologice, Annals of West University Of Timişoara (Series of Chemistry), B. A. S. British and American Studies, BHAUT (Bibliotheca Historica et Archaeologica Universitatis Timisiensis), Caiet de Semiotica, Copiii de azi sunt parintii de mâine, Dialogues Francophones, Geographica Timisiensis, Gender Studies, Journal of Social Informatics—Revista de informatică socială, Paradigme, Probleme de Filologie Slavă, Revart (Specialized Review of Theory and Critique of Art), Review of Historical Geography and Toponomastics, Revista de Ştiinţe ale Educatie, Romanian Journal of Applied Psychology, Romanian Journal of English Studies, Studii de Istorie a Banatului, Studii de Literatură Romana şi Comparată, Studii de Slavistică, Temeswarer Beiträge zur Germanistik, Timişoara Physical Education and Rehabilitation Journal, Translationes*

DEANS

Faculty of Arts and Design: Assoc. Prof. ADRIANA LUCACIU
Faculty of Chemistry, Biology and Geography: Assoc. Prof. Dr GHEORGHE IANOŞ
Faculty of Economics and Business Administration: Prof. Dr MARILEN PIRTEA
Faculty of Law and Administrative Sciences: Prof. Dr RADU I. MOTICA
Faculty of Letters, History and Theology: Prof. Dr OTILIA HEDESAN
Faculty of Mathematics and Informatics: Prof. Dr VIOREL NEGRU
Faculty of Music: Prof. Dr WALTER KINDL
Faculty of Physical Education and Sports: Prof. DORU CIOSICI
Faculty of Physics: Prof. Dr VULCANOV DUMITRU
Faculty of Political Sciences, Philosophy and Communication Sciences: GEORGE CLITAN
Faculty of Sociology and Psychology: Prof. Dr ANCA MUNTEANU

PROFESSORS

Faculty of Arts and Design (Str. Oituz 4, 300086, Timişoara; tel. and fax (256) 59-26-51; e-mail arte@arte.uvt.ro; internet www.arte.uvt.ro):

FÂNTĂNARIU, S., Graphic Arts
FLONDOR, C., Painting
JECZA, P., Sculpture
NUŢIU, R., Painting
SULEA, I., Painting
ZIMAN, M., Textile Arts

Faculty of Chemistry, Biology and Geography (Str. I. Pestalozzi 16, 300115 Timişoara; tel. (256) 59-26-22; fax (256) 59-26-20; e-mail cbg@cbg.uvt.ro; internet www.cbg.uvt.ro):

CHIRIAC, A., Physical Chemistry
DOCA, N., Chemical Engineering
MRACEC, M., Physical Chemistry

NUŢIU, R., Organic Chemistry
TRUŢI, S., Geography

Faculty of Economics and Business Administration (Bdul Pestalozzi 16, 300115 Timişoara; tel. (256) 59-25-05; fax (256) 59-25-00; e-mail secretariat@feaa.uvt.ro; internet www.feaa.uvt.ro):

BĂBĂIŢĂ, I., Political Economy
BĂBĂIŢĂ, V., Accounting
BĂILEŞTEANU, GH., Business Economics
BURTICĂ, M., Macroeconomic Forecasting
CĂTINIANU, FL., Prices and Tariffs
CERNA, S., Currency and Credits
CRĂCIUNESCU, V., Management
CRISTEA, H., Business Finance
DĂNĂIAŢĂ, I., Management
EPURAN, M., Accounting
FALNIŢĂ, E., Science of Commodities
GOIAN, M., Management
IONESCU, GH., Marketing
IVAN, ŞT., Informatics
LĂDAR, L., Marketing
LUPULESCU, M., Computer Programming
MARTIN, I., Microeconomic Analysis
MIHAI, I., Financial Analysis
NEGRUT, C., Agrarian Economics and Policy
OPRIŞ, L., Agrarian Policies in the World
POPOVICI, AL., Programming of Production
PUTZ, E., Transport in Tourism
ROTARIU, I., Management of Foreign Trade
SILAŞI, GR., Regional and World Economy
SOŞDEANU, A., Accounting
TALPOŞ, I., Public Finance
TRANDAFIR, N., Political Economy
VÂRLAN, GH., Economic Forecasting

Faculty of Law and Administrative Sciences (Bdul Eroilor 9A, 300575 Timişoara; tel. (256) 592400; fax (256) 592442; e-mail drept@drept.uvt.ro; internet www.drept.uvt.ro):

DRESSLER, M., Forensic Medicine
MIHAI, GH., Philosophy of Law
MOTICA, R. I., Law
POPA, V., Roman Law, Labour Law

Faculty of Letters, History and Theology (Bdul V. Pârvan 4, 300223 Timişoara, Timiş; tel. and fax (256) 59-21-64; e-mail litere@litere.uvt.ro; internet www.litere.uvt.ro):

BENEA, D., Ancient History
BIRIŞ, I., History of Culture and Civilization
BUCA, M., Russian Language
CHEIE, I., Romanian Literature
CIOCÂRLIE, L., French Literature
EVSEEV, I., Russian Language
FRĂŢILĂ, V., Dialectology
GRECU, C., Philosophy of Logic
GYURCSIK, M., French Literature
HARANGUŞ, C., Ontology
MIOC, S., Romanian Literature
MUNTEANU, I., Modern Romanian History
OANCEA, I., Romance Philology
PÂRLOG, H., English Linguistics
SÂRBU, R., Russian Language
ŢARA, V., History of the Romanian Language

Faculty of Mathematics and Informatics (Bdul V. Pârvan 4, 300223 Timişoara, Timiş; tel. and fax (256) 59-23-16; e-mail secretariat@info.uvt.ro; internet www.math.uvt.ro):

ALBU, A., Differential Geometry
BALINT, Ş., Mathematical Equations
BOROŞ, E., Algebra
CONSTANTIN, GH., Probability Theory
CRAIOVEANU, M., Spectral Geometry
GAŞPAR, D., Functional Analysis, Spectral Theory
IVAN, GH., Algebra
MĂRUŞTER, Ş., Non-Linear Optimization and Computer Science
MEGAN, M., Mathematical Analysis

OBĂDEANU, V., Theoretical Mechanics and Differential Geometry, Operational Research
OPRIȘ, D., Operational Research
PAPUC, D. I., Differential Geometry
PREDA, P., Mathematical Analysis
PUTA, M., Differential Equations in Geometry
RADU, V., Stochastic Analysis and Probability Theory
REGHIȘ, M., Differential Equations
SCHWAB, E., Homological Algebra
STRĂTILĂ, Ș., Mathematical Analysis and Operator Algebras
SUCIU, N., Complex Analysis

Faculty of Music (Bdul V. Piața Libertatii 1, 300077 Timișoara, Timiș; tel. and fax (256) 59-26-54; e-mail muzica@muzica.uvt.ro; internet www.muzica.uvt.ro):

STANCOVICI, F., Piano
VULPE, D., Choral Conducting

Faculty of Physical Education and Sports (Bdul V. Pârvan 4, 300223 Timișoara, Timiș; tel. and fax (256) 59-22-07; e-mail secr_sport@sport.uvt.ro; internet www.sport .uvt.ro):

GÖNCZI-RAICU, M., Gymnastics
IONESCU, I., Football

Faculty of Physics (Bdul V. Pârvan 4, 300223 Timișoara, Timiș; tel. and fax (256) 59-21-08; e-mail secretary@physics.uvt.ro; internet www.physics.uvt.ro):

AVRAM, N., Atomic and Molecular Physics and Spectroscopy
BIRĂU, O., Thermodynamics and Molecular Physics
HRIANCA, I., Electricity and Magnetism
MUSCUTARIU, I., Electricity and Magnetism, Solid State and Semiconductor Physics
NICOARĂ, I., Laser Crystals
SCHLETT, Z., Plasma Physics, Semiconductor Materials and Devices

Faculty of Political Sciences, Philosophy and Communication Sciences (Bdul V. Pârvan 4, 300223 Timișoara, Timiș; tel. (256) 59-21-32; fax (256) 59-23-07; e-mail secr_polsci@polsci .uvt .ro; internet www.polsci.uvt.ro):

COLTESCU, G., Political Sciences

Faculty of Sociology and Psychology (Bdul V. Pârvan 4, 300223 Timișoara, Timiș; tel. and fax (256) 59-23-20; e-mail steb@socio.uvt.ro; internet www.socio.uvt.ro):

DABU, R., Sociology
POENARU, R., Pedagogy, Deontology
VINTILESCU, D., Educational Theory

UNIVERSITATEA DE VEST 'VASILE GOLDIȘ' DIN ARAD
(Vasile Goldis Western University of Arad)

Bdul Revolutiei 94, Arad
Telephone: (257) 28-03-35
E-mail: rectorat@uvvg.ro
Internet: www.uvvg.ro
Founded 1990
Private control
Rector: Prof. Dr AUREL ARDELEAN
Pro-Rectors: Prof. Dr MARTIAN IOVAN, Prof. Dr DELIA PODEA, Prof. Dr GAVRIL ARDELEAN, Prof. Dr CALIN POP, Prof. Dr CORNEL SOMESAN
Library: 1m. vols

DEANS

Faculty of Economics: Prof. Dr FLORIN DUMESCU
Faculty of Informatics: Assoc. Prof. ANTOANELA NAAJI
Faculty of Legal Sciences: Prof. Dr IOAN TRIFA

Faculty of Medicine, Pharmacy and Dentistry: Prof. Dr LIANA MOȘ
Faculty of Natural Sciences: Prof. DORINA CACHIĂȚ

UNIVERSITATEA 'DIMITRIE CANTEMIR' DIN TÂRGU MUREȘ
(Dimitrie Cantemir University of Târgu Mureș)

Str. Bodoni Sandor 3–5, Târgu Mureș
Telephone: (365) 40-11-27
Fax: (365) 40-11-25
E-mail: universitate@cantemir.ro
Internet: www.cantemir.ro
Founded 1991
Private control

Number of teachers: 130

Faculties of law, economic sciences, psychology and educational sciences and geography.

UNIVERSITATEA DIN BUCUREȘTI

Bdul Mihail Kogălniceanu 34–46, sector 5, 050107 Bucharest
Telephone: (21) 307-73-00
Fax: (21) 313-17-60
E-mail: secretariat@unibuc.ro
Internet: www.unibuc.ro
Founded 1864
State control
Academic year: October to July
Rector: Prof. JOHN PANZARU
Dir: MARIA PRUNĂ
Pro-Rectors: Prof. Dr CONSTANTIN BUȘE, Prof. Dr DANA MARINESCU, Prof. Dr IOAN MIHĂILESCU, Prof. Dr ION MUNTEANU
Librarian: Prof. Dr MIRCEA REGNEALĂ
Library: see Libraries and Archives
Number of teachers: 1,490
Number of students: 24,650
Publications: Analele Universității din București (Chemistry, Law, Geology, Geography, History, Romanian Language and Literature, Physics, 1 a year), Euroatlantic Studies (in English, 2 a year), Geography Communications (in French and English, 1 a year), Revue Roumaine d'Egyptologie, Science and Technology of Environmental Protection

DEANS

Dept of Open and Distance Education: Dr BOGDAN LOGOFĂTU
Faculty of Baptist Theology: Prof. Dr OTNIEL IOAN BUNACIU
Faculty of Biology: Prof. Dr TATIANA VASSU DIMOV
Faculty of Chemistry: Prof. Dr DIMITRU OANCEA
Faculty of Foreign Languages and Literature: Prof. Dr ALEXANDRA CORNILESCU
Faculty of Geography: Prof. Dr MIHAI IELENICZ
Faculty of Geology and Geophysics: Prof. Dr Eng VICTOR MOCANU
Faculty of History: Prof. Dr ALEXANDRU BARNEA
Faculty of Journalism and Communication Sciences: Prof. Dr MIHAI COMAN
Faculty of Law: Prof. Dr VIOREL MIHAI CIOBANU
Faculty of Letters: Prof. Dr DAN HORIA MAZILU
Faculty of Mathematics and Computer Science: Prof. Dr VICTOR TIGOIU
Faculty of Orthodox Theology: Prof. Dr NICOLAE NECULA
Faculty of Philosophy: Assist Dr VASILE ROMULUS
Faculty of Physics: Prof. Dr STEFAN ANTOHE
Faculty of Political Science: Prof. Dr CRISTIAN PREDA

Faculty of Psychology and Education: Prof. Dr DAN POTOLEA
Faculty of Public Admin.: Dr MAGDALENA PLATIS
Faculty of Roman Catholic Theology and Social Work: Prof. Dr ISIDOR MARTINCA
Faculty of Sociology and Social Work: Prof. Dr CATALIN BASARAB ZAMFIR

PROFESSORS

Faculty of Baptist Theology (Str. Berzei 29, Bucharest; tel. and fax (21) 224-88-49; e-mail bbts@fx.ro; internet www.unibuc.ro/en/fac_ftb_en):

BUNACIU, I., New Testament
TALPOȘ, V., Old Testament

Faculty of Biology (Splaiul Independenței 91–95, Sector 5, 76201 Bucharest; tel. (21) 411-52-07; fax (21) 411-23-10; e-mail web@bio.bio.unibuc.ro; internet www.bio.unibuc .ro):

BOTNARIUC, N., Ecology
COSTACHE, M., Biochemistry
CRISTUREAN, I., Botany
DINISCHIOTY, A., Biochemistry
FLONTA, M. L., Animal Physiology and Biophysics
GAVRILĂ, L., Plant Genetics
GEORGESCU, D., Anatomy
IGA, D. P., Anatomy
IORDĂCHESCU, D., Biochemistry
LAZĂR, V., Microbiology
MAILAT, I. E., Anatomy
MANOLACHE, V., Animal Biology
MARIN, A., Botany
MEȘTER, L. E., Animal Biology
MIHĂESCU, G., Microbiology
MIȘCALENCU, D., Anatomy
NĂSTĂSESCU, M., Animal Biology
SÂRBU, A., Botany
SESAN, T., Botany
STOIAN, V., Genetics
TEODORESCU, I., Ecology
TESIO, C., Animal Biology
TOMA, N., Botany
VĂDINEANU, A., Ecology
VASSU, T., Genetics
VOICA, C., Plant Physiology
ZĂRNESCU, O., Histology

Faculty of Chemistry (Bdul Regina Elisabeta 4–12, Sector 1, Bucharest; tel. and fax (21) 315-92-49; e-mail chimie_secretariat@yahoo .com; internet www.chimie.unibuc.ro):

ANDRUH, M., Inorganic Chemistry
ANGELESCU, E., Chemical Technology and Catalysis
BACIU, I., Organic Chemistry
BĂIULESCU, G.-E., Analytical Chemistry
BALA, C., Analytical Chemistry
BREZEANU, M., Inorganic Chemistry
CENUȘE, A., Physical Chemistry
CERCASOV, C., Organic Chemistry
CIOACĂ, C., Physics
CIOBANU, A., Organic Chemistry
CIOCĂZANU, I., Physical Chemistry
CIUCU, A., Analytical Chemistry
CONSTANTINESCU, E., Physical Chemistry
CONTINEANU, M., Physical Chemistry
CRISTUREAN, E., Inorganic Chemistry
DĂNEȚ, A. F., Analytical Chemistry
DAVID, V., Analytical Chemistry
DUMITRESCU, V., Analytical Chemistry
FIFIRIG, M., Physics
GĂINAR, I., Physical Chemistry
HILLEBRAND, M., Physical Chemistry
IVAN, L., Organic Chemistry
KRIZA, A., Inorganic Chemistry
LECA, M., Physical Chemistry
MAGEARU, V., Analytical Chemistry
MANDRAVEL, L. C., Physical Chemistry
MARIAN, P., Physics
MARINESCU, D., Inorganic Chemistry
MEDVEDOVICI, A., Analytical Chemistry
MELTZER, V., Physical Chemistry

MIHALCEA, I., Physical Chemistry
MUTIHAC, L., Analytical Chemistry
NEGOIU, D., Inorganic Chemistry
NEGOIU, M., Inorganic Chemistry
NICOLAE, A., Organic Chemistry
OANCEA, D., Physical Chemistry
OLTEANU, M. V., Physical Chemistry
ONCESCU, T., Physical Chemistry
PÂRVULESCU, V., Chemical Technology and Catalysis
PATROESCU, C., Analytical Chemistry
PAULINA, M., Physics
POPA, N., Inorganic Chemistry
ROȘU, T., Inorganic Chemistry
SAHINI, V., Physical Chemistry
SĂNDULESCU, I., Chemical Technology and Catalysis
SEGAL, E., Physical Chemistry
SZABÓ, A., Chemical Technology and Catalysis
TĂNASE, I., Analytical Chemistry
UDREA, I., Organic Chemistry
VÂLCU, R., Physical Chemistry
VLĂDESCU, L., Analytical Chemistry
VOLANSCHI, E., Physical Chemistry

Faculty of Foreign Languages and Literature (Str. Edgar Quinet 5–7, Sector 1, 70106 Bucharest; tel. and fax (21) 312-13-13; e-mail office@limbi-straine.ro; internet www.limbi-straine.ro):

ANGHELESCU, N., Oriental Languages
BACIU, I., English
BĂDESCU, I., French
BĂLUȚĂ-SKULTETY, M., Classical Languages
BARBORICĂ, C., Slovak Language
CĂLIN, G., Slavic Languages
CIZEK, E. A., Classical Languages
CORNILESCU, A., English
CREȚIA, G., Classical Languages
CUNIȚĂ, A., French
DERER, D., Italian
DOBREA, A., Russian
DOBRIȘAN, N., Oriental Languages
DUMITRIU, G., English
GĂMULESCU, D., Serbo-Croat Language
GUȚU, G., German
HOGEA-VELISCU, I., Oriental Languages
IONESCU, A.-I., Slavic Languages
IRIMIA, M. L., English
MICLĂU, P., French
MIHĂILĂ, GH., Slavic Languages
MIHĂILĂ, R., American Literature
MITU, M., Slavic Languages
MOLNAR, S., Hungarian
MURVAI, O., Hungarian
NICOLAESCU, M., English
NICOLESCU, A., English
PANĂ, I., English
PÂNZARU, I., French
PETRICĂ, I., Slavic Languages
REBUȘAPCĂ, I., Slavic Languages
RÎPEANU, S., Romance Languages
ROȘIANU, N., Russian
SANDU, D., German
SĂULESCU, M., English
SLUȘANSCHI, D. M., Classical Languages
ȘOPTEREANU, V., Russian
ȘTĂNESCU, C., German
SURDULESCU, R., English
SZOBOLCS, A., Hungarian
TOMA, D., French
TOMA, R., French
TUPAN, M., English
TUȚESCU, M., French
VIANU, L., English
VISAN, F., Oriental Languages
VIȘAN, V., French
WALD, L., Classical Languages

Faculty of Geography (Bdul Nicolae Bălcescu 1, Sector 1, Bucharest; tel. (21) 315-30-74; fax (21) 315-35-08; e-mail secretariat@geo.unibuc.ro; internet www.geo.unibuc.ro):

BĂLTEANU, D., Geomorphology
CÂNDEA, M., Human and Economic Geography

CIULACHE, S., Meteorology and Hydrology
ERDELI, G., Human and Economic Geography
GEANANĂ, M., Geomorphology and Pedology
GRECU, F., Geomorphology and Pedology
GRIGORE, M., Geomorphology and Pedology
IANOȘ, I., Human and Economic Geography
IELENICZ, M., Geomorphology and Pedology
MARIN, I., Regional Geography
POPESCU, N., Geomorphology and Pedology
VESPREMEANU, E., Meteorology and Hydrology

Faculty of Geology and Geophysics (Str. Traian Vuia 6, Sector 6, Bucharest; tel. (21) 211-31-20; fax (21) 211-73-90; e-mail secr@gg.unibuc.ro; internet www.gg.unibuc.ro):

ANASTASIU, N., Mineralogy
CONSTANTINESCU, E., Mineralogy
DANCHIV, A., Geological Engineering
DINU, C., Geology and Palaeontology
DRĂGĂSTAN, O., Geology and Palaeontology
GEORGESCU, P., Geophysics
GRIGORESCU, D., Geology and Palaeontology
IVAN, M., Geophysics
MĂRUNȚEANU, C., Geological Engineering
MATEI, L., Mineralogy
POPESCU, R., Mineralogy
SCRĂDEANU, D., Geological Engineering
ZAMFIRESCU, F., Geological Engineering

Faculty of History (Bdul Regina Elisabeta 4–12, Sector 5, Bucharest; tel. (21) 314-53-89; fax (21) 310-06-80; e-mail historybucharest@hotmail.com; internet www.unibuc.ro/ro/fac_fistr_ro):

BABEȘ, M., Prehistory and Archaeology
BARNEA, A., Ancient History, Archaeology and Epigraphy
BOIA, I., Historiography and Modern History
BREZEANU, S., Byzantine History
BULEI, I., Modern Romanian History
BUȘE, C., Contemporary History, Euro-Atlantic Studies
CIUCĂ, M., Medieval Romanian History
GIURESCU, D. C., Contemporary Romanian History
ISAR, N., Modern Romanian History
LUKACZ, A., Medieval History
MAIOR, I., Modern Romanian History
MAXIM, M., Ottoman History
MURGESCU, B., Modern and Economic History
NISTOR, V., Ancient Roman History
PANAITE, V., Ottoman History
PETOLESCU, C. C., Ancient Roman History and Epigraphy
PETRE, Z., Ancient Greek History
PIPPIDI, A., Medieval History
RETEGAN, M., Contemporary Romanian History
SCURTU, I., Contemporary Romanian History
ȘTEFĂNESCU, ȘT., Medieval Romanian History
TEOTEOI, T., Medieval Romanian and Byzantine History
VULPE, A., Prehistory and Archaeology
ZBUCHEA, GH., South-east European History

Faculty of Journalism and Communication Sciences (Bdul Iuliu Maniu 1–3, A Building, 6th Floor, Sector 5 Bucharest; tel. (21) 318-15-55; fax (21) 410-06-43; e-mail mcoman53@yahoo.com; internet www.fjsc.unibuc.ro):

COMAN, M., Journalism
FRUMUȘANI, D., Journalism
ZOLTAN, R., Communications

Faculty of Law (Bdul Mihail Kogălniceanu 36–46, Sector 5, 70709 Bucharest; tel. (21) 315-71-87; fax (21) 312-07-19; internet www.drept.unibuc.ro):

ATHANASIU, A., Private Law

BÂRSAN, C., Private Law
BESTELIU, R., Public Law
BIZIM, A., Sports
BUCUR, I., Economic Sciences
CĂRPENARU, ST., Private Law
CIOBANU, V., Private Law
CIOCLEI, V., Criminal Law
CORNESCU, V., Economic Sciences
CREȚOIU, GH., Economic Sciences
FILIPAȘ, A., Criminal Law
IORGOVAN, A., Constitutional Law
MARINESCU, D., Private Law
MITRACHE, C., Criminal Law
MOLCUȚ, E., Public Law
MURARU, I., Public Law
NĂSTASE, A., Public Law
NEAGU, I., Public Law
POPA, N., Public Law
ȘAGUNA, D., Public Law
SITARU, D., Private Law
STANCIU, S., Economic Sciences
STANCU, E., Criminal Law
VOLONCIU, N. D., Criminal Law

Faculty of Letters (Str. Edgar Quinet 5–7, Sector 1, Bucharest; tel. (21) 314-35-08; fax (21) 313-43-36; internet www.lit.unibuc.ro):

ANGELESCU, S., Folklore
ANGHELESCU, M., Romanian Literature
BĂLTĂCEANU, I., Hebrew Studies
BANCIU, D., Communication and Public Relations
BERCIU, A., College of Administration
BIDU VRÂNCEANU, A., Romanian Language
BRÎNCUȘI, GR., Romanian Language
CAZIMIR, ȘT., Romanian Literature
CHIVU, GH., Romanian Language
CONSTANTINESCU, N., Folklore
CORNEA, L. P., Romanian Literature
DINDELEGAN, G., Romanian Language
DINU, M. C., Communication and Public Relations
DOCA, GH., Romanian Language
DOMINTE, C., Romanian Language
FILIPAȘ, E., Romanian Literature
FORASCU, N., Romanian Language
GANĂ, G., Romanian Literature
GRIGORESCU, D., Comparative Literature
GUȚU ROMALO, V., Romanian Language
HANȚA, A., Romanian Literature
HRISTEA, TH., Romanian Language
MANOLESCU, N. A., Romanian Literature
MANZAS, Z., Romanian Language
MARTIN, M. A., Theory of Literature
MAZILU, D. H., Romanian Literature
MELIAN, A., Romanian Literature
MICU, D., Romanian Literature
MIHĂILESCU, F., Romanian Literature
MORARU, M., Romanian Language
MUNTEANU, R., Comparative Literature
NEGRICI, E., Romanian Literature
NICULESCU, F., Romanian Language
REGNEALA, M., Communication and Public Relations
RUXANDOIU, L., Romanian Language
SARAMANDU, N., Romanian Language
ȘERBAN, I. V., European Studies
SIMION, E., Romanian Literature
SLAMA CAZACU, T., Romanian Language
SPIRIDON, M., Communication and Public Relations
STOICA, I., Library and Information Science
TĂNĂSESCU, A., Theory of Literature
VRÂNCEANU, A., Romanian Literature
ZAMFIR, M., Romanian Literature

Faculty of Mathematics and Computer Science (Str. Academiei 14, Sector 1, Bucharest; tel. (21) 314-28-63; fax (21) 315-69-90; e-mail secretariat@fmi.unibuc.ro; internet www.fmi.unibuc.ro):

ALBU, T., Algebra
ATANASIU, A., Theoretical Computer Science
BĂDESCU, L., Geometry
BOBOC, N., Mathematical Analysis
BUCUR, GH., Mathematical Analysis

CAMENSCHI, G., Mechanics and Equations
CĂZĂNESCU, V., Theoretical Computer Science
CHIŢESCU, I., Mathematical Analysis
CRISTEA, M., Mathematical Analysis
CUCULESCU, I., Probability Theory, Statistics and Operational Research
DĂSCĂLESCU, S., Algebra
DINCĂ, G. I., Mechanics and Equations
DUMITRESCU, M., Probability Theory, Statistics and Operational Research
GEORGESCU, G., Theoretical Computer Science
GEORGESCU, H., Computer Science
IANUŞ, S., Geometry
IFTIMIE, V., Mechanics and Equations
ION, I., Algebra
IONESCU, P., Algebraic Geometry
MIHĂILĂ, I., Mechanics and Equations
MILITARU, G., Algebra
MIRICĂ, S., Mechanics and Equations
MITRANA, V., Theoretical Computer Science
NĂSTĂSESCU, C., Algebra
NICOLESCU, L., Geometry
NIŢĂ, C., Algebra
POPA, N., Mathematical Analysis
POPESCU, D., Algebra
POPESCU, I., Information Technology
POPESCU, L., Informatics
PREDA, V., Probability Theory, Statistics and Operational Research
PROPOAIE, G., Geometry
RUDEANU, S. A., Computer Science
SABAC, M., Mathematical Analysis
ŞANDRU, N., Mechanics and Equations
ŞTEFĂNESCU, A., Probability Theory, Statistics and Operational Research
ŞTEFĂNESCU, GH., Computer Science
STRĂTILĂ ŞERBAN, V., Mathematical Analysis
ŢIGOIU, S., Mechanics and Equations
TOMESCU, I., Computer Science
TUDOR, C., Probability Theory, Statistics and Operational Research
VĂDUVA, I., Statistics and Stochastic Models

Faculty of Orthodox Theology (Str. Sfânta Ecaterina 2, Sector 4, 040155 Bucharest; tel. (21) 335-61-17; fax (21) 335-41-83; internet www.unibuc.ro/ro/fac_fto_ro):

CORNIŢESCU, C., Biblical Theology, Cultural Heritage and Church Painting
CORNIŢESCU, E., Biblical Theology, Cultural Heritage and Church Painting
DAVID, P., Systematic Theology
DURA, N., Practical Theology
IONIŢĂ, V., Church History
MOLDOVEANU, N., Practical Theology
NECULA, N., Practical Theology
RĂDUCĂ, P., Systematic Theology
RUS, R., Systematic Theology

Faculty of Philosophy (Splaiul Independenţei 204, Sector 5, 70609 Bucharest; tel. (21) 410-29-74; fax (21) 411-52-89; e-mail matei@fil .unibuc.ro; internet filosofie.unibuc.ro):

BĂNSOIU, I., History of Philosophy and Philosophy of Culture
DUMITRU, M., Logic and Theoretical Philosophy
FLONTA, M., Logic and Theoretical Philosophy
IANOŞI, I., History of Philosophy and Philosophy of Culture
ILIESCU, A., Political and Moral Philosophy
MORAR, V., History of Philosophy and Philosophy of Culture
MUREŞAN, V., Political and Moral Philosophy
PÂRVU, I., Logic and Theoretical Philosophy
STOIANOVICI, D., Logic and Theoretical Philosophy
SURDU, A., History of Philosophy and Philosophy of Culture

TONOIU, V., Logic and Theoretical Philosophy
ŢURLEA, M., Logic and Theoretical Philosophy
VIERU, S., Political and Moral Philosophy
VLĂDUŢESCU, GH., History of Philosophy and Philosophy of Culture

Faculty of Physics (Str. Atomistilor 405, 077125 Platforma Magurele, Bucharest; tel. (21) 457-44-19; fax (21) 457-45-21; e-mail secretariat@fizic.unibuc.ro; internet www .fizica.unibuc.ro):

ALEXANDRU, H., Solid State Physics
ANGELESCU, T., Nuclear Physics and Particle Physics
ANTOHE, ŞT., Electricity, Solid State Physics
ARMEANU, I., Mathematical Physics
BEŞLIU, C., Nuclear Physics
BORŞAN, D., Atmospheric Physics
BRÂNCUŞ, D., Solid State Physics
CIOBANU, GH., Statistical Physics and Thermodynamics
CONSTANTINESCU, A., Nuclear Physics, Computational Physics
CONSTANTINESCU, L. M., Physics of Polymers
COSTESCU, A., Theoretical Physics
COTFAS, N., Mathematical Physics
DOLOCAN, V., Solid State Physics, Electrophysics
DRAGOMAN, D., Solid State Physics
DULIU, O., Nuclear Physics
FLORESCU, V., Quantum Mechanics
GEORGESCU, L., Polymer Physics
GHEORGHE, V., Biophysics
GHIORDĂNESCU, N., Nuclear Physics
GRECU, V., Atomic Physics
IONESCU, A., Atomic Physics
IOVA, I., Optics, Spectroscopy
JIPA, A., Relativistic Nuclear Physics
LAZANU, I., Nuclear Physics
LICEA, I., Solid State Physics
MARIAN, T., Quantum Mechanics
MIHUL, A., Nuclear Physics
MUNTEANU, I., Solid State Physics
MUTIHAC, R., Electricity
NENCIU, GH., Quantum Mechanics
PĂTRAŞCU, ŞT., Earth Physics
PLĂVIŢU, C., Molecular Physics, Polymers
POPA-NIŢĂ, V., Polymer Physics
POPESCU, A., Biophysics
POPESCU, F., Atomic Physics
POPESCU, I., Optics, Spectroscopy, Plasma, Lasers
RĂDUŢĂ, A., Theoretical Physics
REVEICA, I. M., Nuclear Physics
RUXANDRA, V., Electricity
SIMA, O., Nuclear Physics
ŞTEFĂNESCU, D., Mathematical Physics
TOADER, E., Optics, Plasma Physics
TUDOR, T., Optics, Lasers, Holography
TURBATU, S., Mathematical Physics
TURCU, G., Biophysics
VLĂDUCĂ, G., Nuclear Physics

Faculty of Political Science (Str. Sfântul Ştefan 24, Sector 2, Bucharest; tel. (21) 313-90-07; fax (21) 312-53-78; e-mail fspub@fspub .ro; internet www.fspub.ro):

ANDREESCU, Ş., International Relations
BARBU, D., Political Sciences
FIDULU, P., International Relations
MELEŞCANU, T., International Relations
MOTOC, I., International Relations
PREDA, C., Political Sciences
STOICA, G., Political Sciences
VLAD, L., International Relations

Faculty of Psychology and Education (Bdul Iuliu Maniu 1–3, A Building, 5th Fl., Sector 6, Bucharest; tel. (314) 25-34-52; fax (21) 411-68-90; internet www.fpse.ro):

CREŢU, T., Psychology
CRISTEA, S., Teacher Training
ENĂCHESCU, S., Special Education

FĂTU, S., Teacher Training
LERGHIT, I., Education
MITROFAN, I., Psychology
MITROFAN, N., Psychology
NEACŞU, I., Education
NICOLESCU, V., Education
PĂUN, E., Education
POPESCU, E., Education
POTOLEA, D., Education
RĂSCANU, R., Psychology
ROCO, M., Psychology
SCHIOPU, U., Psychology
STANCIU, I., Education
TOMŞA, G., Education
VERZA, E., Special Education
ZLATE, M., Psychology

Faculty of Public Administration (tel. (21) 312-49-31; fax (21) 312-16-50; e-mail mihaela .dutulescu@drept.unibuc.ro):

BUCUR, I., Public Administration
CORNESCU, V., Public Administration

Faculty of Roman Catholic Theology and Social Work (Str. General Berthelot 19, Sector 1, Bucharest; tel. and fax (21) 314-86-10; internet www.unibuc.ro/ro/fac_ftrcas_ro):

FERENŢ, E., Theology
MĂRTINCĂ, I., Theology
PETERCĂ, V., Theology
ROBU, I., Theology

Faculty of Sociology and Social Work (Str. Schitu Magureanu 9, Sector 5, Bucharest; tel. and fax (21) 315-83-91; e-mail secretar@ sas.unibuc.ro; internet www.sas.swork .unibuc.ro):

ABRAHAM, P., Social Work
ANGHEL, P., Social Work
BĂDESCU, I., Sociology
CHELCEA, S., Sociology
DRĂGAN, I., Sociology
GEANĂ, GH., Sociology
GHEŢĂU, V., Sociology
LARIONESCU, M., Sociology
MĂRGINEAN, I., Sociology
MIHĂILESCU, I., Sociology
SANDU, D., Sociology
VOINEA, M., Sociology
ZAMFIR, C., Sociology
ZAMFIR, E., Social Work

UNIVERSITATEA DIN CRAIOVA

Str. A. I. Cuza 13, 200585 Craiova
Telephone: (251) 41-43-98
Fax: (251) 41-16-88
E-mail: relint@central.ucv.ro
Internet: www.central.ucv.ro

Founded 1947
State control
Academic year: October to July

Rector: ION VLADIMIRESCU
Vice-Rectors: NICU PANEA, DUMITRU TOPAN, DAN POPESCU, MARCEL DRACEA, COSTEL PETCU
Scientific Sec.: EDMOND-GABRIEL OLTEANU
Gen. Sec.: MIRCEA ZĂVĂLEANU
Librarian: MIHAI COSOVEANU

Library: see Libraries and Archives
Number of teachers: 1,084
Number of students: 32,000

Publications: *Revista Arhivele Olteniei, Revista de Ştiinţe Juridice, Revista Forum Geografic—Studii şi Cercetari de Geografie şi Protectia Mediului, Studii si Cercetari de Onomastica, University Bulletin* (1 a year, in 16 series according to subject), *Viitorul*

DEANS

Faculty of Agriculture: MARIN SOARE
Faculty of Automatics, Computers and Electronics: EUGEN BOBAŞU
Faculty of Chemistry: CEZAR SPÎNU

Faculty of Economic Sciences and Business Administration: LUCIAN BUSE

Faculty of Electrotechnology: ELEONOR STOENESCU

Faculty of Technological System Engineering and Management: ION CIUPITU

Faculty of Engineering for Electromechanics, Environment and Industrial Informatics: SORIN ENACHE

Faculty of Horticulture: ION MITREA

Faculty of Law and Administration: DAN CLAUDIU DANISOR

Faculty of Letters: GABRIEL COSOVEANU

Faculty of Mathematics and Computer Science: NICOLAE ȚANDAREANU

Faculty of Mechanics: NICOLAE DUMITRU

Faculty of Physical Education and Sports: MARIAN DRAGOMIR

Faculty of Physics: DAN RADU CONSTANTINESCU

Faculty of Socio-Human Sciences: DUMITRU OTOVESCU

Faculty of Theology: IRINEU IOAN POPA

PROFESSORS

Faculty of Agriculture:

GĂNGIOVEANU, I., Agrotechnology
IONESCU, I., Meadow Cultivation
MARIN, N., Agrochemistry
MATEI, I., Agrotechnics
MOCANU, R., Agrochemistry
NICOLESCU, M., Phytotechnics
PANĂ, D., Management
POP, L., Agrotechnics
ȘOROP, G., Pedology
VASILE, D., Pedology
VOICA, N., Genetics

Faculty of Automatics, Computers and Electronics:

BĂDICĂ, C., Computers and Information Technology
BÎZDOACĂ, N., Mechatronics and Robotics
BOBASU, E., Automatics
BREZOVAN, M., Computers and Information Technology
BURDESCU, D., Computers and Information Technology
COJOCARU, D., Mechatronics and Robotics
DIACONU, I., Mechatronics and Robotics
IANCU, E., Automatics
IONETE, C., Automatics
IVANESCU, M., Mechatronics and Robotics
LUNGU, M., Computers and Information Technology
MARIAN, G., Computers and Information Technology
MARIN, C., Automatics
MOCANU, M., Computers and Information Technology
NICULESCU, E., Simulation
NITULESCU, M., Mechatronics and Robotics
PETRE, E., Automatics
POPESCU, D., Automatics
POPESCU, D., Mechatronics and Robotics
PURCARU, D., Electronic Structures for Measuring and Monitoring
RASVAN, V., Automatics
SELISTEANU, D., Automatics
STANESCU, L., Computers and Information Technology
STOIAN, Mechatronics and Robotics
VÎNATORU, M., Automatics

Faculty of Chemistry (Calea București 107, 200479 Craiova; tel. (251) 54-46-21; fax (251) 44-66-30; e-mail negrum@mecanica.ucv.ro; internet chimie.ucv.ro):

BRĂTULESCU, G., Organic Chemistry
POPESCU, A., Analytical Chemistry
PREDA, M., Physical Chemistry
SPÎNU, C., Inorganic Chemistry

Faculty of Economic Sciences and Business Administration (tel. and fax (251) 41-13-17; e-mail stec@central.ucv.ro; internet stec.central.ucv.ro):

AVRAM, M., Accounting
AVRAM, V., Currency and Credits
BĂNDOI, A., Price and Competitiveness
BERCEANU, D., Corporate Finance
BURLEA-SCHIOPOIU, A., Management
BUSE, L., Economic and Financial Analysis
CONSTANTINESCU, D., Management
CRĂCIUN, L., Marketing
DOMNISORU, S., Accounting
DRĂCEA, M., Public Finance
GEORGESCU, V., Statistics
GIURGITEANU, N., Informatics
GRUESCU, R., Economics
IACOB, C., Accounting
IONASCU, C., Statistics
LITOIU, V., Informatics
LOLESCU, E., Economics
MIHAI, M., Accounting
NETOIU, L., Currency and Credits
NISTORESCU, T., Marketing
OPRITESCU, M., Currency and Credits
PETCU, C., Economics
PÎRVU, C., Accounting
PÎRVU, G., Economics
POPA, S., Informatics
SICHIGEA, N., Corporate Finance
SIMINICĂ, M., Economic and Financial Analysis
SITNIKOV, C., Management
SOAVĂ, G., Informatics
SPULBĂR, C., Banking Management
ZAHARIA, C., Management

Faculty of Electrotechnology (Bdul Decebal 107, Craiova; tel. and fax (251) 43-64-47; e-mail decanat@elth.ucv.ro; internet elth.ucv.ro):

BROJBOIU, M., Electrical Engineering
CIONTU, M., Energetic Engineering
DIGĂ, S., Energetic Engineering
GOSEA, I., Energetic Engineering
LUNGU, R., Aerospace Engineering
MĂNESCU, L., Energetic Engineering
MIRCEA, I., Energetic Engineering
NICOLAE, P., Electrical Engineering
PASĂRE, S., Electrical Engineering
POPA, I., Electrical Engineering
TOPAN, D., Electrical Engineering
TUSALIU, P., Electrical Engineering

Faculty of Engineering for Electromechanics, Environment and Industrial Informatics:

BITOLEANU, A., Electrotechnics
IVANOV, S., Electrotechnics
MANOLEA, G., Electromechanics
MIHAI, D., Electrotechnics
NICOLA, A., Electrotechnics
POPESCU, M., Electrotechnics
ROSCA, D., Mechanics
VLAD, I., Electrotechnics

Faculty of Horticulture (Str. A. I. Cuza 13, 200585 Craiova; tel. and fax (251) 41-45-41; e-mail horticultura@central.ucv.ro; internet cis01.central.ucv.ro/facultatea_horticultura):

ACHIM, G., Fruit Farming
ANTON, D., Floriculture
BACIU, A., Fruit Farming
BOTU, I., Amelioration
BOTU, M., Fruit Farming
CHILOM, P., Vegetable Farming
CORNEANU, G., Genetics
DINCĂ, F., Biology
GAVRILESCU, E., Pollution and Pollutants
GHEORGHIȚĂ, M., Oenology
GIUGEA, N., Viticulture
IACOBESCU, F., Geometry
MITREA, I., Entomology
MITREA, R., Phytopathology
NOUR, V., Food Production
OLTEANU, I., Viticulture
PARASCHIVU, M., Phytopathology
POPA, A., Microbiology

POPA, D., Microbiology

Faculty of Law and Administration (e-mail secretariat@drept.ucv.ro; internet drept.ucv.ro):

CERCEL, S., Civil Law
DĂNIȘOR, D., Political Institutions, Constitutional Law
GĂINĂ, V., Commercial Law
NICULEANU, C., General Criminal Law
OLTEANU, G., Intellectual Property Law
SÂMBRIAN, T., Roman Law
SANDU, A., Political Economy
SCURTU, S., International Commercial Law
TURCULEANU, I., Civil Law Succession

Faculty of Letters (tel. (251) 41-44-68; fax (251) 41-66-88; e-mail litere@central.ucv.ro; internet www.ucv.ro):

AFANA, E., Stylistics, Poetics, Semiotics, Theory of Communication
BUCIU, M., Romanian Literature
BURDESCU, F., English Literature
COSTĂCHESCU, A., French Linguistics, Pragmatics
MURAR, I., English Linguistics
PANEA, N., Anthropology, Romanian Literature
RĂDULESCU, A., French Linguistics, Theory of Translation
SCURTU, G., French Linguistics, General Linguistics
SÎRBULESCU, E., English Literature
TEODORESCU, C., French Linguistics, Theory of Communication
TROCAN, L., French Literature

Faculty of Mathematics and Computer Science (tel. (251) 41-37-28; fax (251) 41-26-73; e-mail facmatinf@central.ro; internet inf.ucv.ro):

BUSNEAG, D., Algebra
DINCĂ, A., Algebra
IANCU, I., Artificial Intelligence
MICU, S., Numarical Analysis
NICULESCU, C., Mathematical Analysis
RĂDULESCU, V., Partial Differential Equations
ȚĂNDĂREANU, N., Artificial Intelligence
VLADIMIRESCU, I., Probability and Statistics

Faculty of Mechanics:

ASTEFANEI, I., Fluid Mechanics
BĂGNARU, D., Mechanics
BICĂ, M., Thermotechnics and Thermic Machines
CĂTĂNEANU, A., Machineries
CERNĂIANU, A., Advanced Production Systems
CHERGHINA, G., Technical Drawing and Infographics
CIOLACU, F., Chip Tooling Theory
CREȚU, S., Machineries
DUMITRU, C., Engineering and Design of Products
DUMITRU, N., Machine Elements
GEORGESCU, I., Steel Armed Concrete Buildings
ILINCIOIU, D., Materials Resistance
MARIN, M., Materials Resistance
NANU, G., Mechanics
OȚĂT, V., Automotive Dynamics
RINDERU, P., Mechanical Vibrations
ROȘCA, V., Materials Resistance
STANIMIR, A., Technology of Machine Construction
TĂRÂȚĂ, D., Material Science
TARNIȚĂ, D., Statistics
VINTILĂ, D., Mechanics
ZAMFIRACHE, M., Mechanicals Works

Faculty of Physical Education and Sports (Str. Brestei 156, Craiova; tel. and fax (251) 42-27-43; e-mail efs_kineto@sport.ucv.ro; internet cis01.central.ucv.ro/educatie_fizica-kineto/):

AVRAMESCU, T., Sport Medicine

CĂTĂNEANU, S., Physical Education and
Sports
DĂNOIU, M., Sport Medicine
DRAGOMIR, M., Physical Education and
Sports
DRAGOMIR, M., Physical Education and
Sports
ORTĂNESCU, C., Physical Education and
Sports
ORTĂNESCU, D., Physical Education and
Sports
RUSU, L., Sport Medicine

Faculty of Physics (tel. and fax (251) 41-50-
77; e-mail fizica@central.ucv.ro; internet
fizica.ucv.ro):

BIZDADEA, C., Classical Mechanics
CONSTANTINESCU, R., Electrodynamics
SALIU, S., Constrained Dynamics
SOCACIU, M., Liquid Crystals, Dielectrics
URSACHE, M., Optics

Faculty of Socio-Human Sciences (tel. and
fax (251) 41-85-15; e-mail ifgcraiova@yahoo
.com; internet www.ucv.ro):

AVRAM, C., History
CIOBOTEA, D., History
DEACONESCU, I., Philology
GHERGHE, P., History
LUNGU, M., History
OSIAC, V., History
OTOVESCU, D., Sociology
PITURCĂ, A., History-Philosophy
TOMESCU, V., Geography

Faculty of Technological System Engineering
and Management:

BENGA, G., Fundamentals of Cutting Technologies, Machining Technologies
CIUPITU, I., Cold Plastic Deformation
GÎNGU, O., Material Science and Engineering
MANGRA, M., Material Science and Engineering

Faculty of Theology:

CHIRILĂ, P., Pastoral Medicine and
Bioethics
ISVORANU, A., Old Testament Study
PĂTULESCU, C., Universal Church History
POPA, I., Orthodox Dogmatics
RESCEANU, Ş., Religions History

UNIVERSITATEA DIN ORADEA
(University of Oradea)

CP 114, OP 1, Str. Universităţii 1, Oradea
Telephone: (259) 40-81-05
Fax: (259) 43-37-89
E-mail: rectorat@uoradea.ro
Internet: www.uoradea.ro
Founded 1990
State control
Languages of instruction: English, Romanian
Academic year: October to July
Rector: Prof. Dr CONSTANTIN BUNGĂU
Pres. of the Senate: Prof. Dr SORIN CURILĂ
Vice-Rector: Prof. Dr GHEORGHE TARA
Vice-Rector: Prof. Dr MARCELA PRADA
Vice-Rector: Prof. Dr SIMONA TRIP
Vice-Rector: Prof. Dr SORIN CURILĂ
Vice-Rector: Prof. Dr SORIN ŞIPOŞ
Pres. of the Senate: Prof. Dr SORIN CURILĂ
Gen. Dir: Prof. Dr MIRCEA GORDAN
Registrar: VASILE CĂUŞ

Library of 280,000 vols
Number of teachers: 1,139
Number of students: 22,419
Publications: Analele Universităţii din Oradea, Fascicula Agricultură-Horticultură,
Analele Universităţii din Oradea, Fascicula Biologie (bioresearch.ro/bioresearch/
revistaen.htm), Analele Universităţii din
Oradea, Fascicula Chimie, Analele Universităţii din Oradea, Fascicula Constructii si Instalatii Hidroedilitare
(www.arhiconoradea.ro/JAES/Journal_-
Archives.htm), Analele Universităţii din
Oradea, Fascicula Drept, Analele Universităţii din Oradea, Fascicula Ecotoxicolo-
gie, Zootehnice si Tehnologii de Industrie
Alimentara (protmed.uoradea.ro/facultate/
anale/ecotox_zooteh_ind_alim/ecotox_zoo-
teh_ind_alim.htm), Analele Universităţii
din Oradea, Fascicula Educaţie Fizică şi
Sport, Analele Universităţii din Oradea,
Fascicula Istorie-Arheologie, Analele Universităţii din Oradea, Fascicola Kinetoterapie, Analele Universităţii din Oradea,
Fascicula Limba şi Literatura Română,
Analele Universităţii din Oradea, Fascicula Limbi şi Literaturi Străine: Engleza,
Franceza, Germana, Analele Universităţii
din Oradea, Fascicula Matematica (stiin-
te.uoradea.ro/en/auofm.htm), Analele Universităţii din Oradea, Fascicula Psihologie
(socioumane.ro/blog/fasciculapsihologie/),
Analele Universităţii din Oradea, Fascicula Protecia Mediului (protmed.uora-
dea.ro/facultate/anale/protectia_mediului/
protectia_mediului.htm), Analele Universităţii din Oradea, Fascicula Silvicultură,
Analele Universităţii din Oradea, Fascicula Sociologie-Fiolosie-Asistenta Sociala,
Analele Universităţii din Oradea, Fizica,
Annals of the Oradea University, Fascicle
of Management and Technological Engineering (imtuoradea.ro/auo.fmte), Annals of
the University of Oradea, Fascicle of Tex-
tiles-Leatherwork (textile.webhost.uora-
dea.ro/Conferinta.html), Analele
Universităţii din Oradea, Seria Geografie
(istgeorelint.uoradea.ro/Reviste/Anale/
anale.htm), Analele Universităţii din Oradea, Seria Relatii International si Studii
Europene, Analele Universităţii din Oradea, Stiinte Economice (steconomice.uora-
dea.ro/anale), Biharean Biologist (biologie-
oradea.xhost.ro/BihBiol/index.html), Ceta-
tea Bihariei, Eurolimes (iser.rdsor.ro/euro-
limes.htm), Geojournal of Tourism and
Geosites, Herpetologica Romanica (herpe-
tofauna.uv.ro/herprom.html), Journal of
Computer Science and Control Systems
(electroinf.uoradea.ro/reviste/default.htm),
Journal of Electrical and Electronics
Engineering (electroinf.uoradea.ro/reviste/
default.htm), Journal of Identity and
Migration Studies, Journal of Sustainable
Energy (www.energy-cie.ro), North-West-
ern Journal of Zoology (herp-or.uv.ro/
nwjz), Orizonturi Teologice, Revista Medicala Oradeana, Revista Română de Geografie Politică (rrgp.uoradea.ro), Revista
Romana de Kinetoterapie

DEANS

Faculty of Architecture and Construction:
Prof. Dr RAMONA NOVICOV
Faculty of Arts: Prof. Dr AGNETA MARCU
Faculty of Economics: Prof. Dr ALINA BĂDU-
LESCU
Faculty of Electrical Engineering and
Informatics: Prof. Dr Eng. TEODOR LEUCA
Faculty of Energy Engineering and Indus-
trial Management: Prof. Dr. GABRIEL
BENDEA
Faculty of Environmental Protection: Prof.
Dr IOAN MINTAŞ
Faculty of Geography, Tourism and Sport:
Prof. Dr OCTAVIAN BÂC
Faculty of History, International Relations,
Information and Communication Sciences:
Prof. Dr IOAN HORGA
Faculty of Humanities: Prof. Dr ADRIAN
HATOS
Faculty of Law: Prof. Dr VALENTIN MIRIŞAN
Faculty of Letters: Prof. Dr ION SIMUŢ
Faculty of Management and Technological
Engineering: Prof. Dr TIBERIU VESSELENYI
Faculty of Medicine and Pharmacy: Prof. Dr
GHEORGHE BUMBU
Faculty of Orthodox Theology: Prof. Dr NICU
DUMITRAŞCU
Faculty of Political Science and Communica-
tion Sciences: Prof. Dr LIA POP
Faculty of Science: Prof. Dr SANDA MONICA
FILIP
Faculty of Technological and Management
Engineering: Prof. Dr CONSTANTIN BUNGĂU
Faculty of Textiles and Leatherwork: Prof.
Dr Ing. VASILE ANTON
Faculty of Visual Arts: Prof. Dr IOAN PANTEA
Teacher Training Dept: Prof. Dr VASILE
MARCU
Univ. College of Education: Dr IOAN SABĂU
Univ. College of Technology, Economics and
Administration: Prof. Dr Ing. DINU MIRCEA
FODOR
Univ. Medical College: Prof. Dr MIRCEA IFRIM

UNIVERSITATEA DIN PETROŞANI
(University of Petroşani)

Str. Universităţii 20, 332006 Petroşani,
Hunedoara
Telephone: (254) 54-25-80
Fax: (254) 54-34-91
E-mail: m_georgescu@upet.ro
Internet: www.upet.ro
Founded 1864; became Coal Institute 1948,
Mining Institute 1957 and Technical Univ.
of Petroşani 1991; present name 1995
State control
Academic year: October to July
Rector: Prof. Dr Ing. EMIL POP
Vice-Rectors: Ing. ILIE MITRAN, Prof. Dr Ing.
VIOREL VOIN, Dr ILIE RASCOLEAN
Chancellor: Dr Ing. MARIUS MARCU
Scientific Sec.: Assoc. Prof. Dr Eng. Ec. IOAN
CUCU
Chief Registrar: MARIA ZAPARTAN
Librarian: Eng. LUMINIŢA DANCIU

Library of 305,172 vols
Number of teachers: 215
Number of students: 6,341
Publications: Annals of Economics (1 a year),
Annals of Electrical Engineering (1 a year),
Annals of Mechanical Engineering (1 a
year), Annals of Mining Engineering (1 a
year), Annals of Physics (1 a year), Annals
of Social Sciences (1 a year), Informative
Gazette (12 a year), Library's Informative
Gazette (4 a year), Mining Magazine (12 a
year)

DEANS

Faculty of Machine and Electrical Engineer-
ing: Prof. Dr Eng. ARON POANTA
Faculty of Mining: Prof. Dr Eng. IOAN
DUMITRESCU
Faculty of Science: Assoc. Prof. Dr Eng. ILIE
MITRAN
Univ. College: Prof. Dr Eng. MIHAI PASCU-
LESCU (Dir)

UNIVERSITATEA DIN PITEŞTI

Piteşti Str. Targu din Vale 1, 110040 Arges
Telephone: (348) 45-31-00
Fax: (348) 45-31-23
E-mail: info@upit.ro
Internet: www.upit.ro
Founded 1962, present name and status 1991
State control
Rector: BARBU GHEORGHE
Rector of Social Affairs and Students: CRIVAC
GHEORGHE
Rector of Int. Relations and European Inte-
gration: CHIRLESAN DUMITRU
Vice-Rector for Scientific Research: SERBAN
GHEORGHE
Rector of Quality Education and Investment:
TABACU ION

DEANS

Faculty of Economics Sciences: Prof. Dr CONSTANTIN DRAGHICI

Faculty of Educational Sciences: Prof. Dr CONSTANTIN TIBRIAN

Faculty of Electronics, Communications and Computers: Prof. Dr Ing. SILVIU IONITA

Faculty of Law and Administrative Sciences: Prof. Dr EUGENE CHELARU

Faculty of Letters: Prof. Dr ALEXANDRINA MUSTATEA

Faculty of Mathematics and Computer Science: Dr PAUL-CORNELIU RADOVICI-MARCU-LESCU

Faculty of Mechanics and Technology: Prof. Dr VIOREL NICOLAE

Faculty of Orthodox Theology: Prof. Dr ION POPESCU

Faculty of Physical Education and Sport: Prof. Dr NICULESCU MUGUREL

Faculty of Sciences: Dr AUREL POPESCU

Faculty of Social Sciences: Prof. Dr GEANINA CUCU-CIUHAN

UNIVERSITATEA 'DUNAREA DE JOS' DIN GALAŢI

Str. Domnească 47, 800008 Galaţi
Telephone: (336) 13-01-09
Fax: (236) 46-13-53
Internet: www.ugal.ro
Founded 1948, Univ. status 1974
State control
Languages of instruction: English, French, Romanian
Academic year: October to July

Rector: VIOREL MINZU
Pro-Rectors: TOADER MUNTEANU, MIRELA PRAISLER, IULIAN GABRIEL BIRSAN, VICTOR CRISTEA, DANIELA ANCUTA SARPE
Registrar: DANA MIOARA ROTARU
Librarian: MIOARA VONCILA

Number of teachers: 679
Number of students: 15,164

DEANS

Faculty of Arts: TOADER NITA
Faculty of Computer Science: ADRIAN FILI-PESCU
Faculty of Economic Sciences: COSTEL NISTOR
Faculty of Electronics and Electrical Engineering: DOREL AIORDACHIOAIE
Faculty of Engineering (in Brăila): ADRIAN GOANTA
Faculty of Food Science and Engineering: PETRU ALEXE
Faculty of History, Philosophy and Theology: IVLAMPIE IVAN
Faculty of Legal, Social and Political Sciences: OPREA RADUCAN
Faculty of Letters: NICOLAE IOANA
Faculty of Mechanical Engineering: CATALIN FETECAU
Faculty of Medicine and Pharmacy: AUREL NICHITA
Faculty of Metallurgy and Materials Science: NICOLAE CANANAU
Faculty of Naval Architecture: ADRIAN LUNGU
Faculty of Physical Education and Sport: ALEXANDRU PACURARU
Faculty of Sciences: PUIU LUCIAN GEORGESCU

PROFESSORS

Faculty of Arts:
BULANCEA, G., History of Music, Aesthetics, Folklore
DUMITRIU, M., History of Theatre
NITA, T., Vocal Interpretation

Faculty of Computer Science:
DUMITRIU, L., Applied IT and Computer Science
FILIPESCU, A., Industrial IT and Automation
PUSCASU, G., Industrial IT and Automation

SEGAL, C., Applied IT and Computer Science

Faculty of Economic Sciences:
BUHOCIU, F., Finances
PUSCASU, V., Economy
NISTOR, C., Business Communication
SARPE, D., Economy

Faculty of Electronics and Electrical Engineering:
AIORDACHIOAIE, D., Data Compression and Signals
BADEA, N., Electrical Equipment
MINZU, V., Automatic control systems
MUNTEANU, T., Electrotechnical Materials

Faculty of Engineering (in Brăila):
CIUREA, A., Technical Equipment
GOANTA, A., Computer-aided Graphics
OPROESCU, GH., Technical Equipment
PICU, M., Fundamental Sciences

Faculty of Food Science and Engineering:
ALEXE, P., Biochemistry
BAHRIM, G., Bioengineering
CRISTEA, V., Fishery
NICOLAE, A., Bioengineering
VIZIREANU, C., Biochemistry

Faculty of History, Philosophy and Theology:
IVAN, I., History of Contemporary Philosophy
LICA, V., History
SISCANU, I., History
TOFAN, S., Philosophy

Faculty of Legal, Social and Political Sciences:
RADUCAN, O., Law of Internal Combustion Engines
VICTOR, I., Public Administration

Faculty of Letters:
CROITORU, E., Law of Internal Combustion Engines
GATA, A., Public Administration
IOANA, N., Law of Internal Combustion Engines
MILEA, D., Law of Internal Combustion Engines
PRAISLER, M., Law of Internal Combustion Engines

Faculty of Mechanical Engineering:
ANDREI, G., Machine-parts Design and Graphics
BIRSAN, I., Machine-parts Design
CHIRICA, I., Structures Strength
FETECAU, C., Machine Manufacturing and Robotics
MEREUTA, E., Applied Mechanics

Faculty of Medicine and Pharmacy:
FIRESCU, D., General Surgery, Low-invasive Surgery
MUSAT, C., Physiology and Sports Medicine
NICHITA, A., Paediatrics, Physiology

Faculty of Metallurgy and Materials Science:
BENEA, L., Environmental and Materials Engineering
CANANAU, N., Plastic Deformation and Heat Treatment
MUSAT, V., Plastic Deformation and Heat Treatment
RADU, T., Environmental and Materials Engineering
VLAD, M., Environmental and Materials Engineering

Faculty of Naval Architecture:
DOMNISORU, L., Naval Structures
LUNGU, A., Naval Structures
OBREJA, C., Naval Hydrodynamics

Faculty of Physical Education and Sport:
LIUSNEA, S., Body Building
NICOLAE, P., Athletics
PACURARU, A., Sport Games and Physical Education

Faculty of Sciences:
CARAC, G., Chemistry
GEORGESCU, L., Chemistry
GEORGHIES, C., Physics
MORARU, L., Physics
PRAISLER, M., Physics

UNIVERSITATEA ECOLOGICA DIN BUCURESTI
(Ecological University of Bucharest)

Bdul Vasile Milea 1G, Sector 6, 061341 Bucharest
Telephone: (21) 316-79-32
Fax: (21) 316-63-37
E-mail: ecoueb@gmail.com
Internet: www.ueb.ro
Founded 1990
Private control

Rector: Prof. Dr ALEXANDRU TICLEA
Pro-Rectors: CAMELIA CAMASOIU, VLADIMIR ROJANSCHI, NICOLAE GALDEAN
Chancellor: CONSTANTIN DANCIULESCU
Library of 9,820 vols.

UNIVERSITATEA 'EFTIMIE MURGU' REŞIŢA

Piaţa Traian Vuia 1–4, 320085 Reşiţa
Telephone: (255) 21-02-27
Fax: (255) 21-02-30
E-mail: rector@uem.ro
Internet: www.uem.ro
Founded 1992
State control

Rector: Prof. Eng. DOINA FRUNZAVERDE
Rector for Education: Prof. Eng. GILBERT-RAINER GILLICH
Rector for Image and Communication: Prof. Dr MARIAN MICHAEL
Pres.: Prof. Dr Eng. ION VELA
Scientific Sec.: Prof. Eng. VIOREL CAMPIAN

DEANS

Faculty of Engineering: Prof. Dr Eng. SAVA IANICI
Faculty of Economics and Administrative Sciences: Prof. Dr GHEORGHE POPOVICI

UNIVERSITATEA EMANUEL DIN ORADEA
(Emanuel University of Oradea)

Str. Nufarului 87, 410597 Oradea
Telephone and fax (259) 42-66-92
E-mail: contact@emanuel.ro
Internet: www.emanuel.ro
Founded 1990
Private control
Language of instruction: Romanian
Academic year: October to July

Rector: Prof. Dr CORNELIU C. SIMUŢ
Pres. of the Admin. Council: Prof. Dr PAUL NEGRUŢ

Library of 61,000 vols
Number of teachers: 50
Number of students: 500

Publication: Perichoresis the theological journal of Emanuel University (4 a year)

DEANS

Faculty of Management: Dr SEBASTIAN VĂDUVA
Faculty of Theology: Dr MARIUS CRUCERU

UNIVERSITATEA EUROPEANĂ 'DRĂGAN' DIN LUGOJ
(Dragan European University of Lugoj)

Str. Ion Huniade 2, 305500 Lugoj, Timiş
Telephone: (256) 35-91-98
E-mail: rectorat@deu.ro

Internet: www
.universitateaeuropeanadragan.ro
Founded 1991
Private control
Academic year: October to September

Rector: Prof. Dr NICU TRANDAFIR
Pro-Rector: Prof. Dr PERSIDA CECHIN-CRISTA
Chancellor: Prof. Dr LIVIUS BERCEA
Dir: FLORIN MIHAI

DEANS

Faculty of Economics: Prof. Dr DĂNUȚ RADA
Faculty of Law: Dr DUMITRU CORNEAN

UNIVERSITATEA 'GEORGE BACOVIA' DIN BACĂU
(George Bacovia University of Bacău)

Str. Pictor Aman 96, 600164 Bacău
Telephone: (234) 56-26-00
Fax: (234) 51-64-48
E-mail: rectorat@ugb.ro
Internet: www.ugb.ro
Founded 1992
Private control

Rector: Prof. Dr TOADER GHERASIM
Pro-Rector: Prof. Dr DUMITRU BONTAS
Chancellor: Prof. Dr LIVIU DRUGUS

DEANS

Faculty of Accounting and Business Data
  Processing: Prof. CONSTANTIN COJOCARU
Faculty of Business Administration: Assoc.
  Prof. ANDREIA MELNIC
Faculty of Management: Prof. TATIANA PUIU

UNIVERSITATEA 'LUCIAN BLAGA' SIBIU
(Lucian Blaga University of Sibiu)

Bdul Victoriei 10, 550024 Sibiu
Telephone: (269) 21-60-62
Fax: (269) 21-04-92
E-mail: ccom@ulbsibiu.ro
Internet: www.ulbsibiu.ro
Founded 1990
State control
Academic year: October to June

Rector: Prof. Eng. CONSTANTIN OPREAN CIO-
  COI-POP
Vice-Rector: Assoc. Prof. RODICA MICLEA
Vice-Rector: Prof. LUIGI DUMITRESCU
Vice-Rector: Prof. DAN-MANIU DUSE
Vice-Rector: Prof. ALEXANDRU BACACI
Vice-Rector: Prof. MIHAI LEONIDA NEAMTU
Scientific Sec.: Prof. DORIN STOICESCU
Dir-Gen.: Econ. VASILE MOȚOC
Scientific Sec. to the Senate: Prof. Dr
  GHEORGHE DORIN STOICESCU

Library of 600,000 vols, 14,000 periodicals
Number of teachers: 486
Number of students: 20,000

DEANS

Faculty of Agriculture, Food Industry and
  Environmental Protection: IOAN DANCIU
Faculty of Economics: Prof. Dr CARMEN
  COMĂNICIU
Faculty of Engineering 'Hermann Oberth':
  Prof. Dr IOAN BONDREA
Faculty of Food and Textile Processing Tech-
  nology: Prof. Dr VASILE JĂȘCANU
Faculty of History and Patrimony 'Nicolae
  Lupu': Dr SORIN RADU
Faculty of Journalism: ION DUR
Faculty of Law 'Simion Bărnuțiu': Prof. Dr
  IOAN LEĂȘ
Faculty of Letters and Arts: Prof. Dr ALEX-
  ANDRA MITREA
Faculty of Medicine 'Victor Papilian': Prof.
  Dr MANUELA MIHALACHE
Faculty of Political Science, International
  Relations and European Studies: VASILE
  TABĂRĂ

Faculty of Sciences: Prof. Dr DUMITRU BATÂR
Faculty of Theology 'Andrei Șaguna': Prof. Dr
  LAURENȚIU STREZA
Univ. College: Prof. Dr NICOLAE TODERICIU
  (Dir)

UNIVERSITATEA 'MIHAIL KOGALNICEANU' DIN IAȘI
(Mihail Kogalniceanu University of Iași)

Str. Băluşescu 2, 700309 Iași
Telephone: (232) 21-24-16
Fax: (232) 27-98-21
E-mail: secretariat@umk.ro
Internet: www.umk.ro
Founded 1990
Private control
Language of instruction: Romanian
Academic year: October to July

Rector: Prof. Dr GENOVEVA VRABIE
Pro-Rector: Dr CRISTIAN SANDACHE
Library of 12,300 vols
Number of teachers: 40
Number of students: 1,000

Publication: B+ category

DEANS

Faculty of Law: Prof. Dr AURORA CIUCA

UNIVERSITATEA NAȚIONALĂ DE ARTE BUCUREȘTI
(National University of Arts Bucharest)

Str. Gen. Budişteanu 19, 010773 Bucharest 1
Telephone and fax (21) 312-54-29
E-mail: rectorat@unarte.ro
Internet: www.unarte.ro
Founded 1864 as Scoala Naţionala de Arte
  Frumoase
Academic year: October to June
State control

Rector: Dr RUXANDRA DEMETRESCU
Chancellor: Dr CATALIN BALESCU
Library: see Libraries and Archives
Number of teachers: 274
Number of students: 1,000

Depts of ceramics, glass and metal, design
(industrial and graphic), graphic fine art,
history and theory of art, mural art, painting,
pedagogy of art, photography, video and new
media, sculpture, stage design and scenography, textile arts, work of art restoration

DEANS

Faculty of Applied Arts and Design: ALEXAN-
  DRU GHILDUS
Faculty of Art History and Theory: CORINA
  POPA
Faculty of Fine Arts: MIHAIL MANESCU

UNIVERSITATEA NAȚIONALĂ DE EDUCAȚIE FIZICĂ ȘI SPORT
(National University of Physical Education and Sport)

Str. Constantin Noica 140, Sector 6, 060057
  Bucharest
Telephone: (21) 316-41-07
Fax: (21) 312-04-00
E-mail: rector@anefs.edu.ro
Internet: www.anefs-edu.ro
Founded 1922
State control

Rector: Prof. Dr VIOREL COJOCARU
Pro-Rector: Prof. Dr CORINA TIFREA
Pro-Rector: Dr TUDOR VIRGIL
Library of 102,222 vols, 3,963 titles
Number of teachers: 99
Number of students: 887

Publication: Discobolul

DEANS

Faculty of Physical Education and Sport:
  ALINA DANIELA MOANTA
Faculty of Physical Therapy: MARIANA COR-
  DUN

UNIVERSITATEA NAȚIONALĂ DE MUZICĂ DIN BUCUREȘTI

Str. Ştirbei Vodă 33, Sector 1, 010102
  Bucharest
Telephone and fax (21) 314-63-41
E-mail: international@unmb.ro
Internet: www.unmb.ro
Founded 1864
State control
Language of instruction: English, French,
  German, Romanian
Academic year: October to June

Rector: Prof. Dr DAN DEDIU
Chair.: Prof. Dr DOREL PAȘCU RĂDULESCU
Pro-Rectors: Prof. Dr DANA BORȘAN, Prof. Dr
  TEODOR ȚUȚUIANU
Library of 249,000 vols
Number of teachers: 210
Number of students: 1,250 (full-time)

Publication: Musicology Today

DEANS

Faculty of Composition, Musicology and
  Musical Education: Prof. Dr SMARANDA
  MURGAN
Faculty of Performing Arts: Assoc. Prof. Dr
  BIANCA LUIGIA MANOLEANU

PROFESSORS

BARBU BUCUR, SEBASTIAN, Byzantine Music
BORSAN, DANA, Piano
BUCIU, MAGDA, Music Theory
DANCEANU, LIVIU, Musicology
ENACHESCU, ELEONORA, Singing
IONOAIA, FLORENEL, Wind Instruments
PASCU-RADULESCU, DOREL, Conducting
RATIU, OCTAVIAN, Violin
ROTARU, DOINA, Composition
VOICU-ARNAUTOIU, RALUCA, Chamber Music

UNIVERSITATEA 'NICOLAE TITULESCU' DIN BUCUREȘTI
(Nicolae Titulescu University of Bucharest)

Calea Văcărești 185, Sector 4, 040051
  Bucharest
Telephone: (21) 330-90-32
Fax: (21) 330-86-06
E-mail: office@univnt.ro
Internet: www.univnt.ro
Founded 1990
Private control

Rector: Prof. Dr ION NEAGU

Faculties of banking and finance, law, public
administration, sociolology

Publications: Lex et Scientia magazine B
  plus, Romanian Journal of Intellectual
  Property Law.

UNIVERSITATEA OVIDIUS CONSTANȚA

Bdul Mamaia 124, 900527 Constanţa
Telephone and fax (241) 60-64-65
Fax: (241) 51-15-12
E-mail: rectorat@univ-ovidius.ro
Internet: www.univ-ovidius.ro
Founded 1990
State control

Rector: Prof. Dr VICTOR CIUPINĂ
Vice-Rector for Institutional Devt Issues and
  Regional Cooperation: Prof. VICTOR PLOAE
Vice-Rector for Admin. and Students' Social
  Problems: Prof. NICULAE PERIDE

Scientific Sec.: Assoc. Prof. LUCIAN CRISTIAN PETCU

Number of teachers: 857
Number of students: 16,702

DEANS

Faculty of Arts: Prof. Dr CARMEN CRISTESCU
Faculty of Dental Medicine: Prof. Dr AMARIEI CORNELIU
Faculty of Economic Sciences: Prof. Dr EPURE DĂNUȚ TIBERIUS
Faculty of General Medicine: VIRGIL BREABAN
Faculty of History and Political Science: Dr DANIEL FLAUT
Faculty of Law and Public Admin.: Prof. Dr ANA RODICA STĂICULESCU
Faculty of Letters: Prof. Dr ADINA CIUGUR-EANU
Faculty of Mathematics and Informatics: MACEDON TEODOSIE
Faculty of Mechanical Engineering, Industrial and Maritime: Prof. Dr PETRU BORDEI
Faculty of Medicine: Prof. Dr Ing ZAGAN REMUS
Faculty of Natural and Agricultural Sciences: Prof. Dr DRAGOMIR COPREAN
Faculty of Pedagogy: FLORENTA MARINESCU
Faculty of Petroleum Technology: MARIAN COJOC
Faculty of Pharmacy: Prof. Dr GHEORGHE ȚARĂLUNGĂ
Faculty of Physics, Chemistry, Electronics and Oil Technology: MIHAI GÎRȚU
Faculty of Psychology and Educational Sciences: Prof. Dr ANCA DRAGU
Faculty of Sports: IONEL NICOLAE
Faculty of Theology: Prof. Dr TEODOSIE PETRESCU
School of Construction: Prof. Dr Ing VIRGIL BREABĂN

UNIVERSITATEA 'PETRE ANDREI' DIN IAȘI
(Petre Andrei University of Iași)

Str. Grigore Ghica Voda 13, 700469 Iași
Telephone: (232) 21-04-74
Fax: (232) 21-48-58
E-mail: office@upa.ro
Internet: www.upa.ro
Private control
Language of instruction: Romanian
Academic year: October to July

Rector: Prof. Dr N. NICULESCU

DEANS

Faculty of Communication Sciences: Prof. Dr ODETTE ARHIP
Faculty of Economics: Prof. Dr BOGDAN CONSTANTIN ANDRONIC
Faculty of Medicine: Prof. Dr CARMEN STADO-LEANU
Law School: Prof. Dr CONSTANTIN ANDRONO-VICI

UNIVERSITATEA 'PETROL-GAZE' DIN PLOIEȘTI

Bdul București 39, POB 52, 100680 Ploiești
Telephone: (244) 57-31-71
Fax: (244) 57-58-47
E-mail: rectorat@upg-ploiesti.ro
Internet: www.upg-ploiesti.ro
Founded 1948 as Institutul de Petrol și Gaze; present name 1994
State control
Academic year: October to July
Pres.: Prof. Dr Ing. VLAD ULMANU
Vice-Rector for Scientific Research: Prof. Dr Ing. ION BOLOCAN
Vice-Rector for Academic Affairs: Prof. Dr Ing. DRAGOS CIUPARU
Vice-Pres. for Admin. Affairs: Prof. Dr Ing. MIHAI PASCU COLOJA

Vice-Rector for Int. Relations: Prof. Dr Ing. LIVIU DUMITRAȘCU
Scientific Sec.: Prof. Dr IONUT LAMBRESCU
Library of 259,542 vols, 2,879 periodicals
Number of teachers: 726
Number of students: 11,544

Publication: Bulletin of Petroleum Gas University of Ploiesti (series on Philology, Mathematics-Informatics, Physics, Economics, Educational Sciences, Law and Social Sciences)

DEANS

Faculty of Economical Sciences: Prof. Dr ION IARCA
Faculty of Letters and Sciences: Assoc. Prof. Dr CHRISTIAN MARINOIU
Faculty of Mechanical and Electrical Engineering: Prof. Dr Ing. MIHAIL MINESCU
Faculty of Petroleum and Gas Engineering: Prof. Dr Ing. IULIAN NISTOR
Faculty of Petroleum Technology and Petrochemistry: Assoc. Prof. Dr Ing. PAUL ROSCA

PROFESSORS

ANGHEL, A.
ANTONESCU, L.
ANTONESCU, N. N.
AVRAM, L.
BADOIU, D.
BALU, I.
BOLOCAN, I.
BUCUR, C.
CARTOAJE, V.
COLOJA, M. P.
CUTU, I.
DUDA, G.
DUMITRASCU, L.
FRUZESCU, D.
GEORGESCU, D.
GEORGESCU, O.
GHEORGHITOIU, M.
GRIGORE, N.
IARCA, I.
IONESCU, M.
IORDACHE, G.
MALUREANU, I.
MARIN, C.
MINESCU, F.
MINESCU, M.
NISTOR, I.
OPREA, M.
PANAIT, G.
PARASCHIV, N.
PATARLAGEANU, M.
PETCU, A.
POPA, C.
ROSCA, P.
SIRO, B.
SOARE, A.
STEFAN, G.
STOICESCU, C. C.
STRATULA, C.
TALLE, V.
TOMESCU, D.
TUDOR, I.
ULMANU, V.
VASILESCU, S.
VOICU, I.
ZECHERU, G.

UNIVERSITATEA 'PETRU MAIOR' DIN TÂRGU MUREȘ
(Petru Maior University of Târgu Mureș)

Str. Nicolae Iorga 1, 540088 Târgu Mureș, Mureș
Telephone and fax (265) 16-22-75
E-mail: rectorat08@upm.ro
Internet: www.upm.ro
Founded 1960
State control
Academic year: October to July

Rector: Prof. Dr. Eng. CALIN ENACHESCU
Vice-Rector: Assoc. Prof. Dr TATIANA DANESCU
Vice-Rector: Prof. Dr CALIN MOLDOVAN
Pres.: Prof. Dr CORNEL SIGMIREAN
Library of 120,000 vols
Number of teachers: 190 (154 full-time, 36 part-time)
Number of students: 4,130
Publications: Buletinul Științific (1 a year), Studia Universitatis—Filologia (1 a year), Studia Universitatis—Istoria (1 a year)

DEANS

Faculty of Economics and Admin. Sciences: Prof. LIVIU MARIAN
Faculty of Engineering: Prof. Dr NICOLAE CHIRILA
Faculty of Sciences and Letters: Prof. Dr IULIAN BOLDEA
Univ. College: Assoc. Prof. Dr MARIA GEORGESCU

UNIVERSITATEA ROMÂNĂ DE ȘTIINȚE ȘI ARTE 'GHEORGHE CRISTEA'
(Gheorghe Cristea Romanian University of Sciences and Arts)

Bdul Energeticienilor 9E, bloc M1, et. 1, Sector 3, Bucharest
E-mail: ugc_rei@ugc.ro
Internet: www.ugc.ro
Founded 1990
Private control
Rector: Prof. Dr Ing. LIDIA CRISTEA
Faculties of arts and sciences, business, legal and administration
Library of 60,000 vols

UNIVERSITATEA ROMÂNO-AMERICANA DIN BUCUREȘTI
(Romanian-American University of Bucharest)

Bdul Expozitiei 1B, Sector 1, 012101 Bucharest
Telephone: (21) 202-95-18
Fax: (21) 318-35-66
Internet: www.rau.ro
Founded 1991
Private control
Rector: Prof. Dr ION SMEDESCU.

UNIVERSITATEA ROMÂNO-GERMANĂ DIN SIBIU
(Romanian-German University of Sibiu)

Calea Dumbravii 28–32, 550324 Sibiu
Telephone: (269) 23-35-68
Fax: (269) 23-35-76
E-mail: rectorat@roger-univ.ro
Internet: www.roger-univ.ro
Founded 1998
Private control
Rector: Prof. Dr HORTENSIA GORSKI
Pro-Rector: Prof. Dr GHEORGHE BICHICEAN
Scientific Sec.: Prof. Dr IOAN CONSTANTIN PETCA
Library of 18,000 vols, 11,500 Romanian, 5,000 German, 1,280 English, 220 other languages

DEANS

Faculty of Economics: Dr Ing. ELENA SIMA
Faculty of Law and Administrative Science: Dr TITUS SEREDIUC

UNIVERSITATEA 'SPIRU HARET' DIN BUCURESTI
(Spiru Haret University of Bucharest)

Str. Ion Ghica 13, Sector 3, 030045 Bucharest
Telephone: (21) 314-00-75
Fax: (21) 314-39-08
E-mail: info@spiruharet.ro
Internet: www.spiruharet.ro
Founded 1991
Private control
Language of instruction: Romanian
Academic year: October to July

Rector: Prof. Dr AURELIAN A. BONDREA
Vice-Rector: Prof. Dr GHEORGHE BICA, Prof. Dr DOINEL DINUICA, Prof. Dr IOAN GAFDEAC, Prof. Dr ELENA DOVAL, Assoc. Prof. Dr MANUELA EPURE, Assoc. Prof. Dr EDUARD IONESCU

Number of teachers: 1,264
Number of students: 90,565

Library of 675,464 vols, 4,738 journals

Publications: *Annals of Spiru Haret, Economic Series, Annals of Spiru Haret University, Filology Series—Foreign Languages, Annals of Spiru Haret University, Geography Series, Annals of Spiru Haret University, Journalism Studies, Annals of Spiru Haret University, Mathematics-Informatics Series, Annals of Spiru Haret University, Music Series, Annals of Spiru Haret University, Veterinary Medicine Series*

DEANS

Department of Finance and Banking: Prof. Dr GHEORGHE PISTOL
Department of Marketing and International Business: Prof. Dr LUMINITA PISTOL
Department of Theatre: Prof. Dr LUCIA MUREȘAN
Faculty of Architecture: Prof. Dr EMIL CREANGĂ
Faculty of Arts: Assoc. Prof. Dr GEORGE GRIGORE
Faculty of Accounting and Finance, Câmpulung-Muscel: Assoc. Prof. Dr ODI MIHAELA ZARNESCU
Faculty of Accounting and Finance, Râmnicu-Vâlcea: Assoc. Prof. Dr LUMINITA IONESCU
Faculty of Economic Sciences, Blaj: Prof. Dr EMIL POPA
Faculty of Financial and Accounting Management, Constanţa: Assoc. Prof. Dr DRAGOS MIHAI IPATE
Faculty of Financial and Accounting Management, Craiova: Assoc. Prof. Dr ION VIOREL MATEI
Faculty of Financial and Accounting Management, Constanţa: Assoc. Prof. Dr DRAGOS MIHAI IPATE
Faculty of Foreign Languages and Literatures: Prof. Dr ELENA BĂLAN
Faculty of Geography: Dr GHEORGHE HERISANU
Faculty of Geography and Tourism: Dr CORNELIA MARIN
Faculty of History, Museology and Archival Science: Prof. Dr DUŢU ALEXANDRU
Faculty of International Relations, History and Philosophy: Prof. Dr GHEORGHE ONIȘORU
Faculty of Journalism, Communication and Public Relations: Assoc. Prof. Dr SOFIA BRATU
Faculty of Law and Public Administration: Prof. Dr LAZĂR CARJAN
Faculty of Law and Public Administration, Constanta: Assoc. Prof. Dr GHEORGHE DINU
Faculty of Law and Public Administration, Craiova: Assoc. Prof. Dr BUJOR FLORESCU
Faculty of Law and Public Administration, Ramnicu Valcea: Assoc. Prof. Dr CONSTANTIN PLETEA

Faculty of Legal and Administrative Sciences, Brașov: Prof. Dr ALEXANDRU IONAS
Faculty of Letters: Dr TAMARA CEBAN
Faculty of Management, Brașov: Prof. Dr STELIAN PANZARU
Faculty of Mathematics and Informatics: Prof. Dr GRIGORE ALBEANU
Faculty of Music: Prof. Dr PETRU STOIANOV
Faculty of Philosophy, Political Science and Cultural Studies: Prof. Dr IOAN N. ROȘCA
Faculty of Physical Education and Sport: Assoc. Prof. Dr GEORGETA NICULESCU
Faculty of Psychology and Pedagogy, Brașov: Prof. Dr PETRE LISIEVICI
Faculty of Romanian Language and Literature: Dr VALERIU MARINESCU
Faculty of Sociology-Psychology: Prof. Dr FLORIN TUDOSE
Faculty of Veterinary Medicine: Assoc. Prof. Dr DANUT TURCU
Financial and Accounting Management Faculty: Assoc. Dr EUGEN GHIORGHIȚĂ

UNIVERSITATEA 'ŞTEFAN CEL MARE'
(Ştefan Cel Mare University)

Str. Universității 13, 720229 Suceava
Telephone: (230) 52-00-81
Fax: (230) 52-00-80
E-mail: rectorat@usv.ro
Internet: www.usv.ro
Founded 1963 as Pedagogical Institute, became Institute of Higher Education 1976, univ. status 1990
State control
Language of instruction: Romanian
Academic year: October to July

Rector: Prof. VALENTIN POPA
Vice-Rector for Didactical Activity and Quality Assurance: Prof. MIRCEA DIACONU
Vice-Rector for Univ. Image, Int. Relations and European Devt: Prof. STEFAN PURICI
Vice-Rector for Material Resources and Students Issues: Prof. GABRIELA PRELIPCEAN
Gen. Admin. Dir: Ing. CATALIN VELICU
Registrar: Ing. MARIA MUSCĂ
Library Dir: Prof. VASILE DOSPINESCU

Library of 268,700 vols, 3,207 periodicals
Number of teachers: 360
Number of students: 11,500

Publications: *Acta Tribologica* (1 a year), *Annals* (philosophy and socio-human disciplines, geography, philology (literature), philology (linguistics), mechanics, electrical engineering, forestry, economic sciences and public admin., education; annals of univ. college, 1 a year), *Atelier de Traduction* (2 a year), *ISTECFILO* (2 a year), *La Lettre 'R'* (2 a year)

DEANS

Faculty of Economic Sciences and Public Administration: Prof. Dr CARMEN NASTASE
Faculty of Education Sciences: Dr OTILIA CLIPA
Faculty of Electrical Engineering and Computer Science: Prof. Dr STEFAN-GHEORGHE PENTIUC
Faculty of Food Engineering: Prof. Dr SONIA AMARIEI
Faculty of Forestry: Assoc. Prof. Dr SERGIU ANDREI HORODNIC
Faculty of History and Geography: Prof. Dr VASILE EFROS
Faculty of Letters and Communication Sciences: Assoc. Prof. Dr LUMINITA TURCU
Faculty of Mechanical Engineering, Mechatronics and Management: Prof. Dr ROMEO IONESCU
Faculty of Physical Education and Sport: Assoc. Prof. Dr PETRU GHERVAN

PROFESSORS

Faculty of Economic Sciences and Public Administration (tel. (230) 52-29-78; fax (230) 52-02-73; e-mail secretariat@seap.usv.ro; internet www.seap.usv.r):
  BOSTON, I., Financial Control
  BURCIU, A., Management
  HAPENCIUC, C.-V., Enterprise Economy, Economic Statistics
  HLACIUC, E., Accounting, Accounting Expertise
  IFTIME, E., Law
  LUPU, V., Informatics
  PAVALEANU, V., Law
  PETRIS, R., Accounting, Financial-Accounting Audit
  PRELIPCEAN, G., Management, Capital Markets
  PRISACARIU, G., Management
  SANDU, G., Finance

Faculty of Education Sciences (tel. and fax (230) 52-04-65):
  NAGY, R., Contemporary Romanian Language, History of Literary Language

Faculty of Electrical Engineering and Computer Science (Str. Universității 13, 720229 Suceava; tel. and fax (230) 52-48-01; e-mail secretariat@eed.usv.ro; internet www.eed.usv.ro):
  CERNOMAZU, D., Inventics and Design
  GAITAN, V., Computer Networks; Operating Systems; Computing Systems Architecture
  GRAUR, A., Electronics; Electronic Devices
  PENTIUC, GH., Computer Programming and Programming Languages; Programming of Distributed Systems
  PENTIUC, R., Industrial Consumers' Power Alimentation
  POPA, V., Applied Electronics; System Input/Output; Identification Systems
  POTORAC, A., Computer Networks; Digital Integrated Circuits
  TURCU, C., Systems Theory; Intelligent Systems; Theory of Automatic Regulation

Faculty of Food Engineering (Str. Universității 9, 720225 Suceava; tel. (230) 21-61-47; fax (230) 52-02-67; e-mail gutts@usv.ro; internet www.fia.usv.ro):
  GUTT, G., Materials Engineering
  GUTT, S., Food Engineering
  SOLOMON, N., Equipment for Food Industry, Refrigeration Machinery, Operations and Devices in Food Industry

Faculty of Forestry (Str. Universității 13, 720229 Suceava; tel. and fax (230) 52-29-78; fax (230) 52-16-64; e-mail silvic@usv.ro; internet www.silvic.usv.ro):
  CENUSA, R., Forestry
  GIURGIU, V., Dendrometry
  HOREANU, C., Botanics
  MILESCU, I., Forest Economy, Law and Forest Legislation

Faculty of History and Geography (Str. Universității 13, 720229 Suceava; tel. (230) 21-61-47; fax (230) 52-37-42; e-mail stefanp@atlas.usv.ro; internet atlas.usv.ro):
  BRANDUS, C., Regional Geography of Romania, Geomorphology
  EFROS, N., Economic Geography, Geography of Tourism, Geography of Industry, Transport and Trade
  GULICIUC, E., History of Contemporary Philosophy
  GULICIUC, V., Theory and Practice of Communication, Semiotics
  IACOBESCU, M., Contemporary History, History of Bucovina
  MAXIM, T., Moral and Political Philosophy, History of Romanian Philosophy

PURICI, S., Slav History, History of Basarabia, European and Euroatlantic Integration

RADOANE, M., Geomorphology, Modern Methods in Geomorphology

RADOANE, N., Physical Geography of Romania, Geomorphology

SANDRU, D., Contemporary History, International Relations in the 20th Century

Faculty of Letters and Communication Sciences (Str. Universității 13, 720229 Suceava; tel. (230) 21-61-47; fax (230) 52-40-97; e-mail secretariat@litere.usv.ro; internet www.litere.usv.ro):

ARDELEANU, S.-M., Discourse Analysis, Language Semiotics

BARLEANU, I.-H., History of Communication, Actual Publishing Language, Introduction in Communication Sciences

CONSTANTINESCU, M., History of French Literature, Translation

DIACONU, M., Ideology and Exile, Romanian Post-war Poetry, Modernism after Modernism

DOSPINESCU, V., Contemporary French Language, Didactic Semiotics

OPREA, I., European Culture and Languages, Fundamentals of Lexical Theory

STEICIUC, E.-B., Translation, French Literature

Faculty of Mechanical Engineering, Mecatronics and Management (Str. Universității 9, 720225 Suceava; tel. and fax (230) 52-37-43; e-mail secretariat@fim.usv.ro; internet www.fim.usv.ro):

AMARANDEI, D., Manufacturing Technologies

BANCESCU, N., Materials Technology, Thermic Treatments

CEFRANOV, E., Quality Management, Manufacturing Technologies

CIOBANU, M., Metalworking, Quality Assurance

DIACONESCU, E., Tribology; Mechanical Contact

FRUNZA, G., Equipment Maintenance and Repair, Machines Manufacturing Technology

GLOVNEA, M., Mechanical Contact, Elasticity and Strength of Materials

GRAMATICU, M., Materials Science, Thermic Treatments

IACOB, D., Statistics, Quality Statistic Control

IONESCU, R., Robots and Flexible Systems, Industrial Automations

MIHAI, I., Thermodynamics and Thermic Machines

MUSCA, I., Numerical Analysis, Mechanisms and Machines Design, Tribology

RATA, V., Machines Manufacturing Technology, Equipment Maintenance and Repair

SEVERIN, L., Cold Plastic Deformation, Management

UNIVERSITATEA 'TIBISCUS' DIN TIMIŞOARA
(Tibiscus University of Timişoara)

Str. Lascăr Catargiu 4–6, 300559 Timişoara
Telephone and fax (256) 22-06-89
E-mail: rectorat@tibiscus.ro
Internet: www.tibiscus.ro
Private control

Rector: Prof. Dr CORNEL HARANGUŞ
Pro-Rector: Prof. Dr CRĂCIUN SABĂU
Chancellor: DAN LACRĂMĂ
Library of 135,000 vols

DEANS

Department of Psychology: Prof. Dr RADU RĂDUCAN

Faculty of Computer Science and Applied Information Technology: Dr LUCIAN LUCA
Faculty of Design, Music: Dr TIBERIU MARIUS KARNYANSZKY
Faculty of Economics: Prof. Dr ADRIAN COJOCARIU
Faculty of Education and Sports: Dr CORINA MUŞUROI
Faculty of Law and Public Administration: Dr DUMITRU VLĂDUŢ

UNIVERSITATEA 'TITU MAIORESCU'
(Titu Maiorescu University)

Str. Dâmbovnicului 22, Sector 4, 040441 Bucharest
Telephone and fax (213) 16-16-43
E-mail: rectorat@utm.ro
Internet: www.utm.ro
Founded 1990
Private control
Language of instruction: Romanian
Academic year: October to June

Rector: Prof. SMARANDA ANGHENI
Pro-Rector: Prof. Dr DUMITRU GHEORGHIU
Pro-Rector: Prof. Dr MAGDALENA NEGRUŢIU
Pro-Rector: Prof. VALENTIN CORNELIU PAU
Scientific Sec. of the Senate: Prof. MADALINA VOICULESCU

Library of 1,500,000 vols (central library; there are also separate faculty libraries)
Number of teachers: 500
Number of students: 15,000

DEANS

Faculty of Dental Medicine (Bucharest): Prof. LUCIA GHERGIC
Faculty of Economics (Bucharest): Dr FLORIN VADUVA
Faculty of Economics (Târgu Jiu): Prof. Dr ION NEAMTU
Faculty of Informatics (Bucharest): Prof. IUSTIN PRIESCU
Faculty of Law (Bucharest): Prof. GABRIEL LIVIU ISPAS
Faculty of Law (Târgu Jiu): Dr ANICA MERISESCU
Faculty of Medicine (Bucharest): Prof. MINERVA GHINESCU
Faculty of Psychology (Bucharest): Prof. VIOREL TANASE
Faculty of Social and Political Science (Bucharest): Prof. MARIANA COJOC

UNIVERSITATEA 'TRANSILVANIA' DIN BRAŞOV

Bdul Eroilor 29, 500036 Braşov
Telephone: (268) 41-20-88
Fax: (268) 41-05-25
E-mail: rectorat@unitbv.ro
Internet: www.unitbv.ro
Founded 1971 by merger of Polytechnical and Pedagogical Institutes of Braşov
State control
Language of instruction: English, French, German, Romanian
Academic year: October to July

Rector: Prof. Dr Ing. IOAN VASILE ABRUDAN
Vice-Rector for Scientific Research and IT: Prof. Dr Ing. DORU TALABA
Vice-Rector for Liaison with Economic, Social and Cultural Environment: Prof. Dr EMIL STOICA
Vice-Rector for Quality Assurance and Int. Evaluation: Prof. Dr Ing. SIMONA LACHE
Vice-Rector for Student Activities: Prof. Dr Ing. DANIEL MUNTEANU
Vice-Rector for Public Relations: Prof. Dr LILIANA ROGOZEA
Registrar: Ing. ALINA POPESCU
Library Dir: Prof. Dr Ing. ELENA HELEREA
Library: see Libraries and Archives
Number of teachers: 785

Number of students: 21,122
Publication: *Buletinul Universității 'Transilvania' din Braşov*

DEANS

Faculty of Civil Engineering: Prof. Dr Ing. IOAN TUNS
Faculty of Economic Sciences and Business Administration: Prof. Dr GABRIEL BRATUCU
Faculty of Electrical Engineering and Computer Science: Assoc. Prof. Dr Ing. CARMEN GERIGAN
Faculty of Food and Tourism: Prof. Dr Ing. CAROL CSATLOS
Faculty of Letters: Assoc. Prof. Dr ADRIAN LACATUS
Faculty of Law: Prof. Dr CRISTINEL MURZEA
Faculty of Materials Science and Engineering: Prof. Dr Ing. TEODOR PISU-MACHEDON
Faculty of Mathematics and Computer Science: Prof. Dr MARIN MARIN
Faculty of Mechanical Engineering: Prof. Dr Ing. ION CALIN ROSCA
Faculty of Medicine: Assoc. Prof. Dr MARIUS MOGA
Faculty of Music: Prof. Dr STELA DRAGULIN
Faculty of Physical Education and Mountain Sports: Prof. Dr MIRCEA NEAMTU
Faculty of Product Design and Environment: Prof. Dr Ing. OLIMPIU MUNTEANU
Faculty of Psychology and Education Sciences: Assoc. Prof. Dr TEODOR PALASAN
Faculty of Silviculture and Forest Engineering: Assoc. Prof. Dr Ing. LUCIAN CURTU
Faculty of Sociology and Communication: Prof. Dr SILVIU COPOSESCU
Faculty of Technological Engineering and Industrial Management: Prof. Dr Ing. VLADIMIR MARASCU-KLEIN
Faculty of Wood Engineering: Prof. Dr Ing. MIHAI ISPAS

PROFESSORS

Faculty of Economic Sciences and Business Administration (Colina Universității 1, 500036 Braşov; tel. (268) 41-93-04; fax (268) 41-93-04; e-mail f8-economic@unitbv.ro; internet econ.unitbv.ro):

BĂCANU, V. B., Finance, Accounting and Economic Theory
BRÂNZAN, I., Management and Computing
BRĂTUCU, G., Marketing and Tourism
DUGULEANĂ, L., Management and Computing
FORIŞ, T., Management and Computing
LEFTER, C., Marketing and Tourism
LIXĂNDROIU, D. I., Management and Computing
OPREI, I., Management and Computing
POPA, M., Management and Computing
POPESCU, M., Management and Computing
SAON, S., Finance, Accounting and Economic Theory

Faculty of Electrical Engineering and Computer Science (Str. Politehnicii 1, 500024 Braşov; tel. (268) 47-47-18; fax (268) 47-47-18; e-mail f4-electro@unitbv.ro; internet www.vega.unitbv.ro):

ANDONIE, R., Electronics
BIDIAN, D. Ş., Electrical Engineering
BORZA, P. N., Electronics
CERNAT, M., Electrical Engineering
DAN, ŞT., Automation
FRATU, A., Automation
GEORGESCU, M., Electrical Engineering
GOGIOIU, A., Electrical Engineering
HELEREA, E., Electrical Engineering
MĂRGINEANU, I., Automation
MARINESCU, C., Electrical Engineering
MATLAC, I. V., Electrical Engineering
NICOLAIDE, A. C., Electrical Engineering
OLTEAN, I. D., Electronics
PEŞTEANU, O., Electrical Engineering
SCUTARU, GH., Electrical Engineering
SISAK, F., Automation

STOIA, D. D., Electrical Engineering
SZABO, W., Electronics
SZEKELY, I., Electronics
ȚAȚA, M. S., Electrical Engineering
TOACȘE, GH., Electronics
TOPA, I., Automation

Faculty of Law (Bdul Eroilor 25, 500030 Brașov; tel. and fax (268) 47-40-17):

BUJDOIU, N., Sociology, Philosophy and Law
CHIRIȚĂ, R., Sociology, Philosophy and Law
POENARU, E., Sociology, Philosophy and Law

Faculty of Materials Science and Engineering (Colina Universității 1, 500068 Brașov; tel. and fax (268) 47-16-26; fax (268) 47-16-26; e-mail f3-simat@unitbv.ro; internet www.unitbv.ro):

ANDREESCU, F. G., Welding Equipment
BEJAN, V., Technology of Fabrication and Maintenance of Equipment
BOT, D., Heating Equipment, Foundry Technology
CÂNDEA, V. N., Welding Technology
CHICHERNEA, F., Technological Equipment and Materials Science
CIOBANU, I., Fundamentals of Foundry
CONSTANTINESCU, A., Foundry Equipment
CRIȘAN, A., Technological Equipment and Materials Science
DUȚĂ-CAPRĂ, A., Chemistry
EFTIMIE, L., Welding Technology
ENE, V., Special Proceedings for Foundry
FĂTU, S., Study of Metals
FLOREA, R. G., Welding Technology
GEAMÂN, V., Technological Equipment and Materials Science
GIACOMELLI, I., Equipment and Technologies for Thermal Treatments
IOVANĂȘ, R., Technology of Welding by Pressing
LUCA, V., Study of Metals
MACHEDON, T., Welding Equipment, Non-Destructive Testing, Hydraulic and Pneumatic Engines
MARKOS, Z., Welding Technology
MILOȘAN, I.
MUNTEANU, A., Thermal Treatments and Heat Processing
NOVAC, GH., Welding Equipment
PAȚACHIA, S., Chemistry
POPA, A., Technology of Plastic Deformation
POPESCU, R. M., Welding Technology
SAMOILĂ, C., Furnaces and Equipment for Heating
SCOROBEȚIU, L., Fundamentals of Welding Processes
ȘERBAN, C., Study of Metals
ȚICĂ, E.-R., Chemistry
ȚIEREAN, M., Welding Technology
TRIF, N., Mechanization, Automation and Robots for Welding Processing
TUDORAN, P., Study of Metals
VARGA, B., Technological Equipment
VEȚELEANU, A.

Faculty of Mathematics and Computer Science (Str. Iuliu Maniu 50, 500091 Brașov; tel. and fax (268) 41-40-16; e-mail f-mate-info@unitbv.ro; internet cs.unitbv.ro):

ATANASIU, GH., Geometry
CIUREA, E., Computing
COCAN, M., Computing
LUPU, M., Differential Equations
MARIN, M., Differential Equations
MARINESCU, C., Differential Equations
MUNTEANU, GH., Differential Equations
ORMAN, G., Mathematical Analysis and Probability
OVESEA, H., Mathematical Analysis and Probability
PASCU, N., Mathematical Analysis and Probability
PESCAR, V., Geometry

PITIȘ, GH., Differential Equations
RADOMIR, I., Mathematical Analysis and Probability
SCHEIBER, E., Computing
TIȚA, N., Mathematical Analysis and Probability

Faculty of Mechanical Engineering (Str. Politehnicii 1, 500036 Brașov; tel. and fax (268) 47-47-61; e-mail f-mecanica@unitbv.ro; internet mecanica.unitbv.ro):

ABĂITĂNCEI, D., Automotive Technology
BĂCANU, GH., Physics
BALCU, I., Strength of Materials and Vibration
BENCHE, V., Heat Engineering and Fluid Mechanics
BIȚ, C. S., Strength of Materials and Vibration
BOBESCU, GH., Automotive Technology
BOLFA, T. E., Strength of Materials and Vibration
BRĂTUCU, GH., Agricultural and Food-processing Machinery
CÂMPIAN, V., Automotive Technology
CÂNDEA, I., Mechanics
CHIRIACESCU, T. S., Strength of Materials and Vibration
CHIRU, A., Automotive Technology
CIOFOAIA, V., Strength of Materials and Vibration
CIOLAN, GH., Automotive Technology
COFARU, C., Automotive Technology
CONSTANTIN, F., Mechanics
CRISTEA, L., Precision Engineering and Mechatronics
CURTU, T. I., Strength of Materials and Vibration
DELIU, GH., Mechanics
DUMITRIU, A., Precision Engineering and Mechatronics
FETCU, D., Heat Engineering and Fluid Mechanics
GOIA, A.I, Strength of Materials and Vibration
IONESCU, EMIL GH., Precision Engineering and Mechatronics
IONESCU, ENACHE, Agricultural and Food-processing Machinery
MUNTEANU, GH. M., Strength of Materials and Vibration
MUREȘAN, M., Heat Engineering and Fluid Mechanics
NAGY, T., Automotive Technology
NĂSTĂSOIU, S., Automotive Technology
OLTEANU, C., Precision Engineering and Mechatronics
POPA, V. A., Strength of Materials and Vibration
POPARAD, H., Precision Engineering and Mechatronics
POPESCU, S., Agricultural and Food-processing Machinery
POSTELNICU, A., Heat Engineering and Fluid Mechanics
PREDA, I., Automotive Technology
RADU, GH. A., Automotive Technology
RADU, N. GH., Strength of Materials and Vibration
ROȘCA, ILEANA C., Strength of Materials and Vibration
ROȘCA, IOAN C., Precision Mechanics and Mechatronics
RUS, F., Agricultural and Food-processing Machinery
SĂLĂJAN, C., Automotive Technology
SECARA, E. M., Mechanics
SEITZ, N., Automotive Technology
ȘERBĂNOIU, N., Heat Engineering and Fluid Mechanics
SOARE, I., Automotive Technology
ȘOVA, M., Heat Engineering and Fluid Mechanics
ȘOVA, V., Heat Engineering and Fluid Mechanics

SZÁVA, I., Strength of Materials and Vibration
ȚANE, N., Agricultural and Food-processing Machinery
TOFAN, M., Mechanics
ȚUREA, N., Automotive Technology
ULEA, M., Strength of Materials and Vibration
UNGUREANU, V. B., Heat Engineering and Fluid Mechanics
VEȘTEMEAN, N., Heat Engineering and Fluid Mechanics
VLASE, S., Mechanics

Faculty of Medicine (Str. N. Bălcescu 56, 500019 Brașov; tel. and fax (268) 41-21-85; e-mail f-medicina@unitbv.ro; internet www.unitbv.ro/faculties/medicina):

COMAN, GH., Preclinical Medicine
LEAȘU, T., Specialized Medicine
RĂDOI, M., Internal Medicine
RADU, I., Preclinical Medicine

Faculty of Music (Str. Andrei Saguna 2, Brașov; tel. (268) 47-88-84; fax (268) 41-05-25; e-mail f-muzica@unitbv.ro; internet www.unitbv.ro/muzica):

BICA, N., Teaching Music
DRĂGULIN, S. D., Instrumental Interpretation
IACOBESCU, L., Instrumental Interpretation

Faculty of Silviculture and Forest Engineering (Șirul Beethoven 1, 500123 Brașov; tel. (268) 47-57-05; fax (268) 47-57-05; e-mail f5-silvic@unitbv.ro; internet www.unitbv.ro/silvic):

ALEXANDRU, V. M., Forest Exploitation
BELDEANU, E., Forest Exploitation
BOȘ, N.
CHIȚEA, GH., Biostatistics
CIORTUZ, I., Silviculture
CIUBOTARU, A., Forest Exploitation
CLINCIU, I., Flood Control
COSTEA, C.
DANCIU, M. A., Silviculture
FLORESCU, I. I., Silviculture
IONAȘCU, GH., Forest Exploitation
KISS, A., Topography
LEAHU, I., Dendrometry
MARCU, M., Silviculture
MARCU, O., Silviculture
NEGRUȚIU, A., Silviculture
NEGRUȚIU, F., Silviculture
OLTEANU, N., Forest Exploitation
OPREA, I., Forest Exploitation
PARASCAN, D., Silviculture
POPESCU, I., Forest Exploitation
RUSU, A.
SIMON, D., Silviculture
ȘOFLETEA, N., Silviculture
SPÂRCHEZ, GH., Silviculture
TAMAȘ, Ș., Operations Research
TÂRZIU, D., Silviculture
UNGUREANU, ȘT., Forest Exploitation

Faculty of Technological Engineering and Industrial Management (Str. Colina Universității 1, 500036 Brașov; tel. and fax (268) 41-46-90; e-mail f2-itehn@unitbv.ro; internet www.unitbv.ro/tech):

ALEXANDRU, P., Mechanisms
BOBANCU, Ș., Mechanisms
BONCOI, GH., Automatic Machine Tools
BRANA, M. A., Descriptive Geometry and Technical Drawing
BUZATU, C., Automation of Technological Processes
CALEFARIU, G.
CHIȘU, E., Machine Components
CIOBOTĂ, M., Precision Mechanics
CRUCIAT, P., Technical Measurements
DAJ, I., Machine Components
DEACONESCU, T.
DELIU, M.
DIACONESCU, D. V., Mechanisms
DIȚU, V., Car Construction Technology
DUDIȚĂ, F., Mechanisms

DUMITRU, S., Physics
GAGIONEA, E. L., Descriptive Geometry and Technical Drawing
INȚA, I., Physics
IVAN, M., Machine Tools and Dimensional Control
IVAN, N. V., Machine Engineering Technology
JULA, A., Machine Elements
LUPULESCU, N.-B., Car Construction Technology
MĂNIUȚ, P.
MĂRĂSCU KLEIN, V., Unconventional Materials, Computer-Aided Production Systems Design
MARTINESCU, I., Technology of Cold-pressing
MOGAN, GH. L., Machine Elements
MOLDOVEAN, GH., Machine Elements
NEDELCU, A.
OBACIU, GH., Electric Drive and Machine Tools
PĂUNESCU, T., Car Construction Technology
POPESCU, I., Technical Measurement and Tolerance
ROȘCA, D. M., Metal-cutting Theory
SĂVESCU, D., Machine Elements
SECARĂ, GH., Metal Cutting, Tool Design
SOFONEA, L., Physics
STAREȚU, I., Machine Components
STROE, I., Machine Components
TALABĂ, D., Machine Components
TĂNĂSESCU, I., Machine Elements and Mechanisms
TUREAC, I., Machines for Processing by Deformation
URSUȚIU, D., Physics
VĂSÎI-ROȘCULEȚ, S., Design of Devices
VELICU, D., Descriptive Geometry and Technical Drawing
VIȘA, I., Mechanisms

Faculty of Wood Engineering (Str. Colina Universității 1, 500068 Brașov; tel. (268) 41-53-15; fax (268) 41-53-15; e-mail f-ilemn@unitbv.ro; internet www.unitbv.ro/il):

BĂDESCU, L. A.-M., Wood-processing Machinery
BARBU, M. C., Wood Technology
BUDĂU, G., Wood-processing Machinery
CISMARU, I., Wood Technology
DOGARU, V., Wood-processing Machinery
ISTRATE, V., Wood Technology
LĂZĂRESCU, C., Wood-processing Machinery
MIHAI, D., Wood Technology
MITIȘOR, A., Wood Technology
NĂSTASE, V., Wood Technology
PETROVICI, V., Wood Technology
ȚĂRAN, N., Wood-processing Machinery
TUDOR, E., Wood-processing Machinery
ZLATE, GH., Wood Technology

UNIVERSITATEA 'VALAHIA' DIN TÂRGOVIȘTE

Bdul Regele Carol I 2, 130024 Târgoviște
Telephone: (245) 20-61-01
Fax: (245) 21-76-92
E-mail: rectorat@valahia.ro
Internet: www.valahia.ro
Founded 1989

Rector: Prof. Dr ION CUCUI
Pro-Rectors: Prof. Dr MARIN CIRCIUMARU, Prof. Dr CONSTANTIN GHITA, Prof. Dr GHEORGHE IONITA
Librarian: Prof. AGNES ERICH

Number of teachers: 400
Number of students: 10,000

DEANS

Faculty of Arts and Sciences: Dr LAURA MONICA GORGHIU

Faculty of Economic Sciences: Dr LEONARDO BADEA
Faculty of Environmental Engineering and Biotechnology: Prof. Dr STEFANIA IORDACHE
Faculty of Electrical Engineering: Dr Ing. HENRI GEORGE COANDA
Faculty of Humanities: Prof. Dr CONSTANTIN PEHOIU
Faculty of Law: Dr LIVIA MOCANU
Faculty of Material Sciences, Mechatronic Engineering and Robotics: Prof. Dr VASILE BRATU
Faculty of Theology: Prof. Dr MIHAITA NIFON

DIRECTORS OF COLLEGES

Univ. College of Economics and Admin.: Dr VIRGIL POPA
Univ. College of Education: (vacant)
Univ. College of Technology: Dr CORNEL MARIN

UNIVERSITATEA 'VASILE ALECSANDRI' DIN BACĂU
('Vasile Alecsandri' University Of Bacău)

Calea Marașești 157, 600115 Bacău
Telephone: (234) 54-24-11
Fax: (234) 54-57-53
E-mail: rector@ub.ro
Internet: www.ub.ro

Founded 1961 as Pedagogical Institute, became Bacău Institute of Higher Education 1974, 1990 became Univ. of Bacău, present name and status 2009
State control
Languages of instruction: English, French, Romanian
Academic year: October to July

Rector: Prof. VALENTIN NEDEFF
Vice-Rector for Economical and Quality Strategies: Assoc. Prof. Dr CORNELIA MARCELA DANU
Vice-Rector for Educational Programmes and Student activities: Prof. Dr ADRIANA-GERTRUDA ROMEDEA
Vice-Rector for Research Programmes and Int. Relations: Assoc. Prof. Dr ELENA NECHITA
Vice-Rector for Univ. Image and Media Relation: Prof. Dr CĂTĂLINA ABABEI
Gen.-Man.: Eng. IOAN-CIPRIAN DRUGĂ
Registrar and Chief Sec.: Eng. ADRIAN APĂVĂLOAIE
Head of Int. Relations: SILVIA LEONTE
Chief Librarian: Eng. CECILIA ANGHEL

Library of 176,830 vols, 58,459 periodicals
Number of teachers: 242
Number of students: 5,792

Publications: *Actes du Colloque Franco-Roumain de Chimie Appliquée, Cultural Perspectives—Journal for Literary and British Cultural Studies in Romania* (1 a year), *Gymnasium* (2 a year), *Interstudia* (2 a year), *Journal of Engineering Studies and Research* (4 a year), *Junimea studențească băcăuană, Kinetostud, Reste a voir, Ro-Brit, Scientific Study & Research—Chemistry and Chemical Engineering, Biotechnology, Food Industry* (4 a year), *Scientific Studies and Research—Economic Sciences series, Scientific Studies and Research—Mathematics* (12 a year), *Scientific Studies and Research—Series Mathematics and Informatics* (2 a year), *Studențimea băcăuană, Studii și Cercetări—Seria Biologie* (2 a year), *Voxstud*

DEANS

Faculty of Economic Sciences: Prof. Dr Ing. OVIDIU-LEONARD TURCU
Faculty of Engineering: Prof. Dr Ing. CAROL SCHNAKOVSZKY

Faculty of Letters: Assoc. Prof. Dr SIMINA MASTACAN
Faculty of Movement, Sport and Health Sciences: Assoc. Prof. Dr DĂNUȚ NICU MÂRZA DĂNILĂ
Faculty of Sciences: Prof. Dr MIHAI TĂLMACIU

Technological Universities

IULIU HAȚIEGANU UNIVERSITY OF MEDICINE AND PHARMACY CLUJ-NAPOCA

Str. Emil Isac 13, 400023 Cluj-Napoca
Telephone: (264) 59-72-56
Fax: (264) 59-72-57
E-mail: rectoratumf@umfcluj.ro
Internet: www.umfcluj.ro

Founded 1872
Public control
Languages of instruction: Romanian, English, French
Academic year: October to July (2 semesters)

Rector: Prof. Dr CONSTANTIN CIUCE
Pres.: Prof. Dr MARIUS BOJIȚĂ
Vice-Rector for Academic Affairs: Prof. Dr SORIN DUDEA
Vice-Rector for Management and Academic Development: Assoc. Prof. Dr DORIN FARCĂU
Vice-Rector for Scientific Affairs: Assoc. Prof. Dr ALEXANDRU IRIMIE
Vice-Rector for Academic Evaluation and Quality Assurance: Prof. RADU OPREAN
Vice-Rector for Postgraduate Studies: Prof. Dr GRIGORE BACIUT
Gen. Man.: IOAN POP
Registrar in Chief: MIHAI GUDEA
Library Dir: IOANA ROBU

Library of 270,850 vols
Number of teachers: 750
Number of students: 9,000

Publications: *Acta Dermatologica Transilvanica, Acta Neurologica Transilvanicae, Anuarul Universității, Applied Medical Informatics, Biology and Therapy of Cancer Cell, Chirurgia, Clujul Medical, Cosmetic Dentistry—Beauty and Science, Diabetes Management, Diabet, Nutritie, Risc Cardiometabolic, Journal of Clinical Anatomy and Embriology, Journal of Clinical Oncology, Journal of Gastrointestinal and Livers Diseases, Journal of Radiotherapy & Medical Oncology, Jurnalul de Diabet, Jurnalul Roman de Anestezie și Terapie Intensiva, Jurnalul Roman de Pediatrie, Medical Ultrasonography, Minimally Invasive Surgery, Obstetrica si Ginecologia, Palestrica Mileniului III—Civilizatie si sport, Pediatria.ro, Quo Vadis, Radiology and Medical Oncology, Revista de Recuperare, Medicina Fizica si Balneologie, Revista Romana de Chirurgie Rino-sinusala, Romanian Journal of Angiology and Vascular Surgery, Romanian Journal of Gastroenterology, Romanian Journal of Hand and Reconstructive Microsurgery, Romanian Journal of Pathology, The Heart, Transilvania Stomatologica*

DEANS

Faculty of Dental Medicine: Prof. Dr ALIN SERBANESCU
Faculty of Medicine: Prof. Dr ANCA DANA BUZOIANU
Faculty of Pharmacy: Prof. Dr FELICIA LOGHIN

PROFESSORS

Faculty of Medicine:

ACALOVSCHI, I., Anaesthesiology and Intensive Care

ANDERCOU, A., Surgery
BADEA, R., Medical Imaging
BÂRSAN, M., Cardiology
BENGA, G., Cellular and Molecular Biology
BENGA, I., Paediatric Neurology
BOCȘAN, I., Epidemiology
BOLOSIU, H. D., Internal Medicine
CĂLUGĂRU, M., Ophthalmology
CĂPÂLNEANU, R., Cardiology
CÂRSTINA, D., Infectious Diseases
COCÂRLĂ, A., Occupational Health
COSTIN, N., Gynaecology
DEJICA, D., Clinical Immunology
DRAGHICI, A., Internal Medicine
DUNCEA, C., Internal Medicine
FUNARIU, GH., Surgery
GHERMAN, M., Nephrology
GHILEZAN, N., Oncology
GRIGORESCU-SIDO, F., Anatomy
GRIGORESCU-SIDO, P., Paediatrics
HANCU, N., Nutrition and Metabolic Diseases
IONUȚ, C., Hygiene
JEBELEANU, GH., Biochemistry
KORY, S., Neurology
LAZĂR, L., Oncology
LUCAN, M., Urology
MACREA, R., Paediatric Psychiatry
MAIER, N., Dermatology
MIU, N., Paediatrics
MUREȘAN, A., Physiology
NANULESCU, M., Paediatrics
OLINIC, N., Internal Medicine
OLINICI, C., Morphopathology
PARAIAN, N., Paediatric Surgery
PASCU, O., Gastroenterology
PLESCA-MANEA, L., Physiopathology
POPESCU, A., Neonatology
SANDOR, V., Pharmacology
SASCA, C., Microbiology
SURCEL, I. V., Gynaecology
ȚIGAN, S., Medical Informatics
TOADER RADU, M., Histology
TOMESCU, E., Otorhinolaryngology
TURDEANU, N., Surgery
VLAD, L., Surgery
ZAMORA, C., Pneumophthisiology
ZDRENGHEA, D., Cardiology

Faculty of Pharmacy:

BOJIȚĂ, M., Drug Control
COMAN, M., Drug Industry
LEUCUȚA, S., Pharmaceutical Technology
MOLDOVAN, M., Dermatopharmacy and Cosmeticology
ONIGA, I., Pharmacognosy
ONIGA, O., Pharmaceutical Chemistry
OPREAN, L., Inorganic Chemistry
POLICINENCU, C., Pharmaceutical Legislation, Marketing and Management
PRODAN, A., Informatics
SĂNDULESCU, R., Analytical Chemistry
TĂMAȘ, M., Pharmaceutical Botany
TĂRMURE, C., Biochemistry

Faculty of Stomatology:

BĂCUIȚ, G., Oral and Maxillofacial Surgery
BORZEA, D., Stomatological Propaedeutics
COCÂRLĂ, E., Orthodontics, Paedodontics
FILDAN, F., Oral Radiology
NEGUCIOIU, M., Dental Propaedeutics
POPA, S., Dental Propaedeutics
ROTARU, A., Oral and Maxillofacial Surgery

UNIVERSITATEA DE ARHITECTURA ȘI URBANISM 'ION MINCU'

Str. Academiei 18–20, 010014 Bucharest
Telephone: (21) 307-71-12
Fax: (21) 307-71-09
E-mail: rectorat.uauim@gmail.com
Internet: www.uauim.ro

Founded 1892 by the Romanian Soc. of Architects as a private school of architecture, present name and status 2000
State control

Academic year: October to July

Chair.: Prof. Dr EMIL BARBU POPESCU
Rector: Prof. Dr ȘTEFAN SCAFA UDRISTE
Rector for Professional Issues: Prof. Dr RODICA CRIȘAN
Rector for Students: Prof. Dr DAN CORNELIUS ȘERBAN
Chancellor: Prof. Dr NICOLAE LASCU
Dir of Library: GABRIELA TABACU

Library of 170,000 vols, 50 Periodicals
Number of teachers: 267 (incl. 150 part-time)
Number of students: 3,280

Publications: *Analele Arhitecturii*, *Arhitext Design*

DEANS

Faculty of Architecture: Prof. Dr ZENO BOGDĂNESCU
Faculty of Interior Architecture: Dr IULIUS IONESCU
Faculty of Urbanism: Prof. Dr ALEXANDRU M. SANDU

DIRECTORS

Univ. College: Prof. Dr NICULAE GRAMA
School of Advanced Studies: Prof. Dr HANNA DERER

UNIVERSITATEA DE MEDICINĂ ȘI FARMACIE 'CAROL DAVILA' (Carol Davila University of Medicine and Pharmacy)

Str. Dionisie Lupu 37, Bucharest
Telephone: (21) 318-07-18
Fax: (21) 318-07-19
Internet: www.univermed-cdgm.ro

Founded 1857 (fmrly Institutul de Medicina și Farmacie, renamed 1990)

Rector: Prof. Dr FLORIAN POPA
Pro-Rectors: Prof. Dr CONSTANTIN VIRGILIU ARION, Prof. Dr ION FULGA, Prof. Dr IOAN LASCAR, Prof. Dr MONICA DANIELA POP, Prof. Dr IOANEL SINESCU

Library of 388,614 vols, 1,690 periodicals
Number of teachers: 2,323
Number of students: 8,436

DEANS

Faculty of Dentistry: Prof. Dr DRAGOȘ STANCIU
Faculty of Medicine: Prof. Dr VICTOR STOICA
Faculty of Pharmacy: Prof. Dr DUMITRU LUPULIASA

UNIVERSITATEA DE MEDICINĂ ȘI FARMACIE DIN CRAIOVA

Str. No Petru Rares 2, 200349 Craiova
Telephone: (251) 52-24-58
Fax: (251) 59-30-77
E-mail: rectorship@umfcv.ro
Internet: www.umfcv.ro
Academic year: October to July
Founded 1998

Rector: Prof. Dr ADRIAN SAFTOIU
Vice-Rectors for Academic and Scientific Affairs: TUDOREL CIUREA, Prof. Dr AUGUSTIN CUPSA ION GEORGESCU
Vice-Rector for Student Affairs: Prof. Dr TUDOR UDRISTOIU
Scientific Sec.: Prof. Dr FLORINEL BĂDULESCU
Head of Library Services: Prof. ALINA CROITORU

Library of 70,000 vols, 59 periodicals
Number of teachers: 453
Number of students: 4,478

Publications: *Craiova Medicala* (4 a year), *Journal of Pharmacology* (4 a year), *Romanian Journal of Morphology and Embriology*

DEANS

Faculty of Dentistry: Prof. Dr VERONICA MERCUT
Faculty of Medicine: Prof. Dr ION ROGOVEANU
Faculty of Midwifery and Nursing: Assoc. Prof. IULIANA NICOLESCU
Faculty of Pharmacy: Prof. Dr JOHNY NEAMTU

PROFESSORS

Faculty of Dentistry:

BANIȚA, I.
CALOTĂ, F.
MANOLESCU, I.
MERCUȚ, V.
PETCU, P.
STOICESCU, I.
SURPĂTEANU, M.

Faculty of Medicine:

ANUȘCA, D.
BADEA, M.
BĂDULESCU, F.
BISTRICEANU, M.
BRĂILA, M.
BUTEICĂ, E.
CÂRSTEA, D.
CERNEA, N.
CIUREA, P.
CIUREA, T.
CRĂIȚOIU, S.
CUPȘA, A.
DINCĂ, M.
ENĂCHESCU, V.
GĂMAN, G.
GEORGESCU, E.
GEORGESCU, I.
IANCĂU, M.
IONESCU, D.
IONIȚA, E.
MARINESCU, D.
MIXICH, F.
MOGOANTĂ, L.
MOGOȘ, D.
MOȚA, E.
MOȚA, I.
NOVAC, L.
PLEȘEA, I.
POPESCU, R.
PREJBEANU, I.
ROGOVEANU, I.
ROȘU, A.
ROȘU, L.
SABETAY, C.
SĂFTOIU, A.
SBÂRCEA, V.
SIMIONESCU, C.
STANCIU, P.
STOICA, Z.
TĂRÂȚĂ, M.
TOMA, I.
UDRIȘTOIU, T.
VASILE, I.
VRABETE, M.
ZAHARIA, C.
ZĂVOI, R.

Faculty of Midwifery and Nursing:

MERCUȚ, D.
NICOLESCU, I.
TRAȘCĂ, E.

Faculty of Pharmacy:

AVRAMESCU, C.
BĂNICERU, M.
GOFIȚA, E.
GORUNESCU, F.
NEAMȚU, J.
PISOSCHI, C.
RADU, S.
TIȚA, I.

UNIVERSITATEA DE MEDICINĂ ȘI FARMACIE 'GR. T. POPA'

Str. Universității 16, 700115 Iași
Telephone: (232) 30-16-00

Fax: (232) 21-18-20
E-mail: rectorat@umfiasi.ro
Internet: www.umfiasi.ro
Founded 1879
State control
Languages of instruction: English, French, Romanian
Academic year: October to July
Rector: Prof. Dr VASILE ASTARASTOAE
Vice-Rector: Prof. TRAIAN MIHAESCU
Vice-Rector: Prof. IOAN COSTEA
Vice-Rector: Prof. MARIA STAMATIN
Vice-Rector: Prof. DRAGOS PIEPTU
Registrar: GEANINA CARMEN UNGUREANU
Library Man.: Prof. VIORICA SCUTARU
Library of 264,243 vols
Number of teachers: 900
Number of students: 9,824

DEANS

Faculty of Dentistry: Prof. Dr NORINA FORNA
Faculty of Medical Bioengineering: Dr DAN ZAHARIA
Faculty of Medicine: Prof. Dr DOINA AZOICAI
Faculty of Pharmacy: Prof. Dr MONICA HANCIANU

PROFESSORS

Faculty of Medical Bioengineering (Str. Kogalniceanu 9–13, Iaşi; tel. and fax (232) 21-35-73; e-mail pflocea@bioing.umfiasi.ro; internet www.umfiasi.ro):

APOSTOL, I., Clinical Physiology
BALTAG, O., Exact, Metrological and Informatics Sciences
CHIRIAC, H., Biomedical Engineering
DIACONU, I., Exact, Metrological and Informatics Sciences
GROSU, I., General and Applied Physics
PETRESCU, GH., General Management and Marketing
POEATA, I., Biomaterials and Techniques of Prosthetic Systems
UGLEA, C., Applied Chemistry and Physical Chemistry
UNGUREANU, M., Synthetic and Bioactive Substances

Faculty of Medicine (Str. Universitatii 16, 700115 Iaşi; tel. (232) 30-16-15; fax (232) 30-16-33; e-mail gcuciureanu@medgen.umfiasi.ro; internet www.umfiasi.ro):

ALDEA, A. S., Thoracic Surgery
ANTOHE, D. S., Anatomy
ARSENESCU, C., Internal Medicine
ASTARASTOAIE, V., Forensic Medicine
BĂDESCU, A., Histology
BĂDESCU, M., Physiopathology
BALAN, G., Internal Medicine
BILD, E., Oncology and Radiotherapy
BOISTEANU, P., Psychiatry
BRĂNIŞTEANU, D., Physiology
BRUMARU, O., Paediatrics
BUIUC, D., Microbiology
CARASIEVICI, E., Immunology
CHIRIAC, R. M., Rheumatology and Balneo-physiotherapy
CHIRIŢA, V., Psychiatry
CHISĂLIŢA, D., Ophthalmology
CIORNIA, T., Forensic Medicine
COLEV, V., Physiopathology
COMAN, G., Microbiology
COSOVANU, A., Internal Medicine
COSTĂCHESCU, GH., Obstetrics and Gynaecology
COSTINESCU, V., Otorhinolaryngology
COTRUTZ, C., Cell Biology
COTUŢIU, C., Histology
COVIC, M., Genetics
COVIC, M., Internal Medicine
DANIIL, C., Radiology
DATCU, G., Internal Medicine
DATCU, M. D., Internal Medicine
DIACONU, C., Surgery
DIMITRIU, A. G., Paediatrics

DRAGOMIR, C., Infant Care
DRAGOMIR, C., Surgery
DRAGOMIR, D., Obstetrics and Gynaecology
FRÎNCU, D. L., Anatomy
FRÎNCU, D. L., Physical Education
GAVĂT, V., Hygiene
GEORGESCU, G., Internal Medicine
GEORGESCU, N. M., Orthopaedics and Traumatology
GHEORGHIŢĂ, N., Biochemistry
GOŢIA, D. G., Paediatric Surgery
GOŢIA, S., Paediatrics
IANOVICI, N., Neurosurgery
IONESCU, C., History of Medicine
IVAN, A., Epidemiology
LUCA, M., Parasitology and Mycoses
LUCA, V., Infectious Diseases
LUCA, V., Physiopathology
MĂTĂSARU, S., Paediatrics
MIHAIESCU, T., Pneumopthisiology
MIHAILOVICI, M. S., Pathological Anatomy
MIHALACHE, C., Occupational Medicine
MIHALACHE, ST., Surgery
MOGOŞ, V., Endocrinology
MORARU, D., Paediatrics
MORARU, E., Paediatrics
MUNGIU, C. O., Pharmacology
PANDELE, G. I., Internal Medicine
PETRESCU, GH., Physiology
PETRESCU, Z., Dermatology
PETROVANU, R., Family Practice Medicine
PLAHTEANU, M., Forensic Medicine
PLEŞA, C., Surgery
POPESCU, D. C., Neurobiology
PRELIPCEAN, C., Internal Medicine
PRICOP, F., Obstetrics and Gynaecology
PRICOP, M., Obstetrics and Gynaecology
RADULESCU, D., Pathological Anatomy
RUSU, V., Biophysics
SINIŢCHI, G., Family Practice Medicine
SLĂTINEANU, S., Physiology
STAN, M., Internal Medicine
STANCIU, C., Internal Medicine
ŞTEFANACHE, F., Neurology
STOIAN, M., Surgery
STRATONE, A., Exploration Physiology
TÎRCOVEANU, E., Surgery
TOPOLICEANU, F., Exploration Physiology
UNGUREANU, G., Internal Medicine
ZAMFIR, M., Anatomy
ZBRANCA, E., Endocrinology

Faculty of Pharmacy (Str. Universitati 16, 700115 Iaşi; tel. (232) 30-16-23; fax (232) 21-18-20; e-mail eonica@farmacie.umfiasi.ro; internet www.umfiasi.ro):

CARAMAN, C., Inorganic Chemistry
CUCIUREANU, R., Environmental Chemistry
DĂNILĂ, GH., Pharmaceutical Chemistry
DORNEANU, M., Organic Chemistry
DORNEANU, V., Analytical Chemistry
GAFIŢEANU, E., Pharmaceutical Technology
HRISCU, A., Pharmacodynamics
LAZAR, M., Drug Control
PĂDURARU, I., Pharmaceutical Biochemistry
PAVELESCU, M. D. G., Pharmacology
POPOVICI, I., Pharmaceutical Technology
PROCA, M., Toxicology
SCUTARIU, M. D., Anatomy and Physiology
STAN, M., Analytical Chemistry
STĂNESCU, U. H., Pharmacognosy
ŞTEFĂNESCU, E., Organic Chemistry

UNIVERSITATEA DE MEDICINĂ ŞI FARMACIE TÂRGU MUREŞ

Gh. Marinescu 38, 540000 Târgu Mureş
Telephone: (265) 21-55-51
Fax: (265) 21-04-07
E-mail: rectorat@umftgm.ro
Internet: www.umftgm.ro
Founded 1948
State control
Languages of instruction: English, Hungarian, Romanian

Academic year: October to September
Rector: Prof. Dr CONSTANTIN COPOTOIU
Vice-Rectors: Assoc. Prof. Dr KLARA BRÎNZA-NIUC, Prof. Dr ÖRS ŞTEFAN NAGY
Chief Sec.: ELENA NISTOR
Scientific Sec.: Prof. Dr AUREL NIREŞTEAN
Int. Relations Officer: ANNAMÁRIA GYÖRFI
Librarian: FLORIN DAMIAN
Library of 184,600 vols
Number of teachers: 422
Number of students: 3,530

Publication: *Revista de Medicină şi Farmacie/Orvosi és Gyógyszerészeti Szemle* (4 a year)

DEANS

Faculty of Dentistry: Prof. Dr MIRCEA SUCIU
Faculty of General Medicine: Dr DAN DOBREANU
Faculty of Pharmacy: Prof. Dr DANIELA-LUCIA MUNTEAN

PROFESSORS

Faculty of Dentistry (tel. (265) 21-55-51 ext. 130; fax (265) 21-04-07; e-mail decanatstoma@umftgm.ro):

KOVÁCS, D.
PĂCURAR, M., Paedodontics and Orthodontics
POPŞOR, S.
SZEKELY, M., Teeth and Dental Arches Morphology

Faculty of General Medicine (tel. (265) 21-55-51 ext. 110; fax (265) 21-04-07; e-mail decanatmg@umftgm.ro):

ABRAM, Z., Hygiene
AZAMFIREI, L., Intensive Care
BANCU, S., Surgery
BOJA, R., Urology
BORDA, A., Histology
BRASSAI, Z., Internal Medicine
BRATU, D., Internal Medicine
BURIAN, M., Radiology
CARASCA, E., Internal Medicine
COPOTOIU, C., Surgery
DEAC, R., Cardiac Surgery
DRAŞOVEANU, C., Otorhinolaryngology
EGYED, Z., Pathomorphology
GEORGESCU, C., Internal Medcine
GEORGESCU, L., Physiotherapy
HOBAI, S., Biochemistry
INCZE, A., Internal Medicine
JUNG, I., Pathology
KIKELI, P. I., Family Medicine
KUN, I. Z., Endocrinology
MATHE, I., Biochemistry
MONEA, M., Pharmacology
MUNTEANU, I., Paediatrics
NAGY, Ö., Orthopaedics
NICOLAESCU, I., Biophysics
NIRESTEAN, A., Psychiatry
OLTEANU, G., Internal Medicine
SABĂU, M., Epidemiology
TOGĂNEL, R., Paediatrics

Faculty of Pharmacy (tel. (265) 21-55-51 ext. 111; fax (265) 21-04-07; e-mail rectorat@umftgm.ro):

DOGARU, M. T.
DUDUCZ, G., Medicinal Biotechnology
GYÉRESI, A., Pharmaceutical Chemistry
IMRE, S., Drugs Analysis
KINCSES-AJTAI, M., Toxicology
MUNTEAN, D. L., Drugs Analysis
OROIAN, S.

UNIVERSITATEA DE MEDICINĂ ŞI FARMACIE 'VICTOR BABEŞ'

Piaţa Eftimie Murgu 2, 300041 Timişoara
Telephone: (256) 20-44-00
Fax: (256) 49-06-26
E-mail: rectorat@umft.ro
Internet: www.umft.ro

Founded 1945 as Institutul de Medicină
Languages of instruction: English, French,
Romanian
Academic year: October to July
Rector: Prof. Dr MARIUS RAICA
Vice-Rector: Prof. Dr SIMONA DRAGAN
Vice-Rector: Prof. Dr OCTAVIAN CRETU
Vice-Rector: Prof. Dr EUGEN BOIA

Library of 150,000 vols, 31,000 journals
Number of teachers: 770
Number of students: 5,500

Publications: *Cercetări Medico-Chirurgicale*
(4 a year), *Fiziologia-Physiology* (4 a year),
Timişoara Medicală (4 a year)

DEANS

Dental Medicine: Prof. Dr MIHAI ROMINU
Medicine: Prof. Dr DORU ANASTASIU
Pharmacy: Dr CRISTINA DEHELEAN

UNIVERSITATEA DE ŞTIINŢE AGRICOLE ŞI MEDICINĂ VETERINARĂ A BANATULUI DIN TIMIŞOARA
(Banat's University of Agricultural Sciences and Veterinary Medicine, Timişoara)

Calea Aradului 119, 300645 Timişoara

Telephone: (256) 49-40-23
Fax: (256) 20-02-96
E-mail: usabtm@mail.dnttm.ro
Internet: www.usab-tm.ro

Founded 1945
State control
Academic year: September to September
Languages of instruction: English, Romanian
Rector: Prof. PAUL PÎRŞAN
Vice-Rector for Economic and Social Problems: Prof. OLIMPIA IORDĂNESCU
Vice-Rector for Educational Issues and Int. Relations: Prof. GHEORGHE DĂRĂBUŞ
Vice-Rector for Scientific Research: Prof. Dr TEODOR TRAŞCĂ
Gen. Admin. Dir: Assoc. Prof. TRAIAN BERAR
Head of Int. Relations Office: Prof. Dr H. C. HORIA CERNESCU
Univ. Registrar: ENIKO NĂDĂŞAN
Librarian: Prof. CONSTANTIN MATEESCU

Library of 368,307 vols, 45 periodicals
Number of teachers: 332
Number of students: 7,040

Publications: *Didactica*, *Journal of Agroalimentary Processes and Technologies*, *Journal of Horticulture, Forestry and Biotechnology*, *Journal of Linguistic Studies*, *Research Journal of Agricultural Science*, *Scientific Papers: Animal Sciences and Biotechnologies*, *Scientific Papers: Farm Management*, *Scientific Papers: Veterinary Medicine*, *Scientific Papers of Young Researchers*

DEANS

Faculty of Agriculture: Prof. COSMIN POPESCU
Faculty of Animal Husbandry and Biotechnologies: Prof. Dr NICOLAE PĂCALĂ
Faculty of Farm Management: Prof. Dr VASILE GOŞA
Faculty of Food Processing Technologies: Prof. Dr ADRIAN RIVIŞ
Faculty of Horticulture and Forestry: Prof. Dr ALIN DOBREI
Faculty of Veterinary Medicine: Prof. Dr VIOREL HERMAN

PROFESSORS

Faculty of Agriculture (Calea Aradului 119, 300645 Timişoara, Timiş; tel. (256) 27-70-07; fax (256) 27-71-26; internet www.agricultura .usab-tm.ro):

ADRIAN, B., Phytopathology
DORIN, A., Land Evaluation

DORU, P., Entomology
FLORIAN, B., Biodiversity
GICU GABRIEL, A., Botanics
HORTENSIA, R., Policies and Environmental Depopulation Techniques
IACOB, B., General Ecology and Environmental Protection
IOANA, G., Entomology
RADU, P., Comparative Anatomy and Etology
SILVICA, O., Land Improvement
VALERIA, C., Topography

Faculty of Animal Husbandry and Biotechnologies (Calea Aradului 119, 300645 Timişoara, Timiş; tel. and fax (256) 27-71-10; e-mail info@animalsci-tm.ro; internet www.animalsci-tm.ro):

ADRIAN, G., Aquaculture
BENONI, L., Animal Hygiene
CORNELIA, V., Processing and Animal Products Control
DAN, D., Biotechnologies in Animal Nutrition
EUGENIE, G., Management
GHORGHE, N., Animal Husbandry and Nutrition
IOAN, P., Sheep Breeding Technologies
LAVINIA, A., Animal Nutrition
MARIAN, B., Breeding of Fur-Bearing Animals, Bees and Small Animals
NECULAI, D., Fodder Production and Preservation
NICOLAE, P., Animal Reproduction
STELIAN, A., Bovine Breeding Technologies

Faculty of Farm Management:

CORNELIA, P., Growth of Products through Processing
IOAN, C., Rural Services
IOAN, P., Production Systems Modulation and Simulation
LIVIU, S., Production Management
NICOLETA, M., Agricultural Policies
PĂUN ION, O., Durable Development Management
VASILE, G., Financial Management

Faculty of Food Processing Technologies (Calea Aradului 119, 300645 Timişoara, Timiş; tel. (256) 27-70-04; fax (256) 27-73-26; e-mail secretariattpa@yahoo.com; internet tpa .usab-tm.ro):

ADRIAN, C., Organic Chemistry
ADRIAN, R., Food Contaminants
CONSTANTIN, M., Applied Physics
DOREL, P., Physical and Coloidal Chemistry
ERSILIA, A., Vegetable Origins Food Technologies
IONEL-VASILE, J., Food Industry General Technologies
IOSIF-IOAN, G., Agro-alimentary Products Analysis
MIHAI, D., Food Quality Control
TEODOR-IOAN, T., Food Industry Machines

Faculty of Horticulture and Forestry (Calea Aradului 119, 300645 Timişoara, Timiş; tel. (256) 27-70-06; internet www.horticultura .usab-tm.ro):

ALIN, D., Viticulture
ARSENIE, H., Special Vegetable Crops
AUREL, L., Agrotechnology
DAGMAR, V., Dendrology
DORICA, B., Industrial Biotechnologies
EMILIAM, M., Plant Improvement
GHORGHE, C., Soil Work Management
IRINA, P., Genetics
MARIA, B., Floriculture
MIHAELA, C., Genetics
OLIMPIA, I., Fruit Growing
RADU, A., Vegetable Physiology
SIMION, A., Soil Work Maintenance and Preparation Techniques
SORIN, C., Experimental Techniques
VIOREL, B., General Vegetable Crops

Faculty of Veterinary Medicine (Calea Aradului 119, 300645 Timişoara, Timiş; tel. (256) 27-71-18; fax (256) 27-70-08; e-mail office@ fmvt.ro; internet usab-tm.ro):

ALEXANDRA, T., Toxicology
CARMEN, G., Anatomy
CORNEL, I., Surgery Diseases
EMIL, T., Immunology
EUGENIU, C., Nutrition and Fodder Control
GHEORGHE, D., Parasitology
GHORGHE, B., Medical Genetics
HOREA, S., Physiology
HORIA, C., Reproduction, Obstetrics, Gynecology
IOAN, A., Entomology
IOAN, O., Forensics
ION, O., Animal Biology and Ecology
MARIAN, C., Pathological Anatomy
MIHAI, D., Animal Protection
NICOLAE, C., Infectious Diseases
ROMEO, C., Pharmacology
TEODOR, M., Medical Pathology
VASILE, A., Reproduction, Obstetrics, Gynaecology
VIOREL, H., Infectious Diseases

UNIVERSITATEA DE ŞTIINŢE AGRICOLE ŞI MEDICINĂ VETERINARĂ CLUJ-NAPOCA

Calea Mănăştur 3–5, 400372 Cluj-Napoca

Telephone: (264) 59-63-84
Fax: (264) 59-37-92
E-mail: contact@usamvcluj.ro
Internet: www.usamvcluj.ro

Founded 1869 as Institutul Agronomic; present name and status 1992
Rector: Prof. Dr DORU PAMFIL
Pres.: Prof. Dr LIVIU AL. MĂRGHITAŞ
Vice-Rector for Academic Affairs: Prof. Dr CORNEL CATOI
Vice-Rector for Admin. Affairs: Prof. Dr SEVASTIŢA MUSTE
Vice-Rector for Scientific Research: Prof. Dr AUGUSTIN VLAIC
Gen. Dir: VIOREL PORUŢIU

Library of 170,000 vols, 10,000 documents
Number of teachers: 267
Number of students: 6,202

Publications: *Agriculture* (magazine), *Bulletin of USAMV Cluj Napoca, Agriculture series* (B+), *Bulletin of USAMV Cluj Napoca, Animal Science and Biotechnology series* (B+), *Bulletin of USAMV Cluj Napoca, Horticulture series* (B+), *Bulletin of USAMV Cluj Napoca, Veterinary Medicine series* (B+), *Clujul Medical Veterinar*, *Hops and Medical Plants* (magazine), *Index Seminum, Notulae Botanicae Horti Agrobotanici Cluj Napoca (ISI), Scientia parasitological*

DEANS

Faculty of Agriculture: Prof. Dr IOAN ROTAR
Faculty of Animal Science and Biotechnology: Prof. Dr VIOARA MIRESAN
Faculty of Horticulture: Prof. Dr RADU SESTRAS
Faculty of Veterinary Medicine: Prof. Dr IOAN STEFAN GROZA

UNIVERSITATEA DE ŞTIINŢE AGRICOLE ŞI MEDICINĂ VETERINARĂ 'ION IONESCU DE LA BRAD' DIN IAŞI

Aleea Mihail Sadoveanu 3, 700490 Iaşi

Telephone: (232) 27-49-33
Fax: (232) 26-06-50
E-mail: rectorat@univagro-iasi.ro
Internet: www.univagro-iasi.ro

Founded 1912; present name 1990
Rector: Prof. Dr GERARD JITĂREANU

Vice-Rector for Didactic Activity: Prof. Dr VASILE VÎNTU

Vice-Rector for Social and Students' Issues: Prof. Dr GHEORGHE SAVUŢA

Vice-Rector for Scientific Activity: Prof. Dr VALERIU V. COTEA

Library of 112,597 vols, incl. 105,942 books and 6,655 periodicals

Publications: *Cercetari Agronomice in Moldova, Lucrări Ştiinţifice Editura* (1 a year)

DEANS

Faculty of Agriculture: Prof. Dr CONSTANTIN LEONTE

Faculty of Animal Science: Prof. Dr BENONE PĂSĂRIN

Faculty of Horticulture: Prof. Dr GICĂ GRĂDINARIU

Faculty of Veterinary Medicine: Prof. Dr OCTAVIAN ZAHARIE OPREAN

UNIVERSITATEA DE ŞTIINŢE AGRONOMICE ŞI MEDICINĂ VETERINARĂ DIN BUCUREŞTI
(University of Agricultural Sciences and Veterinary Medicine in Bucharest)

Bdul Mărăşti 59, 011464 Bucharest

Telephone: (21) 318-22-66
Fax: (21) 318-28-88
E-mail: post@info.usamv.ro
Internet: www.usab.ro

Founded 1852 as Institutul Agronomic 'N. Bălcescu'

Rector: Prof. Dr STEFAN DIACONESCU
Pres.: Prof. Dr IOAN-NICULAE ALECU

Library: see Libraries and Archives
Number of teachers: 495
Number of students: 4,573 (4,298 undergraduate, 275 postgraduate)

Publication: *Lucrări Ştiinţifice* (1 a year)

DEANS

Department of Land Improvement and Environmental Engineering: SORIN CÎMPEANU

Faculty of Agriculture: Prof. Dr COSTICĂ CIONTU

Faculty of Biotechnology: Prof. Dr PETRU NICULIŢĂ

Faculty of Horticulture: Prof. Dr DOREL HOZA

Faculty of Veterinary Medicine: Prof. Dr GABRIEL PREDOI

Faculty of Zoology: Prof. Dr VAN ILIE

UNIVERSITATEA MARITIMĂ DIN CONSTANŢA

Str. Mircea cel Bâtrân 104, 900663 Constanţa

Telephone: (241) 66-47-40
Fax: (241) 61-72-60
E-mail: info@imc.ro
Internet: www.cmu-edu.eu

Founded 1972
State control
Languages of instruction: English, Romanian
Academic year: October to June

Rector: Dr VIOLETA VALI CIUCUR
Vice-Rector for Academic Activity: Prof. Dr ELIODOR CONSTANTINESCU
Vice-Rector for Institutional Devt and Int. Relations: Prof. Dr CORNEL PANAIT
Vice-Rector for Research and Scientific Innovation: Dr EMIL OANŢĂ
Librarian: TANASE RALUCA

Library of 71,000 vols, 20 periodicals
Number of teachers: 96
Number of students: 6,407

Publications: *Constanta Maritime University Annals, Journal of Maritime Technology, Journal of Maritime Transport*

DEANS

Faculty of Naval Electromechanics: Prof. Dr GHEORGHE BORDEA

Faculty of Navigation and Naval Transport: Dr COSTEL STANCA

UNIVERSITATEA 'POLITEHNICA' DIN BUCUREŞTI

Splaiul Independenţei 313, 060042 Bucharest

Telephone: (21) 402-91-00
Fax: (21) 318-10-01
E-mail: relatii.publice@upb.ro
Internet: www.pub.ro

Founded 1818
State control
Academic year: October to July (2 semesters)

Rector: Prof. Dr Eng. ECATERINA ANDRONESCU
Vice-Rector for Financial Affairs: Prof. Dr MIHAI OCTAVIAN POPESCU
Vice-Rector for Graduate Education: Prof. Dr MARIN DRAGULINESCU
Vice-Rector for Int. Relations, European Integration and Partnership: Prof. Dr MARIAN GHEORGHE
Vice-Rector for Scientific Research: Prof. Dr SERBAN RAICU
Vice-Rector for Undergraduate Education: Prof. Dr DUMITRU CEZAR IONESCU
Scientific Sec.: Prof. Dr IULIAN RIPOSAN
Chief Admin. Officer: Prof. Dr GABRIEL IACOBESCU
Dir of the Int. Cooperation Dept: (vacant)
Librarian: Dr DUMITRU RADU POPESCU

Library: see Libraries and Archives
Number of teachers: 1,590
Number of students: 22,000

DEANS

Faculty of Aerospace Engineering: Prof. VIRGIL STANCIU

Faculty of Applied Sciences: Prof. CONSTANTIN UDRISTE

Faculty of Automatic Control and Computer Science: Prof. Dr DUMITRU POPESCU

Faculty of Biotechnical Systems Engineering: Prof. Dr GIGEL PARASCHIV

Faculty of Electrical Engineering: Prof. CLAUDIA POPESCU

Faculty of Electronics and Telecommunications: Prof. Dr TEODOR PETRESCU

Faculty of Engineering and Management of Technological Systems: Prof. Dr Ing. GHEORGHE AMZA

Faculty of Engineering Sciences Taught in Modern Languages: Prof. Dr Ing. ADRIAN VOLCEANOV

Faculty of Industrial Chemistry: Prof. Dr HORIA IOVU

Faculty of Materials Science and Engineering: Prof. Dr RAMI SABAN

Faculty of Mechanical Engineering: Prof. Dr Ing. TUDOR PRISECARU

Faculty of Power Engineering: Prof. GEORGE DARIE

Faculty of Transport Engineering: Prof. Dr CORNELIU MIHAIL ALEXANDRESCU

DIRECTORS

Technical College No. 1 (Mechanical College): Prof. Dr GHEORGHE SOLOMON

Technical College No. 2 (Electrical College): Dr ISTVAN SZTOJANOV

PROFESSORS

Faculty of Aerospace Engineering (Str. George Polizu, nr. 1, sector 1, 011061 Bucharest; tel. and fax 402-38-14; e-mail s_galetuse@aero.pub.ro; internet www.aero.pub.ro):

BERBENTE, C., Aircraft Engineering
GĂLETUŞE, S., Aircraft Engineering
STANCIU, V., Aircraft Engineering

Faculty of Automatic Control and Computer Science (Splaiul Independenţei 313, Sector 6, 060042 Bucharest; tel. (21) 402-94-94; fax (21) 410-10-14; e-mail dpopescu@indinf.pub.ro; internet www.acs.pub.ro):

ATHANASIU, I., Computer Science
BORANGIU, T., Robotics
CRISTEA, V., Computer Science
CUPCEA, N., Computer Science
DUMITRACHE, I., Control Engineering
GIUMALE, C., Computer Science
ILIESCU, S., Control Engineering
IONESCU, T., Control Engineering
IORGA, V., Computer Science
MOISA, T., Computer Science
NIŢU, C., Control Engineering
PETRESCU, A., Computer Science
POPEEA, C., Control Engineering
POPESCU, D., Control Engineering
STANESCU, A., Control Engineering
TĂPUŞ, N., Computer Science

Faculty of Biotechnical Systems Engineering (Splaiul Independenţei 313, Sector 6, 060042 Bucharest; tel. (21) 402-96-49; fax (21) 318-10-18; e-mail paraschiv2005@yahoo.com; internet www.isb.pub.ro):

DAVID, L., Agricultural Machines
MURAD, E., Agricultural Machines
PAUNESCU, I., Agricultural Machines

Faculty of Electrical Engineering (Splaiul Independenţei 313, Sector 6, body EA 123, 060042 Bucharest; tel. (21) 402-91-49; fax (21) 410-43-55; e-mail elth@electro.pub.ro; internet www.upb.ro):

CRĂCIUNESCU, A., Drive Systems
CRISTEA, P., Basic Electrical Engineering
FLUERAŞU, C., Basic Electrical Engineering
GALAN, N., Electrical Machines
GAVRILĂ, H., Basic Electrical Engineering
GOLOVANOV, C., Theory and Design of Electrical Apparatus
HĂNŢILĂ, I. F., Basic Electrical Engineering
IOAN, C. D., Basic Electrical Engineering
IONESCU, F., Theory and Design of Electrical Apparatus
MĂGUREANU, R., Micromachines and Drive Systems
MOREGA, AL., Electrical Materials
NOŢINGHER, P., Electrical Materials
POPESCU, M. O., Theory and Design of Electrical Apparatus
SPINEI, F., Basic Electrical Engineering
TĂNĂSESCU, F., Electrical Engineering
TOMESCU, F., Basic Electrical Engineering
TRUŞCĂ, V., Theory and Design of Electrical Apparatus

Faculty of Electronics and Telecommunications (Bdul Iuliu Maniu 1–3, Sector 6, 061071 Bucharest; tel. (21) 402-46-18; fax (21) 411-33-73; e-mail decanat@electronica.pub.ro; internet www.electronica.pub.ro):

BĂNICĂ, I., Telecommunications
BODEA, M., Electronic Devices and Circuits
BORCOCI, E., Telecommunications
BREZEANU, GH., Electronic Devices and Circuits
BURILEANU, L., Telecommunications
BUZULOIU, V., Information Theory
CONSTANTIN, I., Telecommunications
DASCĂLU, D., Electronic Devices and Circuits
DRAGULANESCU, N., Reliability
DRAGULIMISCU, M., Reliability
IANCU, O., Reliability
LĂZĂRESCU, V., Information Theory
MANOLESCU, A., Electronic Devices and Circuits
MANOLESCU, A. M., Electronic Devices and Circuits
PROFIRESCU, M., Electronic Devices and Circuits
RUSU, A., Electronic Devices and Circuits
STRUNGARU, R., Medical Engineering

SVASTA, P., Reliability

Faculty of Engineering and Management of Technological Systems (Splaiul Independenţei 313, Sector 6, 060042 Bucharest; tel. (21) 402-95-20; fax (21) 411-42-67; e-mail amza@camis.pub.ro; internet www.imst.pub.ro):

ANTONESCU, P., Mechanism Theory
AURITE, T., Machine Tools
CONSTANTINESCU, I., Strength of Materials
DORIN, A., Machine Tools
GHEORGHE, M., Machine-Building Technology
ILIESCU, N., Strength of Materials
ISPAS, C., Machine Tools
MINCIU, C., Machine Tools
NEAGU, C., Machine-Building Technology
POPESCU, I., Machine-Building Technology
RADEŞ, M., Strength of Materials
ZGURĂ, GH., Technology of Materials

Faculty of Industrial Chemistry (Str. Polizu 1, Bucharest; tel. and fax (21) 223-09-03):

ANDRONESCU, E., Silicate and Oxide Compounds Chemistry
BANCIU, M., Organic Chemistry
BOZGA, GH., Chemical Reactors
CONSTANTINESCU, I., Inorganic Chemical Technology
DIMONIE, M., Polymer Science
FILIPESCU, L., Inorganic Chemical Technology
GEANĂ, D., Physical Chemistry
GEORGESCU, M., Silicate and Oxide Compounds Chemistry
GURAN, C., Inorganic Chemistry
JINESCU, GH., Chemical Engineering
JITARU, I., Inorganic Chemistry
MEGHEA, A., Physical Chemistry
MUNTEAN, M., Silicate and Oxide Compounds Chemistry
RADU, C., Management in the Chemical Industry
RADU, D., Silicate and Oxide Compounds Chemistry
ROŞCA, S., Organic Chemistry
TARABAŞANU, C., Dyes
VASILESCU, D. S., Polymer Science
VIŞAN, T., Physical Chemistry and Electrochemical Technology
WOINAROSCHY, E. A., Chemical Engineering

Faculty of Materials Science and Engineering (Splaiul Independenţei 313, Sector 6, 060042 Bucharest; tel. (21) 402-96-24; fax (21) 410-39-85; e-mail decanat@sim.pub.ro; internet www.sim.pub.ro):

BOJIN, D., Metallurgy of Non-Ferrous Metals
BRATU, C., Forge and Foundry Technology
BUNEA, D., Forge and Foundry Technology
COJOCARU, M., Metallurgy of Non-Ferrous Metals
MOLDOVAN, P., Metallurgy of Non-Ferrous Metals
PANAIT, N., Metallurgy of Non-Ferrous Metals
RIPOŞAN, I., Forge and Foundary Technology
TALOI, D., Metallurgy of Non-Ferrous Metals
ZAMFIR, S., Metallurgy of Non-Ferrous Metals

Faculty of Mechanical Engineering (Splaiul Independenţei 313, Sector 6, 060042 Bucharest; tel. (21) 402-94-35; fax (21) 410-42-51; e-mail tudor.prisecaru@upb.ro; internet www.mecanica.home.ro):

ALEXANDRESCU, N., Fine Mechanics
BRĂTIANU, C., Thermomechanical Equipment
JINESCU, V., Thermomechanical Equipment
MARINESCU, M., Thermodynamics
MICU, C., Fine Mechanics
MIHAIESCU, L., Thermomechanical Equipment
PANA, C., Internal Combustion Engines
PASCOVICI, M., Machine Elements
PASCU, A., Fine Mechanics
PETRESCU, S., Thermodynamics
TUDOR, A., Machine Elements

Faculty of Power Engineering (Splaiul Independenţei 313, Sector 6, 060042 Bucharest; tel. (21) 402-94-33; fax (21) 410-43-50; e-mail facultatea.energetica@gmail.com; internet www.energ.pub.ro):

ATHANASOVICI, V., Electric Power Plants
BADEA, A., Electric Power Plants
COATU, S., High Voltage Technology
CRISTESCU, D., High Voltage Technology
EREMIA, M., High Voltage Technology
GOLOVANOV, N., High Voltage Technology
HURDUBETIU, S., High Voltage Technology
IONESCU, D. C., Reliability
ISBĂŞOIU, E., Hydraulics
NISTREANU, V., Hydraulics
PANAITESCU, V., Hydraulics
POSTOLACHE, P., High Voltage Technology
ROBESCU, D. N., Hydraulics
SETEANU, I., Hydraulics
VASILIU, N., Hydraulics

Faculty of Transport Engineering (Splaiul Independenţei 313, Sector 6, 060042 Bucharest; tel. (21) 402-95-68; fax (21) 411-16-59; e-mail cma@eltrans.pub.ro):

ALEXANDRESCU, C., Remote Controls and Electronics
FRĂŢILĂ, GH., Automotive Engineering
NEGRUŞ, E., Automotive Engineering
RAICU, Ş., Transport Engineering
SEBEŞAN, I., Railway Vehicles
STOICESCU, A., Automotive Engineering
TANASUICA, I., Transport Engineering

UNESCO Department (tel. (21) 402-94-75; fax (21) 402-93-87; e-mail leca@eeee.unesco.pub.ro):

LECA, A., Environment

Basic Training:

BLANDU, M., Modern Languages
CRAIU, M., Mathematical Analysis
ENESCU, N., Mechanics
FLONDOR, P., Mathematical Analysis
STAICU, M., Mechanics
STĂNĂŞILĂ, O., Algebra, Mathematical Analysis
UDRIŞTE, C., Special Mathematics

UNIVERSITATEA 'POLITEHNICA' DIN TIMIŞOARA

Piaţa Victoriei 2, 300006 Timişoara
Telephone: (256) 40-30-00
Fax: (256) 40-30-21
E-mail: rector@rectorat.upt.ro
Internet: www.upt.ro
Founded 1920; attached to The Romanian Agency for Quality Assurance in Higher Education
State control
Language of instruction: English, French, German, Romanian
Academic year: October to July
Rector: Prof. Dr Eng. NICOLAE ROBU
Vice-Rector: Prof. Dr Eng. VIOREL-AUREL SERBAN
Vice-Rector: Prof. Dr Eng. CORNELIU DAVIDESCU
Vice-Rector: Prof. Dr Eng. SEVASTEAN IANCA
Scientific Sec.: Prof. Dr Eng. RADU VASIU
Chief Sec.: Prof. A. GASPAR
Admin. Dir: Dr Eng. FLORENTIU STAICU
Dir of the Library: ERICA OTESTEANU
Library of 500,000 vols
Number of teachers: 887
Number of students: 15,000
Publication: *Research Report* (1 a year)

DEANS

Centre for Continuing Education: VASILE RUSET
Dept of Mathematics: Prof. Dr OCTAVIAN LIPOVAN
Dept of Physical Foundations of Engineering: Prof. Dr DUMITRU TOADER
E-learning Centre: Dr DIANA ANDONE
Faculty of Architecture: Prof. Dr SMARANDA BICA
Faculty of Civil Engineering: GHEORGHE LUCACI
Faculty of Communication Sciences: Prof. Dr RODICA SUPERCEANU
Faculty of Computers and Automatization: Prof. Dr Eng. OCTAVIAN PROŞTEAN
Faculty of Electronics and Telecommunications: Prof. Dr Eng. MARIUS OTEŞTEANU
Faculty of Electrotechnical Engineering: Prof. Dr Eng. PETRU ANDEA
Faculty of Engineering (Hunedoara): TEODOR HEPUT
Faculty of Hydrotechnical Engineering: Prof. Dr Eng. TEODOR EUGEN MAN
Faculty of Industrial Chemistry and Environmental Engineering: Prof. Dr Eng. LUCIAN RUSNAC
Faculty of Management in Production and Transportation: Prof. Dr Ing. MONICA IZVERCIANU
Faculty of Mechanical Engineering: Prof. Dr Eng. LIVIU BERETEU

PROFESSORS

Faculty of Civil Engineering:

BĂNCILĂ, R., Steel Structures
BOB, C., Chemistry and Construction Materials
BOTICI, A., Statics, Stability and Dynamics of Constructions
CADAR, I., Reinforced Concrete Structures
CARABA, I., Steel Structures
CIOBANU, G., English
CLIPII, T., Reinforced Concrete Structures
COSTESCU, I., Road Design and Construction
CUTEANU, E., Strength of Materials
DIMOIU, I., Earthquake Engineering
DUBINA, D., Construction
FURDUI, C., Civil Construction
GĂDIANU, L., Steel Structures
GAVRA, C. S., History of Architecture
GHEORGHIU, T., Urbanism, Architecture Design
GIONCU, V. M., Structures
GRUIA, A., Soil Mechanics and Foundation Engineering
HAIDA, V., Soil Mechanics and Foundation Engineering
IANCA, S., Civil Engineering, Architecture and Urbanism
IVAN, M., Statics, Stability and Dynamics
JIVA, C., Concrete Bridges
MARIN, M., Soil Mechanics and Foundation Engineering
MERCEA, G., Steel Structures
NEAMŢU, M., Topography
PATCAS, I., Steel Structures
PODRUMAR, D. G., Heating Installations
REGEP, Z., Steel Structures
RETEZAN, A., Installations
SÂRBU, I., Numerical Methods in Installations Optimization
SCHEIN, T., Soil Mechanics and Foundation Engineering
STOIAN, V., Civil Construction
TOMA, A., Technologies and Mechanization in Civil Engineering
TUDOR, D., Civil Construction

Faculty of Computers and Automatization (Bdul Vasile Pârvan 2, 300223 Timişoara; tel. (256) 40-32-11; fax (256) 40-32-14; e-mail secretariat@ac.upt.ro; internet www.ac.upt.ro):

BREABAN, F., Biomedical Engineering

CIOCARLIE, H., Numerical Processing of Signals
CRETU, V., Advanced Data Structures and Programming Techniques
CRIȘAN, M., Artificial Intelligence
DRAGOMIR, T.-L., Systems Theory
ELES, P., Programming Techniques
HOLBAN, S., Basis of Artificial Intelligence
JIAN, I., Database Design and Use
JURCĂ, I., Operating Systems Design
PREITL, S., Automatic Adjustment Engineering
PROSTEAN, O., System Identification
ROBU, N., Neuronal Networks
STRATULAT, M., Creation of Interfaces, Circuits
STRUGARU, C., Peripheral Devices and Data Transmission
VLĂDUTIU, M., Computer Reliability

Faculty of Electronics and Telecommunications (Bdul Vasile Pârvan 2, 300223 Timișoara; tel. (256) 40-32-91; fax (256) 40-32-95; internet www.etc.upt.ro):

BOGDANOV, I., Robotics
CARSTEA, H., Electronic Equipment Testing and Control
CHIVU, M., Electric and Electronic Measurements
CIUGUDEAN, M., Integrated Circuits and Electronics
CRISAN, S., Electronic Measurements
IGNEA, A., Electric and Electronic Measurements
IONEL, S., Statistics Processing of Signals
ISAR, A., Signals, Circuits, Systems
MUREȘAN, T., Integrated Circuits and Electronics
NAFORNIȚĂ, I., Signals Processing
NAFORNIȚA, M., Data Transfer, Modern Communications Networks
OTESTEANU, M., Television
POLICEC, A., Communications Systems and Techniques
POPESCU, V., Power Electronics
TĂNASE, M., Electronics
TIPONUT, V., Electronic Devices
TOMA, C., Television
TOMA, L., Data Acquisition Systems

Faculty of Electrotechnical Engineering (Bdul V. Pârvan 2, 300223 Timișoara; tel. (256) 40-33-81; fax (256) 40-33-84; e-mail decanat@et.upt.ro; internet www.et.upt.ro):

ANDEA, P., Electrical Apparatus Technology
ATANASIU, G., Special Electrical Machines
BABESCU, M., Electrical Machines
BANZAR, T., Mathematics
BARTZER, S., Technology of Electrical Products
BIRIESCU, M., Electromechanical Systems Testing
BOJA, N., Mathematics
BOLDEA, I., Electrical Machines
BUTTA, A., Power Delivery
CONSTANTIN, I., Mathematics
CRĂCIUN, P., Physics
CRISTEA, M., Physics
DABA, D., Theoretical Electrotechnics
DELESEGA, I., Electrical Apparatus and Equipment Testing
DOBRE, S., Electrotechnics
DUȘA, V., Optimization Techniques in Industrial Energetics
GHEJU, P., Industrial Power Systems and Networks
HEINRICH, I., Stations and Transformation Posts
HELER, A., Electrotechnics and Electric Machines
IVASCU, C., Automation and Power Systems Protection
KILYENI, S., Numerical Methods in Engineering
LIPOVAN, O., Mathematics

LUSTREA, B., Basis of Energetics and Energy Conversion
MARCU, C., Physics
MIHALCA, I., Physics
MOGA, B., Microprocessors in Electroenergetics
MOLDOVAN, L., Electric Equipment
NEAGU, M., Mathematics
NEGRU, V., High-Voltage Engineering
NEMEȘ, M., Electrical Power Systems
NICA, E., Electrical Machines
POPOVICI, D., Electrical Drives
RADU, D., Non-linear Electrotechnics
SORA, I., Electroheat, Electrotechnology, Electrical Lighting
TOADER, D., Electromechanical Engineering
VASILIEVICI, A., Electrical Equipment
VELICESCU, C., Power Systems and Network Viability
VETRES, I., Basis of Electrotechnics

Faculty of Engineering (Hunedoara) (Str. Revoluției 5, 331128 Hunedoara; tel. (254) 20-75-02; fax (254) 20-75-01; e-mail decan@fih.upt.ro; internet www.fih.upt.ro):

ILCA, I., Technology of Plastic Deformation
SAIMAC, A., Electrotechnics

Faculty of Hydrotechnical Engineering (George Enescu St 1A. 300022 Timișoara; tel. (256) 40-40-81; fax (256) 40-40-83; e-mail decan@hidro.upt.ro; internet www.hidro.upt.ro):

CIOMOCOS, F., Strength of Materials
CRETU, G., Hydrology, Water Resources Supply
DANILESCU, A., Statics, Stability and Dynamics of Construction
DAVID, A., Hydraulics, Transport, Groundwater Pollution Modelling
DOANDES, V., Topography, Road Topography
ION, M., Hydrotechnical Construction
IONESCU, N., Machines for Construction, Irrigation and Drainage
MAN, E. T., Irrigation and Drainage
MARTON, A., Ecology, Ecotoxicology
MIREL, I., Water Supply and Town Drainage
NICOARĂ, T., Hydraulics
POPA, G., Hydrotechnical Construction
PRELUSCHEK, E., Hydrotechnical Construction
ROGOBETE, G., Improvement of Soils and Polluted Areas
WEHRY, A., Irrigation and Drainage

Faculty of Industrial Chemistry and Environmental Engineering (Piața Victoriei 2, 300006 Timișoara; tel. (256) 40-30-63; fax (256) 40-30-60; e-mail secretar.sef@chim.upt.ro; internet www.chim.upt.ro):

BURTICA, G., Mineral Salts Technology
CSUNDERLIK, C., Organic Chemistry
DAESCU, C., Pharmaceutical Products
IOVI, A., Technology of Mineral Fertilizers
LAZĂU, I., Physical Chemistry
LUPEA, A. X., Pharmaceutical Products
NUȚIU, M., Organic Chemistry
OPRESCU, D., General Chemistry
PERJU, D., Process Modelling
PETCA, G., Technology of General Chemistry, Water and Waste Water Technology
PUGNA, I., Chemical Industry

Faculty of Management in Production and Transportation (Str. Remus 14, 300289 Timișoara; tel. (256) 40-42-84; fax (256) 40-42-87; e-mail office@mpt.upt.ro; internet www.mpt.upt.ro):

DĂNILĂ, C., Harvesting Machines
DUMITRESCU, C., Ergonomics, Quality Engineering
GLĂVAN, S., Agrobiological Basis of Agricultural Mechanics
IZVERCIAN, M., Management
NICA, C., Zootechnical Machines

POCINOG, G., Modelling, Simulation and Study of Production
POPA, H., Management and Industrial Engineering
SABAU, C., Finances, Accounting, Ergonomic Analysis, Management
ȘTEFAN, C., Agricultural Engineering
TAROATA, A., Marketing, Industrial Engineering

Faculty of Mechanical Engineering (Bdul Mihai Viteazu 1, 300222 Timișoara; tel. (256) 40-35-21; fax (256) 40-35-23; e-mail cab_robu@rectorat.upt.ro; internet www.mec.upt.ro):

ANCUSA, V., Fluid Mechanics, Transport Phenomena
BABEU, T., Theory of Elasticity and Strength of Materials
BACRIA, V., Mechanics
BAGIU, L., Electromechanical Engineering
BALAȘOIU, V., Hydropneumatic Equipment
BALEKICS, M., Machine Elements
BĂRGLĂZAN, M., Hydraulic Turbines
BRESTIN, A., Technology of Materials
BRÎNDEU, L., Mechanics and Vibration
BUDĂU, V., Materials, Quality Control
CARTE, I., Hydraulic Machines
CARTIS, I., Heat Treatment
CHIRIAC, A., Robotics and Automation in the Textile Industry
CRISTUINEA, C., Theory of Elasticity
CRUDU, M., Mechanisms
CUCURUZ, L., Materials, Casting
DAVID, I., Tolerances
DOBRE, I., Theory of Elasticity and Strength of Materials
DOLGA, V., Mechanical Engineering
DRĂGHICI, G., Manufacturing Engineering
DRĂGULESCU, D., Mechanical Engineering
DUMITRU, I., Technical Mechanics, Strength of Materials
DUNGAN, M., Calculus and Construction of Weight-bearing Structures of Railway Rolling Stock
FAUR, N., Elasticity and Strength of Materials
FLESER, T., Quality Control
GHEORGHIU, M., Mechanics of Fluids and Hydraulic Machines
GLIGOR, O., Components for Precision Mechanics Devices
GLIGOR, T., Mechanics
GLITA, G., Non-Conventional Welding Technologies
HEGEDUS, A., Mechanics
HERMAN, R., Technology Systems and Adjustments
HOANCĂ, V., Thermal Engines
ICLĂNZAN, T., Plastics Manufacturing
IONEL, I., Combustion and Environmental Impact of Stationary Combustion Facilities
IONESCU, N., Mechanisms
IORGA, D., Internal Combustion Engines
JADANEANȚ, M., Thermotechnics
KOVACS, A., Mathematics
LĂNCRĂNGEAN, Z., Technology of Materials
MĂDĂRAS, L., Machine Elements
MANIU, I., Dynamics, Construction and Design of Robotic Systems
MARCUSANU, A., Tolerances
MARINA, M., Mechanisms
MARINCA, V., Mechanics
MESAROȘ, A., Mechatronics, Mechanics
MILOȘ, L., Welding
MITELEA, I., Materials Science
NAGI, M., Thermic Devices, Heat and Mass Transfer
NEGREA, V. D., Internal Combustion Engines
NEGUT, N., Elasticity and Strength of Materials
NICA, C. M., Basic Experimental Research
NICHICI, A., Technology of Materials
NICOARĂ, I., Optical Devices

OPREA, M., Anti-Corrosive Protection Technologies, Materials Technology
PERJU, D., Mechanisms
POMMERSHEIM, A., Programming Languages
POPOVICI, I., Technology of Materials
POPOVICI, V., Welding Equipment
RADULESCU, C., Robotics, Industrial Robots
SAFTA, V., Welding Control and Welded Constructions
SANTĂU, I., Pumping Services
SAVII, G., Computer-Aided Design
SERBAN, V., Materials and Primary Technologies
SMICALĂ, I., Mechanics
SPOREA, I., Materials Technology
SURU, P., Management and Marketing, Computer-Aided Design
TOADER, M., Mechanics
TUCU, D., Technologies and Machines for the Food Industry
URDEA, G., Machine Tools
VACARESCU, I., Biomedical Apparatus

UNIVERSITATEA TEHNICĂ DE CONSTRUCȚII BUCUREȘTI
(Bucharest Technical University of Civil Engineering)

Bdul Lacul Tei 122–124, Sector 2, 020396 Bucharest

Telephone: (21) 242-12-08
Fax: (21) 242-07-81
E-mail: secretariat@utcb.ro
Internet: www.utcb.ro

Founded 1864

Rector: Prof. Dr Ing. JOHAN NEUNER
Pro-Rectors: Prof. Dr Ing. ANTHONY CHIRITA, Prof. Dr Ing. ANTON ANTON, Prof. Dr Ing. MICHAEL TOMA
Scientific Sec.: Prof. Dr RADU DROBOT

Library of 560,000 vols
Number of teachers: 530
Number of students: 6,964

Publication: Științific Journal (Scientific Bulletin, 4 a year)

DEANS

Faculty of Bridges, Roads and Railways: Prof. Dr Ing. MIHAI DICU
Faculty of Civil, Industrial and Agricultural Buildings: Prof. Dr Ing. DANIELA PREDA
Faculty of Engineering in Foreign Languages: Prof. Dr Ing. NICOLETA RADULESCU
Faculty of Geodesy: Prof. Dr Ing. DUMITRU ONOSE
Faculty of Hydrotechnic: Prof. Dr Ing. IOAN BICA
Faculty of School Equipment: Prof. Eng. SERBAN LAZAR
Faculty of Technological Equipment: Prof. Dr Ing. ION DAVID

UNIVERSITATEA TEHNICĂ DIN CLUJ-NAPOCA

St Memorandumului 28, 4000114 Cluj-Napoca

Telephone: (264) 40-12-00
Fax: (264) 59-16-90
E-mail: int.rel.office@staff.utcluj.ro
Internet: www.utcluj.ro

Founded 1948

Languages of instruction: English, German, Romanian
Academic year: October to July

Rector: Prof. Dr Eng. RADU MUNTEANU
Deputy Rector: Prof. Dr Eng. AUREL VLAICU
Deputy-Rector: Prof. Dr Eng. MIRCEA PETRINA
Deputy Rector: Prof. Dr Eng. IOAN ABRUDAN
Deputy Rector: Prof. Dr Eng. TIBERIU RUSU
Deputy Rector: Prof. Dr Eng. MIHAIL ABRUDEAN

Registrar: Dr Eng. LIA CHIOREAN
Library: see Libraries and Archives
Number of teachers: 660
Number of students: 15,000

Publications: ACAM-Automation, Computer Science and Applied Mathematics, Acta Technica Napocensis, Logi A, Scientific Bulletin of the Cluj-Napoca Technical University (1 a year)

DEANS

Faculty of Architecture and Urban Planning: Prof. Dr Eng. ADRIANA MATEI
Faculty of Automation and Computer Science: Prof. Dr Eng. SERGIU NEDEVSCHI
Faculty of Building Services: Prof. Dr. Eng. GHEORGHE BADEA
Faculty of Civil Engineering: Prof. Dr Eng. MIHAI ILIESCU
Faculty of Electrical Engineering: Prof. Dr Ing. RADU CIUPA
Faculty of Electronics and Telecommunications: Prof. Dr MARINA TOPA
Faculty of Machine Building: Prof. Dr Eng. PETRU BERCE
Faculty of Materials Science and Engineering: Prof. Dr Eng. VIDA SIMITI
Faculty of Mechanical Engineering: Prof. Dr Eng. NICOLAE BURNETE

PROFESSORS

Faculty of Architecture and Urban Planning (Str. Observator 72–76, 3400 Cluj-Napoca; tel. (264) 59-18-12; fax (264) 59-09-13; e-mail moldovanms@hotmail.com; internet www.utcluj.ro/utcn/arch):

MATEI, A., Architectural Composition
MOLDOVAN, M., History of World Architecture, Aesthetics, History of Arts
MURADIN, C., Styles of Furniture
SZABO, B., Theory of Structures and Renovation of Constructions

Faculty of Automation and Computer Science (Str. G. Barițiu 26–28, 400027 Cluj-Napoca; tel. (264) 40-12-18; fax (264) 19-48-35; internet ac.utcluj.ro):

CĂMPEANU, V., Mathematical Analysis
COLOSI, T., Theory of Systems, Automation
COROVEI, I., Algebra, Special Mathematics
CRIVEI, I., Algebra, Mathematical Analysis
DĂDÂRLAT, T., Digital Circuits
FEȘTILĂ, C., Control Structures and Algorithms
GANSCA, I., Mathematical Analysis
GAVREA, I., Calculus
GORGAN, D., Fundamentals of Computer Graphics
IGNAT, I., Operating Systems
IVAN, D. M., Numerical Analysis, Mathematical Analysis
LAZEA, GH., Theory of Robot Control
LEȚIA, I. A., Real Time Control
LUNG, N., Special Mathematics
NEDEVSCHI, S., Design with Microchips
OPRIȘ, GH., Special Mathematics, Differential Equations
PUSZTAI, K., Computer Networks
RASA, I., Numerical Mathematics
SALOMIE, I., Design Techniques
TOADER, GH., Mathematical Analysis
VORNICESCU, N., Differential Equations, Mathematical Analysis

Faculty of Civil Engineering (Str. G. Baritiu 25, 400027 Cluj-Napoca; tel. (264) 40-12-49; fax (264) 59-49-67; internet constructii.utcluj.ro):

ALEXA, P., Theoretical Mechanics, Structural Dynamics, Structural Stability
ANDREICA, H., Timber Structures
BADEA, G., Water Supplies and Sewerage
BÂRSAN, G., Theoretical Mechanics, Structural Dynamics, Structural Stability
BIA, C., Strength of Materials, Theory of Elasticity

BORȘ, I., Theoretical Mechanics, Numerical Methods
BRUMARU, M., Buildings
BUCUR, I., Reinforced Concrete Structures
CĂTĂRIG, A., Structural Analysis
CHIOREAN, T., Economics of the Construction Industry, Management and Organization
CHISĂLIȚĂ, A., Theoretical Mechanics, Numerical Methods, Cable and Hinged Structures, Non-Linear Analysis
COMȘA, E., Buildings
CORDOȘ, GH., Sociology
DOMȘA, J., Construction Technology
DUMITRAȘ, M., Buildings
HOSSU, T., Management in Civil Engineering
ILIESCU, M., Road Engineering
IOANI, A., Strength of Materials, Theory of Elasticity
IONESCU, A., Reinforced Concrete Structures
JURCĂU, N., Psychology
KOPENETZ, L., Computer-Aided Engineering and Design, Structural Analysis, Lightweight Structures
MĂGUREANU, C., Reinforced and Prestressed Concrete
MARȚIAN, I., Strength of Materials, Theory of Elasticity
MOGA, A., Construction Technology
MOGA, I., Thermotechnology
MOGA, P., Metal Bridges
NISTOR, I., History of Culture and Civilization
OLARIU, I., Structural Analysis
ONEȚ, T., Reinforced and Prestressed Concrete
OPRIȚOIU, A., Heat Engineering
PĂCURAR, V., Steel Structures
PANTEL, E., Strength of Materials, Theory of Elasticity, Numerical Methods
PETRINA, M., Structural Analysis, Computer Programming
POP, F., Electric Installation
POP, I., Seismic Engineering
POPA, A., Soil Mechanics and Foundations
VERDEȘ, D., Agricultural Buildings, Physics of Construction
VIOREL, G., Concrete Bridges

Faculty of Electrical Engineering (Str. G. Barițiu 26–28, 400027 Cluj-Napoca; tel. (264) 40-12-28; e-mail decanatet@utcluj.ro; internet ie.utcluj.ro):

BĂLAN, H., Electrical Equipment
BIRO, K., Electrical Machines
CATANĂ, D., Marketing
CATANĂ, GH., Marketing
CHINDRIȘ, M., Technological Design of Management Systems
CIUPA, R., Principles of Electronics
DARIE, S., Electrical Power Stations, Electrical Apparatus
DRAGOMIR, N., Electrical Measuring
IANCU, V., Electrical Machines
IMECS, M., Theory of Automatic Control Systems
IUGA, A., Electrotechnical Engineering
MAIER, V., Electrothermics
MAN, E., Elements of Electrotechnics
MARSCHALKO, R., Electronics
MICU, D., Electrical Engineering
MUNTEANU, R., Data Acquisition, Sensors and Control
RĂDULESCU, M., Electrical Drives
SIMION, E., Non-linear Circuits, Basic Electrical Engineering
TÂRNOVAN, I. G., Electronic Measurements
TODORAN, GH., Electrical Measurements
TRIFA, V., Applied Informatics and Microprocessor Systems
VIOREL, A., Electrical Machines

Faculty of Electronics and Telecommunications (Str. G. Barițiu 26–28, 400027 Cluj-Napoca; tel. and fax (264) 59-16-89; e-mail

aurel.vlaicu@com.utcluj.ro; internet www
.utcluj.ro/utcn/eltc):

BORDA, M., Information Theory
DOBROTĂ, V., Telecommunications
FEȘTILĂ, L., Analogical Integrated Circuits
LUNGU, Ș., Electronics
MIRON, C., Electronics
PITICĂ, D., Applied Electronics
RUSU, C., Signal Processing
TODEREAN, G., Communications Engineering
VAIDA, M., Informatics
VLAICU, A., Multimedia Systems
VOICULESCU, E., Optoelectronics
ZĂHAN, S., Telecommunications

Faculty of Machine Building (Bdul Muncii
103–105, 3400 Cluj-Napoca; tel. (264) 41-50-
51; fax (264) 41-50-54; e-mail gheorghe
.achimas@tcm.utcluj.ro; internet zeus.east
.utcluj.ro/mb):

ABRUDAN, I., Production Systems
ACHIMAȘ, GH., Metal Forming
ANTAL, A., Machine Components
ARGHIR, M., Computer Programming
BANABIC, D., Manufacturing Technologies
BERCE, P., Manufacturing Technologies
BLEBEA, I., Industrial Robots
BOJAN, I., Management Information Systems
CÂNDEA, D., Industrial Management
CĂZILĂ, A., Machine Components
CREȚU, M., Machine Tools and Industrial Robots
DEACU, L., Hydraulics
GALIȘ, M., Design of Machine Tools
GYENGE, CS., Manufacturing Technologies
IANCĂU, H., Plastics
ISPAS, V., Mechanics, Robotics
ITU, T., Technical Measurements
MORAR, L., Numerical Control
NEGREAN, L., Mechanics
OLTEANU, R., Manufacturing Technology
PLITEA, N., Mechanics
POP, D., Machine Components
POP, I., Hydraulics
POPA, M., Unconventional Technologies
POPESCU, S., Mechanics
PRUNEA, P., Economics
ROȘ, O., Manufacturing Technologies
SUCALĂ, F., Machine Components
URSU-FISCHER, N., Computer Programming

Faculty of Materials Scienceand Engineering
(Bdul Muncii 103–105, 400641 Cluj-Napoca;
tel. (264) 41-50-51; fax (264) 41-50-54; e-mail
trusu@sim.east.utcluj.ro; internet www
.utcluj.ro/utcn/facsim):

ARGHIR, G., Crystallography
BICSAK, E., Science of Materials, Welded Constructions Technology
BIRIȘ, I., Heat Processes in Metallurgical Furnaces
CÂNDEA, V., Materials Science
CANTA, T., Plastic Deformation Theory
COMAN, S., Mechanical Engineering, Mechanical Technology
COSMA, I., Physics
CULEA, E., Physics
DEMCO, D., Physics
DOMȘA, S., Materials Technology
IANCU, D., Heat and Thermochemical Treatment Technologies
LUCACI, P., Physics
LUPȘA, I., Physics
MILEA, I., Physics
MILITARU, V., Physics
NAGY, E., Steel Casting
NAȘCU, H., Chemistry
ORBAN, R., Materials Technology
PICĂ, M., Chemistry
POP, O., Physics
RUSU, T., Quality Management, Environmental Protection
SOPORAN, V., Technology for Casting Alloys

SPÂRCHEZ, Z., Composite Materials, Metallurgical Physics
VERMEȘAN, G., Heat and Thermochemical Treatment Technologies
VIDA, S., Materials Manufacturing Technology

Faculty of Mechanical Engineering (Bdul
Muncii 103–105, 400641 Cluj-Napoca; tel.
(264) 41-50-51; fax (264) 41-54-90; e-mail
cordos_n@yahoo.fr; internet www.east.utcluj
.ro/mec):

APAHIDEAN, B., Thermodynamics
BĂȚAGĂ, N., Heat Machines
BEJAN, M., Strength of Materials
BRÂNZAȘ, P., Management and Marketing
BURNETE, N., Automobiles and Tractors
CORDOȘ, N., Vehicle Dynamics
CREȚU, A., Strength of Materials
HĂRDĂU, M., Strength of Materials
MĂDĂRĂȘAN, T., Thermodynamics and Thermal Machines
MĂTIEȘ, V., Mechanics
ROȘ, V., Forming Machines

UNIVERSITATEA TEHNICĂ 'GHEORGHE ASACHI' DIN IAȘI
('Gheorghe Asachi' Technical University of Iași)

Strada Prof. Dr. Docent Dimitrie Mangeron, 700050 Iași

Telephone: (232) 27-86-83
Fax: (232) 21-16-67
E-mail: international@tuiasi.ro
Internet: www.tuiasi.ro

Founded 1937, present name and status 1993
State control
Languages of instruction: English, French, Romanian
Academic year: October to October

Rector: Prof. Dr Ing. ION GIURMA
Vice-Rector for Academic Affairs: Prof. Dr MIRCEA DAN GUȘĂ
Vice-Rector for Scientific Research: Prof. Dr CARMEN TEODOSIU
Vice-Rector for International Relations and University Image: Prof. Dr HORIA-NICOLAI TEODORESCU
Scientific Sec.: Prof. Dr DAN GELU GALUȘĂ
Registrar: GABRIELA IURCAN
Librarian: MIHAELA ȘTIRBU

Library: see Libraries and Archives
Number of teachers: 1,164
Number of students: 10,117

Publications: *Environmental Engineering and Management Journal*, *Review Magazine* (2 a year), *Scientific Bulletin* (2 a year), *The Bulletin of the Polytechnic Institute of Iași*

DEANS

Cross-Border Faculty of Engineering (in collaboration with Technical University of Moldova): Prof. GH. NISTOR
Faculty of Architecture 'G. M. Cantacuzino': Prof. Dr Arch. VIRGILU CAȘCAVAL
Faculty of Automatic Control and Computer Engineering: Prof. Dr Ing. VASILE MANTA
Faculty of Chemical Engineering and Environmental Protection: Prof. Dr Ing. DAN CAȘCAVA
Faculty of Civil Engineering and Building Services: Prof. Dr Ing. NICOLAE TĂRANU
Faculty of Electrical Engineering: Prof. Dr Ing. ALEXANDRU SALCEANU
Faculty of Electronics, Telecommunications and Information Technology: Prof. Dr Ing. ION BOGDAN
Faculty of Hydrotechnical Engineering, Geodesy and Environmental Engineering: Prof. Dr Ing. DORIN COTIUSCA
Faculty of Machine Manufacturing and Industrial Management: Prof. Dr Ing. GHEORGHE NAGÎȚ

Faculty of Materials Science and Engineering: Prof. Dr Ing. IULIAN IONIĂȚ
Faculty of Mechanical Engineering: Prof. Dr Ing. VIOREL CHIRILĂ
Faculty of Textiles and Leather Engineering and Industrial Management: Prof. Dr Ing. CARMEN LOGHIN

PROFESSORS

Faculty of Architecture 'G. M. Cantacuzino'
(Bdul Dimitrie Mangeron 43, 700050 Iași; tel.
(232) 27-86-80; fax (232) 21-15-95; e-mail
arhitect@ce.tuiasi.ro; internet www.tuiasi
.ro):

BLIUC, I., Building Elements
ONOFREI, V., Architectural Theory

Faculty of Chemical Engineering and Environmental Protection (Bdul Dimitrie Mangeron 73, 700050 Iași; tel. (232) 27-86-83;
fax (232) 27-13-11; e-mail decanat@ch.tuiasi
.ro; internet www.ch.tuiasi.ro):

AELENEI, N., Physical Chemistry
APOSTOLESCU, M., Mineralogy
BALASANIAN, I., Technology of Inorganic Substances
BEZDADEA, M., General Chemistry
BOBU, E., Equipment in the Pulp and Paper Industry
BULACOVSCHI, V., Macromolecular Chemistry
CIOVICĂ, S., Paper Technology
CRISTIAN, GH., Equipment for Organic Industry
DĂRÂNGĂ, M., Physical Chemistry of Polymers
DUMITRIU, E., Organic Technology
GAVRILESCU, D., Pulp and Paper Technology
GORDUZA, V., Technology of Dyes
GRIGORIU, I., Equipment for Inorganic Technology
IVĂNOIU, M., Physical Chemistry of Polymers
LAZĂR, D., Electrochemistry
LUCA, C., General Chemistry
LUNGU, M., Rheology of Polymers
MACOVEANU, M., General Technology
MIHĂILESCU, C., Physico-Chemistry of Polymers
NICU, M., Technology of Polymers
NICU, V., General Technology
OBROCEA, P., Pulp and Paper Technology
ONISCU, C., Technology of Synthetic and Biosynthetic Drugs
ONU, P., General Chemistry
OPREA, CL., Mechano-chemistry of Polymers, Monomers and Polymer Technology
OPREA, SP., Chemical Organic Technology
PETRESCU, S., Materials Science
POPA, I. M., Physical Chemistry
POPA, M., Polymer Technology
POPA, V., Wood Chemistry
ROȘCA, I., Inorganic Chemistry
RUSU, M., Rubber and Plastic Materials Processing
SCUTARU, D., Organic Chemistry
SIMINICEANU, I., Technology of Inorganic Substances
SIMIONESCU, B., Physical Chemistry of Polymers
SÎRGHIE, I., Analytical Chemistry
STANCU, A., Transport Phenomena in the Chemical Industry
SZEP, A., Technology of Inorganic Substances
UNGUREANU, ȘT., Automation in the Chemical Industry
VĂTĂ, M., Organic Chemistry

Faculty of Civil Engineering and Building
Services (Bdul Dimitrie Mangeron 43,
700050 Iași; tel. (232) 27-86-83; fax (232)
23-33-68; e-mail decanat@ce.tuiasi.ro;
internet www.ce.tuiasi.ro):

AMARIEI, C., Structural Mechanics, Plastic Design
ANDREI, R., Transport Infrastructure
ATANASIU, M. G., Structural Mechanics, Computer-Aided Design, Earthquake Engineering
AXINTE, E., Steel Structures
BOBOC, V., Road Engineering
BROŞTEANU, M., Buildings
BUDESCU, M., Structural Mechanics, Computer-Aided Design, Earthquake Engineering
CIONGRADI, I., Structural Mechanics, Computer-Aided Design, Earthquake Engineering
CIORNEI, AL., Buildings
COROBCEANU, S., Concrete and Reinforced Concrete Construction
COSOSCHI, B., Road Engineering
DUMITRAŞ, A., Structural Mechanics
FLOREA, N., Hydrotechnical Structures
GAVRILAŞ, I., Construction
GIUŞCĂ, N., Construction Technology
GORBĂNESCU, D., Strength of Materials, Theory of Elasticity and Plasticity
GRECU, V., Soil Mechanics and Foundation Engineering
GROLL, L., Building Materials
GUGIUMAN, G., Road Engineering
HAGIU, V., Management of Construction Works
HIRHUI, I., Building Materials
IGNAT, J., Electrical Installations
IONESCU, C., Structural Mechanics, Earthquake Engineering
ISOPESCU, D., Wooden Constructions, Composite Structures
JANTEA, C., Bridge Engineering
MATEESCU, TH., Water Supply and Sewerage Installations, Installations for Buildings
MIHALACHE, N., Strength of Materials, Theory of Elasticity and Plasticity, Numerical Methods
MUŞAT, V., Soil Mechanics and Foundation
NOUR, S., Concrete and Reinforced Concrete Constructions
PESCARU, V., Steel Structures
POPOVICI, D., Highways
PRECUPANU, D., Strength of Materials, Theory of Elasticity and Plasticity
RĂILEANU, P., Soil Mechanics and Foundations
SECU, AL., Industrial and Agricultural Constructions
ŞERBANOIU, I., Managerial Analysis of the Building Process, Management of Construction Work
STANCIU, A., Soil Mechanics and Foundations
ŞTEFĂNESCU, D., Buildings
ŢĂRANU, N., Industrial Buildings and Composite Structures, Steel Structures
UNGUREANU, N., Strength of Materials, Theory of Elasticity and Plasticity, Numerical Methods
VARLAM, F., Concrete Bridge Engineering
VELICU, C., Thermal Engineering, Rehabilitation of Buildings
VEREŞ, AL., Buildings and Architectural Acoustics
VLAD, I., Strength of Materials, Theory of Elasticity and Plasticity
VLAD, N., Road Technology Engineering

Faculty of Control Systems and Computer Engineering (Bdul Dimitrie Mangeron 53A, 700050 Iaşi; tel. (232) 23-13-43; fax (232) 21-42-90; e-mail decanat@ac.tuiasi.ro):

BALABAN, E., Digital Control Systems, Control of Electrical Drives
BOŢAN, C., Optimization Techniques, Optimal Control
BOTEZ, C., Databases and Computer Programming, Software Engineering
GÂLEA, D., Artificial Intelligence

GANCIU, T., Systems Identification, Data Processing
HOZA, F., Digital Computers, Microcontrollers
HUŢANU, C., Multiprocessor Systems, Microprocessor Systems
ILINCA, M., Computer Programming
LAZĂR, C., Control Engineering, Data Transmission
OLAH, I., Electrical and Electronic Control Equipment, Servomechanisms
PAL, C., Robot Control Systems
PĂNESCU, A. D., Knowledge-Based Systems, Robot Control Systems
PĂSTRĂVANU, O. C., Discrete Event Systems, Neural Networks in Control Engineering
VALACHI, A., Digital Logic Design, Digital Systems Design
VOICU, M., Systems Theory, Principles of Feedback Control

Faculty of Electrical Engineering (Bdul Dimitrie Mangeron 51–53, 700050 Iaşi; tel. and fax (232) 27-86-83; fax (232) 23-76-27; e-mail secretariat@ee.tuiasi.ro; internet www.ee.tuiasi.ro):

ADAM, M., Electrical Equipment
ALEXANDRESCU, V., Power Systems
ANDRONE, C., Principles of Electrical Engineering
ASAFTEI, C., Power Plants
ASANDEI, D., Power Plants
BALAN, T., Electrical Materials
BALUTA, GH., Principles of Electrical Engineering
BARABOI, A., Electrical Equipment, EMC, Power Electronics
CANTEMIR, L., Electric Traction, Uses of Electrical Energy in Modelling, Electrical Drives, Systems Theory, Intelligent Control
CÂRŢÎNĂ, GH., Optimal Control and Computer Applications in Energetics
CIOBANU, L., Electrical Drives of Robots, Reliability
CIOBANU, R. C., Electrical Materials
CREŢU, A., Electrical Engineering
CREŢU, M., Electrical Measurements and Transducers
DIACONESCU, M., Electrical Drives, Electronics and Power Electronics
GAVRILAŞ, M., Power Plants
GEORGESCU, GH., Power Networks
GRAUR, I., Power Electronics, Vector Control of AC Drives
GUŞĂ, M., High-Voltage Engineering
HNATIUC, E., Electrical Apparatus Design, Environmental Protection
IVAS, D., Power Systems Reliability
LEONTE, P., Electrical Equipment
LIVINŢ, GH., Systems Theory, Automatic Control
MITREA, S., Principles of Electrical Engineering
MUNTEANU, F., Power Systems Reliability
NEMESCU, M., Systems Theory and Industrial Automation
OLAH, R., Overvoltages and Insulation Engineering
OLARU, R., Industrial Automation
POPESCU, I., Fundamentals of Electrical Engineering
SIMION, A., Electrical Machines
SUCHAR, I., Electrical Engineering and Electronics
TEODORU, E., Electrical Machines and Drives

Faculty of Electronics, Telecommunications and Information Technology (Bdul Carol I 11, 700506 Iaşi; tel. (232) 21-37-37; fax (232) 21-77-20; e-mail decanat@etc.tuiasi.ro; internet www.tuiasi.ro):

ALEXA, D., Microwave Engineering, Power Electronics

ALEXANDRU, D. N., Telecommunications, Communications Systems
BÂRSAN, T., Mathematics
BEJANCU, A., Mathematics
BOGDAN, I., Mobile Communications, Antennas
CASSIAN, I., Fibre-optic Communications, Microwave Technology
CEHAN, V., Radio Transmitters, Satellite Communications
CIOBANU, GH., Mathematics
CORDUNEANU, A., Mathematics
COTAE, P., Digital Communication
CRĂCIUN, I., Mathematics
DIMITRIU, L., Electronic Measurement and Control Apparatus, Automotive Electronics
DUMA, P., Microprocessors, Microcontrollers, Electronic Telephone Exchanges
FETECĂU, C., Mathematics
GORAS, L., Signals, Circuits and Systems
GRIGORAS, V., Signals, Circuits and Systems
LUCANU, M., Industrial Electronics, PWM Techniques for Converters
MUNTEANU, V., Information Theory
NEAGU, AL., Mathematics
NEGOESCU, N., Mathematics
PAPAGHIUC, N., Mathematics
SAVA, V., Mathematics
SÎRBU, A., Software Engineering, Computer-Aided Design
STIURCĂ, D., Analogue Integrated Circuits
TALPALARU, P., Mathematics
TARNICERIU, D., Signal Processing
TEODORESCU, H., Medical Electronics, Image Processing, Neural Networks and Fuzzy Systems

Faculty of Hydrotechnical Engineering, Geodesy and Environmental Engineering (Bdul Dimitrie Mangeron 65, 700050 Iaşi; tel. and fax (232) 27-08-04; e-mail decanat@hidro .tuaisi.ro; internet www.tuiasi.ro):

ALEXANDRESCU, O., Pumping Installations
AXINTE, S., Ameliorative Agriculture
BÂRSAN, E., Water Supply
BARTHA, I., Hydraulics
BLĂGOI, O., Hydraulics
CISMARU, C., Irrigation and Drainage
COJOCARU, I., Irrigation and Drainage
DIMA, M., Sewerage, Waste Water Treatment
GIURMĂ, I., Hydrology and Water Management
HOBJILĂ, V., Construction Technology
LUCA, M., Hydraulics
MANOLOVICI, M., Hydrotechnical Constructions
NISTOR, GH., Surveying
NIŢESCU, E., Work Technology and Mechanization in Land Reclamation
PATRAŞ, M., Reinforced Concrete
POPESCU, ST., Numerical Methodology, Dispersion
POPOVICI, N., Soil Erosion Control, Regulation and Management of Watercourses
STĂTESCU, F., Soil Science

Faculty of Machine Engineering (Bdul Dimitrie Mangeron 63, 700050 Iaşi; tel. (232) 24-21-09; fax (232) 21-16-67; e-mail secretariat@ tcm.tuiasi.ro):

AGOP, M., Physics
BOHOSIEVICI, C., Technology of Machine Building
BRAHA, V., Mechanical Engineering
CĂLUGĂRU, GH., Physics
CARATA, E., Machine Tools
CHIRILĂ, V., Technology of Machine Building
CIUBOTARIU, C., Physics
CONSTANTINESCU, C., Machine Tools
COZMÎNCĂ, M., Metal Cutting
DUSA, P.
FETECĂU, C., Theoretical Mechanics

GHERGHEL, N., Design of Mechanical Devices

GRĂMESCU, TR., Technology of Machine Building

IBĂNESCU, I., Theoretical Mechanics

LUNGU, GH., Machine Tools

MUSCĂ, G., Computer-Aided Manufacturing

NEAGU, E., Physics

NEAGU, R., Physics

PANAIT, S., Metal Cutting

PARASCHIV, DR., Machine Repairing Technology

PLĂHTEANU, B., Machine Tools

RUSU, E., Theoretical Mechanics

SLĂTINEANU, L., Machine Building Technology

UNGUREANU, GH., Computer-Aided Design

URSU, D., Physics

ZET, GH., Physics

ZETU, D., Design of Automatic Machine Tools

Faculty of Materials Science and Engineering (Bdul Dimitrie Mangeron 61A, 700050 Iaşi; tel. and fax (232) 23-00-09; e-mail decanat@sim.tuiasi.ro):

ALEXANDRU, I., Technology of Materials

BACIU, C., Technology of Materials

BULANCEA, V., Rolling

CARCEA, I., Composites

COJOCARU FILIPIUC, V., Metallurgy

DIMA, A., Technology and Applied Metallurgy

FLORESCU, A., Materials Technology

GĂLUSCĂ, D. G., Technology of Thermal Treatment

MĂLUREANU, I., Technology of Metals

MUNTEANU, C., Materials Technology

PETRUŞ, O., Computational Metallurgy

SUSAN, M., Applied Metallurgy

Faculty of Machine Manufacturing and Industrial Management (Bdul Dimitrie Mangeron 59A, Et. 1, 700050 Iaşi; tel. and fax (232) 24-21-09; e-mail secretariat@tcm.tuiasi.ro):

AMARIEI, N., Strength of Materials

ATANASIU, V., Mechanical Transmissions

BÂRSĂNESCU, P., Strength of Materials

BERCEA, M., Machine Design

COMANDAR, C., Strength of Materials

COZMA, D., Agricultural Machines

CRĂCIUN, V., Agricultural Machines

CREŢU, SP., Machine Design, Tribology and Vibration

DĂSCĂLESCU, D., Internal Combustion Engines

DRĂGAN, B., Machine Vibrations

DUCA, C., Mechanisms

DUMITRAŞCU, GH., Thermotechnics and Heat Engines

GAFIŢANU, M., Machine Design, Tribology and Vibration

GAIGINSCHI, R., Internal Combustion Engines

GRIGORAS, S., Machine Design and Reliability

HAGIU, GH., Machine Design and Vibration

HORBANIUC, G., Thermotechnology and Heat Engines

HOSTIUC, L., Machine Design

LEON, D., Strength of Materials

LOZONSCHI, GH., Thermotechnics and Heat Engines

MERTICARU, V., Machine Dynamics

MOCANU, F., Strength of Materials

NECULĂIASA, V., Agricultural Machines

OLARU, D., Tribology and Machine Design

OPRIŞAN, C., Mechanisms

PALIHOVICI, VAL., Strength of Materials

POPOVICI, A., Mechanisms

RACOCEA, C., Machine Design

RECEANU, D., Mechanisms

ŢENU, I., Equipment for the Food Industry

ŽUBCU, V., Gas and Steam Turbines

Faculty of Textiles and Leather Engineering and Industrial Management (Bdul Dimitrie Mangeron 29, 700050 Iaşi; tel. and fax (232) 23-04-91; e-mail decanat@tex.tuiasi.ro; internet www.tuiasi.ro/facultati/tex):

ANTONIU, GH., Textile Raw Materials

AVRAM, D., Structure of Textile Yarns

BADEA, N., Leather and Furs Chemistry and Technology

BORDEIANU, D., Technology and Equipment for Spinning Mills

BRUDARU, O., Fuzzy Systems

BUCEVSCHI, D., Technology of Leather Substitutes

BUDULAN, C., Equipment and Automation in the Knitwear Industry

BUTNARU, R., Chemistry and Technology of Textile Materials

CIOCOIU, M., Weaving Process and Machinery, Statistical Methods in Textiles

CONDUCARCHE, GH., Management

DRĂGOI, L., Weaving Machinery Design and Automation

GRIBINCEA, V., Textile Raw Materials

GRIGORIU, A., Special Technologies of Textile Products Finishing

ILIESCU, E., Principles of Chemical Technology

IRIMIA, M., Economics and Accountability

LEONTE, R., Marketing

LIUŢE, D., Preparatory Weaving Processes, Weaving Technology

LUCA, G., Management

MĂLUREANU, G., Footwear Design

MITU, S., Clothing

MUNTEANU, A., Marketing and Economics

MUNTEANU, V., Marketing

MUREŞAN, A., Equipment for Textile Finishing

MUSTAŢĂ, A., Bast Fibre Spinning

NECULĂIASA, M., Textile Metrology, Textile Quality Control

PINTILIE, E., Computer-Aided Design in Ready-Made Clothing, Design of Ready-Made Clothing Machinery

RUSU, C., Total Quality Management, Human Resources Management

VÎLCU, M., Theoretical Bases of Spinning

VITAN, F., Transfer Phenomena and Equipment

VOICU, M., Interpersonal Communication

Other Institutes of Higher Education

Academia de Arte Vizuale 'Ioan Andreescu' (Academy of Visual Arts 'Ioan Andreescu'): Piaţa Unirii 31, 400098 Cluj-Napoca; tel. (264) 19-15-77; fax (264) 19-28-90; f. 1950; faculties of fine arts, decorative arts and design; library: 52,000 vols; 75 teachers; 553 students; Rector IOACHIM NICA.

Academia de Muzică 'Gheorghe Dima': Str. Ion. C. Brătianu 25, 400079 Cluj-Napoca; tel. (264) 59-12-41; fax (264) 59-38-79; e-mail conscluj@gmail.com; internet www.amgd.ro; f. 1819, reorganized 1919, present name 1990; faculties of instrumental performance, music theory, singing and stage art; library: 188,000 vols; 250 teachers; 1,182 students; Rector Prof. Dr ADRIAN POP; Prorector Prof. Dr GABRIEL BANCIU; Scientific Sec. Dr ELENA CHIRCEV; publs *Intermezzo* (magazine), *Lucrări de Muzicologie* (Musicology Articles, 1 a year).

Academia de Studii Economice (Academy of Economic Studies): Piaţa Romană 6, sector 1, 010374 Bucharest; tel. (21) 319-19-00; fax (21) 319-18-99; e-mail rectorat@ase.ro; internet www.ase.ro; f. 1913; faculties of management, economics, agricultural and food production, economy and administration, finance and banking, administration and accounting, cybernetics, statistics and computer science for economics, trade, international economic relations, economic studies in foreign languages; college of economics at Buzău; library: see Libraries and Archives; 765 teachers; 49,000 students; Rector Prof. Dr ION GH. ROSCA; Vice-Rector for Bachelors and Masters programmes Prof. NICOLAE DARDAC; Vice-Rector for Int. Relations and European Integration Prof. VIOREL LEFTER; Vice-Rector for Scientific Research and PhD programmes Prof. ION STANCU; Scientific Sec. Prof. RAZVAN ZAHARIA; publs *Economic Journal* (in Romanian and English, 4 a year), *Informatica Economică* (4 a year).

Attached Centre:

Bulgaria–Romania Interuniversity Europe Centre/BRIE–Giurgiu: Str. Mircea cel Batran 36, 080036 Giurgiu; tel. (21) (246) 21-91-61; fax (21) 312-95-49; e-mail brie@ase.ro; internet www.brie.ase.ro; f. 2001; operates through collaboration between Rusenski Universitet 'Angel Kanchev' (see Bulgaria chapter) and the Academia de Studii Economice; Dir Prof. Dr CONSTANTIN APOSTOL.

Academiei Naţionale de Informaţii 'Mihai Viteazul': Şoseaua Odăi 20, sector 1, Bucharest; tel. (21) 410-65-60; fax 31-04-750; e-mail ani@sri.ro; internet www.sri.ro; training intelligence officers; offers Bachelors, Masters and doctoral courses.

Institutul Teologic Baptist din Bucureşti: Str. Berzei, 29, sector 1, 010251 Bucharest; tel. (21) 315-91-08; fax (21) 318-15-93; e-mail bbtseminary@yahoo.com; internet www.itb.ro; f. 1921; Rector Prof. Dr VASILE TALPOS.

Institutul Teologic Protestant Cluj: Piaţa Avram Iancu 13, 400124 Cluj-Napoca; tel. and fax (264) 59-13-68; internet proteo.cj.edu.ro; f. 1568; offers Bachelors, Masters and doctoral courses.

Institutul Teologic Romano-Catolic 'Sf. Losif' Iaşi: Str. Th. Văscăuţeanu 6, 700462 Iaşi; tel. (232) 41-04-19; fax (232)21-14-76; e-mail decan@itrc.ro; internet www.itrc.ro; f. 1886; Rector Dr WILHELM DANCĂ; Vice-Rector Dr ŞTEFAN LUPU; Dean Dr MIHAI PATRAŞCU; publs *Dialog Teologic*, *Drumuri Deschise*, *Educatorul Creştin*, *Lasati Copiii Sa Vina La Mine*.

RUSSIA

The Higher Education System

In March 1917 the last Tsar of the Romanov dynasty, which had ruled Russia as an autocracy since 1613, was forced to abdicate and a liberal Provisional Government took power. The Bolsheviks overthrew the Provisional Government in November of the same year and the Russian Soviet Federative Socialist Republic (RSFSR) was proclaimed. In 1922 the RSFSR joined the Union of Soviet Socialist Republics (USSR), which disintegrated in 1991, when the Russian Federation, as the RSFSR was formally renamed, was founded. The oldest current institutions of higher education date from the 18th century, notably St Petersburg State University (founded 1724) and Moscow State University 'M. V. Lomonsov' (founded 1755). Several specialist institutions were founded during the reign of Catherine the Great (1762–96). Major institutions founded during the 19th century include Moscow Agricultural Academy 'K. A. Tirmiyazev' (founded 1865), Tomsk Polytechnic University (founded 1896) and Nizhnii Novgorod State Technical University (founded 1898 in Warsaw, Poland). Universal education was a fundamental Bolshevik principle, and during the period of Soviet rule (1917–91) more than 340 institutions of higher education were founded. In 2009/10 there were 7,419,000 students enrolled in 1,114 institutions of higher education. Under Soviet rule all educational institutions were state-owned but a wide range of independent schools and colleges were created in the early 1990s. In 2008/09 there were 474 independent higher education institutions.

Higher education institutions are categorized as Academies, Universities, Institutes and Conservatories. Universities are sub-divided by subject area: Agriculture, Humanities and Sciences, Medical, Pedagogical and Technical. The Ministry of Education and Science has overall responsibility for higher education, particularly the licensing and accreditation of institutions. Russia participates in the Bologna Process to establish a European Higher Education Area, the first phase of which is to adopt a credit-based system of comparable degrees with two main cycles (undergraduate and graduate). In 2007 Russia enacted a law that replaced the traditional five-year model of education with a two-tiered approach: a four-year Bachelors degree followed by a two-year Masters. This system was to have been fully implemented by 2010.

Admission was formerly made on the joint basis of the Certificate of Secondary Education (Attestat o srednem obrazovanii) and performance in a competitive entrance examination. However, a system of Single Entry University Examinations was gradually adopted by the administrative regions (48 by 2003), testing students in a range of compulsory and designated subjects (the latter depending on the institution's requirements). In 2007 the Unified State Examination (USE), a standardized common university admission examination replacing the state final school attestation and entrance examinations, was introduced by law. Since 2009 the USE has been adopted nationwide and is compulsory for all applicants. However, in 2009 24 universities received the right to administer their own entrance exams and in 2010 a further 11 Russian universities were allowed to do this as well. The undergraduate degree is the Bakalavr (Bachelors), a four-year programme of study divided into two years of general studies and two years of specialized studies. Graduates holding the Bachelors are eligible to study for the Magistr (Masters), the first postgraduate degree, which is either a one-year taught course or a two-year period of research. Doctoral-level studies have a two-tiered structure, comprising the Aspirantura and Doktorantura. Aspirantura is a period of study following the Masters lasting a minimum of three years and culminating with the defence of a thesis and the award of the title Kandidat Nauk (Candidate of Sciences). Following Aspirantura, Doktorantura lasts for an unspecified period of time that, upon completion, results in the title Doktor Nauk (Doctor of Sciences).

Technical and vocational education is largely offered by specialist institutions and technical colleges at the upper secondary level. The primary qualifications are the Diplom ob okanchanii proftekhuchilishcha (Diploma of Completed Vocational-Technical Education) and the Diplom ob okanchanîi srednego spetsial'nogo uchebnogo zavedeniya (Diploma of Completed Specialized Secondary Education—available at both basic and advanced levels). Basic level courses last between two and three years, while advanced level courses generally last an additional year.

The Federal Service for Supervision in Education and Science carries out quality control, licensing, certification and state accreditation of educational institutions. In November 2010 the Government approved a new federal programme for 2011–15 intended to improve the quality of higher education, primarily focusing on Russia's universities. Expected to cost some 137,000m. rubles (US $4,100m.), the programme was to include improving the quality of teaching staff, the introduction of new technologies and upgrading the infrastructure at the country's leading federal universities.

Regulatory and Representative Bodies

GOVERNMENT

Ministry of Culture and the Mass Media: 109074 Moscow, Kitaigorodskii proyezd 7; tel. (495) 625-11-95; internet www.mkmk.ru; Minister ALEKSANDR S. SOKOLOV.

Ministry of Education and Science: 125993 Moscow, ul. Tverskaya 11; tel. (495) 629-70-62; internet www.mon.gov.ru; Min. ANDREI A. FURSENKO.

ACCREDITATION

Agency for Higher Education Quality Assurance and Career Development (AQA): 101000 Moscow, Myasnitskaya ul., 24, Bldg 1, Office 79; tel. (495) 628-05-09; fax (495) 628-47-79; e-mail akkork@akkork.ru; internet www.akkork.ru; f. 2005; carries out ind. analysis, evaluation and assurance of the quality of education provided by higher education instns; Dir-Gen. Dr VYACHESLAV SAMOILOV.

ENIC Russia: 117198 Moscow, Nat. Information Centre for Academic Recognition and Mobility, Mikluho-Maklaya St 6, RUDN; Moscow, Ordzhonikidze St 3; tel. (495) 958-28-81; fax (495) 433-15-11; e-mail russianenic@sci.pfu.edu.ru; internet www.russianenic.ru; f. 1999; Dir Dr GENNADY LUKICHEV.

Federal Service for Supervision in Education and Science: 115998 Moscow, ul. Shabolovka 33; tel. (495) 208-68-38; internet www.obrnadzor.gov.ru; provides supervision and guidance in the sphere of education and science; monitors the quality of education in instns; organizes licensing, attestation and accreditation of educational instns; Head VIKTOR ALEKSANDROVICH BOLOTOV.

National Accreditation Agency: 424000 Yoshkar-Ola, 3 Lenin Sq.; tel. (8362) 41-61-94; fax (8362) 41-38-84; e-mail umo@nica.ru; internet www.nica.ru; f. 1995; supports higher-education instns, vocational-training establishments and the educational authorities in carrying out their state accreditation procedures; Dir Prof. VLADIMIR NAVODNOV.

NATIONAL BODIES

Association of Non-State Higher Education Establishments: 107005 Moscow, Radio St 22; tel. (495) 105-03-83; fax (495) 105-03-81; e-mail va_zernov@mtu-net.ru; Pres. VLADIMIR ZERNOV.

Association of Russian Higher Education Institutions: 105064 Moscow, 4 Gorokhovsky per.; tel. (499) 261-31-52; fax (499) 267-46-81; e-mail svp@miigaik.ru; Pres. VIKTOR SAVINYKH.

Federal Agency for Education: 115998 Moscow, Lyusinovskaya ul. 51; tel. (495) 237-97-63; fax (495) 236-01-71; e-mail bicab@ed.gov.ru; internet www.ed.gov.ru; manages state property, implements education and training policies, funds higher-education instns; Head NIKOLAI IVANOVICH BULAEV.

Russian Academy of Education: 119121 Moscow, Pogodinskaya ul. 8; tel. (495) 245-16-41; fax (495) 246-81-77; f. 1943; br. depts of philosophy of education and theoretical pedagogy, psychology and physiology in education, general secondary education, culture and education, basic vocational training, higher education; regional depts: Northwest (St Petersburg), Siberia (Krasnoyarsk), Southern (Rostov-on-Don), Central (Moscow), Povolzhskoe (Kazan), Urals (Ekaterinburg); 4 experimental schools, 30 research institutes; see Research Institutes; library: see Libraries and Archives; Pres. Prof. Dr N. D. NIKANDROV; Chief Learned Sec. Prof. Dr I. V. ROBERT; publs *Defektologiya* (Defectology, 6 a year), *Izvestiya RAO* (News, 4 a year), *Pedagogika* (Pedagogics, 12 a year), *Voprosy Psikhologii* (Problems of Psychology, 12 a year).

Russian Rectors' Union: 119991 Moscow, V-234, Vorobievy Gory, Lomonosov Moscow State Univ., Glavnoe Zdanie, Rooms 1001–1003; tel. and fax (495) 939-20-32; e-mail office@rsr-online.ru; internet rsr-online.ru/english; f. 1992; c. 1,000 mems; Pres. VIKTOR A. SADOVNICHY; Sec. Gen. OLGA V. KASHIRINA.

Learned Societies

GENERAL

Russian Academy of Natural Sciences: 113105 Moscow, Varshavskoye shosse 8; tel. (495) 954-26-11; fax (495) 954-73-05; e-mail presidium@raen.ru; internet www.raen.ru; f. 1990; organizes and coordinates pure and applied research; sections: Mathematics; Physics; Chemistry; Earth Sciences; Mining and Metallurgy; Issues in Education; Informatics; Biomedicine; Biology and Ecology; Russian Encyclopedia; Economics and Sociology; Issues in Macroeconomics; Geopolitics and Security; Noosphere Knowledge and Technology; Humanities and Creative Work; Interbranch Ecological and Economic Systems Research; Environmental Sciences; depts: St Petersburg Branch for Education and Science Development; Oil and Gas; Forest Sciences; Eurasia Concept and Culture; Ecology, Hydrogeology, Engineering Geology and Geocryology; Applied Mathematics and Mathematical Physics; Class and National Traditions; 2,500 mems (incl. 100 hon., 250 foreign); Pres. Prof. Dr OLEG L. KUZNETSOV; Chief Scientific Sec. LIDA V. IVANITSKAYA.

Russian Academy of Sciences: 119991 Moscow, Leninsky pr. 14; tel. (495) 954-29-05; fax (495) 954-33-20; e-mail uvs@pran.ru; internet www.pran.ru; f. 1724; depts of mathematics (Academician-Sec. L. D. FADEYEV), physics (Academician-Sec. A. F. ANDREEV), power engineering, mechanics and control processes (Academician-Sec. V. E. FORTOV), information science and computer technology (Academician-Sec. E. P. VELIKHOV), chemistry and materials (Academician-Sec. V. A. KABANOV), biology (Academician-Sec. A. I. GRIGORIEV), earth sciences (Academician-Sec. O. A. BOGATIKOV), social sciences (Academician-Sec. V. L. MAKAROV), history and philology (Academician-Sec. A. P. DEREVYANKO); Siberian division (Pr. Akademika Lavrenteva 17, 630090 Novosibirsk; tel. 30-05-67; Chair. N. L. DOBRETSOV), incl. centres in Krasnoyarsk, Irkutsk, Kemerovo, Omsk, Tomsk and Tumen; Far Eastern division (Svetlanskaya 50, 690600 Vladivostok; tel. 2-25-28; Chair. V. J. SERGIENKO); Urals division (Pervomaiskaya 91, 620219 Ekaterinburg; tel. 74-02-23; Chair. V. A. CHERESHNEV), incl. centres in Perm and Komi; additional centres in Makhachkala, Petrozavodsk, Kazan, Nalchik, Ufa and Apatity; attached research institutes: see Research Institutes; libraries and archive: see Libraries and Archives; 1,429 mems (501 academicians, 720 corresp. mems, 208 foreign mems); Pres. YU. S. OSIPOV; Chief Learned Sec. V. V. KOSTYUK; publs *Izvestiya Rossiiskoi Akademii Nauk* (Bulletin of the Russian Academy of Sciences, in 16 series: Biology, Geography, Literature and Language, Mathematics, Metals, Economics and Society, Mechanics of Liquids and Gases, Solid State Mechanics, Technical Cybernetics, Energy and Transport (6 a year); Geology, Inorganic Materials, Physics of Atmosphere and Ocean, Earth Physics, Physics, Chemistry (12 a year)), *Doklady Rossiiskoi Akademii Nauk* (Proceedings of the Academy, 36 a year), *Izvestiya Sibirskogo otdeleniya Rossiiskoi Akademii Nauk* (Bulletin of the Siberian Branch of the Russian Academy of Sciences, in 5 series: Biological and Medical Sciences, History, Philology and Philosophy, Economics and Applied Sociology (4 a year); Technical Sciences, Chemical Sciences (6 a year)), *Nauka v Rossii* (Science in Russia, in Russian and English, 6 a year), *Vestnik Rossiiskoi Akademii Nauk* (Journal of the Russian Academy of Sciences, 12 a year), *Vestnik Dalnevostochnogo otdeleniya RAN* (Journal of the Far Eastern Division of the Russian Academy of Sciences).

UNESCO Office Moscow: 119331 Moscow, ul. Mytnaya 1; tel. (495) 230-10-65; fax (495) 238-60-85; e-mail moscow@unesco.org; internet www.unesco.ru; designated Cluster Office for Armenia, Azerbaijan, Belarus, Moldova and Russia; Dir BADARCH DENDEV.

Union of Scientific and Engineering Associations: 119034 Moscow, Kursovoi per. 17; tel. (495) 290-62-86; fax (495) 291-85-06; Pres. Acad. I. GULIAEV; Learned Sec. S. V. PRYANISHNIKOV; Sec.-Gen. V. SITSEV.

AGRICULTURE, FISHERIES AND VETERINARY SCIENCE

Russian Academy of Agricultural Sciences: 107814 Moscow, Bolshoi Kharitonevsky per. 21; tel. (495) 207-39-42; f. 1992; depts of plant breeding and genetics (Academician-Sec. V. S. SHEVELUKHA), arable farming and the use of agricultural chemicals (Academician-Sec. I. P. MAKAROV), feed and fodder crops production (Academician-Sec. (vacant)), plant protection (Academician-Sec. N. M. GOLYTSIN), livestock production (Academician-Sec. (vacant)), veterinary science (Academician-Sec. V. P. SHISHKOV), mechanization, electrification and automation in farming (Academician-Sec. G. E. LISTOPAD), forestry (Academician-Sec. V. N. VINOGRADOV), the Economics and Management of agricultural production (Academician-Sec. (vacant)), land reform and the organization of land use (Academician-Sec. (vacant)), land reclamation and water resources (Academician-Sec. B. B. SHUMAKOV), the storage and processing of agricultural products (Academician-Sec. (vacant)); regional depts in St Petersburg (Non Black Soil Zone), Novosibirsk (Siberia), Khabarovsk (Far East); 150 mems; 128 corresp. mems; 73 foreign corresp. mems; attached research institutes: see Research Institutes; library: see Libraries and Archives; Pres. A. A. NIKONOV; Chief Learned Sec. V. P. SHISHKOV; publs *Doklady* (Proceedings), *Mekhanizatsiya i elektrificatsiya selskogo khozyaistva* (Mechanization and Electrification of Agriculture), *Selektsiya i Semenovodstvo* (Selection and Seed Science), *Selskokhozyaistvennaya biologiya* (Agricultural Biology), *Sibirskii vestnik selskokhozyaistvennoi nauki* (Siberian Agricultural Science Journal), *Vestnik selskokhozyaistvennoi nauki* (Agricultural Science Journal).

Society of the Timber and Forestry Industry: 103062 Moscow, Ul. Chernyshevskogo 29; tel. (495) 923-95-70; Chair. YU. A. YAGODNIKOV.

Soil Science Society: 109017 Moscow, Pyzhevskii per. 7; tel. (495) 231-43-59; attached to Russian Acad. of Sciences; Pres. G. V. DOBROVOLSKY.

ARCHITECTURE AND TOWN PLANNING

Union of Russian Architects: 123001 Moscow, Granatni per. 22; tel. (495) 291-55-78; fax (495) 202-81-01; e-mail sarrus@rambler.ru; f. 1981; 12,000 mems; Pres. YU. P. GNEDOVSKIY; publ. *Vesti SAR* (4 a year).

ECONOMICS, LAW AND POLITICS

Association of International Law: 119841 Moscow, ul. Frunze 10; attached to Russian Acad. of Sciences; Chair. Prof. G. I. TUNKIN.

Association of Orientalists: 103753 Moscow, ul. Rozhdestvenka 12; tel. (495) 928-57-64; attached to Russian Acad. of Sciences; Chair. M. S. KAPITSA.

Association of Political Sciences: 118941 Moscow, ul. Znamenka 10; attached to Russian Acad. of Sciences; Pres. Dr G. K. SHAKHNAZAROV.

Economics Society: 117259 Moscow, B. Cheremushkinskaya ul. 34; tel. (495) 120-13-21; Chair. V. S. PAVLOV.

Municipal Economy and Services Society: 103001 Moscow, Trekhprudny per. 11/13; tel. (495) 299-83-00; Chair. A. F. PORYADIN.

Russian Association of Sinologists: 117218 Moscow, Nakhimovsky pr. 32; tel. (495) 124-08-35; fax (495) 310-70-56; e-mail ifes@cemi.rssi.ru; f. 1992; 700 mems; attached to Russian Acad. of Sciences; Pres. V. S. MYASNIKOV.

EDUCATION

All-Russia 'Znanie' Society: 101990 Moscow, Novaya pl. 3/4; tel. (495) 621-90-58; fax (495) 625-42-49; e-mail znanie@znanie.org; internet www.znanie.org; f. 1947; co-founder of 30 non-govt instns of higher education and 40 instns or centres of additional education; publishes science-popular brochures and books, educational and methodical literature books for children and parents (incl. those on problems of prevention of drug addiction and AIDS), magazines; 120,000 mems; Pres. Prof. OLEG N. SMOLIN; publ. *New Knowledge* (online, 4 a year).

FINE AND PERFORMING ARTS

Russian Academy of Arts: 119034 Moscow, Ul. Prechistenka 21; tel. and fax (495) 201-39-71; f. 1757; depts of Painting (Academician-Sec. E. N. MAXIMOV), Sculpture (Academician-Sec. A. A. BICHUKOV), Graphic Art (Academician-Sec. M. P. MITURICH-KHLEBNIKOV), Decorative Arts (Academician-Sec. L. A. SOKOLOVA), Architecture and Monumental Art (Academician-Sec. M. M. POSOKHIN); attached research institutes: see Research Institutes; 218 mems (100 ordinary, 118 corresp.); library: see Libraries and Archives; Pres. Z. K. TSERETELY; Chief Learned Sec. M. M. KURILKO-RYUMIN; publ. *Informatsionny Byulleten* (Information Bulletin, 4 a year).

Russian Union of Composers: 125009 Moscow, per. Bryusova 8/10; tel. (495) 629-52-18; fax (495) 629-08-67; e-mail ubioncomposers@mail.ru; internet www.soyuzkompozitorov.ru; f. 1960; organizes music competitions and festivals; 1,600 mems; Chair. VLADISLAV KAZENIN; publs *Musical Life, Muzikalnaya Akademia.*

Theatre Union of the Russian Federation: 103009 Moscow, ul. Gorkogo 16/2; tel. (495) 229-91-52; 30,124 mems; library of 300,000 vols; Chair. M. A. ULYANOV; publ. *Problems of Contemporary Theatre.*

Union of Arts of the Russian Federation: 103062 Moscow, ul. Pokrovka 37.

Union of Russian Filmmakers: 123056 Moscow, Vasilevskaya 13; tel. (495) 251-53-70; e-mail unikino3@aha.ru; internet www.unikino.ru; Chair. NIKITA MIKHALKOV.

HISTORY, GEOGRAPHY AND ARCHAEOLOGY

Russian Geographical Society: 190000 St Petersburg, tsentr, per. Grivtsova 10; tel. (812) 315-85-35; fax (812) 315-63-12; e-mail rgo@spb.org.ru; internet spb.org.ru/rgo/; f. 1845; attached to Russian Acad. of Sciences; 20,000 mems; library of 470,000 vols, archive of 600,000 units; Pres. Prof. SERGEI B. LAVROV; publ. *Izvestiya RGS* (6 a year).

LANGUAGE AND LITERATURE

Alliance Française: 191186 St Petersburg, ul. Zhukovskogo 16; tel. (812) 272-08-60; e-mail info@af.spb.ru; internet www.af.spb.ru; offers courses and exams in French language and culture and promotes cultural exchange with France; attached offices in Ekaterinburg, Irkutsk, Kazan, Nizhnii Novgorod, Novosibirsk, Rostov-on-Don, Samara and Yakutsk; Dir of School GALINA DRAGAN.

British Council: 109189 Moscow, ul. Nikoloyamskaya 1; tel. (495) 782-02-00; fax (495) 782-02-01; e-mail bc.moscow@britishcouncil.ru; internet www.britishcouncil.ru; teaching centre; offers courses and exams in English language and British culture and promotes cultural exchange with the UK; attached centres in Ekaterinburg, Irkutsk, Krasnoyarsk, Nizhnii Novgorod, Novosibirsk, Rostov-on-Don, Samara, Sochi, Tomsk, Yaroslavl and Yuzhno-Sakhalinsk; Dir ADRIAN GREER; Training Centre Man. CLARE JEFFS.

Instituto Cervantes: 121069 Moscow, Novinski bul. 20 bl. 1–2; tel. (495) 937-19-52; fax (495) 937-19-51; e-mail cenmos@cervantes.es; internet moscu.cervantes.es; offers courses and exams in Spanish language and culture and promotes cultural exchange with Spain and Spanish-speaking Latin and Central America; library of 12,000 vols; Dir JUAN CARLOS VIDAL GARCÍA.

International Community of Writers' Unions: 121825 Moscow, Povarskaya ul. 52; tel. (495) 291-63-07; f. 1992; 7,000 mems; Chair. G. M. MARKOV; First Sec. TIMUR PULATOV; publs *Inostrannaya Literatura* (12 a year), *Literaturnaya Gazeta* (52 a year), *Novyi Mir* (12 a year).

Press Society: 103051 Moscow, Petrovka 26; tel. (495) 921-82-98; Chair. B. A. KUZMIN.

Russian Association for Comparative Literature: 121069 Moscow, ul. Vorovskogo 25A; tel. (495) 290-17-09; attached to Russian Acad. of Sciences; Chair. Acad. YU. B. VIPPER.

Russian Linguistics Society: 103009 Moscow, ul. Semashko 1/12; attached to Russian Acad. of Sciences; Chair. Acad. T. V. GAMKRELIDZE.

Russian PEN Centre: 107031 Moscow, ul. Neglinnaya 18/1, str. 2; tel. (495) 625-27-18; fax (495) 625-35-73; e-mail penrussian@mail.ru; internet www.penrussia.org; f. 1989; protection of freedom of expression, int. exchange; writers in prison cttee; 355 mems; Pres. ANDREI BITOV; Dir MIKHAIL DEMCHENKOV; Deputy Dir EKATERINA TURCHANINOVA.

Union of Writers of the Russian Federation: 119087 Moscow, Komsomolsky pr. 13; tel. (495) 246-43-50.

MEDICINE

Federation of Anaesthesiologists and Reanimatologists: 125284 Moscow, POB 87, Botkin Hospital K. 14; tel. and fax (495) 945-97-25; e-mail admin@far.org.ru; internet far.org.ru; f. 1991 (fmrly All-Union Society, f. 1959); 600 mems; Chair. I. MOLCHANOV.

International Society for Pathophysiology: 125315 Moscow, ul. Baltiiskaya 8; tel. (095) 151-17-56; fax (095) 151-95-40; e-mail 4909.g23@g23.relcom.ru; internet home.ptt.ru/pathophysiology; f. 1991; 1,200 mems; Pres. Prof. OSMO HÄNNINEN; Sec.-Gen. L. SZOLLAR; publ. *Pathophysiology* (4 a year).

National Immunological Society: 115478 Moscow, Kashirskoe shosse 24/2; tel. (499) 611-83-33; fax (499) 616-10-27; f. 1983; 500 mems; Chair. R. V. PETROV; Gen. Sec. S. YU. SIDOROVICH; publ. *Immunologiya* (6 a year).

National Medical and Technical Scientific Society: 129301 Moscow, ul. Kasatkina 3; tel. (495) 283-97-84; fax (495) 187-37-34; f. 1968; 55,000 mems and 512 orgs; library: Central State Scientific Medical Library of 3m. vols; Pres. B. I. LEONOV; Chief Learned Sec. B. E. BELOUSOV; publ. *Biomedical Engineering* (6 a year).

National Ophthalmological Society: 103064 Moscow, ul. Sadovo-Chernogryazskaya 14/19; Chair. E. S. AVETISOV; Chief Learned Sec. T. I. FOROFONOFA; publ. *Vestnik oftalmologii* (6 a year).

National Pharmaceutical Society: 117418 Moscow, ul. Krasikova 34; Chair. M. T. ALYUSHIN; Chief Learned Sec. R. S. SKULKOVA.

National Scientific Medical Society of Anatomists, Histologists and Embryologists: 117869 Moscow, ul. Ostrovityanova 1; Chair. V. V. KUPRIYANOV; Chief Learned Sec. V. V. KOROLEV.

National Scientific Medical Society of Endocrinologists: 117036 Moscow, ul. Dm. Ulyanova 11; Chair. V. G. BARANOV; Chief Learned Sec. N. T. STARKOVA.

National Scientific Medical Society of Haematologists and Transfusiologists: 125167 Moscow, Novozykovskii pr. 4-a; Chair. V. N. SHABALIN; Chief Learned Sec. M. P. KHOKHLOVA.

National Scientific Medical Society of the History of Medicine: 101838 Moscow, Petrovirigskii per. 6/8; Chair. YU. P. LISITSYN; Chief Learned Sec. I. V. VENGROVA.

National Scientific Medical Society of Hygienists: 103064 Moscow, Mechnikova per. 5; Chair. G. N. SERDYUKOVSKAYA; Chief Learned Sec. A. G. SUKHAREV.

National Scientific Medical Society of Infectionists: 125284 Moscow, 1 Botkinskii pr. 3; Chair. V. N. NIKIFOROV; Chief Learned Sec. N. M. BELYAEVA.

National Scientific Medical Society of Nephrologists: 119021 Moscow, ul. Rossolimo 11-A; tel. (495) 248-53-33; f. 1969; holding of conferences, congresses, symposia; 1,200 mems; Chair. N. A. MUKHIN; Chief Learned Sec. S. O. ANDROSOVA.

National Scientific Medical Society of Obstetricians and Gynaecologists: 113163 Moscow, ul. Shabolovka 57; Chair. G. M. SAVELEVA; Chief Learned Sec. T. V. CHERVAKOVA.

National Scientific Medical Society of Oto-Rhino-Laryngologists: 119435 Moscow, Bol. Pirogovskaya 6; Chair. N. A. PREOBRAZHENSKII; Chief Learned Sec. N. P. KONSTANTINOVA.

National Scientific Medical Society of Paediatricians: 117963 Moscow, Lomonosovskii pr. 2/62; Chair M. YU. STUDENIKIN; Chief Learned Sec. G. V. YATSYK.

National Scientific Medical Society of Phthisiologists: 107564 Moscow, platforma Yauza, ul. 6 km Severnoi Zheleznoi Dorogi; Chair. A. G. KHOMENKO; Chief Learned Sec. V. V. EROKHIN.

National Scientific Medical Society of Physical Therapists and Health-Resort Physicians: 121099 Moscow, Kalinina pr. 50; Chair. A. N. OBROSOV; Chief Learned Sec. V. D. GRIGOREVA.

National Scientific Medical Society of Physicians-Analysts: 123242 Moscow, ul. Sadovaya-Kudrinskaya 3; Chair. B. F. KOROVKIN; Chief Learned Sec. R. L. MARTSISHEVSKAYA.

National Scientific Medical Society of Physicians in Curative Physical Culture and Sports Medicine: 117963 Moscow, Lomonosovskii pr. 2/62; Chair. S. V. KRUZSHEV; Chief Learned Sec. A. V. SOKOVA.

National Scientific Medical Society of Roentgenologists and Radiologists: 117837 Moscow, ul. Profsoyuznaya 86; Chair. A. S. PAVLOV; Chief Learned Sec. V. Z. AGRANAT.

National Scientific Medical Society of Stomatologists: 119435 Moscow, ul. Pogodinskaya 5; Chair. N. N. BAZHANOV; Chief Learned Sec. V. M. BEZRUKOV.

National Scientific Medical Society of Surgeons: 119874 Moscow, Abrikosovskii per. 2; Chair. B. V. PETROVSKII; Chief Learned Sec. M. I. PERELMAN.

National Scientific Medical Society of Therapists: 121500 Moscow, 3 Cherepkovskaya 15; Chair. A. S. SMETNEV; Chief Learned Sec. B. A. SIDORENKO.

National Scientific Medical Society of Traumatic Surgeons and Orthopaedists: 125299 Moscow, ul. Priorova 10; tel. (495) 450-24-72; fax (495) 154-31-39; f. 1921; Chair. S. P. MIRONOV; Chief Learned Sec. V. V. TROTSENKO; publ. *N. N. Priorov Journal of Traumatology and Orthopaedics* (4 a year).

National Scientific Medical Society of Urological Surgeons: 105483 Moscow, ul. 3-ya Parkovaya 51; tel. (495) 367-62-62; fax (495) 164-76-60; e-mail urology@cdromclub.ru; f. 1925; 5,506 mems; Chair. N. A. LOPATKIN; Chief Learned Sec. L. M. GORILOVSKI; publ. *Urology and Nephrology* (6 a year).

National Scientific Medical Society of Venereologists and Dermatologists: 107076 Moscow, Korolenko str. 3, bldg 6; tel. and fax (495) 964-26-20; e-mail info@cnikvi.ru; f. 1921; Chair. A. A. KUBANOVA; Chief Learned Sec. I. N. LESNAYA.

Russian Academy of Medical Sciences: 109801 Moscow, ul. Solyanka 14; tel. (095) 298-21-37; fax (095) 921-56-15; e-mail orlov@ramn.ru; f. 1944; depts of Preventive Medicine (Academician-Sec. N. F. IZMEROV), Clinical Medicine (Academician-Sec. E. I. GUSEV), Medical and Biological Sciences (Academician-Sec. K. V. SUDAKOV); Siberian dept

(Academician-Sec. V. A. TRUFAKIN), North-west dept (Academician-Sec. B. I. TKA-CHENKO); 496 mems (191 ordinary, 232 corresp., 73 foreign); 60 specialist research ccls; attached research institutes: see Research Institutes; library: see Libraries and Archives; Pres. V. I. POKROVSKY; Gen. Sec. V. A. TUTELIAN; publs *Vesti Meditsyny* (Medical News), *Vestnik Rossiiskoi Akademii Meditsinskikh Nauk* (Journal of the Russian Academy of Medical Sciences), *Arkhiv Patologii* (Pathology Archive), *Byulleten Eksperimentalnoi Biologii i Meditsiny* (Bulletin of Experimental Biology and Medicine), *Voprosy Virusologii* (Problems in Virology), *Voprosy Meditsinskoi Khimii* (Problems in Medical Chemistry), *Immunologiya* (Immunology), *Meditsinskaya Radiologiya* (Medical Radiology and Radiation Safety), *Morfologia* (Morphology), *Patologicheskaya Fiziologiya i Eksperimentalnaya Terapiya* (Pathological Physiology and Experimental Therapy), *Eksperimentalnaya i Klinicheskaya Pharmakologiya* (Experimental and Clinical Pharmacology), *Byulleten Sibirskogo Otdeleniya Rossiiskoi AMN* (Bulletin of the Siberian Division of the Russian Academy of Medical Sciences).

Russian Gastroenterological Association: 119881 Moscow, ul. Pogodinskaya 5; tel. (495) 248-38-00; fax (495) 248-36-10; f. 1995; 2,500 mems; Pres. Prof. Dr V. T. IVASHKIN; Sec. Dr A. S. TRUKHMANOV; publs *Journal of Gastroenterology, Hepatology and Coloproctology* (6 a year).

Russian Medical Association: 125315 Moscow, ul. Baltiskaya 10/3; tel. (495) 151-27-67; fax (495) 151-55-25; e-mail rmass@online.ru; internet www.rmass.ru; f. 1993; 262,000 mems; Chair. Prof. A. G. SARKISIAN; Learned Sec. Dr LEV MALYSHEV; publ. *Vrachebnaya Gazeta* (12 a month).

Russian Neurosurgical Association: 603600 Nizhnii Novgorod, Verkhne-Volskaya nab. 18; tel. (8312) 46-36-48; fax (8312) 36-05-95; Pres. A. P. FRAERMAN; Sec. S. N. KOLESOV.

Russian Oncological Society (St Petersburg branch): 197758 St Petersburg, pos. Pesochnyi-2, ul. Leningradskaya 68; tel. (812) 596-86-54; fax (812) 596-89-47; f. 1954; 460 mems; Chair. Prof. Dr VLADIMIR F. SEMIGLAZOV; Sec.-Gen. Dr EVGENIA V. TSYRLINA; publ. *Voprosi oncologii* (6 a year).

Russian Pharmacology Society: 125315 Moscow, ul. Baltiyskaya 8; tel. (495) 151-18-81; fax (495) 151-12-61; f. 1958 (fmrly All-Union Scientific Medical Soc. of Pharmacologists); 295 mems; library of 10,000 vols; Chair. SERGEY SEREDENIN; Sec.-Gen. ELENA VALDMAN; publ. *Russian Journal of Experimental and Clinical Pharmacology* (in Russian).

Russian Rheumatological Association: 115522 Moscow, Kashirskoye shosse 34A; tel. (495) 114-44-90; fax (495) 114-44-68; e-mail sokrat@irramn.ru; internet www.rheumatolog.ru; f. 1928; 1,860 mems; library of 102,000 vols; Chair. E. NASONOV; Gen. Sec. I. ALEXEEVA; publ. *Clinical-practical Rheumatology* (6 a year).

Russian Society of Medical Genetics: 115478 Moscow, Moskvorechie ul. 1; tel. (499) 612-86-07; fax (499) 324-07-02; e-mail mgnc@med-gen.ru; internet www.med-gen.ru; f. 1993; human genetics, medical genetics, cytogenetics, clinical genetics, genetic counselling, experimental genetics, ecogenetics, human molecular genetics; 500 mems; Chair. Prof. E. K. GINTER; Chief Learned Sec. V. L. IZHEVSKAYA; publ. *Medical Genetics* (12 a year).

Russian Society of Toxicologists: 117105 Moscow, 19A, Varshavskoye shosse; tel. (495) 633-95-90; fax (495) 633-16-84; e-mail khalidiya@yandex.ru; internet www.rpohv.ru; f. 1996; represents Russian toxicologists in int. orgs; contributes information on advanced studies and achievements among toxicologists in Russia; 200 mems; Chair. Dr B. A. KURLYANDSKIY; Exec. Sec. Dr KHALIDYA KHAMIDULINA; publ. *Toxicological Review*.

Scientific Medical Society of Anatomists-Pathologists: 109801 Moscow, ul. Bolshaya Serpuhovskaya 27; Chair. D. S. SARKISOV.

Society of Cardiology: 101953 Moscow, Petroverigskii ul. 10; tel. (495) 623-86-36; e-mail info@cardiosite.ru; internet www.cardiosite.ru; f. 1963; cardiology, diagnosis, treatment and prevention of cardiovascular disease; training courses; 188 mems; Pres. Dr RAFAEL OGANOV; Sec.-Gen. Prof. SVETLANA A. SHALNOVA; publs *Cardiovascular Therapy and Prevention* (6 a year), *Russian Journal of Cardiology* (6 a year).

NATURAL SCIENCES
General

Moscow House of Scientists: 119821 Moscow, Kropotkinskaya ul. 16; tel. (495) 201-45-55; attached to Russian Acad. of Sciences; Dir A. I. DERGACHEV.

St Petersburg M. Gorky House of Scientists: 191065 St Petersburg, Dvortsovaya nab. 26; tel. (812) 315-88-14; attached to Russian Acad. of Sciences; Dir L. M. ANISIMOVA.

Biological Sciences

Biochemical Society: c/o Prof. M. B. Agalarova, Ovchinnikov Institute of Bio-organic Chemistry, 117871 Moscow, Miklukho-Maklaya 16/10; tel. and fax (495) 724-81-44; e-mail biosoc@mail.ibch.ru; f. 1959; attached to Russian Acad. of Sciences; 6,500 mems; Pres. Acad. A. G. GABIBOV; Sec. Gen. MARIA B. AGALAROVA.

Biotechnology Society: 109044 Moscow, Bol. Kommunisticheskaya ul. 27; tel. (495) 272-67-49; Chair. V. E. MATVEYEV.

Hydrobiological Society: 103050 Moscow, Tverskaya ul. 27; tel. (495) 299-65-04; attached to Russian Acad. of Sciences; Pres. L. M. SUSHCHENYA.

Interregional Russian Microbiological Society: 117312 Moscow, pr. 60-letiya Oktyabrya 7, korp. 2; tel. (499) 135-01-80; fax (499) 135-65-30; e-mail microbsociety@inmi.host.ru; internet www.inmi.ru/microbsociety/news.htm; f. 2004; attached to Russian Acad. of Sciences; 580 mems; Pres. V. F. GALCHENKO; Exec. Sec. NATALY GALCHENKO.

Moscow Society of Naturalists: 125009 Moscow, ul. Bolshaya Nikitskaya 6; tel. (495) 629-48-36; internet www.moipros.ru; f. 1805; sections for biophysics, botany, genetics, geography, geology, gerontology, hydrobiology, palaeontology, zoology; 1,500 mems; library of 500,000 vols; Chair Prof. Dr VICTOR A. SADOVNICHY; publ. *Byulleten Moskovskogo Obshchestva Ispytatelei prirody* (6 a year).

Palaeontological Society: 199106 St Petersburg, Sredny Prospect 74; tel. (812) 328-91-56; fax (812) 321-30-23; e-mail po_ran@vsegei.ru; f. 1916; attached to Russian Acad. of Sciences; 700 mems; Pres. B. S. SOKOLOV.

Russian Botanical Society: 197376 St Petersburg, ul. Prof. Popova 2; tel. (812) 346-47-53; fax (812) 234-45-12; attached to Russian Acad. of Sciences; Pres. R. V. KAMELIN.

Russian Entomological Society: 199034 St Petersburg, Universitetskaya nab. 1; tel. (812) 328-12-12; fax (812) 114-04-14; e-mail reo@zisp.spb.su; f. 1859; attached to Russian Acad. of Sciences; 2,000 mems; library of 80,000 vols; Pres. G. S. MEDVEDEV; publs *Chtenia pamyati N.A. Kholodkovskogo* (1 a year), *Entomologicheskoe obozrenie* (4 a year), *Trudy Russkogo Entomologicheskogo Obschestva* (irregular).

Russian Society of Geneticists and Breeders: 117312 Moscow, ul. Fersmana 11, korp. 2; tel. (495) 124-59-52; attached to Russian Acad. of Sciences; Pres. Acad. V. A. STRUNNIKOV.

Society of Helminthologists: 117259 Moscow, Bol. Cheremushkinskaya 28; attached to Russian Acad. of Sciences; Pres. A. S. BESSONOV.

Society of Ornithologists: c/o Russian Academy of Sciences, 117901 Moscow, Leninsky pr. 14; attached to Russian Acad. of Sciences; Pres. V. D. ILICHEV.

Society of Protozoologists: 194064 St Petersburg, Tikhoretsky pr. 4; tel. (812) 247-18-36; fax (812) 247-03-41; e-mail tamara@tb10336.spb.edu; f. 1968 as All-Union Society of Protozoologists; present name 1991; attached to Russian Acad. of Sciences; 200 mems; Pres. (vacant); Sec.-Gen. Prof. Dr TAMARA V. BEYER; publs *Protistology* (4 a year), *Tsitologiya* (Cytology, in Russian with English summaries, 12 a year).

Physical Sciences

Astronomical and Geodesical Society: 103001 Moscow, Sadovo-Kudrinskaya ul. 24; attached to Russian Acad. of Sciences; Pres. YU. D. BULANZHE.

Ferrous Metallurgy Society: 129812 Moscow, pr. Mira 101; tel. (495) 287-83-80; Chair. N. I. DROZDOV.

Gubkin, Acad. I. M., Petroleum and Gas Society: 117876 Moscow, 12-ya Parkovaya ul. 5; tel. (495) 463-93-72; Chair. S. T. TOPLOV.

Mendeleev, D. I., Chemical Society: 101907 Moscow, Krivokolennyi per. 12; tel. (495) 928-43-51; fax (495) 928-43-54; f. 1868; 45 regional orgs; 1,800 mems; Sec.-Gen. NATATYA KOSSINOVA; publs *Chemistry in Russia* (12 a year bulletin), *Russian Chemical Journal* (6 a year).

Russian Geological Society: 113191 Moscow, 2-aya Roshinskaya ul. 10; tel. (495) 954-96-34; fax (495) 954-96-22; f. 1988; 1,025 mems; Pres. V. P. ORLOV.

Russian Mineralogical Society: 199026 St Petersburg, 21st line 2; tel. and fax (812) 328-86-40; e-mail rmo@minsoc.ru; internet www.minsoc.ru; f. 1817; attached to Russian Acad. of Sciences; mineralogy and adjacent sciences; 1,200 mems; library of 85,000 vols; Pres. Prof. DMITRY RUNDQVIST; Vice-Pres. Prof. YURI MARIN; publ. *Zapiski RMO (Proceedings of the Russian Mineralogical Society)*.

Society of Non-Ferrous Metallurgy: 103001 Moscow, Sadovaya-Kudrinskaya ul. 18; tel. (495) 291-29-87; Chair. V. S. LOBANOV.

PHILOSOPHY AND PSYCHOLOGY

Russian Philosophical Society: 119991 Moscow, ul. Volhonka 14, Room 102; tel. (495) 609-90-76; e-mail rphs@iph.ras.ru; internet www.dialog21.ru; f. 1971; attached to Russian Acad. of Sciences; 6,131 mems; Pres. V. S. STEPIN; Vice-Pres. A. N. CHUMAKOV; publ. *Bulletin of the Russian Philosophical Society*.

Society of Psychologists: 129366 Moscow, Yaroslavskaya ul. 13; tel. (495) 282-45-03; attached to Russian Acad. of Sciences; Chair. E. V. SHOROKHOVA.

RELIGION, SOCIOLOGY AND ANTHROPOLOGY

Russian Society of Sociologists: 117259 Moscow, ul. Krzhizhanovskogo 24/35 str. 5; tel. (495) 719-09-71; fax (495) 719-07-40; e-mail mansurov@isras.rssi.ru; internet www.isras.rssi.ru; f. 1989; attached to Russian Acad. of Sciences; 1,350 mems; Chair. VALERY A. MANSUROV.

TECHNOLOGY

Aircraft Building Society: 125040 Moscow, Leningradskii pr. 24a; tel. (495) 214-22-88; Chair. A. M. BATKOV.

Civil Engineering Society: 103062 Moscow, Podsosensky per. 25; tel. (495) 297-07-29; Chair. I. I. ISHENKO.

Computers and Informatics Society: 127486 Moscow, Deguninskaya ul. 1, korp. 4; tel. (495) 487-31-61; Chair. I. N. BUKREYEV.

Mapping and Prospecting Engineering Society: 117801 Moscow, ul. Krzhizhanovskogo 14, korp. 2; tel. (495) 124-35-60; Chair. A. A. DRAZHNYUK.

Mechanical Engineering Society: 109004 Moscow, ul. Zemlyanoi Val 64, korp. 1; tel. (495) 297-93-00; Chair. B. N. SOKOLOV.

Mining Engineers' Society: 103006 Moscow, Karetnyi ryad 10/18; tel. (495) 299-88-15; Chair. A. P. FISUN.

Popov, A. S., Radio Engineering, Electronics and Telecommunications Society: 103897 Moscow, Kuznetskii Most 20/6; tel. (495) 921-71-08; Chair. YU. V. GULYAEV.

Power and Electrical Power Engineering Society: 191025 St Petersburg, Stremyannaya ul. 10; tel. (812) 311-32-77; Chair. N. N. TIKHODEYEV.

Scientific-Technical Association: 198103 St Petersburg, pr. Ogorodnikova 26; tel. (812) 251-28-50; attached to Russian Acad. of Sciences; General Dir M. L. ALEKSANDROV.

Shipbuilding Engineering Society: 191011 St Petersburg, Nevskii pr. 44; tel. (495) 315-50-27; Chair. I. V. GORYNIN.

Society of the Food Industry: 103031 Moscow, Kuznetskii Most 19, pod. 2; tel. (495) 924-49-30; Chair. A. N. BOGATYREV.

Society of the Instrument Manufacturing Industry and Metrologists: 103009 Moscow, Tverskaya ul. 12, str. 2; tel. (495) 209-47-98; Chair. G. I. KAVALEROV.

Society of Light Industry: 117846 Moscow, ul. Vavilova 69; tel. (495) 134-90-01; Chair. R. A. CHAYANOV.

Vavilov, S. I., Society of Instrument Manufacturers: 121019 Moscow, Mokhovaya ul. 17, str. 2; tel. (495) 203-34-65.

Water Transport Society: 103012 Moscow, Staropansky per. 3; tel. (495) 921-18-12; Chair. (vacant).

Research Institutes

AGRICULTURE, FISHERIES AND VETERINARY SCIENCE

Adygea Agricultural Research Institute: 352764 Krasnodar krai, Maikop, Podgornoe; attached to Russian Acad. of Agricultural Sciences.

Afanasev, V. A., Research Institute of Fur-Bearing Animals and Rabbits: 140143 Moscow oblast, Ramensky raion, p/o Rodniki; tel. and fax (495) 501-53-55; e-mail niipzk@mail.ru; f. 1932; attached to Russian Acad. of Agricultural Sciences; Dir N. A. BALAKIREV.

Agrarian Institute: 103064 Moscow, Bol. Kharitonevskaya per. 21, korp. 2, POB 34; tel. (495) 207-70-75; fax (495) 928-22-90; e-mail agrin@glas.apc.org; f. 1990; attached to Russian Acad. of Agricultural Sciences; Dir Dr A. V. PETRIKOV.

Agricultural Research Institute for the Central Areas of the Non-Black Soil (Nechernozem) Zone: 143104 Moscow oblast, Odintsovsky raion, Nemchinovka, ul. Agrokhimikov 6; tel. (495) 591-83-91; attached to Russian Acad. of Agricultural Sciences.

Agrophysical Research Institute: 195220 St Petersburg, Grazhdanskii Pr.14; tel. (495) 543-46-30; e-mail office@agrophys.ru; attached to Russian Acad. of Agricultural Sciences; Dir I. B. USKOV.

All-Russia Horticulture Institute for Breeding, Agrotechnology and Nursery: 115598 Moscow, Birulevo-Zagorie, ul. Zagorievskogo; tel. and fax (495) 329-51-66; e-mail vstisp@vstisp.org; internet www.vstisp.org; attached to Russian Acad. of Agricultural Sciences; Dir IVAN KULIKOV; publ. *Fruit Trees and Small Fruits of Russia* (2 a year).

All-Russia Institute of Plant Protection: 196608 St Petersburg, Pushkin, shosse Podbelskogo 3; tel. (812) 470-43-84; fax (812) 470-51-10; e-mail vizrspb@mail333.com; internet www.vizrspb.chat.ru; f. 1929; attached to Russian Acad. of Agricultural Sciences; Dir V. A. PAVLYUSHIN; publ. *Plant Protection News* (3 a year).

All-Russia Legumes and Pulse Crops Research Institute: 302502 Orel, p/o Streletskoe; tel. (0862) 403-224; fax (0862) 403-130; e-mail office@vniizbk.orel.ru; internet vniizbk.ru; attached to Russian Acad. of Agricultural Sciences; Dir Prof. V. I. ZOTIKOV.

All-Russia Maize Research Institute: 860022 Nalchik, ul. Mechnikova 130A; tel. (86622) 5-03-16; attached to Russian Acad. of Agricultural Sciences.

All-Russia Meat Research Institute: 109316 Moscow, ul. Talilikhina 26; tel. (495) 276-95-11; fax (495) 276-95-51; e-mail vniimp@glasnet.ru; f. 1930; attached to Russian Acad. of Agricultural Sciences; Dir L. A. BORISOVICH.

All-Russia Potato Research Institute: 140052 Moscow oblast, Lyuberetsky raion, pos. Korenevo, ul. Lorkha; tel. and fax (495) 557-10-11; f. 1930; attached to Russian Acad. of Agricultural Sciences; library of 500,000 vols; Dir Prof. A. V. KORSHUNOV.

All-Russia Poultry Research and Technology Institute: Moscow oblast, Sergiev pos.; attached to Russian Acad. of Agricultural Sciences.

All-Russia Research and Technological Institute for Chemical Land Reclamation: 189520 St Petersburg, Pushkin, ul. Lermontova 9; tel. (812) 465-58-75; attached to Russian Acad. of Agricultural Sciences.

All-Russia Research and Technological Institute for Chemicalization in Agriculture: 143013 Moscow oblast, Odinstsovsky raion, Nemchinovka, ul. Agrokhimikov 6; tel. (495) 591-91-73; attached to Russian Acad. of Agricultural Sciences.

All-Russia Research and Technological Institute for Mechanization in Livestock Raising: 142004 Moscow oblast, Podolsky raion, p/o Znamya Oktyabrya; tel. (495) 119-74-97; fax (495) 119-75-17; f. 1969; attached to Russian Acad. of Agricultural Sciences; Dir N. M. MOROZOV; publ. *Scientific Research Problems of Mechanization and Automation of Livestock Farming.*

All-Russia Research Institute for Agricultural Biotechnology: 127550 Moscow, Timiryazevskaya ul. 42; tel. (495) 976-65-44; fax (495) 977-09-47; e-mail iab@iab.ac.ru; internet www.agrobiotech.ru; f. 1974; attached to Russian Acad. of Agricultural Sciences; Dir P. N. KHARCHENKO.

All-Russia Research Institute for Agricultural Economics and Standards and Norms: 344006 Rostov on Don, pr. Sokolova 52; tel. (8632) 65-31-81; fax (8632) 64-89-61; f. 1980; attached to Russian Acad. of Agricultural Sciences; Dir Dr VLADIMIR V. KUZNETSOV.

All-Russia Research Institute for Beef Cattle Breeding and Production: Orenburg, Yanvarskaya ul. 29; attached to Russian Acad. of Agricultural Sciences.

All-Russia Research Institute for Biological Control: 350039 Krasnodar, a/ya 39; tel. (8612) 50-81-91; attached to Russian Acad. of Agricultural Sciences.

All-Russia Research Institute for Cybernetics in the Agro-industrial Complex: 117218 Moscow, ul. Krzhizhanovskogo 14/1; tel. (495) 124-76-02; attached to Russian Acad. of Agricultural Sciences.

All-Russia Research Institute for Economics, Labour and Management in Agriculture: 111621 Moscow, Orenburgskaya ul. 15; tel. (495) 550-06-71; attached to Russian Acad. of Agricultural Sciences.

All-Russia Research Institute for Electrification in Agriculture: 109456 Moscow, 1-i Veshnyakovskii pr. 2; tel. (499) 171-19-20; fax (499) 170-51-01; e-mail viesh@dol.ru; internet www.viesh.ru; f. 1930; attached to Russian Acad. of Agricultural Sciences; rural energy and electrification, solar energy biomass and wind energy; library of 135,000 vols; Dir Acad. D. S. STREBKOV; publ. *Scientific Proceedings* (2 a year).

All-Russia Research Institute for Farm Animal Genetics and Breeding: 196600 St Petersburg-Pushkin, Moskovskoye shosse 55a; tel. (812) 470-76-63; fax (812) 465-99-89; e-mail spbvniigen@mail.ru; attached to Russian Acad. of Agricultural Sciences; Dir Acad. P.N. PROCHORENKO.

All-Russia Research Institute for Floriculture and Subtropical Crops: 354002 Sochi, Jan Fabriziusa str. 2/28; tel. (8622) 96-40-21; fax (8622) 46-80-16; e-mail subplod@mail.ru; f. 1894; attached to Russian Acad. of Agricultural Sciences; library of 77,000 vols.

All-Russia Research Institute for Horse Breeding: 391105 Ryazan oblast, Rybnoyek raion; tel. and fax (912) 24-02-65; e-mail vniik08@mail.ru; internet www.ruhorses.ru; f. 1930; attached to Russian Acad. of Agricultural Sciences; library of 47,000 vols; Dir Prof. Dr V. V. KALASHNIKOV; publs *Scientific Works* (1 a year), *Stud Book* (every 4 years, with 1 a year supplement).

All-Russia Research Institute for Irrigated Arable Farming: 400002 Volgograd, Timiryazevskaya ul. 9; tel. (8442) 43-49-79; fax (8442) 43-34-75; e-mail vniioz@avtlg.ru; f. 1967; attached to Russian Acad. of Agricultural Sciences; library of 138,000 vols; Dir Dr V. V. MELIKHOV.

All-Russia Research Institute for Irrigated Horticulture and Vegetable Crops Production: 416300 Astrakhan oblast, Kamyziak, ul. Lubicha 13; attached to Russian Acad. of Agricultural Sciences.

All-Russia Research Institute for Mechanization in Agriculture: 109389 Moscow, 1-i Institutskii pr. 5; tel. (495) 171-19-33; attached to Russian Acad. of Agricultural Sciences; Dir Acad. V. A. KUIBYSHEV.

All-Russia Research Institute for Sheep and Goat Breeding: 355014 Stavropol, Zootekhnichesky per. 15; tel. and fax (8652) 34-76-88; f. 1932; attached to Russian Acad.

of Agricultural Sciences; Dir Prof. VASILY MOROZ.

All-Russia Research Institute for the Agricultural Use of Reclaimed and Improved Land: 170530 Tver oblast, Emmaus; tel. (0822) 37-15-46; fax (0822) 36-07-63; e-mail vniimz@mail.ru; internet www .vniimz.newmail.ru; f. 1977; attached to Russian Acad. of Agricultural Sciences; library of 20,000 vols; Dir Dr N. KOVALEV.

All-Russia Research Institute for the Biosynthesis of Protein Substances: 109004 Moscow, Bol. Kommunisticheskaya 27; tel. (495) 912-70-09; fax (495) 911-39-23; e-mail belok@rutenia.ru; attached to Russian Acad. of Agricultural Sciences; Dir Dr ALEXANDER P. ZAKHARYCHEV.

All-Russia Research Institute for Vegetable Breeding and Seed Production: 143080 Moscow oblast, Odintsovsky raion, Lesnoi gorodok; tel. (495) 599-24-42; fax (495) 599-22-77; e-mail vniissok@cea.ru; f. 1920; attached to Russian Acad. of Agricultural Sciences; Dir Prof. VICTOR F. PIVOVAROV.

All-Russia Research Institute for Veterinary Sanitation, Hygiene and Ecology: 123022 Moscow, Zvenigorodskoe shosse 5; tel. (495) 256-35-81; attached to Russian Acad. of Agricultural Sciences.

All-Russia Research Institute of Agricultural Microbiology: 189620 St Petersburg, Pushkin 8, shosse Podbelskogo 3; tel. (812) 470-51-00; fax (812) 470-43-62; f. 1930; attached to Russian Acad. of Agricultural Sciences; Dir Prof. I. A. TIKHONOVICH.

All-Russia Research Institute of Animal Husbandry: 142023 Moscow oblast, Podolskii raion, pos. Dubrovitsy; tel. (495) 546-63-35; attached to Russian Acad. of Agricultural Sciences; Dir Acad. A. P. KALASHNIKOV.

All-Russia Research Institute of Arable Farming and Soil Erosion Control: 305021 Kursk, ul. Karla Marksa 70B; tel. (0712) 53-42-56; fax (0712) 53-67-29; e-mail vnizem@kursknet.ru; f. 1970; attached to Russian Acad. of Agricultural Sciences; library of 20,000 vols, 40 periodicals; Dir G. N. CHERKASOV.

All-Russia Research Institute of Economics in Agriculture: 123007 Moscow, Khoroshevskoe shosse 35, korp 3; tel. (495) 195-60-16; attached to Russian Acad. of Agricultural Sciences; Dir I. G. USHCHACHEV.

All-Russia Research Institute of Information, Technological and Economic Research on the Agro-Industrial Complex: c/o Russian Academy of Agricultural Sciences, 107814 Moscow, Bolshoi Kharitonevsky per. 21; attached to Russian Acad. of Agricultural Sciences; Dir Acad. V. I. NAZARENKO.

All-Russia Research Institute of Marine Fisheries and Oceanography: 107140 Moscow, Verkhnyaya Krasnoselskaya 17; tel. (495) 264-93-87; Dir A. S. BOGDANOV.

All-Russia Research Institute of Medicinal and Aromatic Plants: 113628 Moscow, ul. Grina 7; tel. (495) 382-83-18; attached to Russian Acad. of Agricultural Sciences.

All-Russia Research Institute of Organic Fertilizers and Peat: 601390, Vladimir obl., Sudogodskiy region, Vyatkino; tel. (22) 42-60-14; fax (22) 42-60-10; e-mail vnion@vtsnet.ru; f. 1981; attached to Russian Acad. of Agricultural Sciences; Dir Dr LUKIN SERGEY MICHAILOVICH.

All-Russia Research Institute of Phytopathology: 143050 Moscow oblast, Vyazemy; tel. (495) 592-92-87; e-mail vniif@vniif .ru; attached to Russian Acad. of Agricultural Sciences.

All-Russia Research Institute of Pond Fishery: 141821 Moscow oblast, Dmitrovsky raion, p/o Rubnoe; tel. (495) 587-21-98; attached to Russian Acad. of Agricultural Sciences.

All-Russia Research Institute of Tobacco, Makhorka and Tobacco Products: 350072 Krasnodar, Moskovskaya ul. 42; tel. (861) 252-08-82; e-mail vniitti1@mail .kuban.ru; attached to Russian Acad. of Agricultural Sciences; Dir V. A. SALOMATIN.

All-Russia Rice Research Institute: 353204 Krasnodar krai, Dinskoi raion, pos. Belozernoe; tel. (8612) 56-65-96; fax (8612) 50-91-24; e-mail arri_kub@mail.ru; attached to Russian Min. of Agriculture; Dir Prof. E. P. ALESHIN.

All-Russia Vegetable Production Research Institute: 141018 Moscow oblast, Mytishchi, Novomytishchinsky pr. 82; tel. (495) 582-00-15; attached to Russian Acad. of Agricultural Sciences.

All-Russia Veterinary Research Institute for Poultry Diseases: St Petersburg, Moskovsky pr. 99; attached to Russian Acad. of Agricultural Sciences.

All-Russian Plant Quarantine Centre: 140150 Bykovo, Ramenskoe region, Moscow oblast, Pogranichnaya 32; tel. (499) 271-38-24; fax (495) 785-76-13; e-mail vniikr@mail .ru; internet www.vniikr.ru; f. 1979; plant quarantine research and diagnostics; library of 10,000 vols; Dir Dr ULLUBY MAGOMEDOV; Deputy Dir Dr NATALYA SHEROKOLAVA; Deputy Dir Dr MUZAFAR ABASOV; Deputy Dir Dr VERA IAKOVLEVA; publ. *Plant Quarantine Issues*.

All-Russian Rapeseed Research Institute: 398037 Lipetsk, Boevoy proezd 26; tel. and fax (4742) 34-63-61; e-mail rapeseed@ yandex.ru; internet rapslipetsk.ru; f. 1986; attached to Russian Acad. of Agricultural Sciences; Head VLADIMIR VLADIMIROVICH KARPACHEV.

All-Russian Scientific Research Institute of Agroforest Reclamation: 400062 Volgograd, Universitetsky pr. 97; tel. (8442) 46-25-67; fax (8442) 46-25-13; e-mail vnialmi@avtlg.ru; internet www.vnialmi.ru; f. 1931; attached to Russian Acad. of Agricultural Sciences; research on reclamation of agricultural lands by methods of forest and phytomelioration; combats desertification processes; ecological investigations; library of 93,700 vols; Dir KONSTANTIN N. KULIK; publ. *Scientific Papers* (2 a year).

All-Russian Williams Fodder Research Institute: 141055 Moscow oblast, Lobnya Nauchniy gorodok; tel. (495) 577-73-37; fax (495) 577-71-07; e-mail vniicormov@nm.ru; internet www.vniikormov.ru; f. 1922; attached to Russian Acad. of Agricultural Sciences; scientific research in fields of agriculture, biology, genetics, breeding and seed multiplication of forage crops; grasslands management, fodder production, fodder preservation and utilization; library of 15,000 vols of books, scientific journals, methodological recommendations, brochures, patents, dissertations; Dir Prof. Dr VLADIMIR KOSOLAPOV; publ. *Adaptive Fodder Production (AFP)* (4 a year, online (www.adaptagro.ru)).

Altai Experimental Farm: 659739 Altai krai, Gorno-Altaisky autonomous oblast, Shebalinsky raion, selo Cherga; attached to Russian Acad. of Sciences; Dir YU. S. ZEMIROV.

Bashkir Research and Technological Institute for Animal Husbandry and Feed Production: Bashkortostan, 450025 Ufa, Pushkinskaya ul. 86; tel. (3472) 22-17-23; attached to Russian Acad. of Agricultural Sciences.

Bashkir Research Institute for Arable Farming and Field Crops Breeding: 450059 Ufa, ul. Zorge 19; tel. (3472) 24-07-08; attached to Russian Acad. of Agricultural Sciences.

Caspian Research Institute for Arid Arable Farming: 431213 Astrakhan, Solenoe zaimishche; tel. (851) 24-38-36; fax (851) 192-17-00; f. 1991; attached to Russian Acad. of Agricultural Sciences; library of 30,000 vols.

Chelyabinsk Agricultural Research Institute: 436404 Chelyabinsk oblast, Chebarkulsky raion, Timiryazevsky; tel. (35168) 33-23-16; attached to Russian Acad. of Agricultural Sciences.

Dagestan Agricultural Research Institute: 367014 Makhachkala, pr. K. Marksa, Nauchnyi park; tel. (8722) 3-66-60; attached to Russian Acad. of Agricultural Sciences.

Don Zone Agricultural Research Institute: 346714 Rostov oblast, Aksai raion, Rassvet; attached to Russian Acad. of Agricultural Sciences.

Flax Research Institute: 172060 Tverskii raion, Torzhok, ul. Lunacharskogo 35; tel. (08251) 5-16-45; fax (08251) 5-44-58; e-mail vniil@tver.dep.ru; f. 1930; library of 50,000 vols; Dir ANATOLI N. MARCHENKOV; publ. *Trudy VNIL* (1 a year).

Forest Research Institute of the Karelian Research Centre: 185910 Petrozavodsk, Pushkinskaya ul. 11; tel. and fax (8142) 76-81-60; e-mail forest@krc.karelia .ru; internet forestry.krc.karelia.ru; f. 1957; attached to Russian Acad. of Sciences; Dir Dr VITALY KRUTOV.

Institute of Forest Research: 143030 Moscow oblast, Odintsovsky raion, p/o Uspenskoe; tel. and fax (495) 419-52-57; f. 1958; attached to Russian Acad. of Sciences; library of 51,400 vols; Dir Prof. S. E. VOMPERSKY; publ. *Lesovedenie* (Russian Forest Science, 6 a year).

Institute of Forestry: 620134 Ekaterinburg, Bilimbaevskaya ul. 32A; tel. (3432) 52-08-80; attached to Russian Acad. of Sciences; Dir S. A. MAMAEV.

Institute of Soil Science and Agrochemistry: 630099 Novosibirsk, Sovetskaya St. 18; tel. (3832) 22-50-88; fax (3832) 22-76-52; e-mail go2siberia@gmail.com; internet www .siberia-eco.org; f. 1968; attached to Russian Acad. of Sciences; education and research soil science, plant nutrition, pedology, soil chemistry, soil microbiology, int. field courses, summer schools in Siberia, int. annual soil-ecological excursions in Siberia; Dir Dr KONSTANTIN S. BAYKOV; Scientific Sec. for Int. Cooperation Dr PAVEL A. BARSUKOV.

Kovalenko, Ya. R., All-Russia Institute of Experimental Veterinary Science: 109472 Moscow, Kuzminki; tel. (495) 377-29-79; attached to Russian Acad. of Agricultural Sciences; Dir G. F. KOROMYSLOV.

Krasnodar Scientific Research Institute of the Storage and Processing of Agricultural Produce: 350072 Krasnodar, Topolinaya Alley St 2; tel. (8612) 52-15-93; fax (8612) 57-01-56; e-mail kisp@kubannet .ru; internet www.kniihpsp.ru; attached to Russian Acad. of Agricultural Sciences.

Krasnodar Scientific Research Institute of Vegetable and Potato Production: 350921 Krasnodar Belozerny; tel. (8612) 229-54-90; f. 1931; attached to Russian Acad. of Agricultural Sciences; library of 10,000 vols.

Kursk Research Institute of the Agro-industrial Complex: 307026 Kursk oblast, Cheremushki; attached to Russian Acad. of Agricultural Sciences.

Lukianenko, P. P., Krasnodar Agricultural Research Institute: 350012 Krasnodar; tel. (8612) 56-28-15; attached to Russian Acad. of Agricultural Sciences.

Michurin, I. V., All-Russia Research Institute for Genetics and Breeding in Horticulture: 393740 Tambov oblast, Michurinsk; tel. (47545) 5-78-87; fax (47545) 5-79-29; e-mail cglm@rambler.ru; attached to Russian Acad. of Agricultural Sciences; Dir SAVELYEV NIKOLAI IVANOVICH.

Michurin, I. V., All-Russia Research Institute for Horticulture: 393740 Tambov oblast, Michurinsk, ul. Michurina 30; tel. and fax (47545) 2-07-61; e-mail vniis@pochta.ru; f. 1931; attached to Russian Acad. of Agricultural Sciences; Dir Prof. Dr YURI TRUNOV.

N.I. Vavilov All Russian Research Institute of the Plant Industry: 190000 St Petersburg Bolshaya Morskaya St42–44; tel. (812) 315-50-93; fax (812) 311-87-62; e-mail vir@vir.nw.ru; internet vir.nw.ru; f. 1894; attached to Russian Acad. of Agricultural Sciences; departments: computerized information systems; plant biochemistry and molecular biology; laboratory for long-term storage of seeds; rye, barley and oats; fruit crops; industrial crops; experimental stations: Astrakhan, Daghestan, Far East, Krymsk, Kuban, Maikop, Moscow, Pavlovsk, Polar, Volgograd, Yekaterinino, Zeya; herbarium of 250,000 specimens; Dir Prof. Dr NIKOLAI I. DZYUBENKO.

Nizhne-Volzhsky Agricultural Research Institute: 404013 Volgograd oblast, Nizheznensky; attached to Russian Acad. of Agricultural Sciences.

North Caucasus Mountains and Foothills Agricultural Research Institute: 363110 North Ossetia, Prigorny raion, Mikhailovskoe; attached to Russian Acad. of Agricultural Sciences.

North Caucasus Research Institute for Horticulture and Viticulture: 350029 Krasnodar, ul. 40-letiya Pobedy 9; tel. (8612) 54-06-74; attached to Russian Acad. of Agricultural Sciences.

Orenburg Agricultural Research Institute: 460051 Orenburg, ul. Gagarina 27/1; tel. (3532) 3-86-94; attached to Russian Acad. of Agricultural Sciences.

Pacific Fisheries Research Centre (TINRO): 690950 Vladivostok, ul. Shevchenko 4; tel. (4232) 400921; fax (4232) 300752; e-mail tinro@tinro.ru; f. 1925; ichthyology, oceanography, commercial invertebrates, commercial marine algae, parasitology of marine animals, commercial fisheries, mechanization of fish processing, technology of fish and marine production, aquaculture (marine and freshwater), study of marine pollution; brs at Amur (Khabarovsk) and Chukotka; library of 61,500 vols, 11,000 MSS; Dir Dr L. N. BOCHAROV; publ. *Izvestiya TINRO* (1–3 a year).

Potapenko, Ya. I., All-Russia Research Institute for Viticulture and Winemaking: Rostovsky raion, 346421 Novocherkassk, pr. Baklanovsky 166; tel. (86352) 6-70-88; fax (86352) 6-64-59; e-mail ruswine@yandex.ru; internet www.rusvine.com; f. 1936; attached to Russian Acad. of Agricultural Sciences; Dir Dr LEONID VASILIEVICH KRAVCHENKO.

Povolzhsky Research Institute for the Economics and Development of the Agro-industrial Complex: 410020 Saratov, ul. Shekhurdina 12; tel. (8452) 64-06-47; attached to Russian Acad. of Agricultural Sciences.

Pryanishnikov, D. N., All-Russia Research Institute of Agrochemistry: 127550 Moscow, ul. Pryanishnikova 31A; tel. (495) 976-37-50; fax (495) 976-37-39; e-mail info@vniia-pr.ru; internet www .vniia-pr.ru; f. 1931; attached to Russian Acad. of Agricultural Sciences; coordination of field experiments with Fertilizers Network, Scientific and Methodical Center of Agrochemical Service, Official Registration Agency for Chemicals and Soils; theory of crop nutrition, soil fertility monitoring of agricultural lands, strategy of fertilizers and chemicals application, geographical principles of fertilizers efficiency, new fertilizers; updating of agrochemical service, integration of agrochemical data; Dir V. G. SYCHEV.

Pustovoit, V. S., All-Russia Research Institute of Oil Crops: 350038 Krasnodar, ul. Filatova 17; tel. (861) 255-59-33; fax (861) 254-27-80; e-mail vniimk-center@mail.ru; internet www.vniimk.ru; f. 1912; attached to Russian Acad. of Agricultural Sciences; breeding and seed growing of oil crops: sunflower, soybean, flax, mustard, rapeseed; library of 100,300 vols; Gen. Dir Dr VYACHESLAV M. LUKOMETS; publ. *Oil Crops Scientific Bulletin* (2 a year).

Research and Technological Institute for Agricultural Biotechnology: 410020 Saratov, ul. Tulaikova 7; tel. (8452) 64-04-31; attached to Russian Acad. of Agricultural Sciences.

Research Institute for Animal Nutrition: Moscow oblast, Dmitrovsky raion, pos. Ermolovo.

Research Institute for Breeding and Diversity in Horticulture: 303130 Orel, Zhilina; attached to Russian Acad. of Agricultural Sciences.

Research Institute of Chemical Means of Plant Protection: 109088 Moscow, Ugreshskaya 31; tel. (495) 679-55-40; Dir B. P. VASILENKOV.

Research Institute of Farm Animal Physiology, Biochemistry and Nutrition: 249010 Kaluzhskaya oblast, Borovsk; tel. (495) 996-34-15; fax (48438) 42088; e-mail bifip@kaluga.ru; internet bifip2006 .narod.ru; f. 1960; attached to Russian Acad. of Agricultural Sciences; library of 55,000 vols; Dir Dr A. SH. USHAKOV; publ. *Problems of Productive Animal Biology* (4 a year).

Research Institute of Non-infectious Animal Diseases: Moscow oblast, Istrinsky raion.

Research Institute of Technological Studies in Agricultural Cybernetics: c/o Russian Academy of Agricultural Sciences, 107814 Moscow, Bolshoi Kharitonevsky per. 21; attached to Russian Acad. of Agricultural Sciences.

Research Institute of the Economics and Development of the Agro-industrial Complex in the Central Black Soil (Chernozem) Zone: 394042 Voronezh, ul. Sarafimovicha 26A; tel. and fax (4732) 22-99-40; e-mail niieoapk@mail.ru; internet niieoapk.ru; f. 1930; attached to Russian Acad. of Agricultural Sciences; Dir I. HITSKOV.

Research Institute of Veterinary Entomology and Arachnology: 625010 Tyumen, Institutskaya ul. 2; e-mail adm@vniier .ru; attached to Russian Acad. of Agricultural Sciences; Dir V. Z. YAMOV.

Russian Institute of Agricultural Radiology and Agroecology: 249032 Kaluga oblast, Obninsk, Kievskoe shosse 109 km; tel. (48439) 6-48-02; fax (48439) 6-80-66; e-mail riarae@riar.obninsk.org; f. 1971; attached to Russian Acad. of Agricultural Sciences; library of 70,000 vols; Dir RUDOLF M. ALEXAKHIN; Deputy Dir NATALYA I. SANZHAROVA.

St Petersburg Forestry Research Institute: 194021 St Petersburg, Institutsky pr. 21; tel. (812) 552-80-21; fax (812) 552-80-42; e-mail spbfriin@nm10043.spb.edu; internet www.spbniilh.ru; f. 1929; 130 mems; library of 90,000 vols; Dir ALEXANDER B. EGOROV (acting).

State Scientific Institution Voronezh Scientific Research Institute of Agriculture: 397463 Voronezh, p/o Institute Dokuchaev, oblast, Talovya raion; e-mail niishi1c@mail.ru; internet www.niidokuchaeva.ru; attached to Russian Acad. of Agricultural Sciences.

Samoilov, Ya. V., Research Institute of Fertilizers and Insectofungicides: 119333 Moscow, Leninsky pr. 55/1, bld. 1; tel. (495) 232-96-89; fax (495) 956-19-02; e-mail info@niui.ru; internet www.niuif.ru; f. 1919; technology for production of phosphate fertilisers, sulphuric, phosphoric and nitric acid, and feed phosphates; Gen. Dir V. V. DAVYDENKO; publ. *Mir Sery i NPK (The World of Sulphur & NPK)*.

Skryabin, K. I., All-Russia Institute of Helminthology: 117259 Moscow, Bol. Cheremushkinskaya, 28; tel. (495) 124-56-55; attached to Russian Acad. of Agricultural Sciences; Dir Acad. V. S. ERSHOV.

South-East Agricultural Research Institute: 410020 Saratov, ul. Tulaykova 7; tel. and fax (8452) 64-76-88; f. 1910; attached to Russian Acad. of Agricultural Sciences; library of 350,000 vols; Dir NIKOLAI I. KOMAROV.

South Urals Agricultural Research Institute: 454002 Chelyabinsk, Shershni; tel. (3512) 42-42-01; attached to Russian Acad. of Agricultural Sciences.

Stavropol Agricultural Research Institute: 356200 Stavropol krai, Shpakovskoe; attached to Russian Acad. of Agricultural Sciences.

Tula Agricultural Research Institute: 301053 Tula oblast, Molochnye dvory; tel. (08752) 5-23-41; fax (08752) 2-30-15; f. 1956; attached to Russian Acad. of Agricultural Sciences; Dir Prof. V. I. SEVEROV.

Tulaikov, M. M., Samara Agricultural Research Institute: 446080 Samara oblast, Bezenchuk, ul. K. Marksa 41; attached to Russian Acad. of Agricultural Sciences.

Ulyanovsk Agricultural Research Institute: 433115 Ulyanovsk oblast, Timiryazevskoe; tel. (8422) 31-78-58; e-mail ulniish@mv .ru; attached to Russian Acad. of Agricultural Sciences.

V. N. Sukachev Forest Institute: 660036 Krasnoyarsk, Akademgorodok 50, Bldg 28; tel. and fax (3912) 43-36-86; e-mail institute_forest@ksc.krasn.ru; f. 1944; attached to Russian Acad. of Sciences; library of 143,731 vols; Dir ALEXANDER A. ONUCHIN.

V. V. Dokuchaev Soil Science Institute: 109017 Moscow, Pyzhevsky per. 7; tel. (495) 951-50-37; e-mail info@esoil.ru; internet www.esoil.ru; f. 1927; attached to Russian Acad. of Agricultural Sciences; research in field of soil science; Dir ANDREY IVANOV; Vice-Dir IGOR SAVIN.

ARCHITECTURE AND TOWN PLANNING

Central Research and Design Institute of Dwellings: 127434 Moscow, Dmitrovskoe shosse 9, korp. 8; tel. (495) 976-28-19; fax (495) 976-37-82; f. 1962; Dir STANISLAV V. NIKOLAEV.

Central Research and Design Institute of Town Planning: 117944 Moscow, pr. Vernadskogo 29; tel. (495) 138-28-06; fax (495) 133-11-29; f. 1963; library of 25,000 vols; Dir YU. N. MAXIMOV.

Kucherenko, V. A., State Central Research and Experimental Design Institute for Complex Problems of Civil Engineering and Building Structures: 109428 Moscow, 2-ya Institutskaya 6; tel. (495) 171-26-50; fax (495) 171-28-58; f. 1927; Dir VASIL GORPINCHENKO; publs *Earthquake Engineering* (6 a year), *Investigation into Building Structures* (1 a year), *Investigations into Structural Earthquake Resistance* (every 2 years), *Large-Panel and Masonry Structures* (every 3 years), *New Forms and Strength of Metal Structures* (very 3 years), *Numerical Methods of Analysis and Optimization of Building Structures* (every 2 years), *Phosphate Materials* (1 a year), *Strength and Reliability of Structures* (every 2 years), *Structural Dynamics* (every 2 years), *Timber Structures* (every 2 years).

Panfilov, K. D., Academy of Municipal Economics: 123371 Moscow, Volokolamskoe shosse 116; tel. (495) 490-31-66; fax (495) 490-36-00; f. 1931; depts of scientific-technical co-ordination, municipal electrical supply, urban electric transport, anti-corrosion protection of underground metal structures, urban roads maintenance, municipal sanitation, urban landscaping, housing and municipal buildings, information, automation of technological processes, ecology; 5 research institutes (Moscow, St Petersburg, Rostov on Don, Tomsk, Ekaterinburg); 2 experimental factories (Moscow, St Petersburg); library of 740,000 vols; Dir V. F. PIVOVAROV; Scientific Sec. A. N. PROKHOROV.

Research Institute of Foundations and Underground Structures: 109428 Moscow, 2-ya Institutskaya 6; tel. (495) 171-22-40; fax (495) 171-37-01; f. 1931; Dir Prof. V. A. ILYICHEV; publ. *Soil Mechanics and Foundation Engineering* (6 a year).

Scientific and Research Institute for Architecture and Town Planning Theory: 121019 Moscow, pr. Vozdvizhenka 5; tel. and fax (495) 290-36-80.

BIBLIOGRAPHY, LIBRARY SCIENCE AND MUSEOLOGY

All-Russia Research Institute of Restoration: 109172 Moscow, Krestyanskaya ul. 10; tel. (495) 276-99-90.

Book Research Institute: 103473 Moscow, 2-i Volkonsky per. 10; tel. (495) 281-72-58; Dir A. I. SOLOVEV.

Library Association of Dagestan: 367026 Dagestan, ul. Batyraya 1; tel. (8722) 68-02-74; Pres. KAZIM OMAROV.

ECONOMICS, LAW AND POLITICS

All-Russia Research and Design Institute of the Statistical Information System: 127486 Moscow, Deguninskaya ul. 1/3; tel. (495) 488-14-04.

All-Russia Research Institute of Economic Problems in Development of Science and Technology: 111024 Moscow, Aviamotornaya ul. 26/5; tel. (495) 273-52-31; f. 1986; library of 15,000 vols.

Bank Credit and Finance Research Institute: 103016 Moscow, ul. Alekseya Tolstogo 30/1; tel. (495) 925-61-18.

Central Economics and Mathematics Institute: 117418 Moscow, Nakhimovsky pr. 47; tel. (495) 129-16-44; fax (495) 310-70-15; e-mail director@cemi.rssi.ru; internet www.cemi.rssi.ru; f. 1963; attached to Russian Acad. of Sciences; Dir V. L. MAKAROV; publs *Economics and Mathematical Methods* (4 a year), *Economics of Contemporary Russia* (4 a year).

Central Economics Research Institute: 119898 Moscow, Smolensky bul. 3/5; tel. (495) 246-84-63.

Central Laboratory of Socio-Economic Measurements: c/o Russian Academy of Sciences, 117418 Moscow, ul. Krasikova 32; attached to Russian Acad. of Sciences; Dir A. YU. SHEVYAKOV.

Centre for the Study of Nationality Problems: 117036 Moscow, ul. Dm. Ulyanova 19; tel. (495) 123-90-61; attached to Russian Acad. of Sciences; Head M. N. GUBOGLO.

Federal Service of State Statistics: 107450 Moscow, ul. Myasnitskaya 39; tel. (495) 207-49-02; fax (495) 207-40-87; e-mail stat@gks.ru; internet www.gks.ru; f. 1918 as Central Statistical Board; present name 1991; provides demographic and economic statistical information and analysis to state authorities, the scientific community and commercial and international organizations; Dir VLADIMIR SOKOLIN.

Financial Research Institute: 103006 Moscow, Nastasinsky per. 3 korp. 2; tel. (495) 299-74-14; fax (495) 299-31-69; f. 1937.

Institute for African Studies: 123001 Moscow, ul. Spiridonovka 30/1; tel. (495) 290-27-52; fax (495) 202-07-86; e-mail dir@inafr.ru; f. 1959; attached to Russian Acad. of Sciences; Dir A. M. VASILIEV; publs *Asia and Africa Today* (jtly with Institute of Oriental Studies, 12 a year), *Vostok-Orience* (jointly with Institute of Oriental Studies, 6 a year).

Institute for Comparative Political Studies: 101831 Moscow, Kolpachnyi per. 9a; tel. (495) 916-37-03; fax (495) 916-03-01; f. 1966; attached to Russian Acad. of Sciences; library of 50,000 vols; Dir T. T. TIMOFEEV; publs *Forum* (1 a year), *Polis* (6 a year).

Institute for Economics and Mathematics at St Petersburg: Tchaikovski ul. 1, St Petersburg 191187; tel. and fax (812) 273-7953; e-mail emi@emi.nw.ru; internet emi.nw.ru; f. 1990; attached to Russian Acad. of Sciences; Dir Prof. LEONID A. RUKHOVETS.

Institute for International Economic and Political Studies: 117418 Moscow, Novocheremushkinskaya 46; tel. (495) 128-91-57; fax (495) 120-83-71; internet www.transecon.ru; f. 1960; attached to Russian Acad. of Sciences; Dir Prof. Dr RUSLAN GRINBERG; publ. *The World of Transformations* (4 a year).

Institute for Legislation and Comparative Law: 103728 Moscow, Vozdvizhenka 4/22; tel. (495) 291-02-07; fax (495) 290-58-56; f. 1925 (fmrly All-Union Research Institute of Soviet Legislation); library of 180,000 vols; Dir LEV A. OKUNKOV; publs *Commentary on New Russian Legislation* (1 a year), *Legislation of Foreign Countries* (6 or 7 a year), *Materials of Foreign Legislation and International Private Law* (1 a year), *Problems of Perfecting Legislation* (3 a year).

Institute for Socio-Economic Studies of Population: 117218 Moscow, Nakhimovsky pr. 32; tel. (495) 129-04-00; fax (495) 129-08-01; e-mail isesp_ras@mtu-net.ru; internet www.cemi.rssi.ru/isesp; f. 1988; attached to Russian Acad. of Sciences; Dir NATALIA RIMASHEVSKAYA; publ. *Population* (4 a year).

Institute of Economic and Social Problems of the North: 167610 Syktyvkar, Kommunisticheskaya ul. 26; tel. and fax (8212) 42-42-67; e-mail iespn@ksc.komi.ru; attached to Russian Acad. of Sciences; Dir V. N. LAZHENTSEV.

Institute for Economic Studies: 184209 Murmansk oblast, Apatity, ul. Fersmana 24A; tel. (81555) 7-64-72; fax (81555) 7-48-44; e-mail iep@iep.kolasc.net.ru; internet www.ksc.ru; f. 1986; attached to Kola Science Centre (Russian Acad. of Sciences); Dir Prof. FIODOR D. LARICHKIN; publ. *Sever i rynok*

(The North and the Market, 3 a year, in Russian).

Institute of Economic Research: 680042 Khabarovsk, Tikhookeanskaya ul. 153; tel. (421) 272-48-88; fax (421) 272-48-07; e-mail minakir@ecrin.ru; internet www.ecrin.ru; f. 1976; attached to Russian Acad. of Sciences; Dir Acad. P. A. MINAKIR; publ. *Spatial Economics* (4 a year).

Institute of Economics: 620219 Ekaterinburg, Moskovskaya ul. 29; tel. and fax (3432) 51-45-36; e-mail green@uran.ru; f. 1971; attached to Russian Acad. of Sciences; Dir A. I. TATARKIN.

Institute of Economics: 119991 Moscow, Leninskii Av. 14; tel. (495) 938-03-09; fax (495) 954-33-20; attached to Russian Acad. of Sciences; Dir Acad. RUSLAN S. GRINBERG.

Institute of Europe: 103873 Moscow, Mokhovaya 8–3; tel. (495) 203-73-43; fax (495) 200-42-98; f. 1988; attached to Russian Acad. of Sciences; library of 3,000 vols; Dir VITALY V. ZHURKIN.

Institute of Far Eastern Studies: 117218 Moscow, Nakhimovsky pr. 32; tel. (495) 124-01-17; fax (495) 310-70-56; e-mail ifes@cemi.rssi.ru; f. 1966; attached to Russian Acad. of Sciences; Dir M. L. TITARENKO; publ. *Far Eastern Affairs* (6 a year).

Institute of Foreign Economic Research: c/o Russian Academy of Sciences, 117418 Moscow, ul. Krasikova 32; attached to Russian Acad. of Sciences; Dir S. A. SITARYAN.

Institute of National Economic Forecasting: 117418 Moscow, Nakhimovsky pr. 47; tel. (495) 129-34-33; fax (495) 718-97-71; e-mail office@ecfor.ru; internet www.ecfor.ru; f. 1986; attached to Russian Acad. of Sciences; undertakes macroeconomic analysis; short-, medium-, and long-term forecasting of the Russian economy; Dir Prof. VICTOR V. IVANTER; publs *Problemy Prognozirovaniya* (in Russian, 6 a year), *Studies on Russian Economic Development* (in English, 6 a year).

Institute of Philosophy and Law: 620144 Ekaterinburg, ul. 8 Marta 68; tel. (3432) 22-23-46; attached to Russian Acad. of Sciences; Dir S. S. ALEKSEEV.

Institute of Problems of Assimilation of the North: 625003 Tyumen, a/ya 2774; tel. (3452) 7-82-76; attached to Russian Acad. of Sciences; Dir V. P. MELNIKOV.

Institute of Problems of the Marketplace: 117418 Moscow, Nakhimovsky pr. 47; tel. (495) 129-10-00; attached to Russian Acad. of Sciences; Dir N. YA. PETRAKOV.

Institute of Social Sciences: 670042 Ulan-Ude, ul. Marii Sakhyanovoi 6; tel. (3012) 3-66-25; attached to Russian Acad. of Sciences; Dir V. T. NAIDAKOV.

Institute of Socio-Economic Problems of the Development of the Agroindustrial Complex: 401600 Saratov, pr. Lenina 94; tel. (8452) 24-25-38; attached to Russian Acad. of Sciences; Dir V. B. OSTROVSKY.

Institute of Socio-Political Research: 119991 Moscow, Leninsky pr. 32A; tel. and fax (495) 938-53-70; e-mail ispr@ras.ru; internet www.ispr.ru; f. 1991; attached to Russian Acad. of Sciences; Dir Prof. Dr GENNADY OSIPOV; publs *Eurasia* (1 a year), *Science, Culture, Society* (4 a year), *Social and Demographic Policies*.

Institute of State and Law: 119841 Moscow, ul. Znamenka 10; tel. (495) 291-33-81; attached to Russian Acad. of Sciences; Dir B. N. TOPORNIN.

Institute of the Economics of the Comprehensive Assimilation of the Natural Resources of the North: 677891 Yakutsk, ul. Petrovskogo 2; tel. (4112) 3-52-46; attached to Russian Acad. of Sciences; Dir N. V. IGOSHIN.

Institute of USA and Canada Studies: 121814 Moscow, Khlebnyi per. 2/3; tel. (495) 291-20-52; fax (495) 200-12-07; e-mail iskran@glasnet.ru; attached to Russian Acad. of Sciences; Dir SERGEI ROGOV; publs *Ideology* (12 a year), *Policy*, *US: Economy*.

Institute of World Economics and International Relations: 117957 Moscow, Profsoyuznaya 23; tel. (495) 120-43-32; fax (495) 120-65-75; e-mail imemoran@imemo.ru; internet www.imemo.ru; attached to Russian Acad. of Sciences; 545 mems; Dir Prof. SIMONIA A. NODARI (acting); publs *World Economics and International Relations* (12 a year, in Russian), *Russian Economic Barometer* (4 a year, in English).

International Research Institute for Management Sciences: 117312 Moscow, Pr. 60-letiya Oktyabrya 9; tel. (495) 137-28-57.

Latin America Institute: 115035 Moscow, Bol. Ordynka 21; tel. (495) 951-53-23; fax (495) 953-40-70; e-mail ilac-zan@mtu-net.ru; internet www.mtu-net.ru/ilaran; f. 1961; attached to Russian Acad. of Sciences; Dir Dr V. M. DAVYDOV; publ. *Iberoamerica* (in Spanish, 4 a year).

Peace Research Center of IMEMO: 117859 Moscow, ul. Profsoyuznaya 23; tel. (495) 128-93-89; fax (495) 120-65-75; e-mail imemoran@online.ru; attached to Russian Acad. of Sciences; Dir A. K. KISLOV; publ. *Ways to Security* (in Russian, 2 or 3 a year).

Pricing Research Institute: 107078 Moscow, Kirovsky pr-d 4/3; tel. (495) 925-50-56.

Research Institute for the Strengthening of the Legal System and Law and Order: 123805 Moscow, GSP 2-ya Zvenigorodskaya ul. 15; tel. (495) 256-54-63.

Research Institute of Planning and Normatives: 125319 Moscow, Kochnovsky pr. 3; tel. (495) 152-45-91; attached to Russian Acad. of Sciences; Dir B. V. GUBIN (acting).

Sochi Research Centre: 354000 Sochi, Teatralnaya 8a; tel. (862) 92-37-71; fax (862) 292-44-11; e-mail snic@sochi.ru; f. 1988; attached to Russian Acad. of Sciences; research into management of the development of recreational areas and tourism; Dir M. M. AMIRKHANOV.

Survey Technique and Applied Research (STAR) Centre of the Institute of Sociology: 117259 Moscow, ul. Krzhizhanovskogo 24/35, str. 5; tel. (495) 719-09-71; fax (495) 719-07-40; e-mail valman@socio .msk.su; f. 1983; attached to Russian Acad. of Sciences; opinion survey design, data collection; Dir Prof. V. MANSUROV.

EDUCATION

Central Sports Research Institute: 107005 Moscow, Elizavetinsky per. 10; tel. (499) 261-50-76.

Centre for Pre-School Education: 113035 Moscow, ul. Osipenko 21; tel. (495) 231-49-28; attached to Russian Acad. of Education; Dir A. S. SPIVAKOVSKAYA.

Centre for Social Pedagogics: 119905 Moscow, Pogodinskaya ul. 8; tel. (495) 246-44-58; attached to Russian Acad. of Education; Dir V. G. BOCHAROVA.

Institute for Advanced Training: 109180 Moscow, ul. Bol. Polyanka 58; tel. (095) 237-31-51; attached to Russian Acad. of Education; Dir Y. A. ROODIE.

Institute for Educational Innovation: 117449 Moscow, ul. Vinokurova 3-B; tel.

(095) 126-26-30; attached to Russian Acad. of Education; Dir V. I. SLOBODCHIKOV.

Institute for School Development in Siberia, the Far East and the North: 634050 Tomsk, ul. Gertsena 68; tel. (3822) 21-28-21; attached to Russian Acad. of Education; Dir G. V. ZALEVSKY.

Institute for the Occupational Training of Youth: 119903 Moscow, Pogodinskaya ul. 8; tel. (495) 245-05-13; attached to Russian Acad. of Education; Dir V. A. POLYAKOV.

Institute of Developmental Physiology: 119869 Moscow, ul. Pogodinskaya 8, korp. 2; tel. (495) 245-04-33; attached to Russian Acad. of Education; Dir Dr M. M. BEZRUKIKH.

Institute of Higher Education: 111024 Moscow, Tretya Kabelynaya ul. 1; tel. (495) 273-48-19; e-mail sav@niivo.hetnet.ru; attached to Russian Acad. of Education; Dir ALEXANDER SAVELIEV.

Institute of National Problems of Education: 105077 Moscow, Pervomayskaya 101; tel. (495) 461-92-45; fax (495) 461-92-45; f. 1991; (fmrly Research Institute of National Schools, f. 1949); Dir Prof. M. N. KOUZMIN; publ. *Uchenye Zapiski* (1 a year).

Institute of Secondary Education: 119906 Moscow, ul. Pogodinskaya 8; tel. (495) 245-37-33; attached to Russian Acad. of Education; Dir. V. S. LEDNEV.

Institute of Secondary Specialized Education: Tatarstan, 420039 Kazan, ul. Isayeva 12; tel. (8432) 42-63-24; fax (8432) 42-46-80; f. 1976; attached to Russian Acad. of Education; Dir G. V. MUKHAMETZYANOVA; publ. *Professional Education* (4 a year).

Institute of Teaching and Learning Resources: 119903 Moscow, ul. Pogodinskaya 8; tel. (495) 246-35-90; attached to Russian Acad. of Education; Dir T. S. NAZAROVA.

Institute of Theoretical Pedagogics and International Research in Education: 129278 Moscow, ul. Pavla Korchagina 7; tel. (495) 283-09-55; attached to Russian Acad. of Education; Dir B. S. GERSHUNSKY.

Institute of Vocational Education: 119186 St Petersburg, nab. Moiki 48; tel. (812) 311-60-88; attached to Russian Acad. of Education; Dir A. P. BELYAEVA.

Psychological Institute: 125009 Moscow, Mokhovaya ul. 9, Bldg 4; tel. (495) 695-88-76; fax (495) 695-81-28; e-mail pirao@list.ru; internet www.pirao.ru; f. 1912; attached to Russian Acad. of Education; library of 60,000 vols; Dir Prof. VITALY V. RUBTSOV; Vice-Dir for science Prof. SERGEY MALYKH; publs *New trends in Psychology* (4 a year, in Russian), *Theoretical and Experimental Psychology* (4 a year, in Russian).

Research Centre for Aesthetic Education: 119034 Moscow, Kropotkinskaya nab. 15; tel. (495) 202-25-97; attached to Russian Acad. of Education; Dir B. P. YUSOV.

Research Centre for the Teaching of Russian: 119903 Moscow, Pogodinskaya ul. 8; tel. (495) 246-05-59; attached to Russian Acad. of Education; Dir E. A. BYSTROVA.

Research Institute of Remedial Education: 119869 Moscow, ul. Pogodinskaya 8, korp. 1; tel. (495) 245-04-52; attached to Russian Acad. of Education; Dir N. N. MALOFEEV.

Siberian Institute of Educational Technologies: 630098 Novosibirsk, Primorskaya ul. 22; tel. (3832) 45-18-32; fax (3832) 45-87-51; f. 1985; attached to Russian Acad. of Education; Dir I. M. BOBKO; publ. *Information Technologies in Education* (2 a year).

Family and Education Institute: 119121 Moscow, ul. Pogodinskaya 8; tel. (499) 255-26-06; fax (499) 255-24-77; e-mail niisv@mail

.ru; internet www.niisv.ru; f. 1998; attached to Russian Acad. of Education; Dir Acad. SERGEI VLADIMIROVICH DARMODECHIN.

FINE AND PERFORMING ARTS

Scientific-Research Museum of the Russian Academy of Fine arts: St Petersburg, Universitetskaya nab. 17; tel. (812) 328-27-19; fax (812) 323-61-69; e-mail sekretar@ nimrah.ru; internet www.nimrah.ru; f. 1758; attached to Russian Acad. of Arts; casts, masterpieces of antique sculpture and models of antique architecture monuments made in 18th century of cork in workshop of Chichi, Roman patternmaker and sculptor; history of Russian artistic school; works of Losenko, Borovikovsky, Bryullov, P.P. Chistyakov, Kustodiyev, Brodsky, A.P. Ostroumova-Lebedeva, sculptors Shubin, Kozlovsky, Shchedrin, Prokofyev, Antokolsky; Saint Petersburg architecture of the 18th–19th centuries in patterns, paintings and drawings; Dir LUDMILA KONDRATENKO.

Research Institute of Film Art: 125009 Moscow, Degtyarny per. 8; tel. and fax (095) 299-56-79; e-mail cineaste@mail.ru; f. 1974; research in the field of history and theory of film and monitoring of the situation in Russian and world cinema; 65 mems; library of 60,000 vols; still photos archive; Dir LIUDMILA BUDYAK; Deputy Dirs DMITRY KARAVAEV, MARK ZAK; publs *Kinograph* (almanac), *Kinovedcheskie Zapisky* (Film Notebooks, 4 a year).

Research Institute of the Theory and History of Fine Arts: 119034 Moscow, ul. Prechistenka 21; tel. (495) 201-42-91; attached to Russian Acad. of Arts; Dir V. V. VANSLOV.

State Institute for Art Studies: 125000 Moscow, Kozitsky per. 5; tel. (495) 200-03-71; fax (495) 785-24-06; e-mail institut@sias.ru; internet www.sias.ru; f. 1944; research in fine art, theatre, music, architecture, folklore, mass media; studies in sociology, economics and the politics of culture; library of 70,000 vols; Dir Dr A. I. KOMECH; publs *Cultural Transactions* (every 2 years), *Occidental Art of the 20th Century* (every 2 years), *Theory of Culture* (1 a year), *World of Arts* (1 a year).

HISTORY, GEOGRAPHY AND ARCHAEOLOGY

Institute of Archaeology: 117036 Moscow, ul. Dm. Ulyanova 19; tel. (495) 126-47-98; fax (495) 126-06-30; e-mail ia.ras@mail.ru; internet archaeolog.ru; f. 1919; attached to Russian Acad. of Sciences; Dir N. A. MAKAROV; publ. *Russiyskaya Archeologia* (4 a year).

V. B. Sochava Institute of Geography: 664033 Irkutsk, Ulanbatorskaya 1; tel. (3952) 42-61-00; fax (3952) 42-27-17; e-mail postman@irigs.irk.ru; internet www.irigs.irk .ru; f. 1957; attached to Russian Acad. of Sciences; the state and devt of Siberia's regions; landscape science; devt of the geographical framework for territorial org. of production, and population formation; systemic mapping; creation of the theoretical foundation for forecasting, monitoring and controlling the geosystem; library of 52 vols; Dir Dr VICTOR M. PLYUSNIN.

Institute of Geography: 109017 Moscow, Staromonetnii per. 29; tel. (495) 959-00-32; fax (495) 959-00-33; e-mail igras@igras .geonet.ru; internet www.igras.ru; f. 1918; attached to Russian Acad. of Sciences; research on interaction between nature and society at global, regional, and national scales; evolutionary analysis of environment and its components for forecast of global and regional changes; monitors and evaluates efficiency of natural resource utilization; elaboration of ecological and geographical bases of sustainable devt at global, regional, and nat. levels; library of 10,000 vols; Dir Acad. V. M. KOTLYAKOV; publs *Ekologicheskoe Planirovanie i Upravlenie* (6 a year), *Geomorphology* (4 a year), *Izvestiya Akademii Nauk – Seriya Geograficheskaya* (6 a year), *Lyod i Sneg* (2 a year), *Problemy regionalnoi Ekologii* (6 a year).

Institute of History and Archaeology: 620219 Ekaterinburg, ul. R. Lyuksemburg 56; tel. (3432) 22-14-02; fax (3432) 22-42-30; e-mail istor@uran.ru; internet www.uran.ru/structure/institutions/history/index.htm; f. 1988; attached to Russian Acad. of Sciences; Dir Prof. V. V. ALEKSEEV; publ. *Ural Historical Journal* (1 a year).

Institute of History, Language and Literature: 450054 Ufa, pr. Oktyabrya 71; tel. (3472) 35-60-50; fax (3472) 35-60-77; e-mail rihll@anrb.ru; internet rihll.ru; f. 1932; attached to Russian Acad. of Sciences; Dir Prof. Dr FIRDAUS G. KHISAMITDINOVA.

Institute of History, Philology and Philosophy: 630090 Novosibirsk, pr. Akad. Lavrenteva 17; tel. (3832) 35-05-37; fax (3832) 35-77-91; attached to Russian Acad. of Sciences; Dir Acad. A. P. DEREVYANKO.

Institute of Language, Literature and Arts: 367025 Makhachkala 25, ul. Magomeda Gadjieva 45; tel. and fax (872) 267-06-21; f. 1924; attached to Russian Acad. of Sciences; library of 160,000 vols; Dir M. I. MAGOMEDOV.

Institute of Language, Literature and History: 167610 Syktyvkar, Kommunisticheskaya ul. 26; tel. (8212) 24-55-64; fax (8212) 44-21-97; e-mail smetanin@mail.komisc.ru; internet www.komisc.ru/illh; f. 1970; attached to Russian Acad. of Sciences; Dir ALEXANDR F. SMETANIN.

Institute of Linguistics, Literature and History: 185610 Petrozavodsk, Pushkinskaya ul. 11; tel. (8142) 77-44-96; attached to Russian Acad. of Sciences; Dir YU. A. SAVVATEEV.

Institute of Military History: 117330 Moscow, Universitetskii pr. 14; tel. (495) 147-45-65; attached to Russian Acad. of Sciences; Dir A. N. BAZHENOV.

Institute of Oriental Manuscripts: 191186 St Petersburg, Dvortsovaya 18; tel. (812) 315-87-28; fax (812) 312-14-65; e-mail iom@orientalstudies.ru; internet www.orientalstudies.ru; f. 1818; attached to Russian Acad. of Sciences; specialized collns of MSS and early printed books of countries of East; archive of Orientalists; Dir IRINA F. POPOVA; publ. *Pismennye pamyatniki Vostoka* (2 a year).

Institute of Research in the Humanities: 677007 Sakha Republic, Yakutsk, Petrovskaya ul. 1; tel. and fax (4112) 35-49-96; f. 1935; attached to Acad. of Sciences of the Sakha Republic; history, language and culture of the peoples of the Sakha Republic; Dir VASILY N. IVANOV; publ. *Yakutsky arkhiv* (12 a year).

Institute of Russian History: 117036 Moscow, ul. Dm. Ulyanova 19; tel. (495) 126-94-49; fax (495) 126-39-55 br. at St Petersburg: 197110 St Petersburg, Petrozavodskaya 7; tel. (812) 235-41-98; fax (812) 235-64-85; attached to Russian Acad. of Sciences; Dir A. N. SAKHAROV.

Institute of Slavonic Studies: 117334 Moscow, Leninsky pr. 32A; tel. (495) 938-17-80; fax (495) 938-00-96; e-mail ritlen@mail.ru; f. 1947; attached to Russian Acad. of Sciences; Dir V. K. VOLKOV; publ. *Slavyanovedeniye* (4 a year).

Institute of the History, Archaeology and Ethnography of the Peoples of the Far East: 690950 Vladivostok, ul. Pushkinskaya 89; tel. (4232) 22-05-07; fax (4232) 26-82-11; internet www.febras.ru/~ihae; f. 1971; attached to Russian Acad. of Sciences; Dir Dr V. L. LARIN; publ. *Russia and the Pacific* (in Russian, 4 a year).

Institute of the History of Material Culture: 191065 St Petersburg, Dvortsovaya nab. 18; tel. (812) 312-14-84; attached to Russian Acad. of Sciences.

Institute of World History: 117036 Moscow, ul. Dm. Ulyanova 19; tel. (495) 126-94-21; attached to Russian Acad. of Sciences; Dir A. O. CHUBARYAN.

Krasovsky, F. N., Central Research Institute for Geodesy, Aerial Photography, and Cartography: 125413 Moscow, Onezhskaya 26; tel. (495) 456-95-31.

Oceanography Research Institute: 190121 St Petersburg, nab. Moiki 120; Dir I. S. GRAMBERG.

Pacific Institute of Geography: 690041 Vladivostok, ul. Radio 7; tel. (4232) 32-06-72; fax (4232) 31-21-59; f. 1971; attached to Russian Acad. of Sciences; library of 28,000 vols; Dir Prof. P. YA. BAKLANOV; publ. *Zov Taigi*.

State Oceanography Institute: 119838 Moscow, Kropotkinskii per. 6; tel. (095) 246-72-88 199026 St Petersburg, V.O., 23-ya liniya 2-a; tel. (812) 218-81-23; Dir F. S. TERZIEV.

Udmurt Institute of History, Language and Literature: 426004 Izhevsk, ul. Lomonosova 4; tel. (3412) 75-53-21; fax (3412) 75-39-94; f. 1931; attached to Russian Acad. of Sciences; library of 60,000 vols; Dir KUZMA I. KULIKOV.

LANGUAGE AND LITERATURE

Gorky, A. M., Institute of World Literature: 121069 Moscow, ul. Vorovskogo 25A; tel. (495) 290-50-30; attached to Russian Acad. of Sciences; Dir F. F. KUZNETSOV.

Ibragimov, G., Institute of Language, Literature and Art: 420503 Kazan, ul. Lobachevskogo 2/31; tel. (8432) 38-70-59; fax (8432) 38-74-79; attached to Acad. of Sciences of the Republic of Tatarstan; Dir M. Z. ZAKIEV.

Institute for Linguistic Studies: 199053 St Petersburg, Tuchkov per. 9; tel. (812) 328-16-11; fax (812) 328-46-11; e-mail iliran@mail.ru; internet iling.spb.ru; f. 1921; attached to Russian Acad. of Sciences; research on all aspects of language; library of 140,000 vols; Dir Prof. Dr NIKOLAY N. KAZANSKY; publs *Acta Linguistica Petropolitana* (3 a year), *Indoevropeyskoe yazykoznaniye i klassicheskaya filologiya* (1 a year).

Institute of Linguistics: 125009 Moscow, ul. Bol. Kislovsky per. 1, st. 1; tel. (495) 690-35-85; fax (495) 690-05-28; e-mail iling@iling-ran.ru; internet www.iling-ran.ru; f. 1950; attached to Russian Acad. of Sciences; Dir V. A. VINOGRADOV; Vice-Dir M. ALEKSEYEV; publs *Ural-Altaic Studies* (2 a year), *Voprosy Filologii* (3 a year), *Voprosy Psikholingvistiki* (2 a year).

Institute of Russian Literature (Pushkin House): 199034 St Petersburg, nab. Makarova 4; tel. (812) 328-19-01; fax (812) 328-11-40; e-mail irli@mail.ru; f. 1905; attached to Russian Acad. of Sciences; Dir N. N. SKATOV; publ. *Russian Literature* (4 a year).

Russian Institute for Cultural Research: 119072 Moscow, Bersenevskaya nab. 20; tel. (495) 959-09-08; fax (495) 959-10-17; e-mail riku@dol.ru; internet www.ricur.ru; f. 1932; attached to Min. of Culture and the Mass Media; research in theory and history of culture, humanities, applied cultural research; organizes conferences, publs, workshops and festivals; br. in Omsk; library: library of 67,000 books and periodicals; Dir Prof. KIRILL E. RAZLOGOV; Deputy Dir Prof. ELEONORA A. SHOULEPOVA; Deputy Dir Assoc. Prof. ALEXEI G. VASILIEV; Deputy Dir Prof. YURI M. REZNIK; publ. *Journal of Cultural Research* (online).

Vinogradov Institute of the Russian Language: 121019 Moscow, Volkhonka 18/2; tel. (495) 202-65-40; fax (495) 291-23-17; f. 1944; attached to Russian Acad. of Sciences; library of 110,000 vols; Dir Dr A. M. MOLDOVAN; publs *Rusistics Today* (4 a year), *Russian Speech* (6 a year).

MEDICINE

All-Russia Antibiotics Research Institute: 113105 Moscow, Nagatinskaya ul. 3a; tel. (499) 611-42-38; fax (495) 118-93-66; f. 1947; library of 65,000 vols; br. in Penza; Dir Prof. S. M. NAVASHIN; publ. *Antibiotics and Chemotherapy*.

All-Russia Research Institute of Eye Diseases: 119021 Moscow, ul. Rossolimo 11; tel. (495) 248-01-25; f. 1973; micro-surgery of the eye, therapeutic ophthalmology, laser ophthalmology, new technical equipment in ophthalmology; Chief Officers ALEKSEEV, KRASNOV, KUZNETSOVA, MUSTAEV; publ. *Vestnik Oftalmologii* (6 a year).

All-Russia Research Institute of Pharmaceutical Plants: 113628 Moscow, ul. Grina 7; tel. (495) 382-83-18; Dir P. T. KONDRATENKO.

All-Russia Research Institute of the Technology of Blood Substitutes and Hormonal Preparations: 109044 Moscow, per. Lavrov 6; tel. (495) 276-43-60.

Allergen State Unitary Enterprise: 355019 Stavropol, Biologicheskaya ul. 20; tel. (8652) 24-40-84; fax (8652) 25-31-46; f. 1918; vaccines and sera, allergens, nutrient media, pharmaceuticals; library of 39,500 vols and periodicals; Dir-Gen. V. V. ERMELOV.

Anokhin, P. K., Institute of Normal Physiology: Russian Academy of Medical Sciences 125009, Moscow, Mokhovaya St, 11 Blvd a; tel. (495) 629-70-45; fax (495) 629-71-82; e-mail s-sudakov@mail.ru; attached to Russian Acad. of Medical Sciences; Dir S. K. SUDAKOV.

Bakulev Scientific and Research Centre for Cardiovascular Surgery: 117049 Moscow, Leninskii pr. 8; tel. (495) 236-13-61; fax (495) 237-21-72; e-mail leoan@online.ru; internet www.bakoulev.sovintel.ru; f. 1956; attached to Russian Acad. of Medical Sciences; Head Acad. L. A. BOCERIA; publs *Journal of Thoracic and Cardiovascular Surgery* (in Russian, 6 a year), *Annals of Surgery* (in Russian, 6 a year), *Annals of Arrhythmology* (in Russian, 6 a year).

Blokhin, N. N., Cancer Research Center: Kashirskoe shosse 24, 115478 Moscow; tel. (495) 324-11-14; fax (495) 323-53-55; e-mail info@eso.ru; internet www.cancercenter.ru; f. 1951; attached to Russian Acad. of Medical Sciences; Dir MIKHAIL V. DAVYDOV; publs *Herald of Moscow Cancer Society* (12 a year), *Journal* (4 a year), *Journal of Biotherapy* (24 a year), *Pediatric Oncology* (24 a year).

Attached Institutes:

Research Institute of Carcinogenesis: Kashirskoe shosse 24, 115478 Moscow; tel. (495) 324-14-70; attached to Russian Acad. of Medical Sciences; Dir DAVID G. ZARIDZE.

Research Institute of Experimental Therapy and Tumour Diagnosis: Kashirskoe shosse 24, 115478 Moscow; tel. (495) 324-22-74; attached to Russian Acad. of Medical Sciences; Dir ANATOLY Y. BARYSHNIKOV.

Research Institute of Pediatric Oncology: Kashirskoe shosse 24, 115478 Moscow; tel. (495) 324-43-09; attached to Russian Acad. of Medical Sciences; Dir LEV A. DURNOV.

Russian Institute of Clinical Oncology: Kashirskoe shosse 24, 115478 Moscow; tel. (495) 324-44-16; attached to Russian Acad. of Medical Sciences; Dir MIKHAIL I. DAVYDOV.

Blood Transfusion Research Institute: 125167 Moscow, Novozykovsky pr-d 4A; tel. (495) 212-45-51; fax (495) 212-42-52.

Burdenko Neurosurgical Institute: 125047 Moscow, ul. Fadeeva 5; tel. (0495) 251-65-26; fax (495) 250-93-51; attached to Russian Acad. of Medical Sciences; Dir A. N. KONOVALOV.

Cardiological Research Centre: 121552 Moscow, 3°, Cherepkovskaya ul. 15; tel. (495) 415-13-47; fax (495) 415-29-62; attached to Russian Acad. of Medical Sciences; Dir E. I. CHAZOV.

Attached Institutes:

Institute of Experimental Cardiology: 121552 Moscow, 3 Cherepkovskaya ul. 15A; tel. (495) 415-00-35; attached to Russian Acad. of Medical Sciences; Dir V. N. SMIRNOV.

Myasnikov, A. L., Institute of Cardiology: 121552 Moscow, 3°, Cherepkovskaya ul. 15a; tel. (495) 415-52-05; fax (499) 414-54-00; e-mail c34h@cardio.ru; f. 1945 as Institute of Experimental and Clinical Therapy, present name 1966; attached to Russian Acad. of Medical Sciences; Dir Prof. Dr IRINA YE. CHAZOVA.

Central Institute of Traumatology and Orthopaedics: 125299 Moscow, ul. Priorova 10; tel. (495) 450-24-72; fax (495) 154-31-39; f. 1921; 12 clinics; library of 40,000 vols; Dir Prof. S. P. MIRONOV; publ. *N. N. Priorov Journal of Traumatology and Orthopaedics* (4 a year).

Central Research Institute for the Evaluation of Working Capacity and Vocational Assistance to Disabled Persons: 127486 Moscow, ul. Susanina 3; tel. (495) 906-18-31; fax (495) 906-18-32; f. 1930; library of 50,000 vols; Dir D. I. LAVROVA.

Central Research Institute of Dermatology and Venereal Diseases: 107076 Moscow, ul. Korolenko 3; tel. (495) 964-26-20; fax (495) 964-43-22; e-mail info@cnikvi.ru; internet www.cnikvi.ru; f. 1921; attached to Federal Agency for High Technology Medical Care; Dir Prof. ALEXEI KUBANOV; publ. *Vestnik Dermatologii i Venerologii* (Journal of Dermatology and Venereology, 6 a year).

Central Research Institute of Epidemiology: 111123 Moscow, Novogireevskaya 3-a; tel. (495) 176-02-19; Dir A. SUMAROKOV.

Central Research Institute of Gastroenterology: 111123 Moscow, shosse Enthuziastov 86; tel. and fax (495) 304-19-42; e-mail gastroenter@rambler.ru; internet www.cniig.ru; f. 1973; Dir Prof. LEONID LAZEBNIK; publ. *Experimental and Clinical Gastroenterology* (12 a year).

Central Research Institute of Roentgenology and Radiology: 197758 St Petersburg, Pesochny, ul. Leningradskaya 70/4; tel. (812) 596-84-62; fax (812) 596-67-05; e-mail crirr@peterlink.ru; internet www.private .peterlink.ru/crirr; f. 1918; Dir Prof. ANATOLY

M. GRANOV; publ. *Volume of Conference Reports* (1 a year).

Central Tuberculosis Research Institute: 107564 Moscow, Yauzskaya alleya 2; tel. (499) 785-90-19; fax (499) 785-91-08; e-mail cniit@cniitramn.ru; internet www .cniitramn.ru; f. 1921; attached to Russian Acad. of Medical Sciences; Dir Prof. V. V. EROKHIN.

Centre for the Chemistry of Drugs—All-Russia Chemical and Pharmaceutical Research Institute: 119815 Moscow, ul. Zubovskaya 7; tel. (495) 246-97-68; fax (495) 246-78-05; f. 1920; research on drugs; library of 150,000 items; Dir R. G. GLUSHKOV; publ. *Collection of Proceedings* (1 a year).

Chumakov, M. P., Institute of Poliomyelitis and Virus Encephalitis: 142782 Moscow oblast, Kievskoe shosse, 27 km; tel. (495) 439-90-07; attached to Russian Acad. of Medical Sciences; Dir S. G. DROZDOV.

Chuvash Eye Diseases Research Institute: 428028 Cheboksary, Traktorostroitelei 10; tel. (8350) 26-05-75; fax (8350) 26-52-13; f. 1987; Dir Dr NIKOLAI PASHTAEV.

Dagestan Medical Research Centre: 367020 Makhachkala, ul. Gorikogo 53; tel. (87200) 7-49-97; attached to Russian Acad. of Medical Sciences; Dir S.-M. A. OMAROV.

Eastern Siberian Research Centre: 664003 Irkutsk, ul. Timiryazeva 16; tel. (3952) 27-54-48; fax (3952) 27-48-13; e-mail scippnw@sbamsr.irk.ru; attached to Russian Acad. of Medical Sciences; Chair. of Presidium Acad. S. I. KOLESNIKOV.

Attached Institutes:

Institute of Epidemiology and Microbiology: 664000 Irkutsk, ul. Karla Marksa 3; tel. (3952) 33-34-23; fax (3952) 33-34-45; attached to Russian Acad. of Medical Sciences; Dir Prof. V. I. ZLOBIN.

Institute of Industrial Medicine and Human Ecology: 665827 Irkutskaya oblast, Angarsk 27, a/ya 1170; tel. (218) 55-90-70; fax (218) 55-40-77; e-mail rvc@ iimhe.irk.ru; attached to Russian Acad. of Medical Sciences; Dir V. S. RUKAVISHNIKOV.

Institute of Paediatrics and Human Reproduction: 664003 Irkutsk, ul. Timiryazeva 16; tel. (3952) 34-73-67; fax (3952) 27-48-13; e-mail scippnw@sbamsr.irk.ru; attached to Russian Acad. of Medical Sciences; Dir Acad. S. I. KOLESNIKOV.

Institute of Surgery: 664047 Irkutsk, Yubileiny mikroraion 100; tel. and fax (3952) 38-53-31; attached to Russian Acad. of Medical Sciences; Dir Prof. E. G. GRIGOREV.

Institute of Traumatology and Orthopaedics: 664003 Irkutsk, ul. Bortsov Revolyutsii 1; tel. and fax (3952) 27-54-30; attached to Russian Acad. of Medical Sciences; Dir Prof. A. P. BARABASH.

Ekaterinburg Institute of Restorative Surgery, Traumatology and Orthopaedics: Ekaterinburg, Bankovsky per. 7.

Ekaterinburg Region Institute of Dermatology and Venereal Diseases: Ekaterinburg, ul. K. Libknekhta 9.

Ekaterinburg Viral Infections Research Institute: 620030 Ekaterinburg, Letnyaya ul. 23; tel. (3432) 61-99-60; e-mail virus@etel .ru; f. 1920; Dir Prof. NINA P. GLINSKIKH; publ. *Viral Infections: Urgent Problems* (1 a year).

Endocrinology Research Centre: 117036 Moscow, ul. Dm. Ulyanova 11; tel. (495) 500-00-90; fax (495) 718-05-22; e-mail science@ endocrincentr.ru; internet www .endocrincentr.ru; f. 1925; attached to Russian Acad. of Medical Sciences; Dir I. I.

DEDOV; publ. *Diabetes Mellitus* (in Russian, 4 a year).

Attached Institutes:

Institute of Clinical Endocrinology: Institute of Clinical Endocrinology: Moscow; tel. (495) 129-01-24; fax (495) 718-05-22; e-mail endocrin@endocrincentr.ru; f. 1988; Dir J. A. MELNICHENKO.

Institute of Experimental Endocrinology: 112255 Moscow, ul. Moskvorechie 1; tel. (495) 324-93-25; f. 1965; Dir V. N. BABICHEV.

Institute of Diabetes: Moscow; tel. (495) 1244500; fax (495) 7180522; f. 1988; Dir M. I. BALABOLKIN.

Ersman Hygiene Research Institute: 141000 Mytishchi, ul. Semashko 2; tel. (495) 583-82-14.

Far Eastern Scientific Center of Physiology and Pathology of Respiration: 675000 Blagoveshchensk, ul. Kalinina 22; tel. and fax (4162) 53-35-45; e-mail cfpd@ amur.ru; internet www.people.amursu.ru/ cfpd/win; f. 1981; attached to Russian Acad. of Medical Sciences; Dir Prof. Dr VICTOR P. KOLOSOV; Vice-Dir Prof. Dr YULIY M. PERELMAN; publ. *Bulletin Physiology and Pathology of Respiration*.

Federal Bureau for Medical and Social Expertise: 127486 Moscow, ul. Ivana Susanina 3; tel. (495) 487-57-11; fax (495) 487-81-81; e-mail fbmse@inbox.ru; f. 2000 as Federal Scientific and Practical Centre for Medico-Social Expertise and Rehabilitation of Invalids (formed by merger of Central Research Institute of Prosthetics and Prosthesis Design and Central Research Institute for the Evaluation of Working Capacity and Vocational Assistance to Disabled Persons); present name 2005; library of 45,000 vols; Dir Prof. Dr S. N. PUZIN; publ. *Journal of Medical and Social Expertise and Rehabilitation* (4 a year).

Federal Research Institute for Health Education and Health Promotion: 103101 Moscow, ul. A. Mitskevicha 3; tel. (495) 202-18-13; fax (495) 202-54-08; f. 1927; library of 10,000 vols; Dir Dr V. A. POLESKY.

Federal Research Institute of Paediatric Gastroenterology: 603950 Nizhnii Novgorod, ul. Semashko 22; tel. (8312) 36-66-35; fax (8312) 36-56-59; e-mail niidegastro@mail.ru; f. 1929; Dir Prof. Dr ANATOLY I. VOLKOV.

Gamalei, N. F., Institute of Epidemiology and Microbiology: 123098 Moscow, ul. Gamalei 18; tel. (495) 193-30-01; fax (495) 305-67-38; attached to Russian Acad. of Medical Sciences; Dir S. V. PROZOROVSKII.

Haematological Research Centre: 125167 Moscow, Novozykovsky pr-d 4A; tel. (495) 212-21-23; fax (495) 212-42-52; attached to Russian Acad. of Medical Sciences; Dir A. I. VOROBIEV.

Herzen, P. A., Moscow Cancer Research Institute: 125284 Moscow, 2-i Botkinsky pr-d 3; tel. (495) 945-19-35; f. 1903; library of 19,336 vols; Dir Prof. V. I. CHISSOV.

Mother and Child Care Institute: 680022 Khabarovsk, ul.Voronezgskaya, 49, bldg 1; tel. (4212) 98-02-15; fax (4212) 98-03-35; e-mail zdorovye@mail.redcom.ru; f. 1986 collaboration with Far-Eastern State Medical Univ. and other medical instns of the whole Russia and foreign countries (USA, Japan, China, Germany and others); attached to Russian Acad. of Medical Sciences; scientific activities incl. ecological-medical, molecular mechanisms investigations in aspects of the children and adolescents healthcare in the Far-Eastern region of Russia, estimation of viral and bacterial infections influence for the reproductive function and foetus formation and infants loss; the formation and support of tissue homeostasis at the early stages of ontogenesis; investigations of the immune-dependent peculiarities for pathologic states among children and adolescents at the Far-Eastern region of Russia; Dir V. K. KOZLOV.

Scientific Research Institute of Biochemistry: 630117 Novosibirsk, Academician Timakov St. 2; tel. (383) 332-27-35; fax (383) 333-67-58; e-mail ibch@soramn.ru; internet www.ibch.soramn.ru; f. 1988; attached to Russian Acad. of Medical Sciences; Dir L. E. PANIN.

Institute of Biomedical Chemistry: 119121 Moscow, ul. Pogodinskaya 10; tel. (495) 246-69-80; fax (495) 245-08-57; internet www.ibmc.msk.ru; f. 1944; attached to Russian Acad. of Medical Sciences; library of 136,000 vols; Dir Prof. ALEXANDER IVANOVICH ARCHAKOV; publ. *Voprosy meditsinskoy khimii* (6 a year).

Institute of Biomedical Problems: 123007 Moscow, Khoroshevskoe shosse 76A; tel. (495) 195-23-63; fax (495) 195-22-53; f. 1963; environmental effects on the human body, with emphasis on the effect of space flights; library of 80,000 vols; Dir ANATOLY I. GRIGORIEV; publ. *Aerospatial and Environmental Medicine* (6 a year).

Institute of Biomedical Research and Therapy: 113149 Moscow, Simferopolsky bul. 8; tel. (495) 113-23-51; Dir A. V. KARAULOV.

Institute of Clinical and Experimental Lymphology: 630117 Novosibirsk, ul. Timakova 2; tel. (383) 333-64-09; fax (383) 333-51-22; f. 1991; attached to Russian Acad. of Medical Sciences; library of 1,000 vols; Dir V. I. KONENKOV.

Institute of Clinical and Preventive Cardiology: 625026 Tyumen, ul. Melnikaite 111, POB 4312; tel. (3452) 22-76-08; fax (3452) 22-53-49; f. 1985; attached to Russian Acad. of Medical Sciences; Dir V. A. KUZNETSOV.

Institute of Clinical Immunology: 630091 Novosibirsk, ul. Yadrintsovskaya 14; fax (3832) 22-70-28; attached to Russian Acad. of Medical Sciences; Dir V. A. KOZLOV.

Institute of Epidemiology and Microbiology: 690028 Vladivostok, ul. Selskaya 1; tel. (4232) 29-43-03; attached to Russian Acad. of Medical Sciences; Dir N. N. BESEDNOVA.

Institute of Experimental Medicine: 197376 St Petersburg, ul. Akad. Pavlova 12; tel. (812) 234-54-01; fax (812) 234-94-89; e-mail iem@iemrams.ru; internet www.iemrams.spb.ru; f. 1890; attached to Russian Acad. of Medical Sciences; library of 500,000 vols; Dir GENRIKH A. SOFRONOV; Librarian ARINA DZENISKEVICH.

Institute of Eye Diseases: 119021 Moscow, ul. Rossolimo 11; tel. (495) 248-78-92; fax (495) 248-01-25; attached to Russian Acad. of Medical Sciences; Dir M. M. KRASNOV.

Institute of General Pathology and Pathophysiology: 125315 Moscow, ul. Baltiiskaya 8; tel. (499) 151-17-56; fax (495) 601-23-66; attached to Russian Acad. of Medical Sciences; Dir A. A. KUBATIEV; Scientific Sec. LARISA N. SKURATOVSKAYA.

Institute of Human Morphology: 117418 Moscow, ul. Tsyuryupy 3; tel. (495) 120-80-65; fax (495) 120-14-56; attached to Russian Acad. of Medical Sciences; Dir N. K. PERMYAKOV.

Institute of Immunology: 142380 Moscow oblast, Chekhovsky raion, Lyubuchany; tel.

and fax (495) 546-15-55; f. 1980; library of 2,800 vols; Dir V. P. ZAVYALOV.

Institute of Immunology: 115478 Moscow, Kashirskoe shosse 24, korp. 2; tel. (499) 611-83-01; fax (499) 616-10-27; Dir R. M. KHAITOV.

Institute of Influenza: 197022 St Petersburg, ul. Prof. Popova 15/17; tel. (812) 234-58-75; fax (812) 234-01-50; attached to Russian Acad. of Medical Sciences; Dir O. I. KISELEV.

Institute of Internal Medicine: 630089 Novosibirsk, ul. Bogatkova 175/1; tel. and fax (3832) 64-25-16; e-mail office@iimed.ru; f. 1981; attached to Russian Acad. of Medical Sciences; Dir Prof. M. I. VOEVODA; publ. *Interpress* (4 a year).

Institute of Medical and Biological Cybernetics: 630117 Novosibirsk, ul. Akad. Timakova 2; tel. (3832) 32-12-56; fax (3832) 32-55-58; f. 1992; attached to Russian Acad. of Medical Sciences; Dir M. B. SHTARK; publ. *Biofeedback* (every 3 years).

Institute of Medical Climatology and Rehabilitation: 690025 Vladivostok, Sadgorod 25; tel. (4232) 33-05-22; fax (4232) 25-11-83; f. 1984; attached to Russian Acad. of Medical Sciences; library of 20,000 vols; Dir Prof. Dr E. M. IVANOV.

State Scientific Research Institute on Medical Problems of the Far North of Russian Academy of Medical Sciences: 629730 Tyumen oblast, Yamalo-Nenets Autonomous Okrug, Nadym, km 107; tel. (34995) 3-03-20; fax (34995) 9-74-53; e-mail nii-mpks@mail.ru; internet mpks.ptline.ru; f. 1994; attached to Russian Acad. of Medical Sciences; health service and scientific researches in cardiology, pulmonology, pediatrics, gastroenterology, immunology, genetics, ecology and some other biological and medical brs taking into account the unfavourable conditions of the Far North and influence of extreme northern factors upon people's health; library of 2,000 vols on medical and biological sciences; Dir Prof. A. A. BUGANOV; publ. *Questions of Polar Medicine* (2 a year).

Institute of Medical Problems of the North: 660022 Krasnoyarsk, ul. Partizana Zheleznyaka 3G; fax (3912) 23-19-63; f. 1976; attached to Russian Acad. of Medical Sciences; Dir VALERY T. MANCHUK.

Institute of Nutrition: 109240 Moscow, Ustinskii pr-d 2/14; tel. (495) 917-44-85; attached to Russian Acad. of Medical Sciences; Dir M. N. VOLGAREV.

Institute of Occupational Health: 105275 Moscow, pr. Budennogo 31; tel. (495) 365-02-09; fax (495) 366-05-83; e-mail niimt@niimt.ru; internet www.niimt.ru; f. 1923; attached to Russian Acad. of Medical Sciences; devt of theoretical basis establishing laws and mechanisms of factors responsible for industrial, general and working process on workers health; aims to find out efficient prevention, diagnosis and treatment of work-related and occupational diseases; research into socio-medical problems and health dynamics of workers due to demographic shifts, changing working conditions, environmental and migration processes; devt and improvement of preventive technologies; Dir Prof. I. V. BUKHTIYAROV; publs *Meditsina Truda i Promyshlennaia Ekologiia* (12 a year), *Occupational Health and Industrial Ecology*.

Institute of Paediatrics: 117296 Moscow, Lomonsovskii pr. 2/62; tel. (495) 134-03-61; fax (495) 134-13-08; attached to Russian Acad. of Medical Sciences; Dir M. YA. STUDENIKIN.

Institute of Paediatrics and Child Surgery of the Ministry of Public Health of

the Russian Federation: 127412 Moscow, Taldomskaya ul. 2; tel. (495) 484-02-92; fax (495) 438-62-32; Dir Prof. YURI E. VELTISCHEV; publ. *Vestnik* (Annals of Perinatology and Paediatrics).

Institute of Pharmacology: 125315 Moscow, ul. Baltiiskaya 8; tel. (495) 151-18-41; fax (495) 151-12-61; attached to Russian Acad. of Medical Sciences; Dir S. B. SEREDENIN.

Institute of Physiology: 630117 Novosibirsk, ul. Akad. Timakova 4; fax (3832) 32-42-54; attached to Russian Acad. of Medical Sciences; Dir V. A. TRUFAKIN.

Institute of Regional Pathology and Pathomorphology: 630117 Novosibirsk, ul. Timakova 2; tel. (3833) 34-84-38; fax (3833) 33-48-45; e-mail pathol@soramn.ru; internet www.pathomorphology.soramn.ru; f. 1992; attached to Russian Acad. of Medical Sciences; diagnostic and training centre; diagnostics of viral hepatitis, tumours, lung, heart, kidney, gastrointestinal chronic diseases; Dir L. M. NEPOMNYASHCHIKH; Deputy Dir for Science and Research ELENA L. LUSHNIKOVA.

Institute of the Brain: 107120 Moscow, per. Obukha 5; tel. (495) 917-80-07; fax (495) 916-05-95; attached to Russian Acad. of Medical Sciences; Dir N. N. BOGOLEPOV.

Institute of the Molecular Pathology and Biochemistry of Ecology: 630117 Novosibirsk, ul. Akad. Timakova 2; fax (3832) 32-31-47; attached to Russian Acad. of Medical Sciences; Dir V. V. LYAKHOVICH.

Institute of Viral Preparations: 109088 Moscow, 1 Dubrovskaya ul. 15; tel. (495) 274-81-45; fax (495) 274-57-10; attached to Russian Acad. of Medical Sciences; Dir O. G. ANDZHAPARIDZE.

Irkutsk Antiplague Research Institute of Siberia and the Far East: 664047 Irkutsk, ul. Trilissera 78; tel. (3952) 22-01-35; fax (3952) 22-01-40; e-mail adm@chumin.irkutsk.ru; internet www.irkutsk.ru/chumin; f. 1934; library of 55,000 vols; Dir Prof. E. P. GOLUBINSKY.

Irkutsk Institute of Orthopaedics and Traumatology: 664003 Irkutsk, ul. Bortzov Revoliutsii 1; tel. (3952) 27-54-30; f. 1946; diseases of the skeleton and bone tissue regeneration; library of 32,000 vols; Dir Prof. A. P. BARABASH.

Irkutsk Research Institute of Epidemiology and Microbiology: 664000 Irkutsk, ul. Karla Marksa 3; tel. (3952) 24-42-30; Dir V. I. ZLOBIN.

Ivanovskii, D. I., Institute of Virology: 123098 Moscow, Gamalei 16; tel. (499) 190-28-74; fax (499) 190-28-67; attached to Ministry of Health and Soc. Devt of the Russian Federation; Dir DMITRY K. LVOV.

Kazan Institute of Epidemiology, Microbiology and Hygiene: 420015 Kazan, Bol. Krasnaya ul. 67; tel. (8432) 32-25-80; Dir F. Z. KAMALOV.

Kazan State Institute of Orthopaedics and Traumatology: 420015 Kazan, ul. Gorkogo 3; tel. (8432) 38-59-05; f. 1945; library: 13,500 units; publ. *Transactions* (1 a year).

Khabarovsk Research Institute of Epidemiology and Microbiology of Rospotrebnadzor: Khabarovsk, Shevchenko 2, 680610; tel. and fax (4212) 32-54-13; e-mail bovlad@email.kht.ru; internet www.hniiem.rospotrebnadzor.ru; f. 1925; microbiological and epidemiological studies; Head of Institute OLGA E. TROTSENKO; publ. *The Far Eastern Journal of Infectious Pathology* (2 a year).

Laboratory of Experimental Biological Models: 143412 Moscow oblast, p/o Otradnoe, pos. Svetlye Gory; tel. (495) 561-53-70; attached to Russian Acad. of Medical Sciences; Dir T. I. ZAITSEV.

Laboratory of Polar Medicine: 663310 Norilsk 10, ul. Talnakhskaya 7A, p/ya 625; fax (3919) 34-47-19; attached to Russian Acad. of Medical Sciences; Dir L. A. NADTOCHII.

Martsinovsky, I. E., Institute of Medical Parasitology and Tropical Medicine: 119435 Moscow, Mal. Pirogovskaya ul. 20; tel. (495) 246-80-49; fax (495) 246-90-47; f. 1920; library of 70,000 vols; Dir Prof. V. P. SERGIEV; publ. *Medical Parasitology and Parasitic Diseases* (4 a year).

Mechnikov I. I., Institute of Vaccines and Sera: 103064 Moscow, Mal. Kazenny per. 5A; tel. (495) 917-49-00; fax (495) 917-54-60; f. 1919; attached to Russian Acad. of Medical Sciences; Dir B.F. SEMENOV.

Medical Research Centre for Preventive Medicine and the Protection of the Health of Industrial Workers: 620014 Ekaterinburg, ul. Popova 30; tel. (3432) 71-87-54; fax (3432) 71-87-40; e-mail mrc@etel.ru; f. 1929; Dir SERGEY V. KUZMIN; publs *Balneology and Physiotherapy* (1 a year), *Urgent Issues of Preventive Medicine in the Urals* (1 a year).

Moscow G. N. Gabrichevskii Institute of Epidemiology and Microbiology: 125212 Moscow, ul. Admirala Makharova 10; tel. (495) 452-18-16; fax (495) 452-18-30; f. 1895; library of 8,922 vols; Dir Prof. BORIS A. SHENDEROV; publ. *Medical Aspects of Microecology* (1 a year).

Moscow Helmholtz Research Institute of Eye Diseases: 103064 Moscow, ul. Sadovaya-Chernogryazskaya 14/19; tel. (495) 207-23-19; fax (495) 975-24-00; f. 1900; library of 69,445 vols; Dir ALEXANDER M. YUZHAKOV.

Moscow Municipal Research First Aid Institute: 129010 Moscow, Sukharevskaya pl. 3; tel. (495) 925-38-97; f. 1923; library of 30,000 vols; Dir Prof. B. D. KOMAROV.

Moscow Research Institute of Psychiatry: 107076 Moscow, Poteshnaya ul. 3; tel. (495) 963-76-26; fax (495) 963-09-97; e-mail krasnov@mtu-net.ru; internet www.mniip.org; f. 1920; social and biological psychiatry; treats mental illness, alcohol and drug addiction; Dir VALERY KRASNOV; publ. *Social and Clinical Psychiatry* (in Russian, 4 a year).

Nizhnii Novgorod Institute for Skin and Venereal Diseases: Nizhnii Novgorod, ul. Kovalikhinskaya 49; f. 1930; library of 10,000 vols; Dir Prof. T. A. GLAVINSKAYA.

Nizhnii Novgorod Institute of Industrial Hygiene and Occupational Diseases: Nizhnii Novgorod, ul. Semashko 20.

Nizhnii Novgorod Research Institute of Traumatology and Orthopaedics: 603155 Nizhnii Novgorod, V. Volzhskaya nab. 18; tel. (8312) 36-01-60; fax (8312) 36-05-91; e-mail gito@pop.sci-nnov.ru; internet www.nniito.ru; f. 1945; 222 mems; library of 38,035 vols; Dir Prof. V. AZOLOV.

Novosibirsk Institute of Tuberculosis: Novosibirsk, ul. Chaplygina 75.

Omsk Research Institute of Naturally Occurring Infections: 644080 Omsk 80, pr. Mira 7; tel. (3812) 65-06-33; Dir A. A. MATUSHENKO.

Ott, D. O., Research Institute of Obstetrics and Gynaecology: 199034 St Petersburg, Mendeleevskaya liniya 3; tel. (812) 328-14-02; fax (812) 328-23-61; f. 1797; attached to Russian Acad. of Medical Sciences; Dir Prof. EDWARD K. AILAMAZYAN.

Pharmacy Research Institute: 117418 Moscow, ul. Krasikova 34; tel. (495) 128-57-88; Dir A. I. TENTSOVA.

Plague Prevention Research Institute for the Caucasus and Transcaucasia: 355106 Stavropol, Sovetskaya ul. 13; tel. (8652) 3-13-12; Dir V. I. EFREMENKO.

Research Centre for Medical Genetics: 115478 Moscow, Moskvorechie 1; tel. (499) 612-86-07; fax (499) 324-07-02; e-mail ekginter@mail.ru; internet www.med-gen.ru; f. 1969; attached to Russian Acad. of Medical Sciences; medical genetics, molecular genetics, cytogenetics, genetics of populations, clinical genetics, genetic counselling, hereditary metabolic diseases, prenatal diagnostics; library of 37,500 vols; Dir EVGENY K. GINTER; Deputy Dir VERA IZHEVSKAYA; publ. *Medical Genetics* (12 a year).

Attached Institutes:

> **Institute of Clinical Genetics:** Moscow; tel. (499) 611-85-94; attached to Russian Acad. of Medical Sciences; Dir Prof. EVGENY K. GINTER.

> **Institute of Human Genetics:** Moscow; tel. (499) 611-85-87; attached to Russian Acad. of Medical Sciences; Dir S. S. SHISHKIN.

Research Centre for Molecular Diagnostics and Therapy: 117638 Moscow, Simferopolsky bul. 8; tel. (495) 113-23-51; fax (495) 113-26-33; e-mail e.severin@mtu-net.ru; f. 1985; Dir E. S. SEVERIN; publs *Molecular Medicine* (4 a year), *Problems of Biological, Medical and Pharmaceutical Chemistry* (4 a year).

Research Centre for Obstetrics, Gynaecology and Perinatology: 117815 Moscow, GSP-7, ul. Akademika Oparina; tel. (495) 438-51-71; internet www.pregnancy.ru; Dir Prof. VLADIMIR I. KULAKOV; Scientific Sec. Dr TATYANA V. LEOPATINA.

Research Centre of Medical Radiology: 249020 Kaluga oblast, Obninsk, ul. Koroleva 4; tel. (495) 956-14-39; fax (495) 956-14-40; f. 1958; attached to Russian Acad. of Medical Sciences; library of 121,000 vols; Dir A. F. TSYB; publ. *Radiation and Risk* (2 a year).

Research Centre of Mental Health: 115552 Moscow, Kashirskoe shosse 34; tel. (499) 616-61-83; fax (495) 952-89-40; attached to Russian Acad. of Medical Sciences; Dir A. S. TIGANOV.

Research Centre of Neurology: 125367 Moscow, Volokolamskoe shosse 80; tel. (495) 490-20-02; fax (495) 490-22-10; e-mail center@neurology.ru; internet www.neurology.ru; f. 1945; attached to Russian Acad. of Medical Sciences; Dir Z. A. SUSLINA.

Research Centre of Obstetrics, Gynaecology and Perinatology: 117815 Moscow, ul. Akad. Oparina 4; tel. (495) 438-18-00; fax (495) 438-18-00; attached to Russian Acad. of Medical Sciences; Dir VLADIMIR KULAKOV.

Research Centre of Surgery: 119991 Moscow, Abrikosovski per. 2; tel. (499) 246-95-63; fax (499) 246-89-88; e-mail nrcs@med.ru; internet med.ru; attached to Russian Acad. of Medical Sciences; Dir SERGEY L. DZEMESHKEVICH.

Research Institute BIF Rheumatology: 115552 Moscow, Kashirskoe shosse 34-a; tel. (495) 114-44-90; fax (495) 114-44-68; e-mail sokrat@irramn.ru; f. 1959; attached to Russian Acad. of Medical Sciences; br. at Volgograd; Dir EL NASONOV; publ. *Scientific Practical Rheumatology* (6 a year).

Research Institute for Complex Problems of Hygiene and Occupational Diseases: 654041 Novokuznetsk, ul. Kutuzova 23; tel. (3843) 79-69-79; fax (3843) 79-66-69; e-mail zacharenkov@nvkz.kuzbass.net;

internet www.ni-kpg.ru; f. 1976; attached to Russian Acad. of Medical Sciences; Dir Dr V. V. ZAKHARENKOV.

Research Institute of Children's Infections: 197022 St Petersburg, ul. Prof. Popova 9; tel. (812) 234-18-62; f. 1927; library of 25,000 vols; Dir V. V. IVANOVA; publ. *Infectious Diseases of Childhood* (1 or 2 a year).

Research Institute of Epidemiology and Microbiology: 603600 Nizhnii Novgorod, Gruzinskaya ul. 44; tel. (8312) 33-40-07; fax (8312) 35-64-80; f. 1929; library of 10,000 vols; Dir I. N. BLOKHINA; publ. *Annual Collection of Research Articles*.

Research Institute of Forensic Medicine: 123242 Moscow, ul. Sadovaya-Kudrinskaya 3, Korp. 2; tel. (495) 254-32-49; Dir Prof. V. I. PROZOROVSKY.

Research Institute of Haematology and Intensive Therapy: 125167 Moscow, Novozykovsky pr-d 4A; tel. (495) 212-45-51; fax (495) 212-42-52; f. 1926; library of 50,000 vols; publ. *Sovremennye Problemy Gematologii i Perelivaniya Krovi* (12 a year).

Research Institute of Laser Medicine: 121165 Moscow, Studencheskaya ul. 40; tel. (495) 249-39-05.

Research Institute of Medical Primatology: 354376 Sochi-Adler, Veseloye 1; tel. (8622) 41-68-62; fax (8622) 41-62-39; e-mail primatologia@ramn.ru; f. 1927; attached to Russian Acad. of Medical Sciences; principal research programmes: primatology, maintaining and breeding primates, primate models of human diseases, endocrinology, immunology and cell biology, pathomorphology, comparative pathology, infectious pathology, infectious virology; library of 7,300 vols; Dir Prof. Acad. BORIS ARKADIEVICH LAPIN; Deputy Dir Dr OLEG VYSHEMIRSKI.

Research Institute of Occupational Safety under the auspices of the Independent Russian Trade Unions: 191187 St Petersburg, ul. Gagarinskaya 3; tel. (812) 279-08-13; fax (812) 275-42-48; f. 1927; noise control, respiratory protection, air conditioning, ventilation, air pollution analysis, hygiene and VDUs, certification of personal protective equipment and workplaces; library of 47,000 vols; Dir E. A. KOLODIN.

Research Institute of Radiation Hygiene: 197101 St Petersburg, ul. Mira 8; tel. (812) 233-53-63; fax (812) 233-26-12; e-mail irii@ek6663.spb.edu; f. 1956.

Research Institute of the Technology and Safety of Medicines: 142450 Moscow oblast, Noginsky raion, pos. Staraya Kupavna, ul. Kirova 23; tel. (495) 524-09-36; attached to Russian Acad. of Sciences; Dir YU. V. BUROV.

Research Institute of Traditional Methods of Treatment: 103051 Moscow, Petrovsky bul. 8; tel. (495) 200-27-91.

Research Institute of Transplants and Artificial Organs: 123436 Moscow, Shchukinskaya ul. 1; tel. (495) 190-29-71.

Research Institute of Vaccines and Sera: 614089 Perm, GSP, NIIVS.

Research Institute of Vaccines and Sera: 634004 Tomsk, ul. Lenina 32; tel. (3822) 22-45-12; Dir N. B. CHERNY.

Rostov Institute of Radiology and Oncology: Rostov-on-Don, Voroshilovsky pr. 119; affiliated to the Chelyabinsk Radiation Hygiene Institute.

Rostov Region Paediatric Research Institute: Rostov-on-Don, Dolomanovsky per. 142.

Rostov Research Institute for Plague Control: 344007 Rostov on Don, ul. M. Gorkogo 117; tel. (8632) 66-57-03; fax (8632)

34-13-76; f. 1934; library of 52,300 vols; Dir Prof. YU. M. LOMOV.

Russian Anti-plague Research Institute 'Microbe': 410005 Saratov, ul. Universitetskaya 46; tel. (8452) 26-21-31; fax (8452) 51-52-12; e-mail microbe@san.ru; internet www.microbe.ru; f. 1918; library of 100,000 vols; Dir Dr Prof. V. V. KUTYREV; publ. *Problems of Particularly Dangerous Infections* (4 a year).

Russian Institute of Medical Parasitology: Rostov-on-Don, Moskovskaya 67.

Russian Polenov, A. L., Neurosurgical Institute: 191104 St Petersburg, ul. Mayakovskogo 12; tel. (812) 272-98-79; fax (812) 275-56-03; f. 1926; library of 36,000 vols; Dir V. P. BERSNEV; publ. *Neurosurgery* (1 a year).

Russian Research Centre of Rehabilitation and Physiotherapy: 121099 Moscow, Novy Arbat 32; tel. (495) 252-18-83; fax (495) 292-65-11; f. 1920; library of 73,500 vols; Dir Dr V. M. BOGOLYUBOV; publs *Problems of Health Resorts, Physiotherapy and Exercise Therapy* (6 a year).

Russian Research Institute of Haematology and Transfusiology: 191024 St Petersburg, 2-a Sovetskaya ul. 16; tel. (812) 274-56-50; fax (812) 274-92-27; e-mail bloodscience@mail.ru; internet www.bloodscience.ru; f. 1932; Dir Dr E. A. SELIVANOV.

Research Institute of Phthisiopulmonology of the First Moscow Sechenov Medical University: 127994 Moscow, ul. Dostoevskogo 4; tel. (495) 281-84-22; fax (495) 281-59-88; e-mail tbcripp@mail.ru; f. 1918; research in area of identification, diagnostics, treatment of pulmonary and extrapulmonary tuberculosis and sarcoidosis in children, adolescents and adults; epidemiological surveys and assistance in organization of anti-tuberculosis aid; library of 54,517 vols; Dir Dr SERGEY V. SMERDIN; publ. *Tuberculosis and Ecology* (6 a year).

Russian Research Institute of Traumatology and Orthopaedics 'Vreden, R. R.': 195427 St Petersburg, ul. Akademika Baykova, dom 8; tel. (812) 670-89-05; fax (812) 670-95-68; e-mail info@rniito.org; internet www.rniito.org; f. 1906; orthopaedic clinical research centre; postgraduate training; library of 57,000 vols; Dir Prof. RASHID TIKHILOV; publ. *Travmatologia i Ortopedia Rossii* (Traumatology and Orthopaedics of Russia, 4 a year).

Russian Scientific Centre of Roentgenoradiology: 117837 Moscow, ul. Profsoyuznaya 86; tel. (495) 333-94-39; fax (495) 334-79-24; e-mail mailbox@rncrr.rssi.ru; internet www.space.ru/rncrr; f. 1924; laser diagnosis and treatment of malignant tumours; library of 51,700 vols; Dir Prof. V.P. KHARCHENKO.

St Petersburg Artificial Limb Research Institute: St Petersburg, pr. K. Marxa 9/12.

St Petersburg Institute of Ear, Throat, Nose and Speech: St Petersburg, Bronnitskaya 9; tel. (812) 292-54-29; f. 1930; library of 45,000 vols; Dir A. A. LANTSOV.

St Petersburg Institute of Eye Diseases: St Petersburg, Mokhovaya 38.

St Petersburg Institute of Phthisiopulmonology: 193036 St Petersburg, Ligovsky pr. 2–4; tel. (812) 279-25-54; fax (812) 279-25-73; f. 1923; library of 26,000 vols; Dir Prof. ALEXANDR V. VASILEV.

St Petersburg Institute of Tuberculosis: 193130 St Petersburg, Ligovsky pr. 2/4.

St Petersburg Institute of Vaccines and Sera: 198320 Krasnoe Selo, ul. Svobody 52; tel. (812) 741-19-78; fax (812) 741-10-53; e-mail reception@spbniivs.ru; internet www.spbniivs.ru; Dir R. N. RODIONOVA.

St Petersburg Pasteur Institute of Epidemiology and Microbiology: 197101 St Petersburg, ul. Mira 14; tel. (812) 233-20-92; fax (812) 232-92-17; e-mail intdeppi@ok7368.spb.edu; internet www.pasteur-nii.spb.ru; f. 1923; library of 60,000 vols; Dir Prof. ANATOLY ZHEBRUN.

St Petersburg Petrov, N. N., Research Institute of Oncology: 188646 St Petersburg, Pesochny 2, St Petersburgskaya ul. 68; tel. (812) 237-89-94.

St Petersburg Research Institute of Industrial Hygiene and Occupational Diseases: 193036 St Petersburg, 2-a Sovetskaya ul. 4; tel. (812) 279-40-11; f. 1924.

Samara Institute of Epidemiology, Microbiology and Hygiene: Samara, Chapaevskaya 87.

Saratov Institute of Restorative Surgery, Traumatology and Orthopaedics: Saratov, ul. Chernyshevskogo 148.

Scientific Centre of Clinical and Experimental Medicine: ul. Akad. Timakova 2, 630117 Novosibirsk; tel. (3832) 33-64-56; fax (3832) 33-64-56; e-mail sck@cyber.ma.nsc.ru; f. 1970; attached to Russian Acad. of Medical Sciences; Dir Dr V. A. SHKURUPY; publ. *Siberian Consilium* (medical pharmaceuticals, 6 a year).

Scientific Research Institute for General Reanimatology: 103031 Moscow, ul. Petrovka 25; tel. (495) 200-27-08; fax (495) 209-96-77; e-mail miiorramn@mediann.ru; f. 1936; attached to Russian Acad. of Medical Sciences; Dir Prof. V. V. MOROZ; br. at Novokuznetsk.

Scientific Research Institute for the Investigation of New Antibiotics: 119867 Moscow, Bol. Pirogovskaya 11; tel. (495) 246-99-80; fax (495) 245-02-95; attached to Russian Acad. of Medical Sciences; Dir YU. V. DUDNIK.

Semashko, N. A., Research Institute of Social Hygiene, Health Service Economics and Management: 103604 Moscow, ul. Vorontsovo Pole 12; tel. (495) 917-48-86; fax (495) 916-03-98; f. 1944; attached to Russian Acad. of Medical Sciences; Dir O. P. SHCHEPIN; publ. *Journal of Social Hygiene and the History of Medicine*.

Serbsky National Research Centre for Social and Forensic Psychiatry: 119034 Moscow, Kropotkinsky per. 23; tel. (495) 201-52-62; fax (495) 201-72-31; internet www.psi.med.ru/sspcen.htm; f. 1921; forensic psychiatry, social and clinical issues of psychiatry; library of 74,000 vols; Dir T. B. DMITRIEVA; publ. *Russian Psychiatric Journal* (contents and summaries in English, 6 a year).

Sochi Health Research Institute: Sochi, Kurortny pr. 110.

State Institute of Natural Curative Factors: 357500 Pyatigorsk, pr. Kirova 30; tel. (87933) 50-050; fax (87933) 55-618; f. 1920; neurology, rheumatology, pain assessment and management, behavioural therapy; library of 120,000 vols; Dir Prof. KRIVOBOROV.

State Research Institute for the Standardization and Control of Drugs: 117246 Moscow, Nauchni pr-d 14a; tel. (495) 128-26-32; Dir Prof. YU. F. KRYLOV.

State Scientific Research Institute of Medical Polymers: 117246 Moscow, Nauchni pr-d 10; tel. (495) 120-21-62; fax (495) 120-05-61; internet www.medpol.ru; f. 1966; library of 15,000 vols; Dir Prof. G. A. MATJUSHIN.

Sysin, A. N., Institute of Human Ecology and Environmental Hygiene: 119833 Moscow, ul. Pogodinskaya 10; tel. (495) 246-58-24; fax (495) 247-04-28; f. 1931; attached

to Russian Acad. of Medical Sciences; Dir G. I. SIDORENKO.

Tarasevich, L. A., State Research Institute for the Standardization and Control of Medical Biological Preparations: 121002 Moscow, Sivtsev-Vrazhek 41; tel. and fax (495) 241-39-22; e-mail gisk@glasnet.ru; f. 1919; library of 20,000 vols; Dir Prof. N. V. MEDUNTSIN.

Technological Research Institute for Antibiotics and Medical Enzymes: 198020 St Petersburg, Ogorodnikov pr. 41; tel. (812) 251-19-44; f. 1956; antifungal antibiotics, enzymes for medical use, nucleoside preparation of cardiovascular action; library of 55,000 vols; Dir Dr B. V. MOSKVICHEV.

Tomsk Institute of Physiotherapy and Spa Treatment: Tomsk, ul. Rosa Luxembourg 1.

Tomsk Research Centre: 634012 Tomsk, Kievskaya ul. 111/2; fax (3822) 44-50-57; attached to Russian Acad. of Medical Sciences; Chair. of the Presidium R. S. KARPOV.

Attached Institutes:

Institute of Cardiology: 634012 Tomsk, Kievskaya ul. 111/2; tel. (3822) 44-33-97; attached to Russian Acad. of Medical Sciences; Dir R. S. KARPOV.

Institute of Medical Genetics: 634050 Tomsk, pos. Sputnik, nab. Ushaika 10; tel. (3822) 22-22-28; attached to Russian Acad. of Medical Sciences; Dir V. P. PUZYREV.

Cancer Research Institute: 634050 Tomsk, Kooperativnyi st 5; tel. (3822) 51-10-39; fax (3822) 51-40-97; e-mail nii@oncology.tomsk.ru; internet www.oncology.tomsk.ru; f. 1979; attached to Siberian Br. Russian Acad. of Medical Sciences; studies on cancer prevalence and carcinogenesis on the territory of Siberia and the Russian Far E; detects endogenous and exogenous factors in tumour devt; investigates biochemical and molecular-genetic factors reflecting the mechanisms of carcinogenesis and tumour progression for assessing cancer risk and disease prognosis; develops new efficient programmes of the combined modality treatment for cancer patients using high-technology approaches; improves reconstructive plastic and organ-preserving surgeries and approaches for medical-social rehabilitation; Dir EVGENY L. CHOYNZONOV; publ. *Siberian Journal of Oncology* (6 a year).

Institute of Pharmacology: 634028 Tomsk, pr. Lenina 3; fax (3822) 41-83-79; attached to Russian Acad. of Medical Sciences; Dir E. D. GOLDBERG.

Laboratory of Experimental Biomedical Models: 634009 Tomsk, Kooperativny per. 7B; tel. (3822) 22-36-26; attached to Russian Acad. of Medical Sciences; Dir S. A. KUSMARTSEV.

Mental Health Research Institute: 634014 Tomsk, Sosnovy Bor, Aleutskaya St, 4; tel. (3822) 72-43-79; fax (3822) 72-44-25; e-mail redo@mail.tomsknet.ru; internet tomskinstitute.mental-health.ru; f. 1981; attached to Siberian Br., Russian Acad. of Medical Sciences; library of 8,120 vols; Dir Acad. VALENTIN SEMKE; Deputy Dir Prof. NIKOLAYF BOKHAN; publ. *Siberian Journal of Psychiatry and Addiction Psychiatry* (6 a year).

Institute of Toxicology: 192019 St Petersburg Bekhtereva St 1; tel. and fax (812) 365-06-80; e-mail info@toxicology.ru; internet www.toxicology.ru; f. 1935; attached to Federal Medico-Biological Agency of Russia Federal State Scientific Institution; Dir SERGEY P. NECHIPORENKO; Deputy Dir for Research Affairs EVGENY YU. BONITENKO.

Turner Scientific Research Institute of Child Orthopaedics and Traumatology: 189620 St Petersburg, ul. Parkovaya 64–68; tel. (812) 465-28-57; f. 1932; library of 33,600 vols; Dir Prof. V. L. ANDRIANOV; publ. scientific papers (2–3 a year).

Ufa Eye Research Institute: 450077 Ufa, 90 Pushkin str.; tel. (347) 272-37-75; fax (347) 272-08-52; e-mail eye@anrb.ru; internet www.ufaeyeinstitute.ru; f. 1926; attached to Acad. of Sciences of Republic of Bashkortostan; Dir Prof. M. M. BIKBOV; publ. *Collected Articles* (1 a year).

Ufa Research Institute of Occupational Health and Human Ecology: 450106 Ufa, ul. Kuvykina 94; tel. (3472) 28-53-19; fax (3472) 28-49-16; f. 1955; complex development of scientific fundamentals of labour hygiene and physiology, industrial toxicology, occupational pathology, environmental hygiene and aspects of hygiene in juvenile vocational training and the workplace in the oil, petrochemical, gas and microbiological industries; library of 63,000 vols; Dir A. B. BAKIROV; publ. *Production and Environmental Hygiene: Workers' Health Care in Oil and Gas Extracting and Petrochemical Industries* (1 a year).

Ufa Skin and Venereal Diseases Institute: Ufa, ul. Frunze 43.

Urals Research Institute of Maternity and Childhood Care: 620028 Ekaterinburg, ul. Repina 1; tel. (3432) 51-42-02; fax (3432) 51-22-12; f. 1877; library of 30,000 vols; Dir Dr G. A. CHERDANTSEVA.

Urals Research Institute of Phthisiopulmonology: 620039 Ekaterinburg, ul. 22 Partsezda 50; tel. (3432) 32-72-20; fax (3432) 31-80-41; e-mail urniif@mail.ur.ru; internet www.urniif.okb1.mplik.ru; f. 1931; library of 5,000 vols; Dir V. A. SOKOLOV.

Urology Research Institute: 105425 Moscow, 3-ya Parkovaya ul. 51; tel. and fax (495) 367-62-62; e-mail urology@cdromclub.ru; f. 1979; Dir Acad. NIKOLAI A. LOPATKIN.

Vishnevsky, A. V., Institute of Surgery: 113811 Moscow, Bol. Serpukhovskaya 27; tel. (495) 236-72-90; fax (495) 237-08-14; attached to Russian Acad. of Medical Sciences; Dir V. D. FEDOROV.

Volgograd Plague Prevention Research Institute: 400131 Volgograd, Golubinskaya ul. 7; tel. (8442) 37-37-74; fax (8442) 32-33-36; e-mail vari2@sprint-v.com.ru; f. 1970; library of 13,320 vols; Dir V. V. ALEKSEEV.

Voronezh Region Radiological and Oncological Institute: Voronezh, ul. Kalyaeva 2.

NATURAL SCIENCES

General

Arctic and Antarctic Research Institute: 199397 St Petersburg, ul. Beringa 38; tel. (812) 352-00-96; fax (812) 352-26-88; Dir I. YE. FROLOV.

Institute of Economic and International Problems of the Assimilation of the Ocean: 690600 Vladivostok, ul. Sukhanova 5-a; tel. (4232) 5-77-31; attached to Russian Acad. of Sciences; Dir R. SH.-A. ALIEV.

Institute of Global Climate and Ecology: 107258 Moscow, Glebovskaya 20B; tel. (495) 169-01-43; attached to Russian Acad. of Sciences; Dir YU. A. IZRAEL.

Institute of Limnology: 196199 St Petersburg, ul. Sevastyanova 9; tel. (812) 297-22-97; attached to Russian Acad. of Sciences; Dir V. A. RUMYANTSEV.

Institute of Natural Sciences: 670042 Ulan-Ude, ul. M. Sakhyanovoi 6; tel. (3012) 3-01-62; attached to Russian Acad. of Sciences; Dir K. A. NIKIFOROV.

Institute of the History of Science and Technology 'S. I. Vavilov': 109012 Moscow, Staropanskii per. 1/5; tel. and fax (495) 925-22-80; e-mail postmaster@ihst.ru; internet www.ihst.ru; f. 1953; attached to Russian Acad. of Sciences; research in history of natural sciences and technology (history of maths, physics, mechanics, biology, chemistry, social studies, Earth sciences, ecology and history of space); library of 70,000 vols; Dir Dr YURY M. BATURIN; publ. *Voprosy istorii estestvoznaniya i tekhniki* (4 a year).

Branch:

Institute for the History of Science and Technology—St Petersburg Branch: Universitetskaya nab. 5, 199034 St Petersburg; tel. (812) 328-47-12; fax (812) 328-46-67; e-mail ihst@ihst.nw.ru; internet www.ihst.nw.ru; Dir Prof. EDUARD I. KOLCHINSKY; publs *Sociology of Science and Technology*, *Studies in the History of Biology*.

Limnological Institute: 664033 Irkutsk, Ulan-Batorskaya ul. 3; tel. (3952) 42-65-04; fax (3952) 42-54-05; e-mail info@lin.irk.ru; internet www.lin.irk.ru; attached to Siberian Br., Russian Acad. of Sciences; Dir M. A. GRACHEV.

Mountain Taiga Station: 692533 Primorskii krai, Ussuriisky raion, pos. Gornotaezhnoe; tel. (42341) 9-11-10; attached to Russian Acad. of Sciences; Dir P. S. ZORIKOV.

North-East Interdisciplinary Scientific Research Institute FEB RAS: 685000 Magadan, Portovaya 16; tel. and fax (4132) 63-00-51; e-mail secretary@neisri.ru; internet www.neisri.ru; f. 1960; attached to Russian Acad. of Sciences; geology, geophysics, metallogeny, history, archaeology, economics; library of 450,000 vols; Dir Prof. Dr NIKOLAI ANATOLYEVICH GORYACHEV; Scientific Sec. PLYASHKEVICH ANNA ALEKSEEVNA; publ. *Vestnik NESC* (4 a year).

Pushchino Scientific Centre: 142290 Moscow oblast, Pushchino, pr. Nauki 3; tel. and fax (495) 923-80-03; e-mail nazarova@psn.ru; internet www.psn.ru; f. 1963; attached to Russian Acad. of Sciences; Dir VLADIMIR A. SHUVALOV.

Shirshov, P. P., Institute of Oceanology: 117997 Moscow, Nakhimovsky pr. 36; tel. (495) 124-59-96; fax (495) 124-59-83; e-mail office@ocean.ru; internet www.ocean.ru; f. 1946; attached to Russian Acad. of Sciences; brs in Kaliningrad, Gelendzhik, St Petersburg; Dir Prof. S. S. LAPPO.

V. I. Il'ichev Pacific Oceanological Institute: 690041 Vladivostok, Baltiiskaya ul. 43; tel. (423) 231-14-00; fax (423) 231-25-73; e-mail pacific@vlad.ru; internet www.poi.dvo.ru; f. 1973; attached to Russian Acad. of Sciences; comprehensive hydrophysical, hydrochemical and hydrobiological studies of water masses in seas and oceans; energy-mass exchange and the interaction of ocean and atmosphere; marine ecosystems state; studies of geology, geophysics and geochemistry of the Pacific Ocean and its mineral resources; devt of new methods and creation of technical means to study the ocean and atmosphere; devt and application of remote control methods; creation and analysis of oceanography data bases; Dir Prof. Acad. V. A. AKULICHEV.

Biological Sciences

All-Russia Research Institute for Nature Conservation: 113628 Moscow, Znamenskoe-Sadki, VNII Priroda; tel. (495) 423-03-22; fax (495) 423-23-22; f. 1981; research, general methodology, environmental protection strategy and coordination at home and internationally; 5 depts: animal protection, plant protection, ecosystem protection and recovery (incl. aquatic ecosystems), utilization of natural resources and nature reserves; library (books, journals, theses); Dir Prof. V. A. KRASILOV.

All-Russia Research Institute of Applied Microbiology: 142279 Moscow oblast, Serpukhovsky raion, Obolensk; tel. (0967) 2-77-61; Dir N. N. URAKOV.

Bakh, A. N., Institute of Biochemistry: Leninsky Pr. 33, 119071 Moscow; tel. (495) 952-34-41; fax (495) 952-27-32; e-mail inbi@inbi.ras.ru; internet www.inbi.ras.ru; attached to Russian Acad. of Sciences; 255 mems; Dir Prof. V. O. POPOV; Vice-Dir Prof. B. B. DZANTIEV; publs *Applied Biochemistry and Microbiology* (6 a year), *Uspekhi Biologicheskoi Khimii* (Progress of Biological Chemistry, in Russian, 1 a year).

Bioengineering Research Centre: 117984 Moscow, ul. Vavilova 34/5; tel. (495) 135-73-19; fax (495) 135-05-71; attached to Russian Acad. of Sciences; Dir K. G. SKRYABIN.

Biotechnical Research Institute: 119034 Moscow, ul. Prechistenka 38; tel. (495) 246-16-56; Dir A. M. KARPOV.

Biotechnologia JSC: 117246 Moscow, Nauchny pr-d 8; tel. (495) 332-34-20; fax (495) 331-01-01; f. 1993 as private company (fmrly state enterprise, f. 1986); biotechnology, pharmaceuticals; Gen. Dir RAIF G. VASILOV.

Borissiak Palaeontological Institute of Russian (PIN RAS): 117647 Moscow, Profsoyuznaya 123; tel. (495) 339-05-77; fax (495) 339-12-66; e-mail admin@paleo.ru; internet www.paleo.ru; f. 1930; attached to Russian Acad. of Sciences; library of 20,000 vols; attached museum: see Museums and Art Galleries; Dirs Acad. A. YU. ROZANOV, Prof. S. V. ROZHNOV, Prof. A. V. LOPATIN; publs *Paleontological Journal* (6 a year, in English and Russian), *Transactions* (3 or 4 a year).

Engelhardt Institute of Molecular Biology: 117984 Moscow, ul. Vavilova 32; tel. (495) 135-23-11; fax (495) 135-14-05; attached to Russian Acad. of Sciences; Dir Acad. A. D. MIRZABEKOV.

Institute of Biological Problems of the North: 685000 Magadan, pr. K. Marksa 24; tel. (41322) 2-47-30; fax (41322) 2-01-66; f. 1972; attached to Russian Acad. of Sciences; Dir Prof. F. B. CHERNYAVSKY.

Institute of Biology: 630091 Novosibirsk, ul. Frunze 11; tel. (3832) 20-96-14; attached to Russian Acad. of Sciences; Dir V. I. EVSIKOV.

Institute of Biology: 185610 Petrozavodsk, Pushkinskaya ul. 11; tel. (8142) 7-36-15; attached to Russian Acad. of Sciences; Dir S. N. DROZDOV.

Institute of Biology: 167610 Syktyvkar, Kommunisticheskaya ul. 28; tel. (8212) 42-52-02; fax (8212) 42-01-63; f. 1962; attached to Russian Acad. of Sciences; Dir Dr A. I. TASKAEV.

Institute of Biology: 450054 Ufa, 25, pr. Oktyabrya 69; tel. (3472) 34-34-01; attached to Russian Acad. of Sciences; Dir V. M. KORSUNOV.

Institute of Biology: 670047 Ulan-Ude, ul. M. Sakhyanovoi 6; tel. (3012) 43-45-75; attached to Russian Acad. of Sciences; Dir L. L. UBUGUNOV.

Institute of Biology: 677891 Yakutsk, pr. Lenina 41; tel. (4112) 2-77-81; attached to Russian Acad. of Sciences; Dir. N. G. SOLOMONOV.

Institute of Biology and Soil Science: 690022 Vladivostok, pr. Stoletiya Vladivostoka 159; tel. (4232) 31-04-10; fax (4232) 31-01-93; internet www.ibss.febras.ru; f. 1962;

attached to Russian Acad. of Sciences; library of 80,000 vols; Dir Prof. YU. N. ZHURAVLEV; publ. *Proceedings* (in Russian, 1 a year).

Institute of Biophysics: 660036 Krasnoyarsk, Akademgorodok; tel. (3912) 43-15-79; fax (3912) 43-34-00; internet www.ibp.ru; f. 1981; attached to Russian Acad. of Sciences; Dir Dr A. G. DEGERMENDZHY; Scientific Sec. Dr EGOR ZADEREEV.

Institute of Biophysics: 123182 Moscow, Zhivopisnaya ul. 46; tel. (495) 190-56-51; fax (495) 190-35-90; e-mail ibphgen@rcibph.dol .ru; f. 1946; radiobiology, radiation protection, health physics, medical radiology, non-ionizing radiation; Dir L. A. ILYIN.

Institute of Cell Biophysics: 142290 Moscow oblast, Pushchino, Institutskaya ul. 3; tel. (495) 625-59-84; fax (496) 733-05-09; f. 1991; attached to Russian Acad. of Sciences; Dir Prof. EVGENII FESENKO.

Institute of Chemical Bioload Fundamental Medicine SB RAS: 630090 Novosibirsk, pr. Akad. Lavrenteva 8; tel. (383) 363-51-50; fax (383) 363-51-53; e-mail vvv@ niboch.nsc.ru; internet www.niboch.nsc.ru; f. 1984; attached to Russian Acad. of Sciences; Dir Prof. V. V. VLASOV; Academic Sec. Dr MARSEL KABILOV.

Institute of Cytology: 194064 St Petersburg, Tikhoretsky pr. 4; tel. (812) 247-18-29; fax (812) 247-03-41; attached to the Soc. of Protozoologists, affiliated with the Russian Acad. of Sciences; Dir Prof. Dr VLADIMIR N. PARFENOV.

Institute of Cytology and Genetics: 630090 Novosibirsk, pr. Akad. Lavrienteva 10; tel. (3832) 363-49-80; fax (3832) 333-12-78; internet www.bionet.nsc.ru; f. 1957; attached to Russian Acad. of Sciences; Dir Acad. N. A. KOLCHANOV; Scientific Sec. G. V. ORLOVA.

Institute of Food Substances: c/o Russian Academy of Sciences, 117901 Moscow, Leninsky pr. 14; attached to Russian Acad. of Sciences; Dir M. N. MANAKOV.

Institute of Higher Nervous Activity and Neurophysiology: 117865 Moscow, ul. Butlerova 5a; tel. (495) 334-70-00; attached to Russian Acad. of Sciences; Dir Acad. P. V. SIMONOV.

Institute of Marine Biology: Petropavlovsk-Kamchatskii; attached to Russian Acad. of Sciences; Dir (vacant).

Institute of Marine Biology: 690041 Vladivostok, ul. Palchevskogo 17; tel. (423) 231-09-05; fax (423) 231-09-00; e-mail inmarbio@ mail.primorye.ru; internet www.imb.dvo.ru; f. 1970; attached to Russian Acad. of Sciences; library of 40,000 vols; Dir ANDREY V. ADRIANOV; publs *Biologiya morya* (6 a year), *Russian Journal of Marine Biology* (7 a year, online).

Institute of Microbiology: 117811 Moscow, pr. 60-letiya Oktyabrya 7, korp. 2; tel. (495) 135-45-66; attached to Russian Acad. of Sciences; Dir Acad. M. V. IVANOV.

Institute of Molecular Biology of the Gene: 117333 Moscow, ul. Vavilova 34/5; tel. (495) 135-60-89; attached to Russian Acad. of Sciences; Dir Acad. G. P. GEORGIEV.

Institute of Molecular Genetics: 123182 Moscow, pl. Kurchatova 2; tel. (499) 196-00-00; fax (499) 196-02-21; e-mail img@img.ras .ru; internet www.img.ras.ru; f. 1978; attached to Russian Acad. of Sciences; Dir Prof. SERGEY V. KOSTROV.

Institute of Parasitology: 117071 Moscow, Leninskii pr. 33; tel. (495) 952-57-46; attached to Russian Acad. of Sciences; Dir M. D. SONIN.

Institute of Physicochemical and Biological Problems in Soil Science: 142290

Moscow oblast, Pushchino; tel. (4967) 73-18-96; fax (4967) 33-05-95; e-mail soil@issp .serpukhov.su; internet www.issp.psn.ru; f. 1999; attached to Russian Acad. of Sciences; Dir Prof. V. N. KUDEYAROV.

Institute of Physiologically Active Substances: 142432 Moscow oblast, Noginskii raion, p/o Chernogolovka; tel. (096) 524-50-62; attached to Russian Acad. of Sciences; Dir Acad. N. S. ZEFIROV.

Institute of Physiology: c/o Russian Academy of Sciences, 117901 Moscow, Leninsky pr. 14; attached to Russian Acad. of Sciences; Dir O. G. GAZENKO.

Institute of Physiology: 167982 Syktyvkar, Pervomayskaya str. 50; tel. and fax (8212) 24-10-01; e-mail ovoys@physiol .komisc.ru; internet www.physiol.komisc.ru; f. 1988; attached to Russian Acad. of Sciences; Urals br. of the Russian Acad. of Sciences; Dir Prof. Dr Y. S. OVODOV.

Institute of Plant and Animal Ecology, Ural Division of Russian Academy of Sciences: 620144 Ekaterinburg, 8 Marta St 202; tel. (343) 260-82-55; fax (343) 260-65-00; e-mail common@ipae.uran.ru; internet www .ipae.uran.ru; f. 1944; attached to Russian Acad. of Sciences; investigations on regularities of org., functioning, dynamics and stability of living systems on population, community and ecosystem levels incl. palaeoreconstructions of late quaternary ecosystems of the Urals mountains and adjacent territories (N Eurasia); elaboration of theoretical foundations of rational nature management ecological regulation, bio-indication, ecotoxicology and radioecology; library of 150,000 vols; Dir Acad. VLADIMIR N. BOLSHAKOV; Deputy Dir VLADIMIR D. BOGDANOV; Deputy Dir EUGENE L. VOROBEICHIK; publ. *Russian Journal of Ecology* (6 a year).

Institute of Problems of the Industrial Ecology in the North (INEP KSC): 184209 Murmansk region, Apatity Fersman St, 14; tel. (81555) 6-10-93; fax (81555) 7-49-64; e-mail vandysh@inep.ksc.ru; internet inep .ksc.ru; f. 1989; attached to Kola Science Centre, Russian Acad. of Sciences; library of 400,000 vols; Dir Prof. Dr VLADIMIR A. MASLOBOEV.

Institute of Protein Research: 142292 Moscow oblast, Serpukhovskii raion, Pushchino; tel. and fax (495) 924-04-93; e-mail protres@sun.ipr.serpukhov.su; attached to Russian Acad. of Sciences; Dir Prof. A. S. SPIRIN.

Institute of the Biochemistry and Physiology of Micro-organisms: 142292 Moscow oblast, Serpukhovskii raion, Pushchino; tel. (277) 3-05-26; attached to Russian Acad. of Sciences; Dir A. M. BORONIN.

Institute of the Biochemistry and Physiology of Plants and Micro-organisms: 410049 Saratov, pr. Entuziastov 13; tel. (8452) 97-04-44; fax (8452) 97-03-83; e-mail institute@ibppm.sgu.ru; internet www .ibppm.saratov.ru; f. 1980; attached to Russian Acad. of Sciences; library of 30,000 vols; Dir V. V. IGNATOV.

Institute of the Biology of Inland Waters: 152742 Yaroslavskaya oblast, Nekouzsky raion, p/o Borok; tel. and fax (8547) 24-042; e-mail ibiw@mail.ru; internet www.ibiw.yaroslavl.ru; f. 1956; attached to Russian Acad. of Sciences; Dir Dr SERGEI I. GENKAL; publ. *Biology of Inland Waters* (3 a year).

Institute of the Ecology and Genetics of Micro-organisms: 614081 Perm, ul. Goleva 13; tel. (3422) 44-67-12; fax (3422) 44-67-11; internet www.ecology.psu.ru; f. 1988; attached to Russian Acad. of Sciences; library

of 3,000 vols; Dir V. A. CHERESHNEV; publ. *Proceedings of Scientific Research* (1 a year).

Institute of the Ecology of the Volga Basin: 445003 Togliatti; tel. (8469) 23-54-78; fax (8469) 48-95-04; attached to Russian Acad. of Sciences; Dir G. S. ROZENBERG.

Institute of Theoretical and Experimental Biophysics: 142290 Moscow oblast, Serpukhovsky raion, Pushchino; tel. (495) 632-78-69; fax (496) 733-05-53; e-mail office@ iteb.ru; attached to Russian Acad. of Sciences; Dir Prof. G. R. IVANITSKY; Asst Dir A. NAUMOV.

Institute of Water and Ecological Problems: 680063 Khabarovsk, ul. Kim Yu Chena 65; tel. (4212) 22-75-73; fax (4212) 22-70-85; f. 1968; attached to Russian Acad. of Sciences; Dir Dr B. A. VORONOV; publ. *Biogeochemical and Hydroecological Peculiarities of the Amur River Watershed Ecosystems* (1 a year).

Institute for Water and Environmental Problems: 656038 Barnaul, Molodyozhnaya ul. 1; tel. (3852) 66-64-60; fax (3852) 24-03-96; e-mail iwep@iwep.asu.ru; internet www .iwep.asu.ru; f. 1987; research into hydrology, physical geography, cartography, biogeochemistry, geomorphology, limnology, air and water quality, mathematical modelling of contaminant transport in the environment; attached to Russian Acad. of Sciences; library of 37,000 vols; Dir Prof. YURI I. VINOKUROV; publ. *Polzunovsky Vestnik* (in Russian, 6 a year).

Kazan Institute of Biology: 420111 Kazan, ul. Lobachevskogo 2/31; tel. (8432) 32-64-91; attached to Russian Acad. of Sciences; Dir Dr A. I. TARCHEVSKY.

Koltsov, A. N., Institute of Developmental Biology: 117808 Moscow, ul. Vavilova 26; tel. (495) 135-64-83; attached to Russian Acad. of Sciences; Dir N. G. KHRUSHCHOV.

Komarov, V. L., Botanical Institute: 197376 St Petersburg, ul. Prof. Popova 2; tel. (812) 234-12-37; fax (812) 234-45-12; e-mail binadmin@ok3277.spb.edu; internet www.binran.spb.ru; f. 1713; attached to Russian Acad. of Sciences; 460 mems; Dir V. T. YARMISHKO; publs *Botanichesky Zhurnal* (12 a year), *Rastitelnost Rossii* (2 or 3 a year).

Murmansk Marine Biological Institute: 183010 Murmansk, Vladimirskaya ul. 17; tel. (8152) 25-39-63; fax (8152) 25-39-94; e-mail mmbi@mmbi.info; internet www.mmbi.info; f. 1935; attached to Russian Acad. of Sciences; oldest instn of the Kola Scientific Centre of the Russian Acad. of Sciences; conducts complex investigations of Nordic seas from Iceland to the Laptev Sea; studies southern seas: the Barents Sea and the Sea of Azov are the focus of ecosystem investigations; addresses problems of climate, marine peri-glacial, quaternary and current ecology, aquaculture, bioresources and environmental safety; monitors the ecosystem of the northern sea route, atomic fleet bases, and other water areas exposed to anthropogenic impacts; develops marine biotechnologies and prediction models for oceanologic processes, and environmental and engineering strategies to be applied to Arctic and southern sea; library of 70,000 vols; Dir Acad. GENNADY MATISHOV.

Pacific Institute of Bio-organic Chemistry: 690022 Vladivostok, pr. 100-letiya Vladivostoka 159; tel. (4232) 31-14-30; fax (4232) 31-40-50; f. 1964; attached to Russian Acad. of Sciences; Dir Prof. A. STONIK.

Pavlov Institute of Physiology: 199034 St Petersburg, nab. Makarova 6; tel. (812) 328-07-01; fax (812) 328-05-01; e-mail krylov@ infran.ru; internet www.infran.ru; f. 1925;

attached to Russian Acad. of Sciences; Dir Prof. D. P. DVORETSKY.

Research Institute for Monitoring Land and Ecosystems: 101000 Moscow, Bolshevistaky per. 11; tel. (495) 924-55-52.

Research Institute for the Biological Testing of Chemical Compounds: Moscow oblast, Kupavna, ul. Kirova 23; Dir L. A. PIRUZYAN.

Research Institute for the Genetics and Selection of Industrial Micro-organisms: 113545 Moscow, 1-i Dorozhnyi per. 1; tel. (495) 315-37-47; Dir V. G. DEBABOV.

Research Institute of Food Biotechnology: 109033 Moscow, Samokatnaya 4B; tel. (495) 362-44-95.

Scientific Centre of Biological Research: Moscow oblast, Serpukhovskii raion, Pushchino; attached to Russian Acad. of Sciences; Dir E. L. GOLOVLEV.

Sechenov, I. M., Institute of Evolutionary Physiology and Biochemistry: 194223 St Petersburg, pr. M. Toreza 44; tel. (812) 552-79-01; attached to Russian Acad. of Sciences; Dir Acad. V. L. SVIDERSKY.

Severtsov, A. N., Institute of Ecology and Evolution: 119071 Moscow, Leninskii pr. 33; tel. (495) 952-20-88; fax (495) 954-55-34; e-mail admin@sevin.ru; attached to Russian Acad. of Sciences; Dir Acad. DMITRI S. PAVLOV; publs *Russian Journal of Aquatic Ecology* (2 a year), *Lutreola* (2 a year).

Shemyakin-Ovchinnikov Institute of Bio-organic Chemistry: 117871 Moscow, ul. Miklukho-Maklaya 16/10; tel. (495) 335-01-00; fax (495) 310-70-07; f. 1959; attached to Russian Acad. of Sciences; library of 250,000 vols; br. at Pushchino; Dir Prof. V. T. IVANOV; publ. *Journal of Bio-organic Chemistry* (in Russian and English, monthly).

Siberian Institute of Plant Physiology and Biochemistry: 664033 Irkutsk 33, POB 317; tel. (3952) 42-67-21; fax (3952) 51-07-54; e-mail matmod@sifibr.irk.ru; internet sifibr .irk.ru; f. 1961; attached to Russian Acad. of Sciences; researches on plant physiology and biochemistry, microbiology and soil science, entomology, botany, geobotany and forestry; Dir Dr VICTOR VOINIKOV; publ. *Journal of Stress Physiology & Biochemistry*.

State Research Centre of Virology and Biotechnology (Vector): 630559 Novosibirsk oblast, Koltsovo; tel. (3832) 36-60-10; fax (3832) 36-74-09; e-mail vector@vector.nsk .su; internet www.vector.nsc.ru; f. 1974; library of 90,000 vols; Dir Acad. LEV S. SANDAKHCHIEV.

State Research Institute of Highly Pure Biopreparations (IHPB): 197110 St Petersburg, Pudozhskaya St 7; tel. (812) 235-12-25; fax (812) 230-49-48; e-mail onir@ hpb-spb.com; internet www.hpb-.spb.com; f. 1974; basic research and applied activities using the latest advances in molecular biology, microbiology, virology, and biotechnology; Dir Prof. VALERIY DOBRITSA.

Timiryazev, K. A., Institute of Plant Physiology: 127276 Moscow, Botanicheskaya 35; tel. (495) 977-80-22; fax (495) 977-80-18; e-mail ifr@ippras.ru; internet www .ippras.ru; f. 1890; attached to Russian Acad. of Sciences; library of 83,000 vols; Dir Prof. VL. V. KUZNETSOV; publ. *Russian Journal of Plant Physiology* (6 a year).

Vavilov Institute of General Genetics: 119991 Moscow, ul. Gubkina 3; tel. (495) 135-62-13; fax (495) 135-12-89; e-mail iogen@vigg .ru; internet www.vigg.ru; f. 1966; attached to Russian Acad. of Sciences; library of 5,000 vols; Dir Prof. YU. P. ALTUKHOV; publs *Rus-*

sian Journal of Genetics (12 a year), *Advances in Current Biology* (6 a year).

Zoological Institute: 199034 St. Petersburg, Universitetskaya nab. 1; tel. (812) 328-03-11; fax (812) 328-29-41; e-mail admin@zin.ru; internet www.zin.ru; f. 1832; attached to Russian Acad. of Sciences; Dir O. N. PUGACHEV; Vice-Dir ALEXEY TIKHONOV.

Mathematical Sciences

Euler, L., International Institute of Mathematics: 197022 St Petersburg, Pesochnaya nab. 10; tel. (812) 234-05-74; fax (812) 234-58-19; e-mail admin@euler .pdmi.ras.ru; internet www.pdmi.ras.ru/ eimi; f. 1988; attached to Russian Acad. of Sciences; Dir Acad. L. D. FADDEEV.

Institute of Mathematics: 450057 Ufa, ul. Tukaeva 50; tel. (3472) 22-59-36; attached to Russian Acad. of Sciences; Dir V. V. NAPALKOV.

Sobolev Institute of Mathematics: 630090 Novosibirsk, pr. Akad. Koptyuga 4; tel. (3833) 33-28-92; fax (3833) 33-25-98; e-mail im@math.nsc.ru; internet www.math .nsc.ru; f. 1957; attached to Russian Acad. of Sciences; library of 120,000 vols; Dir Acad. YU. L. ERSHOV; Scientific Sec. YURIY VOLKOV; publs *Diskretny Analiz i Issledovanie Operatsii* (6 a year), *Matematicheskie Trudy* (2 a year), *Siberian Electronic Mathematical Reports*, *Sibirsky Matematichesky Zhurnal* (6 a year), *Sibirsky Zhurnal Industrialnoy Matematiki* (4 a year).

Steklov, V. A., Institute of Mathematics: 119991 Moscow, ul. Gubkina 8; tel. (495) 135-22-91; fax (495) 135-05-55; e-mail steklov@mi .ras.ru; internet www.mi.ras.ru; attached to Russian Acad. of Sciences; Dir Acad. YU. S. OSIPOV.

St Petersburg Department of V. A. Steklov Mathematical Institute: 191023 St Petersburg, nab. Fontanki 27; tel. (812) 312-40-58; fax (812) 310-53-77; e-mail admin@pdmi.ras.ru; internet www.pdmi.ras .ru; f. 1940, ind. instn; attached to Russian Acad. of Sciences; Dir Acad. S. V. KISLYAKOV; Exec. Academic Sec. Dr MAXIM VSEMIRNOV; publs *Journal of Mathematical Sciences* (11 a year), *St Petersburg Math Journal* (24 a year).

Physical Sciences

All-Russia Geological Oil Research Institute (VNIGNI): 105819 Moscow, shosse Entuziastov 36; tel. (495) 273-26-51; fax (495) 273-55-38; f. 1953; library of 80,000 vols; Dir Dr K. A. KLESCHEV; publs *Geology of Oil and Gas* (1 a year), *Proceedings* (6 a year).

All-Russia Research Institute for the Geology and Mineral Resources of the World's Oceans: 190121 St Petersburg, Angliisky 1; tel. (812) 113-83-79; fax (812) 114-14-70; f. 1948; library of 60,500 vols; Dir Prof. I. S. GRAMBERG.

All-Russia Research Institute of Chemical Technology: 115409 Moscow, Kashirskoe shosse 33; tel. (495) 324-61-55.

All-Russian Research Institute of Geological, Geophysical and Geochemical Systems (VNIIgeosystem): 117105 Moscow, Varshavskoe shosse 8; tel. (495) 954-53-50; fax (495) 958-37-11; e-mail geosys@ geosys.ru; internet www.geosys.ru; f. 1961; fundamental and applied scientific research; experimental design and technological research in earth sciences and geological exploration; library of 38,000 vols; Dir LEONID E. CHESALOV; Sec. OLGA LYUBIMOVA; publ. *Geoinformatika* (6 a year).

All-Russia Research Institute of Hydrolysis: 198099 St Petersburg, ul. Kalinina 13; tel. (812) 186-29-22; Dir O. I. SHAPOVALOV.

All-Russia Research Institute of Natural Gases and Gas Technology: 142717 Moscow oblast, Leninsky raion, pos. Razvilka; tel. (495) 355-92-06; fax (495) 399-16-77; e-mail samsr@gazprom.ru; f. 1948; library of 100,000 vols.

All-Russia Research Institute of Optical and Physical Measurements: 103031 Moscow, ul. Rozhdestvenka 27; tel. (495) 208-41-83; attached to Russian Acad. of Sciences; Gen. Dir I. G. BARANNIK.

All-Russia Research Institute of Physical-Technical and Radiotechnical Measurements: 147570 Moscow oblast, Solnechnogorsky raion, p/o Mendeleevo; tel. (495) 535-92-78; attached to Russian Acad. of Sciences; Dir B. I. ALSKIN.

All-Russia Scientific Research Institute of Mineral Resources: 109017 Moscow, Staromonetni per. 31; tel. (495) 231-50-43; fax (495) 238-19-21; f. 1918; prospecting for and estimating ore deposits, research in processing; library of 345,000 vols; Dir Prof. A. N. EREMEEV.

Amur Complex Research Institute: 675000 Amur oblast, Blagoveshchensk, per. Relochnyi 1; tel. (4162) 42-72-32; fax (4162) 42-59-31; f. 1980; attached to Russian Acad. of Sciences; geology, minerals; library of 26,000 vols; Dir V. G. MOISEENKO.

Andreev Acoustics Institute: 117036 Moscow, ul. Shvernika 4; tel. (495) 126-74-01; fax (495) 126-84-11; e-mail dubrov@akin.ru; internet www.akin.ru; f. 1953; attached to Russian Acad. of Sciences; Dir N. A. DUBROVSKY.

Arbuzov, A. E., Institute of Organic and Physical Chemistry: 420088 Kazan, ul. Akad. Arbuzova 8; tel. (8432) 73-93-65; fax (8432) 73-22-53; e-mail arbuzov@iopc.kcn.ru; internet www.iopc.kcn.ru; f. 1965; attached to Russian Acad. of Sciences; Dir O. G. SINYASHIN.

Baikov, A. A., Institute of Metallurgy: 117911 Moscow, Leninskii pr. 49; tel. (495) 135-86-11; attached to Russian Acad. of Sciences; Dir Acad. N. P. LYAKISHEV.

Bardin, I. P., Central Research Institute of Ferrous Metallurgy: 107005 Moscow, 2-ya Baumanskaya 9/23; tel. (495) 265-72-04; fax (499) 267-48-27; e-mail ferrum.sc@online .ru; f. 1944; library of 65,000 vols; Dir-Gen. VLADIMIR I. MATORIN.

Bochvar, A. A., All-Russia Research Institute of Inorganic Materials: 123060 Moscow, ul. Rugova 5a; tel. (495) 190-82-97; fax (495) 196-41-68; e-mail post@bochvar.ru; internet www.bochvar.ru; f. 1945; Dir-Gen. ALEKSANDR VIKTOROVICH VATULIN; publ. *Materialovedeniye i Novye Materialy* (Materials Science and New Materials, 1 a year).

Boreskov Institute of Catalysis: 630090 Novosibirsk, pr. Akad. Lavrenteva 5; tel. (383) 330-82-69; fax (383) 330-47-19; e-mail bic@catalysis.ru; internet www.catalysis.ru; attached to Russian Acad. of Sciences; Dir V. N. PARMON.

Central Aerological Observatory: 141700 Moscow, 3 Pervomayskaya St., Dolgoprudny; tel. (495) 408-61-48; fax (495) 575-33-27; e-mail caohead@cao-rhms.ru; internet www .cao-rhms.ru; f. 1941; atmospheric physics and chemistry up to 100 km, study and monitoring of ozone layer, cloud physics, applied meteorology, weather modification; use of aircraft, rockets, satellites and radar for atmospheric studies.; library of 61,000 vols; Dir A. A. IVANOV; publ. *CAO Proceedings*.

Central Seismological Observatory: Obninsk; attached to Russian Acad. of Sciences.

Chita Institute of Natural Resources: 672014 Chita, ul. Nedorezova 16, POB 147; tel. and fax (302) 221-25-82; internet www .chita.ru/public_htm/cinr/cinr.htm; f. 1981; attached to Russian Acad. of Sciences; library of 6,000 vols; Dir A. B. PTITSYN; publ. *Report on Environmental Conditions in Zabailkalye* (1 a year).

Far Eastern Institute of Geology: 690022 Vladivostok, pr. Stoletiya Vladivostoka 159; tel. (4232) 31-87-50; fax (4232) 31-78-47; e-mail fegi@online.marine.su; f. 1959; attached to Russian Acad. of Sciences; Dir A. I. KHANCHUK.

Federal G. G. Devyatykh Institute of the Chemistry of High-Purity Substances: 603950 Nizhnii Novgorod, ul. Tropinina 49; tel. (831) 462-56-70; fax (831) 462-56-66; e-mail victor@ihps.nnov.ru; internet www .ihps.nnov.ru; f. 1988; attached to Russian Acad. of Sciences; fundamental and applied research of high-purity substances; production of zinc selenide, quartz and chalcogenide optical fibres; Dir Prof. MIKHAIL CHURBANOV; publs *Journal of Optoelectronics and Advanced Materials, Optical Letters.*

General Physics Institute: 119991 Moscow, ul. Vavilova 38; tel. (495) 135-82-96; fax (495) 234-31-96; e-mail director@gpi.ru; internet www.gpi.ru; f. 1983; attached to Russian Acad. of Sciences; brs in Tarusa and Troitsk; Dir Prof. IVAN A. SHCHERBAKOV.

Geological Institute: 670047 Ulan-Ude, ul. Sakhyanova 6A; tel. and fax (3012) 43-30-24; e-mail gin@gin.bscnet.ru; internet geo.stbur .ru; f. 1973; attached to Siberian Br., Russian Acad. of Sciences; study of structure, history of devt and matter composition of earth crust in the Buryatia and Chita regions by geological, geophysical and geochemical methods; Dir GENNADI TATKOV.

Geological Institute of Kola Science Centre: 184209 Murmansk oblast, Apatity, ul. Fersmana 14; tel. (81555) 79656; fax (81555) 76481; e-mail geoksc@geoksc.apatity .ru; internet geoksc.apatity.ru; f. 1951; attached to Russian Acad. of Sciences; Dir YURY L. VOYTEKHOVSKY.

Graphite Research Institute: 111524 Moscow, Elektrodnaya 2; tel. (495) 176-13-06; fax (495) 176-12-63; Dir V. I. KOSTIKOV.

Grebenshchikov, I. V., Institute of Silicate Chemistry: 199155 St Petersburg, ul. Odoevskogo 24, korp. 2; tel. (812) 350-65-16; fax (812) 328-54-01; e-mail ichsran@isc.nw .ru; attached to Russian Acad. of Sciences; Dir Acad. V. J. SHEVCHENKO.

High-Mountain Geophysical Institute: 360030 Nalchik, pr. Lenina 2; tel. (866) 247-00-31; fax (866) 247-00-24; e-mail vgikbr@ rambler.ru; f. 1963; meteorology, climatology, glaciology, geophysics, ecology; library of 17,230 vols, 26,288 periodicals; Dir Dr VALERY O. TAPASKHANOV.

Institute for Geothermal Research: 367030 Makhachkala, Shamil pr. 39-A; tel. and fax (8722) 62-93-57; e-mail geoterm@ mail.ru; internet www.ipgdncran.ru; f. 1980; attached to Russian Acad. of Sciences; fundamental scientific research on heat physics, hydrodynamics and heat exchange in geothermal systems, mathematical and information models in geothermy, renewable energy; Dir Prof. A. B. ALKHASOV; publ. *Proceedings of the Scientific Training 'Actual problems of renewable energy resources development'* (2 a year).

Institute for High-Energy Physics: 142281 Moscow oblast, Protvino; tel. (4967) 74-04-56; fax (4967) 74-49-37; e-mail yury .ryabov@ihep.ru; internet www.ihep.ru; f. 1963; high energy physics; proton accelerators; library of 300,000 vols; Dir NIKOLAI TYURIN.

Institute for Metals Superplasticity Problems of RAS: 450001 Ufa, 39 St Khalturina; tel. (347) 223-64-07; fax (347) 282-37-59; e-mail imsp@anrb.ru; f. 1985; attached to Russian Acad. of Sciences; library of 8,700 vols; Dir R. R. MYLYUKOV.

Institute of Applied Astronomy: 197110 St Petersburg, ul. Zhdanovskaya 8; tel. (812) 275-11-18; fax (812) 275-11-19; e-mail ipa@ ipa.nw.ru; internet www.ipa.nw.ru; f. 1988; attached to Russian Acad. of Sciences; Dir Prof. A. V. IPATOV; publs *Trudy IPA RAN* (2 a year, in Russian), *Communications* (10 a year, in Russian and English).

Institute of Applied Physics: 603600 Nizhny Novgorod, ul. Ulyanova 46; tel. (831) 436-58-10; attached to Russian Acad. of Sciences; Dir Acad. A. G. LITVAK.

Institute of Astronomy: 109017 Moscow, Pyatnitskaya ul. 48; tel. (495) 951-54-61; fax (495) 951-55-57; e-mail admin@inasan.rssi .ru; internet www.inasan.rssi.ru; f. 1936; attached to Russian Acad. of Sciences; Dir Prof. BORIS M. SHUSTOV.

Institute of Atmospheric Optics: 634055 Tomsk, Akademicheskii pr. 1; tel. (382) 249-27-38; fax (382) 249-20-86; e-mail mgg@iao .ru; internet www.iao.ru; f. 1969; research and development in physics, laser engineering, aerosol technology and ozone; attached to Siberian br. of the Russian Acad. of Sciences; Dir Prof. GENNADY GRIGOREVICH MATVIENKO.

Institute of Atmospheric Physics: 119017 Moscow, Pyzhevskii per. 3; tel. (495) 951-55-65; fax (495) 953-16-52; e-mail mail_adm@ omega.ifaran.ru; f. 1956; attached to Russian Acad. of Sciences; library of 4,000 vols, 40 periodicals; Dir Acad. G. S. GOLITSYN; publ. *Izvestiya—Atmospheric and Oceanic Physics* (6 a year).

Institute of Chemical Kinetics and Combustion: 630090 Novosibirsk, Institutskaya 3; tel. (3832) 34-41-50; fax (3832) 34-23-50; f. 1957; attached to Russian Acad. of Sciences; library of 88,000 vols; Dir Prof. YU. D. TSVETKOV.

Institute of Chemistry: 690022 Vladivostok, pr. Stoletiya Vladivostoka 159; tel. (4232) 31-25-90; fax (4232) 31-18-89; e-mail chemi@online.ru; f. 1971; attached to Russian Acad. of Sciences; library of 5,000 vols; Dir Prof. Dr V. YU. GLUSHCHENKO.

Institute of Coal and Coal Chemistry: 650610 Kemerovo GSP, ul. Rukavishnikova 21; tel. (3842) 28-14-33; fax (3842) 21-18-38; e-mail pvp@kemsc.ru; internet www.kemsc .ru; f. 1983; attached to Russian Acad. of Sciences; library of 40,000 vols; Dir G. I. GRITSKO; publ. *Coalbed Methane* (4 a year).

Institute of Earthquake Prediction Theory and Mathematical Geophysics: 117997 Moscow, Profsoyuznaya str. 84/32; tel. (495) 333-45-13; fax (495) 333-41-24; e-mail mitpan@mitp.ru; internet www.mitp .ru; f. 1990; attached to Russian Acad. of Sciences; predicts earthquakes and geological disasters in complex systems; risk analysis and optimization of disasters preparedness; identification of earthquake-prone areas; theory of seismic waves; inverse problems of geophysics computational geodynamics; inverse retrospective problems of thermal evolution of the Earth's interior; magnetohydrodynamics problems; modelling of dynamics of lithosphere blocks and seismicity; socio-economic predictions; library of 10,400 vols; Dir Dr A. A. SOLOVIEV; Deputy Dir Dr IGOR KUZNETSOV; Scietific Sec. Dr

ALEXANDER GORSHKOV; publ. *Computational Seismology* (1 a year).

Yu. G. Shafer Institute of Cosmophysical Research and Aeronomy: 677980 Yakutsk, pr. Lenina 31; tel. (4112) 39-04-00; fax (4112) 39-04-50; e-mail ikfia@ysn.ru; internet ikfia.ysn.ru; f. 1962; attached to Russian Acad. of Sciences; scientific research in field cosmic ray physics and solar-terrestrial physics incl. upper atmosphere physics; library of 40,000 vols; Dir Dr EVGENY G. BEREZHKO.

Institute of Electrophysics: 620219 Ekaterinburg, Amundsena ul. 106; tel. (3432) 67-87-96; fax (3432) 67-87-94; attached to Russian Acad. of Sciences; Dir V.G. SHPAK; Scientific Sec. E. E. KOKORINA.

Institute of Energy Problems of Chemical Physics: 117829 Moscow, Leninskii pr. 38, korp. 2; tel. (495) 137-34-79; attached to Russian Acad. of Sciences; Dir V. L. TALROZE.

Institute of Experimental Meteorology: Obninsk; Dir M. A. PETROSYANTS.

Institute of Experimental Mineralogy: 142432 Moscow oblast, Noginskii raion, Chernogolovka, Institutskaya ul. 4; tel. (496) 524-44-25; fax (496) 524-96-87; e-mail shap@iem.ac.ru; internet www.iem.ac.ru; f. 1969; attached to Russian Acad. of Sciences; 206 mems; Dir YURI B. SHAPOVALOV; publ. *Experiments in Geosciences* (1 a year).

Institute of Geochemistry: 664033 Irkutsk, ul. Favorskogo 1a; tel. (3952) 46-05-00; attached to Russian Acad. of Sciences; Dir M. I. KUZMIN.

Institute of Geology: 367025 Makhachkala, ul. Gadzhieva 45; attached to Russian Acad. of Sciences; Dir V. V. SUETNOV.

Institute of Geology: 109017 Moscow, Pyzhevskii per. 7; tel. (495) 230-80-29; fax (495) 231-04-43; f. 1930; attached to Russian Acad. of Sciences; Dir Y. G. LEONOV.

Institute of Geology of Karelian Research Centre: 185910 Petrozavodsk, Pushkinskaya ul. 11; tel. (8142) 78-06-02; fax (8142) 77-06-02; e-mail geology@krc .karelia.ru; internet geoserv.krc.karelia.ru; f. 1946; attached to Russian Acad. of Sciences; Dir V. V. SHCHIPTSOV (acting).

Institute of Geology: 167982 Syktyvkar, Pervomaiskaya ul. 54; tel. (8212) 24-00-37; fax (8212) 24-09-70; f. 1958; attached to Russian Acad. of Sciences; Dir A. M. ASKHABOV; publs *Vestnik* (12 a year), *Proceedings* (4 a year).

Institute of Geology: 450000 Ufa 25, ul. K. Marksa 16/2; tel. (3472) 22-82-56; fax (3472) 23-03-68; attached to Russian Acad. of Sciences; Dir V. N. PUCHKOV.

Diamond and Precious Metal Geology Institute of the Siberian Branch of the Russian Academy of Sciences (DPMGI SB RAS): 677890 Yakutsk, pr. Lenina 39; tel. (4112) 33-58-64; fax (4112) 33-57-08; e-mail geo@yakutia.ru; internet www .diamond.ysn.ru; f. 1957; attached to Russian Acad. of Sciences; tectonics and geodynamics of Siberian platform and Verkhoyansk-Kolyma folded region; kimberlite magmatism, formation and disposition laws for deposits of diamond, gold, silver, MPG and other; investigation of diamonds; paleontology and stratigraphy of Phanerozoic era; Dir Dr ALEXANDER P. SMELOV.

Institute of Precambrian Geology and Geochronology: 199034 St Petersburg, 2 nab. Makarova; tel. (812) 328-47-01; fax (812) 328-48-01; e-mail a.b.vrevsky@ipgg.ru; internet www.ipgg.ru; f. 1967; attached to Russian Acad. of Sciences; Dir Dr A. B. VREVSKY; Sec. for Science S. G. SKUBLOV.

Institute of Geomechanics: c/o Russian Academy of Sciences, 117333 Moscow, ul. Vavilova 44 (korp. 2, komn. 86); attached to Russian Acad. of Sciences.

Institute of Geophysics: 620016 Ekaterinburg, ul. Amundsena 100; tel. (343) 267-88-68; attached to Russian Acad. of Sciences; Dir P. S. MARTYSHKO.

Institute of High-Pressure Physics: 142092 Moscow oblast, Troitsk; tel. (495) 334-00-10; fax (495) 334-00-12; internet www.hppi.troitsk.ru; f. 1958; attached to Russian Acad. of Sciences; Dir Prof. S. M. STISHOV.

Institute of High-Temperature Electrochemistry: 620219 Ekaterinburg, S. Kovalevskaya 22; tel. (343) 374-50-89; fax (343) 374-59-92; e-mail head@ihte.uran.ru; internet www.ihte.uran.ru; f. 1958; attached to Russian Acad. of Sciences; Dir Prof. V. A. KHOKHLOV.

Institute of High-Temperature Physics: 127412 Moscow, Izhorskaya 13/19; tel. (495) 485-83-45; attached to Russian Acad. of Sciences; Dir V. M. BATENIN.

Institute of Hydrodynamics: 630090 Novosibirsk, pr. Akad. Lavrenteva 15; tel. and fax (383) 333-16-12; e-mail igil@hydro.nsc.ru; internet www.hydro.nsc.ru; f. 1957; attached to Russian Acad. of Sciences; library of 87,000 vols; Dir Prof. ANATOLY VASILYEV; publs *Combustion Explosions and Shock Waves* (6 a year), *Continuum Dynamics* (1 or 2 a year), *Journal of Applied Mechanics and Technical Physics* (6 a year).

Institute of Macro-Molecular Compounds: 199004 St Petersburg, Bolshoi pr. 31; tel. (812) 213-10-70; fax (812) 218-68-69; attached to Russian Acad. of Sciences; Dir E. F. PANARIN.

Institute of Marine Geology and Geophysics: 693002 Yuzhno-Sakhalinsk, ul. Nauki 5; tel. (4242) 2-21-28; attached to Russian Acad. of Sciences; Dir K. F. SERGEEV.

Institute of Metal Physics: 620041 Ekaterinburg, GSP-170, ul. Sofia Kovalevskaya 18; tel. (343) 374-02-30; fax (343) 374-52-44; e-mail physics@imp.uran.ru; internet www.imp.uran.ru; f. 1932; attached to Russian Acad. of Sciences; library of 18,000 vols, 92,000 periodicals; Dir Prof. Dr V. V. USTINOV; publs *Fizika metallov i metallovedenie* (Physics of Metals and Metallography, 12 a year), *Defectoscopiya* (Journal of Non-Destructive Testing, 12 a year).

Institute of Metallo-organic Chemistry: 603600 Nizhnii Novgorod, ul. Tropinina 49; tel. (8312) 66-27-09; fax (8312) 66-14-97; f. 1989; attached to Russian Acad. of Sciences; library of 50,000 vols; Dir G. A. ABAKUMOV.

Institute of Metallurgy: Ural Br., 620016 Ekaterinburg, 101, Amundsen St; tel. (343) 2679-124; fax (343) 2679-186; e-mail admin@imet.mplik.ru; internet www.imet-uran.ru; f. 1955; attached to Russian Acad. of Sciences; devt of physicochemical principles of high temperature processes in ferrous and nonferrous metallurgy; library of 35,000 vols; Dir Dr E. N. SELIVANOV; Scientific Sec. V. I. PONOMAREV; publ. *Rasplavy* (6 a year).

Institute of Metrology named after D. I. Mendeleyev (VNIIM): 190005 St Petersburg, Moskovskii pr. 19; tel. (812) 251-76-01; fax (812) 713-01-14; e-mail info@vniim.ru; internet www.vniim.ru; f. 1842; attached to Fed. Agency of Technical Regulation and Metrology (Rosstandart); centre of scientific and practical metrology; measurements in metrology; centre of nat. measurement standards in Russia; library of 40,000 vols; Dir Dr N. I. KHANOV.

Institute of Mineralogy: 456301 Chelyabinsk oblast, Miass; tel. (35135) 5-35-62; attached to Russian Acad. of Sciences; Dir V. N. ANFILOGOV.

Institute of New Chemical Problems: 142432 Moscow oblast, Noginsky raion, Chernogolovka; tel. (495) 524-50-24; attached to Russian Acad. of Sciences; Dir V. N. TROITSKII.

Institute of Nuclear Physics: 630090 Novosibirsk, pr. Akad. Lavrenteva 11; tel. (3832) 35-97-77; fax (3832) 35-21-63 br. in Protvin; attached to Russian Acad. of Sciences; Dir Acad. A. N. SKRINSKY.

Institute of Nuclear Research: 117312 Moscow, pr. 60-letiya Oktyabrya 7A; tel. (499) 135-77-60; attached to Russian Acad. of Sciences; Dir Dr V. A. MATVEEV.

Institute of Organic Chemistry: 630090 Novosibirsk, Akademgorodok, pr. Akad. Lavrenteva 9; tel. (3832) 35-16-52; attached to Russian Acad. of Sciences; Dir Acad. G. A. TOLSTIKOV.

Institute of Organic Chemistry: 450054 Ufa, pr. Oktyabrya 71; tel. and fax (347) 235-60-66; e-mail valeev@anrb.ru; internet w3.chem.anrb.ru; attached to Russian Acad. of Sciences; Dir Acad. M. S. YUNUSOV.

Institute of Organic Synthesis: 620219 Ekaterinburg, S. Kovalevskoi 20; tel. and fax (3432) 74-11-89; e-mail chupakhin@ios.uran.ru; f. 1993; attached to Russian Acad. of Sciences; Dir Prof. OLEG N. CHUPAKHIN.

Institute of Petroleum Chemistry: 634021 Tomsk, Akademicheskii pr. 4; tel. (3822) 49-16-23; fax (3822) 49-14-57; e-mail canc@ipc.tsc.ru; internet www.ipc.tsc.ru; f. 1970; attached to Siberian Br., Russian Acad. of Sciences; chemistry of Russian oils, physicochemical fundamentals of enhanced oil recovery, transformations of oils and their natural components; Dir Prof. Dr LYUBOV K. ALTUNINA; publs *Journal Russian Chemical Reviews, Kinetics and Catalysis*.

Institute of Physical Chemistry: 117915 Moscow, Leninskii pr. 31; tel. (495) 955-46-36; attached to Russian Acad. of Sciences; Dir YU. M. POLUKAROV.

Institute of Physics: 367003 Makhachkala 3, ul. 26 Bakinskikh Komissarov 94; tel. (8722) 2-51-60; attached to Russian Acad. of Sciences; Dir I. K. KAMILOV.

Institute of Problems of Chemical Physics: Chernogolovka; tel. (495) 993-57-07; fax (496) 524-96-76; e-mail sma@icp.ac.ru; internet www.icp.ac.ru; attached to Russian Acad. of Sciences; fundamental research in chemistry, chemical physics, biology, applied research; Dir SERGEY ALDOSHIN.

Institute of Semiconductor Physics: 630090 Novosibirsk, pr. Akad. Lavrenteva 13; tel. (383) 333-39-50; fax (383) 333-27-71; f. 1962; attached to Russian Acad. of Sciences; Dir Prof. A. L. ASEEV.

Institute of Solid State Chemistry: 620219 Ekaterinburg, ul. Pervomaiskaya 91; tel. (3432) 74-52-19; fax (3432) 74-44-95; e-mail server@ihim.uran.ru; internet www.uran.ru/structure/institutions/chimtt/issc.htm; f. 1932; attached to Russian Acad. of Sciences; Dir V. G. BAMBUROV.

Institute of Solid State Physics: 142432 Moscow oblast, Chernogolovka; tel. (495) 962-80-54; fax (496) 524-97-01; e-mail adm@issp.ac.ru; internet www.issp.ac.ru; f. 1963; attached to Russian Acad. of Sciences; Dir Prof. V. V. KVEDER.

Institute of Solution Chemistry: 153045 Ivanovo, Akademicheskaya ul. 1; tel. (0932) 37-85-21; fax (0932) 37-85-09; e-mail adm@isc-ras.ru; internet www.isc-ras.ru; f. 1981; attached to Russian Acad. of Sciences; library of 70,000 vols; Dir Prof. ANATOLY ZAKHAROV; publs *Chemical Thermodynamics and Thermochemistry* (2 a year), *Problems of Solution Chemistry* (4 a year), *Proceedings* (1 a year), *Textile Chemistry* (2 a year).

Institute of Space Physics Research and the Diffusion of Radio Waves: 684034 Kamchatka obl., Elizovsky raion, Paratunka, Mirnaya ul. 7; tel. (41531) 9-31-93; attached to Russian Acad. of Sciences; Dir I. N. AMIANTOV.

Institute of Space Research: 117997 Moscow, Profsoyuznaya 84/32; tel. (495) 333-20-88; fax (495) 310-12-48; internet www.iki.rssi.ru; f. 1965; attached to Russian Acad. of Sciences; Dir Prof. Dr L. M. ZELENYI.

Institute of Spectroscopy: 142092 Moscow oblast, Troitsk; tel. (495) 334-05-79; fax (495) 334-08-86; attached to Russian Acad. of Sciences; Dir E. A. VINOGRADOV.

Institute of Strength Physics and Materials Science: 634021 Tomsk, Akademicheskii pr. 2/1; tel. (3822) 25-94-81; fax (3822) 25-95-76; internet www.ispms.tsc.ru; f. 1984; attached to Russian Acad. of Sciences; Dir Acad. V. E. PANIN; publ. *Physical Mesomechanics* (6 a year).

Institute of Structural Macrokinetics and Materials Science: 142342 Moscow oblast, Chernogolovka, Institutskiy 8; tel. (495) 962-80-01; fax (495) 962-80-70; e-mail director@ism.ac.ru; internet www.ism.ac.ru; f. 1988; attached to Russian Acad. of Sciences; studies on macroscopic kinetics of chemical reactions; Dir Prof. YURI GORDOPOLOV.

Institute of Tectonics and Geophysics: 680022 Khabarovsk, ul. Kim Yu Chena 65; tel. (4212) 22-71-89; fax (4212) 22-76-84; attached to Russian Acad. of Sciences; Dir N. P. ROMANOVSKY; publ. *Tikhookeanskaya Geologiya* (in Russian and English, 6 a year).

Institute of Terrestrial Magnetism, the Ionosphere and Radio Wave Propagation: 142092 Moscow oblast, Troitsk; tel. (495) 334-01-20; fax (495) 334-01-24; f. 1940; attached to Russian Acad. of Sciences; library of 100,000 vols; br. in St Petersburg; Dir Prof. VICTOR N. ORAEVSKY.

Institute of the Chemistry and Technology of Rare Elements and Mineral Raw Materials: 184200 Apatity, ul. Fersmana 26a; tel. (81555) 7-95-49; fax (81555) 7-94-14; e-mail office@chemy.kolasc.net.ru; internet www.kolasc.net.ru/chemy; f. 1957; attached to Russian Acad. of Sciences; Dir V. T. KALINNIKOV.

Institute of the Earth's Crust: 664033 Irkutsk, ul. Lermontova 128; tel. (3952) 42-70-00; fax (3952) 42-69-00; e-mail drf@crust.irk.ru; internet www.crust.irk.ru; f. 1949; attached to Russian Acad. of Sciences; 3 sections: geology, geophysics and recent geodynamics, hydrogeology and engineering geology; research areas incl. recent endo and exogeodynamics, geological medium and seismic process, resources and dynamics of underground waters and geoecology, internal structure, paleogeodynamics, endogenous processes and fluid dynamics of the continental lithosphere; library of 400,000 vols; Dir Dr DMITRY P. GLADKOCHUB; publs *American Journal of Sciences, Geodynamics & Tectonophysics, Tectonics*.

Institute of the Geology of Ore Deposits, Petrography, Mineralogy and Geochemistry: 119017 Moscow, Staromonetnyi per. 35; tel. (495) 951-45-79; fax (495) 230-21-79; e-mail director@igem.ru; internet www.igem.ru; f. 1955; attached to Russian Acad. of Sciences; Dir NIKOLAY BORTNIKOV.

Institute of the Mineralogy, Geochemistry and Crystal Chemistry of Rare Elements: 121357 Moscow, ul. Veresaeva 15; tel. (495) 443-84-28; fax (495) 443-90-43; f. 1956;

attached to Russian Acad. of Sciences and Min. of Natural Resources; Dir A. A. KREME-NETSKY; publ. *Applied Geochemistry* (1 a year).

Institute of Theoretical and Experimental Physics: 117218 Moscow, Bol. Cheremushkinskaya ul. 25; tel. (495) 123-02-88; fax (495) 123-30-28; e-mail director@itep.ru; internet www.itep.ru; f. 1945; Dir M. V. DANILOV.

Institute of Thermal Physics: 620016 Ekaterinburg, Amundsena 106; tel. (3432) 67-88-01; fax (3432) 67-88-00; e-mail itp@itp .uran.ru; f. 1988; attached to Russian Acad. of Sciences; Dir V. G. BAIDAKOV.

Institute of Thermophysics: 630090 Novosibirsk, pr. Akad. Lavrenteva 1; tel. (3833) 30-70-50; fax (3833) 30-84-80; e-mail web@itp .nsc.ru; internet www.itp.nsc.ru; f. 1957; attached to Russian Acad. of Sciences; undertakes research in the fields of heat and mass transfer, physical hydrodynamics and gas dynamics, thermal physics of ionized gases and physics of low-temperature plasma; library of 100,000 vols; Dir Dr S. V. ALEKSEENKO; publs *Thermophysics and Aeromechanics* (4 a year), *Journal of Engineering Thermophysics* (4 a year).

Institute of Volcanology and Seismology: 683006 Petropavlovsk-Kamchatsky, bul. Piipa 9; tel. (4152) 25-95-13; fax (4152) 25-47-23; e-mail volcan@kcs.iks.ru; internet www.kcs.iks.ru; 130 mems; attached to Russian Acad. of Sciences; Dir EVGENY I. GORDEEV.

Institute of Water Problems: 107078 Moscow, Novaya Basmannaya ul. 10, POB 231; tel. (495) 265-97-57; fax (495) 265-18-87; e-mail iwapr@iwapr.msk.su; f. 1968; attached to Russian Acad. of Sciences; library of 35,000 vols; Dir M. G. KHUBLARYAN; publ. *Water Resources* (6 a year).

Institute of Water Problems of the North: Petrozavodsk, pr. Uritskogo 50; tel. (8142) 5-34-71; attached to Russian Acad. of Sciences; Head N. N. FILATOV (acting).

Irkutsk Institute of Chemistry 'A. E. Favorsky': 664033 Irkutsk, 1 Favorsky Stu; tel. (3952) 51-14-31; fax (3952) 41-93-46; e-mail irk_inst_chem@irioch.irk.ru; internet www.inchemistry.irk.ru; f. 1957; attached to Russian Acad. of Sciences; research and devt in organic chemistry; elemento-organic chemistry; chemistry of polymers; wood chemistry; library of 10,000 vols, 55,000 periodicals; Dir Prof. BORIS A. TROFIMOV.

Joint Institute for Nuclear Research: 141980 Moscow oblast, Dubna; tel. (9621) 65-059; fax (9621) 65-146; e-mail post@jinr .ru; internet www.jinr.ru; f. 1956; conducts studies on the structure of matter, high- and low-energy physics, condensed matter, heavy ion and neutron physics; education programme; library of 434,000 vols; Dir V. A. MATVEEV; publs *Journal of Elementary Particles and the Atomic Nucleus* (6 a year), *Particles and Nuclei—Letters* (7 a year).

Kapitza, P. L., Institute of Physical Problems: 117973 Moscow, GSP-1, ul. A. N. Kosygina 2; tel. (495) 137-32-48; fax (495) 938-20-30; e-mail andreev@kapitza.ras.ru; attached to Russian Acad. of Sciences; Dir Acad. A. F. ANDREEV.

Karpinsky, A. P., All-Russia Geological Research Institute: 199106 St Petersburg, Vasilevsky ostrov, Sredny pr. 74; tel. (812) 321-57-06; fax (812) 321-30-23; e-mail vsegei@vsegei.ru; internet www.vsegei.ru; f. 1882; Dir O. V. PETROV; publ. *Regional Geology and Metallogeny* (2 a year).

Karpov Institute of Physical Chemistry: ul. Vorontsovo Pole 10, 105064 Moscow; tel.

(495) 917-32-57; fax (495) 975-24-50; e-mail center@cc.nifhi.ac.ru; internet www.nifhi.ac .ru; f. 1918; 900 mems; library of 38,000 vols; Exec. Dir Prof. ALEXANDER PAVLOVICH SIMONOV.

Khlopin, V. G., Radium Institute: 194021 St Petersburg, 2-i Murinskiy pr. 28; tel. (812) 247-56-41; fax (812) 247-57-81; e-mail moshkov@atom.nw.ru; f. 1922; radiochemistry, nuclear physics; library of 170,000 vols; Dir Dr ALEXANDER A. RIMSKY-KORSAKOV; publ. *Radiochemistry* (in Russian, 6 a year).

Kirensky Institute of Physics: 660036 Krasnoyarsk; tel. (3912) 43-26-35; fax (3912) 43-89-23; e-mail dir@iph.krasn.ru; internet www.kirensky.ru; f. 1956; attached to Russian Acad. of Sciences; 300 mems; main fields of activity: physics, magnetic phenomena and magnetic materials; condensed matter physics and materials for electronics; design and engineering of new active elements; components and devices for radio-electronics, acousto-electronics, opto-electronics and quantum electronics; training of higher level material science specialists; Dir Acad. Prof. VASILY F. SHABANOV; Scientific Sec. Dr KIRILL A. SHAIKHUTDINOV.

Konstantinov, B. P., St Petersburg Institute of Nuclear Physics: 188350 Leningrad oblast, Gatchina, Orlova Roscha; tel. (812) 297-91-25; fax (812) 713-71-96; attached to Russian Acad. of Sciences; Dir ANSELM.

Krylov, A. P., All-Russia Oil and Gas Research Institute: 125422 Moscow, Dmitrovsky pr. 10; tel. (495) 976-83-01.

Kurchatov, I. V., Institute of Atomic Energy: 123182 Moscow, ul. Kurchatova 46; tel. (495) 196-61-07; fax (495) 943-00-74; Dir Acad. EVGENII P. VELIKHOV.

Kurnakov, N. S., Institute of General and Inorganic Chemistry: 117907 Moscow, Leninskii pr. 31; tel. (495) 952-07-87; fax (495) 954-12-79; f. 1918; attached to Russian Acad. of Sciences; Dir Acad. NIKOLAI T. KUZNETSOV.

Landau, L. D., Institute of Theoretical Physics: 117940 Moscow V-234, ul. A. N. Kosygina 2; tel. (495) 137-32-44; fax (495) 938-20-77; attached to Russian Acad. of Sciences; Dir Acad. I. M. KHALATNIKOV.

Lebedev, P. N., Physics Institute: 117924 Moscow, Leninskii pr. 53; tel. (495) 135-14-29; fax (495) 135-85-33; attached to Russian Acad. of Sciences; br. in Kuibyshev; Dir Acad. L. V. KELDYSH.

Lithosphere Institute: 109180 Moscow, Staromonetnyi per. 22; tel. (495) 233-55-88; attached to Russian Acad. of Sciences; Dir N. A. BOGDANOV.

Main Astronomical Observatory: 196140 St Petersburg, Pulkovo; tel. (812) 297-98-41; attached to Russian Acad. of Sciences; br. in Nikolaev oblast; Dir V. K. ABALAKIN.

Melnikov Permafrost Institute: 677010 Yakutsk, ul. Merzlotnaya 36; tel. and fax (4112) 33-44-76; e-mail mpi@ysn.ru; internet mpi.ysn.ru; f. 1961; attached to Russian Acad. of Sciences, Siberian Br.; permafrost research; library of 42,000 vols; Dir MIKHAIL ZHELEZNYAK.

Moscow Radiotechnical Institute: 117519 Moscow, Varshavskoe shosse 132; tel. (495) 315-31-11; fax (495) 314-10-53; e-mail mrti@mrtiran.ru; internet www .mrtiran.ru; f. 1946; attached to Russian Acad. of Sciences; devt of particle accelerators for industrial and medical applications; high-power SHF and x-ray technologies and installations; plasma technologies and installations; computer control and data-processing systems for applications such as

accelerators, medicine, ecology and safety; Dir Dr BORIS ALEKSANDROVICH.

Nesmeyanov, A. N., Institute of Elementary Organic Compounds: 119991 Moscow V-334, GSP 1, Vavilova str. 28, INEOS; tel. (495) 135-61-66; fax (495) 135-50-85; e-mail larina@ineos.ac.ru; f. 1954; attached to Russian Acad. of Sciences; Dir Prof. YU. N. BUBNOV.

Nikolaev Institute of Inorganic Chemistry: 630090 Novosibirsk, pr. Akad. Lavrenteva 3; tel. (383) 330-94-90; fax (383) 330-94-89; e-mail niic@niic.nsc.ru; internet www .niic.nsc.ru; f. 1957; attached to Russian Acad. of Sciences; Dir Prof. Dr VLADIMIR P. FEDIN; Scientific Sec. OLGA GERASKO; publ. *Journal of Structural Chemistry* (6 a year).

Noginsk Research Centre: c/o Institute of Solid State Physics, 142342 Moscow oblast, Chernogolovka; attached to Russian Acad. of Sciences; Chair. Acad. YU. A. OSIPYAN.

Oil and Gas Research Institute: 119333 Moscow, Gubkin St, 3; tel. (499) 135-73-71; fax (499) 135-54-65; e-mail a.dmitrievsky@ ipng.ru; internet www.ipng.ru; f. 1987; attached to Russian Acad. of Sciences; Dir Prof. Dr A. N. DMITRIEVSKIY.

Polar Geospace Physics Observatory 'Tiksi': 678400 Bulunsky raion, Tiksi, Leninskaya ul. 25; tel. (41167) 2-17-89; fax (41167) 5-39-94; e-mail common@pgo.ysn.ru; attached to Russian Acad. of Sciences; Dir V. N. MEDVEDEV.

Polar Institute of Geophysics: 183023 Murmansk, ul. Khalturina 15; tel. (8152) 6-58-29; attached to Russian Acad. of Sciences; br. in Apatity; Dir V. G. PIVOVAROV.

Radiophysical Research Institute: 603950 Nizhny Novgorod, Bol'shaya Pecherskaya ul. 25/12a; tel. (831) 436-72-94; fax (831) 436-99-02; e-mail rf@nirfi.sci-nnov.ru; internet www.nirfi.ru; f. 1956; library of 250,000 vols; Dir Dr SERGEY SNEGIREV; Acad. Sec. Dr VLADIMIR FRIDMAN; publ. *Izvestiya vysshikh uchebnykh zavedenii-Radiofizika* (12 a year).

Research Centre for the Study of Properties of Surfaces and Vacuums: c/o Russian Academy of Sciences, 117901 Moscow, Leninsky pr. 14; attached to Russian Acad. of Sciences; Dir L. E. LAPIDUS.

Research Institute of Experimental Physics: 607190 Nizhegorodskaya oblast, Sarov, pr. Mira 37; tel. (83130) 4-44-68; fax (83130) 5-38-08; e-mail osv@dc.vniief.ru; f. 1946; Dir Dr RADY I. ILKAEV; publs *Questions of Atomic Science and Technics* (4 a year), *Atom* (4 a year).

Research Institute of Geophysical Research on Exploration Wells: Bashkortostan, 452620 Oktyabrsky, ul. Gorkogo 1; tel. (34767) 5-30-24; fax (34767) 5-50-16; e-mail vniigis@poikc.bashnet.ru; internet www.vniigis.bashnet.ru; f. 1956; geophysical well logging; library of 177,000 vols; Dir A. P. POLIAKOV.

Research Institute of Geophysical Shock Waves: Moscow oblast, Ramenskoe, Pryamolineinaya ul. 26.

Research Institute of Gold and Rare Metals: Magadan, ul. Gagarina 2.

Research Institute of the Geochemistry of the Biosphere: 353918 Novorossiisk, Leninsky pr. 54; tel. and fax (8617) 23-03-03; e-mail niigb@mail.kubtelecom.ru; f. 1992; attached to Rostov on Don State University; Dir V. A. ALEKSEENKO; publs *Ecology: Experience, Problems* (irregular), *Geochemistry of the Biosphere* (1 a year).

Russian Research Institute for Integrated Water Management and Protection: 620062 Ekaterinburg, ul. Mira 23; tel.

and fax (343) 374-26-79; e-mail wrm@wrm .ru; internet www.wrm.ru; f. 1969; 98 mems; library of 30,000 vols; Dir Prof. Dr N. B. PROKHOROVA; Deputy Dir Y. A. PODZINA; publs *Water of Russia* (12 a year), *Water Sector of Russia* (6 a year).

Semenov, N. N., Institute of Chemical Physics: 117977 Moscow, ul. A. N. Kosygina 4; tel. (495) 939-72-00; fax (495) 651-21-91; e-mail icp@chph.ras.ru; internet www.chph .ras.ru; f. 1931; attached to Russian Acad. of Sciences; Dir A. A. BERLIN; publ. *Khimicheskaya fizika* (12 a year).

Shmidt Institute of Earth Physics: 123995 Moscow, Bol. Gruzinskaya ul. 10; tel. (495) 252-07-26; fax (495) 255-60-40; e-mail ifz@ifz.ru; internet www.ifz.ru; f. 1928; attached to Russian Acad. of Sciences; fundamental and applied research in internal structure and physical processes in the Earth's interior; global and regional geodynamics, stresses in the Earth's crust and mantle; seismisity, seismic risk assessment and earthquake prediction; magnetic, electromagnetic, gravity and other measurements and analysis of the Earth's physical fields; mathematical geophysics and geoinformatics; Dir ALEXANDER GLIKO.

Shubnikov, A. V., Institute of Crystallography: 117333 Moscow, Leninskii pr. 59; tel. (495) 135-63-11; fax (495) 135-10-11; attached to Russian Acad. of Sciences; br. in Kaluga; Dir V. I. SIMONOV (acting).

Siberian Research Institute of Geology, Geophysics and Mineral Raw Materials: 630104 Novosibirsk, Krasny pr. 67; tel. (3832) 22-45-03.

Special Astrophysical Observatory: 369167 Karachai-Cherkessian Republic, pos. Nizhnii Arkhyz; tel. and fax (901) 498-29-31; e-mail adm@sao.ru; internet www.sao.ru; f. 1966; attached to Russian Acad. of Sciences; library of 205,247 vols; Dir YU. YU. BALEGA.

State Hydrological Institute: 199053 St Petersburg, V.O., 2-ya liniya 23; tel. (812) 213-89-16; Dir I. A. SHIKLOMANOV.

State Research Institute of Non-ferrous Metals: 129515 Moscow, ul. Akad. Koroleva 13; tel. (495) 215-61-73; fax (495) 215-34-53; e-mail gin@gintsvet.msk.ru; f. 1918; library of 500,000 vols; Dir ANDREI TARASOV; publ. *Gintsvetmet Proceedings* (1 a year).

The Institute of Solar-Terrestrial Physics: 664033 Irkutsk, ul. Lermontova 126A; tel. (3952) 42-82-65; fax (3952) 42-55-57; e-mail uzel@iszf.irk.ru; internet www.iszf .irk.ru; f. 1960; attached to Siberian Br., Russian Acad. of Sciences; current problems in astronomy, astrophysics, and research into outer space, incl. solar physics, physics of interplanetary medium, near-Earth environment, ionosphere, and atmosphere; research into solar-terrestrial rels, devt of methods and facilities for investigations in the field of astrophysics and geophysics; library of 115,000 books, brochures, periodicals, MSS; Dir Acad. ALEXANDER P. POTEKHINS.

Titanium Research Institute: 117393 Moscow, ul. Obrucheva 52; tel. (495) 332-95-55.

Troitsk Research Centre: 142092 Moscow oblast, Troitsk, Yubileinaya 3; tel. (495) 334-06-35; fax (495) 334-06-32; e-mail laptev@inr .troitsk.ru; attached to Russian Acad. of Sciences; Chair. Acad. VICTOR A. MATVEEV.

United Institute of Geology, Geophysics and Mineralogy: 630090 Novosibirsk, pr. Akad. Koptyuga 3; tel. (3832) 33-26-00; fax (3832) 33-27-92; attached to Russian Acad. of Sciences; Dir-Gen. Acad. N. L. DOBRETSOV.

Vernadsky, V. I., Institute of Geochemistry and Analytical Chemistry: 119991 Moscow, ul. A. N. Kosygina 19; tel. (495) 137-14-84; fax (495) 938-20-54; e-mail geokhi .ras@relcom.ru; internet www.geokhi.ru; f. 1947; attached to Russian Acad. of Sciences; library of 33,000 vols, 230 periodicals; Dir Prof. ERIC M. GALIMOV; publs *Geochemical International* (12 a year), *Journal of Analytical Chemistry* (12 a year).

Voeikov, A. I., Main Geophysical Observatory: 194018 St Petersburg, ul. Karbysheva 7; tel. (812) 297-01-03; fax (812) 297-86-61; f. 1849; climatology, atmospheric physics, air pollution; library of 380,000 vols; Dir Dr V. M. KATTSOV; publ. *Trudy GGO*.

A. N. Zavaritzky Institute of Geology and Geochemistry: 620075 Ekaterinburg, Pochtovy per. 7; tel. (343) 371-19-97; fax (343) 371-52-52; e-mail director@igg.uran.ru; internet www.igg.uran.ru; f. 1939; attached to Russian Acad. of Sciences; scientific research and applications in geology, geochemistry and geo-ecology; library of 90,000 vols; Dir SERGEY L. VOTYUAKOV; Deputy Dir ELENA V. ANIKINA; publ. *Lithosphere* (6 a year).

Zelinsky, N. D., Institute of Organic Chemistry: 119991 Moscow, Leninsky pr. 47; tel. (499) 137-29-44; fax (499) 135-53-28; e-mail secretary@ioc.ac.ru; internet www.ioc .ac.ru; f. 1934; attached to Russian Acad. of Sciences; fundamental research in organic chemistry; library of 213,300 vols; Dir Prof. MIKHAIL P. EGOROV; publs *Mendeleev Communication* (6 a year), *Russian Chemical Bulletin* (12 a year), *Russian Chemical Reviews* (12 a year).

PHILOSOPHY AND PSYCHOLOGY

Institute of Philosophy: 119991 Moscow, Volkhonka ul. 14; tel. (495) 697-92-17; fax (495) 609-93-50; e-mail iph@iph.ras.ru; internet www.iph.ras.ru; f. 1929; attached to Russian Acad. of Sciences; 300 mems; library of 89,500 vols; Dir A. A. GUSEINOV; Acad. Sec. B. O. NIKOLAICHEV; publs *Epistemology and Philosophy of Science* (4 a year), *Personality, Culture, Society* (4 a year), *Philosophical journal* (2 a year).

Institute of Psychology: 129366 Moscow, Yaroslavskaya ul. 13; tel. (495) 282-51-49; attached to Russian Acad. of Sciences; Dir A. V. BRUSHLINSKY.

RELIGION, SOCIOLOGY AND ANTHROPOLOGY

Institute of Sociology: 117259 Moscow, ul. Krzhizhanovskogo 24/35, korp. 5; tel. (495) 128-91-09 br. in St Petersburg: 198147 St Petersburg, ul. Serpukhovskaya 38; tel. (812) 292-27-65; fax (812) 292-29-29; attached to Russian Acad. of Sciences; Dir V. A. YADOV.

Miklukho-Maklai, N. N., Institute of Ethnology and Anthropology: 117334 Moscow, Leninsky pr. 32A; tel. (495) 938-17-47; fax (495) 938-06-00; e-mail anthpub@iea .ras.ru; internet www.iea.ras.ru; f. 1933; attached to Russian Acad. of Sciences; library of 60,000 vols; Dir V. A. TISHKOV; publs *Etnograficheskoe obozrenie* (Ethnographic Review, 6 a year), *Bulletin of Ethnological Monitoring* (6 a year).

Research and Training Centre for Problems of Human Activity: 117279 Moscow, ul. Profsoyuznaya 83B; tel. (495) 333-01-02; attached to Russian Acad. of Sciences; Gen. Dir V. A. SHESTAKOV.

TECHNOLOGY

Accounting Machine Building Research Institute: 115230 Moscow, Varshavskoe shosse 42; tel. (499) 611-51-61.

All-Russia Electrotechnical Institute (VEI): 111250 Moscow, Krasnokazarmennaya ul. 12; tel. (495) 362-55-08; fax (495) 362-56-17; e-mail vkozlov@online.ru.

All-Russia Logachev Scientific Research Institute of Exploration Geophysics (VIRG-Rudgeofizika): 193019 St Petersburg, Fayansovaya ul. 20; tel. (812) 567-68-03; fax (812) 567-87-41; internet www.virg .spb.ru; f. 1945; devt of instruments and technology for predicting, exploring, evaluating and mining ores and diamonds, drilling for oil and gas; solving environmental problems; provision of services in these areas; library of 54,000 vols; Dir G. N. MIKHAILOV; publs *Geophysical Instruments* (2 a year), *Russian Journal of Geophysics* (2 a year).

All-Russia Oil Geological Prospecting Institute: 191104 St Petersburg, Liteinyi pr. 39; tel. (812) 273-43-83; fax (812) 273-73-87.

All-Russia Railway Transport Research Institute: 107996 Moscow, 3-ya Mytishchinskaya str. 10; tel. (495) 687-64-23; fax (495) 687-65-48; e-mail mnts@vniizht.ru; internet www.vniizht.ru; f. 1917; Dir-Gen. Dr BORIS LAPIDUS; Deputy Dir-Gen. ALEXANDER KASSAY; publ. *Vestnik VNIIZhT* (12 a year).

All-Russia Research and Design Institute for Atomic Power Station Equipment: 125171 Moscow, ul. Volkova Kosmonavta 6A; tel. (495) 150-83-55.

All-Russia Research and Design Institute for Problems of the Development of Oil and Gas Resources on the Continental Shelf: 107078 Moscow, Kalanchevskaya ul. 11; tel. (495) 971-51-03; fax (495) 280-23-57; Dir I. B. DUBIN.

All-Russia Research and Design Institute of Electroceramics: 111024 Moscow, shosse Entuziastov 17; tel. (495) 273-13-34.

All-Russia Research and Design Institute of Metallurgical Engineering: 109428 Moscow, Ryazansky pr. 8A; tel. (495) 174-37-00; attached to Russian Acad. of Sciences; Gen. Dir V. M. SINITSKY.

All-Russia Research and Design Institute of the Oil-Refining and Petrochemical Industry: 107005 Moscow, ul. Fridrikha Engelsa 32; tel. (499) 261-96-26; fax (499) 261-66-44; e-mail vnipineft@ vnipineft.ru; internet www.vnipineft.ru; f. 1929; Dir V. M. NIKITIN.

All-Russia Research, Design and Technological Institute of Lighting Technology: 129626 Moscow, pr. Mira 106; tel. (495) 287-13-52; fax (495) 287-08-91; f. 1953.

All-Russia Research Institute for Nuclear Power Plant Operation: 109507 Moscow, Ferganskaya 25; tel. (495) 376-15-43; fax (495) 376-83-33; f. 1979; Dir-Gen. Prof. A. A. ABAGYAN.

All-Russia Research Institute for Oil Refining JSC: 111116 Moscow, Aviamotornaya ul. 6; tel. (499) 261-52-02; fax (499) 261-02-95; f. 1933; Dir E. F. KAMINSKY; publ. *Mir Nefteproduktov* (The World of Oil Products, 4 a year).

All-Russia Research Institute for the Canned and Vegetable Dry Products Industry: 142703 Moscow oblast, Vidnoe, Shkolnaya 78; tel. (495) 541-08-72; attached to Russian Acad. of Agricultural Sciences.

All-Russia Research Institute for the Dairy Industry: 113093 Moscow, Lyusinovskaya 35; tel. (495) 236-31-64; attached to Russian Acad. of Agricultural Sciences.

All-Russia Research Institute for the Protection of Metals from Corrosion: 125209 Moscow, Baltiiskaya ul. 14; tel. (495) 151-55-01.

All-Russia Research Institute for the Refrigeration Industry: 125422 Moscow, ul. Kostyakova 12; tel. (495) 216-00-04; attached to Russian Acad. of Agricultural Sciences; Dir V. F. LEBEDEV.

All-Russia Research Institute of Electrical Insulating Materials and Foiled Dielectrics: 111250 Moscow, Krasnokazarmennaya ul. 12; tel. (495) 273-24-78.

All-Russia Research Institute of Electromechanics (VNIIEM): 101000 Moscow, Glavpochtamt Box 496 VNIIEM, Khoromny Tupik 4; tel. (495) 208-84-67; fax (495) 207-49-62; f. 1941; research and devt in space technology, monitoring and control systems for nuclear reactors, electromechanical systems, devices and materials; library of 200,000 vols; Dir Dr S. A. STOMA; publ. *Trudy VNIIEM* (proceedings, 3 a year).

All-Russia Research Institute of Exploration Geophysics: 101000 Moscow, ul. Pokrovka 22; tel. (495) 925-45-13; fax (495) 956-39-38; f. 1944; library of 50,000 vols; Dir A. V. MIKHALTSEV; publs *Prikladnaya Geofizika* (2 a year), *Razvedochnaya Geofizika*.

All-Russia Research Institute of Fibre-Optic Systems of Communication and Data Processing: 107066 Moscow, Khiznyaya Krasnoselskaya ul. 13, korp. 1; tel. (499) 267-20-31.

All-Russia Research Institute of Food Biotechnology: 109033 Moscow, Samokatnaya ul. 4B; tel. (495) 362-44-95; attached to Russian Acad. of Agricultural Sciences.

All-Russia Research Institute of Fuel and Energy Problems (VNIIKTEP): 117259 Moscow, Bol. Cheremushkinskaya 34; tel. (495) 128-90-14; fax (495) 128-85-91; f. 1975; library of 63,000 vols; Dir N. K. PRAVEDNIKOV; publ. *The Fuel and Energy Complex of Russia* (1 a year).

All-Russia Research Institute of Helium Technology: 119270 Moscow, Luzhnetskaya nab. 10A; tel. (495) 242-50-77; fax (495) 234-91-11.

All-Russia Research Institute of Mineral Resources and the Use of the Subsurface: 123007 Moscow, 3-ya Magistralnaya 38; tel. and fax (495) 259-69-88; fax (495) 259-91-25; e-mail info@viems.ru; internet www.viems.ru; f. 1964; attached to Russian Acad. of Sciences and Russian Min. of Natural Resources; Dir-Gen. M. A. KOMAROV.

All-Russia Research Institute of Organic Synthesis (VNIIOS): 105005 Moscow, ul. Radio 12; tel. (499) 261-96-88; fax (499) 261-07-77; e-mail vniios@aha.ru; internet www.vniios.ru; f. 1949; Dir-Gen. V. K. S. CHERNYKH.

All-Russia Research Institute of Problems of Computer Technology and Information Science: 113114 Moscow, 2-i Kozhevnichesky per. 4/6; tel. (495) 235-58-09; Dir V. ZAKHAROV.

All-Russia Research Institute of Radiotechnology: 107055 Moscow, Bol. Pochtovaya ul. 55–59; tel. (499) 267-66-04.

All-Russia Research Institute of Refractory Metals and Hard Alloys: 115430 Moscow, Varshavskoe shosse 56; tel. (495) 113-55-72.

All-Russia Research Institute of Starch Products: 140052 Moscow oblast, pos. Korenevo, ul. Nekrasova; tel. (495) 557-15-00; attached to Russian Acad. of Agricultural Sciences.

All-Russia Research Institute of Television and Radio Broadcasting JSC: 123298 Moscow, 3-ya Khoroshevskaya ul. 12; tel. (495) 192-90-02; fax (495) 943-00-06; e-mail vniitr@online.ru; internet www.vniitr

.com; f. 1934; Gen. Dir ALEXANDER S. MKRTUMOV; publ. *Teleraidoveshchaniye* (4 a year).

All-Russia Research Institute of the Cable Industry: 111112 Moscow, shosse Entuziastov 5; tel. (495) 278-02-16.

All-Russia Research Institute of Trunk Pipeline Construction: 105058 Moscow, Okruzhnoi pr-d 19; tel. (495) 366-68-39.

All-Russia Scientific Research Institute for Exploration Methods and Engineering: 199106 St Petersburg, Veselnaya ul. 6; tel. (812) 322-78-53; fax (812) 322-79-37; e-mail vitr@spb.cityline.ru; f. 1955; drilling equipment and techniques for minerals and water; library of 30,000 vols, patents; Dir IVAN S. AFANASYEV; publ. *Collection of Scientific Works* (4–6 a year).

All-Russian Scientific Research Institute of Aviation Materials (VIAM): 105005 Moscow, ul. Radio 17; tel. (499) 261-86-77; fax (499) 267-86-09; e-mail admin@viam.ru; internet www.viam.ru; f. 1932; Dir-Gen. EVGENY N. KABLOV; publ. *Aircraft Materials and Technology* (1 a year).

All-Russia Scientific Research Institute of Fats: 191119 St Petersburg, ul. Chernyakovskogo 10; tel. (812) 164-15-24; fax (812) 112-25-74; e-mail wniig@peterlink.ru; f. 1933; attached to Russian Acad. of Agricultural Sciences; Dir ALEXANDER N. LISITSYN; publ. *Trudy* (works, irregular).

All-Russia Scientific Research Institute of Natural and Synthetic Diamonds and Tools: 129110 Moscow, ul. Giliarovskogo 65; tel. (495) 281-59-07; fax (495) 288-99-42; f. 1948; library of 25,000 vols; Dir N. A. KOLCHEMANOV; publ. *Works of VNIIALMAZ* (1 a year).

All-Russian Scientific Research Institute of Technical Physics and Automation: 115230 Moscow, Varshavskoe shosse 46; tel. (499) 611-2522; fax (499) 611-5344; e-mail kancelaria@vniitfa.ru; internet www.vniitfa.ru; f. 1960 as Research Institute of Radiation Technology; Dir NIKOLAY KUZELEV.

Blagonravov, A. A., Institute of Machine Science: 101830 Moscow, ul. Griboedova 4; tel. (495) 924-98-00; attached to Russian Acad. of Sciences; brs in St Petersburg, Samara, Saratov, Nizhnii Novgorod; Dir Acad. K. V. FROLOV.

Budnikov, P. P., All-Russia Research Institute of Construction Materials and Structures: 140080 Moscow, pos. Kraskovo, ul. Karla Marksa 117; tel. (495) 557-30-66; fax (495) 557-30-09; f. 1931; library of 180,000 vols; Dir YU. GUDKOV; publs *Autoclaved Materials* (1 a year), *Ceramic Materials* (1 a year), *Gypsum Binders and Products* (1 a year).

Burenie Scientific and Production Co.: 350624 Krasnodar, ul. Mira 34; tel. (8612) 62-23-34; fax (8612) 62-23-34; f. 1970; drilling and maintenance of wells; library of 100,000 vols; Gen. Dir Dr SERGEI A. RYABOKON.

Central Boiler and Turbine Institute: 194021 St Petersburg, Politekhnicheskaya ul. 24; tel. (812) 277-95-64; fax (812) 277-40-95; e-mail ckti@neva.spb.ru; internet www.ckti.ru; f. 1927; Dir-Gen. E. K. CHAVCHANIDZE.

Central Design and Research Institute of the Standard and Experimental Design of Livestock Units for the Production of Milk, Beef and Pork: 121002 Moscow, Maly Mogiltsevsky per. 3; tel. (495) 241-36-82.

Central Diesels Research and Development Institute: 196158 St Petersburg, Moskovskoe shosse 25, korp. 1; tel. (812) 291-65-81; fax (812) 291-22-73; f. 1924;

library of 62,000 vols; Dir V. BORDUKOV; publ. *Dvigatelestroynie* (4 a year).

Central Electronics Research Institute: 117415 Moscow, pr. Vernadskogo 39; tel. (495) 432-93-30; fax (495) 431-58-86; f. 1964; Dir B. N. AVDONIN.

Central Institute of Aviation Engines: 111116 Moscow, Aviamotornaya ul. 2; tel. (495) 361-64-81; fax (499) 267-13-54; f. 1930; Dir V. SKIBIN.

Central Marine Research and Design Institute Ltd (CNIIMF): 193015 St Petersburg, Kavalergardskaya ul. 6; tel. (812) 271-12-83; fax (812) 274-38-64; f. 1929; shipbuilding, marine equipment, navigation, transport technology; library of 312,000 vols; Dir VSEVOLOD I. PERESYPKIN; publ. *Transactions*.

Central Paper Research Institute: 141290 Moscow oblast, Pushkinsky raion, pos. Pravdinsky, ul. Lenina 15/1; tel. (495) 584-36-23; fax (495) 292-65-11; f. 1918; library of 90,000 vols; Dir B. V. OREKHOV; publs *Board* (12 a year), *Paper*, *Pulp*, *Research Papers of ZNIIB* (1 a year).

Central Research and Design Institute of Fuel Apparatus and Vehicle and Tractor Engines and Stationary Engines: 192102 St Petersburg, Volkovskii pr-d 102; tel. (812) 166-91-11.

Central Research Institute for Machine Building: 141070 Moscow oblast, Korolev, Pionyerskaya ul. 4; tel. (495) 513-50-00; fax (495) 187-03-22; f. 1946; spacecraft and rocket engineering, aero and gas dynamics, heat and mass exchange, strength of materials, reliability, mission control for spacecraft and space stations; library of 100,000 vols; Dir NIKOLAI A. ANFIMOV; publs *Astronautics and Rocket Engineering* (3 or 4 a year), *Rocketry and Space Technology* (52 a year).

Central Research Institute of Coating Materials and Artificial Leathers: 113184 Moscow, ul. Bakhrushina 11; tel. (495) 953-23-55; fax (495) 951-39-27; e-mail cniipik@mail.ru; Dir Dr C. N. KOZLOV.

Central Research Institute of Engineering Technology: 109088 Moscow, Sharikopodshipnikovskaya ul. 4; tel. (495) 275-83-00.

Central Research Institute of Geological Prospecting for Base and Precious Metals: 117545 Moscow, Varshovskoe shosse 129B; tel. and fax (495) 313-18-18; e-mail tsnigri@tsnigri.ru; internet www.tsnigri.ru; f. 1935; forecasting, prospecting, exploration and assessment of deposits of base and precious metals; library of 200,000 vols; Dir Dr IGOR MIGACHEV; publs *Otechestvennaya Geologia* (6 a year, in Russian with English abstracts), *Rudy i Metally* (6 a year, in Russian with English abstracts).

Central Research Institute of Telecommunications: 111141 Moscow, 1-i pr-d Perova Polya 8; tel. (495) 304-57-97; fax (495) 274-00-67.

Central Research Institute of the Ministry of Defence: 141090 Moscow oblast, Bolshevo, V/Ch 25840; tel. (495) 472-92-12; Dir L. I. VOLKOV.

Central Research Laboratory for the Introduction of Personal Computers: c/o Russian Academy of Sciences, 117901 Moscow, Leninsky pr. 14; attached to Russian Acad. of Sciences; Dir A. N. ILIN.

Central Scientific Research and Design Institute of the Wood Chemical Industry: 603603 Nizhnii Novgorod, Moskovskoe shosse 85, GSP 703; tel. (8312) 41-36-98; fax (8312) 41-36-90; f. 1932; library of 146,000 vols; Dir VICTOR YA. BONDAREV; publ. *Scientific Works* (1 a year).

Concrete and Reinforced Concrete Research Design and Technological

Institute: 109428 Moscow, Vtoraya Institutskaya ul. 6; tel. (495) 171-26-69; fax (495) 174-77-24; e-mail niizhb@niizhb.ru; internet www.niizhb.ru; f. 1927; devt of standards and norms for concrete construction and design; certification testing; postgraduate courses; 400 mems; library of 200,000 vols; Dir Dr A. I. ZVEZDOV; Deputy Dir Dr V. FALIKMAN; Scientific Dir Dr T. MOUKHAMEDIEV; publs *Beton i Zhelezobeton* (Concrete and Reinforced Concrete, 6 a year), *Proceedings of NIIZLB* (1 a year).

Design and Research Institute of the Synthetic Rubber Industry: 105318 Moscow, ul. Ibragimova 15; tel. (495) 366-43-44; fax (495) 369-52-55; Dir S. I. KARTASHOV.

Design and Technological Institute of Monocrystals: 630058 Novosibirsk, Russkaya ul. 43; tel. (3832) 33-22-39; fax (3832) 33-22-59; f. 1978; attached to Russian Acad. of Sciences; Head ANATOLY I. CHEPUROV.

Dollezhal, N. A. Research and Development Institute of Power Engineering: 101000 Moscow, POB 788; tel. (499) 263-73-88; fax (499) 788-20-52; e-mail nikiet@nikiet .ru; internet www.nikiet.ru; f. 1952; nuclear power, thermal physics and hydrodynamics; radiation, nuclear and environmental safety of nuclear reactors; strength, reliability and material science; conversion of nuclear technologies; library of 200,000 vols; Dir B. A. GABARAEV.

Dorodnicyn Computing Centre of the Russian Academy of Sciences (CC RAS): 119333 Moscow, ul. Vavilova 40; tel. (499) 135-24-89; e-mail wcan@ccas.ru; internet www.ccas.ru; f. 1955; attached to Russian Acad. of Sciences; scientific divs: mechanics and mathematical physics, informatics and mathematical cybernetics, mathematical systems and decisions modelling, mathematical and programming software, computational technique; Dir Prof. YU. G. EVTUSHENKO; Scientific Sec. SHURSHALOV LEV.

Efremov, D. V., Institute of Electrophysical Apparatus: 196641 St Petersburg, Sovetsky pr. 1; tel. (812) 464-89-63; fax (812) 464-79-79; e-mail glukhikh@niiefa.spb .su; internet www.niiefa.spb.su; f. 1945; Dir V. A. GLUKHIKH; publ. *Plasma Devices and Operations*.

Electronic Control Machines Research Institute: 117812 Moscow, ul. Vavilova 24; tel. (495) 135-32-21; Dir N. L. PROKHOROV.

Energy Systems Institute: 664033 Irkutsk, Lermontova ul. 130; tel. (3952) 42-47-00; fax (3952) 42-44-44; e-mail root@isem .sei.irk.ru; internet www.sei.irk.ru; f. 1960; attached to Russian Acad. of Sciences; Dir N. I. VOROPAI.

Ershov, A. P., Institute of Informatics Systems: 630090 Novosibirsk, pr. Akad. Lavrenteva 6; tel. (3832) 35-56-52; fax (3832) 32-34-94; f. 1990; attached to Russian Acad. of Sciences; library of 100,000 vols; Dir Prof. ALEXANDER G. MARCHUK; publ. *Systems Informatics* (1 a year).

Experimental Factory for Analytical Instrumentation: 198510 St Petersburg, Lomonosov, ul. Fedyuninskogo 3; tel. (812) 473-06-48; attached to Russian Acad. of Sciences; Dir V. I. STEPANOV.

Experimental Factory for Scientific Instrumentation: 142342 Moscow oblast, Noginsk raion, p/o Chernogolovka; tel. (495) 524-50-05; attached to Russian Acad. of Sciences; Dir L. P. KOKURIN.

Experimental Research Institute of Metal-Cutting Machine Tools: 117419 Moscow, 5-i Donskoi pr-d 21B; tel. (495) 952-39-63; Dir V. S. BELOV.

Far Eastern Research Institute of Mineral Raw Materials: 680005 Khabarovsk, ul. Gerasimova 31; tel. (4212) 34-28-43; Dir YU. I. BAKULIN.

Federal State Unitary Enterprise Central Scientific Research Automobile and Engine Institute of the Russian Federation: 125438 Moscow, Avtomotornaya st. 2; tel. (495) 456-30-81; fax (495) 456-31-32; e-mail admin@nami.ru; internet www.nami .ru; national automobile manufacturing and testing; f. 1918; library of 106,000 vols, spec. colln 93,600 vols; Gen. Dir Prof. A. IPATOV; publ. various journals.

Fedorov, E. K., Institute of Applied Geophysics: 129128 Moscow, Rostokinskaya ul. 9; tel. (495) 181-37-14; Dir S. I. AVDYUSHIN.

Gubkin Russian State University of Oil and Gas: 119991 Moscow, Leninsky pr. 65; tel. (499) 233-92-25; fax (499) 135-88-95; e-mail com@gubkin.ru; internet www .gubkin.ru; f. 1930, present status 2010; educational and research and devt programmes through the full process chain of petroleum engineering, 330 journals; library: 1.5m. vols incl. rare monographs, MSS theses and specialized journals; Rector Prof. VICTOR G. MARTYNOV; publs *Chemistry & Technology of Fuels and Oils, Oil, Gas & Business, Proceedings of Gubkin Russian State University of Oil and Gas*.

High-Technology Ceramics Research Centre: 119361 Moscow, Ozernaya ul. 48; tel. (495) 430-77-70; fax (495) 437-98-93; attached to Russian Acad. of Sciences; Dir V. YA. SHEVCHENKO.

Hydrochemical Institute: 344090 Rostov on Don, pr. Stachki 198; tel. and fax (8632) 22-44-70; e-mail ghi@aaanet.ru; f. 1920; library of 40,000 vols; Dir A. M. NIKANOROV; publ. *Gidrokhimicheskiye Materialy* (3 a year).

Image Processing Systems Institute: 443001 Samara, ul. Molodogvardeiskaya 151; tel. (846) 332-56-20; fax (846) 332-27-63; e-mail ipsi@smr.ru; internet www.ipsi .smr.ru; f. 1988; attached to Russian Acad. of Sciences; diffractive optics, nanophotonics, image processing and pattern recognition; library of 1,000 vols; Dir Prof. V. A. SOIFER; publ. *Computer Optics* (in Russian, 4 a year).

Institute for Systems Analysis: 117312 Moscow, pr. 60-letia Oktyabrya 9; tel. (495) 135-42-22; fax (495) 938-22-09; e-mail isa@ isa.ru; internet www.isa.ru; f. 1976; attached to Russian Acad. of Sciences; Dir YU. S. POPKOV.

Institute of Analytical Instrumentation: 190103 St Petersburg, Rizhsky pr. 26; tel. (812) 251-86-00; fax (812) 251-70-38; e-mail iap@ianin.spb.su; internet www.iai.rssi.ru; f. 1977; attached to Russian Acad. of Sciences; fundamental and applied research aimed at development of new methods, instruments and technologies in the areas of elemental phase and structural analysis; nanotechnology and surface diagnostics; biotechnology, ecology and medicine; Dir Prof. V. E. KUROCHKIN; publ. *Scientific Instrumentation* (4 a year).

Institute of Applied Mathematics: 690041 Vladivostok, ul. Radio 7; tel. (4232) 31-33-30; fax (4232) 31-18-56; f. 1988; attached to Russian Acad. of Sciences; library of 21,000 vols; Dir Prof. N. V. KUZNETSOV.

Institute of Applied Mechanics: c/o Russian Academy of Sciences, 119991 Moscow, Leninsky pr.; tel. (495) 938-18-45; fax (495) 938-07-11; attached to Russian Acad. of Sciences; Dir YU G. YANOVSKY; publ. *Journal on Composite Materials and Design* (4 a year).

Institute of Applied Mechanics: 426067 Izhevsk, T. Baramzinoy 34; tel. (3412) 50-88-10; fax (3412) 50-79-59; e-mail foipm@udm .ru; internet www.udman.ru; f. 1989; attached to Russian Acad. of Sciences; physics and mechanics of heterogenous media; problems of mechanics of deformed solid and material tribo-technology; new materials; Dir Acad. ALEXEY LIPANOV; publ. *Chemical Physics and Mezoscopy* (4 a year).

Institute of Automation and Control Processes: 690041 Vladivostok, ul. Radio 5; tel. (4232) 31-04-39; fax (4232) 31-04-52; e-mail director@iacp.vl.ru; internet www .dvo.ru/iacp; f. 1971; attached to Russian Acad. of Sciences; Dir V. P. MYASNIKOV.

Institute of Automation and Electrometry: 630090 Novosibirsk, Universitetskii pr. 1; tel. (3832) 35-10-52; fax (3832) 35-48-51; e-mail malinovsky@iae.nsk.su; attached to Russian Acad. of Sciences; Dir Prof. S. T. VASKOV.

Institute of Biological Instrumentation: 123373 Moscow, Volokalamskoe shosse 91; tel. (495) 491-73-72; Dir V. N. ZLOBIN.

Institute of Chemistry and Chemical Technology: 660049 Krasnoyarsk, ul. K. Marksa 42; tel. (3912) 27-38-31; fax (3912) 23-86-58; e-mail chem@krsk.info; internet krsk.info/icct; f. 1981; attached to Russian Acad. of Sciences; Dir Prof. G. L. PASHKOV; publs *Proceedings of Workshops* (every 3 years), *Siberian Gold* (symposium proceedings, every 2 years).

Institute of Computational Technologies: 630090 Novosibirsk, pr. Akad. Lavrenteva 6; tel. (383) 330-61-50; fax (383) 330-63-42; e-mail shokin@ict.nsc.ru; internet www .ict.nsc.ru; f. 1990; attached to Russian Acad. of Sciences, Siberian br.; designs and implements informational-telecommunication technologies in decision-making problems; applies mathematical modelling and computational algorithm devt to a wide range of problems arising in mechanics of continuous media, physics and ecology; Head YURI SHOKIN; publ. *Journal of Computational Technologies* (6 a year).

Institute of Continuous Media Mechanics: 614013 Perm, ul. Akad. Koroleva 1; tel. (3422) 33-07-21; fax (3422) 33-69-57; e-mail mvp@admin.icmm.perm.su; f. 1971; attached to Russian Acad. of Sciences; Dir V. P. MATVEYENKO.

Institute of Control Sciences, Automation and Telemechanics: 117806 Moscow, ul. Profsoyuznaya 65; tel. (495) 334-89-10; fax (495) 334-93-40; e-mail vasmac@ipu.rssi .ru; attached to Russian Acad. of Sciences; Dir Acad. I. V. PRANGISHVILI.

Institute of Electronic Measurement 'Kvarz': 603009 Nizhnii Novgorod, pr. Gagarina 176; tel. (8312) 66-70-93; fax (8312) 66-55-62; e-mail nnipi_kvarz@sinn .ru; internet www.kvarz.ru; f. 1949; research, development and manufacture of electronic measurement equipment; 1,200 mems; Dir-Gen. A. M. KUDRIAVTSEV; publ. *Electronic Measurements* (in Russian, 1 a year).

Institute of Energy Research: 117333 Moscow, ul. Vavilova 44, korp. 2; tel. (495) 127-48-34; attached to Russian Acad. of Sciences; Dir A. A. MAKAROV.

Institute of Engineering Science: 620219 Ekaterinburg, Komsomolskaya ul. 34, GSP-207; tel. (343) 374-47-25; fax (343) 374-53-30; e-mail ges@imach.uran.ru; internet www .imach.uran.ru; f. 1986; attached to Russian Acad. of Sciences; research into mechanics of solids and structures, advanced materials and technologies; automated systems of measurements, nondestructive testing and diagnostics of machine life; mechanics and control of transportation and traction machines; creation of basic algorithms, software and hardware for systems of automated control of compound objects; library of 16,700 vols; Dir Prof. E. S. GORKUNOV.

Institute of High Current Electronics: 634055 Tomsk, pr. Akademichesky 2–3; tel. (3822) 49-15-44; fax (3822) 49-24-10; e-mail contact@hcei.tsc.ru; internet www.hcei.tsc.ru; f. 1977; attached to Russian Acad. of Sciences; library of 50,000 vols; Dir Acad. SERGEI D. KOROVIN.

Institute of Informatics and Mathematical Modelling of Technological Processes: 184200 Murmansk oblast, Apatity, ul. Fersmana 24A; tel. (81555) 7-40-50; fax (81555) 7-42-26; e-mail putilov@iimm.kolasc.net.ru; f. 1989; attached to Russian Acad. of Sciences; Dir Dr V. A. PUTILOV; publ. *Computer-Aided Simulation.*

Institute of Informatics Problems of the Russian Academy of Sciences (IPIRAN): 119333 Moscow, ul. Vavilova 44-2; tel. (499) 137-34-94; fax (495) 930-45-05; e-mail sshorgin@ipiran.ru; internet www.ipiran.ru; f. 1983; attached to Russian Acad. of Sciences; fundamental and applied research and devt in integrated information-telecommunication networks and systems and stochastic systems; theoretical problems and applied technologies in accumulation, processing and representation of information; creation of computerized information systems; Dir Acad. IGOR SOKOLOV; Deputy Dir SERGEY SHORGIN; publs *Informatics and Applications* (4 a year), *Systems and Means of Informatics* (2 a year).

Institute of Information Science and Automation: 199178 St Petersburg, 14 liniya 39; tel. (812) 218-03-82; attached to Russian Acad. of Sciences; Dir V. M. PONOMAREV.

Institute of Information Transmission Problems (Kharkevich Institute): 127994 Moscow 19/1, Bol. Karetny per.; tel. (495) 650-42-25; fax (495) 650-05-79; e-mail director@iitp.ru; internet www.iitp.ru; f. 1961; attached to Russian Acad. of Sciences; Dir ALEXANDER KULESHOV; publs *Automation and Remote Control* (12 a year), *Information Processes, Problems of Information Transmission* (4 a year).

Institute of Laser and Information Technology: 140700 Moscow oblast, Shatura, Svyatoozerskaya ul. 1; tel. (496) 452-59-95; fax (496) 452-25-32; e-mail center@laser.ru; internet www.laser.ru; f. 1979; attached to Russian Acad. of Sciences; library of 35,000 vols; Dir Prof. V. YA. PANCHENKO.

Institute of Mathematics and Mechanics: 620219 Ekaterinburg, ul. S. Kovalevskoi 16; tel. (3432) 374-83-32; fax (3432) 374-25-81; e-mail bvi@imm.uran.ru; internet www.imm.uran.ru; f. 1956; attached to Ural Branch of the Russian Acad. of Sciences; Dir Prof. V. I. BERDYSHEV.

Institute of Medical Instrument Making: 125422 Moscow, Timiryazevskaya ul. 1; tel. (495) 211-09-65; fax (495) 200-22-13; attached to Russian Acad. of Medical Sciences; Dir V. A. VIKTOROV.

Institute of Mining, Khabarovsk: 680000 Khabarovsk, ul. Turgeneva 51; tel. (4212) 33-79-27; attached to Russian Acad. of Sciences; Dir G. V. SEKISOV.

Institute of Mining, Novosibirsk: 630091 Novosibirsk, Krasny pr. 54; tel. (3832) 17-05-36; fax (3832) 17-06-78; e-mail admin@misd.nsc.ru; internet www.misd.nsc.ru; f. 1944; attached to Russian Acad. of Sciences; library of 40,000 vols; Dir OPARIN VICTOR NIKOLAEVICH; Academic Sec. TARASIK T. MIKHAILOVNA; publ. *Journal of Mining Science* (6 a year).

Institute of Mining of the North: 677018 Yakutsk, ul. Lenina 43; tel. and fax (4112) 44-59-30; f. 1980; attached to Russian Acad. of Sciences; Dir Dr M. D. NOVOPASHIN.

Institute of Mining, Perm: 614007 Perm, Sibirskaya ul. 78A; tel. (3422) 16-75-02; fax (3422) 16-09-69; e-mail arc@mi-perm.ru; f. 1988; attached to Russian Acad. of Sciences; library of 3,000 vols; Dir Prof. ARKADI E. KRASNO-SHTEIN; publs *Collection of Scientific and Research Works* (1 a year), *Mining Echo* (4 a year), *Proceedings* (1 a year).

Institute of Monitoring of Climatic and Ecological Systems: 634055 Tomsk, Akademicheskii pr. 10/3; tel. (3822) 492265; fax (3822) 491950; e-mail post@imces.ru; internet www.imces.ru; f. 1972, fmrly the Institute of Optical Monitoring; attached to Russian Acad. of Sciences; scientific and technological basis for monitoring and modelling climatic and ecosystem changes under impact of natural and anthropogenic factors; Dir V. A. KRUTIKOV; Scientific Sec. for Foreign Relations ELENA YURIEVNA GENINA.

Institute of Petrochemistry and Catalysis: 450075 Bashkortostan, Ufa, pr. Oktyabrya 141; tel. and fax (3472) 31-27-50; e-mail ink@anrb.ru; internet www.anrb.ru/ink/index.html; f. 1992; Dir USAIN M. DZHEMILEV.

Institute of Petroleum Refining and Petrochemistry: 450065 Bashkortostan, Ufa, Initsiativnaya ul. 12; tel. (3472) 43-31-17; fax (3472) 43-31-17; e-mail ipnhp@anrb.ru; f. 1956; Dir E. G. TELIASHEV.

Institute of Physical and Technical Problems of the North: 677891 Yakutsk, Oktyabrskaya ul. 1; tel. and fax (4112) 44-66-65; attached to Russian Acad. of Sciences; f. 1970; Dir Acad. V. P. LARIONOV.

Institute of Physics and Power Engineering: Bondarenko pl. 1, 249033 Kaluga oblast, Obninsk; tel. (08439) 98250; fax (08439) 58545; e-mail avzrod@ippe.obninsk.ru; internet www.ippe.ru; f. 1946; nuclear systems for civil and defence purposes; nuclear, laser and reactor physics; thermal physics, hydro-, gas and plasma-dynamics, liquid-metal coolant technologies; radiation material science; 3,800 mems; library of 320,000 vols; Dir-Gen. ANATOLY V. ZRODNIKOV.

Institute of Problems in Cybernetics: 117312 Moscow, ul. Vavilova 37; tel. (495) 124-77-67; attached to Russian Acad. of Sciences; Dir (vacant).

Institute of Problems in the Complex Utilization of Mineral Resources: 111020 Moscow, Kryukovskii tupik 4; tel. and fax (495) 360-89-60; e-mail info@ipkonran.ru; internet www.ipkonran.ru; f. 1977; attached to Russian Acad. of Sciences; Dir V. A. CHANTURIA.

Institute of Problems in the Safe Development of Nuclear Energy: 115191 Moscow, Bol. Tulskaya; tel. (495) 952-24-21; attached to Russian Acad. of Sciences; Dir L. A. BOLSHOV.

Institute of Problems of Marine Technology: 690600 Vladivostok, ul. Sukhanova 5A; tel. (4232) 22-64-16; fax (4232) 22-64-51; f. 1988; attached to Russian Acad. of Sciences; Dir M. D. AGEEV.

Institute of Problems of Mechanics: 119526 Moscow, pr. Vernadskogo 101; tel. (495) 434-32-38; fax (495) 938-20-48; f. 1965; attached to Russian Acad. of Sciences; library of 150,000 vols; Dir Prof. F. L. CHERNOUSKO.

Institute of Programmable Systems: 152140 Pereslavl-Zalesskii; tel. (08535) 9-81-21; attached to Russian Acad. of Sciences; Dir A. K. AILAMAZYAN.

Institute of Radio Engineering and Electronics: 103907 Moscow, Mokhovaya ul. 8; pr. K. Marksa 18; tel. (495) 203-52-93; fax (495) 200-52-58; attached to Russian Acad. of Sciences; br. in Saratov; Dir Acad. YU. V. GULYAEV.

Institute of Regional Systems Research: Birobidzhan; attached to Russian Acad. of Sciences; (in process of formation).

Institute of Remote Sensing Methods for Geology (VNIIKAM): 199034 St Petersburg, Birzhevoi pr-d 6; tel. (812) 218-28-01; fax (812) 218-39-16; Dir ALEXEI V. PERTSOV.

Institute of Solid State Chemistry and Mechanochemistry: 630128 Novosibirsk, Kutateladze ul. 18; tel. (383) 332-96-00; fax (383) 332-28-47; e-mail root@solid.nsc.ru; internet www.solid.nsc.ru; f. 1944; attached to Russian Acad. of Sciences; topo-chemical, radiation chemical and mechano-chemical methods of the control of the reactivity of solids; chemistry of supramolecular systems; reactions of intercalation; transport properties of composite materials; processes of electro-deposition and electro-dissolution of solid metallic electrodes in water solutions; devt of methods for nano-sized and high-dispersed materials preparation; mechanical alloying and mechano-chemical interaction in organic systems; synthesis of bismuth compounds of high purity and reactivity; library of 50,000 vols; Dir Prof. N. Z. LYAKHOV; publ. *Chemistry for Sustainable Development* (6 a year).

Institute of Synthetic Polymer Materials: 117393 Moscow, Profsoyuznaya 70; tel. (495) 335-91-00; attached to Russian Acad. of Sciences; Dir (vacant).

Institute of Technical Chemistry: 614013 Perm, ul. ak. Koroleva, 3; tel. (342) 237-82-72; fax (342) 237-82-62; e-mail international@itch.perm.ru; internet www.itch.perm.ru; f. 1985; attached to Ural Br. of Russian Acad. of Sciences; areas of research: synthesis of organic monomers, devt of new polymers and composite materials based thereupon, design of chemical processes based on new catalytic systems; library of 17,000 vols (incl. books and journals); Dir Dr V. N. STRELNIKOV; publs *Colloid Polym Sci, Journal of Molecular Structure, Microporous and Mesoporous Materials.*

Institute of the Automation of Design: 123056 Moscow, 2-ya Brestskaya; tel. (495) 250-02-62; attached to Russian Acad. of Sciences; Dir O. M. BELOTSERKOVSKY.

Institute of the Economics and Organization of Industrial Production: 630090 Novosibirsk, pr. Akad. Lavrenteva 17; tel. (3832) 35-05-36; fax (3832) 35-55-80; attached to Russian Acad. of Sciences; Dir (vacant).

Institute of the Geology and Exploitation of Fossil Fuels: 117312 Moscow, ul. Fersmana 50; tel. (495) 124-91-55; attached to Russian Acad. of Sciences; Dir N. KRYLOV.

Institute of Theoretical and Applied Mechanics: 630090 Novosibirsk, Institutskaya ul. 4/1; tel. (3832) 33-35-34; fax (3832) 34-22-68; e-mail fomin@itam.nsc.ru; internet www.itam.nsc.ru; f. 1957; attached to Russian Acad. of Sciences; library of 87,000 vols; Dir Prof. V. M. FOMIN; publs *Combustion, Explosion and Shock Waves* (a year), *Journal of Applied Mechanics and Technical Physics* (6 a year), *Physical Mesomechanics* (4 a year), *Thermophysics and Aeromechanics* (4 a year).

Institute of Trade Machinery: 127521 Moscow, Scheremetevskaya ul. 47; tel. (495) 218-51-47; fax (495) 219-73-21; f. 1961; Dir VYACHESLAV LVOVICH UMANSKY.

Ioffe, Acad. A. F., Physical-Technical Institute: 194021 St Petersburg, Politeckhnicheskaya ul. 26; tel. (812) 247-21-45; fax (812) 247-10-17; attached to Russian Acad. of

Sciences; br. in Shuvalovo; Dir Acad. ZH. I. ALFEROV.

Joint Russian-Vietnamese Tropical Research and Technological Centre: 119071 Moscow, Leninsky pr. 33; tel. (495) 954-12-19; f. 1987; attached to Russian Acad. of Sciences; long-term health consequences of Agent Orange, ecology, tropical resistance of materials and equipment; Head Acad. D. S. PAVLOV.

Kargin, V. A., Polymer Research Institute: 606006 Nizhegorodskaya oblast, Dzerzhinsk; tel. (8313) 25-50-00; fax (8313) 33-13-18; e-mail niip@kis.ru; internet www.advtech.ru/nipolymer/nipolymer1.htm; f. 1949; library of 142,000 vols; Gen. Dir Prof. V. V. GUZEEV.

Kazan Physical-Technical Institute: 420029 Kazan, ul. Sibirskii trakt 10/7; tel. (8432) 76-50-44; attached to Russian Acad. of Sciences; Dir K. M. SALIKHOV.

Keldysh, M.V., Institute of Applied Mathematics: 125047 Moscow, Miusskaya pl. 4; tel. (495) 972-37-14; attached to Russian Acad. of Sciences; Dir S. P. KURDYUMOV.

Kostyakov, A. N., All-Russian Research Institute of Hydraulic Engineering and Land Reclamation: 127550 Moscow, Bol. Akademicheskaya 44; tel. (499) 153-72-70; fax (499) 729-35-00; library of 8,000 vols; Dir Prof. Dr B. M. KIZYAEV (acting); publ. *Transactions* (1 or 2 a year).

Krylov Shipbuilding Research Institute: 196158 St Petersburg, Moskovskoe shosse 44; tel. (812) 727-93-48; fax (812) 727-93-49; e-mail krylov@krylov.spb.ru; internet www.krylov.com.ru; f. 1894; Science Prin. and Dir V. M. PASHIN; publ. *Proceedings* (1 a year).

Krzhizhanovsky, G. M., State Energy Research Institute: 117927 Moscow, Leninsky pr. 19; tel. (495) 954-37-32; attached to Russian Acad. of Sciences; Dir E. P. VOLKOV.

Lebedev, S. A., Institute of Precision Mechanics and Computing Technology: 117333 Moscow, Leninsky pr. 51; tel. (495) 137-15-67; attached to Russian Acad. of Sciences; Dir G. G. RYABOV.

Lebedev, S. V., All-Russia Synthetic Rubber Research Institute: 198035 St Petersburg, Gapsalskaya ul. 1; tel. (812) 251-40-28; fax (812) 251-48-13; f. 1928; synthetic elastomeric materials, production processes, applications; Dir Prof. VITALY A. KORMER.

Mining Institute: 184209 Murmansk oblast, Apatity, ul. Fersmana 24; tel. (81555) 7-43-42; fax (81555) 7-46-25; e-mail root@goi.kolasc.net.ru; internet www.goikolasc.ru; attached to Russian Acad. of Sciences; Dir Acad. N. N. MELNIKOV.

Mints, Acad. A. L., Institute of Radio Technology JSC: 127083 Moscow, ul. 8 Marta 10/1; tel. (495) 214-04-51; fax (495) 214-06-62; e-mail spz@newmail.ru; Gen. Dir V. I. SHUSTOV.

Moscow Scientific-Industrial Association 'Spektr': 119048 Moscow, ul. Usacheva 35; tel. (495) 245-56-56; fax (495) 246-88-88; f. 1964; attached to Russian Acad. of Sciences; research, devt and manufacture of non-destructive-testing equipment and instruments; Gen. Dir V. V. KLYUEV.

National Institute of Aviation Technology: 127051 Moscow, Petrovka 24; tel. (495) 311-05-41; fax (495) 311-03-23; e-mail info@niat.ru; internet www.niat.ru; f. 1920; Dir. O. S. SIROTKIN; publ. *Aviation Industry* (in Russian and English).

Paper Research Institute: 194018 St Petersburg, pr. Shvernika 49; tel. (812) 247-17-03; Dir A. IVANOV.

Pechora Research and Design Institute for the Oil Industry: 169400 Komi, Ukhta, Oktyabrskaya ul. 11; tel. (82147) 6-16-63; fax (82147) 6-03-36; Dir A. N. ILIN.

Physical-Technical Institute: 42600 Izhevsk, ul. Kirova 132; tel. (3142) 43-02-03; fax (3142) 25-06-14; e-mail fti@fti.udm.ru; internet fti.udm.ru; attached to Russian Acad. of Sciences; Dir Dr VLADIMIR LADYANOV.

Plastics Research Institute: 111112 Moscow, Perovskii pr. 35; tel. (495) 361-64-21; Dir V. I. ILICH.

Polymer Plastics Research Institute: St Petersburg, Polyustrovskii pr. 32; Dir Z. N. POLYAKOV.

Polzunov, I. I., Scientific and Development Association for Research and Design of Power Equipment JSC: 191167 St Petersburg, Atamanskaya str. 3/6; tel. (812) 578-87-13; fax (812) 717-43-00; e-mail general@ckti.ru; f. 1927; attached to Russian Acad. of Sciences; Dir YU. K. PETRENYA; publ. *Proceedings*.

Republic Engineering-Technical Centre for the Restoration and Strengthening of Components of Machines and Mechanisms: 634067 Tomsk, Khim ploshchadka; tel. (3822) 1-45-04 br. at Novosibirsk: 630055 Novosibirsk, ul. Musy Dzhalilya 9; tel. (3832) 32-12-49; attached to Russian Acad. of Sciences; Dir V. F. PINKIN (Tomsk); Dir V. M. NEZAMUTDINOV (Novosibirsk).

Research and Design Institute for the Mechanical Processing of Minerals: 199026 St Petersburg, V. O., 21-ya liniya 8A; tel. (812) 321-97-29; fax (812) 325-62-02; f. 1920; Dir VASILY ARSENTIEV; publ. *Obogashcheniye Rud* (Mineral Processing Journal, 6 a year).

Research and Design Institute of Artificial Fibres: 141009 Moscow oblast, Mytishchi, ul. Kolontsova 5; tel. (495) 284-44-78; Dir V. SMIRNOV.

Research and Design Institute of Autogenous Engineering: 109004 Moscow, Shelaputinsky per. 1; tel. and fax (495) 915-09-60; e-mail vniiautogen@newmail.ru; f. 1944; equipment for thermal cutting and spraying; Dir NIKOLAI I. NIKIFOROV; publ. *Research Work* (irregular).

Research and Design Institute of Chemical Engineering: 125015 Moscow, Bol. Novodmitrovskaya 14; tel. (495) 685-56-74; fax (495) 685-29-23; e-mail info@niichimmash.ru; internet niichimmash.ru; f. 1943; Gen. Dir A. TSYGANKOV.

Research and Design Institute of Management Information Technology: 125083 Moscow, ul. Yunnatov 18; tel. (495) 212-60-60.

Research and Design Institute of Metallurgical Engineering: 109428 Moscow, Ryazanskii pr. 8A; tel. (495) 174-37-00.

Research and Design Institute of Polymer Construction Materials: 117419 Moscow, 2-i Verkhny Mikhailovsky pr. 9; tel. (495) 952-30-68; fax (495) 954-40-91; attached to Polymerstroymateriali JSC; Dir ALEXANDER V. POGORELOV.

Research and Design Institute of the Bearings Industry: 109088 Moscow, 2-ya ul. Mashinostroeniya 27; tel. (495) 275-11-59.

Research and Design Institute of Woodworking Machinery: 107082 Moscow, Rubtsovskaya nab. 3; tel. (495) 261-16-73; f. 1948; library of 50,000 vols; publ. *Catalogue of Woodworking Machines* (1 a year).

Research and Design Technological Institute of Heavy Engineering: Ekaterinburg, pl. 1-i Pyatiletki.

Research and Experimental Design Institute of Machinery for the Food Industry: 123308 Moscow, pr. Marshala Zhukova 1.

Research Centre for Fundamental Problems of Computer Technology and Control Systems: 117218 Moscow, ul. Krasikova 25A; tel. (495) 125-77-09; attached to Russian Acad. of Sciences; Chair. of Presidium K. A. VALIEV.

Attached Institutes:

Institute of Computer Technology Problems: 150007 Yaroslavl, Universitetskaya 21; tel. (0852) 35-52-83; attached to Russian Acad. of Sciences; Dir YU. A. MAMATOV.

Institute of Microelectronics Technology and High-purity Materials: 142432 Moscow oblast, Chernogolovka vul. Institutskay 6; tel. (495) 962-80-74; fax (495) 962-80-47; e-mail general@iptm.ru; internet www.iptm.ru; attached to Russian Acad. of Sciences; Dir V. A. TULIN.

Microelectronics Institute: 150007 Yaroslavl, Universitetskaya 21; tel. (0852) 11-65-52; attached to Russian Acad. of Sciences; Dir V. A. KURCHIDIS.

Physical Technological Institute: 117218 Moscow, ul. Krasikova 25-A; tel. (495) 125-77-09; attached to Russian Acad. of Sciences; Dir K. A. VALIEV.

Research Institute of Systems of Automated Designing of Radioelectronic Apparatus and Very Large Scale Integrated Circuits: 103681 Moscow, Zelenograd, ul. Sovetskaya 3; tel. (495) 531-56-45; attached to Russian Acad. of Sciences; Dir A. L. STEMPKOVSKY.

Special Design Bureau for Microelectronics and Computer Technology: 15007 Yaroslavl, Universitetskaya 21; tel. (0852) 11-81-73; attached to Russian Acad. of Sciences; Dir A. M. GLUSHKOV.

Research Centre for Space Probes: 117810 Moscow, Profsoyuznaya ul. 84/32; attached to Russian Acad. of Sciences; Head N. A. DOLGIKH (acting).

Research, Design and Technological Institute of Electrothermic Equipment: 109052 Moscow, Nizhegorodskaya 29; tel. (495) 278-75-09.

Research Design-Technological Institute for Coal Machinery: 109193 Moscow, ul. Petra Romanova 7; tel. (495) 279-47-66.

Research Institute for Food Concentrates and Food Technologies and Special Food Technology: 117279 Moscow, Miklukho-Maklaya ul. 32; tel. and fax (495) 429-04-11; e-mail niispt@yandex.ru; internet www.niippspt.ru; f. 1981; attached to Russian Acad. of Agricultural Sciences; develops food concentrates, cereal snacks; food rations for Armed Forces and cosmonauts; tea and coffee products, infant foods; library of 7,000 vols; Dir Dr VICTOR F. DOBROVOLSKY; publ. *Tea and Coffee in Russia* (4 a year).

Research Institute for Instrumentation: 125124 Moscow, ul. Raskovoi 20; tel. (495) 214-55-88.

Research Institute for Systems Research: 109280 Moscow, Avtozavodskaya 23; tel. (495) 277-87-31; attached to Russian Acad. of Sciences; Dir V. B. BETELIN.

Research Institute for the Bakery and Confectionery Industry: 107553 Moscow, Bol. Cherkizovskaya ul. 26A; tel. (495) 161-41-44; attached to Russian Acad. of Agricultural Sciences.

Research Institute for the Beer, Soft Drinks and Wine Industry: 119021 Moscow, ul. Rossolimo 7; tel. (495) 246-67-69;

attached to Russian Acad. of Agricultural Sciences.

Research Institute for the Organization, Management and Economics of the Oil and Gas Industry: 117420 Moscow, ul. Nametkina 14; tel. (495) 332-00-22.

Research Institute for the Processing of Casing Head Gas: 350550 Krasnodar, Krasnaya ul. 118; tel. (8612) 55-85-52; Dir N. I. KORSAKOV.

Research Institute of Abrasives and Grinding: 197342 St Petersburg, Beloostrovskaya ul. 17; tel. (812) 245-33-05; fax (812) 245-47-90; f. 1931; library of 62,000 vols; Dir S. MOLCHANOV.

Research Institute of Agricultural Engineering: 127427 Moscow, Dmitrovskoe shosse 107; tel. (495) 485-55-81.

Research Institute of Applied Automated Systems: 103009 Moscow, ul. Nezhdanovoi 2A; tel. (495) 229-78-46; attached to Russian Acad. of Sciences; Dir O. L. SMIRNOV.

Research Institute of Atomic Reactors: Ulyanovsk oblast, 433510 Dimitrovgrad; tel. (84235) 3-20-21; fax (84235) 3-56-48; e-mail adm@niiar.ru; internet www.niiar.ru; f. 1956; library of 150,000 vols; Dir Dr A. V. BYCHKOV.

Research Institute of Automobile Electronics and Electrical Equipment: 105187 Moscow, Kirpichnaya 39–41; tel. (495) 365-25-66.

Research Institute of Automobile Industry Technology: 115333 Moscow, pr. Andropova 22/30; tel. (495) 118-20-00; Dir S. V. PODOBLYAEV.

Research Institute of Building Ceramics: 143980 Moscow oblast, Zheleznodorozhnyi-1; tel. (495) 527-73-73.

Research Institute of Chemical Fibres and Composite Materials: 195030 St Petersburg, ul. Khimikov 28; tel. (812) 227-61-48; Dir P. E. MIKHAILOV.

Research Institute of Chemical Reagents and Ultrapure Chemical Substances: 107258 Moscow, Bogorodskii val 3; tel. (495) 963-70-70; Dir E. A. RYABENKO.

Research Institute of Chemicals for Polymer Materials: 392680 Tambov, ul. Montazhnikov 3; tel. (0752) 29-51-52; attached to Syntez joint-stock company; Dir B. N. GORBUNOV.

Research Institute of Construction and Road Machinery: 123424 Moscow, Volokolamskoe shosse 73; tel. (495) 491-10-33.

Research Institute of Construction Physics: 127238 Moscow, Lokomotivny pr. 21; tel. (495) 482-40-76; fax (495) 482-40-60; e-mail niisf@ipc.ru; f. 1956; library of 2,000 vols; Dir G. L. OSIPOV.

Research Institute of Current Sources: 129626 Moscow; tel. (495) 287-97-42; attached to Russian Acad. of Sciences; Dir YU. V. SKOKOV.

Research Institute of Drilling Technology: 117957 Moscow, Leninsky pr. 6; tel. (495) 236-01-70; Dir A. V. MNASHCHAKOV.

Research Institute of Earthmoving Machinery: c/o VNIIZEMMASH, 198005 St Petersburg, Petrovskii pr. 2; tel. and fax (812) 235-57-84; attached to VNIIZEMMASH; Dir V. P. KORNEEV.

Research Institute of Elastic Materials and Products: 119048 Moscow, Mal. Trubetskaya ul. 28; tel. (495) 242-53-42; fax (495) 245-62-10; Dir S. V. REZNICHENKO.

Research Institute of Electrical Engineering: 191186 St Petersburg, Dvortsovaya nab. 18; tel. and fax (812) 387-55-22; e-mail jandan@peterlink.ru; f. 1992; attached to Russian Acad. of Sciences; Dir Acad. Y. B.

DANILEVICH; publs *Electrichestvo* (12 a year), *Energetics News of RAS* (6 a year).

Research Institute of Electro-welding Technology: 194100 St Petersburg, Litovskaya ul. 10; tel. (812) 245-40-95; Dir V. V. SMIRNOV.

Research Institute of Electromeasuring Equipment: 195267 St Petersburg, pr. Prosveshcheniya 85; tel. (812) 559-51-41.

Research Institute of Foundry Machinery and the Technology and Automation of Foundry Production: 123557 Moscow, Presnenskii val 14; tel. (495) 252-27-25; Dir E. KRAKOVSKII.

Research Institute of Gas Use in the Economy and Underground Storage of Oil, Oil Products and Liquefied Gases: 123298 Moscow, ul. Berzarina 12; tel. (499) 946-89-11.

Research Institute of Hydrogeology and Engineering Geology (VSEGINGEO): 142452 Moscow oblast, Noginskii raion, p/o Kupavna, pos. Zelenyi; tel. (495) 521-20-00; fax (495) 913-51-26; e-mail gvartany@online .ru; f. 1939; Dir Acad. G.S. VARTANYAN.

Research Institute of Instrumentation Technology: 113191 Moscow, Gamsonovskii per. 9; tel. (495) 232-10-41.

Research Institute of Light Alloys: Moscow, ul. Gorbanova 20; Dir N. I. KORYAGINA.

Research Institute of Light and Textile Machinery: 113105 Moscow, Varshavskoe shosse 33; tel. (499) 611-00-30; fax (495) 958-58-41; e-mail vniiltek@mail.magelan.ru; internet www.vimi.ru/vniiltekmash; f. 1932; library of 30,000 vols; Dir Prof. Dr R. M. MALAFEYEV.

Research Institute of Organizational Technology: 119146 Moscow, Komsomolskii pr. 9A; tel. (495) 246-41-21.

Research Institute of Road Traffic Safety: 109389 Moscow, Mal. Lubyanka 16/4.

Research Institute of Rubber and Latex Products: 107564 Moscow, Krasnobogatyrskaya ul. 42; tel. (495) 161-02-92; fax (495) 963-49-11; Dir V. A. BERESTENEV.

Research Institute of Rubber Technical Products: 141300 Moscow oblast, Sergievsky Posad; tel. (496) 544-57-59; fax (0496) 544-10-52; f. 1960; library of 15,000 vols; Dir V. V. SHVARTS.

Research Institute of Special Engineering: 107082 Moscow, Cheshikhinsky pr-d 18/20; tel. (499) 261-50-76.

Research Institute of Synthetic Fibres: 170613 Tver, ul. Pashi Savelevoi 45; tel. (08222) 5-36-10; Dir V. F. LOSKUTOV.

Research Institute of Technical Physics: 454070 Chelyabinsk oblast, Chelyabinsk 70; Dir V. Z. NECHAI.

Research Institute of the Cement Industry OJSC (NIICement): 107014 Moscow, 3-i Luchevoy prosek 12; tel. (495) 268-27-21; fax (495) 268-27-26; e-mail riicement@mtu-net.ru; f. 1947; formerly State Research Institute of the Cement Industry; Dir-Gen. Prof. Dr V.I. SHUBIN.

Research Institute of the Chemistry and Technology of Organoelement Compounds: 105118 Moscow, shosse Entuziastov 38; tel. (495) 673-49-53; fax (495) 913-25-38; e-mail eos2004@inbox.ru; internet www .eos.su; f. 1945; Gen.-Dir P. A. STOROZHENKO.

Research Institute of the Clock and Watch Industry: 125315 Moscow, Chasovaya 24/1; tel. (495) 151-15-01.

Research Institute of the Factory Technology of Prefabricated Reinforced Concrete Structures and Items: 111524

Moscow, ul. Plekhanova 7; tel. (495) 176-27-04.

Research Institute of the Gas Industry: 142700 Moscow oblast, Vidnoe.

Research Institute of the Metrology Service: 119361 Moscow, G-361, Ozernaya ul. 46; tel. (495) 437-55-77; fax (495) 437-56-66; e-mail office.vniims@relcom.ru; attached to Russian Acad. of Sciences; Dir V. V. SAZHIN.

Research Institute of the Tyre Industry: 105118 Moscow, ul. Burakova 27; tel. (495) 273-69-01; fax (495) 176-37-42; Dir A. A. VOLNOV.

Research Institute of Tooling: 105023 Moscow, Bol. Semenovskaya 49; tel. (495) 366-94-11.

Research Institute of Transport Construction: 129329 Moscow, Kolskaya 1; tel. (495) 180-20-42; fax (495) 189-72-53; e-mail mail@tsniis.com; internet www.tsniis.com; f. 1935; research on bridges, tunnels, railways and associated structures, and development of standards and codes of practice; Dir-Gen. ANATOLY SYCHEV.

Research Institute of Vehicle and Tractor Materials: 113184 Moscow, Ozerkovskaya nab. 22/24; tel. (495) 230-94-59.

Research-Training Centre 'Robototekhnika': 105037 Moscow, Izmailovskaya pl. 7; tel. (495) 165-17-01; fax (495) 367-06-36; e-mail robot@bmstu.ru; internet www.robot .bmstu.ru; f. 1983; attached to Russian Acad. of Sciences and Bauman Moscow State Technical University; Head Prof. A. S. YUSCHENKO.

Russian Research, Design and Technological Institute for Crane and Traction Electrical Equipment: 109280 Moscow, ul. Masterkova 4; tel. (495) 275-61-66; fax (495) 275-49-03; f. 1960; library of 160,000 vols; Dir ANATOLY D. MASHIKHIN.

Russian Research Institute of Industrial Design: 129223 Moscow, pr. Mira, VVTs, korp. 312; tel. (495) 216-90-10; fax (495) 216-88-10; f. 1962; Dir LEV A. KUZMICHEV; publs *Tekhnicheskaya Estetika* (2 a year), *Designer's Library* (2 a year).

Russian Research Institute of Information Technology and Automated Design Systems: 129090 Moscow, ul. Shchepkina 22; tel. (495) 288-19-24.

Russian Scientific Centre of Applied Chemistry: 197198 St Petersburg, pr. Dobrolyubova 14; tel. (812) 325-66-45; fax (812) 325-66-48; f. 1919; library of 500,000 vols; Gen. Dir Prof. G. F. TERESHCHENKO; publ. *Annual Proceedings*.

Science Production Association 'Orgstankinprom': 105264 Moscow, 5-ya Parkovaya 37, korp. 2; tel. (495) 164-56-53.

Scientific and Engineering Centre 'SNIIP': 123060 Moscow, ul. Raspletina 5; tel. (499) 198-97-64; fax (499) 943-00-63; e-mail support@sniip.ru; internet www.sniip .ru; attached to Rosatom (State Atomic Energy Corporation); systems and instrumentation connected with nuclear power production, electronics and space research; library of 83,000 research vols; Dir-Gen. Dr ALEXANDER F. PELEVIN; publ. *Proceedings* (1 a year).

Scientific and Research Institute for Standardization and Certification in the Engineering Industry: 123007 Moscow, ul. Shenogina 4; tel. (495) 256-04-49; fax (495) 943-00-78; f. 1957; standardization, certification of products.

Scientific and Research Institute of Motor Transport: 123514 Moscow, ul. Geroev-Panfilovtsev 24; tel. (495) 496-55-23; fax (495) 496-61-36; e-mail niiat@niiat.ru; internet www.niiat.ru; f. 1930; research and devt in field of motor transport operation, incl. transport and traffic management, traffic safety, urban transport, transport and the environment, transport economy; library of 250,000 vols.

Scientific and Technical Complex 'Progress': 119034 Moscow, Kropotkinskaya ul. 13/7; tel. (495) 301-23-25; attached to Russian Acad. of Sciences; Gen. Dir L. N. LUPICHEV.

Scientific Centre of Complex Transportation Problems: 113035 Moscow, Sofiiskaya nab. 34, korp. V; tel. (495) 233-89-13; fax (495) 231-14-54; f. 1955; Dir V. ARSENOV.

Scientific-Experimental Centre for the Automation of Air Traffic Control: 123182 Moscow, Volokolamskoe shosse 26; tel. (495) 190-42-18; attached to Russian Acad. of Sciences; Head T. G. ANODINA.

Scientific Research Institute for Systems Studies: 117218 Moscow, pr. Nakhimovsky 36, korp. 1; tel. (495) 719-76-51; fax (495) 719-76-81; e-mail betelin@sistyd.msk .su; internet www.niisi.ru; f. 1989; attached to Russian Acad. of Sciences; Dir V. B. BETELIN; publs *Issues in Cybernetics* (1 a year), *Issues of SRISA* (2 a year).

Scientific Research Institute of Comprehensive Engineering Problems in Animal Husbandry and Fodder Production (VNIIKOMZH): 101509 Moscow, Lesnaya 43; tel. (495) 250-37-90; fax (495) 978-91-38; f. 1974; library of 40,000 vols; Dir-Gen. I. V. ILIN; publ. *Scientific Research Works of VNIIKOMZH* (1 a year).

Scientific Research Institute of Multiprocessor Computer Systems of the Taganrog State University of Radio Engineering: 347928 Taganrog, ul. Chekhova 2; tel. (86344) 36-07-57; fax (86344) 36-03-76; internet www.mvs.tsure.ru; f. 1972; attached to Russian Acad. of Sciences; Dir I. A. KALIAEV; publ. *Multiprocessor Computer Structures* (1 a year).

Scientific-Technical Co-operative 'Problems of Mechanics and Technology': 109180 Moscow, ul. Bol. Polyanka 2/10; tel. (495) 251-52-08; attached to Russian Acad. of Sciences; Chair. Acad. V. V. STRUMINSKY.

Siberian Research Institute of the Oil Industry: 625016 Tyumen, ul. 50-let Oktyabrya 118; tel. (3452) 21-19-16; Dir R. I. KUZOVATKIN.

Skochinsky Institute of Mining: 140004 Moscow, Lyubertsy 4; tel. (495) 554-85-13; fax (495) 554-52-47; e-mail igd@igd.ru; internet www.igd.ru; f. 1927; attached to Russian Acad. of Sciences; technology of opencast and underground coal mining; certification of mine electrical equipment and explosion-proof equipment; library of 40,000 vols; Dir ANATOLY DMITRIEVICH RUBAN; publs *Economics of the Coal Industry* (1 or 2 a year), *Technology of Opencast and Underground Coal Mining* (4 a year).

Special Design Bureau for Applied Geophysics: 630058 Novosibirsk, Russkaya ul. 35; tel. (3832) 32-36-45; e-mail geophys@ hydromet.ru; attached to Russian Acad. of Sciences; Head N. P. RASHENTSEV.

Special Design Bureau for Automation of Marine Research: 693023 Yuzhno-Sakhalinsk, ul. Gorkogo 25; tel. and fax (424) 255-49-66; e-mail skb-sami@sakhalin .ru; f. 1972; attached to Russian Acad. of Sciences; Head ANATOLY E. MALASHENKO.

Special Design Bureau for High Capacity Electronics: 634055 Tomsk, Akademicheskii pr. 4; tel. (3822) 1-84-59; attached to Russian Acad. of Sciences; Head A. P. KHUZEEV.

Special Design Bureau for Hydroimpulse Technology: 630090 Novosibirsk, ul. Tereshkovoi 29; tel. (3832) 35-72-91; attached to Russian Acad. of Sciences; Head A. A. DERIBAS.

Special Design Bureau for Scientific Instruments: 630058 Novosibirsk, Russkaya ul. 41; tel. (3832) 35-30-41; attached to Russian Acad. of Sciences; Head YU. V. CHUGUI.

Special Design-Technological Bureau for Special Electronics and Analytical Instrumentation: 630090 Novosibirsk, ul. Akad. Nikolaeva 8; tel. (3832) 32-24-40; attached to Russian Acad. of Sciences; Head K. K. SVITASHCHEV.

Special Design-Technological Bureau 'Nauka': 66049 Krasnoyarsk, pr. Mira 53; tel. (3912) 27-29-12; attached to Russian Acad. of Sciences; Head V. V. MOSKVICHEV.

State Design and Research Institute for the Design of Research Institutes, Laboratories and Research Centres of the Academy of Sciences: 117971 Moscow, ul. Gubkina 3; tel. (495) 135-73-01; fax (495) 135-02-20; e-mail gp@gpran.msk.ru; f. 1938; attached to Russian Acad. of Sciences; Dir A. S. PANFIL.

State Design and Research Institute of Power Systems and Electricity Networks: 107884 Moscow, 2-ya Baumanskaya 7; tel. (499) 261-98-21.

State Institute of Mined Chemical Raw Materials: 140000 Moscow oblast, Lyubertsy, Oktyabrsky pr. 259; tel. (495) 554-42-46.

State Research and Project Development Institute of Maritime Transport: 125319 Moscow, Bol. Koptevsky pr-d 6; tel. (495) 152-36-51; fax (495) 152-09-16; f. 1939; design of port structures and ship repair yards; economic problems of maritime transport; maritime law; Dir FELIX G. ARAKELOV.

State Research Institute for the Nitrogen Industry and the Products of Organic Synthesis: 109815 Moscow, Zemlyanoi val 50; tel. (495) 227-00-04; Dir N. D. ZAICHKO.

State Research Institute for the Operation and Repair of Civil Aviation Equipment: Moscow, ul. Krzhizhanovskogo 7.

State Research Institute of Civil Aviation: 103340 Moscow oblast, Sheremetevo Airport; tel. (495) 578-48-01.

State Research Institute of the Rare Metals Industry: 109017 Moscow, Bol. Tolmachevsky per. 5; tel. (495) 239-90-66.

'Submicron' Research Institute: 103482 Moscow, Zelenograd, korp. 331A; tel. (495) 536-26-17.

Topchiev, A. V., Institute of Petro-Chemical Synthesis: 117912 Moscow, Leninskii pr. 29; tel. (495) 954-22-92; attached to Russian Acad. of Sciences; Dir Acad. N. A. PLATE.

Tractor Research and Development Institute: 125040 Moscow, Verkhnyaya 34; tel. (495) 257-01-10; fax (495) 973-20-23; e-mail nati@ccas.ru; f. 1925; Dir NIKOLAI A. SHCHELTSIN.

Vavilov State Optical Institute: 199034 St Petersburg, Birzhevaya Liniya 12; tel. (812) 328-48-92; fax (812) 328-37-20; e-mail leader@soi.spb.ru; internet soi.srv.pu.ru; f. 1918; library of 600,000 vols; Dir Dr G. PETROVSKY; publ. *Journal of Optical Technology* (12 a year).

'VNIPIenergoprom' Association JSC: 105094 Moscow, Semenovskaya nab. 2/1; tel. (495) 360-76-40; fax (495) 366-36-25; internet www.vnipiep.ru; f. 1942; design,

research and devt of energy transmission systems, combined heating and power plants, project management, devt of heat and power-supply schemes for municipal areas, principally Moscow.

Vologdin, V. P., Research Institute of High-Frequency Currents: 197376 St Petersburg, ul. L. Tolstogo 7; tel. (812) 594-81-23; fax (812) 594-81-27; e-mail vniitvch@ mail.ru; internet www.vniitvch.spb.ru; f. 1947; Dir F. V. BEZMENOV.

Zhukovsky, N. E., Central Aero- and Hydro-dynamics Institute: 140160 Moscow oblast, Zhukovsky 3; tel. (495) 556-41-79; Dir G. P. SVISHCHEV.

Libraries and Archives

Arkhangelsk

Dobroliubov Arkhangelsk Regional Research Library: 163061 Arkhangelsk, ul. Loginova 2; tel. (8182) 65-11-28; fax (8182) 43-97-39; internet www.dvinalend.ru; Dir OLGA STIUPINA.

Barnaul

Altai State University Library: 656099 Barnaul, Sotsialisticheskii pr. 68; 159,000 vols; Dir GALINA TRUSHNIKOVA.

Cheboksary

Chuvash State University Library: 428034 Cheboksary, Universitetskaya 38; tel. (8835) 49-79-88; e-mail library@chuvsu .ru; internet library.chuvsu.ru; 1,703,091 vols; Dir NINA D. NIKITINA.

Ekaterinburg

Scientific Library of Ural State University 'M. Gorky': 620083 Ekaterinburg, 51, Lenina ave; tel. and fax (343) 350-75-65; e-mail library@usu.ru; internet lib.usu.ru; f. 1920; incl. rare book dept; institutional repository; 1,261,687 vols; Dir K. P. KUZNET-SOVA.

Elista

Kalmyk State University Library: Elista, ul. R. Luksemburg 4; c. 350,000 vols; Dir P. A. DOLINA.

Grozny

Chechen State University Library: 364907 Grozny, ul. N. Buachidze 34/96; 460,000 vols; Dir R. M. NAZARETYANI.

Ingushetia

National Library of Ingushetia: 366700 Ingushetia, Sunezhsky district, ul. Lunacharskogo 106; Dir RADIMA GAZDIEVA.

Irkutsk

Irkutsk State University Library: 664695 Irkutsk, bul. Gagarina 24; 3.2m. vols; Dir R. V. PODGAICHENKO.

Ivanovo

Ivanovo State University Library: 153377 Ivanovo, ul. Ermaka 37; 410,000 vols; Dir A. N. KRUPPA.

Library of Ivanovo State Chemistry and Technology University: 153460 Ivanovo, ul. Fridrikha Engelsa 7; tel. (0932) 32-73-54; fax (0932) 32-95-02; Dir VERA DMITRIEVA.

Izhevsk

Udmurt State University Library: 426034 Izhevsk, Universitetskaya ul. 1; tel. (3412) 52-60-89; fax (3412) 75-58-66; e-mail admin@lib.udsu.ru; internet lib.udsu.ru; f. 1932; 970,647 vols; Librarian L. P. BESKLINS-KAYA.

Kaliningrad

Immanuel Kant Baltic Federal University Library: 236040 Kaliningrad, Universitetskaya ul. 2; tel. (4012) 53-31-29; fax (4012) 53-36-08; e-mail eafilippova@kantiana.ru; internet lib.kantiana.ru; f. 1968; 624,212 vols; Dir A. N. CHERNYAKOV; Deputy Dir FILIPPOVA ELENA.

Kazan

Kazan Federal University N. I. Lobachevsky Library: 420008 Kazan, Kremlevskaya 35; tel. (843) 264-47-54; e-mail lsl@ksu.ru; internet www.lsl.ksu.ru; f. 1804; 6,099,966 vols; Dir Dr EUGENE N. STROUKOV; publs *Opisaniya rukopisei*, *Retrospektivnye bibliograficheskie ukazately*.

Kemerovo

Kemerovo State University Library: 650043 Kemerovo, Krasnaya ul. 6; tel. (3842) 23-14-26; f. 1928; 350,000 vols; Librarian N. P. KONOVALOVA.

Krasnodar

Kuban State University Library: 350049 Krasnodar, Stavropolskaya ul. 149; tel. (8612) 69-95-52; fax (8612) 69-95-17; e-mail gsol@pop.kubsu.ru; internet www.library.kubsu.ru; f. 1920; 1,253,824 vols; Dir G. V. SOLOVEVA.

Krasnoyarsk

Krasnoyarsk State University Library: 660049 Krasnoyarsk, ul. Maerchaka 6; tel. (3912) 21-03-17; 166,000 vols; Librarian E. G. KRIVONOSOVA.

Makhachkala

Dagestan State University Library: 367008 Makhachkala, Batir ul. 1; tel. (8722) 68-02-74; e-mail alieva_li@mail.ru; internet elib.dgu.ru; 780,000 vols; Dir A. M. SHAKHSHAEVA.

Moscow

'All-Russia Patent and Technical Library' of Federal Institute of Industrial Property of Federal Service for Intellectual Property, Patents and Trademarks (Rospatent): 123995 Moscow, Berezhkovskaya nab. 24; tel. (499) 240-64-25; fax (499) 240-44-37; e-mail omobp@rupto.ru; internet www1.fips.ru/wps/wcm/connect/content_ru/ru/activity_lines/fonds/; f. 1896; the only Russian library which receives Russian and all foreign patents; copies of 117,986,700 patent documents; Dir V. I. AMELKINA; publs *Guidebook to funds of Division 'All-Russia Patent and Technical Library'*, *Thematic bibliographic indexes of the literature*.

All-Russia Scientific and Research Institute of Patent Information (VNIIPI): 113035 Moscow, Raushskaya nab. 4; tel. (495) 959-33-13; fax (495) 959-33-04; f. 1964; Dir V. D. ZINOVIEV; publs *Inventions* (36 a year), *Service Marks. Appellations of Origin of Goods* (12 a year), *Trademarks, Utility Models. Industrial Designs* (12 a year).

Archives of the Russian Academy of Sciences: 117218 Moscow, Novocheremushkinskaya ul. 34; tel. (499) 129-19-10; fax (499) 129-19-66; e-mail academ_archive@mail.ru; f. 1728; 9,000 vols; Dir V.Y. AFIANI; publs *Proceedings*, *Scientific Heritage*.

Central Library of the Academy of Medical Sciences: 125874 Moscow, Baltiiskaya ul. 8; tel. (495) 155-47-93; f. 1935; 640,000 vols; acts as an enquiry, loan, research and guide centre for 42 libraries in the institutes and laboratories of the Academy of Medical Sciences; Dir G. I. BAKHEREVA.

Central Scientific Agricultural Library of the Russian Academy of Agricultural Sciences: 107139 Moscow,Orlikov byst, 3-B; tel. (495) 607-54-48; fax (495) 607-89-72; e-mail dir@cnshb.ru; internet www.cnshb.ru; f. 1930; centre for bibliographical information on national and foreign agricultural literature, and for scientific and methodological work of agricultural libraries in Russia; 3m. vols, 3,300 periodicals; Dir BUNIN MIKHAIL STANISLAVOVICH; publs *Bibliographic Information* (52 a year), *Selskoe khozyaistvo* (12 a year), *Selskokhozyaistvennaya literatura* (12 a year), *Subject Bibliographic Lists* (15 a year).

Central State Archives: 125212 Moscow, Vyborgskaya 3; tel. (495) 159-73-83; Dir A. PROKOPENKO.

Centre for the Preservation of Historical Documentary Collections: Moscow, Vyborgskaya ul. 3; tel. (495) 159-74-71; Dir V. BONDAREV; formerly Central State Archive of the USSR (TsGA SSSR) Special Archive.

Federal Archival Agency: 103132 Moscow, ul. Ilyinka 12; tel. (495) 606-35-31; fax (495) 606-55-87; e-mail rosarhiv@archives.ru; internet www.rusarchives.ru; f. 1991; Head ANDREY ARTIZOV; publ. *Otechestvenniye archivy* (6 a year).

Gorky, A. M., Archives: 121069 Moscow, ul. Vorovskogo 25A; tel. (495) 291-19-23; fax (495) 200-32-16; f. 1937; Dir VLADIMIR S. BARAKHOV.

Institute for Scientific Information on the Social Sciences of the Russian Academy of Sciences: 117418 Moscow, ul. Krasikova 28/21; tel. (495) 128-88-81; fax (495) 420-22-61; f. 1969; sections on philosophy, history, economics, sociology, politology, culturology, global problems and international relations, law, science of sciences, linguistics, theory of literature; 13,500,000 vols; Dir V. A. VINOGRADOV; publs *The Human Being: Image and Essence* (1 a year), *Theory and Practice of Information in Social Sciences* (1 a year), various periodicals on social sciences and other subjects.

Institute of Scientific and Technical Information: 125219 Moscow, ul. Usievicha 20A; tel. (495) 155-43-96; attached to Russian Acad. of Sciences; Dir P. V. NESTEROV.

International Centre for Scientific and Technical Information: 125252 Moscow, ul. Kuusinena 21 B; tel. (495) 198-70-21; fax (495) 943-00-89; e-mail alsor@icsti.su; internet www.icsti.su; f. 1969; Dir Dr ZURAB A. YAKOBASHVILI.

Library for Natural Sciences of the Russian Academy of Sciences: 119992 Moscow GSP-2, ul. Znamenka 11/11; tel. (495) 291-22-89; fax (495) 291-91-93; e-mail osiat@benran.ru; internet www.benran.ru/ben_ne2.htm; f. 1973; 12,549,000 items in main and associated libraries; Dir Prof. Dr N. E. KALENOV; publ. *Libraries of Academies of Sciences* (in Russian, 1 a year).

Library of the State A. S. Pushkin Museum of Fine Arts: 119019 Moscow, ul. Volkhonka 12; tel. (495) 697-97-28; fax (495) 697-32-08; e-mail bib@artsmuseum.ru; f. 1898; mem of Russian Library Asscn; holds encyclopaedic collns, European art, Egyptian, Greek and Roman art, numismatic, archaeology; art education, architecture, world history, museology; supports research activities; 280,000 vols of books (17th–21st centuries), 405,000 periodicals of 19th–21st centuries, 100,000 reproductions on paper and canvas, 120,000 negatives and photographs, 70,000 slides; Dir OLGA B. MALINKOVSKAYA; publ. *Bulletin of the New Acquisitions* (2 a year, spec. issue for researchers).

Library of the State Central Museum of the Contemporary History of Russia: 103050 Moscow, Tverskaya ul. 21; tel. (495) 299-52-17; fax (495) 299-85-15; e-mail sovrhistory@mtu-net.ru; internet www.sovr.ru; f. 1917 as Museum of the Russian Revolution; 360,000 vols, 825,000 periodicals; Chief Librarian TATYANA N. EREMEEVA.

Library of the State Literature Museum: Moscow, Rozhdestvenskii bul. 16; f. 1926; collection of 180,000 books, 27,644 periodicals; Russian and foreign works from 16th to 20th centuries; letters and autographed works; folklore works; periodical collection; Dir ANNA IVANOVNA NIKULINA.

Library of the State Museum of Oriental Arts: 103064 Moscow, Vorontsovo pole 16A; tel. and fax (495) 916-34-29; e-mail dinagnw@rambler.ru; f. 1918; 75,000 vols; Dir DIANA VAKHTANGOVA; publ. *Scientific Reports* (1 a year).

Library (Book Fund Department) of the State Theatrical A. A. Bakhrushin Museum: 115054 Moscow, Bakhrushin St. 31/12; tel. (495) 953-48-48; fax (495) 953-54-48; e-mail gctm@gctm.ru; internet www.gctm.ru; f. 1894; colln of 1.5m. objects reflecting history of theatre in Russia from 17th century until present day; 120,000 vols on theatrical art; Head TITANIA BONILYA; Gen. Dir RODIONOV DMITRY.

Library of the Tolstoy State Museum: 119034 Moscow, ul. Prechistenka 11; tel. (495) 202-78-51; fax (495) 202-93-38; f. 1911; 76,000 vols, 86,000 newspaper cuttings; Dir L. M. LUBIMOVA.

The M. I. Rudomino, All-Russia State Library for Foreign Literature: 109189 Moscow, Nikoloyamskaya St 1; tel. (495) 915-36-21; fax (495) 915-36-37; e-mail vgbil@libfl.ru; internet www.libfl.ru; f. 1922; research and public library; cultural centre; exchange arrangements with 500 libraries, publishing houses and univs in 90 countries; 4,428,000 vols in 140 foreign languages; Dir E. YU. GENIEVA; publ. *'Otkrytyj Dostup: Biblioteki za rubezhom'* (Open Access: Libraries around the World).

Moscow State University Scientific Library: 103009 Moscow, Mokhovaya 10.

Russian National Public Library for Science and Technology: 103031 Moscow, Kuznetskii Most 12; tel. (495) 925-92-88; fax (495) 921-98-62; e-mail root@gpntb.ru; internet www.gpntb.ru; f. 1958; permanent contacts with 7,000 enterprises in Russia and other republics of the former USSR; 8m. books, periodicals and documents on natural sciences, technology, agriculture and medicine; special collection of domestic literature of limited distribution; 24 original databases; Dir Dr A. I. ZEMSKOV; publs *Journal of Research, Scientific and Technical Libraries*, *Proceedings of Crimea Conferences*.

Russian Peoples' Friendship University Library: 117198 Moscow, Miklukho-Maklaia 6; tel. (495) 434-86-32; fax (495) 433-15-11; e-mail lib.rudn@gmail.com; internet lib.rudn.ru; f. 1960, present status 2008; organizes Russian language programme, books and art exhibitions; 1.8m. vols, 280 periodicals; Dir ELENA LOTOVA; Deputy Dir SVETLANA FOMICHEVA.

Russian State Archive of Modern History: 103132 Moscow, ul. Ilinka 12; tel. (495) 206-50-06; fax (495) 206-23-21; f. 1991; based on the Archive of the General Department of the Communist Party of the fmr USSR; Dir N. G. TOMILINA.

Russian State Archives of Old Documents: 119992 GSP-2 Moscow, G-435, Bolshaya Pirogovskaya ul. 17; tel. (495) 580-87-23; fax (8) 499-30-98; e-mail rgada@archives

.ru; annals, charts of grand dukes and independent princes, legal documents of Early Russia (11th–18th centuries), documents of central and patrimonial archives of nobility and gentry, archives of church establishments and the largest monasteries of Russia; Dir MIKHAIL R. RYZHENKOV.

Russian State Archive of Social-Political History: 109999 Moscow, Bol. Dmitrovka 15; tel. (495) 629-97-26; fax (495) 692-90-17; e-mail rgaspi@inbox.ru; internet www.rgaspi.ru; f. 1920s; 10,000 vols; incl. colln from Central Archive of Komsomol; Dir Dr OLEG VLADIMIROVICH NAUMOV; publ. *Scientific Information Bulletin* (1 a year).

Russian State Archives of Sound Recording: 107005 Moscow, 2-ya Baumanskaya ul. 3; tel. (495) 261-13-00; f. 1932; sound recordings from 1902 of artistic and documentary nature; Dir V. A. KOLIADA.

Russian State Archives of the National Economy: 119435 Moscow, Bol. Pirogovskaya ul. 17; tel. (495) 245-26-64; documents of the state bodies in charge of management of industries, agriculture, transportation, communication, construction and of central bodies of financing, planning and statistics (1917–); Dir E. A. TYURINA.

Russian State Army Archives: 125212 Moscow, ul. Admirala Makarova 29; tel. (495) 159-80-91; documents of military authorities of the RSFSR and the USSR, of the military areas, detachments, units and establishments of the Soviet Army and Frontier Guards (1918–40); Dir V. D. ZAPOROZHNICHENKO.

Russian State Art Library: 107031 Moscow, Bol. Dmitrovka 8/1; tel. and fax (495) 692-06-53; e-mail bisk@liart.ru; internet www.liart.ru; f. 1922; 1,701,000 items (books, periodicals, press cuttings, engravings, sketches, postcards, photographs, posters); Dir A. A. KOLGANOVA.

Russian State Library for the Blind: 129090 Moscow, Protopopovsky per. 9; tel. and fax (495) 680-26-14; e-mail admin@rgbs.ru; internet www.rgbs.ru; f. 1920; acts as methodical, coordinating and resources centre for special libraries throughout Russia; 1,320,000 vols; Dir T. N. ELFIMOVA; publs *The Visually-impaired and Society* (12 a year), *Correspondence School for the Parents* (2 a year).

Russian State Literature and Art Archives: 125212 Moscow, Vyborgskaya 3, korp. 2; tel. (499) 159-76-85; fax (499) 159-73-86; e-mail rgali@list.ru; internet rgali.ru; f. 1941; MSS, art works and documents of prominent Russian and Soviet writers, composers, artists, theatrical and cinema workers; documents of state and public organizations concerned with the arts (18th century–present day); 1,503,825 vols; Dir T. M. GORYAEVA; publ. *Vstrechi s proshlym* (irregular).

Russian State Military Historical Archives: 107005 Moscow, ul. 2-ya Baumanskaya 3; tel. (495) 261-20-70; fax (495) 267-18-66; f. 1797; documents of central and district military administrations and establishments of the Russian Army, private collections of prominent generals, military leaders and historians (end 17th century–1918); Dir I. O. GARKUSHA.

Scientific Library of the State Tretyakov Gallery: 113035 Moscow, 1-i Kadashevskii per. 14; tel. (495) 953-41-85; fax (495) 953-10-51; f. 1899; stock relating to Russian and Soviet art; 400,000 vols; Dir Z. P. SHERGINA.

Scientific S. I. Taneev Library of the Moscow P. I. Tchaikovsky State Conservatoire: 125009 Moscow, ul. B. Nikitskaya 13/6; tel. and fax (495) 629 6062; e-mail rassina@lib.mosconsv.ru; internet www.taneevlib.ru; f. 1866; Russian and foreign music and books on music; complete files of many Russian and foreign musical periodicals; 1,250,941 vols; Dir E. B. RASSINA.

State Archives of the Russian Federation: 119992 Moscow, Bol. Pirogovskaya ul. 17; tel. and fax (495) 245-12-87; e-mail garf@online.ru; internet www.garf.narod.ru; f. 1992; 5,513,107 items; Dir SERGEY V. MIRONENKO; publ. *Archive of Contemporary Russian History* (3 series: catalogues, documents, research).

State Central Polytechnic Library: 101000 Moscow, Politekhnicheskii pr-d 2; tel. (495) 928-64-65; f. 1964; 3m. vols, incl. periodicals; Dir N. G. REINBERG.

State Medical Library of Russia: 117418 Moscow, Nakhimovskaya ul. 49; tel. (495) 128-33-46; fax (495) 128-87-39; e-mail loginov@server.scsml.rssi.ru; f. 1919; 3m. vols; Dir Dr B. R. LOGINOV; publs *Medicine and Public Health* (bibliographical index), *New Medical Books*.

State Public Historical Library of Russia: 101990 Moscow, Starosadskii per. 9; tel. (495) 925-65-14; fax (495) 928-02-84; e-mail maf@shpl.ru; internet www.shpl.ru; f. 1938; 3,229,696 vols, including 74,695 in the Department of Rare Books, 1,107,604 items in the Serials Department; special collection of 10,119 unofficial publications; Dir Dr MIKHAIL AFANASIEV.

Turgenev Library No. 13: 101000 Moscow, Bobrov per. 6, str. 2; tel. (495) 921-00-52; fax (495) 921-99-17; e-mail biblioteka@turgenev.ru; Dir TATYANA KOROBKINA.

Institution of Russian Academy of Education Ushinsky State Pedagogical Library: 119017 Moscow, Bol. Tolmachevskii per. 3; tel. (495) 951-05-85; fax (495) 953-22-61; e-mail gnpbu@gnpbu.ru; internet www.gnpbu.ru; f. 1925; 2m. units; Dir TAMARA S. MARKAROVA (acting); publ. *Literatura po pedagogicheskim naukam i narodnomu obrazovaniyu* (4 a year).

Nalchik

Kabardino-Balkar State University Library: 360004 Nalchik, ul. Chernyshevskogo 173; 738,000 vols; Dir E. D. MIGUCHKINA.

Nizhnii Novgorod

Nizhnii Novgorod N. I. Lobachevsky State University Central Library: 603091 Nizhnii Novgorod, pr. Gagarina 23; tel. (8312) 31-11-54; 1,210,470 vols; Dir A. I. SAVENKOV.

Novosibirsk

Novosibirsk State University Library: 630090 Novosibirsk, Akademgorodok; tel. (3832) 65-62-60; 450,000 vols; Dir L. G. TORSHENOVA.

Scientific—Technical Centre for Chemical Information: 630090 Novosibirsk, pr. Akad. Lavrenteva 9; tel. (383) 330-96-62; attached to Russian Acad. of Sciences; Head Prof. I. A. GRIGORR'EV.

State Public Scientific and Technical Library of the Siberian Department of the Russian Academy of Sciences: 630200 Novosibirsk, Voskhod 15; tel. (3832) 66-18-60; fax (3832) 66-33-65; e-mail office@spsl.nsc.ru; internet www.spsl.nsc.ru; f. 1918; acts as reference, loan, research and coordinating centre for 65 academic institutes located in Siberia and the Far East; 14m. vols; Dir Prof. B. S. ELEPOV.

Omsk

Omsk State University Library: 644077 Omsk, pr. Mira 55A; 182,000 vols; Dir L. A. BALAKINA.

Perm

Perm State University Scientific Library: 614990 Perm, ul. Bukireva 15; tel. (3422) 39-64-80; e-mail library@psu.ru; internet www.library.psu.ru; f. 1916; 1,467,000 vols; Dir NATALIA YAKSHINA.

Petrozavodsk

Petrozavodsk State University Library: 185640 Petrozavodsk, pr. Lenina 33; tel. (8142) 71-10-44; 850,000 vols; Dir MARINA P. OTLIVANCHIK.

Rostov-on-Don

'Yu. A. Zhdanov' Zone Scientific Library at Southern Federal University: 344006 Rostov-on-Don, Pushkinskaya 148; tel. and fax (8632) 64-08-56; e-mail zaharova@sfedu.ru; internet www.library.sfedu.ru; f. 1915; attached Museum of the History of Books; 2,515,102 vols; Dir SVETLANA A. BONDARENKO; publ. *Donskaya Speech*.

St Petersburg

All-Russian Geological Library: 199106 St Petersburg, Srednii pr. 74; tel. and fax (812) 321-72-12; e-mail vgb@vsegei.ru; f. 1882; scientific and technical literature; 1m. books, monographs, periodicals and special maps; Dir OLGA K. ERMILOVA; publ. *Geologicheskaya literatura* (Geological Literature, 1 a year).

Department of the Art and Museum Book Collections of the State Russian Museum: 191186 St Petersburg, Inzhenernaya ul. 4; tel. (812) 595-42-08; fax (812) 314-41-53; e-mail library@rusmuseum.ru; internet library.rusmuseum.ru; f. 1898; 185,000 vols; Dir YULIA JURKINA.

Library of the National Pushkin Museum: 191186 St Petersburg, nab. Moiki 12; tel. (812) 571-06-19; fax (812) 315-73-79; e-mail vmp@mail.admiral.ru; internet www.museumpushkin.ru; f. 1953; collections of works by Russian authors incl. Pushkin, V. A. Krylov and S. Mazkov; 80,000 vols; Dir M. V. BOKARIUS.

Library of the Russian Academy of Sciences: 199034 St Petersburg, Birzhevaya liniya 1; tel. (812) 328-35-92; fax (812) 328-74-36; e-mail ban@rasl.nw.ru; internet www.ban.ru; f. 1714; 20,353,000 vols; collection of 19,000 MSS, 250,000 rare books, including 834 incunabula; 123,000 maps, 1.8m. publications of the Russian Academy of Sciences; acts as inter-library loan and reference service, exchange centre and book publisher; conducts research in library science, bibliography, palaeography and conservation; coordinates network of 31 specialized libraries in the Academy's research institutes; Dir Dr VALERII P. LEONOV; publs *Bibliography of Publications of the Russian Academy of Sciences* (1 a year), *Book in Russia* (1 a year), *Quarterly Bibliography*.

Library of the State Hermitage Museum: St Petersburg, Dvortsovaya nab. 34; f. 1762; over 500,000 vols; on painting, sculpture and all branches of graphic arts throughout the centuries; Dir MAKAROVA.

Mariinsky Theatre library: 190000 St Petersburg, Teatralnaya pl., 1; tel. (12) 326-4164; e-mail cml@mariinsky.ru; contains one of the largest collns in the world of Russian music in MSS, single copies, first edns, etc., 1,500 copies of Russian vaudeville scores, 200 MSS of ballet scores, and a large collection of opera scores incl. 1,000 foreign operas; Dir Prof. Dr MARIA N. SHCHERBAKOVA.

Music Library of the St Petersburg Conservatoire: St Petersburg, Teatralnaya pl. 3; tel. (812) 571-32-23; fax (812) 312-89-74; e-mail admlib@conservatory.ru; internet biblio.conservatory.ru; f. 1862; 583,000 vols, incl. 187,000 Russian and foreign works on music, 338,000 scores, 7,600 MSS, 490 incunabula; Dir HELLEN NEKRASOVA; publs *Musicus* (4 a year), *Opera Musicologica* (4 a year).

Music Library of the St Petersburg Dmitri Shostakovich State Philharmonic Society: 191011 St Petersburg, Mikhailovskaya ul. 2; f. 1882; 200,000 scores and books on music, 40,000 engravings, lithographs and paintings of musicians, composers, etc; 1m. newspaper cuttings; Dir G. L. RETROVSKAYA.

National Library of Russia: 191069 St Petersburg, Sadovaya ul. 18; tel. (812) 310-98-50; fax (812) 310-61-48; e-mail office@nlr.ru; internet www.nlr.ru; f. 1795; 32,064,000 items, including a large collection of incunabula and MSS; Dir VLADIMIR N. ZAITSEV; publ. *PNB-Informazia* (12 a year).

Russian State Historical Archives: 190000 St Petersburg, Angliiskaya nab. 4; tel. (812) 311-09-26; fax (812) 311-22-52; f. 1918; documents of central state bodies of the Russian Empire, state and private banks, railways, industrial, trade and other companies; private collections of prominent political and public figures, etc. (18th century–1917); 350,000 vols; Dir A. R. SOKOLOV; publ. *Herald* (irregular).

Russian State Naval Archives: St Petersburg, Millionnaya ul. 36; tel. (812) 315-90-54; f. 1724; documents of central institutions of the Russian pre-revolutionary and Soviet Navy and prominent naval officers (17th century–1940); 1,219,454 vols; Dir V. G. MISHANOV.

St Petersburg State University M. Gorky Scientific Library: 199034 St Petersburg, Universitetskaya nab. 7/9; tel. and fax (812) 328-27-41; e-mail marina@lib.pu.ru; internet www.lib.pu.ru; f. 1783; 7m. vols, 100,000 rare books, 1,000 MSS; Dir N. A. SHESHINA; publs *Pravovedenie* (6 a year), *Vestnik St. Petersburg* (24 a year).

St Petersburg Theatrical Library: St Petersburg, ul. Zodchego Rossi 2; f. 1756; 800,000 vols of plays and works on theatrical subjects, department of French works with first editions of Corneille; MSS and letters by Chekhov, Turgenev, Diaghilev, Fokine; department of stage designs by Bakst, Benoit, etc; department of classical and contemporary fiction; Dir ANASTASIYA G. GAI.

Scientific Library attached to the Russian Institute for the History of Arts: 190000 St Petersburg, Isaakievskaya pl. 5; tel. (812) 315-55-87; fax (812) 315-72-02; f. 1912; 300,000 books and periodicals on theatre, music, cinematography, history of literature and art, fiction, philosophy, aesthetics, folklore; Chief Librarian I. V. KYTMANOVA.

Scientific Library of the Russian Academy of Arts: 199034 St Petersburg, Universitetskaya nab. 17; Moscow Branch: 119034 Moscow, ul. Prechistenka 21; f. 1757; 471,445 vols on art, architecture, applied and folk arts, including rare 16th- and 17th-century vols and a notable collection of 18th-century works on architecture; Dir L. S. POLAYKOVA; Dir N. V. KOMAROVA.

Samara

Russian State Scientific and Technical Archives: 443096 Samara, ul. Michurina 58; tel. (846) 336-17-81; fax (846) 336-17-85 also: Moscow, Profsoyuznaya ul. 82; tel. (495) 335-00-95; f. 1964; documentation of research and devt projects in industry, construction, transport and communications; invention applications; Dir IRINA N. DAVYDOVA.

Samara State University Library: 443086 Samara, ul. Potapova 64/163; 245,000 vols; Dir N. I. PARANINA.

Saransk

Mordovian N. P. Ogarev State University Library: 430000 Saransk, Bolshevistskaya ul. 68; tel. (8342) 4-49-91; f. 1931; 1,954,861 vols; Dir Doc. A. V. SMOLYANOV.

Saratov

V. A. Artisevich Zonal Scientific Library: 410000 Saratov, Universitetskaya ul. 42; tel. (845) 227-14-80; fax (845) 251-40-00; e-mail library@sgu.ru; internet library.sgu.ru/nbsgu; f. 1909; 2,861,763 vols; Dir IRINA V. LEBEDEVA.

Syktyvkar

Syktyvkar State University Library: 167001 Syktyvkar, Oktyabrskii pr. 55; tel. (8212) 43-94-51; fax (8212) 43-72-86; f. 1972; 560,980 vols; 812 MSS and books published in Russia before the 18th century; 22 personal archives of scientists; Dir NONNA F. AKOPOVA; publs *Rubezh* (4 a year), *Vestnik* (1 a year).

Tomsk

Russian State Historical Archive of the Far East: Tomsk, ul. K. Marksa 26; tel. (3822) 2-29-15; formerly Central State Archive of the RSFSR of the Far East (TsGA RSFSR DV).

Tomsk State University Library: 634010 Tomsk, Leninskii pr. 34a; tel. (3822) 2-44-69; 3,320,000 vols; Dir E. SYNTIN.

Tver

Tver State Medical Academy Library: 170000 Tver, ul. Sovetskaya 4; tel. (822) 33-27-26; fax (822) 33-43-09; f. 1954; 468 vols; Dir O. V. TULTSEVA.

Tyumen

Tyumen State University Library: 625036 Tyumen, ul. Volodarskogo 38; 382,000 vols; Dir L. P. KRYUKOVA.

Ufa

Bashkir State University Library: 450074 Ufa, ul. Zaki Validi 32; tel. (3472) 73-66-26; fax (3472) 73-67-78; e-mail jane@ic.bashedu.ru; internet www.bashlib.ru; f. 1909; 1,405,779 vols; Dir E. G. GELVANOVSKAYA.

National Library of Bashkortostan: 450000 Ufa, ul. Lenina 4; tel. and fax (3472) 22-04-89; e-mail bashnl@mail.ru; internet bashnl.ru; f. 1836; collecting, processing, storage, use of information resources; 3.3m. vols; Dir AZAT IBRAGIMOV.

Vladikavkaz

North-Ossetian State University Library: 362000 Vladikavkaz, ul. Vatutina 46; 76,000 vols; Dir K. L. KOCHISOV.

Vladimir

Central State Archives of the Nation's Documentary Films and Photographs: Vladimir, Letneperevozinskaya ul. 9; tel. (0922) 2-79-95 also: Moscow oblast, Krasnogorsk, Rechnaya ul. 1; tel. (495) 563-08-45; topical films, newsreels and historical material which was not included in finished films, negatives of documentary photographs (1854–); Dir L. P. ZAPRYAGAEVA.

Vladivostok

Far Eastern State University Central Library: 690652 Vladivostok, Okeanskii pr. 37/41; 700,000 vols; Dir A. G. TRETYAKOVA.

Voronezh

Scientific Library of Voronezh State University: 394000 Voronezh, pr. Revolyutsii 24; tel. (473) 255-35-59; fax (473) 220-82-58; e-mail minakov@lib.vsu.ru; internet www.lib.vsu.ru; f. 1918; 3,176,406 vols; Dir ARKADY MINAKOV; Chief Librarian LYUBOV KATZ.

Yakutsk

Scientific Library of North-Eastern Federal University: 677018 Yakutsk, Belinsky St 58; tel. (4112) 36-38-82; fax (4112) 35-62-95; e-mail libr.ysu@mail.ru; internet www.ysu.ru/library; f. 1934; compiles and publishes bibliographic indexes; 1,129,971 vols; Dir MAXIMOVA TATIANA SEMENOVNA; Deputy Dir TARABUKINA SARGYLANA KHRISTOPHOROVNA.

Yalutorovsk

Centre for the Preservation of the Reserve Collection: Tyumen oblast, Yalutorovsk, Ishimskaya ul. 136; tel. (34535) 2-29-87; formed from Central State Archive Reserve Collection of Documents of the State Archive Collection of the USSR (TsGA SF SSSR).

Yaroslavl

P. G. Demidov Yaroslavl State University Library: 150000 Yaroslavl, ul. Sovetskaya 14; tel. (4852) 79-16-34; internet www.uniyar.ac.ru; 774,324 vols; Dir I. V. DENEZHKINA.

Museums and Art Galleries

Arkhangelsk

Arkhangelsk State Museum: 163061 Arkhangelsk, pl. V. I. Lenina 2; tel. (8182) 3-66-79; f. 1737; contains 150,000 items featuring the history of the North coast area of Russia, since ancient times; large collection of archaeology, ethnography, documents and photographs; library of 30,000 vols; Dir YU. P. PROKOPEV.

Arkhangelsk State Museum of Fine Arts: 163061 Arkhangelsk, nab. Lenina 79; tel. (8182) 3-26-73; e-mail m1444@mail.museum.ru; internet www.museum.ru/m1444; contains over 150,000 items of ancient North and Western European art; library of 30,000 vols; Dir M. V. MITKEVICH.

Ashaga-stal

Stalsky Memorial Museum: 368765 Dagestan, Suleiman-Stalskii raion, Ashaga-stal; internet www.museum.ru/m1802; f. 1950; exhibits on the history of Dagestan literature, former home of poet Suleiman Stalskii; library of 20,000 vols; Dir LIDIYA M. STALSKAYA.

Astrakhan

Astrakhan State B. M. Kustodiev Gallery: Astrakhan, ul. Sverdlova 81; tel. and fax (8512) 22-66-65; f. 1918; fine arts; library of 15,000 vols; Dir L. J. ILINA.

Barnaul

State Art Museum of Altai Territory: Barnaul, pr. Lenina 88; tel. (3852) 61-25-10; fax (3852) 61-06-70; e-mail muzei@ab.ru; internet muzei.ab.ru; f. 1959; large collection since 16th century, of icons, paintings, sculptures, wood carvings, ceramics, national costumes; library of 13,526 vols; Dir I. K. GALKINA.

Belinsky

Belinsky, V. G., State Museum: Penza oblast, Belinsky, ul. Belinskogo 11; f. 1938; 31,280 exhibits on the life and work of the literary critic V. G. Belinsky; Curator I. A. GERASEKIN.

Borodino

Borodino State War and History Museum: 143240 Moscow oblast, Mozhaisk, selo Borodino; tel. (963) 86-32-23; fax (963) 86-32-22; e-mail pr@borodino.ru; internet www.borodino.ru; f. 1839; researches into 1812 campaign, the Battle of Borodino and the 1941–45 war; 60,000 exhibits incl. material on the Battle of Borodino; library of 12,100 vols; Dir MIKHAIL R. CHEREPASHENETS; Curator GALINA N. NEVSKAYA.

Bryansk

Bryansk State Museum of Soviet Fine Arts: Bryansk, ul. Gagarina 19; Dir B. F. FAENKOV.

Cheboksary

Chuvash Art Museum: 428008 Cheboksary, Kalinina 60; tel. (8352) 22-07-04; f. 1939; 12,000 exhibits, mainly modern Russian, Soviet and Chuvash artists and traditional Chuvash decorative art; library of 15,000 vols; Dir N. SADYUKOV.

Chelyabinsk

Chelyabinsk State Picture Gallery: Chelyabinsk, ul. Truda 92A; 5,000 items; Dir I. F. TKACHENKO.

Ekaterinburg

Ekaterinburg Picture Gallery: Ekaterinburg, ul. Vainera 11; f. 1746; Western European, Russian and Soviet artists and objects from the Kishisk foundries; Dir E. V. KHAMTSOV.

State Amalgamated Museum of the Writers of the Urals: 620075 Ekaterinburg, Tolmacheva ul. 41; tel. (343) 371-46-52; f. 1940 (amalgamated 1980); study and popularization of the heritage of the writers of the Urals, collns incl. the personal belongings and archives of Mamin-Sibiryak, Bazhov and other Ural writers, illustrations to edns of their works and various other artworks, 34,723 items in all; incorporates the House of D. N. Mamin-Sibiryak in Ekaterinburg, the House of P. P. Bazhov, the House of F. M. Reshetnikov; library of 37,700 vols; Dir V. P. PLOTNIKOV.

Ural Geological Museum: 620144 Ekaterinburg, ul. Kuibysheva 30; tel. (343) 257-31-09; fax (343) 257-48-38; f. 1937; Dir YURI A. POLENOV.

Gagarin

Yurii Gagarin Memorial Museum: 215010 Gagarin, ul. Gerzena 7; tel. (08135) 4-88-37; fax (08135) 4-88-37; f. 1970; exhibits depicting the life and career of Yurii Alekseevich Gagarin (the first man in space) and other early Soviet cosmonauts, and the designers of the spaceships; Dir MARIA STEPANOVA.

Ivanovo

Ivanovo Museum of Art: 153002 Ivanovo, pr. Lenina 33; tel. (0932) 32-65-04; f. 1960; Greek, Roman and Ancient Egyptian art, icons, 18th–20th-century Russian art; library of 7,500 vols; Dir L. W. WOLOWENSKAYA.

Kaluga

Kaluga Museum of Art: Kaluga, ul. Lenina 104; 2,700 exhibits; Dir. A. V. KAZAK.

Tsiolkovsky, K. E., State Museum of the History of Cosmonautics: Kaluga, ul. Koroleva 2; tel. and fax (842) 57-43-33; e-mail director@mkosmos.kaluga.ru; internet www.museum.ru/gmik; f. 1967; contains K. E. Tsiolkovsky's scientific works, history of rocket technique and cosmonautics, large collection of objects relating to astronautics and rocket technology, including the first experimental rocket launched in 1933, the *Sputniks* and *Luniks*, models of orbital stations; library of 35,600 vols; Dir EVGENY KOUZIN.

Kazan

Kazan State A. M. Gorky Memorial Museum: Kazan, ul. Gorkogo 10; exhibits illustrating Gorky's life in the flat where he lived and wrote.

National Museum of the Republic of Tatarstan: Tatarstan, 420111 Kazan, Kremlevskaya ul. 2; tel. (8432) 92-71-62; fax (8432) 92-14-84; e-mail tatar_museum@mail.ru; internet www.tatar.museum.ru; f. 1894; history, archaeology, ethnography, natural resources and decorative applied art of Tatarstan, Russia and other countries; library of 12,000 vols; 54 brs; Gen. Man. G. S. MYKHANOV.

State Museum of Fine Arts of the Republic of Tatarstan: 420015 Kazan, ul. K. Marksa 64; tel. (8432) 36-69-21; fax (8432) 36-18-65; internet www.kcn.ru/tat_en/culture/art_museum/home.htm; f. 1958; large collections of Russian, Western European and Soviet paintings; 10,000 exhibits; Dir ANATOLIY A. SLASTUNIN.

Tatar Historical Museum (House of V. I. Lenin): Tatarstan, Kazan, ul. Ulyanova 58; 10,000 exhibits including documents, photographs, works of art and other exhibits relating to Lenin's life.

Kirov

Kirov Victor and Apollinaris Vasnetsov Museum: 610000 Kirov, ul. K. Marksa 70; tel. (8332) 62-26-46; f. 1910; Russian and Western European sculpture, paintings, engravings and decorative arts; library of 14,000 vols; Dir ALLA A. NOSKOVA.

Kirovsk

Polar Alpine Botanical Garden Institute: 184230 Murmansk region, Kirovsk; tel. (81555) 63350; fax (81555) 79448; e-mail pabgi@aprec.ru; attached to Russian Acad. of Sciences; Dir Prof. VLADIMIR K. ZHIROV.

Klin

Tchaikovsky House-Museum: 141600 Klin, ul. Tchaikovskogo 48; tel. (49624) 5-81-96; fax (49624) 5-84-67; e-mail gdmch@dol.ru; internet www.russianmuseums.info/m443; f. 1894; composer's last residence and first Russian musical museum; contains 216,108 documents and museum treasures associated with the life and work of Tchaikovsky and other Russian musicians; library of 57,375 vols; Dir GALINA I. BELONOVICH.

Komsomolsk-on-Amur

Komsomolsk-on-Amur Museum of Soviet Fine Arts: Komsomolsk-on-Amur, pr. Mira 50; 5,000 exhibits; Dir E. Y. TURCHINSKAYA.

Konchanskoe-Suvorovskoe

Suvorov Museum: 174435 Novogorodskaya oblast, Borovichskii raion, selo Konchanskoe-Suvorovskoe; tel. (81664) 9-85-33; internet www.museum.ru/m669; the museum fea-

tures the main periods in the life of General A. V. Suvorov; Dir V. P. MALYSHEVA.

Kostroma

Kostroma Museum of Fine Arts: Kostroma, pr. Mira 5; f. 1913; 5,700 items; collecting, exhibitions, sales, scientific and historical Russian art research, art restoration; library of 6,410 vols; special collections of Ancient Russian religious books and the work of Y. Chestnyakov; Dir V. Y. IGNATEV.

Krasnoyarsk

Krasnoyarsk Arts Museum: 660097 Krasnoyarsk, Parizhskoi Kommuny ul. 20; tel. (3912) 27-25-58; f. 1958; Russian art (including icons), Russian pre-revolutionary applied art, Siberian folk art and Soviet art; painting, sculpture, graphic art, applied arts; library of 7,700 vols; Dir A. F. EFIMOVSKII; publ. *Surikov Readings* (2 a year).

Krasnoyarsk Museum and Historical Centre: Krasnoyarsk, pl. Mira 1; tel. (3912) 23-82-02; f. 1987; Dir MIKHAIL SHUBSKY.

Kursk

Kursk Art Gallery: 305016 Kursk, ul. Sovetskaya 3; tel. and fax (4712) 54-87-21; e-mail gallery@sovtest.ru; internet www.kursk.amr-museum.ru; f. 1935; Russian, Soviet and European painting and sculpture; library of 50,000 vols; Dir I. A. PRIPACHKIN.

Lermontovo

Lermontov State Museum 'Tarkhany': 442280 Penza oblast, Belinskii raion, Lermontovo; tel. and fax (84153) 2-07-99; e-mail muslerm@sura.ru; internet www.tarhany.ru; f. 1939; life and work of M. Yu. Lermontov; library of 15,000 vols; Dir TAMARA MIKHAILOVNA MELNIKOVA; publ. *Tarkhansky vestnik* (bulletin, 1 a year).

Makhachkala

Dagestan Museum of Fine Arts: Makhachkala, ul. Markova 45; 7,000 exhibits.

Maloyaroslavets

Maloyaroslavets Museum of Military History of 1812: 249050 Maloyaroslavets, Moskovskaya ul. 27; tel. (08431) 2-27-11; f. 1939; collection and study of exhibits of the 1812 war; library of 1,100 vols; Dir N. V. KOTLYAKOVA; publ. *Nashe Nasledie* (Our Heritage, 6 a year).

Melikhovo

Chekhov, A. P. State Literature and Memorial Museum-Reserve: 142326 Melikhovo, Chekhovsky region, Moscow oblast; tel. (496) 723-64-53; fax (499) 270-79-91; e-mail melikhovo@mail.ru; internet www.chekhov-melikhovo.com; f. 1944; house where the writer lived and worked during 1892–99; library of 28,514 vols; Dir K. V. BOBKOV.

Miass

Natural Science Museum of the Ilmen State Reserve: 456301 Chelyabinsk oblast, Miass 1; tel. (35135) 5-48-90; fax (35135) 5-02-86; e-mail founds@imin.urc.ac.ru; f. 1930; the museum shows the mineralogical resources of the Ilmen State Reserve, the grounds of which contain more than 250 minerals; library of 17,000 vols; Dir Dr S. N. NIKANDROV; publs *Trudy Ilmenskogo Zapovednika, Uralsky mineralogichesky Sbornik*.

Moscow

Anuchin Institute and Museum of Anthropology of Moscow State University: 125009 Moscow Mokhovaya str. 11; tel. (495) 629-44-49; fax (495) 629-75-21; e-mail anthropos.msu@mail.ru; internet www .antropos.msu.ru; f. 1879; 5 depts: laboratories of anthropogenesis, human diversity, anthropo-ecology, human auxology, human morphology and the Museum of Anthropology; about 470,000 items; anthropology and archaeology of the Stone Age; collns from outstanding Russian explorers; Mousterian Man from Teshik-Tash and Staroseliye; Mesolithic burials from the Dnieper Region in the Ukraine; library of 30,000 vols; Dir Prof. Dr ALEXANDRA BUZHILOVA; publs *Antropologia*, *Vestnik MGU*.

Central Museum of Aviation and Cosmonautics: 125167 Moscow, Krasnoarmeiskaya 4; tel. (495) 212-73-01; f. 1924; to record the national development of aeronautics and astronautics; contains original full-size aircraft, spacecraft, recovered space exploration vehicles, instruments, flight clothing, accessories of technical, historical and biographical interest; library of 15,800 vols; Dir P. F. VYALIKOV.

Central Museum of Armed Forces: 129110 Moscow, I-110, ul. Sovetskoi Armii 2, a/ya 125; tel. and fax (495) 681-18-80; e-mail cmvs-secretariat@mail.ru; internet www.cmaf.ru; f. 1919; military exhibits; library of 90,000 vols; Dir ALEXANDER K. NIKONOV.

Chekhov, A. P., House-Museum: 103001 Moscow, Sadovaya-Kudrinskaya 6; tel. (495) 291-61-54; f. 1954; flat where the writer lived from 1886–1890; branch of the State Literature Museum.

Dostoevsky, F. M., Museum: 127473 Moscow, ul. Dostoyevskogo 2; tel. (495) 681-10-85; fax (495) 680-30-17; e-mail litmuz@arc .ru; f. 1928; affiliated to the State Literature Museum; exhibits illustrating Dostoyevsky's life, organized in the flat where he lived until sixteen years old; Dir GALINA B. PONOMAREVA.

Fersman Mineralogical Museum: 119071 Moscow, Leninsky pr. 18, korp. 2; tel. (495) 954-39-00; fax (495) 952-48-50; e-mail mineral@fmm.ru; internet www.fmm.ru; f. 1716; attached to Russian Acad. of Sciences; 150,000 mineral samples from throughout the world; library of 16,700 vols; Dir Prof. V. K. GARANIN; publ. *New Data on Minerals* (1 a year).

'Glinka, M. I.', State Central Museum of Musical Culture: 125047 Moscow, ul. Fadeeva 4; tel. (495) 972-32-37; fax (495) 972-32-55; internet www.museum.ru/glinka; f. 1943; based on the Museum of the Moscow Conservatoire; collects archives, MSS and memorabilia; musical instruments; musical iconography; records and tape recordings; music, books, posters, programmes—in all, 800,000 items; exhibits: musical instruments of the world; Russian musical culture; Dir-Gen. A. D. PANIUSHKIN.

Gogol, N. V., House-Museum and Gogol Study Centre: 121019 Moscow, Nikitsky bul. 7; tel. and fax (495) 291-15-50; e-mail vik@systel.ru; f. 1974; exhibits illustrating life and work of Gogol; library of 200,000 vols, Gogol spec. colln of 600 vols and MSS; Dir VERA P. VIKULOVA.

Gorky, A. M., Memorial Museum: Moscow 121069, Malaya Nikitskaya ul. 6/2; tel. (495) 290-05-35; f. 1965 in the house where the author lived; contains Gorky's private library of 10,000 vols, and his collection of Oriental arts (ivory); Dir L. P. BYKOVTSEVA.

Gorky, A. M., Museum: 121069 Moscow, ul. Povarskaya 25A; tel. (495) 291-51-30; f. 1937; 44,500 items, including literary and photographic documents, works of art, memorabilia; Dir L. P. BYKOVTSEVA.

Moscow Kremlin Museums: 103073 Moscow, Kremlin; tel. (495) 695-89-23; fax (495) 621-63-23; e-mail head@kremlin.museum.ru; internet www.kreml.ru; f. 1806; monuments built from late 15th to 20th centuries; incl. cathedrals-museums: Assumption Cathedral, Archangel Cathedral, Annunciation Cathedral, Church of Deposition of Robe of the Holy Virgin, Palace of Patriarch of 17th century with Church of Twelve Apostles, bell tower of Ivan the Great with the belfry and the State Armoury Chamber-treasury; collns of State Historical and Cultural Museum-Preserve comprise more than 60,000 historical, cultural and artistic monuments; library of 49,000 vols; Dir YELENA GAGARINA.

Attached Sites:

Armoury: 103073 Moscow, Kremlin; f. 1857; Museum since 1806; 3,500 artworks: ancient state regalia, diplomatic gifts to Russian Tsars, vestments of Russian Church hierarchs of 14th–18th centuries, coronation suits of Russian Emperors and dresses of Empresses, artworks by Russian gold and silversmiths of 12th–20th centuries, monuments of Byzantine and Western European art of 15th–19th centuries, ceremonial weapons, and ancient carriages.

Kremlin Cathedrals: 103073 Moscow, Kremlin; The cathedrals around the Cathedral Square (Sobornaya ploshchad) include, among others, the following: Cathedral of the Assumption (f. 1479); icons of the 14th–17th centuries; throne of Ivan the Terrible; Cathedral of the Annunciation (f. 1489); iconostasis by leading artists of the 14th–15th centuries. Archangel Cathedral (1508); tombs of Ivan Kalita and other Russian Grand Dukes and Czars. Rizpolozhenskii Cathedral (f. 1485). Cathedral of the Twelve Apostles and Patriarch's Palace; 17th-century items of applied decorative art.

Main Botanical Garden 'N. V. Tsitsin': 127276 Moscow, Botanicheskaya ul. 4; tel. (495) 977-90-44; fax (495) 977-91-72; e-mail info@gbsad.ru; internet www.gbsad.ru; f. 1945; attached to Russian Acad. of Sciences; br. in Cheboksary; Dir Dr ALEXANDER S. DEMIDOV; publs *Bulletin* (2 a year), *Newsletter* (2 a year).

Marx-Engels Museum: c/o Russian State Archive of Modern History, 103132 Moscow, ul. Ilinka 12; f. 1962; 2,000 exhibits descriptive of the lives of Marx and Engels; Dir V. N. KUZNETSOV.

Moscow Arts Theatre Museum: 103009 Moscow, pr-d Khudozhestvennogo Teatra 3A; tel. (495) 229-00-80; f. 1923; Dir V. S. DAVIDOV.

Attached Museums:

Nemirovich-Danchenko, V., Flat-Museum: 103009 Moscow, Ul. Nemirovicha-Danchenko 5/7, kv. 52; tel. (495) 209-53-91; f. 1944; illustrating career of Nemirovich-Danchenko.

Stanislavsky, K. S., House-Museum: 103009 Moscow, Ul. Stanislavskogo 6; tel. (495) 229-28-55; f. 1948; attached to Theatre Museum; deals with Stanislavsky's work and the theatrical career of People's Artist, M. P. Lilina.

Moscow State University Museum of Zoology: 125009 Moscow, ul. Bol. Nikitskaya 6; tel. (495) 203-64-93; fax (495) 203-27-17; e-mail zmmu@zmmu.msu.ru; internet zmmu.msu.ru; f. 1791; systematics, speciation, zoogeography, fauna research, phylogenetics; library of 190,000 vols; Dir Dr OLGA L. ROSSOLIMO; publs *Archives* (1 a year), *Zoologicheskie Issledovania (Zoological Research)*.

The Earth Science Museum of the Moscow State M. V. Lomonosov University: 119992 Moscow, GSP-2, MGU; tel. (495) 939-14-15; fax (495) 939-29-76; e-mail info@mes .msu.ru; internet www.museum.msu.ru; f. 1955; includes material on the origin of the face of the earth, its geospheres, surface and underwater landscapes, earth crust, climates, waters, soils, plants, animals, economic resources; on the conservation, utilization and reconstruction of nature; complex geological and geographical characteristics of Russia and of the earth; science-teaching museum for students of the geological, geographical, biological soil science et al depts of Moscow University; 48000 samples; library of 5,000 vols in library; Dir Prof. A. V. SMUROV; publ. *Zhizn Zemli* (The Life of the Earth, 1 vol. every 1–2 years).

Museum of Frontier Guards: Moscow, ul. Bol. Bronnaya 23; 110,000 exhibits featuring the history of Soviet frontier guards.

Museum of the History of the City of Moscow: 103012 Moscow, Novaya pl. 12; tel. and fax (495) 924-31-45; f. 1896; Dir G. I. VEDEZNIKOVA.

Museum of the Palaeontological Institute: 117647 Moscow, Profsoyuznaya ul. 123; tel. (495) 339-05-77; fax (495) 339-12-66; e-mail admin@paleo.ru; internet www.paleo .ru; f. 1930; attached to Russian Acad. of Sciences; library of 20,000 vols; Dir A. YU. ROZANOV.

Museum of the State Academic Malyi Theatre: 103009 Moscow, Malyi teatr, Teatralnaya pl. 1/6; tel. (495) 921-85-48; f. 1932, being developed out of 1927 exhibition; illustrates and studies history of the Theatre; Dir YU. M. STRUTINSKAYA.

Nikolai Rubinstein Museum: 125009 Moscow, Bol. Nikitskaya 13; tel. and fax (495) 629-90-98; e-mail museumrub@mail.ru; internet www.mosconsv.ru; f. 1992; colln incl. musical instruments and portraits and sculptures of Russian composers; documents, photographs, phonographs, antique furniture; Dir Dr EVGENIA GUREVICH.

Novodevichii Monastery Museum: 119435 Moscow, Novodevichii pr. 1; tel. (495) 246-22-01; fax (495) 246-85-26; e-mail m337@mail.museum.ru; internet www.shm .ru/filials/novodev/fil_nov.htm; Smolensky Cathedral (1524) and other monuments of Russian architecture form the architectural ensemble of the monastery; Russian fine and decorative art (16th and 17th centuries); Dir IRINA G. BORISENKO.

Obraztsov Puppet Museum of the Central State Academic Puppet Theatre: 123473 Moscow Sadovaya-Samotechnaya ul. 3; tel. (495) 699-55-53; fax (495) 699-89-10; e-mail museum@obraztsov.ru; internet www .puppet.ru/museum; f. 1937; Central Puppet Theatre; 5,600 dolls from 50 countries; puppet theatres of the fmr USSR and many other countries; colln of cartoons, sketches, MSS and other documents; library of 15,000 books; Vice-Dir Dr BORIS GOLDOVSKY.

Permanent Tchaikovsky Exhibition in the Tchaikovsky Concert Hall: 125047

Moscow, pl. Triumfalnaya 4/31; exhibits of the composer's life and works.

Petrographic Museum: 109017 Moscow, Staromonetnyi per. 35; tel. (495) 230-82-92; fax (495) 230-21-79; internet www.museum .ru/m417; f. 1934; Dir V. A. PAVLOV.

Pharmaceutical Museum of the Central Drug Research Institute: 117418 Moscow, ul. Krasikova 34; tel. (495) 120-91-51; unique collection of about 6,000 items on the history of pharmacy in Russia and the fmr USSR; Dir B. M. SALO.

Polytechnic Museum: 101000 Moscow, Novaya Sq. 3/4; tel. (495) 625-06-14; fax (495) 625-12-90; e-mail info@polymus.ru; internet www.polymus.ru; f. 1872; over 200,000 exhibits; features history and latest devts in science and technology; belongs to the Ministry of Culture; library: 35m. vols; Dir-Gen. BORIS SALTYKOV.

Rublev, Andrei, Central Museum of Ancient Russian Culture and Art: 107120 Moscow, Andronevskaya pl. 10; tel. (495) 678-14-67; fax (495) 678-50-55; e-mail rublevmuseum@aha.ru; internet www .rublev-museum.ru; f. 1947; Russian art, icons, applied art, manuscripts, old printed books; library of 23,000 vols; Dir Dr G. V. POPOV.

Shchukin, B. V., Museum-Room: Moscow, Flat 11, ul. Shchukina 8; contains material he had about him during his lifetime as a great actor at the Vakhtangov Theatre.

Shchusev State Museum of Architecture: 121019 Moscow, Vozdvizhenka 5/25; tel. (495) 691-21-09; fax (495) 690-14-31; e-mail info@muar.ru; internet www.muar .ru; f. 1934; study, collection, care and popularization of historical architecture, outstanding contemporary work, monumental sculpture and painting; collection and care of documents on architecture and town planning; over 70,000 sheets of architectural drawings; over 300,000 negatives and 400,000 photographs of architectural monuments throughout the world; library of 50,000 vols; Dir IRINA KOROBINA; Curator I. V. SEDOVA.

Skryabin, A. N., Museum: 121002 Moscow, ul. Vakhtangova 11; tel. (495) 241-19-01; f. 1919, opened in 1922 in flat where the composer lived and died; MSS, letters, Skryabin's personal library and magnetic-tape archive of Skryabin's compositions performed by the composer and famous artists; excursions, lectures and concerts; library of 287 vols in Skryabin's personal library, 2,149 vols in scientific library; Dir RYBAKOVA.

State Academic Bolshoi Theatre Museum: 103009 Moscow, Bolshoi Teatr, Okhotnyi Ryad 8/2; tel. (495) 292-00-25; f. 1920; objects: documentation of the work of the Bolshoi Theatre, collection of materials and documents on its history and work, study of history of the theatre; Dir V. I. ZARUBIN.

State Central Museum of Contemporary Russian History: 125009 Moscow, Tverskaya ul. 21; tel. (495) 299-52-17; fax (495) 299-85-15; e-mail 9055.g23@g23.relcom.ru; internet www.sovr.ru; f. 1917; social and political history of Russia since 1850; library of 360,000 vols and 825,000 periodicals; Dir Dr TAMARA SHUMNAYA; publ. *Trudy* (Proceedings).

State Central Theatrical Museum 'A. A. Bakhrushin': 115054 Moscow, ul. Bakhrushina 31/12; tel. (495) 953-48-48; fax (495) 953-54-48; e-mail gctm@gctm.ru; internet www.gctm.ru; f. 1894; collects, houses, studies and exhibits varied materials on history and theory of theatre; approx. 1.5m. exhibits; archives of original MSS of Ostrovsky, Lensky, Stanislavsky, Meyerhold, etc.;

library of 120,000 vols; Dir-Gen. DMITRY V. RODIONOV.

State Darwin Museum: 117292 Moscow, Vavilova 57; tel. (495) 135-33-76; fax (495) 135-33-84; e-mail darwin@museum.ru; internet www.darwin.museum.ru; f. 1907; natural history and evolution; total holdings of 360,065 items; library of 30,000 vols; Dir A. I. KLUKINA.

State Historical Museum: 103012 Moscow, Krasnaya pl. 1/2; tel. (495) 924-45-29; fax (495) 925-95-27; e-mail shkurko@shm.ru; internet www.shm.ru; f. 1872; 4.5m. exhibits covering Russian history from pre-history to the present; colln of birch-bark writings; library of 229,000 vols, 29,000 MSS, 25,000 rare books; Dir-Gen. ALEXANDER SHKURKO; publs *Ezhegodnik GIM*, *Numizmaticheskii sbornik* (irregular), *Trudy GIM*.

State Literature Museum: 103051 Moscow, Petrovka ul. 28; tel. (495) 921-38-57; fax (495) 923-30-22; f. 1934; the museum is a research and educational centre which collects, studies and publishes material on the history of Russian and Soviet literature; br. (museums of Lermontov, Herzen, Dostoevsky, Chekhov, Tolstoy, Pasternak, Prishvin, Aksakov and Bryusov); library of 250,000 vols; Gen. Dir NATALYA V. SHAKHALOVA.

State Museum of Ceramics (country-seat Kuskovo): 111402 Moscow Yunosti ul. 2; tel. (495) 370-01-50; fax (495) 918-65-40; internet www.kuskovo.ru; large collection of Russian art: paintings, furniture, porcelain, pottery; collection of Western European art, tapestries, furniture, paintings, porcelain, pottery, etc.; Dir YELENA S. YERITSYAN.

State Museum of Oriental Art: 107120 Moscow, Nikitsky bul. 12A; tel. (495) 291-96-14; fax (495) 202-48-46; internet www .orientalart.ru; f. 1918; large collection of Middle and Far Eastern art, art of the fmr Soviet Central Asian Republics and Transcaucasia, carpets, fabrics, ceramics, etc.; Dir-Gen. V. A. NABACHIKOV.

State Pushkin Museum: 119034 Moscow, ul. Prechistenka 12/2; tel. and fax (495) 202-43-54; f. 1958; 200,000 exhibits; maintains br. in Pushkin's former home (Arbat 53); library of 51,000 vols; Dir E. BOGATYREV.

State Pushkin Museum of Fine Arts: 121019 Moscow, Volkhonka 12; tel. (495) 203-58-09; fax (495) 203-46-74; e-mail finearts@gmii.museum.ru; internet www .museum.ru/gmii; f. 1912; about 558,000 items of ancient Eastern, Graeco-Roman, Byzantine, European and American art; numismatic colln of 200,000 items; library of 200,000 vols; Dir I. A. ANTONOVA; Chief Conservator GALINA ERSHOVA.

State Tretyakov Gallery: 117049 Moscow, Lavrushinskii per. 10; tel. (495) 230-77-88; fax (495) 231-10-51; e-mail tretyakov@ tretyakov.ru; internet www.tretyakov.ru; f. 1856; collection of 130,000 Russian icons and works of Russian and Soviet painters, sculptors and graphic artists since 11th century; also 3,200 items from the former Pyotr Zakharov Fine Arts Museum in Grozny; new building at Krymskiy Val houses an exhibition of Russian art from 20th century; Dir VALENTIN A. RODIONOV.

State V. V. Mayakovsky Museum: 101000 Moscow, pr. Serova 3/6; tel. (095) 921-93-87; f. 1974 in the building where Mayakovsky lived 1919–30; manuscripts, documentary material, notebooks, memorial items; library and reading room with c. 200,000 vols, including periodicals; Dir S. E. STRIZHNIKOVA.

S. T. Morozov Folk-Art Museum: 103009 Moscow, Leontyevskii per. 7; tel. (495) 290-52-22; f. 1885; three sections devoted to (a)

handicrafts connected with peasant daily life; (b) applied arts both ancient and contemporary; (c) experimental decorative applied art; about 800,000 exhibits; under the jurisdiction of the Russian Council of Local Industries; Dir G. A. YAKOVLEVA.

Timiryazev, K. A., Apartment Museum: 103009 Moscow, Romanovski per. 2, str. 2, kv. 29; tel. (495) 202-80-64; fax (495) 976-29-10; f. 1942; cultural and historical memorial to K. A. Timiryazev; 7,545 exhibits and archives on his life and work; library: personal library of 4,871 vols; Dir A. A. DRUCHEK.

Timiryazev State Museum of Biology: 123242 Moscow, Mal. Gruzinskaya 15; tel. (499) 252-55-42; fax (499) 255-63-21; e-mail gbmt@gbmt.ru; internet www.gbmt.ru; f. 1922; origin and evolution of life on earth; library of 70,000 vols; Dir E. A. CHUSOVA.

Tolstoy Residence Museum: 119021 Moscow, ul. Lva Tolstogo 21; tel. (495) 246-94-44; rooms arranged as they were when the author lived there; 4,200 exhibits; Dir A. V. SALOMATIN.

Leo Tolstoy State Museum: 119021 Moscow, ul. Prechistenka 11/8; tel. (499) 766-93-28; e-mail tolstoy@museum.comsat.ru; internet www.tolstoymuseum.ru; f. 1911; MSS section contains 400,000 items of Tolstoy's writings and nearly 600,000 MSS and archive material on Tolstoy and his circle; library of 76,800 works by or about Tolstoy; nearly 87,000 newspaper cuttings, and over 42,000 exhibits in the form of painting, sculpture, photographs, etc.; 4 brs: Literary Museum, urban estate 'Khamovniki', exhibition hall and Leo Tolstoy museum 'Astapovo'; Dir VITALY REMIZOV.

Vakhtangov Theatre Museum: Moscow; history of the Vakhtangov Theatre; Dir I. L. SERGEEVA.

Vernadsky State Geological Museum: 103009 Moscow, Mokhovaya ul. 11, korp. 2; tel. (495) 203-52-87; fax (495) 203-47-98; e-mail info@sgm.ru; internet www.sgm.ru; f. 1755; Dir Prof. D. V. RUNDQVIST.

Zhukovskii, N. E., Memorial Museum: 107005 Moscow, ul. Radio 17; tel. (495) 267-50-54; 25,000 items feature the work of N. E. Zhukovskii, and Soviet contributions to aviation and astronautics; Dir V. I. MASLOV.

Nalchik

Kabarda-Balkar Art Museum: Nalchik, pr. V. I. Lenina 35; 3,500 exhibits; Dir I. Z. BATASHOV.

Nizhnii Novgorod

Nizhnii Novgorod Historical Museum: Nizhnii Novgorod, nab. Zhdanova 7; 160,000 exhibits including collections of archaeology, featuring the history of the Central Volga area since ancient times.

Nizhnii Novgorod State Museum of Art: 603082 Nizhnii Novgorod, korp. 3 Kremlya; tel. (8312) 39-08-55; fax (8312) 19-20-85; e-mail art@museum.nnov.ru; internet www .museum.nnov.ru/art; f. 1896; Dir VALENTINA N. KRIVOVA.

State A. M. Gorky Museum of Literature: 603155 Nizhnii Novgorod, ul. Minina 26; tel. and fax (8312) 36-15-29; e-mail danco6@ yandex.ru; internet www.museum.nnov.ru/ danco; f. 1928; 102,000 exhibits, illustrating the life and work of the writer; library of 40,000 vols; Dir T. A. RIZHOVA.

Novocherkassk

Novocherkassk Museum of the History of the Don Cossacks: 346430 Rostov oblast, Novocherkassk, Atamanskaya ul. 38; tel. (86352) 4-80-59; e-mail m838@mail.museum

.ru; internet www.doncossacks.ru; f. 1899; deals with the traditions and exploits of the Don Cossacks; collections of porcelain and painting; library of 17,000 vols; Dir SVETLANA A. SEDINKO.

Novosibirsk

Central Siberian Botanical Garden: 630090 Novosibirsk, Zolotodolinskaya ul. 101; tel. (3832) 30-41-01; fax (3832) 30-19-86; e-mail root@botgard.nsk.su; internet www.cbsg.narod.ru; f. 1946; attached to Russian Acad. of Sciences; Dir Prof. V. P. SEDELNIKOV.

Omsk

Omsk Fine Art Museum: Omsk, ul. Lenina 23; 3,780 exhibits; Dir A. A. GERZON.

Orel

Turgenev, I. S., State Literary Museum: 302000 Orel, ul. Turgeneva 11; tel. (08622) 6-27-37; f. 1918; library of 60,000 vols; Dir V. V. SAFRONOVA.

Branch museums:

Andreev Leonid, House Museum: Orel, Pushkarnaya 41; tel. (4862) 76-48-24; f. 1991; Man. O. V. VOLOGINA.

Bunin Museum: 302000 Orel, Oktyabrsky pr. 1; tel. (08622) 6-07-74; f. 1991; Man. I. A. KOSTOMAROVA.

Granovsky, T. N., Museum: Orel, ul. 7 Noyabrya 24; tel. (08622) 6-34-65; f. 1985; devoted to public figures born in Orel; Man. E. A. IVUSHKINA.

Leskov, N. S., House Museum: 301028 Orel, ul. Oktyabrskaya 9; tel. (08622) 6-33-04; f. 1974; Man. L. S. KAMYSHALOVA.

Literary Museum: 302000 Orel, ul. Turgeneva 11; tel. (08622) 6-35-28; f. 1957; devoted to writers born in Orel; Man. L. E. URAKOVA.

Orenburg

Orenburg Fine Art Museum: Orenburg, ul. Pravdy 6; 3,500 items; Dir L. B. POPOVA.

Palekh

State Museum of Palekh Art: 155620 Ivanovo oblast, Palekh ul. Bakanova 50; tel. (49334) 2-20-54; fax (49334) 2-26-41; e-mail m1571@mail.museum.ru; internet www.museum.ru/m1571; f. 1934; library of 16,000 books, photographs and film docs; Dir ALEVTINA G. STRAKHOVA.

Pavlovsk

The State Museum 'Pavlovsk': 196621 St Peterburg Pavlovsk, ul. Sadovaya 20; tel. (812) 452-21-55; fax (812) 465-11-04; e-mail palace@pavlovskmuseum.ru; internet www.pavlovskmuseum.ru; f. 1918; many examples of Russian garden architecture, antique sculpture and sculpture by 18th-century Italian and French masters; European paintings of the 16th to 19th centuries; Russian portraits of the 18th century, Russian decorative art of the 18th and 19th centuries; furniture, porcelain, bronzes and textiles; library of 17,000 vols; Dir N. S. TRETYAKOV.

Penza

Penza Picture Gallery: 660026 Penza, Sovetskaya ul. 3; tel. (8412) 66-64-00; f. 1892; library of 3,200 vols; 7,700 exhibits; also 3 memorial museums; Dir VALERYI SAZONOV.

Perm

Perm State Art Gallery: 614045 Perm, Komsomolskyi Ave 4; tel. (342) 212-95-24; fax (342) 212-22-50; e-mail pghg@mail.ru; internet www.gallery.permonline.ru; f. 1922;

coll'n management (conservation, restoration, art expertise); academic work (research, exhibitions, confs, seminars, publs, scholarly exchange); adult and children education (guide tours, programmers, actions); information technologies; devt and fund raising, PR support; coll'n stocks 50,000 works of art of the 15th–21st centuries; Russian and foreign art: paintings, graphic, decorative and applied art objects; the Stroganovs school icons and Perm wood carving cult sculptures; library of 28,900 vols; Dir JULYA B. TAVRIZYAN.

Petrodvorets

Peterhof State Museum Reserve: 198516 St Petersburg, Petrodvorets, ul. Rasvodnaya 2; tel. (812) 427-74-25; fax (812) 427-93-30; e-mail admin@peterhof.org; internet www.peterhof.org; f. 1918; 18th- to 20th-century architecture, painting and landscape gardening; 18th- and 19th-century sculpture, furniture, porcelain, clocks and jewellery; library of 21,000 books, special collection of 2,000 rare books, 7,000 Russian book-plates, 1,300 printed graphics; Dir V. V. ZNAMENOV.

Petrozavodsk

Karelian Museum of Fine Arts: 185035 Republic of Karelia, Petrozavodsk, pr. K. Marksa 8; tel. (8142) 77-98-60; fax (8142) 78-25-78; e-mail pictures@sampo.ru; internet artmuseum.karelia.ru; f. 1960; Karelian iconic paintings from 15th–19th centuries, Karelian folk art, modern Karelian art, Russian art from the 18th century to present, western European art; library of 21,000 vols; Dir NATALIA I. VAVILOVA.

Karelian State Regional Museum: 185035 Republic of Karelia, Petrozavodsk, pl. Lenina 1; tel. (8142) 78-02-40; fax (8142) 78-02-40; e-mail kgkm@karelia.ru; internet karelia.ru/~kgkm; f. 1871; history, economy, science, culture, and natural history of the area; 3 brs; library of 25,700 vols; Dir ELENA ZARINA; publs *Museum Herald* (1 a year), *Museums of Karelia* (4 a year), *Vestnik* (1 a year).

Kizhi State Open-Air Museum of History, Architecture and Ethnography: 185035 Republic of Karelia, Petrozavodsk, 10A, Kirov Sq.; tel. (8142) 78-32-52; fax (8142) 78-35-91; e-mail olga@kizhi.karelia.ru; internet kizhi.karelia.ru; f. 1961; wooden architecture, history, ethnography, early Russian and Karelian painting and folklore; library of 10,227 vols; Dir E. V. AVERYANOVA.

Pushkin

Tsarskoe Selo State Museum: 189690 Leningrad oblast, Tsarskoe Selo, Sadovaya ul. 7; tel. (812) 466-66-69; fax (812) 465-21-96; e-mail tzar@spb.cityline.ru; internet www.tzar.ru; f. 1918; former imperial summer residence, incl. Catherine and Alexander Palaces; park and garden architecture and 100 architectural ornaments from 18th to 20th centuries, esp. in Baroque and Classical styles; library of 18,041 vols including collection of rare books of 2,375 vols; Dir I. P. SAUTOV.

Pushkinskie Gory

State Memorial Museum-Reserve of A. S. Pushkin 'Mikhailovskoye': 181370 Pskovskaya oblast, Pushkinskie Gory, Novorzhevskaya 21; tel. and fax (81146) 2-19-50; e-mail pgmuseum@ellink.ru; internet www.pushkin.ellink.ru; f. 1922; 33,000 exhibits on the life in exile of the poet, Aleksandr Pushkin (1799–1837); the preserve incl. the family lands at Mikhailovskoe, Trigorskoe and Petrovskoe, the ancient towns of Voronich and Savkina Gorka and

the grave of Pushkin; library of 21,000 vols; Dir GEORGY VASILEVICH.

Pyatigorsk

State Lermontov Literary Memorial Museum: Pyatigorsk, Lermontovskaya ul. 4; tel. (87933) 5-27-10; f. 1912; exhibits feature the life and work of M. Yu. Lermontov in the Caucasus; library of 14,000 vols; Dir L. MOROZOVA.

Roslavl

Roslavl Historical Museum: Roslavl, ul. Proletarskaya 63; tel. (08134) 3-18-49; f. 1920; collection tracing the history, economy and culture of Russian people from the earliest times; library of 1,300 vols; Dir M. I. IVANOVA.

Rostov-on-Don

Rostov Museum of Fine Art: 344002 Rostov-on-Don, ul. Pushkinskaya 115; tel. and fax (8632) 69-10-88; e-mail romii@mail.ru; f. 1938; old Russian, Soviet and foreign descriptive art; library of 16,697 vols; Dir KRUZE SVETLANA VALEREVNA; publ. *Khudozhnik*.

Ryazan

Ryazan Kremlin Historical and Architectural Museum Reserve: Ryazan, Kreml 118; tel. (0912) 27-60-65; fax (0912) 21-56-70; e-mail root@riamz.ryazan.ru; internet www.ryazankreml.ru; f. 1884; over 220,000 items describing the history, culture and art of the peoples of Russia; Dir LUDMILA MAKSIMOVA; publs *Yakhontovsky's Readings* (every 2 years), *Scientific Works* (every 5 years).

Ryazan Regional Art Museum: Ryazan, Svoboda st. 57; tel. and fax (4912) 28-04-24; f. 1913; old Russian (15th–20th centuries), European (16th–19th centuries) and Soviet art; library of 17,000 vols; Dir M. A. KOTOVA.

St Petersburg

Acad. F. N. Chernyshev Central Scientific Research Geological and Prospecting Museum (CNIGR museum): 199106 St Petersburg, Vasilevskii ostrov, Srednii pr. 74; tel. and fax (812) 321-53-99; e-mail cnigr_museum@vsegei.ru; internet www.vsegei.com; f. 1882, opened 1930; attached to A. P. Karpinsky Russia Geological Research Institute (VSEGEI); c. 1m. geological specimens incl. examples of mineral deposits from all over the fmr USSR; monographic and palaeontological coll'ns; popularization of geological knowledge; Dir Dr ALEKSEY SOKOLOV.

Botanical Museum: 197022 St Petersburg, ul. Prof. Popova 2; tel. (812) 234-84-39; f. 1823; over 60,000 specimens; br. of V. L. Komarov Botanical Institute of Academy of Sciences; Dir L. YU. BUDANTSEV.

Central Museum of Railway Transport of Russia: St Petersburg, Sadovaya ul. 50; fax (812) 315-14-76; e-mail cmrt1813@yandex.ru; internet www.railroad.ru/cmrt; f. 1813; traces the history of railway transport in Russia; incl. unique coll'n of miniature models of engines and carriages; Dir G. ZAKREVSKAYA.

Central Naval Museum: 199034 St Petersburg, Birzhevaya pl. 4; tel. (812) 328-27-02; fax (812) 328-27-01; e-mail museum@mail.admiral.ru; internet www.museum.navy.ru; f. 1709; relics and other materials from the Russian and Soviet Navies; departments of history of the Russian Navy, history of the Soviet Navy, history of the Navy in the 1941–45 period, history of the Navy in the post-war period; responsible for Kronstadt Fortress, cruiser Aurora and submarine Narodovolets; library of 16,000 vols; Dir E. N. KORCHAGIN.

Dokuchaev Central Soil Museum: St Petersburg, Birzhevoi pr-d 6; tel. (812) 328-54-02; fax (812) 328-56-02; e-mail soilmuseum@bk.ru; internet www.soil-museum.ru; f. 1904; about 5,000 specimens of soil from nearly every soil zone in the world; library of 14,000 vols (Dokuchaev personal library); Dir Dr B. F. APARIN.

Dostoevsky Memorial Museum: 191002 St Petersburg, Kuznechnyi per. 5/2; tel. (812) 571-40-31; e-mail ashimbaeva@md.spb.ru; internet www.md.spb.ru; f. 1971; the house where the author lived 1878–81; MSS, documentary material, memorial items; library of 23,000 vols; Dir Dr NATALIA ASHIMBAEVA.

Literary Museum of the Institute of Russian Literature: 199034 St Petersburg, Pushkinskii Dom, nab. Makarova 4; tel. (812) 328-05-02; fax (812) 328-11-40; e-mail irliran@mail.ru; internet www.pushkinhouse.spb.ru; f. 1905; based on the material of the Pushkin Anniversary Exhibition of 1899; contains 95,000 exhibits and over 120,000 items of reference material; 7 halls containing permanent exhibitions devoted to G. R. Derzhavin, A. S. Pushkin, M. Y. Lermontov, N. V. Gogol, F. M. Dostoevsky, I. S. Turgenev, L. N. Tolstoy and other Russian writers and poets; Dir L. G. AGAMALIAN.

Lomonosov, M. V., Museum: 199164 St Petersburg, Universitetskaya nab. 3; tel. (812) 328-10-11; internet www.kunstkamera.ru/en/museums_structure/research_departments/mv_lomonosov_museum; f. 1947; attached to Museum of Anthropology and Ethnography (Kunstkamera); 3,000 exhibits; Head MARGARITA F. KHARTONOVICH.

Military Medical Museum: 191180 St Petersburg, Lazaretny per. 2; tel. (812) 315-53-58; fax (812) 310-20-25; e-mail m170@mail.museum.ru; internet www.museum.ru/m170; f. 1942; history of Russian and Soviet military medicine; library: research library of 50,000 vols, also collections of rare books; 60m. archive docs on citizens of 45 countries in Europe, Asia, America and Africa; Dir Prof. Dr A. A. BUDKO; publs *History of Medicine in St Petersburg* (1 a year), *History of Military Medicine in Russia* (1 a year), *Memorial Dates of Military Medicine* (1 a year), *Military Medicine Abroad* (6 a year), *Review of the History of Military Medicine* (1 a year).

Mining Museum of the St Petersburg State Mining Institute (Technical University): 199106 St Petersburg, 21-ya liniya 2; tel. (812) 328-84-29; fax (812) 327-73-59; e-mail rectorat@spmi.ru; internet www.gorny-ins.ru; f. 1773; specimens of minerals, rocks, ores, fossils, meteorites; historical mining techniques illustrated by models of the 19th and early 20th century; colln of edged weapons from the Zlatoust Arms Factory; Dir J. POLYARNAYA.

Museum of Artillery, Engineers and Signal Corps: 197046 St Petersburg, Aleksandrovsky park 7; tel. and fax (812) 238-47-04; f. 1703; library of 115,000 vols; Dir Col V. M. KRYLOV.

Museum of Sculpture: St Petersburg, pl. A. Nevskogo 1; largest collection of Russian sculpture, collection and care of documents on architecture and town planning; over 150,000 sheets of architectural drawings; Dir N. H. BELOVA.

Museum of the Gorky Bolshoi Drama Theatre: St Petersburg, ul. Fontanka 65.

Museum of the History of Religion: 191186 St Petersburg, Kazanskaya pl. 2; fax (812) 311-94-83; f. 1932; 186,000 exhibits on Russian Orthodox Church, Roman Catholic and other Christian churches, Judaism, Islam and Buddhism; library of 170,000 vols; Dir S. A. KUCHINSKY; publ. *Theses* (1 a year).

Library of the Mariinsky State Academic Theatre of Opera and Ballet: 190000 St Petersburg, ul. Zodchego Rossi 2, Teatralnaya pl. 1; tel. (812) 326-41-64; e-mail cml@mariinsky.ru; library: consists of repertoire and archive sections; Dir Prof. Dr MARIA N. SHCHERBAKOVA.

Museum of the St Petersburg Mussorgsky Academic Opera and Ballet Theatre: St Petersburg, pl. Iskusstv 1; tel. (812) 595-43-13; fax (812) 314-36-53; internet www.reserve.sp.ru; f. 1935; colln of materials (sketches, posters, photographs, costumes) depicting the history of the theatre and its work; Dir M. KORTUNOVA.

Museum of Zoology: 199034 St Petersburg, Universitetskaya nab. 1; tel. (812) 328-01-12; fax (812) 328-29-41; e-mail museum@zin.ru; internet www.zin.ru; f. 1832; over 30,000 items describe the origin and evolution of the animal world; attached to Zoological Institute of the Russian Acad. of Sciences (see under Research Institutes); Chief ALEXEI TIKHONOV; publ. *Proceedings of the Zoological Institute.*

National Pushkin Museum: 191186 St Petersburg, nab. Moiki 12; tel. (812) 571-38-01; fax (812) 315-73-79; e-mail vmp@mail.admiral.ru; internet www.museumpushkin.ru; f. 1879; under supervision of Ministry of Culture; exhibits illustrating the life and work of the poet and his epoch; Dir S. M. NEKRASOV.

Annexes:

Lyceum Museum: 196600 Pushkin, Sadovaya 2; tel. (812) 476-64-11; fax (812) 315-73-79; e-mail vmp@mail.admiral.ru; internet www.museumpushkin.ru; f. 1949; Chief Curator M. N. PETAI.

Main Literary Exposition–Life and Creative Work of Alexander Pushkin: 191186 St Petersburg, nab. Moiki 12; tel. (812) 314-00-07; fax (812) 315-73-79; e-mail vmp@mail.admiral.ru; internet www.museumpushkin.ru; f. 1999; Chief Curator N. L. PETROVA.

Museum of Derzhavin and Russian Literature of the 18th Century: 198005 St Petersburg, nab. Fontanki 118; tel. (812) 713-07-17; fax (812) 315-73-79; e-mail vmp@mail.admiral.ru; internet www.museumpushkin.ru; f. 2003; Chief Curator N. P. MOROZOVA.

Nekrasov Apartment Museum: 191104 St Petersburg, Liteiny per. 36; tel. (812) 272-01-65; fax (812) 315-73-79; e-mail vmp@mail.admiral.ru; internet www.museumpushkin.ru; f. 1946; Chief Curator E. YU. GLEVENKO.

Pushkin Apartment Museum: 191186 St Petersburg, nab. Moiki 12; tel. (812) 117-35-31; fax (812) 315-73-79; e-mail vmp@mail.admiral.ru; internet www.museumpushkin.ru; f. 1925; Chief Curator G. M. SEDOVA.

Pushkin Country House Museum: 196607 Pushkin, Pushkinskaya ul. 2; tel. (812) 476-69-90; fax (812) 315-73-79; e-mail vmp@mail.admiral.ru; internet www.museumpushkin.ru; f. 1958; Chief Curator T. I. GALKINA.

Permanent Exhibition of Musical Instruments: St Petersburg, 5 Isaakievskaya pl.; about 3,000 exhibits, including a large collection of instruments made by outstanding Russian and foreign craftsmen: Batov, Leman, Nalimov, Krasnoshchekov, Fedorov, Amati, Villaume, Tilke and Denner.

Peter the Great Museum of Anthropology and Ethnography (Kunstkamera): 199034 St Petersburg, Universitetskaya nab. 3; tel. (812) 328-07-12; fax (812) 328-08-11; e-mail info@kunstkamera.ru; internet www.kunstkamera.ru; f. 1714; attached to Russian Acad. of Sciences; ethnographical, archaeological, and anthropological material on the native peoples of all continents; anatomical colln; scientific instruments; Dir Prof. YURI K. CHISTOV; publs *Etnograficheskiye tetradi* (1 a year), *Forum for Anthropology and Culture* (2 in Russian, 1 in English and 2 online), *Kuryer* (2 a year), *Mauscripta Orientalia* (4 a year), *Sbornik MAE* (1 a year).

Popov, A. S., Central Museum of Communications: 190000 St Petersburg, Pochtamtskaya ul. 7; tel. and fax (812) 315-48-73; e-mail bakayutova@telecommuseum.sp.ru; internet www.rustelecom-museum.ru; f. 1872; over 8m. items representing the development of all types of communication used in Russia and the former USSR; includes the national postage stamp collection; Dir L. BAKAYUTOVA.

Russian Ethnographic Museum: St Petersburg, Inzhenernaya ul. 4/1; tel. (812) 210-47-68; fax (812) 315-85-02; e-mail rme@infopro.spb.ru; internet www.ethnomuseum.ru; f. 1902; 150,000 photographs; library of 105,000 vols; Dir V. M. GRUSMAN; publ. *Collected Articles* (2 a year).

Russian State Museum of the Arctic and the Antarctic: 191040 St Petersburg, ul. Marata 24A; tel. (812) 713-19-98; fax (812) 764-68-18; e-mail boyarsky@norpolex.com; internet www.polarmuseum.ru; f. 1930; exploration, history and environment of polar regions; library of 6,362 vols; Dir Dr VICTOR I. BOYARSKY; Scientific Deputy Dir Dr M. V. DUKALSKAYA.

St Petersburg State Museum of Theatre and Music: 191011 St Petersburg, pl. Ostrovskogo 6; tel. (812) 315-52-43; fax (812) 314-77-46; e-mail theatre@museums.org.ru; internet www.theatremuseum.ru; f. 1918; over 440,000 exhibits depicting the history of Russian, Soviet and foreign theatre; 31,000 stage designs, 7,000 prints, 900 sculptures, 240,000 photographs, 24,000 MSS and documents, 62,000 posters and programmes, 4,000 theatre costumes; library of 5,000 vols; museum branches: *Rimsky-Korsakov Museum:* f. 1971; memorial museum in house where the composer lived; *F. I. Chaliapin Museum:* f. 1975; museum of history of Russian opera, in former house of Chaliapin; *Music Museum at the Sheremetev Palace:* f. 1991; museum of music incl. 3,000 instruments, and international music centre; *Samoilov Family Museum:* f. 1994; museum of a dynasty of Russian actors; Dir IRINA V. YEVSTIGNEYEVA.

State Circus Museum: 191011 St Petersburg, ul. Fontanka 3; tel. (812) 313-44-13; fax (812) 314-80-59; e-mail circusmuseum@aport.ru; internet www.circus.spb.ru; f. 1928; 80,000 exhibits of plans, sketches, paintings; section on the circus in Western Europe since 18th century and on Russian and fmr Soviet state circus; library of 4,000 items, Russian and foreign works; 300 videocassettes of circus material; Dir NATALIA KUZNETSOVA.

State Hermitage Museum: 190000 St Petersburg, Dvortsovaya nab. 34; tel. (812) 110-90-79; e-mail chancery@hermitage.ru; internet www.hermitagemuseum.org; f. 1764 as a court museum; opened to public 1852; richest collection in fmr USSR of the art of pre-historic, ancient Eastern, Graeco-Roman and medieval times; preserves 2.8m. *objets d'art*, including 600,000 drawings and engravings; works by Leonardo da Vinci, Raphael, Titian, Rubens and Rembrandt; collection of coins, weapons and applied art; Dir MIKHAIL PETROVSKY.

State Museum of the History of St Petersburg: 197046 St Petersburg, Petropavlovskaya krepost 3; tel. (812) 498-05-11; fax (812) 498-02-43; internet www .spbmuseum.ru; f. 1957; more than 1.5m. exhibits; shows history and architectural devt of St Petersburg; 7 brs: Peter and Paul Fortress, 'Oreshek' Fortress, Alexander Blok Museum, Museum of Printing, Sergey. Kirov Museum, Monument to Heroic Defenders of Leningrad, Rumyantsev Mansion; Dir ALEXANDER KOLYAKIN.

State Museum of the Political History of Russia: 197046 St Petersburg, ul. Kuybysheva 2–4; tel. (812) 233-70-48; fax (812) 233-73-00; e-mail polithist@cards.lanck.net; internet www.museum.ru/museum/ polit_hist; f. 1919; history of Russia in the 19th and 20th centuries with particular reference to political and social development; Dir E. G. ARTEMOV.

State Russian Museum: 191186 St Petersburg, Inzhenernaya ul. 4; tel. (812) 595-42-40; fax (812) 314-41-53; e-mail info@ rusmuseum.ru; internet www.rusmuseum .ru; f. 1895; Russian icons, folk and applied arts, painting, sculpture, 10th–21st-century drawings; Dir Dr V. A. GUSEV.

Summer Garden and Museum Palace of Peter the Great: 191186 St Petersburg, Letny Sad; tel. (812) 312-77-15; fax (812) 312-96-66; e-mail m126@mail.museum.ru; f. 1934; 18th-century architecture and sculpture; Dir T. D. KOZLOVA.

Samara

Samara A. M. Gorky Memorial Museum: Samara, ul. S. Razina 126; f. 1946; literary museum devoted to the life and work of Gorky; exhibits in the house and furniture which belonged to him; Chief Curator YELENA KOTELNIKOVA.

Samara Art Museum: 443001 Samara 10, pl. Kuibysheva, Palace of Culture; f. 1897; fine arts museum with 11,000 exhibits; library of 7,000 vols; Dir ANNETA YU. BASS.

Saransk

Mordovian Republic S. D. Erzi Museum of Fine Arts: 430000 Mordoviya Saransk, Kommunisticheskaya ul. 61; tel. and fax (8342) 17-56-38; e-mail m1451@mail .museum.ru; internet www.museum.ru/ m1451; f. 1960; painting, sculpture, prints, decorative arts; library of 10,000 vols; Dir M. N. BARANOVA.

Saratov

Chernyshevsky Memorial Museum: 410002 Saratov, ul. Chernyshevskogo 142; tel. (8452) 26-35-83; fax (8452) 26-33-67; f. 1920; study of N. G. Chernyshevsky's life, times and literary inheritance; library of 14,232 vols; Dir GALINA P. MURENONA; publs *Propagandist Velikovo Naslediya* (Publicist of the Great Inheritance, every 5 years), *N. G. Chernyshevsky Articles, Investigations and Materials* (every 3 years).

Saratov A. N. Radishchev State Art Museum: 410031 Saratov, Pervomaiskaya 75; tel. and fax (8452) 26-12-09; e-mail radmuseumart@radmuseumart.ru; internet www.radmuseumart.ru; f. 1885; library of 34,000 vols; brs: Victor Borisov-Musatov and Pavel Kuznetsov memorial museums (Saratov), Kuzma Petrov-Vodkin memorial museum (Khvalynsk, Saratov region), Balakovo art gallery (Balakovo, Saratov region), A. A. Mylnikov Engels Art Gallery (Engels, Saratov region); Dir T. V. GRODSKOVA.

Sergievsky Posad

Sergiev Posad State History and Art Museum: 141300 Moscow oblast, Sergiev Posad, pr. Krasnoi Armii 144; tel. and fax (09654) 4-13-58; e-mail sergiev@divo.ru; internet www.musobl.divo.ru; f. 1920; items dealing with the development of Russian art from the 14th century to the present; icons, embroidery, jewellery, porcelain, glass, vestments; secular applied arts, folk arts; library of 17,000 vols; Dir FELIKS KH. MAKOYEV; Scientific Sec. Dr S. V. NIKOLAEVA.

Starki

Far Eastern State Marine Reserve: 690601 Vladivostok, o. Popova, pos. Starki, Olkhovaya 11; tel. (4232) 9-66-82; attached to Russian Acad. of Sciences; Head V. V. GORLACH.

Stavropol

Stavropol Museum of Fine Arts: Stavropol, ul. Dzerzhinskogo 115–119; tel. and fax (8652) 26-54-78; e-mail izomuz@iskra .stavropol.ru; internet www.museum.ru/ m1608; f. 1962; Dir Z. A. BELAYA.

Syktyvkar

National Gallery of the Komi Republic: 167981 Komi Republic, Syktyvkar, ul. Kirova 44; tel. and fax (8212) 42-60-66; e-mail nrgk@ online.ru; internet www.komi.com/ngall; f. 1943; Komi, Russian, Soviet and Western European fine art; Dir SVETLANA BELYAEVA.

Taganrog

Chekhov, A. P., Museum: Taganrog, ul. Oktyabrskaya 9; tel. (86344) 6-27-45; rooms arranged as they were when Chekhov lived there in his childhood.

Tambov

Tambov Picture Gallery: 392000 Tambov, Sovetskaya ul. 97; tel. (0752) 2-36-95; f. 1960; 3,500 exhibits; library of 7,000 vols; Dir T. N. SHESTAKOVA.

Tikhvin

Rimsky-Korsakov House-Museum: 187500 Leningrad oblast, Tikhvin, ul Rimskogo Korsakova 12; tel. (81267) 1-15-09; f. 1944 in house where composer was born; main exhibition devoted to composer's childhood; also material on his later life; special collections: original scores, etc.

Tobolsk

Tobolsk Picture Gallery: Tobolsk, Krasnaya pl. 2; 1,800 items.

Tula

Tula Art Museum: 300012 Tula, ul. Engelsa 64; tel. and fax (872) 35-42-72; f. 1919; library: specialist art library of 15,000 vols; Dir M. N. KUSINA.

Tula Museum of Regional Studies: Tula, ul. Sovetskaya 68; tel. (0872) 36-22-08; f. 1919; natural sciences, archaeology, literature, architecture, art, history of Tula region; library of 10,806 vols; Dir N. B. NEMOVA.

Tver

Tver Art Gallery: 170640 Tver, ul. Sovetskaya 3; tel. and fax (822) 33-25-61; e-mail art@tversu.ru; internet www.gallery.tversu .ru; f. 1937; library of 33,000 vols; Dir TATYANA S. KUYUKINA.

Tyumen

Tyumen Picture Gallery: Tyumen, ul. Republiki 29; Dir I. S. TERENTEV.

Uglich

Uglich Historical Museum: Uglich, Kreml 3; tel. (08532) 5-17-57; fax (08532) 5-36-78; e-mail uglmus@yaroslavl.ru; f. 1892; exhibits on the history of the Russian people; Dir VALERY DENISOV.

Vladikavkaz

North-Ossetian K. L. Khetagurov Memorial Museum: Vladikavkaz, Butirina 19; tel. (86722) 3-62-22; f. 1979; collection of materials on Caucasian poetry and literature; Dir E. A. KESAYEVA.

Vladivostok

Botanical Garden FEB RAS: 690024 Vladivostok, ul. Makovskogo 142; tel. and fax (4232) 38-80-41; e-mail gardens@yandex.ru; internet botsad.ru; f. 1949; attached to Russian Acad. of Sciences; research in botany, plant ecology, plant cultivation, plant resources, investigation of biological diversity of the Russian Far East; environmental education; maintaining exhibits of living plants; landscaping and design; library of 22,000 vols, attached to FEB RAS Central Academical Library, Vladivostok; Dir Dr PAVEL KRESTOV; Deputy Dir Dr OLGA KHRAPKO; publ. *Bulletin of Botanical Garden FEB RAS* (online (botsad.ru/journal)).

Oceanarium of the Pacific Research Fisheries Centre: 690950 Vladivostok, Batareinaya ul. 4; tel. (4232) 40-19-65; fax (4232) 30-07-52; e-mail oceanariumtinro@ mail.ru; internet www.tinro-center.ru; f. 1991; freshwater aquarium; 2,500 exhibits of flora and fauna of the Pacific Ocean; marine museum, 1,950 exhibits; study of hydrobiology and aquaculture; maintenance of zoological colln; library of 3,242 rare vols; Dir B. K. RAZUVAEV.

Voeikovo

Meteorological Museum of the Central Geophysical Observatory: Leningrad oblast, Vsevolozhskii raion, Voeikovo; Dir A. A. VASILIEV.

Volgograd

Volgograd State Museum and Panorama of the Battle of Stalingrad: 400053 Volgograd, ul. Marshal Chuykov 47; tel. (8442) 34-72-72; fax (8442) 34-72-41; e-mail panorama@volgadmin.ru; internet www .volgadmin.ru/panorama; f. 1937; exhibits feature the defence of the city during the Civil War (1918–20) and the Battle of Stalingrad (1942–43); library of 14,450 vols; Dir B. G. USIK.

Vologda

Vologda Picture Gallery: Vologda, Kremlevskaya pl.; 6,500 exhibits; Dir S. G. IVENSKII.

Vologda State Museum—Preserve of History, Architecture and Decorative Arts: 160000 Vologda, 15 S. Orlov St; tel. and fax (8172) 72-22-83; e-mail museum .admin@vologda.ru; internet vologdamuseum.ru; f. 1885; history, archaeology, ethnography, nature, literature, handicrafts, folk art, decorative and applied art, old Russian painting, modern art of the Vologda region, architecture; library of 27,000 vols, incl. books on history, art, ethnography and archeology; Dir-Gen. ALEXANDR SUVOROV.

Voronezh

Voronezh Art Museum: Voronezh, pr. Revolyutsii 18; tel. (0732) 55-28-43; f. 1933; 22,065 exhibits; library of 18,800 vols; Dir VLADIMIR Y. USTINOV.

Yakutsk

Yakutsk Museum of Fine Arts: 677000 Yakutsk, ul. Khabarova 27; tel. (4112) 2-77-98; f. 1928; folk art, Western European, Russian and Soviet art of 17th to 20th centuries; Dir N. M. VASILEVA.

Yaroslavl

Yaroslavl Historical and Architectural Museum: 150000 Yaroslavl, pl. Bogoyavlenskaya 25; tel. (0852) 30-56-30; fax (0852) 30-57-55; e-mail mp@yarmp.yar.ru; internet www.yarmp.yar.ru; f. 1865; over 370,000 exhibits on the history of the Russian people from ancient times to the present; library of 42,000 vols; Dir YELENA A. ANKUDINOVA; publ. *Kraevedcheskiye Zapiski* (irregular).

Yasnaya Polyana

Leo Tolstoy Museum and Estate: 301214 Tula Region, Shchekino Dist., Yasnaya Polyana; tel. and fax (4872) 38-67-10; e-mail yaspol@tula.net; internet yasnayapolyana.ru; f. 1921; memorial house and estate belonging to L. N. Tolstoy; over 33,000 original objects in the Tolstoy House; literary museum devoted to his life and work; estate with park and forest; library of 22,000 vols in Tolstoy's personal library (in the Tolstoy House); c. 60,000 vols in museum library; Dir VLADIMIR I. TOLSTOY; publ. *Yasnaya Polyana* (Writers' Meetings, 1 a year).

Universities

AGRICULTURAL UNIVERSITIES

ALTAI STATE AGRARIAN UNIVERSITY

656099 Barnaul, Krasnoarmeisky pr. 98
Telephone and fax (3852) 62-83-96
E-mail: rector@asau.ru
Internet: www.asau.ru
Founded 1943 as Altai Agricultural Institute, present name and status 1991
Depts: accounting, agronomy, animal production, economics, irrigation and land reclamation, management, mechanization, veterinary, zoology
Rector: Prof. SERGEI V. ZOLOTAREV
Library of 360,430 vols
Number of teachers: 508
Number of students: 10,010

BASHKIR STATE AGRARIAN UNIVERSITY

450001 Ufa, 50 let Oktyabrya ul. 34
Telephone and fax (3472) 28-08-98
E-mail: bgau@ufanet.ru
Internet: www.bsau.ru
Rector: Prof. VLADIMIR D. NEDOREZKOV
Number of teachers: 685

CHELYABINSK STATE AGRO-ENGINEERING UNIVERSITY

454080 Chelyabinsk, Lenina Ave 75
Telephone: (3512) 66-65-30
Fax: (3512) 66-65-35
E-mail: kbv@agroun.urc.ac.ru
Internet: www.csaa.ru
Founded 1930
Training of engineers, economists, agronomists, teachers and agroecologists for state and private farms and businesses; bachelors and masters for agro-engineering
Rector: YURY B. CHETYRKIN
Library of 550,000 vols
Number of teachers: 350
Number of students: 5,600
Publications: *Trudy Chimeskh*, *Vestnik Akademii*, *Vestnik Universiteta*.

DON STATE AGRARIAN UNIVERSITY

346493 Rostov oblast, Oktyabrsky r-n, pos. Persianovsky
Telephone and fax (86360) 35-150
E-mail: dgau-web@mail.ru
Internet: www.dongau.ru
Founded 1840
State control
Language of instruction: Russian
Rector: Prof. ANATOLY I. BARANIKOV
Library of 540,000 vols
Number of teachers: 414
Number of students: 3,152
Fields of study: agronomy, animal husbandry, biotechnology, economy, processing of agricultural products, veterinary science.

FAR EAST STATE AGRARIAN UNIVERSITY

675005 Blagoveshchensk, Politekhnicheskaya ul. 86
Telephone: (4162) 42-32-06
Fax: (4162) 42-31-79
E-mail: dgu@inbox.ru
Founded 1950
Institutes of agronomy, mechanization, finance and economics, civil engineering, technology, veterinary science and animal husbandry, electrification and the automation of agriculture, forestry, humanities; research institutes of stockbreeding, selection and technology in plant breeding, construction, systems of machinery, technology of the processing of agricultural production
Rector: BORIS I. KASHPURA
Library of 398,000 vols
Number of teachers: 570
Number of students: 8,000
Publications: *Amur Researcher* (2 a year), *Collection of Scientific Publications* (separate series published by each of 14 institutes, each 1 or 2 a year), *Science to Production* (conference report, 1 a year), *Students' Research to Production* (1 a year).

GORSKY STATE AGRICULTURAL UNIVERSITY

362040 Vladikavkaz, ul. Kirova 37
Telephone: (8672) 3-23-04
Fax: (8672) 53-90-04
Library of 208,000 vols
Rector: BORIS B. BASAEV
Number of teachers: 412
Number of students: 6,500
Fields of study: agronomy, animal husbandry, mechanization, economics and management, accounting.

KRASNOYARSK STATE AGRARIAN UNIVERSITY

660049 Krasnoyarsk, 90 Mira pr.
Telephone and fax (3912) 27-03-86
E-mail: info@kgau.ru
Internet: www.kgau.ru
Founded 1952
State control
Language of instruction: Russian
Academic year: September to June
Rector: Prof. Dr NIKOLAY V. TSUGLENOK
Vice-Rector for Int. Relations and Chief Administrative Officer: Dr GALINA I. TSUGLENOK
Chief Administrative Officer: Dr VASILY V. MATYUSHEV
Chief Librarian: RAISA ZORINA
Library of 360,442 vols
Number of teachers: 636

Number of students: 5,695

KUBAN STATE AGRARIAN UNIVERSITY

350044 Krasnodar, ul. Kalinina 13
Telephone: (8612) 56-49-42
Fax: (8612) 50-29-35
E-mail: inform@kubagro.ru
Internet: www.kubagro.ru
Founded 1922
Library of 635,000 vols
Number of teachers: 1,070
Number of students: 17,496
Rector: Dr IVAN T. TRUBILIN
Fields of study: agrochemistry and soil science, agronomy, tropical and sub-tropical agriculture, veterinary, horticulture and viticulture, animal husbandry, mechanization, plant protection, electrification, construction, law, economics and management, accountancy.

MICHURINSK STATE AGRARIAN UNIVERSITY

393760 Tambov oblast, Michurinsk Internationalnaya 101
Telephone and fax (47545) 5-26-35
E-mail: info@mgau.ru
Internet: www.mgau.ru
Founded 1931
Language of instruction: Russian
Rector: ALEXANDR V. NIKITIN
Library of 300,000 vols
Number of teachers: 395
Number of students: 7,000
Fields of study: fruit and vegetable production, viticulture, agronomy, selection and genetics of crops, storing and processing of agricultural produce, agroecology, commodity research, horticulture, economics and management of agricultural enterprises, livestock production, commerce, accounting and auditing, banking and finance, catering technologies, municipal management, landscape design
Publication: *Herald of Michurinsk State Agrarian University*.

MOSCOW STATE AGRO-ENGINEERING UNIVERSITY, V. P. GORYACHKIN

127540 Moscow, ul. Timiryazevskaya 58
Telephone: (495) 976-36-40
Fax: (495) 976-78-74
E-mail: rkt@mail.msau.ru
Internet: www.msau.ru
Founded 1930
State control
Language of instruction: Russian
Academic year: September to June
Pres. and Rector: MIKHAIL N. EROKHIN
Library: 1m. vols
Number of teachers: 400
Number of students: 5,500
Publication: *Vestnik*

DEANS
Agricultural Education: VASILIY P. KOSYREV
Economics: VLADIMIR T. VODYANNIKOV
Energy: VLADIMIR I. ZAGINAILOV
Processes and Machines in Agribusiness: ANATOLIY N. SKOROHODOV
Technical Service in Agro-Industrial Complex: SERGEY P. KAZANCEV

MOSCOW STATE UNIVERSITY OF LAND MANAGEMENT

105064 Moscow, ul. Kazakova 15
Telephone: (495) 261-31-46
Internet: www.guz.ru
Founded 1779
Faculties of architecture, correspondence, further training, land management, land tenure, law, municipal land tenure, retraining
Rector: Prof. SERGEI N. VOLKOV
Library of 220,000 vols
Publications: *Land Boundary Register* (1 a year), *Rural Architecture* (1 a year).

NOVOSIBIRSK STATE AGRARIAN UNIVERSITY

630039 Novosibirsk, ul. Dobrolyubova 160
Telephone: (3832) 67-38-11
Fax: (3832) 67-39-22
E-mail: public@nsau.edu.ru
Internet: www.nsau.edu.ru
Rector: Prof. ANATOLY F. KONDRATOV
Library of 252,000 vols
Number of teachers: 437
Number of students: 9,400
Fields of study: agronomy, plant protection, mechanization, economics and management, accounting.

OMSK STATE AGRARIAN UNIVERSITY

644008 Omsk, Institutskaya pl. 2
Telephone: (3812) 65-17-72
Fax: (3812) 65-10-72
E-mail: adm@omgau.ru
Internet: www.omgau.ru
Founded 1918
Faculties of agricultural engineering, agrochemistry, agronomy, dairy production technology, mathematics and social studies, soil science and environment, water resource engineering, humanities; institute of economics and finance, institute of land use planning and tenure, institute of veterinary medicine institute of part-time and continued education
Rector: NIKOLAI M. KOLYCHEV
Library of 622,000 vols
Number of teachers: 979
Number of students: 10,357
Publications: *Kirovets* (12 a year), *Vestnik OmGAU* (4 a year).

OREL STATE AGRARIAN UNIVERSITY

302019 Orel, ul. Generala Rodina 69
Telephone: (0862) 29-40-50
Fax: (0862) 29-40-79
E-mail: pnv@orel.ru
Internet: www.orelsau.ru
Founded 1975 as Orel Agricultural Institute; present name and status 1999
Rector: Prof. NIKOLAI V. PARAKHIN.

ORENBURG STATE AGRARIAN UNIVERSITY

460014 Orenburg, ul. Leninskaya 59
Telephone and fax (3532) 77-52-30
E-mail: orensau@mail.ru
Internet: www.orensau.ru
Founded 1930
Faculties of agronomy, biotechnology, economics and law, forestry, information technology, mechanization of agriculture, veterinary medicine
Rector: VLADIMIR V. KARAKULEV

Library of 842,127 vols
Number of teachers: 601
Number of students: 8,210
Publication: *Works*.

ST PETERSBURG STATE AGRARIAN UNIVERSITY

189620 St Petersburg, Pushkin, Peterburgskoe shosse 2
Telephone: (812) 470-04-22
Fax: (812) 465-05-05
Founded 1904
Br. in Polessk; depts of agroecology and soil science, agronomy, animal husbandry, economics, engineering, farm electrification, law, plant protection, vegetable growing
Rector: VLADIMIR S. SHKRABAK
Library of 782,700 vols
Number of teachers: 473
Number of students: 7,865
Publication: *Collection of Scientific Research Works* (8 a year).

SARATOV STATE AGRARIAN UNIVERSITY, N. I. VAVILOV

410034 Saratov, Teatralnaya pl. 1
Telephone: (8452) 26-32-92
Fax: (8452) 72-30-42
E-mail: rector@ssau.saratov.ru
Internet: www.ssau.saratov.ru
Founded 1997
Fields of study: agricultural electrification and automation, agricultural mechanization, agronomy, amelioration and village arrangement, biotechnology, economics, forestry, mechanization of farm production processing, plant protection, technical service, technology, veterinary
Rector: NIKOLAI I. KUZNETSOV
Library: 1.5m. vols
Number of teachers: 1,189
Number of students: 19,036

STAVROPOL STATE AGRARIAN UNIVERSITY

355017 Stavropol, Zootekhnichesky per. 12
Telephone: (8652) 35-22-82
Fax: (8652) 34-58-70
E-mail: rector@stgau.ru
Internet: www.stgau.ru
Founded 1930
Languages of instruction: English, Russian
Academic year: September to June
Rector: Prof. VLADIMIR IV. TRUKHACHEV
Vice-Rector for Education: Dr IVAN V. ATANOV
Library: 3m. vols
Number of teachers: 1,500
Number of students: 17,500
Publication: *Collection of Scientific Works* (1 a year)

DEANS
Accounting and Finance: Prof. IGOR SKLYAROV
Agricultural Mechanization: Dr MIKHAIL DANILOV
Agronomy: Prof. ALEXANDR ESAULKO
Economics: Prof. OLGA KUSAKINA
Electrical Engineering: Dr IVAN ATANOV
Plant Protection: Prof. ALEXANDR ESAULKO
Technological Management: Prof. MARINA SELIONOVA
Veterinarian Medicine: Dr VALERY BELYAEV

VORONEZH STATE AGRARIAN UNIVERSITY, K. D. GLINKA

Telephone and fax (732) 52-86-31

E-mail: an@vsau.ru
Internet: www.vsau.ru
Founded 1913
Fields of study: agribusiness, agricultural economics, agricultural engineering, agrochemistry and soil science, agronomy, animal sciences, food-processing technology, land surveying, veterinary science
Rector: VLADIMIR E. SHEVCHENKO
Library of 870,000 vols
Number of teachers: 528
Number of students: 8,663
Publication: *Zapiski* (Notes).

HUMANITIES AND SCIENCES UNIVERSITIES

ADYGHE STATE UNIVERSITY

352700 Republic of Adygheya, Maykop, ul. Universitetskaya 208
Telephone and fax (8772) 27-02-73
E-mail: adsu@adygnet.ru
Internet: www.adygnet.ru
State control
Founded 1941, present name and status 1993
Brs in Apsheronsk, Belorechensk, Eisk, Novokubansk, Sochi and Koshekhabl
Rector: Prof. RASHID D. KHUNAGOV
Library of 529,000 vols
Number of teachers: 550
Number of students: 7,547

DEANS
Faculty of Economics: RAMAZAN M. TESHEV
Faculty of Foreign Languages: SUSANNA K. BEDANOKOVA
Faculty of Law: AZAMAT M. SHADZHE
Faculty of Pedagogy: FATIMA P. KHAKNOVA
Faculty of Philology: UCHUZHUK M. PANESH

ALTAI STATE UNIVERSITY

656049 Altai Krai, Barnaul, pr. Lenina 61
Telephone: (3852) 66-75-84
Fax: (3852) 66-76-26
E-mail: rector@asu.ru
Internet: www.asu.ru
Founded 1973
State control
Language of instruction: Russian
Academic year: September to June
Rector: Prof. SERGEI ZEMLYUKOV
Vice-Rector for Academic Affairs: Prof. IRINA ROTANOVA
Vice-Rector for Finance: Prof. VITALY MISHCHENKO
Vice-Rector for Strategic Programs and Int. Cooperation: IGOR DUBINA
Vice-Rector for Science and Innovations: YURI LADYGIN
Librarian: GALINA TRUSHNIKOVA
Library: 1m. vols, 1,400 periodicals
Number of teachers: 750
Number of students: 18,000
Publications: *Chemistry of Vegetative Raw Materials* (4 a year, online), *Proceedings* (8 a year), *Turchaninovia* (4 a year, online)

DEANS
Faculty of Arts: L. NEKHVYADOVICH
Faculty of Biology: G. SOKOLOVA
Faculty of Chemistry: N. BAZARNOVA
Faculty of Distance Learning: D. PAPIN
Faculty of Economics: O. MAMCHENKO
Faculty of Geography: G. BARYSHNIKOV
Faculty of History: E. DEMCHIK
Faculty of Journalism: V. MANSUROVA
Faculty of Law: V. SOROKIN
Faculty of Mathematics: A. PETROVA
Faculty of Pedagogical Education: O. KUNGOROVA
Faculty of Philology: N. BUGORSKAYA

Faculty of Physics and Technology: V. POLY-
AKOV
Faculty of Political Science: E. PRITCHINA
Faculty of Public Relations: N. KUZNETSOVA
Faculty of Preliminary Training: N. YAKOV-
LEVA
Faculty of Psychology and Philosophy: L.
DEMINA
Faculty of Sociology: O. KOLESNIKOVA

PROFESSORS

ALGAZIN, G., Mathematical Methods in Soci-
ology
BARUSHNIKOV, G., Geography
BAZARNOVA, N., Chemistry
BELYAEV, V., Marketing
BEZNOSUK, S., General Physics
BOBROV, M., Sociology
BUDKIN, A., Algebra and Mathematical Logic
BUKATY, V., General Physics
BURDASOV, V., Biology
CHERNUSHOV, Y., Ancient History
CHERVYAKOV, V., Economic Geography
CHUVAKIN, A., Philology
DEMCHIK, E., Sociology
DEMINA, L., Psychology and Philosophy
ELCHANINOV, V., Philosophy
FEDYUKIN, V., Philosophy
GAVLO, V., Criminology
GLUSHANIN, E., History
GOLEV, N., Russian Language
GRIGORYEV, S., Sociology
GUBAR, A., Economics
GUSLYAKOVA, L., Social Work
IVANOV, A., Philosophy
IVOLGIN, A., Political Science
KHALINA, N., Linguistics
KIRUSHIN, Y., Archaeology
KISELEV, V., Human and Animal Physiology
KOMAROV, S., Radio Physics
KOZLOVA, S., Philology
KUPRIYANOV, A., Biology
LAGUTIN, A., Theoretical Physics
LAVRENTIEV, G., Education
MALOLETKO, A., Nature Management
MALTSEV, Y., Algebra and Mathematical
Logic
MAMCHENKO, O., Information Systems
MEDVEDEV, N., Algebra and Mathematical
Logic
MELNIKOV, A., Philosophy
MELNIKOVA, L., Regional Economics
MIRONOV, V., Radiophysics
MISCHENKO, V., Regional Economics
MOISEEV, V., Oriental History
NEVINSKY, V., Constitutional Law
OSKORBIN, N., Cybernetics and Applied
Mathematics
PETROV, B., Analytical Chemistry
POLYAKOV, V., Applied Physics
RASTOV, Y., Empiric Sociology
RAZGON, V., History
REVYAKIN, V., Geography
REVYAKINA, N., Geography
ROGOVSKY, E., Management
SAGALAKOV, A., Experimental Physics
SEMILET, T., Psychology
SENKO, Y., Education
SHAIDUK, A., General Physics
SHELEPOVA, L., Philology
SKUBNEVSKY, V., History
STARTSEV, O., Applied Physics
STEPANSKAYA, T., Art
TROTSKOVSKY, A., Theory of Economics
TRUKHINA, V., Art
TSUB, S., History
USHAKOVA, E., Philosophy
VASILYEV, V., Biochemistry
YELCHANINOV, V., Philosophy
ZEMLYUKOV, S., Criminal Law

AMUR STATE UNIVERSITY

675027 Amur Region, Blagoveshchensk,
Ignatevskoye shosse 21
Telephone: (4162) 39-46-86
Fax: (4162) 39-45-25
E-mail: master@amursu.ru
Internet: www.amursu.ru
Founded 1975
State control
Language of instruction: Russian
Academic year: September to July
Pres.: ELENA S. ASTAPOVA
Vice-Pres.: VICTOR V. PROKAZIN
Pro-Rectors: LUDMILA N. GERASIMOVA,
ANDREW P. ZABEAKO
Chief Admin. Officer: TATYANA V. ASTAFUR-
OVA
Librarian: LUDMILA A. PROKAZINA
Library of 232,000 vols
Number of teachers: 600
Number of students: 8,500
Publication: *Bulletin* (3 a year)

DEANS

Applied Arts: ALEXANDER M. MEDVEDEV
Economics: NATALIA A. BABKINA
Engineering and Physics: VERA F. ULYANY-
CHEVA
International Relations: SVETLANA S. KOSI-
KHINA
Law: SERGEY V. CHERDAKOV
Mathematics and Computer Science: SVE-
TLANA G. SAMOKHVALOVA
Philology: IRINA I. LEIFA
Power Engineering: NATALIA V. SAVINA
Social Sciences: NELLE K. SCHEPKINA

BASHKIR STATE UNIVERSITY

450074 Bashkortostan, Ufa, Z. Validie 32
Telephone: (3472) 72-63-70
Fax: (3472) 73-66-80
E-mail: interdpt@bsu.bashedu.ru
Internet: www.bsunet.ru
Founded 1909
State control
Language of instruction: Russian
Academic year: September to June
Rector: Prof. AHAT G. MUSTAFIN
Vice-Rector for Education: Prof. YAUDAT T.
SULTANAEV
Vice-Rector for Academic Affairs: Prof. NIKO-
LAI D. MOROZKIN
Vice Rector for Science: Prof. RIFKAT TALIPOV
Vice-Rector for Int. Cooperation: ALEXANDR I.
SHABRIN
Univ. Library Dir: EVGENIYA GELVANOVSKAYA
Library: 2m. vols
Number of teachers: 1,325
Number of students: 22,300

DEANS

Faculty of Biology: Prof. RINAT I. IBRAHIMOV
Faculty of Chemistry: Prof. RINAT M.
AHMETHANOV
Faculty of Economics: Prof. FANIYA S. ISKHA-
KOVA
Faculty of Geography: Prof. INBER M. YAP-
PAROV,
Faculty of History: Prof. MARAT M. KULSHAR-
IPOV
Faculty of Mathematics: Prof. TAGIR G.
AMALGILDIN
Faculty of Philology: Prof. ALEXANDER A.
FEDOROV
Faculty of Philosophy and Sociology: Prof.
DAMIR A NURIEV
Faculty of Physics: Prof. ROBERT A. YAKSHI-
BAEV
Faculty of Romance and Germanic Philology:
Prof. RAKHIM Z. MURYASSOV

BELGOROD STATE UNIVERSITY

308015 Belgorod, ul. Pobedy 30
Telephone: (0722) 30-12-11
Fax: (0722) 30-10-12
E-mail: info@bsu.edu.ru
Internet: www.bsu.edu.ru
State control
Founded 1876 as Belgorod Teaching Insti-
tute; 1939–1957 as Belgorod State Teach-
ing Institute; 1957–1994 as Belgorod State
Pedagogical Institute; as Belgorod State
Pedagogical Univ. 1994–1996; present
name and status 1996
Rector: Prof. LEONID YA. DYATCHENKO
First Pro-Rector for Admin., Finance and
Security: MIKHAIL V. KOSTROV
First Pro-Rector and Pro-Rector for Science:
TATYANA M. DAVYDENKO
Pro-Rector for Academic Affairs: VIKTOR N.
TKACHEV
Pro-Rector for Distance and Evening Educa-
tion: VLADIMIR A. SHAPOVALOV
Chief Accountant: NATALYA P. KOZYREVA
Brs in Alekseevka and Stary Oskol, both f.
1999.
Library of 987,987 vols
Number of teachers: 717
Number of students: 13,015

DEANS

Faculty of Biology and Chemistry: GENNADY
M. FOFANOV
Faculty of Computer Science and Telecom-
munications: EVGENY G. ZHILYAKOV
Faculty of Economics: VLADIMIR I. BOLTENKOV
Faculty of Geology and Geography: ALEXAN-
DER N. PETIN
Faculty of History: ELENA YU. PROKOFIEVA
Faculty of Law: EVGENY E. TONKOV
Faculty of Management and Business: VIK-
TORIA B. TARABAEVA
Faculty of Medicine: YURI I. AFANASEV
Faculty of Pedagogy: NIKOLAI V. PODDUBNY
Faculty of Philology: SVETLANA P. GRINEVA
Faculty of Physical Culture: VASILY V.
SOKOREV
Faculty of Physics and Mathematics: OLEG
M. PENKIN
Faculty of Psychology: NADEZHDA I. ISAEVA
Faculty of Romance and Germanic Philology:
OLGA N. PROKHOROVA
Faculty of Socio-Theology: SERGEI A. KOLES-
NIKOV
International Faculty: MIKHAIL A. TRUBITSYN

BELGOROD UNIVERSITY OF CONSUMER CO-OPERATIVES

308023 Belgorod, ul. Sadovaya 116A
Telephone: (0722) 6-08-48
Fax: (0722) 6-49-65
E-mail: bupk@intbel.ru
Internet: www.bupk.ru
Faculties of economics, trade management;
br. in Stavropol
Rector: VITALY I. TEPLOV
Number of teachers: 326
Number of students: 8,030

BRATSK STATE UNIVERSITY

665709 Bratsk, Makarenko ul. 40
Telephone and fax (3953) 33-20-08
E-mail: rector@brstu.ru
Internet: www.brstu.ru
Founded 1980 as Bratsk Industrial Institute,
present name and status 2004
State control
Language of instruction: Russian
Academic year: September to June
Rector: Prof. Dr SERGEY V. BELOKOBYLSKY

Pro-Rector for Education: Prof. Dr LEONID A. MAMAYEV

Pro-Rector for Economics and Univ. Devt: Prof. YELENA I. LUKOVNIKOVA

Pro-Rector for Innovation: Prof. VALERY A. LYUBLINSKY

Pro-Rector for Secondary Professional Education: VLADIMIR P. KALINNIKOV

Pro-Rector for Science: Prof. Dr PETR M. OGAR

Library of 633,114 vols
Number of teachers: 324
Number of students: 8,673

Publications: *Issues of Social-Economic Development of Siberia* (4 a year), *Systems. Methods. Technologies* (4 a year)

DEANS

Faculty of Building Engineering: Assoc. Prof. ALEXANDER A. ZINOVYEV

Faculty of Correspondence Education: Prof. OLEG V. KULIKOV

Faculty of Economics and Management: Prof. MIKHAIL P. GLEBOV

Faculty of Forestry Engineering: Prof. GARIK D. GASPARYAN

Faculty of Humanities and Pedagogical Sciences: Assoc. Prof. SERGEY A. SOLDATOV

Faculty of Intensive Specialists' Training: Assoc. Prof. VLADIMIR B. KASHUBA

Faculty of Masters Degree Programmes: Assoc. Prof. YELENA A. CHEVSKAYA

Faculty of Mechanics: Assoc. Prof. SERGEY A. ZENKOV

Faculty of Natural Sciences: Assoc. Prof. ALLA D. SINEGIBSKAYA

Faculty of Power Engineering and Automation: Assoc. Prof. SVETLANA M. IGNATYEVA

BRYANSK STATE UNIVERSITY

241036 Bryansk, Bezhitskaya ul. 14

Telephone: (083) 246-65-38
Fax: (083) 246-63-53
Internet: www.bgunet.com
State control

Founded 1974

Rector: Prof. ANDREI V. ANTYUKHOV
Pro-Rector of Academic Affairs: Prof. VLADIMIR V. SHLYK

Number of teachers: 515
Number of students: 15,712

BURYAT STATE UNIVERSITY

670000 Ulan-Ude, ul. Smolina 24A

Telephone: (3012) 21-15-80
Fax: (3012) 21-05-88
E-mail: univer@bsu.ru
Internet: www.bsu.ru

Founded 1932 as Buryat State Teacher Training Institute, present name and status 1995
State control
Languages of instruction: Buryat, Russian
Academic year: August to June

Rector: Prof. Dr STEPAN V. KALMYKOV
First Pro-Rector: Prof. Dr TSYDYPZHAP Z. DORZHIYEV
Pro-Rector for Academic Affairs: Assoc. Prof. ANDREY K MORDOVSKOY
Pro-Rector for Admin.: Assoc. Prof. ALEXANDER G. SHARGAEV
Pro-Rector for Research: Prof. Dr ALEXANDER S. BULDAEV
Pro-Rector for Social Policy and Extra-Curricular Activities: Assoc. Prof. ANDREY V KOZULIN
Academic Ccl's Sec.: Asoc. Prof. TATIANA V. PALIKOVA

Library of 1,150,000 vols
Number of teachers: 985
Number of students: 10,000

DEANS

Faculty of Biology and Geography: ERDENI N. ELAEV

Faculty of Chemistry: GALINA N. BATOROVA

Faculty of Eastern Studies: POLINA P. DASHINIMAYEVA

Faculty of Economics and Management: MARIYA V. BADMAEVA

Faculty of Foreign Languages: NINA A. BOKHACH

Faculty of History: ANNA A. BURKINA

Faculty of Law: JAMILYA K. CHIMITOVA

Faculty of Medicine: VLADIMIR E. KHITRIKHEEV

Faculty of Physics and Technology: VALENTINA M. KHALTANOVA

Faculty of Socio-Psychology: TATIYANA S. BAZAROVA

Faculty of Philology: VERA V. BASHKEEVA

Faculty of Physical Culture, Sport and Tourism: GENNADY P. PETRENKO

Institute of Mathematics and Computer Science: IVAN K. SHARANKHAYEV

National Institute: BATOR B. ZANDARAEV

Pedagogical Institute: NINA Z. DAGBAEVA

CHELYABINSK STATE UNIVERSITY

454021 Chelyabinsk, ul. Bratev Kashirinykh 129

Telephone: (3512) 42-05-31
Fax: (3512) 42-09-25
E-mail: postmaster@csu.ru
Internet: www.csu.ru

Founded 1976
Academic year: September to July

Rector: Prof. V. D. BATUKHTIN
Registrar: A. YU. SHATIN
Librarian: L. M. KISELYOVA

Number of teachers: 1,760 (1,410 full-time, 350 part-time)
Number of students: 14,369 (7,800 full-time, 6,569 correspondence)

Publication: *Vestnik*

DEANS

Faculty of Access to Higher Education: E. A. MARTYNOVA

Faculty of Biology: A. L. BURMISTROVA

Faculty of Chemistry: A. V. BELIK

Faculty of Continuing Education: V. A. BURMISTROV

Faculty of Ecology: S. G. AGEEV

Faculty of Economics: T. A. VERESHCHAGINA

Faculty of Eurasia and the East: G. V. SACHKO

Faculty of History: G. A. GONCHAROV

Faculty of Journalism: B. N. KIRSHIN

Faculty of Law: V. A. LEBEDEV

Faculty of Linguistics and Translation: L. A. NEFYODOVA

Faculty of Management: L. A. KUZNETSOVA

Faculty of Mathematics: O. N. DEMENTIEV

Faculty of Original Professions: T. M. KUYASHEVA

Faculty of Philology: I. YU. KARTASHOVA

Faculty of Physics: V. D. BUCHELNIKOV

Institute of Psychology and Pedagogics: S. A. REPIN

PROFESSORS

ABRAMOVSKY, A. P., History
AKHMEDZIANOV, M. G., Physical Education
ALEEV, Physics and Mathematics
ALEVRAS, N. N., History
AZNACHEEVA, E. N., Linguistics
BALYKIN, V. P., Chemistry
BATUKHTIN, V. D., Mathematical Theory of Optimization and Control
BELANKOV, Physics and Mathematics
BELIK, A. V., Chemistry
BENT, M. I., Philology
BLUDENOV, A. F., Economics

BUCHELNIKOV, V. D., Physics and Mathematics
BURMISTROV, V. A., Physics and Mathematics
BURMISTROVA, A. L., Biology
BYCHKOV, I. V., Physics and Mathematics
CHERNETSOV, P. I., Education
DARANKOV, A. Y., Economics
DEMENTIEV, O. N., Physics and Mathematics
DUDOROV, A. Y., Physics and Mathematics
GALIULINA, G. S., History
GOLIKOV, A. A., Economics
GOLOVANOV, V. I., Technology
GORSHKOV, A. V., Economics
GRUDZINSKY, V. V., History
ILYIN, A. M., Physics and Mathematics
JEYT, Physics and Mathematics
KOLOSOVA, O. S., Medicine
KORNEV, N. I., Economics
LAPPA, A. V., Physics and Mathematics
LEBEDEV, V. A., Law
LEZHNEVA, Pedagogics
MARTYNOVA, Pedagogics
MATUSHKIN, S. I., Didactics
MATVEEV, S. V., Topology
MIKHNUKEVICH, V. A., Philology
NARSKY, I. V., History
NEFYODOVA, L. A., Linguistics
NEVELEV, A. B., Philosophy
PAVLENKO, V. N., Physics and Mathematics
PISCHCLIULIN, Pedagogics
PITINA, S. A., Linguistics
PLOKHIKH, N. A., Geology and Mineralogy
POPOV, V. I., Law
POPOVA, N. B., Philology
PRIVEZENTSEV, A. P., Physics and Mathematics
RATANOV, N. E., Physics and Mathematics
REPIN, S. A., Didactics
ROZKOV, A. V., Physics and Mathematics
SABITOV, P. A., Law
SEDOV, V. V., Political Economy
SHATIN, A. YU., Economics
SHISHMARENKOVA, G. YA., Education
SHKATOVA, L. A., Russian Language
SINYAVSKY, V. A., Geology and Mineralogy
SMIRNOV, S. S., History
SOLOVIEV, A. A., Physics and Mathematics
SUKHANOV, K. N., Philosophy
SUROV, Physics and Mathematics
SVIRIDUK, G. A., Physics and Mathematics
TANANA, V. P., Mathematics
TYUMENTSEV, V. A., Physics and Mathematics
UCHOBOTOV, V. I., Physics
YALOVETS, A. P., Physics
YARTSEV, V. M., Physics and Mathematics
ZAGIDULLINA, M. V., Linguistics

CHECHEN STATE UNIVERSITY

Chechnya, 364907 Groznyi, ul. Sheripova 32

Telephone: (87322) 23-40-89

Founded 1972

Faculties of chemistry and biology, economics, geography, history, mathematics, philology, physics, romance and Germanic philology

Rector: ADNAN D. KHAMZAYEV

Number of teachers: 620
Number of students: 8,000

CHEREPOVETS STATE UNIVERSITY

162600 Cherepovets, ul. Lunacharskogo 5

Telephone: (8202) 55-65-97
Fax: (8202) 55-70-49
E-mail: chsu@chsu.ru
Internet: www.chsu.ru

Founded 1919

Rector: Prof. VLADIMIR S. GRYZLOV
First Pro-Rector: Prof. EVGENY V. ERSHOV

Library of 437,168 vols.

CHITA STATE UNIVERSITY

672039 Chita, Aleksandro-Zavodskaya ul. 30
Telephone and fax (3022) 41-64-44
E-mail: root@chitgu.ru
Internet: www.chitgu.ru

Founded 1966 as a br. of Irkutsk State Polytechnic Institute
State control
Language of instruction: Chinese, English, French, Russian
Academic year: September to June (2 semesters)

Rector: Prof. YURI N. REZNIK
Vice-Rector: Prof. SERGEY A. IVANOV
Librarian: NINA V. OKUNEVA

Library of 828,057 vols
Number of teachers: 845
Number of students: 12,377

Publications: *ChSU Journal* (6 a year, scientific), *Science: XX1 Century* (1 a year, scientific), *Social Anthropology of North-East Asia* (SCANEA journal, 4 a year, scientific)

DEANS

Automobile Transportation: SERGEI P. OZORNIN
Civil Engineering: A.V. KUYDIN
Computer Science and Economics: TATYANA A. PLYUSNINA
Ecology: VLADIMIR V. ZVYAGINTSEV
Economics: S. V. VASILIEVA
Geology: SERGEI V. SMOLICH
International Law: D. S. LUKONIN
Law: V. V. BESSONOVA
Management: N. P. KALASHNIKOVA
Mining: LUDMILA G. NIKITINA
Power Technology: YURI V. ERMOLAEV
Professional Development: M. G. MELKOYAN
Social Policy and Cultural Studies: E. E. KOVALENOK
Social Systems and Regional Forecasting: A. A. RUSANOVA
Technology: VITALY V. GRUSHEV

PROFESSORS

ABAKUMOV, Y., Mathematics
ABRAMOV, V., Philosophy
ABRAMOVA, N., Oriental Studies
BALANDIN, O., Constructing Engineering
BEIDINA, T., Political Studies
BERNUKEVICH, T., Social Philosophy
BORODIN, V., Law
BUKIN, A., Anthropology
CHERKASOV, V., Mining
ERDYNEEVA, K., Psychology
FATIANOV, A., Mining Engineering
FOMINA, M., Philosophy
GARMAEV, Y., Law
GERASIMOV, V., Geotechnology
GLAZYRINA, I., Economy
IMETINOV, N., Civil Engineering
IVANOV, S., Power Engineering
KARASEV, K., Chemistry
KOGAN, E., Mathematics
KONDRATIEV, V., Geocryology
KOSTROMIN, M., Mining Engineering
KUZNETSOV, O., Ethnography
LETUNOV, V., Chemistry
LIZUNKIN, V., Geotechnology
LUBIMOVA, L., Linguistic
MAKAROV, A., Law
MALYSHEV, E., Economy
MYAZIN, V., Mining Engineering
OVESHNIKOV, Y., Geoecology
OVSEYCHUK, V., Geotechnology
POLUTOVA, M., Pedagogy
REZNIK, Y., Geotechnology
ROMANOVA, N., Sociology
SEKISOV, G., Geotechnology
SHVETSOV, M., Pedagogy
SUVOROV, I., Engineering
SVININ, V., Engineering
TEREKHOVA, T., Pedagogy

TRUBACHEV, A., Mining Engineering
VASILIEVA, K., Philosophy
VORONOV, E., Geotechnology
ZASLONOVSKY, V., Hydrology

CHUVASH STATE UNIVERSITY

428015 Chuvash Autonomous Republic, Cheboksary, Moskovsky pr. 15
Telephone: (8352) 24-03-79
Fax: (8352) 42-80-90
E-mail: office@chuvsu.ru
Internet: www.chuvsu.ru

Founded 1967
State control
Languages of instruction: Chuvash, Russian
Academic year: September to July

Rector: Prof. Dr LEV P. KURAKOV
First Vice-Rector: NIKOLAI F. GRIGORIEV
Vice-Rector for Academic Affairs: VSEVOLOD G. AGAKOV
Librarian: NINA D. NIKITINA

Library: see Libraries and Archives
Number of teachers: 1,270
Number of students: 19,391

Publications: *Chuvash segodny*, *Ulyanovets* (52 a year)

DEANS

Faculty of Arts: M. N. YACLASHKYN
Faculty of Chemistry: O. Y. NOSAKIN
Faculty of Chuvash Philology and Culture: V. G. RODIONOV
Faculty of Construction: Y. V. CHERNOV
Faculty of Economics: A. E. YAKOVLEV
Faculty of Electrical and Power Engineering: N. A. KOKOREV
Faculty of Electrical Engineering: N. A. KOKOREV
Faculty of Geography: I. N. SHIROKOV
Faculty of History: A. V. ARSENTEVA
Faculty of Journalism: A. P. DANILOV
Faculty of Law: N. V. IVANZOVA
Faculty of Mathematics: V. G. AGAKOV
Faculty of Medicine: V. E. VOLKOV
Faculty of Philology: G. E. KORNILOV
Faculty of Physics: L. K. MYTRUCHIN
Faculty of Psychology and Administration: E. N. KADISHEV
Faculty of Stomatology and Pediatrics: E. V. BUSHUEVA
Higher Business School: L. P. KURAKOV (Dir)
Higher School For Training Engineers: V. A. CHEDRIN (Dir)

DAGESTAN STATE UNIVERSITY

Dagestan, 367000 Makhachkala, 43A Gadzhiyev St
Telephone and fax (8722) 68-23-26
E-mail: dgu@dgu.ru
Internet: www.dgu.ru

Founded 1931
State control
Language of instruction: Russian
Academic year: September to July

Rector: Prof. M. KH. RABADANOV
Vice-Rector for Academic Affairs: Prof. M. M. GASANOV
Vice-Rector for Research and Innovation: Prof. N. A. ASHURBEKOV
Librarian: L. I. ALIEVA

Library: 2.5m. vols
Number of teachers: 1,100
Number of students: 20,000

Publication: *Herald of Dagestan State Universiy*

DEANS

Faculty of Biology: Dr R. A. KHALILOV
Faculty of Chemistry: Dr A. SH. RAMAZANOV
Faculty of Culture: Dr N. K. ADZHAMATOVA

Faculty of Ecology and Geography: Dr G. M. ABDURAKHMANOV
Faculty of Economics: Dr D. K. DZHAVATOV
Faculty of Foreign Languages: Dr T. I. ASHURBEKOVA
Faculty of History: Dr B. B. BULATOV
Faculty of Information and Information Technologies: Dr S. A. AKHMEDOV
Faculty of International and Pre-University Training: Dr K. G. KHALIKOV
Faculty of Law: Dr SH. B. MAGOMEDOV
Faculty of Mathematics and Computer Science: Dr A. K. RAMAZANOV
Faculty of Oriental Studies: Dr A. R. MAGOMEDOV
Faculty of Philology: Dr SH. A. MAZANAEV
Faculty of Physical Training and Sport: Dr A. SH. RAMAZANOV
Faculty of Physics: Dr V. S. KURBANISMAILOV
Faculty of Professional Development of Teachers: Dr N. SH. ZAGIROV
Faculty of Psychology and Philosophy: Dr M. Y. YAKHIAEV
Faculty of Social Studies: Dr I. I. MAGOMED-SULTANOV

ELETS STATE UNIVERSITY 'I. A. BUNIN'

399770 Lipetsk Region, Elets, ul. Kommunarov 28
Telephone: (07467) 2-21-93
Fax: (07467) 2-04-63
E-mail: main@elsu.ru
Internet: www.elsu.ru

Founded 1939
State control

Rector: VALERY P. KUZOVLEV
First Pro-Rector for Academic Affairs: ANDREY A. ZAITSEV
Second Pro-Rector for Academic Affairs: OLGA N. SARYCHEVA
Pro-Rector for Admin. and Finance: STANISLAV A. KLEIMENOV

DEANS

Faculty of Design: NADEZHDA P. LOGINOVA
Faculty of Economics: SVETLANA A. VOROTYNTSEVA
Faculty of Engineering and Physics: NATALYA A. FORTUNOVA
Faculty of Foreign Languages: IRINA V. ZAITSEVA
Faculty of Further Pedagogic Training: EKATERINA V. CHERNYKH
Faculty of History: DENIS A. LIAPIN
Faculty of Law: SERGEY S. FOMENKO
Faculty of Pedagogy and Primary Education: IRINA A. YELETSKICH
Faculty of Pedagogy and Psychology: TATIANA D. KRASOVA
Faculty of Philology: OLGA A. MESHCHERIAKOVA
Faculty of Physics and Mathematics: ELENA I. TROFIMOVA
Faculty of Sport: VLADIMIR V. MAKAROV

FAR EASTERN STATE UNIVERSITY

690600 Vladivostok, ul. Sukhanova 8
Telephone: (4232) 26-12-80
Fax: (4232) 25-72-00
E-mail: office@dip.dvgu.ru
Internet: www.dvgu.ru

Founded 1899
State control
Language of instruction: Russian
Academic year: September to June

Rector: V. I. KURILOV
Pro-Rectors: V. P. DIKAREV, N. M. PESTEREVA, B. L. REZNIK, R. M. SAMIGULIN, R. P. SHEPELEVA, G. S. VOROPAYEV
Librarian: N. N. GAIDARENKO
Library: see Libraries

Number of teachers: 993
Number of students: 16,000
Publications: *News of the Institute of International Studies* (4 a year), *News of the Institute of Oriental Studies* (1 a year), *The Russian Far East* (4 a year)

DEANS

Chemistry and Chemical Ecology: A. A. KAPUSTINA
Correspondence Programme: L. I. ROMANOVA
Economics: R. V. SABITOVA
Entrepreneurial Law: A. S. SHEVCHENKO
German Philology: L. P. BONDARENKO
History and Philosophy: O. V. SIDORENKO
Information Technology: I. V. SOPPA
International Economic Relations and Management: A. A. KHAMATOVA
International Law: V. V. GAVRILOV
International Relations: T. D. KHUZIYATOV
Investigation and Public Prosecution: A. F. REKHOVSKY
Japanese Studies: A. G. SHNYRKO
Journalism: V. V. BAKSHIN
Jurisprudence: A. G. KORCHAGIN
Law (in Petropavlovsk-Kamchatsky): L. A. ZAKHOZHY
Law (in Yuzhno-Sakhalinsk): M. G. SEREBRENNIKOV
Management and Business: S. B. GOLOVACHEV
Mathematics and Computer Science: V. B. OSIPOV
Physics: P. N. KORNYUSHIN
Physics and Engineering: V. G. LIFSHITS
Political Science and Public Administration: A. M. KUZNETSOV
Psychology and Social Work: A. V. STETSIV
Romance Philology: N. S. MOREVA
Russian Philology: V. I. SHESTOPALOVA
Sinology: O. V. KUCHUK
State Law: V. F. SHEKHOVTSOV
Academy of Ecology, Marine Biology and Biotechnology: V. A. KUDRYASHOV
Higher College of Korean Studies: V. V. VERKHOLYAK (Dir)
Institute of Environment: YU. B. ZONOV (Dir)
Institute of Foreign Languages: L. P. BONDARENKO (Dir)
Institute of International Tourism and Hospitality: N. M. PESTEREVA (Dir)
Institute of Law: V. I. KURILOV (Dir)
Institute of Management and Business: A. A. BELUSOV (Dir)
Institute of Military Programmes: S. A. BOGATYRENKO (Dir)
Institute of Oriental Studies: A. A. KHAMATOVA (Dir)
Institute of Physics and Information Technology: V. I. BELOKON (Dir)
Institute of Pre-University Training: N. A. SMAL (Dir)
Institute of Professional Development and In-Service Training: E. M. CHUKHRAYEV (Dir)
Institute for Training Highly Qualified Specialists: B. L. REZNIK (Dir)
Pacific Institute of Distance Education and Technology: V. I. VOVNA (Dir)
Research Institute of Chemistry: N. P. SHAPKIN (Dir)
Research Institute of Regional Studies: B. K. STAROSTIN (Dir)
Vladivostok Institute for International Studies of the Asia-Pacific Region: M. YU. SHINKOVSKY (Dir)
FESU branch in Artem: P. V. KHARITONSKY (Dir)
FESU branch in Hakodate: S. N. ILYIN (Dir)
FESU branch in Nakhodka: A. I. RAZGONOV (Dir)

PROFESSORS

ABAKUMOV, A. I., Mathematics
ABRAMOVA, L. A., Economics

AFINOGENOV, YU. A., Law
AKIMOVA, L. V., Economics
AKIMOVA, T. I., Chemistry
ALEXANDROVSKAYA, L. V., Economics
ALEXEYEV, G. V., Mathematics
ANIKONOV, D. S., Mathematics
ANISIMOV, A. P., Biology
ANISIMOV, N. A., Mathematics
ASHCHEPKOV, L. T., Mathematics
BAKLANOV, P. YA., Physical Geography
BAKSHIN, V. V., Journalism
BELOKON, V. I., Physics
BELOUSOV, A. A., Economics
BEREZNIKOV, K. P., Geophysics
BESSONOVA, V. I., Chemistry
BINDER, A. I., Economics
BINEVSKY, A. A., Philosophy
BONDARENKO, L. P., English Philology
BRESLAVETS, T. I., Japanese Philology
BRODYANSKY, D. L., History
BROVKO, P. F., Geography
BUKIN, O. A., Physics
CHEBOTKEVICH, L. A., Physics
CHIZHOV, L. N., Management
CHUVAKIN, A. A., Russian Philology
DASHKO, N. A., Geophysics
DERBENTSEVA, A. M., Biology
DROZDOV, A. L., Chemistry
DUBININ, V. N., Mathematics
DYUZHIKOVA, E. A., English
EFIMENKO, V. F., Physics
ELANTSEVA, O. P., History
ELYAKOV, G. B., Chemistry
FISENKO, I. I., Economics
FROLOV, N. N., Mathematics
GALKINA, L. V., Korean Philology
GAVRILOVA, T. L., Mathematics
GERASIMENKO, M. D., Physics
GLUSHCHENKO, I. I., History
GRAMM-OSIPOV, L. M., Chemistry
GRAMM-OSIPOV, V. N., Chemistry
IGNATYUK, V. A., Physics
ILYUSHIN, I. A., Journalism
ISAYEVA, T. S., Law
ISAYEVA, V. V., Biology
IVANKOV, V. N., Biology
IVLEV, A. M., Biology
KAMINSKY, V. A., Chemistry
KAPUSTINA, A. A., Chemistry
KARTAVTSEV, YU. F., Biology
KHAMATOVA, A. A., International Economic Relations and Management
KHRISTOFOROVA, N. K., Biology
KILMATOV, T. R., Oceanology
KLESHCHEV, A. S., Mathematics
KNYAZEV, S. D., Law
KOCHETKOV, V. P., English Language
KOGAN, B. I., Mathematics
KOMAROVA, T. A., Biology
KONDRIKOV, N. B., Chemistry
KORNYUSHIN, P. N., Physics
KOROBEYEV, A. I., Law
KOROTKY, A. M., Physical Geography
KOSTETSKY, E. YA., Biology
KRIVSHENKO, S. F., Russian Philology
KUDRYASHOV, V. A., Biology
KULEBYAKIN, YE. V., Social Work
KULESHOV, YE. L., Physics
KURILOV, V. I., Law
KUSAKIN, O. G., Biology
KUZNETSOV, A. M., Political Science
KUZNETSOV, N. V., Mathematics
KUZNETSOVA, N. V., Economy and Finance of Asian Pacific Countries
LEBEDKO, M. G., English
LIFSHITS, V. G., Physics
MEDVEDEVA, E. S., Economics
MEDVEDEVA, K. A., Russian Philology
MEGRABOVA, E. G., English
MELNIKOVA, T. N., English
MIKHAILOV, V. S., International Law
MIKHEEV, R. I., Law
MIRONETS, YU. A., English
NEDOLUZHKO, A. V., Biology
NELEZIN, A. D., Oceanology
NEMOV, R. S., Psychology

NESTERENKO, A. D., Economics
NOMOKONOV, V. A., Law
NURMINSKY, YE. A., Mathematics
OSIPOV, V. B., Mathematics
OSTANIN, V. A., Economics
OVRAKH, G. P., Political Science
PAK, G. K., Mathematics
PECHERITSA, V. F., International Relations
PESTEREVA, N. M., Geophysics
PRIYATKINA, A. F., Russian Philology
PROSHINA, Z. G., English
PSCHENICHNIKOV, B. F., Biology
RAGULIN, P. G., Economics
REZNICHENKO, I. M., Law
REZNIK, B. L., Physics
ROMANOVA, L. I., Law
SABITOVA, R. G., Economics
SAMIGULIN, R. M., History
SARANIN, A. A., Physics
SAZONOV, V. G., International Economics
SEROV, V. M., Japanese Studies
SHAKHOV, V. N., Economics
SHAPKIN, N. P., Chemistry
SHASHKOV, N. I., Philosophy
SHAVKUNOV, E. V., History
SHCHETINNIKOV, P. S., Economics
SHEKHOVTSOV, V. A., Law
SHEPELEVA, R. P., Mathematics
SHEVCHENKO, A. S., Law
SHEVCHENKO, D. K., Mathematics
SHISHMARYOV, YU. E., Mathematics
SHLYK, V. A., Mathematics
SHNYRKO, A. A., Japanese Studies
SOLONITSYNA, A. A., Sociocultural Service and Tourism
SONIN, V. V., Law
SOVASTEEV, V. V., History
STARODUMOVA, YE. A., Russian Philology
STONIK, V. A., Chemistry
SUKHANOV, V. V., Biology
SVYATETSKAYA, T. K., Law
TEREKHOVA, E. V., Foreign Languages
TITOV, A. I., Physics
TKACHEV, V. A., Journalism
TSITSIASHVILI, G. SH., Mathematics
TURCHIN, D. A., Law
VANEEVA, L. A., Law
VASKOVSKY, V. E., Chemistry
VELIKAYA, N. I., Russian Philology
VERISOTSKAYA, YE. V., Japanese Studies
VOLOSHIN, G. YA., Mathematics
VOVNA, V. I., Physics
VYSOTSKY, V. I., Chemistry
YACHIN, S. E., Philosophy
YAKUNIN, L. P., Oceanology
YAROVENKO, V. V., Law
YELANTSEVA, O. P., Economics
YERMAKOVA, E. V., History
YUDIN, V. V., Physics
YUDINA, L. A., Physics
ZAKHOZHY, L. A., Law
ZAYATS, T. S., Chinese Philology
ZHARIKOV, E. P., International Economics
ZHIRMUNSKY, A. V., Biology
ZHURAVLEV, YU. N., Biology
ZOLOTAR, G. YA., Chemistry
ZONOV, YU. B., Geophysics
ZUS, L. B., Law

GORNO-ALTAISK STATE UNIVERSITY

Altai Republic, 649000 Gorno-Altaisk, Lenkina ul. 1

Telephone: (3882) 22-64-39
Fax: (3882) 22-67-35
E-mail: office@gasu.ru
Internet: www.gasu.ru

Founded 1949, present name and status 1993
Public control
Language of instruction: Russian
Academic year: September to January, February to June

Rector: Prof. VALERY G. BABIN
Vice-Rector for Academic Affairs: EUGENIY E. SHVAKOV

Vice-Rector for Educational Work: Prof. BORIS V. PAKHAYEV
Vice-Rector for Science and Innovations: Prof. YURY V. TABAKAYEV
Librarian: NATALYA N. VAKHRENEVA
Library of 345,763 vols, 312 periodicals
Number of teachers: 430
Number of students: 5,443 (incl. 2,015 external)

DEANS

College of Agriculture: YELENA V. PIVOVAROVA
Faculty of Agriculture: LUDMILA I. SURTAEVA
Faculty of Biology and Chemistry: VERA N. ALEYNIKOVA
Faculty of Economics: JULIA G. GAZUKINA
Faculty of Foreign Languages: TATYANA V. DERBENEVA
Faculty of Geography: ALEXEI V. BONDARENKO
Faculty of History: TATYANA S. PUSTOGACHEVA
Faculty of Law: VERA S. KRASHENININA
Faculty of Philology: TATYANA N. NIKONOVA
Faculty of Physics and Mathematics: IVAN B. DAVYDKIN
Faculty of Psychology and Pedagogy: OLGA V. OSTAPOVICH

IMMANUEL KANT BALTIC FEDERAL UNIVERSITY

236041 Kaliningrad,14 A. Nevskogo Str.
Telephone: (4012) 59-55-77
Fax: (4012) 33-83-22
E-mail: rector@kantiana.ru
Internet: www.kantiana.ru
Founded 1967
State control
Languages of instruction: English, Russian
Academic year: September to June
Rector: Prof. Dr ANDREY KLEMESHEV
Pro-Rector: Dr V. N. KHUDENKO
Librarian: A. D. SHKITSKAYA
Library: see under Libraries and Archives
Number of teachers: 1,000
Number of students: 15,000
Publications: *Kantovsky sbornik*, *Vestnik of IKBFU*

DEANS

Faculty of Bioecology: Prof. Dr VIKTOR DEDKOV
Faculty of Economics: Dr ANATOLY CHUIKIN
Faculty of Geography and Geoecology: Dr FATIMA TSEKOEVA
Faculty of History: Dr VALERY GALTSOV
Faculty of Informatics and Applied Mathematics: Prof. Dr SERGEY ISHANOV
Faculty of Law: Dr OLEG ZAYACHKOVSKY
Faculty of Linguistics and Cross-Cultural Communication: Prof. Dr IRINA IERONOVA
Faculty of Medicine: Prof. Dr SERGEY KORENEV
Faculty of Philology and Journalism: Dr NATALYA LIKHINA
Faculty of Physical Culture and Sports: Prof. Dr VIKTOR PELMENEV
Faculty of Physics and Technology: Prof. Dr ALEKSEY IVANOV
Faculty of Psychology and Social Work: Prof. Dr IRINA SIMAEVA
Faculty of Services: Prof. Dr SERGEY KORYAGIN
Institute of Modern Educational Technologies: Dr NATALYA NIKULINA

INGUSH STATE UNIVERSITY

Republic of Ingushetia, 366700 Magas, Aleksandro-Zavodskaya ul. 30
Telephone and fax (8734) 55-12-64
Founded 1994
Rector: ARSAMAK MARTAZANOV

First Pro-Rector: AKHMED MATIYEV
Pro-Rector for Int. Relations: ZAHIDAT SULTYGOVA
Number of teachers: 316
Number of students: 2,752

IRKUTSK STATE UNIVERSITY

664003 Irkutsk, 3, K. Marksa ul. 1
Telephone: (3952) 24-34-53
Fax: (3952) 24-22-38
E-mail: rector@isu.ru
Internet: www.isu.ru
Founded 1918
State control
Language of instruction: Russian
Academic year: September to May
Rector: Prof. ALEXANDER I. SMIRNOV
Vice-Rector for Academic Affairs: I. GUTNIK
Vice-Rector for Devt: V. SAUNIN
Vice-Rector for Finance and Gen. Affairs: V. I. GLEBETS
Vice-Rector for Scientific Research: A. V. ARGUCHINTSEV
Librarian: R. V. PODGAICHENKO
Library: 3m. vols
Number of teachers: 900
Number of students: 17,230
Publications: *Collected Short Scientific Papers*, *Proceedings of the Applied Physics Research Institute*, *Proceedings of the Biological Research Institute*, *Proceedings of the Oil and Coal Products Research Institute*, *Transactions*

DEANS

Baikal School of International Business: V. N. SAUNIN
Faculty of Biology and Soil Sciences: Asst Prof. A. N. MATVEYEV
Faculty of Chemistry: Prof. Dr A. YU. SAFRONOV
Faculty of Geography: Asst Prof. A. V. ARGUCHINTSOVA
Faculty of Geology: Asst Prof. S. P. PRIMINA
Faculty of History: Prof. YU. A. ZULYAR
Institute of Law: Assoc. Prof. O. P. LICHICHAN
Faculty of Philology: Prof. A. S. SOBENNIKOV
Faculty of Physics: Prof. YU. V. AGRAPHONOV
Faculty of Psychology: Asst Prof. I. A. KOPONAK
Faculty of Service and Advertisment: Asst Prof. V. K. KARNAUKHOVA
Siberian-American Faculty of Management: Asst Prof. A. V. DIOGENOV
Institute of Social Sciences: Prof. V. A. RASHETNIKOV
Institute of Mathematics, Economics and Information Science: Prof. YU. D. KOROLKOV
International Institute of Economics and Linguistics: Asst Prof. V. YA. ANDRUKHOVA

IVANOVO STATE UNIVERSITY

153025 Ivanovo, ul. Ermaka 39
Telephone: (932) 32-62-10
Fax: (932) 32-46-77
E-mail: rector@ivanovo.ac.ru
Internet: www.ivanovo.ac.ru
Founded 1974
State control
Faculties of biology and chemistry, economics, history, law, mathematics, philology, physics, romance and Germanic philology
Number of teachers: 429
Number of students: 7,919 (4,452 full-time, 3,467 correspondence)
Rector: Prof. VLADIMIR N. YEGOROV
Pro-Rector for Academic Affairs: ALEXEY I. SCHEGLOV
Pro-Rector for Admin. and Finance: Dr VLADIMIR S. RADNYUK

Pro-Rector for Distance Learning and Further Education: Dr VLADIMIR I. NAZAROV
Pro-Rector for Int. Affairs: Dr NADEZHDA V. USOLTSEVA
Pro-Rector for Public Relations: Dr OLGA M. KARPOVA
Pro-Rector for Scientific Affairs: Dr DMITRY I. POLYVYANNY.

KABARDINO-BALKARIAN STATE UNIVERSITY

360004 Kabardino-Balkar Republic, Nalchik, ul. Chernyshevskogo 173
Telephone and fax (095) 337-99-55
E-mail: kodzokov@kbsu.ru
Internet: www.kbsu.ru
Founded 1932
State control
Language of instruction: Russian
Academic year: September to June
Rector: BARASBI S. KARAMURZOV
Vice-Rector for Extramural Studies and Postgraduate Studies: MUSLIM BARAZBIEV
Vice-Rector for Head of Studies: ARTUR KAZHAROV
Vice-Rector for Scientific Studies and Int. Affairs: ALEKSEY P. SAVINTSEV
Registrar: I. SHOMAKHOVA
Librarian: ROSA N. UNACHEVA
Library: see Libraries and Archives
Number of teachers: 950
Number of students: 20,635

DEANS

Faculty of Biology: A. M. PARITOV
Faculty of Chemistry: T. KH. LYGIDOV
Faculty of Computer Science and Systems Control: A. S. KSENOFONTOV
Faculty of Economics: R. V. GURFOVA
Faculty of Law: M. KH. GUKEPSHOKOV
Faculty of Mathematics: M. ABREGOV
Faculty of Mechanical Engineering: V. D. BATYROV
Faculty of Medicine: R. M. ZAKHOKHOV
Faculty of Microelectronics: R. SH. TESHEV
Faculty of Pedagogy and Methods of Primary Education: A. ZH. NASIPOV
Institute of Philology: L. A. KHARAEVA
Faculty of Physical Education and Sport: A. TKHAZEPLOV
Faculty of Physics: A. A. AKHUBEKOV
Institute of Social Sciences and Humanities: KH. B. MAMSIROV

KALMYK STATE UNIVERSITY

358000 Elista, ul. Pushkina 11
Telephone: (84722) 5-34-31
Fax: (84722) 5-37-29
E-mail: uni@kalmsu.ru
Internet: www.kalmsu.ru
Founded 1970
Faculties of general engineering, philology, biology, physics, mathematics, oriental studies and agriculture
Rector: G. M. MANDZHIYEVICH
Vice-Rector for Academic Affairs: Prof. ANATOLY V. RUDENKO
Vice-Rector for Admin. and Finance: Prof. VLADIMIR V. UCHUROV
Vice-Rector for Scientific Affairs: Prof. ALEKSANDR A. SOLOVEV
Vice-Rector for Social-Economic Affairs: Prof. VALERY U. MANDZHIEV
Vice-Rector for Univ.–Industry Liaison: Prof. ARKADY K. NATYROV
Number of students: 5,000

UNIVERSITIES   RUSSIA

KAZAN (VOLGA REGION) FEDERAL UNIVERSITY

420008 Tatarstan, Kazan, 18 Kremlevskaya St

Telephone: (843) 292-76-00
Fax: (843) 292-74-18
E-mail: public.mail@ksu.ru
Internet: www.kpfu.ru

Founded 1804
State control
Languages of instruction: English, Russian, Tatar
Academic year: September to June

Pres.: Prof. MYAKZYUM KH. SALAKHOV
Rector: Prof. ILSHAT R. GAFUROV
Vice-Rector for Admin. Affairs: Dr ANDREY N. KHASHOV
Vice-Rector for Economic Affairs: LENAR S. SAFIULLIN
Vice-Rector for Economic and Strategic Devt: Dr MARAT R. SAFIULLIN
Vice-Rector for Education: Prof. RIYAZ G. MINZARIPOV
Vice-Rector for Finance: RAISA R. MULLA-KAEVA
Vice-Rector for Innovations: Prof. NAIL F. KASHAPOV
Vice-Rector for Int. Relations: Dr LINAR N. LATYPOV
Vice-Rector for Research: Prof. DANIS K. NURGALIEV
Vice-Rector for Social Education: ARIF M. MEZHVEDILOV
Head of Library: Dr EVGENIY N. STRUKOV

Library: 6.1m. vols
Number of teachers: 3,100
Number of students: 36,000

Publications: *Education and Self-Development, Environmental Radioecology and Applied Ecology, Georesources, Philology and Culture, Proceedings of Higher Education Institutions: Mathematics* (print and online)

DEANS

A. Butlerov Institute of Chemistry: Prof. VLADIMIR I. GALKIN
Faculty of Biology and Soil: Dr RUSHAN M. SABIROV
Faculty of Journalism and Sociology: Prof. VASIL Z. GARIFULLIN
Faculty of Law: Prof. ILDAR A. TARKHANOV
Faculty of Philosophy: Prof. MIKHAIL D. SCHELKUNOV
Higher School of Information Technologies and Information Systems: Dr AIRAT F. KHASIYANOV
Institute for Comparative Studies of Modernity: Dr IRINA B. KUZNETSOVA-MORENKO
Institute of Computer Mathematics and Information Technologies: Prof. RUSTAM KH. LATYPOV
Institute of Ecology and Geography: Prof. OLEG P. ERMOLAEV
Institute of Economics and Finance: Prof. SHAMIL M. VALITOV
Institute of Geology and Petroleum Technology: Prof. DANIS C. NURGALIEV
Institute of History: Prof. RAMIL R. KHAYR-UTDINOV
Institute of Management and Territorial Development: Prof. NAILYA G. BAGAITDI-NOVA
Institute of Pedagogy and Psychology: Prof. AIDAR M. KALIMULLIN
Institute of Philology and Arts: Prof. RADIF R. ZAMALETDINOV
Institute of Physical Education, Sport and Restorative Medicine: Dr ISKANDER SH. GALEEV
Institute of Physics: Prof. ALBERT V. AGANOV
Institute of Oriental Studies and International Relations: Dr LINAR N. LATYPOV

N. Lobachevsky Institute of Mathematics and Mechanics: Prof. VLADIMIR A. CHUGU-NOV

PROFESSORS

AGANOV, A. V., Physics
AKHMADULLIN, A. G., Philology
ALATYREV, V. I., Physiology
ANDRAMONOVA, N. A., Russian Philology
ANDREEV, V. I., Education
ARSLANOV, M. M., Mathematics
BAKHTIN, A. I., Mineralogy
BALALYKINA, E. A., Philology
BARABANSHIKOV, B. I., Genetics
BASHKIROV, SH. SH., Physics
BUDNIKOV, G. K., Chemistry
BUKHARAEV, R. G., Cybernetics
BUROV, B. V., Lithology
BUSYGIN, E. P., History
BUTAKOV, G. P., Geomorphology
CHERKASOV, R. A., Chemistry
ERMOLAEV, I. P., History
FARUKSHIN, M. H., Sociology
GABDULKHAEV, B. G., Mathematics
GALIULLIN, T. N., Philology
GOLUBEV, A. I., Zoology
KAIGORODOV, V. R., Physics
KHAIRUTDINOV, R. G., History
KHAKOV, V. H., Turkic Languages
KHALYMBADYA, V. G., Palaeontology
KHOKHLOVA, L. P., Plant Physiology
KOCHELAEV, B. I., Physics
KONOPLEV, YU. G., Mechanics
KOPOSOV, G. F., Soil Studies
KURDYUKOV, G. I., Law
KUZNETSOV, V. A., Ichthyology
LESHCHINSKAYA, I. B., Microbiology
LIASHKO, A. D., Computing Mathematics
LITVIN, A. L., History
LYUBARSKI, E. L., Botany
MAKLAKOV, A. I., Physics
MALKOV, V. P., Law
NAFIGOV, R. I., History
NEPRIMEROV, N. N., Electronics
NIKOLAEV, G. A., Philology
PEREVEDENTSEV, YU. P., Meteorology
RAKHMATULLIN, E. S., Sociology
RESHETOV, YU. S., Law
RYABOV, A. A., Law
SADYKOV, M. B., Philosophy
SAKHIBULLIN, N. A., Astrophysics
SALNIKOV, YU. I., Chemistry
SEMENOV, V. F., Political Economy
SHARIFYANOV, I. I., History
SHERSTNEV, A. N., Mathematics
SHIROKOV, A. P., Geometry
SIDOROV, V. V., Radiophysics
TAGIROV, I. R., History
TEPLOV, M. A., Physics
TEPTIN, G. M., Meteorology
TORSUEV, N. P., Geomorphology
TROFIMOV, A. M., Geomorphology
TUMASHEVA, D. G., Turkic Languages
USMANOV, M. A., History
YEGALOV, V. I., Differential Equations
YIGUNIN, V. D., History
ZABOTIN, YA. I., Computing Mathematics

KEMEROVO STATE UNIVERSITY

650043 Kemerovo, Krasnaya ul. 6
Telephone: (3842) 23-12-26
Fax: (3842) 23-30-34
E-mail: rector@kemsu.ru
Internet: www.kemsu.ru

Founded 1974
State control
Language of instruction: Russian
Academic year: September to July

Faculties of biology, chemistry, economics, foreign languages, history, law, mathematics, philology, physics, social sciences and sport

Rector: YU. A. ZAKHAROV

Pro-Rectors: K. E. AFANASIEV, T. M. CHUR-EKOVA, B. P. NEVZOROV, T. M. PANINA, B. A. SECHKARYOV, V. A. VOLCHEK
Librarian: N. P. KONOVALOVA
Number of teachers: 780
Number of students: 8,834

KHAKASSIA STATE UNIVERSITY 'N. F. KATANOV'

Khakassia Republic, 655000 Abakan, Lenina pr. 90
Telephone: (3902) 24-53-29
Fax: (3902) 24-33-64
E-mail: univer@khsu.ru
Internet: www.khsu.ru
State control

Founded 1994
Accredited by Fed. Service of Supervision in Education and Science of Nat. Accreditation Agency of Russia

Rector: Prof. GENNADY STANISLAVOVICH SUR-VILLO
First Vice-Rector, Vice-Rector of Scientific Work: ANDREY ANATOLYEVICH POPOV
Vice-Rector of Quality Control and Devt: VASILY VASILJEVICH ANJUSHIN
Vice-Rector of Teaching and Organizational Work: SVETLANA MIKHAILOVNA KUBRINA
Vice-Rector of Pedagogical Work: SVETLANA AFANASYEVNA SUBRAKOVA
Vice-Rector of Admin. Work: YURY VASILYE-VICH RYBALCHENKO

Library: more than 1m. vols in 9 libraries and 15 reading-halls; more than 700 periodicals
Number of teachers: 591
Number of students: 17,459 , of whom 7,501 external

Publications: *Herald of Katanov State University of Khakassia, Yearbook of the Institute of Sajan-Altay Turkology*

DEANS AND DIRECTORS

Agrarian Dept: ALEXEY NIKOLAEVICH KADY-CHEGOV
Centre of Socio-Political and Humanitarian Education: TATYANA SERGEEVNA TCHIVERS-KAJA
College of Agriculture: GALINA ALEKSAN-DROVNA MINYUHINA
College of Medicine: OLGA VLADIMIROVNA SHTYGASHEVA
College of Music: NINA NIKOLAEVNA KUSHNIR
College of Pedagogical Education, Computer Science and Law: NADEZHDA VIKTOROVNA NADEEVA
College of Service Technologies: NINA VIKTOR-OVNA SLICHNAYA
Dept of Physical Training: ALEXANDER VIC-TOROVICH FOMINYKH
Engineering and Technical Dept: OLEG NICO-LAEVICH KHEGAY
Institute of Arts: NINA NIKOLAEVNA KUSHNIR
Institute of Computer Science and Telematics: SERGEY VIKTOROVICH SHWETZ
Institute of Continuing Pedagogical Education: LYUDMILA ANATOLJEVNA MINDIBEKOVA
Institute of Economics and Management: NINA FEDOTOVNA DITZ
Institute of History and Law: VLADIMIR GEORGEVICH KICHEEV
Institute of Medicine, Psychology and Social Sciences: OLGA VLADIMIROVNA SHTYGA-SHEVA
Institute of Natural Sciences and Mathematics: IRINA VICTOROVNA KARPUKHINA
Institute of Philology: IVAN IVANOVICH KRE-MICH
Institute of Sajan-Altay Turkology: TAMARA GERASIMOVNA BORGOYAKOVA
Institute of Service and Design Technologies: MARINA VICTOROVNA KHORTOVA

1869

Institute of Upgrading Skills and Staff Retraining: LIDIA NIKOLAEVNA CHAIRKINA
Veterinary Medicine Dept: VICTOR YURYEVICH TCHUMAKOV

KOSTROMA STATE NEKRASSOV UNIVERSITY

156961 Kostroma, ul. Pervogo Maya 14
Telephone: (4942) 31-82-91
Fax: (4942) 31-13-22
E-mail: rgc@ksu.edu.ru
Internet: www.ksu.edu.ru

Founded 1918
State control
Language of instruction: Russian
Academic year: September to July

Rector: Prof. NIKOLAI M. RASSADIN
First Pro-Rector: ANATOLY G. KIRPICHNIK
Pro-Rector for Academic Affairs: IRINA G. ASADULINA
Pro-Rector for Computerisation: VLADIMIR N. ERSHOV
Pro-Rector for Household Affairs: VYACHE-SLAV V. ROGACHEV
Pro-Rector for Int. Relations: LIDIA N. VAU-LINA
Pro-Rector for Science: ALEXANDER R. NAU-MOV
Pro-Rector for Social Affairs: ALEXEI E. PODOBIN
Librarian: NATALIA A. SMIRNOVA
Library of 614,200 vols
Number of teachers: 500
Number of students: 7,000

Publications: *Educational economic, Vestnik KSU*

DEANS

Faculty of Art: MARINA A. ALEKSEEVA
Faculty of Foreign Languages: MARGARITA M. KAPLINA
Faculty of History: ANDREI M. BELOV
Faculty of Music: ANDREI I. SAKHAROV
Faculty of Natural Science: IGOR G. KRINITSIN
Faculty of Philology: MADINA A. FOKINA
Faculty of Physical Education: LILIA M. BOCHKOVA
Faculty of Physics and Mathematics: DENIS L. LEGOTIN
Faculty of Service and Technologies: NATALIA B. TARASOVA
Institute of Economics: VLADIMIR V. BULATOV
Institute of Pedagogics and Psychology: ANDREI I. TIMONIN

KUBAN STATE UNIVERSITY

350040 Krasnodar, ul. Stavropolskaya 149
Telephone: (8612) 69-95-02
Fax: (8612) 69-95-17
E-mail: rector@kubsu.ru
Internet: www.kubsu.ru

Founded 1924
State control
Languages of instruction: Russian, English
Academic year: September to July

Pres.: VLADIMIR A. BABESHKO
Chief Vice-Pres. and Vice-Pres. for Information: ALEXANDER G. IVANOV
Vice-Pres. for Academic Affairs: NATALYA V. KRASNOVA
Vice-Pres. for Additional Education: ELENA A. ZHURAVLEVA
Vice-Pres. for Capital Construction and Repairs: ELENA N. SAVENKO
Vice-Pres. for Distance Education: IGOR D. BREGEDA
Vice-Pres. for Science and Research: ALEX-ANDER A. GAVRILOV
Vice-Pres. for Social Affairs: VIKTOR V. MOMOTOV
Sec. of the Univ. Academic Ccl: TATYANA M. BELOKON

Librarian: G. V. SOLOVIEVA
Number of teachers: 1,000 (incl. 144 professors and 506 associate professors)
Number of students: 16,770

Publications: *Ekologichesky vestnik nauch-nykh tsentrov TchES* (Letters of BSEC Research centres, 4 a year), *Ekonomika* (1 a year), *Filologiya* (Philology, 2 a year), *Golos Minuvshego* (The Voice of the Past, 4 a year), *Obshchestvo i Chelovek* (Society and Mankind, 4 a year), *Priroda* (Nature, 4 a year), *Terra Incognita* (2 a year), *Uprav-leniye* (Management, 1 a year)

DEANS

Faculty of Applied Mathematics: YU. V. KOLTSOV
Faculty of Architecture and Design: S. YU KOCHETKOVA
Faculty of Biology: V. YA. NAGALEVSKY
Faculty of Chemistry: V. D. BUYKLISKY
Faculty of Economics: I. V. SHEVCHENKO
Faculty of Geography: M. YU. BELIKOV
Faculty of Graphic Art: YU. V. KOROBKO
Faculty of History, Sociology and International Relations: G. M. ACHAGU
Faculty of Journalism: V. V. ROUNOV
Faculty of Law: I. A. NIKOLAYCHUK
Faculty of Management: A. M. ZHDANOVSKY
Faculty of Mathematics: G. F. SOKOL
Faculty of Philology: V. P. ABRAMOV
Faculty of Physics and Technics: N. A. YAKOVENKO
Faculty of Romano-Germanic Philology: V. I. TKHORIK

KURGAN STATE UNIVERSITY

640669 Kurgan, ul. Gogolya 25
Telephone: (3522) 43-26-52
Fax: (3522) 43-20-51
E-mail: rektor@kgsu.ru
Internet: www.kgsu.ru

Founded 1952

Faculties of mathematics and information technology, natural sciences, history, law, philology, economics, health protection, psychology and sport, pedagogy, technology, transport systems

Rector: Prof. OLEG I. BUKHTOYAROV

Library of 1,000,000 vols
Number of teachers: 700
Number of students: 8,000

KURSK STATE UNIVERSITY

305000 Kursk, ul. Radischeva 33
Telephone: (4712) 70-05-38
Fax: (4712) 51-36-49
E-mail: info@kurksu.ru
Internet: www.kurksu.ru

Founded 1934 as Kursk State Pedagogical Institute
Public control
Language of instruction: Russian
Academic year: September to June

Rector: Prof. VYACHESLAV V. GVOZDEV
First Vice-Rector: NIKOLAI N. GREBENKOV
Vice-Rector for Academic Affairs: Dr VLADI-MIR V. ZAKHAROV
Vice-Rector for Int. Relations: Dr ELENA I. MIKHAILINA
Vice-Rector for Science and Research: Dr VITALIY A. KUDINOV
Vice-Rector for Technical Support: IGOR O. SHULGIN
Chief Accountant: GALINA E. KLOCHKOVA
Library of 65,000 vols
Number of teachers: 900
Number of students: 12,000 (of which 9,000 internal and 3,000 external students)

DEANS

Faculty of Art and Design: VIKTOR I. ZHILIN
Faculty of Computer Science: Dr VITALIY A. KUDINOV
Faculty of Economy and Management: Dr VIKTOR A. KRIULIN
Faculty of Foreign Languages: NIKOLAI A. SMAKHTIN
Faculty of Geography: IRINA P. BALABINA
Faculty of History: PLAKSIN
Faculty of Law: Dr VLADIMIR V. ZAKHAROV
Faculty of Philology: YURI L. PHILIPPOV
Faculty of Physics and Mathematics: VYA-CHESLAV V. MELENTYEV
Faculty of Psychology and Pedagogics: MAR-INA A. LUKINA
Faculty of Sport and Physical Education: Dr TATYANA V. SKOBLIKOVA
Faculty of Theology and Religion Studies: ANATOLIY A. KORZINKIN

LENINGRAD STATE UNIVERSITY 'A. S. PUSHKIN'

196605 St Petersburg, Pushkin, Peterburgs-koe shosse 10
Telephone: (812) 466-65-58
Fax: (812) 466-49-99
E-mail: pushkin@infos.ru
Internet: www.lgu-edu.spb.ru
State control

Founded 1992 as Leningrad Regional Peda-gogical Institute; as Leningrad State Regional Univ. 1996–1999; as A. S. Push-kin Leningrad State Regional Univ. 1999–2003; present name and status 2003

Rector: Prof. VYACHESLAV N. SKVORTSOV
First Pro-Rector: Prof. GALINA P. CHEPUR-ENKO
Pro-Rector for Academic Affairs: Prof. TATYANA V. MALTSEVA
Pro-Rector for Economic and Int. Affairs: Dr LEONID L. BUKIN
Pro-Rector for External and Further Profes-sional Education: Prof. TATYANA S. KOMIS-SAROVA
Pro-Rector for Science: Dr EKATERINA S. NERYSHKINA
Number of teachers: 361
Number of students: 13,403

DEANS

Faculty of Arts: Dr SVETLANA I. NAZAROVA
Faculty of Foreign Languages: Prof. SVYATO-SLAV I. ALATORTSEV
Faculty of Law: Prof. GALINA P. CHEPURENKO
Faculty of Mathematics, Physics and Infor-mation Science: Dr SERGEI D. BORONENKO
Faculty of Natural Sciences, Geography and Tourism: Dr ANATOLY M. MAKARSKY
Faculty of Philology: Prof. TATYANA V. MAL-TSEVA

MAGNITOGORSK STATE UNIVERSITY

455043 Magnitogorsk, Lenina pr. 114
Telephone and fax (3511) 35-15-32
E-mail: masu@masu.ru
Internet: www.masu.ru

Founded 1932
State control

Rector: Prof. VALENTIN F. ROMANOV
First Pro-Rector: Prof. VLADIMIR P. SEMENOV
Librarian: LUDMILA V. KOTELNIKOVA
Library of 443,335 vols

DEANS

Faculty of Advancement of Qualifications and Training of Specialists: Prof. LUDMILA A. MIROSHNICHENKO
Faculty of Art and Design: Prof. VLADIMIR M. BELY
Faculty of History: Prof. MIKHAIL G. ABRAM-ZON

Faculty of Information Technology: Prof. ELMIRA R. IPATOVA

Faculty of Linguistics and Translation: Prof. GALINA I. VASINA

Faculty of Pedagogy and Methods of Primary Education: Prof. YURI D. KOROBKOV

Faculty of Philology: Prof. LYUBOV D. PONOMAREVA

Faculty of Physics and Mathematics: Prof. VIKTOR A. KUZNETSOV

Faculty of Pre-School Education: Prof. BORIS D. KULANIN

Faculty of Psychology: Prof. ELENA D. PETROVA

Faculty of Social Work: Prof. FLYURA A. MUSTAEVA

MARI STATE UNIVERSITY

424001 Mari-El Republic, Yoshkar-Ola, pl. Lenina 1

Telephone: (8362) 12-59-20
Fax: (8362) 45-45-81
E-mail: postmaster@marsu.ru
Internet: www.marsu.ru

Founded 1972
State control
Academic year: September to July

Rector: V. I. MAKAROV
Vice-Rector: V. I. CHEMODANOV
Chief Admin. Officer: L. N. STRELNIKOVA

Number of teachers: 384
Number of students: 4,055

Publication: *Arkheografichesky vestnik* (Archaeological News, 2 a year)

DEANS

Faculty of Agriculture: G. S. YUNUSOV

Faculty of Biology and Chemistry: M. G. GRIGORIEV

Faculty of Culture and Arts: R. L. YASHMETOVA

Faculty of Economics: K. V. SHAKIROV

Faculty of Electric Power Technology: L. M. RIBAKOV

Faculty of History and Philology: A. N. CHIMAEV

Faculty of Law: A. M. LOMONOSOV

Faculty of Linguistics and Intercultural Communication: Z. G. ZORINA

Faculty of Physics and Mathematics: G. A. SITNIKOV

MORDOVIAN STATE UNIVERSITY

430005 Mordovia, Saransk, Bolshevistskaya ul. 68

Telephone: (8342) 24-48-88
Fax: (8342) 32-75-27
E-mail: vice-rector@adm.mrsu.ru
Internet: www.mrsu.ru

Founded 1957
State control
Academic year: September to June

Rector: Prof. SERGEY M. VDOVIN

First Vice-Rector for Academic Studies: Prof. N. E. FOMIN

Vice-Rector for Extracurricular Activities: Prof. MARINA D. MARTYNOVA

Vice-Rector for Financial Admin.: Prof. N. D. KULIKOV

Vice-Rector for Further Training and Professional Devt Programmes: ANTONINA M. AKHMETOVA

Vice-Rector for Innovative Research and Devt Activities: PETR V. SENIN

Vice-Rector for Logistics Accomplishment: Prof. SERGEI V. KARGIN

Vice-Rector for Major Construction Work: STEPAN P. GUDOZHNIKOV

Vice-Rector for Science and Research: Prof. V. D. CHERKASOV

Vice-Rector for Security: Prof. ALEKSANDR I. EKIMOV

Registrar: MIKHAIL M. GOUDOV
Librarian: I. V. OTSTAVNOVA

Library of 2,196,381 vols, 731 periodicals
Number of teachers: 1,689
Number of students: 39,787

Publications: *Integration of Education* (4 a year), *Regionologiya* (4 a year), *Vestnik Mordovskogo Universiteta* (4 a year)

DEANS

Faculty of Biology: Prof. V. W. REVIN

Faculty of Economics: Prof. N. D. GUSKOVA

Faculty of Electronics: I. V. GULAYEV

Faculty of Foreign Languages: Prof. NATALIA V. BURENINA

Faculty of Geography: ANATOLY A. YAMASHKIN

Faculty of Industrial and Civil Construction: Prof. V. T. EROFEYEV

Faculty of Law: Prof. YULIA N. SUSHKOVA

Faculty of Mathematics: Prof. I. I. CHUCHAYEV

Faculty of Medicine: Prof. ANNA A. USANOVA

Faculty of National Culture: B. S. BRYZHINSKY

Faculty of Philology: Prof. M. V. MOSIN

Faculty of Lighting Engineering: Prof. OLGA E. ZHELEZNIKOVA

Folk Culture Institute: TATYANA N. SIDORKINA

DIRECTORS

Institute of Agrocomplex: SAMIL I. AKHMETOV

Institute of Economics: NIKOLAI P. MAKARKIN

Institute of Man and Light: LUDMILA V. ABRAMOVA

Science and Research Institute of Ecology: VICTOR N. MASKAIKIN

Science and Research Institute of Industrial and Civil Construction: VLADIMIR P. SELYAYEV

Science and Research Institute of Mathematics: EVGENY V. VOSKRESENSKY

Science and Research Institute of Regional Studies: ALEXANDR I. SUKHAREV

MOSCOW STATE REGIONAL UNIVERSITY

107005 Moscow, ul. Radio 10A

Telephone and fax (495) 261-22-28
E-mail: mgou@mgou.ru
Internet: www.mgou.ru

Founded 1923 as Moscow State Pedagogical Technical College
State control
Language of instruction: Russian
Academic year: September to June

Faculties of business and technology, decorative arts, economics, further education for higher education specialists, law, linguistics, mathematics and physics, military education, pedagogy, physical education and philology, politics, translation; summer school of Russian language, summer school of Arts

Rector: Prof. PAVEL KHROMENKOV

First Pro-Rector for Academic Affairs and Int. Cooperation: Dr VLADIMIR KLICHNIKOV

Pro-Rector for Education and Youth Politics: VYACHESLAV KHORIHIN

Pro-Rector for Science: Dr MARINA LEVCHENKO

Pro-Rector for Education and Youth Politics: Dr MIKHAIL V. YUDIN

Pro-Rector for Scientific and Int. Cooperation: Prof. YURI I. YAMALOV

Number of teachers: 800
Number of students: 13,000

Publication: *Vestnik MSRU.*

MOSCOW STATE UNIVERSITY 'M. V. LOMONOSOV'

119991 Moscow, GSP-1, Leninskie Gory

Telephone: (495) 939-10-00
Fax: (495) 939-01-26
E-mail: info@rector.msu.ru
Internet: www.msu.ru

Founded 1755
Academic year: September to June

Rector: Acad. VIKTOR SADOVNICHY

Vice-Rector for Academic Policy and Degree Programs Man.: PYOTR VRZHESHCH

Vice-Rector for Educational Standards, Curricula and Syllabi: IGOR KOTLOBOVSKY

Vice-Rector for Innovations, Informatization and Int. Scientific Cooperation: ALEXEI KHOKHLOV

Vice-Rector for Int. Cooperation: NIKOLAY SYOMIN

Vice-Rector for Research Policy and Research Man.: VLADIMIR BELOKUROV

Vice-Rector for Social Services and Facilities Devt: ALEXANDER CHERNYAEV

Vice-Rector: NIKITA ANISSIMOV (acting)
Vice-Rector: YURI BELENKOV
Vice-Rector: ALEXEY REYMERS (acting)
Vice-Rector: VICTOR TROFIMOV

Number of teachers: 10,441
Number of students: 40,756

Publications: *Moscow State University* (52 a year), *Vestnik MGU* (20 series, 2 a year)

DEANS

Faculty of Bioengineering and Bioinformatics: VLADIMIR SKULACHEV

Faculty of Biology: MIKHAIL KIRPICHNIKOV

Faculty of Chemistry: VALERY LUNIN

Faculty of Computational Mathematics and Cybernetics: YEVGENY MOISEEV

Faculty of Economics: VASSILI KOLESOV

Faculty of Educational Studies: NIKOLAI ROZOV

Faculty of Fine and Performing Arts: ALEXANDER LOBODANOV

Faculty of Foreign Languages and Area Studies: SVETLANA TER-MINASOVA

Faculty of Fundamental Medicine: VSEVOLOD TKACHUK

Faculty of Geography: NIKOLAI KASIMOV

Faculty of Geology: DMITRY PUSHCHAROVSKY

Faculty of Global Processes: V. I. ILIYIN (acting)

Faculty of History: SERGEY KARPOV

Faculty of Journalism: YASEN ZASURSKY

Faculty of Law: ALEXANDER GOLICHENKOV

Faculty of Material Sciences: YURI TRETYAKOV

Faculty of Mechanics and Mathematics: VLADIMIR CHUBARIKOV (acting)

Faculty of Philology: MARINA REMNYOVA

Faculty of Philosophy: VLADIMIR MIRONOV

Faculty of Physical Chemistry: SERGEY ALDOSHIN

Faculty of Physics: VLADIMIR TRUKHIN

Faculty of Political Science: A. YU. SHUTOV (acting)

Faculty of Psychology: YURI ZINCHENKO

Faculty of Public Administration: (vacant)

Faculty of Sociology: VLADIMIR DOBRENKOV

Faculty of Soil Science: SERGEY SHOBA

Faculty of World Politics: ANDREI KOKOSHIN

Graduate School of Innovative Business: DMITRY KOSHUG

Graduate School of Management and Innovation: VLADIMIR VASSILIEV

School of Business Administration: OLEG VIKHANSKY

School of Comtemporary Social Sciences: G. V. OSIPOV

Moscow School of Economics: ALEXANDER NEKIPELOV (Dir)

School of Television: VITALY TRETYAKOV

School of Translation and Interpretation: NIKOLAI GARBOVSKY

Institute of Asian and African Studies: MIKHAIL MEYER

MOSCOW UNIVERSITY OF CONSUMER COOPERATIVES

141014 Moscow oblast, Mytischi, ul. V. Voloshinoi 12

Telephone: (495) 582-97-37
Fax: (495) 582-93-10
E-mail: muller@mupk.ru
Internet: www.mupk.ru
Founded 1913
Areas of study: accounting and auditing, commerce, commodity science, economics, economic information systems, finance and credit, global economics, jurisprudence, management, marketing
Pres. and Rector: Prof. MARIA V. SEROSHTAN
Number of teachers: 500
Number of students: 12,000

NIZHNII NOVGOROD STATE UNIVERSITY 'N. I. LOBACHEVSKY'

603950 Nizhnii Novgorod, pr. Gagarina 23

Telephone: (831) 462-30-90
Fax: (831) 462-30-85
E-mail: unn@unn.ru
Internet: www.unn.ru
Founded 1916
State control
Language of instruction: Russian
Academic year: September to June
Rector: Prof. EVGENY V. CHUPRUNOV
Vice-Rector for Academic Affairs: Assoc. Prof. ALEXANDER V. PETROV
Vice-Rector for Research: Prof. SERGEI N. GURBATOV
Vice-Rector Int. Relations and Innovations in Education: Prof. ALEXANDER O. GRUDZINSKY
Pres.: Prof. ROMAN G. STRONGIN
Librarian: Dr YURI M. SOROKIN
Number of teachers: 1,350
Number of students: 32,000
Publication: *Vestnik of the Nizhnii Novgorod University*

DEANS

Advanced School of General and Applied Physics: Dr M. D. TOKMAN
Faculty of Biology: Dr A. P. VESELOV
Faculty of Business and Management: Dr A. O. GRUDZINSKY
Faculty of Chemistry: Dr A. V. GUSHCHIN
Faculty of Computer Science and Cybernetics: Dr V. P. GERGEL
Faculty of Economics: Dr YU. V. TRIFONOV
Faculty of Finance: Dr V. N. YASENEV
Faculty of History: Dr E. A. MOLEV
Faculty of International Relations: Dr O. A. KOLOBOV
Faculty of Law: Dr V. I. TSYGANOV
Faculty of Mechanics and Mathematics: Dr A. K. LYUBIMOV
Faculty of Philology: Dr L. I. RUCHINA
Faculty of Physical Training and Sport: Dr V. G. KUZMIN
Faculty of Physics: Dr K. A. MARKOV
Faculty of Radiophysics: Dr A. V. YAKIMOV
Faculty of Social Sciences: Dr V. A. BLONIN

NORTH-EASTERN FEDERAL UNIVERSITY

Republic of Sakha (Yakutia), 677000 Yakutsk, ul. Belinskogo 58

Telephone: (4112) 35-20-90
Fax: (4112) 32-13-14
E-mail: oip-yakutsk@mail.ru
Founded 1956
State control
Languages of instruction: Russian, Yakut

Academic year: September to July
Chancellor: EVGENIYA I. MIKHAYLOVA
Vice-Chancellor: VASILY I. VASILYEV
Librarian: ANATOLY P. SEMENOV
Number of teachers: 950
Number of students: 10,000
Publication: *Nauka i obrazovaniye* (4 a year)

DEANS

Faculty of Biology and Geography: ANATOLY N. NIKOLAEV
Faculty of Civil Engineering: TERENTY A. KORNILOV
Faculty of Geology and Survey: BORIS I. POPOV
Faculty of History: YURI D. PETROV
Faculty of Law: PETR V. GOGOLEV
Faculty of Mining: BORIS N. ZAROVNYAEV
Faculty of Philology: GALINA E. ZHONDOROVA
Faculty of Pre-Undergraduate Education: SVETLANA V. FEDOROVA
Faculty of Road Construction: MIKHAIL F. SEMENOV
Institute of Finances and Economics: NATALIA V. OKHLOPKOVA
Institute of Foreign Languages and Regional Studies: OLGA A. MELNICHUK
Institute of Languages and Cultures of the Peoples of the North-East: GAVRIL G. FILIPPOV
Institute of Mathematics and Information Science: VERA I. AFANASYEVA
Institute of Medicine: PALMIRA G. PETROVA
Institute of Physics and Technologies: NADEZHDA A. SAVVINOVA
Institute of Psychology: ANASTASIA P. OKONESHNIKOVA
Institute of Sports and Physical Education: DMITRY N. PLATONO
Teacher Training Institute: ANTONINA A. GRIGORYEVA
Technological Institute: GENNADIY I. MUGUEV

PROFESSORS

ALEXEEV, A. N., History
ANDREEV, V. S., Engineering
ANISIMOV, V. M., Education
ANTONOV, N. K., Philosophy
BASHARIN, K. G., Medicine
BEGIEV, V. G., Medicine
BLOKHIN, I. P., Biology
BURTSEV, A. A., Philology
BURYANINA, N. S., Geology
BUSHKOV, P. N., Surgery
CHEMEZOV, E. N., Geology
DANILOV, D. A., Pedagogics
DIACHKOVSKY, N. D., Yakut Language and Literature
DOBROVOLSKY, G. N., Engineering
EGOROV, I. E., Mathematics
FEDOROV, M. M., Law
FOMIN, M. M., Pedagogics
FRIDOVSKY, V. Y., Geology
GOGOLEV, A. I., General History
GOGOLEV, M. P., Medicine
ILLARIONOV, V. V., Philology
IVANOV, A. I., Medicine
IVANOVA, A. V., Education
IZAKSON, V. Y., Mathematics
KERSHENGOLTS, B. M., Biology
KHANDY, M. V., Medicine
KHATYLAEV, M. M., History
KOCHNEV, V. P., Education
KOLODEZNIKOV, I. I., Geology and Mineralology
KORNILOVA, A. G., Education
KOZHEVNIKOV, N. N., Philosophy
KYCHKIN, I. S., Theoretical Physics
KYLACHANOV, A. P., Engineering
LUKOVTSEV, V. S., Philosophy
MAKAROV, V. M., Medicine
MAKHAROV, Y. M., Philosophy
MAKSIMOV, G. N., Philosophy
MIKHAILOV, V. D., Philosophy
MISHLIMOVICH, M. Y., Philology

MORDOSOV, I. I., Biology
NEUSTROEV, N. D., Education
NIKOLAEV, N. S., Engineering
NOVIKOV, A. G., Philosophy
OKONESHNIKOVA, A. P., Psychology
PETROV, E. E., Mathematics
PETROV, N. E., Philology
PETROVA, P. G., Medicine
PETROVA, S. M., Education
POPOV, A. A., Economics
POPOV, B. N., Philosophy
PROKOPIEVA, S. M., Philology
SAMOKHIN, A. V., Mining
SAMSONOV, N. G., Philology
SHAMAEV, N. R., Education
SHEPELEV, V. S., Geology
SIVTSEV, I. S., History
SLASTENA, YU. L., Geology
SMIRNOV, V. P., Engineering
SOLOMONOV, N. G., Biology
STOGNY, V. V., Geology
TAZLOVA, R. S., Psychiatry
TIKHONOV, D. G., Medicine
TOBUROKOV, N. N., Linguistics
TOLSTIKHIN, O. N., Permafrost
TOMSKY, I. E., Economics
TYRLYGIN, M. A., Medicine
VASILIEV, E. P., Medicine
VASILIEV, V. I., Mathematics
VASILIEVA-KRALINA, I. I., Biology
VIKULOV, M. A., Engineering
VINOGRADOV, A. V., Chemistry
YAKIMOV, O. D., Journalism
ZAROVNYAEV, B. N., Geology

NORTHERN INTERNATIONAL UNIVERSITY

685014 Magadan, ul. Portovaya 13

Telephone: (41322) 3-00-21
Fax: (41322) 3-42-37
Internet: www.niu.ru.

NORTH OSSETIAN STATE UNIVERSITY

362025 Vladikavkaz, ul. Vatutina 46

Telephone: (8672) 53-09-04
Fax: (8672) 74-05-79
E-mail: webmaster@nosu.ru
Internet: www.nosu.ru
Founded 1969
Language of instruction: Russian
Academic year: September to June
Rector: AKHURBEK M. MAGOMETOV
First Pro-Rector, Pro-Rector for Academic Affairs: ANATOLY V. RAITSEV
Pro-Rector for Int. Affairs: OLEG S. KHATSAYEV
Pro-Rector for Science: VALERY G. SOZNANOV
Librarian: KLARA K. KOKAYEVA
Number of teachers: 833
Number of students: 11,718

DEANS

Faculty of Arts and Design: V. N. TSALAGOV
Faculty of Biology and Soil Studies: R. G. ZANGIONOVA
Faculty of Chemistry and Technology: N. I. KALOYEV
Faculty of Economics: Z. G. TEDEEV
Faculty of Education and Elementary Education: V. K. KOCHISOV
Faculty of Foreign Languages: T. T. KAMBOLOV
Faculty of Geography: B. M. BEROYEV
Faculty of History: A. I. ABAYEV
Faculty of Law: E. G. PLIYEV
Faculty of Management: V. G. TSOGOYEV
Faculty of Mathematics: A. A. AZIYEV
Faculty of Ossetian Philology: R. Z. KOMAYEVA
Faculty of Philology: L. M. BESOLOV
Faculty of Physical Education and Sports: F. G. KHAMIKOYEV

Faculty of Physics: A. P. BLIYEV

NOVGOROD STATE UNIVERSITY

173003 Veliky Novgorod, St Petersburgskaya ul. 41

Telephone: (8162) 62-72-44
Fax: (8162) 62-41-10
E-mail: novsu@novsu.ru
Internet: www.novsu.ru

Founded 1993
Academic year: September to June

Faculties of administration, agricultural engineering, agricultural production technology, architecture, arts and design, arts and technology, biology, chemistry and environmental science, child education and psychology, economics, engineering and technology, finance, foreign languages, higher nursing education, history, law, medicine, pharmacy, philosophy, physics and technology, stomatology

Rector: Prof. Dr VIKTOR VEBER

Number of teachers: 896
Number of students: 14,000

Publications: *Chelo* (History and Literature, 4 a year), *Vestnik Novgorodskogo Gosudarstvennogo Universiteta* (Research, 4 a year).

NOVOSIBIRSK STATE UNIVERSITY

630090 Novosibirsk, ul. Pirogova 2

Telephone: and fax (3832) 39-73-78
E-mail: inter@nsu.ru
Internet: www.nsu.ru

Founded 1959
State control
Language of instruction: Russian
Academic year: September to June

Rector: Prof. NIKOLAY S. DIKANSKY
Vice-Rector for Int. Activities: ELENA M. LISMAN
Vice-Rector for Research: Prof. GENNADY YU. SHVEDENKOV
Vice-Rector for Studies: Prof. NATALIA V. DULEPOVA
Registrar: N. I. BOIKOVA
Librarian: L. A. LYAGUSHINA

Library of 815,051 vols
Number of teachers: 2,226
Number of students: 6,038

Publications: *Algebra and Logics* (6 a year), *Critics and Semiotics* (1 a year), *Philosophy of Science* (4 a year), *Siberian Philological Journal* (2 a year), *Vestnik NGU* (3 a year)

DEANS

Department of Economics (tel. (3832) 39-72-42; e-mail dekeko@lab.nsu.ru; f. 1967):
  Prof. GAGIK M. MKRTCHAN

Department of Foreign Languages:
  Prof. G. G. KURKINA

Department of Geology and Geophysics (tel. (3832) 39-72-18; e-mail shatsky@uiggm.nsu.ru; internet ggd.nsu.ru; f. 1962):
  Prof. VLADISLAV S. SHATSKY

Department of the Humanities (tel. (3832) 30-08-62; e-mail info@gf.nsu.ru; internet www.gf.nsu.ru; f. 1962):
  Prof. LEONID G. PANIN

Department of Information Technologies (tel. (3832) 39-77-95; e-mail dekanat@ccfit.nsu.ru; internet www.fit.nsu.ru; f. 2000):
  Dr MIKHAIL M. LAVRENTIEV

Department of Mechanics and Mathematics (tel. (3832) 39-75-81; e-mail mmf@msu.ru; internet mmfd.nsu.ru):
  Prof. SERGEY S. GONCHAROV

Department of Natural Sciences (tel. (3832) 39-74-30; e-mail decan@fen.nsu.ru; internet www.fen.nsu.ru; f. 1959):
  Prof. VLADIMIR A. REZNIKOV

Department of Physics (tel. (3832) 39-78-00; e-mail dean@phys.nsu.ru; internet www.phys.nsu.ru; f. 1961):
  Prof. ANDREY V. ARZHANNIKOV

OMSK STATE UNIVERSITY

644077 Omsk, pr. Mira 55A

Telephone: (3812) 67-01-04
Internet: www.omsu.ru

Founded 1974
State control
Language of instruction: Russian
Academic year: September to June

Rector: Prof. GENNADY I. GERING
Pro-Rectors: Dr MIKHAIL V. KHOROSHEVSKY, Dr VALERY V. DUBITSKY (Academic), Dr VLADIMIR P. AVILOV (Finance and Admin.), Dr VLADIMIR I. STRUNIN (Scientific)
Librarian: LYUDMILA A. BALAKINA

Number of teachers: 640
Number of students: 10,000

Publications: *Omsky Universitet* (28 a year), *Vestnik Omskogo Universiteta* (4 a year)

DEANS

Faculty of Arts and Culture: NINA M. GENOVA
Faculty of Chemistry: IRINA V. VLASOVA
Faculty of Economics: LYUDMILA N. IVANOVA
Faculty of Foreign Languages: NATALYA G. GICHEVA
Faculty of History: ALEXEY V. YAKUB
Faculty of International Business: YURI P. DRUS
Faculty of Law: MAXIM S. FOKIN
Faculty of Mathematics: VLADIMIR B. NIKOLAEV
Faculty of Philology: NIKOLAI N. MISYUROV
Faculty of Physics: KLIMENTY N. YUGAI
Faculty of Psychology: LYUDMILA I. DEMENTY
Faculty of Theology and World Culture: DMITRY P. SINELNIKOV

PROFESSORS

ADEEV, G. D., Theoretical Nuclear Physics
AKELKINA, E. A., Literature
AZAROV, V. A., Law
BAOURIN, S. N., Law
BORBAT, V. F., Chemistry and Technology of Non-ferrous and Noble Metals
DUBENSKY, U. P., Pedagogics
ELOVIKOV, L. A., Methodology of Local Labour Management
FAIZULLIN, R. T., Mathematics
FISYUK, A. S., Chemistry
FOMENKO, S. V., History
GERING, G. I., Physics
GOOTS, A. K., Geometry
GRIN, A. G., Mathematics
GRINBERG, M. S., Criminal Law
GRISHKOV, A. N., Mathematics
ISSERS, O. S., Linguistics
KASANNIK, A. I., Ecological Law
KLEIMENOV, M. P., Law
KUKIN, G. P., Algebra
KUZMINA, N. A., Linguistics
LAVROV, E. I., Political Economy
MATYUSCHENKO, V. I., Archaeology
MILLER, A. E., Economy
NOVATOROV, V. E., Pedagogics
OSIPOV, B. I., Linguistics
OSTROVSKY, N. M., Chemistry
OVSIANNIKOVA, I. N., Philosophy
PERTSEV, N. V., Mathematics
POSDNIAKOV, N. K., Politology
PRUDNIKOV, V. V., Physics
RAZUMOV, V. I., Philosophy
REMNEV, A. V., History
ROMANKOV, V. A., Mathematics
ROY, O. M., Sociology

SAGITULLIN, R. S., Chemistry of Heterocyclic Compounds
SEMIKOLENOVA, N. A., Physics
SHIROKOV, I. V., Physics
SKOBELKIN, V. V., Labour Law
SOROKIN, U. A., History
STRUGOV, U. F., Mathematics
TIPUKHIN, V. N., Philosophy
TOLOCHKO, A. P., Pre-Revolutionary Native History
TOMILOV, N. A., Ethnography
VERSHININ, V. I., Analytical Chemistry
YUGAI, K. N., Physics
ZOLOTARYOV, I. D., Physics

OREL STATE UNIVERSITY

302015 Orel, Komsomolskaya ul. 95

Telephone: (0862) 77-73-18
Fax: (0862) 77-73-32
Internet: www.osu.edu.ru
State control
Founded 1974

Rector: Prof. FEDOR S. AVDEEV
Pro-Rector for Academic Affairs: Prof. NADEZHDA A. ILYINA
Pro-Rector for External Education and Int. Relations: Prof. NADEZHDA A. ILYINA
Pro-Rector for Science: Prof. GENNADY P. VERKEENKO

Number of teachers: 668
Number of students: 11,203

ORENBURG STATE UNIVERSITY

460018 Orenburg, pr. Pobedy 13

Telephone: (3532) 77-67-70
Fax: (3532) 72-37-01
E-mail: oms@mail.osu.ru
Internet: www.osu.ru

Founded 1971
Public control
Language of instruction: Russian
Academic year: September to July

Rector: Dr VLADIMIR KOVALEVSKIY
Pro-Rector for Scientific Research: Dr SERGEY N. LETUTA
Pro-Rector for Academic Affairs: ALEXANDER D. PROSKURIN
Pro-Rector for Academic Methodology: TATYANA P. PETUKHOVA
Pro-Rector for Admin. Maintenance and Capital Construction: VLADIMIR P. KOLGANOV
Pro-Rector for Int. Students Affairs: BALAZHAN M. KARCHAEVA
Pro-Rector for Social and Educational Affairs: TATYANA A. NOSOVA
Pro-Rector for Informatization and Security: VICTOR V. BIKOVSKY

Library: 1m. vols
Number of teachers: 2,659
Number of students: 39,865

PACIFIC NATIONAL UNIVERSITY

680035 Khabarovsk, ul. Tikhookeanskaya 136

Telephone and fax (4212) 72-07-12
E-mail: info@khstu.ru
Internet: www.khstu.ru

Founded 2005, fmrly Khabarovsk State Univ. (f. 1958)
State control
Language of instruction: Chinese, English, Japanese, Korean, Russian
Academic year: September to June

Depts: engineering and construction, nature management and ecology, architecture and design, automation and informational technology, transport and technology, economics and management, social studies and humanities, law, computer and fundamental sciences, extramural training, extension and parallel training, further professional education

Rector: SERGEI N. IVANCHENKO

Library: 1.2m. vols
Number of teachers: 950
Number of students: 25,000

PACIFIC STATE UNIVERSITY OF ECONOMICS

690950 Vladivostok, Okeansky pr. 19

Telephone: (4232) 26-62-21
E-mail: web@psue.ru
Internet: www.psue.ru
State control

Founded 1964

Rector: Prof. VIKTOR G. BELKIN.

PENZA STATE UNIVERSITY

440026 Penza, Krasnaya ul. 40

Telephone and fax (8412) 66-29-27
E-mail: cnit@stup.ac.ru
Internet: www.stup.ac.ru
State control

Founded 1943, present name and status 1998

Rector: Prof. VLADIMIR VOLCHIKHIN
First Pro-Rector: VICTOR A. MESCHERYAKOV
Pro-Rector for Academic Affairs: VICTOR B. MEKHANOV
Pro-Rector for Admin. and Finance: BORIS V. MALSANOV
Pro-Rector for Governance and Personnel: YURI V. KLOCHKOV
Pro-Rector for Science: MIKHAIL A. SCHERBAKOV

Number of teachers: 725
Number of students: 13,895.

UNIVERSITY BRANCH

Serdobsk Branch: Penza Region, 442890 Serdobsk, Lenina ul. 285A; Dir IVAN I. IVANOV.

PEOPLES' FRIENDSHIP UNIVERSITY OF RUSSIA

117198 Moscow, Miklukho-Maklaya ul. 6

Telephone: (095) 434-70-27
Fax: (095) 433-15-11
E-mail: druzhba@rudn.ru
Internet: www.rudn.ru

Founded 1960 as Patrice Lumumba Peoples' Friendship Univ.

Self-governing
Language of instruction: Russian
Academic year: September to July

Rector: Prof. VLADIMIR M. FILIPPOV (acting)
Vice-Rectors: N. A. CHICHULIN, A. D. GLADUSH, V. F. PONYKA, V. D. PROTSENKO, E. L. SHESHNYAK, G. G. SOKOLOV, N. V. VENSKOVSKY, A. P. YEFREMOV
Librarian: A. N. SHUMILOV

Number of teachers: 2,112
Number of students: 4,000

Publications: *Druzhba* (52 a year, university newspaper), *Vestnik Rossiiskogo Universiteta Druzhby Narodov* (4 a year)

DEANS

Faculty of Agriculture: Prof. V. V. GORCHAKOV
Faculty of Ecology: Prof. S. N. SIDORENKO
Faculty of Economics: Prof. N. P. GUSAKOV
Faculty of Engineering: Prof. N. K. PONOMAREV
Faculty of Foreign Languages and General Educational Disciplines: Prof. V. V. YAKUSHEV
Faculty of Humanities and Social Sciences: Prof. N. S. KIRABAEV

Faculty of Law: Prof. A. Y. KAPUSTIN
Faculty of Medicine: Prof. V. A. FROLOV
Faculty of Philology: Prof. V. N. DENISENKO
Faculty of Physical, Mathematical and Natural Sciences: Prof. V. V. DAVYDOV
Academic and Scientific Institute of Information Technology in Physics and Chemistry: Prof. S. N. SIDORENKO
Institute of Distance Learning: Prof. G. A. KRASNOVA
Institute of Foreign Languages: Prof. N. L. SOKOLOVA
Institute of Hotel Business and Tourism: Prof. S. V. DIKHTYAR
Institute of World Economy and Business (International School of Business): Prof. N. P. GUSAKOV

PERM STATE UNIVERSITY

614600 Perm, GSP, ul. Bukireva 15

Telephone: 33-61-83
Fax: 33-80-14
Internet: www.psu.ru

Founded 1916
State control
Language of instruction: Russian
Academic year: September to June

Faculties of biology, chemistry, economics, geology, geography, history, law, mechanics and mathematics, philology, physics

Rector: V. V. MALANIN
Vice-Rectors: Prof. V. I. KACHEVROVSKY, Prof. V. I. KOSTYTSIN, Prof. B. M. OSOVETSKY
Librarian: R. N. ROGALNIKOVA

Number of teachers: 683
Number of students: 9,167

Publications: *Caves Research Problems* (1 a year), *Computer Systems and Processes Modelling* (1 a year), *Geophysical Methods of Oil and Gas Exploration* (1 a year), *Mechanics of Controlled Movement Problems* (1 a year), *Radiospectroscopy* (1 a year), *Statistical Methods of Verifying and Estimating Hypotheses* (1 a year), *Uchenye Zapiski* (Transactions).

PETROZAVODSK STATE UNIVERSITY

185640 Republic of Karelia, Petrozavodsk, Ave Lenina 33

Telephone: (8142) 78-51-40
Fax: (8142) 71-10-00
E-mail: rectorat@psu.karelia.ru
Internet: petrsu.ru

Founded 1940
State control
Languages of instruction: English, Russian
Academic year: September to June

Rector: Prof. ANATOLY VORONIN
Pres.: Prof. VICTOR VASILYEV
Vice-Rector for Admin. and Economic Work: LJUDMILA BEZLATNAYA
Vice-Rector for Education: Prof. VLADIMIR SYUNEV
Vice-Rector for Innovation and Production Activities: Prof. ILYA SHEGELMAN
Vice-Rector for Organizational Work: Prof. SERGEY KORZHOV
Vice-Rector for Pre-Univ. Training and Career Guidance: Assoc. Prof. ANATOLY LOPUHA
Vice-Rector for Research: Prof. Dr ELMIRA ZILBER
Head of Directorate for Int. Cooperation: LYUDMILA KULIKOVSKAYA
Librarian: MARINA OTLIVANCHIK

Library of 1,179,042 vols
Number of teachers: 905
Number of students: 18,616

Publications: *Trudy* (Works, 1 a year), *Uche-niye Zapiski* (1 a year)

DEANS

Faculty of Agriculture: NIKITA ONISCHENKO
Faculty of Baltic and Finnish Philology and Culture: TAMARA STARSHOVA
Faculty of Ecology and Biology: ERNEST IVANTER
Faculty of Economics: VLADIMIR AKULOV
Faculty of Forest Engineering: ALEXANDER PITUKHIN
Faculty of History: SERGEY VERIGIN
Faculty of Improvement of Professional Skills: TATYANA AGARKOVA
Faculty of Industrial and Civil Engineering: YURY MARKADANOV
Faculty of Law: SERGEY CHERNOV
Faculty of Mathematics: ALEKSEI VARFOLOMEEV
Faculty of Medicine: ALEKSANDR BALASHOV
Faculty of Mining and Geology: VLADIMIR AMINOV
Faculty of Philology: ANDREY KUNILSKY
Faculty of Physical Engineering: DMITRI BALASHOV
Faculty of Political and Social Sciences: VALENTINA MAKSIMOVA

POMORSKY STATE UNIVERSITY 'M. V. LOMONSOV'

163002 Arkhangelsk, Lomosova pr. 4

Telephone and fax (8182) 28-07-80
E-mail: dit@pomorsu.ru
Internet: www.pomorsu.ru

Founded 1991, present name and status 1996
State control

Rector: Prof. VLADIMIR N. BULATOV
First Pro-Rector: YURI V. KUDRYASHOV
Pro-Rectors for Academic Affairs: IRINA R. LUGOVSKAYA, LEONID N. SHESTAKOV
Pro-Rector for Admin. and Finance: ALEXANDER G. LESCHIKOV
Pro-Rector for External Academic Affairs: ANATOLY A. SEMIN
Pro-Rector for Int. Affairs: ALEXANDER S. KRYLOV
Pro-Rector for Science: VLADISLAV I. GOLDIN

Library of 700,000 vols
Number of students: 12,419

ROSTOV STATE UNIVERSITY OF ECONOMICS (RINKH)

344007 Rostov-on-Don, Bol. Sadovaya ul. 69

Telephone: (8632) 66-51-23
Fax: (8632) 65-45-21
E-mail: rector@rseu.ru
Internet: www.rseu.ru

Founded 1931

Rector: VLADIMIR S. ZOLOTAREV

Library of 750,000 vols
Number of teachers: 400
Number of students: 15,830

Publications: *Bulletin* (4 a year), *Scientific Notes* (4 a year).

RUSSIAN STATE SOCIAL UNIVERSITY

107150 Moscow, ul. Losinoostrovskaya 24
Moscow, ul. Vilgelma Pika ul., korp. 1

Telephone: (495) 187-60-25
Fax: (495) 783-71-25
E-mail: info@mgsu.info
Internet: www.rgsu.net

Founded 1991 as Russian State Social Institute; accredited with univ. status as Moscow State Social Univ. 1994; present name 2004

Rector: Prof. VASILY I. ZHUKOV
Vice-Rector: GENNADY V. SAENKO

DEANS

Faculty of Foreign Languages: IRINA N. TUPITSYNA

Faculty of Further Education: TAMARA S. SUMSKAYA

Faculty of Humanities: LEONID G. LAPTEV

Faculty of Law: DIMITRY V. ILYAKOV

Faculty of Personnel Training and Qualification Improvement: TATYANA V. SHELYAG

Faculty of Socioeconomics: NIKOLAI N. PILIPENKO

Faculty of Social Information Technologies: VITALY M. ARISTOV

Faculty of Social Insurance and Finance: ALEXANDER A. GRUNIN

Faculty of Social Management: OLGA A. URZHA

Faculty of Social Medicine and Rehabilitation Technologies: VALENTINA V. CHESHIKHINA

Faculty of Sociology: DINA T. KABDULLINOVA

Faculty of Social Work, Pedagogy and Psychology: VLADISLAV A. NIKITIN

Faculty of Work and Employment Security: YURI G. SOROKIN

RUSSIAN STATE TRADE AND ECONOMICS UNIVERSITY

125993 Moscow, ul. Smolnaya 36

Telephone: (499) 458-94-79

Fax: (499) 458-72-47

E-mail: mail@rsute.ru

Internet: www.rsute.ru

Founded 1930

Language of instruction: Russian

Academic year: September to July

Rector: Prof. Dr SERGEY N. BABURIN

Library of 868,960 vols

Number of students: 65,000

Publications: *Caucasian research notes* (scientific journal), *Science Horizons*, *Vestnik of RSUTE*

DEANS

Faculty of Computing Technologies: Prof. DMITRY NECHAEV

Faculty of Commerce and Marketing: Prof. TATYANA PARAMONOVA

Faculty of Finance and Economics: Prof. ALEKSANDR LITVINYUK

Faculty of Hospitality, Restaurant Business and Services: Prof. MIKHAIL MOROZOV

Faculty of Law: Prof. OLEG SAULYAK

Faculty of Social Technologies: Prof. ALEKSEY CHERNYSHOV

Faculty of Tax and Taxation: Prof. DMITRY RAZUMOVSKY

Faculty of Management: Prof. LYUDMILA NIKITINA

Faculty of World Economics and Trade: Prof. ELENA VAVILOVA

RUSSIAN STATE UNIVERSITY FOR THE HUMANITIES

125267 Moscow, Miusskaya pl. 6

Telephone: (495) 250-61-18

Fax: (495) 250-51-09

E-mail: afn@rggu.msk.su

Internet: www.rsuh.ru

Founded 1991

Rector: Prof. YURI N. AFANASYEV

Library: 1.5m. vols

Number of teachers: 484

Number of students: 4,120

ST PETERSBURG STATE UNIVERSITY

199034 St Petersburg, Universitetskaya nab. 7/9

Telephone: (812) 328-20-00

Fax: (812) 328-04-02

E-mail: office@inform.pu.ru

Internet: www.spbu.ru

Founded 1724

State control

Academic year: September to June (2 terms)

Rector: Prof. NIKOLAY M. KROPACHEV

Vice-Rector: I. A DEMENTYEV

Vice-Rector for Academics: Prof. IGOR A. GORLINSKY

Vice-Rector for Academic Affairs: Prof. NIKOLAY V. KALEDIN

Vice-Rector for Admission: Prof. VALERY S. KATKALO

Vice-Rector for Economics: Prof. IVAN I. BOYKO

Vice-Rector for Economy and Social Devt: Prof. STANISLAV G. EREMEEV

Vice-Rector for Innovative Devt Projects: ILYA A. DEMENTYEV

Vice-Rector for Int. Affairs: Prof. KONSTANTIN K. KHUDOLEY

Vice-Rector for Legal Issues: MIKHAIL N. KUDILINSKY

Vice-Rector for Philology and Arts: Prof. SERGEY I. BOGDANOV

Vice-Rector for Research: Prof. NIKOLAY G. SKVORTSOV

Librarian: MAXIM GORKY

Library: see Libraries and Archives

Number of teachers: 6,000

Number of students: 32,400

Publications: *Jurisprudence*, *Vestnik St. Petersburg University* (Journal, in 7 series)

DEANS

Faculty of Applied Mathematics: Dr LEON A. PETROSIAN

Faculty of Arts: VALERY A. GERGIEV

Faculty of Asian and African Studies: Prof. EVGENIY I. ZENELEV

Faculty of Biology and Soil Science: Prof. IGOR A. GORLINSKY

Faculty of Chemistry: Prof. ALEXANDER YU. BILIBIN

Faculty of Economics: Prof. IVAN P. BOYKO

Faculty of Geography and Geo-Ecology: Prof. NIKOLAY V. KALDENIN

Faculty of Geology: Prof. IGOR V. BULDAKOV

Faculty of History: Prof. ANDREY YU. DVORNICHENKO

Faculty of International Relations: Prof. KONSTANTIN K. KHUDOLEY

Faculty of Journalism: Prof. ANATOLY S. PUYU

Faculty of Law: Prof. NIKOLAY M. KROPACHEV

Faculty of Management: Prof. VALERY S. KATKALO

Faculty of Mathematics and Mechanics: Prof. GENNADY. A. LEONOV

Faculty of Medicine: Prof. PETR K. YABLONSKY

Faculty of Oriental Studies: Dr I. M. STEBLIN-KAMENSKY

Faculty of Philology: Prof. LUDMILA A. VERBITSKAYA

Faculty of Philosophy: Prof. YURY N. SOLONIN

Faculty of Physics: Dr ALEXANDER S. CHIRTSOV

Faculty of Political Science: Prof. STANISLAV G. EREMEEV

Faculty of Psychology: Dr LARISSA A. TSVETKOVA

Faculty of Sociology: Dr NIKOLAY G. SKVORTSOV

ATTACHED INSTITUTES

Institute of Astronomy: Dir Dr V. V. VITYAZEV.

Botanical Gardens: Dir V. N. NIKITINA.

Institute of Applied Mathematics: Dir Dr D. A. OVSIANNIKOV.

Institute of Biology: Dir Dr D. V. OSIPOV.

Institute of Chemistry: Dir Dr YU. E. ERMOLENKO.

Institute of Complex Social Research: Dir Dr V. E. SEMENOV.

Institute of Geography: Dir Dr A. I. CHISTOBAEV.

Institute of the Earth's Crust: Dir Dr V. V. KURILENKO.

Institute of Mathematics and Mechanics: Dir Dr G. A. LEONOV.

Institute of Physics: Dir Dr YE. I. RYUMTSEV.

Institute of Physiology: Dir Dr I. YE. KANUNIKOV.

Institute of Radiophysics: Dir O. V. SOLOVIEV.

Institute of Information Technology: Dir Dr A. N. TEREKHOV.

Institute of Laser Research: Dir Dr YU. S. TVERIANOVICH.

ST PETERSBURG STATE UNIVERSITY OF CINEMA AND TELEVISION

191126 St Petersburg, ul. Pravdy 13

Telephone: (812) 315-74-83

E-mail: info@gukit.ru

Internet: www.gukit.ru

Founded 1918

Study areas incl. art of cinema and television, economics, electrical engineering, film equipment, film and photographic materials

Rector: Prof. ALEXANDER A. BELUSOV

Library of 500,000 vols

Number of students: 4,500

Publication: *Proceedings*.

ST PETERSBURG STATE UNIVERSITY OF ECONOMICS AND FINANCE

191023 St Petersburg, ul. Sadovaya 21

Telephone: (812) 310-38-23

Fax: (812) 110-56-74

E-mail: rector@finec.ru

Internet: www.finec.ru

Founded 1930, present name and status 1997

Faculties of accounting, banking, economic theory, finance, industrial economics, international economic relations, management, marketing, statistics; also comprises a Higher Economics School

Rector: LEONID S. TARASEVICH

Number of teachers: 2,000

Number of students: 12,000

Library: 1m. vols.

SAKHALIN STATE UNIVERSITY

693008 Yuzhno-Sakhalinsk, ul. Lenina 290

Telephone: (424) 42-43-57

E-mail: admin@sakhgu.sakhalin.ru

Internet: www.sakhgu.ru

State control

Founded 1949 as teacher training institute, reorganized into Yuzhno-Sakhalinsk State Pedagogical Institute in 1954; present name and status 1998

Rector: Dr BORIS R. MISIKOV

Library of 613,099 vols

Number of teachers: 350

Number of students: 7,483

Publications: *Law Journal, Maymanovsky Readings, Philological Journal, Regional Studies Bulletin*.

SAMARA STATE UNIVERSITY

443011 Samara, ul. Akademika Pavlova 1

Telephone: (8462) 34-54-02

Fax: (8462) 34-54-17

E-mail: avn@ssu.samara.ru

Internet: www.ssu.samara.ru

Founded 1969
State control
Language of instruction: Russian, English
Academic year: September to June

Rector: GENNADY P. YAROVOY
First Pro-Rector: PETR S. KABYTOV
Pro-Rector for Education: VITALY P. GARKIN
Pro-Rector for Science: YURI N. GORELOV
Chief Librarian: GALINA A. BARSUKOVA

Library of 900,000 vols
Number of teachers: 820
Number of students: 14,000

Publications: *Bulletin* (8 a year), *Physics of Wave Processes and Radio-Technical Systems* (4 a year), *Samara Zemsky Collection* (4 a year)

DEANS

Faculty of Biology: G. L. RYTOV
Faculty of Chemistry: S. V. KURBATOVA
Faculty of History: U. N. SMIRNOV
Faculty of Languages and Literature: A. A. BEZRUKOVA
Faculty of Law: A. A. NAPREENKO
Faculty of Mathematics and Mechanics: V. M. KLIMKIN
Faculty of Physics: V. V. IVAKHNIK
Faculty of Psychology: K. S. LISETSKY
Faculty of Sociology: V. YA. MACHNEV

PROFESSORS

ASTAFIEV, V. I., Mechanics
BLATOV, V. A., Inorganic Chemistry
BREUSOV, Y. G., Economics
BULANOVA, A. V., General Chemistry and Chromatography
FILATOV, O. P., Equations of Mathematical Physics
GIZATULLIN, M. H., Physics and Mathematics
GOLUBKOV, S. A., Russian and Foreign Literature
GORELOV, Y. N., Differential Equations
KABYTOV, P. S., History of Russia
KHRAMKOV, I. V., History of Russia
KLIMKIN, V. M., Functional Analysis
KOMOV, A. N., Electronics
KONEV, V. A., Philosophy of the Humanities Faculties
KOZENKO, B. D., World History
KOZHEVNIKOV, Y. N., Physics and Mathematics
LEONOV, M. I., Russian History
LOBACHEV, A. L., Chemistry and Chromatography
MATVEEV, N. M., Ecology, Botany and Environmental Protection
MERKULOVA, N. A., Human and Animal Physiology
MOLEVICH, E. F., Sociology and Political Science
PLAKSINA, T. I., Ecology, Botany and Environmental Protection
PODKOVKIN, V. G., Biochemistry
PURYGIN, P. P., Organic Chemistry
RUDNEVA, T. I., Education
RYMAR, N. T., Russian and Foreign Literature
SARAEV, L. A., Mathematics and Computers
SEREZHKIN, V. N., Inorganic Chemistry
SEREZHKINA, L. B., Inorganic Chemistry
SHEIFER, S. A., Criminal Court Proceedings and Investigation
SHESTAKOV, A. A., Philosophy
SIKORA, P. E., State and Administrative Law
SKOBELEV, V. P., Russian and Foreign Literature
SKOBLIKOVA, Y. S., Philology, Russian Language
SOBOLEV, V. A., Differential Equations
SOLODYANNIKOV, Y. V., Functional Analysis and Theory of Functions
VOSKRESENSKY, V. E., Algebra and Geometry
YAROVOY, G. P., Radiophysics and Computers
ZAGUZOV, I. S., Mechanics

SARATOV STATE UNIVERSITY 'N. G. CHERNYSHEVSKY'

410012 Saratov, Astrakhanskaya ul. 83

Telephone: (2) 26-16-96
Fax: (2) 27-85-29
E-mail: rector@sgu.ru
Internet: www.sgu.ru

Founded 1909
State control
Academic year: September to July

Br. in Astrakhan; colleges and institutes: College of Radioelectronics, P. N. Yablochkov; Geological College; College of Management and Service; Pedagogical Institute in Balashov.

Rector: Dr LEONID YU. KOSSOVICH
Vice-Rector for Academic Affairs: Dr ELENA G. YELINA
Vice-Rector for Int. Cooperation: DIMITRY N. KONAKOV
Vice-Rector for Science: Dr DIMITRY A. USANOV
Registrar: IRINA V. FEDUSENKO
Librarian: IRINA V. LEBEDEVA

Library of 2,903,504 vols
Number of teachers: 982
Number of students: 16,000

Publications: *Applied Nonlinear Dynamics, Contemporary Herpetology, Ecological magazine in the Volga Region, Electrochemical Energetics, Entomological and Parasitological Research in the Volga Region, Hetero-magnetic Electronics, Numbers Theory Research, Problems of Applied Physics*

DEANS

Biology: Dr GENNADIY V. SHLYAKHTIN
Chemistry: Dr OLGA V. FEDOTOVA
Computer Sciences and Information Technologies: ANTONINA G. FEDOROVA
Geography: Dr VLADIMIR Z. MAKAROV
Geology: ELENA N. VOLKOVA
History: Prof. TATYANA V. CHEREVICHKO
Humanities and Social Sciences: Dr SERGEY YU. SHENIN
Mechanics and Mathematics: Dr ANDREY M. ZAKHAROV
Non-Linear Processes: Dr YURIY I. LEVIN
Philology: Dr VALERY V. PROZOROV
Philosophy: MIKHAIL O. ORLOV
Physics: Dr VALERIY M. ANIKIN
Psychology: Dr LIUDMILA N. AKSENOVSKAYA
Sociology: Dr GENNADIY V. DYLNOV

SOUTH URAL STATE UNIVERSITY

454080 Chelyabinsk, 76 Lenin Ave

Telephone: (351) 267-94-56
Fax: (351) 265-65-04
E-mail: susuniversity@yandex.ru
Internet: www.susu.ac.ru

Founded 1943, fmrly Chelyabinsk State Technical Univ., present name and status 1997
State control
Academic year: September to June

Rector: Prof. ALEXANDER SHESTAKOV
First Vice-Rector for Academics: Prof. MAJOROV VLADIMIR I.
Vice-Rector for Academics: Prof. CHUMANOV ILYA V.
Vice-Rector for Int. Affairs: Prof. VICTOR M. KATOCHKOV
Vice-Rector for Scientific Affairs: Prof. VAULIN SERGEY D.
Registrar: IGOR V. SIDOROV
Dir of Int. Relations Dept: SERGEY G. BARYSHNIKOV
Dir of Library: IRINA P. BERGER

Library: 3m. vols
Number of teachers: 5,000
Number of students: 55,000

DEANS

Architectural and Civil Engineering Faculty: VLADIMIR V. SPASIBOZHKO
Architectural Faculty: SALAVAT G. SHABIEV
Faculty of Chemistry: VYACHESLAV V. AVDIN
Faculty of Computing Mathematics and Computer Science: LEONID B. SOKOLINSKY
Faculty of History: NATALIA V. PARFENTIEVA
Faculty of Journalism: LUDMILA P. SHESTERKINA
Faculty of Physical Education and Sport: EVGENY V. BYKOV
Faculty of Psychology: NIKOLAY A. BATURIN
Instrument-Making Faculty: LEV S. KAZARINOV
International Faculty: VLADIMIR P. GORSHENIN
Law and Finance Faculty: BORIS I. ROVNY
Law Faculty: ALEXANDER N. CLASSEN
Linguistics Faculty: TAMARA N. KHOMUTOVA
Mechanics and Engineering Faculty: VIKTOR I. GUZEEV
Mechanics and Mathematics Faculty: ALEXANDR D. DROZIN
Motor and Tractor Faculty: YURI V. ROZHDESTVENSKY
Physical and Metallurgical Faculty: GENNADY G. MIKHAYLOV
Physical Faculty: NATALIA D. KUNDIKOVA
Power Engineering Faculty: YURI I. KHOKHLOV
Service and Tourism Faculty: VICTOR A. LIVSHITS
Trade and Economics Faculty: IRINA U. OKOLNISHNIKOVA

SOUTHERN FEDERAL UNIVERSITY

344006 Rostov-on-Don, Bolshaya Sadovaya Str. 105/42

Telephone: (863) 263-32-36
Fax: (863) 263-87-23
E-mail: info@sfedu.ru
Internet: sfedu.ru

Founded 2006 by merger of Rostov State Acad. of Architecture and Arts, Rostov State Pedagogical Univ. and Taganrog State Radio Engineering Univ. to the Rostov State Univ.
State Control
Languages of instruction: English, Russian
Academic year: September to June

11 Research institutes and design centres, 22 education and research centres

Rector: Dr Sc. Prof. VLADISLAV G. ZAKHAREVICH
Sr Vice-Rector for Academic Affairs: Prof. IGOR M. UZNARODOV
Sr Vice-Rector for Research and Innovation: EVGENY K. AYDARKIN
Vice-Rector for Curriculum and Social Affairs: Prof. IRINA V. MOSTOVAYA
Vice-Rector for Economics: ALEKSEY Y. ARHIPOV
Vice-Rector for Int. Relations and Regional Policy: Assoc. Prof. SERGEY A. DUZHIKOV
Vice-Rector for Human Resources and Security: VITALIY P. PERETOKIN
Academic Sec.: Dr VALENTINA N. CHYBAROVA

Library of 3,998,616 vols, (incl. 2,515,102 vols of the main library, 552,741 vols of Pedagogical Institute, 28,809 vols of Institute of Architecture and Arts and 901,964 vols of Taganrog Technological Institute), 32,619 e-books
Number of teachers: 4,109 (2,876 full-time, 1,233 part-time)
Number of students: 43,183 (23,309 full-time, 19,874 part-time)

DEANS

Faculty of Biological Sciences: VITOLD G. PARSHIN
Faculty of Chemistry: VLADIMIR E. GUTERMAN

Faculty of Economics: Prof. VALERY A. ALE-SHIN

Faculty of Geology and Geography: Prof. NIKOLAY I. BOYKO

Faculty of High Technologies: ANATOLY E. PANICH

Faculty of History: VIKTOR YU. APRYSH-CHENKO

Faculty of Information Security: SVETLANA M. LYAH

Faculty of Law: Assoc. Prof. SVETLANA M. LYAKH

Faculty of Mathematics, Mechanics and Computer Science: Prof. MIKHAIL I. KAR-YAKIN

Faculty of Philology and Journalism: Assoc. Prof. ELENA V. GRIGORYEVA

Faculty of Philosophy and Culture Studies: Prof. GENNADY V. DRACH

Faculty of Physics: VYACHESLAV S. MALY-SHEVSKY

Faculty of Psychology: Prof. PAVEL N. ERMA-KOV

Faculty of Regional Studies: ANTON V. SER-IKOV

Faculty of Social and Political Science: VIKTOR I. FILONENKO

SFEDU INSTITUTES

Institute of Architecture and Art

344082 Rostov-on-Don, Budennovsky pr. 39

Telephone: (8632) 39-09-62

E-mail: rai@aaanet.ru

Founded 1988

Architecture, environmental design, arts and crafts, history of art, fashion design, management in architecture

Library of 300,000 vols

Number of teachers: 181

Number of students: 1,091

Rector: V. A. KOLESNIK

Publication: *Problems of Architectural Education* (1 a year)

SFU Pedagogical Institute

Rostov oblast, 347928 Taganrog, GSP-17a, Nekrasovsky pr. 44

Telephone: (863) 4431-05-98

Fax: (863) 446-05-19

E-mail: rspu@rspu.edu.ru

Internet: www.rspu.edu.ru

Founded 1869 as Rostov State Pedagogical Univ.

Academic year: September to June

Dir: Dr Sc. Prof. VLADIMIR I. MAREEV

Number of students: 1,746

Taganrog Institute of Technology

Rostov oblast, 347928 Taganrog, GSP-17a, Nekrasovsky pr. 44

Telephone: (863) 439-30-29

Fax: (863) 431-05-98

E-mail: rector@tsure.ru

Internet: www.tsure.ru

Founded 1952 as Taganrog Institute of Radio Engineering, renamed Taganrog State Univ. of Radio Engineering 1993, present status 2006

Academic year: September to June

Head: ALEKSANDER IVANOVICH SUKHINOV

First Deputy Head: VICTOR ALEKSANDROVICH OBUKHOVETS

Deputy Head for Int. Relations: VADIM P. POPOV

Library of 980,000 vols

Number of teachers: 804

Number of students: 11,300

ACADEMIC INSTITUTES AND RESEARCH INSTITUTES

Institute of Economics and Foreign Economic Relations: 344002 Rostov-on-Don, Soborny 26; tel. and fax (863) 244-15-02; e-mail iecier@sfedu.ru.

Inter-regional Institute of Social Science: 344006 Rostov-on-Don, Bol. Sadovaya 105; e-mail narezhni@mis.sfedu.ru; internet www.rostov.iriss.ru; Acad. Dir ANATOLY IVA-NOVICH NAREZHNY.

ATTACHED RESEARCH CENTRES

Research and Educational Centre 'Nanotechnologies': integration of education and research as well as improvement of cooperation with scientific orgs and institutes of South Federal Dist.

Research Centre for Nanoscale structure of Matter: 344090 Rostov-on-Don, Sorge 5; tel. (8632) 97-53-26; e-mail asoldatov@phys.rsu.ru; internet www.nano.sfedu.ru; study of 3D local atomic nanoscale geometry and electronic structure in various types of advanced novel materials; Dir Prof. ALEXANDER V SOLDATOV.

14 attached research institutes.

STATE UNIVERSITY FOR THE HUMANITIES

119334 Moscow, Leninsky pr-t, 32A

Telephone: (495) 938-10-09

Fax: (495) 938-22-88

E-mail: gugn@gugn.info

Internet: www.gugn.ru

State control

Founded 1992 as the Republican Centre for Humanities Education; present name 1998

Institutes of advancement of qualifications and teacher training, economics, culture, history, law, literary culture and management, philosophy, politology, psychology, sociology, world politics

Rector: Prof. ALEXANDER O. CHUBARYAN

First Pro-Rector: Prof. NATALYA N. NIKITINA

Pro-Rector for Gen. Affairs: GEORGY N. KRASNOV

Pro-Rector for Science: Prof. MIKHAIL V. BIBIKOV

Academic Sec.: DENIS V. FOMIN-NILOV.

STATE UNIVERSITY OF MANAGEMENT

109542 Moscow, Ryazansky pr. 99

Telephone: (495) 371-13-22

Fax: (495) 174-62-81

E-mail: rectorat@guu.ru

Internet: www.guu.ru

Founded 1919

Rector: ANATOLY G. PORSHNEV

Library of 280,000 vols

Number of teachers: 700

Number of students: 10,000

STAVROPOL STATE UNIVERSITY

355009 Stavropol, ul. Pushkina 1

Telephone: (8652) 35-72-65

Fax: (8652) 35-40-33

E-mail: stavsu@stavsu.ru

Internet: www.stavsu.ru

State control

Founded 1930 as Stavropol Agro-Pedagogical Institute; 1932–1994 as Stavropol Pedagogical Institute, 1994–1996 as Stavropol State Pedagogical Univ., present name 1996

Academic year: September to June

Rector: Prof. VLADIMIR ALEXANDROVICH

Vice-Rector for Capital Construction: LUBE-NETS YURIY PETROVICH

Vice-Rector for Curriculum: Prof. BELOZEROV VITALY SEMENOVICH

Vice-Rector for Economic Issues and Additional Educational Programmes: Prof. EROKHIN ALEKSEY MIKHAILOVICH

Vice-Rector for Maintenance: VASILENKO ANA-TOLIY KUZMICH

Vice-Rector for Research: Prof. LIKHOVID ANDREY ALEXANDROVICH

Vice-Rector for Security: Assoc. Prof. TER-ESCHENKO NIKOLAY VIKTOROVICH

Dean of Extra Mural and Externship Dept: Prof. TARANOVA TATYANA NIKOLAEVNA

Dir for Studies: Assoc. Prof. VOLKOVA VALEN-TINA IVANOVNA

Dir for Univ. Scientific Library: KUZMINA ELENA ANATOLIEVNA

Library: 1.2m. vols, 382 periodicals

Number of teachers: 900

Number of students: 15,000

Publication: *Stavropol State University Vestnik*

DEANS

Advanced Training: Prof. GUROV VALERIY NIKOLAEVICH

Arts: Assoc. Prof. MARKOV ALEKSANDR IVANO-VICH

Economics: Prof. AKININ PETR VIKTOROVICH

Geography: Prof. SCHITOVA NATALYA ALEK-SANDROVNA

History: Prof. KUDRYAVSTEV ALEXANDER ABA-KAROVICH

Law: Assoc. Prof. SCHERBAKOVA LUDMILA MIKHAILOVNA

Medicine Biology and Chemistry: Prof. IVA-NOV ALEXANDER LVOVICH

Philology and Journalism: Assoc. Prof. SER-BRYAKOV ANATOLY ALEKSEEVICH

Physical Education: Prof. MAGIN VLADIMIR ALEKSEEVICH

Physics and Mathematics: Assoc. Prof. AGI-BOVA IRINA MARKOVNA

Psychology: Prof. AKHVERDOVA OLGA ALBER-TOVNA

Romance and Germanic Languages: Prof. LOMTEVA TATYANA NIKOLAEVNA

SURGUT STATE UNIVERSITY

628400 Tyumen oblast, Surgut, ul. Energeti-kov 30

Telephone: (3462) 52-47-00

Fax: (3462) 52-47-29

E-mail: info@inao.surgu.ru

Internet: www.surgu.ru

Founded 1993

Private control

Rector: Prof. GEORGY I. NAZIN

Vice-Rector for Academic Affairs: Prof. YURI V. KUZNETSOV

Vice-Rector for Admin. and Finance: Dr BORIS U. SERAZETDINOV

Vice-Rector for Capital Construction: KON-STANTIN S. MOKHOV

Vice-Rector for Distance Learning: Prof. SERGEI F. KOZHUKOV

Vice-Rector for Economic and Social Affairs: VIKTOR I. LYUTY

Vice-Rector for Information Resources: Dr NIKOLAI G. SHEVCHENKO

Vice-Rector for Science: Dr VIKTOR P. SAMSO-NOV

Vice-Rector for Student Affairs: Dr BORIS U. SERAZETDINOV

Librarian: VALENTINA N. SHEVCHENKO

Library of 282,354 vols

DEANS

Biology: VLADIMIR P. STARIKOV

Economics: LEONID A. AVDEEV

Engineering and Physics: NIKOLAI N. BADU-LIN

History: ALEXANDER I. PRISCHEPA

Information Technology: FEDOR F. IVANOV

Law: VLADIMIR V. CHERUSHEV

Linguistics: SVETLANA G. KULAGINA
Medicine: LUDMILA V. KOVALENKO
Physical Culture: SERGEI M. OBUKHOV
Psychology: IRINA P. GREKHOVA

SYKTYVKAR STATE UNIVERSITY

167001 Syktyvkar, Oktyabrskii pr. 55
Telephone and fax (8212) 43-68-20
E-mail: ssu@syktsu.ru
Internet: www.syktsu.ru

Founded 1972
State control
Languages of instruction: Russian, Komi
Academic year: September to July

Rector: VASILY N. ZADOROZHNY
Vice-Rector: NIKOLAI A. TIKHONOV
Chief Admin. Officer: OLGA P. ZBOROVSKAYA
Librarian: V. PROKURATOVA

Number of teachers: 330
Number of students: 4,250

Publications: *Rubezh* (4 a year), *Vestnik* (1 a year)

DEANS

Faculty of Arts: LUDMILA V. GURLENOVA
Faculty of Chemistry and Biology: IRINA V. PIYR
Faculty of Finance and Economics: EVGENIA A. BADOKINA
Faculty of History: LUBOV A. MAKSIMOVA
Faculty of Humanities: ELENA G. TONKOVA
Faculty of Information Systems and Technologies: DMITRIY A. BELYAEV
Faculty of Law: DMITRIY I. PINAEVSKIY
Faculty of Mathematics: VYACHESLAV G. ANTONOV
Faculty of Management: LUDMILA I. BUSHUEVA
Faculty of Philology: MIKHAIL V. MELIKHOV
Faculty of Physics and Engineering: YURIY N. BELYAEV
Faculty of Physical Training and Sports: SERGEI A. SOKOLOV
Faculty of Psychology and Social Work: LUDMILA I. BYKOVSKAYA

PROFESSORS

ARAPOV, N., Jurisprudence
BOLOTOV, S., Management
BRACH, B., Chemistry
IRZHAK, L., Physiology
KNJAZEVA, G., Finance
MIKHAILOVSKY, E., Computer Science
NAGAEV, V., Psychology
NIKETENKOV, V., Mathematics
NOVIKOV, Y., Management
POROSHKIN, A., Mathematical Analysis
SEMENOV, V., History
TIKHOMIROV, A., Mathematics
VITYAZEVA, V., Economics
ZADOROZHNIY, V., Economics
ZOLOTAREV, V., History

TAMBOV STATE UNIVERSITY 'G. R. DERZHAVIN'

392000 Tambov, Internatsionalnaya ul. 33
Telephone: (0752) 72-12-29
Fax: (0752) 72-36-31
E-mail: priem1@tsu.tmb.ru
Internet: tsutmb.ru

Founded 1994, on the basis of Tambov State Pedagogical Institute and Tambov State Institute of Culture
State control
Languages of instruction: English, French, Russian
Academic year: September to June

Rector: Prof. VLADISLAV YURIEV
Vice-Rector for Int. Relations: Prof. TATIANA OSADCHAYA
Vice-Rector for Academic Affairs: Prof. VLADIMIR MAMONTOV

Pro-Rector for Research: Prof. NIKOLAY BOLDYREV
Vice-Rector for Educational Policy and Innovation: Prof. MARINA CHVANOVA

Library: 1.5m. vols
Number of teachers: 900
Number of students: 15,000

Publications: *Issues of Cognitive Linguistics, Social-Economic Phenomena and Processes, Vestnik Tambovskogo Universiteta (Tambov University Reports)* (Series: Natural and Technical Sciences; the Humanities).

TOGLIATTI STATE UNIVERSITY

445667 Togliatti, Belorusskaya ul. 14
Telephone: (8482) 54-63-99
Fax: (8482) 53-95-22
E-mail: office@tltsu.ru
Internet: www.tltsu.ru

Founded 1951, as Togliatti Polytechnic Institute; present name and status 2001 following merger with Togliatti State Pedagogical Univ. (f. 1988)
Public conrol
Language of instruction: Russian
Academic year: September to June

Rector: Prof. Dr MIKHAIL M. KRISHTAL
First Vice-Rector: Assoc Prof. Dr NADEZHDA G. PUDOVKINA

Library of 1,093,941 vols
Number of teachers: 570
Number of students: 13,000

Publications: *Herald of the Humanities, Vector of Science*

DEANS

Faculty of Electrical Engineering: Assoc. Prof. Dr VLADIMIR SHAPOVALOV
Faculty of Fine, Decorative and Applied Arts: Assoc. Prof. Dr ALEXANDER KOZLYAKOV
Faculty of Mathematics and Informatics: Prof. Dr PETR ZYBROV
Faculty of Physical Education and Sport: Assoc. Prof. Dr VALENTINA BALASHOVA
Law Faculty: Prof. Dr RUDOLF KHACHATUROV
Teachers Training Faculty: Prof. Dr IRINA NEPROKINA

TOMSK STATE UNIVERSITY

634050 Tomsk, pr. Lenina 36
Telephone: (3822) 52-95-58
Fax: (3822) 52-95-85
E-mail: rector@tsu.ru
Internet: www.tsu.ru

Founded 1878
State control
Academic year: September to June

Faculties of applied mathematics and cybernetics, biology and soil science, chemistry, computer science, economics, foreign languages, geology and geography, history and international relations, journalism, law, mechanics and mathematics, philology, philosophy, physics, political science, psychology, sociology and radio-physics, technical physics; Institute of Culture; International Faculty of Public and Business Administration

Rector: Prof. GEORGY V. MAYER
Sr Vice-Rector: Dr MIKHAIL D. BABANSKY
Vice-Rector for Academic Affairs: Prof. ALEXANDER S. REVUSHKIN
Vice-Rector for Int. Affairs: Dr SERGEY N. KIRPOTIN
Vice-Rector For Research and Postgraduate Studies: Prof. GRIGORY E. DUNAEVSKY
Registrar: N. BUROVA
Librarian: EVGENY N. SYNTIN

Library: see Libraries and Archives
Number of teachers: 1,410

Number of students: 14,000 (10,000 full-time, 4,000 part-time)

Publications: *Krylovia: Siberian Botanical Journal* (2 a year), *Physics* (4 a year), *Vestnik* (4 a year).

TVER STATE UNIVERSITY

170100 Tver, ul. Zhelyabova 33
Telephone: (4822) 32-11-95
Fax: (4822) 32-12-74
E-mail: rector@tversu.ru
Internet: university.tversu.ru

Founded 1971
State control
Language of instruction: Russian
Academic year: September to June

Rector: ANDREY VLADLENOVICH BELOTSERKOVSKY
Pro-Rector: LIUDMILA NIKOLAEVNA SKAKOVSKAYA
Librarian: OLGA V. VERSHININA

Library: 1m. vols
Number of teachers: 720
Number of students: 10,000

DEANS

Applied Mathematics and Cybernetics: Prof. ALEXANDER YAZENIN
Economics: Prof. DAVID MAMAGULASHVILI
Foreign Languages and International Communication: Prof. LARISA SAPOZHNIKOVA
History: Prof. TATIANA LEONTIJEVA
Law: Prof. LIDIA TUMANOVA
Management and Sociology: Prof. LARISA MOSHKOVA

TYUMEN STATE UNIVERSITY

625003 Tyumen, ul. Semakova 10
Telephone: (3452) 46-01-41
Fax: (3452) 46-19-30
E-mail: international@utmn.ru
Internet: www.utmn.ru

Founded 1930 as Tyumen Pedagogical Institute, present name 1973

Faculties of chemistry and biology, economics, geography, history, philology, physics and mathematics, romance and Germanic philology

Rector: Prof. Dr CHEBOTAREV GENNADY NIKOLAEVITCH
Pres.: Prof. Dr KUTSEV GENNADY PHILIPOVITCH

Number of teachers: 929
Number of students: 40,000

Publications: *Philological Discourse, Siberian Historical Journal, The Journal of Tyumen State University.*

UDMURT STATE UNIVERSITY

426034 Udmurt, Izhevsk, Universitetskaya ul. 1
Telephone: (3412) 68-16-10
Fax: (3412) 68-58-66
E-mail: adm@uni.udm.ru
Internet: www.udsu.ru

Founded 1931
State control
Language of instruction: Russian
Academic year: September to June

Rector: Prof. GALINA MERZLYAKOVA
Chief Vice-Rector: Assoc. Prof. SEMEN BUNTOV
Vice-Rector for Academic Affairs: Assoc. Prof. MIKHAIL KIBARDIN
Vice-Rector for Finance, Economics and Investments: GERMAN SERGEEV
Vice-Rector for Int. Relations: MARIA I. BESNOSOVA

Vice-Rector for Public Relations: Assoc. Prof. VLADIMIR A. BAYMETOV

Vice-Rector for Research and Innovation: Dr IGOR MENSHIKOV

Vice-Rector for Social and Educational Work and Extra Curricular Activities: SERGEY V. VOSTROKUTNOV

Head of Int. Relations Office: Assoc. Prof. MARIA BEZNOSOVA

Dir for Library: LYUDMILA BESKLINSKAYA

Library of 1,000,000 vols, 40 periodicals, 50 newspapers

Number of teachers: 1,000

Number of students: 25,000

Publications: *Management: Theory and Practice* (4 a year), *Nonlinear Dynamics* (4 a year), *Problems of Regional Economics* (4 a year), *Quantum, Computers and Computing* (1 a year), *Regular and Chaotic Dynamics*) (English version, 6 series a year), *Udmurt University* (12 a year), *Univer.ru* (12 a year), *Vestnik UdSU* (2 a year, 6 series)

DEANS

Faculty of Biology and Chemistry: NIKOLAY ZUBTSOVSKY

Faculty of Geography: IVAN RYSSIN

Faculty of History: NADEZHA STARKOVA

Faculty of Journalism: VLADIMIR BAYMETOV

Faculty of Mathematics: NIKOLAY PETROV

Faculty of Medical Biotechnology: ALEXEY BARSUKOV

Faculty of Philosophy and Sociology: Prof. MARINA MAKAROVA

Faculty of Physical Education and Sport: ALEXANDER ALABUZHEV

Faculty of Physics and Energetics: VLADIMIR BOVIN

Faculty of Professional Foreign Language Study: RAISA SHISHKINA

Faculty of Russian Philology: ELENA PODSHIVALOVA

Faculty of Udmurt Philology: LUBOV FYODOROVA

Institute of Arts and Design: MARINA BOTYA

Institute of Civil Defence: VLADIMIR KOLODKIN

Institute of Economics and Management: ANATOLY ANOSHIN

Institute of Foreign Languages and Literature: OLGA GOLUBKOVA

Institute of Law, Social Management and Security: VLADIMIR IVSHIN

Institute of Oil and Gas: ALEXEY VOLKOV

Institute of Psychology, Pedagogics and Social Technology: Prof. ALEXANDER BARANOV

Institute of Social Communications: LARISA BATALOVA

PROFESSORS

Faculty of Biology and Chemistry (tel. (3412) 75-56-48; fax (3412) 75-58-66; e-mail bhf@uni .udm.ru):

BARANOVA, O., Botany and Plant Ecology

KORNEV, V., Inorganic and Analytic Chemistry

MAKAROVA, L., Physical and Organic Chemistry

PRONICHEV, I., Anatomy and Human and Animal's Physiology

TUGANAEV, V., General Ecology

Faculty of Geography (tel. (3412) 916070; e-mail rvsin@uni.udm.ru):

RYSSIN, I. I., Physical Geography and Landscape Ecology

STURMAN, V. I., Natural Use and Geo-Ecological Cartography

Faculty of History (tel. (3412) 916184; e-mail history@udsu.ru):

EFREMOVA, T., Native History of newer time

GOLDINA, R., Archeology and the History of Primitive Society

SANNIKOV, N., New History and International Relations

SHISHKINA, N., Ancient World and the Middle Ages

VLADYKIN, V. E., Ethnology and Regional Study

Faculty of Information Technology and Computer Engineering (tel. (3412) 916131; e-mail rodionov@uni.udm.ru):

BELTYUKOV, A., Theoretical and Informatic Basis

ISLAMOV, G., Computation and Parallel Programming

KOLODKIN, V., Mathematical Modelling and Forecasting

NIKOLAY, N., Theory and Methodology of Informatics

Faculty of Mathematics (tel. (3412) 916086; e-mail dekanmf@udsu.ru):

BELTYUKOV, A., Mathematical Provision for Computers and Software

DERR, V., Mathematical Analysis

GRYZLOV, A., Algebra and Topology

ISLAMOV, G., Calculus Mathematics

KARPOV, A., Computer Techniques

KONDRATYEV, B., Astronomy and Topology

TONKOV, E., Differential Equation

Faculty of Physics and Energetics (tel. (3412) 916129; e-mail bovin@uni.udm.ru):

TARPEZNIKOV, V., Surface Physics

Faculty of Philology (tel. (3412) 916154; e-mail ktl@udm.ru):

DONETSKIK, L., Contemporary Russian Language and History

PODSHIVOLAVA, E., Russian Literature of the 20th Century and Folklore

SHEIDAEVA, S., Language Theory and Speech

VOROZHTSOVA, I., Lingual Didactics

Faculty of Professional Foreign Languages (tel. (3412) 685557; e-mail profin@udm.ru):

MERZLYAKOVA, A., Romance Languages

Faculty of Sociology and Philosophy (tel. (3412) 916020):

KRUTKIN, V., Philosophy and Sociology of Culture

LADYZHETZ, N., Sociology

Faculty of Udmurt Philology (tel. (3412) 755920):

KELMAKOV, V. K., General and Finno-Ugric Linguistics

SHUTOV, A. F., Udmurt Language and Pedagogy

TARAKANOV, I. V., Udmurt Language and Pedagogy

VLADIKINA, T. G., Russian Philology

Institute of Economics and Management (tel. (3412) 916062; e-mail ier@inem.uni.udm.ru):

BOTKIN, O. I., Economic Theory

LETCHIKOV, A. V., Mathematical Methods in Economics

MATVEEV, V. V., Business Economics

PEREVOSCHIKOV, YU. S., Business Economics

Institute of Foreign Languages and Literature (tel. (3412) 916179; e-mail ifl@pils.uni .udm.ru):

PUSHINA, N. I., Grammar and History of English

UTEKHINA, A. N., German Philology

Institute of Law, Social Management and Security (tel. (3412) 916002; e-mail lawfak@ uni.udm.ru; internet www.ipsub.udsu.ru):

IAKOVLEV, V., Ecological and Agrarian Law and Law of Natural Resources

KAMINSKY, M. K., Criminology and Court Examination

POSKONINA, O. V., Philosophy and Sociology of Law

VOYTOVICH, V. YU., Legal Basis of State and Municipal Services

ZINATULLIN, Z. Z., Criminal Procedure

Institute of Pedagogic Philosophy and Social Technology (tel. (3412) 916119; e-mail baranov@ppf.uni.udm.ru):

BARANOV, A., Developmental Psychology and Differential Psychology

KHOTINETS, U., General Psychology

LEONOV, N., Social Psychology

Institute of Social Communications (tel. (3412) 916035; e-mail pr@udsu.ru):

RODIONOV, B., Sociology of Communications

YEROHIN, A., Publishing and Book Studies

ULYANOVSK STATE UNIVERSITY

432700 Ulyanovsk, ul. L. Tolstogo 42

Telephone: (8422) 41-20-88

Fax: (8422) 41-23-40

E-mail: contact@ulsu.ru

Internet: www.ulsu.ru

State control

Founded 1974

Rector: Prof. YURI V. POLYANSKOV

First Pro-Rector and Pro-Rector for Academic Affairs: TOFIK Z. BIKTIMINOV

Pro-Rector for Admin. and Finance: VALERY V. NEFEDKIN

Pro-Rector for Economic and Legal Affairs: NATALYA N. LOMOVYEVA

Pro-Rector for New Information and Teaching Technologies: DIMITRY YU. SHABALKIN

Pro-Rector for Pre-Univ. Education: SERGEI N. MITIN

Pro-Rector for Research: SERGEI V. BULYARSKY

Pro-Rector for Social Devt, Internal Communication and Marketing: TATYANA E. NIKITINA

Number of teachers: 635

Number of students: 10,695

URALS FEDERAL UNIVERSITY

620002 Yekaterinburg, 19 Mira St

Telephone and fax (343) 374-03-62

E-mail: rectorat@ustu.ru

Internet: www.urfu.ru

Founded 1920

State control

Languages of instruction: English, Russian

Academic year: September to July

Pres.: Dr. STANISLAV NABOYCHENKO

Rector: Dr VICTOR KOKSHAROV

First Vice-Rector: Dr ANATOLY MATERN

First Vice-Rector: Dr DMITRY BUGROV

Vice-Rector for Academic Affairs: Dr SERGEY KNYAZEV

Vice-Rector for Economics and Strategic Devt: Dr DANIIL SANDLER

Vice-Rector for General Affairs: VASILY KOZLOV

Vice-Rector for Int. Relations: Dr MAXIM KHOMYAKOV

Vice-Rector for Research: Dr ARTEMY POPOV

Librarian: KLAVDIYA P. KUZNETSOVA

Library of 3,067,719 vols

Number of teachers: 4,674

Number of students: 44,323

DEANS

Faculty of Accelerated Education: Dr DMITRY MATYUNIN

Faculty of Professional Development and Professional Retraining of Staff Members: BORIS SEMENOV

Graduate School of Economics and Management: Prof. Dr SERGEY KADOCHNIKOV

Institute of Chemical Engineering: Prof. Dr VLADIMIR RUSINOV

Institute of Civil Engineering: Dr VLADIMIR ALEKHIN
Institute of Continuing Education and Professional Retraining: Dr VLADIMIR SHVEYKIN
Institute of Fundamental Studies: Dr OLEG OKHOTNIKOV
Institute of Humanities and Arts: Dr DMITRY BUGROV
Institute of Information Educational Technologies: Dr ALEXEY TSVETKOV
Institute of Mathematics and Computer Sciences: Prof. Dr ALEXEY IVANOV
Institute of Material Science and Metallurgy: Dr VICTOR MALTSEV
Institute of Mechanics and Machine Building: Dr OLEG BLINKOV
Institute of Military Training and Security: Dr VICTOR BATMAZOV
Institute of Natural Sciences: Dr VLADIMIR KRUZHAEV
Institute of Physical Culture, Sport and Youth Policy: Dr NINA SEROVA
Institute of Physical Engineering: Prof. Dr VLADIMIR RYCHKOV
Institute of Public Administration and Entrepreneurship: Dr ALEXEY KLUYEV
Institute of Radioelectronics and Information Technologies: Dr SERGEY KNYAZEV
Institute of Social and Political Studies: Prof. Dr MAXIM KHOMYAKOV
Ural Institute of Energetics: Dr YURI BRODOV

PROFESSORS

Faculty of Art Criticism and Culture:
  GOLINETS, S. V., History of Art
  MIKHAILOV, S. A., Cultural Studies
  PIVOVAROV, D. V., History and Philosophy of Religion
  TROSHINA, T. M., Museology

Faculty of Biology:
  BIBIN, I. A., Human and Animal Physiology
  MUKHIN, V. A., Botany
  NOVOZHENOV, Y. I., Zoology
  PYANKOV, V. I., Plant Physiology

Faculty of Chemistry:
  NEUCHADINA, L. N., Analytical Chemistry
  NEYMAN, A. YA., Inorganic Chemistry
  PETROV, A. N., Physical Chemistry
  SUVOROVA, A. I., Higher Molecular Compounds
  VSHIVKOV, A. A., Organic Chemistry

Faculty of Economics:
  AKBERDINA, R. A., Economics
  GREBENKIN, A. V., History and Theory of Management
  IVANTSOV, G. B., Theory of Economics
  MAZUROV, V. D., Economic Models and Information
  NESTEROVA, D. V., Economic History and World Economics
  SEMYAKIN, M. N., Economics and Law

Faculty of History:
  CHERNUKHOV, A. V., Archives
  CHEVTAEV, A. G., Modern History
  MIKHAILENKO, V. I., Theory and History of Foreign Affairs
  MINENKO, N. A., Ethnology and Special Historical Sciences
  POLYAKOVSKAYA, M. A., Ancient and Medieval History
  ROMANCHUK, A. I., Archaeology
  SHASHKOV, A. G., Russian History

Faculty of Journalism:
  BRODSKY, I. S., Television, Radio and Technical Methods of Journalism
  KOVALEVA, M. M., History of the Press
  LAZAREVA, E. H., Stylistics and Russian Language
  OLESHKO, V. F., Periodical Press

Faculty of Mathematics and Mechanics:
  ALBREKHT, E. G., Applied Mathematics

ARESTOV, V. V., Mathematical Analysis and Theory of Functions
ASANOV, M. O., Mathematics for Economics
IVANOV, A. O., Mathematical Physics
PROKOPIEV, V. P., Theoretical Mechanics
RYASHKO, L. V., Computational Mathematics
SHEVRIN, L. N., Algebra of Discrete Mathematics
TRETYAKOV, V. E., Computer Information Science and Management Processes

Faculty of Philology:
  BABENKO, L. G., Modern Russian Language
  BLAZHES, V. V., Folklore
  BIKOV, L. P., Criticism of 20th-century Literary Theory
  MATVEEV, A. V., General Linguistics
  MIKHAILOVA, O. A., Rhetoric and Stylistics of Russian Language
  PAVERMAN, V. M., Foreign Literature
  SIDOROVA, O. G., Romance and Germanic Philology

Faculty of Philosophy:
  BRYANIK, N. V., Ontology and Theory of Cognition
  EREMEEV, A. P., Ethics, Aesthetics, History and Theory of Culture
  KEMEROV, V. E., Social Philosophy
  LYUBUTIN, K. N., History of Philosophy

Faculty of Physics:
  BABUSHKIN, A. N., Low-Temperature Physics
  BARANOV, N. V., Condensed Matter
  BORISOV, S. F., General and Molecular Physics
  GULYAEV, S. A., Astronomy and Geodesy
  IVANOV, O. A., Magnetic Phenomena
  MOSKVIN, A. S., Theoretical Physics
  ZVEREV, L. P., Semiconductor Physics, Radiospectroscopy

Faculty of Psychology:
  GLOTOVA, G. A., General Psychology and Psychology of Personality
  LUPANDIN, V. I., Psychophysiology

Faculty of Sociology and Politics:
  BAGIROV, B. B., Social Politics
  BARAZGOVA, E. S., Theory and History of Sociology
  MERENKOV, A. V., Sociology
  MIRONOV, D. A., History of Politics

URAL STATE UNIVERSITY OF ECONOMICS

620219 Yekaterinburg, ul. 8 Marta 62
Telephone: (343) 257-96-15
Fax: (343) 257-71-47
E-mail: start@usue.ru
Internet: www.usue.ru

Founded 1967
Academic year: September to June

Rector: Prof. Dr MIKHAIL FEDOROV

Library of 624,800 vols, 9,000 periodicals
Number of teachers: 590
Number of students: 26,500

VLADIMIR STATE UNIVERSITY NAMED AFTER ALEXANDER AND NIKOLAY STOLETOVS

600000 Vladimir, Gorkogo St 87
Telephone: (4922) 47-77-79
Fax: (4922) 47-97-79
E-mail: prorms@vlsu.ru
Internet: www.vlsu.ru

Founded 1958
Public control
Languages of instruction: English, Russian
Academic year: September to June

Rector: Prof. VALENTIN V. MOROZOV
First Vice-Rector: Dr VALERIY G. PROKOSHEV

Vice-Rector for Methodological Work and Int. Cooperation: Prof. VLADIMIR A. NEMONTOV
Vice-Rector for Capital Building and Material Resources: Dr IGOR A. GANDELSMAN
Vice-Rector for Economics: Prof. SVETLANA M. BASHARINA
Vice-Rector for Education and Social Policy: Dr ANZOR M. SARALIDZE
Vice-Rector for Gen. Affairs: Dr ALEXANDER V. CHUB
Vice-Rector for Innovations and Strategic Devt: Prof. SERGEY M. ARAKELYAN
Vice-Rector for Research: Prof. SERGEI G. MOSIN

Number of teachers: 1,100
Number of students: 27,000

DEANS

Faculty of Architecture and Building: Prof. SERGEY N. AVDEEV
Faculty of Automobile Transport: Prof. YURI V. BAZHENOV
Faculty of Chemistry and Ecology: Prof. JURI T. PANOV
Faculty of Economics: Prof. SERGEY A. MAXIMOV
Faculty of History: Dr MICHAEL A. BARASHEV
Faculty of Information Technologies: Dr ALEXANDER A. GALKIN
Faculty of Mechanical Engineering: Dr ELENA A. NOVIKOVA
Faculty of Philosophy and Social Sciences: NATALYA M. MARKOVA
Faculty of Physics and Applied Mathematics: NIKOLAI D. DAVIDOV
Faculty of Radiophysics, Electronics and Medical Engineering: Prof. ALEXANDER G. SAMOILOV
Faculty of Correspondence and Distance Learning: Prof. ILYA E. ZHIGALOV
Institute of Law and Psychology: Dr OKSANA V. BOGATOVA
Institute of Small and Medium Business: Dr OLGA P. POLOTSKAYA
Institute of Staff Development and Re-training: Prof. VLADIMIR P. LEGAEV

VLADIVOSTOK STATE UNIVERSITY OF ECONOMICS AND SERVICE

690600 Vladivostok, 41 Gogolya Str.
Telephone: (423) 245-08-53
Fax: (423) 240-41-50
E-mail: international@vvsu.ru
Internet: www.vvsu.ru

Founded 1967
State control
Language of instruction: Russian
Academic year: September to May

Areas of study: business administration, culture, fashion and design, information technology and technical systems, politics and law of Asian-Pacific countries, service, social and political studies, tourism and hospitality

Rector: Prof. GENNADY I. LAZAREV

Library of 258,170 vols
Number of teachers: 410
Number of students: 24,000

Publication: *Russia—21st Century* (4 a year).

VOLGOGRAD STATE UNIVERSITY

400062 Volgograd, Pr. Universitetsky 100
Telephone and fax (8442) 43-81-24
E-mail: oms@volsu.ru
Internet: www.volsu.ru

Founded 1980
State control
Languages of instruction: English, French, Russian
Academic year: September to June

Rector: Prof. Dr OLEG V. INSHAKOV
Deputy Rector: Dr VASILY V. TARAKANOV

Vice-Rector for Academic Affairs: Dr SERGEI G. SIDOROV
Vice-Rector for Research and Innovations: Dr ALLA E. KALININA
Librarian: LARISA E. YAKOVLEVA
Library of 900,000 vols
Number of teachers: 612
Number of students: 13,545
Publications: *Archaeological Vestnik of the Lower Volga* (1 a year), *Economic History of Russia* (1 a year), *Junior Faculty and Students' Papers and Reports* (1 a year), *Proceedings of the Annual Scientific Conference* (1 a year), *Proceedings of International Conferences* (5 a year), *Strezhen* (1 a year), *The Region's Economic Development: Problems, Searches, Prospects* (2 a year), *Vestnik VolGU* (10 series, 1 a year)

DEANS

Faculty of Continuing Education: Dr ALBINA V. GUKOVA
Faculty of Law: Dr ILYA S. DIKAREV
Faculty of Management and Regional Economy: Dr VIKTOR O. MOSEYKO
Faculty of Mathematics and Informational Technologies: Dr ALEXANDER G. LOSEV
Faculty of Natural Sciences: Dr ALEXANDER B. MULIK
Faculty of Philosophy, History, International Relations and Social Technologies: Prof. Dr OLGA Y. REDKINA
Institute of Philology and Intercultural Communication: Dr NIKOLAI L. SHAMNE
Institute of Physics and Telecommunications: KONSTANTIN M. FIRSOV (Dir)
Institute of World Economy and Finances: Dr ELENA G. RUSSKOVA

VORONEZH STATE UNIVERSITY

394006 Voronezh, Universitetskaya pl. 1
Telephone: (0732) 20-75-22
Fax: (0732) 20-87-55
E-mail: office@main.vsu.ru
Internet: www.vsu.ru
Founded 1918
State control
Academic year: September to July
Rector: Prof. IVAN I. BORISOV
First Vice-Rector: SERGEY A. ZAPRYAGAEV
Vice-Rector: VLADIMIR T. TITOV
Vice-Rector for Admin. and Finance: ANATOLY N. PODOBEDOV
Vice-Rector for Information Services: ALEXANDER P. TOLSTOBROV
Vice-Rector for Major Construction Projects: ANATOLY I. BIRYUKOV
Vice-Rector for Organizational and Legal Matters: VALERY P. TROFIMOV
Vice-Rector for Pre-Univ. Training: VLADIMIR N. GLAZYEV
Vice-Rector for Research: ALEXANDER S. SIDORKIN
Librarian: SVETLANA V. YANTS
Library: 3m. vols
Number of teachers: 1,300
Number of students: 21,000
Publication: *Vestnik Voronezhskogo Universiteta*

DEANS

Faculty of Applied Mathematics and Mechanics: A. I. SHASHKIN
Faculty of Biology and Soil Science: V. G. ARTYUKHOV
Faculty of Chemistry: YU. P. AFINOGENOV
Faculty of Computer Science: E. A. ALGAZINOV
Faculty of Economics: V. P. BOCHAROV
Faculty of Geography and Geo-Ecology: V. I. FEDOTOV
Faculty of Geology: V. M. NENAKHOV
Faculty of History: A. Z. VINNIKOV

Faculty of Journalism: V. V. TULUPOV
Faculty of Law: V. A. PANYUSHKIN
Faculty of Mathematics: V. A. KOSTIN
Faculty of Pharmaceutics: A. I. SLIVKIN
Faculty of Philology: V. M. AKATKIN
Faculty of Philosophy and Psychology: YU A. BUBNOV
Faculty of Physics: A. M. VOROBEV
Faculty of Romance and Germanic Philology: N. A. FENENKO

YAROSLAVL STATE UNIVERSITY

150000 Yaroslavl, ul. Sovetskaya 14
Telephone: (0852) 72-51-38
Fax: (0852) 30-75-15
E-mail: depint@uniyar.ac.ru
Internet: www.uniyar.ac.ru
Founded 1970
Academic year: September to July
Rector: Prof. G. S. MIRONOV
First Vice-Rector: A. I. RUSAKOV
Vice-Rector (Economy): R. P. USATYUK
Vice-Rector (Education): I. M. LOKHANINA
Vice-Rector (Innovation): S. A. KASHCHENKO
Vice-Rector (Science): Y. A. BRUKHANOV
Registrar: V. P. ISAYEVA
Librarian: I. V. DENEZHKINA
Number of teachers: 530
Number of students: 6,500
Publications: *Aktualnye Problemy Fiziki* (Current Problems of Physics, 1 a year), *Ekonomichesky Vestnik* (Bulletin on Economics, 1 a year), *Modelirovaniye i Analiz Informatsionnykh System* (Modelling and Analysis of Information Systems, 1 or 2 a year), *Ocherki po Torgovomy Pravu* (Sketches on Trade Law, 1 or 2 a year), *Problemy Novoi i Noveishei Istorii* (Issues of Modern and Contemporary History), *Put v Nauku* (Road to Science, 1 a year), *Sovremennye Problemy Matematiki i Informatiki* (Modern Problems of Mathematics and Informatics, 1 a year), *Yuridicheskiye zapiski* (Judicial Notes, 1 a year)

DEANS

Faculty of Biology: A. V. EREMEISHVILI
Faculty of Economics: L. B. PARFIONOVA
Faculty of History: N. P. RYAZANTSEV
Faculty of Information Science and Computing Technology: A. V. ZAFIEVSKY
Faculty of Law: N. N. TARUSINA
Faculty of Mathematics: V. G. DURNEV
Faculty of Physics: V. P. ALEKSEYEV
Faculty of Psychology: A. V. KARPOV
Faculty of Social Sciences: G. M. NAZHMUTDINOV

YUGORSKY STATE UNIVERSITY

628012 Khanty-Mansiysk, ul. Chekhova 16
Telephone: (34671) 35-77-13
E-mail: ugrasu@ugrasu.ru
Internet: www.ugrasu.ru
State control
Founded 2001
Rector: Prof. YURI I. REUTOV
First Pro-Rector: TATIANA D. KARMINSKAYA
Pro-Rector for Academic Affairs: OLGA F. SHAPKINA
Pro-Rector for Research: VLADIMIR Z. KOVALEV (acting)
Librarian: NINA I. SMIRNOVA
Library of 170,000 vols, 248 periodicals
Number of teachers: 521
Number of students: 5,138
Publication: *Vestnik of YuSU* (scientific journal)

DEANS

Applied Mathematics, Computer Science and Control: YURIY V. KOLOKOLOV

Economics and Finance: ALEXEY P. ERMILOV
Engineering: VLADIMIR Z. KOVALEV
Further Education: ARKADY V. KRASILNIKOV
Geology, Oil and Gas: TATIANA I. ROMANOVA
Humanities: VLADIMIR A. MISHCHENKO
Language, History and Culture of the Peoples of Yugra: VICTORIA I. SPODINA
Law: STANISLAV V. ROZENKO
Sports and Tourism: SERGEY V. BARBASHOV

MEDICAL UNIVERSITIES

ALTAI STATE MEDICAL UNIVERSITY

656038 Barnaul, pr. Lenina 40
Telephone: (3852) 36-88-48
Fax: (3852) 36-60-91
E-mail: rector@mail.ru
Internet: www.agmu.ru
Founded 1954
Language of instruction: Russian
Rector: VALERY M. BRYUKHANOV
Library of 542,000 vols
Number of teachers: 536
Number of students: 5,079

DEANS

Faculty of General Medicine: Prof. V. G. LICHEV
Faculty of Paediatrics: Prof. G. E. VYKHODTCEVA
Faculty of Pharmaceuticals: Prof. Y. F. ZVEREV
High Qualified Nurses' Education: Assoc. Prof. I. E. GOSSEN
Medico—Preventive Faculty: Prof. E. L. BOBROVSKY

BASHKIR STATE MEDICAL UNIVERSITY

450092 Bashkortostan, Ufa, ul. Lenina 3
Telephone: (3472) 22-41-73
Fax: (3472) 22-37-51
E-mail: admin@bsmu.anrb.ru
Internet: www.bsmu.anrb.ru
Founded 1932
Rector: VIL M. TIMERBULATOV
Library of 600,000 vols
Number of teachers: 650
Number of students: 4,175

IRKUTSK STATE MEDICAL UNIVERSITY

664003 Irkutsk, ul. Krasnogo Vosstaniya 1
Telephone: (3952) 24-38-25
Fax: (3952) 34-03-36
E-mail: rector_ismu@bk.ru
Internet: www.ismu.baikal.ru
Founded 1919
Rector: Prof. ASKOLD A. MAIBORODA.

KAZAN STATE MEDICAL UNIVERSITY

420012 Kazan, 49 Butlerov St
Telephone: (843) 236-05-43
Fax: (843) 236-03-93
E-mail: info@kazansmu.com
Internet: www.kazansmu.com
Founded 1814
State control
Languages of instruction: English, Russian
Academic year: September to June
Faculties of dentistry, general medicine, graduate nursing, medical biochemistry, medical biophysics, paediatrics, pharmacy, prophylactic medicine, social work
Rector: Prof. ALEXEY SOZINOV
Vice-Rector for Int. Affairs: Prof. AYRAT ZIGANSHIN
Library of 20,000 vols
Number of teachers: 500

Number of students: 4,500

Publication: *Kazan Medical Journal* (6 a year).

KURSK STATE MEDICAL UNIVERSITY

305041 Kursk, ul. Karla Marksa 3

Telephone: (0712) 58-81-32

Fax: (0712) 56-73-99

E-mail: main@kgmu.kursknet.ru

Internet: www.kgmu.kursknet.ru

Founded 1935

Rector: Prof. A. LAZAREVA

Library of 320,214 vols.

MOSCOW STATE MEDICAL-STOMATOLOGICAL UNIVERSITY

127473 Moscow, ul. Delegatskaya 20/1

Telephone: (495) 631-25-44

Fax: (495) 973-37-26

E-mail: mmsi@online.ru

Internet: www.msmsu.ru

Founded 1922

Academic year: September to June

Faculties of advanced training in dentistry, clinical psychology, general medicine, postgraduate education, stomatology; Institute of Orthodontics, State Stomatological Research Institute

Rector: Prof. NIKOLAI D. YUSHCHUK

Library of 549,979 vols

Number of teachers: 1,147

Number of students: 6,000

NORTHERN STATE MEDICAL UNIVERSITY

163001 Arkhangelsk, Troitsky pr. 51

Telephone: (8182) 21-00-00

E-mail: info@nsmu.ru

Internet: www.nsmu.ru

Founded 1932 as Arkhangelsk State Medical Institute, present name and status 2000

Faculties of adaptive physical training, ecology, general practice, medical clinical psychology, medical management, paediatrics, pharmaceutics, prophylactic medicine, social work, stomatology; institutes: management, medical education, information technology

Rector: PAVEL I. SIDOROV

Library of 400,000 vols

Number of students: 5,500

Publications: *Human Ecology* (4 a year), *Medik Severa* (12 a year).

ROSTOV STATE MEDICAL UNIVERSITY

344022 Rostov-on-Don, Nakhichevansky per. 29

Telephone: (863) 265-23-91

Fax: (863) 253-06-11

Internet: www.rgmu.al.ru

Founded 1931

Rector: Prof. VIKTOR N. CHERNYSHOV

Library of 340,000 vols.

RUSSIAN STATE MEDICAL UNIVERSITY

117869 Moscow, ul. Ostrovityanova 1

Telephone: (495) 434-03-29

Fax: (495) 434-47-87

E-mail: rgmu@rsmu.ru

Internet: www.rsmu.ru

Founded 1906, present name and status 1991

Faculties of biomedicine, medicine, paediatrics

Rector: Prof. Dr VLADIMIR N. YARYGIN

Library of 900,000 vols

Number of teachers: 1,200

Number of students: 6,300

Publication: *Vestnik* (4 a year).

ST PETERSBURG STATE MEDICAL UNIVERSITY 'ACAD. I. P. PAVLOV'

197022 St Petersburg, ul. L. Tolstogo 6/8

Telephone: (812) 238-71-12

Fax: (812) 234-08-97

E-mail: admission@spmu.rssi.ru

Internet: www.spmu.runnet.ru

Founded 1897

Areas of study: basic sciences, dentistry, medicine, sports medicine

Rector: Prof. NIKOLAI A. YAITSKY

Vice-Rector for Academic Affairs: Prof. U. D. IGNATOV

Vice-Rector for Int. Affairs: Prof. S. H. AL-SHUKRI

Vice-Rector for Research: Prof. E. E. ZVARTAU

Dean of Faculty of Gen. Medicine: Prof. N. N. PETRISHEV

Dean of Foreign Students Affairs: Prof. M. SH. VAKHITOV

Library: 1m. vols

Publications: *Arterial Hypertension* (4 a year), *Nephrology* (4 a year), *Scientific Items* (4 a year), *St Petersburg Medical News* (6 a year).

SAMARA STATE MEDICAL UNIVERSITY

443099 Samara, ul. Chapaevskaya 89

Telephone: (8462) 32-16-34

Fax: (8462) 33-29-76

E-mail: info@samsmu.ru

Internet: samsmu.ru

Founded 1919

Fields of study: cardiology, dentistry, general medicine, gerontology, healthcare, ionizing radiation, medical management, medical prophylactics, military medicine, nursing, paediatrics, pharmaceutics, psychology, surgery, therapy, traumatology; tissue bank

Rector: Prof. Dr GENNADY P. KOTELNIKOV

Library of 570,183 vols

Number of teachers: 700

Number of students: 6,500

Publications: *Annals of Traumatology and Orthopaedics* (6 a year), *Aspirant Herald of Volga Region* (12 a year), *Older Generation* (12 a year), *Samara Medical Archive* (6 a year), *Transregional Association 'Povolzhye Healthcare' Herald* (12 a year).

SARATOV STATE MEDICAL UNIVERSITY

410012 Saratov, Bol. Kazachya 112

Telephone: (8452) 27-33-70

Fax: (8452) 51-15-34

E-mail: meduniv@sgmu.ru

Internet: www.sgmu.ru

Founded 1909

Rector: Dr PETR V. GLYBOCHKO

Library of 950,000 vols.

SIBERIAN STATE MEDICAL UNIVERSITY

534050 Tomsk, Moskovsky Trakt 2

Telephone: (3822) 53-04-23

Fax: (3822) 53-33-09

E-mail: office@ssmu.net.ru

Internet: www.ssmu.ru

Founded 1888

Faculties of biological medicine, medicine, military medicine, nursing, paediatrics, pharmaceutics, postgraduate education, preparatory education; institutes: cardiology, genetics, oncology, pharmacology, psychiatric health; attached hospital

Pres.: Prof. Dr VYACHESLAV V. NOVITSKY

Library of 500,000 vols

Number of teachers: 676

Number of students: 3,445

Publications: *Bulletin of Siberian Healthcare* (4 a year), *Questions of Reconstructive and Plastic Surgery* (4 a year), *Siberian Magazine of Gastroenterology and Haematology* (4 a year).

VLADIVOSTOK STATE MEDICAL UNIVERSITY

690600 Vladivostok, pr. Ostryakova 2

Telephone: (4232) 45-16-24

Fax: (4232) 45-17-19

E-mail: webadmin@vgmu.ru

Internet: www.vgmu.ru

Founded 1958

Faculties of therapeutics, medicine and prophylaxis, paediatrics, qualification improvement

Rector: Prof. YURI V. KAMINSKY

Number of teachers: 400

Number of students: 2,717

VOLGOGRAD STATE MEDICAL UNIVERSITY

400066 Volgograd, pl. Pavshikh Bortsov 1

Telephone and fax (8442) 38-50-05

E-mail: cved@volgmed.ru

Internet: www.volgmed.ru

Founded 1935

Colleges of advanced and continuing education, clinical psychology, general medicine, dentistry, medical biology, paediatrics, pharmacy, social work

Rector: Prof. VLADIMIR I. PETROV

Number of teachers: 657

Number of students: 5,070

PEDAGOGICAL AND LINGUISTIC UNIVERSITIES

BARNAUL STATE PEDAGOGICAL UNIVERSITY

656031 Altai Region, Barnaul, ul. Molodezhnaya 55

Telephone: (3852) 22-85-52

Fax: (3852) 26-08-36

E-mail: rector@bspu.secna.ru

Internet: www.bspu.secna.ru

Rector: Prof. VLADIMIR N. LOPATKIN

Number of teachers: 563

Number of students: 8,534

BLAGOVESHCHENSK STATE PEDAGOGICAL UNIVERSITY

675000 Blagoveshchensk, Amur oblast, ul. Lenina 104

Telephone and fax (4162) 52-41-64

E-mail: rektorat@bgpu.ru

Internet: www.bgpu.ru

State control

Languages of instruction: French, Russian

Academic year: September to July

Founded 1930, present status 1996

Rector: Prof. Dr YURI P. SERGIENKO

First Vice-Rector: Dr YURY MALINOVSKY

Dir of the Foreign Affairs Office: Dr NIKOLAY KUKHARENKO

Library of 700,000 vols

Number of teachers: 449

Number of students: 6,200

Publications: *Geographical Aspects of Upper Amur Area*, *Regional Studies of Amur Area* (in Russian, French, Chinese and English), *Salut! Ça va?*

DEANS

Dept of Foreign Languages: NATALIA KUTCH-ERENKO

Dept of History and Philology: DMITRY BOLO-TIN

Dept of Industry and Pedagogics: IRINA KIYASHKO

Dept of Natural Sciences and Geography: IRINA TROFIMOVA

Dept of Pedagogics and Elementary Education: TATIANA PLOTNIKOVA

Dept of Physical Culture and Sports: YURY KRETOV

Dept of Physics and Mathematics: VALENTINA NEMILOSTEVYKH

Dept of Psychology and Pedagogics: SVE-TLANA ZUEVA

Int. Dept: VERA PIRKO

IRKUTSK STATE LINGUISTIC UNIVERSITY

664000 Irkutsk, ul. Lenina 8

Telephone: (3952) 20-03-61

E-mail: islu@islu.irk.ru

Internet: www.islu.ru

Founded 1948

Faculties of eastern languages, English language, foreign languages and social science, German language, Romance languages, training of foreign students and advancement of qualifications; external faculty

Rector: Prof. GRIGORY D. VOSKOBOYNIK.

MOSCOW STATE LINGUISTICS UNIVERSITY

119837 Moscow, ul. Ostozhenka 38

Telephone: (495) 246-86-03

Fax: (495) 246-83-66

E-mail: info@linguanet.ru

Internet: www.linguanet.ru

Founded 1930, present name and status 1990

Fields of study: humanities and applied science, English, German and French teaching, interpretation and translation, international economics, management, law, international relations, political studies, public relations, cultural studies, regional studies; in-service training for foreign-language teachers and advanced training for interpreters; Interdisciplinary In-Service Training Institute; Foreign Language Methodology Centre for Non-Philological Universities; Russian language programmes.

Rector: Prof. IRINA I. KHALEEVA

Library: 1m. vols

Number of teachers: 1,500

Number of students: 10,000

NIZHNII NOVGOROD STATE LINGUISTICS UNIVERSITY 'N. A. DOBROLYUBOV'

603155 Nizhnii Novgorod, ul. Minina 31A

Telephone: (8314) 36-15-75

Fax: (8314) 36-20-49

E-mail: admdep@lunn.ru

Internet: www.lunn.sci-nnov.ru

Founded 1937

Faculties of business administration, economics, international relations, law, office management, pedagogy, philology, public relations, translation and interpreting, Russian language and culture

Rector: Prof. BORIS A. ZHIGALEV

Library of 405,000 vols

Number of teachers: 350

Number of students: 3,500

PYATIGORSK STATE LINGUISTIC UNIVERSITY

357532 Pyatigorsk, pr. Kalinina 9

Telephone: (8793) 400-505

Fax: (8793) 400-527

E-mail: ums@pglu.ru

Internet: www.pglu.ru

Founded 1939

Educational programmes: English, French, German, Spanish, Italian, Polish, Turkish, Arabic and Chinese languages, Russian as a foreign language, oriental studies, govt and public admin, business admin, hospitality and tourism management, int. relations, public relations, int. journalism, law, conflict resolution, psychology, theology (Christian and Islam), customs management and advertising

State control

Languages of instruction: English, Russian

Academic year: September to June

Rector: Prof. ALEXANDER P. GORBUNOV

Vice-Rector: Prof. YURI Y. GRANKIN

Dir for Int. Office: Dr VICTOR E. MISHIN

Chief Librarian: SVETLANA A. CHERNOMOR-DOVA

Library of 850,000 vols

Number of teachers: 562

Number of students: 5,500

Publications: *PSLU Bulletin*, *PSLU Herald* (4 a year, research journal).

RUSSIAN STATE VOCATIONAL PEDAGOGICAL UNIVERSITY

620012 Ekaterinburg, ul. Mashinostroitelei 11

Telephone: (343) 338-44-47

Fax: (343) 338-44-42

E-mail: mail@rsvpu.ru

Internet: www.rsvpu.ru

Founded 1979

Rector: GENNADY M. ROMANTSEV

Library of 333,800 vols

Number of teachers: 441

Number of students: 18,124

Publications: *Bulletin of Teaching Research* (2 a year), *Bulletin of the Association of Russian Educational Institutions on Vocational Pedagogics* (1 a year), *Improvement of Educational Processes in Vocational Schools* (1 a year), *Innovations in Industry and Education* (1 a year), *Integrational Processes in Pedagogical Theory and Practice* (1 a year), *Problems of Public Development in the Fields of Sociology and Economics*.

SIBERIAN FEDERAL UNIVERSITY

660041 Karsnoyarsk, Svobodny pr. 79,

Telephone: (391) 244-82-13

Fax: (391) 244-86-24

E-mail: rector@sfu-kras.ru

Internet: www.sfu-kras.ru

Founded 2006, reorganised Karsnoyarsk State Univ., Karsnoyarsk State technical Univ., Karsnoyarsk State Academy of Architecture and Civil Construction, State Univ. of Non-Ferrous Metals and Gold

State Control

Language of instruction: Russian

Academic year: September to July

Rector: EVGENY A. VAGANOV

Vice-Rector: SERGEY V. VERKHOVETS

Vice-Rector: VLADIMIR I. KOLMAKOV

Vice-Rector: PAVEL M. VCHERASHINY

Vice-Rector: SERGEY A. PODLESNYI

Vice-Rector: VLADISLAV YU. PANCHENKO

Vice-Rector: VALENTIN M. ZURAVLEV

Vice-Rector: NIKOLAY N. DOVZHENKO

Librarian: EVEGINYA G. KRIVONOSOVA

Library: 3.7m.

Number of teachers: 3,300

Number of students: 43,000

Publications: *New University Life* (48 a year), *Scientific Journal of Siberian Federal University* (4 a year, 5 series).

URALS STATE PEDAGOGICAL UNIVERSITY

620219 Ekaterinburg, GSP 135, pr. Kosmonavtov 26

Telephone: (343) 34-12-59

Fax: (343) 34-97-71

E-mail: root@uspu.ru

Internet: www.uspu.ru

Founded 1930 as Urals Industrial Pedagogical Institute; as Urals State Pedagogical Institute 1932–1993; present name and status 1994

State control

Rector: Prof. VLADIMIR D. ZHAVORONKOV

Number of teachers: 720

Number of students: 7,600

VOLGOGRAD STATE SOCIO—PEDAGOGICAL UNIVERSITY

400005 Volgograd pr. V. I. Lenina 27

Telephone: (8442) 30-28-12

Fax: (8442) 24-13-68

E-mail: vspu@vspu.ru

Internet: www.vspu.ru

State control

Academic year: September to June

Rector: Dr NIKOLAY K. SERGEEV

Number of teachers: 800

Number of students: 10,500

VORONEZH STATE PEDAGOGICAL UNIVERSITY

394043 Voronezh, ul. Lenina 86

Telephone: (0732) 55-19-49

Fax: (0732) 55-17-50

E-mail: rector@vspu.ac.ru

Internet: www.vspu.ac.ru

Founded 1930

State control

Rector: Prof. VYACHESLAV V. PODKOLZIN

Library of 600,000 vols

Number of teachers: 473

TECHNICAL UNIVERSITIES

ARKHANGELSK STATE TECHNICAL UNIVERSITY

163002 Arkhangelsk, Severnaya Dvina nab. 17

Telephone and fax (8182) 28-76-14

E-mail: public@agtu.ru

Internet: www.agtu.ru

Founded 1929

Academic year: September to June

Faculties of chemical technology, construction, distance learning, forestry, industrial power engineering, law, mechanical engineering, mechanical wood technology, natural resources, re-training and preparatory studies; institutes of chemical technology, economics, finance and business, information technology, law and entrepreneurship, oil and gas; colleges of business, information technology, law; centres of innovative technologies and information science; brs in Naryan-Mar, Kotlas, Velsk, Novodvinsk and Mirny

Rector: ALEXANDER L. NEVZOROV

Library of 720,000 vols, 380 periodicals
Number of teachers: 515
Number of students: 12,040

Publication: *Lesnoi Zhurnal* (Forestry Journal, 6 a year).

ASTRAKHAN STATE TECHNICAL UNIVERSITY

414025 Astrakhan, ul. Tatishcheva 16

Telephone: (8512) 25-09-23
Fax: (8512) 25-73-68
E-mail: astu@astu.org
Internet: www.astu.org

Founded 1930
Public control
Language of instruction: Russian
Academic year: September to June

Rector: Prof. Y. T. PIMENOV (acting)

Library of 700,000 vols
Number of teachers: 450
Number of students: 12,000

Publications: *ASTU Herald* (1 a year), *Proceedings*

DEANS

Construction Faculty: Prof. Dr RAMAZAM ABDULMUMINOVICH NABIEV
Faculty of Law: Prof. Dr IVAN VLADIMIROVICH MAKSIMOV
Institute of Economics: Assoc. Prof. TAMARA FEDOROVNA LOKTEVA
Institute of Fisheries, Biology and Nature Management: Prof. Dr ALEXANDR NIKOLAEVICH NEVALENNYI
Institute of Humanities: Dr ELVIRA ZELETDINOVA
Institute of Information Technologies and Communications: Dr IRINA YURIEVNA KVYATKOVSKAYA
Institute of Oil and Gas: Assoc. Prof. NATALIA NIKOLAEVNA LETICHEVSKAYA
Institute of Marine Sciences, Energy and Transport: SERGEY VLADIMIROVICH VINOGRADOV
Institute of Mechanics and Engineering: Prof. ANATOLY VIKTOROVICH KARABLIN
Preparatory Faculty for Foreign Citizens: NATALIA VITALIEVNA SHTEINIKOVA

BALTIC STATE TECHNICAL UNIVERSITY 'D. F. USTINOV' (VOENMEKH)

198005 St Petersburg, ul. 1-ya Krasnoarmeiskaya 1/21

Telephone: (812) 316-26-13
E-mail: zag@insu.ru
Internet: www.insu.ru

Founded 1930

Depts of aerospace, applied mechanics and automation, guidance systems, humanities, international industrial management, natural sciences, rocketry and aircraft

Rector: Prof. YURI V. ZAGASHVILI

Library: 1.1m. vols
Number of teachers: 600
Number of students: 5,300

BELGOROD STATE TECHNOLOGICAL UNIVERSITY 'V. G. SHUKOV'

308012 Belgorod, ul. Kostyukova 46

Telephone: (722) 54-20-87
Fax: (722) 25-71-39
E-mail: rektor@intbel.ru
Internet: www.bstu.ru

Founded 1970
Academic year: September to June

Institutes of building materials, economics and management, mechanical equipment in the building industry; depts: architecture and building technologies, civil engineering, engineering and ecology, highways, machine building, production automation and information technologies; 4 brs across Russia

Rector: Prof. ANATOLY M. GRIDCHIN

Library of 600,000 vols
Number of teachers: 540
Number of students: 9,152

Publication: *Tekhnolog* (newspaper, 6 a year).

BRYANSK STATE TECHNICAL UNIVERSITY

241035 Bryansk, bul. 50-let. Oktyabrya 7

Telephone: (4832) 56-09-05
Fax: (4832) 56-24-08
E-mail: rector@tu-bryansk.ru
Internet: www.tu-bryansk.ru

Founded 1929

Rector: Prof. ALEXANDER V. LAGEREV

Library of 705,668 vols
Number of teachers: 1,131
Number of students: 8,859

Publication: *Vestnik BGTU*.

DAGHESTAN STATE TECHNICAL UNIVERSITY

367015 Makhachkala, 70 Imama Shamil pr.

Telephone and fax (8722) 62-37-61
E-mail: dstu@dstu.ru
Internet: www.dstu.ru

Founded 1960 as Daghestan Polytechnic Institute
Academic year: September to July

Rector: Prof. TAGIR A. ISMAILOV
Vice-Rector for Academics: Prof. KADI A. GASANOV
Vice-Rector for Humanities and Educational work: Prof. YUSUP N. ABDULKADYROV
Vice-Rector for Economy: Prof. NURMAGOMED S. SURAKATOV
Vice-Rector for Science: SHIRALIE A. YUSUFOV
Vice-Rector for Administration: ALIMAGOMED G. MIRZEMAGOMEDOV
Head Librarian: TAMILA A. RAGHIMOVA

Library of 818,231 vols, 68,725 periodicals
Number of teachers: 800
Number of students: 14,000

Publications: *Herald of DSTU* (technical sciences, humanities), *Thematic Collected Scientific Papers*

DEANS

Architecture and Construction: Prof. GADGIMAGOMED N. KHADGISHALAPOV
Engineering and Economics: Prof. ELENA I. PAVLYUCHENKO
Finance and Audit: Prof. AMMAKADI R. RABADANOV
Humanities and Social Science: Prof. GYULNARA ALIEVA
Informatics and Management: Assoc. Prof. ARSLAN MUSTAFAEV
Information Systems: Prof. TADZHIDIN E. SARKAROV
Law and Customs Affairs: Assoc. Prof. NADIR K. SANAEV
Oil, Gas and Environmental Devt: Assoc. Prof. MARINA KOTENKO
Public and Municipal Management: Assoc. Prof. KHADGIMURAD KHALIMBEKOV
Radio Engineering: Assoc. Prof. GAMID IRZAEV
Skill Improvement and Personnel Retraining: Asst Prof. AISHAT R. SHAKHMAEVA
Technology: Assoc. Prof. MAGOMED AKHMEDOV
Transport: Asst Prof. GUSEIN M. MAGOMEDOV

DON STATE TECHNICAL UNIVERSITY

344010 Rostov-on-Don, pl. Gagarina 1

Telephone: (822) 38-15-25
Fax: (822) 32-79-53
E-mail: root@sintez.rud.su

Founded 1930 as Rostov Institute of Agricultural Engineering, present name 1992

Rector: Prof. Dr ANATOLY A. RYZHKIN

Library of 837,000 vols
Number of teachers: 650
Number of students: 6,000

EASTERN SIBERIAN STATE UNIVERSITY OF TECHNOLOGY

670013 Ulan-Ude, ul. Klyuchevskaya 40B

Telephone: (3012) 37-56-00
Fax: (3012) 44-14-15
E-mail: office@esstu.ru
Internet: www.esstu.ru

Founded 1962

Fields of study: mechanics and technology of light industry, construction, mechanical engineering, electrical engineering, power engineering, preparatory faculty; institutes: sustainable development, economics and law, food industry and biotechnology; postgraduate courses, Russian language courses, Russian language summer school, pre-university training courses

Rector: Prof. VLADIMIR E. SAKTOYEV

Library of 715,246 vols
Number of teachers: 868
Number of students: 10,640

FAR EASTERN NATIONAL TECHNICAL UNIVERSITY

690990 Vladivostok, ul. Pushkinskaya 10

Telephone: (4232) 26-51-18
Fax: (4232) 26-69-88
E-mail: festu@festu.ru
Internet: www.festu.ru

Founded 1899

Institutes of architecture, automatics and advanced technologies, civil engineering, continuing and distance education, economics and management, engineering, humanities, information science, maritime engineering, mechanics, mining engineering, natural sciences, oriental studies, politics and law, radioelectronics and electrical engineering, social ecology; brs in Nakhodka, Arseniev, Petropavlovsk-Kamchatsky, Dalnegorsk, Dalnerechensk, Bolshoi Kamen, Artyom, Lesozavodsk, Yuzhno-Sakhalinsk and Kirovsky

Pres.: ANVIR A. FATKULIN

Library of 2,328,000 vols, 300 periodicals
Number of teachers: 109
Number of students: 25,000

Publications: *Pacific Science Review* (jtly with Kangnam Univ., Republic of Korea, annual), *Proceedings* (1 a year).

FAR EASTERN STATE TECHNICAL FISHERIES UNIVERSITY

690600 Vladivostok, ul. Lugovaya 52B

Telephone: (4232) 44-03-06
Fax: (4232) 44-24-32
E-mail: support@dalrybvtuz.ru
Internet: www.dalrybvtuz.ru

Founded 1930

Rector: Prof. GEORGY N. KIM

Library of 450,000 vols
Number of teachers: 266
Number of students: 6,264

Publications: *Dalrybvtuz* (2 a year), *Scientific Papers* (2 a year).

FAR EASTERN STATE TRANSPORT UNIVERSITY

680021 Khabarovsk, ul. Serysheva 47
Telephone: (4212) 40-72-00
Fax: (4212) 40-73-21
E-mail: root@festu.khv.ru
Internet: www.festu.khv.ru

Founded 1937
State control
Languages of instruction: English, Russian
Academic year: September to July

Rector: Prof. BORIS E. DYNKIN (acting)
Vice-Rector: ANDREY N. GANUS (acting)

Library of 960,000 vols
Number of teachers: 520
Number of students: 25,000

Publication: *Social and Humanity Sciences at the Far East*

DEANS

Institute of Economics: Prof. YULIA A. TYUR-INA

GAGARIN STATE TECHNICAL UNIVERSITY, SARATOV (SSTU)

410054 Saratov, Politekhnicheskaya St 77
Telephone: (8452) 99-87-09
Fax: (8452) 99-87-10
E-mail: international@sstu.ru
Internet: www.sstu.ru

Founded 1930
State control
Language of instruction: Russian
Academic year: September to June

Rector: Prof. IGOR PLEVE

Library: 1.5m. vols
Number of teachers: 2,000
Number of students: 25,000

Publications: *The Journal of Innovation Activity* (4 a year), *The Journal of Innovations and Publicity* (4 a year), *The Journal of Saratov State Technical University* (4 a year), *The Journal of Social Policy Studies* (4 a year)

DEANS

Applied Information Technology: Assoc. Prof. OLGA DOLININA
Architecture and Road Construction: Prof. YURIY IVASHCHENKO
Automotive Engineering: Prof. IGOR DANILOV
Ecology and Service: Prof. ALEXEY IVANOV
Economics and Management: Prof. VLADIMIR TREGUBOV
Electronics and Instrumentation Engineering: Prof. MARINA BROVKOVA
Humanities and Social Sciences: Prof. DMITRIY MIKHEL
Mechanical Engineering: Prof. OLEG DAVYDENKO
Physical and Technical Sciences: Prof. ALEXANDER GOROKHOVSKIY
Power Engineering: Assoc. Prof. PAVEL ANTROPOV

GUBKIN RUSSIAN STATE UNIVERSITY OF OIL AND GAS

119991 Moscow, Leninsky pr. 65
Telephone: (4959) 137-81-08
Fax: (499) 135-88-95
E-mail: com@gubkin.ru
Internet: www.gubkin.ru

Founded 1930
State control
Academic year: September to June

Faculties of automation and computer science, construction and operation, chemical and environmental engineering, economics and management and law, liberal arts and humanities, mechanical engineering, natural science studies, oil and gas fields devt, petroleum geology and geophysics, pipeline network design, reservoir engineering; brs in Ashgabat, Orenburg, Tashkent

Rector: Prof. VICTOR G. MARTYNOV
Vice-Rector for Academic Affairs: Prof. VLADIMIR N. KOSHELEV
Vice-Rector for Int. Affairs: Prof. ANATOLY B. ZOLOTUKHIN

Library: 1.5m. vols
Number of teachers: 900
Number of students: 8,500

Publications: *Chemistry & Technology of Fuels and Oils, Oil, Gas & Business, Proceedings of Gubkin Russian State University of Oil and Gas.*

IVANOVO STATE ENERGY UNIVERSITY

153548 Ivanovo, ul. Rabfakovskaya 34
Telephone: (0932) 32-72-43
Fax: (0932) 38-57-01
E-mail: nvn@ispu.ru
Internet: www.ispu.ru

Faculties of electrical engineering, heat and power engineering, industrial heat and power engineering, power engineering

Rector: VLADIMIR N. NUZHDIN

Number of teachers: 1,500
Number of students: 8,000

IVANOVO STATE UNIVERSITY OF CHEMISTRY AND TECHNOLOGY

153460 Ivanovo, pr. F. Engelsa 7
Telephone: (0932) 32-92-41
Fax: (0932) 41-79-95
E-mail: rektor@isuct.ru
Internet: www.isuct.ru

Founded 1918 as Ivanovo-Vosnessensk Polytechnic Institute, Ivanovo Institute of Chemistry and Technology 1930–92, as Ivanovo State Acad. of Chemistry and Technology 1992–98, present name and status 1998

Faculties of inorganic chemistry technology, organic chemistry, silicates and engineering

Rector: OSCAR I. KOIFMAN.

KALASHNIKOV IZHEVSK STATE TECHNICAL UNIVERSITY

426069 Izhevsk, Studencheskaya St 7
Telephone: (3412) 59-25-55
Fax: (3412) 58-88-52
E-mail: inter@istu.ru
Internet: www.istu.ru

Founded 1952
State control
Languages of instruction: English, Russian
Academic year: September to July

Faculties of advanced technologies and automobiles, advertising and design, civil engineering, computer science, economics, heat engineering, instrumentation engineering, law and humanities, management and marketing, mathematics and natural sciences, mechanical engineering, quality management, sports; brs in Glazov, Kambarka, Sarapul, Tchaikovsky, Votkinsk

Rector: Prof. BORIS YAKIMOVICH

Library of 800,000 vols
Number of teachers: 800
Number of students: 22,000

KALININGRAD STATE TECHNICAL UNIVERSITY

236000 Kaliningrad, Sovietsky pr. 1
Telephone: (0112) 27-22-55
Fax: (0112) 27-95-11
E-mail: ivanov@klgtu.ru
Internet: www.klgtu.ru

Founded 1930
Academic year: September to June

Faculties of biological resources and water usage, commercial fisheries, economics and humanities, mechanics and technology, naval and power engineering, production automation and control

Rector: Prof. VICTOR E. IVANOV

Library of 530,000 vols
Number of teachers: 560
Number of students: 7,000

Publication: *Izvestiya KGTU* (12 a year).

KAZAN STATE TECHNICAL UNIVERSITY 'A. N. TUPOLEV'

420111 Kazan, ul. K. Marksa 10
Telephone and fax (8432) 31-02-44
E-mail: icd@kai.ru
Internet: www.kai.ru

Founded 1932, present name and status 1992

Rector: Prof. YURIY GORTYSHOV

Library: 3m. vols
Number of teachers: 1,800
Number of students: 24,000

Publications: *Aviatsionaya Tekchnika: Izvestia VUZov* (Russian Aeronautics, in Russian and English, 4 a year), *Non-Linear Analysis Problems in Engineering Systems* (in English, 2 a year), *Problemy Nelineinogo Analiza v Inzhenernykh Sistemakh* (Non-Linear Analysis Problems in Engineering Systems, in Russian and English, 2 a year), *Russian Aeronautics* (in English, 4 a year), *Radioelectronnye Ustroistva* (Radioengineering Devices, in Russian, 2 a year), *Vestnik KGTU* (Proceedings of KSTU, in Russian, 4 a year).

KAZAN STATE TECHNOLOGICAL UNIVERSITY

420015 Kazan, ul. K. Marksa 68
Telephone: (8432) 38-56-94
Fax: (8432) 19-42-16
E-mail: office@kstu.ru
Internet: www.kstu.ru

Founded 1919

Faculties of light industry engineering, mechanics, chemical engineering, oil and oil refining, polymers, chemical technology, energy engineering and technological engineering, power machinery construction and process equipment, management and automation, humanities and food technology; br. at Nizhnekamsk

Rector: SERGEI G. DYAKONOV

Library: 1.6m. vols
Number of teachers: 950
Number of students: 25,000

Publications: *Economy of Industrial Production, Heat and Mass Transfer in Chemical Engineering.*

KAZAN STATE UNIVERSITY OF ARCHITECTURE AND CIVIL ENGINEERING

420043 Kazan, ul. Zelenaya 1
Telephone: (843) 510-46-10
Fax: (843) 238-79-72
E-mail: rector@kgasu.ru
Internet: www.kgasu.ru

Founded 1930 as Kazan Engineering and Civil Engineering Institute; later Kazan State Acad. of Architecture and Civil Engineering; present name 2005
Academic year: September to June

Rector: RASHIT K. NIZAMOV

Vice-Rector: ILFAC E. VILDANOV
Vice-Rector for Academic Affairs: DAMIR K. SHARAFUTDINOV

Library of 583,000 vols
Number of teachers: 540
Number of students: 6,799

DEANS

Architecture: ALEXANDER D. KULIKOV
Building Science Engineering: VLADIMIR S. AGAFONKIN
Construction Technologies: DMITRIY A. SOLDATOV
Design: SERGEY M. MIKHAILOV
Economics: GUZEL M. HARISOVA
Engineering: MUNIR A. VALIULLIN
Engineering Basics: NAIL K. TUKTAMISHEV
Engineering Systems and Ecology: RAIS S. SAFIN
General Architectural and Art Training: HANIFA G. NADIROVA
Part-time and Extended Studies: VICTOR YA. ORLOV
Transport Engineering: ILVERA N. HABIBULLINA

KOMSOMOLSK-ON-AMUR STATE TECHNICAL UNIVERSITY

681013 Komsomolsk-on-Amur, pr. Lenina 27
Telephone: (4217) 53-23-04
Fax: (4217) 53-61-50
E-mail: office@knastu.ru
Internet: www.knastu.ru
Founded 1955
Rector: Prof. YURI KABALDIN
Number of students: 3,500

KOSTROMA STATE TECHNOLOGICAL UNIVERSITY

156005 Kostroma, ul. Dzerzhinskogo 17
Telephone: (4942) 31-48-14
Fax: (4942) 31-70-08
E-mail: info@kstu.edu.ru
Internet: www.kstu.edu.ru

Founded 1932, as Kostroma Textile Institute, as Kostroma Technological Institute 1962, present name and status 1995

Rector: ANDREI P. BOLOTNY
Vice-Rector for International Links: VICTOR P. KALASHNIK

Library of 608,000 vols
Number of teachers: 430
Number of students: 6,520

KUBAN STATE TECHNICAL UNIVERSITY

350072 Krasnodar, ul. Moskovskaya 2
Telephone: (861) 255-84-01
Fax: (861) 257-65-92
E-mail: adm@kgtu.kuban.ru
Internet: www.kubstu.ru
Founded 1918

Faculties of chemical engineering, civil engineering, computer technology and automated systems, economics, food technology, gas and power engineering, highway engineering, oil, mechanical engineering, technology of grain products; Institute of Mechanical Engineering in Armavir, br. in Novorossiisk

Rector: Prof. A. A. PETRIK

Library of 720,000 vols
Number of teachers: 800
Number of students: 13,000

Publications: *Izvestiya Vuzov, Pishevaya Teckhnologiya* (Food Technology, 6 a year).

KURSK STATE TECHNICAL UNIVERSITY

305040 Kursk, ul. 50-letiya Oktyabrya 94
Telephone: (0712) 22-57-43
Fax: (0712) 56-18-85
E-mail: rector@kstu.kursk.ru
Internet: www.kstu.kursk.ru
Founded 1964

Faculties of civil and industrial construction engineering, computer engineering and automation systems, economics, environmental protection, finance and auditing, law, management, machine-building, textile technology

Rector: Prof. IVAN S. ZAKHAROV

Library of 536,000 vols
Number of teachers: 530
Number of students: 4,400

Publication: *Izvestia* (2 a year).

KUZBASS STATE TECHNICAL UNIVERSITY NAMED AFTER T.F. GORBACHEV

650026 Kemerovo, ul. Vesennyaya, 28
Telephone: (3842) 58-33-83
Fax: (3842) 58-33-80
E-mail: rector@kuzstu.ru
Internet: www.kuzstu.ru
Founded 1950
Public control
Language of instruction: Russian
Academic year: September to June
Rector: Dr VLADIMIR A. KOVALEV

Library of 650,000 vols
Number of teachers: 761
Number of students: 8,660

DEANS

Chemical Technology: Prof. Dr TATYANA G. CHERKASOVA
Economics and Service: Prof. Dr VALERIY N. BOBRIKOV
Machinery Engineering: Prof. Dr ALEXANDER N. KOROTKOV
Mining and Electrical Engineering: Prof. Dr VENIAMIN G. KASHIRSKIH
Mining Engineering: Prof. Dr ALEXEY A. RENEYV
Surface and Underground Construction: Prof. Dr ANDREY V. UGLYANITCA

LIPETSK STATE TECHNICAL UNIVERSITY

398055 Lipetsk, ul. Moskovskaya 30
Telephone: (0742) 25-00-61
Fax: (0742) 31-04-73
E-mail: mailbox@stu.lipetsk.su
Internet: www.stu.lipetsk.ru
Founded 1956

Rector: Prof. MIKHAIL P. KUPRYANOV

Number of teachers: 500
Number of students: 5,000

MAGNITOGORSK STATE TECHNICAL UNIVERSITY 'G. I. NOSOV'

455000 Magnitogorsk, pr. Lenina 38
Telephone: (3519) 22-12-87
Fax: (3519) 29-84-26
E-mail: mgtu@magtu.ru
Internet: www.magtu.ru
Founded 1932
Rector: Dr BORIS A. NIKIFOROV
Library of 846,656 vols
Br. in Beloretsk.

MARI STATE TECHNICAL UNIVERSITY

424024 Yoshkar-Ola, 3 Lenin pl.
Telephone: (8362) 41-08-72
E-mail: rector@marstu.net
Internet: www.marstu.net
Founded 1932
Rector: EVGENY M. ROMANOV
Library: 1m. vols
Number of teachers: 591
Number of students: 12,406

MOSCOW AVIATION INSTITUTE (STATE TECHNICAL UNIVERSITY)

125993 Moscow, A-80, GSP-3, Volokolamskoe shosse 4
Telephone: (495) 158-04-65
Fax: (495) 158-29-77
E-mail: aet@mai.ru
Internet: www.mai.ru
Founded 1930

Schools of aerospace engineering, aircraft engineering, applied mathematics and physics, applied mechanics, control systems, economics and management, flight vehicle engines, humanities and preparatory studies, informatics and electric power engineering, robotics and intelligent systems, vehicle flight radioelectronics

Rector: Prof. Dr ALEXANDR M. MATVEENKO

Library of 909,000 vols
Number of teachers: 2,000
Number of students: 14,000

MOSCOW ENGINEERING PHYSICS INSTITUTE (STATE UNIVERSITY)

115409 Moscow, Kashirskoe shosse 31
Telephone: (495) 324-74-91
Fax: (495) 324-85-20
E-mail: degnn@mephi.ru
Internet: www.mephi.ru
Founded 1942
Rector: Prof. BORIS N. ONYKY
Library: 1m. vols
Number of teachers: 880
Number of students: 6,000

MOSCOW INSTITUTE OF PHYSICS AND TECHNOLOGY (STATE UNIVERSITY)

141700 Moscow oblast, Dolgoprudny, Institutsky per. 9
Telephone: (495) 408-57-00
Fax: (495) 408-68-69
E-mail: rector@mipt.ru
Internet: www.mipt.ru
Founded 1951

Depts of aeromechanics and flight engineering (located in Zhukovsky), aerophysics and space research, applied mathematics and economics and problems of physics and power engineering, general and applied physics, molecular and biological physics, physical and quantum electronics, radio engineering and cybernetics

Rector: Prof. NIKOLAY N. KUDRYAVTSEV

Library of 733,000 vols
Number of teachers: 470 full-time, 1,090 part-time
Number of students: 3,500

MOSCOW STATE ACADEMY OF FINE CHEMICAL TECHNOLOGY 'M. V. LOMONOSOV'

117571 Moscow, pr. Vernadskogo 86
Telephone: (495) 434-71-55
Fax: (495) 434-87-11

E-mail: mitht@mitht.ru
Internet: www.mitht.ru
Founded 1930
Rector: Prof. ALLA K. FROLKOVA
Library of 220,000 vols

DEANS

Faculty of Biotechnology and Organic Synthesis: Prof. A. F. MIRONOV
Faculty of Chemistry and Technology Polymer Processing: Prof. E. E. POTAPOV
Faculty of Chemistry and Technology of Rare Elements and Materials for Electronic Technology: Prof. D. V. DROBOT
Faculty of Engineering: Prof. G. I. LAPSHENKOV
Faculty of Management, Ecology and Economics: Doc. I. H. ROZDIN
Faculty of Natural Sciences: Prof. E. M. KARTASHOV
Preparatory Faculty: V. B. MARGULIS
Evening Classes: Doc. A. P. PETRUSENKO

MOSCOW STATE AUTOMOBILE AND ROAD TECHNICAL UNIVERSITY

125829 Moscow, Leningradsky pr. 64
Telephone: (495) 151-03-71
E-mail: info@madi.ru
Internet: www.madi.ru
Founded 1930
Faculties of building and technological machines, correspondence learning, economics, energy and ecology, design and mechanical engineering, foreign citizen preparation, humanities, management, military training, motor transport, natural sciences, pre-admission preparation, road, road building; institute for the improvement of professional skills and retraining of personnel in the transport and road infrastructure; Moscow Transport Institute; Centre of Engineering Pedagogy; Centre of Innovations in Engineering Education
Rector: Prof. VYACHESLAV M. PRIKHODKO
Library: 1m. vols
Number of teachers: 850
Number of students: 10,000

MOSCOW STATE FORESTRY UNIVERSITY

141005 Moscow oblast, Mytischi, 1-ya Institutskaya ul. 1
Telephone: (495) 588-55-78
E-mail: mgul@mgul.ac.ru
Internet: www.mgul.ac.ru
Founded 1919
Faculties of forestry, mechanical and chemical wood technology, electronics and technical systems, economics and foreign relations, humanities, landscape architecture, International School of Business and Management
Rector: Prof. VIKTOR G. SANAEV
Library of 550,000 vols
Number of teachers: 627
Number of students: 10,000

MOSCOW STATE INDUSTRIAL UNIVERSITY

115280 Moscow, ul. Avtozavodskaya 16
Telephone: (495) 675-52-37
Fax: (495) 674-63-92
E-mail: topstaff@msiu.ru
Internet: www.msiu.ru
Founded 1960
State control
Faculties of applied mathematics and engineering physics, automotive engineering,

information technology and law, management
Rector: Prof. VALERY KOSHKIN
Number of teachers: 790
Number of students: 7,000

MOSCOW STATE INSTITUTE OF ELECTRONICS AND MATHEMATICS (TECHNICAL UNIVERSITY)

109028 Moscow, Bolshoi Trekhsvyatitelsky per. 1-3/12
Telephone: (495) 917-90-89
Fax: (495) 916-28-07
E-mail: lenor@miem.edu.ru
Internet: www.miem.edu.ru
Founded 1962
Rector: Dr DMITRY V. BYKOV
Library of 600,000 vols
Number of students: 5,000

MOSCOW STATE INSTITUTE OF RADIO ENGINEERING, ELECTRONICS AND AUTOMATION (TECHNICAL UNIVERSITY)

119454 Moscow, pr. Vernadskogo 78
Telephone: (495) 433-00-44
Fax: (495) 434-86-65
E-mail: rector@mirea.ru
Internet: www.mirea.ru
Founded 1947
Academic year: September to June
Languages of instruction: Russian, English
Rector: ALEXANDER S. SIGOV
Library: 1.5m. vols
Number of teachers: 1,200
Number of students: 16,000
Publication: *Proceedings of MIREA* (irregular)

DEANS

Faculty of Cybernetics: Prof. MIKHAIL ROMANOV
Faculty of Economy and Management: Prof. ALEXANDER BOLSHAKOV
Faculty of Electronics: Prof. YURI FETISOV
Faculty of Information Technologies: Prof. ANDREY PETROV
Faculty of Radioengineering: Prof. GENNADY KULIKOV
International Faculty of Informatics: Prof. ALEKSEY LOBUZOV

MOSCOW STATE MINING UNIVERSITY

117049 Moscow, Leninsky pr. 6
Telephone: (495) 236-94-80
Fax: (495) 237-31-63
Internet: www.msmu.ru
Founded 1918
Faculties of applied physics, coal mining and underground construction, mining automation and control, mining electrification and mechanization, mining of mineral and non-mineral deposits
Rector: Prof. Dr LEV A. PUCHKOV
Library of 800,000 vols
Number of teachers: 540
Number of students: 5,270
Publications: *Gornyatskaya Smena* (52 a year), *Scientific Papers* (2 a year).

MOSCOW STATE TECHNICAL UNIVERSITY 'MAMI'

107023 Moscow, ul. Bol. Semenovskaya 38
Telephone: (495) 369-91-53
Fax: (495) 918-29-75
E-mail: decinter@mami.ru

Founded 1865
Faculties of automation and control, design and technology, economics and engineering economics, machine-building, mechanical engineering, motor vehicles and tractors, power engineering
Rector: Prof. ANATOLY L. KARUNIN
Library: 1m. vols
Number of teachers: 800
Number of students: 7,500

MOSCOW STATE TECHNICAL UNIVERSITY OF CIVIL AVIATION

125838 Moscow, GSP-47, Kronshtadtsky bul. 20
Telephone: (495) 459-07-07
Fax: (495) 457-12-01
E-mail: rectorat@mail.mstuca.ru
Internet: www.mstuca.ru
Founded 1971 as Moscow Institute of Civil Aviation Engineers, present name and status 1992
Faculties of applied mathematics, computer systems and networks, maintenance of aircraft and engines, maintenance of aircraft electrical systems and avionics, maintenance of transport radio equipment, management, technological processes and safety in the aviation industry
Rector: Prof. VLADIMIR G. VOROBIEV
Library: 1.1m. vols
Number of teachers: 300
Number of students: 5,300
Publication: *Proceedings* (1 a year).

MOSCOW STATE TECHNICAL UNIVERSITY 'N. E. BAUMAN'

107005 Moscow, 2-ya Baumanskaya ul. 5
Telephone: (495) 261-40-55
Fax: (495) 267-98-93
E-mail: irina@interd.bmstu.ru
Founded 1830
Faculties of basic sciences, electronics and laser technology, engineering business, humanities, informatics and control systems, management, materials and technology, power engineering, robotics and complex automation, special machinery; br. in Kaluga
Rector: Prof. IGOR B. FEDOROV
Library: 3m. vols
Number of teachers: 2,500
Number of students: 18,000
Publications: *Izvestiya Vuzov* (mechanical engineering), *Vestnik MGTU* (issues each on instrumental engineering and mechanical engineering).

MOSCOW STATE TECHNOLOGICAL UNIVERSITY, STANKIN

101472 Moscow, Vadkovsky per. 3-a
Telephone: (495) 973-30-66
Fax: (495) 973-38-85
E-mail: rector@stankin.ru
Internet: www.stankin.ru
Founded 1930
Faculties of economics, information technology, innovation technology management, mechanics and control, metrological informatics, technology
Rector: Prof. YURY M. SOLOMENTSEV
Library of 700,000 vols
Number of teachers: 677
Number of students: 5,873

MOSCOW STATE TEXTILE UNIVERSITY

119991 Moscow, ul. Malaya Kaluzhskaya 1
Telephone: (495) 954-70-73
Fax: (495) 952-14-40
E-mail: office@msta.ac.ru
Internet: www.msta.ac.ru
Founded 1919
Faculties of mechanical technology, textile machinery, chemical technology, applied arts, economics and management, information, automation and energetics
Rector: SERGEI D. NIKOLAEV
Library of 780,000 vols
Number of teachers: 530
Number of students: 5,000
Publication: *Vestnik MGTU* (2 a year).

MOSCOW STATE UNIVERSITY OF CIVIL ENGINEERING

129337 Moscow, Yaroslavskoe shosse 26
Telephone: (495) 183-44-38
Fax: (495) 183-48-01
E-mail: kanz@mgsu.ru
Internet: www.mgsu.ru
Founded 1921
Faculties of constructional technology, economics organization and management of construction, heat and power construction, heat and ventilation, hydraulic engineering, industrial and civil construction, mechanization and automation of construction, urban construction and services, water and sewerage
Rector: Prof. VALERY I. TELICHENKO
Library: 1.6m. vols
Number of teachers: 1,300
Number of students: 11,000
Publication: *Proceedings of MSUCE* (4 a year).

MOSCOW STATE UNIVERSITY OF ENGINEERING ECOLOGY

105066 Moscow, ul. Staraya Basmannaya 21/4
Telephone: (495) 267-07-01
Fax: (495) 261-49-61
Internet: www.msuie.ru
Founded 1920 as Moscow State Acad. of Chemical Engineering; present name and status 1997
Faculties of chemical and biological engineering and economics, chemical apparatus manufacture, chemical machine building, cryogenic technology, technical cybernetics and automation of technological processes
Rector: Prof. MIKHAIL B. GENERALOV
Library of 650,000 vols
Number of teachers: 400
Number of students: 3,000

MOSCOW STATE UNIVERSITY OF ENVIRONMENTAL ENGINEERING

127550 Moscow, ul. Pryanishnikova 19
Telephone and fax (495) 976-10-46
E-mail: mailbox@msuee.ru
Internet: www.msuee.ru
Founded 1930
Rector: Prof. DMITRY V. KOZLOV
Vice-Rector for Academic Affairs: VLADIMIR F. STORCHEVOY
Vice-Rector for Int. Affairs: ANDREI SOROKIN
Vice-Rector for Research: VALENTIN N. KRAS-NOSHCHEOKOV
Number of teachers: 400
Number of students: 3,700

Publication: *Environmental Engineering* (in Russian).

MOSCOW STATE UNIVERSITY OF GEODESY AND CARTOGRAPHY

105064 Moscow, Gorokhovsky per. 4
Telephone: (495) 261-31-52
Fax: (495) 267-46-81
E-mail: rector@miigaik.ru
Internet: www.miigaik.ru
Founded 1779
Academic year: September to June
Faculties of applied cosmonautics, cartography, geodesy, humanities, optical instrument manufacture, space surveying and photogrammetry, territorial economics and land management
Rector: Prof. VIKTOR P. SAVINYKH
Library of 800,000 vols
Number of teachers: 400
Number of students: 5,000
Publication: *Geodeziya i Aerofotosiomka* (6 a year).

MOSCOW STATE UNIVERSITY OF RAILWAY ENGINEERING

103055 Moscow, ul. Obraztsova 15
Telephone: (495) 681-31-77
Fax: (495) 681-13-40
E-mail: mgups@online.ru
Internet: www.miit.ru
Founded 1896, present name and status 1993
Faculties of mechanical engineering, mechanical engineering technology, railway automation, telemechanics and communication, technical cybernetics, industrial and civil construction, traffic management, electrification of railways, railway construction, bridges and tunnels engineering and economics
Rector: Prof. BORIS A. LEVIN
Library: 2m. vols
Number of teachers: 1,300
Number of students: 12,000
Publications: *Inzhener Transporta*, *MREI* (colln of works).

MOSCOW TECHNICAL UNIVERSITY OF COMMUNICATION AND INFORMATICS

111024 Moscow, ul. Aviamotornaya 8A
Telephone: (495) 957-77-09
Fax: (495) 274-00-32
E-mail: mtuci@mtuci.ru
Internet: www.mtuci.ru
Founded 1921 as Moscow Institute of Electrical Engineering and Communications; present name and status 1992
Faculties of radio communication and radio and television broadcasting, multi-channel communications, postal services automation, automatic telecommunications and engineering and economics; brs in Rostov-on-Don, Nizhnii Novgorod
Rector: Prof. VAGAN V. SHAKHGILDYAN
Library: 1.3m. vols
Number of teachers: 850
Number of students: 14,000

MURMANSK STATE TECHNICAL UNIVERSITY

183010 Murmansk, Sportivnaya ul. 13
Telephone: (8152) 45-46-09
E-mail: webmaster@mstu.edu.ru
Internet: www.mstu.edu.ru
Founded 1950
Rector: Dr ALEXANDER ERSHOV

Library of 350,000
Number of teachers: 394
Number of students: 4,458

NATIONAL RESEARCH IRKUTSK STATE TECHNICAL UNIVERSITY

664074 Irkutsk, ul. Lermontova 83
Telephone: (3952) 40-52-00
Fax: (3952) 40-51-00
E-mail: oms@istu.edu
Internet: www.istu.edu
Founded 1930
State control
Language of instruction: Russian
Academic year: September to June
Rector: Prof. Dr IVAN GOLOVNYKH
Vice-Rector for Int. Relations: Dr ANDREY TANAEV
Library: 1.5m. vols
Number of teachers: 1,450
Number of students: 31,000
Publications: *Geology, Search and Prospecting for Oil and Mineral Deposits*, *Higher Educational Institutes' News: Geoscience*, *ISTU Bulletin*, *Ore Dressing*, *Problems of the Development of Eastern Siberia's Mineral Base*

DEANS

Faculty of Chemical Engineering and Metallurgy: Prof. SVETLANA DYACHKOVA
Faculty of Computer Sciences: Prof. ALEXANDER PETROV
Faculty of Power Engineering: Dr VADIM FEDCHISHIN
Institute of Architecture and Civil Engineering: Prof. VIKTOR R. CHUPIN
Institute of Aviation Mechanical Engineering and Transport: Dr RASHID AKHATOV
Institute of Economics, Management and Law: Prof. GENNADIY DYKUSOV
Institute of Fine Arts, Social Sciences and Humanities: Dr OLGA IGNATIEVA
Institute of Mineral Resource Management and Processing: Prof. BORIS L. TALGAMER
Int. Faculty: Dr VITALIY EFREMOV
Physical and Engineering Institute: Prof. KONSTANTIN KAZAKOV

NATIONAL RESEARCH UNIVERSITY 'MOSCOW POWER ENGINEERING INSTITUTE'

111250 Moscow, ul. Krasnokazarmennaya 14
Telephone: (495) 362-56-45
Fax: (495) 362-89-18
E-mail: uvs@mpei.ru
Internet: www.mpei.ru
Founded 1930
Public control
Languages of instruction: English, Russian
Academic year: September to June
Rector: Prof. SERGEY SEREBRIANNIKOV
Vice-Rector for Int. relations: Prof. VLADIMIR ZAMOLODCHIKOV
Library: 2m. vols
Number of teachers: 1,500
Number of students: 15,000
Publication: *Vestnik MPEI* (6 a year).

NATIONAL RESEARCH UNIVERSITY OF ELECTRONIC TECHNOLOGY

124498 Moscow, Zelenograd, pr-d 4806, 5
Telephone: (499) 720-8933
Fax: (499) 734-3453
E-mail: netadm@miee.ru
Internet: www.miet.ru
Founded 1965
Public control
Language of instruction: Russian
Academic year: September to June

Rector: Prof. YURI A. CHAPLYGIN

Vice-Rector for International Affairs and Information Technology: Prof. SERGEY V. UMNYASHKIN

Dean of Computer Science and Telecommunications: Prof. Dr ALEXANDER GUREEV

Library of 680,000 vols
Number of teachers: 530
Number of students: 6,400

Publication: *Collection of Research Work* (12 a year)

DEANS

Electronics and Computer Technologies: Prof. MIKHAIL G. PUTRYA

Electronic Technologies, Materials and Equipment: Prof. VLADIMIR M. ROSHIN

NIZHNII NOVGOROD STATE TECHNICAL UNIVERSITY

603600 GSP 41, Nizhnii Novgorod, ul. Minina 24
Telephone: (8312) 36-23-25
Fax: (8312) 36-05-69
E-mail: nntu@nntu.nnov.ru
Internet: www.nntu.nnov.ru

Founded 1898 in Warsaw as Warsaw Polytechnic Institute; relocated to Moscow 1916, then Nizhnii Novgorod in 1917; reestablished as Nizhnii Novgorod Polytechnic Institute; present name and status 1992

Rector: VLADIMIR P. KIRIENKO

Number of teachers: 1,166
Number of students: 12,310

NIZHNII NOVGOROD STATE UNIVERSITY OF ARCHITECTURE AND CIVIL ENGINEERING

603950 Nizhnii Novgorod, ul. Ilyinskaya 65
Telephone: (8312) 33-82-47
Fax: (8312) 33-73-66
E-mail: srec@nngasu.ru
Internet: www.nngasu.ru

Founded 1930
State control
Academic year: September to June

Fields of study: architecture, design, urban development, environmental engineering, economics, law, industrial management, environmental management and occupational safety; distance learning programmes

Rector: Prof. VALENTIN V. NAIDENKO
Vice-Rector for Int. Relations: Dr ALEXANDER PALEEV

Library of 800,000 vols
Number of teachers: 890
Number of students: 8,000

Publication: *Collected Papers and Proceedings of Scientific Conferences* (2 a year).

NORTH CAUCASIAN INSTITUTE OF MINING AND METALLURGICAL (STATE TECHNOLOGICAL UNIVERSITY)

362021 North-Ossetian Republic, Vladikavkaz, ul. Kosmonavta Nikolaeva 44
Telephone: (8672) 74-93-79
Fax: (8672) 74-99-45
E-mail: skgtu@skgtu.ru
Internet: www.skgtu.ru

Founded 1931 as the North Caucasian Institute of Non-Ferrous Metals

Faculties of construction, electromechanical, electronic engineering, metallurgical, mining, management

Rector: Dr VLADIMIR S. VAGIN

Library of 520,000 vols
Number of teachers: 500

Number of students: 4,000
Publications: *Izvestiya Vuzov, Tsvetnaya Metallurgia* (6 a year).

NORTH CAUCASIAN STATE TECHNICAL UNIVERSITY

362021 Stavropol, pr. Kulakova 2
Telephone and fax (8652) 95-68-08
E-mail: info@ncstu.ru
Internet: www.ncstu.ru
Founded 1958
Rector: Prof. BORIS M. SINELNIKOV.

NORTH-WEST STATE TECHNICAL UNIVERSITY

191186 St Petersburg, ul. Millionnaya 5
Telephone and fax (812) 312-94-84
E-mail: office@nwpi.ru
Internet: www.nwpi.ru
Founded 1930
Rector: ALEXANDER A. KONDRATYEV
Library of 1,544,698 vols
Number of teachers: 400

NOVOSIBIRSK STATE TECHNICAL UNIVERSITY

630092 Novosibirsk, pr. Karla Marksa 20
Telephone: (3832) 46-50-01
Fax: (3832) 46-02-09
Internet: www.nstu.ru
Founded 1953
11 Faculties; 80 depts
Rector: Prof. NIKOLAI V. PUSTOVOI
Number of teachers: 1,105
Number of students: 9,354

NOVOSIBIRSK STATE UNIVERSITY OF ARCHITECTURE AND CIVIL ENGINEERING

630008 Novosibirsk-8, ul. Leningradskaya 113
Telephone: (3832) 66-41-25
Fax: (3832) 16-11-07
E-mail: uungas@sibstrin.ru
Internet: www.sibstrin.ru
Founded 1930

Faculties of architecture and construction, building specialists refresher programmes and further training, construction technology, environmental engineering, first stage of higher education, part-time and correspondence education, preliminary training, training of overseas students; institutes: architecture and civil engineering, economics and management, general and basic education, humanities

Rector: Prof. ARKADY P. YANENKO
Library of 553,000 vols
Number of teachers: 580
Number of students: 6,700

Publication: *Izvestiya vuzov—Stroitelstvo* (Higher School News—Civil Engineering, 12 a year).

OBNINSK STATE TECHNICAL UNIVERSITY FOR NUCLEAR POWER ENGINEERING (TECHNICAL UNIVERSITY)

249020 Kaluga oblast, Obninsk, Studgorodok 1
Telephone: (08439) 7-01-31
Fax: (08439) 7-08-22
E-mail: priem@iate.obninsk.ru
Internet: www.iate.obninsk.ru

Founded 1953 as a br. of Moscow Engineering and Physics Institute; as Obninsk

Institute for Nuclear Power Engineering 1985–2002, present name and status 2002

Faculties of advanced education, cybernetics, distance education, economics, evening education, natural science, physics and power engineering

Rector: Prof. NIKOLAI L. SALNIKOV
Library of 140,000 vols
Number of teachers: 340
Number of students: 2,100

OMSK STATE TECHNICAL UNIVERSITY

644050 Omsk, Mira pr. 11
Telephone: (3812) 65-33-89
Fax: (3812) 65-26-98
E-mail: info@omgtu.ru
Internet: inter.omgtu.ru
Founded 1942
Public control
Academic year: September to June

Rector: Prof. VICTOR SHALAY
Vice-Rector for Education: Prof. ALEXANDER MYSHLYAVTSEV
Vice-Rector for Research: Prof. ANATOLY KOSYKH

Library of 1,281,294 vols
Number of teachers: 1,000
Number of students: 17,000 (incl. 500 int. students)

Publications: *Analysis and Synthesis of Mechanical Systems* (1 a year), *International conference: Dynamics of Machines and Mechanisms* (every 2 years), *Omsk Scientific Bulletin* (12 a year)

DEANS

Economics and Management Faculty: Prof. VERA POTUDANSKAYA
Energy Institute: Prof. VLADIMIR GORYUNOV
Humanitarian Education Faculty: Prof. MIKHAIL MASHKARIN
Information Technologies and Computer Systems Faculty: Prof. ANNA ZYKINA
Mechanical Engineering Institute: Prof. EVGENIY EREMIN
Petrochemical Institute: Prof. VLADIMIR YUSHA
Radio Engineering Faculty: Prof. VALERIY LEVCHENKO
Transport, Oil and Gas Faculty: Prof. VALENTIN BELKOV

OMSK STATE TRANSPORT UNIVERSITY

644046 Omsk, pr. Karla Marksa 35
Telephone and fax (3812) 31-42-13
E-mail: omgups@omgups.ru
Internet: www.omgups.ru
Founded 1930

Faculties of locomotives, railway rolling stock, electric transport, power supply for railways, automation, telemechanics and communication facilities for railway vehicles, technology of machine-building, heat and power engineering, control and information technology in technical systems, information systems, world economy, management, marketing, finance and credit, quality control

Rector: Prof. ILKHAM I. GALIEV
Library of 700,000 vols
Number of teachers: 310
Number of students: 6,000

PENZA STATE UNIVERSITY OF ARCHITECTURE AND CONSTRUCTION

440028 Penza, ul. Titova 28
Telephone: (8412) 48-74-76

Fax: (8412) 48-27-77
E-mail: relay@gasa.penza.com.ru
Internet: www.gasa.penza.com.ru
Founded 1958
Faculties of architecture, automotive engineering, construction, economics and management, engineering ecology, technology
Rector: ALEXANDER I. EREMKIN
Library of 370,000 vols
Number of teachers: 395
Number of students: 5,735

PERM STATE TECHNICAL UNIVERSITY

614600 Perm, Komsomolsky pr. 29A
Telephone: (3422) 12-87-53
Fax: (3422) 12-11-47
E-mail: rector@pstu.ac.ru
Internet: www.pstu.ac.ru
Founded 1953 as Perm Mining Institute
Faculties of aerospace technology, applied mathematics and mechanics, chemical technology, construction, electrical engineering, humanities, mining, road transport
Rector: VASILY YU. PETROV
Library: 1.4m. vols
Number of teachers: 932
Number of students: 12,500

PETERSBURG STATE TRANSPORT UNIVERSITY

190031 St Petersburg, Moskovsky pr. 9
Telephone: (812) 310-25-21
Internet: www.pgups.ru
Founded 1809
Faculties of bridge and tunnel construction, construction, electrical engineering, electrification, mechanics, traffic management; br. in Velikie Luki
Rector: Prof. VALERY I. KOVALEV
Library: 1.5m. vols
Number of teachers: 700
Publication: *Proceedings* (1 a year).

POLZUNOV ALTAI STATE TECHNICAL UNIVERSITY

656038 Barnaul, Lenina pr. 46
Telephone: (3852) 26-05-42
Fax: (3852) 36-78-64
E-mail: nikonov@mail.altstu.ru
Internet: www.altstu.ru
Founded 1942
State control
Language of instruction: Russian
Academic year: September to August
Faculties of automotive, part-time studies, civil engineering, extramural education, food and chemical engineering, humanities, information technologies, innovation technologies in machine building, military training, natural science, power engineering, second degree education, social science and tourism; institutes of architecture and design, economics and management, further professional education devt, intensive education, textile and light industry; brs: Biysk Technological Institute, Rubtsovsk Industrial Institute
Rector: Prof. OLEG I. KHOMUTOV
Dean of Faculty of Foreign Students: Prof. ALEXEY T. EVTUSHENKO
Library of 992,456 vols
Number of teachers: 1,500
Number of students: 21,000
Publication: *Polzunovsky Vestnik*.

ROSTOV STATE UNIVERSITY OF CIVIL ENGINEERING

344022 Rostov-on-Don, Sotsialisticheskaya ul. 162
Telephone: (8632) 65-50-76
Fax: (8632) 65-57-31
E-mail: rgsu@jeo.ru
Internet: www.rgsu.ru
Founded 1943
Institutes of civil engineering technology and materials, economics, environmental engineering, highways and transport, industrial and civil engineering, management
Rector: VIKTOR I. SHUMEIKO
Library of 710,000 vols
Publication: *Izvestiya* (4 a year).

ROSTOV STATE UNIVERSITY FOR RAILWAY TRANSPORTATION

344038 Rostov-on-Don, pl. Narodnogo Opolcheniya 2
Telephone and fax (8632) 45-06-13
E-mail: rek@rgups.ru
Internet: www.rgups.ru
Founded 1929
Areas of study: automation and telemechanics, power engineering, electromechanical engineering, railway construction, traffic and transport management, road building machinery, humanities; Institute of Management and Law
Rector: VLADIMIR I. KOLESNIKOV
Library of 980,000 vols
Number of teachers: 550
Number of students: 5,000

RUSSIAN STATE HYDROMETEOROLOGICAL UNIVERSITY

195196 St Petersburg, Malookhtinsky pr. 98
Telephone: (812) 444-41-63
Fax: (812) 444-60-90
E-mail: rector@rshu.ru
Internet: www.rshu.ru
Founded 1930
Languages of instruction: English, Russian
Academic year: September to July
Rector: Prof. LEV N. KARLIN
Vice-Rector for Academic Asscns: Prof. ANDREI V. BELOTSERKOVSKY
Vice-Rector for Int. Relations: Dr ANATOLY I. BOGUSH
Vice-Rector for Research: VLADIMIR N. VOROBYEV
Vice-Rector for Undergraduate and Graduate Education: Dr VLADIMIR M. SAKOVICH
Library of 408,000 vols
Number of teachers: 250
Number of students: 5,500
Publication: *Proceedings* (4 a year)

DEANS

Correspondence Education: Prof. VADIM G. ORLOV
Economic and Social-Humanitarian Faculty: Prof. MIKHAIL M. GLAZOV
Faculty of Ecology and Natural Physics: Dr ANNA L. SKOBLIKOVA
Faculty of Information Systems and Geo-Technologies: Prof. Dr EVGENY P. ISTOMIN
Hydrological Faculty: Dr ARKADY DOGANOVSKY
Meteorological Faculty: Prof. LEONID DIVINSKY
Oceanological Faculty: Dr ALEXANDER S. AVERKIYEV

BRANCHES

RSHU Aleksin: 301351, Tula oblast, Aleksin District, Kolosovo; tel. (8753) 7-34-17; Dir VALERY M. BORTYAKOV.
RSHU Rostov-on-Don: 344025 Rostov-on-Don, 31-aya Liniya 4; tel. (8632) 91-41-05; Dir SERGEY S. ANDREEV.
RSHU Tuapse: 352800 Krasnodar oblast, Tuapse, ul. Morskaya 4; tel. (8616) 72-37-63; Dir YARVANT O. YAILY.

RUSSIAN STATE OPEN TECHNICAL UNIVERSITY OF RAILWAY TRANSPORT

125993 Moscow, ul. Chasovaya 22/2
Telephone: (495) 151-14-51
Fax: (495) 151-18-37
E-mail: org@rgotups.ru
Internet: www.rgotups.ru
Founded 1951
Faculties of Railway Traffic and Management, Railway Construction and Civil Engineering, Economics and General Technology; brs in Nizhnii Novgorod, Voronezh, Yaroslavl, Smolensk, Saratov, Bryansk, Tula, Novomoskovsk, Ryazan, Murom, Elets, Vologda, Vladimir, Kirov, Izhevsk, Lisky, Kotlas, Kaliningrad, Orel, Rtitshevo, Labytnangy, Astrakhan, Volgograd, Uhta
Rector: Prof. Dr A. T. DEMCHENKO
Vice-Rector: Prof. Dr V. I. APATZEV
Library of 930,453 vols
Number of teachers: 508
Number of students: 21,573

RUSSIAN STATE TECHNOLOGICAL UNIVERSITY 'K. E. TSIOLKOVSKY' (MATI)

103767 Moscow, ul. Orshanskaya 3
Telephone: (495) 141-18-40
Fax: (495) 141-19-50
E-mail: intdep@intedu.mati.msk.ru
Internet: www.mati.ru
Founded 1932
Faculties of aerospace engineering and technology, applied mathematics and mechanics, avionics, computer science, economics and business, ecology, materials science and technology, satellite communications and technology
Rector: ANATOLY P. PETROV
Library of 800,000 vols
Number of teachers: 1,103
Number of students: 9,000

RUSSIAN UNIVERSITY OF CHEMICAL TECHNOLOGY 'D. MENDELEEV'

125047 Moscow, Miusskaya pl. 9
Telephone: (495) 978-87-33
Fax: (495) 200-42-04
E-mail: rector@muctr.edu.ru
Internet: www.muctr.edu.ru
Founded 1920
Faculties of chemical technology of inorganic substances, chemical technology of organic substances, chemical technology engineering, chemical technology of polymers, cybernetics of chemical technological processes, ecological engineering, physical chemistry engineering, general engineering and economics; br. in Novomoskovsk
Rector: Dr PAVEL D. SARKISOV
Library: 1.7m. vols
Number of teachers: 1,003
Number of students: 8,416
Publication: *Trudy* (6 a year).

ST PETERSBURG ELECTROTECHNICAL UNIVERSITY 'LETI' (ETU)

197376 St Petersburg, ul. Prof. Popova 5

Telephone: (812) 234-35-53

Fax: (812) 346-27-58

E-mail: fordep@eltech.ru

Internet: www.eltech.ru

Founded 1886

Academic year: September to June

Faculties of electrical engineering and automatics, electronics, computing and information technologies, humanities, measurement and biotechnical systems, radio engineering and telecommunications

Chancellor: VLADIMIR M. KUTUZOV

Library of 1,063,000 vols

Number of teachers: 1,000

Number of students: 9,000

Publications: *Izvestiya ETU* (10 a year), *Izvestiya Vuzov Rossii—Radioelektronika* (6 a year).

ST PETERSBURG STATE MARINE TECHNICAL UNIVERSITY

190008 St Petersburg, ul. Lotsmanskaya 3

Telephone: (812) 114-41-68

Fax: (812) 318-52-27

E-mail: inter@smtu.ru

Internet: www.smtu.ru

Founded 1930

Faculties of natural and social sciences and humanities, naval architecture and ocean engineering, marine engineering, marine electronics and control systems, business and management

Rector: Dr KONSTANTIN P. BORISENKO

Library of 862,380 vols

Number of teachers: 600

Number of students: 5,500

ST PETERSBURG STATE MINING INSTITUTE (TECHNICAL UNIVERSITY)

199026 St Petersburg, Vasilevskii ostrov, 21-ya Liniya 2

Telephone: (812) 213-60-78

Fax: (812) 327-73-59

E-mail: rectorat@spmi.ru

Internet: www.spmi.ru

Founded 1773

Rector: Prof. VLADIMIR S. LITVINENKO

Library of 1,209,266 vols

Number of students: 8,000

ST PETERSBURG STATE POLYTECHNICAL UNIVERSITY

195251 St Petersburg, Politekhnicheskaya ul. 29

Telephone: (812) 247-1616

Fax: (812) 552-6080

E-mail: rector@stu.neva.ru

Internet: www.spbstu.ru

Founded 1899

State control

Languages of instruction: Russian, English

Academic year: September to July

Faculties of computer science and engineering, biomedical engineering, electrical engineering, economics and management, humanities, hydraulic engineering, industrial engineering, mechanical engineering, physical science and engineering, physics and mechanical sciences, power engineering, radiophysical science and engineering, technology and materials science; brs at Pskov, Cherboksary and Orsk

Pres.: Prof. MIKHAIL P. FIODOROV

Library: 2.5m. vols

Number of teachers: 2,000

Number of students: 16,000

Publications: *Scientific and Engineering News*, *Transactions.*

ST PETERSBURG STATE TECHNOLOGICAL UNIVERSITY OF PLANT POLYMERS

198095 St Petersburg, ul. Ivan Chernykh 4

Telephone: (812) 786-57-44

Fax: (812) 786-86-00

E-mail: zsv@gturp.spb.ru

Internet: www.gturp.spb.ru

Founded 1931, present name and status 1993

Academic year: September to June

Integrated training of specialists for enterprises in the pulp and paper industry and the fuel and power sector; depts of automated control systems, chemical engineering, economics and management, environmental engineering, heat and power engineering, mechanical, part-time studies

Rector: VYACHESLAV A. SUSLOV (acting)

Vice-Rector for Economics and Devt: ALEXANDER L. ASHKALUNIN

Vice-Rector for Innovations: ALEXANDER N. IVANOV

Vice Rector for Int. Relations: NADEZHDA V. KHODYREVA

Vice-Rector for Research: VICTOR S. KUROV

Vice-Rector for Studies: PAVEL V. LUKANIN

Library of 740,000 vols

Number of teachers: 300

Number of students: 5,000

Publications: *JPPS*, *Pulp Paper Board Magazine*, *TAPPI.*

ST PETERSBURG STATE UNIVERSITY OF ARCHITECTURE AND CIVIL ENGINEERING

190005 St Petersburg, 2nd Krasnoarmeiskaya ul., 4

Telephone: (812) 316-58-72

Fax: (812) 575-05-34

E-mail: rector@spbgasu.ru

Internet: www.spbgasu.ru

Founded 1832

Advanced training and retraining institute; faculties of architecture, civil engineering, automobile and road building, environment engineering, economics and management, urban construction and public utilities, correspondence faculty

Rector: Prof. YEVGENY I. RYBNOV

Library of 855,000 vols

Number of teachers: 870

Number of students: 8,775

Publications: *Masterok* (4 a year), *Za stroitel'nye kadry* (12 a year).

ST PETERSBURG STATE UNIVERSITY OF INFORMATION TECHNOLOGY, MECHANICS AND OPTICS

197101 St Petersburg, ul. Sablinskaya 14

Telephone: (812) 233-00-89

Fax: (812) 232-23-07

E-mail: rector@mail.ifmo.ru

Internet: www.ifmo.ru

Founded 1900

Rector: Prof. VLADIMIR N. VASILEV

Library of 900,000 vols

Number of teachers: 500

Number of students: 4,000

Publication: *Izvestiya Vuzov (Priborostroenie)* (4 a year).

ST PETERSBURG STATE UNIVERSITY OF REFRIGERATION AND FOOD ENGINEERING

191002 St Petersburg, ul. Lomonosova 9

Telephone and fax (812) 315-36-17

E-mail: refr@gunipt.spb.ru

Internet: www.gunipt.edu.ru

Founded 1931

Academic year: September to June

Rector: ALEXANDER V. BARANENKO

Vice-Rector for Int. Contacts: OLGA N. RUMYANTSEVA

Library: 1m. vols

Number of teachers: 337

Number of students: 6,344

DEANS

Faculty of Correspondence and Extramural: Prof. DMITRY P. MALYAVKO

Faculty of Cryogenics and Conditioning Systems: Dr IGOR V. BARANOV

Faculty of Economics and Environmental Management: Dr VICTOR L. VASILYONOK

Faculty of Food Manufacturing Facilities: Prof. ELENA V. VERBOLOZ

Faculty of Food Technologies: Dr ALEXANDER L. ISHEVSKY

Faculty of Refrigeration Engineering: Prof. VLADIMIR A. KOROTKOV

ST PETERSBURG STATE UNIVERSITY OF TECHNOLOGY AND DESIGN

191186 St Petersburg, Bol. Morskaya ul. 18

Telephone and fax (812) 315-12-10

E-mail: international@sutd.ru

Internet: www.sutd.ru

Founded 1828, present name and status 1992

Academic year: September to June

Rector: Prof. ALEXEY V. DEMIDOV

Head of Library: O. TEROVA

Library of 1,245,684 vols

Number of teachers: 900

Number of students: 12,000 (incl. 6,500 full-time)

DEANS

Faculty of Applied Chemistry and Ecology: Prof. N. NOVOSELOV

Faculty of Information Technologies and Machine Science: Prof. V. ENTIN

Faculty of Natural Sciences and Humanities: S. IVANOVA

Faculty of Textiles and Clothing: Prof. E. SURZHENKO

ST PETERSBURG STATE UNIVERSITY OF TELECOMMUNICATIONS 'PROF. M. A. BONCH-BRUYEV'

191065 St Petersburg, nab. Moiki 61

Telephone: (812) 315-01-18

Fax: (812) 315-32-27

E-mail: rector@sut.ru

Internet: www.sut.ru

Founded 1930

Faculties of biomedical electronics, economics and management, multi-channel telecommunication systems, radio broadcasting and television, radio communication, switching systems and computer technology, telecommunication networks, telecommunication technologies

Rector: Prof. ALEXANDER A. GOGOL

Library of 90,000 vols.

SAINT PETERSBURG STATE UNIVERSITY OF WATERWAY COMMUNICATIONS

198035 St Petersburg, ul. Dvinskaya 5/7

Telephone: (812) 251-12-21

Fax: (812) 251-01-14
E-mail: rector@spbuwc.ru
Internet: www.spbuwc.ru
Founded 1809
State control
Rector: Prof. SERGEY BARYSHNIKOV
Library of 950,663 vols
Number of teachers: 376
Number of students: 7,353 (3,953 full-time, 3,400 correspondence)

DEANS

Evening and Correspondence Study: Dr YURI EZHOV
Faculty of Arts and Social Sciences: OLEG CHULKOV
Faculty of Economics and Finance: Dr IGOR RASTORGUEV
Faculty of Information Technologies: Dr EVGENIY BARSCHEVSKIY
Faculty of Law: Prof. OLEG KARATAEV
Faculty of Navigation: Dr KIRILL SLATIN
Hydrotechnical Engineering Faculty: SERGEY GOLOVKOV
Marine Engineering: Dr YURI LOPAREV
Port Facilities and Electrical Engineering: Dr EVGENIY ANDRIANOV
Regional and Distant Learning: Dr LARISA ALPEEVA

SAMARA STATE AEROSPACE UNIVERSITY 'S. P. KOROLEV'

443086 Samara, Moskovskoye shosse 34
Telephone and fax (846) 334-57-22
E-mail: intdep@ssau.ru
Internet: www.ssau.ru
Founded 1942
State control
Language of instruction: Russian
Academic year: September to June
Rector: EVGENIY SHAKHMATOV
Library of 1,092,955 vols
Number of teachers: 750
Number of students: 11,790

DEANS

Aircraft Design: Prof. VICTROR KIRPICHEV
Aircraft Engines Design: Prof. ALEXANDER ERMAKOV
Aircraft Maintenance: Assoc. Prof. ALEKSEI TIKHONOV

SAMARA STATE TECHNICAL UNIVERSITY

443010 Samara, ul. Molodogvardeiskaja 244
Telephone: (846) 278-43-00
Fax: (846) 278-44-00
E-mail: postman@samgtu.ru
Internet: www.samgtu.ru
Founded 1914
State control
Language of instruction: Russian
Faculties of automation and information technology, chemical technology, economics and humanities, electrotechnology, engineering technology, machine building, oil technology, physical technology, thermal power
Rector: Prof. DMITRY BYKOV
Number of teachers: 2,500
Number of students: 18,000
Publication: *Vestnik SamGTU.*

SAMARA STATE UNIVERSITY OF ARCHITECTURE AND CIVIL ENGINEERING

443001 Samara, Molodogvardeiskaya ul. 194
Telephone: (8462) 42-17-84
Fax: (8462) 32-19-65
E-mail: sgasu@sgasu.smr.ru

Internet: www.sgasu.smr.ru
State control
Languages of instruction: Russian, English
Academic year: September to June
Founded 1930 as Samara State Acad. of Architecture and Civil Engineering, present name and status 2004
Rector: Prof. MIKHAIL I. BALZANNIKOV
Pres.: VSEVOLOD A. SHABANOV
Vice-Rector: NATALYA G. CHUMACHENKO
Library Dir: LYUDMILA I. KORYTINA
Library: 1m. vols, incl. 300,000 specialist books
Number of teachers: 420
Number of students: 8,000

DEANS

Centre for Linguistic Training and Translation/Interpretation: Prof. EUPHYM G. VYSHKIN
Construction Institute: Prof IGOR S. KHOLOPOV
Faculty of Architecture: Assoc. Prof ELINA V. DANILOVA
Faculty of Construction Engineering: Assoc. Prof. KONSTANTIN S. GALITSKOV
Faculty of Design: Assoc. Prof SVETLANA G. MALYSHEVA
Faculty of Engineering Economics: Assoc. Prof VALERY A. PROTSENKO
Faculty of Engineering Systems and Environment Protection Construction: Assoc. Prof. MIKHAIL V. SHUVALOV
Faculty of Industrial and Civil Engineering: Assoc. Prof VALERY M. KAZAKOV
Faculty of Information Systems and Technologies: Prof. SEMYON A. PIYAVSKIY
Faculty of Transport and Town Development: Assoc. Prof. TATYANA E. GORDEYEVA
Institute of Architecture and Design: Prof. YELENA A. AKHMEDOVA
Institute of Ecology and Engineering Life Support Systems: Prof. ALEKSANDR K. STRELKOV
Institute of Economics and Management: Prof. IRINA P. SCHEGOLEVA

SIBERIAN STATE AEROSPACE UNIVERSITY 'M. F. RESHETNEV'

660014 Krasnoyarsk, 31 Krasnoyarsky Rabochy pr.
Telephone: (391) 264-00-14
Fax: (391) 264-47-09
E-mail: info@sibsau.ru
Internet: www.sibsau.ru
Founded 1959
State control
Languages of instruction: Russian, English
Academic year: September to June
Rector: Prof. IGOR V. KOVALEV
Vice-Rector for Academic Affairs: ANNA A. LUKIANOVA
Vice-Rector for Devt: VLADIMIR A. KURESHOV
Vice-Rector for Research and Innovations: YURIY Y. LOGINOV
Vice-Rector for Pre-univ. Training and Educational work: VADIM V. KOLGA
Vice-Rector for General Affairs and Public Relations: BORIS V. VERBENKO
Vice-Rector for Int. Cooperation and Additional Education: ANNA A. VOROSHILOVA
Vice-Rector for Admin. and Social Affairs: SERGEY N. SKOTNIKOV
Library of 858,424 vols, 427 titles
Number of teachers: 808
Number of students: 11,403
Publication: *Vestnik Sibsau*

DEANS

Faculty of Distance and Additional Learning: LILIYA V. ERYGINA
Faculty of Economics and Finance: YURIY V. ERYGIN

Faculty of Humanities: SVETLANA Y. PISKORSKAYA
Faculty of Physical Education and Sport: IGOR A. TOLSTOPYATOV
Faculty of Professional Devt of Teaching Staff: VALERIY A. LEVKO
Faculty of Retraining and Professional Devt of Specialists: GRIGORIY B. DOBRETSOV
Institute of Civil Aviation: VLADIMIR L. MEDVEDEV
Institute of Information Science and Telecommunication: ALEKSEY M. POPOV
Institute of Machine Science and Innovation: EVGENIY V. SUGAK
Institute of Space Technology: NIKOLAY A. TEREKHIN
Institute of Space Research and High Technologies: VASILIY F. SHABANOV
Int. Higher School of Innovating Business and Admin.: OLGA E. PODVERBNYKH
Military Institute: EVGENIY I. DOBRYAKOV

SIBERIAN STATE TECHNOLOGICAL UNIVERSITY

660049 Krasnoyarsk, pr. Mira 82
Telephone: (391) 227-63-82
Fax: (391) 227-44-40
E-mail: repyakh@sibstu.kts.ru
Internet: www.sibstu.kts.ru
Founded 1930
Faculties of automation and robot technology, chemical technology, engineering economics, engineering for chemical technology, forestry, humanities and mechanics, woodworking technology, timber technology and equipment; brs in Lesosibirsk and 5 representative offices in major Siberian cities
Rector: Prof. EDUARD S. BUKA
Library of 243,000 vols
Number of teachers: 682
Number of students: 12,912

SIBERIAN STATE UNIVERSITY OF TELECOMMUNICATIONS AND INFORMATICS

630102 Novosibirsk, ul. Kirova 86
Telephone: (3832) 66-10-38
Fax: (3832) 66-10-39
E-mail: rectorat@neic.nsk.ru
Internet: www.sibsutis.ru
Founded 1953
Faculties of automatic electrical communication, engineering economics and informatics, multi-channel electrical communication, radio communication and broadcasting; brs in Khabarovsk, Ekaterinburg, Ulan-Ude
Rector: Prof. VALERY P. BAKALOV
Library of 463,638 vols
Number of teachers: 650
Number of students: 10,000

SIBERIAN TRANSPORT UNIVERSITY

630023 Novosibirsk, ul. D. Kovalchuk 191
Telephone: (3832) 28-74-70
Fax: (3832) 26-79-78
Founded 1932
Faculties of accounting and auditing, bridges and tunnels, civil engineering, construction and track machinery, economics and building management, economics and transport management, management and world economics, railway construction, railway traffic management, water supply and sewerage
Rector: Dr VLADIMIR D. VERESKUN
Library of 773,000 vols
Number of teachers: 600
Number of students: 12,000
Publication: *Proceedings* (5 or 6 a year).

SOUTH RUSSIA STATE TECHNICAL UNIVERSITY (NOVOCHERKASSK POLYTECHNIC INSTITUTE)

346428 Novocherkassk, ul. Prosveshcheniya 132

Telephone: (8635) 25-55-14
Fax: (8635) 22-72-69
E-mail: ngtu@novoch.ru
Internet: www.npi-tu.ru

Founded 1907
State control
Language of instruction: Russian
Academic year: September to June

Rector: Prof. VLADIMIR G. PEREDERIY
Vice-Rector: Prof. NIKOLAY I. GORBATENKO
Vice-Rector for Admin. Work: URIY I. KLIMENKO
Vice-Rector for Educational Activities: Prof. LIDIA I. SHERBAKOVA
Vice-Rector for Research and Innovation: Prof. ALEXANDER V. PAVLENKO
Vice-Rector for Strategic Devt: Dr VALERY V. SHMATKOV

Library of 3,162,689 vols, 300 periodical titles
Number of teachers: 2,111
Number of students: 24,616
Publications: *Izvestiya SK NC Visshey Shkoly* (4 a year), *Izvestiya Vuzov Severo-Cavkazskogo regiona: Elektromekhanika* (12 a year)

DEANS

Department of Electromechanics: Prof. Dr BORIS N. LOBOV
Department of Energy: Prof. Dr VLADIMIR I. NAGAY
Department of Geology, Mining and Petroleum Engineering: Prof. Dr URIY I. RAZARENOV
Department of Innovation and Production Organization: Prof. Dr EVGENIY B. KOLBYSHEV
Department of Open and Distance Learning: Prof. Dr VLADIMIR S. ISAKOV
Faculty of Automation and Control: Prof. Dr VALERIY L. KANDRASHOV
Faculty of Chemical Technology: Prof. Dr ELENA A. YACENKO
Faculty of Civil Engineering: Prof. Dr GENADIY M. SKIBIN
Faculty of Information Technology: Prof. Dr VALERIY M. GRINSHENKOV
Faculty of Mechanical Engineering: Prof. Dr VITALIY M. BERDNIK
Faculty of Physics and Mathematics: Prof. Dr VIKTOR V. NEFEDOV

STATE EDUCATIONAL INSTITUTION OF HIGHER PROFESSIONAL EDUCATION ULYANOVSK STATE TECHNICAL UNIVERSITY

432027 Ulyanovsk, ul. Severny Venets 32

Telephone: (8422) 43-06-43
Fax: (8422) 43-02-37
E-mail: rector@ulstu.ru
Internet: www.ulstu.ru

Founded 1957 as Ulyanovsk Evening Polytechnic Institute; reorganized into Ulyanovsk Polytechnic Institute 1962, renamed Ulyanovsk State Technical University 1994, present name and status 2002

Rector: Prof. Dr ALEXANDER D. GORBOKONENKO
Vice-Rector: N. YARUSHKINA
Librarian: TAMARA M. SMIRNOVA

Library of 1,411,507 vols
Number of teachers: 637
Number of students: 13,318
Publication: *Vestnik Ulyanovsk State Technical University* (4 a year)

Faculties of information systems and technology, radio engineering, power engineering, civil engineering, mechanical engineering, aircraft engineering, humanities, economics, mathematics, correspondent (evening) studies, open education centres and distance education; open business school at Dimitrovgrad.

TAMBOV STATE TECHNICAL UNIVERSITY

392000 Tambov, Sovetskaya ul. 106

Telephone: (4752) 63-10-19
Fax: (4752) 63-02-16
E-mail: tstu@admin.tstu.ru
Internet: www.tstu.ru

Founded 1958
Public control
Language of instruction: Russian
Academic year: September to July

Rector: Prof. Dr SERGEY V. MISCHENKO
Vice-Rector: Dr VYACHESLAV F. KALININ
Vice-Rector: Dr NIKOLAY S. POPOV
Librarian: IRINA V. SCHUKINA

Library: 1.5m. vols
Number of teachers: 700
Number of students: 12,000
Publications: *Problems of Contemporary Science and Practice* (4 a year), *TSTU Transactions* (4 a year)

DEANS

Architecture and Civil Engineering: PAVEL MONASTYREV
Correspondence Study and External Studies: VALERIY ODNOLKO
Economics: BORIS GERASIMOV
Information Technologies: YURIY GROMOV
International Education: MAXIM PROMOTOV
Motor Transport: OLEG DMITRIEV
Nanotechnologies: ALEXANDER MAYSTRENKO
Noosphere Safety and Law: SERGEY YESIKIV
Power Engineering: TATYANA CHERNYSHEVA
Pre-University Training: VLADIMIR PLOTNIKOV

PROFESSORS

BELYAEV, P.
BRUSENTOV, Y.
BYKOVSKIY, V.
CHERNYSHEVA, T.
CHERNYSHEV, V. N.
DEMIN, O. B.
DMITRIEV, O.
DVORETSKIY, S. I.
DZUBA, S.
FROLOV, S.
GATAPOVA, N. T.
GERASIMOV, B. I.
GROMOV, Y.
KALININ, V. F.
KILIMNIK, A.
KLIMOV, A. M.
KLINKOV, A.
KONOVALOV, V.
KULIKOV, G.
KULIKOV, N.
KUROCHKIN, I. M.
LAZAREV, S.
LEDENEV, V.
LEONTYEVA, A. I.
MAKEEVA, M.
MALYGYN, E.
MARTEMYANOV, Y. F.
MATVEYKIN, V.
MOLOTKOVA, N
MILOVANOV, I. V.
MISCHENKO, S. V.
MOLOTKOV, N.
NIKULIN, V. V.
ODNOLKO, V. G.
PARKHOMENKO, L.
PENKOV, V.

PERSHIN, V.
PODOLSKIY, V. Y.
POPOVA, I.
POPOV, N. S.
PROMTOV, M. A.
PUCHKOV, N. P.
PUDOVKIN, A.
ROMANOV, A. P.
SHAMKIN, V. N.
SLEZIN, A.
TKACHEV, A.
VANIN, V.
VOROBYEV, Y.
VORONKOVA, O.
YESIKOV, S. A.
ZHARIKOV, V.
ZHUKOV, N. P.

TOMSK POLYTECHNIC UNIVERSITY

634050 Tomsk, 30 Lenin Ave

Telephone: (3822) 70-17-77
Fax: (3822) 56-38-65
E-mail: tpu@tpu.ru
Internet: www.tpu.ru

Founded 1896
State control
Languages of instruction: English, Russian
Academic year: September to July

Rector: Prof. PETR CHUBIK

Library: 2.7m. vols
Number of teachers: 2,300
Number of students: 22,800

DEANS

Institute of Cybernetics: Prof. MIKHAIL SONKIN
Institute of High Technology Physics: Prof. ALEXEY YAKOVLEV
Institute of Natural Resources: Prof. ANDREY DMITRIEV
Institute of Non-Destructive Testing: Prof. VASILIY KLIMENOV
Institute of Physics and Technology: Prof. VALERI KRIVOBOKOV
Institute of Power Engineering: Prof. YURI BOROVIKOV

TOMSK STATE UNIVERSITY OF CONTROL SYSTEMS AND RADIOELECTRONICS

634050 Tomsk, pr. Lenina 40

Telephone: (3822) 51-05-30
Fax: (3822) 51-32-62
E-mail: office@tusur.ru
Internet: www.tusur.ru

Founded 1962
State control

Pres.: ANATOLY V. KOBZEV
Rector: YURY A. SHURYGIN

Library of 620,000 vols
Number of teachers: 600
Number of students: 13,000

DEANS

Faculty of Advanced Training: Prof. VYACHESLAV I. EFANOV
Faculty of Computer Systems: Assoc. Prof. MIKHAIL V. CHERKASHIN
Faculty of Control Systems: Assoc. Prof. PAVEL V. SENCHENKO
Faculty of Distance Learning: IRINA P. LEVSHENKOVA
Faculty of Economics: Prof. Dr ARKADY G. BUIMOV
Faculty of Electronic Engineering: Assoc. Prof. VIKTOR M. GERASIMOV
Faculty of Extramural and Evening Education: Assoc. Prof. IGOR V. OSIPOV
Faculty of Human Sciences: Prof. Dr TATYANA I. SUSLOVA
Faculty of Innovation Technologies: Assoc. Prof. YURI M. LIRMAK

Faculty of Law: Assoc. Prof. SERGEY L. KRASINSKY

Higher College of Informatics, Electronics and Management: Prof. Dr VYACHESLAV M. DMITRIEV

Radio Design Faculty: Assoc. Prof. DENIS V. OZERKIN

Radio Engineering Faculty: Assoc. Prof. ANATOLY Y. DEMIDOV

TULA STATE UNIVERSITY

300600 Tula, pr. Lenina 92
Telephone: (0872) 35-21-55
Fax: (0872) 33-13-05
E-mail: info@tsu.tula.ru
Internet: www.tsu.tula.ru
Founded 1930
Faculties of mechanics and control systems, mechanics and mathematics, applied physics, engineering, cybernetics, mining and construction, medicine, natural sciences, humanities, economics and law, technological, physical culture, sport and tourism, int. students' faculty
Rector: Prof. MIKHAIL V. GRYAZEV
Library: 1m. vols
Number of teachers: 1,386
Number of students: 17,000
Publication: *Izvestiya* (4 a year).

TVER STATE TECHNICAL UNIVERSITY

170026 Tver, nab. A. Nikitina 22
Telephone: (0822) 31-15-09
Fax: (0822) 31-43-07
E-mail: common@tstu.tver.ru
Internet: www.tstu.tver.ru
Founded 1922
Faculties of machine building, automatic control systems, civil and industrial engineering, environmental engineering, humanities, postgraduate, evening and distance education
Rector: Prof. VYACHESLAV A. MIRONOV
Library: 2m. vols.

TYUMEN STATE OIL AND GAS UNIVERSITY

625000 Tyumen, ul. Volodarskogo 38
Telephone: (3452) 25-08-61
Fax: (3452) 25-08-25
E-mail: general@tgngu.tyumen.ru
Internet: www.tgngu.tyumen.ru
Founded 1963
Faculties of geology and geoinformatics, oil and gas fields, pipeline engineering, transport, technical cybernetics, oil and gas refining, management, drilling and mechanical engineering
Rector: NIKOLAI N. KARNAUKHOV
Library of 677,000 vols
Number of teachers: 1,230
Number of students: 30,000

UFA STATE AVIATION TECHNICAL UNIVERSITY

450000 Bashkortostan, Ufa, ul. K. Marksa 12
Telephone and fax (347) 256-96-93
E-mail: root@admin.ugatu.ac.ru
Internet: www.ugatu.ac.ru
Founded 1932
Faculties of aircraft engines, aircraft machine building technology, aircraft technological systems, general sciences, informatics and robotics, economics, management and finance, social sciences
Rector: Prof. MURAT B. GUZAIROV

Library of 700,000 vols
Publication: *Higher School Collections on Research* (irregular).

UFA STATE PETROLEUM TECHNOLOGICAL UNIVERSITY

450062 Bashkortostan, Ufa, ul. Kosmonavtov 1
Telephone: (3472) 42-03-70
Fax: (3472) 43-14-19
E-mail: info@rusoil.net
Internet: www.ugntu.ru
Founded 1941
Faculties of oil and mining, pipeline transport, petrochemical, oil equipment, construction, technology, economics and management, automation of production processes, humanities, military studies; brs in Oktyabrsky, Salavat, Sterlitamak
Rector: AYRAT M. SHAMMAZOV
Library of 1,031,930 vols
Number of teachers: 802
Number of students: 14,000

URALSKIY GOSUDARSTVENNYY LESOTEHNICHESKIY UNIVERSITET (Ural State Forest Engineering University)

260100 Ekaterinburg, ul. Sibirsky Trakt 37
Telephone: (343) 254-65-06
Fax: (343) 254-62-25
E-mail: general@usfeu.ru
Internet: www.usfeu.ru
Founded 1930
State control
Language of instruction: Russian
Academic year: September to June
Rector: Prof. ANDREY V. MEKHRENTSEV
Pro-Rector for Educational Work: SERGEY I. KOLESNIKOV
Pro-Rector for Innovation Activity and Int. Cooperation: NATALIA A. SHPAK
Pro-Rector for Scientific Work: Prof. SERGEY V. ZALESOV
Librarian: LUDMILA K. BUKVAREVA
Library of 878,000 vols, 260 periodical titles
Number of teachers: 473
Number of students: 8,400

DEANS

Faculty of Complementary Education: Prof. LEO G. SHVAMM
Faculty of Correspondence: Prof. ANATOLY V. KAPRALOV
Faculty of Ecological Engineering: Prof. ALESJA V. VURASKO
Faculty of Economics and Management: Prof. VICTOR P. CHASOVSKIH
Faculty of Forestry: Prof. ZUFAR YA. NAGIMOV
Faculty of Forestry Engineering: Prof. EDWARD F. GUERZ
Faculty of Humanities: IRINA G. SVETLOVA
Faculty of Mechanical Engineering: Prof. VALERY P. SIVAKOV
Faculty of Professional Education: OLGA A. UDACHINA
Faculty of Wood Technology: Prof. YURY I. TRAKALO

URALS STATE MINING UNIVERSITY

620144 Ekaterinburg, ul. Kuibysheva 30
Telephone: (3432) 22-25-47
Fax: (3432) 29-48-38
E-mail: office@usmga.ru
Internet: www.usmga.ru
Founded 1914 as Ekaterinburg Mining Institute; as Sverdlovsk Mining Institute 1934–1993; as Urals State Acad. of Mining and Geology 1993–2004; present name and status 2004

Faculties of economics, environmental engineering, geology, geophysics, mining engineering, mining technology
Rector: Prof. NIKOLAI P. KOSAREV
Library of 800,000 vols
Number of teachers: 1,500
Number of students: 6,000

URALS STATE TECHNICAL UNIVERSITY

620002 Ekaterinburg, ul. Mira 19
Telephone: (343) 374-54-34
Fax: (343) 374-38-84
E-mail: inter@inter.ustu.ru
Internet: www.ustu.ru
Founded 1920
Faculties of chemical technology, civil engineering, construction materials, economics and management, electrical engineering, heat and power engineering, mechanical engineering, metallurgy, physical engineering, humanities, physical training and sport, radio engineering
Rector: Prof. STANISLAV S. NABOICHENKO
Library of 2m. vols
Number of teachers: 2,233
Number of students: 35,000

URALS STATE UNIVERSITY OF RAILWAY TRANSPORT

620034 Ekaterinburg, ul. Kolmogorova 66
Telephone and fax (343) 245-34-67
E-mail: rector@usart.ru
Internet: www.usart.ru
Founded 1956
State control; attached to the Min. of Transport of the Russian Federation
Academic year: September to June
Faculties of construction, economics, electrical engineering, electrification, mechanics, traffic management
Rector: Prof. ALEXANDER V. EFIMOV
Vice-Rector for Int. Affairs: BORIS M. GOTLIB
Library of 600,000 vols
Number of teachers: 580
Number of students: 10,186 ; 6,000 full-time, 4,186 correspondence
Publication: *Research Reviews* (every 2 years).

VOLGOGRAD STATE TECHNICAL UNIVERSITY

400131 Volgograd, pr. Lenina 28
Telephone: (8442) 23-66-35
Fax: (8442) 23-41-21
E-mail: rector@vstu.ru
Internet: www.vstu.ru
Founded 1930
Academic year: September to June
Faculties: automobile transport, chemical technology, construction materials technology, economics and business administration, electronics and computer science, evening faculty (Kirovsky district), machine building, preparatory faculty for foreign students, preparatory training faculty, training and retraining evening faculty (Traktorzavodsky district)
Rector: Prof. IVAN A. NOVAKOV
Vice-Rector for Int. Relations and Cooperation: Prof. ALEXANDER A. CHUGUNOV
Library of 1,235,810 vols
Number of teachers: 1,112
Number of students: 18,000
Publication: *Polytekhnik* (26 a year)

DEANS
A. V. BELOV
A. E. GODENKO
V. F. KABLOV
VASILIY G. KARABAN
YURI Y. KOMAROV
OLEG D. KOSOV
S. M. LEDENEV
A. P. MANTOROSHIN
YURI P. MUKHA
YURI I. OSADSHY
O. P. OTCHENASHEV
A. N. SAVKIN
N. I. ZUBAN

VOLGOGRAD STATE UNIVERSITY OF ARCHITECTURE AND CIVIL ENGINEERING

400074 Volgograd, Akademicheskaya ul. 1

Telephone: (8442) 97-48-72
Fax: (8442) 97-49-33
E-mail: info@vgasu.ru
Internet: www.vgasu.ru

Founded 1952, present name and status 2003

5 Br. institutes: Institute of Architecture and Civil Engineering, Institute of Traffic Engineering, Institute of Economics and Law, Institute of Ecology, Institute of Distance Education; attached institute: Volzhsky Institute of Civil Engineering and Technologies

Rector: SERGEY YU. KALASHNIKOV

Library: 1.1m. vols
Number of teachers: 879
Number of students: 12,026

VOLOGDA STATE TECHNICAL UNIVERSITY

160000 Vologda, ul. Lenina 15

Telephone: (8172) 72-46-45
E-mail: rector_s@mh.vstu.edu.ru
Internet: www.vstu.edu.ru

Founded 1975 as Vologda Polytechnic Institute

Brs in Cherepovets and Veliky Ostyug

Rector: Prof. RUSLAN V. DERYAGIN

Library: 1.2m. vols.

VORONEZH STATE TECHNICAL UNIVERSITY

394026 Voronezh, Moskovsky pr. 14

Telephone: (0732) 21-09-19
Fax: (0732) 78-38-91
E-mail: rector@vorstu.ru
Internet: www.vorstu.ru

Faculties of automation and mechanization of engineering, aviation, automation and electrical engineering, engineering economics, radio engineering, physical engineering

Rector: Prof. VADIM N. FROPOV

Library of 700,000 vols.

VYATKA STATE TECHNICAL UNIVERSITY

610601 Kirov, GSP (Centre), Moskovskaya ul. 36

Telephone and fax (8332) 62-65-71
E-mail: root@kpicnit.vyatka.su

Founded 1963

Faculties of electrical engineering, automation and computer technology, chemical technology, construction engineering, socioeconomics and machine engineering

Rector: Prof. VASILY M. KONDRATOV

Library: 1m. vols

Publication: *Transactions.*

YAROSLAVL STATE TECHNICAL UNIVERSITY

150053 Yaroslavl, Moskovsky pr. 88

Telephone: (0852) 44-15-19
E-mail: webmaster@ystu.ru
Internet: www.ystu.ru

Founded 1944; present name and status 1994

Rector: Prof. YURI A. MOSKVICHEV
Number of students: 5,000

Academies

ARCHITECTURE AND CIVIL ENGINEERING

Ivanovo Academy of Civil Engineering and Architecture: 153002 Ivanovo, ul. 8 Marta 20; tel. (0932) 32-85-40; fax (0932) 30-00-74; e-mail post@iisi.asinet.ivanovo.su; f. 1981; facilities: construction technology, economics, architecture; library: 250,000 vols; Rector Prof. Dr S. V. FEDOSOV.

Tomsk State Academy of Civil Engineering: 634003 Tomsk, Solyanaya pl. 2; tel. 75-39-30; fax 75-33-58; f. 1952; faculties: architecture, civil and industrial construction engineering, road building, mechanical engineering, technology; library: 638,000 vols; 458 teachers; 5,086 students; Rector G. M. ROGOV.

Tyumen Civil Engineering and Architectural Academy: 625001 Tyumen, ul. Lunacharskogo 2; tel. (3452) 46-10-10; fax (3452) 46-23-90; e-mail tumgasa@sbtx.tmn.ru; internet www.tumgasa.ru; f. 1971; faculties: construction, engineering networks and systems, road building, economics and management; 360 teachers; 5,000 students; Rector Dr TCHIKICHEV.

Ural State Academy of Architecture and Arts: 620075 Ekaterinburg, ul. Karla Libknekhta 23; tel. (3432) 51-33-69; fax (3432) 51-95-32; e-mail vgafurov@usaaa.ru; internet www.usaaa.ru; f. 1972 (fmrly Sverdlovsk Architectural Institute); depts of architecture, applied decorative art, design, fashion design, monumental decorative art, urban planning; library: 80,000 vols; 1,100 students; Rector A. A. STARIKOV; publ. *Architecton* (4 a year).

Voronezh State University of Architecture and Civil Engineering: 394006 Voronezh, 20-Letiya Oktyabrya ul. 84; tel. (0732) 71-52-68; fax (0732) 71-58-54; e-mail rectorat@vgasu.vrn.ru; internet www.vgasu.vrn.ru; f. 1930; academic year September to July; faculties of arts, automation and information systems, architecture, construction, construction technology, engineering economics, engineering systems and buildings, mechanical engineering and highway construction; distance learning courses available; Rector IGOR S. SUROVTSEV; library: 500,000 vols; 485 teachers; 7,981 students; publ. *Scientific Bulletin* (colln of scientific articles, 1 a year).

AGRICULTURE AND VETERINARY SCIENCE

Belgorod State Agricultural Academy: 309103 Belgorod oblast, pos. Maiskii, Vavilova ul. 1; tel. (0722) 39-21-79; fax (0722) 39-11-74; e-mail bsaa@csn.ru; internet www.bsaa.edu.ru; f. 1978; 490 teachers; 4,500 students; Rector ALEXANDR V. TURIANSKY.

Bryansk State Agricultural Academy: 243365 Bryansk oblast, Vygonichesky r-n, pos. Kokino; tel. (8341) 2-43-21; e-mail bgsha@bitmcnit.bryansk.su; internet www.bgsha.com; f. 1980; library: 385,000 vols, 150 periodicals; Rector Prof. NIKOLAI M. BELUS;

publ. *Collection of Scientific Papers* (1 a year).

Buryat State Agricultural Academy: 670024 Ulan-Ude, Pushkina ul. 8; tel. (3012) 34-26-11; fax (3012) 34-22-54; e-mail bgsha@eastsib.ru; f. 1932; depts: animal husbandry, agronomy, veterinary medicine, economics, farm mechanization, land tenure regulations, accounting, management; library: 582,000 vols; 325 teachers; 4,800 students; Rector Prof. ALEXANDER P. POPOV.

Chuvash State Agricultural Academy: 428000 Cheboksary, K. Marksa ul. 29; tel. (8352) 22-23-34; depts: agronomy, mechanization, animal husbandry; library: 83,000 vols; Rector NIKOLAI K. KIRILLOV.

Dagestan State Agricultural Academy: 367032 Makhachkala, M. Gadzhieva ul. 180; tel. (8722) 68-24-70; f. 1932; Rector MAGOMED M. DZHAMBULATOV; library: 200,000 vols; publ. *Works*; fields of study: zootechnics, veterinary, fruit and vegetable growing, accountancy.

Irkutsk State Agricultural Academy: 664038 Irkutsk, pos. Molodozhny; tel. (3952) 39-93-30; fax (3952) 39-94-18; e-mail rector@ishi.baikal.ru; internet www.irgsha.narod.ru; f. 1934; depts at main campus: economics, accounting, computer engineering, agronomy, agroecology, soil management, energy engineering, mechanization, zoological engineering, veterinary science, wildlife management; Chita campus: economics, accounting, agronomy, mechanization, zoological engineering; library: 504,814 vols; 357 teachers; 7,736 students; br. in Chita; Rector ALEXANDER A. DOLGOPOLOV.

Ivanovo Agricultural Academy: 153012 Ivanovo, Sovetskaya ul. 45; tel. and fax (0932) 32-81-44; e-mail ivgsha@tpi.ru; f. 1918; depts: agronomy, zootechnics, veterinary medicine, mechanization in agriculture, service and exploitation of farm machines and equipment, land use and land distribution, economics and management in rural production, agroecology; library: 260,364 vols; 211 teachers; 3,328 students; Rector V.F. TSARYOV.

Izhevsk State Agricultural Academy: Udmurt Republic, 426069 Izhevsk, Studencheskaya ul. 11; tel. (3412) 58-99-48; fax (3412) 58-99-47; e-mail root@isa.udm.ru; internet isa.udm.ru; f. 1954; depts: agronomy, animal husbandry, veterinary science, forestry, mechanization, bookkeeping and agricultural analysis, economics, mechanization of the processing of farm produce; library: 500,000 vols; 357 teachers; 6,038 students; extra-mural faculty; Pres. Prof. V. V. FOKIN.

Kazan State Academy of Veterinary Medicine 'N. E. Bauman': Tatarstan, 420074 Kazan, Sibirsky trakt ul.; tel. (8432) 76-15-05; f. 1873; advanced training of veterinary and animal husbandry specialists; library: 410,000 vols; 230 teachers; 3,700 students; Rector Acad. G. Z. IDRISOV; publ. *Nauchnye Trudy* (4–5 a year).

Kazan State Agricultural Academy: 420015 Kazan, Karla Marksa ul. 65; tel. (8432) 36-65-22; fax (8432) 36-66-51; internet www.ksha.ru; fields of study: agronomy, mechanization, economics and management, accounting; library: 135,000 vols; Rector Prof. DZHAUDAT I. FAIZRAKHMANOV.

Kostroma State Agricultural Academy: 156530 Kostroma, p/o Karavaevo; tel. (942) 54-12-63; fax (942) 54-34-23; e-mail mobot@ksaa.edu.ru; internet www.ksaa.edu.ru; f. 1949; depts of agronomy, zootechnics, veterinary science, farm mechanization, automobiles and automobile facilities, service and operation of vehicles and machines, electrifi-

cation and automation of agricultural production, application of computers, architecture, industrial and civil engineering,
economics and management, accountancy
and auditing, finance and credit, fundamentals of law in agriculture, agricultural management; library: 510,000 vols; 370 teachers;
5,100 students; Rector V. I. VOROBEV.

**Kursk State Agricultural Academy 'I. I.
Ivanov':** 305034 Kursk, Karla Marksa ul. 70;
tel. (0712) 33-06-05; fax (0712) 23-13-30;
e-mail academy@kgsha.ru; internet www
.kgsha.ru; f. 1956; fields of study: agronomy,
plant protection, zootechnics, mechanization,
economics and management, accounting,
agroecology, veterinary medicine, seed processing and storage; library: 130,000 vols;
Rector VLADIMIR D. FLOUR.

**Moscow Agricultural Academy 'K. A.
Timiryazev':** 127550 Moscow, Timiryazevskaya ul. 49; tel. (495) 976-04-80; fax (495)
976-29-10; e-mail info@timacad.ru; internet
www.timacad.ru; f. 1865; faculties of agricultural chemistry, agronomy, agropedagogy,
horticulture, economics, soil science and
ecology, zootechnics; 33 attached research
stations and 5 experimental and instructional farms; br. in Kaluga; library: 1.5m.
vols; 650 teachers; 10,000 students; Rector
Prof VLADIMIR M. BAUTIM; publs *Papers of
TSHA* (1 a year), *Proceedings of TSHA* (6 a
year).

**Moscow State Academy of Veterinary
Medicine and Biotechnology 'K. I.
Skryabin':** 100472 Moscow, Akad. K. I.
Skryabina 23 ul.; tel. (495) 377-91-17; f.
1919; faculties: veterinary biological science,
animal husbandry, pedagogical, animal products; library: 500,000 vols; 360 teachers;
3,500 students; Rector Acad. A. D. BELOV.

**Nizhnii Novgorod State Agricultural
Academy:** 603078 Nizhnii Novgorod pr.
Gagarina 97; tel. (8312) 66-07-30; fax (8312)
66-06-84; f. 1930; fields of study: accounting,
agrochemistry, agronomy, animal husbandry, mechanization, veterinary medicine;
library: 500,000 vols; 5,000 students; Rector
ALEZEY GALKIN; publ. *Scientific Works* (1 a
year).

Penza State Agricultural Academy:
440014 Penza, Botanicheskaya ul. 30; tel.
and fax (841) 259-63-54; e-mail psaca@penza
.com.ru; internet pgsha.penza.com.ru; f.
1951; fields of study incl. agronomy, agroecology, animal husbandry, mechanization of
agriculture, machine repairing, book-keeping
and auditing, economics, administration,
farm production technology, motor vehicles
and motor vehicle management; library:
264,000 vols; 264 teachers; 3,500 students;
Rector Prof. VLADIMIR D. KOROTNEV.

**Perm Agricultural Academy 'Acad. D. N.
Pryanishnikov':** 614600 Perm, Kommunisticheskaya ul. 23; tel. and fax (3422) 12-53-
94; e-mail pgsha@permregion.ru; f. 1918;
depts: agrochemistry and soil science, agronomy, animal husbandry, mechanization, economics and management, accounting,
forestry, food technology, applied informatics; library: 320,000 vols; 376 teachers; 9,000
students; Rector YU. N. ZUBAREV.

Primorsky State Agricultural Academy:
692510 Ussuriisk, pr. Blyukhera 44; tel.
(42341) 6-33-91; fax (42341) 6-03-13; e-mail
agracad@hotbox.ru; internet www.primacad
.ru; institutes: land management and farming, animal husbandry and veterinary medicine, forestry, economics and business, farm
mechanization, staff upgrading and retraining for the agro-industrial complex; f. 1957;
library: 380,000 vols; 500 teachers; 5,000
students; Rector A. A. DYOMIN.

Ryazan State Agricultural Academy:
390044 Ryazan, Kostycheva ul. 1; tel. (0912)

55-35-01; fax (0912) 55-10-70; e-mail rsaa@
narod.ru; internet www.rsaa.narod.ru; fields
of study: agronomy, animal husbandry,
mechanization, economics and management,
accounting; library: 94,000 vols; Rector GEN-
NADY M. TUNIKOV.

**St Petersburg Academy of Forestry
Technology:** 194018 St Petersburg, Institutsky per. 5; tel. (812) 550-07-00; fax (812)
550-08-15; f. 1803; faculties of chemical
technology, engineering economics, forest
machinery, forestry, forestry engineering,
mechanical technology of timber; br. in
Syktyvkar; library: 1.4m. vols; 613 teachers;
9,000 students; Rector Prof. V. I. ONEGIN;
publ. *Nauchnye trudy* (1 a year).

Tyumen State Agricultural Academy:
625003 Tyumen, Respubliki ul. 7; tel. and
fax (3452) 46-16-50; e-mail acadagro@tmn
.ru; internet www.tgsha.ru; f. 1879; attached
institutes of agronomy and ecology, finance
and management, veterinary medicine and
aquaculture; library: 700,000 vols; 250 teachers; 5,000 students; Rector Dr NIKOLAI V.
ABRAMOV.

Ulyanovsk State Agricultural Academy:
432601 Ulyanovsk, bul. Novy Venets 1; tel.
and fax (88422) 31-42-72; e-mail academy@
mv.ru; internet www.academy.mv.ru; f.
1943; depts of agronomy, animal husbandry,
mechanization, veterinary, medicine, economics; library: 452,000 vols; 312 teachers;
4,248 students; Rector B. I. ZOTOV.

**Urals State Academy of Veterinary
Medicine:** 457100 Chelyabinsk oblast,
Troitsk, Gagarina ul. 13; tel. (3516) 32-00-
10; fax (3516) 32-04-72; internet www.ugavm
.boom.ru; f. 1929; library: 200,000 vols; 180
teachers; 1,434 students; Rector Prof. V.
LAZARENKO.

Urals State Agricultural Academy:
620219 Ekaterinburg, K. Libknekhta ul. 42;
tel. (3432) 51-33-63; fax (3432) 51-24-80;
e-mail academy@usaca.ru; internet www
.usaca.ru; f. 1940; library: 450,000 vols; 700
teachers; 2,500 students; Rector ALEXANDER
N. SEMIN.

**Velikie Luki State Agricultural Acad-
emy:** 182100 Pskov oblast, Velikie Luki, pl.
V. I. Lenina 1; tel. (81153) 3-77-28; fax
(81153) 3-26-73; e-mail vgsha@mart.ru; f.
1958; depts: agronomy and ecology, economics, animal husbandry, engineering; library:
390,000 vols; 291 teachers; 4,114 students;
Rector Prof. V. P. SPASOV; publ. *Works* (1 a
year).

Volgograd State Agricultural Academy:
400041 Volgograd, Institutskaya ul. 8; tel.
(8442) 43-08-45; fax (8442) 43-18-07; f. 1944;
depts: agronomy, animal husbandry, farm
mechanization, farm electrification, ecology
and land reclamation, accounting; library:
568,000 vols; 4,000 students; Rector Acad. A.
M. GAVRILOV; publ. *Scientific Information* (2
a year).

**Vologda State Dairy Academy 'N. V.
Vereschagin':** 160555 Vologda pos. Moloch-
noe, Shmidta ul. 2; tel. (8172) 76-17-30; fax
(8172) 76-10-69; e-mail rector@molochnoe.ru;
internet www.molochnoe.ru; f. 1911; library:
420,000 vols; 270 teachers; 4,000 students;
Rector Dr VLADIMIR N. OSTRETSOV; publ.
Works.

**Voronezh State Academy of Forestry
Engineering:** 394613 Voronezh, Timiryazeva ul. 8; tel. (0732) 53-74-98; fax (0732)
53-86-10; e-mail postmaster@julygb.vsi.ru;
internet vglta.vrn.ru; f. 1918; faculties: forest
engineering, forestry, wood-processing technology, motor-vehicle engineering, forest
industry economics and management, furniture design, forest machinery and equipment, safety traffic regulation, landscape

gardening, gamekeeping and national parks
management, international wood trade,
industrial process automation; library:
568,000 vols; 397 teachers; 5,500 students;
Rector Prof. V. K. POPOV.

Vyatka State Agricultural Academy:
610017 Kirov, Oktyabrsky pr. 133; tel.
(8332) 62-97-19; fax (8332) 62-23-17; e-mail
vsaa@vit.kirov.ru; f. 1930; depts: agronomy,
biology, economics, veterinary medicine,
mechanization; library: 407,000 vols; Rector
A. K. BOLOTOV.

ECONOMICS, LAW AND POLITICS

Academy of Social Sciences: 117606 Moscow, pr. Vernadskogo 84; tel. (95) 436-93-30;
f. 1946; library: 2m. vols; Rector R. G.
YUNOVSKII.

**Finance Academy under the Govern-
ment of the Russian Federation:** 125468
Moscow, Leningradsky pr. 49; tel. (495) 943-
98-55; fax (495) 157-70-70; e-mail academy@
fa.ru; internet www.fa.ru; f. 1918; institutes
and depts: finance, credit, financial management, insurance, taxes and taxation,
accounting and audit, international economic
relations, mathematical methods in economics and crisis management, tax police, evening school, distance learning, short-term retraining and skill development; 21st-Century
International Finance University; MBA
Business School; 650 teachers; 10,000 students; Rector A. G. GRYAZNOVA.

Irkutsk State Academy of Economics:
664001 Irkutsk, ul. Lenina 11; tel. (3952) 24-
10-55; fax (3952) 24-28-38; e-mail kvm@cc
.isea.baikal.ru; f. 1930; faculties: law, world
economics, finance, economics of mining
industry and construction, economics of
engineering and road transport, accounting,
information systems, labour economics, public administration, management, economics
of using natural resources; library: 530,000
vols; Rector M. A. VINOKUROV.

**Khabarovsk State Academy of Econom-
ics and Law:** 680042 Khabarovsk, Tikhookeanskaya ul. 134; tel. (4212) 35-87-37; fax
(4212) 72-79-14; auditing and accounting,
finance, management, commerce, law, foreign economic relations; library: 400,000
vols; 220 teachers; 7,000 students; Rector
Prof. V. A. LIKHOBABIN.

Polar Academy: 192007 St Petersburg,
Voronezhskaya ul. 79, A/Ya 533; tel. (812)
167-04-52; fax (812) 167-08-50; f. 1992; Mas-
ter-level training of students from native
Siberian peoples, who are expected to be
appointed to high administrative posts in
northern and far eastern Siberia; 60 teachers; 100 students; Rector AZURGET CHAUKEN-
VAEVA; publ. *Polarnaya Akademia* (2 a year).

**Russian Academy of Economics 'G. V.
Plekhanov':** 115998 Moscow M-54, Stre-
myannyi per. 36; tel. (095) 237-85-17; fax
(095) 237-95-18; e-mail inter@rea.ru;
internet www.rea.ru; f. 1907; faculties: general economics, finance, taxation, national
economy, trade in commodities, economics
and mathematics, economics and engineering, international economic relations; graduate school; library: 815,000 vols; 1,000
teachers; 12,000 students; Rector V. I. VIDYA-
PIN.

**St Petersburg State Academy of Engin-
eering and Economics:** 191002 St Petersburg, ul. Marata 27; tel. (812) 112-06-33; fax
(812) 112-06-07; e-mail oms@engec.ru;
internet www.engec.ru; f. 1930; institutes:
industrial economics and management,
regional economics and management, transport economics and management, management information systems, general
management of business and finance, tour-

ism and hotel management; library: 370,000 vols; 310 teachers; 3,540 students; Rector A. I. MIKHAILUSHKIN; publ. *Scientific Proceedings of the Institute* (1 a year).

Samara State Academy of Economics: 443090 Samara, ul. Sovetskoi Armii 141; tel. (8462) 22-15-42; fax (8462) 22-09-53; f. 1931; faculties: finance, industrial economics, commerce and marketing, agribusiness, law, management, accounting; library: 596,000 vols; Rector Prof. A. I. NOSKOV.

Saratov State Academy of Law: 410720 Saratov, Chernyshevskogo ul. 104; tel. (8452) 25-04-86; fax (8452) 25-32-78; e-mail post@sgap.ru; internet www.sgap.ru; f. 1931; library: 500,000 vols; 300 teachers; 3,000 students; Rector FEDOR A. GRIGORYEV; publ. *Vestnik Saratovskoi gosudarstvennoi academii prava.*

Urals State Academy of Law: 620066 Ekaterinburg, Komsomolskaya ul. 21; tel. (3432) 74-43-63; fax (3432) 74-50-34; e-mail rektorat@usla.ru; internet www.usla.ru; f. 1931; library: 850,000 vols; 327 teachers; 7,310 students; Rector Prof. VIKTOR D. PEREVALOV; publ. *Russian Law Journal* (4 a year).

Volgograd Academy of Public Administration: 400131 Volgograd Gagarina ul. 8; tel. (8442) 33-58-39; fax (8442) 36-29-51; e-mail rector@vags.ru; internet www.vags .ru; f. 1992 to prepare and develop qualified administrators for government and non-profit positions; br. in Astrakhan; 250 teachers; 3,000 students; Rector MIKHAIL A. SUKIASYAN.

ENGINEERING AND INDUSTRY

Ivanovo State Textile Academy: 153000 Ivanovo, pr. F. Engels 21; tel. (0932) 32-85-45; fax (0932) 41-21-08; e-mail rector@igta .ru; internet www.igta.ru; f. 1918; Rector Prof. VLADIMIR V. ZRYUKIN; Vice-Rectors Prof. ALEXANDER A. TUVIN (Complementary Education), Prof. ALEXANDER N. SMIRNOV (Information and Int. Relations), Prof. GRIGORY I. CHRISTOBORODOV (Scientific and Industrial Activity), Prof. VLADIMIR V. LYUBIMTSEV (Studies); library 740,911 vols; 388 teachers (incl. 51 professors); 8,488 students; publ. *Technology of Textile Industry* (6 a year).

Moscow State Academy of Light Industry: 113127 Moscow, ul. Osipenko 33; tel. (495) 231-58-01; faculties: chemical technology, sewn goods technology, mechanical, leather goods technology, engineering economics; br. in Novosibirsk; library: 392,000 vols; Rector V. A. FUKIN.

Siberian State Academy of Mining and Metallurgy: 654007 Kemerovo oblast, Novokuznetsk, pr. Kirova 42; tel. (3843) 46-35-02; fax (3843) 46-57-92; faculties: mining, metallurgy, electrometallurgy, foundry work, mechanical, technology, construction; library: 1,010,000 vols; 620 teachers; 6,000 students; Rector N. M. KULAGIN.

MEDICINE

Astrakhan State Medical Academy: 414000 Astrakhan, Bakinskaya ul. 121; tel. (8512) 22-70-16; fax (8512) 39-41-30; e-mail agma@astranet.ru; internet www.agma .astranet.ru; f. 1918; library: 700,000 vols; 520 teachers; 3,500 students; Rector Prof. VALENTIN M. MIROSHNIKOV.

Blagoveshchensk State Medical Academy: 675006 Blagoveshchensk, Gorkogo ul. 95; tel. (4162) 2-27-13; tel. (4162) 2-28-68; 264 teachers; 1,681 students.

Chelyabinsk State Medical Academy: 454092 Chelyabinsk, Vorovskogo ul. 64; tel. (3512) 34-16-86; fax (3512) 34-03-36; internet www.vita.chel.su; library: 500,000 vols; 3,000 students; Rector Prof. YURI S. SHAMUROV.

Chita State Medical Academy: 672090 Chita, Gorkogo ul. 39A; tel. (3022) 23-41-63; fax (3022) 32-30-58; e-mail macadem@mail .chita.ru; f. 1953; library: 387,000 vols; 311 teachers; 2,400 students; Rector VLADIMIR N. IVANOV.

Dagestan State Medical Academy: 367025 Dagestan Autonomous Republic, Makhachkala, pl. Lenina 6; tel. (8722) 67-07-94; fax (8722) 68-12-80; e-mail dgma@iwt .ru; internet www.dgma.ru; Rector ABDUR-AKHMAN O. OSMANOV.

Ivanovo State Medical Academy: 153462 Ivanovo, pr. F. Engelsa 8; tel. (0932) 30-17-66; fax (0932) 32-66-04; e-mail adm@isma .ivanovo.ru; internet www.isma.ivanovo.ru; f. 1930; library: 545,059 vols; 578 teachers; 2,084 students; Rector Prof. RUDOLF R. SHILYAEV.

Izhevsk State Medical Academy: 426034 Udmurt Republic, Izhevsk, Revolyutsion-naya ul. 199; tel. (3412) 52-62-01; fax (3412) 65-81-67; e-mail rector@igma.udm.ru; internet www.igma.udm.ru; f. 1933; library: 402,000 vols; 387 teachers; 2,500 students; Rector Prof. NIKOLAI S. STRELKOV.

Kemerovo State Medical Academy: 650029 Kemerovo, Voroshilova ul. 22A; tel. and fax (3842) 73-48-55; e-mail ksma@ksma .kuzstu.ac.ru; internet www.ksma.kuzstu.ac.ru; f. 1956; library: 390,681 vols; 461 teachers; 3,573 students; Rector ALEXANDER YA. EVTUSHENKO.

Krasnoyarsk State Medical Academy: 660022 Krasnoyarsk, Partizana Zheleznyaka ul. 1; tel. (3912) 27-49-24; fax (3912) 23-78-35; e-mail onmpi@krsk.infotel.ru; internet www.krasgma.ru; f. 1942; library: 472,000 vols; 609 teachers; 3,270 students; Rector Prof. VICTOR I. PROKHORENKOV; publ. *Medical Man* (12 a year).

Kuban State Medical Academy: 350614 Krasnodar, Sedina ul. 4; tel. and fax (8612) 68-34-57; e-mail corpus@ksma.kubannet.ru; internet www.ksma.ru; f. 1920, present name and status 1994; library: 560,000 vols; 600 teachers; 5,000 students; Rector BORIS G. ERMOSHENKO.

Nizhnii Novgorod State Medical Academy: 603005 Nizhnii Novgorod, pl. Minina i Pozharskogo 10/1; tel. and fax (8312) 39-06-43; e-mail nnsma@sandy.ru; internet www .n-nov.mednet.com; f. 1920; 645 teachers; 3,542 students; library: 480,000 vols; publ. *Zhurnal* (4 a year); Rector Prof. VYACHESLAV V. SHKARIN.

North Ossetia State Medical Academy: 362019 North Ossetia, Vladikavkaz, Push-kinskaya ul. 40; tel. (8672) 53-42-21; fax (8672) 53-03-97; e-mail nosma@dol.ru; f. 1796; 278 teachers; library: 265,000 vols; Rector Prof. KAZBEK D. SALBIEV.

Novosibirsk State Medical Academy: 630091 Novosibirsk, Krasnyi pr., 52; tel. and fax (3832) 22-32-04; e-mail rector@ medin.nsc.ru; internet www.medin.nsc.ru; f. 1935; academic year September to June (2 semesters); faculties of clinical psychology, ecology, international physicians, laboratory medicine, medicine, paediatrics, physicians' and professors' improving and retraining and preparatory studies, nurses' training, pharmaceutical science, social activity, stomatology, traditional medicine; evening lyceum, institute of public health economics and management; library: 400,000 specialized vols and periodicals; 784 teachers; 4,500 students; Rector Prof. ANATOLY V. EFREMOV; publs *Eksperimentalnaya klinicheskaya medicina* (Experimental Clinical Medicine, 4 a year), *Meditsinskaya Gazeta* (Medical Newspaper, 26 a year).

Omsk State Medical Academy: 644099 Omsk, Lenina ul. 12; tel. (3812) 23-32-89; fax (3812) 23-14-57; e-mail osma@omsk-osma .ru; internet www.omsk-osma.ru; f. 1921; faculties: therapeutic and preventive medicine, paediatrics, stomatology; library: 573,199 vols; Rector Prof. ALEXANDER I. NOVIKOV.

Orenburg State Medical Academy: 460014 Orenburg, Sovetskaya ul. 6; tel. (3532) 77-61-03; fax (3532) 77-94-08; library: 160,000 vols; Rector SERGEI A. PAVLOVICHEV.

Perm State Medical Academy: 614600 Perm, Kuybyshevskaya ul. 39; tel. (3422) 90-44-53; fax (3422) 33-84-55; e-mail med@ psma.ru; internet www.psma.ru; library: 541,000 vols; Rector Prof. VLADIMIR A. CHERKASSOV.

St Petersburg State Academy of Paediatric Medicine: 194100 St Petersburg, Litovskaya ul. 2; tel. (812) 245-06-46; fax (812) 245-40-85; f. 1925; library: 600,000 vols; Rector V. V. LEVANOVICH.

St Petersburg State Chemical-Pharmaceutical Academy: 197376 St Petersburg, ul. Professora Popova 14; tel. (812) 234-57-29; fax (812) 234-60-44; e-mail rector@spcpa .ru; internet www.spcpa.ru; f. 1919; faculties: drug industry technology, pharmacy, further education; library: 334,200 vols; 250 teachers; 2,000 students; Rector G.P. YAKOVLEV.

St Petersburg State Medical Academy 'I. I. Mechnikov': 195067 St Petersburg, Piskarevsky pr. 47; tel. (812) 543-50-14; fax (812) 140-15-24; e-mail mechnik@westcall .net; internet www.mechnik.spb.ru; f. 1907; faculties: pre-medical training, general medical, preventative medicine, advanced nursing, foreign students, further training, advanced training; library: 556,000 vols; 361 teachers; 4,500 students; Rector Prof. ALEXANDER V. SHABROV.

Smolensk State Medical Academy: 214019 Smolensk, Krupskoi ul. 28; tel. and fax (812) 55-26-92; e-mail admsgma@sci .smolensk.ru; internet www.sgma.ru; library: 207,000 vols; Rector Prof. VLADIMIR G. PLESHKOV.

Stavropol State Medical Academy: 355017 Stavropol, Mira ul. 310; tel. (8652) 37-06-92; fax (8652) 37-06-42; e-mail sgma@ statel.stavropol.ru; internet www.stgma.ru; f. 1937; languages of instruction: English, Russian; academic year September to July; Faculties: General Medicine, Stomatology, Paediatrics, Medical College Teaching Skills, Nursing, Postgraduate Studies; 2 attached museums; clinics of ophthalmology, neurology and vertebraneurology; library: 345,000 vols; 525 teachers; 3,500 students; Rector Prof. B. D. MINAEV; publ. *South Russia Medical Magazine* (6 a year).

Tver Medical Academy: 170642 Tver, Sovetskaya ul. 4; tel. (0822) 33-17-79; fax (0822) 33-57-59; library: 446,000 vols; Rector BORIS N. DAVYDOV.

Tyumen Medical Academy: 625023 Tyumen, Odesskaya ul. 54; tel. (3452) 22-62-00; fax (3452) 25-23-19; e-mail tgma@tgma.info; internet www.tgma.info; f. 1963; 515 teachers; 3,256 students.

Urals State Medical Academy: 620219 Ekaterinburg, Repina ul. 3; tel. (3432) 51-14-90; fax (3432) 51-64-00; e-mail info@usma .ru; internet www.usma.ru; f. 1931; areas of study: anaesthesiology, dentistry, epidemiology, gynaecology, obstetrics, ophthalmology, otolaryngology, paediatric surgery, pathology, surgery paediatrics, therapeutics; library: 600,000 vols; Rector Prof. ANATOLY P. YASTREBOV; publ. *Herald* (12 a year).

Voronezh State Medical Academy 'N. N. Burdenko': 394036 Voronezh, Studencheskaya ul. 10; tel. and fax (0732) 53-03-98; e-mail foreign@vsma.ac.ru; internet www.vsma.ac.ru; f. 1918; academic year September to June (two semesters); library: 500,000 vols; 1,105 teachers; 3,850 students; Rector Prof. Dr I. E. YESAULENKO; publs *Applied Informational Aspects in Medicine* (4 a year), *Medical Staff* (12 a year).

Yaroslavl State Medical Academy: 150000 Yaroslavl, Revolutsionnaya ul. 5; tel. (0852) 30-56-41; fax (0852) 30-50-13; e-mail rector@yma.ac.ru; internet www.yma.ac.ru; Rector YURI V. NOVIKOV.

SCIENCE AND TECHNOLOGY

Moscow State Academy of Applied Biotechnology: 109029 Moscow, ul. Talalikhina 33; tel. (495) 276-19-10; fax (495) 276-14-23; f. 1931; faculties: dairy industry technology, meat industry technology, food production, automation, plastics processing, low-temperature technology, veterinary sanitation, book-keeping, management; library: 611,000 vols; Rector IOSIF A. ROGOV.

Moscow State Academy of Food Industry: 125080 Moscow, Volokolamskoe shosse 11; tel. and fax (495) 158-03-71; f. 1931; food technology, chemical engineering and biotechnology, information systems in economics, management and marketing, machinery, informatics, power engineering, agricultural engineering; 500 teaching staff; library: 1m. vols; 6,000 students; Pres. Prof. V. I. TUZHILKIN.

Moscow State Academy of Instrumentation and Informatics: 107076 Moscow, ul. Stromynka 20; tel. (495) 268-01-01; faculties: automation in instrument making, engineering, transport and power machine building; library: 250,000 vols; Rector Prof. BORIS M. MIKHAILOV.

Moscow State Geological Prospecting Academy: 117873 Moscow, ul. Miklukho-Maklaya 23; tel. (495) 433-62-56; fax (495) 433-56-33; faculties: geology, geophysics, hydrogeology, prospecting engineering and mining, economics; library: 410,335 vols; 439 teachers; 3,964 students; Rector L. G. GRABCHAK; publ *Geology and Prospecting* (6 a year).

Ryazan State Radio Engineering Academy: 390005 Ryazan, ul. Gagarina 59/1; tel. (0912) 72-18-44; fax (0912) 72-22-15; f. 1951; faculties: automation and telemechanics, computer technology, electronics, engineering economics, humanities, radio engineering, radio equipment design; library: 720,000 vols; Rector V. K. ZLOBIN.

Rybinsk State Academy of Aviation Technology: 152934 Rybinsk, ul. Pushkina 53; tel. (0855) 52-09-90; fax (0855) 21-39-64; e-mail root@rgata.adm.yar.ru; internet www.rgata.yaroslavl.ru; f. 1955; faculties: aerotechnology, informatics, radioelectronics, rocket technology; library: c. 500,000 vols; 230 teachers; 4,000 students; Rector Prof. V. F. BEZYAZICHNY; publs *Scientific Notes* (1 a year), *Vestnik* (1 a year).

St Petersburg Academy of Civil Aviation: 196210 St Petersburg, ul. Pilotov 38; tel. (812) 291-28-43; faculty: air traffic control; Rector P. V. KARTAMYSHEV.

St Petersburg State Academy of Aerospace Instrumentation: 190000 St Petersburg, Bol. Morskaya ul. 67; tel. (812) 117-15-22; fax (812) 313-70-18; e-mail common@aanet.ru; internet www.suai.ru; areas of study: automation, informatics and computer systems, information systems in economics, instrumentation, law, management, radio engineering; Rector Prof. ANATOLY A. OVO-

DENKO; library: 1m. vols; publ. *V polet* (12 a year).

St Petersburg State Academy of Refrigeration and Food Technology: 191002 St Petersburg, ul. Lomonosova 9; tel. (812) 315-36-17; fax (812) 315-05-35; depts of refrigeration engineering, equipment for food manufacturing and commerce, cryogenics and conditioning systems; faculties: refrigeration equipment, equipment for food industry, trade and public catering, cryogenic technology and conditioning; library: 850,000 vols; Rector A. V. BARANENKO.

Siberian State Academy of Geodesy: 630108 Novosibirsk, Plakhotnogo ul. 10; tel. (3832) 43-39-37; fax (3832) 44-30-60; e-mail rektorat@ssga.ru; internet www.ssga.ru; f. 1932; faculties: geodesy and economics, aerial phototopography, cadastre and regional planning, management and regulation of land relations, optics and optoelectronic instruments, correspondence, evening, preliminary training; institutes: surveying and management, cadastre and geographic information systems, remote sensing and natural resources management, optics and optical technologies, distance education; library: 267,000 vols; 345 teachers; 9,500 students; Rector Prof. IVAN V. LESNYKH.

Volga Region State Academy of Telecommunications and Informatics: 443010 Samara, ul. L. Tolstogo 23; tel. and fax (8462) 33-58-56; internet www.psati.ru; f. 1956; faculties: radio engineering, radio communication and television, general engineering, economics, telecommunications and informatics, electrical communication, continuing education, extra-mural; Telecom College of PSATI, regional telecommunications training centre; brs in Stavropol and Orenburg; library: 461,000 vols; 298 teachers; 4,100 students; Rector VLADIMIR A. ANDREEV.

Voronezh State Technological Academy: 394000 Voronezh, pr. Revolyutsii 19; tel. and fax (732) 55-42-67; e-mail rector@vgta.vrn.ru; internet www.vgta.vrn.ru; f. 1930, present name and status 1994; faculties: mechanical, automation, chemical, technological, technology of meat and dairy products; library: 850,000 vols; 491 teachers; 4,800 students; Rector VITALY K. BITYUKOV.

TRANSPORT

Admiral Makarov State Maritime Academy: 199026 St Petersburg, Vasilevskii ostrov, Kosaya Liniya 15A; tel. (812) 217-19-34; fax (812) 217-07-82; f. 1876; faculties: arctic, navigation, radio engineering, international transport management, electrical engineering, marine engineering; brs in Arkhangelsk, Murmansk; library: 762,000 vols; 380 teachers; 4,400 students; Pres. IVAN I. KOSTYLEV.

Baltic Fishing Fleet State Academy: 236029 Kaliningrad oblast, Molodezhnaya ul. 6; tel. (0112) 21-72-04; fax (0112) 51-66-90; e-mail rector@bga.gazinter.net; f. 1966; faculties: economics, marine engineering, navigation, radio engineering; library: 165,426 vols; 253 teachers; 3,000 students; Dir Prof. A. PIMOSHENKO; publ. *Research Work* (1 a year).

Far-Eastern State Maritime Academy: Vladivostok, Verkhneportovaya ul. 50A; tel. (4232) 22-49-58; fmrly Far Eastern Higher School of Marine Engineering; faculties: navigation, ship engineering, management of marine transport, electrical engineering, practical psychology; library: 360,000 vols; Rector V. I. SEDYKH.

Kamchatka State Fishing Fleet Academy: 683003 Petropavlovsk-Kamchatsky,

Klyuchevskaya ul. 35; tel. and fax (41500) 22-45-38; e-mail rektor@marine.kamchatka.su; f. 1987; trains specialists for the fishing industry, navigators, marine engineers, electrical engineers, radio engineers, technologists and refrigeration engineers; library: 70,000 vols; 250 teachers; 2,000 students; Rector BORIS I. OLEINIKOV; publ. *Conference Papers* (1 a year).

Moscow State Academy of Water Transport: 115407 Moscow, ul. Sudostroitelnaya 46; tel. (495) 116-30-88; fax (495) 118-31-11; f. 1980; faculties: marine engineering, operations, navigation, mechanization and automation of ports, hydrotechnical construction, engineering economics, legislation, international economic management for water wransport; library: 106,000 vols; 5,000 students; Rector Prof. N. P. GARANIN.

Novorossiisk State Maritime Academy: 353918 Novorossiisk, pr. Lenina 93; tel. (8617) 23-03-93; fax (8617) 23-22-95; f. 1975; trains specialists in navigation, ship power plant operation, ship electrical and automated equipment operation, ship radio equipment operation, economics and management for the merchant marine; library: 267,000 vols; Dir VASILY GUTSULYAK.

Novosibirsk State Academy of Water Transport: 630099 Novosibirsk, Ul. Shchetinkina 33; tel. (3832) 22-24-28; fax (3832) 22-49-76; e-mail vyacheslavh@mail.ru; f. 1951; faculties: hydroengineering for waterways and ports, navigation and operation of water transport, ship engineers, electrical engineering, water transport management and economics; library: 450,000 vols; 380 teachers; 10,000 students; Dir I. A. RAGULIN.

Volga State Academy of Water Transport: 603600 Nizhnii Novgorod, ul. Nesterova 5; tel. (8312) 36-37-80; fax (8312) 32-17-91; courses in: transport operation and navigation, shipbuilding and ocean technology, land transport systems, electromechanics, electrical engineering, hydrotechnical construction, economics, business management, law; library: 500,000 vols.

Institutes of Higher Education

ARCHITECTURE AND CIVIL ENGINEERING

Moscow Architectural Institute: 103754 Moscow Centre GSP, ul. Rozhdestvenka 11; tel. (495) 924-79-90; fax (495) 921-12-40; e-mail marhi@marhi.ru; internet www.miarch.ru; f. 1866; library: 400,000 vols; 400 teachers; 2,000 students; Pres. ALEKSANDR P. KUDRYAVTSEV.

Moscow Institute of Municipal Economy and Construction: 109807 Moscow, Srednyaya Kalitnikovskaya ul. 30; tel. (495) 278-32-05; fax (495) 278-15-10; f. 1944; faculties of construction, technology, mechanical engineering, urban construction, ecology and sanitary engineering, engineering, management and economics, commerce; 500 teachers; 13,000 students; library: 600,000 vols; Rector N. V. KOLKUNOV.

Novosibirsk Architectural Institute: 630008 Novosibirsk, Belinskogo 151; tel. and fax (3832) 66-42-64; f. 1989; architecture, design; library: 50,000 vols.

AGRICULTURE AND VETERINARY SCIENCE

All-Russian Extra-Mural Agricultural Institute: 143900 Moscow oblast, Balashikha 8; tel. (095) 521-24-64; fax (095) 521-24-

56; f. 1930; depts: agriculture, economics and management, electrification, information technology in economics and law, mechanization, zoological engineering; library: 517,000 vols; Rector L. Y. KISELEV; publ. collections of scientific works of the institute (1 a year).

Azov-Black Sea Institute of Agricultural Mechanization: 347720 Rostov oblast, Zernograd, ul. Lenina 21; tel. (08536) 3-18-31; library: 192,000 vols; Rector B. M. TITOV.

Kabardino-Balkar Land Improvement Institute: 360004 Nalchik, ul. L. Tolstogo 185; tel. (86600) 5-69-43.

Kurgan Agricultural Institute: 641311 Kurgan oblast, Ketovskii raion, selo Lesnikovo; tel. (35222) 9-41-40; f. 1944; depts: agronomy, zootechnics, economics, mechanization, industrial and civil construction; library: 358,600 vols; Rector V. D. PAVLOV.

Omsk Veterinary Institute: 664007 Omsk, Oktyabrskaya ul 92; tel. and fax (3812) 24-15-35; f. 1918; library: 205,000 vols; 229 teachers; 2,600 students; Dir Prof. GENNADY A. KHONIN.

St Petersburg Veterinary Institute: 196006 St Petersburg, Moskovskii pr. 112; tel. (812) 298-36-31; f. 1919; library: 194,000 vols; 140 teachers; 1,340 students; Rector G. S. KUZNETSOV; publ. *Trudy* (Works).

Samara Agricultural Institute: 446400 Kinel, Poselok Ust-Kinelskii; tel. (8462) 4-68-72; f. 1919; depts: agronomy, animal husbandry, mechanization; library: 215,000 vols; 210 teachers; 3,500 students; Rector N. S. SHIBRAEV.

Saratov Animal Husbandry and Veterinary Institute: 410071 Saratov, Bol. Sadovaya 220; tel. (8452) 24-45-32; f. 1918; library: 376,500 vols; 213 teachers; 4,500 students; Rector V. I. VOROBYEV.

Saratov Institute of Agricultural Engineering: 410740 Saratov, Sovetskaya ul. 60; tel. (8452) 24-37-66; f. 1932; library: 550,000 vols; 320 teachers; 3,500 students; Rector A. G. RYBALKO.

Tver Agricultural Institute: 171314 Tver, p/o Sakharovo; tel. (822) 39-92-32.

Yakutsk Agricultural Institute: 677891 Yakutsk, ul. P. Morozova 2; tel. (41122) 2-23-20.

ECONOMICS, LAW AND POLITICS

All-Russian Distance Institute of Finance and Economics: 121807 Moscow, ul. Oleko Dundicha 23; tel. (95) 144-85-19; fax (95) 144-86-19; faculties: finance and credit, accounting, management, marketing; depts and brs in 21 Russian cities; library: 1.5m. vols.

Far Eastern Institute of Trade: 690600 Vladivostok, Okeanskii pr. 19; tel. (4232) 2-50-89; f. 1964; faculties: economics, accounting, foodstuffs and non-foodstuffs sciences, technology, organization of public catering; library: 220,000 vols; 572 teachers; 2,760 students; Rector Prof. L. S. PUZYREVSKY.

Institute of Business Studies: 117571 Moscow, pr. Vernadskogo 82; tel. (495) 434-92-53; fax (495) 434-11-48; e-mail ibs@ane.ru; f. 1989; independent; library: 10,500 vols; 182 teachers (32 full-time, 150 part-time); 1,500 students; Pres. Dr SERGEI MIASOEDEV.

Kazan Finance and Economics Institute: 420012 Tatarstan, Kazan, ul. Butlerova 4; tel. (8432) 36-54-41; fax (8432) 38-30-54; e-mail rector@kfei.kcn.ru; internet kfei .kcn.ru; f. 1932; faculties: general economics, business economics, finance and credit, distance learning, advanced training for profes-

sionals; 240 teachers; 5,000 students; library: 330,000 vols; Rector N. G. KHAIRULLIN.

Krasnoyarsk Institute of Commerce: 660049 Krasnoyarsk, ul. L. Prushinskoi 14; tel. (3912) 21-93-33; f. 1989; library: 205,835 vols; Chief Officers Y. L. ALEXANDROV, B. K. GUSEV.

Moscow Institute of Economics, Statistics and Informatics: 119501 Moscow, Nezhinskaya ul. 7; tel. (495) 442-65-77; fax (495) 442-65-88; e-mail office@rector.mesi.ru; internet www.mesi.ru; f. 1932; faculties: economics and finance, management, law and humanities, statistics and economics, computer technology, Masters programmes; MBA; Open Education and Distance Learning Systems; Institute of Professional Development; library: 269,000 vols; 6,110 teachers (425 in Moscow, 5,685 in Russian regions); 65,000 students (10,000 in Moscow, 55,000 in Russian regions); Rector Prof. VLADIMIR P. TIKHOMIROV.

Moscow State Institute of International Relations: 117454 Moscow, pr. Vernadskogo 76; tel. (495) 434-91-74; fax (495) 434-90-66; internet www.mgimo.ru; f. 1944; faculties: international relations, international economic relations, international law, international business and business administration, international journalism, political science; library: 750,000 vols; 974 teachers; 2,848 students; Rector A. V. TORKUNOV.

Novosibirsk Institute of Commerce: 630087 Novosibirsk, pr. K. Marksa 26; tel. (3832) 46-58-52; f. 1956; faculties: trade economics, trade, accounting, technology; library: 197,000 vols; 240 teachers; 7,500 students; br. in Chita; Rector N. N. PROTOPOPOV.

Novosibirsk Institute of National Economy: 630070 Novosibirsk, Kamennaya ul. 56; tel. (3832) 24-27-22; f. 1968; faculties of industrial economics, economics and planning of supply, financial economics, accounting and statistics; library: 250,000 vols; 4,800 students; Rector V. N. SHCHUKIN.

St Petersburg Institute of Trade and Economics: 194018 St Petersburg, Novorossiiskaya 50; tel. (812) 247-78-06; f. 1930; faculties: trade economics, accounting, trade in industrial goods, trade in foodstuffs, technology; library: 595,300 vols; br. in Krasnoyarsk; Rector V. A. GULIAEV.

Saratov Institute of Economics: 410760 Saratov, ul. Radishcheva 89; tel. (8452) 26-38-50; f. 1918; faculties: industry, agriculture, credit and economics, accounting; library: 255,000 vols; 160 teachers; 4,000 students; Rector K. I. BABAYTSEV.

ENGINEERING AND INDUSTRY

Grozny State Oil Institute: 364051 Grozny, pl. Ordzhonikidze 100; tel. and fax (8712) 22-31-20; f. 1920; faculties: geology, petroleum technology, mechanical engineering, construction engineering, automation and applied informatics; library: 175,864 vols; 340 teachers; 5,565 students; Rector I. A. KERIMOV.

Moscow Institute of Printing: 127550 Moscow, ul. Pryanishnikova 2A; tel. (495) 216-07-46; faculties: printing equipment, printing technology, engineering economics, book trade, layout; br. in St Petersburg.

Norilsk Industrial Institute: 663310 Norilsk, ul. 50-let Oktyabrya 7; tel. (3919) 42-16-31; fax (3919) 42-17-41; f. 1961; faculties: mining, metallurgy, economics, mechanical technology, civil and electrical engineering; library: 300,000 vols; 500 teachers; 3,500 students; Rector A. A. KOLEGOV.

Novocherkassk Institute of Engineering Amelioration: 346409 Novocherkassk, Pushkinskaya 111; tel. (86352) 5-57-56; f. 1907; depts: irrigation and land reclamation, forestry; library: 170,000 vols; 250 teachers; 5,100 students.

Rostov-on-Don Automation and Mechanical Engineering Institute: 344023 Rostov-on-Don, pl. Strany Sovetov 2; tel. (8632) 52-93-51; fax (8632) 54-84-11; f. 1960; faculties: agricultural engineering, mechanical engineering, automation and robotics; library: 237,424 vols; 565 teachers; 1,730 students; Rector N. G. CHEREDNICHENKO; publ. *Economics and Industrial Management.*

Rubtsovsk Industrial Institute: 658207 Rubtsovsk, Traktornaya ul. 2/6; tel. (38557) 3-26-29; fax (38557) 3-54-22; e-mail rii@inst .rubtsovsk.ru; f. 1946; br. of Altai State Technical University; machine technology, motor car and tractor construction, motor vehicles and vehicle equipment, foundry machinery and technology, applied mathematics, management, industrial and civil engineering; library: 130,000 vols; 193 teachers; 1,950 students; Rector S. A. GURCHENKOV.

St Petersburg Institute of Engineering (LMZ-VTUZ): 195197 St Petersburg, Polyustrovsky pr. 14; tel. (812) 540-01-54; fax (812) 540-01-59; f. 1930; faculties: mechanical engineering, Nuclear power engineering, turbine manufacture, management; library: 185,000 vols; 350 teachers; 5,000 students; Rector Prof. M. A. MARTYNOV.

Ukhta Industrial Institute: 169400 Komi Autonomous Republic, Ukhta, Pervomaiskaya ul. 13; tel. (82147) 6-06-10.

MEDICINE

Khabarovsk State Pharmaceutical Institute: 680000 Khabarovsk, ul. K. Marksa 30; tel. (4210) 34-68-26.

Perm Pharmaceutical Institute: 614600 Perm, GSP-277, ul. Lenina 48; tel. (3422) 12-34-45; fax (3422) 12-94-76; e-mail pfa@ degacom.ru; f. 1937; library: 80,000 vols; 220 teachers; 3,500 students; Rector Prof. Y. OLESHKO.

Pyatigorsk Pharmaceutical Institute: 357533 Pyatigorsk, pr. Kalinina 11; tel. (8790) 9-44-74; f. 1943; library: 370,000 vols; 308 teachers; 2,300 students; Rector V. G. BELIKOV.

SCIENCE AND TECHNOLOGY

Bryansk Technological Institute: 241037 Bryansk, ul. Stanke Dimitrova 3; tel. (0832) 1-19-12; faculties: forestry engineering, forestry machinery, forestry management, timber technology.

Kemerovo Institute of Food Science and Technology: 650056 Kemerovo, bul. Stroitelei 47; tel. (3842) 73-40-40; fax (3842) 73-41-03; e-mail office@kemtipp.ru; internet www.kemtipp.ru; f. 1972; divs of mechanics, refrigeration machines, food products technology, meat and dairy products, technology and organisation of public catering; 480 teachers; 10,000 students; Rector VLADIMIR PETROVITCH YUSTRATOV.

Moscow State Food Institute: 109803 Moscow, Zemlynoi Val 73; tel. (495) 915-03-40; fax (495) 915-08-77; f. 1953; faculties: bread products, fish breeding and biotechnology, industrial economics, mechanical engineering; brs in Krasnoyarsk, Vyazma and Rostov; 211 teachers; library: 380,000 vols; Rector O. K. FILATOV.

Moscow Technological Institute: 141220 Moscow oblast, Pushkinskii raion, pos. Cherkizovo 1, Glavnaya ul. 99; tel. (495) 584-30-86; faculties: art and technology, chemical technology, engineering economics, mechanical and radio engineering; brs in St Petersburg, Ufa and Tolyatti.

Omsk Technological Institute for Service Industries: 644099 Omsk, Krasnogvardeiskaya 9; tel. (3812) 24-16-93; faculties: Art and Technology, Engineering Economics.

Penza Technological Institute: 440600 Penza, pr. Baidukova 1A; tel. (8412) 55-60-86; e-mail rector@vmis.pti.ac.ru; faculties: mechanical engineering, computer science, economics; library: 140,000 vols; Rector Prof. V. B. MOISEEV.

Russian Extra-Mural Institute of the Textile and Light Industries: 123298 Moscow, ul. Narodnogo Opolcheniya 38, korp. 2; tel. (095) 943-63-59; f. 1932; faculties: textile industry technology, light industry technology, chemical technology, electrical engineering, engineering economics; brs in Barnaul, Ufa, Kemerovo and Omsk; library: 780,000 vols; 350 teachers; 13,000 students; Rector V. S. STRELYAEV.

Shakhty Technological Institute for Service Industries: 346500 Rostov oblast, Shakhty, ul. Shevchenko 147; tel. (08536) 2-20-37; f. 1969; courses in fields of municipal finance and planning, light industry, service industries,; library: 370,000 vols, 250,000 patent documents; 300 teachers; 2,000 full-time students; Rector Prof. VICTOR ROMANOV; publ. *Sbornik rabot instituta* (collected works, 1 a year).

TRANSPORT

Irkutsk Institute of Railway Engineers: 664074 Irkutsk, ul. Chernyshevskogo 15; tel. (3952) 28-27-12; faculties: electromechanical, construction, traffic management; library: 116,000 vols; 497 teachers; Rector L. P. SURKOV.

Samara Institute of Railway Engineers: 443066 Samara 9, Pervyi Bezymyannyi per. 18; tel. (8462) 51-75-09; fax (8462) 51-77-90; faculties: construction, electromechanical, electrotechnical, operating; library: 260,000 vols; 6,000 students; Rector Prof. V. V. IVANOVICH.

Siberian Motor and Highway Institute: 644080 Omsk, pr. Mira 5; tel. (38112) 65-03-02; fax (38112) 65-03-23; e-mail info@sibadi.omsk.ru; internet www.sibadi.omsk.ru; f. 1930; faculties: road-building machinery, highway and airport building, bridges and tunnels, industrial and civil engineering, vehicles and vehicle services, traffic organization and services management, road transport economics and management; library: 747,000 vols; 500 teachers; 5,000 students; Rector V. A. SALNIKOV.

Schools of Art and Music

CONSERVATOIRES AND SCHOOLS OF MUSIC

Astrakhan State Conservatoire: 414000 Astrakhan, Sovetskaya ul. 23; tel. (8510) 2-93-11; f. 1969; courses: choral conducting, orchestral instruments, piano, folk instruments, singing, musicology; 450 students; Rector GEORGI I. SLAVNIKOV.

Kazan State Conservatoire: 420015 Tatarstan, Kazan, Bol. Krasnaya ul. 38; tel. (8432) 36-55-33; fax (8432) 36-56-41; f. 1945; piano, organ, orchestral and folk instruments, composition, singing, choral conducting, musicology; library: 223,000 vols; 178

teachers; 659 students; Rector R. K. ABDUL-LIN.

Moscow State Conservatoire 'P. I. Tchaikovsky': 103871 Moscow, ul. Bolshaya Nikitskaya 13; tel. (495) 229-06-41; fax (495) 229-96-59; internet www.mosconsv.ru; f. 1866; faculties: piano, orchestral instruments, singing, operatic and symphonic conducting, choral conducting, composition, musicology; 386 teachers; 865 students; library: 1,244,412 vols; Rector M. A. OVCHIN-NIKOV (acting).

Nizhnii Novgorod State Conservatoire 'M. I. Glinka': 603600 Nizhnii Novgorod GSP-30, ul. Piskunova 40; tel. (8312) 36-45-27; fax (8312) 36-42-37; f. 1946; piano, orchestral and folk instruments, singing, choral conducting, opera and symphony conducting, composition, musicology; library: 130,000 vols; 170 teachers; 700 students; Rector E. B. FERTELMEISTER.

Novosibirsk State Conservatoire 'M. I. Glinka': 630099 Novosibirsk, Sovetskaya ul. 31; tel. (3832) 22-25-22; fax (3832) 23-95-37; f. 1956; piano, orchestral and folk instruments, singing, symphony and choral conducting, composition, musicology; library: 104,000 vols; Rector Prof. Dr E. G. GURENKO.

Rostov State Conservatoire 'S. V. Rakhmaninov': 344008 Rostov-on-Don, Budennovsky pr. 23; tel. (8632) 62-36-14; fax (8632) 62-35-84; e-mail rostcons@aaanet.ru; internet www.rostcons.aaanet.ru; f. 1967 (fmrly Rostov Musical Pedagogical Institute, present name 1992); courses: piano, orchestral instruments, folk instruments, singing, choral conducting, orchestral conducting, composition, musicology, jazz; library: 204,000 vols; 124 teachers; 630 students; Prin. Prof. A. S. DANILOV.

Russian State Academy of Music 'Gnesins': 121069 Moscow, Povarskaya ul. 30–36; tel. (495) 291-15-54; fax (495) 290-17-65; f. 1944; 476 teachers; 1,337 students; Prin. Prof. S. M. KOLOBKOV.

St Petersburg State Conservatoire 'N. A. Rimsky-Korsakov': 190000 St Petersburg, Teatralnaya pl. 3; tel. (812) 314-96-93; fax (812) 311-82-88; e-mail info@conservatory.ru; internet www.conservatory.ru; f. 1862; piano, orchestral instruments, singing, operatic, symphonic and choral conducting, composition, musicology, opera and ballet direction, musical comedy, folk instruments; library: 462,000 vols, 2,431 incunabula, 7,000 MSS of Russian and European composers; 266 teachers; 1,000 students; Rector S. P. ROLDUGIN; publ. *Teatralnaya ploshchad* (6 a year).

Saratov State Conservatoire 'L. V. Sobinov': 410600 Saratov, pr. Kirova 1; tel. (8452) 26-06-38; fax (095) 975-09-33; piano, orchestral and folk instruments, choral conducting, singing, composition, musicology, theatre and cinema acting, musical comedy acting; library: 54,065 vols; Rector Prof. VALERY P. LOMAKO.

Urals State Conservatoire 'M. P. Mussorgsky': 620014 Ekaterinburg, pr. Lenina 26; tel. and fax (343) 271-21-80; e-mail mail@uscon.ru; internet www.uscon.ru; f. 1934; piano, orchestral and folk instruments, singing, choral conducting, composition, musicology, sound production; library: 130,000 vols; 190 teachers; 700 students; Rector Prof. MIKHAIL V. ANDRIANOV.

SCHOOLS OF ARTS AND CULTURE

Altai State Institute of Culture: 656055 Barnaul, ul. Yurina 277; tel. (3852) 44-57-09; tel. (3852) 44-54-57; librarianship, cultural and educational work; br. in Omsk.

Chelyabinsk State Institute of Art and Culture: 454091 Chelyabinsk, ul. Ordzhonikidze 36A; tel. (3512) 33-89-32; f. 1968; training in theatre direction, choreography, ballet, conducting, library science; library: 301,000 vols; 508 teachers; 2,700 students; Rector A. P. GRAI.

Eastern Siberian State Institute of Culture: 670005 Buryat Autonomous Republic, Ulan-Ude, ul. Tereshkovoi 1; tel. (31022) 3-33-22; f. 1960; faculties: library science, bibliography; library: 420,000 vols.

Far-Eastern State Academy of Arts: 690600 Vladivostock, Petr Veliky 3; tel. (4232) 26-49-22; fax (4232) 26-44-88; e-mail dvgii@fastmail.vladivostock.ru; f. 1962; piano, orchestral instruments, folk instruments, singing, choral conducting, musicology, drama, painting, directing; library: 102,000 vols; 100 teachers; 450 students.

Kazan State Institute of Culture: 420059 Kazan, Orenburgskii trakt 3A; tel. (8432) 37-31-27; librarianship, cultural and educational work.

Kemerovo State Academy of Culture and Arts: 650029 Kemerovo, ul. Voroshilova 17; tel. (3842) 73-29-67; fax (3842) 73-28-08; e-mail kemgaki@mail.ru; internet www.art.kemerovonet.ru; f. 1969; library sciences, information technology, social education, music, theatre, video art, design, art management, worldwide art studies; library: 249,000 vols; 210 teachers; 3,000 students; Rector Prof. EKATERINA L. KUDRINA.

Khabarovsk State Institute of Culture: 680045 Khabarovsk, Krasnorechenskaya ul. 112; tel. (4210) 36-30-39; dept: library science.

Krasnodar State Institute of Culture and Art: 350072 Krasnodar, ul. 40-letiya Pobedy 33; tel. (8612) 55-30-63; f. 1967; depts: library science, folk culture; library: 152,500 vols; 267 teachers; 2,800 students; Dir IRINA I. GORLOVA.

Krasnoyarsk State Institute of Fine Arts: 660049 Krasnoyarsk, ul. Lenina 22; tel. (3912) 23-35-02; courses: piano, orchestral instruments, folk instruments, singing, choral conducting, musicology, theatre and cinema acting.

Moscow Higher School of Industrial Art: 125080 Moscow A-80, Volokolamskoe shosse 9; tel. (495) 158-01-33; f. 1825; refounded 1945; faculties: industrial arts, decorative and applied art, interior design, monumental art; library: 50,000 vols; 1,300 students; Rector A. S. KVASOV.

Moscow Literary Institute of the Union of Writers 'M. Gorky': 103104 Moscow, Tverskoi bul. 25; tel. (495) 291-22-66; library: 106,000 vols.

Moscow State Art Institute 'V. I. Surikov': 109004 Moscow, Tovarishchesky per. 30; tel. (495) 912-39-32; fax (495) 912-18-75; e-mail artinst@online.ru; f. 1843; depts: architecture, graphic arts, painting, sculpture, theory and history of art; library: 154,000 vols; 103 teachers; 450 students; Dir A. A. BICHUKOV.

Moscow State Institute of Culture: 141400 Moscow oblast, Khimki 6, Bibliotechnaya ul. 7; tel. (495) 570-31-33; f. 1930; librarianship, bibliography, information science, cultural studies, museum studies; library: 786,814 vols; 6,000 students; Rector L. P. BOGDANOV.

Perm State Institute for Arts and Culture: 614000 Perm, ul. Gazety 'Zvezda' 18; tel. and fax (3422) 12-45-93; f. 1975; educational and cultural work; 156 teachers; 1,814 students; library: 170,000 vols; Rector Y. A. MALYANOV.

Samara State Institute of Culture: 443010 Samara, ul. Frunze 167; tel. (8462) 32-76-54; f. 1971; librarianship, educational and cultural work; library: 239,100 vols; 200 teachers; Dir Prof. I. M. KUZMIN; publs *Culture, Creative Activity, Humanity*.

St Petersburg Academy of Art and Design: 191028 St Petersburg, Solyanoi per. 13; tel. (812) 273-38-04; fax (812) 272-84-46; f. 1876 (fmrly St Petersburg V. I. Mukhina Higher Industrial Art School, present name 1992); faculties: decorative and applied art, monumental arts, design; library: 140,000 vols; 230 teachers; 1,100 students; Rector Prof. A. Y. TALASCHUK.

St Petersburg Institute of Painting, Sculpture and Architecture 'I. E. Repin': 199034 St Petersburg, Universitetskaya nab. 17; tel. (812) 213-61-89; fax (812) 213-65-48; f. 1757; attached to the Acad. of Arts of Russia; depts: painting, sculpture, graphic art, architecture, theory and history of art; library: 500,000 vols; 160 teachers; 1,370 students; Rector Prof. O. A. YEREMEYEV.

St Petersburg State Institute of Culture: 191065 St Petersburg, Dvortsovaya nab. 4; tel. (812) 314-11-21; f. 1918; librarianship, cultural, musical and theatrical studies, cinema and television; library: 600,000 vols; 492 teachers; 5,000 students; Rector Prof. P. A. PODBOLOTOV; publ. *Trudy Instituta* (Proceedings).

Ufa State Institute of Fine Arts: 450025 Bashkortostan, Ufa, ul. Lenina 14; tel. (3472) 23-49-56; depts: piano, orchestral instruments, folk instruments, choral conducting, singing, composition, musicology, theatre and cinema acting, folk theatre, painting; Rector Prof. Z. A. NURGALIN.

Voronezh State Institute of Fine Arts: 394088 Voronezh, ul. Lizyukova 42; tel. (0732) 13-14-81; tel. (0732) 13-08-90; piano, orchestral instruments, folk instruments, singing, choral conducting.

SCHOOLS OF FILM AND THEATRE

Drama School attached to the E. B. Vakhtangov State Theatre 'B. V. Shchukin': 121002 Moscow, ul. Vakhtangova 12a; tel. (495) 241-56-44; theatre and cinema acting.

Drama School attached to the Maly Theatre 'M. S. Shchepkin': 103012 Moscow, Pushechnaya ul. 2/6; tel. (495) 923-18-80; tel. (495) 924-38-89; theatre and cinema acting.

Ekaterinburg State Theatrical Institute: 620151 Ekaterinburg, ul. K. Libknechta 38; tel. (3432) 51-36-90; f. 1985; 350 students; Rector Prof. V. BABENKO.

Moscow Choreographic Institute: 119146 Moscow, 2-ya Frunzenskaya ul. 5; tel. (495) 247-37-80.

Russian Academy of Theatre Arts: 103888 Moscow, Mal. Kislovsky per. 6; tel. (495) 291-91-92; fax (495) 290-05-97; e-mail info@gitis.net; internet www.gitis.net; f. 1878; faculties and depts: acting, directing (directing dramatic theatre, circus direction), musical theatre (musical theatre direction and acting), theatre history and criticism (world theatre history, Russian theatre history), ballet-master faculty (choreography), variety theatre (variety arts), theatre management and production (performing arts management), set design; inter-faculty deps: voice and speech training, vocal training, dance training, movement training, history

of the arts, history and theory of music and musical performance, history, philosophy and literature, foreign languages, Russian as a foreign language; Rector Prof. MARINA KHMELNITSKAYA.

St Petersburg State Theatre Arts Academy: 192028 St Petersburg, ul. Mokhovaya 34; tel. (812) 273-15-81; fax (812) 272-17-89; e-mail international@tart.spb.ru; internet www.tart.spb.ru; f. 1779; drama and cinema acting, rock opera acting, puppet theatre, stage directing, theatre planning and organization, theatrical equipment and stage planning; research dept; library: 350,000 vols; 150 teachers; 1,160 students; Rector Prof. Dr L. G. SOUNDSTREM.

State Institute of Cinematography: 129226 Moscow, ul. Vilgelma Pika 3; tel. (495) 181-38-68; f. 1919; direction, shooting, screen play and script writing, cinema studies, economics of cinematography, arts; library: 300,000 vols; 200 teachers; 1,550 students; Rector ALEXANDER NOVIKOV; publs *Tvorchestvo Molodykh* (Creations of Young Artists), etc.

Studio-School of the Moscow Arts Theatre 'V. I. Nemirovich-Danchenko': 103009 Moscow, Tverskaya ul. 6, str. 7; tel. (495) 229-39-36; fax (495) 200-42-41; f. 1943; drama and cinema acting, theatre directing, theatre technology, set and costume design, theatre management; library: 20,000 vols; 80 teachers; 230 students; Rector Prof. O. P. TABAKOV.

Yaroslavl State Theatre Institute: 150000 Yaroslavl, Pervomaiskaya ul. 43; tel. and fax (0852) 22-23-11; f. 1980; theatrical art; library: 25,300 vols; 300 students; Rector Prof. STANISLAV KLITIN.

RWANDA

The Higher Education System

Rwanda became independent from Belgium in 1962, and in 1963 the Université Nationale du Rwanda, its oldest institution of higher education, was founded. However, the vast majority of higher education institutions were founded after 1994. Three new major institutions were opened in the late 1990s: Institut des Sciences, Technologie et de Gestion de Kigali (Kigali Institute of Science, Technology and Management), Institut Supérieur de Santé de Kigali (Kigali Health Institute) and Institut Supérieur Pédagogique de Kigali (Kigali Institute of Education). In 2008/09 there were 55,213 students enrolled in tertiary education; there are nine public, 11 private higher education institutions and 10 technical and vocational colleges. In 2011 the Government was considering a proposal to merge public universities that were performing under par, in order to raise standards and create a more streamlined and coherent higher education system. Some students attend universities abroad, particularly in Belgium, France and Germany.

The Ministry of Education is the national coordinating body for higher education. The Minister of Education is the Chairman of the Governing Council of the Université Nationale du Rwanda. The Council's leading officers, including the Rector and Vice-Rectors, are government appointees. The operating environment for all higher education institutions, both public and private, is defined by the Higher Education Act of 2005. From 2007 all programmes have been revised according to the Rwanda National Qualifications Framework For Higher Education, which was introduced at the beginning of that year by the National Council of Higher Education (NCHE). Within the new system, all qualifications, with the exception of Doctorate and some (research-based) Masters degrees, are credit-based.

Accreditation of higher education providers is granted by the Ministry of Education, based on a detailed report submitted by the NCHE, which also serves as the quality assurance agency for higher education.

The Certificat du Cycle supérieur de l'enseignement secondaire (Advanced General Certificate of Secondary Education) is required for admission to higher education. The primary undergraduate qualification is the Bachelors degree, which is generally awarded after three years' study, although some courses are longer in duration (e.g. medicine, which lasts six years). Bachelors degrees with Honours are available, following the successful completion of between four and five years' study; all Honours programmes require the submission of a dissertation. Subsequent to the Bachelors degree, students may undertake a Postgraduate Certificate, which lasts up to one year, or a Postgraduate Diploma, which generally lasts for one year. Masters degrees require a minimum of 18 months' study, and the completion of a dissertation. Master of Philosophy and Master of Letters degrees require a minimum of two years' study, and the completion of a dissertation, which must be presented and defended in front of an examining panel. Doctorate degrees require a minimum of three years' additional study and research and the completion of a thesis, which must demonstrate an independent and original contribution to the studied subject, and which must be presented and defended in front of an examining panel.

The universities and specialist institutes offer post-secondary technical and vocational education. Courses last two to three years and students receive (usually) the Diplôme de Technicien Supérieur, Diplôme d'Ingénieur Technicien or Diplôme d'Ingénieur des Travaux.

Regulatory Bodies

GOVERNMENT

Ministry of Education: BP 622, Kigali; tel. 583051; fax 582161; e-mail info@mineduc.gov.rw; internet www.mineduc.gov.rw; Minister DAPHROSE GAHAKWA.

Ministry of Youth, Sports and Culture: BP 1044, Kigali; tel. 583527; fax 583518; e-mail minicult@rwanda1.com; internet www.mijespoc.gov.rw; Minister JOSEPH HABINEZA.

Learned Society

GENERAL

UNESCO Office Kigali: BP 2502, Kigali; MINEDUC Compound, Kigali; tel. 513845; fax 513844; e-mail kigali@unesco.org; Programme Specialist CONSTANTINO CONSTATINI.

Research Institutes

GENERAL

Institut de Recherche Scientifique et Technologique: BP 227, Butare; tel. 530395; fax 530939; f. 1989; pharmacology, energy, social sciences; library of 9,500 vols; Dir-Gen. Prof. Dr CHRYSOLOGUÉ KOURANGUIÉ; Dir of Pharmacology Centre POLYCARPE NYETERO; Dir of Energy Centre DÉO NKRORUMZIZA; Dir of Centre for Rwanda Studies JEAN MARARA.

AGRICULTURE, FISHERIES AND VETERINARY SCIENCE

Institut des Sciences Agronomiques du Rwanda (ISAR): BP 138, Butare; tel. 530145; fax 530642; internet www.isar.cgiar.org; f. 1962; attached to Min. of Agriculture; 1,000 personnel; library of 2,500 vols; Dir Dr ELIE MUGUNGA MUHINDA; publ. Technical Letters.

Attached Research Stations:

Agricultural Research Institute of Rwanda–Ruhande Station: BP 617, Butare; forestry; Dir ATHANASE MUKURARINDA.

Centre de Sélection Bovine de Songa: BP 138, Butare; stockbreeding (cattle, sheep, poultry); Dir (vacant).

Station ISAR/PNAP: BP 73, Ruhengeri; Dir GERVAIS NGERERO.

Station Karama: BP 121, Kigali; plant breeding (living plants, irrigation), stockbreeding (cattle, goats); Dir Ir LAMBERT MAYALA.

Station Rubona: BP 138, Butare; laboratories (chemistry, technology, phytopathology), environmental studies, phytotechnics (living plants, cash crops: coffee, tobacco), zootechnics.

Station Rwerere: BP 73, Ruhengeri; high-altitude cultures (wheat, peas, potatoes); Dir C. SEHENE.

Station Tamira: BP 69, Gisenyi; high-altitude cultures (pyrethrum); Dir C. NTAMBABAZI.

TECHNOLOGY

Direction des Mines et de la Géologie: Ministère de l'Energie, de l'Eau et des Resources Naturelles, BP 447, Kigali; tel. 570496; f. 1962; geological services to the Government and private industry; to prepare a geological map of Rwanda; prospecting; library of 6,000 vols; Dir EMMANUEL BIZIMANA; publ. Bulletin du Service Géologique (1 a year).

Libraries and Archives

Butare

Bibliothèque Universitaire: Université Nationale du Rwanda, BP 117, Butare; tel. 530330; fax 530210; e-mail nurlibrary@nur.ac.rw; internet www.lib.nur.ac.rw; f. 1964; 206,000 vols; Dir EMMANUEL SERUGENDO.

Kigali

Archives Nationales du Rwanda: BP 1044, Kigali; tel. 83525; fax 83518; f. 1979; 7 staff; 600 vols; Dir ELIAS KIZARI; publ. Presidential Speeches (1 a year).

Bibliothèque Nationale du Rwanda: BP 1044, Kigali; tel. 572730; fax 83518; f. 1989; 6,000 vols; Dir SÉVERIM SEKUBUMBA.

Universities

INSTITUT DES SCIENCES, TECHNOLOGIE ET DE GESTION DE KIGALI (KIST) (Kigali Institute of Science, Technology and Management (KIST))

Ave de l'Armée, BP 3900, Kigali

Telephone: 574696

Fax: 571924

E-mail: info@kist.ac.rw

Internet: www.kist.ac.rw

Founded 1997

Academic year: February to November

Rector: Prof. Dr SILAS LWAKABAMBA

Vice-Rector for Academic Affairs: Ing. ALBERT BUTARE

Vice-Rector for Finance and Admin.: Dr NELSON LUJARA

Dir of Academic Services: Prof. ELIPHAZ BISANDA

Dir of Admin.: ANSELME SANO

Dir of Finance: CALISTUS OBIERO

Chief Librarian: ALPHONSE NGABONZIZA

Number of teachers: 165

Number of students: 2,416

DEANS

Centre for Continuing Education: ANTONIA MUTORO NSANGANO

Faculty of Management: Dr IBRAHIM MUSOBO

Faculty of Science: Dr DESIRÉ KARANGWA

Faculty of Technology: Prof. GRANT MONNEY

School of Language Studies: TEMBWE Z. WA OLOLO

UNIVERSITÉ NATIONALE DU RWANDA

BP 56, Butare

Telephone: 530122

Fax: 530121

E-mail: rector@nur.ac.rw

Internet: www.nur.ac.rw

Founded 1963

Languages of instruction: French, English

State control

Academic year: January to October (2 semesters)

Rector: Dr EMILE RWAMASIRABO

Vice-Rector for Academic Affairs: Prof. SILAS MURERAMANZI

Vice-Rector for Admin. and Finance: CANISIUS KARURANGA

Library: see Libraries

Number of teachers: 384

Number of students: 7,240

Publications: *Annuaire, Etudes Rwandaises* (2 a year), *Revue Juridique*

DEANS

Faculty of Agriculture: Dr CANISIUS KANANGIRE

Faculty of Arts and Humanities: DÉO BYANAFASHE

Faculty of Economics, Social Sciences, and Management: Dr JEAN BOSCO MUTAJOGIRE

Faculty of Education: Dr JEAN-PIERRE DUSINGIZEMUNGU

Faculty of Law: Dr NGAGI ALPHONSE

Faculty of Medicine: Dr ALEXIS NYAKAYIRO

School of Journalism: JEAN-PIERRE GATSINZI

School of Modern Languages: DEO HODARI

School of Public Health and Nutrition: Dr JOSEPH NTAGANIRA

Colleges

Institut Africain et Mauricien de Statistique et d'Economie Appliquée: BP 109, Kigali; tel. 84989; f. 1975 by the OCAM states; 3-year diploma course; library: 9,184 vols; 7 teachers; 38 students; Dir SÉRIGNE T. DIASSE; publ. *Rapport d'enquête* (1 a year).

Institut Supérieur des Finances Publiques (ISFP): BP 1514, Kigali; tel. 574302; f. 1987; attached to the Ministry of Finance; offers 2-year courses in the financial aspects of public administration; library; Dir JEAN-BAPTISTE BYILINGIRO.

SAINT CHRISTOPHER AND NEVIS

The Higher Education System

The islands of St Christopher and Nevis were settled by the British in the 1620s and remained under British control until 1983, when they jointly became an independent state and joined the Commonwealth as a full member. The College of Further Education was founded in 1988 as an amalgamation of previously existing institutions and was renamed Clarence Fitzroy Bryant College in 1996. In 2000 a privately financed 'offshore' medical college, the Medical University of the Americas, opened in Nevis. The country is also affiliated to the University of the West Indies, which offers distance learning programmes through its School of Continuing Studies in Basseterre. In 2007/08 there were 859 students in tertiary education. One national and four private institutions offer a number of degree programmes recognized and accredited by the Accreditation Board of the Ministry of Education.

Admission to Bachelors degree courses requires sufficient passes in the Caribbean Examinations Council Secondary Education Certificate or GCE A-Level examinations. Some professional certificates and diplomas are also acceptable for entry. The Bachelors degree at the University of the West Indies lasts three to four years, although some medical degrees may last five years. The Masters degree takes between one and two years and requires the submission of a thesis. Following completion of the Masters, the Doctorate requires two to four years of further study, culminating in the submission and defence of a thesis; some courses also require students to undertake a period of internship relevant to their chosen field of study.

Clarence Fitzroy Bryant College and other colleges offer post-secondary vocational and technical education, leading to the award of qualifications such as Diplomas, Technician Diplomas and Associate degrees.

Regulatory and Representative Bodies

GOVERNMENT

Ministry of Education: Church St, POB 333, Basseterre; tel. 465-2521; internet www.moeskn.org; Minister SAM TERRENCE CONDOR.

Ministry of Tourism, Culture and Sport: POB 878, Port Zante, Basseterre; tel. 465-2521; fax 465-7075; e-mail culture@sisterisles.kn; Minister Dr DENZIL LLEWELLYN DOUGLAS.

ACCREDITATION

Accreditation Board: Min. of Education and Youth, POB 333, Lockhart St, Basseterre; tel. 466-8610; fax 466-3322; e-mail board_acc@hotmail.com; Chair. Dr HERMIA MORTON-ANTHONY; Sec. EVAN HARVEY.

Accreditation Commission on Colleges of Medicine (ACCM): see under Ireland.

Learned Societies

HISTORY, GEOGRAPHY AND ARCHAEOLOGY

Nevis Historical and Conservation Society: POB 563, Charlestown, Nevis; tel. 469-5786; fax 469-0274; e-mail museums@nevis-nhcs.org; internet www.nevis-nhcs.org; f. 1980; administers Nevis Field Study Centre, Museum of Nevis History (birthplace of Alexander Hamilton), Horatio Nelson Museum; 650 mems; library: materials on history and culture of Nevis, St Kitts and West Indies, Alexander Hamilton, Horatio Nelson, and Amerindians; Archives of Nevis, newspapers, and civil, parish and government records, maps; Pres. HALSTEAD BYRON; Sec. SUZANNE GORDON; Exec. Dir JOHN GUILBERT.

LANGUAGE AND LITERATURE

Alliance Française: 1 Orchid St, Greenlands, POB 93, Basseterre, St Kitts; tel. 465-9415; fax 465-0478; e-mail allfrskn@caribsurf.com; offers courses and exams in French language and culture and promotes cultural exchange with France.

Library
Charlestown

Nevis Public Library: Prince William St, Charlestown, Nevis; tel. 469-0421; fax 469-1207; e-mail nepublib@caribsurf.com; Librarian HAZEL FRANCIS (acting).

Universities and Colleges

Clarence Fitzroy Bryant College: Burdon St Campus, POB 268, Basseterre, St Kitts; tel. 465-2856; fax 465-8279; e-mail info@cfbc.edu.kn; internet www.cfbc.edu.kn; f. 1988 as College of Further Education by merger of 4 instns; present name 1996; Prin. MARILYN ROGERS (acting); Registrar VENETTA MILLS; Librarians LORREL BRADSHAW, LEAH LIBURD.

Medical University of the Americas: POB 701, Charlestown, Nevis; tel. 469-9177; fax 469-9180; e-mail admissions@mua.edu; internet www.mua.edu; f. 1998; Private control; library: 2,950 books, 110 periodicals; 80 teachers; 600 students (postgraduate); Pres. Dr DAVID L. FREDRICK; Exec. Dean Dr SEWELL DIXON; Dean, Basic Sciences Dr RAY LASH.

University of the West Indies Branch: Basseterre; tel. 465-6583; fax 465-2190; e-mail ewiskn@caribsurf.com; Dir OLIVIA EDGECOMBE-HOWELL.

SAINT LUCIA

The Higher Education System

The island became a British colony in 1814 and remained under British rule until 1979, when it became independent (but remaining within the Commonwealth). Tertiary education is principally offered by the Sir Arthur Lewis Community College (founded 1985) and a branch campus of the University of the West Indies. In 2006/07 there were 1,395 students enrolled in adult education. In 2011/12 there were 1,599 students enrolled at the Sir Arthur Lewis Community College. The Ministry of Education and Culture is the government agency responsible for higher education.

Admission to higher education courses at the Sir Arthur Lewis Community College requires sufficient passes in the Caribbean Examinations Council Secondary Education Certificate or GCE A-Level examinations. It offers qualifications at the upper-secondary and tertiary levels. Certificate programmes last between one and two years, while Diploma courses are two years in duration. The Associate degree is a two- or three-year programme of study, depending on the subject. Undergraduate Bachelors and postgraduate Masters degrees are available at the University of the West Indies.

Regulatory Body

GOVERNMENT

Ministry of Education and Culture: Francis Compton Bldg, Waterfront, Castries; tel. 468-5203; fax 453-2299; e-mail mineduc@candw.lc; internet www.education.gov.lc; Minister ARSENE VIGIL JAMES.

Learned Societies

EDUCATION

National Research and Development Foundation: La Clery, POB 3067, Castries; tel. 452-4253; fax 453-6389; e-mail info@nrdf.org.lc; internet www.nrdf.org.lc; f. 1983 to promote research and the expansion of economic devt in St Lucia; provides technical assistance, training and consultancy; offers short courses in business management and admin.; Exec. Dir GERALD MORRIS.

HISTORY, GEOGRAPHY AND ARCHAEOLOGY

St Lucia Archaeological and Historical Society: Vigie, POB 3060, La Clery, Castries; f. 1954; organizes public lectures, exhibitions and educational activities; Pres. FORTUNA ANTHONY; Admin. Sec. ERIC BRANFORD.

LANGUAGE AND LITERATURE

Alliance Française: La Pyramide, Pointe Séraphine, POB 898, Castries; tel. 452-6602; fax 452-1871; e-mail alliancefrancaise@candw.lc; internet www.af-antilles.org; f. 1994; offers courses and examinations in French language and culture, and promotes cultural exchange with France; library of 3,792 vols; Dir CLAUDE GONIN.

NATURAL SCIENCES

Biological Sciences

St Lucia Naturalists' Society: POB 783, Castries; tel. 451-6957; conservation and educational activities; Chair. CRISPIN D'AUVERGNE.

RELIGION, SOCIOLOGY AND ANTHROPOLOGY

Folk Research Centre: Mount Pleasant, POB 514, Castries; tel. 453-1477; fax 451-9365; e-mail frc@candw.lc; internet www.stluciafolk.org; f. 1973; preserves and promotes the cultural heritage of St Lucia; Chair. HILARY LaFORCE; Exec. Dir KENTRY D. JnPIERRE.

Libraries and Archives

Castries

Central Library of St Lucia: POB 103, Castries; tel. 452-2875; internet www.educ.gov.lc; f. 1847; dept of Min. of Education and Culture; government public library; 160,000 vols; Dir of Library Services JOHN ROBERT LEE.

National Archives of St Lucia: POB 3060, La Clery, Castries; tel. 452-1654; fax 453-1405; e-mail stlunatarch_mt@candw.lc; internet www.stluciaarchives.org; f. 1995; 6,000 vols; unselected govt records; spec. historical collns, multimedia; Archivist MARGOT THOMAS.

Museum

Castries

St Lucia National Trust: POB 595, Castries; tel. 452-5005; fax 453-2791; internet www.slunatrust.org; f. 1975; responsible for the protected areas of Pigeon Island (history, archaeology, geology, natural history), Fregate Islands Nature Reserve and the proposed Praslin Protected Landscape (archaeology, history, coastal resources, geology, flora and fauna), the Anse Galet Nature Reserve (flora and fauna, history) and several offshore islands (bird nesting sites) and other sites; 600 mems; Dir BISHNU TULSIE; publ. *Conservation News* (4 a year).

College

University of the West Indies, School of Continuing Studies: University Centre, POB 306, The Morne, Castries; tel. 452-3866; fax 452-4080; e-mail uwislu@candw.lc; f. 1948; continuing education; houses the University's Distance Education Centre (UWIDEC) linking the university campuses with eight university centres; Resident Tutor and Head MATTHEW VERNON ROBERTS.

SAINT VINCENT AND THE GRENADINES

The Higher Education System

From the 18th century the islands were under British control until they became fully independent, within the Commonwealth, as Saint Vincent and the Grenadines in 1978. The Vincentian education system is modelled on the British system. Post-secondary education is provided through the Kingstown Medical College, a campus of St George's University (Grenada), located near Kingstown. The University maintains affiliations with hospitals in the USA, the United Kingdom and the Caribbean for clinical programmes. There are also teacher-training, technical, nursing and community colleges, with total enrolment in 2000 of 904 students. The Ministry of Education is the national body responsible for higher education. The establishment and management of higher education institutions is governed by the Education Act of 2005.

Regulatory Bodies

GOVERNMENT

Ministry of Education: Halifax St, Kingstown; tel. 456-1877; fax 457-1114; Minister GIRLYN MIGUEL.

Ministry of Urban Development, Labour, Culture and Electoral Matters: Marion House Bldg, Ground Floor, Murray's Rd, Kingstown; tel. 457-1789; fax 485-6737; e-mail office.elections@mail.gov.vc; Minister RENÉE MERCEDES BAPTISTE.

Learned Societies

ARCHITECTURE AND TOWN PLANNING

Saint Vincent and the Grenadines National Trust: POB 1538, Heritage Hall, Carnegie Bldg, Kingstown; tel. 451-2921; e-mail svgntrust@vincysurf.com; f. 1969; concerned with the preservation of the architectural, cultural and environmental heritage of St Vincent and the Grenadines; educational workshops on conservation and preservation values and skills; advises govt and private sector on sustainable devt policies and legislation; restores and preserves bldgs and objects of archaeological, architectural, artistic, historic, scientific or traditional merit; lists historical bldgs, sites, flora and fauna; maintains photographic inventories of historical and natural sites; 200 mems; Man. Dir RACHEL MOSES.

FINE AND PERFORMING ARTS

Saint Vincent and the Grenadines Visual Arts Society: POB 2303, Kingstown; tel. 457-4454; f. 2003 to encourage the local devt of the visual arts; organizes exhibitions and other events; Sec. CÉCILE COMBLEN.

LANGUAGE AND LITERATURE

Alliance Française: POB 560, Kingstown; Old Public Library Bldg, Kingstown; tel. and fax 456-2095; e-mail afsvg@vincysurf.com; f. 1969; organizes French classes, confs, exhibitions, seminars, films and lectures; Dir VANESSA DEMIRCIYAN.

Libraries and Archives

Kingstown

Department of Libraries, Archives and Documentation Services: Richmond Hill, Kingstown; tel. and fax 457-2022; e-mail publiclibrary@vincysurf.com; f. 1893; attached to Min. of Education; oversees 20 br. libraries containing 262,000 vols; Dir JOAN L. JOB MOSES (acting); Librarian DANA NEVERSON.

Principal Attached Centres:

Documentation Centre: Richmond Hill, Kingstown; tel. 456-1689; e-mail document@caribsurf.com; f. 1989; 15,000 vols; Librarian TRISHA-ANN MOSES.

National Archives: Richmond Hill, Kingstown; tel. 450-0485; e-mail archives@vincysurf.com; f. 1990; 15,000 vols; Archivist TRISHA-ANN JOB; Librarian DANA NEVERSON.

National Public Library, Archives and Documentation Services: Richmond Hill, Kingstown; tel. and fax 457-2022; e-mail publiclibrary@vincysurf.com; f. 2011; 20 br. libraries; 5,200 vols; Dir MICHELLE KING; Librarian DANA NEVERSON; Librarian DONNA MASON-McLEAN; Librarian TRISHA-ANN MOSES.

Museums and Galleries

Kingstown

Botanical Gardens: New Montrose, Kingstown; tel. 457-1003; f. 1763; the oldest botanical gardens in the western hemisphere; conservation of rare species of plants; aviary containing St Vincent parrots; Dir EMMETT DOYLE.

Dr Cecil Cyrus Museum: Montrose, Kingstown; tel. 457-8981; fax 457-0812; e-mail cyrusclinic@caribsurf.com; f. 2002; colln of medical exhibits, 1,000 pathological specimens, 3,000 photographs; memorabilia of Vincentian life and history, historical maps; Keeper Dr A. CECIL CYRUS.

Fort Charlotte: Berkshire Hill, Kingstown; f. 1806; contains a museum depicting the history of the Black Caribs.

College

Kingstown Medical College: POB 585, Ratho Mill, Kingstown; tel. 456-4832; fax 456-9670; e-mail sgu_info@mssl.com; internet www.sgu.edu; f. 1979; preclinical school affiliated to St George's Univ., Grenada; Dean Dr EDWARD S. JOHNSON.

SAMOA

The Higher Education System

In 1962 Western Samoa (as it was then known) gained independence, having been governed by New Zealand since 1919, first as a League of Nations mandate and then as a UN Trust Territory. The current name was adopted in 1997. There are two higher education institutions in Samoa: the National University of Samoa (founded 1984, and into which the Samoa Polytechnic—founded 1993—was merged in 2006) and a branch campus of the University of the South Pacific, which specializes in agricultural studies. The National University of Samoa has eight faculties and schools , in which an estimated 2,000 students were enrolled in 2010.

Admission to non-university-level higher education is on the basis of the Samoa School Certificate, while admission to university-level higher education requires completion of Senior Secondary school and award of the Pacific Senior Secondary School Certificate. The National University of Samoa and the University of the South Pacific also offer one-year pre-university preparation and foundation courses. Sub-degree level qualifications include one-year Certificates and one- or two-year Diplomas. Undergraduate Bachelors degrees at the National University of Samoa and the University of the South Pacific last three years and qualify students for the postgraduate Masters, which requires an additional two years of study.

Regulatory Body

GOVERNMENT

Ministry of Education, Sports and Culture: POB 1869, Apia; tel. 21911; fax 21917; e-mail education@mesc.gov.ws; internet www.mesc.gov.ws; Minister MAGELE MAUI-LIU.

Learned Societies

GENERAL

UNESCO Office Apia: POB 615, Mata'utu-Uta, Apia; tel. 24276; fax 26593; e-mail apia@unesco.org; internet www.unesco.org/apia/; f. 1984; designated cluster office for Australia, Cook Islands, Fiji, Kiribati, Marshall Islands, Federated States of Micronesia, Nauru, New Zealand, Niue, Palau, Papua New Guinea, Samoa, Solomon Islands, Tonga, Tuvalu and Vanuatu; documentation centre; Dir VISESIO PONGI.

BIBLIOGRAPHY, LIBRARY SCIENCE AND MUSEOLOGY

Library Association of Samoa: POB 1622, Apia; tel. 20072; fax 22440; e-mail libraryassociationofsamoa@gmail.com; internet www.las.org.ws; f. 1986 as Library Asscn of Western Samoa (LAWS), present name 1997; promotes libraries, literacy, education, reading for pleasure, internet and computer use across Samoa; provides training for all Samoan librarians; preserves Samoan culture, history and literature; Pres. AVALOGO TOGI TUNUPOPO; Sec. RACHELLE HICKS; Treas. OMAR BURGESS.

Research Institute

AGRICULTURE, FISHERIES AND VETERINARY SCIENCE

Scientific Research Organisation of Samoa: POB 6597, Nafanua, Apia; tel. 20664; fax 27769; e-mail enquiries@sros.org.ws; internet www.sros.org.ws; f. 2006, fmrly Research and Devt Institute of Samoa (RDIS); assists farmers and businesses through scientific and technical research; CEO TILAFONO LEATIOGIE DAVID JOSEPH HUNTER.

Libraries and Archives

Apia

Avele College Library: POB 45, Apia; tel. 20831; 5,000 vols serving 520 students.

Nelson Memorial Public Library: POB 598, Apia; tel. and fax 21208; e-mail jpgodinet@lesamoa.net; f. 1959; 1 br. library on Savaii island; 1 bookmobile; spec. collns: R. L. Stevenson, Samoa and Pacific; 92,000 vols; Sr Librarian JACINTA P. GODINET.

Museums

Apia

Museum of Samoa: POB 1869, Apia; tel. 26036; e-mail saphoe@mesc.gov.ws; attached to Min. of Education Sports and Culture; displays lifestyles, culture, history and environment of Samoans and the Pacific; photographic colln from early missionaries; traditional forms of art and wildlife; artefacts from other Pacific people, donated during the Arts Festival in Apia.

Robert Louis Stevenson Museum: POB 850, Apia; tel. 20798; fax 25428; e-mail info@rlsm.ws; f. 1990; writer Robert Louis Stevenson's (1850–1894) restored house and estate; library of 400 vols; Gen. Man. LUFILUFI RASMUSSEN.

University

IUNIVESITE AOAO O SAMOA
(National University of Samoa)

POB 1622, Apia
Telephone: 20072
Fax: 25489
E-mail: secretariat@nus.edu.ws
Internet: www.nus.edu.ws
Founded 1984

Motootua campus incl. faculty of nursing and health sciences

Languages of instruction: English, Samoan

Academic year: February to November

Vice-Chancellor and Pres.: Prof. LE'APAI TU'UA 'ILAOA ASOFOU SO'O

Deputy Vice Chancellor: Dr EMMA KRUSE VAAI

Registrar: LUAGALAU FOISAGAASINA ETEUATI SHON

Univ. Librarian: AVALOGO TOGI TUNUPOPO

Number of teachers: 140

Number of students: 2,500

Publications: *Jafnus* (1 a year), *Prismcs* (1 a year), *The Journal of Sāmoan Studies*

DEANS

Faculty of Arts: MARIA KERSLAKE

Faculty of Business and Entrepreneurship: Dr WOOD SALELE

Faculty of Education: EPENESA LAFI ESERA

Faculty of Nursing and Health Science: FULISIA PITA-UO AIAVAO

Faculty of Science: Dr IOANA CHAN MOW

Colleges

Avele College: POB 45, Apia; tel. 20831; e-mail avelecollege@lesamoa.net; f. 1924; attached to Min. of Education, Sports and Culture; 5-year courses; 520 students, incl. students from the Tokelau Islands; Prin. LAFAITELE AIGA ESERA.

University of the South Pacific, Alafua Campus: PMB, Apia; tel. 21671; fax 22933; e-mail enquiries@samoa.usp.ac.fj; internet www.usp.ac.fj/soa; f. 1977; school of agriculture and food technology incl. applied sciences and agribusiness (see also Fiji chapter); academic year February to December; library: 15,000 vols, 1,000 periodicals; 19 teachers; 200 students; Head and Campus Dir Dr EKPO MMAH OSSOM (acting); Sr Librarian ANGELA JOWITT; publs *IRETA South Pacific Agriculture News* (12 a year), *Journal of South Pacific Agriculture* (4 a year), *South Pacific Agricultural Teacher* (4 a year).

SAN MARINO

The Higher Education System

San Marino evolved as a city state in the early Middle Ages and is the sole survivor of the numerous independent states that existed in Italy before its unification in the 19th century. A treaty of friendship and cooperation with Italy was signed in 1862, renewed in March 1939 and revised in September 1971. The only institution of higher education is the state-run Università degli Studi della Repubblica di San Marino (founded 1985). In 2009/10 43 students attended the Università, and another 832 students were attending courses outside San Marino.

The Secretariat of State for Education, Culture and the University is the national body responsible for higher educa-

tion. The university's senior administrative and academic officer is the Rector, who is responsible for its internal affairs and external relations. The Departments, Centres and Schools constitute the university's academic division, while the Administrative Directorate deals with its financial affairs.

Admission to the university requires students to hold the Diploma di Maturità (secondary school leavers' certificate). The university employs a three-tier system of education. The first cycle is the Laurea di Primo Livello (Bachelors), which lasts three years and is followed by the Laurea Magistrale (Masters), which lasts between one and two years. The highest academic qualification is the Dottorato di Ricerca (Doctorate), which requires a minimum of three years' additional study.

Regulatory and Representative Bodies

GOVERNMENT

Secretariat of State for Education, Culture and the University: Contrada Omerelli, 47890 San Marino; tel. 0549-882548; fax 0549-882301; e-mail segreteria.ic@gov.sm; internet www.educazione.sm; Secretary of State Dott. ROMEO MORRI.

ACCREDITATION

ENIC/NARIC San Marino: Dipartimento Pubblica Istruzione, Contrada Omerelli 23, 47890 San Marino; tel. 0549-882550; fax 0549-882301; e-mail segr.pub-istr@omniway.sm; Coordinator FILIBERTO BERNARDI.

Learned Society

LANGUAGE AND LITERATURE

Alliance Française: Centro Social Dogana, Piazza Tini, 47891 Dogana, San Marino; e-mail alliancefrsm@yahoo.fr; internet www.alliancefrancaise.sm; offers courses and exams in French language and culture and promotes cultural exchange with France.

Library

San Marino

Biblioteca di Stato: Palazzo Valloni 13, Contrada Omerelli, 47890 San Marino; tel.

0549-882248; fax 0549-882295; e-mail biblioteca@omniway.sm; internet www .bibliotecadistato.sm; f. 1839; 120,000 vols, 77 periodicals, collns of posters, photographs and MSS; Dir ELISABETTA RIGHI IWANEJKO.

Museums

San Marino

Museo delle Curiosità: Salita all Rocca 26, Centro Storico, 47890 San Marino; tel. 0549-992437; fax 0549-991075; e-mail info@ museodellecuriosita.sm; internet www .museodellecuriosita.sm; colln of curiosities and highly unusual objects.

Museo di San Francesco: Via Basilicius, 47890 San Marino; tel. 0549-885132; internet www.museidistato.sm/museo_trad/msf; f. 1966; exhibits of the artistic heritage of the monastery and other Franciscan churches; panel paintings, canvases, vestments, furnishings, sculptures.

Museo di Stato: Sede Espositiva, Piazzetta del Titano 1, 47890 San Marino; tel. 0549-882670; fax 0549-882679; e-mail info@ museidistato.sm; internet www.museidistato .sm; f. 1899; reorganized as autonomous entity 1982; 5,000 objects; archaeological finds from the Neolithic to early Middle Ages; architectural remains of the ancient Basilica; paintings and objects from the 17th-century convent of the Clarisse; works of art of the Republic; San Marino coins and medals (1865–1938); Egyptian, Etruscan and Roman archaeological finds donated to the State; Dir Dott. FRANCESCA MICHELOTTI.

University

UNIVERSITÀ DEGLI STUDI DELLA REPUBBLICA DI SAN MARINO

Antico Monastero Santa Chiara, Contrada Omerelli 20, 47890 San Marino

Telephone: 378-882541
Fax: 378-882545
E-mail: rettorato@unirsm.sm
Internet: www.unirsm.sm
Founded 1985
State control
Rector: Prof. GIORGIO PETRONI
Admin. Dir: Avv. MARIA SCIARRINO
Librarian: Dott. GABRIELLA LORENZI
Library of 45,000 vols, 500 periodicals
Publication: *L'Ateneo del Citano* (1 a year)

DEANS

Department of Biomedical Studies: Prof. VINCENZO GASBARRO
Department of Communication: Prof. PATRIZIA VIOLI
Department of Economics and Technology: Prof. ANGELO MARCELLO TARANTINO
Department of Education and Training: Prof. LUIGI GUERRA
Department of Historical Studies: Prof. LUCIANO CANFORA
Department of Law Studies: Prof. PIER GIORGIO PERUZZI

SÃO TOMÉ E PRÍNCIPE

The Higher Education System

The Democratic Republic of São Tomé and Príncipe is a group of islands lying in the Gulf of Guinea, off the west coast of Africa. It achieved independence from Portugal in 1975. The Government has made higher education a national priority; however, São Tomé e Príncipe is a small, poor and isolated nation, and consequently faces many challenges in progressing towards its strategic goals. The Instituto Universitario de Contabilidade, Administração e Informatica was founded in 1994; it is a private institution that primarily provides vocational training.

The Instituto Superior Politécnico de São Tomé e Príncipe was founded in 1997 and is administered by the Government; it offers Bachelors degrees, particularly in teacher training, although its curriculum has recently expanded to include areas such as business administration, languages, literature and technology. The country's first university, Universidade Lusíada, was inaugurated in 2006. In 2009/10 766 students were enrolled within tertiary education. The higher education sector is administered by the Ministry of Education, Culture and Vocational Training.

Regulatory Body

GOVERNMENT

Ministry of Education, Culture and Vocational Training: Rua Misericórdia, CP 41, São Tomé; tel. 222861; fax 221466; e-mail mineducal@cstome.net; Minister MARIANA RUTE LEAL.

Learned Society

LANGUAGE AND LITERATURE

Alliance Française: CP 974, São Tomé; tel. 242300; fax 242309; e-mail alliancefr@cstome.ne.

Libraries and Archives

São Tomé

Arquivo Histórico de São Tomé e Príncipe: CP 87, São Tomé; tel. 222306; fax 224201; e-mail ahstp@cstome.net; f. 1969; 60,000 boxes of documents; 5,000 vols of bibliography; Dir MARIA NAZARÉ DE CEITA.

Biblioteca do Ministério de Agricultura e Pesca: CP 47, São Tomé; tel. 224657; f. 1973; 1,750 vols; Librarian TOMÉ DE SOUSA DA COSTA.

Biblioteca Municipal: São Tomé.

Centro de Documentação Técnica e Científica: São Tomé; 45,000 vols of specialized documents on agriculture, fisheries, economics; 2,000 periodicals; Dir MARIA ROSÁRIO ASSUNÇÃO.

Museum

São Tomé

Museu Nacional: CP 87, São Tomé; tel. 221874; history, ethnography, religious art.

University

UNIVERSIDADE LUSÍADA DE SÃO TOMÉ E PRÍNCIPE

Rua da Caixa, 188, 1031
Telephone: 225209
E-mail: ulstp@lis.ulusiada.pt
Internet: stp.ulusiada.pt

Founded 2006
Academic year: October to July
Private control

Courses in economics and business, foreign languages and informatics,.

College

Instituto Superior Politécnico de São Tomé e Príncipe: Endereço Ministério da Educação, Quinta de Santo António, CP 41, Príncipe; tel. and fax 223896; e-mail isptsp@cstome.net; internet www.stome.net/educa/isp.htm; f. 1997; Dir LÚCIO LIMA VIEGAS PINTO.

SAUDI ARABIA

The Higher Education System

The Kingdom of Saudi Arabia was proclaimed in 1932 following the unification of the central Najd (Nejd) and western Hedjaz regions of the Arabian peninsula under the rule of Ibn Sa'ud, who also established the current ruling Saudi dynasty. The oldest existing institution of higher education is the Madrasat Ahl Al-Hadith (founded 1933), a school of Islamic studies. King Saud University (founded 1957; current name 1982) was the first university-level institution. Universities mostly consist of colleges, and male and female students are often segregated. In 2008 there were an estimated 659,887 students enrolled in higher education. Higher education institutions in 2010 included 21 state universities, 24 private universities and colleges, 37 health institutes and colleges, 12 technical colleges, 80 teacher-training colleges for women and 18 teacher-training colleges for men. The Higher Education Council is the supreme national body of post-secondary, non-military education. Responsibility for female higher education (as well as primary and secondary education) is delegated to the General Presidency for Girls' Education. Quality assurance and accreditation is undertaken by the National Commission for Academic Accreditation and Assessment (founded 2002). In late 2009 the Government announced a 25-year higher education initiative, which was intended, inter alia, to increase women's access to higher education and to improve private and teacher education. As part of the initiative, the Princess Nora bint Abdulrahman University was opened in Riyadh in May 2011; the university was expected eventually to cater for around 50,000 female students, rendering it the largest women's university in the world.

Admission to higher education is based on the award of the Tawjihiyah (General Secondary Education Certificate) and performance in the Qudrat (General Aptitude Test). The Associate degree and undergraduate Diploma are pre-university qualifications offered by community colleges and are four-semester (two-year) programmes of study. Saudi degrees are awarded on a 'credit–semester' system, whereby students are required to accrue a specified number of credits each semester in order to graduate. Both the Associate degree and the undergraduate Diploma require 48–70 credits for graduation. The undergraduate Bachelors degree is often a four-year programme of study, although degrees in professional fields of study such as dentistry, medicine and pharmacy last upwards of five years. The minimum number of credits required for graduation ranges between 128 and 204, depending on the course. Graduates holding the Bachelors degree are eligible for admission to the postgraduate Diploma or Masters degree. The postgraduate Diploma lasts one year (30 credits) and the Masters degree is a two-year course (42 credits), including submission of a dissertation. The highest university degree is the Doctorate, which requires a minimum of three years of study and research, culminating in the public defence of a dissertation.

Post-secondary technical and vocational education is supervised by the Technical and Vocational Training Corporation, and admission is based on the Tawjihiyah. Institutions offering technical and vocational education include Colleges of Technology, Higher Technical Institutes, Pre-Vocational and Vocational Training Centres, Trade Schools and Junior Health Colleges. Colleges of Technology provide two-year courses of education leading to the award of the Technical College Certificate; Higher Technical Institutes offer a Diploma programme; Trade Schools specialize in programmes of study relating to trades and professions; and Junior Health Colleges train technicians for the health services profession. In 2008 a total of 83,347 students attended 101 technical and vocational institutes.

There are also eight military institutions, which are under the supervision of either the Ministry of Defence, the Ministry of the Interior or the Saudi Arabian National Guard. These institutions do not have degree-awarding powers.

Regulatory and Representative Bodies

GOVERNMENT

Ministry of Culture and Information: Intercontinental Rd, Riyadh 11112; tel. (1) 401-4440; fax (1) 402-3570; internet www.moci.gov.sa; Minister Dr ABD AL-AZIZ IBN MOHI EL-DIN KHOJA.

Ministry of Education: POB 3734, Airport Rd, Riyadh 11148; tel. (1) 404-2888; fax (1) 401-2365; internet www.moe.gov.sa; Minister PRINCE FAISAL IBN ABDULLAH IBN MUHAMMAD AL SA'UD.

Ministry of Higher Education: POB 225085, Riyadh 11324; tel. (1) 441-5555; fax (1) 441-9004; e-mail contact@mohe.gov.sa; internet www.mohe.gov.sa; Minister Dr KHALID IBN MUHAMMAD AL-ANGARI.

ACCREDITATION

National Commission for Academic Accreditation and Assessment: POB 8252, Riyadh 11482; fax (1) 212-0666; internet www.ncaaa.org.sa; 17 mems; Chair. THE MINISTER OF HIGHER EDUCATION.

Learned Societies

BIBLIOGRAPHY, LIBRARY SCIENCE AND MUSEOLOGY

Arab Regional Branch of the International Council on Archives (ARBICA): Institute of Public Administration, POB 205, Riyadh 11141; tel. (1) 476-1600, ext. 462; close collaboration with ICA, UNESCO and other int. orgs; mems: 20 Arab countries; Pres. A. TAMINI (Tunisia); Sec.-Gen. FAHD AL-ASKAR (Saudi Arabia); publ. *Arab Archives Journal* (1 a year).

LANGUAGE AND LITERATURE

British Council: C-14, Third Fl., Al-Fazari Sq., Diplomatic Quarter, POB 58012, Riyadh 11594; tel. (1) 483-1818; fax (1) 483-1717; e-mail enquiry.riyadh@sa.britishcouncil.org; internet www.britishcouncil.org/saudiarabia; teaching centre (men's and women's sections); offers courses and examinations in English language and British culture and promotes cultural exchange with the UK; attached teaching centres in Jeddah and Dammam; Country Dir ALAN SMART; Teaching Centre Man. (Men's section) MALCOLM JARDINE; Teaching Centre Man. (Women's section) HELEN GLENN.

NATURAL SCIENCES

Biological Sciences

Saudi Biological Society: King Saud University, POB 2455, Riyadh 11451; tel. (1) 467-5835; fax (1) 467-5833; f. 1975; 350 mems; Pres. Dr I. A. IRIF; Sec.-Gen. Dr F. AL-MANA; publ. *Journal of the Saudi Biological Society*.

Geographical Sciences

Saudi Geographical Society: POB 2456, Riyadh 11451; tel. (1) 467-8798; fax (1) 467-7732; e-mail sgs@ksu.edu.sa; internet www.saudigs.org; Chair. Prof. MOHAMMAD MAKKI; Sec.-Gen. Dr ABDALLAH H. AL-SOLAI.

Research Institutes

GENERAL

King Faisal Centre for Research and Islamic Studies: POB 51049, Riyadh 11543; tel. (1) 465-2255; fax (1) 465-9993; e-mail kfcrisinfo@kff.com; internet www.kfcris.com; f. 1983; part of King Faisal Foundation; research in various fields of Islamic civilization; library of 85,000 books, 2,400 periodicals, 23,833 original MSS, 13,000 microfilm and microfiche; audiovisual library of 10,000 vols; children's library of 17,000 vols; Chair. HRH Prince TURKI AL-FAISAL; Sec.-Gen. Dr

YAHYA MAHMOUD AL-JUNAID; publs *Al-Faisal* (12 a year), *Journal of Linguistic Studies* (in Arabic, 6 a year).

ECONOMICS, LAW AND POLITICS

Islamic Research and Training Institute: POB 9201, Jeddah 21413; tel. (2) 636-1400; fax (2) 637-8927; e-mail irti@isdb.org; internet www.irti.org; f. 1982; part of Islamic Development Bank; research to enable the economic and financial activities of the IDB's mem. countries to conform to the Islamic Shari'a; research into all aspects of mem. countries' economic and financial systems; training of personnel (but no formal teaching courses); language of instruction: Arabic; library of 9,000 vols; Dir Prof. Dr MABID ALI AL-JARHI.

EDUCATION

Centre for Research in Islamic Education: POB 1034, Mecca; tel. (2) 556-5677; fax (2) 558-6707; f. 1980 by the Organization of the Islamic Conference, affiliated 1982 to Umm Al-Qura University; aims to promote Islamic values in education through research, devt and training; Dir Dr ABDURRAZZAK AHMED ZAFAR.

HISTORY, GEOGRAPHY AND ARCHAEOLOGY

King Abdulaziz Research Centre: POB 2945, Riyadh 11461; tel. (1) 441-2316; fax (1) 441-7020; e-mail ibnsaud@saudinf.com; f. 1972 in memory of the late King; historical research, preservation of historical documents, photographs and other cultural material; library of 28,000 vols, 200 periodicals; also the private library of the late King (2,000 vols); historical archive incl. documents in various languages, esp. Turkish and English, and Arabic MSS; King Abdulaziz Memorial Hall shows events in the late King's life, esp. his military battles; Sec.-Gen. Dr FAHD AL-SEMMARI.

MEDICINE

Saudi–German Institute for Nursing and Allied Health Sciences: POB 2550, Jeddah 21461; e-mail webmaster@sgnursing .com; internet www.sgna-sa.com; Pres. Dr SOBHI IBRAHIM BATTERJEE.

TECHNOLOGY

Bureau de Recherches Géologiques et Minières (BRGM): POB 1492, Jeddah 21431; tel. (2) 665-1104; see main entry under France.

King Abdulaziz City for Science and Technology: POB 6086, Riyadh 11442; tel. (1) 481-4329; fax (1) 481-6730; e-mail public@ kacst.edu.sa; internet www.kacst.edu.sa; nat. science agency; Pres. Dr MOHAMMAD IBN IBRAHIM AL-SUWAIYEL.

Libraries and Archives
Jeddah
Educational Library: General Directorate of Broadcasting, Press and Publications, Jeddah.

Mecca
Abbas Kattan Library: Mecca; 7,800 vols, 200 MSS.
Library of Alharam: Mecca; 6,000 vols.
Madrasat Ahl Al-Hadith Library: Mecca.

Medina
Islamic University Library: POB 170, Medina; tel. (4) 847-4080; fax (4) 847-4560;

f. 1961; consists of a central library and 11 brs; 143,000 vols, 27,772 MSS, 8,761 microfilms, 3,247 theses.
King Abdulaziz Library: Medina; tel. (4) 823-2134; fax (4) 823-2126; f. 1983; 120,000 vols and MSS; Dir D. ABDULRAHMAN BIN SULIMAN ALMUZINY.

Riyadh
Institute of Public Administration Library: POB 205, Riyadh 11141; tel. (1) 476-8888; fax (1) 479-2136; e-mail library@ ipa.edu.sa; internet www.ipa.edu.sa; f. 1961; 240,000 vols in Arabic, English and French, 1,088 periodical titles, 55,000 Saudi public records, 4,953 official publs., 33,420 microforms, 712 CD-ROMs; Dir-Gen. EN MOSTAFA SADHAN.
King Abdulaziz City for Science and Technology Library: POB 6086, Riyadh 11442; tel. (1) 488-3555; fax (1) 488-3118; 50,000 vols, 75,000 technical reports; Dir of Information Systems HAMAD AL-SADOUN.
King Abdulaziz Public Library: POB 86486, Riyadh 11622; tel. (1) 434-7805; fax (1) 491-1949; e-mail hyami@kapl.org.sa; internet www.kapl.org.sa; f. 1985; 275,000 vols (Arabic and non-Arabic), 1,100 current periodicals, 2,500 MSS, 53,000 historic documents on microform, 5,000 audiovisual items, doctoral dissertations; equestrian information; Supervisor-Gen. Dr. FAISAL A. AL-MUAAMMAR.
King Fahad National Library: POB 7572, Riyadh 11472; tel. (1) 462-4888; fax (1) 464-5341; e-mail headoffice@kfnl.gov.sa; internet www.kfnl.gov.sa; f. 1968; 37,000 vols in Arabic, English, French; 150 MSS; Dir ABDUR RAHMAN AL-SARRA.
King Saud University Libraries: POB 22480, Riyadh 11495; tel. (1) 467-3404; fax (1) 467-6127; e-mail itlibrary@ksu.edu.sa; internet www.ksu.edu.sa; f. 1957; central library and 11 brs incl. Prince Salman Central Library, Central Library for Girls (Malaz), Univ. Studies Centre for girls (Ulayshah), Faculty of Medicine, King Abdulaziz Univ. Hospital, College of Dentistry, College of Applied Medical Sciences, College of Community Services, Library of Preparatory year, Library of Teachers College; 1.54m. vols, 4,500 periodicals, 22,000 MSS, 150,400 govt publs, 24,000 microfilm items, 4,000 microfiche items, 18,000 audiovisual items; Dean Dr SAUD LEILY AL ROWAILY; Vice-Dean Dr ABDUL RAHMAN A. AL-SHAMMARI.
Saudi Arabian Standards Organization Information Centre: POB 3437, Riyadh 11471; tel. (1) 452-0000; fax (1) 452-0086; f. 1972; 10,000 vols, 650,000 nat., int. and foreign standards; Dir MOHAMMAD ALMESHARI.

Museums
Al-Ahsa
Al-Hafouf Museum: Al-Ahsa; tel. (3) 580-2639; f. 1991; regional folklore and archaeological collns.

Al-Baha
Al-Baha Museum: Al-Baha; tel. (7) 725-5251; fax (7) 725-5212; f. 2003; regional archaeological and heritage collns.

Al-Jouf
Al-Jouf Museum: Al-Jouf; tel. (4) 622-2151; f. 2004; regional archaeological collns; next to ancient Mraid Castle.

Al-Ola
Museum of Al-Ola Antiquities: Medina Al-Munwarrah, Al-Ola; tel. (4) 884-1536; fax (4) 884-1536; f. 1991; archaeological colln.

Dammam
Dammam Museum: Dammam 31158; tel. (3) 826-6056; e-mail offica18@school.adst.net; f. 1985; antiquities and heritage collns.

Hail
Al-Qushlah Museum: Hail; tel. (6) 533-1684; f. 2004; regional archaeological collns.

Jazan
Jazan Museum: Jazan province, Subia; tel. (7) 326-1193; f. 1991; regional archaeological collns; next to Al-Adareisa archaeological site.

Jeddah
Al-Khozam Palace Museum: Jeddah; tel. (2) 636-4271; fax (2) 636-4271; f. 1995; Saudi history from Stone Age to Islamic Age; folklore colln.

Najran
Najran Museum: Al-Okhdood; f. 1995; housed on archaeological site of ancient city of Najran; regional folklore and archaeological collns; restoration laboratory.

Riyadh
National Museum, Riyadh: POB 3734 Riyadh 11481; tel. (1) 403-0104; fax (1) 404-1391; f. 1999; Saudi history, archaeology, geology, trade, social life and ethnography, and man's relationship with the Universe; Dir-Gen. Dr ALI SALEH AL-MOGHANNAM.

Taif
Shobrah Palace Museum: Taif; tel. (2) 732-1033; f. 1995; Saudi history from Stone Age to Islamic Age.

Universities
AL-FAISAL UNIVERSITY

POB 50927, Riyadh 11533

Telephone: (1) 440-2000
Fax: (1) 462-3508
E-mail: info@alfaisal.edu
Internet: www.alfaisal.edu

Founded 2004
Private control
Academic year: September to July

Provost: Dr FAISAL ALMUBARAK (acting)
Vice-Pres. for Research and Graduate Studies: Dr MATHEUS GOOSEN
Vice-Pres. for Advancement: Prof. AHMED AL OBAID (acting)
Dean for Student Affairs: Dr MOHAMMED ALOWAYED
Vice-Provost for Accreditation and Quality Assurance: Prof. ALA AL-BAKRI
Librarian: Prof. THOMAS L. WILLIAMS

DEANS

College of Business: Dr EARL NAUMANN
College of Engineering: Dr ABDULMAJEED MOHAMMED
College of Medicine: Prof. KHALED AL-KATTAN
College of Science and General Studies: Dr NORMAN SWAZO

AL-IMAM MUHAMMAD IBN SAUD ISLAMIC UNIVERSITY

POB 5701, Riyadh 11432

Telephone: (1) 258-0812
Fax: (1) 259-0271
E-mail: admission@imamu.edu.sa

Internet: www.imamu.edu.sa
Founded 1953, Univ. status 1974
State control
Language of instruction: Arabic
Academic year: August to June
Rector: HE Prof. Dr SULIMAN A. ABA AL-KHAIL
Vice-Rector: Dr ABDULLAH ASH-SHETHRY
Vice-Rector for Shari'a Institute Affairs: Dr BANDAR F. AS-SUWAILAM
Vice-Rector for Higher Studies and Scientific Research: Dr ABDULLAH H. AL-KHALAF
Vice-Rector for Studies, Devt, and Academic Accreditation: Dr ABDUR-RAHMAN H. AD-DAWUD
Vice-Rector for Community Service and Continuing Education: AHMAD Y. A. AD-DRIWEESH (acting)
Vice-Rector for Female Student Affairs: Dr KHALID SAAD AL-MEGREN
Dean of Academic Research: Dr ABDULLAH IBN ABDULLRAHMAN AL-RABEE
Dean of Admissions and Registrations: Dr SAAD A. AL-GUSAIBY
Dean of Admissions and Students Affairs in Qassim: Dr MEZAYAD IBN IBRAHIM AL-MEZAYAD
Dean of Admissions and Students Affairs in the South: Dr SAAD IBN HUSAIN OTHMAN
Dean of Higher Studies: Dr KHALID A. AL-MESHAL
Dean of Institute Affairs Abroad: Dr IBRAHIM A. AS-SAADAN
Dean of Libraries: Dr MUSAED S. AT-TAIYAR
Dean of Students: Dr MEGREN S. AL-MEGREN
Dean of Univ. Centre for Community Service and Continuing Education: Dr ABDULLAH M. AR-REZAIN

Number of teachers: 1,648
Number of students: 39,938

DEANS

Arabic Language Teaching Institute (Riyadh): Dr ABDULAZIZ I. AL-ESAILY
College of Arabic and Social Sciences (Qassim): Dr MOHAMMAD IBN SULAIMAN-RAJHI
College of Arabic and Social Sciences (in the South): Dr ALI IBN MUHAMMAD ARISH
College of Arabic Language: Dr MOHAMMED A. AS-SEHABEAIN
College of Computer and Information: Dr ABDULLAH A. AT-TAMIM (acting)
College of Dawa and Mass Communication: Dr ABDULLAH AL-MAJALY
College of Economics and Administrative Sciences: Dr KHALID AL-MEGREN
College of Fundamentals of Religion: Dr FAHD S. AL-FUHAID
College of Islamic Call Dawa (Medina): Dr MOSTAFA IBN OMAR HALABI
College of Islamic Law and Fundamentals of Religion (Al-Qassim): Dr ABDUL RAHMAN AL-MEZAINI (acting)
College of Islamic Law and Fundamentals of Religion (in the South): Dr ABDULAZIZ IBN ALI AL-GHAMDI
College of Language and Translation: Dr MOHAMMED S. AL-ALAM
College of Medicine: Prof. Dr KHALID A. AL-ABDUL-RAHMAN
College of Science: Dr MOHAMMED A. AL-QADI (acting)
College of Shari'a and Islamic Studies (Al-Ihsa): Dr MOHAMMED A. AL-JABR
College of Social Science: Dr FAWZAN A. AL-FAWAZAN
Female University Study Centre: Dr MOHAMMED I. AL-AJLAN
Shari'a College: Dr ABDULLAH E. AL-ESA
Supreme Jurisdiction Institute: Dr ABDULLAH AS-SELAMAY (acting)

AL-YAMAMAH UNIVERSITY

POB 45180, Riyadh 11512
Telephone: (1) 224-2222
Fax: (1) 224-1111
E-mail: info@alyamamah.edu.sa
Internet: www.yu.edu.sa
Founded 2001 as Al-Yamamah College; Univ. status in 2008
Private control
Accredited by Saudi Ministry of Higher Education
Pres.: Dr AHMED M. AL-EISA (acting)
Vice-Pres. for Academic Affairs: Dr OWEN F. CARGOL
Dean of Women's College: Dr HESSAH M. AL-SHEIK
Dir of Student Affairs: RAMI AL-SHARAFEEN
Dir of Library: MOHAMMAD ASSIM
Colleges of Business Admin., Computing and IT.

ISLAMIC UNIVERSITY IN MEDINA

POB 170, Medina
Telephone: (1) 847-4080
Fax: (1) 827-4560
Internet: www.iu.edu.sa
Founded 1961
State control
Language of instruction: Arabic
Chancellor: Dr ABDULLAH BIN SALAH AL-ABID
Vice-Rector: ABDUL MUHSIN BEN HAMAD AL-ABBAD
Number of teachers: 620
Number of students: 3,140

DEANS

College of Prophet Sayings (Hadeith) and Islamic Studies: (vacant)
College of the Holy Koran and Islamic Studies: (vacant)
Faculty of Arabic Language: A. D. ABDUL RAZAK BIN FARRAJ ALSAIDI
Faculty of Dawa and the Fundamentals of Islam: (vacant)
Faculty of Islamic Law (Shari'a): D. AHMED ABDULLAH

JAZAN UNIVERSITY

POB 114, Jazan
Telephone: (7) 321-0869
Fax: (7) 321-1052
Internet: www.jazanu.edu.sa
Founded 2006
State control
Pres.: Prof. MOHAMMED A. AL-HAYAZA (acting)
Faculties of applied medical science, architecture and design, arts and humanities, business administration, computer and information systems, dentistry, education, engineering, health sciences, medicine, pharmacy, science, science and arts (in Al-Darb, Farasan, Samtah); Girls faculty of health sciences, Community college.

KING ABDULAZIZ UNIVERSITY

POB 1026, Jeddah 21441
Telephone: (2) 695-1995
Fax: (2) 640-5974
Internet: www.kau.edu.sa
Founded 1967
State control
Languages of instruction: Arabic, English
Academic year: September to June
Pres.: Prof. USAMA SADIQ TAYEB
Vice-Pres.: (vacant)
Vice-Pres. for Graduate Studies and Academic Research: Prof. FOUAD M. GHAZALI

Vice-Pres. for Post-Graduate Studies and Scientific Research: Prof. ABDULLA OMAR BAFAIL
Supervisor-Gen. for Admin. and Financial Affairs: Dr SAMIR A. MURSHID
Librarian: Dr MOFAKHAR H. KHAN
Library of 500,000 vols
Number of teachers: 1,145
Number of students: 30,773
Publication: research publs, bulletins

DEANS

Faculty of Applied Medical Sciences: Prof. GHAZI DAMANHOURI
Faculty of Arts and Humanities: Dr M. A. ABOZEID
Faculty of Computing and Information Technology: A. D. KHALID BIN ABDULLAH FAKIH
Faculty of Dentistry: Prof. TAREK LOUTFI AL-KHATEEB
Faculty of Earth Sciences: Prof. MOHAMMED R. MOUFTI
Faculty of Economics and Administration: Prof. HUSSAM A. AL-ANGARI
Faculty of Education: Dr A. I. HAFIZ
Faculty of Engineering: Dr FAISAL ISKANDER-ANI
Faculty of Marine Sciences: Dr O. A. HASHIM
Faculty of Medicine: Dr ADNAN ABDULLA ALMAZROA
Faculty of Meteorology, Environment and Arid Land Agriculture: Dr ABDUL REHMAN KHALAF M. AL-KHALAF
Faculty of Pharmacy: Dr HISHAM A. M. MOSLI
Faculty of Science: Prof. ABDULLAH YOUSIF ABDULLAH OBAID

PROFESSORS

Faculty of Arts and Humanities:
  AL-BAGHDADI, M. M., Arabic Literature
  AL-DIGS, K. S., Islamic Literature
  AL-JERASH, M. A., Climatology and Quantitative Methods
  AL-KHERIJI, A. M., Social Development
  AL-ZEID, I. M., History
  ANQAWI, A. A., Medieval Islamic History
  BAGADER, A. A., Social Changes
  OMER, M. Z., Modern History
  TASHKANDI, A. S., Arabic Manuscripts

Faculty of Dentistry:
  ABDULRAHMAN, A., Paediatric Dentistry
  AL-JEYAR, I. L., Operative
  AL-KHATEB, M. M., Fixed Prosthodontics
  AL-SABBAGH, A. M., Oral Surgery
  FARGHALY, M. M., Dental Public Health
  KAMAR, A. A., Dental Biomaterials
  KATALDO, A., Oral Pathology
  MASOUD, A. J., Endodontics
  MOHAMED, M. A., Operative
  MOUSTAFA, M. A., Removable Prosthodontics, Partial Dentures
  NADA, A. M., Removable Prosthodontics, Partial Dentures
  OMAR, T. A., Oral Pathology
  SAMAH, A., Paediatric Dentistry
  SHARQAWI, M. M., Operative
  SHOUKRY, M. M. S., Periodontics

Faculty of Earth Sciences:
  ALLOUSH, M. A., Building Materials
  AL-MAHDI, O. R., Mineral Resources
  AL-NASSER, H. S., Geophysics
  AL-SHANTI, A. M., Mineralogy
  BASAHEL, A. N., Structural Geology
  MARZOUKI, M. H., Petrology and Mineralogy
  NASSIEF, A. O., Petrology and Mineralogy
  RADEEN, A. A., Petrology and Mineralogy
  SHAREEF, F. A., Petroleum and Stratigraphy
  SHEHATA, W. M., Engineering Geology

Faculty of Economics and Administration:
  AL-AMRI, B. O., Civil Law

ALAKI, M. A., Administration and Management Relations
AL-JEFRI, Y. A., Business Administration
ALSABBAB, A. A., Administration and Management Relations
AL-SOBIANI, A. A., Administration and Management Planning
BAIOUMI, A. M., Cost and Management Accounting
BAMOKHRAMA, A. S., Economics
FADEL, S. Y., International Relations
HASANAIN, O. S., Cost Accounting
MADANI, G. O., Finance and Investment
OMRAN, O. A., Law
SOFI, A. A., Financial Administration
ZA'ED, M. E., Cost Accounting
ZOBAIR, M. O., Monetary Theory

Faculty of Education:

ABDULRADHI, H. M., Physics and Theory
AL-MOJADDADI, M. H. M., Shari'a and Legal System
AL-OQABI, A. H., Modern History
AL-SHATAIRI, B. A., Chemistry
BADAWI, A. A., History
BADAWI, F. A., Ancient History
BAMASHMOOS, S. M., Educational Planning
BEDAIR, A. H. M., Biochemistry
HAMID, M. A. I., Weaving
HASSAN, N. M. A., Psychology
JALLOON, A. D., Archery
KHALIL, M. S. M., Fish Anatomy
KHATIR, K. I. M., Tradition of the Prophet
KHOGALI, M. M., Human Geography
MADBROOK, N. A., Principles of Language
REDWAN, M. N., Wrestling
SHAIKH, A. A., English Language Teaching Methods
SHEHATAH, M. N., Entomology

Faculty of Engineering:

ABD. EL-LATIF, A. K., Mechanical Design and Stress Analysis
ABDEL RAHMAN, M. M., Aerodynamics
ABDIN, M. F., Metrology and Advanced Manufacturing Technology
ABDUL-MAJID, S., Nuclear Instrumentation
ABOKHASHABA, A., Metal Cutting and Spare Parts
ABOLANIN, G. M., Heat and Energy Transfer
ABOLFARAJ, W. H., Industrial Engineering
ABORAZIZAH, O. S., Civil Engineering
AHMED, K. M., Structure and Construction
AKYURT, M., Mechanisms and Robotics
AL-IDRISI, M. M., Operational Research
AL-NOURY, S. I., Structure
ALP, T. Y., Physical Metallurgy
ALY, S. E., Desalination Technology and Two-Phase Flow
AWAD, A. E., Biotechnology, Floriculture
DARWISH, M. A., Rock Blasting
ELGILLANI, D. A., Mineral Processing and Metallurgy
EL-NAGGAR, M. M., Extractive Metallurgy
FATHALAH, K., Heat and Mass Transfer
FATTAH, A. A., Nuclear Reactor Safety and Nuclear Desalination
FOUAD, A. A., Nuclear Desalination
GHAZALI, F. M., Geotechnics
HAQUE, M. Z., Mine Management and Mining Law
KUTBI, I. I., Nuclear Desalination
MOHAMED, S. E., Electrical Power Engineering
MOUSSA, H. A., Electrical Power Engineering
NAHHAS, M. N., Aviation Engineering
NAJJAR, Y., Gas Turbines, Engines and Energy Systems
NAWAIR, M. H., Human Factors
RAIH, M. A., Aviation Engineering
RUSHDI, A. M., Computer Engineering and Electrical Communication
SABBAGH, J. A., Heat and Energy Transfer
WAFA, F. F., Structural Engineering
WANAS, M. A., Electronics

YORULMAZ, Y. K., Petroleum Refining and Petrochemicals

Faculty of Marine Sciences:

AHMAD, F., Residual and Tidal Currents
BEHAIRY, A. K. A., Modern Marine Sediments
EL-NAKKADI, A. N., Biochemistry
KHAFAJI, A. K., Marine Plant Physiology
NIAZ, G. R., Marine Biochemistry

Faculty of Medicine:

ABDULMONAM, N. A., Community Medicine
AHMAD, A. O., Haematology
AJABNOOR, M. A., Biochemistry
AL-ARDAWI, M. S., Biochemistry
AL-AWWAD, A. M., Chemistry
AL-BADWI, A. A., Surgery
AL-JOHARI, K. M., Anatomy
AL-KHATEEB, A. M., Physics
AL-MATRAWI, U. M., Parasitology
AL-QADASI, A. A., Biochemistry
AL-SHAIKH, S. A., Paediatrics
ALI, F. M., Medical Technology
ATTALLAH, A. A., Physiology
BASALAMAH, A. H., Obstetrics and Gynaecology
FATANI, H. H., Medicine
ISLAM, S. I., Pharmacology
KHAN, N. M., Anatomy
MATIX, F. A., Microbiology
MUKHTAR, A. M., Surgery
OSMAN, O. O., Pharmacology
RAFFAH, H. M., Surgery
RAZIK, S. M., Surgery
SAJINEE, S. A., Haematology
SALAMA, H. S., Biology
SALMAN, KH. M., Surgery
SHARIF, M. A., Radiology
SHARIF, M. T., Anatomy
SHOBOKSHI, O. A., Medicine
SIRAJ, A. A., E.N.T.
SOLIMAN, S. A., Chemistry
SUKKAR, M. Y., Physiology
SULAIMAN, N. K., Community Medicine
TAYEB, O. S., Pharmacology
TILMISANY, A. M., Pharmacology
YOUSIF, K. M., Surgery
ZAFAR, M. N., Radiology
ZAHRAN, F. M., E.N.T.

Faculty of Meteorology, Environment and Arid Land Agriculture:

ABDURAZZAK, M. G., Water Resources
ABOHASSAN, A. A., Forest Management
AL-HASHIM, G. M., Environmental Toxicology and Health
AL-HIFNY, A. M., Entomology (Bees)
ARAFA, A. S., Environmental Health
EL-AGAMY, S. A., Horticulture
GOKNIL, M. H., Air Pollution
SAMARRAI, S. M., Genetics and Plant Breeding
SHAHEEN, M. A., Genetics and Fruit Breeding

Faculty of Science:

ABOU-ZAID, A. A., Fermentation
AHMAD, I., Theoretical Nuclear Physics
AL-DESSOUKI, T. A., Laser Optics
ALHARBI, M. A., Theoretical Nuclear Physics
AL-SAYAD, G. M., Statistics
BAESHIN, N. A., Genetics
BAGHLAF, A. O., Chemistry
BANAGAH, A. A., Parasitology
BASAHEL, S. N., Chemistry
ELDIN, H. M., Environmental Microbiology
EL-MASHAK, E. M., Biophysics
EZMIRLI, T. S., Chemistry
FARAG, A. A., Vertebrate Zoology
GHANEM, K. M., Biotechnology
KHOJA, S. M., Enzymes and Metabolic Regulation
MAGHRABI, Y. M., Plant Physiology
MELIBARI, A. A., Biology
RAFI, M., Experimental Molecular Physics
SABBAK, O. A., Chemistry

SAHAB, S. M., Mathematics
SEJININ, M. J., Plant Pathology
SHAHAB, F., Theoretical Particle Physics
SOLEIMAN, A. H., Chemistry
TAHER, M. O., Entomology (Bionomics)
TAWFIK, K. A., Plant Pathology

ATTACHED RESEARCH INSTITUTES

Centre for Nanotechnology: POB 80216, Jeddah 21589; tel. (2) 695-1399; fax (2) 695-1566; e-mail cnt@kau.edu.sa; Dir Dr SAMI S. HABIB.

Centre of Excellence in Environmental Studies: POB 80216, Jeddah 21589; tel. (2) 640-0200; fax (2) 640-2000; e-mail cees@kau.edu.sa; Dir GHAZI A. JAMJOOM.

Centre of Excellence in Genomic Medicine Research: POB 80216, Jeddah 21589; tel. (2) 640-1000; fax (2) 695-2521; e-mail cegmr.info@kau.edu.sa; internet www.kau.edu.sa/centers/cegmr; Exec. Dir Dr MOHAMMED H. ALQAHTANI.

FAH Research Centre: POB 80202, Jeddah 21589; tel. (2) 695-2353; fax (2) 695-1732; e-mail rca_kaau@hotmail.com; internet www.kau.edu.sa/rca/rca; Pres. Dr AYMAN BIN ABDULLAH HABIS.

Islamic Economics Research Centre: POB 80214, Jeddah 21589; tel. (2) 695-2751; fax (2) 695-2404; e-mail cn-crie@kau.edu.sa; Dir Dr M. A. ELGARI.

King Fahd Medical Research Centre: POB 80216, Jeddah 21589; tel. (2) 640-0000; fax (2) 695-2076; e-mail kfmrc@kau.edu.sa; internet www.kau.edu.sa/kfmrc; Dir GHAZI A. JAMJOOM (acting).

Water Research Centre: POB 80160, Jeddah 21589; tel. (2) 695-2507; fax (2) 695-1403; e-mail wrc@kau.edu.sa; internet wrc.kau.edu.sa; Dir Dr ABDULLAH S. AL-GHAMDI.

KING ABDULLAH UNIVERSITY OF SCIENCE AND TECHNOLOGY

POB 55455, 4700 KAUST Thuwal 23955-6900

Internet: www.kaust.edu.sa

Founded 2009

Pres.: CHOON FONG SHIH
Provost: BRIAN MORAN
Dir of Libraries: JOSEPH J. BRANIN
Library of 25,000 books, 2,000 journals (incl. 1,500 e-journals), 10 online research databases

DEANS

Chemical and Life Sciences and Engineering: KEN MINNEMAN
Mathematical and Computer Sciences and Engineering: DAVID KEYES
Physical Sciences and Engineering: (vacant):

KING FAHD UNIVERSITY OF PETROLEUM AND MINERALS

POB 5082, Dhahran 31261
Telephone: (3) 860-0000
Fax: (3) 860-3018
E-mail: registrar@kfupm.edu.sa
Internet: www.kfupm.edu.sa
Founded 1963, Univ. status 1975
State control with semi-autonomous operation under a Board of the Univ.
Languages of instruction: English, Arabic
Academic year: September to June (summer semester: June to August)
Chair. of Board of Trustees: HE The Minister of Higher Education Dr KHALID M. AL-ANGARY
Rector: HE Dr KHALID S. AL-SULTAN
Vice-Rector for Academic Affairs: Dr ABDULAZIZ A. AL-SUWAYAN

Vice-Rector for Applied Research and Scientific Research and Graduate Studies: Dr SALEH N. ABDULJAUWAD

Vice-Rector for Technology Devt and Industrial Relations: Dr FALEH ABDULLAH AL-SULAIMAN

Dean of Admissions and Registration: Dr MAMDOUH M. NAJJAR

Dean of Library Affairs: Dr IBRAHIM M. AL-JABRI

Library of 355,700 vols
Number of teachers: 950
Number of students: 8,155

Publication: *Arabian Journal for Science and Engineering* (6 a year)

DEANS

Computer Science and Engineering: Dr UMAR AL-TURKI

Dammam Community College: TARIQ AL-JUFRI

Educational Services: Dr MUHAMMAD S. AL-MULHEM

Engineering Sciences and Applied Engineering: Dr SAMIR A. AL-BAIYAT

Environmental Design: Dr ABDULAZIZ BUB-SHAIT

Industrial Management: Dr AREF A. AL-ASHBAN

Sciences: Dr WALID S. AL-SABAHI

Scientific Research: Dr OSAMA A. JANNADI

Graduate Studies: Dr OSAMA A. JANNADI

KING FAISAL UNIVERSITY

POB 380, Al-Hassa 31982
and POB 1982, Dammam 31441
Telephone: (Dammam) (3) 587-7000
Fax: (Dammam) (3) 587-6748
Telephone: (Al-Hassa) (3) 850-0000
Fax: (Al-Hassa) (3) 580-1243
Internet: www.kfu.edu.sa

Founded 1975
State control
Languages of instruction: Arabic, English
Academic year: September to June

Pres.: Prof. Dr YUSSUF M. AL-GINDAN

Vice-Pres.: Dr ABDULAZIZ AL-SAATI (Dammam)

Vice-Pres. for Academic Affairs: Dr SAAD M. AL-HAREKY (Al-Hassa)

Vice-Pres. for Graduate Studies and Scientific Research: Dr ABDULLAH I. AL-SAADAT (Al-Hassa)

Sec.-Gen.: Dr SAAD MUHAMMAD AL-HAREKY

Librarian: Dr FADEL M. HOUSAWI (Al-Hassa)

Number of teachers: 717
Number of students: 12,880

Publications: *Basic and Applied Sciences* (2 a year), *Humanities and Management Sciences* (2 a year)

DEANS

College of Agricultural and Food Sciences (Al-Hassa): Dr ABDULLAH S. AL-GAMDI

College of Applied and Community Service (Al-Hassa): Dr ADNAN AL-MULHIM

College of Applied Medical Sciences (Dammam): Dr BASIL A. AL-SHIAKH

College of Architecture and Planning (Dammam): Dr MOHAMMAD MASOUD AL-ABDUL-LAH

College of Clinical Pharmacy (Al-Hassa): Dr AHMED A. AL-SHAOIBY

College of Computer Science and Information Technology (Al-Hassa): Dr BADIR AL-GOHAR

College of Dentistry (Dammam): Dr ABDUL-SALAM A. AL-SULIAMAN

College of Education (Al-Hassa): Dr MOHAM-MAD AL-OMARE

College of Management Sciences and Planning (Al-Hassa): Dr HASSAN AL-HAJHOOJ

College of Medicine (Al-Hassa): Dr ALI AL-SULTAN

College of Medicine (Dammam): Dr ABDUL-LAH M. AL-ROBIASH

College of Nursing (Dammam): Dr NAIF I. AL-AWAAD

College of Science (Al-Hassa): Dr SHAR A. AL-SHIHRY

College of Veterinary Medicine and Animal Resources (Al-Hassa): Dr ABDULLAH AL-AZRAGY

KING KHALID UNIVERSITY

Abha 418, Asir Province
Telephone: (7) 339-0641
Fax: (7) 339-0531
E-mail: kku@kku.edu.sa
Internet: www.kku.edu.sa

Founded 1998
State control

Rector: Dr ABDULLAH AL-RASHID

Faculties of Arabic Language, Computer Science, Dentistry, Engineering, Science and Shari'a Law; Colleges of Education, Medicine and Medicinal Science and Pharmacy; Institute of English and Translation.

KING SAUD UNIVERSITY

POB 2454, Riyadh 11451
Telephone: (1) 467-0000
Fax: (1) 467-8301
E-mail: rectoroffice@ksu.edu.sa
Internet: www.ksu.edu.sa

Founded 1957 as Riyadh Univ., present name 1982
State control
Language of instruction: Arabic (English in Medicine and Engineering)
Academic year: October to June

Rector: Prof. ABDULLAH A. AL-OTHMAN

Vice-Rector: Prof. ABDULAZIZ SALEM AL-RUWAIS

Dean of Admissions and Registrations: Dr ABDULLAH AL-SALMAN

Dean of Student Affairs: Dr FAHED ABDUL-MUHSEN AL-MISNED (acting)

Dean of Library Affairs: Dr SULIMAN SALEH AL-AQLAA

Library: see Libraries and Archives
Number of teachers: 2,768
Number of students: 37,324

Publications: *Journal of King Saud University, Statistical Yearbook*

DEANS

Arabic Language Institute: Dr NASSER A. ALGHALI

Centre of Female Scientific and Medical Colleges: Dr AMAL JAMIL FATANI

College of Administrative Sciences: Dr ABDULLAH BIN MOHAMMAD AL-FAISAL

College of Agriculture and Veterinary Medicine: Dr AHMED BIN ALI AL-RUGEIBAH

College of Applied Medical Sciences: Dr ABDULLAH Z. AL-OTAIBI

College of Applied Studies and Community Service: Dr FAHAD N. AL-FAHAD

College of Architecture and Planning: Prof. ABDUL AZIZ S. H. AL MOGREN

College of Arts: Dr FAHAD M. AL-KOLIBI

College of Arts and Sciences in Wady Addwaser: Dr MUBARAK MOHAMMED EL HAMAD

College of Business Administration: Dr AHMED BIN SALEM AL AMERI

College of Computer and Information Sciences: Dr SAMI SALEH AL-WAKEEL

College of Dentistry: Prof. ABDULLAH S. AL-YAHYA

College of Education: KAHID BIN FAHAD AL-HUTHAIFI

College of Engineering: Prof. ABDULAZIZ A. AL-HMAID

College of Engineering in Al-Kharj: Dr AWAD KH. AL-ASMARI

College of Food and Agricultural Sciences: Dr HASSAN A. AL-KAHTANI

College of Higher Studies: Dr AHMAD SULAI-MAN AL-OBAID

College of Languages: Dr SAAD ALHASHASH

College of Law and Political Science: Dr FAHAD HAMOUD ALANAZI

College of Medicine: Prof. MUSSAAD AL-SAL-MAN

College of Medicine in Al-Kharj: Prof. ABDUL-LAH M. AL-BEKAIRI

College of Nursing: Dr MOHAMMED S. AL-NAIF

College of Pharmacy: Dr YOSEF A. ASIRI

College of Pharmacy in Al-Kharj: Dr SALEH I. ALQASOUMI

College of Science: Prof. AWAD BIN MUTAIRIK AL-JOHANI

College of Science and Humanitarian Studies in Al-Kharj: Dr ABDULRAHMAN AL-KHED-HAIRI

College of Teaching: Prof. ALI ABDULLAH AL-AFNAN

College of Tourism and Archaeology: Prof. SAID AL-SAID

Community College in Al-Afalj: Dr RASHED BEN MUBARAK AL-RUSHOUD

Community College in Al-Majma'ah: Dr ABDULLAH ALDAHASH

Community College of Al-Quwayiyah: Dr NASER OREIFI

Community College in Al-Riyadh: Prof. SAAD M. ALSHEHRI

Olyashah Centre for Girls: Dr JAZI BINT MOHAMMED BIN FAHD ALCBIKI

KING SAUD UNIVERSITY FOR HEALTH SCIENCES

Riyadh
Telephone: (1) 252-0088
Internet: www.ksau-hs.edu.sa
Founded 2008
Campuses in Jeddah and Al-Hassa

Pres.: Dr BANDAR ABDULMOHSEN AL-KNAWY (acting)

Vice-Pres. for Academic Affairs: Prof. YOUS-SEF ABDULLAH AL-EISSA

Vice-Pres. for Postgraduate Education: Prof. RASHED SULAIMAN AL-RASHED

Dean of Student Affairs: Prof. ALI SULAIMAN AL-TUWAIJRI

DEANS

College of Applied Medical Sciences: MOHAM-MAD ABDULLAH AL-KHAZIM

College of Medicine (Jeddah): Dr HASSAN SAEED BA'AQEEL

College of Nursing (Al-Hassa): Dr ABDULATIF ABDULLAH AL-FARAID

College of Nursing (Jeddah): Dr WAFIKA ABDULRAHEM SULAIMAN

College of Nursing (Riyadh): Dr HAYA MOHAMMAD AL-FOZAN

College of Public Health and Health Informatics: Dr MAJID MOHAMMED AL-TUWAIJRI

NAIF ARAB UNIVERSITY FOR SECURITY SCIENCES

POB 6830, Riyadh 11452
Telephone: (1) 246-3444
Fax: (1) 246-4713
E-mail: info@nauss.edu.sa
Internet: www.nauss.edu.sa.

PRINCE MOHAMMAD BIN FAHD UNIVERSITY

POB 1664, Al-Khobar 31952
E-mail: info@pmu.edu.sa
Internet: www.pmu.edu.sa

Founded 2006
Private control

Rector: Dr ISSA AL-ANSARI (acting)
Vice-Rector for Academic Affairs: Dr NASSAR M. SHAIKH
Vice-Rector for Business Devt: Dr MASHARY AL-NAIM
Dir of Libraries: Dr JAMIL AHMAD QURESHY

BSc and Masters degree level; Colleges of Business, Engineering, IT.

PRINCE SULTAN UNIVERSITY

POB 66833, Riyadh 11586
Telephone: (1) 494-8000
Fax: (1) 454-8317
E-mail: info@psu.edu.sa
Internet: www.psu.edu.sa
Founded 1999 as Prince Sultan Private College; Univ. status in 2003
Private control

Rector: Dr AHMED AL-YAMANI (acting)
Vice-Rector for Academic Affairs: Dr ABDUL HAFEEZ FEDA
Vice-Rector for Admin. and Financial Affairs: Dr SAAD SALEH AL-RWAITA
Dean of College for Women: Dr FADIA SAUD ALSALEH
Dir of Libraries: Prof. Dr FOUAD H. R. FARSUNI

DEANS

College of Business Admin.: Dr YAHYA N. AL-SERHAN
College of Computer and Information Sciences: Dr ELTAYEB SALIH ABUELYAMAN

QASSIM UNIVERSITY

POB 6677, Buraydah, Qassim 51452
Telephone: (6) 380-3373
Fax: (6) 380-1152
E-mail: syhya@qec.edu.sa
Internet: www.qu.edu.sa
Founded 2004
Number of students: 40,000

Colleges of Agricultural and Veterinary Sciences, Applied Medical Sciences, Arabic and Social Sciences, Computer Science, Dentistry, Economics, Engineering, Medicine, Pharmacy, Science, Shari'a; Community Colleges, Girls' Education Colleges.

TAIBAH UNIVERSITY

Madinah
Telephone: (4) 846-0008
Fax: (4) 846-0020
E-mail: dar@taibahu.edu.sa
Internet: www.taibahu.edu.sa

Pres.: Prof. MANSOUR BIN MOHAMMED AL-NOUZHA (acting)
Vice-Pres. for Academic Affairs: Dr OSAMAH BIN ISMAEL ABDULAZIZ
Vice-Pres. for Graduate Studies and Research: Prof. TALA BIN OMAR HALAWANI

Colleges of Applied Medical Sciences, Computer Science and Engineering, Dentistry, Education, Engineering, Finance and Admin., Medicine, Pharmacy, Science.

UMM AL-QURA UNIVERSITY

POB 715, Mecca
Telephone: (2) 557-4644
Fax: (2) 556-4560
E-mail: info@uqu.edu.sa
Internet: www.uqu.edu.sa
Founded 1979 from existing faculties of King Abdulaziz Univ.

Rector: Prof. WALEED HUSSAIN ABULFARAJ
Deputy Rector: Dr HASHIM BAKR MOHAMMED HARIRI

Deputy Rector for Graduate Studies and Scientific Research: Prof. HASHIM BAKR MOHAMMED HARIRI
Dean of Admission and Registration: Dr ABDULLAH AHMED ABDULLAH
Dean of Graduate Studies: Dr THAMIR HAMDAN JABIR AL-HARBI
Dean of Libraries Affairs: Dr ADNAN MOHAMMED FAIZ AL-HARTHI
Dean of Students Affairs: Dr SALIH HASAN AL-MAB'UTH

Library of 450,000 vols
Number of teachers: 1,408
Number of students: 32,000

Publications: *Journal of Arabic Language and Sharia Sciences, Journal of Engineering, Medicine and Applied Sciences, Journal of Social Sciences and Education*

DEANS

Faculty of Applied Sciences: Dr AHMED ALI AL-KHAMMASH
Faculty of Arabic Language and Literature: Dr ABDULLAH NASIR AL-GARNI
Faculty of Dawa: Dr ABDULLAH OMAR AL-DUMEIGI
Faculty of Education (Makkah): Dr ZOHAIR AHMED ALI AL-KADMI
Faculty of Education (Taif): Dr SUBHI ABDULHAFEEZ QADI
Faculty of Engineering and Islamic Architecture: Dr TARIG MOHAMMAD AHMED NAHAAS
Faculty of Medicine and Medical Studies: Prof. ABDUL-RAZZAG MOHAMMED NUR SULTAN
Faculty of Science (Taif): Dr BAKHIT NAFIE AL-MATRAFI
Faculty of Shari'a and Islamic Studies: Dr SAUD IBRAHIM AL-SHEREAM
Faculty of Social Sciences: Dr AHMED YAHIA AL-GHAMDI
Institute of the Custodian of the Two Holy Mosques for Haj Research: Dr USAMA FADL AL-BAR
Institute of Scientific Research and Revival of Islamic Heritage: MOHAMMED HAMZA AL-SULEIMANI
Institute of Teaching Arabic for Non-native Speakers: Dr SALIH KHAILD DERRI

ATTACHED CAMPUS

Umm Al-Qura University, Taif Campus

Al-Saddad Rd, Shihar, Taif
Telephone: (2) 749-1917
Fax: (2) 746-3008
Founded 1981

Pres.: Dr RASHID BIN RAJIH
Vice-Pres.: Dr MUHAMMAD IBRAHIM AHMED ALI, Higher Studies and Research: Dr SAAD AL-SOBAI, Finance and Admin.
Registrar: ALI F. AL-FAER
Librarian: MOHD ADIL USMANI

Library of 50,000 vols
Number of teachers: 90
Number of students: 2,000

DEANS

Faculty of Education: Dr ABDULLAH ABDUL KARIM AL-ABBADI
Faculty of Library Studies: Dr HAMMAD MUHAMMAD AL-SOMALI

UNIVERSITY OF HA'IL

Ha'il City
Telephone: (6) 531-2500
Fax: (6) 531-0900
E-mail: al-ghazi@uoh.edu.sa
Internet: www.uoh.edu.sa
Founded 1998 as Ha'il Community College; Univ. status in 2005

Rector: Dr AHMED M. AL-SAIF (acting)

Vice-Rector for Academic Affairs: Dr MOHAMMAD A. AL-NAAFA
Dir of Admissions: SAUD ABDULLAH AL-GAHZI
Number of students: 16,000

DEANS

College of Computer Science and Engineering: Dr SALAH A. ZUGAIL
College of Engineering: Dr MOHAMMAD A. AL-NAAFA
College of Sciences: Dr ALI A. AL-QARAWI

Institutes of Higher Education

College of Business Administration: POB 110200, Jeddah 21361; tel. (2) 215-9000; fax (2) 656-3175; e-mail info@cba.edu.sa; internet www.cba.edu.sa; Private control; degree level; Dean Prof. HUSSEIN AL-ALAWI.

Dar Al-Hekma College: POB 34801, Jeddah 21478; tel. (2) 630-3333; e-mail officeofthedean@dah.edu.sa; internet www.daralhekma.edu.sa; private control; f. 1999; accredited by Accrediting Ccl for Ind. Colleges and Schools; to Bachelor degree level; Dean Dr SUHAIR HASSAN AL-QURASHI.

Dr Soliman Fakeeh College for Nursing and Medical Science: POB 2537, Jeddah 21461; tel. (2) 665-5000; fax (2) 660-4332; e-mail college@drfakeehhospital.com; internet www.dsf-nursingcollege.com; private control; f. 2003; women's nursing college to Bachelor degree level; Chair. Dr MAZIN FAKEEH.

Effat College: POB 34689, Jeddah 21478; tel. (2) 636-4300; fax (2) 637-7447; e-mail admissions@effatcollege.edu.sa; internet www.effatcollege.edu.sa; private control; degree level; colleges of business, engineering, humanities and social sciences; Dean Dr HAIFA JAMAL AL-LAIL.

English Language Teaching Institute: POB 58012, Al Mousa Bldg, Olaya Main Rd, Riyadh 11594; tel. (1) 462-1818; fax (1) 462-0663; f. 1969 by Min. of Education and directed by the British Ccl; brs in Jeddah and Dammam; Direct Teaching Operations Man. KEVIN SMITH.

Ibn Sina National College for Medical Studies: Jeddah; tel. (2) 637-4566; fax (2) 637-6630; internet www.ibnsina.edu.sa; private control; under supervision of Ministry of Higher Education; MMS, BDS and Pharm-D qualifications; medicine, dentistry, pharmacy; Dean Dr RASHID HASSAN HABIBULLA KASHGARI.

Institute of Public Administration: POB 205, Riyadh 11141; tel. (1) 476-7305; fax (1) 479-2136; e-mail esl@ipa.edu.sa; internet www.ipa.edu.sa; f. 1961; conducts training courses for govt and private-sector employees; researches into and offers advice on admin. problems; Dir-Gen. HAMAD I. AL-SALLOOM; publ. *PA Journal* (4 a year, in Arabic).

Jeddah College of Technology: King Khaled St, Jeddah 17608; tel. (2) 637-0387; fax (2) 637-8376; internet www.jct.edu.sa.

Jeddah Health Institute: Jeddah; provides basic medical training; similar Institutes at Riyadh and Hofouf.

Jubail Industrial College: POB 10099, Jubail Industrial City 31961; tel. (3) 340-2000; fax (3) 341-1258; internet www.jic.edu.sa; f. 1982; private control; BSc degrees in chemical, electrical, mechanical engineering.

King Abdulaziz Military Academy: POB 5969, Riyadh; tel. (1) 465-4244; f. 1955;

courses given in modern languages, incl. English, French and Hebrew, science and military subjects; library: 20,000 vols; 1,300 students; publ. *Journal*.

King Fahd Security College: POB 2511, Riyadh 11461; tel. (1) 246-4444; fax (1) 246-4320; internet www.kfsc.edu.sa.

Madrasat Ahl Al-Hadith: Mecca; f. 1933; the institute provides instruction in the Hadith, Koran, Fiqh, Tawheed and other Islamic religious studies; Prin. Sheikh MUHAMMAD ABDUL RAZZAQ; Sec. MUHAMMAD OMAR ABDULHADI.

Prince Sultan College of Tourism and Business: POB 7307, Jeddah 21462; tel. (2) 667-0110; fax (2) 668-5977; internet www .pscabha.edu.sa; private control, King Faisal Foundation; accredited by Ministry of Higher Education; BSc degrees in business admin., hospitality management, management information systems, travel and tourism.

Saad College of Nursing and Allied Health Sciences: POB 30353, Al-Khobar 31952; tel. (3) 801-3555; fax (3) 801-1940; e-mail college@saad.com.sa; internet www .saadcollege.com; private control, Saad

Group; attached to Univ. of Ulster; Bachelor of Science nursing degree.

Technical Institute: Riyadh; f. 1964; 1,000 students.

Yanbu Industrial College: POB 30436, Madinat Yanbu Al-Sinaiyah; tel. (4) 394-6111; fax (4) 392-0213; e-mail yic.dir@rc-ynb .com; internet www.yic.edu.sa; f. 1989; engineering technology; library: 11,570 vols; 127 teachers; 1,400 students; Man. Dir BASSAM ABDULLAH YAMANI; Registrar HAMZA ATIK.

SENEGAL

The Higher Education System

Senegal was a French colony from the 17th century until independence was achieved in 1960. The first institution of higher education, a school of medicine, was founded in 1915; this later became an institute of higher education in 1950 and was incorporated into the new Université Cheikh Anta Diop de Dakar in 1957. Université Cheikh Anta Diop de Dakar is one of the three public universities, the others being Université de Saint-Louis (or Université de Gaston-Berger—founded 1990) and Université du Sahel (founded 1998). Other institutions of higher education, which mirror the French system, include schools of science and veterinary medicine, agriculture and health. In 2008/09 there were 94,400 students in tertiary education. Higher education is largely state funded, although some funding is provided by major international organizations such as United States Agency for International Development (USAID), the European Union (EU) and the World Bank. In mid-2011 the World Bank approved funding of some US $100m. for an initiative intended to improve the management of Senegal's higher education sector, including the development of an information communications technology (ICT) network.

The national body responsible for higher education is the Ministry of Higher Education, Universities and Scientific Research, while technical and vocational education is overseen by the Ministry of Technical and Professional Training.

The secondary school Baccalauréat is the main qualification required for admission to higher education, although applicants without the Baccalauréat can sit an alternative entrance examination. Legislation passed in February 2011 provided for the implementation of a new three-tier LMD (Licence–Master–Doctorat) system of university degrees, bringing the Senegalese system closer in line with the European systems under the Bologna Process in a bid to harmonize degree structures, credit systems and quality assurance procedures in all higher education programmes and institutions in Senegal, as well as in the other seven member states of the West African Economic and Monetary Union, all of which have implemented, or have pledged to implement by 2013, the LMD degree system. Under the new simplified system, the first cycle is the undergraduate Licence (Bachelors) degree, which generally lasts three years. The second cycle leads to award of a Master degree after two years' study. Finally, the third cycle consists of a further three years' study and leads to the conferring of a Doctorat qualification.

The primary qualification for post-secondary technical and vocational education is currently the Brevet de Technicien Supérieur en Maintenance.

Regulatory Bodies

GOVERNMENT

Ministry of Culture, Protected National Heritage, National Languages and Francophone Affairs: Bldg Administratif, ave Léopold Sédar Senghor, BP 4001, Dakar; tel. 33-822-4303; fax 33-822-1638; internet www.culture.gouv.sn; Minister MAME BIR-AME DIOUF; Office Dir PAPE MASSÈNE SENE.

Ministry of Education: rue Docteur Calmette, BP 4025, Dakar; tel. 33-849-5454; fax 33-822-1463; internet www.education.gouv.sn; Minister Prof. MOUSTAPHA SOURANG.

Learned Societies

BIBLIOGRAPHY, LIBRARY SCIENCE AND MUSEOLOGY

Association Sénégalaise de Bibliothécaires, Archivistes et Documentalistes: ASBAD, BP 3252, Dakar; tel. 33-864-2773; fax 33-824-2379; internet www.ebad.ucad.sn/asbad; f. 1988; 200 mems; Pres. DJIBRIL NDIAYE; Sec. BERNARD DIONE; publ. Canal I. S. T. (3 a year).

EDUCATION

UNESCO Regional Office in Dakar: BP 3311, Dakar; 12 ave L. S. Senghor, Dakar; tel. 33-849-2323; fax 33-823-8393; e-mail dakar@unesco.org; internet www.unesco.org/dakar; f. 1970; designated Cluster Office for Burkina Faso, Cape Verde, Gambia, Guinea-Bissau, Liberia, Mali, Niger and Senegal; Dir ARMOOGUM PARSURAMEN.

LANGUAGE AND LITERATURE

Alliance Française: 3, Rue Parchappe, BP 1777, Dakar; tel. 33-821-0822; fax 33-822-1225; e-mail alliancefg@gamtel.gm; internet www.alliancefr-senegalgambie.org; offers courses and exams in French language and culture and promotes cultural exchange with France; attached teaching centres in Kaolack, St Louis, Tambacounda and Ziguinchor; also responsible for operations in Gambia; Dir of Office and of Operations in Senegal and Gambia SERGE AYASSE.

British Council: 34–36 Blvd de la République, Immeuble Sonatel, BP 6232, Dakar; tel. 33-822-2015; fax 33-821-8136; e-mail postmaster@britishcouncil.sn; internet www.britishcouncil.org/senegal; teaching centre; offers courses and examinations in English language and British culture and promotes cultural exchange with the UK; library of 3,500 vols; Dir ANDREW MCNAB.

Goethe-Institut: Rue de Diourbel angle Piscine Olympique, Dakar; tel. 33-869-8880; fax 33-825-1371; e-mail prog@dakar.goethe.org; internet www.goethe.de/dakar; f. 1978; offers courses and examinations in German language and culture and promotes cultural exchange with Germany; Dir UWE RIEKEN.

Research Institutes

GENERAL

Institut de Recherche pour le Développement, Centre de Dakar (IRD): BP 1386, Route des Pères Maristes, Dakar; tel. 33-832-3480; fax 33-832-4307; e-mail durand@orstom.sn; internet www.ird.sn; f. 1950; soil biology, pedology, medical entomology, hydrology, geology, nematology, demography, economics, zoology, botany, agronomy, geography, sociology, nutrition, marine fisheries, public health, tree viruses, vegetal ecology, geophysics, microbiology; library of 10,000 vols; Dir J. R. DURAND; see main entry under France.

Institut Fondamental d'Afrique Noire Cheikh Anta Diop: BP 206, Université Cheikh Anta Diop de Dakar, Dakar; tel. 33-824-1652; fax 33-824-4918; e-mail bifan@ucad.sn; internet www.refer.sn; f. 1936, reconstituted 1959; scientific and humanistic studies on Black Africa; library and museums (see below); Dir DJIBRIL SAMB; publs Bulletin de l'IFAN, Série A—Sciences Naturelles, Série B—Sciences Humaines, Notes Africaines (4 a year), Mémoires de l'IFAN, Initiations et Etudes Africaines.

AGRICULTURE, FISHERIES AND VETERINARY SCIENCE

Institut Sénégalais de Recherches Agricoles (ISRA): BP 3120, Route des Hydrocarbures, Bel-Air, Dakar; tel. 33-832-2420; e-mail dgisra@isra.sn; internet www.isra.sn; f. 1974; research in all fields of agriculture, forestry and pisciculture; Dir Dr MOUSSA BAKHAYOKHU.

Attached Centres:

Centre de Recherche Agronomique de Djibélor: BP 34, Ziguinchor; tel. 33-991-1205; fax 33-991-1293; Dir SAMBA SALL.

Centre de Recherche Agronomique de Kaolack: BP 199, Kaolack; tel. 33-941-2916; fax 33-941-2902; Dir Dr MODOU SENE.

Centre de Recherche Agronomique de Saint-Louis: BP 240, Richard-Toll; tel. 33-961-1751; fax 33-961-1891; Dir Dr SIDY SECK.

Centres de Recherches Océanographiques de Dakar-Thiaroye (CRODT): BP 2241, Dakar; tel. 33-834-0536; f. 1956 for the study of oceanographic physics and biology; 67 scientists; library of 450 vols and 74 periodicals; Dir DIAFARA TOURE.

Centre de Recherches Zootechniques de Dahra-Djoloff: BP 01, Dahra-Djoloff; tel. 33-968-6111; fax 33-968-6271; f. 1950; amelioration of local bovine and ovine breeds, rearing and cross-breeding; Dir TAMSIR DIOP.

Centre de Recherches Zootechniques de Kolda: BP 53, Kolda; tel. 33-996-1152; fax 33-996-1152; f. 1972; amelioration of local bovine and ovine breeds; fodder cultivation; Dir Dr DEMBA FARBA MBAYE.

Centre National de Recherches Agronomiques (CNRA): BP 53, Bambey; tel. 33-973-6050; fax 33-973-6052; f. 1921; applied agricultural research; stations at Louga and Thilmakha; 45 research mems; library of 6,700 vols; Dir Dr DOGO SECK; publs *Rapport de synthèse, Annuaire analytique des travaux de l'IRAT au Sénégal.*

Centre pour le Développement de l'Horticulture (CDH): BP 2619, Dakar; tel. 33-835-0610; fax 33-835-1075; f. 1972; market garden research; Dir Dr ALAIN MBAYE.

Direction des Recherches sur les Productions Forestières: BP 2313, Route des Pères Maristes, Dakar-Hann; tel. 33-832-3219; fax 33-832-9617; Dir Dr PAPE NDIENGOU SALL.

ECONOMICS, LAW AND POLITICS

Institut Africain de Développement Economique et de Planification des Nations Unies (United Nations African Institute for Economic Development and Planning): BP 3186, Dakar; tel. 33-823-1020; fax 33-822-2964; f. 1962 under the aegis of the Economic Comm. for Africa; financed jointly by African states, the UN, and bilateral and multilateral partners; provides training through the org. of courses, seminars, etc., and undertakes research; library of 25,000 vols, 1,400 periodicals; Dir Dr JEGGAN C. SENGHOR.

MEDICINE

Institut d'Hygiène Sociale: Ave Blaise-Diagne, Dakar.

Institut Pasteur: BP 220, Dakar; tel. 33-839-9200; fax 33-839-9210; e-mail pasteur.dakar@pasteur.sn; internet www.pasteur.sn; f. 1896; medical research, microbiology, virology, immunology; library of 2,030 vols, 88 periodicals; Dir Dr ANDRÉ SPIGEL; Exec. Sec. CAMILLE ABBEY.

Organisme de Recherches sur l'Alimentation et la Nutrition Africaines (ORANA): BP 2089, 39 ave Pasteur, Dakar; tel. 33-822-5892; f. 1956; research into African foods and nutritional values, investigations, documentation, teaching; 30 mems; Dir Dr AMADOU MAKHTAR NDIAYE.

TECHNOLOGY

African Regional Centre for Technology/Centre Régional Africain de Technologie: BP 2435, Dakar; tel. 33-823-7712; fax 33-823-7713; f. 1977 as an intergovernmental institution under the auspices of the OAU and UNECA; aims to promote the use of technology to improve the socio-economic development of Africa; advises and sets up national institutions, holds training seminars and workshops; activities include food science and technology, energy technology, technological consulting and advisory services, training and information and documentation; 31 mem. states; library of 6,000 vols, patents, microfiches, video cassettes; Exec. Dir Dr OUSMANE KANE; publs *African Technodevelopment Bulletin* (English and French, 2 a year), *Alert Africa Newsletter* (4 a year), *Infonet* (irregular).

Bureau de Recherches Géologiques et Minières (BRGM): BP 268, Dakar; tel. 33-822-7219; mining, hydrogeology, irrigation;

also directs research in Mali and Mauritania; Dir D. FOHLEN.

Libraries and Archives
Dakar

Archives du Sénégal: Immeuble administratif, Ave Léopold Sédar Senghor, Dakar; tel. 33-823-5072; fax 33-822-5126; e-mail pmarchi@primature.sn; f. 1913; 26,000 vols, 1,500 periodicals, 8,000 official publs, 12 km of documents; Dir SALIOU MBAYE; publ. *Bibliographie du Sénégal* (2 a year).

Bibliothèque Centrale, Université Cheikh Anta Diop de Dakar: BP 2006, Dakar; tel. 33-824-6981; fax 33-824-2379; e-mail hsene@ucad.sn; internet www.bu.ucad.sn; f. 1952; higher education, human and social sciences, law and economics, medicine and pharmacy, science and technology, veterinary science, information science; 353,000 vols, 5,000 periodicals (of which 1,000 are current); Dir HENRI SENE.

Bibliothèque de l'Alliance Française: BP 1777, 2 rue Assane Ndoye, Dakar; tel. 33-821-0822; f. 1948; 12,000 vols; Dir PATRICK MANDRILLY.

Bibliothèque de l'Institut Fondamental d'Afrique Noire: BP 206, Dakar; tel. 33-825-0090; f. 1936; research in humanities and natural sciences; 70,000 vols, 8,200 brochures, 4,036 collections of periodicals, 1,600 microfilms, 2,566 maps, 32,000 photographs, 2,100 slides, 12,200 files of documents; Librarian GORA DIA.

Centre National de Documentation Scientifique et Technique (CNDST): Ministère de la Recherche Scientifique et de la Technologie (MRST), 61 Blvd Djily Mbaye, BP 3218, Dakar; tel. 33-822-9619; fax 33-822-6144; f. 1977; maintains a database each of research institutions, researchers, research projects and research results, and a socioeconomic databank on Senegal; Dir MOHAMED FADHEL DIAGNE; publs *Répertoire des sources d'information sur l'environnement, Répertoire des organismes de documentation au Sénégal, Répertoire des textes législatifs et réglementaires dans le domaine de l'environnement au Sénégal* (1 a year), *Répertoire des textes législatifs et réglementaires au Sénégal* (1 a year).

Centre Régional de Recherche et de Documentation pour le Développement Culturel (CREDEC) (Regional Research and Documentation Centre for Cultural Development): 13 ave du Pdt Bourguiba, Dakar; tel. 33-827-8059; fax 33-821-7515; f. 1976; mems: 20 African states; part of African Cultural Institute (see under International); 3,200 vols, spec. collns on African crafts; Coordinator FALILOU DIALLO; publ. *ICA-Information* (4 a year).

Museums and Art Galleries
Dakar

Musée d'Art Africain de Dakar: BP 6167, Dakar-Étoile; f. 1936; administered by Institut Fondamental d'Afrique Noire; ethnography and African art; Curator Dr TAHIROU DIAW.

Gorée

Musée de la Mer: Gorée; f. 1959; administered by Institut Fondamental d'Afrique Noire; sea sciences, oceanography, fishing; Curator Dr SECK.

Musée Historique: Gorée; administered by Institut Fondamental d'Afrique Noire; Curator Dr ABDOULAYE CAMARA.

Universities
UNIVERSITÉ CHEIKH ANTA DIOP DE DAKAR

BP 5005, Dakar-Fann

Telephone: 33-825-7528
Fax: 33-825-3724
E-mail: info@ucad.sn
Internet: www.ucad.sn

Founded 1915 as École de Médecine, became Institut des Hautes Études 1950, univ. status 1957
State control
Language of instruction: French
Academic year: October to July

Rector: ABDEL KADER BOYE
Vice-Pres.: MOUSTAPHA SOURANG
Sec.-Gen.: ALIOUNE BADARA DIAGNE
Librarian: HENRI SENE

Library: see under Libraries and Archives
Number of teachers: 700
Number of students: 22,000

Publications: *Annuaire, Dakar médical* (3 a year), *Journal de la Faculté des Sciences et Techniques* (2 a year), *Notes Africaines, Revue de l'Ecole Normale Supérieure* (2 a year), *Revue de la Faculté des Lettres*

DEANS

Faculty of Arts and Humanities: MAMADOU KANDJI
Faculty of Economics and Management: MOUSTAPHA KASSE
Faculty of Law and Political Science: MOUSTAPHA SOURANG
Faculty of Medicine, Pharmacy and Odonto-Stomatology: RENÉ NDOYE
Faculty of Science and Technology: LIBASSE DIOP

UNIVERSITÉ DU SAHEL

BP 5355 33, Sotrac-Mermoz, Dakar

Telephone: 33-860-9975
Fax: 33-860-9975
E-mail: unis@refer.sn
Internet: www.unis.sn

Founded 1998
State control

Pres.: ISSA SALL

Number of teachers: 80
Number of students: 400

Publications: *Les Annales du Sahel, Le Sahalien* (12 a year)

DIRECTORS

School of Economics and Administration: MOUSTAPHA THIOUINE
School of Educational Sciences: BADARA SALL
School of Humanities and Civilization: BADARA SALL
School of Law and Political Science: MARIE-PIERRE TRAORÉ SARR
School of Science, Engineering and Technology: KHADIR DIOP
School of Social Sciences: MAME DEMBA THIAM

UNIVERSITÉ DE SAINT-LOUIS
(Université Gaston-Berger)

BP 234, Saint-Louis

Telephone: 33-961-1906
Fax: 33-961-1884
E-mail: webmaster@ugb.sn
Internet: www.ugb.sn

Founded 1990
State control
Language of instruction: French
Academic year: October to July

Rector: Prof. NDIAWAR SARR
Sec.-Gen.: PAPA SÉKOU SONKO
Librarian: MAMADOU LAMINE NDOYE

Library of 18,500 vols
Number of teachers: 237
Number of students: 2,663

HEADS OF TEACHING AND RESEARCH UNITS

Applied Mathematics and Computer Science:
  MARY TEUW NIANE
Arts and Humanities: GORA MBODJ
Economics and Management: ADAMA DIAW
Law: SAMBA TRAORÉ

Colleges

Ecole Inter-Etats des Sciences et Méde-cine Vétérinaires (EISMV): BP 5077, Dakar; tel. 33-865-1008; fax 33-825-4283; e-mail mariamd@eismv.refer.sn; internet www.refer.sn/sngal_ct/edu/eismv/eismv.htm; f. 1968; representing 13 French-speaking African countries; 36 teachers (17 full-time, 19 part-time); 232 students; Dir Prof. FRAN-ÇOIS ADÉBAYO ABIOLA.

Ecole Nationale d'Administration du Sénégal: BP 5209, Dakar; f. 1959; Dir A. N'DENE N'DIAYE.

Ecole Nationale d'Economie Appliquée: BP 5084, Dakar/Fann; tel. 33-824-7928; f. 1963; library: 4,500 vols; 147 students; Dir SAMBA DIONE; publ. *Bulletin de Recherche Appliquée.*

Ecole Nationale Supérieure d'Agricul-ture: BP A 296, Thiès; tel. 33-951-1257; fax 33-951-1551; e-mail ensath@sentoo.sn;

internet www.refer.sn/ensa/accueil.htm; f. 1980; 5-year courses in agricultural engin-eering; training for mems of the agricultural sector; library: 6,000 vols; 10 full-time teachers; 132 students; Dir Prof. PAPA IBRA SAMB.

Ecole Supérieure Polytechnique: BP 5085, Dakar; tel. 33-825-0879; fax 33-825-5594; e-mail esp@ucad.sn; internet www.esp.sn; 2nd campus in Thiès; f. 1994; 5-year diploma courses in engineering; library: 22,378 vols; 116 teachers; 2,105 students, (913 undergraduate, 1,192 postgraduate); Dir ABIB NGOUM; Registrar MARIE NOËLLE MBENGUE; Vice-Dean MAMADOU ADJ; Librar-ians PHILOMÈNE FAYE, EMMANUEL CABOU.

Institut de Technologie Alimentaire: BP 2765, Hann, Dakar; tel. 33-832-0070; fax 33-832-3295; e-mail ita@metissacana.sn; internet www.ita.sn; f. 1963; Dir Dr AMADOU TIDIANE GUIRO.

SERBIA

The Higher Education System

Following the dissolution of the Socialist Federal Republic of Yugoslavia in 1992, Serbia became part of the Federal Republic of Yugoslavia, which was renamed the State Union of Serbia and Montenegro in 2003. In 2006 Montenegro declared independence from the State Union of Serbia and Montenegro. There are seven state universities in Serbia, the oldest of which is Univerzitet u Beogradu (University of Belgrade—founded 1808), and seven private universities. Serbian is the main language of instruction, but Hungarian is also used at Univerzitet u Novum Sadu (University of Novi Sad). In addition to the universities, higher education is offered by university faculties, specialist institutes and high schools. In 2008/09 235,940 students were enrolled in 193 institutes of higher education.

The Ministry of Education is the national body responsible for higher education. The New University Law (2002) initiated several new reforms, including adoption of the European Credit Transfer System (ECTS) and increased autonomy for universities; additionally, Serbia participates in the Bologna Process to establish a European Higher Education Area, the first phase of which was to adopt a credit-based system of comparable degrees with two main cycles (undergraduate and graduate). Following passage of a new Law on Higher Education in 2005, the practical implementation of the Bologna Process formally began in 2006/07, including changes to quality assurance in higher education and the introduction of a three-cycle structure, which involved a complete redesign of university curricula. The new legislation also established the Commission for Accreditation and Quality Evaluation , and introduced the mandatory use of the ECTS. Universities are autonomous establishments, administered by a rector and a university council; management of university faculties is entrusted to faculty councils and deans, who are elected every two years.

Under the old system, admission to higher education was based on completion of general secondary education and award of the Diploma o Zavrsenoj Srednjoj Skoli (Secondary School Leaving Diploma), or completion of a four-year vocational certificate programme. Universities also set their own entrance examinations. The new undergraduate Bachelors degree (three to four years) replaces the old-style awards of Diplom Višeg Obrazovanje (two to three years) and Diplom Visokog Obrazovanja (four to six years). The Magistarska Nauka (Masters) is a one- to two-year programme of study following the Bachelors. Finally, the Doktorat Nauka (Doctorate) is the highest university-level degree and is awarded after a period of research culminating with defence of a thesis.

Technical and vocational education has also undergone reforms in recent years. The aims of the reforms, started in 2002, included creating a centre to develop occupational standards and profiles, teacher-training initiatives and new qualifications. Previously, two- to three-year post-secondary vocational schools offered vocational qualifications, regarded as final qualifications, with the potential to allow access to second- or third-year university undergraduate education. Through reforms along Bologna lines, post-secondary vocational schools have now been transformed into higher education professional (vocational) colleges, offering higher education courses that combine theoretical knowledge with occupational skills.

Regulatory and Representative Bodies

GOVERNMENT

Ministry of Culture: Vlajkovićeva 3, 11000 Belgrade; tel. and fax (11) 303-2112; e-mail kabinet@kultura.gov.rs; internet www .kultura.sr.gov.yu; Min. NEBOJS BRADIC.

Ministry of Education: Nemanjina 24, 11000 Belgrade; tel. (11) 361-6489; fax (11) 361-6491; e-mail kabinet@mp.gov.rs; internet www.mps.sr.gov.rs; Min. Dr ŽARKO OBRADOVIĆ.

ACCREDITATION

ENIC/NARIC Serbia: ENIC Centre of Serbia, Ministry of Education, Nemanjina 22–26, 1000 Belgrade; tel. (11) 361-6607; fax (11) 361-6514; e-mail enic@mps.sr.gov.rs; internet www.mps.sr.gov.rs; Contact MILENA DAMJANOVIC.

Learned Societies

GENERAL

Matica srpska (Serbian Cultural and Scientific Association): Matice Srpske 1, 21000 Novi Sad; tel. (21) 527-622; fax (21) 528-901; e-mail ms@maticasrpska.org.rs; internet www.maticasrpska.org.rs; f. 1826; literary, scientific, cultural and publishing soc.; 2,830 mems; library of 3,000,000 vols; Pres. BOŽIDAR KOVAČEK; Sec. DRAGAN STANIĆ; publs Letopis Matice srpske (literary magazine), Proceedings (in the following series: natural sciences, history, social sciences, literature and language, philology and linguistics, art, Slavonic studies, theatre and music, classical studies).

Srpska Akademija Nauka i Umetnosti (Serbian Academy of Sciences and Arts): Knez Mihailova 35, 11001 Belgrade; tel. (11) 2027-200; fax (11) 219-2825; e-mail sasadir@sanu.ac.rs; internet www.sanu.ac .rs; f. 1886; sections of mathematics, physics and geosciences (Sec. DRAGOŠ CVETKOVIĆ), chemical and biological sciences (Sec. MIROSLAV GAŠIĆ), technical sciences (Sec. PETAR MILJANIĆ), medical sciences (Sec. VESELINKA SUŠIĆ), literature and language (Sec. PREDRAG PALAVESTRA), social sciences (Sec. VOJISLAV STANOVČIĆ), historical sciences (Sec. LJUBOMIR MAKSIMOVIĆ), fine arts and music (Sec. MILAN LOJANICA); 139 mems (89 ordinary, 50 corresp.); library of 1,200,000 vols (incl. 650,000 vols of periodicals); Pres. NIKOLA HAJDIN; Gen. Sec. DIMITRIJE STEFANOVIĆ; Exec. Dir BUDIMIR LONČAR; publs Ekonomski zbornik (Collection of Economic Works), Galerija (Gallery), Glas (Review), Godišnjak (Yearbook), Iz teorije prava (Theory of Law), Muzička izdanja (Musical Editions), Naučni skupovi (Scientific Conferences), Posebna izdanja (Monographs), Spomenik (Monument), Srpski dijalektološki zbornik (Serbian Dialectology Collection), Srpski etnografski zbornik (Serbian Ethnographic Collection).

BIBLIOGRAPHY, LIBRARY SCIENCE AND MUSEOLOGY

Bibliotekarsko društvo Srbije (Serbian Library Association): Skerlićeva 1, 11000 Belgrade; tel. (11) 451-242; fax (11) 452-952; e-mail milun67@gmail.com; internet www .bds.rs; f. 1947 as Society of Library Workers of Serbia; 2,000 mems; Pres. Dr ŽELJKO VUČKOVIĆ; Sec. VESNA CRNOGORAC; publ. Bibliotekar (The Librarian, 2 a year).

ECONOMICS, LAW AND POLITICS

Association of Jurists of Serbia: Proleterskih brigada 74, Belgrade; f. 1946; Pres. Prof. Dr MIODRAG ORLIĆ; publ. Pravni život.

Drustva sudija Srbije (Judges' Association of Serbia): Alekse Nenadovća 24, Belgrade; tel. (11) 344-3132; fax (11) 344-3505; e-mail jaserbia@verat.net; internet www.sudije.rs; f. 1997; non-govt, non-profit org.; works towards advancement of regulations, strengthening respect, professional ethics; dignity of judges; Pres. DRAGANA BOLJEVIC; Pres. MARKO SARIC; Pres. DUSKO MARTIC; publ. Informator.

Economists' Society of Serbia: Nusićeva 6/III, POB 490, Belgrade; f. 1944; Pres. BOGOLJUB STOJANOVIĆ; publ. Ekonomika preduzeća (12 a year).

EDUCATION

Pedagoško društvo Srbije (Pedagogical Society of Serbia): Terazije 26, 11000 Belgrade; tel. and fax (11) 268-7749; e-mail drustvo@pedagog.rs; internet www.pedagog .rs; f. 1924, reorganized 1949 and 1977; training programmes; devt and project planning; 2,000 mems; Pres. SONJA ŽARKOVIĆ; Sec. MILENA DJOKIĆ; publs *Nastava i vaspitanje* (Teaching and Education, 5 a year), *Pedagoška Biblioteka* (Pedagogical Library, irregular).

FINE AND PERFORMING ARTS

Akademija umetnosti (Academy of Arts): Nemanjina 28, Belgrade; tel. and fax (11) 361-8715; fax (11) 361-8716; e-mail info@ akademijaumetnosti.edu.rs; internet www .akademijaumetnosti.edu.rs; f. 1998; offers undergraduate, graduate academic, specialist academic and doctoral studies in drama and audiovisual arts, music and performing arts, arts, applied art and design; library of 4,000 vols; Dean Prof. MIRJANA KARANOVIC; Pres. DUŠAN ĐOKOVIĆ.

HISTORY, GEOGRAPHY AND ARCHAEOLOGY

Historical Society of Serbia: Faculty of Philosophy, Čika Ljubina 18–20, Belgrade; f. 1948; 1,500 mems; Pres. Dr LJUBOMIR MAKSIMOVIĆ; publ. *Istoriski glasnik* (2 a year).

Srpsko geografsko drustvo (Serbian Geographical Society): Studenski trg 3/III, Belgrade; tel. (11) 2184-065; fax (11) 2184-065; e-mail info@sgd.org.rs; internet www.sgd.org .rs; f. 1910; 1,500 mems; library of 4,500 vols; Pres. Prof. Dr STEVAN M. STANKOVIĆ; Sec. DUSAN KIĆOVIĆ; publs *Editions Spéciales* (1 or 2 a year), *Géographique Actualité*, *Glasnik* (4 a year), *Globus* (1 a year), *Mémoires*, *Terre et Hommes* (1 a year).

LANGUAGE AND LITERATURE

British Council: Terazije 8/II, 11000 Belgrade; tel. (11) 302-3800; fax (11) 302-3898; e-mail info@britishcouncil.rs; internet www .britishcouncil.rs; f. 1940 as Yugoslav–British Institute, present name 2001; teaching centre; offers courses and exams in English language and British culture; conducts seminars and workshops; promotes cultural exchange with the UK; attached centres in Priština and Podgorica (Montenegro); library of 9,000 vols, 30 periodicals; Dir ANDREW GLASS.

Društvo za Srpski Jezik i Književnost (Society of Serbian Language and Literature): University, Studenski trg 1, Belgrade; f. 1910; Pres. P. STEVANOVIĆ; Sec. D. PAVLOVIĆ; publ. *Pritozi za knjizevnost, jezik, istorija i folklor*.

Goethe-Institut: Knez Mihailova 50, POB 491, 11000 Belgrade; tel. (11) 262-2823; fax (11) 263-6746; e-mail info@belgrad.goethe .org; internet www.goethe.de/belgrad; f. 1970; offers courses and exams in German language and culture; promotes cultural exchange with Germany; organizes exhibitions and seminars; library of 12,000 vols; Dir VOLKER MARWITZ.

Serbian PEN Centre: 29/II Terazije St, 11000 Belgrade; tel. (11) 334-4607; fax (11) 334-4427; e-mail pencent@bitsyu.net; f. 1926, re-f. 1962; 83 mems; Pres. VIDA OGNJENOVIC; Sec. NEDA BOBIC; publ. *Relations* (4 a year, in English, with Asscn of Serbian Writers).

Srpska književna zadruga (Serbian Literary Association): Kralja Milana 19, 11000 Belgrade; tel. (11) 3230-305; e-mail skz@ beotel.rs; internet www .srpskaknjizevnazadruga.com; f. 1892; publishing of literary, historical and other learned works; 2,500 mems; library of 12,000 vols; spec. colln of 19th-century periodicals; Pres. SLOBODAN RAKITIC; Sec.-Gen. RADIVOJE KONSTANTINOVIĆ; publ. *Glasnik* (1 a year).

MEDICINE

Serbian Society for Fight against Cancer: Pasterova 14 St, 11000 Belgrade; tel. (11) 2656-386; fax (11) 2656-386; e-mail serbca@ncrc.ac.yu; internet www .serbiancancer.org; f. 1927; voluntary nonprofit org.; raises awareness; supports health professionals and orgs; 30,000 mems; Chair. Prof. Dr SLOBODAN ČIKARIĆ; Vice-Chair. Dr PREDRAG BRZAKOVIĆ; Sec. Dr ANA JOVICEVIC; Sec. Dr VESNA LUKIC; publ. *Bolje Sprečiti nego Lečiti* (The Best Cure is Prevention, 4 a year).

NATURAL SCIENCES

Mathematical Sciences

Society of Mathematicians of Serbia: Knez Mihailova 35, POB 791, Belgrade; tel. (11) 638-263; f. 1948; Pres. Dr DJORDJE KARAPANDŽIĆ; publ. *Matematički Vesnik* (4 a year).

Physical Sciences

Serbian Chemical Society: Karnegijeva 4, 11120 Belgrade; tel. and fax (11) 337-0467; e-mail shd@shd.org.rs; internet www.shd.org .rs; f. 1897; promotes chemical research and education; 850 mems; library of 24,300 vols; Pres. Prof. Dr IVANKA POPOVIĆ; Vice-Pres Prof. Dr SLAVICA RAŽIĆ; Vice-Pres. Prof. Dr VLATKA VAJS; Sec. Prof. Dr ALEKSANDRA PERIĆ-GRUJIĆ; Sec. Prof. Dr RADA BAOŠIĆ; publs *Hemijski Pregled* (6 a year, in Serbian), *Journal of the Serbian Chemical Society* (12 a year, in English).

Srpsko Geološko Društvo (Serbian Geological Society): Kamenička 6, POB 227, 11000 Belgrade; e-mail nsgd@verat.net; internet www.nsgd.org; f. 1891; sections for history of geology; stratigraphy, palaeontology and tectonics; mineralogy, petrology, geochemistry and sedimentology; hydrogeology; engineering geology; oil geology and geophysics; economic geology and the study of ore deposits; organizes symposia and other scientific and professional meetings; 300 mems (active and inactive); library of 3,500 vols; Pres. Dr NENAD BANJAC; Vice-Pres. MIODRAG BANJEŠEVIĆ; Sec. ALEKSANDRA MARAN; Treas. LJUBINKO SAVIĆ; publ. *Zapisnici srpskog geološkog društva* (reports, 1 a year).

TECHNOLOGY

Nikola Tesla Society: POB 359, Belgrade; e-mail boris@tesla-society.org; internet www .tesla-society.org; f. 1936 reorg. 1993; organizes int. festival of scientific and technical films, held every 2 years; conducts study tours and scientific meetings; publishing.

Savez inženjera i tehničara Srbije (Union of Engineers and Technicians of Serbia): Kneza Miloša 7, 11000 Belgrade; tel. and fax (11) 323-0067; e-mail office@sits .rs; internet www.sits.org.rs; f. 1868; voluntary, non-govt, non-profit, professional, scientific org.; 44 mem. orgs; Pres. Prof. Dr ČASLAV LAČNJEVAC; Vice-Pres. Dr IGOR MARIĆ; Sec.Gen. BRANISLAV VUJINOVIĆ; publ. *Tehnika* (scientific and technical magazine).

Research Institutes

GENERAL

Ethnographic institute of the Serbian Academy of Sciences and Arts: Knez Mihailova 36 /IV, 11000 Belgrade; tel. (11) 263-6804; e-mail eisanu@ei.sanu.ac.rs; internet www.etno-institut.co.rs; promotes theoretical and methodological knowledge in the field of ethnology; organizes ethnolo-

gical research, scientific conferences, lectures, study visits; cooperates with related cultural institutions in the country and abroad; Dir DRAGANA RADOJIČIĆ; Sec. NEVENKA SPASOJEVIC; publ. *Proceedings of the EI SASA* (bulletin, 1 a year).

Matematički Institut SANU (Mathematical Institute SANU): Kneza Mihaila 36, 11001 Belgrade; tel. (11) 263-0170; fax (11) 218-6105; e-mail office@mi.sanu.ac.rs; internet www.mi.sanu.ac.rs; f. 1961; organizes seminars and colloquiums; int. collaborations; Dir Dr ZORAN MARKOVI; Deputy Dir Dr ZORAN OGNJANOVIĆ; Pres. MILAN BOŽIĆ; publs *Publications de l'Institut Mathematique* (2 a year), *Visual Mathematics* (4 a year, online).

AGRICULTURE, FISHERIES AND VETERINARY SCIENCE

Institute for Agricultural Mechanization: Zemun, POB 41, Belgrade; f. 1947; 30 mems; library of 6,000 vols; Dir DJORDJE DJURDJEVIĆ; publ. *Poljoprivredna Tehnika* (Agricultural Engineering, 1 a year).

Institute for Plant Protection and the Environment: T. Drajzera 9, POB 936, 11000 Belgrade; tel. (11) 266-9860; fax (11) 266-9860; e-mail izbisfu@beotel.yu; f. 1945; depts of biological control, environmental protection, phytopathology, phytopharmacy, toxicology; library of 7,000 books, 12,650 periodicals; Dir Dr DIMITRIJE MATIJEVIĆ; publ. *Zaštita bilja* (Plant Protection, 4 a year).

BIBLIOGRAPHY, LIBRARY SCIENCE AND MUSEOLOGY

Republički zavod za zaštitu spomenika kulture (Institute for the Protection of Cultural Monuments of Serbia): Božidara Adžije 11, 11118 Belgrade; tel. (11) 454-786; fax (11) 344-14-30; e-mail rzzsk@eunet.yu; f. 1947; research, documentation, conservation and restoration, legal protection and maintenance of central registers of immovable cultural property; specialized training of personnel; publication of books and periodicals; Dir MILETA MILIĆ; Head, Architecture Dept BRANA STOJKOVIĆ PAVELKA; Head, Paintings Dept RADIŠA ŽIKIĆ; Head, Physical and Chemical Laboratory (vacant); Head of Dept of History of Art, Ethnology and Archaeology RADOJKA ZARIĆ; depts of law, documentation, photographic laboratory; library of 21,000 vols; publ. *Saopštenja* (Communications).

ECONOMICS, LAW AND POLITICS

Institute of International Politics and Economics: POB 750, Makedonska 25, 11000 Belgrade; tel. (11) 337-3824; fax (11) 337-3835; e-mail iipe@diplomacy.bg.ac.yu; internet www.diplomacy.bg.ac.yu; f. 1947; int. relations; world economy; int. law; social, economic and political devt in all countries; library of 150,000 vols; Dir DUŠKO DIMITRIJEVIĆ; publs *International Problems* (4 a year), *Medjunarodna Politika* (4 a year), *Pregled evropskog zakonodavstva* (Survey of European Legislations, 6 a year), *Review of International Affairs* (4 a year).

FINE AND PERFORMING ARTS

Institute of Musicology of the Serbian Academy of Sciences and Arts: Knez Mihailova 36, 11000 Belgrade; tel. and fax (11) 2639-033; e-mail music_inst@music .sanu.ac.rs; f. 1948; history of Serbian and Yugoslav music, Balkan folk music, medieval and traditional Orthodox church music, music theory and aesthetics; library of 5,500 vols; Dir Prof. Dr DANICA PETROVIĆ; publs *Musicology* (1 a year), *Sources for the History of Serbian Music* (1 a year).

HISTORY, GEOGRAPHY AND ARCHAEOLOGY

Arheološki Institut (Archaeological Institute): Knez Mihailova 35/IV, Belgrade; tel. (11) 637-191; fax (11) 180-189; e-mail institut@ai.sanu.ac.yu; internet www.ai.sanu.ac.rs; f. 1947; study of prehistoric, classical and medieval archaeology in the Central Balkan area; library of 13,000 books, 23,000 vols of periodicals; Dir Dr MILOJE VASIĆ; Admin. Sec. OLIVERA ILIĆ; publs *Djerdapske sveske – Cahiers des Portes de Fer*, *Singidunum* (irregular), *Starinar* (1 a year).

Geographical Institute 'Jovan Cvijić': Đure Jakšića 9, 11000 Belgrade; tel. (11) 263-6276; fax (11) 263-7597; e-mail general@gi.sanu.ac.rs; internet www.gi.sanu.ac.rs; f. 1947; physical geography; social geography; regional geography; cartography with GIS; environmental studies; spatial planning; Head Dr MILAN RADOVANOVIĆ; publ. *Journal of the Geographical Institute* (1 a year).

Institute for Balkan Studies Serbian Academy of Sciences and Arts: Knez Mihailova 35/IV, 11000 Belgrade; tel. (11) 263-9830; fax (11) 263-8756; e-mail balkinst@bi.sanu.ac.rs; internet www.balkaninstitut.com; f. 1934 started as Institut des Études Balkaniques; present name 1969; Balkans studies from prehistory to the modern age; incl. archaeology, ethnography, anthropology, history, culture, art, literature, law; multidisciplinary approach; Dir Acad. NIKOLA TASIĆ; Vice-Dir DUŠAN T. BATAKOVIĆ; Librarian VALENTINA BABIC; publ. *Balcanica*.

Institute for Byzantine Studies of the Serbian Academy of Sciences and Arts: Knez-Mihailova 35, 11000 Belgrade; tel. (11) 263-7095; fax (11) 328-8441; e-mail inst.byz@vi.sanu.ac.rs; internet www.vi.sanu.ac.rs; f. 1948; research in modern Byzantine studies; int. cooperation; library of 21,000 vols; Dir Prof. LJUBOMIR MAKSIMOVIĆ; Deputy Dir BOJANA KRSMANOVIĆ; publ. *Zbornik radova Vizantoloskog instituta (ZRVI)*.

LANGUAGE AND LITERATURE

Institute for Serbian Language SASA: Đure Jaksic 9, 11000 Belgrade; tel. (11) 218-1383; fax (11) 218-3175; e-mail isj@isj.sanu.ac.yu; internet www.isj.sanu.ac.rs; f. 1947, present name 1992; processing old Serbian written monuments; etymological research dialectological research; description and Serbian language standardization; scientific meetings; lectures; Pres. PREDRAG PIPER.

MEDICINE

Institut za javno zdravlje Srbije (Institute of Public Health of Serbia): Dr Subotića 5, 11000 Belgrade; tel. (11) 268-4566; fax (11) 268-5735; e-mail info@batut.org.rs; internet www.batut.org.rs; f. 1924 as Central Institute of Hygiene, present name 2006; epidemiology, microbiology, hygiene and human ecology, social medicine; health care orgs and services; health education; library of 40,000 vols; Dir Dr TANJA KNEZEVIC; publ. *Glasnik* (2 a year).

NATURAL SCIENCES

Biological Sciences

Botanical Institute and Garden of the University of Belgrade: Takovska 43, 11000 Belgrade; tel. (11) 767-988; fax (11) 638-500; f. 1874; library of 7,000 vols; Dir Prof. Dr JELENA BLAŽENČIĆ; publ. *Bulletin* (1 a year).

Physical Sciences

Astronomska Opservatorija (Astronomical Observatory): Volgina 7, 11060 Belgrade; tel. and fax (11) 241-9553; e-mail contact@aob.rs; internet www.aob.rs; f. 1887, reformed 1932; astrometry, astrophysics, astrodynamics, cosmology, astrobiology, astronomy and planetology; library of 15,000 vols; Dir Dr ZORAN KNEŽEVIĆ; Chief Officer SRETEN STEPANOVIĆ; publs *Publications of the Astronomical Observatory of Belgrade* (irregular), *Serbian Astronomical Journal* (2 a year).

Hidrometeorološki Zavod Republike Srbije (Hydrometeorological Service of Serbia): Kneza Višeslava 66, 11000 Belgrade; tel. (11) 3050-923; fax (11) 3050-847; e-mail office@hidmet.gov.rs; internet www.hidmet.gov.rs; f. 1888; forecasts weather and issues severe weather warnings; Dir MILAN DACIĆ; Deputy Dir. DANICA SPASOVA.

Attached observatory:

Meteorološka opservatorija Beograd (Belgrade Meteorological Observatory): Bul. JNA 8, 11000 Belgrade; tel. (11) 685-770; fax (11) 685-840; f. 1887; Chief Officer SLOBODAN HADŽIVUKOVIĆ; publ. *Observations Météorologiques à Belgrade*.

Seismological Institute: Tasmajdanski park bb, POB 16, 11120 Belgrade; tel. (11) 322-7013; e-mail seismo@seismo.sr.gov.yu; internet www.seismo.gov.rs; f. 1906; Dirs Dr B. A. SIKOŠEK, Dr M. N. VUKAŠINOVIĆ; Gen. Man. SLAVITZA RADOVANOVITCH; Sec. SLADYANA MAKSIN-JOKSIMOVITCH; 12 mems; publs *Annuaire macroséismique et microséismique*, *Bulletin mensuel*, *Studies*.

TECHNOLOGY

Institut za nuklearne nauke 'Vinča' (Vinča Institute of Nuclear Sciences): Mike Petrovića Alasa 12–14, Belgrade; tel. (11) 243-8906; fax (11) 344-2420; e-mail office@vin.bg.ac.rs; internet www.vin.bg.ac.rs; f. 1948; multidisciplinary scientific research; basic and applied research in natural, technological and nuclear sciences; consulting and research programmes in physics, chemistry, physical chemistry, biology, technical sciences, nuclear energy, electronics, computing, material sciences; production and application of radio isotopes; information systems and data processing; library of 30,000 vols; Dir Dr JOVAN NEDELJKOVIĆ; Pres. Prof. Dr DRAGAN MITRAKOVIC; Exec. Sec. MAJA MILANOV.

Institut za Tehnologiju Nuklearnih i Drugih Mineralnih Sirovina (Institute for Technology of Nuclear and Other Mineral Raw Materials): Franše D'Epere 86, POB 390, 11000 Belgrade; tel. (11) 3691-581; fax (11) 3691-583; e-mail itnms@itnms.ac.rs; internet www.itnms.ac.rs; f. 1948; research and application of technology in the field of processing nuclear, metallic and non-metallic mineral raw materials; environmental protection; training; 168 staff; library of 4,000 vols, 40,000 periodicals; Dir-Gen. Prof. ZVONKO GULISIJA.

Institute of Technical Sciences of The Serbian Academy of Sciences and Arts: Knez-Mihailova 35/IV, POB 377, 11000 Belgrade; tel. (11) 218-5437; fax (11) 218-5263; e-mail its@itn.sanu.ac.rs; internet www.itn.sanu.ac.rs; f. 1947; centres for fine particles processing and nanotechnologies; metallic constructions in civil engineering; scientific and research programmes; publishing and conferences; int. cooperation; Dir Dr DRAGAN P. USKOKOVIĆ; Sec. ALEKSANDRA STOJIČIĆ.

Libraries and Archives

Belgrade

Arhiv Jugoslavije: Vase Pelagića 33, POB 65, 11000 Belgrade; tel. (11) 369-0252; fax (11) 306-6635; e-mail arhivyu@arhivyu.rs; internet www.arhivyu.rs; f. 1950; documents regarding Yugoslav history; offers professional training in archival theory and practice; archival literature; exhibits; 26,621 vols, 18,200 reference books and 8,900 periodicals; Dir MILOŠEVIĆ MILADIN (acting); publ. *Arhiv* (1 a year).

Arhiv Srbije (Archives of Serbia): Karnegijeva 2, 11000 Belgrade; tel. (11) 337-0781; fax (11) 337-0246; e-mail office@archives.org.rs; internet www.archives.org.rs; f. 1898, present name 1969; history of Serbia; protection of cultural heritage, professional guidance and education; assignment of professional titles; devt and promotion of archival activities; 75,000 vols; Dir Dr MIROSLAV PERIŠIĆ; publ. *Arhivski pregled* (1 a year).

Biblioteka grada Beograda (Belgrade City Library): Knez Mihailova 56, Belgrade; tel. (11) 202-4000; internet www.bgb.rs; f. 1929, present bldg 1986; 2m. vols; depts of arts, children's periodicals, cultural programmes, local history; Dir JOVAN RADULOVIC.

Biblioteka Srpske akademije nauka i umetnosti (Library of the Serbian Academy of Sciences and Arts): Knez Mihailova 35, 11000 Belgrade; tel. (11) 2639-120; fax (11) 2639-120; e-mail katalog@bib.sanu.ac.rs; internet www.sanu.ac.rs; f. 1842 by the Serbian Learned Society; present name 1960; information service, inter-library loan scheme; prepares bibliographies and edits spec. publs; primarily for mems; 1,200,000 vols (incl. 550,000 books and 650,000 vols of periodicals); Dir NIKŠA STIPČEVIĆ; publ. *Izdanja biblioteke*.

Narodna biblioteka Srbije (National Library of Serbia): Skerlićeva 1, 11000 Belgrade; tel. (11) 245-1242; fax (11) 245-1289; e-mail nbs@nb.rs; internet www.nb.rs; f. 1832; large fed. copyright and deposit library; nat. agency for CIP, ISBN, ISSN, ISMN, DOI numbers; centre for nat. current bibliography; nat. centre for conservation and preservation; nat. digital library centre; 5,500,000 vols, incl. electronic titles; large colln of medieval Cyrillic MSS; Dir SRETEN UGRIČIĆ; publs *Arheografski prilozi* (1 a year), *Glasnik narodne biblioteke Srbije* (Herald of the Nat. Library of Serbia, 1 a year), *Srpska bibliografija* (Serbian nat. bibliography, 17 volumes).

Univerzitetska biblioteka 'Svetozar Marković' (University Library 'Svetozar Marković'): Bulvr Kralja Aleksandra 71, 11000 Belgrade; tel. (11) 337-0512; fax (11) 337-0354; e-mail pitajbibliotekara@unilib.bg.ac.rs; internet www.unilib.bg.ac.rs; f. 1921 as successor to the library of the Serbian Lyceum (1838); centre of the network of univ. libraries in Serbia; exhibits; inter-library loan scheme; 1,448,245 vols (books, periodicals, newspapers), 548 Serbian and other MSS 12th–18th century, 5,000 old documents; Dir Dr STELA FILIPI MATUTINOVIĆ; Deputy Dir BOGOLJUB MAZIĆ; publ. *Infoteka* (2 a year).

Čacak

Gradska biblioteka Vladislav Petković Dis (Public library 'Vladislav Petkovic Dis'): Gospodar Jovanova 6, 32000 Čačak; tel. (32) 340-960; fax (32) 223-608; e-mail biblioteka@cacak-dis.rs; internet www.cacak-dis.rs; f. 1848 as Asscn for Reading Serbian–Slavonic Newspapers in Čačak, present name 1998; incl. scientific dept; depts for adults, children; inter-library loans; 150,000 vols; Dir DANICA OTAŠEVIĆ.

Kragujevac

Narodna biblioteka (Public Library): Kragujevac; f. 1866; 50,000 vols.

Niš

Narodna Biblioteka 'Stevan Sremac' (National Library 'Stevan Sremac'): Borivoje Gojkovic no. 9, 18000 Niš; tel. (18) 511-410; fax (18) 250-188; e-mail n.vasic09@yahoo .com; internet www.nbss.rs; f. 1879; collns of the Serbian Acad. of Sciences and Arts and Serbian graphics; depts of ancient and rare books; local history; 250,000 vols, 950 titles, 200 original graphic prints; Dir NEBOJŠA VASIĆ; Sec. SONJA SUKOVIĆ; Librarian SLAVICA KRIVOKUĆA.

Novi Sad

Arhiv Vojvodine (Archives of Vojvodina): Dunavska 35, 21000 Novi Sad; tel. (21) 489-1800; fax (21) 522-332; e-mail info@ arhivvojvodine.org.rs; internet www .arhivvojvodine.org.rs; f. 1926 as State archives in Novi Sad, present name 1970; 30,000 vols; Dir STEVAN RAJČEVIĆ; publs *Izveštaji o naučno-istraživačkom radu u inostranstvu* (Research reports from archives abroad), *Naučno-informativna sredstva o arhivskoj gradji u arhivima Vojvodine* (Scientific information on the Vojvodina archives, 4 a year).

Biblioteka Matice srpske (Matica Srpska Library): Ul. Matice srpske 1, 21000 Novi Sad; tel. (21) 420-199; fax (21) 528-574; e-mail bms@bms.ns.ac.rs; internet www .bms.rs; f. 1826 in Budapest, opened 1838, present location 1864; copyright and deposit library for Serbia; regional information centre of Science and Technology Information Network; depository library for FAO and UNESCO; 3m. vols (incl. books and periodicals), 17 incunabula, 671 MSS, 500 palaeotype, 35,000 old and rare books, 700,000 units of spec. library material (maps, posters, leaflets, music records, cassettes, etc.); Dir MIRO VUKSANOVIĆ; Deputy Dir NOVKA SOKICA ŠUVAKOVIĆ.

Požarevac

Narodna biblioteka (Public Library): Drinska 2, 12000 Požarevac; tel. (12) 221-957; fax (12) 221-029; e-mail bibliotekapo@ ptt.yu; f. 1847; 112,000 vols.

Sabac

Narodna biblioteka 'Žika Popovič' (Public Library 'Žika Popovič'): Masarikova 18, 15000 Sabac; f. 1847; 200,000 vols.

Museums and Art Galleries

Belgrade

Etnografski muzej u Beogradu (Ethnographical Museum of Belgrade): Studentski trg. 13, p.p. 357, Belgrade; tel. (11) 328-1888; fax (11) 328-2944; e-mail info@ etnografskimuzej.rs; internet www .etnografskimuzej.rs; f. 1901; permanent and temporary exhibits; collns incl. nat. costumes, jewellery, embroidery and lace, textile household items, devices and contrivances for productions of textiles, elements of nat. architecture, rural household, urban architecture, urban household, agriculture, crafts, pottery, traffic and transport of goods, hunting and fishing, music instruments, custom items, folk knowledge and belief, warriors' equipment, measures and tally, glass, tuxedo outfits, children's toys, photographs and negatives, art, video records, items of European and other cultures, archives; library of 60,000 vols; Dir VILMA NIŠKANOVIĆ (acting);

Deputy Dir VESNA DUSKOVIC; Curator JELENA SAVIC; publ. *Glasnik etnografskog muzeja* (1 a year).

Istorijski muzej Srbije (Historical Museum of Serbia): Đure Jaksic 9, Belgrade; tel. (11) 328-7242; fax (11) 328-7243; e-mail istorijskimuzej@imus.org.yu; internet www .imus.org.rs; f. 1844 as National Museum, present name and status 1963; Dir Dr ANA STOLIĆ; Sr Curator ANDREJ VUJNOVIĆ; publs *Proceedings of the Historical Museum of Serbia, Zbornik* (1 a year).

Museum of Contemporary Art: Ušće 10, blok 15, 11070 Belgrade; tel. (11) 367-6288; fax (11) 367-6291; e-mail msub@msub.org.rs; internet www.msub.org.rs; f. 1958; opened 1965, exhibits Serbian and foreign art; library of 5,200 vols, 25,500 catalogues; Dir BRANISLAVA ANDJELKOVIC DIMITRIJEVIC; Exec. Dir SLOBODAN NAKARADA; publ. *World Art Critics* (1 a year).

Muzej afričke umetnosti: zbirka Vede i dr Zdravka Pečara (Museum of African Art: the Veda and Dr Zdravko Pechar Collection): 14, Andre Nikolića St, 11000 Belgrade; tel. and fax (11) 265-1654; fax (11) 265-1269; e-mail africanmuseum@gmail.com; internet www.museumofafricanart.org; f. 1977; displays traditional arts of W Africa; collns incl. masks, sculptures in wood and bronze, gold weights, ceramics, musical instruments, textiles, jewellery, objects of everyday use; organizes exhibitions, workshops, lectures; Dir and Curator NARCISA KNEŽEVIĆ ŠIJAN; Chair. Dr MIROSLAVA LUKIĆ KRSTANOVIĆ; publ. *AFRIKA-Studies in Art and Culture, Journal of the Museum of African Art.*

Muzej grada Beograda (Belgrade City Museum): Zmaj Jovina St 1, 11000 Belgrade; tel. (11) 263-8744; fax (11) 328-3504; e-mail office@mgb.org.rs; internet www.mgb.org.rs; f. 1903; Belgrade from prehistory to the present; depts of archaeology, art, history, literature, numismatics, science; documentation centre; conservation laboratory; library of 23,091 vols, 305 rare books; Dir DANICA JOVOVIC PRODANOVIC; publ. *Godišnjak Grada Beograda* (1 a year).

Muzej istorije Jugoslavije (Museum of Yugoslav History): Botićeva 6, 11000 Belgrade; tel. (11) 367-1485; fax (11) 266-0170; e-mail info@mij.rs; internet www.mij.rs; f. 1996 by merger of Josip Broz Tito Memorial Centre and Museum of Revolution of Nations and Nationalities of Yugoslavia; history of the people of the fmr Yugoslavia; the life and work of Josip Tito (1892–1980), Pres. of Yugoslavia 1953–80; research, art and educational programmes; library of 200,000 items; Dir KATARINA ZIVANOVIC (acting); Curator ANA PANIC.

Muzej Nikole Tesla (Nikola Tesla Museum): Krunska 51, 11000 Belgrade; tel. (11) 243-3886; fax (11) 243-6408; e-mail info@ tesla-museum.org; internet www .tesla-museum.org; f. 1952; preserves legacy of the engineer and inventor, Nikola Tesla (1856–1943); contains biographical and scientific works; library of 786 vols, 323 magazines, 155,000 pages of Nikola Tesla's original documents and 1,000 of his personal items; Dir VLADIMIR JELENKOVIĆ; Curators BRATISLAV STOJILJKOVIĆ, IVANA ZORIĆ.

Muzej Pozorišne Umetnosti Srbije (Serbian Museum of Theatre): Gospodar Jevremova 19, 11000 Belgrade; tel. (11) 262-6630; fax (11) 262-8920; e-mail office@mpus.org.rs; internet www.mpus.org.rs; f. 1950; documents, photographs, newspaper cuttings on the theatre, costumes, decorations, audiovisual documentation; colln of art and memorial objects, theatrical programmes and posters; archives; library of 7,500 vols; Dir

KSENIJA RADULOVIĆ; Sec.-Treas. LJILJANA BANOVIC; Sr Curator MIRJANA ODAVIĆ; publ. *Teatron* (4 a year, print and online).

Muzej primenjene umetnosti (Museum of Applied Art): Vuka Karadžića 18, 11000 Belgrade; tel. (11) 262-6841; fax (11) 262-9121; e-mail info@mpu.rs; internet www .mpu.rs; f. 1950; collects, conserves, studies, publishes works of applied art; exhibits incl. ceramics, porcelain, glass, metalwork, jewellery, period furniture, woodwork, textiles and costume, photography, book layout, modern architecture and design, contemporary applied art, fashion and clothing; library: 2m. books, 960 periodicals; Dir IVANKA ZORIĆ; Sec. SLAĐANA TOMIĆ; Sr Curator MILICA ĆUKIĆ; publ. *Journal* (1 a year).

Narodni muzej u Beogradu (National Museum in Belgrade): Trg Republike 1A, 11000 Belgrade; tel. (11) 330-6000; fax (11) 262-7721; e-mail pr@narodnimuzej.rs; internet www.narodnimuzej.rs; f. 1844 as Museum Srbski, present name and bldg 1952; archaeological and historical art collns (medieval, Yugoslav and foreign collns), numismatics; conducts exhibitions; library of 85,000 vols; Dir TATJANA CVJETIĆANIN; publs *Glasnik društva prijatelja Narodnog muzeja, Kovčežić, Numizmatičar, Zbornik Narodnog muzeja.*

Prirodnjački muzej u Beogradu (Natural History Museum Belgrade): Njegoševa 51, POB 401, 11000 Belgrade; tel. (11) 344-2147; fax (11) 344-6580; e-mail nhmbeo@nhmbeo .rs; internet www.nhmbeo.rs; f. 1895 as Jestastvenički Museum of Serbian Land; botanical, environmental, geological, mineralogical, palaeontological, petrological and zoological studies and collns; library: 21,554 books, 1,183 journal titles, 1,005 maps and 226 MSS; Dir Dr SLAVKO SPASIĆ; Sec. for Admin. and Technical affairs MARIJA VUCETIC; publ. *Bulletin* (separate series on biology and geology).

Vojni Muzej (Military Museum): Kalemegdan bb, 11000 Belgrade; tel. (11) 334-3441; fax (11) 334-3915; e-mail vojnimuzej@mod .gov.rs; internet www.muzej.mod.gov.rs; f. 1878; military history of Serbia, incl. collns of arms, medals, flags, uniforms; archaeological and art colln; archive of 100,000 photographs; 30,000 objects in 12 collns; library of 15,000 vols, 5,000 magazines; Chief Col MIROSLAV KNEŽEVIĆ; publ. *Vesnik* (1 a year).

Zeljeznicki Muzej (Railway Museum of Serbia): 6 Nemanjina ul., 11000 Belgrade; tel. (11) 361-4811; fax (11) 361-6722; e-mail medijacentar@srbrail.rs; internet www .zeleznicesrbije.com; f. 1950; library of 20,000 vols; Dir MILAN RADIVOJEVIĆ.

Novi Sad

Galerija Matica Srpska (Art Gallery of Matica Srpska): Trg Galerija 1, 21000 Novi Sad; tel. (21) 489-9000; fax (21) 489-9000; e-mail ms@maticasrpska.org.rs; internet www.maticasrpska.org.rs; f. 1847; fine art; paintings, graphics, sculptures and drawings from the 16th to 20th centuries; Dir LEPOSAVA SELMIĆ.

Muzej Vojvodine (Museum of Vojvodina): Dunavska 35–37, 21000 Novi Sad; tel. (21) 420-566; fax (21) 520-135; e-mail muzejvojvodine1@nscable.net; internet www .muzejvojvodine.org.rs; f. 1947; sections: archaeology, ethnology, history, applied art; organizes lectures, workshops, exhibits; library of 80,000 vols; Dir Prof. Dr VLADIMIR MITROVIĆ; publs *Posebna izdanja* (irregular), *Rad Muzeja Vojvodine* (1 a year).

Subotica

Gradski muzej—Városi Múzeum (Municipal Museum of Subotica): Trg Sinagoge 3, 24000 Subotica; tel. (24) 555-128; fax (24) 555-228; e-mail muzejsubotica@open.telekom .rs; internet www.gradskimuzej.subotica.rs; f. 1892; sections: archaeology, local history, art, ethnology (collns from Africa and SE Asia and Oceania), biology, coins (Hungarian and Roman); library of 12,000 vols; Dir HULLÓ ISTVÁN.

Universities

DRŽAVNI UNIVERZITET U NOVOM PAZARU
(State University in Novi Pazar)

Vuk Karadzic bb, Novi Pazar
Telephone: (20) 317-754
Fax: (20) 337-669
E-mail: rektorat@np.ac.rs
Internet: www.np.ac.rs
Founded 2006
State Control
Rector: Prof. ĆEMAL DOLIĆANIN (acting)

Offers Bachelors, Masters and doctoral courses in depts of arts; biochemical and medical sciences; legal and economic sciences; mathematical, physical and information sciences; philosophical-philological sciences; technical and technological sciences.

MEGATREND UNIVERZITET
(Megatrend University)

8 Goce Delceva, 11070 Belgrade
Telephone: (11) 220-3029
E-mail: info@megatrend.edu.rs
Internet: www.megatrend-edu.net
Founded 1989
Private Control
Rector: Prof. Dr MICA JOVANOVIC
Pres.: WALTER SCHWIMMER
Vice-Rector for Teaching and Internal Organization: Prof. Dr VESNA MILANOVIC
Vice-Rector for Int. Cooperation: Prof. SLOBODAN PAJOVIC
Vice-Rector for Research Work: Prof. DRAGANA GNJATOVIĆ
Number of students: 26,000

Publication: *Megatrend Review* (applied economics)

DEANS

Faculty of Bio-farming in Backa Topola: Prof. JELENA BOŠKOVIĆ
Faculty of Business Studies: Prof. Dr GORDANA KOMAZEC
Faculty of Culture and Media: Prof. Dr MILIVOJE PAVLOVIC
Faculty of Management in Zajecar: Prof. Dr NEDELJKO MAGDALINOVIĆ
Faculty of Public Administration: Prof. Dr MILOMIR MINIĆ
Geoeconomic Faculty: Prof. Dr BRANISLAV PELEVIĆ
Graduate School of Arts and Design, Belgrade: Prof. MILOS SOBAJIC
Graduate School of Bio-farming, Backa Topola: Prof. JELENA BOSKOVIC
Graduate School of Business Economy, Valjevo: Prof. MILAN GRUJIC
Graduate School of Business Studies, Belgrade: Prof. ANA LANGOVIC
Graduate School of Business Studies, Požarevac: Prof. DRAGAN KOSTIC
Graduate School of Business Studies, Vrsac: Prof. MILAN MILANOVIC
Graduate School of Computer Science, Belgrade: Prof. MILAN TUBA

Graduate School of Culture and Media, Belgrade: Prof. MILIVOJE PAVLOVIC
Graduate School of International Economy, Belgrade: BRANISLAV PELEVIC
Graduate School of Management, Zajecar: Prof. NEDELJKO MAGDALINOVIC
Graduate School of Public Admin.: Prof. MILOMIR MINIC
Management and Business College, Professional Studies, Zajecar: DRAGAN MIHAJLOVIC (Dir)
Megatrend Basketball College Borislav Stankovic: Prof. TOMISLAV OBRADOVIC
Megatrend Business College, Professional Studies, Belgrade: NATASA SIMIC (Dir)
Megatrend Virtual Univ., MTVU: Prof. VELJKO SPASIC

UNIVERZITET SINGIDUNUM
(Singidunum University)

Danijelova 32, Belgrade
Telephone: (11) 309-3209
Fax: (11) 309-3294
E-mail: mstanisic@singidunum.ac.rs
Internet: www.singidunum.ac.rs
Founded 2005
Private Control
Languages of instruction: English, Serbian
Rector: Prof. Dr MILOVAN STANIŠIĆ
Sec.-Gen.: LJILJANA STANCIC-BUKVIC

Publication: *Singidunum Show* (Journal of Theory and Practice)

DEANS

Faculty of Applied Ecology: Dr GORDANA DRAZIC
Faculty of Business (Belgrade): Dr DANIJEL CVJETICANIN
Faculty of Business (Valjevo): Dr OLIVERA NIKOLIC
Faculty of Economics, Finance and Administration: Prof. Dr MIHAILO CRNOBRNJA
Faculty of European law, Political Studies: Dr ILIJA BABIC
Faculty of Informatics and Computing: Dr MLADEN VEINOVIĆ
Faculty of Management: Dr DRAGAN CVETKOVIC
Faculty of Media and Communications: NADA POPOVIC-PERISIC
Faculty of Tourism and Hospitality Management: Dr KRUNOSLAV ČAĆIĆ

UNIVERZITET U BEOGRADU
(University of Belgrade)

Studentski trg 1, 11000 Belgrade 6
Telephone: (11) 263-5153
Fax: (11) 263-8912
E-mail: officebu@rect.bg.ac.rs
Internet: www.bg.ac.rs
Founded 1808 as the College of Velika škola, reorganized 1905 and 1954
State Control
Academic year: October to September
Rector: Dr BRANKO KOVAČEVIĆ
Vice-Rector for Education: Dr NEDA BOKAN
Vice-Rector for Finances and Organization: Dr NEVENKA ŽARKIĆ-JOKSIMOVIĆ
Vice-Rector for International Relations: Dr VOJISLAV LEKOVIĆ
Vice-Rector for Science: Dr MARKO IVETIĆ
Sec.-Gen.: SLAVICA KAPETANOVIĆ
Librarian: DEJAN AJDAČIĆ

Library of 700,000 vols, 10,000 periodicals
Number of teachers: 2,552
Number of students: 92,652 (90,152 undergraduate, 2,500 postgraduate)

Publications: *Acta Veterinaria*, *Annals of the Faculty of Law* (in Serbian), *Annals of the Faculty of Philology*, *Bulletin Astronomique de Belgrade*, *Collection of Works of the Faculty of Mining and Geology* (in Ser-

bian), *Collection of Works of the International Slavistics Centre*, *Contemporary Research in Physics* (in Serbian), *Contributions to Language, Literature and Folklore*, *Economic Annals* (in Serbian, 4 a year), *Education – the Theory and the Practice* (in English, Russian and Serbian), *Gazette of the Faculty of Forestry* (2 a year), *Geological Annals of the Balkan Peninsula* (in Serbian), *Germanica Belgradensia*, *Headmaster* (in Serbian), *Information Bulletin* (Faculty of Agriculture, in Serbian, 12 a year), *Innovations in the Field of Instruction* (in Serbian), *Italica Belgradensia*, *Journal of Automatic Control* (in English), *Journal of Mining and Metallurgy* (in Serbian), *Lectures in Physical Sciences, Management, Mathematics* (in Serbian), *Medical Research* (in Serbian), *Medical Students*, *Miscellaneous Studies of the Faculty of Philosophy* (series A: culture and history; series B: social sciences), *October Symposium of Miners and Metallurgists* (1 a year, colln of works, in Serbian), *Philosophical Yearbook* (in Serbian), *Philosophy and Society* (in Serbian), *Physical Education, Physical Engineering* (in English), *Population, Power Engineering* (in English), *Problems of Ethnology and Anthropology, Psychological Research, Review of Research Work at the Faculty of Agriculture* (in English), *Sociological Review, Studies of Adult Education Topics, The Veterinary Herald* (in Serbian), *Transactions* (mechanical engineering, in Serbian and English, 2 a year), *Transport and Traffic in Cities* (in Serbian), *Underground Works* (in Serbian), *Yugoslav Journal of Operations Research* (in English), *Zograf* (iconography)

DEANS

Faculty of Agriculture: Dr NEBOJŠA RALEVIĆ
Faculty of Architecture: Dr VLADIMIR MAKO
Faculty of Biology: Dr JELENA KNEŽEVIĆ-VUKČEVIĆ
Faculty of Chemistry: Dr BRANIMIR JOVANČIĆEVIĆ
Faculty of Civil Engineering: Dr ĐORĐE VUKSANOVIĆ
Faculty of Defectology: Dr JASMINA KOVAČEVIĆ
Faculty of Economics: Dr MARKO BACKOVIĆ
Faculty of Forestry: Dr MILAN MEDAREVIĆ
Faculty of Geography: Dr SRBOLJUB STAMENKOVIĆ
Faculty of Law: Dr MIRKO VASILJEVIĆ
Faculty of Mathematics: Dr MIODRAG MATELJEVIĆ
Faculty of Mechanical Engineering: Dr MILORAD MILOVANČEVIĆ
Faculty of Mining and Geology: Dr VLADICA CVETKOVIĆ
Faculty of Organizational Sciences: Dr MILAN MARTIĆ
Faculty of Pharmacy: Dr NADA KOVAČEVIĆ
Faculty of Philology: Dr SLOBODAN GRUBAČIĆ
Faculty of Philosophy: Dr VESNA DIMITRIJEVIĆ
Faculty of Physical Chemistry: Dr ŠĆEPAN ŠĆEPAN
Faculty of Physics: Dr LJUBIŠA ZEKOVIĆ
Faculty of Political Sciences: Dr ILIJA VUJAČIĆ
Faculty of Security Studies: Dr VLADIMIR CVETKOVIĆ
Faculty of Sports and Physical Education: Dr DUŠAN MITIĆ
Faculty of Stomatology: Dr DRAGOSLAV STAMENKOVIĆ
Faculty of Teacher Training: Dr ALEKSANDAR JOVANOVIĆ
Faculty of Technology and Metallurgy: Dr IVANKA POPOVIĆ
Faculty of Transport and Traffic Engineering: Dr SLOBODAN SLOBODAN
Faculty of Veterinary Medicine: Dr VELIBOR STOJIĆ

School of Electrical Engineering: Dr MIODRAG
   POPOVIĆ
School of Medicine: Dr VLADIMIR BUMBAŠIRE-
   VIĆ
Technical Faculty in Bor: Dr MILAN ANTONI-
   JEVIĆ

PROFESSORS
Faculty of Agriculture (Nemanjina 6, 11080
Belgrade-Zemun; tel. (11) 261-5315; fax (11)
219-3659; e-mail office@agrif.bg.ac.rs;
internet www.agrifaculty.bg.ac.rs):

BLAGOJEVIĆ, S., Agricultural Chemistry
ČANAK, M., Mathematics
ČOROVIĆ, M., Market and Turnover of
   Agricultural and Agroindustrial Prod-
   ucts
ELEZOVIĆ, I., General Phytopharmacy
ERCEGOVIĆ, Ð., Elements and Agricultural
   Machinery Mechanics
GLAMOČLIJA, Ð., Crop Farming
GRUBIĆ, G., Ruminant Nutrition
IVANOVIĆ, M., Plant Mycosis
JAKOVLJEVIĆ, M. D., Soil and Water Chem-
   istry
JANKOVIĆ, M., Cooling Technology
JELIĆ, M. P., Mathematics
KOSI, F., Thermodynamics and Thermo-
   technics
KOSTIĆ, N. M., Agrogeology
KOVAČEVIĆ, D., General Crop Farming
LATINOVIĆ, D., Population Genetics and
   Fertilization of Domestic Animals
LESKOŠEK ČUKALOVIĆ, I., Malt and Beer
   Technology
MAČEJ, O., Milk Proficiency and Prepar-
   ation
MITROVIĆ, S., Zootechnics
MRATINIĆ, E., Special Fruit Growing
NEDIĆ, M. J., Special Crop Farming
OBRADOVIĆ, D. B., Technological Microbiol-
   ogy
OSTOJIĆ, M., Milk Production
PAVASOVIĆ, V. L., Technological Operations
PEKIĆ, S., Botany
PERIĆ, V. T., Meat Proficiency and Prepar-
   ation
PEŠIĆ, R., Macroeconomic Analysis
PETANOVIĆ, R., Acarology
PETKOVIĆ, S., Hydraulics
PETROVIĆ, M., Cattle Breeding
RADOVANOVIĆ, R. M., Meat Industry Fol-
   low-Up Products Technology
RAIČEVIĆ, D., Agricultural Machinery
RALEVIĆ, N., Statistics
RALEVIĆ LJUBANOVIĆ, I., Statistics and
   Operational Research
RISTIĆ, N., Organic Chemistry
RUDIĆ, D. V., Drainage
ŠESTOVIĆ, M. B., Special Phytopharmacy
ŠEVRALIĆ, M., Field and Cooperative Move-
   ment Economics
ŠINŽAR, B. C., Botany
SKALICKI, Z., Zootechnics
SPALEVIĆ, B., Soil and Water Conservation
SPASIĆ, R., Special Entomology
STEVANOVIĆ, Ð., Sociology
STEVANOVIĆ, D. R., Agrochemistry
ŠTIKIĆ, R., Plant Physiology
ŠURLAN MOMIROVIĆ, G., Genetics
TODOROVIĆ, M. S., Thermodynamics
VASIĆ, G., Reclamation Systems Produc-
   tion and Maintenance
VELIČKOVIĆ, M., General Fruit Growing
VEREŠ, M., Plant Products Technology
VITOROVIĆ, S. L., Agricultural Toxicology
VUKIĆ, Ð., Agricultural Electrical Technol-
   ogy
VUKŠA, P., Plant Protection Technology
ŽEŽELJ, M., Wheat and Flour Technology

Faculty of Architecture (Blvr Kralja Aleksandra 73/II, 11000 Belgrade; tel. (11) 322-5254;
fax (11) 337-0193; e-mail fakultet@arh.bg.ac
.rs; internet www.arh.bg.ac.rs):

BADOVINC, P., Urban Functions

BAJIĆ BRKOVIĆ, M., Urban and Regional
   Planning
CAGIĆ, P. R., Architectural Design, Design
   Studio
ÐORDEVIĆ, D., Construction Management
   and Utilities Management in Architec-
   ture
JOVANOVIĆ POPOVIĆ, M., Architectural Con-
   struction and Principles of Bioclimatic
   Design
KRUNIĆ, S., Design Studio
KUJUNDŽIĆ, V. B., Wood and Metal Struc-
   tures
KURTOVIĆ FOLIĆ, N., History of Architec-
   ture and Settlements
LAZAREVIĆ BAJEC, N., Urban Structures
   and Zoning
LOJANICA, M. M., Design Studio, Process in
   Architectural Design
MARUŠIĆ, D. M., Architectural Design,
   Design Studio
MIHAJLOVIĆ, M., Physics and Materials in
   Architectural Building Physics
MIHALJEVIĆ, G. P., Built Environment Eco-
   nomics
MITROVIĆ, B., Architectural Design, Design
   Studio
NESTOROVIĆ, M., Structural Systems, Spa-
   tial Structures
PEROVIĆ, M. R., History of Modern Archi-
   tecture and Town Planning
RAJIĆ, D., Mechanics and Strength of
   Materials
RAJOVIĆ, S., Architectural and Urban
   Design
RAKOČEVIĆ, M., Architectural Design
RIBAR, M., Architectural Design, Specific
   Design Problems
RISTIĆ, M., Analysis of Metal Structures

Faculty of Biology (Studentski trg 16, 11000
Belgrade; tel. (11) 218-6635; fax (11) 263-
8500; e-mail dekanat@bio.bg.ac.rs; internet
www.bio.bg.ac.rs):

ANÐELKOVIĆ, M. L., Population Genetics
ČURČIĆ, B., Pedology and Pedobiology with
   Soil Protection
CVIJIĆ, G., Experimental Physiology
KALEZIĆ, M., Vertebrate Comparative
   Morphology
KEKIĆ, V., Behavioural Genetics
KONJEVIĆ, R., Plant Physiology
PETKOVIĆ, B., Plant Morphology, General
   Botany, Botany with Mycology
RADOVIĆ, I., Principles of Ecology
ROMAC, S., Eucaryote Molecular Biology
SIMIĆ, D., Microbiology, Microbiology and
   Microbial Ecology Genotoxicology, Water
   Microbiology
STEVANOVIĆ, B., Plant Ecology and Phyto-
   geography, Plant Ecology, Physiology
   and Physiological Ecology of Plants,
   Plant Adaptive Types, Physiological
   Ecology of Plants, Aquatic Botany
STEVANOVIĆ, V., Plant Ecology and Phyto-
   geography, Principles of Ecology, Biogeo-
   graphy, Biodiversity Protection and
   Revival, Ecosystems of Yugoslavia and
   the Balkan Peninsula
TOPISIROVIĆ, LJ., Biochemistry
TUĆIĆ, N., Organic Evolution Theory

Faculty of Chemistry (Studentski trg 12–16,
11000 Belgrade; tel. (11) 328-2111; fax (11)
638-785; e-mail dekan@chem.bg.ac.rs;
internet www.chem.bg.ac.rs):

BOJOVIĆ, S., Chemical Education
DOŠEN-MIĆOVIĆ, L., Organic Chemistry
GRŽETIĆ, I., Applied Chemistry
JANKOV, R., Biochemistry
JOVANČIĆEVIĆ, B., Applied Chemistry
JURANIĆ, I., Organic Chemistry
MARKOVIĆ, R., Organic Chemistry
MILOSAVLJEVIĆ, S., Organic Chemistry
NIKETIĆ, S., Inorganic Chemistry
NIKETIĆ, V., Biochemistry
PAVLOVIĆ, V., Organic Chemistry

ŠAIČIĆ, R., Organic Chemistry
SOLAJA, B., Organic Chemistry
SOVILJ, S., Inorganic Chemistry
TEŠIĆ, Ž., Analytical Chemistry
VRVIĆ, M., Biochemistry
VUČKOVIĆ, G., Inorganic Chemistry

Faculty of Civil Engineering (Blvr Kralja
Aleksandra 73/I, 11000 Belgrade; tel. (11)
321-8524; fax (11) 337-0223; e-mail lilja@grf
.bg.ac.rs; internet www.grf.bg.ac.rs):

ANÐUS, V., Road Design
BAJIĆ, D., Concrete Structures
BRČIĆ, S., Engineering Mechanics and
   Strength of Materials
BUÐEVAC, D., Metal Structures
ĆORIĆ, B., Theory of Structures
CVETANOVIĆ, A., Elements of Transporta-
   tion, Roads
ÐORDJEVIĆ, B., Water Power Engineering,
   Water Resource Systems
DUNICA, Š., Engineering Mechanics and
   Strength of Materials
GEORGIJEVIĆ, V., Technical Physics, Build-
   ing Physics, Introduction to Electronics
IVKOVIĆ, B., Construction Management
   and Technology, Construction Project
   Management
JOKSIĆ, D., Geodesy, Geodesy on Roads and
   Railways, Engineering, Geodesy in City
   Infrastructure Systems, Photogramme-
   try, Remote Sensing
JOVANOVIĆ, M., River Engineering, Water-
   ways and Ports
KLEM, N., Automatic Data Processing in
   Geodesy
KOLUNDŽIJA, B., Structural Theory
LJUBISAVLJEVIĆ, D., Municipal Hydraulic
   Engineering, Water Quality
MAKSIMOVIĆ, Č., Fluid Mechanics,
   Hydraulic Measurement, Engineering
MAKSIMOVIĆ, M., Soil Mechanics
MALETIN, M., Urban Streets
MURAVLJOV, M., Building Materials
NADJANOVIĆ, D., Concrete Structures
OPRICOVIĆ, S., Systems Optimization
PEROVIĆ, G., Calculus, Congruence Theory
PRAŠĆEVIĆ, Ž., Construction Management
   and Technology, Special Construction
   Problems
ŠEKULOVIĆ, M., Structural Theory
ŠUMARAC, D., Engineering Mechanics and
   Strength of Materials
VRAČARIĆ, K., Geodesy
VUKSANOVIĆ, Ð., Structural Theory

Faculty of Defectology (Visokog Stevana 5,
11000 Belgrade; tel. (11) 218-3036; fax (11)
218-3081; e-mail info@fasper.bg.ac.rs;
internet www.fasper.bg.ac.rs):

ANDREJEVIĆ, I., Professional and Occupa-
   tional Training of Persons with Mental
   Retardation, Professional Training of
   Deaf and Hard of Hearing Persons
ANIČIĆ, L., Pedagogy of Mentally Retarded
   Persons, Methodology of Preschool Work
   with Mentally Retarded Persons
GOLOBOVIĆ, S., Clinical Logopaedia
ILANKOVIĆ, V., Basics of Kinesitherapy
ISPANOVIĆ RADOJKOVIĆ, V., Neurology and
   Psychiatry, Neuropsychiatry with Re-
   educational Methods
JOVANOVIĆ, T., Medical Psychology with
   Basics of Anatomy
KAŠIĆ, Z., Phonetics, Linguistics
KRAJGER GUZINA, A., Neurology and Psych-
   iatry
MATEJIĆ ÐURIČIĆ, Ž., Developmental Psych-
   ology, Psychology of Blind and Low
   Vision Persons
MILANDINOVIĆ, V., Serbian Language
   Methodology for Children with Mental
   Retardation, Mathematical Methodology
   for Children with Mental Retardation
POPOVIĆ KANDIĆ, Z., Criminal Law

RADOMAN, V., Psychology of Deaf and Hard of Hearing Persons, Psychology of Persons with Speech Disturbances
RADOVANOVIĆ, D., Psychology of Persons with Behavioural Disturbances
RADULOVIĆ, K., Psychology of Persons with Mental Retardation, Psychology of Physically Challenged Persons
RAPAIĆ, D., Clinical Somatopaedia
STANKOV, B., Basics of Strabology with Orthoptics and Pleoptics
TREBJEŠANIN, Ž., General Psychology with Personality Psychology

Faculty of Economics (Kamenička 6, 11000 Belgrade; tel. (11) 302-1240; fax (11) 263-9560; e-mail ekof@ekof.bg.ac.rs; internet www.ekof.bg.ac.rs):

ANIČIĆ, R. M., Methods of Economic Analysis
ARSENIĆ, Ž., Vehicle Design, Experimental Methods
BABIĆ, S. L., Price Theory, Industrial Organization
BAJEC, J. M., Contemporary Economic Systems, Public Sector Economy
BAKIĆ, O., Tourism Marketing, Tourist Organization Business Operations
BORIČIĆ, B., Mathematics, Program Languages
BOŽIĆ, V. S., Transport Economics, Marketing Logisitics
ČAČIĆ, K. T., Tourism and Catering Business Management, Tourism Economics, Tourism Marketing
CEROVIĆ, B. D., Transition Economics
CVIJETIĆANIN, D., Operational Research, Economic and Mathematical Methods and Models
DEVETAKOVIĆ, S. R., National Economy, Technological Development and Policy, Agrarian Policy
ĐOLEVIĆ, V. R., Economic Statistics, Bases of Statistical Analysis
ĐUKIĆ, Đ., Banking, Securities Trading
ĐURIČIN, D., Strategic Management
EREMIĆ, M. B., Market Research, Bases of Statistical Analysis, Theoretical Statistics
ILIĆ, B. B., Political Economy
IVANIŠEVIĆ, M., Business Finance, Business Financial Restructuring
JAKŠIĆ, M. P., Development and Contemporary Economic Thought, Macroeconomic Analysis
JOKSIMOVIĆ, L., Contemporary Economic Systems, Public Sector Economics
JOVANOVIĆ GAVRILOVIĆ, B., National Economy, Development Theory and Planning, Industrial Economics
JOVANOVIĆ GAVRILOVIĆ, P. R., Yugoslav Economic Relations with Foreign Countries, International Business Finance, International Financing
JOVIČIĆ, M. M., Econometry, Times Series Analysis
KOČOVIĆ, J., Financial and Actuary Mathematics, Insurance, Insurance Tariffs
KOVAČ, O., International Finances, Yugoslav Economic Relations with Foreign Countries, European Union Economics
LOVRETA, S. M., Trade and Sales Management, Trade Economics
LOVRIĆ, M., Bases of Statistical Analysis
MALENOVIĆ, N., Business Economics
MARIČIĆ, B. R., Marketing, Consumer Behaviour
MEDOJEVIĆ, B. V., Political Economy
MILOVANOVIĆ, M. R., Price Theory, Macroeconomic Analysis
NIKOLIĆ, M. M., Business Economic, Energy Economics
PAVLIČIĆ, D., Bases of Statistical Analysis, Decision Making Theory

PETKOVIĆ, M., Business Organization, Human Resources Management, Organizational Development
PETKOVIĆ, V. V., Sociology with Labour Sociology, Tourism Sociology
PETROVIĆ, L., Samples Theory and Experiment Planning, Mathematics, Theoretical Statistics
PETROVIĆ, P. D., Econometry, Open Economy Macroeconomics
RIKALOVIĆ, G., National Economy, Agrarian Economics, Transport Economics
ŠKARIĆ JOVANOVIĆ, K. I., Financial Accounting, Balance Theory and Policy, Special Balances
STANIŠIĆ, M., Accounting Information Systems, Auditing Theory, Auditing
STEVANOVIĆ, N., Cost Accounting Systems, Management Accounting
ŠUVAKOVIĆ, DJ. M., Price Theory, Production Theory
TODOROVIĆ, J. B., Marketing Research and Marketing Information Systems, Management Information Systems, Price Theory
ZARIĆ, S., Economic Analysis Methods, Market and Market Institutions

Faculty of Forestry (Kneza Višeslava 1, 11000 Belgrade; tel. (11) 305-3990; fax (11) 254-5485; e-mail sf.bg@sezampro.rs; internet www.sfb.bg.ac.rs):

BAJIĆ, V., Forest Utilization, Forestry Mechanization
BANKOVIĆ, S. V., Dendrometry, Geodesy
DANON, G., Basics of Mechanical Engineering, Wood Processing Tool Machinery
ĐOROVIĆ, M., Agricultural Field Improvement
ISAJEV, V., Seed Production, Nursery Practice and Afforestation, Genetics with Plant Breeding
JAIĆ, M., Surface Wood Processing
JOKSIMOVIĆ, V., Erosion Control Agroecosystems
KARADŽIĆ, D., Forest Phytopathology, Ornamental Plant Diseases
KOLIN, B., Hydrothermic Wood Processing, Veneers and Composite Boards
KOSTADINOV, S., Torrents and Erosion
KOSTADINOVIĆ, A., Sociology
KRSTIĆ, M., Silviculture, Forest Improvement
LETIĆ, L., Woodland Water Exploitation, Forest Hydrology
MARJANOV, M., Engineering Mechanics
MATIĆ, V., Materials in Erosion Control Works, Ecological Materials
MIHAJLOVIĆ, L., Forest Protection, Forest Entomology
MILJKOVIĆ, J. P., Chipboards, Particle Boards and Wood-Based Materials
NEŠIĆ, M., Wood Processing Production Management, Change Control, Wood Processing Management
PETKOVIĆ, S. D., Hydraulics with Hydrology, Water Management Basics
RANKOVIĆ, N., Forest Economics, Forest Organization and Management, Timber Trade, Forest Economic Geography
SKAKIĆ, D., Final Wood Processing, Timber Construction
SOKOLOVIĆ, S., Design, Furniture Design
SOŠKIĆ, B. M., Wood Properties, Mill Conversion of Wood
STOJANOVIĆ, L., Silviculture, Forest Improvement
ŠULETIĆ, R., Wood Processing Enterprise Design, Project and Investment Management, Enterprise Development Management
TODOROVIĆ, P. S., Wood Industry Control System Technology, Engineering Physics

TODOROVIĆ, T. N., Geotechnics in Flood Control, Geodynamics, Hydrogeology with Geomorphology
TOMIĆ, Z. S., Dendrology, Forest Phytocenology
VOJKOVIĆ, L., Landscape Design, History of Landscape Architecture
VUČKOVIĆ, M., Increment Study
VUKIĆEVIĆ, M., Wood Processing Production Organization, Operational Research

Faculty of Geography (Studentski trg 3/III, 11000 Belgrade; tel. (11) 218-3537; fax (11) 218-2889; e-mail dekanat@gef.bg.ac.rs; internet www.gef.bg.ac.rs):

DERIĆ, B., Regional Planning
GRČIĆ, M., Political Geography, Industrial and Transport Geography
KUKRIKA, M., Computing, Information Technology
LJEŠEVIĆ, M., Environment
MANOJLOVIĆ, P., Geomorphology, Mathematical Geography
PAVLOVIĆ, M., Yugoslav Geography, Yugoslav Regional Geography
SPASOVSKI, M., Population Geography, Demography
STAMENKOVIĆ, S., Urban Geography, Applied Urban Geography
STANKOVIĆ, S. M., Tourism Geography, World Tourism Geography
STOJKOV, B., Spatial Planning Analysis and Synthesis Methods, Urban and Rural Spatial Planning
ŽIVKOVIĆ, D., Cartography, Topical Mapping

Faculty of Law (Blvr Kralja Aleksandra 67, 11000 Belgrade; tel. (11) 302-7600; fax (11) 322-1299; e-mail pravni@ius.bg.ac.rs; internet www.ius.bg.ac.rs):

ANTIĆ, O., Succession Law
AVRAMOVIĆ, S. D., General History of Law
BASTA, D. N., Legal Philosophy
BESAROVIĆ, V. M., Commercial Law, Copyright and Intellectual Property Law
BRAJIĆ, V. M., Labour Law
ČAVOŠKI, K. S., Introduction to Law
ĐUKIĆ VELJOVIĆ, Z., Constitutional Law
IGNJATOVIĆ, Đ., Criminology and Penology
JANJIĆ KOMAR, M., Family Law
JEKIĆ, Z. M., Criminal Procedure
KOŠUTIĆ, B. P., Introduction to Law
KREĆA, M. D., International Public Law
LABUS, M. Z., Political Economy
LILIĆ, S., Administrative Law and Governance
MARKOVIĆ, R. Č., Constitutional Law, Administrative Law
MARKOVIĆ, S., Copyright and Intellectual Property Law
MILIĆ, V. B., Sociology
MITROVIĆ, D., Introduction to Law, Autonomy Law
MITROVIĆ, M., Sociology
ORLIĆ, M. V., Introduction to Civil Law, Real Law
POPOVIĆ, D. M., Public Finances and Financial Law
POPOVIĆ, D. M., General History of Law
STOJANOVIĆ, Z., Criminal Law
SUNDEROVIĆ, B., Labour Law
TABOROŠI, S. A., Law of the Economic System
TODOROVIĆ, M., Sociology
TRKULJA, J., Political Systems
VASILJEVIĆ, M. S., Commercial Law and Traffic Law
VUKADIN, E., Economic Policy

Faculty of Mathematics (Studentski trg 16, 11000 Belgrade; tel. (11) 202-7801; fax (11) 263-0151; e-mail matf@matf.bg.ac.rs; internet www.matf.bg.ac.rs):

ANGELOV, T., Stellar Astronomy, Stellar Structure and Evolution
BOKAN, N., Differential Geometry

JARIĆ, J. P., Continuum Mechanics, Tensor Calculus

JEVTIĆ, M. J., Complex Analysis

JOVANOVIĆ, B. S., Numerical Analysis

KADELBURG, Z. L., Analysis

KNEŽEVIĆ, J., Differential Equations

KUZMANOVSKI, M., Positional Astronomy

LAŽETIĆ, N., Analysis

MATELJEVIĆ, M. S., Complex Analysis

MIJAJLOVIĆ, Ž. D., Algebra, Mathematical Logic

PAVLOVIĆ, M., Complex and Functional Analysis

RADOJČIĆ, M., Algebra, Mathematical Logic

VREĆICA, S., Topology

Faculty of Mechanical Engineering (K. M. Arias Raljić 1, 11120 Belgrade; tel. (11) 337-0266; fax (11) 337-0364; e-mail dekan@mas.bg.ac.rs; internet www.mas.bg.ac.rs):

ADŽIĆ, M., Fuels, Industrial Water, Lubricants, Combustion

BENIŠEK, M. H., Hydraulic Machinery, Measurement Techniques

BLAGOJEVIĆ, Đ., Rocket Propulsion, Flight Dynamics with Aerodynamics

BOGNER, M. G., Process Equipment Mechanical Design and Selection

BOJANIĆ, P. O., Computer Graphics

BRKIĆ, L. D., Steam Boilers, Thermal Power

ČANTRAK, S., Hydraulics and Pneumatics, Hydromechanics

ČOVIĆ, V. M., Mechanics

DEBELJKOVIĆ, D. L., Linear System Design, Object and Process Dynamics

ĐORDEVIĆ, S., Mechanism Design

ĐORDJEVIĆ, V. D., Fluid Mechanics

DUBOKA, Č. V., Vehicle Maintenance Technology, Experimental Methods

DUBONJIĆ, R. R., Economy

GAJIĆ, A., Turbomachinery, Hydraulic Torque Converters

GEORGIJEVIĆ, D., Mathematics

GOLUBOVIĆ, Z., Mechanics

HOFMAN, M., Ship Theory, Ship Behaviour in Waves

IVANOVIĆ, G., Theory of Vehicle Motion, Theory of Effectiveness

JAĆIMOVIĆ, B., Process Planning, Heat and Mass Transfer Equipment

JANKES, G., Industrial Furnaces and Boilers, Furnace Design

JANKOVIĆ, J., Aircraft Equipment and Systems

JANKOVIĆ, M., Fundamentals of Machine Design

JARAMAZ, S., Interior Ballistics, Projectile Design

JOJIĆ, B. Ž., Aircraft Propulsion, Rocket Propulsion

KALAJDŽIĆ, M. J., Production Process Automation

KLARIN, M. M., Production Organization, Terotechnology

KORUGA, D., Bioautomatic Control

KOZIĆ, Đ., Thermodynamics, Heat and Mass Transfer

KRIVOŠIĆ, I. N., Aircraft Structure

KUBUROVIĆ, M., Environmental Engineering, Drying Equipment

MAJSTOROVIĆ, V., Quality Management

MARKOSKI, M. J., Cooling Devices, Pipelines

MARKOVIĆ, D., Agricultural Machines

MILINOVIĆ, M., Rocket and Launcher Design, Fire Control Systems

MILOSAAVLJEVIĆ, A., Engineering Materials

MILUTINOVIĆ, D., Manufacturing Technology, Industrial Robots

MLADENOVIĆ, N., Mechanics

NEDELJKOVIĆ, M., Hydraulic Machinery, Pumps and Fans

OGNJANOVIĆ, M., Machine Elements, Machine Design

PAVLOVIĆ, M., Fluid Mechanics, Gas Dynamics

PEŠIĆ, S., Aerodynamics, Propellers and Rotors

PETKOVIĆ, Z., Material Handling Machines, Steel Structures

PETROVIĆ, S. V., Internal Combustion Engine Theory and Design

PETROVIĆ, Z., Computer-Aided Design, Aircraft Armament

PILIPOVIĆ, M., Manufacturing Systems, Production Process Automation

PLAVŠIĆ, N. I., Machine Elements, Fundamentals of Machine Design

POKRAJAC, S., Sociology, Industrial Management

RAC, A. A., Tribology

RADENOVIĆ, S., Mathematics

RADOJČIĆ, D., Resistance, Propulsion Steering of Ships

RADOVANOVIĆ, M. R., Fuels, Industrial Water, Lubricants

RAŠUO, B., Aircraft Maintenance, Flight Mechanics

RIBAR, Z., Pneumoelectric Control Systems, Hydroelectric Control Systems

RUŽIĆ, D. B., Strength of Materials

SAVIĆ, B., Heat Turbomachines, Thermal Power Plants

SEDMAK, A., Engineering Materials

SEKULIĆ, A., Mechanism Design, Technical Drawing with Engineering Design Graphics

ŠIJAČKI ŽERAVČIĆ, V., Engineering Materials

SPASIĆ, Ž., Computer-Integrated Manufacturing

STEFANOVIĆ, Z., Aerodynamic Construction

STUPAR, S., Computer-Aided Design, Aircraft Armament

TANOVIĆ, L., Tools and Tooling, Manufacturing Technology

TOMIĆ, M., Internal Combustion Engines, Internal Combustion Engine Equipment

TOPIĆ, R., Agricultural Machinery Design and Construction

TOŠIĆ, S., Conveyors and Lifting Devices, Material Handling System Design

VELJIĆ, M., Agricultural Machinery Design and Construction

VUKOVIĆ, J. U., Mechanics

ZEKOVIĆ, D., Mechanics

ŽIVANOVIĆ, T., Power Steam Boilers, Plant Boilers

Faculty of Mining and Geology (7 Djušina Str., 11000 Belgrade; tel. (11) 323-8832; fax (11) 323-5539; e-mail dean@rgf.bg.ac.rs; internet www.rgf.bg.ac.rs):

BABIĆ, D., Genetic Mineralogy, Mineralogy, Technical Mineralogy

BATALOVIĆ, V., Hydraulic and Pneumatic Machines in Mining, Boring Machines and Equipment, Exploitation and Oil and Gas Transport

BLEČIĆ, N., Coal Deposits, Mining Geology

ĆALIĆ, N. M., Theoretical Bases of Mineral Processing, Mineral Processing

ČOKORILO, V., Underground Mining Mechanization

ĆORIĆ, S., Geostatic Calculation

CVETKOVIĆ MRKIĆ, S., Ground Improvement Methods and Engineering Geology

ĐAJIĆ, N., Thermodynamics, Heat Engines and Energy Plants, Automation and Process Control

DANGIĆ, A. V., Geochemistry, Mineral Raw Material Deposits, Geology and Environmental Protection

DEUŠIĆ, S., Mineral Processing Machinery and Equipment

DIMITRIJEVIĆ, S., Surveying, Mining Photogrammetry

ĐOKOVIĆ, I. M., Geological Mapping, Environmental Geology

DRAGIŠIĆ, V., Mineral Deposit Hydrogeology, General Hydrogeology

GAGIĆ, D., Methods and Technology for Underground Excavation of Bedded Deposits, Underground Excavation Methods

GRUBOR, D., Physics

GRUJIĆ, M., Mine Transport and Hoisting

GRŽETIĆ, I., Physical Chemistry of Ore Deposits, Geology and Environmental Protection, Laboratory Investigation of Mineral Resources

ILIĆ, M. M., Exploration of Building Material Deposits, Nonmetallic Mineral Deposits

IVIĆ, A. P., Mathematics

IVKOVIĆ, S. Ž., Elements of Machines, Machine Design, Metalworking

JANIČEVIĆ, D., Historical Geology, Geology of Yugoslavia

JELENKOVIĆ, R., Metallic Mineral Deposits, Mineral Deposits

JEVREMOVIĆ, D., Engineering Geological Investigation, Geological Construction Materials

KARANOVIĆ, L., X-Ray Structural Analysis, Applied Crystallography

KNEŽEVIĆ, S., Historical Geology, Quaternary Geology, Stratigraphy of Yugoslavia

KOSTIĆ PULEK, A., Chemistry

LAZIĆ, M., Special Hydrogeology, Exploratory Drilling

LILIĆ, N., Mine Ventilation, Mine Safety, Environmental Impact of Surface Drilling

LOGAR, M., Silicate Classification, Industrial Product Mineralogy, Geology and Environmental Protection, Mineral Raw Materials in Technology

LOKIN, P. M., Principles of Geotechnics, Geotechnical Investigation Methods

MARINKOVIĆ, S., Chemistry, Oil Chemistry with Basic Refining

MAROVIĆ, M. S., Neotectonics, Geotectonics, Geology of Yugoslavia

MIHAJLOVIĆ, Đ., Palaeobotany, Palaeoecology, Evolutionary Palaeontology, Fossil Organism Comparative Morphology, Micropalaeontology

MILIČIĆ, M., Mathematics, Numerical Analysis

MILOVANOVIĆ, D. J., Metamorphic Rock Petrology, Technical Petrology, Yugoslav Rock Formation Geology

MITROVIĆ, V., Reservoir Physics, Fluid Mechanics, Oil and Gas Reservoir Engineering

PAVLOVIĆ, V., Open Pit Exploitation Technology, Open Pit Exploration Technology, Removal of Water in Open Pit Mining

PEŠIĆ, L., Essentials of Geology, Principles of Geology

PETKOVIĆ, Z., Basics of Deposit Exploitation, Mineral Resource Deposit Exploitation

POHARAC LOGAR, V., Instrumental Mineralogy, Mineralogy

POPOV, S. R., Physical Chemistry, Fundamentals of Inorganic Chemistry

PROHASKA, S. J., Hydrogeology

PURTIĆ, N. M., Drilling and Blasting

PUŠIĆ, M., Ground Water Dynamics and Hydrology

RABRENOVIĆ, D., Historical Geology, Palaeogeography

RADOJEVIĆ, J. R., Rock Mechanics, Geomechanics, Rock and Soil Mechanics

SIMEUNOVIĆ, D. M., Underground Mine Design, Mine Organization, Underground Excavation Methods

SIMIĆ, R., Surface Mining Methods, Removal of Water in Open Pit Mining

STAJEVIĆ, B., Solid Mineral Deposit Prospecting and Exploration, Geological and Geochemical Prospecting

STARČEVIĆ, M., Gravity Methods for Investigation, Geophysical Investigation Methodology, Seismology, Geophysical Electronic Instruments, Geophysics
STEVANOVIĆ, Z., Hydrogeological Investigation Methods, Hydrogeological Investigation
SUDAR, M., Micropalaeontology, Palaeontological and Biostratigraphic Research Methodology
SUNARIĆ, D., Engineering Geology, Engineering Geodynamics
TANSKOVIĆ, T., Mining Equipment Maintenance, Thermodynamic Machinery
TOMANEC, R., Raw Material Testing Methods for Mineral Processing Technology
TOMIĆ, V., Hydrogeological Mapping
TRIFUNOVIĆ, P., Mining Materials Technology
VUJASINOVIĆ, S. O., Ground Water Protection, Geology and Environmental Protection
VUJIĆ, S. B., Application of Computers in Mining, Programming
ZAJIĆ, B., Hoisting Equipment

Faculty of Organizational Sciences (Jove Ilića 154, 11040 Belgrade; tel. (11) 395-0893; fax (11) 461-221; e-mail dekanat@fon.bg.ac.rs; internet www.fon.bg.ac.rs):
ĆAMILOVIĆ, S. V., Human Resources Management
ČANGALOVIĆ, M., Operations Research, Discrete Mathematics
ĆIRIĆ, V. V., Computer Program Design Principles
ČUPIĆ, M. E., Decision Making Theory, Decision Support Systems
DABIĆ, S., Stock Exchanges and Shareholding
DAJOVIĆ, S. V., Mathematics
DRAKULIĆ, M., Information Systems and Law, Business Law
DULANOVIĆ, Ž., Basics of Organization, Organization Projects
FILIPOVIĆ, V., Marketing, Strategic Marketing
JOVANOV, Đ., Mathematics, Numerical Analysis
KOSTIĆ, K., Management Systems
KRČEVINAC, S. B., Operations Research, Econometric Methods
LAZAREVIĆ, B. J., Information System Design
LEVI JAKŠIĆ, M. I., Technology Management
MILIĆEVIĆ, V., Management Economics and Business Planning, International Management
MITROVIĆ, Ž. V., Quality Management, Quality Control
PEŠALJEVIĆ, M., Quality Management, Standardization Systems, Metrology Systems
PETROVIĆ, B. M., Work Studies
PETROVIC, M. M., Manpower Planning
RADENKOVIĆ, B., Simulation and Simulation Languages
RADOVIĆ, M. K., Fundamentals of Production Systems, Production Systems
STARČEVIĆ, D., Distributed Information Systems
TODOROVIĆ, J. M., Production Management
VUČIĆ, V. V., Mathematics, Operations Research
VUJOŠEVIĆ, M., Optimization Methods
VUKOVIĆ, N. A., Probability and Statistics
ŽARKIĆ JOKSIMOVIĆ, N., Financial Management and Accounting, Management Accounting

Faculty of Pharmacy (Vojvode Stepe 450, 11221 Belgrade; tel. (11) 247-3224; fax (11) 397-2840; e-mail info@pharmacy.bg.ac.rs; internet www.pharmacy.bg.ac.rs):
AGBABA, D., Pharmaceutical Chemistry

DIMITRIJEVIĆ, M., Immunology
ĐURIĆ, Z., Pharmaceutical Technology with Biopharmacy, Industrial Pharmacy with Cosmetology
JANČIĆ, R., Botany
JELIĆ IVANOVIĆ, Z., Medicinal Biochemistry and Clinical Chemistry
JELIKIĆ STANKOV, M., Analytical Chemistry
JOVANOVIĆ, M., Pharmaceutical Technology with Biopharmacy, Industrial Pharmacy with Cosmetology
JOVANOVIĆ, T., General and Inorganic Chemistry
KORIĆANAC, Z, General and Inorganic Chemistry
KRSTIĆ, S., Pharmacology
LEPOSAVIĆ, G., Pathophysiology
MAJKIĆ SINGH, N., Medicinal Biochemistry and Clinical Enzymology
MALEŠEV, D., Physical Chemistry, Instrumental Methods, Chemical Laboratory Methods
MEDENICA, M., Physical Chemistry, Instrumental Methods, Chemical Laboratory Methods
MILETIĆ, I., Bromatology, Quality and Food Safety Control
POKRAJAC, M., Analytical Chemistry
RISTOVSKI, L., Physics
SPASIĆ, S., Medical Biochemistry, Statistics in Pharmacy
SPASOJEVIĆ KALIMANOVSKA, V., Medicinal Biochemistry and Clinical Chemistry
STOJANOV, M., General Biochemistry and Medicinal Biochemistry
STUPAR, M., Pharmaceutical Technology with Biopharmacy, Industrial Pharmacy with Cosmetology
UGREŠIĆ, N., Pharmacology
VLADIMIROV, S., Pharmaceutical Chemistry
VULETA, G., Industrial Pharmacy with Cosmetology
ŽIVANOVIĆ, L., Drugs Analysis

Faculty of Philology (Studentski trg 3, 11000 Belgrade; tel. (11) 263-8622; fax (11) 263-0039; e-mail info@fil.bg.ac.rs; internet www.fil.bg.ac.rs):
BOGOSAVLJEVIĆ, S., German Literature
BOJOVIĆ, Z., Yugoslav Literature from the Renaissance to Romanticism
BOZOVIĆ, R. N., Arabic Language and Literature
BOZOVIĆ, Z. N., Russian Literature
ĆORIĆ, B., History of the Serbian Language
DERETIĆ, J. R., Serbian and South-Slav Literature
DESIĆ, M. P., Serbo-Croat Language Teaching Methodology
DJINDJIĆ, S. M., Albanian Studies
GRUBAČIĆ, S. K., German Language
HLEBEC, B., English Language
IVANIĆ, D., Modern Serbian Literature
JANIČEVIĆ, J., Cultural Studies
JANKOVIĆ, V. D., Literary Theory
JEREMIĆ, L., World Literature and Literary Theory
JOVANOVIĆ, G. M., Polish Literature
KOJEN, L., Aesthetics and Literary Theory
MAROJEVIĆ, R. N., Russian Literature
NESKOVIĆ, R. R., Philosophical Fundamentals of Marxism
NIKOLIĆ, M., Contemporary Serbian Language
NOVAKOVIĆ, J. R., French Literature
PETKOVIĆ, N. B., Modern Yugoslav Literature, Twentieth Century Literature
PETROVIĆ, S. D., Sociology of Culture and Art
PIPER, P. J., Russian Literature
POLOVINA, V., General Linguistics
RADIĆ DUGONJIĆ, M., Russian Language
SIMIĆ, R. D., Contemporary Serbo-Croatian Language with Stylistics
STANKOVIĆ, B. D., Russian Language

STOJANOVIĆ, D. S., World Literature with Literary Theory
TANASKOVIĆ, D. R., Arabic Language and Literature
TRNAVCI, H. I., Albanian Language and Literature
VUKOBRAT, S., English Literature

Faculty of Philosophy (Čika Ljubina 18–20, 11000 Belgrade; tel. (11) 263-9119; fax (11) 263-9356; e-mail info@f.bg.ac.rs; internet www.f.bg.ac.rs):
ALIBABIĆ, Š., Theory of Educational Organization
BANDIĆ, D. I., Ethnology of Yugoslavia (Spiritual Culture)
BOGDANOVIĆ, M. I., Social Research Methodology
BOGOSAVLJEVIĆ, S., Statistics in Psychology
BOJANOVIĆ, R. Ž., Psychology of Interpersonal Relations
BOLČIĆ, S. I., Sociology of Work
BULATOVIĆ, R. N., Andragogy of Work
ČUPURDIJA, B., Social Anthropology
DENEGRI, J., History of Modern Art
DIMIĆ, L., Yugoslav History
DOŠEN, K., Philosophy
DUŠANIĆ, S. S., Ancient History
ELAKOVIĆ, S., History of Philosophy
HRNJICA, S., General Psychology with Personality Psychology
JELIĆ, V., History of Greek Literature
KAČAVENDA RADIĆ, N., Andragogy of Free Time
KOCIĆ, L. P., General Pedagogy
KOVAČEVIĆ, I., Methodology of Ethnology and Anthropology
KULJIĆ, T., Political Sociology
KUZMANOVIĆ, B., Social Psychology
LAZIĆ, M., Sociology
LJUSIĆ, R., National History of the New Age
LOMA, A., Historical Grammar of the Greek Language
MAKSIMOVIĆ, L. M., Byzantine History
MEDIĆ, S., Family Andragogy
MIKIĆ, Ž. M., Physical Anthropology
MILIĆ, A., Family Sociology
MILIN, M., Introduction to the Classics
MIMICA, A., History of Social Theory
MITROVIĆ, A., General History of the New Age
OPALIĆ, P., Social Pathology
PAJEVIĆ, D., Work Psychology
PEŠIĆ, M., Preschool Pedagogy
RADOŠ, K., Educational Psychology
RICL, M., Ancient History
RISTOVIĆ, M., General Modern History
ŠARANOVIĆ BOŽANOVIĆ, N., General Pedagogy
SPREMIĆ, M. M., General History of the Middle Ages
STANKOVIĆ, Dj. Dj., Yugoslav History
ŠUPUT, M., History of Architecture
TODIĆ, B., Introduction to Art History
TRNAVAC, N., School Pedagogy
VOJVODIĆ, M. S., General History of the New Age
VUJOVIĆ, S., Urban Sociology
ZEC, N., Introduction to Economics
ZUROVAC, M. M., Aesthetics

Faculty of Physical Chemistry (Studentski trg 12–16, 11000 Belgrade; tel. (11) 218-7133; fax (11) 218-7133; e-mail ffh@ffh.bg.ac.rs; internet www.ffh.bg.ac.rs):
ANIĆ, S., Physical Chemistry
BAČIĆ, G., Physical Chemistry of Fluids, Nuclear Spectrometry
DONDUR, V., Chemical Kinetics, Catalysis
HOLCLAJTNER ANTUNOVIĆ, I., General Physical Chemistry, Plasma Physical Chemistry
JEREMIĆ, M., Physical Chemistry
MARKOVĆ, D., Physical Chemistry, Physical Chemistry in Environmental Protection

MENTUS, S. V., Electrochemistry, Physical Chemistry of Solid Electrolytes

MILJANIĆ, Š., Radiochemistry and Nuclear Chemistry

MIOČ, U., Physico-Chemical Analysis, Applied Spectroscopy

PERIĆ, M. N., Quantum Chemistry and Molecular Structures, Spectra and Structures

Faculty of Physics (Studentski trg 12, 11000 Belgrade; tel. (11) 263-0152; fax (11) 328-2619; e-mail dekanat@ff.bg.ac.rs; internet www.ff.bg.ac.rs):

ANIČIN, I., Nuclear Physics

BELIĆ, D. S., Atomic and Molecular Physics, Applied Physics

ĆURIĆ, M. B., Dynamic Meteorology, Cloud Physics

DAMNJANOVIĆ, M., Quantum and Mathematical Physics, Condensed Matter Physics

ĐENIŽE, S. I., Ionized Gas and Plasma Physics, Atomic and Molecular Physics

DRNDAREVIĆ, S., Nuclear Physics, Particle and Field Physics

JANJIĆ, Z. I., Dynamic Meteorology

KNEŽEVIĆ, M., Statistical Physics

KONJEVIĆ, N., Classical and Quantum Optics, Lasers

KRPIĆ, D., Nuclear Physics, Particle and Field Physics

MILOŠEVIĆ, S., Statistical Physics

PURIĆ, J. M., Ionized Gas and Plasma Physics

SAVIĆ, I., Nuclear Physics, Condensed Matter Physics

SREKOVIĆ, A., Ionized Gas and Plasma Physics

STAMATOVIĆ, A. S., Applied Physics, Atomic and Molecular Physics

ZEKOVIĆ, L., Applied Physics, Condensed Matter Physics

Faculty of Political Sciences (Jove Ilića 165, 11000 Belgrade; tel. (11) 397-6422; fax (11) 249-1501; e-mail fpn@fpn.bg.ac.rs; internet www.fpn.bg.ac.rs):

DAMJANOVIĆ, M. D., Organization and Management Studies

JEVTIĆ, M., Religious and Political Studies

KECMANOVIĆ, N., Family Sociology

LAKIĆEVIĆ, M., Social Development and Planning

MILOSAVLJEVIĆ, M. V., Social Pathology

PAVLOVIĆ, V. D., Political Sociology of Modern Society

PEŠIĆ, M. D., General Sociology

PODUNAVAC, M. L., Theory of Political Systems

RADOJKOVIĆ, M. J., Communication Studies

SAMARDŽIĆ, S., European Relations and European Union Studies

SIMEUNOVIĆ, D., Foundations of Political Science

SIMIĆ, M., Rehabilitation of Disabled Persons, Public Health

SLAVUJEVIĆ, Z., Political Marketing and Public Relations

SOKIĆ, S. R., Yugoslav Economy, National Economic Studies

ŠTAMBUK, V. Z., Cybernetics and Informatics

TRGOVČEVIĆ, L., Contemporary Political History

VASILJEVIĆ, B., Contemporary Political Economy

VESELINOV, D. S., Political Ecomony

VIDANOVIĆ, I., Social Case Work

VUKOVIĆ, D., Systems of Social Welfare

Faculty of Security Studies (Gospodara Vučića 50, 11000 Belgrade; tel. (11) 645-1843; fax (11) 645-7-685; e-mail dekanat@fb.bg.ac.rs; internet www.fb.bg.ac.rs):

CVETKOVIĆ, M., Contemporary Combat Systems and Devices

KANDIĆ, D., Introduction to Philosophy and Ethics, Ethics

MILAŠINOVIĆ, R., Conflict Theory

MIŠOVIĆ, S., Violent Conflict Theory

PLAVŠIĆ, M., Macroeconomics

Faculty of Sports and Physical Education (Blagoja Parovića 156, 11000 Belgrade; tel. (11) 353-1000; fax (11) 353-1100; e-mail dekanat@dif.bg.ac.rs; internet www.dif.bg.ac.rs):

ALEXSIĆ, V., Football

BOKAN, B., Physical Culture Theory

ČIRKOVIĆ, Z., Martial Arts

ILIĆ, N., Physiology

JOVANOVIĆ, S., Martial Arts

KARALEJIĆ, M., Basketball

KUKOLJ, M., General Anthropology

LAZAREVIĆ, L., Psychology

NIKOLIĆ, Z., Physiology

PETROVIĆ, Z., Physical Culture Facilities

RADISAVIJEVIĆ, L., Rhythmic-Sports Gymnastics

RADISAVIJEVIĆ, M., Corrective Gymnastics

RADOJEVIĆ, J., Sports Gymnastics

ŠTAKIĆ, Đ., General Sociology and Physical Culture Sociology

STEFANOVIĆ, Đ., Athletics

UGARKOVIĆ, D., Human Development Biology with Elements of Sports Medicine

Faculty of Stomatology (Dr Subotića 8, 11000 Belgrade; tel. (11) 268-5288; fax (11) 685-361; e-mail dekan@stomf.bg.ac.rs; internet www.stomf.bg.ac.rs):

BELOICA, D. Ć., Paediatrics, Preventive Dentistry

DAPČEVIĆ, B., Internal Medicine

DERGENC, R, Otorhinolarnygology

DIMITRIJEVIĆ, B. B., Periodontology, Oral Medicine

DIMITRIJEVIĆ, B. R., Maxillofacial Surgery

GAVRIĆ, M. M., Maxillofacial Surgery

IVANOVIĆ, V., Conservation Dentistry Endodontics

JANKOVIĆ, L., Periodontology, Oral Medicine

KONTIĆ, M., General Surgery

LEKOVIĆ, V. M., Periodontology, Oral Mechine

MIJANOVIĆ, B., General Surgery

MIKOVIĆ, M. D., Forensic Medicine

MILENKOVIĆ, P. B., Pathophysiology

NIKODIJEVIĆ, M., General Surgery

NIKOLIĆ, L., Ophthalmology

PAP, K., Conservation Dentistry Endodontics

POTIĆ, J. B., Neurology and Psychiatry

SJEROBABIN, I., Maxillofacial Surgery

STAMENKOVIĆ, D., Prosthodontics

STANIŠIĆ-SINOBAD, D. N., Prosthodontics

STOJIĆ, D., Pharmacology, Toxicology

TODOROVIĆ, L. M., Oral Surgery

URSU MAGIDU, I., Periodontology, Oral Medicine

VRANJEŠ, D., Neurology and Psychiatry

VULOVIĆ, M. D., Paediatric Preventive Dentistry

ZELIĆ, O. B., Periodontology, Oral Medicine

Faculty of Teacher Training (Narodnog frontna 43, 11000 Belgrade; tel. (11) 361-5225; fax (11) 264-1060; e-mail dekanat@uf.bg.ac.rs; internet www.uf.bg.ac.rs):

BANDJUR, V. B., Didactics

JOVANOVIĆ, A., Literature

KECMANOVIĆ, N., Sociology

Faculty of Technology and Metallurgy (Karnegijeva 4, 11000 Belgrade; tel. (11) 337-0460; fax (11) 337-0387; e-mail tmf@tmf.bg.ac.rs; internet www.tmf.bg.ac.rs):

IVANIĆ, L., Casting, Theory of Casting

MAGADALINOVIĆ, D., Comminution and Classification

MARKOVIĆ, D., Materials Testing

MILIĆEVIĆ, Ž., Underground Mining Technology

MILJKOVIĆ, M., Mine Ventilation, Technical Safety Precautions

RAJČIĆ VUJASINOVIĆ, M., Hydro- and Electrometallurgical Process Theory

STANKOVIĆ, R., Transport and Haulage, Transport in Mineral Technologies

STANKOVIĆ, V., Metallurgical Operations

STANKOVIĆ, Z., Physical Chemistry

STANOJLOVIĆ, R., Physical Methods of Concentration, Mineral Processing

STAVRIĆ, B. J., Economics and Production Organization

ŽIVKOVIĆ, Ž., Nonferrous Metal and Alloy Metallurgy, Pyrometallurgical Process Theory

Faculty of Transport and Traffic Engineering (Vojvode Stepe 305, 11000 Belgrade; tel. (11) 309-1234; fax (11) 246-6294; e-mail dean@sf.bg.ac.rs; internet www.sf.bg.ac.rs):

BABIĆ, O., Air Traffic Control, Air Cargo Transport

BAKMAZ, M. R., Telecommunications Switching Technology, Telecommunications Traffic and Networks

BOJKOVIĆ, Z. S., Electrical Engineering, Basic Telecommunications Technology, Telecommunications Traffic Exploitation

BUKUMIROVIĆ, M. M., Cybernetics, Cybernetics in Transport and Traffic, Computer Simulation, System Modelling on Computer, Programming Languages in Postal and Telecommunications Traffic

ČOLIĆ, V., Ships and Vessels, Ship Resistance and Propulsion, Basics of Water Transport

CVETKOVIĆ, P. A., Fluid Mechanics, Mechanics, Materials Strength

KUZMANOVIĆ, D., Mechanics

LAZOVIĆ, S. M., Telecommunication Systems

MANDIĆ, D., Railway Traction, Urban Rail Systems, Rail Traffic Operation, Application of Telematics and Process Automation in Railway Traffic

MILORADOVIĆ, S., Mathematics

PANTELIĆ VUJANIĆ, S., Sociology, Traffic and Transport Engineering Law, Navigable Waterways Law, Air Transport Law, Traffic Law, Postal and Telecommunications Law, Railway Transport Law

PAPIĆ, V., Motor Vehicle Maintenance, Transport Vehicles and Maintenance

POPOVIĆ, J., Probability and Statistics, Operations Research

PUTNIK, N. D., Terminals

RADMILOVIĆ, Z., Port Planning and Design, Fleet Operation and Management, Water Transport Basics

RADOJKOVIĆ, Z., Roads, Civil Engineering Basics

ŠELMIĆ, R. R., Elements of Transport Devices and Installations, Thermodynamics

SRETENOVIĆ, M., Materials Handling, Fundamentals in Materials Handling

TOŠIĆ, V. S., Airports

VEŠOVIĆ, V. B., Transport and Traffic Organization and Management, Transport and Traffic, Transport and Traffic Work Organization, Postal and Telecommunications Organization and Management

VUJANIĆ, M., Traffic Safety, Accident Prevention, Accident Reconstruction

VUKANOVIĆ, S. V., Traffic Management and Control, Intelligent Transport Systems

VUKOBRAT, M. D., Mechanics

ŽEŽELJ, S., Motor Vehicles

Faculty of Veterinary Medicine (Blv Oslobođenja 18, 11000 Belgrade; tel. (11) 361-5436; fax (11) 268-5936; e-mail podrska@vet.bg.ac.rs; internet www.vet.bg.ac.rs):

ALEKSIĆ, Z., Forensic Veterinary Medicine

AŠANIN, R. M., Microbiology and Immunology

BALGOJEVIĆ, Z., Anatomy

BALTIĆ, M., Fish, Crab and Shellfish Food Quality and Hygiene

BOŽIĆ, T., Pathophysiology

BUNIČIĆ, O., Meat Hygiene and Meat Technology

DJURIČIĆ, B., Infectious Diseases of Domestic Animals

DOBRIĆ, Đ., Infectious Diseases of Domestic Animals

DREKIĆ, D. M., Anatomy

GLEDIĆ, D. S., Histology and Embryology

IVANOV, I., Ruminant and Swine Diseases, Clinical Diagnostics

JEZDIMIROVIĆ, M., Pharmacology and Toxicology

JOVANOVIĆ, M., General Pathology and Pathological Morphology

JOVANOVIĆ, S. J., Animal Breeding

KATIĆ, V., Dairy Product Hygiene

KATIĆ RADIVOJEVIĆ, S., Parasitology

KNEŽEVIĆ, M. A., General Pathology and Pathological Morphology

KULIŠIĆ, Z., Parasitology

LAZAREVIĆ, M., Physiology

MIJAČEVIĆ, Z. M., Dairy Product Technology

NIKOLIĆ, Z., Anatomy

NIKOLOVSKI STEFANOVIĆ, Z., Equine and Small Animal Disease, Clinical Propaedeutics

PALIĆ, T. D., Avian Diseases, Equine and Small Animal Diseases

PAVLOVIĆ, V., Domestic Animal Reproduction, Artificial Insemination

PEJIN, I., Statistics

PETRUJKIĆ, T., Domestic Animal Reproduction, Artificial Insemination

POPOVIĆ, D., Biophysics

POPOVIĆ, N., Wild Animal Diseases, Equine and Small Animal Diseases

RADENKOVIĆ DAMNJANOVIĆ, B., Animal Hygiene and General Hygiene

ŠAMANC, H., Ruminant and Swine Diseases

ŠĆEPANOVIĆ, D., Sociology and Ethics

ŠIMIĆ, M., Histology and Embryology

SINOVEC, Z., Animal Nutrition Physiology and Pathology

SMILJANIĆ, D., Unit Operations

STOJANOVIĆ, L. V., Dairy Product Hygiene

STOJIĆ, V., Physiology

TRAILOVIĆ, D., Cattle Production Economics and Organization, Health Care, Cattle and Food Marketing and Transfer, Equine and Small Animal Diseases, Clinical Propaedeutics

VASIĆ, J., Surgery, Orthopaedics, Ophthalmology

VICKOVIĆ, D., Forensic Veterinary Medicine

VUKOVIĆ, I., Meat Technology

School of Electrical Engineering (Blvr Kralja Aleksandra 73, 11120 Belgrade; tel. (11) 324-8464; fax (11) 324-8681; e-mail dekanat@etf.rs; internet www.etf.bg.ac.rs):

CVETKOVIĆ, D. M., Mathematics

ĐORDJEVIĆ, A. R., Microwave Technology, Electromagnetics, Fundamentals of Electrical Engineering

DRAJIĆ, D. B., Statistical Telecommunication Theory, Computer Telecommunications, Digital Transfer Techniques, Transfer and Recording Codes

DUKIĆ, M., Signal Processing and Transfer, Telecommunications, Radio Systems

ĐURIĆ, M., Power System Components, Power Engineering System Regulation, Replay Protection, Power Stations and Distribution Plants

KOSTIĆ, M., Electrical Lighting, Electrical Installations with Lighting

KOVAČEVIĆ, B. D., Automatic Control, Stochastic Systems and Estimation

LACKOVIĆ, I. B., Mathematics

LAZIĆ, B., Fundamentals of Computer Technology, Computer Architecture, Operating Systems

MARJANOVIĆ, S. N., Electronics

MATAUŠEK, M. R., Optimal Process Control, Automatic Control Systems, Process Control, Process Identification

MERKELE, M., Mathematics, Probability and Statistics

MIKIČIĆ, D. J., Technical Mechanics with Hydraulics, Fundamentals of Mechanical Engineering

MILANOVIĆ, V., Quantum Mechanics, Electronic Device Components, Solid State Physical Electronics, Semiconducting Microstructures

MILUTINOVIĆ, V., Microprocessing Systems, Computer VLSI Systems

OSMOKROVIĆ, P., Electrical Engineering Materials, Dosimetry and Radiation Protection, Nuclear Physics

PAUNOVIĆ, Đ., Radio Systems, Telecommunication Electronics, Radio Relay Systems, Design and Simulation Methods, Radiotechnics

PETROVIĆ, D., A.C. Electrical Machinery, Electromechanical Power Conversion

PETROVIĆ, G., Digital Telecommunications, Digital Telephone Exchange Design, Telecommunication Networks, Digital Transfer Technology, Communication System Simulation, Computational Systems

PETROVIĆ, T., Simulation and Modelling, Non-linear Control Systems, Automatic Control Robust Systems Regulation

PETROVIĆ, Z., Satellite Systems, Fundamentals of Telecommunications, Integrated Telecommunications Networks

POPOVIĆ, B. D., Electrical Measurements, Biomedical Engineering, Biomedical Instrumentation

POTKONJAK, V. N., Robots and Automation

PRAVICA, P. B., Telecommunications

RADUNOVIĆ, J. B., Materials Physics, Optoelectronic Devices and Systems, Optoelectronic and Laser Systems, Electro-optics, Statistical Physics

RAJAKOVIĆ, N., Distributive and Industrial Networks, Power Systems Analysis, Power Systems Exploitation, Power Systems Analysis

RAKOVIĆ, D., Materials Physics, Biophysics

RAMOVIĆ, R., Microelectronics, Electronic Device Components, Semiconductor Analysis and Modelling

REIJIN, B., Electrical Circuit Theory, Medical Informatics, Digital Information Processing, Electrical Circuit Theory

SAVIĆ, M. S., High Voltage Technology, High Voltage Equipment

ŠIMIĆ, S. K., Mathematics

ŠKOKLJEV, I., General Power Engineering, Power Engineering System Planning

SREĆKOVIĆ, M., Laser Technics, Quantum Electronics

STANKOVIĆ, D. K., Sensors and Converters, Physico-Technical Measurement, Sensors and Actuators

STANKOVIĆ, S. S., Stochastic Signal Processing, Artificial Intelligence and Neural Networks, Automatic Control Systems, Digital Signal Processing

STOJIĆ, M. R., Automatic Control, Digital Control Systems

VASILJEVIĆ, D. M., Digital System Design

VELAŠEVIĆ, D. M., Programming Compilers, Expert Systems, Digital Programming

ŽIVKOVIĆ, D. B., Computer System Control, Pulse and Digital Electronics

ZLATANOVIĆ, M. D., Sensors and Convertors, Atomic and Molecular Spectroscopy, Fundamentals of Mechanical Engineering

School of Medicine (Dr Subotica 8, 11000 Belgrade; tel. (11) 363-6368; fax (11) 363-6368; e-mail boca@med.bg.ac.rs; internet www.med.bg.ac.rs):

ALEKSANDRIĆ, B., Forensic Medicine

ANTUNOVIĆ, V., Surgery

APOSTOLSKI, S., Neurology

ARSOV, V. J., Surgery

ASIĆ RADOSAVLJEVIĆ, G., Internal Medicine

AVRAMOVIĆ, D. M., Internal Medicine

BACETIĆ, D., Pathological Anatomy

BANIĆEVIĆ, M., Paediatrics

BLAGOTIĆ, M. Ž., Anatomy

BOGDANOVIĆ, R., Paediatrics

BOŠKOVIĆ, D., Internal Medicine

BOŠNJAK, V. I., Internal Medicine

BOŽANIĆ, M., Internal Medicine

BOŽIĆ, M., Infectious Diseases

BRKIĆ POPOVIĆ, V., Internal Medicine

BULAJIĆ, M., Internal Medicine

BUMBAŠIREVIĆ, V., Histology and Embryology

BUNJEVAČKI, G., Paediatrics

ĐUTKOVIĆ, I., Surgery

ČEBEŠEK, R., Internal Medicine

ČEMERIKIĆ, D. A., Pathological Physiology

ČOLOVIĆ, M., Internal Medicine

ČOLOVIĆ, R., Surgery

CUCIĆ, V. S., Social Medicine

CVEJIĆ, V., Biochemistry

CVETKOVIĆ, D. H., Pathological Anatomy

CVETKOVIĆ, M., Gynaecology and Obstetrics

DENIĆ DJORDJEVIĆ, G., Pathological Physiology

ĐERIĆ, D., Otolaryngology and Maxillofacial Surgery

DJORDJEVIĆ, L. V., Anatomy

DJURIČIĆ, B., Biochemistry

ĐORĐEVIĆ, M., Surgery

ĐORĐEVIĆ, P., Internal Medicine

DOTLIĆ, R., Statistics and Informatics in Medicine

DRAŠKOVIĆ MAŠIREVIĆ, G., Physiology

DREZGIĆ, M., Internal Medicine

ĐUKIĆ, P., Surgery

ĐUKIĆ, V., Surgery

DUNJIĆ, D., Forensic Medicine

ERIĆ MARINKOVIĆ, J., Statistics and Informatics in Medicine

GANOVIĆ, R., Gynaecology and Obstetrics

GLEDOVIĆ, Z., Epidemiology

GLIŠIĆ, S., Surgery

GOLUBOVIĆ, G., Internal Medicine

GOLUBOVIĆ, S., Ophthalmology

GRBOVIĆ, L. C., Pharmacology and Toxicology

GRUJIĆ, M., Internal Medicine

HADŽI ĐOKIĆ, J. B., Surgery

HAN, R., Nuclear Medicine

HAVELKA, M., Pathological Anatomy

IGNAJČEV, M., Ophthalmology

ILANKOVIĆ, N., Psychiatry

ILIĆ, A. B., Anatomy

JAKOVIĆ, M., Surgery

JANIĆIJEVIĆ, M., Surgery

JANKOVIĆ, S., Epidemiology

JANOŠEVIĆ, L., Otolaryngology and Maxillofacial Surgery

JANOŠEVIĆ, S., Statistics and Informatics in Medicine

JAREBINSKI, M. S., Epidemiology

JAŠOVIĆ, M., Psychiatry

JEVREMOVIĆ, I., Epidemiology

JORGA, I., Physiology

JORGA, V., Hygiene and Medical Ecology

JOVANOVIĆ, T. M., Physiology

JOVANOVIĆ, T. P., Microbiology and Immunology

KALEZIĆ, V., Surgery

KAŽIĆ, T. M., Pharmacology and Toxicology

KOCIJANČIĆ, M., Internal Medicine

KOCIJANČIĆ, R., Hygiene and Medical Ecology

KONTIĆ, Đ., Ophthalmology

KOSTIĆ, V., Neurology
KOVAČEVIĆ, N., Internal Medicine
KOVAČEVIĆ, S. J., Forensic Medicine
LABAN, A. I., Pathological Anatomy
LAČKOVIĆ, V. B., Histology and Embryology
LASTIĆ, S. S., Anatomical Pathology
LATKOVIĆ, Z., Ophthalmology
LONČAR STEVANOVIĆ, H., Physiology
LOTINA, S., Surgery
LUKIĆ, V. S., Neurology
MAGLAJIĆ, S., Paediatrics
MAKSIMOVIĆ, Ž., Surgery
MANČIĆ, J., Paediatrics
MARIĆ, J., Psychiatry
MARINKOVIĆ, S. V., Anatomy
MARŠEVALSKI, A., Physical Medicine and Rehabilitation
MARTINOVIĆ, Ž., Neurology
MATIĆ, M., Internal Medicine
MICIĆ, D., Internal Medicine
MICIĆ, S., Surgery
MIJAČ, M., Anatomy
MILENKOVIĆ, S., Ophthalmology
MILIČEVIĆ, N., Histology and Embryology
MILIČEVIĆ, R., Surgery
MILIČEVIĆ, Ž., Histology and Embryology
MILIKIĆ MITIĆ, M., Internal Medicine
MILOVIĆ, I., Surgery
MILUTINOVIĆ, D., Surgery
MIMIĆ OKA, J. I., Biochemistry
MISITA, V., Ophthalmology
MITROVIĆ, M. M., Surgery
MUJOVIĆ, V. M., Physiology
MUNJIZA, M., Psychiatry
NEDELKJOV, V., Pathological Physiology
NEŠIĆ, V., Internal Medicine
NIKOLIĆ, G., Physical Medicine and Rehabilitation
NIKOLIĆ, P. L., Infectious Diseases
NIKOLIĆ, S., Infectious Diseases
OBRADOVIĆ, M., Forensic Medicine
OBRADOVIĆ, V., Nuclear Medicine
OCIĆ, G., Neurology
OSTOJIĆ, M., Internal Medicine
OŠTRIĆ, V., Internal Medicine
PANTELIĆ ATANACKOVIĆ, M., Pathological Anatomy
PANTIĆ, S., Histology and Embryology
PAOVIĆ STANOJEVIĆ, A., Ophthalmology
PAPOVIĆ, R., Biology and Human Genetics
PAUNOVIĆ, V., Psychiatry
PAVLOVIĆ, M. D., Infectious Diseases
PAVLOVIĆ, M. R., Physiology
PAVLOVIĆ, M. Ž., Occupational Medicine
PAVLOVIĆ, S., Nuclear Medicine
PEJOVIĆ, M., Psychiatry
PERIŠIĆ, M., Internal Medicine
PERIŠIĆ, V., Paediatrics
PEŠIĆ, B., Pathological Physiology
PETKOVIĆ, S., Gynaecology and Obstetrics
PILIPOVIĆ, N., Internal Medicine
PLEĆAŠ, D., Hygiene and Medical Ecology
POPOVIĆ, G., Physical Medicine and Rehabilitation
POPOVIĆ, M. R., Surgery
POTIĆ VESOVIĆ, V., Physical Medicine and Rehabilitation
PROSTRAN, M., Anatomy
PROSTRAN, M., Pharmacology and Toxicology
RADEVIĆ, B., Surgery
RADONJIĆ, V., Anatomy
RADULOVIĆ, N., Paediatrics
RADULOVIĆ, R., Otolaryngology and Maxillofacial Surgery
RAMIĆ, Z., Microbiology and Immunology
RANKOVIĆ, A., Anatomy
REBIĆ, P., Internal Medicine
REPAC, R. M., Surgery
RISTIĆ, M., Surgery
RUNIĆ, S., Gynaecology and Obstetrics
SAMARDŽIĆ, M., Surgery
SAMARDŽIĆ, R. G., Pharmacology and Toxicology
ŠAŠIC, M., Infectious Diseases
SAVIĆ DJURKOVIĆ, R. M., Biochemistry

ŠEFEROVIĆ, P., Internal Medicine
ŠIKIĆ, B., Pathological Physiology
SIMEUNOVIĆ, S. D., Paediatrics
SIMIĆ, S., Social Medicine
SINĐELIĆ, R., Surgery
SKENDER, M., Pathological Anatomy
SLAVKOVIĆ, S., Surgery
STANIMIROVIĆ, B., Gynaecology and Obstetrics
STARČEVIĆ, V., Physiology
STAROVIĆ, D., Surgery
STEFANOVIĆ, B., Histology and Embryology
STEVOVIĆ, D. M., Surgery
STOJKOVIĆ MOSTARICA, M., Microbiology and Immunology
SUBOTIĆ, S. L., Surgery
SUZIĆ, S., Physiology
TALIĆ, B. S., Surgery
TEOFILOVSKID, G. E., Anatomy
TIMOTIJEVIĆ, I., Psychiatry
TODOROVIĆ, S., Neurology
TRPINAC, D., Histology and Embryology
VASILJEVIĆ, J., Pathological Anatomy
VASILJEVIĆ, Z., Internal Medicine
VELIMIROVIĆ, D., Surgery
VELIMIROVIĆ, D., Pathological Anatomy
VELJKOVIĆ, S. D., Forensic Medicine
VIDAKOVIĆ, A. R., Occupational Medicine
VLAHOVIĆ ŠVABIĆ, M., Microbiology and Immunology
VLAJINAC, H. D., Epidemiology
VUČKOVIĆ, V., Physiology
VUČOVIĆ, D., Surgery
VULOVIĆ, D. M., Pathological Physiology
VULOVIĆ, Z., Chemistry in Medicine
ZAMAKLAR, D., Surgery
ZEC KRANJČIĆ, I., Microbiology and Immunology
ŽIVKOVIĆ, S., Surgery

Technical Faculty in Bor (Vojske Jugoslavije 12, 19210 Bor; tel. (30) 424-555; fax (30) 421-078; e-mail office@tf.bor.ac.rs; internet www .tf.bor.ac.rs):

IVANIĆ, L., Casting, Theory of Casting
MAGDALINOVIĆ, N. M., Comminution and Classification
MARKOVIĆ, D., Metals Testing
MILIĆEVIĆ, Ž. M., Underground Mining Technology
MILJKOVIĆ, M. A., Mine Ventilation, Technical Safety Precautions
RAJČIĆ VUJASINOVIĆ, M., Theory of Hydro- and Electrometallurgical Processes
STANKOVIĆ, R., Transport and Haulage, Transport in Mineral Technologies
STANKOVIĆ, V., Metallurgical Operations
STANKOVIĆ, Z. D., Physical Chemistry
STANOJLOVIĆ, R. D., Physical Concentration Methods, Mineral Processing
ŽIVKOVIĆ, Ž. D., Metallurgy of Non-Ferrous Metals and Alloys, Pyrometallurgical Process Theory

UNIVERZITET U KRAGUJEVCU
(University of Kragujevac)

Jovana Cvijica bb, 34000 Kragujevac
Telephone: (34) 370-270
Fax: (34) 370-168
E-mail: unikg@kg.ac.rs
Internet: www.kg.ac.rs
Founded 1976
State control
Academic year: October to June
Rector: Prof. Dr SLOBODAN ARSENIJEVIC
Vice-Rector for Finance: Prof. Dr BRANISLAV JEREMIC
Vice-Rector for Education: Prof. Dr ZORA ARSOVSKI
Vice-Rector for Science and Research: Prof. Dr ZIVADIN BUGARCIC
Gen. Sec.: ZORICA AVRAMOVIC
Librarian: RUŽICA IGNJATOVIĆ
Library of 100,000 vols

Number of teachers: 1,000
Number of students: 14,000
Publication: *LIPAR* (cultural and literary themes, 4 a year)

DEANS

Faculty of Agriculture in Čačak: Prof. Dr MIROSLAV SPASODEVIĆ
Faculty of Economics in Kragujevac: Prof. Dr SLOBODAN MALINIĆ
Faculty of Law in Kragujevac: Prof. Dr PREDRAG STOJANOVIC
Faculty of Mechanical Engineering in Kragujevac: Prof. Dr MIROSLAV BABIĆ
Faculty of Mechanical Engineering in Kraljevo: Dr NOVAK NEDIĆ
Faculty of Medicine in Kragujevac: Dr NEBOJSA ARSENIJEVIĆ
Faculty of Philology and Arts in Kragujevac: Prof. FREE ŠTETIĆ
Faculty of Science and Mathematics in Kragujevac: Assoc. Prof. Dr DRAGOSLAV NIKEZIĆ
Faculty of Technology in Čačak: Prof. Dr JEROSLAV ŽIVANIĆ
Teacher-Training Faculty in Jagodina: Prof. SRETKO DIVLJAN
Teacher-Training Faculty in Užice: Prof. Dr KRSTIVOJE ŠPIJUNOVIĆ

UNIVERZITET U NIŠU
(University of Niš)

Univerzitetski trg 2, 18000 Niš
Telephone: (18) 257-970
Fax: (18) 257-950
E-mail: uniuni@ni.ac.rs
Internet: www.ni.ac.rs
Founded 1965
State control
Rector: Prof. Dr DAGAN ANTIC (acting)
Vice-Rector for Teaching: Prof. Dr VLASTIMIR DJOKIC (acting)
Vice-Rector for Scientific Work: Prof. Dr DRAGAN DÖNITZ (acting)
Vice-Rector for International Cooperation: Prof. Dr VESNA LOPICIC (acting)
Vice-Rector for Finance: Prof. Dr SLOBODAN ANTIC (acting)
Sec.-Gen.: DRAGOSLAV DJOKIĆ
Number of teachers: 1,514
Number of students: 25,844
Publications: *Facta Universitatis* (scientific journal, irregular), *Teme* (journal for social theory and practice, 4 a year)

DEANS

Faculty of Arts: Prof. DRAGOSLAV ACIMOVIC (acting)
Faculty of Civil Engineering and Architecture: Prof. Dr DRAGAN ARANDJELOVIĆ
Faculty of Economics: Dr EVICA PETROVID
Faculty of Electronic Engineering: Prof. Dr DRAGAN ANTIĆ
Faculty of Law: Prof. Dr NEVENA PETRUSIC
Faculty of Mechanical Engineering: Prof. Dr VLASTIMIR NIKOLIĆ
Faculty of Medicine: Prof. Dr MILAN VIŠNJIĆ
Faculty of Occupational Safety: Prof. Dr LJILJANA ŽIVKOVIĆ
Faculty of Philosophy: Prof. Dr MOMCILO STOJKOVIC
Faculty of Science and Mathematics: Prof. Dr DRAGAN S. ĐORDEVIĆ
Faculty of Sports and Physical Education: Prof. Dr DOBRICA ŽIVKOVIĆ
Faculty of Technology in Leskovac: Prof. Dr JAKOV STAMENKOVIĆ
Teacher-Training Faculty in Vranje: Prof. Dr STANA SMILJKOVIC

PROFESSORS

Faculty of Arts (Knjeginje Ljubice 10, 18000 Niš; tel. and fax (18) 522-396; fax (18) 513-272; e-mail info@artf.ni.ac.rs; internet www.artf.ni.ac.rs):

CEKIĆ, N., Forms Design

Faculty of Civil Engineering and Architecture (Aleksandra Medvedeva 14, 18000 Niš; tel. (18) 588-200; fax (18) 588-200; e-mail gaf@gaf.ni.ac.rs; internet www.gaf.ni.ac.rs):

ANDJELKOVIĆ, H., Descriptive Geometry
ANDJELKOVIĆ, M., Industrial Facilities Design, Public Facilities Design
ARANDJELOVIĆ, D., Hydraulic Engineering
CEKIĆ, N., Public Facilities Design, Essential Designing
DAMNJANOVIĆ, M., Architectural Structures, Metal Structures, Metal Structures in Buildings
DRENIĆ, D., Structure Testing, Coupled and Special Structures
IGIĆ, T., Strength of Materials, Structure Plasticity and Limitation Analysis
ILIĆ, Č., Railway Engineering, Superstructures and Stations
ILIĆ, D., Housing Design, Project Development
MARKOVIĆ, M., Descriptive Geometry
MARKOVIĆ, V., Dams and Water Potential Utilization
MILENKOVIĆ, S., Urban Water Supply and Sewerage Systems Engineering
MITKOVIĆ, P., Urbanism, Area Planning
PETKOVIĆ, D., Concrete Structures, Concrete Bridges
POPOVIĆ, B., Structure Plasticity and Limitation Analysis, Structure Statics
PROLOVIĆ, V., Foundation Engineering
PROTIĆ, P., Mathematics
RADIVOJEVIĆ, G., Statics of Architectural Structures, Construction Systems
SPASOJEVIĆ, N., Concrete Bridges, Concrete Structures
STOJIĆ, D., Timber Structures and Scaffolds, Timber and Masonry Structures
TRAJKOVIĆ, D., Organization of Construction Works
VELIČKOVIĆ, D., Metal Structures
ZDRAVKOVIĆ, S., Structural Stability and Dynamics, Theory of Surface Girders
ŽIVKOVIĆ, D., Hydrotechnical Structures
ZLATANOVIĆ, M., Organization of Construction Works, Elements of Road Engineering

Faculty of Economics (Trg Kralja Aleksandra Ujeditelja 11, 18000 Niš; tel. (18) 528-601; fax (18) 523-859; e-mail ekonomski@eknfak.ni.ac.rs; internet www.eknfak.ni.ac.rs):

ARANDJELOVIĆ, Z., Yugoslav Economy, Economic Policy
BARAC, N., Business Logistics Management
BOGDANOVIĆ, S., Mathematics
ĆUZOVIĆ, S., Trade Economics, Trade Management
CVETANOVIĆ, S., Theory and Policy of Economic Development
DJEKIĆ, S., Agricultural Economics, Agricultural Management
FIGAR, N., Business Economics
GLIGORIJEVIĆ, Ž., Industrial Economics, Industrial Management
GROZDANOVIĆ, D., Business Economics
HAFNER, P., Sociology
JOVANOVIĆ, R., Informatics
KITANOVIĆ, D., Political Economy
KOSTIĆ, V., Russian Language
KRSTIĆ, B., Banking, Banking Management
KRSTIĆ, J., Financial Accounting, Auditing
NIKOLIĆ, S., Business Organization
NOVIĆEVIĆ, B., Managerial Accounting
PREDIĆ, B., Business Planning and Development Policy

SEKULOVIĆ, M., Economic Doctrines, Transition Economics
STANKOVIĆ, L., Marketing, International Marketing
TODOROVIĆ, E., Business Finance
TODOROVIĆ, O., Operations Research, Financial Mathematics
ZDRAVKOVIĆ, D., Theory of Prices and Pricing Policy

Faculty of Electronic Engineering (Aleksandra Medvedeva 14, 18000 Niš; tel. (18) 529-105; fax (18) 588-399; e-mail efinfo@elfak.ni.ac.rs; internet www.elfak.ni.ac.rs):

ARSIĆ, M., Measurements in Electronics, Telemetry
DAMNJANOVIĆ, M., VLSI Design, Electronic System Design
DANKOVIĆ, B., Methods of Intelligent Control, Process Control, Process Identification
DELETIĆ, S., Theory of Social Development
DIMITRIJEVIĆ, B., Electrical Measurement, Intelligent Instrumentation, Measurement in Microelectronics
DJORDJEVIĆ, B., Digital Electronics, Electronic Circuits
DJORDJEVIĆ KAJAN, S., Computer Graphics, Systems Software, Data Structures and Databases, Software Engineering
GMITROVIĆ, M., Network Synthesis and Signal Processing
JANKOVIĆ, N., Power Components and Circuits, Sensors and Convertors
KOCIĆ, LJ., Mathematics, Numerical Mathematics
KOVAČEVIĆ, M., Mathematics, Numerical Mathematics
KRSTIĆ, D., Wireless Engineering, High-Frequency Electronics
LITOVSKI, V., Electronics, Neural Networks, Electronic Circuit Design
MARKOVIĆ, V., Microwave Electronics, Satellite Communications
MILOSAVLJEVIĆ, Č., Elements of Automatic Control, EMP Regulation
MILOŠEVIĆ, M., Electroacoustics, Audiotechnics
MILOVANOVIĆ, B., Microwave Technology, Microwave Systems, Mobile Telecommunications
MILOVANOVIĆ, D., Electronics, Analogue Electronics
MILOVANOVIĆ, G., Mathematics, Mathematical Methods, Numerical Mathematics
MILOVANOVIĆ, I., Mathematics, Discrete Mathematics
MITIĆ, D., Elements of Electrical Engineering, Electromagnetics
NAUMOVIĆ, M., SAU Design, Automatic Control Theory, Intelligent Control Methods
NIKOLIĆ, Z., Quality and Reliability
NIKOLIĆ, Z., Mobile Telecommunications, Basic Telecommunications, Telecommunications in Electronic Power Engineering
PEJČIĆ, M., Philosophy and Sociology
PEJOVIĆ, M., Physics
PETKOVIĆ, M., Mathematics
PETKOVIĆ, P., Computer-Aided Design, Electronics Circuit Design, Integrated Circuit Design
RADENKOVIĆ, V., Electrical Measurement, Measurement in Electric Power Engineering
RANČIĆ, P., Electrical Installations and Illumination, Special Electrical Installations
RISTIĆ, S., Electronic Components, Semiconducting Components, Power Components and Circuits
STANKOVIĆ, M., Basic Computer Technology, Programming Languages, Assemblers

STANKOVIĆ, R., Logic Design, Pattern Recognition
STEFANOVIĆ, D., Optoelectronics
STEFANOVIĆ, M., Optic Telecommunications, Telecommunication Theory, Digital Telecommunications, Telecommunication System Design, Radar Systems and Radiolocation
STOJADINOVIĆ, N., Quality and Reliability, Physical Electronics, Failure Physics and Diagnostics, Components Characterization, Basic Microelectronics
STOJANOVIĆ, V., Circuit Theory, Television Systems, Television, Digital Picture Processing
STOJČEV, M., Microprocessing Technology, Microprocessing Systems
STOJILKOVIĆ, S., Low Temperature Electronics
TOKIĆ, T., Microcomputers and Programming, Microcomputer Systems and I/O Devices
VELIČKOVIĆ, D., Electromagnetics, Basic Electrical Engineering
ŽIVKOVIĆ, LJ., Materials for Electronics

Faculty of Law (Trg Kralja Aleksandra 11, 18000 Niš; tel. (18) 500-201; fax (18) 4523-747; e-mail pravni@prafak.ni.ac.rs; internet www.prafak.ni.ac.rs):

BOŽIĆ, M., Economic Policy
ĆIRIĆ, A., International Trade Law
DJURDJIĆ, V., Criminal Procedural Law with Crime Investigation and Law Enforcement
GORČIĆ, J., Financial Law
KONSTANTINOVIĆ-VILIĆ, S., Criminology, Penology
KOVAČEVIĆ-KUŠTRIMOVIĆ, R., Introduction to Civil and Property Law
MIJAČIĆ, M., Law of Obligation
MILENOVIĆ, D., Trade Law
NIKOLIĆ, D., General Legal History
PETROVIĆ, M., Administrative Law, Management Science with Legal Informatics
RADIVOJEVIĆ, Z., Public International Law
ROČKOMANOVIĆ, M., Private International Law
SERJEVIĆ, V., Political Economy
SIMIĆ, M., Introduction to Law
STANIMIROVIĆ, D., Sociology
STANKOVIĆ, G., Civil Procedural Law, Arbitration Law
STOJANOVIĆ, D., Constitutional Law
STOJIČIĆ, S., National Legal History

Faculty of Mechanical Engineering (ul. Aleksandra Medvedeva 14, 18000 Niš; tel. (18) 588-229; fax (18) 588-244; e-mail info@masfak.ni.ac.rs; internet www.masfak.ni.ac.rs):

BLAGOJEVIĆ, B., Aeration and Ventilators, Cooling Techniques
BOGDANOVIĆ, B., Hydro-Power Transmitters, Compressors and Ventilators, Piping
BORIČIĆ, Z., Fluid Mechanics, Hydraulic and Pneumatic Systems of Automatic Control
ĆOJBAŠIĆ, LJ., Basic Processing Technology, Prime Materials
DJOKIĆ, V., Theory and Methods of Mechanical Systems Design, Elements of Construction Theory, Construction Methods, Welded Constructions, Rubber Construction Machines
DJORDJEVIĆ, D., Sociology and Philosophy of Natural Sciences, Basic Labour Sociology and Economics
DJURDJANOVIĆ, M., Welding, Welding Technology, Machine Systems Tribology
DOMAZET, D., Modelling and Optimization of Production Systems, Computer-Aided Production Design
HEDRIH, K., Elastodynamics
ILIĆ, G., Measurement Technology, Thermodynamics

JEVTIĆ, V., Technical Logistics, Mining and Building Machinery, Continuous Transport Machinery, Mining Mechanization, Driving System Dynamics, Fundamentals of Technical Logisitics

JOVANOVIĆ, M., Computer-Aided Design, Information Technologies, Structure Analysis, Geometric Modelling, Metal Construction

LAKOVIĆ, S., Thermal Plants, Thermal Power Plants, Boilers

LAZAREVIĆ, D., Tools, Non-Conventional Methods, Polymer Modelling Tools

MARINKOVIĆ, V., Machining, Processing Tribology

MILENKOVIĆ, D., Turbomachine Theory and Fundamentals, Hydraulic Machines, Special Pumps

MILOVANČEVIĆ, D., Mathematics

MILTENOVIĆ, V., Machine Parts, Reliability of Machine Systems, Integral Product Development, Machine System Supervision and Protection

NIKODIJEVIĆ, D., Fluid Mechanics, Oil Hydraulics and Pneumatics, Hydraulic Components, Hydro-Pneumatic Elements in Mechatronics, Physics

NIKOLIĆ, V., Automatic Control, Automatic Control Discrete Systems, Systems of Control in Mechatronics, Optimal Control, Nonlinear Control Systems, Neural and Fuzzy Modelling and Control

PAVLOVIĆ, N., Mechanisms in Mechatronics, Micromechanics, Elements of Fine Mechanics, Optical Elements in Mechatronics

PAVLOVIĆ, R., Mechanics, Plate and Shell Theory

PETKOVIĆ, LJ., Mathematics, Numerical Mathematics and Programming

PETROVIĆ, T., Measurement Techniques, Basic Mechatronics, Mechanical Elements in Mechatronics, Mechatronic System Design, Special Design Methods

RADOJKOVIĆ, N., Thermodynamics, Thermal and Diffusing Apparatus

STEFANOVIĆ, A., Internal Combustion Engines

STOJILJKOVIĆ, M., Automation of Production, Packing Machines, Pneumatic and Hydraulic Components, Assembling and Packing Technology, Digital Control Techniques

STOJILJKOVIĆ, V., Production Management, Processing by Plastic Deformation, Management in Mechanical Engineering, Production Process Statistical Control

TASIĆ, Ž., Electrical Engineering and Electronics, Basic Mechatronics

TEMELJKOVSKI, D., Machines for Processing by Deformation

VULIĆ, A., Power Conveyors, Quality of Machine Systems, Technical Diagnostics, Special-Purpose Machines, Agricultural Machines

ŽIVKOVIĆ, D., Hydromechanics of Mixtures, Thermal Turbomachines

ŽIVKOVIĆ, Ž., Theory of Machines and Mechanisms, Technical Drawing, Mechatronic System Modelling

Faculty of Medicine (Blvr Dr Zorana Đinđića 81, 18000 Niš; tel. (18) 457-0029; fax (18) 423-8770; e-mail contact@medfak.ni.ac.rs; internet www.medfak.ni.ac.rs):

ANTIĆ, M., Medical Sociology
BABIĆ, M., Neurosurgery
BAŠIĆ, H., Pathological Anatomy
BJELAKOVIĆ, G., Biochemistry
BOGIĆEVIĆ, M., Nuclear Medicine
BOŠNAKOVIĆ, P., Radiology
BURAZOR, M., Internal Medicine, Cardiology
DAČIĆ-SIMONOVIĆ, D., Dental Pathology
DENOVIĆ, B., Forensic Medicine
DIMOV, D., Pathological Anatomy

DJORDJEVIĆ, D., Internal Medicine, Pneumophysiology
DJORDJEVIĆ, V., Biochemistry
DJORDJEVIĆ, V., Internal Medicine, Nephrology
FILIPOVIĆ, S., Elements of Clinical Oncology
IGIĆ, A., Prosthodontics
IGIĆ, S., Prosthodontics
ILIĆ, R., Pathological Anatomy
ILIĆ, S., Internal Medicine, Cardiology
ILIĆ, SL., Nuclear Medicine
JEREMIĆ, M., Surgery, General Surgery
JOVANOVIĆ, D., Physiology
JOVČIĆ, S., Paediatric Surgery
KAMENOV, B., Paediatrics
KATIĆ, V., Pathological Anatomy
KOCIĆ, B., Microbiology and Immunology
KOJOVIĆ, Z., Physical Medicine and Rehabilitation
KONSTANTINOVIĆ, LJ., Infectology
KOSTIĆ, V., Infectology
KOSTIĆ, Ž., Hygiene and Medical Ecology
KRSTIĆ, M., Infectology
KUTLEŠIĆ, Č., Pathological Anatomy
LOVIĆ, B., Internal Medicine, Cardiology
MALOBABIĆ, Z., Pharmacology and Toxicology
MARKOVIĆ, V., Internal Medicine, Cardiology
MARKOVIĆ, Z., Internal Medicine, Rheumatology
MIHAJLOVIĆ, D., Pathological Anatomy
MIHAJLOVIĆ, M., Physiology
MIHAJLOVIĆ, P., Physics
MILADINOVIĆ, P., Gynaecology and Obstetrics
MILATOVIĆ, S., Radiology
MILENKOVIĆ, Z., Surgery, Neurosurgery
MILIĆEVIĆ, R., Paediatric Surgery
MILJKOVIĆ, S., Psychiatry with Medical Psychology
MILOSAVLJEVIĆ, LJ., Otorhinolaryngology
MILOSAVLJEVIĆ, M., Gynaecology and Obstetrics
MIRKOVIĆ, B., Oral and Periodontal Diseases
MITIĆ, N., Dental Pathology
MITIĆ, S., Dental Pathology
MITROVIĆ, M., Surgery, Orthopaedics
MITROVIĆ, R., Hygiene, Medical Ecology
NIKOLIĆ, J., Biochemistry
NOVAK, D., Paediatrics
ORLOV, S., Oral and Periodontal Diseases
PARAVINA, M., Dermatovenereology
PAVLOVIĆ, D., Biochemistry
PEROVIĆ, M., Histology and Embryology
POP-TRAJKOVIĆ, Ž., Gynaecology and Obstetrics
RADENKOVIĆ, S., Pathological Physiology
RADIĆ, S., Pathological Physiology
RAIČEVIĆ, R., Internal Medicine, Nephrology
RANKOVIĆ, Ž., Infectology
SAVIĆ, M., Paedodontics and Preventive Stomatology
SAVIĆ, V., Pathological Anatomy
SKOČAJIĆ, S., Dental Pathology
SPALEVIĆ, M., Forensic Medicine
SPASIĆ, M., Epidemiology
STAMENKOVIĆ, I., Internal Medicine, Gastroenterology
STANIŠIĆ, V., Medical Statistics and Informatics
STANKOVIĆ, A., Internal Medicine, Rheumatology
STANKOVIĆ, D., Prosthodontics
STEFANOVIĆ, N., Anatomy
STEFANOVIĆ, V., Internal Medicine, Nephrology
STOJILJKOVIĆ, M., General Surgery
STOJILJKOVIĆ, S., Pathological Physiology
TIODOROVIĆ, B., Epidemiology
VELJKOVIĆ, S., Physiology
VIŠNJIĆ, M., Plastic Surgery
VUČETIĆ, D., Gynaecology and Obstetrics

VUČETIĆ, R., Anatomy
VUJIČIĆ, B., Oral Surgery
ZLATANOVIĆ, G., Opthalmology
ŽIVKOVIĆ, DJ., Internal Medicine, Pneumophysiology

Faculty of Occupational Safety (Čarnojevića 10A, 18000 Niš; tel. (18) 529-701; fax (18) 249-962; e-mail dekanat@znrfak.ni.ac.rs; internet www.znrfak.ni.ac.rs):

ANDJELKOVIĆ, B., Protection against Fire in Technical Processes, Introduction to Working and Living Environment Protection, Technological Processes in the Living Environment

CVETKOVIĆ, D., Noise and Vibrations, Noise in the Living Environment

DJORDJEVIĆ, J., Sociology, Social Ecology

IVANJAC, M., Labour Law

JANKOVIĆ, Ž., Safety at Work with Machines and Devices, Fire Extinguishing Processes and Methods

JOVANOVIĆ, D., Protection against Fire and Explosions, Uncontrolled Combustion Processes

MITIĆ, D., Ignition and Combustion Theory, Engineering Materials

NEDELJKOVIĆ, V., Ventilation and Air-Conditioning Systems, Energy and Living Environment

SPASIĆ, D., Economics of Occupational Safety, Economics of Environmental Protection

STANKOVIĆ, M., Mathematics, Mathematical Modelling

ŽIVKOVIĆ, LJ., Safety at Work with Thermal Plants

ŽIVKOVIĆ, N., Systems and Equipment for Industrial Waste Treatment, Air Protection

Faculty of Philosophy (Ćirila i Metodija 2, 18000 Niš; tel. (18) 514-312; fax (18) 514-310; internet www.filfak.ni.ac.rs):

BOGDANOVIĆ, N., History of Serbian Language, Dialectology

BUTIGAN, Z., Sociology of Politics

DJORDJEVIĆ, Z., Introduction to History with Methodology

DJUROVIĆ, R., Serbian Language (Phonology with Accentology)

IVKOVIĆ, M., Sociology of Education, Social Sciences Teaching Methods

MAŠOVIĆ, D., Introduction to American Studies, American Literature

MILOSAVLJEVIĆ, LJ., History of Social Theories, Introduction to Philosophy

MITROVIĆ, LJ., General Sociology

NAUMOVIĆ, M., Sociology of Rural Areas, Sociology of Urban Areas

NEŠIĆ, B., Pedagogical Psychology

NEŠIĆ, V., Social Psychology

PETROVIĆ, C., Political Economy with Elements of Economic Systems

RISTIĆ, R., Introduction to Canadian and Australian Studies

STOJADINOVIĆ, M., Yugoslav Literature

STOJANOVIĆ, M., Yugoslav Literature

STOJKOVIĆ, M., Sociology of Morals, Labour Sociology

VELIČKOVIĆ, D., Russian Language

VIDANOVIĆ, DJ., English Morphology and Teaching Methods

ŽUNIĆ, D., Sociology of Art, Sociology of Culture and Arts with Serbian Cultural History

Faculty of Science and Mathematics (Višegradska 33, 18000 Niš; tel. (18) 223-430; fax (18) 533-014; e-mail dragan@pmf.ni.ac.rs; internet www.pmf.ni.ac.rs):

ĆIRIĆ, M., Mathematical Logic, Computer Technology Teaching Methods, Philosophy and History of Mathematics

DIMITRIJEVIĆ, P., Electromagnetism and Optics, Physics

JANKOVIĆ, S., Differential and Integral Equations, Theory of Probability and Random Processes

KOČINAC, LJ., Linear Algebra and Analytical Geometry, Topology

MILETIĆ, G., Instrumental Analytical Chemistry

MILJKOVIĆ, LJ., Solid State Physics, Physics of Materials

NIKOLIĆ, R., Higher Inorganic Chemistry

NOVAKOVIĆ, N., Physics, Plasma Physics

OBRADOVIĆ, M., Physical Chemistry

PALIĆ, R., Organic Chemistry

PAVLOTIĆ, T., Mechanics and Thermodynamics, Physics of Surfaces and Thin Layers

PECEV, T., Analytical Chemistry

PREMOVIĆ, P., General and Inorganic Chemistry

PURENOVIĆ, M., Industrial Chemistry

RADOVANOVIĆ, B., Instrumental Methods of Structural Analysis, Mechanisms of Organic Reactions

RAKOČEVIĆ, V., Functional Analysis, Theory of Measures and Integrals

STANIMIROVIĆ, P., Programming Languages, Mathematical Programming

URSIĆ-JANKOVIĆ, J., Biochemistry

Faculty of Sports and Physical Education (Čarnojevića 10A, 18000 Niš; tel. (18) 510-900; fax (18) 42-482; e-mail info@ffk.ni.ac.rs; e-mail faksfiz@ni.ac.rs):

BUBANJ, R., Biomechanics

DJURAŠKOVIĆ, R., Biology of Human Development with Sports Medicine

JOKSIMOVIĆ, S., Football, Skiing

KOSTIĆ, R., Dancing

KOSTIĆ, R., Volleyball

PETKOVIĆ, D., Sports Gymnastics

POPOVIĆ, R., Rhythmical and Sports Gymnastics

VUČKOVIĆ, S., Recreation Theory and Teaching Methods, Activities in Nature

ŽIVANOVIĆ, N., Theory and History of Physical Education

ŽIVKOVIĆ, D., Theory of Corrective Gymnastics, Corrective Gymnastics Teaching Methods

Faculty of Technology in Leskovac (Blvr oslobodjenja 124, 16000 Leskovac; tel. (16) 247-203; fax (16) 242-859; e-mail info@tehfin.tehfak.ni.ac.rs):

CAKIĆ, M., Physical Chemistry, Instrumental Analysis

CVETKOVIĆ, D., Organic Chemistry, Organo-Chemical Technology

CVETKOVIĆ, LJ., Production Management and Basic Marketing, Product Management

DJORDJEVIĆ, G., Mathematics

DJORDJEVIĆ, S., Organic Chemistry

GLIGORIJEVIĆ, V., Planning of Textile Processes, Knitting Technology

ILIĆ, P., General Chemistry

KOCIĆ, M., Physics

MARKOVIĆ, D., Instrumental Analysis, Organic Analysis, Chemical-Engineering Thermodynamics

NOVAKOVIĆ, M., Dyeing and Printing Technology

STANKOVIĆ, M., Biochemistry, Technology of Natural Organic Products

STANKOVIĆ, S., Analytical Chemistry

STOJILJKOVIĆ, D., Elements of Equipment in Processing Industry, Engineering Drawing, Mechanics

STOJILJKOVIĆ, S., Thermodynamics and Thermotechnics, Construction Materials, Process Analysis and Simulation, Chemical-Engineering Thermodynamics

TRAJKOVIĆ, C., Clothing Production Technology, Textile Quality Control and Testing

VELJKOVIĆ, V., Unit Operations in Chemical Engineering

Teacher-Training Faculty in Vranje (Partizanska 14, 17500 Vranje; tel. (17) 431-960; fax (17) 421-633; e-mail ucfaxvranje@yahoo.com; internet www.ucfak.ni.ac.rs):

CENIĆ, S., General Pedagogy, History of Pedagogy

MALINOVIĆ, T., Mathematics, Mathematical Teaching Methods

UNIVERZITET U NOVOM PAZARU
(University of Novi Pazar)

Demetrius Tucovića bb, 36300 Novi Pazar

Telephone: (20) 316-634

Fax: (20) 337-322

E-mail: info@uninp.edu.rs

Internet: www.uninp.edu.rs

Founded 2002

Private Control

Language of instruction: Bosnian, English, German, Serbian

Academic year: October to July

Pres.: MUFTI MUAMER EF. ZUKORLIĆ

Rector: Prof. Dr MEVLUD DUDIC

Pro-Rector: Dr AMELA LUKAČ

Gen. Man.: Dr NUSRET NICEVIĆ

Man.: ALEKSANDAR IVANOVIĆ

Library of 10,000 vols

Number of teachers: 270

Number of students: 2,500

Publications: *AGROBIZ*, *Pravni izazovi na početku XXI veka*, *Univerzitetska misao*

DEANS

Dept of Art: Prof. Dr FEHIM HUSKOVIĆ

Dept of Economics: Prof. Dr BEĆIR KALAC

Dept of Legal Science: Prof. Dr MUAMMER NICEVIĆ

Dept of Natural and Technical Sciences: Prof. Dr CAMIL SUKIĆ

Dept of Pedagogical and Psychological Science: Dr ADMIR MURATOVIĆ

Dept of Philological Sciences: Dr SAMINA DAZDAREVIĆ

UNIVERZITET U NOVOM SADU
(University of Novi Sad)

Trg Dositeja Obradovića 5, 21000 Novi Sad

Telephone: (21) 6350-622

Fax: (21) 450-418

E-mail: rektorat@uns.ac.rs

Internet: www.uns.ac.rs

Founded 1960

State control

Languages of instruction: Hungarian, Serbian

Academic year: October to July

Rector: Prof. MIROSLAV VESKOVIĆ

Vice-Rector for Education: Prof. MILAN SIMIĆ

Vice-Rector for Finance: Prof. RADOVAN PEJANOVIĆ

Vice-Rector for International Relations and Science: Prof. PAVLE SEKERUŠ

Vice-Rector for Students: GORAN RADIĆ

Gen. Sec.: ANĐELKA STANOJEVIĆ

Library of 15,000 vols, 450 theses, 400 periodicals

Number of teachers: 3,297

Number of students: 48,415

Publication: *Glas Univerziteta* (newspaper, 12 a year)

DEANS

Academy of Arts: Prof. ZORAN TODOVIĆ

Faculty of Agriculture: Prof. Dr MILAN KRAJINOVIĆ

Faculty of Civil Engineering: Prof. Dr DRAGAN MILAŠINOVIĆ

Faculty of Economics: Prof. Dr NENAD VUNJAK

Faculty of Education: Prof. Dr ALEKSANDAR PETOJEVIĆ

Faculty of Law: Prof. Dr RANKO KEČA

Faculty of Medicine: Prof. Dr NIKOLA GRUJIĆ

Faculty of Natural Sciences and Mathematics: Prof. Dr NEDA MIMICA-DUKIĆ

Faculty of Philosophy: Prof. Dr LJILJANA SUBOTIĆ

Faculty of Sport and Physical Education: Prof. Dr MILENA MIKALAČKI

Faculty of Technical Sciences: Prof. Dr ILIJA ĆOSIĆ

Faculty of Technology: Prof. Dr ZOLTAN ZAVARGO

'Mihajlo Pupin' Technical Faculty: Prof. Dr MILAN PAVLOVIĆ

Teacher Training Faculty in Hungarian: Prof. Dr KATALIN KAIĆ

PROFESSORS

Academy of Arts (Akademija Umetnosti, Djure Jakšića 7, 21000 Novi Sad; tel. (21) 422-177; fax (21) 420-187; e-mail aofarts@uns.ac.rs; internet www.akademija.uns.ac.rs):

BLANUŠA, M., Painting and Painting Technology

ČERNOGUBOV, B., Choir

DENKOVIĆ, LJ., Sculpture

DOBANOVAČKI, B., Poster Arts

DRAŠKOVIĆ, B., Acting, Directing

DJAK, Ž., Graphics and Graphic Technology

GILIĆ, V., Directing

HORVAT, L., Viola

JANKETIĆ, M., Acting

JOVANOVIĆ, V., Elements of Vocal Technique

JOVANOVIĆ, Z., Chamber Music

KATUNAC, D., History of Music, History of Performing

KINKA, R., Piano

KLEMENC, I., Stage Movement

KNEŽEVIĆ, S., Graphics and Graphic Technology

LAZIĆ, R., History and Aesthetics of Directing

MARINKOVIĆ, O., Diction

MIŠIĆ, LJ., Dance

OGNJENOVIĆ, V., Acting

OSTOJIĆ, N., Tone Syllable

OSTOJIĆ, T., Conducting

PREDOJEVIĆ-MILOVANOVIĆ, V., Voice Technique

RAKIDŽIĆ, J., Painting and Painting Technology

RNJAK, D., History of World Drama and Theatre

SIMONOVIĆ, M., Voice Technique

SRDIĆ, N., Clarinet

STANOJEV, M., Graphics and Graphic Technology

STAŠEVIĆ, M., Drawing and Drawing Technology

SUBOTIĆ, I., History of Art

ŠTATKIĆ, M., Composition

TODOROVIĆ, D., Painting and Painting Technology

UZELAC, M., Aesthetics

VARGA, I., Cello

Faculty of Agriculture (Poljoprivredni Fakultet, Trg Dositeja Obradvića 8, 21000 Novi Sad; tel. (21) 485-3500; fax (21) 459-761; e-mail dean@polj.ns.ac.rs; internet polj.uns.ac.rs):

ALMAŠI, R., Special Entomology

ANTOV, G., Cattle Breeding, Animal Husbandry

BABIĆ, LJ., Drying and Storage, Basic Agricultural Engineering

BAJKIN, A., Agricultural Machinery

BALAŽ, F., Mycoses of Plants, Plant Protection

BALAŽ, J., Mycoses and Bacterioses of Plants

BELIĆ, S., Water Management, Irrigation and Drainage Engineeering

BOGDANOVIĆ, D., Agrochemistry

BOŠNJAK, DJ., Crop Irrigation

BOŽIDAREVIĆ, D., Marketing of Agricultural and Food Products

BRKIĆ, M., Elements of Agricultural Technology, Thermotechnology in Agriculture

ÇINDRIĆ, P., Fruit Growing and Viticulture

ČOBANOVIĆ, K., Statistics, Statistical Methods

DJUKIĆ, D., Forage Crop Production

DJUKIĆ, NI., Agricultural Machinery

DJUROVKA, M., Vegetable Crop Production

ERIĆ, P., Forage Crops

GOVEDARICA, M., Microbiology

GVOZDENOVIĆ, D., Pomology, Picking and Storage of Fruit

HADŽIĆ, V., Pedology

JARAK, M., Microbiology

JASNIĆ, S., Plant Pathology, Plant Viruses

JOVANOVIĆ, M., Economics of Agricultural Estates, Economics of Agricultural Engineering

KEVREŠAN, S., Chemistry

KNEŽEVIĆ, A., Botany

KONSTANTINOVIĆ, B., Special Phytopharmacy, Control of Weeds

KORAĆ, M., Pomology, Viticulture

KOVČIN, S., Nutrition of Nonruminant Animals

KRAJINOVIĆ, M., Animal Husbandry

KRALJEVIĆ-BALALIĆ, M., Genetics

LAZIĆ, B., Vegetable Crop Production

LAZIĆ, V., Agricultural Machinery

MALETIN, S., Agricultural Zoology

MALINOVIĆ, N., Agricultural Machinery

MARINKOVIĆ, B., Arable Crop Production, Agronomy

MARKOVIĆ, V., Vegetable Crop Production

MIHAILOVIĆ, D., Meteorology

MIHAJLOVIĆ, L., Agricultural Cooperative Economics, Agrarian Policy

MIHALJEV, I., Seed Production

MILIĆ, D., Organization of Fruit and Vine Production, Business Organization and Economics

MOLNAR, I., Agronomy

NIKOLIĆ, R., Agricultural Tractors, Agricultural Machinery

NOVKOVIĆ, N., Planning Theory and Methodology of Organization

OBRENOVIĆ, D., Business Analysis, Bookkeeping

PAPRIĆ, DJ., General Viticulture

PEJANOVIĆ, R., Economy

PEJIĆ, N., Nutrition of Ruminant Animals

PEKANOVIĆ, V., Botany

PETRIĆ, D., General Entomology

PETROVIĆ, N., Plant Physiology, Protection of Ecosystems

PETROVIĆ, S., Genetics

POKRIĆ, V., Land Reclamation

POPOVIĆ, M., Plant Biochemistry, Biochemistry of Farm Animals

POTKONJAK, S., Economics of Melioration and Mechanization, Economics of Water Resources

POTKONJAK, V., Mechanization in Animal Breeding, Means of Transportation in Agriculture

RATAJAC, R., Agricultural Zoology, Ecology

SAVIĆ, S., Fodder, Feeding Technology

SRDJEVIĆ, B., Informatics

STAJNER, D., Chemistry

STANČIĆ, B., Breeding of Farm Animals

STARČEVIĆ, LJ., Arable Crop Production

STEVANOVIĆ, M., Agronomy

STOJANOVIĆ, S., Botany

ŠTRBAC, P., Special Entomology, Plant Protection

SUPIĆ, B., Poultry Production, Animal Husbandry

TEODOROVIĆ, M., Pig Breeding

UBAVIĆ, M., Agrochemistry

VIDOVIĆ, V., Improvement of Farm Animals

ŽIVANOVIĆ, M., Special Phytopharmacy

Faculty of Civil Engineering (Gradjevinski Fakultet, Kozaračka 2A, 24000 Subotica; tel. (24) 554-300; fax (24) 554-580; e-mail dekanat@gf.su.ac.rs; internet www.gf.uns.ac.rs):

BENAK, J., Water Refinement and Water Quality

ĆULIBRK, R., Earthworks, Elements of Traffic Arteries

DELEVIĆ, K., Organization in Building

GOSTOVIĆ, M., Engineering Geodesy

KLEIN, R., Architecture

MEŠTER, DJ., Technical Mechanics

MIHAILOVIĆ, V., Concrete Structures

MILAŠINOVIĆ, D., Resistance of Materials, Theory of Surface Bearers

SAM, A., Social Sciences

STOJKOVIĆ, S., Watercourses, Flood Management

VLAJIĆ, LJ., Experimental Analysis of Construction

ZELENHASIĆ, E., Hydrology and Elements of Hydrotechnology

Faculty of Economics (Ekonomski Fakultet, Segedinski put 9–11, 24000 Subotica; tel. (24) 628-000; fax (24) 546-486; e-mail dekanat@ef.uns.ac.rs; internet www.ef.uns.ac.rs):

ACIN, DJ., International Economic Relations

ACIN SIGULINSKI, S., International Trade, Management in International Trade

ADŽIĆ, S., Economic System and Economic Policy, National Economy

AHMETAGIĆ, E., Theory of an Organization

ANDRIĆ, M., Accountancy and Revision, Financial Control and Revision

BALABAN, N., Principles of Informatics, Support Systems in Decision Making

BALJ, B., Philosophy

BANDIN, J., Accountancy and Bookkeeping

BANDIN, T., Business Economics

ČILEG, M., Operational Research

DJURKOVIĆ, J., Principles of Informatics, Analysis and Planning of Information Systems

DMITROVIĆ, LJ., Management Accounting

GABRIĆ MOLNAR, I., Sociology

JAKOVČEVIĆ, K., Business Economics

JOSIFIDIS, K., Macroeconomics

KALINIĆ, V., Trade Company Management, Marketing in Trade

KIŠ, T., Econometrics

KONČAR, J., Economics of Domestic Commerce and Commercial Politics

KRMPOTIĆ, T., Agrotechnology

LEKIĆ, T., Development of Technology and Commercial Recognition of Goods

LEKOVIĆ, B., Principles of Management

LJUBOJEVIĆ, Č., Marketing Services

LOVRE, K., Programming of Agricultural Development

MALEŠEVIĆ, DJ., Analysis of Business Enterprise Operations

MESAROŠ, K., Mathematics for Economists

ŠAGI, A., Microeconomics

SALAI, S., Marketing of Research, Market Communications

STOJKOVIĆ, M., Statistics

SUŠNJAR, G., Human Resources Management

ŠUVAKOV, T., Microeconomics

TODOSIJEVIĆ, R., Strategic Management, Investments

TOT, A., History of Economic Thought

VASILJEV, S., Marketing

VUGDELIJA, D., Mathematics for Economists

VUNJAK, N., Finance, Banking

Faculty of Education (Pedagoški Fakultet, Podgorička 4, 25000 Sombor; tel. (25) 460-595; fax (25) 26461; e-mail dekanat@pef.uns.ac.rs; internet www.pef.uns.ac.rs):

BERBER, S., School Hygiene with Ecology

DJURIĆ, DJ., Social Psychology, Educational Psychology

ERAKOVIĆ, T., Defectology

GRHOVAC, S., Teaching Methods in Serbian Language and Literature, Performing Arts

JANKOVIĆ, P., General Pedagogy

LIPOVAC, M., Pedagogy, Didactics

LJUBOJEV, P., Mass Communication, Film and Television Culture

MALEŠEVIĆ, J., Elements of Natural Sciences

NENADIĆ, M., General Sociology, Sociology of Education

PETROVIĆ, N., Mathematics and Teaching Methods in Mathematics

PINTER, J., Teaching Methods in Mathematics, Informatics in Education

Faculty of Law (Pravni Fakultet, Trg Dositeja Obradovića 1, 21000 Novi Sad; tel. (21) 485-3040; fax (21) 450-427; e-mail dekanat@pf.ns.ac.rs; internet www.pf.uns.ac.rs):

ARSIĆ, Z., Economic Law

BOŠKOVIĆ, M., Criminology, Penology

CARIĆ, S., Economic Law

CVEJIĆ-JANČIĆ, O., Family Law, Inheritance Law

DJURDJEV, A., Constitutional Law

DJURDJEV, D., International Public Law

ETINSKI, R., International Public Law

GRUBAČ, M., Criminal Procedural Law

JOVANOVIĆ, PA., Contemporary Political Systems

JOVANOVIĆ, PR., Labour Law

KEČA, R., Civil Procedural Law

KRKLJUŠ, LJ., History of Yugoslav State and Law

MALENICA, A., Roman Law

MARJANOVIĆ, M., Sociology

MILKOV, D., Administrative Law

PAJVANČIĆ, M., Constitutional Law

PERIĆ, O., Criminal Law

PIHLER, S., Criminal Law

POPOV, DJ., Principles of Economics

POPOVIĆ, M., Theory of State and Law

SALMA, J., Law of Obligation

ŠARKIĆ, S., History of State and Law

SOGOROV, S., Economic Law

STANKOVIĆ, F., Principles of Economics

VRANJEŠ, M., Financial Law

VUČKOVIĆ, M., Law of Obligation

VUKADINOVIĆ, G., Theory of State and Law

VUKIĆEVIĆ, M., Introductory Economics

Faculty of Medicine (Medicinski Fakultet, Hajduk Veljkova 3, 21000 Novi Sad; tel. (21) 420-677; fax (21) 662-4153; e-mail dekanmf@uns.ac.rs; internet www.medical.uns.ac.rs):

ALEKSIĆ, S., Gynaecology and Obstetrics

AVRAMOV, S., Surgery

BABIĆ, LJ., Pathology

BALTIĆ, V., Internal Medicine

BUDAKOV, P., Pathology

BUJAS, M., Gynaecology and Obstetrics

BORIŠEV, V., Surgery

BOROTA, J., Biochemistry

ČIKOŠ, J., Internal Medicine

ĆURIĆ, S., Internal Medicine

CVEJANOV, M., Surgery

DJAKOVIĆ-SVARCER, K., Pharmacology and Toxicology

DJILAS-TODOROVIĆ, LJ., Internal Medicine

DOKMANOVIĆ-DJORDJEVIĆ, M., Gynaecology and Obstetrics

DŽOLEV, A., Maxillofacial Surgery

ERI, Ž., Pathology

FILIPOVIĆ, D., Physiology

GEBAUER, E., Paediatrics

GRUJIĆ, N., Physiology

GRUJIĆ, V., Social Medicine

GUDOVIĆ, R., Anatomy

GUDURIĆ, B., Surgery

HADŽIĆ, B., Pathology
HADŽIĆ, M., Pathology
IVETIĆ, V., Physiology
IVKOVIĆ-LAZAR, T., Internal Medicine
JANJIĆ, DJ., Surgery
JERANT-PATIĆ, V., Microbiology with Parasitology and Immunology
JEŠIĆ-VINDIŠ, M., Internal Medicine
JOVANOVIĆ, J., Infectious Diseases
KNEŽEVIĆ, A., Psychiatry and Medical Psychology
KOVAČEVIĆ, Z., Biochemistry
KRISTIFOROVIĆ-ILIĆ, M., Hygiene
KRSTIĆ, A., Paediatrics
KRSTIĆ-BOŽIĆ, V., Biology
KULAUZOV, M., Pathological Physiology
KULAUZOV, M., Microbiology with Parasitology and Immunology
LATINOVIĆ, S., Ophthalmology
LAŽETIĆ, B., Physiology
LUČIĆ, A., Pathological Physiology
LUČIĆ, Z., Radiology
LUKAČ, I., Radiology
MAČVANIN, N., Occupational Medicine
MARTINOV-CVEJIN, M., Social Medicine
MIHALJ, M., Anatomy
MIHALJEV-MARTINOV, J., Neurology
MIKOV, M., Pharmacology and Toxicology
MILIČIĆ, A., Surgery
MIROSAVLJEV, M., Hygiene
MILOŠEVIĆ, D., Otorhinolaryngology
MILUTINOVIĆ, B., Physiology
MIRKOVIĆ, M., Surgery
MIROSAVLJEV, M., Hygiene
OBRADOVIĆ, D., Anatomy
PAVLOV-MIRKOVIĆ, M., Gynaecology and Obstetrics
PAVLOVIĆ, S., Internal Medicine
PEJIN, D., Internal Medicine
PJEVIĆ, M., Gynaecology and Obstetrics
PJEVIĆ, M., Surgery
POLZOVIĆ, A., Anatomy
POPOV, I., Psychiatry, Medical Psychology
POPOVIĆ, D., Forensic Medicine
POPOVIĆ, J., Pharmacology and Toxicology
POPOVIĆ, LJ., Surgery
POPOVIĆ, M., Chemistry
RISTIĆ, J., Maxillofacial Surgery
RONČEVIĆ, N., Paediatrics
SABO, A., Pharmacology and Toxicology
SAVIĆ, K., Medical Rehabilitation
SAVIĆ, M., Occupational Medicine
SĆEKIĆ, V., Internal Medicine
SEDLAK-VADOC, V., Pathological Physiology
SEGEDI, D., Obstetrics and Gynaecology
SEGULJEV, Z., Epidemiology
ŠIMIČ, M., Forensic Medicine
SLJAPIĆ, N., Pathology
SOMER, LJ., Histology and Embryology
SOMER, T., Surgery
STANKOVIĆ, S., Biophysics
STANULOVIĆ, M., Pharmacology and Toxicology
STOJANOVIĆ, S., Surgery
STOJKOV, J., Surgery
STOJSIĆ, DJ., Internal Medicine
TASIĆ, M., Forensic Medicine
TOPALOV, V., Internal Medicine
VADOC-SEDLAK, V., Pathological Physiology
VOJINOVIĆ-MILORADOV, M., Chemistry
VUKADINOVIĆ, S., Surgery
VUKOVIĆ, B., Epidemiology
ŽAMUROVIĆ, A., Medical Rehabilitation
ŽIKIĆ, M., Neurology
ZORIČIĆ, D., Surgery

Faculty of Natural Sciences and Mathematics (Prirodno-Matematički Fakultet, Trg Dositeja Obradovića 3, 21000 Novi Sad; tel. (21) 455-630; fax (21) 455-662; e-mail dekanpmf@uns.ac.rs; internet www.pmf.uns .ac.rs):

ABRAMOVIĆ, B., Microanalysis
ACKETA, D., Informatics and Numerical Mathematics
BIKIT, I., Nuclear Physics

BJELICA, L., Physical Chemistry
BOGDANOVIĆ, Ž., Physical Geography
BOŽIĆ-KRSTIĆ, V., Biology with Human Genetics
BUDIMAC, Z., Informatics and Numerical Mathematics
BUDINČEVIĆ, M., Analysis and Geometry
BUGARSKI, D., Geography
ČRVENKOVIĆ, S., Mathematics
ČURČIĆ, S., Social Geography
CVETKOVIĆ, LJ., Informatics and Numerical Mathematics
DALMACIJA, B., Chemical Technology and Environmental Protection
DAVIDOVIĆ, R., Regional Geography
DIVJAKOVIĆ, V., Physics of Condensed Matter
DJURDJEV, B., Social Geography
DJUROVIĆ, S., Atomic Physics, Physical Electronics
GAAL, F., Analytical Chemistry
GAJIĆ, LJ., Analysis and Probability
GAJIN, S., Microbiology
GRUBOR-LAJŠIĆ, G., Biochemistry, Physiology, Histology
HADŽIĆ, O., Probability and Statistics, Mathematics
HALAŠI, R., Organic Analysis
HERCEG, D., Numerical Mathematics
JANJIĆ, J., Physics
JOVANOVIĆ, LJ., Chemistry
KAPOR, A., Physics of Condensed Matter
KAPOR, D., Theoretical Physics
KARLOVIĆ, E., Chemical Technology and Environmental Protection
KOSANIĆ, M., General Chemistry
KOVAČEVIĆ, R., Biochemistry
KRSTIĆ, B., Plant Physiology
KUHAJDA, K., Chemistry of Natural Products
LEOVAC, V., Inorganic Chemistry
LOZANOV-CRVENKOVIĆ, Z., Analysis and Probability
MADARASZ-SZILAGYI, R., Algebra and Mathematics
MAŠKOVIĆ, LJ., Classical Theoretical Mechanics
MATAVULJ, M., Microbiology
MERKULOV, LJ., Botany, Plant Anatomy and Morphology
MILJKOVIĆ, LJ., Physical Geography
MILJKOVIĆ, N., Physical Geography
NIKOLIĆ, A., Physical Chemistry
OBADOVIĆ, D., Physics, Physics of Liquid Crystals
PAP, E., Mathematics, Analysis and Geometry
PAUNIĆ, DJ., Informatics and Numerical Mathematics
PENOV-GAŠI, O., Organic Chemistry
PERIŠIĆ-JANJIĆ, N., General and Inorganic Chemistry
PETROVIĆ, D., Biophysics, Medical Physics
PETROVIĆ, J., Organic Chemistry
PETROVIĆ, O., Microbiology, Bacteriology
PETROVIĆ, V., Algebra and Mathematics
PILIPOVIĆ, S., Analysis and Probability
POPSAVIN, V., Chemistry of Natural Products
ŠEŠELJA, B., Mathematical Logic and Algebra, Mathematical Elements of Informatics
ŠETRAJČIĆ, J., Theoretical Physics
ŠIMIĆ, S., Biology, Zoology
ŠKRINJAR, M., Theoretical Physics
STANKOVIĆ, S., Biophysics, Medical Physics
STANKOVIĆ, Ž., Plant Physiology
STEVANOVIĆ, D., Morphology and Taxonomy of Invertebrates
STOJAKOVIĆ, Z., Linear Algebra
STOJANOVIĆ, S., Theoretical Mechanics and Electrodynamics
ŠURANJI, T., Analytical Chemistry
SURLA, D., Computer Science
SURLA, K., Numerical Mathematics
TAKAČI, A., Mathematics

TAKAČI, DJ., Mathematics, Analysis and Geometry
TERZIĆ, M., Atomic and Isotopic Molecular Spectroscopy
TOMIĆ, P., Geography
TOŠIĆ, B., Theoretical Physics
TOŠIĆ, R., Combinatorics
VAPA, LJ., Biochemistry, Physiology, Histology, Genetics
VOJINOVIĆ-MILORADOV, M., General Chemistry
VOJVODIĆ, G., Algebra and Logic
VRBAŠKI, Ž., Chemical Technology
VUČKOVIĆ, M., Botany, Plant Ecology, Ecology of Medicinal Herbs
VUJIČIĆ, B., Physical Electronics
ŽDERIĆ, M., Biology
ŽIGRAI, I., Analytical Chemistry

Faculty of Philosophy (Filozofski Fakultet, Dr Zorana Đinđića 2, 21000 Novi Sad; tel. (21) 450-690; fax (21) 450-929; e-mail dekanat@unsff.ns.ac.rs; internet www.ff.uns .ac.rs):

BANJAI, J., Literary Theory
BEKIĆ, T., German Literature
BERIĆ, V., History of German Language
BIRO, M., Elements of Clinical Psychology, Elements of Psychotherapy and Consulting
BOŠNJAK, I., Hungarian Literature
BURZAN, M., Serbian Language
ČAKI, P., Introduction to Expert and Scientific Work, Library Science
ČELOVSKI, S., Slovak Studies
ĆOVIĆ, B., Russian Literature
DINIĆ-KNEŽEVIĆ, D., Medieval History of Yugoslav Nations
DJOŠIĆ, D., Demography with Statistics
DUDOK, D., History of Slovak Language and Literature
EGERIĆ, M., Modern Serbian Literature
GADJANSKI-MARICKI, K., Classical Languages, Ancient History
GENC, L., Genetics and Educational Psychology
GEROLD, L., Hungarian Literature
GORDIĆ, S., Serbian and Yugoslav Literature, Serbian Critics
GRANDIĆ, R., Theory of Education, Family Pedagogy
GRKOVIĆ, M., History of Serbian and Comparative Grammar of Slavic Languages
HARPANJI, M., Slovak Literature, Literary Theory
IGNJATOVIĆ, I., General Psychology, Psychology of Personality
IVANOVIĆ, R., History of Yugoslav Literature
JUKIĆ, S., Elements of Pedagogy, Methodical Bases of Educational Work
JUNG, K., Ethnology, Hungarian Folk Literature
KAIĆ, K., History of Hungarian Culture
KAMENOV, E., Pre-School Education
KAPOR-STANULOVIĆ, P., Development of Psychology, Mental Health
KARANOVIĆ, Z., Serbian Folk Literature
KLEUT, M., Serbian Literature
KOKOVIĆ, D., Sociology and Sociology of Culture
KOSANOVIĆ, B., Russian Literature
KULIĆ, M., Philosophy
LANC, I., Introduction to General and Hungarian Linguistics
MATIĆ, LJ., French Literature
MATIJAŠEVIĆ, J., Modern Russian Language
MILOSAVLJEVIĆ, P., Methodology of Literary Studies
MILOŠEVIĆ, B., Introduction to Sociology, Occupational Sociology
MLADENOVIĆ, U., Pedagogic Psychology, Genetic and Pedagogic Psychology

MOLNAR-ČIKOŠ, L., Syntax of Hungarian Language, Phonetics of Hungarian Language

MOMČILOVIĆ, B., English Literature

OLJAČA, M., Educational System

PEROVIĆ, M., Philosophy

PETROVIĆ, D., Dialectology of Serbian and Standard Serbian Language

PIŽURICA, M., History of Serbian Language

POPOV, Č., Modern History

PUŠIĆ, LJ., Urban Sociology

RADOVANOVIĆ, M., General Linguistics

RADOVIĆ, M., Comparative Literature

RAMAČ, J., Ruthenian Language, Ukrainian Language

REDJEP, J., Medieval Literature

RISTIĆ, Ž., Methodology of Psychology

RODIĆ, R., School Education

ROKAI, P., Medieval History

SAVIĆ, S., Sociolinguistics and Discourse Analysis

SIMEUNOVIĆ, V., Philosophy

STEFANOVIĆ, M., Literary Theory, Serbian Literature

STEPANOV, R., Theory of Law and Politics

STOJAKOV, S., Introduction to Education Science

ŠIPKA, M., Statistical Psychology

STRAJNIĆ, N., Comparative Literature

TAMAŠ, J., Ruthenian Literature, Ukrainian Literature

TOČANAC, D., Modern French Language

TRIPKOVIĆ, M., Sociology and Sociological Theories

UTAŠI, Č., History of Hungarian Literature

VUKOVIĆ, G., Modern Serbian Language

Faculty of Sport and Physical Education (Fakultet sporta i fizičkog vaspitanja, Lovćenska 16, 21000 Novi Sad; tel. (21) 450-188; fax (21) 450-199; e-mail admin@fsfv.ac.rs; internet www.fsfvns.rs):

BALA, G., Kinesiology of Individual Sports

BJELICA, S., Sociological and Psychological Elements of Kinesiology

DIMOVA, K., Kinesiology of Individual Sports

DUNDJEROVIĆ, R., Kinesiology of Individual Sports

KALAJDŽIĆ, J., Kinesiology of Sports Games

KRSMANOVIĆ, B., Theory and Methods of Physical Education

LUKAČ, D., Sports Medicine

MALACKO, J., Kinesiology of Sports

NIĆIN, DJ., Kinesiology

RADOSAV, M., Football

RAIČ, A., Economical and Political Elements of Kinesiology

SAVIĆ, M., Martial Sports

TONČEV, I., Kinesiology of Individual Sports

ULIĆ, D., Kinesitherapy

Faculty of Technical Sciences (Fakultet Tehničkih Nauka, Trg Dositeja Obradovića 6, 21000 Novi Sad; tel. (21) 485-2055; fax (21) 458-133; e-mail ftndean@uns.ac.rs; internet www.ftn.uns.ac.rs):

ATANACKOVIĆ, T., Material Resistance

BABIN, N., Transport Machines

BAČLIĆ, B., Mechanics and Thermodynamics of Continuum

BANJANIN, M., Theory of Communications

BAŠIĆ, DJ., Thermoprocessing Systems

BOROVAC, B., Industrial Robots

BUKUROV, Ž., Fluid Mechanics

ČASNJI, F., Motor Vehicles

ĆIRIĆ, D., Physics

ČOMIĆ, I., Mathematics

COSIĆ, I., Planning of Production Systems

CVETIĆANIN, L., Mechanics

DIMIĆ, M., Mass Transfer, Heat Apparatus

DJORDJEVIĆ, R., Construction Theory

DJORDJEVIĆ, T., Theory of Traffic Flow and Capacity

DJUKIĆ, DJ., Mechanics

DOROSLOVAČKI, R., Discrete Mathematics

DOVNIKOVIĆ, L., Descriptive Geometry

FOLIĆ, R., Concrete Structures and Structural Theory

GAJIĆ, V., Logistics of Enterprise

GALOGAŽA, M., Technology of Prediction, Marketing and Enterprise

GATALO, R., Machine Tools, Flexible Technological Systems

GEORGIJEVIĆ, M., Storage, Equipment and Simulations

GERIĆ, LJ., Distributive Installations

GRKOVIĆ, V., Turbines

GVOZDENAC, D., Thermal Energy and Measurement in Thermal Engineering

HAJDUKOVIĆ, M., Architecture of Computer Systems

HODOLIĆ, J., Productive Engineering Equipment

INIĆ, M., Traffic Safety

KAKAŠ, D., Heat Treatment

KISIN, S., Metal Constructions

KLINAR, I., Motor Equipment

KOPIĆ, DJ., Technology of Railway Transport

KOVAČ, P., Welding

KOVAČ, R., Casting Technology

KOVAČEVIĆ, I., Mathematics

KOVAČEVIĆ, V., Logical Planning of Computing Systems

KOZIMIDIS-LUBURIĆ, U., Physics

KOZIMIDIS-PETROVIĆ, A., Physics

KUZMANOVIĆ, S., Mechanical Elements

LIČEN, H., Automation of Measuring Processes

LUKIĆ, S., Elements of Building Planning

MALBAŠA, V., Electronic Systems and Communication Networks

MALBAŠKI, D., Elements of Computer Programming and Programme Languages

MARIĆ, M., Heat Science, Drying Technology

MARINIĆ, I., Sociology and Economy

MARTINOV, M., Agricultural Machines

MILIDRAG, S., Motor Vehicles

MILIKIĆ, D., Treatment Methods by Material Removal

MILINSKI, N., Physics

MILOŠEVIĆ, V., Digital Telecommunication

MOGIN, P., Databases

NIKIĆ, J., Mathematics

NOVAK, L., Circuit and Systems Theory

OBRADOVIĆ, D., Digital Communications

OBRADOVIĆ, M., Intercomputer Communications

PEKARIĆ-NADJ, N., Principles of Electrical Engineering

PERUNOVIĆ, P., Boilers

PEŠALJEVIĆ, M., Engineering Communications and Logistic Control

PETROVAČKI, D., Automatic Control

PLANČAK, M., Technology of Plasticity and Cold Extrusion

POPOVIĆ, D., Synthesis of Complex Systems in Automatic Control

PRODANOVIĆ, M., City and Spatial Planning

RADIVOJEVIĆ, R., Sociology, Sociology of Work

RADOVIĆ, R., Urban Planning, Contemporary Architecture

SABO, B., Welding Technology

SATARIĆ, M., Physics

ŠAVIĆ, V., Logistic Technical Systems

ŠEŠIĆ, Ž., Internal Combustion Engines

ŠIDJANIN, L., Materials Science, Engineering Materials

SOVILJ, B., Technoeconomic Optimization

STANIVUKOVIĆ, D., Reliability of Mechanical Systems

STOJAKOVIĆ, M., Mathematics, Statistical Methods in Planning

STREZOSKI, V., Elements of Electroenergetics

TEŠIĆ, M., Agricultural Machinery

TODIĆ, V., Technological Processes

TOROVIĆ, T., Internal Combustion Engine

UZELAC, Z., Mathematical Methods

VILOTIĆ, D., Plasticity Technology

VLADIĆ, J., Uninterrupted and Automatic Transport

VLAHOVIĆ, M., Recognition of Goods in Transport

VUKOVIĆ, S., Architectural Construction

VUKOVIĆ, V., Fluid Mechanics

ŽIVANOV, LJ., Microelectronics, Principles of Electronics

ZLOKOLICA, M., Theory of Mechanisms and Machines

ŽUPUNSKI, I., Electrical Measurements

Faculty of Technology (Tehnološki Fakultet, Blvr Cara Lazara 1, 21000 Novi Sad; tel. (21) 485-3600; fax (21) 450-413; e-mail deantf@uns.ac.rs; internet www.tf.uns.ac.rs):

CARIĆ, M., Milk and Dairy Technology

CURAKOVIĆ, M., Wrapping and Packaging

DJILAS, S., Organic Chemistry

DJURIĆ, M., Engineering Thermodynamics

DOKIĆ, P., Chemistry and Technology of Emulsions and Cosmetics, Colloid Chemistry

GRUJIĆ-IVKOV, O., Malt and Beer Technology

JAKOVLJEVIĆ, J., Starch Technology

KIŠ, I., Physical Chemistry, Catalysis

LOMIĆ, G., Physical Chemistry, Catalysis

MARINKOVIĆ-NEDUČIN, R., Physical Chemistry, Catalysis

MARJANOVIĆ, N., Food Analysis

PAUNOVIĆ, R., Mathematical Modelling in Industrial Processes

PEJIN, D., Yeast and Alcohol Technology, Industrial Microbiology

PERIČIN, D., Biochemistry, Industrial Enzymology

PERUNIČIĆ, M., Process Dynamics and Control, Process Control Systems

PETROVIĆ, LJ., Meat Processing Technology

POPOV-RALJIĆ, J., Ready-Made Food Technology

PRIBIŠ, V., Meat Processing Technology, Sensory Evaluation of Food

RADONJIĆ, LJ., Construction Materials, Inorganic Materials

RANOGAJEC, J., Ceramics Technology, Inorganic Raw Materials and Products

RAZMOVSKA, R., Yeast and Alcohol Technology

RUŽIĆ, N., Technology of Wine Production

SEĆEROV-SOKOLOVIĆ, R., Industrial Processes Design, Environmental Protection in the Chemical Industry

ŠKRBIĆ, B., Natural Gas Engineering

ŠKRINJAR, M., Food Microbiology

SOKOLOVIĆ, S., Petroleum Refining Technology, Petrochemical Products Applications

SOVILJ, M., Unit Operations, Measurement Techniques

SOVILJ, V., Colloid Chemistry, Physical Chemistry of Macromolecules

STOILJKOVIĆ, D., Physical Chemistry of Polymer Materials, Plastics Materials Technology

TEKIĆ, M., Design of Equipment for the Chemical Industry, Separation Processes

TOJAGIĆ, S., Ready-Made Food Technology

'Mihajlo Pupin' Technical Faculty (Tehnički Fakultet 'Mihajlo Pupin', Djure Djakovića bb, 23000 Zrenjanin; tel. (23) 550-515; fax (23) 550-520; e-mail dekanat@tf.zr.ac.rs; internet www.tfzr.uns.ac.rs):

ADAMOVIĆ, Ž., Mechanics, Maintenance, Hydraulics and Pneumatics

ČERNIČEK, I., Theory of Systems, Theory of Management and Decision Making

DJARMATI, Z., Chemistry with Chemical Technology, Chemistry and Biochemistry

HOTOMSKI, P., Informatics

LAMBIĆ, M., Mechanical Engineering, Energetics

MITROVIĆ, Ž., Mathematics
SOTIROVIĆ, V., Informatics
STOJADINOVIĆ, V., Industrial Engineering
ŠUNJKA, S., Textile Technology

There are research institutes attached to each faculty

UNIVERZITET UMETNOSTI U BEOGRADU
(University of Arts in Belgrade)

Kosančićev venac 29, 11000 Belgrade
Telephone: (11) 262-5166
Fax: (11) 262-9785
E-mail: rektorat@arts.bg.ac.rs
Internet: www.arts.bg.ac.rs

Founded 1957 as Acad. of Arts, present status 1973
Academic year: October to September

Rector: Prof. Dr LJILJANA MRKIĆ POPOVIĆ
Pres.: Prof. SLAVENKO SALETOVIC
Vice-Pres.: Prof. Dr DIMITRIJE GOLEMOVIĆ
Vice-Pres.: Prof. ANDJELKA BOJOVIĆ
Vice-Pres.: Prof. MARINA NAKIĆENOVIĆ
Sec.-Gen.: OLGA STANKOVIĆ

Library of 200,000 vols
Number of teachers: 500
Number of students: 2,500

Publication: *Bilten INFO* (dramatic arts, 12 a year)

DEANS

Faculty of Applied Arts: Prof. VLADIMIR KOSTIĆ DIVAČ
Faculty of Dramatic Arts: ZORAN S. POPOVIĆ
Faculty of Fine Arts: Prof. SLOBODAN ROK-SANDIĆ
Faculty of Music: Prof. Dr DUBRAVKA JOVIČIĆ (acting)

PROFESSORS

Faculty of Applied Arts (Kralja Petra 4, 11000 Belgrade; tel. and fax (11) 218-2047; e-mail fpu@eunet.rs; internet www.fpu.edu.rs):

ANĐELKOVIĆ, M.
BAJIĆ, M.
BLAŽINA, Z.
BOČINA, R.
BOŽOVIĆ, N.
BULAJIĆ, Z.
ĆIRIĆ, R.
ĆIRIĆ-KRSTIĆ, G.
CVIJANOVIĆ, S.
DENIĆ, D.
DIMITRIJEVIĆ, D.
ĐOLIĆ, S.
DRAGOVIĆ, J.
DRAGUTINOVIĆ, A.
DRAGUTINOVIĆ, M.
DRAGUTINOVIĆ-KOMATINA, S.
DRAMIĆANIN, M.
ĐULIZAREVIĆ, S.
ĐURIČKOVIĆ, S.
FULGOSI, D.
GAVRIĆ, Z.
GLOGOVAC, M.
HULJEV, I.
IVANOVIĆ, Z.
IZVONAR, D.
JANKOVIĆ, Z.
JANKOVIĆ-NEDELKOV, T.
KAJTEZ, S.
KARANOVIĆ, B.
KNEŽEVIĆ, I.
KNEŽEVIĆ, N.
KOMAD-ARSENIJEVIĆ, G.
KOSTIĆ, M.
KOSTIĆ, V.
KRSMANOVIĆ, K.
KUZMANOVIĆ, B.
KUZMANOVIĆ-NOVOVIĆ, I.

LAĐUŠIĆ, M.
LALIĆ, R.
LAZIĆ, T.
LAZOVIĆ, M.
LUKOVIĆ, M.
MANOJLOVIĆ, D.
MANOJLOVIĆ, S.
MANOJLOVIĆ, T.
MARCIKIĆ, I.
MIĆANOVIĆ, Z.
MIJATOVIĆ, A.
MILIĆEVIĆ, I.
NAKIĆENOVIĆ, M.
NANOVIĆ, B.
NEŠIĆ, D.
NIKOLIĆ, S.
NINČIĆ, O.
NOVAKOVIĆ, M.
OGNJANOVIĆ, M.
PETKOVIĆ, Z.
PETROVIĆ, G.
PETROVIĆ, L.
PETROVIĆ, M.
POPOVIĆ, Z.
RAKIĆ, I.
RUSALIĆ, D.
SAMARDŽIĆ, R.
ŠAVIĆ, S.
ŠĆEPANOVIĆ, V.
SEKULIĆ, T.
SIMONOVIĆ, J.
STAMENKOVIĆ, M.
STOJADINOVIĆ, O.
STOJANOVIĆ, D.
ŠTRBAC, V.
TATAREVIĆ, V.
TIKVEŠA, L.
TODIĆ, M.
TOMAŠEVIĆ, M.
TRNINIĆ, M.
VELJOVIĆ, I.
VIĆENTIĆ, N.
VLAHOVIĆ, J.
VUČKOVIĆ, M.
VUJOVIĆ-STOJANOVIĆ, M.
VUKIĆEVIĆ, V.
VUKSAN, D.
ZARIĆ, G.
ZEČEVIĆ, S.
ŽIKIĆ, S.
ŽIVKOVIĆ, M.

Faculty of Dramatic Arts (Blvr umetnosti 20, 11070 Belgrade; tel. (11) 214-0419; fax (11) 213-0862; e-mail fduinfo@eunet.rs; internet www.fdubg.com):

ALEKSIC, B.
BAJIC, D.
BOGOEVA SEDLAR, LJ.
COLAKOVIC, M.
COLIC BILJANOVSKI, D.
DAKOVIC, N.
DAUTOVIC, F.
DEJANOVIC, V.
DESPOT, B.
DIMITRIJEVIC, A.
DJOKIC, J.
DJUKIC, A.
DJUKIC, V.
DRAGICEVIC SESIC, M.
GADJANSKI, M.
GLUSICA, M.
IMAMI, P.
IVANOVIC, S.
JEVTIC, N.
JEVTOVIC, V.
JEZERKIC, V.
JOVANOVIC, D.
JOVICEVIC, A.
KARAJICA, F.
KARANOVIC, S.
KNEZEVIC, R.
MANDIC, A.
MANDIC, T.
MARIC, G.
MARICIC, N.

MARKOVIC, G.
MARKOVIC, M.
MILETIN, M.
MRKIC POPOVIC, L.
PAJKIC, N.
PAVLOVIC, M.
PEKOVIC, G.
POPOV, D.
POPOVIC, Z.
PROKIC, N.
RANKOVIC, R.
SALETOVIC, S.
SAVIN, E.
SAVKOVIC, M.
SIJAN, S.
SIMJANOVIC, Z.
TABACKI, M.
TERZIC, G.
TODOROVIC, R.
VESELINOVIC, D.
VOLK, M.
VUJIC, I.

Faculty of Fine Arts (Pariska br. 16, 11000 Belgrade; tel. (11) 263-0635; fax (11) 218-1214; e-mail dekanat@flu.bg.ac.rs; internet www.flu.bg.ac.rs):

ANTONIJEVIĆ, R.
BAJIĆ, M.
BISENIĆ, D.
BOJOVIĆ, A.
DIMOVSKI, Z.
DRAGOJLOVIĆ, M.
DRAGOJLOVIĆ, M.
GRAOVAC, Z.
GRBA, D.
ILIĆ, D.
JOKSIMOVIĆ, A.
JOKSIMOVIĆ, Z.
JOVANOVIĆ, D.
KAĆIĆ, D.
KALIĆ-KUMANUDI, J.
KNEŽEVIĆ, R.
KNEŽEVIĆ, V.
KRSTIĆ, V.
LALIĆ, V.
MILINKOVIĆ, Z.
MLADENOVIĆ, A.
MLAĐOVIĆ, M.
MOMIROV, D.
NIKOLIĆ, G
NOVAKOVIĆ, Z.
PANTIĆ, A.
PECIĆ, D.
PETROVIĆ, D.
POPTSIS, M.
PRODANOVIĆ, M.
RADOJEV, N.
RAJČEVIĆ, S.
RAKOVIĆ, B
ROKSANDIĆ, S.
SIMEONOVIĆ ĆELIĆ, I.
ŠIVAČKI, J.
ŠKORC, B.
SMILJANIĆ, Z.
STANAĆEV, D.
ŠUICA, N.
TODOROVIĆ, J.
TODOROVIĆ, Z.
VASIĆ, C.
VELJAŠEVIĆ, V.
VUKOSAVLJEVIĆ, N.
VUKOVIĆ, B.
VUKOVIĆ, Z.
ZARIĆ, K.
ŽIVKOVIĆ, V.

Faculty of Music (Kralja Milana 50, 11000 Belgrade; tel. (11) 265-9466; fax (11) 264-3598; e-mail fmuinfo@fmu.bg.ac.rs; internet www.fmu.bg.ac.rs):

BELIĆ, S.
BOŽIĆ, S.
ĆETKOVIĆ, Z.
ĐORĐEVIĆ, M.
ERIĆ, Z.
GOLEMOVIĆ, D.

GRGIN, A.
HOFMAN, S.
IGNJATOVIĆ, N.
ISAESKI, M.
JOKANOVIĆ, M.
JOVANOVIĆ, L.
JOVIČIĆ, D.
KARLOVIĆ, M.
KOSANOVIĆ, M.
KRŠIĆ–SEKULIĆ, V.
MAKSIMOVIĆ-VESELINOV, J.
MARINKOVIĆ, S.
MEZEI, L.
MIHAILOVIĆ, J.
MILANKOVIĆ, V.
MLAĐENOVIĆ, D.
NIKOLIĆ, M.
OGRIZOVIĆ, V.

PERIĆ, D.
PETROVIĆ, M.
POPOVIĆ, L.
POPOVIĆ, N.
RAŠKOVIĆ, F.
SERDAR, A.
SINADINOVIĆ, D.
SUĐIĆ, B.
ŠUVAKOVIĆ, M.
TOŠIĆ, S.
TOŠIĆ, V.
TRAJKOVIĆ, V.
VASIĆ, O.
VESELINOVIĆ–HOFMAN, M.
VUJIĆ, A.
ŽIVKOVIĆ, N.

College

Belgrade Business School: Kraljice Marije 73 (27 Marta 149), 11000 Belgrade; tel. (11) 240-1888; fax (11) 242-4069; e-mail info@bbs.edu.rs; internet www.bbs.edu.rs; f. 1956 as Junior Commercial-Business College, present name and status 2002; offers three-year diploma courses in finance, accounting, marketing, foreign and domestic trade, commerce, management, business informatics and computers, banking and insurance, customs, taxes and budget; int. studies programme; distance studies; library: 20,000 vols; 90 teachers (60 full-time, 30 part-time); 2,000 students; Dir Prof. Dr ILIJA SAMARDŽIĆ (acting).

SEYCHELLES

The Higher Education System

The Republic of Seychelles comprises some 115 islands in the western Indian Ocean. Seychelles achieved full independence from Britain, as a sovereign republic within the Commonwealth, in 1976. The University of Seychelles was established in October 2009; in 2011 there were around 300 students enrolled on 12 degree programmes delivered though the University of London International Programmes. The University, which is governed by the Chancellor, Senate and University Board, was expected eventually to be able to cater for approximately 1,500 students, and a distance education programme was to be introduced. The Seychelles Polytechnic (founded 1983) offers one- to three-year Diploma and Certificate courses, and the National College of the Arts (founded 1997) offers one- and two-year programmes of study. There are several professional institutes of training and an Adult Learning and Distance Education Centre. There were 2,280 students in post-secondary (non-tertiary) education in 2010.

The Ministry of Education is responsible for post-secondary, tertiary and adult education. The Ministry offers scholarships for students wishing to pursue tertiary education overseas. Under the Higher Education Act, the Ministry has instigated reforms in the education system in five priority areas to increase its effectiveness. A number of reforms were carried out during 2009–11. In November 2011 the National Assembly voted unanimously to approve the Tertiary Education Act (2011), which was intended further to develop tertiary and post-secondary education within Seychelles. Upon implementation, the legislation would provide for, inter alia, the establishment of a Tertiary Education Commission and a number of higher education institutions.

Regulatory Bodies

GOVERNMENT

Ministry of Community Development and Sports: Oceangate House, POB 731, Victoria; tel. 4225477; fax 4224081; e-mail oplg@seychelles.net; internet www.localgovernment.gov.sc; Minister VINCENT MERITON.

Ministry of Education: POB 48, Mont Fleuri; tel. 283283; fax 224859; e-mail pamedu@seychelles.net; internet www.education.gov.sc; Min. BERNARD SHAMLAYE.

Learned Societies

LANGUAGE AND LITERATURE

Alliance Française: Ave Bois de Rose, BP 210, Victoria; tel. 282424; fax 225172; internet www.alliancefr.sc; offers courses and exams in French language and culture and promotes cultural exchange with France.

British Council: see chapter on Mauritius.

Research Institute

GENERAL

National Heritage: POB 573, Victoria, Mahé; tel. 321333; fax 322531; e-mail heritage@seychelles.net; f. 1987; controlled by Culture Division of the Min. of Education; carries out research into the cultural heritage of Seychelles; Advisor MARCEL BARRY ROSALIE.

Libraries and Archives

Victoria

Seychelles National Archives: POB 720, 5th June Ave, Victoria, Mahé; tel. 321333; fax 322481; e-mail archives@seychelles.net; internet www.sna.gov.sc; Dir ALAIN LUCAS.

Seychelles National Library: POB 45, Francis Rachel St, Victoria, Mahé; tel. and fax 321333; e-mail natlib@seychelles.net; internet www.national-library.edu.sc; f. 1910 as Carnegie Library; 75,000 vols (incl. 3 br. libraries & 2 regional reading centres); 3 brs; spec. collns: documents on Indian Ocean region, FAO, UNESCO, IMO and ILO publs; Prin. Librarian ANNE-MARY ROBERT; Sr Librarian CHRISTIANE ADELINE.

Museum

Victoria

National Museum: POB 720, La Bastille, Victoria, Mahé; tel. (248) 321333; e-mail mizenasyonal@gmail.com; f. 1964; Dir CECILLE KALEBI.

Polytechnic

SEYCHELLES POLYTECHNIC

POB 77, Anse Royale, Victoria
Telephone: 371188
Fax: 371545
E-mail: info@seypoly.edu.sc
Internet: www.seypoly.edu.sc

Founded 1983
State control
Language of instruction: English
Academic year: January to December

Dir: JEAN RASSOOL
Asst Dir for Admin.: HELENE BELMONT
Asst Dir for Studies: AUDREY NANON
Sr Librarian: MARIE-FRANCE LOZÉ

Library of 9,500 vols
Number of teachers: 56
Number of students: 578

School of Music

National College of the Arts: Ministry of Education, POB 1383, Mahé; tel. 224777; fax 321591; e-mail acollart@hotmail.com; f. 1997; depts of music, dance, visual arts, drama; 33 teachers (28 full-time, 5 part-time); 720 students (120 full-time, 600 part-time); Dir DAVID CHETTY.

SIERRA LEONE

The Higher Education System

Formerly a British colony and protectorate, Sierra Leone gained independence from the United Kingdom in 1961. Fourah Bay College (founded 1827), a constituent college of the University of Sierra Leone (founded 1967), is the oldest current institution of higher education. Before joining the University, degrees from Fourah Bay College were awarded by the University of Durham (United Kingdom). In 2011 there were three degree-awarding institutions in Sierra Leone—the University of Sierra Leone, Njala University (formerly the Njala University College of the University of Sierra Leone; current status adopted in 2005) and the Milton Margai College of Education and Technology (founded 2000). In 2001/02 a total of 9,041 students were enrolled in tertiary education.

The Ministry of Education, Science and Technology is responsible for higher education. The Tertiary Education Commission Act, approved in 2001, established a Commission to ensure that higher education academic programmes were effectively monitored, and set regulations for the approval and establishment of new higher education institutions.

Admission to higher education is on the basis of the West African Senior School Certificate examination. One-year Certificate and two- to three-year Diploma courses are available in mostly professional fields of study, such as agriculture, engineering and marine biology. The undergraduate Bachelors is either a three- to four-year 'General' degree or a four- to five-

year 'Honours' degree. At postgraduate level, students first take the Masters degree, which is awarded after one year following the Bachelors (Honours) or two years following the Bachelors (General) and requires submission of a dissertation or project. The Master of Philosophy requires an additional two years of study in certain subjects following award of a Masters degree, and also requires submission of a dissertation. The Doctor of Philosophy is the highest university degree, requiring three years of research leading to submission of a thesis.

The evaluation and certification of technical and vocational education is the responsibility of the National Council for Technical, Vocational and other Academic Awards (NCTVA—founded 2001); in 2011 the NCTVA was in the process of establishing a national framework for vocational qualifications. Post-secondary technical and vocational education is available from technical institutes in Kenema and Freetown and the Institute of Public Administration and Management attached to the University of Sierra Leone. The technical institutes offer a range of British-accredited qualifications, including City and Guilds certificates, London Chamber of Commerce and Industry examinations and Royal Society of Arts secretarial examinations, although increasingly these are being replaced by courses certified by the NCTVA. The Institute of Public Administration and Management (founded 1980) specializes in continuing education and workplace-based training.

Regulatory Bodies

GOVERNMENT

Ministry of Education, Science and Technology: New England, Freetown; tel. (22) 240881; fax (22) 240137; Minister Dr MINKAILU BAH.

Ministry of Tourism and Cultural Affairs: Ministerial Bldg, George St, Freetown; tel. (22) 222588; Minister HINDOLO TRYE.

Learned Societies

BIBLIOGRAPHY, LIBRARY SCIENCE AND MUSEOLOGY

Sierra Leone Association of Archivists, Librarians and Information Scientists: 7 Percival St, Freetown; f. 1970; 90 mems; Pres. OLATUNGIE CAMPBELL; Sec. AGNES MOROVIA; publ. *SLAALIS Bulletin* (4 a year).

HISTORY, GEOGRAPHY AND ARCHAEOLOGY

Historical Society of Sierra Leone: c/o Dept of History, Fourah Bay College, University of Sierra Leone, Freetown; f. 1975; 30 mems; Pres. G. S. ANTHONY; publ. *Journal* (2 a year).

LANGUAGE AND LITERATURE

Alliance Française: 30 Howe St, POB 510, Freetown; tel. (76) 683523; e-mail alliancefreetown@yahoo.fr; offers courses and exams in French language and culture and promotes cultural exchange with France.

British Council: Tower Hill, POB 124, Freetown; tel. (22) 222223; fax (22) 224123; e-mail info.enquiry@sl.britishcouncil.org;

internet www.britishcouncil.org/sierraleone; offers courses and exams in English language and British culture and promotes cultural exchange with the UK; Dir RAJIV BENDRE.

MEDICINE

Sierra Leone Medical and Dental Association: POB 850, Freetown; tel. (22) 229825; fax (22) 228430; f. 1961; 220 mems; library of 3,000 vols (shared with main hospital); Pres. Dr S. U. M. JAH; Sec. Dr DESMOND WRIGHT; publ. *Journal* (1 a year).

NATURAL SCIENCES

General

Sierra Leone Science Association: c/o Dept of Physics, Fourah Bay College, University of Sierra Leone, Freetown; tel. (22) 231617; fax (22) 224439; f. 1960; Hon. Pres. Prof. Dr ERNEST H. WRIGHT; Hon. Sec. (vacant).

Research Institutes

GENERAL

Institute of African Studies: c/o University of Sierra Leone, Fourah Bay College, Freetown; f. 1962; undertakes research in sociology, history and culture of Sierra Leone; offers undergraduate and postgraduate courses in cultural studies; Dir Dr ARTHUR ABRAHAM; publ. *Africana Research Bulletin* (2 a year).

NATURAL SCIENCES

Biological Sciences

Institute of Marine Biology and Oceanography: Fourah Bay College, University of

Sierra Leone, Freetown; tel. (22) 250775; f. 1966; 4-year degree programme in marine science, undergraduate diploma in aquatic biology and fisheries; research and training in oceanography, marine algae and ecology, fishery biology and management, aquaculture, marine pollution, estuarine dynamics, and coastal processes; Dir Dr I. W. O. FINDLAY; publ. *Annual Bulletin*.

Physical Sciences

Geological Survey Division: Ministry of Mines, Youyi Bldg, Brookfields, Freetown; f. 1918 to locate mineral deposits and to advise on all matters relating to the Earth; library of 16,000 vols including periodicals; Dir A. H. GABISI; publs *Bulletin* (1 a year), *Short Papers* (1 a year).

Libraries and Archives

Freetown

Fourah Bay College Library: Univ. of Sierra Leone, Freetown; tel. (22) 229471; e-mail fbclibrary2005@yahoo.com; internet www.daco-sl.org/encyclopedia/1_gov/1_7fourahbay.htm; f. 1827; 200,000 vols, 300 current periodicals; Sr Librarian OLIVER HARDING.

Public Archives of Sierra Leone: c/o Fourah Bay College, Freetown; f. 1965; 63,000 linear ft of records; Sr Archivist ALBERT MOORE.

Sierra Leone Library Board: POB 326, Rokel St, Freetown; tel. (22) 226993; e-mail sielib2002@yahoo.com; f. 1959; nationwide public library service; also acts as a nat. library (legal deposit); 1 central library (HQ), 3 regional libraries, 14 br. and district libraries; 110,000 vols; Chief Librarian SALLIEU TURAY; publs *Children's magazine*,

Golden Jubilee Souvenir, Sierra Leone Publications (1 a year).

Museum
Freetown

Sierra Leone National Museum: Cotton Tree Building, POB 908, Freetown; tel. (22) 223555; fax (22) 224439; e-mail cabnicol70@yahoo.co.uk; historical, ethnographical and archaeological collection; Curator CELIA NICOL.

University
UNIVERSITY OF SIERRA LEONE

PMB, Freetown
Telephone: (22) 226859
Founded 1967
State control
Language of instruction: English
Academic year: October to June
Chancellor: THE PRESIDENT OF THE REPUBLIC OF SIERRA LEONE
Vice-Chancellor: Prof. ERNEST H. WRIGHT
Pro-Chancellor: Dr ARTHUR PORTER
Pro-Vice-Chancellor: Prof. A. M. ALGHALI
Sec. and Registrar: J. A. G. THOMAS
Librarian: GLADYS JUSU-SHERIFF
Number of teachers: 301
Number of students: 4,310 (full-time)
Publications: *African Research Bulletin* (2 a year), *Calendar and Prospectus* (1 a year), *Varsity Update* (12 a year).

CONSTITUENT COLLEGES

Fourah Bay College

POB 87, Mount Aureol, Freetown
Telephone: (22) 227924
Internet: fbcusl.8k.com
Founded 1827, affiliated to the Univ. of Durham in 1876, became a constituent college of the univ. in 1966
Prin.: Prof. V. E. H. STRASSER-KING
Vice-Prin.: Prof. A. J. G. WYSE

DEANS

Faculty of Arts: Rev. Dr L. E. T. SHYLLON

Faculty of Economic and Social Sciences: Prof. A. ABRAHAM
Faculty of Engineering: Prof. O. R. DAVIDSON
Faculty of Law: Prof. H. M. JOKO-SMART
Faculty of Pure and Applied Science: Prof. V. E. GODWIN
Postgraduate Studies: Prof. A. J. G. WYSE

PROFESSORS

Faculty of Arts:
  WYSE, A. J. G., History
Faculty of Economic and Social Sciences:
  ABRAHAM, A., Institute of African Studies
Faculty of Engineering:
  DAVIDSON, O. R., Mechanical Engineering
Faculty of Pure and Applied Science:
  AWUNOR-RENNER, E. R. T., Physics
  COLE, N. H. A., Botany
  STRASSER-KING, V. E. H., Geology
  WILLIAMS, M. O., Zoology

College of Medicine and Allied Health Sciences

Telephone: (22) 240884
Founded 1987
Prin.: Prof. A. M. TAQI
Vice-Prin.: Assoc. Prof. F. D. R. LISK

DEANS

Faculty of Basic Medical Sciences: Dr J. K. GEORGE
Faculty of Clinical Sciences: Dr L. GORDON-HARRIS
Faculty of Pharmaceutical Sciences: Prof. E. AYITEY-SMITH

PROFESSORS

Faculty of Basic Medical Sciences:
  GEORGE, J. K., Anatomy
Faculty of Clinical Sciences:
  TAQI, A. M., Paediatrics
Faculty of Pharmaceutical Sciences:
  AYITEY-SMITH, E., Pharmacology

Njala University College

Telephone: (22) 228788
E-mail: nuc@sierratel.sl
Internet: www.nuc-online.com
Founded 1964

Prin.: Prof. A. M. ALGHALI
Vice-Prin.: P. K. SAIDU

DEANS

Faculty of Agriculture: Prof. E. R. RHODES
Faculty of Education: Dr T. M. DUGBA
Faculty of Environmental Sciences: Dr G. M. T. ROBERT

PROFESSORS

Faculty of Agriculture:
  KOROMA, J. P. C., Crop Science
  RHODES, E. R., Soil Science
Faculty of Education:
  BOMAH, A. K., Geography and Rural Development.

OFF-CAMPUS INSTITUTES

Institute of Education: PMB, Tower Hill, Freetown; tel. (22) 226874; Dir MELISSA F. JONAH (acting).

Institute of Library Studies: Mount Aureol, Freetown; tel. (22) 240290; Dir GLADYS JUSU-SHERIFF.

Institute of Public Administration And Management: PMB, Tower Hill, Freetown; tel. (22) 224801; Dir I. I. MAY-PARKER.

Colleges

Milton Margai College of Education and Technology: Goderich, nr Freetown; f. 1960; trains secondary school teachers; library: 23,000 vols; 55 teachers; 624 students; Prin. Dr DENIS KARGBO; Registrar J. U. WRIGHT (acting).

Paramedical School: POB 50, Bo; f. 1979 with funds from the Govt and the EEC; trains primary health workers; Prin. Dr V. O. COLE.

Technical Institute: Congo Cross, Freetown; tel. (22) 231368; fax (22) 231368; f. 1952; 80 teachers; 980 students; City and Guilds Craft and Technical Courses and Commercial Education; certificate, diploma and higher diploma courses in engineering, business, secretarial work and education; focal point for the UNEVOC project; Prin. MOHAMED A. JALLOH.

Technical Institute: Kenema; vocational courses.

SINGAPORE

The Higher Education System

In 1826 the East India Company formed the Straits Settlements by the union of Singapore and the dependencies of Penang and Malacca on the Malay Peninsula. They came under British rule in 1867. In 1946 Singapore became a separate crown colony, and in 1959 achieved complete internal self-government. After seceding from the Federation of Malaysia in 1965, Singapore became an independent republic. There are three public universities—National University of Singapore (founded 1980), Nanyang Technological University (founded as Nanyang Technological Institute in 1981; current status 1991) and Singapore Management University (founded 2000). Combined enrolment at the public universities totalled 72,710 students in 2009. In 2005 the Open University Centre (founded 1992), affiliated with the Open University (United Kingdom), was elevated to university status and renamed SIM University; it is a private institution specializing in adult education and correspondence courses. In the late 2000s the number of higher education institutions increased with the opening of, among others, the Singapore University of Technology and Design and the Singapore Institute of Technology. There were also several private institutions operating in conjunction with universities overseas—in particular in Germany and the USA. In 2009 the total number of students enrolled at the country's five polytechnics amounted to 80,635, while a further 24,846 students were enrolled at the Institute of Technical Education (ITE) and 4,934 students were enrolled at the National Institute of Education.

At the higher education level, the Ministry of Education primarily offers policy guidance and quality assurance, as well as providing funding. Adult and technical training is the responsibility of the Ministry of Manpower.

Admission to university undergraduate degrees is on the basis of results in A-Level examinations; some institutions also run entrance examinations and interviews. The undergraduate Bachelors degree lasts three years at 'Pass' level and four years at 'Honours' level, although degrees in certain professional fields of study, such as dentistry, law, engineering and construction, last longer. Both postgraduate Diplomas and Masters degrees are one- or two-year programmes of study, and the Doctor of Philosophy, the highest university degree, requires at least a further three years.

Post-secondary technical and vocational education is offered by the polytechnics and the Institute of Technical Education. The five polytechnics offer three levels of qualification, Certificate, Diploma and Advanced Diploma, in a range of professional fields of study. The ITE (founded 1992) replaced the former Vocational and Industrial Training Board and is under the control of the Ministry of Education. Consisting of 10 centres on two campuses, it specializes in full- and part-time training, workplace-based apprenticeships and continuing education. The two main qualifications offered by the ITE are the National ITE Certificate (NITEC) and the Higher NITEC.

Regulatory Body

GOVERNMENT

Ministry of Education: 1 North Buona Vista Drive, MOE Bldg, Singapore 138675; tel. 68722220; fax 67755826; e-mail contact@moe.edu.sg; internet www.moe.gov.sg; Minister NG ENG HEN; Permanent Sec. TAN CHING YEE.

Learned Societies

GENERAL

Singapore National Academy of Science: 1st Floor, Singapore Science Centre Building, off Jurong Town Hall Rd, Singapore 2260; established to promote the advancement of science and technology and to represent the mem. societies, institutes and other founder/affiliate mems of the Academy; Pres. Prof. LEO TAN WEE HIN; Sec. Dr CHIA WOON KIM.

Singapore Society of Asian Studies: Kent Ridge, POB 1076, Singapore 9111; f. 1982 to promote the study of Asian culture and heritage, with special emphasis on the South-East Asian region; 130 mems; Pres. LIM GUAN HOCK; Sec. Dr YEO MANG THONG; publ. *Asian Culture* (1 a year).

ARCHITECTURE AND TOWN PLANNING

Singapore Institute of Architects: 79 Neil Rd, Singapore 088904; tel. 62262668; fax 62262663; e-mail info@sia.org.sg; internet www.sia.org.sg; f. 1923; 1,000 mems; Pres. EDWARD D'SILVA; Hon. Sec. JOHNNY TAN; publs *SIA Year Book*, *Singapore Architect* (4 a year).

BIBLIOGRAPHY, LIBRARY SCIENCE AND MUSEOLOGY

Library Association of Singapore: Bukit Merah Central, POB 0693, Singapore 9115; internet www.las.org.sg; f. 1955; 328 mems; Pres. CHOY FATT CHEONG; Hon. Sec. LIM-YEO PIN PIN; publs *Singapore Libraries* (2 a year), *Singapore Libraries Bulletin* (4 a year).

ECONOMICS, LAW AND POLITICS

Singapore Institute of International Affairs: 2 Nassim Rd, Singapore 258370; tel. 67349600; fax 67336217; e-mail research@siiaonline.org; f. 1961; organizes talks, conferences, etc.; commissions research on East Asian economic integration, sustainable development and governance issues, and peace and development in South-East Asia; 379 mems; Chair. Assoc. Prof. SIMON TAY; Dir YEO LAY HWEE.

FINE AND PERFORMING ARTS

Singapore Art Society: 6001 Beach Rd, No. 18–08, Golden Mile Tower, Singapore 0719; tel. 62924244; f. 1949 to foster the practice and appreciation of art in Singapore; 325 mems; Pres. HO KOK HOE; Hon. Sec. QUEK KIAN GUAN.

LANGUAGE AND LITERATURE

Alliance Française: 1 Sarkies Rd, Singapore 258130; tel. 67378422; fax 67333023; e-mail afsing@alliancefrancaise.org.sg; internet www.alliancefrancaise.org.sg; offers courses and examinations in French language and culture and promotes cultural exchange with France; Exec. Dir YVES CORBEL.

British Council: 30 Napier Rd, Singapore 258509; tel. 64731111; fax 64721010; e-mail enquiries@britishcouncil.org.sg; internet www.britishcouncil.org.sg; f. 1947; teaching centre; offers courses and exams in English language and British culture and promotes cultural exchange with the UK; attached teaching centres in Holland Village, Marsiling and Tampines; Dir LES DANGERFIELD; Dir, Teaching Centre MARTIN HOPE.

Goethe-Institut: 163 Penang Rd 05-01, Winsland House II, Singapore 238463; tel. 67354555; fax 67354666; internet www.goethe.de/so/sin/deindex.htm; offers courses and examinations in German language and culture and promotes cultural exchange with Germany; library of 8,000 vols; Dir Dr ULRICH NOWAK.

MEDICINE

Academy of Medicine, Singapore: College of Medicine Bldg, Level 1, Left Wing, 16 College Rd, Singapore 0316; tel. 62238968; fax 62255155; f. 1957; professional corporate body of medical and dental specialists; also involved in the postgraduate training of doctors; Master Dr N. C. TAN; Chief Administrator Y. L. LAM; publ. *Annals* (4 a year).

Singapore Medical Association: Level 2, 2 College Rd, Alumni Medical Centre, Singapore 169850; tel. 62231264; fax 62247827; e-mail sma@sma.org.sg; internet www.sma.org.sg; f. 1959; 3,900 mems; Pres. Prof. C. H. LOW; Hon. Sec. Dr W. M. YUE; publ. *Singapore Medical Journal* (12 a year).

NATURAL SCIENCES

General

Singapore Association for the Advancement of Science: 1st Floor, Singapore Science Centre Bldg, off Jurong Town Hall Rd, Singapore 2260; f. 1976 for the dissemination of science and technology; Pres. Prof. ANG KOK PENG; Sec. Dr LEO TAN WEE HIN.

Mathematical Sciences

Singapore Mathematical Society: Mathematics Dept, National University of Singapore, Kent Ridge, Singapore 119260; tel. 68742394; fax 67795452; e-mail smsuser@math.nus.edu.sg; internet sms.math.nus.edu.sg; f. 1952; aims to maintain the status and advance the interests of the profession of mathematics, to improve the teaching of mathematics, and to provide means of interaction between students, teachers and others interested in mathematics; 620 mems; Pres. Prof. TAN ENG CHYE; Sec. Prof. TANG WEE KEE; publ. *Mathematical Medley* (2 a year).

Physical Sciences

Institute of Physics, Singapore: c/o Dept of Physics, National University of Singapore, Kent Ridge, Singapore 119260; tel. 67722604; fax 67776126; f. 1973; promotes study of and research in physics in Singapore; organizes confs, talks, seminars, exhibitions, visits to industrial and commercial establishments and educational tours abroad; 180 mems; Pres. Prof. BERNARD TAN; Sec. Assoc. Prof. ANDREW T. S. WEE; publs *Physics Update* (2 a year), *Singapore Journal of Physics* (2 a year).

Research Institutes

ECONOMICS, LAW AND POLITICS

Asian Media Information and Communication Centre: Jurong Point, POB 360, Singapore 916412; tel. 67927570; fax 67927129; e-mail enquiries@amic.org.sg; internet www.amic.org.sg; f. 1971; non-profit regional documentation centre; works in cooperation with UNESCO and other int. orgs to promote the understanding and devt of communication and its application in the Asia-Pacific region with regard to economic, social and cultural progress; publishes media journals and books; organizes seminars, capacity building workshops; convenes confs; conducts communication research; library of 35,000 records in databases, 350 journals; regional centre for Japan Prize Circulating Library; Sec.-Gen. Prof. SUNDEEP R. MUPPIDI; publs *AMCB* (6 a year), *Asian Communication Handbook* (every 3–4 years), *Asian Journal of Communication* (6 a year), *Media Asia* (4 a year).

Institute of Southeast Asian Studies: Heng Mui Keng Terrace, Pasir Panjang, Singapore 119614; f. 1968; undertakes research on SE Asia, esp. problems of devt, modernization, political and social change; library of 400,000 vols; Dir TAN CHIN TIONG; Librarian ZALEHA TAMBY; publs *ASEAN Economic Bulletin* (3 a year), *Contemporary Southeast Asia* (3 a year), *Regional Outlook*, *Social Issues in Southeast Asia* (2 a year), *SOJOURN*, *Southeast Asian Affairs* (1 a year).

EDUCATION

East Asian Institute (EAI): 469A Bukit Timah Rd, Tower Block, 06–01, Singapore 259770; tel. 65163715; fax 67793409; e-mail eaizyn@nus.edu.sg; internet www.eai.nus.edu.sg; f. 1997; attached to Nat. Univ. of Singapore; promotes both academic and policy-oriented research on East Asian devt; focuses on political, economic and social devt of contemporary China (incl. Hong Kong and Taiwan) and China's growing economic relations with the region and the world, incl. Japan, Korea, ASEAN; library of 27,892 vols, incl. colln of yearbooks and 359 journals, periodicals and newspapers from the People's Republic of China, Hong Kong and Taiwan; Chair. Prof. GUNGWU WANG; Dir Prof. YONG-

NIAN ZHENG; publs *China: An International Journal (CIJ)*, *East Asian Policy (EAP)* (4 a year).

Institute of Technical Education (ITE): 10 Dover Drive, Singapore 138683; tel. 67757800; fax 67762172; e-mail itehq@ite.edu.sg; internet www.ite.edu.sg; Chair. ERIC GWEE TECK HAI; Dir Dr LAW SONG SENG; publ. *The Quality Workforce* (6 a year).

Libraries and Archives

Singapore

National Archives of Singapore: National Heritage Board, 1 Canning Rise, Singapore 179868; fax 63393583; e-mail nhb_nasreg@nhb.gov.sg; f. 1968; 3,400 vols, 43 current periodicals, 1.5m. photographs, 128,200 building plans, 6,630 maps, 66,427 microfilm rolls, 18,000 cassettes of recorded interviews; Senior Dir LILY TAN.

National Library Board: 100 Victoria St, 14-01, Nat. Library Bldg, Singapore 188064; tel. 63323133; fax 63323332; e-mail helpdesk@nlb.gov.sg; internet www.nlb.gov.sg; f. 1995; oversees management of Nat. Library and network of public libraries, also 1 community children's library and 17 libraries belonging to govt agencies, schools and instns; 1.2m. vols, collns in languages of English, Chinese, Malay, Tamil; 119,838 serial titles; 115,977 spec. materials such as microfilm, audiovisuals and 1.2m. book titles available in Malay, Chinese, Tamil and English colln; Chief Exec. Dr N. VARAPRASAD; publs *Books about Singapore* (online), *Singapore National Bibliography* (CD-ROM, 2 a year), *Singapore Periodicals Index* (1 a year).

National University of Singapore Libraries: 12 Kent Ridge Crescent, Singapore 119275; tel. 65162069; fax 67771272; e-mail clbsec@nus.edu.sg; internet www.lib.nus.edu.sg; f. 1905; 2.4m. vols (Central Library 1.1m. vols; Japanese Resources 51,955 vols; Chinese Library 465,644 vols; C. J. Koh Law Library 157,087 vols; Hon Sui Sen Memorial Library 90,992 vols; Medical Library 170,040 vols; Science Library 286,221 vols), 23,844 electronic titles, 27,423 audiovisual items, 24,266 microforms; Dir., NUS Libraries SYLVIA YAP; publ. *Guide to NUS Libraries* (1 a year).

Museums and Art Galleries

Singapore

National Heritage Board: 93 Stamford Rd, Singapore 78897; tel. 63361460; fax 63323568; f. 1849; consists of Asian Civilizations Museum, Singapore History Museum, Singapore Art Museum, Children's Discovery Gallery; library of 25,000 vols; history and oral history archives; CEO LIM SIAM KIM.

Singapore Art Museum: 71 Bras Basah Rd, Singapore 189555; tel. 63323222; fax 63347919; internet www.museum.org.sg/sam/sam.shtml; f. 1996; modern and contemporary South-East Asian art.

Singapore Botanic Gardens: National Parks Board, Cluny Rd, Singapore 259569; tel. 64717361; fax 64674832; internet www.nparks.gov.sg; f. 1859; botanical and horticultural research with particular reference to South-East Asia and the tropics; library of 30,000 vols; CEO POON HONG YUEN; Dir for Gdns Dr NIGEL TAYLOR; Keeper of Herbarium and Library Dr WONG KHOON MENG; publ. *The Gardens Bulletin Singapore* (2 a year).

Universities

NANYANG TECHNOLOGICAL UNIVERSITY

50 Nanyang Ave, Singapore 639798

Telephone: 67911744
Fax: 67911604
E-mail: adm_intnl@ntu.edu.sg
Internet: www.ntu.edu.sg

Founded 1981 as Nanyang Technological Institute; present name and status 1991
Academic year: July to July

Pres.: Dr SU GUANING
Provost: Prof. BERTIL ANDERSSON
Sr Assoc. Provost: Prof. ER MENG HWA
Assoc. Provost for Graduate Education and Special Projects: Prof. LAM KHIN YONG
Assoc. Provost for Innovation: JEFFREY NADISON
Assoc. Provost for Research: Prof. MICHAEL KHOR
Sec.: ANTHONY TEO
Chief Planning Officer and Registrar: CHAN KWONG LOK
Chief Financial Officer: GOH BOON HUAT
Chief Human Resource Officer: ANGELA LIM SAU TING
Chief Univ. Advancement Officer: CHEW KHENG CHUAN
Dir of Corporate Communications: Dr VIVIEN CHIONG
Librarian: CHOY FATT CHEONG
Number of teachers: 1,635
Number of students: 33,087

Publications: *Asian Business Law Review* (4 a year), *Asian Journal of Communication* (3 a year), *Asian Mass Communication Bulletin* (6 a year), *Asia Pacific Journal of Education* (2 a year), *Electrical and Electronic Engineering Bulletin* (1 a year), *Mechanical and Aerospace Engineering Research Bulletin* (1 a year), *Media Asia* (4 a year), *Nanyang Business Review* (2 a year), *Pedagogies: An International Journal* (2 a year), *School of Computer Engineering Research Report* (1 a year), *Singteach* (4 a year), *Teaching Education* (4 a year), *Technical Reports* (12 a year)

DEANS

College of Engineering: Prof. PAN TSO-CHIEN
College of Humanities, Arts and Social Sciences: Prof. ALAN CHAN KAM-LEUNG
College of Science: Prof. MARK FEATHERSTONE
Cornell-Nanyang Institute of Hospitality Management: Dr RUSSELL ARTHUR SMITH
Nanyang Business School: Prof. GILLIAN YEO HIAN HENG
School of Art, Design and Media: Prof. VIBEKE SORENSEN
School of Biological Sciences: Prof. ALEX LAW SAI KIT (acting)
School of Chemical and Biomedical Engineering: Prof. CHING CHI BUN
School of Civil and Environmental Engineering: Assoc. Prof. EDMOND LO YAT-MAN
School of Computer Engineering: Prof. THAMBIPILLAI SRIKANTHAN
School of Electrical and Electronic Engineering: Prof. KAM CHAN HIN
School of Humanities and Social Sciences: Prof. EUSTON QUAH (acting)
School of Materials Science and Engineering: Prof. FREDDY BOEY YING CHIANG (acting)
School of Mechanical and Aerospace Engineering: Prof. LING SHIH FU (acting)
School of Physical and Mathematical Sciences: Prof. LING SAN
S. Rajaratnam School of Int. Studies: Ambassador BARRY DESKER
Wee Kim Wee School of Communication and Information: Assoc. Prof. BENJAMIN HILL DETENBER

PROFESSORS

College of Engineering (Block S3.2, Level B1, 50 Nanyang Ave, Singapore 639798; tel. 67906706; fax 67912523; e-mail d-coe@ntu .edu.sg; internet www.ntu.edu.sg/coe):

LIM, E. N.
LIM, M. K.

Nanyang Business School (Block S3, 50 Nanyang Ave, Singapore 639798; tel. 67904636; fax 67913697; e-mail wwwnbs@ ntu.edu.sg; internet www.nbs.ntu.edu.sg):

ANG, S., Strategy, Management and Organization
DUFEY, G., Banking and Finance
HONG, H.
NEO, B. S.
SETHI, V., Information Technology and Operations Management
SIGUAW, J. A., Cornell-Nanyang Institute of Hospitality Management
TAN, H. T., Accounting
WEE, C. H., Strategy, Management and Organization
WILLIAMS, J. J., Accounting
YEO, F. H. H., Accounting

National Institute of Education (1 Nanyang Walk, Singapore 637616; tel. 67903888; fax 68968874; e-mail niepr@nie.edu.sg; internet www.nie.edu.sg):

CHEW, C. H.
GAN, L. H.
GOH, K. C.
GOPINATHAN, S.
HOGAN, D. J.
LEE, S. K.
LUKE, A. A. J.
MATTHEWS, J. S.
TAN, L. W. H.
XU, S. Y.

School of Biological Sciences (60 Nanyang Dr., SBS-01n-21, Singapore 637551; tel. 63162800; fax 67913856; e-mail d-sbs@ntu .edu.sg; internet www.ntu.edu.sg/sbs):

LAW, A. S. K., Molecular and Cell Biology
LUN, K. C., Structural and Computational Biology
NORDENSKLÖLD, L., Structural and Computational Biology
TAM, J. P. K.

School of Chemical and Biomedical Engineering (Block 1 Innovation Centre, 16 Nanying Dr., Unit 100, Level 1, Singapore 637722; tel. 67906743; fax 67947553; e-mail cbe@ntu .edu.sg; internet www.ntu.edu.sg/cbme):

CHING, C. B.

School of Civil and Environmental Engineering (Block N1, 50 Nanyang Ave, Singapore 639798; tel. 67905265; fax 67910676; e-mail d-cee@ntu.edu.sg; internet www.ntu.edu.sg/ cee):

CHIEW, Y. M., Environmental and Water Resources Engineering
CHOA, V. C. E., Geotechnical Engineering
CHOI, E. C. C., Construction Technology and Management
FAN, H. S. L., Transportation Engineering
FAN, S. C., Structures and Mechanics
PAN, T. C., Structures and Mechanics
RAHARDJO, H., Geotechnical and Transportation Engineering
SOH, C. K., Structures and Mechanics
TAY, J. H., Environmental and Water Resources Engineering

Wee Kim Wee School of Communication and Information (31 Nanyang Link, Singapore 637718; tel. 67904577; fax 67943662; e-mail wwwsci@ntu.edu.sg; internet www.ntu.edu .sg/sci):

FOO S. B., Information Studies
KUO C. Y. E., Communication Research

School of Computer Engineering (Block N4, 2A-32, Nanyang Ave, Singapore 639798; tel.

67905786; fax 67926559; e-mail wwwsce@ntu .edu.sg; internet www.ntu.edu.sg/sce):

GOH, A. E. S., Information Systems

School of Electrical and Electronic Engineering (Block S2.1, 50 Nanyang Ave, Singapore 639798; tel. 67905367; fax 67912687; e-mail wwweee@ntu.edu.sg; internet www.ntu.edu .sg/eee):

CHOI, S. S., Power Engineering
DO, M. A., Circuits and Systems
ER, M. H.
GAY, R. K. L., Information Communication Institute of Singapore
KAM, C. H., Microelectronics
KOH, S. N., Communication Engineering
KOT, C. C., Information Engineering
LIM, Y. C., Information Engineering
SOH, Y. C., Control and Instrumentation
SUNDARARAJAN, N., Control and Instrumentation
XIE, L. H., Control and Administration
YOON, S. F., Microelectronics
ZHU, W. G., Microelectronics

School of Humanities and Social Sciences (Block S3.2, Level B2, 50 Nanyang Ave, Singapore 639798; tel. 67906983; fax 67942830; e-mail d-hss@ntu.edu.sg; internet www.hss.ntu.edu.sg):

CHEW, S. B., Economics
KOH, T. A., English
KUO, C. O. E., Sociology
LIM, C. Y., Economics
REISMAN, D. A., Economics

School of Materials Science and Engineering (Block N4.1, #01-30, Nanyang Ave, Singapore 639798; tel. 67904142; fax 67909081; e-mail wwwsme@ntu.edu.sg; internet www .ntu.edu.sg/sme):

BOEY, F. Y. C.

School of Mechanical and Aerospace Engineering (Block N3, 50 Nanyang Ave, Singapore 639798; tel. 67905486; fax 67911859; e-mail wwwmae@ntu.edu.sg; internet www .ntu.edu.sg/mae):

ASUNDI, A. K., Engineering Mechanics
HELANDER, M. E. G., Systems and Engineering Management
KHOO, L. P., Mechatronics and Design
KHOR, K. A., Manufacturing Engineering
LAM, Y. C., Manufacturing Engineering
LIEW, K. M., Engineering Mechanics
LIM, L. E. N., Manufacturing Engineering
LIM, M. K., Engineering Mechanics
LING, S. F., Engineering Mechanics
LYE, S. W., Manufacturing Engineering
MEGUID, S. A., Engineering Mechanics
SHANG, H. M., Engineering Mechanics
TAM, K. C., Manufacturing Engineering
YUE, C. Y.

School of Physical and Mathematical Sciences (Block 5, Level 3, 1 Nanyang Walk, Singapore 637616; tel. 67906983; fax 67906984; e-mail spms-v1@ntu.edu.sg; internet www.ntu.edu.sg/spms/home):

LEE, S. Y.
LEUNG, P. H., Physical and Mathematical Sciences
LING, S., Mathematical Sciences
LOH, T. P., Chemistry and Biological Chemistry

ATTACHED RESEARCH INSTITUTES

Advanced Materials Research Centre: tel. 67904626; fax 67909081; e-mail d-amrc@ntu.edu.sg; Dir Assoc. Prof. SUBODH MHAISALKAR.

Bioinformatics Research Centre: tel. 63162957; fax 67912274; internet www.ntu .edu.sg; Dir Assoc. Prof. SUBBU S. VENKATRAMAN.

BioMedical Engineering Research Centre: Dir Assoc. Prof. LIM CHU SING DANIEL.

Centre for Advanced Numerical Engineering Simulations: Dir Prof. LIEW KIM MEOW.

Centre for Financial Engineering: tel. 67904758; fax 67937440; e-mail mfe@ntu.edu .sg; Dir Assoc. Prof. BUEN SIN LOW.

Centre for Graphics and Imaging Technology: Dir Assoc. Prof. WONG KOK CHEONG.

Centre for High-Performance Embedded Systems: tel. 67906638; fax 67920774; e-mail chipes@ntu.edu.sg; internet www.chipes .ntu.edu.sg; Dir Prof. THAMBIPILLAI SRIKANTHAN.

Environmental Engineering Research Centre: Dir Assoc. Prof. STEPHEN TAY TIONG LEE.

Maritime Research Centre: tel. 67905321; fax 67906620; e-mail d-mrc@ntu.edu.sg; Dir Assoc. Prof. TAN SOON KEAT.

Nanyang Technopreneurship Centre: tel. 67906675; fax 67920467; e-mail ntc@ntu .edu.sg; Dir Assoc. Prof. TAN TENG KEE.

Network Technology Research Centre: tel. 67905019; fax 67904685; e-mail ntrc@ntu .edu.sg; internet www.ntu.edu.sg/ntrc; Dir Assoc. Prof. PING SHUM.

NTU-BCA Centre for Advanced Construction Studies: Dir Assoc. Prof. TING SENG KIONG.

NTU-MINDEF Protective Technology Research Centre: tel. 67905285; fax 67910046; e-mail ptrc@ntu.edu.sg; internet www.ntu.edu.sg/ptrc; Dir Prof. TSO-CHIEN PAN.

Positioning and Wireless Technology Centre: tel. 67917326; fax 6793318; e-mail d-pwtc@ntu.edu.sg; internet www.ntu.edu .sg/centre/pwtc; Dir Assoc. Prof. CHOI LOOK LAW.

Robotics Research Centre: tel. 67905568; e-mail d-rrc@ntu.edu.sg; internet www.ntu .edu.sg/mae/centres/rrc; Dir Assoc. Prof. GERALD SEET.

NATIONAL UNIVERSITY OF SINGAPORE

21 Lower Kent Ridge Rd, Singapore 119077
Telephone: 65166666
Internet: www.nus.edu.sg
Founded 1980 by merger of fmr Univ. of Singapore and Nanyang Univ.
State control
Language of instruction: English
Academic year: July to June (2 semesters)
Pres.: Prof. TAN CHORH CHUAN
Deputy Pres. for Acad. Affairs and Provost: Prof. TAN ENG CHYE
Deputy Pres. for Research and Technology: Prof. BARRY HALLIWELL
Deputy Pres. for Admin.: JOSEPH P. MULLINIX
Vice-Pres. for Campus Infrastructure: Prof. YONG KWET YEW
Vice-Pres. for Human Resources: DANIEL CHO KWONG CHOW
Vice-Pres. for Univ. and Global Relations: Prof. LILY KONG
Vice-Pres. for Research Strategy: Prof. SEERAM RAMAKRISHNA
Vice-Pres. for Endowment and Institutional Devt: WEE SIN THO
Vice-Provost for Academic Personnel: Prof. LAI CHOY HENG
Vice-Provost for Education: Prof. TAN THIAM SOON
Vice-Provost for Student Life: Prof. TAN TAI YONG
CEO: Dr LILY CHAN
Registrar: CHRISTINE CHEN (acting)

Librarian: JILL QUAH
Library: see under Libraries and Archives
Number of teachers: 2,207
Number of students: 33,741
Publication: *Knowledge Enterprise* (10 year)

DEANS

Duke-NUS Graduate Medical School Singapore: TONY CHEW (Chair.)
Faculty of Arts and Social Sciences: Prof. BRENDA YEOH
Faculty of Dentistry: Assoc. Prof. GRACE ONG HUI LIAN
Faculty of Engineering: Prof. CHAN ENG SOON
Faculty of Law: Prof. TAN CHENG HAN
Faculty of Science: Prof. ANDREW WEE
Lee Kwan Yew School of Public Policy: Prof. KISHORE MAHBUBANI
NUS Business School: Prof. BERNARD YEUNG
NUS Graduate School for Integrative Sciences and Engineering: Prof. LI BAOWEN (Exec. Dir)
School of Computing: Prof. BENG CHIN OOI
School of Design and Environment: Prof. HENG CHYE KIANG
Yong Loo Lin School of Medicine: Prof. JOHN WONG
Yong Siew Toh Conservatory of Music: Prof. BERNARD LANSKEY (Dir)

PROFESSORS

Faculty of Arts and Social Sciences:

CHAN, H. C., Political Science
KAPUR, B. K., Economics
MOHANAN, K. P., English Language and Literature
MUKUL, A., Public Policy
NG, C. K., History
QUAH, S. T. J., Political Science
SIDLE, R. C., Geography
SINGH, R., Social Work and Psychology
SURYADINATA, L., Political Science
WANG, G. W., East Asian Institute
WONG, K. L. C. A., Sociology
WONG, Y. W., Chinese Studies

Faculty of Business Administration:

KAU, A. K., Marketing
LEONG, S. M., Marketing
TAN, C. H., Management and Organization
WONG, K. A., Finance and Accounting

Faculty of Dentistry:

CHEW, C. L., Restorative Dentistry
LOH, H. S., Oral and Maxillofacial Surgery

Faculty of Engineering:

ANG, B. W., Industrial and Systems Engineering
ARUN, S. M., Mechanical Engineering
CHAN, S. H. D., Electrical and Computer Engineering
CHEONG, H. F., Civil Engineering
CHEW, Y. T., Mechanical Engineering
CHING, C. B., Chemical and Environmental Engineering
CHOW, Y. K., Civil Engineering
CHUA, S. J., Electrical and Computer Engineering
CHUNG, T. S. N., Chemical and Environmental Engineering
FWA, T. F., Civil Engineering
GOH, T. N., Industrial and Systems Engineering
HANG, C. C., Electrical and Computer Engineering
KAM, P. Y., Electrical and Computer Engineering
KANG, E. T., Chemical and Environmental Engineering
KOOI, P. S., Electrical and Computer Engineering
LAM, K. Y., Mechanical Engineering
LEE, T. H., Electrical and Computer Engineering

LEONG, M. S., Electrical and Computer Engineering
LI, M. F., Electrical and Computer Engineering
LIEW, A. C., Electrical and Computer Engineering
LIM, S. C., Mechanical Engineering
LIM, Y. C., Electrical and Computer Engineering
LING, C. H., Electrical and Computer Engineering
LOW, T. S., Electrical and Computer Engineering
LYE, K. M., Electrical and Computer Engineering
NEE, Y. C. A., Mechanical Engineering
NEOH, K. G., Chemical and Environmental Engineering
NG, W. J., Civil Engineering
NHAN, P. T., Mechanical Engineering
PARAMASIVAM, P., Civil Engineering
PHANG, C. H. J., Electrical and Computer Engineering
POO, A. N., Mechanical Engineering
SHANG, H. M., Mechanical Engineering
SHANKAR, N. J., Civil Engineering
SHANMUGAM, N. E., Civil Engineering
SHIH, C. F., Engineering
TAN, T. C., Chemical and Environmental Engineering
TAY, A. O. A., Electrical and Computer Engineering
TOYOAKI, N., Civil Engineering
VISWANADHAM, N., Mechanical Engineering
WIJEYSUNDERA, N. E., Mechanical Engineering
WONG, L., Electrical and Computer Engineering
YAP, M., Chemical and Environmental Engineering
YEO, S. P., Electrical and Computer Engineering
YONG, K. Y., Civil Engineering

Faculty of Law:

JAYAKUMAR, S.
KOH, T. B. T.
PINSLER, J.
SORNARAJAH, M.
TAN, Y. L.
WOON, C. M. W.

Yong Loo Lin School of Medicine:

AW, T. C., Pathology
BOSE, K., Orthopaedic Surgery
CHAN, H. L., Medicine
CHAN, S. H., Microbiology
CHIEW, Y. C., Medicine
GOPALAKRISHNAKONE, P., Anatomy
GWEE, M., Pharmacology
HALLIWELL, B., Biochemistry
HWANG, L. H. P., Physiology
KOH, S. Q. D., Community, Occupational and Family Medicine
KUA, E. H., Psychological Medicine
LEE, E. H., Orthopaedic Surgery
LEE, H. P., Community, Occupational and Family Medicine
LEE, J. D. E., Pharmacology
LEE, T. L., Anaesthesia
LEE, Y. S., Pathology
LIM, P., Medicine
LING, E. A., Anatomy
LIU, E., Medicine
LOW, P. S., Paediatrics
NG, S. C., Obstetrics and Gynaecology
OH, M. S. V., Medicine
ONG, C. N., Community, Occupational and Family Medicine
PHO, W. H. R., Orthopaedic Surgery
PRASAD, R. N. V., Obstetrics and Gynaecology
SATKUNANANTHAM, K., Orthopaedic Surgery
SHAMAL, D. D., Orthopaedic Surgery
SIT, K. H., Anatomy
SIT, K. P., Biochemistry

TAN, C. C., Medicine
TAN, K. A. L., Diagnostic Radiology
TAN, W. C., Medicine
TAN, Y. H., Medicine
WEE, A., Pathology
WONG, E. L. J., Medicine
YAP, H. K., Paediatrics

Faculty of Science:

BAI, Z., Statistics and Applied Probability
BERRICK, A. J., Mathematics
CHAN, S. O. H., Chemistry
CHEN, H. Y. L., Mathematics
CHONG, C. T., Mathematics
CHOU, L. M., Biological Sciences
CHOW, S. N., Mathematics
DING, J. L., Biological Sciences
GOH, S. H., Chemistry
HEW, C. L., Biological Sciences
HOR, T. S. A., Chemistry
IP, Y. K. A., Biological Sciences
KOH, K. M., Mathematics
LAI, C. H., Physics
LAM, T. J., Biological Sciences
LEE, C. K., Chemistry
LEE, S. L., Mathematics
LEE, S. Y., Chemistry
LI, F. Y. S., Chemistry
LIM, C. S., Mathematics
LIM, H., Physics
NIEDERREITER, H., Mathematics
OH, C. H., Physics
ONG, C. K., Physics
ONG, P. P. P., Physics
PHILPOTT, M. R., Materials Science
SY, H. K., Physics
TANG, S. H., Physics
TANG, S. M., Physics
TRUONG, Y. K.-N., Statistics and Applied Probability
WATT, F., Physics

School of Computing:

JAFFAR, J., Computer Science
LING, T. W., Computer Science
LU, H. J., Computer Science
OOI, B. C., Computer Science
PNG, P. L. I., Information Systems
WEI, K. K., Information Systems
YUEN, C. K., Computer Science

School of Design and Environment:

BROWN, G. R., Real Estate
OFORI, G., Building

SIM UNIVERSITY

461 Clementi Rd, Singapore 599491
Telephone: 62489777
Fax: 67639077
E-mail: student_recruitment@unisim.edu.sg
Internet: www.unisim.edu.sg

Founded 1992, present name and status 2005
Private control

Chair.: Prof. CHAM TAO SOON
Pres.: CHEONG HEE KIAT
Registrar: Assoc. Prof YIP WOON KWONG

DEANS

School of Arts and Social Sciences: Dr GENICE NGG (acting)
School of Business: Prof. TAN NGOH TIONG
School of Human Development and Social Services: Prof. TAN NGOH TIONG
School of Science and Technology: Assoc. Prof. PHILIP CHEANG HONG NING (acting)

SINGAPORE INSTITUTE OF TECHNOLOGY

25 N Bridge Rd, EFG Bank Bldg 03–01, Singapore 179104
Telephone: 65921189
E-mail: adm.intl@singaporetech.edu.sg
Internet: www.singaporetech.edu.sg

Founded 2009

State control
Chair.: NG YAT CHUNG
Deputy Chair.: NG CHER PONG
Pres.: Prof. TAN CHIN TIONG
Deputy Pres. for Academics: Dr TING SENG KIONG
Deputy Pres. for Operations: TAN CHEK MING.

SINGAPORE MANAGEMENT UNIVERSITY

Tanglin, POB 257, Singapore 912409
Bukit Timah Campus, 469 Bukit Timah Rd, Oei Tiong Ham Bldg, Singapore 259756
Telephone: 68220100
Fax: 68220101
E-mail: enquire@smu.edu.sg
Internet: www.smu.edu.sg
Founded 2000
Private control
Pres.: HOWARD HUNTER
Provost: Prof. CHIN TIONG TAN
Registrar: TAN LEE CHUAN
Chief Librarian: KOH BEE CHIN

DEANS

Lee Kong Chian School of Business: Prof. DAVID B. MONTGOMERY
School of Accountancy: Assoc. Prof. PANG YANG HOONG
School of Economics and Social Sciences: Prof. ROBERTO S. MARIANO
School of Information Systems: STEVEN MILLER

PROFESSORS

Lee Kong Chian School of Business (Business Bldg, 469 Bukit Timah Rd, Singapore 259756; e-mail dmontgomery@smu.edu.sg; internet www.business.smu.edu.sg):

LIM, K. G.
MONTGOMERY, D.
PANG, E. F.
PHANG, A.
TAN, C. T.
YANG, K. K.

School of Accountancy (Accountancy Bldg, 469 Bukit Timah Rd, Singapore 259756; tel. 68220610; fax 68220600; e-mail adelineheng@smu.edu.sg; internet www .accountancy.smu.edu.sg):

TAN, T. M.
YOUNG, K. K.

School of Economics and Social Sciences (The Federal Bldg, 469 Bukit Timah Rd, Singapore 259756; tel. 68220832; fax 68220833; e-mail sess@smu.edu.sg; internet www.sess.smu.edu.sg):

KUEN, T. S.
MARIANO, R. S.

School of Information Systems (Raffles Bldg, 469 Bukit Timah Rd, Singapore 259756; tel. 68220903; fax 68220919; e-mail sis@smu.edu.sg; internet www.sis.smu.edu.sg):

DENG, R. H.
LEE, J. K.

SINGAPORE UNIVERSITY OF TECHNOLOGY & DESIGN (SUTD)

287 Ghim Moh Rd, 04-00, Singapore 279623
Telephone: 63036600
E-mail: enquiry@sutd.edu.sg
Internet: www.su.edu.sg
Offers courses in architecture and sustainable design, engineering product development, engineering systems and design, information systems technology and design
Chair.: PHILIP NG
Pres.: TOM MAGNANTI
Provost: Prof. CHONG TOW CHONG

Assoc. Provost: Prof. PEY KIN LEONG.

Polytechnics

NANYANG POLYTECHNIC

180 Ang Mo Kio Ave 8, Singapore 569830
Telephone: 64515115
Internet: www.nyp.edu.sg
Founded 1992
Pres.: TAN PHENG HOCK
Prin. and CEO: LIN CHENG TON
Deputy Prin. for Academic Affairs and Registrar: CHAN LEE MUN
Deputy Prin. for Devt: BRUCE POH GEOK HUAT
Deputy Prin. for Technology: EDWARD HO SZE LEUNG
Chief Librarian: WONG CHIEW AUN

DIRECTORS

School of Business Management: V. SESHAMANI
School of Chemical and Life Sciences: Dr JOEL LEE
School of Engineering: CHAN YEW MENG
School of Health Sciences: LONG CHOOI FONG
School of Information Technology: JOHN TAN

NGEE ANN POLYTECHNIC

535 Clementi Rd, Singapore 599489
Telephone: 64666555
Fax: 64687326
E-mail: asknp@np.edu.sg
Internet: www.np.edu.sg
Founded 1963
State control
Language of instruction: English
Academic year: April to March
Chair.: KIN FEI TANG
Prin.: MIA CHIANG CHIA
Deputy Prin.: WEE BENG FOO
Sr Dir: CHOO MIN LIM
Registrar: JEANNE LIEW
Library Dir: CAROLINE CHOON KHENG PHUA
Library of 200,000 vols, 900 periodicals, 35,000 online books, 40 databases, 41,000 audiovisual items
Number of teachers: 897
Number of students: 17,927
Publications: eXtra, Hype, NP Tribune (online magazine), SGNewWave, Urban Wire.

REPUBLIC POLYTECHNIC

1 Kay Siang Rd, Singapore 248922
Telephone: 63768000
Fax: 64151310
E-mail: gsm@rp.edu.sg
Internet: www.rp.edu.sg
Founded 2002
Prin. and Chief Exec.: Prof. LOW TECK SENG
Deputy Registrar: SEAN TAY
Library Man.: YEE WAI FUN.

SINGAPORE POLYTECHNIC

500 Dover Rd, Singapore 139651
Telephone: 67751133
Fax: 67806189
E-mail: info@sp.edu.sg
Internet: www.sp.edu.sg
Founded 1954
Language of instruction: English
Academic year: April to February (4 terms)
Chair.: TAN KAY YONG
Prin.: TAN HANG CHEONG
Deputy Prin. for Admin.: EDWARD QUAH KOK WAH

Deputy Prin. for Corporate Devt: HEE JOH LIANG
Registrar: TAN PENG ANN
Librarian: FANG SIN GUEK
Library of 266,000 vols, periodicals and multimedia and 60,000 electronic resources
Number of teachers: 857
Number of students: 17,443 (15,523 full-time, 1,920 part-time)
Publications: fullstop (8 a year), inSPire (1 a year), RIOT (1 a year)

DIRECTORS

School of Architecture and the Built Environment: LIM CHER YAM
School of Business: V. MAHEANTHARAN
School of Chemical and Life Sciences: Dr CHAI MIN SEN
School of Communication, Arts and Social Sciences: LAM YOKE
School of Design and the Environment: JEFFREY HO KIAT
School of Electrical and Electronic Engineering: NG WENG LAM
School of Info-communications Technology: TIMOTHY CHAN WAI KUEN
School of Mechanical and Manufacturing Engineering: NG ENG HONG
Singapore Maritime Academy: ROLAND TAN

TEMASEK POLYTECHNIC

21 Tampines Ave 1, Singapore 529757
Telephone: 67882000
Fax: 67898220
E-mail: corpcomm@tp.edu.sg
Internet: www.tp.edu.sg
Founded 1990
Prin. and CEO: BOO KHENG HUA
Registrar: SOH ENG KHIM
Library Dir: ESTHER ONG
Library of 218,000 vols, 1,900 periodicals
Number of teachers: 801
Number of students: 16,005
Publications: In Tempo (4 a year, online), Temasek Journal, T's (2 a year).

Institutes of Technical Education

DIGIPEN INSTITUTE OF TECHNOLOGY—SINGAPORE

PIXEL Bldg, 10 Central Exchange Green, 01-01, Singapore 138649
Telephone: 65771900
Fax: 65771908
E-mail: singapore@digipen.edu
Internet: singapore.digipen.edu
Founded 2008
Private control
Bachelors in arts (game design), fine arts (production animation), science (game design, real-time interactive simulation).

GERMAN INSTITUTE OF SCIENCE AND TECHNOLOGY—TUM ASIA (GIST—TUM ASIA)

10 Central Exchange Green, 03-01, Pixel Bldg, Singapore 138649
Telephone: 67777407
Fax: 67777236
E-mail: admin@gist.edu.sg
Internet: www.gist.edu.sg
Private control
Offers Bachelors and Masters programmes in aerospace engineering, electrical engineering and information technology, industrial chem-

istry, integrated circuit design, microelectronics, transport and logistics; br. of Technische Universität München, Germany

Publication: *GIST—TUM Asia Digest*.

INSTITUTE OF TECHNICAL EDUCATION

10 Dover Dr., Singapore 138683
Telephone: 65902288
Fax: 65902578
E-mail: itehq@ite.edu.sg
Internet: www.ite.edu.sg

Founded 1992 as Post-Secondary Technical Education Institution

State control

3 Colleges: ITE College Central, ITE College East, ITE College West; courses in applied and health sciences, automotive engineering, business and services, design and media, electronics and info-comm technology, engineering, machine technology

Chair.: BOB TAN BENG HAI
Deputy Chair.: HENG CHIANG GNEE
Dir and CEO: BRUCE POH GEOK HUAT

Publications: *ignITE* (2 a year), *iLink*, *infinITE*, *Transforming Lives—The ITE Story*.

Schools of Art and Music

LASALLE College of the Arts: 1 McNally St, Singapore 187940; tel. 64965000; fax 64965353; e-mail enquiries@lasalle.edu.sg; internet www.lasalle.edu.sg; f. 1984 as St Patrick's Arts Centre, present status 2004, present name and location 2007; attached to LASALLE Foundation Limited; design, fine art, media, performing arts; 2,300 students; Pres. Prof. ALASTAIR PEARCE; Provost and Chief Academic Officer VENKA PURUSHOTHAMAN; Chair. PETER SEAH.

Nanyang Academy of Fine Arts: 80 Bencoolen St, Singapore 189655; tel. 65124000; fax 63373920; e-mail president@nafa.edu.sg; internet www.nafa.edu.sg; f. 1938 as Nanyang Fine Arts College, present name 1990; offers diploma, Bachelors and Masters degrees; depts of 3D design, arts management and education, dance, design and media, fashion studies, fine art, music, theatre; library: 80,000 vols of books and journals; 2,200 students; Chair. Prof. CHAM TAO SOON; Vice-Chair. POH CHOON ANN; Vice-Chair. Prof. PHUA KOK KHOO; Pres. CHOO THIAM SIEW; Vice-Pres. LIEW CHIN CHOY.

New York University Tisch School of Arts Asia: 3 Kay Siang Rd, Singapore 248923; tel. 65001700; fax 65001719; e-mail tisch.asia@nyu.edu; internet www.tischasia.nyu.edu.sg; f. 2007; offers Masters degree in animation and digital arts, dramatic writing, film production; Dean and Chair. MARY SCHMIDT CAMPBELL; Artistic Dir OLIVER STONE; Pres. PARI SARA SHIRAZI; Chair. of Graduate Dept of Dramatic Writing RICHARD WESLEY; Chair. of Graduate Dept of Film DAVID K. IRVING; Exec. Dir ANNIE STANTON; Exec. Dir GERARD I. BUENO; Dir of Admin. JASON SETH BECKERMAN; Dir for Graduate Dept of Animation and Digital Arts JEAN-MARC GAUTHIER; Dir of Public Affairs and Marketing TIMOTHY TAN.

Colleges

ESSEC Business School: 100 Victoria St, 13-02, Nat. Library Bldg, Singapore; tel. 68849780; fax 68849781; e-mail mailtaxe@nullessec.fr; internet www.essec.edu; f. 2006; offers Bachelors, Masters and PhD; courses in business administration, finance and asset management, financial techniques, hospitality management, information systems and telecommunication networks, international business law and management, international food industry management, international luxury brand management, international supply chain management, logistics and supply chain management, management, management of technological projects, marketing management, strategy and management of international business, urban environmental and services management, executive MBA, executive education; Dean JEAN-MARC XUEREB.

INSEAD: 1 Ayer Rajah Ave, Singapore 138676; tel. 67995388; fax 67995399; internet www.insead.edu; f. 2000; offers MBA, Exec. MBA, PhD programmes; Dean FRANK BROWN.

S. P. Jain Center of Management: 10 Hyderabad Rd, off Alexandra Rd, Singapore 119579; tel. 62704748; fax 68385406; e-mail admissionssg@spjain.org; internet www.spjain.org; f. 2006; banking and international finance, business strategy, communications, economics, entrepreneurship, financial management, human resource management, information technology management, international business, international management, leadership, logistics, marketing management, mergers and acquisitions, operations management, organizational behaviour, portfolio management, quantitative methods, services management, supply chain management; Head Prof. SUBBARAMAN IYER; Dean Dr MICHAEL J. BARNES; Deputy Dean Dr PARVINDER ARORA; Dean for Global Bachelor of Business Admin. Programme Dr DAWN DEKLE.

The University of Chicago Booth School of Business: 101 Penang Rd, Singapore 238466; tel. 68356482; fax 68356483; e-mail asia.inquiries@chicagobooth.edu; internet www.chicagobooth.edu; f. 2000; offers Exec. MBA programmes; Dean (vacant); publ. *Chicago Booth Magazine* (3 a year).

William F. Harrah College of Hotel Administration: 100 Victoria St, Nat. Library Bldg 11–02, Singapore 188064; tel. 63329538; fax 63329531; e-mail admissions@unlv.edu.sg; internet www.unlv.edu.sg; f. 2006; attached to Univ.of Nevada, Las Vegas, USA; Dean STUART H. MANN.

SLOVAKIA

The Higher Education System

Many of Slovakia's higher education institutions predate the foundation of the former Czechoslovakia in 1918, with the oldest being the Univerzita Komenského v Bratislave (Comenius University in Bratislava—founded 1465). The next oldest university is the Univerzita Pavla Jozefa Šafárika v Košiciach (Šafárik University of Košice—the history of which can be traced back to the foundation of Academia Cassoviensis by Benedikt Kishdy, Bishop of Eger, in 1657). In 1990, following the removal of the communist Government which had been in power since 1948, Czechoslovakia was replaced by the Czech and Slovak Federative Republic (CzSFR). In turn, the CzSFR was dissolved in 1993 and the Czech Republic and Slovakia became independent sovereign states. In addition to the universities, higher education is offered by academies of art, military and police academies, technical universities, universities of economics and universities of pedagogy. In 2009 there were 33 institutions of higher education, with a total enrolment of 144,018 students. There has been a marked increase in the number of postgraduate students in recent years; in 2008/09 there were 10,417 Slovak and 754 foreign students studying for a PhD in Slovakia.

Higher education is administered according to the Higher Education Act (No. 172) of 1990; following ratification of later legislation in 2002, Slovakia now participates in the Bologna Process to establish a European Higher Education Area, the first phase of which is to adopt a credit-based system of comparable degrees with two main cycles (undergraduate and postgraduate). Since 2005/06 the use of European Credit Transfer and Accumulation System (ECTS) has been obligatory in all higher education institutions, although some had already begun the implementation before then. Since 2008/09 Diploma Supplements have been issued automatically to all graduates. The Accreditation Commission of the Slovak Republic is an independent agency that advises the Government and monitors the quality of higher education in Slovakia through evaluation, accreditation and recognition of quality assurance systems, institutions and study programmes. At 2011 there was no official national qualifications framework in place.

The Vysvedcenie o Maturitnej Skúške (Secondary School Leaving Certificate) is the main requirement for admission to higher education; additionally, many institutions administer entrance examinations. The Bakalár (Bachelors) is the undergraduate degree and is awarded after three or four years' study, depending on the subject. Graduates holding the Bakalár are eligible for admission to the first postgraduate degree, the Magister (Masters) or Inzinier (Engineer), which lasts between one and three years. Doctoral-level studies last at least three years, require submission of a dissertation and lead to the award of the Doktor (Doctorate).

Regulatory and Representative Bodies

GOVERNMENT

Ministry of Culture: nám. SNP 33, 813 31 Bratislava; tel. (2) 59-39-11-55; fax (2) 59-39-11-74; e-mail mksr@culture.gov.sk; internet www.culture.gov.sk; Minister Mgr MAREK MAĎARIČ; State Secs Mgr IVAN SEČÍK, Dr AUGUSTÍN JOZEF LANG.

Ministry of Education: Stromová 1, 813 30 Bratislava; tel. (2) 59-37-41-11; fax (2) 59-37-43-35; e-mail kancmin@minedu.sk; internet www.minedu.sk; Minister Prof. Ing. JÁN MIKOLAJ; State Secs Mgr BIBIÁNA OBRIM-ČÁKOVÁ, Dr Ing. JOZEF HABÁNIK.

ACCREDITATION

Akreditačná komisia (Accreditation Commission): Stromová 1, 813 30 Bratislava; tel. (2) 59-23-81-19; fax (2) 59-23-81-18; e-mail contact@akredkom.sk; internet www .akredkom.sk; f. 1990; ind. body set up to monitor and evaluate the quality of education, research and other activities in Slovak univs; 21 mems; Chair. Prof. PAVOL NÁVRAT.

ENIC/NARIC Slovakia: Centre for the Recognition of Diplomas, Ministry of Education, Stromová 1, 813 30 Bratislava 1; tel. (2) 59-23-81-21; fax (2) 59-23-81-24; e-mail naric@minedu.sk; Dir Prof. PETER PLAVCAN.

NATIONAL BODIES

Slovenská akademická asociácia pre medzinárodnú spoluprácu (Slovak Academic Association for International Co-operation): Staré grunty 52, 842 44 Bratislava 4; tel. (2) 65-42-43-83; fax (2) 65-42-44-83; e-mail tajomnik@saaic.sk; internet www .saaic.sk/saaic/eng; f. 1992; ind. NGO providing information to univs and other instns about participation in educational and research activities through int. programmes; Pres. Doc. PhDr JANA LENGHARDTOVÁ.

Slovenská akademická informačná agentúra (Slovak Academic Information Agency): Nám. slobody 23, 812 20 Bratislava 1; tel. (2) 54-41-14-26; fax (2) 54-41-14-29; e-mail saia@saia.sk; internet www.saia.sk; f. 1990; ind. NGO assisting in internationalization of education and research in Slovakia; supports the mobility of students, university teachers and researchers from public and private research orgs; nat. scholarship programme; Chair. PhDr HELENA WOLEKOVÁ; Exec. Dir KATARÍNA KOŠŤÁLOVÁ.

Slovenská rektorská konferencia (Slovak Rectors' Conference): Inštitút Slovenskej rektorskej konferencie, Konventná 1, 812 02 Bratislava; tel. (2) 57-29-45-21; fax (2) 57-29-45-22; e-mail srk@srk.sk; internet www.srk .sk; f. 1993; Pres. Prof. Dr LIBOR VOZÁR; Gen. Sec. Ing. DENISA VOKÁROVÁ.

Learned Societies

GENERAL

Slovenská Akadémia Vied (Slovak Academy of Sciences): Štefánikova 49, 814 38 Bratislava; tel. (2) 52-49-56-34; fax (2) 52-44-49-28; internet www.savba.sk; f. 1953; depts of exact and technical sciences, natural sciences and chemistry, social sciences; attached research institutes: see Research Institutes; library: see Libraries and Archives; Pres. STEFAN LUBY; publs *Acta Hydrologica* (2 a year), *Acta Montanistica Slovaca* (4 a year), *Acta Physica Slovaca* (6 a year), *Acta Virologica* (4 a year), *Architektúra a urbanizmus* (4 a year), *ARS* (3 a year), *Asian and African Studies* (2 a year), *Biologia* (6 a year), *Building Research Journal* (4 a year), *Computing and Informatics* (6 a year), *Contributions of the Astronomical Observatory Skalnaté Pleso* (4 a year), *Contributions to Geodesy and Geophysics* (4 a year), *Časopis pre Politické Vedy* (2 a year), *Človek a Spoločnosť* (e-journal), *Ekológia* (4 a year), *Ekonomický časopis* (10 a year), *Endocrine Regulations* (4 a year), *Entomological Problems* (6 a year), *Filozofia* (10 a year), *Folia Œcologica* (2 a year), *General Physiology and Biophysics* (4 a year), *Geografický časopis* (4 a year), *Geographia Slovaca* (1–2 a year), *Geologica Carpathica* (6 a year), *Geologica Carpatica Clays* (2 a year), *Helminthologia* (4 a year), *Historický časopis* (4 a year), *Human Affairs* (2 a year), *Chemical Papers* (6 a year), *Jazykovedný časopis* (2 a year), *Journal of Electrical Engineering* (12 a year), *Journal of Hydrology and Hydromechanics* (4 a year), *Kovové materiály* (6 a year), *Kultúra slova* (6 a year), *Mathematica Slovaca* (5 a year), *Neoplasma* (6 a year), *Organon F* (4 a year), *Power Metallurgy Progress* (4 a year), *Právny obzor* (6 a year), *Slavica Slovaca* (2 a year), *Slovak Review* (2 a year), *Slovenská archeológia* (2 a year), *Slovenská literatúra* (6 a year), *Slovenská reč* (6 a year), *Slovenské divadlo* (4 a year), *Slovenské štúdie* (2 a year), *Slovenský národopis* (4 a year), *Sociológia* (6 a year), *Studia Psychologica* (4 a year), *Systematische Musikwissenschaften* (2 a year), *Tatra Mountains—Mathematical Publications* (3 a year), *Zivotné prostredie* (6 a year).

AGRICULTURE, FISHERIES AND VETERINARY SCIENCE

Slovenská spoločnosť pre polnohospodárske, lesnícke a potravinárske vedy (Slovak Society for Agriculture, Forestry and Food): Radlinskeho 9, 812 37 Bratislava; tel. (2) 52-92-60-55; fax (2) 52-49-31-89; f. 1968; 564 mems; Pres. Prof. Dr A. DANDAR; Sec. Assoc. Prof. Dr M. TAKÁCSOVA.

ARCHITECTURE AND TOWN PLANNING

Spolok architektov Slovenska (Slovak Architects' Society): Panská 15, 811 01 Bratislava; tel. (2) 54-43-14-31; fax (2) 54-43-57-44; e-mail sas@euroweb.sk; internet www.archinet.sk; 1,900 mems; library of 2,700 vols; Pres. Prof. Dr Ing. Arch. ŠTEFAN SLACHTA; Dir Dr FRANTIŠEK KYSELICA; publs *Projekt* (review of Slovak architecture, 6 a year), *Fórum architektúry* (12 a year).

EDUCATION

Slovenská pedagogická spoločnost' (Slovak Education Society): Filozofická fakulta UPJŠ, 080 01 Prešov; internet www.ucm.sk/ff/slovensky/sps; f. 1965; 365 mems; Pres. Prof. Mgr LADISLAV MACHÁČEK; Sec. Doc. PhDr JÁN DANEK.

FINE AND PERFORMING ARTS

Slovenská výtvarná únia (Slovak Union for the Visual Arts): Dostojevskeho rad 2, 811 09 Bratislava; tel. (2) 52-96-24-02; e-mail svu@svu.sk; internet www.svu.sk; f. 1990; 1,800 mems; Pres. PAVOL KRAL; publs *Profil*, *Výtvarný život*.

HISTORY, GEOGRAPHY AND ARCHAEOLOGY

Slovenská archeologická spoločnost' (Slovak Archaeological Society): Akademická 2, 949 21 Nitra; tel. (37) 733-57-38; fax (37) 733-56-18; e-mail nrauklku@savba.savka.sk; f. 1956; 300 mems; library of 860 vols; Pres. Dr JAN RAJTÁR; Sec. Dr KLÁRA KUZMOVÁ; publs *Bibliografia Slovensky Archeologie* (irregular), *Informator* (2 a year).

Slovenská geografická spoločnost' pri Slovenskej akadémii vied (Slovak Geographical Society at the Slovak Academy of Sciences): Štefánikova 49, 814 73 Bratislava; tel. (2) 57-51-02-09; e-mail geognovo@savba.sk; internet www.sgs.sav.sk; f. 1945; 250 mems; Pres. Prof. RENÉ MATLOVIČ; Treas. Dr JÁN NOVOTNÝ; Sec. FRANTIŠEK KRIŽAN.

Slovenská historická spoločnost' pri SAV (Slovak Historical Society): Klemensova 19, 813 64 Bratislava 1; tel. (2) 52-92-57-53; fax (2) 52-96-16-45; e-mail viliam.cicaj@savba.sk; internet www.shs.sav.sk; f. 1946; sections devoted to modern history, economic history, urban history, military history, gender studies, literature, history of religion; regional divisions in Trenčín, Topolčany, Košice, Banská Bystrica and Prešov; 280 mems; Pres. PhDr VILIAM ČICAJ; Sec. PhDr KATARÍNA HRADSKÁ.

LANGUAGE AND LITERATURE

Alliance Française: 812 83 Bratislava 1, Palais Kutscherfeld, Sedlarska 7, POB 152; tel. (2) 59-34-77-77; fax (2) 59-34-77-05; internet slovaquie.alliance.free.fr; offers courses and exams in French language and culture and promotes cultural exchange with France; Dir JEAN-PIERRE MEULLENET.

British Council: 814 99 Bratislava, Panská 17, POB 68; tel. (2) 54-43-10-74; fax (2) 54-43-47-05; e-mail info.bratislava@britishcouncil.sk; internet www.britishcouncil.org/slovakia; teaching centre; offers courses and exams in English language and British culture and promotes cultural exchange with the UK; attached centres in Banská Bystrica and Košice; Dir HUW JONES.

Goethe-Institut: Panenská 33, 814 82 Bratislava; tel. (2) 54-43-31-30; fax (2) 54-43-31-34; e-mail info@bratislava.goethe.org; internet www.goethe.de/bratislava; offers courses and exams in German language and culture and promotes cultural exchange with Germany; library of 12,500 vols; Dir Dr WOLFGANG FRANZ.

Slovenská jazykovedná spoločnost' (Slovak Linguistics Society): Panská 26, 813 64 Bratislava; tel. (2) 54-33-17-61; fax (2) 54-33-17-56; e-mail mirod@juls.savba.sk; f. 1957; 266 mems; Pres. Prof. PhDr MIROSLAV DUDOK; Sec. Mgr GABRIELA MÚCSKOVÁ; publs *Spisy SJS, Varia, Zápisník slovenského jazykovedca.*

Spoločnost' učitelov nemeckého jazyka a germanistov Slovenska (SUNG) (Verband der Deutschlehrer und Germanisten der Slowakei/Union of German Teachers and Germanists of Slovakia): Tomášikova 4, POB 14, 820 09 Bratislava 29; tel. (2) 43-42-22-53; fax (2) 48-20-94-28; internet www.sung.sk; f. 1991 as the successor organization to Krúžok moderných filológov (Union of Modern Philology); Pres. Prof. Dr HELENA HANULJAKOVÁ; Gen. Sec. NADEŽDA ZEMANÍKOVÁ; publs *Begegnungen* (1 or 2 a year), *Zeitschrift für Germanistische Sprach-Literaturwissenschaft in der Slowakei*, *Zeitschrift Mosaik* (1 a year).

Spolok slovenských spisovatel'ov (Slovak Writers' Society): Laurinská 2, 815 84 Bratislava 1; tel. (2) 54-41-86-70; fax (2) 54-43-53-71; e-mail spolspis@stonline.sk; f. 1923; 350 mems; Pres. Mgr art. PAVOL JANÍK; Sec. JOZEF ZAVARSKÝ; publs *Dotyky* (literature by young writers), *Literárny týždenník* (Literary Weekly).

MEDICINE

Slovenská parazitologická spoločnost' (Slovak Society for Parasitology): Hlinkova 3, 040 01 Košice; tel. (55) 633-44-55; fax (55) 633-14-14; e-mail pausav@saske.sk; internet www.saske.sk/~pauwww/helminth.htm; f. 1993; 92 mems; Pres. Prof. Dr P. DUBINSKÝ; Sec. Prof. Dr V. LETKOVÁ; publ. *Správy slovenskej parazitologickej spoločnosti* (irregular).

NATURAL SCIENCES

General

Rada vedeckých spoločností (Council of Scientific Societies): Štefánikova 49, 814 38 Bratislava; tel. (2) 52-49-61-48; fax (2) 52-49-61-48; f. 1990; 45 Slovak mem. socs; Pres. Dr Dipl. Ing. JAN KNOPP.

Biological Sciences

Slovenská biologická spoločnost' (Slovak Biological Society): Sasinkova 4, 811 08 Bratislava; f. 1967; 180 mems; Pres. Asst Prof. Dr IGOR M. TOMO; publ. *Bulletin* (2 a year).

Slovenská botanická spoločnost' pri SAV (Slovak Botanical Society): Botanický ústav SAV, Dúbravská cesta 9, 841 01 Bratislava 4; fax (2) 54-77-19-48; e-mail pavol.mereda@savba.sk; internet www.sbs.sav.sk; f. 1955; attached to Slovac Acad. of Sciences; 390 mems; Pres. MILAN VALACHOVIČ; Sec. Dr PAVOL MEREDA.

Slovenská ekologická spoločnost' (Slovak Ecological Society): c/o Institute of Botany, Dúbravská cesta 14, 845 23 Bratislava; tel. (25) 477-35-07; fax (25) 477-19-48; e-mail viera.vitekova@savba.sk; internet ibot.sav.sk; f. 1992; 192 mems; Pres. Prof. Ing. IVAN VOLOŠČUK; Sec. Ing. BRANISLAV OLAH; publs *Ekologické Štúdie* (Ecological Studies, 1 a year), *SEKOS Bulletin* (2 a year).

Slovenská entomologická spoločnost' (Slovak Entomology Society): c/o Dept of Zoology, Univerzita Komenského, Mlynská dolina, 842 15 Bratislava 4; tel. (2) 60-29-62-49; internet www.ses.sav.sk; f. 1957; 235 mems; Pres. Dr STANISLAV KALUZ; Sec. Dr LADISLAV ROLLER; publs *Entomofauna carpathica* (4 a year), *Entomological Problems* (2 a year).

Slovenská spoločnost' pre biochémiu a molekulárnu biológiu (Slovak Society for Biochemistry and Molecular Biology): Vlárska 3, 833 06 Bratislava 3; internet www.ssbmb.sav.sk; f. 1959; 220 mems; Pres. Dr JÁN TURŇA; Sec. Ing. Dr ALBERT BREIER.

Slovenská zoologická spoločnost' pri SAV (Slovak Zoological Society): Mlynská dolina B-2, 842 15 Bratislava; tel. (2) 60-29-66-80; e-mail talka@zoznam.sk; internet www.szs.sav.sk; f. 1956; 200 mems; Pres. Mgr JÁN KAUTMAN; Sec. Dr LUCIA KRŠKOVÁ; publ. *Správy Slovenskej zoologickej spoločnosti* (1 a year).

Mathematical Sciences

Jednota slovenských matematikov a fyzikov (Union of Slovak Mathematicians and Physicists): Faculty of Mathematics, Physics and Informatics, Univerzita Komenského, Mlynská dolina F2, 842 48 Bratislava; tel. (2) 60-29-51-111; fax (2) 65-41-23-05; e-mail sd@fmph.uniba.sk; internet www.fmph.uniba.sk/index.php?id=1743; f. 1969; 1,500 mems; Pres. Assoc. Prof. MARTIN KALINA; Sec. Dr MAREK HYČKO; publ. *Obzory matematiky, fyziky a informatiky* (4 a year).

Physical Sciences

Slovenská astronomická spoločnost' (Slovak Astronomical Society): 059 60 Tatranská Lomnica; tel. (52) 787-91-48; fax (52) 446-76-56; e-mail sas@ta3.sk; internet www.ta3.sk/sas; f. 1959; 160 mems; Pres. RNDr JURAJ ZVERKO; Sec. RNDr LADISLAV HRIC.

Slovenská chemická spoločnost' (Slovak Chemical Society): Radlinského 9, 812 37 Bratislava; tel. (2) 59-32-52-99; fax (2) 52-49-52-05; e-mail schs@chtf.stuba.sk; internet www.schems.sk; f. 1929; 874 mems; Pres. Dr MILAN DRÁBIK; Sec. Dr DALMA GYEPESOVÁ; publ. *Chemti* (2 a year).

Slovenská geologická spoločnost' (Slovak Geological Society): Mlynská dolina 1, 817 04 Bratislava; tel. (2) 59-37-53-78; fax (2) 54-19-40; e-mail ladislav.simon@geology.sk; internet dionysos.gssr.sk/sgs; f. 1965; 300 mems; Pres. Dr L. SIMON; Sec. Dr Z. NEMETH; publ. *Mineralia slovaca* (4 a year).

Slovenská meteorologická spoločnost' (Slovak Meteorological Society): c/o Slovenský hydrometeorologický ústav, Jeséniova 17, 833 15 Bratislava; tel. (2) 54-77-20-04; fax (2) 54-77-20-34; f. 1960; 175 mems; Pres. PAVEL ŠT'ASTNÝ; Sec. MARIAN OSTROŽLÍK.

PHILOSOPHY AND PSYCHOLOGY

Slovenské filozofické združenie (Slovak Philosophical Association): Klemensova 19, 813 64 Bratislava; tel. (2) 52-92-64-48; fax (2) 52-92-12-15; e-mail sfz@sfz.sk; internet www.sfz.sk; f. 1990; 292 mems; Pres. Mgr Dr SLAVOMÍR GÁLIK; Sec. Mgr PhDr ERIKA LALÍKOVÁ.

RELIGION, SOCIOLOGY AND ANTHROPOLOGY

Národopisná spoločnost' Slovenska (Slovak Ethnography Society): Klemensova 19, 813 64 Bratislava; tel. and fax (2) 52-96-47-07; e-mail nss@savba.sk; internet net.sav.sk/nss; f. 1958; 250 mems; Chair. Dr HANA HLOSKOVA; Scientific Sec. Dr KATANRA NOVAKOVA; publ. *Etnologické rozpravy* (Ethnological Review, 2 a year).

Slovenská antropologická spoločnost' (Slovak Anthropological Society): Mlynská dolina B2, 842 15 Bratislava; e-mail benus@fns.uniba.sk; f. 1965; 117 mems; Pres. Doc. MILAN THURZO; Sec. EVA NESCAKOVA; Sec. SILVIA BODORIKOVA; Treas. Doc. RADOSLAV BENUS; publ. *Slovenska Antropologia*.

Slovenská orientalistická spoločnosť' (Slovak Society for Oriental Studies): Klemensova 19, 813 64 Bratislava; tel. (2) 52-92-63-26; fax (2) 52-92-63-26; e-mail koholla@klemens.savba.sk; f. 1960; 42 mems; Pres. Doc. Dr KAROL SORBY; Sec. Dr GABRIEL PIRICKÝ; publs *Asian and African Studies* (2 a year), *Human Affairs* (2 a year).

Slovenská sociologická spoločnosť' (Slovak Sociological Association): Klemensova 19, 813 64 Bratislava; tel. (2) 52-96-43-55; fax (2) 52-96-23-15; e-mail bednarik@sspr.gov.sk; internet www.sociologia.eu.sk; f. 1964; 270 mems; Pres. Dr RASTISLAV BEDNÁRIK; Scientific Sec. Dr MARGITA MINICHOVÁ; publs *Sociologicky Zapisník* (4 a year), *Spravodajca SSS* (2 a year).

TECHNOLOGY

Slovenská spoločnosť' pre mechaniku (Slovak Society for Mechanics): Dúbravská cesta 9, 845 03 Bratislava; tel. (2) 54-78-86-62; fax (2) 54-77-35-48; e-mail usarslad@savba.sk; internet mppserv.utc.sk; f. 1967; 252 mems; Pres. Dr J. SLADEK; Sec. Ing. O. IVANKOVA.

Research Institutes

ARCHITECTURE AND TOWN PLANNING

Institute of Construction and Architecture: Dúbravská cesta 9, 845 03 Bratislava; tel. and fax (2) 54-77-35-48; e-mail usarslad@savba.sk; f. 1953; attached to Slovak Acad. of Sciences; Dir Dr JAN SLADEK; publs *Architektura a urbanizmus* (4 a year), *Building Research Journal* (4 a year).

ECONOMICS, LAW AND POLITICS

Ekonomický ústav SAV (Institute of Economic Research): Šancova 56, 811 05 Bratislava; tel. (2) 52-49-82-14; fax (2) 52-49-51-06; e-mail milan.sikula@savba.sk; internet www.ekonom.sav.sk; f. 1953; attached to Slovak Acad. of Sciences; library of 32,000 vols, 1,400 periodicals; Dir Prof. Ing. Dr MILAN ŠIKULA; publ. *Ekonomický Časopis* (Journal of Economics, 10 a year).

Institute of Political Science: Dúbravská cesta 9, 813 64 Bratislava; tel. (2) 54-78-97-24; fax (2) 54-78-97-26; internet nic.savba.sk/sav/inst/poli; f. 1990; attached to Slovak Acad. of Sciences; Dirs PhDr JOZEF JABLONICKÝ, PhDr MIROSLAV PEKNÍK; publ. *Politické vedy* (Political Sciences, 4 a year).

Institute of State and Law: Klemensova 19, 813 64 Bratislava; tel. (2) 52-96-18-33; fax (2) 52-96-23-25; e-mail usap@klemens.savba.sk; internet klemens.savba.sk/usap; f. 1953; attached to Slovak Acad. of Sciences; Dir JUDr EDUARD BARÁNY; publ. *Právny odbor* (6 a year).

Prognostický ústav Slovenskej Akadémie Vied (Institute for Forecasting of the Slovak Academy of Sciences): Sancova 56, 811 05 Bratislava; tel. (2) 52-49-51-14; fax (2) 52-49-50-29; e-mail progasis@savba.sk; internet www.prog.sav.sk; f. 1989; attached to Slovak Acad. of Sciences; behavioural economy, physical and space planning, prognostics environmental economy; Dir Ing. Dr EDITA NEMCOVÁ; Deputy Dir Dr Mgr TATIANA KLUVÁNKOVÁ-ORAVSKÁ; Scientific Sec. Dr Ing. VIERA GAJOVÁ; publs *Ekonomický časopis/Economic Magazin*, *Prognostické práce/Forecasting Papers*.

EDUCATION

Ústav informácií a prognóz školstva (Institute of Information and Prognoses of Education): Staré grunty 52, 842 44 Brati-slava 4; tel. (2) 69-29-51-01; fax (2) 65-42-61-80; e-mail uips@uips.sk; internet www.uips.sk; f. 1976; library of 4,691 vols; Dir ROMAN BARANOVIČ; Librarian VIEROSLAVA CHUDIKOVÁ; publs *Academia* (4 a year), *Mládež a spoločnosť'* (Youth and Society, 4 a year), *Informatika v škole* (Informatics in Education, 2 a year), *Prevencia* (Prevention, 4 a year).

FINE AND PERFORMING ARTS

Institute of Art History: Dúbravská cesta 9, 841 04 Bratislava; tel. and fax (2) 54-79-38-95; e-mail dejusekr@savba.sk; internet www.dejum.sav.sk; f. 1953 as Dept for Theory and History of Art of the Institute of History of the Slovak Acad. of Sciences, present name 1990; attached to Slovak Acad. of Sciences; researches into history of Slovak art and architecture since Middle Ages; Dir Dr IVAN GERÁT; Sec. ERIKA OKRUHLICOVA; publ. *ARS* (2 a year).

Institute of Musicology: Dúbravská cesta 9, 841 04 Bratislava; tel. and fax (2) 54-77-35-89; e-mail musicology@savba.sk; internet www.uhv.sav.sk; f. 1943; attached to Slovak Acad. of Sciences; Dir Prof. PhDr ArtD JURAJ LEXMANN; publs *Musicologica Slovaca et Europaea* (irregular), *Ethnomusicologicum* (irregular).

Institute of Theatre and Film (Kabinet divadla a filmu SAV): Dúbravská cesta 9, 841 04 Bratislava; tel. (2) 54-77-71-93; fax (2) 54-77-35-67; internet www.kadf.sav.sk; f. 1953; attached to Slovak Acad. of Sciences; Dir PhDr MILOŠ MISTRIK; publ. *Slovenské divadlo* (4 a year).

HISTORY, GEOGRAPHY AND ARCHAEOLOGY

Institute of Archaeology: Akademická 2, 949 21 Nitra; tel. (37) 733-56-17; fax (37) 733-56-18; e-mail nraurut@savba.sk; internet www.sav.sk; attached to Slovak Acad. of Sciences; Dir Prof. PhDr ALEXANDER RUTTKAY; publs *AVANS* (1 a year), *Slovenská archeológia* (2 a year), *Študijné zvesti AÚ SAV* (6 a year), *Východoslovenský pravek* (irregular), *Slovenská numizmatika* (jtly with Nat. Numismatic Cttee, every 2 years).

Institute of Geography: Štefánikova 49, 814 73 Bratislava; tel. (2) 57-51-01-87; fax (2) 52-49-13-40; e-mail geogsekr@savba.sk; internet www.geography.sav.sk; f. 1943; attached to Slovak Acad. of Sciences; basic and strategic applied research in human geography, regional geography, physical geography and geoinformatics; library of 15,570 vols, 118 series of journals; Dir Prof. Dr VLADIMÍR IRA; publs *Geografický časopis* (Geographical Journal, 4 a year), *Geographia Slovaca* (1 a year), *Geomorphologia Slovaca et Bohemica* (2 a year).

Institute of Historical Studies: Klemensova 19, 813 64 Bratislava; tel. (2) 52-92-63-21; fax (2) 52-96-16-45; e-mail histor@klemens.savba.sk; internet klemens.savba.sk/husav/prac.htm; f. 1942; attached to Slovak Acad. of Sciences; library of 75,000 vols; Dir PhDr VALERIAN BYSTRICKÝ; publs *Forum Historiae* (www.forumhistoriae.sk; 2 a year), *Historický časopis* (Journal of History, 4 a year), *Historické štúdie* (Historical Studies, 1 a year), *Human Affairs* (2 a year), *Slovanské štúdie* (Slavonic Studies, 2 a year), *Studia Historica Slovaca* (1 a year), *Z dejín vied a techniky* (Studies in the History of Science and Technology, 1 a year).

LANGUAGE AND LITERATURE

Institute of Slovak Literature: Konventná 13, 813 64 Bratislava; tel. and fax (2) 54-41-60-25; e-mail usllnada@savba.sk; internet www.uslit.sav.sk; f. 1943; attached to Slovak Acad. of Sciences; library of 50,000 vols; Dir Doc. PhDr JELENA PASTEKOVA; Sec. Doc. PhDr NADEŽDA BUGÁROVÁ; publ. *Slovenská literatúra* (6 a year).

Institute of World Literature: Konventná 13, 813 64 Bratislava; tel. (2) 54-41-33-91; fax (2) 54-43-19-95; e-mail usvlust@savba.sk; internet www.usvl.sav.sk; f. 1991; attached to Slovak Acad. of Sciences; basic research of phenomena and processes of world literature in these major fields: developmental tendencies of modern literary movements, theoretical and methodological questions of general literary process, history of literary translation in Slovakia, theoretical and methodological questions of translation, interdisciplinary research of major cultural epochs; 29 mems; library of 52,866 vols; Dir ADAM BŽOCH; publs *Slovak Review of World Literature Research* (2 a year), *World Literature Studies* (4 a year).

Ľudovít Štúr Institute of Linguistics: Panská 26, 813 64 Bratislava; tel. (2) 54-43-17-61; fax (2) 54-43-17-56; e-mail slavo@juls.savba.sk; f. 1943; attached to Slovak Acad. of Sciences; library of 22,000 vols; Dir PhDr SLAVO ONDREJOVIČ; publs *Jazykovedný časopis* (2 a year), *Kultúra slova* (6 a year), *Slovenská reč* (6 a year).

MEDICINE

Cancer Research Institute: Vlárska 7, 833 91 Bratislava; tel. (2) 59-32-72-46; fax (2) 59-32-72-50; e-mail exonalt@savba.sk; internet www.exon.sav.sk; f. 1946; attached to Slovak Acad. of Sciences; cancer genetics, carcinogenesis, molecular oncology, tumor immunology, stem cells chemoprevention; Dir Dr JAN SEDLAK; Scientific Sec. Dr ALENA GABELOVA; publ. *Neoplasma* (6 a year).

Institute of Experimental Endocrinology: Vlárska 3, 833 06 Bratislava; tel. (2) 54-77-28-00; fax (2) 54-77-42-47; e-mail ueenregu@savba.sk; internet www.elis.sk; f. 1969; attached to Slovak Acad. of Sciences; Dir RNDr RICHARD KVETŇANSKÝ; publ. *Endocrine Regulations* (4 a year).

Institute of Experimental Pharmacology: Dúbravská cesta 9, 842 16 Bratislava; tel. (2) 54-77-35-86; fax (2) 54-77-59-28; e-mail exfastol@savba.sk; internet nic.savba.sk/sav/insl/exfa/index.html; f. 1969; attached to Slovak Acad. of Sciences; Scientific Sec. Ing. MÁRIA DURIŠOVÁ.

Institute for Heart Research: Dúbravská cesta 9, 842 33 Bratislava; tel. (2) 54-77-44-05; fax (2) 54-77-66-37; e-mail usrdsekr@savba.sk; internet www.usrd.sav.sk; attached to Slovak Acad. of Sciences; Dir Dr JAN STYK; Scientific Sec. Dr MIROSLAV BARANČÍK.

Institute of Neurobiology: Šoltésovej 4, 040 01 Košice; tel. (55) 678-50-69; fax (55) 678-50-74; internet www.saske.sk/inb; f. 1977; attached to Slovak Acad. of Sciences; Dir Dr IVO VANICKÝ.

Institute of Normal and Pathological Physiology: Sienkiewiczova 1, 813 71 Bratislava; tel. (2) 52-92-66-18; fax (2) 52-96-85-16; e-mail postmast@unpf.savba.sk; internet nic.savba.sk/sav/inst/unpf/index.html; f. 1953; attached to Slovak Acad. of Sciences; Dir MUDr FEDOR JAGLA.

Institute of Parasitology: Hlinkova 3, 040 01 Košice; tel. (55) 633-44-55; fax (55) 633-14-14; e-mail pausav@saske.sk; internet www.saske.sk/~pauwww/helminth.htm; f. 1953; attached to Slovak Acad. of Sciences; library of 8,000 vols; Dir Assoc. Prof. Dr B. PEŤKO; publ. *Helminthologia* (4 a year).

Institute of Virology: Dúbravská cesta 9, 842 46 Bratislava; tel. (2) 54-77-42-68; fax (2)

54-77-42-84; e-mail virufcem@savba.savba
.sk; internet www.nic.savba.sk/sav/ins/viru;
f. 1953; attached to Slovak Acad. of Sciences;
Dir Doc. MUDr FEDOR ČIAMPOR; publ. *Acta
Virologia* (6 a year).

NATURAL SCIENCES

Biological Sciences

**Institute of Animal Biochemistry and
Genetics:** Moyzesova 61, 900 28 Ivanka pri
Dunaji; tel. (2) 45-94-30-52; fax (2) 45-94-39-
23; e-mail greksak@ubgz.savba.sk; f. 1990;
attached to Slovak Acad. of Sciences; Dir Doc.
RNDr MILOSLAV GREKSÁK.

Institute of Animal Physiology: Šoltésovej 4, 040 01 Košice; tel. (55) 728-78-41;
fax (55) 728-78-42; e-mail ufhzsav@saske.sk;
internet www2.saske.sk/iap; f. 1964;
attached to Slovak Acad. of Sciences; Dir
MVDr JURAJ KOPPEL.

Institute of Botany S. A. S.: Dúbravská
cesta 9, 845 23 Bratislava; tel. (2) 59-42-61-
11; fax (2) 54-77-19-48; e-mail botuinst@
savba.sk; internet ibot.sav.sk; f. 1953 by
merger of the Laboratory of Geobotany and
Floristics and Laboratory of Plant Biology;
attached to Slovak Acad. of Sciences; strategic and applied research in biological and
ecological sciences; nat. nature protection
and environment management; library of
22,500 vols; Dir IVAN JAROLÍMEK; publ. *Biologia* (6 a year).

**Institute of Experimental Phytopathol-
ogy and Entomology:** Nádražná 52, 900 28
Ivanka pri Dunaji; tel. (2) 45-94-33-31; fax (2)
45-94-34-31; internet nic.savba.sk/sav/inst/
uefe/informatclip.htm; f. 1953; attached to
Slovak Acad. of Sciences; Dir Doc. Ing. ANTON
JANITOR; publ. *Entomological Problems* (2 a
year).

Institute of Forest Ecology: Štúrova 2,
960 53 Zvolen; tel. (45) 533-09-14; fax (45)
547-94-85; internet www.savzv.sk; f. 1983;
attached to Slovak Acad. of Sciences; Dir
Prof. Ing. JOZEF VAĽKA; publ. *Folia Oecolo-
gica*.

Institute of Landscape Ecology: Štefánikova 3, POB 254, 814 99 Bratislava; tel.
(2) 52-49-38-82; fax (2) 52-49-45-08; e-mail
director@uke.savba.sk; attached to Slovak
Acad. of Sciences; Dir Ing. JÚLIUS OSZLÁNYI;
publs *Ecology* (4 a year), *Životné postredie* (6
a year).

Institute of Molecular Biology:
Dúbravská cesta 9, 842 51 Bratislava; tel.
(2) 59-30-74-11; fax (2) 59-30-74-16; internet
imb.savba.sk; f. 1976; incorporated Institute
of Microbiology 2000; attached to Slovak
Acad. of Sciences; Dir Prof. Ing. Dr JOZEF
TIMKO; Scientific Sec. RNDr GABRIELA
BUKOVSKA; publ. *Biologia*.

**Institute of Molecular Physiology and
Genetics:** Vlárska 5, 833 34 Bratislava; tel.
(2) 54-77-52-66; fax (2) 54-77-36-66; e-mail
usrdtylo@savba.savba.sk; internet nic.savba
.sk/sav/inst/umfg; f. 1990; attached to Slovak
Acad. of Sciences; library of 1,000 vols; Dir
Dr ALBERT BREIER; publ. *General Physiology
and Biophysics* (4 a year).

**Institute of Plant Genetics and Biotech-
nology:** Akademická 2, POB 39A, 950 07
Nitra; tel. (37) 733-66-59; fax (37) 733-66-60;
internet pribina.savba.sk/ugbr/sk; f. 1990;
present name 1998; attached to Slovak
Acad. of Sciences; research activities are
focused on plant reproduction and breeding,
as well as molecular biology and biotechnology of plant processes; Dir Dr JÁN SALAJ;
Scientific Sec. ILDIKÓ MATUŠÍKOVÁ.

Institute of Zoology: Dúbravská cesta 9,
842 06 Bratislava; tel. (2) 59-30-26-01; fax (2)
59-30-26-46; internet www.zoo.sav.sk;
attached to Slovak Acad. of Sciences; Dir

RNDr MILAN LABUDA; publs *Biologia* (6 a
year), *Entomological Problems* (2 a year).

Mathematical Sciences

Institute of Mathematics: ul. Štefánikova
49, 814 73 Bratislava; tel. (2) 57-51-04-14; fax
(2) 52-49-73-16; internet www.mat.savba.sk;
f. 1959; attached to Slovak Acad. of Sciences;
research in mathematics, applied mathematics, computer science; undergraduate and
graduate studies; cooperation with home
and foreign scientific and research instns;
publishing of scientific journals and books;
scientific information providing for the institutes and citizens of Slovakia; cooperation
with univs and supporting education on
univs; science popularization; brs in Košice,
Banská Bystrica; library of 25,589 vols; Dir
Prof. RNDr ANATOLIJ DVUREČENSKIJ; Scientific Sec. KAROL NEMOGA; publs *Mathematica
Slovaca* (6 a year), *Tatra Mountains Mathematical Publications*, *Uniform Distribution
Theory*.

Physical Sciences

Astronomical Institute: Slovak Acad. of
Sciences, 059 60 Tatranská Lomnica; tel. (52)
787-91-11; fax (52) 446-76-56; e-mail
astrinst@astro.sk; internet www.astro.sk; f.
1943; attached to Slovak Acad. of Sciences;
astronomical and astrophysical research,
incl. sun, interplanetary matter, star systems, exoplanets; library of 9,280 vols, 6,040
vols of periodicals; Dir ALEŠ KUČERA;
Deputy Dir Assoc. Prof. JÁN SVOREŇ; Scientific Sec. Dr DRAHOMÍR CHOCHOL; publ. *Contributions of the Skalnaté Pleso Observatory*
(2 a year).

Institute of Chemistry: Dúbravská cesta 9,
845 38 Bratislava; tel. (2) 54-77-20-80; fax (2)
59-41-02-22; e-mail chemsekr@savba.sk;
internet chem.sav.sk; f. 1953; attached to
Slovak Acad. of Sciences; Dir Dr JÁN HIRSCH;
publ. *Chemical Papers* (6 a year).

Institute of Experimental Physics: Watsonova 47, 040 41 Košice; tel. (55) 792-22-01;
fax (55) 633-62-92; e-mail sekr@saske.sk;
internet www.saske.sk/uef/index.php; f.
1969; attached to Slovak Acad. of Sciences;
research into the fields of sub-nuclear physics, condensed-matter physics, space physics,
theoretical physics and biophysics; Dir Doc.
RNDr PETER KOPČANSKÝ.

Institute of Geology: Dúbravská cesta 9,
842 26 Bratislava; tel. (2) 54-77-39-41; fax (2)
54-77-70-97; e-mail geolinst@savba.savba.sk;
internet nic.savba.sk/sav/inst/geol/index
.html; f. 1952; attached to Slovak Acad. of
Sciences; Dir Dr JOZEF MICHALÍK; publ.
Geologica Carpathica (6 a year).

Institute of Geophysics: Dúbravská cesta
9, 845 28 Bratislava; tel. (2) 59-41-06-26; fax
(2) 59-41-06-26; e-mail geoflabi@savba.sk;
internet gpi.savba.sk; f. 1953; attached to
Slovak Acad. of Sciences; Dir Dr IGOR TUNYI;
publ. *Contributions to Geophysics and Geodesy* (4 a year).

Institute of Geotechnics: Watsonova 45,
043 53 Košice; tel. (55) 633-40-49; fax (55)
632-34-02; e-mail ugtsekr@saske.sk; f. 1957;
attached to Slovak Acad. of Sciences; Dir Dr
VITÁZOSLAV KRÚPA.

Institute of Hydrology: Račianska 75, 831
02 Bratislava 3; tel. and fax (2) 44-25-94-04;
e-mail supervisor@uh.savba.sk; internet
www.ih.savba.sk; f. 1955 as Water Management Laboratory; present name 1989;
attached to Slovak Acad. of Sciences; Dir Dr
V. STEKAUEROVA; publ. *Journal of Hydrology
and Hydromechanics* (produced jtly with the
Institute of Hydrodynamics of the Academy
of Sciences of the Czech Republic, 6 a year).

Institute of Inorganic Chemistry:
Dúbravská cesta 9, 845 36 Bratislava; tel.

(2) 59-41-04-01; fax (2) 59-41-04-44; e-mail
uachsekr@savba.sk; internet www.uach.sav
.sk; f. 1953; attached to Slovak Acad. of
Sciences; Dir Prof. PAVOL ŠAJGALÍK; Sec.
ZDENA KAPISINSKA.

Institute of Materials Research: Watsonova 47, 040 01 Košice; tel. (55) 792-24-02;
fax (55) 792-24-08; internet www.imr.saske
.sk; f. 1955; attached to Slovak Acad. of
Sciences; develops new materials and technologies; conducts research on the nature of
transformations and transport processes that
occur within the structures of materials of
varying chemical character (metals, ceramics, plastics, etc.) and internal composition
(crystalline, amorphous, composite, etc.); also
conducts research on the mechanical and
physical properties of materials; Dir Dr
PETER SEVC; Deputy Dir JÁN MIHALIK; Scientific Sec. Dr KAREL SAKSL; publs *Kovové
materiály* (online (www.kovmat.sav.sk)),
Powder Metallurgy Progress (online
(www.imr.saske.sk/pmp/index.htm)), *Acta
Metallurgica Slovaca* (online (www.ams.tu-
ke.sk)).

Institute of Measurement Science:
Dúbravská cesta 9, 841 04 Bratislava; tel.
(2) 54-77-40-33; fax (2) 54-77-59-43; e-mail
umersekr@savba.sk; internet www.um.savba
.sk; f. 1953; attached to Slovak Acad. of
Sciences; scientific depts: optoelectronic
measuring methods, magnetometry, theoretical methods, imaging methods, biomeasurements; 76 mems; library of 8,000 vols;
Dir Assoc. Prof. MILAN TYSLER; Scientific
Board Chair. Assoc. Prof. VIKTOR WITKOVSKY;
publ. *Measurement Science Review* (online
(www.measurement.sk)).

Institute of Physics: Dúbravská cesta 9,
845 11 Bratislava; tel. (2) 59-41-05-00; fax (2)
54-77-60-85; e-mail fyzihaso@nic.savba.sk;
internet www.fu.sav.sk; f. 1955; attached to
Slovak Acad. of Sciences; Dir Prof. Ing. IVAN
STICH; publ. *Acta Physica Slovaca* (6 a year).

Institute of Polymer Research:
Dúbravská cesta 9, 842 36 Bratislava; tel.
(2) 54-77-34-48; fax (2) 54-77-59-23; e-mail
upolsekr@savba.sk; internet www.savba.sk/
polymer; f. 1963; attached to Slovak Acad. of
Sciences; Dir RNDr PAVOL HRDLOVIČ.

PHILOSOPHY AND PSYCHOLOGY

Institute of Experimental Psychology:
Dúbravska cesta 9, 813 64 Bratislava; tel. (2)
54-77-56-25; fax (2) 54-77-55-84; e-mail ida
.prokopcakova@savba.sk; internet www
.psychologia.sav.sk; f. 1955; attached to Slovak Acad. of Sciences; Dir Prof. Dr VIERA
BAČOVÁ; publ. *Studia Psychologica* (4 a year).

Institute of Philosophy: Klemensova 19,
813 64 Bratislava; tel. (2) 52-96-15-27; fax (2)
52-92-12-15; e-mail filosekr@savba.sk;
internet sav.sk; f. 1946; attached to Slovak
Acad. of Sciences; Dir Prof. TIBOR PICHLER;
publs *Filozofia* (10 a year), *Organon F* (4 a
year).

RELIGION, SOCIOLOGY AND ANTHROPOLOGY

**Department of Social and Biological
Communication:** Klemensova 19, 813 64
Bratislava; tel. (2) 54-77-56-83; fax (2) 54-77-
34-42; e-mail kvsbk@savba.sk; internet
kvsbk.sav.sk; f. 1990; attached to Slovak
Acad. of Sciences; Dirs Assoc. Prof. PhDr
GABRIEL BIANCHI, Assoc. Prof. PhDr OLGA
ZAPOTOCNA; publs *Human Affairs* (2 a year),
Human Communication Studies (1 a year).

Institute of Ethnology: Klemensova 19,
813 64 Bratislava; tel. (2) 52-96-47-07; fax (2)
52-96-47-07; e-mail gabriela.kilianova@savba
.sk; internet www.uet.sav.sk/en/index.htm; f.
1946; attached to Slovak Acad. of Sciences;

library of 10,000 vols, 63 periodicals; Dir Dr GABRIELA KILIÁNOVÁ; publs *Etnologické rozpravy* (2 a year), *Slovenský národopis* (5 a year).

Institute of Oriental Studies: Klemensova 19, 813 64 Bratislava; tel. (2) 52-92-63-26; fax (2) 52-92-63-26; e-mail kaoreast@savba.sk; internet www.orient.sav.sk; f. 1960; attached to Slovak Acad. of Sciences; history, linguistics, literature, religion, ethnography, philosophy; library of 14,008 vols; Dir Dr DUŠAN MAGDOLEN; publ. *Asian and African Studies* (2 a year).

Institute of Social Sciences: Karpatská 5, 040 00 Košice; tel. (55) 625-58-56; fax (55) 625-58-56; e-mail gajdosm@saske.sk; f. 1975; attached to Slovak Acad. of Sciences; library of 7,000 vols; Dir Dr MARIÁN GAJDOŠ; publ. *International Journal of Transdisciplinary Studies* (4 a year).

Institute of Sociology: Klemensova 19, 813 64 Bratislava; tel. (2) 52-96-43-55; fax (2) 52-96-23-15; e-mail sociolog@savba.sk; internet www.sociologia.sav.sk; f. 1990; attached to Slovak Acad. of Sciences; Dir Dr ROBERT KLOBUCKÝ; publ. *Sociológia—Slovak Sociological Review* (6 a year, in Slovak and English).

TECHNOLOGY

Institute of Electrical Engineering: Dúbravská cesta 9, 842 39 Bratislava; tel. (2) 54-77-58-06; fax (2) 54-77-58-16; e-mail elusav@savba.sk; internet www.elu.sav.sk; f. 1963; attached to Slovak Acad. of Sciences; Dir Dr KAROL FROHLICH; publ. *Journal of Electrical Engineering* (12 a year).

Institute of Informatics: Dúbravská cesta 9, 845 07 Bratislava; tel. (2) 54-77-10-04; fax (2) 54-77-10-04; e-mail upsysekr@savba.sk; internet www.ui.sav.sk; f. 1991; attached to Slovak Acad. of Sciences; research and education in informatics, nano- and micro-technology, cybernetics; Dir Dr LADISLAV HLUCHÝ; publ. *Computing and Informatics* (6 a year).

Institute of Materials and Machine Mechanics: Račianska 75, 831 02 Bratislava 3; tel. (2) 44-25-47-51; fax (2) 44-25-33-01; e-mail ummjerz@savba.sk; internet www .immm.sav.sk; f. 1980; attached to Slovak Acad. of Sciences; library of 13,000 vols; Dir Dr FRANTIŠEK SIMANČÍK; publs *Kovové materiály* (Metallic Materials, 6 a year), *Strojnícky časopis* (Journal of Mechanical Engineering, 6 a year).

Transport Research Institute, Inc.: Veľký Diel 3323, 010 08 Žilina; tel. (41) 565-28-19; fax (41) 565-28-83; e-mail management@vud.sk; internet www.vud.sk; f. 1954; Man. Dir Ing. LUBOMIR PALČÁK; publ. *Horizonty dopravy* (4 a year).

Vúje Trnava Inc.: Okružná 5, 918 64 Trnava; tel. (33) 599-13-56; fax (33) 599-11-93; e-mail vuje@vuje.sk; internet www.vuje .sk; f. 1977; library: of 23,000 items; engineering design and research; Man. Dir Ing. MATEJ KOREC; publ. *Spravodajca VÚJE* (1 a year).

Libraries and Archives
Banská Bystrica
Štátna vedecká knižnica (State Scientific Library): Lazovná 9, POB 205, 975 58 Banská Bystrica; tel. (48) 415-51-11; fax (48) 412-40-96; e-mail svkbb@svkbb.sk; internet www.svkbb.sk; f. 1924; 2m. vols; Dir Mgr Dr OĽGA LAUKOVÁ.

Bratislava
Archív hlavného mesta SR Bratislavy (Archives of the Capital of the Slovak Repub-

lic, Bratislava): Markova 1, 850 05 Bratislava; POB 40, 850 05 Bratislava; tel. (2) 54-43-32-48; fax (2) 54-43-08-48; e-mail archiv@ samb.vs.sk; f. 13th century (archives); 1923 (library); attached to Min. of Interior; 95,000 vols; Dir Dr ANNA BUZINKAYOVÁ.

Centrum vedecko-technických informácií Slovenskej republiky (Slovak Centre for Scientific and Technical Information): Nám. Slobody 19, 812 23 Bratislava; tel. (2) 36-24-19; fax (2) 32-35-27; e-mail cvti@cvtisr .sk; internet www.cvtisr.sk; f. 1938; 362,000 books, 144,000 vols of periodicals, 28,000 trade publs, 239,000 patents, 90,000 standards; Dir ULRICH KOLOMAN; publs *Bulletin Centra VTI SR* (4 a year), *Euro-Info* (10 a year), *Infotrend* (4 a year), *Signálne informácie* (12 a year).

Mestská knižnica Bratislava (Bratislava Municipal Library): Klariská 16, 814 79 Bratislava; tel. (2) 54-43-32-44; fax (2) 54-43-51-48; e-mail bratislava@mestskakniznica .sk; internet www.mestskakniznica.sk; f. 1900; 310,000 vols; Dir PhDr ELENA VEĽASOVÁ.

Slovenská ekonomická knižnica Ekonomickej univerzity v Bratislave (Slovak Economic Library): Dolnozemská cesta 1/a, 852 35 Bratislava; tel. (2) 67-29-14-14; fax (2) 67-29-11-61; e-mail sek@sekba.euba.sk; internet www.sek.euba.sk; f. 1948, present name 1993; specialized material in field of economic sciences and interdisciplinary sciences; 364,757 vols, 297 periodicals; Dir JITKA KMEŤOVÁ.

Slovenská pedagogická knižnica (Slovak Education Library): Hálova 16, 851 01 Bratislava 5; tel. (2) 62-41-09-92; fax (2) 62-41-09-92; e-mail postmast@spgk.sk; internet www.spgk.sk; f. 1956; 296,000 vols; Dir PhDr HELENA PANGRÁCOVÁ.

Univerzitná knižnica v Bratislave (University Library of Bratislava): Michalská 1, 814 17 Bratislava 1; tel. (2) 59-80-42-22; fax (2) 54-43-42-46; e-mail ukb@ulib.sk; internet www.ulib.sk; f. 1919; 2.4m. vols; Dir PhDr TIBOR TRGIŇA.

Ústredná knižnica Slovenskej akadémie vied (Central Library of the Slovak Academy of Sciences): Klemensova 19, 814 67 Bratislava; tel. (2) 52-92-17-33; fax (2) 52-92-17-33; e-mail andrea.doktorova@savba.sk; internet www.uk.sav.sk; f. 1953; 520,000 vols; Dir Mgr ANDREA DOKTOROVÁ.

Košice
Štátna vedecká knižnica (State Scientific Library): Hlavná 10, 042 30 Košice; tel. (55) 622-67-24; fax (55) 622-23-31; e-mail svkk@ ke.sanet.sk; f. 1657; 3.4m. vols; Dir Mgr DANIELA DŽUGANOVÁ; publs *Zoznam zahraničných časopisov objednaných na východné Slovensko* (1 a year), *Súpis bibliografií a rešerší vypracovaných v SVK Košice* (1 a year).

Verejná knižnica Jána Bocatia (Ján Bocatius Public Library): Hlavná 48, 042 61 Košice; tel. (55) 622-32-91; fax (55) 622-32-92; f. 1924; 476,000 vols; Dir Dr KLÁRA KERNEROVÁ.

Martin
Matica slovenská (Slovak National Library): Nám. J. C. Hronskeho 1, 036 52 Martin; tel. (43) 430-18-03; fax (43) 430-18-02; e-mail snk@snk.sk; internet www.snk.sk; f. 1863; 4.5m. vols; literary archives and museum documents, and complete Slovak printed production; Dir Dr DUŠAN KATUŠEÁK; publs *Biografické štúdie* (1 a year), *Genealogicko-heraldický hlas* (2 a year), *Inventar rukopisov ALÚ MS* (1 a year), *Knižnica* (Library, 12 a year), *Slovenská národná*

bibliografia (CD-ROM, 4 a year; print, 1 a year).

Nitra
Slovenská poľnohospodárska knižnica (Slovak Agricultural Library): Štúrova 51, 949 59 Nitra; tel. (37) 641-50-37; fax (37) 651-77-43; e-mail slpk@uniag.sk; internet www .slpk.sk; f. 1946; 525,000 vols; Dir Mgr Dr BEÁTA BELLÉROVÁ.

Prešov
Štátna vedecká (State Scientific Library): Hlavná ul. 99, 081 89 Prešov; tel. (51) 772-49-60; fax (51) 772-49-60; e-mail kniznica@svkpo .sk; internet www.svkpo.sk; f. 1952; 450,000 vols; Dir PhDr ANNA HUDÁKOVÁ.

Zvolen
Slovenská lesnícka a drevárska knižnica (Slovak Library for Forestry and Wood Technology): Masarykova 20, 961 02 Zvolen; tel. (45) 520-66-41; fax (45) 547-99-42; e-mail sldk@sldk.tuzvo.sk; internet sldk.tuzvo.sk; f. 1952; attached to the Technical Univ. in Zvolen; 360,000 vols; Dir Ing. ALENA POLÁČIKOVÁ; publs *Bibliography of the Technical University in Zvolen* (1 a year), *Ecology Bulletin* (6 a year), *Forestry Bulletin* (12 a year), *Wood Sciences Bulletin* (12 a year).

Museums and Art Galleries
Banská Bystrica
Múzeum Slovenského národného povstania (Slovak National Uprising Museum): Kapitulská č. 23, 974 00 Banská Bystrica; tel. (48) 415-20-70; fax (48) 412-37-16; e-mail muzeumsnp@isternet.sk; internet www .muzeumsnp.sk; f. 1955; anti-fascist struggle of the Slovak people during the Second World War; library of 17,000 vols; Dir Dr JÁN STANISLAV.

Stredoslovenské múzeum (Central Slovakia Museum): Nám. Slovenského národného povstania 4, 974 00 Banská Bystrica; tel. (48) 412-58-97; fax (48) 415-50-77; e-mail smbb@ stonline.sk; internet www .stredoslovenskemuzeum.sk; f. 1889; natural sciences, history, ethnography; library of 12,000 vols; Dir Dr ZUZANA DRUGOVÁ; publs *Katalog chladných zbraní*, *Katalog fajky a fajčiarske potreby*, *Stredné Slovensko* (1 a year).

Banská Štiavnica
Slovenské banské múzeum (Slovak Mining Museum): Kammerhofská 2, 969 01 Banská Štiavnica; tel. (45) 694-94-22; e-mail sbm@muzeumbs.sk; internet www .muzeumbs.sk; f. 1900; library of 21,000 vols; Dir Dr JOZEF LABUDA; publ. *Zborník SBM* (bulletin).

Bratislava
Galéria mesta Bratislavy (Municipal Gallery of Bratislava): Mirbachov palác, Františkánske nám. 11, 815 35 Bratislava; tel. (2) 54-43-51-02; fax (2) 54-43-26-11; e-mail gmb@gmb.sk; internet www.gmb.sk; f. 1961; Slovak and Central European art; library of 12,000 vols; Dir Dr IVAN JANČÁR.

Mestské muzeum v Bratislave (Bratislava City Museum): Primaciálne nám. 3, 815 18 Bratislava; tel. (2) 54-43-47-42; fax (2) 54-43-46-31; e-mail mmba@bratislava.sk; f. 1868; archaeology, history, art history, applied arts, numismatics, history of pharmacy, ethnography; library of 21,000 vols; Dir PhDr PETER HYROSS.

Slovenská národná galéria (Slovak National Gallery): Riečna 1, 815 13 Bratislava; tel. (2) 20-47-60-81; fax (2) 20-47-63-97; e-mail info@sng.sk; internet www.sng.sk; f. 1948; art, applied art; library of 100,710 vols, 80,000 documents; Dir-Gen. Dr ALEXANDRA KUSÁ.

Slovenské národné múzeum (Slovak National Museum): Vajanského nábrežie č 2, POB 13, 810 06 Bratislava 16; tel. (2) 59-34-91-11; fax (2) 52-92-43-44; e-mail riaditel@snm.sk; internet www.snm.sk; f. 1893; history, natural history, art, archaeology; Dir PhDr PETER MARÁKY; publs *História* (1 a year), *Prírodné vedy* (1 a year), *Etnografia* (1 a year), *Archeológia* (1 a year), *Annotationes Zoologicae et Botanicae, Pamiatky a múzeá* (Cultural Heritage Review, 4 a year), *Múzeum* (guidance for museum and art gallery workers, 4 a year).

Košice

Východoslovenské múzeum (Museum of Eastern Slovakiá): Hviezdoslavová 3, 041 36 Košice; tel. (55) 622-03-09; fax (55) 622-86-96; f. 1872; history, natural sciences, art, ethnography; library of 53,000 vols; Dir PhDr RÓBERT POLLÁK; publs *Historica Carpatica* (1 a year), *Natura Carpatica* (1 a year).

Kremnica

NBS—Múzeum mincí a medailí (National Bank of Slovakia—Museum of Coins and Medals): Štefánikovo nám. 11/21, 967 01 Kremnica; tel. (45) 678-03-01; fax (45) 674-21-21; e-mail muzeum@nbs.sk; internet www .nbs.sk/en/museum-of-coins-and-medals; f. 1890; Dir MARIANA NOVOTNÁ.

Piešťany

Balneologické múzeum (Museum of Balneology): Beethovenova 5, 921 01 Piešťany; tel. and fax (33) 772-28-75; e-mail krupa .vladimir@zupa-tt.sk; internet www .balneomuzeum.sk; f. 1928; history of Slovak spas, regional history; Dir Dr VLADIMÍR KRUPA.

Svidník

Múzeum ukrajinsko-rusínskej kultúry (Museum of Ukrainian-Ruthenian Culture): Centrálna 258, 089 01 Svidník; tel. (54) 752-13-65; fax (54) 752-15-69; f. 1956; history and culture of the Ukrainians and Ruthenians in Slovakia; library of 44,354 vols; Dir PhDr MIRÓSLAV SOPÓLIGA.

Vojenské historické múzeum (Military Historical Museum): Bardejovská 14, 089 01 Svidník; tel. (54) 752-13-98; f. 1965; history of the military in eastern Slovakia 1914-1945; library of 3,225 vols; Dir Dr JOZEF RODÁK.

Tatranská Lomnica

Múzeum Tatranského národného parku (Tatras National Park Museum): 059 60 Tatranská Lomnica; tel. (52) 446-79-51; fax (52) 446-79-58; e-mail sl@tanap.sk; f. 1957; geology, botany, zoology, natural history; ethnography, history; library of 19,520 vols; Dir Ing. MIKULÁŠ MICHELČIK.

Universities

EKONOMICKÁ UNIVERZITA V BRATISLAVE
(University of Economics in Bratislava)

Dolnozemská cesta 1/B, 852 35 Bratislava 5
Telephone: (2) 62-41-14-78
Fax: (2) 62-24-73-48
E-mail: komunikacia@euba.sk
Internet: www.euba.sk
Founded 1940, became State School 1945

State control
Language of instruction: English, French, German, Slovak
Academic year: September to June,
Rector: Prof. Dr RUDOLF SIVÁK
Vice-Rector: Assoc. Prof. Dr ANETTA ČAPLÁNOVÁ
Vice-Rector: Prof. Dr FERDINAND DAŇO
Vice-Rector: Assoc. Prof. Dr JANA LENGHARTOVÁ
Vice-Rector: Assoc. Prof. Dr JANA MIKOCZIOVÁ
Vice-Rector: Assoc. Prof. Dr ĽUBOMÍR STRIEŠKA
Head of Univ. Admin. and Finance: MÁRIA DZIUROVÁ
Librarian: Dr JITKA KMEŤOVÁ
Number of teachers: 650
Number of students: 11,583

Publications: *Acta oeconomica Cassoviensia* (2 a year), *Almanac: current issues of World Economics and Politics* (2 a year), *Business review* (2 a year), *Economic Review* (4 a year), *Economics and Management* (3 a year), *Economics and Informatics* (2 a year), *Economics of Tourism and Business* (4 a year), *Ekonóm* (5 a year), *International relations*, *Nová ekonomika* (4 a year), *Studia commercialita Bratislavensia* (4 a year)

DEANS

Faculty of Applied Language: Prof. Dr LÍVIA ADAMCOVÁ
Faculty of Business Economics (in Košice): Prof. Dr MICHAL TKÁČ
Faculty of Business Management: Prof. Dr LUBOSLAV SZABO
Faculty of Commerce: Dr ŠTEFAN ŽÁK
Faculty of Economic Informatics: Dr MICHAL FENDEK
Faculty of International Relations: Prof. Dr LUDMILA LIPKOVÁ
Faculty of National Economy: Prof. Dr JÁN LISÝ

KATOLÍCKA UNIVERZITA V RUŽOMBERKU
(Catholic University in Ružomberok)

Nám. Andreja Hlinku 60, 034 01 Ružomberok
Telephone: (44) 431-62-00
Fax: (44) 431-62-07
E-mail: rektorat@ku.sk
Internet: www.ku.sk
Founded 2000
Jt control of Slovak state and the Catholic Church
Language of instruction: Slovak
Rector: Prof. Dr BORIS BANÁRY
Vice-Rectors: Prof. Dr JÁN KURUCZ, Prof. Dr DALIBOR MIKULÁS, Prof. Dr ĽUBOMÍR STANČEK
Librarian: Mag. PETER DVORSKÝ
Library of 17,000 vols
Number of teachers: 300
Number of students: 3,000
Publication: *Disputationes Scientificae Universitatis Catholicae in Ružomberok*

DEANS

Faculty of Health Service: Dr ANTON LACKO
Faculty of Pedagogy: Prof. Dr AMANTIUS AKIMJAK
Faculty of Philosophy: Prof. Dr IMRICH VAŠKO
Faculty of Theology: ANTON KONEČNY

PREŠOVSKÁ UNIVERZITA V PREŠOVE
(University of Prešov)

Ul. 17. novembra 15 080 01 Prešov
Telephone: (51) 756-31-00
Fax: (51) 756-31-43

E-mail: erasmus@unipo.sk
Internet: www.unipo.sk
Founded 1997
State control
Academic year: September to June
Rector: Prof. Dr RENÉ MATLOVIČ
Vice-Rector for Academic Affairs: Prof. Dr MILAN PORTIK
Vice-Rector for Devt: Doc. Ing. PETER ADAMIŠIN
Vice-Rector for Int. Relations: Dr IVANA CIMERMANOVÁ
Vice-Rector for Science and Research: Prof. Dr PETER KÓNYA
Library of 300,000 vols
Number of students: 12,000

DEANS

Faculty of Arts: Prof. Dr VASIL GLUCHMAN
Faculty of Education: Dr JANA BURGEROVÁ
Faculty of Greek Catholic Theology: Prof. Dr PETER STURÁK
Faculty of Health: Dr ANNA ELIAŠOVÁ
Faculty of Humanities and Natural Sciences: Dr NADEŽDA KRAJČOVÁ
Faculty of Orthodox Theology: Prof. JÁN SAFIN

SLOVENSKÁ POĽNOHOSPODÁRSKA UNIVERZITA V NITRE
(Slovak University of Agriculture in Nitra)

Tr. A. Hlinku 2, 949 76 Nitra
Telephone: (37) 641-55-33
Fax: (37) 653-43-93
E-mail: verejnost@uniag.sk
Internet: www.uniag.sk
Founded 1946 as Vysoká Škola Poľnohospodárska; new name c. 1996
Public control
Languages of instruction: Slovak, English
Academic year: September to June
Rector: Prof. Dr Ing. PETER BIELIK
Vice-Rectors: Prof. ZDENKA GÁLOVÁ, Prof. Ing. MARIÁN BRESTIČ, Prof. Dr Ing. ELENA HORSKÁ, Dr Ing. ZUZANA PALKOVÁ
Chancellor: Ing. ANNA BOŽIKOVÁ
Bursar: Dr Ing. OĽGA ROHÁČIKOVÁ

Library: see 'Slovenská poľnohospodárská knižnica', under Libraries and Archives
Number of teachers: 474
Number of students: 10,300

Publications: *Acta fytotechnica et zootechnica* (4 a year), *Acta Horticulturae et regioecturae* (4 a year), *Acta regionalia et enviromentalica* (4 a year), *Acta oeconomica et informatica* (4 a year), *Acta Zootechnica* (1 a year)

DEANS

Faculty of Agricultural Engineering: Assoc. Prof. Dr Ing. ZDENKO TKÁČ
Faculty of Agrobiology and Food Resources: Prof. Dr Ing. DANIEL BÍRO
Faculty of Biotechnology and Food Sciences: Prof. Ing. JÁN TOMÁŠ
Faculty of Economics and Management: Prof. Dr Ing. IVETA ZENTKOVÁ
Faculty of European Studies and Regional Devt: Prof. Dr ANNA BANDLEROVÁ
Faculty of Horticulture and Landscape Engineering: Assoc. Prof. Ing. KAROL KALÚZ

PROFESSORS

Faculty of Agricultural Engineering (tel. (37) 651-32-44; fax (37) 741-70-03; e-mail dekmf@uniag.sk):

BALLA, J., Agricultural Engineering
JECH, J., Technology and Mechanization of Agriculture

LOBOTKA, J., Technology and Mechanization of Agriculture
PÁLTIK, J., Technology and Mechanization of Agriculture
PETRANSKÝ, I., Technology and Mechanization of Agriculture
SEMETKO, J., Technology and Mechanization
ŠESTÁK, J., Technology and Mechanization of Agriculture
ȚOLNAI, R., Agricultural Engineering
ŽIKLA, A., Technology and Mechanization

Faculty of Agronomy (tel. (37) 651-12-44; fax (37) 741-14-51; e-mail dekaf@uniag.sk):

BEŽO, M., Plant Genetics
BULLA, J., Fundamental Zootechnics
FECENKO, J., Special Plant Production
GÁLIK, R., Fundamental Zootechnics
HALAJ, M., Special Zootechnics
HANES, J., Pedology
HOLÚBEK, R., Special Plant Production
KOVÁČ, L., Fundamental Zootechnics
KOVÁČIK, J., General Zootechnics
KÚBEK, A., Fundamental Zootechnics
KULICH, J., Plant Production
LÍŠKA, E., General Plant Production
MICHALÍK, I., Plant Production
MICHALÍKOVÁ, A., Plant Protection
PAJTÁŠ, M., General Zootechnics
PAŠKA, I., Special Zootechnics
PIVKO, J., General Zootechnics
POLÁČEK, S., Plant Production
PRASLIČKA, J., Plant Protection
ŠŤASTNÝ, P., Fundamental Zootechnics

Faculty of Economics and Management (tel. (37) 651-11-51; fax (37) 651-15-89; e-mail dekfem@uniag.sk):

BANDLEROVÁ, A., Economics and Management
BIELIK, P., Food Industry Management
GOZORA, V., Economics and Management
HRONEC, O., Management
HRUBÝ, J., Economics
HUDÁK, J., Sectorial Economics
KABÁT, L., Economics
KUZMA, F., Economics
OKENKA, I., Economics and Management
PODOLÁK, A., Economics
ŘEPKA, I., Economics
ŠIMO, D., Economics
VIŠŇOVSKÝ, J., Economics
ZOBORSKÝ, I. M., Economics

Faculty of Gardening and Landscape Engineering (Ul. Tulipanová 7, 949 76 Nitra; tel. (37) 652-27-41; fax (37) 652-27-41; e-mail dekfzki@uniag.sk):

ANTAL, J., Land Improvement
DEMO, M., Plant Production
HRICOVSKY, I., Plant Production
HRUBÍK, P., Horticulture
HUSKA, D., Land Improvement
MACHOVEC, J., Horticulture
ŠPÁNIK, F., Special Plant Production
STREĎANSKY, J., Land Improvement
SUPUKA, J., Phytopathology
VREŠTIAK, P., Special Plant Production

SLOVENSKÁ TECHNICKÁ UNIVERZITA V BRATISLAVE
(Slovak University of Technology in Bratislava)

Vazovova 5, 812 43 Bratislava
Telephone: (2) 52-49-71-96
Fax: (2) 57-29-43-33
E-mail: rector@stuba.sk
Internet: www.stuba.sk
Founded 1938
State control
Languages of instruction: Slovak, English
Academic year: September to September
Rector: Assoc. Prof. Dr ROBERT REDHAMMER

Vice-Rector for Economy and Devt: Prof. Dr MILAN SOKOL
Vice-Rector for Education: Prof. JÁN KALUŽNÝ
Vice-Rector for Int. Relations: Prof. Dr. MARIÁN PECIAR
Vice-Rector for Science and Research: Prof. Dr STANISLAV BISKUPIČ
Bursar: Ing. HELENA ZIDEKOVA
Librarian: VIERA POLČÍKOVÁ

Number of teachers: 1,170
Number of students: 18,900

Publications: *Almanach Znalca* (in Slovak, 4 a year), *ALFA—Architektonické listy FA STU* (in Slovak with summary in English, 4 a year), *Acta Chimica Slovaca* (in English, 4 a year), *AT & P Journal* (in Slovak with summary in English, 12 a year), *Computing and Informatics* (in English, 4 a year), *EE—Journal for Electrical and Power Engineering* (in Slovak with summary in English, 6 a year), *Formation Sciences and Technologies- Bulletin of the ACM Slovakia* (2–4 a year), *Journal of Electrical Engineering* (in English, 6 a year), *Journal of Cybernetics and Informatics* (e-journal for control community, in English), *Kovové materiály* (in Slovak, 12 a year), *Mathematical Publications* (in English, 2–3 a year), *Scientific Proceedings of FME STU in Bratislava* (in English), *Slovak Journal of Civil Engineering* (in English, 4 a year), *Spektrum-Informative Journal of STU* (in Slovak, 10 a year), *Tatra Mountains*

DEANS

Faculty of Architecture: Assoc. Prof. Ing. Dr LUBICA VITKOVA
Faculty of and Food Technology: Prof. Dr JAN SAJBIDOR
Faculty of Civil Engineering: Prof. Ing. ALOJZ KOPACIK
Faculty of Electrical Engineering and Information Technology: Assoc. Prof. Dr GABRIEL JUHAS
Faculty of Informatics and Information Technology: Prof. Dr LUDOVIT MOLNAR
Faculty of Materials Science and Technology: Prof. Dr Ing. OLIVER MORAVCIK
Faculty of Mechanical Engineering: Prof. Ing. LUBOMIR SOOS

PROFESSORS

Faculty of Architecture:

DULLA, M., Architecture
KEPPL, J., Architecture
KOVÁČ, B., Town Planning
PETELEN, I., Industrial Design
PETRÁNSKY, L'., Theory and History of Art Design
ŠPAČEK, R., Architecture
VODRÁŽKA, P., Architecture

Faculty of Chemical and Food Technology:

BAJUS, M., Fuel Technology
BAKOŠ, D., Macromolecular Chemistry and Engineering
BÁLEŠ, V., Chemical Engineering and Process Control
BOČA, R., Inorganic Chemistry
BOSKUPIČ, S., Physical Chemistry and Chemical Physics
BREZOVA, V., Chemical Physics
BUSTIN, D., Analytical Chemistry
CIK, G., Technology of Macromolecular Substances
FELLNER, P., Technology of Inorganic Chemistry
FIŠERA, L., Organic Chemistry
GRACZA, T., Organic Chemistry
HIVES, J., Technology of Inorganic Chemistry and Materials
HRONEC, M., Organic Technology
KOMAN, M., Inorganic Chemistry
KRUPČÍK, J., Analytical Chemistry

LABUDA, J., Analytical Chemistry
LEHOTAY, J., Analytical Chemistry
LOKAJ, J., Material Engineering
MALÍK, F., Biochemical Technology
MARCHALIN, S., Organic Chemistry
MARKOS, J., Chemical Engineering and Process Control
MESZAROS, A., Chemical Engineering and Process Control
MIKLEŠ, J., Technical Cybernetics
MOCÁK, J., Analytical Chemistry
MRAVEC, D., Organic Technology and Fuel Technology
ŠAJBIDOR, J., Biochemical Technology
SCHMIDT, S., Food Chemistry and Technology
ŠIMA, J., Inorganic Chemistry
ŠIMON, P., Physical Chemistry
STASKO, A., Physical Chemistry
VALACH, F., Physical Chemistry and Chemical Physics
VALKO, L., Physical Chemistry
VARECKA, L., Biochemistry

Faculty of Civil Engineering:

AGÓCS, Z., Steel and Timber Structures
BAJZA, A., Non-Metallic Materials and Construction Materials
BALÁŽ, L., Construction Engineering
BALIAK, F., Construction Engineering
BANÍK, I., Physics
BARTOŠ, P., Geodesy and Cartography
BEDNÁROVÁ, E., Hydraulic Engineering
BETKO, B., Engineering Theory and Construction Engineering
BEZÁK, B., Transport Engineering
BIELEK, M., Building Construction
BILČÍK, J., Construction Engineering
CHMÚRNY, I., Engineering Theory and Construction Engineering
DUŠIČKA, P., Hydraulic Engineering
FILLO, L., Construction Engineering
GAŠPARÍK, J., Construction Technology
GSCHWENDT, I., Transport Engineering
HEFTY, J., Geodesy and Cartography
HRAŠKA, J., Engineering Theory and Construction Engineering
HULLA, J., Geotechnology
KLEPSATEL, F., Building Construction
KOMORNÍKOVÁ, M., Applied Mathematics
KOPÁČIK, A., Geodesy and Cartography
KRIŠ, J., Construction in Health-care Sector
LAPOS, J., Construction Engineering
LOVÍŠEK, J., Mechanics of Solid and Pliable Bodies
MACURA, V., Landscaping
MAJDÚCH, D., Concrete Structures and Bridges
MELICHER, J., Geodesy and Cartography
MESIAR, R., Applied Mathematics
MIKULA, K., Applied Mathematics
MUDRONČÍK, M., Bulding Structures and Architecture
OHRABLO, F., Building Construction
OLÁH, J., Building Construction
PETRÁŠ, D., Engineering Theory and Construction Engineering
PUŠKÁR, A., Engineering Theory and Construction Engineering
RAVINGER, J., Applied Mechanics
ROUSEKOVÁ, I., Non-Metallic Materials and Construction Materials
ŠIRÁŇ, J., Applied Mathematics
SOKOL, M., Applied Mechanics
SOKOL, Š., Geodesy and Cartography
ŠOLTÉSZ, A., Hydraulic Engineering
STANĚK, V., Geodesy and Cartography
ŠUMEC, J., Building Construction
ŠVEDA, M., Non-Metallic Materials and Construction Materials
SZOLGAY, J., Hydrology and Water Management
TOMAŠOVIČ, P., Engineering Theory and Construction Engineering
TURČEK, P., Building Construction

VALÁŠEK, J., Building Construction
ZAJAC, J., Building Construction
ZAPLETAL, I., Technology and Materials Engineering

Faculty of Electrical Engineering and Information Technology:

BALLO, I., Physical Engineering
BAROŇÁK, I., Telecommunication
BOCK, I., Applied Mathematics
BREZA, J., Electronics
CIRÁK, J., Physical Engineering
DONOVAL, D., Electronics
DURAČKOVÁ, D., Electronics
DURNÝ, R., Solid State Physics
FARKAŠ, P., Telecommunication
GROŠEK, O., Applied Informatics
HUBA, M., Automation
JANÍČEK, F., Electrical Energy
JASENEK, J., Theory of Electromagnetism
JURIŠICA, L., Technical Cybernetics
KOVÁČ, J., Electronics
KOZÁK, Š., Automation and Control
MIGLIERINI, M., Solid State Physics
MURGAŠ, J., Cybernetics
MURÍN, J., Applied Mechanics
NEČAS, V., Nuclear Energy
PODHRADSKÝ, P., Telecommunications
POLEC, J., Telecommunications
SITEK, J., Condensed Matter Physics and Acoustics
SLUGEŇ, V., Nuclear Energy
SMIEŠKO, V., Measurement Engineering
SMOLA, A., Electrical Energy
STOPJAKOVÁ, V., Electronics
TVAROŽEK, V., Electronics
UHEREK, F., Electronics
ŽALMAN, M., Automation and Control

Faculty of Informatics and Information Technology:

BIELIKOVA, M., Software Engineering
HORVATH, P., Applied Informatics
KOLESAR, M., Computer Engineering
KVASNICKA, V., Artificial Intelligence
MOLNAR, L., Informatics
NAVRAT, P., Information Systems
POSPICHAL, J., Applied Informatics
SAFARIK, J., Informatics

Faculty of Materials Science and Technology in Trnava:

BAČA, J., Mechanical Engineering Technology
BALOG, K., Occupational Health and Safety
BARÁNEK, I., Production Technologies, Machine Technologies and Materials
BLAŠKOVITŠ, P., Mechanical Engineering Technology
BLEHA, T., Materials
ČAMBÁL, M., Industrial Engineering
ČAUS, A., Production Technologies, Machine Technologies and Materials
CYRUS, P., Teacher Training of Vocational Subjects and Practical Training for Didactics
DRIENSKY, D., Engineering Education
DUSZA, J., Materials
GRGAČ, P., Materials Engineering
HRIVŇÁK, I., Physical Metallurgy and Materials Engineering
HRIVŇÁKOVÁ, D., Physical Metallurgy
HUSAR, P., Automation, Applied Informatics
JAHNÁTEK, L., Industrial Engineering
JANAČ, A., Machinery
JANOVEC, J., Materials
JOEHNK, P., Industrial Engineering
KALUŽNÝ, J., Materials Engineering
KIPS, M., Teacher Training of Vocational Subjects and Practical Training
KOLITSCH, A., Materials
KOŠTURIAK, J., Quality of Production
KOVÁČ, J., Physics
KOZÍK, T., Teacher Training of Vocational Subjects and Practical Training for Didactics

KUPČA, L., Materials
LINCZÉNYI, A., Quality of Production
LIPA, Z., Production Technologies
LOKAJ, J., Materials
MORAVČÍK, O., Applied Information Science and Automation in Industry
MUDRONČÍK, D., Automation and Applied Information Science
MURGAŠ, M., Industrial Engineering
OŽVOLD, M., Materials
PETERKA, J., Production Technologies, Machine Technologies and Materials
POKUSA, A., Production Technologies
RICHTER, V., Automation
SABLIIK, J., Quality of Production
SAKÁL, P., Industrial Engineering
SCHREIBER, P., Automation and Applied Informatics
ŠVRČEK, D., Production Technology
TURŇA, M., Welding and Welding Machines
ULRICH, K., Production Technologies, Machine Technologies and Materials
URBAN, M., Materials
VELÍSEK, K., Production Technology
VRBAN, A., Applied Information Science and Automation

Faculty of Mechanical Engineering:

BENKO, B., Production Technology and Materials
BUKOVECZKY, J., Transportation Machines and Equipments
DEDIK, L., Instrumentation, Informatics and Automation Technology
ELESZTOS, P., Applied Mechanics
GODNAR, E., Production Technology and Materials
GULAN, L., Machines and Equipments for Building, Processing and Agriculture
HAVELSKY, V., Thermal Power Engineering and Environmental Technology
HEKELOVA, E., Production Quality and Technological Systems Safety
HULKO, G., Instrumentation, Informatics and Automation Technology
KRESEK, A., Manufacturing Systems with Industrial Robots and Manipulators
MOLNAR, V., Power Engineering
PALENCAR, R., Instrumentation, Informatics and Automation Technology
PECIAR, M., Machines and Equipment for Chemical and Food Industries
ROHLA-ILKIV, B., Instrumentation, Informatics, Mechatronic and Automation Technology
SKAKALA, J., Instrumentation, Informatics and Automation Technology
SLADEK, J., Applied Mechanics
SOOS, L., Production Machines
STAREL, L., Applied Mechanics
TICHY, J., Transport Technology
TOLNAY, M., Mechanical Engineering Technologies
URBAN, J., Transport Technology
VALCUHA, Š., Construction of Manufacturing Machines
VARCHOLA, M., Hydraulic and Pneumatic Machines and Equipment
VAVRO, K., Power Engineering
VERES, M., Machine Parts and Mechanisms
ZAHOREC, O., Applied Mechanics

Institute of Engineering Studies:

MESZAROS, A., Chemical Engineering and Process Control

Institute of Management:

FINKA, M., Spatial Planning
IVANICKA, K., Management
ROCH, I., Spatial Planning
SCHOLICH, D., Spatial Planning

SLOVENSKÁ ZDRAVOTNÍCKA UNIVERZITA
(Slovak Medical University)

Limbová 12, 883 03 Bratislava
Telephone: (2) 59-37-01-11
E-mail: info@szu.sk
Internet: www.szu.sk

Founded 2002
State control
Language of instruction: Slovak
Rector: Prof. JÁN ŠTENCL
First Pro-Rector and Pro-Rector for Educational Affairs: Prof. Dr DANA FARKAŠOVÁ
Pro-Rector for Int. Relations: Prof. Dr JURAJ ŠVEC
Vice-Rector for Pedagogical and Academic Affairs: Assoc. Prof. Dr JAROSLAV HINŠT
Pro-Rector for Curative and Preventive Activity: Prof. Dr JÁN BREZA
Pro-Rector for Public Relations: Prof. Dr VILIAM FISCHER
Pro-Rector for Research: Assoc. Prof. Dr KATARÍNA ŠEBEKOVÁ
Bursar: Ing. MILAN CAGÁŇ
Librarian: ZUZANA ONDEROVÁ
Library of 19,311 vols, 150 periodicals
Number of teachers: 397
Number of students: 16,535

DEANS

Faculty of Health Care (Banskej Bystrici): Prof. Dr SVETOZÁR DLUHOLUKCÝ
Faculty of Medical Specialization Studies: Prof. TIBOR SAGÁT
Faculty of Nursing and Health Professional Studies: Prof. Dr DANA FARKAŠOVÁ
Faculty of Public Health: Assoc. Prof. ROMAN KOVÁČ

PROFESSORS

Faculty of Health Care:

DLUHOLUCKÝ, S., Paediatrics
KRALINSKÝ, K., Urgent Medical Care

Faculty of Medical Specialization Studies:

BREZA, J., Urology
ČERNÁK, A., Ophthalmology
FISCHER, V., Cardiosurgery
GÚTH, A., Physiology, Balneology, and Medical Rehabilitation
HARUŠTIAK, S., Surgery and Thoracic Surgery
HATALA, R., Cardiology
HOLOMÁŇ, J., Clinical Pharmacology
KOTHAJ, P., Gastroenterological Surgery
KOVÁČ, G., Clinical Biochemistry and Laboratory Medicine
KOZA, I., Clinical Oncology
KRAJČÍK, S., Geriatrics
KRESÁNEK, J., Adolescent Medicine
KRISTÚFEK, P., Functional Diagnostics
KUKUMBERG, P., Neuropsychiatry
LECHTA, V., Logopaedia
LISÝ, L., Neurology
MASARIK, J., Biophysics
PECHAN, J., Surgery
RIEČANSKÝ, I., Cardiology and Angiology
ROVENSKÝ, J., Rheumatology
ŠABÓ, A., Biology
SAGÁT, T., Paediatric Anaesthiology and Intensive Medicine
ŠAKALOVÁ, A., Haematology
ŠEFRÁNEK, V., Vascular Surgery
ŠIMKO, P., Injury-related Surgery
ŠTENCL, J., Obstetrics and Gynaecology
ŠTEŇO, J., Neurosurgery
TÓTH, K., Medical Law
VAVREČKA, A., Gastroenterology
VOJTAŠŠÁK, J., Orthopaedics

Faculty of Nursing and Health Professional Studies:

FARKAŠOVÁ, D., Nursing
MALÝ, M., Physiotherapy
ŠVEC, J., Oncology

Faculty of Public Health:
  ḤEGYI, L., Medical Teaching
  ŠAJTER, V., Theoretical Science
  SULCOVÁ, M., Health in the Workplace

TECHNICKÁ UNIVERZITA V KOŠICIACH
(Technical University of Košice)

Letná 9, 042 00 Košice
Telephone: (55) 602-11-11
Fax: (55) 633-27-48
E-mail: rektor@tuke.sk
Internet: www.tuke.sk

Founded 1952
State control
Languages of instruction: Slovak, English
Academic year: September to August

Rector: Prof. Dr JURAJ SINAY
Vice-Rector for Devt: Prof. Dr DUŠAN MAL-INDŽÁK
Vice-Rector for Education: Assoc. Prof. Dr VLADIMÍR PENJAK
Vice-Rector for Informatics: Prof. Dr ANTON ČIŽMÁR
Vice-Rector for Science, Research and Int. Relations: Prof. Dr KAROL FLÓRIÁN
Questor: Ing. GABRIEL FISCHER
Librarian: Dr VALÉRIA KROKAVCOVÁ
Number of teachers: 850 (820 full-time, 30 part-time)
Number of students: 13,351
Publications: Acta Electrotechnica et Informatica (4 a year), Acta Mechanica Slovaca (4 a year), Acta Metallurgica Slovaca (4 a year), Acta Montanistica Slovaca (4 a year), Halo TU (12 a year)

DEANS

Faculty of Arts: Assoc. Prof. Dr JAROSLAV JAREMA
Faculty of Civil Engineering: Prof. Dr STA-NISLAV KMEŤ
Faculty of Economics: Prof. Dr TOMÁŠ SABOL ŠOLTÉS
Faculty of Electrical Engineering and Informatics: Assoc. Prof. Dr DUŠAN KOCUR
Faculty of Mechanical Engineering: Prof. Dr MIROSLAV BADIDA
Faculty of Metallurgy: Prof. Dr KAREL TOMÁŠEK
Faculty of Mining, Ecology, Control and Geotechnology: Prof. Dr PAVOL RYBÁR
Faculty of Production Technology: Assoc. Prof. Dr SLAVKO PAVLENKO

PROFESSORS

Faculty of Arts (tel. and fax (55) 602-21-77; e-mail dekan.fuu@tuke.sk; internet www.fu.tuke.sk):
  BARTUSZ, J., Fine Art

Faculty of Civil Engineering (Vysokoškolská 4, 042 00 Košice; tel. (55) 633-53-11; fax (55) 623-32-19; e-mail stanislav.kmet@tuke.sk; internet svfweb.tuke.sk):
  HORNIAKOVÁ, L., Theory of Construction of Overground Buildings
  HUDÁK, J., Theory of Construction of Engineering Structures
  JUHÁS, P., Theory of Construction of Engineering Structures
  KMEŤ, S., Theory of Construction of Engineering Structures
  ŠTEVULOVÁ, N., Environmental Studies
  TKÁČOVÁ, K., Mineralogy and Ecotechnology

Faculty of Economics (B. Němcovej 32, 040 01 Košice; tel. and fax (55) 633-09-83; e-mail ekfdec@tuke.sk; internet www.tuke.sk/ekf/ekf.html):
  ŠAMSON, Š., Economic Theory
  ŠOLTÉS, V., Mathematics

Faculty of Electrical Engineering and Informatics (tel. (55) 632-24-83; fax (55) 633-01-15; e-mail dusan.kocur@tuke.sk):
  BANSKÝ, J., Radio Electronics, Electronic Technology
  ČIŽMÁR, A., Electronics and Telecommunications Engineering
  HUDÁK, Š., Computers and Informatics
  JELŠINA, M., Electronic Computers
  KOLCUM, M., Energetics, High Voltage Engineering
  KOVÁČ, D., Energetics, High Voltage Engineering
  KROKAVEC, D., Technology and Automation
  KROKAVEC, M., Computers and Informatics
  LEVICKÝ, D., Radio Electronics
  MADARÁSZ, L., Technical Cybernetics
  MARCHEVSKÝ, S., Electronics and Telecommunications Engineering
  MARTON, K., Energetics, High Voltage Engineering
  MICHAELI, L., Radio Electronics
  MIHALÍK, J., Electronics and Telecommunications Engineering
  SARNOVSKÝ, J., Technical Cybernetics
  SINČÁK, P., Artificial Intelligence
  ŠOMORA, M., Materials Engineering
  ŠPÁNY, V., Radio Electronics
  TIMKO, J., Electrical Engineering
  TURÁN, J., Radio Electronics
  ZBORAY, L., Electrical Engineering

Faculty of Mechanical Engineering (tel. (55) 625-78-25; fax (55) 633-47-38; e-mail miroslav.badida@tuke.sk; internet www.sjf.tuke.sk):
  BADIDA, M., Environmental Protection
  BIGOŠ, P., Construction of Transport Machinery
  ČOP, V., Robots and Manipulators
  HAJDUK, M., Manufacturing Systems with Robots and Manipulators
  HRIVŇÁK, A., Technology of Mechanical Engineering
  IMRIŠ, I., Non-Ferrous Metallurgy
  KAŽIMÍR, I., Technology of Mechanical Engineering
  KLIMO, V., Machine Parts
  KNIEWALD, D., Technology of Mechanical Engineering
  KOVÁČ, J., Automation and Management
  KOVÁČ, M., Robots and Manipulation Devices
  LACHVÁČ, J., Production Machines and Equipment
  LIBERKO, I., Industrial Engineering and Management
  MAJERNÍK, M., Environmental Studies
  POLLÁK, L., Technology of Mechanical Engineering
  RITÓK, Z., Machine Parts
  SALOKY, T., Automation and Control in Mechanical Engineering
  ŠIMŠÍK, D., Automation and Management
  SINAY, J., Transport and Manipulation
  SMRČEK, J., Manufacturing Systems with Robots and Manipulators
  SPIŠÁK, E., Engineering Technology and Materials
  TAKÁČ, K., Technology of Mechanical Engineering
  TREBUŇA, F., Mechanics

Faculty of Metallurgy (tel. (55) 633-18-14; fax (55) 633-70-48; e-mail dhf@hfnov.tuke.sk; internet www.tuke.sk/tu/hf):
  BURŠÁK, M., Physical Metallurgy and Materials Science
  FLÓRIÁN, K., General and Analytical Chemistry
  HAVLIK, T., Non-Ferrous Metallurgy
  HOLOUBEK, D., Thermal Power Engineering
  KRAKOVSKÁ, E., Analytical Chemistry
  KVAČKAJ, T., Ferrous Metallurgy

  LUKÁČ, I., Physical Metallurgy and Materials Science
  MICHEL', J., Materials Science
  MIHOK, L., Ferrous Metallurgy
  STOFKO, M., Non-Ferrous Metallurgy
  TOMÁŠEK, K., Non-Ferrous Metallurgy
  VARGA, A., Thermal Power Engineering
  VIRČÍKOVÁ, E., Non-Ferrous Metallurgy
  ZRNÍK, J., Physical Metallurgy and Materials Science

Faculty of Mining, Ecology, Control and Geotechnology (tel. (55) 633-00-18; fax (55) 633-66-18; e-mail pavol.rybar@tuke.sk; internet www.tuke.sk/fberg):
  BOROŠKA, J., Mining, Mechanization, Transport and Deep Well Drilling
  DOJČÁR, O., Mining
  FABIÁN, J., Mining
  FARYAD, S. W., Mining Geology and Geological Prospecting
  JACKO, S., Geological Prospecting, Geological Engineering
  KOŠTIAL', I., Production Control
  KOSTÚR, K., Control of the Acquiring and Processing of Raw Materials
  KUNÁK, L., Mining Surveying and Geodesy
  LEŠKO, M., Minerals Processing
  MALINDŽÁK, D., Control of Acquiring and Processing of Raw Materials
  PINKA, J., Mining, Mechanization, Transport and Deep Well Drilling
  PODLUBNÝ, I., Control of Acquiring and Processing of Raw Materials
  RYBÁR, P., Mining and Geotechnology
  SASVÁRI, T., Mining Geology and Geological Prospecting
  ŠEKULA, F., Mining
  STROFFEK, E., Mining, Mining Mechanization
  ŠÚTTI, J., Three-Dimensional Geodesy
  VODZINSKÝ, V., Economy and Management
  WEISS, G., Mining Surveying and Geodesy
  ZÁBRANSKÝ, F., Petrology

Faculty of Production Technology (Plzenská 10, 080 01 Prešov; tel. (51) 772-30-12; fax (51) 773-34-53; e-mail pavlenko.slavko@fvt.sk; internet www.tuke.sk/fvtpo):
  NOVÁK-MARCINČIN, P., Production Engineering
  RAGAN, E., Mechanical Technology
  VASILKO, K., Mechanical Technology

TECHNICKÁ UNIVERZITA VO ZVOLENE
(Technical University in Zvolen)

T. G. Masaryka 24, 960 53 Zvolen
Telephone: (45) 520-61-03
Fax: (45) 533-00-27
E-mail: rektor@vsld.tuzvo.sk
Internet: www.tuzvo.sk

Founded 1807, reorganized 1952 as Univ. of Forestry and Wood Technology, renamed 1991
State control
Languages of instruction: Slovak, Czech; for graduate studies, also English, German and Russian
Academic year: September to June

Rector: Prof. Ing. JÁN TUČEK
Vice-Rectors: Assoc. Prof. JURAJ MAHÚT, Assoc. Prof. JÁN ŠIMKO, Prof. ŠTEFAN ŽIHLAVNÍK
Questor: Dr MÁRIA BÍZIKOVÁ
Librarian: Dr LUBICA LUDVIGHOVÁ
Library of 359,000 vols
Number of teachers: 243
Number of students: 2,200
Publications: Acta Facultatis Forestalis (1 a year), Acta Facultatis Xylologiae (1 a year), Proceedings of Research Works of the Faculty of Ecology and Environmental Sci-

ences (1 a year), *Scientific and Pedagogical News* (1 a year)

DEANS

Faculty of Ecology and Environmental Science: Assoc. Prof. Dr IMRICH BESEDA
Faculty of Environmental and Manufacturing Technology: Assoc. Prof. JÁN ZELENÝ
Faculty of Forestry: Assoc. Prof. MILAN HLADÍK
Faculty of Wood Sciences and Technology: Assoc. Prof. MIKULÁŠ ŠUPÍN

PROFESSORS

Faculty of Ecology and Environmental Science:

CHRAPAN, J., Radioecology
KOŠTÁLIK, J., Physical Geography
MIDRIAK, R., Landscape Ecology
MIKLOS, L., Landscape Ecology
SUPUKA, J., Landscape Ecology

Faculty of Environmental and Manufacturing Technology:

DANKO, M., Processes and Technology of Forest Production
MIKLEŠ, M., Processes and Technology of Forest Production

Faculty of Forestry:

BUBLINEC, E., Nature and Environment
GARAJ, P., Forest Protection and Game Management
HLADÍK, M., Forest Management
KODRÍK, J., Forest Protection and Game Management
KOLENKA, I., Forest Economics
PAGAN, J., Silviculture
PAULE, L., Forest Genetics
ŠANIGA, M., Silviculture
ŠMELKO, S., Biometry and Forest Management
VALTÝNI, J., Forest Hydrology—Torrent Control
ŽIHLAVNÍK, S., Geodesy and Photogrammetry

Faculty of Wood Sciences and Technology:

BOROTA, J., Management of Tropical Forests
BUČKO, J., Chemistry and Chemical Technology
DEKRÉT, A., Mathematics
DUBOVSKÁ, R., Metal Processing Technology
HORSKÝ, D., Mechanical Technology of Wood
KURJATKO, S., Wood Science
LIPTÁKOVÁ, E., Wood Products Manufacturing
MARČOK, M., Physics and Applied Mechanics
OSVALD, A., Fire Protection
PETRANSKY, L., Design
RAJČAN, E., Physics and Applied Mechanics
REINPRECHT, L., Wood Technology Engineering
ŠUPÍN, M., Forestry Policy, Trade, Marketing
TREBULA, P., Technology of Wood
VINCÚR, P., Economics

TRENČIANSKA UNIVERZITA ALEXANDRA DUBČEKA
(Alexander Dubček University in Trenčín)

Študentská 2, 911 50 Trenčín
Telephone: (32) 740-01-08
Fax: (32) 740-01-02
E-mail: slabeycius@tnuni.sk
Internet: www.tnuni.sk

Founded 1997
State control
Academic year: September to June

Rector: IVAN KNEPPO

Vice-Rector for Education: Dr ERNEST BROSKA
Vice-Rector for Investment and Devt: Assoc. Prof. IGNÁC PRNO
Vice-Rector for Science, Research and Int. Cooperation: Prof. JURAJ SLABEYCIUS
Vice-Rector for Social Care: Dr ERNEST BROSKA
Chief Librarian: Mgr MÁRIA REHUŠOVÁ
Library of 13,663 vols
Number of teachers: 245
Number of students: 5,393
Publications: *Socialno-ekonomicka Revue* (4 a year), *TnU Trendy* (4 a year)

DEANS

Faculty of Industrial Technology: Assoc. Prof. Dr ONDREJ NEMČOK
Faculty of Mechatronics: Prof. Dr DUŠAN MAGA
Faculty of Social and Economic Relations: Prof. Dr MIROSLAV MEČÁR
Faculty of Special Technologies: Prof. BOHUMIL BÁTORA

PROFESSORS

Faculty of Industrial Technology:

CAPEK, I.
JAMBRICKY, M.
KOPECKY, M.
KOSTIAL, P.
LETKO, I.
MACKO, V.
SLABEYCIUS, J.
STEFANIK, J.
YONA, E.

Faculty of Mechatronics:

BORSC, M.
KNEPPO, I.
KNEPPO, P.
PLANDER, I.
RACEK, V.
TKAC, M.
WAGNER, J.

Faculty of Social and Economic Relations:

ALEXY, J.
BARÁNIK, M.
BARTAK, P.
BENCO, J.
BLAZEJ, A.
CAMPAI, O.
LIPTAK, J.
STRAZOVSKA, H.
VOJTOVIC, S.

Faculty of Special Technologies:

BATORA, B.
DUBOVSKA, R.
VARKOLY, L.

TRNAVSKÁ UNIVERZITA
(Trnava University)

Hornopotočná 23, 918 43 Trnava
Telephone: (33) 593-92-03
Fax: (33) 551-11-29
E-mail: rektor@truni.sk
Internet: www.truni.sk

Founded 1992
State control
Academic year: October to August

Rector: Prof. JUDr PETER BLAHO
Vice-Rector for Academic Affairs: Doc. ThDr ANDREJ FILIPEK
Vice-Rector for Devt and Foreign Relations: Prof. MVDr ALEXANDER SABÓ
Vice-Rector for External Relations and Continuing Education: Doc. PhDr Dr Prof. JANA BÉREŠOVÁ
Vice-Rector for Information Systems and Publishing: Doc. PhDr Dr MILAN KATUNINEC
Vice-Rector for Science and Research: Prof. JUDR. IVAN ŠIMOVČEK
Librarian: Ing. ZUZANA MARTINKOVIČOVÁ

Library of 68,073 books, 241 periodicals
Number of teachers: 350
Number of students: 7,677

DEANS

Faculty of Arts: Doc. PhDr MARTA DOBROTKOVÁ
Faculty of Education: Doc. RNDr PAVEL HÍC
Faculty of Health and Social Work: Prof. MUDr FRANTIŠEK MATEIČKA
Faculty of Law: Prof. JUDr HELENA BARANCOVÁ
Faculty of Theology: Doc. PhDr ThLic. JURAJ DOLINSKÝ

UNIVERZITA J. SELYEHO V KOMÁRNE/SELYE JÁNOS EGYETEM, KOMÁROM
(University of J. Selyeho in Komárno)

Bratislavská cesta 3322, 945 01 Komárno
Telephone: (35) 773-30-73
Fax: (35) 773-30-72
E-mail: info@selyeuni.sk
Internet: www.selyeuni.sk

Founded 2004
State control
Language of instruction: Hungarian

Rector: Dr. JÁNOS TÓTH
Vice-Rector: Dr MELINDA NAGY
Vice-Rector: Dr PETER CSIBA
Vice-Rector: Prof. Ing. VERONIKA STOFFOVA

Library of 150,000 vols, 40 periodicals
Number of teachers: 86
Number of students: 3,000

DEANS

Faculty of Economy: Prof. Dr habil SIKOS T. TAMÁS
Faculty of Pedagogy: Dr MARGITY ERDÉLYI
Faculty of Reformed Theology: Dr JÁNOS MOLNÁR

UNIVERZITA KOMENSKÉHO V BRATISLAVE
(Comenius University in Bratislava)

Šafárikovo nám. 6, 818 06 Bratislava 16
Telephone: (2) 52-92-15-94
Fax: (2) 52-96-38-36
E-mail: kr@rec.uniba.sk
Internet: www.uniba.sk

Founded 1465 as Academia Istropolitana; reopened with present name 1919
State control
Languages of instruction: Slovak, English
Academic year: October to June

Rector: Prof. PhDr FRANTIŠEK GAHÉR
Vice-Rector for Devt: Assoc. Prof. RNDr IVAN OSTROVSKÝ
Vice-Rector for Education: Prof. RNDr PAVEL SŮRA
Vice-Rector for Int. Relations: MUDr PETER OSUSKÝ
Vice-Rector for Legislation and Public Relations: JUDr MÁRIA DURAČINSKÁ
Vice-Rector for Science: Prof. RNDr DUŠAN MLYNARČÍK
Bursar: Ing. ZORA DOBRÍKOVÁ

Number of teachers: 2,092
Number of students: 27,000

Publication: numerous faculty publications

DEANS

Faculty of Education: Prof. RNDr OTO MAJZLAN
Faculty of Law: Assoc. Prof. JUDr MARIÁN VRABKO
Faculty of Management: Prof. RNDr JOZEF KOMORNIK
Faculty of Mathematics, Physics and Informatics: Assoc. Prof. RNDr JÁN BOD'A
Faculty of Medicine in Bratislava: Prof. MUDr PAVEL TRAUBNER

Jessenius Faculty of Medicine in Martin:
Prof. MUDr Ján Danko
Faculty of Natural Sciences: Assoc. Prof.
RNDr Anton Gáplovský
Faculty of Pharmacy: Assoc. Prof. RNDr
Jozef Seginko
Faculty of Philosophy: Assoc. Prof. PhDr
Anton Eliáš
Faculty of Physical Education and Sport:
Assoc. Prof. PedDr Dušan Kutlík
Faculty of Protestant Theology: Prof. ThDr
Igor Kiss
Faculty of Roman Catholic Theology: Prof.
ThDr Viliam Judák
Faculty of Social and Economic Sciences:
Prof. Ing. Ladislav Kabát

PROFESSORS

Faculty of Education (Račianska 59, 813 34
Bratislava; tel. (2) 44-25-49-60; fax (2) 44-25-
49-56; e-mail sd@fedu.uniba.sk; internet
www.fedu.uniba.sk):

Blanár, V., Slovak Language
Čižmár, J., Teaching of Mathematics
Cvrkal, I., Modern Non-Slavonic Phil-
ology, German Literature
Kačala, J., Slovak Language
Kováč, D., Educational Psychology
Kusin, V., Philosophy
Lechta, V., Special Education
Majzlan, O., Ecology
Marčok, V., Theory and History of Slovak
Literature
Mistrík, E., Synthetic Philosophy
Obdržálek, Z., Education
Ondreička, K., Graphics
Pažitka, M., Modern Non-Slavonic Phil-
ology
Pikálek, Š., Social Work
Povchanič, Š., Modern Non-Slavonic Phil-
ology
Požár, L., Psychology
Raninec, J., Music Education
Repka, R., Linguistics of Concrete Lan-
guage Groups
Šedivý, O., Descriptive Geometry
Sliacky, O., Theory and History of Slovak
Literature
Štraus, F., Theory and History of Slovak
Literature
Šulka, R., Descriptive Geometry
Šupšáková, B., Arts and Crafts
Švec, M., Mathematics
Trup, L., Modern Non-Slavonic Philology
Vašek, Š., Special Education
Vietorová, N., Modern Non-Slavonic Phil-
ology
Zelina, M., Education

Faculty of Law (tel. (2) 59-24-41-03; fax (2)
59-24-42-16; e-mail sd@flaw.uniba.sk;
internet www.flaw.uniba.sk):

Cúth, J., International Law
Husár, E., Penal Law
Klimko, J., History of State and Law
Mamojka, M., Commercial Law
Mathern, V., Penal Law
Ovečková, O., Economic and Financial
Law
Planková, O., Civil Law
Posluch, M., State Law
Škultéty, P., Administrative Law
Straka, J., Czechoslovak History

Faculty of Management (POB 95, Odbojárov
10, 820 05 Bratislava; tel. (2) 55-56-67-02; fax
(2) 55-56-67-03; e-mail sd@fm.uniba.sk;
internet www.fm.uniba.sk):

Hlavatá, I., Finance
Komorník, J., Probability and Mathemat-
ical Statistics
Korček, L., Economics
Piškanin, A., Economics and Industrial
Management
Ralbovský, M., Finance
Rudy, J., Business Management

Zapletal, V., Economics

Faculty of Mathematics, Physics and Informatics (Mlynská dolina, 842 48 Bratislava; tel.
(2) 65-42-67-20; fax (2) 65-42-58-82; e-mail
sd@fmph.uniba.sk; internet www.fmph
.uniba.sk):

Bezák, V., Condensed Matter Physics
Brunovský, P., Mathematics
Chorvát, D., Biophysics
Čižmár, J., Teaching Mathematics
Dubničková, A., Physics
Gruska, J., Informatics
Hianík, T., Biophysics
Hubač, I., Biophysics
Kabát, L., Economics
Kačur, J., Mathematics
Katriňák, T., Mathematics
Kodnár, R., Mathematics
Kostyrko, P., Mathematics
Lukáč, P., Plasma Physics
Masarik, J., Physics
Medveď, M., Mathematics
Moczo, P., Physics
Noga, M., Theoretical Physics
Pázmán, A., Mathematics
Pišút, J., Theoretical Physics
Plesník, J., Mathematics
Povinec, P., Physics
Prešnajder, P., Physics
Rovan, B., Informatics
Ružička, J., Physics
Šalát, T., Mathematics
Šáro, S., Nuclear Physics
Sitár, B., Physics
Skalný, J., Physics
Štrba, A., Experimental Physics
Tomlain, J., Meteorology and Climatology

Faculty of Medicine in Bratislava (Špitálska
24, 813 72 Bratislava; tel. (2) 52-96-17-36; fax
(2) 59-35-72-70; e-mail sd@fmed.uniba.sk;
internet ww.fmed.uniba.sk):

Ághová, L., Public Health
Bada, V., Internal Medicine
Bakoss, P., Epidemiology
Balažovjech, I., Internal Medicine
Bálint, O., Infectious Diseases
Beniak, M., Social Medicine
Beňuška, J., Normal Anatomy, Histology
and Embryology
Bergendi, L., Biochemistry
Bilický, J., Radiology
Borovský, M., Gynaecology and Obstetrics
Breza, J., Urology
Buc, M., Immunology
Buchvald, J., Dermatovenereology
Cársky, J., Medicinal Chemistry and Bio-
chemistry
Danihel, L., Pathological Anatomy and
Forensic Medicine
Ďuračková, Z., Biochemistry
Ďuriš, I., Internal Medicine
Ferenčík, M., Immunology and Immuno-
chemistry
Gerinec, A., Ophthalmology
Holomáň, K., Gynaecology and Obstetrics
Horňák, M., Urology
Hulín, L., Normal and Pathological Anat-
omy
Jakubovský, J., Pathological Anatomy and
Forensic Medicine
Kapellerová, A., Paediatrics
Kotulová, D., Microbiology
Kovács, L., Paediatrics
Kriška, M., Pharmacology
Makai, F., Orthopaedics and Traumatology
Michalková, D., Paediatrics
Mikeš, Z., Internal Medicine, Cardiology
Mráz, P., Anatomy
Oláh, Z., Ophthalmology
Ondruš, D., Oncology
Pontuch, P., Internal Medicine
Profant, M., Otorhinolaryngology
Redhammer, R., Internal Medicine
Remková, A., Internal Medicine
Satko, I., Stomatology

Šiman, J., Surgery
Šimko, F., Normal and Pathological Physi-
ology
Štrmeň, P., Ophthalmology
Štvrtinová, V., Internal Medicine
Šuška, P., Gynaecology and Obstetrics
Švec, J., Oncology
Traubner, P., Neurology
Turčáni, M., Normal and Pathological
Physiology
Turčáni, P., Neurology
Varsík, P., Neurology
Vaško, J., Stomatology
Vojtassak, J., Surgery
Zaviačič, M., Pathological Anatomy and
Forensic Medicine
Zlatoš, J., Normal Anatomy, Histology
and Embryology
Zlatoš, L., Normal and Pathological Physi-
ology
Žucha, L., Psychiatry

Jessenius Faculty of Medicine in Martin
(POB 34, Záborského 2, 036 45 Martin; tel.
(43) 413-33-05; fax (43) 413-63-32; e-mail sd@
jfmed.uniba.sk; internet www.jfmed.uniba
.sk):

Bánovčin, P., Paediatrics
Buchancová, J., Internal Medicine
Buchanec, J., Paediatrics
Danko, J., Gynaecology and Obstetrics
Drobný, M., Neurology
Hajtman, A., Otorhinolaryngology
Hanáček, J., Physiology and Pathophysiol-
ogy
Jakuš, J., Pathophysiology
Javorka, K., Physiology and Pathophysiol-
ogy
Jurko, A., Paediatrics
Kliment, J., Urology
Korpáš, J., Pathological Physiology
Kubisz, P., Internal Medicine
Lehotský, J., Biochemistry
Mazúch, J., Surgery
Meško, D., Internal Medicine
Mézeš, V., Medicinal Biochemistry
Mokáň, D. M., Internal Medicine
Nosálová, G., Pharmacology
Novomeský, F., Forensic Medicine
Péč, J., Dermatovenereology
Plank, L., Pathological Anatomy
Sámel, M., Epidemiology
Straka, S., Epidemiology
Stránsky, A., Physiology and Pathophy-
siology
Tatár, M., Normal and Pathological Physi-
ology
Zibolen, M., Paediatrics

Faculty of Natural Sciences (Mlynská dolina,
842 15 Bratislava; tel. (2) 60-29-66-71; fax (2)
65-42-90-64; e-mail sd@fns.uniba.sk; internet
www.fns.uniba.sk):

Adamčíková, L., Physical Chemistry and
Chemical Physics
Ebringer, L., Microbiology
Grolmus, J., Genetics
Hensel, K., Zoology
Holba, V., Physical Chemistry
Hovorka, D., Petrology
Hudák, J., Plant Physiology
Jedlička, L., Zoology
Juráni, B., Pedology
Kellö, V., Physical Chemistry and Chem-
ical Physics
Kettner, M., Microbiology
Kminiak, M., Ecology
Kolarov, J., Biochemistry
Kollárová, M., Biochemistry and Molecu-
lar Biology
Kováč, L., Biochemistry
Kováč, M., Stratum Geology, Geology and
Palaeontology, Applied Geophysics
Kraus, I., Applied Geophysics
Krcho, J., Cartography
Macášek, F., Nuclear Chemistry
Masarovičová, E., Plant Physiology

MATYS, M., Engineering Geology
MIADOKOVÁ, E., Genetics
MLÁDEK, J., Human and Regional Geography
ONDRÁŠIK, R., Hydrology and Engineering Geology
ORSZÁGH, L., Zoology
PAULOV, J., Human and Regional Geography
ROJKOVIČ, I., Stratum Geology, Geology and Palaeontology, Applied Geophysics
SCHWENDT, P., Inorganic Chemistry
ŠEFARA, J., Stratum Geology, Geology and Palaeontology, Applied Geophysics
ŠEVČÍK, P., Physical Chemistry
SILNÝ, P., Theory of Teaching Chemistry
SOJÁK, L., Analytical Chemistry
ŠOMŠÁK, L., Botany
ŠUBÍK, J., Biochemistry
ŠUCHA, V., Stratum Geology
TOMA, Š., Organic Chemistry
URBAN, M., Chemical Physics
VLČEK, D., Genetics
VOZÁROVÁ, A., Mineralogy, Petrology and Geochemistry
ZAŤKO, M., Geography
ŽÚRKOVÁ, L'., Inorganic Chemistry

Faculty of Pharmacy (Odbojárov 10, 832 32 Bratislava; tel. (2) 55-57-20-22; fax (2) 55-57-20-65; e-mail sd@fpharm.uniba.sk; internet www.fpharm.uniba.sk):

BALGAVÝ, P., Physics
ČIŽMÁRIK, J., Pharmaceutical Chemistry
DEVÍNSKY, F., Pharmaceutical Chemistry
FOLTÁN, V., Public Health
GRANČAI, D., Pharmacognosis
HAVRÁNEK, E., Pharmaceutical Chemistry
KOVÁCS, P., Biochemistry
MLYNARČÍK, D., Galenic Pharmacy
PŠENÁK, M., Biochemistry
RAK, J., Galenic Pharmacy
REMKO, M., Physical Chemistry and Chemical Physics
SARKA, K., Physical Chemistry and Chemical Physics
ŠPRINGER, V., Social Pharmacy
SVEC, P., Pharmacology

Faculty of Philosophy (Gondova 2, 818 01 Bratislava; tel. (2) 52-92-10-78; fax (2) 52-96-60-16; e-mail sd@fphil.uniba.sk; internet www.fphil.uniba.sk):

BAĎURÍK, J., History
BAJZÍKOVÁ, E., Slovak Language
BAKOŠ, J., Fine Art
CHALUPKA, L., Music
DOLNÍK, J., General Linguistics
DUDOK, M., Slavonic Philology
HERETÍK, A., Psychology
HOLEC, R., History
HRČKOVÁ, N., Music
HVIŠČ, J., Slavonic Philology
KIMLIČKA, Š., Librarianship and Information Science
KOLLÁRIK, T., Psychology
KREKOVIČ, E., Archaeology
KUKLICA, P., Classical Philology
KUSÝ, M., Philosophy
MARCELLI, M., Philosophy
MÉSZÁROS, O., Modern Non-Slavonic Philology
MICHÁLEK, J., Ethnography
MIKULA, V., Slovak Literature
MLACEK, J., Slovak Language
PAULÍNY, J., Modern Non-Slavonic Philology
PERHÁCS, J., Pedagogy
POTZLOVÁ-MALIKOVÁ, M., Fine Art
POVCHANIČ, Š., Modern Non-Slavonic Philology
PŠENÁK, J., Pedagogy
SCHENK, J., Sociology
SOKOLOVSKÝ, L., History
ŠVEC, Š., Pedagogy
SZOMOLÁNYIOVÁ, S., Political Science

TANDLICHOVÁ, E., Theory of English Language Teaching
TUŠER, A., Journalism
VOJTEK, J., General History
ŽAMBOR, M., Philosophy
ŽIGO, M., Philosophy
ŽIGO, P., Slovak Language
ŽILINEK, M., Pedagogy

Faculty of Physical Education and Sport (Nábrežie arm. generála L. Sobodu, 814 69 Bratislava; tel. (2) 54-41-19-09; fax (2) 54-41-33-27; e-mail sd@fsport.uniba.sk; internet www.fsport.uniba.sk):

GREXA, J., History
HAMAR, D., Sport Kinanthropology
HELLEBRANDT, V., Sport Kinanthropology
KAMPMILLER, T., Sport Kinanthropology
KASA, J., Sport Kinanthropology
MORAVEC, R., Sport Kinanthropology
ŠTULRAJTER, V., Physiology

Faculty of Protestant Theology (Bartókova 8, 811 02 Bratislava; tel. (2) 67-28-82-50; fax (2) 62-80-39-51; e-mail sd@fevth.uniba.sk; internet www.fevth.uniba.sk):

BÁNDY, J., Protestant Theology
KIŠŠ, L., Protestant Theology

Faculty of Roman Catholic Theology (Kapitulska 26, 814 58 Bratislava; tel. (2) 54-43-51-09; fax (2) 54-43-51-09; e-mail sd@frcth.uniba.sk; internet www.frcth.uniba.sk):

BOŠMÁNSKY, K., Catholic Theology
ĎURICA, M., Catholic Theology
JUDÁK, V., Catholic Theology
KUTARŇA, J., Theology
VRAGAŠ, Š., Catholic Theology

Faculty of Social and Economic Sciences (Odbojárov 10A, 820 05 Bratislava; tel. (2) 55-56-67-18; fax (2) 55-42-36-02; e-mail sd@fses.uniba.sk; internet www.fses.uniba.sk):

KABÁT, L., Economics
KLEIN, F., Therapeutics and Special Education
KOLLÁRIK, T., Psychology
KUSÝ, M., Philosophy
KVASNIČKA, V., Informatics

UNIVERZITA KONŠTANTÍNA FILOZOFA V NITRE (Constantine the Philosopher University in Nitra)

Trieda A. Hlinku 1, 949 74 Nitra
Telephone: (37) 640-80-01
Fax: (37) 640-80-20
E-mail: ukf@ukf.sk
Internet: www.ukf.sk
Founded 1959 as Pedagogical Institute, univ. status 1992, present name 1996
State control
Language of instruction: English, French, German, Hungarian, Italian, Russian, Slovak, Spanish
Academic year: September to August
Rector: Prof. Dr LIBOR VOZÁR
Vice-Rector for Academic Affairs: Dr RUŽENA ŽILOVÁ
Vice-Rector for Implementation of Information Technology: Mgr Dr JÁN SKALKA
Vice-Rector for Int. Relations: Prof. Dr EVA MALÁ
Vice-Rector for Lifelong Learning: Dr MARCELA VEREŠOVÁ
Vice-Rector for Public Relations and Social Affairs: Doc. Dr MIROSLAV TVRDOŇ
Vice-Rector for Science and Research: Prof. Dr MÁRIA BAUEROVÁ
Bursar: Ing. LUBICA EHRENHOLDOVÁ
Librarian: ANEŽKA STRIHOVÁ
Library of 244,527 vols, 344 periodical titles
Number of teachers: 532
Number of students: 12,208 (8,361 full-time, 3,847 part-time)

DEANS

Faculty of Arts: Prof. Dr BERNARD GARAJ
Faculty of Central European Studies: Dr ATTILA KOMZSÍK
Faculty of Education: Prof. Dr EVA SZÓRÁDOVÁ
Faculty of Natural Sciences: Prof. Dr ĽUBOMÍR ZELENICKÝ
Faculty of Social Sciences and Health Care: Prof. Dr EVA SOLLÁROVÁ

PROFESSORS

Faculty of Arts (Štefánikova 67, 949 74 Nitra; tel. (37) 640-84-44; fax (37) 640-85-00; e-mail dekanatff@ukf.sk; internet www.ff.ukf.sk):

BUJNA, J.
ČUKAN, J.
DIATKA, C.
FARKAŠ, P.
FRANEK, L.
GADUŠOVÁ, Z.
GÁLIK, S.
GARAJ, B.
GERO, Š.
GLOVŇA, J.
GROMOVÁ, E.
HAJKO, D.
HEČKOVÁ, J.
INŠTITORISOVÁ, D.
KAPSOVÁ, E.
KERUĽOVÁ, M.
KOLI, F.
KOPRDA, P.
KRALČÁK, Ľ
KRNO, S.
LEIKERT, J.
MEŠŤAN, P.
MIŠŠÍKOVÁ, G.
MÜGLOVÁ, D.
ONDREJKOVIČ, P.
PAVELKA, J.
PLESNÍK, Ľ
POKRIVČÁK, A.
RADIČOVÁ, I.
ROMSAUER, P.
SOKOLOVÁ, J.
SWIATKIEWICZ, W.
TUČNÁ, E.
VAŇKO, J.
VITÉZOVÁ, E.
WIEDERMANN, E.
ZELENICKÁ, E.
ŽILKOVÁ, M.

Faculty of Central European Studies (Drážovská 2, 949 74 Nitra; tel. and fax (37) 640-88-53; e-mail dkss@ukf.sk; internet www.fss.ukf.sk):

KÁRPÁTI, A.
LÁSZLÓ, B.
NAGY, G.
POSPÍŠIL, I.
PUSZTAY, J.
ZELENKA, M.
ŽILKA, T.

Faculty of Education (Drážovská 2, 949 74 Nitra; tel. (37) 640-82-18; fax (37) 640-82-61; e-mail dpf@ukf.sk; internet www.pf.ukf.sk):

BITTEROVÁ, M.
HAŠKOVÁ, A.
KOMLÓSI, L.
KOZÍK, T.
KURINCOVÁ, V.
MALÁ, E.
PERHÁCS, J.
PETROVÁ, G.
SEIDLER, P.
SIMONEK, J.
SZÓRÁDOVÁ, E.

Faculty of Natural Sciences (Tr. A. Hlinku 1, 949 74 Nitra; tel. (37) 640-85-55; fax (37) 640-85-56; e-mail dfpv@ukf.sk; internet www.fpv.ukf.sk):

BAUEROVÁ, M.
BÍLEK, M.

CHRENEK, P.
FULIER, J.
HEGEDÜSOVÁ, A.
HETÉNYI, L.
HRAŠKA, S.
HREŠKO, J.
KECSKÉS, A.
KLUVANEC, D.
KMEŤ, T.
KONEČNÝ, M.
KOREC, P.
KRAUS, I.
LAUKO, V.
LAURINČÍK, J.
MIKULECKÝ, P.
RÓZOVÁ, Z.
ŠEDIVÝ, O.
STEHLÍKOVÁ, B.
TIRPÁKOVÁ, A.
TURČÁNI, M.
VALKO, M.
VOZÁR, L.
ZELENICKÝ, Ľ.

Faculty of Social Sciences and Health Care
(Kraskova 1, 949 74 Nitra; tel. (37) 640-87-51; fax (37) 640-87-63; e-mail dekanatfsv@ukf.sk; internet www.fsv.ukf.sk):

BAKOŠ, E.
LÍŠKOVÁ, A.
LOHNERT, J.
LUŽICA, R.
MAZUR, S.
MLYNČEK, M.
ŘEHULKA, E.
RUISEL, I.
SOLLÁROVÁ, E.
SVAČINA, Š.
TKÁČ, V.

UNIVERZITA MATEJA BEL
(Matej Bel University)

Národná 12, 974 01 Banská Bystrica

Telephone: (48) 446-11-52
Fax: (48) 415-31-80
Internet: www.umb.sk

Founded 1992 following merger of Pedagogic
Faculty and School of Economics
Academic year: September to June

Rector: Doc. Ing. MILAN MURGAŠ
Vice-Rector for Education and Devt: Prof.
Ing. JOZEF BENČO
Vice-Rector for Research and Int. Relations:
Doc. PaedDr PAVOL ODALOŠ
Number of students: 7,500

DEANS

Faculty of Economics: Prof. Ing. MILOTA
VETRÁKOVÁ
Faculty of Finance: Prof. Ing. JURAJ NEMEC
Faculty of Humanities: Doc. PhDr VLADIMÍR
VARINSKÝ
Faculty of Law: Prof. JuDR MOJMÍR MAMOJKA
Faculty of Natural Sciences: Doc. RnDR
STANISLAV HOLEC
Faculty of Pedagogy: Prof. PhDr BEATA
KOSOVÁ
Faculty of Philology: Doc. PhDr FRANTIŠEK
ALABÁN
Faculty of Political Sciences and International Relations: Doc. PhDr PETER KULAŠIK

UNIVERZITA PAVLA JOZEFA ŠAFÁRIKA V KOŠICIACH
(Šafárik University of Košice)

Šrobárova 2, 041 80 Košice

Telephone: (55) 622-26-08
Fax: (55) 622-81-09
E-mail: zahrodd@kosice.upjs.sk
Internet: www.upjs.sk

Founded 1657 as Academia Cassoviensis by
Benedikt Kishdy, bishop of Eger, present
name and status 1959
State control
Languages of instruction: Slovak, English
Academic year: September to July

Rector: Prof. Dr DUŠAN PODHRADSKÝ
Pro-Rectors: Prof. Dr IGOR PALÚŠ, Doc. Dr
PAVOL PETROVIČ, Doc. Dr LEONARD SIEG-FRIED, Prof. Dr JÚLIUS VAJÓ
Registrar: Dr Ing. JOZEF LOKŠA
Librarian: Dr DARINA KOŽUCHOVÁ

Number of teachers: 400
Number of students: 4,100

Publications: Acta iuridica Cassoviensia,
Folia Facultatis Medicae Universitatis
Šafarikianae Cassoviensia, Thaiszia

DEANS

Faculty of Law: Doc. Dr PETER VOJČÍK
Faculty of Medicine: Doc. Dr LADISLAV MIR-OSSAY
Faculty of Natural Sciences: Prof. Dr ALEX-ANDER FEHER
Faculty of Public Administration: Doc. Dr
LADISLAV LOVAŠ

PROFESSORS

Faculty of Law:

GAŠPAR, M., Administrative Law
PALÚŠ, I., Administrative Law

Faculty of Medicine:

JURKOVIČ, I., Pathology
KAFKA, J., Psychiatry
KALINA, I., General Biology
KOHÚT, A., Pharmacology
MYDLÍK, M., Internal Medicine
PAČIN, J., Gynaecology and Obstetrics
ŠAŠINKA, A., Paediatrics
ŠULLA, I., Neurosurgery
TOMORI, Z., Physiology
VAJÓ, J., Surgery

Faculty of Natural Sciences:

AHLERS, I., General Biology
AHLERSOVÁ, E., Animal Physiology
BUKOVSKÝ, L., Mathematics
CHALUPKA, S., Theoretical Physics
FEHER, A., Physics
GÁLOVÁ, M., Analytical Chemistry
GYÖRYOVÁ, K., Inorganic Chemistry
HONČARIV, R., Genetics
JENDROĽ, S., Mathematics
KRISTIÁN, F., Organic Chemistry
MIŠUROVÁ, E., General Biology
PODHRADSKÝ, D., Biochemistry
SÍLEŠ, E., Physics

Department of Languages:

RYBÁK, J., Slavonic Languages

UNIVERZITA SV. CYRILA A METODA V TRNAVE
(University of Saints Cyril and Methodius in Trnava)

Námestie Jozefa Herdu 2, 917 01 Trnava

Telephone: (33) 556-51-11
Fax: (33) 556-51-20
E-mail: info@ucm.sk
Internet: www.ucm.sk

Founded 1997
State control
Academic year: October to June

Rector: Assoc. Prof. Dr EDUARD KOSTOLANSKÝ
Vice-Rector for Education: Dr DAGMAR
VALENTOVIČOVÁ
Vice-Rector for Int. Relations: Assoc. Prof. Dr
JÁN DANEK
Vice-Rector for Investment and Devt: Assoc.
Prof. Ing. ERNEST ŠTURDÍK
Vice-Rector for Research: Prof. Dr RASTISLAV
TOTH

Number of teachers: 221

Number of students: 3,130

DEANS

Faculty of Mass Media and Communications:
Doc. Dr VIERA GAŽOVÁ
Faculty of Natural Sciences: Prof. Dr Ing.
JOZEF OBOŇA
Faculty of Philosophy: Assoc. Prof. Dr
RUŽENA KOZMOVÁ

UNIVERZITA VETERINÁRSKEHO LEKÁRSTVA A FARMÁCIE V KOŠICIACH
(University of Veterinary Medicine and Pharmacy in Košice)

Komenského 73, 041 81 Košice

Telephone and fax (55) 632-52-93
E-mail: rektor@uvlf.sk
Internet: www.uvlf.sk

Founded 1949
State control
Languages of instruction: Slovak, English
Academic year: September to June

Chancellor: Mgr ĽUDMILA KUNDRÍKOVÁ
Rector: Prof. Dr EMIL PILIPČINEC
Vice-Rector: Prof. Dr JANA MOJŽIŠOVÁ
Vice-Rector: Prof. Dr Ing. OĽGA ONDRAŠOVI-ČOVÁ
Vice-Rector: Prof. Dr JAROSLAV LEGÁTH
Vice-Rector: Assoc. Prof. Dr PETER KORIM
Chief Admin. Officer: SILVIA ROLFOVÁ
Librarian: Assoc. Prof. Dr LIBUŠA BODNÁROVÁ
Library of 91,133 vols, 114 periodicals
Number of teachers: 220
Number of students: 2,020

Publications: Folia Veterinaria (4 a year),
Slovenský veterinársky časopis (6 a year)

PROFESSORS

BAJOVÁ, V., Infectious Diseases
BÍREŠ, J., Internal Diseases of Ruminants
and Swine
BLAHOVEC, J., Biochemistry
CABADAJ, R., Food Hygiene and Food Technology
DANKO, J., Anatomy and Histology
KAČMÁRIK, J., Obstetrics and Gynaecology
KOVÁČ, G., Internal Diseases of Ruminants
and Swine
LEGÁTH, J., Toxicology
LENARTOVÁ, V., Chemistry and Biophysics
LEŠNÍK, F., Biology
LEVKUT, M., Pathological Anatomy
MARÁČEK, I., Physiology
MARETTA, M., Anatomy and Histology
MESÁROŠ, P., Andrology
MIKULA, I., Microbiology and Immunology
PAULÍK, Š., Infectious Diseases
VAJDA, V., Nutrition and Veterinary Dietetics
VÁRADY, J., Comparative Physiology
ZIBRÍN, M., Anatomy and Histology

ŽILINSKÁ UNIVERZITA
(University of Žilina)

Univerzitná 1, 010 26 Žilina

Telephone: (41) 513-51-30
Fax: (41) 513-50-56
E-mail: peter.fabian@rekt.uniza.sk
Internet: www.uniza.sk

Founded 1953 as Vysoká Škola Dopravy a
Spojov, present name 1996
State control
Languages of instruction: English, Slovak
Academic year: September to June

Rector: Prof. Ing. Dr TATIANA ČOREJOVÁ
Vice-Rector for Devt: Prof. Ing. Dr MILAN
MALCHO
Vice-Rector for Education: Assoc. Prof. Ing.
Dr MILAN TRUNKVALTER
Vice-Rector for Foreign and Public Relations:
Assoc. Prof. Ing. Dr PETER FABIÁN

Vice-Rector for Science and Research: Prof. Ing. Dr Ján Čelko

Registrar: Jana Gjašíková

Dir of Univ. Library: Dr Marta Sakalová

Library of 216,025 vols

Number of teachers: 696

Number of students: 10,154

Publications: *Komunikácie–vedecké listy ŽU* (Communications–Scientific Letters, 4 a year), *Krizový Manažment* (Crisis Management), *Materiálové inžinierstvo* (Materials Engineering, 1 a year), *Pokrok v Elektrickom a Elektromikrom Inžinigrstve* (Advances in Electrical and Electronic Engineering), *Práce a štúdie ŽU* (Works and Studies, 1 a year), *Zborník z konferencie TRANSCOM* (Proceedings of the TRANSCOM Conf., every 2 years), *Zborník z vedeckých konferencií ŽU* (Proceedings of the Scientific Confs, every 5 years), *Žnalectvo-Cestná doprava, elektrotechnika, strojarstvo* (Expertise in Road Transport, Electrotechnology and Mechanical Engineering, 4 a year), *Znalectvo-Stavebníctvo a Podnikové Hospodárstvo* (Expertise in Civil Engineering and Economics of Enterprise, 4 a year)

DEANS

Faculty of Civil Engineering: Prof. Ing. Dr Ján Vičan

Faculty of Electrical Engineering: Prof. Ing. Dr Milan Dado

Faculty of Management Science and Informatics: Prof. Ing. Dr Karol Matiaško

Faculty of Mechanical Engineering: Prof. Ing. Dr Štefan Medvecký

Faculty of Operation and Economics of Transport and Communications: Assoc. Prof. Dr Anna Križanová

Faculty of Science: Assoc. Prof. Dr Vlasta Cabanová

Faculty of Special Engineering: Prof. Ing. Dr Ladislav Simák

PROFESSORS

Faculty of Civil Engineering (Komenského 52, 010 26 Žilina; tel. (41) 513-55-01; fax (41) 723-35-02; e-mail education@fstav.utc.sk; internet svf.utc.sk):

Benčat, J., Structural Mechanics

Bujňák, J., Theory and Construction of Engineering Structures

Čelko, J., Theory and Construction of Engineering Structures

Čorej, J., Theory and Construction of Engineering Structures

Kovařík, K., Theory and Construction of Engineering Structures

Melcer, J., Structural Mechanics

Mikolaj, J., Theory and Construction of Engineering Structures

Moravčík, M., Applied Mechanics

Schlosser, F., Theory and Construction of Engineering Structures

Vičan, J., Theory and Construction of Engineering Structures

Faculty of Electrical Engineering (Univerzitná 1, 010 26 Žilina; tel. (41) 513-20-51; fax (41) 513-15-15; e-mail education@fel.utc.sk; internet fel.utc.sk):

Blunár, K., Communications Engineering

Bury, P., Physics of Condensed Matter and Acoustics

Čápová, K., Theoretical Electrotechnology

Dado, M., Telecommunications

Dobrucký, B., Electric Traction and Electric Drives

Hrabovcová, V., Electric Traction and Electric Drives

Neveselý, M., Theoretical Electrotechnology

Trstenský, D., Communications Engineering

Vittek, J., Electric Traction and Electric Drives

Faculty of Management Science and Informatics (Univerzitná 1, 010 26 Žilina; tel. (41) 513-40-51; fax (41) 565-20-44; e-mail education@fri.utc.sk; internet www.fri.utc.sk):

Alexík, M., Information and Control Systems

Cenek, P., Transport and Communications Technology

Hittmár, Š., Management in Transport

Janáček, J., Transport and Communications Technology

Manuliak, I., Information and Control Systems

Marček, D., Management

Skýva, L., Technical Cybernetics

Faculty of Mechanical Engineering (Univerzitná 1, 010 26 Žilina; tel. (41) 513-25-00; fax (41) 565-29-40; e-mail education@dsjf.utc.sk; internet fstroj.utc.sk):

Bokuvka, O., Materials Engineering

Dzimko, M., Machine Elements and Mechanisms

Gregor, M., Industrial Engineering and Management

Hlavňa, V., Transportation and Handling Technologies

Honner, K., Workplace Arrangement

Konečná, R., Material Engineering

Košturiak, J., Industrial Engineering and Management

Kukuča, P., Transportation and Handling Technologies

Kuric, I., Mechanical Engineering

Málik, L., Machine Elements and Mechanisms

Medvecký, Š., Machine Elements and Mechanisms

Meško, J., Mechanical Engineering

Mičieta, B., Industrial Management

Obmaščík, M., Mechanical Engineering

Palček, P., Materials Engineering

Skočovský, P., Materials Engineering

Sládek, G., Mechanical Engineering

Zvolenský, P., Transport and Handling Technologies

Faculty of Operation and Economics of Transport and Communications (Univerzitná 1, 010 26 Žilina; tel. (41) 513-30-50; fax (41) 565-14-99; e-mail education@fpedas.utc.sk; internet fpedas.utc.sk):

Čisko, Š., Economics

Čorejová, T., Transport and Communications Technology

Gnap, J., Economics

Havel, K., Transport and Communications Technology

Hollarek, T., Transport Engineering

Kazda, A., Transport and Communications Technology

Kevický, D., Transport and Communications Technology

Královenský, J., Economics

Kříž, J., Transport and Communications Technology

Liščák, Š., Transport and Communications Technology

Nedelka, M., Transport and Communications Technology

Sedláček, B., Economics

Štofková, J., Economics

Surovec, P., Transport and Communications Technology

Voleský, K., Transport and Communications Technology

Faculty of Science (Hurbanova 15, 010 26 Žilina; tel. (41) 513-61-01; fax (41) 564-30-85; e-mail education@fpv.utc.sk; internet www.fpv.utc.sk):

Baják, I., Physics

Boichuk, O., Mathematics

Čáp, I., Physics

Diblík, J., Applied Mathematics

Konvit, M., Transport and Communications Technology

Kurcz, J., Musicology

Oberuč, J., Education and Psychology

Polonský, D., Education and Psychology

Volf, I., Teaching of Physics

Faculty of Special Engineering (Ul. 1. mája 32, 011 17 Žilina; tel. (41) 513-66-01; fax (41) 513-66-20; e-mail education@fsi.utc.sk; internet www.utc.sk/fsi):

Maca, A., Operational Research, Stochastic Dynamics of Systems

Mikolaj, J., Transport Economics

Poledňák, P., Fire Protection

Seidl, M., Logistics, Transport Technology

Šimák, L., Crisis Management

Schools of Art and Music

VYSOKÁ ŠKOLA MÚZICKÝCH UMENÍ (Academy of Music and Dramatic Arts)

Ventúrska 3, 813 01 Bratislava

Telephone: (2) 54-43-21-72

Fax: (2) 54-43-01-25

E-mail: rektorat@vsmu.sk

Internet: www.vsmu.sk

Founded 1949

Academic year: September to June

Rector: Prof. Ondrej Šulaj

Library of 65,000 vols

Number of teachers: 220

Number of students: 880

DEANS

Faculty of Drama and Puppetry: Assoc. Prof. Juraj Letenay

Faculty of Film and Television: Prof. Stanislav Párnický

Faculty of Music and Dance: Prof. Ján Vladimír Michalko

VYSOKÁ ŠKOLA VÝTVARNÝCH UMENÍ V BRATISLAVE (Academy of Fine Arts and Design Bratislava)

Hviezdoslavovo nám. 18, 814 37 Bratislava

Telephone: (2) 59-42-85-02

Fax: (2) 59-42-85-03

E-mail: rektor@vsvu.sk

Internet: www.afad.sk

Founded 1949

Public control

Language of instruction: Slovak

Academic year: October to July

Rector: Prof. Stanislav Stankoci

Vice-Chancellor for Academic Affairs: Asst Prof. Jozef Kovalčík

Vice-Chancellor for Foreign Relations: Asst Prof. Silvia Seneši Lutherová

Vice-Chancellor for Devt, Science and Research: Prof. Ivan Csudai

Registrar: Ing. Lýdia Macurová

Library of 37,300 vols

Number of teachers: 108

Number of students: 667

Konzervatórium: Timonova 2, 042 03 Košice; tel. (55) 622-19-67; fax (55) 622-20-92; e-mail kon-ke@stonline.sk; internet www.cassovia.sk/konzervatorium; f. 1951; library: 20,185 vols, 3,079 records; 103 teachers; 262 students; Dir Mag. Bartolomej Buráš.

SLOVENIA

The Higher Education System

Slovenia's higher education institutions predate the foundation of the former Yugoslavia in 1918, with the oldest being Univerza v Ljubljani (University of Ljubljana—founded 1595). In 1991 Slovenia declared independence from the Socialist Federal Republic of Yugoslavia. In 2006/07 91,229 undergraduates were enrolled in 49 higher education institutions. There are four universities, the oldest of which is the Univerza v Ljubljani (founded 1919).

Higher education is organized according to the terms of the Higher Education Act (1994, amended 2004 and 2006). In addition to the universities, other institutions of higher education include fakultet (university faculties), urnetniske akademije (art academies), and professional institutes. The Council for Higher Education was founded in 1993 as the main accreditation body and since 2006 has been responsible for quality assurance. A 'credit' system for awarding postgraduate degrees was introduced in 1998 and was extended to undergraduate degrees in 2002. Following amendments to the Higher Education Act in 2004, Slovenia now participates in the Bologna Process to establish a European Higher Education Area, the first phase of which is to adopt a credit-based system of comparable degrees with two main cycles (undergraduate and graduate). Since 2005/06 Diploma Supplements have been issued automatically to all graduates. The Professional and Scientific Titles Act (2006) laid out the new system of degrees and titles to be awarded in accordance with the principles of the Bologna Process; since 2009/10 all offerings have been Bologna-style programmes.

In 2010 the Government announced the National Higher Education Master Plan for the period 2011–20, which was intended significantly to improve the quality of the higher education system. The initiative included, inter alia, plans to establish polytechnics by 2020 (these would be the only institutions at which professional higher education study programmes would be available); an increase in the total levels of funding available for the higher education sector, and the introduction of a performance-related system of financing whereby higher education institutions would be allocated funding on the basis of their quality, development and efficiency, rather than on the basis of the number of students enrolled; and measures to bolster links between higher education institutions and the economic and public sectors. At 2011 an eight-level national qualification framework was under development.

The Matura (secondary school leavers' diploma) is the main requirement for admission to higher education. University places are offered on a quota basis. Higher education degrees are now divided into three cycles. The first cycle consists of either academic or professional undergraduate degrees, equivalent to Bachelors, requiring 180–240 credits during two to four years of study. The second cycle degree is the Magister (Masters), lasting up to two years and requiring 60–120 credits. The Doctorat (Doctorate) constitutes the third cycle of university degrees and lasts a minimum of three years (180 credits).

Post-secondary technical and vocational education is provided by višje strokovne šole (vocational colleges). The primary qualification is the Post-Secondary Diploma, which usually requires two years' study. Quality standards are set by the national accreditation bodies, but higher vocational education is administered by the Ministry of Education and Sport and regulated by the Higher Vocational Education Act (2004).

Regulatory and Representative Bodies

GOVERNMENT

Ministry of Education, Sport, Culture and Science: Masarykova 16, 1000, Ljubljana; tel. (1) 400-54-00; fax (1) 400-53-29; e-mail gp.mss@gov.si; internet www.mizks.gov.si; Minister Dr ŽIGA TURK; State Sec ALEKSANDER ZORN; State Sec. MOJCA SKRINJA.

Ministry of Higher Education, Science and Technology: Kotnikova 38, 1000 Ljubljana; tel. (1) 478-46-00; fax (1) 478-47-19; e-mail gp.mvzt@gov.si; internet www.mvzt.gov.si; Minister GREGOR GOLOBIČ; State Sec. Dr JÓZSEF GYÖRKÖS.

ACCREDITATION

Council for Higher Education: trg OF 13, 1000 Ljubljana; tel. (1) 400-57-71; fax (1) 400-57-79; e-mail gp.svs@gov.si; internet www.svs.gov.si; f. 1993; approves higher education study programmes and assesses teaching and research quality; Minister GREGOR GOLOBIČ.

ENIC–NARIC Slovenia: Min. of Education, Science, Culture and Sport, ENIC-NARIC centre Slovenia, Masarykova cesta 16, 1000 Ljubljana; tel. (1) 478-46-00; fax (1) 478-47-19; e-mail enicnaric-slovenia.mvzt@gov.si; internet www.mvzt.gov.si/si/delovna_podrocja/enic_naric_center_slovenija; Head Mag. ALENKA LISEC.

NATIONAL BODY

Association of Rectors of Slovenia: University of Nova Gorica, 5000 Nova Gorica; tel. (5) 331-52-61; fax (5) 331-52-24; internet www.ung.si; Pres. Prof. Dr DANILO ZAVRTANIK.

Learned Societies

GENERAL

Slavistično društvo Slovenije (The Society for Slavic Studies of Slovenia): Aškerčeva 2/II, 1000 Ljubljana; internet www.ff.uni-lj.si/slovjez/sds/sds.html; f. 1935; a forum for professional Slavists, to provide a link between research and professional practice, to nurture cultural values regarding Slovene language and literature and awareness of Slovene history; to organize support for and publish Slavic research in academic and popular books and periodicals; 900 mems; Chair. IRENA NOVAK POPOV; Sec. MATJAŽ ZAPLOTNIK; publs *Jezik in slovstvo* (Language and Literature, 6 a year), *Kronike Slavističnega Društva* (12 a year, online), *Slavistična revija* (Slavonic Review, 4 a year).

Slovenska Akademija Znanosti in Umetnosti (Slovenian Academy of Sciences and Arts): Novi trg 3, 1000 Ljubljana; tel. (1) 470-61-00; fax (1) 425-34-23; e-mail sazu@sazu.si; internet www.sazu.si; f. 1938; promotes and contributes to the devt of scientific thought and artistic creativity; 70 full mems, 30 assoc. mems; library: see under Libraries and Archives; Pres. Prof. Dr JOŽE TRONTELJ; Vice-Pres. TADEJ BAJD; Vice-Pres. MARKO MARIJAN MUŠIČ; Sec.-Gen. Prof. Dr ANDREJ KRANJC; Dir ZORAN MEZEG; publs *Acta Archaeologica, Acta Carsologica, Acta Geographica, Opera, Traditiones*.

BIBLIOGRAPHY, LIBRARY SCIENCE AND MUSEOLOGY

Zveza bibliotekarskih društev Slovenije (Union of Associations of Slovene Librarians): Turjaška 1, 1000 Ljubljana; tel. (1) 200-11-93; fax (1) 251-30-52; e-mail zveza-biblio.ds-nuk@guest.arnes.si; internet www.zbds-zveza.si; f. 1947; 1,000 mems, coordinates activities with 8 regional library assocs; Pres. MELITA AMBROŽIČ; Vice-Pres. MARTINA KEREC; Sec. LILI HUBEJ; Treas. ZDENKA RUDOLF; publ. *Knjižnica* (Library, 4 a year).

ECONOMICS, LAW AND POLITICS

Society of Jurists of Slovenia: Dalmatinova 4, Ljubljana; f. 1947; 1,073 mems; Pres. JOŽE PAVLIČIČ; publ. *Jurist*.

FINE AND PERFORMING ARTS

Društvo slovenskih skladateljev (Society of Slovene Composers): trg francoske revolucije 6, 1000 Ljubljana; tel. (1) 241-56-60; fax (1) 241-56-66; e-mail info@dss.si; internet www.dss.si; f. 1945; represents and promotes Slovene composers; promotes the creation of new Slovene music; organizes concerts of contemporary Slovene music; 114 mems; Pres. NENAD FIRST; publ. *Edicije DSS* (printed scores, etc., of its mems).

Slovensko umetnostnozgodovinsko društvo (Slovenian Art History Society): Aškerčeva cesta 2, 1000 Ljubljana; tel. (1) 241-12-10; fax (1) 241-12-11; e-mail suzd@ suzd.si; internet www.suzd.si; f. 1921; excursions, symposia, congresses; 300 mems; library of 22,000 vols; Chair. Assoc. Prof MATEJ KLEMENCIC; Vice-Pres. Dr MATEJA KOS; Sec. METKA DOLENEC ŠOBA; publs *Bilten SUZD* (5 a year, online), *Zbornik za umetnostno zgodovino* (Art History Journal, 1 a year, print and online).

HISTORY, GEOGRAPHY AND ARCHAEOLOGY

Zveza geografov Slovenije (Association of Slovenian Geographers): Filozofska fakulteta, Aškerčeva 2, 1000 Ljubljana; tel. (1) 241-12-1248; fax (1) 425-77-93; e-mail lucija .mikliccvek@ff.uni-lj.si; internet zgs.zrc-sazu .si; f. 1922; supports professional research, stimulates and directs modernization of teaching; organizes professional confs, lectures, publs and field works; 700 mems; Pres. STANKO PELC; Vice-Pres. VLADIMIR DROZG; Sec. LUCIJA MIKLIČ CVEK; publs *Geografski obzornik* (4 a year), *Geografski vestnik* (2 a year).

Zveza zgodovinskih društev Slovenije (Slovenian Historical Association): Aškerčeva 2, 1000 Ljubljana; tel. (1) 241-12-01; fax (1) 241-11-97; e-mail zzds@ff.uni-lj.si; internet www.ff.uni-lj.si/drustva/zzds; f. 1839; 1,649 mems; library of 5,215 vols; Pres. Dr EGON PELIKAN; Vice-Pres. Dr NEVENKA TROHA; Vice-Pres. BORUT BATAGELJ; publs *Casopis za zgodovino in narodopisje* (2 a year), *Kronika* (3 a year), *Prispevki za novejšo zgodovino* (Contributions to Contemporary History, 1 a year), *Zgodovinski časopis* (Historical Review, 4 a year).

LANGUAGE AND LITERATURE

Goethe-Institut: Bleiweisova 30, 1000 Ljubljana; tel. (1) 300-00-11; fax (1) 300-03-19; e-mail info@ljubljana.goethe.org; internet www.goethe.de/ljubljana; offers courses and exams in German language and culture; promotes cultural exchange with Germany; Dir HENDRIK KLONINGER.

Slovenska Matica (Slovenian Society): Kongresni trg 8, 1000 Ljubljana; tel. (1) 422-43-40; fax (1) 422-43-44; e-mail drago .jancar@siol.net; internet www .slovenska-matica.si; f. 1864; literary and publishing soc.; 2,800 mems; library of 10,000 vols; Pres. Prof. Dr MILČEK KOMELJ; Sec. DRAGO JANČAR.

NATURAL SCIENCES
General

Društvo matematikov, fizikov in astronomov Slovenije (Society of Mathematicians, Physicists and Astronomers of Slovenia): Jadranska ul. 19, 1000 Ljubljana; tel. (1) 476-65-59; fax (1) 251-72-81; e-mail tajnik@dmfa.si; internet www.dmfa.si; f. 1949; 1,050 mems; Chair. Prof. Dr SANDI KLAVŽAR; Vice-Pres. NADA RAZPET; Sec. JANEZ KRUSIC; publs *Obzornik mat. fiz.* (6 a year), *Presek* (6 a year).

Prirodoslovno Društvo Slovenije (Natural History Society of Slovenia): Salendrova ul. 4, 1573, 1001 Ljubljana; tel. (1) 252-19-14; fax (1) 421-21-21; e-mail prirodoslovno .drustvo@guest.arnes.si; internet www .proteus.si; f. 1934; 2,500 mems; Pres. RADOVAN KOMEL; Sec.-Gen. JANJA BENEDIK; publ. *Proteus* (10 a year).

Physical Sciences

Jamarska zveza Slovenije (Speleological Association of Slovenia): Lepi pot 6, POB 2544, 1109 Ljubljana; tel. and fax (1) 428 34 44; e-mail predsedstvo@jamarska-zveza.si; internet www.jamarska-zveza.si; f. 1889; 43 caving socs and research groups with a total of 1,000 mems; Pres. VIDKO KREGAR; Sec IRENA STRAŽAR; publs *Jamar* (1 a year), *Naše jame* (2 a year).

Research Institutes
GENERAL

Inštitut za Antropološke in Prostorske Študije ZRC SAZU (Institute of Anthropological and Spatial Studies ZRC SAZU): Novi trg 2, 1000 Ljubljana; tel. (1) 470-64-95; fax (1) 425-77-95; e-mail iaps@zrc-sazu.si; internet iaps.zrc-sazu.si; f. 1994; attached to Scientific Research Centre of SASA (ZRC SAZU); Dir Dr IVAN ŠPRAJC.

Kmetijski inštitut Slovenije (Agricultural Institute of Slovenia): Hacquetova ul. 17, 1000 Ljubljana; tel. (1) 280-52-62; fax (1) 280-52-55; e-mail info@kis.si; internet www.kis .si; f. 1898; library of 32,000 vols; Dir Dr ANDREJ SIMONČIČ; publ. *Raziskave in Studije* (Research and Studies).

Zavod za gradbeništvo Slovenije (Slovenian National Building and Civil Engineering Institute): Dimičeva 12, 1000 Ljubljana; tel. (1) 280-42-50; fax (1) 280-44-84; e-mail info@zag.si; internet www.zag.si; f. 1949; research and devt in the field of building and civil engineering; Dir Dr ANDRAŽ LEGAT.

Znanstvenoraziskovalni Center SAZU (ZRC SAZU) (Scientific Research Centre of SASA): Novi trg 2, 1000 Ljubljana; tel. (1) 470-63-54; fax (1) 425-77-93; e-mail zrc@ zrc-sazu.si; internet odmev.zrc-sazu.si/zrc; f. 1981 by Slovenian Acad. of Sciences and Arts; network of research institutes (listed individually in this section of Research Institutes) in the humanities and natural sciences; Dir Dr OTO LUTHAR.

BIBLIOGRAPHY, LIBRARY SCIENCE AND MUSEOLOGY

Inštitut za Kulturno zgodovino ZRC SAZU (Institute for Cultural History at ZRC SAZU): Novi trg 5, 1000 Ljubljana; tel. (1) 470-61-00; fax (1) 425-52-53; e-mail ibb@ zrc-sazu.si; internet odmev.zrc-sazu.si/ instituti/ikz; f. 1999, as Inštitut za Biografiko in Bibliografijo (Institute of Biographical and Bibliographical Studies), current name 2007; attached to Scientific Research Centre of SASA (ZRC SAZU); biographical research and studies; research of modern Slovenian and European history; Head Prof. IGOR GRDINA; publ. *Življenja in dela-Lives and Works* (book series).

FINE AND PERFORMING ARTS

Glasbenonarodopisni Inštitut ZRC SAZU (Institute of Ethnomusicology ZRC SAZU): Novi trg 2, 1000 Ljubljana; tel. (1) 470-62-65; fax (1) 425-77-53; e-mail gni@ zrc-sazu.si; internet gni.zrc-sazu.si; f. 1934; attached to Scientific Research Centre of SASA (ZRC SAZU); conducts ethnomusicological and ethnochoreological research; Dir Prof. Dr MARJETKA GOLEŽ KAUČIČ; Sec. ANJA SEREC HODŽAR; publ. *Traditiones* (2 a year).

Muzikološki inštitut ZRC SAZU (Institute of Musicology at ZRC SAZU): Novi trg 2, 1000 Ljubljana; tel. (1) 470-61-96; fax (1) 425-77-99; internet mi.zrc-sazu.si; f. 1972; attached to Scientific Research Centre of SASA (ZRC SAZU); library of 7,000 vols; Head Dr METODA KOKOLE; publs *De Musica Disserenda* (2 a year), *Monumenta Artis Musicae Sloveniae* (2 a year).

Umetnostnozgodovinski inštitut Franceta Steleta ZRC SAZU (France Stele Institute of Art History at ZRC SAZU): Novi trg 2, POB 306, 1001 Ljubljana; tel. (1) 470-61-00; fax (1) 425-78-00; e-mail umzg@ zrc-sazu.si; internet uifs.zrc-sazu.si; f. 1972; attached to Scientific Research Centre of SASA (ZRC SAZU); library of 17,000 vols; Dir Dr BARBARA MUROVEC (acting); Sec. ROMANA ZAJC; publs *Acta historiae artis Slovenica* (1 a year), *Umetnosta Kronika* (4 a year).

HISTORY, GEOGRAPHY AND ARCHAEOLOGY

Geografski inštitut Antona Melika ZRC SAZU (Anton Melik Geographical Institute at ZRC SAZU): Gosposka ul. 13, 1000 Ljubljana; tel. (1) 470-63-60; fax (1) 425-77-93; e-mail gi@zrc-sazu.si; internet giam2 .zrc-sazu.si; f. 1946; attached to Scientific Research Centre of Slovenian Acad. of Sciences and Arts (ZRC SAZU); depts of physical, social, regional geography, natural disasters, geographical information system, thematic cartography, environmental protection; geographical museum and library; also houses a cartographic colln and 3 spec. geographical collns: Landscapes of Slovenia, Settlements of Slovenia and Glaciers of Slovenia; HQ of the Comm. for the Standardization of Geographical Names; library of 42,000 vols and periodicals; Dir Dr DRAGO PERKO; Asst Dir Dr MATIJA ZORN; Asst Dir Dr. MIMI URBANC; publs *Geografija Slovenije* (Geography of Slovenian, book series, in Slovene, 2 a year), *Geografski zbornik* (Acta Geographica Slovenica, scientific journal, in English and Slovenian, 2 a year), *Georithem* (in Slovenian, 2 to 5 a year), *GIS v Sloveniji* (GIS in Slovenia, book series, in Slovenian, every 2 years), *Naravne nesreče* (Natural Disasters, book series, in Slovene, every 3 years), *Regionalni razvoj* (Regional Devt, book series, in Slovene, every 2 years).

Inštitut za arheologijo ZRC SAZU (Institute of Archaeology at ZRC SAZU): Novi Trg 2, 1000 Ljubljana; tel. (1) 470-63-80; fax (1) 425-77-57; e-mail iza@zrc-sazu.si; internet iza.zrc-sazu.si; f. 1947; attached to Scientific Research Centre of SASA (ZRC SAZU); library of 50,000 vols; Dir Dr JANA HORVAT; publs *Arheološki vestnik* (Acta Archaeologica, 1 a year), *Opera Instituti archaeologici Sloveniae*.

Zgodovinski inštitut Milka Kosa ZRC SAZU (Milko Kos Historical Institute at ZRC SAZU): Novi trg 2, 1000 Ljubljana; tel. (1) 470-62-00; fax (1) 425-78-01; e-mail zi@ zrc-sazu.si; internet zimk.zrc-sazu.si; f. 1947; attached to Scientific Research Centre of SASA (ZRC SAZU); Head Prof. Dr PETRA SVOLJŠAK.

LANGUAGE AND LITERATURE

Inštitut za slovenski jezik Frana Ramovša ZRC SAZU (Fran Ramovš Institute of the Slovenian Language at ZRC SAZU): Novi trg 2, p.p. 306, 1001 Ljubljana; tel. (1) 470-61-60; fax (1) 425-77-96; e-mail isj@zrc-sazu.si; internet isjfr.zrc-sazu.si; f. 1945; attached to Scientific Research SAZU (ZRC SAZU); Slovenian lexicography; library of 25,000 vols; Head Prof. Dr MARKO SNOJ; Sec. ALENKA LAP; publs *Jezikoslovni zapiski* (2 a year), *Slovenski jezik* (Slovene Linguistic Studies, every 2 years).

Inštitut za slovensko literaturo in literarne vede ZRC SAZU (Institute of Slovenian Literature and Literary Studies at ZRC SAZU): Novi trg 2, 1000 Ljubljana; tel. (1) 470-63-00; fax (1) 425-77-54; e-mail lit@zrc-sazu.si; internet isllv.zrc-sazu.si/#/v; f. 1947; attached to Research Centre of the

Slovenian Academy of Sciences and Arts (ZRC SAZU); research on Slovenian literature, comparative literature, literary theory, digital humanities, textual criticism and cultural studies; library of 37,000 vols; Dir Prof. Dr MARKO JUVAN; Sec. ALENKA MAČEK; publs *Studia litteraria*, *Zbrana dela slovenskih pesnikov in pisateljev* (Collected Works of Slovenian Writers and Poets).

MEDICINE

Družbenomedicinski inštitut ZRC SAZU (Sociomedical Institute at ZRC SAZU): Novi trg 2, 1000 Ljubljana; tel. (1) 470-61-00; fax (1) 426-14-93; e-mail imv@zrc-sazu.si; internet dmi.zrc-sazu.si; f. 1981 as Inštitut za medicinske vede; social sciences, humanities and medical sciences; sociological and social-anthropological interpretation of classical demographic models and concepts, social-anthropological theory of ethnicity and nationalism, personality, psychosocial, neuropsychological and neurobiological theories of social behaviour; attached to Scientific Research Centre of SASA (ZRC SAZU); Dir Dr DUŠKA KNEŽEVIĆ HOČEVAR.

NATURAL SCIENCES
Biological Sciences

Biološki inštitut Jovana Hadžija ZRC SAZU (Jovan Hadži Institute of Biology at ZRC SAZU): Novi trg 5, 1000 Ljubljana; tel. (1) 470-63-10; fax (1) 425-77-97; e-mail bio@zrc-sazu.si; internet bijh.zrc-sazu.si; f. 1950; attached to Scientific Research Centre of SASA (ZRC SAZU); Chair. Dr MATJAŽ KUNTNER.

Paleontološki inštitut Ivana Rakovca ZRC SAZU (Ivan Rakovec Institute of Palaeontology at ZRC SAZU): Novi trg 2, p.p. 306, 1001 Ljubljana; tel. (1) 470-63-71; fax (1) 425-77-55; e-mail spela@zrc-sazu.si; internet piir.zrc-sazu.si; f. 1949; attached to Scientific Research Centre of the Slovenian Acad. of Sciences and Arts (ZRC SAZU); Dir Dr ŠPELA GORIČAN.

Physical Sciences

Inštitut za matematiko, fiziko in mehaniko Jezik (Institute of Mathematics, Physics and Mechanics): Jadranska 19, 1000 Ljubljana; tel. (1) 426-71-77; fax (1) 426-71-78; internet www.imfm.si; f. 1960; research and technical activities in fields of Mathematics, Physics, Mechanics and Theoretical Computer Science; Dir Prof. Dr JERNEJ KOZAK; Deputy Dir TANJA CVEK; publ. *Ars Mathematica Contemporanea* (2 a year).

Institut Jožef Stefan (Jožef Stefan Institute): Jamova 39, 1000 Ljubljana; tel. (1) 477-39-00; fax (1) 251-93-85; e-mail info@ijs.si; internet www.ijs.si; f. 1949; basic and applied research in the fields of natural sciences and technology; Dir Prof. Dr JADRAN LENARČIČ.

Geološki Zavod Slovenije (Geological Survey of Slovenia): Dimičeva ul. 14, 1000 Ljubljana; tel. (1) 280-97-00; fax (1) 280-97-53; e-mail www@geo-zs.si; internet www.geo-zs.si; f. 1946; geology, geotechnology, geophysics, mining, soil and rock mechanics, drilling and blasting, manufacturing and maintenance of drilling equipment; 1,300 mems; library of 15,000 vols, 300 periodicals, 30,000 reports; Dir Dr MARKO KOMAC; publ. *Geologija* (2 a year).

Inštitut za raziskovanje krasa ZRC SAZU (Karst Research Institute at ZRC SAZU): Titov trg 2, 6230 Postojna; tel. (5) 700-19-00; fax (5) 700-19-99; e-mail izrk@zrc-sazu.si; internet kras.zrc-sazu.si; f. 1947; karstology and speleology; attached to Scientific Research Centre of SASA (SRC SAZU); Dir Dr TADEJ SLABE; Sec. SONJA STAMENKO-

VIĆ; publs *Acta Carsologica* (2 a year), *Annotated Bibliography of Karst Publications* (1 a year).

PHILOSOPHY AND PSYCHOLOGY

Filozofski inštitut ZRC SAZU (Institute of Philosophy at ZRC SAZU): Novi trg 2, POB 306, 1001 Ljubljana; tel. (1) 470-64-70; fax (1) 425-77-92; e-mail fi@zrc-sazu.si; internet fi2.zrc-sazu.si/en/predstavitev#v; f. 1979; attached to Scientific Research Centre at SASA (ZRC SAZU); research on encounters between philosophy and psychoanalysis, science, politics and art; library of 5,000 vols; Head Dr RADO RIHA; Sec. MATEJ AŽMAN; publ. *Filozofski vestnik* (3 a year).

RELIGION, SOCIOLOGY AND ANTHROPOLOGY

Inštitut za narodnostna vprašanja (Institute for Ethnic Studies): Erjavčeva 26, 1000 Ljubljana; tel. (1) 200-18-72; fax (1) 251-09-64; e-mail inv@inv.si; internet www.inv.si; f. 1925; study of inter-ethnic relations in Slovenia and abroad and of Slovene ethnic minorities in neighbouring countries; sociolinguistics, human rights, migration, general ethnic issues; library of 38,000 vols; Pres. ŽARKO BOGUNOVIČ; Dir SONJA NOVAK LUKANOVIC; publ. *Razprave in gradivo* (Treatises and Documents, 3 a year).

Inštitut za slovensko izseljenstvo in migracije ZRC SAZU (Slovenian Migration Institute ZRC SAZU): Novi trg 2, 1000 Ljubljana; tel. (1) 470-64-85; fax (1) 425-78-02; e-mail isi@zrc-sazu.si; internet isi.zrc-sazu.si; f. 1986; attached to Scientific Research Centre of SASA (ZRC SAZU); interdisciplinary research of migration processes in Slovenia and in the international environment; Head Dr MARINA LUKŠIČ-HACIN; publs *Bilten* (Newsletter, 1 a year), *Dve Domovini* (Two Homelands, 2 a year).

Inštitut za slovensko narodopisje ZRC SAZU (Institute of Slovenian Ethnology at ZRC SAZU): Novi trg 2, 1000 Ljubljana; tel. (1) 470-42-92; fax (1) 425-77-52; internet isn.zrc-sazu.si; f. 1951; attached to Scientific Research Centre SASA (ZRC SAZU); research in ethnology and folklore studies; library of 19,000 vols; Head INGRID SLAVEC GRADIŠNIK; Sec. BOŽENA GABRIJELČIČ; Documentarian, Archivist STANKA DRNOVŠEK; Documentarian, Archivist MIHA PECE; Librarian VANJA HUZJAN; publs *Studia Mythologica Slavica* (1 a year), *Traditiones* (2 a year).

Libraries and Archives
Celje

Osrednja knjižnica Celje (Public Library of Celje): Muzejski trg 1A, 3000 Celje; tel. (3) 426-17-10; e-mail sikce@knjiznica-celje.si; internet www.ce.sik.si; f. 1946; 365,000 vols; Librarian BRANKO GOROPEVŠEK; Deputy Librarian MARTINA ROZMAN SALOBIR.

Koper

Osrednja knjižnica Srečka Vilharja (Srečko Vilhar Public Library): trg Brolo 1, 6000 Koper; tel. (5) 663-26-00; fax (5) 663-26-15; e-mail info@kp.sik.si; internet www.kp.sik.si; f. 1951; 300,000 vols; Librarian Prof. IVAN MARKOVIĆ.

Ljubljana

Arhiv Republike Slovenije (Archives of the Republic of Slovenia): Zvezdarska 1, p.p. 21, 1127 Ljubljana; tel. (1) 241-42-00; fax (1) 241-42-69; e-mail ars@gov.si; internet www.arhiv.gov.si; f. 1887; colln of important archives, esp. those connected with the ter-

ritory populated by Slovenes since 12th century; archive of Slovene film production since 1905; Dir Dr JOŽE DEŽMAN (acting); Librarian ALENKA HREN.

Biblioteka Slovenske akademije znanosti in umetnosti (Library of the Slovenian Academy of Sciences and Arts): Novi trg 3–5, POB 323, 1000 Ljubljana; tel. (1) 470-62-46; fax (1) 425-34-62; e-mail sazu-biblioteka@sazu.si; internet www.sazu.si/biblioteka.html; f. 1938; 520 vols; Librarian MARIJA FABJANČIČ; publs *Kratko poročilo o delu v letu* (1 a year), *Mesečni seznam novosti* (12 a year), *Objave* (irregular).

British Library: 1000 Ljubljana, Center Tivoli, Tivolska 30; tel. (1) 300-20-30; fax (1) 300-20-44; e-mail info@britishcouncil.si; internet www.britishcouncil.si; offers courses and exams in English language and British culture and promotes cultural exchange with the UK; 400 vols; Dir STEVE GREEN.

Centralna ekonomska knjižnica (Central Economic Library): Kardeljeva ploščad 17, 1000 Ljubljana; tel. (1) 589-25-91; fax (1) 589-26-98; e-mail cek@ef.uni-lj.si; internet www.ef.uni-lj.si/cek; f. 1946; library and information centre for business, economics and related sciences; European documentation centre; 242,000 vols; 301 current periodicals (print), 11,000 e-journals; 9,000 mems; Head IVAN KANIČ; publ. *Mesečni pregled novih knjig* (12 a year).

Centralna medicinska knjižnica, Medicinska fakulteta (Central Medical Library, Faculty of Medicine): Vrazov trg 2, 1000 Ljubljana; tel. (1) 543-77-35; fax (1) 543-77-45; e-mail infocmk@mf.uni-lj.si; internet www.mf.uni-lj.si/cmk; f. 1945; central library for the Faculty of Medicine, Slovene healthcare orgs and biomedical research instns; literature of biomedicine; 210,000 books and periodicals, 1,100 e-journals and 150 ebooks; Dir Dr ANAMARIJA ROŽIĆ-HRISTOVSKI.

Centralna tehniška knjižnica Univerze v Ljubljani (Central Technical Library of the University of Ljubljana): trg republike 3, 1000 Ljubljana; tel. (1) 200-34-00; fax (1) 425-66-67; e-mail post@ctk.uni-lj.si; internet www.ctk.uni-lj.si; f. 1949; central technical library for the university; specialized information centre for engineering, civil engineering and standards; information and referral centre for science and technology; inter-library loan centre; 230,000 vols, research papers, standards, regulations; Dir Dr MIRO PUŠNIK; publ. *New Books Accession List* (4 a year).

Knjižnica Narodnega Muzeja Slovenije (Library of the National Museum of Slovenia): Prešernova 20, POB 1967, 1000 Ljubljana; tel. (1) 241-44-68; fax (1) 241-44-00; e-mail anja-dular@nms.si; internet www.nms.si/anj/odd/knj/knj.html; f. 1821; spec. colln of Slovene prints from 16th century; 200,000 vols; Librarian Doc. Dr ANJA DULAR; publs *ARGO* (journal on museology), *Viri–monograph series* (Topics in Slovenian Material Culture).

Knjižnica Pravne fakultete (Library of the Faculty of Law): Poljanski Nasip 2, 1000 Ljubljana; tel. (1) 420-32-31; fax (1) 420-32-82; e-mail knjiznica@pf.uni-lj.si; internet www.pf.uni-lj.si/knjiznica-in-zalozba; f. 1920; 123,000 vols; Head Librarian MARIJAN PAVČNIK.

Narodna in univerzitetna knjižnica (National and University Library): Turjaška 1, POB 259, 1000 Ljubljana; tel. (1) 200-11-88; fax (1) 425-72-93; e-mail uprava@nuk.uni-lj.si; internet www.nuk.uni-lj.si; f. 1774; incorporates state copyright and deposit library, Nat. Slovene library, Univ. of Ljubljana library, library promotion and consultancy centre, permanent education centre and library research centre; UNESCO deposit library; Information and Documentation Centre on the Council of Europe, and EU Colln; 2.5m. vols, incl. 1.2m. books, 324,000 serials, 80,000 printed music items, 23,700 sound recordings, 13,800 audiovisual items, 7,400 MSS (incl. 85 parchments and 508 incunabula), 74,000 maps, 170,000 pictorial items, 3,800 microforms; Dir MATEJA KOMEL SNOJ; publs *Knjižničarske novice* (12 a year, print; online), *Signalne informacije* (12 a year, print; online), *Slovenska bibliografija* (4 a year, print; online).

Mestna knjižnica Ljubljana (Ljubljana City Library): Kersnikova ul. 2, 1000 Ljubljana; tel. (1) 600-13-00; fax (1) 600-13-32; e-mail info@mklj.si; internet www.mklj.si; f. 2008 as Slovanska knjižnica Ljubljana (Slavic Library); language, literature, history and culture of the Slavs; 1.6m. vols; Dir Mag. JELKA GAZVODA.

Maribor

Univerzitetna knjižnica Maribor (University of Maribor Library): Gospejna ul. 10, 2000 Maribor; tel. (2) 250-74-00; fax (2) 252-60-87; e-mail ukm-tajnistvo@uni-mb.si; internet www.ukm.si; f. 1903; 960,000 vols; Dir Dr. ZDENKA PETERMANEC (acting); publ. *Časopis za zgodovino in narodopisje* (Journal of History and Ethnology, 1 a year).

Novo Mesto

Knjižnica Mirana Jarca Novo Mesto ('Miran Jarc' Regional Public Library): Rozmanova ul. 28, 8000 Novo Mesto; tel. (7) 393-46-00; fax (7) 393-46-01; e-mail knjiznicanm@nm.sik.si; internet www.nm.sik.si; f. 1946; 600,000 vols; Dir CLAUDIA JERINA MESTNIK.

Museums and Art Galleries

Brežice

Posavski muzej (Regional Museum): Cesta prvih borcev 1, 8250 Brežice; tel. (7) 496-12-71; fax (7) 466-05-16; e-mail ivan.kastelic@guest.arnes.si; internet www.posavski-muzej.si; f. 1949; colln of archaeological exhibits from Neolithic times to the early Middle Ages; also ethnographical colln; historical section: from Slovene-Croat peasants' revolt of 1573 to the present; Baroque festival hall with frescoes (1703) and Baroque gallery; memorial room of painter Franjo Stiplovšek; library of 7,350 vols, 35 periodicals; Dir Dr. TOM TEROPŠIČ; Curator IVAN KASTELIČ.

Celje

Pokrajinski muzej Celje (Celje Regional Museum): trg Celjskih knezov 8, 3000 Celje; tel. (3) 428-09-50; fax (3) 428-09-66; e-mail info@pokmuz-ce.si; internet www.pokmuz-ce.si; f. 1882 as City Museum; present status 1965; collns of archaeology, art and cultural history, ethnography and history; library of 8,456 vols; Dir DARJA PIRKMAJER.

Ljubljana

Mednarodni Grafični Likovni Center (MGLC) (International Centre of Graphic Arts): Grad Tivoli, Pod turnom 3, 1000 Ljubljana; tel. (1) 241-38-00; fax (1) 241-38-21; e-mail lili.sturm@mglc-lj.si; internet www.mglc-lj.si; f. 1986; permanent colln of contemporary int. graphics, artists' books and printed ephemera; organizes the int. Biennial of Graphic Arts; exhibitions of prints, drawings, artists' books and printed ephemera; print workshops; Dir Dr BARBARA SAVENC.

Mestni muzej Ljubljana (City Museum of Ljubljana): Gosposka 15, 1000 Ljubljana; tel. (1) 241-25-00; fax (1) 241-25-40; e-mail info@mgml.si; internet www.mgml.si; f. 1935; cultural history museum of Ljubljana; collns incl. archaeological dept, containing articles from lake dwellings of the chalcolithic period, cemeteries of the Illyrian-Celtic period and of Roman domination (Emona), and from the Old Slavic period; cultural historical colln; modern history; also fine arts exhibitions; information centre about the cultural and natural heritage in the Ljubljana area; publs various guides; library of 9,324 vols; Dir BLAŽ PERŠIN.

Moderna galerija (Museum of Modern Art): Tomšičeva 14, 1000 Ljubljana; tel. (1) 241-68-00; fax (1) 251-41-20; e-mail info@mg-lj.si; internet www.mg-lj.si; f. 1948; incl. Museum of Contemporary Art; permanent colln of modern and contemporary Slovene and int. art from the Impressionists to the present day; organizes regular art exhibitions, lectures and events; library: art library of 52,000 vols; Dir ZDENKA BADOVINAC.

Muzej novejše zgodovine slovenije (National Museum of Contemporary History): Celovška cesta 23, 1001 Ljubljana; tel. (1) 300-96-10; fax (1) 433-82-44; e-mail uprava@muzej-nz.si; internet www.muzej-nz.si; f. 1948; important archives, museum objects and library material of Slovene history since 1914; Dir Dr KAJA ŠIROK.

Narodna galerija (National Gallery): Puharjeva 9, 1000 Ljubljana; tel. (1) 241-54-34; fax (1) 241-54-03; e-mail info@ng-slo.si; internet www.ng-slo.si; f. 1918; colln of Gothic sculptural arts, medieval frescoes and copies of Gothic frescoes from Slovenia; colln of Slovenian Renaissance, Baroque and 19th-century paintings and sculptures; paintings by Slovenian impressionists; European painters since the 14th century; colln of Slovenian graphic arts from the 18th to the early 20th centuries; photo-documentation of works of art from Slovenia; library of 34,000 vols; Dir Dr BARBARA JAKI.

Narodni muzej Slovenije (National Museum of Slovenia): Prešernova ul. 20, POB 1967, 1000 Ljubljana; tel. (1) 241-44-00; fax (1) 241-44-22; e-mail info@nms.si; internet www.nms.si; f. 1821; depts of archaeology; history and applied arts; coins and medals; graphic arts; conservation and restoration; library of 220,000 vols; brs: National Museum of Slovenia (Metelkova); Sneznik Castle Museum; Museum of Bled (medieval castle); Dir Prof. Dr PETER KOS; publs *Argo* (2 a year), *Catalogi et Monographiae* (1 a year), *Situla* (1 a year), *Viri* (irregular).

Prirodoslovni muzej Slovenije (Slovenian Museum of Natural History): Prešernova 20, POB 290, 1001 Ljubljana; tel. (1) 241-09-40; fax (1) 241-09-53; e-mail uprava@pms-lj.si; internet www2.pms-lj.si; f. 1821; zoology, botany, geology; library of 12,500 vols of books and periodicals; Dir BREDA CINC JUHANT; publs *Acta Entomologica Slovenica* (2 a year), *Illiesia–International Journal of Stonefly Research* (1 a year, print and online), *Scopolia* (3 a year).

Slovenski etnografski muzej (Slovenian Ethnographical Museum): Metelkova 2, 1000 Ljubljana; tel. (1) 300-87-00; fax (1) 300-87-36; e-mail etnomuz@etno-muzej.si; internet www.etno-muzej.si; f. 1923; Slovenian and non-European ethnographic collns; library of 30,000 vols; Dir Dr BOJANA ROGELJ ŠKAFAR; publs *Etnolog* (1 a year), *Knjižnica Slovenskega etnografskega muzeja* (library newsletter, 1 or 2 a year).

Slovenski šolski muzej (Slovenian School Museum): trg Plečnikov 1, 1000 Ljubljana; tel. and fax (1) 251-30-24; e-mail solski.muzej@guest.arnes.si; internet www.ssolski-muzej.si; f. 1898; school documents and educational books since 16th century; exhibition about the devt of schools in Slovenia; library of 59,000 vols, 542 fascicules; 17,084 documents for all schools in Slovenia; Dir Mag. STANKO OKOLIŠ; publ. *Šolska kronika* (School Chronicle, 2 a year).

Zemljepisni muzej Geografskega inštituta Antona Melika ZRC SAZU (Geographical Museum of the Anton Melik Geographical Institute at ZRC SAZU): Gosposka ul. 13, 1000 Ljubljana; tel. (1) 470-63-58; e-mail giam@zrc-sazu.si; internet www.zrc-sazu.si; f. 1946; attached to the Anton Melik Geographical Institute at ZRC SAZU; maps and atlases of Slovenia, geographical collns; Head PRIMOŽ GAŠPERIČ; Dir Dr DRAGO PERKO.

Maribor

Pokrajinski muzej Maribor (Regional Museum of Maribor): Grajska ul. 2, 2000 Maribor; tel. (2) 228-35-51; fax (2) 252-77-77; e-mail info@pmuzej-mb.si; internet www.pmuzej-mb.si; f. 1903 from collns of the Maribor Museum, the historical socs and the Episcopal Museum; archaeological, ethnological, historical, fine and applied art, costume colln exhibits; library of 12,000 vols; Dir MIRJANA KOREN.

Piran

Obalne Galerije Piran (Coastal Galleries of Piran): Tartinijev trg 3, 6330 Piran; tel. (5) 671-20-80; fax (5) 671-20-90; internet www.obalne-galerije.si; f. 1975; group of galleries; display contemporary art of Slovenian coast; Dir TONI BILOSLAV.

Pomorski Muzej Sergej Mašera (Maritime Museum Sergej Masera): Cankarjevo nabrežje 3 p.p. 103, 6330 Piran; tel. (5) 671-00-40; fax (5) 671-00-50; e-mail muzej@pommus-pi.si; internet www2.arnes.si/~kppomm; f. 1954 as the Civic Museum of Piran, present name 1967; colln and study of the maritime past of the Slovene coast, Slovene naval history and related economic activities; archaeological, maritime and art-history collns; an anthropological study and colln of items used in salt-making and fishing; library of 14,000 vols; Dir MARTINA GAMBOZ.

Ptuj

Pokrajinski muzej Ptuj (Ptuj Regional Museum): Muzejski trg 1, 2250 Ptuj; tel. (2) 787-92-30; fax (2) 787-92-45; e-mail muzej-ptuj.uprava@siol.net; internet www.pok-muzej-ptuj.si; f. 1893; history, archaeology, art, ethnography, numismatics, musical instruments, lapidary; reconstructions of 4 temples of Mithras; library of 17,000 vols; Dir Prof. ALEŠ ARIH; publs *Archaeologia Poetovionensis, Zbornik*.

Škofja Loka

Loški Muzej (Loški Museum): Grajska pot 13, 4220 Škofja Loka; tel. (4) 517-04-00; fax (4) 517-04-12; e-mail loski.muzej@guest.arnes.si; internet www.loski-muzej.si; f. 1939 by the Museum Asscn of Skofja Loka; special colln of exhibits relating to the Freising dominion (973–1803); ethnographic, topographic, natural history and historical exhibits; records of altars since 17th century, exhibits of medieval guilds; relics of the struggle for national liberation; art gallery; open-air museum; library of 18,000 vols; Pres. JANA MLAKAR; publ. *Loški razgledi*.

Universities

UNIVERZA NA PRIMORSKEM
UNIVERSITA' DEL LITORALE
(University of Primorska)

Titov trg 4, 6000 Koper
Telephone: (5) 611-75-00
Fax: (5) 611-75-30
E-mail: info@upr.si
Internet: www.upr.si
Founded 2003
State control
Languages of instruction: Slovenian, English
Academic year: October to September

Rector: Prof. DRAGAN MARUŠIČ
Vice-Rector for Education: Assoc. Prof. NADJA PLAZAR
Vice-Rector for Science and Research: Assoc. Prof. ŠTEFKO MIKLAVIČ
Sec.-Gen.: INGRID KOCJANČIČ
Vice-Rector for Economics and Finance: Assoc. Prof. ROK STRAŠEL
Library of 40,000 vols, 400 periodicals across 5 libraries
Number of teachers: 328
Number of students: 6,499

DEANS

Faculty of Education: Dr MARA COTIČ
Faculty of Health Sciences: Dr ANDREJ CÖR
Faculty of Humanities: Dr GORAZD DREVENŠEK
Faculty of Management: Dr ANITA TRNAVČEVIČ
Faculty of Mathematics, Science and Information Technology: Dr KLAVDIJA KUTNAR
Faculty of Tourism Studies (Turistica): Dr ANTON GOSAR

UNIVERZA V LJUBLJANI
(University of Ljubljana)

Kongresni trg 12, 1000 Ljubljana
Telephone: (1) 241-85-00
Fax: (1) 241-86-60
E-mail: rektorat@uni-lj.si
Internet: www.uni-lj.si
Founded 1595, reconstituted 1809, reopened 1919
State control
Languages of instruction: Slovene, English
Academic year: October to September (2 terms)

Rector: Prof. Dr RADOVAN STANISLAV PEJOVNIK
Vice-Rector: Prof. Dr JULIJANA KRISTL
Vice-Rector: Prof. Dr MIHA JUHART
Vice-Rector: Prof. Dr ANDREJ KOVAČIČ
Vice-Rector: Prof. Dr ALEŠ VALIC
Sec.-Gen.: ANDREJA KERT
Librarian for Central and Technical Library: MIRO PUŠNIK
Librarian for Nat. and Univ. Library: MATEJA KOMEL SNOJ

Library: 3m. vols
Number of teachers: 4,088
Number of students: 66,000

Publications: Seznam predavanj (1 a year), University of Ljubljana, Welcome

DEANS

Academy of Fine Arts: Prof. BOJAN GORENC
Academy of Music: Prof. ANDREJ GRAFENAUER
Academy of Theatre, Radio, Film, Television: Prof. ALEŠ VALIC
Faculty of Architecture: Prof. PETER GABRIJELČIČ
Faculty of Arts: Prof. Dr VALENTIN BUCIK
Faculty of Biotechnology: Prof. Dr MIHAEL JOŽEF TOMAN
Faculty of Chemistry,Chemical Technology: Prof. Dr ANTON MEDEN

Faculty of Civil and Geodetic Engineering: Prof. Dr MATJAŽ MIKOŠ
Faculty of Computer, Information Science: Prof. Dr NIKOLAI ZIMIC
Faculty of Economics: Prof. DUSAN MRAMOR
Faculty of Education: Prof. JANEZ KREK
Faculty of Electrical Engineering: Prof. Dr JANEZ NASTRAN
Faculty of Health Sciences: Prof. Dr FRANCE SEVŠEK
Faculty of Law: Prof. Dr PETER GRILC
Faculty of Maritime Studies, Transport: Prof. ELEN TWRDY
Faculty of Mathematics, Physics: Prof. ANDREJ LIKAR
Faculty of Mechanical Engineering: Prof. Dr JOŽE DUHOVNIK
Faculty of Medicine: Prof. Dr DUŠAN ŠUPUT
Faculty of Natural Sciences, Engineering: Prof. JAKOB LIKAR
Faculty of Pharmacy: Prof. Dr STANISLAV GOBEC
Faculty of Public Administration: Prof. Dr STANKA SETNIKAR CANKAR
Faculty of Social Sciences: Prof. Dr ANTON GRIZOLD
Faculty of Social Work: Prof. Dr BOGDAN LEŠNIK
Faculty of Sports: Prof. Dr MILAN ŽVAN
Faculty of Theology: Prof. Dr STANKO GERJOLJ
Faculty of Veterinary Medicine: Prof. Dr MARJAN KOSEC

UNIVERZA V MARIBORU
(University of Maribor)

Slomškov trg 15, 2000 Maribor
Telephone: (2) 235-52-80
Fax: (2) 235-52-11
E-mail: rektorat@uni-mb.si
Internet: www.uni-mb.si
Founded 1975
State control
Language of instruction: Slovene
Academic year: October to September

Rector: Prof. Dr IVAN ROZMAN
Vice-Rector for Int. and Inter-Univ. Cooperation: Assoc. Prof. Dr MARKO MARHL
Vice-Rector for Scientific Research and Business Cooperation: Prof. Dr MILAN MARČIČ
Vice-Rector for Legal and General Affairs: Prof. Dr BOJAN SKOF
Vice-Rector for Students: DANIEL VUK
Sec.-Gen.: BOŠTJAN BRUMEN
Librarian: Dr ZDENKA PETERMANEC

Number of teachers: 1,800
Number of students: 24,600

Publications: Časopis za zgodovino in narodopisje, Naše gospodarstvo (6 a year, published by the Faculty of Business and Economics), Organizacija in Kadri (10 a year, published by the Faculty of Organizational Sciences), Univerzitetna revija, Znanstvena revija

DEANS

Faculty of Agricultural Sciences and biosystems: Dr JERNEJ TURK
Faculty of Arts: Prof. Dr MARKO JESENŠEK
Faculty of Business and Economics: Prof. Dr SAMO BOBEK
Faculty of Chemistry and Chemical Engineering: Prof. Dr ŽELJKO KNEZ
Faculty of Civil Engineering: Prof. Dr MIROSLAV PREMROV
Faculty of Criminal Justice: Prof. Dr GORAZD MESKO
Faculty of Education: Prof. Dr SAMO FOŠNARIČ
Faculty of Electrical Engineering,Computer Science: Prof. Dr IGOR TIČAR
Faculty of Energy: Prof. Dr ANDREJ PREDIN

Faculty of Health Sciences: Prof. Dr PETER KOKOL
Faculty of Law: Prof. Dr RAJKO KNEZ
Faculty of Logistics: Prof. Dr MARTIN LIPIČNIK
Faculty of Mechanical Engineering: Prof. Dr NIKO SAMEC
Faculty of Medicine: Prof. Dr IVAN KRAJNC
Faculty of Natural Sciences and Mathematics: Prof. Dr NATAŠA VAUPOTIČ
Faculty of Organizational Sciences: Dr FERJAN MARKO

PROFESSORS

Faculty of Agriculture (Pivola 10, 2311 Maribor; tel. (2) 320-90-00; fax (2) 616-11-58; e-mail fk@uni-mb.si; internet fk.uni-mb.si):

BAVEC, F., Organic Farming, Crops, Vegetables and Ornamental Plants
CENCIČ, A., Microbiology, Biochemistry, Molecular Biology and Biotechnology
IVANCIC, A., Genetics and Breeding of Plants
KRAJNČIČ, B., Plant Physiology, Biology, Botany
KRAMBERGER, B., Grass and Fodder Production
LAKOTA, M., Engineering biosystems
LEŠNIK, M., Phytomedicine
LEŠNIK, M., Foreign Languages Expert
NEMEC, J., Mathematical Methods, Informatics and Statistics in agriculture
ŠKORJANC, D., Animal Genetics and Breeding
SLEKOVEC, M., Chemistry, Agrochemistry and Pedology
TOJNKO, S., Fruit and Fruit Processing
TURK, J, Agricultural Economics and Rural Devt
VOLK, M., Physiology, Anatomy and Animal Health
VRŠIC, S., Viticulture and Enology

Faculty of Business and Economics (Razlagova 14, 2000 Maribor; tel. (2) 229-00-00; fax (2) 229-02-17; e-mail epf@uni-mb.si; internet www.epf.uni-mb.si):

BOBEK, D., Business Administration in Banking
BELAK, J., Economics
FILIPIČ, D., Finance
GUSEL, L., Yugoslav Import-Export System
HAUC, A., Project Management
INDIHAR, S., Mathematics
KENDA, V., International Trade
KOKOTEC-NOVAK, M., Economics
KOLETNIK, F., Accounting, Auditing
MULEJ, M., Dialectical Theory of Systems
MUSIL, V., Polymeric Materials
OVIN, R., Economic Policy
PAUKO, F., Tourism
PIVKA, H., Business Law
RADONJIČ, D., Market Research
SAVIN, D., Political Economy
SRUK, V., Sociology, Philosophy and Political Science
ŽIŽMOND, E., Economic Policy

Faculty of Chemistry and Chemical Engineering (Smetanova ul. 17, 2000 Maribor; tel. (2) 229-44-01; fax (2) 252-77-74; e-mail fkkt@uni-mb.si; internet www.atom.uni-mb.si):

DOBČNIK, D., Analytical Chemistry
DOLEČEK, V., Physical Chemistry
DROFENIK, M., Inorganic Chemistry
GLAVIČ, P., Inorganic Technology
KNEZ, Ž, Separation Process
KROPE, J., Thermoenergetics

Faculty of Civil Engineering (Smetanova ul. 17, 2000 Maribor; tel. (2) 229-43-02; fax (2) 252-41-79; e-mail fg@uni-mb.si; internet kamen.uni-mb.si):

CVIKL, B., Physics
LEP, J., Mathematics
PŠUNDER, M., Building Economics

ŠKRABL, S., Materials
TRAUNER, L., Soil Mechanics, Geotechnics
UMEK, A., Earthquake Engineering

Faculty of Education (Koroska 160, 2000 Maribor; tel. (2) 229-36-00; fax (2) 251-81-80; internet www.pfmb.uni-mb.si):

BELEC, B., Geography
BOKOR, J., Hungarian Linguistics
BREŠAR, M., Mathematics
BRUMEN, M., Physics
FLERE, S., Sociology
JAUŠOVEC, N., Psychology
JUTRONIĆ-TIHOMIROVIĆ, D., English Linguistics
KLAVŽAR, S., Mathematics
KLEMENČIČ, M., Contemporary History
MIŠČEVIĆ, N., History of Philosophy
MLINARIČ, J., History of Middle Ages
PANDUR, L., Painting Design
ROZMAN, F., History of Southeast Europe
VAUHNIK, J., Special Didactics of Sports Education
VUKMAN, J., Mathematics
ZORKO, Z., History of Language, Dialectology

Faculty of Electrical Engineering and Computer Science (Smetanova ul. 17, 2000 Maribor; tel. (2) 220-70-00; fax (2) 251-11-78; e-mail feri@uni-mb.si; internet www.feri.uni-mb.si):

BREŠAR, F., Mathematics
DOLINAR, D., Electro-Mechanical Control Systems
GRČAR, B., Control and Regulation Systems
GUID, N., Computer Graphics
HORVAT, B., Computing and Microcomputer Systems
JEZERNIK, K., Robotics
KUMPERŠČAK, V., Physics
ROZMAN, I., Information Systems
ZAGRADIŠNIK, I., Electrical Machines
ZAZULA, D., Systems Software
ŽUMER, V., Programming Languages

Faculty of Law (Mladinska 9, 2000 Maribor; tel. (2) 250-42-00; fax (2) 252-32-45; e-mail info.pf@uni-mb.si; internet www.pf.uni-mb.si):

DEVETAK, S., Public International Law
FLERE, S., Sociology
GEČ-KOROŠEC, M., Family Law

IVANJKO, Š., Company Law, Insurance Law
KRANJC, J., Roman Law
OJNIK, S., History of Law
PERNEK, F., Financial Law
RUPNIK, J., Constitutional Law
TOPLAK, L., International Business Law

Faculty of Mechanical Engineering (Smetanova ul. 17, 2000 Maribor; tel. (2) 220-75-00; fax (2) 220-79-90; e-mail fs@uni-mb.si; internet www.fs.uni-mb.si/en):

ALUJEVIĆ, A., Mechanics, Thermodynamics
BALIČ, J., Manufacturing Technologies, Theory of Systems, Computer Integrated Manufacturing, Manufacturing Systems
FLAŠKER, J., Machine Elements II, Mechanical Design of Devices I, Technical Regulations
JEZERNIK, A., CAD/CAM
KRIŽMAN, A., Industrial Engineering, Metal Heat Processing
MAJCEN LE MARECHAL, A., Chemistry, Organic Chemistry I
OBLAK, M., Mechanics and Hydrodynamics
POLAJNAR, A., Work Study and Manufacturing Systems Planning
ŠKERGET, L., Fluid Mechanics and Heat Transfer, Transport Phenomena, Eco-Engineering in Manufacturing
ŠOSTAR, A., Technological Measurements

Faculty of Organizational Sciences (Kidričeva cesta 55A, 4000 Kranj; tel. (4) 237-42-00; fax (4) 237-42-99; e-mail dekanat@fov.uni-mb.si; internet www.fov.uni-mb.si):

FLORJANČIČ, J., Personnel Administration
GRIČAR, J., Analysis and Design of Organizational Systems
JEREB, J., Human Resources Management
JESENKO, J., Quantitative Methods
JUG, J., Andragogy and Human Relations, Human Resources
KLJAJIĆ, M., Systems Theory
RAJKOVIĆ, V., Management Information Systems
VILA, A., Production Process Management
VRŠEC, E., Production Systems

Faculty of Health Sciences (Zitna 15, 2000 Maribor; tel. (2) 300-47-00; fax (2) 300-47-47; e-mail vzs@uni-mb.si; internet sola.vzdr.uni-mb.si):

BERVAR, M., Surgery

BORKO, E., Gynaecology and Obstetrics
BRUMEC, V., Physiology
GOLOUH, R., Pathology
HREN-VENCELJ, H., Microbiology, Parasitology
KAJZER, Š., Elements of Administration and Management
KRAJNC-SIMONETTI, S., Social Medicine and Statistics in Health Care
MULEJ, M., Anaesthesiology and Reanimatology
POKORN, D., Medical Dietetics
RAIŠP, I., Internal Medicine

UNIVERZA V NOVI GORICI
(University of Nova Gorica)

Vipavska 13, Rožna Dolina, 5000 Nova Gorica

Telephone: (5) 331-53-97
Fax: (5) 331-53-81
E-mail: info@ung.si
Internet: www.ung.si
Founded 1995
Autonomous

Pres.: Prof. Dr DANILO ZAVRTANIK
Vice-Pres. for Research: Prof. Dr GVIDO BRATINA
Vice-Pres. for Education: Prof. Dr MLADEN FRANKO
Sec.: ERICA GOJKOVIĆ

Library of 10,000 vols, 100 periodicals, 200 non-book materials and e-edition of scientific journals
Number of students: 800

DEANS

Business School of Engineering: Prof. Dr TANJA URBANČIČ
College of Arts: BOŠTJAN POTOKAR
College of Viticulture, Enology: Prof. DANILO ZAVRTANIK
Faculty of Applied Sciences: Prof. Dr GVIDO BRATINA
Faculty of Environmental Sciences: Prof. Dr POLONCA TREBŠE
Faculty of Humanities: Dr FRANC MARUŠIČ
Faculty of Postgraduate studies: Prof. IZTOK ARCON

SOLOMON ISLANDS

The Higher Education System

Formerly a British protectorate since 1900, Solomon Islands became independent within the Commonwealth in 1978. The Solomon Islands College of Higher Education (founded 1984) and the University of the South Pacific Solomon Islands Centre (founded 1971) are the principal institutions of higher education. Scholarships are available for higher education at various universities overseas. In October 2010 the Government announced a Strategic Framework for National Distance Education and Flexible Learning, which outlined a range of measures intended to improve and expand the provision of distance education and flexible learning in Solomon Islands, and proposed the eventual development of a national qualifications framework. Higher education is the responsibility of the Ministry of Education and Human Resources Development.

The Pacific Senior Secondary Certificate or the Solomon Islands School Certificate is the main requirement for admission to the University of the South Pacific (and also to the University of Papua New Guinea). Preliminary and Foundation programmes, both of which last for one year, are available to prepare students for admission to degree courses. The Bachelors is the main undergraduate degree, and lasts for three years in most subjects; however, some courses are longer in duration—for example, medicine, which lasts four years and is taught at the Fiji School of Medicine—while the University of Papua New Guinea offers four-year Bachelors, with an additional year for 'Honours' degrees. After the Bachelors, the first postgraduate degree is the one- to two-year Masters, which is followed by the Doctorate, the highest university degree, which requires a minimum of two years' additional study. In addition to Bachelors, Masters and Doctoral degrees, the University of the South Pacific also offers courses leading to professional and in-service qualifications, while the University of Papua New Guinea offers Postgraduate Diploma qualifications.

The Solomon Islands College of Higher Education (comprising seven schools) is an autonomous institution primarily offering technical and vocational education via Certificate and Diploma courses. As with degree-level education, some students intending to enrol on Certificate and Diploma courses first elect to take a preparatory one-year Foundation course.

Regulatory Bodies

GOVERNMENT

Ministry of Culture and Tourism: POB G26, Honiara; tel. 26848; fax 26875; Minister SAMUEL MANETOALI.

Ministry of Education and Human Resources Development: POB G28, Honiara; tel. 23900; fax 20485; Minister DICKSON HA'AMORI.

Learned Societies

GENERAL

Commonwealth Secretariat: POB 1681, Honiara; tel. 38374; fax 38377; e-mail regionaldirector@cypsp.org.sb; internet www.thecommonwealth.org/cyppacific; provides young citizens of the Commonwealth with knowledge, skills and opportunities; encourages citizens to participate in the devt and governance of their communities and socs; Dir AFU LEAH BILLY.

Libraries and Archives

Honiara

Solomon Islands College of Higher Education Library: Kukum Campus, Prince Philip Highway, Honiara; tel. 39016; fax 30390; e-mail library@siche.edu.sb; internet www.siche.edu.sb/library.html; f. 1987; 4 brs in Honiara (capital), and 1 in the Western Province (Solomon Islands); 80,000 vols, 26 serial titles, 20 current serial titles; Man. NELSON B. MANERARA; Principal Librarian NICHOLAS RUBOSA.

Solomon Islands National Archives: Min. of Education and Human Resources Devt, POB 781, Honiara; tel. 21426; f. 1979; British Solomon Islands Protectorate records 1900–78, Solomon Islands Govt records since 1978; colln of records, microfilm, film and sound recordings on Solomon Islands and Western Pacific; Govt Archivist JOSEPH P. WALE.

Solomon Islands National Library: POB 165, Min. of Education and Human Resources Devt, Watts St, Honiara; tel. 21601; fax 25366; e-mail nls@welkam.solomon.comb.sb; f. 1974; Solomon Islands colln and central reference colln; 2 br. libraries at Solomon Islands Centre of the Univ. of the South Pacific and Solomon Islands Nat. Museum and Cultural Centre; 120,000 vols; Dir EDDIE MARAHARE.

Museum

Honiara

Solomon Islands National Museum and Cultural Centre: POB 313, Honiara; tel. 24896; fax 23492; e-mail loafoa@yahoo.com; f. 1969; attached to Min. of Culture and Tourism; colln began in 1950s, permanent site 1969; research into all aspects of Solomon's culture (prehistory, language, oral tradition, music, dance and architecture); promotes traditional crafts, music and dance; art, heritage, photography, archaeology, natural history (animal specimens, wet and dry), contemporary, technology, audiovisual material, books, journals, posters, pamphlets, documents, outdoor sculptures, art, monuments; houses relics of Second World War; Dir LAWRENCE FOANA'OTA; publs *Custom Stories, Journal.*

Colleges

Solomon Islands College of Higher Education: POB R113, Honiara; tel. 30111; fax 30390; e-mail siche@solomon.com.sb; internet www.siche.edu.sb; f. 1984; 4 campuses: Kukum, Panatina, Ranadi, Poitete; offers Bachelor of nursing; library: see under Libraries and Archives; 135 teachers; 1,200 students; Dir DONALD MALASA; Dean of Academic Services NORMAN HATIGEVA.

University of the South Pacific Solomon Islands Centre: POB 460, Honiara; tel. 21307; fax 24024; e-mail usuramo_j@usp.ac.fj; internet www.usp.ac.fj; f. 1971; responsible for providing USP courses through extension; developing nat. continuing education courses; promoting research on subjects of nat. interest; library: 15,000 vols; 4 teachers; 600 students (mostly distance-learning); Dir JOHN USURAMO; Librarian TONY DADALO.

SOMALIA

The Higher Education System

The union of former British and Italian Somaliland took effect in 1960, when the independent Somali Republic (Somalia) was proclaimed. In 1954 the Italian Government established institutes of law, economics and social studies, and in 1969 these institutions were incorporated into the National University of Somalia. In 1990 there were an estimated 10,400 students enrolled in higher education and in 1991 there were 4,640 university students. However, in the early 1990s the campus of the National University of Somalia in Mogadishu was largely destroyed during a civil war that effectively brought the higher education sector to a standstill. The University of Qaran was established in 2000, and at 2011 it was the sole operating public university in Somalia; based in Mogadishu, the University has four other branch campuses in the country. A number of private universities have been founded since the mid-1990s, including Amoud University (founded 1996), Mogadishu University (founded 1997), University of Hargeisa (founded 2000), Benadir University (founded 2002), Puntland State University and Burao University (both founded 2004); more recently, Kismayo University was founded in 2007 and East Somali University opened its doors in 2010.

Owing to security concerns, the Somali Government was based in Nairobi, Kenya, until mid-2005; hence, there was no direct government control over higher education prior to this. Today, higher education institutions are government-funded, but not all are under the supervision of the Ministry of Education, Culture and Higher Education. In May 2011 the Government announced a National Education Plan, which sought to address ongoing shortcomings within the education sector in the wake of the civil war; inter alia, the initiative included plans to establish a National Education Commission, to implement quality assurance and accreditation schemes, and further to develop and expand the provision of technical and vocational education.

The Secondary School Certificate is the main requirement for admission to higher education; other criteria include two years' national youth service and a competitive entrance examination. The Laurea (Bachelors) is the main undergraduate degree, and lasts four years. There are numerous institutions of professional education offering post-secondary vocational and technical qualifications, which require between one and four years' study.

Research Institutes

MEDICINE

Institute for the Preparation of Serums and Vaccines: Mogadishu.

Laboratory of Hygiene and Prophylaxis: Mogadishu; sections of medicine and chemistry.

NATURAL SCIENCES

Physical Sciences

Geological Survey Department: Ministry of Water Development and Mineral Resources, POB 744, Mogadishu; library of 500 vols; Dir V. N. KOZERENKO.

Libraries and Archives

Mogadishu

National Library of Somalia: POB 1754, Mogadishu; tel. (1) 22758; f. 1970; research, legal deposit; 30,000 vols, 75 periodicals; training in library science; Dir HASSAN NOOR FARAH.

Somali Institute of Public Administration Library: Mogadishu.

Museum

Mogadishu

Somali National Museum: Corso Republica, POB 6917, Mogadishu; tel. 21041; f. 1934; ethnographical, historical and natural science collections; library of 3,000 vols; Dir AHMED FARAH.

Universities

AMOUD UNIVERSITY

Borama, Awdal
Internet: amouduniversity.org
Private control
Pres.: Prof. SULEIMAN AHMED GULAID
Vice Pres. for External Affairs: Prof. ABDILLAHI HASHI ABIB
1st Vice-Pres. for Planning and Registrar: Prof. AHMED HASHI ABIB
2nd Vice-Pres. for Academic Affairs and Students: Prof. AHMED A. BOQORE
Librarian: QABUL NUH ALI

Library: main campus library: 65,000 vols, all subjects; Borama City campus: 30,000 vols, all subjects; medical and allied health sciences library of 20,000 vols

DEANS

Faculty of Agriculture and Environmental Sciences: Prof. ABUBAKAR SH. ABDI
Faculty of Business and Public Administration: Prof. HASSAN OMAR HALAS
Faculty of Education: Prof. FARAH ABDILLAHI FARID
Faculty of Medicine and Allied Health Sciences: Dr SAEED WALHAD

NATIONAL UNIVERSITY OF SOMALIA

POB 15, Mogadishu
Telephone: (1) 80404
Founded 1954, Univ. status 1969
Languages of instruction: Somali, Arabic, Italian, English
Rector: MOHAMED GANNI MOHAMED
Vice-Rector for Academic Affairs: MOHAMED ELMI BULLALE
Registrar: NUREYN SHEIKH ABRAR
Librarian: Mrs SIRAD YUSUF ISMAIL
Number of teachers: 549
Number of students: 4,640

DEANS

Faculty of Agriculture: MOHAMED ALI MOHAMED
Faculty of Economics: MOHAMED ISMAIL SHEIKH
Faculty of Education: HUSSEIN MUSA ALI
Faculty of Engineering: ABDULLAHI JIMALE MOHAMED
Faculty of Geology: MOHAMMOUD ABDI ARUSH
Faculty of Industrial Chemistry: AHMED MAYE ABDURAHMAN
Faculty of Islamic and Arabic Studies: SHARIF MOHAMED ALI ISAAK
Faculty of Journalism: MOHAMOUD ISMAIL ABDIRAHMAN
Faculty of Languages: (vacant)
Faculty of Law: ABUD MUSAD ABUD
Faculty of Medicine: ABDI AHMED FARAH
Faculty of Political Science: ADEN ABDULLAHI NUR
Faculty of Technical Teacher Education: ABDULLAHI MOHAMUD WARSAMME
Faculty of Veterinary Medicine: ABDULHAMID HAJI MOHAMED
Somali Institute of Development Administration and Management: IBRAHIM MOHAMUD ABYAN

UNIVERSITY OF HARGEISA

University Ave Rd, Hargeisa
Telephone: (2) 422166
E-mail: contact@hargeisauniversity.net
Internet: www.hargeisauniversity.net
Founded 2000
Private control
Academic year: September to July, two semesters
Vice-Pres. for Admin.: MOHAMED MOHAMUD FARAH
Registrar: YUSUF AINAB
Library of 15,000 vols.

Colleges

School of Industrial Studies: Mogadishu; depts of radio, carpentry, mechanics, electricity, building construction.

School of Islamic Disciplines: Mogadishu; incl. a faculty of law.

School of Public Health: Mogadishu.

School of Seamanship and Fishing: Mogadishu; 170 students.

Technical College: Burgo; f. 1965; 4-year courses.

Veterinary College: Mogadishu; 10 teachers; 30 students; Projects Dir Dr J. NEILSEN.

SOUTH AFRICA

The Higher Education System

Higher education institutions predate the formation of the Union of South Africa in 1910, with the oldest being the University of Cape Town (formerly South African College), which was founded in 1829. The development of the higher education system in the 20th century was affected by the 'apartheid' (segregation) laws imposed by the National Party in the period 1948–91, which resulted in the emergence of historically 'white' and 'black' universities and universities of technology (tertiary education institutions offering technological and commercial vocational training, formerly known as technikons). In 1986 the 'quota clause' of the governing Universities Act was abolished and institutions were free to admit students regardless of race or ethnicity; by 1991 all the apartheid laws had been repealed. In 1999 there were 21 universities and 15 universities of technology. In 2004–05 the number of universities was reduced to 11, while the number of universities of technology was reduced to six, and four comprehensive institutions and two national higher education institutes were created. In 2009 there were 837,779 students enrolled in 23 public institutions of higher education and 420,475 in 49 public institutions of further education and training.

Higher education is principally funded by the Government and administered by the Department of Higher Education and Training (formed when the Ministry of Education was controversially split in two in 2009), under the terms of the Higher Education Act (1997). Public higher education institutions operate autonomously with the right to establish their own programmes of study; private institutions must register with the Department of Higher Education and Training and apply for programme accreditation from the South African Qualifications Authority. A constitutional amendment transferring responsibility for further education and training from provincial governments to the Department of Higher Education and Training was approved in September 2011; it was hoped that the amendment would enable the consolidation, alignment and proper coordination of further education and training colleges, and thereby to help to address South Africa's ongoing national skills shortage. The government of a University is the duty of the Council, which comprises senior officers, such as the Vice-Chancellor, staff representatives, students, alumni and local government officials, among others. The Senate is the supreme academic body, and is made up of Heads of Department and Professors. Faculty Boards are subordinate to the Senate. The Vice-Chancellor, Rector or Principal is the chief executive officer. The government budget and students' tuition fees are the main sources of higher education funding.

The Senior Certificate was gradually phased out in favour of the National School Certificate as the main criterion for admission to higher education and this process was completed by 2009. Undergraduate admissions are administered by the Matriculation Board of Higher Education South Africa (formed in 2005 from the amalgamation of the South African Universities Vice-Chancellors Association and the Committee of Technikon Principals). The main undergraduate degree is the 'Ordinary' or 'Honours' Bachelors, which is usually a three-year programme of study, although some professionally related fields of study, such as architecture, dentistry, law and medicine, last between four and six years. A Bachelors with 'Honours', or a professional degree, is required for admission to the postgraduate Masters degree, a one- or two-year course of research. The Doctorate is the highest university degree; it requires a minimum research period of two years after the award of the Masters, and students must submit a thesis.

Tertiary-level technical and vocational education is principally offered by the universities of technology. In addition to non-university Certificates and Diplomas, universities of technology offer university-level degrees with a professional or technical focus. The Bachelor of Technology is a four-year undergraduate degree, the Master of Technology is a one- or two-year postgraduate research degree and the Doctor of Technology is a two-year research project following the award of the Master of Technology.

The Council on Higher Education (CHE) was established under the terms of the Higher Education Act (1997) and is responsible for quality assurance in higher education and training by accrediting private providers and programmes. Within the CHE, the Higher Education Quality Committee (HEQC) sets the quality assurance criteria with which both public and private higher education institutions must comply; the HEQC is also responsible for the accreditation (in terms of both institutions and study programmes) of private institutions.

Regulatory and Representative Bodies

GOVERNMENT

Ministry of Arts and Culture: Private Bag X899, Pretoria 0001; 481 Church St, 10th Floor, cnr Church and Beatrix Sts, Kingsley Centre, Arcadia, Pretoria; tel. (12) 441-3709; fax (12) 440-4485; e-mail sandile.memela@dac.gov.za; internet www.dac.gov.za; Minister Dr Z. PALLO JORDAN; Dir-Gen. THEMBINKOSI PHILEMON WAKASHE.

Ministry of Education: Private Bag X895, Pretoria, 0001; Sol Plaatje House, 123 Schoeman St, Pretoria 0002; tel. (12) 312-5911; fax (12) 321-6770; e-mail webmaster@doe.gov.za; internet www.education.gov.za; Minister G. NALEDI PANDOR; Dir-Gen. DUNCAN HINDLE.

ACCREDITATION

Council for Quality Assurance in General and Further Education and Training: Post Net Suite 102, Private Bag X1, Queenswood, Pretoria 0121; 37 General Van Ryneveld St, Persequor Techno Park, Pretoria; tel. (12) 349-1510; fax (12) 349-1511; e-mail info@umalusi.org.za; internet www.umalusi.org.za; monitors and improves the quality of gen. and further education and training in SA; Chair. Prof. JOHN D. VOLMINK; CEO Dr PELIWE LOLWANA.

Higher Education Quality Committee (HEQC): POB 13354, The Tramshed, Pretoria 0126; Didacta Bldg, 211 Skinner St, Pretoria 0001; tel. (12) 392-9100; fax (12) 392-9110; e-mail admin@che.ac.za; internet www.che.ac.za/heqc/heqc.php; the HEQC is in the process of implementing new audit and accreditation systems as well as supporting capacity devt in a number of areas; CEO Prof. CHERYL DE LA REY.

NATIONAL BODIES

Council on Higher Education: POB 13354, The Tramshed, Pretoria 0126; Didacta Bldg, 211 Skinner St, Pretoria 0001; tel. (12) 392-9100; fax (12) 392-9110; e-mail admin@che.ac.za; internet www.che.ac.za; f. 1998; aims to contribute to the devt of a higher education system characterized by quality and excellence, equity, responsiveness to economic and social devt needs, and effective and efficient provision, governance and management; CEO Prof. CHERYL DE LA REY.

Higher Education South Africa: POB 27392, Sunnyside, Pretoria 0132; UNISA Sunnyside Campus, Bldg 3, Level 1, cnr Rissik and Mears St, Sunnyside, Pretoria; tel. (12) 481-2842; fax (12) 481-2843; e-mail admin@hesa.org.za; internet www.hesa.org.za; f. 2005; works to enhance the role and contribution of higher education in society; aims to contribute to nat. devt goals through critical enquiry, and scholarly and intellectual leadership; 23 mems (public univs and univs of technology); Chair. Dr T. ELOFF; CEO Prof. DUMA MALAZA.

International Education Association of South Africa: POB 27394, Sunnyside, Pretoria 0132; Room 2–11, Level 1, Bldg 3,

UNISA Sunnyside Campus Cnr. Rissik & Mears Sts, Sunnyside, Pretoria 0002; tel. (12) 481-2908; fax (12) 649-1247; e-mail admin@ ieasa.studysa.org; internet www.ieasa .studysa.org; f. 1997; advocates, promotes and supports internationalization of higher education by providing a professional forum for instns and individuals to address challenges and develop opportunities in int. education; Pres. MERLE HODGES; Exec. Dir Dr ROSHEN KISHUN.

Matriculation Board: POB 3854, Pretoria 0001; Ground Fl., Bldg 3, Unisa Sunnyside North Campus, cnr Rissik and Mears St, Sunnyside, Pretoria; tel. (12) 481-2848; fax (12) 481-2922; e-mail exemption@hesa-enrol .ac.za; internet www.hesa-enrol.ac.za/mb; f. 1997; advisory cttee on minimum gen. univ. admission requirements to Higher Education South Africa; Chair. HUGH AMOORE (acting).

National Association of Distance Education and Open Learning in South Africa (NADEOSA): POB 31822, Braamfontein, Johannesburg 2017; tel. (11) 403-2813; fax (11) 403-2814; e-mail info@saide .org.za; internet www.nadeosa.org.za; f. 1996; 55 mem. orgs; Pres. RACHEL PRINSLOO.

Learned Societies
GENERAL

Royal Society of South Africa: 4.17 P. D. Hahn Bldg, Rhodes Gift 7700; tel. (21) 650-2543; fax (8) 651-73674; e-mail royalsociety@ uct.ac.za; internet www.royalsocietysa.org .za; f. 1877; promotes science; research and scholarship; advances all aspects of science; publishes scientific journal; public lectures; organises confs, colloquia; expeditions; 487 mems (212 fellows, 35 hon. fellows, 240 ordinary mems); library of 33,000 vols of scientific periodicals; Pres. Prof. DON COWAN; Gen. Sec. Prof. JANE CARRUTHERS; Foreign Sec. Prof. M. N. BRUTON; publ. *Transactions of the Royal Society of SA* (3 a year).

South African Academy for Science and Arts/Suid-Afrikaanse Akademie vir Wetenskap en Kuns: Private Bag X11, Arcadia, Pretoria 0007; tel. (12) 328-5082; fax (12) 328-5091; e-mail akademie@ akademie.co.za; internet www.akademie.co .za; f. 1909; promotes science, technology, arts and the Afrikaans language; 1,000 mems; Chair. Prof. W. A. M. CARSTENS; CEO Dr D. PRINSLOO; Sec. NELLIE ENGELBRECHT; publs *Nuusbrief* (4 a year), *SA Tydskrif vir Natuurwetenskap en Tegnologie* (4 a year), *Tydskrif vir Geesteswetenskappe* (3 a year).

AGRICULTURE, FISHERIES AND VETERINARY SCIENCE

South African Society for Animal Science/Suid-Afrikaanse Vereniging vir Veekunde: POB 13884, Hatfield, Pretoria 0028; tel. (12) 420-5017; fax (12) 420-3290; e-mail secretary@sasas.co.za; internet www .sasas.co.za; f. 1961; advances animal science and promotes viable animal production systems; 400 mems; Pres. E. C. WEBB; Sec. Prof. J. B. J. VAN RYSSEN; publs *Applied Animal Husbandry & Rural Development*, *South African Journal of Animal Science* (4 a year).

South African Society of Dairy Technology: POB 1853, Silverton, 01217; tel. (12) 991-4164; fax (12) 991-4134; e-mail dairy-foundation@pixie.co.za; f. 1967; 300 mems; Pres. STEPHAN STEPHYN; Sec. Y. E. STEYN.

Southern African Institute of Forestry/Suider-Afrikaanse Instituut van Boswese: Postnet Suite 329, P/Bag X4, Menlo Park 0102; tel. (12) 348-1745; fax (12) 348-1745; e-mail forestry@mweb.co.za; internet www.saif.org.za; f. 1937; aims to collect and publish information on all aspects of forestry, to conserve the forest estate, to encourage the practice of scientific forestry, to create a forum for discussion of topics related to forestry; 560 mems; Chair. G. MARAIS; Sec.-Treas. C. VILJOEN; publ. *Southern African Forestry Journal* (3 a year).

ARCHITECTURE AND TOWN PLANNING

South African Institute of Architects: Private Bag X10063, Randburg 2125; Bouhof, 31 Robin Hood Rd, Robindale, Randburg; tel. (11) 782-1315; fax (11) 782-8771; e-mail admin@saia.org.za; internet www.saia.org .za; f. 1996 by merger of existing organizations; professional voluntary association of architects; 2,600 mems; Exec. Officer S. LINNING; publs *Architecture South Africa* (6 a year), *Digest of South African Architecture* (1 a year).

BIBLIOGRAPHY, LIBRARY SCIENCE AND MUSEOLOGY

Library and Information Association of South Africa (LIASA): POB 1598, Pretoria 0001; LIASA House, 228 Proes St, Pretoria Central; tel. (12) 323-4912; fax (12) 323-1033; e-mail liasa@liasa.org.za; internet www.liasa .org.za; f. 1997; advocates, supports and promotes the provision of efficient, user-orientated library and information services; develops library and information services profession; offers networking, education, training and devt and professional recognition opportunities; 3,000 mems; Pres. NAOMI HAASBROEK; Pres.-Elect UJALA SATGOOR; publ. *South African Journal of Libraries and Information Science* (2 a year).

South African Museums Association: POB 12413, Central Hill, Port Elizabeth 6006; tel. (11) 936-7754; fax (86) 503-4521; e-mail sama@futurserve.co.za; internet www .samaweb.org.za; f. 1936; membership-based professional nat. museums asscn; 400 mems incl. 150 institutional mems; Pres. ISHMAEL MBHOKODO; publs *Samab Conference Bulletin* (1 a year), *Samantics* (Newsletter, 4 a year).

ECONOMICS, LAW AND POLITICS

Economic Society of South Africa: Department of Economics, University of South Africa, POB 302, Pretoria 0001; tel. (11) 429-4878; internet www.essa.org.za; f. 1925 to promote the thorough discussion of and research into economic questions, in particular those affecting South Africa; 550 mems, incl. 6 honorary mems, 14 life members, 22 foreign members; brs in Bloemfontein, Cape Town, Eastern Cape, Johannesburg, Kwazulu-Natal, Limpopo, North-West, Pretoria and Stellenbosch; Pres. Prof. ELSABÉ LOOTS; publ. *The South African Journal of Economics* (4 a year).

Institute of Bankers in South Africa: POB 61420, Marshalltown 2107; 1st Fl., Sunnyside Ridge Bldg, Sunnyside Office Park, 32 Princess of Wales Terrace, Parktown; tel. (11) 481-7000; fax (11) 484-8716; e-mail iobinfo@iob.co.za; internet www.iob.co .za; f. 1904; 20,000 mems; Chief Exec. PHIL MNISI; Pres. T. A. BOARDMAN; publ. *South African Banker* (4 a year).

South African Institute of International Affairs: POB 31596, Braamfontein, Johannesburg 2017; Jan Smuts House, East Campus, University of the Witwatersrand, Johannesburg; tel. (11) 339-2021; fax (11) 339-2154; e-mail saiiagen@global.co.za; internet www.saiia.org.za; f. 1934 to promote understanding of international issues among South Africans; 3,500 mems; library: Jan Smuts Library; 10,000 books, 2,000 journals; spec. collns incl. UN depository colln, World Bank regional depository library, Martin Edmonds colln; Chair. of the Nat. Ccl FRED PHASWANA; Nat. Dir ELIZABETH SIDIROPOULOS; publs *eAfrica* (online, 12 a year), *SADC Barometer* (online, 12 a year), *South African Foreign Policy Monitor* (online, 6 a year), *South African Journal of International Affairs* (2 a year), *South African Yearbook of International Affairs*.

FINE AND PERFORMING ARTS

Federasie van Afrikaanse Kultuurvereniginge (Association of Afrikaans Cultural Societies): POB 2655, Brooklyn Sq. 0075; Gerard Moerdykhuis, Voortrekkermonmentterrein Eeufeesweg, Pretoria; tel. (12) 301-1777; fax (12) 301-1767; e-mail fak@ mweb.co.za; internet www.fak.org.za; f. 1929; 2,300 affiliated socs; Chair. Prof. DANIE GOOSEN; Dir Dr CAREL STANDER.

South African National Association for the Visual Arts (SANAVA): POB 6188, Pretoria 0001; tel. (12) 460-5862; fax (12) 323-1275; f. 1851 as the Cape Fine Arts Society; became the South African Fine Arts Asscn in 1871; became the South African Asscn of Arts in 1945; mem. of Int. Asscn of Art; present name 1998; encourages visual arts nationally and internationally; 23 autonomous brs with individual galleries, management cttees, as well as 22 affiliated orgs; 5,500 mems; Nat. Pres. ANTON LOUBSER; Vice-Pres LYNETTE DEN KROODEN, HELEN WELDRICK; Hon. Consultant for Social Devt AVITHA SOOFUL; Treas. BASIE BOTHA.

HISTORY, GEOGRAPHY AND ARCHAEOLOGY

Genealogical Society of South Africa: Suite 143, Postnet X2600, Houghton 2041; e-mail tesourier@ggsa.info; internet www .ggsa.info; tel. (86) 672-2412; f. 1964; promotes and facilitates interest in genealogy and family history; brs in Bloemfontein, Cape Town, Durban, Johannesburg, Pietermaritzburg, Port Elizabeth, Potchefstroom, Pretoria, Vanderbijlpark, Western Gauteng; 900 mems; Pres. JOHANN JANSE VAN VUUREN; Sec. MARILYN COETZEE; publ. *Familia* (4 a year).

Nederlands Cultuurhistorisch Instituut: University of Pretoria, Pretoria 0002; tel. (12) 420-2808; fax (12) 362-5100; e-mail pieter.vandermerwe@up.ac.za; internet www .up.ac.za; f. 1931; offers books and information on Dutch culture, history and art; 250 mems; library of 32,000 vols; Dir ROBERT MOROPA.

Society of South African Geographers: Dept of Geography (53), POB 339, Univ. of the Free State, Bloemfontein 9301; tel. (51) 401-2184; fax (51) 401-3816; e-mail britss@ ufs.ac.za; internet www.ssag.org.za; f. 1994 by merger of existing orgs; 400 mems; Pres. Prof. CECIL SEETHAL; Hon. Sec. Dr SAGIE NARSIAH; publ. *South African Geographical Journal* (2 a year).

South African Archaeological Society: POB 15700, Vlaeberg 8018; tel. (21) 481-3886; fax (21) 481-3993; e-mail archsoc@iziko .org.za; internet www.archaeology.org.za; f. 1945; 1,000 mems; library of 1,000 vols, 5,000 periodicals; Hon. Sec. J. DEACON; publs *Goodwin Series* (irregular), *South African Archaeological Bulletin* (2 a year), *The Digging Stick* (3 a year).

Van Riebeeck Society: POB 15151, Vlaeberg 8018; Centre for the Book, 62, Queen Victoria St, Cape Town 8000; tel. (21) 423-8424; fax (86) 670-9828; e-mail vanriebk@ mweb.co.za; internet www .vanriebeecksociety.co.za; f. 1918; publishes and republishes original and rare documents, books and pamphlets relating to the history of Southern Africa; 1,075 mems; Chair. Prof. H. PHILLIPS; Sec. P. E. WESTRA; Sec. Dr CORA OVENS.

LANGUAGE AND LITERATURE

Alliance Française: POB 72067, Parkview 2122; 17 Lower Park Dr., Cnr Kerry Rd, Johannesburg; tel. (11) 646-1169; fax (11) 646-4521; e-mail info@alliance.org.za; internet www.alliance.org.za; f. 1936; offers courses and exams in French language and culture and promotes cultural exchange with France; attached teaching centres in Bloemfontein, Bosmont, Cape Town, Diepkloof, Durban, East London, Florida Hills, Klersdorp, Lowveld, Mitchell's Plain, Nelspruit, Parkview, Pietermaritzburg, Port Elizabeth, Potchefstroom, Pretoria, Somerset West, Soweto, Stellenbosch, Vaal Triangle, Vanderbiljpark, Vlaeberg and Welkom; also responsible for Alliance Française operations in Botswana, Lesotho and Swaziland.

British Council: Ground Fl., Forum 1, Braampark, 33 Hoofd St, Braamfontein, Johannesburg; tel. (11) 718-4300; fax (11) 718-4400; e-mail information@britishcouncil.org.za; internet www.britishcouncil.org/africa-south-africa.htm; offers courses and exams in English language and British culture and promotes cultural exchange with the UK; attached offices in Johannesburg (teaching centre), Cape Town and Durban; responsible for British Council activities in Botswana, Lesotho, Malawi, Mauritius, Mozambique, Namibia, Swaziland, Zambia and Zimbabwe; Regional Dir, Southern Africa ROSEMARY ARNOTT; Dir of Operations, South Africa DAVID HIGGS.

Classical Association of South Africa: c/o Academia Latina, Univ. of Pretoria, Pretoria 0002; tel. (12) 420-2368; fax (12) 420-4008; internet www.casa-kvsa.org.za; f. 1965 to promote the study and appreciation of classical antiquity; 350 mems; Chair. J. L. HILTON; Sec. M. R. DIRCKSEN; publs *Acta Classica* (1 a year), *Akroterion* (1 a year).

English Academy of Southern Africa: POB 124, WITS, Johannesburg 2050; tel. (11) 717-9339; fax (11) 717-9339; e-mail englishacademy@societies.wits.ac.za; internet www.englishacademy.co.za; f. 1961; concerned with all forms and uses of English; promotes education, research and debate; organizes lectures and promotes creative, critical and scholarly talents of users of English in Southern Africa; awards the English Academy Medal, the Olive Schreiner Prize, the Percy FitzPatrick Prize, the Sol Plaatje Prize for Translation and the Thomas Pringle Awards for translation; over 300 mems; Pres. Prof STANLEY RIDGE; Hon. Sec. DAVID ROBINSON; publ. *The English Academy Review: Southern African Journal of English Studies* (2 a year, online).

Goethe-Institut: 119 Jan Smuts Ave, Parkwood 2193, Johannesburg; tel. (11) 442-3232; fax (11) 442-3738; e-mail info@johannesburg.goethe.org; internet www.goethe.de/johannesburg; f. 1995; offers courses and exams in German language and culture and promotes cultural exchange with Germany; attached centre in Cape Town; project space in Johannesburg CBD; library of 7,600 vols incl. books, magazines, newspapers, audio and video tapes and DVDs; Regional Dir for Sub-Saharan Africa Dr KATHARINA VON RUCK-TESCHELL-KATTE.

South African PEN Centre: POB 732, Constantia 7848; e-mail rudebs@icon.co.za; internet www.sapen.co.za; f. 1960; 165 mems (155 full, 10 assoc.); Sec. DEBORAH HORN-BOTHA.

MEDICINE

Association of Surgeons of South Africa/Chirurgiese Vereniging van Suid-Africa: POB 1105, Johannesburg, Cramerview 2132; tel. (11) 706-4815; fax (11) 463-1041; e-mail surgicom@worldonline.co.za; internet www.surgeon.co.za; f. 1945; 250 mems; Pres. Prof. M. R. Q. DAVIES; Chair. Dr S. S. PILLAY; publ. *South African Journal of Surgery*.

Colleges of Medicine of South Africa: 17 Milner Rd, Rondebosch 7700; tel. (21) 689-9533; fax (21) 685-3766; e-mail admin@colmedsa.co.za; internet www.collegemedsa.ac.za; f. 1954; provides postgraduate examinations in all brs of medicine for all doctors and dentists in South Africa; small archive and reference library; 12,000 mems; CEO and Sec. BERNISE BOTHMA; publ. *Transactions* (2 a year).

Nutrition Society of Southern Africa: POB 1697, Brits 0250; tel. (82) 667-4723; fax (12) 521-3510; internet www.nutritionsociety.co.za; f. 1955 to advance the scientific study of nutrition; 235 mems; Pres. Prof. ESTÉ VORSTER; Chair. Dr MARIUS SMUTS; Sec. P. M. N. KUZWAYO; publ. *The South African Journal of Food Science and Nutrition*.

South African Medical Association: Private Bag X1, Pinelands 7430, Cape Town; Block F, Castle Walk, Office Park, Nossob St, Erasmuskloof Ext. 3, Pretoria; tel. (21) 481-2000; fax (21) 481-2100; e-mail online@samedical.org; internet www.samedical.org; f. 1998 from existing organizations; 16,000 mems; professional org. for medical practitioners in South Africa; Pres. Prof. RALPH KIRSCH; Chair. (vacant); publs *Continued Medical Education* (12 a year), *South African Medical Journal* (12 a year).

South African Pharmacology Society: Box 16, Pharmacology, North-West Univ., Potchefstroom 2520; tel. (18) 299-2304; fax (18) 299-2447; e-mail office@sapharmacol.co.za; internet www.sapharmacol.co.za; f. 1966; promotes and develops interest in teaching and research in basic and clinical pharmacology; promotes communication and cooperation between socs and industry representing pharmacology and related disciplines; creates forums to present and exchange ideas with state and provincial depts, local and other authorities; 154 mems; Pres. Prof. WIM DU PLOOY; Vice-Pres. CHRISTIAAN BRINK; Sec. Prof. VANESSA STEENKAMP.

South African Society of Obstetricians and Gynaecologists: POB 363, Tongaat 4400; tel. (83) 944-1308; e-mail biggles@ispace.co.za; internet www.sasog.co.za; f. 1946; 571 mems; Pres. Dr A. B. KOLLER; Sec. Dr M. PILLAY.

NATURAL SCIENCES

General

Associated Scientific and Technical Societies of South Africa: POB 93480, Yeoville 2143; located at: 18A Gill St, Observatory 2198; tel. (11) 487-1512; fax (11) 648-1876; f. 1920; to promote the interests of scientific, professional and technical societies; to advance the knowledge of scientific and technical subjects; to assist in raising the standard of mathematics and science for underprivileged scholars; to raise awareness of career prospects in technology; and to provide secretarial, liaison, and meeting facilities, etc., for its member societies; 60,000 mems in 51 mem. socs; Pres. A. S. MEYER; Man. ERROL H. VAN ROOY.

Southern Africa Association for the Advancement of Science: POB 366, Irene

0062; tel. and fax (12) 667-2544; e-mail s2a3@global.co.za; internet s2a3.up.ac.za; f. 1902; 83 mems; Pres. Dr I. RAPER; Hon. Sec. S. A. KORSMAN.

Biological Sciences

BirdLife South Africa: POB 515, Randburg 2125, Johannesburg; 239 Barkston Dr., Blairgowrie, Johannesburg; tel. (11) 789-1122; fax (11) 789-5188; e-mail info@birdlife.org.za; internet www.birdlife.org.za; f. 1930; 6,000 mems; Pres. Prof. PETER RYAN; Dir M. D. ANDERSON; publs *Africa Birds and Birding* (6 a year), *Ostrich* (4 a year).

Botanical Society of South Africa: Private Bag X10, Claremont 7735; tel. (21) 797-2090; fax (21) 797-2376; e-mail info@botanicalsociety.org.za; internet www.botanicalsociety.org.za; f. 1913; 15,000 mems; promotes the conservation, cultivation, wise use and study of the indigenous flora of Southern Africa; Pres. Adv. A. B. MEIRING; Dir ZAITOON RABANEY; publ. *Veld and Flora* (4 a year).

Herpetological Association of Africa: Dept of Herpetology, National Museum, POB 266, Bloemfontein 9300; e-mail herp@nasmus.co.za; internet www.wits.ac.za/haa; promotes the study and conservation of reptiles and amphibians, especially African species; Chair. MICHAEL F. BATES; Sec. ROSE SEPHTON-POULTNEY; publs *African Herp News*, *African Journal of Herpetology*.

South African National Biodiversity Institute: Head Office: Private Bag X101, Pretoria 0001; tel. (12) 843-5000; fax (12) 804-3200; e-mail info@sanbi.org; internet www.sanbi.org; f. 1913 as the Nat. Botanical Institute; present name 2004; promotes the conservation, sustainable use and appreciation of South Africa's biodiversity; library: libraries at Pretoria and Kirstenbosch with 15,500 vols; Chief Exec. SUNJIT SINGH (acting); publs *Bothalia* (2 a year), *Flowering Plants of Africa* (2 a year), *Strelitzia* (irregular).

Southern African Society of Aquatic Scientists: c/o Dr Nico Smit, Centre for Aquatic Research, Department of Zoology, University of Johannesburg, POB 524, Auckland Park 2006; tel. (11) 559-2457; fax (11) 559-2286; e-mail nicos@uj.ac.za; internet www.riv.co.za/sasaqs; f. 1964 as Limnological Society of South Africa; holds annual congresses and general meetings; 250 mems; Pres. Prof. WYNAND VLOK; Hon. Sec. and Treas. Dr PAUL FOUCHE; Vice-Pres. Dr JAN ROOS; publ. *African Journal of Aquatic Science* (3 a year).

South African Society of Biochemistry and Molecular Biology: c/o Dept of Biochemistry, Microbiology and Biotechnology, Rhodes Univ,. Grahamstown 6140; tel. (46) 603-8262; fax (46) 622-3984; e-mail g.blatch@ru.ac.za; internet www.sasbmb.org.za; f. 1973; 450 mems; Pres. Prof. GREG BLATCH; Sec. FOURIE JOUBERT.

South African Society for Microbiology: Dept of Biotechnology, University of the Free State, POB 339, Bloemfontein 9300; tel. (51) 401-2223; fax (51) 444-3219; internet www.sasm.za.net; 420 mems; Pres. Dr KOOS ALBERTYN; Sec. Dr EVODIA SETATI.

Southern African Wildlife Management Association: POB 217, Bloubergstrand 7436; tel. (21) 554-1297; fax (86) 672-9882; e-mail elma@mweb.co.za; internet www.sawma.co.za; f. 1970; 370 mems; Pres. Dr CHRISTO MARAIS; Vice-Pres. and Treasurer JULIUS KOEN; publ. *South African Journal of Wildlife Research*.

WESSA—Wildlife and Environment Society of South Africa: 1 Karkloof Rd, POB 394, Howick 3290; tel. (33) 330-3931;

fax (33) 330-4576; e-mail marketing@wessa
.co.za; internet www.wessa.org.za; f. 1926;
5,500 mems; Chair. Dr RICHARD LEWIS; Hon.
Treas. FRANK VAN HEERDEN; publs *Enviro-
Kids* (4 a year, in English), *Environment* (4 a
year, in English).

Physical Sciences

**Astronomical Society of Southern
Africa:** POB 9, Observatory 7935; tel. (21)
447-0025; e-mail assa@saao.ac.za; internet
assa.saao.ac.za; f. 1922; 250 mems; Pres.
MICHAEL POLL; Hon. Sec. LAURIE SIMONE;
publs *Monthly Notes* (6 a year), *SkyGuide
Africa South* (1 a year).

Geological Society of South Africa: POB
61809, Marshalltown 2107; Chamber of
Mines Bldg, 5th Fl., 5 Hollard St, Marshalltown; tel. (11) 492-3370; fax (11) 492-3371;
e-mail info@gssa.org.za; internet www.gssa
.org.za; f. 1895; promotes the study of the
earth sciences, facilitates the professional
devt of its members, and advances the use
of geoscience in the academic, professional,
and public sectors; 2,700 mems, incl. 500
student mems; Exec. Man. CRAIG SMITH;
publs *Geobulletin* (4 a year), *South African
Journal of Geology* (4 a year).

South African Chemical Institute: POB
407, Witwatersrand 2050; Humphrey Raikes
Bldg, Rm 500, Wits Campus, Witwatersrand;
tel. (11) 717-6741; fax (11) 717-6779; e-mail
saci@aurum.wits.ac.za; internet www.saci.co
.za; f. 1912; promotes chemistry and chemical
industry in South Africa; 755 mems; Pres.
Prof. IVAN GREEN; Vice-Pres. Prof. JAMES
DARKWA; publ. *South African Journal of
Chemistry* (4 a year).

South African Institute of Physics: Postnet Suite 165, Private Bag X025, Lynnwood
Ridge 0040; tel. (12) 841-2627; fax (86) 648-
8474; e-mail secretary@saip.org.za; internet
www.saip.org.za; f. 1955; 540 mems; Pres.
Prof. SIMON CONNELL; Council Sec. Dr JACKIE
NEL; Exec. Officer BRIAN MASARA.

RELIGION, SOCIOLOGY AND ANTHROPOLOGY

**South African Institute of Race Rela-
tions:** Private Bag X13, Marshalltown, 2107
Johannesburg; tel. (11) 492-0600; fax (11)
492-0588; e-mail sairr@sairr.org.za; internet
www.sairr.org.za; f. 1929; research, publishing, bursary admin.; library: J. H. Hofmeyer
Library specializing in South African current
affairs incl. 120 journals, historical documents, statistics, biographies; Pres. J. D.
JANSEN; Chief Exec J. S. KANE-BERMAN; publs
Fast Facts (12 a year), *South Africa Survey* (1
a year).

TECHNOLOGY

**Aeronautical Society of South Africa
(AeSSA):** POB 14717, Sinoville 0129; tel.
and fax (12) 808-1359; internet www.aessa
.org.za; f. 1911 to advance the growth and
scientific study of aeronautics; merged with
South African Institute of Aerospace Engineering and the Royal Division of AeSSA 2001,
to form Royal Aeronautical Society of South
Africa (RAeSSA); present name 2005 (while
retaining Royal Division status); theoretical
and practical research; offers advice, instruction and facilities for those studying the
subject; organizes meetings, lectures, etc.;
20,000 mems; Chair. Dr ROB HURLIN; Hon.
Sec. Dr C. LAW.

**Chartered Institute of Transport in
Southern Africa:** POB 95327, Grant Park
2051; tel. (11) 888-1813; fax (11) 782-8265;
e-mail citsa@global.co.za; f. 1993; 700 mems;
Pres. MALCOLM F. MITCHELL; Exec. Man. C.
LARKIN; publs *CITSA Handbook* (1 a year),
Pegasus (4 a year).

**Institution of Certificated Mechanical
and Electrical Engineers, South Africa:**
POB 93480, Yeoville 2143; 18A Gill St,
Observatory, Johannesburg 2198; tel. (11)
487-1683; fax (8667) 18533; e-mail icmee@
pixie.co.za; internet www.icmeesa.com; f.
1912; 1,444 mems; Pres. CHRIS SCHNEHAGE;
Hon. Treas. ROBBY HOLMWOOD; publ. *Vector
Magazine* (12 a year).

**South African Institute of Agricultural
Engineers/Suid-Afrikaanse Instituut
van Landbou-Ingenieurs:** POB 912-719,
Silverton 0127; tel. (12) 804-1540; fax (12)
804-0753; f. 1964; 500 mems; meetings, lectures, symposia, etc.; awards study bursaries; Pres. Prof. P. W. L. LYNE; Sec. F. B.
REINDERS; publ. *Agricultural Engineering in
South Africa* (1 a year).

South African Chemical Institute: The
Secretary, South African Chemical Institute,
POB 407, Witwatersrand 2050; e-mail saci
.chem@wits.ac.za; f. 1919; upholds the status
and interests of the profession of assaying in
all its brs; 900 mems; Administrator L.
SMITH; publ. *South African Journal of Chemistry* (online).

**South African Institute of Electrical
Engineers:** POB 751253, Gardenview 2047;
Innes House, 18A Gill St, Observatory,
Johannesburg; tel. (11) 487-3003; fax (11)
487-3002; e-mail info@saiee.org.za; internet
www.saiee.org.za; f. 1909; 5,000 mems; Pres.
MIKE CARY; Sr Sec. GERDA GEYER; Dir STAN
BRIDGENS; publs *SAIEE Africa Research
Journal* (4 a year), *WATTnow* (12 a year).

**South African Institute of Mining and
Metallurgy:** POB 61127, Marshalltown
2107; 5th Fl., Chamber of Mines Bldg, 5
Hollard St, Johannesburg; tel. (11) 834-1273;
fax (11) 838-5923; e-mail carina@saimm.co
.za; internet www.saimm.co.za; f. 1884;
3,000 mems; Pres. Dr WILLEM VAN NIEKERK;
Man. CARINA REYNDERS; publ. *Journal* (6 a
year).

**South African Institution of Civil Engin-
eering (SAICE):** Private Bag X200, Halfway
House 1685; Building 19, Thornhill Office
Park, Bekker St, Vorna Valley, Midrand; tel.
(11) 805-5947; fax (11) 805-5971; e-mail
civilinfo@saice.org.za; internet www.civils
.org.za; f. 1903; represents the civil engineering profession in South Africa; 6,571
mems; Exec. Dir D. B. BOTHA; publs *Civil
Engineering* (magazine, 11 a year), *Journal*
(technical journal for research papers, 4 a
year).

**South African Institution of Mechanical
Engineering:** POB 511, Bruma 2026; tel.
(11) 615-5660; fax (11) 388-5356; e-mail
saimeche@iafrica.com; internet www
.saimeche.org.za; f. 1892; 4,500 mems; Pres.
Prof. H. L. T. JEFFERY; Hon. Treasurer G.
BARBIC; publs *R&D Journal* (4 a year), *SA
Mechanical Engineer* (12 a year).

Research Institutes

GENERAL

Africa Institute of South Africa: POB
630, Pretoria 0001; Embassy House, cnr of
Edmond St and Bailey Lane, Arcadia, Pretoria; tel. (12) 304-9760; fax (12) 323-8153;
e-mail ai@ai.org.za; internet www.ai.org.za;
f. 1960; applied research and the colln of
information in the fields of politics, socio-
economics, devt and int. relations on the
African continent and its diaspora; CEO Dr
MATLOTLENG P. MATLOU; publs *Africa Insight*
(4 a year), *Inside AISA* (newsletter, 6 a year).

**Council for Scientific and Industrial
Research (CSIR):** POB 395, Pretoria 0001;
Meiring Naudé Rd, Brummeria, Pretoria; tel.

(12) 841-2911; fax (12) 841-4326; e-mail
callcentre@csir.co.za; internet www.csir.co
.za; f. 1945; directed and multi-disciplinary
research in areas of biosciences, built environment, defence, emerging research areas of
nanotechnology, materials science and
manufacturing, mobile autonomous intelligent systems, natural resources and the
environment, peace, safety and security,
synthetic biology; provides consulting and
analytical services incl. engineering forensics, environmental testing, fires and explosion testing, food and beverage analysis,
forensic fire investigations, mechanical testing, project management, sports technology
and analysis, wire rope testing; library: see
under Libraries and Archives; Pres. and CEO
Dr SIBUSISO SIBISI; Chief Financial Officer
EBIE MAYET; Group Exec. for Operations
HOFFIE MAREE; Exec. Dir Services RAYNOLD
ZONDO; Group Exec. for Research and Devt
Outcomes and Strategic Human Capital Devt
KHUNGEKA NJOBE; publs *ScienceScope* (4 a
year), research reports.

AGRICULTURE, FISHERIES AND VETERINARY SCIENCE

Agricultural Research Council: POB
8783, Pretoria 0001; 1134 Park St, Hatfield,
Pretoria; tel. (12) 427-9700; fax (12) 342-
3948; e-mail nkami@arc.agric.za; internet
www.arc.agric.za; f. 1992; Pres. and CEO Dr
N. TAU-MZAMANE.

Attached Research Institutes:

Agrimetrics Institute: Private Bag
X5013, Stellenbosch 7599; tel. (12) 342-
9968; fax (12) 342-9969; interdisciplinary
service of biometrical and datametrical
input to all institutes of the Agricultural
Research Ccl; planning of scientific experiments, analysis and interpretation of
research results; datametric service for
devt and application of scientific data and
management of computer systems; Dir Dr
PIET JOOSTE.

Animal Improvement Institute, Irene:
ARC Livestock Division, Private Bag X2,
Irene 0062; tel. (12) 672-9055; fax (12) 665-
1550; e-mail andrew@arc.agric.za; internet
www.arc.agric.za; research and devt in
animal breeding and genetics; nutrition
and food science; library of 10,000 vols; Dir
Dr M. A. MAGADLELA.

**Animal Nutrition and Animal Prod-
ucts Institute, Irene:** Private Bag X2,
Irene 1675; tel. (12) 672-9111; fax (12) 665-
1609; research and devt in animal nutrition, meat and dairy products; Dir Dr
HEINZ MEISSNER.

ARC Infruitec-Nietvoorbij: Private Bag
X5026, Stellenbosch 7599; tel. (21) 809-
3100; fax (21) 809-3400; e-mail breedtk@
arc.agric.za; internet www.arc.agric.za; f.
1960; research on the cultivation and post-
harvest technology of deciduous fruit, on
all aspects of cultivation of table, raisin
and wine grapes, and on production of wine
and brandy; library of 5,000 vols; Research
Man. Dr JOHAN VAN ZYL.

ARC Institute for Industrial Crops:
Private Bag X82075, Rustenburg 0300;
tel. (14) 5363150; fax (14) 5363113; e-mail
infoiic@arc.agric.za; internet www.arc
.agric.za; basic and applied research on
tobacco cotton and industrial crops; Sr
Man. Dr GRAHAM THOMPSON; Sr Sec. KAREN
SMOOK.

ARC Small Grain Institute: Private Bag
X29, Bethlehem 9700; tel. (58) 307-3400;
fax (58) 307-3519; e-mail kilianj@arc.agric
.za; internet www.arc.agric.za; f. 1947;
research on improvement and cultivation

of wheat and small grain crops; Man. Dr COBUS LE ROUX.

Grain Crops Institute: Private Bag X1251, Potchefstroom 2520; tel. (18) 299-6100; fax (18) 294-7146; f. 1981; research on grain crops and oil and protein seeds; Dir Dr P. J. A. VAN DER MERWE.

Institute for Agricultural Engineering: Private Bag X519, Silverton 0127; tel. (12) 842-4000; fax (12) 804-0753; f. 1961; research on agricultural mechanization, farm structures, irrigation, resource conservation, energy, aquaculture and product processing; Dir Prof. TIMOTHY SIMALONGA.

Institute for Soil, Climate and Water: Private Bag X79, Pretoria 0001; tel. (12) 310-2500; fax (12) 323-1157; e-mail iscwinfo@arc.agric.za; f. 1902; soil science, agrometeorology, water utilization, remote sensing, analytical services; library of 10,000 vols; Research and Technology Man. Dr M. MAILA; Librarian REJAENE VAN DYK.

Institute of Tropical and Subtropical Crops: Private Bag X11208, Nelspruit 1200; tel. (13) 753-2071; fax (13) 752-3854; f. 1926; research on fruit, cocoa, and exotic crops; Dir Dr JOHANN VAN ZYL.

Onderstepoort Veterinary Institute: Private Bag X5, Onderstepoort 0110, Pretoria; tel. (12) 529-9111; fax (12) 565-6573; e-mail ovi-info@arc.agric.za; internet www.arc.agric.za; f. 1908; research on animal diseases; production of vaccines; diagnostic service; library of 96,000 vols; Dir Dr DAAN VERWOERD; Research Institute Man. Prof. TONY MUSOKE; publ. *Onderstepoort Journal of Veterinary Research* (4 a year).

Plant Protection Research Institute: Private Bag X134, Pretoria 0001; tel. (12) 808-0952; fax (12) 808-1489; promotes economically and environmentally acceptable pest control and sustainable farming; research on invertebrates, fungi, bacteria and viruses; advisory service on aspects of biological control; library of 9,000 vols; Dir MIKE WALTERS.

Range and Forage Institute: Private Bag X05, Lynn East, Pretoria 0039; tel. (12) 841-9611; fax (12) 808-2155; research on sustainable livestock and rangeland management systems; Head Dr AIMIE AUCAMP.

Roodeplaat Vegetable and Ornamental Plant Institute: Private Bag X293, Pretoria 0001; tel. (12) 841-9611; fax (12) 808-0844; f. 1949; research on vegetables, and on cut flowers, pot plants and other ornamental plants; Dir Dr SONJA VENTER.

Attached Unit:

Plant Genetic Resources Unit: c/o The Division Manager, Private Bag X05, Lynn East 0039; tel. (12) 841-9716; fax (12) 808-1001; centralizes and co-ordinates plant genetic resources activities within the plant science institutes and liaises with regional and int. agencies; responsible for documenting Agricultural Research Council germplasm and for arranging safety base collection facilities; Man. Dr ROGER ELLIS.

MEDICINE

National Health Laboratory Service: POB 1038, Johannesburg 2000; 1 Modderfontein Rd, Sandringham, Johannesburg; tel. (11) 386-6000; fax (11) 386-6002; e-mail info@nhls.ac.za; internet www.nhls.ac.za; f. 1912, formerly South African Institute for Medical Research; national network of approx 250 regional pathology laboratories, situated in all provinces except KwaZulu-Natal; co-ordi-

nates diagnostic pathology services, research, teaching, training and production of anti-snake sera, reagents and media; member institutions include the pathology departments and laboratories of the medical schools of the universities of the Witwatersrand, Pretoria, Cape Town, Free State and Transkei and the Medical University of South Africa; library of 17,500 vols, 250 periodical titles, 5,000 reprint titles of staff papers; Chair. of Board of Management SESI BALOYI; CEO JOHN ROBERTSON; Head of Dept of Anatomical Pathology Prof. A. PATTERSON; Head of Dept of Chemical Pathology (vacant); Head of Dept of Clinical Microbiology and Infectious Diseases Prof. A. DUSE; Head of Dept of Haematology Prof. WENDY STEVENS; Head of Dept of Human Genetics Prof. D. VILJOEN; Head of Dept of Immunology Prof. A. A. WADEE; Head of Dept of Medical Entomology Prof. M. COETZEE; publ. *South African Journal of Epidemiology and Infection.*

South African Brain Research Institute: 6 Campbell St, Waverley, Johannesburg 2090; tel. (11) 786-2912; fax (11) 786-1766; e-mail mag@iafrica.com; internet www.sabri.org.za; f. 1981; all aspects of pure and applied brain research; library of 10,000 vols; CEO Prof. M. A. GILLMAN.

South African Medical Research Council: POB 19070, Tygerberg 7505; located at: Francie van Zijl Drive, Parowvallei, Western Cape; tel. (21) 938-0911; fax (21) 938-0200; e-mail info@mrc.ac.za; internet www.mrc.ac.za; f. 1969; nat. research programmes: environment and development, health systems and policy, infection and immunity, molecules to disease, non-communicable diseases, and women and child health; Pres. Prof. ANTHONY MBEWU.

NATURAL SCIENCES

Biological Sciences

Municipal Botanic Gardens: 70 St Thomas Rd, Durban, KwaZulu-Natal; tel. (31) 201-1303; fax (31) 201-7382; e-mail sandig@prcsu.durban.gov.za; internet www.durbanbotanicgardens.org.za; f. 1849, for the propagation, display and landscape of ornamental, exotic and Southern African indigenous flora, and as a place for the study of and instruction in botany and horticulture and potential agricultural crops; extensive collections of orchids, cycads, palms and bromeliads; herb garden; garden for the blind; water lily pond, fern garden; indigenous medicinal plants; Chair. Prof. DONAL McCRACKEN; Curator, Durban Botanic Gardens C. G. M. DALZELL.

National Zoological Gardens of South Africa: POB 754, Pretoria 0001; located at: 232 Boom St, Pretoria 0001; tel. (12) 328-3265; fax (12) 323-4540; e-mail zoologic@cis.co.za; internet www.zoo.ac.za; f. 1899; attached to National Research Foundation; library of 4,000 vols, 40 periodicals; CEO WILLIE LABUSCHAGNE; publ. *Zoön.*

Physical Sciences

Council for Geoscience: Private Bag X112, Pretoria 0001; 280 Pretoria St, Silverton, Pretoria 0001; tel. (12) 841-1911; fax (12) 841-1221; internet www.geoscience.org.za; f. 1912; applied and fundamental geological research, mapping; library of 200,000 books, 10,000 maps; CEO THIBEDI RAMONTJA; publs bulletins, biographies, handbooks, *Groundwater Series, Memoirs, Seismological Series.*

Hartebeesthoek Radio Astronomy Observatory: POB 443, Krugersdorp 1740; tel. (12) 326-0742; fax (12) 326-0756; e-mail info@hartrao.ac.za; internet www.hartrao.ac.za; f. 1961, since 1988 a national facility

under Foundation for Research Development (now National Research Foundation); radio telescope 26 m in diameter used for observations of Local Galaxy, spectroscopy of interstellar and circumstellar atoms and molecules, masers, pulsars, quasars and active galaxies; collaborates in global VLBI Networks; library of 1,000 vols, 75 periodicals; Dir Prof. ROY BOOTH.

NECSA (South African Nuclear Energy Corporation): POB 582, Pretoria 0001; located at: Church St W Extension, Pelindaba, Brits District; tel. (12) 305-4911; fax (12) 305-3111; e-mail webmaster@necsa.co.za; internet www.necsa.co.za; f. 1982 as Atomic Energy Corporation of South Africa Ltd (AEC); 10 mems; operates UF6 conversion, fuel fabrication facilities, isotope production centre, hot cell facility and food radurization plant; enrichment research; operates 20- MW ORR type research reactor (SAFARI-1); 3.75- MV Van der Graaff accelerator; CEO Dr ROB ADAM.

Satellite Applications Centre: Division of Microelectronics and Communications Technology, CSIR, POB 395, Pretoria 0001; tel. (12) 841-9211; fax (12) 349-1153; e-mail callcentre@csir.co.za; internet www.csir.co.za/sac; f. 1961 as part of US Satellite Tracking and Data Network; since 1975 part of CSIR; receives, archives and processes METEOSAT, LANDSAT, NOAA and SPOT data; online LANDSAT data catalogue; 45 staff; library of 500 vols, 30 periodicals; Operations Man. RAOUL HODGES.

South African Astronomical Observatory: POB 9, Observatory 7935; POB 25, Sutherland 6920; tel. (21) 447-0025; fax (21) 447-3639; e-mail enquiries@saao.ac.za; internet www.saao.ac.za; f. 1972 by a merger of Royal Observatory Cape of Good Hope and Republic Observatory, Johannesburg; equipment incl. 11-, 1.9-, 1.0-, 0.75- and 0.5-m reflectors; library of 30,000 vols; Dir Prof. P. A. CHARLES; Librarian SHIREEN DAVIS.

RELIGION, SOCIOLOGY AND ANTHROPOLOGY

Human Sciences Research Council (HSRC): Private Bag X41, Pretoria 0001; 134 Pretorius St, Pretoria 0002; tel. (12) 302-2000; fax (12) 302-2001; e-mail helpdesk@hsrc.ac.za; internet www.hsrc.ac.za; f. 1969; promotes, supports and coordinates research in the human and social sciences; advises the govt on research priorities; disseminates research findings; promotes the training of people for research work and makes available to all South Africans the full range of disciplines in the human sciences; library of 60,000 vols, 700 current periodicals; Pres. and CEO Dr OLIVE SHISANA; publ. *HSRC Review* (4 a year).

Institute for the Study of Mankind in Africa: School of Anatomical Sciences, University of the Witwatersrand Medical School, 7 York Rd, Parktown 2193; tel. (11) 717-2405; e-mail science.pg@wits.ac.za; f. 1960 to perpetuate the work of Prof. Raymond A. Dart on the study of mankind in Africa, past and present, in health and disease; serves as a centre of anthropological and medical field work; it functions partly through the auspices of the University of the Witwatersrand; Pres. Prof. J. N. MAINA.

TECHNOLOGY

MINTEK: PMB X3015, Randburg 2125; tel. (11) 709-4111; fax (11) 793-2413; e-mail info@mintek.ac.za; internet www.mintek.co.za; f. 1934; research, devt and technology transfer to promote mineral technology and to foster the establishment and expansion of industries in the fields of minerals and mineral products; investigates all aspects of mineral beneficiation, especially areas such as new alloys and chemical products; divs specializing in analytical and process chemistry, analytical science, hydrometallurgy, measurement and control, mineralogy, minerals eng., physical metallurgy, pyrometallurgy; sponsors univ. research groups; library of 30,000 vols; CEO Dr PAUL JOURDAN; publs *Mintek Bulletin* (12 a year), *Research Reports* (irregular).

South African Bureau of Standards: Private Bag X191, 1 Dr Lategan Rd, Groenkloof, Pretoria 0001; tel. (12) 428-7911; fax (12) 344-1568; e-mail info@sabs.co.za; internet www.sabs.co.za; f. 1945; draws up national standards, administers the SABS mark and listing schemes; Pres. M. J. KUSCUS (acting); publ. *Standards Bulletin: Official information* (online).

Libraries and Archives
Alice
University of Fort Hare Library: Private Bag X1322, Alice 5700; tel. (40) 602-2612; fax (40) 653-1423; f. 1916; 165,000 vols; contains the Howard Pim Library of Rare Books; University Librarian YOLISA K. SOUL.

Bloemfontein
Free State Library and Information Services: Private Bag X20606, Bloemfontein 9300; tel. (51) 405-4680; fax (51) 403-3567; e-mail jacomien@majuba.ofs.gov.za; internet mangaung.ofs.gov.za; f. 1948; 3m. books; serves 135 public libraries; Dir T. A. LUBBE; publ. *Free State Libraries* (4 a year).

Mangaung Library Services: POB 1029, Bloemfontein 9301; tel. (51) 405-8241; fax (51) 405-8604; f. 1875; Legal Deposit, National Drama Library, and Public Library; 500,000 vols, 65,000 plays; Man., Education, Library, Arts and Culture N. L. MOHLAODI; publ. *Catalogue of the National Drama Library*.

University of the Free State Library and Information Services: POB 301, Bloemfontein 9300; tel. (51) 401-3488; fax (51) 444-6343; e-mail eisterkb@ufs.ac.za; internet www.ufs.ac.za; f. 1904; colln incl. rare pamphlets and other early South African publs of Dreyer-Africana Colln and items on South African War; 576,000 vols (3,000 periodicals); Dir K. B. EISTER.

Cape Town
Cape Town City Libraries: POB 4728, Cape Town 8000; tel. (21) 462-4400; fax (21) 461-5981; f. 1952; free municipal public library service; central library and 32 suburban brs, travelling, hospital, old age homes, homebound library services; 1.5m. vols; special art, music and business collections; Librarian H. C. F. HEYMANN.

Library and Information Unit of Parliament: POB 18, Cape Town 8000; located at: Ground Fl., NCOP Wing, Parliament St, Cape Town 8000; tel. (21) 403-2140; fax (21) 461-4331; e-mail library@parliament.gov.za; internet www.parliament.gov.za; f. 1857; provides general and legislative reference services and a press-cutting service to members and officers of Parliament; legal deposit library and depository for UN publs; 350,000 items, including the Mendelssohn Africana Collection; 2,700 current periodicals; local and foreign government and parliamentary publs; Librarian ALBERT NTUNJA.

Royal Society of South Africa Library: 4.17 P D Hahn Bldg, c/o Univ. of Cape Town, Rhodes Gift 7700; tel. (21) 650-2543; e-mail

royalsociety@uct.ac.za; internet www.royalsocietysa.org.za; f. 1877, Royal Charter 1908; 33,000 vols of scientific periodicals, held by Univ. of Cape Town Library; Hon. Librarian Prof. J. R. E. LUTJEHARMS; publ. *Transactions of the Royal Society of South Africa* (3 a year).

South African Library: POB 496, Cape Town 8000; 5 Queen Victoria St, POB 496, Cape Town 8000; tel. (21) 424-6320; fax (21) 423-3359; e-mail info@nlsa.ac.za; internet www.nlsa.ac.za; f. 1818; nat. reference and preservation library with legal deposit privileges; 750,000 books and official publs, 200,000 bound periodicals, 8,000 current periodicals, 45,000 bound newspapers, 300 current newspapers, 20,000 maps, 100,000 iconographic items; MS collections of Cape and early SA; comprehensive Africana collection pertaining to South Africa, with materials on neighbouring Southern African countries; UN and World Bank depository library; special collections incl. Grey Collection of 115 medieval MSS, 5,000 vols incl. incunabula and early South African imprints; Dessinian (17th–18th century); Nourse Cromwelliana (17th century); Fairbridge (19th century); reference room for research; regular exhibitions of library material; microfilming, photographic and copying services; Dir JOHN KGWALE TSEBE; publs *Grey Bibliographies*, *Quarterly Bulletin*.

University of Cape Town Libraries: Private Bag X3, Rondebosch, Cape Town 7701; tel. (21) 650-3134; fax (21) 650-2965; e-mail libraries@uct.ac.za; internet www.lib.uct.ac.za; f. 1905; comprises Chancellor Oppenheimer Library and brs: Special Collns, Bolus Herbarium Library, Brand van Zyl Law Library, Built Environment Library, Health Sciences Library, Hiddingh Hall Library (fine arts and drama), Institute of Child Health Library, Jewish Studies Library, WH Bell Music Library; spec. collns incl. archives of the Black Sash (Cape Western region) and other human rights orgs, African language collns, African Studies colln (incl. pre-1925 Africana, local imprints from the African continent, and grey literature), Bolus colln (antiquarian botanical works), govt publs, rare books (with fore-edge paintings), Kipling colln, literary collns incl. C. Louis Leipoldt, medical history colln, MSS and archives (incl. Bleek and Lloyd colln), MSS music scores of South African composers, original material relating to South African political and social history, Pauline Smith and Olive Schreiner, collns of South African architects, records of the Jewish community in the W Cape, Van Zyl colln (antiquarian legal works); 1.2m. vols, 100,600 journal titles and 190 online database; Exec. Dir GWENDA THOMAS; Head Librarian FIONA JONES.

Western Cape Education Library and Information Service (EDULIS): Private Bag X9099, Cape Town 8000; tel. (21) 957-9618; fax (21) 948-0748; e-mail edulis@pgwc.gov.za; internet edulis.pgwc.gov.za; f. 1859; 8,000 mems; 60,000 vols, 150 current periodicals; Head LYNE MCLENNAN.

Western Cape Provincial Library Service: POB 2108, Cape Town 8000; cnr of Chiappinni and Hospital Sts, Cape Town 8001; tel. (21) 483-2273; fax (21) 483-2031; e-mail capelib@pgwc.gov.za; internet www.capegateway.gov.za/library; f. 1945; 15 regional libraries, 316 affiliated libraries; library promotion; training of public librarians; selection, buying and distribution of library material; central reference service; computerized library and information system; 5.7m. vols; collns of art prints, phonographic records, CDs, audio cassettes, 16mm

films, video cassettes, DVDs; Dir, Library and Archival Services NOMAZA DINGAYO; publ. *Cape Librarian / Kaapse Bibliotekaris* (6 a year).

Durban
eThekwini Municipal Library Service: City Hall, Smith St, POB 917, Durban 4000; tel. (31) 311-2444; fax (31) 311-2410; e-mail masingat@durban.gov.za; internet www.durban.gov.za; f. 1853; spec. collns of African Studies and Shakespearean; 89 brs; 1.5m. vols; Dir R. NYONGWANA (acting); Dir TREVOR MASINGA (acting).

University of KwaZulu-Natal Library: King George V Ave, Glenwood, Durban 4041; tel. (31) 260-2317; fax (31) 260-1084; e-mail buchanan@ukzn.ac.za; internet www.library.und.ac.za; f. 2004; five main libraries in two centres, four in Durban and one in Pietermaritzburg and several br. libraries; 1,321,971 vols; Dir of Library Services NORA BUCHANAN.

East London
Buffalo City Municipal Library Service: Gladstone St, POB 652, East London; tel. (43) 722-4991; fax (43) 743-1729; f. 1876; 30,000 mems; 225,000 vols; Librarian Mrs M. M. DAVIDSON.

Grahamstown
Grahamstown Public Library: POB 180, Grahamstown 6140; tel. (46) 603-6040; fax (46) 622-9488; e-mail library@makana.gov.za; internet www.makana.gov.za; f. 1842; 81,053 vols; Librarian P. VUBELA.

National English Literary Museum: Private Bag 1019, Grahamstown 6140; tel. (46) 622-7042; fax (46) 622-2582; e-mail nelm@ru.ac.za; internet www.rhodes.ac.za/nelm; f. 1980, fmrly Thomas Pringle Colln for English in Africa; collns of literary MSS, books, photographs, journal articles, academic theses and press cuttings; educational programmes, exhibitions, lectures; 31,000 vols; Dir BEVERLEY THOMAS; Sr Librarian DEBBIE S. LANDMAN; Head Archivist ANN TORLESSE; publ. *NELM News* (2 a year).

Rhodes University Library: Rhodes Univ., POB 184, Grahamstown 6140; tel. (46) 603-8436; fax (46) 603-7310; e-mail library@ru.ac.za; internet www.ru.ac.za/library; f. 1904; 400,000 vols; Dir for Library Services UJALA SATGOOR.

Johannesburg
City of Johannesburg Library and Information Services: Central Reference Library, Market Sq., Johannesburg; tel. (11) 870-1227; e-mail joburgconnect@joburg.org.za; f. 1890; 1.9m. vols; Regional Man. (vacant); publ. *Local Government Library Bulletin* (12 a year).

Library of the South African Institute of Race Relations: POB 291722, Melville 2109; 2 Clamart Rd Richmond, Johannesburg 2092; tel. (11) 482 7221; fax (11) 482 7690; e-mail prisca@sairr.org.za; internet www.sairr.org.za; f. 1929; valuable archival and documentary material; newspaper clippings from 1930 on race relations, politics, labour and economics; bibliographies on race relations; 7,030 vols; Information Dir T. DIMANT.

University of the Witwatersrand Library: Private Bag XI, PO Wits, 2050; tel. (11) 717-1901; fax (11) 717-1946; e-mail felix.ubogu@library.wits.ac.za; internet www.wits.ac.za/library; f. 1922; 1.2m. vols, access to 46,000 e-journal titles; 2 central libraries (undergraduate and research), also br. libraries: architecture, biological and physical sciences, education and commerce, engineering, geological and mathematical sciences, health sciences, law, management, nuclear sciences; spec. collns incl. Africana, Hebraica and Judaica, Archaeology and Egyptology, Early Printed Books, Historical and Literary Papers (incl. Church of the Province of South Africa), Portuguese; Librarian FELIX N. UBOGU.

Kimberley

Kimberley Public Library: POB 627, Kimberley 8300; tel. (53) 830-6241; fax (53) 833-1954; internet home.global.co.za/~afrilib; f. 1882; 127,000 vols; Africana Library of 20,000 vols, 545 MSS, 1,145 photographs (North Cape and Diamond Fields); Judy Scott Library of 43,000 vols; Librarian F. VAN DYK.

Mmabatho

North-West Provincial Library Services: Private Bag X2044, Mmabatho 2735; tel. (18) 392-2060; f. 1978; under Dept of Arts, Culture and Sport; 75 public libraries, 7 college libraries, 1,000 school libraries, 7 govt dept libraries; 1.6m. vols; Deputy Dir N. B. NOMNGA.

Pietermaritzburg

KwaZulu-Natal Provincial Library Service: Private Bag X9016, Pietermaritzburg; tel. (33) 341-3000; fax (33) 394-2237; e-mail frenchl@plho.kzntl.gov.za; f. 1952; consists of central org. and reference library at Pietermaritzburg; 4 regional offices for Coast, S Coast, Midlands and N areas, serving 172 public libraries; 3.4m. vols, 21,000 CDs, 32,000 video cassettes, 6,500 DVDs; Man. CAROL SLATER; Asst Man., Central Reference Library LINDY FRENCH; publ. KZN Librarian (4 a year).

Natal Society Library: Churchill Sq., Church St, Pietermaritzburg 3200, Natal; tel. (33) 345-2383; fax (33) 394-0095; f. 1851; lending, children's, reference, legal deposit, school assignments, music, special collections, map collns, Africana colln; 6 brs, hospital, housebound and travelling library services; 600,000 vols; 6,332 current legal deposit periodicals and newspapers, 122 current overseas periodicals, numerous bound legal deposit and overseas periodicals and newspapers; Dir J. C. MORRISON; publs AIDS Bibliography, Natalia (1 a year).

University of KwaZulu-Natal Library, Pietermaritzburg Campus: Private Bag X014, Scottsville 3209; tel. (33) 260-6194; fax (33) 260-5260; e-mail sukram@ukzn.ac.za; internet www.library.unp.ac.za; f. 1909; 375,000 vols; Librarian PRAVERSH SUKRAM (acting).

Port Elizabeth

Nelson Mandela Metropolitan Libraries: POB 66, Port Elizabeth 6000; tel. (41) 506-1373; fax (41) 506-1390; e-mail kdeklerk@mandelametro.gov.za; f. 1901; public library with extensive Africana, genealogical and maritime collns; research and orientation workshops for scholars; 500,000 vols; Head of Libraries BONGIWE CHIGUMBU.

Nelson Mandela Metropolitan University Library and Information Services: POB 77700, Port Elizabeth 6000; tel. (41) 504-2281; fax (41) 504-2280; internet www.nmmu.ac.za; f. 1964; 507,356 vols; L. C. Steyn Collection of Roman Dutch Law; Director MARJORY EALES.

Potchefstroom

Ferdinand Postma Library, North-West University: Private Bag X05, Noordbrug 2522; tel. (18) 299-2000; fax (18) 299-2999; e-mail fpbalg@nwu.ac.za; internet www.nwu.ac.za/library; f. 1869; 547,035 vols, 1,694 current periodicals; Main Library (Ferdinand Postma Library), Library of the Theological School of the Reformed Churches in South Africa (Jan Lion Cachet Library), Music Library, Natural Sciences Library, Vaal Triangle Campus Library at Vanderbijlpark; special collections: Carney Africana Collection, Hertzog Law Collection, Collection of the Institute for Research in Children's Literature; Dir TOM LARNEY.

Pretoria

Council for Scientific and Industrial Research (CSIR) Information Services: POB 395, Pretoria 0001; tel. (12) 841-2911; fax (12) 841-4405; e-mail callcentre@csir.co.za; internet www.csir.co.za; f. 1945; provides scientific, technical and business management information services to CSIR research staff and to external clients; 90,000 bound vols, 4,000 serial titles and 22,000 pamphlets; Man. Dr MARTIE VAN DEVENTER; publ. Technobrief.

Department of Agriculture, Fisheries & Forestry Information Centre: Private Bag X388, Pretoria 0001; tel. (12) 319-6872; fax (12) 319-7245; e-mail daleenk@daff.gov.za; internet www.daff.gov.za; f. 1910; library services, distribution of departmental publs; 40,000 vols, 50 current periodicals, 140,000 pamphlets; Asst Dir DALEEN KOEN.

Department of Arts, Culture, Science and Technology Library: Private Bag X894, Pretoria 0001; tel. (12) 314-6033; fax (12) 323-2720; special collections: library science, science planning, state language services, national terminology services; 42,000 vols; 153 current periodicals; Librarian D. E. MOHLAKWANA.

Department of Education Library: Private Bag X895, Pretoria 0001; tel. (12) 312-5265; fax (12) 325-1475; f. 1994; Asst Dir REGINAH BAMUZA.

Gauteng Library Information Policy and Archiving Services: Private Bag X33, Marshalltown 2000; tel. (11) 355-2500; fax (11) 355-2565; e-mail koekie.meyer@gpg.gov.za; internet www.srac.gpg.gov.za; f. 1995; consists of Head Office in Johannesburg, and 4 Regional Libraries; provides library and information service to 324 public and community libraries and depots in Gauteng Province; 3.5m. vols; Dir J. M. MEYER (acting).

Mary Gunn Library, South African National Biodiversity Institute: Private Bag X101, Pretoria 0001; tel. (12) 843-5042; fax (12) 804-8740; e-mail potgietere@sanbi.org; internet www.sanbi.org; f. 1916; 17,642 vols; Chief Exec. Dr T. ABRAHAMSE.

National Archives and Heraldic Services: Private Bag X236, Pretoria 0001; tel. (12) 323-5300; fax (12) 323-5287; e-mail arg02@dacst4.pwv.gov.za; provides a comprehensive archives service to all government offices and local authorities; processes and stores archive material; makes archives and facilities available to researchers; National Archivist for the Republic of South Africa Dr G. A. DOMINY.

State Library: POB 397, Pretoria 0001; tel. (12) 321-8931; fax (12) 325-5984; f. 1887; national and legal depository library, and depository library for US Government and UN publications; 684,000 vols, 9,600 current serials; responsible for compiling the national bibliography; international and national interlending centre; Southern African Book Exchange Centre; ISBN and ISSN centre for South Africa; Dir Dr PETER J. LOR; publs South African National Bibliography (4 a year and 1 a year cumulations, paper and machine-readable format), Index to South African Periodicals (CD-ROM and machine-readable format), RSA Government Gazette (4 a year, microfiche), South African Newspapers on Microfilm, Bibliography of the Xhosa Language, Northern Sotho Bibliography, Directory of South African Publishers.

Transvaal Education Department, Education Media Service: 328 Van der Walt St, Private Bag X290, Pretoria 0001; tel. (12) 322-7685; fax (12) 322-7699; f. 1951; 385,000 vols, 600 periodicals, 3,000 video cassettes; Dir J. A. BIERMAN.

University of Pretoria Libraries: Academic Information Service, University of Pretoria, Pretoria 0002; tel. (12) 420-4111; fax (12) 362-5182; e-mail jaboon@up.ac.za; internet www.up.ac.za/asservices/ais/ais.htm; f. 1908; 1.2m. vols, pamphlets, govt publs, 5,698 periodicals, etc., 8,000 gramophone records, 26,000 items of sheet-music, 2,250 CDs; Dir J. A. BOON.

University of South Africa Library: POB 392, UNISA 0003; tel. (12) 429-3131; fax (12) 429-2925; e-mail mbambtb@unisa.ac.za; internet www.unisa.ac.za/library; f. 1947; 2m. vols, 335,000 bound serials; science library and law colln specializing in foreign and comparative law; brs in Cape Town, Durban, Pretoria Johannesburg, Rustenburg, Addis Ababa and Polokwane; Exec. Dir Dr MBAMBO-THATA; publ. Mousaion (irregular).

Sovenga

University of Limpopo Library: Private Bag X1112, Sovenga, Limpopo 0727; tel. (15) 268-2656; fax (15) 268-2198; internet www.ul.ac.za/library; 80,000 vols, 581 periodicals; Exec. Dir. MAKGABELA CHUENE; Librarian PATEKA MATSHAYA.

Stellenbosch

Stellenbosch University Library and Information Service: Stellenbosch University, Private Bag X5036, Stellenbosch 7599; tel. (21) 808-4876; fax (21) 808-3723; e-mail etise@sun.ac.za; internet www.sun.ac.za/library; f. 1895; 701,853 books; Sr Dir ELLEN TISE.

Museums and Art Galleries

Bloemfontein

National Museum: POB 266, Bloemfontein 9300; 36 Aliwal St, Bloemfontein 9301; tel. (51) 447-9609; fax (51) 447-6273; e-mail ornito@nasmus.co.za; internet www.nasmus.co.za; f. 1877; main focus is on natural and cultural history (incl. Florisbad human fossil skull); also social and local history; library of 10,000 vols, 1,730 serial titles, 11,000 pamphlets; Dir R. J. NUTTALL; publs Navorsinge van die Nasionale Museum / Researches of the National Museum, Praktikum.

Cape Town

Iziko Museums of Cape Town: POB 61, Cape Town 8000; tel. (21) 481-3800; fax (21) 481-3993; internet www.iziko.org.za; f. 1999; CEO Prof. H. C. BREDEKAMP.

Art Sites:

Iziko—Michaelis Collection: POB 61, Cape Town 8000; The Old Town House, Greenmarket Sq., Cape Town; tel. (21) 481-3933; fax (21) 424-6441; internet www.iziko.org.za/michaelis; f. 1916; Dutch and Flemish paintings, drawings and prints of the 16th century to the early 20th century; Dutch and colonial furniture; library of 1,500 vols; Dir, Art Collns M. H. MARTIN.

Iziko—Natale Labia Museum: POB 61, Cape Town 8000; 192 Main Rd, Muizenberg, Cape Town 7945; tel. (21) 788-4106; fax (21) 788-3908; internet www.iziko.org .za/natale; f. 1988; built 1929 as residence of first Italian Minister Plenipotentiary in SA, Prince Natale Labia; elaborate Italianate furnishings with 18th- and 19th-century British and European art; Dir for Art Collns M. H. MARTIN.

Iziko—South African National Gallery Library: POB 61, Cape Town 8001; tel. (21) 467-4660; fax (21) 467-4680; e-mail info@iziko.org.za; internet www.iziko.org .za/sang; f. 1871; collns of South African, African, British, French, Dutch and Flemish art; also photography, sculpture, beadwork, textiles and architecture; library of 10,000 vols, journals and pamphlets; public access by appointment; Dir for Art Collns RAISON NAIDOO; Librarian MAUREEN CHIWARE.

Natural History Sites:

Iziko—Planetarium: 25 Queen Victoria St, Cape Town 8000; tel. (21) 481-3900; fax (21) 481-3990; e-mail tferreira@iziko.org .za; internet www.iziko.org.za/ planetarium; f. 1987; organizes shows; holiday workshops and astronomy courses; Man. THEO FERREIRA.

Iziko—South African Museum: 25 Queen Victoria St, Cape Town 8000; tel. (21) 481-3900; fax (21) 481-3990; internet www.iziko.org.za/sam; f. 1825; collns incl. ethnography, applied arts, philately, transport, weaponry, toys; library of 12,000 vols, 4,000 periodicals; Dir, Natural History Collns Dr H. ROBERTSON; publ. *African Natural History* (1 a year).

Iziko—West Coast Fossil Park: POB 42, Langebaanweg, Cape Town 7375; R27 Langebaanweg, Cape Town 7375; tel. (22) 766-1606; fax (22) 766-1765; e-mail info@ iziko.org.za; internet www.iziko.org.za/ iziko/partners/wcfp.html; f. 1998; Dir for Natural History Collns Dr P. HAARHOFF.

Social History Sites:

Iziko—Bertram House: Hiddingh Campus, Orange St, Cape Town 8000; tel. (21) 481-3940; fax (21) 481-3941; internet www .iziko.org.za/bertram; f. 1984; early 19th-century Georgian townhouse; displays of Georgian furniture, Chinese and English porcelain, and English silver and kitchenware; Dir for Social History Collns Dr P. J. DAVISON.

Iziko—Bo-Kaap Museum: 71 Wale St, Cape Town 8000; tel. (21) 481-3939; fax (21) 481-3938; internet www.iziko.org.za/ bokaap; f. 1978; focuses on the social history of the local community; Dir for Social History Collns Dr P. J. DAVISON.

Iziko—Groot Constantia: Groot Constantia Estate, Constantia, Cape Town 8000; tel. (21) 795-5140; fax (21) 795-5150; internet www.iziko.org.za/grootcon; f. 1927; 17th-century wine estate and manor house; art colln; wine museum; Dir for Social History Collns Dr P. J. DAVISON.

Iziko—Koopmans-De Wet House: 35 Strand St, Cape Town 8000; tel. (21) 481-3935; fax (21) 424-6441; internet www .iziko.org.za/koopmans; f. 1914; early 18th-century townhouse; colln of Cape furniture, Chinese and Japanese ceramics, Dutch Delft ware, paintings, glass and silverware; Dir for Social History Collns Dr P. J. DAVISON.

Iziko—Rust-en-Vreugd: 78 Buitenkant St, Cape Town 8000; tel. (21) 464-3280; fax (21) 461-9620; internet www.iziko.org.za/ rustvreugd; f. 1965; 18th-century Cape Dutch house with colln of African water-

colours and prints from the William Fehr Colln; Dir for Art Collns M. H. MARTIN.

Iziko—Slave Lodge: 49 Adderley St, Cape Town 8000; tel. (21) 467-7229; fax (21) 461-2960; internet www.iziko.org.za/ slavelodge; f. 1966 as South African Cultural History Museum, present name 1998; slavery, human rights, nat. and local history, illustrating life in 18th and 19th centuries; library of 14,000 vols; Dir for Social History Collns J. L. MELTZER; Curator for Social History Collns F. H. CLAYTON.

Iziko—South African Maritime Museum: Victoria and Albert Waterfront, Table Bay Harbour, Cape Town 8000; tel. (21) 405-2880; fax (21) 405-2882; internet www.iziko.org.za/maritime; f. 1990; focuses on fishing and shipping industry; colln of ships; floating exhibition: SAS *Somerset*, boom defence vessel built in 1942; Dir for Social History Collns Dr P. J. DAVISON.

Iziko—William Fehr Collection: POB 61, Cape Town 8000; The Castle of Good Hope, Buitenkant St, Cape Town 8000; tel. (21) 464-1260; fax (21) 464-1280; internet www.iziko.org.za/castle; f. 1965; colln of paintings and decorative arts of relevance to Cape region; Dir for Social History Collns P. J. DAVISON.

Museum of Coast and Anti-Aircraft Artillery: Fort Wynyard, POB 14068, Green Point 8051; tel. (21) 419-1765; internet www .museum.com/jb/museum?id=24015; f. 1987; coast and anti-aircraft guns and relics displayed in a restored coast artillery battery.

Durban

Durban Museums: City Hall, POB 4085, Durban 4000; tel. (31) 300-6911; fax (31) 300-6308; e-mail mnikathib@prcsu.durban.gov .za; internet www.durban.gov.za; f. 1887; South African fauna, flora, ethnography, archaeology, paintings, graphic art, porcelain, sculptures, local history; Dir of Durban Art Gallery C. BROWN; Dir of Local History Museums R. OMAR; Dir of Natural Science Museum Q. B. HENDEY; publ. *Novitates* (1 a year).

Local History Museums: Old Court House Museum, Aliwal St, Durban; tel. (31) 311-2223; fax (31) 311-2224; f. 1966; local and KwaZulu Natal-historical collns, restored Natal colonial public building; Dir M. NGUBANE.

Attached Museums:

Bergtheil Museum: c/o Old Court House Museum, Aliwal St, Durban; e-mail mnikathib@prcsu.durban.gov.za; collections related to local communities, particularly early German settlers.

Cato Manor Heritage Centre: c/o Old Court House Museum, Aliwal St, Durban; e-mail mnikathib@prcsu.durban.gov.za; interpretative centre featuring the history of Cato Manor, including aspects related to forced removals and the Apartheid era.

Kwa Muhle Museum: 130–132 Ordnance Rd, Durban; tel. (31) 311-1111; fax (31) 311-2224; f. 1994; urban life in the Apartheid era, with emphasis on the 'Durban System' of administering the African population 1884–1986.

Old House Museum: c/o Old Court House Museum, Aliwal St, Durban; e-mail mnikathib@prcsu.durban.gov.za; a replica of the Robinson Home, a house belonging to the founder of the city's first morning newspaper; contains displays of early domestic life.

Pinetown Museum: c/o Old Court House Museum, Aliwal St, Durban; e-mail

mnikathib@prcsu.durban.gov.za; collections related to the Pinetown area.

Port Natal Maritime Museum: c/o Old Court House Museum, Aliwal St, Durban; f. 1988; Natal and Durban maritime history, 2 tugs and a minesweeper; Site Supervisor PHILLIP LABUSCHAGNE.

East London

East London Museum: POB 11021, Southernwood, East London 5213; 319 Oxford St, Southernwood, East London 5201; tel. (43) 743-0686; fax (43) 743-3127; e-mail rachel@ tsamail.co.za; f. 1931; collns of conchology, ichthyology, ornithology of the Eastern Cape Province, cultural history of the Border region and ethnography of the Southern Nguni peoples; houses specimen of Coelacanth (primitive fish) and world's only dodo egg; administers Victorian house museum; library: library holds books, journals, video cassettes, cartographic material, microfiches, microfilms, photographs, reprints, slides; Museum Dir MCEBISI MAGADLA (acting); Museum Librarian RACHEL WILLIAMS; publ. *Annals of the Eastern Cape Museums* (jtly with 4 other museums).

Franschhoek

Huguenot Memorial Museum and Monument: Lambrechts St, POB 37, Franschhoek 7690; tel. (21) 876-2532; fax (21) 876-3649; e-mail hugenoot@museum.co.za; internet www.museum.co.za; f. 1967; research into Cape Huguenot history, exhibition of over 400 Huguenot artefacts and documents; Chair. L. CYSTER; Curator E. A. JOHANNES; publ. *Bulletin of the Huguenot Society of South Africa*.

Grahamstown

Albany Museum: Somerset St, Grahamstown 6139; tel. (46) 622-2312; fax (46) 622-2398; e-mail l.webley@ru.ac.za; internet www.ru.ac.za/albany-museum; f. 1855; archaeology, terrestrial entomology, freshwater ichthyology, freshwater invertebrates, botany, palaeontology, ornithology, history and material cultures of the peoples of the Eastern Cape Province; library of 2,000 vols, 1,400 periodicals; Librarian A. PANTSI; publs *Annals of the Eastern Cape Provincial Museums* (jtly with 3 other museums, irregular), *Southern African Field Archaeology* (1 a year).

Johannesburg

Apartheid Museum: POB 82283, Southdale, 2135 Johannesburg; Northern Parkway and Gold Reef Rd, Ormonde 2001; tel. (11) 309-4700; fax (11) 309-4726; e-mail info@ apartheidmuseum.org; internet www .apartheidmuseum.org; f. 2001; film footage, photographs and artefacts illustrating the rise and decline of the apartheid system; Chair. Dr JOHN KANI.

City of Johannesburg Museums and Galleries: internet www.joburg.org.za/arts/ arts_heritage.stm#museums; Dir of Arts, Culture and Heritage Services STEVEN SHACK.

Branch Museums:

Adler Museum of Medicine: Faculty of Health Sciences, Univ. of the Witwatersrand, 7 York Rd, Parktown, Johannesburg 2193; tel. (11) 717-2081; fax (86) 553-2484; e-mail adler.museum@wits.ac.za; internet www.wits.ac.za/health/adlermuseum; f. 1962; history of medicine, dentistry, optometry and pharmacy; colln of medical, dental and surgical instruments and equipment; reconstructions of early 20th-century pharmacy, doctor's and dentist's surgeries, herbalist shop and traditional medicine display, incl. unani/tibb, ayurveda, western herbal medicine and homoeopathy, traditional healing; guided tours exhibits and public lectures; facilities of medical historical research; library of 10,000 vols; Curator ROCHELLE KEENE; publ. *Adler Museum Bulletin* (2 a year).

Bensusan Museum of Photography and Library: MuseuMAfricA, 121 Bree St, Newtown, Johannesburg; tel. (11) 833-5624; fax (11) 833-5636; e-mail photographiclibrary@joburg.org.za; f. 1968; colln incl. rare and valuable precision-made photographic equipment, incl. early Daguerre camera bought in 1839; Collector's Gallery; colln of pictures from the earliest wet-plate prints to digital images and experiments in 3 dimensions, such as stereoscopic views and holograms; specializes in preserving the work of South African photographers; Curator JONATHAN FROST.

Bernberg Fashion Museum: c/o Museum Africa, POB 517, Newtown 2113, Johannesburg; 121 Bree St, Newtown, Johannesburg; tel. (11) 833-5624; fax (11) 833-5636; e-mail museumafrica@joburg .org.za; internet www.joburg.org.za/ culture/museums-galleries/museumafrica; f. 1973; costume and accessories since the 17th century; collns housed in Museum Africa and displayed in temporary exhibitions; Man. DIANA WALL; Costume and Textile Curator (vacant).

Hector Pieterson Museum: 8288 Maseko St, Orlando West 1804; tel. and fax (11) 536-0611; named after one of the first fatalities of the march through Soweto on 16 June 1976, when police were ordered to shoot at a crowd of demonstrating students; commemorates the day's events, incl. television footage of the uprising and coverage of the anti-apartheid struggle generally; museum is next to the Pieterson Memorial, and the area has been declared a nat. heritage site; Curator ALI HLONGWANE.

James Hall Museum of Transport: Pioneers' Park, Rosettenville Rd, La Rochelle 2190, Johannesburg; tel. (11) 435-9485; fax (11) 435-9821; e-mail curator@jhmt.org.za; internet www.jhmt .org.za; f. 1964; largest and most comprehensive land transport museum in South Africa; land transport in all its forms: oxwagons, coaches and carts, bicycles, motorbikes, tractors, fire engines, buses, trams, trains, and cars from the Model T Ford to electric cars; Curator PETER HALL.

Johannesburg Art Gallery: POB 30951, Braamfontein 2017, Johannesburg; tel. (11) 725-3130; fax (11) 720-6000; e-mail job@joburg.org.za; internet www.joburg .org.za; f. 1910; colln of 9,000 artworks comprising contemporary S African art; traditional Southern African art and modern int. art; print colln and historical European paintings and sculptures; extensive public programmes; library of 9,500 vols; Dir ANTOINETTE MURDOCH.

MuseuMAfricA: 121 Bree St, Newtown, Johannesburg; tel. (11) 833-5624; fax (11) 833-5636; e-mail museumafrica@joburg .org.za; permanent displays show urban life in Johannesburg and its place in South Africa's history; themes incl. the gold miner, life in a shack and township jazz; coverage of Mahatma Gandhi's and Nelson Mandela's time in the city; displays on early man, stone-age and iron-age communities, San rock art in a reconstructed shelter, lifestyle of the first white settlers in the Johannesburg area; Chief Curator DAWN ROBERTSON.

Roodepoort Museum: Civic Centre, Christiaan de Wet Rd, Florida Park 1709; tel. (11) 761-0225; fax (11) 674-4043; e-mail annes@joburg.org.za; internet www.joburg .org.za; f. 1963; permanent displays illustrate the changes brought about by the discovery of gold in the area, incl. reconstructed 19th-century farmhouse, late Victorian home, 1920s and 1930s interiors; exhibition of decorative arts; guided tours; curriculum-based school programme; open by appointment only; Curator ANNE SMART.

Kimberley

McGregor Museum: Atlas St, POB 316, Kimberley 8300; tel. (53) 839-2700; fax (53) 842-1433; e-mail cfortune@museumsnc.co.za; internet www.museumsnc.co.za; f. 1907; archaeology and rock art, history (incl. Anglo-Boer War of 1899–1902), geology, zoology and herbarium of N Cape; ethnological collection housed in Duggan-Cronin Gallery, incorporates Magersfontein Battlefield Museum, Rudd House, Dunluce and Memorial to the Pioneers of Aviation; Dir C. FORTUNE.

King William's Town

Amathole Museum: Cnr Albert Rd and Alexandra Rd, POB 1434, King William's Town 5600; tel. (43) 642-4506; fax (43) 642-1569; e-mail amathole@museum.za.net; internet www.museum.za.net; f. 1884 as a naturalist soc.; studies, collects, houses and exhibits Southern Africa mammalogy, Xhosa ethnography, local history, Eastern Cape missionary history and Eastern Cape German settler history; library of 8,200 vols, 150 current periodicals; spec. collns incl. Kitton Colln of Africana; Dir FRED KIGOZI; publ. *Cape Provincial Museums Annals* (jtly with 4 other museums).

Attached Museum:

Missionary Museum: Berkeley St, POB 1434, King William's Town 5600; tel. (43) 642-4506; fax (43) 642-1569; e-mail stephanie.v@museum.za.net; internet www.museum.za.net; f. 1972; satellite museum; missionary history in E Cape; missionary library; Dir FRED KIGOZI; Curator of History STEPHANIE VICTOR; publ. *Imvubu*.

Pietermaritzburg

Natal Museum: Private Bag 9070, Pietermaritzburg 3200; 237 Ndlovu St, Pietermaritzburg 3201; tel. (33) 345-1404; fax (33) 345-0561; internet www.nmsa.org.za; f. 1904; collns incl. entomology, mollusca, archaeology, historical anthropology, mammals, arachnology, earthworms, herpetology, palaentology, local history; library of 12,000 books, 2,500 periodicals, 61,000 pamphlets, 8,000 photographs, 900 maps, 8,000 slides; Dir (vacant); publs *Annals*, *Natal Museum Journal of Humanities* (1 a year).

Tatham Art Gallery (Municipal): Chief Albert Luthuli Rd (Commercial Rd), Opposite City Hall, Pietermaritzburg; tel. (33) 392-2801; fax (33) 394-9831; e-mail brendan.bell@ msunduzi.gov.za; internet www.tatham.org .za; f. 1903; British and French painting since 19th century, sculpture and graphics, Southern African painting, sculpture, ceramics, prints and ethnic objects d'art; library of 2,300 vols; Dir BRENDAN BELL.

Port Elizabeth

Bayworld (incorporating Port Elizabeth Museum, Snake Park, Oceanarium and No. 7 Castle Hill Historical Museum): POB 13147, Humewood, Port Elizabeth 6013; tel. (41) 584-0650; fax (41) 584-0661; e-mail pr@ bayworld.co.za; internet www.bayworld.co .za; f. 1856; research on maritime history, marine biology, marine mammalogy, herpetology, marine ornithology and local history; Museum: marine life, maritime history, birds, dinosaurs, costume and local history; Snake Park: African colln of reptiles; library of 20,000 vols; Dir SYLVIA VAN ZYL.

Nelson Mandela Metropolitan Art Museum: 1 Park Drive, Port Elizabeth; tel. (41) 586-1030; fax (41) 586-3234; e-mail artmuseum@artmuseum.co.za; internet www.artmuseum.co.za; f. 1956 as King George VI Art Gallery; municipal art museum; collections of South African and British art, Indian miniatures, international graphics, Chinese textiles; library of 5,460 vols; Dir Dr MELANIE HILLEBRAND.

Pretoria

Ditsong National Museum of Natural History: Paul Kruger St, POB 413, Pretoria; tel. (12) 322-7632; fax (12) 322-7939; e-mail perregil@ditsong.org.za; internet www .ditsong.org.za; f. 1893, fmrly Transvaal Museum, present status 1964; taxonomy, ecology, zoo-geography and evolutionary studies with main emphasis on Southern Africa; mammals, birds, herpetology, palaeontology (incl. mammal-like reptiles and early hominids), Coleoptera, Lepidoptera, Orthoptera, invertebrates, archaeo-zoology and education; library of 11,000 vols, 2,000 periodicals and 80,000 reprints; rare book colln; Dir BONA NYAWOSE; publs *Annals of the Ditsong National Museum of Natural History* (1 a year), *Transvaal Museum Monographs* (irregular).

National Cultural History Museum: POB 28088, Sunnyside 0132; tel. and fax (12) 328-5173; e-mail nchm@nfi.org.za; internet www .nfi.org.za; f. 1892; exhibitions; research, education and conservation; library; special collns: Jansen, ethnography, archaeological, furniture and ceramics; library of 17,500 vols, 200 periodicals; Man. NEO MALAO; publ. *Nasko Navorsing* (research by the museum, 1 a year).

Pretoria Art Museum (Municipal Art Museum): POB 40925, Arcadia, Pretoria 0007; Cnr Schoeman and Wessels Sts, Arcadia Park, Pretoria 0083; tel. (12) 344-1807; fax (12) 344-1809; e-mail art.museum@ tshwane.gov.za; internet www .pretoriaartmuseum.co.za; f. 1964; South African art, small colln of int. graphic art, some 17th-century Dutch and Flemish art, colln of traditional and contemporary African art; Head DIRK OEGEMA (acting); Curator HANNELIE DU PLESSIS.

Stellenbosch

Stellenbosch Museum: Private Bag X5048, Stellenbosch 7599; Erfurthuis, Ryneveld St 37, Stellenbosch 7600; tel. (21) 887-2948; e-mail stelmus@mweb.co.za; internet www .stelmus.co.za; f. 1962; comprises 18th-century powder magazine (weaponry, Stellenbosch military history); Village Museum (bldgs illustrating life from 1690–1890), Toy and Miniature Museum; reference library; Man. W. SCHOLTZ.

Universities and Colleges

CAPE PENINSULA UNIVERSITY OF TECHNOLOGY

POB 1906, Belleville 7535

Telephone: (21) 959-6911
Fax: (21) 959-6069
E-mail: info@cput.ac.za
Internet: www.cput.ac.za

Founded 2005 by merger of Cape Technikon and Peninsula Technikon

Vice-Chancellor: Prof. L. VUYISA MAZWI-TANGA

Campuses at Cape Town, Granger Bay, Mowbray, Wellington

DEANS

Faculty of Applied Sciences: Prof. O. FATOKI
Faculty of Business: Prof. S. BAYAT
Faculty of Education and Social Sciences: Prof. M. ROBINSON
Faculty of Engineering: Dr O. FRANKS
Faculty of Health and Wellness Sciences: Dr D. GIHWALA
Faculty of Informatics and Design: Prof. J. CRONJE

RESEARCH CENTRES

Centre for Instrumentation Research: POB 652, Cape Town 8000; tel. (21) 460-4281; fax (21) 460-3705; e-mail cir@cput.ac.za; Dir Prof. JEVON DAVIES.

Fundani Centre for Higher Education Development: Dir Dr NOMATHAMSANQA TISANI.

Water Supply and Sanitation Unit (WSSU): tel. (21) 959-6111; fax (21) 959-6786; e-mail brandc@cput.ac.za; Dir Prof. ALVIN LAGARDIEN.

CENTRAL UNIVERSITY OF TECHNOLOGY, FREE STATE

PMB X20539, Bloemfontein 9300
Pres. Brand St 20, Bloemfontein 9301
Telephone: (51) 507-3911
Fax: (51) 507-3019
E-mail: cajvr@cut.ac.za
Internet: www.cut.ac.za
Founded 1981
Academic year: January to December
Vice-Chancellor and Prin.: Prof. T. Z. MTHEMBU
Deputy Vice-Chancellor for Academic Affairs: Prof. M. D. R. RALEBIPI-SIMELA
Deputy Vice-Chancellor for Institutional Planning, Partnerships and Communications: Prof. T. G. SCHULTZ
Deputy Vice-Chancellor for Resources and Operations: Prof. M. E. RALEKHETHO (acting)
Registrar: Dr M. J. G. VINGER
Welkom Campus Man.: Dr S. MAKOLA
Dir of Library: J. M. KABAMBA
Library of 143,354 vols
Number of teachers: 1,500
Number of students: 12,000

DEANS

Faculty of Engineering and Information-Technology: Prof. Y. E. WOYESSA (acting)
Faculty of Health and Environmental Sciences: Prof. L. DE JAGER
Faculty of Humanities: Prof. D. NGIDI
Faculty of Management Sciences: Prof. A. STRYDOM

DURBAN UNIVERSITY OF TECHNOLOGY

41–43 Centenary Rd, Durban 4001
E-mail: webmaster@dit.ac.za
Internet: www.dit.ac.za
Founded 2002 following merger of M. L. Sultan Technikon (f. 1946) and Technikon Natal (f. 1907); incorporated Umlazi Campus of University of Zululand 2004; univ. status and incorporated Mangosuthu Technikon 2006
Chancellor: PATRICIA DE LILLE
Vice-Chancellor: Prof. DAN J. NCAYIYANA
Chief Librarian: ROY RAJU.

CAMPUSES

M. L. Sultan Campus

41–43 Centenary Rd, Durban 4001
Telephone: (31) 308-5111
Fax: (31) 308-5194
E-mail: info@mlsultan.ac.za
Internet: www.mlsultan.ac.za
Deputy Vice-Chancellor: UJEN PURMASIR
Library Man.: SIZA RODABE
Library: B. M. Patel Memorial Library of 55,000 books, 900 journals, 4,000 video and audio cassettes
Faculties of arts, commerce, engineering, science.

Steve Biko Campus
(formerly Technikon Natal)

70 Mansfield Rd, Berea, Durban 4001
Telephone: (31) 204-2111
Fax: (31) 204-2663
E-mail: postmaster@ntech.ac.za
Internet: www.ntech.ac.za
Vice-Chancellor and Prin.: Prof. B. KHOAPA
Vice-Prin. for Academic Affairs: Prof. LOUIS DU PREEZ
Vice-Prin. for Admin.: Dr REGINALD THABEDE
Vice-Prin. for Student Affairs and Devt: Adv. REAGAN JACOBUS
Asst Vice-Prin. for Undergraduate Studies: Prof. NQABOMZI GAWE
Academic Registrar: DAVID HELLINGER
Registrar (Pietermaritzburg): Prof. SAM ZOND
Library of 81,000 vols, 1,001 periodical titles

DEANS

Faculty of Arts: A. R. STARKEY
Faculty of Commerce: T. DAGNALL-QUINN
Faculty of Engineering and Science: M. STEWART
Faculty of Health: A. MILNE

MANGOSUTHU TECHNIKON

POB 12363, Jacobs 4026
Mangosuthu Highway, Umlazi, Durban
Telephone: (31) 907-7111
Fax: (31) 907-2892
E-mail: miken@julian.mantec.ac.za
Internet: www.mantec.ac.za
Founded 1978
Academic year: January to December
Prin. and Vice-Chancellor: Prof. A. M. NDLOVU
Vice-Prin. for Academic Affairs: Prof. E. C. ZINGU
Vice-Prin. for Admin.: Dr Y. L. MBELE
Academic Registrar: S. NAIDOO
Library of 54,454 vols
Number of teachers: 150
Number of students: 10,000

DEANS

Faculty of Engineering: S. MALINGA
Faculty of Management Sciences: Prof. E. C. ZINGU
Faculty of Natural Sciences: Prof. ALLAN FEMI LANA

NELSON MANDELA METROPOLITAN UNIVERSITY

POB 77000, Port Elizabeth 6031
Telephone: (41) 504-1111
Fax: (41) 583-1558
E-mail: info@nmmu.ac.za
Internet: www.nmmu.ac.za
Founded 2005 by merger of Univ. of Port Elizabeth, PE Technikon and the Port Elizabeth Campus of Vista Univ.
Public control
Language of instruction: English
Academic year: February to November
Vice-Chancellor and CEO: Prof. DERRICK SWARTZ
Deputy Vice-Chancellor: Prof. PIET NAUDE
Deputy Vice-Chancellor: Dr SIBONGILE MUTHWA
Deputy Vice-Chancellor: Prof. THOKOZILE MAYEKISO
Campus Prin. for George Campus: Prof. CHRISTO FABRICIUS
Campus Prin. for Missionvale Campus: Prof. IONA WANNENBURG
Dean of Students: KHAYA MATISO
Library: see Libraries and Archives
Number of teachers: 1,500
Number of students: 25,000

DEANS

Faculty of Arts: Prof. VELILE NOTSHULWANA
Faculty of Business and Economic Sciences: Prof. NIEKIE DORFLING
Faculty of Education: Prof. DENISE ZINN
Faculty of Engineering: Prof. HENK DE JAGER
Faculty of Health Sciences: Prof. D. EXNER
Faculty of Law: Prof. VIVIENNE LAWACK-DAVIDS
Faculty of Science: Prof. ANDREW LEITCH

NORTH-WEST UNIVERSITY

Mafikeng Campus, PMB X2046, Mmabatho 2735
Telephone: (18) 389-2111
Fax: (18) 392-5775
E-mail: motabogis@uniwest.ac.za
Internet: www.uniwest.ac.za
Founded 1980 as Univ. of North-West; merged with Potchefstroom Univ. and incorporated Sebokeng Campus of Vista Univ. 2004
Autonomous control
Languages of instruction: Afrikaans, English
Academic year: February to November
Chancellor: Dr POPO MOLEFE
Vice-Chancellor: Dr THEUNS ELOFF
Chair. of the Ccl: L. NYHONYA
Vice-Prin.: Dr M. N. TAKALO
Registrar: Prof. C. F. C. VAN DER WALT
Librarian: DUDU NKOSI
Library of 90,000 vols
Number of teachers: 588 (Potchefstroom and Vaal Triangle Campus 226 full-time, 7 part-time (incl. 99 professors); Mafikeng Campus 172 full-time, 183 part-time)
Number of students: 40,702 (Potchefstroom Campus 28,390; Vaal Triangle Campus 2,836; Mafikeng Campus 9,476)
Publications: *Didaktikom* (4 a year), *Fokus* (4 a year), *In die Skriflig* (4 a year), *Koers* (4 a year), *Literator* (3 a year), *Woord en Daad* (4 a year)

DEANS

Mafikeng Campus:
  Faculty of Agriculture, Science and Technology: Dr S. H. TAOLE
  Faculty of Commerce and Admin.: G. D. STESETSE
  Faculty of Education: L. M. E. M. SEHLARE
  Faculty of Human and Social Sciences: Dr R. M. MANYANE
  Faculty of Law: R. L. KETTLES
Potchefstroom Campus:
  Faculty of Arts: Prof. A. L. COMBRINK
  Faculty of Economic and Management Sciences: Prof. G. J. DE KLERK
  Faculty of Educational Sciences: Prof. H. J. STEYN
  Faculty of Engineering: Prof. J. I. J. FICK
  Faculty of Health Sciences: Prof. H. A. KOELEMAN
  Faculty of Law: Prof. F. VENTER
  Faculty of Natural Sciences: Prof. D. J. VAN WYK

Faculty of Theology: Prof. A. LE R. DU PLOOY

Vaal Triangle Campus:

Faculty of the Vaal Triangle: Prof. A. M. C. THERON

PROFESSORS

Mafikeng Campus (Private Bag X2046, Mmabatho 2735; tel. (18) 389-2111; fax (18) 392-5575; e-mail travisk@uniwest.ac.za; internet www.uniwest.ac.za):

Faculty of Agriculture, Science and Technology:

BEIGHLE, D. E., Animal Health
FUNNAH, S. M., Plant Production
KHALIQUE, C. M., Mathematical Sciences
TAOLO, S. H., Mathematical Sciences

Faculty of Human and Social Sciences:

CHIKULO, B. C., Development Studies
KALULE-SABITI, I., Population Training and Research Unit
MANSON, A., History
MOGEKWU, M., Communication

Faculty of Law:

MBAO, M. L. M., Public Law and Legal Philosophy

Potchefstroom Campus (Private Bag X6001, Potchefstroom 2520; tel. (18) 299-1111; fax (18) 299-2799; internet www.puk.ac.za):

Faculty of Arts:

CARSTENS, W. A. M., School of Languages (Dir)
COMBRINK, A. L., Dean
DE LANGE, A. M., English and Literature
DU PISANI, J. A., History
DU PLESSIS, H. G. W., ATKV Writing School
DU PLOOY, H. J. G., Afrikaans and Dutch
JOOSTE, S. J., Music
MOLLER, P. H., Sociology
SCHUTTE, P. J., Communication Studies
VAN DER WALT, J. L., English and Literature
VAN WYK, W. J., School of Social Studies (Dir)
VENTER, J. J., Philosophy

Faculty of Economic and Management Sciences:

BISSCHOFF, C. A., Potchefstroom Business School
COETSEE, L. D., Potchefstroom Business School
COETZEE, K., Chartered Accountant Training
COETZEE, W. N., Potchefstroom Business School
DE KLERK, G. J., Dean
DU PLESSIS, J. L., Potchefstroom Business School
DU TOIT, A., Chartered Accountant Training
ELOFF, T., School of Accounting Sciences (Dir)
GERICKE, J. S., Chartered Accountant Training
JANSEN VAN RENSBURG, L. R., Entrepreneurship, Marketing and Tourism Management
JORDAAN, K., Chartered Accountant Training
KOTZE, J. G., Potchefstroom Business School
KROON, J., Entrepreneurship, Marketing and Tourism Management
NAUDE, W. A., Decision-making and Management for Economic Development
PRETORIUS, J. P. S., Potchefstroom Business School
RADEMEYER, A., Chartered Accountant Training
ROTHMAN, S., Industrial Psychology
SAAYMAN, M., Tourism

SCHOLTZ, P. E., School of Human Resource Sciences (Dir)
VAN HEERDEN, J. H. P., School of Economics, Risk Management and International Trade (Dir)
VISSER, S. S., Management Accountant Training
VIVIERS, W., Economics, Risk Management and International Trade

Faculty of Educational Sciences:

DREYER, C., Postgraduate School of Education
MENTZ, P. J., Education and Training
MONTEITH, J. L. D. K., Postgraduate School of Education
SPAMER, E. J., Teachers' Centre
STEYN, H. J., Dean
VAN DER WESTHUIZEN, P. C., Postgraduate School of Education

Faculty of Engineering:

DE KOCK, J. A., Electrical and Electronic Engineering
DU TOIT, C. G. D. K., Mechanical and Material Engineering
FICK, J. I. J., Dean
GREYVENSTEIN, G. P., Mechanical and Material Engineering
HELBERG, A. S. J., Electrical and Electronic Engineering
HOFFMAN, A. J., Electrical and Electronic Engineering
MATHEWS, E. H., Centre for Research and Commercialization
ROUSSEAU, P. G., Energy Systems
WAANDERS, F. B., Chemical and Mineral Engineering

Faculty of Health Sciences:

BERGH, J. J., Pharmaceutical Chemistry
BONESCHANS, B., CENQAM
BREYTENBACH, J. C., Pharmaceutical Chemistry
DE RIDDER, J. H., Human Movement Studies
DEKKER, T. G., Industrial Pharmacy
DU PLESSIS, J., Drug Research and Development
GREEF, M., Nursing
HARVEY, B. H., Pharmacy
KOELEMAN, H. A., Dean
KOTZÉ, A. F., Pharmaceutics
KOTZE, G. J., Social Work
LIEBENBERG, W., Institute for Industrial Pharmacy
MALAN, D. D. J., Human Movement Studies
MALAN, N. T., Physiology, Nutrition and Consumer Sciences
OLIVER, D. W., Pharmacy
STRYDOM, H., Social Work
THOMAS, A. J., Pharmacy
VENTER, C. A., Physiology
VENTER, D. P., Pharmacology
WISSING, M. P., Psycho-social Behavioural Science

Faculty of Law:

DU PLESSIS, W., Legal Pluralism and Legal History
FERREIRA, G. M., Public Law and Legal Philosophy
PIENAAR, G. J., Private Law
ROBINSON, J. A., Private Law
STANDER, A. L., Private Law
VENTER, F., Dean

Faculty of Natural Sciences:

BOUWMAN, H., Zoology
BREET, E. L. J., Chemistry
BRUINSMA, O. S. L., Separation Sciences and Technology
BURGER, R. A., Space Physics
DE JAGER, O. C., Physics
DE JONGH, D. C. J., Centre for Business Mathematics and Informatics

DE JONGH, P. J., Centre for Business Mathematics and Informatics
DE KLERK, J. H., Mathematics
DE VILLIERS, A. B., Geography and Environmental Studies
DU TOIT, G. J., Environment Sciences and Management
FOURIE, J. H., Computer, Statistical and Mathematical Sciences
GEYSER, H. S., Town and Regional Planning
GROBLER, J. J., Business Mathematics and Informatics
KOTZÉ, H. F., Biochemistry
MORAAL, H., Physics
PETERSEN, M. A., Mathematics
PIENAAR, J. J., Chemistry and Biochemistry
PIETERSE, A. J. H., Life Sciences
POTGIETER, M. S., Physics
RAUBENHEIMER, B. C., Space Physics
RIEDEL, K. J., Microbiology
STEYN, T., Computer Sciences and Information
STYGER, P., Centre for Business Mathematics and Informatics
SWANEPOEL, J. W. H., Statistics and Operational Research
THERON, P. D., Zoology
VAN DER WALT, D. J., Physics
VAN HAMBURG, H., Environment Sciences and Development
VAN WYK, D. J., Dean
VOSLOO, H. C. M., Chemistry

Faculty of Theology:

DE KLERK, B. J., Practical Theology
DU PLOOY, A. LE R., Dean
JANSE VAN RENSBURG, J. J., New Testament
JORDAAN, G. J. C., New Testament
LOTTER, G. A., Practical Theology
VAN ROOY, H. F., Theology and the Development of the South African Society
VENTER, J. M., Practical Theology
VORSTER, J. M., Ecclesiology

Vaal Triangle Campus (Private Bag X6001, Potchefstroom 2520; tel. (16) 910-3710; fax (16) 910-3103; e-mail dvdamct@puknet.puk.ac.za; internet www.puk.ac.za):

Faculty of the Vaal Triangle:

DE KLERK, P., History
JORDAAN, D. B., Modelling Sciences
LUCOUW, P., Economic Sciences
PRETORIUS, J. B., Business Management
THERON, A. M. C., Dean
VERHOEF, M. M., Languages

RHODES UNIVERSITY

POB 94, Grahamstown 6140

Telephone: (46) 603-8101
Fax: (46) 603-8127
E-mail: registrar@ru.ac.za
Internet: www.ru.ac.za

Founded 1904; East London Campus incorporated into Univ. of Fort Hare 2004
State control
Language of instruction: English
Academic year: February to November (4 terms)

Chancellor: Prof. G. J. GERWEL
Chair. of the Ccl: Hon. Mr Justice R. J. W. JONES
Prin. and Vice-Chancellor: D. R. WOODS
Vice-Prin. and Pro-Vice-Chancellor: C. T. JOHNSON
Dean of Research: J. R. DUNCAN
Dean of Students: M. A. MOTARA
Registrar: S. FOURIE
Librarian: M. A. E. KENYON

Library: see Libraries and Archives
Number of teachers: 305
Number of students: 6,155

Publications: English in Africa (1 a year), Journal of Contemporary African Studies

(2 a year), *New Coin Poetry* (2 a year), *Philosophical Papers* (2 a year), *Rhodes Journalism Review* (irregular)

DEANS

Faculty of Commerce: A. C. M. WEBB
Faculty of Education: G. J. EUVRARD
Faculty of Humanities: F. T. HENDRICKS
Faculty of Law: J. R. MIDGLEY
Faculty of Pharmacy: I. KANFER
Faculty of Science: P. D. TERRY

PROFESSORS

ADENDORFF, R., English Language and Linguistics
ADESINA, J. O. T., Sociology and Industrial Sociology
ANTROBUS, G. G., Economics
BERGER, G. J. E. G., Journalism and Media Studies
BERNARD, R. T. F., Zoology
BLATCH, G. L., Biochemistry, Microbiology and Biotechnology
BOTHA, C. E. J., Botany
CHARTERIS, J., Human Kinetics and Ergonomics
CLAYTON, P. G., Computer Science
COETZEE, J. K., Sociology and Industrial Sociology
CRAIG, A. T. F., Zoology and Entomology
DAVIES-COLEMAN, M. T., Chemistry
DAYA, S., Pharmacy
DE KLERK, V. A., Linguistics and English Language
DE WET, C. J., Anthropology
DUNCAN, J. R., Biochemistry
EDWARDS, D. J. A., Psychology
EUVRARD, G. J., Education
FABRICIUS, C., Environmental Science
FAURE, P., Economics
FOX, R. C., Geography
GORDON, G. E., Drama
GOUWS, J. S., English
HAIGH, J. M., Pharmacy
HARVEY, N., Management
HENDRICKS, F. T., Sociology and Industrial Sociology
HEPBURN, H. R., Entomology
HODGSON, A. N., Zoology and Entomology
HUGHES, D. A., Water Research
IRWIN, P. R., Education
JACOB, R. E., Geology
JAQUES, F. E., School of Languages
JONAS, J. L., Physics and Electronics
KANFER, I., Pharmaceutics
KAYE, P. T., Organic Chemistry
LEWIS, C. A., Geography
MABIZELA, S. G., Pure and Applied Mathematics
MARSH, J. S., Geology
MAYLAM, P. R., History
McQUAID, C. D., Zoology
MIDGLEY, J. R., Law
MØLLER, V., Social and Economic Research
MOORE, J. M., Exploration Geology
MQEKE, R. B., Law
NEL, E. L., Geography
NEL, H., Economics
NYOKONG, T., Chemistry
RADLOFF, S. E., Statistics
ROSE, P. D., Biotechnology
ROWNTREE, K. M., Geography
SCARR, D. T., Music and Musicology
SCHMAHMANN, B. L., Fine Art
SCOTT, P. A., Human Kinetics and Ergonomics
SEWRY, D. A., Information Systems
SKELTON, P., Aquatic Biodiversity
STACK, E. M., Accounting
STAUDE, G. E., Management
STONES, C. R., Psychology
TERRY, P. D., Computer Science
VALE, P. C. J., Political and International Studies
WALTERS, P. S., English
WEBB, A. C. M., Economics

WENTWORTH, E. P., Computer Science
WRIGHT, L. S., Study of English in Africa

TSHWANE UNIVERSITY OF TECHNOLOGY

PMB X 680, Pretoria 0001
Telephone: (12) 318-5911
Fax: (12) 318-5114
E-mail: general@tut.ac.za
Internet: www.techpta.ac.za

Founded 2004 by merger of Technikon Pretoria, Technikon North Gauteng and Technikon North West

Vice-Chancellor and Rector: Prof. REGGIE NGCOBO
Exec. Mans and Deputy Vice-Chancellors: Prof. N. P. DU PREEZ, Prof. H. H. DÜRRHEIM, Prof. J. G. PRETORIUS
Registrar: N. J. V. D. M. STOFBERG
Library Dir: Dr A. SWANEPOEL

Library of 70,000 vols
Number of students: 40,000

Publication: *Peritus* (4 a year)

DEANS

Faculty of Agriculture, Horticulture and Nature Conservation: Prof. J. J. BOTHA
Faculty of Arts: E. R. DINKELMANN
Faculty of Economic Sciences: Prof. M. J. VAN DER MERWE
Faculty of Engineering: Prof. F. OTIENO
Faculty of Health Sciences: Prof. M. M. J. LOWES
Faculty of Information and Communication Technology: Dr J. ZAAIMAN
Faculty of Natural Sciences: Prof P. J. J. G. MARAIS
Faculty of Social Development Sciences: Prof. S. N. IMENDA

UNIVERSITY OF CAPE TOWN

Private Bag X3, Rondebosch 7701
Telephone: (21) 650-9111
Fax: (21) 650-2138
E-mail: int-iapo@uct.ac.za
Internet: www.uct.ac.za

Founded 1829 as South African College; univ. status 1918
Autonomous, state-subsidized
Language of instruction: English
Academic year: February to December (2 semesters)

Chancellor: GRAÇA MACHEL
Vice-Chancellor: Dr MAX PRICE
Deputy Vice-Chancellor: Prof. C. SOUDIEN
Deputy Vice-Chancellor: Prof. D. VISSER
Deputy Vice-Chancellor: Prof. J. BEALL
Deputy Vice-Chancellor: Prof. T. NHLAPO
Registrar: HUGH AMOORE
Librarian: JOAN RAPP

Library: see Libraries and Archives
Number of teachers: 1,980
Number of students: 23,500

Publications: *Acta Juridica* (1 a year), *Contributions from the Bolus Herbarium* (irregular), *Journal of Energy in Southern Africa* (4 a year), *Pretexts* (4 a year), *Responsa Meridiana* (1 a year), *Sea Changes* (2 a year), *Selected Energy Statistics: Southern Africa* (4 a year), *Social Dynamics* (2 a year), *UCT Research Report* (1 a year)

DEANS

Faculty of Commerce: Prof. DON ROSS
Faculty of Engineering and the Built Environment: Prof. FRANCIS PETERSEN
Faculty of Health Sciences: Prof. MARIAN JACOBS
Faculty of Humanities: Prof. PAULA ENSOR
Faculty of Law: Prof. PAMELA JANE SCHWIKKARD

Faculty of Science: Prof. KATHY DRIVER
Graduate School of Business: Prof. WALTER BAETS
Centre for Higher Education Devt: Prof. NAN YELD

PROFESSORS

Faculty of Commerce (tel. (21) 650-2694; fax (21) 650-2696; e-mail comsec@commerce.uct.ac.za):

ABEDIAN, I., Economics
BARR, G. D. I., Statistical Sciences
BRADFIELD, D., Statistical Sciences
DORRINGTON, R. E., Management Studies
EVERINGHAM, G. K., Accounting
FAULL, N. H. B., Graduate School of Business
HORWITZ, F., Graduate School of Business
KAHN, S. B., Economics
KANTOR, B. S., Economics
KAPLAN, D., Economics
LICKER, P. S., Information Systems
NATTRASS, N., Economics
SIMPSON, J. D., Business Science
SMITH, D. C., Information Systems
SULCAS, P., Graduate School of Business
TROSKIE, C. G., Statistical Sciences
UNDERHILL, L. G., Statistical Sciences
WILSON, F. A. H., Economics

Faculty of Engineering and the Built Environment (tel. (21) 650-2699; fax (21) 650-3782; e-mail engsec@eng.uct.ac.za):

ABBOTT, J., Civil Engineering
ALEXANDER, M. G., Civil Engineering
ALLEN, C., Mechanical Engineering
BALL, A., Mechanical Engineering
BENNETT, K. F., Mechanical Engineering
BOWEN, P. A., Construction Economics and Management
BRAAE, M., Electrical Engineering
DE JAGER, G., Electrical Engineering
DEWAR, D., School of Architecture and Planning
DOWNING, B. J., Electrical Engineering
EKAMA, G. A., Civil Engineering
GRYZAGORIDAS, T., Mechanical Engineering
HANSFORD, G. S., Chemical Engineering
NURICK, G. N., Mechanical Engineering
O'CONNOR, C. T., Chemical Engineering
REDDY, B. D., Centre for Research in Computational and Applied Mechanics
REINECK, K. M., Electrical Engineering
RÜTHER, H., Geomatics
STEVENS, A. J., Construction Economics and Management

Faculty of Health Sciences (tel. (21) 406-6346; fax (21) 447-8955; e-mail medfac@curie.uct.ac.za):

BAQWA, D., Primary Health Care
BATEMAN, E. D., Medicine
BEATTY, D. W., Paediatrics and Child Health
BENATAR, S. R., Medicine
BENINGFIELD, S. J., Radiology
BONNICI, F., Medicine
BORNMAN, P. C., Surgery
COMMERFORD, P. J., Medicine
CRUSE, J. P., Anatomical Pathology
DAVIDSON, J., Chemical Pathology
DENT, D. M., Surgery
ELS, W. J., Anatomy and Cell Biology
FOLB, P. I., Pharmacology
GEVERS, W., Medical Biochemistry
HALL, P., Anatomical Pathology
HARLEY, E. H., Chemical Pathology
JACOBS, M. E., Paediatrics and Child Health
JAMES, M. F. M., Anaesthetics
KIRSCH, R. E., Medicine
KNOBEL, G. J., Forensic Medicine and Toxicology
LOUW, J., Medicine
MOLTENO, C. D., Psychiatry
MURRAY, A. D. N., Ophthalmology

MYERS, J. E., Community Health
NOAKES, T. D., Physiology
NOVITZKY, N., Haematology
PADAYACHEE, G. N.
PARKER, M. I., Medical Biochemistry
PETER, J. C., Neurosurgery
POWER, D. J., Paediatrics and Child Health
RAMESAR, R., Human Genetics
ROBERTSON, B. A., Psychiatry
RODE, H., Paediatric Surgery
SEGGIE, J., Medicine
SELLARS, S. L., Otorhinolaryngology
STEYN, L. M., Medical Microbiology
VAN DER SPUY, Z. M., Obstetrics and
  Gynaecology
VAN NIEKERK, J. P., Medicine
VAUGHAN, C. L., Biomedical Engineering
VILJOEN, J. F., Anaesthesia
VON OPPEL, U., Cardiothoracic Surgery
WALTERS, J., Orthopaedic Surgery
WERNER, I. D., Radiation Oncology
WILSON, E. L., Immunology
ZILLA, P., Cardiovascular Research

Faculty of Humanities (tel. (21) 650-4216; fax
(21) 686-9840; e-mail artsec@beattie.uct.ac
.za):

BRINK, A., English Language and Litera-
  ture
BUNTING, I., Philosophy
CHIDESTER, D. S., Religious Studies
COCHRANE, J. R., Religious Studies
COETZEE, J. M., English Language and
  Literature
COOPER, B., Centre for African Studies
CORNILLE, J.-L., French Language and
  Literature
DE GRUCHY, J., Religious Studies (Gradu-
  ate School of Humanities)
DU TOIT, A. B., Political Studies
FOSTER, D. H., Psychology
GITAY, Y., Hebrew and Jewish Studies
GODBY, M. A. P., Historical Studies
HAYNES, D. J., Drama
KLATZOW, P., Music
LASS, R. G., Linguistics
LOUW, J., Psychology
MAMA, A., African Gender Institute
MAREE, J., Sociology
MAY, J., South African College of Music
MESTHRIE, R., Linguistics and Southern
  African Languages
MULLER, J. P., Education
NASSON, W., History
NOYES, J., German Language and Litera-
  ture
REYNOLDS, P. F., Social Anthropology
SALAZAR, PH.-J., French Language and
  Literature (Graduate School of Human-
  ities)
SATYO, S. C., African Languages
SAUNDERS, C. C., Historical Studies
SCHRIRE, R. A., Political Studies
SEEGERS, A., Political Studies
SHAIN, M., Hebrew and Jewish Studies
SKOTNES, P., Fine Art
SNYMAN, H. J., Afrikaans and Netherlandic
  Studies (Graduate School of Humanities)
TAYOB, A. I., Religious Studies
UNDERWOOD, P. G., School of Librarianship
VAN HEERDEN, E. R., Afrikaans and Neth-
  erlandic Studies
WEST, M., Social Anthropology
WHITAKER, R. A., Classics
WORDEN, N. A., Historical Studies
YOUNG, D. N., Education
YOUNGE, G., Fine Art

Faculty of Law (tel. (21) 650-3086; fax (21)
686-2577; e-mail lawnv@law.uct.ac.za):

BENNETT, T. W., Public Law
BLACKMAN, M. S., Commercial Law
BURMAN, S. B., Private Law
CHEADLE, M. H., Public Law
CORDER, H. M., Public Law
DEVINE, D. J., Public Law
HUTCHISON, D. B., Private Law

JOOSTE, R. D., Commercial Law
MALUWA, T., Public Law
MURRAY, C. M., Public Law
VAN BUEREN, G., Law
VISSER, D. P., Private Law

Faculty of Science (tel. (21) 650-2712; fax (21)
650-2710; e-mail scifac@psipsy.uct.ac.za):

ASCHMAN, D. G., Physics
BARR, G. D. I., Statistical Sciences
BECKER, R. I., Mathematics and Applied
  Mathematics
BOND, W., Botany
BRADFIELD, D., Statistical Sciences
BRANCH, G. M., Zoology
BRUNDRIT, G. B., Oceanography
BULL, J., Chemistry
BUTTERWORTH, D. S., Mathematics and
  Applied Mathematics
CLEYMANS, J. W. A., Physics
DE WIT, M. J., Geological Sciences
DOMINGUEZ, C. A., Physics
DU PLESSIS, M., Zoology
ELLIS, G. F. R., Mathematics and Applied
  Mathematics
FAIRALL, A. P., Astronomy
FIELD, J. G., Zoology
FUGGLE, R. F., Environmental and Geo-
  graphical Science
GÄDE, G., Zoology
GURNEY, J. J., Geological Sciences
HALL, M. J., Archaeology
KHAM, M. J., Mathematics, Science and
  Technology Education
KLUMP, H. H., Biochemistry
KRITZINGER, P. S., Computer Science
KURTZ, D. W., Astronomy
LE ROEX, A. P., Geological Sciences
LUTJEHARMS, J. R. E., Oceanography
MACGREGOR, K. J., Computer Science
MOSS, J. R., Chemistry
NASSIMBENI, L. R., Chemistry
PARKINGTON, J. E., Archaeology
PEREZ, S. M., Physics
REDDY, B. D., Mathematics and Applied
  Mathematics
SILLEN, A., Archaeology
STEWART, T. J., Statistical Sciences
THOMSON, J. A., Microbiology
TROSKIE, C. G., Statistical Sciences
UNDERHILL, L. G., Statistical Sciences
VAN DER MERWE, N. J., Archaeology
VIOLLIER, R. D., Physics
WARNER, B., Astronomy
WEBB, J. H., Mathematics and Applied
  Mathematics

UNIVERSITY OF FORT HARE

Private Bag X1314, Alice 5700
Telephone: (40) 602-22011
Fax: (40) 653-1023
E-mail: dmc@ufh.ac.za
Internet: www.ufh.ac.za

Founded as 'South African Native College' in
  1916 by the United Free Church of Scot-
  land; transferred to the Dept of Bantu
  Education in 1960 to cater specifically for
  the Xhosa ethnic group; present name
  1970; incorporated Medical School of
  Univ. of Transkei and East London Cam-
  pus of Rhodes Univ. 2004
Language of instruction: English
Academic year: February to December
Chancellor: Prof. S. M. BHENGU
Vice-Chancellor and Rector: Prof. DERRICK
  SWARTZ
Deputy Vice-Chancellor for Admin. and
  Finance: R. OLANDER
Dean of Students: N. MORRISON
Librarian: Y. K. SOUL

Library: see Libraries
Number of teachers: 239
Number of students: 2,869

Publications: *Ardrinews*, *Fort Hare Papers*,
The Fort Harian

DEANS

Faculty of Agricultural and Environmental
  Studies: Prof. J. RAATS
Faculty of Arts: Prof. C. R. BOTHA
Faculty of Economic Sciences: Prof. T. M.
  JORDAN
Faculty of Education: Prof. P. M. FIHLA
Faculty of Law: Prof. J. ROBBERTSON
Faculty of Medicine and Health Sciences:
  Prof. E. L. MAZWAI
Faculty of Science and Technology: Dr D. O.
  OKEYO
Faculty of Social Sciences: Prof. SOBAHLE
Faculty of Theology: Prof. S. P. ABRAHAMS

PROFESSORS

Faculty of Agricultural and Environmental
Studies:

BESTER, B. J., Agricultural Economics
IGODAN, C. O., Agricultural Extension and
  Rural Development
MNKENI, P. N. S., Crop Science
MZAMANE, N., Agronomy
RAATS, J. G., Livestock and Pasture Sci-
  ence
TROLLOPE, W. S. W., Livestock and Pasture
  Science

Faculty of Arts:

AUCAMP, J. C., History
BOTHA, C. R., African Languages
BROUWER, P., Political Science and Public
  Administration
DE WET, G., Communication
ELS, J. M., Classical Languages
ETSIAH, A. K., Political Science and Public
  Administration
HALLIER, M. G. T., Fine Arts
LOSAMBE, L., English
LOUW, T. J. G., Philosophy
PRINS, M. J., Afrikaans and Dutch
SIRAYI, G. T., Centre for Cultural Studies
VERHAGE, H. M., Psychology

Faculty of Economic Sciences:

JORDAN, T. M., Accountancy
SWARTZ, D. I., Intergovernmental Relations
VAN DAALEN, H. J., Industrial Psychology

Faculty of Education:

DARGIE, D. J., Music
DREYER, J. N., Foundations of Education
FILHA, P. M., Educational Psychology
JIYA, M. A. Y., Curriculum Studies and
  Didactics
LINDEQUE, B. R. G., Curriculum Studies
  and Didactics

Faculty of Law:

DU PLESSIS, P. A., Mercantile Law
IYA, P. F., African and Comparative Law
LABUSCHAGNE, J., Constitutional and Pub-
  lic International Law
REMBE, N. S., Oliver Tambo Chair of
  Human Rights

Faculty of Science and Technology:

BRAND, J. M., Biochemistry and Microbiol-
  ogy
FATOKI, O. S., Chemistry
MAKUNGA, O. H. D., Plant Sciences
SADIMENKO, A., Chemistry
SANYAL, D. K., Chemistry
SERETIO, J. R., Physics
TYLER, J. C., Statistics
VAN DYK, T. J., Mathematics
VAN HEERDEN, J. W. A., Zoology
WAGENER, P. C., Applied Mathematics

Faculty of Theology:

ABRAHAMS, S. P., Old Testament and Hebrew
THOM, G., Historical and Contextual Theology

UNIVERSITY OF JOHANNESBURG

POB 524, Auckland Park, Johannesburg 2092

Telephone: (11) 559-4555
Fax: (11) 559-2191
Internet: www.uj.ac.za

Founded 2005 by merger of Rand Afrikaans Univ. and Technikon Witwatersrand
State control
Languages of instruction: Afrikaans, English
Academic year: January to November

Chancellor: WENDY LUHABE
Vice-Chancellor: Prof. IHRON RENSBURG
Pro-Vice-Chancellor: Prof. DEREK VAN DER MERWE
Deputy Vice-Chancellor for Academic Affairs: Prof. ANGINA PAREKH
Deputy Vice-Chancellor for Finance: Prof. HENK KRIEK
Deputy Vice-Chancellor for Research, Innovation and Advancement: Prof. ADAM HABIB

Library of 452,273 vols
Number of teachers: 350
Number of students: 49,000

DEANS

Faculty of Art, Design and Architecture: MARIAN SAUTHOFF
Faculty of Economic and Financial Science: Prof. AMANDA DEMPSEY
Faculty of Education: Prof. SARAH GRAVETT
Faculty of Engineering and the Built Environment: Prof. TSHILIDZI MARWALA
Faculty of Health: Prof. ANDRE SWART
Faculty of Humanities: Prof. RORY RYAN
Faculty of Law: Prof. PATRICK O'BRIEN
Faculty of Management: Prof. STEPHEN KRUGER
Faculty of Natural Science: Prof. KINTA BURGER

PROFESSORS

ABRAHAMSE, H., Biomedical Technology
ALBERTS, V., Physics
ALEXANDER, P., Centre for Sociological Research
AMORY, A., Mathematics, Science, Technology and Computer Education
ANKIEWICZ, P., Mathematics, Science, Technology and Computer Education
ANNEGARN, H., Geography and Environmental Management and Energy Studies
AURIACOMBE, C., Public Governance
BERNDT, A., Marketing Management
BEUKES, N., Geology
BOESSENKOOL, A., Business Management
BROERE, I., Mathematics
BUHLUNGU, S., Sociology
BURGER, W., Afrikaans
BURNETT-LOUW, C., Sport and Movement Studies
CAIRNCROSS, B., Geology
CASE, M., Power and Control Engineering Technology
CHABELI, M., Professional Nursing Practice
CLOETE, G., Public Governance
COETSEE, D., Accountancy
COETZEE, J., Biblical and Religious Studies
COETZEE, J., Industrial Psychology and People Management
COETZEE, P., Chemistry
CONNELL, S., Geography and Environmental Management and Energy Studies
CONRADIE, C., Afrikaans
CONRADIE, W., APB Entrepreneurship
CORNELIUS, S., Private Law
CROUS, F., Industrial Psychology and People Management
DARKWA, J., Chemistry
DE BRUIN, G., Industrial Psychology and People Management
DE BRUYN, H., Business Management
DE KLERK, N., Communication
DE VILLIERS, D., Criminal Law and Procedure

DE WET, D., Humanities Dean's Office
DEMPSEY, A., Economic and Financial Sciences Dean's Office
DU RAND, J., Biblical and Religious Studies
DU TOIT, A., Information and Knowledge Management
DU TOIT, S., Mercantile Law
DUBERY, I., Biochemistry
EHLERS, E., Academy for Information Technology
ESACK, F., Psychology
FERREIRA, H., Electrical and Electronic Engineering Science
FERREIRA, J., Optometry
FRANGOS, C., Statistics
GELDENHUYS, D., Politics
GREYLING, L., Economics and Econometrics
GRUNDLINGH, L., Historical Studies
HAARHOFF, J., Civil Engineering Science
HAMILTON, L., Politics
HARRIS, W., Optometry
HOLLANDER, W., Sport
JACOBS, G., Division for Institutional Planning and Quality Promotions
JANSE VAN RENSBURG, J., Semitic Languages
JANSE VAN VUREN, J., Zoology
JOHL, C., Linguistics and Literary Theory
JOOSTE, C., Marketing Management
JOOSTE, K., Professional Nursing Practice
KATZ, Z., Mechanical Engineering Science
KRUGER, G., Chemistry
KRUGER, S., Management Dean's Office
LANDSBERG, C., Politics
LOMBARD, F., Statistics
LOTTER, H., Philosophy
MACKENZIE, C., English
MAINA, A., SWC Chemistry
MALHERBE, E., Public Law
MANS, K., Accountancy
MARWALA, T., Engineering and the Built Environment Dean's Office
MARX, B., Accountancy
METZ, T., Philosophy
MOORE, D., Anthropology and Development Studies
MYBURGH, C., Educational Psychology
NEELS, J., Private Law
NEL, A., Mechanical Engineering Science
NIEUWENHUIZEN, C., Business Management
NOLTE, A., Maternal and Child Nursing
NURICK, A., Mechanical Engineering Science
O'BRIEN, P., Law Dean's Office
OLDEWAGE, A., Zoology
OLIVIER, L., Accountancy
OTTO, J., Private Law
PATEL, L., Social Work
PIENAAR, M., Afrikaans
PILLAY, J., Educational Psychology
POGGENPOEL, M., Psychiatric Nursing
POSTHUMUS, L., African Languages
PRETORIUS, J., Electrical and Electronic Engineering Science
PRINSLOO, G., Transport and Supply Chain Management
RAUBENHEIMER, H., Mathematics
RAUTENBACH, I., Law Dean's Office
RENSLEIGH, C., Information and Knowledge Management
ROODT, G., Industrial Psychology and People Management
RUTTKAMP, E., Philosophy
SADIE, A., Politics
SAUTHOFF, M., APB Art, Design and Architecture Dean's Office
SCHERZINGER, K., English
SMIT, N., Mercantile Law
SMITH, D., Industrial Psychology and People Management
SNYMAN, J., Philosophy
SONNEKUS, J., Private Law
STEEB, W., Applied Mathematics
STONES, C., Psychology
STRYDOM, A., Physics
STRYDOM, H., Public Law
THOMAS, A., Business Management
TRIEGAARDT, J., Social Work

UYS, J., Industrial Psychology and People Management
UYS, J., Sociology
VAN DER BANK, F., Zoology
VAN DER LINDE, K., Mercantile Law
VAN DER WESTHUIZEN, D., Mathematics, Science, Technology and Computer Education
VAN LILL, D., Tourism and Hospitality Management
VAN ROOYEN, H., Curriculum and Instruction
VAN TONDER, C., Industrial Psychology and People Management
VAN VUUREN, L., Industrial Psychology and People Management
VAN WYK, B., Botany and Plant Biotechnology
VAN ZYL, G., Economics and Econometrics
VELDSMAN, T., Industrial Psychology and People Management
VENTER, A., Politics
VERHOEF, G., Accountancy
VERWEY, S., Communication
VILJOEN, K., Geology
VILLET, C., Applied Mathematics
VIVIERS, H., Biblical and Religious Studies
VON SOLMS, S., Academy for Information Technology
VOOGT, T., Accountancy
WALTERS, J., Transport and Supply Chain Management
WATNEY, M., Criminal Law and Procedure
WEPENER, V., Zoology
WHITEHEAD, C., Botany and Plant Biotechnology
WILLIAMS, D., Chemistry
WINKLER, H., Physics
WOLMARANS, J., Greek and Latin Studies
ZIMPER, A., Economics and Econometrics

UNIVERSITY OF KWAZULU-NATAL

Westville Campus, PMB X54001, Durban 4000

Telephone: (31) 260-7111
Fax: (31) 204-4383
E-mail: enquiries@ukzn.ac.za
Internet: www.ukzn.ac.za

Founded 2004 by merger of Univ. of Natal and Univ. of Durban-Westville
Language of instruction: English
Autonomous control
Academic year: February to December (4 terms)

Chancellor: Judge ZAC M. YACOOB
Vice-Chancellor and Prin.: Prof. M. W. MAKGOBA
Deputy Vice-Chancellor for Finance and Admin.: Prof. HILTON STANILAND
Deputy Vice-Chancellor for Research and Devt: Prof. SALIM S. ABDOOL KARIM

Publication: Con-text (irregular)

DEANS

Faculty of Education: Prof. TUNTUFYE MWAMWENDA
Faculty of Engineering: Prof. DENYS SCHREINER
Faculty of Health Sciences: Prof. LEANA UYS
Faculty of Humanities, Devt and Social Science: (vacant)
Faculty of Law: Prof. L. GERING
Faculty of Management Studies: Prof. KANTILAL BHOWAN (Asst Dean)
Faculty of Nursing: Prof. OLUYINKA ADEJUMO (Head of School)
Faculty of Science and Agriculture: Prof. P. J. K. ZACHARIAS

BRANCH CAMPUSES

Edgewood Campus: cnr Richmond Rd and Marionhill Rd, Pinetown 3605; tel. (31) 260-3414; e-mail connawayn@ukzn.ac.za.

Howard College Campus: University KZN, Durban 4041; tel. (31) 260-2212.

Medical School Campus: Umbilo Rd, Durban 4013; tel. (31) 260-4248; e-mail undergrad@ukzn.ac.za.

Pietermaritzburg Campus: King Edward Ave, Scottsville, Pietermaritzburg 3209; tel. (33) 260-5212; e-mail naidoo@ukzn.ac.za.

UNIVERSITY OF LIMPOPO

PMB X1106, Sovenga 0727
Telephone: (15) 268-3061
Fax: (15) 268-3567
Internet: www.ul.ac.za
Founded 2005 by the merger of Medical University of Southern Africa and Univ. of the North
Academic year: January to December
Vice-Chancellor: Prof. MOKGALONG (acting)
Campus Prin.: K. NHLANE (acting)
Registrar: Prof. P. FRANKS (acting)
Library: see Libraries and Archives
Number of teachers: 400
Number of students: 12,000.

CONSTITUENT CAMPUSES

Medunsa Campus

POB 189, Medunsa 0204
Telephone: (12) 521-4111

DEANS

Faculty of Dentistry: Prof. T. S. GUGUSHE
Faculty of Medicine: Prof. C. F. VAN DER MERWE (acting)
Faculty of Sciences: Prof. J. V. GROENEWALD
National School of Public Health: Prof. A. A. HERMAN

Turfloop Campus

PMB X1106, Sovenga, Limpopo 0727
Telephone: (15) 268-9111
Fax: (15) 267-0152

DEANS

Faculty of Humanities: Prof. L. J. TEFFO
Faculty of Management Sciences and Law: Prof. P. E. FRANKS
Faculty of Sciences, Health and Agriculture: Dr N. M. MOKGALONG

DIRECTORS

Faculty of Humanities:
School of Education: Prof. J. KUIPER
School of Languages and Communication Studies: Prof. S. LOUW
School of Social Sciences: Dr N. C. KIRK

Faculty of Management Sciences and Law:
School of Economics and Management: Prof. A. DE VILLIERS
School of Law: Prof. M. C. OKBPALUBA
Graduate School of Leadership: Prof. L. G. BUBERWA

Faculty of Sciences, Health and Agriculture:
School of Agricultural and Environmental Sciences: Prof. N. M. MOLLEL
School of Computational and Mathematical Sciences: Prof. B. W. BECKER
School of Health Sciences: Prof. P. A. VENTER
School of Physical and Mineral Sciences: Dr W. P. MASHELA (acting)

UNIVERSITY OF PRETORIA

Pretoria 0002
Telephone: (12) 420-4111
Fax: (12) 362-5168
E-mail: csc@up.ac.za
Internet: www.up.ac.za
Founded 1908 as Transvaal Univ. College; granted Charter as Univ. of Pretoria 1930
Private control
Languages of instruction: Afrikaans, English

Academic year: February to December (2 semesters)
Chancellor: Dr C. L. STALS
Vice-Chancellor and Prin.: Prof. C. W. I. PISTORIUS
Advisor to the Prin.: Prof. A. P. MELCK
Vice-Prins: Prof. C. R. DE BEER, Prof. R. M. CREWE, Prof. N. C. MANGANYI, Prof. R. A. MOGOTLANE
Exec. Dirs: Prof. A. M. DE KLERK, J. S. J. NEL, Prof. S. VIL-NKOMO
Head of the Secretariat: M. G. VILJOEN
Registrar: Prof. N. J. GROVÉ
Dir for Academic Admin.: Dr D. D. MARAIS
Dir of Academic Information Service: Prof. J. A. BOON
Dir of Client Services Centre: Dr K. LAZENBY
Dir for Corporate Communication and Marketing: Dr K. LAZENBY
Dir of Facilities Planning and Services: D. MOKOTEDI
Dir of Financial Admin.: T. G. KRUGER
Dir of Human Resources: Prof. A. VAN ASWEGEN
Dir of Dept of Information Technology: Dr J. A. PRETORIUS
Dir of Institutional Research and Planning: Prof. P. J. VERMEULEN
Dir of Mamelodi Campus: E. SMITH
Dir of Management Services: Prof. Q. VORSTER
Dir of Telematic Learning and Education Innovation: Prof. J. A. BOON
Dir of TuksSport: J. K. VAN DER WALT
Dean of Students: Prof. M. T. SPECKMAN
Library: see Libraries and Archives
Number of teachers: 1,385
Number of students: 39,000

Publications: *Ad Destinatum: Gedenkboek van die Universiteit van Pretoria, Huldigingsbundels* (irregular), *Openbare Fakulteitslesings* (irregular), *Opvoedkundige Studies* (Educational Studies, 3 or 4 a year), *Publikasies van die Universiteit van Pretoria—Nuwe Reeks* (Publications of the University of Pretoria—New Series (I) Research, 1 a year), *Tukkie-Werf* (4 a year)

DEANS

Faculty of Economic and Management Sciences: Prof. C. KOORNHOF
Faculty of Education: Prof. J. D. JANSEN
Faculty of Engineering, Built Environment and Information Technology: Prof. R. F. SANDENBERGH
Faculty of Health Sciences: Prof. T. J. MARIBA
Faculty of Humanities: Prof. M. E. MULLER
Faculty of Law: Prof. D. G. KLEYN
Faculty of Natural and Agricultural Sciences: Prof. A. STRÖH
Faculty of Theology: Prof. C. A. VOS
Faculty of Veterinary Science: Prof. N. P. J. KRIEK
School of Dentistry: Prof. A. J. LIGTHELM (Chair.)

PROFESSORS

Faculty of Economic and Management Sciences:
ALBERTS, N. F., Tourism Management
BASSON, J. S., Human Resources Management
BLIGNAUT, J. N., Economics
BRAND, H. E., Human Resources Management
BRYNARD, P. A., School of Public Management and Administration
DE BEER, J. J., Human Resources Management
DE JAGER, H., Auditing
DE LA REY, J. H., Financial Management
DE VILLIERS, C. J., Financial Management
DE WET, J. M., Marketing and Communication Management

DE WIT, P. W. C., Business Management
DU PLESSIS, P. J., Marketing and Communication Management
FOURIE, D. J., School of Public Management and Administration
GLOECK, J. D., Auditing
GOUWS, D. G., Financial Management
HALL, J. H., Financial Management
HARMSE, C., Economics
HEATH, E. T., Tourism Management
HOOLE, C. R., Human Resources Management
KOORNHOFF, C., Accounting
KUYE, J. O., School of Public Management and Administration
LAMBRECHTS, H. A., Financial Management
MAASDORP, E. F. DE V., Business Management
MARX, A. E., Business Management
OOST, E. J., Financial Management
SCHOEMAN, N. J., Economics
STEYN, F. G., Economics
THORNHILL, C., School of Public Management and Administration
VAN DER SCHYF, D. B., Auditing
VAN HEERDEN, J. H., Economics
VERMEULEN, L. P., Human Resources Management

Faculty of Education:
ALANT, E., Augmentative and Alternative Communication
BECKMANN, J. L., Education Management and Policy Studies
BOUWER, A. C., Educational Psychology
CRONJÉ, J. C., Curriculum Studies
FRASER, W. J., Curriculum Studies
MAREE, J. G., Curriculum Studies
NKOMO, M., Educational Management and Policy Studies
ONWU, G. O. M., Science, Mathematics and Technology Education
VAN ROOYEN, L., Curriculum Studies

Faculty of Engineering, Built Environment and Information Technology (University of Pretoria, Pretoria 0002; tel. (12) 420-2005; fax (12) 362-5173; e-mail dean@eng.up.ac.za; internet www.up.ac.za/ebit):
BOTHMA, T. J. D., Information Science
BRÜMMER, D. G., Construction Economics
CLAASEN, S. J., Industrial and Systems Engineering
CRIMSEHL, U. H. J., Chemical Engineering
DE VILLIERS, C., Informatics
ELOFF, J. H. P., Computer Science
FISHER, R. C., Architecture
GRIMSEHL, U. H. J., Chemical Engineering
HORAK, E., Civil and Biosystems Engineering
LEUSCHNER, F. W., Electrical, Electronic and Computer Engineering
MEYER, J. P., Mechanical and Aeronautical Engineering
ORANJE, M. C., Town and Regional Planning
PISTORIUS, P. C., Materials Science and Metallurgical Engineering
POURIS, A., Institute for Technological Innovation
PRETORIUS, M. W., Engineering and Technology Management
VAN DER MERWE, J. N., Mining Engineering

Faculty of Health Sciences:
ANDERSON, R., Immunology
BARTEL, P. R., Neurology
BECKER, J. H. R., Surgery
BLITZ-LINDEQUE, J. J., Family Medicine
BUCH, E., School of Health Systems and Public Health
DIPPENAAR, N. G., Physiology
DREYER, L., Anatomical Pathology
DU PLESSIS, D. J., Cardiothoracic Surgery
GREY, S. V., Health Sciences General
KER, J. A., Internal Medicine
KRUGER, M., Paediatrics

LEVINSON, I. P., Urology
LINDEQUE, B. G., Obstetrics and Gynaecology
MAFOJANE, N. A., Neurology
MARITZ, N. G. J., Orthopaedics
MATHIVHA, T. M., Cardiology
MEDLEN, C. E., Pharmacology
MEIRING, J. H., Anatomy
MEYER, H. P., Internal Medicine
MOKOENA, T. R., Surgery
MULDER, A. A. H., Ear, Nose and Throat Medicine
MWANTEMBE, O., Internal Medicine
PATTINSON, R. C., Obstetrics and Gynaecology
RANTLOANE, J. L. A., Anaesthesiology
REIF, S., Urology
RHEEDER, P., Clinical Epidemiology
ROOS, J. L., Psychiatry
ROUX, P., Ophthalmology
SAAYMAN, G., Forensic Medicine
SCHOLTZ, M. E., Radiology
SCHUTTE, C.-M., Neurology
SNYMAN, J. R., Pharmacology
STEYN, M., Anatomy
SWART, J. G., Otorhinolaryngology
VAN GELDER, A. L., Internal Medicine
VAN PAPENDORP, D. H., Physiology
VAN WYK, N. C., Nursing Science
VERMAAK, W. J. H., Chemical Pathology
VILJOEN, M., Physiology
WITTENBERG, D. F., Paediatrics

Faculty of Humanities:

ANTONITES, A., Philosophy
BERGH, J. S., Historical and Heritage Studies
BOTHA, P. J., Ancient Languages
CARSTENS, A., Afrikaans
DU PLESSIS, A., Political Sciences
FOURIE, E., Music
GOSLIN, A. E., Biokinetics
GRAY, R. A., English
GROBBELAAR, J., Sociology
HAGEMANN, F. R., Drama
HARRIS, K. L., Historical and Heritage Studies
HOUGH, M., Political Sciences
KRUGER, P. E., Biokinetics, Sport and Leisure Sciences
LOMBARD, A., Social Work
LOUW, B., Communication Pathology
MARCHETTI-MERCER, M. C., Psychology
MAREE, D. J. F., Pyschology
MEDALIE, D., English
MITI, K. N., Political Science
MLAMBO, A. S., Historical and Heritage Studies
NEOCOSMOS, M., Sociology
NIEHAUS, I. A., Anthropology and Archaeology
NZEWI, M. E., Music
OHLHOFF, C. H. F., Afrikaans
PEETERS, L. F. H. M. C., Modern European Languages
POTGIETER, J. H., Ancient Languages
PRETORIUS, F., Historical and Heritage Studies
PRETORIUS, R., Criminology
PRINSLOO, D. J., African Languages
PRINSLOO, G. T. M., Ancient Languages
ROODT, P. H., Afrikaans
SAUTHOFF, M. D., Visual Arts
SCHOEMAN, J. B., Psychology
SCHOEMAN, M. M. E., Political Sciences
SHARP, J. S., Anthropology and Archaeology
STANDER, H. F., Ancient Languages
STANFORD, H. J., Music
STEYN, B. J. M., Biokinetics
VAN DER MERWE, A., Communication Pathology
VAN DER MESCHT, H., Music
VAN NIEKERK, C., Music
VAN WYK, G. J., Biokinetics, Sport and Leisure Sciences

VILJOEN, W. D., Music
WALTON, C. R., Music
WEBB, V. N., Afrikaans
WEIDEMAN, A. J., Unit for Language Skills Development
WESSELS, J. A., English
WILLEMSE, H. S. S., Afrikaans

Faculty of Law (tel. (12) 420-2412; fax (12) 362-5184; e-mail duard.kleyn@up.ac.za):

BORAINE, A., Procedural Law
BOTHA, C. J., Public Law
BURDETTE, D. A., Centre for Practical and Continuing Legal Education
CARSTENS, P. A., Public Law
DAVEL, C. J., Private Law and Centre for Child Law
DELPORT, P. A., Mercantile and Labour Law
HANSUNQULE, K. M., Centre for Human Rights
HAUPT, F. S., Law Clinic
HEYNS, C. H., Centre for Human Rights
KLOPPER, H. B., Mercantile and Labour Law
KOTZE, D. J. L., Procedural Law
LOTZ, D. J., Mercantile Law
MAITHUFI, I. P., Private Law
NAGEL, C. J., Mercantile Law
NICHOLSON, C. M. A., Legal History, Comparative Law and Legal Philosophy
SCHOEMAN, M. C., Private Law
SCOTT, T. J., Private Law
THOMAS, P. J., Legal History, Comparative Law and Legal Philosophy
VAN ECK, B. P. S., Mercantile Law
VAN JAARSVELD, S. R., Mercantile Law
VAN MARLE, K., Legal History, Comparative Law and Legal Philosophy
VAN SCHALKWYK, L. N., Private Law
VILJOEN, F. J., Legal History, Comparative Law and Legal Philosophy
VISSER, P. J., Private Law

Faculty of Natural and Agricultural Sciences (Room 2-32, Agricultural Sciences Building, University of Pretoria, Pretoria 0002; tel. (12) 420-3201; fax (12) 420-3890; internet www.up.ac.za/science):

ALBERTS, H. W., Physics
AURET, F. D., Physics
BEAVON, K. S. O., Geography and Geoinformatics
BENNETT, N. C., Zoology and Entomology
BESTER, M. N., Zoology and Entomology
BRAUN, M. W. H., Physics
BREDENKAMP, G. J., Botany
BRINK, D. J., Physics
CASEY, N. H., Animal and Wildlife Sciences
CLOETE, T. E., Microbiology and Plant Pathology
COUTINHO, T. A., Microbiology and Plant Pathology
CROWTHER, N. A. S., Statistics
DE KLERK, H. M., Consumer Science
DE WAAL, S. A., Geology
HUISMANS, H., Genetics
KIRSTEN, J. F., Agricultural Economics, Extension and Rural Development
KUNERT, K. J., Botany
LOTZ, S., Chemistry
LOUW, A. I., Biochemistry
MALHERBE, J. B., Physics
MEYER, J. J. M., Botany
MILLER, H. G., Physics
MINNAAR, A., Food Sciences
NEITZ, A. W. H., Biochemistry
NICOLSON, S. W., Zoology and Entomology
PLASTINO, A. R., Physics
REINHARDT, C. F., Plant Production and Soil Science
ROHWER, E. R., Chemistry
SCHOLTZ, C. H., Zoology and Entomology
STRÖH, A., Mathematics and Applied Mathematics
VAN AARDE, R. J., Zoology and Entomology

VAN ROOYEN, C. J., Agricultural Economics, Extension and Rural Development
VAN WYK, A. E., Botany
VERSCHOOR, J. A., Biochemistry
VLEGGAAR, R., Chemistry

Faculty of Theology:

DE VILLIERS, D. E., Dogmatics and Christian Ethics
DREYER, Y., Practical Theology
HOFMEYR, J. W., Church History and Church Policy
HUMAN, D. J., Old Testament Studies
LE ROUX, J. H., Old Testament Studies
MEIRING, P. G. J., Science of Religion and Missiology
MÜLLER, J. C., Practical Theology
VAN AARDE, A. G., New Testament
VAN DER MERWE, P. J., Science of Religion and Missiology
VAN DER WATT, J. G., New Testament Studies
VENTER, P. M., Old Testament Studies
WETHMAR, C. J., Dogmatics and Christian Ethics

Faculty of Veterinary Science (Private Bag X04, Ondestepoort 0110; tel. (12) 529-8000; fax (12) 529-8300; e-mail dean@op.up.ac.za; internet www.up.ac.za/academic/veterinary):

BERTSCHINGER, H. J., Wildlife Unit
BOOMKER, J. D. F., Veterinary Tropical Diseases
BOOTH, K. K., Anatomy and Physiology
COETZER, J. A. W., Veterinary Tropical Diseases
GROENEWALD, H. B., Anatomy and Physiology
GUTHRIE, A. J., Centre for Equine Research
KIRBERGER, R. M., Companion Animal Clinical Studies
LOURENS, D. C., Production Animal Studies
McCRINDLE, C. M., Paraclinical Sciences
PENZHORN, B. L., Veterinary Tropical Diseases
RAUTENBACH, G. H., Production Animal Studies
STADLER, P., Companion Animal Clinical Studies
SWAN, G. E., Paraclinical Sciences
TERBLANCHE, W. M., Deputy Dean

School of Dentistry:

BOTHA, S. J., Centre for Stomatological Research
BUCH, B., Diagnostics and Röntgenology
BÜTOW, K. W., Maxillofacial and Oral Surgery
DE WET, F. A., Prosthetics and Dental Mechanics
JACOBS, F. J. (acting), Maxillofacial and Oral Surgery
KEMP, P. L., Prosthetics and Dental Mechanics
VAN HEERDEN, W. F. P., Oral Pathology and Oral Biology
VAN WYK, P. J., Community Dentistry
VERWAYEN, F. D., Periodontics and Oral Medicine

UNIVERSITY OF SOUTH AFRICA

POB 392, Unisa 0003

Telephone: (12) 429-3111
Fax: (12) 429-3221
E-mail: artes@unisa.ac.za
Internet: www.unisa.ac.za

Founded 1873, Royal Charter 1877; merged with Technikon Southern Africa and incorporated Vista Univ. 2004
Languages of instruction: Afrikaans, English
Academic year: February to November

Chancellor: Justice BERNARD MAKGABO NGOEPE
Vice-Chancellor: Prof. BARNEY PITYANA
Chair. of the Ccl: Dr MATTHEWS PHOSA
Pro-Vice-Chancellor: Prof. NEO MATHABE

Deputy Vice-Chancellor and Vice-Prin. for Operations: Prof. D. L. MOSOMA (acting)

Vice-Prin. for Academic Affairs: Prof. C. F. SWANEPOEL

Vice-Prin. for Finance: Prof. G. J. DE J. CRONJE (acting)

Vice-Prin. for Learner Support: Prof. A. H. LOUW

Vice-Prin. for Research and Planning: Prof. N. BAIJNATH

Vice-Prin. for Student and Alumni Affairs: Prof. R. C. BODIBE

Registrar: Prof. T. H. LINKS

Academic Registrar: Prof. L. MOLAMU (acting)

Librarian: Prof. J. WILLEMSE

Number of teachers: 1,074

Number of students: 200,000

Publications: *Africanus* (2 a year), *Ars Nova* (1 a year), *Codicillus* (2 a year), *Communicatio* (2 a year), *De Arte* (2 a year), *Educare* (1 a year), *Kleio* (1 a year), *Language Matters* (1 a year), *Mousaion* (2 a year), *Musicus* (2 a year), *Politeia* (3 a year), *Scrutiny*^{2} (2 a year), *Unisa Bulletin* (5 a year), *Unisa News* (4 a year), *Unisa Psychologia* (2 a year)

DEANS

College of Agriculture and Environment Sciences: (vacant)

College of Economics and Management Sciences: Prof. MRAD SHAHIA

College of Human Sciences: Prof. M. S. MAKHANYA

College of Law: Prof. RITA MARE'

College of Science, Engineering and Technology: Prof. G. J. SUMMERS

Graduate School of Business Leadership: Prof. H. C. NGAMBI (Executive Director)

PROFESSORS

ABRIE, A., Accounting
ACKERMANN, P. L. S., Graduate School of Business Leadership
ADLEM, W. L. J., Public Administration
AILOLA, D. A., Mercantile Law
BADENHORST, J. A., Business Management
BARROW, J. E., Computer Science
BEATY, D. T., Graduate School of Business Leadership
BECKER, H. M. R., Applied Accountancy
BEGEMANN, E., Business Management
BEKKER, P. M., Criminal and Procedural Law
BESTER, G., Educational Studies
BEYERS, E., Psychology
BISHOP, N. T., Mathematics, Applied Mathematics and Astronomy
BODENSTEIN, H. C. A., Educational Studies
BOOT, G., Accounting
BOOYENS, S. W., Advanced Nursing Sciences
BOOYSE, J. J., Further Teacher Training
BOOYSEN, H., Constitutional and International Law
BORNMAN, C. H., Computer Science
BOTHA, J. E., New Testament
BOTHA, N. J., Constitutional and International Law
BOTHA, P. J. J., New Testament
BRITS, J. P., History
BRYNARD, D. J., Public Administration
BURNS, Y. M., Constitutional and International Law
CALITZ, E., Economics
CANT, M. C., Business Management
CARPENTER, G., Constitutional and International Law
CHURCH, J., Jurisprudence
CILLIERS, C. H., Criminology
CILLIERS, F. VAN N., Industrial Psychology
COETZER, I. A., Educational Studies
CONRADIE, H., Criminology
CRONJE, D. S. P., Private Law
CRONJE, G. J. DE J., Business Management
CRONJE, P. M., Accounting

CROUS, S. F. M., Educational Studies
DADOO, Y., Semitics
DE BEER, C. S., Information Science
DE BEER, F. C., Anthropology and Archaeology
DE BEER, F. C., Development Administration
DE JONGH, M., Anthropology and Archaeology
DEMBETEMBE, N. C., African Languages
DICK, A. L., Information Science
DREECKMEYER, M., Secondary School Education
DREYER, J. M., Advanced Nursing Sciences
DU PISANIE, J. A., Economics
DU PLESSIS, I. J., New Testament
DU PLESSIS, P. J., Graduate School of Business Leadership
DU TOIT, C. W., Research Institute for Theology and Religion
DU TOIT, G. S., Business Management
ENGELBRECHT, J., New Testament
ERASMUS, B. J., Business Management
FARIS, J. A., Criminal and Procedural Law
FAURE, A. M., Political Sciences
FINLAYSON, R., African Languages
FOURIE, D. P., Psychology
FOURIE, L. J., Economics
FOURIE, P. J., Communication
FRANZSEN, R. C. D., Mercantile Law
GELDENHUYS, D. G., Musicology
GHYOOT, V. G., Business Management
GRÄBE, R. C., Theory of Literature
GROBBELAAR, A. F., Accounting
GROBBELAAR, J. I., Sociology
GROBLER, G. M. M., African Languages
GROBLER, P. A., Business Management
GRUNDLINGH, A. M., History
HAVENGA, M. K., Mercantile Law
HAVENGA, P. H., Mercantile Law
HAWTHORNE, L., Private Law
HEIDEMA, J., Mathematics, Applied Mathematics and Astronomy
HENDRIKSE, A. P., Linguistics
HIGGS, P., Educational Studies
HOFMEYR, K. B., Graduate School of Business Leadership
HOUGH, J., Business Management
HUBBARD, E. H., Linguistics
HUGO, P. J., Political Sciences
HUGO, W. M. J., Graduate School of Business Leadership
JANSE VAN RENSBURG, J. B., Applied Accountancy
JORDAAN, W. J., Psychology
JOUBERT, J. J., Criminal and Procedural Law
JULYAN, F. W., Accounting
KATKOVNIK, V., Statistics
KLERCK, W. G., Graduate School of Business Leadership
KRIEK, D. J., Political Science
KRITZINGER, J. N. J., Missiology
KRUGER, E. G., Secondary School Teacher Education
KRÜGER, J. S., Religious Studies
LANDMAN, A. A., Mercantile Law
LEMMER, E. M., Further Teacher Training
LESSING, A. C., Educational Studies
LIEBENBERG, E. C., Geography
LIGTHELM, A. A., Bureau for Market Research
LOMBARD, D. B., Classics
LÖTTER, S., Criminal and Procedural Law
LOUWRENS, L. J., African Languages
LÜBBE, J. C., Semitics
LUCAS, G. H. A., Business Management
McKAY, V. I., Institute for Adult Basic Education and Training
McLEARY, F., Graduate School of Business Leadership
MADER, G. J., Classics
MARAIS, A. DE K., Business Management
MARE, E. A., History of Art, Fine Art
MARÉ, M. C., Criminal and Procedural Law
MAREE, M. C., Romance Languages
MARKHAM, R., Statistics
MARTINS, J. A., Bureau for Market Research
MARX, J., Business Management

MISCH, M. K. E., German
MOHR, P. J., Economics
MOTLHABI, M. B. G., Systematic Theology and Theological Ethics
MSIMANG, C. T., African Languages
MYNHARDT, C. M., Mathematics, Applied Mathematics and Astronomy
NAUDE, C. M. B., Criminology
NELL, V., Social and Health Sciences
NESER, J. J., Criminology
NTULI, D. B., African Languages
OBERHOLZER, M. O., Educational Studies
OLIVIER, A., Primary School Education
ORR, M. A., English
PALMER, P. N., Business Management
PAUL, S. O., Chemistry
PAUW, J. C., Public Administration
PELSER, G. P. J., Graduate School of Business Leadership
PIETERSE, H. J. C., Practical Theology
PLUG, C., Psychology
POTGIETER, C., Further Teacher Education
POTGIETER, J. M., Private Law
POTGIETER, T. J. E., Graduate School of Business Leadership
POULOS, G., African Languages
PRETORIUS, E. A. C., New Testament
PRETORIUS, J. T., Mercantile Law
PRETORIUS, L., Sociology
PRINSLOO, E. D., Philosophy
RABINOWITZ, I. A., English
RADEMEYER, G., Psychology
REYNHARDT, E. C., Physics
ROELOFSE, J. J., Communication
ROOS, H. M., Afrikaans
RUTHERFORD, B. R., Mercantile Law
RYAN, P. D., English
SADLER, E., Applied Accountancy
SALBANY, S. DE O., Applied Mathematics, Mathematics and Astronomy
SCHEFFLER, E. H., Old Testament
SCOTT, S. J., Private Law
SEBOTHOMA, W. A., New Testament
SERUDU, S. M., African Languages
SHAHIA, M., Transport Economics and Logistics
SMIT, B. F., Criminology
SMIT, P. J., Business Management
SMITH, J. DU P., Economics
SMITH, K. W., History
SMUTS, C. A., Transport Economics and Logistics
SNYDERS, F. J. A., Psychology
SNYMAN, C. R., Criminal and Procedural Law
SNYMAN, J. W., African Languages
SOFIANOS, S. A., Physics
SÖHNGE, W. F., Educational Studies
STEENEKAMP, T. J., Economics
STEFFENS, F. E., Statistics
STEYN, B. L., Accounting
STRIKE, W. N., Romance Languages
STRYDOM, J. W., Business Management
SUMMERS, G. J., Chemistry
SWANEPOEL, C. F., African Languages
SWANEPOEL, C. H., Institute for Educational Research
SWANEPOEL, C. J., Quantitative Management
SWANEPOEL, F. A., C. B. Powell Bible Centre
SWANEPOEL, P. H., Afrikaans
SWANEVELDER, J. J., Accounting
SWART, G. J., Mercantile Law
SWEMMER, P. N., Auditing
TERBLANCHE, S. S., Criminal and Procedural Law
THOMASHAUSEN, A. E. A. M., Institute for Foreign and Comparative Law
TORR, C. S. W., Economics
TROSKIE, R., Advanced Nursing Sciences
VAKALISA, N. C. G., Secondary School Education
VAN ASWEGEN, A., Private Law
VAN BILJON, R. C. W., Social Work
VAN BLERK, A. E., Jurisprudence
VAN DELFT, W. F., Social Work
VAN DEN BERG, P. H., Graduate School of Business Leadership

VAN DER MERWE, C. A., Quantitative Management
VAN DER MERWE, D. P., Criminal and Procedural Law
VAN DER WALT, A. J., Private Law
VAN DYK, P. J., Old Testament
VAN HEERDEN, B., Auditing
VAN NIEKERK, E., Systematic Theology, Theological Ethics
VAN NIEKERK, J. P., Mercantile Law
VAN ROOY, M. P., Educational Studies
VAN WYK, A. M. A., Private Law
VAN WYK, C. W., Jurisprudence
VAN WYK, D. H., Constitutional and International Law
VAN WYK, H. DE J., Bureau for Market Research
VAN ZYL, A. E., Educational Studies
VILJOEN, H. G., Psychology
VISSER, C. J., Mercantile Law
VISSER, P. S., Educational Studies
VORSTER, H. J. S., Auditing
VORSTER, J. N., New Testament
VORSTER, L. P., Indigenous Law
VORSTER, S. J. R., Mathematics, Applied Mathematics and Astronomy
WATKINS, M. L., Industrial Psychology
WEINBERG, A. M., English
WESSELS, W. J., Old Testament
WHELPTON, F. P. VAN R., Indigenous Law
WIECHERS, E., Educational Studies
WIECHERS, N. J., Private Law
WILLIAMS, G., Applied Accountancy
WOLFAARDT, J. A., Practical Theology
WOLFAARDT, J. B., Industrial Psychology
WOLVAARDT, J. S., Quantitative Management
YADAVALLI, V. S. S., Statistics

UNIVERSITY OF STELLENBOSCH

PMB X1, Matieland 7602, Cape Province
Telephone: (21) 808-9111
Fax: (21) 808-4499
E-mail: webinfo@maties.sun.ac.za
Internet: www.sun.ac.za

Founded 1918, dental faculty incorporated into Univ. of the Western Cape 2004
Language of instruction: Afrikaans
Academic year: February to December (4 terms)
Chancellor: Prof. ELIZE BOTHA
Prin. and Vice-Chancellor: Prof. C. H. BRINK
Vice-Prin. for Academic Affairs: Prof. H. R. BOTMAN
Vice-Prin. for Operations: Prof. J. F. SMITH
Vice-Prin. for Research: Prof. W. T. CLAASSEN
Registrar: J. A. ASPELING
Sr Dir of Library Services: ELLEN TISE
Number of teachers: 745
Number of students: 22,000

Publications: *Maatskaplike Werk* (Social Work, 4 a year), *Matieland*, *Opinion Survey Report* (Bureau of Economic Research, 4 a year), *Research Report* (1 a year), *Survey of Contemporary Economic Conditions and Prospects* (1 a year)

DEANS

Faculty of Agriculture and Forestry: Prof. L. VAN HUYSTEEN
Faculty of Arts: Prof. H. J. KOTZÉ
Faculty of Economic and Management Sciences: Prof. J. U. DE VILLIERS
Faculty of Education: Prof. T. PARK
Faculty of Engineering: Prof. A. SCHOONWINKEL
Faculty of Health Sciences: Prof. W. L. VAN DER MERWE
Faculty of Law: (vacant)
Faculty of Military Science: Prof. D. J. MALAN
Faculty of Science: Prof. A. S. VAN JAARSVELD
Faculty of Theology: Prof. A. E. J. MOUTON

PROFESSORS

Faculty of Agriculture and Forestry (tel. (21) 808-4792; fax (21) 808-2001; e-mail lvh@maties.sun.ac.za; internet www.sun.ac.za/agric):

AGENBAG, G. A., Agronomy and Pastures
BREDENKAMP, B. V., Forestry Science
BRITZ, T., Food Science
FEY, M. V., Soil Science
GOUSSARD, P. G., Oenology and Viticulture
HOLZ, G., Plant Pathology
MARAIS, G. F., Genetics
SAMWAYS, M. J., Entomology
THERON, K. I., Horticulture
VAN HUYSSTEEN, L., Soil Science
VAN WYK, G., Forestry Science
VINK, N., Agricultural Economics
WARNICH, L., Genetics

Faculty of Arts (tel. (21) 808-2138; fax (21) 808-2123; e-mail hjk@maties.sun.ac.za; internet www.sun.ac.za/arts):

BEKKER, S. B., Sociology
BOTHA, R. P., Linguistics
CILLIERS, F. P., Philosophy
CORNELIUS, I., Ancient Studies
DU TOIT, P. V. D. P., Political Science
GAGIANO, A. H., English
GOUWS, A., Political Science
GOUWS, R. H., Afrikaans and Dutch
GREEN, S., Social Work
GROVÉ, I. J., Music
GRUNDLINGH, A. M., History
HATTINGH, J. P., Philosophy
HAUPTFLEISCH, T., Drama
KAGEE, S. A., Psychology
KINGHORN, J., Biblical Studies
KLOPPER, D. C., English
KLOPPER, S., Fine Arts
KOTZE, H. J., Political Science
KRITZINGER, A. S., Sociology
MOUTON, J., Sociology
NAIDOO, A. V., Psychology
RABE, L., Journalism
ROOSENSCHOON, H., Music
SWARTZ, L. P., Psychology
THOM, J. C., Ancient Studies
VAN DER MERWE, W. L., Philosophy
VAN DER WAAL, C. S., Sociology
VAN NIEKERK, A. A., Philosophy
VILJOEN, L., Afrikaans and Dutch
VON MALTZAN, C. H., Modern Foreign Languages
ZIETSMAN, H. L., Geography and Environmental Studies
ZULU, N. S., African Languages

Faculty of Economic and Management Sciences (tel. (21) 808-2225; fax (21) 808-2409; e-mail calitz@maties.sun.ac.za; internet www.sun.ac.za/economy):

AUGUSTYN, J. C. D., Industrial Psychology
BIEKPE, N. B., Business Administration
BROWN, W., Accounting
BURGER, A. P., Public and Development Management
CLOETE, G. S., Public and Development Management
DE VILLIERS, J. U., Business Management
DE WET, T., Statistics and Actuarial Science
GEVERS, W. R., Business Management and Administration
HOUGH, J., Business Management
LEIBOLD, M., Business Management
MOSTERT, F. J., Business Management
OLIVIER, P., Accounting
OOSTHUIZEN, H., Business Administration
PIENAAR, W. J., Logistics
SCHOOMBEE, G. A., Economics
SCHWELLA, E., Public and Development Management
SLATTERY, P. G., Statistics and Actuarial Science
SMIT, B. W., Economics
SMIT, E. VAN DER M., Business Management and Administration
STEEL, S. J., Statistics and Actuarial Science
SWILLING, M., Public and Development Management
TERBLANCHE, N. S., Business Management
VAN DER BERG, S., Economics
VAN SCHALKWYK, C. J., Accounting

Faculty of Education (tel. (21) 808-2258; fax (21) 808-2269; e-mail tp@maties.sun.ac.za; internet www.sun.ac.za/education):

BERKHOUT, S. J., Educational Policy Studies
BITZER, E. M., Didactics
CARL, A. E., Didactics
KAPP, C. A., Centre for Higher and Adult Education
LE GRANGE, L. L. L., Didactics
PARK, T., Didactics
SCHREUDER, D. R., Didactics
SWART, R. E., Educational Psychology
WAGHID, Y., Educational Policy Studies

Faculty of Engineering (tel. (21) 808-4203; fax (21) 808-4206; e-mail schoonwinkel@maties.sun.ac.za; internet www.sun.ac.za/eng):

ALDRICH, C., Chemical Engineering
BASSON, A. H., Mechanical Engineering
BASSON, G. R., Civil Engineering
BESTER, C. J., Civil Engineering
BRADSHAW, S. M., Chemical Engineering
BURGER, A. J., Chemical Engineering
CLOETE, J. H., Electrical and Electronic Engineering
DAVIDSON, D. B., Electrical and Electronic Engineering
DUNAISKI, P. E., Civil Engineering
DU PLESSIS, J. P., Applied Mathematics
DU PREEZ, N. D., Industrial Engineering
HERBST, B. M., Applied Mathematics
JENKINS, K. J., Civil Engineering
KAMPER, M. J., Electrical and Electronic Engineering
KNOETZE, J. H., Chemical Engineering
LORENZEN, L., Chemical Engineering
LOURENS, J. G., Electrical and Electronic Engineering
MEYER, P., Electrical and Electronic Engineering
PEROLD, W. J., Electrical and Electronic Engineering
READER, H. C., Electrical and Electronic Engineering
SCHOONWINKEL, A., Electrical and Electronic Engineering
STEYN, W. H., Electrical and Electronic Engineering
VAN NIEKERK, J. L., Mechanical Engineering
VON BACKSTRÖM, T. W., Mechanical Engineering
WEIDEMAN, J. A. C., Applied Mathematics

Faculty of Health Sciences (tel. (21) 938-9200; fax (21) 938-9558; e-mail wvdmerwe@maties.sun.ac.za; internet www.sun.ac.za/med.fac):

BEYERS, N., Paediatrics and Child Health
BRINK, P. A., Internal Medicine
CHIKTE, U. M. E., Associate Dean
COETZEE, A. R., Anaesthesiology
DE VILLIERS, B., Associate Dean
DE VILLIERS, M. R., Family Medicine and Primary Care
DE VILLIERS, P. J. T., Family Medicine and Primary Care
DOUBELL, A. F., Internal Medicine
DU TOIT, D., Anatomy and Histology
EMSLEY, R. A., Psychiatry
ERASMUS, R. T., Chemical Pathology
HEYNS, C. F., Urology
HOUGH, F. S., Internal Medicine
KOESLAG, J. H., Medical Physiology and Biochemistry

KRUGER, T. F., Obstetrics and Gynaecology
LABADARIOS, D., Human Nutrition
LIEBOWITZ, L. D., Medical Microbiology
LOOCK, J. W., Otorhinolaryngology
MANSVELT, E. P., Haematology
MEYER, D., Ophthalmology
MOORE, S. W., Surgery
ROSSOUW, G. J., Cardiothoracic Surgery
SCHER, A. T., Radiation Oncology
SCHNEIDER, J. W., Anatomical Pathology
SEEDAT, S., Psychiatry
THERON, G. B., Obstetrics and Gynaecology
VAN DER BIJL, P., Pharmacology
VAN DER MERWE, W. L., Medical Physiology and Biochemistry
VAN HEERDEN, B. B., Head of School of Medicine
VERNIMMEN, F. J. A. I., Radiation Oncology
VLOK, G. J., Orthopaedic Surgery
WARREN, B. L., Surgery
WELMANN, E. B., Nursing Science
WRIGHT, C. A., Anatomical Pathology

Faculty of Law (tel. (21) 808-4853; fax (21) 886-6235; e-mail jsaf@maties.sun.ac.za; internet www.sun.ac.za/law):

BUTLER, D. W., Mercantile Law
DE VOS, W., Private Law and Roman Law
DE WAAL, M. J., Private Law and Roman Law
DU PLESSIS, J. E., Private Law and Roman Law
DU PLESSIS, L. M., Public Law
ERASMUS, M. G., Public Law
HUGO, C. F., Mercantile Law
HUMAN, C. S., Private Law and Roman Law
LIEBENBERG, S., Public Law
LOUBSER, M. M., Private Law and Roman Law
LUBBE, G. F., Private Law and Roman Law
PIENAAR, J. M., Private Law and Roman Law
SUTHERLAND, P. J., Mercantile Law
VAN DER MERWE, S. E., Public Law
VAN DER WALT, A. J., Public Law

Faculty of Science (tel. (21) 808-3072; fax (21) 808-3608; e-mail asvanj@maties.sun.ac.za; internet www.sun.ac.za/science):

CHOWN, S. L., Plant and Animal Science
CROUCH, A. M., Chemistry
DE VILLIERS, J. M., Mathematics
DICKS, L. M. T., Microbiology
DILLEN, J. L. M., Chemistry
EGGERS, H. C., Chemistry
GEYER, H. B., Physics
GREEN, B. W., Mathematics
HAPGOOD, J. P., Biochemistry
HOFMEYR, J. H. S., Biochemistry
KOCH, K. R., Chemistry
KOSSMANN, J. M., Zoology
KRZESINSKI, A. E., Computer Science
LAURIE, D. P., Mathematics
MUCINA, L., Plant and Animal Science
MYBURGH, K. H., Physiological Sciences
PRIOR, B. A., Microbiology
PRODINGER, H., Mathematics
RAUBENHEIMER, H. G., Chemistry
RAWLINGS, D. E., Microbiology
REINECKE, A. J., Plant and Animal Science
RICHARDSON, D. M., Plant and Animal Science
ROBINSON, T. J., Plant and Animal Science
ROZENDAAL, A., Geology
SANDERSON, R. D., Polymer Science
SCHOLTZ, F. G., Physics
SMITH, V. R., Plant and Animal Science
SNOEP, J. L., Biochemistry
STEVENS, G., Geology
SWART, P., Biochemistry
VAN JAARSVELD, A. S., Plant and Animal Science
VAN WYK, L., Mathematics
VAN ZYL, W. H., Microbiology
VON BERGMANN, H. M., Physics

Faculty of Theology (tel. (21) 808-3255; fax (21) 808-3251; e-mail djl@maties.sun.ac.za; internet www.sun.ac.za/theology):

BOSMAN, H. L., Old and New Testament
HENDRIKS, H. J., Practical Theology and Missiology
MOUTON, A. E. J., Old and New Testament
SMIT, D. J., Systematic Theology

UNIVERSITY OF THE FREE STATE

POB 339, Bloemfontein 9300
Telephone: (51) 401-9111
Fax: (51) 401-2117
E-mail: info@stiq.ufs.ac.za
Internet: www.uovs.ac.za
Founded 1855, fmrly a constituent college of the Univ. of South Africa, became ind. as Univ. of the Orange Free State 1950, present name 2003, incorporated Bloemfontein Campus of Vista Univ. 2004
Languages of instruction: Afrikaans, English
Academic year: February to November

Chancellor: Dr FRANKLIN SONN
Vice-Chancellor and Rector: Prof. JONATHAN JANSEN
Vice-Rector for Academic Operations: Prof. TEUNS VERSCHOOR
Vice-Rector for Academic Planning: Prof. MAGDA FOURIE
Vice-Rector for Student Affairs: Dr RALETSATSI EZEKIEL MORAKA
Dean of Students: Dr NATIE LUYT
Registrar: Prof. IZAK STEYN
Dir of Library and Information Services: CLEMENCE NAMPONYA
Number of teachers: 476
Number of students: 20,000

DEANS

Faculty of Economic and Management Sciences: Prof. TIENIE CROUS
Faculty of Health Sciences: Prof. LETTICIA MOJA
Faculty of Humanities: Prof. GERHARDT DE KLERK
Faculty of Law: Prof. JOHAN HENNING
Faculty of Natural and Agricultural Sciences: Prof. HERMAN VAN SCHALKWYK
Faculty of Theology: Prof. HERMIE VAN ZYL

ATTACHED CAMPUS

University of the Free State, Qwaqwa Campus

PMB X13, Phuthaditjhaba 9866
Telephone: (58) 713-0211
Fax: (58) 713-0158
Founded 1982
Chancellor: Dr N. R. MANDELA
Vice-Chancellor and Prin.: Prof. N. NDEBELE
Vice-Prin.: Prof. Dr W. MÖDINGER
Registrars: A. T. KGABO, T. P. MASIHLEHO, N. T. MOSIA
Librarian: C. J. KOK
Library of 30,000 vols
Number of teachers: 85
Number of students: 2,500

DEANS

Faculty of Arts: Prof. L. J. FERREIRA
Faculty of Education: L. E. MOFOKENG
Faculty of Management Sciences: P. C. MOJET
Faculty of Mathematics and Natural Sciences: Prof. Dr P. C. KEULDER
Faculty of Theology: Dr S. P. BOTHA

PROFESSORS

Faculty of Arts:

FERREIRA, L. J., Political Science
JONES, H. J., Afrikaans
MOOLMAN, J. P. F., History

Faculty of Education:

MOLETSANE, R. I. M., Comparative Education

Faculty of Management Sciences:

CLOETE, N., Commercial Law
JONKER, L. J. G., Business Economics
VENTER, A. P., Industrial Psychology
WEBSTER, S. A., Accounting

Faculty of Mathematics and Natural Sciences:

DE HAAS, W., Physics
DEN HEYER, J., Zoology
JORDAAN, D. B., Computer Science
KEULDER, P. C., Botany
LUYT, A. S., Chemistry
MOFFETT, R. O., Botany
MTHEMBU, T. Z., Mathematics

UNIVERSITY OF THE WESTERN CAPE

Private Bag X17, Bellville 7535
Telephone: (21) 959-2911
Fax: (21) 959-3627
Internet: www.uwc.ac.za
Founded 1960
Languages of instruction: Afrikaans, English
Academic year: February to December

Chancellor: (vacant)
Vice-Chancellor and Rector: Prof. BRIAN O'CONNELL
Vice-Rector for Academic Affairs: Prof. RAMESH BHARUTHRAM (acting)
Deputy Vice-Chancellor and Vice-Rector for Student Affairs: Prof. L. TSHIWULA
Registrar: Dr INGRID MILLER
Librarian: P. P. NTSHUNTSHE-MATSHAYA
Library of 297,756 vols, 1,280 journals, 41,333 electronic journals
Number of teachers: 910
Number of students: 17,500
Publications: Journal of Community Health (staff research publication, 1 a year), KRONOS: Journal of Cape History, Law, Democracy and Development (4 a year)

DEANS

Faculty of Arts: Prof. DUNCAN BROWN (acting)
Faculty of Community and Health Sciences: Prof. RATIE MPOFU
Faculty of Dentistry: Prof. Y. OSMAN
Faculty of Economics and Management Sciences: Prof. CHRIS TAPSCOTT
Faculty of Education: Prof. ZUBEIDA DESAI
Faculty of Law: Prof. JULIA SLOTH-NIELSEN
Faculty of Natural Science: Prof. JAN VAN BEVERDONKER

UNIVERSITY OF THE WITWATERSRAND, JOHANNESBURG

PMB X3, Wits 2050
Telephone: (11) 717-1054
Fax: (11) 717-1059
E-mail: studysa.international@wits.ac.za
Internet: www.wits.ac.za
Founded 1922
State-subsidized, but functions under its own charter
Language of instruction: English
Academic year: February to November

Chancellor: Dep. Chief Justice DIKGANG MOSENEKE
Vice-Chancellor and Prin.: Prof. LOYISO NONGXA
Vice-Prin. and Deputy Vice-Chancellor for Academic Affairs: Prof. YUNUS BALLIM
Deputy Vice-Chancellor for Partnerships and Advancement: Prof. ROB MOORE
Deputy Vice-Chancellor for Research: Prof. BELINDA BOZZOLI
Registrar: Dr DEREK SWEMMER
Exec. Dir: Rev. LULAMILE MBETE (acting)
Univ. Librarian: FELIX OBOGU

Library: see Libraries and Archives
Number of teachers: 1,766
Number of students: 27,722
Publications: *African Studies* (2 a year), *English Studies in Africa* (2 a year), *Palaeontologia Africana* (1 a year), *Perspectives in Education* (4 a year), *Philosophical Papers* (3 a year), *The Industrial Law Journal* (6 a year), *The Research Report* (1 a year)

DEANS

Faculty of Commerce, Law and Management: Prof. KATHERINE MUNRO (acting)
Faculty of Engineering and the Built Environment: Prof. BEATRYS LACQUET
Faculty of Health Sciences: Prof. HELEN LABURN
Faculty of Humanities: Prof. TAWANA KUPE
Faculty of Science: Prof. ANDREW CROUCH

PROFESSORS

Faculty of Education:

ENSLIN, P. A.
PENDLEBURY, S. A.
SKUY, M. S.

Faculty of Engineering:

BRYSON, A. W., Chemical Engineering
ERIC, R. H., Metallurgy and Materials Engineering
FOURIE, A., Civil Engineering
GLASSER, D., Chemical Engineering
HANRAHAN, H. E., Electrical Engineering
HILDEBRANDT, D., Process and Materials Engineering
IWANKIEWICZ, R. M., Applied Mathematics
LANDY, C. F., Electrical Engineering
MacLEOD, I. M., Control Engineering
McCUTCHEON, R. T., Project and Construction Management
ONSONGO, W. M., Undergraduate Engineering Education
PHILLIPS, H. R., Mining Engineering
REYNDERS, J. P., Electrical Engineering
SHEER, T. J., Mechanical Engineering
SKEWS, B. W., Mechanical Engineering
STEPHENSON, D., Hydraulic Engineering

Faculty of Engineering and the Built Environment:

BREMNER, L., Architecture
MULLER, J. G., Town and Regional Planning
SCHLOSS, R. I., Construction Economics and Management

Faculty of Health Sciences:

ALLWOOD, C., Psychiatry
ALTINI, M., Oral Pathology
CARMICHAEL, T., Ophthalmology
CARR, L., Prosthetic Dentistry
CLEATON-JONES, P. E., Experimental Odontology
COOPER, P. A., Paediatrics
CREWE-BROWN, H., Medical Microbiology
CRONJE, S. L., Cardiothoracic Surgery
DAVIES, M. R. Q., Paediatric Surgery
ERKEN, E. H. W., Orthopaedic Surgery
EVANS, W. G., Orthodontics
FELDMAN, C., Medicine
FRITZ, V. U., Neurology
GEORGE, J. A., Orthopaedic Surgery
GRAY, I. P., Chemical Pathology
HAVLIK, I., Pharmacology
HOFMEYR, G. J., Obstetrics and Gynaecology
HUDDLE, K., Medicine
JOFFE, B. I., Medicine
KALK, W. J., Clinical Endocrinology
KEW, M. C., Medicine
KLUGMAN, K. P., Clinical Microbiology
KRAMER, B., Anatomical Sciences
LABURN, H. P., Physiology
LOWNIE, J. F., Maxillofacial and Oral Surgery
MACPHAIL, A. P., Medicine

MAINA, J. N., Anatomical Sciences
MANGA, P., Cardiology
MCINTOSH, W., Ear, Nose and Throat Surgery
MEYERS, A. M., Nephrology
MILNE, F. J., Medicine
MITCHELL, D., Physiology
MITCHELL, G., Physiology
OWEN, P., Prosthetic Dentistry
PANTANOWITZ, D., Surgery
PATERSON, A. C., Anatomical Pathology
PETIT, J.-C., Oral Medicine and Periodontology
PETTIFOR, J. M., Paediatrics
PICK, W., Community Health
RAMSAY, M., Human Genetics
REES, D., Occupational Health
RUDOLPH, M. J., Community Medicine
SARELI, P., Cardiology
SCHOUB, B. D., Virology
SHIPTON, E. A., Anaesthesia
SPARKS, B. L. W., Family Health
SUR, R., Radiation Oncology
VAN GELDEREN, C. J., Obstetrics and Gynaecology
VILJOEN, D., Human Genetics
WADEE, A. A., Immunology

Faculty of Humanities and Faculty of Science:

ADLER, J., Mathematics Education Development
ALEXANDER, J. J., Microbiology
ANHAEUSSER, C. R., Geology
ASHER, A., Statistics and Actuarial Science
BEICHELT, F., Statistics and Actuarial Science
BONNER, P. L., History
BOZZOLI, B., Sociology
BRADLEY, J. D., Chemistry
BUNN, D., History of Art
CAWTHORN, R. G., Geology
COCK, J., Sociology
COMINS, J. D., Physics
COPLAN, D. B., Social Anthropology
COVILLE, N. J., Organo-Metallic Chemistry
CRUMP, A., Fine Arts
DABBS, E., Genetics
DELIUS, P. S., History
DIRR, H. W., Biochemistry
DRIVER, K., Mathematics
DU PLESSIS, P., Physics
EVERY, A. G., Physics
FABIAN, B. C., Zoology
FATTI, L. P., Statistics
FISHER, J., Psychology
GLASSER, L., Physical Chemistry
HEISS, W. D., Theoretical Physics
HOCH, M. J. R., Solid State Physics
HOFMEYR, I., African Literature
HUFFMAN, T. N., Archaeology
HUNT, J. H. V., Mathematics
LODGE, T., Political Studies
LOWTHER, J. E., Physics
LUBINSKY, D. S., Mathematics
MAAKE, N. P., African Languages
McCARTHY, T. S., Geology
McKENDRICK, B. W., Social Work
McLACHLAN, D. S., Electronic Properties of Solids
MARQUES, H., Chemistry
MASON, D. P., Applied Mathematics
MICHAEL, J. P., Organic Chemistry
MOYS, M., School of Process and Materials Engineering
MURRAY, B. K., Edwardian British History
OLIVIER, G., Afrikaans and Dutch
OWEN-SMITH, N., Zoology
PENDLEBURY, H., Philosophy
PENN, C., Speech Pathology and Audiology
PIENAAR, R. N., Botany
PRODINGER, H., Mathematics
ROBB, L. J., Geology
RODRIGUES, J. A. P., Physics
ROGERS, K. H., Botany
ROGERSON, C. M., Geography

ROLLNICK, M., College of Science
RUBIDGE, B. S., Palaeontology
SCURRELL, M. S., Chemistry
STADLER, A. W., Political Studies
STREMLAU, J. J., International Relations
TAYLOR, J., Dramatic Art
TYSON, P. D., Climatology
VILJOEN, M. J., Mining Geology
VON HOLY, A., Microbiology
WEBSTER, E. C., Sociology
WRIGHT, C., Geophysics
WRIGHT, C. J., Computational and Applied Mathematics

UNIVERSITY OF VENDA FOR SCIENCE AND TECHNOLOGY

PMB X5050, Thohoyandou 0950, Limpopo
Telephone: (15) 962-8000
Fax: (15) 962-4749
E-mail: prd@univen.ac.za
Internet: www.univen.ac.za
Founded 1982 as Univ. of Venda by Venda Parliament; nat. status as Univ. of Venda 1996; non-statutory name Univ. of Venda for Science and Technology
State control

Schools: agriculture, environmental sciences and engineering; health sciences; human and social sciences; management sciences and law; mathematics and natural sciences; postgraduate and integrated studies; rural development and forestry

Prin. and Vice-Chancellor: Prof. G. M. NKONDO
Library of 90,871 vols, 823 periodicals
Number of teachers: 301
Number of students: 9,500

Publication: *Journal of Educational Studies* (2 a year)

EXECUTIVE DEANS

Faculty of Health, Agriculture and Rural Development: Prof. N. S. MAHOKO
Faculty of Human and Social Sciences, Management Sciences and Law: Prof. M. D. R. RALEBIPI-SIMELA
Faculty of Natural and Applied Sciences: Prof. P. H. OMARA-OJUNGU

PROFESSORS

Faculty of Human and Social Sciences, Management Sciences and Law:

AKINNUSI, D. M.
AYURU, R. N.
BAYONA, E. L. M.
GYEKE, A. B.
LUKHAIMANE, E. K.
MIREKU, O.
SIMUKONDA, H. P. M.
SPENCER, J. P.
STEYN, J. N.

Faculty of Natural and Applied Sciences:

AGBONJINMI, A. P.
AMUSA, L. O.
DU TOIT, P. J.
KHOZA, L. B.
KIRUNDA, E. F.
MAKINDE, M. O.
MBHENYANE, X. G.
OGOLA, J. S.
OLE-MEILUDI, R. E.
OLORUNDA, A. O.
OMARA-OJUNGU, P. H.
ONI, S. A.
SHAI-MAHOKO, N. S.
SIMALENGA, T. E.
VAN DER WAAL, B. C. W.
VAN REE, T.

UNIVERSITY OF ZULULAND

PMB X1001, KwaDlangezwa, KwaZulu-Natal 3886

Telephone: (35) 902-6000
Fax: (35) 793-3735
Internet: www.uzulu.ac.za

Founded 1960; Umlazi Campus incorporated into Durban Institute of Technology 2004
State control
Language of instruction: English
Academic year: February to December

Chancellor: Dr JACOB ZUMA
Vice-Chancellor and Rector: Prof. RACHEL GUMBI
Vice-Rector for Academic Affairs and Research: Prof. L. M. MAGI
Chief Financial Officer: M. GOUINDSAMY
Dean of Students: M. M. HLONGWANE
Registrar: G. S. MAPHISA
Librarian: L. VAHED

Number of teachers: 293
Number of students: 7,978

Publications: *Journal of Psychology, Paidonomia, Unizul*

DEANS

Faculty of Arts: Prof. L. Z. M. KHUMALO
Faculty of Commerce and Administration: Prof. T. R. SABELA
Faculty of Education: Prof. R. V. GABELA
Faculty of Law: Prof. R. SONI
Faculty of Science and Agriculture: Prof. M. F. COETSEE
Faculty of Theology and Religious Studies: Prof. J. A. LOUBSER

PROFESSORS

Faculty of Arts (tel. (35) 902-6087; e-mail bbishop@pan.uzulu.ac.za):

BUIJS, G. C. U., Anthropology
DALRYMPLE, L. I., Drama
DE VILLIERS, J., History
EDWARDS, S. D., Psychology
GLASS, H. G. L., Sociology
GUMBI, T. A. P., Social Work
HOOPER, M. J., English
KHUMALO, L. Z. M., African Languages
KLOPPER, R. M., Afrikaans
MAKHANYA, E. M., Geography
MEIHUIZEN, N. C. T., English
MERSHAM, G. M., Communication Science
NZIMAKWE, D. P., Nursing Science
OCHOLLA, D. N., Library and Information Science
POTGIETER, P. J., Criminal Justice
WAIT, E. C., Philosophy
ZUNGU, B. M., Nursing Science

Faculty of Commerce and Administration (tel. (35) 902-6173; fax (35) 793-3583; e-mail sbooysen@pan.uzulu.ac.za):

CLOETE, J., Business Management
LIVINGSTONE, M., Accountancy and Auditing
NAIDOO, I. U., Accountancy and Auditing
SABELA, T. R., Public Administration and Political Science
SHRESTHA, B. C., Economics

Faculty of Education (tel. (35) 902-6258; fax (35) 793-3149; e-mail rvgabela@pan.uzulu.ac.za):

COETSEE, M. F., Human Movement Science
DLAMINI, E. T., History of Education and Comparative Education
GABELA, R. V., Educational Planning and Administration
JACOBS, M., Didactics
SIBAYA, P. T., Educational Psychology
URBANI, G., Educational Psychology

Faculty of Law (tel. (35) 902-6212; fax (35) 793-3529; e-mail sjclarke@pan.uzulu.ac.za):

SONI, R., Constitutional Law

Faculty of Science and Agriculture (tel. (35) 902-6649; fax (35) 793-3162; e-mail lorraine@pan.uzulu.ac.za):

BEESHAM, A., Mathematical Sciences
BERMANSEDER, N., Engineering
COETSEE, M. F., Human Movement Science
CYRUS, D. P., Zoology
DAVIDSON, A. T., Physics
DJAVOVA, T., Biochemistry
FERREIRA, D. P., Botany
JURY, M. R., Geography
KELBE, B. E. M.-L., Hydrology
KOLAWOLE, G. A., Chemistry
NDWANDWE, M. O., Physics

Faculty of Theology and Religious Studies (tel. (35) 902-6716; fax (35) 793-3159; e-mail asong@uzulu.ac.za; internet www.uzulu.ac.za/the/the.html):

LOUBSER, J. A., Bibliological Studies
SONG, A., Missiology, Religious Studies and Practical Theology

VAAL UNIVERSITY OF TECHNOLOGY

PMB X021, Vanderbijlpark, 1900 Gauteng
Telephone: (16) 950-9000
Fax: (16) 950-9787
E-mail: international@vut.ac.za
Internet: www.vut.ac.za

Founded 1966, present name 1979

Vice-Chancellor and Rector: Prof. A. T. MOKADI
Vice-Rector for Academic Affairs: Prof. ROY DU PRÉ
Vice-Rector for Admin.: Dr PRAKASH NAIDOO
Librarian: A. J. GOZO

Library of 42,000 vols, 4,480 periodicals
Number of teachers: 311 full-time, 551 part-time
Number of students: 12,434

Publications: *Sediba sa Thuto* (academic journal, 1 a year), *Tempo* (communications journal, 2 a year)

Faculties of applied and computer sciences, engineering and technology, humanities and management sciences.

WALTER SISULU UNIVERSITY FOR TECHNOLOGY AND SCIENCE, EASTERN CAPE

Founded 2005 by merger of Eastern Cape Technikon, Border Technikon and Univ. of Transkei.

CONSTITUENT INSTITUTION

University of Transkei

PMB X1, Unitra
Telephone: (47) 502-2111
Fax: (47) 532-6820
E-mail: postmaster@getafix.utr.ac.za
Internet: www.utr.ac.za

Founded 1976 as br. of Fort Hare Univ., ind. 1977
State control
Language of instruction: English
Academic year: January to December

Chancellor: (vacant)
Administrator: Prof. N. I. MORGAN
Vice-Prin.: Prof. J. M. NORUWANA
Registrar: Prof. P. N. LUSWAZI
Chief Librarian: P. E. OFORI

Number of teachers: 357
Number of students: 4,551

Publications: *Journal of Humanities* (2 a year), *Perspectives in Education* (1 a year)

DEANS

Faculty of Arts: Prof. N. MIJERE
Faculty of Economic Sciences: Prof. M. MAHABIR
Faculty of Education: Prof. S. V. S. NGUBENTOMBI
Faculty of Law: Prof. V. DLOVA
Faculty of Medicine and Health Sciences: Prof. E. L. MAZWAI
Faculty of Natural Sciences: Prof. B. S. NAKANI

PROFESSORS

Faculty of Arts:

ALABI, G. A., Information Science
COETSER, A., Afrikaans
MIJERE, N., Sociology

Faculty of Economic Sciences:

MAHABIR, M., Business Management

Faculty of Education:

LWANGA-LUKWAGO, J., Social Studies Education
NGUBENTOMBI, S. V. S., Educational Foundations

Faculty of Law:

DLOVA, V., Mercantile Law

Faculty of Medicine and Health Sciences:

ERASMUS, R. T., Chemical Pathology
IPUTO, J. E., Physiology
MAZWAI, E. L., Surgery
MEISSNER, O., Pharmacology
MFENYANA, K., Family and Community Medicine
NGANWA-BAGUMAH, A. B., Anatomy
STEPHEN, A., Pathology

Faculty of Natural Sciences:

EMMERSON, W., Zoology
FANIRAN, J. A., Science Foundation Year Programme
JACOBS, T. V., Botany
MISHRA, S. N., Mathematics

SOUTH SUDAN

The Higher Education System

South Sudan gained its independence in July 2011, after a six-year post-war political transition that had entailed semi-autonomy from Sudan's government. Both the transition and independence have had huge implications for South Sudan's higher education sector. On the positive side, the end of the 22-year north-south civil war in 2005 and the achievement of semi-autonomous status catalyzed significant donor support, much of it centred on state building, including the establishment of a Ministry of Higher Education, Science and Technology. However, independence has also brought substantial negative implications, most notably the end of any prospect of financial support for higher education institutions by Sudan's government.

The two prolonged periods of civil war in pre-secession Sudan (in 1953–72 and 1983–2005), during which a significant number of higher education institutions in the south and west were badly damaged or destroyed, prompted a number of southern universities to relocate to the north. In late 2010 such institutions were returned to the south during a five-day repatriation exercise orchestrated by Sudan's Ministry of Higher Education and Scientific Research.

Less than a year after independence, South Sudan found itself in a financial crisis arising from a dispute over a post-secession sharing of oil revenues with Sudan. South Sudan's public universities too were in a state of crisis. The University of Northern Bahr el Ghazal, in Aweil, was unable to open its doors to students. The Government acknowledged in March 2012 that it simply didn't have enough money to support the two-year-old institution, despite its public status. Also in March 2012, staff at the University of Bahr el Ghazal, which is located in Wau and opened in the early 1990s, announced that they were going on strike, claiming that the Government was three months behind in paying wages.

The University of Juba, the country's principal institution of higher learning, has also been hampered by financial problems. Underlining the extent of internal ethnic tensions in the new country, the Juba campus was also affected by inter-group tensions in the year after independence. In late March 2012, the university was temporarily closed down, after pitched battles between students from the dominant Dinka community and various other ethnic groups. Earlier that month, Juba had become the second public institution of higher learning in South Sudan to ban tribal associations, following the lead of the Doctor John Garang de Mabior Memorial University of Science and Technology. The latter institution is based in Bor, the capital of Jonglei State, where hundreds of people were killed in clashes between the Lou Nuer and Murle communities in late 2011 and early 2012.

Given the financial constraints faced by the public sector and the relative freedom generated by the end of Sudan's harsh Islamist rule, private universities have begun to spring up in South Sudan, competing with their public counterparts for students and non-government funding. However, in March 2012, Minister of Higher Education, Science and Technology Dr Peter Adwok Nyaba gave notice of his department's intention to reform universities, in a drive that would target both public and private institutions. He claimed that some new private centres of learning were masquerading as universities and lacked accreditation by the Government. Further, he stated that the Ministry would seek the closure of offending institutions and the prosecution of proprietors. According to a policy framework document published by the Ministry soon after independence, there were, at that stage, over 35 private institutions. While accreditation laws for the private sector had yet to be confirmed, an inspection process was underway in early 2012. Meanwhile, with regard to public sector reform, the Ministry was overseeing a commission to rationalize the universities of Juba, Upper Nile, Bahr el Ghazal, Rumbek and the Dr. John Garang de Mabior Memorial University of Science and Technology. The closure and merger of departments were some of the ideas being considered, in a context of the ongoing funding crisis.

In order to qualify for an undergraduate position in public sector universities in South Sudan, a four-year secondary school education is required. One of the main private institutions—The Bridge University, in Juba—requires at least seven passes in the country's Secondary School Certificate for relevant subjects, while for diplomas at least five passes are required, together with 'proficiency in written and spoken English'.

Only a miniscule proportion of South Sudan's population receives a university education, owing largely to the effect of more than two decades of north-south civil war on its territories' infrastructure and school system. During the 1983–2005 civil war (and the preceding conflict that lasted from 1956 to 1972), hundreds of thousands of people missed out on primary and secondary school education. As independence dawned, the legacy of the conflict—together with a tendency among some cattle herding communities to eschew formal education—was an adult literacy rate of just 27%, according to the United Nations Development Programme. The literacy rate for women was just 16%, while 42% of civil servants lacked a secondary school education, according to the same source. For the 2011/12 academic year, the four main public universities—Juba, Bahr el Ghazal, Upper Nile and Rumbek—approved a total intake of 2,722 students, out of just over 4,500 applications, according to the Ministry of Higher Education, Science and Technology. By contrast, there were over 215,000 applicants to Sudan's universities for the same period.

In the final intake (2011/12) before South Sudan achieved independence from Sudan (July 2011), the number of approved applicants for the main public universities were as follows; University of Juba, 1,310; University of Bahr el Ghazal, 599; Upper Nile, 441; Rumbek, 372.

The John Garang De Mabior Memorial University of Science and Technology and the University of Northern Bahr el Ghazal were missing from the list. With regard to the former, Vice-Chancellor Prof. Aggrey Ayuen Majok told the press that his institution was ready to host 160 students (40 in each of its four faculties), but South Sudan's Ministry of Higher Education, Science and Technology had not notified the admissions board in Khartoum. Meanwhile, the University of Northern Bahr el Ghazal had yet to receive any funding, from either Khartoum or Juba, despite having been bestowed university status by Sudan's President Omar-al Bashir in 2010. South Sudan's President Salva Kiir officially cut the ribbon to open this institution in March 2012. Even at that late stage, Kiir underlined that the university was still 'not budgeted for' in the national accounts, although he pledged that his government would attempt to secure a funding avenue.

In 2011 it was reported that South Sudan had requested assistance in developing its higher education system from the Kenyan Government. The South Sudanese Government's development plans included proposals to establish new private universities as well as to attract foreign professors and other academic staff in order to address a local shortfall within the fledgling nation.

Regulatory Bodies

GOVERNMENT

Ministry of Culture, Youth and Sports: Juba; internet www.goss-online.org/magnoliapublic/en/ministries/culture--youth-and-sport.html; Minister Hon. Dr CIRINO HITENG OFUHO.

Ministry of Higher Education, Science and Technology: Juba; tel. (955) 107417; e-mail sistootim@yahoo.com; internet www.goss-online.org/magnoliapublic/en/ministries/high-education--research--science-and--technology.html; Minister Hon. Dr PETER ADWOK NYABA.

Library

Juba

University of Juba Library: POB 82, Juba; tel. (155) 888489; f. 1977; 38,700 vols, 664 periodicals; depository library for UN, UNESCO, WHO, FAO and World Bank; Librarian OKENY A. ADALA (acting).

Universities

DOCTOR JOHN GARANG DE MABIOR MEMORIAL UNIVERSITY OF SCIENCE AND TECHNOLOGY

POB, Bor, Jonglei State
Telephone: (955) 363752
E-mail: info@jgmust-edu.org
Internet: jgmust-edu.org
Founded 2007 as an institute, univ. status 2010
State control
Faculties: Faculty of Agriculture; Faculty of Economics and Management Sciences; Faculty of Education; Faculty of Environmental Studies; Faculty of Humanities; Faculty of Law; Faculty of Science and Technology
Vice-Chancellor: Prof. AGGREY AYUEN MAJOK
Deputy Vice-Chancellor: Dr MELHA ROUT BIEL.

RUMBEK UNIVERSITY

c/o Rumbek Secondary School, Rumbek, Rumbek Central County, Lakes State
Founded 2010
State control
Faculties: Faculty of Education; Faculty of Economic and Social Sciences
Vice-Chancellor: Prof. MICHAEL MAKER MANGONY (acting)
Number of teachers: 40
Number of students: 500

SAINT MARY'S UNIVERSITY IN JUBA

Juba, Central Equatoria State
Founded 2009

Private control
Faculties of arts, education, science and computer studies, social studies
Vice-Chancellor: PAULINO LUKUDU LORO.

THE BRIDGE UNIVERSITY

POB 434, Juba
Telephone: (955) 235665
E-mail: magijude@yahoo.com
Internet: www.thebridgeuniversity.com
Founded 2009
Private control
Language of instruction: English
Faculties: Faculty of Business Administration and Management; Faculty of Education; Faculty of Humanities and Social Sciences; Faculty of Science
Vice-Chancellor: Dr ANDREW ANTHONY CULA
University Secretary: JUDE MAGINOT
Academic Registrar: MOSES OKWII
Bursar: PHILEMON BWANGA
Administrator: IVAN FRED TABAN
Dean of Students: PADDY TUMUHIMBISE
Number of teachers: 65
Number of students: 3,000

UNIVERSITY OF BAHR EL-GHAZAL

Wau, Wau County, Western Bahr Al-Ghazal State
E-mail: ubgzal@sudanmail.net
Founded 1991
State Control
Languages of instruction: Arabic, English
Faculties of economics, education, medicine and health sciences, veterinary sciences; institute of public health
Vice-Chancellor: TIMOTHY TELAR
Number of students: 1,000

UNIVERSITY OF JUBA

POB 82, Juba
Telephone: (155) 888405
E-mail: info@juba.edu.sd
Internet: www.juba.edu.sd
Founded 1975 with financial help from the EEC; first student admission 1977
State control
Language of instruction: English
Academic year: March to December (two semesters)
Vice-Chancellor: Prof. AGGREY ABATE
Principal: WANI SULE
Sec.-Gen.: Prof. MOSES MACAR KACUOL
Librarian: ALFRED D. LADO (acting)
Number of teachers: 220
Number of students: 16,565
Publications: *Juvarsity* (12 a year), *Library News* (12 a year)

DEANS

College of Applied and Industrial Sciences: Prof. TARIG OSMAN KHIDIR

College of Arts and Humanities: Prof. ABDEL-RAHIM MOHAMMED KHABIR
College of Arts, Music and Drama: Prof. MOHAMMED EL-AMIN ALI
College of Community Studies and Rural Development: SHADIA MOHAMED IDRIS
College of Computer Science and Information Technology: Dr MOHAMMED HASSAN MUDAWI
College of Education: Dr AMIRA MOHAMMED FADALALLA
College of Engineering and Architecture: Dr IBRAHIM AHMED MOHAMMED KHALID
College of Law: DENG AWUR WANYIN
College of Medicine: Dr ABDELAYE KUNNA MAJOUB
College of Natural Resources and Environmental Studies: (vacant)
College of Social and Economic Studies: SAMSON SAMUEL WASSARA

UNIVERSITY OF NORTHERN BAHR EL-GHAZAL

Mathiang, Aweil
Telephone: (123) 106510
E-mail: info@unbeg.edu.sd
Internet: www.unbeg.edu.sd
Founded 2010
State control
Language of instruction: English
Academic year: December to August
Chancellor: PRES. OF THE REPUBLIC OF SOUTH SUDAN
Vice-Chancellor: Prof. JOHN APURUOT AKEC
Prin.: Prof. KARLO AYUEL KUCGOR
Academic Sec.: Dr SALIM GIBRIL AHMED (acting)

DEANS

Faculty of Architecture and Physical Planning: Prof. ADIL MUSTAFA AHMAD (acting)
Faculty of Health Sciences and Medical Technology: Dr ROSE AJACK KOSTA (acting)
Faculty of Petroleum, Engineering and Earth Sciences: Dr ABDALLA KODI (acting)
Faculty of Preparatory, Human Resource Development and Vocational Studies: BEDA DIING AMOI (acting)

UPPER NILE UNIVERSITY

Malakal, Upper Nile State
Telephone: (183) 220825
Founded 1991
State control
Language of instruction: Arabic
Academic year: November to June
Faculties: Faculty of Agriculture; Faculty of Animal Production; Faculty of Arts and Humanities; Faculty of Computer Science; Faculty of Education; Faculty of Forestry; Faculty of Medicine and Public Health; Faculty of Nursing; Faculty of Science; Faculty of Social Science; Faculty of Veterinary Medicine; Faculty of Vocational Medicine
Vice-Chancellor: Prof. BOL DENG CHOL
Library of 23,000 vols.

SPAIN

The Higher Education System

Institutions of higher education pre-date the consolidation of the Kingdom of Spain within the Iberian peninsula in the early 16th century, with the oldest being Universidad Pontificia de Salamanca, which was founded in 1134. Spain participates in the Bologna Process to establish a European Higher Education Area, the first phase of which is to adopt a credit-based system of comparable degrees with two main cycles (undergraduate and graduate). Little progress was made until 2005, when a royal decree was passed establishing the new degree structure. Higher education is provided by public and private universities, higher technical colleges (escuelas técnicas superiores), university colleges (colegios universitarios), university faculties (facultades universitarias) and university schools (escuelas universitarias). An estimated 1,404,115 students were attending university in 200/10. In 2005/06 there were 72 universities, including the open university (UNED—founded 1972).

The Ministry of Education has overall responsibility for higher education, although much of the administration has been devolved to the 17 Autonomous Communities. Universities were granted the right to become autonomous under the law on University Reform (1983), although very few have chosen to do so. The 1983 legislation was supplemented by further reforms enacted under the terms of the Spanish Universities Act (2001), covering university governance, entrance examinations, quality assurance, accreditation and staff recruitment. At 2011 a national qualifications framework was under development.

The main requirements for admission to higher education are the Bachillerato (secondary school certificate) and the Prueba de Acceso Universidad (university entrance examination). Under the new system, university degrees are divided into three cycles. The first cycle, Título de Grado (Bachelors degree), lasts four years, following which students may progress to the second cycle, the Título de Máster (Masters degree), which lasts between one and two years. The third cycle, the Doctorado (Doctorate), constitutes the highest level of university degree and requires an additional three or four years of classwork and research, culminating with the submission and defence of a thesis. Pre-Bologna qualifications (which included the Diplomado, Diplomatura, Licenciado, Licenciatura and professional titles) are in the process of being phased out, with new students no longer being admitted onto such courses and the final existing students enrolled on such programmes due to graduate in 2014.

The main qualification offered in vocational and technical education is the Técnico Superior (higher certificate), awarded after one-and-a-half to two years of study. Occupational training is also available; students are awarded the Certificados de Profesionalidad (vocational certificate).

The Agencia Nacional de Evaluación de la Calidad y Acreditación (National Agency for Quality Assessment and Accreditation), which was founded in 2002 following the Spanish Universities Act, is responsible for accrediting programmes of study, providing quality assurance and acting as the inter-agency coordinating body for Spanish higher education.

Regulatory and Representative Bodies

GOVERNMENT

Ministry of Culture: Plaza del Rey 1, 28004 Madrid; tel. (91) 7017000; fax (91) 7017352; e-mail contacte@mcu.es; internet www.mcu.es; Minister ÁNGELES GONZÁLEZ-SINDE REIG.

Ministry of Education: Alcalá 36, 28071 Madrid; tel. (91) 7018098; fax (91) 7018648; e-mail prensa@educacion.es; internet www.educacion.es; Minister ÁNGEL GABILONDO PUJOL.

Ministry of Science and Innovation: Albacete 5, 28027 Madrid; tel. (91) 4959554; e-mail informa@micinn.es; internet www.micinn.es; Minister CRISTINA GARMENDIA MENDIZÁBA.

ACCREDITATION

Agencia Nacional de Evaluación de la Calidad y Acreditación (National Agency for Quality Assessment and Accreditation): Calle Orense 11, 7°, 28020 Madrid; tel. (91) 4178230; e-mail informacion@aneca.es; internet www.aneca.es; f. 2002; contributes to the quality improvement of the higher education system through the assessment, certification and accreditation of univ. degrees, programmes, teaching staff and instns; Dir ZULIMA FERNÁNDEZ.

ENIC/NARIC Spain: Centro NARIC España Ministerio de Educación, Cultura y Deporte Subdirección General de Títulos y Reconocimiento de Cualificaciones, Paseo del Prado, 28 28014 Madrid; tel. (91) 5065593; fax (91) 5065706; e-mail naric@mecd.es; internet www.educacion.gob.es/naric; offers information about the processes of academic recognition and professional recognition of qualifications in Spain and in other countries; provides information about the existing recognition processes; Technical Adviser ISABEL BARRIOS; Technical Adviser JUAN CARLOS PARODI.

FUNDING

Fundación Juan March: Castelló 77, 28006 Madrid; tel. (91) 4354240; fax (91) 5763420; e-mail info@march.es; internet www.march.es; f. 1955; awards scholarships and research grants to Spanish profs and scholars in molecular biology and other fields; organizes cultural, artistic and musical activities; library dealing with modern Spanish theatre and contemporary Spanish music; Pres. JUAN MARCH DELGADO; Dir JAVIER GOMÁ LANZÓN; publ. *Revista de la Fundación Juan March* (9 a year).

NATIONAL BODIES

Asociación Iberoamericana de Educación Superior a Distancia (Ibero-American Association for Open and Distance Higher Education): Calle Bravo Murillo 38, 7°, 28015 Madrid; tel. (91) 3986549; fax (91) 3986587; e-mail aiesad@adm.uned.es; internet www.aiesad.org; f. 1981; network for the devt of distance education in Spanish-speaking Latin America; biannual int. seminars, joint projects and electronic newsletter; 43 mems; library of 50 vols; bibliography of distance- and open-education in Spanish-speaking Latin America; Pres. Dr JUAN A. GIMENO ULLASTRES; Permanent Sec. Dra MARÍA TERESA AGUADO ODINA; publ. *Revista Iberoamericana de Educación a Distancia* *(RIED)* (scientific review, available electronically).

Conferencia de Rectores de las Universidades Españolas (CRUE) (Spanish Universities' Rectors' Conference): Plaza de las Cortes 2, 7°, 28014 Madrid; tel. (91) 3601200; fax (91) 3601201; e-mail info@crue.org; internet www.crue.org; f. 1994; fosters links between the univs, studies and analyses univ. problems, acts as link between the Univ. Council and the state univs; 74 mems; Pres. FEDERICO GUTIÉRREZ-SOLANA SALCEDO; Gen. Sec. MARÍA TERESA LOZANO MELLADO.

Conferencia General de Política Universitaria (National Conference of University Policy): c/o Alcalá 36, 28071 Madrid; f. 2007, together with Consejo de Universidades (*q.v.*), to replace Consejo de Coordinación Universitaria (f. 1983); coordinating, cooperative and consultative body for matters concerning higher education policy; chaired by the Min. of Education.

Consejo de Universidades (University Council): c/o Alcalá 36, 28071 Madrid; f. 2007, together with Conferencia General de Política Universitaria (*q.v.*), to replace Consejo de Coordinación Universitaria (f. 1983); advises and promotes coordination in the univ. system; chaired by the Min. of Education; mems incl. (among others) the Rectors of the state univs.

Consejo General de Colegios Oficiales de Doctores y Licenciados en Filosofía y Letras y en Ciencias (National Council of Official Colleges of Doctors and Licentiates in Arts and Science): Bolsa 11, 28012 Madrid; tel. and fax (91) 5224597; e-mail secretaria@consejogeneralcdl.es; internet www.consejogeneralcdl.es; f. 1945; protects and represents education professionals, and seeks to promote initiatives that contribute to improving the quality of education in Spain; 60,000 mems; Pres. JOSEFINA CAMBRA GINÉ; Gen. Sec. JESÚS BONALS CODINA; publ. *Trivium* (4 a year).

Learned Societies

GENERAL

Agencia Española de Cooperación Internacional para el Desarrollo (AECID) (Spanish Agency for International Development Cooperation): Avda Reyes Católicos 4, Ciudad Universitaria, 28040 Madrid; tel. (91) 5838100; fax (91) 5838310; internet www .aecid.es; f. 1946; contributes to peace, freedom, human security and the eradication of poverty; promotes respect for human rights and devt of democratic systems; promotes the role of culture and knowledge in development; Pres. MARÍA SORAYA RODRÍGUEZ RAMOS; Dir ELENA MADRAZO HEGEWISCH; publ. *Cooperación Española* (4 a year).

Attached Institutes:

Instituto de Cooperación con el Mundo Arabe, Mediterráneo y Países en Desarrollo (Institute for Cooperation with the Arab World, the Mediterranean and Developing Countries): Avda Reyes Católicos 4, Ciudad Universitaria, 28040 Madrid; tel. (91) 5838565; fax (91) 5838219; technical assistance, economic cooperation, cultural activities, research grants, scholarships; library of 65,000 vols, 800 periodicals; Dir SENÉN FLORENSA PALAU; publs *Arabismo* (4 a year), *Awraq* (1 a year).

Instituto de Cooperación Iberoamericana (Institute for Ibero-American Cooperation): Avda Reyes Católicos 4, Ciudad Universitaria, 28040 Madrid; tel. (91) 5838100; fax (91) 5838310; f. 1946; promotes cultural understanding between Spain and the USA by organizing conferences, congresses, cultural exhibitions and university exchanges, scholarships for students; finances programmes of cultural, scientific, economic and technical cooperation; information department; Centre for Advanced Hispanic Studies; organizes programmes to diffuse the Spanish language and culture in the USA; radio, cinema and theatre unit; large library open to students; Spanish Library: see Libraries; Pres. FERNANDO VILLALONGA; Dir-Gen. JESÚS MANUEL GRACIA ALDAZ; publs *Cuadernos Hispanoamericanos* (12 a year), *Pensamiento Iberoamericano* (2 a year).

Casa de Velázquez: Calle Paul Guinard 3, Ciudad Universitaria, 28040 Madrid; tel. (91) 4551580; fax (91) 5446879; e-mail info@ casadevelazquez.org; internet www .casadevelazquez.org; f. 1928; French school for research into all aspects of Iberia; grants sr fellowships to French artists or scholars to work in Spain; 34 mems; library of 100,000 vols, 1,700 current periodicals; Dir JEAN-PIERRE ÉTIENVRE; Sec.-Gen. DOMINIQUE DUMAS; publ. *Mélanges de la Casa de Velázquez* (4 a year).

Dirección General de Relaciones Culturales y Científicas (Cultural and Scientific Relations Department): Agencia Española de Cooperación Internacional, Avda Reyes Católicos 4, 28040 Madrid; tel. (91) 5838100; internet www.maec.es; f. 1926; promotes Spanish culture and science in foreign countries; int. cultural and scientific agreements, exchange of professors and lec-

turers, scholarships, etc.; Dir-Gen. ANTONIO NICOLUA MARTÍ.

Fundación Instituto de Estudios Norteamericanos (Institute of North American Studies): Vía Augusta 123, 08006 Barcelona; tel. (93) 2405110; fax (93) 2020690; e-mail ien@ien.es; internet www.ien.es; f. 1951; cultural exchange programmes, lectures, discussions, musical events, theatre, cinema, art exhibitions, seminars, etc.; courses in English and in American Studies; runs an academic counselling service and is the official centre for examinations for students entering US universities; 400 mems; 18,000 students; library of 10,000 vols, 100 periodicals; Pres. ROBERT M. MANSON; Exec. Dir CARLES DOMINGO.

Institut d'Estudis Catalans (Institute of Catalan Studies): Carrer del Carme 47, 08001 Barcelona; tel. (93) 2701620; fax (93) 2701180; e-mail informacio@iec.cat; internet www.iec.cat; f. 1907; incorporates sections on history and archaeology, science and technology, philology, philosophy and social sciences, biology; 183 mems (125 ordinary, 58 corresp.), 28 affiliated scientific socs; Pres. SALVADOR GINER DE SAN JULIÁN; Sec.-Gen. ROMÀ ESCALAS I LLIMONA; publs *Acta Numismàtica, Anuari de la Societat Catalana d'Economia, Anuari de la Societat Catalana de Filosofia, Anuari de la Societat Catalana d'Estudis Jurídics, Arxiu de Textos Catalans Antics, Butlletí de la Institució Catalana d'Història Natural, Butlletí de la Societat Catalana d'Estudis Històrics, Butlletí de la Societat Catalana de Matemàtiques, Butlletí de la Societat Catalana de Musicologia, Butlletí de la Societat Catalana de Pedagogia, Cinematògraf, Dossiers Agraris, Educació i Història: Revista d'Història de l'Educació, Estudis Romànics, Gazeta, Lambard, Llengua i Literatura, Memòria, Miscellània Litúrgica Catalana, Notícies de la Societat Catalana de Matemàtiques, Quaderns Agraris, Periodística, Recursos de Física, Revista Catalan de Dret Privat, Revista Catalan de Física, Revista Catalana de Micologia, Revista Catalan de Musicologia, Revista Catalan de Pedagogia, Revista Catalan de Sociologia, Revista de Dret Històrica Català, Revista de la Societat Catalana de Química, Sessió Conjunta d'Entomologia, Tamid, Tecnologia i Ciència dels Aliments (TECA), Trabades d'Història de la Ciència i la Tècnica, Treballs de Comunicació, Treballs de Física, Treballs de la Societat Catalana de Biologia, Treballs de la Societat Catalana de Geografia, Treballs de Sociolingüística Catalana.*

Instituto Cervantes: Alcalá 49, 28014 Madrid; tel. (91) 4367600; fax (91) 4367691; e-mail informa@cervantes.es; internet www .cervantes.es; f. 1991; promotes Spanish language and the culture of Spain and Spanish-speaking Latin and Central America globally; operates in 26 countries; maintains teaching centres in Sofia (Bulgaria), Zagreb (Croatia), Belgrade (Serbia) and Hanoi (Viet Nam); Dir CARMEN CAFFAREL SERRA; Gen. Sec. CARMEN PÉREZ-FRAGERO RODRÍGUEZ DE TEMBLEQUE.

Instituto de España (Institute of Spain): San Bernardo 49, 28015 Madrid; tel. (91) 5224885; fax (91) 5210654; e-mail secretaria@insde.es; internet www.insde.es; f. 1938; the Institute's constituent academies form a 'Senado de la Cultura Española'; Pres. GONZALO ANES Y ÁLVAREZ DE CASTRILLÓN; Sec.-Gen. PEDRO GARCÍA BARRENO.

Constituent Academies:

Real Academia de Bellas Artes de San Fernando (San Fernando Royal Academy of Fine Arts): Calle Alcalá 13, 28014 Madrid; tel. (91) 5240864; fax (91)

5231599; e-mail director@rabasf.org; internet rabasf.insde.es; f. 1752; attached museum: see under Museums and Art Galleries; 57 mems; library of 40,000 vols, 1,100 periodicals; Dir ANTONIO BONET CORREA; Vice-Dir ISMAEL FERNÁNDEZ DE LA CUESTA; Sec.-Gen. FERNANDO DE TERÁN TROYANO.

Real Academia de Ciencias Exactas, Físicas y Naturales (Royal Academy of Exact, Physical and Natural Sciences): Valverde 22 y 24, 28004 Madrid; tel. (91) 7014230; fax (91) 7014232; e-mail secretaria@rac.es; internet www.rac.es; f. 1847; sections of exact sciences, natural sciences, physical and chemical sciences; 43 mems, 90 Spanish corresp. mems; Pres. MIGUEL ÁNGEL ALARIO FRANCO; publs *Revista* (4 a year), *Serie A: Matemáticas* (4 a year).

Real Academia de Ciencias Morales y Políticas (Royal Academy of Moral and Political Sciences): Plaza de la Villa 2, 28005 Madrid; tel. (91) 5481330; fax (91) 5481975; e-mail biblioteca@racmyp.es; internet www.racmyp.es; f. 1857; 89 mems (44 ordinary, 14 Spanish corresp., 35 foreign corresp.); library of 125,000 vols, 340 periodicals; Pres. MARCELINO OREJA AGUIRRE; Sec. JULIO IGLESIAS DE USSEL; publs *Anales* (1 a year), *Papeles y Memorias* (4 a year).

Real Academia de Jurisprudencia y Legislación (Royal Academy of Jurisprudence and Law): Calle Marqués de Cubas 13, 28014 Madrid; tel. (91) 5222069; fax (91) 5234021; e-mail secretaria.rajyl@insde .es; internet rajyl.insde.es; f. 1730; 38 mems; library of 40,000 vols; Pres. LANDELINO LAVILLA ALSINA; Sec.-Gen. RAFAEL NAVARRO-VALLS; publ. *Anales*.

Real Academia de la Historia (Royal Academy of History): Calle León 21, 28014 Madrid; tel. (91) 4290611; fax (91) 3694636; e-mail direccion@rah.es; internet www.rah.es; f. 1738; 33 mems, 370 corresp. mems; library of 350,000 vols, 180,000 MSS; Dir GONZALO ANES Y ÁLVAREZ DE CASTRILLÓN; Permanent Sec. ELOY BENITO RUANO.

Real Academia Española (Royal Spanish Academy): Calle de Felipe IV 4, 28014 Madrid; tel. (91) 4201478; fax (91) 4200079; e-mail secretaria@rae.es; internet www.rae.es; f. 1713; 40 ordinary mems, 3 elected mems; Dir VICTOR GARCÍA DE LA CONCHA; Sec. DARÍO VILLANUEVA.

Real Academia Nacional de Farmacia (Royal National Academy of Pharmacy): Calle de la Farmacia 9–11, 28004 Madrid; tel. (91) 5310307; fax (91) 5310306; e-mail secretaria@ranf.com; internet www.ranf .com; f. 1589; 44 mems; library of 30,000 vols; Pres. MARÍA TERESA MIRAS PORTUGAL; Permanent Sec. LUIS ANTONIO DOADRIO VILLAREJO; publ. *Anales* (4 a year).

Real Academia Nacional de Medicina (Royal National Academy of Medicine): Calle Arrieta 12, 28013 Madrid; tel. (91) 5470318; fax (91) 5470320; internet www .ranm.es; f. 1733; 46 mems, 81 Spanish corresp. mems, 82 foreign corresp. mems; library of 100,000 vols; Pres. MANUEL DÍAZ-RUBIO GARCÍA; Sec.-Gen. MIGUEL LUCAS TOMÁS; publ. *Anales* (4 a year).

Instituto Egipcio de Estudios Islámicos (Egyptian Institute of Islamic Studies): Calle Francisco de Asís Méndez Casariego 1, 28002 Madrid; tel. (91) 5639468; fax (91) 5638640; e-mail secretaria@institutoegipcio.com; internet www.institutoegipcio.com; f. 1950; 14 mems; library of 38,000 vols, 1,200 periodicals; Dir Dr ELSAYED IBRAHIM SOHEIM; Sec. ALMUDENA GARCÍA; publ. *Revista* (1 a year).

Real Academia de Bellas Artes y Ciencias Históricas de Toledo (Toledo Royal Academy of Fine Arts and Historical Sciences): Calle Esteban Illán 9, 45002 Toledo; tel. and fax (92) 5214322; internet www .realacademiatoledo.es; f. 1916; 24 mems, 26 corresp. mems; library of 4,000 vols; Dir RAMÓN SÁNCHEZ GONZÁLEZ; Sec. JOSÉ LUIS ISABEL SÁNCHEZ; publ. *Toletum*.

Real Academia de Ciencias y Artes de Barcelona (Barcelona Royal Academy of Science and Arts): Rambla de los Estudios 115, 08002 Barcelona; tel. (93) 3170536; fax (93) 3011656; e-mail info@racab.es; internet www.racab.es; f. 1764; 75 mems; attached observatory: see Research Institutes; library of 150,000 vols; Pres. Dr RAMON PASCUAL DE SANS; Sec.-Gen. Dr JOAN JOFRE I TORROELLA; Vice-Pres. Dra MERCÉ DURFORT I COLL; publ. *Memòries*.

Real Academia de Doctores (Royal Academy of Doctors): Calle de San Bernardo 49, 28015 Madrid; tel. (91) 5319522; fax (91) 5240027; e-mail rad@radoctores.es; internet www.radoctores.es; f. 1920; sections of architechture, commerce, economics, engineering, law, literature, medicine, pharmacy, philosophy, politics, veterinary science, sciences; 4 hon. mems, 100 mems, 110 national corresp., 90 foreign corresp. mems; Pres. Dr LUIS MARDONES SEVILLA; Sec.-Gen. Dra ROSA MARÍA GARCERÁN PIQUERAS; publs *Anales* (irregular), *Anuario*.

Real Academia Galega (Royal Galician Academy): Rúa Tabernas 11, 15001 A Coruña; tel. (981) 207308; fax (981) 216467; e-mail secretaria@realacademiagalega.org; internet www.realacademiagalega.org; f. 1905; promotes Galician language and literature; 29 mems; library of 65,000 vols, incl. valuable colln of books on Galicia; Pres. MÉNDEZ FERRÍN XOSÉ LUÍS; Sec. AXEITOS AGRELO XOSÉ LUÍS; publs *Boletín da Real Academia Galega* (Galician literature and history), *Cadernos de Lingua* (Galician language: grammar, phonetics, lexicography, sociolinguistics).

Real Academia Hispano-Americana (Royal Spanish-American Academy): Paseo Carlos III 9, 1°, 11003 Cadiz; tel. (95) 6221680; fax (95) 6221224; e-mail raha@ raha.es; internet www.raha.es; f. 1910; library of 120,000 vols; 25 mems, 6 hon. mems; Dir MARÍA DEL CARMEN CÓZAR NAVARRO; Sec.-Gen. FERNANDO SÁNCHEZ GARCÍA; publ. *Anuario*.

AGRICULTURE, FISHERIES AND VETERINARY SCIENCE

Institut Agrícola (Agricultural Institute): Plaça Sant Josep Oriol 4, 08002 Barcelona; tel. (93) 3011636; fax (93) 3173005; e-mail info@institutagricola.org; internet www .institutagricola.org; f. 1851; 2,000 mems; library of 16,000 vols, 200 periodicals; Pres. BALDIRI ROS I PRAT; Sec. MATEU COMALRENA DE SOBREGRAU; publ. *La Drecera* (6 a year).

Real Academia de Ciencias Veterinarias (Royal Academy of Veterinary Sciences): c/o Prof. Dr Mariano Illera Martín, Maestro Ripoll 8, 28006 Madrid; tel. (91) 5611799; fax (91) 3943864; e-mail info@racve.es; internet www.racve.es; f. 1975; 38 mems, 5 hon. mems, 32 corresp. mems in Spain, 81 corresp. mems abroad; Pres. CARLOS LUIS DE CUENCA Y ESTEBAN; Sec.-Gen. JULIO SALVIO JIMÉNEZ PÉREZ; publ. *Anales* (1 a year).

ARCHITECTURE AND TOWN PLANNING

Col·legi d'Arquitectes de Catalunya (Association of Catalan Architects): Plaça Nova 5, 08002 Barcelona; tel. (93) 3015000; fax (93) 3186029; e-mail coac@coac.net; internet www.coac.net; f. 1931; 9,000 mems;

library of 80,000 vols; Dean LUÍS-XAVIER COMERÓN I GRAUPERA; Sec. ASSUMPCIÓ PUIG I HORS; publ. *Quaderns d'Arquitectura i Urbanisme*.

BIBLIOGRAPHY, LIBRARY SCIENCE AND MUSEOLOGY

Amics dels Museus de Catalunya (Friends of the Catalan Museums): Palau de la Virreina, La Rambla 99, 08002 Barcelona; tel. (93) 3014379; fax (93) 3189421; e-mail amics@amicsdelsmuseus.org; internet www .amicsdelsmuseus.org; f. 1933; 800 mems, 6 hon., 81 associates, 52 others; Pres. FAUSTO SERRA DE DALMASES; Sec.-Gen. MARINA GÓMEZ CASAS.

Federación Española de Asociaciones de Archiveros, Bibliotecarios, Arqueólogos, Museólogos y Documentalistas (Spanish Federation of Associations of Archivists, Librarians, Archaeologist, Museums and Archives): Calle Recoletos 5, 3°, 28001 Madrid; tel. (91) 5751727; fax (91) 5781615; e-mail anabad@anabad.org; internet www .anabad.org; f. 1949; more than 1,500 mems; groups all specialists working in the country's archive services, libraries, museums and documentation services; has regional branches in Aragón, Castilla-La Mancha, Galicia, La Rioja and Murcia; Pres. ANTONIO CASADO POYALES; Sec. RAMÓN VILLA GONZÁLEZ.

ECONOMICS, LAW AND POLITICS

Centro de Estudios Políticos y Constitucionales (Centre for Political and Constitutional Studies): Plaza de la Marina Española 9, 28071 Madrid; tel. (91) 5401950; fax (91) 5419574; e-mail cepc@cepc .es; internet www.cepc.es; f. 1977, by merger with Instituto de Estudios Políticos; organizes courses and seminars on politics and constitutional law; 100 mems; library of 85,500 vols; Dir Dra PALOMA BIGLINO CAMPOS; Man. JOSÉ ÁNGEL MANZANO GARCÍA; publs *Anuario Iberoamericano de Justicia Constitucional* (1 a year), *Derecho Privado y Constitución* (1 a year), *Historia y Política* (2 a year), *Revista de Administración Pública* (3 a year), *Revista de Derecho Comunitario Europeo* (3 a year), *Revista de Estudios Políticos* (4 a year), *Revista Española de Derecho Constitucional* (3 a year).

Col·legi de Notaris de Catalunya (College of Catalan Notaries): Carrer Notariat 4, Barcelona; tel. (93) 3174800; fax (93) 3026331; e-mail info@catalunya.notariado .org; internet www.colnotcat.es; f. 1932; 500 mems; Dir ÁNGEL SERRANO DE NICOLÁS; Sec. ESTEBAN CUYAS HENCHE; publ. *La Notaría*.

Il·lustre Col·legi d'Advocats de Barcelona (Barcelona Bar Association): Calle Mallorca 283, 08037 Barcelona; tel. (93) 4961880; fax (93) 4871589; e-mail icab@icab .es; internet www.icab.es; f. 1832; 20,000 mems; library: see Libraries and Archives; Dean PEDRO L.YÚFERA SALES; Sec. LUIS ANTONIO SALES CAMPRODON; publs *Món Jurídic* (12 a year), *Revista Jurídica de Catalunya* (8 a year).

Instituto Nacional de Administración Pública (National Institute of Public Administration): Atocha 106, 28012 Madrid; tel. (91) 2739281; fax (91) 2739287; e-mail direccion@inap.es; internet www.inap.map .es; f. 1940; library of 150,000 vols, 3,000 periodicals; Sec.-Gen. MARÍA SOL SERRANO ALONSO; Dir ÁNGEL MANUEL MORENO MOLINA; publs *Cuadernos de Derecho Público* (3 a year), *Documentación Administrativa* (3 a year), *Gestión y Análisis de Políticas Públicas* (3 a year), *Revista de Estudios de Administración Local* (3 a year), *Revista Internacional de Administrativas* (4 a year).

Instituto Nacional de Estadística (National Statistical Office): Paseo de la Castellana 183, 28071 Madrid; tel. (91) 5839100; fax (91) 5839158; e-mail biblioteca@ine.es; internet www.ine.es; f. 1945; library of 170,000 vols, 125,000 microfiches; Pres. JAUME GARCÍA VILLAR; Sec.-Gen. NATIVIDAD DOMÍNGUEZ CALAVERAS; publs *Anuario Estadístico de España* (1 a year), *Boletín Mensual de Estadística* (data on short-term indicators, 12 a year), *Boletín Trimestral de Coyuntura* (national accounts and other indicators, 4 a year), *Censos de la Población y de la Vivienda* (every 10 years), *Dirce* (number of enterprises by sector and breakdown by number of workers and activity), *Encuesta Anual de Comercio* (data on trade, 1 a year), *Epa* (employment), *España en Cifras* (main statistical indicators and data, in Spanish or English), *Estadística Española* (statistical theory and methodology, 3 a year), *Estadística Industrial* (data on production and business turnover, 1 a year), *Nomenclaturas y Metodología*.

Real Sociedad Económica de Amigos del País de Tenerife (Royal Economic Society of Friends of Tenerife): Calle San Agustín 23, 38201 San Cristóbal de La Laguna, Tenerife, Canary Islands; tel. (922) 250010; fax (922) 257735; e-mail secretaria@rseapt.com; internet www.rseapt.com; f. 1777; 500 mems; library of 12,000 vols; Dir ANDRÉS M. DE SOUZA IGLESIAS; Sec. MARÍA LUISA DE CÓRDOVA SANTANA.

EDUCATION

Fundación José Ortega y Gasset: Calle Fortuny 53, 28010, Madrid; tel. (91) 7004100; fax (91) 7003530; e-mail comunicacion@fog .es; internet www.ortegaygasset.edu; f. 1978; organizes cultural activities and undertakes debate and research in the fields of the social sciences and humanities; attached institute in Toledo offers courses in Hispanic, Latin American and European Studies (incl. anthropology, archaeology, politics, economics, geography, history, art, Spanish language, literature), designed specifically for foreign students; Pres. JOSÉ VARELA ORTEGA; Dir-Gen. JESÚS SÁNCHEZ LAMBÁS; publs *Revista de Estudios Orteguianos* (2 a year), *Revista de Occidente* (12 a year).

FINE AND PERFORMING ARTS

Asociación Española de Pintores y Escultores (Association of Spanish Artists and Sculptors): Calle Infantas 30, 2°, 28004 Madrid; tel. (91) 5224961; fax (91) 5225508; e-mail administracion@aepe.e.telefonica.net; internet www.apintoresyescultores.es; f. 1910; 1,000 mems; Pres. JOSÉ GABRIEL ASTUDILLO LÓPEZ; Sec. MARÍA ISABEL MORENO GONZÁLEZ; publ. *Gaceta de las Bellas Artes* (12 a year).

Ateneo Científico, Literario y Artístico (Scientific, Literary and Artistic Athenaeum): Sa Rovellada de Dalt 25, 07703 Mahón, Minorca, Balearic Islands; tel. 971-36-05-53; f. 1905; library of 15,000 vols; 630 mems; Pres. JOSÉ ANTONIO FAYAS JANER; Sec. CATALINA SEGUI DE VIDAL; publ. *Revista de Menorca* (4 a year).

Ateneo Científico, Literario y Artístico de Madrid (Scientific, Literary and Artistic Athenaeum in Madrid): Calle Prado 21, 28014 Madrid; tel. (91) 4291750; fax (91) 4297901; e-mail admonateneo@telefonica .net; internet www.ateneodemadrid.com; f. 1820; 7,000 mems; library of 500,000 vols; Pres. CARLOS PARÍS AMADOR; Sec. CARLOS GARCÍA; publ. *El Ateneno* (1 a year).

Ateneu Barcelonès (Barcelona Athenaeum): Calle de la Canuda 6, 08002 Barcelona; tel. (93) 3436121; fax (93) 3171525;

e-mail info@ateneubcn.org; internet www
.ateneubcn.org; f. 1860; library: see Libraries; 4,000 mems; Pres. ORIOL BOHIGAS GUAR-
DIOLA; Sec. MERCÈ ÀLVAREZ.

Consejo General de la Música (General
Council on Music): Calle Davallada 12,
Planta Baixa, 08870 Sitges; tel. (93)
8949990; fax (93) 8948996; e-mail consejo@
musicae.org; mem. of Int. Music Council
(q.v.); Pres. MANUEL VALLRIBERA I MIR.

Institut Amatller d'Art Hispànic (Amatller Institute of Hispanic Art): Passeig de
Gràcia 41, 08007 Barcelona; tel. (93)
2160175; fax (93) 4670194; e-mail
administracio@amatller.org; internet www
.amatller.org; f. 1941; library of 26,000 vols;
colln of 350,000 photographs; Pres. MONTSER-
RAT BLANCH ALMUZARA; Sec. JACINT BEREN-
GUER I CASAL.

Institut del Teatre (Theatrical Institute):
Plaça Margarida Xirgu s/n, 08004 Barcelona;
tel. (93) 2273900; fax (93) 2273939; e-mail i
.teatre@diba.es; internet www
.institutdelteatre.org; f. 1913; drama and
dance school; documentation and research
information centre; library of 150,000 vols;
Dir JORDI FONT I CARDONA.

**Real Academia de Bellas Artes de la
Purísima Concepción** (Royal Academy of
Fine Arts): Casa de Cervantes, Calle del
Rastro s/n, 47001 Valladolid; tel. (983)
398004; fax (983) 390703; e-mail info@
realacademiaconcepcion.net; internet www
.realacademiaconcepcion.net; f. 1779; 32
mems; Pres. JOAQUÍN DÍAZ GONZÁLEZ; Sec.
JESÚS URREA FERNÁNDEZ.

**Real Academia de Bellas Artes de San
Telmo** (Royal Academy of Fine Arts, San
Telmo): Málaga; internet www
.realacademiasantelmo.org; f. 1849 as Aca-
demia de Bellas Artes de Málaga; present
name adopted 1883; 34 mems; Pres. MANUEL
DEL CAMPO Y DEL CAMPO; Sec. FRANCISCO
CABRERA PABLOS; publ. Anuario.

**Real Academia de Bellas Artes de Santa
Isabel de Hungría** (Royal Academy of Fine
Arts, Santa Isabel de Hungría): Abades 14,
Casa de los Pinelo, 41004 Seville; tel. and fax
(95) 4221198; e-mail rabasih@insacan.org;
internet www.insacan.org/rabasih/
rabasihsede.html; f. 1660; research, courses
and exhibitions; 40 mems; library of 3,900
vols; Pres. ISABEL DE LEÓN BORRERO; Gen.
Sec. Dr FERNANDO FERNÁNDEZ GÓMEZ; publs
Boletín de Bellas Artes (1 a year), Temas de
Estética y Arte (1 a year).

**Real Academia de Nobles y Bellas Artes
de San Luis** (Royal Academy of Noble and
Fine Arts of San Luis): Plaza de los Sitios 6,
50001 Zaragoza; tel. (97) 6217969; fax (97)
6222378; e-mail rasanluis@rasanluis.es;
internet www.rasanluis.es; f. 1792; comprises 5 sections (architecture, sculpture,
painting, music, literature) and 3 permanent
cttees; 38 mems; library of 5,500 vols; Pres.
Dr DOMINGO JESÚS BUESA CONDE; Vice-Pres.
FERNANDO ALVIRA BANZO; Vice-Pres. MIGUEL
CABALLÚ ALBIAC; Gen. Sec. JAVIER SAURAS
VIÑUALES.

Real Sociedad Fotográfica (Royal Photographic Society): Apdo 7238, 28080 Madrid;
Calle de los Tres Peces 2, 28012 Madrid; tel.
(91) 5397579; e-mail info@rsf.es; internet
www.rsf.es; f. 1899; 1,400 mems; library of
3,800 vols; Pres. ENRIQUE SANZ RAMÍREZ; Sec.-
Gen. MARÍA ANTONIA GARCÍA DE LA VEGA; publ.
Boletín (4 a year).

HISTORY, GEOGRAPHY AND ARCHAEOLOGY

**Arxiu Històric de la Ciutat de Barce-
lona:** Casa de l'Ardiaca, Carrer Santa Llúcia
1, 08002 Barcelona; tel. (93) 3181195; fax (93)

3178327; e-mail arxiuhistoric@bcn.cat;
internet www.bcn.es/arxiu/arxiuhistoric; f.
1917; archives of municipal records and local
press; the Archives undertake historical
research on Barcelona, organize courses,
lectures, exhibitions; library: see Libraries
and Archives; Dir XAVIER TARRAUBELLA MIR-
ABET; publs Barcelona Quaderns d'Història (2
a year), Història, Antropología, y Fuentes
Orales (2 a year), Quaderns del Seminari
d'Història de Barcelona (irregular).

Deutsches Archaeologisches Institut
(German Archaeological Institute): Serrano
159, 28002 Madrid; tel. (91) 4110163; fax (91)
5640054; e-mail sekretariat@madrid.dainst
.org; internet www.dainst.de; f. 1943; library
of 65,000 vols; archive of photographs; Dir
Prof. Dr HANS-JOACHIM GEHRKE; publs Hispania Antiqua, Iberia Archaeologica, Madrider Beiträge, Madrider Forschungen,
Madrider Mitteilungen (1 a year), Studien
über frühe Tierknochenfunde von der Iber-
ischen Halbinsel.

Instituto de Historia y Cultura Naval
(Institute of Naval History and Culture):
Calle Juan de Mena 1, 28014 Madrid; tel.
(91) 3795050; fax (91) 3795945; f. 1942 as
Instituto Histórico de la Marina, present
name adopted 1976; associated with the
Consejo Superior de Investigaciones Cien-
tíficas; for library see entry under Museo
Naval; Dir Contralmirante TEODORO DE
LESTE CONTRERAS.

Instituto Geográfico Nacional (National
Geographical Institute): Calle del General
Ibáñez de Ibero 3, 28003 Madrid; tel. (91)
5979453; fax (91) 5532913; e-mail ign@mfom
.es; internet www.mfom.es/ign; f. 1870; 1,200
mems; library of 28,000 vols; geodesy and
geophysics, cartography, map printing, seismology, astronomy, runs the Nat. Astronomical Observatory (see under Research
Institutes); Dir-Gen. ALBERTO SERENO
ÁLVAREZ; publs Boletín Astronómico, Anuario
del Observatorio Astronómico, Anuario de
Geomagnetismo, Boletines Sísmicos.

Real Sociedad Geográfica (Royal Geographic Society): Calle Monte Esquinza 41,
28010 Madrid; tel. (91) 3082477; fax (91)
3082478; e-mail secretaria@
realsociedadgeografica.com; internet www
.realsociedadgeografica.com; f. 1876; geography and earth sciences; 450 mems; library
of 11,000 vols, 12,700 booklets, 110 periodicals; Pres. JUAN VELARDE FUERTES; Perm.
Sec. Dr JOAQUÍN BOSQUE MAUREL.

**Reial Societat Arqueològica Tarraco-
nense** (Royal Archaeological Society in Tarragona): POB 573, 43080 Tarragona; Carrer
Major 35, 43003 Tarragona; tel. and fax (977)
23-37-89; e-mail informacio@arqueologica
.org; internet www.arqueologica.org; f. 1844;
Iberian, Roman and early Christian archaeology; ancient, medieval, modern and contemporary history of Tarragona; 600 mems;
library of 4,000 vols, 18,000 vols of periodicals; Pres. RAFAEL GABRIEL COSTA; Sec. JORDI
ROVIRA SORIANO; publ. Butlletí Arqueològic (4
a year).

**Servicio de Investigación Prehistórica
de la Excelentísima Diputación Provincial** (Prehistoric Research Society of the
Province of Valencia): Calle de la Corona
36, 46003 Valencia; tel. (96) 3883587; fax (96)
3883536; e-mail sip@dival.es; internet www
.museoprehistoriavalencia.es; f. 1927;
palaeolithic, neolithic, Bronze and Iron
Ages, Iberian and colonial exhibits, prehistoric Americana; 30 mems; library of 60,000
vols; Curator MARÍA JESÚS DE PEDRO MICHÓ;
publs Serie de Trabajos Varios, Archivo de
Prehistoria Levantina.

Societat Arqueològica Lul·liana (Lulli-
ana Archaeological Society): Calle Monti-

Sion 9, 07001 Palma de Mallorca, Balearic
Islands; tel. (971) 713912; e-mail info@
arqueologicaluliana.com; internet www
.arqueologicaluliana.com; f. 1880; 600 mems;
library of 20,000 vols; museum; Pres. ANTO-
NIO PLANAS ROSSELLÓ; Sec. MARIA ANTÒNIA
SEGURA BONNÍN; publ. Bolletí de la Societat
Arqueològica Lul·liana: Revista d'estudis
històrics (1 a year).

LANGUAGE AND LITERATURE

Alliance Française: Calle Marqués de la
Ensenada 10, 28004 Madrid; tel. (91)
7007736; fax (91) 7007707; e-mail secaf@
alliancefrancaise.es; internet www
.alliancefrancaise.es; offers courses and
exams in French language and culture and
promotes cultural exchange with France;
attached offices in Alicante, Burgos, Cartagena, Gijon, Girona, Granada, Granollers, La
Coruña, Las Palmas, Lerida, Lleida, Málaga,
Oviedo, Palma de Mallorca, Sabadell, Sama
de Langreo, Santa Cruz de Tenerife, Santander, Santiago de Compostela, Valladolid,
Vigo and Vitoria.

**Asociación de Escritores y Artistas
Españoles** (Spanish Writers' and Artists'
Association): Calle de Leganitos 10, 1° Dere-
cha, 28013 Madrid; tel. (91) 5599067; fax (91)
5424467; e-mail secretaria@aeae.es; internet
www.aeae.es; f. 1871; 527 mems; library of
3,000 vols; Pres. JUAN VAN-HALEN; Dir and
Sec.-Gen. JOSÉ LÓPEZ MARTÍNEZ.

British Council: Paseo del General Martínez, Campos 31, 28010 Madrid; tel. (91)
3373500; fax (91) 3373573; e-mail prensa@
britishcouncil.es; internet www
.britishcouncil.es; offers courses and examinations in English language and British culture and promotes cultural exchange with
the United Kingdom in 13 centres across
Spain (7 in Madrid, 2 in Barcelona, and 1
each in Bilbao, Valencia, Segovia and Plama
de Mallorca); Dir CHRIS HICKEY.

**Euskaltzaindia/Real Academia de la
Lengua Vasca** (Royal Academy of the
Basque Language): Plaza Barria 15, 48005
Bilbao; tel. (94) 4158155; fax (94) 4158144;
e-mail info@euskaltzaindia.net; internet
www.euskaltzaindia.net; f. 1919; research
into and conservation of the Basque language; 30 full mems, 33 hon. mems, 135
assoc. academic mems; library of 70,000 vols
specializing in philology and linguistics,
principally of the Basque language; Pres.
ANDRÉS URRUTIA BADIOLA; Vice-Pres. AURELIA
ARKOTXA MORTALENA; Sec. XABIER KINTANA
URTIAGA; Treas. JOSE LUIS LIZUNDIA
ASKONDO; publs Erlea, Euskera (3 a year),
Euskaltzainak Bilduma (irregular), Euskalt-
zaindiaren Arauak (3 a year), Euskararen
Lekukoak, Iker, Jagon, Mendaur bilduma
(irregular), Onomasticon Vasconiae, Plaza-
berri (irregular).

Goethe-Institut: Calle Zurbarán 21, 28010
Madrid; tel. (91) 3913944; fax (91) 3913945;
e-mail info@madrid.goethe.org; internet
www.goethe.de/madrid; offers courses and
exams in German language and culture and
promotes cultural exchange with Germany;
attached centres in Alcalá de Henares,
Colmenarejo, Colmenar Viejo, Getafe,
Leganés, Villanueva de la Cañada, Granada
and San Sebastián; library of 15,000 vols; Dir
MARGARETA HAUSCHILD; Sec. REBECA CASTEL-
LANO.

**Real Academia Sevillana de Buenas
Letras** (Seville Royal Academy of Belles
Lettres): Calle Abades 14, 41004 Seville; tel.
(95) 4225200; e-mail secretariarasbl@
infonegocio.com; internet www
.academiasevillanadebuenasletras.org; f.
1751; 29 mems, 7 hon., 100 corresp.; library
of 20,000 vols; Dir MANUEL GONZÁLEZ JIMÉ-

NEZ; Sec. ENRIQUETA VILA VILAR; publ. *Boletín* (1 a year).

Reial Acadèmia de Bones Lletres (Royal Academy of Belles Lettres): Carrer del Bisbe Caçador 3, 08002 Barcelona; tel. and fax (93) 3102349; e-mail bones-lletres@bonesletres .cat; internet www.bonesletres.cat; f. 1700; 36 mems; Pres. EDUARD RIPOLL; Sec. ALBERT CORBETO LÓPEZ; publ. *Boletín*.

Sociedad General de Autores y Editores (General Society of Authors and Publishers): Fernando VI 4, 28004 Madrid; tel. (91) 3499550; internet www.sgae.es; f. 1932; 95,000 mems; library of 25,000 vols, relating to the theatre, music (scores) and cinema only; Pres. JOSÉ LUIS BORAU MORADELL; publ. *Boletín* (4 a year).

MEDICINE

Academia de Ciencias Médicas de Bilbao (Academy of Medical Sciences, Bilbao): Lersundi 9, 5°, 48009 Bilbao; tel. (94) 4233768; fax (94) 4232161; e-mail academiacmb@gruponahise.com; internet www.icombi.org/academiacm.htm; f. 1895; more than 1,200 mems; library of 10,000 vols; Pres. Dr JUAN IGNACIO GOIRIA ORMAZA-BAL; Sec.-Gen. Prof. Dr RICARDO FRANCO VICARIO; publ. *Gaceta Médica de Bilbao* (4 a year).

Acadèmia de Ciències Mèdiques de Catalunya i de Balears (Academy of Medical Sciences and Health of Catalonia and the Balearic Islands): Paseo de la Bonanova 51, 08017 Barcelona; tel. (93) 4188729; e-mail academia@academia.cat; internet www .acmcb.es; f. 1872; 20,000 mems; Pres. JOSEP ANTONI BOMBÍ LATORRE; publ. *Annals de Medicina* (4 a year).

Academia Española de Dermatología y Venereología (Spanish Academy of Dermatology and Venereology): Calle Ferraz 100, 1° izq, 28008 Madrid; tel. (91) 5446284; fax (91) 5494145; e-mail contacto@aedv.es; internet www.aedv.es; f. 1909; brs: Andalusia; Asturias, Cantabria and Castille Leon; Balearic Islands; Canary Islands; Catalonia; Centro; Euskadi, Navarre, La Rioja and Aragon; Galicia; Murcia; Valencia; 450 mems, 50 hon., 3 corresp.; library of 1,000 vols; Pres. Dr JOSÉ CARLOS MORENO GIMÉNEZ; Sec. Dr HUGO ALBERTO VÁZQUEZ VEIGA; publ. *Actas Dermosifiliográficas* (12 a year).

Academia Médico-Quirúrgica Española (Spanish Academy of Medicine and Surgery): Calle Villanueva 11, 28001 Madrid; f. 1844; 500 mems; Pres. Prof. LUIS ORTIZ QUINTANA; Sec. Dr JULIO MÚÑIZ GONZÁLEZ; publ. *Anales*.

Consejo General de Colegios Oficiales de Farmacéuticos (General Council of Official Colleges of Pharmacists): Calle Villanueva 11, 7°, 28001 Madrid; e-mail buzon@ redfarma.org; internet www.portalfarma .com; f. 1942; 13,500 mems; Pres. ERNESTO MARCO CAÑIZARES; publ. *Farmacéuticos* (9–12 a year).

Organización Médica Colegial—Consejo General de Colegios Oficiales de Médicos de España (Spanish General Council of Official Medical Colleges): Plaza de las Cortes 11, 28014 Madrid; tel. (91) 4317780; fax (91) 4319620; e-mail administrador@ cgcom.org; internet www.cgcom.org; f. 1930; 52 mems; Pres. Dr JUAN JOSÉ RODRÍGUEZ SENDÍN; Sec.-Gen. Dr SERAFÍN ROMERO AGÜIT; publs *Europa al Día* (26 a year), *Periódico OMC* (12 a year).

Real Academia de Medicina y Cirugía de Palma de Mallorca (Royal Academy of Medicine and Surgery, Palma de Mallorca): Calle Morey 8, 07001 Palma de Mallorca; tel. (971) 721230; f. 1831; 19 mems; Pres. JOSÉ

TOMÁS MONSERRAT; Sec. SANTIAGO FORTEZA FORTEZA.

Sociedad de Pediatría de Madrid y Castilla-La Mancha (Paediatrics Society of Madrid and Castilla La Mancha): Calle Cea Bermúdez 39, Bajo, 28003 Madrid; tel. (91) 4358031; e-mail spmycm@mcmpediatria .org; internet www.mcmpediatria.org; f. 1913; 750 mems; Pres. Dr JOSÉ GARCÍA-SICILIA LÓPEZ; Sec.-Gen. Dr JUAN JOSÉ JIMÉ-NEZ GARCÍA; publ. *MCM—Pediatría* (3 a year).

Sociedad Española de Patología Digestiva (Society of Digestive Diseases): Francisco Silvela 69, 2° C, 28028 Madrid; tel. (91) 4021353; fax (91) 4027691; e-mail sepd@sepd .es; internet www.sepd.es; f. 1933; 800 mems; Pres. Dr JUAN ENRIQUE DOMÍNGUEZ MUÑOZ; Sec. Dr FEDERICO ARGÜELLES ARIAS; publs *G.I. & Hepatology News*, *Revista Española de las Enfermedades Digestivas* (12 a year).

Sociedad Española de Radiología Médica (Spanish Society of Medical Radiology): Gran Vía 1, 28013 Madrid; tel. (91) 5752613; fax (91) 5763279; e-mail secretaria@seram .es; internet www.seram.es; f. 1946; 3,500 mems; 200 founder mems; Pres. Dr EDUARDO FRAILE MORENO; Sec.-Gen. Dr MIGUEL ANGEL LÓPEZ PINO; publs *Diagnóstico por la Imagen* (4 a year), *Radiología* (6 a year).

NATURAL SCIENCES
General

Real Academia de Ciencias Exactas, Físicas, Químicas y Naturales de Zaragoza (Royal Academy of Exact, Physical, Chemical and Natural Sciences in Zaragoza): Facultad de Ciencias, Calle Pedro Cerbuna 12, 50009 Zaragoza; tel. (976) 761128; fax (976) 761125; e-mail acz@posta.unizar.es; internet www.unizar.es/acz; f. 1916; comprises sections on Exact Sciences, Physics and Chemistry, and Natural Sciences; Pres. LUIS JOAQUÍN BOYA BALET; Sec. JOSÉ F. CARIÑENA MARZO; 40 mems, 44 corresp. mems; publ. *Revista* (1 a year).

Sociedad de Ciencias 'Aranzadi' Zientzia Elkartea (Aranzadi Society of Sciences): Calle del Alto de Zorroaga 11, 20014 San Sebastián; tel. (943) 466142; fax (943) 455811; e-mail idazkaritza@ aranzadi-zientziak.org; internet www .aranzadi-zientziak.org; f. 1947; encourages interest in various brs of natural science, prehistory and ethnology; 1,540 mems; library of 28,000 vols, 2,181 periodicals; Pres. FRANCISCO ETXEBERRIA; Sec. JAVIER CANTERA; publs *Aranzadiana* (1 a year), *Aranzadi Berriak*, *Boletín de Astronomía* (4 a year), *Munibe Antropologia—Arkeologia* (1 a year), *Munibe Ciencias Naturales—Natur Zientziak* (1 a year).

Biological Sciences

Asociación Española de Entomología (Spanish Entomological Association): c/o Dr Eduardo Galante Patiño, Centro Iberoamericano de Biodiversidad, Universidad de Alicante, Apdo 99, 03080 Alicante; e-mail galante@ua.es; internet www.entomologica .es; f. 1977; Pres. Dr EDUARDO GALANTE PATIÑO; Sec. Dr JOSÉ MARÍA HERNÁNDEZ DE MIGUEL; publ. *Boletín* (2 a year).

Real Sociedad Española de Historia Natural (Royal Spanish Natural History Society): Facultades de Biología y Geología, Universidad Complutense de Madrid, 28040 Madrid; tel. and fax (91) 3945000; e-mail rsehno@bio.ucm.es; internet rshn.geo.ucm .es; f. 1871; biological and geological sciences; 800 mems; library of 10,000 vols, 2,500 current periodicals; Pres. Dr JOSÉ LUIS VIEJO MONTESINOS; Sec.-Gen. Dr ALFREDO BARATAS

DÍAZ; publs *Boletín: Sección Biológica* (4 a year), *Boletín: Sección Geológica* (4 a year).

Sociedad Española de Etología (Spanish Ethological Society): Museu Ciències Naturals, P° Picasso s/n, Parc Ciutadella, 08003 Barcelona; tel. (93) 2562217; fax (93) 3104999; e-mail larroyo@bcn.cat; internet www.etologia.org; f. 1984; 350 mems; Pres. Dr JUAN CARRANZA; Sec. Dr JUAN CARLOS SENAR; publs *Acta Etohologica* (2 a year), *EtoloGUIA* (2 a year).

Mathematical Sciences

Real Sociedad Matemática Española (Royal Spanish Mathematical Society): Despacho 525, Facultad de Matemáticas, Universidad Complutense, 28040 Madrid; tel. (91) 3944937; fax (91) 3945027; e-mail secretaria@rsme.es; internet www.rsme.es; f. 1911; 1,500 mems; Pres. ANTONIO CAMPILLO LÓPEZ; Sec. HENAR HERRERO SANZ; publs *La Gaceta* (3 a year), *Revista Matemática Iberoamericana* (4 a year).

Physical Sciences

Asociación Nacional de Químicos de España (Spanish National Association of Chemists): Calle Lagasca 27, 28001 Madrid; tel. (91) 4310703; fax (91) 5765279; e-mail anquejg@mail.ddnet.es; internet www.anque .es; f. 1945; 10,000 mems; mem. of the int. Fed. of Mediterranean Asscns and of the European Fed. of Chemical Engineering; Pres. BALDOMERO LÓPEZ PÉREZ; Sec. IGNACIO RAMÍREZ CUESTA; publ. *Química e Industria* (12 a year).

Real Sociedad Española de Física (Royal Spanish Society of Physics): Facultad de Ciencias Físicas, Universidad Complutense, Ciudad Universitaria, s/n, 28040 Madrid; tel. (91) 3944350; fax (91) 3944362; e-mail rsef@ fis.ucm.es; internet www.rsef.org; f. 1903; 800 mems; Pres. Prof. MARÍA ROSARIO HERAS CELEMÍN; Sec.-Gen. Prof. CARMEN MARÍA PEREÑA FERNÁNDEZ; publs *Revista Iberoamericana de Física* (1 a year), *Revista Española de Física* (4 a year).

Real Sociedad Española de Química (Royal Spanish Society of Chemistry): Facultad de Ciencias Químicas, Universidad Complutense, Ciudad Universitaria, s/n, 28040 Madrid; tel. (91) 3944361; fax (91) 5433879; e-mail secretario.general@rseq.org; internet www.rseq.org; f. 1903; 3,578 mems; Pres. Prof. NAZARIO MARTÍN LEÓN; Sec.-Gen. JESÚS JIMÉNEZ BARBERO; publ. *Anales* (4 a year).

Sociedad Española de Astronomía (Spanish Astronomical Society): Universitat de Barcelona, Facultad de Física, Avda Martí Franquès 1, 08028 Barcelona; tel. (93) 4034986; fax (93) 4021133; e-mail secretaria@sea.am.ub.es; internet www .sea-astronomia.es; f. 1991; lectures, courses, etc.; 500 mems; library of 3,000 vols; Pres. EMILIO ALFARO; Sec. RUTH CARBALLO FIDALGO.

Sociedad Geológica de España (Geological Society of Spain): Facultad de Ciencias, Universidad de Salamanca, Plaza de la Merced, s/n, 37008 Salamanca; tel. (923) 294752; e-mail sge@usal.es; internet www .sociedadgeologica.es; f. 1985; 1,000 mems; Pres. ANA CRESPO BLANC SORANDO; Sec. JOSÉ EUGENIO ORTIZ MENÉNDEZ; Treas. GABRIEL GUTIÉRREZ-ALONSO; publs *Geogaceta* (2 a year), *Geo-Temas* (irregular), *Revista* (4 a year).

RELIGION, SOCIOLOGY AND ANTHROPOLOGY

Federación Española de Religiosos de Enseñanza—Centres Catholiques (FERE-CECA)/Escuelas Católicas (Spanish Federation of Religious Institutions in Education—Catholic Centres): Calle

Hacienda de Pavones 5, 1°, 28030 Madrid; tel. (91) 3288000; fax (91) 3288001; e-mail escuelascatolicas@escuelascatolicas.es; internet www.escuelascatolicas.es; f. 1957 as Federación Española de Religiosos de Enseñanza (FERE); groups all the centres of elementary, secondary and higher education of the Catholic Church; 2,635 centres; library of 7,000 vols, 150 periodicals; Pres. INMACULADA TUSET GARÍN; Sec.-Gen. JUAN ANTONIO OJEDA ORTIZ; publs *Educadores* (Teachers' Review, 4 a year), *Revista EC* (6 a year).

Institución 'Fernando el Católico', Excma Diputación Provincial de Zaragoza (Institution of Ferdinando the Catholic): Plaza de España 2, 50071 Zaragoza; tel. (976) 288878; fax (976) 288869; e-mail ifc@dpz.es; internet www.ifc.dpz.es; f. 1943 as Institución 'Fernando el Católico'; present name adopted 2006; part of CSIC; sections: linguistics and literature, Aragonese art, history, geography and ecology, economic and social studies, law, music for young people, ancient music; Council of 12 representing the univ. and municipality; library of 83,000 vols; Pres. JAVIER LAMBÁN MONTAÑÉS; Sec. JESÚS COLÁS TENAS; publs *Archivo de Filología Aragonesa, Caesaraugusta: Revista de Arqueología, Prehistoria e Historia Antigua, Ciencia Forense: Revista Aragonesa de Medicina Legal, Cuadernos de Aragón, Emblemata, IVS FVGIT: Revista de Estudios Histórico-Jurídicos de la Corona de Aragón, Nassarre: Revista Aragonesa de Musicología, Palaeohispanica: Revista sobre Lenguas y Culturas de la Hispania Antigua, Poesía en el Campus: Editado por Ibercaja y la Universidad de Zaragoza, Revista de Derecho Civil Aragonés, Revista de Historia 'Jerónimo Zurita', Seminario de Arte Aragonés*.

Real Instituto de Estudios Asturianos (Institute of Asturian Studies): Palacio Conde de Toreno, Plaza Porlier 9, 1°, 33003 Oviedo; tel. (98) 4182801; fax (98) 4283391; e-mail ridea@asturias.org; internet ridea.org; f. 1946; 50 mems, 4 hon. mems, 77 corresp. mems; library of 27,000 vols, 250 periodicals; Asturian studies (literature, history, folklore, language); historical archive, archive of 3,000 photographs; Dir JUAN IGNACIO RUIZ DE LA PEÑA SOLAR; Sec. OLGA CASARES ABELLA; publ. *Boletín de Ciencias de la Naturaleza* (1 a year).

Real Sociedad Bascongada de los Amigos del País (Royal Society of Friends of the Basque Country): Calle General Alava 5, 01005 Vitoria-Gasteiz; tel. (945) 147770; fax (945) 155015; e-mail info@bascongada.org; internet www.bascongada.org; f. 1764, the first of such societies in Spain; 25 mems; organized Museo de San Telmo and Museo Naval, also Conservatorio Municipal de Música; f. Editorial Guipuzcoana de Ediciones y Publicaciones, Books in Basque and Biblioteca Vascongada de los Amigos del País, collaborated in archaeological exploration of the prehistoric cave dwellings of the district; the Guipuzcoan Office of the Consejo Superior de Investigaciones Científicas, Madrid (see below); Pres. MIREN SÁNCHEZ ERAUSKIN; Sec. JOSÉ IGNACIO VEGAS; publs *Anuario de Eusko-Folklore Aranzadiana Orria, Boletín* (4 a year), *Boletín de Estudios Históricos sobre San Sebastián* (1 a year), *Boletín de la Cofradía Vasca de Gastronomía, Egan* (literary supplement), *Munibe* (natural sciences supplement).

TECHNOLOGY

Col·legi Oficial d'Enginyers Industrials de Catalunya: Via Laietana 39, 08003 Barcelona; tel. (93) 5572049; fax (93) 3100681; e-mail atencioeic@eic.cat; internet www.eic.cat; f. 1950; 8,000 mems; asscn of engineering graduates of the Schools of Industrial Engineers of Spain; library of 22,000 vols; Dean JOAN VALLVÉ I RIBERA; Sec. JOSEP M. ROVIRA I RAGUÉ; publs *Agenda Dels Enginyers* (24 a year), *Full Dels Enginyers* (12 a year).

Instituto de la Ingeniería de España (Spanish Institute of Engineering): Calle General Arrando 38, 28010 Madrid; tel. (91) 3197417; fax (91) 3103380; e-mail iie@iies.es; internet www.iies.es; f. 1905; 100,000 mems; comprises 10 asscns of higher engineers and the *Aula de Ingeniería* (training centre), offering courses, seminars, etc. for postgraduate students; Pres. MANUEL ACERO GARCÍA; Gen. Sec. ASIS MARTÍN-OAR FERNÁNDEZ DE HEREDIA.

Sociedad Española de Cerámica y Vidrio (Spanish Ceramic and Glass Society): Calle Kelsen 5, 28049 Madrid; tel. (91) 7357860; fax (91) 7355843; e-mail secv@icv.csic.es; internet www.secv.es; f. 1960; promotes technical progress in ceramic and glass work and disseminates info. about manufacture and devts within the field; 750 mems; library of 500 vols; Pres. JORGE J. BAKALI BAKALI; Sec.-Gen. EMILIO CRIADO; publ. *Boletín* (6 a year).

Research Institutes

GENERAL

Consejo Superior de Investigaciones Científicas (CSIC) (Council for Scientific Research): Serrano 117, 28006 Madrid; tel. (91) 5681400; fax (91) 4113077; internet www.csic.es; f. 1940; largest multidisciplinary research body in Spain to serve cultural and technological devt; acts as a creative instrument and forum for Spanish science; has 100 research centres distributed throughout Spain, incl. institutes directly governed by CSIC, those operated jtly by CSIC and univs, and others in association with regional govt or other instns; maintains office for transfer of technology in cooperation with Spanish supervisory agencies for technological devt; journals published by the institutes, scientific and cultural dissemination, scientific publishing house, technical facilities and installations; library of 100,000 vols; Pres. RAFAEL RODRIGO MONTERO; Sec.-Gen. EUSEBIO CARLOS JIMÉNEZ ARROYO; publ. *Arbor* (12 a year).

Attached Research Institutes in the Field of Humanities and Social Sciences:

Centro de Ciencias Humanas y Sociales (Centre for Humanities and Social Sciences): Calle Albasanz 26–28, 28037 Madrid; tel. (91) 6022300; fax (91) 6022971; e-mail director.cchs@csic.es; internet www.cchs.csic.es; f. 2006; research on field of humanities and social sciences; library: 1m. vols; Dir EDUARDO MANZANO MORENO; publs *Al-Qantara* (2 a year), *Anales Cervantinos* (1 a year), *Archivo Español de Arqueología* (1 a year), *Archivo Español de Arte* (4 a year), *Asclepio* (2 a year), *Emerita* (2 a year), *Estudios Geográficos* (2 a year), *Gladius* (1 a year), *Hispania* (3 a year), *Hispania Sacra* (2 a year), *Isegoría* (2 a year), *Revista de Dialectología y Tradiciones Populares* (2 a year, Spanish), *Revista de Filología Española* (2 a year), *Revista de Indias* (3 a year), *Revista de Literatura* (2 a year), *Revista Española de Documentación Científica* (4 a year), *Sefarad* (2 a year), *Trabajos de Prehistoria* (1 a year).

Escuela de Estudios Árabes (School of Arabic Studies): Cuesta del Chapiz 22, 18010 Granada; tel. (958) 222290; fax (958) 224754; e-mail director.eeh@csic.es; internet www.eea.csic.es; Dir JUAN BRACERS CASTILLA.

Escuela de Estudios Hispano Americanos (School of Hispanic-American Studies): Calle Alfonso XII 16, 41002 Seville; tel. (95) 4501120; fax (95) 4500954; e-mail director.eeha@csic.es; internet www.eeha.csic.es; Dir SALVADOR BERNABÉU ALBERT; publ. *Anuario de Estudios Americanos* (2 a year).

Escuela Española de Historia y Arqueología en Roma (CSIC) (Spanish School of History and Archeology in Rome): Via di Torre Argentina 18, 00186 Rome, Italy; tel. (06) 68100021; fax (06) 68309047; e-mail escuela@csic.it; internet www.eehar.csic.es; f. 1910; library of 22,000 vols; Dir FERNANDO GARCÍA SANZ.

Institución Milá y Fontanals: Calle Egipciaques 15, 08001 Barcelona; tel. (93) 4423489; fax (93) 4430071; e-mail director.imf@csic.es; internet www.imf.csic.es; f. 1968; research activities: anthropology, archaeology, medieval studies, ethnography, history of science, musicology and sociology; Dir LUIS CALVO CALVO; library of 60,000 monographs, 2,250 periodicals; publs *Anuario de Estudios Medievales* (2 a year), *Anuario Musical* (12 a year).

Institute of Public Goods and Policies: c/o Albasanz 26–28, 3D, 28037 Madrid; tel. (91) 6023000; fax (91) 5218103; e-mail direccion.ipp@csic.es; internet www.ipp.csic.es; f. 2007; advances knowledge in domain of relationship between the society, the market and the state; Dir LUIS SANZ MENÉNDEZ; Deputy Dir Prof. PABLO CAMPOS; publs *Energy, Energy Policy, Environmental and Resource Economics, Journal of the American Society for Information Science and Technology, Party Politics, Politics & Society, Research Polocy, Scientometrics, West European Politics*.

Instituto de Análisis Económico (Institute of Economic Analysis): UniversitatAutònoma, 08193 Bellaterra (Barcelona); tel. (93) 5806612; fax (93) 5801452; e-mail director.iae@csic.es; internet www.iae.csic.es; f. 1985; econometrics; experimental economics; game theory; industrial org. and regulation; growth and devt; macroeconomics; monetary economics; political economics and public economics; Dir Dr CLARA PONSATI OBIOLS.

Instituto de Economía, Geografía y Demografía: Calle Albasanz 26–28, 28037 Madrid; tel. (91) 6022674; fax (91) 6022971; e-mail director.ieg@csic.es; internet www.cchs.csic.es; f. 1986; Dir Prof. RICARDO MENDEZ GUITÉRREZ DEL VALLE; publ. *Estudios Geográficos* (4 a year).

Instituto de Estudios Documentales sobre Ciencia y Tecnología: Calle Albasanz 26–28, 28037 Madrid; tel. (91) 6022883; fax (91) 3045710; e-mail director.cindoc@csic.es; internet www.cindoc.csic.es; f. 1992, as Centro de Información y Documentación Científica (CINDOC), following merger between Instituto de Información y Documentación en Ciencia y Tecnología (ICYT) and Instituto de Información y Documentación en Ciencias Sociales y Humanidades (ISOC); mainly devoted to the analysis of science, technology and knowledge transfer; Dir Dr LUIS PLAZA; publ. *Revista Española de Documentación Científica* (4 a year).

Instituto de Estudios Gallegos 'Padre Sarmiento': San Roque 2, 15704 Santiago de Compostela (La Coruña); tel. (981) 540220; fax (981) 540222; e-mail director.iegps@csic.es; internet www.iegps.csic.es;

f. 1943; library of 35,000 vols; Dir Prof. EDUARDO PARDO DE GUEVARA Y VALDÉS; publs *Cuadernos de Estudios Gallegos* (1 a year), *Serie de 'Anejos' de Cuadernos de Estudios Gallegos* (1 a year).

Instituto de Estudios Sociales Avanzados: Calle Campo Santo de los Mártires 7, 14004 Córdoba; tel. (957) 760625; fax (957) 760153; e-mail contacto@iesa.csic.es; internet www.iesa.csic.es; Dir EDUARDO MOYANO ESTRADA; publ. *Revista Internacional de Sociología* (3 a year).

Instituto de Filosofía (Institute of Philosophy): Calle Pinar 25, 28006 Madrid; tel. (91) 4117005; fax (91) 5645252; e-mail director.ifs@csic.es; internet www.ifs.csic.es; library of 50,000 vols; Dir JOSÉ MARÍA GONZÁLEZ GARCÍA; publs *Isegoria* (2 a year), *SORITES: Electronic Magazine of Analytical Philosophy* (online).

Instituto de Historia (Institute for History): Calle Albasanz 26–28, 28037 Madrid; tel. (91) 6022300; fax (91) 6022971; e-mail mercedes.aguilar@cchs.csic.es; internet www.ih.csic.es; Dir Dr LEONCIO LÓPEZ-OCÓN CABRERA; publs *Archivo Español de Arqueología* (1 a year), *Archivo Español de Arte* (4 a year), *Asclepio* (2 a year), *Gladius* (1 a year), *Hispania* (3 a year), *Hispania Sacra* (2 a year), *Revista de Indias* (3 a year), *Trabajos de Prehistoria* (2 a year).

Instituto de Historia de la Ciencia y Documentación López Piñero: Palacio Cerveró, Plaza Cisneros 4, 46003 Valencia; tel. (96) 3926229; fax (96) 3919691; internet www.ihmc.uv-csic.es; Dir JOSÉ ANTONIO DÍAZ ROJO.

Instituto de Lengua, Literatura y Antropología: Calle Albasanz 26–28, 28037 Madrid; tel. (91) 6022300; fax (91) 3692971; e-mail director.ile@csic.es; internet www.cchs.csic.es; f. 2007; Dir VIOLETA DEMONTE BARRETO; publs *Anales Cervantinos* (1 a year), *Revista de Dialectología y Tradiciones Populares* (2 a year), *Revista de Filología Española* (2 a year), *Revista de Literatura* (2 a year).

Instituto de Lenguas y Culturas del Mediterráneo y Oriente Próximo: Calle Albasanz 26–28, 28037 Madrid; tel. (91) 6022430; fax (91) 6022970; e-mail maite .ortega@cchs.csic.es; internet www.ilc.csic .es; f. 1984 as Instituto de Filología, integrated within Centro de Ciencias Humanas y Sociales (CCHS) 2008; studies and edns of texts in ancient languages: Arabic, Hebrew, MSS in oriental languages (Arabic, Coptic, Greek, Hebrew and Latin); library: 1m. vols; Research Prof. Dr MARÍA TERESA ORTEGA MONASTERIO; publs *Al-Qantara* (2 a year), *Emerita* (2 a year), *Sefarad* (2 a year).

Instituto Histórico Hoffmeyer: Avda de la Constitución 114, 10400 Jaraiz de la Vera (Cáceres); tel. (927) 170646; fax (927) 170645; e-mail hoffmeyer@iam.csic.es; internet www.hoffmeyer.iam.csic.es; Dir PEDRO MATEOS CRUZ; publ. *Gladius* (1 a year).

Attached Research Institutes in the Field of Biology and Biomedicine:

Centro Andaluz de Biología del Desarrollo: CSIC-Universidad Pablo de Olavide, Carretera de Utrera, Km 1, 41013 Seville; tel. (954) 349399; fax (954) 349376; internet www.cabd.es; Dir EDUARDO SANTERO.

Centro Biológica Molecular Severo Ochoa: Calle Nicolás Cabrera 1, Campus de la Universidad Autónoma, 28049 Madrid; tel. (91) 1964401; fax (91) 1964420; e-mail institucional@cbm.uam

.es; internet www.cbm.uam.es; Dir MANUEL FRESNO ESCUDERO.

Centro de Investigación y Desarrollo: Carrer de Jordi Girona 18–26, 08034 Barcelona; tel. (93) 4006100; fax (93) 2045904; e-mail director@cid.csic.es; internet www.cid.csic.es; f. 1967; library of 30,000 vols; Dir ANGEL MESSEGUER PEYPOCH.

Centro de Investigaciones Biológicas: Ramiro de Maeztu 9, 28040 Madrid; tel. (91) 8373112; fax (91) 5360432; e-mail vlarraga@cib.csic.es; internet www.cib.csic .es; Dir VICENTE LARRAGA RODRÍGUEZ DE VERA.

Centro de Investigaciones Científicas Isla de la Cartuja: Avda Americo Vespucio 49, Isla de la Cartuja, 41092 Seville; tel. (95) 4489501; fax (95) 4460165; e-mail ciccartuja@ciccartuja.es; internet www .ciccartuja.es; Dir MIGUEL ANGEL DE LA ROSA ACOSTA.

Centro Nacional de Biotecnología: UAM, Campus del Cantoblanco, 28049 Cantoblanco (Madrid); tel. (91) 5854500; fax (91) 5854506; e-mail director.cnb@csic .es; internet www.cnb.uam.es; Dir JOSÉ MARÍA VALPUESTA.

Instituto Biomedicina de Valencia: Jaime Roig 11, 46010 Valencia; tel. (96) 3391760; fax (96) 3690800; e-mail director .ibv@csic.es; internet www.ibv.csic.es; f. 1998; research into structural biology (X-ray crystallography), human molecular genetics, molecular/cell biology related to human disease, venomics, inborn errors of urea cycle, signalling cascades related to AMP kinase and to esteroids, molecular biology, genetics and signalling in type 2 diabetes; Dir Prof. VICENTE RUBIO ZAMORA.

Instituto Cajal: Avda Dr Arce 37, 28002 Madrid; tel. (91) 5854750; fax (91) 5854754; e-mail director.incr@csic.es; internet www.cajal.csic.es; f. 1906; neurobiological research; library of 36,000 vols; Dir IGNACIO TORRES ALEMÁN.

Instituto de Biología Molecular 'Eladio Viñuela': c/o Nicolás Cabrera 1, 28049 Cantoblanco (Madrid); tel. (91) 1964401; fax (91) 1964420; e-mail director.ibm@csic .es; internet www.uam.es/institutos/ bmolecular; f. 1975; Dir CÉSAR DE HARO CASTELLA.

Instituto de Biología Molecular de Barcelona: Calle Baldiri Reixac 10–12, 08028 Barcelona; tel. (93) 4034668; fax (93) 4034979; e-mail lcabmc@ibmb.csic.es; internet www.ibmb.csic.es; Dir MARTÍ ALDEA.

Instituto de Biología Molecular y Celular de Plantas 'Eduardo Primo Yúfera': Ingeniero Fausto Elio s/n, 46022 Valencia; tel. (96) 3877856; fax (96) 3877859; e-mail director.ibmcp@csic.es; internet www.ibmcp.upv.es; f. 1994; Dir Prof. VICENTE PALLÁS BENET.

Instituto de Biología Molecular y Celular del Cáncer (CSIC-USAL): Campus Miguel de Unamuno, Universidad de Salamanca, 37007 Salamanca; tel. (923) 294720; fax (923) 294743; e-mail cicancer@ usal.es; internet www.cicancer.org; f. 1997; basic, clinical and translational cancer research; Dir Dr EUGENIO SANTOS.

Instituto de Biología y Genética Molecular: Calle Sanz y Fores, s/n, esq. Real de Burgos, 47003 Valladolid; tel. (983) 184801; fax (983) 184800; e-mail director .ibgm@csic.es; internet www.ibgm.med .uva.es; f. 1998; Dir JOSÉ RAMÓN LÓPEZ LÓPEZ.

Instituto de Bioquímica Vegetal y Fotosíntesis: Avda Americo Vespucio s/

n, Isla de la Cartuja, 41092 Seville; tel. (95) 4489506; fax (95) 4460065; e-mail director@ibvf.csic.es; internet www.ibvf .csic.es; Dir LUIS CARLOS ROMERO GONZÁLEZ.

Instituto de Farmacología y Toxicología: CSIC-Universidad Complutense, Faculted de Medicina, Ciudad Universitaria, 28040 Madrid; tel. (91) 3941469; fax (91) 3941470; e-mail director.ift@csic.es; internet www.csic.es; Dir JUAN TAMARGO MENÉNDEZ.

Instituto de Investigaciones Biomédicas 'Alberto Sols': Calle Arturo Duperier 4, 28029 Madrid; tel. (91) 5854400; fax (91) 5854401; e-mail info@iib.csic.es; internet www.iib.uam.es; f. 1973; Dir Dr LISARDO BOSCÁ GOMAR.

Instituto de Investigaciones Biomédicas de Barcelona: Calle Roselló 161, 6–7°, 08036 Barcelona; tel. (93) 3638300; fax (93) 3638301; e-mail direccion.iibb@csic .es; internet www.iibb.csic.es; f. 1995; multidisciplinary biomedical research in biochemistry, cell biology, neurosciences, pathophysiology with spec. emphasis on translational research; Dir Dr CRISTINA SUÑOL ESQUIROL.

Instituto de Microbiología Bioquímica: Campus Miguel de Unamuno, Universidad de Salamanca, Edif. Departmental, Avda Campo Charro s/n, 37007 Salamanca; tel. (923) 294462; fax (923) 224876; e-mail directorimb@usal.csic.es; internet www.imb.usal-csic.es; Dir Dr DR. ANGEL DURÁN BRAVO.

Instituto de Neurociencias: Apdo de Correos 18, 03550 San Juan (Alicante); tel. (96) 5233700; fax (96) 5919561; e-mail in@umh.es; internet in.umh.es; Dir JUAN LERMA GÓMEZ.

Instituto de Parasitología y Biomedicina 'López Neyra': Parque Tecnológico de Ciencias de la Salud, Avda del Conocimiento s/n, 18100 Armilla (Granada); tel. (95) 8181621; fax (95) 8181632; e-mail director.ipbln@csic.es; internet www.ipb .csic.es; Dir ALFREDO BERZAL HERRANZ.

Unidad de Biofísica: Apdo 644, 48080 Bilbao; tel. (94) 6012625; fax (94) 6013360; e-mail biofisica@lg.ehu.es; internet www .unidaddebiofisica.org; f. 1999; joint centre of the CSIC and the Univ. of the Basque Country; basic research and graduate teaching in biophysics; Dir FÉLIX M. GOÑI.

Attached Research Institutes in the Field of Natural Resources:

Centro de Ciencias Medioambientales: Calle Serrano 115 bis, 28006 Madrid; tel. (91) 7452500; fax (91) 5640800; e-mail director.ccma@csic.es; internet www.ccma.csic.es; Dir ALBERTO FERERES CASTIEL.

Centro de Edafología y Biología Aplicada del Segura: Campus Universitario de Espinardo, 30100 Murcia; tel. (968) 396200; fax (968) 396213; e-mail director .cebas@csic.es; internet www.cebas.csic.es; Dir Dr FRANCISCO TOMÁS BARBERÁN.

Centro de Estudios Avanzados de Blanes: Cala St Francesc 14, 17300 Blanes (Gerona); tel. (972) 336101; fax (972) 337806; e-mail director.ceab@csic.es; internet www.ceab.csic.es; Dir DANIEL MARTÍN SINTES.

Centro de Investigaciones sobre Desertificación: Camí de la Marjal s/n, 46470 Albal (Valencia); tel. (96) 1220540; fax (96) 1270967; e-mail cide@uv.es; internet www.uv.es/cide; f. 1996; Dir Dr PATRICIO GARCÍA-FAYOS.

Estación Biológica de Doñana: Apdo 1056, 41013 Seville; tel. (95) 4232340; fax (95) 4621125; e-mail director.ebd@csic.es; internet www.ebd.csic.es; f. 1964; wetland ecology, evolutionary and molecular ecology, ecological synthesis, conservation biology (incl. biological invasions) and plant–animal interactions; library of 10,000 vols; Dir Prof. FERNANDO HIRALDO CANO; Deputy Dir Prof. JUAN JOSE NEGRO BALMASEDA; publ. *Doñana. Acta Vertebrata* (2 a year).

Estación Experimental de Zonas Áridas: Cuetra de Sacramento s/n, La Cañada de San Urbano, 04120 Almería; tel. (950) 281045; fax (950) 277100; e-mail director .eeza@csic.es; internet www.eeza.csic.es; Dir FRANCISCO VALERA HERNÁNDEZ.

Instituto Agroquímica y Tecnología Alimentos: Apdo 73, 46100 Burjassot (Valencia); tel. (96) 3900022; fax (96) 3636301; e-mail info@iata.csic.es; internet www.iata.csic.es; Dir LORENZO ZACARIAS; publ. *Food Science and Technology International* (6 a year).

Instituto Andaluz de Ciencias de la Tierra: CSIC-Universidad de Granada, Facultad de Ciencias, Avda Fuentenueva s/n, 18002 Granada; tel. (958) 243158; fax (958) 243384; e-mail director.iact@csic.es; internet www.iact.csic.es; Dir ALBERTO LÓPEZ GALINDO.

Instituto Botánico de Barcelona: Passeig del Migdia, Parque de Monjuïc, 08038 Barcelona; tel. (93) 2890611; fax (93) 2890614; e-mail biblioteca@ibb.csic.es; internet www.ibb.bcn-csic.es/institut_cas .html; f. 1917; affiliated to the Botanic Garden of Barcelona, Montjuïc Park; library of 11,000 vols, 80,000 herbarium sheets; Man. JOAN LAMBEA CASTRO; Head Librarian KARINA BARROS FERRADÁS; publ. *Collectanea Botanica* (1 a year).

Instituto de Acuicultura de Torre de la Sal: Calle Ribera de Cabanes s/n, Cabanes, 12595 Castellón; tel. (964) 319500; fax (964) 319509; e-mail director .iats@csic.es; internet www.iats.csic.es; Dir JAUME PÉREZ SÁNCHEZ.

Instituto de Ciencias de la Tierra 'Jaime Almera': Calle Lluis Solé Sabarís, s/n, Apdo 30102, 08028 Barcelona; tel. (93) 4095410; fax (93) 4110012; e-mail director .ictja@csic.es; internet www.ija.csic.es; library of 16,500 vols, 1,050 periodicals; Dir MANEL FERNÁNDEZ I ORTIGA.

Instituto de Ciencias del Mar: Passeig Marítim de la Barceloneta 37–49, 08003 Barcelona; tel. (93) 2309500; fax (93) 2309555; e-mail icmdir@icm.csic.es; internet www.icm.csic.es; Dir ALBERT PALANQUES MONTEYS; publ. *Scientia Marina* (4 a year).

Instituto de Ciencias Marinas de Andalucía: Calle República Saharaui 2, Campus Universitario Río San Pedro, 11519 Puerto Real (Cádiz); tel. (956) 832612; fax (956) 834701; e-mail director .icman@csic.es; internet www.csic.es; f. 1955; Dir MARÍA DEL CARMEN SARASQUETE REIRIZ.

Instituto de Geociencias (CSIC-UCM): Facultad de CC. Geológicas, Universidad Complutense, C/ José Antonio Novais, 2, 3ª 28040 Madrid; tel. (91) 3944786; fax (91) 3944808; e-mail biblioteca@igeo.ucm-csic .es; internet www.igeo.ucm-csic.es; f. 2011 by merger of Instituto de Geología Económica with Instituto de Astronomía y Geodesia; Dir ROSARIO LUNAR HERNÁNDEZ; Librarian LAURA DONADEO NAVALÓN; publs *Estudios Geológicos* (online (estudiosgeol.-revistas.csic.es/index.php/estudiosgeol)),

Journal of Iberian Geology (online (www.ucm.es/info/estratig/journal.htm)).

Instituto de Investigación en Recursos Cinegéticos: Ronda de Toledo s/n, 13071 Ciudad Real; tel. (926) 295450; fax (926) 295451; e-mail irec@irec.uclm.es; internet www.uclm.es/irec; Dir JAVIER VIÑUELA MADURA.

Instituto de Investigaciones Marinas: Calle Eduardo Cabello, 36208 Vigo (Pontevedra); tel. (986) 231930; fax (986) 292762; e-mail direccion@iim.csic.es; internet www .iim.csic.es; f. 1951 as Instituto de Investigaciones Pesqueras de Barcelona, present name adopted 1986; Dir AIDA FERNÁNDEZ RÍOS.

Instituto de Productos Naturales y Agrobiología: Astrofísico Francisco Sánchez 3, 38206 La Laguna (Tenerife); tel. (922) 256847; fax (922) 260135; e-mail director.ipna@csic.es; internet www.ipna .csic.es; f. 1956 as Centro de Edafología y Biología Aplicada de Tenerife, present name 1990; agrobiology, ecology, organic chemistry, volcanology; Dir Dr COSME GARCÍA FRANCISCO.

Instituto de Recursos Naturales y Agrobiología de Salamanca: Apdo 257, 37071 Salamanca; Cordel de Merinas 40–52, 37008 Salamanca; tel. (923) 219606; fax (923) 219609; e-mail secretaria@irnasa.csic .es; internet www.csic.es; f. 1957 as Centro de Edafología y Biología Aplicada de Salamanca, present name 1988; scientific research on agriculture and natural resources; incl. sustainable devt of agri-forest systems, animal pathology, environmental degradation and recovery, and plant abiotic stress; Dir Dr RAFAEL MARTÍNEZ-CARRASCO TABUENCA.

Instituto de Recursos Naturales y Agrobiología de Sevilla: Apdo 1052, Estafeta-Puerto, 41080 Seville; Avda Reina Mercedes 10, 41012 Seville; tel. (954) 624711; fax (954) 624002; e-mail director .irnas@csic.es; internet www.irnase.csic.es; Dir LUIS CLEMENTE SALAS.

Instituto Mediterraneo de Estudios Avanzados: Calle Miquel Marquès 21, 07190 Esporles, Mallorca; tel. (971) 611716; fax (971) 611761; e-mail director .imdea@csic.es; internet www.imedea .uib-csic.es; Dir JOAQUÍN TINTORÉ SUBIRANA.

Instituto Pirenaico de Ecología: Avda Montañana 1005, 50059 Zaragoza; tel. (976) 716034; fax (976) 716019; e-mail director.ipe@csic.es; internet www.ipe.csic .es; f. 1983; Dir BLAS LORENZO VALERO GARCÉS; publ. *Pirineos* (1 a year).

Museo Nacional de Ciencias Naturales: see under Museums and Art Galleries.

Real Jardín Botánico: see under Museums and Art Galleries.

Attached Research Institutes in the Field of Agricultural Sciences:

Instituto de Ganadería de Montaña: Finca Marzanas s/n, 24346 Grulleros, (León); tel. (987) 317064; fax (987) 317161; e-mail director.eae@csic.es; internet www.csic.es; Dir Dr FRANCISCO JAVIER GIRÁLDEZ GARCÍA.

Estación Experimental de Aula Dei: Avda Montañana 1005, 50059 Zaragoza; tel. (976) 716100; fax (976) 716145; e-mail director.eead@csic.es; internet www.eead .csic.es; f. 1944; library of 9,802 vols of book titles, 190,000 e-books, 1,804 journals, 13,000 electronic journals; Dir JESÚS VAL FALCÓN.

Estación Experimental del Zaidín: Apdo 419, 18008 Granada; Calle Professor

Albareda 1, 18008 Granada; tel. (958) 181600; fax (958) 129600; e-mail director .eez@csic.es; internet www.eez.csic.es; library of 4,000 vols, 300 periodicals; Dir NICOLÁS TORO GARCÍA.

Estación Experimental 'La Mayora': 29760 Algarrobo-Costa, (Málaga); tel. (952) 548990; fax (952) 552677; e-mail director.eelm@csic.es; internet www.eelm .csic.es; f. 1968; agronomy, horticulture, pomology, virology, mycology, plant tissue culture; library of 3,000 vols; Dir ENRIQUE MORIONES ALONSO.

Instituto de Agricultura Sostenible: Alameda del Obispo, s/n, Apdo 4084, 14080 Córdoba; tel. (957) 499200; fax (957) 499252; e-mail gerente.ias@csic.es; internet www.ias.csic.es; Dir PABLO J. ZARCO TEJADAL.

Instituto de Agrobiotecnología: Universidad Pública de Navarra, Campus de Arrosadia, 31192 Navarra; tel. (948) 168000; fax (948) 232191; e-mail info@ agrobiotechnologia.es; internet www .agrobiotechnologia.es; f. 1999 as Instituto de Agrobiotecnología y Recursos Naturales, present name 2004; Dir PEDRO APARICIO TEJO.

Instituto de Investigaciones Agrobiológicas de Galicia: Avda de Vigo s/n, Apdo 122, 15780 Santiago de Compostela (La Coruña); tel. (981) 590958; fax (981) 592504; e-mail director.iiag@csic.es; internet www.iiag.csic.es; library of 3,000 vols, 279 periodicals; Dir MARÍA TARSY CARBALLAS FERNÁNDEZ.

Misión Biológica de Galicia: Apdo 28, 36080 Pontevedra; El Palacio, Salcedo, 36143 Pontevedra; tel. (986) 854800; fax (986) 841362; e-mail director.mbg@csic.es; internet www.mbg.csic.es; Dir ROSA ANA MALVAR PINTOS.

Attached Research Institutes in the Field of the Science and Technology of Physics:

Centro de Tecnologías Físicas 'Leonardo Torres Quevedo': Calle Serrano 144, 28006 Madrid; tel. (91) 5618806; fax (91) 4117651; e-mail director.cetef@csic.es; internet www.cetef.csic.es; Dir JUAN ANTONIO GALLEGO JUÁREZ.

Centro Física 'Miguel A. Catalán': Calle Serrano 121, 28006 Madrid; tel. (91) 5616800; fax (91) 5645557; e-mail gerente .cfmac@csic.es; internet www.cfmac.csic .es; Dir FRANCISCO JOSÉ BALTA CALLEJA.

Centro Nacional de Microelectrónica: Campus Universidad Autónoma, 08193 Bellaterra (Barcelona); tel. (93) 5947700; fax (93) 5801496; e-mail info@cnm.es; internet www.cnm.es; f. 1986; research and devt of micro- and nanoelectronics; Dir FRANCISCO SERRA MESTRES.

Centro Técnico de Informática: Calle Pinar 19, 28006 Madrid; tel. (91) 5642963; fax (91) 5616193; e-mail director.cti@csic .es; internet www.cti.csic.es; Dir JOSÉ CARRERO VIVAS.

Instituto de Acústica: Calle Serrano 144, 28006 Madrid; tel. (91) 5618806; fax (91) 4117651; e-mail director.ia@csic.es; internet www.ia.csic.es; Dir Dr CARLOS RANZ GUERRA; publs *ACUSTICA* (12 a year), *Ferroelectrics* (12 a year), *IEEE Transactions on Ultrasonics, Ferroelectrics and Frequency Control* (12 a year), *Journal of Sound and Vibration* (12 a year), *Journal of the Acoustical Society of America, JASA* (12 a year), *Ultrasonics* (12 a year).

Instituto de Astrofísica de Andalucía: Apdo 3004, 18080 Granada; Glorieta de la Astronomía s/n, 18008 Granada; tel. (958) 121311; fax (958) 814530; e-mail director

.iaa@csic.es; internet www.iaa.es/index .html; Dir MATILDE FERNÁNDEZ HERNÁNDEZ.

Instituto de Automática Industrial: Carretera de Campo Real, Km 0.200, 28500 Arganda del Rey (Madrid); tel. (91) 8711900; fax (91) 8717050; e-mail director .iai@csic.es; internet www.iai.csic.es; Dir Dr MANUEL ANGEL ARMADA RODRÍGUEZ (acting).

Instituto de Estructura de la Materia: Calle Serrano 121, 28006 Madrid; tel. (91) 5616800; fax (91) 5645557; e-mail director .iem@csic.es; internet www.iem.csic.es; f. 1976; Dir Dr GUILLERMO ANTONIO MENA MARUGÁN.

Instituto de Física Aplicada: Calle Serrano 144, 28006 Madrid; tel. (91) 5618806; fax (91) 4117651; e-mail director .ifa@csic.es; internet www.ifa.csic.es; Dir FRANCISCO JAVIER GUTIÉRREZ MONREAL.

Instituto de Física Corpuscular: Edificio Institutos de Investigación, Apdo 22085, 46071 Valencia; tel. (96) 3543473; fax (96) 3543488; e-mail director.ific@csic .es; internet ific.uv.es; Dir FRANCISCO J. BOTELLA OLCINA.

Instituto de Física de Cantabria: Edificio Juan Jorda, Avda de los Castros s/n, 39005 Santander; tel. (94) 2201459; fax (94) 2200935; e-mail info@ifca.unican.es; internet www.ifca.es; Dir FRANCISCO MATORRAS.

Instituto de Física Fundamental: Calle Serrano 113–123, 28006 Madrid; tel. (91) 5616800; fax (91) 5854894; e-mail director .iff@csic.es; internet www.iff.csic.es; f. 1992, present name 2009; scientific research in basic physics: theoretical physics of molecules, cluster and extended media, quantum information, dark energy, probabilistic logical inference, physical modelling and entropy, radiation–matter interactions; Dir Dr GERARDO DELGADO BARRIO.

Instituto de Investigación de Inteligencia Artificial: Campus UAB, 08193 Bellaterra Barcelona; tel. (93) 5809570; fax (93) 5809661; e-mail director.iiia@csic.es; internet www.iiia.csic.es; f. 1991; research and devt in Artificial Intelligence (multiagent systems, machine learning, case-based reasoning, data privacy, logic foundations of ai, automated reasoning, search, constraints satisfaction; models of trust and reputation, negotiation algorithms, autonomous and developmental robotics); library of 3,000 vols; Dir Prof. RAMON LÓPEZ DE MÁNTARAS; publ. *Transactions on Data Privacy* (online (www.tdp.cat)).

Instituto de Microelectrónica de Barcelona: Universidad Autónoma, 08193 Cerdanyola del Valles, (Barcelona); tel. (93) 5947700; fax (93) 5801496; e-mail director.imb-cnm@csic.es; internet www .imb-cnm.csic.es; Dir Prof. EMILIO LORA-TAMAYO.

Instituto de Microelectrónica de Madrid: Calle Isaac Newton 8, Tres Cantos, 28760 Madrid; tel. (91) 8060700; fax (91) 8060701; e-mail director .imm-cnm@csic.es; internet www.imm-cnm .csic.es; Dir Prof. LUIS GONZÁLEZ SOTOS.

Instituto de Microelectrónica de Sevilla: Calle Américo Vespucio s/n, 41092 Seville; tel. (95) 4466666; fax (95) 4466690; e-mail director.ims-cnm@csic.es; internet www.imse-cnm.csic.es; f. 1996; Dir Prof. JOSÉ LUIS HUERTAS DÍAZ.

Instituto de Óptica 'Daza de Valdés': Calle Serrano 121, 28006 Madrid; tel. (91) 5616800; fax (91) 5645557; e-mail director .io@csic.es; internet www.io.csic.es; f. 1946; research in visual optics, biophotonics,

image science, non-linear dynamics, fibre optics, nanophotonics, plasmonics, photonics with high energy ions, photonics and nanostructures and ultrafast science; Dir JAVIER SOLÍS CÉSPEDES.

Instituto de Robótica e Informática Industrial: Calle Llorens i Artiges 4–6, 2°, Parc Tecnològic de Barcelona, 08028 Barcelona; tel. (93) 4015751; fax (93) 4015750; e-mail admin-iri@iri.upc.edu; internet www.iri.upc.es; Dir ALBERTO SANFELIU.

Observatorio Física Cósmica de l'Ebro: Horta Alta 38, Apdo 10, 43520 Roquetas (Tarragona); tel. (977) 500511; fax (977) 504660; e-mail biblioteca@ obsebre.es; internet www.obsebre.es; f. 1904; 4 sections: geomagnetism; ionosphere; seismology; meteorology, climate and solar activity; library of 50,000 vols, 2,100 periodicals; Dir Dr JUAN JOSÉ CURTO.

Attached Research Institutes in the Field of Materials Science and Technology:

Centro de Física de Materiales: P. Manuel de Lardizabal 5, 20018 Donostia, San Sebastián; tel. (94) 3018000; fax (94) 3015800; e-mail wapetalap@sq.ehu.es; internet cfm.ehu.es; Dir Prof. JUAN COLMENERO DE LEÓN.

Centro Nacional de Investigaciones Metalúrgicas: Avda Gregorio del Amo 8, 28040 Madrid; tel. (91) 5538900; fax (91) 5347425; e-mail director.cenim@csic.es; internet www.cenim.csic.es; f. 1964; metallurgical research, steel research, new materials, composites, recycling of metals; library of 20,000 vols; Dir MANUEL CARSÍ CEBRIÁN; publ. *Revista de Metalurgia* (6 a year).

Instituto de Cerámica y Vidrio: Campus de UAM, 28049 Madrid; tel. (91) 7355840; fax (91) 7355843; e-mail director .icv@csic.es; internet www.icv.csic.es; Dir Dr JUAN E. IGLESIAS PÉREZ.

Instituto de Ciencia de Materiales de Aragón, CSIC—Universidad de Zaragoza: Facultad San Ciencias, CSIC—Universidad de Zaragoza, Pl. de San Francisco s/n, 50009 Zaragoza; tel. (97) 6761231; fax (97) 6762453; e-mail director.icma@csic.es; internet www.icma.unizar-csic.es/ webicma; f. 1985; Dir Dr RAMÓN BURRIEL LAHOZ.

Instituto de Ciencia de Materiales de Barcelona: Campus Universidad Autónoma, 08193 Cerdanyola del Valles, (Barcelona); tel. (93) 5801853; fax (93) 5805729; e-mail info@icmab.es; internet www.icmab .es; Dir XAVIER OBRADORS.

Instituto de Ciencia de Materiales de Madrid: Cantoblanco, 28049 Madrid; tel. (91) 3349000; fax (91) 3720623; e-mail director.icmm@csic.es; internet www.icmm .csic.es; f. 1986 by merger of 3 centres: Institute of Materials Physics, Solid State Physics Institute and Mineral Physics-Chemistry Institute; personnel from the Inorganic Chemistry 'Elhuyar' Institute joined the ICMM 1987; attached to the Consejo Superior de Investigaciones Científicas (CSIC) (Spanish Nat. Research Ccl); research in material science, aiming at multidisciplinary character and covering theoretical and experimental, basic and applied aspects; Dir Prof. FEDERICO JESÚS SORIA GALLEGO.

Instituto de Ciencia de Materiales de Sevilla: CSIC—Universidad de Sevilla, Americo Vespucio s/n, Isla de la Cartuja, 41092 Seville; tel. (95) 4489527; fax (95) 4460665; e-mail buzon@icmse.csic.es; internet www.icmse.cartuja.csic.es; Dir ALFONSO CABALLERO MARTÍNEZ.

Instituto de Ciencia y Tecnología de Polímeros: Calle Juan de la Cierva 3, 28006 Madrid; tel. (91) 5622900; fax (91) 5644853; e-mail director.ictp@csic.es; internet www.ictp.csic.es; library of 2,000 vols, 40 periodicals; Dir Dra PAULA BOSCH SAROBE.

Instituto de Ciencias de la Construccíon 'Eduardo Torroja': Calle Serrano Galvache 4, 28033 Madrid; tel. (91) 3020440; fax (91) 3020700; e-mail director .ietcc@csic.es; internet www.ietcc.csic.es; Dir VÍCTOR RAMÓN VELASCO RODRÍGUEZ; publs *Informes de la Construcción* (6 a year), *Materiales de la Construcción* (4 a year).

Attached Research Institutes in the Field of Foodstuff Science and Technology:

Instituto de Fermentaciones Industriales: Calle Juan de la Cierva 3, 28006 Madrid; tel. (91) 5622900; fax (91) 5644853; e-mail director.ifi@csic.es; internet www.ifi.csic.es; f. 1967; research in food science and technology; participation in research projects and contracts with companies, nat. and int. confs, scientific symposia; teaching doctorate courses in univs, undergraduate and dipl. courses, masters courses and training teachers for technical college; Dir Dra LOURDES AMIGO GARRIDO.

Instituto de la Grasa: Avda Padre García Tejero 4, 41012 Seville; tel. (95) 4611550; fax (95) 4616790; e-mail director.ig@csic .es; internet www.ig.csic.es; Dir FRANCISCO JAVIER HIDALGO HUERTAS; publ. *Grasas y Aceites* (6 a year).

Instituto de Nutrición y Bromatología: CSIC—Universidad Complutense, Facultad de Farmacia, Cdad Universitaria, 28040 Madrid; tel. (91) 5490038; fax (91) 5495079; e-mail director.inb@csic.es; internet www.csic.es; Dir ASCENSIÓN MARCOS SÁNCHEZ.

Instituto de Productos Lácteos de Asturias: Ctra de Infiesto s/n, 33300 Villaviciosa (Oviedo); tel. (98) 5892131; fax (98) 5892233; e-mail direccion.ipla@ csic.es; internet www.ipla.csic.es; Dir CLARA GONZÁLEZ DE LOS REYES-GAVILÁN.

Instituto del Frío: Calle José Antonio Novais 10, 28040 Madrid; tel. (91) 5492300; fax (91) 5493627; e-mail director .if@csic.es; internet www.if.csic.es; Dir M. P. MONTERO GARCÍA.

Attached Research Institutes in the Field of Chemical Science and Technology:

Centro de Química Orgánica Lora Tamayo: Juan de la Cierva 3, 28006 Madrid; tel. (91) 5622900; fax (91) 5644853; e-mail director.cenquior@csic.es; internet www.cenquior.csic.es; Dir BERNARDO HERRADÓN GARCÍA.

Instituto de Carboquímica: Miguel Luesma Castán 5, 50018 Zaragoza; tel. (97) 6733977; fax (97) 6733318; e-mail director@icb.csic.es; internet www.icb.csic .es; Dir RAFAEL MOLINER ALVAREZ; publ. *Memoria Científica* (every 2 years).

Instituto de Catálisis y Petroleoquímica: Calle Marie Curie 2, 28049 Cantoblanco (Madrid); tel. (91) 5854800; fax (91) 5854760; e-mail director.icp@csic .es; internet www.icp.csic.es; Dir JAVIER SORIA RUIZ.

Instituto de Investigaciones Químicas: Calle Americo Vespucio 49, Isla de la Cartuaja, 41092 Seville; tel. (95) 4489553; fax (95) 4460565; e-mail director .iiq@csic.es; internet www.iiq.cartuja.csic .es; Dir JOSÉ MANUEL GARCÍA FERNÁNDEZ.

Institut de Química Avançada de Catalunya: Calle Jordi Girona 18–26, 08034 Barcelona; tel. (93) 4006100; fax (93) 2045904; e-mail director.cid@csic.es; internet www.iqac.csic.es; Dir Prof. ANGEL MESSEGUER PEYPOCH.

Instituto de Química Física Rocasolano: Calle Serrano 119, 28006 Madrid; tel. (91) 5619400; fax (91) 5642431; e-mail director.iqfr@csic.es; internet www.iqfr .csic.es; Dir JOSÉ ANTONIO GARCÍA DOMÍNGUEZ.

Instituto de Química Médica: Calle Juan de la Cierva 3, 28006 Madrid; tel. (91) 5622900; fax (91) 5644853; e-mail director.iqm@csic.es; internet www.iqm .csic.es; Dir PILAR GOYA LAZA.

Instituto de Química Orgánica General: Calle Juan de la Cierva 3, 28006 Madrid; tel. (91) 5622900; fax (91) 5644853; e-mail director.iqog@csic.es; internet www.iqog.csic.es; f. 1966; research in organic chemistry and related fields, incl. organic synthesis, physical organic chemistry, environmental chemistry, analytical chemistry of organic compounds, carbohydrate chemistry, bio-organic chemistry, biocatalysis, enzyme technology, peptides, proteins, computational chemistry, computational toxicology; library of 3,000 vols; Dir Dr EDUARDO GARCÍA-JUNCEDA.

Instituto de Tecnología Química: CSIC-Universidad Politécnica, Avda de los Naranjos s/n, 46022 Valencia; tel. (96) 3877800; fax (96) 3879444; e-mail director .itq@csic.es; internet itq.webs.upv.es; Dir AVELINO CORMA CANÓS.

Instituto Nacional del Carbón: Calle Francisco Pintado Fe 26, 33080 Oviedo; tel. (98) 5119090; fax (98) 5297662; e-mail director.incar@csic.es; internet www.incar .csic.es; Dir JESÚS A. PAJARES SOMOANO.

Laboratorio de Investigación en Tecnologías de la Combustión (Laboratory for Research in Combustion Technologies): Calle María de Luna 10, 50018 Zaragoza; tel. (976) 506520; fax (976) 506644; e-mail litec@litec.csic.es; internet www.litec.csic .es; f. 1991; research in combustion and fluid mechanics; Dir Dr ANTONIO LOZANO FANTOBA.

Fundació Catalana per a la Recerca i la Innovació (FCRI) (Catalan Foundation for Research and Innovation): Pg Lluís Companys 23, 08010 Barcelona; tel. (93) 2687700; fax (93) 2683768; e-mail fcri@fcri.es; internet www.fcr.es; f. 1986; promotes scientific, sociological and technological research; Pres. JOSEP HUGUET I BIOSCA; Sec. XAVIER QUERALT I BLANCH; publ. Tecno 2000 (6 a year).

Institut d'Estudis Internacionals i Interculturals (Institute for International and Intercultural Studies): Edifici E1, 08193 Bellaterra, Barcelona; tel. (93) 5812111; fax (93) 5813266; e-mail ce.internacionals@uab .es; internet www.uab.es/ceii; attached to Universitat Autònoma de Barcelona; Dir SEÁN GOLDEN.

Instituto CEU de Humanidades Ángel Ayala: Calle Juan XXIII 8, 28040 Madrid; tel. (91) 4568406; e-mail ihuman@ceu.es; internet www.angelayala.ceu.es; attached to Universidad CEU San Pablo; research within the field of the humanities, specifically in the areas of art, history, literature, social doctrine of the Church, thought and philosophy, and the humanistic aspects of the natural sciences; Dir JUAN JOSÉ SANZ JARQUE.

Instituto de Relaciones Europeo-Latinoamericanas (IRELA) (Institute for European-Latin American Relations): Apdo 2600, 28002 Madrid; Pedro de Valdivia 10, 28006 Madrid; tel. (91) 5617200; fax (91) 5626499; e-mail info@irela.org; f. 1984; organization of conferences, etc., for European and Latin American officials, diplomats, journalists, politicians, businessmen, trade unionists and academics on different aspects of European-Latin American relations; collection and systematization of information on relations between the two regions; advisory activities for regional instns in Europe and Latin America; promotion, coordination and pursuit of specific research on relations between the two regions; Dir WOLF GRABENDORFF.

Instituto Interuniversitario de Estudios de Iberoamérica y Portugal (Inter-University Institute of Latin American and Portuguese Studies): Casa del Tratado, 47100 Tordesillas; tel. (98) 3771806; fax (98) 3796338; e-mail ieip@uva.es; internet www3 .uva.es/ieip; attached to Universidad de Valladolid; Dir FELIPE CANO TORRES.

AGRICULTURE, FISHERIES AND VETERINARY SCIENCE

Centro de Investigación Ecológica y Aplicaciones Forestales (Ecological Research and Forestry Centre): Edifici C, Campus de Bellaterra, 08193 Cerdañola del Vallés; tel. (93) 5811312; fax (93) 5814151; e-mail ibec0@uab.es; internet www.creaf.uab .es; f. 1987; attached to Universidad Autónoma de Barcelona; Dir JAVIER RETANA.

Instituto Nacional de Investigación y Tecnología Agraria y Alimentaria (INIA) (National Institute for Food and Agricultural Research and Technology): Carretera de la Coruña, Km 7.5, 28040 Madrid; tel. (91) 3473930; fax (91) 3473931; e-mail direccion@inia.es; internet www.inia.es; f. 1971; library of 30,000 vols, 5,000 periodicals; Sec.-Gen. MARÍA ALARCÓN ALARCÓN; Dir MANUEL NÚÑEZ GUTIÉRREZ; publs Spanish Journal of Agricultural Research (4 a year, in English), Forest Systems (3 a year, in English).

ECONOMICS, LAW AND POLITICS

Centro de Investigaciones Sociológicas: Montalbán 8, 28014 Madrid; tel. (91) 5807600; e-mail cis@cis.es; internet www.cis .es; f. 1977; attached to govt Min. of the Presidency; promotes research in social sciences, arranges courses and seminars, collaborates with similar nat. and int. orgs, and creates databases for relevant material; library of 30,000 vols; Pres. RAMÓN RAMOS TORRE; Sec.-Gen. MARÍA FERNÁNDEZ SÁNCHEZ; publs Clásicos Contemporáneos, Clásicos del Pensamiento Social, Cuadernos Metodológicos (4 a year), Revista Española de Investigaciones Sociológicas (4 a year).

Instituto de Estudios de la Democracia (Institute of Democratic Studies): Calle Julián Romea 23, 28003 Madrid; tel. (91) 4566311; fax (91) 5140141; e-mail id@ceu.es; attached to Universidad CEU San Pablo; Pres. JOSÉ MANUEL OTERO NOVAS.

Instituto de Estudios Fiscales (Institute of Fiscal Studies): Avda Cardenal Herrera Oria 378, 28035 Madrid; tel. (91) 3398800; fax (91) 3398964; e-mail informacion@ief .meh.es; internet www.ief.es; f. 1960; public finance; library of 80,000 vols; Dir-Gen. JOSÉ MARÍA LABEAGA AZCONA; publs Crónica Tributaria (4 a year), Hacienda Pública Española (4 a year), Presupuesto y Gasto Público (3 a year).

Instituto Valenciano de Investigaciones Económicas (Valencian Institute of Economic Research): Calle Guardia Civil 22 esc. 2, 1°, 46020 Valencia; tel. (96) 3190050; fax (96) 3190055; e-mail ivie@ivie.es; internet www.ivie.es; f. 1990; attached to Universidad de Alicante; Dir of Research Prof. Dr FRANCISCO PÉREZ GARCÍA; Man. Dir GERMÁN MOLINA PARDO.

'L. R. Klein' Instituto de Predicción Económica ('L. R. Klein' Institute of Economic Forecasting): Facultad de CC EE. y EE, Módulo E-XIV, 28049 Madrid; tel. and fax (91) 3978670; internet www.uam.es/ otroscentros/klein; f. 1999; Dirs JOSÉ VICÉNS, ANTONIO PULIDO.

EDUCATION

Centro de Investigación y Documentación Educativa (CIDE) (Centre for Educational Research and Documentation): Calle General Oraá 55, 28006 Madrid; tel. (91) 7459400; fax (91) 7459438; internet www .educacion.es/cide; f. 1983; conducts and coordinates educational research; manages the library, archive and documentation centre of the Min. of Education and Science; library of 85,000 vols; publ. Boletín.

Institut de l'Educació (Institute of Education): Edifici del Rectorat, 08193 Bellaterra; tel. (93) 5811708; fax (93) 5812000; e-mail ice@uab.cat; internet www.uab.es/ice; attached to Universitat Autònoma de Barcelona; Dir NEUS SANMARTÍ PUIG.

Institut de Ciències de l'Educació (Institute of Education Sciences): Edifici Ventura i Gassol, Carretera de Valls, s/n, 43007 Tarragona; tel. (97) 7558071; fax (97) 7558072; e-mail gesice@urv.es; internet www.ice.urv .es; f. 1991; attached to Universitat Rovira i Virgili; Dir ANGEL-PÍO GONZÁLEZ SOTO.

Institut de Ciències de l'Educació Josep Pallach (Josep Pallach Institute of Education): Castell de Peralada, 14 Baixos, 17003 Gerona; tel. (972) 418702; fax (972) 484212; e-mail ice@udg.edu; internet www.udg.edu/ ice; attached to Universitat de Girona; Dir MERITXELL ESTEBANELL MINGUELL.

Institut de Creativitat i Innovació Educatives (Institute of Creativity and Educational Innovation): Facultat de Filologia, Traducció i Interpretació, Universidad de Valencia, Avda Blasco Ibáñez 32, 46010 Valencia; tel. (96) 3864132; fax (96) 3983085; e-mail iucie@uv.es; internet www .uv.es/icie; f. 1978; attached to Universidad de Valencia; Dir MARÍA PETRA PÉREZ ALONSO-GETA.

FINE AND PERFORMING ARTS

Instituto del Patrimonio Cultural de España (Institute of Cultural Heritage of Spain): Calle Pintor el Greco 4, Ciudad Universitaria, 28040 Madrid; tel. (91) 5504400; fax (91) 5504444; internet www .mcu.es/patrimonio/mc/iphe; f. 1985 as Instituto de Conservación y Restauración de Bienes Culturales; name subsequently changed to Instituto del Patrimonio Histórico; present name adopted 2008; attached to Min. of Culture; library of 40,000 vols, 1.600 periodicals; archive of 800,000 photographs; publs Revista Bienes Culturales, Revista Patrimonio Cultural de España.

HISTORY, GEOGRAPHY AND ARCHAEOLOGY

Centro de Documentación y Estudios para la Historia de Madrid (Centre of Documentation and Studies on the History of Madrid): Facultad de Formación del Profesorado, Despachos 305–306, Campus de Cantoblanco, 28049 Madrid; tel. (91) 3974201; fax (91) 3974123; e-mail director .cdhm@uam.es; internet www.uam.es/ otroscentros/historiamadrid; f. 1989; attached to Universidad Autónoma de Madrid; Dir VIRGILIO PINTO CRESPO.

Centro de Estudios del Patrimonio Arqueológico de la Prehistoria (Centre for Studies on the Archaeological Heritage of Prehistory): Edifici B, 08193 Bellaterra, (Barcelona); tel. (93) 5813705; fax (93) 5811140; e-mail cepap@uab.es; internet www.uab.es/cepap; attached to Universitat Autònoma de Barcelona; Dir RAFAEL MORA TORCAL.

Instituto Feijoo del Siglo XVIII (Feijoo Institute of Eighteenth-Century Studies): Facultad de Filología, Universidad de Oviedo, Campus de Humanidades, Calle Teniente Alfonso Martínez s/n, 33011 Oviedo; tel. (98) 5104671; fax (98) 5104670; e-mail admifes@uniovi.es; internet www.ifesxviii.es; attached to Universidad de Oviedo; Dir ÁLVARO RUIZ DE LA PEÑA SOLAR.

Instituto Universitario de Historia Simancas (Simancas Institute of History): Calle Real de Burgos s/n, 47011 Valladolid; tel. and fax (98) 3423527; e-mail simancas@uva.es; internet www.uva.es/simancas; f. 1988; attached to Universidad de Valladolid; research projects performance cycle of confs and congresses; historic and cultural exhibitions; graduate school (MA and PhD in Hispanic and World History); Centre for Historical Hispanic Studies "Antonino Fernández y Cinia González"; Dir Dr MARÍA ISABEL DEL VAL VALDIVIESO; Asst Dir Dr HILARIO CASADO ALONSO.

LANGUAGE AND LITERATURE

Centro de Investigaciones Lingüísticas (Linguistics Research Centre): Casa Dorado Montero, Paseo del Rector Esperabé 47, 37008 Salamanca; tel. (92) 3294400; fax (92) 3294655; e-mail cilus@usal.es; internet www.usal.es/cilus; f. 1995; attached to Universidad de Salamanca; Dir MARÍA JESÚS MANCHO DUQUE.

Institut de Llengua i Cultura Catalanes (Institute of Catalan Language and Culture): Plaça Ferrater Mora 1, 17071 Gerona; tel. (97) 2418231; fax (97) 2418230; e-mail ilcc@udg.edu; internet www.udg.edu/ilcc; f. 1986; attached to Universitat de Girona; conducts research in language history, medieval literature, studies on Francesc Eiximenis, literature of the Trobadours (Catalan and Occitan), literature of the modern age, contemporary literature, theory of literature and comparative literature, literary journalism and humanism and literature; library of 5,000 vols; Dir Dr ALBERT ROSSICH ESTRAGÓ; Sec. Dr XAVIER PLA BARBERO; publs *Editorial collections*, *Mot so razo*.

MEDICINE

Centro de Investigación del Cáncer: Campus Miguel de Unamuno, 37007 Salamanca; tel. (92) 3294720; fax (92) 3294743; e-mail cicancer@usal.es; internet www.cicancer.es; attached to Universidad de Salamanca; Dir EUGENIO SANTOS.

Centro Público de Educación Especial María Soriano (Public Centre For Special Educational Needs): Avda de la Peseta 30, 28054 Madrid; tel. (91) 4624600; fax (91) 4628444; e-mail cpee.mariasoriano.madrid@educa.madrid.org; internet www.educa.madrid.org/cpee.mariasoriano.madrid; f. 1922; Dir JULIÁN PALACIOS SÁNCHEZ; Sec. RAQUEL GARZÓN ALONSO.

Escuela Nacional de Medicina del Trabajo (National School of Occupational Medicine): Pabellón 8, Facultad de Medicina, Ciudad Universitaria, 28040 Madrid; tel. (91) 8224012; fax (91) 5437271; e-mail direccion.enmt@isciii.es; internet www.isciii.es; f. 1948; Dir Prof. MANUEL DOMÍNGUEZ CARMONA; publ. *Medicina y Seguridad del Trabajo* (4 a year, print and online).

Institut Universitari d'Investigació en Ciències de la Salut (Institute for Research in Health Sciences): Edif. Cientificotècnic, Campus Universitari, Univ. de les Illes Balears, Carretera de Valldemossa, Km 7.5, 07122 Palma, Mallorca; tel. (97) 1173257; e-mail fgrases@uib.es; internet www.iunics.es; attached to Universitat de les Illes Balears; Dir Dr FELIX GRASES.

NATURAL SCIENCES
General

Instituto Español de Oceanografía (Spanish Institute of Oceanography): Avda de Brasil 31, 28020 Madrid; tel. (91) 5974443; fax (91) 5974770; e-mail ieo@md.ieo.es; internet www.ieo.es; f. 1914; comprises physics, chemistry, pollution, geology, fishery biology and marine biology sections in Madrid; coastal laboratories at Cádiz, Gijón, La Coruña, Málaga, Palma de Mallorca, San Pedro del Pinatar, Santa Cruz de Tenerife, Santander and Vigo; 6 research vessels; library of 12,500 vols, 3,200 periodicals; Dir EDUARDO BALGUERÍAS GUERRA; Sec.-Gen. JOSÉ LUIS DE OSSORNO ALMÉCIJA; publ. *IEO* (4 a year).

Physical Sciences

Agencia Estatal de Meteorología (State Meteorological Agency): Calle Leonardo Prieto Castro 8, Ciudad Universitaria, 28071 Madrid; tel. (91) 5819810; fax (91) 5819811; internet www.aemet.es; f. 2006 to replace Instituto Nacional de Meteorología (f. 1887); 17 meteorological centres, 4,500 stations, 90 observatories; library of 20,000 vols.

Fundación Galileo Galilei (Galileo Galilei Foundation): Rambla José Ana Fernández Pérez 7, Apdo 565, 38712 San Antonio de Breña Baja, La Palma, Canary Islands; tel. (92) 2433666; fax (92) 2420508; e-mail oliva@tng.iac.es; internet www.tng.iac.es; f. 1979; attached to Istituto Nazionale di Astrofisica, Italy; promotes astrophysical research by managing and running the Telescopio Nazionale Galilei (TNG), a 3.58 m optical/infrared telescope located on La Palma; Dir EMILIO MOLINARI.

Instituto de Astrofísica de Canarias (IAC) (Canaries Institute of Astrophysics): Calle Vía Láctea s/n, 38205 La Laguna, Tenerife, Canary Islands; tel. (92) 2605200; fax (92) 2605210; e-mail secadm@iac.es; internet www.iac.es; f. 1982; incl. int. observatories on Tenerife and La Palma; library of 13,000 vols, 360 periodicals; Dir Prof. FRANCISCO SÁNCHEZ MARTÍNEZ; Head. of Admin. RAFAEL ARNAY.

Attached Observatories:

Observatorio del Roque de los Muchachos: Apdo 50, Calle Cuesta de San José s/n, 38712 Santa Cruz de La Palma, Canary Islands; tel. (92) 2405500; fax (92) 2405501; e-mail orm@iac.es; internet www.iac.es; f. 1985; European Northern Observatory; Site Man. Dr JUAN CARLOS PÉREZ ARENCIBIA.

Observatorio del Teide: Calle Vía Láctea s/n, 38205 La Laguna, Tenerife, Canary Islands; tel. (92) 2329100; fax (92) 2329117; e-mail ot@iac.es; internet www.iac.es; f. 1985; European Northern Observatory; Site Man. Dr MIQUEL SERRA RICART.

Observatorio Astronómico Nacional (National Astronomical Observatory): Campus de la Universidad de Alcalá, 28801 Madrid; tel. (91) 5270107; fax (91) 5271935; e-mail spider@oan.es; internet www.oan.es; f. 1790; attached to Instituto Geográfico Nacional; library of 12,000 vols; Dir Dr RAFAEL BACHILLER; publ. *Anuario* (1 a year).

Observatorio Fabra: Camí de l'Observatori, s/n, 08035 Barcelona; tel. (93) 4175736; internet www.fabra.cat; f. 1905; attached to Real Academia de Ciencias y Artes de Barcelona; astronomy, meteorology and seismology; Dir Dr JOSEP MARIA CODINA I VIDAL.

Real Instituto y Observatorio de la Armada (Royal Naval Institute and Observatory): Cecilio Pujazón, s/n, 11110 San Fernando, (Cádiz); tel. (95) 6545590; fax (95) 6599366; e-mail secretaria@roa.es; internet www.roa.es; f. 1753; positional astronomy, ephemerides, time, geophysics and satellite geodesy; collaborates with the British and the American Nautical Almanac Offices, Centre Nat. d'Etudes Spatiales, Le Bureau des Longitudes and Das Astronomische Rechen Institut; library of 29,900 vols, 3,500 maps and plans; Dir Dr FERNANDO BELIZÓN RODRÍGUEZ; publs *Almanaque Náutico* (1 a year), *Anales, Observaciones Meteorológicas, Magnéticas y Sísmicas*, *Efemérides Astronómicas* (1 a year), *Fenómenos Astronómicos* (2 a year).

RELIGION, SOCIOLOGY AND ANTHROPOLOGY

Centro de Investigación en Contabilidad Social y Medioambiental (Centre for Research in Social and Environmental Accounting): Edificio 10, 2°, Despacho 24, Universidad Pablo de Olavide, Ctra de Utrera, Km 1, 41013 Seville; tel. (95) 4349278; fax (95) 4349339; e-mail cicsma@upo.es; internet www.upo.es/cicsma; f. 2003; attached to Universidad Pablo de Olavide; Dir FRANCISCO CARRASCO FENECH.

Instituto Universitario de Estudios de la Mujer (University Institute of Women's Studies): Calle Francisco Tomás y Valiente 5, Edificio de Ciencias Económicas y Empresariales, Módulo VI, Planta Baja, Campus Cantoblanco, 28049 Madrid; tel. (91) 4970034; fax (91) 4975553; e-mail documentacion.iuem@uam.es; internet iuem.jimdo.com; f. 1993; attached to Universidad Autónoma de Madrid; Dir YOLANDA GUERRERO NAVARRETE.

Instituto Universitario de Investigación Ortega y Gasset (Ortega y Gasset University Research Institute): Calle Fortuny 53, 28010, Madrid; tel. (91) 7004149; fax (91) 7003530; e-mail jefatura.estudios@fog.es; internet www.ortegaygasset.edu; f. 1986; attached to Fundación José Ortega y Gasset; affiliated to Universidad Complutense de Madrid; graduate degree programmes and research in social sciences and humanities; library of 50,000 vols, 300 periodicals.

TECHNOLOGY

Centro de Estudios e Investigaciones Técnicas de Gipuzkoa (Centre for Technical Studies and Research, Gipuzkoa): Paseo de Manuel Lardizabal 15, 20018 San Sebastián; tel. (94) 3212800; fax (94) 3213076; e-mail comunicacion@ceit.es; internet www.ceit.es; f. 1982; attached to Universidad de Navarra; areas of research incl. applied mechanics, electronics and communications, environmental engineering, microelectronics and microsystems; Gen. Dir ALEJO AVELLO ITURRIAGAGOITIA.

Centro de Investigaciones Energéticas, Medioambientales y Tecnológicas (Centre for Energy, Environmental and Technological Research): Avda Complutense 22, 28040 Madrid; tel. (91) 3466000; fax (91) 3466005; e-mail contacto@ciemat.es; internet www.ciemat.es; f. 1951; controls and directs research and study of nuclear and new and renewable energies, environmental policy and several advanced technologies; library of 32,000 vols, 300,000 reports, 750,000

microcards, 2,000 periodicals; Dir-Gen. CAYE-
TANO LÓPEZ MARTÍNEZ.

**Instituto Científico y Tecnológico de
Navarra** (Scientific and Technological Institute, Navarre): Avda Pío XII 53, 31008
Pamplona; tel. (94) 8176748; fax (94)
8425223; e-mail ict@unav.es; internet www
.unav.es/ict; f. 1986; attached to Universidad
de Navarra; Dir GUILLERMO GARCÍA DEL
BARRIO.

**Instituto de Biocomputación y Física de
Sistemas Complejos** (Institute of Biocomputation and Physics of Complex Systems):
Edif. I+D, Calle Mariano Esquillor, 50018
Zaragoza; tel. (97) 6762989; fax (97) 6762990;
e-mail info@bifi.es; internet bifi.es; attached
to Universidad de Zaragoza; aims to develop
competitive research in the areas of computing applied to the physics of complex systems
and biological models; Dir JOSÉ FÉLIX SÁENZ
LORENZO.

**Instituto de Investigación en Ingeniería
de Aragón** (Aragón Engineering Research
Institute): I3A Edif. I+D+i, Calle Mariano
Esquillor s/n, 50018 Zaragoza; tel. (97)
6762707; fax (97) 6762043; e-mail i3a@
unizar.es; internet i3a.unizar.es; f. 2002;
attached to Universidad de Zaragoza; contributes to the economic devt of Aragon
through the creation, and exploitation by
industry, of new knowledge and technology;
Dir RAFAEL BILBAO.

Instituto de Robótica (Institute of Robotics): Avda 2085, 46071 Valencia; Parc Cien-
tífic Polígono de La Coma s/n, 46980 Paterna,
Valencia; tel. (9) 63543475; fax (9) 63543550;
internet www.robotica.uv.es; f. 1991;
attached to Universitat de València; research
within the fields of transport and traffic
telematics, computer graphics and virtual
reality simulation of civil equipment, network services and computer security, control
of robotic devices and digital image processing; Dir JUAN JOSÉ MARTÍNEZ DURÁ.

Instituto Geológico y Minero de España
(Spanish Geological and Mining Institute):
Calle Ríos Rosas 23, 28003 Madrid; tel. (91)
3495700; fax (91) 4426216; e-mail igme@igme
.es; internet www.igme.es; f. 1849; attached
to Min. of Science and Innovation; documentation centre of 20,000 items in microfilm;
sections: geology, geophysics, mineral
resources, subterranean hydrology, laboratories, museum; library of 45,000 vols; Pres.
FELIPE PÉTRIZ CALVO; Dir ROSA DE VIDANIA
MUÑOZ; Gen. Sec. AMOR SUÁREZ MUÑOZ; publs
Boletín Geológico y Minero (4 a year), *Revista
Española de Micropaleontología* (3 a year),
geological, metallogenic and hydrogeological
maps.

Libraries and Archives
Barcelona
**Archivo Capitular de la Santa Iglesia
Catedral de Barcelona** (Archive of the
Holy Church of the Cathedral of Barcelona):
Catedral de Barcelona, Pla de la Seu s/n,
08002 Barcelona; tel. (93) 3153156; fax (93)
3100797; f. 9th century; documents since 9th
century; treatises on Holy Scripture, ecclesiastical history and law; religious and economic history; 255 MSS, 200 incunabula and
various printed books from the original
Biblioteca Capitular; 41,000 parchment
documents, 20,000 vols; Archives Prefect
JOSEP BAUCELLS REIG.

Archivo de la Corona de Aragón (Royal
Archives of Aragon): Calle Almogávars 77,
08018 Barcelona; tel. (93) 4854285; fax (93)
3001252; e-mail aca@mcu.es; internet www
.mcu.es/archivos/mc/aca; f. 14th century;

auxiliary 21,000 vols, 870 periodicals; Dir
CARLOS LÓPEZ RODRÍGUEZ.

Arxiu Diocesà de Barcelona (Diocesan
Archives, Barcelona): Palacio Arzobispal,
Calle Obispo Irurita 5, 08002 Barcelona; tel.
(93) 2701017; e-mail dpcarqbcn@filnet.es; f.
11th century; registers (1,200) from 1302;
Diocesan Archivist Dr JOSÉ Ma MARTI BONET;
publ. *El Archivo Diocesano d' Barcelona.*

Biblioteca Balmes (Balmes Library):
Duran i Bas 9, 08002 Barcelona; tel. (93)
3177284; fax (93) 3170498; e-mail biblioteca@
balmesiana.org; internet www.balmesiana
.org; f. 1923; specializes in church studies;
40,000 vols, 345 periodicals; Dir Dr RAMÓN
CORTS BLAY.

**Biblioteca de la Universitat de Barce-
lona** (Barcelona University Library): Baldiri
Reixac 2, 08028 Barcelona; tel. (93) 4035715;
fax (93) 4034592; internet www.bib.ub.es/
biblioteques; f. 1835; network of 19 libraries
attached to the univ.; 1.2m. vols, of which
5,000 date from 16th century, 1,000 incunabula, 2,500 MSS; Dir DOLORS LAMARCA
MORELL.

**Biblioteca de l'Arxiu Històric de la
Ciutat de Barcelona:** Carrer Santa Llúcia
1, 08002 Barcelona; tel. (93) 3181195; fax (93)
3178327; e-mail bibliotecaarxiuhistoric@bcn
.cat; internet www.bcn.cat/arxiu/
arxiuhistoric; f. 1921; gen. works, books
published in Barcelona since the 15th century; the Massana Library, containing works
on iconography and the history of costume;
other libraries donated by private donors,
e.g. Eduardo Toda (British and gen. books);
150,000 vols, divided into several sections;
Dir XAVIER TARRAUBELLA MIRABET.

**Biblioteca de l'Associació d'Enginyers
Industrials de Catalunya** (Library of the
Association of Industrial Engineers of Catalonia): Via Laietana 39, 08003 Barcelona; tel.
(93) 3192366; fax (93) 3198811; e-mail
biblioteca@eic.cat; internet www.eic.cat; f.
1863; 21,200 vols; Librarian FERRAN PUERTA
I SALES.

**Biblioteca del Centre Excursionista de
Catalunya** (Library of the Catalan Alpin
Club): Calle Paradís 10, 08002 Barcelona; tel.
(93) 3152311; fax (93) 3151408; e-mail
direccio.biblioteca@cec.cat; internet
biblioteca.cec.cat; f. 1876; 39,000 vols, 7,000
maps, 300 periodicals; Dir and Librarian
CRISTINA FERRER; Librarian GEBRAN JAMAL;
publs *Espeleòleg* (irregular), *Muntanya* (6 a
year).

**Biblioteca del Collegi de Notaris i Arxiu
Històric de Protocols de Barcelona**
(Library of College of Notaries, Barcelona):
Notariat 4, 08001 Barcelona; tel. (93)
3174800; e-mail info@catalunya.notariado
.org; internet www.colnotcat.es; f. 1862;
specializes in law and the medieval history
of Catalonia; 25,000 vols, 50,000 protocols
since 13th century; Archivist LAUREÀ PAGAR-
OLAS SABATÉ; Librarian MONTSERRAT GÓMEZ;
publs *Estudios Històrics i Documents dels
Arxius de Protocols*, *La Notaría.*

**Biblioteca del Foment del Treball Nacio-
nal** (Library of Department of Trade Development): Via Laietana 32, 08003 Barcelona;
tel. (93) 4841200; fax (93) 4841230; e-mail
foment@foment.com; internet www.foment
.com; f. 1889; 90,000 vols, 2,500 periodicals;
Librarian NURIA SARDÁ; publ. *Horizonte
Empresarial* (12 a year).

**Ilustre Collegi d'Advocats de Barcelona,
Biblioteca** (Barcelona Bar Association
Library): Mallorca 283, 08037 Barcelona;
tel. (93) 4961880; fax (93) 4871128; e-mail
direcciobiblioteca@icab.cat; internet www
.icab.cat; f. 1833; 300,000 vols, 1,500 periodicals; Head PATRICIA SANPERA; publs *Revista*

Jurídica de Catalunya (4 a year), *Món
Jurídic* (10 a year).

**Reial Acadèmia Catalana de Belles Arts
de Sant Jordi** (Royal Catalan Academy of
Fine Arts, Sant Jordi): Casa Llotja, 2°,
Passeig d'Isabel II 1, 08003 Barcelona; tel.
(93) 3192432; fax (93) 3190216; e-mail
biblioteca@racba.org; internet www.racba
.org; f. 1849; 10,000 vols; Pres. JOAN ANTONI
SOLANS HUGUET; Sec. LEOPOLDO GIL NEBOT;
publs *Annuari* (every 2 years), *Butlleti* (1 a
year).

Bilbao
Biblioteca Universitaria de Deusto:
Ramón Rubial 1, 48009 Bilbao; tel. (94)
4139419; fax (94) 4139424; e-mail
biblioteca@deusto.es; internet www
.biblioteca.deusto.es; f. 1886; 1m. vols, 10,000
periodicals; Dir NIEVES TARANCO DEL BARRIO.

Granada
**Archivo de la Real Chancillería de
Granada** (Archives of the Royal Chancery
of Granada): Plaza del Padre Suárez 1, 18009
Granada; tel. (95) 8575757; fax (95) 8575756;
e-mail informacion.arch.gr.ccul@
juntadeaudalucia.es; internet www
.juntadeandalucia.es/cultura/archivos; f.
1494; 13,000 linear metres of conventional
archive material, incl. lawsuits settled by the
Tribunal de la Real Chancillería from 1490 to
1834; also holds documents issued by the
Audiencia Territorial de Granada from 1834
to 1989; Dir DAVID TORRES IBÁÑEZ.

Jerez de la Frontera
**Biblioteca del Museo Arqueológico
Municipal de Jerez** (Jerez Archaeological
Museum Town Library): Plaza del Mercado s/
n, 11408 Jerez de la Frontera; tel. (95)
6149560; fax (95) 6322975; e-mail
museoarq@aytojerez.es; internet www
.museoarqueologico.webjerez.com; f. 1873
(library), 1933 (museum); incunabula,
important collns from 17th to 18th centuries,
local collns on horses, bullfighting, flamenco;
documents dating back to the reconquest of
Jerez by Alfonso El Sabio, documents on the
discovery of America; 100,000 vols; Dirs
RAMÓN CLAVIJO PROVENCIO, CRISTOBAL OREL-
LANA; Librarians CARLA PUERTO CASTRILLÓN,
AMPARO GÓMEZ MARTÍN.

Biblioteca del Campus de Jerez: Avda. de
la Universidad s/n, 11405 Jerez de la Frontera; tel. (95) 6037015; fax (95) 6037077;
e-mail biblioteca.campusjerez@uca.es;
internet biblioteca.uca.es/sbuca/bibcjer.htm;
f. 1979; 93,000 vols, 600 periodicals, 20,000
e-journals; Head Librarian ROSA MARÍA TOR-
IBIO RUIZ.

La Coruña
Arquivo do Reino de Galicia (Archive of
the Kingdom of Galicia): Jardín de San
Carlos s/n, 15001 La Coruña; tel. (98)
1209251; fax (98) 1227094; e-mail arq.reino
.galicia@xunta.es; internet www.xunta.es; f.
1775; comprises a total of 150,926 bundles of
documents dating back to AD 867, the most
important since the 16th century, concerning
disputes and lawsuits of the 'Real Audiencia
de Galicia' and the 'Audiencia Territorial'
relative to the clergy, the nobility, villages
and private persons; 18th- and 19th-century
documents of 'Real Intendencia', concerning
govt and admin. of Galicia; documents 1808–
14 of the 'Junta Superior de Armamento y
Defensa' relative to the Peninsular War;
documents of Provincial Administration of
La Coruña since the 19th century, concerning the govt, police, education, economy,
tourism, finance, health; records of families,
labour unions and churches since the 12th
century; colln of parchment 867–1586; 7,686

maps, plans and drawings since the 16th century; 101,847 photographs and postcards, 1,298 microforms; 25,475 vols, 1,551 periodicals (incl. 23 current) and 929 pamphlets closely related to the archives and of special interest for research; Dir MARÍA CARMEN PRIETO RAMOS.

Lérida (Lleida)

Arxiu Històric de Lleida (Historical Archive of Lleida): Carrer Governador Montcada s/n, 25002 Lleida; tel. (973) 288250; fax (973) 288252; e-mail ahll.cultura@gencat.cat; internet cultura.gencat.cat/arxius/ahl; f. 1952; 10,336 linear m of documents dating from 14th to 21st century; incl. records from Administració de la Generalitat de Catalunya; Dir JOAN FARRÉ VILADRICH.

Madrid

Archivo Central del Ministerio de Trabajo e Inmigración (Central Archive of the Ministry of Labour and Immigration): Calle Agustín de Bethencourt 4, 28003 Madrid; tel. (91) 3630921; e-mail archivocentral@mtin.es; internet www.mtin.es; Head CARMEN CONCEPCIÓN SAIZ GÓMEZ; publ. *Revista del Ministerio de Trabajo e Inmigración* (12 a year).

Archivo General de la Administración Civil del Estado: Paseo de Aguadores 2, 28804 Alcalá de Henares, Madrid; tel. (91) 8892950; fax (91) 8822435; e-mail alfonso .davila@mcu.es; internet www.mcu.es/ archivos/mc/aga; f. 1969; preserves and makes available for information or scientific research documents on public admin. that are no longer of current admin. relevance; 3,000 vols; Dir ALFONSO DÁVILA OLIVEDA.

Archivo Histórico Nacional (National Historical Archives): Calle Serrano 115, 28006 Madrid; tel. (91) 7688500; fax (91) 5631199; e-mail ahn@mcu.es; internet www .mcu.es/archivos/mc/ahn; f. 1866; 400,000 archival items and 30,000 library items, 4,000 ancient monographs and 400 periodicals; Dir CARMEN SIERRA BÁRCENA.

Biblioteca Central de Marina (Central Naval Library): Calle Montalbán 2, 28014 Madrid; tel. and fax (91) 3796024; e-mail bca@fn.mde.es; internet www.portalcultura .mde.es/cultural/bibliotecas/madrid/biblioteca_121.html; f. 1874; 90,000 vols; Dir MARÍA EUGENIA MOREU ABOAL.

Biblioteca Central del Ministerio de Economía y Hacienda (Central Library of the Ministry of Economy and Finance): Calle Alcalá 9, Planta Baja, 28071 Madrid; tel. (91) 5958342; fax (91) 5958431; e-mail biblioteca .alcala@minhac.es; internet www.meh.es/ es-es/publicaciones/bibliotecas; f. 1852; 82,000 vols on economics, finance and government legislation; Librarian ESPERANZA SALÁN PANIAGUA.

Biblioteca Central Militar (Central Military Library): Paseo de Moret 3, , 28008 Madrid; tel. (91) 7808700; fax (91) 3796024; e-mail ftorra@et.mde.es; internet www .portalcultura.mde.es/cultural/bibliotecas/ madrid/biblioteca_107.html; f. 1932; 300,000 vols on military history, civil and military engineering, architecture, science; 1,000 periodicals; rare books, engravings, photographs, maps and plans, microforms; Dir FERNANDO TORRA PÉREZ.

Biblioteca de la Escuela Técnica Superior de Ingenieros de Caminos, Canales y Puertos (Library of the Higher School for Road, Canal and Port Engineers): Ciudad Universitaria, 28040 Madrid; tel. (91) 3366739; internet www.caminos.upm.es; f. 1834; 64,269 vols, 1,384 periodicals (123 current), 3,501 maps, 13,779 microfiches, 587 theses; Head CONCEPCIÓN GARCÍA VIÑUELA.

Biblioteca de la Escuela Técnica Superior de Ingenieros Industriales (Library of the Higher School for Industrial Engineers): Calle José Gutiérrez Abascal 2, 28006 Madrid; tel. (91) 3363076; e-mail biblioteca .industriales@upm.es; internet www.etsii .upm.es/inforgen/biblioteca; f. 1905; 40,000 vols; Dir ISABEL INÉS MENDOZA GARCÍA.

Biblioteca de la Universidad Complutense de Madrid (Complutense University of Madrid Library): Edificio Multiusos 1, Calle Professor Aranguren s/n, 28040 Madrid; tel. (91) 3947985; fax (91) 3947849; e-mail buc@buc.ucm.es; internet www.ucm .es/bucm; f. 1499; 2.7m. vols, 72,879 MSS, 727 incunabula, 181,066 special materials, 50,750 periodicals; Dir JOSÉ ANTONIO MAGÁN WALS.

Biblioteca del Ministerio de Asuntos Exteriores y de Cooperación (Library of the Ministry of Foreign Affairs and Cooperation): Plaza de la Provincia 1, 28012 Madrid; tel. (91) 3799219; fax (91) 3666026; f. 1943; 52,341 vols, 293 periodicals; works on history, geography, international law, political and civil law, and international relations; Dir MARÍA JOSÉ ALBO ALVAREZ.

Biblioteca Hispánica (de la Agencia Española de Cooperación Internacional para el Desarrollo) (Hispanic Library): Avda de los Reyes Católicos 4, Ciudad Universitaria, 28040 Madrid; tel. (91) 5838175; fax (91) 5838525; e-mail biblioteca .hispanica@aecid.es; internet www.aecid.es/ bibliotecas; f. 1947; 550,000 vols and 11,600 periodicals; spec. colln: Latin American incunabula; Dir Dra CARMEN DIEZ HOYO.

Biblioteca Nacional de España (National Library of Spain): Paseo de Recoletos 20, 28071 Madrid; tel. (91) 5807800; fax (91) 5775634; e-mail info@bne.es; internet www .bne.es; f. 1712 as Royal Library; 3.7m. vols, 2.6m. monographs, 152,604 periodicals, 148,320 drawings and photographs, 309,662 audio recordings, 171,725 musical scores, 90,427 video cassettes, 70,156 maps and charts, 28,494 MSS; deposit library; ISSN nat. centre; Dir GLÒRIA PÉREZ-SALMERÓN.

Biblioteca San Dámaso: Calle San Buenaventura 9, 28005 Madrid; tel. and fax (91) 3644010; e-mail biblioteca@fsandamaso.es; internet www.fsandamaso.es/facultad/ biblioteca.htm; f. 1929; comprises sections on theology and philosophy; auxiliary libraries incl. Biblioteca Alemana Görres (studies on German-Spanish cultural relations); 40,000 vols, 672 periodicals; Dir Prof. NICOLÁS ÁLVAREZ DE LAS ASTURIAS; Librarian REGINE BAUMEISTER.

Centro de Información Documental de Archivos Subdirección General de Archivos Estatales Ministerio de Educación, Cultura y Deporte: Paseo de Aguadores, 2-pl. baja, 28871 Madrid; tel. (91) 8838539; fax (91) 8829470; e-mail biblioteca .cida@mcu.es; internet www.mcu.es/ archivos/mc/cida/index.html; f. 1979; archives documentation Centre; 10,000 vols; Dir JOSEFA VILLANUEVA TOLEDO; publ. *Boletín de Información Bibliográfica* (online (www.mcu.es/ccbae/es/inicio/inicio.cmd)).

Hemeroteca Municipal de Madrid (Periodicals Library of the Corporation of Madrid): Calle Conde Duque 9–11, 28015 Madrid; tel. (91) 5885775; fax (91) 5885909; e-mail hemeroteca@munimadrid.es; internet www.madrid.es/hemeroteca; f. 1918; 250,000 vols spanning more than 20,000 titles; the library maintains a microfilm service; Dir CARLOS DORADO FERNÁNDEZ.

Real Biblioteca (Royal Library): Palacio Real, Calle Bailén s/n, 28071 Madrid; tel. (91) 4548700; fax (91) 4548867; e-mail realbiblioteca@patrimonionacional.es; internet www.realbiblioteca.es; f. early 18th century; 250,000 printed vols; fine collns of MSS, incunabula, music, rare editions since 16th century, maps, engravings and drawings; colln of bookbindings; research library; Dir Dr MARÍA LUISA LÓPEZ-VIDRIERO; publ. *Avisos: Noticias de la Real Biblioteca* (4 a year).

Palma de Mallorca

Arxiu del Regne de Mallorca (Archives of the Kingdom of Mallorca): Cuerta de Valldemossa, km 7, Edifici Adduno, Calle de Blaise Pascal, Parc Bit, 07121 Palma de Mallorca, Balearic Islands; tel. (97) 1725999; fax (97) 1177357; e-mail arm@arxregne.caib.es; internet arxregne.caib.es/web/default.htm; f. 1851; 11,000 linear m of documents; public and private archives since 13th century; 15,100 vols, 265 periodicals; Dir RICARD URGELL HERNÁNDEZ.

Peralada

Biblioteca del Palacio de Peralada (Palace of Peralada Library): Plaça del Carmen s/ n, 17491 Peralada (Girona); tel. (97) 2538125; fax (97) 2538087; e-mail inespadrosa@ castilloperalada.com; f. 1882, by the Count of Peralada; confs; exhibitions; lends books for exhibitions; 80,000 vols, 1,200 MSS, 200 incunabula, 10,000 photographs, 20,000 pamphlets and parchments on history; Librarian INÉS PADROSA; Archivist JOSEP CLAVAGUERA.

Sabadell

Arxiu Històric de Sabadell (Historical Archives, Sabadell): Carrer Indústria 32–34, 08202 Sabadell; tel. (93) 7268777; fax (93) 7275703; e-mail ahs@ajsabadell.es; internet www.sabadell.net/websajsab/arxiu; f. 14th century; documents since 1111; MSS of *Arxius Privats* (private records) since 1247, *Fons eclesiàstics* (ecclesiastical archives) since 1334, *Corts Senyorials* (Court of Justice) since 1347, *Escrivania* (notarial archives) since 1400, *Actes* (Proceedings of local council meetings) since 1449, *Hemeroteca oficial* since 1570, *Fons d'empresa* (records of 30 companies) from 19th century; collection of local journals and reviews since 1855; 10,000 vols, 100,000 photographs and 625 audiovisual records; Dir JOAN COMASÒLIVAS I FONT; publ. *Arraona* (1 a year).

San Lorenzo de El Escorial

Real Biblioteca del Monasterio de San Lorenzo de El Escorial (Royal Library of the Monastery of San Lorenzo de El Escorial): 28200 San Lorenzo de El Escorial, Madrid; tel. (91) 8903889; fax (91) 8908369; e-mail real.biblioteca@ctv.es; internet rbme .patrimonionacional.es; f. 1575; 75,000 vols, 477 incunabula, 2,027 engravings, 923 drawings, 10,722 printed books of the 16th century, MSS: 2,000 Arabic, 1,308 Latin, 765 vernacular, 72 Hebrew, 580 Greek; complete copy of the *Biblia Poliglota Complutensis* and of the *Biblia Poliglota* of Antwerp on parchment, and the *Epítome de Anatomía*, by Vesalius, also on parchment; Dir Dr P. JOSÉ LUIS DEL VALLE MERINO.

Santander

Biblioteca Central de Cantabria (Central Library of Cantabria): Ruiz de Alda 19, 39009 Santander; tel. (94) 2241550; fax (94) 2241551; e-mail bcc@gobcantabria.es; internet bcc.cantabria.es; f. 1839 as Biblioteca del Instituto Cántabro para la Enseñanza de la Náutica y el Comercio; present name adopted 1999; present site 2010; Dir JUAN JOSÉ AMADO FERNÁNDEZ.

Biblioteca de Menéndez Pelayo (Menéndez Pelayo Library): Calle Rubio 6, 39001 Santander; tel. (94) 2234534; fax (94)

2373766; e-mail biblioteca-mp@
ayto-santander.es; internet www
.bibliotecademenendezpelayo.org; the private
library of this writer, 45,000 vols, not to be
increased in number, left by him to the town;
opened to the public 1915; inaugurated 1923
by Alfonso XIII; Dir ROSA FERNÁNDEZ-LERA;
publ. *De re Bibliographica* (1 a year).

Seville

Archivo Ducal de Medinaceli (Medinaceli
Archives): Plaza de Pilatos 1, Seville; tel. (95)
4225055; fax (95) 4224677; e-mail
casapilatos@infonegocio.com; internet www
.fundacionmedinaceli.org/archivo; archives of
9th to 20th centuries; more than 5,000 vols;
Dir JUAN MANUEL ALBENDEA SOLÍS; publ.
Histórica.

Archivo General de Indias (Archives of
the Indies): Avda de la Constitución s/n,
Edificio de La Cilla, Calle Santo Tomás 5,
41071 Seville; tel. (95) 4500528; fax (95)
4219485; e-mail agil@mecd.es; internet
www.mcu.es/archivos/mc/agi; f. 1785; documents relating to Spanish colonial administration in America and the Philippines;
36,000 vols, 43,000 files; Dir ISABEL SIMÓ
RODRÍGUEZ; publs incl. *Catálogos de Pasa-
jeros a Indias, Catálogos de Mapas y Planos,
CD-ROM Tesoros del Archivo General de
Indias.*

Biblioteca Capitular y Colombina: Institución Colombina, Calle Alemanes s/n, 41004
Seville; tel. (95) 4560769; fax (95) 4562721;
e-mail bibliotecas@icolombina.es; internet
www.icolombina.es; f. 13th century; 60,000
vols; incl. the 3,500-vol. library of Hernando
Colón, son of the explorer, Cristóbal; Dir
NURIA CASQUETE DE PRADO SAGRERA.

Simancas

Archivo General de Simancas (Simancas
General Archives): Calle Miravete 8, 47130
Simancas (Valladolid); tel. (98) 3590750; fax
(98) 3590311; e-mail eduardo.pedruelo@mcu
.es; internet www.mcu.es/archivos/mc/ags; f.
1540; 70,000 filed documents and 5,000 vols
of documents; 20,000 vols on history; Dir
EDUARDO MARTÍN PEDRUEL.

Toledo

Archivo y Biblioteca Capitulares (Archives and Library of the Cathedral Chapter):
Catedral de Toledo, Hombre de Palo 2, Apdo
295, 45001 Toledo; tel. and fax (925) 212423;
e-mail archivocapitular@catedralprimada.es;
internet www.catedralprimada.es/
archivo_capitular_informacion; f. 1085; the
Archivo Capitular contains c. 6,000 catalogued documents (mostly medieval) since
1085; 127 vols of Chapter's Records (1466-
present); the library (f. 1383); 2,521 MSS and
903 printed books; Dir Dr ANGEL FERNÁNDEZ
COLLADO; Dir Dr RAMON GONZÁLVEZ RUIZ.

Biblioteca de Castilla—La Mancha
(Library of Castilla—La Mancha): Cuesta
de Carlos V, s/n, 45001 Toledo; tel. (92)
5256680; fax (92) 5253642; e-mail
biblioclm@jccm.es; internet www.jccm.es/
biblioclm; f. 1998; 380,000 vols, 4,000 periodicals; spec. collns incl. Borbón-Lorenzana
(more than 100,000 vols 16th–19th centuries,
700 MSS, 414 incunabula), Fondo Regional;
Dirs PALOMA FERNÁNDEZ DE AVILÉS, CARMEN
MORALES MATEO.

Valencia

Archivo del Reino de Valencia (Archive of
United Kingdom of Valencia): Paseo de la
Alameda 22, 46010 Valencia; tel. (96)
3184550; fax (96) 3184527; e-mail arv@gva
.es; internet dglab.cult.gva.es/arxiuregne; f.
1419; 100,000 MSS books (13th century to
present), 50,000 files of MSS, 61,483 charters, deeds, etc., since 13th century; auxiliary

library comprises 13,500 vols, 4,190 pamphlets and 250 periodicals; Dir FRANCESC
TORRES FAUS.

Zaragoza

Biblioteca Ibercaja 'José Sinues': Fernando el Católico 1–3, 50006 Zaragoza; tel.
(97) 6359887; e-mail bjsinues@
ibercajaobrasocial.org; f. 1975; owned by the
Ibercaja credit company; open only to mems;
64,152 vols, 50 periodicals, 250 audiovisual
items; spec. colln: Biblioteca Moncayo of
15,000 vols by Aragonese authors or on the
subject of Aragón.

Museums and Art Galleries

Barcelona

**Museu d'Art Contemporani de Barce-
lona** (Barcelona Museum of Contemporary
Art): Plaça dels Àngels 1, 08001 Barcelona;
tel. (93) 4120810; fax (93) 4124602; e-mail
administracio@macba.es; internet www
.macba.es; f. 1995; modern Catalan and int.
art; Dir BARTOMEU MARÍ.

Museu d'Arqueologia de Catalunya
(Archaeological Museum of Catalonia): Passeig de Santa Madrona 39–41, Parc de
Montjuïc, 08038 Barcelona; tel. (93)
4232149; fax (93) 4254244; e-mail mac
.cultura@gencat.cat; internet www.mac.cat;
f. 1935; collns of prehistoric, Greek, Phoenician, Visigothic and Roman art; library of
40,000 vols; Dir XAVIER LLOVERA MASSANA;
publs *Cypsela* (every 2 years), *Empúries*
(every 2 years).

Museu d'Història de Barcelona: Plaça del
Rei s/n, 08002 Barcelona; tel. (93) 3151111;
fax (93) 3150957; e-mail museuhistoria@bcn
.es; internet www.museuhistoria.bcn.es; f.
1943; 15th-century mansion containing
Roman remains in situ (1st- to 4th-century
Roman wall), 11th- to 15th-century Royal
Palace; documentation centre, information
service; Dir ANTONI NICOLAU MARTÍ; publ.
*Quaderns d'Arqueologia i Història de la
Ciutat de Barcelona.*

Subordinate institutions:

Casa Museu Verdaguer: Carrer Major 7,
08519 Folgueroles; tel. and fax (93)
8122157; e-mail info@verdaguer.cat;
internet www.verdaguer.cat; 18th-century
farmhouse, former home of the poet Jacint
Verdaguer; Dir CARME TORRENTS I BUXÓ.

**Conjunto Monumental de la Plaça del
Rei:** Plaça del Rei s/n, 08002 Barcelona;
tel. (93) 2562100; fax (93) 2680454; e-mail
museuhistoria@bcn.es; internet www.bcn
.cat/museuhistoriaciutat/es/placa_del_rei
.html; 11th-century Count's Palace, later
the residence of the kings of Catalonia and
Aragón; Padellàs House, a Gothic palace;
Roman remains in situ (1st century BC–8th
century AD); Chief Curator JULIA BELTRÁN
DE HEREDIA.

MUHBA Park Güell: Casa del Guarda,
Park Güell, Carrer Olot s/n, 08024 Barcelona; tel. (93) 2562122; fax (93) 2856836;
e-mail museuhistoria@bcn.cat; internet
www.bcn.cat/museuhistoriaciutat/ca/muh-
ba_park_guell.html; information centre;
incl. maps, models, photographs and
audiovisual items on relationships
between Gaudí, Güell (the patron) and
city of Barcelona; Dir Dr JOAN ROCA.

MUHBA Santa Caterina: Plaça del Rei s/
n, 08002 Barcelona; tel. (93) 2562100; fax
(93) 2680454; e-mail museuhistoria@bcn
.cat; internet www.bcn.cat/
museuhistoriaciutat/ca/muhba_santa_ca-

terina.html; f. 1943; depicts the archaeological history of the city of Barcelona
through archaeological sites, medieval
monuments, Gaudí work at Park Güell,
Spanish civil war defences and industrial
bldgs, from the Bronze Age to the latest
examples of contemporary architecture; 12
centres; library of 10,000 vols; Dir Dr JOAN
ROCA; publ. *QUARHIS. Quaderns
d'Arqueologia i Història de la Ciutat de
Barcelona.*

Museu-Monestir de Pedralbes: Baixada
del Monestir 9, 08034 Barcelona; tel. (93)
2039282; fax (93) 2039408; e-mail
monestirpedralbes@bcn.es; f. 1326, opened
to public 1983; Gothic church and monastery; Chief Curator ANNA CASTELLANO I
TRESSERRA.

**Museu de Ciències Naturals de Barce-
lona** (Natural History Museum of Barcelona): Passeig Picasso s/n, 08003 Barcelona;
tel. (93) 3196912; fax (93) 3199312; e-mail
museuciencies@bcn.cat; internet www.bcn
.es/museuciencies; f. 1878; permanent exhibitions on classification of the animal kingdom; honey bees; urban birds; minerals,
rocks and fossils; large collns of coleoptera,
mollusca, fossils and minerals; 2–4 temporary exhibitions annually; research areas incl.
evolutionary ecology, bioespeleology, palaeontology, petrology and the history of science;
library of 20,150 vols, 3,000 periodicals, 3,600
maps; Dir ANNA OMEDES; publs *Animal
Biodiversity and Conservation* (2 a year),
Arxius de Miscelània Zoològica (online),
*Collectanea Botanica, Treballs del Museu de
Geologia* (1 a year).

Subordinate Institution:

**Museu de Ciències Naturals de Barce-
lona—Edifici de Geologia** (Natural History Museum of Barcelona, Geology
Building): Parc de la Ciutadella s/n,
08003 Barcelona; tel. (93) 3196912; fax
(93) 3199312; e-mail museuciencies@bcn
.cat; f. 1882; library: geology library; publ.
*Treballs del Museu de Geologia de Barce-
lona* (1 a year).

Museu de la Música (Museum of Music):
L'Auditori, Calle Lepant 150, 2°, 08013
Barcelona; tel. (93) 2563650; fax (93)
2650102; e-mail museumusica@bcn.cat;
internet www.museumusica.bcn.cat; f. 1946;
valuable collns of antique instruments; phonographs and gramophones, historical early
recordings; archives of Albéniz, Granados
and other Catalan composers; library of
12,000 vols; Dir ROMÀ ESCALAS.

Museu Etnològic (Museum of Ethnology):
Passeig de Sta Madrona 16–22, Parc de
Montjuïc, 08038 Barcelona; tel. (93)
4246807; fax (93) 4237364; e-mail metno@
intercom.es; internet www.museuetnologic
.bcn.es; f. 1948; more than 70,000 artefacts
pertaining to African, Asiatic, American,
Oceanic, and Spanish ethnography and
American archaeology; library of 40,000
vols, more than 1,000 periodicals; Dir JOSEP
FORNÉS I GARCÍA.

**Museu Geològic del Seminari de Barce-
lona** (Geological Museum of Barcelona Seminary): Diputació 231, 08007 Barcelona; tel.
(93) 4541600; e-mail almeracomas@hotmail
.com; internet www.telefonica.net/web2/
pa-ko/mgsb; f. 1874; palaeontology of invertebrates, colln of nearly 70,000 fossils; library
of 13,000 vols; Dir Dr S. CALZADA; publs
Batalleria (1 a year), *Scripta Musei Geologici
Seminarii* (irregular).

Museu Marítim de Barcelona (Barcelona
Maritime Museum): Avda de les Drassanes s/
n, 08001 Barcelona; tel. (93) 3429920; fax
(93) 3187876; e-mail m.maritim@diba.cat;
internet www.mmb.cat; f. 1941; library of
15,000 vols; photographic, cartographic and

documental archives; colln of 158 objects of weaponry; restoration workshop; Dir ROGER MARCET I BARBÉ.

Museu Nacional d'Art de Catalunya (National Art Museum of Catalonia): Palau Nacional, Parc de Montjuïc, 08038 Barcelona; tel. (93) 6220360; fax (93) 6220362; e-mail mnac@mnac.cat; internet www.mnac.cat; f. 1934; incl., on various sites, National Art Museum of Catalonia; educational programmes, debates, lectures and seminars, guided tours; library of 154,000 vols, 2,465 periodicals; Pres. MIQUEL ROCA I JUNYENT; Dir JOSEP SERRA VILLALBA; publs *Butlletí*, *Revista*.

Museu Picasso (Picasso Museum): Carrer Montcada 15–23, 08003 Barcelona; tel. (93) 2563000; fax (93) 3150102; e-mail museupicasso@bcn.cat; internet www.museupicasso.bcn.cat; f. 1963; comprises more than 4,000 paintings, pottery, drawings and engravings by Pablo Picasso (1881–1973), incl. the series 'Las Meninas' and the artist's donation, in 1970, of 940 works of art; library of 4,000 vols; Dir PEPE SERRA; Dir BERNARDO LANIADO-ROMERO.

Bilbao

Guggenheim Bilbao Museoa (Guggenheim Museum, Bilbao): Abandoibarra 2, 48001 Bilbao; tel. (94) 4359000; fax (94) 4359010; e-mail infomacion@guggenheim-bilbao.es; internet www.guggenheim-bilbao.es; f. 1997; modern American and European art; Dir-Gen. JUAN IGNACIO VIDARTE.

Museo de Bellas Artes de Bilbao (Bilbao Museum of Fine Arts): Plaza del Museo 2, 48011 Bilbao; tel. (94) 4396060; fax (94) 4396145; e-mail info@museobilbao.com; internet www.museobilbao.com; f. 1908, opened to public 1914; colln incl. major works by Bermejo, Benson, Mandijn, Vredeman de Vries, De Vos, Moro, Sánchez Coello, El Greco, Pourbus, Gentileschi, Ribera, Zurbarán, Van Dyck, Murillo, Arellano, Meléndez, Bellotto, Goya, Paret, Villamil, Ribot, Zamacois, Madrazo, Gauguin, Cassatt, Sorolla, Guiard, Ensor, Regoyos, Romero de Torres, Zuloaga, Sunyer, Arteta, Gutiérrez Solana, Vázquez Díaz, Lipchitz, Delaunay, González, Gargallo, Bacon, Palazuelo, Oteiza, Chillida, Caro, Millares, Tàpies, Saura, Lüpertz, Kitaj, Blake, Arroyo and Barceló; library of 33,000 vols, 300 periodicals; Dir JAVIER VIAR.

Burgos

Museo de Burgos: Calle Miranda 13, 09002 Burgos; tel. (94) 7265875; fax (94) 7276792; e-mail museo.burgos@jcyl.es; internet www.museodeburgos.com; f. 1871; Casa Miranda: archaeological collns (from Palaeolithic to Visigothic); Casa Angulo: fine arts collns (from Mozarabic to contemporary painting), enamels, ivories, tomb of Juan de Padilla, Tablas Flamencas (Ecce Homo) and 15th- to 20th-century painting, sculpture, altarpieces; library of 3,000 vols, specializing in archaeology and art; Dir Dr J. C. ELORZA Y GUINEA; publ. *Anales*.

Cartagena

Museo Arqueológico Municipal (Archaeological Museum): Calle Ramón y Cajal 45, 30205 Cartagena; tel. (96) 8128967; fax (96) 8128968; e-mail informacionmuseo@ayto-cartagena.es; internet www.museoarqueologicocartagena.es; f. 1943; important collns of Roman remains found in the area, incl. mining, architecture, sculpture, industrial arts exhibits; model sites; Dir Dra MARÍA COMAS GABARRÓN.

Chipiona

Museo Misional de Nuestra Señora de Regla: Colegio de Misioneros Franciscanos, 11550 Chipiona; f. 1939; about 600 exhibits of early Roman Christian relics, ancient Egyptian and other North African objects, antique coins, etc.; Dir R. P. RECTOR DEL COLEGIO.

Córdoba

Museo Arqueológico Provincial de Córdoba: Plaza de Jerónimo Páez 7, 14003 Córdoba; tel. (95) 7355517; fax (95) 7355534; e-mail museoarqueologicocordoba.ccul@juntadeandalucia.es; internet www.juntadeandalucia.es/cultura/museos/maeco; f. 1867; 33,500 exhibits; archaeological, prehistoric and local finds, Roman and medieval collns; library of 13,500 vols; Dir MARÍA DOLORES BAENA ALCANTARA.

Figueres

Teatre-Museu Dalí (Dali Museum): Plaça Gala Dalí 5, 17600 Figueres; tel. (97) 2677500; fax (97) 2501666; e-mail t-mgrups@dali-estate.org; internet www.salvador-dali.org; f. 1974; comprises 1,500 paintings, sculptures and other works by Salvador Dalí, and his private colln of works by other artists; Dir ANTONI PITXOT I SOLER.

Granada

Museo de Bellas Artes (Museum of Fine Arts): Palacio de Carlos V, 18009 Granada; tel. (95) 8575450; fax (95) 8575451; e-mail portaldemuseos@juntadeandalucia.es; internet www.juntadeandalucia.es/cultura/museos/mbagr; f. 1958 (present site); paintings and sculpture by local artists from 16th century to mid-20th century; library of 5,000 vols; Dir RICARDO TENORIO VERA.

Ibiza

Museo Arqueológico dEivissa i Formentera: Via Romana 31, 07800 Ibiza, Balearic Islands; tel. (97) 1301771; fax (97) 1303263; e-mail maef@telefonica.net; internet www.aamaef.org; f. 1907; Phoenician, Carthaginian and Roman remains from the necropolis of Puig des Molins (nat. monument and World Heritage Property); Dir JORGE H. FERNÁNDEZ GÓMEZ; publ. *Treballs del Museu Arqueológic d'Eivissa I Formentera* (2 a year).

Attached Museum:

Museo Monográfico y Necrópolis del Puig des Molins: Via Romana 31, Eivissa (Ibiza); tel. (97) 1301771; fax (97) 1303263; e-mail mmpm@telefonica.net; f. 1966; Phoenicean, Punic and Roman remains from the nat. monument of Puig des Molins, declared as a World Heritage Site by UNESCO in 1999; annual program of activities incl. lectures, courses about archaeology and Phoenicean-Punic archaeology, guided visits to the necropolis for school groups, and activities for children; library of 21,586 vols; Dir and Curator JORGE H. FERNÁNDEZ GÓMEZ; publ. *Treballs del Museu Arqueológic d'Eivissa I Formentera*.

La Escala

Museu d'Arqueologia de Cataluyna—Empúries: Calle Puig i Cadafalch s/n, 17130 L'Escala; tel. (97) 2770208; fax (97) 2775975; e-mail macempuries.cultura@gencat.cat; internet www.mac.cat/cat/seus/empuries; f. 1908; colln of excavations of Graeco-Roman city Empúries; library of 3,500 vols; Dir XAVIER LLOVERA.

Las Palmas

Museo Canario (Canarian Museum): Dr Verneu 2, Vegueta, 35001 Las Palmas de Gran Canaria; tel. (92) 3336800; fax (92) 3336801; e-mail info@elmuseocanario.com; internet www.elmuseocanario.com; f. 1879; local archaeology and anthropology, ethnography and natural sciences; library of 65,000 vols; Dir-Gen. DIEGO LÓPEZ DÍAZ; publ. *El Museo Canario* (1 a year).

Lérida (Lleida)

Gabinet Numismàtic: Institut d'Estudis Ilerdencs, Plaça de la Catedral s/n, 25002 Lérida; tel. (97) 3271500; e-mail iei@fpiei.es; Roman, Iberian, Ibero-Roman, medieval and modern exhibits; local collns.

Museo de la Paeria: Plaça Paeria 1, 25007 Lérida; tel. (90) 2250050; fax (97) 3238953; f. 1963; historical documents and objects belonging to the municipality; archaeological finds of Lérida.

Museu d'Art Jaume Morera: Carrer Major 31, Edifici Casino, 25007 Lérida; tel. (97) 3700419; fax (97) 3700487; e-mail mmorera@paeria.cat; internet www.paeria.cat/mmorera; f. 1917; museum of modern paintings mainly by Catalan artists, incl. works by Morera, C. Haes and others; Dir JESÚS NAVARRO I GUITART.

Museu de Lleida: diocesà i comarcal: Carrer Sant Crist 1, 25002 Lérida; tel. (97) 3283075; fax (97) 3261582; e-mail museu@museudelleida.cat; internet www.museudelleida.cat; f. 1997; medieval sculptures; also sub-section at Rambla de Aragón containing religious paintings, metalwork and vestments; Dir MONTSERRAT MACIÀ I GOU.

Servei d'Arqueologia de la Fundació Pública Institut d'Estudis Ilerdencs (Archaeological Services of the Public Foundation the Institute of Lleida Studies): Apartat de Correus 79, 25080 Lérida; Plaça Catedral s/n, 25002 Lérida; tel. (97) 3271500; fax (97) 3274538; e-mail arqueolo@diputaciolleida.cat; internet www.fpiei.cat; f. 1954; archaeology, excavation; first Trinitarian house of Iberian Peninsula; audiovisual teaching aids; Dir JOAN RAMON GONZÁLEZ PÉREZ.

Madrid

Fundación Lázaro Galdiano (Lázaro Galdiano Foundation): Calle Serrano 122, 28006 Madrid; tel. (91) 5616084; fax (91) 5617793; e-mail secretaria.fundacion@flg.es; internet www.flg.es; f. 1948; 13,000 items: Italian, Spanish and Flemish Renaissance paintings; Primitives; Golden Age, 18th- and 19th-century Spanish paintings; 16th- and 17th-century Dutch paintings; English 18th- and 19th-century colln; Golden Age MSS and incunabula; collns of ivory, enamels, watches, jewellery, furniture, weapons and armour, oriental and Spanish tapestries and cloth; library of 40,000 vols, 1,000 periodicals; Dir ELENA HERNANDO GONZALO; publ. *Goya. Revista de Arte* (3 a year).

Instituto de Valencia de Don Juan (Don Juan Institute of Valencia): Calle Fortuny 43, 28010 Madrid; tel. (91) 3081848; f. 1916; historical archives; museum of ancient Spanish industrial arts; illuminated MS *Les Statuts de la Toison d'Or* with miniatures; library of 10,000 historical and art vols; Dir BALBINA MARTÍNEZ CAVIRO.

Museo Arqueológico Nacional (National Archaeological Museum): Calle Serrano 13, 28001 Madrid; tel. (91) 5777912; fax (91) 4316840; e-mail info.man@mecd.es; internet man.mecd.es; f. 1867; 16th-century miniatures; collns relating to Egyptian, Cypriot, Greek and Etruscan antiquities and to nat. prehistory, Iron Age, Iberian and Hispano-Roman art; from medieval and modern times: ivory carvings, Spanish pottery, Islamic pottery, brocades, tapestries, porcelain, furniture, textiles and a numismatic colln; library of 140,000 vols, 3,000 serial titles; medieval MSS incl. Huesca Bible of 12th century, *Beato de Liébana, Comentarios al Apocalipsis* (12th–13th century), *Martirologio y Regla de S. Benito* (13th century), *Cantorales* (15th century); Dir ROSA CHUMILLAS ZAMORA; Librarian NICOLÁS PÉREZ CÁCERES; publ. *Boletín* (irregular).

Museo Cerralbo: Ventura Rodríguez 17, 28008 Madrid; tel. (91) 5473646; fax (91) 5591171; e-mail mudeo@mcerralbo.mcu.es; internet museocerralbo.mcu.es; f. 1924; the 17th Marquis of Cerralbo left his house to the nation as a museum, together with his colln of 50,000 paintings, drawings, engravings, porcelain, arms, carpets, coins, furniture, incl. paintings by El Greco, Ribera, Titian, Van Dyck, Tintoretto; library of 13,000 vols; Dir LURDES VAQUERO ARGÜELLES.

Museo de Historia (Historical Museum): Calle Fuencarral 78, 28004 Madrid; tel. (91) 7011863; fax (91) 7011686; e-mail smuseosm@madrid.es; internet www .munimadrid.es/museodehistoria; f. 1929, fmrly Museo Municipal de Madrid; historical and artistic evolution of Madrid since 16th century; portraits, paintings, designs, engravings, sculptures, plans, silversmiths' work, coins, ceramics, porcelain; paintings by Berruguete, Maella, Luca Giordano, Bayeu, Castillo, Goya and other contemporary artists, 1830 Madrid scale model, Ramón de Mesonero Romanos and Ramón Gómez de la Serna studies; Dir CARMEN PRIEGO FERNÁNDEZ DEL CAMPO.

Museo de la Farmacia Hispana (Museum of Spanish Medicine): Facultad de Farmacia, Universidad Complutense Madrid, Plaza de Ramón y Cajal s/n, 28040 Madrid; tel. and fax (91) 3941797; e-mail museofar@farm.ucm .es; internet www.ucm.es/info/mhfarhis; f. 1951; library of 10,000 vols; Dir FRANCISCO JAVIER PUERTO SARMIENTO.

Museo de la Real Academia de Bellas Artes de San Fernando (Royal Academy of Fine Arts, San Fernando): Calle Alcalá 13, 28014 Madrid; tel. (91) 5240864; fax (91) 5241034; e-mail museo@rabasf.org; internet rabasf.insde.es; f. 1744; Spanish paintings since 16th century (incl. works by Goya, Zurbarán, Murillo, Ribera and Pereda), European paintings from 16th–18th centuries, Spanish sculpture since 17th century; Dir JOSÉ MARTA LUZÓN NOGUÉ.

Museo del Ejército (Army Museum): Calle Méndez Núñez 1, 28071 Madrid; tel. (91) 5228977; fax (91) 5314624; internet www .ejercito.mde.es/unidades/madrid/ihycm/ museos/ejercito; f. 1803 as Real Museo Militar; 30,000 exhibits; collns of arms, war trophies, flags and tin soldiers; br. museum in Toledo; library of 10,000 vols; Dir-Gen. JOSÉ A. RIVAS OCTAVIO.

Museo del Ferrocarril de Madrid (Madrid Railway Museum): Paseo Delicias 61, 28045 Madrid; tel. (90) 2228822; fax (91) 5068478; e-mail museodelicias@ffe.es; internet www .museodelferrocarril.org; f. 1984; steam, diesel and electric trains, models, exhibitions; photographic archive; library of 35,000 vols; Dir and Curator Dr MIGUEL MUÑOZ RUBIO; publs *Colección de Historia Ferroviaria (Historical Research), Cuadernos del Archivo Histórico Ferroviario, Cuadernos del Museo* (12 a year), *Didactic Handbooks, Railway Museum Bulletin, Monographs, TST (Transports, Services and Telecommunications)*.

Museo Nacional Centro de Arte Reina Sofía: Calle Santa Isabel, 52, 28012 Madrid; tel. (91) 7741000; fax (91) 7741056; e-mail info@museoreinasofia.es; internet www .museoreinasofia.es; f. 1988 by Royal Decree,

permanent colln inaugurated 1992; Spanish and int. modern and contemporary art; library of 184,202 vols, 131,786 monographs, 1,960 periodical publs, 204 MSS, 1,863 audiovisual documents, 1,400 graphic documents and 336 electronic documents; Dir MANUEL J. BORJA-VILLEL; publ. *Carta* (2 a year).

Museo Nacional de Antropología (National Museum of Anthropology): Calle Alfonso XII 68, 28014 Madrid; tel. (91) 5306418; fax (91) 4677098; e-mail antropologico@mcu.es; internet mnantropologia.mcu.es; f. 1910, fmrly a section of the Nat. Museum of Natural Science; colln formed by 30,000 objects and documents from Europe, Asia, the Philippines, Micronesia, Melanesia, Central and S America, the Sahara, Morocco, W and Central Africa, and the fmr Spanish Guinea; organizes temporary exhibitions, workshops for children, families and adults, concerts, lectures; library of 14,000 vols and anthropological periodicals; closed for renovations from Oct. 2010; Dir PILAR ROMERO DE TEJADA Y PICATOSTE; publ. *Anales* (1 a year).

Museo Nacional de Artes Decorativas (National Museum of Decorative Arts): Calle Montalbán 12, 28014 Madrid; tel. (91) 5326845; fax (91) 5232086; e-mail mnad@ mnad.mcu.es; internet mnartesdecorativas .mcu.es; f. 1912; collns of interior decorative arts, especially Spanish from 15th–19th centuries, incl. carpets, furniture, leatherwork, jewellery, tapestries, ceramics, glass, porcelain, textiles; library of 20,000 vols, 500 periodicals; Dir Dr ALBERTO BARTOLOMÉ ARRAIZA.

Museo Nacional de Ciencia y Tecnología (National Museum of Science and Technology): Paseo de las Delicias 61, 28045 Madrid; tel. (91) 6037400; fax (91) 6037423; e-mail infomuseo@muncyt.es; internet www .muncyt.es; f. 1980; library of 13,400 vols, 1,100 periodicals; Dir RAMÓN NÚÑEZ CENTELLA; Librarian JOSEFA PRADOS.

Museo Nacional de Ciencias Naturales (Natural Science Museum): José Gutiérrez Abascal 2, 28006 Madrid; tel. (91) 4111328; fax (91) 5645078; e-mail director.mncn@csic .es; internet www.mncn.csic.es; f. 1771 as Gabinete de Historia Natural by Carlos III; attached to CSIC; valuable natural history and scientific collections, mainly from Iberia, Central and S America, the Philippines and N Africa; library of 63,000 vols, incl. over 2,000 volumes from 15th–18th centuries and 1 incunabulum; 4,300 periodicals, since 1790; Dir ESTEBAN MANRIQUE REOL; publs *Graellsia* (1 a year), *Estudios Geológicos* (3 a year).

Museo Nacional de Reproducciones Artísticas (National Museum of Art Reproductions): Avda Juan de Herrera 2, 28040 Madrid; tel. (91) 5497150; fax (91) 5448004; internet mnreproduccionesartisticas.mcu.es; f. 1877; library of 10,000 vols; more than 3,000 reproductions of Oriental, Greek, Roman and Hispano-Roman statuary, medieval and Renaissance art, classical and medieval sculpture and decorative arts; Dir MARÍA JOSÉ ALMAGRO GORBEA.

Museo Nacional del Prado (National Prado Museum): Paseo del Prado s/n, 28014 Madrid; tel. (91) 3302800; fax (91) 3302856; e-mail museo.nacional@museodelprado.es; internet www.museoprado.es; f. 1819; paintings by Botticelli, Rembrandt, Velázquez, El Greco, Goya, Murillo, Raphael, Bosch, Van der Weyden, Zurbarán, Van Dyck, Tiepolo, Ribalta, Rubens, Titian, Veronese, Tintoretto, Moro, Juanes, Meléndez, Poussin, Ribera; Classical and Renaissance sculpture; jewels and medals; library of 60,000 vols, 700

periodicals; Dir MIGUEL ZUGAZA; publ. *Boletín* (1 a year).

Museo Naval (Naval Museum): Paseo del Prado 5, 28014 Madrid; tel. (91) 5238789; fax (91) 3795056; internet www .museonavalmadrid.com; f. 1843; engravings of sea battles, portraits, nautical instruments and armaments; models of ships since 14th century; more than 6,000 original maps, charts, prints and drawings of many countries since 1600; 70,000 photographs (of which 27,000 are catalogued); library of 20,000 vols, 3,500 vols of MSS; Dir GONZALO RODRÍGUEZ GONZÁLEZ-ALLER; publ. *Revista de Historia Naval* (4 a year).

Museo del Romanticismo (Museum of the Romantic Period): San Mateo 13, 28004 Madrid; tel. (91) 4481045; fax (91) 4456940; e-mail informacion.romanticismo@mcu.es; internet museoromantico.mcu.es; f. 1924 as Museo Romántico, closed 2001, reopened under present name 2009; paintings, furniture, books and decorations of Spanish romantic period; concerts, meetings, family and school programmes, lectures; library of 13,000 vols, 300 periodicals; Dir Dra ASUNCIÓN CARDONA.

Museo de los Orígenes, Casa de San Isidro (Museum of Origins, House of St Isidro): Plaza San Andrés 2, 28005 Madrid; tel. (91) 3667415; fax (91) 3541719; e-mail museodelosorigenes@munimadrid.es; internet www.munimadrid.es/ museodelosorigenes; f. 2000; fmrly Museo de San Isidro; archaeology and history of Madrid and environs; library of 12,000 vols; Dir EDUARDO SALAS VÁZQUEZ; publ. *Estudios de Prehistoria y Arqueología Madrileñas* (1 a year).

Museo Sorolla (Sorolla Museum): General Martínez Campos 37, 28010 Madrid; tel. (91) 3101584; fax (91) 3085925; e-mail museo .sorolla@mecd.es; internet museosorolla.mcu .es; f. 1931; permanent exhibition of some 350 of the artist's works; temporary exhibitions; library of 7,000 vols; Dir CONSUELO LUCA DE TENA NAVARRO.

Museo Thyssen-Bornemisza: Palacio de Villahermosa, Paseo del Prado 8, 28014 Madrid; tel. (91) 3690151; fax (91) 4202780; e-mail mtb@museothyssen.org; internet www.museothyssen.org; f. 1992; paintings and sculpture from 13th–20th centuries; Man. Dir MIGUEL ÁNGEL RECIO CRESPO.

Patrimonio Nacional (National Heritage): Palacio Real, Calle Bailen s/n, 28071 Madrid; tel. (91) 4548700; fax (91) 5426947; e-mail info@patrimonionacional.es; internet www .patrimonionacional.es; f. 1940; state instn responsible for all the museums situated in royal palaces and properties; governed by Admin. Council; Dir MIGUEL ÁNGEL RECIO CRESPO; publ. *Reales Sitios* (4 a year).

Subordinate Institutions:

Abadía Benedictina de la Santa Cruz del Valle de los Caídos: Carretera de Guadarrama-El Escorial, 28209 Valle de Cuelgamuros, (Madrid); tel. (91) 8905611; fax (91) 8905544; internet www .patrimonionacional.es; f. 1957; monument to the fallen, commissioned by Gen. Franco.

Monasterio de las Descalzas Reales: Plaza de las Descalzas s/n, 28013 Madrid; tel. (91) 4548800; fax (91) 5426947; internet www.patrimonionacional.es; f. 1557; combined museum and enclosed convent; 16th- and 17th-century paintings and artefacts.

Monasterio de Santa Maria la Real de las Huelgas: Calle Los Compases s/n, 09001 Burgos; tel. (94) 7201630; fax (94)

7279729; internet www .patrimonionacional.es; f. 1187.

Monasterio de Yuste: 10430 Cuacos de Yuste, (Cáceres); tel. (92) 7172197; fax (92) 7172347; internet www .patrimonionacional.es; f. 1402.

Palacio Real de Aranjuez: Plaza de Parejas, 28300 Aranjuez, (Madrid); tel. (91) 8910740; fax (91) 8921532; internet www.patrimonionacional.es; former royal palace rich in 18th-century art.

Palacio Real de El Pardo: Calle Manuel Alonso s/n, 28048 El Pardo (Madrid); tel. (91) 3761500; fax (91) 3760452; internet www.patrimonionacional.es; f. built for Henry IV in 15th century; rebuilt for Carlos I in 1553 and enlarged in the 18th century by Sabatini; 18th-century tapestries, some by Goya.

Palacio Real de la Almudaina: Palau Reial s/n, 07001 Palma de Mallorca, Balearic Islands; tel. (97) 1214134; fax (97) 1719145; internet www .patrimonionacional.es; built in the middle ages; royal palace; Gothic chapel of St Anne; Arab baths.

Palacio Real de La Granja de San Ildefonso: Plaza de España 17, 40100 La Granja de San Ildefonso (Segovia); tel. (92) 1470019; fax (92) 1471895; internet www .patrimonionacional.es; f. 18th century; built for Philip V; gardens and fountains; colln of furniture and artefacts from the 18th and 19th centuries; tapestry museum.

Palacio Real de Madrid: Calle Bailen s/ n, 28071 Madrid; tel. (91) 4548800; fax (91) 5426947; internet www .patrimonionacional.es; f. 18th century; rooms devoted to 16th- to 18th-century tapestries, clocks, painting and porcelain from the royal palaces and pharmacy; Royal Armoury; rooms with original 18th-century decor; colln of furniture, paintings and porcelain from the 18th and 19th centuries; library: see under Libraries and Archives; archives since the 12th century.

Palacio Real de Riofrío: Bosque de Riofrío, 40420 Navas de Riofrío (Segovia); tel. (92) 1470020; fax (92) 1471895; internet www.patrimonionacional.es; built in 1752.

Real Monasterio de la Encarnación: Plaza de la Encarnación 1, 28013 Madrid; tel. (91) 4548800; fax (91) 5426947; internet www.patrimonionacional.es; f. 1611; combined museum and enclosed convent; 17th- and 18th-century paintings and sculptures; colln of 700 bronze, coral, ivory and fine timber artefacts from Spain, Germany, Italy and the Netherlands.

Real Monasterio de Santa Clara de Tordesillas: 47100 Tordesillas (Valladolid); tel. (98) 3770071; internet www .patrimonionacional.es; f. 1363.

Real Monasterio de Santa Isabel: Calle de Santa Isabel 48, 28012 Madrid; internet www.patrimonionacional.es; f. 16th century; 17th- and 18th-century paintings.

Planetario de Madrid (Planetarium of Madrid): Avda del Planetario, 16, 28045 Madrid; tel. (91) 4673461; fax (91) 4681154; e-mail buzon@planetmad.es; internet www .planetmad.es; f. 1986; exhibition and projection room seating 250 people; Dir ASUNCIÓN SÁNCHEZ JUSTEL.

Real Jardín Botánico (Royal Botanical Garden): Plaza de Murillo 2, 28014 Madrid; tel. (91) 4203017; fax (91) 4200157; e-mail director.rjb@csic.es; internet www.rjb.csic.es; f. 1755; attached to CSIC (q.v.); botanical research; herbarium with more than 1m. specimens; library of 34,000 vols, 2,094 peri-

odicals, 20,000 historical documents, 10,000 botanical drawings; Dir GONZALO NIETO FELINER; publ. Anales (2 a year).

Mérida

Museo Nacional de Arte Romano (National Museum of Roman Art): Calle José Ramón Mélida, s/n, 06800 Mérida Badajoz; tel. (92) 4311690; fax (92) 4302006; e-mail mnar@mnar.es; internet www .museoarteromano.mcu.es; f. 1838, present site 1986; 37,000 artefacts; Roman, Visigoth archaeology; library of 16,000 specialized vols, 695 periodicals; Dir Dr JOSÉ MARÍA ALVAREZ MARTÍNEZ; publs Anas (1 a year), Cuadernos Emeritenses (irregular), Studia Lusitana.

Palma de Mallorca

Museo de Mallorca: Calle Portella 5, 07001 Palma; tel. (97) 1717540; fax (97) 1710483; internet www.museudemallorca.es; f. 1961; history, ethnology, fine arts, prehistory; Dir GUILLERMO ROSSELLÓ BORDOY.

Pontevedra

Museo de Pontevedra: Calle Pasantería 2– 12, 36002 Pontevedra; tel. (98) 6851455; fax (98) 6840693; internet www.museo.depo.es; f. 1927; pottery and ancient industrial and naval history of Galicia; prehistoric jewellery and jet ornaments; Spanish paintings since 15th century; library of 150,000 vols on literature, art and archaeology of Galicia, 6,000 periodicals, 500 maps; Dir Dr JOSÉ CARLOS VALLE PÉREZ; publ. El Museo de Pontevedra (1 a year).

Sabadell

Museu d'Art de Sabadell: Carrer Dr Puig 16, 08202 Sabadell; tel. (93) 7278555; fax (93) 7275507; e-mail mas@ajsabadell.cat; f. 1981; painting, ceramics, photography from early 19th century to 1960s; Dir JOSEP SERRANO; publ. Arraona.

Museu d'Història de Sabadell: Carrer Sant Antoni 13, 08201 Sabadell; tel. (93) 7278555; fax (93) 7266042; e-mail mhs@ ajsabadell.es; f. 1931 as Museu de la Ciutat; present name adopted 1970; prehistoric archaeological, numismatic collections, native handicrafts; Iberico-Roman section, sections on textiles and mineralogy; Dir GENÍS RIBÉ MONGÉ; publ. Arraona (1 a year).

Sabiñánigo

Museo de Dibujo 'Castillo de Larrés': Apdo 25, 22612 Sabiñánigo (Huesca); tel. (97) 4482981; e-mail serrablo@serrablo.org; internet www.serrablo.org/museodibujo; f. 1986 by 'Amigos de Serrablo', a cultural ascn specializing entirely in contemporary Spanish and Spanish-American design; Pres. ALFREDO GAVÍN.

San Roque

Museo Monográfico Municipal de Carteia: Palacio de los Gobernadores, Calle Rubín de Celis 1, 11360 San Roque (Cádiz); tel. (95) 6781587; e-mail prensasanroque@ airtel.net; f. 2001; explains the history of excavations in the town and the historical devt of the ancient settlement of Carteia; Dir RAFAEL CALDELA LÓPEZ.

San Sebastián

Palacio del Mar—Aquarium (Sea Museum and Aquarium): Sociedad de Oceanografía de Guipúzcoa, Plaza Jacques Cousteau 1, 20003 Donostia, San Sebastián; tel. (94) 3440099; fax (94) 3430092; e-mail sog@ aquariumss.com; internet www.aquariumss .com; f. 1928; history of seafaring since 13th century, models of historical ships, portraits of navigators and local fishing tackle; oceano-

graphic museum and marine laboratory; aquarium with Atlantic and tropical fishes; Dir CARMEN ARRAZOLA.

San Telmo Museoa: Andereño Elbira Zipitria 1, 20003 Donostia, San Sebastián; tel. (94) 3481580; fax (94) 3481581; e-mail santelmo@donostia.org; internet www .santelmomuseoa.com; f. 1902; reopened in 2011 to the public as a museum on the Basque Soc. housed in the former Dominican convent of San Telmo, built in the 16th century, and inaugurated 1932 by Alfonso XIII; library of 11,000 vols; Dir SUSANA SOTO.

Santander

Museo de Prehistoria y Arqueología de Cantabria (Prehistoric and Archaeological Museum): Avda Los Castros 65–67, 39005 Santander; tel. (94) 2207106; fax (94) 2207106; internet www.museosdecantabria .com/preh/museo.htm; f. 1941; palaeolithic to Middle Ages in Cantabria; library of 62,000 vols; Curator AMPARO LÓPEZ ORTIZ.

Santiago de Compostela

Museo das Peregrinacións (Pilgrimage Museum): San Miguel 4, 'Casa Gotica', 15704 Santiago de Compostela; tel. (98) 1581558; fax (98) 1581955; e-mail difusion .mdperegrinacions@xunta.es; internet www .mdperegrinacions.com; f. 1951, inaugurated 1965; relics and items related to St James and the Pilgrimages; medieval art and history of the 'Camino de Santiago'; library of 8,246 vols, 350 periodicals; Dir BIEITO PÉREZ OUTEIRIÑO.

Seville

Museo Arqueológico de Sevilla (Archaeological Museum of Sevilla): Plaza de América (Parque de María Luisa) s/n, 41013 Seville; tel. (95) 4786474; fax (95) 4786478; e-mail museoarqueologicosevilla.ccul@juntadeandalucia.es; internet www.juntadeandalucia.es/ cultura/museos/muse/; f. 1880; 60,000 exhibits; Roman statues, mosaics; incorporates municipal collns; treasures of Tarshish; Dir CONCEPCIÓN SAN MARTÍN MONTILLA.

Museo de Bellas Artes de Sevilla (Museum of Fine Arts of Sevilla): Plaza del Museo 9, 41001 Seville; tel. (95) 4786500; fax (95) 4786490; e-mail museobellasartessevilla .ccul@juntadeandalucia.es; internet www .juntadeandalucia.es/cultura/museos/mbase; f. 1835; paintings by local artists from 15th to 20th centuries; Baroque art (esp. Murillo, Zurbarán and Valdés Leal); library of 12,000 vols, 450 periodicals; Dir MARÍA DEL VALME MUÑOZ RUBIO; Curator VIRGINIA MARQUÉS.

Sitges

Museu Cau Ferrat: Calle Fonollar, s/n, 08870 Sitges; tel. (93) 8940364; fax (93) 8948529; e-mail m.sitges@diba.es; internet www.diba.cat/museuslocals/nouwebmuseus/ buscar/cercador_generic.asp; f. 1933; closed for renovations from 2010; house and studio of the painter and writer Santiago Rusiñol; contains drawings and paintings by Rusiñol and his friends and contemporaries, (Casas, Picasso, Utrillo); also woodcarving, sculpture, paintings (El Greco), ceramics (since 14th century), furniture, ironwork (13th– 19th centuries), glass (16th–19th centuries); Dir MARIA-NADAL SAU I GIRALT.

Soria

Museo Numantino: Paseo del Espolón 8, 42001 Soria; tel. (97) 5221397; fax (97) 5229872; f. 1916; prehistoric, ethnological, Roman and medieval archaeological collections, comprising 180,000 objects; library of 10,000 vols; Dir ELÍAS TERÉS NAVARRO.

Tarragona

Museu i Necròpolis Paleocristians: tel. (97) 7211175; fax (97) 7252286; e-mail mnat@mnat.cat; internet www.mnat.es/cat/mnat/necr; f. 1930; objects discovered during excavation of the Roman-Christian necropolis; Dir FRANCESC TARRATS-BOU.

Museu Nacional Arqueològic de Tarragona (National Museum of Archaeology of Tarragona): Plaça del Rei 5, 43003 Tarragona; tel. (97) 7251515; fax (97) 7252286; e-mail mnat@mnat.es; internet www.mnat.es; f. 1834; archaeological, historical, local Roman exhibits; library of 12,000 vols; Dir FRANCESC TARRATS-BOU.

Toledo

Museo del Greco (El Greco Museum): Calle Samuel Leví s/n, 45002 Toledo; tel. (92) 5224405; fax (92) 5224559; e-mail secretaria.greco@telefonica.net; f. 1911; the artist's house; contains important later works by El Greco; works from the Spanish schools of the 17th century; furniture of the 16th–17th century and ceramics from the Talaverana factory; colln of paintings by Spanish artists incl. Francisco de Zurbarán and Bartolomé Esteban Murillo; Dir ANA CARMEN LAVÍN BERDONCES.

Museo de Santa Cruz: Calle Cervantes 3, 45001 Toledo; tel. (92) 5221402; fax (92) 5225862; f. 1958; archaeology, fine arts, industrial and decorative arts; library of 13,000 vols; Dir ALFONSO CABALLERO KLINK; publ. *Memoria del Museo de Santa Cruz* (irregular).

Affiliated Museums:

Museo Casa de Dulcinea en El Toboso: Calle Don Quijote 1, 45820 El Toboso; tel. (92) 5197288; fax (92) 5225862; f. 1967; ethnography of La Mancha area and period reconstruction in the 17th-century Casa Solariega.

Museo de Arte Contemporáneo: Calle de las Bulas s/n, 45002 Toledo; tel. (92) 5227871; f. 1973; closed for renovation until further notice.

Museo de Cerámica 'Ruíz de Luna': Plaça de San Agustín s/n, 45600 Talavera de la Reina; tel. and fax (92) 5800149; f. 1963; local ceramics.

Museo de los Concilios y de la Cultura Visigoda: Calle San Román s/n, 45002 Toledo; tel. (92) 5227872; fax (92) 5225862; f. 1969; Visigothic art and archaeology.

Museo Taller del Moro: Calle Taller del Moro 4, 45002 Toledo; tel. (92) 5224500; fax (92) 5225862; f. 1961; Mudejar art and archaeology.

Museo Sefardi-Sinagoga del Tránsito: Calle Samuel Leví s/n, 45002 Toledo; tel. (92) 5223665; fax (92) 5215831; e-mail museo.msefardi@mcu.es; internet www.museosefardi.mcu.es; f. 1964; Jewish synagogue built in the 14th century by Samuel Ha-Levi, treasurer to King Don Pedro I, 'The Cruel'; given to the Military Order of Calatrava in 1494 by Ferdinand and Isabella; in 18th century became church of Sta María del Tránsito; nat. monument; created Sephardic Museum 1964; archaeology, life and costumes of Sephardic Jews; library of 20,000 vols; Dir SANTIAGO PALOMERO PLAZA.

Valencia

Museo de Bellas Artes de Valencia (Museum of Fine Arts of Valencia): Calle de San Pío V 9, 46010 Valencia; tel. (96) 3870300; fax (96) 3870301; e-mail museobellasartesvalencia@gva.es; internet www.museobellasartesvalencia.gva.es; f. 1839; temporary exhibitions; more than 3,000 paintings; also sculpture, archaeology,

drawing and print sections; library of 24,043 vols on art, 840 periodicals, 7,892 photographs; Dir PAZ OLMOS PERIS.

Museo Nacional de Cerámica 'González Marti': Poeta Querol 2, 46002 Valencia; tel. (96) 3516392; fax (96) 3513512; e-mail difusion.mceramica@mcu.es; internet mnceramica.mcu.es; f. 1947; 26,200 exhibits; a nat. museum of ceramics and decorative arts, set in the Palace of the Marquis of Dos Aguas; library of 25,000 vols; Dir Dr JAUME COLL CONESA; publ. *Materiales y Documentos*.

Museu de Prehistòria de València: Corona 36, 46003 Valencia; tel. (96) 3 883565; fax (96) 3 883536; e-mail sip@dival.es; internet www.museuprehistoriavalencia.es; f. 1927; prehistoric art and culture; Roman era; Iberian culture and coin collns; Valencian archaeology; intense field work in archaeological sites; educational activities, guided tours and workshops; temporary exhibits; courses, confs and workshops; library of 60,000 vols, 1,380 periodicals; Dir HELENA BONET ROSADO; publs *Archivo de Prehistoria Levantina*, *Serie de Trabajos Varios del S.I.P.*

Valladolid

Museo Casa de Cervantes, Valladolid (Cervantes' House Museum, Valladolid): Calle del Rastro s/n, 47001 Valladolid; tel. (98) 3308810; fax (98) 3390703; e-mail informacion@mcervantes.mcu.es; internet museocasacervantes.mcu.es; f. 1948; furniture and possessions of the writer; library of 10,000 vols; Dir AMPARO MAGDALENO DE LA CRUZ.

Museo de Valladolid (Valladolid Museum): Palacio de Fabio Nelli, Plaza de Fabio Nelli s/n, 47003 Valladolid; tel. (98) 3351389; fax (98) 3350422; e-mail museo.valladolid@jcyl.es; f. 1879; archaeology and fine art, articles from palaeolithic times to the 18th century; library: specialized library of more than 15,000 vols, restricted access; Dir ELOISA WATTENBERG GARCÍA.

Museo Nacional Colegio de San Gregorio: Cadenas de San Gregorio 1–3, 47011 Valladolid; tel. (98) 3250375; fax (98) 3259300; e-mail museosangregorio@mcu.es; internet www.museosangregorio.mcu.es; f. 1933 as Museo Nacional de Escultura; present name adopted 2008; housed in the old Colegio de San Gregorio, since late 15th century; works by Alonso Berruguete, Juan de Juni, Gregorio Fernández, Alonso Cano, Felipe Vigarny and others; library of 20,000 vols; Dir MARÍA BOLAÑOS ATIENZA; publ. *Boletín*.

Vic

Museu Episcopal de Vic (Episcopal Museum of Vic): Plaça Bisbe Oliba 3, 08500 Vic; tel. (93) 869360; fax (93) 8869361; e-mail informacio@museuepiscopalvic.com; internet www.museuepiscopalvic.com; f. 1891; medieval arts, provincial Romanesque, Gothic precious metalwork, textiles, embroideries, liturgical vestments, forged iron, etc.; Dir MIQUEL TRESSERRAS.

Zamora

Museo de Zamora (Museum of Zamora): Palacio del Cordón, Plaza de Sta Lucía 2, 49002 Zamora; tel. (98) 0516150; fax (98) 0535064; e-mail museo.zamora@jcyl.es; internet www.museoscastillayleon.jcyl.es/museodezamora; f. 1877; housed in 16th-century palace; collns (300,000 items): palaeontology, prehistory and archaeology, fine arts, ethnography; library of 8,920 vols, 227 periodicals; Dir ROSARIO GARCÍA ROZAS.

Zaragoza

Museo de Zaragoza (Museum of Zaragoza): Plaza de los Sitios 6, 50001 Zaragoza; tel. (97) 6222181; fax (97) 6222378; e-mail museoza@aragob.es; internet www.aragob.es/edycul/patrimo/museos/zaragoza.htm; f. 1848; archaeological; prehistory, Roman, Arab, Gothic, Moorish, Romanesque and Renaissance exhibits; primitive arts and crafts, paintings from 14th–19th centuries, contemporary Aragonese artists; ethnology and ceramics sections are located at Parque Primo de Rivera; library of 31,000 vols; Dir Dr MIGUEL BELTRÁN LLORIS; publs *Boletín* (1 a year), *Guías Didácticas* (2 or 3 a year), *Catálogos Exposiciones*.

Museo Pablo Gargallo: Plaza de San Felipe 3, 50003 Zaragoza; tel. (97) 6392524; fax (97) 6395597; e-mail museogargallo-oficinas@ayto-zaragoza.es; internet www.zaragoza.es/ciudad/museos/es/gargallo; f. 1982; important colln of sculpture, designs and cartoons by Gargallo; research on his life and works, and modern art in gen.; library of 9,000 vols on Gargallo and sculpture in gen.; Dir MARÍA CRISTINA GIL IMAZ.

Universities

ASOCIACIÓN UNIVERSITARIA IBEROAMERICANA DE POSTGRADO

Colegio Arzobispo Fonseca, Calle Fonseca 4, 37002 Salamanca

Telephone: (92) 3210039
Fax: (93) 3214949
E-mail: auip@auip.org
Internet: www.auip.org

Some 100 universities offer 1,500 postgraduate courses under the aegis of the AUIP

Pres.: FRANCISCO GONZÁLEZ LODEIRO
Dir-Gen.: VICTOR CRUZ CARDONA
Deputy Dir-Gen.: FRANCISCO MARTOS PERALES.

I. E. UNIVERSIDAD

Campus de Santa Cruz la Real, 40003 Segovia

Telephone: (92) 1412410
Fax: (92) 1445593
E-mail: university@ie.edu
Internet: www.ie.es

Founded 1992
Private control
Academic year: September to June

Rector: Dr JUAN LUIS MARTÍNEZ SÁNCHEZ
Vice-Rector for Planning: Dr SAMUEL GONZÁLEZ MANCEBO
Vice-Rector for Research and Teaching Staff: SALVADOR CARMONA MORENO
Vice-Rector for Students: Dr MIGUEL LARRAÑAGA ZULUETA
Registrar: Dr ROBERTO RUIZ SALCES
Dir of Academic Org.: ANTONIO DE CASTRO CARPEÑO
Man.: IGNACIO SOTOMAYOR SAEZ
Library Dir: AMADA MARCOS BLÁZQUEZ

Library of 36,000 vols, 4,500 periodicals
Number of teachers: 190
Number of students: 1,400

DEANS

Faculty of Experimental Sciences: JESÚS A. GÓMEZ OCHOA DE ALDA
Faculty of Human, Social and Communication Sciences: SANTIAGO LÓPEZ NAVIA

MONDRAGON UNIBERTSITATEA

Loramendi 4, Apdo 23, 20500 Mondragón
Telephone: (94) 3712185
Fax: (94) 3712193

E-mail: info@mondragon.edu
Internet: www.mondragon.edu
Founded 1997
Private control
Languages of instruction: Basque, Spanish, English
Academic year: September to July

Rector: IOSU ZABALA
Vice-Rector: JOSE MARI AIZEAGA ZUBILLAGA
Academic Vice-Rector: ION ALTUNA
Registrar and Financial Dir: IDOIA PEÑACOBA ETXEBARRIA
Librarian: OBDULIA VELEZ

Library of 80,000 vols, 800 periodicals
Number of teachers: 250
Number of students: 4,000

DEANS

Faculty of Business Studies: LANDER BELOKI
Faculty of Gastronomic Sciences: JOSE MARI AIZEGA (Dir)
Faculty of Humanities and Education: NEKANE ARRATIBEL
Higher Polytechnic School: VICENTE ATXA (Dir)

UNIVERSIDAD ALFONSO X EL SABIO

Campus de Villanueva de la Cañada, Avda Universidad 1, 28691, Madrid

Telephone: (90) 2100868
Fax: (91) 8109101
E-mail: info@uax.es
Internet: www.uax.es
Founded 1993
Academic year: October to June
Pres.: JESÚS NÚÑEZ VELÁZQUEZ

Library of 15,000 vols
Number of teachers: 1,000
Number of students: 10,000

Publications: *A x A* (art and architecture, online), *Linguax* (applied languages, online), *Revista Electrónica Biociencias* (life sciences, online), *Saberes* (law, economics and social sciences, online), *Tecnología y Desarrollo* (science, technology and environment, online)

DEANS

Faculty of Applied Languages: Dr JOAQUÍN GONZÁLEZ IBÁÑEZ
Faculty of Health Sciences: Dr ALFREDO ENTRALA BUENO
Faculty of Social Studies: Dr ANDRÉS TAGLIAVIA LÓPEZ
Polytechnic School: Dr JUAN HERRANZ ARRIBAS

UNIVERSIDAD ANTONIO DE NEBRIJA

Campus de la Berzosa, Hoyo de Manzanares, 28249 Madrid

Telephone: (91) 4521101
E-mail: informa@nebrija.es
Internet: www.nebrija.com
Founded 1995
Private control
Rector: Profa Dra PILAR VÉLEZ MELÓN
Vice-Rector for Academic Affairs: ALBERTO LÓPEZ ROSADO
Vice-Rector for Int. Rels and Registrar: JUAN CAYÓN PEÑA
Vice-Rector for Research: JUAN ANTONIO MAESTRO DE LA CUERDA

Library of 44,000 vols, 300 periodicals
Number of students: 3,500

DEANS

Faculty of Arts and Letters: PABLO ÁLVAREZ DE TOLEDO MÜLLER (Vice-Dean)
Faculty of Communications Science: FERNANDO GONZÁLEZ URBANEJA

Faculty of Social Science: CARLOS CUERVO-ARANGO MARTÍNEZ

UNIVERSIDAD AUTÓNOMA DE MADRID

Ciudad Universitaria de Cantoblanco, Carretera de Colmenar, Km 15, 28049 Madrid

Telephone: (91) 4975100
Fax: (91) 3974123
E-mail: informacion.general@uam.es
Internet: www.uam.es
Founded 1968
State control
Language of instruction: Spanish
Academic year: October to June

Rector: JOSÉ MARÍA SANZ MARTÍNEZ
Vice-Rector for Campus and Environmental Quality: MARÍA ÁNGELES ESPINOSA BAYAL
Vice-Rector for Infrastructure and Technological Devt: JOSÉ MARÍA SANZ MARTÍNEZ
Vice-Rector for Innovation and Technology: JOSÉ RAMÓN DORRONSORO IBERO
Vice-Rector for Institutional Relations and Cooperation: MARGARITA ALFARO AMIEIRO
Vice-Rector for Int. Relations: ASUNCIÓN MARTÍNEZ CEBRÍAN
Vice-Rector for Postgraduate Studies: ÁNGEL RODRÍGUEZ GARCÍA-BRAZALES
Vice-Rector for Research: RAFAEL GARESSE ALARCÓN
Vice-Rector for Students and Continuing Education: ANTONIO ÁLVAREZ-OSSORIO ALVARIÑO
Vice-Rector for Teaching and Research Staff: CARLOS GARCÍA DE LA VEGA
Vice-Rector for Undergraduate Studies: JUAN ANTONIO HUERTAS MARTÍNEZ
Vice-Rector for Univ. Extension and Outreach: VALERIA CAMPORESI
Registrar: JUAN DAMIÁN MORENO
Man.: PEDRO GARCÍA MORENO
Librarian: MIGUEL JIMÉNEZ ALEIXANDRE

Library of 840,000 vols, 18,000 periodicals
Number of teachers: 2,250
Number of students: 35,000

Publications: *Al Sur* (4 a year), *Anuario del Departamento de Filosofía* (4 a year), *Anuario del Departamento de Historia de la Filosofía* (1 a year), *Anuario del Departamento de Historia y Teoría del Arte* (1 a year), *Apuntes de la Autónoma* (irregular), *Boletín del Instituto de Ciencias de la Educación* (irregular), *Boletín Geográfico* (3 a year), *Coyuntura Trimestral* (4 a year, journal of the Laurence R. Klein Institute of Economic Forecasting), *Cuaderno Gris* (3 a year), *Cuadernos de Prehistoria y Arqueología* (1 a year), *Edad de Oro* (1 a year), *Encuentros Multidisciplinares* (Multidisciplinary Research and Debate, 3 a year), *Journal of Human Ecology* (irregular), *La Ecoalternativa* (4 a year), *Manuscrit. CAO* (1 a year), *Narria* (4 a year), *Revista de Cantoblanco* (12 a year), *Revista de Lengua y Literatura Catalana, Gallega y Vasca* (1 a year), *Tarbiya* (educational research and innovation, 3 a year)

DEANS

Faculty of Economics and Business Studies: ANA MARÍA LÓPEZ GARCÍA
Faculty of Law: FERNANDO MOLINA FERNÁNDEZ
Faculty of Medicine: Dr JOSÉ ANTONIO RODRÍGUEZ MONTES
Faculty of Philosophy and Letters: ANTONIO CASCÓN DORADO
Faculty of Psychology: ÁNGELA LOECHES ALONSO
Faculty of Science: ISABEL CASTRO PARGA
Faculty of Teacher Training and Education: ROSALÍA ARANDA REDRUELLO

ATTACHED CENTRES

Escuela Universitaria de Enfermería de la Comunidad de Madrid: Avda Orellana s/n, Recinto Hospital Severo Ochoa, 28911 Leganés, (Madrid); tel. (91) 6931511; e-mail e.u.enfermeria@salud.madrid.org; internet www.eulasalle.com; f. 1948 as teaching institute; courses in educational science, health sciences and management and technology.

Escuela Universitaria de Fisioterapia de la Organización Nacional de Ciegos Españoles: Calle Nuria 42, 28034 Madrid; tel. (91) 5894500; fax (91) 5894498; e-mail euf@once.es; internet euf.once.es; Dir JAVIER SAINZ DE MURIETA Y RODEYRO.

La Salle Centro Universitario: Calle La Salle 10, 28023 Madrid; tel. (91) 7401980; fax (91) 3571730; e-mail sia@lasallecampus.es; internet www.eulasalle.com; f. 1948 as teaching institute; courses in educational science, health sciences and management and technology.

UNIVERSIDAD CAMILO JOSÉ CELA

Castillo de Alarcón 49, Villafranca del Castillo Urb, 28692 Madrid

Telephone: (91) 8153131
Fax: (91) 8153130
E-mail: info@ucjc.edu
Internet: www.ucjc.edu
Founded 2000
Private control

Rector: Dr RAFAEL CORTÉS ELVIRA
Vice-Rector for Academic Affairs and Teaching: ENRIQUE FERNÁNDEZ REDONDO
Vice-Rector for Research and Graduate Affairs
Registrar: JOSÉ LUIS DELSO MARTÍNEZ-TREVIJANO
Dir-Gen.: CONCHA CANOYRA
Library Dir: BELÉN PALOMERO
Number of students: 5,000

Publication: *Revista Edupsykhé* (1 a year)

DEANS

Faculty of Communications: JULIO CÉSAR HERRERO
Faculty of Health Sciences: MIGUEL ÁNGEL PÉREZ NIETO
Faculty of Law and Economics: JESÚS GRACIA SANZ
Faculty of Social Sciences and Education: ESTHER ROBLES SASTRE

UNIVERSIDAD CARLOS III DE MADRID

Calle Madrid 126, 28903 Getafe, Madrid

Telephone: (91) 6246000
Internet: www.uc3m.es
Founded 1989
State control
Language of instruction: Spanish, English
Academic year: September to June

Rector: Prof. DANIEL PEÑA SANCHEZ DE RIVERA
Vice-Rector of Communication, Culture and Sports, and Continuing Education: MONTSERRAT IGLESIAS SANTOS
Vice-Rector of Equality and Cooperation: PILAR AZCÁRATE AGUILAR-AMAT
Vice-Rector of Graduate Programmes and Quality: CARMEN VÁZQUEZ GARCÍA
Vice-Rector of Infrastructure and Environmental Matters: PEDRO ISASI VIÑUELA
Vice-Rector of Int. Relations: ÁLVARO ESCRIBANO SÁEZ
Vice-Rector of Research: CARLOS BALAGUER BERNALDO DE QUIRÓS
Vice-Rector of Student Affairs and Residence Halls: HENAR MIGUÉLEZ GARRIDO
Vice-Rector of Teaching Staff and Depts: JUAN JOSÉ ROMO URROZ

Vice-Rector of the Colmenarejo Campus: MIKEL TAPIA TORRES

Vice-Rector of Undergraduate Studies: ISABEL GUTIÉRREZ CALDERÓN

Registrar: JESÚS RAFAEL MERCADER UGUINA

Man.: JUAN MANUEL MORENO ÁLVAREZ

Library Dir: MARGARITA TALADRIZ MÁS

Number of teachers: 1,666
Number of students: 17,929

Publications: *Boletín Inflación y Análisis Macroeconómico (BIAM), Bulletin EU & US Inflation and Macroeconomic analysis (BIMA), Cuadernos del Instituto Antonio de Nebrija de estudios sobre la Universidad (CIAN), Derechos y libertades: Revista del Instituto Bartolomé de las Casas, Forinf@ Online. Revista Iberoamericana Sobre Servicios de Información, Litterae: Cuadernos Sobre Cultura Escrita, Revista de Historia Económica—Journal of Iberian and Latin American Economic History, Revista de Historiografía, Semanal 3, Universitas: revista de filosofía, derecho y política*

DEANS

Faculty of Social Sciences and Law: Prof. MANUEL ÁNGEL BERMEJO CASTRILLO

Higher Polytechnical School: Prof. EMILIO OLÍAS RUIZ

School of Humanities, Communications and Documentation: JOSÉ MANUEL PALACIO ARRANZ

ATTACHED INSTITUTES

Instituto Alonso Martínez de Justicia y Litigación ('Alonso Martinez' Institute of Justice and Litigation): Calle Madrid 126, 28903 Getafe, Madrid; tel. (91) 6249718; e-mail iam@listserv.uc3m.es; internet www.turan.uc3m.es/uc3m/inst/amj/home.htm; Dir VÍCTOR MORENO CATENA.

Instituto 'Conde de Campomanes' de Iniciativas Empresariales y Empresa Familiar ('Conde de Campomanes' Institute of Entrepreneurship and Family Business): Calle Madrid 126, 28903 Getafe, Madrid; tel. (91) 6249345; fax (91) 6245707; e-mail organizaciondeempresas@uc3m.es; internet www.uc3m.es/portal/page/portal/instituto_iniciativas_emp_empresa_familiar/conde_-camp_institute; Dir ZULIMA FERNÁNDEZ RODRÍGUEZ.

Instituto de Cultura y Tecnología 'Miguel de Unamuno' ('Miguel de Unamuno' Institute of Culture and Technology): Calle Madrid 126, Edif. Concepción Arena, 28903 Getafe, Madrid; tel. (91) 6249258; fax (91) 6249212; e-mail buforn@pa.uc3m.es; internet turan.uc3m.es/uc3m/inst/mu/dpmu.html; Dir Prof. Dr ANTONIO RODRÍGUEZ DE LAS HERAS.

Instituto de Derecho Público Comparado 'Manuel García Pelayo' ('Manuel García Pelayo' Institute of Comparative Public Law): Calle Madrid 126, Despacho 11.07, 28903 Getafe, Madrid; tel. (91) 6249714; fax (91) 6249517; e-mail imgp@der-pu.uc3m.es; internet turan.uc3m.es/uc3m/inst/mgp/portada.htm; Dir Prof. Dr MIGUEL REVENGA SÁNCHEZ.

Instituto de Documentación y Gestión de la Información 'Agustín Millares' ('Agustin Millares' Institute for Documentation and Information Management): Calle Madrid 126, Edif. 14, Oficina 14.2.52, 28903 Getafe, Madrid; tel. (91) 6249252; fax (91) 6249212; e-mail instituto-millares@bib.uc3m.es; internet iamc.uc3m.es; Dir Profa. Dra MERCEDES CARIDAD SEBASTIÁN.

Instituto de Derechos Humanos 'Bartolomé de las Casas' ('Bartolomé de las Casas' Institute of Human Rights): Calle Madrid 126, Despacho 11.1.03. CP, 28903 Getafe,

Madrid; tel. (91) 6249834; fax (91) 6248923; e-mail idhbc@pa.uc3m.es; internet turan.uc3m.es/uc3m/inst/bc; Dir Prof. Dr RAFAEL DE ASIS ROIG.

Instituto de Estudios Internacionales y Europeos 'Francisco de Vitoria' ('Francisco de Vitoria' Institute of International and European Studies): Calle Madrid 126, 28903 Getafe, Madrid; tel. (91) 6249843; fax (91) 6249517; e-mail fvitoria@der-pu.uc3m.es; internet turan.uc3m.es/uc3m/inst/fv/dpfv.html; Dir Prof. Dr FERNANDO MARIÑO MENÉNDEZ.

Instituto de Historiografía 'Julio Caro Baroja' (The 'Julio Caro Baroja' Institute for Histography): Calle Madrid 126, 28903 Getafe, Madrid; e-mail ijcarobaro@uc3m.es; internet turan.uc3m.es/uc3m/inst/jcb; Dir JAIME ALVAR EZQUERRA.

Instituto de Política y Gobernanza ('Fermin Caballero' Institute of Politics and Government): Calle Madrid 126, 28903 Getafe, Madrid; tel. (91) 6245728; fax (91) 6245848; e-mail ipoliticagobernanza@uc3m.es; internet www.uc3m.es/portal/page/portal/inst_pol_gob_fermin_caballero; Dir ANTONIO NATERA PERAL.

Instituto de Seguridad Social 'Juan Luis Vives' ('Juan Luis Vives' Institute of Social Security): Calle Madrid 126, Edif. Luis Vives, Despacho 11.07, 28903 Getafe, Madrid; tel. (91) 6249371; fax (91) 6249517; e-mail ijlv@pa.uc3m.es; internet turan.uc3m.es/uc3m/inst/iuss/dpiuss.html; Dir Prof. Dr SANTIAGO GONZÁLEZ ORTEGA.

Instituto de Seguridad de los Vehículos Automóviles 'Duque de Santo Mauro' (Institute of Automotive Vehicle Safety): Avda de la Universidad 30, Edif. Agustín de Betancourt, Despacho 1.1.C.05, 28911 Leganés, Madrid; tel. (91) 6249460; e-mail celtia@pa.uc3m.es; internet turan.uc3m.es/uc3m/inst/isva/home.htm; Dir Prof. Dr VICENTE DÍAZ LÓPEZ.

:Instituto 'Figuerola' de Historia y Ciencias Sociales ('Laureano Figueroa' Institute of Economic History and Institutions): Calle Madrid 126, 28903 Getafe, Madrid; tel. (91) 6249620; fax (91) 6249574; e-mail laureano_figuerola@uc3m.es; internet turan.uc3m.es/uc3m/inst/lf; Dir JUAN CARMONA PIDAL.

Instituto 'Flores de Lemus' ('Flores de Lemus' Institute of Advanced Studies in Economics): Calle Madrid 126, Laboratorio Predicción y Análisis Macroeconómico, 28903 Getafe, Madrid; tel. (91) 6249889; fax (91) 6249305; e-mail laborat@est-econ.uc3m.es; internet turan.uc3m.es/uc3m/inst/fl; Dir Prof. Dr ANTONI ESPASA TERRADES.

Instituto Interuniversitario para la Comunicación Cultural (Interuniversity Institute for Cultural Communication): Calle Madrid 126, Despacho 15.1.5.9, 28903 Getafe, Madrid; tel. (91) 6245781; fax (91) 6249517; e-mail icultura@pa.uc3m.es; internet turan.uc3m.es/uc3m/inst/iudc; Dir Prof. Dr JESÚS PRIETO DE PEDRO.

Instituto 'Juan Velázquez de Velasco' de Investigación en inteligencia para la Seguridad y la Defensa ('Juan Velázquez de Velasco' Institute for Research and Intelligence for Security and Defence): Avda de la Universidad Carlos III 22, Edif. Miguel de Unamuno, 1.2.B10, 28270 Colmenarejo, Madrid; tel. (91) 8561275; fax (91) 6249212; e-mail institutodeinteligencia@uc3m.es; internet www.institutodeinteligencia.uc3m.es; Dir DIEGO NAVARRO BONILLA.

Instituto 'Lucio Anneo Séneca' de Estudios Clásicos sobre la Sociedad y la Política ('Lucio Anneo Séneca' Institute for Classic Studies on Society and Politics): Calle

Madrid 133, Edif. 17 Ortega y Gasset, Despacho 17.02.43, 28903 Getafe, Madrid; tel. (91) 6245868; fax (91) 6249212; e-mail seneca@hum.uc3m.es; internet institutolucioanneoseneca.com; Dir Prof. FRANCISCO LISI BERETERBIDE; publ. *Manuscritos de Salamanca (Library of Salamanca University)* (online (institutolucioanneoseneca.com/es/recursos/manuscritos-de-salamanca/fondo.html)), *Platón, Leyes (Plato's Laws)* (online (institutolucioanneoseneca.com/es/recursos/las-leyes-de-platon-y-las-leyes-de-las-ciudades-griegas.html)), *Res Publica Litterarum* (online (institutolucioanneoseneca.com/es/el-instituto3/publicaciones/revistas/res-publica-litterarum.html)).

Instituto 'Pascual Madoz' del Territorio, Urbanismo y Medio Ambiente ('Pascual Madoz' Institute of Territorial, Urban and Environmental Studies): Calle Madrid 126, Edif. Luis Vives, 28903 Getafe, Madrid; tel. (91) 6249838; fax (91) 6249212; e-mail cruiz@pa.uc3m.es; internet turan.uc3m.es/uc3m/inst/pm/dppm.html; Dir Prof. Dr LUCIANO JOSÉ PAREJO ALFONSO.

Instituto Tecnológico de Química y Materiales 'Álvaro Alonso Barba' ('Álvaro Alonso Barba' Technological Institute of Chemistry and Materials): Avda de la Universidad 30, Edif. Agustín de Betancourt, 28911 Leganés, Madrid; tel. (91) 6249990; e-mail fvelasco@ing.uc3m.es; internet turan.uc3m.es/uc3m/inst/aab/principal.html; Dir Prof. Dr FRANCISCO JAVIER VELASCO LÓPEZ.

Instituto Universitario de Derecho y Economía (Institute of Law and Economics): Calle Madrid 126, 28903 Getafe, Madrid; tel. (91) 6249846; fax (91) 6249802; e-mail iudec@eco.uc3m.es; internet turan.uc3m.es/uc3m/inst/de; Dir DAVID CAMINO BLASCO.

Instituto Universitario de Economía (Institute of Economics): Calle Madrid 126, 28903 Getafe, Madrid; tel. (91) 6249287; fax (91) 6249872; e-mail instituto.economia@uc3m.es; internet www.institutoeconomiauc3m.es.

Instituto Universitario 'Pedro Juan de Lastanosa' de Desarrollo Tecnológico y Promoción de la Innovación ('Pedro Juan de Lastanosa' Institute of Technological Development and the Promotion of Innovation): Avda de la Universidad 30, 28911 Leganés, Madrid; e-mail lastanosa@uc3m.es; internet turan.uc3m.es/uc3m/inst/pl; Dir Prof. Dr FERNANDO LÓPEZ MARTÍNEZ.

Instituto Universitario sobre Modelización y Simulación en Fluidodinámica, Nanociencia y Matemática Industrial 'Gregorio Millán Barbany': Ave. de la Universidad s/n, Madrid 28916; internet www.uc3m.es/portal/page/portal/instituto_univ_gregorio_millan_barbany.

Instituto sobre Desarrollo Empresarial 'Carmen Vidal Ballester' ('Carmen Vidal Ballester' Institute of Business Development): internet turan.uc3m.es/uc3m/inst/cvb.

UNIVERSIDAD CEU CARDENAL HERRERA

Edificio Seminario, Avda Seminario s/n, 46113 Moncada (Valencia)

Telephone: (96) 1369000
Fax: (96) 1395272
E-mail: informa@uch.ceu.es
Internet: www.uch.ceu.es

Founded 1999
Private control

Rector: JOSÉ MARÍA DÍAZ Y PÉREZ DE LA LASTRA

Vice-Rector for Academic Affairs and Teaching Staff: FRANCISCO BOSCH MORELL

Vice-Rector for Centre at Elche: CÉSAR CASIMIRO ELENA

Vice-Rector for Institutional Relations: Dr PILAR PARICIO ESTEBAN

Vice-Rector for Research: JUAN MANUEL CORPA ARENAS

Vice-Rector for Strategic Action Plan Coordination: HIGINIO MARÍN PEDREÑO

Vice-Rector for Student Affairs and Univ. Extension: RAFAEL FAYOS FEBRER

Registrar: ROSA VISIEDO CLAVEROL

Man.: BARTOLOMÉ SERRA MARQUÉS

Library Dir: ELENA SAURÍ RODRIGO

Library of 90,000 vols, 2,019 periodicals

DEANS

Faculty of Communication Science: ELIAS DURÁN DE PORRAS

Faculty of Health Sciences: FRANCISCO JAVIER ROMERO GÓMEZ

Faculty of Law, Business and Politics: ROSA PASCUAL SERRATS (acting)

Faculty of Veterinary Science: SANTIAGO VEGA GARCÍA

ATTACHED SCHOOL

San Pablo Business School: Palacio de Colomina, Calle Almudín 1, 46003 Valencia; tel. (96) 3156306; fax (96) 3918684; e-mail env@env.ceu.es; internet www.env.ceu.es; Dir CARMEN MARCILLA CUBELLS.

UNIVERSIDAD CEU SAN PABLO

Julián Romea 23, 28003 Madrid

Telephone: (91) 4566300

E-mail: ceu.sec.vrrii@ceu.es

Internet: www.uspceu.com

Founded 1993

Private control

Languages of instruction: Spanish, English

Academic year: September to June

Rector: RAFAEL SÁNCHEZ SAUS

Vice-Rector for Academic and Graduate Affairs: AGUSTÍN PROBANZA LOBO

Vice-Rector for Int. Relations: ALFONSO MARTÍNEZ-ECHEVARRÍA Y GARCÍA DE DUEÑAS

Vice-Rector for Research: ELENA POSTIGO SOLANA

Vice-Rector for Student Affairs: CARMEN FERNÁNDEZ DE LA CIGOÑA CANTERO

Vice-Rector for Teaching Staff: MANUEL ALEJANDRO RODRÍGUEZ DE LA PEÑA

Registrar: MARTA VILLAR EZCURRA

Man.: EUGENIO UBIETA BRAVO

Library Dir: JOSÉ MORILLO-VELARDE SERRANO

Library of 230,000 vols

Number of teachers: 923

Number of students: 7,998

DEANS

Faculty of Business and Economics: Dra CRISTINA ELORZA ARANZÁBAL

Faculty of Humanities and Communication Sciences: Dr JOSÉ FRANCISCO SERRANO OCEJA

Faculty of Law: Dr JUAN MANUEL BLANCH NOUGUÉS

Faculty of Medicine: Dra INMACULADA CASTILLA DE CORTÁZAR LARREA

Faculty of Pharmacy: BEATRIZ DE PASCUAL-TERESA FERNÁNDEZ

Higher Polytechnic School: FELIX HERNANDO MANSILLA (Dir)

UNIVERSIDAD COMPLUTENSE DE MADRID

Ciudad Universitaria, Avda Seneca 2, 28040 Madrid

Telephone: (91) 4520400

Fax: (91) 3943400

E-mail: infocom@ucm.es

Internet: www.ucm.es

Founded 1499

State control

Languages of instruction: English, Spanish

Academic year: September to June

Rector: Prof. JOSÉ CARRILLO MENÉNDEZ

Vice-Rector for Academic Management: EUMENIO ANCOCHEA SOTO

Vice-Rector for Degree Studies: SILVIA IGLESIAS RECUERO

Vice-Rector for Economic Affairs: JUAN ANTONIO MAROTO ACÍN

Vice-Rector for Int. and Institutional Relations: JUAN FERRERA CUESTA

Vice-Rector for Innovation: MANUEL MAÑAS BAENA

Vice-Rector for Organization and Communication: FRANCISCO JAVIER DEL RÍO ESTEBAN

Vice-Rector for Postgraduate and Continuing Education: JOSÉ MARÍA ALUNDA RODRÍGUEZ

Vice-Rector for Quality Evaluation: ELENA GALLEGO ABAROA

Vice-Rector for Research: JOAQUÍN PLUMET ORTEGA

Vice-Rector for Students: MARÍA ENCINA GONZÁLEZ MARTÍN

Gen. Sec.: MATILDE CARLÓN RUIZ

Man.: BEGOÑA AÍSA PEINÓ

Library: see under Libraries and Archives

Number of teachers: 6,000

Number of students: 85,505

Publications: *Memoria de la UCM*, *Gaceta Complutense*, *Tribuna Complutense*

DEANS

Faculty of Biological Sciences: ANTONIO TORMO GARRIDO

Faculty of Chemical Sciences: REYES JIMÉNEZ APARICIO

Faculty of Computer Science: DANIEL MOZOS MUÑOZ

Faculty of Dentistry: MARIANO SANZ ALONSO

Faculty of Economics and Business: MARÍA BEGOÑA GARCÍA GRECIANO

Faculty of Education: MARÍA JOSÉ FERNÁNDEZ DÍAZ

Faculty of Fine Arts: JOSU LARRAÑAGA ALTUNA

Faculty of Geography and History: LUIS ENRIQUE OTERO CARVAJAL

Faculty of Geological Sciences: JOSÉ RAMÓN MAS MAYORAL

Faculty of Information Science: MARÍA DEL CARMEN PÉREZ DE ARMIÑÁN GARCÍA-FRESCA

Faculty of Law: RAÚL LEOPOLDO CANOSA USERA

Faculty of Mathematics: FRANCISCO JAVIER MONTERO DE JUAN

Faculty of Medicine: JOSÉ LUIS ÁLVAREZ-SALA WALTHER

Faculty of Pharmacy: RAFAEL LOZANO FERNÁNDEZ

Faculty of Physical Sciences: MARÍA LUISA LUCÍA MULAS

Faculty of Philology: DÁMASO LÓPEZ GARCÍA

Faculty of Philosophy: RAFAEL VALERIANO ORDEN JIMÉNEZ

Faculty of Politics and Sociology: HERIBERTO CAIRO CAROU

Faculty of Psychology: CARLOS GALLEGO LÓPEZ

Faculty of Veterinary Science: PEDRO LUIS LORENZO GONZÁLEZ

ATTACHED INSTITUTES

Complutense Institute of Administrative Science: Facultad de Ciencias Políticas y Sociología, Departamento de Derecho Administrativo II, 3°, Martillo 5°, Campus de Somosaguas, 28223 Pozuelo de Alarcón (Madrid); tel. (91) 3942893; fax (91) 3942620; Dir JOSÉ VICENTE GÓMEZ RIVAS.

Complutense Institute of Economic Analysis: Facultad de Ciencias Económicas y Empresariales, Pabellón prefabricado, 1°, ala Norte, Campus de Somosaguas, 28223 Pozuelo de Alarcón (Madrid); tel. (91) 3942611; fax (91) 3942613; e-mail icaesec@ccee.ucm.es; internet www.ucm.es/icae; Dir ANTONIO ABADÍA CASELLES.

Complutense Institute of Industrial and Financial Analysis: Facultad de Ciencias Económicas y Empresariales, Pabellón Central, 1°, Campus de Somosaguas, 28223 Pozuelo de Alarcón (Madrid); tel. and fax (91) 3942456; e-mail joost@ccee.ucm.es; internet www.ucm.es/bucm/cee/iaif; Dir MIKEL BUESA BLANCO.

Complutense Institute of Morphofunctional and Sport Sciences: Facultad de Medicina, Pabellón 6, Plantas Baja, Ciudad Universitaria, 28040 Madrid; tel. (91) 3941339; fax (91) 3941342; Dir JOSÉ RAMÓN MÉRIDA VELASCO.

Higher Centre for Studies on Management, Analysis and Evaluation: Finca Mas Ferré, Edificio B, Campus de Somosaguas, 28223 Pozuelo de Alarcón (Madrid); tel. (91) 3942958; fax (91) 3942956; e-mail csegae05@cseg.ucm.es; internet www.ucm.es/info/csegae; Dir JUAN GÓMEZ CASTAÑEDA.

Institute of Bromatology and Nutrition: Facultad de Farmacia, 2°, Ciudad Universitaria, 28040 Madrid; tel. (91) 3941799; fax (91) 3941732; Dir ESPERANZA TORIJA ISASA.

Institute of Education: Calle Santísima Trinidad 37, 28010 Madrid; tel. (91) 3946707; fax (91) 3946695; e-mail captutor@edu.ucm .es; internet www.ice.ucm.es; Dir MARÍA DEL CARMEN CHAMORRO PLAZA.

Institute of Environmental Science: Manuel Bartolomé Cossio s/n, 1°, 28040 Madrid; tel. and fax (91) 5491075; e-mail lopezal@pdi.ucm.es; internet www.ucm.es/info/iuca; Dir ALEJANDRO LÓPEZ LÓPEZ.

Institute of Meat Science and Technology: Facultad de Veterinaria, 2°, Ciudad Universitaria, 28040 Madrid; tel. (91) 3943749; fax (91) 3943743; e-mail icamber@vet.ucm.es; Dir ISABEL CAMBERO RODRÍGUEZ.

Instituto Universitario de Investigación Ortega y Gasset (Ortega y Gasset University Research Institute): see under Learned Societies—Education.

UNIVERSIDAD DE ALCALÁ

Plaza de San Diego s/n, 28801 Alcalá de Henares (Madrid)

Telephone: (91) 8854000

Fax: (91) 8854095

E-mail: ciu@uah.es

Internet: www.uah.es

Founded 1977

State control

Language of instruction: Spanish

Academic year: September to June

Rector: FERNANDO GALVÁN REULA

Vice-Rector for Academic Organization and Teaching Staff: JOSÉ VICENTE SAZ PÉREZ

Vice-Rector for Coordination and Communication: JOSÉ SANTIAGO FERNÁNDEZ VÁZQUEZ

Vice-Rector for Guadalajara Campus: NAZARETH PÉREZ DE CASTRO

Vice-Rector for Innovation and New Technology: JOSÉ ANTONIO GUTIÉRREZ DE MESA

Vice-Rector for Int. Relations: ELENA LÓPEZ DÍAZ-DELGADO

Vice-Rector for Postgraduate and Continuing Education: JUAN RAMÓN VELASCO PÉREZ

Vice-Rector for Research: MARÍA LUISA MARINA ALEGRE

Vice-Rector for Students and Sports: CARMELO PÉREZ GARCÍA

Vice-Rector for Teaching Quality and Innovation: LEONOR MARGALEF GARCÍA

Vice-Rector for Univ. Extension and Institutional Relations: JAVIER RIVERA BLANCO

Registrar: MIGUEL RODRÍGUEZ BLANCO

Gen. Man.: RUBÉN GARRIDO YSERTE

Library Dir: CARMEN FERNÁNDEZ-GALIANO PEYROLÓN

Number of teachers: 1,762 (947 full-time, 815 part-time)

Number of students: 28,909

Publications: *Barataria, Cairón, Encuentro, Estudios de Historia Económica y Social de América, Henares, Idagación, Las Comarcas Agrarias de España, Polis, Quodlibelt, Quórum Revista de Pensamiento Iberoamericano, Reale, Reden, Revista, Signo, Teatre*

DEANS

Faculty of Biology: CARMEN BARTOLOMÉ ESTEBAN

Faculty of Chemistry: MELIA RODRIGO LÓPEZ

Faculty of Documentation: M. PILAR LACASA DÍAZ

Faculty of Economics and Business: EMMA CASTELLÓ TALIANI

Faculty of Environmental Sciences: ROSA VICENTE LAPUENTE

Faculty of Law: ALFONSO CARLOS GARCÍA-MONCÓ MARTÍNEZ

Faculty of Medicine: M. JULIA BUJÁN VARELA

Faculty of Pharmacy: JULIO ÁLVAREZ-BUILLA GÓMEZ

Faculty of Philosophy and Arts: JOSÉ IGNACIO RUIZ RODRÍGUEZ

UNIVERSIDAD DE ALICANTE

Carretera San Vicente del Raspeig, s/n, 03690 Alicante

Telephone: (96) 5903400

Fax: (96) 5903464

E-mail: informacio@ua.es

Internet: www.ua.es

Founded 1979

State control

Languages of instruction: Spanish, Valenciano

Academic year: October to July

Pres.: Dr IGNACIO JIMÉNEZ RANEDA

Vice-Pres. for Academic Org. and Teaching Staff: Dr JESÚS PRADELLS NADAL

Vice-Pres. for Economic Planning: Dr MARÍA BEGOÑA SUBIZA MARTÍNEZ

Vice-Pres. for Extracurricular Activities: Dra JOSEFINA BUENO ALONSO

Vice-Pres. for Infrastructure, Space Management and Environment: Dr VICENTE MONTIEL LEGUEY

Vice-Pres. for Institutional Relations: Dr ARÁNZAZU CALZADA GONZÁLEZ

Vice-Pres. for Int. Relations and Cooperation: Dr MARÍA BEGOÑA SAN MIGUEL DEL HOYO

Vice-Pres. for Research, Devt and Innovation: Dr MANUEL PALOMAR SANZ

Vice-Pres. for Strategic Planning and Quality: Dra CECILIA GÓMEZ LUCAS

Vice-Pres. for Students: Dr JOSÉ VICENTE CABEZUELO PLIEGO

Vice-Pres. for Technology and Educational Innovation: Dr FARAÓN LLORENS LARGO

Registrar: NURIA FERNÁNDEZ PÉREZ

Man.: ÁLVARO A. BERENGUER BERENGUER

Library Dir: REMEDIOS BLANES

Number of teachers: 1,600

Number of students: 30,000

Publication: *Anales*

DEANS

Faculty of Arts: JORGE OLCINA CANTOS

Faculty of Economics and Business Administration: JUAN LLOPIS TAVERNER

Faculty of Education: MARÍA ÁNGLES MARTÍNEZ RUIZ

Faculty of Law: ÁFRICA GARCÍA MORENO

Faculty of Sciences: NURIA GRANÉ TERUEL

UNIVERSIDAD DE ALMERÍA

Ctra Sacramento s/n, La Cañada de San Urbano, 04120 Almería

Telephone: (95) 0015000

E-mail: aagg@ual.es

Internet: www.ual.es

Founded 1993

State control

Rector: PEDRO ROQUE MOLINA GARCÍA

Vice-Rector for Academic Org. and Teaching Staff: JOSÉ JUAN CARRIÓN MARTÍNEZ

Vice-Rector for Culture, Sport and Univ. Extension: JOSÉ ANTONIO GUERRERO VILLALBA

Vice-Rector for Graduate Affairs and Continuing Education: MARÍA TRINIDAD ANGOSTO TRILLO

Vice-Rector for Information and Communication Technology: MANUEL BERENGUEL SORIA

Vice-Rector for Infrastructure and Campus Sustainability: JUAN FRANCISCO PÉREZ CANO

Vice-Rector for Int. Relations and Devt Cooperation: MARÍA SAGRARIO SALABERRI RAMIRO

Vice-Rector for Planning, Quality and Social Participation: LUÍS FRANCISCO FERNÁNDEZ-REVUELTA PÉREZ

Vice-Rector for Research, Devt and Innovation: JOSÉ LUÍS MARTÍNEZ VIDAL

Vice-Rector for Students and Employment: RAFAEL QUIROSA-CHEYROUZE MUÑOZ

Registrar: MARÍA LUISA TRINIDAD GARCÍA

Man.: ANTONIO MIGUEL POSADAS CHINCHILLA

Library Dir: ENCARNACIÓN FUENTES MELERO

Publications: *Nimbus* (2 a year, climatology and meteorology), *Odisea* (1 a year, English studies)

DEANS

Faculty of Economics and Business: JOSÉ JOAQUÍN CÉSPEDES LORENTE

Faculty of Education: JUAN FERNÁNDEZ SIERRA

Faculty of Experimental Sciences: ENRIQUE DE AMO ARTERO

Faculty of Health Sciences: GENOVEVA GRANADOS GÁMEZ

Faculty of Humanities: MANUEL LÓPEZ MUÑOZ

Faculty of Law: FERNANDO FERNÁNDEZ MARÍN

Faculty of Psychology: JUAN GARCÍA GARCÍA

UNIVERSIDAD DE BURGOS

Hospital del Rey s/n, 09001 Burgos

Telephone and fax (94) 7258736

E-mail: intl@ubu.es

Internet: www.ubu.es

Founded 1994

Rector: ALFONSO MURILLO VILLAR

Vice-Rector for Academic Affairs: MANUEL PÉREZ MATEOS

Vice-Rector for Finance, Planning and Technological Innovation: JOSÉ LUIS PEÑA ALONSO

Vice-Rector for Infrastructure: JESÚS ÁNGEL MENESES VILLAGRÁ

Vice-Rector for Int. Relations and Cooperation: INÉS PRAGA TERENTE

Vice-Rector for Quality and Accreditation: ARÁZAZU MENDÍA JALÓN

Vice-Rector for Research: JORDI ROVIRA CARBALLIDO

Vice-Rector for Student Affairs, Employment and Univ. Extension: RENÉ JESÚS PAYO HERNANZ

Registrar: JOSÉ MARÍA GARCÍA-MORENO GONZALO

Man.: ENRIQUE DE SIMÓN GARCÍA-VICENTE

Library Dir: FERNANDO MARTÍN RODRÍGUEZ

Library of 100,000 vols, 1,500 periodicals

Number of teachers: 700

Number of students: 9,000

DEANS

Faculty of Economics and Business: MARÍA BEGOÑA PRIETO MORENO

Faculty of Humanities and Education: RAQUEL DE LA FUENTE ANUNCIBAY

Faculty of Law: AMABLE CORCUERA TORRES

Faculty of Sciences: JOSÉ MIGUEL GARCÍA PÉREZ

UNIVERSIDAD DE CÁDIZ

Calle Ancha 16, 11001 Cádiz

Telephone: (956) 015000

E-mail: jose.palao@uca.es

Internet: www.uca.es

Founded 1979

Academic year: October to July

Rector: DIEGO SALES MÁRQUEZ

Deputy Rector: FRANCISCO ALVAREZ GONZÁLEZ

Vice-Rector for Bahía de Algeciras Campus: FRANCISCO TRUJILLO ESPINOSA

Vice-Rector for Graduate and Continuing Education: MARÍA LUISA GONZÁLEZ DE CANALES GARCÍA

Vice-Rector for Information Technology and Educational Innovation: EDUARDO BLANCO OLLERO

Vice-Rector for Int. Relations and Cooperation: ALEJANDRO DEL VALLE GÁLVEZ

Vice-Rector for Planning and Quality: JOSÉ MARÍA RODRÍGUEZ-IZQUIERDO GIL

Vice-Rector for Research, Technological Devt and Innovation: FRANCISCO ANTONIO MACÍAS DOMÍNGUEZ

Vice-Rector for Students: DAVID ALMORZA GOMAR

Vice-Rector for Teaching and Academic Management: MARÍA JOSÉ RODRÍGUEZ MESA

Vice-Rector for Univ. Extension: MARIETA CANTOS CASENAVE

Sec.-Gen.: ANA MARÍA RODRÍGUEZ TIRADO

Man.: ANTONIO VADILLO IGLESIAS (acting)

Library Dir: MIGUEL DUARTE BARRIONUEVO (acting)

Number of teachers: 1,052

Number of students: 18,202

DEANS

Faculty of Economics and Business: FERNANDO MARTÍN ALCÁZAR

Faculty of Educational Science: JOSÉ MARÍA MARISCAL CHICANO

Faculty of Labour Sciences: FRANCISCA FUENTES RODRÍGUEZ

Faculty of Law: ROCÍO DOMÍNGUEZ BARTOLOMÉ

Faculty of Marine and Environmental Sciences: RAFAEL MAÑANES SALINAS

Faculty of Medicine: MARÍA FELICIDAD RODRÍGUEZ SÁNCHEZ

Faculty of Nautical Science: JUAN MORENO GUTIÉRREZ

Faculty of Nursing: ÁNGELES MARTELO BARO

Faculty of Philosophy and Letters: MANUEL ARCILA GARRIDO

Faculty of Science: MANUEL GARCÍA BASALLOTE

UNIVERSIDAD DE CANTABRIA

Avda de los Castros s/n, 39005 Santander

Telephone: (94) 2201500

Fax: (94) 2201103

E-mail: informacion.general@unican.es

Internet: www.unican.es

Founded 1972 as Universidad de Santander

State control

Language of instruction: Spanish

Academic year: September to July

Rector: JOSÉ CARLOS GÓMEZ SAL

Vice-Rector for Academic Affairs: FERNANDO ETAYO GORDEJUELA

Vice-Rector for Culture, Participation and Dissemination: ELENA MARTÍN LATORRE

Vice-Rector for Institutional Relations and Coordination of the Campus of Excellence: JUAN ENRIQUE VARONA ALABERN

Vice-Rector for International Relations: CONCEPCIÓN LÓPEZ FERNÁNDEZ

Vice-Rector for Research and Knowledge Transfer: ÁNGEL PAZOS CARRO

Vice-Rector for Spaces, Services and Sustainability: ÁNGELA DE MEER LECHA-MAZO

Vice-Rector for Student Affairs, Employment and Entrepreneurship: RAFAEL TORRES JIMÉNEZ

Vice-Rector for Teaching: FERNANDO CANIZAL BERINI

Registrar and Sec.-Gen.: JOSÉ IGNACIO SOLAR CAYÓN

Man.: ENRIQUE ALONSO DÍAZ

Library Dir: MARÍA JESÚS SÁIZ

Library of 399,372 vols, 7,036 online magazines, 4,034 e-books, 23,764 e-magazines

Number of teachers: 1,218

Number of students: 12,489

DEANS

Doctoral School: ALBERTO RUIZ

Faculty of Economics and Business Studies: BEGOÑA TORRE OLMO

Faculty of Education: JOSÉ MANUEL OSORO SIERRA

Faculty of Humanities: FIDEL GÓMEZ OCHOA

Faculty of Industrial and Telecommunication Engineering: EDUARDO MORA MONTE

Faculty of Law: JUAN BARÓ PAZOS

Faculty of Medicine: FRANCISCO JAVIER LLORCA DÍAZ

Faculty of Mines and Energy Engineering: JULIO MANUEL DE LUIS

Faculty of Navigation: CARLOS PÉREZ

Faculty of Nursing: MARÍA MADRAZO

Faculty of Sciences: ERNESTO ANABITARTE CANO

UNIVERSIDAD DE CASTILLA–LA MANCHA

Calle Altagracia 50, 13071 Ciudad Real

Telephone: (902) 204100

Fax: (902) 204130

E-mail: informacion@uclm.es

Internet: www.uclm.es

Founded 1982

State control

Language of instruction: Spanish

Academic year: October to June

Rector: Prof Dr ERNESTO MARTÍNEZ ATAZ

Vice-Rector for Academic Affairs and Continuing Education: Profa Dra FÁTIMA GUADAMILLAS GÓMEZ

Vice-Rector for Coordination and Communication: Prof. Dr FRANCISCO ALÍA MIRANDA

Vice-Rector for Cultural Cooperation and Ciudad Real Campus: Profa Dra MAIRENA MARTÍN LÓPEZ

Vice-Rector for Entrepreneurial Projects and Albacete Campus: Prof. Dr ANTONIO RONCERO SÁNCHEZ

Vice-Rector for Finance and Planning: Prof. Dr JESÚS FERNANDO SANTOS PEÑALVER

Vice-Rector for Infrastructure and Corporate Relations: Prof. Dr JUAN JOSÉ HERNÁNDEZ ADROVER

Vice-Rector for Institutional Relations and Toledo Campus: Profa Dra EVANGELINA ARANDA GARCÍA

Vice-Rector for Int. Relations and Devt Cooperation: Prof. Dr JUAN JOSÉ RUBIO GUERRERO

Vice-Rector for Research: Prof. Dr FRANCISCO JOSÉ QUILES FLOR

Vice-Rector for Students: Profa Dra CARMEN LÓPEZ BALBOA

Vice-Rector for Studies and Programmes: Prof. Dr MIGUEL ÁNGEL COLLADO YURRITA

Vice-Rector for Teaching Staff: Prof. Dr PABLO CAÑIZARES CAÑIZARES

Vice-Rector for Univ. Extension and Cuenca Campus: Prof. Dr JOSÉ IGNACIO ALBENTOSA HERNÁNDEZ

Registrar: Profa Dra MARÍA CÁNDIDA GUTIÉRREZ GARCÍA

Man.: JOSÉ LUIS MORAGA ALCAZAR

Librarian: FRANCISCO ALIA MIRANDA

Library of 952,268 vols, 22,252 periodicals

Number of teachers: 2,396

Number of students: 28,026

Publication: *Info-Campus* (12 a year)

DEANS

Faculty of Arts (Ciudad Real): MATIAS BARCHINO PÉREZ

Faculty of Chemical Sciences (Ciudad Real): ÁNGEL RÍOS CASTRO

Faculty of Economics and Business Sciences (Albacete): ÁNGEL TEJADA PONCE

Faculty of Education (Albacete: PEDRO LOSA SERRANO

Faculty of Education (Ciudad Real: EMILIO NIETO LÓPEZ

Faculty of Education (Cuenca: MARTÍN MUELAS HERRAÍZ

Faculty of Education (Toledo: ERNESTO GARCÍA SANZ

Faculty of Education Sciences and Humanities (Cuenca): MARÍA DEL CARMEN POYATO HOLGADO

Faculty of Environmental Sciences and Biochemistry (Toledo): MARÍA JOSÉ RUIZ GARCÍA

Faculty of Fine Arts (Cuenca): ANA NAVARRETE TUDELA

Faculty of Humanities (Albacete): FRANCISCO CEBRIÁN ABELLÁN

Faculty of Humanities (Toledo): RICARDO IZQUIERDO BENITO

Faculty of Law (Albacete): DIEGO JOSÉ GÓMEZ INIESTA

Faculty of Law and Social Sciences (Ciudad Real): JUAN RAMÓN DE PÁRAMO ARGÜELLES

Faculty of Law and Social Sciences (Toledo): PEDRO J. CARRASCO PARRILLA

Faculty of Medicine (Albacete): JOSÉ MARTÍNEZ PÉREZ

Faculty of Medicine (Ciudad Real): EMILIO FELIU ALBIÑANA

Faculty of Nursing (Albacete): ANGEL LÓPEZ GONZÁLEZ

Faculty of Nursing (Ciudad Real): CARMEN PRADO LAGUNA

Faculty of Nursing (Cuenca): MARÍA ROSARIO OLMO GASCÓN

Faculty of Pharmacy (Albacete): JORGE DE LAS HERAS IBAÑEZ

Faculty of Social Sciences (Cuenca): MARÍA ÁNGELES ZURILLA CARIÑANA

Faculty of Sport Sciences (Toledo): SUSANA MENDIZABAL ALBIZU

UNIVERSIDAD DE CÓRDOBA

Alfonso XIII 13, 14071 Córdoba

Telephone: (95) 7218000

Fax: (95) 7218030

E-mail: secretaria.rector@uco.es

Internet: www.uco.es

Founded 1972

Language of instruction: Spanish

Academic year: October to June

Rector: JOSÉ MANUEL ROLDÁN NOGUERAS

Vice-Rector for Academic Affairs and Teaching Staff: JOSÉ NARANJO RAMÍREZ

Vice-Rector for Communication and Institutional Coordination: MANUEL TORRALBO RODRÍGUEZ

Vice-Rector for Information Technology and Communications: JUAN ANTONIO CABALLERO MOLINA

Vice-Rector for Infrastructure: MARÍA DEL PILAR DORADO PÉREZ

Vice-Rector for Innovation and Educational Quality: MARÍA TERESA SÁNCHEZ PINEDA DE LAS INFANTAS

Vice-Rector for Int. Relations and Cooperation: CARMEN GALÁN SOLDEVILLA

Vice-Rector for Policy Development: PEDRO GÓMEZ CABALLERO

Vice-Rector for Postgraduate and Continuing Education: JOSÉ CARLOS GÓMEZ VILLAMANDOS

Vice-Rector for Science Policy: ENRIQUE AGUILAR BENÍTEZ DE LUGO

Vice-Rector for Students and Culture: MANUEL TORRES AGUILAR

Registrar: JULIA ANGULO ROMERO

Man.: ANTONIO CUBERO ATIENZA

Librarian: MARÍA DEL CARMEN LIÑÁN MAZA

Library of 460,000 vols, 10,000 periodicals

Number of teachers: 1,250

Number of students: 20,000

DEANS

Faculty of Education: FRANCISCO VILLAMANDOS DE LA TORRE

Faculty of Labour Relations: Prof. Dr FEDERICO NAVARRO NIETO

Faculty of Law and Economics: Prof. Dr MIGUEL J. AGUDO ZAMORA

Faculty of Medicine: Prof. Dr RAFAEL SOLANA LARA

Faculty of Philosophy and Letters: Prof. Dr EULALIO FERNÁNDEZ SÁNCHEZ

Faculty of Science: Prof. Dr MANUEL BLÁZQUEZ RUIZ

Faculty of Veterinary Science: Prof. Dr LIBRADO CARRASCO OTERO

UNIVERSIDAD DE DEUSTO

Apdo 1, 48080 Bilbao

Avda de las Universidades 24, 48007 Bilbao

Telephone: (94) 4139000

Fax: (94) 4139098

E-mail: secretaria.general@deusto.es

Internet: www.deusto.es

Founded 1886

Private control, directed by the Jesuits

Languages of instruction: Basque, English, Spanish

Academic year: September to July

Chancellor: R. P. ADOLFO NICOLÁS PACHÓN, S. J.

Deputy-Chancellor: R. P. JUAN JOSÉ ETXEBERRIA SAGASTUME, S. J.

Vice-Chancellor: R. P. JAVIER LÓPEZ ARÍZTEGUI, S.J.

Rector: R. P. JAIME ORAÁ ORAÁ, S. J.

Vice-Rector for Academic Organization and Educational Innovation: MARÍA BEGOÑA ARRIETA HERAS

Vice-Rector for Communication, Multilingualism and Social Affairs: ROBERTO SAN SALVADOR DEL VALLE DOISTUA

Vice-Rector for Int. Relations: ÁLVARO DE LA RICA ASPIUNZA

Vice-Rector for Research, Innovation and Knowledge Transfer: JOSÉ LUIS DEL VAL ROMÁN

Vice-Rector for Research: JOSÉ LUIS AVILA ORIVE

Vice-Rector for San Sebastián Campus and Univ. Community and Identity: R. P. JOSÉ JAVIER PARDO IZAL, S. J.

Registrar: MARÍA BEGOÑA ARRIETA HERAS

Librarian: NIEVES TARANCO DEL BARRIO

Library: see Libraries and Archives

Number of teachers: 1,818

Number of students: 13,173

Publications: *ADOZ Boletín del Centro de Documentación en Ocio* (4 a year), *Anuario de Estudios Cooperativos* (1 a year), *Anuario del Instituto Ignacio de Loyola* (1 a year), *Boletín Asociación Internacional de Derecho Cooperativo* (6 a year), *Boletín de Estudios Económicos* (3 a year), *Cuadernos Europeos de Deusto* (2 a year), *Enseiukarrean* (1 a year), *ESIDE* (1 a year), *Estudios de Deusto* (2 a year), *Estudios Empresariales* (3 a year), *Letras de Deusto* (4 a year), *Mundaiz* (2 a year), *Revista de Derecho y Genoma Humano* (2 a year), *Revista Noticias UD Berriak* (4 a year), *RAS* (2 a year)

DEANS

Faculty of Economics and Business Studies (Bilbao): ANTONIO YABAR MAISTERRENA
Faculty of Economics and Business Studies (San Sebastián): VÍCTOR URCELAY YARZA
Faculty of Engineering: JOSU SOLABARRIETA EIZAGUIRRE
Faculty of Law: JOSÉ LUIS ÁVILA ORIVE
Faculty of Psychology and Education: JOSU SOLABARRIETA
Faculty of Social and Human Sciences: JOSÉ ANGEL ACHÓN INSAUSTI
Faculty of Theology: VICENTE VIDE RODRÍGUEZ

UNIVERSIDAD DE EXTREMADURA

Avda de Elvas, s/n, 06071 Badajoz
Plaza de los Caldereros 1, 10071 Cáceres
Telephone: (924) 289369 (Badajoz)
Fax: (924) 276367 (Badajoz)
E-mail: rector@unex.es
Internet: www.unex.es
Founded 1973
State control
Language of instruction: Spanish
Academic year: October to June
Rector: Prof. Dr JUAN FRANCISCO DUQUE CARRILLO
Vice-Rector for Academic Planning: Prof. JAVIER GRANDE QUEJIGO
Vice-Rector for Economic Planning: AGUSTÍN GARCÍA GARCÍA
Vice-Rector for Information and Communications Technology: JUAN MANUEL MURILLO RODRÍGUEZ
Vice-Rector for Institutional Relations and Cultural Outreach: Prof. FERNANDO SÁNCHEZ FIGUEROA
Vice-Rector for Quality and Continuing Education: Dra MARÍA JOSÉ MARTÍN DELGADO
Vice-Rector for Research, Devt and Infrastructure: Prof. JUAN MANUEL SÁNCHEZ GUZMÁN
Vice-Rector for Student Affairs and Employment: ANTONIO JAVIER FRANCO RUBIO
Vice-Rector for Teaching Staff: ANTONIO HIDALGO GARCÍA
Registrar: Prof. FRANCISCO ÁLVAREZ ARROYO
Man.: LUCIANO CORDERO SAAVEDRA
Number of teachers: 1,995
Number of students: 23,862
Publication: *Boletín*

DEANS

Faculty of Business Studies and Tourism (Cáceres): JOSÉ ANTONIO PÉREZ RUBIO
Faculty of Economics and Business (Badajoz): ANTONIO FERNÁNDEZ FERNÁNDEZ
Faculty of Education (Badajoz): Ma. ROSA LUENGO GONZÁLEZ
Faculty of Law (Cáceres): EMILIO CORTÉS BECHIARELLI
Faculty of Library Science (Badajoz): ANTONIO PULGARÍN GUERRERO
Faculty of Medicine (Badajoz): PEDRO BUREO DACAL
Faculty of Philosophy and Letters (Cáceres): LUIS MERINO JEREZ

Faculty of Science (Badajoz): MANUEL GONZÁLEZ LENA
Faculty of Sports Science (Cáceres): FERNANDO DEL VILLAR ÁLVAREZ
Faculty of Teacher Training (Cáceres): BEATRIZ MARTÍN MARÍN
Faculty of Veterinary Science (Cáceres): PEDRO LUIS RODRÍGUEZ MEDINA

UNIVERSIDAD DE GRANADA

Avda del Hospicio s/n, 18071 Granada
Telephone: (95) 8243000
Fax: (95) 8243066
E-mail: informa@ugr.es
Internet: www.ugr.es
Founded 1526, charter granted 1531, est. 1536
State control
Language of instruction: Spanish
Academic year: October to May
Rector: FRANCISCO GONZÁLEZ LODEIRO
Vice-Chancellor for Academic Organization and Teaching Staff: LUIS M. JIMÉNEZ DEL BARCO JALDO
Vice-Chancellor for Campus Infrastructure: BEGOÑA MORENO ESCOBAR
Vice-Chancellor for Environmental Quality, Welfare and Sport: PEDRO ESPINOSA HIDALGO
Vice-Chancellor for Int. Relations: DOROTHY KELLY
Vice-Chancellor for Quality Assurance: MARÍA JOSÉ LEÓN GUERRERO
Vice-Chancellor for Undergraduate and Postgraduate Teaching: LOLA FERRE CANO
Vice-Rector for Science Policy and Research: MARÍA DOLORES SUÁREZ ORTEGA
Vice-Chancellor for Student Affairs: INMACULADA MARRERO ROCHA
Vice-Chancellor for the Health Sciences Technoogical Park: MOLINA PINEDA DE LAS INFANTAS
Vice-Chancellor for Univ. Extension and Devt: MIGUEL GÓMEZ OLIVER
Registrar: ROSSANA GONZÁLEZ GONZÁLEZ
Man.: ANDRÉS NAVARRO GALERA
Librarian: JOSE ARIZA RUBIO
Library of 686,300 vols, 15,338 periodicals, 35 incunabula
Number of teachers: 3,650
Number of students: 60,000
Publications: *Anales de la Cátedra Francisco Suarez, Arenal: Revista de Historia de Mujeres, Chronica Nova: Revista de Historia Moderna, Cuadernos de Arte, Cuadernos de Estudios Medievales, Cuadernos de Estudios Medievales y Ciencias y Técnicas Historiográficas, Cuadernos de Prehistoria, Cuadernos Geográficos, Dynamis: Acta Hispanica ad Medicinae: Scientiarumque Historiam Ilustrandam, Florentia Iliberritana, Miscelánea de Estudios Arabes y Hebraicos, Revista de Educación, Revista de la Facultad de Derecho de la Universidad de Granada, Sendebar: Boletín de la Facultad de Traducción e Interpretación, Zoologica Baetica*

DEANS

Faculty of Communication and Documentation: ANTONIO ÁNGEL RUIZ RODRÍGUEZ
Faculty of Dentistry: Dr ALBERTO RODRÍGUEZ ARCHILLA
Faculty of Economic and Business Administration: Dra MARÍA DEL MAR HOLGADO MOLINA
Faculty of Education and Humanities (Ceuta): RAMÓN GALINDO MORALES
Faculty of Education and Humanities (Melilla): JUAN GRANDA VERA ROMERO
Faculty of Educational Sciences: Dr JOSÉ ANTONIO NARANJO RODRÍGUEZ

Faculty of Fine Arts: Dr VÍCTOR MEDINA FLÓREZ
Faculty of Health Sciences (Ceuta): Dr RAFAEL GUISADO BARRILAO
Faculty of Labour Sciences: Dr ANTONIO DELGADO PADIAL
Faculty of Law: Prof. Dr JUAN LÓPEZ MARTÍNEZ
Faculty of Nursing (Melilla): Dra BIBINHA BENBUNAN BENTATA
Faculty of Medicine: Dr RAMÓN GALINDO MORALES
Faculty of Pharmacy: LUÍS RECALDE MANRIQUE
Faculty of Philosophy and Literature: Dra MARIA ELENA MARTIN-VIVALDI CABALLERO
Faculty of Physical Education and Sports Sciences: AURELIO UREÑA ESPA
Faculty of Political Science and Sociology: Dra SUSANA CORZO FERNÁNDEZ
Faculty of Psychology: Dr ANTONIO MALDONADO LÓPEZ
Faculty of Sciences: Dr ANTONIO RÍOS GUADIX
Faculty of Translation and Interpretation: Dra EVA MUÑOZ RAYA

AFFILIATED INSTITUTIONS

Institute of Nutrition and Food Technology: Edif. Fray Luís de Granada, C/ Ramón y Cajal 4, 18071 Granada; tel. (95) 8244174; fax (95) (8248326); internet www.ugr.es/%7ewinyta; Dir EMILIO MARTÍNEZ DE VICTORIA MUÑOZ.

Andalusian Institute of Earth Sciences: Facultad de Ciencias, Universidad de Granada, Campus Fuentenueva s/n, 18002 Granada; tel. (95) 8243158; fax (95) 8243384; e-mail offiact@ugr.es; internet www.iact.csic .es; Dir ANDRES MALDONALDO LÓPEZ.

Andalusian Institute of Geophysics and Prevention of Seismic Disasters: Campus Universitario de Cartuja s/n, 18071 Granada; tel. (95) 8243557; fax (95) 8160907; e-mail morales@iag.ugr.es; internet www.ugr.es/%7eiag; Dir JOSÉ MORALES SOTO.

Biotechnology Institute: Facultad de Ciencias, Universidad de Granada, Campus Fuentenueva s/n, 18002 Granada; tel. (95) 8200686; e-mail info@biotec.ugr.es; internet biotec.conzepto.com/index.asp; Dir Dr ANTONIO OSUNA CARRILLO DE ALBORNOZ.

'Carlos I' Institute of Theoretical and Computational Physics: Facultad de Ciencias, Universidad de Granada, Campus de Fuentenueva, 18071 Granada; tel. (95) 8242860; fax (95) 8242862; e-mail carlos1@ ugr.es; internet www.ugr.es/%7ecarlos1; Dir PEDRO L. GARRIDO GALERA.

Institute of Neurosciences 'Federico Oloriz' Granada: Avda de Madrid 11, Facultad de Medicina, Universidad de Granada, 18012 Granada; tel. (95) 8244033; fax (95) 8246187; e-mail ineurociencias@ugr.es; internet ineurociencias.ugr.es; Dean and Dir Dr FRANCISCO VIVES MONTERO.

Interuniversity Andalusian Institute of Criminology: Sección Universidad de Granada, Edificio Centro de Documentación Científica, C/ Rector López Argüeta s/n, 18071 Granada; tel. (95) 8243150; fax (95) 8243095; e-mail criminol@ugr.es; internet www.ugr .es/%7ecriminol; Dir Prof. Dr JESÚS BARQUÍN SANZ.

'La Inmaculada' University College of Teacher Training: Carretera de Murcia s/ n, 18010 Granada; tel. (95) 8205861; fax (95) 8287469; internet www.lainmaculada.com; Pres. and Dir ANTONIO ALMENDROS GALLEGO.

Regional Development Institute: Universidad de Granada, Edificio Centro de Documentación Científica, C/ Rector López Argüeta s/n, 18071 Granada; tel. (95) 8243083; fax (95) 8248967; e-mail idesareg@

azahar.ugr.es; internet www.ugr.es/%7eidr; Dir Dr Francisco Rodríguez Martínez.

University Institute of Peace and Conflict: Edificio de Documentación Científica, C/ Rector López Argüeta s/n, 18071 Granada; tel. (95) 8244142; fax (95) 8248974; e-mail eirene@ugr.es; internet www.ugr.es/%7eeirene; Dir Prof. Mario López Martínez.

University Institute of Studies on Women: Edificio de Documentación Científica, C/ Rector López Argüeta s/n, 18071 Granada; tel. (95) 8248366; fax (95) 8242828; e-mail insmujer@azahar.ugr.es; internet www.ugr.es/%7eiem; Dir Dra María Eugenia Fernández Fraile.

Water Institute: Edif. Fray Luis de Granada, C/ Ramon y Cajal 4, 18071 Granada; tel. (95) 8243093; fax (95) 8243094; e-mail javicruz@instagua.ugr.es; internet www.ugr.es/%7ejjcruz/instagua.htm; Dir Luis Cruz Pizarro.

UNIVERSIDAD DE HUELVA

Calle Dr Cantero Cuadrado 6, 21071 Huelva
Telephone: (95) 9218001
Fax: (95) 9218080
E-mail: rector@uhu.es
Internet: www.uhu.es
Founded 1993
State control
Rector: Prof. Dr Francisco José Martínez López
Vice-Rector for Academic Organization and Teaching Staff: Prof. Dr Juan José García del Hoyo
Vice-Rector for Infrastructure and Services: Prof. Dr Emilio Manuel Romero Macías
Vice-Rector for Int. Relations: Prof. Dr Enrique Bonsón Ponte
Vice-Rector for Lifelong Learning and Innovation: Profa Dra María Carmen Fonseca Mora
Vice-Rector for Research: Prof. Dr Jesús Damián de la Rosa Díaz
Vice-Rector for Student Affairs, Employment and Business Administration: Profa Dra Isabel María Rodríguez García
Vice-Rector for Technology and Quality: Prof. Dr José Ignacio Aguaded Gómez
Vice-Rector for Univ. Extension: Prof. Dr Manuel José de Lara Ródenas
Registrar: Profa Dra María Luisa Pérez Guerrero
Man.: Antonio Morilla Frías
Librarian: María Antonia Álvarez Álvarez
Library of 259,839 vols, 4,755 periodicals
Number of teachers: 700
Number of students: 14,500

DEANS

Faculty of Business Studies: Profa Dra María Asunción Grávalos Gastaminza
Faculty of Education: Francisco José Morales Gil
Faculty of Experimental Sciences: Gabriel Ruiz de Almodóvar Sel
Faculty of Humanities: Prof. Dr Zenón Luis Martínez
Faculty of Labour Relations: Prof. Dr Agustín Galán García
Faculty of Law: Prof. Dr Salvador Ramírez Gómez

UNIVERSIDAD DE JAÉN

Campus Las Lagunillas, 23071 Jaén
Telephone: (95) 3012121
Fax: (95) 3012239
E-mail: info@ujaen.es
Internet: www.ujaen.es
Founded 1993
State control

Rector: Manuel Parras Rosa
Vice-Rector for Academic Org., Educational Innovation and Teaching Staff: Juan Carlos Castillo Armenteros
Vice-Rector for European Convergence, Postgraduate Studies and Life Long Learning: Joaquín Tovar Pescador
Vice-Rector for Information and Communication Technology: Francisco Roca Rodríguez
Vice-Rector for Infrastructure and Campus Devt: Nicolás Ruíz Reyez
Vice-Rector for Institutional Relations and Communication: Esther López Zafra
Vice-Rector for Int. Relations and Cooperation: Victoria López Ramón
Vice-Rector for Research, Technological Devt and Innovation: María Angeles Peinado Herreros
Vice-Rector for Strategic Planning and Quality Management: Jorge Delgado García
Vice-Rector for Student and Labour Orientation: Mozas Moral
Vice-Rector for Univ. Extension: Ana Ortiz Colón
Registrar: José Cuesta Revilla
Man.: Armando Moreno Castro
Library Dir: Sebastián Jarillo Calvarro
Library of 205,000 vols, 4,356 periodicals
Number of teachers: 1,000
Number of students: 16,000

DEANS

Faculty of Experimental Sciences: Dr María Isabel Torres López
Faculty of Health Sciences: Manuel Linares Abad
Faculty of Humanities and Education: Dr Antonio Bueno González
Faculty of Law and Social Sciences: Dr Jorge Lozano Miralles
Faculty of Social Work: Dra Yolanda de la Fuente Robles

ATTACHED INSTITUTIONS

Andalusian Centre of Iberian Archaeology: Paraje las Lagunillas s/n, 23071 Jaén; tel. (95) 3012132; fax (95) 3012287; e-mail caai@ujaen.es; internet www.ujaen.es/centros/caai; Dir Dr Arturo Carlos Ruiz Rodríguez.

University School of Teacher Training in Úbeda: Avda Cristo Rey 25, 23400 Úbeda (Jaén); tel. (95) 3796102; e-mail magisterio@safa.edu; internet magisterio.safa.edu; Dir Francisco Javier Muñoz Delgado.

UNIVERSIDAD DE LA LAGUNA

Pabellón de Gobierno, Calle Molinos de Agua s/n, 38207 La Laguna, Tenerife, Canary Islands
Telephone: (92) 2319000
Fax: (92) 2319544
E-mail: ccti@ull.es
Internet: www.ull.es
Founded 1792
State control
Language of instruction: Spanish
Academic year: October to June

Rector: Eduardo Doménech Martínez
Vice-Rector for Academic Affairs: José María Palazón López
Vice-Rector for Cultural Affairs and Infrastructure: Pablo González Vera
Vice-Rector for Economic Planning: Lilibeth Fuentes Medina
Vice-Rector for Int. Relations: María Gracia Rodríguez Brito
Vice-Rector for Institutional Quality and Educational Innovation: Justo Roberto Pérez Cruz
Vice-Rector for Research, Technological Devt and Innovation: Lorenzo Moreno Ruiz

Vice-Rector for Student Affairs: Roberto Rodríguez Guerra
Vice-Rector for Teaching Staff: Carmen Dolores Sosa Castilla
Vice-Rector for Univ. and Society Relations: María Nélida Rancel Torres
Vice-Rector for Univ. Services: Rosa María Aguilar Chinea
Man.: Francisco Calero García
Registrar: Fernando Rosa González
Librarian: Fernando Rodríguez Junco
Library of 637,202 vols, 12,025 periodicals
Number of teachers: 1,794
Number of students: 23,167

Publications: *Anales de la Facultad de Derecho* (1 a year), *Clepsidra* (1 a year), *Cuadernos de Cemyr* (1 a year), *Latente* (1 a year), *Revista Canaria de Estudios Ingleses* (2 a year), *Revista de Bellas Artes* (1 a year), *Revista de Filología* (1 a year), *Revista de Historia Canaria* (1 a year), *Revista Fortunatae* (1 a year), *Revista Laguna* (2 a year), *Tempora* (1 a year)

DEANS

Faculty of Biology: Juan Felipe Pérez Francés
Faculty of Chemistry: Ana María Afonso Perera
Faculty of Economics and Business Administration: Carlos Rodríguez Fuentes
Faculty of Education: Olga María Alegre de la Rosa
Faculty of Fine Arts: Alfonso Ruiz Rallo
Faculty of Geography and History: Manuel de Paz Sánchez
Faculty of Information Science: Carmen Rodríguez Wangüemert
Faculty of Law: Marcel Manuel Bonnet Escuela
Faculty of Mathematics: Antonio Martinón Cejas
Faculty of Medicine: Emilio Sanz Álvarez
Faculty of Pharmacy: Enrique Martínez Carretero
Faculty of Philology: Juan Ignacio Oliva Cruz
Faculty of Philosophy: Ángela Sierra González
Faculty of Physics: Teodoro Roca Cortés
Faculty of Political and Social Sciences: Carmen Marina Barreto Vargas
Faculty of Psychology: Pedro Avero Delgado

ATTACHED INSTITUTES

Andrés Bello Institute of Linguistics: C/ Juan de Vera 13, La Laguna; Dir Manuel Almeida Suárez.

Antonio González University Institute of Bio-Organics: Avda Astrofísico Fco. Sánchez 2, La Laguna; tel. (92) 2318570; fax (92) 2318571; e-mail iubo@ull.es; internet www.iubo.ull.es; Dir Víctor Sotero Martín García.

Astrophysics Institute of the Canary Islands: Avda Astrofísico Francisco Sánchez s/n, 38206 La Laguna; tel. (92) 2318121; fax (92) 2318123; e-mail mcv@ll.iac.es; internet www.ull.es/departamento; Dirs Manuel Mas García, Antonio Aparicio Juan.

University Business Institute: Avda 25 de Julio 9, 38004 Santa Cruz de Tenerife; tel. (92) 2319708; fax (92) 2319709; e-mail iude@ull.es; Dir Dr José Antonio Lastres Segret.

University Institute of Political and Social Sciences: Facultad de Derecho, módulo D-02, Campus de Guajara, 38071 La Laguna; tel. (92) 2317306; fax (92) 2317308; e-mail inucps@ull.es; Dir Ma. Teresa González De La Fe.

University Institute of Regional Development: Facultad de Económicas, Campus de Guajara s/n, 38071 La Laguna; tel. (92)

2317112; Dir ROSA MARINA GONZÁLEZ MAR-RERO.

University Institute of Tropical Diseases and Public Health of the Canaries: Unidad de Parasitología, Facultad de Farmacia, Avda Astrofísico Fco. Sánchez s/n, 38071 La Laguna; tel. (92) 2318486; e-mail jcastilo@ull.es; Dir JOSÉ ANTONIO DEL CASTILLO REMIRO.

UNIVERSIDAD DE LA RIOJA

Avda de La Paz 93, 26006 Logroño

Telephone: (94) 1299100
Fax: (94) 1299120
E-mail: informacion@unirioja.es
Internet: www.unirioja.es

Founded 1992
State control
Academic year: September to July

Rector: JOSÉ MARÍA MARTÍNEZ DE PISÓN CAVERO
Vice-Rector for Academic Org. and Teaching Staff: JOSÉ IGNACIO EXTREMIANA ALDANA
Vice-Rector for Infrastructure and Technology: ELISEO VERGARA GONZÁLEZ
Vice-Rector for Int. and Institutional Relations: SYLVIA SASTRE I RIBA
Vice-Rector for Planning and Quality: RODOLFO SALINAS ZÁRATE
Vice-Rector for Research: EDUARDO J. FERNÁNDEZ GARBAYO
Vice-Rector for Student Affairs: MARÍA DEL MAR ASENSIO AROSTEGUI
Registrar: ISABEL MARTÍNEZ NAVAS
Man.: GUILLERMO BRAVO MENÉNDEZ-RIVAS
Librarian: MARTA MAGRIÑÁ CONTRERAS

Library of 250,000 vols, 6,000 periodicals
Number of teachers: 430
Number of students: 7,500

Publications: *Anuario Jurídico de La Rioja* (1 a year), *Brocar: Cuadernos de Investigación Histórica* (1 a year), *Contextos Educativos* (1 a year, education review), *Cuadernos de Gestión* (2 a year), *Cuadernos de Investigación Filológica* (1 a year), *Cuadernos de Investigación Geográfica* (1 a year), *Iberia: Revista de la Antigüedad* (1 a year), *Journal of English Studies* (1 a year)

DEANS

Faculty of Arts and Education: JOSÉ ANTONIO CABALLERO LÓPEZ
Faculty of Business Sciences: EDUARDO RODRÍGUEZ OSÉS
Faculty of Law and Social Sciences: MARIOLA URREA CORRES
Faculty of Sciences, Agriculture Studies and Computer Engineering: SUSANA CABREDO PINILLOS

ATTACHED INSTITUTIONS

University School of Labour Relations: Edificio Quintiliano, La Cigüeña 60, 26004 Logroño; tel. (94) 1299100; fax (94) 1299259; internet www.unirioja.es/facultades_escuelas/relaciones_laborales.shtml; Dir MANUEL GARCÍA-MIGUEL GARCÍA-ROSADO.

University School of Nursing: Calle Donantes de Sangre, s/n, 26004 Logroño; tel. and fax (94) 1261443; internet www.unirioja.es/facultades_escuelas/enfermeria.shtml; Dir ROSARIO ARÉJULA BENITO.

University School of Tourism: Calle Quintiliano 5–7, 26005 Logroño; tel. (94) 1257372; fax (94) 1248506; internet www.escuela-turismo-larioja.com; Gen. Dir YOLANDA MONFORTE MORÚA; Academic Dir MERCEDES GONZÁLEZ MARIJUÁN.

UNIVERSIDAD DE LAS PALMAS DE GRAN CANARIA

Calle Juan de Quesada 30, 35001, Las Palmas de Gran Canaria, Canary Islands

Telephone: (92) 8451000
Fax: (92) 8451022
E-mail: universidad@ulpgc.es
Internet: www.ulpgc.es

Founded 1980
State control
Language of instruction: Spanish
Academic year: October to September

Rector: Dr JOSÉ REGIDOR GARCÍA
Vice-Rector for Academic Org. and European Higher Education Convergence: Dr LUIS ÁLVAREZ ÁLVAREZ
Vice-Rector for Culture and Sport: Dra ISABEL PASCUA FEBLES
Vice-Rector for Int. and Institutional Relations: Dra ROSARIO BERRIEL MARTÍNEZ
Vice-Rector for Quality and Educational Innovation: Dra RAQUEL ESPINO ESPINO
Vice-Rector for Research, Devt and Innovation: Dr FERNANDO REAL VALCÁRCEL
Vice-Rector for Student Affairs and Univ. Extension: Dr NICOLÁS DÍAZ DE LEZCANO SEVILLANO
Vice-Rector for Teaching Staff: Dr GUSTAVO MONTERO GARCÍA
Registrar: CARMEN SALINERO ALONSO
Man.: CONRADO DOMÍNGUEZ TRUJILLO
Library Dir: MARÍA DEL CARMEN MARTÍN MARICHAL

Library of 477,251 vols, 9,634 periodicals
Number of teachers: 1,500
Number of students: 25,000

DEANS

Faculty of Computer Science: MANUEL GONZÁLEZ RODRÍGUEZ
Faculty of Economics and Business: SERGIO J. MARTÍN MACHÍN
Faculty of Geography and History: JOSEFA DOMÍNGUEZ MUJICA
Faculty of Health Sciences: JUAN CABRERA CABRERA
Faculty of Law and Social Sciences: IGNACIO DÍAZ DE LEZCANO SEVILLANO
Faculty of Marine Sciences: JOSÉ MIGUEL PACHECO CASTELAO
Faculty of Philology: EUGENIO PADORAO NAVARRO
Faculty of Physical Activity Science and Sport: FERNANDO AMADOR RAMÍREZ
Faculty of Teacher Training: GERMÁN HERNÁNDEZ RODRÍGUEZ
Faculty of Translating and Interpreting: MA. JESÚS GARCÍA DOMÍNGUEZ
Faculty of Veterinary Science: ANSELMO GRACIA MOLINA

ATTACHED INSTITUTES

Innovation Centre for the Information Society: Edificio Central del Parque Científico y Tecnológico, Campus Universitario de Tafira, 35017 Las Palmas de Gran Canaria; tel. (92) 8451045; fax (92) 8451492; e-mail info@cicei.com; internet www.cicei.com; Dir Prof. Dr ENRIQUE RUBIO ROYO.

Institute for Cybernetic Science and Technology: Campus Universitario de Tafira, 35017 Las Palmas de Gran Canaria; tel. (92) 8457100; e-mail mperez@ciber.ulpgc.es; internet www.iuctc.ulpgc.es.

Institute of Applied Microelectronics: Edificio de Electrónica y Telecomunicación, Campus Universitario de Tafira, 35017 Las Palmas de Gran Canaria; tel. (92) 8451233; fax (92) 8451243; e-mail carballo@iuma.ulpgc.es; internet www.iuma.ulpgc.es; Dir ANTONIO NÚÑEZ ORDÓÑEZ.

Marine Biotechnology Centre: Muelle de Taliarte, s/n, 35214 Telde, Las Palmas de Gran Canaria; tel. (98) 72912581; fax (98) 72912671; e-mail ggarcia@dbio.ulpgc.es; internet www.cbm.ulpgc.es; Dir Prof. GUILLERMO GARCÍA REINA.

UNIVERSIDAD DE LEÓN

Edif. Rectorado, Pabellón de Gobierno, Avda de la Facultad 25, 24004 León

Telephone: (98) 7291607
Fax: (98) 7291939
E-mail: rectorado@unileon.es
Internet: www.unileon.es

Founded 1979
State control
Language of instruction: Spanish
Academic year: October to September

Rector: JOSÉ ÁNGEL HERMIDA ALONSO
Vice-Rector for Academic Org.: MATILDE SIERRA VEGA
Vice-Rector for Campus Infrastructure: MARÍA VICTORIA SECO FERNÁNDEZ
Vice-Rector for Economic Affairs: ÁNGELES MARÍN RIVERO
Vice-Rector for Int. and Institutional Relations: JOSÉ LUIS CHAMOSA GONZÁLEZ
Vice-Rector for Ponferrada Campus: VICTORIA SECO FERNÁNDEZ
Vice-Rector for Quality and Accreditation: JUAN CARLOS REDONDO CASTÁN
Vice-Rector for Research: ALBERTO JOSÉ VILLENA CORTÉS
Vice-Rector for Student Affairs: JOSÉ MANUEL GONZALO ORDEN
Vice-Rector for Teaching Staff: JOSÉ LUIS FANJUL SUÁREZ
Registrar: PIEDAD GONZÁLEZ GRANDA
Man.: JOSÉ LUIS MARTÍNEZ JUAN
Library Dir: MARÍA MARSÁ VILA

Library of 458,170 vols, 13,815 periodicals
Number of teachers: 898
Number of students: 15,072

Publications: *Contextos, De Arte, Estudios Humanísticos: Filología, Estudios Humanísticos: Historia, Lancia: Revista de Arqueología, Prehistoria e Historia Antigua, Polígonos, Silva: Estudios de Humanismo y Tradicción Clásica*

DEANS

Faculty of Biology and Environmental Sciences: BLANCA RAZQUÍN PERALTA
Faculty of Economics and Business: MARÍA JESÚS MURES QUINTANA
Faculty of Education: JOSÉ MARÍA SANTAMARTA LUENGOS
Faculty of Labour Studies: GERMÁN BARREIRO GONZÁLEZ
Faculty of Law: Dr TOMÁS QUINTANA LÓPEZ
Faculty of Philosophy and Letters: CARLOS FERNÁNDEZ RODRÍGUEZ
Faculty of Physical Education and Sport: Dra MARTA ZUBIAUR GONZÁLEZ
Faculty of Veterinary Science: JOSÉ GABRIEL FERNÁNDEZ ÁLVAREZ

ATTACHED INSTITUTES

Institute of Automation and Manufacturing: Dir for Automation Section DAVID MARCOS MARTÍNEZ; Dir for Automation Section MANUEL DOMÍNGUEZ GONZÁLEZ; Dir for Imaging Section ÁNGEL ALONSO ÁLVAREZ; Dir for Manufacturing Engineering Section JULIO LABARGA.

Institute of Biomedical Research: Departamento de Fisiología, Campus de Veganaza, 24071 León; tel. (98) 7291258; fax (98) 7291267; e-mail dfijgg@unileon.es; Dir Dr JAVIER GONZÁLEZ GALLEGO.

Institute of Cattle Development: Campus de Veganaza, 24071 León; tel. (98) 7291928; fax (98) 7291638; e-mail dbbmfg@unileon.es; Dir (vacant).

Institute of Food Science and Technology: Calle La Serna 56, 24007 León; tel. (98) 7243123; e-mail dhtjfb@unileon.es; Dir Dr JOSÉ MARÍA FRESNO BARO.

Institute of Natural Resources: Campus de la Escuela T y S de Agrónomos, Avda de Portugal 42, 24071 León; tel. (98) 7291844; fax (98) 7291839; e-mail dfqamp@unileon.es; Dir Dr ANTONIO MORÁN PALAO.

Institute of the Environment: Calle La Serna 56, 24007 León; tel. (98) 7291568; e-mail degelc@unileon.es; Dir Dr ESTANISLAO LUIS CALABUIG.

Institute of Toxicology: Avda Real 1, 24006 León; tel. (98) 7210083; fax (98) 7210091; e-mail dftdoe@unileon.es; Dir Dr DAVID ORDÓÑEZ ESCUDERO.

Instituto de Biotecnología de León (Institute of Biotechnology): Avda Real 1-Parque Científico de León, 24006 León; tel. (98) 7210308; fax (98) 7210388; e-mail inbiotec@inbiotec.com; internet www .inbiotec.com; Gen. and Scientific Dir Dr ELÍAS FERNANDO RODRÍGUEZ FERRI; Gen. and Scientific Dir Dr RAFAEL BALAÑA FOUCE.

UNIVERSIDAD DE MÁLAGA

El Ejido s/n, 29071 Málaga
Telephone: (95) 2131000
Fax: (95) 2263858
E-mail: informacion@uma.es
Internet: www.uma.es
Founded 1972
State control
Language of instruction: Spanish
Academic year: October to July
Rector: ADELAIDA DE LA CALLE MARTÍN
Vice-Rector for Academic Affairs: ANA LOZANO VIVAS
Vice-Rector for Academic Org.: ANA CAÑIZARES LASO
Vice-Rector for Culture and Institutional Relations: ANA MARÍA SÁNCHEZ TEJEDA
Vice-Rector for Infrastructure and Sustainability: RAFAEL MORALES BUENO
Vice-Rector for Int. Relations: MARÍA DEL ROSARIO CABELLO PORRAS
Vice-Rector for Quality, Strategic Planning and Social Responsibility: CARLOS A. BENAVIDES VELASCO
Vice-Rector for Research: JOSÉ ÁNGEL NARVÁEZ BUENO
Vice-Rector for Student Affairs: JUAN ANTONIO PERLES ROCHEL
Vice-Rector for Teaching, Training and Coordination: ENRIQUE CARO GUERRA
Vice-Rector for Technological Devt and Innovation: MARÍA VALPUESTA FERNÁNDEZ
Vice-Rector for Univ. Business Relations: ANA MARÍA SÁNCHEZ TEJEDA
Vice-Rector for Welfare and Equality: MARÍA TERESA PRIETO RUZ
Registrar: MIGUEL PORRAS FERNÁNDEZ
Manager: JOSÉ ANTONIO MOLINA RUIZ
Library Coordinator: GREGORIO GARCÍA RECHE
Library of 921,364 vols, 23,706 periodicals
Number of teachers: 1,600
Number of students: 36,000
Publications: *Boletín de Arte* (1 a year), *Filosofía Malacitana* (1 a year), *Histología Médica* (2 a year)

DEANS

Faculty of Communication: JUAN ANTONIO GARCÍA GALINDO
Faculty of Economic and Business Studies: Dr EUGENIO JOSÉ LUQUE DOMÍNGUEZ
Faculty of Education: JOSÉ FRANCISCO MURILLO MAS
Faculty of Fine Arts: CARMEN OSUNA LUQUE

Faculty of Law: ALEJANDRO J. RODRÍGUEZ CARRIÓN
Faculty of Medicine: ALFREDO BLANES BERENGUEL
Faculty of Philosophy and Letters: SEBASTIÁN FERNÁNDEZ LÓPEZ
Faculty of Psychology: JULIÁN ALMARAZ CARRETERO
Faculty of Science: JOSÉ JOAQUÍN QUIRANTE SÁNCHEZ

PROFESSORS

Faculty of Economic and Business Studies:

AGUIRRE SADABA, A., Economics and Business Administration
GARCÍA LIZANA, A., Applied Economics (Political)
GONZÁLEZ PAREJA, A., Applied Economics (Mathematics)
MOCHON MORCILLO, F., Economic Analysis
OTERO MORENO, J. M., Applied Economics (Statistics and Econometrics)
PINO ARTACHO, J. DEL, State Law and Sociology
REQUENA RODRÍGUEZ, J. M., Financial Economics and Accountancy
SÁNCHEZ MALDONADO, J., Applied Economics (Structure and Public Finance)

Faculty of Law:

AURIOLES MARTIN, A., Private Law
CARRETERO LESTON, J. L., Public Law
ORTEGA CARILLO DE ALBÓRNOZ, A., Civil, Ecclesiastical and State Law
ROBLES GARZÓN, J. A., Political Science, International Law

Faculty of Medicine:

BROTAT ESTER, M., Radiology, Physical and Psychiatric Medicine
CASTILLA GONZALO, J., Normal and Pathological Morphology
FERNÁNDEZ-CREHUET NAVAJAS, J., Preventative Medicine and Public Health
OCAÑA SIERRA, J., Medicine
SÁNCHEZ DE LA CUESTA Y ALARCÓN, F., Physiology, Pharmacology and Paediatrics
SÁNCHEZ DEL CURA, G., Surgery, Obstetrics and Gynaecology

Faculty of Philosophy and Letters:

ALVAR EZQUERRA, M., Spanish and Romance Philology
CUEVAS GARCÍA, C., Spanish Philology and Theory of Literature
ESTEVE ZARAZAGA, J. M., Theory and History of Education
GARCÍA DE LA FUENTE, O., Classical Philology and Arabic and Islamic Studies
LAVIN CAMACHO, E., English and French Philology
MARTÍNEZ FREIRE, P., Philosophy
MORALES FOLGUERAS, J. M., History of Art
NADAL SÁNCHEZ, A., Modern History
OCANA OCANA, M. C., Geography
PÉREZ GÓMEZ, A., Didactics
RODRIGUEZ OLIVA, P., Prehistory and Science of Antiquity and Middle Ages
TRAINES TORRES, M. V., Psychology

Faculty of Science:

ARENAS ROSADO, J. F., Physical Chemistry
CABEZUDO ARTERO, B., Plant Biology
CANO PAVÓN, J. M., Analytical Chemistry
CUENCA MIRA, J. A., Algebra, Geometry and Topology
FERNÁNDEZ-FIGARES PÉREZ, J. M., Cellular and Genetic Biology
FERNÁNDEZ JIMÉNEZ, C., Applied Physics
GARCÍA RASO, E., Animal Biology
JIMÉNEZ LÓPEZ, A., Inorganic Chemistry, Crystalography and Mineralogy
RODRÍGUEZ JIMÉNEZ, J. J., Chemical Engineering
RODRÍGUEZ ORTIZ, C., Applied Mathematics and Statistics

SERRANO LOZANO, L., Ecology and Geology
SUAU SUÁREZ, R., Biochemistry, Molecular Biology and Organic Chemistry

University School of Teacher Training:

DEL CAMPO Y DEL CAMPO, M., Didactics of Expression, Music
GARCÍA ESPAÑA, J., Didactics, Social Science, Experimental Science
MANTECON RAMÍREZ, B., Didactics of Language and Literature

University Polytechnic:

OLLERO BATURONE, A., Systems Engineering, Information Science, Electronics
RUIZ MUNOZ, J. M., Electrical Engineering, Electronic Technology
SIMON MATA, A., Mechanical Engineering, Engineering Graphics
TROYA LINERO, J. M., Language and Science of Computing

UNIVERSIDAD DE MURCIA

Avda Teniente Flomesta 5, 30003 Murcia
Telephone: (96) 8363000
Fax: (96) 8363603
E-mail: siu@um.es
Internet: www.um.es
Founded 1915
State control
Language of instruction: Spanish
Academic year: September to June
Rector: JOSÉ ANTONIO COBACHO GÓMEZ
Vice-Rector for Academic Staff: JOSÉ MARÍA RUIZ GÓMEZ
Vice Rector for Coordination and Communication: MARÍA ANGELES ESTEBAN ABAD
Vice-Rector for Finance and Infrastructure: ANTONIO CALVO-FLORES SEGURA
Vice-Rector for Int. Relations and Innovation: PILAR ARNAIZ SÁNCHEZ
Vice-Rector for Research: JUAN MARÍA VÁZQUEZ ROJAS
Vice Rector for Strategic Devt and Training: FERNANDO MARTÍN RUBIO
Vice-Rector for Students and Employment: MARÍA ISABEL SÁNCHEZ-MORA MOLINA
Vice-Rector for Studies: CONCEPCIÓN R. PALACIOS BERNAL
Vice Rector for Univ. Extension: GUILLERMO DÍAZ BAÑOS
Registrar: NATALIA EGEA DÍAZ
Man.: JORGE NAVARRO OLIVARES
Library Dir: LOURDES COBACHO GÓMEZ
Library of 718,276 vols, 9,416 periodicals, 14,625 e-journals
Number of teachers: 2,101
Number of students: 34,483
Publications: *Anales de Biología* (1 a year), *Antigüedad y Cristianismo* (1 a year), *Daimon* (2 a year, philosophy), *Historia Agraria* (4 a year), *Myrtia* (2 a year, classical philology), *Papeles de Geografía* (2 a year)

DEANS

Faculty of Arts: JOSÉ MARÍA JIMÉNEZ CANO
Faculty of Biology: JOSÉ MESEGUER PEÑALVER
Faculty of Chemistry: M. GLORIA SÁNCHEZ GÓMEZ
Faculty of Communication and Documentation: JOSÉ VICENTE RODRÍGUEZ MUÑOZ
Faculty of Computer Science: JOSÉ MANUEL GARCÍA CARRASCO
Faculty of Economics and Business Studies: MARÍA PILAR MONTANER SALAS
Faculty of Education: CONCEPCIÓN MARTÍN SÁNCHEZ
Faculty of Fine Arts: JUAN ROMERA AGULLÓ
Faculty of Labour Relations: DOMINGO A. MANZANARES MARTÍNEZ
Faculty of Law: FAUSTINO CAVAS MARTÍNEZ
Faculty of Mathematics: FRANCISCO ESQUEMBRE MARTÍNEZ

Faculty of Medicine: JOAQUÍN GARCÍA-ESTAÑ LÓPEZ

Faculty of Optometry: PALOMA SOBRADO CALVO

Faculty of Philosophy: ANTONIO CAMPILLO MESEGUER

Faculty of Psychology: JUAN JOSÉ LÓPEZ GARCÍA

Faculty of Social Work: ENRIQUE PASTOR SELLER

Faculty of Veterinary Studies: ANTONIO ROUCO YÁÑEZ

ATTACHED INSTITUTIONS

Institute of Ageing: Campus Universitario de Espinardo, 30100 Espinardo (Murcia); tel. (96) 8363499; e-mail maemedina@um.es; internet www.um.es/estructura/institutos/iupe; Dir MANUEL E. MEDINA TORNERO.

Institute of Education: Edificio D, 3°, Campus de Espinardo, 30100 Murcia; tel. (96) 8363926; fax (96) 8363925; e-mail ice@um.es; internet www.um.es/ice; Dir JUAN MANUEL ESCUDERO MUÑOZ.

Institute of Financial and Fiscal Studies: Dept Hacienda y Economía del Sector Público, Despacho B109, Campus de Espinardo, 30100 Murcia; tel. (96) 8367798; e-mail inueff@um.es; internet www.um.es/inueff; Dir GLORIA ALARCÓN GARCÍA.

Institute of Sport Science: Facultad de Educación, Campus Universitario de Espinardo, 30100 Espinardo (Murcia); tel. (96) 8364052; fax (96) 8364146; e-mail icd@um.es; internet www.um.es/icd; Dir ARTURO DÍAZ SUÁREZ.

Institute of University Teaching: Calle Real 80, Cartagena (Murcia); tel. (96) 8505313; internet www.um.es/isen; Dir MA. DOLORES FONTES BASTOS.

Institute of Water and the Environment: Edificio D, Campus de Espinardo, 30100 Murcia; tel. (96) 8364910; fax (96) 8363389; e-mail inuama@um.es; internet www.um.es/inuama; Dir ALBERTO BARBA NAVARRO.

Inter-university Institute of the Ancient Near East: Antigua Escuela de Empresariales, Calle Actor Isidoro Máiquez 8, Vistalegre, 30007 Murcia; tel. and fax (96) 8363890; e-mail ipoa@um.es; internet www.um.es/ipoa.

University School of Nursing in Cartagena: Plaza San Agustín 3, 30201 Cartagena (Murcia); tel. (96) 8326696; fax (96) 8326695; internet www.um.es/eu-enfermeria-ct; Dir CARMEN SÁNCHEZ TRIGUEROS.

University School of Tourism: Paseo de Malecón 5, 30004 Murcia; tel. (96) 8293624; fax (96) 8291096; e-mail eutm@um.es; Academic Dir BERNARDINO BENITO LÓPEZ.

UNIVERSIDAD DE NAVARRA

Campus Universitario, 31080 Pamplona
Telephone: (94) 8425600
Fax: (94) 8425619
E-mail: relint@unav.es
Internet: www.unav.es

Founded 1952
Private control
Languages of instruction: Spanish, English
Academic year: September to June

Chancellor: JAVIER ECHEVARRÍA
Vice-Chancellor: Mgr RAMÓN HERRANDO
Rector: Prof. ANGEL JOSÉ GÓMEZ MONTORO
Vice-Rector for Academic Org. and Educational Innovation: Prof. BORJA LÓPEZ-JURADO
Vice-Rector for Academic Staff: Prof. CONCEPCIÓN NAVAL-DURÁN
Vice-Rector for Corporate Communication: Prof. JUAN MANUEL MORA

Vice-Rector for Int. Relations: Prof. ALFONSO SÁNCHEZ-TABERNERO
Vice-Rector for Research: Prof. LUIS MONTUENGA-BADIA
Vice-Rector for Student Affairs and Univ. Extension: Prof. MARÍA IRABURU-ELIZALDE
Registrar: Dr GONZALO ROBLES GONZÁLEZ
Man.: XABIER AIZPURUA TELLERÍA
Admin. Dir: IGOR ERRASTI
Library Dir: VÍCTOR SANZ SANTACRUZ
Library of 1,200,000 vols, 60,000 journals
Number of teachers: 1,791 (900 full-time, 891 part-time)
Number of students: 13,197 (11,198 full-time, 1,999 part-time)
Publications: *Anuario de Derecho Internacional* (1 a year), *Anuario Filosófico* (3 a year), *Comunicación y Sociedad* (2 a year), *Ius Canonicum* (2 a year), *Nuestro Tiempo* (12 a year), *Persona y Derecho* (2 a year), *Redacción* (4 a year), *Revista de Edificación* (4 a year), *Revista de Medicina* (4 a year), *RILCE* (2 a year), *Scripta Theologica* (4 a year)

DEANS

Faculty of Architecture: MARIANO GONZALEZ-PRESENCIO
Faculty of Canon Law: JORGE MIRAS POUSO
Faculty of Communication: MONICA HERRERO
Faculty of Economics: REYES CALDERÓN
Faculty of Engineering: ALEJO AVELLO
Faculty of Humanities and Social Sciences: JAUME AURELL
Faculty of Law: PABLO SÁNCHEZ-OSTIZ
Faculty of Medicine: JORGE IRIARTE
School of Nursing: MERCEDES PÉREZ-DIEZ DEL CORRAL
Faculty of Pharmacy: ADELA LÓPEZ DE CERAIN
Faculty of Sciences: IGNACIO LÓPEZ GOÑI
Faculty of Theology: JUAN CHAPA
IESE School of Business Administration: Professor JORDI CANALS-MARGALEF
Univ. Hospital: JOSE A. GÓMEZ-CANTERO

PROFESSORS

Faculty of Canon Law:

BAÑARES PARERA, J. I., Family Law
CALVO-ÁLVAREZ, J., Administrative Canon Law
FUENTES ALSONSO, J. A., Administrative Canon Law
GÓMEZ-IGLESIAS, V., Constitutional Canon Law
MIRAS POUSO, J. M., Administrative Canon Law
MOLANO GRAGERA, E., Constitutional Canon Law
OTADUY, J., Ecclesiastical Law
OTADUY GUERIN, J., General and Personal Law
RINCÓN, T., Administrative Canon Law
RODRÍGUEZ-OCAÑA, R., Procedural Canon Law
VIANA TOMÉ, A., Ecclesiastical Organization
VILADRICH BATALLER, P. J., Canon Law

Faculty of Communication:

AMOEDO CASAIS, A., Journalistic Projects
ARRESE RECA, A., Media Business
ARTÁZCOZ LÓPEZ, M. A., Journalistic Projects
AZURMENDI ADARRAGA, A., Public Communication
BARRERA DEL BARRIO, C., Public Communication
BRINGUÉ SALA, J., Media Business
CODINA BLASCO, M., Public Communication
CUEVAS ÁLVAREZ, E., Audiovisual Communication
DE LA RICA ARANGUREN, A., Audiovisual Communication
DE LOS ÁNGELES VILLENA, J., Media Business

ECHART ORÚS, P., Audiovisual Communication
ETAYO PÉREZ, C., Media Business
FAUS BELAU, A., Audiovisual Communication
GARCÍA AVILÉS, J. A., Journalistic Projects
GARCÍA-NOBLEJAS LINIERS, J. J., Audiovisual Communication
JIMENO LÓPEZ, M. A., Journalistic Projects
LA PORTE FERNÁNDEZ-ALFARO, M. T., Public Communication
LATORRE IZQUIERDO, J., Audiovisual Communication
LEÓN ANGUIANO, B., Journalistic Projects
LÓPEZ PAN, F., Journalistic Projects
LÓPEZ-ESCOBAR FERNÁNDEZ, E., Public Communication
LOZANO BARTOLOZZI, P., Public Communication
MARTÍNEZ COSTA, M. P., Journalistic Projects
MEDINA, M., Media Business
MONTERO DÍAZ, M., Public Communication
MORENO MORENO, E., Journalistic Projects
NAVAS GARCÍA, A., Public Communication
ORIHUELA COLLIVA, J. L., Audiovisual Communication
PARDO FERNÁNDEZ, A., Audiovisual Communication
PÉREZ LATRE, F. J., Media Business
PIQUE I FERNÁNDEZ, A. M., Journalistic Projects
PORTILLA MANJÓN, I., Media Business
REDONDO GÁLVEZ, G., History
SÁDABA CHALEZQUER, R., Media Business
SÁDABA GARRAZA, M. T., Public Communication
SALAVERRÍA ALIAGA, R., Journalistic Projects
SÁNCHEZ ARANDA, J. J., Public Communication
SÁNCHEZ-TABERNERO SÁNCHEZ, A., Media Business
VARA MIGUEL, A., Media Business
VERDERA ALBIÑANA, F., Public Communication
ZORRILLA RUIZ, J., Journalistic Projects

Faculty of Economics and Business:

ABBRITTI, M., Economics
ALFARO TANCO, J. A., Business Admin.
ALVAREZ ARCE, J. L., Economics
ARANDA LEÓN, C., Business Admin.
ARELLANO GIL, J., Business Admin.
BLANCO, B., Business Economics and Quantitative Methods
BLAZSEK, S., Economics
CALDERÓN CUADRADO, R., Business Admin.
CORGNET, B., Economics
CUÑADO EIZAGUIRRE, J., Applied Economics
ELIZALDE, J., Applied Economics
GALERA PERAL, F., Applied Economics
GAVLE, S., Business Economics and Quantitative Methods
GIL ALAÑA, L., Economics
GONZÁLEZ ENCISO, A., Economics
KINATEDEE, M., Economics
LEIVA, R., Business
MARTÍNEZ-ECHEVARRÍA, M. A., Economics
MATEO DUEÑAS, R., Business
MATHEW, A. J., Economics
MENDI GÜEMES, P., Economics
MOLERO GARCÍA, J. C., Applied Economics
MORENO ALMÁRCEGUI, A., Economics
MORENO IBÁÑEZ, A., Economics
PÉREZ DE GRACIA HIDALGO, F., Applied Economics
PUJOL TORRAS, F., Economics
RÁBADE Y HERRERO, L. A., Business
RAVINA BOHORQUEZ, L., Economics
RODRÍGUEZ CARREÑO, I., Economics
RODRÍGUEZ CHACÓN, V., Business
SALVATIERRA, S. M., Quantitative Methods
SAN MARTÍN ECHAURI, C., Quantitative Methods
SEBREK, S., Business

Tolsa Majós, A., Applied Economics
Torres Sánchez, R., Economics
Zaratiegui Laviano, J. M., Economics
Zarco Jasso, H., Business Admin.

Faculty of Law:

Aparisi Miralles, A., Philosophy of Law
Arechederra Aranzadi, L., Civil Law
Blanco Fernández, M., Canon Law
Domingo Oslé, R., Roman Law
Gómez Montoro, A., Constitutional Law
López Sánchez, M. A., Commercial Law
López-Jurado, B., Administrative Law
Muerza Esparza, J., Procedural Law
Sánchez-Ostiz Gutiérrez, P., Criminal Law
Simón Acosta, E., Financial Law
Valpuesta Gastaminza, E., Commercial Law

Faculty of Medicine:

Alberola Gómez-Escolar, I., Internal Medicine
Alcázar Zambrano, J. L., Obstetrics and Gynaecology
Alegría Ezquerra, E., Cardiology
Álvarez-Cienfuegos Suárez, J., General Surgery
Alzina de Aguilar, V., Paediatrics
Amillo Garayoa, S., Orthopaedics Surgery
Aquerreta Beola, A., Radiology
Artieda González-Granda, J., Neurology
Aymerich Soler, M. S., Neurology
Azanza Perea, J. R., Pharmacology
Azcona San Julián, C., Paediatrics
Barba Cosials, J., Cardiology
Bazán Álvarez, A., Plastic Surgery
Beguiristain Gúrpide, J. L., Orthopaedics Surgery
Beloqui Ruiz, Ó., Internal Medicine
Berián Polo, J. M., Urology
Bilbao Jaureguizar, I., Radiology
Bodegas Frías, M. E., Histology
Borrás Cuesta, F., Biochemistry
Burrell Bustos, M. A., Pathological Anatomy
Calabuig Nogués, J., Cardiology
Calvo González, A., Histology
Carrascosa Moreno, F., Anaesthesiology and Resuscitation
Casado Casado, M., Radiology
Cenarruzbeitia Sagarminaga, E., Physiology
Cervera Enguix, S., Psychiatry
Civeira Murillo, M. P., Medical Secretaryship
Colina Lorda, I., Internal Medicine
Coma Canella, I., Cardiology
Corrales Izquierdo, J., Internal Medicine
Cuesta Palomera, B., Haematology
de Castro, P., Neurology
de Miguel Vázquez, C., Biochemistry
Del Pozo León, J. L., Microbiology
Díaz García, R., Microbiology
Diéguez López, I., Allergology
Diez Goñi, N., Physiology
Díez Martínez, J., Internal Medicine
Echarte Alonso, L., Biomedicine
Fernández Alonso, M., Microbiology
Forriol Campos, F., Laboratory Medicine
Frechilla Manso, D., Pharmacology
García-Morato, J. R., Anthropology
Gil Sotres, P., Biomedicine
Honorato Pérez, J., Pharmacology
Hontanilla Catalay, B., Plastic Surgery
Idoate Gastearena, M., Pathological Anatomy
Iraburu Elizalde, M., Biochemistry
Irala Estevez, J. de, Preventive Medicine
Lahortiga Ramos, F., Psychiatry
Lasheras Aldaz, B., Pharmacology
Lázaro Cantero, R., Anthropology
León Sanz, M. P., Biomedicine
López Garacía, M. P., Psychiatry
Lozano Escario, M. D., Pathological Anatomy
Lucas Ros, I., Internal Medicine

Luquin Pulido, M. R., Neurology
Maldonado López, M., Ophthalmology
Manrique Rodríguez, M., Otolaryngology
Manrique Smela, M., Neurology
Martín Algarra, S., Oncology
Martín Trenor, A., General Surgery
Martínez de Tejada de Garaizabal, G., Microbiology
Martínez González, M. A., Epidemiology and Public Health
Martínez Irujo, J. J., Biochemistry
Martínez Lage, M., Neurology
Martínez Monge, R., Radiology
Martínez Regueira, F., General Surgery
Martínez Vila, E., Neurology
Masdeu Puche, J., Neurology
Medina Cabrera, J. F., Internal Medicine
Melero Bermejo, I., Immunology
Mengual Poza, E., Anatomy
Merino Roncal, J., Immunology
Monedero Rodríguez, P., Anaesthesiology and Resuscitation
Montuenga Badia, L., Histology
Moreno Montañés, J., Ophthalmology
Moriyón Uría, I., Microbiology
Muñoz Navas, M. A., General Surgery
Narbona García, J., Paediatrics
Novo Villaverde, J., Genetics
Obeso Inchausti, J., Neurology
Odero de Dios, L., Genetics
Olavide Goya, I., Anaesthesiology
Páramo Fernández, J. A., Haematology
Pardo Caballos, A., Biomedicine
Pardo Mindán, J., Pathological Anatomy
Pastor Muñoz, M. A., Neurology
Peñuelas Sánchez, I., Biochemistry
Pérez Fernández, N., Otolaryngology
Pérez Mediavilla, L. A., Biochemistry
Prensa Sepúlveda, L., Anatomy
Prieto Valtueña, J., Internal Medicine
Prósper, F., Haematology
Purroy Unanua, A., Nephrology
Qian, C., Internal Medicine
Quiroga Vilas, J., Internal Medicine
Redondo, P., Dermatology
Richter Echevarría, J. A., Nuclear Medicine
Rio Zambrana, J., Pharmacology
Robles García, J. E., Urology
Rocha Hernando, E., Haematology
Rodríguez Ortigosa, C., Biochemistry
Rosell Costa, D., Urology
Rouzaut Subirá, A., Biochemistry
Rubio Vallejo, M., Microbiology
Ruiz-Canela López, M., Biomedicine
Salvador Rodríguez, F. J., Endocrinology
Sánchez Ibarrola, A., Immunology
Sangro Gómez-Acebo, B., Internal Medicine
Santidrian Alegre, S., Physiology
Sanz Larruga, M. L., Allergology
Seguí Gómez, M., Internal Medicine
Serrano Martínez, M., Internal Medicine
Sesma Egozcue, P., Pathological Anatomy
Sierrasesúmaga Ariznavarreta, L., Paediatrics
Sola Gallego, J. J., Pathological Anatomy
Torre Buxalleu, W., General Surgery
Ullán Serrano, J., Anatomy
Valentí Nin, J. R., Orthopaedic Surgery
Velayos Jorge, J. L., Anatomy
Villaro Gumpert, A. C., Histology
Villas Tomé, C., Orthopaedic Surgery
Viteri Torres, C., Neurology
Zapata Garcíá, R., Psychiatry
Zornoza Celaya, G., General Surgery
Zubieta Zarraga, J. L., Radiology
Zudaire Bergara, J. J., Urology

Faculty of Pharmacy
(Some professors also serve in the Faculty of Sciences)

Aguirre García, N., Pharmacology
Aldana Moraza, I., Organic Chemistry

Aldaz Pastor, A., Pharmacy and Pharmaceutical Technology
Ansorena, D., Bromatology and Toxicology
Aquerreta González, I., Pharmacy and Pharmaceutical Technology
Astiasarán Anchía, I., Bromatology and Toxicology
Barber Cárcamo, A., Physiology and Nutrition
Beitia Berrotarán, G.
Berjón San Juan, A., Physiology and Nutrition
Blanco, M. J., Pharmacy and Pharmaceutical Technology
Calvo, I., Pharmacy and Pharmaceutical Technology
Cid Canda, C., Bromatology and Toxicology
de Peña Fariza, M. P., Bromatology
Díaz García, J. M., Pharmacy and Pharmaceutical Technology
Dios Viéitez, C., Pharmacy and Pharmaceutical Technology
Espuelas, S., Pharmacy and Pharmaceutical Technology
Idoate García, A., Pharmacy and Pharmaceutical Technology
Fernández de Trocóniz, I., Pharmacy and Pharmaceutical Technology
Font Arellano, M., Organic Chemistry
García del Barrio, G., Pharmacy and Pharmaceutical Technology
Garrido, M. J., Pharmacy and Pharmaceutical Technology
Gil Royo, A. G., Bromatology and Toxicology
Giráldez Deiró, J., Pharmacy and Pharmaceutical Technology
Goñi Leza, M. del M., Pharmacy and Pharmaceutical Technology
Lacasa Arregui, C., Pharmacy and Pharmaceutical Technology
Lasheras Aldaz, B., Pharmacology
Lizarraga Pérez, E., Organic Chemistry
Lobo, J. M., Pharmacy and Pharmaceutical Technology
López de Cerain, A., Bromatology and Toxicology
López Guzmán, J., Biomedicine
Lostao Crespo, P., Physiology and Nutrition
Manuel Irache Garreta, J. M., Pharmacy and Pharmaceutical Technology
Martí del Moral, A., Physiology and Nutrition
Martínez Hernández, A., Physiology and Nutrition
Mohino Sánchez, A., Bromatology and Toxicology
Monge Vega, A., Organic Chemistry
Moreno Aliaga, M. J., Physiology and Nutrition
Muñoz Hornillos, M., Physiology and Nutrition
Ortega Eslava, A., Pharmacy and Pharmaceutical Technology
Palop Cubillo, J. A., Organic Chemistry
Ramírez Gil, M. J., Pharmacology
Recarte Flamarique, F., Pharmacy and Pharmaceutical Technology
Renedo Omaechevarría, M. J., Pharmacy and Pharmaceutical Technology
Romero Cuevas, M., Organic Chemistry
Ruiz de la Heras, A., Bromatology and Toxicology
Sanmartín Grijalba, C., Organic Chemistry
Tros de Ilarduya, C., Pharmacy and Pharmaceutical Technology
Ygartua Ayerra, P., Pharmacy and Pharmaceutical Technology
Zamarreño Arregui, A. M., Pharmacy and Pharmaceutical Technology
Zapelena Iñiguez, M. J., Bromatology and Toxicology
Zulet Alzórriz, M. A., Physiology

Faculty of Sciences:

AGUIRREOLA MORALES, J., Plant Physiology
ALVAREZ CALVIÑO, R., Botany
ALVAREZ GALINDO, J. I., Chemistry and Pedology
ÁLVAREZ JAURRIETA, M. L., Chemistry and Edaphology
ANTOLÍN BELLVER, C., Plant Physiology
AQUERRETA MOLINA, S., Botany
ARDANZA-TREVIJANO, S., Physics and Applied Mathematics
ARIÑO PLANA, A., Zoology and Ecology
AZCÁRATE IRIARTE, R., Chemistry and Edaphology
BAQUERO MARTÍN, E., Zoology and Ecology
BRAGARD, J., Physics and Applied Mathematics
BURGUETE MÁS, F. J., Physics and Applied Mathematics
CALASANZ ABINZANO, M. J., Genetics
CAVERO, Y., Chemistry and Pedology
CHASCO UGARTE, M. J., Physics and Applied Mathematics
CLAVERÍA IRACHETA, V., Botany
DE MIGUEL VELASCO, A., Botany
DÍAZ CALAVIA, E. J., Physics
EDERRA INDURAIN, A., Botany
ESCALA URDAPILLETA, C., Zoology and Ecology
FERNÁNDEZ ALVAREZ, J. M., Chemistry and Pedology
FERNÁNDEZ ASENJO, L., Chemistry and Pedology
GARAYOA POYO, R., Economy
GARCÍA CASADO, P., Chemistry and Pedology
GARCÍA DELGADO, M., Genetics
GARCÍA UNCITI, M. S., Dietetics
GARCÍA ZAMORA, J. M., Chemistry and Pedology
GARCÍA-MINA FREIRE, J. M., Chemistry and Pedology
GARCIMARTÍN, A., Physics and Applied Mathematics
GARDE GARDE, J. M., Zoology and Ecology
GARRIGÓ I REIXACH, J., Chemistry and Pedology
GOICOECHEA PREBOSTE, N., Plant Physiology
GONZÁLEZ, W., Physics and Applied Mathematics
GONZÁLEZ GAITANO, G., Chemistry and Pedology
GUERRERO SETAS, D., Edaphology
HERNÁNDEZ MINGUILLÓN, M. A., Zoology and Ecology
HERRERA MESA, L., Zoology and Ecology
IBÁÑEZ GASTÓN, R., Botany
IRIGOYEN IPARREA, J. J., Plant Physiology
ISASI ALLICA, J. R., Chemistry and Pedology
JORDANA BUTTICAZ, R., Zoology and Ecology
JUARISTI IRANZU, R., Botany
LABAT AYERRA, A., Chemistry and Pedology
LARRAZ AZCÁRATE, M., Zoology and Ecology
LÓPEZ FERNÁNDEZ, M. L., Botany
LÓPEZ GOÑI, I., Microbiology
LÓPEZ MORATALLA, N., Biochemistry
LÓPEZ ZABALZA, M. J., Biochemistry
MANCINI, H., Physics and Applied Mathematics
MARTÍN BACHILLER, C., Chemistry and Pedology
MARTÍNEZ OHARRIZ, C., Chemistry and Pedology
MARTÍNEZ REMÍREZ, M., Physiology
MAZA OZCOIDI, D., Physics and Applied Mathematics
MIRANDA FERREIRO, R., Zoology and Ecology
MORAZA ZORRILLA, L., Zoology and Ecology
NAVARRO BLASCO, I., Chemistry and Pedology
NOVO VILLAVERDE, J., Genetics
ODERO DE DIOS, M. D., Genetics

PALACIOS, C., Physics and Applied Mathematics
PELAEZ LÓPEZ, A., Physics and Applied Mathematics
PEÑAS, F. J., Chemistry and Pedology
PÉREZ GARCÍA, C., Physics and Applied Mathematics
PIUDO AINZINENA, M. J., Botany
PUIG BAGUER, J., Zoology and Ecology
RODÉS NAVARRO, D., Zoology and Ecology
RODRÍGUEZ GARCÍA, J. A., Genetics
RUILOPE PINEDA, R., Chemistry and Pedology
SÁNCHEZ CARPINTERO, I., Chemistry and Pedology
SÁNCHEZ DÍAZ, M., Plant Physiology
SÁNCHEZ GONZÁLEZ, M., Chemistry and Pedology
SÁNCHEZ MONGE, J. M., Chemistry and Pedology
SANTAMARÍA ELOLA, C., Chemistry and Pedology
SANTAMARÍA ULECIA, J. M., Chemistry and Pedology
SERRANO MARTÍNEZ, M., Zoology and Ecology
SIRERA BEJARANO, R., Chemistry and Pedology
VELAZ RIVAS, I., Chemistry and Pedology
VIZMANOS, J. L., Genetics
ZORNOZA CEBEIRO, A., Chemistry and Pedology
ZUDAIRE RIPA, I., Genetics

Faculty of Theology:

ARANDA LOMEÑA, A., Dogmatic Theology
ARANDA PÉREZ, G., Sacred Scripture: New Testament
BASTERO ELEIZALDE, J. L., Dogmatic Theology
IZQUIERDO URBINA, C., Fundamental Theology
MERINO RODRÍGUEZ, M., Patristics
SARANYANA CLOSA, J. I., History of Theology
SARMIENTO FRANCO, A., Moral Theology
VARO PINEDA, F., Sacred Scripture: New Testament

School of Engineering:

ALVAREZ SÁNCHEZ-ARJONA, M. J., Industrial Organization
ARCELUS ALONSO, M., Organization
ARIZTI URQUIJO, F., Fundamental Electronics
AVELLO ITURRIAGAGOITIA, A., Theory of Machines
BAGUER ALCALÁ, A., Organization of Work
BASTERO DE ELEIZALDE, C., Mathematical Methods
BASTERO DE ELEIZALDE, J. M., Mechanics
BERENGUER PÉREZ, R., Electronics
BISTUÉ GARCÍA, G., Electricity
BLANCO DEL PRADO, C., Calculus
BUSTAMANTE MERINO, P., Informatics
CAMPOS CAPELASTEGUI, J., Mechanics
CELIGÜETA LIZARZA, J. T., Computational Mechanics
DE LOS MOZOS VILLAR, L., Mechanics
DE MIGUEL SICILIA, J. J., Anthropology
DE NO LENGARÁN, J., Electricity
FERNÁNDEZ DÍEZ, J., Mechanical Technology
FLAQUER FUSTER, J., Linear Algebra
FLÓREZ ESNAL, J., Robotics
FONTAN AGORRETA, L., Fundamentals of Electronics
FUENTES PÉREZ, M., Metallurgy
GARCÍA RICO, A., Electrical Machines
GARCÍA-ALONSO MONTOYA, A., Electrical Engineering
GARCÍA-ROSALES VÁZQUEZ, C., Materials
GIL NOBAJAS, J. J., Electricity and Electronics
GIL SEVILLANO, J., Metallurgy
GIMÉNEZ ORTIZ, G., Mechanical Technology
GÓMEZ-ACEBO TEMES, T., Thermodynamics

GRACIA GAUDÓ, J., Electronics
GURRUCHAGA VÁZQUEZ, J. M., Technical Drawing
IZU BELLOSO, P., Materials
JIMÉNEZ CONDE, M., General Physics
LÓPEZ DE ARANCIBIA, A., Mechanics
LÓPEZ SORIA, B., Materials
MARTÍN ABREU, F., Mechanics
MARTÍNEZ ESNAOLA, J. M., Mechanics of Continua
MUÑOZ EMPARAN, A., Telecommunications
PARGADA GIL, M., Advanced Mathematics
PÉREZ TOCA, M., Electricity
PUENTE URRUZMENDI, I., Mechanics
RAMOS GONZÁLEZ, J. C., Mechanics
RIVAS NIETO, A., Fluids
RODRÍGUEZ IBABE, J. M., Materials
RUBIO DÍAZ-CORDOVÉS, A. R., Electricity
SANCHO SEUMA, J. I., Electricity
SANTOS GARCÍA, J., Organization
SARRIEGUI DOMÍNGUEZ, J. M., Organization
SERNA OLIVEIRA, M. A., Mechanics
SERRANO BÁRCENA, N., Organization
VERA RODRÍGUEZ, E., Steel Structures
VILES DÍEZ, E., Statistics
VIÑOLAS PRAT, J., Mechanics

ATTACHED INSTITUTES AND SCHOOLS

Higher Institute of Religious Studies: Universidad de Navarra, Edificio de Facultades Eclesiásticas, 31080 Pamplona, (Navarra); tel. (94) 8425716; fax (94) 8425633; e-mail iscr@unav.es; internet www .unav.es/iscr; Dir ENRIQUE MOLINA.

Institute of Advanced Business Studies (IESE): Avda Pearson 21, 08034 Barcelona;- Camino del Cerro del Águila 3 (Ctra. de Castilla km 5.180), 28023 Madrid; tel. (93) 2534200 (Barcelona); fax (93) 2534343 (Barcelona); e-mail info@iese.edu; internet www .iese.edu; f. 1958; business administration; campus at New York, USA; 107 full-time teachers; 1,500 students; library of 51,517 vols, 12,000 periodicals; Dean Prof. Dr JORDI CANALS.

Institute of Anthropology and Ethics: Universidad de Navarra, Edificio Central, 31009 Pamplona; tel. (94) 8425600; e-mail iae@unav.es; internet www.unav.es/iae; Dir SERGIO SÁNCHEZ-MIGALLÓN.

Institute of Enterprise and Humanism: Edificio de Bibliotecas, Campus Universitario s/n, 31080 Pamplona; tel. (94) 8425600; e-mail cosinaga@unav.es; internet www.unav.es/empresayhumanismo; Dir RAFAEL ALVIRA.

Institute of Family Studies: Edificio Los Nogales, Universidad de Navarra, 31080 Pamplona; tel. (94) 8425600; fax (94) 8425640; e-mail icf@unav.es; internet www .unav.es/icf; Dir PEDRO-JUAN VILADRICH BATALLER.

Institute of Food Sciences: Edificio de Ciencias, Universidad de Navarra, C/ Irunlarrea 1, 31008 Pamplona; tel. (94) 8425600; fax (94) 8425649; e-mail icaun@unav.es; internet www.unav.es/icaun.

Institute of Human Rights: Despacho 1731, Edificio de Bibliotecas, Campus Universitario s/n, 31080 Pamplona; tel. (94) 8425600; fax (94) 8425621; e-mail idh@unav .es; internet www.unav.es/idh/default.html; Dir ÁNGELA APARISI MIRALLES.

Institute of Medieval Studies: e-mail saurell@unav.es; internet www.unav.es/ iestmedie; Dir JAUME AURELL.

Institute of Physics: Universidad de Navarra, Irunlarrea, s/n, 31080 Pamplona; e-mail hmancini@fisica.unav.es; internet instituto.fisica.unav.es; Dir HÉCTOR L. MANCINI.

Martín Azpilcueta Institute: Edificio de Bibliotecas, Campus Universitario s/n, 31080

Pamplona; tel. (94) 8425631; fax (94) 8425636; e-mail ima@unav.es; internet www.unav.es/ima; Dir Prof. JORGE OTADUY; Vice-Dir Prof. JOSÉ ANTONIO FUENTES; Vice-Dir Prof. DANIEL CENALMOR; publ. *Ius Canonicum*.

Professional School of Clinical Biochemistry: Dir (vacant).

Professional School of Internal Medicine: Facultad de Medicina; Dir JESÚS PRIETO.

Professional School of Medical-Surgical Dermatology and Venereology: Dir (vacant).

Professional School of Psychiatry: Dir SALVADOR CERVERA.

Professional School of the Digestive Apparatus: Dir FEDERICO CONCHILLO.

School of Legal Practice: Dir FAUSTINO CORDON.

Urban Ecology Studies Centre: Dir MANUEL FERRER.

University Clinic: Avda Pío XII 36, 31008 Pamplona; tel. (94) 8255400; fax (94) 8296500; internet www.cun.es; Gen. Dir AMADOR SOSA LORA; Medical Dir Dr JAVIER ÁLVAREZ-CIENFUEGOS SUÁREZ.

UNIVERSIDAD DE OVIEDO

Calle San Francisco 3, 33003 Oviedo

Telephone: (98) 5104058
Fax: (98) 5104085
E-mail: causi@uniovi.es
Internet: www.uniovi.es

Founded 1608
Language of instruction: Spanish
State control
Language of instruction: English
Academic year: September to July

Rector: Prof. VICENTE GOTOR SANTAMARÍA
Vice-Rector for Campus: Prof. MARÍA PAZ SUÁREZ RENDUELES
Vice-Rector for Economic Planning: SANTIAGO ÁLVAREZ GARCÍA
Vice-Rector for Infrastructure, Campus and Sustainability: Prof. JOSÉ CARLOS RICO FERNÁNDEZ
Vice-Rector for Int. Relations and Devt Cooperation: Prof. ANA MARÍA FERNÁNDEZ GARCÍA
Vice-Rector for IT and Communications: Prof. VÍCTOR GUILLERMO GARCÍA GARCÍA
Vice-Rector for Research: Prof. SANTIAGO GARCÍA GRANDA
Vice-Rector for Students and Employment: Prof. SUSANA LÓPEZ ARES
Vice-Rector for Studies and New Degrees: Prof. COVADONGA BETEGÓN BIEMPICA
Vice-Rector for Teaching Staff, Depts and Centres: Prof. JULIO ANTONIO GONZÁLEZ GARCÍA
Vice-Rector for Univ. Extension, Culture and Sport: Prof. VICENTE JESÚS DOMÍNGUEZ GARCÍA
Gen. Sec.: Prof. JOSÉ FRANCISCO FERNÁNDEZ GARCÍA
Man.: EUSEBIO GONZÁLEZ GARCÍA
Librarian: Dr. RAMÓN RODRÍGUEZ ÁLVAREZ

Library of 1,000,000 vols, 14,000 periodicals
Number of teachers: 2,154
Number of students: 29,000

Publications: *Aljamía, Archivos de la Facultad de Medicina, Asturiensia Medievalia, Brevoria Geológica Astúrica, Ería, Archivum, Liño, Memorias de Historia Antigua y Territorio, Revista de Biología, Revista de Ciencias, Revista de Minas, Sociedad y Poder, Trabajos de Geología* ·

DEANS

Faculty of Biology: TOMÁS EMILIO DÍAZ GONZÁLEZ
Faculty of Chemistry: JOSÉ MANUEL FERNÁNDEZ COLINAS
Faculty of Commerce, Tourism and Social Sciences 'Jovellanos': (vacant)
Faculty of Economics and Business Studies: Prof. MANUEL GONZÁLEZ DÍAZ
Faculty of Geology: LOPEZ CALLEJA ESCUDERO
Faculty of Law: RAMÓN DURÁN RIVACOBA
Faculty of Medicine and Health Sciences: ANTONIO CUETO ESPINAR
Faculty of Philology: JESÚS MENÉNDEZ PELÁEZ
Faculty of Philosophy and Letters: CRISTINA VALDÉS RODRÍQUEZ
Faculty of Psychology: MARCELINO CUESTA IZQUIERDO
Faculty of Science: NORBERTO CORRAL BLANCO
Faculty of Teaching Training and Education: JUAN CARLOS SAN PEDRO VELEDO
Faculty of Trade, Tourism and Social Sciences 'Jovellanos': RAFAEL PÉREZ LORENZO
Higher School of Civil Navy: Prof. RAFAEL GARCÍA MÉNDEZ
Higher Technical School of Mine Engineering: Prof. MARIO MENÉNDEZ ÁLVAREZ
IT Engineering School: Prof. JOSÉ EMILIO LABRA GAYO
Polytechnic School (Mieres): Prof. ANTONIO BERNARDO SÁNCHEZ
Polytechnic School of Egineering (Gijón): Prof. HILARIO LÓPEZ GARCÍA

ATTACHED SCHOOLS AND CENTRES

'Padre Enrique de Ossó' University School of Teacher Training: Calle Prau Picon s/n, 33008 Oviedo; e-mail informa@eupo.es; internet www.eupo.es; Dir FERNANDO PENDAS FERNÁNDEZ.

University School of Industrial Relations: Avda Manuel Llaneza 75, 33208 Gijón; e-mail eurlgijo@correo.uniovi.es; internet www.unioviedo.es/relacioneslaboralesgijon; Dir JULIO RODRÍGUEZ SUÁREZ.

University School of Nursing: Calle Hospital de Cabueñes s/n, 33294 Gijón; e-mail escuelaenfermeria.gae5@sespa.princast.es; Dir CRISTINA FERNÁNDEZ ÁLVAREZ.

University School of Social Work: Calle Fortuna Balnearia 1, 33207 Gijón; e-mail admon@eutsgijon.com; internet www.unioviedo.es/eutsg; Dir MARÍA JOSÉ CAPELLÍN CORRADA.

University School of Tourism in Asturias: Avda de los Monumentos 11, 33012 Oviedo; e-mail escuastur@fade.es; internet www.escuastur.com; Dir COVADONGA VIGIL ÁLVAREZ.

UNIVERSIDAD DE SALAMANCA

Patio de Escuelas Mayores 1, Apdo 20, 37008 Salamanca

Telephone: (92) 3294400
Fax: (92) 3294502
E-mail: informacion@usal.es
Internet: www.usal.es

Founded 1218 by Alfonso IX of León and reorganized 1254 by Alfonso X of Castile
State control
Language of instruction: Spanish
Academic year: October to July

Rector: DANIEL HERNÁNDEZ RUIPÉREZ
Vice-Rector for Economics and Management: RICARDO LÓPEZ FERNÁNDEZ
Vice-Rector for Innovation and Infrastructure: PASTORA VEGA CRUZ
Vice-Rector for Int. and Institutional Relations: NOEMÍ DOMÍNGUEZ GARCÍA
Vice-Rector for Research: MARÍA DE LOS ÁNGELES SERRANO GARCÍA

Vice-Rector for Strategic Planning and Evaluation: MIGUEL PÉREZ FERNÁNDEZ
Vice-Rector for Student Affairs: CRISTINA PITA YAÑEZ
Vice-Rector for Teaching: JOSÉ ÁNGEL DOMÍNGUEZ PÉREZ
Vice-Rector for Teaching Staff: MARIANO ESTEBAN DE VEGA
Registrar: ANA CUEVAS BADALLO
Man.: LUIS J. MEDIERO OSLÉ

Library: 1.05m. vols, 22,706 periodicals
Number of teachers: 2,200
Number of students: 32,000

DEANS

Faculty of Agricultural and Environmental Sciences: FERNANDO SANTOS FRANCÉS
Faculty of Biology: MANUEL ANTONIO MANSO MARTÍN
Faculty of Chemistry: CARMEN MARÍA DEL HOYO MARTÍNEZ
Faculty of Economics and Business: ALBERTO DE MIGUEL HIDALGO
Faculty of Education: MARÍA ESPERANZA HERRERA GARCÍA
Faculty of Fine Arts: JOSÉ MANUEL PRADA VEGA
Faculty of Geography and History: VALENTÍN CABERO DIÉGUEZ
Faculty of Law: RAFAEL DE AGAPITO SERRANO
Faculty of Medicine: JOSÉ CARRETERO GONZÁLEZ
Faculty of Pharmacy: JULIÁN C. RIVAS GONZALO
Faculty of Philology: ROMÁN ÁLVAREZ RODRÍGUEZ
Faculty of Philosophy: PABLO GARCÍA CASTILLO
Faculty of Psychology: JOSÉ CARLOS SÁNCHEZ GARCÍA
Faculty of Sciences: JUAN MANUEL CORCHADO RODRÍGUEZ
Faculty of Social Sciences: PEDRO ANTONIO CORDERO QUIÑONES
Faculty of Translation and Documentation: CARLOS FORTEA GIL

ATTACHED CENTRES AND COLLEGES

Centro de Historia Universitaria Alfonso IX: Colegio Mayor San Bartolomé, Plaza de Fray Luis de León 1–8, 37008 Salamanca; tel. (92) 3294500; fax (92) 3294779; e-mail chuaix@usal.es; internet campus.usal.es/~alfonix; Dir LUIS E. RODRÍGUEZ-SAN PEDRO BEZARES.

College of Industrial Relations: Calle San Torcuato 43, 49014 Zamora; tel. (98) 0531549; fax (98) 0533623; Dir JOSÉ MARÍA GARCÍA SÁNCHEZ.

College of Nursing at Ávila: Calle Canteros s/n, 05005 Ávila; tel. (92) 0253889; fax (92) 0200164; Dir MARÍA DEL PILAR GONZÁLEZ ARRIETA.

College of Nursing at Zamora: Avda de Requejo 21, 1°, 49014 Zamora; tel. (98) 0519343; fax (98) 0519462; Dir MARÍA SOLEDAD SÁNCHEZ ARNOSI.

UNIVERSIDAD DE SEVILLA

Calle de San Fernando 4, 41004 Seville

Telephone: (95) 4551000
Fax: (95) 4212803
E-mail: rector@us.es
Internet: www.us.es

Founded 1505
State control
Language of instruction: Spanish
Academic year: October to July

Rector: Dr JOAQUÍN LUQUE RODRÍGUEZ
Vice-Rector for Academic Affairs: Dr MIGUEL ÁNGEL CASTRO ARROYO
Vice-Rector for Infrastructure: Dr ANTONIO RAMÍREZ DE ARELLANO LÓPEZ

Vice-Rector for Institutional Relations: Dr TERESA GARCÍA GUTIÉRREZ VENTOSA UCERO
Vice-Rector for Int. Relations: Dra LOURDES MUNDUATE JACA
Vice-Rector for Research: Dr MANUEL GARCÍA LEÓ
Vice-Rector for Students: Dra ROSARIO RODRÍGUEZ DÍAZ
Vice-Rector for Teaching: Dra JULIA DE LA FUENTE FERIA
Vice-Rector for Teaching Staff: Dra MARÍA ELENA CANO BAZAGA
Vice-Rector for Technology Transfer: Dr RAMÓN GONZÁLEZ CARVAJAL
Registrar: Dra CONCEPCIÓN HORGUÉ BAENA
Man.: JUAN IGNACIO FERRARO GARCÍA
Library Dir: SONSOLES CELESTINO ANGULO
Number of teachers: 4,478
Number of students: 75,250
Publication: *Anales de la Universidad Hispalense* (1 a year)

DEANS

Faculty of Biology: FRANCISCO JAVIER MORENO ONORATO
Faculty of Chemistry: MARÍA PILAR MALET MAENNER
Faculty of Communication: ANTONIO CHECA GODOY
Faculty of Economics and Business: CARMEN NUÑEZ GARCÍA
Faculty of Education: JUAN DE PABLOS PONS
Faculty of Fine Arts: MARÍA TERESA CARRASCO GIMENA
Faculty of Geography and History: ANTONIO JOSÉ ALBARDONEDO FREIRE
Faculty of Labour Science: MARÍA MILAGRO MARTIN LÓPEZ (acting)
Faculty of Law: ANTONIO MERCHAN ALVAREZ
Faculty of Mathematics: ANTONIO BEATO MORENO
Faculty of Medicine: JUAN RAMÓN LACALLE REMIGIO
Faculty of Nursing, Physical Therapy and Podiatry: JUAN PABLO SOBRINO TOBO
Faculty of Odontology: PEDRO BULLON FERNÁNDEZ
Faculty of Pharmacy: JOSÉ MANUEL VEGA PÉREZ
Faculty of Philology: RAFAEL DE LA CRUZ LÓPEZ-CAMPOS BODINEAU
Faculty of Philosophy: MANUEL BARRIOS CASARES
Faculty of Physics: JOSÉ GÓMEZ ORDÓÑEZ
Faculty of Psychology: ANTONIO AGUILERA JIMÉNEZ
Faculty of Tourism and Finance: JOSÉ LUIS CABALLERO JIMÉNEZ

ATTACHED CENTRES

Andalusian Inter-university Institute of Criminology (Seville Branch): Escuela Técnica Superior de Ingeniería Informática, Avda Reina Mercedes, s/n, 41012 Seville; tel. (95) 4551396; fax (95) 4551397; e-mail iaic@us.es; internet www.iaic.us.es; Dir BORJA MAPELLI CAFFARENA.

'Cardenal Spinola' Centre for Advanced Studies: Campus Universitário, 41930 Bormujos (Seville); tel. (95) 4488000; fax (95) 4488010; e-mail info@ceuandalucia.com; internet www.ceuandalucia.com/indice.html; education and educational psychology; Dir MANUEL GÓMEZ GUILLÉN.

'Cruz Roja Española' University College of Nursing: Avda de la Cruz Roja 1, 41009 Seville; tel. and fax (95) 4350997; e-mail creseue@creseue.infonegocio.com; internet www.infonegocio.com/creseue; Dir FÉLIX JULIO JARA FERNÁNDEZ.

'Francisco Maldonado' University College: Campo de Cipreses 1, (Edif. Antigua Universidad), 41640 Osuna; tel. (95)

5820292; fax (95) 5820289; internet www.euosuna.org; Dir JAVIER MUÑOZ RANGEL.

García Oviedo Institute: Facultad de Derecho, Avda del Cid s/n, 41004 Seville; tel. (95) 4551226; fax (95) 4557899; e-mail instgarciaov@us.es; internet www.us.es/iugo; administrative law; Dir FRANCISCO LÓPEZ MENUDO.

National Accelerators Centre: Parque Tecnológico Cartuja 93, Avda Thomas A. Edison s/n, 41092 Seville; tel. (95) 4460553; fax (95) 4460145; e-mail respaldiza@us.es; internet www.us.es/cna; Dir MIGUEL ÁNGEL RESPALDIZA GALISTEO.

University College of Tourism: Calle Plácido Fernández Viagas 4, 41013 Seville; tel. (95) 4238797; fax (95) 4210278; internet www.eusa.es; language of instruction: Spanish; academic year September to July; Dir FRANCISCO GUERRERO DÍAZ; 1,500 students.

'Virgen del Rocío' University College of Nursing: Avda Manuel Siurot s/n, Edificio de Gobierno, 41013 Seville; tel. (95) 5013434; fax (95) 5013473; e-mail eu.hvr.sspa@juntadeandalucia.es; Dir MERCEDES BUENO FERRÁN.

UNIVERSIDAD DE VALLADOLID

Plaza de Santa Cruz 8, 47002 Valladolid
Telephone: (98) 423283
Fax: (98) 423234
E-mail: relint@uva.es
Internet: www.uva.es
Founded 13th century
Academic year: October to June
Rector: MARCOS SACRISTÁN REPRESA
Vice-Rector for Academic Affairs: LUIS MIGUEL NIETO CALZADA
Vice-Rector for Culture and Infrastructure: ANTONIO ORDUÑA DOMINGO
Vice-Rector for Economy: GUIOMAR MARTÍN HERRÁN
Vice-Rector for Int. Relations: LUIS ANTONIO SANTOS DOMÍNGUEZ
Vice-Rector for Research and Scientific Policy: JOSÉ MANUEL LÓPEZ RODRÍGUEZ
Vice-Rector for Segovia Campus: JOSÉ VICENTE ÁLVAREZ BRAVO
Vice-Rector for Soria Campus: AMELIA RUTH MOYANO GARDINI
Vice-Rector for Students: ROCÍO ANGUITA MARTÍNEZ
Vice-Rector for Teaching: JOSÉ MARÍA MARBÁN PRIETO
Vice-Rector for Teaching and Training: JOSÉ MARÍA MARBÁN PRIETO
Registrar: MIGUEL ÁNGEL GONZÁLEZ REBOLLO
Man.: JOSÉ ANTONIO ANTONA MONTORO
Library Dir: MERCEDES ARRANZ SOMBRÍA
Library of 958,343 vols, 15,725 periodicals and 5,907 audiovisual
Number of teachers: 2,618
Number of students: 26,370

DEANS

Faculty of Arts: MILAGROS ESTILITA ALARIO TRIGUEROS
Faculty of Economics and Business: JOSEFA EUGENIA FERNÁNDEZ ARUFE
Faculty of Education and Social Work: JOSÉ SIXTO OLIVAR PARRA
Faculty of Labour Science (Palencia): JOSÉ ANTONIO OREJAS CASAS
Faculty of Law: LUIS ANTONIO VELASCO SAN PEDRO
Faculty of Medicine: RICARDO JAIME RIGUAL BONASTRE
Faculty of Science: FERNANDO VILLAFAÑE GONZÁLEZ
Faculty of Social, Legal and Communication Sciences (Segovia): JUAN JOSÉ GARCILLÁN GARCÍA

Faculty of Translation and Interpretation (Soria): ANTONIO BUENO GARCÍA

UNIVERSIDAD DE ZARAGOZA

Calle Pedro Cerbuna 12, 50009 Zaragoza
Telephone: (97) 6761000
Fax: (97) 6761009
E-mail: rector@unizar.es
Internet: www.unizar.es
Founded in 1542 by the Emperor Charles V
State control
Language of instruction: Spanish
Academic year: October to June
Rector: MANUEL JOSÉ LÓPEZ PÉREZ
Sec.-Gen. and Registrar: JUAN F. HERRERO PEREZAGUA
Gen. Man.: MARÍA ISABEL LUENGO GASCÓN
Vice-Rector for Academic Policy: FERNANDO ANGEL BELTRÁN BLÁZQUEZ
Vice-Rector for Culture and Social Policy: CONCEPCIÓN LOMBA SERRANO
Vice-Rector for Economic Affairs: FRANCISCO JAVIER TRÍVEZ BIELSA
Vice-Rector for Huesca Campus: JOSÉ DOMINGO DUEÑAS LORENTE
Vice-Rector for Int. Relations and Devt Cooperation: REGINA MARÍA LÁZARO GISTAU
Vice-Rector for Scientific Policy: LUIS MIGUEL GARCÍA VINUESA
Vice-Rector for Students and Employment: FERNANDO ZULAICA PALACIOS
Vice-Rector for Teaching Staff: JOSÉ ANTONIO MAYORAL MURILLO
Vice-Rector for Technological Transfer and Innovation: PILAR ZARAGOZA FERNÁNDEZ
Vice-Rector for Teruel Campus: MARÍA ALEXIA SANZ HERNÁNDEZ
Registrar: JOSÉ DOMINGO DUEÑAS LORENTE
Librarian: RAMÓN ABAD HIRALDO
Library: more than 1m. vols, 20,000 periodicals
Number of teachers: 3,006
Number of students: 35,886
Publications: *Ager: Revista de Estudios sobre Despoblación Rural* (1 a year, rural depopulation), *Anales de la Facultad de Veterinaria, Antigrama: Revista del Departamento de Historia del Arte* (1 a year), *Anuario de pedagogía* (1 a year), *Aragón en la Edad Media, Archivos de la Facultad de Medicina, Arqueología Espacial: Revista del Seminario de Arqueología y Etnología Turolense, Boletín de la Asociación de Demografía Histórica* (2 a year), *Boletín Informativo, Cuadernos Aragoneses de Economía* (2 a year), *Cuadernos de Bioestadística y sus Aplicaciones Informáticas* (2 a year), *El Gnomo: Boletín de Estudios Becquerianos, European Journal of Psychiatry, Geographicalia, Geórgica, Guía, Kalathos: Revista del Seminario de Arqueología y Etnología Turolense* (1 a year), *Llull: Revista de la Sociedad Española de Historia de la Ciencia y de las Técnicas* (3 a year), *Medicina Naturista: Revista Internacional de Difusión Biomédica* (4 a year), *Miscelánea* (1 a year), *Naturaleza Aragonesa: Revista de la Sociedad de Amigos del Museo Paleontológico* (2 a year), *Organización del Conocimiento en Sistemas de Información y Documentación* (2 a year), *Resúmenes de Tesis Doctorales, Revista Aquatic, Revista de Demografía Histórica* (2 a year), *Revista de Desarrollo Rural y Cooperativismo Agrario, Revista de Gestión Pública y Privada* (1 a year), *Revista Española de Filosofía Medieval* (1 a year), *Revista Interuniversitaria de Formación del Profesorado* (3 a year), *Revista Universidad, Riff-Raff: Revista de Pensamiento y Cultura* (3 a year), *Saldvie: Estudios de Prehistoria y Archeología* (1 a year), *Scire:*

Representación y Organización del Conocimiento (2 a year), *Stvdivm: Revista de Humanidades* (2 a year), *Tropelías: Revista de Teoría de la Literatura y Literatura Comparada* (1 a year), *Temas*

DEANS

Faculty of Arts: Dr SEVERINO ESCOLANO UTRILLA

Faculty of Business and Public Management: Dr CARLOS JAVIER RUBIO POMAR

Faculty of Economics and Business Studies: Dr JOSÉ ALBERTO MOLINA CHUECA

Faculty of Education: Dr ENRIQUE GARCÍA PASCUAL

Faculty of Health Sciences and Sport, Huesca: Dr MIGUEL TOMÁS CHIVITE IZCO

Faculty of Health Sciences: Dr JUAN FRANCISCO LEÓN PUY

Faculty of Humanities and Education, Huesca: Dr JOSÉ DOMINGO DUENA LORENTE

Faculty of Law: Dr JUAN GARCÍA BLASCO

Faculty of Medicine: Dr FRANCISCO JAVIER CASTILLO GARCÍA

Faculty of Sciences: Dra ANA ISABEL ELDUQUE PALOMO

Faculty of Social Sciences and Labour: Dr MIGUEL MIRANDA ARANDA

Faculty of Social Sciences and Humanities: Dr MARÍA LUISA ESTEBAN SALVADOR

Faculty of Veterinary Science: Dr JESÚS GARCÍA SÁNCHEZ

Higher Polytechincal School (Huesca): Dr LUIS PARDOS CASTILLO

Polytechnical School of Teruel: Dr GUILLERMO PALACIOS NAVARRO

School of Engineering and Architecture: Dr RAFAEL BILBAO DUÑABEITIA

ATTACHED SCHOOLS

Polytechnic University School La Almunia: Calle Mayor s/n, 50100 La Almunia de Doña Godina (Zaragoza); tel. (97) 6600813; fax (97) 6812379; e-mail info.eupla@unizar.es; internet www.eupla.unizar.es; language of instruction: Spanish; academic year September to June; Engineering, construction civil engineering, industrial management, mechatronics; Dir FERNANDO QUERO SANZ; Chief Administrative Officer SERAFÍN LATORRE CASTILLO; library of 20,034 vols, 40 periodical subscriptions; 66 teachers; 1,728 students.

University College of Nursing, Teruel: Avda América 15, 44002 Teruel; tel. (97) 8620648; fax (97) 8620954; internet www.teruel.unizar.es/enfermeria/enfermeria.html; Dir MARÍA CARMEN GÓRRIZ GONZÁLEZ.

UNIVERSIDAD DEL PAÍS VASCO/EUSKAL HERRIKO UNIBERTSITATEA (University of the Basque Country)

Apdo 1397, 48080 Bilbao

Telephone: (94) 6012000

Fax: (94) 4801590

E-mail: internacional@ehu.es

Internet: www.ehu.es

Founded 1968, reorganized 1980

3 Campuses: Bizkaia Campus, Araba Campus, Gipuzkoa Campus

Basque Regional Govt control

Languages of instruction: Spanish, Basque

Academic year: September to July

Rector: Dr IÑAKI GOIRIZELAIA ORDORIKA

Vice-Rector for Academic Org.: JAVIER GIL GOIKOURIA

Vice-Rector for Araba Campus: EUGENIO RUIZ URRESTARAZU

Vice-Rector for Basque Language and Multilingualism: GIDOR BILBAO

Vice-Rector for Bizkaia Campus: CARMELO GARITAONANDIA

Vice-Rector for Coordination: JUAN JOSE UNZILLA

Vice-Rector for Economic Affairs: EVA FERREIRA GARCÍA

Vice-Rector for Gipuzkoa Campus: CRISTINA URIARTE TOLEDO

Vice-Rector for Int. Relations: ANECA UNIQUAL

Vice-Rector for Quality and Educational Innovation: ITZIAR ALKORTA

Vice-Rector for Research: MIGUEL ÁNGEL GUTIÉRREZ ORTIZ

Vice-Rector for Science and Technology Devt: JOAN SALLÉS

Vice-Rector for Social Responsibility and Community Relations: AMAIA MASEDA

Vice-Rector for Student Affairs: ELENA BERNARAS

Vice-Rector for Teaching Staff: JON IRAZUSTA

Vice-Rector for Univ. Extension: AMAIA MASEDA

Registrar: EVA FERREIRA

Admin. Dir: XABIER AIZPURUA TELLERÍA

Librarian: CARMEN GUERRA

Library: 1m. vols, 17,800 periodicals

Number of teachers: 5,000

Number of students: 49,000

Publications: *Acto de Investidura* (1 a year), *Anuario del Seminario de Filología Vasca 'Julio de Urquijo'* (International Journal of Basque Linguistics and Philology, 1 a year), *Memoria de Actividades* (1 a year), *Memoria Estadística* (1 a year), *Psicodidactics* (The International Journal of Development Biology, 8–10 a year), *Recursos Científicos y Líneas de Investigación* (1 a year), *Resúmenes de Tesis Doctorales* (1 a year)

DEANS

(The letters A, B, G refer to the Araba, Bizkaia and Gipuzkoa campuses)

Faculty of Arts (A): IÑAKI BAZAN

Faculty of Chemistry Sciences (G): IÑIGO LEGORBURU FAUS

Faculty of Computer Science (G): AGUSTÍN ARRUABARRENA

Faculty of Economics and Business Studies (B): ARTURO RODRÍGUEZ CASTELLANOS

Faculty of Fine Arts (B): JOSU REKALDE IZAGIRRE

Faculty of Law (G): FRANCISCO JAVIER QUEL LÓPEZ

Faculty of Medicine and Dentistry (B): AGUSTÍN MARTÍNEZ IBARGÜEN

Faculty of Pharmacy (A): AURORA FERNÁNDEZ ASTORGA

Faculty of Philosophy and Education Science (G): XABIER ETXAGUE ALCALDE

Faculty of Physical Activities and Sport Science (A): MAITE FUENTES

Faculty of Psychology (G): ANA ISABEL VERGARA

Faculty of Sciences and Technology (B): ESTHER DOMÍNGUEZ PÉREZ

Faculty of Social and Communication Sciences (B): ALFONSO UNCETA SATRÚSTEGUI

UNIVERSIDAD EUROPEA DE MADRID (CEES)

Calle Tajo s/n, Urbanización el Bosque, 28670 Villaviciosa de Odón, Madrid

Telephone: (91) 2115200

E-mail: uem@uem.es

Internet: www.uem.es

Founded 1995

Rector: Dra ÁGUEDA BENITO

Vice-Rector for Academic Quality and Innovation: Dr PEDRO JOSÉ LARA

Vice-Rector for Students and Employment: Dra MARTA ARROYO

Vice-Rector for Teaching and Research: Dra MARÍA ADELAIDA PORTELA

Registrar: ELENA DE LA FUENTE

Librarian: ISABEL RICO RODRÍGUEZ

DEANS

Faculty of Biomedical Sciences: Dr JUAN PÉREZ-MIRANDA

Faculty of Communication and Humanities: Dr LUIS CALANDRE

Faculty of Health Sciences: Dr ELENA GAZAPO

Faculty of Physical Education and Sport: Dr JUAN MAYORGA GARCÍA

Faculty of Social Sciences: Dr JOSÉ RAMOS

UNIVERSIDAD INTERNACIONAL DE ANDALUCÍA

Rectorado de la Universidad, Sede de la Cartuja, Monasterio Santa María de las Cuevas, Calle Americo Vespucio 2, Isla de la Cartuja, 41092 Seville

Telephone: (95) 4462299

Fax: (95) 4462288

E-mail: sevilla@unia.es

Internet: www.unia.es

Founded 1994

Rector: Dr JUAN MANUEL SUÁREZ JAPÓN

Vice-Rector for Academic Affairs and Graduate Studies: PLÁCIDO NAVAS LLORET

Vice-Rector for Int. Relations and Cooperation: MARÍA ANTONIA PEÑA GUERRERO

Vice-Rector for Planning and Quality: JULIO TERRADOS CEPEDA

Vice-Rector for Research and Communication Technologies: LLANOS MORA LÓPEZ

Vice-Rector for Univ. Extension and Participation: MARÍA DEL ROSARIO GARCÍA-DONCEL HERNÁNDEZ

Registrar: MARÍA JESÚS GUERRERO LEBRÓN

Man.: LUISA MARGARITA RANCAÑO MARTÍN.

CAMPUSES OF THE UNIVERSITY

Sede Antonio Machado

Palacio de Jabalquinto, Plaza de Santa Cruz s/n, 23440 Baeza (Jaén)

Telephone: (95) 3742775

Fax: (95) 3742975

E-mail: baeza@unia.es

Dir: MARÍA ALCAZAR CRUZ RODRÍGUEZ.

Sede Iberoamericano Santa María de La Rábida

Paraje La Rábida s/n, 21819 Palos de la Frontera (Huelva)

Telephone: (95) 9350452

Fax: (95) 9350158

E-mail: larabida@unia.es

Dir: YOLANDA PELAYO DÍAZ.

Sede de Málaga

Avda Severo Ochoa 16–20, Málaga Business-Park, Edificio Estepona, Parque Tecnológico de Andalucía, 20590 Málaga

Telephone: (95) 2028411

Fax: (95) 2028419

E-mail: malaga@unia.es

Dir: ANTONIO SÁNCHEZ SÁNCHEZ.

UNIVERSIDAD JAUME I DE CASTELLÓN

Campus de Riu Sec, Avda de Vicent Sos Baynat s/n, 12071 Castellón

Telephone: (96) 4728000

Fax: (96)4 729016

E-mail: info@uji.es

Internet: www.uji.es

Founded 1991

State control

Rector: FRANCISCO TOLEDO LOBO

Vice-Rector for Academic Org. and Teaching Staff: Prof. SERAFÍ BERNAT MARTÍ
Vice-Rector for Culture: Profa MARGARITA PORCAR MIRALLES
Vice-Rector for Economic Affairs and Online Services: Prof. MODESTO FABRA VALLÉS
Vice-Rector for Educational Quality and European Harmonization: Profa ROSA MARÍA GRAU GUMBAU
Vice-Rector for Infrastructure and Admin. Services: Prof. VICENTE CERVERA MATEU
Vice-Rector for Institutional Relations and Social Welfare: Prof. MANUEL CHUST CALERO
Vice-Rector for Int. Cooperation and Solidarity: Profa EVA SOLER ALCÓN
Vice-Rector for Postgraduate Studies: Prof. JUAN ANTONIO BARBA
Vice-Rector for Research: Profa ROSA LLUSAR BARELLES
Vice-Rector for Scientific and Technological Promotion: Prof. VICENTE ORTS RÍOS
Vice-Rector for Students and Employment: Profa LEONOR LAPEÑA
Registrar: MARÍA VICTORIA PETIT LAVALL
Library Dir: VICENT FALOMIR DEL CAMPO
Library of 274,444 vols
Number of teachers: 1,022
Number of students: 12,677

DEANS

Faculty of Humanities and Social Sciences: Prof. MANUEL ROSAS ARTOLA
Faculty of Law and Economics: Prof. GERMÁN ORÓN MORATAL

UNIVERSIDAD MIGUEL HERNÁNDEZ DE ELCHE

Edificio de Rectorado y Consejo Social - Avda de la Universidad s/n, 03202 Elche Alicante
Telephone: (96) 6658604
Fax: (96) 6658602
E-mail: rector@umh.es
Internet: www.umh.es
State control
Language of instruction: Spanish
Academic year: September to June
Rector: Dr JESÚS TADEO PASTOR CIURANA
Vice-Rector for Academic Affairs: Dra MARÍA JOSÉ ALARCÓN GARCÍA
Vice-Rector for Culture and Univ. Extension: Dr ESTHER SITGES MACIÁ
Vice-Rector for Economics and Business: Dr FERNANDO VIDAL GIMÉNEZ
Vice-Rector for Human Resources: Dr EVA ALIAGA AGULLÓ
Vice-Rector for Institutional Relations: Dra MARÍA TERESA PÉREZ VÁZQUEZ
Vice-Rector for Int. Relations: Dr MANUEL JORDÁN VIDAL
Vice-Rector for Material Resources: Dr ÓSCAR REINOSO GARCÍA
Vice-Rector for Research and Innovation: Dr FERNANDO BORRÁS ROCHER
Vice-Rector for Student Affairs and Athletics: Dr FRANCISCO JOSÉ MORENO HERNÁNDEZ
Registrar: Dra MARÍA MERCEDES SÁNCHEZ CASTILLO
Man.: RAFAEL GANDÍA BALAGUER
Number of teachers: 1,024
Number of students: 14,500

DEANS

Faculty of Experimental Sciences: JOSÉ LUIS RUIZ GÓMEZ
Faculty of Fine Arts: JOSÉ VICENTE MARTÍN MARTÍNEZ
Faculty of Medicine: ANTONIO COMPAÑ ROSIQUE
Faculty of Pharmacy: JORGE MANZANARES ROBLES
Faculty of Social and Health Sciences: EDUARDO CERVELLÓ GIMENO

Faculty of Social and Legal Sciences of Elche: FERNANDO MIRÓ LLINARES
Faculty of Social and Legal Sciences of Orihuela: JOSÉ ANTONIO CAVERO RUBIO

ATTACHED INSTITUTES

Institute of Bioengineering: Edificio Vinalopó, Avda del Ferrocarril s/n, 03202 Elche; tel. (96) 6658510; fax (96) 6658511; internet bioengenieria.umh.es; Dir BERNAT SORIA ESCOMS.
Institute of Molecular and Cell Biology: Edificio Torregaitán, Avda de la Universidad s/n, 03202 Elche; tel. (96) 6658759; fax (96) 6658758; e-mail biomolcel@umh.es; internet ibmc.umh.es; Dir JOSÉ MANUEL GONZÁLEZ ROS.
Institute of Research into Drug Addiction: Facultad de Medicina, Campus de San Juan, Ctra Alicante-Valencia, Km 87, Apdo no. 18, 03550 San Juan de Alicante; tel. (96) 5919319; fax (96) 5919566; e-mail inid@umh.es; internet inid.umh.es; Dir JOSÉ ANTONIO GARCÍA DEL CASTILLO RODRÍGUEZ.
Neurosciences Institute: Apdo 18, 03550 San Joan d'Alacant; tel. (96) 5919487; fax (96) 5919561; e-mail in@umh.es; internet in .umh.es/index2.htm; Dir CARLOS BELMONTE MARTÍNEZ.
Operational Research Centre: Campus de Elche, Edificio Torretamarit, Avda del Ferrocarril s/n, 03202 Elche; tel. (96) 6658752; fax (96) 6658715; e-mail cio@umh.es; internet cio .umh.es; Dir JESÚS TADEO PASTOR CIURANA.

UNIVERSIDAD NACIONAL DE EDUCACIÓN A DISTANCIA (Open University)

Ciudad Universitaria s/n, 28040 Madrid
Telephone: (91) 3986600
Fax: (91) 3986037
E-mail: infouned@adm.uned.es
Internet: www.uned.es
Founded 1972
State control
Language of instruction: Spanish
Academic year: October to July
Rector: JUAN A. GIMENO ULLASTRES
Vice-Rector for Academic Affairs: ENCARNACIÓN SARRIÁ SÁNCHEZ
Vice-Rector for Associated Centres: ANTONIO FERNÁNDEZ FERNÁNDEZ
Vice-Rector for Continuing Education: JULIO BORDAS MARTÍNEZ
Vice-Rector for Innovation and Teaching Support: MIGUEL SANTAMARÍA LANCHO
Vice-Rector for Int. and Institutional Relations: MARÍA TERESA AGUADO ODINA
Vice-Rector for Planning and Economic Affairs: ANA ISABEL SEGOVIA SAN JUAN
Vice-Rector for Print and Audiovisual Media: IRENE DELGADO SOTILLOS
Vice-Rector for Research: PALOMA COLLADO GUIRAO
Vice-Rector for Student Life, Employment and Culture: ALVARO JARILLO ALDEANUEVA
Vice-Rector for Teaching Staff: MIGUEL ÁNGEL RUBIO ÁLVAREZ
Vice-Rector for Technology: COVADONGA RODRIGO SAN JUAN
Registrar: ANA MARÍA MARCOS DEL CANO
Chief of Admin.: JORDI MONTSERRAT GARROCHO
Librarian: ISABEL BELMONTE MARTÍNEZ
Library: 1.2m. vols
Number of teachers: 1,496
Number of students: 205,931 (incl. 111,310 enrolled on degree and diploma courses)

DEANS

Faculty of Economics and Business Administration: AMELIA PÉREZ ZABALETA

Faculty of Education: LORENZO GARCÍA ARETIO
Faculty of Geography and History: ENRIQUE CANTERA MONTENEGRO
Faculty of Law: ANA ROSA MARTÍN MINGUIJÓN
Faculty of Philology: Dr ANTONIO MORENO HERNÁNDEZ
Faculty of Philosophy: Dr MANUEL FRAIJÓ NIETO
Faculty of Politics and Sociology: MARÍA ELISA CHULIÁ RODRIGO
Faculty of Psychology: Dr MIGUEL ÁNGEL SANTED GERMÁN
Faculty of Sciences: Dr ANTONIO ZAPARDIEL PALENZUELA

UNIVERSIDAD PABLO DE OLAVIDE

Carretera de Utrera, Km 1, 41013 Seville
Telephone: (95) 4349200
Fax: (95) 4349204
Internet: www.upo.es
Founded 1997
State control
Language of instruction: Spanish
Academic year: September to July
Rector: Dr JUAN JIMÉNEZ MARTÍNEZ
Vice-Rector for Graduate Studies: LINA GÁLVEZ MUÑOZ
Vice-Rector for Information Technologies and Communication: Dr ANDRÉS GARZÓN VILLAR
Vice-Rector for International and Institutional Relations: Dr LUIS PÉREZ-PRAT DURBÁN
Vice-Rector for Quality and Planning: Dra ALICIA TRONCOSO LORA
Vice-Rector for Research and Technology Transfer: Dr MANUEL HERRERO SÁNCHEZ
Vice-Rector for Social Participation: Dra ROSALÍA MARTÍNEZ GARCÍA
Vice-Rector for Student Affairs and Sports: Dr FRANCISCO BEDOYA BERGUA
Vice-Rector for Teaching and European Convergence: Dr JUAN MANUEL CORTÉS COPETE
Vice-Rector for Teaching Staff: Dr JOSÉ ANTONIO SÁNCHEZ MEDINA
Registrar: Dr FRANCISCO OLIVA BLÁZQUEZ
Man.: RAFAEL SERRANO AGUILAR
Library of 347,577 vols, 25,284 periodicals, 12,763 audiovisual items
Number of teachers: 1,100
Number of students: 11,500

DEANS

Faculty of Business Sciences: Dr FRANCISCO CARRASCO FENECH
Faculty of Experimental Sciences: Dr ANTONIO GALLARDO CORREA
Faculty of Humanities: Dr GONZALO MALVÁREZ GARCÍA
Faculty of Law: Dr ANDRÉS RODRÍGUEZ BENOT
Faculty of Social Sciences: Dr GUILLERMO DOMÍNGUEZ FERNÁNDEZ
Faculty of Sports: Dr JUAN JOSÉ GONZÁLEZ BADILLO
Polytechnic School: JESÚS SALVADOR AGUILAR RUIZ (Dir)
School of Engineering: Dr JESÚS AGUILAR RUIZ

UNIVERSIDAD PONTIFICIA 'COMILLAS'

Calle Alberto Aguilera 23, 28015 Madrid
Telephone: (91) 5422800
Fax: (91) 5596569
E-mail: oia@oia.upcomillas.es
Internet: www.upcomillas.es
Founded by Pope Leo XIII; classes commencing at Comillas, Santander, in 1890; the right to confer degrees was granted in 1904; moved to Madrid in 1960
Private control

Language of instruction: Spanish
Academic year: October to June
Grand Chancellor: ADOLFO NICOLÁS PACHÓN
Rector: Dr JOSÉ RAMÓN BUSTO SAIZ
Vice-Rector for Academic Affairs and Teaching Staff: Dr ANTONIO OBREGÓN GARCÍA
Vice-Rector for Economic Affairs: Dr CECILIO MORAL BELLO
Vice-Rector for Int. Relations and Services to the Univ. Community: Dr ROMANO GIANNETTI
Vice-Rector for Research, Devt and Innovation: Dr JULIO LUIS MARTÍNEZ MARTÍNEZ
Registrar: Dra CLARA MARTÍNEZ GARCÍA
Librarian: EUSEBIO GIL CORIA
Library of 550,000 vols
Number of teachers: 962
Number of students: 9,804

Publications: *Estudios Eclesiásticos* (4 a year), *ICADE* (4 a year), *Migraciones* (2 a year), *Miscelánea Comillas* (3 a year), *Pensamiento* (3 a year)

DEANS

Faculty of Canon Law and Theology: Dr GABINO URÍBARRI BILBAO
Faculty of Economics and Business: Dra ALFREDO ARAHUETES GARCÍA
Faculty of Human and Social Sciences: Dra BELÉN MERCEDES UROSA SANZ
Faculty of Law: Dra MARÍA CONCEPCIÓN MOLINA BLÁZQUEZ

ATTACHED CENTRES AND INSTITUTES

Centro Teológico de Las Palmas de Gran Canaria: Seminario Mayor, 35001 Las Palmas de Gran Canaria.

Estudio Teológico Agustiniano: Paseo de Filipinos 7, 47007 Valladolid.

Estudio Teológico Claretiano: Juan Alvarez Mendizal 65 Duplicado, 1°, 28008 Madrid.

Estudio Teológico del Seminario Mayor de Córdoba: Amador de los Ríos 1, 14004 Córdoba.

Estudio Teológico del Seminario Mayor de Logroño: Seminario Mayor, Apdo de Correos 150, 26080 Logroño.

Estudio Teológico del Seminario Mayor Diocesano: Carretera de Porzuna s/n, 13002 Ciudad Real.

Estudio Teológico del Seminario Mayor 'Tagaste': Padres Agustinos, Santa Emilia 10, 28409 Los Negrales (Madrid).

Estudio Teológico Monseñor Romero: Apdo Postal (01) 168, San Salvador, El Salvador (Central America).

Instituto Fe y Secularidad: Diego de León 33, 28006 Madrid.

Instituto Internacional de Teología a Distancia: José Ortega y Gasset 62, 1°, 28006 Madrid.

Instituto Superior de Ciencias Morales: Calle Félix Boix 13, 28016 Madrid.

Instituto Superior de Ciencias Religiosas 'San Agustín': José Ortega y Gasset 62, 1°, 28006 Madrid.

ASSOCIATED INSTITUTIONS; THERE ARE OTHER THEOLOGICAL AND PHILOSOPHICAL FACULTIES IN SPAIN CONFERRING DEGREES, WHICH ARE PARTLY ASSOCIATED WITH THE PONTIFICAL UNIVERSITIES, AS FOLLOWS:

Facultad de Teología de Granada (Institución Universitaria de la Compañía de Jesús)

Profesor Vicente Callao, 15 18011 Granada
Telephone: (95) 8185252
Fax: (95) 8162559
E-mail: info@teol-granada.com
Internet: www.teol-granada.com

Founded 1939
Academic year: October to July
Grand Chancellor: RP ADOLFO NICOLÁS PACHÓN
Vice-Grand Chancellor: RP GUILLERMO RODRÍGUEZ-IZQUIERDO
Rector: RP ILDEFONSO CAMACHO LARAÑA
Vice-Rector for Academic Affairs: Prof. JOSÉ LUIS SÁNCHEZ NOGALES
Registrar and Man.: CARLOS JAVIER PALOMEQUE BAENA
Librarian: RP GABRIEL VERD CONRADI
Library of 350,000 vols
Number of teachers: 27
Number of students: 250

Publications: *Archivo Teológico Granadino* (Post-Tridentine theology, 1 a year), *Proyección* (4 a year)

PROFESSORS

ALARCOS MARTÍNEZ, F., Moral Theology
BÉJAR BACAS, J. S., Dogmatic Theology
BERDUGO VILLENA, T., Latin
CAMACHO LARAÑA, I., Moral Theology
CASTÓN BOYER, P., Sociology
DOMÍNGUEZ MORANO, C., Psychology
GRANADO BELLIDO, C., Patrology and Dogmatic Theology
GUEVARA LLAGUNO, M., Scripture
HERNÁNDEZ MARTÍNEZ, J., Dogmatic Theology
JIMÉNEZ ORTIZ, A., Fundamental Theology
LÓPEZ AZPITARTE, E., Moral Theology
LÓPEZ CUERVO, T., Greek
MARTÍN MORILLAS, A., Philosophy
MARTÍNEZ MEDINA, J., Ecclesiastical Art
MOLINA MOLINA, D., Dogmatic Theology
NAVAS GUTIÉRREZ, A., Ecclesiastical History
RODRÍGUEZ CARMONA, A., Scripture
RODRÍGUEZ IZQUIERDO GAVALA, J. M., Liturgy
ROJAS GÁLVEZ, I., Scripture
ROMÁN MARTÍNEZ, M. C., Scripture
RUIZ LOZANO, P., Philosophy
SÁNCHEZ NOGALES, J. L., Philosophy
SICRE DÍAZ, J. L., Scripture
VOLO PÉREZ, R., Scripture
YUBERO SOTO, J., Dogmatic Theology

ATTACHED INSTITUTES

Centro de Estudios Teológicos: Avda Cardenal Buenomonreal 43, 41012 Seville; Rector LUIS F. ALVAREZ.

Centro de Estudios Teológicos: Juan Montilla 1, 23002 Jaén; Rector MANUEL RUIZ CARRERO.

Centro de Estudios Teológicos: Compañía s/n, 11005 Cádiz; Rector JESÚS J. GARCÍA CORNEJO.

Centro de Estudios Teológicos: Carretera de Nijar 61, 04009 Almería; Rector JUAN A. MOYA SÁNCHEZ.

Centro Diocesano de Teología de Málaga: Calle Toquero 20, 29013 Málaga; Rector (vacant).

Instituto Superior de Ciencias Religiosas 'San Pablo': Santa María 20, 29015 Málaga; Rector ILDEFONSO CAMACHO LARAÑA.

Instituto Superior de Ciencias Religiosas 'Tomás Sánchez': Apdo 2002, 18080 Granada; Rector ANTONIO M. NAVAS GUTIÉRREZ.

Institut de Teologia Fonamental

Calle Llaceres 30, Sant Cugat del Vallés Barcelona
Telephone: (93) 6741150
Fax: (93) 5908111
E-mail: itf@jesuites.net
Founded 1964

Jesuit College forming part of the Faculty of Theology of Cataluña; open to non-Jesuit students

Chancellor: Dr LLUÍS MARÍA SISTACH (Archbishop of Barcelona)
General Moderator: LLUÍS MAGRIÑÀ VECIANA
Dir: JOAN CARRERA
Registrar: JORDI ESCUDE
Librarian: ORIOL TUÑI
Library of 350,000 vols, 800 periodicals
Number of teachers: 14
Number of students: 150

Publications: *Actualidad Bibliográfica, Cuadernos de Teología Fundamental, Selecciones de Teología*

PROFESSORS

ALEGRE, X., New Testament Scripture
BOADA, J., Fundamental Theology
CARRERA, J., Fundamental Moral Theology
COLL, J. MA., Fundamental Theology
FLAQUER, J., Fundamental Theology
GARCÍA DONCEL, M., Philosophy of Sciences
GIMÉNEZ, J., Fundamental Theology
GONZÁLEZ FAUS, J. I., Systematic Theology
LATORRE, J., New Testament Scripture
MANRESA, F., Fundamental Theology
MÀRIA, J., Ethical Issues
MELLONI, X., Fundamental Theology
PUIG, LL., Fundamental Theology
RAMBLA, J. MA., Spiritual Theology
SALVAT, I., Fundamental Social Morality
TUÑI, O., New Testament Scripture
VALL, H., Ecumenical Theology

UNIVERSIDAD PONTIFICIA DE SALAMANCA

Calle Compañía 5, Apdo 541, 37002 Salamanca
Telephone: (92) 3277100
Fax: (92) 3277123
E-mail: gabi.com@upsa.es
Internet: www.upsa.es

Founded 1134 as the Ecclesiastical School of Salamanca Cathedral; named a univ. by Alfonso IX of León in 1219; had ceased to function by the end of the 18th century, but restored in 1940 by Pope Pius XII
Private control
Language of instruction: Spanish
Academic year: October to June
Grand Chancellor: Dr RICARDO BLÁZQUEZ PÉREZ
Rector: Dr MARCELIANO ARRANZ RODRIGO
Vice-Rector for Academic Org. and Economy: Dra MA. FRANCISCA MARTÍN TABERNERO
Vice-Rector for Pastoral Affairs, Research and Quality: Dr SANTIAGO GUIJARRO OPORTO
Vice-Rector for Teaching Staff, Student Affairs, Communication and Services: Dra ROSA PINTO LOBO
Registrar: Dr LUIS MIGUEL PEDRERO ESTEBAN
Admin. Coordinator: Lic. MA. TERESA GÓMEZ MARCOS
Dir of Library: Dr ANTONIO GARCÍA MADRID
Library of 500,000 vols and numerous MSS
Number of teachers: 351
Number of students: 8,500

Publications: *Cuadernos Salmantinos de Filosofía, Comunicación y Pluralismo, Diálogo Ecuménico, Familia, Helmántica, Papeles Salmantinos de Educación, Revista Española de Derecho Canónico, Salmanticensis, Sociedad y Utopía*

DEANS

Faculty of Canon Law: Dr FEDERICO RAFAEL AZNAR GIL
Faculty of Communication: Dr ÁNGEL LOSADA VÁZQUEZ
Faculty of Computer Sciences (Madrid): Dr LUIS JOYANES AGUILAR
Faculty of Education: Dr ANTONIO GARCÍA MADRID

Faculty of Insurance, Law and Management (Madrid): Dr ANTONIO GUARDIOLA LOZANO
Faculty of Philosophy: Dr LEONARDO RODRÍGUEZ DUPLÁ
Faculty of Political and Social Sciences (Madrid): Dr JUAN MANUEL DÍAZ SÁNCHEZ
Faculty of Psychology: Dr Mª. PAZ QUEVEDO AGUADO
Faculty of Theology: Dr JOSÉ-RAMÓN FLECHA ANDRÉS

ATTACHED CENTRES

Institute of Biblical Archaeology: tel. (92) 3277143; fax (92) 3277101; e-mail casadesantiago@upsa.es; internet www.ipi .upsa.es; Dir Dr MARCELIANO ARRANZ RODRIGO.

Institute of Education Science: tel. (92) 3277140; fax (92) 3277101; e-mail ice@upsa .es; internet www.ice.upsa.es; Dir Dra MARÍA JESÚS GARCÍA ARROYO.

Institute of European Studies and Human Rights: tel. (92) 3277142; fax (92) 3277101; e-mail europa@upsa.es; internet www.europa.upsa.es; Dir Dr JOSÉ-ROMÁN FLECHA ANDRÉS.

Institute of Family Studies: tel. (92) 3277141; fax (92) 3277101; e-mail cc .familia@upsa.es; Dir Dr ÁNGEL GALINDO GARCÍA.

Institute of Iberoamerican Thought: tel. (92) 3277143; fax (92) 3277101; e-mail ipi@ upsa.es; internet www.ipi.upsa.es; Dir Prof. Dr ILDEFONSO MURILLO MURILLO.

UNIVERSIDAD PÚBLICA DE NAVARRA

Campus de Arrosadía, 31006 Pamplona (Navarre)

Telephone: (94) 8169000
Fax: (94) 8169169
E-mail: infoweb@unavarra.es
Internet: www.unavarra.es

Founded 1987
State control ended Sept. 1993
Languages of instruction: Spanish, Basque, English
Academic year: September to June

Rector: JULIO LAFUENTE LÓPEZ
Vice-Rector for Economic Affairs, Planning and Forecasting: KATRIN SIMON ELORZ
Vice-Rector for Research: ALFONSO CARLOSENA GARCÍA
Vice-Rector for Social and Cultural Projection: CAMINO OSLÉ GUERENDIÁIN
Vice-Rector for Student Affairs and Int. Relations: JAVIER CASALÍ SARASÍBAR
Vice-Rector for Teaching: JESÚS MARÍA PINTOR BOROBIA
Vice-Rector for Teaching Staff: JOSÉ ASIÁIN OLLO
Vice-Rector for Tudela Campus: JOSÉ ASIÁIN OLLO
Registrar: SOLEDAD BARBER BURUSCO
Man.: PEDRO IRAIZOZ MUNÁRRIZ
Library Dir: GUILLERMO SÁNCHEZ MARTÍNEZ
Library of 339,160 vols, 9,309 periodicals
Number of teachers: 800
Number of students: 9,000

Publications: *Anales de Derecho* (1 a year), *Filología y Didáctica de la Lengua, Geografía e Historia* (1 a year), *Psicología y Pedagogía* (1 a year)

DEANS

Faculty of Economics and Business: JOSEBA DE LA TORRE CAMPO
Faculty of Humanities and Social Sciences: MARÍA JESÚS GOIKOETXEA TABAR
Faculty of Law: JOSÉ LUIS GOÑI SEIN

ATTACHED INSTITUTIONS

'Estanislao de Aranzadi' School of Practice in Law: Edificio de El Sario, Módulo 2, 2°, Campus de Arrosadía, 31006 Pamplona; tel. (948) 8169814; e-mail escuela.practica .juridica@unavarra.es; Dir PEDRO CHARRO AYESTARÁN.

Institute of Agrobiotechnology and Natural Resources: Campus de Arrosadía, 31192 Mutilva Baja (Navarra); tel. (94) 8242834; fax (94) 8232191; Dir JAVIER POZUETA ROMERO.

UNIVERSIDAD REY JUAN CARLOS

Calle Tulipán, s/n, 28933 Móstoles (Madrid)

Telephone: (91) 6655060
Fax: (91) 6147120
E-mail: info@urjc.es
Internet: www.urjc.es

Founded 1997
State control
Academic year: October to June

Rector: PEDRO GONZÁLEZ-TREVIJANO SÁNCHEZ
Vice-Rector for Academic Affairs, Teaching Staff and Campus Coordination: FERNANDO SUÁREZ BILBAO
Vice-Rector for European Harmonization and Alignment: JOSÉ MARÍA ÁLVAREZ MONZON-CILLO
Vice-Rector for Information and Communication: FRANCISCO JOSÉ BLANCO JIMÉNEZ
Vice-Rector for Int. Relations, Employment and Devt Cooperation: ANA MARÍA SALAZAR DE LA GUERRA
Vice-Rector for Research: RAFAEL VAN GRIEKEN SALVADOR
Vice-Rector for Student Affairs: MARÍA ANGUSTIAS PALOMAR GALLEGO
Vice-Rector for Univ. Extension and Affiliated Centres: JOSÉ MANUEL VERA SANTOS
Registrar: ANDRÉS GAMBRA GUTIÉRREZ
Gen. Man.: JOSÉ MARÍA BETHENCOURT FONTENLA
Library Dir: RICARDO GONZÁLEZ CASTRILLO
Number of teachers: 900
Number of students: 15,000

DEANS

Faculty of Communication Science: ANTONIO GARCÍA JIMÉNEZ
Faculty of Health Sciences: RAFAEL LINARES GARCÍA-VALDECASAS
Faculty of Law and Social Sciences: CAMILO PRADO FREIRE
Faculty of Tourism: CATALINA VACAS GUERRERO

ATTACHED CENTRES

Higher College of Business Management and Marketing (ESIC): Avda Valdenigrales s/n, 28223 Pozuelo de Alarcón (Madrid); tel. (91) 4524100; fax (91) 3528534; internet www.esic.es; Gen. Dir SIMÓN REYES MARTÍNEZ CÓRDOVA.

Institute of Public Law: Facultad de Ciencias Jurídicas y Sociales, Despacho 2, Campus de Vicálvaro, Paseo de Artilleros s/n, 28032 Vicálvaro (Madrid); tel. (91) 4887792; fax (91) 3718885; e-mail idp@fcjs.urjc.es; Dir Prof. Dr ENRIQUE ÁLVAREZ CONDE.

UNIVERSIDAD VIC

Calle Sagrada Família 7, 08500 Vic (Barcelona)

Telephone: (93) 8861222
Fax: (93) 8891063
E-mail: relin@uvic.es
Internet: www.uvic.es

Founded 1977, present status since 1997

Pres.: JORDI MONTAÑA
Rector: JORDI MONTAÑA I MATOSAS

Vice-Rector for Academic Org. and Teaching Staff: PERE QUER
Vice-Rector for Research and Knowledge Transfer: JOSEP M. SERRAT
Registrar: MONTSERRAT VILALTA
Gen. Man.: PILAR SOLDEVILA
Library Dir: ANNA ANDREU MOLINA
Library of 63,284 vols, 68,000 docs, 1,484 periodicals, 5,170 e-journals
Number of teachers: 544
Number of students: 4,597

DEANS

Faculty of Business and Communication: Dra ANTÒNIA PUJOL
Faculty of Education: FRANCESC CODINA
Faculty of Humanities, Translation and Documentation: CARME SANMARTÍ

ATTACHED CENTRE

BAU College of Design: Calle Pujades 118, 08005 Barcelona; tel. (93) 4153474; fax (93) 3001552; e-mail info@bau.cat; internet www .bau.cat; Academic Dir HUMBERT PLANTADA.

UNIVERSIDADE DA CORUÑA

A Maestranza s/n, 15001 A Coruña

Telephone: (98) 1167000
Fax: (98) 1167011
E-mail: rede@udc.es
Internet: www.udc.es

Founded 1989
Languages of instruction: Spanish, Galician

Rector: JOSÉ MARÍA BARJA PÉREZ
Vice-Rector for Academic Organization: ANA DOROTEA TARRÍO TOBAR
Vice-Rector for Campus at Ferrol and University-Business Relations: LUIS FERNANDO BARRAL LOSADA
Vice-Rector for Culture and Communication: LUÍS CAPARRÓS ESPERANTE
Vice-Rector for Infrastructure and Environmental Management: JOSÉ LUIS MARTÍNEZ SUÁREZ
Vice-Rector for Quality and New Technology: MARÍA ELENA SIERRA PALMEIRO
Vice-Rector for Research: MARÍA CONCEPCIÓN HERRERO LÓPEZ
Vice-Rector for Strategy and Economic Planning: ANGEL FERNÁNDEZ CASTRO
Vice-Rector for Student Affairs and Int. Relations: MARÍA JOSÉ MARTÍNEZ LÓPEZ
Vice-Rector for Teaching Staff: XOSSÉ LUIS ARMESTO BARBEITO
Registrar: CARLOS AMOEDO SOUTO
Man.: MARÍA JESÚS GRELA BARREIRO
Head Librarian: ÁNGELES CAMPOS RODRÍGUEZ
Library of 670,000 vols, 7,600 periodicals
Number of teachers: 1,250
Number of students: 25,000

DEANS

Faculty of Business and Economics: GUSTAVO REGO VEIGA
Faculty of Communication Science: JOSÉ JUAN ANTONI VIDELA RODRÍGUEZ
Faculty of Computing: ALBERTO VALDERRUTEN VIDAL
Faculty of Economics and Business: GUSTAVO REGO VEIGA
Faculty of Education: NARCISO DE GABRIEL FERNÁNDEZ
Faculty of Health Sciences: SERGIO EDUARDO SANTOS DEL RIEGO
Faculty of Humanities: JOSÉ MANUEL RECUERO ASTRAY
Faculty of Labour Relations: MOISES ALBERTO GARCÍA NÚÑEZ
Faculty of Law: JOSÉ MARÍA PENA LÓPEZ
Faculty of Philology: MARÍA TERESA LÓPEZ FERNÁNDEZ
Faculty of Sciences: HORACIO NAVEIRA FACHAL,

Faculty of Sociology: ANTONIO ALVAREZ SOUSA
Faculty of Sports and Physical Education Science: RAFAEL MARTIN ACERO

ATTACHED INSTITUTES

Centre of Educational Training and Innovation: Edificio Facultade de Socioloxía, 1° andar, Campus de Elviña s/n, 15071 A Coruña; tel. (98) 1167189; fax (98) 1167188; e-mail administracion.cufie@udc.es; internet www.udc.es/cufie; Dir ENRIQUE DE LA TORRE FERNÁNDEZ.

Institute of European Studies: Casa de Galería, Campus de Elviña s/n, 15071 A Coruña; tel. (98) 1167000; fax (98) 1167013; e-mail iuee@udc.es; internet www.udc.es/iuee; Dir JOSÉ MANUEL SOBRINO HEREDIA.

Institute of Geology: Edificio de Servicios Centrales de Investigación, Campus de Elviña, 15071 A Coruña; tel. (98) 1167000; fax (98) 1167172; e-mail xeoloxia@udc.es; internet www.iux.es; library of 30,000 vols; Dir Prof. JUAN RAMÓN VIDAL ROMANÍ; publ. *Cadernos do Laboratorio Xeoloxico de Laxe.*

Institute of Health Sciences: Hospital Marítimo de Oza, Area Jubias de Arriba, A Coruña; tel. (98) 1171360; fax (98) 1138714; e-mail iucs@udc.es; internet www.udc.es/cisaude/homepage.html; Dir Dr ALFONSO CASTRO BEIRAS.

Institute of Irish Studies: Edificio Servicios Centrais de Investigación, Campus de Elviña s/n, 15071 A Coruña; tel. (98) 1167000; fax (98) 1167172; e-mail amergin@udc.es; internet www.udc.es/amergin; Dir Dr ANTONIO RAÚL DE TORO SANTOS.

Institute of Maritime Studies: Universidade da Coruña, Campus de Elviña, 15071 A Coruña; tel. (98) 1167000; fax (98) 1167125; e-mail iuem@udc.es; internet www.udc.es/iuem; Dir FERNANDO GONZÁLEZ LAXE.

Institute of the Environment: Pazo de Lóngora 29, Santa Eulalia de Liáns, 15179 Oleiros; tel. (98) 1648569; fax (98) 1648568; e-mail iuma@udc.es; internet www.udc.es/iuma; Dir Prof. Dr DARÍO PRADA RODRÍGUEZ.

Technological Institute of Communication: Paseo de Ronda 47, 15011 A Coruña; tel. (98) 1150100; e-mail info@telematica.org; internet www.telematica.org; Dir Dr ANGEL VIÑA.

UNIVERSIDADE DE SANTIAGO DE COMPOSTELA

Colexio de San Xerome, Praza do Obradoiro s/n, 15782 Santiago de Compostela
Telephone: (98) 1547111
Fax: (98) 1588522
E-mail: reitor@usc.es
Internet: www.usc.es
Founded 1495
State control
Languages of instruction: Spanish, Galician
Rector: JUAN J. CASARES LONG
Vice-Rector: BENITA SILVA HERMO
Vice-Rector: CARMEN FERNÁNDEZ MORANTE
Vice-Rector: FRANCISCO GONZÁLEZ GARCÍA
Vice-Rector: FRANCISCO RAMÓN DURÁN VILLA
Vice-Rector: MERCEDES PINTOS BARRAL
Vice-Rector: PABLO RAMIL REGO
Vice-Rector: PEDRO GARCÍA HERRADÓN
Vice-Rector: SARA CANTORNA AGRA
Vice-Rector: VICTOR MILLET SCHRODER
Registrar: LOURDES NOYA FERREIRO
Man.: MARÍA LOURDES BATÁN AIRA
Librarian: MARÍA ISABEL CASAL REYES
Library: 1.5m. vols, 140 incunabula
Number of teachers: 2,262
Number of students: 27,795

Publications: *Acta Científica Compostelana, Anejos de la revista Verba, Anuario Gallego de Filología, Cursos y Congresos de la Universidad de Santiago de Compostela, Memoria, Trabajos Compostelanos de Biología, Verba*

DEANS
Faculty of Biology: MARÍA LUZ GONZÁLEZ CAAMAÑO
Faculty of Business Administration and Management (Lugo): LUIS E. GAGO GONZÁLEZ
Faculty of Chemistry: JOSÉ RAMON CABANAS ESTÉVEZ
Faculty of Communication Science: JOSÉ FARIÑA PEREIRA
Faculty of Economic and Business Science: MARÍA EMILIA VÁZQUEZ ROZAS
Faculty of Education Science: LUIS FERRADÁS BLANCO
Faculty of Geography and History: JUAN M. MONTERROSO MONTERO
Faculty of Humanities (Lugo): MARÍA ISABEL GONZÁLEZ REY
Faculty of Labour Relations: JUAN J. ARES FERNÁNDEZ
Faculty of Law: LUIS MIGUEZ MACHO
Faculty of Mathematics: VICTORIA M. OTERO ESPINAR
Faculty of Medicine and Dentistry: JUAN GESTAL OTERO
Faculty of Nursing: JESÚS NÚÑEZ IGLESIAS
Faculty of Optics and Optometry: LUZ MARÍA GIGIREY PRIETO
Faculty of Pharmacy: ISABEL M. SANDEZ MACHO
Faculty of Philology: MARÍA JOSÉ LÓPEZ COUSO
Faculty of Philosophy: LUIS MODESTO GARCÍA
Faculty of Physics: LUIS M. VARELA CABO
Faculty of Political Sciences: MARÍA NIEVES LAGARES DÍEZ
Faculty of Psychology: CAROLINA TINAJERO VACAS
Faculty of Sciences (Lugo): JOSÉ MANUEL MARTÍNEZ AGEITOS
Faculty of Veterinary Medicine (Lugo): FRANCISCO RODRÍGUEZ LESTEGÁS
School of Agriculture and Forestry (Lugo): JAVIER BUENO LEMA
School of Engineering: JUAN M. LEMA RODICIO

UNIVERSIDADE DE VIGO

Campus as Lagoas, Marcosende, 36310 Vigo
Telephone: (98) 6812000
Fax: (98) 6813559
E-mail: informacion@uvigo.es
Internet: www.uvigo.es
Founded 1990
State control
Academic year: October to July
Rector: Prof. SALUSTIANO MATO DE LA IGLESIA
Vice-Rector for Academic Org., Teaching Staff and Degrees: Profa MARGARITA ESTÉVEZ TORANZO
Vice-Rector for Economy and Planning: Prof. JOSÉ MANUEL GARCÍA VÁZQUEZ
Vice-Rector for Int. Relations: Prof. MANUEL FERNÁNDEZ IGLESIAS
Vice-Rector for Knowledge Transfer: Prof. JOSÉ ANTONIO VILÁN VILÁN
Vice-Rector for Orense Campus: Profa MARÍA LAMEIRAS FERNÁNDEZ
Vice-Rector for Pontevedra Campus: Profa ANTONIA BLANCO PESQUEIRA
Vice-Rector for Research: Profa MARÍA ASUNCIÓN LONGO GONZÁLEZ
Vice-Rector for Student Affairs, Teaching and Quality: Prof. IGNACIO BARCIA RODRÍGUEZ
Vice-Rector for Univ. Extension: Prof. XOSÉ HENRIQUE COSTAS GONZÁLEZ
Registrar: Profa INMACULADA VALEIJE ÁLVAREZ
Man.: JOSÉ MANUEL FERNÁNDEZ JAUREGUI

Librarian: MARÍA DEL CARMEN PÉREZ PAIS
Library of 180,000 vols
Number of teachers: 1,200
Number of students: 30,000

DEANS
Orense Campus:
Faculty of Business and Tourism: Profa MARÍA ELISA ALÉN GONZÁLEZ
Faculty of Education: Profa MERCEDES SUÁREZ PAZOS
Faculty of History: Profa BEATRIZ COMENDADOR REY
Faculty of Law: Prof. Dr MIGUEL ÁNGEL MICHINEL ÁLVAREZ
Faculty of Science: Prof. PEDRO ARAÚJO NESPEREIRA

Pontevedra Campus:
Faculty of Science Education and Sport: Profa FRANCISCA FARIÑA RIVERA
Faculty of Fine Arts: Prof. JUAN CARLOS MEANA MARTÍNEZ
Faculty of Social Sciences and Communication: Prof. JUAN MANUEL CORBACHO VALENCIA (acting)

Vigo Campus (Lagoas-Marcosende):
Faculty of Biology: Profa MARÍA CRISTINA ARIAS FERNÁNDEZ
Faculty of Chemistry: SOLEDAD GARCÍA FONTÁN
Faculty of Economics and Business: SANTIAGO
Faculty of Law and Labour Science: ANA MARÍA PITA GRANDAL
Faculty of Marine Science: JESÚS SOUZA TRONCOSO
Faculty of Philology and Translation: MARÍA ROSA PÉREZ RODRÍGUEZ

UNIVERSITAT ABAT OLIBA CEU

Calle Bellesguard 30, 08022 Barcelona
Telephone: (93) 2540900
Fax: (93) 4189380
E-mail: info@uao.es
Internet: www.uao.es
Founded 2003
Private control
Languages of instruction: Spanish, English, Catalan
Rector: Dr CARLOS PÉREZ DEL VALLE
Vice-Rector for Research, Graduate Affairs and Quality Control: Dr ENRIQUE MARTÍNEZ
Vice-Rector for Student Affairs: Dr MARCIN KAZMIERCZAK
Gen.-Sec.: Dr CARMEN PARRA
Man.: JUAN ÁLVAREZ
Library of 20,000 vols, 100 periodicals
Number of students: 2,000

Courses in advertising, business admin. and management economics, computer engineering, higher education management, journalism, law, politics, public management, publicity, public relations, psychology

HEADS OF DIVISION
JOAN A. ROCHA, Communication Sciences
FERRAN PORTA, Economic and Social Sciences
MIGUEL A. BELMONTE, Humanities
JOSÉ A. ROZAS, Legal and Political Sciences
MARTÍN ECHAVARRÍA, Psychology

UNIVERSITAT AUTÒNOMA DE BARCELONA

Campus Universitari, 08193 Bellaterra (Barcelona)
Telephone: (93) 5811111
Fax: (93) 5812000
E-mail: informacio@uab.es
Internet: www.uab.es
Founded 1968
Regional govt control

Languages of instruction: Spanish, Catalan
Academic year: September to June
Rector: ANA RIPOLL ARACIL MISSATGE
Vice-Rector for Academic Staff: MIQUEL
ANGEL SENAR ROSELL
Vice-Rector for Academic Policy: MONTSERRAT
FARELL FERRER
Vice-Rector for Economic Policy and Org.:
JOSEP ENRIC LLEBOT RABAGLIATI,
Vice-Rector for Institutional Relations and
Communication: MARÍA JOSÉ RECODER
SELLARÈS
Vice-Rector for Int. Relations: MERCEDES
UNZETA LÓPEZ
Vice-Rector for Research: JOAN GÓMEZ PAL-
LARÈS
Vice-Rector for Social and Cultural Transfer:
BONAVENTURA BASSEGODA HUGAS
Vice-Rector for Strategic Projects and Plan-
ning: CARLES JAIME CARDIEL
Registrar: ISABEL PONT CASTEJÓN
Man.: SANTIAGO GUERRERO BONED
Librarian: JOAN RAMÓN GÓMEZ ESCOFET
Library of 1,114,509 vols, 39,000 periodicals
Number of teachers: 3,566
Number of students: 53,232
Publications: Anàlisi: Quaderns de Comuni-
cació i Cultura, Anuari d'Anglès, Cuader-
nos de Psicología, Cuadernos de
Traducción e Interpretación, Documents
d'Anàlisi Geogràfica, Educar, Enrahonar:
Quaderns de Filosofia, Estudios de la
Antigüedad, Faventia, Medievalia, Orsis:
Organismes i Sistemes, Papers: Revista de
Sociologia, Quaderns de Música Històrica
Catalana, Quaderns de Treball, Recerca
Musicològica

DEANS

Faculty of Communication Science: JOSEP M.
CATALÀ
Faculty of Economics and Business: JOAN
CLAVERA
Faculty of Educational Sciences: ROSA MARÍA
PUJOL
Faculty of Law: JOSEP M. DE DIOS MARCER
Faculty of Medicine: JOAQUIM COLL I DAROCA
Faculty of Philosophy and Letters: TERESA
CABRÉ MONNÉ
Faculty of Political Sciences and Sociology:
SALVADOR CARDÚS I ROS
Faculty of Psychology: MAITE MARTÍNEZ GON-
ZÁLEZ
Faculty of Science: JORDI BARBÉ GARCÍA
Faculty of Translation and Interpretation:
FRANCESC PARCERISAS I VÁZQUEZ
Faculty of Veterinary Medicine: MANEL
LÓPEZ BÉJAR

UNIVERSITAT DE BARCELONA

Gran Via de les Corts Catalanes 585, 08007
Barcelona
Telephone: (93) 4021100
Fax: (93) 3025947
E-mail: comunicacio@ub.edu
Internet: www.ub.es
Founded 1450
State control
Language of instruction: Catalan, English,
Spanish
Academic year: October to September
Rector: Dr DÍDAC RAMÍREZ I SARRIÓ
Vice-Rector for Academic Policy and Quality:
GASPAR ROSSELLÓ NICOLAU
Vice-Rector for Admin.: CARME PANCHÓN
IGLESIAS
Vice-Rector for Arts, Culture and Heritage:
LOURDES CIRLOT VALENZUELA
Vice-Rector for Financial Resources: GON-
ZALO BERNARDOS DOMÍNGUEZ
Vice-Rector for Information and Communi-
cation: PERE QUETGLAS NICOLAU

Vice-Rector for Innovation and Knowledge
Transfer: SÍLVIA ATRIÁN VENTURA
Vice-Rector for Int. Relations and Deputy
Rector: Dr CARLES CARRERAS VERDAGUER
Vice-Rector for Research: Dr JORDI ALBERCH
VIÉ
Vice-Rector for Students and Language Pol-
icy: GEMMA FONRODONA BALDAJOS
Vice-Rector for Teaching and Science Policy:
MARÍA TERESA ANGUERA ARGILAGA (acting)
Vice-Rector for Teaching Staff: MANUEL VILA-
DEVALL SOLÉ
Gen. Sec.: JORDI GARCIA VIÑA
Gen. Man.: VÍCTOR GÓMEZ GÓMEZ
Library Dir: ADELAIDA FERRER TORRENS
Library of 1,650,000 vols
Number of teachers: 5,247
Number of students: 87,486

DEANS

Faculty of Biology: JOAQUÍN GUTIÉRREZ FRUI-
TÓS
Faculty of Chemistry: PERE LLUÍS CABOT
JULIÀ
Faculty of Dentistry: SÍLVIA SÁNCHEZ GONZÁ-
LEZ (acting)
Faculty of Economics and Business: ELI-
SENDA PALUZIE HERNÁNDEZ
Faculty of Education: ANA MARÍA ESCOFET
ROIG
Faculty of Fine Arts: SALVADOR GARCÍA FOR-
TES
Faculty of Geography and History: M.
ÁNGELES DEL RINCÓN MARTÍNEZ
Faculty of Geology: LUIS CABRERA PÉREZ
Faculty of Law: ENOCH ALBERTÍ ROVIRA
Faculty of Library and Information Science:
ERNEST ABADAL FALGUERAS
Faculty of Mathematics: MARIA CARMEN
CASCANTE CANUT
Faculty of Medicine: FRANCESCA CARDELLACH
LÓPEZ
Faculty of Pharmacy: JUAN ESTEVA DE
SAGRERA
Faculty of Philology: ADOLFO SOTELO VÁZQUEZ
Faculty of Philosophy: NORBERT BILBENY
GARCIA
Faculty of Physics: JOAN ÀNGEL PADRÓ CÀR-
DENAS
Faculty of Psychology: MANEL VIADER JUNY-
ENT
Faculty of Teacher Training: ALBERTO
BATALLA FLORES

UNIVERSITAT DE GIRONA

Edifici Les Àligues, Pl. Sant Domènec 3,
17071 Gerona
Telephone: (97) 2418028
Fax: (97) 2418031
E-mail: informacio@udg.es
Internet: www.udg.es
Founded 1992
State control
Academic year: September to June
Rector: Dra ANNA M. GELI
Vice-Rector for Academic Policy: Dr FRAN-
CESC FELIU TORRENT
Vice-Rector for Campus Infrastructure:
LLUÍS ALBÓ RIGAU
Vice-Rector for Int. Policy: Dra MARIA LLUÏSA
PÉREZ CABANÍ
Vice-Rector for Personnel and Social Policy:
Dr TEODOR M. JOVÉ LAGUNAS
Vice-Rector for Planning and Quality: Dr
MARTÍ CASADESÚS FA
Vice-Rector for Regulation Devt: Dr SUSANNA
OROMÍ VALL-LLOVERA
Vice-Rector for Research and Knowledge
Transfer: Dr JOSEP CALBÓ ANGRILL
Vice-Rector for Strategic Projects and
Finance: Dr LIBRADO JESÚS GARCÍA GIL
Vice-Rector for Student Affairs, Cooperation
and Equality: MARIA ROSA TERRADELLAS
PIFERRER

Registrar: Dr CARLES ABELLÀ AMETLLER
Man.: JOSEP M. GÓMEZ PALLARÈS
Librarian: ANTÒNIA BOIX
Library of 372,144 vols, 6,793 periodicals
Number of teachers: 804
Number of students: 12,952

DEANS

Faculty of Arts: JOSÉ LUIS VILLANOVA VALERO
Faculty of Economics and Business Studies:
ANNA GARRIGA RIPOLL
Faculty of Education and Psychology: FRAN-
CISCO JIMÉNEZ MARTÍNEZ
Faculty of Law: GUILLERMO ORMAZABAL SÁN-
CHEZ
Faculty of Medicine: RAMON BRUGADA
Faculty of Science: VICTORIA DE LOS ANGELES
SALVADO MARTIN
Faculty of Tourism: LLUIS MUNDET I CERDAN

ATTACHED SCHOOLS

CETA University School of Tourism: C/
Pàdua 11–13, 08023 Barcelona; tel. (93)
2118074; e-mail informacio@cetaturisme
.com; internet www.cetaturismo.com; Dir Dr
RAMÓN BOSCH.

ESMA University School of Tourism:
Consell de Cent 42, 08014 Barcelona; tel.
(93) 4269988; fax (93) 4267621; e-mail esma@
esma.es; internet www.esma.es; Man. Dir
JOAN B. RENART I MONTALAT.

Euroaula University School of Tourism:
C/ Aragó 208–210, 08011 Barcelona; tel. (93)
4510306; e-mail turisme@euroaula.com;
internet www.euroaula.com.

**Garbí University School of Physiother-
apy:** C/ Ángel Guimerà 108, 17190 Salt,
Gerona; tel. (97) 2405130; e-mail garbi
.girona@udg.es; internet www.fisiogarbi.org;
Dir ANTONIO NARBONA JIMÉNEZ.

**Sant Pol de Mar University School of
Hotel Business and Tourism:** Carretera
N-II s/n, 08395 Sant Pol de Mar, Barcelona;
tel. (93) 7600212; fax (93) 7600985; e-mail
%20mail@euht-santpol.org; internet www
.euht-santpol.org; President RAMON SERRA.

**School of Audiovisual and Multimedia
Production:** Factoria Cultural Coma Cros,
17190 Gerona; tel. (97) 420258; e-mail info@
eramcollege.com; internet www.eramcollege
.com; languages of instruction: English,
Espanol; academic year September to June;
30 teachers; 350 students.

Terrassa University School of Tourism:
Vapor Universitari, Colom 114, 08222 Terrassa; tel. (93) 7311869; fax (93) 7843706;
e-mail info-turisme@fundaciofiac.com;
internet www.fundaciofiac.com.

**University School of Communication
Sciences:** Campus de Montilivi s/n, 17071
Gerona; tel. (97) 2418904; fax (97) 2418732;
e-mail iolanda.vila@pas.udg.es; internet
www.eucc-udg.org; Dir Dra CARMEN ECHA-
ZARRETA SOLER.

UNIVERSITAT DE LES ILLES
BALEARS

Campus Universitari, Cra de Valldemossa,
Km 7.5, 07122 Palma, Mallorca
Telephone: (97) 1173000
Fax: (97) 1172852
E-mail: informacio@uib.es
Internet: www.uib.es
Founded 1978
State control
Languages of instruction: Catalan, Spanish,
English
Academic year: October to September
Rector: Dra MONTSERRAT CASAS AMETLLER
First Vice-Rector for Univ. Planning and
Coordination: Dr MARTÍ X. MARCH CERDÀ

Vice-Rector for Academic Regulation and European Convergence: Dr MATEU SERVERA BARCELÓ
Vice-Rector for Academic Staff and Pedagogical Innovation: Dr JOSEP LLUÍS FERRER GOMILA
Vice-Rector for Cultural Projection: Dr PATRÍCIA TRAPERO LLOBERA
Vice-Rector for Economic and Admin. Planning: Dr ANTONI LLULL GILET
Vice-Rector for Int. Relations and Mobility Programmes: Dra CATALINA NATIVITAT JUANEDA SAMPOL
Vice-Rector for Research: Dr JORDI LALUCAT JO
Vice-Rector for Student and Campus Affairs: Dr CELSO GARCÍA GARCÍA
Vice-Rector for Univ. Infrastructure: Dra RAQUEL HERRANZ BASCONES
Registrar: Dr FEDERICO F. GARAU SOBRINO
Man.: BEGOÑA MOREY AGUIRRE
Librarian: MIQUEL PASTOR TOUS
Number of teachers: 1,202
Number of students: 14,739

Publications: *Annuals of Tourism Research, Educació i Cultura, Mayurqa, Psicología del Deporte, Taula, Treballs de Geografia*

DEANS

Faculty of Economics and Business: MARGALIDA PAYERAS LLODRÀ
Faculty of Education: JOSÉ LUIS OLIVER TORELLÓ
Faculty of Humanities: PERE JOAN BRUNET ESTARELLAS
Faculty of Law: SANTIAGO JOSÉ CAVANILLAS MÚJICA
Faculty of Psychology: ALBERT JOSÉ SESÉ ABAD
Faculty of Sciences: ANTONI MIRALLES SOCÍAS
Faculty of Tourism: MARCO ANTONIO ROBLEDO CAMACHO
Higher Polytechnic University School: GABRIEL OLIVER CODINA
University School of Nursing and Physiotherapy: MARGALIDA MIRÓ BONET

ATTACHED CENTRES

Alberta Giménez University School: Calle de Saragossa 16, Palma, Mallorca; tel. (97) 1792818; fax (97) 1798078; internet www.cesag.org; Dir MARC CARBONELL HUGUET.

Balearic Islands College of Hotel Management: Edif. Arxiduc Lluís Salvador, Campus Universitari, Cra de Valldemossa, Km 7.5, 07702 Palma, Mallorca; tel. (97) 1172608; fax (97) 1172617; e-mail escola.hoteleria@uib.es; internet www.ehib.es/nova; Dir FRANCESC SASTRE ALBERTÍ.

College of Industrial Relations: Via Alemanya 7, 2n dreta, 07003 Palma, Mallorca; tel. (97) 1723268; Dir MARGARITA TARABINI-CASTELLANI AZNAR.

College of Tourism of the Island Council of Ibiza-Formentera: Edif. Polivalent, Cas Serres s/n, 07800 Ibiza; tel. (97) 1392762; fax (97) 1307255; internet euroibiza.org; Dir JOAN B. GARAU VADELL.

Felipe Moreno University School of Tourism (Mahón): Avda Sant Ferran 17, 07702 Mahón, Menorca, Islas Baleares; tel. and fax (97) 1350508; internet www.etb-baleares.es; Dir ONOFRE MARTORELL CUNILL.

Felipe Moreno University School of Tourism (Palma): Calle Sol 1, 07001 Palma, Mallorca; tel. (97) 1721473; fax (97) 1714988; e-mail acapo@etb-baleares.es; internet www.etb-baleares.es; Dir ONOFRE MARTORELL CUNILL.

UNIVERSITAT DE LLEIDA

Plaça de Víctor Siurana 1, 25003 Lleida
Telephone: (97) 3702000
Fax: (97) 3702062
E-mail: pdi@seu.udl.cat
Internet: www.udl.cat
Founded 1991
State control
Language of instruction: Catalan, Spanish, English
Academic year: September to July
Rector: ROBERTO FERNÁNDEZ DÍAZ
Vice-Rector for Campus: JESÚS AVILLA HERNÁNDEZ
Vice-Rector for Cultural Activities and University Outreach: JOAN BISCARRI GASSIÓ
Vice-Rector for International Relations and Cooperation: ASTRID BALLESTA REMY
Vice-Rector for Research: JAUME PUY LLORENS
Vice-Rector for Scientific and Technological Policy: ALBERT SORRIBAS TELLO
Vice-Rector for Students, Postgraduate and Continuing Education: NEUS VILA RUBIO
Vice-Rector for Teaching Staff: DOLORS MAYORAL ARQUÉ
Registrar: Dra ANA MARÍA ROMERO BURILLO
Gen. Sec.: TERESA ARECES PIÑOL
Library Dir: LOLI MANCIÑEIRAS VAZ-ROMERO
Library of 320,341 vols, 4,861 periodicals, 18,747 e-publs
Number of teachers: 966
Number of students: 9,582

Publications: *Arrabal* (1 a Year), *Qualitative Theory of Dynamic Systems* (2 a year), *Revista d'Arqueologia de Ponent* (1 a year), *Sintagma* (1 a year), *Ull Crític* (1 a year)

DEANS

Faculty of Arts: JOAN J. BUSQUETA RIU
Faculty of Educational Sciences: MARI-PAU CORNADÓ TEIXIDÓ
Faculty of Law and Economics: Dra JOAN PERE ENCISO RODRÍGUEZ
Faculty of Medicine: JOAN RIBERA CALVET
Institute of Education: ISABEL DEL ARCO BRAVO
Polytechnic School: FRANCESC GINÉ DE SOLÀ
School of Agricultural Engineering: M. ROSA TEIRA ESMATGES
University School of Nursing: MARÍA LUISA GUITARD SEIN-ECHALUBE

ATTACHED CENTRES

National Institute of Physical Education of Catalonia: Pda de la Caparrella s/n, 25192 Lleida; tel. (97) 3272022; fax (97) 3275941; e-mail inefclleida@inefc.es; internet www.inefc.cat/inefc; Dir CRISTÒFOL SALAS.

University School of Labour Relations: Gran Passeig de Ronda 55–57, 25006 Lleida; tel. (97) 3248993; fax (97) 3221818; e-mail capadministracio@eurl.es; internet www.eurl.es; Dir Dra MARÍA JOSÉ PUYALTO FRANCO.

UNIVERSITAT DE VALÈNCIA

Avda Blasco Ibáñez 13, 46010 Valencia
Telephone: (96) 3864100
Fax: (96) 3864885
E-mail: rectorado@uv.es
Internet: www.uv.es
Founded 1499
State control
Language of instruction: English, Spanish, Valencian (specific programmes)
Academic year: October to September
Rector: Prof. Dr ESTEBAN MORCILLO SÁNCHEZ
Vice-Rector for Academic Org.: Dra MARÍA VICENTA MESTRE ESCRIVÁ
Vice-Rector for Arts, Culture and Heritage: Dr JOSEP LLUÍS SIRERA TURÓ

Vice-Rector for Communications and Institutional Relations: Dra SILVIA BARONA VILAR
Vice-Rector for Community Participation and Outreach: Dr JORGE HERMOSILLA PLA
Vice-Rector for Continuing Education: (vacant)
Vice-Rector for Economics: MÁXIMO FERRANDO BOLADO
Vice-Rector for Infrastructure and Sustainability: Dra CLARA MARTÍNEZ FUENTES
Vice-Rector for Int. Relations and Cooperation: Dra OLGA GIL MEDRANO
Vice-Rector for Planning and Equality: Dr ANTONIO ARIÑO VILLARROYA
Vice-Rector for Postgraduate Studies: Dra ROSA MARÍN SÁEZ
Vice-Rector for Research and Scientific Policy: Dr PEDRO M. CARRASCO SORLI
Vice-Rector for Studies and Language Policy: Dra ISABEL VÁZQUEZ NAVARRO
Registrar: MARÍA JOSÉ AÑÓN ROIG
Man.: JOAN OLTRA VIDAL
Library Dir: JOSEP LLUÍS SIRERA TURÓ
Library of 1,484,000 vols, 17,600 periodicals
Number of teachers: 3,347
Number of students: 46,480 (undergraduates), 4,000 (masters and doctorates)

DEANS

Faculty of Biology: VICENTE ROCA VELASCO
Faculty of Chemistry: PILAR CAMPINS FALCÓ
Faculty of Economics: TRINIDAD CASASÚS ESTELLÉS
Faculty of Geography and History: ELENA GRAU ALMERO
Faculty of Law: SALVADOR MONTESINOS OLTRA
Faculty of Mathematics: RAFAEL CRESPO GARCÍA
Faculty of Medicine and Odontology: ANTONIO PELLICER MARTÍNEZ
Faculty of Pharmacy: MARÍA TERESA BARBER SANCHIS
Faculty of Philology, Translation and Communication: MARÍA JOSÉ COPERÍAS AGUILAR
Faculty of Philosophy and Education: RAMÓN LÓPEZ MARTÍN
Faculty of Physical Activity and Sport: VICTOR TELLA MUÑOZ
Faculty of Physics: JOSÉ ANTONIO PEÑARROCHA GANTES
Faculty of Psychology: JOSÉ RAMOS LÓPEZ
Faculty of Social Sciences: IGNASI LERMA MONTERO

UNIVERSITAT OBERTA DE CATALUNYA

Avda Tibidabo 39–43, 08035 Barcelona
Telephone: (93) 2532300
Fax: (93) 4716495
E-mail: queries@uoc.edu
Internet: www.uoc.edu
Founded 1995
Languages of instruction: Catalan, English, French, Spanish
Rector: IMMA TUBELLA CASADEVALL
Vice-Rector for Academic Policy and Teaching Staff: PERE FABRA ABAT
Vice-Rector for Postgraduate and Continuing Education: JOSEP MARIA DUART MONTOLIU
Vice-Rector for Research and Innovation: TERESA SANCHO
Vice-Rector for Technology: LLORENÇ VALVERDE GARCIA
Gen. Man.: ÒSCAR AGUER BAYARRI
Dir for Academic Services and Library: PEP TORN POCH
Library of 18,000 vols
Number of teachers: 2,346
Number of students: 54,378

Publications: *Journal of Art, Science and Technology* (online (artnodes.uoc.edu)), *Journal of Internet, Law and Politics* (online (idp.uoc.edu)), *Journal of Univer-*

sities and Knowledge Society (online (rus-c.uoc.edu))

DIRECTORS

Arts and Humanities: AGNES VAYREDA

Business Administration and Economics: ANGELS FITO BERTRAN

Communication and Information: LLUÍS PASTOR PÉREZ

Computer Engineering: RAFAEL NADAL MACAU

Health: JOSE ESTEBAN GARCIA

Law and Political Science: AGUSTÍ CERRILLO MARTÍNEZ

Psychology and Educational Sciences: CARLES SIGALES

UNIVERSITAT POMPEU FABRA

Plaça de la Mercè 10–12, 08002 Barcelona
Telephone: (93) 5422000
Fax: (93) 5422002
E-mail: premsa@upf.edu
Internet: www.upf.edu
Founded 1990
State control
Languages of instruction: Catalan, English, Spanish
Academic year: September to June
Rector: Dr JOSEP JOAN MORESO MATEOS
Vice-Rector for Teaching and Academic Devt: Dr JOSEP ELADI BAÑOS DÍEZ
Vice-Rector for Economics, Information Resources and Institutional Relations: Dr DANIEL SERRA DE LA FIGUERA
Vice-Rector for Quality and Institutional Strategy: Dr MIQUEL OLIVER RIERA
Vice-Rector for Int. Relations: Dr JOSEP FERRER RIBA
Vice-Rector for Postgraduate and Doctoral Studies: Dra OLGA VALVERDE GRANADOS
Vice-Rector for Research: Dr ANGEL LOZANO SOLSONA
Vice-Rector for Students: Dr EMMA RODERO ANTÓN
Vice-Rector for Science Politics: Dr JOSÉ GARCÍA MONTALVO
Deputy Gen. Sec.: Dr JOSEP FARGAS FERNÁNDEZ
Man.: RICARD BOIX I JUNQUERA
Librarian: MERCÈ CABO
Library of 600,000 vols of monographs, 12,800 periodicals and 13,800 online periodicals
Number of teachers: 876
Number of students: 11,235 (9,115 undergraduate, 2,120 postgraduate)
Publications: *Línia 14* (in Catalan, 4 a year), *upf.edu* (in Catalan, 2 a year)

DEANS

Faculty of Communication: Dr FRANCISCO JAVIER RUIZ COLLANTES
Faculty of Economics and Business Sciences: Dr VICENTE ORTUN RUBIO
Faculty of Health and Life Sciences: Dr JOAQUIN GEA GUIRAL
Faculty of Humanities: Dr MIREIA TRENCHS PARERA
Faculty of Law: Dr JOSEP MARIA VILAJOSANA RUBIO
Faculty of Political and Social Sciences: Dr DAVID SANCHO ROYO
Faculty of Translation and Interpretation: Dra CRISTINA GELPÍ ARROYO
Institut d'Educació Contínua (IDEC): Dr JAUME CASALS PONS
Polytechnic School (ESUP): ENRIC PEIG OLIVE

UNIVERSITAT RAMÓN LLULL

Claravall 1–3, 08022 Barcelona
Telephone: (93) 6022200
Fax: (93) 6022249

E-mail: info@url.edu
Internet: www.url.es
Founded 1990
Private control
Academic year: September to June
Rector: Dra ESTHER GIMÉNEZ-SALINAS
Vice-Rector for Academic Affairs, Educational Innovation and Quality: Dr JORDI RIERA ROMANÍ
Vice-Rector for Research and Innovation: Dra ANNA BERGA TIMONEDA
Vice-Rector for Students and Int. Relations: Dra ANNA BERGA TIMONEDA
Vice-Rector for Univ. Policy and Registrar: Dr JOSEP M. GARRELL I GUIU
Library: 1.2m. vols, 14,000 periodicals
Number of teachers: 1,494
Number of students: 18,543
Publications: *La URL Informa*, *Signes*

DEANS

Blanquerna Faculty of Communication Sciences: Dr MIQUEL TRESSERRAS MAJÓ
Blanquerna Faculty of Psychology, Educational Sciences and Sport Science: Dr CLIMENT GINÉ I GINÉ
Blanquerna Faculty of Health Sciences: Dr MÀRIUS DURAN HORTOLÀ
Faculty of Economics: Dr JESÚS TRICÀS PRECKLER
Faculty of Law at the Higher School of Business Administration and Management (ESADE): Dr ENRIC BARTLETT CASTELLA
Faculty of Philosophy and Humanities: Dr JOAN MARTÍNEZ PORCELL
Higher School of Business Administration and Management (ESADE): Dr ALFONS SAUQUET ROVIRA
Higher Technical School: Dra ROSA NOMEN RIBÉ
Pere Tarrés Faculty of Social Education and Social Work: FRANCISCO JOSÉ LÓPEZ JIMÉNEZ

UNIVERSITAT ROVIRA I VIRGILI

Carrer de l'Escorxador s/n, 43003 Tarragona
Telephone: (902) 2337878
Fax: (977) 558022
E-mail: contacteu@urv.cat
Internet: www.urv.cat
Founded 1991
State control
Languages of instruction: Catalan, English, Spanish
Academic year: September to June
Rector: Prof. FRANCESC XAVIER GRAU VIDAL
Vice-Rector for Academic and Scientific Policy: Dr JOSEP MANEL RICART PLA
Vice-Rector for Institutional Relations and Society: Dr ENCARNACIÓ RICART MARTÍ
Vice-Rector for Innovation and Transfer: Dr MISERICÒRDIA CARLES LAVILA
Vice-Rector for Int. Relations: Dr ANNA ARDÈVOL GRAU
Vice-Rector for Org. and Resources: Dr XAVIER FARRIOL ROIGÉS
Vice-Rector for Postgraduate and Continuing Education: Dr AURORA RUIZ MANRIQUE
Vice-Rector for Research and Health Instns: Dr ROSA SOLÀ I ALBERICH
Vice-Rector for Students and Univ. Community: Dra MARIA BARGALLÓ ESCRIVÀ
Vice-Rector for Teaching and European Higher Education Convergence: Dr MARIA MARQUÈS I BANQUÉ
Vice-Rector for Teaching Staff and Research Staff: Prof JOSEP PALLARÈS MARZAL
Gen.-Sec.: Dr ANTONI GONZÀLEZ SENMARTÍ
Man.: MANUEL MOLINA CLAVERO
Library of 551,064 vols, 10,232 magazines, 7,415 e-magazines
Number of teachers: 938

Number of students: 17,089 (1,4377 undergraduate, 2,712 postgraduate)
Publications: *URV Magazine* (4 a year), *URV Publications* (4 a year)

DEANS

Faculty of Arts: Dr JOSEP SÁNCHEZ CERVELLÓ
Faculty of Chemistry: Dr JOAN IGUAL RIPOLLÈS
Faculty of Economy and Business Studies: Dr GLÒRIA BARBERÀ MARINÉ
Faculty of Educational Sciences and Psychology: Dr MONTSERRAT GUASCH GARCIA
Faculty of Legal Sciences: Dr ALFONSO GONZÁLEZ BONDIA
Faculty of Medicine and Health Sciences: Dr MONTSERRAT GIRALT BATISTA
Faculty of Nursing: Dr ROSER RICOMÀ MUNTANÉ
Faculty of Oenology: Dr ALBERT MAS BARON
Faculty of Tourism and Geography: SALVADOR ANTON CLAVÉ
School of Architecture: Dr JOSEP BERTRAN ILARI
School of Chemical Engineering: Dr JOSEP BONET ÀVALOS
School of Engineering: Dr XAVIER MAIXÉ ALTÉS

ATTACHED CENTRE

CESDA, Centre for Advanced Studies in Aviation: Carretera de l'Aeroport s/n, 43206 Reus (Tarragona); tel. (97) 7300027; fax (97) 7300028; e-mail cesda@cesda.com; internet www.cesda.com; languages of instruction: English, Spanish; academic year September to July; Dir Dr MARC MEDRANO; 21 teachers.

Polytechnics

UNIVERSIDAD POLITÉCNICA DE CARTAGENA

Plaza del Cronista Isidoro Valverde, Edif. La Milagrosa, 30202 Cartagena (Murcia)
Telephone: (96) 8325400
Fax: (96) 8325972
E-mail: gestion.academica@upct.es
Internet: www.upct.es
Founded 1998
State control
Language of instruction: Spanish
Academic year: September to July
Rector: FÉLIX FAURA MATEU
Vice-Rector for Academic Affairs: JOSEFINA GARCÍA LEÓN
Vice-Rector for Academic Staff: ANTONIO VIGUERAS CAMPUZANO
Vice-Rector for Doctorate and Graduate Affairs: PEDRO SÁNCHEZ PALMA
Vice-Rector for Infrastructure: JUAN PATRICIO CASTRO VALDIVIA
Vice-Rector for New Technology: BÁRBARA ÁLVAREZ TORRES
Vice-Rector for Planning and Coordination: JOSÉ ANTONIO CASCALES PUJALTE
Vice-Rector for Research and Innovation: JOSÉ ANTONIO FRANCO LEEMHUIS
Vice-Rector for Student Affairs and Univ. Extension: FRANCISCO MARTÍNEZ GONZÁLEZ
Registrar: JOSÉ LUJÁN ALCARAZ
Man.: ESTHER NATIVIDAD DULCE
Librarian: MA. ÁNGELES GARCÍA DEL TORO
Library of 50,000 vols, 2,528 periodicals
Number of teachers: 500
Number of students: 7,000.

CONSTITUENT SCHOOLS

Escuela de Arquitectura e Ingeniería de Edificación (School of Architecture and Engineering): Paseo Alfonso XIII 50, 30203 Cartagena; tel. and fax (86) 8071223; e-mail eaie@upct.es; internet www.arquide.upct.es; Dir JOSÉ CALVO LÓPEZ.

Escuela de Ingeniería de Caminos y de Minas (School of Civil Engineering and Mining): Calle Paseo Alfonso XIII 52, 30203 Cartagena; tel. and fax (96) 8325425; fax (96) 8327066; e-mail direccion@euitc.upct.es; internet www.upct.es/~euitc; Dir ANTONIO GARCÍA MARTÍN.

Escuela Técnica Superior de Ingeniería Agronómica (Higher Technical School of Agricultural Engineering): Paseo Alfonso XIII 48, 30203 Cartagena; tel. (96) 8325419; fax (96) 8325793; e-mail direccion@etsia.upct .es; internet www.etsia.upct.es; Dir DON PABLO BIELZA LINO.

Escuela Técnica Superior de Ingeniería Industrial (School of Industrial Engineering): Campus Muralla del Mar, Calle Doctor Fleming s/n, 30202 Cartagena; tel. (96) 8325417; fax (96) 8325420; e-mail etsii@etsii .upct.es; internet www.industriales.upct.es; Dir and Dean Dr LUIS JAVIER LOZANO BLANCO.

Escuela Técnica Superior de Ingeniería de Telecomunicación (Higher Technical School of Telecommunications Engineering): Campus Muralla del Mar, Calle Doctor Fleming s/n, 30202 Cartagena; tel. (96) 8338919; fax (96) 8325338; e-mail etsit@ etsit.upct.es; internet www.teleco.upct.es; Dir LEANDRO JUAN LLÁCER.

Escuela Técnica Superior de Ingeniería Naval y Oceánica (Higher Technical School of Naval and Oceanic Engineering): Paseo Alfonso XIII 52, 30203 Cartagena; tel. and fax (96) 8325422; e-mail secretaria@etsino .upct.es; internet www.upct.es/~etsino; Dir DOMINGO L. GARCÍA LÓPEZ.

Facultad de Ciencias de la Empresa (Faculty of Business Science): Calle Real 3, 30201 Cartagena; tel. (96) 8325569; fax (96) 8325577; e-mail decanato@fce.upct.es; internet www.upct.es/~fcee; Dean ANTONIO GARCÍA SÁNCHEZ.

ATTACHED INSTITUTES

Academia General del Aire (General Air Academy): Calle Coronel López Peña s/n, 30729 Santiago de la Ribera, (Murcia); tel. and fax (96) 8189921; e-mail contacto@cud .upct.es; internet www.cud.upct.es; Dir JOA-QUÍN ROCA DORDA.

Escuela Universitaria de Turismo (University School of Tourism): Calle Ingeniero de la Cierva s/n, Edificio UNED 4°, 30203 Cartagena; tel. and fax (96) 8528027; e-mail escuela.turismo@upct.es; internet www .eutcartagena.es; Dir MARÍA DEL MAR ANDREU MARTÍ.

UNIVERSITAT POLITÈCNICA DE CATALUNYA BARCELONATECH

Calle Jordi Girona 31, 08034 Barcelona

Telephone: (93) 4016200

Fax: (93) 4016210

E-mail: international@barcelonatech.upc.edu

Internet: www.barcelonatech.upc.edu

Founded 1971

Regional govt control

Languages of instruction: Spanish, Catalan, English

Academic year: September to June

Rector: ANTONI GIRÓ ROCA

Vice-Rector for Academic Policy: ANNA SAS-TRE REQUENA

Vice-Rector for Academic Staff: ENRIQUE GARCÍA-BERRO MONTILLA

Vice-Rector for Infrastructure: JOSEP BOSCH ESPELTA

Vice-Rector for Institutional Relations: MAR-ISOL MARQUÉS CALVO

Vice-Rector for Int. Policy: PEDRO DÍEZ MEJÍA

Vice-Rector for Science Policy: FRANCESC XAVIER GIL MUR

Vice-Rector for Teaching and Students: XAVIER COLOM FAJULA

Sec.-Gen.: ANA ABELAIRA TATO

Head of Admin.: CARME LÓPEZ POL

Man.: CARME LÓPEZ I POL

Library: each constituent school has an attached library

Number of teachers: 2,750

Number of students: 30,000

Publications: *Informacions*, *The Mag* (4 a year).

CONSTITUENT SCHOOLS

Faculty of Mathematics and Statistics: Calle Pau Gargallo 5, 08028 Barcelona; tel. (93) 4017298; fax (93) 4015881; internet www-fme.upc.es; Dean SEBASTIÀ XAMBÓ DES-CAMPS.

Faculty of Nautical Studies, Barcelona: Pl. de Palau 18, 08003 Barcelona; tel. (93) 4017936; fax (93) 4017910; internet www.fnb .upc.es; Dean ALEXANDRE MONFERRER DE LA PEÑA.

Higher Polytechnic School, Castellde-fels: Avda del Canal Olímpic s/n, 08860 Castelldefels; tel. (93) 4137000; fax (93) 4137007; e-mail info@epsc.upc.es; internet www-epsc.upc.es; Dir MIGUEL VALERO GAR-CÍIA.

Higher Polytechnic School of Building, Barcelona: Avda Doctor Marañon 44–50, 08028 Barcelona; tel. (93) 4016300; fax (93) 4017700; internet www.epseb.upc.edu; Dir FRANCISCO JAVIER LLOVERA SÁEZ.

Higher Polytechnic School of Engineering, Vilanova i la Geltrú: Avda Víctor Balaguer s/n, 08800 Vilanova i la Geltrú; tel. (93) 8967701; fax (93) 8967700; internet www .upc.edu/epsevg; Dir ANDREU CATALÀ MAL-LOFRÉ.

Higher Technical School of Architecture, Barcelona: Avda Diagonal 649, 08028 Barcelona; tel. (93) 4016359; fax (93) 4015871; internet www.upc.es/etsab; Dir JAUME SANMARTÍ VERDAGUER.

Higher Technical School of Architecture, Vallès: Calle Pere Serra 1–15, 08190 St Cugat del Vallès; tel. (93) 4017900; fax (93) 4017901; e-mail pilar@etsavdaupc.es; internet www.etsavdaupc.es; Dir RAMON SAS-TRE SASTRE.

Higher Technical School of Civil Engineering, Barcelona: Calle Jordi Girona 1–3, Campus Norte, Edif. C2, 08034 Barcelona; tel. (93) 4016900; fax (93) 4016504; internet www.camins.upc.es; Dir FRANCESC ROBUSTÉ I ANTON.

Higher Technical School of Industrial Engineering, Barcelona: Avda Diagonal 647, 08028 Barcelona; tel. (93) 4016700; fax (93) 4016600; e-mail punt_inf@etseib.upc.es; internet www.etseib.upc.es; Dir FERRAN PUERTA SALES.

Higher Technical School of Industrial Engineering, Terrassa: Calle Colom 11, 08222 Terrassa; tel. (93) 7398102; fax (93) 7398101; internet etseit-ct.upc.es; Dir JAUME GIBERT PEDROSA.

School of Informatics, Barcelona: Calle Jordi Girona 1–3, Campus Norte, Edif. B6, 08034 Barcelona; tel. (93) 4017000; fax (93) 4017113; e-mail informacio@fib.upc.es; internet www.fib.upc.es; Dean MARÍA RIBERA SANCHO.

Telecommunications Engineering School of Barcelona: Calle Jordi Girona 1–3, Campus Nord, Edif. B3, 08034 Barcelona; tel. (93) 4016800; fax (93) 4016801; e-mail infoteleco@etsetb.upc.edu; internet

www.etsetb.upc.edu; Dean Prof. FERRAN MARQUÈS.

University Polytechnic School, Manresa: Avda de les Bases de Manresa 61–73, 08240 Manresa; tel. (93) 8777200; fax (93) 8777202; e-mail eupm@eupm.upc.es; internet www.eupm.upc.es; Dir JUAN JORGE SÁNCHEZ.

University School of Industrial Engineering, Terrassa: Calle Colom 1, 08222 Terrassa; tel. (93) 7398132; fax (93) 7398225; internet euetit-ct.upc.es; Dir JUAN ANTONIO GALLARDO LEÓN.

University School of Optics and Optometry, Terrassa: Calle Violinista Vellsolà 37, 08222 Terrassa; tel. (93) 7398300; fax (93) 7398301; internet euoot-ct.upc.es; Dir NÚRIA LUPÓN BAS.

ATTACHED INSTITUTES

Caixa Terrassa Business College: Ctra de Terrassa, Km 3, 08227 Terrassa; tel. (93) 7301900; fax (93) 7301901; internet www .euncet.com; Dir JORDI BALCELLS GENÉ.

Catalan Technical Foundation School of Photography: Calle de la Igualtat 33, 08222 Terrassa; tel. (93) 7398312; fax (93) 7398365; internet www.citm.upc.es; Dir of Centre of the Image and Multimedia Technology MIQUEL MORÓN TARIFA.

College of Agricultural Engineering: Comte d'Urgell 187, 08036 Barcelona; tel. (93) 4137500; fax (93) 4137501; internet www .esab.upc.es; Dir F. XAVIER MARTÍNEZ FARRÉ.

College of Industrial Engineering, Barcelona: Comte d'Urgell 187, 08036 Barcelona; tel. (93) 4137400; fax (93) 4137401; internet www.euetib.upc.es; Dir MARTÍ LLO-RENS MORRAJA.

College of Industrial Engineering, Igualada: Plaça del Rei 15, 08700 Igualada; tel. (93) 8035300; fax (93) 8031589; internet www .euetii.upc.es; Deputy Dir RITA PUIG I VIDAL.

College of Knitted Fabric Engineering: Plaça de la Indústria 1, 08360 Canet de Mar; tel. (93) 7940150; fax (93) 7954817; internet www.diba.es/canet; Dir MIQUEL SOLER LUQUE.

Institute of Education: Calle Jordi Girona 29, Edif. Nexus II, Despatx OD, 08034 Barcelona; tel. (93) 4137643; e-mail info .ice@upc.es; internet www.ice.upc.es; Dir RAFAEL PINDADO RICO.

Institute of Industrial Systems Organization and Control: Avda Diagonal 647, 11°, Edif. H, 08028 Barcelona; tel. (93) 4016653; fax (93) 4016605; e-mail enric .fossas@upc.es; internet www.ioc.upc.es; Dir ENRIC FOSSAS COLET.

Institute of Power Engineering: Avda Diagonal 647, 08028 Barcelona; tel. (93) 4016692; fax (93) 4017149; e-mail ortega@ inte.upc.es; internet www.upc.es/inte/index .html; Dir XAVIER ORTEGA ARAMBURU.

Institute of Textile Research and Industrial Cooperation, Terrassa: Calle Colom 15, 08222 Terrassa; tel. (93) 7398270; fax (93) 7398272; e-mail director-ins@intexter.upc.es; internet www.ct.upc.es/intexter; Dir LLIBERT COLL TORTOSA.

Mataró Technical College: Avda Puig i Cadafalch 101–111, 08303 Mataró; tel. (93) 7574404; fax (93) 7570524; internet www .eupmt.es; Dir JOAN GIL LÓPEZ.

School of Business Administration: Aragó 55, 08015 Barcelona; tel. (93) 2278090; fax (93) 3194436; e-mail eae@eae .es; internet www.eae.es; Dir FERNANDO CASADO JUAN.

School of Multimedia of the UPC Foundation: Calle de la Igualtat 33, 08222 Terrassa.

School of Occupational Hazard Prevention: Calle Dulcet 2–10, 08034 Barcelona; tel. (93) 2804542; fax (93) 2803642; e-mail neus.guardiola@fpc.upc.es; internet www.escuela-prevencion.com.

UNIVERSIDAD POLITÉCNICA DE MADRID

Calle Ramiro de Maeztu 7, 28040 Madrid

Telephone: (91) 3366000

Fax: (91) 3366173

Internet: www.upm.es

Founded 1971

State control

Language of instruction: Spanish

Academic year: October to July

Rector: JAVIER UCEDA ANTOLÍN

Vice-Rector for Academic Administration and Teaching Staff: EMILIO MÍNGUEZ TORRES

Vice-Rector for Academic Affairs and Strategic Planning: CARLOS CONDE LÁZARO

Vice-Rector for Doctorate and Postgraduate Studies: ERNESTINA MENASALVAS RUÍZ

Vice-Rector for Economic Planning: ADOLFO CAZORLA MONTERO

Vice-Rector for Information and Communication: JOSÉ MANUEL PERALES PERALES

Vice-Rector for Int. Relations: JOSÉ MANUEL PÁEZ BORRALLO

Vice-Rector for Research: GONZALO LEÓN SERRANO

Vice-Rector for Student Affairs: LUIS GARCÍA ESTEBAN

Registrar: CRISTINA PÉREZ GARCÍA

Chief Admin. Officer: SIXTO GARCÍA ALONSO

Library: each constituent school has an attached library; 775,000 vols, 11,800 periodicals

Number of teachers: 3,414

Number of students: 41,374.

CONSTITUENT SCHOOLS

Faculty of Computer Science: Campus Montegancedo, Boadilla del Monte, 28660 Madrid; tel. (91) 3367399; fax (91) 3367412; internet www.fi.upm.es; Dean FRANCISCO JAVIER SEGOVIA PÉREZ.

Faculty of Physical Activity and Sport: C/ Martín Fierro s/n, Ciudad Universitaria, 28040 Madrid; tel. (91) 3364000; fax (91) 5441331; internet www.inef.upm.es; Dir JAVIER SAMPEDRO MOLINUEVO.

Higher Technical School of Aeronautical Engineering: Pza Cardenal Cisneros 3, Ciudad Universitaria, 28040 Madrid; tel. (91) 3366300; fax (91) 5439859; internet www.aero.upm.es; Dir MIGUEL ANGEL GÓMEZ TIERNO.

Higher Technical School of Agronomy: Avda Complutense s/n, Ciudad Universitaria, 28040 Madrid; tel. (91) 3365600; fax (91) 5434879; internet www.etsia.upm.es; Dir JESÚS VÁZQUEZ MINGUELA.

Higher Technical School of Architecture: Avda Juan de Herrera 4, Ciudad Universitaria, 28040 Madrid; tel. (91) 3366524; fax (91) 5442481; internet www.aq.upm.es; Dir LUIS MALDONADO RAMOS.

Higher Technical School of Civil Engineering: Ciudad Universitaria, 28040 Madrid; tel. (91) 3363800; fax (91) 5492289; internet www.caminos.upm.es; Dir JUAN ANTONIO SANTAMERA SÁNCHEZ.

Higher Technical School of Forestry: Ciudad Universitaria, 28040 Madrid; tel. (91) 3367073; fax (91) 5439557; internet www.montes.upm.es; Dir ANTONIO NOTARIO GÓMEZ.

Higher Technical School of Industrial Engineering: Calle José Gutiérrez Abascal 2, 28006 Madrid; tel. (91) 3363060; internet www.etsii.upm.es; Dir JESÚS FÉLEZ MINDÁN.

Higher Technical School of Mining Engineering: Ríos Rosas 21, 28003 Madrid; tel. (91) 3367071; internet www.minas.upm.es; Dir BENJAMÍN CALVO PÉREZ.

Higher Technical School of Shipbuilding: Avda Arco de la Victoria s/n, Ciudad Universitaria, 28020 Madrid; tel. (91) 3367140; fax (91) 3367511; internet www.etsin.upm.es; Dean and Dir Asst Prof. Dr JESUS PANADERO PASTRANA.

Higher Technical School of Telecommunications Engineering: Ciudad Universitaria, 28040 Madrid; tel. (91) 3367234; fax (91) 5439652; internet www.etsit.upm.es; Dir GUILLERMO CISNEROS PÉREZ.

Polytechnic School of Higher Education: C/ Ramiro de Maeztu 7, 28040 Madrid; tel. (91) 3365912; fax (91) 3365912; Dir JOSÉ LUIS ENRÍQUEZ ESCUDERO.

University School of Aeronautical Engineering: Pza Cardenal Cisneros s/n, Ciudad Universitaria, 28040 Madrid; tel. (91) 3364166; fax (91) 3367511; internet www.euita.upm.es; Dir MIGUEL ÁNGEL BARCALA MONTEJANO.

University School of Agricultural Engineering: Ciudad Universitaria, 28040 Madrid; tel. (91) 3365400; internet www.agricolas.upm.es; Dir FRANCISCO GONZÁLEZ TORRES.

University School of Architecture: Avda Juan de Herrera, 6, Ciudad Universitaria, 28040 Madrid; tel. (91) 3367636; fax (91) 3367644; internet www.euatm.upm.es; Dir MERCEDES DEL RIO MERINO.

University School of Computer Science: Camino de la Arboleda s/n, Campus Sur, 28031 Madrid; tel. (91) 3367903; internet www.eui.upm.es; Dir JESÚS GARCIA LÓPEZ DELACALLE.

University School of Forestry: Avda Ramiro de Maeztu s/n, Ciudad Universitaria, 28040 Madrid; tel. (91) 3367652; internet www.forestales.upm.es; Dir GERMÁN GLARIA GALCERÁN.

University School of Industrial Engineering: Ronda de Valencia, 3, 28012 Madrid; tel. (91) 3367699; internet www.euiti.upm.es; Dir SARA GÓMEZ MARTÍN.

University School of Public Works: Alfonso XII 3, 28014 Madrid; tel. (91) 3367743; fax (91) 3367958; internet www.op.upm.es; Dir CARLOS DELGADO ALONSO-MARTIRENA.

University School of Telecommunications Engineering: Camino de la Arboleda s/n, Campus Sur, 28031 Madrid; tel. (91) 3367780; fax (91) 3319229; internet www.euitt.upm.es; Dir CESAR SANZ ÁLVARO (acting).

Higher Technical School of Topography, Geodesy and Cartography: Camino de la Arboleda s/n, Campus Sur, 28031 Madrid; tel. (91) 3367915; internet www.euitto.upm.es; Dir ROSA MARIANA CHUECA CASTELO.

ATTACHED INSTITUTES

Higher Centre of Fashion Design: Camino de la Arboleda s/n, Campus Sur, 28031 Madrid; tel. (91) 3310126; fax (91) 3321767; internet www.csdmm.upm.es; Dir DIANA FERNÁNDEZ GONZÁLEZ.

Higher School of Brewing: E. T. S. de Ingenieros Industriales, Laboratorio de Tecnología Química, Calle José Gutiérrez Abascal 2, 28006 Madrid; tel. (91) 3363190; fax (91) 3363009; e-mail eroche@etsii.upm.es; internet www.aetcm.es/escuela/escuela.htm#inicio; Dir ERCARNACIÓN RODRÍGUEZ HURTADO.

Institute of Automobile Research: Ctra de Valencia Km 7, Campus Sur UPM, 28031 Madrid; tel. (91) 3365300; fax (91) 3365302; e-mail insia@insia.upm.es; internet www.insia.upm.es; Dir FRANCISCO APARICIO IZQUIERDO.

Institute of Education: C/ Profesor Aranguren s/n, Ciudad Universitaria, 28040 Madrid; tel. (91) 3366815; fax (91) 3366812; e-mail ice@ice.upm.es; internet www.ice.upm.es; Dir ROSA MARÍA GONZÁLEZ TIRADOS.

Institute of Microgravity 'Ignacio Da Riva': UPM, ETSI Aeronáuticos, 28040 Madrid; tel. (91) 3366353; fax (91) 3366363; e-mail idr@idr.upm.es; internet www.idr.upm.es; Dir JOSÉ MESEGUER RUÍZ.

Institute of Nuclear Fusion: E. T. S. de Ingenieros Industriales, Calle José Gutiérrez Abascal 2, 28006 Madrid; tel. (91) 3363108; Dir JOSÉ MANUEL PERLADO.

Institute of Optoelectronic Systems and Microtechnology: ETSI Telecomunicación (UPM), Ciudad Universitaria, 28040 Madrid; tel. (91) 3367321; fax (91) 5490909; e-mail montse.isom@die.upm.es; internet www.isom.upm.es; Dir ENRIQUE CALLEJA PARDO.

Institute of Solar Energy: E. T. S. de Ingenieros de Telecomunicación, Ciudad Universitaria, 28040 Madrid; tel. (91) 5441060; fax (91) 5446341; e-mail info@ies-def.upm.es; internet www.ies.upm.es; Dir CARLOS DE CAÑIZO NADAL.

Laser Centre: Edif. Tecnológico 'La Arboleda', Campus Sur UPM, Carretera de Valencia Km 7300, 28031 Madrid; tel. (91) 3324280; fax (91) 336906; e-mail jlocana@faii.etsii.upm.es; internet www.upmlaser.upm.es; Dir JOSÉ LUIS OCAÑA MORENO.

UNIVERSIDAD POLITÉCNICA DE VALENCIA

Camino de Vera s/n, 46022 Valencia

Telephone: (96) 3877000

Fax: (96) 3879009

E-mail: informacion@upv.es

Internet: www.upv.es

Founded 1968

State control

Languages of instruction: Spanish, Valencian

Academic year: October to June

Rector: JUAN JULIÁ IGUAL

Vice-Rector for Campus and Infrastructure: SALVADOR LÓPEZ GALARZA

Vice-Rector for Culture, Communication and Institutional Image: JUAN BAUTISTA PEIRÓ LÓPEZ

Vice-Rector for Devt of ITC Technologies: VICENT J. BOTTI NAVARRO

Vice-Rector for Faculty and Academic Planning: JOSÉ LUIS BERNÉ VALERO

Vice-Rector for Int. Relations and Cooperation: JUAN MIGUEL MARTÍNEZ RUBIO

Vice-Rector for Planning and Innovation: FRANCISCO JOSÉ MORA MÁS

Vice-Rector for Quality and Academic Assessment: JUAN JAIME CANO HURTADO

Vice-Rector for Research: AMPARO CHIRALT BOIX

Vice-Rector for Social Affairs and Corporate Social Responsibility: MARÍA PILAR SANTAMARINA SIURANA

Vice-Rector for Sport: ÁNGEL FRANCISCO BENITO BEORLEGUI

Vice-Rector for Student Affairs: VICTORIA VIVANCOS RAMÓN

Vice-Rector for Studies and European Convergence: MIGUEL ANGEL FERNÁNDEZ PRADA

Registrar: VICENT CASTELLANO I CERVERA

Man.: JOSÉ ANTONIO PÉREZ GARCÍA

Librarian: JOSÉ LLORENS SÁNCHEZ

Library of 52,000 vols, 10,000 periodicals

Number of teachers: 2,500

Number of students: 37,500.

CONSTITUENT SCHOOLS

Higher Technical School of Agronomy: Edificio 3H, Camino de Vera s/n, 46022 Valencia; tel. (96) 3877130; fax (96) 3877139; e-mail etsia@etsia.upvnet.upv.es; internet www.etsia.upv.es; Dir NEMESIO FERNÁNDEZ MARTÍNEZ.

Higher Technical School of Architecture: Edificio 2I, Camino de Vera s/n, 46022 Valencia; tel. (96) 3877110; fax (96) 3877119; e-mail etsa@upvnet.upv.es; internet www.arq.upv.es; Dir IGNACIO BOSCH REIG.

Higher Technical School of Applied Computer Science: Edificio 1G, Camino de Vera s/n, 46022 Valencia; tel. (96) 3877210; fax (96) 3877219; e-mail einf_ei@upvnet.upv.es; internet www.eui.upv.es; Dir ANTONIO ROBLES MARTÍNEZ.

Higher Technical School of Building Management: Edificio 1B, Camino de Vera s/n, 46022 Valencia; tel. (96) 3877120; fax (96) 3877943; e-mail euat@upvnet.upv.es; internet www.arq.upv.es; Dir RAFAEL CAPUZ LLADRÓ.

Higher Technical School of Civil Engineering: Edificio 4H, Camino de Vera s/n, 46022 Valencia; tel. (96) 3877150; fax (96) 3877159; e-mail etsiccp@upvnet.upv.es; internet www.iccp.upv.es; Dir JOSÉ AGUILAR HERRANDO.

Higher Technical School of Design Engineering: Edificio 7B, Camino de Vera s/n, 46022 Valencia; tel. (96) 3877180; fax (96) 3877189; e-mail info@etsid.upv.es; internet www.etsid.upv.es; Dir ENRIQUE BALLESTER SARRIAS.

Higher Technical School of Geodesic, Cartographic and Topographic Engineering: Edificio 7E, Camino de Vera s/n, 46022 Valencia; tel. (96) 3877160; fax (96) 3877169; e-mail etsigct@upvnet.upv.es; internet www.top.upv.es; Dir MANUEL CHUECA PAZOS.

Higher Technical School of Industrial Engineering: Edificio 5F, Camino de Vera s/n, 46022 Valencia; tel. (96) 3877170; fax (96) 3877179; e-mail etsii@upvnet.upv.es; internet www.etsii.upv.es; Dir JUAN JAIME CANO HURTADO.

Higher Technical School of Telecommunications Engineering: Edificio 4D, Camino de Vera s/n, 46022 Valencia; tel. (96) 3877190; fax (96) 3877199; e-mail etsitv@upvnet.upv.es; internet www.etsit.upv.es; Dir ELÍAS DE LOS REYES DAVÓ.

Higher Technical School of the Rural Environment and Oenology: Avda Blasco Ibáñez 21, 46010 Valencia; tel. (96) 3877140; fax (96) 3877149; e-mail euita@upvnet.upv.es; internet www.euita.upv.es; Dir SANTIAGO GUILLEM PICÓ.

Faculty of Business Administration and Management: Edificio 8H, Camino de Vera s/n, 46022 Valencia; tel. (96) 3879270; fax (96) 3879279; e-mail ade@upv.es; internet www.upv.es/ade; Dean ENRIQUE DE MIGUEL FERNÁNDEZ.

Faculty of Computer Science: Edificio 1E, Camino de Vera s/n, 46022 Valencia; tel. (96) 3877200; fax (96) 3877924; e-mail finfv@upvnet.upv.es; internet www.fiv.upv.es; Dean EMILIO SANCHÍS ARNAL.

Faculty of Fine Arts: Edificio 3L, Camino de Vera s/n, 46022 Valencia; tel. (96) 3877220; fax (96) 3879229; e-mail fbbaa@upvnet.upv.es; internet www.bbaa.upv.es; Dean ELÍAS MIGUEL PÉREZ GARCÍA.

Higher Polytechnic School, Alcoy: Pl. Ferrándiz Carbonell s/n, 08301 Alcoy (Alicante); tel. (96) 6528400; fax (96) 6528409; e-mail epsa@upvnet.upv.es; internet www

.epsa.upv.es; Dir ENRIQUE JUAN MASIÁ BUADES.

Higher Polytechnic School, Gandía: Carretera Nazaret-Oliva s/n, 46730 Gandía (Valencia); tel. (96) 2849300; fax (96) 2849309; e-mail epsg@upvnet.upv.es; internet www.epsg.upv.es; Dir MARÍA MANUELA FERNÁNDEZ MÉNDEZ.

ATTACHED INSTITUTIONS

Escuela Universitaria Ford España: 46440 Almussafes, (Valencia); tel. (96) 1792246; fax (96) 1792255; e-mail asanramo@ford.com; internet www.escuelaford.com; areas of study: mechanical engineering.

Florida Training Centre: Calle Rei En Jaume I 2, Apdo 15, 46470 Catarroja (Valencia); tel. (96) 1220380; fax (96) 1269933; e-mail info.general@florida-uni.es; internet www.florida.es; aeas of study: mechanics, industrial electronics; Gen. Dir EMPAR MARTÍNEZ BONAFÉ.

Colleges
GENERAL

Schiller International University—Madrid: (For general information, see entry for Schiller International University in Germany chapter) Calle Serrano 156, Plaza de la Republica Argentina, 28002 Madrid; tel. (91) 4482488; fax (91) 4452110; e-mail mad_admissions@schiller.edu; internet www.schiller.edu/campuses/madrid-spain; f. 1967; Dir L. BURGUNDE.

Universidad Internacional Menéndez Pelayo: Calle Isaac Peral 23, 28040 Madrid; tel. (94) 2298800; fax (94) 2298820; internet www.uimp.es; f. 1932; offers long-vacation courses to Spanish and foreign students, and grants fellowships for scientific research; campuses in Santander, Barcelona, Cuenca, Santa Cruz de Tenerife, La Coruña, Seville, Valencia, Formigal (Huesca); library: 16,000 vols; 700 teachers; 15,000 students; Rector SALVADOR ORDÓÑEZ DELGADO.

ECONOMICS AND LAW

ESADE (Escuela Superior de Administración y Dirección de Empresas) (Higher School of Administration and Business Management): Avda Pedralbes 60–62, 08034 Barcelona; tel. (93) 2806162; fax (93) 2048105; e-mail info@esade.edu; internet www.esade.edu; f. 1958; schools of business, law, languages, tourism; 4 campuses: 2 in Barcelona, and 1 each in Madrid and Buenos Aires, Argentina; Dir-Gen. EUGENIA BIETO.

EuroArab Management School (EAMS): Calle Cárcel Baja 3, 18001 Granada; tel. (95) 8805050; fax (95) 8800152; f. 1995, jtly by the EU and the League of Arab States, with support of Spanish Govt; management devt; Dir-Gen. JOAQUÍN ABÓS.

Institut Universitari d'Estudis Europeus: Universitat Autonoma de Barcelona, Edif. E1, 08193 Bellaterra (Barcelona); tel. (93) 5812016; fax (93) 5813063; internet www.iuee.eu; f. 1985; studies in political, economic, cultural, scientific and judicial aspects of modern Europe; participates in conferences on European issues throughout Spain; Dir Dr BLANCA VILÀ.

Instituto de Empresa (Business School): María de Molina 11, 28006 Madrid; tel. (91) 5689600; fax (91) 4115503; e-mail admissions@ie.edu; internet www.ie.edu; f. 1973; 500 teachers; 7,800 students; Dean SANTIAGO IÑÍGUEZ DE OZOÑO.

Real Centro Universitario 'Escorial—María Cristina': Paseo de los Alamillos 2, 28200 San Lorenzo del Escorial, (Madrid); tel. (91) 8904545; fax (91) 8906609; e-mail contacto@rcumariacristina.com; internet www.rcumariacristina.com; f. 1892; private college of the Augustinian Fathers accredited by Universidad Complutense de Madrid; library: 57,000 vols, 500 periodicals; 60 teachers; 1,200 students; Rector EDELMIRO MATEOS MATEOS; publs *Anuario jurídico y económico escurialense* (1 a year), *La Ciudad de Dios* (4 a year), *Nueva Etapa* (1 a year).

MEDICINE

Escuela Andaluza de Salud Pública (Andalusian School of Public Health): Cuesta del Observatorio 4, 18080 Granada; tel. (95) 8027400; fax (95) 8027503; e-mail comunicacion@easp.es; internet www.easp.es; f. 1985; affiliated with Universidad de Granada; Masters degree and other courses in public health management and services; drug information centre; cancer registry; library: 56,000 vols, 1,229 current periodicals; 50 teachers; 2,000 students; Dir HERMINIA MUÑOZ.

MILITARY SCIENCE

Escuela de Guerra del Ejército (Army War College): Santa Cruz de Marcenado 25, 28015 Madrid; tel. (91) 5242000; fax (91) 5425509; f. 1842; library: 140,000 vols; 60 teachers; 180 students; Dir Brig.-Gen. RICARDO MARTÍNEZ ISIDORO.

TECHNOLOGY

Escuela Técnica Superior de Ingenieros Industriales (Higher School for Industrial Engineers): José Gutiérrez Abascal 2, 28006 Madrid; tel. (91) 3363060; fax (91) 5618618; e-mail administrador.industriales@upm.es; internet www.etsii.upm.es; f. 1850; library: see Libraries; 350 teachers; 3,500 students; Dir JESUS FÉLEZ MINDÁN.

ETEA—Institución Universitaria de la Compañía de Jesús: Escritor Castilla Aguayo 4, Apdo 439, 14004 Córdoba; tel. (95) 7222100; fax (95) 7222101; e-mail comunica@etea.com; internet www.etea.com; f. 1963; undergraduate and postgraduate courses in business administration; research institute; extension courses in management; management consultancy services; 150 teachers; library: 50,000 vols; Dir GABRIEL PÉREZ ALCALÁ.

Institut Químic de Sarrià (Sarrià Institute of Chemistry): Universitat Ramon Llull, Calle Via Augusta 390, 08017 Barcelona; tel. (93) 2672000; fax (93) 2056266; e-mail secre@iqs.edu; internet www.iqs.edu; f. 1916; library: 55,000 vols, 780 periodicals; 125 teachers; 1,500 students; Dir-Gen. Dr ENRIC JULIÀ; publs *Afinidad* (6 a year), *IQS* (1 a year).

Schools of Art, Architecture and Music

Conservatori Municipal de Música de Barcelona: Bruc 110–112, 08009 Barcelona; tel. (93) 4584302; fax (93) 4593104; e-mail conservatori@cmmb.cat; internet www.cmmb.cat; f. 1886; library: 27,400 vols and scores, 7,250 items of audio material; 102 teachers; 1,815 students; Pres. ALBERT LLANAS.

Conservatorio Superior de Música de Málaga: Plaza Maestro Artola 2, 29013 Málaga; tel. (95) 1298340; fax (95) 1298341;

e-mail info@conserv-sup-malaga.com; internet www.conserv-sup-malaga.com; f. 1880; Dir MARIANO TRIVIÑO ARREBOLA; publ. *Hoquet* (1 a year).

Conservatorio Superior de Música de Valencia: Calle del Cineasta Ricardo Muñoz Suay s/n, 46013, Valencia; tel. (96) 3605316; fax (96) 3605701; e-mail 46013129@centres .cult.gua.es; internet www.csmvalencia.es; f. 1879; library: 12,000 vols; 40 teachers; 900 students; Pres. and Dir EDUARDO MONTESINOS COMAS; publ. *Memoria* (1 a year).

Conservatorio Superior de Música 'Rafael Orozco' de Córdoba: Calle Angel Saavedra 1, 14003 Córdoba; tel. (95) 7379647; fax (95) 7379653; e-mail oficina@csmcordoba.com; internet www.csmcordoba.com; f. 1902; library: 15,000 vols; 95 teachers; 3,000 students; Dir MANUEL ABELLA FÉRRIZ; publ. *Musicalia*.

Conservatorio Superior de Música 'Manuel Castillo': Calle Baños 48, 41002 Seville; tel. (95) 4915630; fax (95) 4374373; e-mail secretaria@consev.es; internet www .csmsev.es; f. 1933; library: 25,000 books and scores; 120 teachers; 2,400 students; Dir LUIS IGNACIO MARÍN GARCÍA; publ. *Diferencias*.

Conservatorio Superior de Música de Murcia: Paseo del Malecón 9, 30004 Murcia; tel. (96) 8294758; fax (96) 8294756; e-mail info@csmmurcia.com; internet www .csmmurcia.com; f. 1916; library: 1,546 vols, 52 periodicals, 3,914 musical scores, 1,704 audio materials; 85 teachers; 3,000 students; Dir MIGUEL BARÓ BO; publ. *Cadencia* (3 a year).

Subordinate Institute:

   Escuela Superior de Arte Dramático de Murcia: Plaza de los Apóstoles, 30001 Murcia; tel. (96) 8214629; fax (96) 8217636;

internet www.esad-murcia.com; f. 1918 as Conservatorio Provincial de Música y Declamación; changed name to Escuela Superior de Arte Dramático y Danza 1982; present name adopted 1993; Dir JUAN ÁNGEL SERRANO MASEGOSO.

Escuela Superior de Bellas Artes de San Carlos (San Carlos School of Fine Arts): Calle San Pio V 9, 46010 Valencia; f. 1756; library: 5,100 vols; 30 teachers; 300 students; Dir DANIEL DE NUEDA LLISIONA.

Escuela Superior de Música Reina Sofía (Reina Sofía Higher School of Music): Plaza de Oriente s/n, 28013 Madrid; tel. (91) 5230419; fax (91) 5329661; e-mail esmrs@albeniz.com; internet www .escuelasuperiordemusicareinasofia.es; f. 1991; depts of performance, academic studies, artistic studies, and complementary training; library: 1,200 books, 3,600 musical scores, 2,400 CDs, 2,500 LPs, 2,500 video and audio cassettes; Pres. PALOMA O'SHEA.

Escuela Técnica Superior de Arquitectura de Sevilla (Seville School of Architecture): Avda Reina Mercedes 2, 41012 Seville; tel. (95) 4556501; fax (95) 4556534; e-mail directoretsa@us.es; internet www.etsa.us.es; f. 1964; library: 18,000 vols; 160 teachers; 2,200 students; Dir Dr NARCISO-JESÚS VÁZQUEZ CARRETERO.

IES 'Islas Filipinas': Calle Jesús Maestro 3, 28003 Madrid; tel. (91) 5344349; fax (91) 5537592; e-mail ies.islasfilipinas.madrid@educa.madrid.org; internet www .islasfilipinas.com; f. 1968 as Escuela Nacional de Artes Gráfica; name changed to Instituto de Formación Profesional 'Islas Filipinas' 1985; present name subsequently adopted; building and civil engineering, delineation, graphic arts, information tech-

nology; library: 15,000 vols; 110 teachers; 2,000 students; Dir JUSTA ACEDO BARTOLOMÉ.

Musikene—Euskal Herriko Goi-Mailako Musika Ikastegia/Conservatorio Superior de Música del País Vasco: Palacio Miramar, Mirakontxa 48, 20007 Donostia-San Sebastián; tel. (94) 3316778; fax (94) 3316916; e-mail info@musikene.net; internet www.musikene.net; f. 2001; 150 teachers; Gen. Coordinator CARMEN RODRÍGUEZ SUSO; publ. *Ahaire*.

Real Conservatorio Profesional de Música 'Manuel de Falla': Calle Marqués del Real Tesoro 10, 11001 Cádiz; tel. (95) 6243106; fax (95) 6243109; internet www .conservatoriomanueldefalla.es; f. 1860 as Academia Santa Cecilia; 60 professors; 1,000 students; Dir MIGUEL GARRIDO ALDOMAR.

Real Conservatorio Superior de Música de Madrid (Royal Academy of Music, Madrid): Calle Santa Isabel 53, Planta Baja, 28012 Madrid; tel. (91) 5392901; fax (91) 5275822; e-mail secretario.rcsmm@telefonica .net; internet www.educa.madrid.org/web/ csm.realconservatorio.madrid; f. 1830; library: 135,000 vols, incl. 10,000 original 18th- and 19th-century musical scores; 150 teachers; 700 students; Dir ANSELMO IGNACIO DE LA CAMPA DÍAZ; publ. *Musica* (1 a year).

Real Escuela Superior de Arte Dramático (Royal School of Dramatic Art): Avda de Nazaret 2, 28009 Madrid; tel. (91) 5042151; fax (91) 5741138; e-mail secretaria@resad.es; internet www.resad.es; f. 1831; library: 28,300 vols; 50 teachers; 350 students; Dir ÁNGEL MARTÍNEZ ROGER; publ. *Acotaciones* (2 a year).

SRI LANKA

The Higher Education System

Institutions of higher education pre-date the independence of Sri Lanka (formerly Ceylon) from the United Kingdom in 1948, with the oldest being the University of Colombo, which was founded in 1921 (present name 1979). In 1978 an Act of Parliament created the current university system, following which several existing colleges were promoted to university status. In 2010 there was a total of 97,864 students enrolled at 15 universities under the jurisdiction of the University Grants Commission, which supervises and administers all aspects of higher education. The universities are mostly government funded, and although students do not pay tuition fees they are required to pay registration and examination fees. However, students at the Open University (founded 1980) and postgraduate students at private higher education institutions are required to pay tuition fees. Private higher education institutions are not recognized by the state in Sri Lanka. They are not quality assured by the University Grants Commission or other Sri Lankan authorities as they are not considered to offer legal degrees. Consequently, they cannot issue Sri Lankan degrees but operate in conjunction with overseas universities, including British institutions. There are private colleges that award post-secondary qualifications but not degrees. In August 2011 the Ministry of Higher Education announced plans to upgrade six universities, in Colombo, Peradeniya, Moratuwa, Kelaniya, Ruhuna and Sri Jayewardenepura, with US $6m. to be disbursed with a view to improving standards of teaching, research and infrastructure at each of the institutions in a bid to bolster their international reputation.

New regulations regarding university entrance requirements came into effect in 2000, as a result of which students are now required to complete a minimum of three subjects at GCE A-Level in addition to sitting a Common General Paper and a General English Paper, although the Open University (founded 1980) does not have formal entrance requirements. A quota system is in play, whereby 40% of places are awarded on a merit-basis, 55% are divided between the 25 administrative districts according to population size, and 5% are reserved for students from educationally underprivileged districts (primarily in the north, east and south-east of the country). In 2011 the Government introduced a controversial compulsory leadership training programme, which requires all students selected for undergraduate courses at state universities to undergo a three-week period of training at military and police bases managed by the Ministry of Defence and Urban Development. The undergraduate Bachelors degree is classified as either 'General' or 'Special': the former lasts three years and covers three subjects in equal depth, while the latter lasts four years and is a subject-specific programme of study, culminating in a dissertation. Professional degrees, which are offered in technical or practical disciplines such as medicine, engineering and architecture, last four years (or, in the case of medicine, five years plus an additional internship year). Graduates with the Bachelors degree are eligible for the one-year Postgraduate Diploma or the two-year Masters degree, with the latter usually requiring completion of theory examinations and submission of a dissertation. Finally, the Doctorate (mostly PhD) is awarded after a two- or three-year period of research following award of the Masters, culminating in submission of a thesis.

Post-secondary technical and vocational education comprises: short-term training courses of between six and 10 months offered to all school-leavers by various institutions under the control of the Ministry of Education; and courses of two to four years leading to the award of, variously, the National Certificate, National Diploma and Higher National Diploma. City and Guilds qualifications are also available at various institutions and are very popular. The National Vocational Qualifications Framework of Sri Lanka was introduced in 2005 in a bid to unify Technical and Vocational Education and Training (TVET). The framework and skill standards are based on the New Zealand Qualifications Framework. The Tertiary and Vocational Education Commission is the national lead body for the implementation of TVET in Sri Lanka.

Regulatory and Representative Bodies

GOVERNMENT

Ministry of Culture and the Arts: Eigth Fl., Sethsiripaya, Battaramulla, Colombo; tel. (11) 2872001; fax (11) 2872024; e-mail itasst@cultural.gov.lk; internet www.cultural.gov.lk; Min. T. B. EKANAYAKA.

Ministry of Education: 'Isurupaya', Pela-watta, Battaramulla, Colombo; tel. (11) 2785141; fax (11) 2785162; e-mail info@moe.gov.lk; internet www.moe.gov.lk; Min. BANDULA GUNAWARDHANA.

Ministry of Higher Education: 18 Ward Place, Colombo 7; tel. (11) 2694486; fax (11) 2697239; e-mail mohe@mohe.gov.lk; internet www.mohe.gov.lk; Min. S. B. DISSANAYAKE.

ACCREDITATION

Quality Assurance and Accreditation Council of the University Grants Commission: 65/4 Kirula Rd, Colombo; tel. (11) 2368794; fax (11) 2368621; e-mail colinpeiris@qaacouncil.lk; internet www.qaacouncil.lk; f. 2004; ensures quality, continuous devt, accreditation, efficient performance of Sri Lankan higher education instns;

Chair. Prof. M. T. M. JIFFRY; Dir Prof. COLIN N. PEIRIS (acting).

FUNDING

University Grants Commission: 20 Ward Pl., Colombo 7; tel. (11) 2695301; fax (11) 2688045; e-mail secretary@ugc.ac.lk; internet www.ugc.ac.lk; f. 1978; allocates funds to the univs and univ. institutes, serves as the central admissions agency for undergraduate studies; plans, coordinates and monitors activities of the univ. system to maintain academic standards; 8 mems; Chair. Prof. S. V. D. G. SAMARANAYAKE; Sec. TISSA NANDASENA.

NATIONAL BODY

Tertiary and Vocational Education Commission: 'Nipunatha Piyasa', 354/2 Elvitigala Mw Narahenpita, Colombo; tel. (11) 5849291; fax (11) 2555007; e-mail info@tvec.gov.lk; internet www.tvec.gov.lk; f. 1991; apex body for accreditation, policy formulation, planning, quality assurance, coordination, devt of tertiary and vocational education; Chair. Prof. DAYANTHA WIJEYESE-KERA; Dir-Gen. Dr T. A. PIYASIRI.

Learned Societies

GENERAL

Institute of Sinhala Culture: 'Sudarshi' 375 Bauddhaloka Mawatha, Colombo 7; tel. (11) 4687979; e-mail instituteofsinhalaculture@gmail.com; internet instituteofsinhalaculture.lk; f. 1954; preservation and devt of Sinhala culture: art and architecture, drama, dance, music, folklore, arts and crafts, film, research, traditional embroidery, puppetry; presents cultural programmes; holds seminars and workshops; 680 mems; Pres. JEEVAN KUMARANATHUNGA; Sec. Prof. MUDIYANSE DISSANAYAKE.

National Academy of Sciences of Sri Lanka: 120/10 Vidya Mawatha, Colombo 7; tel. (11) 2585038; e-mail zoousa@kln.ac.lk; internet www.nassl.org; f. 1976; promotes advancement and dissemination of scientific knowledge; acts as consultative body to govt of Sri Lanka on matters and activities related to application of science and technology in nat. devt; 110 mems; Pres. Dr K. L. GUNARATNA; Gen. Sec. Prof. U. S. AMARASINGHE.

Royal Asiatic Society of Sri Lanka: Royal Asiatic Society Bldg, 96 Ananda Coomaraswamy Mawatha, Colombo 00700; tel. and fax (11) 2699249; e-mail info@royalasiaticsociety

.lk; internet www.royalasiaticsociety.lk; f. 1845; promotes inquiries into history, religions, languages, literature, arts, sciences and social conditions of the present and fmr inhabitants of Sri Lanka, and connected cultures; library contains one of the largest collns of books on Sri Lanka, and others on Indian and Eastern culture in gen.; library of 11,000 vols, 350 titles; 950 mems; Pres. Dr SUSANTHA GOONATILAKE; Hon. Jt Sec. Prof. A. W. D. RATNASIRI; Hon. Jt Sec. W. STERLING PERERA; publ. *Journal of the Royal Asiatic Society of Sri Lanka* (1 a year).

BIBLIOGRAPHY, LIBRARY SCIENCE AND MUSEOLOGY

Sri Lanka Library Association: Sri Lanka Professional Centre, 275/75 Stanely Wijesundara Mawatha, Colombo 7; tel. and fax (11) 2589103; e-mail slla@sltnet.lk; internet www.slla.org.lk; f. 1960; act as pivotal professional body for library, documentation and information services in Sri Lanka; provides library education programmes; sets professional standards; fosters cooperation between all individuals and orgs interested in the welfare of libraries; acts as forum for exchange of ideas among mems; safeguards and promotes rights, privileges and status of librarians and information scientists; 415 mems; Pres. M. S. U. AMARASIRI; Gen. Sec. INDRANI PONNAMPERUMA; publ. *Sri Lanka Library Review* (1 a year).

University Librarians Association of Sri Lanka: c/o Library, Open Univ. of Sri Lanka, Nawala, Nugegoda; e-mail editor.jula@gmail .com; internet www.ulasl.org; protects and maintains professional status, interests and welfare of univ. librarianship; 100 mems; Pres. Dr PRADEEPA WIJJETUNGE; Gen. Sec. R. MAHESWARAN; publ. *Journal of University Librarians Association* (1 a year).

ECONOMICS, LAW AND POLITICS

Ceylon Institute of World Affairs: c/o Mervyn de Silva, 82B Ward Pl., Colombo 7; f. 1957; Pres. ANTON MUTTUKUMARU.

EDUCATION

National Education Society of Sri Lanka: Faculty of Education, Univ. of Colombo, Colombo 3; 75 mems; publ. *Education*.

FINE AND PERFORMING ARTS

Arts Council of Sri Lanka: 12/1 Polduwa Rd, Battaramulla, Colombo; tel. (11) 2884027; fax (11) 2861420; e-mail artscouncilsl@yahoo.com; internet www .artscouncil.lk; f. 1952; promotes art projects in Sri Lanka; carries out projects in all fields of arts, incl. painting, drama, music, literature, ballet, dancing, folk song, folklore; aims to develop quality of fine art of Sri Lanka; Chair. Prof. CARLO FONSEKA; Gen. Sec. and Exec. Officer KAMAL B. DISSANAYAKE; publ. *Kala Magazine* (4 a year).

Ceylon Society of Arts: Art Gallery, Ananda Coomarassamy Mawatha, Colombo 7; tel. (11) 4693067; f. 1887; Pres. KALAPATHI-P. SUNIL; Hon. Gen. Sec. M. D. S. GUNATHILAKE.

HISTORY, GEOGRAPHY AND ARCHAEOLOGY

Archaeological Society of Sri Lanka: c/o Dept of Archaeology, Sir Marcus Fernando Mawatha, Colombo 7; f. 1966; Pres. Prof. CHANDRA WIKKRAMAGAMAGE; Co-Sec. S. LAKDUSINGHE; Co-Sec. W. H. WIJAYAPALA.

Ceylon Geographical Society: 61 Abdul Caffoor Mawatha, Colombo 3; f. 1938; 100 mems; Pres. Prof. K. KULARATNAM; Sec. Dr K.

U. SIRINANDA; Sec. Dr W. P. T. SILVA; publ. *The Ceylon Geographer* (1 a year).

LANGUAGE AND LITERATURE

Alliance Française de Colombo: 11 Barnes Pl., Colombo 7; tel. (11) 2693467; fax (11) 2688735; e-mail secr@alliancefr.lk; internet www.alliancefr.lk; f. 1954 as Sri Lankan Association, present status 1955; offers courses and exams in French language and culture and promotes cultural exchange with France; attached teaching centres in Kandy and Matara; 600 mems; library of 12,000 vols; Dir KAUSHALYA DIAS; publ. *Rendez-vous* (12 a year).

British Council: 49 Alfred House Gardens, POB 753, Colombo 3; tel. (11) 7521521; fax (11) 2587079; e-mail info.lk@britishcouncil .org; internet www.britishcouncil.org/ srilanka; teaching centre; offers courses and exams in English language and British culture and promotes cultural exchange with the UK; responsible for British Council work in the Maldives; attached teaching centre in Kandy; library of 45,000 vols; Dir TONY REILLY O'BRIEN; Teaching Centre Man. PAUL HILDER.

English Speaking Union of Sri Lanka: 14A, 16K Lane Galle Rd, Colombo 3; tel. (11) 4575843; e-mail upali_iccs@sltnet.lk; f. 1981; library of 3,000 vols; incls an English Language School; Pres. Dr UPALI RATNAYAKE; publ. *Open Mind* (4 a year).

Goethe-Institut: 39 Gregory's Rd, Colombo 00700; tel. (11) 2694562; fax (11) 2693351; e-mail info@colombo.goethe.org; internet www.goethe.de/colombo; f. 1957; offers courses and examinations in German language and culture and promotes cultural exchange with Germany; library of 6,000 vols; Dir RICHARD LANG.

MEDICINE

Sri Lanka Medical Association: Wijerama House, 6 Wijerama Mawatha, Colombo 7; tel. (11) 2693324; fax (11) 2698802; e-mail slma@ eureka.lk; internet www.slma .sharedcarevault.info; f. 1887 as Ceylon Branch of the British Medical Association, present name and status 1972; provides a forum for medical practitioners; 1,200 mems; Pres. Prof. VAJIRA H. W. DISSANAYAKE; Hon. Sec. Dr LASANTHA MALAWIGE; publs *Abstracts of Anniversary Academic Sessions* (1 a year), *Ceylon Medical Journal* (4 a year).

NATURAL SCIENCES

General

Sri Lanka Association for the Advancement of Science: 'Vidya Mandiraya', 120/10 Wijerama Rd, Colombo 7; tel. (11) 2688740; fax (11) 2691681; e-mail hqslaas@gmail.com; internet www.slaas.org; f. 1944; provides systematic direction of scientific enquiry; promotes contact among scientific workers; disseminates scientific knowledge; holds annual session; 7 secs; 6,000 mems; Gen. Pres. Prof. S. W. KOTAGAMA; Gen. Sec. Dr M. M. M. NAJIM; Gen. Sec Prof. NILANTHI BANDARA; publs *Proceedings*, *Vidya Viyapthi*, *Vingnana Murusu*.

PHILOSOPHY AND PSYCHOLOGY

Ceylon Humanist Society: Rutnam Inst. Bldg, Univ. Lane, Jaffna; Pres. J. T. RUTNAM; Sec. O. M. DE ALWIS.

RELIGION, SOCIOLOGY AND ANTHROPOLOGY

Buddhist Academy of Ceylon: 109 Rosmead Pl., Colombo.

Maha Bodhi Society of Sri Lanka: 130 Rev. Hikkaduwe Sri Sumangala Nahimi Mawatha, Colombo 10; tel. and fax (11) 2677626; e-mail banagalaupatissa@gmail .com; f. 1891; propagates Buddhism throughout the world; 900 mems; Pres. BANAGALA UPATISSA NAYAKA THERO; Hon. Sec. VASANTHA DE SILVA; publ. *Sinhala Bauddhaya* (12 a year).

TECHNOLOGY

Institution of Engineers, Sri Lanka: 120/ 15 Wijerama Mawatha, Colombo 7; tel. (11) 2698426; fax (11) 2699202; e-mail es@iesl.lk; internet www.iesl.lk; f. 1956; provides a forum for engineers of all disciplines; promotes advancement of science and practice of engineering; 7,273 mems; library of 12,000 vols; Pres. ANANDA RANASINGHE; Exec. Sec. ARUNDHATI WIMALASURIYA; publs *Engineer* (3 a year), *Sri Lanka Engineering News* (12 a year), *Transactions* (1 a year).

Research Institutes

AGRICULTURE, FISHERIES AND VETERINARY SCIENCE

Coconut Research Institute: Bandirippuwa Estate, Lunuwila 61150; tel. (31) 2255300; fax (31) 2255391; e-mail director@ cri.lk; internet www.cri.lk; f. 1929; quasi-governmental research institute serving coconut industry of Sri Lanka; library: see Libraries and Archives; Chair. Dr NIMAL WEERASINGHE; Dir Dr C. JAYASEKARE; publs *COCOS* (4 a year), *Coco News* (3 a year).

Hector Kobbekaduwa Agrarian Research and Training Institute: 114 Wijerama Mawatha, POB 1522, Colombo 7; tel. (11) 2696981; fax (11) 2692423; e-mail hartilib@sltnet.lk; internet www.harti.lk; f. 1972; attached to Min. of Agriculture; research into and policy analysis on agrarian structures and the economic, social and institutional aspects of agricultural devt; operates training programmes; library: see Libraries and Archives; Dir Prof. PREMALAL DE SILVA; publ. *Sri Lanka Journal of Agrarian Studies* (2 a year, in English and Sinhala).

Horticultural Research and Development Institute: Gannoruwa, Peradeniya; tel. (81) 2288011; fax (81) 2388234; e-mail directorhordi@gmail.com; internet www .agridep.gov.lk; f. 1965; research on fruit, vegetables, roots and tubers, other horticultural crops, ornamental flowers and soya processing; library of 10,854 vols; Dir W. M. K. B. WAHUNDENIYA; publ. *Tropical Agriculturist* (1 a year).

National Aquatic Resources Research and Development Agency: Crow Island, Colombo 15; tel. (11) 2521000; fax (11) 2521922; e-mail dg@nara.ac.lk; internet www.nara.ac.lk; f. 1981; research in fisheries and aquatic resources; library of 350 vols; Chair. Dr S. G. SAMARASUNDARA; Dir-Gen. M. D. I. B. GAMAGE; publ. *NARA Journal* (1 a year).

Rice Research and Development Institute: Batalagoda, Ibbagamuwa; tel. and fax (37) 2222681; e-mail rice@rrdi.ac.lk; f. 1994; Dir S. ABEYSIRIWARDENE.

Rubber Research Institute of Sri Lanka Library: Dartonfield, Agalawatta 12200; tel. (34) 2247426; fax (34) 2247427; internet www .rrisl.lk; f. 1953; Colombo office and laboratories: Telawala Rd, Ratmalana, Mt Lavinia; research and advisory services on rubber planting and manufacture; comprises 10 research depts, biometry section, adaptive research unit, extension dept and economic research unit, specification unit and estate dept; library of 10,500 vols, 275 periodical titles; Dir Dr W. M. G. SENEVIRATNA; publs *Journal* (1 a year), *Rubber Puwath* (1 a year).

Tea Research Institute of Sri Lanka: St Coombs, Talawakelle; tel. (52) 2258201; fax (52) 2258229; e-mail info@tri.lk; internet www.tri.lk; f. 1925; generates and disseminates new technologies related to tea cultivation and processing; library: see Libraries and Archives; Dir I. SARATH B. ABESINGHE; publs *Sri Lanka Journal of Tea Science* (2 a year), *Tea Quarterly, TRI Update* (2 a year).

Veterinary Research Institute: POB 28, Gannoruwa, Peradeniya; tel. (81) 22388312; fax (81) 2387379; e-mail info@vri.lk; internet www.vri.lk; f. 1911 as Veterinary diagnostic laboratory, present name and status 1967; concerned with research and investigations into health and production problems of livestock and poultry; veterinary vaccine production; Dir Dr B. D. R. WIJEWARDHANA; publ. *Sri Lanka Veterinary Journal* (4 a year).

ECONOMICS, LAW AND POLITICS

Economic Research Unit: Business Intelligence Dept, Bank of Ceylon, Colombo; Business Intelligence Officer S. E. A. JAYA-WICKREMA.

Institute of Policy Studies of Sri Lanka: 100/20 Independence Ave, Colombo; tel. (11) 2143100; fax (11) 2665065; e-mail ips@ips.lk; internet www.ips.lk; f. 1988; conducts policy-oriented economic research; Exec. Dir SAMAN KELEGAMA; publ. *Sri Lanka State of the Economy Report* (1 a year).

Marga Institute Centre for Development Studies: 941/1 Jayanthi Mawatha, Kotte Rd, Ethul Kotte 10100; tel. (11) 2888790; fax (11) 2888794; e-mail library@margasrilanka.org; internet www.margasrilanka.org; f. 1972; non-profit multi-disciplinary research org. undertaking critical, non-partisan study of devt issues in Sri Lanka and the wider Asian region; library of 24,800 vols, 50 periodicals; Chair. MANGALA MOONESINGHE; Chair. Emeritus Dr GODFREY GUNATILLEKE; Vice-Chair. MYRTLE PERERA; Head of Library and Information Services DEEPALI TALAGALA; publs *Marga Monograph Series on Ethnic Reconciliation, The Marga Quarterly Journal.*

Wiros Lokh Institute: 81-1A Isipatana Mawatha, Colombo 5; tel. and fax (11) 2580817; e-mail wiroshermes@yahoo.com; internet www.socialreit.org; f. 1981, operationally merged with Capital Markets for the Marginalized Inc. (USA) and Capital for the Marginalized Ltd (Singapore); private research and training foundation; promotes awareness of globalization in the region; spec. projects: innovation in social housing and financing, urban regeneration and sports recreation for urban areas; capital markets, spices, silks and other traditional crafts; 75 mems; library of 20,000 vols; Chair. Dr DARIN GUNESEKERA; Dir of Child Rights Div. CHANDRIKA GUNESEKERA; Gen. Exec. ABHEYAPALA DE SILVA.

EDUCATION

National Institute of Education: POB 21, High Level Rd, Maharagama; tel. (11) 7601601; fax (11) 7601800; e-mail info@nie .lk; internet www.nie.lk; f. 1986; conducts policy research on education; designs and develops curricula for general and teacher education; provides professional devt of educational community; Dir-Gen. Prof. W. M. ABEYRATNE BANDARA.

HISTORY, GEOGRAPHY AND ARCHAEOLOGY

Archaeological Survey Department of Sri Lanka: Sir Marcus Fernando Rd, Colombo 7; tel. (11) 4694727; fax (11) 4696250; e-mail arch@diamond.lanka.net; f. 1890; library of 15,000 vols; Dir-Gen. Dr SENARATH DISSANAYAKE; publs *Administration Report* (1 a year), *Ancient Ceylon* (1 a year), *Memoirs.*

MEDICINE

Institute of Indigenous Medicine: Nawala, Rajagiriya; tel. (11) 2692385; internet iim.cmb.ac.lk; f. 1977; attached to Univ. of Colombo; research areas incl. Ayurveda, Unani, Indigenous system of medicine; library of 28,000 vols; Dir Dr R. A. JAYA-SINGHE.

Medical Research Institute: POB 527, Colombo 8; tel. (11) 2693532; fax (11) 2691495; e-mail director@mri.gov.lk; internet www.mri.gov.lk; f. 1900; research in animal studies, bacteriology, biochemistry, entomology, haematology, histo-pathology, immunology, molecular biology, mycology, nutrition, parasitology, pharmacology, rabies, virology; Dir Dr ANIL SAMARANAYAKE.

NATURAL SCIENCES

Biological Sciences

Department of Wild Life Conservation: 811A, Jayanthipura Rd, Battatamula, Colombo 7; tel. (11) 2888585; fax (11) 2883355; e-mail dg@dwc.gov.lk; internet www.dwc.gov.lk; f. 1950; promotes scientific research relevant to managment of wildlife resources in Sri Lanka; library of 1,962 vols; Dir-Gen. H. D. RATNAYAKE; publs *Sri Lanka Wild Life, Vana Divi* (1 a year), *National Parks of Sri Lanka.*

Physical Sciences

Department of Meteorology: 383 Bauddhaloka, Mawatha, Colombo 7; tel. (11) 2694846; fax (11) 2698311; e-mail meteo@slt .lk; internet www.meteo.gov.lk; f. 1948; climatological data for Sri Lanka; time service; astronomical service; weather forecasting; agrometeorological service; weather services to gen. public, the agricultural, aviation, energy sectors, fisheries, shipping sectors; research in meteorology, climatology, climate change and allied subjects; library of 18,000 vols; Dir Dr G. B. SAMARASINGHE; publs *Agrometeorological Bulletin* (4 a year), *Monthly Weather Review* (12 a year), *Report of the Department of Meteorology* (1 a year).

TECHNOLOGY

Geological Survey and Mines Bureau: Senanayake Bldg, 4 Galle Rd, Dehiwala; tel. (11) 2739307; fax (11) 2735752; e-mail gsmb@ slt.lk; internet www.gsmb.sit.lk; f. 1903; systematic geological mapping of Sri Lanka; identification and assessment of its mineral resources; issues licences to regulate exploration, mining, processing, transport, trading in and export of minerals; Chair. Dr N. P. WIJAYANANDA (acting); Dir-Gen. B. A. PEIRIS; publs *Memoirs, Mineral Year Book.*

Industrial Technology Institute: 363 Bauddhaloka Mawatha, Colombo 7; tel. (11) 2379800; fax (11) 2379850; e-mail info@iti.lk; internet iti.lk; f. 1955 as Ceylon Institute of Scientific and Industrial Research; present name 1998; attached to Min of Technology

and Research; applied technical research in several industrial sectors for government agencies and the public; process research, resource studies, waste material utilization, product testing, standards, calibration and repair of instruments, technical consultation; industrial devt; information services centre; library: see Libraries and Archives; Chair Prof. VIJAYA KUMAR; Dir Dr A. M. MUBARAK.

National Science Foundation: 47/5 Maitland Pl., Colombo 7; tel. (11) 2696771; fax (11) 2694754; e-mail dir@nsf.ac.lk; internet www.nsf.ac.lk; f. 1968 as Nat. Science Ccl, present name and status 1998; attached to Min. of Technology and Research; initiates, facilitates and supports basic and applied scientific research by univs, scientific and technological instns and scientists; fosters the interchange of scientific information among scientists in Sri Lanka and foreign countries; awards scholarships and fellowships for scientific study or work at appropriate instns; provides a central clearing house for the colln and analysis of data on the scientific and technical resources in Sri Lanka; provides information for policy formulation on science and technology; promotes popularization of science; documentation and publs unit; acts as nat. research reports depository on science and technology; library of 7,250 vols; Chair. Prof. SIRIMALI FERNANDO; Exec. Dir SUNETHRA PERERA (acting); publs *Journal of the National Science Foundation* (4 a year), *Sri Lanka Journal of Social Sciences* (2 a year).

Sri Lanka Water Resources Board: 2A Hector Kobbekaduwa Ave, Colombo 7; tel. (11) 2697050; fax (11) 2669294; e-mail wrbmiwm@sltnet.lk; f. 1966; advises the Govt on all matters concerning conservation and utilization of water resources; undertakes hydro geological investigation and groundwater devt projects; library of 4,620 vols, 60 periodicals; Chair. K. YOGANATHAN.

Libraries and Archives

Agalawatta

Rubber Research Institute of Sri Lanka Library: see under Research Institutes.

Colombo

Centre for Development Information: National Planning Dept, Min, of Finance and Planning, POB 1547, Galleface Secretariat, Colombo 1; tel. (11) 2484609; fax (11) 2448063; e-mail cdi@npd.treasury.gov.lk; internet www.treasury.gov.lk/epprm/npd/ cdinew.htm; f. 1979; participates in regional information networks, and maintains an int. exchange programme; nat. focal point for SAARC Documentation Centre, New Delhi, India; coordinates and collates socio-economic information; 25,000 vols, unpublished report colln; Sr Librarian I. HENDAVITHAR-ANA; publs *Bibliography of Economic and Social Development in Sri Lanka, Current Acquisitions* (4 a year), *Guide to current periodical literature in economic and social development* (4 a year), *Register of Development Research in Sri Lanka.*

Colombo National Museum Library: POB 854, Colombo 7; tel. (11) 2693314; f. 1877 (incorporating colln of Govt Oriental Library, f. 1870); depository for Sri Lanka publns since 1885; 12m. vols (incl. 141,703 monographs, 4,500 periodical titles, 3,772 palm leaf MSS in Sinhala and Sanskrit, Pali, Burmese and Cambodian); Chief Librarian I. P. K. KUMARASIRI; publs *Sri Lanka Periodicals Index, Sri Lanka Periodicals Directory, Bibliographical Series.*

Colombo Public Library: 15 Sir Marcus Fernando Mawatha, Colombo 7; tel. (11) 4691968; internet www .colombopubliclibrary.org; f. 1925; 15 brs; five mobile libraries; spec. collns: Sri Lanka, Buddhism, FAO Depository, fine arts, Braille, Japan, Theo Auer colln; 794,088 vols, 2,000 periodical titles; Chief Librarian M. D. H. JAYAWARDHANA; publ. *Administration Report* (1 a year).

Department of National Archives: POB 1414, 7 Philip Gunawardena Mawatha, Colombo 7; tel. (11) 4694523; fax (11) 2694419; e-mail narchive@slt.lk; internet www.archives.gov.lk; f. 1902; contains official records of the Dutch admin. from 1640 to 1796, British admin. from 1796 to 1948; official records of independent Sri Lanka since 1948; few codices of Portuguese admin. prior to 1656 and some documents in French, Sinhalese and Tamil; operates a Presidential Archival Depository and a Reference Service; operates Hon. J. R. Jayewardene Research Centre; deals with documents in private possession; is the legal depository for all printed material in the country, effects the registration of printing presses, printed publs, newspapers; holds copies of books printed since 1885 and newspapers since 1832; Dir Dr SAROJA WETTASINGHE; publs *Administration Report of The National Archives*, *Catalogue of Newspapers* (1 a year), *Catalogue of Printing Presses* (1 a year), *Sri Lanka Archives* (1 a year), *Quarterly Statement of Books printed in Sri Lanka*.

Hector Kobbekaduwa Agrarian Research and Training Institute Library: POB 1522, 114 Wijerama Mawatha, Colombo 7; tel. (11) 4696981; fax (11) 4692423; e-mail hartilib@sltnet.lk; internet www.harti.lk/en/divisions/library; f. 1972; several hundred reports and reprints; spec. colln on Sri Lanka; part of Nat. Centre for Information on Agrarian Devt; 21,000 vols, 20,000 journals; Librarian S. L. KATU-GAMPOLA.

Industrial Technology Institute Information Services Centre: 363 Bauddhaloka Mawatha, Colombo 7; tel. (11) 2379807; fax (11) 2379817; e-mail info@iti.lk; internet iti .lk/information; f. 1955; several thousand reports, reprints, standards; information service to scientists, industrialists and engineers; computer database of books and articles in periodicals; nat. centre of Asian and Pacific Information Network on medicinal and aromatic plants; 35,000 vols, 300 journals; Head of Information Services Centre SURANEE M. SAMARASEKERA; publs *Bibliographical Services*, *State of the Art surveys on spices and essential oilbearing plants*, *News Digest*, *Food Digest*, *S & T News*, *Management Thought*.

Law Library: Hultsdorp, Colombo 12; tel. (11) 4324676; f. 1855; Dir A. COOREY.

National Library and Documentation Centre: 14 Independence Ave, Colombo 7; tel. (11) 2685203; fax (11) 2685201; e-mail libservice@mail.natlib.lk; internet www .natlib.lk; f. 1990; spec. collns: Ola Leaf colln, drama MS colln, library and information science colln, Martin Wickramasinghe colln, folklore colln; ISBN, ISMN and ISSN nat. centres; compiles Nat. Union Catalogue and Online Public Access Catalogue (OPAC); 300,000 vols (incl. govt publs), 500 periodical titles, 6,000 microforms, 1,800 maps, audiovisual items, electronic media; Dir-Gen. N. H. M. CHITHRANANDA (acting); Dir of Documentation Services Div. G. D. AMAR-ASIRI; Dir of Library Services Div. N. MAL-LAWA ARACHCHI; publs *Directory of Government Publications*, *Devolution of Power and Ethnic Problems* (database),

Library News (4 a year), *Index to Postgraduate Theses*, *ISBN Publishers Directory*, *Natnet Lanka Newsletter*, *Periodical Article Index* (4 a year), *Sri Lanka National Bibliography* (12 a year), *Sri Lanka Newspaper Index*.

University of Colombo Library: POB 1698, Colombo 7; tel. and fax (11) 2583043; e-mail sumanaj@lib.cmb.ac.lk; internet www .lib.cmb.ac.lk; f. 1942; 400,000 vols, 970 periodicals; Librarian D. C. KURUPPU (acting); publs *Ceylon Journal of Medical Science* (2 a year), *Colombo Law Review* (1 a year), *Sri Lanka Journal of International Law* (1 a year), *University of Colombo Review* (1 a year).

Lunuwila

Coconut Research Institute Library: Lunuwila; tel. (31) 2253795; fax (31) 2257391; e-mail library@cri.lk; internet www.cri.lk; f. 1929; houses Int. Coconut Information Centre; spec. colln of world literature on the coconut available in hard copy; microfiches, diskettes; 35,000 vols; Librarian P. D. U. C. DHARMAPALA (acting); publ. *Cocos*.

Moratuwa

Centre for Entrepreneurship Development and Consultancy Services: I. D. B., 615 Galle Rd, Katubedda, Moratuwa 10400; tel. (11) 2605372; fax (11) 2607002; e-mail idb@sltnet.lk; internet www.idb.gov.lk; f. 1969; acquisition, processing of library materials, dissemination of industrial information, reference and enquiry services, consultancy services; 20,000 vols, 25 current periodicals; Librarian SWARNA WIJEKOON (acting); publ. *New Arrivals* (12 a year).

Peradeniya

University of Peradeniya Library: POB 35, Peradeniya; Univ. of Peradeniya, Peradeniya 20400; tel. (81) 2392470; fax (81) 2388678; e-mail librarian@pdn.ac.lk; internet www.lib.pdn.ac.lk; f. 1921; collns incl. deposit materials obtained under printers' and publishers' ordinance since 1955, reference colln on Sri Lanka, palm-leaf MSS and rare materials on Sri Lanka, and collns on environmental and religious studies; 1m. vols; Librarian Dr P. WIJETUNGE; publs *Ceylon Journal of Science—Biological Sciences*, *Ceylon Journal of Science—Physical Sciences*, *Sri Lanka Journal of the Humanities*, *Modern Sri Lanka Studies*.

Talawakele

Tea Research Institute Library: St Coombs, Talawakele; tel. (52) 2258201; fax (52) 2258311; e-mail info@tri.lk; internet www.tri.lk; f. 1925; collects and disseminates information on tea and allied subjects; 25,000 vols and 250 periodicals for reference and loan, incl. spec. reference section dealing with tea and allied subjects; Librarian (vacant); publ. *Sri Lanka Journal of Tea Science* (2 a year).

Museums and Art Galleries

Anuradhapura

Anuradhapura Folk Museum: Old Town, Anuradhapura; tel. (25) 2234624; f. 1971; regional museum for North Central Province; Curator L. H. D. M. HETTIARCHCHI.

Colombo

Colombo Dutch Period Museum: Pettah, Colombo; tel. (11) 4448466; f. 1982; period

museum depicting life and times during Dutch rule 1656–1796.

Colombo National Museum: POB 854, Sir Marcus Fernando Mawatha, Colombo 7; tel. (11) 2694366; e-mail ranjith.s.hewage@yahoo .com; f. 1877 as Colombo Museum; nat. colln of art, antiquities and folk culture; research centre; Museum Keeper S. H. RANJITH.

National Museum of Natural History: Ananda Coomaraswamy Mawatha, Colombo 7; tel. (11) 2691399; e-mail nmnh_dnm@ yahoo.com; f. 1986; nat. colln of natural sciences; Museum Keeper K. A. NAYANA DARSHANI PERERA.

Galle

Galle National Museum: Church St, Galle; tel. (91) 2232051; f. 1986; regional museum for Galle Dist.

Kandy

Kandy National Museum: Dharmapala Mawatha, Kandy; tel. (81) 2223867; f. 1942; regional museum for the Central Province; 17th- to 18th-century Kandyan history; Museum Keeper K. D. V. CHANDIMAL.

Peradeniya

Royal Botanic Gardens: Peradeniya; tel. and fax (81) 2388088; e-mail royalbotanicgardens@yahoo.com; internet www.botanicgardens.gov.lk/peradeniya; f. 1821; botanical survey of Sri Lanka, floriculture research and devt; education, training and extension; Deputy Dir K. N. YAPA; Curator A. M. A. S. ATTANAYAKA; Curator P. D. S. WIJERATNE.

Ratnapura

Ratnapura National Museum: Ehelapola Walauwa, Colombo Rd, Ratnapura; tel. (45) 2252451; e-mail pradeep_t@yahoo.com; f. 1988; regional museum for the Sabaragamuwa Province; prehistoric archaeological inventions, natural heritage, geological, anthropological, zoological artefacts and models; Museum Keeper KUMARASIRI THEN-NEGEDARA.

Universities

EASTERN UNIVERSITY

Vantharumoolai, Chenkaladi
Telephone: (65) 2240490
Fax: (65) 2240585
E-mail: aradmin@esn.ac.lk
Internet: www.esn.ac.lk
Founded 1981 as Batticaloa Univ. College, present name 1986
State control
Languages of instruction: English, Tamil
Academic year: January to December
Chancellor: Dr T. VARAGUNAM
Vice-Chancellor: Prof. M. S. MOOKIAH
Registrar: A. D. HARRIS (acting)
Sr Asst Librarian: T. ARULNANDHY
Library of 60,000 vols
Number of teachers: 105
Number of students: 2,423 (1,514 internal, 909 external)

DEANS

Faculty of Agriculture: S. RAVEENDRANATH
Faculty of Arts and Culture: A. MURUGATHAS (acting)
Faculty of Commerce and Management: S. SENTHILNATHAN
Faculty of Science: Dr J. C. N. RAJENDRA

GENERAL SIR JOHN KOTELAWALA DEFENCE UNIVERSITY

Kandawala Estate, Rathmalana
Telephone: (11) 2635268
E-mail: kdudefence@kdu.ac.lk
Internet: www.kdu.ac.lk

Founded 1980, fmrly Gen. Sir John Kotelawala Defence Acad., present name and status 2008
State control
Chancellor: ROHAN DE SILVA DALUWATTE
Vice-Chancellor: MILINDA PEIRIS
Deputy Vice-Chancellor for Academic Affairs: Prof. Dr RAVINDRA LAL WEERARATNE KOGGALAGE
Registrar: H. G. U. KARIYAWASAM
Librarian: T. C. RANAWELLA (acting)

Offers bachelor degree courses in engineering, law, logistic management, management and technical sciences, medicine and surgery.

OPEN UNIVERSITY OF SRI LANKA

POB 21, Nawala, Nugegoda 10250
Telephone: (11) 2881000
Fax: (11) 2853975
E-mail: pio@ou.ac.lk
Internet: www.ou.ac.lk

Founded 1980
State control
Languages of instruction: Sinhala, Tamil, English
Chancellor: SAM S. WIJESINGHE
Vice-Chancellor: Prof. UPALI VIDANAPATHIRANA
Deputy Vice-Chancellor: Dr JANAKA LIYANAGAMA
Registrar: VINDHYA JAYASENA
Librarian: Dr WATHMANEL SENEVIRATNE
Library of 92,000 vols
Number of teachers: 306
Number of students: 19,287
Publication: *Open University Review of Engineering Technology*

DEANS

Faculty of Education: Prof. G. DAYALATHA LEKAMGE
Faculty of Engineering Technology: Prof. W. A. WIMALAWEERA
Faculty of Humanities and Social Sciences: Dr MAHIM MENDIS
Faculty of Natural Sciences: Dr GAYA RANAWAKA

RAJARATA UNIVERSITY OF SRI LANKA

Mihintale
Telephone: (25) 2266650
Fax: (25) 2266511
E-mail: rajalib@sltnet.lk
Internet: www.rjt.ac.lk

Founded 1996
State control
Languages of instruction: Sinhala, English
Chancellor: Prof. A. V. SURAWEERA
Vice-Chancellor: Prof. K. A. NANDASENA
Registrar: A. G. KARUNARATHNE
Librarian: A. S. SIRIWARDHANE
Library of 43,000 vols
Number of teachers: 150
Number of students: 2,500

DEANS

Faculty of Agriculture: Prof. P. A. WEERASINGHE
Faculty of Applied Sciences: Dr M. M. GOONASEKARA
Faculty of Management Studies: Prof. RANJITH WIJEYAWARDANE

Faculty of Social Sciences and Humanities: Prof. A. LAGAMUWA

SABARAGAMUWA UNIVERSITY OF SRI LANKA

POB 02, Belihuloya 70140
Telephone: (45) 2280014
Fax: (45) 2280015
E-mail: ccs@sab.ac.lk
Internet: www.sab.ac.lk

Founded 1996
State control
Language of instruction: English
Chancellor: Prof. KUBURUGAMUWE VAJIRA THERO
Vice-Chancellor: Prof. MAHINDA S. RUPASINGHE
Registrar: K. M. NAVARATHNE BANDA (acting)
Librarian: T. N. NEIGHSOOREI
Library of 116,070 vols, 262 periodical titles
Publications: *Journal of Agricultural Sciences* (3 a year), *Sabaragamuwa University Journal* (1 a year), *Sinhala Journal*

DEANS

Faculty of Agricultural Sciences: Dr ASANGA D. AMPITIYAWATTA
Faculty of Applied Sciences: Dr M. NIRMALI WICKRAMARATHNE
Faculty of Geomatics: Dr K. R. M. U. BANDARA
Faculty of Management Studies: R. M. WASANTHA RATHNAYAKE
Faculty of Social Sciences and Languages: Prof. M. SUNIL SHANTHA

SOUTH EASTERN UNIVERSITY OF SRI LANKA

Univ. Park, Oluvil 32360
Telephone: (67) 2255138
Fax: (67) 2255066
E-mail: vcoffice@seu.ac.lk
Internet: www.seu.ac.lk

Founded 1995 at Addalaichenai as South Eastern Univ. College; present name, status and location 1996
State control
Languages of instruction: English, Tamil
Chancellor: Prof. ACHI. M. ISHAQ
Vice-Chancellor: Dr S. M. MOHAMED ISMAIL
Registrar: H. ABDUL SATHTHAR
Librarian: M. M. RIFAUDEEN (acting)
Library of 45,000 books, 20 periodicals
Number of teachers: 118
Number of students: 1,270
Publication: *Journal of Management* (1 a year)

DEANS

Faculty of Applied Sciences: Dr M. I. S. SAFEENA
Faculty of Arts and Culture: S. M. ALIFF
Faculty of Islamic Studies and Arabic Language: M. S. M. JALALDEEN
Faculty of Management and Commerce: M. B. M. AMJATH

UNIVERSITY OF COLOMBO

94 Cumaratunga Munidasa Mawatha, Colombo 3
Telephone: (11) 2581835
Fax: (11) 2583810
Internet: www.cmb.ac.lk

Founded 1921, present name 1979
State control
Languages of instruction: Sinhala, Tamil, English
Academic year: October to September
Chancellor: Rev. Dr OSWALD GOMIS

Vice-Chancellor: Prof. KSHANIKA HIRIMBUREGAMA
Registrar: T. L. R. SILVA (acting)
Rector of Sripalee Campus: Dr TUDOR WEERASINGHE
Librarian: D. C. KURUPPU (acting)
Library: see Libraries and Archives
Number of teachers: 448
Number of students: 9,158
Publications: *The Ceylon Journal of Medical Science* (2 a year), *University of Colombo Review* (1 a year), *University Calendar* (every 3 years)

DEANS

Faculty of Arts: Prof. INDRALAL DE SILVA
Faculty of Education: Prof. MARIE E. S. PERERA
Faculty of Law: N. SELVAKKUMARAN
Faculty of Management and Finance: H. D. KARUNARATHNE
Faculty of Medicine: Prof. ROHAN JAYASEKARA
Faculty of Science: Prof. T. R. ARIYARATNE
Faculty of Graduate Studies: Prof. SUNIL CHANDRASIRI

UNIVERSITY OF JAFFNA

POB 57, Thirunelvely, Jaffna
Telephone: (21) 2222483
Fax: (21) 2222006
E-mail: ujvc@mail.ewisl.net
Internet: www.jfn.ac.lk

Founded 1974, present name 1978
State control
Languages of instruction: English, Tamil
Academic year: October to July
Chancellor: Prof. M. SIVASURIYA
Vice-Chancellor: Prof. VASANTHY ARASARATNAM
Registrar: V. KANDEEPAN
Librarian: SRIKANTHALUXMY ARULANANTHAM (acting)
Library of 198,960 vols
Number of teachers: 454
Number of students: 5,147
Publications: *Cintanai* (4 a year), *Jaffna Dry Zone Agriculture* (2 a year), *Journal of Business Studies* (2 a year), *Journal of Science and Management* (1 a year), *Journal of South Asian Studies* (1 a year), *Vingnanam*

DEANS

Faculty of Agriculture: Dr SIVAMATHY SIVACHANDRAN
Faculty of Applied Science (Vavuniya Campus): Dr S. KRISHNAKUMAR
Faculty of Arts: Prof. N. GNANAKUMARAN
Faculty of Business Studies (Vavuniya Campus): Dr T. MANGALESWARAN
Faculty of Graduate Studies: Prof. S. SATHIASEELAN
Faculty of Management Studies and Commerce: Prof. T. VELNAMBY
Faculty of Medicine: Dr K. SIVAPALAN
Faculty of Science: Prof. K. KANDASAMY

UNIVERSITY OF KELANIYA

Kelaniya 11600
Telephone: (11) 2909903
Fax: (11) 2913857
E-mail: vcoffice@kln.ac.lk
Internet: www.kln.ac.lk

Founded 1875 as Vidayalankara Pirivena; Univ. status 1959; reorganized 1972 as a campus of Univ. of Sri Lanka; present name 1978
State control
Languages of instruction: English, Sinhala
Chancellor: KUSALA DHAMMA THERO

Vice-Chancellor: Prof. SARATH AMUNUGAMA (acting)
Registrar: W. M. KARUNARATHNE
Librarian: Dr L. A. JAYATISSA
Library of 180,000 vols
Number of teachers: 480
Number of students: 8,423
Publications: *Journal of the Faculty of Humanities* (1 a year), *Journal of the Faculty of Social Science* (1 a year), *Kalyani* (1 a year)

DEANS

Faculty of Commerce And Management Studies: Dr R. P. C. RANJANI
Faculty of Graduate Studies: Prof. M. GUNESEKERA
Faculty of Humanities: Prof. LAKSHMAN SENEVIRATHNE
Faculty of Medicine: Prof. A. R. WICKRAMASINGHE
Faculty of Science: Prof. D. D. S. KULATHUNGA
Faculty of Social Science: Prof. A. H. M. H. ABAYARATHNE

PROFESSORS

CHANDRASENA, L., Biochemistry and Clinical Chemistry
DANGALLE, N., Geography
DE SILVA, H., Medicine
EDIRISINGHE, D., Philosophy
JAYASEKARA, L., Botany
KARUNANANDA, U., History
KUMARASINGHE, K., Sinhala
PATHIRATNE, A., Zoology
SIRIPALA, W., Physics
SUMANAPALA, G., Pali and Buddhist Studies
TILLEKERATNE, K., Mathematics
WIDANAPATHIRANA, S., Microbiology
WIJEYARATNE, M., Zoology

UNIVERSITY OF MORATUWA

Katubedda, Moratuwa
Telephone: (11) 2650441
Fax: (11) 2650622
E-mail: info@mrt.ac.lk
Internet: www.mrt.ac.lk
Founded 1893 as Government Technical School, present name 1978
State control
Language of instruction: English
Academic year: October to September
Chancellor: Dr ROLAND SILVA
Vice-Chancellor: Prof. K. A. K. W. JAYAWARDANE
Deputy Vice-Chancellor: Prof. R. A. ATTALAGE
Registrar: A. L. JOUFER SADIQUE
Librarian: R. C. KODIKARA
Library of 85,000 vols, 300 journals
Number of teachers: 280
Number of students: 5,452
Publications: *Ambalama, Development Planning Review* (4 a year), *Tampitavihara*

DEANS

Faculty of Architecture: Prof. P. K. S. MAHANAMA
Faculty of Engineering: Prof. U. G. A. PUSWEWALA
Faculty of Information Technology: Prof. A. S. KARUNANANDA (acting)

UNIVERSITY OF PERADENIYA

Univ. Park, Peradeniya 20400
Telephone: (81) 2388301
Fax: (81) 2388102
E-mail: vc@pdn.ac.lk
Internet: www.pdn.ac.lk
Founded 1942 by incorporation of Ceylon Medical College (f. 1870) and Ceylon Univ. College (f. 1921); reorganized 1972, present name 1978
State control
Languages of instruction: Sinhala, Tamil, English
Academic year: October to September
Chancellor: Dr PREMADASA UDAGAMA
Vice-Chancellor: Prof. S. B. S. ABAYAKOON
Deputy Vice-Chancellor: Prof. K. PREMARATNE
Registrar: U. D. DODANWELA (acting)
Librarian: Dr P. WIJETUNGE
Library: see Libraries and Archives
Number of teachers: 745
Number of students: 9,500
Publications: *Ceylon Journal of Science, Modern Sri Lanka Studies, Sri Lanka Journal of Biological Science, Sri Lanka Journal of Humanities, Sri Lanka Journal of Physical Science*

DEANS

Faculty of Agriculture: Dr K. SAMARASINGHE
Faculty of Allied Health Sciences: Dr D. B. M. WICKRAMARATNE
Faculty of Arts: Dr A. ABHAYARATNE
Faculty of Dental Sciences: Dr U. B. DISSANAYAKE
Faculty of Engineering: Prof. S. B. WEERAKOON
Faculty of Medicine: Dr G. BUTHPITIYA
Faculty of Science: Prof. S. H. P. P. KARUNARATNE
Faculty of Veterinary Medicine and Animal Science: Prof. P. ABEYNAYAKE

PROFESSORS

Faculty of Agriculture (tel. (81) 2395010; fax (81) 2388041; e-mail deanagri@pdn.ac.lk; internet www.pdn.ac.lk/agri):

BANDARA, J. M. R. S., Agricultural Biology
BOGAHAWATTA, C., Agricultural Economics
CYRIL, H. W., Animal Science
DE COSTA, W. A. J. M., Crop Science
GOONASEKERE, K. G. A., Agricultural Engineering
GUNATHILAKA, H. M., Agricultural Economics
GUNAWARDENA, E. R. N., Agricultural Engineering
IBRAHIM, M. N. M., Animal Science
ILLEPERUMA, D. C. K., Food Science and Technology
JAYAKODY, A. N., Agricultural Soil Science
KUMARAGAMAGE, D., Agricultural Soil Science
MAPA, R. B., Soil Science
PEIRIS, B. C. N., Agricultural Crop Science
PERERA, A. L. T., Agricultural Biology
PERERA, A. N. F., Animal Science
PERERA, E. R. K., Animal Science
SAMARAJEEWA, U., Food Science and Technology
SANGAKKARA, U. R., Agricultural Crop Science
SIVAYOGANATHAN, C., Agricultural Extension
THATTIL, R. O., Crop Science

Faculty of Arts (tel. (81) 2392500; fax (81) 2388933; e-mail deanarts@pdn.ac.lk; internet www.pdn.ac.lk/arts):

AMARASINGHE, Y. R., Political Science
DE SILVA, M. W. A., Sociology
GUNATHILAKE, W. M., Sinhala
HENNAYAKE, H. M. S. K., Geography
KARUNATILAKE, P. V. B., History
LIYANAGE, K., Political Science
MADDEGAMA, U. P., Sinhala
MADDUMA BANDARA, C. M., Geography
NUHUMAN, M. A. M., Tamil
PATHMANATHAN, S., History
PERERA, S. W., English
PREMASIRI, P. D., Pali and Buddhist Studies

SAMARANAYAKE, S. V. D. G., Political Science
SENADHEERA, S., Education
SENEVIRATNE, S. D. S., Archaeology
SILVA, K. T., Sociology
SIRISENA, W. M., Sociology
SIRIWEERA, W. S., History
SIVARAJAH, A., Political Science
WEERAKKODY, D. P. M., Classical Languages
WICKRAMASINGHE, A., Geography

Faculty of Dental Sciences (tel. (81) 2387500; fax (81) 2388948; e-mail deandental@pdn.ac.lk; internet www.pdn.ac.lk/dental):

AMARATUNGE, N. A. DE S., Oral Surgery
EKANAYAKE, A. N. I., Community Dentistry
EKANAYAKE, S. L., Community Dentistry
MENDIS, B. R. R. N., Oral Pathology
NANAYAKKARA, C. D., Basic Science
WIJEYEWEERA, R. L., Community Dentistry

Faculty of Engineering (tel. (81) 2393000; fax (81) 2388158; e-mail deaneng@pdn.ac.lk; internet www.pdn.ac.lk/eng):

AMIRTHANATHAM, G. E., Chemical Engineering
EKANAYAKE, E. M. N., Electrical and Electronic Engineering
HOOLE, S. R. H., Electrical and Electronic Engineering
RANAWEERA, M. P., Civil Engineering
SAMUEL, T. D. M. A., Engineering Mathematics
SENEVIRATNE, K. G. H. C. N., Civil Engineering
SIVASEGARAM, S., Mechanical Engineering

Faculty of Medicine (tel. (81) 2388840; fax (81) 2389106; e-mail deanmed@pdn.ac.lk; internet www.med.pdn.ac.lk):

AMARASINGHE, W. I., Obstetrics and Gynaecology
CHANDRASEKERA, M. S., Anatomy
EDIRISINGHE, J. S., Parasitology
NUGEGODA, D. B., Community Medicine
PERERA, P. A. J., Biochemistry
RATNATUNGE, N. V. I., Pathology
RATNARUNGE, P. C. A., Surgery
SENANAYAKE, N., Medicine
THEVANESAN, V., Microbiology
UDUPIHILLE, M., Physiology
WELGAMA, D. J., Parasitology
WIJESUNDARA, M. K. DE S., Parasitology

Faculty of Science (tel. (81) 2388693; fax (81) 2388018; e-mail deansci@pdn.ac.lk; internet www.pdn.ac.lk/sci):

ADIKARAM, N. K. B., Botany
BANDARA, B. M. R., Chemistry
BANDARA, H. M. N., Chemistry
CAREEM, M. A., Physics
DAHANAYAKE, K. G. A., Geology
DE SILVA, K. H. G. M., Zoology
DE SILVA, P. K., Chemistry
DISSANAYAKE, C. B., Geology
DISSANAYAKE, M. A. K. L., Physics
EDIRISINGHE, J. P., Zoology
GUNATILLAKE, C. V. S., Botany
GUNATILLAKE, I. A. U. N., Botany
GUNAWARDANA, R. P., Chemistry
ILLEPERUMA, O. A., Chemistry
KARUNARATHNA, N. L. V. V., Chemistry
KARUNARATNE, B. S. B., Physics
KARUNARATNE, S. H. P. P., Zoology
KULASOORIYA, S. A., Botany
KUMAR, N. S., Chemistry
KUMAR, V., Chemistry
NAMAL PRIYANTHA, Chemistry
RAJAPAKSHE, R. M. G., Chemistry
SENEVIRATNE, H. H. G., Mathematics
TENNAKOON, D. T. B., Chemistry

Faculty of Veterinary Medicine and Animal Science (tel. (81) 2388205; fax (81) 2389136; e-mail deanvet@pdn.ac.lk; internet www.pdn.ac.lk/vet):

ABEYGUNAWARDENA, H., Farm Animal Production and Health
ABEYNAYAKE, P., Veterinary Pathological Biology
GUNAWARDENA, V. K., Veterinary Basic Science
KURUWITA, V. Y., Veterinary Clinical Science
SILVA, I. D., Veterinary Clinical Science

UNIVERSITY OF RUHUNA

Matara
Telephone: (41) 2222681
Fax: (41) 2222683
E-mail: vcsm@admin.ruh.ac.lk
Internet: www.ruh.ac.lk
Founded 1978 as Ruhuna Univ. College, present name 1984
State control
Languages of instruction: Sinhala, English
Academic year: October to September
Chancellor: PALLATHTHARA SUMANAJOTHI NAYAKA THERO
Vice-Chancellor: Prof. SUSIRITH MENDIS
Deputy Vice-Chancellor: Prof. GAMINI SENANAYAKE
Registrar: P. S. KALUGAMA
Librarian: ANANDA KARUNARATNE
Library of 140,000 vols
Number of teachers: 550
Number of students: 5,500
Publication: *Rohana Research Journal*

DEANS

Faculty of Agriculture: Prof. MANGALA DE ZOYSA
Faculty of Engineering: Dr A. M. N. ALAGIYAWANNA
Faculty of Fisheries and Marine Science and Technology: Dr TILAK P. D. GAMAGE
Faculty of Graduate Studies: Prof. L. P. JAYATISSA
Faculty of Humanities and Social Sciences: Prof. P. HEWAGE
Faculty of Management and Finance: Dr P. A. P. SAMANTHA KUMARA
Faculty of Medicine: Dr SAMPATH GUNAWARDENE
Faculty of Science: Prof. W. G. D. DHARMARATNE

UNIVERSITY OF SRI JAYEWARDENEPURA

Gangodawila, Nugegoda
Telephone: (11) 2802022
Fax: (11) 2801604
E-mail: info@sjp.ac.lk
Internet: www.sjp.ac.lk
Founded 1959 as Vidyodaya Univ. of Ceylon; reorganized 1972 as campus of Univ. of Sri Lanka; present name and status 1978
State control
Languages of instruction: Sinhala, English
Chancellor: Rev. Prof. BELLANWILA WIMALARATNE THERO
Vice-Chancellor: Dr N. L. A. KARUNARATNE
Registrar: K. GNANASIRI BRITTO
Librarian: NAYANA WIJAYASUNDARA
Library of 200,000 vols
Number of teachers: 410
Number of students: 8,400
Publications: *Vidyodaya Journal of Sciences*, *Vidyodaya Journal of Social Sciences*

DEANS

Faculty of Applied Sciences: Prof. SUDANTHA LIYANAGE

Faculty of Humanities and Social Sciences: Prof. P. ATHUKORALE
Faculty of Management Studies: Prof. SAMPATH AMARATUNGA
Faculty of Medical Sciences: Prof. MOHAN DE SILVA
Faculty of Graduate Studies: Prof. SWARNA PIYASIRI

PROFESSORS

ABEYSEKARA, A. M., Chemistry
ARIYARATNE, S., Sinhala
BAMUNUARACHCHI, A., Chemistry
DAYANANDA, R. A., Statistics
DE SILVA, W. M. M., Surgery
DERANIYAGALA, S. P., Chemistry
ENDAGAMA, M., History and Archaeology
FERNANDO, D. J. S., Medicine
FERNANDO, D. P. A., Surgery
FERNANDO, G. H., Pharmacology
FERNANDO, S., Microbiology
FERNANDO, W. S., Chemistry
HETTIARATCHI, S. B., History and Archaeology
JANSZ, E. R., Biochemistry
JAYATISSA, W. A., Social Statistics
JAYAWARDENA, M. A. J., Obstetrics and Gynaecology
JIFFRY, M. T. M., Physiology
JINADASA, J., Zoology
KARIYAWASAM, T., Sinhala
KARUNANAYAKE, M. M., Geography
NANDADASA, H. G., Botany
PERERA, B. A. T., Sociology and Anthropology
PERERA, G. A., Pali and Buddhist Studies
PIYASIRI, S., Zoology
RANASINGHE, D. M. S. H. K., Forestry and Environmental Science
TANTRIGODA, D. A., Physics
WARNASOORIYA, N. D., Paediatrics
WEERAKOON, S., Mathematics
WEERASEKARA, D. S., Obstetrics and Gynaecology
WICKRAMASINGHE, S. M. D. N., Biochemistry
WIJAYARATNE, M. W. W., Sinhula
WIJEBANDARA, W. D. C., Pali and Buddhist Studies
WIJEWARDENA, K. A. K. K., Community Medicine and Family Medicine
WITHANA, R. J., Pathology
YAPA, P. A. J., Botany

UNIVERSITY OF THE VISUAL & PERFORMING ARTS

21 Albert Crescent, Colombo 7
Telephone: (11) 2690240
Fax: (11) 2686071
E-mail: vcuvpa@sltnet.lk
Internet: www.vpa.ac.lk
Founded 2005, fmrly Institute of Aesthetic Studies affiliated to Univ. of Kelaniya (f. 1974)
State control
Vice-Chancellor: Prof. JAYASENA KOTTEGODA
Registrar: B. M. DAYAWANSA
Number of teachers: 82
Number of students: 3,085

DEANS

Faculty of Dance and Drama: R. K. ARIYARATHNA
Faculty of Music: KOLITHA B. DISSANAYAKA
Faculty of Visual Arts: M. G. SUSIRIPALA

UVA WELLASSA UNIVERSITY

Badulla 90000
Telephone: (55) 2226400
Fax: (55) 2226472
E-mail: info@uwu.ac.lk
Internet: www.uwu.ac.lk
Founded 2005
State control

Chancellor: Dr ALUTHWEVA SORATHA NAYAKE THERO
Vice-Chancellor: Prof. RANJITH PREMALAL DE SILVA
Registrar: NILMINI DIYABEDANAGE

DEANS

Faculty of Animal Science and Export Agriculture: Dr G. CHANDRASENA
Faculty of Management: Dr S. G. SIVAGURUNATHAN
Faculty of Science and Technology: Dr S. C. JAYAMANNE

WAYAMBA UNIVERSITY OF SRI LANKA

Lional Jayathilake Mawatha, Kanadulla, Kuliyapitiya
Telephone: (37) 2281412
Fax: (37) 2283614
E-mail: vc@wyb.ac.lk
Internet: www.wyb.ac.lk
Founded 1999
Chancellor: Prof. C. L. V. JAYATHILAKE
Vice-Chancellor: Prof. S. J. B. A. JAYASEKERA
Registrar: E. M. G. EKANAYAKE
Librarian: W. G. P. GAMLATH
Number of students: 1,309

DEANS

Faculty of Agriculture and Plantation Management: Prof. D. P. S. T. G. ATTANAYAKE
Faculty of Applied Sciences: Dr E. M. P. EKANAYAKE
Faculty of Business Studies and Finance: E. S. WICKRAMASINGHE
Faculty of Livestock, Fisheries and Nutrition: Dr K. D. R. R. SILVA

Other Higher Education Institutes

Aquinas University College: 990 Gnanartha Pradeepa Mawatha, Maradana Rd, Colombo 8; tel. (11) 2694014; fax (11) 2678463; e-mail rector@aquinas.lk; internet www.aquinas.lk; f. 1954 as Aquinas College of Higher Studies, present name and status 2004; faculties of agriculture, business and financial management, engineering, hospitality management, information technology, linguistics, marketing and management, nursing, professional studies, theology, undergraduate studies; library: 43,000 vols; 150 teachers; 7,500 students; Rector Rev. Dr PLACIDUS DE SILVA; Vice-Rector Rev. Fr NAMAL FERNANDO; Registrar M. L. FERNANDO; publ. *Aquinas Journal* (1 a year).

Ceylon College of Physicians: 341/1 Kotte Rd, Rajagiriya; tel. (11) 2888146; fax (11) 2888119; e-mail ccp@eureka.lk; internet ceycollphysicians.org; f. 1967; Pres. Prof. SARATH LEKAMWASAM; Joint Sec Dr C. NIRMALA WIJEKOON; Joint Sec. Dr D. U. S. BULUGAHAPITIYA; publ. *Journal of the Ceylon College of Physicians* (1 a year).

Gampaha Wickramarachchi Ayurveda Institute: Univ. of Kelaniya, Kandy Rd, Yakkala; tel. (33) 2222748; fax (33) 2222739; e-mail ayurgmp@sltnet.lk; internet www.kln.ac.lk/institutes/wickramarachchi; f. 1929; attached to Univ. of Kelaniya; offers bachelors of Ayurveda medicine and surgery; library: 20,000 vols; Dir Prof. JANITHA A. LIYANAGE.

In—Service Training Institute: Gannoruwa, POB 21, Peradeniya; tel. (81) 2288146; f. 1965; agricultural education and training; Dir HENRY GAMAGE.

Institute of Biochemistry, Molecular Biology and Biotechnology: 90 Cumaratunga Munidasa Mawatha, Colombo 3; tel. (11) 2552528; fax (11) 2553683; e-mail info@ibmbb.cmb.ac.lk; internet www.ibmbb.lk; f. 2004; attached to Univ. of Colombo; offers courses in molecular life sciences; Dir Prof. KAMANI H. TENNEKOON.

Institute of Human Resource Advancement: Bauddhaloka Mawatha, Colombo; tel. (11) 2503393; e-mail info@ihrauoc.org; internet www.ihra.cmb.ac.lk; attached to Univ. of Colombo; courses offered incl. computer applications in business, driving and road safety instructors training, counselling psychology, geoinformatics, int. business, video editing and media; Dir Dr W. K. HIRIMBUREGAMA.

Institute of Technology: Katubedda, Moratuwa; tel. (11) 2650064; fax (11) 2650622; e-mail tag@civil.mrt.ac.lk; attached to Univ. of Moratuwa; Dir Dr T. A. G. GUNASEKARA.

Jaffna College: Vaddukoddai; tel. (70) 2212531; f. 1823, present name 1872; provides primary, secondary, tertiary and technical education; library: 60,000 vols; 55 teachers; 1,172 students; Prin. ANTHONY A. PAUL; publ. *Jaffna College Miscellany.*

Attached Institutes:

Christian Institute for the Study of Religion and Society: c/o Christian Theological Seminary, Maruthanarmadam, Chunnakam; Dir C. V. SELLIAH.

Evelyn Rutnam Institute for Inter-Cultural Studies: University Lane, Thirunelvely, Jaffna; Dir Rev. ANTHONY A. PAUL.

Institute of Agriculture: Maruthanamadam; 5 teachers; 40 students; Prin. T. KUGATHASAN.

Institute of Technology: Vaddukoddai; 11 teachers; 150 students; Dir H. R. G. HOOLE (acting).

National Centre for Advanced Studies in Humanities & Social Sciences: 6A Sukhastan Gardens, Ward Pl., Colombo 7; tel. (11) 2693974; fax (11) 2693975; e-mail info@ncas.lk; internet www.ncas.lk; f. 2005; offers advanced studies in humanities and social sciences; Dir Dr R. M. K. RATNAYAKE; publ. *Sri Lanka Journal of Advanced Social Studies* (2 a year).

National Institute of Library and Information Science: Univ. of Colombo, Colombo 3; tel. (11) 2507148; fax (11) 2507150; e-mail director@nilis.cmb.ac.lk; internet www.cmb.ac.lk/academic/institutes/nilis; f. 1999; attached to Univ. of Colombo; postgraduate and general training facilities in the field of library and information science; Dir UPALI AMARASIRI.

Postgraduate Institute of Agriculture: POB 55, Old Galaha Rd, Peradeniya; tel. (81) 2386542; fax (81) 2388318; e-mail info@pgia.ac.lk; internet www.pgia.ac.lk; f. 1975; attached to Univ. of Peradeniya; agricultural biology, agricultural economics, agricultural engineering, agricultural extension, animal science, bio-statistics, business admin., crop science, food science and technology, plant protection, soil science; Dir Prof. B. COLIN N. PEIRIS.

Postgraduate Institute of Archaeology: 407 Bauddhaloka Mawatha, Colombo 7; tel. (11) 2694151; fax (11) 2673108; e-mail info@pgiar.lk; internet www.pgiar.lk; f. 1986; attached to Univ. of Kelaniya; postgraduate education, professional training, research in archaeology and related subjects; Dir Prof. JAGATH WEERASINGHE.

Postgraduate Institute of English: POB 21, Nawala, Nugegoda 10250; tel. (11) 2825804; fax (11) 2825805; e-mail pgiedir@gmail.com; internet www.ou.ac.lk/pgie; f. 2005; attached to Open Univ. of Sri Lanka; offers Masters degree and courses related to English and teaching of English; Dir Dr H. RATWATTE (acting).

Postgraduate Institute of Management: 28 Lesley Ranagala Mawatha, Colombo 8; tel. (11) 2689639; fax (11) 2689643; e-mail admin@pim.lk; internet www.pim.lk; f. 1986; attached to Univ. of Sri Jayewardenepura; faculties of arts, applied sciences, graduate studies, management studies and commerce, medical sciences; 4,500 students; Dir Prof. UDITHA LIYANAGE.

Postgraduate Institute of Medicine: 160 Norris Canal Rd, Colombo 7; tel. (11) 2688649; fax (11) 2697757; e-mail pgim_dir@sltnet.lk; internet www.cmb.ac.lk/pgim; f. 1980; attached to Univ. of Colombo; provides specialist training of medical doctors; Dir Prof. JAYANTHA JAYAWARDANA.

Postgraduate Institute of Pali & Buddhist Studies: Sunethra Mahadevi Piriven Vidyayathana Premises, Pepiliyana, Boralesgamuwa, Colombo; tel. (11) 2809321; fax (11) 2809322; e-mail pgipbs@sltnet.lk; internet www.kln.ac.lk/institutes/pgipbs; f. 1975; attached to Univ. of Kelaniya; postgraduate studies in Pali and Buddhist studies; library: 15,000 vols; Dir Prof. Dr G. D. SUMANAPALA.

Postgraduate Institute of Science: POB 25, Peradeniya; tel. (81) 2385660; fax (81) 2389026; e-mail info@pgis.lk; internet www.pgis.lk; f. 1996; Univ. of Peradeniya; offers postgraduate programmes; library: 15,200 vols, 576 journals; Dir Prof. B. S. B. KARUNARATNE.

School of Agriculture: Kundasale; tel. (81) 2420485; f. 1916; library: 5,500 vols; 20 teachers; 253 students; Prin. P. K. K. R. PERERA; publ. *Progress Report* (1 a year).

South Asian Institute of Technology and Medicine: POB 11, Millennium Dr., off Chandrika Kumaratunga Mawatha, Malabe; tel. (11) 2413351; fax (11) 2413332; e-mail info@saitm.edu.lk; internet www.saitm.edu.lk; faculties of engineering, information communications technology, management and finance, medicine; Chair. Prof. NEVILLE FERNANDO.

Sri Lanka College of Technology: POB 542, Olcot Mawatha, Colombo 10; e-mail tdt@sltnet.lk; internet www.srilankatech.net; f. 1893; courses in commerce, trade and engineering; 4,525 students; Dir-Gen. K. A. A. WIJERATHNE.

Sri Lanka Institute of Information Technology: New Kandy Rd, Malabe; tel. (11) 2413900; fax (11) 2413901; e-mail info@sliit.lk; internet www.sliit.lk; f. 1999; offers degrees in the field of information technology; campuses in Colombo, Jaffna, Kandy, Matara; Dir of Academics CHANDRA DE SILVA; Dir of Administration G. L. J. HEWAWASAM.

Sri Lanka Law College: POB 1501, Colombo; 244 Hulftsdorp St, Colombo 12; tel. (11) 2323759; fax (11) 2385847; e-mail locwal@slt.lk; internet www.sllc.ac.lk; f. 1874; run by Ccl of Legal Education; prepares students for admission to the Bar and conducts examinations; library: 11,462 vols; 1,500 students; Prin. Dr W. D. RODRIGO.

University of Colombo School of Computing: UCSC Bldg Complex, 35 Reid Ave, Colombo 7; tel. (11) 2581245; fax (11) 2587239; e-mail info@ucsc.cmb.ac.lk; internet www.ucsc.cmb.ac.lk; attached to Univ. of Colombo; offers undergraduate and postgraduate degree courses in computer science; Dir Prof. G. N. WIKRAMANAYAKE; Deputy Dir Dr D. N. RANASINGHE.

SUDAN

The Higher Education System

Higher education institutions pre-date the independence of Sudan (formerly The Sudan) from the United Kingdom in 1956, with the oldest being Omdurman Islamic University, which was founded in 1912. Gordon Memorial College (founded 1902) has offered degrees since 1945, under the supervision of University of London (United Kingdom), and from 1956 became known as University of Khartoum. The higher education system was severely impacted by two protracted civil wars following independence (in 1955–72 and 1983–2005), during which many educational institutions were badly damaged or completely destroyed in the southern and western parts of the country. In 2000 there were an estimated 200,538 students enrolled in universities (of which 26 were public) and other institutions of higher education. In the 2000s there was a significant increase in the number of public institutions, while a more positive government view of private institutions also led to expansion in this sector. Following a public referendum, South Sudan formally seceded from Sudan in July 2011; higher education statistics for post-secession Sudan were not immediately available.

Higher education is the responsibility of the Ministry of Higher Education and Scientific Research , and is governed by the Higher Education Act (1990) and the Higher Education Regulatory Act (2005). The National Council for Higher Education, which is chaired by the Minister of Higher Education and Scientific Research and which comprises university vice-chancellors and prominent academic figures, is responsible for planning, coordinating, financing and implementing government policies on higher education; this body is also responsible for quality assurance. In 2007 the Arab Network for Quality Assurance in Higher Education was established as a non-profit non-governmental organization, working with the International Network of Quality Assurance Agencies in Higher Education and the Association of Arab Universities. Its member organizations include the Evaluation and Accreditation Commission, part of the Sudanese Ministry of Higher Education and Scientific Research. The President of Sudan is the Chancellor of every university and is also responsible for appointing most of the other senior officers. Each university is operated by a University Council.

Results in the Sudan School Certificate are the main criterion for admission to higher education: students are required to achieve a pass-mark of 50% or higher in seven subjects to be admitted to university, and 50% or higher in five subjects to be admitted to non-university courses. Non-university courses consist principally of Intermediate or General Diplomas and are offered by several public and private institutions. Courses last for three years. The Bachelors is the undergraduate qualification, and may be awarded as either a 'General' (four years) or an 'Honours' (five years) degree. Professional areas of study, such as medicine, dentistry and engineering, may last longer (up to six years). Graduates with either of the Bachelors degrees may be admitted to programmes of study leading to the award of the Postgraduate Diploma, a one- or two-year course. The postgraduate Masters degree is a two- to three-year programme of study open to students holding a Bachelors (Honours) degree. However, students with a Bachelors (General) degree may gain access to the Masters by completing a Postgraduate Diploma. Some Masters programmes also require applicants to sit an entrance examination. The highest university-level degree is the Doctor of Philosophy, a research degree requiring a minimum of an additional three years' study and culminating in submission of a thesis.

Technical and vocational education is principally offered at secondary level, but the Sudan University of Science and Technology and the Sudan Open University (founded 2002) provide correspondence courses and continuing education.

Regulatory Bodies

GOVERNMENT

Ministry of Culture, Youth and Sport: Khartoum; Minister MUHAMMAD YUSSUF ABDALLAH.

Ministry of Education: Khartoum; tel. (183) 772808; e-mail moe-sd@moe-sd.com; internet www.moe-sd.com; Minister HAMID MUHAMAD IBRAHIM.

ACCREDITATION

Evaluation and Accreditation Commission: Ministry of Education, Khartoum; tel. (91) 23126; fax (83) 765986; e-mail evacsud@yahoo.com; f. 2003; Pres. MUHAMMAD SALIM.

Learned Societies

LANGUAGE AND LITERATURE

Alliance Française: POB 465, El Obeid; tel. (183) 23617; e-mail haidaro2000@yahoo.fr; offers courses and exams in French language and culture and promotes cultural exchange with France; attached teaching centre in Wad Medani.

British Council: 14 Abu Sin St, POB 1253, Central Khartoum; tel. (183) 780817; fax (183) 774935; e-mail info@sd.britishcouncil.org; internet www.britishcouncil.org/sudan; offers courses and exams in English language and British culture and promotes cultural exchange with the UK; library of 10,000 vols, 90 periodicals; Dir DAVID CODLING.

Research Institutes

GENERAL

National Centre for Research: POB 2404, Khartoum; tel. (183) 779040; fax (183) 770701; e-mail profsalih@hotmail.com; f. 1991; conducts pure and applied scientific research for the realization of Sudan's economic and social development; incorporates research institutes in renewable energy, environment and natural resources, technology, tropical medicine, medicinal and aromatic plants, economic and social studies, remote sensing, biotechnology and biological engineering; Dir Prof. ABDEL KARIM MOHAMED SALIH.

AGRICULTURE, FISHERIES AND VETERINARY SCIENCE

Agricultural Research Corporation: POB 126, Wad Medani; tel. (511) 842226; fax (511) 843213; e-mail arcdg@sudanmail .net; internet www.arcsudan.sd; f. 1904; part of Ministry of Science and Technology; research centres: Food Research Centre, Land and Water Research Centre, Crop Protection Research Centre, Forestry Research Centre, Date Palm Research Centre; 16 research stations; library: see Libraries; Dir-Gen. Prof. AZHARI ABDELAZIM HAMADA; publ. Sudan Journal of Agricultural Research (2 a year).

Animal Production Corporation, Research Division: POB 624, Khartoum; Dir of Research Dr MUHAMMAD EL TAHIR ABDEL RAZIG; Senior Veterinary Research Officer Dr AMIN MAHMOUD EISA.

Forestry Research Centre: POB 7089, Khartoum; f. 1962; Dir Prof. HASSAN A. MUSNAD.

ECONOMICS, LAW AND POLITICS

Sudan Academy for Administrative Sciences: POB 2003, Khartoum; f. 1980; provides post-service training for government officials; conducts studies on current administrative problems; Dir-Gen. Dr OSMAN ELZUBERI AHMED; publ. Journal of Administration and Development.

MEDICINE

Sudan Medical Research Laboratories: POB 287, Khartoum; f. 1935; Dir MAHMOUD ABDEL RAHMAN ZIADA.

NATURAL SCIENCES
Physical Sciences
Geological Research Authority: POB 410, Khartoum; tel. (183) 777939; fax (183) 776681; e-mail gras@sudanmail.net; internet www.gras-sd.com; f. 1905; attached to Min. of Energy and Mining; applied research and surveys; library: see Libraries and Archives; Dir-Gen. Dr ABDELRAZIG O. M. AHMED.

TECHNOLOGY
Industrial Research and Consultancy Centre: POB 268, Khartoum; tel. (183) 613225; f. 1965 by the Government with assistance from the UN Development Programme; performs tests, investigations, analysis, research and surveys; offers advice and consultation services to industry; General Dir Dr IBRAHIM HASSAN M. EL AMIN.

Libraries and Archives
Khartoum
Antiquities Service Library: POB 178, Khartoum; tel. (183) 780935; fax (183) 786784; f. 1946; 7,200 vols excluding periodicals; Librarian AWATIF AMIN BEDAWI.

Educational Documentation Centre: POB 2490, Khartoum; tel. (183) 71898; f. 1967; 7 mems; 20,000 vols; Dir IBRAHIM M. S. SHATIR; publs Al-Tawitheq El Tarbawi (Educational Documentation, 2 a year), annual reports and educational researches.

Flinders Petrie Library: Sudan Antiquities Service, POB 178, Khartoum; tel. (183) 780935; fax (183) 786784; f. 1946; 6,000 vols.

Geological Research Authority of the Sudan Library: POB 410, Khartoum; tel. (183) 770934; f. 1904; 2,200 vols, 63 periodicals; special collection: geology of the Sudan; Chief Librarian SALAH ABDEL GADIR MOHMED; publ. Bulletin.

Library of the Sudan University of Science and Technology: POB 407, Khartoum; tel. (183) 778922; fax (183) 774559; e-mail library@sustech.edu; f. 1950; 14 libraries on 9 sites; 55,000 vols; Chief Librarian GAWAHIR SIDAHMED EL HASSAN.

National Chemical Laboratories Library: National Chemical Laboratories, Ministry of Health, POB 287, Khartoum; f. 1904; 2,500 vols, 1,600 pamphlets.

National Records Office: POB 1914, Khartoum; f. 1953; 20,000,000 documents covering Sudanese history since 1870; 12,820 vols; Sec.-Gen. Dr M. I. ABU SALEEM; publ. Majallatal Wathaiq (Archives Magazine).

Sudan Medical Research Laboratories Library: POB 287, Khartoum; f. 1904 (as part of Wellcome Tropical Research Laboratories); 7,000 pamphlets, 6,000 vols.

University of Khartoum Library: POB 321, Khartoum; e-mail library@uofk.edu; f. 1945; 333,000 vols, 4,200 periodicals; incl. spec. Sudan and African colln; acts as a depository library for UN, FAO, ILO, WHO and UNESCO publs; Librarian Dr EL-HIBIR YOUSIF.

Omdurman
Omdurman Central Public Library: Omdurman; f. 1951; 17,650 vols.

Wad Medani
Agricultural Research Corporation, Central Library: POB 126, Wad Medani; tel. (511) 842226; fax (511) 843213; e-mail arc.library@arcsudan.sd; internet www.arcsudan.sd; f. 1930; 15,000 vols, 20,000 pamphlets, 250 periodicals, set of The Essential Electronic Agricultural Library (TEEAL) on CD-ROM and LAN version (LanTEEAL); Head Librarian AHLAM ISMAIL MUSA; publs Sudan Journal of Agricultural Research (SJAR) (online), Annual Reports of the ARC research programs, Proceedings of the ARC research programs.

Gezira Research Station Library: Wad Medani; 6,500 vols on agricultural topics.

Museums and Art Galleries
Khartoum
Sudan National Museum: POB 178, Khartoum; tel. (183) 70680; f. 1971; depts of antiquities, ethnology and Sudanese modern history; Dir HASSAN HUSSEIN IDRIS; Curator SIDDIG M. GASM AL-SID; publ. Report on the Antiquities Service and Museums, Kush (1 a year).

Attached Museums:

Ethnographical Museum: POB 178, Khartoum; tel. (183) 77052; f. 1956; collection and preservation of ethnographical objects; Curator MOHAMMED HAMED.

Khalifa's House: Omdurman.

Merowe Museum: Merowe, Northern Province; antiquities and general.

Sheikan Museum: El Obeid; archaeological and ethnographic museum.

Sultan Ali Dinar Museum: El Fasher.

Sudan Natural History Museum: University of Khartoum, POB 321, Khartoum; tel. (183) 81873; f. 1920; library of 801 vols; Dir Dr DAWI MUSA HAMED.

Universities
AL-FASHIR UNIVERSITY
POB 125, Al-Fashir, North Darfur
Telephone: (527) 43394
Fax: (527) 52111
Founded 1975
Vice-Chancellor: ABD ELBAGI MOHAMMED KABIR
Faculties of Education, Environmental Studies and Natural Resources and Medicine and Health Sciences; Centres of Scientific Research and Documentation and Societal Development and Extramural Studies.

AL-NEELAIN UNIVERSITY
POB 12702, Khartoum 12702
Founded 1955 as Khartoum br. of Cairo Univ.; ind. status and present name 1993
State control
Language of instruction: Arabic
Vice-Chancellor: AWAD HAJ ALI AHMED
Number of teachers: 270
Number of students: 36,000
Faculties of agriculture, animal production and fisheries, arts, commerce and socio-economic studies, engineering, graduate studies, law, medicine, optometry and visual sciences, science and technology and statistics, population studies and information technology; Nile Basin Studies Research Centre.

AL-ZAIEM AL-AZHARI UNIVERSITY
POB 1933, Omdurman
Telephone: (15) 560501
Fax: (15) 562536

E-mail: qurashi@sudanmail.net
Founded 1993
State control
Number of teachers: 350
Number of students: 5,109

BAKHET EL-RUDDA UNIVERSITY
POB 1311, Khartoum, Eldewaym
Telephone: (531) 22440
Fax: (531) 20548
Founded 1997
State control
Languages of instruction: Arabic, English
Vice-Chancellor: ANAAS A. EL-HAFEEZ
Number of teachers: 198
Number of students: 4,035

DEANS
Faculty of Agriculture and Natural Resources: GHANIM SABIH
Faculty of Economics and Administration: ILHAM SAADALLAH
Faculty of Education: SALIH NOURIN
Faculty of Medicine: YOUSIF SULTAN
Faculty of Postgraduate Studies: MAHMOUD HASSAN

BLUE NILE UNIVERSITY
POB 143, Damazeen, Blue Nile
Telephone: (183) 785614
Vice-Chancellor: MOHAMMED EL-HASSAN ABDUL EL-RAHMAN
Founded 1995
Faculties of education and engineering; centres of extramural studies and continuing education.

EL-DALANG UNIVERSITY
El-Dalang, South Kordofan
Telephone: (183) 785614
Founded 1990
State control
Vice-Chancellor: KAMESS KAGO KUNDA
Faculties of agriculture, education, social development, teacher training; centres of computer science, peace studies.

EL-GADARIF UNIVERSITY
POB 449, El-Gadarif 32211
Telephone: (441) 43668
Fax: (441) 43120
E-mail: unged@sudanmail.net
Founded 1990; univ. status 1994
State control
Languages of instruction: Arabic, English
Vice-Chancellor: OMER KURDI
Number of teachers: 154
Number of students: 3,845

DEANS
Faculty of Agricultural and Environmental Sciences: ABDEL-AZIZA TAHA
Faculty of Economics and Administrative Science: EL-GUZOLI MOHAMAD
Faculty of Education: SULTAN NOUR
Faculty of Medicine and Medical Sciences: EL-DIRDIRY SALAH

EL-IMAM EL-MAHDI UNIVERSITY
POB 209, Kosti 11588
Telephone: (571) 22545
Fax: (571) 22222
E-mail: abdosm@sudanmail.net
Founded 1993
State control

Vice-Chancellor: ABDELRAHIM OSMAN MOHAMED

Faculties of Arabic and Islamic sciences, arts, engineering and technical studies, law and Islamic law, medicine and health sciences; centres for computer studies, extramural studies.

KASSALA UNIVERSITY

Kassala 266
Telephone: (411) 22095
Fax: (411) 23501
Founded 1990
State control
Vice-Chancellor: MUSTAFA ALI ABASHER

Faculties of agriculture and natural resources, economics and administration, education, medicine and health sciences.

NILE VALLEY UNIVERSITY

POB 1843, Khartoum
E-mail: info@nilevalley.edu.sd
Internet: www.nilevalley.edu.sd
Founded 1990
State control
Language of instruction: Arabic
Academic year: October to June
Vice-Chancellor: Prof. FASIAL A. EL-HAG
Prin.: Dr ATTA A. FADLALLA
Academic Sec.: Prof. MAHMOUD Y. OSMAN
Library of 31,143 books, 76 periodicals
Number of teachers: 240
Number of students: 6,886 (6,796 undergraduate, 90 postgraduate)

DEANS

Faculty of Agriculture: Dr SAIFELDIN M. AL-AMIN
Faculty of Commerce and Business Administration: HAMZA A. HAMZA
Faculty of Education: Dr MOHMED A. MOHAMED
Faculty of Engineering and Technology: IZZELDIN A. ABDALLA
Faculty of Islamic and Arabic Studies: ABDELNABI A. EL-TAYEB
Faculty of Medicine: (vacant)
Teaching-Training College: ABDELGADIR S. HAMAD

NYALA UNIVERSITY

POB 155, Nyala, South Darfur
Telephone: (711) 33122
Fax: (711) 33123
E-mail: nyalauni@yahoo.com
Internet: www.nyalauniversity.net
Founded 1994
State control
Academic year: April to December
Vice-Chancellor
Number of teachers: 151
Number of students: 6,301

Faculties of community development, economics and commerce, education, engineering, law, nursing, technology, veterinary science; Centre for Peace Studies.

OMDURMAN ISLAMIC UNIVERSITY

POB 382, Omdurman
Telephone: (187) 511525
Fax: (187) 511525
Internet: www.oiu.edu
Founded 1912, univ. status 1965
State control
Language of instruction: Arabic
Academic year: October to June
Chair. of Univ. Ccl: Sheikh M. M. SADIQ AL-KAMMOURI

Vice-Chancellor: Prof. MOHAMMED OSMAN SALIH
Sec.-Gen.: Dr HASSAN AHMED HASSAN
Academy Sec.: Prof. HASSAN AHMED EL-HASSAN
Librarian: ABDUL SEED OSMAN
Library of 172,858 vols
Number of teachers: 854
Number of students: 51,636 (47,636 undergraduate, 4,000 postgraduate)
Publications: Faculty of Arts Magazine, Faculty of Islamic Studies Magazine

DEANS

Faculty of Agriculture: Dr M. AL-H. SIDDEEG
Faculty of Arabic Language: Prof. BABEKIR AL-ZACOULT
Faculty of Arts: Prof. H. ABDUL-RAHMAN
Faculty of Basic Medical Sciences: Dr M. SALAH ELDIN
Faculty of Computer Sciences: M. S. MOHAMMED
Faculty of Economics: Dr S. M. MOHAMED
Faculty of Education: Prof. AL-H. OMER HAJ
Faculty of Engineering: Dr H. AL-TAYEB
Faculty of Higher Studies: Dr H. AL-ABBASSI
Faculty of Human Development: Dr IBRAHEEM A. M. AHMED
Faculty of Management Science: Dr A. ABDELRAHD
Faculty of Medicine: Prof. A. I. YOUSSIF
Faculty of Pharmacy: Dr M. AL-H. ABDULLAH
Faculty of Shari'a and Law: Dr A. IBRAHEEM

RED SEA UNIVERSITY

POB 24, Port Sudan
Telephone: (311) 27878
Fax: (311) 27778
Founded 1994
State control
Vice-Chancellor: ABDEL GADIR DAFALLA ELHAG
Number of teachers: 80
Number of students: 800

Faculties of applied sciences, earth sciences, economics and administration, education, engineering, marine science and fisheries, maritime transport economics, medicine and health sciences, teacher training; Institute of Oceanography.

SHENDI UNIVERSITY

POB 142/143, Shendi
Telephone: (261) 5662100
Fax: (261) 872509
E-mail: info@ush.sd
Internet: www.ush.sd
Founded 1990 as Faculty of Nile Valley Univ., present status and title 1994
State control
Language of instruction: Arabic
Academic year: October to August
Vice-Chancellor and Pres.: Prof. YAHIA MOKHTAR
Vice-Pres.: Assoc. Prof. AHMED IBRAHIM
Dean for Graduate Studies and Scientific Research Faculty: Assoc. Prof. YOUSIF YOUSIF
Prin.: Assoc. Prof. SALAH ELHADIA
Dean for Student Affairs: Asst Prof. NADIR SIR ELKHATIM
Dir for Information Technology Center: ABUBAKER ELRAZI AHMED
Number of teachers: 276
Number of students: 5,800
Publication: Journal of Shendi University (scientific, cultural and social topics, 2 a year)

DEANS

Arts Faculty: Asst Prof. HASSAN AWAD ELK-ARIM
Community Development Faculty: Asst Prof. ELYAS ASHWAL
Community Faculty: Assoc. Prof. M. ELHASSAN ELHAFIAN
Economics, Commerce and Business Administration Faculty: Asst Prof. KHALID ABD ELAZIZ
Education Faculty: Asst Prof. YASSIR OSMAN
Health Faculty: Asst Prof. ABD ELSALM DAOOD
Medical Laboratory Science Faculty: Asst Prof. MOHAMMED OSMAN
Medicine and Surgery Faculty: Assoc. Prof. MASOOD ELKHALIFA
Nursing Faculty: Assoc. Prof. NABILA ABD ELALLA
Science and Technology Faculty: Asst Prof. ISAM ELGAILY

SINNAR UNIVERSITY

Sinnar
Telephone: (561) 785614
Fax: (561) 730697
Internet: www.sinnaruniv.edu.sd
Founded 1977; present status 1995
Prin.: MOHAMMED AWAD SALIH

Faculties of agriculture, Arabic and Islamic studies, education, engineering, medicine, natural resources and environment; centre for extramural studies; Da'wah Centre.

SUDAN UNIVERSITY OF SCIENCE AND TECHNOLOGY

POB 407, Khartoum
Telephone: (183) 772508
Fax: (183) 774559
E-mail: sust@sudanet.net
Internet: www.sustech.edu
Founded 1950
State control
Academic year: September to May
Vice-Chancellor: Prof. Dr AHMED ELTAYEB AHMED
Deputy Vice-Chancellor: Prof. Dr GADALLA ABDALLA ELHASSAN
Sec.-Gen.: Dr HASHIM ALI SALIM
Number of teachers: 977
Number of students: 55,924
Publication: Science and Technology (2 a year)

DEANS

College of Agricultural Studies: Dr YOUSIF MOHAMED AHMED
College of Animal Production Science and Technology: Dr HASSAN MOHAMED ADAM
College of Business Studies: Dr MUSA HASAB ELRASOUL KHIER ELSIED
College of Communication Science: Prof. MUKHTAR OSMAN ELSIDDIQ
College of Computer Science and Information Technology: Dr MOHAMED ELHAFIZ MUSTAFA
College of Education: Dr ABDEL RAZEG ABDALLAH ELBONI
College of Engineering: Prof. SHAMBUOL ADLAN MOHAMED
College of Fine and Applied Arts: Dr OMER MOHAMED ELHASSAN
College of Forestry and Range Science: Dr ALI KHALID ALI
College of Graduate Studies: Prof. Dr OSMAN SAAD ALI
College of Languages: Dr SAADIA MOSA OMER
College of Medical Laboratory Science: Dr HUMODI AHMED SAEED
College of Music and Drama: Dr SAAD YOUSIF OBEID

College of Petroleum Engineering and Technology: Dr RASHID AHMED MOHAMMED

College of Physical Education and Sports: Dr HAMID ELSAYED DAFALLAH

College of Medical Radiologic Sciences: Dr ALSAFI AHMED ABD ALLA

College of Sciences: Dr ELFATIH AHMED HASSAN

College of Technology: Dr MUBARAK EL MAHAL AHMED

College of Veterinary Medicine: Prof. Dr AMEL OMER BAKHEIT

College of Water and Environmental Engineering: Dr YOUSIF ALI YOUSIF

UNIVERSITY OF DONGOLA

POB 47, Dongola

Telephone: (241) 21515

Fax: (241) 21514

Founded 1994

State control

Vice-Chancellor: MOHAMMED OSMAN AHMED

Faculties of agriculture, arts, education, law and Islamic law, medicine, mining and earth sciences.

UNIVERSITY OF GEZIRA

POB 20, Wad Medani, 2667 Khartoum

Founded 1975

Language of instruction: English

Vice-Chancellor: (vacant)

Sec.-Gen.: Dr MAHMOUD ABDALLA IBRAHIM

Librarian: ABUEL GAITH SANHOURI

Number of teachers: 140

Number of students: 1,000

DEANS

Faculty of Agriculture: Dr OSMAN ALI SID AHMED

Faculty of Economics and Rural Development: Dr EL TAHIR MOHAMED NUR

Faculty of Education: Prof. ABDEL SALAM MAHMOUD ABDALLA

Faculty of Medicine: Prof. SALAH ELDIN TAHA SALIH

Faculty of Science and Technology: Dr ELNUR KAMAL EL DIN ABU SABAH

Graduate Studies and Academic Affairs: ISAM ABDEL RAHMAN AHMED

Preparatory College: Prof. FAYSAL AWAD

Dean of Students: Dr ABD EL-MUTAAL GIRSHAB

UNIVERSITY OF HOLY QU'RAN AND ISLAMIC SCIENCES

POB 1459, Omdurman

Telephone: (15) 559594

Fax: (15) 559175

Founded 1990 by merger of Holy Qu'ran College and Omdurman Higher Institute

State control

Vice-Chancellor: AHMED KHALID BABIKER

Faculties of Arabic language, community development, media studies, education, educational sciences, the Holy Qu'ran and Islamic law, law; centre for women's studies.

UNIVERSITY OF KHARTOUM

POB 321, 11115 Khartoum

Telephone: (83) 772601

Fax: (83) 780295

E-mail: vc@uofk.edu

Internet: www.uofk.edu

Founded 1956, fmrly Univ. College of Khartoum

State control

Languages of instruction: Arabic, English

Academic year: July to April

Vice-Chancellor: Prof. ELSIDDIG AHMED ELMUSTAFA EL SHEIKH

Deputy Vice-Chancellor: Dr SUMIA MOHAMED AHMED ABU KASHAWA

Prin.: Dr MOHSIN HASSAN ABDALL HASHIM

Academic Sec.: Dr MUSTAFA MOHAMED ALI EL BALLA

Personnel Sec.: Ustaz ABDELRAZIG HASSAN OBEID

Librarian: Prof. AHMED HASSAN FAHAL

Library: see Libraries and Archives

Number of teachers: 1,671

Number of students: 26,088

DEANS

Faculty of Agriculture: Prof. ELAMIN ABDELMAGID EL AMIN

Faculty of Animal Production: Dr IBRAHIM ABDELSALAM YOUSIF

Faculty of Arts: Dr INTISAR SEIGIROUN ELZAIN

Faculty of Dentistry: Dr NADIA AHMED YAHIA

Faculty of Economic and Social Studies: Dr HASSAN ELHAG ALI

Faculty of Education: Prof. ELTYEB AHMED ELMUSTAFA EL SHEIKH

Faculty of Engineering and Architecture: Prof. MOHAMED OSMAN AKODE

Faculty of Forestry: Dr ABDALLA MIRGANI ELTYEB

Faculty of Geography and Environment: Dr AHMED ELFAIEQ

Faculty of Law: Dr ELRASHID HASSAN SAED

Faculty of Mathematical Sciences: Dr MOHSIN HASSAN ABDALLA HASHIM

Faculty of Medical Laboratory Sciences: Prof. NASRELDIN BILAL AHMED

Faculty of Medicine: Prof. AMMAR ELTAHIR AHMED

Faculty of Nursing Sciences: Dr BASHIR ELGAILY

Faculty of Pharmacy: Dr ABUBAKR OSMAN MOHAMED NOOR

Faculty of Public Health and Environmental Hygiene: Dr KAMIL MIRGHANI SHAABAN

Faculty of Science: Dr SALAH BASHIR ABDALLA

Faculty of Technological and Developmental Studies: Dr ABDALLA GUMAA FRWA

Faculty of Veterinary Medicine: Prof. ELGAILANI ALI ELAMIN

Graduate College: Prof. MOHAMED MOHAMED AHMED ELNOUR

School of Management Studies: Prof. ABDELGADIR MOHAMED AHMED

UNIVERSITY OF KORDOFAN

POB 160, El Obeid, North Kordofan 517

Telephone: (611) 23119

Fax: (611) 23108

E-mail: info@uni-kordofan.com

Internet: www.uni-kordofan.com

Founded 1990

State control

Vice-Chancellor: OSMAN ADAM OSMAN

Faculties of commercial studies and business administration; education, engineering and technical science, medicine and health sciences, natural resources, science and humanities, Gum Arabic Research Centre; Institute of Accounting, Banking and Information Systems; Centre for Intermediate Technology in Agriculture.

UNIVERSITY OF WEST KORDOFAN

POB 16722, Khartoum, El-Foula, West Kordofan

Telephone: (183) 785614

Founded 1997

State control

Vice-Chancellor: IBRAHIM MUSA TIBIN

Faculties of economics and community development, education, Islamic and Arabic sciences, natural resources and environmental studies.

UNIVERSITY OF ZALENGEI

Zalengei, West Darfur 6

Telephone: (713) 22013

Fax: (713) 22013

E-mail: uzal@student.net

Founded 1994

State control

Language of instruction: Arabic

Vice-Chancellor: AHMED MOHAMED ABAKER

Number of teachers: 105

Number of students: 1,249

DEANS

Faculty of Agriculture: KUMAL IBRAHIM ADAM

Faculty of Education: ABDUL MUTALIB MOHAMED KHATIR

Holy Koran and Islamic Studies Institute: ABDOUL MUTALIB MOHAMED KHATIR

Colleges and Institutes

Faculty of Hygiene and Environmental Studies: POB 205, Khartoum; tel. 72690; f. 1933; 26 staff; 4 depts; awards BSc and MSc in Environmental Health; Librarian M. MOHD. SALIH; Dean B. M. EL-HASSAN.

Khartoum Nursing College: POB 1063, Khartoum; 3-year diploma course; Prin. A. M. OSMAN.

Yambio Institute of Agriculture: Sud 82/002, c/o UNDP POB 913, Khartoum; f. 1972; library: 5,000 vols; 15 staff; 130 students; 2-year diploma courses; Prin. CHRISTOPHER LADO GALE.

SURINAME

The Higher Education System

Higher education institutions predate the independence of Suriname (formerly Dutch Guiana) from the Netherlands in 1975, with the oldest being Anton de Kom Universiteit van Suriname, which was founded in 1968 and is the sole university in the country. In addition to the university, higher education is offered by six technical and vocational schools. In 2001/02 there were 3,250 students enrolled at the university, with a further 1,936 students enrolled in other institutions of higher education. The Ministry of Education and Community Development is the government agency responsible for higher education.

The Dutch-style Voorbereidend Wetenschappelijk Onderwijs (university preparatory education examination) is the main criterion for admission to higher education. Students holding the Hoger Algemeen Vormend Onderwijs (higher general secondary education examination) may also gain entrance to higher education, via a bridging year of study. The Bachelors is the undergraduate degree at the University and the course lasts four years, with the exception of business administration, which lasts three years. The University does not offer Masters degrees.

The Academie voor Hoger Kunst en Cultuuronderwijs (Academy for Higher Arts and Cultural Education) offers four-year Bachelors degree programmes in arts, journalism and socio-cultural studies, while the other five technical and vocational institutions offer post-secondary Certificates and Diplomas in a variety of professional fields.

Regulatory Body

GOVERNMENT

Ministry of Education and Community Development: Dr Samuel Kafiluddistraat 117–123, Paramaribo; tel. 498383; fax 495083; e-mail minond@sr.net; Minister EDWIN TOEKIDJAN WOLF.

Learned Society

LANGUAGE AND LITERATURE

Alliance Française: Prins Hendrikstraat 8, POB 9209, Paramaribo; tel. 4211305; offers courses and exams in French language and culture and promotes cultural exchange with France.

Research Institutes

AGRICULTURE, FISHERIES AND VETERINARY SCIENCE

Centre for Agricultural Research in Suriname: POB 1914, Paramaribo; tel. 490128; fax 498069; e-mail celos@sr.net; internet www.celos.sr.org; f. 1965; a branch of the University of Suriname; research in tropical agriculture; Dir R. O. RAVENSWAAY; publ. Celos Bulletins.

Landbouwproefstation (Agricultural Experiment Station): POB 160, Paramaribo; tel. 472442; fax 420152; e-mail odlb.ond@sr.net; f. 1903; attached to Min. of Agriculture, Animal Husbandry and Fisheries; agricultural research; library of 28,502 vols, incl. bound periodicals and pamphlets; Dir Drs ELVIS GOEDHART (acting); Librarian R. CHOTOE; publs Bulletins (irregular), Suriname Agriculture (2 to 3 a year).

TECHNOLOGY

Geologisch Mijnbouwkundige Dienst (Geological Mining Service): Lachmonstr. 181, Paramaribo; tel. 434187; fax 434252; f. 1943; publs contributions in Mededelingen, geological maps; library of 20,000 vols; Head M. AUTAR (acting).

Library

Paramaribo

Bibliotheek van het Cultureel Centrum Suriname (Library of the Suriname Cultural Centre): POB 1241, Paramaribo; tel. 473309; fax 476519; e-mail stgccs@yahoo.com; internet www.ccs-suriname.com; f. 1948; 7 brs, 2 book-mobiles; 50,000 vols; Librarian MARCELLA AUGUSTUSZOON; Dir Dr ELVIERA SANDIE.

Museum

Paramaribo

Stichting Surinaams Museum: POB 2306, Abraham Crijnssenweg 1, Paramaribo; tel. 425871; fax 425881; e-mail museum@cq-link.sr; internet www.surinaamsmuseum.net; f. 1947; archaeology, art, history, ethnology; library of 35,000 vols; Dir Drs J. H. J. VAN PUTTEN; publ. Libri Musei Surinamensis.

University

ANTON DE KOM UNIVERSITEIT VAN SURINAME
(Anton de Kom University of Suriname)

Universiteitscomplex Leysweg 86, POB 9212, Paramaribo

Telephone: 465558
Fax: 494697
E-mail: info@uvs.edu
Internet: www.uvs.edu

Founded 1968
Language of instruction: Dutch
Academic year: October to September

Pres.: Dr R. SIDIN
Vice-Pres.: Dr A. LI FO SJOE
Sec.: K. GOENOPAWIRO

Number of teachers: 387
Number of students: 4,496

Publications: Journal of Social Sciences (2 a year), Suriname Medical Bulletin (4 a year)

DEANS

Faculty of Medicine: Dr J. TOELSIE
Faculty of Social Sciences: C. WALLERLEI
Faculty of Technology: C. RAHAN-CHIN

SWAZILAND

The Higher Education System

Higher education institutions pre-date the independence of Swaziland from the United Kingdom in 1968, with the oldest being the University of Swaziland (formerly the University of Botswana, Lesotho and Swaziland), which was founded in 1964. In 2010/11 5,556 students were enrolled at the University of Swaziland, which has two main campuses at Luyengo and Kwaluseni; there are also a number of other institutions of higher education. Plans to establish the Swaziland Christian Medical University, which would become the country's first medical institution, were at an advanced stage in 2011; construction of the university, which was expected to take three years to complete, was to be funded by investors from the Republic of Korea (South Korea). Currently, Swazi students wishing to enter the medical profession are forced to seek training abroad.

GCE A-Levels, the Cambridge Overseas School Certificate or the Cambridge Overseas Higher School Certificate can be used to gain admission to undergraduate courses at the University. The undergraduate Bachelors degree last fours years, divided into two, two-year cycles. Postgraduate Masters degrees are awarded in a restricted number of fields, including arts, sciences and education, and require between one and two years' study.

Post-secondary technical and vocational education is offered by a number of institutions, including Swaziland College of Technology, the Institute of Health Sciences and Swaziland Institute of Management and Public Administration. Swaziland College of Technology offers craft, technician and diploma courses, which generally last between three and five years.

Regulatory Body

GOVERNMENT

Ministry of Education: POB 39, Mbabane; tel. 4042491; fax 4043880; Minister THEMBA MSIBI.

Learned Societies

GENERAL

Royal Swaziland Society of Science and Technology: c/o The University, Private Bag, Kwaluseni; tel. 5284011; fax 5285276; f. 1977 to promote science and technology and relevant research; organizes meetings, seminars, etc.; 100 mems; Pres. Prof. L. P. MAKHUBU; Sec. R. MARTIN; publ. *Swaziland Journal of Science and Technology* (2 a year).

BIBLIOGRAPHY, LIBRARY SCIENCE AND MUSEOLOGY

Swaziland Library Association: POB 2309, Mbabane H100; Elwatini Bldg, cnr Market and Warner Sts, Mbabane; tel. 4042633; fax 4043863; e-mail fmkhonta@uniswacc.uniswa.sz; internet www.swala.sz; f. 1984; 120 mems; Chair. FAITH MKHONTA; Sec. JABULILE DLAMINI; publ. *SWALA Journal* (2 a year).

FINE AND PERFORMING ARTS

Swaziland Art Society: POB 812, Mbabane; tel. 4044136; e-mail artsociety@mailfly.com; internet www.swazilandartsociety.org.sz; f. 1970; classes, workshops, exhibitions, films, discussions, etc.; 60 mems; Chairs HELEN MOIR, ANS VRIEND.

LANGUAGE AND LITERATURE

Alliance Française: Swazi Plaza, POB A266, Mbabane; tel. 4043667; fax 4048340; e-mail mbabane@alliance.org.za; internet www.swaziplace.com/alliancefrancaise/index.html; offers courses and exams in French language and culture and promotes cultural exchange with France.

Research Institutes

AGRICULTURE, FISHERIES AND VETERINARY SCIENCE

Lowveld Experiment Station: POB 11, L312 Matata; tel. 3636311; fax 5283360; f. 1964; agricultural research, cotton breeding, cotton entomology; Chief Research Officer P. MKHATSHWA.

Malkerns Research Station: POB 4, Malkerns; tel. 5283306; fax 5283306; f. 1959; general research on crops, vegetables, fruits and farming systems; 14 research sections; library of 5,000 vols; Chief Research Officer P. D. MKHATSHWA.

Mpisi Cattle Breeding Experimental Station: Mpisi; aims to improve indigenous Nguni cattle; to provide multiplication studs of Brahman, Simmentaler and Friesland cattle for beef, milk and cross breeding; Dir R. A. JOHN; Man. I. A. MORLEY HEWITT.

TECHNOLOGY

Geological Survey and Mines Department: POB 9, Mbabane; tel. 4042411; fax 4045215; e-mail geo.director@swazi.net; f. 1944; activities: mapping of the territory (published at a scale of 1:25,000 and 1:50,000), the investigation of mineral occurrences by prospecting, detailed mapping and diamond drilling, mine and quarry inspections, control of explosives and prospecting; 18 mems; small library; Dir Dr M. MAPHALALA; publ. *Bulletins*.

Libraries and Archives

Mbabane

Swaziland National Archives: POB 946, Mbabane; tel. 4161196; fax 4161241; e-mail kholekilemthethwa@gmail.com; f. 1970; govt records since 1880s; colln of historical photographs, newspapers, maps, reports; oral history and biographies of prominent Swazis; 5,600 vols; Dir D. F. K. MTHETHWA (acting).

Swaziland National Library Service: POB 1461, Mbabane; tel. 4042633; fax 4043863; e-mail snlssz@snls.gov.sz; internet www.gov.sz; f. 1971; operates a public library service throughout the country with branch libraries at Manzini, Mpaka, Lomahasha, Nhlangano, Siteki, Pigg's Peak, Big Bend, Bhunya, Tshaneni, Mankayana, Lavumisa, Hlatikulu and Mhlume; mobile library visits; libraries at secondary schools; 80,000 vols, 150 periodicals; a national library was est. in 1986, which will eventually function as the focal point in Swaziland's documentation and information system; Dir D. J. KUNENE; publs *Accessions List* (irregular), *Index to Swaziland Collection* (irregular).

Museum

Lobamba

Swaziland National Museum: POB 100, Lobamba; tel. 4161178; fax 4161875; f. 1972, under the patronage of the Swaziland National Trust Commission; museum with extra-mural functions, giving information about Swazi culture as well as other Southern African Bantu groups; reference library; Curator ROSEMARY ANDRADE; publ. *Museum Occasional Paper*.

University

UNIVERSITY OF SWAZILAND

Private Bag 4, M201 Kwaluseni
Telephone: 5184011
Fax: 5185276
E-mail: registrar@admin.uniswa.sz
Internet: www.uniswa.sz

Founded 1964 as part of Univ. of Botswana, Lesotho and Swaziland, present name 1982
Language of instruction: English
Academic year: August to May

Chancellor: HM KING MSWATI III
Vice-Chancellor: (vacant)
Pro-Vice-Chancellor: Prof. C. M. MAGAGULA
Registrar: S. S. VILAKATI
Librarian: M. R. MAVUSO

Library of 178,000 vols, 1,500 periodicals
Number of teachers: 303
Number of students: 4,198

Publications: *UNISWA Journal of Agriculture, Science and Health Sciences* (2 a year), *UNISWA Journal of Social Science, Humanities and Education* (2 a year)

DEANS

Faculty of Agriculture: Dr G. N. SHONGWE
Faculty of Commerce: Prof. M. A. KHAN
Faculty of Education: Prof. J. C. B. BIGALA
Faculty of Health Sciences: Dr P. S. DLAMINI
Faculty of Humanities: Dr H. L. NDLOVU
Faculty of Postgraduate Studies: Prof. E. C. L. KUNENE
Faculty of Science: Prof. V. S. B. MTETWA
Faculty of Social Sciences: Prof. A. A. AL-TERAIFI

There is also an Institute of Distance Education

Colleges

Swaziland College of Technology: POB 69, H100 Mbabane; tel. 4042681; fax 4044521; e-mail scot@africaonline.co.sz; f. 1946 as Trade School, present name 1968; diploma courses in mechanical engineering, electrical and electronics engineering, telecommunications engineering, building and civil engineering, hotel and catering, secretarial studies, commercial and technical teaching; certificate courses in accounting, plumbing, block- and bricklaying, carpentry; library: 18,000 vols; 60 teachers; 700 students; Prin. HEBRON T. SUKATI; Registrar ATWELL GULE.

Swaziland Institute of Management and Public Administration: POB 495, Mbabane; tel. 4220740; fax 4220742; e-mail simpa@realnet.co.sz; f. 1965; 21 teachers (15 full-time, 6 part-time); 900 students; Prin. M. N. KHOZA.

SWEDEN

The Higher Education System

The oldest institution of higher education is Uppsala Universitet (Uppsala University), which was founded in 1477; the next oldest is Lunds Universitet (Lund University), which was founded in 1666. Several institutions date from the 19th century, among them Kungliga Tekniska Högskolan (Royal Institute of Technology—founded 1827), Stockholms Universitet (Stockholm University—founded 1878) and Göteborgs Universitet (Gothenburg University—founded 1891). Higher education is offered by universities (universitet), university colleges or institutes of higher education (högskola). In 2003/04 there were 397,679 students enrolled in higher education, and in 2007/08 there were 64 higher education institutions.

Higher education is administered by the Högskoleverket (Swedish National Agency for Higher Education). In 1977 the Higher Education Act classified 100 programmes of undergraduate education by five subject areas (administrative, economic and social science; health; information, communication and fine arts; teacher training; and technical); however, in 1989 responsibility for curriculum-planning was handed over to the universities, and further reforms in 1993 delineated undergraduate programmes into general or professional fields of study. Also in 1993 higher education was decentralized and a new degree system was introduced. Sweden participates in the Bologna Process to establish a European Higher Education Area, the first phase of which is to adopt a credit-based system of comparable degrees with two main cycles (undergraduate and graduate). In 2002 the Ministry of Education and Research established a working group to assess the feasibility of introducing a new degree system to correspond with the criteria of the Bologna Process, and subsequently a new system (see below) was fully implemented in 2007. The Högskoleverket quality-assured all professional degree programmes in the period 2001–06. The new six-year cycle of programme evaluations started in 2007, covering all degrees at first, second and third level. Tuition for domestic and European Union (EU) students is free. However, at the beginning of the 2011/12 academic year Sweden introduced tuition fees for non-EU students; as a result, the number of foreign students was expected to decline substantially.

The main requirement for admission to higher education is completion of secondary education and award of the Avgångsbetyg or Slutbetyg från Gymnasieskola (upper secondary school leaving certificate). Alternatively, applicants can be admitted upon completion of komvux (adult secondary school), completion of folkhögskola (folk high school) or at least four years of professional experience before the age of 25, as well as knowledge of Swedish and English. Specialist programmes of study may have additional criteria. Furthermore, applicants sit either the Högskoleprov (special aptitude test) or Högskoleprovet (national university aptitude test). The newly established university degree system comprises three cycles, each subdivided into two parts; degrees are awarded on a 'credit' basis, and Sweden has adopted the European Credit Transfer System (ECTS). The undergraduate Bachelors degrees is the Kandidatexamen, which lasts three years (180 credits). Yrkesexamen (professional degrees) may last longer. The Masters-equivalent degrees are the Magisterexamen, lasting one year (60 credits), and the Masterexamen, which lasts two years (120 credits). Both the Magisterexamen and the Masterexamen allow access to doctoral-level studies, which consist of the Licentiatexamen, a two-year research degree (120 credits), and the Doktorsexamen, a research degree culminating with submission and defence of a thesis; while it is possible to complete the Doktorsexamen in four years (240 credits), most students take six years.

The Kvalificerad Yrkesutbildning (Advanced Vocational Education—AVE), which was introduced in 1996 on a trial basis and enacted as law in 2002, primarily consists of programmes of study jointly organized by employers and institutions of tertiary education, and lasts between one and three years. The main government provider is the Myndigheten för Yrkeshögskolan (Swedish National Agency for Higher Vocational Education). Yrkeshögskoleutbildning (Higher Vocational Education Courses—HVECs) were introduced in 2009 and will gradually replace the AVE, which is to be phased out by 2013. HVECs last a minimum of six months. HVECs lasting at least one year and including a minimum of 25% workplace-based training as well as submission of a dissertation lead to award of the Yrkeshögskoleexamen (Higher Vocational Education Examination Certificate).

Regulatory and Representative Bodies

GOVERNMENT

Ministry of Culture: Drottninggatan 16, SE-103 33 Stockholm; tel. (8) 405-10-00; fax (8) 21-68-13; e-mail registrator@culture .ministry.se; internet www.sweden.gov.se/sb/ d/8371; Min. of Culture and Sport LENA ADELSOHN LILJEROTH.

Ministry of Education and Research: Drottninggatan 16, SE-103 33 Stockholm; tel. (8) 405-10-00; fax (8) 723-11-92; e-mail registrator@education.ministry.se; internet www.sweden.gov.se/sb/d/2063; Min. of Education JAN BJÖRKLUND; Deputy Min. of Education NYAMKO SABUNI; Min. of Higher Education and Research TOBIAS KRANTZ.

ACCREDITATION

ENIC/NARIC Sweden: Swedish Nat. Agency for Higher Education, POB 7851, SE-103 99 Stockholm; Luntmakargatan 13, SE-111 37 Stockholm; tel. (8) 563-085-00; fax (8) 563-086-50; e-mail hsv@hsv.se; internet www.hsv.se; f. 1995; Head LARS HAIKOLA.

NATIONAL BODIES

Folkhögskolornas informationstjänst (Information Service of the Swedish Folk High Schools): Box 380 74, SE-100 64 Stockholm; Rosenlundsgatan 50, Stockholm; tel. (8) 796-00-50; fax (8) 21-88-26; e-mail info@ folkhogskola.nu; internet www.folkhogskola .nu; Coordinator AGNETA WALLIN.

Myndigheten för Yrkeshögskolan (Swedish National Agency for Higher Vocational Education): Box 145, SE-721 05 Västerås; Ingenjör Bååths gata 19, SE-722 12 Västerås; tel. (10) 209-01-00; fax (21) 13-20-16; e-mail info@yhmyndigheten.se; internet www.yhmyndigheten.se; f. 2009; Gen. Dir PIA ENOCHSSON.

Rådet för högre utbildning (Council for the Renewal of Higher Education): POB 7285, SE-103 89 Stockholm; Luntmakargatan 13, Stockholm; tel. (8) 56-30-88-61; fax (8) 56-30-88-50; e-mail rhu@rhu.se; internet www.rhu.se; f. 1990; Chair. Prof. LARS HAIKOLA.

Skolverket (Swedish National Agency for Education): SE-106 20 Stockholm; Fleminggatan 14, Stockholm; tel. (8) 52-73-32-00; fax (8) 24-44-20; e-mail skolverket@skolverket .se; internet www.skolverket.se; Dir HELÉN ÅNGMO.

Styrelsen för Internationellt Utvecklingssamarbete (Swedish International Development Cooperation Agency): Valhallavägen 199, SE-105 25 Stockholm; tel. (8) 698-50-00; fax (8) 20-88-64; e-mail sida@sida.se; internet www.sida.se; attached to Min. for Foreign Affairs; Dir-Gen. CHARLOTTE PETRI GORNITZKA (acting); Deputy Dir-Gen. BO NETZ.

Svenska institutet (Swedish Institute): Slottsbacken 10, Box 7434, SE-103 91 Stockholm; tel. (8) 453-78-00; fax (8) 20-72-48; e-mail si@si.se; internet www.si.se; Dir-Gen. ANNIKA REMBE.

Sveriges universitets- och högskoleförbund (SUHF) (Association of Swedish Higher Education): Tryckerigatan 8, SE-111 28 Stockholm; tel. (8) 32-13-88; fax (8) 32-93-70; e-mail jennie.reponen@suhf.se; internet www.suhf.se; f. 1995; 40 mems; Chair. PAM

FREDMAN; Vice-Chair. AGNETA STARK; Sec.-Gen. Dr BENGT KARLSSON.

Learned Societies

GENERAL

Finlandsinstitutet (Finnish Cultural Centre): POB 1355, SE-111 83 Stockholm; Snickarbacken 2–4 (vid Birger Jarlsgatan 35), SE-111 83, Stockholm; tel. (8) 54-52-12-00; fax (8) 54-52-12-10; e-mail info@finlandsinstitutet.se; internet www.finlandsinstitutet.se; f. 1995; 1 of 16 Finnish cultural instns worldwide; organizes cultural events, seminars, concerts, art exhibitions, language courses; library of 16,000 vols; cassette books, CDs, video cassettes; Dir BENGT PACKALÉN.

Kungl. Humanistiska Vetenskaps-Samfundet i Uppsala (Royal Society of Humanities at Uppsala): c/o Prof. Staffan Fridell, Dept of Scandinavian Languages, POB 527, SE-751 20 Uppsala; tel. (18) 471-12-73; fax (18) 471-12-72; e-mail info@khvsu.se; internet www.khvsu.se; f. 1889; promotes study of humanities; 5 meetings a year, with lectures and discussion; distributes awards and scholarships; 120 mems (100 Swedish, 20 foreign); Pres. Prof. CARL REINHOLD BRÅKENHIELM; Gen. Sec. Prof. STAFFAN FRIDELL; publs *Acta Westiniana*, *Årsböcker* (Yearbook), *Skrifter* (Proceedings, irregular), *Uppländska domböcker*.

Kungl. Vetenskapsakademien (Royal Swedish Academy of Sciences): POB 50005, SE-104 05 Stockholm; Lilla Frescativägen 4A, SE-114 18 Stockholm; tel. (8) 673-95-00; fax (8) 15-56-70; e-mail info@kva.se; internet kva.se; f. 1739; acts as a forum where researchers can meet across subject borders; supports young researchers; rewards prominent contributions to research; arranges int. scientific contacts; acts as a voice of science and influences research policy priorities; stimulates interest in mathematics and natural sciences in schools; disseminates scientific and popular-scientific information in various forms; 605 mems (430 Swedish, 175 foreign); Pres. Prof. SVANTE LINDQVIST; Vice-Pres. BRITT-MARIE SJÖBERG; Vice-Pres. STEFAN CLAESSON; Vice-Pres. ULF PETTERSSON; Permanent Sec. Prof. STAFFAN NORMARK; publs *Acta Mathematica*, *Acta Zoologica*, *Ambio*, *Arkiv för Matematik*, *ETAI*, *Physica Scripta*, *Zoologica Scripta*.

Kungl. Vetenskaps- och Vitterhets-Samhället i Göteborg (KVVS) (Royal Society of Arts and Sciences in Gothenburg): POB 222, SE-405 30 Gothenburg; tel. (31) 786-14-00; fax (31) 786-55-50; e-mail info@kvvs.se; internet www.kvvs.se; f. 1778; scientific lectures, confs, symposia; cooperation with other scientific academies, domestic and foreign support to long-term scientific research programmes; publs, exchange of publs nationally and internationally; stipends to jr and sr researchers; 331 mems (256 Swedish, 75 foreign); Chair. Prof. PETER JAGERS; Vice-Chair. Prof. BEATA AGRELL; Sec.-Gen. Prof. BIRGER KARLSSON; Treas. Prof. MARTIN FRITZ; Librarian Prof. BO LINDBERG; publ. *Årsbok*.

Kungl. Vetenskaps-Societeten i Uppsala (Royal Society of Sciences of Uppsala): St Lars St 1, SE-753 10 Uppsala; tel. and fax (18) 13-12-70; e-mail kansli@vetenskapssocietetenuppsala.se; internet www.vetenskapssocietetenuppsala.se; f. 1710, charter 1728; promotes research principally in mathematics, natural sciences, medicine, Swedish antiquities and topography by publishing scholarly works, award-ing grants, collecting and making available relevant publs, lectures; 230 mems (130 full mems, 100 foreign mems); library of 600 periodicals; Pres. HM KING CARL XVI GUSTAF; Chair. Prof. LARS ENGWALL; Vice-Chair. Prof. LENNART DENCKER; Sec. Prof. LARS-OLOF SUNDELÖF; Treas. ARNE FORSELL; publs *Matrikel* (1 a year), *Nova Acta Regia Societatis Scientiarum Upsaliensis* (irregular).

Kungl. Vitterhets Historie och Antikvitets Akademien (Royal Swedish Academy of Letters, History and Antiquities): Kungl. Vitterhetsakademien, POB 5622, SE-114 86 Stockholm; tel. (8) 440-42-80; fax (8) 440-42-90; e-mail kansli@vitterhetsakad.se; internet www.vitterhetsakad.se; f. 1753, present name 1786; promotes research and other activities in the fields of humanities, social sciences, religion, law; 169 mems (123 Swedish, 40 foreign, 6 hon.); library: see Libraries and Archives; Pres. Prof. GUNNEL ENGWALL; Vice-Pres. Prof. JAN HJÄRPE; Sec.-Gen. Dr ERIK NORBERG; Deputy Sec. Prof. MATS THELANDER; publs *Arkiv* (archives), *Fornvännen* (journal), *Handlingar* (proceedings).

AGRICULTURE, FISHERIES AND VETERINARY SCIENCE

Kungl. Skogs- och Lantbruksakademien (Royal Swedish Academy of Agriculture and Forestry): POB 6806, SE-113 86 Stockholm; Drottninggatan 95B, SE-113 86 Stockholm; tel. (8) 545-477-00; fax (8) 545-477-10; e-mail akademien@ksla.se; internet www.ksla.se; f. 1813; promotes sustainable devt, agriculture, forestry, horticulture, animal husbandry, hunting, fishing and water management; 556 mems (11 hon., 400 working, 145 foreign); library: see under Libraries and Archives; Pres. Dr KERSTIN NIBLAEUS; Vice-Pres. Prof. BO ANDERSSON; Sec.-Gen. Dr CARL-ANDERS HELANDER; Chief Information Officer YLVA NORDIN; publ. *Kungl. Skogs och Lantbruksakademiens Tidskrift (KSLAT)* (4 a year).

ARCHITECTURE AND TOWN PLANNING

Svenska Teknik & Designföretagen (Swedish Federation of Consulting Engineers and Architects): POB 555 45, SE-102 04 Stockholm; Sturegatan 11, SE-102 04 Stockholm; tel. (8) 762-67-00; fax (8) 762-67-10; e-mail std@std.se; internet www.std.se; f. 2001; focuses on improving the environment for mem. cos that operate both as a commercial party and employer; 740 mem cos; Chair. BENT JOHANNESSON; Man. Dir LENA WÄSTFELT; publ. *Sector Review* (1 a year).

ECONOMICS, LAW AND POLITICS

Centre for the Study of International Relations: Hagtornsvägen 9, Enebyberg, SE-182 47 Stockholm; tel. (8) 612-33-62; fax (8) 758-30-39; e-mail info@cintrel.org; f. 1971; studies social sciences, int. politics, law and economy; ind. of any political party; organizes lectures and confs, research seminars; library; Pres. CLÁES PALME; Vice-Pres. and Dir Prof. Dr RICHARD K. T. HSIEH; Sec. Prof. Dr JACOB W. F. SUNDBERG; Sec. Prof. Dr LARS HJERNER; publ. *Review*.

International Law Association, Swedish Branch: c/o Attorney John Kadelburger AB, Engelbrektsgatan 9–11, SE-114 32 Stockholm; tel. (8) 120-66-132; fax (8) 120-661-10; e-mail sekretariat@ilasweden.se; internet www.ilasweden.se; f. 1922; studies and develops int. law (private and procedural); promotes studies in comparative law; draws up proposals for conflict resolution and unification of measures in int. law; fosters int. understanding and goodwill; Pres. Prof. OVE BRING; Sec. and Treas. JOHN KADELBURGER.

Kungl Krigsvetenskapsakademien (Royal Swedish Academy of War Sciences): Teatergatan 3, 5 tr, SE-111 48 Stockholm; tel. (8) 611-14-00; fax (8) 667-22-53; e-mail info@kkrva.se; internet www.kkrva.se; f. 1796 as Swedish Military Asscn, present status 1805; promotes military sciences, incl. civil defence, economic defence and psychological defence, security and defence policy; 400 mems; Pres. Prof. BO HULDT; Vice-Pres. ERIK ROSSANDER; Sec. BJÖRN ANDERSON; publ. *Kungl Krigsvetenskapsakademiens Handlingar och Tidskrift* (4 a year).

Nationalekonomiska Föreningen (Swedish Economic Association): c/o SOFI, Stockholm Univ., SE-106 91 Stockholm; tel. (8) 16-25-13; fax (8) 15-46-70; e-mail anders.bohlmark@sofi.su.se; f. 1877; study of economics; 1,200 mems; Chair. Dr PEHR WISSÉN; Vice-Chair. Prof. MÅRTEN PALME; Sec. ANDERS BÖHLMARK; publ. *Ekonomisk Debatt* (8 a year).

Utrikespolitiska Institutet (Swedish Institute of International Affairs): POB 27035, SE-102 51 Stockholm; Drottning Kristinas väg 37, SE-102 51 Stockholm; tel. (8) 511-768-00; fax (8) 511-768-99; e-mail info@ui.se; internet www.ui.se; f. 1938; researches on int. affairs; enhances public understanding of current int. affairs; confs, seminars and other events; 250 mems; library of 40,000 vols, 400 periodicals; Pres. MATS BERGQUIST; Dir ANNA JARDFELT; Dir for Admin LARS ÅMAN (acting); Research Dir Dr HANNA OJANEN; publs *Internationella studier*, *Länder i fickformat*, *Research Report*, *UI Papers*, *Världens Fakta*, *Världspolitikens dagsfrågor*.

FINE AND PERFORMING ARTS

Föreningen Svenska Tonsättare (Society of Swedish Composers): POB 27327, SE-102 54 Stockholm; tel. (8) 783-95-90; fax (8) 783-95-40; e-mail katarina.widell@fst.se; internet www.fst.se; f. 1918; promotes contemporary classical music composition; 329 mems; Pres. MARTIN Q. LARSSON; Vice-Pres. CHRICHAN LARSON.

Fylkingen (Society of Contemporary Music and Intermedia Art): Söder Mälarstrand 27, SE-118 25 Stockholm; Torkel Knutssonsgatan 2, Münchenbryggeriet, Stockholm; tel. (8) 84-54-43; fax (8) 669-38-68; e-mail intermedia@fylkingen.se; internet www.fylkingen.se; f. 1933 as a chamber music society; promotes new music and intermedia art; 248 mems; Chair. JOHANNES BERGMARK; publ. *Hz* (online, 2 a year).

Kungliga Akademien för de fria Konsterna (Konstakademien) (Royal Swedish Academy of Fine Arts): POB 16317, SE-103 26 Stockholm; Fredsgatan 12, Jakobsgatan 27C, SE-103 26 Stockholm; tel. (8) 23-29-25; fax (8) 790-59-24; e-mail susanna.sloor@konstakademien.se; internet www.konstakademien.se; f. 1735; promotes devt of painting, sculpture, architecture and allied arts; 145 mems (102 Swedish, 24 foreign, 19 hon.); library of 60,000 vols; Pres. ULLA FRIES; Vice-Pres. STURE KOINBERG; Permanent Sec. SUSANNA SLÖÖR; Head Librarian ULF NORDQVIST.

Kungl. Musikaliska Akademien (Royal Swedish Academy of Music): Blasieholmstorg 8, SE-111 48 Stockholm; tel. (8) 407-18-00; fax (8) 611-87-18; e-mail adm@musakad.se; internet www.musakad.se; f. 1771; promotes and protects the art and science of music; awards Rolf Schock Prize, Christ Johnson Prize and Royal Swedish Acad. of Music Jazz Prize; 170 Swedish mems; 60 foreign mems; Pres. Prof. KJELL INGEBRETSEN; Vice-Pres. THOMAS JENNEFELT; Vice-Pres. ANNA LINDAL; Permanent Sec. Dr ÅKE HOLMQUIST; publs

Årsskrift (yearbook), *Musica Sveciae* (record anthology).

Kulturrådet (Swedish Arts Council): POB 27215, SE-102 53 Stockholm; tel. (8) 519-264-00; fax (8) 519-264-99; e-mail kulturradet@ kulturradet.se; internet www.kulturradet.se; f. 1974; funding, advisory and investigatory body responsible for implementing nat. cultural policy; covers theatre, dance, music, literature, cultural journals, public libraries, art, museums and exhibitions; Chair. KERSTIN BRUNNBERG; Dir-Gen. KENNET JOHANSSON; publ. *Kulturrådet*.

Musikaliska Konstföreningen (Swedish Art Music Society): Sveavägen 12, Saltsjöbaden, SE-111 48 Stockholm; tel. (709) 20-61-96; e-mail sheetmusic@ musikaliskakonstforeningen.se; internet www.musikaliskakonstforeningen.se; f. 1859; publishes and sells works of ancient and contemporary composers; promotes Swedish music; Chair. ERIK LUNDKVIST; Sec. HANS ENFLO; Treas. ALF WESTELIUS.

Svensk Form (Swedish Society of Crafts and Design): POB 204, SE-101 24 Stockholm; Skeppsholmen, Svensksundsvägen 13, SE-111 49 Stockholm; tel. (8) 463-31-30; fax (8) 644-22-85; e-mail info@svenskform.se; internet www.svenskform.se; f. 1845 as Swedish Society for Industrial Design; promotes Swedish designs; 8,000 mems; Chair. JENNY LANTZ; publ. *Form* (6 a year).

Svenska Samfundet för Musikforskning (Swedish Society for Musicology): POB 7448, SE-103 91 Stockholm; tel. (46) 121-027; e-mail jacob.derkert@music.su.se; internet musikforskning.se; f. 1919; unifying forum for musicologists; disseminates knowledge of musicological research in and about Sweden; 87 mems; Chair. JACOB DERKERT; Vice-Chair. EVA GEORGII-HEMMING; Sec. MATTIAS LUNDBERG; Treas. EVA KJELLANDER; publs *Monumenta Musicae Sveciae, Svensk Tidskrift för Musikforskning* (Swedish Journal of Musicology, 1 a year).

Sveriges Allmänna Konstförening (Swedish General Art Association): POB 5343, SE-102 47 Stockholm; Liljevalchs konsthall, Djurgårdsv 60, Stockholm; tel. (8) 10-46-77; fax (8) 20-14-57; e-mail info@ konstforeningen.se; internet www .konstforeningen.se; f. 1832; promotes Swedish contemporary art; organizes exhibitions; 8,000 mems; Pres. EVA SCHÖLD; Vice-Pres. MÅRTEN CASTENFORS; Treas. JAN-ERIK SÖDERHIELM; publ. *Sveriges Allmänna Konstförenings årspublikation* (Swedish General Art Association's annual publication).

HISTORY, GEOGRAPHY AND ARCHAEOLOGY

Karolinska Förbundet: c/o Gidlöf, Hildebergsvägen 16, SE-117 62 Stockholm; tel. (8) 727-02-15; e-mail info@karolinska-forbundet .org; internet www.karolinska-forbundet.org; f. 1910; promotes research and dissemination of knowledge on Caroline era; 1,000 mem companies; Pres. Dr ÅSA KARLSSON; Vice-Pres. Col BERTIL WENNERHOLM; Sec. LEIF GIDLÖF; publ. *Karolinska Förbundets Årsbok*.

Kartografiska Sällskapet (Swedish Cartographic Society): c/o Lantmäteriet, SE-801 82 Gävle; tel. (26) 63-32-37; e-mail ks@ kartografiska.se; internet www .kartografiska.se; f. 1908; promotes and develops cartography and other topics related to mapping or use of maps in Sweden in areas such as photogrammetry, remote sensing, geodesy, geographical information systems, geographic information technology, historical cartography and cartography; 2,000 mems; Pres. PETER WASSTRÖM; Vice-Pres. ANN ERIKSSON; Sec. KARIN GRÅNÄS; Treas. TORBJÖRN OHLSSON; publs *Kart &*

Bildteknik (4 a year), *National Report* (mapping activities, in English, every 4 years), *Sveriges Kartläggning* (mapping of Sweden, every 10 years).

Svenska Museiföreningen (Swedish Museums Association): Åsögatan 90, SE-118 29 Stockholm; tel. (8) 640-43-72; e-mail per .kaks@telia.com; f. 1906; asscn of Swedish museums and mems of staff; debates, etc., concerning practical devt and museum policy issues; mem of Network of European Museum Organizations (NEMO); 1,000 individual mems, 200 institutional mems; Pres. LARS AMREUS; Sec.-Gen. MATS PERSSON; publ. *Svenska Museer* (5 a year).

Svenska Sällskapet för Antropologi och Geografi (Swedish Society for Anthropology and Geography): c/o Madeleine Bonow, School of Life Sciences, Södertörn Univ., SE-141 89 Huddinge; tel. (8) 608-47-08; fax (8) 608-45-10; e-mail ssagmail@yahoo.se; internet www.ssag.se; f. 1873 as Asscn for Anthropology, present name 1877; forwards the devt of anthropology and geography in Sweden, communicates with foreign socs with the same objectives, and supports investigations into anthropology and geography; 900 mems; library of 10,000 vols; Pres. Prof. BRITA HERMELIN; Vice-Pres. Doc. ANNICA DAHLBERG; Sec. Dr MADELEINE BONOW; Treas. Dr THOMAS BORÉN; publs *Årsboken Ymer* (1 a year), *Geografiska Annaler A—Physical Geography* (4 a year), *Geografiska Annaler B—Human Geography* (4 a year), *Ymir* (1 a year).

LANGUAGE AND LITERATURE

Alliance Française: c/o Diana Schwarcz, Sandhamnsgatan 12, SE-11 540 Stockholm; tel. (8) 662-27-35; e-mail info@ alliancefrancaisesthlm.com; internet www .alliancefrancaise-se.com; f. 1889; offers courses and exams in French language and culture and promotes cultural exchange with France; attached offices in Borås, Falun, Gothenburg, Halmstad, Helsingborg, Höglandet, Jönköping, Kalmar, Kristianstad, Linköping, Lund, Norrköping, Nyköping, Örebro, Ornskoldsvik, Östersund, Skaraborg, Skelleftea and Uppsala; Pres. JOHAN STENBERG; Vice-Pres. DANIÈLE BERENHOLT; Sec. DIANA SCHWARCZ; Treas. AKE NILSSON.

British Council: c/o British Embassy, Skarpögatan 6–8, POB 27819, SE-115 93 Stockholm; tel. (70) 671-02-28; e-mail elin .svensson@britishcouncil.se; internet www .britishcouncil.org/sweden; offers courses and exams in English language and British culture and promotes cultural exchange with the UK; Country Man. ELIN SVENSSON.

Goethe-Institut: Bryggargatan 12A, SE-111 21 Stockholm; tel. (8) 459-12-00; fax (8) 459-12-15; e-mail info@stockholm.goethe.org; internet www.goethe.de/stockholm; offers courses and exams in German language and culture and promotes cultural exchange with Germany; attached teaching centre in Gothenburg; library of 3,500 vols, 45 periodicals; Dir and Head of Program Work HEIKE FRIESEL; Dir and Head of Program Work RAINER HAUSWIRTH; Deputy Dir and Head of Language Work BERND ZABEL.

Instituto Cervantes: Bryggargatan 12A, SE-111 21 Stockholm; tel. (8) 440-17-60; fax (8) 21-04-31; e-mail info.stockholm@ cervantes.es; internet www.cervantes.se; f. 2005; offers courses and exams in Spanish language and culture and promotes cultural exchange with Spain and Spanish-speaking Latin and Central America; library of 10,000 vols (books, magazines, CDs, DVDs); Dir JOAN M. ALVAREZ VALENCIA; Librarian JOHNNY PETTERSSON.

Samfundet de Nio (Academy of the Nine): Villagatan 14, SE-114 32 Stockholm; tel. (8) 70-573-44-08; fax (8) 611-22-03; internet www.samfundetdenio.se; f. 1913; Pres. Prof. INGE JONSSON; Sec.and Treas. ANDERS R. ÖHMAN; publ. *De Nios litterära kalender* (1 a year).

Språkrådet (Language Council): POB 20057, SE-104 60 Stockholm; Bjurholmsgatan 10, Stockholm; tel. (8) 442-42-00; fax (8) 455-42-26; e-mail sprakradet@sprakradet.se; internet www.sprakradet.se; f. 2006 by merger of Swedish Language Council, Sweden Finnish Language Council and Plain group in the Cabinet Office; attached to Institute for Language and Folklore; official language planning agency; provides advice on language issues and follows language devt in Sweden; engaged in linguistic research and promotes Swedish and Nordic language of cooperation; Head LENA EKBERG; publs *Kieliviesti* (4 a year), *Klarspråk–bulletin från Språkrådet* (4 a year).

Svenska Akademien (Swedish Academy): POB 2118, SE-103 13 Stockholm; Källargränd 4, Gamla Stan, Stockholm; tel. (8) 555-125-00; fax (8) 555-125-49; e-mail sekretariat@svenskaakademien.se; internet www.svenskaakademien.se; f. 1786; Swedish language and literature; awards Nobel Prize for Literature; 18 mems; library: see Libraries and Archives; Permanent Sec. Prof. PETER ENGLUND; publ. *Svenska Akademiens Handlingar* (1 a year).

Svenska PEN (Swedish PEN): POB 3159, SE-103 63 Stockholm; c/o Albert Bonniers Förlag, Sveavägen 56, SE-103 63 Stockholm; tel. (8) 736-19-40; e-mail ola@larsmo.se; internet www.svenskapen.se; f. 1922; promotes literature; discussion, debates, communication among writers; 600 mems; Chair. BJÖRN LINNELL; Vice-Chair. BIRGITTA ÖHMAN; Pres. OLA LARSMO; Sec. MARTIN KAUNITZ.

Svenska Vitterhetssamfundet: Mariatorget 1C SE-118 48 Stockholm; tel (8) 10-19-69; fax (8) 765-57-71; e-mail vitterhet@gmail .com; internet www .svenskavitterhetssamfundet.se; f. 1907; publishes critical edns by Swedish authors; 311 mems; Sec. PETRA SÖDERLUND.

Sveriges Författarförbund (Swedish Writers' Union): POB 3157, Drottninggatan 88B, SE-103 63 Stockholm; tel. (8) 545-132-00; fax (8) 545-132-10; e-mail sff@ forfattarforbundet.se; internet www .forfattarforbundet.se; f. 1893 as Swedish Asscn of Authors, present name and status 1970; protects intellectual and economic interests of writers and translators; 2,400 mems; Pres. BUNNY RAGNERSTAM; Dir HELENA NELSON-BÜLOW; publ. *Författaren* (6 a year).

MEDICINE

Socialstyrelsen (National Board of Health and Welfare): SE-106 30 Stockholm; Rålambsvägen 3, Stockholm; tel. (8) 75-247-30-00; fax (8) 75-247-32-52; e-mail socialstyrelsen@socialstyrelsen.se; internet www.socialstyrelsen.se; f. 1968 by the merger of Royal Medical Board and Royal Board of Social Affairs; attached to Min. of Health and Social Affairs; public health, medical and social services admin.; Dir-Gen. LARS-ERIK HOLM; Deputy Dir-Gen. HÅKAN CEDER.

Svenska Läkaresällskapet (Swedish Society of Medicine): POB 738, SE-101 35 Stockholm; Klara Östra Kyrkogata 10, SE-101 35 Stockholm; tel. (8) 440-88-60; fax (8) 440-88-99; e-mail sls@sls.se; internet www.sls.se; f. 1808, present bldg 1906; promotes research, education and devt in health care sector; 17,000 mems; Chair. MARGARETA TROEIN TÖLLBORN; Vice-Chair. PETER FRIBERG; Sec.

BRITT NORDLANDER; publ. *Svenska Läkare-sällskapets Handlingar Hygiea*.

NATURAL SCIENCES
General

Kungl. Skytteanska Samfundet (Royal Skytte Society): Humanisthuset, SE-901 87 Umeå; tel. (90) 14-14-28; e-mail skytteanska@adm.umu.se; internet www .skytteanskasamfundet.se; f. 1956; promotes and supports scientific research, particularly that of Norrland interest; Pres. LARS-ERIK EDLUND; Vice-Pres. ERIK LUNDGREN; Sec. ULF WIBERG; publs *Journal of Northern Studies* (2 a year), *THULE* (1 a year).

Svenska Linnésällskapet (Swedish Linnaeus Society): POB 15093, SE-750 15 Uppsala; tel. (18) 471-62-71; fax (18) 471-62-70; e-mail info@linnaeus.se; internet www .linnaeus.se; f. 1917; expands knowledge about Carl Linnaeus and his work; encourages interest in nature and scientific culture; publish writings by and about Carl Linnaeus and his disciples; attached museum; Pres. Doc. ROLAND MOBERG; Sec. EVA NYSTRÖM; publ, *Swedish Linnaeus Society Yearbook (SLÅ)*.

Wenner-Gren Stiftelserna (Wenner-Gren Foundations): Sveavägen 164, 23rd Fl., SE-113 46 Stockholm; tel. (8) 736-98-11; fax (8) 31-33-17; e-mail susanne.falck@swgc.org; internet www.swgc.org; f. 1962; residence and meeting place for foreign and visiting scientists; Chair. Prof. INGE JONSSON; Vice-Chair. KERSTIN ELIASSON; Scientific Sec. Prof. BERTIL DANEHOLT.

Biological Sciences

Kungl. Fysiografiska Sällskapet i Lund (Royal Physiographic Society of Lund): Stortorget 6, SE-222 23 Lund; tel. (46) 13-25-28; fax (46) 13-19-44; e-mail kansli@fysiografen .se; internet www.fysiografen.se; f. 1772 as Acad. of Natural Sciences, Medicine and Technology, present name and status 1778; science, medicine and technology; 500 mems, 100 foreign corresps; Pres. Prof. CHARLOTTE ERLANSON-ALBERTSSON; Vice-Pres. TORBJÖRN FREJD; Dir ULF KÖRNER; Sec.and Treas. PER ALM; publ. *Årsbok* (every 2 years).

Naturskyddsföreningen (Swedish Society for Nature Conservation): POB 4625, Åsögatan 115, 2 tr., SE-116 91 Stockholm; tel. (8) 702-65-00; fax (8) 702-08-55; e-mail medlem@ naturskyddsforeningen.se; internet www .naturskyddsforeningen.se; f. 1909; deals with environmental issues; areas of work incl. climate, oceans, forests, pollution, agriculture; mem. of IUCN; 181,000 mems; Pres. MIKAEL KARLSSON; Vice-Pres. LENA ERIKSSON; Vice-Pres. KARIN ÅSTRÖM; Treas. BO JÖNSON; publ. *Sveriges Natur* (6 a year).

Svenska Bioenergiföreningen (Svebio) (Swedish Bioenergy Association (Svebio)): Torsgatan 12 plan 3, SE-111 23 Stockholm; tel. (8) 441-70-80; fax (8) 441-70-89; e-mail info@svebio.se; internet www.svebio.se; f. 1980; devt of bioenergy in Sweden; 300 mems; Chair. LENA SÖDERBERG; Pres. GUSTAV MELIN.

Mathematical Sciences

Lunds Matematiska Sällskap (Lund Mathematical Society): c/o Matematiska Institutionen, POB 118, SE-221 00 Lund; fax (46) 222-40-10; internet www.matematik .lu.se/lms; f. 1923; promotes greater interest in mathematics and related subjects, both among the gen. public and students; 150 mems; Pres. Prof. NILS DENCKER; Vice-Pres.

ANDERS HOLST; Sec. and Treas. THOMAS EDLUND.

Matematiska Föreningen i Uppsala (Mathematical Society of Uppsala): Dept of Mathematics, Uppsala Univ., POB 480, SE-751 06 Uppsala; tel. (18) 471-32-00; fax (18) 471-32-01; e-mail mans.eriksson@math.uu .se; f. 1853, present name and status 1889; 50 mems; Chair. Dr MÅNS ERIKSSON; Sec. Dr DANIEL STRÖMBOM.

Svenska Matematikersamfundet (Swedish Mathematical Society): c/o Tobias Ekholm, Dept of Mathematics, Uppsala Univ., POB 480, SE-751 06 Uppsala; tel. (46) 471-63-99; fax (46) 471-32-01; e-mail president@swe-math-soc.se; internet www .swe-math-soc.se; f. 1950; meetings, journals, education of mathematics teachers, mathematics competition for students, travel grants for PhD students, research prizes for young mathematicians; 540 mems; Chair. Prof. TOBIAS EKHOLM; Vice-Chair. MIKAEL PASSARE; Sec. Dr WARWICK TUCKER; Treas. MILAGROS IZQUIERDO BARRIOS; publs *Mathematica Scandinavia* (with other Scandinavian mathematical socs), *Nordisk Matematisk Tidskrift* (with other Scandinavian mathematical socs).

Svenska Statistikfrämjandet (Swedish Statistics Promotion): Arenavägen 7, SE-121 88 Stockholm; tel. (8) 688-76-66; e-mail sekrfram@gmail.com; internet www .statistikframjandet.se; f. 2008 by merger of Statistical Society and Swedish Statistician Community; promotes research, devt, education in statistics; provides a forum for its mems; Pres. BERNHARD HUITFELDT; Vice-Pres. SUNE KARLSSON; Sec. ANNA JOHANSSON.

Physical Sciences

Geologiska Föreningen (Geological Society of Sweden): c/o Dept of Geology and Geochemistry, Stockholm Univ., SE-106 91 Stockholm; tel. (8) 674-77-27; fax (8) 674-78-97; e-mail gff@geologiskaforeningen.nu; internet www.geologiskaforeningen.nu; f. 1871 as Geological Society in Stockholm; promotes geology and earth science; 600 mems; Chair. and Sec. Assoc. Prof. VIVI VAJDA (acting); Treas. KARI NIIRANEN; publs *Geologiskt forum* (in Swedish, 4 a year), *GFF* (in English, 4 a year).

Kungl. Örlogsmannasällskapet (Royal Swedish Society of Naval Sciences): Teatergatan 3, 1 tr, SE-111 48 Stockholm; tel. (8) 664-70-18; e-mail akademien@koms.se; internet www.koms.se; f. 1771, reorganized 1777; promotes devts in naval sciences and maritime sciences; library of 15,000 vols, maps, charts, archival records; 400 mems; Pres. THOMAS ENGEVALL; Vice-Pres. Col PER JENVALD; Sec.-Gen. BO RASK; publ. *Tidskrift i Sjöväsendet (TiS)* (4 a year).

Svenska Fysikersamfundet (Swedish Physical Society): Dept of Physics and Astronomy, POB 516, SE-751 20 Uppsala; tel. (13) 28-12-03; fax (13) 13-22-85; e-mail kansliet@fysikersamfundet.se; internet www .fysikersamfundet.se; f. 1920; promotes physics research and applications; spreads knowledge about physics and physics education; stimulates public interest in physics and natural sciences in gen.; 800 mems; Chair. KARL-FREDRIK BERGGREN; Sec. Dr RAIMUND FEIFEL; Treas. LAGE HEDIN; publs *Fysikaktuellt* (4 a year), *Kosmos* (1 a year).

RELIGION, SOCIOLOGY AND ANTHROPOLOGY

Kungl. Gustav Adolfs Akademien för svensk folkkultur (Royal Gustavus Adol-

phus Academy for Swedish Folk Culture): Klostergatan 2, SE-753 21 Uppsala; tel. (18) 71-16-38; fax (18) 54-87-83; e-mail info@kgaa .nu; internet www.kgaa.nu; f. 1932; promotes research on Swedish folk culture; 220 mems (incl. honorary); Pres. Prof. LENNART ELMEVIK; Vice-Pres. Prof. BIRGITTA SKARIN FRYKMAN; Sec. Doc. MAJ REINHAMMAR; Treas. INGEMAR ANDERSÉN; publs *Acta Academiae Regiae Gustavi Adolphi* (irregular), *Arv. Nordic Yearbook of Folklore* (1 a year), *Ethnologia Scandinavica* (1 a year), *Namn och bygd* (1 a year), *Saga och Sed* (1 a year), *Studia Anthroponymica Scandinavica* (1 a year), *Svenska landsmål och svenskt folkliv* (1 a year).

TECHNOLOGY

Kungl. Ingenjörsvetenskapsakademien—IVA (Royal Swedish Academy of Engineering Sciences): POB 5073, SE-102 42 Stockholm; Grev Turegatan 16, SE-102 42 Stockholm; tel. (8) 791-29-00; fax (8) 611-56-23; e-mail info@iva.se; internet www.iva.se; f. 1919; promotes engineering and economic science; acts as a clearing house for scientific information; establishes contacts with foreign research orgs by means of lectures and confs, trade research orgs and research agreements with East European countries, China and the Republic of Korea; library of 10,000 vols; 1,000 Swedish and foreign mems; Pres. Prof. BJÖRN O. NILSSON; Chair. Prof. LENA TRESCHOW TORELL; Vice-Chair. CHARLOTTE BROGREN; Vice-Chair. Assoc. Prof. KARL-OLOF HAMMARKVIST; Vice-Chair. PETER GUDMUNDSON; Vice-Chair. Prof. STAFFAN JOSEPHSON; Sec. PER ÖDLING; publs *IVA-Aktuellt, Meddelanden, Rapporter*.

Svenska Geotekniska Föreningen (Swedish Geotechnical Society): c/o Swedish Geotechnical Institute, SE-581 93 Linköping; tel. (13) 20-18-00; fax (13) 20-19-09; e-mail info@ sgf.net; internet www.sgf.net; f. 1950; soil mechanics, geotechnical engineering, environmental geotechnics; 900 individual mems, 25 corporate mems; Chair. STEFAN ARONSSON; Vice-Chair. ANDERS DAHLBERG; Sec. SARA BLOMBERG; Treas. MATTIAS GUSTAVSSON.

Sveriges Ingenjörer (Swedish Association of Graduate Engineers): POB 1419, SE-111 84 Stockholm; Malmskillnadsgatan 48, Stockholm; tel. (8) 613-80-00; fax (8) 796-71-02; e-mail info@sverigesingenjorer.se; internet www.sverigesingenjorer.se; f. 2007, merger of Civil Engineers and Professional Engineers; mem. of European Metalworker's Fed.; makes employing engineers easier for small and mid-size cos; ensures that engineers receive better salaries; 133,000 mems; Pres. ULF BENGTSSON; Man. Dir RICHARD MALMBORG; publs *Ingenjören* (5 a year), *Ny Teknik-Teknisk Tidskrift* (52 a year).

Research Institutes
GENERAL

Forskningsrådet Formas (Swedish Research Council Formas): POB 1206, SE-111 82 Stockholm; Kungsbron 21, Stockholm; tel. (8) 775-40-00; fax (8) 775-40-10; e-mail registrator@formas.se; internet www.formas .se; f. 2001; govt research funding agency; encourages and supports research related to sustainable devt; programme areas: environment, agriculture (incl. horticulture, fisheries and reindeer husbandry), forestry and the natural environment, the built environment, urban and regional planning; Chair. LARS-ERIK LILJELUND; Dir-Gen. ROLF ANNERBERG; Sec.-Gen. Prof. ANNA LEDIN; publs *Miljö-*

forskning (6 a year, print and online), *Sustainability* (in English, 4 a year, online).

Life & Peace Institute: Sysslomansgatan 7, 1st Fl., SE-753 11 Uppsala; tel. (18) 16-95-00; fax (18) 69-30-59; e-mail info@life-peace .org; internet www.life-peace.org; f. 1985; deals with non-violent conflict transformation and research about role of religion in peace and conflict as well as traditional conflict resolution mechanisms; offices in Congo, Kenya, Sudan, Sweden; Pres. GUSTAF ÖDQVIST; Exec. Dir PETER KARLSSON SJÖGREN; publ. *New Routes* (4 a year).

Stockholm International Water Institute: Drottninggatan 33, SE-111 51 Stockholm; tel. (8) 522-139-60; fax (8) 522-139-61; e-mail siwi@siwi.org; internet www.siwi.org; f. 1997; policy institute on world water crisis; organizes World Water Week; Exec. Dir ANDERS BERNTELL; Deputy Exec. Dir PER BERTILSSON.

Stockholm Resilience Centre: Stockholm Univ., Kräftriket 2B, SE-106 91 Stockholm; tel. (8) 674-70-70; fax (8) 674-70-20; e-mail info@stockholmresilience.su.se; internet www.stockholmresilience.su.se; f. 2007; transdisciplinary research of social-ecological systems; joint initiative between Stockholm Univ., Stockholm Environment Institute and the Beijer International Institute of Ecological Economics; Exec. Dir JOHAN ROCKSTRÖM; Science Dir CARL FOLKE.

Vetenskapsrådet (Swedish Research Council): POB 1035, SE-101 38 Stockholm; Klarabergsviadukten 82, Stockholm; tel. (8) 546-440-00; fax (8) 546-441-80; e-mail vr@vr.se; internet www.vr.se; f. 2001; attached to Dept of Education and Culture; provides support for basic research of highest academic quality within all areas of knowledge; assumed duties of fmr Swedish Ccl for Planning and Co-ordination of Research, Swedish Ccl for Research in the Humanities and Social Sciences, Swedish Medical Research Ccl, Swedish Natural Science Research Ccl, and Swedish Research Ccl for Engineering Sciences; cttees for Culture and the Social Sciences (First Sec. BENGT HANSSON), Medicine (First Sec. OLLE STENDAHL), Natural and Engineering Sciences (First Sec. KÅRE BREMER); Chair. LARS ANELL; Vice-Chair. BRITT-MARIE SJÖBERG; Dir-Gen. Prof. PÄR OMLING.

AGRICULTURE, FISHERIES AND VETERINARY SCIENCE

AgriFood Economics Centre: POB 730, Scheelevägen 15D, SE-220 07 Lund; e-mail info@agrifood.lu.se; internet www.agrifood .se; f. 2009; cooperative venture between Swedish Univ. of Agricultural Sciences (SLU) and Lund Univ.; economic analysis of food, agriculture, fishing and rural devt.

JTI–Institutet för jordbruks- och miljöteknik (JTI—Swedish Institute of Agricultural and Environmental Engineering): POB 7033, SE-750 07 Uppsala; tel. (10) 516-69-00; fax (18) 30-09-56; e-mail info@jti.se; internet www.jti.se; f. 1945, present status 2009; attached to SP Technical Research Institute of Sweden; focuses on research, devt and information in areas of agricultural engineering and environmental technology; Man. Dir KLAS HESSELMAN (acting); Sec. MARI ENGVALL; publ. *JTI Informerar* (8 a year).

Skogforsk (Forestry Research Institute of Sweden): Dag Hammarskjölds Väg 36A, Uppsala Science Park, SE-751 83 Uppsala; tel. (18) 18-85-00; fax (18) 18-86-00; e-mail skogforsk@skogforsk.se; internet www .skogforsk.se; central research body for the Swedish forestry sector; Exec. Dir. JAN FRYK; Deputy Dir. KAJ ROSÉN; publ. *Skogforsks Redogörelser* (6 a year).

Statens Veterinärmedicinska Anstalt (National Veterinary Institute): Ulls Väg 2B, SE-751 89 Uppsala; tel. (18) 67-40-00; fax (18) 30-91-62; e-mail sva@sva.se; internet www.sva.se; f. 1911; research, diagnostic work, consultative work concerning control and prophylaxis of animal diseases; nat. veterinary laboratory; org.: central laboratory, epizootiology unit, animal diseases specialists unit, admin.; library of 27,000 vols; Dir-Gen. ANDERS ENGVALL; Personnel. Dir HÅKAN PALLIN; Dir. for Planning STAFFAN ROS; Sec. GUNILLA LINDGREN; publ. *SVA Vet* (irregular).

Wallenberg Wood Science Centre: Teknikringen 56–58, KTH, Campus Valhallavägen, SE-100 44 Stockholm; tel. (8) 790-81-18; e-mail blund@kth.se; f. 2009; joint research centre at KTH and Chalmers; focus on new materials from trees; Dir LARS BERGLUND; Sec. EWA WAERN-MORATH.

ARCHITECTURE AND TOWN PLANNING

European Network for Housing Research: ENHR, Institute for Housing and Urban Research, Uppsala University, POB 785, SE-801 29 Gävle; tel. (26) 420-65-00; fax (26) 420-65-01; e-mail enhr@ibf.uu.se; internet www.enhr.ibf.uu.se; f. 1988; major int. confs; 20 working groups; smaller conferences; active group of PhD students; Chair. PETER BOELHOUWER; Vice-Chair. IVÁN TOSICS.

Nordregio (Nordic Centre for Spatial Development): POB 1658, SE-111 86 Stockholm; Skeppsholmen, Holmamiralens väg 10, Stockholm; tel. (8) 463-54-00; fax (8) 463-54-01; e-mail nordregio@nordregio.se; internet www.nordregio.se; f. 1997, present status 2000; administered by Nordic Ccl of Mins; demography, global climate change and local adaptation, governance and gender, innovation and knowledge, int. energy policy, regional devt, urban and rural systems; Chair. KIRSTEN VINTERSBORG; Vice-Chair. SVERKER LINDBLAD; Dir OLE DAMSGAARD; publs *European Journal of Spatial Development* (online at www.nordregio.se/ejsd), *Journal of Nordregio* (4 a year).

ECONOMICS, LAW AND POLITICS

Beijerinstitutet för Ekologisk Ekonomi (Beijer Institute of Ecological Economics): Lilla Frescativägen 4A, POB 50005, SE-104 05 Stockholm; tel. (8) 673-95-00; fax (8) 15-24-64; e-mail beijer@beijer.kva.se; internet www.beijer.kva.se; f. 1977; attached to Royal Swedish Academy of Sciences; collaborative research between economists and ecologists and related disciplines; Dir CARL FOLKE; Deputy Dir ANNE-SOPHIE CRÉPIN; publs *Ecology and Society* (e-journals, 2 a year), *Environment and Development Economics* (e-journal).

Ekonomiska Forskningsinstitutet (Economic Research Institute): EFI, The Economic Research Institute at the Stockholm School of Economics, POB 6501, SE-113 83 Stockholm; tel. (8) 736-90-00; fax (8) 31-62-70; e-mail efi@hhs.se; internet www.hhs.se/efi; f. 1929; attached to Stockholm School of Economics; research in economics, business administration, finance and law; 20 centres; library of 150,000 vols, 15,000 e-journals, 60 databases; Dir FILIP WIJKSTRÖM; Chair. CARIN HOLMQUIST; publ. *Forskning i Fickformat* (4 a year).

Entrepreneurship and Small Business Research Institute: Saltmätargatan 9, SE-113 59 Stockholm; tel. (8) 458-78-00; e-mail info@esbri.se; internet www.esbri.se; f. 1996; research on entrepreneurship and small and medium enterprises; founded award for entrepreneurship; Chair. ANDERS FLODSTRÖM; Man. Dir MAGNUS ARONSSON.

Humanistisk-samhällsvetenskapliga (Swedish Council for Humanities and Social Sciences): POB 7120, SE-103 78 Stockholm; tel. (8) 454-43-10; fax (8) 454-43-20; f. 1977; 11 mems; Chair. Dr JANE CEDERQVIST; Sec.-Gen. Prof. ANDERS JEFFNER; Dir BJÖRN THOMASSON.

Institute for International Economic Studies: A-building, 8th Fl., Södra Huset, Univ. of Stockholm, SE-104 05 Stockholm; tel. (8) 16-20-00; fax (8) 16-14-43; internet www.iies.su.se; Dir HARRY FLAM; Deputy Dir JAKOB SVENSSON; publ. *The Review of Economic Studies* (4 a year).

Institute for Security and Development Policy: Västra Finnbodavägen 2, SE-131 30 Nacka; tel. (8) 410-569-60; fax (8) 640-33-70; e-mail info@isdp.eu; internet www.isdp.eu; f. 2007; research on int. conflict, security and devt; especially Eurasia; Dir SVANTE CORNELL; Deputy Dir JOHANNA POPJANEVSKI; publs *The Central Asia-Caucasus Analyst* (web journal), *The China and Eurasia Forum Quarterly* (4 a year), *The Turkey Analyst* (52 a week).

Institutet för Näringslivsforskning (Research Institute of Industrial Economics): POB 55665, SE-102 15 Stockholm; Grevgatan 34, 2nd Fl., SE-102 15 Stockholm; tel. (8) 665-45-00; fax (8) 665-45-99; e-mail info@ifn .se; internet www.ifn.se; f. 1939 as Research Institute of Industries, present name 2006; conducts research on economic and social issues with relevance for industrial devt; 23 research fellows; Chair. Dr BJÖRN HÄGGLUND; Dir Prof. MAGNUS HENREKSON; Deputy Dir Assoc. Prof. LARS PERSSON; publ. *Årsbok* (yearbook).

Institution för Spanska. Portugisiska och Latinamerika Studier (Collections and Swedish National Portrait Gallery, University of Stockholm): Universitetsvägen 10, SE-106 91 Stockholm; tel. (8) 16-34-93; fax (8) 15-85-78; e-mail secretaria@isp.su.se; internet www.isp.su.se; f. 1951, present name and status 1969; research on Spanish, Portuguese, Latin American economic, social and political devt; information, seminars, courses; library of 40,000 vols; Dir Prof. MONA ROSENDAHL; Librarian MARGARETA BJÖRLING; publ. *Ibero-Americana: Nordic Journal of Latin American Studies.*

Nordiska Afrikainstitutet (Nordic Africa Institute): POB 1703, SE-751 47 Uppsala; Kungsgatan 38, Uppsala; tel. (18) 56-22-00; fax (18) 56-22-90; e-mail nai@nai.uu.se; internet www.nai.uu.se; f. 1962; documentation, information and research centre for current African affairs; publ. work, lectures and seminars; library of 68,000 vols, 230 electronic books, 450 print periodicals, 127 online databases (incl. electronic periodicals); Dir CARIN NORBERG; Chief Librarian ÅSA LUND MOBERG; publs *Africa Now, Current African Issues, Discussion Paper, Policy Dialogue, Policy Notes.*

Raoul Wallenberg Institute of Human Rights and Humanitarian Law: Stora Gråbrödersg. 17B, POB 1155, SE-221 05 Lund; tel. (46) 222-12-00; fax (46) 222-12-22; e-mail marie.tuma@rwi.lu.se; internet www.rwi.lu.se; f. 1984; independent academic instn. for human rights promotion through research, training and education; Dir MARIE TUMA; publs *Baltic Yearbook of International Law, Chinese Yearbook of Human Rights, International Journal on Minority and Group Rights* (4 a year), *Nordic Journal of International Law* (4 a year).

Ratio Institute: Sveavägen 59, 4 tr., POB 3203, SE-103 64 Stockholm; tel. (8) 441-59-00; e-mail info@ratio.se; internet www.ratio

.se; f. 2002; researches enterprise and entrepreneurship; conducts research-seminar series; Pres. NILS KARLSON; Vice-Pres. NICLAS BERGGREN.

Statistiska Centralbyrån (Statistics Sweden): POB 24300, SE-104 51 Stockholm; Karlavägen 100, Stockholm; tel. (8) 506-940-00; fax (8) 661-52-61; e-mail scb@scb.se; internet www.scb.se; f. 1858; supplies customers (govt and private sector) with statistics for decision making, debate and research; br. in Örerbo; library: see Libraries and Archives; Dir.-Gen. STEFAN LUNDGREN; publs *Företag—Tidning för Uppgiftslämnare* (1 a year), *Journal of Official Statistics*, *SCB—Kundtidning* (4 a year), *Statistical Abstract of Sweden*, *Statistical Reports*, *Statistical Yearbook of Sweden*, *Survey of Living Conditions*.

Stiftelsen Företagsadministrativ Forskning (Scandinavian Institutes for Administrative Research): c/o Edqvist, Sigtunagatan 5, SE-113 22 Stockholm; tel. (70) 94-44-74; e-mail j.edqvist@gmail.com; internet www.siar.a.se; f. 1966; provides financial support for research in business administration and business economics; Dir CHRISTIAN JUNNELIUS; Sec. JOHAN EDQVIST.

Stockholm Institute for Scandinavian Law: Stockholm Institute for Scandinavian Law, Faculty of Law, University of Stockholm, SE-106 91 Stockholm; tel. (8) 16-25-48; fax (8) 612-90-72; e-mail sisl@juridicum.su.se; internet www.scandinavianlaw.se; f. 1956; attached to Faculty of Law, Stockholm Univ.; spreads knowledge about Scandinavian law and jurisprudence abroad.

Stockholm Institute of Transitional Economics: Sveavägen 65, 9th Fl., A, POB 6501, SE-113 83 Stockholm; tel. (8) 736-96-70; fax (8) 31-64-22; e-mail site@hhs.se; internet www.hhs.se/site; f. 1989; attached to Stockholm School of Economics; research and policy centre on transition in former USSR and Eastern Europe; Chair. MICHAEL SOHLMAN; Dir TORBJÖRN BECKER.

Stockholm International Peace Research Institute: Signalistgatan 9, SE-169 70 Solna; tel. (8) 655-97-51; fax (8) 655-97-33; e-mail cloo@sipri.org; internet www.sipri.org; f. 1966; research in conflict, armaments, arms control and disarmament; library of 50,000 vols; 600 journals; Chair. GÖRAN LENNMARKER; Dir BATES GILL; Deputy Dir DANIEL NORD; publ. *SIPRI Yearbook*.

Swedish Collegium for Advanced Study (SCAS): Linneanum, Thunbergsvägen 2, SE-752 38 Uppsala; tel. (18) 55-70-85; fax (18) 52-11-09; e-mail info@swedishcollegium.se; internet www.swedishcollegium.se; f. 1985; offers 14 fellowships for study at the Collegium each semester; Chair. Prof. LARS MAGNUSSON; Prin. Prof. BJÖRN WITTROCK.

LANGUAGE AND LITERATURE

Institutet för Språk och Folkminnen (Institute for Language and Folklore): POB 135, SE-751 04 Uppsala; von Kraemers allé 2, Arkivcentrum, Uppsala; tel. (18) 65-21-60; fax (18) 65-21-65; internet www.sofi.se; f. 2006; collects, preserves and researches on dialects, place names, personal names and folklore; works on language planning and language policy; Gen.-Dir INGRID JOHANSSON LIND.

MEDICINE

Livsmedelsverket (National Food Administration): POB 622, SE-751 26 Uppsala; Hamnesplanaden 5, Uppsala; tel. (18) 17-55-00; fax (18) 10-58-48; e-mail livsmedelsverket@slv.se; internet www.slv.se; f. 1972; attached to Min. of Agriculture,

Food and Fisheries; central admin. agency in Sweden for foodstuffs and handling of foodstuffs in accordance with the Food Act; library of 11,000 vols; Dir-Gen. INGER ANDERSSON; Deputy Dir-Gen. JAN MOVITZ; publs *Livsmedelsverkets författningar* (The National Food Administration's Regulations), *Livstecknet* (Newsletter), *Vår Föda* (popular scientific).

Ludwig Institute for Cancer Research Ltd: Biomedical Centre, Husargatan 3, Entrance C11, 3rd Fl., POB 595, SE-751 24 Uppsala; tel. (18) 16-04-00; fax (18) 16-04-20; e-mail ludwig@licr.uu.se; internet www.licr.uu.se; f. 1986; non-profit research org. for cancer control; 10 research centres worldwide; in Sweden in Stockholm (Karolinska Institutet) and Uppsala; Dir CARL-HENRIK HELDIN; Sec. INGEGÄRD SCHILLER.

Molecular Infection Medicine Sweden: Laboratory for Molecular Infection Medicine Sweden, University of Umeå, SE-901 87 Umeå; tel. (90) 785-67-60; fax (90) 786-66-76; e-mail eva-maria.diehl@mims.umu.se; internet www.mims.umu.se; f. 2007; Swedish node of the Nordic EMBL Partnership for Molecular Medicine; joint venture between the European Molecular Biology Laboratory (EMBL) and the Univ. of Helsinki, Finland, Univ. of Oslo, Norway and Univ. of Umeå, Sweden; Dir BERNT ERIC UHLIN; Sec. ÅKE FORSBERG.

Statens Folkhälsoinstitut (Swedish National Institute of Public Health): Forskarens väg 3, SE-831 40 Östersund; tel. (63) 19-96-00; fax (63) 19-96-02; e-mail info@fhi.se; internet www.fhi.se; state agency under the Ministry of Health and Social Affairs; Dir Gen. Dr SARAH WAMALA.

Stockholm Brain Institute: Karolinska Institutet, SE-171 77 Stockholm; tel. (8) 517-77-341; e-mail none-marie.kemp@ki.se; internet www.stockholmbrain.se; research on neuroscience; consortium of Karolinska Institutet, Royal Institute of Technology and Stockholm University; Dir HANS FORSSBERG; Sec. NONE-MARIE KEMP.

NATURAL SCIENCES
General

Abisko naturvetenskapliga station (Abisko Scientific Research Station): SE-981 07 Abisko; tel. (980) 400-21; fax (980) 401-71; e-mail ans@ans.kiruna.se; internet www.linnea.com/~ans; f. 1903, present status 1935; attached to Royal Swedish Acad. of Sciences; researches mainly on sub-arctic biology and earth sciences; hosts the Climate Impacts Research Centre (CIRC); Dir Prof. TERENCE V. CALLAGHAN; Deputy Dir CHRISTER JONASSON.

Stockholm Environment Institute: Kräftriket 2B, SE-106 91 Stockholm; tel. (8) 674-70-70; e-mail info@sei-international.org; internet sei-international.org; f. 1989; governed by an international Board; policy-related research on international environmental technology and management issues, incl. acidic deposition co-ordinated abatement strategies, climatic change assessment, energy futures, economics and environmental value, water, sanitation and integrated waste-management, urban environment, common property, energy and development, biotechnology, risk assessment, atmospheric environment, cleaner production, sustainable devt planning and computer tools for integrated management risk and vulnerability; centres in Stockholm, Tallinn (Estonia), Dar Es Salaam (Tanzania), Bangkok (Thailand), York (UK), Oxford (UK), and Boston (USA); Chair. KERSTIN NIBLAEUS; Exec. Dir Adjunct Prof. JOHAN ROCKSTRÖM; publ.

Renewable Energy for Development (4 a year).

Sven Lovén Centrum för Marina Vetenskaper (Sven Lovén Centre for Marine Sciences): Kristineberg 566, SE-450 34 Fiskebäckskil; tel. (523) 185-00; fax (523) 185-02; e-mail katarina.abrahamsson@loven.gu.se; internet www.loven.gu.se; f. 1877 as Kristineberg Marine Research Station, present name and status 2008; attached to Gothenburg Univ.; marine ecology, taxonomic, systematics and biodiversity, morphological, molecular and physiological research on marine animals and plants; laboratory at Tjärnö; Dir KATARINA ABRAHAMSSON.

Biological Sciences

Bergianska stiftelsen (Bergius Foundation): POB 50017, SE-104 05 Stockholm; tel. (8) 545-917-00; fax (8) 612-90-05; e-mail birgitta.bremer@bergianska.se; internet www.bergianska.se/forskning.php; f. 1791; attached to Royal Swedish Acad. of Sciences; botanical and horticultural research; biodiversity projects: Rubiaceae, Rosaleae; Dir Prof. Bergianus BIRGITTA BREMER.

IVL Svenska Miljöinstitutet (IVL Swedish Environmental Research Institute): POB 210 60, SE-100 31 Stockholm; tel. (8) 598-563-00; fax (8) 598-563-90; e-mail info@ivl.se; internet www.ivl.se; f. 1966; Chair. ANNIKA LUNDSTRÖM; Pres. TORD SVEDBERG.

Science for Life Laboratory: Karolinska Institutet Science Park, Tomtebodavägen 23A, SE-171 65 Solna; tel. (70) 326-29-11; fax (85) 248-14-25; e-mail fredrik.sterky@scilifelab.se; internet www.scilifelab.se; national resource centre; research in molecular biosciences and medicine; org. divided into SciLifeLab Stockholm and SciLifeLab Uppsala; SciLifeLab Stockholm between 3 univs: KTH, KI, SU; SciLifeLab Uppsala organized by Uppsala University; Dir (Stockholm) FREDRIK STERKY.

Mathematical Sciences

Institut Mittag-Leffler (Mittag-Leffler Institute): Auravägen 17, SE-182 60 Djursholm; tel. (8) 622-05-60; fax (8) 622-05-89; e-mail info@mittag-leffler.se; internet www.mittag-leffler.se; f. 1916, present status 1919; attached to Royal Swedish Acad. of Sciences; research and postdoctoral training in mathematical sciences; library of 60,000 vols; Chair. Prof. ANDERS BJÖRNER; Vice-Chair. BJÖRN JAHREN; Dir Prof. ARI LAPTEV; Deputy Dir Prof. TOBIAS EKHOLM; publs *Acta Mathematica* (4 a year), *Arkiv för matematik* (2 a year).

Physical Sciences

Institutet för rymdfysik (Swedish Institute of Space Physics): POB 812, SE-981 28 Kiruna; Rymdcampus 1, SE-981 92 Kiruna; tel. (980) 790-00; fax (980) 790-50; e-mail irf@irf.se; internet www.irf.se; f. 1957 as Kiruna Geophysical Observatory, present status 1973, present name 1987; research, education and associated observatory activities in space physics, space technology and atmospheric physics; library of 7,000 vols, 200 journals; Dir Dr LARS ELIASSON; publs *IRF Scientific Report* (irregular), *Kiruna Geophysical Data* (4 a year).

Kungl. Vetenskapsakademiens Institut för Solfysik (Institute for Solar Physics of the Royal Swedish Academy of Sciences): AlbaNova Univ. Centre, Roslagstullsbacken 21, SE-106 91 Stockholm; tel. (8) 16-20-00; fax (8) 553-785-20; e-mail scharmer@astro.su.se; internet www.solarphysics.kva.se; f. 1951 as Research Station for Astrophysics in Italy, reorganized 1978; attached to Royal Swedish Acad. of Sciences; associated with Stockholm Univ.; solar research; operates

Swedish 1-m Solar Telescope (SST) at La Palma; Dir Prof. GÖRAN SCHARMER.

Manne Siegbahnlaboratoriet (MSL) (Manne Siegbahn Laboratory (MSL)): Frescativägen 26, SE-114 18 Stockholm; tel. (8) 16-20-00; fax (8) 16-11-12; internet www.msi .se; f. 1937 as Nobel Institute of Physics, present name 1993, present status 2004; attached to Stockholm Univ.; research in atomic, molecular and surface physics; low-energy ion accelerators (ion sources), accelerator-storage ring for highly charged ions; computer, electronics, and mechanical workshop divs; library of 10,000 vols; Dir SVEN MANNERVIK; Deputy Dir ANDERS KÄLLBERG.

Nordita (Nordic Institute for Theoretical Physics): Nordita, AlbaNova Univ. Centre, Roslagstullsbacken 23, SE-106 91 Stockholm; tel. (8) 553-784-36; fax (8) 553-784-04; e-mail info@nordita.org; internet www.nordita.org; f. 1957, present location 2007; run by Royal Institute of Technology and Stockholm Univ.; main research in astrophysics and astrobiology, condensed matter, statistical and biological physics, high energy and nuclear physics; br. in Copenhagen, Denmark; Dir Prof. LÁRUS THORLACIUS; Deputy Dir Prof. AXEL BRANDENBURG.

Stockholms Observatorium (Stockholm Observatory): SE-106 91 Stockholm; tel. (8) 553-785-01; fax (8) 553-785-10; internet www .astro.su.se; f. 1753; attached to Institutionen för Astronomi, Stockholm Univ.; Dir Prof. GÖRAN ÖSTLIN.

Sveriges Geologiska Undersökning (Geological Survey of Sweden): POB 670, SE-751 28 Uppsala; Villavägen 18, Uppsala; tel. (18) 17-90-00; fax (18) 17-92-10; e-mail sgu@sgu .se; internet www.sgu.se; f. 1858; attached to Min. of Enterprise, Energy and Communications; nat. authority responsible for matters relating to Sweden's geological characteristics and mineral resources management; library of 100,000 vols; Dir.-Gen. JAN MAGNUSSON.

Swedish Meteorological and Hydrological Institute: Folkborgsvägen 1, SE-601 76 Norrköping; tel. (11) 495-80-00; fax (11) 495-80-01; e-mail smhi@smhi.se; internet www .smhi.se; under Min. of Environment; manages and develops information on weather, water and climate; Dir Gen. LENA HÄLL ERIKSSON; Deputy Dir Gen. TORD KVICK.

RELIGION, SOCIOLOGY AND ANTHROPOLOGY

Institute of International Sociology: c/o The Swedish Collegium for Advanced Study, Linneanum, Thunbergsvägen 2, SE-752 38 Uppsala; tel. (18) 55-70-85; fax (18) 52-11-09; e-mail info@iisoc.org; internet www.iisoc.org; f. 1893; oldest continuous sociological asscn; organizes world congress in sociology; Pres. BJÖRN WITTROCK; Sec. Gen. PETER HEDSTRÖM; publs *Annals of the International Institute of Sociology, International Review of Sociology* (3 a year; oldest sociology journal).

Institutet för Social Forskning (Swedish Institute for Social Research): Universitetsvägen 10F, University of Stockholm, SE-106 91 Stockholm; tel. (8) 16-20-00; fax (8) 15-46-70; internet www.sofi.su.se; f. 1972; attached to Stockholm Univ.; research on social policy, welfare, inequality and labour market; Chair. KÅRE BREMER; Dir ANDERS BJÖRKLUND.

TECHNOLOGY

CBI Betonginstitutet AB (Swedish Cement and Concrete Research Institute): SE-100 44 Stockholm; Drottning Kristinas väg 26, SE-114 28 Stockholm; tel. (10) 516-68-00; fax (8) 24-31-37; e-mail cbi@cbi.se; internet www.cbi.se; f. 1942, present status 2008; research and devt; material testing; consulting and training in concrete and rock material field; library of 10,000 vols; Dir Prof. JOHAN SILFWERBRAND; Chair. FREDRIK WINBERG; Deputy Chair. PER-ERIK PETERSSON; Librarian TUULA OJALA; publs *CBI-nytt* (2 a year), *CBI rapporter/report*.

FOI Totalförsvarets Forskningsinstitut (FOI Swedish Defence Research Agency): SE-164 90 Stockholm; Gullfossgatan 6, Stockholm; tel. (8) 555-030-00; fax (8) 555-031-00; e-mail registrator@foi.se; internet www.foi .se; f. 2001; attached to Min. of Defence; conducts research into security-policy studies and analyses of defence and security; systems for control and management of crises; protection against and management of hazardous substances, IT security; brs in Grindsjön, Linköping, Umeå; Chair. SÖREN MELLSTIG; Dir-Gen. JAN-OLOF LIND.

Glafo (Swedish Glass Research Institute): Vejdes Plats 3, SE-352 52 Växjö; tel. (10) 516-63-50; e-mail info@glafo.se; internet www .glafo.se; attached to Technical Research Institute of Sweden; conducts research for the glass industry; Man. Dir MARIANNE GRAUERS.

Innventia AB: POB 5604, SE-114 86 Stockholm; Drottning Kristinas väg 61, Stockholm; tel. (8) 676-70-00; fax (8) 411-55-18; e-mail info@innventia.com; internet www .innventia.com; f. 1942 as STFI-Packforsk, present name 2009; research into pulp, paper, graphic media, packaging and logistics; activities range from basic research to projects into packaging, graphic media and environmentally friendly energy and chemicals; library of 15,000 vols, 500 periodicals; Chair. MATS NORDLANDER; Pres. BIRGITTA SUNDBLAD; Exec. Vice-Pres. ANDERS ENGSTRÖM; publ. *Beyond* (4 a year).

Mobile Life Centre: Electrum Bldg, 6th Fl., Kistagången 16/Isafjordsgatan 22, SE-164 26 Kista; tel. (703) 79-39-64; e-mail oskar@ mobilelifecentre.org; internet www .mobilelifecentre.org; research in mobile services and ubiquitous computing; Chair. MARTIN KÖRLING; Dir OSKAR JUHLIN.

SIK—Institutet för Livsmedel och Bioteknik AB (SIK—Swedish Institute for Food and Biotechnology): POB 5401, SE-402-29 Gothenburg; Frans Perssons väg 6, Delsjömotet; tel. (10) 516-66-00; fax (31) 83-37-82; e-mail webmaster@sik.se; internet www.sik .se; f. 1946; research and devt, documentation and education on production, preservation, food safety, biotechnology, structure and rheology, packaging, information and marketing; library of 7,000 vols; Chair. CHRISTER ÅBERG; Pres. KLAS HESSELMAN; Vice-Pres. HANS LINGNERT; Sec. TINA PETERSSON; publs *SIK-Dokument, SIK-Infood* (in English), *SIK-Publikation, SIK-Rapport*.

SP Sveriges Tekniska Forskningsinstitut (SP Technical Research Institute of Sweden): POB 857, SE-501 15 Borås; Brinellgatan 4, SE-504 62 Borås; tel. (10) 516-50-00; fax (33) 13-55-02; e-mail info@sp.se; internet www.sp.se; f. 1920, fmrly Testing Institute of the Royal Institute of Technology (f. 1896); focuses on calibration, testing, inspection and certification of products and management systems; undertakes applied research and services in technical evaluation, measurement methods, research and devt; library of 17,000 vols; CEO MARIA KHORSAND.

Stålbyggnadsinstitutet (Swedish Institute of Steel Construction): Vasagatan 52, 4th Fl., SE-111 20 Stockholm; tel. (8) 661-02-80; fax (8) 24-54-64; e-mail info@sbi.se; internet www.sbi.se; f. 1967; steel construction research; organizes annual steel construction conference; instituted steel industry award; Chair. JOHAN ANDERSSON; publ. *Stålbyggnad* (4 a year).

Statens Geotekniska Institut (Swedish Geotechnical Institute): Olaus Magnus Väg 35, SE-581 93 Linköping; tel. (13) 20-18-00; fax (13) 20-19-14; e-mail info@swedgeo.se; internet www.swedgeo.se; f. 1944; govt agency responsible for safety issues relating to landslides and coastal erosion; research, information and consulting work in soil mechanics and foundation engineering, environment and energy geotechnology; computerized library retrieval system; brs in Gothenburg, Malmö, Stockholm; library of 100,000 bibliographic records, 10,000 books, 1,600 journals; Deputy Dir-Gen. BO LIND; Sec. KERSTIN CARLSSON; Librarian INGRID GÅRLIN; publs *SGI Information, SGI Report, SGI Varia*.

Swedish ICT: Electrum 233, Isafjordsgatan 22/Kistagången 16, SE-164 40 Kista; tel. (8) 632-78-90; e-mail info@swedish-ict.se; internet www.swedish-ict.se; research and devt on information, communication, technology; group of instns includes Acreo, SICS, Interactive Institute, Imego, Viktoria Institute, Santa Anna IT Research Institute; Chair. ULF WAHLBERG; CEO HANS HENTZELL.

Swerea IVF AB: POB 104, SE-431 22 Mölndal; Argongatan 30, SE-431 53 Mölndal; tel. (31) 706-60-00; fax (31) 27-61-30; e-mail ivf@swerea.se; internet www.swerea.se/ivf; attached to Swerea Group; production engineering, materials applications, textiles, polymers, ceramics; CEO MATS LUNDIN; Sec. INGRID CHRISTOFFERSON; publ. *Teknik & Tillväxt* (Technology & Growth, 6 a year).

Swerea KIMAB AB (Swerea Corrosion and Metals Research Institute AB): POB 55970, SE-102 16 Stockholm; Drottning Kristinas väg 48, SE-114 28 Stockholm; tel. (8) 440-48-00; fax (8) 440-45-35; e-mail kimab@swerea .se; internet www.swereakimab.se; f. 1921, present status 2005; attached to Swerea Group; develops, improves solutions for materials research; areas of research incl.: application of instrumental methods for chemical analysis, welding, brazing and soldering; hot working, cold forming and microscopy; the relationship between microstructure and properties; solidification processes and their industrial applications; continuous casting; powder metallurgy; corrosion problems in connection with microstructure with a special interest in stainless steels; library of 2,000 books, 50 periodicals; Chair. TOMAS THORVALDSSON; Man. Dir STAFFAN SÖDERBERG; Deputy Man. Dir ARNE MELANDER; Librarian ANDERS MÅRTENSON.

Swerea MEFOS: POB 812, SE-971 25 Luleå; tel. (920) 20-19-00; fax (920) 25-58-32; e-mail mefos@swerea.se; internet www .swereamefos.se; research in process metallurgy, heating, metalworking and energy technology; Man. Dir GÖRAN CARLSSON.

Swerea SICOMP: POB 271, SE-941 26 Piteå; tel. (911) 744-01; fax (911) 744-99; e-mail hans.hansson@swerea.se; internet www.swerea.se/sicomp; research in polymer fibre composites; Man. Dir HANS HANSSON.

Swerea SWECAST: POB 2033, SE-553 22 Jönköping; tel. (36) 30-12-00; fax (36) 16-68-66; e-mail swecast@swerea.se; internet www .swerea.se/swecast; research in cast metals; CEO MATS HOLMGREN.

Ytkemiska Institutet (Institute for Surface Chemistry): Drottning Kristinas väg 45, POB 5607, SE-114 86 Stockholm; tel. (10) 516-60-00; fax (8) 20-89-98; e-mail info@yki.se; internet www.yki.se; research in applied surface and colloid chemistry; located on campus of Royal Institute of Technology; library of 5,100 vols; Chair. PER LINDBERG; Sec. PETER ALBERIUS.

Libraries and Archives

Alvesta

Alvesta Bibliotek (Alvesta Library): Allbogatan 17, SE-342 80 Alvesta; tel. (472) 152-69; fax (472) 152-70; e-mail biblioteket@alvesta.se; internet www.alvesta.se; 4 br. libraries, 1 mobile library; Chief Librarian ANN-KATRIN URSBERG.

Borås

Bibliotek & läranderesurser, Högskolan i Borås (University College of Borås Library & Learning Resources): SE-501 90 Borås; Järnvägsgatan 1, Borås; tel. (33) 435-40-50; fax (33) 435-40-04; e-mail biblioteket@hb.se; internet www.hb.se/blr; f. 1972; 117,000 vols, 87,000 e-books, 35,000 e-journals; Dir SVANTE KRISTENSSON; Asst Dir YVONNE OHLSSON.

Borås stadsbibliotek (Borås City Library): POB 856, SE-501 15 Borås; Västerbrogatan 8, Borås; tel. (33) 35-76-20; fax (33) 35-76-75; e-mail boras.stadsbibliotek@boras.se; internet www.boras.se/kultur/stadsbiblioteket; f. 1931, present location 1974; 300,000 vols; Chief Librarian BRITT-INGER LINDQVIST.

Eskilstuna

Eskilstuna stads- och länsbibliotek (Eskilstuna Municipal and County Library): Kriebsensgatan 4, SE-632 20 Eskilstuna; tel. (16) 710-51-10; fax (16) 13-29-49; internet eskilstuna.se/default2____152775.aspx; f. 1925; 550,000 vols; 3 brs in Lagersberg, Torshälla and Årby; Head BARBARA AHLIN; Head KARIN ZETTERBERG.

Gävle

Gävle stadsbibliotek (Gävle City Library): POB 801, SE-801 30 Gävle; Slottstorget 1, Gävle; tel. (26) 17-96-00; fax (26) 61-06-78; e-mail info@gavlebibliotek.nu; f. 1907; 700,000 vols; Dir of Libraries LISBETH FORSLUND.

Gothenburg

Chalmers Bibliotek (Chalmers Library): Chalmers Tvärgata 1, SE-412 96 Gothenburg; tel. (31) 772-37-37; fax (31) 18-35-44; e-mail request.lib@chalmers.se; internet www.lib.chalmers.se; f. 1829; attached to Chalmers Univ. of Technology; 530,000 vols, 620 journals, 7,200 electronic journals; Chair. STEFAN BENGTSSON; Dir ANNIKA SVERRUNG; Asst Dir ANNELIE JANRED.

Attached Libraries:

Arkitekturbiblioteket: Sven Hultins gata 6, SE- 412 96 Gothenburg; tel. (31) 772-24-13; fax (31) 772-24-19; e-mail arch.lib@chalmers.se; Head Librarian ELISABETH KIHLÉN.

Lindholmenbiblioteket: Forskningsgången 6, SE- 412 96 Gothenburg; tel. (31) 772-57-84; fax (31) 772-57-82.

Göteborgs stadsbibliotek (Gothenburg City Library): Götaplatsen, POB 5404, SE-402 29 Gothenburg; tel. (31) 368-33-00; fax (31) 368-35-98; e-mail info.stadsbiblioteket@kultur.goteborg.se; f. 1861; 405,807 vols, incl. 290,000 books; Chief Librarian CHRISTINA PERSSON.

Göteborgs universitetsbibliotek (Gothenburg University Library): POB 222, SE-405 30 Gothenburg; Renströmsgatan 4, Gothenburg; tel. (31) 786-17-49; fax (31) 786-44-11; e-mail universitetsbiblioteket@ub.gu.se; internet www.ub.gu.se; f. 1861; legal deposit library for Swedish publs; spec. collns incl. MSS colln, women's history colln, Snoilsky colln (early Swedish literature), EDC colln, UN colln, Ibero American colln; 2.7m. vols, 5,636 journals, 13,068 e-journals; Dir HAKAN CARLSSON; publs Acta, Qupea.

Halmstad

Halmstads Stadsbibliotek (Halmstad City Library): POB 4083, SE-300 04 Halmstad; Axel Olsons Gata 1, SE-302 27 Halmstad; tel. (35) 13-71-81; fax (35) 13-71-82; e-mail stadsbiblioteket@halmstad.se; f. 2006; public library; 209,000 vols; Chief Librarian ANETTE HAGBERG; Librarian BENEDICTE SÖDERGREN.

Jönköping

Högskolebiblioteket i Jönköping: Högskoleområdet, House C, Gjuterigatan 5, SE-553 16 Jönköping; tel. (36) 10-10-10; fax (36) 10-03-59; internet hj.se/bibl; f. 1914; attached to Jönköping University; 200,000 books, 60,000 e-books, 15,000 journals; Library Dir ANNIKA SWEDÉN.

Stadsbibliotek Jönköpings (Jönköping city library): POB 1029, SE-551 11 Jönköping; Dag Hammarskjölds plats 1, Jönköping; tel. (36) 10-55-75; fax (36) 10-70-44; e-mail stadsbibl@jonkoping.se; internet lingonline.jonkoping.se; f. 1916; 600,000 vols (incl. 700 newspapers and magazines, CDs, DVDs, audio books); Head ULF MOBERG.

Kalmar

Kalmar Stadsbibliotek (Kalmar City Library): Huvudbiblioteket, POB 610, SE-391 26 Kalmar; Tullslätten 4, Kalmar; tel. (480) 45-06-30; fax (480) 45-06-32; e-mail stadsbiblioteket@kalmar.se; f. 1922; 510,000 vols, 300 Swedish periodicals, 25 journals; Chief Librarian SUZANNE HAMMARGREN.

Linnéuniversitetets Biblioteket (Linnaeus University Library): SE-391 82 Kalmar; Nygatan 18A Kalmar; tel. (480) 44-61-00; fax (480) 44-61-15; e-mail kalmar.ub@lnu.se SE- 351 95 Växjö; Universitetsplatsen 2, Växjö; tel. (470) 70-84-00; fax (470) 845-23; e-mail vaxjo.ub@lnu.se; internet lnu.se/ub; 360,000 vols; Library Dir (vacant); Deputy Library Dir ANDERS RYDQVIST.

Karlskrona

Blekinge Tekniska Högskola Library (Blekinge Institute of Technology Library): Library Gräsvik, SE-371 79 Karlskrona; Library Gräsvik, Vallhallavägen 1, Karlskrona; tel. (455) 38-51-01; fax (455) 38-51-07; e-mail biblioteket@bth.se; internet www.bth.se/bib; 2 units: Library Gräsvik, Karlskrona; Library Piren, Karlshamn; incls. learning lab and educational devt; Dir ANNIKA ANNEMARK.

Köpings

Köpings Stadsbibliotek (Köpings City Library): Folkets Hus, SE-731 41 Köpings; tel. (221) 251-82; fax (221) 251-98; e-mail stadsbiblioteket@koping.se; internet www.koping.se; Chief Librarian INGER FELLDIN.

Kristianstad

Högskolan Kristianstad Biblioteket (Kristianstad University College Library): SE-291 39 Kristianstad; Elmetorpsvägen 15, House 7, Kristianstad; tel. (44) 20-30-59; fax (44) 20-30-53; e-mail biblioteket@hkr.se; internet www.hkr.se; Head ANNA BRÜMMER.

Linköping

Linköpings Stadsbibliotek (Linköping City Library): POB 1984, SE-581 19 Linköping; Östgötagatan 5, Linköping; tel. (13) 20-66-01; fax (13) 20-66-50; e-mail stadsbiblioteket@linkoping.se; f. 1926; 666,000 vols; Chief Librarian LENA AXELSSON.

Linköpings Universitetsbibliotek (Linköping University Library): SE-581 83 Linköping; tel. (13) 28-19-10; fax (13) 28-44-24; e-mail hb@bibl.liu.se; internet www.bibl.liu.se; f. 1969; 5 campus libraries; 400,000 books, 2,000 journals, 10,000 e-journals; Dir MARIANNE HÄLLGREN; Asst Dir HELENA WEDBORN; publ. Publikation.

Luleå

Luleå Stadsbiblioteket (Luleå City Library): Skeppsbrogatan 17, SE-971 79 Luleå; tel. (920) 45-59-51; e-mail biblioteket@kulturen.lulea.se; Chief Librarian LENA LUNDBERG VESTERLUND.

Luleå Universitetsbibliotek (Luleå University library): SE-971 87 Luleå; Betahouse, Univ. campus, Porsön, Luleå; tel. (920) 49-15-20; fax (920) 49-20-40; e-mail lulelibrary@ltu.se; internet www.ltu.se/lib; campus libraries at Luleå, Piteå, Skellefteå; research library for Norrbotten County Council; 240,932 vols, 15,663 journals, 66,884 e-books; Chair. ERIK HÖGLUND; Chief Librarian TERJE HÖISETH.

Lund

Landsarkivet i Lund (Lund Regional Archives): POB 2016, SE-220 02 Lund; Dalbyvägen 4, Lund; tel. (10) 476-82-00; fax (10) 476-82-20; e-mail landsarkivet@landsarkivet-lund.ra.se; f. 1903; holds records of govt bodies in S Sweden (counties of Halland, Skåne, Blekinge); spec. collns: estate archives; library: 42,000 shelf m of records, 900 shelf m, mainly genealogy and topography; Chief Archivist JAN DAHLIN.

Universitetsbiblioteket, Lunds Universitet (Lund University Library): POB 3, Helgonabacken, SE-221 00 Lund; tel. (46) 222-00-00; fax (46) 222-42-43; internet www.ub.lu.se; f. 1671; 5,000,000 vols, 129,000 MSS, 120,000 items of microforms; legal deposit library and nat. lending library; MSS incl Necrologium Lundense, the oldest Scandinavian MS; spec. collns: Bibliotheca Gripenhielmiana (6,000 vols 16th- and 17th-century prints), Taussig colln of Schubert MSS, Broman colln of Elsevier prints, De La Gardie colln of prints and MSS; Dir CHRISTINA FRISTRÖM.

Malmö

Malmö Stadsbibliotek (Malmö City Library): SE-205 81 Malmö; Kung Oscars väg 11, SE-211 33 Malmö; tel. (40) 660-85-00; fax (40) 660-86-81; e-mail info.stadsbiblioteket@malmo.se; internet malmo.stadsbibliotek.org; f. 1905; 1,003,469 vols; Librarian ELSEBETH TANK.

Norrköping

Archives for UFO Research Foundation: POB 11027, SE-600 11 Norrköping; tel. (703) 68-32-21; e-mail afu@ufo.se; internet www.afu.info; f. 1973; repositories for UFO data and UFO related folklore; colln of 1,200 m; 15,000 vols; Chair. and Man. ANDERS LILJEGREN.

Norrköpings Stadsbibliotek (Norrköping City Library): POB 2113, SE-600 02 Norrköping; Södra Promenaden 105, Norrköping; tel. (11) 15-26-65; fax (11) 10-38-45; e-mail stadsbiblioteket@norrkoping.se; internet www.nsb.norrkoping.se; f. 1913; 7 br. libraries, 3 bookmobiles; 472,785 vols; Chief Librarian BIRGITTA HJERPE.

Örebro

Örebro stadsbibliotek (City Library and County Library of Örebro län): POB 325 10, SE-701 35 Örebro; Näbbtorgsgatan 12, Örebro; tel. (19) 21-10-00; fax (19) 21-61-62; e-mail biblinfo@orebro.se; f. 1862; 780,000 vols; Chief Librarian CHRISTER KLINGBERG; publ. Samfundet Örebro Stads- och Länsbiblioteks vänner. Meddelande 1929–.

Östersund

Jämtlands Läns Bibliotek (Jämtland's County Library): SE-831 80 Östersund; Råd-

husgatan 25–27, SE-831 80 Östersund; tel.
(63) 14-30-50; e-mail lansbiblioteket@
ostersund.se; internet www.bibliotekmitt.se;
f. 1816, present location 1958; 1 main library,
3 area libraries, 1 mobile library, 2 hospital
libraries; 550,000 vols; Chief Librarian MAJ
ERIKSSON.

Skara
Stifts- och Landsbiblioteket i Skara
(State County and City Library of Skara-
borgs Län): POB 194, SE-532 23 Skara;
Prubbatorget 1, Skara; tel. (511) 32-060; fax
(511) 32-069; e-mail skarabibliotek@skara.se;
f. 1938; 400,000 vols, 200 running m MSS;
Chief Librarian PEMA MALMGREN; publ. *Acta*.

Skövde
Högskolebiblioteket i Skövde (University
College of Skövde Library): POB 408, SE-541
28 Skövde; tel. (500) 44-80-60; fax (500) 44-
80-59; e-mail biblioteket@his.se; internet
www.his.se/biblioteket; 100,000 vols, 8,000
journals, 7,000 e-journals; Library Dir TOMAS
LUNDÉN.

Stockholm
Antikvarisk-topografiska arkivet (Anti-
quarian Topographical Archives): POB 5405,
SE-114 84 Stockholm; Östra stallet, Informa-
tionstorget, Storgatan 41, Stockholm; tel. (8)
519-180-50; fax (8) 519-180-88; e-mail ata@
raa.se; f. 1786; archives of the Collegium
Antiquitatum and the Royal Archives of
Antiquities (1666–1786), archives and collns
of the Royal Academy of Letters, History and
Antiquities (1786–1975) and of the Central
Board of Antiquities and Nat. Historical
Museums, archives of the office of monuments (1918–67) of the Nat. Board of Public
Bldgs; 300 private archives; 120,000 maps
and drawings; 1,100,000 negatives and
photographs; open to the public; Dir Dr ANN
HÖRSELL.

**Handelshögskolans i Stockholm—Bib-
liotek** (Stockholm School of Economics
Library): POB 6501, SE-113 83 Stockholm;
tel. (8) 736-97-02; e-mail library@hhs.se;
internet www.hhs.se/library; f. 1909;
157,000 vols, 15,000 e-journals, 60 databases,
4,500 m of printed materials; provides access
to information within the fields of business,
economics and the social sciences that is
relevant to the teaching and research carried
out at Stockholm School of Economics; Dir
MARIE-LOUISE FENDIN.

**Karolinska Institutet, Universitetsbi-
blioteket** (Karolinska Institute University
Library): POB 200, SE-171 77 Stockholm;
Solna Br.: Solna, Berzelius väg 7B, Stockholm; Huddinge Br.: Huddinge, Alfred
Nobels allé 8, SE- 141 83 Stockholm; tel. (8)
524-840-00; fax (8) 524-843-10; e-mail ub@ki
.se; internet kib.ki.se; f. 1810; Chief Librarian CHRISTER BJÖRKLUND.

**Konstbiblioteket, Nationalmuseum och
Moderna Museet** (Joint Art Library of the
Nationalmuseum and the Museum of Modern Art): POB 16 176, SE-103 24 Stockholm;
Holmamiralens väg 2, Skeppsholmen, Stockholm; tel. (8) 519-543-52; fax (8) 519-543-76;
e-mail konstbiblioteket@nationalmuseum.se;
internet www.nationalmuseum.se; f. late
19th century; 330,000 vols, 247 serials,
2,390,000 cuttings, 900 journal titles; literature on Western art since the Renaissance; jt
library of the Nat. Museum and Moderna
Museet; Librarian MARIA SYLVÉN.

**Kungliga biblioteket—Sveriges natio-
nalbibliotek** (National Library of Sweden):
POB 5039, SE-102 41 Stockholm; Humlegår-
den, Stockholm; tel. (10) 709-30-00; fax (10)
709-39-25; e-mail kungl.biblioteket@kb.se;
internet www.kb.se; f. early 16th century;
Nat. Library of Sweden with most complete

colln of Swedish printed books and
audiovisual material in the world; foreign
holdings in humanities; important collns of
Old Swedish and Icelandic MSS; spec. collns
incl. incunabula, Elzevirs, maps, portraits,
heraldry; responsible for the union catalogue
LIBRIS and for cooperation among scientific
libraries (Nat. Cooperation Dept); 4,000,000
vols; Nat. Librarian Dr GUNNAR SAHLIN;
Deputy Nat. Librarian MAGDALENA GRAM;
publ. *Acta Bibliothecæ regiæ Stockholmiensis*.

**Kungl. Skogs- och Lantbruksakade-
miens Bibliotek** (Royal Swedish Academy
of Agriculture and Forestry Library): POB
6806, SE-113 86 Stockholm; Drottninggatan
95B, Stockholm; tel. (8) 545-477-20; fax (8)
545-477-30; e-mail kslab@ksla.se; internet
www.kslab.ksla.se; f. 1813; 85,000 vols, 400
periodicals; colln of books on rural and
agricultural history, horticulture, forestry
and related fields; Chief Librarian LARS
LJUNGGREN; publs *Miscellanea, Skogs- och
Lantbrukshistoriska Meddelanden* (irregular).

**Kungliga Tekniska Högskolans Biblio-
tek** (Royal Institute of Technology Library):
Osquars Backe 25, SE-100 44 Stockholm;
Osquars Backe 31, Stockholm; tel. (8) 790-70-
88; fax (8) 790-71-22; e-mail sekr@lib.kth.se;
internet www.kth.se/kthb; f. 1827; centre for
computerized information and documentation services in science and technology;
851,299 vols, 125,761 e-books, 8,636,000 e-
journals (incl. br. libraries); Chief Librarian
MATS HERDER; publ. *Stockholm Papers in
History and Philosophy of Science and Technology*.

Kurdiska Biblioteket (Kurdish Library):
POB 13029, SE-103 01 Stockholm; Gustavs-
slundsvägen 170, SE-167 51 Bromma; tel. (8)
679-88-03; fax (8) 679-88-04; e-mail info@
kurdlib.org; internet www.kurdlib.org; f.
1997; collects, preserves and makes available
all printed works written by Kurds or that
have relationship with the Kurds and Kurdi-
stan; 13,000 vols, 700 serials; Chair. ANNE
MURRAY; Vice-Chair. AYCAN BOZARSLAN;
Library Dir and Sec. of Board NEWZAD
HIRORI; Librarian MEHMET TAYFUN.

**Musik- och teaterbiblioteket vid Statens
musiksamlingar** (Music and Theatre
Library of Sweden): POB 16326, SE-103 26
Stockholm; Torsgatan 19, SE-113 21 Stockholm; tel. (8) 519-554-12; fax (8) 519-554-05;
e-mail exp@muslib.se; internet www.muslib
.se; f. 1771, present name and status 2010,
merger of Theatre Library of Sweden (f.
1935); attached to Statens musiksamlingar;
large colln of 18th century music and 19th
century theatre material; about 300 archives
and collns; incl. a documentation centre for
Swedish music; 137,000 books on music and
theatre, 400,000 scores of music, 50,000
plays, 28,000 MSS and about 15,000 letters,
500,000 photographs (theatre colln); Chief
Librarian VESLEMØY HEINTZ; publ. *Dokumen-
terat: bulletin från Musik- och teaterbiblioteket* (online, www.muslib.se/publ/
bulletin.html).

Östasiatiska Biblioteket (Far Eastern
Library — Library of the Museum of Far
Eastern Antiquities): POB 16381, SE-103 27
Stockholm; Tyghusplan, Skeppsholmen,
Stockholm; tel. (8) 519-557-76; fax (8) 519-
557-55; e-mail helena.rundkrantz@
ostasiatiska.se; internet www.ostasiatiska
.se; f. 1986; 3,500 linear m; colln of Chinese
periodicals, Japanese colln of A.E. Nordens-
kiöld, colln of Chinese congshu, colln of
Western-language books on Asia; library is
administered within the MFEA Unit for
Research and Devt (Head: Dr EVA MYRDAL);
Librarian HELENA RUNDKRANTZ.

**Regeringskansliet Utrikesdepartemen-
tets Bibliotek** (Library of the Swedish
Ministry for Foreign Affairs): SE-103 33
Stockholm; tel. (8) 405-10-00; internet www
.regeringen.se; not open to the public; Librarian GRETA QUESADA.

Riksarkivet (National Archives of Sweden):
POB 12541, SE-102 29 Stockholm; Fyrver-
karbacken 13, Stockholm; tel. (10) 476-70-00;
fax (10) 476-71-20; e-mail riksarkivet@
riksarkivet.ra.se; internet www.riksarkivet
.se; f. 1618, present status 2010; 670,000 m
of archival holdings; regional archives at
Gothenburg, Härnösand, Lund, Östersund,
Uppsala, Vadstena, Visby; Military archives
and Research Center SVAR are also
attached; Dir-Gen. BJÖRN JORDEL; publs
Arsbok för Riksarkivet och landsarkiven (1
a year), *Glossarium till medeltidslatinet i
Sverige*, *Skrifter utgivna av Riksarkivet*,
Svenskt diplomatarium.

Riksdagsbiblioteket (Library of the Swedish Parliament): SE-100 12 Stockholm; Stor-
kyrkobrinken 7A; tel. (8) 786-40-00; fax (8)
786-58-70; e-mail biblioteket@riksdagen.se;
internet www.riksdagen.se; f. 1851; serves
the Riksdag, the admin. services and
research; chiefly devoted to political science,
administration, social science and law; open
to the public; 700,000 vols; Chief Librarian
GUNILLA LILIE BAUER; publ. *Fakta om folk-
valda: Riksdagen 1985–* (biographical handbook, every 4 years).

Statistiska Centralbyråns Bibliotek
(Statistics Sweden Library): POB 24300,
SE-104 51 Stockholm; tel. (8) 506-950-66;
fax (8) 661-52-61; e-mail library@scb.se;
internet www.scb.se; f. 1858; research library
for official Swedish statistics; all statistics
published by Statistics Sweden; literature on
statistical theories and methodology; colln of
statistical results from most of the countries
of the world and from 50 int. orgs and the
EU's statistical office Eurostat till 2008;
230,000 vols, 1,400 periodicals; Chief Librarian CHRISTINA CRONSIOE; publ. *Statistics from
International Organizations and other Issuing Bodies* (1 a year).

Stockholms Stadsarkiv (Stockholm City
Archives): POB 22063, SE-104 22 Stockholm;
Kungsklippan 6, Stockholm; tel. (8) 508-283-
00; fax (8) 508-283-01; e-mail stadsarkivet@
stockholm.se; internet www.ssa.stockholm
.se; f. 1930; provincial archives for Stockholm; documents from regional authorities
and the municipal govt of Stockholm; archives on urban history of Stockholm; 130,000
vols, archives: 68,000 shelf m; City Archivist
LENNART PLOOM; publs *Stadsarkivets små-
tryck* (irregular), *Stockholms stadsarkiv.
Årsberättelse* (1 a year), *Stockholms tänke-
böcker från år 1592* (irregular).

Stockholms stadsbibliotek (Stockholm
Public Library): SE-113 80 Stockholm; Oden-
gatan 63, Spelbomskan, Stockholm; tel. (8)
508-311-00; fax (8) 508-312-10; e-mail
stadsbiblioteket@stockholm.se; internet
www.biblioteket.stockholm.se; f. 1927; 40
libraries; 2,225,000 vols; Chief Librarian
INGA LUNDÉN.

Stockholms universitetsbibliotek (Stockholm University Library): SE-106 91 Stockholm; Universitetsvägen 14D, Stockholm; tel.
(8) 16-28-00; fax (8) 15-77-76; internet www
.sub.su.se; f. 1877; 2,500,000 vols; 12 brs;
Librarian Dr CATARINA ERICSON-ROOS.

Svenska Akademiens Nobelbibliotek
(Nobel Library of the Swedish Academy):
POB 2118, SE-103 13 Stockholm; Källargränd 4, Gamla Stan, Stockholm; tel. (8) 555-
125-52; fax (8) 555-125-99; e-mail info@
nobelbiblioteket.se; internet www
.nobelbiblioteket.se; f. 1901; recent works of
literature, literary criticism and linguistics;

assists the Swedish Acad. in evaluations required for the Nobel Prize in Literature; 200,000 vols, 150 journals; Chief Librarian LARS RYDQUIST.

Svenskt Visarkiv (Centre for Swedish Folk Music and Jazz Research): POB 16326, SE-103 26 Stockholm; Torsgatan 19, Stockholm; tel. (8) 519-554-88; fax (8) 519-554-49; e-mail info@visarkiv.se; internet www.visarkiv.se; f. 1951; attached to Swedish Nat. Collns of Music; collects, preserves, publishes material concerning instrumental folk music, folk songs, jazz and traditional music from the end of the 16th century till present; Dir DAN LUNDBERG.

Sveriges Radio Förvaltings AB (Resources of the Swedish Broadcasting Corporation): Oxenstiernsgatan 20, SE-105 10 Stockholm; tel. (8) 784-54-00; fax (8) 660-72-57; internet www.srf.se; f. 1925; documents relating to Swedish public service broadcasting and television; Archivist BJÖRN BLOMBERG.

Vitterhetsakademiens Bibliotek (Library of the Royal Swedish Academy of Letters, History and Antiquities): POB 5405, SE-114 84 Stockholm; Storgatan 41, Stockholm; tel. (8) 519-183-26; fax (8) 663-35-28; e-mail bibl@raa.se; internet www.raa.se/bibliotek; f. 1753, present name 1786; attached to Swedish Nat. Heritage Board; spec. collns on archaeology, medieval art and architecture, numismatics, preservation of cultural heritage; open to the public; affiliated library: Colln of Numismatic Books; 430,000 vols; Head of the Unit of Library Services MIKAEL JAKOBSSON; publ. *Fornvännen*.

Sundsvall

Universitetsbiblioteket, Mittuniversitetet (Mid Sweden University Library): SE-851 70 Sundsvall; Holmgatan 10, Sundsvall; tel. (60) 14-87-50; fax (60) 14-89-66; e-mail bibsvl@miun.se; internet www.bib.miun.se; campus libraries in Härnösand, Östersund; 220,000 vols, 20,000 e-journals, 60 electronic databases; Dir MORGAN PALMQVIST; Library Man. CATHRINE BERGGREN.

Umeå

Umeå stadsbibliotek (Umeå City Library): Rådhusesplanaden 6A, SE-901 78 Umeå; tel. (90) 16-33-00; fax (90) 16-33-04; e-mail stadsbiblioteket@umea.se; internet www.minabibliotek.se; f. 1903; 770,000 vols; Chief Librarian INGER EDEBRO SIKSTRÖM.

Umeå Universitetsbibliotek (Umeå University Library): SE-901 74 Umeå; Social Sciences Bldg, Umeå Univ., Umeå; tel. (90) 786-56-93; fax (90) 786-74-74; e-mail umub@ub.umu.se; internet www.ub.umu.se; f. 1950 as Scientific Library in Umeå, present name and status 1964; academic research; open to public; 1,500,000 vols, 18,000 journals, 12,000 e-journals; Chief Librarian MIKAEL SJÖGREN.

Uppsala

Sveriges lantbruksuniversitets—Bibliotek (Library of the Swedish University of Agricultural Sciences): POB 7071, SE-750 07 Uppsala; Undervisningsplan 10, Uppsala; tel. (18) 67-11-05; fax (18) 67-28-53; e-mail bib-esupport@slu.se; internet www.slu.se/sv/bibliotek; f. 1977; consists of Ultunabiblioteket (main library, in Uppsala) and 8 brs; Dir SNORRE RUFELT; Asst Dir CATHARINA ISBERG; Sr Librarian ULLA ANDERSSON; Librarian CHRISTINA TÖRNQVIST WESTIN.

Uppsala stadsbibliotek (Uppsala City Library): POB 643, SE-751 27 Uppsala; Svartbäcksgatan 17, SE-753 75 Uppsala; tel. (18) 727-17-00; fax (18) 727-06-40; e-mail stadsbibli.inf@uppsala.se; f. 1906;

800,000 vols; Chief Librarian MARIE-LOUISE RITON.

Uppsala universitetsbibliotek (Uppsala University Library): POB 510, SE-751 20 Uppsala; Carolina Rediviva, Dag Hammarskjölds väg 1, Uppsala; tel. (18) 471-39-00; fax (18) 471-39-13; e-mail info@ub.uu.se; internet www.ub.uu.se; f. 1620; consists of 11 subject libraries and cultural heritage collns; 5,500,000 vols, 18,000 e-periodicals, 400,000 e-books, 200 databases, 30 encyclopaedias and 62,000 MSS, incl. the famous *Codex argenteus*, the 'Silver Bible' from the 6th century, a translation of the Gospels into the Gothic language, Swedish and Icelandic medieval MSS, the Bibliotheca Walleriana (medical books), a colln of old music books and MSS, a colln of old maps, engravings and drawings, incl. the *Carta Marina* of 1539 by Olaus Magnus (earliest accurate map of Scandinavia); Dir Prof. ULF GÖRANSON; publs *Acta Bibliothecae R. Universitatis Upsaliensis*, *Scripta Minora Bibliothecae R. Universitatis Upsaliensis*, *Uppsala University Library's exhibition catalogues*.

Varberg

Campusbiblioteket i Varberg (Campus Library in Varberg): Otto Torells gata 18, SE-432 44 Varberg; tel. (340) 69-74-46; fax (340) 69-74-45; e-mail varberg@bib.hh.se; internet www.campusbiblioteket.se; f. 2003; operated jtly by Varberg Kommun and Halmstad Univ.'s Varberg Campus; Librarian CHRISTINA GABRIELSSON; Librarian LENNART ERLING; Librarian VERONICA AASHEIM KVIST.

Varberg Bibliotek: Engelbrektsgatan 7, SE-432 80 Varberg; tel. (340) 886-00; fax (340) 69-70-50; e-mail biblioteket@kommunen.varberg.se; internet www2.varberg.se; 6 br. libraries, 1 mobile library; 250,000 titles; Chief Librarian PER FALK.

Värmland

Värmlandsarkiv (Värmland Archives): POB 475, SE-651 11 Karlstad; Hööksgatan 2, SE-651 11 Karlstad; tel. (54) 61-77-30; e-mail varmlandsarkiv@regionvarmland.se; internet varmlandsarkiv.regionvarmland.se; f. 1970, present status 2001; attached to Nat. Archives of Sweden; colln of 23,000 shelf m from middle ages to present; 25,000 vols.

Västerås

Mälardalens Högskolebiblioteket (Mälardalens University College Library): POB 832, SE-721 22 Västerås; Högskoleplan 1, Västerås; tel. (21) 10-13-44; fax (21) 10-13-40; e-mail biblioteket@mdh.se; internet www.mdh.se/library; 114,364 vols, 46,200 e-books, 318 journals, 10,421 e-journals; Chair. ROLAND SVENSSON; Library Dir ANNSOFIE OSCARSSON.

Västerås stadsbibliotek (Västerås City Library): Biskopsgatan 2, SE-721 87 Västerås; tel. (21) 39-46-01; fax (21) 39-46-80; e-mail stadsbibliotek@vasteras.se; internet www.bibliotek.vasteras.se; f. 1952; 571,000 vols; 6 associated libraries and a mobile library; Chief Librarian EVA MATSSON.

Växjö

Smålands Musikarkiv (Småland's Music Archive): Västergatan 13, SE-352 31 Växjö; tel. (470) 70-03-00; internet www.smalandsmusikarkiv.nu; f. 1992; attached to Musik i Syd; colln incl. music from Småland and adjacent landscape; 2,000 vols; Head MAGNUS GUSTAFSSON.

Växjö Bibliotek (City and County Library, Kronobergs län): POB 1202, SE-351 12 Växjö; Västra Esplanaden 7, SE-351 12 Växjö; tel. (470) 4-14-44; fax (470) 79-69-92; e-mail stadsbiblioteket@vaxjo.se; internet

www.vaxjo.se/bibliotek; f. 1954, present bldg 2003; 460,000 vols; 15 brs; Chief Librarian ANNA-KARIN AXELSSON.

Visby

Almedalsbiblioteket (Almedals Library): POB 1121, SE-621 22 Visby; Cramérgatan 3–5, SE-621 22 Visby; tel. (498) 29-90-00; fax (498) 29-90-11; e-mail almedalsbiblioteket@hgo.se; internet www.almedalsbiblioteket.se; f. 1865; 502,000 vols; Chief Librarian KERSTIN SIMBERG.

Museums and Art Galleries

Falun

Dalarnas Museum: POB 22, SE-791 21 Falun; tel. (23) 76-55-00; fax (23) 283-58; e-mail info@dalarnasmuseum.se; internet www.dalarnasmuseum.se; f. 1962; shows cultural heritage from the Stone Age to present time; exhibits Archaeological Society collection activities from 1862; colln of costume and textiles, folk art, folk music, graphics, Selma Lagerlof's library; Dir. JAN RAIHLE; Deputy Dir ANNA BJÖRKMAN.

Gävle

Länsmuseet Gävleborgs (Gävleborg County Museum): POB 746, SE-801 28 Gävle; Södrastrandgatan 20, Gävle; tel. (26) 65-56-00; e-mail lansmuseetgavleborg@xlm.se; internet www.lansmuseetgavleborg.se; f. 1978 as Gävle Museum; exhibits art, silver and gold metal work, representations of circus life, archaeology of Gävle, selection from Hedvig Ulfsparre's private colln of textiles, devt of modern mass production; Pres. LENNART GARD; Vice-Pres. NILS MALMLÖF.

Sveriges Järnvägsmuseum (Swedish Railway Museum): POB 407, SE-801 05 Gävle; Rälsgatan 1, Gävle; tel. (26) 14-46-15; fax (26) 14-45-98; e-mail jarnvagsmuseum@banverket.se; internet www.banverket.se/en/swedish-railway-museum/; f. 1915; colln of locomotives, carriages, wagons, other railway items; photographs, pictures, historic film material, railway literature, and archival material; br. in Ängelholm; Dir ROBERT SJÖÖ; Admin. GÖRAN JÄDERHOLM.

Gothenburg

Aeroseum: Holmvägen 100, SE-417 46 Gothenburg; Säve Depå, Holmvägen, Gothenburg; tel. (31) 55-83-00; fax (31) 55-13-09; e-mail info@aeroseum.se; internet www.aeroseum.se; f. 1999, present status 2008; history and devt of aviation; preserves ex-military subterranean aircraft hangars; Chair. ROGER ELIASSON.

Göteborgs Konsthall: Gotaplatsen, SE-412 56 Gothenborg; tel. (31) 368-34-50; fax (31) 368-34-59; e-mail goteborgs.konsthall@kultur.goteborg.se; internet www.konsthallen.goteborg.se; f. 1923; exhibits contemporary art; organizes artist talks, tours, seminars and classes; presents group and solo exhibitions of nat. and int. artists; Dir. MIKAEL NANFELDT; Curators STINA EDBLOM, LAURA MOTT.

Göteborgs Naturhistoriska Museet (Gothenburg Museum of Natural History): POB 7283, SE-402 35 Gothenburg; Slottsskogen vid Linnéplatsen, Gothenburg; tel. (31) 775-24-00; fax (31) 12-98-07; e-mail info.naturhistoriska@vgregion.se; internet www.gnm.se; f. 1833, present location 1923; exhibits Swedish animal world and animals from around the world; themes incl. Earth's structure and life history, marine life, environmental problems, humans as biological beings and ecology concepts; specimens date from 18th century; zoological colln: 10m. animals, vertebrate colln: of 100,000 specimens; library of 80,000 vols; Dir Dr ANN STRÖMBERG; publ. *Årstryck*.

Göteborgs Stads Kulturförvaltning (Gothenburg Arts and Culture): Norra Hamngatan 8, SE-411 14 Gothenburg; tel. (31) 368-32-00; fax (31) 368-32-14; e-mail info@kultur.goteborg.se; internet www .goteborg.se/kultur; f. 1993; responsible for cultural activities in Gothenburg; Chair. of Trustees HELENA NYHUS; Vice-Chair. of Trustees LENNART S. WIDING.

Attached Museums:

Göteborgs Konstmuseum (Gothenburg Museum of Art): Götaplatsen, SE-412 56 Gothenburg; tel. (31) 368-35-00; fax (31) 368-35-26; e-mail info.konstmuseum@ kultur.goteborg.se; internet www .konstmuseum.goteborg.se; f. 1925; European paintings, sculpture, prints and drawings from 1400, spec. collns of French art since 1820 and Scandinavian art incl. works by Monet, Picasso, Rembrandt, Van Gogh; art library; Dir ISABELLA NILSSON.

Göteborgs Stadsmuseum (Gothenburg City Museum): Norra Hamngatan 12, SE-411 14 Gothenburg; tel. (31) 368-36-00; fax (31) 774-03-58; e-mail stadsmuseum@ kultur.goteborg.se; internet www .stadsmuseum.goteborg.se; f. 1861, present status 1993; archaeology since prehistoric times, industrial heritage; Dir KARL-GUN-NAR NORDANSTAD.

Röhsska Museet (Röhss Museum of Applied Art and Design): Vasagatan 37–39, SE-400 15 Gothenburg; POB 53178, SE-400 15 Gothenburg; tel. (31) 368-31-50; fax (31) 368-31-78; e-mail info .designmuseum@kultur.goteborg.se; internet www.designmuseum.se; f. 1916, present status 1961; colln incl. 50,000 objects of crafts, applied arts and industrial design; Swedish and European decorative art, Greek and Roman antiquities, material from Japan and China; library of 30,000 vols; Dir TED HESSELBOM; publ. *Röhsska Konstslöjdmuseets årsbok* (Röhsska Museum Yearbook).

Sjöfartsmuseet Akvariet (Maritime Museum and Aquarium): Karl Johansgatan 1–3, SE-414 59 Gothenburg; tel. (31) 368-35-50; fax (31) 368-35-59; e-mail info .sjofartsmuseum@kultur.goteborg.se; internet www.sjofartsmuseum.goteborg.se; f. 1913; permanent exhibitions on world shipping significant for Gothenburg and W Sweden; themes incl. pirates, life at sea; temporary exhibitions and programme activities; library of 20,000 vols; Dir ANNA ROSENGREN; publ. *Unda Maris*.

Kvibergs Museum: Lilla Regementsvägen 33, SE-415 28 Gothenburg; tel. (31) 48-06-02; e-mail kvibergsmuseum@telia.com; internet www.kvibergsmuseum.se; f. 1895; highlights military action in Kviberg area; Dir TORGNY ALLVIN.

Världskulturmuseet (Museum of World Culture): POB 5303, SE-402 27 Gothenburg; Södra vägen 54, Gothenburg; tel. (31) 63-27-00; e-mail info@varldskulturmuseet.se; internet www.varldskulturmuseet.se; f. 2004; exhibitions and programs on contemporary issues around the world; library of 30,000 titles, 900 journals and yearbooks; Dir MARGARETA ALIN.

Hässleholms

Bjärnum Museum och Hembygdssamlingar (Bjärnum Museum and Local Historical Collections): Parkgatan, SE-280 20 Hässleholms; tel. (451) 200-91; e-mail info@

bjarnumsmuseum.se; internet www .bjarnumsmuseum.se; 100,000 articles describing the lifestyle of ancestors; objects covering a period of approx. 11,000 years; Chair. ARNE WIGHAGEN; Sec. ANDERS SVENSSON.

Helsingborg

Dunkers Kulturhus (Arts Centre): Kungsgatan 11, SE-252 21 Helsingborg; tel. (0) 42-10-74-00; fax (0) 42-10-74-10; e-mail dunkerskulturhus@helsingborg.se; internet www.dunkerskulturhus.se; f. 2002; exhibitions with town history, cultural history; contemporary art exhibitions; theatre, ballet, modern dance, jazz, chamber music and world music concerts; Dir ELISABETH ALSHEIMER; Curator BENGT ADLERS.

Grafiska Museet (Printing Museum): c/o Fredriksdal Museums and Gardens, Gisela Trapps väg 5, SE-254 37 Helsingborg; tel. and fax (42) 10-45-24; e-mail info@ grafiskamuseet.se; internet www .grafiskamuseet.se; f. 1990; working printing museum; Chair. BERTIL HAGBERG; Deputy Chair. GIDEON BEIL.

Höganäs

Höganäs Museum och Konsthall: Polhemsgatan 1, SE-263 37 Höganäs; tel. (42) 34-13-35; e-mail hoganas.museum@telia .com; internet www.hoganasmuseum.se; f. 1924, present status 1997; exhibits historical industrial period; art gallery; Chair. SIMON ARNE.

Karlskoga

Nobelmuseet i Karlskoga: Björkbornsvägen 10, SE-691 33 Karlskoga; tel. (46) 586-834-94; fax (46) 586-352-20; e-mail info@ nobelmuseetikarlskoga.se; internet nobelmuseeetikarlskoga.se; exhibits on Alfred Nobel and his home, laboratory on Björkborn Manor.

Karlskrona

Blekinge Museum: Borgmästaregatan 21, SE-371 35 Karlskrona; tel. (455) 30-49-65; fax (455) 30-49-73; e-mail blekingemuseum@ karlskrona.se; internet www .blekingemuseum.se; f. 1899 as preservation society, present status 1983; exhibits history of Blekinge; Dir TULLAN GUNÉR; Librarian CHRISTIN NILSSON.

Museum—The Kulenovic Collection: Stortorget 5, Karlskrona; tel. (455) 25573; e-mail rizah.kulenovic@telia.se; internet www.kulenoviccollection.se; f. 1997, as Museum Lionardo da Vinci Ideale; exhibition of paintings, drawings, etchings and prints, sculptures, artefacts, ceramics; Raphael, Leonardo da Vinci, Rembrandt, Caravaggio, van Gogh and Picasso and others; art objects in the form of figurines, vases and figurines dating from around 3000BC onwards; Dir RIZAH KULENOVIC.

Köpings

Köpings Museum: Östra Långgatan 37, SE-731 30 Köpings; tel. (221) 253-51; fax (221) 179-45; e-mail museum@koping.se; internet www.koping.se; f. 1887; shows Köpings history over 10,000 years; 4,000 glass plates, approx. 8,000 photographs from the 1860s until today; 25,000 magazines; Dir ROY CASSÉ.

Kristianstad

Regionmuseet Kristianstad (Regional Museum in Kristianstad): POB 134, SE-291 22 Kristianstad; Stora Torg, Kristianstad; tel. (44) 13-58-00; fax (44) 21-49-02; e-mail info@regionmuseet.se; internet www .regionmuseet.m.se; has 3 br. museums: Film Museum, Railway Museum and Åhus

Museum; archive and photographic archive; colln incl. archaeological material, natural history: rocks, fossils, animals, military equipment, railway historical stock, movie historical stock, school and teaching materials; agricultural lot, textiles and clothing, business interiors, crafts, furniture, utensils, glass, porcelain, ceramic arts, crafts, toys, musical instruments; art colln by Scanian artists, oils, watercolours, prints and sculptures; Dir BARBRO MELLANDER; Asst Dir OLOF HERMELIN.

Kristinehamn

Kristinehamns Konstmuseum: Dr Enwalls väg 13B, SE-681 84 Kristinehamn; tel. (550) 88 200; fax (550) 180 99; e-mail info .konstmuseum@kristinehamn.se; internet www.kristinehamnskonstmuseum.com; f. 1997; modern and contemporary art; colln of works created by artists connected to Värmland; works of artists Bengt Olson and Stig Olson; Dir ANNA SVENSSON; Curator JOHAN MAGNUSSON.

Jokkmokk

Ájtte Svenskt Fjäll- och Samemuseum (Ajtte Swedish Mountain and Sami Museum): POB 116, SE-962 23 Jokkmokk; Kyrkogatan 3, SE-962 31 Jokkmokk; tel. (971) 170-70; fax (971) 120-57; e-mail info@ ajtte.com; internet www.ajtte.com; exhibits Sami culture; spec. museum of mountain chains, natural and cultural resources, information centre for mountain tourists; Dir KJELL-ÅKE ARONSSON.

Jönköping

Radiomuseet (Radio Museum): Tändsticksgränd 16, SE-553 15 Jönköping; tel. (36) 71-39-59; e-mail radiomuseet@telia.com; internet www.radiomuseet.com; f. 1988; exhibits loudspeaker equipment and microphones, historical radio broadcasting equipment, sound recording devices from Edison's wax cylinders to modern CD.

Landskrona

Tycho Brahe museet (Tycho Brahe Museum): Landsvägen 182, SE-260 13 St Ibb; tel. (418) 72530; e-mail goran.nystrom@ landskrona.se; internet www.tychobrahe .com; f. 2005; colln of films, archaeological finds from field, reconstructed instruments, models, pictures and multimedia; incl. Tycho Brahe's underground observatory Stjärneborg, a reconstructed Renaissance Garden, Tycho Brahe museum, and science centre; Dir GÖRAN NYSTRÖM.

Lidingö

Millesgården: Carl Milles väg 2, SE-181 34 Lidingö; Herserudsvägen 32, Lidingö; tel. (8) 446-75-90; fax (8) 767-09-02; e-mail info@ millesgarden.se; internet www.millesgarden .se; f. 1936; 4 rooms for exhibition: art gallery, artist home and small studio; colln of sculptures made by artists; Dir ONITA WASS; Curator EVELINA JANSSON.

Linköping

Linköpings Slotts- och Domkyrkomuseum: Borggården, SE-582 28 Linköping; tel. (13) 12-23-80; fax (13) 14-23-80; e-mail info@lsdm.se; internet lsdm.se; displays aspects of medieval times, such as episode of bubonic plague, medical practices, status and regalia, pests, family banners.

Lund

Botaniska Museet (Botanical Museum): Östra Vallgatan 18, SE-223 61 Lund; tel. (46) 222-95-59; fax (46) 222-42-34; e-mail museichef@botmus.lu.se; internet www .biomus.lu.se/botaniska-museet; attached to Lund Univ.; colln includes about 2.5m. specimens of plants; fungi, lichens, mosses, vascular plants etc.; Dir Prof. INGVAR KÄRNEFELT.

Historiska museet (Historical museum): Lund University, Krafts torg 1, SE-223 50 Lund; tel. (46) 222-79-44; e-mail info@luhm .lu.se; internet www.luhm.lu.se; f. 1805; exhibits Kilian Stobaeus Cabinet of Curiosities from the 18th century, finds from excavations of the Iron Age city of Uppåkra and artefacts from the Scanian Stone, Bronze and Iron Ages; coin colln; dept of Medieval church art and Antique artefacts; Dir PER KARSTEN.

Kulturen in Lund (Cultural History Museum in Lund): POB 1095, Tegnérsplatsen, SE-221 04 Lund; Tegnérsplatsen, Lund; tel. (46) 35-04-00; fax (46) 30-42-60; e-mail info@kulturen.com; internet www.kulturen .com; f. 1882; ethnography, cultural history, medieval archaeology; open-air museum, town and country houses; applied arts (ceramics, textiles, silver, glass); weapons and uniforms; musical instruments; furniture and fittings; trades; commerce and crafts; fishery; farming; folk art; archaeological finds from medieval Lund; holds more than 30 historical bldgs, around 125,000 items and 1m. archaeological finds from 3000BC to present; Östarp, old farm with inn, 30 km from Lund; library of 35,000 vols; Dir ANKI DAHLIN; publ. *Kulturen* (yearbook).

Lund konsthall: Mårtenstorget 3, SE-223 51 Lund; tel. (46) 35-52-95; fax (46) 18-45-21; e-mail lundkonsthall@lund.se; internet www.lundkonsthall.se; f. 1957; nat. and int. art exhibition; visual and spatial articulation of exhibitions, catalogues, public talks, lectures and discussion events; in charge of producing public art projects for new buildings financed by the City of Lund; Dir ÅSA NACKING; Curator ANDERS KREUGER.

Skissernas Museum (Museum of Sketches): Finngatan 2, SE-223 62 Lund; tel. (46) 222-72-83; e-mail reception@ skissernasmuseum.se; internet www.adk.lu .se; f. 1934; Swedish, Nordic and int. collns; colln of sketches and models; sculpture colln; Dir ELISABET HAGLUND; Curator ANN LANDGREN.

Zoologiska Museet (Zoological Museum): Helgonavägen 3A, SE-223 62 Lund; tel. (46) 222-93-30; fax (46) 222-45-41; e-mail museichef@zool.lu.se; internet www.biomus .lu.se/zoologiska-museet; attached to Lund Univ.; scientific colln; contains approx. 10m objects, mostly insects and other invertebrates; Dir Prof. SVEN-AXEL BENGTSON; publ. *Entomologica scandinavica* (Scandinavian Entomology).

Lycksele

Skogsmuseet (Forestry Museum): POB 176, SE-921 23 Lycksele; Lapland, SE-921 23 Lycksele; tel. (950) 379-45; fax (950) 132-60; internet www.skogsmuseet.se; f. 1983; exhibitions on the manual logging era and the mechanized logging era showing woodland population; Birger Nordin Sami colln of art objects and books; Dir MAARIT KALELA-BRUNDIN.

Malmö

Idrottsmuseet (Sports Museum): Fritidsförvaltningen, POB 8111, SE-200 41 Malmö; Eric Perssons väg, Malmö; tel. (40) 34-26-88; e-mail idrottsmuseet@malmo.se; internet www.malmo.se/idrottsmuseet; material on people who have devoted their lives to sport, active athletes, managers or spectators; publ. *Skånsk Idrotts Historia*.

Malmö Konsthall: S:t Johannesgatan 7, POB 17 127, SE-200 10 Malmö; tel. (40) 34-60-00; fax (40) 30-15-07; e-mail info

.konsthall@malmo.se; internet www .konsthall.malmo.se; f. 1975; exhibits int. and nat. art ranging from the classics of modernism to current experiments; organizes theatre, film, poetry, video installations, multimedia, music, lectures and debates; Dir JACOB FABRICIUS; Chief Curator ANNA HOLMBOM.

Malmö Konstmuseum (Malmö Art Museum): POB 406, SE-201 24 Malmö; Malmöhusvägen 6, Malmö; tel. (705) 77-44-69; fax (708) 87-44-33; e-mail malmokonstmuseum@malmo.se; internet www.malmo.se; f. 1841 as Malmö Museum, reorganized 1932; collns incl. primarily Nordic art, European art, decorative art and design objects from the 1500s to the present; 40,000 works of art; Dir GÖRAN CHRISTENSON.

Malmö Museer (Malmö Museums): POB 406, SE-201 24 Malmö; Malmöhusvägen 6, Malmö; tel. (40) 34-44-00; fax (40) 12-40-97; e-mail malmomuseer@malmo.se; internet www.malmo.se; f. 1841; incl. commander's house, Ebba's house on Snapperupsgatan, Slottsmöllan at Mölleplatsen, Slottsholmen (with hus Castle), Technology & Maritime House, Wowragården in Southern Sallerup; Dir GÖRAN LARSSON.

Teatermuseet (Theatre Museum): Kalendegatan 5C, SE-211 35 Malmö; tel. (40) 12-48-83; e-mail info@teatermuseet.com; internet www.teatermuseet.com; preserves, documents history and traditions of theatre and the performing world; colln incl. Artillery Photographs from Hippodromteatern in Malmö dating from 1924 until closure in 1949, personal letters and photographs of Swedish actors, large colln of press clippings from Swedish newspapers on theatre activities from 1930s onwards, manuscripts from Skåne theatre history.

Mariefred

Swedish National Portrait Gallery: c/o Collections and Swedish National Portrait Gallery, Nationalmuseum, POB 16176, SE-103 24 Stockholm; Gripsholm Castle, Mariefred; tel. (8) 519-543-00; fax (8) 519-544-56; e-mail elk@nationalmuseum.se; internet www.nationalmuseum.se; f. 1822; colln of Swedish portraits from 16th century till present day; Dir Dr MAGNUS OLAUSSON; Curator EVA-LENA KARLSSON.

Mora

Zornmuseet (Zorn Museum): Vasagatan 36, POB 32, SE-792 21 Mora; tel. (250) 59-23-10; fax (250) 184-60; e-mail info@zorn.se; internet www.zorn.se; f. 1939; divided into 4 parts: Zorn Museum, Zorn House, open-air museum Zorn's Gammelgård and Gopsmor; also consists of The Textile Museum; permanent exhibition: 'Midnight' (1891), 'Dairy Maid' (1908), 'Dance in the Gopsmor Cottage' (1913) as well as the 2 self portraits in red and in a wolfskin (both 1915); 'Mormor' (1883) and 'The Misses Salomon' (1888) and water studies; Zorn's etchings and silver collection; Chair. BIRGIT FRIGGEBO; Dir JOHAN CEDERLUND; Sec. KARIN HÖGBERG.

Norrköping

Norrköpings Konstmuseum (Norrköping Art Museum): Kristinaplatsen, SE-602 34 Norrköping; tel. (11) 15-26-00; fax (11) 13-58-97; e-mail konstmuseet@norrkoping.se; internet www.norrkoping.se/kultur-fritid/ museer/konstmuseum; Swedish art from 1600s to present day; int. and nat. graphic colln; print colln consists of works from artists incl. Dürer, Rembrandt and Goya; sculpture park incl. works of Carl Milles, Bror Hjorth and Arne Jones; creative workshops, music, lectures, further training for teachers, corporate events.

Nyköping

Sörmlands museum: POB 314, SE-611 26 Nyköping; tel. (155) 24-57-00; e-mail info .museet@dll.se; internet www .sormlandsmuseum.se; archive of letters, diaries, records, maps, drawings, reports, stories; collns of wedding dresses from the 1700s, home furnishing, textiles; archipelago colln and archaeological colln; organizes courses, lectures, walks, field trips, travelling exhibitions; publishes books; Dir KARIN LINDVALL; Deputy Dir. CARINA WENDEL; Sec. INGER BERG.

Örebro

Örebro Läns Museum: POB 314, SE-701 46 Örebro; tel. (19) 602-87-00; e-mail info@ olm.se; internet www.orebrolansmuseum.se; art colln ranges in time from late 1700s to present; painting; archaeological colln; preserves local history, handicraft, artwork, and cultural heritage sites; organizes lectures, workshops, tours and children's activities; colln of antiques, fine jewellery and clothing, replica of a medieval church interior with altar paintings and shrines; Dir MIKAEL EIVERGÅRD; Admin. Man. LARS NORLING; Asst Dir MARIA UDDÉN.

Rattvik

Folkmusikens hus (Folk Music House): Dalagatan 7, SE-795 31 Rattvik; tel. (48) 79-70-50; fax (48) 129-15; e-mail kontakt@ folkmusikenshus.se; internet www .folkmusikenshus.se; f. 1994; folk music centre; colln of CDs, sheet music and literature; serves as information hub for folk music and dance; organizes exhibitions, concerts, dances, education, archival services; Pres. LARS-ERIK KALLES; Vice-Pres. MATS HULANDER; Man. PER GUDMUNDSON.

Simrishamn

Österlens Museum: Storgatan 24, SE-272 31 Simrishamn; tel. (414) 81-96-70; e-mail osterlens.museum@simrishamn.se; internet www.simrishamn.se/sv/kultur_fritid/osterlens_museum; f. 1917; colln relating to life on Swedish countryside; exhibits native plants, local agriculture, handicraft e.g. lace-making and metal work, fossils and archaeological objects, tools, furniture, clothing and nautical equipment from Eastern Skåne; colln of coins and historical jewellery; Gislövs Forging Museum; Dir LENA ALEBO.

Skara

Västergötlands Museum: POB 253, SE-532 23 Skara; Stadsträdgården, SE- 532 31 Skara; tel. (511) 260-00; fax (511) 260 1999; e-mail kansliet.skaramus@vgregion.se; internet www.vastergotlandsmuseum.se; f. 1863; 3 permanent exhibitions: prehistoric colln of 17 bronze shields buried under water 3,000 years ago, Skara in the Middle Ages, and exposé on 19th-century artist Agnes de Frumerie; exhibits local handicraft and design, traditional games, energy conservation, school projects; Dir GRAZIELLA BELLONI; Curator JOHANNA AUSTRIN.

Skurup

Johanna Museet: POB 85, SE-274 22 Skurup; Sandåkra 6, Skurup; tel. (411) 427-80; fax (411) 425-30; e-mail info@ johannamuseet.se; internet www .johannamuseet.se; f. 1983; objects exhibiting technological devts during the 1900s.

Svaneholms Slottsmuseum (Svaneholm Castle Museum): Svaneholms Slott, SE-274 91 Skurup; tel. and fax (411) 400-12; e-mail svaneholm.museum@telia.com; internet www.svaneholms-slott.se; f. 1935; textile collns of both upper-class and peasant class; colln incl. archaeological finds from the area, works of art, old toys, furniture, photographs and archives; Pres. BRITT-MARIE HANSSON; Vice-Pres. HELGE OLSSON; Treas. LENNART MÖRKING.

Stockholm

Aquaria Vattenmuseum (Aquaria Water Museum): Djurgården, Falkenbergsgatan 2, SE-115 21 Stockholm; tel. (8) 660-90-89; fax (8) 660-70-03; e-mail info@aquaria.se; internet www.aquaria.se; presents physical view of different climates and environments around the world with aquariums and indoor vegetation; centred on 3 themes: the Amazon rain forest, tropical seas, and Nordic waters.

Arkitekturmuseet (Swedish Museum of Architecture): Skeppsholmen, SE-111 49 Stockholm; tel. (8) 58-72-70-00; fax (8) 58-72-70-70; e-mail info@arkitekturmuseet.se; internet www.arkitekturmuseet.se; f. 1962; permanent architecture exhibition, drawings, models and photographs; organizes guided tours, debates, lectures, information, and activities on contemporary issues in architecture, design and planning; acts as platform for architecture, design and sustainable urban devt; library of 25,000 vols; Dir LENA RAHOULT; Asst Dir ULRIKA BEHM.

Biologiska Museet (Biological Museum): POB 27807, SE-115 93 Stockholm; Hazeliusporten, Djurgården, Stockholm; tel. (8) 442-82-15; fax (8) 442-82-98; e-mail bokning@skansen.se; internet www.biologiskamuseet.com; f. 1893; colln of Scandinavian mammals and birds in their natural, ecological habitat; use of dioramas to present natural habitat.

Dansmuseet (Dance Museum): Gustav Adolfs torg 22–24, SE-111 52 Stockholm; tel. (8) 441-76-50; fax (8) 20-06-02; e-mail info@dansmuseet.se; internet www.dansmuseet.se; f. 1933 in Paris as Archives Internationales de la Danse, 1953 in Sweden, present location 1999; performing arts museum; exhibitions of dance, theatre, visual art and photography; material from all over the world, notably Ballets Suédois; videotheque, folk dance dept, Rolf de Maré archive; Dir Dr ERIK NÄSLUND.

Etnografiska Museet (Museum of Ethnography): POB 27140, SE- 102 52 Stockholm; Djurgårdsbrunnsvägen 34, SE-102 52 Stockholm; tel. (8) 519-550-00; fax (8) 519-550-70; e-mail info@etnografiska.se; internet www.etnografiska.se; f. 1880; colln of 150,000 artefacts from Africa, America, Asia, Australia and the Pacific; also houses the Sven Hedin Foundation; library of 45,000 books and journals; Dir ANDERS BJÖRKLUND; Librarian ZSUZSANNA MÜLLER; publs *Ethnos* (4 a year), Monograph Series.

Färgfabriken Contemporary Art Gallery: Lövholmsbrinken 1, SE-117 43 Stockholm; tel. (8) 645-07-07; internet www.fargfabriken.se; f. 1889; ind. foundation; works of art, architecture and community development; Dir RICHARD LESSE.

Fotografiska: Stadsgårdshamnen 22, SE-116 45 Stockholm; tel. (8) 50-90-05-00; e-mail info@fotografiska.eu; internet en.fotografiska.eu; f. 1940; exhibits contemporary photography; organizes seminars and courses; Dir JAN BROMAN; Vice-Pres. CHARLOTTE WIKING; Chief Curator MICHELLE ROY.

Galleri Kontrast: Hornsgatan 8, SE-118 20 Stockholm; tel. (8) 641-49-99; e-mail gkv@gallerikontrast.se; internet www.gallerikontrast.se; f. 1996; documentary photography; exhibits Swedish picture of the year, World Press Photo and work from Nordens Fotoskola; Chair. ROLF ADLERCREUTZ; Curator MIA KLINTEWALL.

Gustav III's Antikmuseum (Gustav III's Museum of Antiquities): Kungliga Slottet, SE-111 30 Stockholm; tel. (8) 402-61-30; fax

(8) 402-61-67; internet www.royalcourt.se/royalpalaces/theroyalpalace/gustaviiismuseumofantiquities; f. 1794; art colln; private sculpture colln of Gustav III; sculptures and artefacts from late 18th century and belonging to Scandinavian region.

Historiska Museet (National Historical Museum): POB 5428, SE-114 84 Stockholm; Narvavägen 13–17, Stockholm; tel. (8) 519-556-00; fax (8) 519-556-40; e-mail info@historiska.se; internet www.historiska.se; comprises Museum of Nat. Antiquities and Royal Cabinet of Coins and Medals; collns comprise archaeological artefacts from Sweden and Swedish ecclesiastical art; Dir.-Gen. LARS AMRÉUS.

Judiska Museet (Jewish Museum): POB 6299, SE-102 34 Stockholm; Hälsingegatan 2, Stockholm; tel. (8) 31-01-43; fax (8) 31-84-04; e-mail info@judiska-museet.se; internet www.judiska-museet.a.se; f. 1987; adaptation of Jews to Swedish society and their contribution to culture, art, literature, trade, industry etc.; culture and religion of Jews, their manners and customs, in the synagogue and in their homes; history of the Swedish Jews; Dir YVONNE JACOBSSON.

Konstnärshuset: Smålandsgatan 7, SE-111 46 Stockholm; tel. (8) 611-10-09; e-mail storagalleriet.konstnarshuset@telia.com; internet www.konstnarshuset.com; f. 1899; exhibits architectural works and contemporary art; Sec. BO L. JOHANSSON.

Kulturhuset: POB 16414, SE-103 27 Stockholm; 7, Sergels torg, SE-103 72 Stockholm; tel. (50) 83-15-08; fax (50) 83-14-09; e-mail info.kulturhuset@stockholm.se; internet www.kulturhuset.stockholm.se; f. 1974; organizes photographic exhibitions, stories for children, concerts, literary discussions, films, debates, theatre; 2 libraries; Dir ERIC SJÖSTRÖM; Curator ESTELLE AF MALMBORG; Curator MARIA PATOMELLA; Curator PIA KRISTOFFERSSON.

Kungl. Myntkabinettet—Sveriges Ekonomiska Museum (Royal Coin Cabinet—National Museum of Economy): Slottsbacken 6, POB 5428, SE-114 84 Stockholm; tel. (8) 519-553-04; e-mail info@myntkabinettet.se; internet www.myntkabinettet.se; f. 1630; coin colln representing all ages; exhibition displays coins, banknotes, tokens, stock certificates, bank materials, wallets, piggy banks and related to economic history; exhibits medal's history and devt; Dir IAN WISÉHN.

Lars Bohman Gallery: Karlavägen 16, SE-114 31 Stockholm; tel. (8) 20-78-07; fax (8) 21-23-66; e-mail info@larsbohmangallery.com; internet www.larsbohmangallery.com; f. 1982; exhibits works of int. contemporary artists that incl. painting, drawing, sculpture, video and photography; Owner JAN HANSEN; Mans. MALIN LEVÉN, PELLE HÖGLUND.

Liljevalchs Konsthall: Djurgårdsvägen 60, SE-115 21 Stockholm; tel. (8) 50-83-13-30; e-mail info.liljevalchs@stockholm.se; internet www.liljevalchs.se; f. 1916; ind. and public art gallery for contemporary art; Head MARTEN CASTENFORS.

Livrustkammaren (Royal Armoury): Royal Palace, Slottsbacken 3, SE-111 30 Stockholm; tel. (8) 402-30-10; fax (8) 20-73-05; e-mail livrustkammaren@lsh.se; internet www.livrustkammaren.se; f. 1628; houses items once in the possession of Swedish monarchs and their families; most artefacts in the colln reflect official occasions such as state ceremonies, weddings, coronations and funerals; historical collns dating from mid-16th century; Swedish royal arms, costumes, jewels, coaches, etc.; library of 43,000 vols; Dir MAGNUS HAGBERG; Curator ELISABETH

WESTIN BERG; Curator LENA RANGSTRÖM; Curator ANN GRÖNHAMMAR; publ. *Livrustkammaren* (Journal of Royal Armour, 1 a year).

Component Sites:

Hallwylska Museet: Hamngatan 4, SE-111 47 Stockholm; tel. (8) 402-30-99; e-mail hallwyl@lsh.se; internet www.hallwylskamuseet.se; f. c. 1900; private residence of Hallwyl family; colln of furniture, paintings, applied art, etc.; Dir HELI HAAPASALO; publ. *Hallwyliana*.

Skoklosters Slott: SE-746 95 Skokloster; tel. (8) 402-30-77; fax (18) 38-64-46; e-mail skokloster@lsh.se; internet sko.lsh.se; baroque castle built in 1654 by Count C. G. Wrangel; contains mainly 17th-century furniture, paintings, applied art and armour; library; library of 20,000 vols; Dir ANN KRISTIN CARLSTRÖM; Curator ELISABETH WESTIN BERG; publ. *Skokloster Studies*.

Magasin 3 Konsthall: Frihamnen, SE-115 56 Stockholm; tel. (8) 54-56-80-40; fax (8) 54-56-80-41; e-mail art@magasin3.com; internet www.magasin3.com; f. 1987; colln of contemporary art; 3-dimensional works, drawings, photographic works and video cassettes; 'Dawning' by James Turrell; Dir DAVID NEUMAN; Chief Curator RICHARD JULIN.

Medelhavsmuseet (Museum of Mediterranean and Near Eastern Antiquities): POB 16008, SE-103 21 Stockholm; Fredsgatan 2, Stockholm; tel. (8) 519-550-50; fax (8) 519-553-70; e-mail info@medelhavsmuseet.se; internet www.medelhavsmuseet.se; f. 1954 by merger of Egyptian Museum and Cyprus colln, present location 1982; archaeological collns of ancient and historical relics from Mediterranean countries; Dir SANNE HOUBY-NIELSEN; Deputy Dir SUZANNE UNGE-SÖRLING; Sec. CLAUDIE WIRÉN.

Moderna Museet (Museum of Modern Art): POB 16382, SE-103 27 Stockholm; Skeppsholmen, Stockholm; tel. (8) 519-552-00; fax (8) 519-552-10; e-mail info@modernamuseet.se; internet www.modernamuseet.se; f. 1958; contemporary paintings and sculptures by Swedish and foreign artists, also photographs and drawings; colln from 1900 to present day; br at Malmö; Dir DANIEL BIRNBAUM; Co-Dir ANN-SOFI NORING.

Museum Tre Kronor: Kungliga Slottet, SE-111 30 Stockholm; tel. (8) 402-61-00; fax (8) 402-61-67; internet www.royalcourt.se/kungligaslotten/kungligaslottet/museumtrekronor; f. 1999; colln of objects rescued from fire of 1697 and newly created models; depicts the Tre Kronor Palace's devt from defence fort to the Renaissance palace of today.

Musik–och Teatermuseet (Stockholm Music and Theatre Museum): POB 16326, SE-103 26 Stockholm; Sibyllegatan 2, Stockholm; tel. (8) 519-554-90; fax (8) 663-91-81; e-mail info-mtm@musikverk.se; internet www.musikochteatermuseet.se; f. 1899 as Musikhistoriska Museet, present location 1979; attached to Music Devt and Heritage Sweden; more than 11,500 art and folk music instruments; theatre collns and marionettes, exhibitions, archives and library; Dir HANS RIBEN.

Nationalmuseum: POB 16176, SE-103 24 Stockholm; Södra Blasieholmshamnen, Stockholm; tel. (8) 519-543-00; fax (8) 519-544-50; e-mail info@nationalmuseum.se; internet www.nationalmuseum.se; f. 1792; 16,000 paintings, sculptures and other objects, 500,000 drawings and prints, 30,000 items of applied art; also administers collns of several royal castles with 23,000 works of art; library: see Libraries and

Archives; Dir Prof. SOLFRID SÖDERLIND; publs *Art Bulletin of Nationalmuseum Stockholm* (1 a year), *Nationalmuseums skriftserie. N. S.*

Naturhistoriska Riksmuseet (Swedish Museum of Natural History): POB 50007, SE-104 05 Stockholm; Frescativägen 40, SE-114 18 Stockholm; tel. (8) 519-540-40; fax (8) 519-540-85; e-mail info@nrm.se; internet www.nrm.se; f. 1739; attached to Min. of Culture; collns and research units: vertebrates, entomology, invertebrates, palaeozoology, phanerogamic botany, cryptogamic botany, palaeobotany, mineralogy, isotope geology, DNA laboratory, contaminants; Dir JAN OLOV WESTERBERG; Dir for Admin. LENNART SANDBERG; Dir for Communication CHRISTINA KÅREMO SKÖLDKVIST; Dir for Public Engagement EWA BERGDAHL; Dir for Science PER ERICSON.

Nobelmuseet (Nobel Museum): POB 2245, SE-103 16 Stockholm; Börshuset, Stortorget, Gamla Stan, Stockholm; tel. (8) 53-48-18-00; fax (8) 23-25-07; e-mail bokning@nobel.se; internet www.nobelmuseet.se; honours Nobel Prize winners by highlighting their achievements and displaying some of their work; organizes lectures, group discussions, games, and interactive exhibitions; permanent colln: children's room educating about the Nobel Prizes in physics, chemistry, medicine, literature, peace, and economics; library of 5,000 vols; Dir OLOV AMELIN; Curator ARON AMBROSIANI.

Nordiska museet (Nordic Museum): POB 27820, SE-115 93 Stockholm; Djurgårdsvägen 6–16, Stockholm; tel. (8) 519-546-00; fax (8) 519-545-80; e-mail nordiska@nordiskamuseet.se; internet www.nordiskamuseet.se; f. 1873, present name and status 1907; nat. museum of cultural history since 16th century ethnological and industrial art collns; 10m. archive and photographic items; library of 250,000 vols; Pres. LARS O. GRÖNSTEDT; Dir CHRISTINA MATTSSON.

Observatoriemuseet (Observatory museum): Drottninggatan 120, SE-113 60 Stockholm; tel. (8) 545-483-90; fax (8) 545-483-95; e-mail observatoriet@kva.se; internet www.observatoriet.kva.se; f. 1991; organizes seminars, visits and excursions; exhibition on building's history; exhibits photographic work; Superintendent INGA EMQVIST SÖDERLUND.

Östasiatiska Museet (Museum of Far Eastern Antiquities): POB 16381, SE-103 27 Stockholm; Tyghusplan, Skeppsholmen, Stockholm; tel. (8) 519-557-50; fax (8) 519-557-55; e-mail info@ostasiatiska.se; internet www.ostasiatiska.se; f. 1926, present status 1999; Chinese paintings, sculptures and ceramics; Chinese pottery and bronze objects; Japanese, Korean, Southeast Asian and Indian collns; Far Eastern Library; Dir ANDERS BJÖRKLUND (acting); Deputy Dir and Curator EVA MYRDAL; Sec. KERSTIN BERGSTRÖM; publ. *Bulletin* (1 a year).

Postmuseum: POB 2002, SE-103 11 Stockholm; Lilla Nygatan 6T, Gamla Stan, Stockholm; tel. (8) 781-17-55; fax (8) 20-90-21; e-mail postmuseum@posten.se; internet www.postmuseum.posten.se; f. 1906; exhibits items connected with the Swedish Post Office and its history; colln of stamps, letter boxes and signs, postal art, furniture, cars, bicycles, stamp cancelling machines, uniforms, postal horns, emblems, mailmen's bags; collns of pictures and documents; philatelic collns; library of 60,000 vols, 180 journals; Dir OLLE SYNNERHOLM.

Prins Eugens Waldemarsudde: POB 16176, SE-103 24 Stockholm; Prins Eugens väg 6, Djurgården, Stockholm; tel. (8) 54-58-

37-00; fax (8) 667-74-59; e-mail bokningen@waldemarsudde.se; internet www.waldemarsudde.se; f. 1995; colln of artwork by Carl Larsson, Anders Zorn, and Karl Nordström, Prince Eugen; sculptures by Carl Eldh, Per Hasselberg, Auguste Rodin, Carl Milles; exhibits sculpture, hand drawing, graphics and art medals; Admin. Man. HELEN WALDENSTRÖM; Chief Sec. CATRIN LUNDEBERG; Curator GÖRAN SÖDERLUND.

Skansen: POB 27807, SE-115 93 Stockholm; Djurgårdsslätten 49–51, SE-115 93 Stockholm; tel. (8) 442-80-00; fax (8) 442-82-82; e-mail info@skansen.se; internet www.skansen.se; f. 1891, present status 1963; open-air museum and zoological garden; Dir JOHN BRATTMYHR; Keeper of Bldgs CORTINA LANGE; Keeper of Zoo TOMAS FRISK.

Statens försvarshistoriska museer (National Swedish Museums of Military History): POB 14095, SE-104 41 Stockholm; Riddargatan 13, Stockholm; tel. (8) 519-563-10; e-mail info@sfhm.se; internet www.sfhm.se; f. 1976, merger of Army Museum in Stockholm, Navy Museum in Karlskrona, Air Force Museum in Linköping and Board of Military Traditions; attached to Min. of Culture; promotes knowledge about Swedish armed forces through the ages and their role in devt of society; responsible for a network of approximately 20 museums relating to particular units and for certain defence facilities of a cultural historical value that previously had been under the auspices of the Swedish armed forces; supports other activities related to the cultural heritage of the armed forces at approximately 30 locations throughout Sweden; Dir-Gen. STAFFAN BENGTSSON; Deputy Dir-Gen. JOHAN ENGSTRÖM.

Statens maritima museer (National Maritime Museums): POB 27131, SE-102 52 Stockholm; Linnégatan 64, SE-114 54 Stockholm; tel. (8) 519-549-00; fax (8) 519-548-94; e-mail registrator@maritima.se; internet www.maritima.se; responsible for museums in Swedish state care that have maritime profile; Dir ROBERT OLSEN.

Component Museums:

Marinmuseum (Naval Museum): POB 48, SE-371 32 Karlskrona; Stumholmen, Karlskrona; tel. (455) 35-93-00; fax (455) 35-93-49; e-mail registrator@maritima.se; internet www.marinmuseum.se; f. 1752; 55,000 exhibits since 17th century; library of 22,000 vols, 4,000 maps and blueprints, 200,000 negatives and photographs; Dir RICKARD BAUER; publ. *Aktuellt-Marinmuseum* (yearbook).

Sjöhistoriska museet (Maritime Museum): POB 27131, SE-102 52 Stockholm; Djurgårdsbrunnsvägen 24, SE-115 27; tel. (8) 519-549-00; fax (8) 519-549-49; e-mail sjohistoriska@maritima.se; internet www.sjohistoriska.se; f. 1938; collns give a view of Swedish naval and merchant history, vessels of the past and of today as well as the history of Swedish shipbuilding; archive of drawings and photographs; colln comprises 100,000 objects, incl. over 1,500 models of ships and boats; library of 60,000 vols; Dir HANS-LENNART OHLSSON; publ. *Sjöhistorisk årsbok* (every 2 years).

Vasamuseet (Vasa Museum): POB 27131, SE-102 52 Stockholm; Galärvarvsvägen 14, Stockholm; tel. (8) 519-548-00; fax (8) 519-548-88; e-mail vasamuseet@maritima.se; internet www.vasamuseet.se; f. 1987; the Swedish warship *Vasa*, lost in 1628 and raised in 1961, and associated exhibits; also steam icebreaker *Sankt Erik* and lightship *Finngrundet*; Dir MARIKA HEDIN.

Stiftelsen Musikkulturens Främjande (Nydahl Collection): Riddargatan 35–37, SE-114 57 Stockholm; tel. and fax (8) 661-71-71; e-mail smf@nydahlcoll.se; internet www.nydahlcoll.se; f. 1920; colln of old music instruments; arranges concerts and lectures; music manuscript colln incl. works of composers Beethoven, Chopin, Donizetti, Mozart, Rossini, Schubert and Schumann, and Swedish and Scandinavian composers; colln of iconographic material, drawings, paintings and photos; a library of scores; colln of music literature belonging to Prof. Ingmar Bengtsson; Curator EDWARD KLINGSPOR; Curator GÖRAN GRAHN; Curator ROBERT HOLMIN.

Stockholms läns museum (Stockholm County Museum): Sickla Industriväg 5B, SE-131 54 Nacka; tel. (8) 586-194-00; e-mail museet@stockholmslansmuseum.se; internet www.stockholmslansmuseum.se; f. 1982; prehistoric finds; architectural and cultural history; library of 10,000 vols; Dir PETER BRATT.

Stockholms Stadsmuseum (Stockholm City Museum): POB 15025, SE-104 65 Stockholm; Ryssgården, Slussen; tel. (8) 508-316-00; fax (8) 508-316-99; e-mail info@stadsmuseum.stockholm.se; internet www.stadsmuseum.stockholm.se; f. 1937; history and devt of Stockholm; archaeology and cultural heritage; colln of photographs, maps, art and artefacts; incl. a library and archives; preserves 300,000 items of historical interest; 20,000 works of art, 3,000 oil paintings, 3m. photographs; library of 40,000 vols; Dir ANN-CHARLOTTE BACKLUND; publs *Blick* (articles covering the activity of the admin.), *Sankt Eriks årsbok* (yearbook).

Affiliated Museum:

Stockholms Medeltidsmuseum (Museum of Medieval Stockholm): SE-100 12 Stockholm; Strömparterren, Norrbro, Stockholm; tel. (8) 508-317-90; fax (8) 508-317-99; e-mail info.medeltidsmuseet@stockholm.se; internet www.medeltidsmuseet.stockholm.se; f. 1986; archaeological remains of Stockholm, reflecting its foundation and history from c. 1250–1550; Dir SOLBRITT BENNETH; Curator LIN ANNERBÄCK.

Strindbergsmuseet (Strindberg Museum): Drottninggatan 85, SE-111 60 Stockholm; tel. (8) 411-53-54; fax (8) 411-01-41; e-mail fornamn@strindbergsmuseet.se; internet www.strindbergsmuseet.se; colln of objects related to Strindberg; collns divided into 7 categories: cultural history, art, theatre, photographs, press clippings, library, audiovisual media; photographic archive with 2,500 photographs; library of 5,000 vols; Dir STEFAN BOHMAN; Curators ERIK HÖÖK, CAMILLA LARSSON.

Tekniska Museet (National Museum of Science and Technology): POB 27842, SE-115 93 Stockholm; Museivägen 7, SE-115 93 Stockholm; tel. (8) 450-56-00; fax (8) 450-56-01; e-mail info@tekniskamuseet.se; internet www.tekniskamuseet.se; f. 1924; history of science and technology; devt of Swedish industry and engineering; mining, iron and steel, steam power and machines, cars and aircraft, history of electricity, chemistry, computers, Polhem's colln of engineering models, mechanical workshop and model railway; Teknorama science centre; Cino4 special effects 3D films, archives of drawings and photographs; library of 50,000 vols; Dir ANN FOLLIN; publ. *Daedalus* (1 a year).

Thielska Gallery: Sjötullsbacken 8, SE-115 25 Stockholm; tel. (8) 662-58-84; fax (8) 544-85-112; e-mail info@thielska-galleriet.se; internet www.thielska-galleriet.se; f. 1926; colln of Nordic Heirloom Art; works of artists Edvard Munch, Carl Larsson, Bruno Liljefors and Eugène Jansson; Curator NINA ÖHMAN.

Vin & Sprithistoriska Museet (Historical Museum of Wines & Spirits): Dalagatan 100, SE-113 43 Stockholm; tel. (8) 51-91-86-50; fax (8) 31-39-28; e-mail ingrid.leffler@ vinosprithistoriska.se; internet www .vinosprithistoriska.se; f. 1967, present status 1992; collns of objects, images, tags from period between late 1800s and present day; alcohol historical archives; colln of wine and liquor bottles; library of 4,500 vols, 150 journal titles; Dir INGRID LEFFLER; Curator EVA LENNEMAN.

Svalöv

Galleri Tapper-Popermajer (Tapper-Popermajer Art Gallery): Bantorget 2, SE-260 20 Teckomatorp; e-mail info@ tapper-popermajer.com; internet www .tapper-popermajer.com; f. 2007; exhibits nat. and int. artists' work; organizes lecturers and musical events; Owner ILONA POPER-MAJER.

Svedala

Statarmuseet i Skåne: Torupsvägen 606-59, SE-230 40 Bara; tel. (40) 44-70-90; fax (40) 41-49-67; e-mail brevladan@ statarmuseet.com; internet www .statarmuseet.com; f. 1995; organizes training courses, seminars, theme days and events with the starting point of the seasons; has archive; exhibits kitchen commons, sleeping accommodation, and tiny garden plot of bonded labours of the time; Dir BARBRO FRANCKIE.

Tjörn

Nordiska Akvarellmuseet (Nordic Watercolour Museum): Södra hamnen 6, SE-471 32 Skärhamn; tel. (304) 60-00-80; e-mail info@ akvarellmuseet.org; internet www .akvarellmuseet.org; f. 1989; Nordic centre for contemporary art, research and training; exhibits works of contemporary int. watercolourists; organizes lectures, theatrical performance, dance, music and discussions; Dir BERA NORDAL.

Umeå

Bildmuseet (Image Museum): c/o Umeå Univ., SE-901 87 Umeå; tel. (90) 786-52-27; fax (90) 786-77-33; e-mail info@bildmuseet .umu.se; internet www.bildmuseet.umu.se; f. 1981; exhibits int. contemporary art and visual culture: photography, design, architecture; combines contemporary perspective with historical flashbacks; Dir KATARINA PIERRE (acting).

Pengsjö nybyggarmuseum (Pengsjö settler's museum): c/o Sven-Eric Nyman, Rönn-bärsstigen 17, SE-903 46 Umeå; tel. (90) 13-05-33; e-mail sven-eric.nyman@ pengsjomuseum.se; internet www .pengsjomuseum.se; exhibits buildings from 17th, 18th and 19th centuries; colln from peasant and Sami culture; Head SVEN-ERIC NYMAN.

Västerbottens museum: POB 3183, SE-903 40 Umeå; tel. (90) 17-18-00; fax (90) 77-90-00; e-mail info@vbm.se; internet www .vbm.se; f. 1886; collns of Sami culture with its gear and clothing; has photo archive; Chair. EVERTH GUSTAVSSON; Dir ULRICA GRUBBSTRÖM; publ. *Västerbotten* (4 a year).

Attached Museums:

Svenska Skidmuseet (Swedish Ski Museum): f. 1928; colln of hand-made ski, snowshoes for both man and horse, prehistoric skis, ski equipment, world's oldest surviving pods, Kalvträsk scabbard.

Fiske- och sjöfartsmuseet (Fishing and Maritime Museum): f. 1975; colln of pictures, models and objects related to boats, ships and sea industries.

Uppsala

Evolutionsmuseet (Museum of Evolution): Norbyvägen 16, SE-752 36 Uppsala; tel. (18) 471-27-39; fax (18) 471-27-94; e-mail info@em .uu.se; internet www.evolutionsmuseet.uu .se; f. 1999; 5m. fossils of animals, plants, fungi, lichens, minerals, dinosaurs; Dir MATS ERIKSSON.

Museum Gustavianum: Akademigatan 3, SE-753 10 Uppsala; tel. (18) 471-75-71; fax (18) 471-75-72; e-mail museum@ gustavianum.uu.se; internet www .gustavianum.uu.se; f. 1997; exhibits Anatomical Theatre, the Augsburg Art Cabinet and objects from Valsgärde; the Antique colln; the Egyptian colln; the Nordic archaeology colln; the physical cabinet; art collns; coin cabinet; Head Curator MARGARETA NIS-SER-DALMAN; Curator ANNA SJÖGREN (acting); Asst Curator JOHAN LUNDBERG.

Upplandsmuseet (Upplands Museum): St Eriksgränd 6, SE-753 10 Uppsala; tel. (18) 16-91-00; fax (18) 69-25-09; e-mail info@ upplandsmuseet.se; internet www .upplandsmuseet.se; f. 1959; provincial cultural history; collns of 750,000 objects and nearly 1.5m. glass negatives, film negatives and prints, extensive archive of topographic data, measurements, records and maps; Chair. ULF SCHMIDT; Vice-Chair. GUNILLA OLTNER; Dir BENT SYSE; Dir HÅKAN LIBY; publ. *Uppland.*

Varberg

Länsmuseet Varberg: Varbergs Fästning, SE-432 44 Varberg; tel. (340) 828-30; e-mail kansli@lansmuseet.varberg.se; internet www.lansmuseet.varberg.se; 50,000 historical items; 20,000 archaeological finds; 200,000 photographs; library of 20,000 vols; Dir AGNES BOQVIST.

Växjö

Kulturparken Småland AB: POB 102, SE-351 04 Växjö; Södra Järnvägsgatan 2, SE-351 04 Växjö; tel. (470) 70-42-00; fax (470) 397-44; e-mail info@kulturparkensmaland .se; internet www.kulturparkensmaland.se; Swedish glass colln; collns incl. objects of cultural historical significance, visual art, textiles, church furnishings, archaeological finds and agricultural history; permanent exhibits on 2 themes: Småland's rural industrial landscape and 5 centuries of Swedish glass; castle ruins of Kronoberg; Kronoberg agricultural museum; numismatic colln; incl. Smålands Museum, The Swedish Glass Museum, The House of Emigrants; Dir ERICA MÅNSSON.

Viken

Beredskapsmuseet: Djuramossavägen 160, SE-260 40 Viken; tel. (42) 22-40-39; fax (42) 22-40-89; e-mail info@beredskapsmuseet .com; internet www.beredskapsmuseet.com; f. 1997; located in a Second World War underground military facility; exhibits Sweden's defences during the Second World War through equipment, photography etc.; Dir JOHAN ANDRÉE.

Universities

GÖTEBORGS UNIVERSITET (Gothenburg University)

POB 100, SE-405 30 Gothenburg
Telephone: (31) 786-00-00
Fax: (31) 786-44-73
E-mail: registrator@gu.se

Internet: www.gu.se
Founded 1891, became state univ. 1954
Academic year: September to June
Vice-Chancellor: PAM FREDMAN
Pro-Vice-Chancellor: LENNART WEIBULL
Pro-Vice-Chancellor: MARGARETA WALLIN PETERSON
Head of Admin.: PER-OLOF REHNQUIST
Librarian: AGNETA OLSSON
Library: see Libraries and Archives
Number of teachers: 2,500
Number of students: 37,000
Publication: *Acta Universitatis Gothoburgensis*

DEANS

Faculty of Arts: Prof. MARGARETA HALLBEERG
Faculty of Education: Prof. MIKAEL ALEXAN-DERSSON
Faculty of Fine, Applied and Performing Arts: Prof. ANNA LINDAL
Faculty of Science: Prof. DAVID TURNER
Faculty of Social Sciences: Prof. HELENA LINDHOLM-SCHULZ
IT Faculty: Prof. JAN SMITH
Sahlgrenska Academy: Prof. OLLE LARKÖ
School of Business, Economics and Law: Prof. ROLF WOLFF
Teacher Training: Prof. ELISABETH HESSLE-FORS-ARKTOFT

PROFESSORS

Faculty of Arts (POB 200, SE-405 30 Gothenburg; tel. (31) 786-00-00; fax (31) 786-11-44; internet www.hum.gu.se):

AGRELL, B., Comparative Literature
AHLBERGER, C., History
AHLSÉN, E., Neurolinguistics
AIJMER, K., English
ALLWOOD, J., General Linguistics
ANDERSSON, L.-G., Modern Swedish
ANDERSSON, S.-G., German
BÄRMARK, J., Theory of Science
BENSON, K., Spanish
BERGH, G., English
BJÖRNBERG, A., Musicology
BORIN, L., Natural Language Processing
BOYD, S., General Linguistics
BYRSKOG, S., New Testament Exegesis
COOPER, R., Computational Linguistics
DAHL, E.-L., History of Science and Ideas
EDSTRÖM, K.-O., Musicology
ENGDAHL, E., Swedish
EKLUND, B.-L., Modern Greek
ERIKSSON, A., Phonetics
FLORBY, G., English Literature
FORSER, T., Comparative Literature
HAGLUND, D., Religious Studies
HALLBERG, M., Theory of Science
HANSSON, S., Comparative Literature
HELDNER, C., French
HOLMQUIST, I., Women Studies
JOHANNESSON, L., History of Art
KRISTIANSEN, K., Archaeology
LAGER, T., Computational Linguistics
LARSSON, L., Comparative Literature
LEGÈRE, K., African Languages
LIEDMAN, S.-E., History of Science and Ideas
LILJA, E., Comparative Literature
LILLIESTAM, L., Musicology
LINDBERG, B., History of Science and Ideas
LINDBERG, I., Swedish as a Second Language
LINDKVIST, T., Medieval History
LJUNGGREN, M., Russian Literature
MALM, M., Comparative Literature
MALMGREN, H., Theoretical Philosophy
MALMGREN, S.-G., Swedish
MALMSTEDT, G., History
MUNTHE, C., Practical Philosophy
NÄSSTRÖM, B.-M., History of Religion
NILSSON, B., History of Christianity
NILSSON, I., History of Science and Ideas

NORDBLADH, J., Archaeology
OHLANDER, S., English
OLAUSSON, L., Conditions in Science and Humanities
OLOFSSON, A., English
OLOFSSON, S., Old Testament Exegesis
PANKOW, C., German
PERSSON, I., Practical Philosophy
PERSSON, L., History
PLATEN, E., German Literature
RALPH, B., Northern Languages
RETSÖ, J., Arabic
SANDBERG, B., German
SJÖGREN, O., Film Studies
SKARIN-FRYKMAN, B., Ethnology
STÅLHAMMAR, M., English Terminology
STRANDBERG-OLOFSSON, M., Classical Archaeology and Ancient History
THUNMAN, N., Japanese
WESTERSTÅHL, D., Theoretical Philosophy
WINBERG, C., History
WISTRAND, M., Latin

Faculty of Education (POB 300, SE-405 30 Gothenburg; tel. (31) 786-00-00; fax (31) 786-22-42; e-mail kansli.ufn@ped.gu.se; internet www.ped.gu.se):

AHLBERG, A., Special Education and Educational Research
ALEXANDERSSON, M., Education and Educational Research—Didactics
ANDERSSON, B., Education and Educational Research—Didactics
BENGTSSON, J., Philosophy of Education
GUNNARSSON, L., Education and Educational Research
GUSTAFSSON, J.-E., Education and Educational Research
HOLMER, J., Work Science
LANDER, R., Education and Educational Research
LASSBO, G., Education and Educational Research
LINDBLAD, S., Education and Educational Research
LINDSTRÖM, B., Education and Educational Research
MARTON, F., Education and Educational Research
MUNCK, J., Education and Educational Research
NILSSON, L., Education and Educational Research
OHLANDER, S., English
OSCARSON, M., Education and Educational Research
OTT, A., Science Education
PATRIKSSON, G., Education and Educational Research
PRAMLING-SAMUELSSON, I., Education and Educational Research
SÄLJÖ, R., Education and Educational Science
SHANAHAN, H., Home Economics
SIMONSON, B., History
THÅNG, P.-O., Education and Educational Research
WENESTAM, C.-G., Education and Educational Research
WERNERSSON, I., Education and Educational Research

Faculty of Fine, Applied and Performing Arts (POB 141, SE-405 30 Gothenburg; tel. (31) 786-00-00; fax (31) 786-13-18; e-mail anna.lindal@konst.gu.se; internet www.konst.gu.se):

DAVIDSSON, H., Organ
DU RÉES, G., Film Directing
EKLUND, B., Trumpet
ELDENIUS, M., Music Theory
FOLKESTAD, G., Research in Music Education
GÅRDFELDT, G., Communication and Performance Skills, Drama
HYBBINETTE, P., Fine Arts in Design
JORMIN, A., Contrabass and Improvisation

LÜTZOW-HOLM, O., Composition
NÄSSEN, E., Voice
NIELSEN, E., Percussion and Contemporary Music
OLSSON, B., Research in Music Education
THORSÉN, S.-M., Music and Society
WASKO, R., Fine Arts
WIKLUND, A., Music Drama

Faculty of Science (POB 460, SE-405 30 Gothenburg; tel. (31) 786-00-00; fax (31) 773-48-39; e-mail info@science.gu.se; internet www.science.gu.se):

ÅBERG, P., Marine Ecology
ABRAMOWICZ, M., Astrophysics
ADLER, L., Marine Microbiology
AHLBERG, E., Inorganic Chemistry
AHLBERG, P., Organic Chemistry
ANDERSSON, L., Hydrosphere Science
ANDERSSON, M., Zooecology
ANDERSSON, S., Animal Ecology
ANDERSSON, S., Physics
ANDREASSON, L.-E., Molecular Biophysics
ARKERYD, L., Applied Mathematics
AXELSSON, M., Comparative Integrative Zoology
BADEN, S. P., Marine Ecology
BILLETER, M., Molecular Biophysics
BJÖRK, G., Polar Oceanography
BJÖRNSSON, B. T., Zoophysiology
BJURSELL, G., Molecular Biology
BLANCK, H., Plant Physiology
BLOMBERG, A., Functional Genomics
BOHLIN, T., Animal Ecology
BRZEZINSKI, J., Mathematics
CAMPBELL, E., Atomic and Molecular Physics
CARLSSON, P., Genetics
CEDERWALL, M., Theoretical Physics
CHEN, D., Physical Meteorology
CLARKE, A., Plant Molecular Biology
CORNELL, D., Geochemistry
DAVE, G., Environmental Protection
ELWING, H., Surface Biophysics
ERSÉUS, C., Evolutionary Morphology and Systematics
FÖRLIN, L., Zoophysiology
FRANZÉN, L., Physical Geography
GÖTMARK, F., Zooecology
HÅKANSSON, M., Organometallic Chemistry
HALL, P., Marine Sediment Diagenesis
HALLENBERG, N., Systematic Biology
HANSTORP, D., Experimental Physics
HELLSING, B., Physics
HERMANSSON, M., Marine Microbiology
HOHMANN, S., Molecular Microbial Physiology
HOLMGREN, S., Zoophysiology
HOLMLID, L., Physical Chemistry, especially Energy-related Basic Research
JAGNER, D., Analytical Chemistry
JOHANNESSON, H., Theoretical Physics
JOHANNESSON, K., Biology, Marine Ecology
JONSON, M., Condensed Matter Physics
JONSSON, P., Marine Ecology
KARLBERG, A.-T., Dermatochemistry and Skin Allergy
KJELLANDER, R., Physical Chemistry
KOMITOV, L., Physics
LARSON, S. A., Geology
LARSSON, Å., Environmental Protection
LEVAN, G., Genetics
LINDHE, U., Zoology (Structural and Animal)
LINDQVIST, O., Inorganic Chemistry
LINDQVIST, S., Physical Geography
LINDVALL, T., Mathematical Statistics
LJUNGSTRÖM, E., Atmospheric Science
LUTHMAN, K., Medicinal Chemistry
MALMGREN, B., Marine Geology
MEHLIG, B., Physics
MOLAU, U., Plant Ecology
NILSSON, S., Zoophysiology
NORDBERG, K., Palaeoceanography
NORDHOLM, S., Physical Chemistry
NYMAN, G., Physical Chemistry

NYSTRÖM, T., Scientific Microbiology
OLSSON, O., Developmental Biology of Plants
OMSTEDT, A., Geosphere Dynamics
ÖSTLAND, S., Solid State Physics
PEDERSEN, K., Biology, Microbiology
PENDRILL, A.-M., Physics
PETTERSSON, J., Environmental Atmospheric Sciences
PIHL, L., Marine Fish Ecology
PLEIJEL, H., Environmental Protection
RODHE, J., Oceanography
ROSEN, A., Molecular Physics
ROSENBERG, R., Marine Ecology
RYDBERG, L., Oceanography
RYDSTRÖM, J., Biochemistry
SANDELIUS, A.-S., Plant Physiology
SELLDÉN, G., Tree Physiology, Influence of Air Pollution
SHCHERBINA, N., Mathematics
SHEKTER, R., Theoretical Physics
SILVERIN, B., Zoology (Structural and Animal)
SJÖGREN, P., Mathematics
SJÖLIN, L., Inorganic Chemistry
STENSON, J., Biology, Aquatic Ecology
STEVENS, R., Environmental and Quaternary Geology
STIGEBRANDT, A., Oceanography
STIGH, J., Bedrock Geology
STOLIN, A., Mathematics
SUNDBÄCK, K., Biology, Marine Botany
SUNDBERG, P., Zoomorphology
SUNDELL, K., Animal Zoophysiology
SUNDQVIST, CH., Plant Physiology
SUNNERHAGEN, P., Eucaryotic Molecular Biology
SVANSTEDT, N., Mathematics
TISELIUS, P., Marine Ecology
TURNER, D. R., Marine Chemistry
WALLENTINUS, I., Marine Botany
WALLIN PETERSSON, M., Zoophysiology
WEDBORG, M., Marine Analytical Chemistry
WERMUTH, N. E., Biostatistics
WETTERBERG, O., Conservation, specializing in integrated conservation of the built environment
WILLANDER, M., Experimental Physics
ZHUKOV, M., Theoretical Physics

Faculty of Social Sciences (POB 720, SE-405 30 Gothenburg; tel. (31) 786-10-00; fax (31) 786-19-40; e-mail lars-olof.karlsson@gu.se; internet www.samfak.gu.se):

ARCHER, T., Psychology
ÅRHEM, K., Social Anthropology
ASP, K., Journalism
BJERELD, U., Political Science
BJÖRNBERG, U., Sociology
BOHOLM, A., Social Anthropology
BROBERG, A., Psychology
BRORSTRÖM, B., Management Economics
BÄCK, H., Public Administration
BÄCK-WIKLUND, M., Social Work
DEMKER, M., Political Science
ESAIASSON, P., Political Science
FURÅKER, B., Sociology
GÄRLING, T., Psychology
GILLJAM, M., Political Science
GLIMELL, H., Science and Technology Studies
GUSTAFSSON, B., Social Work
HANSEN, S., Psychology
HETTNE, B., Peace and Conflict Research
HJELMQUIST, E., Behavioural Studies of Disabilities and Handicap
HÖGLUND, L., Library and Information Science
HOLMBERG, S., Political Science
HWANG, P., Psychology
JOHANSSON, B., Psychology
JONSSON, D., Sociology
LINDAHL, R., Political Science
LUNDQVIST, L. J., Political Science
OLSSON, S., Social Work

PETERSON, A., Sociology
PIERRE, J., Political Science
ROMBACH, B., Management Economics
ROTHSTEIN, B., Political Science
SVENSSON, L. G., Sociology
WEIBULL, L., Mass Communication

IT-Faculty (Forskningsgången 6, SE-412 96 Gothenburg; tel. (31) 786-00-00; fax (31) 772-48-99; e-mail jan.smith@chalmers.se; internet www.itufak.gu.se):

BRENNER, P., Mathematics
COQUAND, T., Computer Science
DAHLBOM, B., Informatics

Sahlgrenska Academy (POB 400, SE-405 30 Gothenburg; fax (31) 786-33-99; e-mail registrator@sahlgrenska.gu.se; internet www.sahlgrenska.gu.se):

AHLMAN, H., Endocrine Surgery
ALBERTSSON-WIKLAND, K., Paediatric Growth Research
ALBREKTSSON, T., Handicap Research
ALLEBECK, P., Social and Preventive Medicine
ÅMAN, P., Tumour Biology
ANDERSSON, O., Medicine
ASHTON, M., Biopharmacy
AXELSSON, G., Hygiene
AXELSSON, R., Psychiatry
BAGGE, U., Anatomy
BARREGÅRD, L., Clinical Environmental Medicine
BENGTSSON, B.-Å, Clinical Endocrinology
BERGBOM, I., Nursing
BERGFELDT, L., Cardiology
BERGGREN, U., Odontological Psychology
BERGLUNDH, T., Parodontology
BERGSTRÖM, T., Clinical Microbiology
BETSHOLTZ, CH., Medical Biochemistry
BIBER, B., Anaesthesiology and Intensive Care
BILLIG, B., Cellular Aging and Apoptosis
BIRKHED, D., Cariology
BJÖRKELUND, C., General Medicine
BLENNOW, K., Clinical Neurochemistry
BLOMSTRAND, C., Neurology
BONDJERS, G., Cardiological Research
BORÉN, J., Cardiovascular Research
BRAIDE, M., Anatomy
BRÄNNSTRÖM, M., Obstetrics and Gynaecology
BREIMER, M., Clinical Molecular Genetics
BRY, K., Paediatrics, especially Neonatology
CARLSSON, J., Physiotherapy
CARLSSON, L., Clinical Metabolic Research
CARLSTEN, H., Rheumatology
DAHLÉN, G., Oral Microbiology
DAHLGREN, C., Medical Microbiology
DAHLGREN, U., Oral Immunology
DAHLSTRÖM, A., Histology
DAMBER, J.-E., Urology
DICKSON, S., Psychology, especially Neuro Endocrinology
EDÉN, S., Physiology, especially Endocrinology
EDENBRANDT, L., Clinical Physiology, especially Nuclear Medicine
EKROTH, R., Thoracic Surgery
EKSTRÖM, J., Pharmacology
ELAM, M., Clinical Neurophysiology
ELIAS, P., Medicinal Biochemistry
EMILSON, C.-G., Cardiology
ENERBÄCK, S., Medical Genetics
ENGEL, J., Pharmacology
ERICSON, L., Anatomy
ERIKSSON, E., Pharmacology
ERIKSSON, P., Neurobiology, especially Stem Cell Research
FÄNDRIKS, L., Integrative Physiology and Pharmacology
FASTH, A., Paediatric Immunology and Rheumatology
FOSSELL-ARONSSON, E., Radiophysics
FREDMAN, P., Neurochemistry
FRIBERG, P., Clinical Physiology

FUNA, K., Medical Cell Biology
GASTON-JOHANSSON, F., Nursing Sciences
GILLBERG, C., Child and Youth Psychiatry and Handicap Research
GRANSTRÖM, G., Otorhinolaryngology
GRÖNDAHL, H.-G., Oral Diagnostic Radiology
GRÖNDAHL, K., Oral Diagnostic Radiology
GUSTAFSSON, B., Neurophysiology
HAGBERG, H., Obstetrics and Gynaecology, especially Periodontology
HAGBERG, M., Occupational Medicine
HAGLID, K., Histology
HAMBERGER, L., Obstetrics and Gynaecology
HANSSON, G., Biochemistry, especially Gastrointestinal Glycobiology
HANSSON, H.-A., Histology
HANSSON, T., Occupational Orthopaedics
HANSSON RÖNNBÄCK, E., Glia Cell Research
HARALDSSON, B., Kidney Medicine with Experimental Alignment
HÄRD, T., Structural Biology, especially Protein Chemistry
HEDNER, T., Clinical Pharmacology
HELLSTRAND, K., Immune Therapy
HELLSTRÖM, A., Paediatric Ophthalmology, especially Growth Factors
HELLSTRÖM, M., Diagnostic Radiology
HJALMARSSON, O., Paediatrics
HOLM, S., Experimental Surgery
HOLMÄNG, A., Laboratory Medicine
HOLMGREN, J., Medical Microbiology
HOLMSTRÖM, H., Plastic Surgery
HULTBORN, R., Oncology
HULTHÉN, L., Clinical Nutrition, especially Human Trace Element Research
ISAKSSON, O., Endocrinology
ISGAARD, J., Hormonal Regulation of the Heart, especially Growth and Repair Processes
IWARSON, S., Infectious Diseases
JACOBSSON, L., Medical Radiophysics
JANSON, P.-O., Obstetrics and Gynaecology
JANSSON, J.-O., Tissue Regeneration
JANSSON, T., Physiology, especially Perinatal Physiology
JERN, C., Neurology, especially Vascular Diseases and Vascular Genetics
JERN, S., Cardiovascular Physiology
JOHANSSON, B. R., Anatomy
JONASON, J., Pharmacology
JONTELL, M., Endocrinology with Oral Diagnostics
KAHNBERG, K.-E., Dental Surgery
KARLSSON, A., Experimental Rheumatology
KARLSSON, J.-O., Histology
KARLSSON, S., Prosthetic Dentistry
KÄRRHOLM, J., Orthopaedic Surgery
KINDBLOM, L.-G., Pathology
LAGERGÅRD, T., Vaccine Research
LARKÖ, O., Dermatology and Venereal Disease
LARSON, G., Laboratory Medicine, especially Glycobiology
LARSSON, S., Pneumology
LEKHOLM, U., Oral Implant Surgery
LINDAHL, A., Cartilage Tissue Regeneration
LINDBLOM, B., Eye Diseases
LINDE, A., Oral Biochemistry
LISSNER, L., Epidemiology
LÖTVALL, J., Clinical Allergology
LUNDHOLM, K., Surgery
LYCKE, N., Clinical Immunology
MAGNUSSON, B., Oral Pathology
MATTSSON, B., General Medicine
MEIS-KINDBLOM, J., Pathology
MELLANDER, L., International Medicine
MILSOM, I., Gynaecology and Obstetrics
MOHLIN, B., Orthodontics
MÖLLER, C., Audiology
NILSSON, O., Pathology
NILSSON, T., Functional Morphology
NISSBRANDT, H., Pharmacology
NORDGREN, S., Surgery

NORÉN, J., Paedodontics
NYGREN, H., Histology
NYSTRÖM, E., Medicine
OHLSSON, C., Hormonal Regulation of Bone Metabolism and Growth
OLAUSSON, M., Clinical Transplantation Surgery
OLDFORS, A., Pathology
OLMARKER, K., Experimental Spinal Pain Research, especially Neuropathic Pain Mechanism
OLOFSSON, S.-O., Medical Biochemistry
OLSSON, J., Odontological Technology
ÖSTMAN-SMITH, I., Paediatric Cardiology
PILHAMMAR-ANDERSSON, E., Nursing Pedagogics
REIT, C., Endodontology
RIDELL, M., Medical Microbiology
RISBERG, B., Surgery
RÖNNBÄCK, L., Neurology
ROSENGREN, A., Epidemiology
ROUPE, G., Dermatology and Venereal Diseases
RYDEVIK, B., Orthopaedic Surgery
RYMO, L., Clinical Chemistry
SAMUELSSON, B., Transfusion Medicine
SANDBERG, M., Biochemistry
SEMB, H., Evolutionary Biology
SENNERBY, L., Handicap Research, especially Experimental and Clinical
SILLÉN, U., Paediatric Surgery
SJÖBERG, B., Medical Biochemistry
SJÖSTRÖM, L., Clinical Research
SJÖVALL, H., Physiology and Pathophysiology of the Digestive and Intestinal Channel
SKOOG, I., Psychiatry, especially Social Psychiatry and Epidemiology
SMITH, U., Medicine
SOUSSI, B., Experimental Medicine, especially NMR Spectroscopy
STEINECK, G., Cancer Epidemiology
STENEVI, U., Ophthalmology
STENMAN, G., Pathology
STRANDVIK, B., Paediatrics
SULLIVAN, M., Psychology
SVENNERHOLM, A.-M., Infectious Diseases and Immunology
SWEDBERG, K., Medicine
TARKOWSKI, A., Rheumatology
THELLE, D., Cardiovascular Epidemiology and Prevention
THOMSEN, P., Medical Biomaterials Research
TYLÉN, U., X-Ray Diagnostics
WAHLSTRÖM, J., Clinical Genetics
WALLERSTEDT, S., Medicine
WALLGREN, A., Radio Therapeutics
WALLIN, A., Geriatric Neuropsychiatry
WENNERBERG, A., Oral Prosthetics
WENNERGREN, G., Paediatrics
WENNSTRÖM, J., Parodontology
WICK, M. J., Clinical and Experimental Immunology
WIGSTRÖM, H., Medical Physics
WIKKELSÖ, C., Neurology
WIKLUND, O., Medicine
WIKSTRÖM, M., Oral Microbiology

School of Business, Economics and Law (POB 600, SE-405 30 Gothenburg; tel. (31) 786-49-48; fax (31) 773-55-20; e-mail info@handels.gu.se; internet www.handels.gu.se):

ALVSTAM, C.-G., International Economic Geography
ANDERSSON, D. T., Marketing
BERGENDAHL, G., Managerial Economics
BIGSTEN, A., Economics
CRAMÉR, P., International Law, European Integration Law
CZARNIAWSKA, B., Business Administration
DOTEVALL, R., Commercial Law
FLOOD, L., Econometrics
FRISÉN, M., Statistics
GADD, C.-J., Economic History
HIBBS, D., Economics

HJALMARSSON, L., Economics
JENSEN, A., Transport Management
JOHANSSON STENMAN, O., Economics
JÖNSSON, S., Business Administration
JONSSON, S., Economic History
LINDBLOM, T., Business Administration
MÅRTENSSON, R., Business Administration
NORBÄCK, L.-E., Business Administration
NORDSTRÖM, L., Human Geography
OLSON, O., Accounting and Finance
OLSSON, U., Economic History
PÅHLSSON, R., Tax Law
POLESIE, T., Accounting and Finance
RAMBERG, C., Commercial Law
SANDELIN, B., Economics
SOLLI, R., Business Administration
STERNER, T., Environmental Economics
STJERNBERG, T., Management and Organization
TÖLLBORG, D., Legal Science
TÖRNQVIST, U., Business Administration
VILHELMSON, B., Human Geography
WESTERHÄLL, V. L., Public Law

KARLSTADS UNIVERSITET
(Karlstad University)

SE-651 88 Karlstad
Universitetsgatan 2, Karlstad
Telephone: (54) 700-10-00
Fax: (54) 700-14-60
E-mail: information@kau.se
Internet: www.kau.se

Founded 1967 as Universitetsfilialen; became Högskolan i Karlstad 1977, present name 1999
State control
Languages of instruction: English, Swedish
Academic year: August to June

Rector: KERSTIN NORÉN
Pro-Rector: THOMAS BLOM
Pro-Rector: GERD LINDGREN
Univ. Dir: ANNE-CHRISTINE LARSEN
Library Dir: EVA ARNDT KLING

Library of 180,000 vols
Number of teachers: 700
Number of students: 12,000

Publications: *Anslaget* (26 a year), *Utbilder* (6 a year)

DEANS

Faculty of Arts and Education: KENNETH NORDGREN
Faculty of Economic Sciences, Communication and IT: JOHN SÖREN PETTERSSON
Faculty of Social and Life Sciences: Prof. CURT RÄFTEGÅRD
Faculty of Technology and Science: JAN VAN STAM

LINKÖPINGS UNIVERSITET
(Linköping University)

SE-581 83 Linköping
Telephone: (13) 28-10-00
Fax: (13) 14-94-03
E-mail: liu@liu.se
Internet: www.liu.se

Founded 1970
Academic year: September to June

Rector: MILLE MILLNERT
Pro-Rector: KARIN FÄLTH-MAGNUSSON
Univ. Dir: CURT KARLSSON

Library: see under Libraries and Archives
Number of teachers: 1,800
Number of students: 25,000

DEANS

Faculty of Arts and Sciences: BO HELLGREN
Faculty of Educational Sciences: KARIN MÅRDSJÖ BLUME
Faculty of Health Sciences: Prof. Dr MATS HAMMAR
Institute of Technology: HELEN DANNETUN

PROFESSORS

Faculty of Arts and Sciences:

ADELSWÄRD, V., Communication Studies
ÅHLUND, A, Ethnicity Studies
ALLARD, B., Water and Environmental Studies
ANSELM, J., Technology and Social Change
ANWARD, J., Language and Culture Studies
ARNESDOTTER, I., Business Law
ARONSSON OTTOSSON, K., Child Studies
BECKMAN, S., Technology and Social Change
BERNER, B., Technology and Social Change
BORGQUIST, L., Health and Society
CARLGREN, I., Education
CARSTENSEN, J., Health and Society
COLLSTE, G., Applied Ethics
DAHLGREN, L.-O., Education
EDQUIST, C., Technology and Social Change
ELLEGÅRD, K., Technology and Social Change
ELLSTÖM, P.-E., Education
ERIKSSON, B. E., Health and Society
FRODI, A., Psychology
GOLDKUHL, G., Information Systems
GRANSTÖM, K., Education
GRIMWALL, A., Statistics
HALLDÉN, G., Child Studies
HELLGREN, B., Management
HJORT AF ORNÄS, A., Water and Environmental Studies
HULTMAN, G., Education
HYDÉN, L.-C., Communication Studies
INGELSTAM, L., Technology and Social Change
JANSSON, J., Transport Economics
JOHANSSON, R., Ethnicity Studies
KYLHAMMAR, J., Communication Studies
LINDKVIST, L., Management
LINELL, P., Communication Studies
LOHM, U., Water and Environmental Studies
LUNDQVIST, J., Water and Environmental Studies
LYKKE, N., Gender Studies
LYXELL, B., Psychology
MYRBERG, M., Education
NÄSMAN, E., Society and Cultural Studies
NELSON, M. C., History
NILSSON, G. B., Technology and Social Change
NORDENFELT, L., Health and Society
NORDIN, I., Health and Society
PETERSON, B., Philosophy
ÖBERG, G., Water and Environmental Studies
QVARSELL, R., Health and Society
RAHM, L., Water and Environmental Studies
RÖNNBERG, J., Psychology
SANDELL, R., Clinical Psychology
SANDIN, B., Child Studies
SJÖGREN, H., Technology and Social Change
SKOGH, G., Economics
SUNDIN, E., Technology and Social Change
SUNDIN, J., Health and Society
SVENSSON, B., Water and Environmental Studies

Faculty of Health Sciences:

ALM-CARLSSON, G., Medical Radiation Physics
ANDERSSON, R., Pharmacology
ARNQVIST, H., Medical Cell Biology
ASPENBERG, P., Orthopaedic Surgery
AXELSON, O., Occupational and Environmental Medicine
BERGDAHL, B., Medicine
BLOMQVIST, A., Pain Research
BORCH, K., Surgery
BRUNK, U., Pathology
CARLSSON, P., Health Technology Assessment
EK, A.-C., Caring Science
EKBERG, K., Work and Rehabilitation

FAGERHOLM, P., Ophthalmology
FORSBERG, P., Infectious Diseases
FORSUM, U., Clinical Microbiology
GERDLE, B., Rehabilitation Medicine
GRANERUS, A.-K., Geriatric Medicine
HAMMAR, M., Obstetrics and Gynaecology
HAMMARSTRÖM, S., Medical Cell Biology
HILDEBRAND, C., Medical Cell Biology
HULTMAN, P., Pathology
KÅGEDAL, B., Clinical Chemistry
KARLBERG, B., Medicine
KINLSTRÖM, E., Clinical Microbiology
LARSSON, S.-E., Orthopaedic Surgery
LENNQUIST, S., Disaster Medicine and Traumatology
LINDSTRÖM, S., Medical Cell Biology
LISANDER, B., Anaesthesiology
LUDVIGSSON, J., Paediatrics
LUNDBLAD, A., Clinical Chemistry
LUNDQUIST, P.-G., Otorhinolaryngology
MAGNUSSON, K.-E., Medical Microbiology
MARAISSON, J., Geriatrics
MÅRDH, S., Cell Biology
MESSNER, K., Skeletal Biology
NILSSON, L., Microbiology
NORDENSKJÖLD, B., Oncology
NORDIN, C., Psychiatry
ÖBERG, A., Medical Engineering (Instrumentation)
ÕBERG, B., Physiotherapy
OLIN, C., Cardiothoracic Surgery
OLSSON, A. G., Internal Medicine
OLSSON, J.-E., Neurology
ÖSTRUP, L., Plastic Surgery
PAULETTE-HULTCRANTZ, E., Otorhinolaryngology
PETERSSON, C., Clinical Pharmacology
RAMMER, L., Forensic Science and Medicine
ROSDAHL, I., Dermatology and Venereology
ROSÉN, A., Inflammation and Tumour Biology
SERUP, J., Dermatology and Venereology
SJÖBERG, F., Critical Care, especially Burn Intensive Care
SMEDBY, Ö., Diagnostic Radiology
SMEDS, S., Surgery
SÖDERFELT, B., Neurology
SÖDERKVIST, P., Cell Biology, especially Medical Genetics
STENDAHL, O., Medical Microbiology
STENMAN, G., Medical Genetics
STRÅLFORS, P., Medical Cell Biology
STRANG, P., Palliative Medicine
SUNDQUIST, T., Medical Microbiology, especially Inflammation
SVANBORG, E., Clinical Neuropsychology
SVANVIK, J., Surgery
TAGESSON, C., Experimental Medicine
THEODORSSON, E., Neurochemistry
TIMPKA, T., Social Medicine and Public Health Sciences
TRELL, E., Primary Health Care and General Practice
WÅLINDER, J., Psychiatry
WASTESON, Å., Medical Cell Biology
WIGERTZ, O., Medical Engineering (Medical Information Processing)
WIJMA, B., Women's Health
WRANNE, B., Clinical Physiology

Institute of Technology:

ABRAHAMSSON, M., Logistics Management
AHRENBERG, L., Computational Linguistics
ANDERSSON, L.-E., Applied Mathematics
ARONSSON, G., Applied Mathematics
ARWIN, H., Applied Optics
ASK, P., Biomedical Engineering
BALTZER, L., Organic Chemistry
BERGGREN, C., Production Management
BERGGREN, K.-F., Theoretical Physics
BORÉN, H., Organic Chemistry
BRANDES, O., Industrial Marketing
BREGE, S., Industrial Marketing
CARLSSON, U., Biochemistry
CHEN, W., Materials Science
DADFAR, H., International Marketing

DAHLBERG, T., Solid Mechanics and Strength of Materials
DAHLGAARD, J. J., Quality Technology and Management
DOHERTY, P., Computer Science
EDGAR, B., Applied Mathematics
EKEDAHL, L.-G., Applied Physics, Catalytic Reactions
EKLUND, J., Industrial Ergonomics
ELDÉN, L., Numerical Analysis
ERICSON, T., Data Transmission
ERICSSON, T., Engineering Materials
FAHLMAN, A., Physics
FRITZSON, P., Computer Science
GLAD, T., Automatic Control
GRANLUND, G., Computer Vision
GRUBBSTRÖM, R. W., Production Economics
GUSTAFSSON, F., Communication Systems
HÄGGLUND, S., Computer Science
HANSSON, G., Experimental Semiconductor Physics
HELMERSSON, U., Thin Film Physics
HOLLNAGEL, E., Industrial Ergonomics
HOLMBERG, K., Optimization
HOLTZ, P.-O., Materials Science
HULTMAN, L., Thin Film Physics
INGANÄS, O., Biomolecular and Organic Electronics
INGEMARSSON, I., Information Theory
JANZÉN, E., Semiconductor Physics
JOHANSSON, L., Materials Science
JONSSON, B. H., Biochemistry
KAMKAR, M., Software Engineering
KARLSSON, B., Energy Systems
KARLSSON, J. M., Telecommunications
KLARBRING, A., Optimization Models in Structural Mechanics
KNUTSSON, H., Medical Informatics
KOSKI, T., Mathematical Statistics
KRUS, P., Fluid Power Technology
KRUSE, B., Digital Images and Media Technology
KVARNSTRÖM, I., Organic Chemistry
LIEDBERG, B., Sensor Science
LINDBERG, P.-O., Optimization
LINUSSON, S., Applied Mathematics
LIU, D., Computer Engineering
LJUNG, L., Automatic Control
LOYD, D., Applied Thermodynamics and Fluid Mechanics
LUND, A., Chemical Physics
LUNDGREN, J., Traffic Systems
LUNDSTRÖM, I., Applied Physics
MALUSZYNSKI, J., Programming Theory
MANDENIUS, C.-F., Biotechnology
MAZ'YA, V., Applied Mathematics
MILLNERT, M., Automatic Control
MONEMAR, B., Condensed Matter Physics
MOSFEGH, B., Energy Systems
MUKHERJEE, S. D., Electronic Production
NIELSEN, L., Vehicle Systems
NILSSON, G., Biomedical Instrumentation
NILSSON, L., Solid Mechanics
NOVAK, A., Production Engineering
ÖBERG, A., Biomedical Engineering
OHLSSON, K., Industrial Ergonomics
PALMBERG, J.-O., Fluid Power Technology
PENG, Z., Computer Systems
PERSSON, J., Medical Technology Assessment
RAPP, B., Economic Information Systems
RAUCH, S., Applied Mathematics
RIKLUND, R., Theoretical Physics
RÖNNQVIST, M., Optimization
RYDBERG, K.-E., Fluid Power Technology
SALANECK, W., Surface Physics and Chemistry
SANDAHL, K., Software Engineering
SANDEWALL, E., Computer Science
SANDKULL, B., Industrial Organization
SERNELIUS, B., Theoretical Physics
SHAHMEHRI, N., Computer Science
SJÖLANDER, S., Zoology
STAFSTRÖM, S., Computational Physics
STRANDBERG, L., Traffic Safety and Environment

SVENSSON, C., Electronic Devices
TENGVALL, P., Applied Physics
UHRBERG, R., Surface and Semiconductor Physics
VÅRBRAND, P., Optimization
WANHAMMAR, L., Electronic Systems
WIGERTZ, O., Medical Informatics

LINNÉUNIVERSITETET
(Linnaeus University)

SE-391 82 Kalmar
Fax: (480) 44-60-32SE-351 95 Växjö
Telephone: (772) 28-80-00
Fax: (470) 832-17
E-mail: registrator@lnu.se
Founded 2010, following merger of Växjö Universitet (f. 1967 as a br. of Lund Univ.) and Högskolan i Kalmar (f. 1977)
State control
Language of instruction: English, Swedish
Academic year: September to June

Rector: STEPHEN HWANG
Pro-Rector: BO BERGBÄCK
Pro-Rector: LENA FRITZÉN
Library Dir: ANDERS RYDQVIST
Library: see Libraries and Archives
Number of teachers: 2,000
Number of students: 34,000 (15,000 full-time, 19,000 part-time)

HEADS OF FACULTY

Faculty of Economics and Design: Prof. HENRIETTE KOBLANCK
Faculty of Education Sciences: Prof. PER GERREVALL
Faculty of Health, Social Work and Behavioural Sciences: HÅKAN JENNER
Faculty of Humanities and Social Sciences: MATS SJÖLIN
Faculty of Science and Technology: Prof. BENGT PERSSON

LULEÅ TEKNISKA UNIVERSITET
(Luleå University of Technology)

SE-971 87 Luleå
Telephone: (920) 49-10-00
Fax: (920) 49-13-99
E-mail: registrator@ltu.se
Internet: www.ltu.se
Founded 1971
State control
Language of instruction: Swedish

Vice-Chancellor: JOHAN STERTE
Deputy Vice-Chancellor: ERIK HÖGLUND
Chief Admin. Officer: STAFFAN SARBÄCK
Univ. Librarian: TERJE HÖISETH

Library of 240,932 vols, 15,663 periodicals
Number of teachers: 650 (incl. researchers)
Number of students: 12,000

PROFESSORS

Department of Applied Physics and Mechanical Engineering:
FREDRIKSSON, S., Physics
GUSTAVSSON, H., Fluid Mechanics
HÖGLUND, E., Machine Elements
JINYUE, Y., Energy Engineering
KAPLAN, A., Systems Engineering
KARLSSON, L., Computer Aided Design
MOLIN, N. E., Experimental Mechanics
ODÉN, M., Engineering Materials
OLDENBURG, M., Solid Mechanics
VARNA, J., Polymer Engineering

Department of Business Administration and Social Sciences:
BERGSTRÖM, I., Management Control
DE RAADT, D., Informatics and Systems Sciences
HÄGERFORS, A., Computer and Systems Sciences

HANSSON, S., Political Science, History and Geography
HÖRTE, S.-Å., Industrial Organization
KLEFSJÖ, B.
LUNDGREN, N.-G., Political Science, History and Geography
MICHANEK, G., Jurisprudence
RADETZKI, M., Economics
SALEHI-SANGARI, E., Industrial Marketing
WIKLUND, H., Quality and Environmental Management

Department of Chemical and Metallurgical Engineering:
BERGLUND, K. A., Biochemical and Chemical Process Engineering
BJÖRKMAN, B., Process Metallurgy
FORSLING, W., Chemistry
FORSSBERG, E., Mineral Processing
STERTE, J., Chemical Technology

Department of Civil and Mining Engineering:
BORGBRANT, J., Construction Management
ELFGREN, L., Structural Engineering
JOHANSSON, B., Steel Structures
KLISINSKI, M., Structural Mechanics
KNUTSSON, S., Soil Mechanics and Foundation Engineering
KUMAR, U., Operation and Maintenance Engineering
LAGERQVIST, O., Steel Structures
LINDQVIST, P.-A., Rock Engineering
NORDLUND, E., Rock Mechanics
OLOFSSON, T., Structural Engineering

Department of Communication and Languages:
MAGNUSSON, U., English
PERSSON, G., English

Department of Computer Science and Electrical Engineering:
DELSING, J., Embedded Internet Systems Laboratory (EISLAB)
MEDVEDEV, A., Automatic Control
WERNERSSON, A., Embedded Internet Systems Laboratory (EISLAB)

Department of Environmental Engineering:
ELMING, S.-Å., Applied Geophysics
HANAEUS, J., Sanitary Engineering
LAGERKVIST, A., Water Science and Technology
NORDELL, B., Renewable Energy
ÖHLANDER, B., Applied Geology
ÖSTMAN, A., Geographical Information Technology
SELLGREN, A., Water Resources Engineering

Department of Human Work Sciences:
ÅGREN, A., Sound and Vibration
ALM, H., Engineering Psychology
JOHANSSON, J., Industrial Work Environment
PETTERSSON, D., Industrial Design

Department of Mathematics:
EULER, M., Applied Mathematics
HEABERG, T., Applied Mathematics
PERSSON, L.-E., Applied Mathematics
STRAESSER, R., Applied Mathematics

Department of Wood Technology:
GRÖNLUND, A., Wood Technology
MORÉN, T., Wood Physics
WESTERMARK, U., Wood Material Science

School of Education:
ALEXANDERSSON, M., Pedagogics

School of Music:
BRÄNDSTRÖM, S., Education and Teaching Methods in Music
ERICSSON, H.-O., Organ
SANDSTRÖM, J., Composition
WESTBERG, E., Choir Singing and Choir Conducting

LUND UNIVERSITY

POB 117, SE-221 00 Lund
Telephone: (46) 222-00-00
Fax: (46) 222-47-20
E-mail: info@rektor.lu.se
Internet: www.lu.se
Founded 1666
State control
Language of instruction: English, Swedish
Academic year: September to June (2 semesters)

Vice-Chancellor: PER ERIKSSON
Pro-Vice-Chancellor: EVA ÅKESSON
Head of Admin.: MARIANNE GRANFELT
Library: see under Libraries and Archives
Number of teachers: 646
Number of students: 47,000

Publication: *LUM* (9 a year)

DEANS

Faculty of Engineering: Prof. ANDERS AXELS-SON
Faculty of Fine and Performing Arts: HÅKAN LUNDSTRÖM
Faculty of Humanities and Theology: Prof. LYNN ÅKESSON
Faculty of Law: Prof. CHRISTINA MOËLL
Faculty of Medicine: Prof. BO AHRÉN
Faculty of Social Sciences: ANN-KATRIN BÄCK-LUND
Faculty of Science: Prof. TORBJÖRN VON SCHANTZ
School of Economics and Mananagement: ALLAN T. MALM

PROFESSORS

Faculty of Humanities and Theology:

ANDERSSON, G., Musicology
ANDRÉN, A., Medieval Archaeology
BJÖRLING, F., Slavic Languages
BLOMQVIST, J., Greek Language and Literature
BROBERG, G., History of Ideas and Sciences
BRUCE, G., Phonetics
EDLUND, B., Musicology
EINARSSON, J., Scandinavian Languages
ENÉVIST, I., Spanish
FLORBY, G., English Literature
FRYKMAN, J., European Ethnology
GÄRDENFORS, P., Cognitive Science
GREATREX, R., Chinese
GUSTAFSSON, H., History
HAETTNER-AURELIUS, E., Literature
HÅKANSSON, G., General Linguistics
HANSSON, B., Theoretical Philosophy
HÅRDH, B., Archaeology
HEDLING, E., Film
HOADLEY, M., Southeast Asian History and Bahasa Indonesia
HOLMBERG, B., Semitic Languages
HORNBORG, A., Human Ecology
IREGREN, E., Historical Osteology
KARLSSON, K.-G., History
LARSSON, B., French
LARSSON, L., Archaeology
LARSSON, L., Literature
LÖFGREN, O., European Ethnology
LÖVKRONA, I., European Ethnology
MOLNÁR, V., German
NORDIN, S., History of Ideas and Science
OLAUSSON, D., Archaeology
OREDSSON, S., History
ÖSTERBERG, E., History
PALM, A., Literature
PERSSON, I., Practical Philosophy
PILTZ, A., Latin
PLATZACK, C., Scandinavian Languages
RABINOWICZ, W., Practical Philosophy
RAGVALD, L., Chinese
RIDDERSTAD, P. S., Book and Library History
RYDÉN, P., Literature
RYSTEDT, E., Classical Archaeology and Ancient History

SAHLIN, N.-E., Theoretical Philosophy
SALOMON, K., International History
SALOMOUSSON, A., European Ethnology
SANDQVIST, S., French
SCHLYTER, S., Romance Languages
SJÖBLAD, C., Literature
SJÖLIN, J.-G., History of Contemporary Art
SONESSON, G., Cultural Semiotics
STEENSLAND, L., Slavic Languages
STRÖMQVIST, S., Language Acquisition
SVANTESSON, J.-O., General Linguistics
SVENSSON, J., Swedish
SVENSSON, L.-H., English Literature
THORMÄHLEN, M., English Literature
VIBERG, Å., General Linguistics
WARREN, B., English
WEIMARCK, T., History of Contemporary Art
WIÉANDER, Ö., Classical Archaeology
WIENBERG, J., Medieval Archaeology

Faculty of Law:

BERGHOLTZ, G., Legal Procedure
BERGSTRÖM, S., Tax Law
BOGDAN, M., Comparative and Private International Law
FAHLBECK, R., Labour Law
GORTON, L., Banking Law
MELANDER, G., Public International Law
MODÉER, K. Å., Legal History
NUMHAUSER-HENNING, A., Private Law
NYSTRÖM, B., Private Law
PECZENIK, A., Jurisprudence
TRÄSKMAN, P. O., Criminal Law
VOGEL, H.-H., Public Law
WESTBERG, P., Legal Procedure

Faculty of Medicine:

ABRAHAMSSON, P.-A., Oncological Urology
AHRÉN, B., Clinical Metabolic Research
ÅKERLUND, M., Obstetrics and Gynaecology
AKERSTROM, M., Medical Chemistry
ALLING, CH., Medical Neurochemistry
ALM, P., Pathology
ANDERSSON, K.-E., Clinical Pharmacology
ANDERSSON, R., Surgery
ANDERSSON, T., Experimental Pathology
ARNER, A., Physiology
BÄCK, O., Dermatology
BELFRAGE, P., Medical Biochemistry
BERGLUND, G., Internal Medicine
BERGLUND, M., Clinical Alcohol Research
BJÖRCK, L., Medical Biochemistry
BJÖRKLUND, A., Histology
BJURSTEN, L.-M., Bio-implant Research
BORGSTRÖM, A., Surgery
BRUNDIN, P., Neuroscience
CARLSTEDT, I., Mucosal Biology
DAHLBÄCK, B., Coagulation Research
DEGERMAN, E., Experimental Diabetes Research
DEHLIN, O., Geriatric Medicine
DILLNER, J., Virology
EHINGER, B., Ophthalmology
EKBLOM, P., Molecular Cell Biology
EKDAHL, C., Physiotherapy
EKHBERG, O., Diagnostic Radiology
ELMESTÅHL, S., Geriatrics
ERLANSON-ALBERTSSON, C.
FÄSSLER, R., Experimental Pathology
FENYÖ, E.-M., Virology
FORSGREN, A., Clinical Bacteriology
FRANSSON, L.-Å., Cell Biology
GERDTHAM, U., Public Health Science
GRÄNDE, P.-O., Anaesthesia and Intensive Care
GROOP, L., Endocrinology
GRUBB, A., Clinical Biochemistry
GULLBERG, U., Haematology
GUSTAFSON, L., Geriatric Psychiatry
HAGANDER, B., Medicine
HAGMAR, L., Environmental Medicine
HÅKANSSON, R., Experimental Endocrinology
HEIJL, A., Ophthalmology
HEINEGÅRD, D., Medical Biochemistry
HELLSTRAND, P., Muscle Research

HERMERÉN, G., Medical Ethics
HESSLOW, G., Neuroscience
HÖGESTÄTT, E., Clinical Pharmacology
HOLMBERG, L., Paediatrics
HOLMDAHL, R., Medical Inflammation Research
HOLMER, N.-G., Biomedical Engineering
HOLM WALLENBERG, C., Molecular Cell Biology
HOLTÅS, S., Neuroradiology
HOVELIUS, B., General Practice
IHSE, I., Surgery
JACOBSEN, S. E., Stem Cell Biology
JANZON, L., Epidemiology
JEPPSSON, B., Surgery
JOHNELL, O., Orthopaedic Surgery
JONSON, B., Clinical Physiology
KARLSSON, S., Gene Therapy in Molecular Medicine
KILLANDER, D., Oncology
LANDBERG, G., Pathology
LEANDERSON, T., Immunology
LEED-LUNDBERG, F., Cellular and Molecular Physiology
LERNMARK, Å., Experimental Diabetes Research
LEVANDER, S., Psychiatry
LIDGREN, L., Orthopaedics
LINDAHL, G., Medical Microbiology and Immunology
LINDGREN, B., Health Economics
LINDGREN, S., Medicine
LINDVALL, O., Restorative Neurology
LJUNGGREN, B., Dermatology and Venereology
LÖFDAHL, C.-G., Lung Disease
LÖFQVIST, A., Logopaedic Phonetics
LOHMANDER, S., Orthopaedics
LÖWENHIELM, P., Forensic Medicine
LUNDBERG, D., Anaesthesiology
LUNDBORG, G., Hand Surgery
LUNDQUIST, I., Pharmacology
LUTHMAN, H., Genetic Epidemiology
McNEIL, T., Medical Behavioural Research
MAGNUSSON, M., Otorhinolaryngology
MALMSTRÖM, A., Medical and Physiological Chemistry
MARSAL, K., Obstetrics and Gynaecology
MATTIASSON, A., Urology
MATTSON, R., Reproduction Immunology
MATTSSON, S., Medical Radiation Physics
MITELMAN, F., Clinical Genetics
NETTELBLÅDT, U., Logopaedics
NILSSON, A., Internal Medicine
NILSSON, J., Experimental Cardiovascular Research
NILSSON-EHLE, P., Clinical Chemistry
NORRBY, R., Infectious Diseases
NORRVING, B., Neurology
ÖHMAN, R. L., Psychiatry
OLBRANT, K., Cell Biology
OLOFSSON, T., Haematology
OLSSON, B., Cardiology
OLSSON, H., Oncology
OLSSON, I., Haematology
OWMAN, CH., Histology
PÅHLMAN, S., Molecular Medicine
PERSSON, B., Medical Radiation Physics
PERSSON, C. G. A., Experimental Clinical Pharmacology
PESONEN, E., Child Cardiology
PETTERSSON, H., Diagnostic Radiology
PRELLNER, K., Otorhinolaryngology
RAHM-HALLBERG, I., Caring Sciences
RÅSTAM, L., Applied Public Health
RENCK, H., Anaesthesiology
RIPPE, B., Nephrology
RISBERG, J., Neuropsychology
RORSMAN, P., Membrane Physiology
ROSÉN, I., Clinical Neurophysiology
SALFORD, L., Neurosurgery
SCHOUENBORG, J., Physiology
SJÖBERG, N.-O., Obstetrics and Gynaecology
SKERFVING, S., Occupational Medicine
STEEN, S., Thoracic Surgery

STENFLO, J., Clinical Chemistry
SUNDLER, F., Histology
SUNDLER, R., Cell Biology
SVANBORG, C., Clinical Immunology
THORNGREN, K.-G., Orthopaedics
TRÄSKMAN BENDZ, L., Psychiatry
WADSTRÖM, T., Bacteriology
WIELOCH, T., Neurobiology
WINGSTRAND, H., Orthopaedics
WOLLMER, P., Clinical Physiology

Faculty of Social Sciences:
AGNÉR SIGBO, G., Informatics
ÅKERSTRÖM, M., Sociology
ALLWOOD, C.-M., Psychology
ALVESSON, M., Business Administration
ANDERSSON, G., Social Work
ANDERSSON, S. I., Psychology
ARWIDI, O., Business Administration
ASHEIM, B. T., Economic Geography
ÅSTRÖM, K., Sociology of Law
BENGTSSON, T., Economic History
BERONIUS, M., Sociology
BORGLIN, A., Public Sector Economics
BRANTE, T., Sociology
CARLSSON, S., Informatics
CARLSSON WETTERBERG, C., Gender Studies
CLARK, E., Social Geography
DAHL, G., Sociology
DAHLGREN, P., Sociology of Communication
DJURFELDT, G., Sociology
EDEBALK, P.-G., Social Work
EDGERTON, D., Econometrics
EHN, P., Information and Computer Sciences
EKHOLM FRIEDMAN, K., Social Anthropology
ELGSTRÖM, O., Political Science
ELIASSON, R.-M., Social Work
ESSEVELD, J., Sociology
FLODGREN, B., Business Law
FRIEDMAN, J., Social Anthropology
GUNNARSSON, CHR., Economic History
HANSSON, B., Economics
HANSSON, G., International Economics
HETZLER, A., Social Policy
HOLMQUIST, B., Statistics
HYDÉN, H., Sociology of Law
JACOBSSON, B., Business Administration
JERNECK, M., Political Science
JOHANSSON, C. R., Industrial and Organizational Psychology
JÖNSSON, CHR., Political Science
LAGNEVIK, M., Business Administration
LANDSTRÖM, H., Entrepreneurship and Small Business
LARSSON, R., Business Administration
LINDBERG, S., Sociology
LINDÉN, A.-L., Sociology
LUNDQUIST, L., Political Science, especially Public Administration
LYTTKENS, C. H., Economics
MALM, A., Business Administration
NORBERG, C., Corporate Law and Tax Law
OHLSSON, R., Modern Economic and Social History
OLANDER, L.-O., Social and Economic Geography
OLERUP, A., Informatics
OLSSON, C.-A., Economic History
OXELHEIM, L., International Business
PERSSON, I., Economics, especially Women's Studies
ROSENBECK, B., Gender Studies
RUNDQUIST, F.-M., Social and Economic Geography
RYDÉN, O., Personality Psychology
SALONEN, T., Social Work
SAMUELSSON, P., Corporate Law and Capital Market Law
SCHÖN, L., Economic History
SELLERBERG, A.-M., Sociology
SÖDERSTRÖM, L., Economics, especially Social Policy
STENELO, L.-G., Political Science
STÅHL, I., Economics

STANKIEWICZ, R., Science and Technology Policy
SUNESSON, S., Social Work
SVENSSON, C., Business Administration
SVENSSON, L., Pedagogy
SVENSSON, L.-G., Economics
SWÄRD, H., Social Work

Faculty of Science:
ADLER, J.-O., Nuclear Physics
AHLBERG, P., Historical Geology and Palaeontology
ÅKESSON, T., Elementary Particle Physics
ALERSTAM, T., Animal Ecology
ALLEN, J. F., Plant Cell Biology
ALMBLADH, C.-O., Physics
ANDERSEN, T., Astronomy
ANDERSSON, B., Theoretical Physics
ANDERSSON, C., Inorganic Chemistry
ANDRÉASSON, P.-G., Mineralogy and Petrology
ARDEBERG, A., Astronomy
ARNASON, U., Evolutionary Genetics
ASMUSSEN, S., Mathematical Statistics
BÅÅTH, E., Microbial Ecology
BENGTSSON, B. O., Genetics
BENGTSSON, G., Chemical Ecology and Ecotoxicology
BENGTSSON, S.-A., Systematic Zoology
BERG, U., Organic Chemistry
BJÖRCK, S., Quaternary Geology
BJÖRN, L. O., Plant Physiology
BRÖNMARK, C., Limnology
CHAO, K., Theoretical Physics
CONSTANTIN, A., Mathematics
DRAVINS, D., Astronomy
EDSTRÖM, A., Zoophysiology
EEROLA, P., Experimental Particle Physics
ELDING, L. I., Inorganic Chemistry
ERIKSSON, M., Physics
EVERITT, E., Microbiology
FAGERSTRÖM, T., Theoretical Ecology
FAHLANDER, C., Physics
FALKENGRENGRERUP, U., Plant Ecology
FREJD, T., Organic Chemistry
GORTON, L., Analytical Chemistry
GRANELI, W., Limnology
GUSTAFSON, G., Theoretical Physics
GUSTAFSSON, H.-Å., High Energy Heavy Ion Physics
HANSSON, B., Chemical Ecology and Ecotoxicology
HANSSON, L.-A., Limnology
HEBERT, H., Molecular Biophysics
HEDENMALM, H., Mathematics
HELLBORG, R., Nuclear Physics
HELLDÉN, U., Physical Geography
HOLM, E., Radiation Physics
HOLMBERG, B., Inorganic Chemistry
HÖSSJER, O., Mathematical Studies
JAKOBSSON, B., Subatomic Physics
JANSSON, H.-B., Microbial Ecology
JARLSKOG, G., Physics
JEPPSSON, L., Historical Geology and Palaeontology
JERGIL, B., Biochemistry
JOHANSSON, S., Atomic Spectroscopy
JÖNSSON, B., Physical Chemistry
JÖNSSON, J.-A., Analytical Chemistry
JÖNSSON, L., Elementary Particle Physics
KANJE, M., Zoological Cell Biology
KANTOR, I., Mathematics
KARLSTRÖM, G., Theoretical Physics
KJELLBOM, P., Plant Biochemistry
KÄRNEFELT, I., Systematic Botany
LARSSON, C., Plant Biochemistry
LARSSON, K., Historical Geology and Palaeontology
LARSSON, P., Chemical Ecology and Ecotoxicology
LARSSON, R., Zoology
LILJAS, A., Molecular Biophysics
LINDAU, I., Synchrotron Light Research
LINDEGREN, L., Astronomy
LINDH, A., Mineralogy and Petrology
LINDMAN, B., Physical Chemistry

LINDROTH, A., Physical Geography
LINGAS, A., Computer Sciences
LINSE, P., Macromolecular Chemistry
LITZÉN, U., Atomic Spectroscopy
LOFSTEDT, C., Ecology, Chemical Communication
LÖRSTAD, B., Elementary Particle Physics
LUNDBERG, P., Theoretical Ecology
MARTINSON, I., Atomic Physics
MATHIASSON, L., Analytical Chemistry
MAX MØLLER, I., Plant Physiology
MELIN, A., Mathematics
MEURMAN, A., Mathematics
NIHLGÅRD, B., Plant Ecology
NILSSON, D. E., Zoology
NILSSON, J.-A., Animal Ecology
NILSSON, N., Mathematics
NILSSON, S. G., Animal Ecology
NYHOLM, R., Synchrotron Radiation Instrumentation
OLSSON, U., Physical Chemistry
OREDSSON, S., Animal Physiology
OSCARSSON, A., Inorganic Chemistry
PEETRE, J., Mathematics
PETERSON, C., Theoretical Physics
PETTERSON, G., Biochemistry
PICULELL, L., Physical Chemistry
PRENTICE, H., Systematic Botany
ROOS, B., Theoretical Chemistry
RUTBERG, B., Microbiology
RUTBERG, L., Microbiology
SANDGREN, P., Quaternary Geology
SCHRÖDER, B., Nuclear Physics
SJÖSTRAND, T., Theoretical Physics
SMITH, H., Animal Ecology
SÖDERGREN, A., Chemical Ecology and Ecotoxicology
SÖDERLIND, G., Numerical Mathematics
SÖDERMAN, O., Physical Chemistry
SÖDERSTRÖM, B., Microbial Ecology
SOMMARIN, M., Plant Biochemistry
STÅHLBERG, F., Magnetic Resonance
STENLUND, E., Cosmic and Subatomic Physics
STRAND, S.-E., Radiation Physics
STYRING, S., Biochemistry
SUNDSTRÖM, V., Chemical Dynamics
SVENSSON, B. E. Y., Theoretical Physics
SYKES, M., Plant Ecology
TJERNELD, F., Biochemistry
TUNLID, A., Microbial Ecology
TYLER, G., Plant Ecology
VON BARTH, U., Physics
VON SCHANTZ, T., Animal Ecology
WENNERSTRÖM, H., Physical Chemistry
WESTRÖM, B., Animal Physiology
WIDELL, S., Plant Physiology

Faculty of Technology:
ÅBERG, S., Mathematical Physics
ADLERCREUTZ, P., Biotechnology
ÅKESSON, B., Applied Nutrition
AKSELSSON, R., Ergonomics
ALAKÜLA, M., Industrial Electrical Engineering
ALDÉN, M., Laser-Based Combustion Diagnostics
ALY, G., Chemical Engineering
ANDERSON, J. B., Digital Communications
ANDERSSON, A., Chemical Engineering, especially Heterogenous Catalysis
ANDERSSON-ENGELS, S., Experimental Physics
ÅRZÉN, K.-E., Automatic Control
ASP, N.-G., Applied Nutrition
ÅSTRÖM, K. J., Mathematics
AXELSSON, A., Chemical Engineering
AXSÄTER, S., Production Management
BARUP, K., Architectural Conservation and Restoration
BENGTSSON, L., Water Resources Engineering
BENGTSSON, P.-E., Laser-Based Combustion Diagnostics
BENGTSSON, R., Mathematical Physics
BERGENSTÅHL, B., Food Technology

BERNDTSSON, R., Water Resources Engineering
BERNHARDSSON, B., Automatic Control
BJELM, L., Engineering Geology
BJÖRK, I., Applied Nutrition and Food Chemistry
BOHGARD, M., Ergonomics and Aerosol Technology
BOLMSJÖ, G., Robotics
BÖRJESSON, P.-O., Signal Processing
BORREBAECK, C., Immunotechnology
BOVIN, J.-O., Materials Chemistry and High-Resolution Electron Microscopy
BÜLOW, L., Biochemistry
DAHLBLOM, O., Structural Mechanics
DAMS, M., Computer Science
DEJMEK, P., Food Engineering
ECKHARDT, C.-C., Industrial Design
EDFORS, O., Radio Communications
EDSTRÖM, M., Architectural Conservation and Restoration
EKHOLM, A., Computer Aided Architectural Design
ELIASSON, A.-C., Cereal Technology
ELMROTH, A., Building Physics
ENGSTRÖM, L., Experimental Physics, especially Atomic Physics and Optics
FAGERLUND, G., Building Materials
FREDLUND, B., Building Science
FUCHS, L., Fluid Mechanics
GONZALEZ, A., Theoretical and Applied Aesthetics
GUSTAFSSON, P. J., Structural Mechanics
HAGANDER, P., Automatic Control
HÄGGLUND, T., Automatic Control
HAHN-HÄGERDAL, B., Applied Microbiology
HALLE, B., Physical Chemistry
HANSON, H., Water Resources Engineering
HANSSON, B., Construction Management
HELSING, J., Scientific Computing
HEYDEN, A., Mathematics
HOLMBERG, B., Traffic Planning
HOLMSTEDT, G., Fire Safety Engineering
HOLST, J., Mathematical Statistics
HOLST, O., Biotechnology
HOLST, U., Mathematical Statistics
HYDÉN, C., Traffic Engineering
JACOBSON, B., Machine Elements
JAMES, P., Proteomics
JARLSKOG, C., Theoretical Particle Physics
JENSEN, L. H., Building Services
JENSEN, U., Real Estate Management
JOHANNESSON, R., Information Theory
JOHANNESSON, T., Materials Engineering
JOHANSSON, B., Combustion Engines
JOHANSSON, G., Ergonomics and Aerosol Technology
JOHANSSON, R., Automatic Control
JOHANSSON, T., Information Theory
JOHANSSON, T.-B., Energy Systems Analysis
JÖNSON, G., Packaging Logistics
JÖNSSON, A. S., Chemical Engineering
JÖNSSON, B., Physical Chemistry
JÖNSSON, B., Rehabilitation Engineering
KARLSSON, A., Electromagnetic Theory
KARLSSON, H., Chemical Engineering, Process Chemistry and Catalysis
KARLSSON, J. M., Communication Systems
KRISTENSSON, G., Electromagnetic Theory
KRÖLL, S., Atomic Physics
KUCHINSKI, K., Computer Science
KÜLLER, R., Environmental Psychology
KÖRNER, U., Communication Systems
L'HUILLIER, A., Atomic Physics
LA COUR JANSEN, J., Water and Waste Water Engineering
LARSON, M., Water Resources Engineering
LARSSON, P.-O., Applied Biochemistry
LAURELL, T., Electrical Measurements
LIDÉN, G., Chemical Reaction Engineering
LIDGREN, K., Environmental Economics
LINDGREN, G., Mathematical Statistics
LINDSTRÖM, K., Electrical Measurements
LUNDHOLM, G., Combustion Engines
MAGNUSSON, B., Software Technology

MAGNUSSON, S.-E., Fire Safety Engineering
MALMQVIST, K., Nuclear Physics
MARTINSSON, B., Aerosol Physics
MATTIASSON, B., Biotechnology
MAURER, F., Polymer Technology
MOLIN, G., Food Hygiene
MOLISCH, A., Radio Communications
MONTELIUS, L., Solid State Physics
NILSSON, S., Technical Analysis Chemistry, especially Microanalytical Chemistry
NYMAN, M., Food Chemistry
ODENBRAND, I., Chemical Engineering, especially Environmental Catalysis
OLSSON, G., Industrial Automation
OMLING, P., Solid State Physics
PAULSSON, M., Dairy Technology
PERSSON, H. W., Electrical Measurements
PETERSON, H., Structural Mechanics
PHILIPSON, L., Computer Systems
PIÓRO, M., Communication Systems
PISTOL, M.-E., Solid State Physics
RÅDBERG, J., Urban Planning
RÅDSTRÖM, P., Applied Microbiology, especially Genetic Applications
RAGNARSSON, I., Mathematical Physics
RANTZER, A., Automatic Control
REUTERSWÄRD, L., Architecture and Development Studies
RISTINMAA, M., Solid Mechanics
RYCHLIK, I., Mathematical Statistics
RYDÉN, T., Mathematical Statistics
SAABYE OTTOSEN, N., Solid Mechanics
SAMUELSSON, L., Solid State Physics
SANDBERG, G., Structural Mechanics
SCHMELING, J., Mathematics
SEIFERT, W., Solid State Physics
SENTLER, L., Structural Engineering
SMEETS, B., Information Theory
SÖDERBERG, J., Construction Management
SÖRNMO, L., Biomedical Signals Processing
SPARR, G., Mathematics
STÅHL, A., Traffic Planning
STÅHL, J.-E., Production and Materials Engineering
STENSTRÖM, S., Chemical Engineering
STERNER, O., Bio-organic Chemistry
SUNDÉN, B., Heat Transfer
SVANBERG, S., Atomic Physics
SVERDRUP, H., Biogeochemistry
SÄRNER, E., Water and Environmental Engineering
THAM, K., Architecture
THELANDERSSON, S., Structural Engineering
THÖRNQVIST, L., Energy Economics and Planning
TORISSON, T., Thermal Power Engineering
TORNBERG, E., Food Engineering
TRÄGÅRDH, C., Food Engineering
TRÄGÅRDH, G., Food Engineering, especially Membrane Technology
WAHLUND, K.-G., Technical Analytical Chemistry
WAHSTRÖM, C.-G., Experimental Physics
WALLENBERG, R., Solid State Chemistry
WANDEL, S., Engineering Logistics
WARFVINGE, P., Biogeochemistry
WERNE, F., Building Functions Analysis
WHITLOW, H. J., Nuclear Physics, especially Ion Physics
WIMMERSTEDT, R., Chemical Engineering
WITTENMARK, B., Automatic Control
WOHLIN, C., Software Systems Engineering
YUAN, J., Circuit Design
ZACCHI, G., Chemical Engineering
ZIGANGIROW, K. S., Telecommunications Theory

MITTUNIVERSITETET
(Mid Sweden University)

SE-851 70 Sundsvall
Telephone: (771) 97-50-00
Fax: (771) 97-50-01
E-mail: info@miun.se

Internet: www.miun.se
Founded 1993 by merger of Univ. Colleges of Sundsvall/Härnösand and Östersund, merger of Sundsvall/Örnsköldsvik and Sundsvall Colleges of Health Sciences 1995, present status 2005
State control
Languages of instruction: English, Swedish
3 Campuses
Vice-Chancellor: ANDERS SÖDERHOLM
Pro-Vice-Chancellor: MATS TINNSTEN
Univ. Dir: YASMINE LINDSTRÖM
Library Dir: MORGAN PALMQVIST
Library: see under Libraries and Archives
Number of teachers: 554
Number of students: 20,000

DEANS

Faculty of Human Sciences: SUSANNA ÖHMAN
Faculty of Science, Technology and Media: HANS-ERIK NILSSON

ÖREBRO UNIVERSITET
(University of Örebro)

SE-701 82 Örebro
Telephone: (19) 30-30-00
Fax: (19) 33-02-38
E-mail: registrator@oru.se
Internet: www.oru.se
Founded 1967 as Högskolan i Örebro, present name and status 1999
State control
Academic year: September to June
Vice-Chancellor: JENS SCHOLLINS
Pro-Vice-Chancellor: GUNILLA LINDSTRÖM
Sec.: MARIANNE ALVELÖV
Univ. Dir: JOHAN LUNDBORG
Head Librarian: PER AHLIN
Library of 325,000 vols, 10,000 periodicals
Number of teachers: 764
Number of students: 16,820

DEANS

Faculty of Economics, Natural and Engineering Sciences: Prof. SUNE KARLSSON
Faculty of Educational Science: Prof. OWE LINDBERG
Faculty of Humanities and Social Sciences: Prof. ÅSA KROON LUNDELL
Faculty of Medicine and Health: Prof. ROBERT BRUMMER

STOCKHOLMS UNIVERSITET
(Stockholm University)

SE-106 91 Stockholm
Bloms hus, Universitetsvägen 16, Stockholm
Telephone: (8) 16-20-00
Fax: (8) 15-95-22
E-mail: press@su.se
Internet: www.su.se
Founded 1878, became State Univ. 1960
State control
Language of instruction: Swedish
Academic year: August to June
Rector: Prof. KÅRE BREMER
Pro-Rector: Prof. LENA GERHOLM
Vice-Rector: ANDERS GUSTAVSSON
Univ. Dir: JENNY GARDBRANT
Library: see Libraries and Archives
Number of teachers: 4,350
Number of students: 28,632
Publication: *Acta Universitatis Stockholmiensis*

DEANS

Faculty of Humanities: Prof. GUNNAR SVENSSON
Faculty of Law: Prof. SAID MAHMOUDI
Faculty of Science: Prof. STEFAN NORDLUND
Faculty of Social Sciences: Prof. GUDRUN DAHL

PROFESSORS

Faculty of Humanities:

ÅMARK, K., History
AILI, H., Latin
ALBERG-JENSEN, P., Slavic Languages
ANDRÉN, A., Archaeology
BARTNING, I., French
BECKER, K., Journalism
BERGLIE, Q., Religion
BERGMAN, B., Sign Language
BILY, M., Slavic Languages
BODIN, P.-A., Slavic Languages
BOLTON, K., English
CARLSHAMRE, S., Theoretical Philosophy
CULLHED, A., Literary History
DAHL, Ö., General Linguistics
DAHLBÄCK, G., History of the Middle Ages
EKECRANTZ, J., Media and Communication
ENGSTRAND, O., Phonetics
FALK, C., Swedish Language
FALK, J., Spanish
FANT, L., Ibero-Romance Languages
FAWKNER, H., English
FERM, O., History
FORSGREN, M., French
GERHOLM, L., Ethnology
GERÖ, E.-C., Greek
GLETE, J., History
HALL, T., Scandinavian and Comparative
  Art History
HEED, S.-A., Theatre Studies
HELANDER, K., Theatre Studies
HELLBERG, S., Scandinavian Languages
HVITFELT, H., Journalism
HYLTENSTAM, K., Bilingualism
INGDAHL KAZMIERA, A., Slavic Languages
IVERSEN, H., Latin
JARRICK, A., History
JOHANNESSON, N.-L., English
KANGERE, B., Baltic Languages
KÖLL, A. M., Baltic Studies
KOPTJEVSKAJA TAMM, M., General Linguistics
KOSKINEN, M., Film Studies
LACERDA, F., Phonetics
LANGE, S., Scandinavian Languages
LARSEN, H., Musicology
LEANDER-TOUATI, A.-M., Ancient Culture
LIDÉN, K., Archaeology
LILJA, S., History
LINDBERG-WADA, G., Japanology
LINDROTH, J., History of Athletics
LJUNGGREN, A., Russian
LODÉN, T., Language and Culture of China
LYSELL, R., History of Literature
MALMNÄS, P.-E., Theoretical Philosophy
MOLIN, K., History
MURDOCH, D., Theoretical Philosophy
NEEDHAM, P., Theoretical Philosophy
NEUGER, L., Polish
NIKOLAJEVA, M., History of Literature
NILSSON, L., History of Municipality
NYSTEDT, J., Italian
OETKE, C., Language and Culture of India
OHLSSON, R., Practical Philosophy
OLSSON, J., Film Studies
PAGIN, P., Theoretical Philosophy
RIAD, T., Scandinavian Languages
RÖHL, M., History of Literature
ROSÉN, S., Language and Culture of Korea
ROSENBERG, T., Gender Studies
ROSENDAHL, M., Latin American Studies
ROSSHOLM, G., History of Literature
ROSSHOLM LAGERLÖF, M., Art History
SAUTER, W., Theatre Studies
SCHEFFER, C., Ancient Culture
SJØVOLD, T., Historical Osteology
SMITH, W., Indology
SÖDERBERGH WIDDING, A., Film Studies
STRAND, H., Swedish
STROUD, C., Bilingualism
SVARTHOLM, K., Swedish as a Second Language for the Deaf
SVENSSON, G., Theoretical Philosophy
TÄNNSJÖ, T., Practical Philosophy

TEODOROWICZ-HELLMAN, E., Polish
TERSMAN, F., Practical Philosophy
TRAUNMÜLLER, H., Auditative Phonetics
VOLK, M., Computer Linguistics
WÅGHALL NIVRE, E., German
WANDE, E., Finnish
WARDINI, E., Arabic
WESTIN, B., History of Literature

Faculty of Law:

BJARUP, J., Jurisprudence
BOHLIN, A., Public Law
BRING, O., International Law
DIESEN, C., Procedure
EBBESSON, J., Environmental Law
EDELSTAM, H., Procedure
EKLUND, R., Private Law, Labour Law
HEUMAN, L., Procedure
KÄLLSTRÖM, K., Private Law
KLEINEMAN, J., Civil Law
LEIJONHUFVUD, M., Penal Law
LEVIN, M., Private Law
MAGNUSSON SJÖBERG, C., Law and Informatics
MAHMOUDI, S., International Law
MELZ, P., Financial Law
PEHRSON, L., Economics and Economic Law
PETERSON, C., Legal History
ROSÉN, J., Civil Law
SANDGREN, C., Civil Law
SANDSTRÖM, M., History of Law
SCHIRATSKY, D., Theoretical Philosophy
SEIPEL, P., Law and Informatics
SILFVERBERG, C., Financial Law
VOGEL, H.-H., Public Law
WAHL, N., European Law
WAHLGREN, P., Law and Informatics
WARNLING-NEREP, W., Public Law
WENNBERG, S., Penal Law

Faculty of Science

Biology Section:

BERGMAN, B., Physiological Botany
BORG, H., Aquatic Environmental Chemistry
BROMAN, D., Aquatic Ecotoxicology
CANNON, B., Animal Physiology
ELMGREN, R., Marine Ecology
ERIKSSON, O., Plant Ecology
FOLKE, C., Management of Natural Resources
GRÄSLUND, A., Biophysics
HAGGÅRD, E., Genetics
ISAKSSON, L., Microbiology
KAUTSKY, N., Marine Ecotoxicology
LINDBERG, U., Zoological Cell Biology
MÖLLER, G., Immunology
NÄSSEL, D., Functional Zoomorphology
RADESÄTER, T., Ethology
RANNUG, U., Toxicological Genetics
SJÖBERG, B.-M., Molecular Biology
WALLES, B., Morphological Botany
WIESLANDER, L., Molecular Genome Research
WIKLUND, C., Ecological Zoology
WULFF, F., Marine Systems Ecology

Chemistry Section:

ANDERSSON, B., Biochemistry
BÄCKVALL, J.-E., Organic Chemistry
BARTFAI, T., Neurochemistry
BERGMAN, Å., Environmental Chemistry
BRZEZINSKI, P., Biochemistry, esp. Molecular Energy Research
DEPIERRE, J., Biochemistry, especially Enzymological Toxicology
HULTH, P.-O., Experimental Physics
JANSSON, B., Chemical Environmental Analysis
JOSEFSSON, B., Analytical Chemistry
KOWALEWSKI, J., Physical Chemistry
LEVITT, M., Chemical Spectroscopy
LIDIN, S., Inorganic Chemistry
NELSON, D., Biochemistry
NORDLUND, P., Structural Biochemistry
NORRESTAM, R., Structural Chemistry

NYGREN, M., Material Chemistry, Electroceramics
ODHAM, G., Analytical Environmental Chemistry
SONNHAMMER, E., Bioinformatics
VON HEIJNE, G., Theoretical Chemistry

Earth and Environmental Studies Section:

BACKMAN, J., General and Historical Geology
HALLBERG, R., Microbial Chemistry
HOLMGREN, K., Physical Geography
IHSE, M., Ecological Geography
INGRI, J., Geochemistry and Petrology
KARLÉN, W., Physical Geography
LUNDÉN, B., Remote Sensing
RINGBERG, B., Quaternary Geology
ROSSWALL, T., Water and Environmental Studies
WASTENSON, L., Remote Sensing

Mathematics-Physics Section:

BARGHOLTZ, C., Nuclear Physics
BJÖRK, J.-E., Mathematics
BOHM, C., Technology of Physical Systems
EKEDAHL, T., Mathematics
FRANSSON, C., Astrophysics
HANSSON, H., Theoretical Physics
HANSSON, H.-C., Air Pollution
HOLMGREN, S.-O., High-Energy Physics
KÄLLEN, E., Dynamic Meteorology
LARSSON, M., Experimental Molecular Physics
MARTIN-LÖF, A., Actuarial Mathematics and Mathematical Statistics
OLOFSSON, H., Astronomy
PALMGREN, J., Biostatistics
PASSARE, M., Mathematics
RODHE, H., Chemical Meteorology
ROOS, J. E., Mathematics
SCHUCH, R., Atomic Physics
SIEGBAHN, P., Theoretical Physics
SUNDQVIST, H., Meteorology
SVENSSON, R., Astrophysics with Cosmology

Faculty of Social Sciences:

AGELL, J., Economics
AHRNE, G., Sociology
ALMKVIST, O., Psychology
ARAI, M., Economics
BACKENROTH-OHSAKO, G., Psychology
BERG, P.-O., Business Administration
BERGLUND, B., Perception and Psychophysics
BERGMARK, A., Social Work
BERNHARDT, E., Demography
BJÖRKUND, A., Economics
CALMFORS, L., International Economics
CHINAPAH, V., International Education
CHRISTIANSSON, S.-Å., Psychology
DAHL, G., Social Anthropology, Development Research
DAHLERUP, D., Political Science
DAUN, H., International Education
EDWARDS, M., Political Science
EKBERG, J., Economics
EKENBERG, L., Computer and Systems Science
ERIKSON, R., Sociology
FÄGERLIND, I., International and Comparative Education
FLAM, H., International Economics
FLYGHED, J., Criminology
FORSBERG, G., Human Geography
FRANK, O., Statistics
GOLDMANN, K., Political Science
GUILLET DE MONTHOUX, P., Business Administration
GUMMESSON, E., Business Administration
HANNERZ, U., Social Anthropology
HART, T., Pacific Asia Studies
HEDBERG, B., Business Administration
HEDSTRÖM, P., Sociology, Population Processes
HESSLE, S., Social Work
HOEM, J., Demography

HORN AF RANTZIEN, H., International Economics
JOHANSSON, G., Working Life Psychology
JONSSON, E., Business Administration, Administrative Economics
KORPI, W., Social Politics
KÜHLHORN, E., Sociological Alcoholic Research
LENNTORP, B., Human and Economic Geography
LUNDBERG, B., Information Administration
LUNDBERG, U., Human Biological Psychology
MONTGOMERY, H., Cognitive Psychology
NILSSON, L.-G., Psychology
NORSTRÖM, T., Sociology, Social Politics
NYSTEDT, L., Psychology, Social Perception
ÖST, L.-G., Clinical Psychology
OVARSELL, B., Education
PALME, J., Computer and Systems Sciences
PALME, M., Social Security
PERSSON, M., International Economics
PERSSON, T., International Economics
PREMFORS, R., Political Science
SAHLIN-ANDERSON, K., Public Organization
SARNECKI, J., Criminology
SIVEN, C.-H., Economics, especially Economic Politics
SKÖLDBERG, K., Business Administration
SÖDERBERG, J., Economic History
SPORRONG, U., Geography, especially Human Geography
SVEDBERG, P., Development Economics
SVENSON, O., Nuclear Power Safety (Psychology)
SVENSSON, L., International Economics
SWEDBERG, R., Economic Sociology
TÅHLIN, M., Sociology
TARSCHYS, D., Political Science, especially Planning and Administration
THAM, H., Criminology
THORBURN, D., Statistics
THORSLUND, M., Social Work
VÅGERÖ, D., Medical Sociology
WADENSJÖ, E., Employment Policy
WESTIN, C., Immigration Research
WIJKANDER, H., International Economics
WIKANDER, U., Economic History
WITTROCK, B., Political Science

SVERIGES LANTBRUKSUNIVERSITET (Swedish University of Agricultural Sciences)

POB 7070, SE-750 07 Uppsala
Telephone: (18) 67-10-00
Fax: (18) 67-20-00
E-mail: registrator@slu.se
Internet: www.slu.se
Founded 1977 by merger of fmr Lantbrukshögskolan, Skogshögskolan and Veterinärhögskolan
Academic year: September to May
Vice-Chancellor: LISA SENNERBY FORSSE
Pro-Vice-Chancellor: LENA ANDERSSON-EKLUND
Pro-Vice-Chancellor: JOHN SCHNUR
Pro-Vice-Chancellor: GÖRAN STÅHL
Chair.: Prof. LARS-ERIK EDQVIST
Univ. Dir: ULF HEYMAN
Chief Librarian: SNORRE RUFELT
Library: see under Libraries and Archives
Number of teachers: 500
Number of students: 3,793 full-time, 712 postgraduate

DEANS

Faculty of Forestry: TOMAS LUNDMARK
Faculty of Natural Resources and Agricultural Science: KRISTINA GLIMELIUS
Faculty of Veterinary Medicine and Animal Science: KERSTIN SVENNERSTEN SJAUNJA

PROFESSORS
(Some professors serve in more than 1 faculty)

Faculty of Forestry:
ÅGREN, G., Systems Ecology
ANDRÉN, H., Conservation Biology
ARNOLD, S. VON, Forest Cell Biology
BERGSTEN, U., Reforestation
BISHOP, K., Environmental Assessment
BORGEFORS, G., Remote Sensing and Image Analysis
CLARHOLM, M., Soil Ecology
DANELL, K., Wildlife Ecology
DANIEL, G., Wood Products
ELFVING, B., Forest Yield Research
ELOWSON, T., Wood Technology
ERICSSON, A., Forest Plant Physiology
ERIKSSON, L.-O., Aquaculture
ERIKSSON, L. O., Forest Planning
FINLAY, R., Forest Microbiology
GEMMEL, P., Forestry
GOBRAN, G., Ecology, Soil Science
GUSTAVSSON, L., Conservation Biology
HÄLLGREN, J.-E., Forest Plant Physiology
HANSSON, L., Population Ecology
HÅNELL, B., Silviculture
HÖGBERG, P., Soil Science
JEGLUM, J., Forest Peatland Science
JOHANSSON, M.-B., Forest Soil Science
JOHANSSON, T., Forest Management
JOHNSSON, R., Aquatic Ecology
KRISTRÖM, B., Natural Resources Economics
LÅNGSTROM, B., Forest Protection from Insects
LARSSON, S., Forest Entomology
LINDER, S., Forest Ecology
LINDGREN, D., Forest Genetics
LOHMANDER, P., Forest Management
LÖNNSTEDT, L., Business Economics
LUNDKVIST, H., Soil Ecology
LUNDQVIST, H., Fish Biology
MAGNHAGEN, C., Aquaculture
MORITZ, T., Forest Plant Physiology
NÄSHOLM, T., Forest Plant Physiology
NILSSON, M.-C., Forest Vegetation Ecology
NILSSON, P.-O., Energy System in Forestry
NILSSON, T., Ultrastructure and Disintegration of Wood
NILSSON, U., Reforestation
NYLINDER, M., Wood Measurement and Cross-Cutting
NYLUND, J.-E., Forest Microbiology
ODÉN, P. C., Forestry Seed Research
OLSSON, H., Remote Sensing applied to Forestry
OLSSON, M., Forest Soil Chemistry
PERSSON, H., Root Ecology
PERSSON, T., Biology of Forest Soils
RANNEBY, B., Forest Survey
ROSEN, K., Forest Soils
SALLNÄS, O., Forest Operations
SANDBERG, G., Morphogenesis of Trees
STÅHL, G., Forest Survey
STENLID, J., Pathology of Forest Trees
SUNDBERG, B., Forest Plant Physiology
VERWIJST, T., Forestry
WÄSTERLUND, I., Forestry Technology
WIBE, S., Forest Economics
WINGSLE, G., Forest Plant Physiology
ZACKRISSON, O., Forest Vegetation Ecology

Faculty of Natural Resources and Agriculture Science:
ÅMAN, P., Plant Products
ANDERSSON, G., Molecular Genetics
ANDERSSON, H., Agricultural Economics
ANDERSSON, I., Plant Biochemistry
ANDRÉN, O., Soil Biology and Agriculture
BENGTSSON, B., International Crop Production Science
BENGTSSON, J., Environmental Science and Conservation
BERGSTRÖM, L., Water Quality Management

BJÖRCK, L., Dairy Products Science
BJÖRNHAG, G., Animal Physiology
BOLIN, O., Economics of Agriculture, International Trade
BOTHMER, R. VON, Genetics and Breeding of Cultivated Plants
BRYNGELSSON, T., Molecular Plant Biology
BUCHT, E., Landscape Planning
BYLUND, A.-C., Meat Science
DANELL, B., Animal Breeding
DANELL, Ö., Reindeer Husbandry
EBBERSTEN, S., Organic Farming/Ecological Farming
EKBOM, B., Entomology
EKLUND, H., Structural Molecular Biology
EMMELIN, L., Environmental Impact Assessment
FLORGÅRD, C., Landscape Architecture
GEBRESENBET, G., Agricultural Engineering
GERHARDSON, B., Plant Pathology
GLIMELIUS, K., Genetics and Plant Breeding
GREN, J.-M., Natural Resource and Environmental Economics
GULLBERG, U., Plant Breeding
GUSTAFSON, A., Water Quality Management
GUSTAFSSON, L., Systems Analysis
GUSTAFSSON, M., Plant Disease Resistance
GUSTAFSSON, P., Landscape Architecture
GUSTAVSSON, R., Planting Design and Management
HANSSON, B. S., Plant Protection Sciences
HAVNEVIK, K., Rural Development
HUSS-DANELL, K., Crop Science
JÄGERSTAD, M., Food Chemistry
JANSSON, C., Molecular Cell Biology
JARVIS, N., Biogeophysics
JENSÉN, P., Horticultural Science
JILAR, T., Horticultural Building and Climate Technology
KENNE, L., Organic Chemistry
KIRCHMANN, H., Soil Fertility
KNIGHT, S., Biochemistry
LARSEN, R., Greenhouse Production, Horticultural Crops
LARSSON, L.-G., Molecular Genetics
LILJENSTRÖM, H., Biometry
LINDBERG, J.-E., Animal Nutrition and Management
LUNDQVIST, P., Work Science
LUNDSTRÖM, K., Meat Science
MÅRTENSSON, A., Soil Fertility
MEIJER, J., Molecular Cell Biology
MERKER, A., Plant Breeding
MOWBRAY, S., Biochemistry
MYRDAL, J., History of Agriculture
NILSSON, C., Building Science
NILSSON, I., Soil Chemistry and Pedology
NILSSON, J., Cooperation
NITSCH, U., Agricultural Communication
NORBERG, T., Inorganic Chemistry
NYBOM, H., Horticultural Genetics and Plant Breeding
NYBRANT, T., Agricultural Control Engineering
ÖBERG, K., Ergonomics
ÖHLMER, B., Agricultural Business Administration
OLOFSSON, C., Entrepreneurial Studies
OLSSON, K., Animal Physiology
OLWIG, K. R., Landscape Planning
PERSSON, I., Inorganic and Physical Chemistry
PETTERSSON, J., Applied Entomology
RABINOWICZ, E., Economic Analysis of Food and Agricultural Systems
RIDDERSTRÅLE, Y., Animal Physiology
RONNE, H., Molecular Genetics
ROSSWALL, T., Water and Environmental Studies
SÄLLVIK, K., Agricultural Building Functions Analysis
SCHNÜRER, J., Food Microbiology

SKÄRBÄCK, E., Comprehensive Landscape Planning
SORTE, G., Landscape Architecture
STYMNE, S., Plant Breeding, Biochemistry
TORSTENSSON, L., Soil Microbiology
UVNÄS-MOBERG, K., Animal Physiology
VALKONEN, J., Virology comprising Plant Viruses
VON ROSEN, D., Statistics
WELANDER, M., Horticultural Science
WIKTORSSON, H., Animal Nutrition and Management
YUEN, J., Plant Pathology

Faculty of Veterinary Medicine and Animal Science (tel. (18) 67-35-70):
ALENIUS, S., Medicine for Ruminants
ALGERS, B., Animal Hygiene
ALM, G., Immunology
ANDERSSON, L., Genetics
BELAK, S., Virology
BJÖRK, I., Medical and Physiological Chemistry
DANIELSSON-THAM, M.-L., Food Hygiene
DREVEMO, S., Anatomy and Histology
EINARSSON, S., Obstetrics and Gynaecology
ENGSTRÖM, W., Pathology
ERIKSSON, S., Medical and Physiological Chemistry
FELLSTRÖM, C., Swine Diseases
FORSBERG, M., Veterinary Diagnostic Endocrinology
GUSTAVSSON, I., Genetics
HEDHAMMER, H., Small Animal Medicine
JENSEN, P., Ethology
JENSEN-WAERN, M., Comparative Medicine
JONES, B., Clinical Chemistry
JÖNSSON, L., Pathology
KINDAHL, H., Obstetrics and Gynaecology
KVART, C., Clinical Physiology
LINDE-FORSBERG, C., Small Animal Reproduction
LINNÉ, T., Virology
LORD, P., Clinical Radiology
LUTHMAN, J., Medicine for Ruminants
MORENO-LOPEZ, J., Virology
NORRGREN, L., Aquatic Ecotoxicology
OSKARSSON, A., Food Hygiene
PLÖEN, L., Anatomy and Histology
PRINGLE, J., Equine Medicine
RODRÍGUEZ-MARTÍNEZ, H., Reproduction Biotechnology
SVENSSON, C., Production Diseases of Farm Animals
SVENSSON, S., Bacteriology
TJÄLVE, H., Toxicology
UGGLA, A., Parasitology

UMEÅ UNIVERSITET
(Umeå University)

SE-901 87 Umeå
Telephone: (90) 786-50-00
Fax: (90) 786-99-95
E-mail: umea.universitet@umu.se
Internet: www.umu.se

Founded 1965
State control
Languages of instruction: English, Swedish
Academic year: September to June

Vice-Chancellor: LENA GUSTAFSON
Pro-Vice-Chancellor: KJELL JONSSON
Deputy Vice-Chancellor for Education: Prof. ANDERS FÄLLSTRÖM
Deputy Vice-Chancellor for Research: MARIANNE SOMMARIN
Vice-Rector for Collaboration and Innovation: Prof. AGNETA MARELL
Univ. Dir: LARS LUSTIG
Head of Admin.: SIV OLOFSSON

Library: see under Libraries and Archives
Number of teachers: 2,125
Number of students: 36,081 (incl. 1,277 postgraduate)

DEANS
Faculty of Arts: Prof. PER-OLOF ERIXON
Faculty of Medicine: Prof. ANDERS BERGH
Faculty of Science and Technology: Prof. ÅSA RASMUSON-LESTANDER
Faculty of Social Sciences: DIETER MÜLLER

PROFESSORS
Faculty of Humanities (internet www.humfak.umu.se):
ANDERSSON, G., Science of Science
BANNERT, R., Phonetics
BRÄNDSTRÖM, A., Historical Demography
EDLUND, L.-E., Scandinavian Languages
EDMAN, M., Philosophy and Science of Humanities
EHN, B., Ethnology
ERICSSON, T., History
FORSGREN, K.-Å., German Language
GENRUP, K., Ethnology
GRANQVIST, R., English Language
GROUNDSTROEM, A., Finnish Language
HATJE, A.-K., History
HENE, B., Swedish Language
JOHANSSON, I., Theoretical Philosophy
JONSSON, K., History of Science and Ideas
LARSSON, T., Archaeology
LILIEQUIST, M., Ethnology
LINDBLAD, I.-B., Media and Communications
LINDSTRÖM, S., Theoretical Philosophy
LUNDGREN, B., Ethnology
PETTERSSON, A., Comparative Literature
POUSSA, P., English Language
RAMQVIST, P., Archaeology
RINGBY, P., Comparative Literature
SJÖBERG TAUSSI, M., History in a Social Historic Perspective
SKÖLD, P., History, Lapp Culture
SMEDS, K., Museology
SÖRLIN, S., Environmental History
SPOLANDER, R., History of Art
STRAARUP, J., Religious Studies
STRANGERT, E., Phonetics
SUNDIN, B., History of Science and Ideas
SVONNI, M., Lapp Language and Culture
WERBART, B., Archaeology
WIKSTRÖM, E., Fine Arts

Faculty of Medicine (tel. (90) 786-64-65; internet www.medfak.umu.se):
ADOLFSSON, R., Psychiatry
ÅHLSTRÖM, K., X-Ray and Diagnostics
ALFREDSSON, H., Sports Medicine
ALSTERMARK, B., Physiology, especially Neurology
ASIKAINEN, S., Oral Microbiology
BÄCKSTRÖM, T., Obstetrics and Gynaecology
BERGENHEIM, T., Neurosurgery
BERGH, A., Pathology
BERGSTRÖM, S., Microbiology
BERNSPÅNG, B., Occupational Therapy
BJÖRNSTIG, U., Surgery, especially Trauma and Civil Defence Medicine
BOMAN, K., Medicine
BORÉN, T., Medical Chemistry
BROSTRÖM, L.-Å., Orthopaedics
BUCHT, G., Geriatrics
DAHLQUIST, G., Paediatrics, especially Diabetes
DAHLQVIST, S., Rheumatology
DANIELSSON, Å., Gastroenterology
DIJKEN, J. VAN, Cariology
DOORN, J. VAN, Logopedics
EDLUND, H., Molecular Development Biology
EDLUND, T., Molecular Genetics
EGELRUD, T., Dermatology and Venereology
EMDIN, S., Surgery
ERIKSSON, A., Forensic Medicine
ERIKSSON, J., Medicine
ERIKSSON, P.-O., Clinical Oral Physiology
FÄLLMAN, M., Medical Microbiology
FISHER, A., Occupational Therapy

FORSGREN, L., Neurology
FOWLER, C., Pharmacology
GOTHEFORS, L., Paediatrics
GRANKVIST, K., Clinical Chemistry, especially Experimental Toxicology
GRÖNBERG, H., Oncology
GROTH, S., Clinical Physiology
GRUNDSTRÖM, T., Tumour Biology
GUNNE, J., Prosthetic Dentistry
GUSTAFSON, Y., Geriatric Medicine
HÄGGLÖF, B., Child and Youth Psychiatry
HALLMANS, G., Nutrition Research
HAMMARSTRÖM, A., Public Health (Gender Perspective)
HAMMARSTRÖM, M.-L., Immunology
HAMMARSTRÖM, S., Immunology
HENRIKSSON, R., Experimental Oncology
HERNELL, O., Paediatrics, especially Nutrition Research
HÖGBERG, U., Obstetrics and Gynaecology
HOLMBERG, D., Molecular Genetics
HULTMARK, D., Medical Molecular Biology
JACOBSSON, L., Psychiatry
JANLERT, U., Public Health
JÄRVHOLM, B., Occupational and Environmental Medicine
JOHANSSON, I., Cariology
JOHANSSON, R., Physiology
JOHANSSON, S., Physiology
KARLSSON, M., Medical Radiation Physics
KELLERTH, J.-O., Anatomy
KULLGREN, G., Psychiatric Epidemiology
LALOS, A., Public Health (Gender Perspective)
LARSÉN, K., Sports Medicine
LERNER, U., Oral Cell Biology
LIBELIUS, R., Clinical Neurophysiology
LINDHOLM, L., Family Medicine
LINDSTRÖM, P., Histology and Cell Biology
LJUNGBERG, B., Urology
LORENTZON, R., Sports Medicine
LUNDGREN, E., Applied Cell Biology
LUNDGREN, S., Oral and Maxillofacial Surgery
LUNDMAN, B., Nursing
MARKLUND, S., Clinical Chemistry
MOLIN, M., Prosthetic Dentistry
NAREDI, P., Surgery
NILSSON, E., Surgery
NORBERG, A., Advanced Nursing
NORDBERG, G., Health and Hygiene
NORGREN, M., Biomedical Laboratory Sciences
NY, T., Medical and Physiological Chemistry
OLIVECRONA, G., Medical Chemistry
OLOFSSON, B.-O., Medicine
OLSSON, K., Physiology
OLSSON, T., Medicine
ROOS, G., Pathology
SANDMAN, P.-O., Advanced Nursing
SANDSTRÖM, T., Pulmonary Medicine
SCHLEUCHER, J., Medical Biophysics
SEHLIN, J., Histology and Cell Biology
SELSTAM, G., Physiology
SJÖLUND, B. H., Rehabilitation Medicine
SJÖSTEDT, A., Clinical Bacteriology
STENLING, R., Pathology
STIGBRAND, T., Immunochemistry
STRÖMBERG, I., Histology and Cell Biology
STRÖMBERG, N., Cardiology
SUNDELIN, G., Advanced Nursing
SUNDVIST, K. G., Clinical Immunology
SVENSSON, O., Orthopaedics
TÄLJEDAL, I.-B., Histology
TÄRNVIK, A., Infectious Diseases
THELANDER, L., Medical and Physiological Chemistry
THORNELL, L.-E., Anatomy
TWETMAN, S., Paedodontics
UHLIN, B. E., Medical Microbiology
WACHTMEISTER, L., Ophthalmology
WADELL, G., Virology
WALDENSTRÖM, A., Cardiology
WALL, S., Epidemiology and Public Health
WESTER, P., Medicine

WESTMAN, G., Family Medicine
WIBERG, M., Anatomy
WIDMARK, A., Oncology
WINKVIST, A., Epidemiology

Faculty of Science and Technology (fax (90) 786-97-96; e-mail teknat@adm.umu.se; internet www.teknat.umu.se):

ANDERSSON, B., Environmental Chemistry
AVONDOGLIO, P., Industrial Design
AXNER, O., Physics
BÅMSTEDT, U., Marine Sciences
BJÖRK, G., Microbiology
BONDESSON, L., Mathematical Statistics
BRODIN, G., Physics
BYSTRÖM, A., Microbiology
CEDERGREN, A., Analytical Chemistry
CEGRELL, U., Mathematics (Complete Analysis)
EDLUND, U., Organic Chemistry
EKLUND, P., Computer Science
ERICSON, L., Plant Ecology
ERIKSSON, E. S., Structural Biology
FRECH, W., Analytical Chemistry
GARDESTRÖM, P., Plant Physiology
GILLBRO, T., Biophysical Chemistry
GUSTAFSSON, P., Plant Molecular Biology
HÄGGKVIST, R., Discrete Mathematics
HEBY, O., Cellular and Developmental Biology
IRGUM, K., Analytical Chemistry
JANLERT, L.-E., Computing Science
JANSSON, M., Physical Geography
JANSSON, S., Plant Biology
JOHANSSON, L., Physical Chemistry
JOHNELS, D., Organic Chemistry
KÅGSTRÖM, B., Numerical Analysis and Parallel Computing
KASTBERG, A., Experimental Optical Physics
KIHLBERG, J., Organic Chemistry
KIRKWOOD, S., Atmospheric Physics
KLECZKOWSKI, L., Plant Physiology
KULLMAN, L., Physical Geography
LARSON, J., Applied Mathematics
LARSSON, J., Plasma Physics
LESTANDER, Å., Genetics
LI, H., Signal Processing
LINDAHL, O., Medical Technology
LINDBLOM, G., Physical Chemistry
LUNDIN, R., Space Physics
MALMQVIST, B., Ecology
MARKLUND, S., Environmental Chemistry
MINNHAGEN, P., Theoretical Physics
NILSSON, C., Landscape Ecology, especially Running Waters
NORDIN, A., Energy Technology
ÖHMAN, L.-O., Inorganic Chemistry
OKSANEN, L., Ecology
OLIVEBERG, M., Biochemistry
ÖQUIST, G., Plant Physiology
OTTO, CH., Animal Ecology
PALMGREN, B., Design
PERSSON, L., Aquatic Ecology
PERSSON, P., Chemistry, Molecular Chemistry
PETTERSSON, L., Inorganic Chemistry
RAMMER, J., Condensed Matter Theory
RENBERG, I., Ecological and Environmental Impact Assessment
RÖNNMARK, K., Theoretical Space Physics
SAMUELSSON, G., Plant Physiology
SANDAHL, I., Space Physics
SAURA, A., Genetics
SCHRÖDER, W., Biochemistry
SELLSTEDT, A., Plant Physiology
SHELANKOV, A., Condensed Matter Physics
SHINGLER, V., Microbiology
SHIRIAEV, A., Automatic Control Engineering
SJÖBERG, S., Inorganic Chemistry
SJÖSTRÖM, M., Inorganic Chemistry
STENFLO, L., Theoretical Plasma Physics
STOTT, M., Interaction Design
SUNDQVIST, B., Condensed Matter Physics
TYSKLIND, M., Environmental Chemistry

WEDIN, P.-Å., Numerical Analysis
WESTLUND, P.-O., Theoretical Chemistry
WOLD, S., Chemometrics
WOLF-WATZ, H., Applied Molecular Biology

Faculty of Social Sciences (fax (90) 786-66-75; internet www.umu.se/samfak):

ÅBERG, R., Sociology
ARMELIUS, B.-Å., Clinical Psychology
ARMELIUS, K., Clinical Psychology
ARONSSON, T., Environmental and Natural Resources Economics
BACKMAN, J., Pedagogics and Educational Psychology
BENGTSSON, M., Business Administration and Economics
BOTER, H., Business Administration and Economics
BRÄNNÄS, K., Econometrics
BRÄNNLUND, R., Economics
BROSTRÖM, G., Statistics
DAHLGREN, L., Medical Sociology
ECKERBERG, K., Political Science
EDSTRÖM, Ö., Legal Science
FRANKE, S., Pedagogics
GUNNARSSON, Å, Legal Science
GUSTAFSSON, G., Political Science
HALLERÖD, B., Sociology
HALLSTRÖM, P., Legal Science
HAMILTON, D., Pedagogics
HENRIKSSON, W., Pedagogics
HOLM, E., Social and Economic Geography, especially Social Community Planning and Financial Control
JOHANSSON, G., Nutritional Studies
JOHANSSON, M., Pedagogics (Sports)
JOHANSSON, O., Political Science
JOHANSSON, S., Social Work
JOHANSSON, U., Pedagogics
KAPTELININ, V., Informatics
LINDQVIST, R., Social Work
LÖFGREN, K.-G., Economics, especially Evaluating Labour Market Research
MALMBERG, G., Social and Economic Geography
MÄNTYLÄ, T., Psychology (Cognitive Science)
MOLANDER, B., Psychology
NIEMI-KIESILÄINEN, J., Legal Science
NILSSON, I., Pedagogics
NYBERG, L., Psychology
NYGREN, L., Social Work
PERSSON, O., Library and Information Science
RÄTHZEL, N., Sociology
SKÖG, L. A., Business Administration
SÖDERHOLM, A., Informatics
STAGE, C., Pedagogics
STOLTERMAN, E., Informatics
SUNDBOM, E., Clinical Psychology
SVALLFORS, S., Sociology
TESAR, G., Business Administration and Economics (Marketing and International Business Administration)
WATERWORTH, J., Informatics
WIBERG, U., Economic Geography, especially the Structural Issues of Sparsely Populated Areas

UPPSALA UNIVERSITET
(Uppsala University)

POB 256, SE-751 05 Uppsala
Telephone: (18) 471-00-00
Fax: (18) 471-20-00
E-mail: info@uadm.uu.se
Internet: www.uu.se

Founded 1477
Academic year: September to June

Vice-Chancellor: Prof. ANDERS HALLBERG
Deputy Vice-Chancellor: KERSTIN SAHLIN
Vice-Rector for Humanities and Social Sciences: MARGARETHA FAHLGREN
Vice-Rector for Medicine and Pharmacy: BRITT SKOGSEID

Vice-Rector for Science and Technology: JOSEPH NORDGREN
Univ. Dir: ANN FUST
Chief Librarian: ULF GÖRANSON
Library: see Libraries and Archives
Number of teachers: 3,600
Number of students: 20,000

Publications: *Acta Universitatis Upsaliensis*, *Multiethnica*, *Universen* (12 a year), *Uppsala Accelerator News*

DEANS

Faculty of Education: Prof. CAROLINE LIBERG
Faculty of History and Philosophy: Prof. JAN LINDEGREN
Faculty of Languages: Prof. BJÖRN MELANDER
Faculty of Law: Prof. TORBJÖRN ANDERSSON
Faculty of Medicine: Prof. GÖRAN MAGNUSSON
Faculty of Pharmacy: Prof. FRED NYBERG
Faculty of Science and Technology: Prof. JOSEPH NORDGREN
Faculty of Social Sciences: Prof. ANDERS MALMBERG
Faculty of Theology: Prof. MIKAEL STENMARK

PROFESSORS

Faculty of History and Philosophy
    I. Historical-Philosophical Division:
ÅHLBERG, L.-O., Aesthetics and Cultural Studies
ALANEN, L., History of Philosophy
ARVASTSON, G., Ethnology
BEACH, H., Cultural Anthropology
BURMAN, L., Rhetoric
DANIELSSON, S. O., Practical Philosophy
FAHLGREN, M., Literature
FRÄNGSMYR, T., History of Science
HERSCHEND, F., Archaeology
IVARSDOTTER, A., Musicology
JANSSON, T., History
JOHANNISSON, K. M., History of Science and Ideas
KJELLBERG, E., Musicology
KYHLBERG, O., Archaeology
LANDGREN, B., Literature
LINDEGREN, J., History
PARKMAN, S., Musicology
PETTERSSON, T., Literature
RUNBLOM, H., History
SANTILLO FRIZELL, B., Archaeology
SINCLAIR, P., African Archaeology
SKUNCKE, M.-C., Literature
SÖDERLIND, S., Art History
SVEDJEDAL, J. O., Literature
TROY, L., Archaeology
    II. Linguistic Division:
EKLUND, S. I., Latin
FRYCKSTEDT, M., English Literature
GREN-EKLUND, G., Indology
GUSTAVSSON, S. R., Slavic Languages
HELANDER, H. O., Latin
ISAKSSON, B., Semitic Languages
JONASSON, K., French Language
KINDSTRAND, J. F., Greek Language and Literature
KROHN, D., German Language
KRONNING, H., French Language
KYTÖ, M., English Language
LARSSON, L.-G., Finno-Ugric Languages
LUNDÉN, R., American Literature
MAIER, I., Russian Language
MELANDER, B., Swedish Language
MULLER, G., German Language and Literature
NORDBERG, B., Sociolinguistics
PACKALEN, A. M., Polish Language
PALM MEISTER, C., German Language
PEDERSEN, O., Assyriology
PETERSON, L., Scandinavian Languages
RAAG, R., Finno-Ugric Languages
ROSENQVIST, J.-O., Byzantine Studies
SÄGVALL-HEIN, A., Computational Linguistics
STRANDBERG, S., Scandinavian Onomastics

SUNDELL, L.-G., French Language
SVANE, B., French Literature
THELANDER, M., Swedish Language
UTAS, B., Iranian Studies
VIBERG, A, Linguistics
WILLIAMS, H., Swedish Language
WOLLIN, L., Scandinavian Languages

Faculty of Law:
ANDERSSON, H., Private Law
ANDERSSON, T., Private Law
CAMERON, I., International Law
ERIKSSON, M., International Law
FRÄNDBERG, Å., History of Law
JÄNTERÄ-JAREBORG, M., International Law
JAREBORG, N., Penal Law
LEHRBERG, B., Penal Law
LINDBLOM, P. H., Judicial Procedure
LINDELL, B., Judicial Procedure
LYSEN, G., International Law
MARCUSSON, L. M., Administrative Law
MATTSSON, N. G., Taxation
MÖLLER, M., Private Law
NYGREN, R. O., History of Law
ÖSTERDAHL, I., International Law
SALDEEN, A., Private Law
THORELL, P. H., Business Law
WESTERLUND, S., Environmental Law

Faculty of Medicine:
ÅKERMAN, K., Cell Physiology
ÅKERSTRÖM, G., Endocrinological Surgery
AKUSJÄRVI, G., Microbiology
ALDSKOGIUS, H., Medical Structural Biology
ALM, A., Ophthalmology
ANDERSSON, A. E. V., Diabetes Research
ANDERSSON, J. H., Immunology
ANNIKO, M., Otorhinolaryngology
AQUILONIUS, S.-M., Neurology
ARNETZ, B., Social Medicine
AXELSSON, O. L., Women's and Children's Health
BERGQVIST, D., Vascular Surgery
BERNE, CH., Medicine
BLOMBERG, J., Clinical Virology
BOBERG, M., Social Medicine
BOMAN, G., Pulmonary Medicine
CARLSSON, J., Biomedical Radiation Science
CLAESSON-WELSH, L., Genetics and Pathology
DAHL, M.-L., Medicine
DAHL, N., Clinical Genetics
DUMANSKI, J., Genetics and Pathology
EBENDAL, T., Developmental Biology
EDLING, C., Occupational Medicine
ERIKSSON, U., Histology
FLEMSTRÖM, G. F., Physiology
FRIES, E., Cell Biology
FRIMAN, G., Infectious Diseases
GEBRE-MEDHIN, M., International Child Care
GERDIN, B., Intensive and Burns Care
GLIMELIUS, B., Oncology
GUSTAFSSON, J., Women's and Children's Health
GYLFE, E., Secretion Research
GYLLENSTEN, U., Medical Molecular Genetics
HAGLUND, U., Surgery
HÄLLGREN, R., Medicine
HAU, J., Comparative Medicine
HEDENSTIERNA, G., Medicine
HEYMAN, B., Genetics and Pathology
HILLERED, L., Clinical Neurochemistry
HOLMBERG, L., Surgery
JOHANSSON, S., Cell Biology
KÄMPE, O., Molecular Medicine
KARLSSON, A., Experimental Endocrinology
KJELLEN, L., Medical Biochemistry and Microbiology
LANDEGREN, U., Molecular Medicine
LARHAMMAR, D. S., Molecular Cell Biology
LARSSON, R., Medicine
LINDAHL, U., Medical Chemistry
LINDGREN, P. G., X-ray Diagnosis

LINDHOLM, D., Neurobiology
LINDMARK, G., International Mother and Child Health
LITHELL, H., Geriatrics
LJUNGHALL, S., Medicine
LÖNNERHOLM, G., Women's and Children's Health
LUNDQVIST, H., Oncology
MAGNUSSON, A., Oncology
MAGNUSSON, G., Molecular Virology
MÅRDH, P.-A., Medicine
NILSSON, K., Cell Pathology
NILSSON, O., Orthopaedics
NISTÉR, M., Experimental Pathology
NORLÉN, B. J., Urology
ÖBERG, K., Oncological Endocrinology
ORELAND, L. A. M., Pharmacology
PÅHLMAN, L., Surgery
PERSSON, E., Physiology
PERSSON, L., Physiology
PETTERSSON, U. G., Medical Genetics
RAININKO, R., Neuroradiology
RASK, L., Medical Biochemistry
RASK-ANDERSEN, H., Surgery
RASTAD, J., Surgery
RAUSCHNING, W., Surgery
ROOMANS, G. M., Medical Ultrastructure
ROSENQVIST, U., Health Services Research
RUBIN, K., Connective Tissue Biochemistry
SALDEEN, T., Forensic Medicine
SANDLER, S., Medical Cell Biology
SCHWARTZ, S., Medical Biochemistry and Microbiology
SEDIN, G., Perinatal Medicine
SIEGBAHN, A., Medicine
SJÖDÉN, P.-O., Nursing and Health Care
SJÖQVIST, M. I. J., Physiology
STJERNSCHANTZ, J., Pharmacology
SVÄRDSUDD, K., Family Medicine
SYVÄNEN, A.-C., Medicine
TOREBJÖRK, E., Pain Research
TÖTTERMAN, T., Clinical Immunology
TURESSON, I., Oncology
TUVEMO, T., Paediatrics
ULMSTEN, U., Obstetrics and Gynaecology
VAHLQUIST, A., Dermatology and Venereology
VENGE, P., Clinical Chemistry
VON KNORRING, A.-L., Child Psychiatry
VON KNORRING, L., Psychiatry
WADELIUS, C., Genetics and Pathology
WALLENTIN, L., Cardiology
WESTERMARK, B. A., Tumour Biology
WESTERMARK, P., Pathology
WESTMAN, J. O., Anatomy
WIESEL, F.-A., Psychiatry
WIKLUND, L., Anaesthesiology

Faculty of Pharmacy:
ALDERBORN, G., Pharmacy
ARTURSSON, P., Pharmacy
BOHLIN, L., Pharmacognosy
BRITTEBO, E. B., Toxicology
DENCKER, L., Toxicology
ENGSTRÖM, S. O. A., Pharmacy
HALLBERG, A., Organic Pharmaceutical Chemistry
HAMMARLUND-UDENAES, M., Pharmacokinetics
ISACSON, D., Pharmacy
KARLSSON, M., Pharmacokinetics
LANG, M., Biochemistry
LENNERNÄS, H., Pharmacy
NYBERG, F., Pharmacological and Biological Research on Drug Dependence
NYSTRÖM, L.-CHR., Pharmacy
OLIW, E., Pharmacological and Biological Research on Drug Dependence
PETTERSSON, C., Analytical Pharmaceutical Chemistry
WESTERLUND, D., Analytical Pharmaceutical Chemistry
WIKBERG, J., Pharmacological and Biological Research on Drug Dependence
WIKVALL, K., Biochemistry

Faculty of Science and Technology:
ÅGREN, J., Ecological Botany
AHLÉN, A., Signal Processing
ALEKLETT, K., Nuclear Physics
ALEXEEV, A., Theoretical Physics
ALMGREN, M., Biochemistry
ANDERSSON, A., Computer Science
ANDERSSON, P., Organic Chemistry
ANDERSSON, S., Evolutionary Biology
ANNERSTEN, H. S., Mineral Chemistry and Petrology
ÅQVIST, J., Evolutionary Biology
ARNESEN, A., Physics
BADELEK, B., Experimental Physics
BENGTSSON, E., Computerized Image Analysis
BENNETT, K. D., Quaternary Geology
BERG, O., Molecular Evolution
BERG, S., Solid State Electronics
BERGER, R., Inorganic Chemistry
BERGLUND, A., Animal Ecology
BERGSTRÖM, Y., Materials Science
BJÖRKLUND, M., Animal Ecology
BOHMAN, O., Organic Chemistry
BOTNER, O., High Energy Physics
BRÄNDAS, E., Quantum Chemistry
BRANDT, I., Ecotoxicology
BRANDT ANDERSSON, Y., Inorganic Chemistry
BREMER, B., Systematic Botany
BREMER, K., Systematic Botany
BRUNSTRÖM, B. O., Ecotoxicology
CARLSSON, B., Systems and Control
CARLSSON, J.-O., Inorganic Chemistry
CHATTOPADHYAYA, J., Bio-organic Chemistry
COORAY, V., Electricity and Lightning
DAHLGREN CALDWELL, K., Surface Biotechnology
DANIELSSON, U., Theoretical Physics
EDWARDS, K., Physical Chemistry
EHRENBERG, M., Molecular Biology with Kinetics
EKELÖF, T., Experimental Elementary Particle Physics
EKMAN, J., Population Biology
ELLEGREN, H., Evolutionary Biology
ENGMAN, L., Organic Chemistry
ENGSTRÖM, P., Physiological Botany
ERICSSON, T., Materials Physics
ERIKSSON, O., Condensed Matter Physics
FÄLDT, G. L., Theoretical Physics
FROELICH, P., Quantum Chemistry
GEE, D. G., Orogenic Dynamics
GELIUS, U., Physics
GESTBLOM, B., Physics
GOSCINSKI, O., Quantum Chemistry
GRANQVIST, C.-G., Solid State Physics
GUNNINGBERG, P., Computer Communication
GUSTAFSSON, B., Numerical Analysis
GUSTAFSSON, B., Theoretical Astrophysics
GUSTAFSSON, L., Animal Ecology
GUT, A., Mathematical Statistics
HAGERSTEN, E., Computer Architecture
HAJDU, J., Biochemistry
HÅKANSSON, L., Sedimentology
HÅKANSSON, P., Ion Physics
HALLDIN, S., Hydrology
HALLGREN, A., Experimental Physics
HEJHAL, D. A., Mathematics
HELLMAN, L., Molecular and Comparative Immunology
HERMANSSON, K. G., Inorganic Chemistry
HILBORN, J., Polymer Chemistry
HÖGLUND, J., Population Biology
HOGMARK, S., Materials Science
HÖISTAD, B., Nuclear Physics
HOLMER, L., Historical Geology and Palaeontology
HUGHES, D., Evolutionary Biology
INGELMANN, G., High Energy Physics
ISRAELSSON, S. O., Meteorology
JACOBSON, S., Materials Science
JANSON, S., Mathematics

JANSSON, U., Inorganic Chemistry
JOHANSSON, B., Condensed Matter Theory
JOHANSSON, S., Materials Science
JOHANSSON, T., Nuclear Physics
JONES, A., Structural Molecular Biology
JONSSON, B., Computer Systems
JUHL-JÖRICKE, B., Mathematics
KAISER, S. G., Mathematics
KÄLLNE, J., Neutron Physics
KARLSSON, L., Experimental Physics
KIRSEBOM, L., Evolutionary Biology
KISELMAN, C. O., Mathematics
KOLSTRUP, E., Physical Geography
LÅNGSTROM, B., Radiopharmaceutical Organic Chemistry
LANSHAMMER, H., Systems and Control
LEIJON, M., Electricity
LIBERMAN, M., Theoretical Statistical Physics
LILJAS, L., Evolutionary Biology
LINDBLAD, P., Evolutionary Biology
LINDER, C., Physical Didactics
LINDGREN, J. B. R., Inorganic Chemistry
LÖTSTEDT, P., Numerical Analysis
LUNDAHL, P., Biochemistry
LUNDBERG, A., Evolutionary Biology
LUNDBERG, B., Solid Mechanics
LUNELL, S. G., Applied Quantum Chemistry
MANNERVIK, B., Biochemistry
MARKIDES, K., Analytical Chemistry
MÅRTENSSON, N., Physics of Metals and Metal Surfaces
MATTSSON, O. L., Organic Chemistry
McGREEVY, R. L., Neutron Research
MILBRINK, G., Animal Ecology
MOLLER, F., Computing Science
NIEMI, A., Theoretical Physics
NIKLASSON, G., Materials Science and Solar Energy
NILSSON, A., Chemical Physics
NILSSON, A., Systematic Botany
NORDBLAD, P., Solid State Physics
NORDGREN, J., Soft X-ray Physics
NYHOLM, L., Analytical Chemistry
OHLSSON, R., Developmental Zoology
OLSSON, E., Experimental Physics
PAMILO, P., Conservation Biology
PAROSH, A., Computer Systems
PAVLENKO, V. P., Astronomy
PEDERSEN, L. B., Solid Earth Physics
PEEL, J. S., Historical Geology and Palaeontology
PETTERSSON, K. I., Evolutionary Biology
PILSTRÖM, L. H., Immunology
PISKOUNOV, N., Astronomy
POSSNERT, G., Accelerator Mass Spectrometry
RIBBING, C.-G., Solid State Physics
RICKMAN, H., Astronomy
ROBERTS, R., Solid Earth Physics
RODHE, A., Hydrology
RONQUIST, F., Systematic Zoology
ROOS, A., Solid State Physics
RYDIN, H., Plant Ecology
SAXENA, S., Theoretical Geochemistry
SCHWEITZ, J.-A., Materials Science
SIEGBAHN, H., Atomic and Molecular Physics
SJÖBERG, S., Organic Chemistry
SKÖLD, K., Neutron Research
SMEDMAN, A.-S., Meteorology
SÖDERHÄLL, K. T., Physiological Mycology
SÖDERSTRÖM, T., Automatic Control
STERNAD, M., Signals and Systems
STOICA, P., Systems Modelling
STOLTENBERG-HANSEN, V., Logic of Mathematics
STRÖMQUIST, L., Applied Environmental Impact Analysis
SUNDQVIST, B. U. R., Ion Physics
SVEDLINDH, P., Solid State Physics
SVENSSON, B. W., Animal Ecology
SVENSSON, S., Physics
TALBOT, C. J., Geodynamics and Tectonics
TAPIA-OLIVARES, O., Physical Chemistry

TÄRNLUND, S. A., Computer Science
TEGELSTRÖM, H., Conservation Biology and Genetics
TEGENFELT, J. S., Inorganic Chemistry
THOMAS, J. O., Solid State Electro-chemistry
THOTTAPPILLIL, R., Electricity
THULIN, M., Systematic Botany
THUNE, M., Scientific Computing
TIBELL, L. B., Systematic Botany
TINTAREV, K., Mathematics
TOTTMAR, O., Comparative Physiology
TRANVIK, L., Limnology
VIRO, O., Mathematics
VIRTANEN, A., Molecular Cell Biology
WAGNER, G., Microbiology
WAHLBERG, C., Astronomy
WANG, Y., Computer Systems
WÄPPLING, R., Physics
ZILITINKEVICH, S., Meteorology

Faculty of Social Sciences:
AGELL, J., Economics
ANDERSSON, R. K. G., Housing and Urban Research
BÄCK, L., Urban Geography
BÄCKMAN, L., Cognitive Psychology
BLOMQUIST, S., Local Public Economics
BOHLIN, G., Developmental Psychology
BORGEGÅRD, L.-E., Urban Geography
BÖRJESSON, E. A., Psychology
BROADY, D., Education
BURNS, T., Sociology
CARLSNAES, W., Political Science
CHRISTOFFERSSON, A. L., Statistics
DIMBERG, U., Psychology
EDIN, P.-A., Labour Market Relations
EKEHAMMAR, B., Psychology
ENGWALL, L., Business Studies
EYERMAN, R., Sociology
FOGELKLOU, A., East European Studies
FORSGREN, M. O., International Business Studies
FREDRIKSON, M., Clinical Psychology
GERNER, K., East European Studies
GOTTFRIES, N., Economics
GUSTAFSSON, C., Education
HADENIUS, A., Political Science
HAGEKULL, B., Developmental Psychology
HÅKANSSON, K. G., Sociology
HALLEN, L., Business Studies
HAMFELT, A., Computer Science
HAMMARSTRÖM, G., Sociology
HANSSON, Å., Computer Science
HEDLUND, S., East European Studies
HEDMAN, L., Media and Communication
HERMANSSON, B. J., Political Science
HOLMLUND, B., Economics
HOPPE, G., Economic Geography
ISACSON, M., Economic History
KEMENY, P. J., Urban Sociology
KLEVMARKEN, A., Econometrics
LEWIN, L., Political Science
LINDBLAD, S., Education
LINDH, T., Economics
LUNDGREN, E., Sociology
LUNDGREN, U. P., Education
MAGNUSSON, L., Economic History
MALMBERG, A., Economic Geography
MELIN, L. G., Clinical Psychology
ÖBERG, S., Social and Economic Geography
OHLSSON, H., Economics
PETERSSOHN, E., Business Administration
RIIS, U., Education
RISCH, T., Computer Science
SAHLIN-ANDERSSON, K., Business Studies
SÖDER, M., Sociology
SÖDERSTEN, J., Economics
SOMMESTAD, L., Economic History
TORNSTAM, L., Sociology
TURNER, B., Housing Economics
VEDUNG, E., Housing Policy
VON HOFSTEN, C., Perceptional Psychology
WALLENSTEEN, P. N., Peace and Conflict
WIGREN, R., Economics

WITTROCK, B., Advanced Study in the Social Sciences
Faculty of Theology:
BÄCKSTRÖM, A., Sociology of Religion
BEXELL, O., Ecclesiology
BRÅKENHIELM, C.-R., Studies of Faiths and Ideologies
BRODD, S.-E., Studies of Churches and Religious Denominations
DE MARINIES, VALERIE, Psychology of Religion
FRANZÉN, R., Church History
GRENHOLM, C.-H., Ethics
HERRMANN, E., Philosophy of Religions
HULTGÅRD, A., History of Religions
NORIN, S., Old Testament Exegesis
PETTERSSON, T., Sociology of Religion
SCHALK, P., History of Religions
SYREENI, K., New Testament Exegesis
WIKSTRÖM, O., Psychology of Religion

University Colleges

Ersta Sköndal Högskola (Ersta Sköndal University College): Stigbergsgatan 30, POB 11189, SE-100 61 Stockholm; tel. (8) 55-50-50; fax (8) 550-050-60; e-mail info@esh.se; internet www.esh.se; f. 1998; studies and research in social work, nursing and health care, psychotherapy, theology and church music; 1,100 students; Rector JAN-HÅKAN HANSSON; Sec. ANN-MARGRET BERGMAN.

Högskola Malmö (Malmö University College): SE-205 06 Malmö; tel. (40) 665-70-00; fax (40) 665-73-05; e-mail intsek@mah.se; internet www.mah.se; f. 1998; faculties of health and society and odontology; schools of arts and communication, international migration and ethnic relations, technology, and culture and society; 1,439 teachers; 25,000 students (full-time and part-time); Vice-Chancellor LENNART OLAUSSON.

Högskolan Dalarna (Dalarna University College): SE-791 88 Falun; tel. (23) 77-80-00; fax (23) 77-80-80; e-mail ioffice@du.se; internet www.du.se; f. 1977; schools of health and social sciences, humanities and media studies, technology and business studies; 666 teachers; 7,380 students; Chair. LARS-OVE STAFF; Vice-Chancellor MARITA HILLIGES; Library Dir MARGARETA MALMGREN.

Högskolan Halmstad (Halmstad University College): POB 823, SE-301 18 Halmstad; tel. (35) 16-71-00; fax (35) 14-85-33; e-mail registrator@hh.se; internet www.hh.se; f. 1983; academic year September to June; library: 125,000 vols, 10,500 e-journals, 500 periodicals; 253 teachers; 14,500 students (5,088 full-time, 9,412 part-time); Rector ROMULO ENMARK.

Högskolan i Borås (University College of Borås): Allégatan 1, SE-501 90 Borås; tel. (33) 435-40-00; fax (33) 435-40-03; e-mail registrator@hb.se; internet www.hb.se; f. 1977; offers courses in behavioural and education sciences, business and informatics, engineering, fashion and textile studies, library and information studies and health sciences; mem. of the European Univ. Asscn; library: see Libraries and Archives; 650 teachers; 15,000 students; Chair. ROLAND ANDERSSON; Rector Prof. LENA NORDHOLM; Head of Central Admin. KARIN CARDELL; Librarian INGER EIDE-JENSEN.

Högskolan i Gävle (Gävle University College): SE-801 76 Gävle; Kungsbackavägen 47, Gävle; tel. (26) 64-85-00; fax (26) 64-86-86; e-mail registrator@hig.se; internet www.hig.se; f. 1977; mathematics, natural sciences, and computer science, technology, humanities and social sciences, teacher training and health care; library: 90,000 vols, 550 periodicals; 500 teachers (incl. 40 profs, 150 senior lecturers); 12,000 students; Rector MAJ-BRITT JOHANSSON.

Högskolan i Jönköping (Jönköping University College): POB 1026, SE-551 11 Jönköping; Gjuterigatan 5, SE-553 18 Jönköping; tel. (36) 10-10-00; fax (36) 15-08-12; e-mail info@hj.se; internet www.hj.se; f. 1977; library: see Libraries and Archives; 500 teachers; 8,595 students; Rector ANITA HANSBO.

Högskolan i Skövde (Skövde University College): POB 408, SE-541 28 Skövde; tel. (500) 44-80-00; fax (500) 44-81-39; e-mail registrator@his.se; internet www.his.se; f. 1977, present status 1983; business administration, economics, engineering science, biosciences, computer science, languages, art, social science, nursing; library: see Libraries and Archives; 312 teachers; 10,904 students (4,381 full-time, 6,523 part-time); Rector SIGBRITT KARLSSON.

Högskolan Kristianstad (Kristianstad University College): Elmetorpsvägen 15, SE-291 88 Kristianstad; tel. (44) 20-30-00; fax (44) 12-96-51; e-mail info@hkr.se; internet www.hkr.se; f. 1977; languages of instruction: Swedish, English; depts of behavioural sciences, business studies, humanities and social sciences, health sciences and mathematics and science; school of engineering; library: see Libraries and Archives; 500 teachers; 12,000 students; Rector LARS CARLSSON.

Högskolan på Gotland (Gotland University): Cramérgatan 3, SE-621 67 Visby; tel. (498) 29-99-00; fax (498) 29-99-62; e-mail info@hgo.se; internet www.hgo.se; f. 1998; primarily business administration and international management and coastal zone management, secondary subjects incl. archaeology, osteology, information technology and business administration, international business relations, technology, art and new media, building restoration, Russian, history, human geography, ethnology, ecology, art history and cross-cultural communication; 150 teachers; 2,396 students; Rector JORGEN THOLIN.

Högskolan Väst (University West): SE-461 86 Trollhättan; tel. (520) 22-30-00; fax (520) 22-30-99; e-mail registrator@hv.se; internet www.hv.se; f. 1990 as Högskolan Trollhättan/Uddevalla, present name 2006; depts of economics and IT, engineering science, nursing, health and culture, social and behavioural studies; 500 teachers; 11,000 students; Vice-Chancellor Prof. LARS EKEDAHL.

Mälardalens Högskola (Mälardalen University College): POB 883, SE-721 23 Västerås; tel. (21) 10-13-00; fax (21) 10-15-44; e-mail info@mdh.se; internet www.mdh.se; f. 1977; library: see Libraries and Archives; 50 teachers; 13,000 students; Chair. MADELEINE CAESAR; Pres. Dr INGEGERD PALMÉR; Vice-Pres. KARIN AXELSSON.

Södertörns Högskola (Sodertorn University College): SE-141 89 Huddinge; Alfred Nobels allé 7, Flemingsberg, Huddinge; tel. (8) 608-40-00; fax (8) 608-40-10; e-mail international@sh.se; internet www.sh.se; f. 1996; faculties of humanities, social sciences and technology, science and teacher training and education studies; library: 119,313 vols; 450 teachers; 12,000 students; Vice-Chancellor Prof. MOIRA VON WRIGHT.

Sophiahemmet Högskola (Sophiahemmet University College): POB 5605, SE-114 86 Stockholm; Lindstedtsvägen 8, Solhemmet, Stockholm; tel. (8) 406-20-00; fax (8) 10-29-09; e-mail info@sophiahemmethogskola.se; internet www.sophiahemmethogskola.se; f. 1884 as Drottningens Sjuksköterskeskola (Queen's School of Nursing); Bachelors and Masters degree courses in nursing science; library: 20,000 vols, 100 periodicals; 1,300 students; Rector JAN ÅKE LINDGREN.

Other Institutes of University Standing

Blekinge Tekniska Högskola (Blekinge Institute of Technology): SE-371 79 Karlskrona; Campus Gräsvik, Karlskrona; tel. (455) 38-50-00; fax (455) 38-50-57; e-mail registrator@bth.se; internet www.bth.se; f. 1989; applied information technology and sustainable devt of industry and soc.; 140 teachers; 7,000 students; Rector URSULA HASS; Deputy Head ANDERS HEDERSTIERNA; Sec. ING-MARIE BILLGREN.

Chalmers Tekniska Högskola (Chalmers University of Technology): SE-412 96 Gothenburg; tel. (31) 772-10-00; fax (31) 772-38-72; e-mail info@adm.chalmers.se; internet www.chalmers.se; f. 1829; depts of applied information technology, applied mechanics, applied physics, architecture, chemical and biological engineering, civil and environmental engineering, computer science and engineering, earth and space sciences, energy and environment, fundamental physics, materials and manufacturing technology, mathematical sciences, microtechnology and nanoscience, product and production devt, shipping and marine technology, signals and systems, technology management and economics; maintains 44 attached centres; language of instruction: Swedish; academic year September to June; library: see Libraries and Archives; 1,590 teachers; 11,000 students; Pres. and CEO Prof. KARIN MARKIDES; First Vice-Pres. Prof. STEFAN BENGTSSON; Libraries Dir L. NELLDE.

Dramatiska Institutet (University College of Film, Radio, Television and Theatre): POB 27090, SE-102 51 Stockholm; Valhallavägen 189, SE-115 53 Stockholm; tel. (8) 55-57-20-00; fax (8) 55-57-20-05; e-mail kansli@draminst.se; internet www .dramatiskainstitutet.se; f. 1970; provides education for professional practice in film, radio, television and theatre; offers univ. diploma in performing arts and media, postgraduate courses and short courses within the field of theatre and media; Rector PER LYSANDER; Pro-Rector BOEL HÖJEBERG; Pro-Rector MARIA HEDMAN HVITFELDT.

Gymnastik- och Idrottshögskolan (Swedish School of Sport and Health Sciences): POB 5626, SE-114 86 Stockholm; Lidingövägen 1, SE-114 33 Stockholm; tel. (8) 402-22-00; fax (8) 402-22-80; e-mail registrator@gih .se; internet www.gih.se; f. 1813, fmrly Stockholm Univ. College of Physical Education and Sports, present name 2005; didactics, human biology, pedagogics, physical education, preventive health, sports coaching; library: 60,000 vols, 6,000 periodicals; 60 teachers; 650 students; Rector Prof. KARIN HENRIKSSON-LARSEN; Vice-Rector KARIN REDELIUS.

Handelshögskolan i Stockholm (Stockholm School of Economics): POB 6501, SE-113 83 Stockholm; Sveavägen 65, Stockholm; tel. (8) 736-90-00; fax (8) 31-81-86; e-mail info@hhs.se; internet www.hhs.se; f. 1909; economics, financial economics, management, marketing, statistics and accounting; library: see under Libraries and Archives; 166 teachers; 2,000 students; Chair. ERIK ÅSBRINK; Pres. Prof. LARS BERGMAN; Vice-Pres. ÖRJAN SÖLVELL.

Högskolan för Design och Konsthantverk (School of Design and Crafts): POB 131, SE-405 30 Gothenburg; Kristinelundsgatan 6–8, SE-405 30 Gothenburg; tel. (31) 786-00-00; fax (31) 786-48-88; e-mail info@hdk.gu.se; internet www.hdk.gu.se; f. 1848; attached to Gothenburg Univ.; product design, interior and graphic design, ceramic art, textile art, jewellery design, film scenography; library: 20,000 vols; 40 teachers; 250 students; Head EVA ENGSTRAND; Librarian KARIN SUNDÉN.

Högskolan för Scen och Musik (Academy of Music and Drama): POB 210, SE-405 30 Gothenburg; Fågelsången 1, Gothenburg; tel. (31) 786-40-20; fax (31) 786-40-30; e-mail kerstin.nilsson@hsm.gu.se; internet www .hsm.gu.se; f. 1916, present status 2005; attached to Göteborgs Univ.; music education, performing, church music, composition, world music, jazz, electro-acoustic composition, music technology; 150 teachers; 600 students; Prin. STAFFAN RYDÉN; Chief Librarian PIA SHEKHTER.

Internationella Handelshögskolan (Jönköping International Business School): POB 1026, SE-551 11 Jönköping; Gjuterigatan 5, Jönköping; tel. (36) 10-10-00; fax (36) 16-50-69; e-mail info@jibs.hj.se; internet hj.se/jibs .html; f. 1994; business administration, economics, political science, business informatics and commercial law; 220 staff (incl. 34 full professors, 10 assoc. professors); 2,100 students (incl. 750 int. students); Man. Dir and Dean Prof. NICLAS ADLER; Exec. Sec. KARIN STENBERG.

Karolinska Institutet: SE-171 77 Stockholm; Solna Br.: Nobels väg 5, Solna, Stockholm; Huddinge Br.: Alfred Nobels Allé 8, Huddinge, Stockholm; tel. (8) 524-800-00; fax (8) 31-11-01; internet www.ki.se; f. 1810; medical univ.; library: see Libraries and Archives; 476 teachers; 6,000 students; Pres. Prof. Dr HARRIET WALLBERG-HENRIKSSON; Vice-Pres. Prof. JAN ANDERSSON; Univ. Dir KARIN RÖDING; Chief Librarian CHRISTER BJÖRKLUND; publs Computerized Publication Register (information on all publs issued by the Institute), Curriculum, Students' Handbook.

Konstfack (University College of Arts, Crafts and Design): POB 3601, SE-126 27 Stockholm; LM Ericssons väg 14, SE-126 27 Stockholm; tel. (8) 450-41-00; fax (8) 450-41-29; e-mail registrator@konstfack.se; internet www.konstfack.se; f. 1844, present bldg 2004; graphic design and illustration, industrial design, interior architecture, furniture design, textile design, ceramics and glass, metalwork design, fine art, art education; library: 110,000 vols; 135 teachers; 900 students; Pres. Dr IVAR BJÖRKMAN.

Konsthögskolan Valand (Valand School of Fine Art): POB 132, SE-405 30 Gothenburg; Vasagatan 50, Gothenburg; tel. (31) 786-51-00; fax (31) 786-51-19; e-mail info@valand.gu .se; internet www.valand.gu.se; f. 1865 as Göteborgs Musei Ritskola, present name 1977, present status 1995; attached to Gothenburg Univ.; fine, applied and performing arts; 14 teachers; 100 students; Dir LESLIE JOHNSON.

Kungl. Konsthögskolan (Royal Institute of Art): POB 163 15, SE-103 26 Stockholm; Flaggmansv. 1, SE-111 49 Stockholm; tel. (8) 614-40-00; fax (8) 679-86-26; e-mail info@kkh .se; internet www.kkh.se; f. 1735, present location 1995, present name 2010; attached to Min. of Education and Research; offers Bachelors and Masters courses in fine arts; library: 60,000 vols; 38 teachers; 230 students; Rector MÅNS WRANGE; Pro-Rector MARIA LANTZ; Librarian ANNAKARIN LINDBERG; Librarian ULF NORDQVIST; publs

Konsthögskolan Elevkatalog, Konsthögskolans Broschyr.

Kungl. Musikhögskolan (Royal College of Music in Stockholm): POB 27711, SE-115 91 Stockholm; Valhallavägen 105, Stockholm; tel. (8) 16-18-00; fax (8) 664-14-24; e-mail info@kmh.se; internet www.kmh.se; f. 1771; classical music, Nordic folk music, music from other cultures, jazz, improvisation, composition, conducting, music and media technology, various forms of music education; 314 teachers; 1,000 students; Prin. JOHANNES JOHANSSON; Vice-Prin. CECILIA RYDINGER ALIN; Vice-Prin. STAFFAN SCHEJA.

Kungliga Tekniska Högskolan (Royal Institute of Technology): SE-100 44 Stockholm; Valhallavägen 79, Stockholm; tel. (8) 790-60-00; fax (8) 790-65-00; e-mail info@kth.se; internet www.kth.se; f. 1827, present location 1917; academic year September to June; offers Bachelors and Masters degrees in architecture, engineering, science; also offers licentiate or doctoral degrees; library: see Libraries and Archives; 479 professors; 14,877 students; Pres. PETER GUDMUNDSON; Deputy Pres. EVA MALMSTRÖM JONSSON; Vice-Pres. for Faculty Devt and Gender Equality GUSTAV AMBERG; Vice-Pres. for Int. Commitments RAMON WYSS; Vice-Pres. for Research

Interactions with Society GUNNAR LANDGREN; Vice-Pres. for Research Structure and Content BJÖRN BIRGISSON; Univ. Dir ANDERS LUNDGREN; Chief Librarian G. LAGER; publs *Catalogue, Study Handbook* (1 a year).

Umeå Institute of Design: SE-901 87 Umeå; Östra Strandgatan 30, Umeå; tel. (90) 786-69-96; fax (90) 786-66-97; e-mail info@dh.umu.se; internet www.dh.umu.se; f. 1989; attached to Umeå Univ.; Bachelors, Masters and Doctoral programmes in industrial design and related specializations; 16 teachers, 76 visiting staff; Rector ANNA VALTONEN.

SWITZERLAND

The Higher Education System

Higher education institutions predate the proclamation of the Helvetic Republic in 1798, with the oldest being the Universität Basel, which was founded in 1460. Other long-standing institutions include the Université de Lausanne (founded 1537), the Université de Genève (founded 1559) and the Universität Luzern (founded 1574; current status since 2000). There are 10 cantonal universities, and the main languages of instruction are French, German or Italian, depending on the canton. However, in 2007 the Swiss Conference of Cantonal Ministers of Education designed an inter-cantonal reform system (HarmoS) that endeavoured to unify the different education systems in the different cantons. At 2011 the agreement had been ratified by 11 cantons (in which it is now legally binding) and was pending in most other cantons. Other institutions of higher education include two federal institutes of technology, and universities of applied sciences (known as Fachhochoshulen, Hautes Ecoles Spécialisées or Scuole Universitarie Professionale). Switzerland participates in the Bologna Process to establish a European Higher Education Area, the first phase of which is to adopt a credit-based system of comparable degrees with two main cycles (undergraduate and graduate). In 2009/10 there were 250,073 students enrolled in higher education, of which 126,940 were enrolled at universities, 69,676 were enrolled at universities of applied sciences and 53,457 were enrolled at vocational institutions.

There is no federal agency for higher education, responsibility for which is divided between the Confederation and the cantons. The cantons are responsible for the universities and are their primary source of funding; they also supervise the universities of applied sciences and many vocational and training institutions. The Confederation supervises and funds the federal institutes of technology; legislates on vocational education and training and the universities of applied sciences; and funds vocational education and training, the universities of applied sciences, as well as providing additional funding for the cantonal universities. The Confederation and cantons cooperate through the Swiss University Conference (SUC), which was established to coordinate the management of the universities.

Either the Federal Maturity Certificate (Maturitätszeugnis, Certificat de Maturité, Baccalauréat or Attestato di Maturità) or the Federally Recognized Cantonal Maturity Certificate (Eidgenössisch anerkanntes kantonales Maturitätszeugnis, Certificat de Maturité cantonal reconnu par la Confédération or Attestato di Maturità cantonale riconosciuto dalla Confederazione) is the main requirement for admission to university. Cantonal Maturity Certificates that do not have federal recognition (Kantonale Maturität, Maturité Cantonale or Maturità Cantonale) give limited access to higher education, while the Vocational Maturity Certificate (Eidgenössisches Berufsmatur-

itätszeugnis, Certificat fédéral de maturité professionelle or Attestato federale di maturità professionale) is required for admission to the Fachhochoshulen, Hautes Ecoles Spécialisées or Scuole Universitarie Professionale, and also allows access to universities when taken in combination with an additional examination (Passarellenprüfung Berufsmaturität, Ergänzungsprüfung, Passerelle maturité professionnelle, examen complémentaire, Passerella maturità professionale or esami complementari). The new Bologna-style degree system, comprising the Bachelors, Masters and Doctorate, was due to have been fully implemented by 2010 . The Bachelors is a three-year degree, equivalent to the old four-year Diplom, Diplôme, Licence or Lizentiat. The first postgraduate degree is the Masters, a one-and-a-half- to two-year programme following the Bachelors. Finally, the highest university degree is the Doctorate (Doktorat, Doctorat), which is only offered by the universities and is awarded after between two and five years of research, culminating with defence of a thesis.

Technical and vocational education is regulated by federal law and implemented by cantonal authorities. Students split their time between the workplace and the classroom, and the primary qualification is the Federal Apprenticeship Certificate or Certificate of Proficiency (Fähigkeitszeugnis, Certificate de Capacité or Attestato di Capacità). There are also Advanced Vocational Schools (Ecoles Professionnelles Supérieures or Scuole Medie Professionale) offering advanced programmes in technical and vocational education.

The Centre of Accreditation and Quality Assurance of the Swiss Universities (OAQ) is an independent body that defines quality assurance requirements and regularly checks compliance with these and prepares guidelines for the national accreditation procedures. In addition, it conducts accreditation procedures as well as other quality assessments such as evaluations and audits on behalf of the Swiss University Conference and the Confederation. The political authorities have mandated the OAQ to undertake quality audits of the universities and federal institutes of technology every four years to determine whether their quality assurance systems are compatible with internationally accepted standards. A system of accreditation has been in place since 2002. It is a voluntary procedure open to academic institutions and their study programmes, both from the public and private sectors. It consists of a three-step procedure comprising self-evaluation, external evaluation and finally decision on accreditation. The accreditation is based on an assessment of compliance with predefined, internationally accepted quality standards as mentioned above. The accreditation decision is made by the Swiss University Conference. An unconditional positive decision is granted for seven years.

Regulatory and Representative Bodies

GOVERNMENT

Staatssekretariat für Bildung und Forschung/Secrétariat d'Etat à l'éducation et à la recherche (State Secretariat for Education and Research): Hallwylstr. 4, 3003 Bern; tel. 313229691; fax 313227854; e-mail info@sbf.admin.ch; internet www.sbf.admin .ch; State Sec. MAURO DELL'AMBROGIO; Deputy Dir JÜRG BURRI.

ACCREDITATION

Organ für Akkreditierung und Quali- tätssicherung der Schweizerischen Hochschulen/Organe d'accréditation et d'assurance de qualité des hautes écoles suisses (Swiss Center of Accreditation and Quality Assurance in Higher Education): Falkenplatz 9, POB 7456, 3001 Bern; tel. 313801150; fax 313801155; e-mail info@oaq .ch; internet www.oaq.ch; f. 2001; promotes quality of teaching and research at univs; develops guidelines and quality standards for academic accreditation and carries out accreditation procedures on basis of guidelines introduced by SUK/CUS; Dir Dr CHRISTOPH GROLIMUND.

Schweizerische Universitätskonferenz/ Conférence universitaire suisse (Swiss University Conference): Sennweg 2, POB 576, 3012 Bern 9; tel. 313066060; fax 313066070; e-mail cus@cus.ch; internet www.cus.ch; f. 1969, present status 2001; coordination of Swiss univs and institutes of higher education; empowered to accredit public or private academic instns and programmes; awards project-specific grants; issues directives on evaluation of teaching and research; 18 mems, representing cantons, univs, Nat. Union of Students, etc.; Pres. Dr BERNHARD PULVER; Sec.-Gen. Dr MARTINA WEISS; Deputy Sec.-Gen. VALÉRIE CLERC BOREL; publ. *SUK Info* (4 a year).

Swiss ENIC—Naric: Rectors' Conf. of the Swiss Univs, POB 607, 3000 Bern 9; tel.

313066042; fax 313066020; e-mail christine .gehrig@crus.ch; internet www.enic.ch; provides information on Swiss and foreign higher education systems and on recognition of qualifications; Head CHRISTINE GEHRIG.

FUNDING

Rat der Eidgenössischen Technischen Hochschulen/Conseil des Ecoles polytechniques fédérales (Board of the Swiss Federal Institutes of Technology): Häldeliweg 15, 8092 Zürich; tel. 446322367; fax 446321190; internet www.ethrat.ch; appointed by Swiss Fed. Council; allocates funds to Swiss Fed. Institutes of Technology in Zurich and Lausanne, the Paul Scherrer Institut, the Swiss Fed. Institute for Forest, Snow and Landscape Research, Materials Science and Technology Research Instn and Swiss Fed. Institute of Aquatic Science and Technology; centre in Bern; Pres. Dr FRITZ SCHIESSER; Vice-Pres. Prof. Dr PAUL L. HERRLING; Exec. Dir Dr MICHAEL KÄPPELI.

Schweizerischer Nationalfonds zur Förderung der wissenschaftlichen Forschung/Fonds national suisse de la Recherche scientifique (Swiss National Science Foundation): Wildhainweg 3, POB 8232, 3001 Bern; tel. 313082222; fax 313013009; e-mail com@snf.ch; internet www.snf.ch; f. 1952; promotes ind. scientific research; supports basic research in all disciplines; supports applied research through Nat. Research Programmes; facilitates and promotes int. engagement for Swiss research community and provides funding opportunities; Pres., Foundation Council GABRIELE GENDOTTI; Dir DANIEL HÖCHLI; publs *Horizons* (4 a year), *SNSFinfo print* (3 a year).

NATIONAL BODIES

EDK/IDES (IDES Information and Documentation Centre): Speichergasse 6, POB 660, 3000 Bern 7; tel. 313095100; fax 313095110; e-mail ides@edk.ch; internet www.edk.ch; f. 1962 (with partial integration of CESDOC 1994); collects information and documents about Swiss education system and makes them accessible; serves cantonal education and training depts; library of 50,000 vols; Pres. ISABELLE CHASSOT; Dir ANNEMARIE STREIT.

Rektorenkonferenz der Schweizer Universitäten (CRUS)/Conférence des Recteurs des Universités Suisses (CRUS) (Rectors' Conference of the Swiss Universities): Sennweg 2, 3012 Bern; tel. 313066036; fax 313066050; e-mail crus@crus.ch; internet www.crus.ch; f. 1904, present status 2001; 12 mem univs; represents Swiss univs in relation with govt and other bodies; responsible for strategic planning and cooperation between univs; coordinates the implementation of the Bologna reform at the doctoral degree awarding univs; provides information service on Swiss and foreign univs; administers bilateral govt scholarships for Swiss students; nat. information service on questions of academic recognition (Swiss ENIC); EURAXESS bridgehead in Switzerland; administers Scientific Exchange Programme between Switzerland and the New Member States of EU (SciexNMSch); library of 4,000 vols; Pres. Prof. Dr ANTONIO LOPRIENO; Sec.-Gen. Dr MATHIAS STAUFFACHER; publs *proff.ch* (online), *Studying in Switzerland: Universities*.

Schweizerische Konferenz der kantonalen Erziehungsdirektoren (EDK)/Conférence suisse des directeurs cantonaux de l'instruction publique (Swiss Conference of Cantonal Ministers of Education): Speichergasse 6, POB 660, 3000 Bern 7; tel. 313095111; fax 313095150;

e-mail edk@edk.ch; internet www.edk.ch; assembly of the 26 cantonal govt ministers responsible for education, training, culture and sport; negotiating partner of federal govt for jt responsibility of education (high school, vocational education, univs) and represents cantons in foreign countries in educational and cultural affairs; centre in Bern; Pres. ISABELLE CHASSOT; Gen. Sec. HANS AMBÜHL.

Schweizerischer Wissenschafts- und Technologierat/Conseil Suisse de la Science et de la Technologie (Swiss Science and Technology Council): Inselgasse 1, 3003 Bern; tel. 313230048; fax 313239547; e-mail swtr@swtr.admin.ch; internet www.swtr.ch; advisory body to govt on all matters relating to science policy; provides and evaluates fundamentals of nat. policy on education, research and technology; Pres. Prof. Dr SUSANNE SUTER; Sec. DENISE WAGNER.

Vereinigung der Schweizerischen Hochschuldozierenden/Association Suisse des Enseignantes d'Université (Swiss University Teachers' Association): Buchhalden 5, 8127 Forch; tel. 446333399; fax 446331105; e-mail vsh-sekretariat@ethz .ch; internet www.hsl.ethz.ch; f. 1971; promotes public understanding of univ. matters and univ. professions; represents interests of univ. lecturers; maintains int. ties among univ. teachers; Pres. Prof. Dr CHRISTIAN BOCHET; Vice-Pres. (vacant); Gen. Sec. Prof. Dr GERNOT KOSTORZ.

Learned Societies
GENERAL

Akademie der Naturwissenschaften Schweiz/Académie des sciences naturelles (Swiss Academy of Sciences): Schwarztorstrasse 9, 3007 Bern; tel. 313104020; fax 313104029; e-mail info@scnat.ch; internet www.scnat.ch; f. 1815, present name 2004; promotes scientific integrity and ethically considered treatment of scientific knowledge and its application; promotes active exchange of opinion between science and society through information and promotional events on new areas of research, support of regional projects and awarding of prizes for outstanding communication of scientific content; 54 mems incl. expert asscns and cantonal and regional asscns; library: see Universitätsbibliothek Bern (Stadtbibliotheken); Pres. Prof. DENIS MONARD; Sec.-Gen. Dr JÜRG PFISTER; Treas. Prof. THIERRY J. L. COURVOISIER; publ. *SCNATinfo*.

Institut National Genevois: Promenade du Pin 1, 1204 Geneva; tel. 223104188; fax 223103453; internet www.inge.ch; f. 1853; divided into four sections: economics, moral and political sciences, fine arts, music and letters and science; encourages advancement and dissemination of science, literature, fine arts, industry, commerce and agriculture; 750 mems; Pres. PIERRE KUNZ; Sec.-Gen. MICHELLE SAUDIN; Treas. JEAN-CLAUDE MEYER; publ. *Mémoires*.

Schweizerische Akademie der Geistes- und Sozialwissenschaften/Académie Suisse des Sciences Humaines et Sociales (Swiss Academy of Humanities and Social Sciences): Hirschengraben 11, POB 8160, 3011 Bern; tel. 313131440; fax 313131450; e-mail sagw@sagw.ch; internet www.sagw.ch; f. 1946; represents concerns of humanities and social sciences to decision makers and authorities and to media and public; provides infrastructure for humanities and social science research; organizes confs and meetings of nat. and int. mem. orgs; 60 mem. socs; Pres. Prof. Dr HEINZ

GUTSCHER; Vice-Pres. Prof. Dr BEATRICE SCHMID; Sec.-Gen. Dr MARKUS ZÜRCHER.

Schweizerische Akademie der Technischen Wissenschaften/Académie Suisse des Sciences Techniques (Swiss Academy of Engineering Sciences): Seidengasse 16, 8001 Zürich; tel. 442265011; fax 442265019; e-mail info@satw.ch; internet www.satw.ch; f. 1981; co-operation with similar socs and acts in advisory capacity to govt; promotes utilization and devt of technology for benefit of soc.; 240 individual mems, 60 mem. orgs; Pres. Prof. Dr RENÉ DÄNDLIKER; Designated Pres. Prof. Dr ULRICH W. SUTER; Vice-Pres. Dr IRENE AEGERTER; Man. Dir Dr ROLF HÜGLI; publ. *Technoscope* (3 a year).

AGRICULTURE, FISHERIES AND VETERINARY SCIENCE

Association des Groupements et Organisations Romands de l'Agriculture—AGORA: Ave des Jordils 5, POB 128, 1000 Lausanne 6; tel. 216140477; fax 216140478; e-mail info@agora-romandie.ch; internet www.agora-romandie.ch; f. 1881, as Fédération des Sociétés d'Agriculture de Suisse Romande (FSASR), present name and status 1996; defends professional interests of Romande agriculture; promotes vocational training and devt of service activities; 21 corporate mems; library of 200 vols; Pres. FRANÇOIS HALDEMANN; Dir WALTER WILLENER; publs *d'arboriculture et d'horticulture* (6 a year), *Revue suisse d'agriculture* (6 a year), *Revue suisse de viticulture*.

Gesellschaft Schweizer Tierärztinnen und Tierärzte/Société des Vétérinaires Suisses: Brunnmattstr. 13, POB 45, 3174 Thörishaus; tel. 313073535; fax 313073539; e-mail info@gstsvs.ch; internet www.gstsvs .ch; f. 1813; represents professional interests of ind. and employed veterinarians; 2,700 mems; Pres. CHARLES TROLLIET; Man. Dir RUEDI HELFER-DÖLKER; publ. *Schweizer Archiv für Tierheilkunde* (12 a year).

ARCHITECTURE AND TOWN PLANNING

Bund Schweizer Architekten/Fédération des Architectes Suisses: Pfluggässlein 3, POB 907, 4001 Basel; tel. 612621010; fax 612621009; e-mail mail@ bsa-fas.ch; internet www.architects-fsa.ch; f. 1908; represents professional interests of architects; provides information on architecture profession and its role in soc.; supports education, training and research of architecture; 858 mems; Pres. PAUL KNILL; Vice-Pres. ALDO NOLLI; Vice-Pres. ELISABETH BOESCH; Vice-Pres. ROLF SEILER; Treas. YVO THALMANN; publ. *Werk, Bauen und Wohnen* (12 a year).

Schweizer Heimatschutz (Swiss Heritage Society): Seefeldstr. 5A, POB 1122, 8032 Zürich; tel. 442545700; fax 442522870; e-mail info@heimatschutz.ch; internet www .heimatschutz.ch; f. 1905; promotes advancement of Switzerland's architectural heritage; preserves important landmarks, develops structural environment, and promotes good architectural design; 27,000 mems; Pres. PHILIPPE BIÉLER; Vice-Pres. RUTH GISI-WILLISEGGER; Vice-Pres. SEVERIN LENEL; Sec.-Gen. ADRIAN SCHMID; publ. *Heimatschutz/Patrimoine* (French and German, 4 a year).

Société Suisse des Ingénieurs et des Architectes/Schweizerischer Ingenieur- und Architektenverein: POB, 8027 Zürich; Selnaustr. 16, 8001 Zürich; tel. 442831515; fax 442831516; e-mail contact@ sia.ch; internet www.sia.ch; f. 1837; promotes sustainable devt and quality of natural and built environment; guards professional interests of its mems; 14,683 mems; Pres. DANIEL

KÜNDIG; Vice-Pres. ANDREAS BERNASCONI; Vice-Pres. LAURENT VULLIET; Sec. Gen. HANS-GEORG BÄCHTOLD; publs *TEC21*, *TRACES* (24 a year).

BIBLIOGRAPHY, LIBRARY SCIENCE AND MUSEOLOGY

Bibliothek Information Schweiz/Bibliothèque Information Suisse/Biblioteca Informazione Svizzera/Biblioteca Infurmaziun Svizra (Swiss National Association of Libraries and Librarians): Hallerstr. 58, 3012 Bern; tel. 313824240; fax 313824648; e-mail info@bis.info; internet www.bis.info; f. 1987, merger of Bibliotheken und der Bibliothekarinnen/Bibliothekare der Schweiz (BBS) and Schweizerische Vereinigung für Dokumentation (SVD) 2008; rep. of mems in politics and public; lobbying of decision makers from education, science and culture in fields of library policy and devt, intellectual, cultural promotion, professional training; organizes training programmes for mems; 1,950 mems incl. instns and professionals; Pres. YOLANDE ESTERMANN WISKOTT; Gen. Sec. CHRISTINE SCHAAD HÜGLI; publ. *ARBIDO* (4 a year).

Genossenschaft der Urheber und Verleger von Musik/Coopérative des auteurs et éditeurs de musique (Cooperative Society of Music Authors and Publishers): Bellariastr. 82, POB 782, 8038 Zürich; tel. 444856666; fax 444824333; e-mail suisa@suisa.ch; internet www.suisa.ch; f. 1923; issues licences authorising its clients to perform, broadcast, disseminate and reproduce music; collects royalties of its members for public use of their works in Switzerland and Liechtenstein; centres in Lausanne and Lugano; 29,000 mems; Pres. HANS ULRICH LEHMANN; Vice-Pres. MARCO ZANOTTA; CEO ANDREAS WEGELIN; Gen. Dir ANDREAS WEGELIN.

Schweizer Diplombibliothekare, -innen/Bibliothécaires diplômé(e)s suisses (Association of Swiss Graduate Librarians): POB 607, 3000 Bern 7; Sekretariat, c/o Martin Rohde, Sportweg 15, 3097 Liebefeld; tel. 4024854-2; e-mail info@sdb-bds.ch; internet www.sdb-bds.ch; f. 1988; promotes professional interests of qualified librarians; regional groups in Aarau, Basel, Bern, Lausanne, Zentralschweiz and Zürich; 500 mems; publ. *SDB/BDS News* (3 a year).

Schweizerische Bibliophilen Gesellschaft/Société Suisse des Bibliophiles: Alte Landstr. 95, POB 151, 8804 Au; e-mail erfueter@gmx.ch; f. 1921; 600 mems; Pres. Dr AGLAJA HUBER; Hon. Treas. EDUARD R. FUETER; publ. *Librarium 58* (3 a year), *Stultifera Navis 44–57*.

Verband der Museen der Schweiz/Association des Musées Suisses: c/o Landesmuseum Zürich, POB, 8021 Zürich; tel. 442186588; fax 442186589; e-mail info@museums.ch; internet www.museums.ch; f. 1966; asscn of Swiss museums and zoological and botanical gardens, to represent their interests; forms a link between Swiss museums and Int. Council of Museums (see International Organizations chapter); organizes annual conf. and work sessions on museology, conservation, restoration and other related topics; jt projects with univs, training; basic program for new museum professionals, spec. courses for guides, security and technical staff, academic museology courses in cooperation with univs; Int. Museum Day; 670 institutional mems; Pres. GIANNA A. MINA; Gen. Sec. DAVID VUILLAUME; publs *Revue museums.ch* (1 a year), *Schweizer Museumsführer/Guide des musées suisses* (irregular).

Verein Schweizerischer Archivarinnen und Archivare/Association des archivistes suisses (Association of Swiss Archivists): c/o Büro Pontri GmbH, Solothurnstr. 13, POB, 3322 Urtenen-Schönbühl; tel. 313122666; fax 313122668; e-mail info@vsa-aas.org; internet www.vsa-aas.org; f. 1922; ensures professionalization of archives; encourages establishment of coordinated archival heritage; represents interests of mems; advanced professional training, confs, lobbying, collaboration and coordination within and for Swiss archival community; 713 mems; Pres. Dr ANNA PIA MAISSEN; Vice-Pres. GREGOR EGLOFF; Sec. DANIEL KRESS; Treas. PHILIPPE KÜNZLER; publ. *ARBIDO* (4 a year).

ECONOMICS, LAW AND POLITICS

Bundesamt für Statistik/Office Fédéral de la Statistique (Federal Statistical Office): Espace de l'Europe 10, 2010 Neuchâtel; tel. 327136011; fax 327136012; e-mail info@bfs.admin.ch; internet www.statistik.ch; f. 1860; nat. centre for public statistics; production and publication of statistics; Dir-Gen. Dr JÜRG MARTI; publ. *Statistical Yearbook* (1 a year).

Gottlieb Duttweiler Institute: Langhaldenstr. 21, POB 531, 8803 Rüschlikon/Zürich; tel. 447246111; fax 447246262; e-mail info@gdi.ch; internet www.gdi.ch; f. 1963; conducts scientific research in social and economic fields; monitoring of social change; organizes confs, seminars and workshops; 35 mems; CEO Dr DAVID BOSSHART; Asst CEO INGRID SCHMID; publ. *GDI Impuls*.

Schweizerische Gesellschaft für Aussenpolitik/L'Association Suisse de Politique Extérieure: c/o Karin Büchli, Netzwerk Müllerhaus, Bleicherain 7, 5600 Lenzburg 1; tel. 628880120; fax 628880101; e-mail info@sga-aspe.ch; internet www.sga-aspe.ch; f. 1968; deals with matters of foreign, int. trade, integration and security policy; organizes lectures, confs and seminars on current foreign policy issues; 800 mems; Pres. HADORN ADRIAN; Sec.-Gen. Dr ULRICH E. GUT.

Schweizerische Gesellschaft für Volkswirtschaft und Statistik/Société Suisse d'Economie et de Statistique (Swiss Society of Economics and Statistics): c/o SNB/BNS, Börsenstr. 15, 8022 Zürich; tel. 446313785; fax 446318390; e-mail mail@sgvs.ch; internet www.sgvs.ch; f. 1864; promotes and advances economic research and improves collaboration between domestic and int. research community, promotes young economists by providing appropriate platform to present their scientific work; awards SSES Young Economist Awards; 600 mems; library: see entry for Schweiz. Wirtschaftsarchiv; Pres. PHILIPPE BACCHETTA; Sec. and Treas. FABIENNE SCHÜRMANN; publ. *Swiss Journal of Economics and Statistics/Schweizerische Zeitschrift für Volkswirtschaft und Statistik/Revue suisse d'économie et de statistique* (4 a year).

Schweizerische Vereinigung für Internationales Recht/Société Suisse de Droit International: c/o Dr Stefan Breitenstein, Lenz & Staehelin, Bleicherweg 58, 8027 Zürich; tel. 442041212; e-mail stefan.breitenstein@lenzstaehelin.com; internet www.svir-ssdi.ch; f. 1914; promotes qualitative implementation of int. law; promotes lawyers working in field of int. and European law; organizes Swiss conf. of int. law; 300 mems; Pres. Prof. CHRISTINE KADDOUS; Vice-Pres. Prof. DANIEL GIRSBERGER; Sec. Dr STEFAN BREITENSTEIN; Treas. Dr MONIQUE JAMETTI GREINER; publs *Schweizerische Zeitschrift für internationales und europäisches Recht* (5 a year), *Swiss Studies in International Law*.

Schweizerischer Anwaltsverband/Fédération Suisse des Avocats/Federazione Svizzera degli Avvocati (Swiss Bar Association): Marktgasse 4, POB 8321, 3011 Bern; tel. 313130606; fax 313130616; e-mail info@swisslawyers.com; internet www.swisslawyers.com; f. 1898; preserves and defends independent legal profession in Switzerland and abroad; represents Swiss law as against federal authorities and int. orgs; fosters relations among cantonal bar asscns; 8,620 mems; Pres. Avv. BRENNO BRUNONI; Vice-Pres. Dr BEAT VON RECHENBERG; Vice-Pres. PIERRE-DOMINIQUE SCHUPP; Gen. Sec. Lic. RENÉ RALL; publs *Anwaltsrevue/Revue de l'Avocat* (12 a year), *Schriftenreihe*.

Schweizerischer Notarenverband/Fédération Suisse des Notaires/Federazione Svizzera dei Notai: Tavelweg 2, 3074 Muri; tel. 313105840; fax 313105841; e-mail info@schweizernotare.ch; internet www.schweizernotare.ch; f. 1920; safeguards interests of freelance notary; rep. of professional notary to authorities and opinion on federal issues associated with exercise of notary in context; maintains relationships follow notary feds of other countries and int. orgs notary; 1,500 mems; Pres. Me PHILIPPE BOSSET; Sec. Me ANDREAS B. NOTTER.

FINE AND PERFORMING ARTS

Berufsverband Visuelle Kunst/Société Des Artistes Visuels (Visual Arts Asscociation): Räffelstrasse 32, 8045 Zürich; tel. 444621030; fax 444621610; e-mail office@visarte.ch; internet www.visarte.ch; f. 1865, present name and status 2001; defends visual artists' interests on political and social levels; seeks to ensure favourable conditions for artistic production and provides counsel to artists; 3,300 mems incl. 2,600 active mems; Pres. HEINRICH GARTENTOR; Vice-Pres. NATALIA SCHMUKI; Man. REGINE HELBLING; publs *Arte Svizzera*, *Art Suisse*, *Schweizer Kunst* (2 a year).

Hindemith Stiftung (Hindemith Foundation): Champ Belluet 41, 1807 Blonay; tel. 219430528; fax 219430529; e-mail administration@hindemith.org; internet www.hindemith.org; f. 1968; promotes and cultivates music, in particular contemporary music; maintains musical and literary heritage of Paul Hindemith; encourages research in field of music and diffusion of research results; awards prizes; Pres. Prof. Dr ANDREAS ECKHARDT; Man. and Vice-Pres. FRANÇOIS MARGOT; publs *Frankfurter Studien*, *Hindemith-Forum* (1 or 2 a year), *Hindemith General Original Edition*, *Les Annales Hindemith* (1 a year).

Attached Institutions:

Hindemith-Institut Frankfurt: Eschersheimer Landstrasse 29–39, 60322 Frankfurt-am-Main, Germany; tel. (69) 5970362; fax (69) 5963104; internet www.paul-hindemith.org; archives of Hindemith's autograph scores and sketches, manuscript versions of musico-theoretical writings, autobiographical catalogues of works and extensive correspondence; Dir Dr SUSANNE SCHAAL-GOTTHARDT.

Centre de Musique Hindemith (Hindemith Centre for Music): Chemin Lacuez 3, 1807 Blonay; tel. 219430520; fax 219430521; internet www.hindemith.org; f. 1978; chamber music master classes; Dir MARCEL LACHAT.

Gesellschaft für Schweizerische Kunstgeschichte/Société d'histoire de l'art en Suisse: Pavillonweg 2, 3012 Bern; tel.

313083838; fax 313016991; e-mail gsk@gsk
.ch; internet www.gsk.ch; f. 1880; studies
and publicizes cultural heritage and diversity of Switzerland dating back to antiquity;
9,500 mems; Pres. Dr BENNO SCHUBIGER;
Vice-Pres. Dr JACQUES BUJARD; Sec. Dr
MATTHIAS EPPENBERGER; Treas. ERICH WEBER;
publs *Beiträge zur Kunstgeschichte der
Schweiz, Die Kunstdenkmäler der Schweiz,
Inventar der neueren Schweizer Architektur,
k+a* (4 a year), *Kunst Architektur in der
Schweiz* (4 a year), *Kunstführer durch die
Schweiz, Schweiz. Kunstführer* (20 a year).

Kunstverein St Gallen: Museumstr. 32,
9000 St Gallen; tel. 712420687; fax
712420672; e-mail kunstverein@
kunstmuseumsg.ch; internet www
.kunstmuseumsg.ch; f. 1827; promotes int.
contemporary art exhibitions; 2,000 mems;
Pres. LORENZ BÜHLER; Man. Dir NADIA VERO-
NESE.

Pro Helvetia (Swiss Arts Council):
Hirschengraben 22, 8024 Zürich; tel.
442677171; fax 442677106; e-mail info@
prohelvetia.ch; internet www.prohelvetia.ch;
f. 1939; promotes artistic creation, fosters
cultural outreach and facilitates cultural
exchange with int. artists; offices in Warsaw,
Cairo, Cape Town, New Delhi, Shanghai and
Paris; Pres. MARIO ANNONI; Dir PIUS KNÜSEL;
publ. *Passagen / Passages* (3 a year).

**Schweizer Blasmusikverband/Associ-
ation Suisse des Musiques** (Swiss Windband Association): Gönhardweg 32, POB,
5001 Aarau; tel. 628228111; fax 628228110;
e-mail info@windband.ch; internet www
.windband.ch; f. 1862; 76,000 mems, 32
associated mem. orgs; Chair. VALENTIN BIS-
CHOF; publ. *Unisono* (26 a year).

**Schweizer Musikrat/Conseil Suisse de la
Musique** (Swiss Music Council): Haus der
Musik, Gönhardweg 32, POB 3839, 5001
Aarau; tel. 628229423; fax 628229407;
e-mail info@musikrat.ch; internet www
.musikrat.ch; f. 1964; mem. of CIM
(UNESCO); mem. of various musical orgs;
rep. of interests of music creators to public
and political bodies at fed. level and in
educational and cultural issues; 61 mem.
orgs; Pres. Dr ISABELLE MILI; Vice-Pres.
MARKUS FLURY; Gen. Sec. HERR KURT HESS;
publs *Guide for Musical Studies in Switzerland, Schweizer Muzikzeitung* (irregular).

**Schweizerische Musikforschende
Gesellschaft/Société Suisse de Musicolo-
gie/Società Svizzera di Musicologia:** Universität Bern, Institut für
Musikwissenschaft, Hallerstr. 5, 3012 Bern;
tel. 316318396; fax 316313459; e-mail info@
smg-ssm.ch; internet www.smg-ssm.ch; f.
1915, present name 1934; supports music
research; organizes lectures, confs and con-
gresses; country rep. of RILM (Répertoire
Int. de Littérature Musicale); 7 sections in
Basel, Bern, Luzern, St. Gallen-Zürich,
Suisse Romande, Svizzera Italiana, Zürich;
awards Glarean Prize for musical research
and Jacques-Handschin Prize; 700 mems;
Pres. Dr THERESE BRUGGISSER-LANKER; Vice-
Pres. Prof. Dr LAURENZ LÜTTEKEN; Treas. Lic.
CHRISTOPH BALLMER; publs *Musik aus
Schweizer Klöstern, Publikationen der
Schweizerischen Musikforschenden
Gesellschaft. Serie II, Schweizer Jahrbuch
für Musikwissenschaft* (1 a year).

**Schweizerischer Kunstverein/Société
Suisse des Beaux-Arts/Società Svizzera
di Belle Arti:** Zeughausstr. 55, 8026 Zürich;
tel. 442983035; fax 44 2983038; e-mail info@
kunstverein.ch; internet www.kunstverein
.ch; f. 1806, present name 1839; promotes
and protects interests of art assocs and art
lovers on fed. level; lobbies and advocacies of
mem. sections on nat. level; 44,000 individual

mems of 34 local and regional art asscns;
Pres. PETER STUDER (acting); publ. *Kunstbul-
letin* (10 a year).

**Schweizerischer Tonkünstlerverein/
Association Suisse des Musiciens:** Ave
du Grammont 11 bis, 1007 Lausanne 13; tel.
216143290; fax 216143299; e-mail info@
asm-stv.ch; internet www.asm-stv.ch; f.
1900; advocates and promotes innovative
music; protects interests of composers, solo-
ists, improvisers, conductors and chorus,
musicologists and music dirs; 950 mems;
Pres. MATTHIAS ARTER; Vice-Pres. WILLIAM
BLANK; Treas. SIMONA RYSER; Dir CSABA
KÉZÉR; publ. *dissonanz/dissonance* (4 a
year).

**Schweizerischer Werkbund/Werkbund
Suisse:** Limmatstr. 118, POB, 8031 Zürich;
tel. 442727176; fax 442727506; e-mail swb@
werkbund.ch; internet www.werkbund.ch; f.
1913; organized into regional groups: Argo-
vie, Bâle, Berne, Grisons, Suisse centrale,
Suisse orientale, Romandie and Zurich; supports professionals from fields of creation, art
and culture; organizes nationwide debates
regarding design creation; 900 mems; Pres.
IWAN RASCHLE; Treas. ALEXANDER ZOANNI;
Sec.-Gen. BERND ZOCHER; publs *SWB-Doku-
mente, SWB-Information* (4 a year).

**Schweizerisches Institut für Kunstwis-
senschaft/Institut Suisse pour l'Etude
de l'Art** (Swiss Institute for Art Research):
Zollikerstr. 32, POB 1124, 8032 Zürich; tel.
443885151; fax 443815250; e-mail sik@
sik-isea.ch; internet www.sik-isea.ch; f. 1951;
registration of Swiss works of art and Swiss
artists; studies in art and technology;
research, documentation, dissemination of
knowledge and information in fields of fine
art, art business and art technology; 1,700
mems; library of 114,000 vols; Pres. ANNE
KELLER-DUBACH; Vice-Pres. and CEO Dr
TONI SCHÖNENBERGER; Treas. Dr ERICH HUN-
ZIKER; Dir Dr ROGER FAYET; publs *Œuvreka-
taloge Schweizer Künstler, Kataloge
Schweizer Museen und Sammlungen,
KUNSTmaterial, Museen der Schweiz, outlines.*

SGD Swiss Graphic Designers: Bahnhofstr. 11, POB 157, 9230 Flawil; tel.
713934535; fax 713934548; internet www
.sgd.ch; f. 1972 by merger of VSG (Verband
Schweizer Grafiker) and BGG (Bund Gestal-
ter Grafische/Graphic Designers Asscn of
AGC), present name 1993; protects and
advances economic and professional interests
of its members and offers advice and assistance; cooperates with nat. and int. orgs and
with partners from economic and scientific
worlds; 600 mems; Pres. DANILO SILVESTRI;
Vice-Pres. MICHAELA VARIN; Sec.-Gen. ERIKA
REMUND; publ. *SGD Information* (4 a year).

**Société Suisse de Pédagogie Musicale/
Società Svizzera di Pedagogia Musicale/
Schweizerische Musikpädagogische
Verband:** Bollstr. 43, 3076 Worb, Bern; tel.
313522266; fax 313522267; e-mail
zentralsekretariat@smpv.ch; internet www
.smpv.ch; f. 1893; 15 regional asscns; promotes musical education and research; 5,000
mems; Pres. BRIGITTE SCHOLL; Sec. LISA
BUCHI; publ. *Agenda du musicien.*

HISTORY, GEOGRAPHY AND
ARCHAEOLOGY

Antiquarische Gesellschaft in Zürich: c/o
Staatsarchiv des Kantons Zürich, POB, 8057
Zürich; tel. 16356911; fax 446356905; e-mail
sekretariat@antiquarische.ch; internet www
.antiquarische.ch; f. 1832; concerned with
history of Zürich and Swiss history in gen.;
organizes lectures, meetings, field trips and
guided tours; 550 mems; Pres. Dr ROLAND
BÖHMER; publs *Mitteilungen der Antiquar-

ischen Gesellschaft in Zürich* (1 a year),
Neujahrsblatt (1 a year).

**Archäologie Schweiz/Archéologie
Suisse/Archeologia Svizzera:** Petersgraben 51, POB 116, 4003 Basel; tel.
612613078; fax 612613076; e-mail info@
archaeologie-schweiz.ch; internet www
.archaeologie-schweiz.ch; f. 1907, present
name 2005; supports research on archaeological heritage and disseminates knowledge;
library of 30,000 vols; 2,200 mems; Pres.
CARMEN BUCHILLER; Treas. WERNER H. GRAF;
Sec. URS NIFFELER; publ. *Archäologie
Schweiz/Archéologie Suisse* (4 a year).

**Geographisch-Ethnographische
Gesellschaft Zürich:** Geographisches Institut der Universität Zürich, Winterthurerstr.
190, 8057 Zürich; tel. 16355111; fax
16356848; e-mail gegz@geo.unizh.ch;
internet www.geo.unizh.ch/gegz; f. 1889, by
merger of Ethnographic Society (f. 1888) and
Geographical Society (f. 1897); promotes
geographical and ethnographic knowledge
and sustainable use of resources; understanding of foreign cultures and global connections; 450 individual and corporate mems;
Pres. Prof. Dr MAX MAISCH; Vice-Pres. Prof.
Dr ULRIKE MÜLLER-BÖKER; Sec. and Treas.
Dr REGULA VOLKART; publ. *Geographica Helvetica* (4 a year).

**Geographisch-Ethnologische
Gesellschaft Basel/Société de Geographie et d'Ethnologie de Bâle:** c/o Geographisches Institut, Klingelbergstr. 27, 4056
Basel; tel. 612673660; fax 612673651; e-mail
info@gegbasel.ch; internet www.gegbasel.ch;
f. 1923; provides knowledge on topics in
geography and anthropology; maintains contact with univs and cultural instns for
research and training; 428 mems; Pres.
Prof. Dr HARTMUT LESER; Hon. Pres. Dr
GEORG BIENZ; Treas. HANSPETER MEIER; publs
Basler Beiträge zur Geographie (irregular),
Basler Beiträge zur Physiogeographie
(irregular), *Regio Basiliensis* (3 a year).

Geographische Gesellschaft Bern: Hallerstr. 12, 3012 Bern; tel. 316318869; fax
316318544; e-mail gb@giub.unibe.ch;
internet www.swissgeography.ch/de/
members/ggb.php; f. 1873; attached to Verband Geographie Schweiz; organizes lectures; 650 mems; Pres. LEKTORIN ELISABETH
BÄSCHLIN; Sec. MONIKA WÄLTI; publs *Berner
Geographische Mitteilungen* (1 a year), *Jahrbuch* (irregular).

**Historische und Antiquarische
Gesellschaft zu Basel:** St. Alban-Vorstadt
5, 4002 Basel; tel. 612058605; fax 612058601;
e-mail a.salvisberg@merianstiftung.ch;
internet pages.unibas.ch/hag; f. 1836; aims
to revive intellectual life in Basel; promotes
historical studies and knowledge; organizes
lectures, seminars and excursions for mems;
450 mems; library of 30,000 vols; Pres. Lic.
ANDRÉ SALVISBERG; publ. *Basler Zeitschrift
für Geschichte und Altertumskunde* (1 a
year).

Historischer Verein des Kantons Bern:
c/o Universitätsbibliothek Bern, Münstergasse 63, 3000 Bern 8; tel. 316319203;
e-mail christian.luethi@ub.unibe.ch;
internet www.hvbe.ch; f. 1846; promotes
studies, dissemination of information and
discussions on history of Bern among its
mems; organizes lectures, publs and excursions for mems; 1,000 mems; Pres. Lic.
CHRISTIAN LÜTHI; Vice-Pres. Lic. HEINRICH
CHRISTOPH AFFOLTER; Vice-Pres. Dr CHAR-
LOTTE GUTSCHER; Treas. SASCHA M. BURKHAL-
TER; publs *Archiv des Historischen Vereins* (1
a year), *Berner Zeitschrift für Geschichte* (4 a
year).

**Historischer Verein des Kantons St
Gallen:** c/o Kantonsbibliothek Vadiana, Not-

kerstr. 22, 9000 St Gallen; e-mail info@hvsg .ch; internet www.hvsg.ch; f. 1859; supports projects on preservation and study of heritage; promotes dialogues on topical issues related to history; demonstrates diversity of cultural history to life through meetings, study tours and film clips; 500 mems; Pres. Dr CORNEL DORA; publs *Neujahrsblatt (NJBL)* (1 a year), *St Galler Kultur und Geschichte* (together with the State Archives St Gallen).

Historischer Verein Obwalden: POB 1314, 6061 Sarnen; tel. 416606522; e-mail info@hvow.ch; internet www.hvow.ch; f. 1877, as Historisch-antiquarischer Verein von Obwalden; promotes understanding and interest in historical issues; preserves historic and ethnographic heritage in Canton; organizes publs, excursions and lectures; Pres. VICTOR BIERI; Vice-Pres. NOTKER DILLIER; Treas. ANNELIS ROHRER; publ. *Obwaldner Geschichtsblätter*.

Schweizerische Gesellschaft für Geschichte/Société Suisse d'Histoire/ Società Svizzera di Storia: Villettemattstr. 9, 3007 Bern; tel. 313813821; e-mail generalsekretariat@sgg-ssh.ch; internet www.sgg-ssh.ch; f. 1841; promotes studies and training related to history; divided in four depts; defends professional interests of historians; rep. of historical branch to int. orgs; 1,400 mems; Pres. Prof. Dr REGINA WECKER; Vice-Pres. SACHA ZALA; Vice-Pres. MAURO CERUTTI; Gen. Sec. Dr ERIKA FLÜCKIGER STREBEL; Treas. MAX HAUCK; publs *ITINERA* (irregular), *Quellen zur Schweizergeschichte*, *Schweizerische Zeitschrift für Geschichte* (1 a year).

Schweizerische Gesellschaft für Kartographie/Société Suisse de Cartographie (Swiss Society of Cartography): Wolfgang-Pauli-Str. 15, 8093 Zürich; tel. 446333031; fax 446331153; e-mail sgk@kartografie.ch; internet www.kartographie.ch; f. 1969; promotes training of theoretical and practical cartography; acts as platform for int. relations with cartographic instns; represents interests of mems; organizes workshops, professional internal training courses, exhibitions and confs; 310 mems; Pres. STEFAN ARN; Sec. STEFAN RÄBER; Treas. MARTIN PROBST; publs *Cartographica Helvetica* (2 a year), *Topographic Maps: Map Graphics ad Generalisation*.

Schweizerische Numismatische Gesellschaft/Société Suisse de Numismatique (Swiss Numismatic Society): c/o J.-P. Righetti, Route de Fribourg 54, 1724 Ferpicloz; tel. 264130216; fax 264130215; e-mail pmzanchi@bluewin.ch; internet www .numisuisse.ch; f. 1879; promotes all branches of numismatic science through its publs dealing with classical, medieval and modern coins, paper money and medals; organizes annual numismatic days Switzerland; 650 mems; Pres. Lic. HORTENSIA VON ROTEN; Vice-Pres. Dr MARKUS PETER; Sec. PIERRE-ANDRÉ ZANCHI; Treas. JEAN-PIERRE RIGHETTI; publs *Schweizer Studien zur Numismatik*, *Schweizerische Numismatische Rundschau* (1 a year), *Schweizer Münzblätter* (4 a year), *Schweizer Münzkatalog*, *Typos*.

Schweizerische Vereinigung für Altertumswissenschaft/Association Suisse pour l'Étude de l'Antiquité: Universität Bern, Historisches Institut, Länggassstr. 49, 3000 Bern 9; tel. 313012326; fax 316314410; e-mail thomas.spaeth@cgs.unibe.ch; internet www.sagw.ch/svaw.html; f. 1943; promotes research and teaching in all areas of classical studies; fosters int. relations with corresponding asscns; 190 mems; Pres. Prof. Dr THOMAS SPÄTH; Treas. Prof. Dr PIERRE SANCHEZ; publs *Museum Helveticum* (2 a year,

online (www.sagw.ch/svaw/publikationen/ museum-helveticum.html)), *Schweizerische Beiträge zur Altertumswissenschaft*.

Società Storica Locarnese: POB 1119, 6601 Locarno; e-mail info@ societastoricalocarnese.ch; internet www .societastoricalocarnese.ch; f. 1954; colln and conservation of documents relating to history of Locarno area; promotes study of history and art of ancient church in the region of Locarno (Locarno and Maggia); organizes exhibitions, confs, and lectures; 150 mems; Pres. RODOLFO HUBER; Vice-Pres. DAMIJANA GRAMIGNA; Sec. ERICA BARLOCCHI; Treas. EMMY FERRARI.

Société d'Egyptologie, Genève: POB 26, 1218 Grand-Saconnex; tel. 227910974; e-mail info@segweb.ch; internet www.segweb.ch; f. 1978; promotes study of Egyptology and related disciplines (coptology, Islamic studies, etc.); organizes confs, seminars and courses; supports research; 400 mems; library of 2,000 vols; Pres. Dr PHILIPPE GERMOND; Vice-Pres. Dr RODOLPHE KASSER; Vice-Pres. JEAN-LUC CHAPPAZ; Sec. SANDRA GUARNORI NICOLLIN; Treas. DANIEL NICOLLIN; publ. *Cahiers* (irregular).

Société d'Histoire de la Suisse Romande: Chemin du Cerisier 1, 1004 Lausanne; e-mail mail@shsr.ch; internet www.shsr.ch; f. 1837; supports historical and archaeological research; organizes seminars and visits; tries to foster interest in history of W Switzerland in public; 530 mems; library: see Bibliothèque Cantonale et Universitaire de Lausanne; Pres. ALAIN CLAVIEN; Vice-Pres. FRANÇOISE DUBOSSON.

Société d'Histoire et d'Archéologie de Genève: c/o Bibliothèque de Genève, 1211 Geneva 4; internet www.shag-geneve.ch; f. 1838; preserves historical and archaeological past of Geneva; promotes research and disseminates results through publs; 440 mems; library of 10,000 vols, 1,000 MSS (contact: c/o Archives de la Ville de Genève, Palais Eynard, 4 rue de la Croix-Rouge, 1211 Geneva 3); Pres. Dr. MATTHIEU DE LA CORBIÈRE; Pres. FRANÇOIS JACOB; Sec. MARTINE PIGUET; Treas. ANDRÉ WAGNIÈRE; publs *Bibliographie genevoise* (1 a year), *Cahiers*, *Mémoires et Documents*.

Société de Géographie de Genève: Route de Malagnou 1, CP 6434, 1211 Geneva 6; tel. 223798347; fax 223798353; e-mail ruggero .crivelli@unige.ch; internet www .geographie-geneve.ch; f. 1858; promotes study advancement and dissemination of geographical science in all its brs; 250 mems; Pres. RUGGERO CRIVELLI; Vice-Pres. RENÉ ZWAHLEN; Sec. CHRISTIAN MOSER; Treas. CHRISTIANE OLSZEWSKI; publ. *Le Globe* (1 a year).

Société Vaudoise d'Histoire et d'Archéologie: 32, rue de la Mouline, 1022 Chavannes-près-Renens; tel. 213163711; fax 213163755; e-mail info@svha-vd.ch; internet www.svha-vd.ch; f. 1902; preserves historic monuments in Canton of Vaud; encourages genealogical research; organizes confs, visits to monuments and exhibitions, excursions and study circles; 800 mems; Pres. LISE FAVRE; Treas. and Sec. RUTH LINIGER; publ. *Revue historique vaudoise* (1 a year).

Verband Geographie Schweiz/Association Suisse de Géographie (Association of Swiss Geographers): Geographisches Institut der Universität Bern, Hallerstrasse 12, 3012 Bern; tel. 316318567; fax 316318511; e-mail pbachmann@giub.unibe.ch; internet www.swissgeography.ch; f. 1990; acts as umbrella asscn of Swiss Geographers; supports research in field of geosciences; rep. of Swiss geography in int. asscns and congresses; coordinates 6 regional and 4 the-

matic socs, and 8 univ. institutes; Central Cttee acts as nat. cttee of IGU; Pres. Prof. HANS-RUDOLF EGLI; Vice-Pres. Prof. CONRADIN A. BURGA; Sec. Dr PHILIPP BACHMANN; Treas. Prof. THOMAS HAMMER; publ. *GeoAgenda (Mitteilungsblatt der ASG)* (6 a year).

Vereinigung der Freunde Antiker Kunst/Association des Amis de l'Art Antique (Association of Friends of Classical Art): c/o Archäologisches Seminar der Universität, Schönbeinstr. 20, 4056 Basel; fax 612673063; tel. 612673068; e-mail editor@ antikekunst.ch; internet www.antikekunst .ch; f. 1956; promotes interest in classical archaeology; offers lectures, guided visits to exhibitions, trips to Classical sites; six regional groups in Basel, Berne-Bienne-Solothurn, Fribourg, Geneva, Lausanne and Zurich; 1,050 mems; Pres. Prof. Dr MARTIN GUGGISBERG; publ. *Antike Kunst* (1 a year).

LANGUAGE AND LITERATURE

Alliance Française de Zurich: Merkurstr. 34, 8032 Zürich; tel. 442619306; fax 442619330; e-mail info@afz.ch; internet www.afz.ch; f. 1883; offers courses and exams in French language and culture and promotes cultural exchange with France; organizes confs, guided tours, lectures, cultural meetings; attached offices in Basel, Berne, Fribourg, Hermance, Locarno, Lucerne, Lugano, Lugnasco and St Gallen.

Autorinnen und Autoren der Schweiz AdS (Swiss Society of Writers): Konradstr. 61, 8031 Zürich; tel. 443500460; fax 443500461; e-mail sekretariat@a-d-s.ch; internet www.a-d-s.ch; f. 2003; supports professional interests of writers in field of political literary, linguistic and cultural asscn, in respect of copyright; creates relationships between AUTRIC, authors, translators, language regions and countries; 940 mems; Pres. RAPHAEL URWEIDER; Dir-Gen. NICOLE PFISTER FETZ.

British Council: Sennweg 2, POB 532, 3000 Bern 9; tel. 315603794; fax 313011459; e-mail britishcouncil@britishcouncil.ch; internet www.britishcouncil.org/ switzerland; offers courses and examinations in English language and British culture; promotes cultural exchange with the UK; Dir CAROLINE MORRISSEY; Deputy Dir SIMON BRIMBLECOMBE.

Centre PEN Suisse Romand (PEN Club of French-speaking Cantons of Switzerland): Ave Krieg 26, 1208 Grand Saconnex; tel. 227882231; e-mail ckrul@bluewin.ch; internet www.penromand.ch; f. 1949; defends freedom of expression and promotes int. cultural exchanges; promotes peace according to the PEN Charter; 70 mems; Pres. CLAUDE KRUL; Sec.-Gen. ZEKI ERGAS; Treas. ALFRED DE ZAYAS; publ. *Pages littéraires*.

Collegium Romanicum: c/o Michele Loporcaro, Romanisches Seminar der, Universität Zürich, Zürichbergstrasse 8, 8032 Zürich; e-mail loporcar@rom.uzh.ch; internet www .sagw.ch/collegium-romanicum; f. 1947; study of Romance languages and literature; 200 mems; Pres. Prof. Dr MICHELE LOPORCARO; Vice-Pres. Prof. Dr YASMINA FOEHR-JANSSENS; Sec. Prof. Dr URSULA BÄHLER; publs *Romanica Helvetica*, *Versants* (2 a year), *Vox Romanica* (1 a year).

Deutschschweizer PEN-Zentrum: c/o Kristin T. Schnider, Russenhaus, 6484 Wassen; tel. 443507070; e-mail office@ pen-dschweiz.ch; internet www .pen-dschweiz.ch; f. 1979; promotes literature and freedom of expression; works by int. PEN charter; 80 mems; Pres. DOMINIK RIEDO; Sec. KRISTIN T. SCHNIDER; publ. *Briefzeitung* (2 a year).

Gesellschaft für deutsche Sprache und Literatur in Zürich: c/o Deutsches Seminar, Schönberggasse 9, 8001 Zürich; e-mail gfdsl@ds.uzh.ch; internet www.ds.uzh.ch/gfdsl; f. 1894; promotes research of linguistics and literary studies; offers courses and lectures; 230 mems; Pres. ZELJKO MEDVED.

Institut dal Dicziunari Rumantsch Grischun: Ringstr. 34, 7000 Chur; tel. 812846642; fax 812840204; e-mail info@drg.ch; internet www.drg.ch; f. 1885; conservation and research into Romansh language; publ. of documented vocabulary of Romansh-speaking people of Switzerland; 1,000 mems; library of 18,000 vols; Pres. Dr CHRISTIAN COLLENBERG; Vice-Pres. CHASPER PULT; publs *Annalas* (1 a year), *Dicziunari Rumantsch Grischun* (2 a year).

Institut et Musée Voltaire: 25 rue des Délices, 1203 Geneva; tel. 224189560; fax 224189561; e-mail institut.voltaire@ville-ge.ch; internet www.ville-ge.ch/imv; f. 1954; research centre, exhibitions, confs; library of 22,000 vols and MSS, 2,500 printed editions of Voltaire's writings; Curator FRANÇOIS JACOB; publs *La Gazette des Délices* (4 a year), *La Ligne d'ombre* (irregular).

Schweizerische Sprachwissenschaftliche Gesellschaft/Société Suisse de Linguistique/Società Svizzera di Linguistica: c/o Dr. Johanna Miecznikowski, Istituto di studi italiani, Università della Svizzera italiana, Via Giuseppe Buffi 13, 6904 Lugano; e-mail johanna.miecznikowskifuenfschilling@usi.ch; f. 1947; 207 mems; Pres. Prof. JACQUES MOESCHLER; Sec. Dr JOHANNA MIECZNIKOWSKI; publs *Bulletin Vals-Asla* (2 a year), *Cahiers Ferdinand de Saussure*.

MEDICINE

Académie Suisse des Sciences Médicales/Schweizerische Akademie der Medizinischen Wissenschaften (Swiss Academy of Medical Sciences): Peterspl. 13, 4051 Basel; tel. 612699030; fax 612699039; e-mail mail@samw.ch; internet www.samw.ch; f. 1943; promotes professional training of scientists, esp. in clinical research; supports research in biomedical and clinical research; clarifies ethical questions in connection with medical devts and their effects on society; 160 mems; Pres. Prof. PETER SUTER; Vice-Pres. Prof. PETER MEIER-ABT; Vice-Pres. Prof. WALTER REINHARD; Gen. Sec. Dr HERMAN AMSTAD; Treas. Dr DIETER SCHOLER.

Schweizerische Gesellschaft für Chirurgie/Société Suisse de Chirurgie: Bahnhofstr. 55, 5001 Aarau; tel. 628362098; fax 628362097; e-mail info@sgc-ssc.ch; internet www.sgc-ssc.ch; f. 1913; promotes scientific activity and generation of academics in field of surgery; rep. of professional interests of mems; 1,202 mems; Pres. Prof. Dr PHILIPPE MOREL; Vice-Pres. Prof. Dr RALPH A. SCHMID; Gen. Sec. Dr FRÉDÉRIC DUBAS; publ. *Swiss Surgery*.

Schweizerische Gesellschaft für Geschichte der Medizin und der Naturwissenschaften/Société Suisse d'Histoire de la Médecine et des Sciences Naturelles (Swiss Society for the History of Medicine and Sciences): c/o Prof. Hans Konrad Schmutz, Naturmuseum Winterthur, Museumstr. 52, 8400 Winterthur; tel. 522675166; fax 522675319; e-mail hubert.steinke@mhi.unibe.ch; internet www.sggmn.ch; f. 1921; promotes history of medicine and sciences; supports young scientists and confers Henry E. Sigerist Prize for promotion of young scholars; 300 mems; Pres. Prof. Dr phil. HANS KONRAD SCHMUTZ; Vice-Pres. Dr

Lic. IRIS RITZMANN; Sec. Dr HUBERT STEINKE; publ. *Gesnerus* (4 a year).

Schweizerische Gesellschaft für Innere Medizin/Société Suisse de Médecine Interne (Swiss Society of General Internal Medicine): POB 422, 4008 Bâle; Solothurnerstr. 68, 4053 Bâle; tel. 612259330; fax 612259331; e-mail info@sgim.ch; internet www.sgim.ch; f. 1932; supports professional and economic interests of Swiss postgraduate internees of management, economics, communication and medical humanities; promotes internal medical research; encourages networking partnership of hospital and ambulatory medicine; 2,100 mems; Pres. Prof. VERENA BRINER; Sec.-Gen. Dr REGULA SIEVERS-FREY.

Schweizerische Gesellschaft für Orthopädie und Traumatologie/Société Suisse d'Orthopédie et de Traumatologie: 15 Ave des Planches, 1820 Montreux; tel. 219632139; fax 219632149; e-mail office@cpconsulting.ch; internet www.sgosso.ch; f. 1942, present name 2006; promotes professional and economic interests of orthopaedic surgeons; promotes specialization in orthopaedics within field of research and teaching; 11 regional groups; 839 mems; Pres. Prof. Dr CHRISTIAN GERBER; Vice-Pres. Prof. Dr BERNHARD CHRISTEN; Sec. Dr THOMAS KEHL; Treas. Dr ANDREAS EGLI.

Schweizerischer Apothekerverband/Société Suisse des Pharmaciens: Stationsstr. 12, POB, 3097 Bern-Liebefeld; tel. 319785858; fax 319785859; e-mail info@pharmasuisse.org; internet www.pharmasuisse.org; f. 1843; promotes interests of pharmacy in areas of teaching, research, policy and practice; 5,528 mems; Pres. DOMINIQUE JORDAN; Vice-Pres. PETER BURKARD; Vice-Pres. CHRISTIAN ROUVINEZ; publs *Apotheken-Handbuch* (1 a year), *Index Nominum*, *Pharmactuel* (6 a year), *Schweizer Apothekerzeitung* (24 a year).

NATURAL SCIENCES

General

Naturforschende Gesellschaft in Basel: c/o Nunzio Putrino, Gartenst. 2, 6300 Zug; tel. 797223913; e-mail sekretariat@ngib.ch; internet www.ngib.ch; f. 1817; promotes natural history; organizes lectures for semester program; 600 mems; library of 74,000 vols; Pres. Prof. Dr ORESTE GHISALBA; Vice-Pres. Prof. Dr RETO BRUN; Sec. PUTRINO NUNZIO; Treas. Dr HANS-PETER SCHÄR; publ. *Mitteilungen der Naturforschenden Gesellschaften beider Basel*.

Naturforschende Gesellschaft in Bern: Universitätsbibliothek, Münstergasse 61, Postfach, 3000 Bern 8; tel. 313203231; fax 313203299; e-mail info@ngbe.ch; internet www.ngbe.ch; f. 1786; attached to Universität Bern; spreads scientific thought and new knowledge from various fields of natural sciences; organizes lecture cycles, field trips; 300 mems; Pres. Dr MARCO HERWEGH; Vice-Pres. Prof. Dr GÜNTER BAARS; Sec. Dr KURT GROSSENBACHER; Treas. MATTHIAS HAUPT; publ. *Mitteilungen* (1 a year).

Naturwissenschaftliche Gesellschaft Winterthur: c/o Peter Lippuner, Geiselweidstr. 6, 8400 Winterthur; internet www.ngw.ch; f. 1884; lectures, field trips, publs of scientific articles to foster understanding of natural sciences; 660 mems; Pres. PETER LIPPUNER; Vice-Pres. Dr HANS KONRAD SCHMUTZ; Sec. Dr SABINE OERTLI; Treas. Dr URS BLUMER; publ. *Mitteilungen* (every 3 years).

Schweizerische Energie-Stiftung/Fondation Suisse pour l'Energie (Swiss Energy Foundation): Sihlquai 67, 8005 Zür-

ich; tel. 442715464; fax 442730369; e-mail info@energiestiftung.ch; internet www.energiestiftung.ch; f. 1976; promotes energy policy suitable for human beings and environment and control of energy consumption; promotes alternative sources of energy and practice of conservation; 3,000 mems; Pres. GERI MÜLLER; Vice-Pres. DIETER KUHN; publs *Energie Umwelt* (4 a year), *SES-Reports* (irregular).

Schweizerische Stiftung für Alpine Forschungen/Fondation Suisse pour Recherches Alpines (Swiss Foundation for Alpine Research): Stadelhoferstr. 42, 8001 Zürich; tel. 442531200; fax 442531201; e-mail mail@alpinfo.ch; internet www.alpinfo.ch; f. 1939; supports scientific studies in field of mountains, mountain people and mountain sports; 11 mems; Pres. ETIENNE GROSS; Man. Dir THOMAS WEBER.

Società Ticinese di Scienze Naturali: c/o Museo cantonale di Storia naturale, viale Cattaneo 4, 6900 Lugano; tel. (91) 8154761; fax (91) 8154769; e-mail stsn-info@scnatweb.ch; internet stsn.ch; f. 1903; promotion and advancement of natural sciences; organizes confs, assembly, courses, exhibitions, excursions; promotes and supports: activities of Cantonal Museum of Natural History and Biology Centre Alpine Piora; 400 mems; Pres. Dr M. TONOLLA; Sec. SIMONA CASATI; publ. *Memorie*.

Société de Physique et d'Histoire Naturelle de Genève: POB 6434, Route de Malagnou, 1211 Geneva 6; tel. 224186300; fax 224186301; internet www.unige.ch/sphn; f. 1790; natural and exact sciences; organizes confs and excursions for mems; 195 mems; Pres. Dr MICHEL GRENON; Vice-Pres. PIERRE KUNZ; Sec. ETIENNE CHAROLLAIS; publ. *Archives des sciences* (2 a year).

Société Vaudoise des Sciences Naturelles: Palais de Rumine, 1005 Lausanne; tel. and fax 213124334; e-mail svsn@unil.ch; internet www.unil.ch/svsn; f. 1819; study, advancement and dissemination of natural sciences and related sciences; publication of research in biology, geology, chemistry, physics, mathematics, and history and methodology of science; 600 mems; library: 1,000 periodicals in library reading-room: see also Bibliothèque Cantonale et Universitaire de Lausanne; Pres. ALAIN MORARD; Vice-Pres. ANNE FREITAG; Treas. JEAN-LUC EPARD; publ. *Mémoires* (irregular).

Biological Sciences

Bernische Botanische Gesellschaft: Altenbergrain 21, 3013 Bern; tel. 313329233; fax 313322059; internet homepage.hispeed.ch/bebege; f. 1918; promotes private or business interest for vegetation science, plant ecology and floristics; organizes lectures on floristic, geobotanical and ecophysiological issues; 380 mems; Pres. BRIGITTA AMMANN; Vice-Pres. STEFAN EGGENBERG; Treas. REGINE BLÄNKNER; Sec. RITA GERBER; publ. *Sitzungsberichte* (1 a year).

Schweizerische Botanische Gesellschaft/Société Botanique Suisse: Institute of Plant Sciences, University of Bern, Altenbergrain 21, 3013 Bern; tel. 316314928; fax 316314942; internet www.botanica-helvetica.ch; f. 1889; encourages plant sciences and initiatives aimed at protecting flora and conservation of its living environment; cultivates exchange of ideas and experiences and friendly relations between Swiss botanists; 700 mems; Pres. Prof. Dr MARKUS FISCHER; Vice-Pres. Prof. Dr PETER LINDER; Sec. CHRISTOPHE BORNAND; Treas. Dr STEFAN EGGENBERG; publ. *Alpine Botany* (2 a year).

Schweizerische Entomologische Gesellschaft/Société Entomologique Suisse: c/o Hannes Baur, Naturhistorisches Museum, Bernastr. 15, 3005 Bern; tel. 313507264; fax 313507499; e-mail hannes .baur@nmbe.ch; internet seg.scnatweb.ch; f. 1858; studies Swiss entomological fauna; develops entomological knowledge; mems are professional or amateur entomologists; 10 local sections Alpstein, Basel, Bern, Freiburg, Geneva, Lucerne, Neuenburg, Waadt, Wallis and Zürich; 293 mems; library of 18,000 vols; Pres. Dr DENISE WYNIGER; Vice-Pres. Dr DANIEL BURCKHARDT; Sec. HANNES BAUR; publ. *Insecta Helvetica / Fauna Helvetica*.

Mathematical Sciences

Schweizerische Mathematische Gesellschaft/Société Mathématique Suisse (Swiss Mathematical Society): Mathematisches Institut, Universität Bern, Sidlerstr. 5, 3012 Bern; tel. 316318834; fax 316318510; e-mail nicolas.monod@epfl.ch; internet www.math.ch; f. 1910; organizes confs and courses of mathematics at schools; 480 mems; Pres. BRUNO COLBOIS; Vice-Pres. CHRISTINE RIEDTMANN; Sec. and Treas. NICOLAS MONOD; publs *Commentarii Mathematici Helvetici* (4 a year), *Elemente der Mathematik* (4 a year).

Physical Sciences

Bundesamt für Meteorologie und Klimatologie (MeteoSchweiz) (Federal Office of Meteorology and Climatology (MeteoSwiss)): Krähbühlstr. 58, 8044 Zürich; tel. 442569111; fax 442569278; internet www .meteoschweiz.ch; f. 1880, present name 1996; meteorological and climatological services; rep. of Switzerland in World Meteorological Org.; three regional centres in Zurich, Geneva and Locarno; 296 mems; library of 40,000 vols; Dir DANIEL K. KEUERLEBER; Librarian GREGOR STORK; publs *Annalen*, *Arbeitsberichte der MeteoSchweiz*, *Veröffentlichung der MeteoSchweiz*.

Schweizerische Astronomische Gesellschaft/Société Astronomique Suisse (Swiss Astronomical Society): c/o Geri Hildebrandt, Mittlere Gstücktstr. 14D, 8180 Bülach; tel. 448601221; e-mail ghildebrandt@hispeed.ch; internet www .astronomie.ch/sag; f. 1938; promotes exchanges of information related to astronomy between mems and gen. public; 2,400 mems; Pres. Dr WALTER KREIN; Vice-Pres. BEAT MÜLLER; Vice-Pres. RAOUL BEHREND; Sec. GERI HILDEBRANDT; publ. *Orion* (6 a year).

Schweizerische Chemische Gesellschaft/Societe Suisse de Chimie (Swiss Chemical Society): Schwarztorstr. 9, 3007 Bern; tel. 313104090; fax 313104029; e-mail info@scg.ch; internet www.scg.ch; f. 1881 as Neue Schweizerische Chemische Gesellschaft, present name 2001; represents chemists and scientists of chemistry related fields in Switzerland and in int. orgs; 2,600 mems; Pres. Prof E. PETER KÜNDIG; Exec. Dir DAVID SPICHIGER; publ. *Chimia* (online (www.chimia.ch)).

Schweizerische Geologische Gesellschaft/Société Géologique Suisse (Swiss Geological Society): c/o Dr Gilles Borel, Musée cantonal de géologie, UNIL-L'Anthropole, 1015 Lausanne; tel. 216924474; fax 216924475; e-mail gilles .borel@unil.ch; internet www.geolsoc.ch; f. 1882; promotes advancement of earth sciences by organizing meetings supported by SCNAT, and by annual reunions of spec. interest groups; 1,000 mems; Pres. Dr GILLES BOREL; Vice-Pres. Dr NEIL MANKTELOW; Treas. Dr ROGERR RÜTTI; Sec. Dr STEPHAN DELL'AGNOLO; publ. *Eclogae geologicae Helvetiae* (Swiss Journal of Geosciences, 3 a year).

Schweizerische Paläontologische Gesellschaft/Société Paléontologique Suisse (Swiss Palaeontological Society): Naturmuseum Solothurn Klosterpl. 2, 4500 Solothurn; tel. (32) 6227021; fax (32) 6227052; e-mail sps@scnatweb.ch; internet spg.scnatweb.ch; f. 1921; attached to Swiss Academy of Sciences (SCNAT); organizes scientific symposia (Swiss Geoscience Meeting), short courses and guided excursions, annual assembly, awards Amanz Gressly-Award for outstanding contributions to Swiss palaeontology; addresses palaeontological questions from geological and biological points of view; 170 mems; Pres. Dr DAMIEN BECKER; Vice-Pres. Dr LIONEL CAVIN; Sec. SILVAN THÜRING; publ. *Swiss Journal of Geosciences* (jtly with Swiss Geological and Mineralogical Socs).

Schweizerische Physikalische Gesellschaft/Société Suisse de Physique (Swiss Physical Society): Dept. Physik, Klingelbergstr. 82, 4056 Basel; fax 612673784; e-mail sps@unibas.ch; internet www.sps.ch; f. 1908; supports exchange of ideas within research community by offering workshops; SPS awards for outstanding achievements of young scientists; offers forum at interface of basic research and applied physics; 1,200 mems; Pres. Dr CHRISTOPHE ROSSEL; Vice-Pres. Dr ANDREAS SCHOPPER; Sec. Dr ANTOINE POCHELON; Treas. Dr PIERANGELO GRÖNING.

PHILOSOPHY AND PSYCHOLOGY

Schweizerische Gesellschaft für Psychologie/Société Suisse de Psychologie: Univ. of Bern, Dept of Psychology, Berne 9, Muesmattstr., 3000 Bern; tel. 789022695; fax 327181391; e-mail sekretariat@ssp-sgp.ch; internet www.ssp-sgp.ch; f. 1943; promotes scientific psychology in education, research and practice; protects professional interests of its mems; 560 mems; Pres. Prof. Dr SABINE SCZESNY (acting); Sec. HEIDI RUPRECHT; publ. *Swiss Journal of Psychology* (4 a year).

Schweizerische Philosophische Gesellschaft/Société Suisse de Philosophie: c/o Christophe Calame, 53 ave de Rumine, 1005 Lausanne; e-mail christophe .calame@bluewin.ch; internet www.sagw.ch/ philosophie; f. 1940; study and discussion of philosophical problems; organizes meetings; 800 mems; Pres. CHRISTOPHE CALAME; Vice-Pres. LEA BÄHLER; Sec. JULIA SCHEIDEGGER; Treas. Lic. HUBERT SCHNÜRIGER; publs *Studia philosophica* (1 a year), *Supplementa* (irregular).

Schweizerischer Berufsverband für Angewandte Psychologie/Association Professionnelle Suisse de Psychologie Appliquée/Associazone Professionale Svizzera della Psicologia Applicata: Vogelsangstr. 15, 8006 Zürich; tel. 432680405; fax 432680406; e-mail info@sbap .ch; internet www.sbap.ch; f. 1952; rep. of professional interests of its members and interests of applied psychology; 1,000 mems; Pres. HEIDI AESCHLIMANN; Sec. MANUELA LISIBACH.

RELIGION, SOCIOLOGY AND ANTHROPOLOGY

Schweizerische Gesellschaft für Afrikastudien/Société Suisse d'Etudes Africaines: Postfach 8212 3001 Bern; tel. 612672742; internet www.sagw.ch/africa; f. 1974; links and coordinates multidisciplinary research on Africa conducted at Swiss univs and research instns; organizes thematic confs and scientific meetings; 200 mems; Co-Pres. ANNE MAYOR; Co-Pres. Dr DIDIER PÉCLARD; Sec. Dr VEIT ARLT.

Schweizerische Gesellschaft für Soziologie/Société Suisse de Sociologie (Swiss Sociological Association): c/o Marie-Eve Zufferey, Département de Sociologie, Université de Genève, Blvd du Pont d'Arve 40, 1211 Geneva; tel. 223798309; fax 716785657; e-mail sss@unige.ch; internet www.sagw.ch/ soziologie; f. 1955; represents interests of Swiss sociology in relation to scientific and political instns; 600 mems; Pres. Prof. ERIC D. WIDMER; Vice-Pres. Prof. Dr KURT IMHOF; Gen. Sec. Prof. Dr CHRISTOPH MAEDER; publ. *Schweizerische Zeitschrift für Soziologie / Revue suisse de sociologie / Swiss Journal of Sociology* (3 a year).

Schweizerische Gesellschaft für Volkskunde/Société Suisse des Traditions Populaires: Spalenvorstadt 2, 4001 Basel; tel. 612671163; fax 612671163; e-mail sgv-sstp@volkskunde.ch; internet www .volkskunde.ch; f. 1896; documents Swiss popular culture in its historical and current forms; supports and promotes ethnographic research; 742 mems; Pres. Prof. Dr WALTER LEIMGRUBER; Sec. ERNST J. HUBER; Treas. HANS-ULRICH VOLLENWEIDER; publs *Schweizer Volkskunde* (4 a year), *Schweizerisches Archiv für Volkskunde* (2 a year).

Schweizerische Theologische Gesellschaft/Société Suisse de Théologie: c/o Prof. Dr Wolfgang Müller, Theologische Fakultät der Universiät Luzern, Gibraltarstr. 3, POB 7763, 6000 Luzern 7; tel. 412286635; e-mail wolfgang.mueller@ unilu.ch; internet www.sagw.ch/sthg; f. 1965; promotes technical and theological debate and scientific research; organizes theological seminars and confs; 272 mems; Pres. Prof. Dr WOLFGANG W. MÜLLER; Vice-Pres. Prof. Dr DENIS MÜLLER; Treas. Prof. Dr PIERRE BÜHLER; Sec. KATHERINE SIEGENTHALER.

Schweizerische Trachtenvereinigung/ Fédération Nationale des Costumes Suisses (Swiss National Costume Association): Rosswiesstr. 29, POB 8608 Bubikon; tel. 552631563; fax 552631561; e-mail info@ trachtenvereinigung.ch; internet www .trachtenvereinigung.ch; f. 1926; maintains and renews different Swiss costumes, folk dance records and descriptions, folk songs, folk music and folk theatre and dialects; organizes projects and courses; 23,400 mems; Pres. ROLAND MEYER-IMBODEN; Vice-Pres. FRITZ BRAND; Vice-Pres. GÉRARD QUELOZ; publ. *Tracht und Brauch / Costumes et Coutumes* (4 a year).

TECHNOLOGY

Fachleute Geomatik Schweiz/Professionnels Geomatique Suisse (Swiss Association of Geomatics): c/o André Franziska, Flühlistr. 30B, 3612 Steffisburg; tel. 334381462; fax 334381464; e-mail admin@ pro-geo.ch; internet www.pro-geo.ch; f. 1929 as Verband Schweizerische Vermessungsfachleute, present name 2005; supports interests of mems professionally and socially; provides apprenticeship training; 11 regional sections in Aargau, Basel, Bern, Fribourg, eastern Switzerland, Rätia, Ticino, Valais, W Switzerland, Central Switzerland, Zürich; 1,450 mems; Pres. CATHY EUGSTER; Vice-Pres. ALESSANDRA BASCIO; Sec. and Treas. FRANZISKA ANDRÉ-HUBER; publs *Geomatik Schweiz* (12 a year), *NotaBene* (2 a year).

Schweizerische Gesellschaft für Automatik/Association Suisse pour l'Automatique (Swiss Federation of Automatic Control): SGA Sekretariat, Christl Vogel, Eggwilstr. 16A, 9552 Bronschhofen; tel. 719118416; fax 719118449; e-mail sekretariat@sga-asspa.ch; internet www

.sga-asspa.ch; f. 1956; promotes and develops knowledge of techniques of measurement, control and calculation, and their application in field of automation; 200 individual mems, 17 corporate mems; Pres. Dr JÜRG KELLER; Sec. CHRISTL VOGEL; publ. *Lernmodule* (4 a year).

Schweizerische Gesellschaft für Mikrotechnik/Association Suisse de Microtechnique: c/o FRSM, Ruelle DuPeyrou 4, CP 2353, 2001 Neuchâtel; tel. 327200900; fax 327200990; e-mail asmt@fsrm.ch; internet www.sgmt-asmt.ch; f. 1962; promotes working in Swiss microtechnology enterprises and instns; offers engineering education in univs, engineering schools; organizes confs, lectures, courses and study tours; 73 mems; Pres. PHILIPP FISCHER; Sec. SUZANNE SCHWENDENER.

Schweizerischer Verband der Ingenieur-Agronomen und der Lebensmittel-Ingenieure/Association suisse des ingénieurs agronomes et des ingénieurs en technologie alimentaire: Länggasse 79, 3052 Zollikofen; tel. 319105075; fax 319105070; e-mail svial@svial.ch; internet www.svial.ch; f. 1901; active in five areas: agricultural production and environment, food and nutrition, management of agricultural and food industry, training and consulting, govt and politics; promotes professional interests of its mems; 2,000 mems; Pres. NICOLAS FELLAY; Sec. ERNST BAUMANN; publ. *Journal* (4 a year).

Swiss Engineering–STV (Association of Engineers and Architects): Weinbergstr. 41, 8006 Zürich; tel. 442683711; fax 442683700; e-mail info@swissengineering.ch; internet www.swissengineering.ch; f. 1905; supports professional interests of mems; encourages engineering education and training and protection of traditional titles; 15,000 mems; Pres. MAURO PELLEGRINI; Sec.-Gen. STEFAN ARQUINT; publs *Revue Technique Suisse, Schweizerische Technische Zeitschrift, Swiss Engineering STZ/Swiss Engineering rts* (10 a year).

Verband Schweizer Abwasser- und Gewässerschutzfachleute/Association suisse des professionnels de la protection des eaux (Swiss Water Association): Europastr. 3, Glattbrugg; tel. 433437070; fax 433437071; e-mail sekretariat@vsa.ch; internet www.vsa.ch; f. 1944; promotes waste-water technology and water pollution control through advanced technical training for its mems through confs, courses and on-the-job exchanges; publication of standards and guidelines; 1,350 mems, 2,400 reps; Pres. WÜRSTEN MARTIN; Vice-Pres. CHAIX OLIVIER.

Research Institutes
GENERAL

European Journalism Observatory: Via G. Buffi 13, 6904 Lugano; tel. 586664126; fax 586664467; e-mail ejo@lu.unisi.ch; internet it.ejo.ch; f. 2004; attached to Univ. della Svizzera Italiana; promotes links between newsrooms and communications research by aiding media managers, analysts, editors and journalists; analyzes research and trends in media industry; Dir Dr STEPHAN RUSS-MOHL; Co-Dir MARCELLO FOA.

Institute of Management: Via G. Buffi 13, 6900 Lugano; fax 586664647; internet www.ima.eco.unisi.ch; attached to Univ. della Svizzera Italiana; research in different fields of management studies: strategic management, clusters and regional competitiveness, entrepreneurship and family business, public administration and health care manage-

ment; programmes at undergraduate and postgraduate levels.

Istituto di Marketing e Comunicazione Aziendale (Institute of Marketing and Communication Management): Via G. Buffi 13, 6900 Lugano; tel. 586664756; fax 58 6664647; e-mail ivan.snehota@usi.ch; internet www.imca.com.usi.ch; attached to Univ. della Svizzera Italiana; scientific and applied research on issues of teaching and communication in field of economic org.; Dir IVAN SNEHOTA.

Istituto Media e Giornalismo (Institute for Media and Journalism): Via G. Buffi 13, 6900 Lugano; tel. 586664738; fax 586664647; e-mail imeg.com@usi.ch; internet www.imeg.com.usi.ch; attached to Univ. della Svizzera italiana; research and teaching activities on two constituent parts of communication: content (text) and their containers (media); main characteristics of media in historical, economic and social context; forms of access and use of media and methods of use content from a variety of audiences; strategies of instns and companies dealing with nat. and int. media; Dir GIUSEPPE RICHERI; Co-Dir STEPHAN RUSS-MOHL.

Laboratorio di Storia delle Alpi: Largo Bernasconi 2, 6850 Mendrisio; tel. 586665819; fax 586665868; e-mail labisalp.arc@usi.ch; internet www.arc.usi.ch/labisalp; f. 2000; attached to Univ. della Svizzera Italiana; research on alpine space, in its economic, social, cultural, demographic, and political aspects; Head LUIGI LORENZETTI; Sec. MONICA BANCALÀ; publ. *Histoire des Alpes/Storia delle Alpi/Geschichte der Alpen* (1 a year).

AGRICULTURE, FISHERIES AND VETERINARY SCIENCE

Office Fédéral de l'Agriculture/Bundesamt für Landwirtschaft (Federal Office for Agriculture): Ministry of Public Economy, Mattenhofstr. 5, 3003 Bern; tel. 313222511; fax 313222634; e-mail info@blw.admin.ch; internet www.blw.admin.ch; centre for federal agricultural research; promotes multifunctional agriculture; implements decisions taken by electorate, Swiss parliament and govt and plays active role in formulating agricultural policy; Dir-Gen. Dr MANFRED BÖTSCH; Deputy Dir Dr JACQUES CHAVAZ; publs *Agrarforschung* (12 a year), *Revue suisse d'agriculture* (12 a year).

Federal Agricultural Research Stations:

Agroscope: Route de Duillier, POB 1012, 1260 Nyon 1; tel. 223634444; fax 223621325; e-mail info@faw.admin.ch; internet www.agroscope.admin.ch; agricultural research for sustained economic activity in agricultural, nutritional and environmental sectors; develops scientific knowledge and technical principles for agricultural and environmental policy decisions and their legal implementation; Dir of Agroscope Changins-Wädenswil Dr JEAN-PHILIPPE MAYOR; Dir of Agroscope Liebefeld-Posieux-Haras Dr MICHAEL GYSI; Dir of Agroscope Reckenholz-Tänikon Dr PAUL STEFFEN; publs *Agrarforschung Schweiz / Recherche Agronomique Suisse, ALP aktuell, Revue suisse de viticulture arboriculture horticulture, Schweizer Zeitschrift für Obst- und Weinbau.*

ARCHITECTURE AND TOWN PLANNING

Fondazione Archivio del Moderno (Archive of the Modern): Largo Bernasconi 2, 6850 Medrisio; tel. 586665500; fax 586665555; e-mail archivio.arc@usi.ch; internet www.arc.usi.ch/archivio.htm; f. 1996; ind. research institute supporting Acad. of Archi-

tecture of Mendrisio, reinforcing its teaching and scholarly activities; acquisition, protection, preservation and exploitation of archives of architecture, urban planning, engineering, design, art and photography; promotes scientific research in fields of history of modern and contemporary architecture, art, design, territory and civil engineering, recognizing their leading role in current state of society; Dir LETIZIA TEDESCHI; Deputy Dir NICOLA NAVONE.

Istituto di Ricerca per il Progetto Urbano Contemporaneo (Institute for the Contemporary Urban Project): Largo Bernasconi 2, 6850 Medrisio; e-mail i.cup@arch.unisi.ch; internet www.arch.unisi.ch/ris_ist_icup; f. 2004; attached to Univ. della Svizzera italiana; research studies on grounds of quantitative parameters: mobility, transport, energetic consumption, sustainability, re-use of existing architectures, effect of new infrastructures, economic capacity of territory; Dir Prof. JOSEP ACEBILLO.

ECONOMICS, LAW AND POLITICS

Center for Comparative and International Studies (CIS) Zürich: Haldeneggsteig 4, 8092 Zürich; tel. 446326385; fax 446321289; e-mail cispostmaster@gess.ethz.ch; internet www.cis.ethz.ch; f. 1997; research centre for comparative politics and int. relations; fosters cooperation in research and education; organizes research seminars, workshops and public events with leading academics and political practitioners; topics of research: democracy, political violence, markets and politics, and sustainable devt; Dir Prof. Dr KATHARINA MICHAELOWA; Vice-Dir Prof. LARS-ERIK CEDERMAN.

Institut Suisse de Droit Comparé/Schweizerisches Institut für Rechtsvergleichung/Istituto Svizzero di Diritto Comparato (Swiss Institute of Comparative Law): 1015 Lausanne; tel. 216924911; fax 216924949; e-mail info@isdc.ch; internet www.isdc.ch; f. 1978; provides Fed. Govt with documents and studies necessary for legislation and for conclusion of int. conventions; participates in int. efforts towards approx. and unification of law; gives information and consultations to courts, admins, attorneys and interested persons; conducts its own scientific research, promotes and co-ordinates studies in Swiss univs and provides researchers in Switzerland with appropriate centre for study; library: see Libraries and Archives; Dir Prof. Dr CHRISTINA SCHMID; Vice-Dir Dr LUKAS HECKENDORN URSCHELER.

Institute for Microeconomics and Public Economics: Via G. Buffi 13, 6904 Lugano; tel. 586664783; fax 586664733; e-mail marisa.clemenz@usi.ch; internet www.mecop.eco.unisi.ch; f. 1998; attached to Univ. della Svizzera italiana; research in fields of public economics and public management; offers graduate and postgraduate courses; Dir MASSIMO FILIPPINI.

Institute of Finance: Via G. Buffi 13, 6900 Lugano; tel. 586664752; fax 586664734; e-mail abf.istfin.eco@usi.ch; internet www.istfin.eco.usi.ch; f. 1999; attached to Univ. della Svizzera Italiana; research about quantitative and institutional themes of financial markets; offers postgraduate studies; Dir GIOVANNI BARONE-ADESI.

Istituto di Diritto (Institute of Law): Via G. Buffi 13, 6900 Lugano; tel. 586664627; fax 586664647; e-mail marco.borghi@usi.ch; internet www.idusi.eco.usi.ch; attached to Univ. della Svizzera Italiana; offers postgraduate training and interdisciplinary activities; research in field law in Ticino; organizes exhibitions; Dir MARCO BORGHI.

Istituto di Ricerche Economiche (Institute for Economic Research): Via Maderno 24, CP 4361, 6904 Lugano; tel. 586664661; fax 586664662; e-mail ire.eco@usi.ch; internet www.ire.eco.usi.ch; attached to Univ. della Svizzera italiana; research on various aspects of regional and urban economics, ranging from regional growth and devt to competitiveness and innovation and from labour market issues to transportation and mobility; Dir RICO MAGGI; Vice-Dir SIEGFRIED ALBERTON.

Schweizerisches Institut für Auslandforschung/Institut Suisse de Recherches Internationales (Swiss Institute of International Studies): Frau Anja Spring Augustinerhof 1, 8001 Zürich; tel. 442121313; fax 442127854; e-mail info@siaf.ch; internet www.siaf.ch; f. 1943; attached to Univ. Zürich; deals with current issues in the fields of politics, economy, society, science and culture and selected for qualified and internationally renowned speakers; gives SIAF Award for outstanding theses, Licentiate and Masters theses at Univ. and ETH Zurich; Pres. KASPAR VILLIGER; Vice-Pres. Dr MARTIN MEYER; Treas. JOSEF MEIER; publ. *Sozialwissenschaftliche Studien* (1 a year).

EDUCATION

Institut de Recherche et de Documentation Pédagogique: Faubourg de l'Hôpital 43–45, CP 556, 2002 Neuchâtel; tel. 328898600; fax 328896971; e-mail secretariat@irdp.ch; internet www.irdp.ch; f. 1970; research in French-speaking Switzerland, into educational methods, organization and administration; creation and analysis of teaching aids; documentation; library of 10,000 vols; Dir MATTHIS BEHRENS; publ. *Le point sur la recherche* (irregular).

Institut Européen de l'Université de Genève: rue Jean-Daniel Colladon 2, 1204 Genève; tel. 223797850; fax 223797852; internet www.unige.ch/ieug; f. 1963; directs, coordinates and promotes educational programs in European studies and research on Europe in interdisciplinary perspective; organizes symposia, seminars, workshops and confs; library of 18,000 vols, 25,000 monographs, 92 periodicals; Dir Prof. NICOLAS LEVRAT; Librarian JEAN-MARC MEMBREZ; publ. *Euryopa*.

Istituto di Studi Italiani: Via Lambertenghi 10A, 6904 Lugano; tel. 586664700; fax 586664259; e-mail ism@usi.ch; internet www.isi.com.usi.ch; f. 2007; attached to Univ. della Svizzera italiana; offers graduate, postgraduate, doctoral studies in language, Italian literature and culture; scientific research projects in tradition of Italian studies; Dir Prof. CARLO OSSOLA.

HISTORY, GEOGRAPHY AND ARCHAEOLOGY

Institut d'Histoire de la Réformation: rue de-Candolle 5, 1211 Geneva 4; tel. 223797128; fax 223797133; e-mail marlene.jaouich@unige.ch; internet www.unige.ch/ihr; f. 1969; attached to Univ. de Genève; promotes research and postgraduate studies in history of ideas, instns and practices of reformation; Dir MARIA-CRISTINA PITASSI; Sec. MARLÈNE JAOUICH.

LANGUAGE AND LITERATURE

Institut de langue et civilisation françaises (Institute of French Language and Civilisation): Faubourg de l'Hôpital 61–63, 2000 Neuchâtel; tel. 327181800; fax 327181801; e-mail ilcf.ce@unine.ch; internet www2.unine.ch/ilcf; f. 1892; attached to Univ. of Neuchâtel; research centre specia-

lized in teaching French; Dir PHILIPPE TERRIER; Sec. BRIGITTE STEINER.

Istituto Linguistico-Semiotico (Institute for Linguistics and Semiotics): Via G. Buffi 13, 6900 Lugano; tel. 586664791; fax 586664647; e-mail ils.com@usi.ch; internet www.ils.com.usi.ch; attached to Univ. della Svizzera italiana; research related to discourse, dialogue, argument, intercultural communication, linguistic structures and processes of interpretation of texts hypermedia; Dir EDDO RIGOTTI; Vice-Dir ANDREA ROCCI.

MEDICINE

Arbeitsstelle für Ethik in den Biowissenschaften (Unit for Ethics in the Biosciences): Univ. of Basel, Schönbeinstr. 20, 4056 Basel; Universität, Missionstr. 24, 4055 Basel; tel. 612601132; fax 612601133; e-mail christoph.rehmann-sutter@unibas.ch; internet www.aeb.unibas.ch; f. 1996; attached to Univ. of Basel; research on bioethics, philosophy of biology and ELSA research in genetics and genomics, esp. the patients' perspectives on gene therapy, genetic tests and societal perceptions of devts in genetics; library of 10,000 vols; Dir Prof. Dr CHRISTOPH REHMANN-SUTTER.

Centre Interfacultaire de Gérontologie (Interfaculty Centre for Gerontology): route de Acacias 54, 1227 Acacias; tel. 223793790; fax 223793787; e-mail cig@unige.ch; internet cig.unige.ch; f. 1992; attached to Univ. de Genève; research on various aspects of ageing, vulnerability and life course; Dir Prof. MICHEL ORIS.

Institut für Sucht- und Gesundheitsforschung Zürich: Konradstr. 32, POB, 8031 Zürich; tel. 444481160; fax 444481170; e-mail isgf@isgf.uzh.ch; internet www.isgf.uzh.ch; f. 1993; attached to Univ. of Zurich; research and service sectors, covering legal and illegal drugs, non substance-related addictive behaviour, health planning and economics, consulting and assessments and transfer of knowledge through training; Pres. Prof. Dr AMBROS UCHTENHAGEN; Vice-Pres. Prof. Dr RAINER HORNUNG.

Institute of Communication and Health: Via G. Buffi 6, 6904 Lugano; tel. 586664487; e-mail teresa.cafaro@usi.ch; internet www.ich.com.usi.ch; attached to Univ. of Lugano; theoretical and applied researches for preservation and improvement of individual health; organizes social and organizational programs for promotion of health, wellness and health policy; offers postgraduate educational programmes in health communication and management; Dir PETER J. SCHULZ.

Schweizerisches Institut für Allergie- und Asthmaforschung (Swiss Institute of Allergy and Asthma Research): Obere Str. 22, 7270 Davos; tel. 814100848; fax 814100840; e-mail siaf@siaf.uzh.ch; internet www.siaf.uzh.ch; f. 1988; attached to Univ. of Zurich; applied and basic research in field of allergies and asthma; Dir Prof. Dr CEZMI A. AKDIS.

Schweizerisches Tropen- und Public Health-institut (Swiss TPH)/**Institut Tropical et de Santé Publique Suisse** (Swiss Tropical and Public Health Institute): Socinstr. 57, 4051 Basel; Socinstr. 55A, Eulerstr. 54, 68, 77 4051 Basel; tel. 612848111; fax 612848101; e-mail library-tph@unibas.ch; internet www.swisstph.ch; f. 1943; present name 2010; provides teaching, research and services in field of int. health devt; library of 7,000 vols, 80 journals, 9,000 monographs, annual reports, reprints, course programs and theses; Pres. Prof. Dr FELIX GUTZWILLER; Vice-Dir JÖRG H. SCHWARZENBACH; Dir Prof.

Dr MARCEL TANNER; Deputy Dir NICOLAUS LORENZ; Deputy Dir NINO KÜNZLI.

NATURAL SCIENCES
General

Collegium Basilea (Institute of Advanced Study): Hochstr. 51, 4053 Basel; tel. 765245846; fax 613619524; e-mail info@colbas.org; internet www.colbas.org; f. 1999; supports interdisciplinary postdoctoral research, mainly in biological, physical and chemical sciences, with emphasis on physicochemical foundations of living systems and in applications of complexity theory; library of 7,000 vols; Pres. Prof. Dr JEREMY J. RAMSDEN; publs *Journal of Biological Physics and Chemistry* (4 a year), *Nanotechnology Perceptions* (review of ultraprecision engineering and nanotechnology, 3 a year).

High Altitude Research Stations Jungfraujoch & Gornergrat Int: Sidlerstr. 5, 3012 Bern; tel. 316314052; fax 316314405; e-mail louise.wilson@space.unibe.ch; internet www.ifjungo.ch; f. 1930; high-altitude research in solar astronomy, astrophysics, environmental sciences, atmospheric physics, atmospheric chemistry, glaciology, meteorology, physics and biology; international foundation run by scientific organizations of Austria, Belgium, Germany, Italy, Switzerland and the UK; Hon. Pres. Prof. Dr HANS BALSIGER; Pres. Prof. Dr ERWIN O. FLÜCKIGER; Treas. KARL MARTIN WYSS; Dir Prof. Dr MARKUS LEUENBERGER; publ. *Review on Activity*.

Space Center: Station 11, 1015 Lausanne; tel. 216936948; fax 216936940; e-mail space.center@epfl.ch; internet space.epfl.ch; attached to Ecole Polytechnique Fédérale de Lausanne; promotes space technology across science, education and industry; Dir Prof. HERBERT SHEA.

Staatssekretariat für Bildung und Forschung SBF/Secretariat d'Etat a l'education et a la recherche SER (State Secretariat for Education and Research SER): Hallwylstr. 4, 3003 Bern; tel. 313229691; fax 313227854; e-mail info@sbf.admin.ch; internet www.sbf.admin.ch; f. 1969; prepares policy decisions for education and science and executes scientific policy; coordinates activities of Fed. bodies concerned with research and education; supports univs and other institutes of higher education and contributes to grants; is responsible for encouragement and general coordination of research and higher education; with other depts deals with int. scientific affairs; Dir MAURO DELL'AMBROGIO; Deputy Dir JÜRG BURRI.

Stiftung für Humanwissenschaftliche Grundlagenforschung/Fondation pour la Recherche de Base dans les Sciences de l'Homme: Kirchgasse 42, 8001 Zürich; tel. 443830922; f. 1970; basic research in human sciences; Pres. Prof. JULES ANGST; Dir Dr WALTER BODMER.

Biological Sciences

Centre d'Imagerie BioMedicale (Centre for Biomedical Imaging): Station 6, 1015 Lausanne; tel. 216934467; fax 216937960; e-mail info@cibm.ch; internet www.cibm.ch; attached to Ecole Polytechnique Fédérale de Lausanne; research on understanding of biomedical processes in health and disease, focusing on mechanisms of normal functioning, pathogenic mechanisms, characterization of disease onset prior to structural damage, metabolic and functional consequences of gene expression, and non-invasive insights into disease processes under treatment; Dir Prof. ROLF GRUETTER.

Conservatoire et Jardin botaniques de la Ville de Genève: POB 60, 1292 Chambésy; tel. 224185133; fax 224185101; e-mail periodiques.cjb@ville-ge.ch; internet www .ville-ge.ch/cjb; f. 1817; systematic botany, taxonomy, floristics, ecology, phytogeography; research in plant systematics, floristics, and population genetics; library of 100,000 vols, 4,1447 periodicals; Dir Prof. PIERRE-ANDRÉ LOIZEAU; publs *Boissiera*, *Candollea*.

Universität Bern Institut für Pflanzenwissenschaften (Institute of Plant Sciences): Altenbergrain 21, 3013 Bern; tel. 316314911; fax 316314942; e-mail ipsinfo@ ips.unibe.ch; internet www.ips.unibe.ch; f. 1862; attached to Univ. Bern; consists of 6 ind. research sections; research covers vegetation ecology, plant ecology, paleoecology, molecular ecology and plant devt, plant breeding, plant nutrition, molecular physiology; teaching at all academic levels; receives c. one-third of budget from the Swiss Nat. Science Foundation, EU and other orgs; Dir Prof. Dr DORIS RENTSCH; Sec. HELGA RODRÍGUEZ.

Botanic Garden:

> **Botanischer Garten Bern:** Altenbergrain 21, 3013 Bern; tel. 316314945; fax 316314993; e-mail info@botanischergarten .ch; internet boga.unibe.ch; f. 1859; Dir Prof. Dr MARKUS FISCHER.

Mathematical Sciences

Centre Interfacultaire Bernoulli (Bernoulli Interfaculty Centre of Mathematics): Station 15, 1015 Lausanne; tel. 216932583; internet cib.epfl.ch; attached to Ecole Polytechnique Fédérale de Lausanne; organizes programmes and symposiums related to research in field of mathematics; Dir TUDOR RATIU.

Physical Sciences

Centre Universitaire d'Ecologie Humaine et des Sciences de l'Environnement: route de Drize 7, 1227 Carouge; tel. 223790875; fax 223790860; internet www .unige.ch/ecohum; f. 1976, present status 2008; attached to Univ. de Genève; research and teaching in natural and social sciences; Dir B. BÜRGENMEIER; publ. *journées du cuepe*.

Eidgenössische Forschungsanstalt für Wald, Schnee und Landschaft (Swiss Federal Institute for Forest, Snow and Landscape Research): Zürcherstr. 111, 8903 Birmensdorf; tel. 447392111; fax 447392215; e-mail wslinfo@wsl.ch; internet www.wsl.ch; attached to ETH Zurich; concerned with use, devt and protection of natural and urban spaces; maintains experimental and research plots for studying rock fall or debris flow, study areas for monitoring effects of climate change on forests and sites damaged by storms or fires for investigating impact of natural hazards; library of 16,000 vols, 4,000 maps of Switzerland, 1,500 journals, 3,000 electronic journals; Dir Prof. Dr JAMES KIRCHNER; Deputy Dir Dr CHRISTOPH HEGG.

Institut für Astronomie: ETH Zürich, Wolfgang-Pauli-Str. 27, 8093 Zürich; tel. 446337608; fax 446331238; e-mail marcella@phys.ethz.ch; internet www.astro .phys.ethz.ch; f. 1864; attached to ETH Zürich; research on astronomy and astrophysics; Chair. Prof. Dr MARCELLA CAROLLO; Vice-Chair. Prof. MICHAEL MEYER.

Observatoire Astronomique de l'Université de Genève: 51 Ch. des Maillettes, 1290 Sauverny–Geneva; tel. 223792200; fax 223792205; e-mail gilbert.burki@obs.unige .ch; internet www.unige.ch/sciences/astro; f. 1772; attached to Univ. de Genève; astronomy, astrophysics research; 115 mems; library of 6,000 vols, 500 periodicals; Dir

Prof. STÉPHANE UDRY; Librarian CLAUDE GUIDI.

Schweizerische Gesellschaft für Astrophysik und Astronomie/Société Suisse d'Astrophysique et d'Astronomie (Swiss Society for Astrophysics and Astronomy): Observatoire de Genève 51, Ch. des Maillettes, 1290 Sauverny; e-mail georges .meynet@unige.ch; internet obswww.unige .ch/ssaa; f. 1968; research in astrophysics and astronomy; training of researchers through courses; Pres. Prof. DANIEL SCHAERER; Vice-Pres. MICHAEL MEYER; Treas. Dr YANN ALIBERT; Sec. Prof. GEORGES MEYNET.

Specola Solare Ticinese, Locarno: Via ai Monti 146, CP 71, 6605 Locarno 5; tel. 917562376; fax 917562375; e-mail scortesi@ specola.ch; internet www.specola.ch; f. 1957; solar observation; determination of Wolf number; data collected sent regularly to SIDC; library of 600 vols; Pres. Prof. Dr PHILIPPE JETZER; Vice-Pres. Dr MARIO CAMANI; Treas. ALBERTO TABORELLI; Sec. Ing. FLAVIO DONATI; publ. *MERIDIANA* (6 a year).

WSL-Institut für Schnee- und Lawinenforschung (SLF) (WSL Institute for Snow and Avalanche Research): Flüelastr. 11, 7260 Davos Dorf; tel. 814170111; fax 814170110; e-mail contact@slf.ch; internet www.slf.ch; f. 1936; attached to Swiss Federal Institute for Forest, Snow and Landscape Research; research on physics and mechanics of snow and snow pack, avalanche formation and mechanics, protective structure, snow and avalanche interaction with forests, and an avalanche warning service; library of 20,000 vols; Dir Prof. Dr JAMES KIRCHNER; Deputy Dir Dr CHRISTOPH HEGG; publs *Mitteilungen*, *Unfallberichte*, *Winterbericht* (1 a year).

Libraries and Archives

Aarau

Aargauer Kantonsbibliothek: Aargauerpl., 5000 Aarau; tel. 628352362; fax 628352369; e-mail kantonsbibliothek@ag.ch; internet www.ag.ch/kantonsbibliothek; f. 1803; oldest document is written parchment from early 9th century; specialized in designed humanities; special collns: Zurlaubiana (history of Switzerland and Europe), Frank Wedekind archive; 700,000 vols, 2,000 periodicals, 850 incunabula, 1,500 MSS; Dir Dr RUTH WÜST; Deputy Dir Lic. ANITA GRESELE.

Staatsarchiv Aargau: Entfelderstr. 22, 5001 Aarau; tel. 628351290; fax 628351299; e-mail staatsarchiv@ag.ch; internet www.ag .ch/staatsarchiv; f. 1803; records of 1027 to 1803 and from district of establishing systematic documentation together until beginning of Canton; divided into dept; 130,000 entries; 70,000 records in Govt Council resolutions from 1971 to 1996, consisting of title and description; State Archivist Lic. ANDREA VOELLMIN; Sec. ANITA MÜLLER.

Basel

Allgemeine Bibliotheken der Gesellschaft für das Gute und Gemeinnützige: Im Schmiedenhof 10, 4051 Basel; tel. 612641111; fax 612641190; e-mail info@ stadtbibliothekbasel.ch; internet www .stadtbibliothekbasel.ch; f. 1807; eight brs; 290,000 vols; central library and 8 br. libraries; Dir KLAUS EGLI; Vice-Dir MARIE-THÉRÈSE BANDERA.

Archiv für Schweizerische Kunstgeschichte: Im Laurenz-Bau, St. Alban-Graben 8, Postfach, 4010 Basel; tel.

612066292; fax 612066297; e-mail info-kunsthist@unibas.ch; internet kunsthist .unibas.ch/seminar/archiv-fuer-schweizer-ische-kunstgeschichte; attached to Universitätsgut; illustrations of monuments, works of painting, sculpture and ancient and modern decorative arts, literature on Swiss art history as reference library, projection images; 6,000 vols; Dir NIKLAUS MEIER.

Bibliothek des Museums der Kulturen Basel: Münsterpl. 20, 4051 Basel; tel. 612665630; fax 612665605; e-mail mkb .biblio@bs.ch; internet www.mkb.ch; f. 1901; specialized literature on ethnology on areas dealt with by museum's collns and scientific history of ethnology; 80,000 vols, 200 journals; Chief Librarian ELISABETH IDRIS-HÖHENER; Librarian ANGELIKA KUTTER.

Schweizerisches Wirtschaftsarchiv/ Archives Economiques Suisses (Swiss Economic Archives): Peter Merian-Weg 6, 4002 Basel; tel. 612673219; fax 612673208; e-mail info@wwzb.unibas.ch; internet www .ub.unibas.ch/wwz-bibliothek-swa; f. 1910; nat. centre for economic information and economic history; open to gen. public; 650,000 vols, incl. business reports, periodicals, statistical publs, reports on social instns and professional socs; 2,500,000 newspaper cuttings; Dir IRENE AMSTUTZ; Sec. BARBARA DÜRR.

Staatsarchiv Basel-Stadt: Martinsgasse 2, 4001 Basel; tel. 612678601; fax 612676571; e-mail stabs@bs.ch; internet www .staatsarchiv.bs.ch; history of canton of Basel and its communities; Dir Lic. ESTHER BAUR; publ. *Quellen und Forschungen zur Basler Geschichte*.

Universitätsbibliothek Basel (University Library of Basel): Schönbeinstr. 18–20, 4056 Basel; tel. 612673100; fax 612673103; e-mail info-ub@unibas.ch; internet www.ub.unibas .ch; f. 1460; 3,300,000 vols, scientific works, 10,000 musical MSS, 3,000 incunabula, 35,000 topographic maps, 100,000 reproductions of portraits; Dir HANNES HUG; Vice-Dir FELIX WINTER; publs *Die Amerbachkorrespondenz*, *Die Matrikel der Universität Basel*, *Die mittelalterlichen Handschriften der Universitätsbibliothek Basel*.

Bern

Bibliothek des Musikschule Konservatorium Bern: Kramgasse 36, 3011 Bern; e-mail office@konsibern.ch; internet www .konsibern.ch; f. 1917; 50,000 vols; Pres. ANNAMARIE ZINSLI.

Burgerbibliothek Bern/Bibliothèque de la Bourgeoisie de Berne: Münstergasse 63, Postfach, 3000 Bern 8; tel. 313203333; fax 313203370; e-mail bbb@burgerbib.ch; internet www.burgerbib.ch; f. 1951; medieval MSS, Bongarsiana-Codices, documents concerning Swiss and Bernese history and bequests of important people such as Albrecht von Haller or Jeremias Gotthelf; acts as archival capacity for Burgergemeinde (civic community), guilds and Burgers' socs; 15,000 vols, 50 periodicals, 2,700 m of historical MSS, of which 50 m medieval MSS; Dir Dr CLAUDIA ENGLER; Sec. ANNELIES HÜSSY; publs *Kataloge der Burgerbibliothek Bern*, *Passepartout*, *Schriften der Burgerbibliothek Bern*.

Schweizerische Nationalbibliothek/Bibliothèque nationale suisse (Swiss National Library): Hallwylstr. 15, 3003 Bern; tel. 313228935; fax 313228408; e-mail info@nb.admin.ch; internet www.nb.admin .ch; f. 1895; contains all publs issued in Switzerland and foreign publs by Swiss authors or concerning Switzerland; Swiss union catalogue, SwissInfoDesk, Swiss Literary Archives, Prints and Drawings Dept,

Swiss ISSN Centre, Centre Dürrenmatt Neuchâtel; 5,400,000 vols, 749,175 bound vols of periodicals, 384,056 engravings, photos and maps, 67,212 musical publs, 14,560 microforms and CD-ROMs, 18,397 audio visual items, 277 collns in the Swiss Literary Archives, 68 collns in the Prints and Drawings Dept; Dir MARIE-CHRISTINE DOFFEY; Vice-Dir ELENA BALZARDI; publs *Bibliographie der Schweizergeschichte / Bibliographie de l'histoire suisse / Bibliografia della storia svizzera*, *Bulletin du Cercle d'études internationales Jean Starobinski*, *Passim* (Bulletin des Schweizerischen Literaturarchivs/Bulletin des Archives littéraires suisses/Bollettino dell'Archivio svizzero di letteratura/Bulletin da l'Archiv svizzer da litteratura), *The Swiss Book / Le Livre suisse/ Das Schweizer Buch / Il libro svizzero* (24 a year), *Quarto* (Zeitschrift des Schweizerischen Literaturarchivs / Revue des Archives littéraires suisses / Rivista dell'Archivio svizzero di letteratura/Revista dell'Archiv svizzer da litteratura).

Schweizerisches Bundesarchiv (Swiss Federal Archives): Archivstr. 24, 3003 Bern; tel. 313228989; fax 313227823; e-mail bundesarchiv@bar.admin.ch; internet www.bar.admin.ch; f. 1798; appraises, secures, describes and provides access to archiveworthy records of Swiss Confederation; Dir ANDREAS KELLERHALS; Deputy Dir P. KUNZLER.

Staatsarchiv des Kantons Bern: Falkenpl. 4, POB 8424, 3001 Bern; tel. 316335101; fax 316335102; e-mail info.stab@sta.be.ch; internet www.sta.be.ch/staatsarchiv; collects, registers and preserves canton's archival heritage; microfilms of parish registers; State Archivist Dr PETER MARTIG; Sec. MADLEN TANNER; publ. *Das Staatsarchiv des Kantons Bern.*

Universitätsbibliothek Bern: Münstergasse 61, 3000 Bern 8; tel. 316319211; fax 316319299; e-mail info@ub.unibe.ch; internet www.ub.unibe.ch; f. 1528; 50 br. libraries; 4,600,000 vols, 17,000 online journals; Chief Librarian MARIANNE RUBLI SUPERSAXO.

Bubendorf

Fondation Bibliotheca Afghanica (Afghanistan Institute in Switzerland): Bruehlstr. 2, 4416 Bubendorf; tel. 619339877; fax 619339878; e-mail info@afghanistan-institut.ch; internet www.afghanistan-institut.ch; f. 1975; research institute and archive; Afghani nature, culture and contemporary history; material on Afghan history, geography, ethnography, religion and politics; German newspaper clippings; Mujahideen and Communist govt publs; 17,000 vols, 40,000 photographs; Dir PAUL BUCHERER-DIETSCHI.

Chur

Staatsarchiv Graubünden: Karlihofpl., 7001 Chur; tel. 812572803; fax 812572001; e-mail info@sag.gr.ch; internet www.sag.gr.ch; f. 1803; written works on history of Graubünden; records of the Canton of Graubünden and its predecessors (Freistaat der drei Bünde); Dir Lic. RETO WEISS; publ. *Quellen und Forschungen zur Bündner Geschichte QBG.*

Cologny

Bibliotheca Bodmeriana (Fondation Martin Bodmer): 19–21 route du Guignard, 1223 Cologny; tel. 227074433; fax 227074430; e-mail info@fondationbodmer.ch; internet www.fondationbodmer.org; f. 1972; 160,000 vols; spec. collns of papyrus, MSS, autographs, incunabula, music MSS, drawings; Dir Prof. CHARLES MÉLA.

Fribourg

Bibliothèque Cantonale et Universitaire de Fribourg/Kantons-und Universitätsbibliothek Freiburg: rue Joseph-Piller 2, 1701 Fribourg; tel. 263051333; fax 263051377; e-mail bcu@fr.ch; internet www.fr.ch/bcuf; f. 1848; special colln of MSS and incunabula of middle ages to present; Heritage Fribourg colln; organizes cultural activities; 3,500,000 vols; Dir Dr MARTIN GOOD.

Geneva

Archives d'etat de Genève: 1 rue de l'Hôtel de Ville, 1211 Geneva 3; tel. 223279320; fax 223279321; e-mail archives@etat.ge.ch; internet www.ge.ch/archives; material on history of Geneva; Dir PIERRE FLÜCKIGER.

Bibliothèque d'Art et d'Archéologie des Musées d'art et d'histoire: 5 Promenade du Pin, 1204 Geneva; tel. 224182700; fax 224182701; e-mail info.baa@ville-ge.ch; internet www.ville-ge.ch/baa; f. 1911; library of Musées d'Art et d'Histoire and public art library; 400,000 vols, 6,200 periodicals, 140,000 exhibition and auction catalogues, CD-ROMs, databases, microforms, video cassettes, iconography; Conservator VÉRONIQUE GONCERUT ESTÈBE; publ. *Geneva* (annual review of Musées d'art et d'histoire).

Bibliothèque de l'ONUG (United Nations Office at Geneva Library): Palais des Nations, 1211 Geneva 10; tel. 229174181; fax 229170028; e-mail library@unog.ch; internet www.unog.ch/library; f. 1919; manages cultural activities at Palais des Nations, organizes c. 40 annual events (concerts, exhibitions, film festivals) in cooperation with Permanent Mission of the UN Member State; manages visits to its premises and research training for UNOG staff members; 1.1m. vols, 4m. documents and publs of UN and its specialized agencies, 500,000 govt documents, 9,000 periodicals; archives of the League of Nations; Chief Librarian Dr DAVID CHIKVAIDZE; publs *Bibliographie Mensuelle* (12 a year), *Catalogue des Publications en Série* (serials catalogue).

Bibliothèque de Genève: Promenade des Bastions, 1211 Geneva 4; tel. 224182800; fax 224182801; e-mail info.bge@ville-ge.ch; internet www.ville-ge.ch/bge; f. 1562; 2,191,000 vols and pamphlets, 70,000 posters, 23,000 maps, 45,000 engravings, 400 painted portraits, 15,000 MSS; Dir JEAN-CHARLES GIROUD.

Bibliothèques Municipales: 10 rue de la Tour-de-Boël, CP 3930 1211 Geneva 3; tel. 224183250; fax 224183251; e-mail webbmu@ville-ge.ch; internet www.ville-ge.ch/bmu; f. 1931; 7 br. libraries, sports library, bookmobile service; 800,000 vols; Dir ISABELLE RUEPP; publ. *AgendaBM.*

International Labour Office Library: 4 route des Morillons, 1211 Geneva 22; tel. 227998675; fax 227996516; e-mail inform@ilo.org; internet www.ilo.org/inform; f. 1919; core repository of ILO publs produced in Geneva and in ILO's offices around world; open to public on request; 2m. vols and pamphlets, 3,000 current periodicals (incl. annuals and official gazettes); computerized data base (LABORDOC), containing 210,000 abstracts, available for online searching worldwide through facilities of ESA-IRS and Questel-ORBIT and on CD-ROM; Dir L. DRYDEN; publ. *ILO Thesaurus: Labour.*

World Health Organization Library and Information Networks for Knowledge: 20 Ave Appia, 1211 Geneva 27; tel. 227912062; fax 227914150; e-mail library@who.int; internet www.who.int/library; f. 1948; WHO permanent colln, int. public health literature, journals and databases, historical colln, govt statistical reports, WHOLIS database; Librarian TOMAS ALLEN.

Grand Saint-Bernard

Bibliothèque de l'Hospice du Grand Saint-Bernard: 1946 Bourg-Saint-Pierre; tel. 277871236; fax 277871107; e-mail hospicestbernard@gsbernard.ch; internet www.gsbernard.ch; library of Austin Canons monastery; works on history, theology, Catholic literature, natural sciences (botany, entomology, zoology, ornithology, mineralogy), applied sciences (physics, arithmetic, chemistry, astronomy), geography and travel, philosophy, law (civil and canon) liturgy and numismatics, ancient MSS and maps; 32,500 vols, 8,000 periodicals.

Lausanne

Bibliothèque & Archives de la Ville de Lausanne: 11 pl. Chauderon, 1003 Lausanne; tel. 213156915; fax 213156007; e-mail bml@lausanne.ch; internet www.lausanne.ch/bibliotheque; f. 1934; 2 main libraries; 4 brs in Chailly, Entre-Bois, Montriond, Grand-Vennes; 4 linear km of municipal archives of admin. and private regional records from 1142 to present; books in French and foreign languages; multimedia collns; 5,000 items of original artwork; 358,000 vols, 150,000 comics research colln; Dir FRÉDÉRIC SARDET.

Bibliothèque cantonale et Universitaire de Lausanne, Riponne-Palais de Rumine: 6, Place de la Riponne, 1014 Lausanne; tel. 213167880; fax 213167870; e-mail info-riponne@bcu.unil.ch; internet www.unil.ch/bcu; f. 1537; br. in Dorigny; legal deposit library of Vaud Canton; regional documentation; 2m. vols, 170 incunabula; 29,500 CDs, 32,000 musical scores, 10,000 audiovisual materials and 2,500 LP records; Dir JEANNETTE FREY; publs *Catalogues des fonds de manuscrits, Catalogues des manuscrits musicaux.*

Bibliothèque de l'EPFL—Rolex Learning Centre: Rolex Learning Centre, Station 20, 1015 Lausanne; tel. 216932156; fax 216935100; e-mail questions.bib@epfl.ch; internet library.epfl.ch; f. 1945; open to public; specializes in fields of study and research at EPFL; organizes confs and publs; science and technology; 550,000 vols, 11,000 electronic journals, 100 databases; Dir DAVID AYMONIN.

Bibliothèque de l'Institut Suisse de Droit Comparé: Dorigny, 1015 Lausanne; tel. 216924911; fax 216924949; internet www.isdc.ch; f. 1982; collects legal material from all countries in all fields of law, incl. int. law; European Documentation Centre; 360,000 vols, 2,000 periodicals, 900 electronic resources; Head SADRI SAIEB.

Bibliothèque Universitaire de Médecine: Centre Hospitalier Universitaire Vaudois, 1011 Lausanne; tel. 213145082; fax 21 3145070; e-mail bdfm@chuv.ch; internet www.chuv.ch/bdfm; f. 1968; colln on different areas of health and medicine; 60,000 vols, 2,000 periodicals, 12,000 electronic journals, microcomputer facilities, audio-visual library; Head Librarian ISABELLE DE KAENEL.

Lucerne

Staatsarchiv des Kantons Luzern: Schützenstr. 9, POB 7853, 6000 Lucerne 7; tel. 412285365; fax 412286663; e-mail staatsarchiv@lu.ch; internet www.staatsarchiv.lu.ch; f. 1803; Siegel colln, seal stamp colln, Clichésammlung, Autograph colln, copy colln, Photo and copy colln, photo negative and microfilm colln, newspapers; 25,000 vols; Archivist Dr JÜRG SCHMUTZ; publ. *Luzerner Historische Veröffentlichungen* (irregular).

Zentral- und Hochschulbibliothek Luzern: Sempacherstr. 10, 6002 Lucerne; tel. 412285312; fax 412108255; e-mail info@zhbluzern.ch; internet www.zhbluzern.ch; f. 1951; incl. Burghers' library, canton library and library of Univ. of Lucerne; Lucerne Documentary Heritage Colln; differentiated spectrum of technical, factual and entertainment media; 960,893 vols, 2,736 MSS, 136,285 engravings, photos and maps, 37,117 microforms; colln of Swiss publs up to 1848; Dir Dr ULRICH NIEDERER; Deputy Dir Dr WILFRIED LOCHBÜHLER.

Lugano

Biblioteca Cantonale: Lugano, Ticino: Viale C. Cattaneo 6, 6901 Lugano; tel. 918154611; fax 918154619; e-mail bclu-segr.sbt@ti.ch; internet www.sbt.ti.ch/bclugano; f. 1852; colln on religion, theology, art, language, philology, linguistics, literature, with particular reference to Italian culture; inc. *Libreria Patria*, special colln of 'Ticinensia', 40,000 vols; Archivio Prezzolini and collns on contemporary culture; 300,000 vols, 1,300 periodicals, 198 incunabula; Dir Prof. GERARDO RIGOZZI.

Neuchâtel

Archives de l'Etat de Neuchâtel: Le Château, 12 rue de la Collégiale, 2000 Neuchâtel; tel. 328896040; fax 328896088; e-mail service.archivesetat@ne.ch; internet www.ne.ch/archives; f. 1898; stores and manages documents of State and private documents relating to history of canton of Neuchâtel; maintains historical library and administrative library; State Archivist LIONEL BARTOLINI; Librarian GÉRALDINE GALFETTI.

Bibliothèque des Pasteurs: Fbg de l'Hôpital 41, 2000 Neuchâtel; tel. 327254666; e-mail carmen.burkhalter@unine.ch; f. 1538; theological library of 90,000 vols, 80,000 monographs; Librarian CECILIA GRIENER HURLEY.

Bibliothèque Publique et Universitaire: 3 pl. Numa-Droz, CP 1916, 2000 Neuchâtel; tel. 327177302; fax 327177309; e-mail secretariat.bpu@unine.ch; internet bpun.unine.ch; f. 1788; 600,000 vols, 1,900 periodicals, 8,000 posters, 40,000 books of information and general knowledge and multimedia documents (DVD, CD-ROMs and audio books); Dir THIERRY CHÂTELAIN; publs *Bibliothèques et musées*, *Revue historique neuchâteloise*, and bulletins of chronometry, geography, and natural sciences.

St Gallen

Kantonsbibliothek Vadiana St Gallen: Notkerstr. 22, 9000 St Gallen; tel. 582292321; fax 582292329; e-mail kb.vadiana@sg.ch; internet www.kb.sg.ch; f. 1551; colln point for St Gallische literature; three specialty divs: Vadian colln, collns of county Library and St Gallen centre for book (Zebu); 800,000 vols; Dir Dr CORNEL DORA; publ. *Veröffentlichungen der Gesellschaft Pro Vadiana*.

Stiftsbibliothek St Gallen: Klosterhof 6D, Postfach, 9004 St Gallen; tel. 712273416; fax 712273418; e-mail stibi@stibi.ch; internet www.stiftsbibliothek.ch; f. 719; library of fmr Benedictine Abbey of St Gall; important colln of MSS from Carolingian and Ottonian periods (8th–11th centuries); colln shows depth of European culture and documents cultural achievements of Abbey of St Gall from 8th century to dissolution of monastery in 1805; 170,000 vols; Dir Prof. Dr ERNST TREMP.

Sion

Médiathèque Valais (Bibliothèque Cantonale)/Mediathek Wallis (Kantonsbibliothek): 18 Ave de Pratifori, CP 182, 1951 Sion; tel. 276064550; fax 276064554; e-mail mv.sion@mediatheque.ch; internet www.mediatheque.ch; f. 1853; 4 brs: Brig, Sion, Martigny, Saint-Maurice; spec. collns on Alps; 840,000 vols; Dir DAMIAN ELSIG.

Solothurn

Bibliomedia Schweiz Suisse Svizzera: Rosenweg 2, 4500 Solothurn; tel. 326249020; fax 326249028; e-mail solothurn@bibliomedia.ch; internet www.buchstart.ch; f. 1920; promotes devt of libraries and promotion of reading; brs at Solothurn, Lausanne and Biasca; 500,000 vols; Dir PETER WILLE; Sec. BÉATRICE AEGERTER; publ. *Le Cri du Hibou* (irregular).

Zentralbibliothek: Bielstr. 39, POB, 4502 Solothurn; tel. 326276262; fax 326276200; e-mail info@zbsolothurn.ch; internet www.zbsolothurn.ch; f. 1930; 800,000 vols, 900 incunabula, 13,200 MSS, 7,000 illustrations and graphics, 18,000 music scores, 42,000 records, 550 current periodicals and series, 30,000 children's books; Dir for Collns Lic. VERENA BIDER; Dir for Admin. PETER PROBST; publs *Kleine Reihe*, *Musik aus der Sammlung der Zentralbibliothek Solothurn* (edns of regional compositions), *Veröffentlichungen der Zentralbibliothek Solothurn*.

Winterthur

Stadtbibliothek: Obere Kirchgasse 6, POB 132, 8402 Winterthur; tel. 522675148; fax 522675140; e-mail stadtbibliothek@win.ch; internet www.winbib.ch; f. 1660; spec. collns of local history, numismatics, music, African languages, MSS, letters and literature; non-lending library book collns, incl. books, music notes and cards from 1465 to 1900; open to public; six brs; 900,000 vols; Dir Dr HERMANN ROMER; publ. *Neujahrsblatt* (1 a year).

Zürich

ETH-Bibliothek (Library of the Swiss Federal Institute of Technology (ETH Zurich)): Rämistr. 101, 8092 Zürich; tel. 446322135; fax 446321087; e-mail info@library.ethz.ch; internet www.library.ethz.ch; f. 1855; specializes in science and technology; colln of architecture, civil engineering, engineering sciences, natural sciences and mathematics, system-oriented natural sciences, management and social sciences; 7.6m. vols and documents, 2.8m. monographs and bound journals, 2.2m. microforms, 1.8m. images, 402,000 maps, 261,000 MSS, 300,000 e-documents, 13,500 e-journals, 5,300 current journals (printed), 145 databases, 86,000 e-books, 144,000 abstracts and indices (NEBIS catalogue); Dir Dr WOLFRAM NEUBAUER; Deputy Dir ANDREAS KIRSTEIN.

Schweizerisches Sozialarchiv/Archives sociales suisses: Stadelhoferstr. 12, 8001 Zürich; tel. 432688740; fax 432688759; e-mail kontakt@sozialarchiv.ch; internet www.sozialarchiv.ch; f. 1906; centre of social documentation; open to public; collects corporate archives of traditional and new social movements and private documents of activists during such movements; 230,000 vols, 1,473 current periodicals, 188,000 brochures and pamphlets, 1.7m. newspaper cuttings, 30,500 archival documents, 102,500 iconic documents, 150 e-journals; Dir Dr ANITA ULRICH; Deputy Dir Dr URS KÄLIN.

Staatsarchiv des Kantons Zürich: Winterthurerstr. 170, 8057 Zürich; tel. and fax 446356911; e-mail staatsarchivzh@ji.zh.ch; internet www.staatsarchiv.zh.ch; f. 1837; archives of canton of Zürich and specialized library (local publs and collns of statutes and numerous pamphlets); archives: 30,000 m; 92,000 vols; Dir Dr BEAT GNÄDINGER.

Zentralbibliothek Zürich: Zähringerpl. 6, 8001 Zürich; tel. 442683100; fax 442683290; e-mail zb@zb.uzh.ch; internet www.zb.uzh.ch; f. 1914; city, cantonal and univ. library, inc. libraries of Naturforschende Gesellschaft in Zürich, Antiquarische Gesellschaft in Zürich, Geographisch-Ethnographische Gesellschaft Zürich, Schweizerischer Alpenclub, Allgemeine MusikGesellschaft Zürich, Bibliotheca Fennica; 5.25m. vols, 106,000 MSS and autographs, 11,260 incunabula, 249,000 maps, and spec. collns of graphic arts (222,000 items), 35,000 records and cassettes; 8,700 current print periodicals, 45,000 electronic periodicals, 190 newspapers; Dir Prof. SUSANNA BLIGGENSTORFER.

Zentrale für Betriebswirtschaft & Zentrale für Wirtschaftsdokumentation, Universität Zürich: Plattenstr. 14, 8032 Zürich; tel. 446343911; fax 446344995; e-mail bfb@business.uzh.ch; internet www.business.uzh.ch/libraries/libraryba.html; f. 1910, present status 1990; attached to Univ. of Zurich; large worldwide colln of annual reports of major companies; periodicals, OECD colln, online library catalogues in fields of business studies and economics, daily newspapers, magazines and statistical material available; 36,000 vols, 122 periodicals; Dir KATHARINA HERTZBERG-SCHILLING.

Museums and Art Galleries

Aarau

Aargauer Kunsthaus: Aargauerpl., 5001 Aarau; tel. 628352330; fax 628352329; e-mail kunsthaus@ag.ch; internet www.aargauerkunsthaus.ch; f. 1959; Swiss painting and sculpture since 1750; colln of paintings by Caspar Wolf (1735–83), Adolf Staebli, and Auberjonois, Brühlmann, Amiet, G. Giacometti, Hodler, Meyer-Amden, Louis Soutter, Vallotton; temporary exhibitions; Dir MADELEINE SCHUPPLI; Deputy Dir and Curator THOMAS SCHMUTZ.

Avenches

Musée Romain Avenches: 1580 Avenches; tel. 265573300; fax 265573313; e-mail musee.romain@vd.ch; internet www.aventicum.org; f. 1824; situated at 2nd century AD Roman amphitheatre; mosaics, funerary stelae and sculptures; excavations of Aventicum; temporary exhibitions; library of 18,000 vols; Pres. Prof. P. DUCREY; Dir Dr MARIE-FRANCE MEYLAN KRAUSE; publ. *Aventicum* (2 a year).

Basel

Antikenmuseum Basel und Sammlung Ludwig: St Alban Graben 5, 4010 Basel; tel. 612011212; fax 612011210; e-mail info@antikenmuseumbasel.ch; internet www.antikenmuseumbasel.ch; f. 1961; exhibition of art and culture of the Mediterranean area; collns of Greek art (2500–100 BC), Roman art (100 BC–AD 300), Etruscan art and Egyptian art, spec. exhibitions; Dir Prof. Dr PETER BLOME; Vice-Dir Dr ANDREA BIGNASCA; Curator Lic. VERA SLEHOFER; Curator Dr ANDRÉ WIESE; Curator Dr ELLA VAN DER MEIJDEN.

Historisches Museum Basel: Verwaltung, Steinenberg 4, 4051 Basel; tel. 612058600; fax 612058601; e-mail historisches.museum@bs.ch; internet www.hmb.ch; f. 1894; 4 brs containing colln of objects from Middle Ages to 20th century, civic culture of Basel in 18th and 19th centuries and colln of old musical instruments, numismatics, coaches and sleighs; library of 21,000 vols, 38 journals, 183 periodicals; Dir Dr MARIE-PAULE JUNG-

BLUT; Librarian DANIEL SUTER; publ. *Basler Kostbarkeiten* (1 a year).

Kunstmuseum Basel: St Albangraben 16, 4010 Basel; tel. 612066262; fax 612066252; internet www.kunstmuseumbasel.ch; f. 1662; pictures from 15th century to present day, notably by Witz, Holbein and contemporary painters; colln incl. Grünewald, Rembrandt, 16th- and 17th-century Dutch painting, Cézanne, Gauguin and Van Gogh; colln of cubist art; sculptures by Rodin and 20th-century artists; American art since 1950; dept of prints and drawings with old Upper Rhine, German and Swiss masters and 20th-century works; library of 150,000 vols, 200 periodicals; Dir Dr BERNHARD MENDES BÜRGI; Man. Dir FAUSTO DE LORENZO; Head of Library RAINER BAUM.

Attached Museum:

Museum für Gegenwartskunst (Museum of Contemporary Art): St Alban-Rheinweg 60, 4010 Basel; tel. 612066262; fax 612066253; internet www .kunstmuseumbasel.ch/en/museum-fuer--gegenwartskunst; f. 1980; contemporary art from collns of Emanuel Hoffmann Foundation and Kunstmuseum; Dir Dr BERNHARD MENDES BÜRGI; Curator NIKOLA DIETRICH.

Museum der Kulturen Basel: Muensterpl. 20, 4051 Basel; tel. 612665600; fax 612665605; e-mail info@mkb.ch; internet www.mkb.ch; f. 1849; ethnographical collections from all parts of the world, esp. from Oceania, Indonesia, South America and Europe; textiles; historic photographs, incl. stocks of fmr Swiss Museum of Ethnology; 300,000 objects; temporary exhibitions; library: see under Libraries and Archives; Dir Dr ANNA SCHMID; Vice-Dir Lic. DOMINIK WUNDERLIN; publs *Basler Beiträge zur Ethnologie*, guides.

Bern

Bernisches Historisches Museum: Helvetiapl. 5, 3005 Bern; tel. 313507711; fax 313507799; e-mail info@bhm.ch; internet www.bhm.ch; f. 1894; Burgundian tapestries, Königsfeld Diptych, Bern's silver treasure, Stone Age, Celts and Romans, art from Asia and Oceania, bronze hydria from Grächwil and series of ethnographic and numismatic collns; colln from early Middle Ages to Ancien Régime; Einstein museum; temporary exhibitions; Dir Dr JAKOB MESSERLI; Vice-Dir Prof. Dr FELIX MÜLLER.

Kunstmuseum (Museum of Fine Arts Bern): Hodlerstr. 8–12, 3000 Bern 7; tel. 313280944; fax 313280955; e-mail info@kunstmuseumbern.ch; internet www .kunstmuseumbern.ch; f. 1879; colln of 3,000 paintings and sculptures incl. Italian paintings from 14th to 16th centuries; works by Swiss masters from 15th to 19th centuries; works illustrating devt of art since 19th century by Manet, Cézanne, Monet, Pissaro, Renoir, Van Gogh, members of 'Blaue Ritter', 'Brücke', and Bauhaus movements, Rothko and Pollock, and other modern works by Hodler and other Swiss, French and German artists; Hermann and Margrit Rupf Foundation, incl. paintings by Picasso, Braque, Léger, Gris and Kandinsky; Adolf Wölfli Foundation; graphic art colln of more than 48,000 drawings, engravings, photographs, video cassettes and films; library of 110,000 vols; Dir Dr MATTHIAS FREHNER; Curator Dr THERESE BHATTACHARYA-STETTLER; Curator Dr KATHLEEN BÜHLER; publ. *Berner Kunstmitteilungen* (4 a year).

Naturhistorisches Museum: Bernastr. 15, 3005 Bern; tel. 313507111; fax 313507499; e-mail contact@nmbe.ch; internet www.nmbe .ch; f. 1832; colln incl. 220 dioramas of Swiss mammals and birds, big game (esp. African), Swiss fish, amphibians and reptiles, minerals of Swiss Alps, invertebrates, hall of skeletons; Earth science exhibition; three depts: Earth sciences, mineralogy and paleontology, invertebrates and vertebrates; promotes research in Univ. of Bern; Dir Prof. Dr MARCEL GÜNTERT; publ. *Contributions to Natural History* (2 a year).

Zentrum Paul Klee Bern: Monument im Fruchtland 3, 3000 Bern 31; tel. 313590101; fax 313590102; e-mail kontakt@zpk.org; internet www.zpk.org; f. 2005; 4,000 works of art by Paul Klee (1879–1940) and collns of biographical material; exhibition space for contemporary artists; children's museum 'Creaviva'; organizes concerts and theatre; CEO URSINA BARANDUN.

Biel

Museum Schwab: Seevorstadt 50, 2502 Biel; tel. 323227603; fax 323233768; e-mail info@muschwab.ch; internet www.bielbienne .ch/ww/de/pub/aktiv/kultur/museen/schwab .cfm; f. 1873; contains prehistoric exhibits, esp. of lake-dwelling culture, New Stone Age, Bronze Age, and 2nd Iron Age; colln of items from Roman period (Petinesca); temporary exhibitions; Dir MADELEINE BETSCHAVT.

Chur

Bündner Kunstmuseum: Postplatz, 7000 Chur; tel. 812572868; fax 812572172; e-mail info@bkm.gr.ch; internet www .buendner-kunstmuseum.ch; f. 1900; colln of works by Swiss artists, Segantini, Hodler, Alberto, Augusto and G. Giacometti, E. L. Kirchner and Angelica Kauffmann; exhibitions of Swiss and foreign art; Dir STEPHAN KUNZ; Curator Dr KATHARINA AMMANN.

Fribourg

Musée d'Art et d'Histoire: 12 rue de Morat, 1700 Fribourg; tel. 263055140; fax 263055141; e-mail mahf@fr.ch; internet www .fr.ch/mahf; f. 1823; housed in Hotel Ratzé (16th century); collns of prehistoric, Roman and medieval exhibits; important collns of Swiss sculpture and painting since 11th century; works from Marcello Foundation; monumental pieces by Jean Tinguely; stained glass gallery; works of art in Freiburg in 19th and 20th centuries; Dir VERENA VILLIGER STEINAUER; Curator STEPHAN GASSER.

Geneva

Fondation Baur, Musée des Arts d'Extrême-Orient (Baur Foundation-Museum of Far Eastern Art): 8 rue Munier Romilly, 1206 Geneva; tel. 227043282; fax 227891845; e-mail musee@fondationbaur.ch; internet fondation-baur.ch; f. 1964; 9,000 Chinese and Japanese art objects; Chinese imperial ceramic ware, jades and snuff bottles from 10th to 19th centuries and Japanese prints, lacquer, netsuke, and sword fittings, Chinese lacquer ware and export ceramics; temporary exhibitions related to Chinese and Japanese artwork; library of 5,500 vols; Dir MONIQUE CRICK; Curator HELEN LOVEDAY.

Musée d'art et d'histoire: 2 rue Charles Galland, 1206 Geneva 3; tel. 224182600; fax 224182601; e-mail mah@ville-ge.ch; internet www.ville-ge.ch/mah; f. 1910; contains local prehistory section; Mediterranean, Egyptian, Near Eastern, Byzantine and Coptic archaeology; Italian, Dutch, Flemish, German, French, English and Swiss (esp. Genevese) paintings, paintings since beginning of 20th century, European sculpture, applied art and numismatic colln; library of 300,000 vols, 5,900 periodicals, 70,000 auction catalogues from 1857 to today; Dir JEAN-YVES MARIN; publs *Genava* (1 a year), *Journal des Musées d'art et d'histoire* (3 a year).

Attached Museums:

Cabinet d'Arts Graphiques: 5 promenade du Pin, 1204 Geneva; tel. 224182770; fax 224182771; e-mail cde@ville-ge.ch; f. 1886, as separate institution, part of Musées d'art et d'histoire 1910; 350,000 items covering five centuries of printmaking; multiples and 20th- and 21st-century artist's books; Keeper Dr CHRISTIAN RÜMELIN.

Maison Tavel: 6 rue du Puits Saint-Pierre, 1204 Geneva; tel. 224183700; fax 224183701; e-mail mah@ville-ge.ch; f. 1986; history of city; exhibits of artifacts and images from 14th to 19th century; Curator CHAIX NATHALIE.

Musée Ariana: 10 ave de la Paix, 1202 Geneva; tel. 224185450; fax 224185451; f. 1884; European and Eastern ceramics and glass; Curator ROLAND BLAETTLER.

Musée d'Histoire des Sciences: 128 rue de Lausanne, 1202 Geneva; tel. 224815060; fax 224815061; f. 1964; scientific instruments; library of 10,000 vols; Curator NINIAN HUBERT VAN BLYENBURGH.

Musée Rath: Pl. Neuve, 1204 Geneva; tel. 224183340; fax 224183351; e-mail mah@ ville-ge.ch; f. 1828; temporary exhibitions; Dir JEAN-YVES MARIN.

Musée d'Art Moderne et Contemporain (Museum of Modern and Contemporary Art): 10 rue des Vieux-Grenadiers, 1205 Geneva; tel. 223206122; fax 227815681; internet www .mamco.ch; f. 1994; specialises in works since 1960; temporary exhibitions; archives of works of art; Dir CHRISTIAN BERNARD; Deputy Dir and Chief Curator FRANÇOISE NINGHETTO; Sec.-Gen. VALÉRIE MALLET.

Musée d'ethnographie de Genève: CP 1549, 1211 Geneva 26; tel. 224184550; fax 224184551; e-mail meg.ethno@ville-ge.ch; internet www.ville-ge.ch/meg; f. 1901; African colln; American colln; Asian colln; European colln; Oceanic colln; musical instruments; 400 film colln; colln of 130,000 historical photographs; also houses Archives Internationales de Musique Populaire; library of 45,000 vols, 1,500 periodicals; Dir Dr BORIS WASTIAU; publ. *Totem* (3 a year).

Muséum d'Histoire Naturelle: Route de Malagnou 1, 1208 Geneva; tel. 224186300; fax 224186301; e-mail info.mhn@ville-ge.ch; internet www.ville-ge.ch/mhng; f. 1820; depts of mammalogy and ornithology, herpetology and ichthyology, invertebrates, arthropods and insects, entomology, archaeozoology, geology and palaeontology, mineralogy; library of 200,000 vols, 40,000 monographs, 4,000 geological and topographical maps, 2,000 periodicals (800 current), also manages Bibliothèque de l'Association Nos Oiseaux and Bibliothèque du Centre de Coordination Ouest pour l'Etude et la Protection des Chauves-souris; Dir Dr DANIELLE DECROUEZ; Librarian CHRISTELLE MOUGIN; publs *Catalogue des Invertébrés de la Suisse*, *Le Rhinolophe* (1 a year), *Revue suisse de Zoologie* (4 a year), *Revue de Paléobiologie* (2 a year).

Glarus

Kunsthaus Glarus: Im Volksgarten, POB 665, 8750 Glarus; tel. 556402535; fax 556402519; e-mail office@kunsthausglarus .ch; internet www.kunsthausglarus.ch; f. 1870; 19th and 20th century Swiss and foreign contemporary art; temporary exhibitions; Pres. KASPAR MARTI; Vice-Pres. THOMAS ASCHMANN; Dir SABINE RUSTERHOLZ.

La Chaux-de-Fonds

Musée des Beaux-Arts: 33 rue des Musées, 2300 La Chaux-de-Fonds; tel. 329676077; fax 327220763; e-mail mba.vch@ne.ch; internet cdf-mba.ne.ch; f. 1864; colln of paintings, sculptures, videos and prints from 19th century (Matisse, Renoir, Van Gogh, Constable, Rouault) to now; works of Swiss artists (Anker, Vallotton, Bailly, Hodler), particularly of Neuchâtel district (Robert, Kaiser, l'Eplattenier, Perrin, Humbert, Le Corbusier, etc.); colln of European and American artists; temporary exhibitions; Dir LADA UMSTÄTTER.

Musée International d'Horlogerie: 29 rue des Musées, 2301 La Chaux-de-Fonds; tel. 329676861; fax 327220761; e-mail mih.vch@ne.ch; internet www.mih.ch; f. 1902; artistic and technical collns of watches, clocks, instruments and objects connected with measurement of time; time research dept; modern carillon; library of 3,000 vols; Curator M. LUDWIG OECHSLIN.

Lausanne

Musée Cantonal des Beaux-Arts: Palais de Rumine, pl. Riponne 6, 1014 Lausanne; tel. 213163445; fax 213163446; e-mail info.beaux-arts@vd.ch; internet www.musees.vd.ch/fr/musee-des-beaux-arts; f. 1841; colln of works since 18th century mainly by Swiss artists; int. exhibitions of classical, modern and contemporary art; has library; Dir BERNARD FIBICHER; Curator CATHERINE LEPDOR; Curator NICOLE SCHWEIZER.

Musée Historique de Lausanne: 4 pl. de la Cathédrale, 1005 Lausanne; tel. 213154101; fax 213154102; e-mail musee.historique@lausanne.ch; internet www.lausanne.ch/mhl; f. 1918; permanent and temporary exhibitions; model of 17th-century Lausanne, collns relating to local and regional history: silver, furniture, paintings and drawings, plans of the town, musical instruments; library; history of city from medieval times to 19th century; colln in three depts: paintings and graphic arts, objects, photographic collns; organizes interactive workshops, meetings, performances and concerts; Dir LAURENT GOLAY; publ. *Mémoire vive* (1 a year).

The Olympic Museum/Le Musée Olympique: 1 Quai d'Ouchy , 1006, Lausanne; tel. 216216511; fax 216216512; internet www.olympic.org/museum; f. 1993; attached to Int. Olympic Cttee; themed exhibitions; philatelic and numismatic exhibition; works of Arnoldi, Berrocal, Botero, Calder, Chillida, Folon, Graham, Niki de Saint Phalle, Tàpies, Mitoraj in bronze, marble and steel to offer their interpretation of sport, athlete and Olympic ideals; library of 23,000 monograph vols, 420 journals, 20,000 historical archival files, 9,500 films, 35,000 hours of film footage, 6,500 hours of sound files, 610,000 photographic documents (120,000 digitized); Dir of the IOC Information Management Dept PHILIPPE BLANCHARD; publ. *Symposium on Olympism – Proceedings* (1 a year).

Ligornetto

Museo Vincenzo Vela: 6853 Ligornetto; tel. 916407044; fax 916473241; e-mail museo.vela@bak.admin.ch; internet www.bundesmuseen.ch/museo_vela; f. 1898; bequests of sculptor Lorenzo Vela and painter Spartaco Vela; colln of 19th-century Lombard and Piemontese paintings, autograph drawings and private collns of photographs; portraits of leading figures of the Risorgimento; landscaped garden; temporary exhibitions; Dir Dr GIANNA A. MINA; Sec. MARIANGELA ROSIELLO-AGNOLA.

Locarno

Museo Civico e Archeologico, Servizi Culturali: Via B. Rusca 5, 6600 Locarno; tel. 917563180; fax 917563268; e-mail servizi.culturali@locarno.ch; f. 1970; 14th-century fortress housing archaeological colln and historical museum; Dir Prof. RICCARDO CARAZZETTI.

Pinacoteca Casa Rusca: Servizi Culturali, Via B. Rusca 5, 6600 Locarno; tel. 917563185; fax 917519871; e-mail servizi.culturali@locarno.ch; f. 1987; restored 17th-century building housing municipal art gallery; incl. Jean Arp colln, and works by Calder, Hans Richter, Van Doesburg, etc.; Dir Prof RICCARDO CARAZZETTI.

Lucerne

Historisches Museum (Museum of History): Altes Zeughaus, Pfistergasse 24, POB 7437, 6000 Lucerne 7; tel. 412285424; fax 412285418; e-mail historischesmuseum@lu.ch; internet www.historischesmuseum.lu.ch; f. 1986; colln of coat of mail worn by Leopold III at battle of Sempach 1386, Milanese round shields from battle of Giornico 1478, column on Weinmarkt fountain by Conrad Lux 1481, gothic altarpieces, baroque sleigh owned by Amrhyn-Göldlin family 1673, Pewter vessels, Swiss costumes, coats of arms in stained glass, industrial products; organizes theatre tours and temporary exhibitions; Dir Dr HEINZ HORAT; Asst Dir and Curator Lic. ALEXANDRA STROBEL; Curator KURT LUSSI; publs *Jahrbuch der Historischen Gesellschaft Luzern, Jahresbericht des Historischen Museums*.

Kunstmuseum Luzern (Museum of Art Lucerne): Europapl. 1, 6002 Lucerne; tel. 412267800; fax 412267801; e-mail info@kunstmuseumluzern.ch; internet www.kunstmuseumluzern.ch; f. 1925; 18th- to 20th-century Swiss landscape painting and portraiture, Swiss art after 1945, foreign contemporary art; temporary exhibitions of contemporary works of art; Dir PETER FISCHER; Curator CHRISTOPH LICHTIN.

Richard Wagner-Museum: Richard Wagner-Weg 27, 6005 Lucerne; tel. 413602370; fax 413602379; e-mail info@richard-wagner-museum.ch; internet www.richard-wagner-museum.ch; f. 1933; home of Richard Wagner from 1866 to 1872; contains original scores of *Siegfried-Idyll, Schusterlied (Meistersinger)*, etchings, paintings, busts and Erard grand piano which accompanied Wagner throughout Europe; maintains image archive; lectures and presentations; Dir KATJA FLEISCHER.

Verkehrshaus der Schweiz (Swiss Transport Museum): Lidostr. 5, 6006 Lucerne; tel. 413704444; fax 413706168; e-mail mail@verkehrshaus.org; internet www.verkehrshaus.org; f. 1959; transport by land, water and air, communication and tourism; transportation archives; IMAX Theatre; planetarium; Dir DANIEL SUTER.

Lugano

Museo Civico di Belle Arti: Villa Ciani, Parco Civico, 6900 Lugano; tel. 588667201; fax 588667497; e-mail museodibellearti@lugano.ch; f. 1903; works by artists of Ticino since 17th century, and by French and Italian artists.

Neuchâtel

Musée d'Art et d'Histoire: Esplanade Léopold Robert 1, 2000 Neuchâtel; tel. 327177920; fax 327177929; e-mail mahn@ne.ch; internet www.mahn.ch; f. 1885; pictures, drawings, prints and sculptures by local and other Swiss artists; French 18th-and 19th-century works (Courbet, Corot, and others);

French Impressionists; furniture, coins and medals; colln of 18th-century automata by Jaquet-Droz; has art library; Curator of Dept of Applied Arts CAROLINE JUNIER; Curator of Numismatic Cabinet GILLES PERRET; Curator of Visual Arts WALTER TSCHOPP.

Attached Gallery:

Galeries de l'Histoire: Ave Du Peyrou 7, 2000 Neuchâtel; tel. 327177920; fax 327177959; e-mail mahn@ne.ch; internet www.mahn.ch; f. 2003; Curator CHANTAL LAFONTANT VALLOTTON.

Musée d'Ethnographie: 4 rue Saint-Nicolas, 2000 Neuchâtel; tel. 327178560; fax 327178569; e-mail secretariat.men@ne.ch; internet www.men.ch; f. 1795; collns incl. Africa, America, Asia, Ancient Egypt, Europe, South Sea Islands, Arctic; musical instruments; library of 25,000 vols, 300 periodicals; music archives of original recordings; Curator MARC-OLIVIER GONSETH.

Muséum d'Histoire Naturelle: Rue des Terreaux 14, 2000 Neuchâtel; tel. 327177960; fax 327177969; e-mail info.museum@unine.ch; internet www.museum-neuchatel.ch; f. 1835; zoological, entomological, geological and botanical collns; Curator CHRISTOPHE DUFOUR; publ. *Ville de Neuchâtel, Bibliothèques et Musées* (1 a year).

Olten

Kunstmuseum Olten: Kirchgasse 8, 4603 Olten; tel. 622128676; fax 622123466; e-mail info@kunstmuseumolten.ch; internet www.kunstmuseumolten.ch; f. 1845; drawings and paintings by Martin Disteli (1802–1844); paintings, drawings and sculptures by Swiss artists; organizes school workshops and temporary exhibitions; library of 500 vols; Curator PATRICIA NUSSBAUM.

St Gallen

Historisches und Völkerkundemuseum: Museumstr. 50, 9000 St Gallen; tel. 712420642; fax 712420644; e-mail info@hmsg.ch; internet www.hmsg.ch; f. 1877, as Historisches Museum; present name 2004 following merger with Völkerkundemuseum; historical-archeological section: prehistoric and early history, history of St-Gall; period rooms from 16th to 19th century, glass paintings, furniture, pewter art, Swiss folk art, porcelain, costumes, fire and light, kitchen, pharmacy, religious art, flags, weapons and uniforms; ethnological section: culture of ancient Egypt, masks and sculptures of Africa, cult objects from Oceania, Inuit cultures of North America, native Indian tribes of north, central and South-America; Islamic cultural area from North Africa to Central Asia; cultural areas of India incl. Sri Lanka, Indochina, Indonesia, China and Japan; children's museum; Dir Dr DANIEL STUDER.

Kunstmuseum: Museumstr. 32, 9000 St Gallen; tel. 712420671; fax 712420672; e-mail info@kunstmuseumsg.ch; internet www.kunstmuseumsg.ch; f. 1877; works by 19th-and 20th-century masters, post-war sculpture, contemporary art; Dir Lic. ROLAND WÄSPE; Deputy Dir and Curator Lic. KONRAD BITTERLI; Curator Lic. MATTHIAS WOHLGEMUTH.

Museum Kirchhoferhaus: Museumstr. 27, 9000 St Gallen; tel. 712447521; fax 712420644; e-mail info@hmsg.ch; prehistoric and historic exhibits; 17th–19th century paintings by Graff, Diogg, Stäbli, Hodler, Corot, Renoir and others; peasant art of eastern Switzerland; furniture, silverware; closed to public; Dir Dr DANIEL STUDER.

Naturmuseum St Gallen: Museumstr. 32, 9000 St Gallen; tel. 712420670; fax 712420672; e-mail info@naturmuseumsg.ch;

internet www.naturmuseumsg.ch; f. 1846; 19th-century exhibits incl. birds, plants and insects; Nile crocodile from 1623 and skeleton of Anatosaurus; colln available for scientific research; library of 2,000 vols; Curator Dr TONI BÜRGIN; publ. *Museumsbriefe*.

Textilmuseum mit Textilbibliothek: Vadianstr. 2, 9000 St Gallen; tel. 712221744; fax 712234239; e-mail info@ textilmuseum.ch; internet www .textilmuseum.ch; f. 1886; colln of tissues of Egyptian graves, historical embroideries from 14th century, handmade lace from major European centres of excellence, ethnographic textiles, historic fabrics and costumes, handmade utensils and objects of contemporary textile art; library of 20,000 vols; special colln of 2m. textile samples; Dir HANSPETER SCHMID; Curator URSULA KARBACHER; Librarian REGULA LÜSCHER.

Schaffhausen

Museum zu Allerheiligen: Baumgartenstr. 6, 8200 Schaffhausen; tel. 526330777; fax 526330788; e-mail admin.allerheiligen@stsh .ch; internet www.allerheiligen.ch; f. 1938; archaeology, history, natural history, numismatic and graphics colln; art of City and Canton of Schaffhausen and of Switzerland; Dir Dr PETER JEZLER.

Solothurn

Kunstmuseum Solothurn: Werkhofstr. 30, 4500 Solothurn; tel. 326244000; fax 326225001; e-mail kunstmuseum@solothurn .ch; internet www.kunstmuseum-so.ch; f. 1902; colln of works by Hans Holbein the younger; int. colln, incl. works by Van Gogh, Klimt, Matisse, Picasso and Braque; Swiss art colln from 1850 to 1990, incl. works by Hodler; paintings, drawings, water-colours; primitive art section; Curator Dr CHRISTOPH VÖGELE; Sec. CHRISTINE KOBEL.

Vevey

Musée Jenisch Vevey: 2 ave de la Gare, 1800 Vevey; tel. 219253520; fax 219253525; e-mail info@museejenisch.ch; internet www .museejenisch.ch; f. 1898; comprises Fine Arts Museum (19th- and 20th-century Swiss and foreign artists, old master drawings, Oskar Kokoschka Foundation, Balthus Foundation) and Cantonal Museum of Prints (16th–20th century prints); Dir DOMINIQUE RODRIZZANI.

Winterthur

Kunstmuseum Winterthur: Museumstr. 52, POB 235, 8402 Winterthur; Museumstr. 52, 8400 Winterthur; tel. 522675162; fax 522675317; e-mail info@kmw.ch; internet www.kmw.ch; f. 1848; painting and sculpture from late 19th century to present, incl. works by Monet, Degas, Picasso, Gris, Léger, Klee, Schlemmer, Magritte, Arp, Kandinsky, Bonnard, Maillol, Van Gogh, Rodin, M. Rosso, Lehmbruck, Brancusi, Morandi, Giacometti, de Staël, Guston, Bishop, Marden, D. Rabinowitch, Richter, Fontana, Manzoni, Merz, Kounellis, Fabro, Paolini; drawings and prints; administered by Kunstverein Winterthur; Pres. Dr JÜRG SPILLER; Dir Dr DIETER SCHWARZ; publ. *Jahresbericht des Kunstvereins Winterthur*.

Museum Oskar Reinhart am Stadtgarten: Stadthausstr. 6, 8400 Winterthur; tel. 522675172; fax 522676228; e-mail museum .oskarreinhart@win.ch; internet www .museumoskarreinhart.ch; f. 1951; public art gallery; exhibits paintings and drawings of Swiss, German and Austrian schools from the 18th to the 20th centuries; Curator Dr MARC FEHLMANN; Curator PETER WEGMANN.

Zürich

Botanischer Garten und Museum der Universität Zürich: Zollikerstr. 107, 8008 Zürich; tel. 446348461; fax 446348404; e-mail botanischer.garten@systbot.uzh.ch; internet www.bguz.uzh.ch; f. 1837; worldwide herbarium, esp. of African and New Caledonian flora; exhibitions on plants; organizes guided tours for public and schools, courses, exhibitions; library of 100,000 vols; Dir Prof. Dr HANS PETER LINDER; Head Curator PETER ENZ.

Graphische Sammlung der ETH Zürich (Collection of Prints and Drawings of ETH Zurich): Rämistr. 101, 8092 Zürich; tel. 446324046; fax 446321168; e-mail info@gs .ethz.ch; internet www.gs.ethz.ch; f. 1867; 150,000 prints and drawings from 15th century to present, with special reference to devt of graphic art in Switzerland; Chief Curator PAUL TANNER; Curator Dr MICHAEL MATILE; Curator and Registrar ALEXANDRA BARCAL.

Kunsthaus Zürich: Postfach, 8024 Zürich; Heimpl. 1, 8001 Zürich; tel. 442538484; fax 442538433; e-mail info@kunsthaus.ch; internet www.kunsthaus.ch; f. 1910; chiefly paintings and sculptures since 19th century by Swiss and foreign artists; selection of old masters; extensive colln covering all brs of graphic art since 16th century; unique Giacometti colln; Monet, Cézanne, van Gogh, Picasso and Chagall; contemporary artists incl. Baselitz, Beuys and Twombly; video colln; library of 250,000 vols, 320 journals; Dir Dr CHRISTOPH BECKER; Curator Dr PHILIPPE BUETTNER; Curator Dr TOBIA BEZZOLA; Curator BICE CURIGER; Curator BERNHARD VON WALDKIRCH; Curator MIRJAM VARADINIS; publ. *Kunsthaus-Magazin* (4 a year).

Musée Suisse/Schweizerisches Landesmuseum (Swiss National Museum): Museumstr. 2, 8021 Zürich; tel. 442186511; fax 442112949; e-mail kanzlei@snm.admin .ch; internet www.landesmuseen.ch; f. 1898; incl. Castle of Prangins, Forum of Swiss History Schwyz and collns centre in Affoltern and Albis; Switzerland's largest colln of objects regarding cultural history of Switzerland; permanent and spec. exhibitions cover all periods from prehistory to the 21st century; library of 90,000 vols, 2,000 periodicals; Pres. MARKUS NOTTER; Dir Dr ANDREAS SPILLMAN; Deputy Dir MARKUS LEUTHARD; publs *Kulturmagazin* (in German and French, 4 a year), *Zeitschrift für Schweizerische Archäologie und Kunstgeschichte* (4 a year).

Museum für Gestaltung Zürich (Museum of Design Zürich): Postfach, 8031 Zürich; Ausstellungsstr. 60, 8005 Zürich; tel. and fax 434466767; e-mail welcome@ museum-gestaltung.ch; internet www .museum-gestaltung.ch; f. 1875; attached to Zurich Univ. of the Arts; design colln, graphic art colln, poster colln; temporary exhibitions, research, education and publishing; library: public library of 90,000 vols; Dir CHRISTIAN BRÄNDLE.

Affiliated Museum:

Museum Bellerive: Höschgasse 3, 8008 Zürich; tel. 434464469; fax 434464503; e-mail welcome@museum-gestaltung.ch; internet www.museum-bellerive.ch; f. 1968; colln of applied and fine arts in glass, ceramics, textiles, marionettes, musical instruments; two or three exhibitions annually exploring art and design, modern classics and recent trends; Man. JACQUELINE GREENSPAN; Asst Curator TANJA TRAMPE.

Museum Rietberg Zürich: Gablerstr. 15, 8002 Zürich; tel. 442063131; fax 442063132; e-mail museum.rietberg@zuerich.ch; internet www.stadt-zuerich.ch/kultur/de/ index/institutionen/museum_rietberg.html; f. 1952; works of art from Asia, Africa, Oceania and Americas; E. von der Heydt colln; organizes tours and educational programmes; Dir Dr ALBERT LUTZ; Deputy Dir KATHARINA EPPRECHT; Chief Curator JOHANNES BELTZ.

Paläontologisches Institut und Museum der Universität: Karl Schmid-Str. 4, 8006 Zürich; tel. 446342339; fax 446344923; internet www.pim.uzh.ch; f. 1991; attached to Univ. Triassic reptiles and fishes, Triassic and Jurassic invertebrates, Tertiary mammals; library of 5,500 vols, 30,000 publs; Curator Dr HEINZ FURRER.

Zoologisches Museum der Universität (Zoological Museum of the University of Zurich): Karl Schmid-Str. 4, 8006 Zürich; tel. 446343838; fax 446343839; e-mail zminfo@zm.uzh.ch; internet www.zm.uzh.ch; f. 1837; research in systematics, taxonomy, and population biology; exhibitions of birds, molluscs and mammals of world and Swiss fauna; public slide shows and films; library of 7,000 vols; Dir LUKAS F. KELLER.

Universities

ÉCOLE POLYTECHNIQUE FÉDÉRALE DE LAUSANNE

1015 Lausanne
Telephone: 216931111
Fax: 216934380
E-mail: mediacom@epfl.ch
Internet: www.epfl.ch

Founded 1853, present status 1969
Language of instruction: French
Federal state control
Academic year: October to July

Pres.: Prof. PATRICK AEBISCHER
Vice-Pres. for Academic Affairs: Prof. PHILIPPE GILLET
Vice-Pres. for Innovation and Technology Transfer: Prof. ADRIENNE CORBOUD FUMAGALLI
Vice-Pres. for Institutional Affairs: Prof. MARIN VETTERLI
Vice-Pres. for Planning and Logistics: Prof. FRANCIS-LUC PERRET
Gen. Sec.: JEAN-FRANÇOIS RICCI (acting)
Library Dir: DAVID AYMONIN
Library: see Libraries and Archives
Number of teachers: 275
Number of students: 6,000

DEANS

College of Human Sciences: Prof. FRANCESCO PANESE (acting)
College of Management of Technology: Dr MARTIN VETTERLI (acting)
School of Architecture, Civil and Environmental Engineering: Prof. MARC PARLANGE
School of Basic Sciences: Prof. THOMAS RIZZO
School of Computer and Communication Sciences: Dr MARTIN VETTERLI
School of Engineering: Prof. DEMETRI PSALTIS
School of Life Sciences: DIDIER TRONO

PROFESSORS

Department of Architecture:

ABOU-JAOUDÉ, G., Computer-Aided Design
BERGER, P., Architecture
CANTAFORA, A., Architecture
CHUARD, P., Building Techniques
DUTRY, G.
LAMUNIÈRE, I., History and Theory of Architecture
LUCAN, J., Architectural Theory
MANGEAT, V., Architecture
MARCHAND, B., History and Theory of Architecture

MESTELAN, P., Architecture
MOREL, C., Building Techniques
ORTELLI, L., Architectural Theory
SCARTEZZINI, J.-L., Solar Energy Research Building
STEINMANN, M., Architecture
THALMANN, P., Economics

Department of Biomedical Engineering:
EBRAHIMI, T., Visual Information Processing
LASSER, T., Biomedical Optics
SALATHE, R., Applied Optics
STERGIOPULOS, N., Cardiovascular Technology
UNSER, M., Biomedical Imaging
ZUPPIROLI, L., Optoelectronics

Department of Chemistry and Chemical Engineering:
BODENHAUSEN, G.
BÜNZLI, J.-C.
DYSON, P.
FREITAG, R., Laboratory of Cellular Biotechnology
GIRAULT, H., Institute of Physical Chemistry
GRAETZEL, M., Institute of Physical Chemistry
JOHNSSON, K.
KROSSING, I.
MERBACH, A.
MUTTER, M.
PITSCH, S.
RENKEN, A., Institute of Chemical Engineering III
RIZZO, T., Institute of Physical Chemistry
RÖTHLISBERGER, U.
ROULET, R.
SEVERIN, K.
VOGEL, H., Laboratory of Polymer Chemistry
VOGEL, P.
VON STOCKAR, U.

Department of Civil Engineering:
BADOUX, M., Institute of Reinforced and Prestressed Concrete
BOVY, P., Institute of Transportation and Planning
BRUEHWILER, E., Maintenance, Construction and Safety of Structures
DESCOEUDRES, F., Road Mechanics
DUMONT, A.-G., Institute of Soils, Rocks and Foundations
FAVRE, R., Institute of Structural Engineering
FREY, FR., Laboratory of Structural and Continuum Mechanics
GRAF, W.-H., Hydraulic Research
HIRT, M., Institute of Steel Structures
JACQUOT, P., Stress Analysis and Measurement
LAFITTE, R., Institute of Hydraulics and Energy
MARCHAND, J.-D., Economics of Infrastructure
NATTERER, J., Timber Construction
PARRIAUX, A., Geology
PERRET, F.-L., Construction Management
PFLUG, L., Optical Stress Analysis Laboratory
RIVIER, R., Institute of Transportation and Planning
SANDOZ, J.-L., Timber Construction
SARLOS, G., Institute of Hydraulics and Energy
SCHLEISS, A., Institute of Hydraulics and Energy
SMITH, I., Institute of Reinforced and Prestressed Concrete
VULLIET, L., Soil Mechanics

Department of Communications Systems:
HUBAUX, J.-P.
KUNT, M.
LE BOUDEC, J.-Y.
NUSSBAUMER, H.

PETITPIERRE, C.
VETTERLI, M.

Department of Computer Science:
BOURLARD, H., Artificial Intelligence Laboratory
CORAY, G., Dir, Theoretical Computer Science Laboratory
COULON, F. DE, Dir, Computer-Aided-Learning Laboratory
FALTINGS, B., Dir, Artificial Intelligence Laboratory
GERSTNER, W., Mini- and Micro-Computer Laboratory
HERSCH, R.-D., Dir, Peripheral Systems Laboratory
LE BOUDEC, J.-Y., Dir, Communication Network Laboratory
MANGE, D., Dir, Logic Systems Laboratory
NICOUD, J.-D., Dir, Mini- and Micro-Computer Laboratory
PETITPIERRE, C., Dir, Data Communication Laboratory
SANCHEZ, E., Logic Systems Laboratory
SCHIPER, A., Dir, Operating Systems Laboratory
SPACCAPIETRA, S., Dir, Databases Laboratory
STROHMEIER, A., Dir, Software Engineering Laboratory
THALMANN, D., Dir, Computer Graphics Laboratory
THIRAN, P., Institute of Data Communication
WEGMANN, A., Industrial Computer Engineering Laboratory
ZAHND, J., Dir, Logic Systems Laboratory

Department of Electrical Engineering:
DECLERCQ, M., Electronics Laboratory
ENZ, C., General Electronics
FAZAN, P., Electronics Laboratory
GERMOND, A., Electrical Installations Laboratory
IONESCU, M.-A., General Engineering
JUFER, M., Electromechanics Laboratory
KAYAL, M., General Electronics
KUNT, M., Signal Processing Laboratory
MLYNEK, D., Electronics Laboratory
MOSIG, J., Electromagnetism and Acoustics
ROBERT, PH., Metrology Laboratory
ROSSI, M., Electromagnetism and Microwaves Laboratory
RUFER, A.-C., Electronics Laboratory
SIMOND, J.-J., Electromechanics and Electrical Machines Laboratory
SKRIVERVIK, A., Electromagnetism and Acoustics
WAVRE, N., Electromechanics and Electrical Machines Laboratory

Department of Environmental Engineering:
BEY, I., Atmospheric Chemistry Modelling
HARMS, H., Pedology
HOLLIGER, C., Environmental Biotechnology
JOLLIET, O., Ecosystem Management
MERMOUD, A., Institute of Development of Earth and Water
MUSY, A., Institute of Agricultural Engineering
PÉRINGER, P., Institute of Environmental Engineering
SCHLAEPFER, R., Soils and Water
TARRADELLAS, J., Institute of Environmental Engineering
VAN DEN BERGH, H., Institute of Environmental Engineering
VÉDY, J.-C., Institute of Agricultural Engineering

Department of Materials Science and Engineering:
HOFMANN, H., Powder Technology Laboratory
JACQUOT, P., Meteorology and Photonics
KURZ, W., Metallurgy
LANDOLT, D., Chemical Metallurgy

MÅNSON, J.-A., Polymer Composite Technology
MATHIEU, H. J., Chemical Metallurgy Laboratory
MORTENSEN, A., Mechanical Metallurgy Laboratory
RAPPAZ, M., Physical Metallurgy Laboratory
SCRIVENER, K., Construction Materials
SETTER, N., Ceramics Laboratory

Department of Mathematics:
BARTHOLDI, L.
BAYER-FLUCKIGER, E.
BEN AROUS, G., Probability Theory
BUSER, P., Geometry
DACAROGNA, B., Analysis
DALANG, R., Probability Theory
DAVISON, A.
DERIGHETTI, A.
JORIS, H.
LIEBLING, T., Operational Research
MADDOCKS, J., Analysis
MORGENTHALER, S., Statistics
MOUNTFORD, T.
OJANGUREN, M., Mathematical Methodology
QUARTERONI, A.
RAPPAZ, J.
RATIU, T. S.
SHOKROLLAHI, A.
STUART, C., Numerical Analysis and Simulation
THÉVENAZ, J.
WERRA, D. DE, Operational Research

Department of Mechanical Engineering:
AVELLAN, F., Institute of Hydraulic Machinery and Fluid Mechanics
BÖLCS, A., Institute of Thermal Engineering
BONVIN, D., Institute of Automatic Control
BOTSIS, J., Applied Mechanics
CURNIER, A., Laboratory of Applied Mechanics
DEVILLE, M., Institute of Hydraulic Machinery and Fluid Mechanics
FAVRAT, D., Laboratory of Industrial Energy Systems
GIOVANOLA, J., Laboratory of Mechanical Systems Design
GLARDON, R., Applied Mechanics and Institute of Machine Design
LONGCHAMP, R., Institute of Automatics
MONKEWITZ, P., Institute of Hydraulic Machinery and Fluid Mechanics
OWEN, R., Fluid Mechanics
THOME, J., Laboratory of Applied Thermodynamics
XIROUCHAKIS, P., Applied Mechanics and Institute of Machine Design
ZYSSET, P., Laboratory of Applied Mechanics

Department of Microengineering:
BLEULER, H., Institute of Microtechnology
CLAVEL, R., Institute of Microtechnology
GIJS, M., Microsystems
HONGLER, M.-O., Microtechnology
JACOT-DESCOMBES, J., Institute of Microtechnology
LEBLEBICI, Y., Microelectronics
NICOLLIER, C., Institute of Microtechnology
PFLUGER, P., Institute of Microtechnology
POPOVIC, R., Institute of Microtechnology
RENAUD, P., Institute of Microtechnology
RYSER, P., Microtechnology
SIEGWART, R., Institute of Microtechnology

Department of Physics:
ANSERMET, J.-P., Experimental Physics Institute
BALDERESCHI, A., Applied Physics Institute
BARÈS, P.-A., Theoretical Physics
BENOIT, W., Nuclear Engineering Institute
BRÜESCH, P., General Physics of Solids
BUTTET, J., Experimental Physics Institute

CHÂTELAIN, A., Experimental Physics Institute
CHAWLA, R., Nuclear Engineering Institute
DEVEAUD-PLEDRAN, B., Micro- and Opto-electronics Institute
FIVAZ, R., Dir, Applied Physics Institute
GRUBER, C., Theoretical Physics Institute
ILEGEMS, M., Dir, Micro- and Opto-electronics Institute
KAPON, E., Micro- and Opto-electronics Institute
KERN, K., Experimental Physics Institute
KUNZ, H., Theoretical Physics Institute
LÉVY, F., Applied Physics Institute
MARGARITONDO, G., Applied Physics Institute
MARTIN, J.-L., Dir, Nuclear Engineering Institute
MARTIN, PH., Theoretical Physics Institute
MEISTER, J.-J., Applied Physics Institute
MONOT, R., Experimental Physics Institute
QUATTROPANI, A., Theoretical Physics Institute
REINHART, F. K., Micro- and Opto-electronics Institute
STERGIOPOULOS, N., Medical Engineering
ZUPPIROLI, L., Nuclear Engineering Institute

EIDGENÖSSISCHE TECHNISCHE HOCHSCHULE ZÜRICH (ETH)
(Swiss Federal Institute of Technology)

8092 Zürich
HG, Rämistr. 101, 8092 Zürich
Telephone: 446321111
Fax: 446321010
E-mail: praesidium@sl.ethz.ch
Internet: www.ethz.ch

Founded 1855
Languages of instruction: French, German
Federal State control
Academic year: October to July (two semesters)

Pres.: Prof. Dr RALPH EICHLER
Rector: Prof. HEIDI WUNDERLI-ALLENSPACH
Vice-Pres. for Research and Corporate Relations: Prof. Dr ROLAND Y. SIEGWART
Vice-Pres. for Finance and Control: Dr ROBERT PERICH
Vice-Pres. for Human Resources and Infrastructure: Prof. Dr ROMAN BOUTELLIER
Sec.-Gen.: HUGO BRETSCHER

Library: see Libraries and Archives
Number of teachers: 400
Number of students: 16,000

Publications: *ETH Globe* (4 a year), *ETH Life* (online magazine), *ETH Life Print* (9 a year)

PROFESSORS

Agriculture and Food Science (D-Agrl, ETH Zentrum, 8092 Zürich; tel. 446323887; fax 446321161; e-mail rutz@agrl.ethz.ch; internet www.agrl.ethz.ch/):

ABDULAI, A., Economics of Nutrition
AMADÒ, R., Food Chemistry
AMRHEIN, N., Plant Science
APEL, K., Plant Science
DORN, S., Applied Entomology
ESCHER, F., Food Technology
FROSSARD, E., Plant Nutrition
GRUISSEM, W., Plant Biotechnology
HURRELL, R. F., Human Nutrition
KREUZER, M., Animal Nutrition
KÜNZI, N., Animal Breeding
LANGHANS, W., Physiology and Animal Husbandry
LEHMANN, B., Farm and Agrobusiness Management
MCDONALD, B., Phytopathology
PUHAN, Z., Dairy Science
RIEDER, P., Agricultural Market and Policy
STAMP, P., Agronomy and Plant Breeding

STRANZINGER, G., Breeding Biology
TEUBER, M., Food Microbiology
WENK, C., Biology of Nutrition
WINDHAB, E., Food Engineering

Applied Biosciences (D-Anbi, Uni Irchel, Winterthurerstr. 110, 8057 Zürich; tel. 446356042; fax 446356883; e-mail wyrsck@anbi.ethz.ch; internet www.pharma.ethz.ch):

BOUTELLIER, U., Exercise Physiology
FOLKERS, G., Pharmaceutical Chemistry
MERKLE, H. P., Galenic Pharmacy
MÖHLER, H., Pharmacology
MÜNTENER, M., Anatomy
MURER, K.
NERI, D., Protein Engineering
SCHUBIGER, P. A., Radiopharmacy
STICHER, O., Pharmacognosy and Phytochemistry
WUNDERLI-ALLENSPACH, H., Biopharmacy

Architecture (D-Arch, ETH Honggerberg, 8093 Zürich; tel. 446332885; fax 446331053; e-mail michel@arch.ethz.ch; internet www.arch.ethz.ch):

ANGÉLIL, M., Architecture and Design
CAMINADA, G. A., Architecture and Design
CAMPI, M., Architecture and Design
DANIELS, K., Building Systems
DE MEURON, P., Architecture and Design
DEPLAZES, A., Architecture and Technology
DIENER, R., Architecture and Design
EBERLE, D., Architecture and Design
ENGELI, M., Architecture and Computer-Aided Architectural Design
FLÜCKIGER, H., Spatial Development
HERZOG, J., Architecture and Design
HOVESTADT, L., Computer-Aided Architectural Design
JENNY, P., Visual Design
KELLER, B., Building Physics
KÖHLER, B., History and Theory of Architecture
KOLLHOFF, H., Architecture and Technology
KRAMEL, H. E., Architecture and Technology
KRUCKER, B., Architecture and Design
KÜNZLE, O., Building Structures
LYNN, G., Spatial Conception and Exploration
MAGNAGO LAMPUGNANI, V., History of Urbanism
MEILI, M., Architecture and Design
MEYER, A., Architecture and Design
MEYER, P., Architecture and Building Realization
MÖRSCH, G., Preservation of Historical Monuments and Sites
OECHSLIN, W., History of Art and Architecture
OSWALD, F., Architecture and Urbanism
RUCHAT-RONCATI, F., Architecture and Design
RÜEGG, A., Architecture and Design
SCHETT, W., Architecture and Design
SCHMID, W. A., Regional Planning and Methodology
SCHMITT, G., Computer-Aided Architectural Design
SIK, M., Architecture and Design
THIERSTEIN, A., Spatial Development

Biology (D-Biol, ETH Zentrum, 8092 Zürich; tel. 446325942; fax 446321151; e-mail ulrich@biol.ethz.ch; internet www.biol.ethz.ch):

AEBI, M., Microbiology
BAILEY, J. E., Biotechnology
BARRAL, Y., Biochemistry
DIMROTH, P., Microbiology
EPPENBERGER, H. M., Cell Biology
FELDON, J., Behavioural Neurobiology
GLOCKSHUBER, R., Molecular Biology and Biophysics
HELENIUS, A., Biochemistry

HENGARTNER, H., Experimental Immunology
HENNECKE, H., Microbiology
KUTAY, U., Biochemistry
LEISINGER, TH., Microbiology
MANSUY, I., Neurobiology
MARTIN, K. A. C., Systematic Neurophysiology
RICHMOND, T. J., Molecular Biology and Biophysics
SCHWAB, M. E., Neuroscience
SUTER, U., Cell Biology
THÖNY-MEYER, L., Molecular Microbiology
WERNER, S., Cell Biology
WINKLER, F. K., Structural Biology
WITHOLT, B., Biotechnology
WÜRGLER, F. E., Genetics
WÜTHRICH, K., Molecular Biology and Biophysics

Chemistry (D-Chem, ETH Zentrum, 8093 Zürich; tel. 446323055; fax 446321058; e-mail hauser@chem.ethz.ch; internet www.chem.ethz.ch):

BAIKER, A., Chemical Engineering and Catalysis
CARREIRA, E. M., Organic Chemistry
CHEN, P., Physical-organic Chemistry
DIEDERICH, F., Organic Chemistry
GRÜTZMACHER, H., Inorganic Chemistry
GÜNTHER, D., Analytical Chemistry
HILVERT, D., Organic Chemistry
HÜNENBERGER, PH. H., Physical Chemistry
HUNGERBÜHLER, K., Safety and Environmental Protection
KOPPENOL, W. H., Bioinorganic Chemistry
MEIER, B. H., Physical Chemistry
MERKT, F., Physical Chemistry
MORBIDELLI, M., Chemical Reaction Engineering
NESPER, R., Inorganic Chemistry
PRINS, R., Industrial Chemistry
QUACK, M., Physical Chemistry
RÖTHLISBERGER, U., Computer-Aided Inorganic Chemistry
RYS, P., Technical Chemistry
SCHWEIGER, A., Physical Chemistry
SEEBACH, D., Organic Chemistry
TOGNI, A., Organometallic Chemistry
VAN GUNSTEREN, W. F., Computer-Aided Chemistry
VASELLA, A. T., Organic Chemistry
WILD, U. P., Physical Chemistry
WOKAUN, A., Chemistry
ZENOBI, R., Analytical Chemistry

Civil, Environmental and Geomatics Engineering (D-Baug, ETH Honggerberg, 8093 Zürich; tel. 446332691; fax 446331088; e-mail altenburger@baug.ethz.ch; internet www.baum.ethz.ch):

AMANN, P., Soil Engineering and Soil Mechanics
ANDERHEGGEN, E., Applied Computer Science
AXHAUSEN, K. W., Traffic Engineering
BACCINI, P., Material Flux and Waste Management
BÖHNI, H., Materials Science
BRÄNDLI, H., Traffic Engineering
BURLANDO, P., Hydrology and Water Resource Management
CAROSIO, A., Geodesy
FABER, M., Structural Engineering
FONTANA, M., Structural Engineering
GIGER, CH., Geographic Information Systems
GIRMSCHEID, G., Construction Management and Process Technology
GRÜN, A., Photogrammetry
GUJER, W., Sanitary Engineering
HERMANNS STENGELE, R., Geotechnics
HURNI, L., Cartography
INGENSAND, H., Geodesy
KAHLE, H.-G., Geodesy
KINZELBACH, W., Hydromechanics
KOVARI, K., Tunnelling

MARTI, P., Structural Engineering
MINOR, H.-E., Hydraulic Structures
SCHALCHER, H.-R., Planning and Construction Management
SCHMID, W. A., Rural Engineering and Planning
SPRINGMAN, S., Geotechnical Engineering
VIRTANEN, S., Metallic High-Performance Materials
VOGEL, TH., Structural Engineering
WITTMANN, F. H., Materials Science

Computer Science (D-Infk, ETH Zentrum, 8092 Zürich; tel. 446327220; fax 446321620; e-mail haeni@inf.ethz.ch; internet www.inf .ethz.ch):

ALONSO, G., Information Systems
BIERE, A., Computer Systems
GANDER, W., Scientific Computing
GONNET, G. H., Scientific Computing
GROSS, M., Computer Graphics
GROSS, TH., Computer Systems
GUTKNECHT, J., Computer Systems
MATTERN, F., Information Systems
MAURER, U., Theoretical Computer Science
NAGEL, K., Scientific Computing
NIEVERGELT, J., Theoretical Computer Science
NORRIE, M., Information Systems
RICHTER-GEBERT, J., Theoretical Computer Science
SCHEK, H.-J., Information Systems
SCHIELE, B., Scientific Computing
STÄRK, R., Theoretical Computer Science
STRICKER, TH. M., Computer Systems
WELZL, E., Theoretical Computer Science
WIDMAYER, P., Theoretical Computer Science
ZEHNDER, C. A., Information Systems

Earth Sciences (D-Erdw, ETH Zentrum, 8092 Zürich; tel. 446325647; fax 446321112; e-mail bonadurer@erdw.ethz.ch; internet www.erdw.ethz.ch):

BURG, J.-P., Structural Geology
GIARDINI, D., Seismology and Geodynamics
GREEN, A. G., Applied Geophysics
HALLIDAY, A. N., Isotope Geochemistry
HEINRICH, CH. A., Mineral Resources and Processes of the Earth's Interior
KUNZ, M., Crystallography
LÖW, S., Engineering Geology
LOWRIE, W., Geophysics
MCKENZIE, J., Earth System Sciences
SEWARD, T. M., Geochemistry
STEURER, W., Crystallography
THIERSTEIN, H. R., Micropalaeontology
THOMPSON, A. B., Petrology
TROMMSDORFF, V., Petrography

Electrical Engineering (D-Elek, ETH Zentrum, 8092 Zürich; tel. 446325002; fax 446321492; e-mail marcel.kreuzer@ee.ethz .ch; internet www.itet.ethz.ch):

ANDERSSON, G., Electrical Energy Systems and Processes
BÄCHTOLD, W., Electromagnetic Fields and Microwaves
DAHLHAUS, D., Mobile Radio Communication
EGGIMANN, F., Signal and Information Processing
ERLEBACH, TH., Theory of Communication Networks
FICHTNER, W., Integrated Systems
FRÖHLICH, K., Electric Power Transmission and High Voltage Technology
GUT, J., Military Security Technology
HUANG, Q., Integrated Systems
HUBBELL, J. A., Biomedical Engineering and Medical Informatics
HUGEL, J., Electrical Engineering Design
JÄCKEL, H., Electronics
KÜNDIG, A., Computer Engineering and Communication Networks
LAPIDOTH, A., Information Theory
LEUTHOLD, P., Communication Technology

LOELIGER, H.-A., Signals Processing
MORARI, M., Automatic Control
NIEDERER, P., Biomedical Engineering and Medical Informatics
PLATTNER, B., Computer Engineering and Communications Networks
SCHAUFELBERGER, W., Automatic Control
STILLER, B., Communication Systems
THIELE, L., Computer Engineering
TRÖSTER, G., Electronics
VAHLDIECK, R., Field Theory
VAN GOOL, L., Computer Vision

Environmental Sciences (D-Umnw, ETH Zentrum, 8092 Zürich; tel. 446322523; fax 446321309; e-mail secretariat@umnw.ethz .ch; internet www.env.ethz.ch):

DAVIES, H. C., Atmospheric Physics, Dynamic Meteorology
EDWARDS, P., Plant Ecology
EWALD, K., Nature and Landscape Protection
FLÜHLER, H., Soil Physics
IMBODEN, D., Environmental Physics
KAISER, F. G., Human–Environmental Relations
KRETZSCHMAR, R., Soil Chemistry
MIEG, H. A., Human–Environmental Relations
OHMURA, A., Climatology
PETER, TH., Atmospheric Chemistry
ROY, B. A., Plant Biodiversity
SCHÄR, C., Hydrology and Climatology
SCHMID-HEMPEL, P., Experimental Ecology
SCHOLZ, R. W., Environmental Sciences
SCHULIN, R., Soil Protection
SCHWARZENBACH, R., Organic Environmental Chemistry
WALDVOGEL, A., Atmospheric Physics
WARD, J. V., Aquatic Ecology
WEHRLI, B., Aquatic Chemistry
ZEHNDER, A. J. B, Environmental Biotechnology
ZEYER, J., Soil Biology

Forest Sciences (D-Fowi, ETH Zentrum, 8092 Zürich; tel. 446326194; fax 446321575; e-mail benz@fowi.ethz.ch; internet www.fowi.ethz .ch):

BACHMANN, P., Forest Inventory and Planning
BUGMANN, H., Mountain Forest Ecology
HEINIMANN, H. R., Forestry Engineering
HOLDENRIEDER, O., Forest Pathology and Dendrology
KISSLING-NÄF, I., Forest Resource Economics
SCHMITHÜSEN, F., Forestry Policy and Economics
SCHÜTZ, J.-PH., Silviculture

Humanities, Social and Political Sciences (D-Gess, ETH Zentrum, 8092 Zürich; tel. 446322308; fax 446321027; e-mail margelisch@gess.ethz.ch; internet www.gess .ethz.ch):

BERNAUER, T., International Relations
BESOMI, O., Italian Language and Literature
BUCHMANN, M., Sociology
DÄLLENBACH, L., French Language and Literature
EISNER, M., Sociology
FREY, K., Education
GABRIEL, J. M., International Relations
GUGERLI, D., History of Technology
HERTIG, G., Law
HOLENSTEIN, E., Philosophy
KAPPEL, R., Problems of Developing Countries
NEF, U. CH., Law
NOWOTNY, H., Philosophy and Social Studies
RIS, R., German Language and Literature
RUCH, A., Law
SCHIPS, B., Economics
SCHUBERT, R., Economics

SPILLMAN, K. R., Security Studies and Conflict Research
SUTER, CH., Sociology
TOBLER, H. W., General History
VICKERS, B., English Language and Literature
WENGER, A., Swiss and International Security Policy

Industrial Management and Manufacturing Engineering (D-Bepr, ETH Zentrum, 8092 Zürich; tel. 446325718; fax 446321047; e-mail wismer@bepr.ethz.ch; internet www.bepr .ethz.ch/main.htm):

ABELL, D. F., Technology and Management
FAHRNI, F., Technology Management
GROTE, G., Work Psychology
HUBER, F., Industrial Engineering and Management
KOLLER, TH., Hygiene and Applied Physiology
KRUEGER, H., Ergonomics
MEYER, U., Textile Machinery
REISSNER, J., Forming Technology
SCHÖNSLEBEN, P., Industrial Engineering and Management
TSCHIRKY, H., Industrial Engineering and Management
WEHNER, T., Work and Organizational Psychology

Materials Sciences (D-Werk, ETH Zentrum, 8092 Zürich; tel. 446322520; fax 446321028; e-mail krombach@ifp.mat.ethz.ch; internet www.mat.ethz.ch):

GAUCKLER, L. J., Non-metallic Materials
LUISI, P. L., Macromolecular Chemistry
ÖTTINGER, H. CH., Polymer Physics
SMITH, P., Polymer Technology
SPEIDEL, M. O., Metals and Metallurgy
SPENCER, N. D., Surface Technology
STÜSSI, E., Biomechanics
SUTER, U. W., Macromolecular Chemistry
WINTERMANTEL, E., Biocompatible Materials

Mathematics (D-Math, ETH Zentrum, 8092 Zürich; tel. 446325615; fax 446321085; e-mail mathdept@math.ethz.ch; internet www .math.ethz.ch):

BÜHLMANN, P. L., Mathematics
BURGER, M., Mathematics
DELBAEN, F., Financial Mathematics
EMBRECHTS, P., Mathematics
FEICHTNER, E. M., Mathematics
FELDER, G., Mathematics
GROTE, M. J., Mathematics
HAMPEL, F., Statistics
ILMANEN, T., Mathematics
JELTSCH, R., Applied Mathematics
KIRCHGRABER, U., Mathematics
KNÖRRER, H., Mathematics
KNUS, M. A., Mathematics
KÜNSCH, H. R., Mathematics
LANFORD, O. E., III, Mathematics
LANG, U., Mathematics
LÜTHI, H.-J., Operations Research
MISLIN, G., Mathematics
NUCINKIS, B. E. A., Mathematics
OSTERWALDER, K., Mathematics
PINK, R., Mathematics
SALAMON, D. A., Mathematics
SALMHOFER, M., Mathematics
SCHWAB, CH., Applied Mathematics
STAMMBACH, U., Mathematics
STRUWE, M., Mathematics
SZNITMAN, A.-S., Mathematics
TRUBOWITZ, E., Mathematics
WÜSTHOLZ, G., Mathematics
ZEHNDER, E., Mathematics

Mechanical and Process Engineering (D-Mavt, ETH Zentrum, 8092 Zürich; tel. 446322596; fax 446321483; e-mail vonrohr@ mavt.ethz.ch; internet www.mavt.ethz.ch):

ABHARI, R., Turbomachinery
DUAL, J., Mechanics

EBERLE, M., Internal Combustion Engines and Combustion Technology
ERMANNI, P., Composites and Structures
FILIPPINI, M., Economics and Energy Policy
GEERING, H. P., Measurement and Control
GUZZELLA, L., Internal Combustion Engines
JOCHEM, E., Economics and Energy Policy
KLEISER, L., Fluid Dynamics
KOUMOUTSAKOS, P., Fluid Dynamics
KRÖGER, W., Safety Technology
MAZZOTTI, M., Process Engineering
MEIER, M., Product Development
MEYER-PIENING, H.-R., Lightweight Structures and Ropeways
POULIKAKOS, D., Thermodynamics in Emerging Technology
PRATSINIS, S. E., Process Engineering
RÖSGEN, TH., Fluid Dynamics
RUDOLF VON ROHR, PH., Process Engineering
SAYIR, M., Mechanics
SCHWEITZER, G., Robotics
SEILER, A., Engineering and Management
STEINER, M., Control Systems
STEINFELD, Renewable Energy Carriers
STEMMER, A., Nanotechnology
YADIGAROGLU, G., Nuclear Engineering

Physics (D-Phys, ETH Hönggerberg, 8093 Zürich; tel. 446332585; fax 446331106; e-mail rafailidis@phys.ethz.ch; internet www.phys.ethz.ch):

BALTES, H., Quantum Electronics
BATLOGG, B., Solid State Physics
BLATTER, J. W., Theoretical Physics
DEGIORGI, L., Solid State Physics
DOUGLAS, R. J., Theoretical Neuroinformatics
EICHLER, R., Experimental Particle Physics
ENSSLIN, K., Solid State Physics
FRÖHLICH, J., Theoretical and Mathematical Physics
GRAF, G. M., Theoretical Physics
GÜNTER, P., Quantum Electronics
HEPP, K., Theoretical Physics
HOFER, H., Experimental Particle Physics
HUNZIKER, W., Theoretical Physics
KELLER, U., Quantum Electronics
KOSTORZ, G., Applied Physics
LANDOLT, M., Solid State Physics
LANG, J., Experimental Particle Physics
MARTIN, K. A. C., Systematic Neurophysiology
OTT, H. R., Solid State Physics
PAUSS, F., Experimental Particle Physics
PESCIA, D., Solid State Physics
RICE, TH. M., Theoretical Physics
RUBBIA, A., Experimental Particle Physics
SCHMID, CH., Theoretical Physics
STENFLO, J. O., Astrophysics
VAN ER VEEN, J. F., Experimental Particle Physics

UNIVERSITÀ DELLA SVIZZERA ITALIANA
(University of Lugano)

Via Lambertenghi 10, 6904 Lugano
Telephone: (58) 6664000
Fax: (58) 6664647
E-mail: info@usi.ch
Internet: www.usi.ch
Founded 1996
State control
Language of instruction: Italian
Academic year: September to June

2 Campuses at Lugano and Mendrisio

Pres.: PIERO MARTINOLI
Gen. Sec.: Lic. phil. ALBINO ZGRAGGEN
Head Librarian for Lugano Campus: Dr GIUSEPPE ORIGGI
Head Librarian for Mendrisio Campus: SERGIO STEFFEN

Library of 70,000 vols

Number of teachers: 743
Number of students: 2,852

DEANS

Academy of Architecture: MARIO BOTTA
Faculty of Communication Sciences: Prof. Dr LORENZO CANTONI
Faculty of Economics: Prof. RICO MAGGI
Faculty of Informatics: MAURO PEZZÈ

UNIVERSITÄT BASEL

Peterspl. 1, 4003 Basel
Telephone: 612671298
Fax: 612673013
E-mail: studienberatung@unibas.ch
Internet: www.unibas.ch
Founded 1460
Languages of instruction: German, English
Academic year: August to July

Rector: Prof. Dr ANTONIO LOPRIENO
Vice-Rector for Research and Professional Devt: Prof. Dr PETER MEIER-ABT
Vice-Rector for Devt: Prof. Dr ALEX N. EBERLE
Vice-Rector for Teaching: Prof. Dr HEDWIG J. KAISER
Exec. Dir: CHRISTOPH TSCHUMI
Librarian: H. HUG

Library: see under Libraries and Archives
Number of teachers: 1,300
Number of students: 11,360

DEANS

Faculty of Business and Economics: Prof. Dr. MANFRED BRUHN
Faculty of Humanities: Prof. Dr C. OPITZ-BELAKHAL
Faculty of Law: Prof. Dr PETER JUNG
Faculty of Medicine: Prof. Dr ALBERT URWYLER
Faculty of Psychology: Prof. Dr MICHAELA WÄNKE
Faculty of Science: Prof. Dr MARTIN SPIESS
Faculty of Theology: Prof. Dr ALFRED BODENHEIMER

PROFESSORS

Faculty of Humanities:

HOLL, U., Media Sciences
MAASEN, SABINE, Social Studies of Science

Faculty of Economics (Wirtschaftswissenschaftliches Zentrum (WWZ), Petersgraben 51, 4003 Basel):

BORNER, S., Political Economics
BRUHN, M., Marketing and Management
KUGLER, P., Monetary Macroeconomics
MÜLLER, W. R., Business Administration
SCHIERENBECK, H., Business Administration
WEDER, R., Economics
ZIMMERMANN, H., Finance Theory

Faculty of Law (Peter Merian-Weg 8, 4056 Basel; tel. 612672531; fax 612672508; e-mail dekanat-ius@unibas.ch; internet www.ius.unibas.ch):

BEHNISCH, U., Public Law
GLESS, S., Criminal Law
HANDSCHIN, L., Private Law
KRAMER, E. A., Civil Law
NADAKAVUKAREN SCHEFER, K., Public Law
PETERS, A., Public Law, Swiss National Law
PIETH, M., Penal Law
RIVA, E., Public Law
SCHEFER, M., Swiss National Law
SCHWENZER, I., Civil Law
SEELMANN, K., Penal Law, Philosophy of Law
STÖCKLI, F., Private Law
SUTTER-SOMM, T., Civil Law and Civil Procedural Law
THURNHERR, D., Public Law

TOBLER, C., Public Law

Faculty of Medicine (Klingelbergstr. 61, 4056 Basel; tel. 612652050; fax 612652230; internet www.medizin.unibas.ch):

ACKERMANN-LIEBRICH, U., Social and Prophylactic Medicine
BETTLER, B., Physiology
BÜHLER, F. R., Pharmaceutical Medicine
CHRISTOFORI, G., Biochemistry and Genetics
DE GEEST, S., Nursing
DICK, W., Orthopaedics
DITTMANN, V., Legal Medicine
ECKSTEIN, F., Cardiology
FLAMMER, J., Ophthalmology
GASSER, TH., Urology
GRATWOHL, A., Internal Medicine
HESS, C., Ambulant Internal Medicine
HOLLÄNDER, G., Paediatric Molecular Medicine
ITIN, P., Dermatology and Venereology
KAPPOS, L., Neurology
KRAPF, R., Internal Medicine
KÜNZLE, N., Social and Preventive Medicine
LAMBRECHT, J. TH., Dentistry
LUIGI, M., Neurosurgery
MARINELLO, C. P., Dentistry
MIHATSCH, M. J., General and Special Pathology
MORONI, CHR., Medical Microbiology
MÜLLER, V., Internal Medicine
MÜLLER-SPAHN, F. S., Adult Psychiatry
OERTLI, D., General Surgery
OSSWALD, S., Cardiology
PALMER, E., Experimental Transplantation Immunology and Nephrology
PFISTERER, M., Cardiology
PÜHSE, U., Science of Sports Medicine
QUERVAIN, D., Cognitive Neurosciences
RIECHER-RÖSSLER, Adult Psychiatry
ROLINK, A., Immunology
SCHAAD, U. B., Paediatrics
SCHEIDEGGER, D. H., Anaesthetics
SCHIFFERLI, J., Internal Medicine
SCHMIDT-TRUCKSÄSS, A., Sports Medicine
SKODA, R., Molecular Medicine
STEIGER, J., Internal Medicine
STEINBRICH, W., Medical Radiology
TOLNAY, M., Pathology
TYNDALL, L. A., Rheumatology
WEIGER, R., Dentistry
ZEILHOFER, H.-F., Reconstructive Surgery
ZELLER, R., Anatomy and Embryology
ZIMMERLI, W., Internal Medicine

Faculty of Philosophy and History (Bernoulistr. 28, 4056 Basel):

ANGEHRN, E., Philosophy
ARLT, W., Musicology
BERGMAN, M., Sociology
BEYER, A., Modern History of Art
BIERL, A., General Philology
BOEHM, G., History of Art
BURGHARTZ, S., History of the 14th–16th centuries
ENGLER, B., English Philology
FÖRSTER, T., Ethnology
GLAUSER, J., Nordic Philology
GUSKI, S., Slavonic Philology
HÄCKI BUHOFER, A., German Philology
HARICH-SCHWARZBAUER, H., Latin Philology
HAUMANN, H., History of Eastern Europe
HONOLD, A., Modern German Literature
KOPP, R., Romance Philology
KREBS, A., Philosophy
KREIS, G., Modern General History and Swiss History
LEIMGRUBER, W., Folklore, European Ethnology
LOPRIENO, A., Egyptology
LÜDI, G., Romance Philology
MÄDER, U., Sociology
MILLET, O., French Philology
MOOSER, J., History of the 20th Century

OPITZ-BELAKHAL, C., History of the 17th and 18th Centuries
PILLER, I., Sociolinguistics and Sociology of English as a Global Language
SCHAFFNER, M., Swiss History and Recent General History
SCHELLEWALD, B., History of Art
SCHMID, B., Ibero-Romance Philology
SCHNELL, R., German Philology
SCHOELER, G., Islamic Studies
SIEGMUND, F., Prehistory and Early History
SIMON, R., German Literary Studies
STÄHELI, U., Sociology
STUCKY, R., Classical Archaeology
TERZOLI, M. A., Romance Philology
THOLEN, G. C., Media Science
VON GREYERZ, K., Recent General History and Swiss History
VON MÜLLER, A, Medieval History
VON UNGERN-STERNBERG, J, Ancient History

Faculty of Psychology (Missionsstr. 60–62, 4055 Basel; tel. 612673528; fax 612673526; e-mail info-psycho@unibas.ch; internet www.unibas.ch/psycho):
GROB, A., Developmental Psychology
MARGRAF, J., Clinical Psychology
OPWIS, K., General Psychology and Methodology
WÄNKE, M., Social and Business Psychology

Faculty of Science (Pharmazentrum, Klingelbergstr. 50, 4056 Basel; tel. 612673053; fax 612671434; internet www.unibas.ch/philnat):
A'CAMPO, N., Mathematics
AEBI, U., Structural Biology
AFFOLTER, M., Neurobiology and Developmental Biology
ALEWELL, CH., Environmental Earth Sciences
BARDE, Y. A., Neurobiology
BICKLE, T. A., Microbiology
BOLLER, TH., Botany
BRUDER, C., Theoretical Physics
CONSTABLE, E., Inorganic Chemistry
CORNELIS, G., Microbiology
EBERT, D., Zoology
ENGEL, A., Structural Biology
ERNST, B., Molecular Pharmaceutics
FOLKERS, G., Pharmaceutical Chemistry
GASSER, S., Molecular Biology
GEHRING, W. J., Physiology of Development and Genetics
GIESE, B., Organic Chemistry
GROTE, M. S., Mathematics
GRZESIEK, S., Structural Biology
GÜNTHERODT, H.-J., Experimental Physics
HALL, M., Biochemistry
HAMBURGER, M. O., Pharmacy
HAURI, H., Cell Biology
IM HOF, H.-CHR., Mathematics
KELLER, W., Cell Biology
KÖRNER, CHR., Botany
KRAFT, H., Mathematics
LE TENSORER, J.-M., Pre- and Early History
LESER, H., Physical Geography
LEUENBERGER, H., Pharmaceutical Technology
LOSS, D., Theoretical Physics
MAIER, J. P., Physical Chemistry
MASSER, D., Mathematics
MEIER, W., Chemistry
PARLOW, E., Meteorology and Climatology
PFALTZ, A., Organic Chemistry
PHILIPPSEN, P., Applied Microbiology
REICHERT, H., Zoology
RÜEGG, M., Neurobiology
SCHMID, S. M., Geology and Palaeontology
SCHNEIDER-SLIWA, R., Human Geography
SCHÖNENBERGER, CH., Experimental Physics
SEELIG, J., Structural Biology
SPIESS, M., Biochemistry

TANNES, M., Epidemiology and Medical Parasitology
THIELEMANN, F. K., Theoretical Physics
TSCHUDIN, CH., Applied Information Technology
VETTER, T., Applied Information Technology
WIEMKEN, A. M., Botany
ZUBERBÜHLER, A., Inorganic Chemistry

Faculty of Theology (Nadelberg 10, 4051 Basel; tel. 612672901; fax 612672902; internet theolrel.unibas.ch):
BERNHARDT, R., Systematic Theology, Dogmatics
BRÄNDLE, R., New Testament, History of the Early Church
GÄBLER, U., Ecclesiastical and Dogmatic History
GRÖZINGER, A., Practical Theology
LIENEMANN, CH., Ecumenical Movement and Mission
MATHYS, H.-P., Old Testament and Semitic Languages
MOHN, J., Science of Religion
PFLEIDERER, G., Systematic Theology, Ethics
STEGEMANN, E., New Testament
WALRAFF, M., History of the Church and of Theology

Institute for Jewish Studies (Leimenstr. 48, 4051 Basel; tel. 612051636; fax 612051640; e-mail institut-judaistik@unibas.ch; internet www.jewishstudies.unibas.ch):
BODENHEIMER, A., Jewish Literature and History
PICARD, J., Modern Jewish History and Culture

UNIVERSITÄT BERN

Hochschulstr. 4, 3012 Bern
Telephone: 316318111
Fax: 316318008
E-mail: info@imd.unibe.ch
Internet: www.unibe.ch
Founded 1834, (inc. Theological School, f. 1528)
State control
Language of instruction: German
Academic year: September to August
Rector: Prof. Dr URS WÜRGLER
Vice-Rector for Research: Prof. Dr MARTIN TÄUBER
Vice-Rector for Univ. Education: Prof. Dr GUNTER STEPHAN
Admin. Dir: Dr DANIEL ODERMATT
Chief Librarian: Prof. Dr ROBERT BARTH
Number of teachers: 3,552
Number of students: 14,300
Publications: uniaktuell (online magazine), UniPress–Forschung und Wissenschaft

DEANS

Faculty of Economics and Social Science: Prof. Dr HARLEY KROHMER
Faculty of Humanities: Prof. Dr HEINZPETER ZNOJ
Faculty of Human Sciences: Prof. Dr ROLAND SEILER
Faculty of Law: Prof. Dr STEPHAN WOLF
Faculty of Medicine: Prof. Dr PETER EGGLI
Faculty of Science: Prof. Dr SILVIO DECURTINS
Faculty of Theology: Prof. Dr SILVIA SCHROER
Vetsuisse Faculty: Prof. Dr ANDREAS ZURBRIGGEN

UNIVERSITÄT LUZERN
(University of Lucerne)

Pfistergasse 20, 6003 Luzern
Frohburgstr. 3, POB 4466, 6002 Lucerne 7
Telephone: 412295000
Fax: 412295001

E-mail: iro@unilu.ch
Internet: www.unilu.ch
Founded 1574, univ. status 2000
Languages of instruction: English, French, German
Academic year: August to July
Rector: Prof. Dr PAUL RICHLI
Vice-Rector: Prof. Dr MARTIN BAUMANN
Vice-Rector for Education and Int. Relations: Prof. Dr MARKUS RIES
Admin. Sec.: JUSTINA SCHMIDLIN
Librarian: Dr WOLFRAM LUTTERER
Number of teachers: 148
Number of students: 2,600

DEANS

Faculty of Culture and Social Sciences: Prof. Dr CHRISTOPH A. SCHALTEGGER
Faculty of Law: Prof. Dr FELIX BOMMER
Faculty of Theology: Prof. Dr MONIKA JAKOBS

UNIVERSITÄT ST GALLEN
(University of St Gallen)

Dufourstr. 50, 9000 St Gallen
Telephone: 712242111
Fax: 712242816
E-mail: info@unisg.ch
Internet: www.unisg.ch
Founded 1898, present name 2011
State control
Languages of instruction: German, English
Academic year: April to March
Pres.: Prof. Dr THOMAS BIEGER
Vice-Pres.: Lic. WERNER GÄCHTER
Exec. Dir: Lic. MARKUS BRÖNNIMANN
Library Dir: Dr XAVER BAUMGARTNER
Number of teachers: 2,223
Number of students: 6,726
Publications: Aussenwirtschaft (6 a year), Electronic Markets (4 a year), Thexis (6 a year)

DEANS

School of Economics and Political Science: Prof. MONIKA BÜTLER
School of Finance: Prof. Dr KARL FRAUENDORFER
School of Humanities and Social Sciences: Prof. ULRICH SCHMID
School of Management: Prof. WALTER BRENNER
Law School: Prof. LUKAS GSCHWEND

PROFESSORS

ANDEREGG, J., German Language and Literature
BACK, A., Information Processing
BAUDENBACHER, C., Private, Commercial and Economic Law
BAUMER, J.-M., Development Policy
BEHR, G., Business Administration
BELZ, C., Marketing
BERNET, B., Business Administration, Banking
BIEGER, T., Business Administration, Tourism
BOURQUI, C., Business Administration
BURMEISTER, K. H., History of Law
CHONG, L., Business Administration
DACHLER, P., Psychology
DOPFER, K., Foreign Trade and Development Theory
DRUEY, J. N., Civil and Commercial Law
DUBS, R., Business Pedagogy
DYLLICK, T., Business Administration
EHRENZELLER, B., Public Law
FICKERT, R., Business Administration
FISCHER, G., Economics
FRAUENDORFER, K., Operations Research
GÄRTNER, M., Economics
GEISER, T., Civil and Commercial Law
GOMEZ, P., Business Administration
GROSS, P., Sociology

GRÜNBICHLER, A., Finance
HALLER, M., Insurance and Business Admin-
istration, Risk Management
HAUSER, H., Foreign Trade Theory and Policy
HILB, M., Business Administration
INGOLD, F. P., Russian Language and Litera-
ture
JAEGER, F., Economic Policy
KAUFMANN, V., French Language and Litera-
ture
KEEL, A., Statistics
KIRCHGÄSSNER, G., Economics
KLEY, R., Political Science
KOLLER, A., Civil and Commercial Law
LECHNER, M., Empirical Economic Research
and Econometrics
LEUENBERGER, T., Modern History
MANELLA, J., Business Administration
MARTINONI, R., Italian Language and Litera-
ture
MASTRONARDI, P., Public Law
MEIER, A., Economics
MEIER-SCHATZ, C., Civil and Commercial Law
METZGER, CH., Business Administration
MOHR, E., Economics
MÜLLER, H., Mathematics
MÜLLER-STEWENS, G., Business Administra-
tion
NOBEL, P., Private, Commercial and Eco-
nomic Law
OESTERLE, H., Information Processing
PLEITNER, H. J., Business Administration
REETZ, N., Economics
RIKLIN, A., Political Science
ROBERTO, V., Private, Commercial and Eco-
nomic Law
ROBINSON, A. D., English Language and
Literature
RUIGROK, W., International Management
RUUD, F., Accounting
SCHEDLER, K., Public Management
SCHMID, B., Information Processing
SCHMID, H., Economics
SCHUH, G., Technology
SCHWANDER, I., Civil Law
SCHWEIZER, R., Public Law
SILES, J. R., Spanish Language and Litera-
ture
SPREMANN, K., Business Administration
STÄHLY, P., Operations Research
STIER, W., Empirical Social Research and
Applied Statistics
TOMCZAK, T., Business Administration
TRECHSEL, ST., Criminal Law and Criminal
Case Law
ULRICH, P., Economic Ethics
VALLENDER, C., Public Law and Law of
Taxation
VON KROGH, F., Business Administration
WALDBURGER, R., Taxation Law
WINTER, R., Information Processing
WUNDERER, R., Business Administration
ZIMMERMANN, H., Financial Market Analysis

UNIVERSITÄT ZÜRICH

Rämistr. 71, 8006 Zürich
Telephone: 446341111
Fax: 446344901
Internet: www.uzh.ch
Founded 1833, as Universitas Turicensis,
univ. status 1912
State control
Language of instruction: German
Academic year: October to July (2 semesters)
Pres.: Prof. Dr ANDREAS FISCHER
Vice-Pres. for Arts and Social Sciences: Prof.
Dr OTTFRIED JARREN
Vice-Pres. for Medicine and Natural Sci-
ences: Prof. Dr DANIEL WYLER
Vice-Pres. for Law and Economics: Prof. Dr
EGON FRANCK
Admin. Dir. and Dir of Finance: Dipl.-Ing.
STEFAN SCHNYDER
Sec.-Gen.: Dr KURT REIMANN

Librarian: Dr HEINZ DICKENMANN
Number of teachers: 512
Number of students: 25,854
Publications: *unijournal* (6 a year), *unim-
agazin* (4 a year), *unireport* (1 a year)

DEANS

Faculty of Arts: Prof. Dr BERND ROECK
Faculty of Economics: Prof. Dr JOSEF FALK-
INGER
Faculty of Law: Prof. Dr WOLFGANG WOHLERS
Faculty of Medicine: Prof. Dr KLAUS GRÄTZ
Faculty of Science: Prof. Dr MICHAEL HEN-
GARTNER
Faculty of Theology: Prof. Dr CHRISTOPH
UEHLINGER
Vetsuisse Faculty: Prof. Dr FELIX R. ALTHAUS

PROFESSORS

Centre for Dentistry, Oral and Maxillary
Medicine (Plattenstr. 11, 8028 Zürich; tel.
446343203):
GRÄTZ, K., Oral Surgery
HÄMMERLE, C., Crowns and Bridges
IMFELD, T., Preventive Dentistry, Period-
ontology, Cardiology
PALLA, S., Dental Prosthesis
PELTOMÄKI, T., Children's Dentistry

Faculty of Economics (tel. 446342314; e-mail
dekanatww@zuv.uzh.ch; internet www.oec
.uzh.ch):
BACKES-GELLNER, U., Business Admin.
BERNSTEIN, A., Dynamic and Distributed
Application Systems
CHESNEY, M., Quantitative Finance
DIETL, H., Service and Operation Manage-
ment
DITTRICH, K. R., Computer Science
EWERHART, C., Information Economy
FALKINGER, J., Finance and Macroeconom-
ics
FEHR, E., Economics
FRANCK, E., Business Admin.
GALL, H. C., Software Engineering
GEIGER, H., Banking and Finance
GIBSON-ASNER, R., Financial Economics
GLINZ, M., Informatics
HABIB, M., Corporate Finance Theory
HENS, T., Financial Economics
HOFFMANN, M., Int. Trade and Finance
HOTZ-HART, B., Economics
JANSSEN, M., Financial Economics
KLATTE, D., Mathematics and Economics
MEYER, C., Accountancy and Financial
Control
OSTERLOH, M., Business Admin.
PAJAROLA, R., Multimedia
PAOLELLA, M., Empirical Finance
PFAFF, D., Accountancy and Financial Con-
trol
PFEIFER, R., Computer Science
RUUD, F., Accountancy and Financial Con-
trol
SAEZ-MARTI, F., Microeconomics
SCHAUER, H., Computer Science
SCHENKER-WICKI, A., Business Manage-
ment
SCHERER, A. G., Business Admin.
SCHMUTZLER, A., Economics
SCHWABE, G., Information Management
STAFFELBACH, B., Business Admin.
STILLER, B., System and Communication
VOLKART, R., Banking and Finance
WEHRLI, H. P., Business Admin.
WINKELMANN, R., Empirical Economics
WOITEK, U., History of Economics and
National Economy
ZILIBOTTI, F., National Economics
ZWEIFEL, P., Political Economy
ZWEIMÜLLER, J., Macroeconomics

Faculty of Law (tel. 446342233; e-mail
dekrwf@ius.uzh.ch; internet www.jur.uzh
.ch):
BIAGGINI, G., State, Administrative and
European Law
BREITSCHMID, P., Private Law
BÜCHLER, A., Private Law
DONATSCH, A., Criminal Law
ERNST, W., Roman Law
FÖGEN, M. T., Roman Law and Compara-
tive Law
FORSTMOSER, P., Trade Law
GÄCHTER, TH., State, Administrative and
Securities Law
GRIFFEL, A., State and Administrative Law
HEINEMANN, A., Economic Law
HILTY, R., Private Law
HONSELL, H., Swiss and European Civil
Law, Roman Law
HUGUENIN, C., Private Economic Law and
European Law
JAAG, T., State and Administrative Law
JOSITSCH, D., Criminal Law
KAUFMANN, C., State and Administrative
Law, Law of Nations
KELLER, H., State Law
KILLIAS, M., Criminal Law
KLEY, A., State Law
MEIER, I., Civil Case Law, Bankruptcy Law
NOBEL, P. J., Swiss and European Trading
and Economic Law
OBERHAMMER, P., Civil Case Law
OTT, W., Philosophical and Swiss Civil Law
PORTMANN, W., Private and Industrial Law
RAUSCH, H., Environmental and Adminis-
trative Law
REICH, M., Tax, Fiscal and Administrative
Law
REY, H., Swiss Civil Law
SCHNYDER, A., Private Economic Law
SENN, M., Philosophical Law
TAG, B., Criminal Law
THIER, A., History of Law
THÜRER, D., Law of Nations, State and
Administrative Law
UHLMANN, F., State and Administrative
Law
VON DER CRONE, H. C., Private and Busi-
ness Law
WEBER, R., European Law
WEBER-DÜRLER, B., State and Administra-
tive Law
WOHLERS, P., Private, Economic and Euro-
pean Law
ZOBL, D., Civil Law, Banking and Secur-
ities Law

Faculty of Medicine (Zürichbergstr. 14, 8091
Zürich; tel. 446341071; e-mail renate.gay@
usz.ch; internet www.med.uzh.ch):
AGUZZI, A., Neuropathology
AKDIS, C., Immunology
ARAND, M., Pharmacology
ATTIN, TH., Preventive Dentistry
BÄR, W., Forensic Medicine
BASSETTI, C., Neurology
BERGER, E. G., Physiology
BERGER, W., Medical Molecular Genetics
BILLER-ANDORNO, N., Biomedical Ethics
BOLTSHAUSER, E., Paediatrics
BORGEAT, A., Anaesthesiology
BÖSIGER, P., Biomedical Technology
BÖTTGER, E. C., Medical Microbiology
BOUTELLIER, U., Physiology
BUCHER, H. U., Neonatology
BUCK, A., Nuclear Medicine
BUDDEBERG, C., Social Psychology
CLAVIEN, P. A., Abdominal Surgery
DIETZ, V., Paraplegology
FEHR, J., Haematology
FINK, D. A., Gynaecology
FONTANA, A., Clinical Immunology
FRENCH, L., Dermatology
FRIED, M., Gastroenterology
FRITSCHY, J. M., Neuropharmacology
GAY, S., Experimental Rheumatology

GENONI, M., Heart Surgery
GERBER, C., Orthopaedics
GIOVANOLI, P., Surgery
GRÄTZ, K., Pathology
GROSCURTH, P., Anatomy
GRÜTTER, M. G., Biochemistry, Macromolecular Crystallography
GUTZWILLER, F., Social and Preventive Medicine
HÄMMERLE, CH., Dentistry
HELD, L., Biostatics
HELL, D., Clinical Psychiatry
HELMCHEN, F., Neurology
HENGARTNER, H., Experimental Pathology
HENNET, TH., Human Biology
HOCK, C., Biological Pharmacology
HODLER, J., Radiology
HUG, E., Radiology
IMFELD, TH., Preventive Dentistry
IMTHURN, B., Gynaecological Endocrinology
JENNI, R., Cardiology
JIRICNY, J., Molecular Radiology
KAISSLING, B., Anatomy
KNUTH, A., Oncology
KOLLIAS, S., Radiology
KULLAK-UBLICK, G. A., Clinical Pharmacology
LANDAU, K., Ophthalmology
LIPP, H. P., Anatomy
LOFFING, J., Anatomy
LÜSCHER, T. F., Cardiology
LÜTOLF, U. M., Radiotherapy
MANSUY, I., Neurology
MARINCEK, B., Diagnostic Radiology
MEULI, M., Surgery
MICHEL, B., Rheumatology
MITSIADIS, TH., Oral Biology
MOCH, H., Pathology
MODESTIN, J., Clinical Psychiatry
MÖLLING, K., Virology
MURER, H., Physiology
NADAL, D., Paediatrics
NEUHASS, S., Neurobiology
NITSCH, R. M., Psychiatry
NOLL, G., Molecular Biology
PALLA, S., Prosthetics
PELTOMÄKI, T., Maxillary Orthopaedics
PLÜCKTHUN, A., Biochemistry
PRÊTRE, R., Children's Cardiac Surgery
PROBST, R. R., Otorhinolaryngology
PRUSCHY, M., Molecular Biology
REINECKE, M., Anatomy
ROGLER, G., Internal Medicine
RÖSSLER, W., Clinical Psychiatry
ROTH, J., Cell Molecular Pathology
RUDIN, M., Pharmacology
RUSSI, E., Internal Medicine
RÜTTIMANN, B., History of Medicine
SALLER, R., Naturopathy
SCHINZEL, A., Medical Genetics
SCHMID, E., Anaesthesia
SCHMID, S., Otorhinolaryngology
SCHNYDER, U., Psychiatry
SCHÖNLE, E., Paediatrics
SCHWAB, M. E., Neurology and Anatomy
SEGER, R., Children's Medicine, Immunology and Haematology
SENNHAUSER, F. H., Paediatrics
SONDEREGGER, P., Biochemistry
SPAHN, D. R., Anaesthesiology
SPINAS, G. A., Endocrinology, Diabetology and Pathophysiology
STEINHAUSEN, H.-C., Child and Youth Psychiatry
STEINMANN, B. U., Paediatrics
STEURER, J., Internal Medicine
SULSER, T., Urology
TRENTZ, O., Accident Surgery
VALAVANIS, A., Neuroradiology
VERREY, F., Physiology
VETTER, W., Internal Medicine
VON ECKARDSTEIN, A., Clinical Chemistry
VON SCHULTHESS, G. K., Nuclear Medicine
WAGNER, A., Bioinformatics
WEBER, R., Clinical Infectology
WEDER, W., Thorax Surgery

WENGER, R. H., Physiology
WIESER, H.-G., Neurology, Special Epileptology
WOGGON, B., Pharmacotherapy
WOLFER, D., Anatomy
WÜTHRICH, B., Dermatology and Venereology
ZEILHOFER, H. U., Pharmacology
ZIMMERMANN, R., Obstetrics and Gynaecology
ZINKERNAGEL, R. M., Experimental Pathology
ZÜND, G., Surgery

Faculty of Philosophy (tel. 446342234; fax 446344966; e-mail heidi.moor@access.unizh.ch; internet www.uzh.ch/fakultaet/phil):

BONFADELLI, H., Journalism
BOOTHE, B., Clinical Psychology
BORNSCHIER, V., Economic Sociology
BOSKOVSKA, N., History of Eastern Europe
BOSSONG, G., Romance Philology
BRANDSTÄTTER, V., General Psychology
BRONFEN, E., English and American Literature
BUCHMANN, M., Sociology
CLAUSSEN, P. C., Art History of the Middle Ages
CRIVELLI, T., Special Romance Literature
DELLA CASA, PH., History of Medieval Art
DESCOEDRES, G., History of Medieval Art
DUNKEL, G. E., Comparative Indo-German Linguistics
DURSCHEID, CH., German Language
EBERLE, F., Pedagogy
EBERT, K. H., General German Philology
EHLERT, U., Psychology
EIGLER, U., Classical Philology
ESSER, F., Journalism
ESTERHAMMER, A., English Literature
FATKE, R., Pedagogy, Special Social Pedagogics
FINKE, P., Ethnology
FISCH, J., General Modern History
FISCHER, A., English Philology
FREUD, A., Applied Psychology
FRIES, U., English Philology
FRÖHLICHER, P., History of French Literature
GASSMANN, R. H., Sinology
GESER, H., Sociology
GILOMEN, H. J., General Economic and Social History, Swiss History
GLASER, E., German Philology
GLAUSER, J., Nordic Philology
GLESSGEN, M.-D., Romance Philology
GLOCK, H.-J., Philosophy
GONON, P., Pedagogy
GRODDECK, W., New German Literature
GÜNTHER, H., History of Modern Art
GUTSCHER, H., Social Psychology
GYR, U., Folklore
HAUG, H.-J., Psychiatry
HAUSENDORF, H., German Language
HELBLING, J., Ethnology
HESS, M., Computer Linguistics
HEUSSER, M., English Literature
HINRICHSEN, H.-J., Musicology
HIRSIG, R., Psychological Methods
HORNUNG, R., Social Psychology
HUG, S., Political Science
IMHOF, K., Journalism
JÄNCKE, L., Neuropsychology
JARREN, O., Publicity Science
JONAS, K., Social Psychology
JUCKER, A., English Philology
KELLNER, B., Old German Literature
KIENING, C., German Literature
KLEINMANN, M., Psychology
KOHLER, G., Philosophy, Political Philosophy
KOLB, G., Ancient History
KRIESI, H., Political Science
KRÜGER, G., Modern History
KYBURZ-GRABER, R., Pedagogy

LA FAUCI, N., Romance Philology, Italian Linguistics
LABARTHE, P., Romance Literature
LEIST, A., Ethics
LIENHARD, M., Spanish
LINKE, W. A., German Literature
LOETZ, F., History
LOPEZ GUIL, I., Iberoromanic Literature
LOPORCARO, M., Romance Philology, History of Italian
LÜTTEKEN, L., Musicology
MAERCKER, A., Psychopathology
MAREK, CH., Ancient History
MARTIN, M., Gerontology
MARX, W., General Psychology
MICHAELOWA, K., Politology
MICHEL, P., Ancient German Literature
MOOS, C., General and Swiss Modern History
MÜLLER NIELABA, D., German Literature
NÄF, B., Ancient History
NAUMANN, B., German Literature
OELKERS, J., Pedagogy
OPPITZ, M., Ethnology
PETERS, J.-U., Slavic Philology
PICONE, M., Italian Literature
RANDERIA, S., Ethnology
REDDICK, A., English Literature
REUSSER, K., Pedagogy
RIATSCH, C., Romance Literature
RIEDWEG, C., Classical Philology, Ancient Greek Studies
RIEMENSCHNITTER, A., Chinese Philology
ROECK, B., General and Swiss History
ROSSI, L., Romance Literature
RUCH, W., Psychology
RUDOLPH, U., Islamic Sciences
RUF, U., Pedagogy
RULOFF, D., Political Science
SAPORITI, K., Philosophy
SARASIN, P., General and Swiss Modern History
SCHABER, P., Philosophy
SCHNEIDER, S., German Literature
SCHREIER, D., English Language
SCHREINER, P., Indology
SCHULTHESS, P., Philosophical Theory
SIEGERT, G., Journalism
STOTZ, P., Middle Latin Philology
SZYDLIK, M., Sociology
TANNER, J., General and Swiss Modern History
TEUSCHER, S., Medieval Studies
TRÖHLER, M., Cinema Studies
URSPRUNG, PH., Modern Art
WAGNER, K., German Literature
WEISS, D., Slavonic Languages
WILKENING, F., General Psychology
WIRTH, W., Publicity Science
ZEY, C., History

Faculty of Science (Winterthurerstr. 190, 8057 Zürich; tel. 446344002; fax 446346806; e-mail dekanat@mnf.uzh.ch; internet www.mnf.uzh.ch):

ACBERSOLD, R., Functional Genomics
ALBERTO, R., Inorganic Chemistry
AMSLER, C., Experimental Physics
BALDRIDGE, K., Computer-supported Chemistry
BARBOUR, A. D., Biomathematics
BASLER, K., Zoology, Molecular Development Genetics
BERKE, H. G. H., Inorganic Chemistry
BOLTHAUSEN, E., Mathematics, esp. Applied Mathematics
BRODMANN, M., Mathematics
BUCHER, H. F. R., Palaeontology
BURG, J.-P., Geology
CAFLISCH, A., Computer-supported Structural Biology
CATTANEO, A. S., Mathematics
CHIPOT, M. M., Mathematics
CONTI, E., Systematic Biology
DE LELLIS, C., Pure Mathematics
DOUGLAS, R., Neuroinformatics

EBERL, L., Microbiology
ENDRESS, P. K., Systematic Botany
FABRIKANT, S. I., Geography, esp. Geographical Information Science
FINK, H.-W., Experimental Physics
GEHRMANN, T., Theoretical Physics
GREBER, U., Zoology
GROSSNIKLAUS, U., Biology
HAEBERLI, W., Geography
HAHNLOSER, R., Neuroinformatics
HAMM, P., Physical Chemistry
HEINRICH, C. A., Crystallography and Petrography
HENGARTNER, M. O., Molecular Biology
HUTTER, J., Physical Chemistry
ITTEN, K. I., Geography
KAPPELER, T., Mathematics
KELLER, B., Plant Molecular Biology
KELLER, H., Physics of Condensed Matter
KÖNIG, B., Zoology, Behavioural Biology
KRESCH, A., Pure Mathematics
LAKE, G., Theoretical Physics
LEHNER, C. F., Developmental Biology
LINDER, H. P., Systematic Biology
MARTIN, K. A., Neurophysiology Systems
MARTINOIA, E., Plant Biology
MOORE, B., Theoretical Physics
MÜLLER-BÖKER, U., Anthropogeography
NOLL, M., Molecular Biology
OKONEK, CH., Mathematics
OSTERWALDER, J., Experimental Physics
REYER, H.-U., Zoology
ROBINSON, J. A., Organic Chemistry
ROSENTHAL, J. J., Mathematics
SAUTER, S. A., Mathematics
SCHAFFNER, W., Molecular Biology
SCHILLING, A., Experimental Physics
SCHMID, B., Environmental Science
SCHMIDT, M., Physical Geography
SCHMIDT, M. W., Crystalline Geology
SCHROEDER, V., Mathematics
SEEGER, S., Physical Chemistry
SELJAK, U., Theoretical Physics
SIEGEL, J. S., Organic Chemistry
STEINMANN-ZWICKY, M., Zoology
STENFLO, J. O., Astronomy
STEURER, W., Crystallography
STOECKLI, E., Neurobiology
STRAUMANN, U., Physics
THIERSTEIN, H. R., Micro-Palaeontology
THOMPSON, A. B., Petrology
VAN SCHAIK, C. P., Anthropology
VON MERING, CH., Bioinformatics
WARD, P., Zoology, Ecology
WEIBEL, R., Geography
WYLER, D., Theoretical Physics
ZOLLIKOFER, CH., Zoology

Faculty of Theology (Kirchgasse 9, 8001 Zürich; tel. 446344721; e-mail dekanat@theol.uzh.ch):

BERGIAN, S., History of Church and Dogma
BÜHLER, P., Systematic Theology
CAMPI, E., History of Church and Dogma
DALFERTH, I. U., Systematic Theology
FISCHER, J., Theological Ethics
KRÜGER, T., Old Testament
KUNZ, R., Practical Theology
SCHMID, K., Old Testament
UEHLINGER, C., History and Science of Religions
VOLLENWEIDER, S., New Testament
ZUMSTEIN, J., New Testament

Faculty of Veterinary Medicine (Winterthurerstr. 252, 8057 Zürich; tel. 446358121; fax 446358902; e-mail dekanat@vetadm.uzh.ch; internet www.vet.uzh.ch):

ACKERMANN, M., Virology
ALTHAUS, F., Pharmacology and Toxicology
AUER, J. A., Veterinary Surgery
BRAUN, U., Internal Medicine of Ruminants
BÜRKI, K., Laboratory Animal Science
DEPLAZES, P., Parasitology
EHRENSPERGER, F., Immunopathology
GASSMAN, M., Veterinary Physiology

HATT, J. M., Small Animals
HOTTIGER, M., Molecular Biology
HÜBSCHER, U., Biochemistry
KÄHN, W., Reproductive Medicine
LUTZ, H., Internal Medicine
LUTZ, TH., Physiology
MONTAVON, P. M., Surgery of Small Domestic Animals
NAEGELI, H. P., Toxicology
POSPISCHIL, A., Pathology
REUSCH, C., Internal Medicine (Small Animals)
SPIESS, B., Veterinary Ophthalmology
STEPHAN, R., Foodstuff Security
WANNER, M., Animal Nutrition
WITTENBRINK, M. M., Veterinary Bacteriology

UNIVERSITÉ DE FRIBOURG/ UNIVERSITÄT FREIBURG

1700 Fribourg
Telephone: 263007111
Fax: 263009700
E-mail: rectorat@unifr.ch
Internet: www.unifr.ch

Founded 1889
State control
Languages of instruction: French, German, English
Academic year: July to August

Rector: Prof. G. VERGAUWEN
Vice-Rector: Prof. A. EPINEY
Vice-Rector: Prof. J.-L. GURTNER
Vice-Rector: Prof. F. MÜLLER
Vice-Rector: Prof. J. PASQUIER
Librarian: M. GOOD
Library: 2.4m. vols
Number of teachers: 200
Number of students: 10,000

Publications: Uni Reflets (6 a year), Universitas Friburgensis (4 a year)

DEANS

Faculty of Arts: Prof. THOMAS AUSTENFELD
Faculty of Economics and Social Sciences: Prof. M. WIDMER
Faculty of Law: Prof. MARCEL ALEXANDER NIGGLI
Faculty of Science: Prof. ROLF INGOLD
Faculty of Theology: Prof. MARIANO DELGADO

PROFESSORS

Faculty of Arts (Ave Europe 20, 1700 Fribourg; tel. 263007500; fax 263009709; e-mail lettres@unifr.ch; internet www.unifr.ch/lettres):

AUSTENFELD, T., American Literature
BERRENDONNER, A., French Linguistics
BERTHELE, R., Multilingualism
BILLERBECK, M., Classical Philology
BLESS, G., Therapeutic Pedagogy
BUDOWSKI, M., Social Policy
CASASUS, G., Contemporary History
CHRISTEN, H., Germanic Linguistics
CLAVIEN, A., General and Swiss Contemporary History
DARMS, G., Rhaeto-Romance Language and Culture
FRICKE, H., Modern German Literature
GHOSE, I., English Literature
GIORDANO, C., Ethnology
GURTNER, J.-L., General Pedagogy
HAUSER, C., General and Swiss Contemporary History
HERLTH, J., Slavistic Studies
HUBER, O., General Psychology
HUNKELER, T., French Literature
KARFIK, P., Philosophy of Antiquity
KRONIG, W., Special Education
KURMANN, P., History of Art
LAMBERT, J., Therapeutic Pedagogy
LUTZ, E., German Philology
MARTINI, A., Italian Literature

NIDA RUEMELIN, M., Philosophy
PEÑATE RIVERO, J., Spanish Literature
PERREZ, M., Clinical Psychology
PIÉRART, M., Ancient History
PYTHON, F., General and Swiss Contemporary History
REICHERTS, M., Clinical Psychology
REINHARDT, V., Early Modern History of Europe and Switzerland
SCHMIDT, H.-J., Medieval History of Europe and Switzerland
SCHMIDT, T., Classical Philology
SOLDATI, G., Modern and Contemporary Philosophy
SOULET, M., Social Work
SPIESER, J.-M., Early Christian Archaeology
STAMM, M., Education Science
STOICHITA, V., History of Art
SUAREZ NANI, T., Medieval Philosophy, Ontology
TURCHETTI, M., Early Modern History of Europe and Switzerland
VIEGNES, M., French Literature
WOLF, J.-C., Ethical and Political Philosophy
ZOPPELLI, L., History of Music

Faculty of Economics and Social Sciences (Blvd de Pérolles 90, 1700 Fribourg; tel. 263008200; fax 263009725; e-mail decanat-ses@unifr.ch; internet www.unifr.ch/economics):

BORTIS, H., History of Economic Theory
BOSSHART, L., Media and Communication
BOURGEOIS, D., Media and Communication
BRACHINGER, H.-W., Statistics
DAFFLON, B., Public Finance
DAVOINE, E., Administration of Human Resources
DESCHAMPS, P., Econometrics
EICHENBERGER, R., Public Finance
FRIBOULET, J.-J., Economic History
GMÜR, M., Management, NPO–Management
GÖX, R., Finance and Controlling
GRÖFLIN, H., Information Systems
GROSSMANN, V., Macro Economy
GRÜNIG, R., Management
GUGLER, P., Social and Political Economy
ISAKOV, D., Financial Management
MEIER, A., Informatics
MORSCHETT, D., International Management
PASQUIER-ROCHA, J., Informatics
ROSSI, S., Macro Economy
SCHÖNHAGEN, P., Media and Communication
TEUFEL, S., International Telecommunications Management
VANETTI, M., Marketing
WALLMEIER, M., Financial Management
WIDMER, M., Decision Support Systems
WOLFF, R., Economic Theory and Empirical Research

Faculty of Law (Ave Europe 20, 1700 Fribourg; tel. 263008000; fax 263009719; e-mail droit-decanat@unifr.ch; internet www.unifr.ch/droit):

AMSTUTZ, M., Private Law
BELSER, M., Private Law
BESSON, S., International Public Law, European Law
BORGHI, M., Swiss Public Law
BORS, M., Roman Law
EPINEY, A., Constitutional Law, International Public Law, European Law
HÄNNI, P., Constitutional and Administrative Law
HINNY, P., Tax Law
HÜRLIMANN-KAUP, B., Private Law
HURTADO POZO, J., Criminal Law
LE ROY, Y., History of Law, Canon Law
MURER, E., Labour and Social Insurance Law
NIGGLI, M., Criminal Law

PAHUD DE MORTANGES, R., History of Law
PICHONNAZ, P., Private Law
QUELOZ, N., Criminal Law
RUMO-JUNGO, A., Private Law
STEINAUER, P.-H., Civil Law
STÖCKLI, H., Civil Law, Trade Law
STOFFEL, W., International Private Law, Trade Law
TORRIONE, H., Tax Law and Philosophy of Law
VOLKEN, P., International and Commercial Law
WALDMANN, B., Public Law
WERRO, F., Private Law
ZUFFEREY, J. B., Public Law

Faculty of Science (Ch. du Musée 9, Pérolles, 1700 Fribourg; tel. 263008111; fax 263009729; e-mail science@unifr.ch; internet www.unifr.ch/sciences):

AEBI, P., Physics
BAERISWYL, D., Theoretical Physics
BERNHARD, C., Experimental Physics
BERRUT, J.-P., Mathematics
BERSIER, L.-F., Ecology and Evolution
BOCHET, C., Organic Chemistry
CELIO, M., Histology
CONZELMANN, A., Biochemistry
DESSAI, A., Mathematics
DE VIRGILIO, C., Biochemistry
FROMM, K., Inorganic Chemistry
HAUCK, C., Physical Geography
HIRSBRUNNER, B., Computer Science
HÖLZLE, M., Physical Geography
HUGHES, K., Microbiology
INGOLD, R., Computer Science
KELLERHALS, R., Mathematics
MAZZA, C., Statistics and Theory of Probability
MÉTRAUX, J.-P., Plant Biology
MONTANI, J.-P., Physiology
MÜLLER, F., Zoology
ROUILLER, E., Physiology
RÜEGG, C., Pathology
SCHEFFOLD, F., Experimental Physics
WEDER, C., Polymer Chemistry
WEIS, A., Experimental Physics
ZHANG, Y.-C., Theoretical Physics

Faculty of Theology (Ave Europe 20, 1700 Fribourg; tel. 263007370; fax 263009708; e-mail decanat-theol@unifr.ch; internet www.unifr.ch/theo):

DELGADO, M., History of Church
EMERY, G., Dogmatic Theology
HALLENSLEBEN, B., Dogmatic Theology
HOLDEREGGER, A., Moral Theology
KLÖCKENER, M., Moral Theology
KÜCHLER, M., New Testament Exegesis

UNIVERSITÉ DE GENÈVE

rue du Général-Dufour 24, 1211 Geneva 4
Telephone: 223797111
Fax: 223791134
E-mail: secretariat-rectorat@unige.ch
Internet: www.unige.ch
Founded 1559, univ. status 1873
Language of instruction: French
Academic year: October to July

Rector: Prof. JEAN-DOMINIQUE VASSALLI
Vice-Rector: Prof. ANIK DE RIBAUPIERRE
Vice-Rector: Prof. YVES FLÜCKIGER
Vice-Rector: Prof. PIERRE SPIERER
Sec.-Gen.: Dr STÉPHANE BERTHET
Library: see under Libraries and Archives
Number of teachers: 3,569
Number of students: 14,500
Publication: Campus

DEANS

Faculty of Arts: Prof. ERIC WEHRLI
Faculty of Economics and Social Science: Prof. BERNARD MORARD
Faculty of Law: Prof. CHRISTIAN BOVET

Faculty of Medicine: Prof. JEAN-LOUIS CARPENTIER
Faculty of Psychology and Educational Sciences: Prof. JEAN-PAUL BRONCKART
Faculty of Science: Prof. JEAN-MARC TRISCONE
Faculty of Theology: ANDREAS DETTWILER
School of Translation and Interpretation: LANCE HEWSON

PROFESSORS

Faculty of Arts (3 rue de Candolle, 1211 Geneva 4; tel. 223797111; fax 223791029; internet www.unige.ch/lettres):

ADAMZIK-BEVAND, K., German Literature and Civilization
ALVAR, C., Spanish Language and Literature
BARDAZZI, G., Romance Literature
BERELOWITCH, W., History
BOCCADORO, B., Musicology
BOLENS-JEANNERET, G., English Language and Literature
BORGEAUD, P., History of Ancient Religions
CAVIGNEAUX, A., Oriental Languages
CERUTTI, M., General History
CONRAD, C., History
DARBELLAY, E., Musicology
DE LIBERA, A., Philosophy
DESCOEUDRES, J.-P., Archaeology
FOEHR-JANSSENS, Y., Medieval French Literature
GAJO, G., Romance Literature
GAMBONI, L., Linguistics
GENEQUAND, C., Muslim and Arab Civilization
GROSRICHARD, A., French Literature
HAEBERLI, E., English Literature
HELG, A., General History
HURST, A., Classical Greek
JACCARD, J.-P., Russian Language
JENNY, L., French Literature
KOT, S., General History
LASSITHIOTAKIS, M., Modern Greek
LOMBARDO, P., French Literature
MADSEN, D., English Language and Literature
MANZOTTI, E., Italian Linguistics
MÉLA, CH., Medieval Romance Languages and Literature
MOESCHLER, J., General Linguistics
MORENZONI, F., History
MULLIGAN, K., Philosophy
NAEF, S., Arabic Language
NATALE, M., History of Art
NELIS, D., Latin Literature
PERUGI, M., Medieval Latin Language and Literature
PONT, J.-C., History of Sciences
PORRET, M., Modern History
POT, O., French Literature
RIGOLI, J., French Literature
SCHRADER, H. J., German Literature and Civilization
SCHUBERT, P., Modern Greek
SHLONSKY, UR., Linguistics
SOUYRI, P.-F., Japanese
SPURR, D. A., Modern English Literature
TALENS, C. J., Spanish Language and Literature
TILLIETTE, J.-Y., Medieval Latin Language and Literature
VALLOGGIA, M., Egyptology
WALTER, F., General History
WEHRLI, E., French Linguistics and Computer Science
WETZEL, R., German Literature and Civilization
WINKLER, M., German Literature and Civilization
WIRTH, J., History of Art in the Middle Ages
ZUFFEREY, Chinese Studies

Faculty of Economics and Social Science (40 blvd du Pont-d'Arve, 1211 Geneva 4; tel.

223797111; fax 223799919; internet www .unige.ch/ses):

ALLAN, P., Political Science
ANTILLE GAILLARD, G., Economics and Social Science
BALLMER-CAO, T.-H., Political Science
BENDER, A., Industrial Organization
BERGADAA DELMAS, M., Marketing
BRAILLARD, P., European Globalization
BURGENMEIER, B., Political Economy
CARLEVARO, F., Econometrics
CASSIS, Y., Economic History
CATTACIN, S., Sociology
CURZON-PRICE, V., Economics
DE BLASIS, J. P., Industrial Organization
DE LA GRANDVILLE, O., Political Economy
DE MELO, J., Political Economy
DEBARBIEUX, B., Geography
DENIS, J. E., Industrial Organization
DUMONT, P.-A., Industrial Organization
DUMONTIER, P., Accountancy
FLUECKIGER, Y., Political Economy
GILLI, M., Computer Science, Econometrics
HOESLI, M. E. R., Real Estate Financing
HORBER, E., Sociology
HUSSY, C., Geography
JARILLO, J.-C., Economic Strategy
KELLERHALS, J., Sociology
KONSTANTAS, D., Information Systems
KRISHNAKUMAR, J., Econometrics
LANE, J. E., Political Science
LAWRENCE, R. J., Human Ecology
LEFOLL, J., Industrial Organization
LEONARD, M., Computer Science applied to Business
LOUBERGÉ, H., Political Economy
MAGNENAT THALMANN, N., Information Systems
MIRONESCO, C., Political Science
MORARD, B., Accountancy
MÜLLER, T., Econometrics
ORIS, M., Economic History
OSSIPOW, W., Political Science
PROBST, G., Industrial Organization
RAFFOURNIER, B., Accountancy
RECORDON, P. A., Contracts
RITSCHARD, G., Econometrics
RONCHETTI, E., Industrial Organization
ROYER, D., Statistics
SAUVAIN, C., Demography
SCAILLET, O., Statistics and Probability
SCHMITT, N., Political Economy
SCIARINI, P., Political Science
SCHNEIDER, S. C., Industrial Organization
SCHULTHEISS, F., Sociology
THOENIG, M., Political Economy
VERLEY, P., Economic History
VERNEX, J. C., Geography
VIAL, J.-PH., Industrial Organization
VIALLON, P., Sociology
VICTORIA FESER, M.-P., Statistics and Probability
WEBER, L., Political Economy
WINDISCH, U., Sociology

Faculty of Law (40 blvd du Pont-d'Arve, 1211 Geneva 4; tel. 223797111; fax 223799916; internet www.unige.ch/droit):

AUBERT, G., Administrative Law
AUER, A., Constitutional Law
BADDELEY, M., Civil Law
BELLANGER, F., Fiscal Law
BOISSON DE CHAZOURNES, L., Public International Law
BOVET, C., Fiscal Law
BUCHER, A., Civil Law
CASSANI, U., Penal Law
CHAPPUIS, C., Business Law
DELLEY, J.-D., Constitutional Law
FLUECKIGER, A., Constitutional Law
FOEX, B., Civil Law
GREBER, P. Y., Administrative Law
HOTTELIER, M., Constitutional Law
JEANDIN, N., Civil Law
KADDOUS, C., Public International Law
KADNER, T., Civil Law

KAUFMANN-KOHLER, G., Private International Law
KELLER, A., History of Institutions and Law
LEVRAT, N., Public International Law
MALINVERNI, G., Constitutional Law, Introduction to the Science of Law
MANAÏ-WEHRLI, D., Civil Law
MONNIER, V., History of Institutions and Law
OBERSON, X. B., Fiscal Law
PETER, H., Civil Law
PETITPIERRE-SAUVAIN, A., Commercial Law
ROBERT, C. N., Penal Law, Criminology
ROTH, R., Penal Law
SASSOLI, M., Public International Law
STAUDER, B., German Commercial Law
STETTLER, M., Civil Law
TANQUEREL, T., Constitutional Law
THÉVENOZ, L., Civil Law
TRIGO TRINDADE, R. M., Business and Commercial Law
WINIGER, B., European and Civil Law

Faculty of Medicine (C.M.U., 1 rue Michel-Servet, 1211 Geneva 4; tel. 223795111; fax 223473334; internet www.unige.ch/medecine):

ANTONORAKIS, S., Genetics and Microbiology
ASSIMACOPOULOS, F., Medical Biochemistry
BADER, C., Oto-neuro-ophthalmology
BAEHNI, P., Dentistry
BAERTSCHI, A. J., Physiology
BAIROCH, A., Medical Biochemistry
BARRAZZONE, C., Paediatrics
BECKER, C., Radiology
BEGHETTI, M., Paediatrics
BELIN, D., Pathology
BELLI, D. C., Paediatrics
BELSER, U., Dentistry
BERNER, M., Paediatrics
BERNHEIM, L., Physiology
BERTRAND, D., Physiology
BERTSCHY, G., Psychiatry
BISCHOF, P. A., Gynaecology and Obstetrics
BORISCH, B., Pathology
BOUNAMEAUX, H., Medicine
CAPPONI, A., Endocrinology
CARPENTIER, J.-L., Morphology
CAVERZASIO, J., Medicine
CHARDOT, C., Paediatrics
CHEVROLET, J.-C., Medicine
CLERGUE, F., Cardiology
COLLART BUCKHARD, M., Medical Biochemistry
COSSON, P., Morphology
DAYER, J.-M., Medicine
DAYER, P., Pharmacology
DE TRIBOLET, N., Oto-neuro-ophthalmology
DEMAUREX, N., Physiology
DUBUISSON, J.-S., Gynaecology and Obstetrics
FANTINI, B., Medicine
FASEL, J., Morphology
FERRERO, F., Pharmacology
FRENCH, L., Oto-neuro-ophthalmology
GABAY, C., Medicine
GEISSBUHLER, A., Radiology
GENTA, R., Pathology
GEORGOPOULOS, C. P., Medical Biochemistry
GIANNAKOPOULOS, P., Psychiatry
GIRARDIN, E., Paediatrics
GOLAY, A., Medicine
GUYOT, J., Oto-neuro-ophthalmology
HADENGUE, A., Medicine
HALBAN, PH., Medicine
HARDING, T., Legal Medicine
HOCHSTRASSER, D., Medical Biochemistry
HOESSLI, D., Pathology
HOFFMEYER, P., Surgery
HUEPPI, P., Paediatrics
IMHOF, B., Pathology
ISELIN, C., Surgery
IZUI, S., Pathology

KATO, A. C., Oto-neuro-ophthalmology
KAYSER BENGT, E. J., Sports Medicine
KILIARIDIS, S., Orthodontics
KISS, J. Z., Morphology
KOLAKOFSKY, D., Microbiology
KRAUSE, K. H., Medicine
KREJCI, I., Dentistry
LANDIS, T., Oto-neuro-ophthalmology
LE COULTRE, C., Surgery
LERCH, R., Medicine
LEW, D. P., Microbiology
LINDER, P., Medical Biochemistry
LÜSCHER, C., Oto-neuro-ophthalmology
MAGISTRETTI, P., Psychiatry
MALAFOSSE, A., Psychiatry
MARTIN, P.-Y., Nephrology
MAURON, A., Clinical Ethics
MEDA, P., Morphology
MENTHA, G., Surgery
MICHEL, C., Oto-neuro-ophthalmology
MICHEL, J.-P., Geriatrics
MOMBELLI, A., Orthodontics
MONTESANO, R., Morphology
MORABIA, A., Social Medicine
MOREL, D., Cardiology
MOREL, PH., Surgery
MUHLETHALER, M., Neurophysiology
MÜLLER, D., Pharmacology
MÜLLER, F., Dental Prosthesis
PALACIO-ESPASA, F., Psychiatry
PANIZZON, R., Oto-neuro-ophthalmology
PELIZZONE, M., Oto-neuro-ophthalmology
PERNEGER, T., Social Medicine
PERRIER, A., Medicine
PETER, R., Surgery
PHILIPPE, J., Medicine
PITTET, D., Medicine
PITTET-CUENOD, B., Surgery
PRALONG, F., Medicine
RAPIN, CH.-H., Gerontology
RATIB, O., Radiology
REITH, W., Genetics, Microbiology
RICHTER, M. W., Surgery
ROCHAT, T., Medicine
ROSE, K., Medical Biochemistry
ROUGEMONT, A., Social Medicine
ROUX, L., Genetics, Microbiology
RUEFENACHT, D., Radiology
RUIZ-ALTABA, A., Stem Cells
SAFRAN, A.-B., Oto-neuro-ophthalmology
SAMSON, J., Dentistry
SAPPINO, P., Oncology
SAURAT, J.-H., Dermatology
SCHLEGEL, W., Medicine
SCHNIDER, A., Oto-neuro-ophthalmology
SIEGRIST, C.-A., Paediatrics
SIGWART, U., Medicine
SOLDATI-FAVRE, D., Genetics, Microbiology
STALDER, J., Medicine
STRUBIN, M., Genetics, Microbiology
SUTER, P., Surgery
SUTER, S., Paediatrics
VAN DER GOOT GRUNBERG, F., Genetics, Microbiology
VASSALLI, J.-D., Morphology
VILLEMURE, J.-G., Oto-neuro-ophthalmology
VU, NU. V., Medicine
WOLLHEIM, C., Medicine
ZUBLER, R., Medicine

Faculty of Protestant Theology (3 rue de Candolle, 1211 Geneva 4; tel. 223797111; fax 223797430; e-mail info@theologie.unige.ch; internet www.unige.ch/theologie):

BACKUS, I., History of the Reformation
BENEDICT, J., History of the Reformation
DERMANGE, F., Ethics
DETTWILER, A., New Testament Exegesis
GRANDJEAN, M., History of Christianity
NORELLI, E., New Testament Exegesis
PITASSI, M. C., History of the Reformation

Faculty of Psychology and Educational Sciences (40 blvd du Pont-d'Arve, 1211 Geneva 4; tel. 223797111; fax 223799020; internet www.unige.ch/fapse):

Section of Psychology:

BARISUKOV, K., Psychology of Mental Deficiency
BETRANCOURT, M., Training Technologies
CASPAR, F., Psychology
DE RIBAUPIERRE, A., Differential Psychology
EID, M., Data Analysis
FRAUENFELDER, U. H., Psycholinguistics
GENDOLLA, G., Psychology
GILLIÈRON-PALÉOLOGUE, C., Psychology, Epistemology
HAUERT, C.-A., Psychology of Development
KAISER, S., Verbal and Non-Verbal Communication
KERZEL, D., Cognitive Psychology
LORENZI-CIOLDI, F., Social Psychology
MOUNOUD, P., Psychology of Personality Development
MUGNY, G., Social Psychology
ROBERT-TISSOT, C., Child Psychotherapy
SCHERER, K., Social Psychology
VAN DER LINDEN, M., Psychopathology
VANHULLE, S., Psychology
VIVIANI, P., Statistics and Modelling in Psychology
ZESIGER, P. E., Language Disorders

Section of Educational Sciences:

ALLAL, L., Pedagogical Evaluation
AUDIGIER, F., Teaching of Social Science and Humanities
BAYER, E., Research Techniques in Education
BELLIER, S., Educational Sciences
BRONCKART, J.-P., Introduction to Language Theories
BUCHEL, F., Cognitive Education
CHATELANAT, G., Educational Sciences
CIFALI, M., Psycho-pedagogy
CRAHAY, M., Educational Sciences
DASEN, P., Introduction to Educational Sciences
DOLZ-MESTRE, J., Educational Sciences
DURAND, M., Adult Education
GIORDAN, A., Psycho-pedagogy in Sciences
HANHART, S., Education
HOFSTETTER-ROSET, R., Educational Sciences
JOBERT, G., Adult Education
MAGNIN, C. F., History of Education
PAYET, J. P., Sociology of Education
PERAYA, D., Educational Sciences
PERREGAUX, C., Cultural and Linguistic Diversity at School
PERRENOUD, P., General Pedagogy
SAADA-ROBERT, M., Learning Process
SCHNEUWLY, B., Introduction to Language Theories
SCHUBAUER, M.-L., Social Psychology
SCHURMANS BRONCKART, M. N., Social Construction of Knowledge

Faculty of Science (30 quai Ernest-Ansermet, 1211 Geneva 4; tel. 223796111; fax 223796698; internet www.unige.ch/sciences):

ALEXAKIS, A, Organic Chemistry
ALEXEEV, A., Mathematics
AUGUSTYNSKI, J., Applied Mineral Chemistry
BALLIVET, M., Biochemistry
BENY, J.-L., Animal Biology
BESSE, M., Anthropology, Ecology
BLECHA, A., Astronomy
BLONDEL, A., Nuclear Physics
BORKOVEC, M., Applied Mineral Chemistry
BOURQUIN, M., Nuclear Physics
BROUGHTON, W. J., Botany
BUCHS, D., Electronic Computing
BUETTIKER, M., Theoretical Physics
BUFFLE, J., Mineral Chemistry
BURKI, G., Astronomy
CARRUPT, P. A., Pharmacy
CHOPARD, B., Electronic Computing
CLARK, A. G., Nuclear Physics
CORAY, D., Mathematics

COURVOISIER, TH., Astronomy
DAVAUD, E. J., Geology
DE LA HARPE, P., Mathematics
DOELKER, E., Pharmacy
DOMINIK, J., History and Philosophy of Science
DROZ, M., Theoretical Physics
DUBOULE, D., Animal Biology
DUNGAN, M., Mineralogy
DURRER, R., Theoretical Physics
ECKMANN, J. P., Theoretical Physics and Mathematics
EDELSTEIN, S., Biochemistry
FISCHER, Ø., Physics
FONTBOTÉ, L., Mineralogy
GANDER, M.-J., Mathematics
GEOFFROY, M., Physical Chemistry
GIAMARCHI, T., Solid State Physics
GISIN, N., Theoretical Physics
GORIN, G. E., Geology
GRENON, M., Astronomy
GRUENBERG, J., Biochemistry
GULAÇAR, F., Physical Chemistry
GURNY, R., Pharmacy
HAIRER, E., Mathematics
HAUSER, A., Physical Chemistry
HOCHSTRASSER, D., Pharmacy
HOPFGARTNER, G., Pharmacy
HOSTETTMANN, K., Pharmacy
IZZAURRALDE, E., Molecular Biology
JEAN-PETIT-MATILE, S., Organic Chemistry
KIENZLE, M.-N., Solid State Physics
KINDLER, P., Geology and Palaeontology
KRAEMER BILBE, A., Cell Biology
KUNDIG, E. P., Organic Chemistry
LACHAL, B. M., Problems of Energy
LACHAVANNE, J.-B., Anthropology
LACOUR, J., Organic Chemistry
LANGANEY, A., Anthropology
LELUC, C., Nuclear Physics
MAEDER, A., Astronomy
MAGGIORE, M., Theoretical Physics
MARTINOU, J.-C., Cell Biology
MAYOR, M., Astronomy
MONOD, N., Mathematics
PALAZZO ROLIM, J., Electronic Computing
PASZKOWSKI, J., Vegetal Biology
PELLEGRINI, CH., Computer Science
PENEL, C., Botany
PFENNIGER, D., Astronomy
PICARD, D., Biology
PIGUET, C., Mineral Chemistry
POHL, M., Nuclear Physics
PONT, J.-C., History and Philosophy of Science
PUN, T., Computer Science
RAPIN, D., Nuclear Physics
RIEZMAN, H., Biochemistry
ROCHAIX, J.-D., Biology
RODRIGUEZ, I., Animal Biology
RONGA, F., Mathematics
RUEGG, U.-T., Pharmacy
SANCHEZ-MAZAS DE ABREU, A., Anthropology
SCAPPOZZA, L., Pharmacy
SCHALTEGGER, U., Mineralogy
SCHIBLER, U., Molecular Biology
SHORE, D., Molecular Biology
SMIRNOV, S., Mathematics
SPIERER, P., Animal Biology
STRASSER, R., Botany
STREIT, F., Mathematics
TRISCONE, J.-M., Solid State Physics
VAN DER MAREL, D., Solid State Physics
VAUTHEY, E., Physical Chemistry
VEUTHEY, J.-L., Pharmaceutical Chemistry
WANNER, G., Mathematics
WERNLI, R., Micropalaeontology
WILDI, W., Geology
WILLIAMS, A. F., Applied Mineral Chemistry
WITTWER, P., Theoretical Physics
WOLF, J.-P., Physics
WOLFENDER, J. L., Pharmacy
YVON, K., Structural Crystallography
ZANINETTI, L., Zoology and Palaeontology

Institute of Architecture (7 route de Drize, 1227 Carouge; tel. 223790799; fax 223799789; e-mail info@archi.unige.ch; internet www.unige.ch/ia):

CÊTRE, J.-P., Materials and Structures
MARIANI, R., Urban History
REICHLIN, B., Theory of Architecture
SCHEIWILLER, A., Architectural Design and Arts and Crafts
SIMONNET, C., Culture and History of Architecture and Arts and Crafts
WEBER, W., Architecture

School of Translation and Interpretation (40 blvd du Pont-d'Arve, 1211 Geneva 4; tel. 223797111; fax 223798750; internet www.unige.ch/eti):

ABDEL HADI, M., Arabic
ARMSTRONG, S., Use of Computers
BOCQUET, C.-Y., French
DANIEL, M., Translation with Computer Assistance
DE BESSÉ, B., Terminology
FANTUZZI, M., Italian
GEMAR, J.-C., French
GRIN, F., French
HEWSON LANCE, S. F., English
LEE-JAHNKE, H., German
MARCHESINI, G., Italian
MOSER-MERCER, B., German
SETTON, R. A. M., Interpretation
WEIBEL, L., French

ATTACHED SCHOOLS

École d'Education Physique et de Sport (School of Physical Education and Sport): tel. 223797722; attached to Faculty of Medicine; Dir P. HOLENSTEIN.

École de Langue et de Civilisation Françaises (School of French Language and Culture): tel. 223797111; fax 223797681; internet www.unige.ch/lettres/elcf; attached to Faculty of Arts; teaching activities, research and services in areas of French language (FLE), applied linguistics and multilingualism; Dir Prof. LAURENT GAJO.

ASSOCIATED INSTITUTES

Institut Oecuménique de Bossey (Ecumenical Institute): Château de Bossey, POB 1000, 1299 Crans-près-Céligny;Château de Bossey, Chemin Chenevière 2, Bogis-Bossey; tel. 229607300; fax 229607367; e-mail bossey@wcc-coe.org; internet www.wcc-coe.org/bossey; f. 1946; Dir IOAN SAUCA.

UNIVERSITÉ DE LAUSANNE

1015 Lausanne
Telephone: 216921111
Fax: 216922615
E-mail: immat.bachelor@unil.ch
Internet: www.unil.ch

Founded 1537, present name and status 1890
State control
Languages of instruction: English, French
Academic year: September to July

Rector: Prof. DOMINIQUE ARLETTAZ
Vice-Rector for Junior Faculty Devt and Diversity: Prof. FRANCISKA KRINGS
Vice-Rector for Quality and Human Resources: Dr JACQUE LANARÈS
Vice-Rector for Research and Int. Relations: Prof. PHILIPPE MOREILLON
Vice-Rector for Sustainability and Campus: BENOÎT FRUND
Vice-Rector for Teaching and Student Affairs: Prof. DANIELLE CHAPERON
Gen. Sec.: MARC DE PERROT

Library: see under Libraries and Archives
Number of teachers: 865
Number of students: 12,091

Publications: *Allez Savoir!, La Recherche, Uniscope*

DEANS

Faculty of Arts: Prof. FRANÇOIS ROSSET
Faculty of Biology and Medicine: Prof. BÉATRICE DESVERGNE
Faculty of Business and Economics: Prof. THOMAS VON UNGERN-STERNBERG
Faculty of Geosciences and Environment: Prof. JEAN RUEGG
Faculty of Law and Criminal Justice: Prof. BETTINA KAHIL
Faculty of Social and Political Science: Prof. FABIEN OHL
Faculty of Theology and Religious Studies: Prof. JÖRG STOLZ

PROFESSORS

Faculty of Biology and Medicine (Rue du Bugnon 21, 1005 Lausanne; tel. 216925000; fax 216925005; e-mail info.fbm@unil.ch; internet www.unil.ch/fbm):

ACHA-ORBEA, H., Biochemistry
AGUET, M., ISREC
ANSERMET, F., Child and Adolescent Psychiatry
BARRANDON, Y., Experimental Surgery
BARRAS, V., History of Medicine and Public Health
BECKMANN, J., Medical Genetics
BESSON, J., Community Psychiatry
BILLE, J., Medical Bacteriology
BIOLLAZ, J., Clinical Pharmacology
BISCHOF-DELALOYE, A., Nuclear Medicine
BOSMAN, F. T., Pathology
BULA, C., Geriatrics
BURNIER, M., Nephrology
CALANDRA, T., Infectious Diseases
CHIOLERO, R. L., Intensive Surgical Care
CLARKE, S., Neuropsychology and Neurorehabilitation
DANUSER, B., Work Health
DEMARTINES, N., Visceral Surgery
DESVERGNE, B., Genomics
DOTTO, G.-P., Biochemistry
EGLOFF, D. V., Surgery
FANCONI, S., Paediatrics
FARMER, E. E., Molecular Biology
FARRON, A., Orthopedics
FRACKOWIAK, R., Neurology
FRANCIOLI, P., Preventive Hospital Medicine
GAILLARD, R. C., Endocrinology and Metabolism
GRUETTER, R., Biomedical Imagery
GUEX, P., Psychiatry of Liaison
GUILLOU, L., Pathology
HAALFON, O., Infant and Adolescent Psychiatry
HAAS, D., Basic Microbiology
HERNANSEZ, N., Genomics
HERR, W., Genomics
HOHLFELD, P., Obstetrics
HORNUNG, J.-P., Cell Biology and Morphology
JICHLINSKI, P., Urology
KELLER, L., Ecology and Evolution
KERN, C. G., Anesthesiology
LAUNOIS, J., Biochemistry
LEHR, H.-A., Pathology
LEVI, F. G., Social and Preventive Medicine
LEVIVIER, M., Neuro-Surgery
LEYVRAZ, P.-F., Locomotive Device
MAGISTRETTI, P., Psychiatric Neurosciences
MANGIN, P., Forensic Medicine
MAYER, A., Biochemistry
MERMOD, N., Biotechnology
MEULI, R., Radiodiagnostic and Radiology Intervention
MICHAUD, P.-A., Adolescent Health
MICHETTI, P., Gastroenterology and Hepatalogy
MIRIMANOFF, R.-O., Radiotherapy

MOESSINGER, A. C., Neonatology and Paediatrics
MONNIER, P., Otorhinolaryngology
MORADPOUR, D., Gastroenterology and Hepatalogy
MOREILLON, P., Basic Microbiology
NICOD, L., Pneumology
NICOD, P., Internal Medicine
PACCAUD, F. M., Social and Preventive Medicine
PANIZZON, R., Dermatology
PANTALEO, G., Allergology and Immunology
PASCUAL, M., Transplantation
PÉCOUD, A., General Medicine
PERRIN, N., Ecology and Evolution
RIS, H.-B. F., Thoracic and Vascular Surgery
SAURAT, J. H., Dermatology
SCHENK, F., Physiology
SCHILD, L., Pharmacology and Toxiology
SCHNYDER, P.-A., Radiodiagnostics and Radiology Intervention
SO, A., Rheumatology, Physical Medicine and Rehabilitation
STAMENKOVIC, I., Pathology
STIEFEL, F., Psychiatry of Liaison
TAPPY, L., Physiology
TELENTI, A., Microbiology
THORENS, B., Genomics
TISSOT, J.-D., Haematology
TSCHOPP, J., Biochemistry
VOLTERRA, A., Cellular Biology, Morphology
VON SEGESSER, L.-K., Cardiovascular Surgery
WAEBER, B., Clinical Physiopathology
WAEBER, G., Internal Medicine
WAHLI, W., Genomics
ZOGRAFOS, L., Ophthalmology

Faculty of Geosciences and Environment (tel. 216923500; fax 216923505; internet www .unil.ch/gse):

BAUMGARTNER, P. O., Institute of Geology and Palaentology
ERKMAN, S., Institute of Territorial Politics and Human Ecology
HOLLIGER, K., Institute of Geophysics
JABOYEDOFF, M., Institute of Geomatics and Risk Analysis
MUNTENER, O., Institute of Mineralogy and Geochemistry
REYNARD, E., Institute of Geography

Faculty of Law and Criminal Justice (tel. 216922740; fax 21692745; internet www.unil .ch/droit):

BIERI, L., Law of Obligation
BONOMI, A., Comparative Civil Law and International Private Law
BRIDEL, P., Political Economics, Centre Walras-Pareto
DONGOIS, N., Penal Law
FAVRE, A.-CH., Environment Law
HAHN, M., European Law
KAHIL-WOLFF, B., Social Security
KUHN, A., Criminology
MARGOT, P., Criminal Investigation
MARTENET, V., Constitutional Law
MEIER, PH., Civil Law
MOREILLON, L., Penal Law
MORIN, A., Law of Obligation
NOEL, Y., Tax Law
PETER, H., Roman Law, Bankruptcy Law
PIOTET, D., Civil Law
POLTIER, E., Administrative Law
RAPP, J.-M., Commercial Law
SCHULZE, G., German Law
TAPPY, D., Private Law, History of Public Institutions and Sources, Civil Procedure
ZIEGLER, A., Foreign Trade Law and International Public Law

Faculty of Letters (BFSH2, 1015 Lausanne; tel. 216922978; fax 216922905; internet www .unil.ch/lettres):

ADAM, J.-M., French Linguistics
ALBERA, F., History of Cinema
BÉRARD, C., Classical Archaeology
BERTHOUD, A.-C., Applied Linguistics
BOUVIER, D., Greek Language and Literature
BRONKHORST, J., Sanskrit, Indian Studies
CÉLIS, R., Philosophy
DUCREY, P., Ancient History
EBERENZ, R., Spanish Linguistics and Philology
ESFELD, M. A., Philosophy
FORSYTH, N., English Literature
HALTER, P., American Literature
HART-NIBBRIG, C., German Language and Literature
HELLER, L., Modern Russian Literature
HOFMANN, E., History
JEQUIER, F., Modern History
JOLIVET, R., Theoretical Linguistics, Sociolinguistics
JOST, H.-U., Modern Swiss History
KAEMPFER, J., French Literature
KELLER, E., Computing for the Humanities
LARA POZUELO, A., Spanish Language and Literature
MAGGETTI, D., French Literature
MARCHAND, J.-J., Italian Language and Literature
MICHEL, C., History of Art
MÜHLETHALER, J.-C., Medieval French
NESCHKE HENTSCHKE, A., Philosophy
PARAVICINI, A., Medieval History
PRALORAN, M., Italian Linguistics
REICHLER, C., French Language and Literature
ROMANO G. DI STURMECK, S., History of Art
SCHWARZ, A., German Linguistics
SCHWYTER, J., English Linguistics
SERIOT, P., Russian Linguistics and Philology
TILLEMANS, T., Oriental Languages and Civilizations
TOSCATO-RIGO, D., Modern History
UTZ, P., German Language and Literature
VAN MAL-MAEDER, D., German Language and Literature
WYSS, A., Modern French Language and Literature

Faculty of Social and Political Science (BFSH2, 1015 Lausanne; tel. 216923100; fax 216923115; internet www.unil.ch/ssp):

BATOU, J., European Political and Social History
BRAUN, D., Political Sciences
BUTERA, F., Social Psychology
DAUWALDER, J.-P., Psychology
FILLIEULE, O., Study of Social and Political Movements
FONTANA, B., History of Political Theory
GRAZ, J.-C., International Relations
GROSSEN, M., Clinical Psychosociology
HOFMANN, E., History and Social Sciences
KAUFMANN, L., Sociology of Communication and Culture
KILANI, M., Cultural and Social Anthropology
KNUSEL, R., Social Policy
LE FEUVRE, N., Sociology of Work and Employment
MERRIEN, F. X., Sociology, Social Policy
MORO, C., Developmental and Educational Psychology
MUNSCH, S., Child and Adolescent Clinical Psychology
OHL, F., Sociology of Sport
PAPADOPOULOS, I., Public Policy
PETITAT, A., Sociology, Education
ROMAN, P., Clinical Psychology
ROSSIER, J., Career Counselling and Vocational Psychology
SANTIAGO, M., Health Psychology
SCHENK, F., Neurosciences, Psychophysiology
VOLKEN, H., Applied Mathematics

Faculty of Theology and Religious Studies (BFSH2, 1015 Lausanne; tel. 216922700; fax 216922700; e-mail secretariattheologie@unil .ch; internet www.unil.ch/theol):

AMSLER, F., History of Christianity
BURGER, M., Science of Religions
EHRENFREUND, J., History of Jews and Judaism
GISEL, P., Dogmatics and Fundamental Theology
MULLER, D., Ethics
ROMER, TH., Old Testament
STOLZ, J., Religious Sociology

Business School (BFSH1, 1015 Lausanne; tel. 216923300; fax 216933005; internet www .hec.unil.ch):

ANTONAKIS, J., Organizational Behaviour
AUTIO, E., Strategic Technology Management
BERGMANN, A., Organizational Behaviour
BRÜLHART, M., International Economics, Applied Econometrics
BÜTLER, M., Economics, Public Finance
CADOT, O., International Economy
CATRY, B., Business Policy
CESTRE, G., Marketing
DANTHINE, J.-P., Monetary Theory and Policy, Macroeconomics, Quantitative Methods
DE TREVILLE, S., Productivity in Operations Management
DUBEY, A., Actuarial Mathematics
DUFRESNE, F., Economic and Actuarial Mathematics
DUPARC, J., Theoretical Computer Science
GARBINATO, B., Programming
GERBER, H.-U., Economic and Actuarial Mathematics
GHERNAOUTI HÉLIE, S., Information Systems
HAMERI, A., Operations Management
HOFFRAGE, U., Risk Theory
HOLLY, A., Econometrics
IMBS, J., Macroeconomics
JONDEAU, E., Finance
LIMAYEM, M., Information Technology
MATTEI, A., Microeconomics and Statistics
MORELLEC, E., Finance
MUNARI, S., System Management
OYON, D., Accounting
PIGNEUR, Y., Information Systems
RACINE, J.-B., Geographical Structures
ROCKINGER, M., Finance
ST-AMOUR, P., Macroeconomics
STETTLER, A., Financial Accounting
USUNIER, J.-C., International Marketing
VAN ACKERE, A., Decision Science
VON UNGERN, T., Analysis of Industrial Structures, Macroeconomics
WEISS, L., Financial Accounting
WENTLAND FORTE, M., Knowledge Management

School of Criminal Sciences (tel. 216924600; fax 216924605; e-mail info.esc@unil.ch; internet www.unil.ch/esc):

AEBI, M.F., Criminology and Penal Law
CHAMPOD, C., Scientific Police
MARGOT, P., Criminal Science

School of French as a Foreign Language (tel. 216923080; fax 216923085; e-mail efle@unil .ch):

ANDISON, L.
BLANC, G.
BREYMANN, T.
BUCHS, A.
CAPRÉ, R.
CERNUSCHI, A.
CORDONIER, D.
DE VRIES DE HECKELINGEN, B.
DELACRÉTAZ MAGGETTI, A. L.
FLÜTSCH, C.
GENOUD, I.
GIROUD, A.
GONZALEZ, A.

JAQUEROD, P.
KILANI SCHOCH, M.
MARCELLI, A.
NICOLLERAT GILLARD, M.
PANDAZIS-RUDER, A. C.
PFERSICH, H.
REYMOND, C.

UNIVERSITÉ DE NEUCHÂTEL

ave du 1er Mars 26, 2000 Neuchâtel
Telephone: 327181000
Fax: 327181001
E-mail: contact@unine.ch
Internet: www2.unine.ch
Founded 1838
State control
Languages of instruction: French, English
Academic year: September to June

Rector: Dr MARTINE RAHIER
Vice-Rector for Education: Prof. PHILIPPE
TERRIER
Vice-Rector for Quality: Prof. CLAIRE JAQUIER
Vice-Rector for Research Devt: Prof. NATHA-
LIE TISSOT
Sec.-Gen.: PHILIPPE JEANNERET
Librarian: LAURENT GOBAT

Number of teachers: 196
Number of students: 4,378
Publications: *Recueils, 'La Chair et le Souffre'*
(Theology) (1 a year)

DEANS

Faculty of Economics: GERALD REINER
Faculty of Humanities: PATRICK VINCENT
Faculty of Law: FLORENCE GUILLAUME
Faculty of Science: Prof. PETER KROPF
Faculty of Theology: Prof. FÉLIX MOSER

PROFESSORS

Faculty of Economics (ave du 1er-Mars 26,
2000 Neuchâtel; tel. 327181500; fax
327181501; e-mail secretariat.seco@unine
.ch; internet www.unine.ch/seco):

BANGERTER, A.
BARANZINI, R.
BELKONIENE, A.
BLILI, S.
CADOT, O.
DAL ZOTTO, C.
DE BOND, W.
DUBOIS, M.
FARSI, M.
GRETHER, J.
KOSTECKI, M.
MELFI, G.
RAMACIOTTI, D.
REINER, G.
SALVA LOPEZ, C.
SCHATT, A.
SCHMID MAST, M.
SCHOENENBERGER, A.
STANOEVSKA-SLABEVA, K.
STARICA, C.
STOFFEL, K.
TILLE, Y.
TSCHAN SEMMER, F.
ZARIN-NEJADAN, M.

Faculty of Humanities (1 Espace Louis-
Agassiz, 2000 Neuchâtel; tel. 327181700;
fax 327181701; internet www.unine.ch/
lettres):

ACHERMANN, C.
ANDRES-SUAREZ, I.
AUBERT, J.
BANDELIER, A.
BEGUELIN, M.
BONNEFOIT, R.
CHAPPUIS SANDOZ, L.
CHRISTIN, O.
CLÉMENT, F.
CORBELLARI, A.
COTELLI, S.
CREVOISIER, O.

D'AMATO, G.
DAHINDEN, J.
DE SAUSSURE, L.
DE WECK, G.
DEBARY, O.
DIEMOZ, F.
DRIDI, H.
DUBOIS, M.
FILLIEULE, O.
FOSSARD, M.
FRESIA, M.
GASSER, J.
GESLIN, P.
GHASARIAN, C.
GILOMEN, H.
GLAUSER, R.
GREMAUD, G.
GRIENER, P.
HAINARD, F.
HERMAN, T.
HERTZ WERRO, E.
HONEGGER, M.
IANNACCONE, A.
JAQUIER KAEMPFER, C.
KAESER, M.
KAMBER, A.
KLAUSER, F.
KRISTOL, A.
LUESCHER, J.
LUGINBUEHL, M.
MAILLAT, D.
MARIAUX, P.
MARRO, P.
MCINTYRE, A.
MERONI, B.
MIEVILLE, D.
MOREROD, J.
MOSER, L.
NEDELCU, M.
NÄF, A.
PEKAREK DOEHLER, S.
PERRET, J.
PERRET-CLERMONT, A.
PETER, P.
PETRIS, L.
PIGUET, E.
REBETEZ, M.
RUPP, K.
RYTZ, F.
SANGSUE, D.
SCHNYDER, P.
SCHRAMM, T.
SCHULTHESS, D.
SCHWEIZER, V.
SKUPIEN DEKENS, C.
SOUGY, N.
SUTER, C.
SÁNCHEZ MÉNDEZ, J.
SÖDERSTRÖM, O.
TERRIER, P.
TISSOT, L.
TUDEAU-CLAYTON, M.
VAN ELSLANDE, J.
VIBERT, D.
VINCENT, P.
VUILLEMIN, N.
WERLY, S.
ZITTOUN, T.

Faculty of Law (26 ave du 1er Mars, 2000
Neuchâtel; tel. 327181200; fax 327181201;
e-mail secretariat.droit@unine.ch; internet
www.unine.ch/droit):

AMARELLE, C.
BOHNET, F.
CARRON, B.
CHENAUX, J.
CLERC, E.
DANON, R.
DISTEFANO, G.
DUNAND, J.
GUILLAUME, F.
GUILLOD, O.
GUY-ECABERT, C.
JEANNERET, Y.
JONGE, F.

KRAUS, D.
KUHN, A.
MAHON, P.
MARCHAND, S.
MAVROIDIS, P.
MUELLER, C.
NGUYEN, M.
OSWALD, D.
RIGOZZI, A.
RUMLEY, P.
SALVADE, V.
SPRUMONT, D.
TISSOT, N.

Faculty of Science (11 rue Emile-Argand,
2000 Neuchâtel; tel. 327182100; fax
327182103; e-mail secretariat.sciences@
unine.ch; internet www.unine.ch/sciences):

AEBI, P.
BALLIF, C.
BELBAHRI, L.
BENAIM, M.
BESSON, O.
BETSCHART, B.
BLAU, M.
BSHARY, R.
COLBOIS, B.
DE ROOIJ, N.
DERENDINGER, J.
DESCHENAUX, R.
FARINE, P.
FELBER, F.
FELBER, F.
FOELLMI, K.
FREI HALLER, B.
GERMOND, J.
GERN, L.
GOBAT, J.
GROEBLI, Y.
GUERIN, P.
HERZIG, H.
HUNKELER, D.
JOB, D.
JOLISSAINT, P.
JUNIER, P.
KALT, A.
KESSLER, F.
KRAUS, D.
KROPF, P.
LE BAYON, R.
MAUCH-MANI, B.
MILETI, G.
MITCHELL, E.
MONTANDON, P.
MONTANI, J.
NEIER, R.
NEUHAUS, J.
PERROCHET, P.
PFISTER, K.
RAEBER, P.
RENARD, P.
ROUILLER, E.
SAVOY, J.
SCHILL, E.
SCHIRMER, M.
SCHLENK, F.
SIEGRIST, H.
SUESS-FINK, G.
SÜDMEYER, T.
THERRIEN, B.
TURLINGS, T.
VALETTE, A.
VANNOTTI, M.
VERRECCHIA, E.
VOORDOUW, M.
VUATAZ, F.
VUILLEUMIER, J.
WILLI, Y.
ZUBER, M.
ZUBERBUEHLER, K.
ZWAHLEN, F.

Faculty of Theology (41 Faubourg de l'Hôpital, 2000 Neuchâtel; tel. 327181900; fax
327181901; e-mail secretariat.factheol@
unine.ch; internet www.unine.ch/theol):

BASSET, L.

MOSER, F.
ROSE, M.

Other Institutes of Higher Education

INSTITUT DE HAUTES ÉTUDES EN ADMINISTRATION PUBLIQUE (IDHEAP)
(Swiss Graduate School of Public Administration)

Quartier UNIL Mouline, 1015 Lausanne
rue de la Mouline 28, 1022 Chavannes-près-Renens
Telephone: 215574000
Fax: 215574009
E-mail: idheap@idheap.unil.ch
Internet: www.idheap.ch
Founded 1981
Pres.: Dr BARBARA HAERING
Dir: Prof. JEAN-LOUP CHAPPELET
Gen. Sec.: JACQUES-ANDRÉ VULLIET
Library of 10,000 vols and 100 periodicals
Number of teachers: 12
Number of students: 384

INSTITUT DE HAUTES ÉTUDES INTERNATIONALES ET DU DÉVELOPPEMENT
(Graduate Institute of International and Development Studies)

rue de Lausanne 132, CP 136, 1211 Geneva 21
Telephone: 229085700
Fax: 229085710
E-mail: prospective@graduateinstitute.ch
Internet: graduateinstitute.ch
Founded 2008 by merger of Institut universitaire de hautes études internationales (f. 1927) and Institut universitaire d'études du développement (f. 1961)
Private control
Languages of instruction: English, French
Academic year: September to June
Dir: Prof. PHILIPPE BURRIN
Deputy Dir: Prof. ELISABETH PRÜGL
Dean of Studies: Prof. BRUNO ARCIDIACONO
Library of 300,000 vols, 850 journals, 5,500 DVDs and videotapes
Number of teachers: 50
Number of students: 810
Publications: *Journal International Relations* (in French), *International Development Policy* (in English and French).

INSTITUT UNIVERSITAIRE KURT BÖSCH
(Kurt Bösch University Institute)

CP 4176, 1950 Sion 4
Chemin de l'Institut 18, 1967 Bramois
Telephone: 272057300
Fax: 272057301
E-mail: institut@iukb.ch
Internet: www.iukb.ch
Founded 1989, present status 1992
Language of instruction: French
Academic year: September to June
Dir: Prof. PHILIP D. JAFFÉ
Vice-Dir: Prof. STÉPHANE NAHRATH.

UNIVERSITÄRE FERNSTUDIEN SCHWEIZ/FORMATION UNIVERSITAIRE À DISTANCE
(Distance Learning University)

Überlandstr. 12, POB 265, 3900 Brig
Telephone: 279223180
Fax: 279223185
E-mail: admin@fernuni.ch
Internet: www.fernuni.ch
Founded 2005, by merger of three regional study centres: Brig Study Centre of the Distance Learning University Switzerland, Brig VS, Pfäffikon Study Centre of the Distance Learning University Switzerland, Pfäffikon SZ and French-Swiss Distance Learning Centre CRED, Sierre VS
Public control
Languages of instruction: French, German
Rector: Prof. Dr PAUL VOLKEN
Dir for Service Centre and Coordination: STÉPHANE PANNATIER
Dir for Planning, Cooperation and e-Learning: Dr KURT GRÜNWALD
Number of students: 2,190

Universities of Applied Sciences

BERNER FACHHOCHSCHULE/HAUTE ÉCOLE SPÉCIALISÉE BERNOISE
(Bern University of Applied Sciences)

Hallerstr. 10, 3012 Berne
Telephone: 318483300
Fax: 318483303
E-mail: office@bfh.ch
Internet: www.bfh.ch
Founded 1997
Languages of instruction: English, French, German
Pres.: Dr RUDOLF GERBER
Number of teachers: 1,945 f.t.e.
Number of students: 5,673

FACHHOCHSCHULE NORDWESTSCHWEIZ
(University of Applied Sciences of Northwestern Switzerland)

Schulthess-Allee 1, POB 235, 5200 Brugg
Telephone: 564624911
Fax: 564624401
Internet: www.fhnw.ch
Founded 2006, by merger of three Univs of applied sciences (Aargau, Basel-Stadt and Basel-Landschaft, and Solothurn), School of Education of Solothurn and School of Education and Social Sciences of Basel-Stadt and Basel-Landschaft and Acad. of Music Basel
State control
Languages of instruction: English, German
Pres.: PETER SCHMID-SCHEIBLER
Vice-Pres.: PETER KOFMEL
Number of teachers: 1,265
Number of students: 9,231

FACHHOCHSCHULE OSTSCHWEIZ/ HAUTE ECOLE SPÉCIALISÉE DE LA SUISSE ORIENTALE
(University of Applied Sciences of Eastern Switzerland)

Bogenstr. 7, 9000 St. Gallen
Telephone: 712808383
Fax: 712808389
E-mail: info@fho.ch
Internet: www.fho.ch
Founded 1999
State control
Languages of instruction: English, German
Pres.: STEFAN KÖLLIKER
Vice-Pres.: MARTIN JÄGER
Head of Library: CRISTINA CARLINO
Number of students: 3,300

Publication: *Zeitschrift der Fachhochschule Ostschweiz* (2 a year).

HAUTE ÉCOLE SPÉCIALISÉE DE SUISSE OCCIDENTALE/ FACHHOCHSCHULE WESTSCHWEIZ
(University of Applied Sciences Western Switzerland)

Rue de la Jeunesse 1, CP 452, 2800 Delémont 1
Telephone: 324244900
Fax: 324244901
E-mail: info@hes-so.ch
Internet: www.hes-so.ch
Founded 1997
State control
Languages of instruction: English, French
Pres.: MARC-ANDRÉ BERCLAZ
Vice-Pres.: MARTIN KASSER
Number of students: 15,500

HOCHSCHULE LUZERN
(Lucerne University of Applied Sciences and Arts)

Frankenstr. 9, POB 2969, 6002 Lucerne
Telephone: 412284242
Fax: 412284243
E-mail: info@hslu.ch
Internet: www.hslu.ch
Founded 1997
State control
Rector: Prof. SABINE JAGGY
Exec. Dir: ANDREAS KALLMANN
Number of teachers: 661
Number of students: 8,438
Publication: *Hochschule Luzern – Das Magazin* (3 a year).

KALAIDOS FACHHOCHSCHULE

Wirtschaft AG, Hohlstr. 535, 8048 Zürich
Telephone: 442001919
Fax: 442001915
E-mail: info@kalaidos-fh.ch
Internet: www.kalaidos-fh.ch
Founded 1995
Private control
Rector: Lic. JÜRG EGGENBERGER
Number of teachers: 75
Number of students: 1,729
Publication: *Kalaidoskop*.

LES ROCHES-GRUYÈRE UNIVERSITY OF APPLIED SCIENCES

rue du Lac 118, 1815 Clarens
Telephone: 219892600
Fax: 219892645
E-mail: info@lrguas.ch
Internet: www.lrguas.ch/les_roches_gruyere
Founded 2008, by merger of Les Roches Int. School of Hotel Management and Glion Institute of Higher Education
Private control
Dir-Gen.: Dr DEBORAH PRINCE.

SCUOLA UNIVERSITARIA PROFESSIONALE DELLA SVIZZERA ITALIANA
(University of Applied Sciences and Arts of Southern Switzerland)

Le Gerre, 6928 Manno
Telephone: 586666000
Fax: 586666001
E-mail: info@supsi.ch
Internet: www.supsi.ch
Founded 1997
Public control

Pres.: ALBERTO COTTI
Dir: FRANCO GERVASON
Number of teachers: 652
Number of students: 5,000

ZÜRCHER FACHHOCHSCHULE

Walchepl. 2, POB, 8090 Zürich
Telephone: 432592348
Fax: 432595161
E-mail: info@zfh.ch
Internet: www.zfh.ch
State control
Languages of instruction: English, German
Gen. Sec.: Dr RETO THALER
Number of teachers: 1,322
Number of students: 14,000

Colleges

C. G. Jung Institute Zürich: Hornweg 28, 8700 Küsnacht; tel. 449141040; fax 449141050; e-mail cg@junginstitut.ch; internet wwww.junginstitut.ch; f. 1948; private teaching and research institute for analytical psychology as conceived by psychoanalyst, Carl Gustav Jung (1875–1961); clinical and professional training programme leading to Diploma; courses and seminars in German and English for qualified auditors; special training in child-psychotherapy (for German-speaking students); several further education programmes; counselling centre; int. picture archive and library: 15,000 vols; 100 teachers; 150 students; Pres. Dipl. DANIEL BAUMANN; Dir of Studies Lic. URSULA WEISS.

Eidgenössische Hochschulinstitut für Berufsbildung/Institut Fédéral des Hautes Études en Formation Professionnelle/Istituto Universitario Federale per la Formazione Professionale (Swiss Federal Institute for Vocational Education and Training): Kirchlindachstr. 79, 3052 Zollikofen; tel. 319103700; fax 319103701; internet www.ehb-schweiz.ch; f. 1972, present name 2007; regional campuses in Lugano, Lausanne and Zurich; teaching and research in areas of vocational pedagogy, vocational and professional education and training and career devt; Chair. Prof. Dr STEFAN C. WOLTER; Dir Dr DALIA SCHIPPER; Deputy Dir Dr ALEXANDER ETIENNE.

Facoltà Di Teologia Di Lugano: Via G. Buffi 13, CP 4663, 6904 Lugano; tel. 586664555; fax 586664556; e-mail info@teologialugano.ch; internet www.teologialugano.ch; f. 1993; research and teaching in liberal arts, particularly in fields of theology, canon law and philosophy; Rector AZZOLINO CHIAPPINI; Sec. Gen. and Treas. LUCA MATTIOLO; publ. *Rivista Teologica di Lugano (RTLu)* (in French, German and Italian).

Franklin College Switzerland: Via Ponte Tresa 29, 6924 Sorengo (Lugano); tel. 919852260; fax 919944117; e-mail info@fc.edu; internet www.fc.edu; f. 1969; language of instruction: English; academic year September to May; mem. of Asscn of American Int. Colleges and Univs, Ccl of Ind. Colleges; accredited by Middle States Asscn; 11 accredited undergraduate degree courses; library: 36,000 vols, 150 periodicals; 50 teachers; 450 students; Pres. ERIK O. NIELSEN.

Haute Ecole Pédagogique des Cantons de Berne, du Jura et de Neuchâtel—BEJUNE: Rue du Banné 23, 2900 Porrentruy; tel. 844886996; e-mail info@hep-bejune.ch; internet www.hep-bejune.ch; f. 2001; campuses at Bienne and La Chaux-de-Fonds;

courses in teaching at pre-school, primary, secondary and further education level; Rector JEAN-PIERRE FAIVRE; publ. *Revue Académique Electronique* (1 a year).

Pädagogische Hochschule: Baslerstr. 43, 5201 Brugg; tel. 848012210; fax 564600609; e-mail info.ph@fhnw.ch; internet www.fhnw.ch/ph; courses in pre-school, primary and secondary teaching, special psychology and pedagogy and research and development in applied pedagogy; 2,000 students; Dir Prof. Dr HERMANN FORNECK; Exec. Sec. KATJA MINI.

Pädagogische Hochschule Bern: Weltistr. 40, 3006 Bern; tel. 313092711; fax 313092199; e-mail iinfo-iwb@phbern.ch; internet www.phbern.ch; f. 2005; institutes of pre-school and primary-level teaching, secondary-level teaching I and II, remedial pedagogy, further training and of educational media; 2,000 students; Rector Prof. Dr MARTIN SCHÄFER; Sec. ERICH SCHMID; Gen. Sec. Dr MONIKA PÄTZMANN.

Pädagogische Hochschule des Cantons St Gallen: Notkerstr. 27, 9000 St Gallen; tel. 712439400; fax 712439496; e-mail phs_sekretariat@unisg.ch; internet www.phsg.ch; f. 1983; campus at Gossau; courses in secondary-level teaching; 210 teachers; 810 students; Rector Prof. Dr ERWIN BECK; Exec. Dir MARKUS SEITZ.

Schiller International University—Switzerland: (For general information, see entry for Schiller International University in Germany chapter).

Campuses:

Schiller International University—American College of Switzerland: 1854 Leysin; tel. 244930309; fax 244930300; e-mail siuacsadmissions@bluewin.ch; internet www.american-college.com; f. 1963; degree courses in liberal arts and business administration; French and English Language Institute for EFL/ESL students (programme certificate); library of 48,000 vols; Pres. WALTER LEIBRECHT.

Schiller International University—Engelberg: Dorfstr. 40, 6390 Engelberg; tel. 416397474; fax 416397475; e-mail info@schiller-university.ch; internet www.schiller-university.ch; f. 1978; Dir ROBERTA LO.

Staatsunabhängige Theologische Hochschule Basel (Basel Theological Seminary (State Independent)): Mühlestiegrain 50, 4125 Riehen BS; tel. 616468080; fax 616468090; e-mail info@sthbasel.ch; internet www.sthbasel.ch; f. 1970; masters and doctoral degree programmes in theology; distance-learning courses in Hebrew and Greek; excavation project in Israel; Rector Prof. Dr JACOB THIESSEN.

Theologische Hochschule Chur: Alte Schanfiggerstr. 7, 7000 Chur; tel. 812549999; fax 812549998; e-mail sekretariat@priesterseminar-thc.ch; internet www.thchur.ch; f. 1807, present status 2006; courses in philosophy and theology; library: 50,000 vols; Rector Prof. Dr EVA-MARIA FABER; Head of Library Prof. Dr MICHAEL DURST.

Schools of Art and Music
ART

Centre de Formation Professionnelle Arts Appliqués: 2 rue Necker, 1201 Geneva; tel. 223885000; fax 223885059; internet edu

.ge.ch/cfpaa; f. 1876 as École des Arts Industriels; jewellery, ceramics, stylism, interior architecture, dressmaking, graphic art, art expression; 7 bldgs; library: 11,000 vols, 70 periodicals; 125 teachers; 600 students; Dir GUY MÉRAT.

École Çantonale d'Art de Lausanne/ Haute École d'Art et de Design (University of Art and Design Lausanne): ave du Temple 5, CP 555, 1001 Lausanne; ave du Temple 5, 1020 Lausanne; tel. 213169933; fax 213169266; e-mail ecal@ecal.ch; internet www.ecal.ch; f. 1821; depts of fine arts, audiovisual studies, graphic design, multimedia and industrial design, film studies; 227 teachers; 574 students incl. exchange students; Dir PIERRE KELLER.

École Cantonale d'Art du Valais: rue Bonne-Eau 16, 3960 Sierre; tel. 274565511; fax 274565530; e-mail ecav@ecav.ch; internet www.ecav.ch; f. 1948; present name 1997; courses in graphic design and visual arts; organizes summer acad. and workshops; library: 12,000 vols, 40 periodicals, 900 DVDs, VHS, CD-ROM and music CDs; 200 students; Dir SIBYLLE OMLIN.

Haute École d'Art et de Design-Genève (Geneva University of Art and Design): 15 blvd James-Fazy, 1201 Geneva; tel. 223885100; fax 223885159; e-mail info.head@hesge.ch; internet head.hesge.ch; f. 2006, by merger of École Supérieure des Beaux-arts (f. 1748) and Haute École d'Arts Appliqués (HEAA); courses in fine arts, cinema specialization and design; library: 7,000 vols, 2,500 CDs and DVDs, 50 periodicals, 4,500 exhibition catalogues; 97 teachers; 670 students; Dir JEAN-PIERRE GREFF; Deputy Dir MARC PICCAND; Exec. Sec. DIANE CHRISTINAZ.

MUSIC

Conservatoire de Fribourg: 8 route Louis Braille, CP 88, 1763 Granges-Paccot; tel. 263059940; fax 263059941; e-mail conservatoire@fr.ch; internet www.fr.ch/cof; f. 1904; attached to Dept of Culture, Directorate of Education, Culture and Sport (SCID); vocal and instrumental music, dance and drama; library: 12,000 vols, 20,000 printed music; 207 teachers; 5,000 students; Dir GIANCARLO GEROSA; Librarian CHRISTIANE ANTONIAZZA-TORCHE.

Conservatoire de Musique: 12 rue de l'Arquebuse, CP 5155, 1211 Geneva; tel. 223196060; fax 223196062; e-mail cmg@cmusge.ch; internet www.cmusge.ch; f. 1835; 7 educational centres; all brs of music, dramatic art and classical ballet; library: 70,000 vols, music scores and 10,000 vols; 144 teachers; 2,400 (full-time) students; Dir EVA AROUTUNIAN; Librarian JACQUES TCHAMKERTEN.

Conservatoire de Musique de Neuchâtel: 21 Espace de l'Europe, 2000 Neuchâtel; tel. 328896912; fax 328891510; e-mail conservatoire.ne@cmne.ch; internet www.cmne.ch; f. 1918; pre-vocational courses, courses in all fields of music; library: 2,000 vols, 800 CDs, 20,000 scores; 2,100 students; Dir FRANÇOIS HOTZ; Librarian JOËLLE EICHENBERGER; publ. *Le Journal* (2 a year).

HEMU Lausanne (High School of Music in Lausanne): 2 rue de la Grotte, CP 5700, 1002 Lausanne; tel. 213213535; fax 213213536; e-mail info@hemu-cl.ch; internet www.hemu.ch; f. 1861; research and courses in classical and jazz; library: 20,000 scores and 4,000 reference books; 120 teachers; 1,400 students; Dir-Gen. HERVÉ KLOPFENSTEIN.

Konservatorium Winterthur: Tössertobelstr. 1, 8400 Winterthur; tel. 522681580; fax 522681501; e-mail info@konservatorium.ch; internet www.konservatorium.ch; f.

1873; courses and workshops related to music and musical instruments; lessons for children, adolescents and adults with disabilities; 105 teachers; 224 students; Dir HANS-ULRICH MUNZINGER.

Musik Akademie Basel: 6 Leonhardsstr., 4003 Basel; tel. 612645757; fax 612645713; e-mail info@mab-bs.ch; internet www .musik-akademie.ch; f. 1867; comprises 3 institutes: music school providing non-pro-

fessional musical education, conservatory providing professional musical education, Schola Cantorum Basiliensis providing specialized education in early music; library: 100,000 vols; 430 staff; 9,000 students; Rector Dr ANDRÉ BALTENSPERGER; Exec. Dir MARC DE HALLER.

Musikschule Konservatorium Bern: Kramgasse 36, 3000 Bern 8; tel. 313265353; fax 313122053; e-mail office@konsibern.ch;

internet www.konsibern.ch; f. 1858; library: 50,000 vols; 140 teachers; Dir GERHARD MÜLLER; Deputy Dir MARKUS PLATTNER.

Zürich Konservatorium Klassik und Jazz: Hirschengraben 1, 8001 Zürich; tel. 442504600; fax 442504601; e-mail info@konsi .ch; internet www.konsi.ch; f. 1875; 125 teachers; 2,700 students; Man. DANIEL KNECHT; Admin. Dir CHRISTINE GISLER.

SYRIA

The Higher Education System

Higher education institutions predate Syria's independence from France in 1946, with the oldest being the University of Damascus, which was founded in 1903 (when Syria was part of the Ottoman Turkish Empire). There were 279,614 students enrolled in higher education (excluding private universities) in 2006/07, with another 6,000 at private universities. A further 2,500 were enrolled at the Syrian Virtual University (established in 2002, offering degree courses via the internet).

The Ministry of Higher Education is responsible for the universities, intermediate institutes (also attached to other ministries) and higher institutes, and the Council of Higher Education is the coordinating body. Higher education policy is planned centrally but implementation is decentralized. The intermediate institutes, of which there are around 190, are supervised by the Supreme Council of Intermediate Institutes. Legislative Decree No. 36 (2001) authorized the establishment of private institutions of higher education. The Ministry of Higher Education is, in theory, the agency responsible for quality assurance in Syria, although in practice there are no formal procedures in place and the Ministry does not often directly intervene. Higher Council Decision 154 (2005) established the legal basis for quality assurance, and plans for a quality assurance and accreditation agency were under discussion at 2011.

Applicants are legally required to possess the General Secondary Certificate to be admitted to university. The specific grade requirements for admission to programmes are determined by the Council of Higher Education. The Bachelors (*Licence*—French, or *Ijâza fi*—Arabic) is often a four-year degree, although some disciplines are longer in duration, such as architecture, dentistry, engineering, pharmacy and veterinary medicine (all five years) and medicine (six years). The first postgraduate degree is the Diploma of Higher Studies or Postgraduate Diploma, a full-time course of a professional nature lasting one or two years. Additionally, there is a Diploma of Qualification and Specialization, which is a professional qualification in commerce, medicine and teacher-training. Following the award of the Diploma of Higher Studies, the Masters degree is a two-year course consisting of both taught and research elements. Finally, the highest university degree is the Doctor of Philosophy (PhD), which usually requires an additional three years' study, comprises both taught and research elements, and culminates in submission and defence of a thesis.

The intermediate institutes are the main institutions for the provision of post-secondary technical and vocational education. Courses last two years and are administered either by the Ministry of Higher Education or one of the relevant ministries. Upon completion of the course, students are awarded the Certificate of Assistant Bachelor.

Regulatory and Representative Bodies

GOVERNMENT

Ministry of Culture: rue George Haddad, Rawda, Damascus; tel. (11) 3331556; fax (11) 3342606; e-mail info@moc.gov.sy; internet www.moc.gov.sy; Minister MUHAMMAD RIYAD HUSSEIN ISMAT.

Ministry of Education: rue Shahbander, al-Masraa, Damascus; tel. (11) 3313206; fax (11) 4420435; e-mail info@syrianeducation .org.sy; internet www.syrianeducation.org .sy; Minister SALEH AL-RASHED.

Ministry of Higher Education: BP 9251, place Mezzeh Gamarik, Damascus; tel. (11) 2119865; fax (11) 2128919; e-mail mhe@mhe .gov.sy; internet www.mhe.gov.sy; Minister ABD AL-RAZZAQ SHEIKH ISSA.

NATIONAL BODY

Council of Higher Education: BP 9355, Damascus; tel. (11) 2126336; fax (11) 2129298; regulates and oversees the higher education system; Minister GHIATH BARAKAT; Sec-Gen. RIAD AL-AJLANI.

Learned Societies

GENERAL

Arabic Language Academy of Damascus: BP 327, Damascus; tel. (11) 3713103; fax (11) 3733363; f. 1919; Arabic Islamic legacy and linguistic studies and terminology; 20 mems; Chair. Dr MARWAN AL-MAHASINI; Sec.-Gen. Dr A. WASSEK CHAHID; publ. *Majallat Majmaa al-Lughah al-Arabiyyah bi-Dimashq* (review, 4 a year).

LANGUAGE AND LITERATURE

British Council: Maysaloun St, Shalaan, BP 33105, Damascus; tel. (11) 3310631; fax (11) 3321467; e-mail info@sy.britishcouncil .org; internet www.britishcouncil.org/syria; f. 1974; information services; Education UK teaching centre; offers courses and exams in English language and British culture and promotes cultural exchange with the UK; library of 7,000 vols; additional electronic resources and audiovisual materials; Dir PAUL DOUBLEDAY; Teaching Centre Man. AMIR RAMZAN.

Goethe-Institut: Adnan Malki St 8, BP 6100, Damascus; tel. (11) 3719435; fax (11) 3719437; e-mail info@damascus.goethe.org; internet www.goethe.de/damaskus; offers courses and exams in German language and culture and promotes cultural exchange with Germany; library of 5,200 vols; Dir MANFRED EWEL; Librarian REGINA ABBOUD.

Instituto Cervantes: 10 Malek Abdel Aziz al Saud St, Sebki, Damascus; tel. (11) 3737061; fax (11) 3737062; e-mail cendam@ cervantes.es; internet damasco.cervantes.es; offers courses and exams in Spanish language and culture and promotes cultural exchange with Spain and Spanish-speaking Latin and Central America; library of 10,000 vols; Dir PABLO MARTIN ASUERO.

Research Institutes

GENERAL

Institut Français du Proche-Orient: BP 344, Damascus; tel. (11) 3330214; fax (11) 3327887; e-mail f.burgat@ifporient.org; internet www.ifporient.org; f. 1922 as Institut Français d'études Arabes de Damas (Ifead); 2003 merged with Centre d'études et de recherches sur le Moyen-Orient con-temporain (Cermoc) and L'Institut français d'archéologie de Beyrouth; archaeological research, study of the classical Arab world, Islamic civilization, and history and studies of modern Syria; library of 100,000 vols, 1,500 periodicals; Dir FRANÇOIS BURGAT; Gen. Sec. EMMANUEL RATTIN; Librarian MARTINE GILLET; publ. *Bulletin d'Etudes Orientales* (1 a year).

AGRICULTURE, FISHERIES AND VETERINARY SCIENCE

Arab Centre for the Study of Arid Zones and Dry Lands: BP 2440, Damascus; tel. (11) 5743087; fax (11) 5743063; e-mail email@acsad.org; internet www.acsad.org; f. 1968 by the Arab League; studies problems of management conservation and devt of agricultural resources, incl. water, soil, plant and animal resources; emphasis on resources survey and assessment, causes of degradation and desertification, processes of conservation and devt, economic evaluation and social implications, proper management through appropriate technologies, technical training, processing and dissemination of pertinent scientific and technical knowledge and information; mems: 16 Arab states; library of 1,500 vols, 152 periodicals, 65,000 references; Dir-Gen. Dr HASSAN SEOUD; publs *Agriculture and Water in Arid Regions of the Arab World* (2 a year), *The Camel Newsletter* (2 a year).

EDUCATION

Arab Centre for Arabization, Translation, Authorship and Publication: Al-Afif St, 2 Senbul Jadet, BP 3752, Damascus; tel. (11) 3334876; fax (11) 3330998; e-mail acatap@net.sy; internet www.acatap .htmlplanet.com; f. 1989; attached to the Arab League Educational, Cultural and Scientific Organization (ALECSO); translates and prints recent educational, medical and scientific titles in Arabic; organizes seminars and workshops; library of 3,500 items; Dir Prof. Dr ZAID IBRAHEEM AL ASSAF; publ. *Arabization* (2 a year).

Libraries and Archives

Aleppo

Al Maktabah Al Wataniah: Bab El-Faradj, Aleppo; tel. (21) 236130; fax (21) 229184; f. 1924; Librarian YOUNIS ROSHDI.

Damascus

Al Zahiriah (Public Library): Bab el Barid, Damascus; f. 1919; main subjects are miscellaneous sciences, literature and language, history, biography, religion; 100,000 vols, 50,000 periodicals; spec. colln: rare pre-1900 Arabic books; Librarian SAMA EL MAHASSINI; publ. brochure of new additions (4 a year).

Assad National Library: Malki St, BP 3639, Damascus; tel. (11) 3320803; e-mail anl@alassad-library.gov.sy; internet www .alassad-library.gov.sy; f. 1984; nat. deposit library; publishes National Bibliography, trains librarians; 280 staff; 147,124 vols, 19,000 Arabic MSS; Gen. Dir GHASSAN LAHHAM; publs *Analytical Index of Syrian Periodicals, Index of Syrian University Theses, National Bibliography* (1 a year).

University of Damascus Library: BP 3003, Damascus; tel. (11) 33924406; fax (11) 33924407; e-mail library@damasuniv.edu.sy; internet www.damascusuniversity.edu.sy/library; f. 1903; 32 brs; 250,000 vols, 2,700 periodicals; Library Dir Dr MOHAMMAD ZUHEIR BAKLEH.

Homs

Dar al-Kutub al-Wataniah (Public Library): Homs.

Latakia

Public Library of Latakia: Latakia; f. 1944; 12,000 vols; Dir MOHAMAD ALI NTAYFI.

Museums and Art Galleries

Aleppo

Aleppo National Museum: BP 6581, Aleppo; tel. (21) 212400; f. 1931; archaeology and modern art; spec. colln of Iron Age artefacts; library of 4,000 vols; Head Curator Dr SHAWQI SHAATH.

Busra

Busra Museum: Busra; tel. (15) 790105; traditional arts and crafts; Dir of Archaeological Research Dr SULEIMAN MOGHDAD.

Damascus

Adnan Malki Museum: Adnan Malki Sq., Damascus; dedicated to Lt Col. Malki, assassinated in 1955 failed Syrian Socialist Nationalist Party coup.

Agricultural Museum: Halbouni, Damascus; colln of agricultural tools; paintings of rural life.

Military Museum: Takeih Suleimanieh, Damascus; depictions of famous battles; colln of weapons.

Museum of Arabic Epigraphy: Jakmakieh Madressa, Damascus; tel. (11) 2219746; f. 1974; examples of calligraphy from different periods and colln of tools used in writing Arabic script; Dir FAYEZ HOMSI.

National Museum: Syrian University St, Damascus 4; tel. (11) 2219148; fax (11) 2247983; f. 1919; Sections: Prehistory; Ancient Oriental; Greek, Roman and Byzantine; Arab and Islamic; Modern Art; of special interest is the reconstruction of the Palmyrene Hypogeum of Yarhai (2nd century AD), of the Dura Synagogue (3rd century AD), of the Umayyad Qasr El-Hair El-Gharbi (8th century AD) and of the Damascus Hall (18th century AD); houses the Directorate-General of Antiquities and Museums, established by decree in 1947 to conserve Syrian antiquities and to supervise the archaeological museums and the excavations; Dir-Gen. of Antiquities and Museums ALI AL-KAYYEM; publs *Les Annales Archéologiques Arabes Syriennes, Les Chroniques Archéologiques en Syrie.*

Popular Traditions Museum Qasrelazem: Bzourieh St, Damascus; tel. (11) 2225418; f. 1954; traditions and crafts; library of 3,000 vols; Curator HASSAN KAMAL.

Deir ez-Zor

Deir ez-Zor Museum: Pl. du Président, Deir ez-Zor; tel. (51) 222530; f. 1974; archaeology; library of 1,000 vols; Dir ASSAD MAHMOUD; publ. *Les Annales Archéologiques de Syrie.*

Hama

Hama Museum: rue Abou al-Fida'a Hama; tel. (33) 224550; f. 1956; history and folklore; Dir ABDEL RAZZAQ ZAGZOUQ.

Homs

Homs Museum: rue al-Koutli, Homs dar Al-Thakafa; tel. (33) 220002; f. 1974; archaeology, folk and modern art; Curator MAJED EL MOUSSLI.

Palmyra

Palmyra National Museum: Palmyra; tel. (31) 910573; f. 1961; archaeological finds from prehistory to 16th century; attached is the museum of Syrian desert folklore, traditional handicraft industry and agriculture; Dir KHALED AL As'AD.

Sweida

Sweida Museum: rue de Qanawat, Sweida; tel. (16) 232035; artefacts from Roman, Nabatean and Islamic periods; Curator M. HOUSSEIN ZEIN EL-DIN.

Tartos

Tartos Museum: Tartos; tel. (43) 220541; Islamic history; Curator RAMIZ HOUCHE.

Universities

AL-BAATH UNIVERSITY

BP 77, Homs
Telephone: (31) 431847
Fax: (31) 426716
E-mail: baath-univ@net.sy
Internet: www.albaath-univ.edu.sy
Founded 1979
State control
Language of instruction: Arabic
Academic year: September to June
Pres.: Prof. Dr YASSER HOURI
Vice-Pres. for Admin. and Student Affairs: Prof. Dr HOUSAM BARAKAT
Vice-Pres. for Scientific Affairs: Prof. Dr AUODI SALHA
Admin. Officer: KASSEM HAMMOUD
Dir of Int. Relations: ABDUL ILAH AL-ABDOU
Librarian: LINA MAASRANI

Library of 63,000 vols
Number of teachers: 802
Number of students: 26,730

DEANS

Faculty of Agriculture: Dr ABDULA AL-ISA
Faculty of Chemical and Petroleum Engineering: Dr SHARIF SADIQ
Faculty of Civil Engineering and Architecture: Dr MOHAMED HAKEMI (Architecture)
Faculty of Civil Engineering and Architecture: Dr BASSAM IBRAHIM (Civil Engineering)
Faculty of Dentistry: Dr MOUHAMED SABEH ARAB
Faculty of Education: Dr IBRAHIM KHADOUR
Faculty of Informatics: Dr MUHAMAD AL-RAJAB
Faculty of Literature: Dr AHMAD DAHMAN
Faculty of Mechanical and Electrical Engineering: Dr RADWAN AL-MASRI
Faculty of Medicine: Dr ISA TUMI
Faculty of Pharmacy: Dr IMAD HADAD
Faculty of Sciences: Dr MALEK ALI
Faculty of Veterinary Science (in Hama): Dr MOHAMED ALI AL-IMADI
Intermediate Institute of Computer Engineering: Dr MOHAMED AL-HAG YOUNES
Intermediate Institute of Engineering: Dr MOUFAK FAKHOURI
Intermediate Institute of Industry: Dr HASSAN FARAH
Intermediate Institute of Veterinary Medicine: Dr ASAD AL-ABID

TISHREEN UNIVERSITY
(University of October)

POB 2230, Latakia
Telephone and fax (41) 445290
E-mail: inter-rel@tishreen.shern.net
Internet: www.tishreen.edu.sy
Founded 1971 as Univ. of Latakia
State control
Language of instruction: Arabic
Academic year: September to June
Rector: Prof. Dr MOHAMMAD YAHIA MOUALLA
Vice-Rector for Academic Affairs: Prof. Dr EBRAHEM SULAIMAN
Vice-Rector for Admin. and Students Affairs: Prof. Dr HANI SHABAAN
Vice-Rector for Open Learning: Prof. Dr RAFIK JIBLAWI
Vice-Rector for Scientific Research and Postgraduate Studies: Prof. Dr BASSAM HASSAN
Provost and Registrar: SALAH SHABAAN
Vice-Provost: IBRAHIM AL-SAWA
Vice-Provost: MOUSTAFA FAWAL
Librarian: MOUHAMMAD NAJIB SAKER

Library of 60,214 vols, 468 periodicals
Number of teachers: 1,281
Number of students: 100,438

Publications: *Journal of Agriculture, Journal of Arts and Humanities, Journal of Basic Science, Journal of Law and Economics, Journal of Medical Science, Journal of Studies and Scientific Research*

DEANS

Faculty of Agriculture: Dr AHMAD JALLOUL
Faculty of Architecture: Dr NUHAD ABDALLA
Faculty of Arts: Dr MOHAMMAD JALAL OSMAN
Faculty of Civil Engineering: Dr ALI TURIKIEH
Faculty of Dentistry: Dr NAZIH ISSA
Faculty of Economics: Dr ALI HISMEH
Faculty of Education: Dr GHASSAN SALEH
Faculty of Electrical and Mechanical Engineering: Dr JARKAS TAJE DINE
Faculty of Medicine: Dr IBRAHIM SULAIMAN
Faculty of Nursing: NAJWA KERDOGHLI
Faculty of Pharmacology: Dr MARROUF AL KHAYER
Faculty of Physical Education: NOURI BARAKAT
Faculty of Science: Dr DAIFALLAH NASSOUR

UNIVERSITY OF ALEPPO

Aleppo
Telephone: (21) 2671200
Fax: (21))2229184
E-mail: alepuniv@alepuniv.edu.sy
Internet: www.alepuniv.edu.sy

Founded 1958
State control
Languages of instruction: Arabic, English, French
Academic year: September to June

Pres.: Dr ABED YAKAN
Vice-Pres. for Academic Affairs: Dr AMMAR KAADAN
Vice-Pres. for Admin. and Student Affairs: Dr KHDER OURFALI
Vice-Pres. for Open Education: Dr MOHAMED GHASSAN DAHHAN
Vice-Pres. for Research and Postgraduate Studies: Dr NAJAH TANNOUS
Sec.: Dr ABDUL KADER HABBACHE
Registrar: AHMAD BAZAR
Librarian: MARWAN ABSI

Number of teachers: 4,042
Number of students: 130,772

Publications: *Aleppo's Adiyat, Journal for the History of Arabic Science, Medical Scholarly Journal Magazine, Research Journal of Aleppo University* (comprises the following series: Arts and Humanities; Medical Sciences; Agricultural Sciences; Basic Sciences; Engineering Sciences; *Adiyat Halab*)

DEANS

Faculty of Administration Sciences (Idleb): Dr KAMAL DISHLI
Faculty of Agriculture: Dr AHMAD ALSHEIKH KADDOUR
Faculty of Agriculture II (Idleb): Dr ABBAS ALSHEIKH
Faculty of Applied Fine Arts: Dr ABDEL ALHAKEEM ALHOSAINI
Faculty of Architecture: Dr LAMIS HERBLE
Faculty of Arts and Humanities: Dr AHMED KADDOUR
Faculty of Arts and Humanities II (Idleb): FAROUK SLEEM
Faculty of Civil Engineering: Dr MOHAMAD AMIN CHAGHALE
Faculty of Dentistry: Dr MOHAMAD SULTAN
Faculty of Economics: Dr ALAA EDDIN JABAL
Faculty of Education: Dr MOHAMED ABDULLAH KASIM
Faculty of Education II (Idleb): Dr AHMAD ABORASS
Faculty of Electrical and Electronic Engineering: Dr LOUAY CHACHATI
Faculty of Informatics: Dr MOHAMED ALHAMID
Faculty of Law: Dr OMAR FARES
Faculty of Law II (Idleb): Dr AHMAD AL ISSA
Faculty of Mechanical Engineering: Dr NABHAN KHYATTA
Faculty of Medicine: Dr RIAD NOR EDDIN ELASFARI

Faculty of Nursing: Dr NIZAR HAMMAD
Faculty of Pharmacy: Dr AHMAD KHALIL
Faculty of Sciences: Dr SAFWAN ASHOUR
Faculty of Sciences II (Idleb): Dr NAWRAS HASSOUN
Faculty of Shariaa: Dr AHMAD ALOMAR
Faculty of Technological Engineering: Dr NABIL SHEIKH KOROSH
Faculty of Veterinary Medicine (Idleb): Dr YAHYA KHANJI
Higher Institute for the History of Arabic Sciences: Dr SAKHER OLABI
Higher Institute of Languages: Dr ABDUL JABBAR OUAYED
Technical Agricultural Institute: Dr ZOHEIR ABBASSI
Technical Agricultural Institute (Idleb): Dr ABDUL HAMID ALI AGHA
Technical Engineering Institute: YOUSEF KEBBIEH
Technical Institute for Financing and Accounting: Dr MOH FADI ALKARAAN
Technical Institute for Financing and Accounting (Idleb): Dr ABDUL AZIZ ALDGAIM
Technical Institute for Veterinary Medicine (Idleb): Dr MOTAAZ MERIE
Technical Institute of Computer: Dr AHMAD RAJAB BOSHNAAK
Technical Institute of Computer (Idleb): Dr TAYSEER ALZAMEL
Technical Institute of Dentistry: Dr GHASSAN JRADEH
Technical Institute of Marketing and Business Administration: Dr HASAN KATALO
Technical Institute of Mechanical and Electrical Engineering: Dr MOUFID MOUWAKEH
Technical Medical Institute: Dr ADNAN JALKHI

UNIVERSITY OF DAMASCUS

Damascus
Telephone: (11) 2232152
Fax: (11) 2236010
E-mail: w-mualla@scs-net.org
Internet: www.damascusuniversity.edu.sy

Founded 1903
State control
Language of instruction: Arabic
Academic year: September to June

Pres.: Dr WAEL MUALLA
Vice-Pres. for Academic Affairs: Dr MOHAMMAD SALEM AL-RIKAB
Vice-Pres. for Admin. and Student Affairs: Prof. Dr TAREK AL-KHAIR
Vice-Pres. for Postgraduate Studies and Scientific Research: Dr RAKAN RAZOUK
Registrar: YOUSEF KAHELEH
Librarian: KAIS SHAHEEN

Library of 51,500 vols, 70,000 vols in libraries of faculties
Number of teachers: 2,688
Number of students: 120,000 (60,000 distant learning)

Publications: *Dirasat Tarikhiyyah* (historical review, 4 a year), *Journal for Agricultural Studies* (4 a year), *Journal for Basic and Applied Sciences* (4 a year), *Journal for the Arts, Humanities and Sciences* (4 a year), *Journal for the Economic and Legal Sciences* (4 a year), *Journal for the Medical Sciences* (4 a year), *Statistical Collections* (1 a year), *University Journal* (4 a year)

DEANS

Faculty of Agriculture: Prof. Dr HAMZEH BLAL
Faculty of Architecture: Dr PIERRE NANO
Faculty of Arts and Humanities: Prof. Dr WAHAB ROUMIEH
Faculty of Civil Engineering: Prof. Dr AMJAD ZENO
Faculty of Computer Science: Dr AMMAR KHEIR-BEK
Faculty of Dentistry: Prof. Dr M. HASAN YOUSEF
Faculty of Economics: Prof. Dr MUSTAFA AL-KAFRI
Faculty of Fine Arts: Prof. Dr MAHMOUD SHAHEEN
Faculty of Law: Prof. Dr MOHAMED AL-HUSEIN
Faculty of Mechanical and Electrical Engineering: (vacant)
Faculty of Medicine: Prof. Dr NEZAR ASSAD
Faculty of Pharmacy: Prof. Dr ANTOIN LAHHAM
Faculty of Political Science: Prof. Dr OMAR ABDULLAH
Faculty of Science: Prof. Dr ESSAM KASSEM
Faculty of Sharia: Prof. MOHAMED AL-HASAN AL-BOGHAA
Faculty of Tourism: Dr REEM RAMADAN

Colleges

Arab Conservatory of Music: Sabil near Kalimeh Hospital, Aleppo; tel. (21) 2672600; fax (21) 2672600; f. 1963; depts of classical (Western) and Oriental (Middle Eastern) music; children's choir, chamber orchestra; 28 teachers; 600 students; Dir NABIL GHREWATI.

Higher Institute of Applied Sciences and Technology: BP 31983, Barzeh, Damascus; tel. (11) 5140520; fax (11) 2237710; e-mail info@hiast.edu.sy; internet www.hiast.edu.sy; f. 1983; awards BSc, MSc, PhD; depts of informatics, systems engineering, mathematics, physics, electronics, management, mechanics; language of instruction: Arabic; 120 teachers; 400 students; Dir Prof. Dr OMRAN KOUBA.

Higher Institute of Political Science: Al-Tall, Damascus; tel. (11) 5911704; fax (11) 5911526; f. 1976; depts of administration and public relations, international relations and political studies; library: 15,000 vols; 25 teachers; 434 students; Dean HUSEIN AL-SAYED HUSEIN.

TAIWAN

The Higher Education System

In 1945, following Japan's defeat in the Second World War, Taiwan became one of the provinces of the Republic of China, which was then ruled by the Kuomintang (KMT, Nationalist Party). However, having been defeated on the mainland by the Communist revolution (which led to the proclamation of the People's Republic of China), in 1949 the KMT Government was forced to remove itself to Taipei, the capital of Taiwan, where it established a KMT regime and declared itself to be the rightful Chinese Government, as well as its intention ultimately to recover control of the mainland from the Communists. The population is mainly Chinese in origin, and the official language is Mandarin (Guoyu); Taiwanese, Hakka and English are also spoken. Most universities in Taiwan have been founded since 1949, but some were formerly mainland institutions that either relocated during the Communist takeover or were refounded; these include Fu-Jen Catholic University (founded in 1925 in Beijing), National Central University (originally based in Nanking), National Chiao Tung University (founded in 1896 in Shanghai), National Tsing Hua University (founded in 1911 in Beijing), and Soochow University (founded in 1900 in the mainland province of Jiangsu). In 1987 the nine teachers' junior colleges were upgraded to teachers' colleges. These admit senior secondary graduates for a four-year course. High-school teachers are trained at normal universities. In 2009/10 there were 164 universities, junior colleges and independent colleges, most of which offer postgraduate facilities; total enrolment in higher education in that year was 1,336,592 students. Higher education is highly centralized and the Constitution places great emphasis on the importance of education. The higher education system is based on the US model.

The Ministry of Education supervises the Universities and Colleges Joint Entrance Examination, which is required for admission to higher education. Students, however, may also gain admission through two other methods, either by applying directly to the institution in question and meeting that institution's entry requirements, or through recommendation on grounds of academic excellence.

Junior colleges, which provide two- or five-year Junior College Diploma programmes, are the first level of higher education. Two-year junior colleges admit graduates from Senior and Senior Vocational High Schools, while five-year junior colleges accept students from Junior High Schools. The majority of junior colleges are privately run. Institutes of technology operate on a similar basis: two-year institutes admit junior college graduates and four-year institutes admit senior vocational school graduates. There are also 'Open' universities, which specialize in adult education.

The Bachelors degree is the main university undergraduate qualification, and usually lasts four years, although some specialist programmes are longer in duration, including civil engineering, dentistry, law and medicine, which take between five and seven years. At postgraduate level, the Masters degree requires one to four years' study, while the final qualification, the Doctorate, requires two to seven years' study following the Masters. Technical and vocational education and training is provided by senior vocational schools and junior colleges. Periods of study vary between two to five years.

Legislative amendments allowing mainland Chinese students to enrol at Taiwanese universities for the first time since 1949 were approved by the Taiwanese parliament in August 2010; however, mainland Chinese would remain unable to enrol at university departments related to Taiwan's national security. The first mainland students were admitted in 2011.

Regulatory Bodies

GOVERNMENT

Bureau of International Cultural and Educational Relations: Min. of Education, 13F, 5 Syujhou Rd, Jhongjheng Dist., Taipei 100; tel. (2) 23565608; fax (2) 23976978; e-mail cschang@mail.moe.gov.tw; internet english.moe.gov.tw; f. 1947; assists colleges and univs to enter into academic co-operation with foreign instns of higher learning; sponsors int. scholar exchange programmes; organizes bilateral confs on higher education; encourages Taiwan specialists, academics and doctoral students to participate in int. academic confs abroad; provides Taiwan Scholarships to encourage exceptional foreign students to pursue degrees in Taiwan; works with govts, cultural and educational instns and commercial enterprises to obtain scholarships for Taiwan students; Dir-Gen. Dr CHIN-SHENG CHANG.

Ministry of Education: 5 Chung Shan South Rd, Taipei 10051; tel. (2) 23566051; fax (2) 23976978; internet www.moe.gov.tw; Min. TU CHENG-SHENG.

Research, Development and Evaluation Commission: 6/F, 2-2 Chi Nan Rd, Sec. 1, Taipei 10051; tel. (2) 23419066; fax (2) 23969990; e-mail service@rdec.gov.tw; internet rdec.gov.tw; Minister SHIH NING-JYE.

Learned Societies

GENERAL

Academia Sinica: 128 Academia Rd, Section 2, Nankang, Taipei 11529; tel. (2) 27822120; fax (2) 27853847; internet www .sinica.edu.tw; f. 1928; 220 mems; attached research institutes: see Research Institutes; library of 2,236,000 vols; Pres. Dr YUAN-TSEH LEE; Dir-Gen. Dr YIH-HSIUNG YEH; Chief of Secretariat Dr CHI-CHIUNG LO; publs *Academia Economic* (papers), *Academia Sinica* (2 a year), *Asia-Major* (2 a year), *Asia-Pacific Forum* (4 a year), *Botanical Bulletin* (4 a year), *Bulletin of the Institute of Ethnology*, *Bulletin of the Institute of History and Philosophy*, *Bulletin of the Institute of Mathematics*, *Bulletin of the Institute of Modern History* (4 a year), *Disquisitions of the Past and Present* (2 a year), *EurAmerica Quarterly*, *Journal of Social Sciences and Philosophy*, *Language and Linguistics* (4 a year), *Mathmedia* (4 a year), *Research on Women in Chinese History* (1 a year), *Statistica Sinica* (4 a year), *Taiwan Economic Forecasts and Policies Academia Economic Papers*, *Taiwan Historical Research* (2 a year), *Taiwan Journal of Anthropology* (2 a year), *Taiwanese Sociological Review* (2 a year), *Zoological Studies* (4 a year).

China Academy: Hwa Kang, Yang Ming Shan; f. 1966; private instn for sinological studies, consisting of 20 academic asscns and research institutions and Chinese and foreign mems; 591 acads, 312 hon. acads, 1,815 fellows; library of 450,000 vols; Pres. CHANG CHI-YUN; Sec.-Gen. PAN WEI-HO; publs *Beautiful China Pictorial Monthly* (bilingual Chinese and English), *Chinese Culture* (in English, 4 a year), *Renaissance Monthly* (in Chinese), *Sino-American Relations* (in English, 4 a year), *Sinological Monthly* (in Chinese), *Sinological Quarterly* (in Chinese).

China National Association of Literature and the Arts: 4 Lane 22, Nuigpo St W, Taipei.

China Society: 7 Lane 52, Wenchow St, Taipei; f. 1960; centre for Chinese studies; 100 mems; Pres. Dr CHEN CHI-LU; publ. *Journal* (1 a year).

AGRICULTURE, FISHERIES AND VETERINARY SCIENCE

Agricultural Association of China: 14 Wenchow St, Taipei; tel. (2) 23636681; f. 1917; mems: 159 instns, 2,554 individuals; Pres. TSONG-SHIEN WU; publ. *Journal* (4 a year).

Chinese Forestry Association: 2 Sec. 1, Hang-chow South Rd, Taipei 100; tel. (2) 33221299; fax (2) 33221099; e-mail cfa@forest .gov.tw; internet www.forestry.org.tw; f. 1967; 1,219 mems; Chair. JEN-TEH YEN; publ. *Quarterly Journal of Chinese Forestry*.

BIBLIOGRAPHY, LIBRARY SCIENCE AND MUSEOLOGY

Library Association of the Republic of China (Taiwan): 20 Chungshan S Rd,

Taipei 10001; tel. (2) 23312475; fax (2) 23700899; e-mail lac@ncl.edu.tw; internet www.lac.org.tw; f. 1953; 2,060 mems; Pres. HSUEH-HUA CHEN; Sec.-Gen. WEI PENG; publs *Journal of Library and Information Science Research* (2 a year), *Library Association of the Republic of China (Taiwan) e-NEWs* (12 a year).

ECONOMICS, LAW AND POLITICS

Chinese National Foreign Relations Association: Third Fl., 94 Nanchang St, Sec. 1, Taipei; Pres. HUANG KUO-SHU.

National Bar Association: 124 Chungking South Rd, Sec. 1, Taipei.

HISTORY, GEOGRAPHY AND ARCHAEOLOGY

Academia Historica (Academy of History): 406 Sec. 2, Pei Yi Rd, Hsintien, Taipei; tel. (2) 22175500; fax (2) 22170317; internet www.drnh.gov.tw; f. 1947; responsible for researching and compiling material on Taiwanese national history; 175 mems; library of 10,000,000 items (nat. archives, books, documents); Pres. CHANG YEN HSIEN; Sec.-Gen. Prof. LI CHUNG KUANG; publs *Bulletin* (2 a year), *Journal* (2 a year).

LANGUAGE AND LITERATURE

British Council: 2F-1, 106 XinYi Rd, Sec. 5, Taipei 110; tel. (2) 87221000; fax (2) 87860985; e-mail enquiries@britishcouncil.org.tw; internet www.britishcouncil.org/taiwan; teaching centre; offers courses and exams in English language and British culture and promotes cultural exchange with the UK; attached office in Kaohsiung; Dir GORDON SLAVEN.

Chinese Language Society: c/o Taiwan Normal Univ., Hoping E Rd, Taipei; f. 1953; Dir MAO TZU-SHUI; publ. *Chinese Language Monthly.*

MEDICINE

Chinese Medical Association: 201 Shih-Pai Rd, Sec. II, Taipei; f. 1915; 1,672 mems; Pres. Dr KWANG-JUEI LO; Sec.-Gen. Dr YANG-TE TSAI; publ. *Chinese Medical Journal* (12 a year).

NATURAL SCIENCES
Mathematical Sciences

Chinese Statistical Association: 1 Nan Chung Rd, Sec. 1, Taipei; f. 1941; 1,082 mems; Pres. C. C. LEE; publ. *Chinese Statistical Journal.*

Mathematical Society of the Republic of China: Dept of Mathematics, Nat. Cheng Kung Univ., Tainan 70101; fax (6) 2743191; Pres. LEE YUH-JIA; Sec. HUANG YOUNG-YE.

Physical Sciences

Chemical Society: POB 1-18, Nankang, Taipei 115; tel. (2) 27898574; fax (2) 26530440; e-mail ccswww@gate.sinica.edu.tw; internet www.ccs.sinica.edu.tw; f. 1932; 3,000 mems; Sec.-Gen. LING-KANG LIU; publs *Hua Hsueh* (in Chinese, 4 a year), *Journal* (in English, 6 a year).

Committee on the Promotion of the Peaceful Uses of Atomic Energy: 110 Yenping South Rd, Taipei; Pres. MILTON J. T. SHIEH.

Physical Society of China: POB 23-30, Taipei.

PHILOSOPHY AND PSYCHOLOGY

Confucius-Mencius Society of the Republic of China: 45 Nanhai Rd, Taipei; f. 1960; spreads knowledge about Confucius and Mencius, seeks the improvement of public morals and the creation of a better society; 3,900 mems; Chair. Dr CHEN LI-FU; Sec. HUA CHUNG-LIN; publ. *Confucius-Mencius Monthly*, *Journal of Confucius-Mencius Society.*

RELIGION, SOCIOLOGY AND ANTHROPOLOGY

Chinese Association for Folklore: 422 Fulin Rd, POB 68-1292, Shihlin, Taipei; f. 1932; Chinese and Asian folklore; 47 mems; library of 1,000 vols and MSS; Chair. Prof. LOU TSU-KUANG; Sec. AMY LOU.

TECHNOLOGY

Chinese Institute of Civil and Hydraulic Engineering: 4th Fl., 1 Jen Ai Rd, 2 Taipei; tel. (2) 23926325; fax (2) 23964260; e-mail ciche@ciche.org.tw; internet www.ciche.org.tw; f. 1973; 7,500 mems; Pres. YU CHENG; publs *Journal of Civil and Hydraulic Engineering* (4 a year), *Journal of the Chinese Institute of Civil and Hydraulic Engineering* (4 a year).

Chinese Institute of Engineers: Fl. 3, No. 1 Ren-ai Rd, Sec. 2, Taipei 10055; tel. (2) 23925128; fax (2) 23973003; e-mail secretariat@cie.org.tw; internet www.cie.org.tw; f. 1912; 18,125 individual mems and 78 group mems; library of 7,500 vols, 60 periodicals; Sec. FENZA CHIANG; publs *Journal of the Chinese Institute of Engineers* (8 a year), *Newsletter* (4 a year), *Transactions* (6 a year).

Research Institutes
GENERAL

National Institute for Compilation and Translation: 179 Heping E Rd, Sector 1, Da-An District, Taipei City 10644; tel. (2) 33225558; fax (2) 33225559; e-mail trcnews@mail.nict.gov.tw; internet www.nict.gov.tw; f. 1932; translates foreign books, examines and approves textbooks, standardizes scientific and technical terms; 75 mems; library of 100,000 vols; Dir-Gen. PAN WEN-CHUNG; publs *Compilation and Translation Review* (print and online), *Journal of Textbook Research* (print and online).

AGRICULTURE, FISHERIES AND VETERINARY SCIENCE

Council of Agriculture: 37 Nanhai Rd, Taipei; tel. (2) 23812991; fax (2) 23310341; e-mail coa@mail.coa.gov.tw; internet www.coa.gov.tw; f. 1984; govt agency under the Exec. Yuan, with ministerial status; administers nat. agriculture, forestry, fisheries, livestock farming and food; library of 18,000 vols; Min. Dr WU-HSIUNG CHEN.

Taiwan Agricultural Research Institute: 189 Zhongzheng Rd, Wufeng, Taichung 41362; tel. (4) 23302301; fax (4) 23338162; e-mail mwf-doc@wufeng.tari.gov.tw; internet www.tari.gov.tw; f. 1895; insect colln; Dir JUNNE-JIH CHEN; publ. *Journal of Taiwan Agricultural Research* (4 a year).

Taiwan Fisheries Research Institute: 199 Hou-Ih Rd, Keelung 220; tel. (2) 24622101; fax (2) 24629388; f. 1933; library of 16,000 vols; Dir-Gen. I-CHIU LIAO; publs *Journal*, research reports.

Taiwan Forestry Research Institute: 53 Nan-Hai Rd, Taipei, 10066; tel. (2) 23039978; fax (2) 23142234; e-mail service@serv.tfri.gov.tw; internet www.tfri.gov.tw; f. 1896; library of 33,000 vols; Dir-Gen. STAR HUANG; Sec.-Gen. YIN-SHENG WANG; publ. *Journal of Forest Science* (4 a year).

Taiwan Sugar Research Institute: 54 Sheng Chan Rd, Tainan; tel. (6) 2671911; fax (6) 2685425; e-mail tsc02@taisugar.com.tw; f. 1902; supported by Taiwan Sugar Corpn; library of 46,800 vols; Dir LONG-HUEI WANG; publs *Extension Bulletin*, *Report* (in Chinese, 4 a year, English summary), *Technical Bulletin.*

ECONOMICS, LAW AND POLITICS

Co-operative League of the Republic of China: 11-2 Fu Chow St, Taipei; tel. (2) 23219343; fax (2) 23517918; f. 1940; cooperative business research and education; Chair. YANG CHIA-LIN; Exec. Dir and Sec.-Gen. HSU WEN-FU; publs *CLC Co-operative News* (1 a year), *Co-operative Economics* (4 a year).

Institute of Economics: c/o Academia Sinica, Nankang, Taipei 11529; tel. (2) 27822791; fax (2) 27853946; internet www.sinica.edu.tw/~econ; f. 1962; attached to Academia Sinica; Dir Dr CHUNG-MING KUAN; publs *Academia Economic Papers* (4 a year), *Taiwan Economic Forecast and Policy* (2 a year).

FINE AND PERFORMING ARTS

National Taiwan Arts Education Centre: 47 Nan Hai Rd, Taipei; tel. (2) 23110574; fax (2) 23122555; internet www.arte.gov.tw; f. 1957; in charge of the research, extension and guidance of art education in Taiwan; Dir JOSEPH TSU-SHENG WU; publs *Journal of Aesthetic Education* (6 a year), *Newsletter of Arts Education* (12 a year), *The International Journal of Arts Education* (2 a year).

HISTORY, GEOGRAPHY AND ARCHAEOLOGY

Institute of History and Philology: c/o Academia Sinica, Nankang, Taipei 11529; tel. (2) 27829555; fax (2) 27868834; internet www.ihp.sinica.edu.tw/english; attached to Academia Sinica; Dir Prof. TUNG-KUEI KUAN.

Institute of Modern History: c/o Academia Sinica, Nankang, Taipei 11529; tel. (2) 27824166; attached to Academia Sinica; Dir Prof. KO-WU HUANG; Sec. SHU-LING CHIANG.

MEDICINE

Institute of Biomedical Sciences, Preparatory Office: c/o Academia Sinica, Nankang, Taipei 11529; attached to Academia Sinica; Dir Dr CHENG-WEN WU.

NATURAL SCIENCES
General

National Science Council: 106 Ho-ping E Rd, Section 2, Taipei 106; tel. (2) 27377981; fax (2) 27377672; e-mail klchou@nsc.gov.tw; internet www.nsc.gov.tw; f. 1959; br. of central govt; promotes nat. science and technology devt, supports academic research and establishes industrial parks; Sr Systems Coordinator K. L. CHOU; publs *East Asian Science, Technology and Society* (in English, 4 a year), *Indicators of Science and Technology* (in Chinese and English, 1 a year), *International Journal of Science and Mathematics Education* (in English, 4 a year), *Journal of Biomedical Science* (in English, 6 a year, open access journal since January 2009), *National Science Council Review* (in English and Chinese, 1 a year), *Science Development* (in Chinese, 12 a year).

Biological Sciences

Central Laboratory of Molecular Biology, Preparatory Office: c/o Academia Sinica, Nankang, Taipei 11529; attached to Academia Sinica; Dir Dr CHIEN HO.

Institute of Biological Chemistry: c/o Academia Sinica, Nankang, Taipei 11529;

attached to Academia Sinica; Dir Dr WEN-CHANG CHANG (acting).

Institute of Botany: c/o Academia Sinica, Nankang, Taipei 11529; tel. (2) 27899590; fax (2) 27827954; e-mail boplshaw@ccvax.sinica.edu.tw; internet www.botany.sinica.edu.tw; f. 1929; attached to Academia Sinica; Dir Dr JEI-FU SHAW; publ. *Botanical Bulletin of Academia Sinica* (4 a year).

Institute of Zoology: c/o Academia Sinica, Nankang, Taipei 11529; attached to Academia Sinica; Dir Dr JEN-LEIH WU.

Mathematical Sciences

Institute of Mathematics: c/o Academia Sinica, Nankang, Taipei 11529; attached to Academia Sinica; Dir Dr KO-WEI LIH.

Institute of Statistical Science: c/o Academia Sinica, 128 Academia Rd Sec. 2, Taipei 11529; tel. (2) 27835611; fax (2) 27831523; internet www.stat.sinica.edu.tw; f. 1982; attached to Academia Sinica; Dir Dr KER-CHAU LI; publ. *Statistica Sinica* (4 a year).

Physical Sciences

Atomic Energy Council: 67 Lane 144, Keelung Rd, Sec. 4, Taipei 106; tel. (2) 23634180; fax (2) 23635377; f. 1955; govt agency for the peaceful application of atomic energy; library of 11,000 vols, deposit library at the Nat. Tsing Hua Univ. of 36,000 vols and 424,000 microcards; Chair. Dr YIH-YUN HSU; Sec.-Gen. KUANG-CHI LIU; publs *Nuclear Climate* (12 a year), *Nuclear Science Journal* (6 a year).

Central Geological Survey: POB 968, Taipei 100; tel. (2) 29462793; fax (2) 29429291; e-mail cgs@linx.moeacgs.gov.tw; internet www.moeacgs.gov.tw; f. 1946; maps; library of 50,000 vols and periodicals; Dir CHAO-CHUNG LIN; publs *Bulletin*, *Ti-Chih* (geology, 2 a year).

Institute of Atomic and Molecular Sciences, Preparatory Office: c/o Academia Sinica, Nankang, Taipei 11529; attached to Academia Sinica; Dir Dr CHAO-TIN CHANG.

Institute of Chemistry: c/o Academia Sinica, Nankang, Taipei 11529; attached to Academia Sinica; Dir Dr SUNNEY I. CHAN.

Institute of Earth Sciences: Academia Sinica, Nankang, Taipei 11529; tel. (2) 27839910; fax (2) 27839871; attached to Academia Sinica; Dir Dr BOR-MING JAHN.

Institute of Information Science: c/o Academia Sinica, Nankang, Taipei 11529; attached to Academia Sinica; Dir Dr YUE-SUN KUO (acting).

Institute of Nuclear Energy Research: POB 3, Lung-Tan 32500; tel. (2) 3651717; fax (3) 4711064; f. 1968; research in peaceful uses of atomic energy; Dir Dr HSIA DER-YU (acting); publ. *INER report series*.

Institute of Physics: c/o Academia Sinica, Nankang, Taipei 11529; attached to Academia Sinica; Dir Dr TUNG-MIN HO (acting).

PHILOSOPHY AND PSYCHOLOGY

Sun Yat-sen Institute for Social Sciences and Philosophy: c/o Academia Sinica, Nankang, Taipei 11529; tel. (2) 27821693; fax (2) 27854160; e-mail issp@www.issp.sinica.edu.tw; internet www.issp.sinica.edu.tw; f. 1981; attached to Academia Sinica; Dir Dr ANGELA KI CHE LEUNG; publ. *Journal of Social Sciences and Philosophy* (4 a year).

RELIGION, SOCIOLOGY AND ANTHROPOLOGY

Institute of Ethnology: c/o Academia Sinica, Nankang, Taipei 11529; tel. (2) 26523300; fax (2) 26523436; e-mail tja@gate.sinica.edu.tw; internet www.sinica.edu.tw/

ioe; f. 1955; attached to Academia Sinica; main field of research: social and cultural anthropology; Dir Prof. HUANG SHU-MIN; publs *Field Materials*, *Taiwan Journal of Anthropology* (2 a year).

Institute of European and American Studies: Academia Sinica, Nankang, Taipei 11529; attached to Academia Sinica; Dir Dr WEN-CHING HO; publ. *EurAmerica* (4 a year).

TECHNOLOGY

Industrial Technology Research Institute: 195 Chung Hsing Rd, Sec. 4, Chu-Tung, Hsinchu; tel. (35) 820100; fax (35) 820045; f. 1973; library of 130,000 vols; Pres. Dr OTTO C. C. LIN; publs *Chemical Industry Notes*, *Electro-optics Development Journal*, *Energy-Resources and Environment* (in Chinese, 4 a year), *Materials and Society*, *Mechatronics Journal*, *Metrology Information* (in Chinese, 6 a year), *Mining Technology*, *MRL Bulletin of Research and Development* (in English, 2 a year), *Opto-Electronics and Systems*, *Reports of Center for Measurement Standards* (in Chinese, 12 a year), *Superconductor Applications News*, *UCL Chemical Information Digest*.

Research Laboratories:

Centre for Aviation and Aerospace: Hsinchu; Dir Dr RICHARD Y. H. LIN.

Centre for Industrial Safety and Health Technology: Hsinchu; Dir Dr ADA W. S. MA.

Centre for Measurement Standards: Hsinchu; Dir Dr CHANG HSU.

Centre for Pollution Control Technology: Hsinchu; Dir Dr LING-YUAN CHEN.

Computer and Communication Research Laboratories: Hsinchu; Dir Dr STEVEN CHENG.

Electronics Research and Service Organization: Hsinchu; Dir Dr DAVID C. T. HSING.

Energy and Resources Laboratories: Hsinchu; Dir Dr ROBERT J. YANG.

Materials Research Laboratories: Hsinchu and Kaohsiung; Dir Dr LI-CHUNG LEE.

Mechanical Industry Research Laboratories: Hsinchu; Dir Dr C. RICHARD LIU.

Opto-Electronics and Systems Laboratories: Hsinchu; Dir Dr MIN-SHYONG LIN.

Union Chemical Laboratories: Hsinchu; Dir Dr JOHN-SEE LEE.

National Bureau of Standards: Min. of Economic Affairs, 3rd Floor, 185 Hsinhai Rd, Sec. 2, Taipei 106; tel. (2) 27380007; fax (2) 27352656; f. 1947; nat. standards, weights and measures, patents, trademarks; library of 20,000 vols, 500 periodicals; Dir-Gen. MING-BANG CHEN; publs *Catalogue of Chinese National Standards* (1 a year), *Chinese National Standards* (irregular), *Official Gazette for Patents* (36 a year), *Official Gazette for Standards* (12 a year), *Official Gazette for Trademarks* (24 a year).

Libraries and Archives
Tainan

National Cheng Kung University Library: 1 Ta Hsueh Rd, Tainan 70101; tel. (6) 2757575; fax (6) 2378232; internet www.lib.ncku.edu.tw; f. 1927; 1,685,049 vols, 12,676 periodicals; Dir MING-TZONG YANG; publ. *Bulletin* (4 a year).

Taipei

Agricultural Science Information Centre: POB 7-636, Taipei 106; tel. (2) 23626222; internet www.asic.org.tw; f. 1977; 11,000 vols, 638 periodicals, databases; Dir WAN-JIUN WU.

Dr Sun Yat-sen Library: 2F, 505 Jen Ai Rd, Sec. 4, Taipei; tel. (2) 27297030; fax (2) 27582460; f. 1929; 299,345 vols on Dr Sun Yat-sen's writings and studies on San Min Chu Yih and modern Chinese history; Curator SHAW MING-HUANG; publ. *Modern China* (6 a year).

Fu Ssu-nien Library, Institute of History and Philology: 130 Yen Chiu Yuan Rd, Sec. 2, Nankang, Taipei 11521; tel. (2) 27829555; fax (2) 27868834; f. 1928; 420,000 vols, 3,000 periodicals; spec. collns incl. 33,889 stone and bronze rubbings, 13,100 folk plays, 310,000 cabinet records of Ming and Ch'ing dynasties; Dir JUEI-HSIU WU.

National Central Library: 20 Chung Shan South Rd, Taipei 100; tel. (2) 23619132; fax (2) 23110155; e-mail iechief@ncl.edu.tw; internet www.ncl.edu.tw; f. 1933; 4,198,475 vols, incl. 190,000 rare books, stone rubbings and historical material; Dir-Gen. Dr TSENG SHU-HSIEN; publs *Chinese National Bibliography* (12 a year), *Index to Chinese Periodicals* (4 a year), *NCL Bulletin* (2 a year), *NCL News Bulletin* (4 a year).

Branch Library:

Taiwan Branch Library, National Central Library: 1 Hsinshen South Rd, Sec. 1, Taipei; tel. (2) 27724724; internet www.ncltb.edu.tw; f. 1915; 592,023 vols; spec. collns incl. Taiwan and Southern Asia; Dir LIN WEI-JEI; publs *Catalogue of Materials for the Blind*, *Catalogue of NCL Taiwan Branch Collection on Southeast Asia*, *Catalogue on China in Japanese Languages*, *Catalogue on China in Western Languages*, *Index to Taiwan-Related Periodical Literature Collected in NCL Taiwan Branch*, *List of Non-Chinese Serials in NCL Taiwan Branch*, *The Annotative Catalogue of Taiwan Documents*, *Union Catalogue of Taiwan-Related Bibliographies*.

National War College Library: Yangmingshan, Taipei; 156,639 vols on political subjects; Librarian LO MOU-PIN.

Parliamentary Library, Legislative Yuan: 1 Chung Shan S Rd, Taipei 10051; tel. (2) 23585278; fax (2) 23585290; internet npl.ly.gov.tw; f. 1947; gen. reference, govt publs, legal documents; 248,235 vols; Dir Dr SHOW-RONG WANG; publs *Chinese legislative news review index* (12 a year), *Chinese legislative news reviews series* (irregular), *Code Amendment Cyclopedia* (irregular), *Code and reference book catalogue* (irregular), *Code resource pathfinder* (6 a year), *Collection of Interpellation Records* (irregular), *Gazette*, *Index to Chinese Legislative Literature* (6 a year), *Index to Legal Periodicals* (irregular), *Index of Legislative Records* (every 3 years), *LEGISIS thesaurus* (irregular), *Legislative Decision Support Service* (12 a year), *Legislative Microform Catalogue* (irregular), *Library Communications Quarterly*, *Newsletter of books and documentation* (4 a year), *Proceedings and Serials Catalogue* (irregular), *Selective Abstracts of US Congressional Records* (irregular), *Selected Dissemination of Information Series* (6 a year), *Subject Guide to Chinese Code* (irregular), *The Legislative Yuan Library Catalogue* (irregular).

Taipei City Library: 46 Chinan Rd, Sec. 2, Taipei; f. 1952; 125,000 vols; 4 brs; Dir CHIH-SHIH YANG; publ. *Taipei Municipal Library Annals*.

Museums and Art Galleries

Kaohsiung

Kaohsiung Museum of Fine Arts: 80 Meishukuan Rd, Kaohsiung; tel. (7) 5550331; fax (7) 5550307; e-mail service@kmfa.gov.tw; internet www.kmfa.gov.tw; f. 1994; Dir PEI-NI BEATRICE HSIEH.

Taichung

National Taiwan Museum of Fine Arts: 2, Sec. 1, Wu Chuan West Rd, Taichung 403; tel. (4) 23723552; fax (4) 23721195; e-mail artnet@art.ntmofa.gov.tw; internet www.ntmofa.gov.tw; f. 1986; mostly works of Taiwan artists; library of 70,000 vols; Dir TSAI-LANG HUANG; publ. *Journal of National Taiwan Museum of Fine Arts* (4 a year).

Taipei

Chinese Postal Museum: 45 Chungking South Rd, Sec. 2, Taipei 100; tel. (2) 23945185; fax (2) 23518773; e-mail musol@mail.post.gov.tw; internet www.post.gov.tw/museum.htm; f. 1966; library of 27,000 vols; Dir SUSAN TENG-KUEI YU.

Hwa Kang Museum: 55 Hwa Kang Rd, Chinese Culture Univ., Yang Ming Shan, Taipei 111; tel. (2) 28610511; fax (2) 28621918; e-mail cuch@staff.pccu.edu.tw; internet www2.pccu.edu.tw/cuch; f. 1971; Chinese folk arts, pottery, porcelain, calligraphy and paintings; Dir MARGARET CHEN LEE.

National Museum of History: 49 Nan Hai Rd, Taipei 10066; tel. (2) 23610270; fax (2) 23610171; internet www.nmh.gov.tw; f. 1955; Chinese and Taiwanese historical and archaeological artefacts; library of 30,000 vols; Dir YUNG-CHUAN HUANG; publs *Bulletin of the National Museum of History* (in Chinese, 12 a year), *Journal of the National Museum of History* (in Chinese, 2 a year).

National Palace Museum: Wai-shuanghsi, Shih-lin, Taipei; tel. (2) 28812021; fax (2) 28821440; internet www.npm.gov.tw; f. 1925; colln consists chiefly of historic and archaeological treasures brought from mainland China; library of 155,136 vols, 624 periodical titles, 200,907 rare books, 395,335 Ch'ing documents; Dir SHIH SHOU-CHIEN; publs *National Palace Museum Monthly of Chinese Art* (12 a year), *Research Quarterly* (4 a year).

National Taiwan Museum: 2 Siang-yang Rd, Taipei 100; tel. (2) 23822699; fax (2) 23822684; e-mail ntmmail@ntm.gov.uk; internet www.ntm.gov.uk; f. 1908; anthropology, earth sciences, zoology and botany; Dir HSIAO TSUNG-HUANG; publs *Journal of Taiwan Museum* (in English), *Taiwan Natural Science*.

National Taiwan Science Education Centre: 41 Nan Hai Rd, Taipei; tel. (2) 23116734; f. 1958; planetarium, science exhibitions, lectures and films; Dir SHIH-BEY CHEN; publ. *Science Study Monthly*.

Shung Ye Museum of Formosan Aborigines: 282 Chishan Rd Section 2, Shi-Lin Dist, Taipei 11143; tel. (2) 28412611; fax (2) 28412615; e-mail shungye@gate.sinica.edu.tw; internet www.museum.org.tw; f. 1994; holds a colln of artefacts of Taiwan's indigenous peoples; promotes understanding between ethnic groups and undertakes research and preservation of Aboriginal cultural works; Museum Curator and Dir ERIC H. Y. YU.

Taipei Astronomical Museum: 363 Kee-Ho Rd, Taipei 111; tel. (2) 28314551; fax (2) 28314405; e-mail tam001@tam.gov.tw; internet www.tam.gov.tw; f. 1996; exhibits hall, cosmic adventure, IMAX and 3D theatre, observation area; organizes lectures, astronomer workshops and programmes, teacher training; Pres. GUO-GUANG CIOU; Gen. Sec. CHING-HSIUNG WANG; publs *Astronomical Almanac* (1 a year), *Journal Taipei Astronomical Museum*, *Report on Sunspot Observations* (1 a year), *Taipei Skylight* (4 a year).

Taipei Fine Arts Museum: 181, Sec. 3, Zhong Shan N Rd, Taipei 10461; tel. (2) 25957656; fax (2) 25944104; e-mail info@tfam.gov.tw; internet www.tfam.gov.tw; f. 1983; modern art; Dir TSAI-LANG HSIAO (acting); publs *Journal* (2 a year), *Modern Art* (6 a year).

Universities

CHINESE CULTURE UNIVERSITY

55 Hwa Kang Rd, Yang Ming Shan, Taipei
Telephone: (2) 28610511
Fax: (2) 28615031
Internet: www.pccu.edu.tw
Founded 1962
Private control
Colleges of agriculture, arts, business, engineering, foreign languages and literature, journalism and mass communication, law, liberal arts, science; graduate and evening schools
Pres.: LIN TSAI-MEI
Library of 630,000 vols, 3,500 periodicals
Number of teachers: 531
Number of students: 20,013

CHUNG YUAN CHRISTIAN UNIVERSITY

Chung Li
Telephone: (3) 4563171
Fax: (3) 4563160
Internet: www.cycu.edu.tw
Founded 1955
Private control
Academic year: August to July
Colleges of business, design, engineering, science; evening dept
Pres.: Dr SAMUEL K. C. CHANG
Library of 250,000 vols
Number of teachers: 12,491
Number of students: 11,798
Publications: *Chung Yuan Journal*, *CYCU News*.

FENG CHIA UNIVERSITY

100 Wenhwa Rd, Seatwen, Taichung 40724
Telephone: (4) 24517250
Fax: (4) 24514907
E-mail: linkages@fcu.edu.tw
Internet: www.fcu.edu.tw
Founded 1961
Private control
Languages of instruction: Chinese, English
Academic year: September to June
Pres.: AN-CHI LIU
Vice-Pres.: YUAN-TONG LEE
Sec.-Gen.: HAI-PING HSIEH
Chief Librarian: HSIANG-HOO CHING
Library of 590,000 vols
Number of teachers: 1,107
Number of students: 19,124 (17,517 undergraduate, 1,607 postgraduate)
Publications: *Accounting Journal*, *Architecture Quarterly*, *Banking and Insurance*, *Civil Engineering Journal*, *Computer Science*, *Co-operative Research*, *FCU Weekly*, *Finance Research*, *Industrial Engineering*, *International Trade*, *Mechanical Engineering*, *Statistics Journal*, *Textile Science*

DEANS
College of Business: PAO-LONG CHANG
College of Construction and Devt: BING-JEAN LEE
College of Continuing Education: YOU-REN SHIAU
College of Engineering: TONG-MIIN LIOU
College of Humanities and Social Studies: YEN CHU
College of Information and Electrical Engineering: CHUANG-CHIEN CHIU
College of Sciences: TAI-LEE HU

DIRECTORS OF GRADUATE INSTITUTES
Accounting and Taxation: YU-CHI LIN
Aeronautical Engineering: WEN-SHYONG KOU
Applied Mathematics: JIANN-CHERNG YANG
Architecture and Urban Planning: MEI-JUNG LAI
Automatic Control Engineering: CHERN-SHENG LIN
Business Administration: MEI-YANE CHUNG
Chemical Engineering: CHYI-TSONG CHEN
Chinese Literature: JIANN-HWA SONG
Civil and Hydraulic Engineering: YU-MIN KANG
Communications Engineering: CHENG-HO HSIN
Economics: CHI-CHU CHOU
Electrical and Communications Engineering: CHUANG-CHIEN CHIU
Electrical Engineering: CHANG-CHOU HWANG
Electronic Engineering: WEN-LUH YANG
Environmental Science and Engineering: JYA-JYUN YU
Finance: CHE-PENG LIN
History and Cultural Heritage Management: CHIH-CHIA HU
Industrial Engineering: ANGUS JEANG
Information Engineering: DON-LIN YANG
Insurance: GOW-NING YUAN
International Trade: TING-JI LIN
Land Management: JING-CHZI HSIEH
Materials Science: HSIN-CHIH LIN
Mechanical Engineering: JIN-HUANG HUANG
Optical Physics: YING-TE LEE
Statistics and Actuarial Science: WOAN-SHU CHEN
Textiles Engineering: TIEN-WEI SHYR
Traffic and Transportation Engineering and Management: TA-YIN HU

FU-JEN CATHOLIC UNIVERSITY

510 Chungcheng Rd, Hsin-Chuang, Taipei
Telephone: (2) 29031111
Fax: (2) 29017391
E-mail: fjuweb@mails.fju.edu.tw
Internet: www.fju.edu.tw
Founded 1925 in Beijing; re-opened in Taiwan 1961
Academic year: August to July
Pres.: Dr JOHN NING-YUEAN LEE
Vice-Pres.: Dr PERRY C. CHIU, Dr PETER SHANG-SHING CHOU, Rev. LOUIS GENDRON
Sec.-Gen.: JOHN SHIANG-YANG HWANG
Dean of Academic Affairs: Dr YIU-LUNG CHEN
Dean of Gen. Affairs: Prof. ZERMAN HU
Dean of Research and Devt: Dr SHIH-MING KO
Dean of Student Affairs: Dr HUNG YAN CHEN
Registrar: TZU-CHI LI
Librarian: Dr H. H. CHENG
Library of 828,000 vols
Number of teachers: 1,591
Number of students: 23,658
Publications: *Catholic Observer*, *Fu Jen Philosophical Studies*, *Fu Jen Studies* (4 a year)

DEANS
College of Fine Arts: Dr MING-JIAN FANG

College of Foreign Languages: Dr NICHOLAS KOSS
College of Human Ecology: Dr SHAU-YEN HUANG
College of Law: Dr AH-YEE LEE
College of Liberal Arts: Dr THOMAS FU-BEING CHEN
College of Management: Dr DENG-YUAN HUANG
College of Medicine: Dr VINCENT HAN-SUN CHIANG
College of Science and Engineering: Dr JOSEPH L. G. HWA
Holistic Education Centre: Dr DAMIANUS JEN-LUNGKAO
School of Continuing Education: Dr CAJUS CHI-CHI LIN

NATIONAL CENTRAL UNIVERSITY

Chung-Li 320
Telephone: (3) 4227151
Fax: (3) 4226062
Internet: www.ncu.edu.tw
Founded 1968 as re-establishment of Nat. Central Univ. (Nanking)
Academic year: February to January
Pres.: Prof. CHAO-HAN LIU
Vice-Pres.: KUANG-FU CHENG
Dean of Academic Affairs: KUAN-CHING LEE
Dean of Gen. Affairs: EDMOND LIU-WU HOURNG
Dean of Research and Devt: WEI-LING CHIANG
Dean of Student Affairs: DYI-HWA TSENG
Dir of Secretariat: JIEN-MING JUE
Librarian: CHIEU-YIUG WANG
Number of teachers: 450
Number of students: 7,813
Publications: *Bulletin of Geophysics* (2 a year), *Journal of Humanities East/West* (2 a year)

DEANS

College of Earth Sciences: YI-BEN TSAI
College of Engineering: KUO-SHONG WANG
College of Information Technology and Electrical Engineering: SHING-TSAAN HUANG
College of Liberal Arts: JEH-HANG LAI
College of Management: JING-TWEN CHEN
College of Science: WING-HUEN IP

NATIONAL CHENG KUNG UNIVERSITY

1 Ta-Hsueh Rd, Tainan 70101
Telephone: (6) 2757575
Fax: (6) 2368660
E-mail: em50000@mail.ncku.edu.tw
Internet: www.ncku.edu.tw
Founded 1931 as Tainan Technical College, renamed Taiwan Provincial College of Engineering 1946, present name 1971
State control
Language of instruction: Chinese, some English
Academic year: September to June
Pres.: Dr CHIANG KAO
Dean of Academic Affairs: Dr YAN-KUIN SU
Registrar: SHIN-FU HUANG
Librarian: Dr JEN-FA MIN
Number of teachers: 1,200
Number of students: 19,000
Publications: *Bulletin of National Cheng Kung University* (1 a year), *Journal of National Cheng Kung University* (1 a year)

DEANS

College of Design: Dr MING-FU HSU
College of Electrical Engineering and Computer Science: Dr CHING-TING LI
College of Engineering: Dr WEN-TENG WU
College of Liberal Arts: Dr KAO-PING CHANG

College of Management Science: Dr WANN-YIH WU
College of Medicine: Dr RUEY-JEN SUNG
College of Sciences: Dr SHU-CHENG YU
College of Social Sciences: Dr JENN-YEU CHEN

Graduate institutes are attached to the College of Engineering, the College of Liberal Arts, the College of Management Science, the College of Medicine, the College of Sciences and the College of Social Sciences

NATIONAL CHENGCHI UNIVERSITY

64 Zhinan Rd Sec. 2, Wenshan 116, Taipei
Telephone: (2) 29393091
Fax: (2) 29379611
E-mail: oic@nccu.edu.tw
Internet: www.nccu.edu.tw
Founded 1927, univ. status 1946; state-funded
Public control
Languages of instruction: Chinese, English
Academic year: September to June (2 semesters)
Pres.: SE-HWA WU
Vice-Pres. and Dean of Academic Affairs: LIEN-KONG TSAI
Dean of General Affairs: TAI-MING BEN
Dean of Student Affairs: MEI-LIE CHU
Dir of Library: JYI-SHANE LIU
Library of 2,106,128 vols
Number of teachers: 684 (full- and part-time)
Number of students: 16,038

DEANS

College of Commerce: CHUEN-LUNG CHEN
College of Communication: CHIH-YU CHAN
College of Education: WEI-WEN CHUNG
College of Foreign Languages: NAI-MING YU
College of Int. Affairs: CHUNG-CHIAN TENG
College of Law: KAI-LIN FAUNG
College of Liberal Arts: WHEI-MING CHOU
College of Science: ARBEE CHEN
College of Social Sciences: SONG-LING YANG

NATIONAL CHIAO TUNG UNIVERSITY

1001 Ta Hsueh Rd, Hsinchu
Telephone: (35) 712121
Fax: (35) 721500
Internet: www.nctu.edu.tw
Founded 1896, re-established in Hsinchu 1958
Languages of instruction: Chinese, English
Academic year: August to July (2 semesters)
Pres.: Dr CHI-FU DEN
Dean of Academic Affairs: Dr LONG-ING CHEN
Dean of Gen. Affairs: Dr CHUNG-BIAU TSAY
Dean of the Research and Devt Ccl: Dr CHUNG-YU WU
Dean of Student Affairs: Dr FU-WHA HAN
Chief Sec.: Prof. HSIN-SEN CHU
Registrar: Assoc. Prof. CHIN-SHYONG CHEN
Chief Librarian: Dr RUEI-CHUAN CHANG
Library of 170,329 vols, 2,373 periodicals
Number of teachers: 415 (full-time)
Number of students: 4,896
Publications: *Chiao Ta Management Review*, *List of Publications of Faculty Members*, abstracts of papers and research reports

DEANS

College of Electrical Engineering and Computer Science: Dr CHE-HO WEI
College of Engineering: Dr TAI-YAN KAM
College of Management: Dr PAO-LONG CHANG
College of Science: Dr DER-SAN CHUU

DIRECTORS OF GRADUATE INSTITUTES

Applied Arts (Design and Music): Dr MING-CHUEN CHUANG

Applied Chemistry: Dr CHAIN-SHU HSU
Applied Mathematics: Dr GERARD J. CHANG
Biological Science and Technology: Dr CHENG ALLEN CHANG
Civil Engineering: Dr YUNG-SHOW FANG
Communication Engineering: Dr CHUNG-JU CHANG
Communication Studies: Dr SHIN-MIN CHEN
Computer and Information Science: Dr RONG-HONG JAN
Computer Science and Information Engineering: Dr SHU-YUEN HWANG
Control Engineering: Dr DER-CHERNG LIAW
Electronics: Dr TAN-FU LEI
Electro-Optical Engineering: Dr CI-LING PAN
Electrophysics: Dr MING-CHIH LEE
Environmental Engineering: Dr JEHNG-JUNG KAO
Industrial Engineering: Dr CHAO-TON SU
Information Management: Dr CHI-CHUN LO
Management Science: Dr SOUSHAN WU
Management Technology: Dr SHANG-JYH LIU
Materials Science and Engineering: Dr TZENG-FENG LIU
Mechanical Engineering: Dr HSIN-SEN CHU
Physics: Dr JSIN-FU JIANG
Statistics: Dr CHAO-SHENG LEE
Traffic and Transportation: Dr YUAN-CHING HSU

DIRECTORS OF RESEARCH CENTRES

Centre for Telecommunications Research: Dr SIN-HORNG CHEN
Computer Centre: Dr RUEI-CHUAN CHANG
Microelectronics and Information Science and Technology Research Centre: Dr MING SZE
National Nano Device Centre: Dr CHUN-YEN CHANG
Semiconductor Research Centre: (vacant)

NATIONAL CHUNG HSING UNIVERSITY

250 Kuokuang Rd, Taichung
Telephone: (4) 2872991
Fax: (4) 2853813
Internet: www.nchu.edu.tw
Founded 1961
Pres.: Dr CHENG-CHANG LI
Sec.-Gen.: MU-CHIOU HUANG
Librarian: WOEI LIN
Number of teachers: 980
Number of students: 17,625

DEANS

College of Agriculture: MING-TSAO CHEN
College of Engineering: SHIH-SHYN WU
College of Law and Commerce: SEN-TIAN WU
College of Liberal Arts: CHUNG-HSUAN TUNG
College of Life Science: SCHENG-MING TSCHEN
College of Science: TENG-KUEI YANG

HEADS OF INSTITUTES

Institute of Agricultural Biotechnology: FENG-NAN HOU
Institute of Agricultural Extension and Education: CHING-YING HUANG
Institute of Biochemistry: JUNGYIE KAO
Institute of Computer Science: SYING-JYAN WANG
Institute of Library and Information Science: WOEI LIN
Institute of Materials Engineering: FUN-SHENG SHEIU
Institute of Molecular Biology: LIANG-JWU CHEN
Institute of Natural Resource Management: DAIGEE SHAW
Institute of Urban Planning: HSUEH-TAO CHIEN
Institute of Veterinary Microbiology: LONG-HUW LEE
Institute of Veterinary Pathology: CHENG-I LIU

NATIONAL OPEN UNIVERSITY

172 Chung Cheng Rd, Lu Chow, Taipei 24702

Telephone: (2) 22829355
Fax: (2) 22831721
E-mail: elec007@mail.nou.edu.tw
Internet: www.nou.edu.tw

Founded 1986
Language of instruction: Chinese
Academic year: September to June

Pres.: Dr SHENG-SHIUNG HUANG
Registrar: LI-CHI HSIEH
Dean of Academic Affairs: Dr CHIA-SHING YANG

Number of teachers: 2,037 (88 full-time, 1,949 part-time)
Number of students: 40,000

Publication: *National Open University Learning Journal* (24 a year)

CHAIRMEN OF DEPARTMENTS
Arts in Commerce: JIN-HO YUAN
General Affairs: TSAI HSIANG-HUEI
General Studies: SZE-LU NA
Instructional Media: DWO-YAN CHANG
Liberal Arts: YUAN-JEN FANG
Living Sciences: WEN-CHIN CHOU
Management and Information: SUNG-BO CHEN
Public Administration: SHIH-PEI LAI
Research and Development: JUDY HUANG
Social Sciences: JEHNG OUYANG
Student Affairs: JESSE C. CHOU

NATIONAL PINGTUNG UNIVERSITY OF SCIENCE AND TECHNOLOGY

1 Hseuh-Fu Rd, Nei Pu Hsiang, Pingtung Hsien 912

Telephone: (8) 7703660
Fax: (8) 7702226
E-mail: choumasa@mail.npust.edu.tw
Internet: www.npust.edu.tw

Founded 1954 as Taiwan Provincial Institute of Agriculture; became National Pingtung Institute of Agriculture 1981 and National Pingtung Polytechnic Institute 1991; present name and status 1997

Pres.: CHANG-HUNG CHOU
Library of 227,198 vols
Number of teachers: 324
Number of students: 9,000

Publication: *Bulletin* (1 a year)

Colleges of agriculture, engineering, management and humanities, social sciences.

NATIONAL TAIWAN NORMAL UNIVERSITY

162 East Ho Ping Rd, Sec. 1, Taipei 10610

Telephone: (2) 23625101
Fax: (2) 23922673
Internet: www.ntnu.edu.tw

Founded 1946
Language of instruction: Chinese
State control
Academic year: August to July (2 semesters)

Pres.: MAW-FA CHIEN
Vice-Pres.: CHUNG-YANG TSAI
Sec.-Gen.: HSI-PING WANG
Dean of General Affairs: DAR-CHIN RAU
Dean of Internship Supervision and Placement: (vacant)
Dean of Research and Devt: LILLIAN MEEI-JIN HUANG
Dean of Students: HU-HSIUNG LI
Dean of Studies: C. H. GEORGE KAO
Registrar: AN-PAN LIN
Library Dir: HARRY LIANG

Number of teachers: 1,131
Number of students: 9,716

Publications: *A-V Education* (6 a year), *Bulletin, NTNU Alumni* (12 a year), *Secondary Education* (6 a year), graduate institutional and departmental journals

DEANS
College of Education: WU-TIEN WU
College of Fine and Applied Arts: CHING-LANG CHANG
College of Liberal Arts: WEN-HSING WU
College of Sciences: CHU-NAN CHANG
College of Sports and Recreation: YAO-HUI CHIEN
College of Technology: LUNG-SHERN LEE
Extension Division: SUZ-WEI YANG

NATIONAL TAIWAN OCEAN UNIVERSITY

2 Pei-Ning Rd, Keelung

Telephone: (2) 24622192
Fax: (2) 24623563
Internet: www.ntou.edu.tw

Founded 1953 (fmrly Nat. Taiwan College of Marine Science and Technology)
Language of instruction: Mandarin
Academic year: August to July

Pres.: KUO-TIEN LEE
Vice-Pres.: SAN-SHYAN LIN
Vice-Pres.: CHING-FONG CHANG
Dean of Academic Affairs: KUO-KAO LEE
Dean of General Affairs: KUO-CHENG YANG
Dean of Research and Devt: HSUAN-HSIH LEE
Dean of Student Affairs: TAN-KIN WANG
Librarian: YIN-HWANG LIN

Library of 423,000 vols, 3,000 periodicals
Number of teachers: 325
Number of students: 7,731

Publication: *Journal of Marine Science and Technology* (4 a year)

DEANS
Electrical Engineering and Computer Science: CHUNG-CHENG CHANG
Engineering: JIAHN-HORNG CHEN
Life and Resource Science: DENG-FWU HWANG
Maritime Science and Management: CHIH-CHING CHANG
Ocean Science and Resource: MING-AN LEE

NATIONAL TAIWAN UNIVERSITY

1 Roosevelt Rd, Section 4, Taipei 10617

Telephone: (2) 3366-3366
Fax: (2) 2362-7651
E-mail: secretor@ntu.edu.tw
Internet: www.ntu.edu.tw

Founded 1928 during the Japanese occupation as the Taihoku Imperial Univ.; taken over and renamed by Chinese Govt in 1945
Language of instruction: Chinese
Academic year: August to July (2 semesters)

Pres.: Dr SI-CHEN LEE
Vice-Pres. for Academic Affairs: Dr TAI-JEN GEORGE CHEN
Vice-Pres. for Admin. Affairs: TZONG-HO BAU
Vice-Pres. for Financial Affairs: MING-JE TANG
Dean of Academic Affairs: BEEN-HUANG CHIANG
Dean of Gen. Affairs: Dr HONG-KI HONG
Dean of Int. Affairs: TUNG SHEN
Dean of Research and Devt: JI-WANG CHERN
Dean of Student Affairs: JOYCE YEN FENG
Library Dir: SHIUE-HUA CHEN

Library of 3,000,000 vols
Number of teachers: 3,509
Number of students: 33,416

Publications: *Acta Botanica Taiwania, Acta Geologica Taiwanica, Acta Oceanographica Taiwanica*

DEANS
College of Bio-Resources and Agriculture: BAO-JI CHEN
College of Electrical Engineering and Computer Science: SOO-CHANG PEI
College of Engineering: HUAN-JANG KEH
College of Law: MING-CHEN TSAI
College of Liberal Arts: KUO-LIANG YEH
College of Life Science: GRACE CHU-FANG LO
College of Management: MAO-WEI HUNG
College of Medicine: PAN-CHYR YANG
College of Public Health: DUNG-LIANG JIANG
College of Science: CHING-HUA LU
College of Social Sciences: YUNG-MAU CHAO
School of Dentistry: CHUN-PIN LIN
School of Professional and Continuing Studies: RUEI-SHIANG GUO
School of Veterinary Medicine: CHEN-HSUAN LIU (Chair.)

DIRECTORS OF GRADUATE INSTITUTES
Accounting: SHU-HSING LI
Agricultural Chemistry: DAR-YUAN LEE
Agricultural Economics: SHIH-HSUN HSU
Agronomy: YUN-MING PONG
Anatomy and Cell Biology: KUO-SHYAN LU
Animal Science and Technology: LEANG-SHIN WU
Anthropology: YUAN-CHAO TUNG
Applied Mechanics: MAO-KUEN KUO
Applied Physics: YEE-BOB HSIUNG
Art History: MING-LIANG HSIEH
Astrophysics: YEE-BOB HSIUNG
Atmospheric Sciences: CHUN-CHIEH WU
Biochemical Sciences: GEEN-DONG CHANG
Biochemistry and Molecular Biology: LU-PING CHOW
Bioenvironmental Systems Engineering: HUNG-PIN HUANG
Bio-Industrial Mechatronics Engineering: TA-TE LIN
Bio-Industry Communication and Development: ER-ROU LAI
Biomedical Electronics and Bioinformatics: PAI-CHI LI
Biomedical Engineering: TAI-HORNG YOUNG
Biotechnology: HUU-SHENG LUR
Building and Planning: CHU-JOE HSIA
Business Administration: SHU-CHENG STEVE CHI
Chemical Engineering: LI-JEN CHEN
Chemistry: PI-TAI CHOU
Chinese Literature: YU-YU JENG
Civil Engineering: KUO-CHUN CHANG
Clinical Dentistry: CHUN-PIN LIN
Clinical Laboratory Sciences and Medical Biotechnology: CHUN-NAN LEE
Clinical Medicine: PEI-JER CHEN
Clinical Pharmacy: FE-LIN LIN
Communications Engineering: HUEI WANG
Computer Science and Information Engineering: YUH-DAUH LYUU
Drama and Theatre: WEI-JAN CHI
Economics: CHIEN-FU CHOU
Electrical Engineering: JENN-GWO HWU
Electronics Engineering: SHEY-SHI LU
Engineering Science and Ocean Engineering: JING-FA TSAI
Entomology: CHENG-JEN SHIH
Environmental Engineering: SHIAN-CHEE WU
Environmental Health: GEN-SHUH WANG
Epidemiology: WEN-CHUNG LEE
Finance: MING-SHEN CHEN
Fisheries Science: WANN-NIAN TZENG
Food Science and Technology: AN-I YEH
Foreign Languages and Literature: YAN-WING LEUNG
Forensic Medicine: YAO-CHANG CHEN
Forestry and Resource Conservation: HANN-CHUNG LO
Geography: SUE-CHING JOU
Geosciences: HONGEY CHEN
Health Care Organization Administration: MING-CHIN YANG
Health Policy and Management: LAN LEE

History: HUAI-CHEN KAN
Horticulture: YANN-JOU LIN
Immunology: PING-NING HSU
Industrial Engineering: ARGON CHEN
Information Management: CHING-CHIN CHERN
Interdisciplinary Legal Studies: TAY-SHENG WANG
International Business: HSIOU-WEI LIN
Japanese Language and Literature: SHING-CHING SHYU
Journalism: DENNIS WENG-JENG PENG
Law: MING-CHENG TSAI
Library and Information Science: CLARENCE TSA-KANG CHU
Linguistics: HINTAT CHEUNG
Materials Science and Engineering: JER-REN YANG
Mathematics: GERARD-JENNHWA CHANG
Mechanical Engineering: SHUO-HUNG CHANG
Microbiology: SHOW-LIN CHEN
Microbiology and Biochemistry: TZU-MING PAN
Molecular and Cellular Biology: HUAI-JEN TSAI
Molecular Medicine: FANG-JEN LEE
Musicology: YING-FEN WANG
National Development: RONG-JEO CHIU
Networking and Multimedia: YI-PING HUNG
Nursing: LIAN-HUA HUANG
Occupational Medicine and Industrial Hygiene: TSUN-JEN CHENG
Occupational Therapy: KEH-CHUNG LIN
Oceanography: LING-YUN CHIAO
Oral Biology: YEN-PING KUO
Pathology: CHUNG-WU LIN
Pharmacology: CHING-CHOW CHEN
Pharmacy: SHOEI-SHENG LEE
Philosophy: HSIAO-CHIH SUN
Photonics and Optoelectronics: SHENG-LUNG HUANG
Physical Therapy: SUH-FANG JENG
Physics: YEE-BOB HSIUNG
Plant Biology: KAI-WUN YEH
Plant Pathology and Microbiology: CHAO-YING CHEN
Political Science: TSAI-TSU SU
Political Science and Engineering: WEN-CHANG CHEN
Preventive Medicine: WEI-CHU CHIE
Psychology: LI-JEN WENG
Physiology: KUO-CHU CHANG
Public Health: WEI-JIAN CHEN
Social Work: YEUN-WEN KU
Sociology: HOLIN LIN
Taiwan Literature: CHIA-LING MEI
Toxicology: SHING-HWA LIU
Veterinary Clinical Science: LI-SEN YEH
Veterinary Medicine: ZHEN-XUAN LIU
Zoology: JIUN-HONG CHEN

NATIONAL TAIWAN UNIVERSITY OF SCIENCE AND TECHNOLOGY

43 Keelung Rd, Sec. 4, Taipei
Telephone: (2) 27376101
Fax: (2) 27376107
E-mail: president@mail.ntust.edu.tw
Internet: www.ntust.edu.tw

Founded 1974
Academic year: August to July (2 semesters)
Pres.: SHUN-TYAN CHEN
Dean of Studies: CHENG-SEEN HO

Library of 279,326 vols
Number of teachers: 315
Number of students: 8,106

NATIONAL TSING HUA UNIVERSITY

101, Sec. 2, Kuang Fu Rd, Hsinchu 30013
Telephone: (3) 5715131
Fax: (3) 5710582
E-mail: presid@my.nthu.edu.tw
Internet: www.nthu.edu.tw

Founded 1911, re-established in Hsinchu 1956
Language of instruction: Chinese
Academic year: August to July
Pres.: Dr LIH J. CHEN
Librarian: HSIAO-CHIN HSIEH

Number of teachers: 635
Number of students: 12,050

Publication: Tsing Hua Journal of Chinese Studies (Sinology, Literature and History and Philosophy, 4 a year)

DEANS

College of Electrical Engineering and Computer Science: KEH-YUNG CHENG
College of Engineering: NYAN-HWA TAI
College of Humanities and Social Sciences: Dr WEI-AN CHANG
College of Life Science: YEN-CHUNG CHANG
College of Nuclear Science: RUEY-AN DOONG
College of Science: HUAN-CHIU KU
College of Technology Management: CHAO-HSI HUANG
Commission of General Education: HSIAO-CHIN HSIEH

SOOCHOW UNIVERSITY

70 Linhsi Rd, Shihlin, Taipei 111
Telephone: (2) 28819471
Fax: (2) 28829310
E-mail: secretary@scu.edu.tw
Internet: www.scu.edu.tw

Founded 1900
Private control
Languages of instruction: Chinese, English
Academic year: September to June (2 semesters)

Pres.: CHAO-SHUIAN LIU
Vice-Pres.: CHUN-MEI MA
Vice-Pres. for Academic Affairs: MAO-TING CHIEN
Registrar: CHENG-TSUN LIN
Librarian: YUAN-JEE DING

Library of 692,767 vols
Number of teachers: 1,149 (including part-time teachers)
Number of students: 15,085

Publications: Journal of Chinese Studies (1 a year), Journal of Economics and Business (4 a year), Journal of Foreign Languages and Cultures (1 a year), Journal of History (1 a year), Journal of Japanese Language Teaching (1 a year), Journal of Mathematics (1 a year), Journal of Philosophical Studies (2 a year), Journal of Political Science (2 a year), Journal of Sociology (2 a year), Law Review (2 a year)

DIRECTORS

School of Arts and Social Sciences: SIU-KEUNG WONG
School of Business: YUNG-HO CHIU
School of Foreign Languages and Cultures: TSONG-MINN LIN
School of Law: WEI-DA PAN
School of Science: HIN-CHUNG WONG
Extension School: PING-WEN LIN

TAIPEI NATIONAL UNIVERSITY OF THE ARTS

1 Hsueh Yuan Rd, Kuan-Tu, Taipei 112
Telephone: (2) 28961000
Fax: (2) 28945124
E-mail: www@www.tnua.edu.tw
Internet: www.tnua.edu.tw

Founded 1982 as National Institute of the Arts, present name 2001
Pres.: Prof. JU TZONG-CHING
Vice-Pres.: Prof. CHUNG-SHIUAN CHANG
Dean of Academic Affairs: Prof. CHUNG-SHIUAN CHANG

Dean of General Affairs: YUE-HUNG CHEN
Dean of Research and Devt: Assoc. Prof. SHAW-REN LIN
Dean of Student Affairs: Assoc. Prof. HUEI-TENG CHAN
Sec.-Gen.: MEY-JUANE KUO

Library of 438,967 vols
Number of teachers: 154
Number of students: 2,816

Publications: Arts Review (2 a year), Guandu Music Journal (2 a year), Journal of Cultural Resources (1 a year), Journal of Fine Arts (1 a year), Kuandu General Education Journal (1 a yera), Taipei Theatre Journal (2 a year)

DEANS

Faculty of Culture Resources: SUNG-SHAN WANG
Faculty of Dance: HENG PING
Faculty of Fine Art: CHENG-JEN CHANG
Faculty of Film and New Media: TEH-I CHU
Faculty of Music: HWEI-JIN LIU
Faculty of Theatre: CHYI-WEN YANG

TAMKANG UNIVERSITY

151 Ying-Chuan Rd, Tamsui, Taipei 25137
Telephone: (2) 26215656
Fax: (2) 26237384
Internet: www.tku.edu.tw

Founded 1950 (formerly Tamkang College of Arts and Sciences)
Private control
Languages of instruction: Chinese, English
Academic year: August to July

Pres.: Dr HORNG-JINH CHANG
Vice-Pres. for Academic Affairs: Dr CHAO-KANG FENG
Vice-Pres. for Admin.: Dr FLORA CHIA-I CHANG
Sec.-Gen.: Dr TUN-LI CHEN
Dean of Academic Affairs: Dr HIS-JEN FU
Dean of General Affairs: Prof. CHING-JEN HUNG
Dean of Student Affairs: Dr HUAN-CHAO KEH
Librarian: Prof. HONG-CHU HUANG

Library of 753,911 vols, 6,901 periodicals
Number of teachers: 2,033
Number of students: 26,600

Publications: Educational Media and Library Science, International Journal of Information and Management Science, Journal of Future Studies, Tamkang Journal, Tamkang Journal of International Affairs, Tamkang Mathematics, Tamkang Review

DEANS

Business: Dr JONG-RONG CHIOU
Engineering: Dr SHI-CHIH CHU
Extension Education Centre: Prof. YAO-LUNG HAN
Foreign Languages and Literature: Dr YAOFU LIN
International Studies: Dr WOU WEI
Liberal Arts: Dr SHIH-HSION HUANG
Management: Dr LIANG-YU OUYANG
Science: Dr KAN-NAN CHEN
Technocracy: Prof. HSIN-FU TSAI

TUNGHAI UNIVERSITY

181 Taichung Harbour Rd, Sec. 3, Taichung 40704
Telephone: (4) 23590200
Fax: (4) 23590361
E-mail: kpwang@mail.thu.edu.tw
Internet: www.thu.edu.tw

Founded 1955 under the auspices of the United Board for Christian Higher Education in Asia
Languages of instruction: Chinese, English

Academic year: September to July (2 semesters)

Pres.: KANG-PEI WANG
Dean of Academic Affairs: CHENG-TUNG LIN
Dean of General Affairs: I-CHAO HSIAO
Dean of Student Affairs: HUNG-DER FU
Librarian: CHUNG-LIN LU

Number of teachers: 826
Number of students: 14,500

Publications: *The Vineyard, Tunghai Bulletin, Tunghai Journal, Tunghai News*

DEANS

College of Agriculture: TSUN-CHUNG TSAI
College of Arts: HAI-YUN HUANG
College of Engineering: JEN-TENG TSAI
College of Management: TSAI-DING LIN
College of Science: CHING-SHENG CHEN
College of Social Sciences: JENN-HWAN WANG

Colleges and Institutes

China Medical College: 91 Hseuh Shih Rd, Taichung 404; tel. (4) 2057153; f. 1958; Private control; 2 campuses (in Taichung and Peikang), 6 graduate institutes, 12 undergraduate schools, Chiang Kai-shek Medical Center, 2 teaching hospitals; 4,666 students; Pres. MASON CHEN.

Kaohsiung Medical University: 100 Shih Chuan 1st Rd, Kaohsiung 807; tel. (7) 3117820; fax (7) 3212062; internet www .kmu.edu.tw; f. 1954; Private control; colleges of medicine, dental medicine, pharmacy, nursing, health sciences, life sciences; undergraduate division of 19 schools; 12 postgraduate institutes; 7 research centres: health and social services, industrial hygiene, gender studies, tropical medicine, orthopaedics, genomics, proteomics; 428 teachers; 6,106 students; library: 175,802 vols, 2,970 periodicals; Pres. Dr GWO-JAW WANG; publ. *Kaohsiung Journal of Medical Sciences* (12 a year).

National Kaohsiung University of Applied Sciences: 415 Chien-Kung Rd, Kaohsiung 807; tel. (7) 3814526; fax (7) 3838435; f. 1963; depts of accounting, applied foreign languages, business administration, chemical, civil, cultural industries development, electrical, electronic, finance, human resource development, industrial management, information management, international trade, mechanical, mould- and die-making engineering, taxation and finance, tourism; graduate institutes of civil engineering and disaster prevention, commerce, electrical energy and control, electronic and information engineering, finance and information, mechanical and precision engineering, tourism management; library: 171,674 vols; 415 teachers; 10,727 students; Pres. Dr REN-YIH LIN; publ. *Journal* (1 a year).

Taipei Institute of Technology: 3, Sec. 1, Shin-sheng South Rd, Taipei; f. 1912; 8,973 students; library: 112,000 vols; Pres. Dr CHIH TANG.

Taipei Medical University: 250 Wu Hsing St, Taipei, 110; tel. (2) 27361661; fax (2) 27387795; f. 1960; Private control; undergraduate and graduate programmes; 1,000 teachers incl. full-time and part-time; 6,000 students; library: 132,015 vols, 650 periodicals; Pres. Prof. WEN-TA CHIU; Vice-Pres. Prof. TA-LIANG CHEN; publ. *Journal* (2 a year).

Tatung University: 40 Chungshan N Rd, Sec. 3, Taipei; tel. (2) 25925252; fax (2) 25941371; e-mail registrar@ttu.edu.tw; internet www.ttu.edu.tw; f. 1956; private control; depts of applied mathematics, bioengineering, business management, chemical engineering, computer science and engineering, electrical engineering, industrial design, information management, materials engineering, mechanical engineering; graduate institutes in electro-optical engineering and communications engineering; 200 teachers; 2,500 students; library: 159,683 vols; Pres. T. S. LIN; Dean of Studies JAN-CHEN HONG.

School of Art and Music

National Taiwan College of Arts: Panchiao, Taipei; tel. (2) 22722181; fax (2) 29687563; internet www.ntca.edu.tw; f. 1955; Chinese music, cinema, dance, drama, fine arts, graphic arts, industrial arts, music, painting, radio and television; sculpture; 364 teachers; 2,300 students; library: 104,000 vols; Pres. MING-SHEAN WANG.

TAJIKISTAN

The Higher Education System

Higher education institutions predate the independence of Tajikistan (formerly Tajik SSR) from the USSR in 1991, with the oldest being Tajik State Pedagogical University S. Aini and Tajik Agricultural University, both of which were founded in 1931. In 2000 the Presidents of Kazakhstan, Kyrgyzstan and Tajikistan co-signed a charter of foundation for a new University of Central Asia, which was to be established in Khorog (in Kuhistoni Badakhshon Autonomous Viloyat) and administered by the Aga Khan Development Network, based in Geneva, Switzerland; this began admitting students in 2006. Higher education is provided by three types of higher education institutions; as well as the universities (donishgoh), there are also academies (akademiya) and institutes (donishkada). In 2003 constitutional amendments abolished free higher education. In 2009/10 some 157,800 students were enrolled at 36 institutes of higher education.

The National Strategy for Education Development for the period 2006–15 was initiated by the Government in August 2005 with a view to improving and reforming a number of key issues within educational management, finance and quality assurance. The Office for the Attestation of Education Institutions, which comprises representatives of the Ministry of Education together with teachers and researchers, is the agency responsible for accreditation and quality assurance within the higher education sector.

The Certificate of Completed Secondary Education or the Diploma of Completed Vocational Education are the main requirements for admission to higher education. Most universities and academies have adopted a three-cycle system of Bakalavr (Bachelor), Magister (Masters) and Doctorontura (Doctorate) degrees, but the Darajai Mutakhassis (Specialist Diploma)—a Soviet-style undergraduate degree lasting five or six years and allowing students to enter directly into doctoral-level studies upon successful completion—is still offered in professional fields such as engineering, medicine and pharmacy. The Bakalavr degree is a four-year programme of study, after which a graduate may study for the Magister, the first postgraduate degree. The Magister is a two-year course culminating in the submission of a thesis; students who have successfully completed the Magister may undertake doctoral-level studies. As well as the European-style Doctorontura (which is the highest academic qualification available), the Soviet-style Kandidat Nauk (Candidate of Science) is also available; both are awarded after two to three years of independent research. The Doctorontura is a purely academic degree, aimed at students who wish to pursue a career in academia or research, and must be completed within a maximum of three years.

Technical and vocational education at the post-secondary level consists of two-year programmes of study, which are open to holders of the Certificate of Completed Secondary Education or the Diploma of Completed Vocational Education and lead to the title of Junior Specialist.

Regulatory and Representative Bodies

GOVERNMENT

Ministry of Culture: Xiyoboni Rudaki 34, 734025 Dushanbe; tel. (372) 210305; fax (372) 214701; Min. MIRZOSHOHRUKH ASROROV.

Ministry of Education: Kuchai Chexov 13A 734025 Dushanbe; tel. (372) 214605; fax (372) 217041; Min. NURIDDIN SAIDOV.

Learned Societies

GENERAL

Academy of Science of the Republic of Tajikistan: 33 Rudaki Ave, 734025 Dushanbe; tel. (372) 215083; fax (372) 214911; e-mail info@anrt.tj; internet anrt.tj; f. 1951; divs of Physical-Mathematical, Chemical and Geological Sciences (Chair. S. ODINAEV, Scientific Sec. R. I. KOSTOVA), Biological and Medical Sciences (Chair. M. YAKUBOVA, Scientific Sec. M. QURBANOVA), Social Sciences (Chair. K.OLIMOV, Scientific Sec. SH. UMAROVA); attached research institutes: see Research Institutes; 79 mems (36 full, 43 corresp.); library: see Libraries and Archives; Pres. Prof. MAMADSHO ILOLOV; Vice-Pres. Prof. KAROMATULLO OLIMOV; Vice-Pres. Prof. SAIDMUHAMMAD ODINAEV; Vice-Pres. Prof. MUHIBA YAKUBOVA; Gen. Sec. Dr KHAKIM AHMEDOV; publs Proceedings (each div. publishes its own edn, 4 a year), Doklady (Reports), Problemy gastroenterologii, Izvestiya (bulletins: Physical-Engineering and Geological Sciences, Biological Sciences, History and Philology, Philosophy, Economics and Law).

LANGUAGE AND LITERATURE

British Council: see chapter on Uzbekistan.

RELIGION, SOCIOLOGY AND ANTHROPOLOGY

Red Crescent Society of Tajikistan: 120 Umar Khayom str., 734017 Dushanbe; tel. (372) 240374; fax (372) 244433; e-mail zmuhabbatov@redcrescent.tj; prevents and mitigates human suffering in compliance with complete impartiality and non-discrimination based on ethnicity, race, age, gender, religious beliefs, class and political views; promotes mutual understanding and friendship among people; contributes to peace all over the world; Pres. GHIESIDDIN MEROJEV; Sec-Gen. ZAFAR MUHABBATOV.

Tajikistan Association of Professional Social Workers: 137 Rudaki St, Fifth Fl., Ste 50, 734003, Dushanbe; tel. (372) 243461; e-mail info@tapsw.org.tj; internet www .tapsw.org.tj; f. 2009; promotes and enhances social work education; assists in devt of social work knowledge, practice, services; develops social work standards in Tajikistan.

Research Institutes

GENERAL

Khatlon Scientific Centre: Kulob; tel. (332) 223636; f. 1985; attached to Acad. of Sciences of the Republic of Tajikistan; Dir TILLO BOBOEV.

Khujand Scientific Centre: ul. Syrdarinskaya 26, 735714 Khudzhand; tel. (379) 251774; attached to Acad. of Sciences of the Republic of Tajikistan; Chair. M. R. DZHALILOV; Scientific Sec. M. SUBKHONOV.

ARCHITECTURE AND TOWN PLANNING

Institute of Geology, Earthquake Engineering and Seismology: ul. Aini 121, 734029 Dushanbe; tel. (372) 250669; fax (372) 244383; e-mail tisss@iscuk.td.silk.org; f. 1951; attached to Acad. of Sciences of the Republic of Tajikistan; library of 6,000 vols, 40 periodicals; Dir SOBIT KH. NEGMATULLAEV; Sec. PULAT A. YASUNOV; publs Prognoz zemletryasenii (1 a year, in Russian), Zemletryaseniya Sredney Azii i Kazakhstana (1 a year, in Russian).

BIBLIOGRAPHY, LIBRARY SCIENCE AND MUSEOLOGY

Institute of Language, Literature, Oriental Studies and Written Heritage named after Rudaki: Kirov 35, 734025 Dushanbe; tel. (372) 273404; attached to Acad. of Sciences of the Republic of Tajikistan; Dir D. NAZRIYEV.

ECONOMICS, LAW AND POLITICS

Institute of Economy and Demography: ul. Aini 44, 734000 Dushanbe; tel. (372) 216750; fax (372) 215765; f. 1951; attached to Acad. of Sciences of the Republic of Tajikistan; Dir R. K. RAKHIMOV.

Institute of State and Law: Pr. Rudaki 19, 734025 Dushanbe; tel. and fax (372) 216572; e-mail isalanrt@rambler.ru; f. 2005; attached to Acad. of Sciences of the Republic of Tajikistan; library of 5,000 vols; Dir SAITUM-

BAR ADINAEVICH RAJABOV; publ. *Izvestiya Akademii Nauk RT, seriya Philosophiya i Pravo.*

HISTORY, GEOGRAPHY AND ARCHAEOLOGY

Institute of History, Archaeology and Ethnography named after A. Donish: Pr. Rudaki 33, 734025 Dushanbe; tel. (372) 223742; f. 1932; attached to Acad. of Sciences of the Republic of Tajikistan; Dir R. M. MASOV.

LANGUAGE AND LITERATURE

Institute of Language, Literature, Oriental Studies and Written Heritage named after Rudaki: Pr. Rudaki 21, 734025 Dushanbe; tel. (372) 216011; f. 1932; attached to Acad. of Sciences of the Republic of Tajikistan; Dir A. M. MANIYAZOV.

MEDICINE

Institute of Gastroenterology: Parvin 12, 734002 Dushanbe; tel. (372) 217782; fax (372) 234917; e-mail mansurov@academy.td .silk.org; f. 1959; attached to Acad. of Sciences of Republic of Tajikistan; library of 5,000 vols; Dir Prof. G. MIRODJEV; publ. *Problems of Gastroenterology* (4 a year).

NATURAL SCIENCES

Biological Sciences

Institute of Botany, Physiology and Genetics: Ul. Karamova 27, 734017 Dushanbe; tel. (372) 247188; f. 1941; attached to Acad. of Sciences of the Republic of Tajikistan; Dir U. I. ISMOILOV.

Institute of Plant Physiology and Genetics: Ul. Aini 299/2, 734063 Dushanbe; tel. (372) 252644; e-mail akotibbm@ac.tajik.net; f. 1964; attached to Acad. of Sciences of the Republic of Tajikistan; Dir Prof. KHURSHED KARIMOV.

Institute of Zoology and Parasitology named after E. N. Pavlovskii: Post Office 70, 734025 Dushanbe; tel. (372) 255871; f. 1941; attached to Acad. of Sciences of the Republic of Tajikistan; Dir A. K. GAFUROV.

Pamir Biological Institute: Kholdorov St 1, 736002 Khorog; tel. (352) 204182; fax (372) 217087; e-mail pamir@eco.khorugh.td.silk .org; internet pbi.narod.ru; f. 1969; attached to Acad. of Sciences of the Republic of Tajikistan; Dir Dr OGONAZAR AKNAZAROV.

Mathematical Sciences

Institute of Mathematics: Ul. Aini 299/1, 734063 Dushanbe; tel. (372) 258089; e-mail usmanov@ac.tajik.net; f. 1973; attached to Acad. of Sciences of the Republic of Tajikistan; Dir Z. D. USMANOV.

Physical Sciences

Institute of Astrophysics: Ul. Bukhoro 22, 734042 Dushanbe; tel. (372) 274614; e-mail astro@ac.tajik.net; f. 1958; attached to Acad. of Sciences of the Republic of Tajikistan; Dir KHURSAND I. IBADINOV; publ. *Bulletin* (2 a year).

Institute of Chemistry named after V. I. Nikitin: Ul. Aini 299/2, 734063 Dushanbe; tel. (372) 252604; e-mail sarvar@ac.tajik.net; f. 1946; attached to Acad. of Sciences of the Republic of; Dir U. M. MIRSAYIDOV.

Institute of Geology: Ul. Aini 267, 734063 Dushanbe; tel. (372) 253267; f. 1941; attached to Acad. of Sciences of the Republic of Tajikistan; Dir M. R. DHALILOV.

Institute of Water Problems, Hydropower and Ecology: Parvin 12, 734002 Dushanbe; tel. and fax (372) 245231; e-mail kobuliev@mail.ru; f. 2002; attached to Acad.

of Sciences of the Republic of Tajikistan; Dir Prof. ZAINALOBUDIN KOBULIEV.

PHILOSOPHY AND PSYCHOLOGY

Institute of Philosophy, Political Sciences and Law named after A. M. Bahovaddinov: Pr. Rudaki 33, 734025 Dushanbe; tel. (372) 237796; e-mail noibprez@ac.tajik .net; attached to Acad. of Sciences of the Republic of Tajikistan; f. 1991; Dir M. DINORSHOYEV.

RELIGION, SOCIOLOGY AND ANTHROPOLOGY

Institute of Economics and Demographics: Ayni 44, 734024 Dushanbe; tel. (372) 218939; e-mail inst.demography.tj@ gmail.com; internet www.demography.tj; f. 2003 as Institute of Demography, present name and status 2011; attached to Acad. of Sciences of the Republic of Tajikistan; population, fertility, mortality, family issues, internal and external migration processes, policy making; library of 100 vols; Dir Prof. BOBOEV OLIMJON BOBOEVICH.

Institute of Humanities: Lenin 35, 736000 Khorog; tel. (352) 226755; f. 1991; attached to Acad. of Sciences of the Republic of Tajikistan; Dir SHODIKHON YUSUFBEKOV.

Institute of Oriental Studies and Written Heritage: Kiroka 35, 734025 Dushanbe; tel. (372) 272336; e-mail ogonazar@ac.tajik .net; f. 1958; attached to Acad. of Sciences of the Republic of Tajikistan.

TECHNOLOGY

Nuclear and Radiation Safety Agency: 17A Khamza Khakimzoda St, 734003 Dushanbe; tel. (372) 2247797; fax (372) 2245578; e-mail info@nrsa.tj; internet www.nrsa.tj; f. 2003; attached to Acad. of Sciences of the Republic of Tajikistan; Dir ULMAS MIRSAIDOV.

S. U. Umarov Physical-Technical Institute of Academy of Sciences of Rebublic of Tajikistan: Ul. Aini 299/1, 734063 Dushanbe; tel. (37) 2258092; fax (37) 2257914; e-mail muminov@phti.tj; internet www.phti .tj; f. 1964; attached to Acad. of Sciences of the Republic of Tajikistan; theoretical and mathematical physics (classical and quantum statistics, field theory, non-linear science); materials science (crystal physics, polymer science); nanoscience and nanotechnology; lasers and infrared spectroscopy; cryophysics; mathematical modelling of climate and climate change; application of nuclear physics methods; instrumentation and detectors; radiation safety and ecology; renewable energy sources; Dir Dr KHIKMAT KH. MUMINOV; Vice-Dir Dr ALIMAHMAD KHOLOV.

Libraries and Archives

Dushanbe

Central Scientific Library of the Academy of Sciences of the Republic of Tajikistan: Pr. Rudaki 33, 734025 Dushanbe; tel. (372) 224224; f. 1933; 1.5m. vols; Dir Dr A. A. ASLITDINOVA.

Firdavsi Tajik National Library: Pr. Rudaki 36, 734025 Dushanbe; tel. (372) 274726; 3m. vols; Dir SH. TOSHEW.

State Patent and Technical Library of Republic of Tajikistan: Ul. Aini 14A, 734042 Dushanbe; tel. (372) 275877; fax (372) 217154; f. 1965; 148m. vols (incl. 14m. patents); Dir BOBOJON BOYZODA.

Tajik State University Library: Pr. Rudaki 17, 734016 Dushanbe; tel. (372)

233981; f. 1948; 1m. vols; Dir R. YARBABAYEV; publ. *Vestnik* (1 a year).

Museum

Dushanbe

Tajik State Historical Museum: Ul. Aini 31, 734012 Dushanbe; tel. (372) 231544; history, culture, art; library of 14,000 vols; Dir M. MAKHMUDOV.

Universities

AVICENNA TAJIK STATE MEDICAL UNIVERSITY

139 Rudaki Ave, 734003 Dushanbe

Telephone: (372) 241253
Fax: (372) 243687
E-mail: info@tajmedun.tj
Internet: www.tajmedun.tj

Founded 1939 as Tajik Medical Institute, fmrly Tajik Abu-Ali Ibn-Cina State Medical Institute, present name 2009
State control
Languages of instruction: Tajik, Russian, English
Academic year: September to July

Rector: Prof. UBAIDULLO KURBANOV

Library of 515,035 vols
Number of teachers: 855
Number of students: 6,222

DEANS

Dentistry Faculty: SAID SHARIPOV
Medical Faculty: MUHIDDIN TABAROV
Pharmaceutical Faculty: ERAHMAD KHOLOV
Public Health Faculty: SHAROFIDDIN MATINOV

BOBOJON GAFUROV KHUJAND STATE UNIVERSITY

B. Mavlonbekova 1, 735700 Khujand

Telephone: (342) 265273
Fax: (342) 265137
E-mail: hgu-rector@khujandi.com
Internet: www.hgu.tj

Founded 1932
State control
Language of instruction: English, Russian, Tajik, Uzbek

Rector: VAHOB NABIEV

Library of 500,000 vols
Number of teachers: 465
Number of students: 10,600

DEANS

Art: G. JURAYEV
Cybernetics and World Economics: A., ABDULLOYEV
Drawing and Graphics: S. OLOV
Eastern Languages (Arabic and Persian): U. GAFFOROVA
Economics: A., ABDULLOYEV
Finance and Marketing: A. MAJIDOV
Foreign Languages: M. AZIMOVA
History: U. GAFFOROV
Law: IKROM KASIMOV
Mathematics: A. KASHIDOV
Natural Sciences: S. KARIMOV
Pedagogy: S. SHAROPOV
Physics and Technology: S. YAKUBOV
Russian and Literature: A. AZIZOV
Tajik Philology: N. F. FAIZULLAYEV
Uzbek Language: I. MAVLONBERDIYEV

CENTRAL INSTITUTE OF ADVANCED QUALIFICATION OF TEACHERS

Chechova 13, 734013 Dushanbe
Telephone: (372) 215457
Fax: (372) 271627
E-mail: ciftmail@tajnet.com
Founded 1935
State control
Rector: ABUNAZAR A. SOIBOV
Vice-Rector: ABDUHALIM GAFFAROV
Faculties of economics, educational administration, foreign languages education, pedagogy, psychology, science education and teacher training
Number of students: 2,000

FISCAL—LEGAL INSTITUTE

Drujby Narodov 96, 734013 Dushanbe
Telephone: (3772) 215948
Fax: (3772) 217459
State control
Rector: D. G. GULMIRZOYEV
Faculties of economics and law.

HIGHER SCHOOL OF THE MINISTRY OF THE INTERIOR

Vose 123, 734025 Dushanbe
Telephone: (372) 270607
Fax: (372) 217221
State Control
Faculties of history, law.

INSTITUTE OF ENTREPRENEURSHIP AND SERVICE OF TAJIKISTAN

Borbad Ave 48/5, 734055 Dushanbe
Telephone: (372) 348800
Fax: (372) 348802
E-mail: dsx_ips@mail.ru
Internet: www.dsx.tj
Founded 1991
State control
Languages of instruction: Russian, Tajik
Academic year: September to June
Rector: Prof. Dr DILOVAR QODIROV
Deputy Rector for Education: BAHRIDDIN B. JABBOROV
Deputy Rector for Science and Int. Relations: Prof. Dr SAID A. AHMADOV
Deputy Rector for Teaching: SHERMAHMAD B. JONMAMMADOV
Librarian: JAMILA PULODOVNA KHOLOVA
Library of 34,877 vols
Number of teachers: 170
Number of students: 3,250
Publications: *Payom* (1 a year), *Sohibkor* (12 a year)

DEANS

Accounting and Management: IZATULLO NASIRDINOV
Entrepreneurship and Management: ZOIRJON RAHMONOV
Financial Services: ISLOMBEK KHORKASHEV
Information Services and Marketing: ABDURAHIM ISMOILOV
Tourism and Custom's Services: FAIZIDDIN QODIROV

KHOROG INSTITUTE OF SOCIAL SCIENCES

Khorog
Telephone and fax (352) 225886
E-mail: jangibekov@land.ru
State control
Languages of instruction: English, Russian
Academic year: September to June
Rector: SH. YUSUFBEKOV

Number of teachers: 280
Number of students: 5,005

KHOROG STATE UNIVERSITY

736000 Khorog
Telephone: (342) 202218
Fax: (342) 204399
Founded 1992
State control
Rector: IMOMYORBEK QALANDARBEKOV
Faculties of economics, history, mathematics, natural sciences and philology.

KULYAB STATE UNIVERSITY

Safarov 26, 735360 Kulyab
Telephone: (332) 223507
E-mail: kgu@mail.tj
State control
Faculties of economics, history, mathematics, pedagogy, philology and physics.

MODERN HUMANITARIAN UNIVERSITY

Microraion 17, 735700 Khujand
Telephone: (342) 221958
Fax: (342) 261991
Founded 1998
State control
Language of instruction: Russian
Rector: M. I. BAKIYEV
Number of teachers: 36
Number of students: 380

DEANS

Faculty of Computer Science: U. V. SIT
Faculty of Languages: SH. D. KHODJAYEV
Faculty of Law: N. T. RAKHIMOV
Faculty of Management: G. A. USUPOVA

REPUBLICAN INSTITUTE OF ADVANCED TEACHERS' STUDIES

Chehova 13, 734013 Dushanbe
Telephone: (372) 216467
State control.

RUSSIAN-TAJIK SLAVONIC UNIVERSITY

M. Tursunzade 30, 734032 Dushanbe
Telephone: (372) 223550
Fax: (372) 210579
Internet: www.rtsu-slavist.tj
Founded 1996
State control
Faculties of economics, history, international relations, law and philology
Rector: Prof. MAHMADUSUF S. IMOMOV
Library of 42,208 vols.

TAJIK AGRARIAN UNIVERSITY NAMED AFTER SHIRINSHO SHOTEMUR

Pr. Rudaki 146, 734003 Dushanbe
Telephone and fax (372) 247207
E-mail: rectortau31@mail.ru
Internet: www.tajagroun.tj
Founded 1931
State control
Languages of instruction: Tajik, Russian
Academic year: September to June
Rector: Dr SATTORI IZZATULLO
Pro-Rector for Cultural Upbringing: Doc. HASANOV NAHTULLO RAHMATOVICH
Pro-Rector for Economy: KAMOLJON MAHMUDOV
Pro-Rector for Education: Prof. SALIMOV AMONULLO FAIZULLOEVICH

Pro-Rector for Int. Relations: KODIROV TURA ABDULLOEVICH
Pro-Rector for Science: Prof. Dr SARDOROV MAHMADIYOR NAIMOVICH
Head of Educational Dept: MAKSATULLO ISMOILOV
Dir of Library: ODINA DAVLATOV
Library of 356,434 vols, 63 periodicals
Number of teachers: 536
Number of students: 8,121
Publication: *Kishovarz* (Peasant)

DEANS

Faculty of Accounting and Finance: Prof. Dr SAMANDAROV ISKANDAR HUSEINOVICH
Faculty of Agrobusiness: Prof. Dr NOROV MASTIBEK SAMADOVICH
Faculty of Agronomy: HAYDAROV ZIKRIYOKHON YOKUBOVICH
Faculty of Animal Science: KOSIMOV RAJABEK BOBORAJABOVICH
Faculty of Economy: BAEVA NODIRA KHOLMURADOVNA
Faculty of Horticulture and Agricultural Biotechnology: Prof. Dr KARIMOV MUZAFFAR KARIMOVICH
Faculty of Hydromeliorative: ABDUGAFFOR AKRAMOV
Faculty of Mechanization of Agriculture: AHMADOV BAHROM RAJABOVICH
Faculty of Veterinary Medicine: Prof. Dr HABIBOV ABDUJALIL KHALILOVICH

TAJIK INSTITUTE OF MANAGEMENT

Kairakkum
Telephone: (344) 322485
State control
Rector: YU. MADJIDOV
Faculties of management and marketing.

TAJIK ISLAMIC UNIVERSITY

Shodmoni 58, 734001 Dushanbe
Telephone: (372) 249261
State control
Rector: ABDUJALOL ALIZODA
Faculties of general studies, Islamic law and religious studies.

TAJIK OPEN UNIVERSITY

Rudaki 108, 735500 Penjikent
Telephone: (347) 555309
Fax: (347) 554050
E-mail: tou@pnjk.tajik.net
Founded 1991
State control
Languages of instruction: Russian, Tajik
Divs of computing and programming, law and management
Prin.: AHMADJON HOTAMOV
Number of teachers: 138 (full-time)
Number of students: 413

TAJIK STATE INSTITUTE OF FINE ARTS

Ul. Borbada 73A, 734032 Dushanbe
Telephone: (372) 314545
E-mail: tgii@tajnet.com
Founded 1967
Rector: Prof. TALABKHUJA SATTOROV
Faculties of cultural science, performing arts, library science and information, musical-pedagogical studies and theatre
Library of 70,000 vols
Number of students: 1,500

TAJIK STATE INSTITUTE OF LANGUAGES

F. Muhammadiyeva 13, 734064 Dushanbe
Telephone: (372) 329529
Fax: (372) 329515
E-mail: mabdullaeva@yandex.ru
Founded 1980
State control
Languages of instruction: Tajik, Russian
Rector: MAVLUDA ABDULLAYEVA
Vice-Rector: KHURSHED ZIYOYEV
Library of 113,000 vols
Number of teachers: 65
Number of students: 763

DEANS

Faculty of Foreign Languages: KHALIDA ASTANOVA
Faculty of Philology: KAHHOR AVAZOV

TAJIK STATE NATIONAL UNIVERSITY

Pr. Rudaki 17, 734025 Dushanbe
Telephone: (372) 217711
Fax: (372) 214884
E-mail: tgnu@mail.ru
Internet: www.tgnu.tarena.tj
Founded 1948, present status 1997
State control
Languages of instruction: Tajik, Russian
Academic year: September to July
Rector: Prof. KH. S. SAFIEV
Vice-Rector for Educational Affairs: Prof. D. KH. SAFAROV
Vice-Rector for Int. Relations: N. N. JUMAEV
Vice-Rector for Scientific Affairs: A. A. AMIN-JANOV
Librarian: R. I. YARBABAEV
Number of teachers: 1,228
Number of students: 13,060
Publications: *Guli murod* (Government and Law, 4 a year), *Science* (1 a year), *Vestnik* (4 a year)

DEANS

Faculty of Accounting: D. U. UROKOV
Faculty of Biology: Dr M. GIYOSOV
Faculty of Chemistry: L. KUDRATOVA
Faculty of Economics and Management: Prof. T. B. GANIEV
Faculty of Finance and Credit: SH. D. DUSTBOEV
Faculty of History: Prof. N. M. MIRZOEV
Faculty of Journalism and Translation Studies: Prof. A. SAIDULLOEV (acting)
Faculty of Law: M. A. MAKHMUDOV
Faculty of Mechanics and Mathematics: Dr R. M. MUSTAFOKULOV
Faculty of Mountain Geology: M. M. PHOZI-LOV

Faculty of Oriental Languages: S. SH. SHUK-ROEVA
Faculty of Philosophy: Prof. A. MUKHABATOV (acting)
Faculty of Physics: K. K. KOMILOV
Faculty of Tajik Philology: M. S. IMOMOV

TAJIK STATE PEDAGOGICAL UNIVERSITY NAMED AFTER S. AINI

Pr. Rudaki 121, 734001 Dushanbe
Telephone: (37) 2248993
Fax: (37) 2241383
E-mail: info@tgpu.tj
Internet: www.tgpu.tj
Founded 1931
State control
Faculties of economics and management, finance and accountancy, history, law, mechanics and mathematics, pedagogics, philology
Rector: NURIDDIN ABDUJABBOR RAHMONOV

TAJIK STATE UNIVERSITY OF COMMERCE

Dehoti 1/2, 734055 Dushanbe
Telephone: (372) 348546
Fax: (372) 348394
E-mail: kaa77@tajik.net
Internet: www.tguk.tj
Founded 1991
State control
Languages of instruction: Russian, Tajik
Academic year: September to June
Rector: MUMIN SHARIPOV
Vice-Rector for Academic Affairs: TOLIBOV KOBIL KOSIMOVICH
Vice-Rector for Int. Affairs: ZARRINA HALI-MOVNA KADIROVA
Library of 107,000 vols
Number of teachers: 168
Number of students: 2,380

DEANS

Faculty of Customs: KHAMID MADJIDOV
Faculty of Distance Education: MUKHIDDIN KHOMIDOV
Faculty of Economics and Management: SAFIULLO HABIBOV
Faculty of World Economics and Financing: ZUYORATSHO AKOBIROV

TAJIK STATE UNIVERSITY OF LAW, BUSINESS AND POLITICS

17 micro region, Bldg 1, Sugd, 735700 Khujand
Telephone and fax (342) 223811
E-mail: tsulbp-dia@rambler.ru
Internet: www.tsulbp.tj

State control
Rector: H. R. PULATOV
Faculties of business and management, computer technology and accounting, finance, innovation and commercial technology, law, political science and int. relations.

TAJIK TECHNICAL UNIVERSITY NAMED AFTER ACADEMICIAN M. OSIMI

Pr. Acad Rajabovs 10, 734042 Dushanbe
Telephone: (372) 213511
Fax: (372) 217135
E-mail: ttu@ttu.tj
Internet: www.ttu.tj
Founded 1956
State control
Languages of instruction: Tajik, Russian
Number of teachers: 530
Number of students: 6,000
Rector: ABDURASULOV ANVAR

DEANS

Business Engineering: S. KAMOLIDDINOV
Chemical Technology and Metallurgy: A. SHARIFOV
Construction and Architecture: A. FAZILOV
Energy Engineering: R. JALILOV
Mechanical Technology: S. ZULFANOV
Transport and Road Engineering: A. TURSU-NOV

TECHNOLOGICAL UNIVERSITY OF TAJIKISTAN

N. Narabayev 63/3, 734061 Dushanbe
Telephone: (372) 347987
Fax: (372) 347988
E-mail: rektorat@tat.tajik.net
Founded 1992
State control
Languages of instruction: Tajik, Russian, English
Academic year: September to June
Rector: AMIR H. KATAYEV
Vice-Rector: NURALI N. SHOYEV
Library of 70,000 vols
Number of teachers: 158
Number of students: 1,050
Publications: *Collection of Scientific Works* (2 a year), *Herald of Ecology* (12 a year)

DEANS

Faculty of Industrial Informatics: MIRZO YUSUPOV
Faculty of International Studies: NASRULLO HOJAYOROV
Faculty of Textile Technology and Mechanical Engineering: VALIJON M. MIRAKILOV

TANZANIA

The Higher Education System

Higher education institutions predate the formation of the United Republic of Tanzania (by a merger of the independent states of Tanganyika and Zanzibar) in 1964, with the oldest being St Augustine University of Tanzania (formerly Nyegezi Social Training Centre), which was founded in 1960. In 2008 there were 64,664 students enrolled in 71 public institutions of higher education (which comprised 34 teacher-training colleges, 16 technical colleges, eight full universities, three constituent universities and 10 other higher institutions), with a further 17,865 students enrolled at 51 private institutions (which comprised 40 teacher-training colleges and 11 universities). Higher education is administered by the Ministry of Education and Vocational Training. Quality assurance within university-level education is overseen by the Tanzania Commission for Universities (formerly the Higher Education Accreditation Council; current name adopted in 2005). The regulatory authority for non-university higher education institutions is the National Council for Technical Education. A 10-stage Tanzanian Qualifications Framework was under development at 2011, and was expected to include the introduction of a credit-based degree system.

Students are required to gain three passes in the Advanced Certificate of Secondary Education and five passes at Certificate of Secondary Education level in order to gain admission to higher education. Examinations are administered by the National Examinations Council of Tanzania. Undergraduate Certificate and Diploma courses are available in a number of study areas and last between one and two years. Undergraduate Bachelors degrees usually last three years, although programmes in mainly professional fields of study last longer, such as engineering, nursing, pharmacy (four years) and medicine (five years). Following the award of the Bachelors, graduates may take the one-year Postgraduate Diploma or the Masters degree, which lasts one to three years and requires submission of a thesis. The highest university degree is the Doctor of Philosophy (PhD), which requires a minimum of two years' research, culminating with the submission of a thesis.

The National Council for Technical Education was established in 1997 to create a national system of post-secondary, non-university education. Post-secondary technical and vocational education is organized within the Framework of Technical and Vocational Education and Training Qualifications (also known as the National Technical Awards Framework), and qualifications include the Technician Certificate, the Diploma and the Higher Diploma. There are also a number of institutions offering semi-professional training, in fields such as accountancy, agricultural studies and nursing; such institutions are administered by the relevant government ministry.

Regulatory Bodies

GOVERNMENT

Ministry of Education and Vocational Training: POB 9121, Dar es Salaam; tel. (22) 2120403; fax (22) 2113271; e-mail psmoevt@moe.go.tz; internet www.moe.go.tz; Minister Prof. JUMANNE ABDALLAH MAGHEMBE; Permanent Sec. HAMISI O. DIHENGA.

Ministry of Information, Culture and Sports: Dar es Salaam; internet www.hum.go.tz; Minister GEORGE MKUCHIKA.

Learned Societies

GENERAL

Tanzania Society: POB 511, Dar es Salaam; f. 1936; a non-profit society catering for the geographical, ethnological, historical, and general scientific interests of Tanzania; 1,200 mems; publ. *Tanzania Notes and Records* (1 a year).

UNESCO Dar es Salaam Cluster Office: POB 31473, Dar es Salaam; Plot 127c, Mafinga St (off Kinondoni Rd), Dar es Salaam; tel. (22) 2666623; fax (22) 2666927; e-mail dar-es-salaam@unesco.org; designated Cluster Office for Comoros, Madagascar, Mauritius, Seychelles and Tanzania; library of 2,500 vols; Dir and Rep. VIBEKE JENSEN.

AGRICULTURE, FISHERIES AND VETERINARY SCIENCE

Tanzania Veterinary Association: POB 3174, Chuo Kikuu Morogoro; tel. (23) 2604979; fax (23) 2604647; e-mail deanfvm@suanet.ac.tz; f. 1968; 350 mems; Chair. Prof. D. M. KAMBARAGE; publs *Annual Proceedings of the Tanzania Veterinary Association Sci-*entific Conferences, *Tanzania Veterinary Journal.*

BIBLIOGRAPHY, LIBRARY SCIENCE AND MUSEOLOGY

Tanzania Library Association: POB 33433, Dar es Salaam; tel. and fax (22) 2775411; e-mail tla_tanzania@yahoo.com; internet www.tlatz.org; f. 1965 as a br. of the East African Library Association, reorganized 1973 as an independent body; 200 mems; Chair. Dr ALLI MCHARAZO; Sec. P. MUNUBHI; publ. *Matukio* (Newsletter, irregular).

ECONOMICS, LAW AND POLITICS

East Africa Law Society: POB 6240, Arusha; 64 Haile Selassie Rd, Arusha; tel. (27) 2503135; fax (27) 2508707; e-mail eals@habari.co.tz; f. 1996; 5,000 mems; CEO DONALD DEYA; publs *The East African Human Rights Report* (1 a year), *The East African Lawyer* (4 a year).

HISTORY, GEOGRAPHY AND ARCHAEOLOGY

Historical Association of Tanzania: c/o Department of History, University of Dar es Salaam, POB 35050, Dar es Salaam; tel. (22) 2410397; f. 1966; 2,000 mems; Chair. Prof. K. I. TAMBILA; Sec. Dr E. P. A. N. MIHANJO; publ. *Tanzania Zamani.*

LANGUAGE AND LITERATURE

Alliance Française: Ali Hassan Mwinyi Rd (behind Las Vegas Casino), Upanga, POB 2566, Dar es Salaam; tel. (22) 2111331; fax (22) 2666576; offers courses and exams in French language and culture and promotes cultural exchange with France; attached teaching centre in Arusha.

British Council: Samora Ave/Ohio St, POB 9100, Dar es Salaam; tel. (22) 2116574; fax (22) 2112699; e-mail info@britishcouncil.or.tz; internet www.britishcouncil.org/tanzania; teaching centre; offers courses and exams in English language and British culture and promotes cultural exchange with the UK; Dir TOM COWIN.

Research Institutes

GENERAL

Tanzania Commission for Science and Technology: POB 4302, Dar es Salaam; tel. (22) 2700745; fax (22) 2775313; e-mail costech@costech.or.tz; internet www.costech.or.tz; f. 1986; 73 mems; library of 8,000 vols; Dir-Gen. Dr HASSAN MSHINDA; publ. *Tanzania Science and Technology Newsletter* (4 a year).

AGRICULTURE, FISHERIES AND VETERINARY SCIENCE

Agricultural Research Institute (Mlingano): ARI Mlingano, POB 5088, Tanga; tel. (27) 2647647; fax (27) 2642577; e-mail mlingano@iwayafrica.com; internet www.kilimo.go.tz/research-training/mlingano.htm; f. 1934; research on cultivation of sisal and other crops, soils, resourcing of efficient farming methods, horticulture; germplasm collection of tropical and subtropical fruits, spices and essential oils; Dir Dr A. NYAKI.

Forestry and Beekeeping Division: c/o Ministry of Natural Resources and Tourism, POB 426, Dar es Salaam; tel. (22) 2864249; e-mail dfob@mnrt.go.tz; internet www.nfp.co.tz; forest surveying, mapping, industrial development, economics, management and education as part of the National Forest Policy and National Beekeeping Policy (both adopted 1998); library of 2,500 vols; Dir Dr FELICIAN KILAHAMA.

Mikocheni Agricultural Research Institute: POB 6226, Kinondoni District, Dar es Salaam; tel. (22) 2700552; fax (22) 2775549; e-mail mari@mari.or.tz; integrated pest management, with emphasis on biological control of coconut pests; Dir Dr ALOIS KULLAYA.

National Livestock Research Institute: POB 202, Mpwapwa, Dodoma; tel. and fax (26) 2320853; f. 1905; research in dairy science, breeding and nutrition of livestock, Mpwapwa cattle and Malya goats, pastural agronomy and multidisciplinary research; Nat. Livestock Research Institute; research information documentation and dissemination; library of 4,000 vols, 40 periodicals; Dir Dr REGINALD P. MBWILE; publ. *Progressive Stockman* (4 a year).

Tanzania Forestry Research Institute: Silviculture Research Centre, POB 95, Lushoto; f. 1951; library of 3,000 vols; Officer-in-Charge T. H. MSANGI; publs *TAFORI Newsletter, Tanzania Silviculture Research Notes* (4 a year), *Technical Notes*.

Tanzania Wildlife Research Institute: POB 661, Arusha; tel. (27) 2509871; fax (27) 2548240; e-mail info@tawiri.org; internet www.tawiri.org; research into wildlife, with the objective of providing scientific information and advice to the Govt of Tanzania and local wildlife management authorities on the sustainable conservation of wildlife; Chair Prof. PETER MSOLLA.

Tropical Pesticides Research Institute: POB 3024, Arusha; tel. (27) 2548813; fax (27) 2548217; e-mail tpri@habari.co.tz; internet www.habari.co.tz/tpri; f. 1962; research into all aspects of pesticide application and behaviour; library of 5,000 vols; Dir Dr GRATIAN BAMWENDA.

HISTORY, GEOGRAPHY AND ARCHAEOLOGY

Geological Survey of Tanzania: c/o Min. of Energy and Minerals, POB 903, Dodoma; tel. (26) 2324943; e-mail madini-do@gst.go.tz; internet www.gst.go.tz; f. 1925; attached to Min. of Energy and Minerals; regional mapping, mineral exploration and assessment; supporting laboratory facilities; reprints, bulletins, memoirs, books and maps; library of 4,000 books; Chief Exec., Geological Survey of Tanzania Prof. A. H. MRUMA (acting); Librarian/Information Officer E. LUHOKO; publs *Bulletins, Records of the Geological Survey of Tanzania*.

LANGUAGE AND LITERATURE

Eastern African Centre for Research on Oral Traditions and African National Languages (EACROTANAL): POB 600, Zanzibar; f. 1979 as a regional and intergovernmental organization to encourage research and develop means of collection, analysis, conservation and diffusion of oral traditions and promotion of national languages; provides short-term training courses on these subjects; library of 3,000 vols (incl. 148 old Arabic MSS from Zanzibar); one of 3 African regional centres, set up by Burundi, Comoros, Ethiopia, Madagascar, Mauritius, Mozambique, Somalia, Sudan, Tanzania; Exec. Dir KHATIB MAKAME OMAR (acting); publs annotated bibliography of the Arabic MSS (every 2 years), *Paukwa Pakawa* (traditional tales, 1 a year).

Institute of Kiswahili Research: POB 35110, Dar es Salaam; tel. (22) 2410757; e-mail tuki@ikr.udsm.ac.tz; internet www .udsm.ac.tz/ikr/; f. 1970; initiates and conducts fundamental research in all aspects of Kiswahili language; cooperates with local

public authorities and int. organizations; promotes the standardization of orthography and the development of language generally; preparing new standard dictionary, technical dictionaries, grammars, monographs on oral literature; library of 3,000 vols; Dir Prof. M. M. MULOKOZI; publs *Kiswahili* (1 a year), *Mulika* (1 a year).

MEDICINE

National Institute for Medical Research (NIMR): Headquarters, Ocean Rd, POB 9653, Dar es Salaam; tel. (22) 2121400; fax (22) 2121360; e-mail headquarters@nimr.or .tz; internet www.nimr.or.tz; f. 1949 at Muheza as the Malaria Unit; investigation into human vector-borne diseases, especially malaria, bancroftian filariasis, and onchocerciasis; Dir Dr ANDREW KITUA.

National Institute for Medical Research, Mwanza Centre: POB 1462, Mwanza; tel. (28) 250189; f. 1949; investigations into various tropical diseases with emphasis on bilharziasis, and other soil-transmitted helminths, bacterial diseases, sanitation and water, diarrhoeal diseases, sexually transmitted diseases, HIV/AIDS; library of 2,300 vols; Dir Dr R. M. GABONE; publs *NIMR Bulletin, Proceedings of the Annual NIMR Joint Scientific Conference*.

Libraries and Archives
Dar es Salaam

Tanzania Information Services Department: POB 9142, Dar es Salaam; tel. (22) 2122771; fax (22) 2113814; e-mail maelezo@ pmo.go.tz; reference books on Tanzania, journalism, photography, social sciences, geography and history; newspapers and periodicals.

Tanzania Library Services Board: Bibi Titi Mohamed Rd, POB 9283, Dar es Salaam; tel. (22) 2150048; fax (22) 2151100; e-mail tlsb@africaonline.co.tz; internet www.tlsb.or .tz; f. 1964; 16 brs; Dir-Gen. ELIEZER A. MWINYIMVUA.

Tanzania National Archives: Vijibweni St, POB 2006, Dar es Salaam; tel. (22) 2151279; fax (22) 2150634; e-mail dram@ intafrica.com; internet www.tanzania.go.tz/ psrp/record1.html; f. 1963; German and British colonial archives, post-independence archives; Dir J. M. KARUGILA; publ. *Guide to Archives*.

University of Dar es Salaam Library: POB 35092, Dar es Salaam; tel. and fax (22) 2410241; e-mail director@libis.udsm.ac.tz; internet www.udsm.ac.tz/library; f. 1961; legal deposit library; 600,000 vols, 280 journals, spec. collns: E Africana Colln, UN Colln, Law Colln; 8,000 periodicals; Dir JANGAWE MSUYA.

Morogoro

Sokoine National Agricultural Library: POB 3022, Morogoro; tel. (23) 2604639; fax (23) 2604388; e-mail library@suanet.ac.tz; internet www.suanet.ac.tz; f. 1964 as library for the College of Agriculture, library for Faculty of Agriculture, Forestry and Veterinary Medicine of the Univ. of Dar es Salaam 1972, Sokoine Univ. of Agriculture Library 1984, present name and status 1991; attached to Sokoine Univ. of Agriculture; learning, teaching, research, consultancy and outreach services; 75,000 vols, 100 periodicals; Library Dir Dr DORIS. S. MATOVELO.

Mwanza

Ladha Meghji Indian Public Library: POB 70, Mwanza; tel. (28) 2500482; fax (28)

2500222; e-mail desaitz@yahoo.com; f. 1935; 11,130 vols; runs English, French, oriental language and computer classes; Librarian RAMAN DESAI.

Zanzibar

Agricultural Department Library: POB 159, Zanzibar; 1,100 vols, 50 periodicals.

Museum Research Library: c/o Dept of Antiquities, Archives and Museum, Zanzibar National Archives, POB 116, Zanzibar; tel. (22) 30342; e-mail dama@zitec.org; f. 1930; reference library; 15,000 vols and 1,000 periodicals; Head of the Library SULEIMAN SEIF.

Zanzibar National Archives: POB 116, Zanzibar; tel. and fax (22) 35241; e-mail dama@zitec.org; f. 1956; history and administration; 3,500 vols; Archivist HAMAD OMAR.

Museums and Art Galleries
Dar es Salaam

National Museums of Tanzania: POB 511, Dar es Salaam; tel. (22) 2122030; internet www.museum.or.tz; f. 1937 as King George V Memorial Museum, name changed 1963; ethnography, palaeoanthropology, history and marine biology; houses the *Zinjanthropus* skull and other material from Olduvai Gorge and other Palaeolithic sites; also houses reference library; Dir-Gen. Dr N. A. KAYOMBO.

Branch Museums:

Arusha Declaration Museum: POB 7423, Arusha; tel. (27) 2507800; e-mail adm-arusha@habari.co.tz; internet www .arushamuseum.ac.tz; f. 1977; preservation and exhibition of political, social and economic history; Curators CONSTANTINUS MISAGO NYAMABONDO, FABIAN LYIMO.

Arusha Natural History Museum: POB 2160, Arusha; tel. (27) 2507540; e-mail nnhm@habari.co.tz; internet www .museum.or.tz; Curator FELISTA MANGALU.

Village Museum: POB 511, Dar es Salaam; tel. (22) 2700437; e-mail villagemuseum@raha.com; f. 1967; traditional house styles and crafts; Curator JACKSON M. KIHIYO.

Zanzibar

Zanzibar Government Museum: POB 116, Zanzibar; tel. (24) 2230342; fax (24) 2235241; e-mail dama@zitec.org; internet www.museum.com/jb/museum?id=24191; f. 1925; operates House of Wonders Museum at Forodhani (history and culture of Zanzibar and Swahili Coast civilization, f. 2001), Palace Museum at Mizingani (history of the Zanzibar sultans, f. 1994), Peace Memorial Museum at Mnazi Minoja (history, ethnography, natural history and archaeology of Zanzibar, f. 1925), Pemba Museum at Chake (history of Pemba Island, f. 2000); Dir H. H. OMAR.

Universities
HUBERT KARIUKI MEMORIAL UNIVERSITY

POB 65300, 322 Regent Estate, Dar es Salaam
Telephone: (22) 2700021
Fax: (22) 2775591
E-mail: secvc@hkmu.ac.tz
Internet: www.hkmu.ac.tz

Founded 1997; univ. status 2000
Language of instruction: English
Academic year: September to August
Vice-Chancellor: Prof. KETO E. MSHIGENI
Deputy Vice-Chancellor for Finance, Planning and Admin.: Prof. PASCHALIS RUGARABAMU
Dir of Postgraduate Studies and Research Institute: Prof. SYLVESTER L. B. KAJUNA
Dean of Students: Dr ALPHAGE LIWA
Sr Librarian: STANSLAUS NGADAYA

DEANS

Faculty of Medicine: Dr FELICIAN RUTACHUNZIBWA
Faculty of Nursing: Prof. PAULINE P. MELLA

PROFESSORS

LUTAHOIRE, S., Medicine
MELLA, P., Nursing
MSAMATI, B. C., Medicine
MWAIKAMBO, E., Medicine

INTERNATIONAL MEDICAL AND TECHNOLOGICAL UNIVERSITY

Mbeze Beach area, New Bagamoyo Rd, POB 77594, Dar es Salaam
Telephone: (22) 2647036
Fax: (22) 2647038
E-mail: imtu@costech.or.tz
Internet: www.imtu.edu
Founded 1995 by Vignan Educational Foundation (India) and Tanzanian Govt
Number of teachers: 23
Vice-Chancellor: Dr V. P. KIMATI
Deputy Vice-Chancellor for Academic Affairs: V. S. RAKESH
Dir of Finance: P. B. KUMAR
Dean of Students: Dr RENJU THOMAS.

MZUMBE UNIVERSITY
(Chuo Kikuu Mzumbe)

POB 1, Mzumbe, Morogoro
Telephone: (23) 2604380
Fax: (23) 2604382
E-mail: mu@mzumbe.ac.tz
Internet: www.mzumbe.ac.tz
Founded 1972 as Institute of Devt Management; present name and univ. status 2001
State control
Language of instruction: English
Academic year: October to June
Chancellor: Hon. Judge (retd) BARNABAS SAMATTA
Vice-Chancellor: Prof. JOSEPH ANDREW KUZILWA
Deputy Vice-Chancellor for Academic Affairs: Prof. MAGISHI NKWABI MGASA
Deputy Vice-Chancellor for Admin. and Finance: Prof. FAUSTIN KAMUZORA
Dir of Information and Communications Technology: ALMAS MAGUYE
Dir of MU Mbeya campus: ROSS KINEMO
Dir of Research and Postgraduate Studies: Dr AGGREY KIHOMBO
Registrar: Prof. HAMISI I. MAHIGI
Dir of Library and Technical Services: MATILDA KUZILWA
Library of 50,000 books, 900 current periodicals
Number of teachers: 270
Number of students: 3,551
Publications: *Economics and Development Papers*, *Journal of Public Policy and Administration*, *Uongozi Journal of Management and Development Dynamics* (4 a year)

DEANS

Dar es Salaam Business School: Dr ANDREW MBWAMBO

Faculty of Commerce: Dr JOSEPH A. KIMEME
Faculty of Law: ELEUTER G. MUSHI
Faculty of Public Administration and Management: Prof. JOSEPHAT ITIKA
Faculty of Science and Technology: Prof. Dr PHILBERT NDUNGURU
Faculty of Social Science: Prof. Dr EULALIA I. TEMBA

ATTACHED RESEARCH INSTITUTES

Institute of Continuing Studies: POB, Mzumbe; tel. (23) 2604380; fax (23) 2604382; e-mail ics@mzumbe.ac.tz; Dir ALOYCE MAZIKU.
Institute of Development Studies: POB 83, Mzumbe; tel. (23) 2604380; fax (23) 2604382; e-mail ids@mzumbe.ac.tz; Dir Dr IDDI MAKOMBE.
Institute of Public Administration: POB 2, Mzumbe; tel. (23) 2604380; fax (23) 2604382; e-mail ipa@mzumbe.ac.tz; Dir Dr EMMANUEL MATIKU.

OPEN UNIVERSITY OF TANZANIA

Kawawa Rd, Kinondoni Municipality, POB 23409, Dar es Salaam
Telephone: (22) 2668992
Fax: (22) 2668759
E-mail: vc@out.ac.tz
Internet: www.out.ac.tz
Founded 1992
State control
Languages of instruction: English, Kiswahili
Academic year: January to December
Chancellor: Dr JOHN SAMWEL MALECELA
Vice-Chancellor: Prof. TOLLY S. A. MBWETTE
Deputy Vice-Chancellor for Academic Affairs: Prof. DONATUS A. KOMBA
Registrar: Prof. USWEGE M. MINGA
Librarian: A. S. SAMZUGI
Library of 5,000 vols
Number of teachers: 113 (33 full-time, 80 part-time)
Number of students: 12,945
Publication: *HURIA Journal*

PROFESSORS

AMAA, K. O., Business Management
KIWANGA, C. A., Science, Technology and Environmental Studies
KOMBA, D. A., Education
MASENGE, R. W. P., Science, Technology and Environmental Studies
MUKOYOGO, M. C., Law
TEMU, A. J., Arts and Social Sciences
23 regional centres and 69 study centres

ST AUGUSTINE UNIVERSITY OF TANZANIA

POB 307, Mwanza
Telephone: (28) 2552725
Fax: (28) 2550167
E-mail: saut@saut.ac.tz
Internet: www.saut.ac.tz
Founded 1960 as Nyegezi Social Training Centre; present status and name 1998
Private control (Catholic Church)
Language of instruction: English
Academic year: October to June
Vice-Chancellor: Prof. CHARLES KITIMA
Library of 15,000 vols, 30 periodicals
Number of teachers: 44
Number of students: 404

DEANS

Faculty of Business Administration: ILDEFONS CHONYA (acting)
Faculty of Humanities and Mass Communication: JOSEPH MLACHA (acting)

SOKOINE UNIVERSITY OF AGRICULTURE

POB 3000, Chuo Kikuu, Morogoro
Telephone: (23) 2603511
Fax: (23) 2604651
E-mail: sua@suanet.ac.tz
Internet: www.suanet.ac.tz
Founded 1984, previously a faculty of Univ. of Dar es Salaam
State control
Language of instruction: English
Academic year: September to June
Chancellor: AL NOOR KASSUM
Vice-Chancellor: Prof. G. C. MONELA
Deputy Vice-Chancellor for Academic Affairs: Prof. D. M. KAMBARAGE
Deputy Vice-Chancellor for Admin. and Finance: Prof. A. E. PEREKA
Dir, Solomon Mahlangu Campus: Assoc. Prof. N. D. URIO
Registrar: Assoc. Prof. H. O. DIHENGA
Librarian: D. S. MATOVELO
Library: see Libraries and Archives
Number of teachers: 452
Number of students: 3,619 (2,925 undergraduate, 694 postgraduate)

DEANS

Faculty of Agriculture: Prof. B. P. TIISEKWA
Faculty of Forestry and Nature Conservation: Prof. P. R. GILLAH
Faculty of Science: Dr Y. C. MUZANILA
Faculty of Veterinary Medicine: Assoc. Prof. P. N. WAMBURA

PROFESSORS

ABELI, W., Forest Engineering
ASSEY, R., Veterinary Anatomy
BALTHAZARY, S., Physiology, Biochemistry, Pharmacology and Toxicology
BATAMUZI, E., Surgery and Theriogenology
BITEGEKO, S., Surgery and Theriogenology
CHAMSHAMA, S., Forest Biology
GWAKISA, P., Microbiology and Parasitology
HAMZA, K., Wood Utilization
ISHENGOMA, R., Wood Utilization
KAJEMBE, G., Forest Mensuration and Management
KAMBARAGE, D., Veterinary Medicine and Public Health
KASSUKU, A., Veterinary Microbiology and Parasitology
KAZWALA, R., Veterinary Medicine and Public Health
KESSY, B., Veterinary Surgery and Theriogenology
KIFARO, G., Animal Science
KILONZO, B., Veterinary Microbiology and Parasitology
KIMAMBO, A., Animal Science
KINABO, L., Veterinary Physiology, Biochemistry, Pharmacology and Toxicology
KURWIJILA, R., Animal Science
LASWAI, G., Animal Science
LASWAI, H., Food Science and Production
LEKULE, F., Animal Science
LULANDALA, L., Forest Biology
LWOGA, A., Crop Science and Production
MABAGALA, R., Crop Science and Production
MACHANG'U, R., Veterinary Microbiology and Parasitology
MADOFE, S., Forest Biology
MALIMBWI, R., Forest Mensuration
MALIONDO, S., Forest Biology
MASELLE, R., Veterinary Pathology
MATOVELO, J., Veterinary Pathology
MBASSA, G., Veterinary Anatomy
MDOE, N., Agricultural Economics and Agribusiness
MGASA, M., Veterinary Surgery and Theriogenology
MGONGO, F., Veterinary Surgery and Theriogenology
MISANGU, R., Crop Science and Production

MLAMBITI, M., Agricultural Economics and Agribusiness

MLANGWA, J., Veterinary Medicine and Public Health

MLOZI, M., Agricultural Education and Extension

MONELA, G., Forest Economics

MOSHA, R., Veterinary Physiology, Biochemistry, Pharmacology and Toxicology

MSANYA, B., Soil Science

MTAMBO, M., Veterinary Medicine and Public Health

MTENGA, L., Animal Science

MUHIKAMBELE, V., Animal Science

MUNISHI, P., Forest Biology

MUTAYOBA, B., Veterinary Physiology, Biochemistry, Pharmacology and Toxicology

NGOMUO, A., Veterinary Physiology, Biochemistry, Pharmacology and Toxicology

NYARUHUCHA, C., Food Science

PEREKA, A., Veterinary Physiology, Biochemistry, Pharmacology and Toxicology

REUBEN, S., Crop Science and Production

RUTATORA, D., Agricultural Education and Extension

SEMOKA, J., Soil Science

SEMUGURUKA, W., Veterinary Pathology

SENKONDO, E., Agricultural Economics and Agribusiness

SHAYO, N., Food Science and Production

SHEM, M., Animal Science

SIBUGA, K., Crop Science and Production

SILAYO, R., Veterinary Microbiology and Parasitology

TARIMO, A., Agricultural Engineering and Land Planning

TIISEKWA, B., Food Science and Production

ATTACHED CENTRES

Computer Centre: POB 3218, Chuo Kikuu, Morogoro; e-mail ccentre@suanet.ac.tz; Dir Prof. S. D. TUMBO.

Development Studies Institute: POB 3024, Chuo Kikuu, Morogoro; e-mail dsi@suanet.ac.tz; Dir Prof. A. Z. MATTEE.

Directorate of Research and Postgraduate Studies: POB 3151, Morogoro; tel. and fax (23) 2604388; e-mail drpgs@suanet.ac.tz; Dir Prof. J. A. MATOVELO.

Institute of Continuing Education: POB 3044, Morogoro; tel. (23) 2604549; fax (23) 2603718; e-mail ice@suanet.ac.tz; Dir Assoc. Prof. G. G. KIMBI.

SUA Centre for Sustainable Rural Development: POB 3035, Morogoro; tel. (23) 2604360; fax (23) 2604758; e-mail suajica@suanet.ac.tz; Dir Prof. D. F. RUTATORA.

SUA Pest Management Centre: POB 3110, Morogoro; tel. (23) 2604621; e-mail pestman@suanet.ac.tz; Dir Prof. R. H. MAKUNDI.

TUMAINI UNIVERSITY

POB 55, Usa River, Arusha

Telephone: (27) 2541144

Fax: (27) 2541146

E-mail: tu@kilinet.co.tz

Internet: www.tumainiuniversity.ac.tz

Founded 1996, present status 2001

Private control (Evangelical Lutheran Church in Tanzania)

Language of instruction: English

Vice-Chancellor: Prof. JOHN F. SHAO

Number of teachers: 400

Number of students: 9,000

Publication: *Tumaini Hill* (Newsletter, 4 a year).

CONSTITUENT COLLEGES

Iringa University College

POB 200, Iringa

Telephone: (26) 2720900

Fax: (26) 2720904

Founded 1993

Provost: NICOLAS BANGU

Deputy Provost for Academic Affairs: Rev. Dr RICHARD LUBAWA

DEANS

Faculty of Arts and Social Sciences: EGIDIO Y. CHAULA

Faculty of Business and Economics: EMMANUEL LUVANDA

Faculty of Law: THOMAS MWAHOMBELA

Faculty of Theology: PETER FUE

Kilimanjaro Christian Medical University College

POB 2240, Moshi

Telephone: (27) 2754377

Fax: (27) 2751351

E-mail: info@kcmuco.ac.tz

Internet: www.kcmuco.ac.tz

Founded 1997

Provost: EGBERT M. KESSI

Deputy Provost for Academic Affairs: Prof. NOEL SAM

DEANS

Faculty of Medicine: KIEN MTETA

Faculty of Nursing: MARCELINA H. MSUYA

Faculty of Rehabilitative Science: HAROLD G. SHANGALI

Makumira University College

POB 55, Usa River, Arusha

Telephone: (27) 2541034

Fax: (27) 2541030

E-mail: provost@makumira.ac.tz

Internet: www.makumira.ac.tz

Founded 1954

Provost: Rev. Prof. JOSEPH W. PARSALAW

Deputy Provost for Academic Affairs: Prof. ISMAEL R. MBISE

Dean of Students: ZAKARIA MATINDA

Dean of Students: Rev. Dr E. A. MUNGURE

DEANS

Faculty of Humanity and Social Sciences: APOLO A. MUGYENYI

Faculty of Law: DANIEL PALLANGYO

Faculty of Theology: Rev. HABAKUKI LWENDO

Sebastian Kolowa University College

POB 370, Lushoto

Telephone: (27) 2640114

Fax: (27) 2640107

E-mail: admin@sekuco.org

Internet: www.sekuco.org

Provost: Rev. Dr ANNETH MUNGA

DEANS

Faculty of Education: PAUL O. NWAOGU

Faculty of Law: MUTABAZI LUGAZIYA (acting)

Faculty of Science: NATHAN MUNYIAMBA (acting)

Stefano Moshi Memorial University College

POB 881, Moshi

Telephone: (27) 2757070

Fax: (27) 2757880

E-mail: masoka@kilinet.co.tz

Provost: ARNOLD TEMU (acting)

Deputy Provost for Academic Affairs: Prof. PETER CHONJO (acting)

DEANS

Faculty of Business and Management: ERNEST KASHESHI (acting)

Faculty of Education: ISMAIL NKYA (acting)

Faculty of Science and Technology: (vacant)

Tumaini University Dar es Salaam College

POB 77588, Lushoto

Telephone: (22) 2760335

Fax: (22) 2760432

E-mail: provost@tumainidsm.ac.tz

Internet: www.tumainidsm.ac.tz

DEANS

Faculty of Arts and Social Sciences: ROBERT MFUGALE

Faculty of Business Administration: GILLIARD LOTH

Faculty of Law: MASUMBUKO LAMWAI

UNIVERSITY OF BUKOBA

POB 1725, Bukoba

Telephone: (28) 2220691

Fax: (28) 2222341

E-mail: uobtz@yahoo.com

Internet: uobtz.tripod.com

Founded 1999

State control

Language of instruction: English

Academic year: October to June

Chancellor: C. G. KAHAMA

Vice-Chancellor: Prof. M. HODD

Deputy Vice-Chancellor: Prof. ISRAEL KATOKE

Registrar: SAMUEL MUTASA

Library of 1,000 vols

Number of teachers: 20

Number of students: 50

DEANS

Faculty of Commerce and Management: JOSEPH MWABUKI

Faculty of Social and Natural Science: CHRISTOPHER RWIZA (acting)

UNIVERSITY OF DAR ES SALAAM

POB 35091, Dar es Salaam

Telephone: (22) 2410500

Fax: (22) 2410078

E-mail: vc@admin.udsm.ac.tz

Internet: www.udsm.ac.tz

Founded 1961; univ. status 1970

Language of instruction: English

Academic year: October to June (two semesters)

Chancellor: Ambassador F. KAZAURA

Vice-Chancellor: Prof. RWEKAZA MUKANDALA

Deputy Vice-Chancellor for Academic Affairs: Prof. M. A. H. MABOKO

Deputy Vice-Chancellor for Admin.: Prof. Y. D. MGAYA

Dir for Postgraduate Studies: Prof. B. M. MWINYIWIWA

Dir for Research: Prof. J. V. TESHA

Library: see Libraries and Archives

Number of teachers: 1,172

Number of students: 19,650

Publication: *Research Bulletin* (2 a year)

DEANS

College of Arts and Social Sciences: B. B. MAPUNDA

College of Engineering Technology: J. H. Y. KATIMA

College of Natural and Applied Sciences: Prof. F. S. S. MAGINGO

Dar es Salaam University College of Education: Prof. S. B. MISANA

Mkwawa University College of Education: Prof. P. A. K. MUSHI

School of Education: Prof. E. P. BHALALUSESA

School of Informatics and Communication Technologies: Prof. J. R. IKINGURA
School of Journalism and Mass Communication: Dr B. KILLIAN
School of Law: P. J. KABUDI

PROFESSORS

CHAMBEGA, D., Electrical Power Engineering
CHAMI, F., History and Archaeology
FIMBO, G., Economic Law
GALABAWA, J., Educational Planning and Administration
ISHUMI, A., Educational, Management, Foundations and Lifelong Studies
JOHN, G., Energy Engineering
KIMAMBO, I., History and Archaeology
LUHANGA, M., Electrical and Computer Systems Engineering
MAGHIMBI, S., Sociology and Anthropology
MASANJA, V., Mathematics
MASSAMBA, D., Institute of Kiswahili Research
MBAGO, M., Statistics
MBUNDA, F., Educational Psychology and Curriculum Studies
MLAWA, H., Institute of Development Studies
MOSHA, H., Educational Management, Foundations and Learning
MPANGALA, G., Institute of Development Studies
MSAKI, P., Physics
MSAMBICHAKA, L., Economics
MTALO, F., Water Resources Engineering
MUHONGO, S., Geology
MUNISHI, G., Political Science and Public Administration
MUSHI, P., Adult Education and Extension
MUSHI, S., Political Science and Public Administration
MUTAHABA, G., Political Science and Public Administration
MUTAKYAHWA, M., Geology
NGANA, J., Institute of Resource Assessment
NGWARE, S., Institute of Development Studies
NJAU, E., Physics
NYICHOMBA, B., Design and Production Engineering
OMARI, I., Curriculum and Teaching
OSORO, E., Economic Development
PETER, C., Private Law
RUGUMAMU, S., Institute of Development Studies
RUGUMAMU, W., Geography
RUTASHOBYA, L., Marketing
SHISHIRA, E., Institute of Resource Assessment
SHIVJI, I., Chairs

ZANZIBAR UNIVERSITY

POB 2440, Zanzibar
Telephone: (77) 3901217
Fax: (77) 3901218
E-mail: info@zanvarsity.ac.tz
Internet: www.zanvarsity.ac.tz
Founded 1998

State control
Language of instruction: English
Vice-Chancellor: Prof. MUSTAFA A. A. ROSHASH (acting)
Library of 4,000 vols, 1,000 e-books
Number of teachers: 32
Number of students: 1,977

DEANS

Faculty of Arts and Social Sciences: MOHAMMED JIDDAWY
Faculty of Business Administration: AHMAD MAJID ALI
Faculty of Law and Shariah: SOWED JUMA MAYANJA

Colleges

College of African Wildlife Management, Mweka: POB 3031, Moshi; tel. (27) 2756451; fax (27) 2756414; e-mail mweka@mwekawildlife.org; internet www.mwekawildlife.org; f. 1963; professional and technical training, research and consultancy services in African wildlife management; qualifications awarded include certificate, diploma, advanced diploma and postgraduate diploma in wildlife management; library: 10,000 vols; 16 teachers; 150 students; Prin. DEO-GRATIAS M. GAMASSA.

College of Business Education: POB 1968, Dar es Salaam; tel. (22) 2150177; e-mail principalcbe@yahoo.com; f. 1965; 55 teachers; 1,300 students; two- and three-year diploma courses in business administration and metrology; certificate course in business administration; postgraduate course in business administration; Prin. S. M. HYERA.

Dar es Salaam Institute of Technology: Private Bag 2958, Dar es Salaam; tel. (22) 2150174; fax (22) 2152504; e-mail principaldit@intafrica.com; internet www.dit.ac.tz; f. 1957; civil, mechanical, electrical, electronics and telecommunications engineering courses; science and laboratory technology and computing studies courses; library: 27,000 vols; 180 teachers; 3,600 students (1,200 full-time, 2,400 part-time); Prin. Prof. J. W. A. KONDORO.

Eastern and Southern African Management Institute: POB 3030, Arusha; tel. (27) 2508384; fax (27) 2508285; e-mail esamihq@esamihq.ac.tz; internet www.esami-africa.org; f. 1974, reconstituted 1980; country offices in Kenya, Malawi, Mozambique, Namibia, Swaziland, Tanzania, Uganda, Zambia, Zimbabwe; conducts management development programmes; programmes in corporate entrepreneurship, energy and environment management, finance and banking, gender development and management, governance and public sector management, human resource management, information technology, transport and infrastructure development, health services management and administration; also Executive MBA and MBA in Transport Economics and Logistics Management; 44 teachers (24 full-time, 20 associate); library: 12,000 vols, 15,000 pamphlets; Dir-Gen. Dr BONARD MWAPE; publs *African Management Development Forum* (2 a year), *ESAMI Newsletter* (4 a year).

Institute of Finance Management: Shaaban Robert St, POB 3918, Dar es Salaam; tel. (22) 2112931; fax (22) 2112935; e-mail principal@africaonline.co.tz; internet www.ifm.ac.tz; f. 1972; courses incl. certificates in insurance, social security administration, information technology and computer science; library: 32,000 vols, 100 periodicals; 80 teachers; 1,710 students; Chief Exec. Prof. JOSHUA DORIYE (acting); Dir of Studies Dr ISAYA JAIRO (acting); publ. *African Journal of Finance and Management* (2 a year).

Kivukoni Academy of Social Sciences: POB 9193, Dar es Salaam; tel. (22) 2820041; fax (22) 2820816; e-mail kass@kasstz.org; internet www.kasstz.org; f. 1961; two-year diploma courses in social sciences, economic development and gender issues in development; one-year certificate in youth work; library: 27,000 vols; 30 teachers; 250 students; Prin. Dr JOHN M. J. MAGOTTI.

Moshi University College of Cooperative and Business Studies: POB 474, Sokoine Rd, Moshi; tel. (27) 2751183; fax (27) 2750806; e-mail moshiuniversity@yahoo.com; internet www.muccobs.ac.tz; f. 1963; library: 37,000 vols; Gender Documentation Centre on cooperatives and development; Health Information Centre; 90 teachers; 900 students; Prin. Prof. S. A. CHAMBO; publs *Journal of Cooperative and Business Studies* (2 a year), *Research Abstracts* (every 3 years), *Research Report Series*.

National Social Welfare Training Institute: POB 3375, Dar es Salaam; tel. (22) 2700918; f. 1974; 20 teachers; 180 students; library: 7,172 vols; Prin. T. F. NGALULA; publ. *Jamii Journal*.

University College of Lands and Architectural Studies: POB 35176, Dar es Salaam; tel. (22) 2775004; fax (22) 27755391; e-mail uclas@uclas.ac.tz; internet www.uclas.ac.tz; f. 1996; architecture, building economics, land management and valuation, land surveying, geomatics, environmental engineering, urban and rural planning; Centre for Information Communication Technology (geographic information systems, remote sensing and ICT Studies); Institute of Human Settlements Studies (applied research and documentation services in housing, building, planning and environmental management); library: 20,000 vols; spec. collns of UN publications, theses and masterplans; 111 teachers; 1,060 students; Prin. Prof. IDRIS KIKULA; publ. *Journal of Building and Land Development* (3 a year).

THAILAND

The Higher Education System

The oldest institution of higher education is Chulalongkorn University, which was founded in 1917. In 2005 there were 1,950,892 students enrolled in 156 institutions under the authority of the Office of the Higher Education Commission, and a further 615,548 students enrolled in 408 institutions under the authority of the Office of the Vocational Education Commission.

Following the National Education Act (1999; amended 2002) and the Act for Streamlining of Ministries and Government Agencies (2003), the Ministry of Education, the Ministry of University Affairs and the Office of the National Education Commission were incorporated into a supra-Ministry of Education. Higher education is the responsibility of the Ministry of Education's Higher Education Commission. The University Personnel Act (2004; amended 2008) allowed for the decentralization of authority within the university sector, enabling universities to formulate their own rules and procedures. A roadmap for higher education quality development was launched for the period 2005–08, following which a six-level, credit-based National Qualifications Framework for Higher Education was established in 2009. A 15-Year Long Range Plan on Higher Education covering the period 2008–22 was instigated with a view to bolstering quality standards within the Thai higher education sector by, inter alia, reforming university-level education and financing so as to enhance efficiency, and strengthening university governance.

The main requirements for admission to higher education are 12 years of secondary school education and the MAW 6 (M6)

certificate. Applicants to state institutions must sit the Written Entrance Examination, and private institutions may also require applicants to fulfil additional criteria for admission. A two-year Advanced Diploma course often leads onto the Bachelors, which is the principal undergraduate degree and is a four-year programme of study, although degrees in mainly professional fields of study may last longer, such as architecture, dentistry, pharmacy (all five years) and medicine (six years). The one-year Graduate Diploma offers a further level of specialization after the Bachelors and is generally offered in professional fields. The main postgraduate degree is the Masters, which usually lasts two years (although can take up to five years to complete) and may be either a taught or a research degree. Following the Masters, some students go on to take the Higher Graduate Diploma, which is a one-year course that aims to develop professional expertise in the chosen subject of study. The highest university degree is the Doctor of Philosophy (PhD), which requires a minimum of three years and a maximum of eight years of classwork and research.

Post-secondary vocational and technical education is overseen by the Ministry of Education's Office of the Vocational Education Commission. Qualifications offered include the Diploma in Vocational Education, Higher Certificate (Technician Level) and Higher Diploma of Technical Education (all two years). Private vocational institutes exist, some of which follow curricula devised by the Ministry of Education and some of which devise their own syllabus; qualifications awarded by the latter are not recognized by the Ministry, but are recognized by some employers.

Regulatory and Representative Bodies

GOVERNMENT

Ministry of Culture: Thanalongkorn Bldg, Thanon Boromrachanonnee, Bangplud, Bangkok 10700; tel. (2) 522-8888; e-mail webmaster@m-culture.go.th; internet www .m-culture.go.th; Minister ANUSORN WONG-WAN.

Ministry of Education: Wang Chankasem, Thanon Ratchadamnoen Nok, Bangkok 10300; tel. (2) 281-9809; fax (2) 281-9241; e-mail website@emisc.moe.go.th; internet www.moe.go.th; Min. CHINNAWORN BOONYA-KIAT.

NATIONAL BODIES

Association of Private Higher Education Institutions of Thailand: Siam Univ., 235 Petchkasem Rd, Phasi-charoen, Bangkok 10160; tel. (2) 354-5689; fax (2) 457-3982; e-mail webmaster@siam.edu; internet www .apheit.com; f. 1976; Pres. Assoc. Prof. Dr CHIRADET OUSAWAT.

Commission on Higher Education: 328 Si Ayutthay Rd, Ratchathewi, Bangkok 10400; tel. (2) 610-5200; fax (2) 354-5524; e-mail pr_mua@mua.go.th; internet www.mua.go .th/default1.html; part of Min. of Education; makes policy recommendations, sets standards and plans devt in higher education; devises criteria and guidelines for the allocation of resources; tests and assesses academic and professional standards for purposes of quality assurance; coordinates and promotes research activities; Chair. THE

MIN. OF EDUCATION ; Sec.-Gen. Dr SUMATE YAMNOON; publ. *Thai Higher Education Review* (4 a year).

Council of University Presidents of Thailand (CUPT): 333 Moo 1, Muang Dist., Chiangrai 57100; tel. (53) 706-175; fax (53) 706-174; e-mail postmaster@mua.go .th; internet www.mfu.ac.th; f. 1972; 24 mem. univs and institutes of higher learning; Pres. Assoc. Prof. Dr WANCHAI SIRICHANA.

Rectors' Conference of Thailand: Planning Division, Ministry of University Affairs, Si-Ayuthya Rd, Bangkok 10400; f. 1971; to exchange ideas and discuss problems of common concern to univs; 14 mems; Chair. Prof. Dr NATTH BHAMARAPRAVATI; Sec. Asst Prof. Dr UTHAI BOONPRASERT.

Learned Societies

GENERAL

Office of the National Culture Commission: Ratchadapisek Rd, Huay Khwang, Bangkok 10320; tel. (2) 247-0013; fax (2) 248-5841; internet www.culture.go.th; f. 1979; advises the Ministerial Council on cultural policy, and promotes coordination and cooperation in cultural activities (e.g. ASEAN projects, UNESCO programmes, intraregional music workshop, cultural exchanges, varied research); 300 mems; library of 30,000 vols; Sec.-Gen. ARTORN CHANDAVIMOL; publ. *Thai Culture Magazine* (52 a year).

Royal Institute: The Royal Grand Palace Grounds, Thanon, Na Phra Lan Rd, Bangkok 10200; tel. (2) 221-4822; fax (2) 224-9910;

e-mail royal_institute@mozart.inet.co.th; f. 1933; promotes investigation and encouragement of all branches of knowledge, the exchange of knowledge and advises the Government; 151 mems; library of 25,000 vols; Pres. Prof. Dr PRAYOON KANCHANADUL; Sec.-Gen. CHAMNONG TONGPRASERT.

Siam Society under Royal Patronage: 131 Soi 21 (Asoke), Asokemontri Rd, Wattana, Bangkok 10110; tel. (2) 661-6470; fax (2) 258-3491; e-mail info@siam-society.org; internet www.siam-society.org; f. 1904; promotes the preservation of Thai heritage, culture, art, flora and fauna; 2,000 mems; library of 35,000 vols; Pres. M. R. CHAKRAROT CHITRABONGS; Hon. Sec. MONITA SINGHAKO-WIN; publs *Journal, Natural History Bulletin* (2 a year).

BIBLIOGRAPHY, LIBRARY SCIENCE AND MUSEOLOGY

Thai Library Association: 273 Vibhavadee Rangsit Rd, Phyathai, Bangkok 10400; tel. (2) 271-2084; f. 1954; 1,524 mems; Pres. M. CHAVALIT; Sec. K. SUCKCHAROEN; publs *TLA Bulletin, The World of Books*.

EDUCATION

UNESCO Office Bangkok and Asia and Pacific Regional Bureau for Education: Prakanong Post Office, POB 10110, Bangkok; located at: 920 Sukhumvit Rd, Bangkok 10110; tel. (2) 391-0577; fax (2) 391-0866; e-mail bangkok@unesco.org; internet www .unesco.org/bangkok; f. 1961; designated Cluster Office for Cambodia, Laos, Myanmar, Thailand and Viet Nam; Dir SHELDON SHAEFFER.

LANGUAGE AND LITERATURE

Alliance Française: 29 Thanon Sathorn Tai, Bangkok 10120; tel. (2) 670-4200; fax (2) 670-4200; e-mail bangkok@ alliance-francaise.or.th; internet www .alliance-francaise.or.th; offers courses and exams in French language and culture and promotes cultural exchange with France; attached teaching centres in Chiang Mai, Chiang Rai and Phuket; Dir of Operations, Thailand ANDRÉ SCHMITT.

British Council: 254 Chulalongkorn Soi 64, Siam Sq., Phayathai Rd, Pathumwan, Bangkok 10330; tel. (2) 652-5480; fax (2) 253-5312; e-mail info@britishcouncil.or.th; internet www.britishcouncil.or.th; teaching centre; offers courses and exams in English language and British culture and promotes cultural exchange with the UK; attached teaching centres in Chiang Mai, Ladprao, Pinklao and Srinakarin; Dir PETER UPTON.

Goethe-Institut: 18/1 Soi Goethe, Sathorn 1 Rd, Bangkok 10120; tel. (2) 287-0942; fax (2) 287-1829; e-mail info@bangkok.goethe.org; internet www.goethe.de/bangkok; f. 1960; offers courses and exams in German language and culture and promotes cultural exchange with Germany; library of 8,000 vols; Dir Dr NORBERT SPITZ.

MEDICINE

Medical Association of Thailand: 3 Silom St, Bangkok; f. 1921; 3,057 mems; Pres. Prof. Dr SONGKRANT NIYOMSEN; Hon. Sec. Prof. Dr SANONG UNAKOL; publ. *Journal*.

NATURAL SCIENCES

General

Science Society of Thailand: Faculty of Science, Chulalongkorn University, Phyathai Rd, Bangkok 10330; tel. and fax (2) 252-7987; f. 1948; aims to promote education and research in all branches of natural science; 2,500 mems; Pres. Prof. Dr MONTRI CHULAVATNATOL; Sec.-Gen. Dr PIAMSOOK PONGSAWASDI; publs *Journal* (4 a year, in English), *Science* (26 a year).

Research Institutes

AGRICULTURE, FISHERIES AND VETERINARY SCIENCE

Fishery Technological Development Division: Dept of Fisheries, Ministry of Agriculture and Co-operatives, Charoen Krung Rd, Yannawa, Bangkok 10120; tel. (2) 211-1261; f. 1954; fish handling, processing and utilization; analytical and sanitary certificate for export; Dir UDOM SUNDRARAVIPAT.

Forest Products Research and Development Division: Royal Forest Dept, Ministry of Agriculture and Co-operatives, 61 Paholyothin Rd, Jatujak, Bangkok 10900; f. 1935; wood and non-wood products research and utilization; library of 20,000 vols; Dir of Division WANIDA SUBANSENEE.

Rubber Research Centre: Hat Yai, Songkhla, Dept of Agriculture, Ministry of Agriculture and Co-operatives, Bangkok.

NATURAL SCIENCES

Biological Sciences

Marine Biology Centre: Marine Fisheries Division, 89/1 Sapanpla, Yanawa, Bangkok 12; f. 1968; research and training of marine biologists; Dir DEB MENASWETA.

RELIGION, SOCIOLOGY AND ANTHROPOLOGY

Buddhist Research Centre: Wat Benchamabopitr, Bangkok; f. 1961; sponsored by Department of Religious Affairs, Ministry of Education; publs *Pali-Thai-English Dictionary, vol. 1*.

TECHNOLOGY

Department of Alternative Energy Development and Efficiency: Kasatsuk Bridge, Rama I Rd, Bangkok 10330; tel. (2) 223-0021; fax (2) 226-1416; e-mail dede@dede .go.th; internet www.dede.go.th; f. 1953; conducts research and inspection, surveys and gathers data on energy resources; lays down safety regulations, sets up standards for the sale of energy, promotes the use of energy to improve the economy; library of 13,000 vols; Dir-Gen. SIRIPORN SAILASUTA; publs *Electric Power in Thailand* (1 a year), *Oil and Thailand* (1 a year), *Thailand Alternative Energy Situation* (1 a year), *Thailand Energy Situation* (1 a year).

Department of Mineral Resources: Ministry of Industry, Rama VI Rd, Bangkok 10400; geological mapping, mineral prospecting, mining, mineral dressing and metallurgical research; Dir-Gen. Dr PRABHAS CHAKKAPHAK.

Department of Science Service: Rama VI Rd, Bangkok 10400; tel. 246-1387; f. 1891; testing, calibration and analysis services; research in food technology, industrial fermentation, pulp and paper raw materials, chemical engineering processes, air and water pollution control; research in ceramics; scientific and technological information service; library: see under Libraries and Archives; Dir-Gen. CHODCHOI EIUMPONG; publ. *Journal* (3 a year).

Office of Atomic Energy for Peace: Vibhavadi Rangsit, Chatuchuk, Bangkok 10900; tel. 579-5230; fax 561-3013; f. 1961; 401 staff; library of 11,000 vols, 265 periodicals; Sec.-Gen. KRIENGSAK BHADRAKOM; publ. *OAEP Newsletter* (4 a year).

Thailand Institute of Scientific and Technological Research: Technopolis Klong 5, Klong Luang, Pathumthani, Bangkok 10120; tel. (2) 577-4157; fax (2) 577-4160; e-mail tistr@tistr.or.th; internet www.tistr.or .th; f. 1963; principal govt research agency; research depts: pharmaceuticals and natural products, food industry, chemical industry, biotechnology, building technology, electronics industry, engineering industry, materials technology, agricultural technology, energy technology, environmental and resources management, ecological research, Thai packaging centre; 690 staff; Governor Dr SURAPOL VATANAWONG (acting).

Libraries and Archives

Bangkok

Asian Institute of Technology Library: POB 4, Klong-Luang, Pathumthani 12120; tel. (2) 524-5853; fax (2) 524-5870; e-mail ref@ait.ac.th; internet www.library.ait.ac.th; f. 1959; provides services and training in library and information services; 250,000 vols, 900 periodicals; Head of Library BOONTHAREE PHOONCHAI.

Chulalongkorn University, Center of Academic Resources: Phyathai Rd, Bangkok 10330; tel. (2) 218-2905; fax (2) 215-3617; internet www.car.chula.ac.th; f. 1910; Central Library (995,264 vols), Thailand Information Center (73,400 vols), Audio Visual Center (14,269 vols), International Information Center (20,147 vols), Academic Development and Service Center; Dir Dr KAMALES SANTIVEJKUL (acting).

Kasetsart University, Main Library: Bangkok 10900; tel. (2) 940-5834; fax (2) 561-1369; e-mail lib@ku.ac.th; internet www .lib.ku.ac.th; f. 1943; 279,465 vols, 647 periodicals, 48,218 theses, 107,631 jackets, 9,408 titles of audiovisual materials; Dir Mrs AREE THUNKIJJANUKIJ; publ. *Buffalo Bulletin* (4 a year).

Knowledge Centre: 35 Mu 3 Tambon Klong Ha, Amphoe Khlong Luang, Pathum Thani 12120; tel. (2) 577-9294; fax (2) 577-9084; e-mail klc@tistr.or.th; internet klc.tistr.or.th; f. 1961; documentation services to science and technology; 55,443 vols monographs in Thai, 19,287 vols monographs in English, 37,156 vols periodicals (111 in English, 178 in Thai); Dir Dr NARUMOL RUENWAI; Librarian SAIVAROON KLOMJAI.

Library of the Scientific and Technological Information Division, Department of Science Service: Ministry of Science, Technology and Environment, Rama VI Rd, Ratchathewi District, Bangkok 10400; tel. (2) 245-5271; fax (2) 247-9468; internet www.dss.moeste.go.th; f. 1918; 450,000 vols; spec. library and technical information services incl. patents, standards and trade literature; Dir MAYUREE PONGPUDPUNTH.

National Archives of Thailand: Fine Arts Dept, Samsen Rd, Bangkok 10300; tel. (2) 281-1599; fax (2) 281-5341; e-mail taweta2001@yahoo.com; f. 1952; historical and research resources services for official agencies, scholars and public; 5 major classes of documentary material: textual (10,274 ft), audiovisual (24,508 glass plates, 442,149 photographs, 808,693 film negatives and slides, 19,840 maps, drawings and blueprints, 2,496 posters, 4,427 calendars, 4,467 audio tapes, 3,941 video cassettes, 962 microfilm rolls, 734 CDs, 34 digital tapes), bound vols, govt publs and rare books (42,418 titles), documents, memory records and contemporary records (1,867 titles), clippings and news items (677,112 titles); Dir SUREERAT WONGSANGIM.

National Library of Thailand: Samsen Rd, Bangkok 10300; tel. (2) 281-7927; fax (2) 281-7543; e-mail nlt@nlt.go.th; internet www .nlt.go.th; f. 1905; nat. research library; depository for UN publs and UNESCO documents and collns; controls Int. Standard Serial Number (ISSN–Thailand), ISSN Regional Centre for Southeast Asia (ISSN-SEA); 2.5m. vols, unique and rare collns: 163,607 rare books, 355,172 MSS, 132,239 indexes, 336,000 bibliographies, digitized materials: 53,655 rare books, 26,420 MSS, 221,839 microfilms, depository colln: 263,878 books, 325,246 periodicals, 738,449 newspapers, 11 nat. and spec. databases; Dir WILAWAN SAPPHANSAEN; publs *ISSN-SEA Bulletin, Thai National Bibliography*.

Neilson Hays Library: 195 Suriwongse Rd, Bangkok; tel. (2) 233-1731; fax (2) 233-4999; e-mail neilson@loxinfo.co.th; internet www .neilsonhays.com; f. 1869; Librarian PRAPHEN CHITRAKDI.

Siriraj Medical Library, Mahidol University: Siriraj Hospital, Bangkok 10700; tel. (2) 411-3112; fax (2) 412-8418; e-mail silib@diamond.mahidol.ac.th; f. 1897; 159,600 vols, 3,918 periodicals; Librarian K. CHOLLAMPE; publs *Journal of the Medical Association of Thailand, Siriraj Hospital Gazette*.

Srinakharinwirot University, Central Library: Sukhumvit 23, Wattana, Bangkok 10110; tel. 258-4002; fax 260-4514; e-mail library@swu.ac.th; internet lib.swu.ac.th; f. 1954; audiovisual centre; campus in Ongkarak, Nakornnayok; 492,123 vols, 78,600 theses and dissertations, 14,910 periodicals; Dir Asst Prof. NONGNATH CHAIRAT; publ. *New Books of the Month—A Bibliography*.

Thammasat University Libraries: 2 Prachand Rd, Bangkok 10200; tel. (2) 623-5171; fax (2) 623-5173; e-mail tulib@tu.ac.th; internet www.library.tu.ac.th; f. 1934; 11 br. libraries; 2.1m. vols (social sciences and humanities, medical science, science and technology), 4,782 periodicals, 63 databases, 75,538 audiovisual items; Dir SRICHAN CHANCHEEWA; publ. *Dom That* (2 a year).

United Nations Economic and Social Commission for Asia and the Pacific Library: United Nations Bldg, Rajdamnern Ave, Bangkok 10200; tel. (2) 288-1360; fax (2) 288-1000; e-mail escap_libref.unescap@un .org; internet www.unescap.org/unis/library/ weblib.htm; economic and social development; 150,000 vols; Chief Librarian EVELYN DOMINGO-BARKER; publs *Asian and Pacific Bibliography* (1 a year), *ESCAP Documents and Publications* (1 a year).

Museum
Bangkok

National Museum Bangkok: Na Phra That Rd, Phra Borom Maha Ratchawang, Phra Nakhon, Bangkok 10200; tel. and fax (2) 224-1396; internet www .bangkok-museum.go.th; f. 1874; permanent exhibitions on Thai history, archaeology and art history of Thailand from the prehistoric period to the Bangkok period, decorative arts and ethnology; prehistoric artefacts, bronze and stone sculptures, costumes, textiles, ancient weapons, coins, wood-carvings, ceramics, royal regalia, theatrical masks and dresses, marionettes, shadow-play figures, funeral chariots, illustrated books, musical instruments, monuments, historic bldgs; lectures on Thai art and culture; library; Dir SOMCHAI NA NAKHONPANOM; publs *Guide to Old Sukhothai, Guide to the National Museum, Official Guide to Ayutthaya and Bang Pa-in, Thai Cultural Series*.

Universities and Technical Institutes

ASIAN INSTITUTE OF TECHNOLOGY
POB 4, Klong Luang, Pathumthani 12120
Telephone: (2) 516-0110
Fax: (2) 516-2126
E-mail: provost@ait.ac.th
Internet: www.ait.ac.th

Founded 1959
Language of instruction: English
Academic year: January to December
Ind. graduate institute, open to graduates from all countries; 2 semesters per year leading to Diploma; 4 semesters (2 years) course leading to a Masters degree; further 3 years leading to Doctoral degree
Pres.: Prof. MARIO T. TABUCANON (acting)
Provost: Prof. MARIO T. TABUCANON
Dir of Promotion Activities: SANJEEV JAYASINGHE
Sec.: KARMA RANA
Library: see under Libraries and Archives
Number of teachers: 110
Number of students: 2,000

DEANS

School of Advanced Technologies: Prof. M. T. TABUCANON (acting)

School of Civil Engineering: Prof. CHONGRAK POLPRASERT (acting)
School of Environment, Resources and Development: Prof. CHONGRAK POLPRASERT
School of Management: Dr NAZRUL ISLAM (acting)

ASIAN UNIVERSITY
POB 15, Baan Amphur Post Office, Baan Amphur, Chonburi 20250
89 Moo 1, Highway 331 Rd, Huayyai, Banglamung, Chonburi 20260
Telephone: (38) 253-700
Fax: (38) 253-747
E-mail: admissions@asianust.ac.th
Internet: www.asianust.ac.th

Founded 1993
Private control
Language of instruction: English
Academic year: August to July (2 semesters)
Pres.: Dr VIPHANDH ROENGPITHYA
Vice-Pres. for Admin.: PANIT NILUBOL
Registrar: LADDA THIRAPORN
Librarian: PREEYAGARN JAISA-ARD

Number of teachers: 43
Number of students: 200

DEANS

Faculty of Business: Dr VIPHANDH ROENGPITHYA
Faculty of Engineering: Asst. Prof. Dr APICHAT TUNGTHANGTHUM
Faculty of Liberal Arts: CHARURAT TANTRAPORN

ASSUMPTION UNIVERSITY
Hua Mak Campus, 682 Ramkhamhaeng 24 Rd, Hua Mak, Bangkapi, Bangkok 10240
Bang Na Campus, 88 Moo 8, K. M. 26 Bang Na-Trad Rd, Samutprakarn 10540
Telephone: (2) 300-4543
Fax: (2) 300-4563
E-mail: abac@au.edu
Internet: www.au.edu

Founded 1969, became university in 1990, formerly Assumption Business Administration College
Private control (Catholic: Brothers of St Gabriel)
Language of instruction: English
Academic year: June to March
Pres.: Rev. Bro. BANCHA SAENGHIRAN
Vice-Pres. for Academic Affairs: Rev. Bro. VISITH SRIVICHAIRATANA
Vice-Pres. for Admin. Affairs: Dr CHAVALIT MEENNUCH
Vice-Pres. for Financial Affairs: Rev. Bro. ANUPATT P. YUTTACHAI
Vice-Pres. for Information Technology: Prof. Dr SRISAKDI CHARMONMAN
Vice-Pres. for Research Affairs: Asst Prof. Dr JIRAWAT WONGSWADIWAT
Vice-Pres. for Student Affairs: Rev. Bro. LOECHAI LAVASUT
Registrar: KAMOL KITSAWAD
Dir of Central Library: SUPRATA SINCHAISUK
Library of 500,000 vols
Number of teachers: 1,233
Number of students: 20,000

Publications: *ABAC Journal, ABAC Today, AU Journal of Technology, English Teacher, Galaxy, International Journal of Computer and Engineering Management (IJCEM), Journal of Risk Management and Insurance, Prajna-Vihara (The Journal of Philosophy and Religion)*

DEANS

Graduate School of Business: Rev. Bro. VINAI VIRIYADIDHAYAVONGS

Graduate School of Computer Engineering Management (MS Programme): Dr CHAMNONG JUNGTHIRAPANICH
Graduate School of Computer Information Systems (MS Programme): Air Marshal Dr CHULIT MEESAJJEE
Graduate School of Computer Information Systems (PhD Programme): Asst Prof. Dr VICHIT AVATCHANAKORN
Graduate School of Counselling Psychology: Dr DOLORES DE LEON
Graduate School of Education: Assoc. Prof. Dr METHI PILANTHANANOND
Graduate School of Internet and E-Commerce Technology: Rear Admiral PRASART SRIBHADUNG
Graduate School of Philosophy and Religion: Asst Prof. Dr WARAYUTH SRIWARAKUEL
School of Architecture: PISIT VIRIYAVADHANA
School of Arts: Dr PIMPORN CHANDEE
School of Biotechnology: Dr CHURDCHAI CHEOWTIRAKUL
School of Business: Dr CHERDPONG SIBANRUANG
School of Communication Arts: CHALIT LIMPANAVECH
School of Engineering: Dr SUDHIPORN PATUMTAEWAPIBAL
School of Law: Assoc. Prof. PORNCHAI SOONTHORNPAN
School of Nursing Science: Dr NANTHAPHAN CHINLUMPRASERT
School of Risk Management and Industrial Services: BANCHA THEERASATIANKUL (acting)
School of Science and Technology: Asst Prof. SUPAVADEE NONTAKAO

BANGKOK UNIVERSITY
Rama 4 Rd, Klong-Toey, Bangkok 10110
Telephone: (2) 350-3500
Fax: (2) 249-6274
E-mail: buiao@bu.ac.th
Internet: www.bu.ac.th

Founded 1962 as Thai Polytechnic Institute, present status 1984
Private control
Languages of instruction: Thai, English
Academic year: August to May,June to March (2 semesters)
Pres.: Asst Prof. Dr MATHANA SANTIWAT
Advisor to the Pres.: Prof. Dr POTE SAPIANCHAI
Vice-Pres. for Academic Affairs: Asst Prof. Dr TIPARATANA WONGCHAROEN
Vice-Pres. for Admin. Affairs: Assoc. Prof. LAKSANA SATAWEDIN
Vice-Pres. for External Affairs: Dr SUPONG LIMTHANAKOOL
Vice-Pres. for Financial Affairs: NARUMON OSATHANUGRAH
Vice-Pres. for Int. Affairs: Dr UTTAMA SAVANAYANA
Vice-Pres. for Information Resources and Technology: SOMCHIT LIKHITTAWORN
Vice-Pres. for Student Affairs: SOMMAI DOKMAI
Dir of Library: Dr SHANANA RODSOODTHI
Library of 400,000 vols
Number of teachers: 1,104
Number of students: 26,884

Publications: *BU Academic Journal* (2 a year), *Executive Journal* (4 a year)

DEANS

Graduate School: Asst Prof. Dr SIVAPORN WANGPIPATWONG
International College: Assoc. Prof. Dr TIPCHAN WONGCHANTA
School of Accounting: Dr SUTHA JIARANAIKULVANICH
School of Business Administration: Asst Prof. Dr VEERAPONG MALAI

School of Communication Arts: Asst Prof. Dr PEERAYA HANPONGPANDH
School of Economics: Dr UKRIST TUCHINDA
School of Engineering: Dr NATTHAPHOB NIMPITIWAN
School of Fine and Applied Arts: Asst Prof. SANSERN MILINDASUTA
School of Humanities: Asst. Prof. Dr SOMYOT WATTANAKAMOLCHAI
School of Law: Asst Prof. Dr AUNYA SINGSAN-GOB
School of Science and Technology: Dr WUTNIPONG WARAKRAISAWAT

BURAPHA UNIVERSITY

169 Saen Sook, Muang Chonburi 20131
Telephone: (38) 745-900
Fax: (38) 390-049
Internet: www.adm.buu.ac.th
Founded 1955
State control
Language of instruction: Thai
Academic year: June to March
Pres.: Prof. Dr SUCHART UPATHAM
Vice-Pres. for Academic Affairs: Assoc. Prof. Dr RENA PONRUENGPHANT
Vice-Pres. for Admin.: Assoc. Prof. BOONSERM POOHSANGUAN
Vice-Pres. for Finance and Property Affairs: Assoc. Prof. SUDA SUWANNAPIROM
Vice-Pres. for Int. Relations: Asst Prof. PICHAN SAWANGWONG
Vice-Pres. for Planning and Devt: VIRAT KARAVAPITTAYAKULA
Vice-Pres. for Research Affairs: Prof. Dr SOMSAK PHANTUWATTANA
Vice-Pres. for Student Affairs: Asst Prof. BOOMKA THAIKRA
Librarian: Dr KWANCHADIL PHISALPHONG
Library of 231,635 vols
Number of teachers: 657
Number of students: 10,000 (8,000 undergraduate, 2,000 postgraduate)
Publication: *Journal of Science, Technology and Humanity*

DEANS
Faculty of Education: Assoc. Prof. Dr CHALONG TUBSEE
Faculty of Engineering: Asst Prof. Dr WIRONGA RUENGPHRATHUENGSUKA
Faculty of Fine and Applied Arts: Prof. THESAKAI THONANOPKONG
Faculty of Humanities and Social Sciences: Assoc. Prof. Dr CHARAN CHAKANDANG
Faculty of Marine Technology: Dr PINCHAI SONCHAENG
Faculty of Nursing: Asst Prof. Dr SUNTHARAWADEE THEMPICHET
Faculty of Public Health: Assoc. Prof. Dr SASTRI SAOWAKONTHA
Faculty of Science: Assoc. Prof. Dr KASHANE CHALERMWAT
Faculty of Science and Art: Asst. Prof. RANOP PRAVATNGAM
Graduate School: Assoc. Prof. Dr PRATOOM MUONGMEE

CHIANG MAI UNIVERSITY

239 Huay Keaw Rd, Muang Dist., Chiang Mai 50200
Telephone: (53) 943-661
Fax: (53) 942-670
E-mail: irdcmu@chiangmai.ac.th
Internet: www.cmu.ac.th
Founded 1964
Private control
Languages of instruction: Thai, English
Academic year: June to May (3 semesters)
Pres.: Prof. Dr PONGSAK ANGKASITH
Vice-Pres. for Academic and Educational Quality Affairs: Prof. WIPADA KUNIVIKTIKUL

Vice-Pres. for Gen. Admin., Human Resource Management and Univ. Council Affairs: Asst Prof. SUPHACHAI CHUARATANAPHONG
Vice-Pres. for Int. Relations and Alumni Affairs: Asst Prof. Dr NAT SIRITHUNYALUG
Vice-Pres. for Physical and Campus Management: Asst Prof. Dr PRAYOTE OUNCHANUM
Vice-Pres. for Planning, Financial and Property Management: Assoc. Prof. Dr PAIROTE WIRIYACHAREE
Vice-Pres. for Research and Academic Services: Asstn Prof. JAKKAPAN VORAYOS
Vice-Pres. for Student Devt and Spec. Affairs: Assoc. Prof. Dr AMNAT YOUSUKH
Vice-Pres. for Univ. Ccl Affairs and Information Technology: Asst Prof. SUPHACHAI CHUARATANAPHONG
Registrar: Asst Prof. TODSAPORN PICHAIYA
Librarian: WARARAK PATTANAKIATPONG
Number of teachers: 2,174
Number of students: 39,399 (623 int. students)
Publications: *Arts Journal* (2 a year), *Chiang Mai Journal of Science* (4 a year), *Chiang Mai Medical Journal* (4 a year), *Chiang Mai University Journal of Natural Sciences* (2 a year), *Chiang Mai University Journal of Social Sciences and Humanities* (1 a year), *Chiang Mai Veterinary Journal* (2 a year), *CM Dental Journal* (2 a year), *Determination* (1 a year), *Educational Research Journal* (1 a year), *Engineering Journal Chiang Mai University* (3 a year), *Graduate Research Conference Proceeding*, *Journal of Agriculture* (3 a year), *Journal of East Review* (1 a year), *Journal of Economics* (3 a year), *Journal of Education* (2 a year), *Journal of Human Sciences* (1 a year), *Journal of Social Sciences* (1 a year), *Nursing Journal* (4 a year), *The Thai Feminist Review* (1 a year)

DEANS
Chiang Mai Univ. Int. College: Assoc. Prof. Dr ANNOP PONGWAT
College of Arts, Media and Technology: Dr PITIPONG YODMONKON
Faculty of Agriculture: Assoc. Prof. THEERA VISITPANICH
Faculty of Agro-Industry: Asst Prof. Dr CHARIN TECHAPUN
Faculty of Architecture: Dr EKKACHAI MAHAEK
Faculty of Associated Medical Sciences: Asst Prof. Dr WASNA SIRIRUNGSI
Faculty of Business Administration: BOONSAWART PRUGSIGANONT
Faculty of Dentistry: Assoc. Prof. THONGNARD KUMCHAI
Faculty of Economics: Dr PISIT LEEAHTAM
Faculty of Education: Assoc. Prof. Dr PONGSAK PANKAEW
Faculty of Engineering: Assoc. Prof. Dr SERMKIAT JOMJUNYONG
Faculty of Fine Arts: Assoc. Prof. PONGDEJ CHAIYAKUT
Faculty of Humanities: Assoc. Prof. Dr SUMALEE SAWATDIRAKPONG
Faculty of Law: Dr CHATREE RUENGDETNARONG
Faculty of Mass Communications: Assoc. Prof. JIRAPORN WITAYASAKPUN
Faculty of Medicine: Assoc. Prof. NIWES NANTACHIT
Faculty of Nursing: Assoc. Prof. Dr THANARUK SUWANPRAPISA
Faculty of Pharmacy: Assoc. Prof. WANDEE TAESOTIKUL
Faculty of Political Science and Public Admin.: Assoc. Prof. PAIRAT TRAKARNSIRINONT
Faculty of Social Sciences: Dr SIDTHINAT PRABUDHANITISARN
Faculty of Veterinary Medicine: Assoc. Prof. Dr LERTRAK SRIKITJAKARN

Graduate School: Assoc. Prof. Dr SURASAK WATANESK

CHULALONGKORN UNIVERSITY

254 Phayathai Rd, Pathumwan, Bangkok 10330
Telephone: (662) 215-0871
Fax: (662) 215-4804
E-mail: info@chula.ac.th
Internet: www.chula.ac.th
Founded 1917
State control
Language of instruction: Thai
Academic year: June to March
Pres.: Prof. PIROM KAMOLRATANAKUL
Vice-Pres. for Academic Affairs: Asst Prof. M. R. KALAYA TINGSABADH
Vice-Pres. for Admin.: Assoc. Prof. CHESADA SANGSUBHAN
Vice-Pres. for Finance: Assoc. Prof. DUNUJA KUNPANITCHAKIT
Vice-Pres. for Information Technology: Asst Prof. BOONCHAI SOWANWANICHCHAKUL
Vice-Pres. for Int. Relations: Prof. KUA WONGBOONSIN
Vice-Pres. for Physical Resources Management: Assoc. Prof. LERSOM STHAPITANONDA
Vice-Pres. for Property Management: Assoc. Prof. Gr. Capt. PERMYOT KESOLBHAND
Vice-Pres. for Research and Innovations: Prof. KUA WONGBOONSIN
Vice-Pres. for Strategy and Planning: Assoc. Prof. Dr SITTICHAI TUDSRI
Vice-Pres. for Student Affairs: Assoc. Prof. TANIT TONGTHONG
Registrar: Assoc. Prof. PRADISTHA INTARAKOSIT
Library: see under Libraries and Archives
Number of teachers: 2,427
Number of students: 31,896 (20,419 undergraduate, 11,477 postgraduate)
Publications: *Chula Samphan* (26 a year), *Data on Freshmen Entering Chulalongkorn University, Fact Book* (1 a year), 'Pra Keaw' Students' Handbook (1 a year), *Research Journal* (1 a year)

DEANS
College of Population Studies: Assoc. Prof. VIPAN PRACHUABMOH
College of Public Health Science: Prof. Dr SURASAK TANEEPANICHSKUL
Faculty of Allied Health Sciences: Asst Prof. Dr VANIDA NOPPONPUNTH
Faculty of Architecture: Prof. Dr BUNDIT CHULASAI
Faculty of Arts: Asst Prof. Dr PRAPOD ASSAVAVIRULHAKARN
Faculty of Commerce and Accountancy: Assoc. Prof. Dr ANNOP TANLAMAI
Faculty of Communication Arts: Assoc. Prof. Dr YUBOL BENJARONGKIJ
Faculty of Dentistry: Assoc. Prof. WACHARAPORN TASACHAN
Faculty of Economics: Prof. Dr TEERANA PONGMAKAPAT
Faculty of Education: Prof. Dr SIRICHAI KANJANAWASEE
Faculty of Engineering: Assoc. Prof. Dr BOONSOM LERDHIRUNWONG
Faculty of Fine and Applied Arts: Assoc. Prof. Dr SUPPAKORN DISATAPUNDHU
Faculty of Law: Assoc. Prof. Dr SAKDA THANITCUL
Faculty of Medicine: Prof. Dr ADISORN PATRADUL
Faculty of Nursing: Asst Prof. Capt. YUPIN AUNGSUROCH
Faculty of Pharmaceutical Sciences: Assoc. Prof. PINTIP PONGPECH
Faculty of Political Science: Prof. Dr CHARAS SUWANMALA

Faculty of Psychology: Asst Prof. Dr KAKA-
NANG MANEESRI
Faculty of Science: Prof. Dr SUPOT HANNONG-
BUA
Faculty of Veterinary Science: Prof. Dr
MONGKOL TECHAKUMPHU
Graduate School: Assoc. Prof. Dr PORNPOTE
PIUMSOMBOON
Petroleum and Petrochemical College: Asst
Prof. POMTHONG MALAKUL
School of Sport Science: Assoc. Prof. Dr VIJIT
KANUNGSUKKASEM

DHURAKIJPUNDIT UNIVERSITY

110/1-4 Prachacheun Rd, Laksi, Bangkok
10210
Telephone: (2) 954-7300
Fax: (2) 954-7904
E-mail: dpuic@dpu.ac.th
Internet: www.dpu.ac.th
Founded 1968
Private control
Languages of instruction: Chinese, English,
Thai
Academic year: June to February (2 semes-
ters)
Pres.: Assoc. Prof. Dr VARAKORN SAMAKOSES
Registrar: BUPHA ANUNTARASIRICHAI
Librarian: SUWAKHON SIRIWONGWORAWAT
Library of 220,304 vols
Number of teachers: 529
Number of students: 28,952
Publication: *Sudhiparidhasna* (Univ. jour-
nal)

DEANS

Faculty of Accounting: Dr PATTANAN PETCH-
CHERDCHOO
Faculty of Arts and Sciences: Assoc. Prof.
PREEYA UNARATANA
Faculty of Business Administration: Assoc.
Prof. Dr UPATHAM SAISANGJAN
Faculty of Communication Arts: Asst Prof.
Dr THANTAKARN DUANGRAT
Faculty of Economics: THAMMARAK KARNPISIT
Faculty of Engineering: Dr CHAIYAPORN KHA-
MAPATAPHAN
Faculty of Fine and Applied Arts: Assoc. Prof.
Dr SULUCK SRIBURI
Faculty of Information Technology: Assoc.
Prof. Dr NUTCHAREE PREMCHAISAWADI
Faculty of Law: Prof. Dr PRASIT EKABUTRA
Faculty of Public Admin.: POONSAK PRANOOT-
NARAPARN
Int. College: Asst Prof. Dr HARALD KRAUS
Language Institute: Asst Prof. Dr PEANSIRI
EKNIYOM

HUACHIEW CHALERMPRAKIET UNIVERSITY

18/18 Bangna-Trad Rd, Bangplee Dist.,
Samutprakarn 10540
Telephone: (2) 312-6300
Fax: (2) 312-6237
E-mail: regist@hcu.ac.th
Internet: www.hcu.ac.th
Founded 1942 as Midwifery School; became a
college 1981; present name and status
1992
Private control
Language of instruction: Thai
Academic year: June to May
Pres.: Assoc. Prof. Dr PRACHAK POOMVISES
Vice-Pres.: PISANU RIENMAHASARN
Vice-Pres. for Academic Affairs: Asst. Prof.
Dr URAIPAN JANVANICHYANONT
Vice-Pres.: SANGUANSRI KENGKIJKOSOL
Vice-Pres.: Assoc. Prof. Dr CHANTRA SHAIPA-
NICH (acting)
Vice-Pres. for Planning and Devt: Assoc.
Prof. Dr CHIRADET OUSAWAT

Vice-Pres. for Student Affairs: KANOGWAN
CHANTHANAMONGKOL
Dir of Library and Information Centre:
SUCHANYA CHIRABANDHU
Library of 209,803 books, 1,157 periodicals
Number of teachers: 476
Number of students: 8,934 (8,620 under-
graduate, 226 postgraduate, 88 certificate)

DEANS

Faculty of Business Administration: Prof. Lt-
Gen. PISANU RIENMAHASARN
Faculty of Communication Arts: Asst. Prof.
Dr URAIPAN JANVANICHYANONT
Faculty of Law: Lt.-Gen. SUPHOT NA BANG-
CHANG
Faculty of Liberal Arts: Assoc. Prof. Dr
SUREERAT MARAPO
Faculty of Medical Technology: Asst Prof.
ISAYA JANWITHYANUCHIT
Faculty of Nursing: Assoc. Prof. Dr JARIYA-
WAT KOMPAYAK
Faculty of Pharmaceutical Science: Assoc.
Prof. Dr CHANTRA SHAIPANICH
Faculty of Physical Therapy: BOONRAT NGOW-
TRAKUL
Faculty of Public and Environmental Health:
Asst. Prof. Dr SAOVALUG LUKSAMIJARULKUL
Faculty of Science and Technology: Assoc.
Prof. RACHNEE RUKVEERADHUM
Faculty of Social Work and Social Welfare:
NUANYAI WATTANAKOON
Faculty of Traditional Chinese Medicine:
UDOM CHANTHARAKSRI
Graduate School: Asst Prof. PANNARAI SANG-
VICHIEN

KASETSART UNIVERSITY

Bangkhen Campus: 50 Phahonyothin Rd,
Chatuchak, Bangkok 10900
*Chalermprakiat Sakon Nakhon Province
Campus*: 59 Moo 1, Chiangkrua, Muang,
Sakonnakhon 47000
Kamphaeng Saen Campus: 1 Moo 6, Tambon
Kamphaeng Saen, Amphur Kamphaeng
Saen, Nakhon Pathom 73140
Si Racha Campus: 199 Moo 6, Sukhumvit
Rd, Tambon Tungsukla, Amphur Si Racha,
Changwat Chon Buri 20230
Telephone: (2) 942-8171
Fax: (2) 942-8170
E-mail: fro@ku.ac.th
Internet: www.ku.ac.th
Founded 1943
State control
Languages of instruction: Thai, English
Academic year: June to March (2 semesters)
Pres.: Assoc Prof. VUDTECHAI KAPILAKAN-
CHANA
Vice-Pres. for Academic Affairs: Assoc. Prof.
Dr PANIT KHEMTHONG
Vice-Pres. for Central Management: Asst
Prof. MAYUREE THESPOL
Vice-Pres. for Chalermprakiat Sakon Nakorn
Campus: Assoc. Prof. Dr PONGSAK SURIYA-
VANAGUL
Vice-Pres. for Financial and Property Man-
agement: PREUNGBOON CHAKKAPHAK
Vice-Pres. for Information Technology: Assoc
Prof. YUEN POOVARAWAN
Vice-Pres. for Int. Affairs: Assoc. Prof. Dr
SORNPRACH THANISAWANYANGKURA
Vice-Pres. for Kamphaeng Saen Campus:
Assoc. Prof. Dr CHAWALIT HONGPRAYOON
Vice-Pres. for Quality Assurance: Assoc. Prof.
KAMOLPUN NAMWONGPROM
Vice-Pres. for Research: Assoc. Prof. Dr
SAMAKKEE BOONYAWAT
Vice-Pres. for Si Racha Campus: Assoc. Prof.
Dr CHAIWAT CHAIKUL
Vice-Pres. for Spec. Projects: Asst Prof.
THANWA JITSANGUAN
Vice-Pres. for Student Affairs and Physical
Devt: NIPHON LIMLEAMTHONG

Registrar: Assoc. Prof. SAKDA INTRRAVICHAI
Librarian: AREE THUNKIJJANUKIJ
Library: see under Libraries and Archives
Number of teachers: 3,166
Number of students: 57,116 (45,810 undergraduate, 11,306 postgraduate)
Publications: *Kasetsart Journal* (4 a year,
natural sciences edn; 3 a year, social
sciences edn), *Knowledge of the Land* (1 a
year, university's academic affairs, in English)

DEANS

College of Environment: KASEM CHUNKAO
College of Graduate Studies (Si Racha): SRI-
ON SOMBOONSUP
Faculty of Agriculture: VICHAN VICHUKIT
Faculty of Agriculture (Kamphaeng Saen):
VORAVIT SIRIPHOLVAT
Faculty of Agro-Industry: SIREE CHAISERI
Faculty of Architecture: RATCHOT CHOMPU-
NICH
Faculty of Business Administration: SAMPAN
HANPAYON
Faculty of Economics: SAROJ AUNGSUMALIN
Faculty of Education: PORNTIP CHAISO
Faculty of Education and Development Sci-
ences: BUNJOB PIROMKAM
Faculty of Engineering: NONTAWAT JUNJAR-
EON
Faculty of Engineering (Kamphaeng Saen):
BANCHA KWANYUEN
Faculty of Engineering (Si Racha): KIATYUTH
KVEEYARN
Faculty of Fisheries: SURIYAN TUNKIJJANUKIJ
Faculty of Forestry: WANCHAI ARUNPRAPARUT
Faculty of Humanities: WILAISAK KINGKHAM
Faculty of Natural Resources and Agro-
Industry: NITSRI SANGDUEN
Faculty of Resources and Environment: RUJA
ARUNBANJERDKUL
Faculty of Science: SURAPOL PATHARAKORN
Faculty of Science and Engineering: SUPAKIT
NONTANANANDH
Faculty of Social Science: MANITPOL URABUN-
NUALCHAT
Faculty of Sport Sciences: SIRIPORN SASIMON-
TONKUL
Faculty of Veterinary Medicine: THAVAJCHAI
SAKPUARAM
Faculty of Veterinary Technology: WORAWUT
RERKAMNUAYCHOKE
Graduate School: GUNJANA THEERAGOOL
International Maritime College: SUPIT
UMNUAY

PROFESSORS

ATTATHOM, T., Entomology
CHANDRAPATYA, A., Entomology
CHAREONVIRIYAPHAP, T., Entomology
HORMCHAN, P., Entomology
KAMDEE, D., Philosophy and Religion
KANCHANALAI, T., Civil Engineering
KETSA, S., Horticulture
LAOHAKOSOL, V., Mathematics
LIMTONG, S., Microbiology
LIMTRAKUL, J., Chemistry
MAKARABHIROM, K., English Literature
NAIVIKUL, O., Food Science and Technology
NA-NAKORN, U., Aquaculture
PANICHSAKPATANA, S., Soil Science
PONGTONGKAM, P., Genetics
ROADRANGKA, V., Education
ROJANARIDPICHED, C., Agronomy
RUJOPAKARN, W., Transportation Engineer-
ing
SIRIPHANICH, J., Horticulture
SRINIVES, P., Agronomy
SUPRASERT, A., Anatomy
TASANACHAIKUL, N., Political Science and
Public Administration
TUDSRI, S., Agronomy
YINGJAJAVAL, S., Soil Physics
YONGSMITH, B., Microbiology

KHON KAEN UNIVERSITY

123 Mitraparb Rd, Amphur Muang, Khon Kaen 40002

Telephone: (4) 300-9700
Fax: (4) 324-1216
Internet: www.kku.ac.th

Founded 1964
State control
Language of instruction: Thai
Academic year: June to March (2 semesters)

Pres.: Assoc. Prof. Dr SUMON SAKOLCHAI
Vice-Pres. for Academic and Int. Affairs: Assoc. Prof. Dr KUTHILDA TUAMSUK
Vice-Pres. for Admin. Affairs: Assoc. Prof. DUMRONG HORMDEE
Vice-Pres. for Planning and Information Technology: Asst Prof. AROM TATAWASART
Vice-Pres. for Research: Asst Prof. PUSAN SIRITHORN
Vice-Pres. for Spec. Affairs: Asst Prof. WICHAI NEERATANAPHAN
Vice-Pres. for Student Affairs: Asst Prof. Dr ANAN HIRANSALEE
Vice-Pres. for Student Devt: Assoc. Prof. LIKHIT AMARTTAYAKONG
Vice-Pres. for Univ. Facilities: SURACHET MANGMEESRI

Library of 339,614 vols
Number of teachers: 1,810
Number of students: 18,457

Publications: *Architecture Journal* (4 a year), *Bulletin of Medical Technology and Physical Therapy* (4 a year), *Humanities and Social Sciences Journal* (4 a year), *Information* (2 a year), *I-San Journal of International Medicine* (4 a year), *Journal of Library and Information Science* (4 a year), *Journal of Learning and Teaching Competency* (4 a year), *Journal of Learning and Teaching Innovation* (4 a year), *Journal of Medical Technology and Physical Therapy* (4 a year), *Journal of Mekong Societies* (4 a year), *Journal of Nursing* (4 a year), *Kaen Kaset* (4 a year), *Khon Kaen Agriculture Journal* (6 a year), *KKU Dental Journal* (2 a year), *KKU Engineering Journal* (4 a year), *KKU Engineering Quarterly*, *KKU Health Sciences Center Bulletin* (6 a year), *KKU Journal of Education* (4 a year), *KKU Journal of Management Science* (1 a year), *KKU Quality Assurance Journal* (2 a year), *KKU VET Journal* (2 a year), *Science Journal* (4 a year), *Srinagarind Medical Journal* (4 a year)

DEANS

Faculty of Agriculture: Asst Prof. ASSANEE PRACHINBURAVAN
Faculty of Architecture: Asst. Prof. TANOO POLWAT
Faculty of Associated Medical Sciences: Assoc. Prof. YUPA UAVIJTIAROON
Faculty of Dentistry: Asst Prof. Dr NIWUT JUNTAVEE
Faculty of Education: Assoc. Prof. Dr SAMPAN PANPURK
Faculty of Engineering: Assoc. Prof. Dr WINIT CHINSUWAN
Faculty of Fine and Applied Arts: Assoc. Prof. Dr CHALERMSAK PIKULSRI
Faculty of Humanities and Social Sciences: Assoc. Prof. SRIPANYA CHAIYAI
Faculty of Management Sciences: Assoc. Prof. SUMETH KAENMANEE
Faculty of Medicine: Asst Prof. SUCHART AREEMITR
Faculty of Nursing: Asst Prof. Dr WANAPA SRITANYARAT
Faculty of Pharmaceutical Sciences: Assoc. Prof. SUMON SAKOLCHAI
Faculty of Public Health: Assoc. Prof. AROON JIRAWATKUL
Faculty of Sciences: Asst Prof. Dr WANCHAI SOOMLEG

Faculty of Technology: Asst Prof. Dr KRIENGSAK SRISUK
Faculty of Veterinary Medicine: Assoc. Prof. PRACKAK PUAPERMPOONSRI
Graduate School: Assoc. Prof. Dr SOMMAI PRIPREM

KING MONGKUT'S INSTITUTE OF TECHNOLOGY LADKRABANG

Chalongkrung Rd, Ladkrabang District, Bangkok 10520

Telephone: (2) 326-9157
Fax: (2) 326-7333
E-mail: inter@kmitl.ac.th
Internet: www.kmitl.ac.th

Founded 1960
State control
Academic year: June to March

Pres.: Assoc. Prof. PRAKIT TANGTISANON
Vice-Pres. for Academic Affairs: SUCHEEP SUKSUPATH
Vice-Pres. for Admin.: KITTI TIRASESTH
Vice-Pres. for Chumporn Campus: SURAPOL SETHABUTR
Vice-Pres. for Devt: AMNOUY PANITKULPONG
Vice-Pres. for Finance and Property: WILAIWAN WONYODPUN
Vice-Pres. for Int. Affairs: DUSANEE THANABORIPAT
Vice-Pres. for Planning: KULTHORN LUERNSHAVEE
Vice-Pres. for Student Affairs: PACHERNCHAI CHAIYASITH
Admin. Officer: RUAMPORN INTARAPRASONG
Dir of Central Library: OUEN PIN-NGERN

Library of 67,000 vols
Number of teachers: 808
Number of students: 15,052

Publications: *IT Journal* (2 a year), *Journal* (2 a year), *Journal of Science—Ladkrabang* (2 a year), *Ladkrabang Engin* (4 a year), *Research Abstracts* (irregular)

DEANS

Faculty of Agricultural Technology: JUTARAT SETHAKUL
Faculty of Architecture: EKAPHONG CHULASANIE
Faculty of Engineering: TAWIL PAUNGMA
Faculty of Industrial Education: PREEYAPORN WONGANUTROHD
Faculty of Information Technology: SURASIT VANNAKRAIROJN
Faculty of Science: THEERAWAT MONGKOLAUSSAWARATNA
Graduate School: MANAS SANGWORASIL

KING MONGKUT'S INSTITUTE OF TECHNOLOGY NORTH BANGKOK

1518 Pibulsongkram Rd, Bangsue, Bangkok 10800

Telephone: (2) 913-2500
Fax: (2) 587-4350
E-mail: iro@kmitnb.ac.th
Internet: www.kmitnb.ac.th

Founded 1959
State control
Languages of instruction: Thai, English
Academic year: June to March

Pres.: Prof. Dr TERAVUTI BOONYASOPON
Vice-Pres. for Academic Affairs: Assoc. Prof. Dr CHANASAK BAITIANG
Vice-Pres. for Admin. and Int. Affairs: Asst Prof. WATANA PINSEM
Vice-Pres. for Finance: Asst Prof. ACHARA SUNGSUWAN
Vice-Pres. for Prachinburi Campus: Asst Prof. WORAWIT CHATURAPANICH
Vice-Pres. for Research and Quality Assurance: Assoc. Prof. CHARN THANADNGARN
Vice-Pres. for Student Affairs: Asst Prof. WITTAYA WIPAWIWAT

Vice-Pres. for Univ. Devt and Promotion: ARUN PUTHAYANGKURA
Registrar: SANGOB KONGKA
Dir of Central Library: MONTREE KHEMRACH

Number of teachers: 626
Number of students: 16,445

Publications: *Journal of King Mongkut's Institute of Technology North Bangkok* (in Thai, 6 a year), *Technical Education Development* (in Thai, 4 a year)

DEANS

College of Industrial Technology: Asst Prof. PREECHA ONG-AREE
Faculty of Agro-Industry: Asst Prof. MALEE SIMSRISAKUL (acting)
Faculty of Applied Arts: Assoc. Prof. SURAPHI TONSIENGSOM (acting)
Faculty of Applied Science: Asst Prof. WICHAI SURACHERDKIATI
Faculty of Engineering: Asst Prof. Dr SIRISAK HARNCHOOWONG
Faculty of Information Technology: Assoc. Prof. Dr MONCHAI TIANTONG (acting)
Faculty of Technical Education: Asst Prof. Dr PISIT METHAPATARA
Faculty of Technology and Industrial Management: PEERASAK SAREKUL
Graduate College: Asst Prof. Dr VIBOON CHUNKAG

KING MONGKUT'S UNIVERSITY OF TECHNOLOGY THONBURI

126 Pracha-utit Rd, Bangmod, Thungkruh, Bangkok 10140

Telephone: (2) 470-8000
Fax: (2) 427-9860
E-mail: int.off@kmutt.ac.th
Internet: www.kmutt.ac.th

Founded 1960 as Thonburi Technical Institute, combined with two other Institutes to form King Mongkut's Institute of Technology 1971, but regained autonomy as King Mongkut's Institute of Technology Thonburi 1986, present name and status 1998
State control
Languages of instruction: Thai, English
Academic year: June to March

Pres.: Assoc. Prof. Dr SAKARINDR BHUMIRATANA
Senior Vice-Pres. for Academic Affairs: Assoc. Prof. Dr SUVIT TIA
Senior Vice-Pres. for Admin. Affairs: Assoc. Prof. PRASERT KANTHAMANON
Vice-Pres. for Human Resources: Asst Prof. SUPANEE LERTTRILUCK
Vice-Pres. for Planning and Information: THANITSORN CHIRAPORNCHAI
Vice-Pres. for Property and Finance: Asst Prof. Dr TIPPAWAN PINANICHKUL
Vice-Pres. for Research: Asst Prof. Dr BUNDIT FUNGTAMMASAN
Vice-Pres. for Student Devt: Assoc. Prof. Dr CHAOWALIT LIMMANEEVICHITR
Registrar: APAKORN PADUNGSATAYAWONG

Library of 120,000 books, 2,200 periodicals, 2,000 CD-ROMs, 14 online databases
Number of teachers: 576
Number of students: 12,453

Publication: *Research and Development Journal* (4 a year)

DEANS

Faculty of Engineering: Assoc. Prof. Dr BUNCHAREON SIRINAOWAKUL
Faculty of Science: Assoc. Prof. Dr WORANUJ KIRDSINCHAI
Graduate School of Management and Innovation: Asst. Prof. Dr PASIT LORTERAPONG
Joint Graduate School of Energy and Environment: Assoc. Prof. Dr BUNDIT FUNGTHAMMASAN

School of Architecture and Design: MICHAEL PAIRPOL

School of Bioresources and Technology: Assoc. Prof. NARUMON JEYASHOKE

School of Energy, Environment and Materials: Dr PATTANA RAKKAWAMSUK

School of Industrial Education and Technology: Assoc. Prof. Dr SITTICHAI KAEWKUE-KOOL

School of Information Technology: Asst Prof. Dr BORWORN PAPASRATORN

School of Liberal Arts: Asst Prof. Dr PORNA-PIT DARASAWANG

PROFESSORS

CHUCHEEPSAKUL, S., Civil Engineering

CHULLABODHI, C., Energy Management Technology

JIRARATANANON, R., Chemical Engineering

SOPONRONNARIT, S., Energy Technology

WONGWISES, S., Mechanical Engineering

KRIRK UNIVERSITY

43/1111 Ram-Indra Rd, Bangkhem, Bangkok 10220

Telephone: (2) 552-3500

Fax: (2) 552-3511

E-mail: phakaphan@krirk.ac.th

Internet: www.krirk.ac.th

Founded 1952

Private control

Academic year: June to May

President: DHATTONG VIRIYAVEJAKUL

Vice-Presidents: BENJA MANGALAPRUEK, Assoc. Prof. Dr MANOON PAHIRAH

Library of 68,000 books, 419 periodicals

Number of teachers: 130

Number of students: 3,445 (2,955 undergraduate, 490 postgraduate)

DEANS

Faculty of Business Administration: SANONG DEPRADIT

Faculty of Communication Arts and Liberal Arts: Prof. Maj.-Gen. SANITPONG KHEM-TONG

Faculty of Economics: Asst Prof. Dr BUNSERM BUNCHAROENPOL

Faculty of Law: Pol. Maj.-Gen. Dr SAWADI SORALUM

Graduate School: Assoc. Prof. Dr MANOON PAHIRAH (acting)

MAE FAH LUANG UNIVERSITY

333 Moo 1, Muang Dist., Chiangrai 57100

Telephone: (53) 916-000

Fax: (53) 916-031

E-mail: pr@mfu.ac.th

Internet: www.mfu.ac.th

Founded 1998

Public Autonomous University

Academic year: June to March (2 semesters)

Schools of agricultural technology, biotechnology, information technology, liberal arts, management science and science.

Pres.: Assoc. Prof. Dr VANCHAI SIRICHANA (acting)

Vice-Pres.: Assoc. Prof. Dr TED TESPRATEEP, Asst Prof. PRITANA PRADIPASEAN, PORNTHIP PHUTIYOTHIN, Assoc. Prof. NAREEWAN CHINTAKANOND, Assoc. Prof. GANNAGA SATITTADA, Assoc. Prof. Group Capt. YUTANA TRA-NGARN

Library Dir: Dr PATHA SUWANNARAT

Library of 200,000 vols

Number of teachers: 350

Number of students: 9,186 (59 diploma, 8,183 undergraduate, 944 postgraduate)

DEANS

School of Agro-Industry: Assoc. Prof. Dr ORAPIN BHUMIBHAMON

School of Anti-Ageing and Regenerative Medicine: Prof. Dr THAMTHIWAT NARARAT-WANCHAI

School of Cosmetic Science: Assoc. Prof. Dr PANVIPA KRISDAPHONG

School of Health Science: Dr SAMRUENG KANJANAMETHAKUL

School of Information Technology: Group Capt. Dr THONGCHAI YOOYATIVONG

School of Law: Assoc. Prof. Dr CHALOR WONGWATTANAPHIKULA

School of Liberal Arts: Assoc. Prof. CHAKRA-PAND WONGBURANAVART

School of Management: Assoc. Prof. Dr CHUTA MANUSPHAIBOON

School of Nursing: Assoc. Prof. SUPRANEE ATHASERI

School of Science: Prof. Dr SIRIWAT WONGSIRI

MAEJO UNIVERSITY

Sansai, Chiang Mai 50290

Telephone: (53) 873-000

Fax: (53) 498-861

Internet: www.mju.ac.th

Founded 1934, present name 1992 (fmrly Maejo Institute of Agricultural Technology)

State control

Language of instruction: Thai

Academic year: June to March

Pres.: Prof. Dr THEP PHONGPARNICH

Vice-Pres. for Admin.: Prof. ARKORN KANJA-NAPHACHOT, Asst. Prof. Dr CHAMNIAN YOSRAJ

Vice-Pres. for Assets and Spec. Affairs: PRAMOTE KLIBNGERN

Vice-Pres. for Education Quality Standards: Asst. Prof. PRASAN WONGMANEERUNG

Vice-Pres. for Information Technology and Communications: Asst. Prof. Dr. SIRICHAI UNSRISONG

Vice-Pres. for Planning and Int. Affairs: Prof. Dr NUMCHAI THANUPON

Vice-Pres. for Research and Academic Affairs: Assoc. Prof. Dr CHALERMCHAI PUNYADEE

Vice-Pres. for Student Devt and Alumni Relations: Prof. MANAS GUMPUKUL, Assoc. Prof. ARKOM KANJANAPHACHOTE (acting)

Registrar: KRISSADA BHACKDEE

Librarian: WASSANA PHONGPAL

Library of 1,357 vols, 1,032 periodicals

Number of teachers: 1,190

Number of students: 12,925

Publications: *Journal of Agricultural Research and Extension* (6 a year, in Thai, with English summaries), *Maejo International Journal of Science and Technology*, *Maejo Journal* (6 a year, in Thai)

DEANS

Faculty of Agricultural Business: Asst. Prof. Dr PRAPHANT OSATHAPHANT

Faculty of Architecture and Environmental Design: SIRICHAI HONGVITYAKORN

Faculty of Business Admin.: BOONSOM SUKHA-JIT

Faculty of Economics: Asst Prof. THANARUG MECKHAYAI

Faculty of Engineering and Agro-Industry: RACHATA CHEUVIROJ

Faculty of Fisheries Technology and Aquatic Resources: Assoc. Prof. Dr KRIANGSAK MENG-AMPAN

Faculty of Information and Communication: Assoc. Prof. Dr WITTAYA DAMRONGKIATTISAK

Faculty of Liberal Arts: Asst Prof. Dr SAOWA-LUCK CHAYTAWEEP

Faculty of Science: Asst Prof. PHUENGPORN NIUMSUP

School of Admin. Science: PRADTANA YOSSUCK

School of Tourism Devt: Assoc. Prof. Dr WEERAPON THONGMA

MAHANAKORN UNIVERSITY OF TECHNOLOGY

51 Cheum Sampan Rd, Nong Chok, Bangkok 10530

Telephone: 988-3655

Fax: 988-3687

E-mail: www@mut.ac.th

Internet: www.mut.ac.th

Founded 1990 as Mahanakorn College

Depts of accountancy, anatomy, business communication arts, business computer, chemical engineering, chemistry, civil engineering, computer engineering, control and instrument engineering, electrical engineering, electrical power engineering, finance and banking, industrial management, management, marketing, mathematics, mechanical engineering, microbiology, parasitology, pathology, pharmacology, physics, physiology, telecommunication engineering

Chancellor: Prof. Dr YONGYUT SATJAVANIT

Vice-Chancellor: YOUNGSAK KANATANAVANIT

Pres.: Assoc. Prof. Dr SITTHICHAI POOKAIYAU-DOM

Publication: *Engineering Transactions* (3 a year).

MAHASARAKHAM UNIVERSITY

Tambon Kamriang, Kantarawichai Dist., Maha Sarakham 44150

Telephone and fax (43) 75-4241

E-mail: iroffice@msu.ac.th

Internet: www.inter.msu.ac.th

Founded 1968 as Mahasarakham College of Education, became Mahasarakham campus of Srinakharinwirot Univ. in 1974, present name and status 1994

State control

Academic year: June to March

Languages of instruction: Thai, English

Pres.: Asst Prof. Dr SUPACHAI SAMAPPITO

Vice-Pres. for Academic Affairs and Research: Assoc. Prof. Dr PREECHA PRATHE-PHA

Vice-Pres. for Admin.: Asst Prof. THIENSAK MAKKAPAN-OPAS

Vice-Pres. for Gen. Management: Asst Prof. PIYAPUN SANTAVEESUK

Vice-Pres. for Personnel Devt and Univ. Ccl Affairs: Assoc. Prof. THIENSAK MEKKAPAN-OPAS

Vice-Pres. for Spec. Affairs: Assoc. Prof. SURACHA AMORNPAN

Vice-Pres. for Student Affairs: Asst Prof. Dr SUJIN BUTDISUWAN

Dir of Academic Resource Centre: Dr SUR-ITHONG SRISA-ARD

Library of 424,705 books, 2,171 periodicals

Number of teachers: 991

Number of students: 39,117

DEANS

College of Graduate Studies: Assoc. Prof. Dr PAITOOL SUKSRINGARM

College of Music: Assoc. Prof. Dr SUPANNEE LEAUBOONSHOO

College of Politics and Governance: Assoc. Prof. SIDA SORNSRI

Faculty of Accounting and Management: Assoc. Prof. PHAPRUKE USSAHAWANITCHAKIT

Faculty of Architecture, Urban Design and Creative Arts: PUANGPEN WIBOONSAWAT

Faculty of Education: Assoc. Prof. PRAWIT ERAWAN

Faculty of Engineering: Prof. Dr PRADIT TERDTOON

Faculty of Environment and Resource Studies: Assoc. Prof. Dr CHALEE NAWANUKHROH

Faculty of Fine and Applied Arts: NONTHI-VATHN CHANDHANAPHALIN

Faculty of Hotel and Tourism Management: YUWADEE TAPANEEYAKORN

Faculty of Humanities and Social Sciences: Asst Prof. Dr SOMKIET POOPATWIBOON

Faculty of Informatics: Assoc. Prof. WIRAT PONGSIRI

Faculty of Medicine: Prof. Dr SOMPORN PHOTHINAM

Faculty of Nursing: Assoc. Prof. WALAIPORN NUNSUPHAWAT

Faculty of Pharmacy: Asst Prof. Dr CHANTIP KANCHANASIN

Faculty of Public Health: Prof. Dr SOMJIT SUPANNATAS

Faculty of Science: Assoc. Prof. JEERAPAN SUKSRINGARM

Faculty of Technology: Asst Prof. Dr RAMPAI KENSAKOO

Faculty of Tourism and Hotel Management: Asst Prof. SURACHET CHETTAMART

Faculty of Veterinary Medicine and Animal Science: Assoc. Prof. SAELI DONKAEWBUA

MAHIDOL UNIVERSITY

999 Phuttamonthon 4 Rd, Salaya, Phutta-monthon, Nakorn Pathom 73170

Telephone: (2) 849-6230

Fax: (2) 849-6237

E-mail: opinter@mahidol.ac.th

Internet: www.mahidol.ac.th

Founded 1888, as Siriraj Medical School; present name 1969

State control

Pres.: Prof. PIYASAKOL SAKOLSATAYADORN

Vice-Pres.: Prof. NAPATAWN BANCHUIN

Vice-Pres. for Academic Infrastructures Devt: Assoc. Prof. SUPACHAI TANGWONGSAN

Vice-Pres. for Admin. and Univ. Ccl Sec.: Prof. PASSIRI NISALAK

Vice-Pres. for Amnaj Charoen Campus: BOONSANONG BOONMEE

Vice-Pres. for Campus Devt: Asst Prof. NAKORN HAMAH

Vice-Pres. for Collaboration and Networking: Assoc. Prof. CHURNRURTAI KANCHANACHITRA

Vice-Pres. for Education: Assoc. Prof. SUNANTA VIBULJAN

Vice-Pres. for Finance and Assets: Assoc. Prof. SATIT HOTRAKITYA

Vice Pres. for Human Resources and Quality Devt: Prof. PRASIT WATANAPA

Vice Pres. for Int. Relations: Assoc. Prof. EMORN WASANTWISUT

Vice-Pres. for Law and Regulation Devt: Asst Prof. SINGHAPAN TONGSAWAS

Vice-Pres. for Nakhon Sawan Campus: Dr SOMPONG YOONGTONG

Vice-Pres. for Policy and Informatics Technology: Assoc. Prof. SORANIT SILTHARM

Vice-Pres. for Research and Academic Affairs: Prof. SANSANEE CHAIYAROJ

Vice-Pres. for Student and Univ. Affairs: Assoc. Prof. PREECHA SOONTRANAN

Library of 540,118 vols, 186,663 bound periodicals, 4,247 current periodicals, 15,961 audiovisual units, 97,786 theses, 79 online databases; 38,193 e-journals and 65,976 e-books, 21 libraries

Number of teachers: 3,598 (168 full profs, 791 assoc. profs, 822 asst profs and 1,817 lecturers)

Number of students: 25,129

Publications: *Environment and Natural Resources Journal* (2 a year), *Journal of Applied Animal Science* (3 a year), *Journal of Health Education* (3 a year), *Journal of Language and Culture* (2 a year), *Journal of Nursing Science* (3 a year), *Journal of Population and Social Studies* (2 a year), *Journal of Public Health* (3 a year), *Journal of Public Health Admin.* (2 a year), *Journal of Public Health and Devt* (3 a year), *Journal of Public Health Nursing* (3 a year), *Journal of Ratchasuda College for Research and Development of Persons with Disabilities* (2 a year), *Journal of Religion and Culture* (2 a year), *Journal of Sahasat* (2 a year), *Journal of Tropical Medicine and Parasitology* (2 a year), *Mahidol Journal* (2 a year), *Mahidol Dental Journal* (3 a year), *Mahidol University Journal of Pharmaceutical Sciences* (4 a year), *MUMJ-Mahidol University Music Journal* (2 a year), *Music Journal* (12 a year), *Quality of Life and Law Journal* (2 a year), *Pacific Journal of Allergy and Immunology* (4 a year), *Ramathibodi Medical Journal* (4 a year), *Ramathibodi Nursing Journal* (4 a year), *ScienceAsia—Journal of the Science Society of Thailand* (4 a year), *Siriraj Medical Journal* (12 a year), *Southeast Asian Journal of Tropical Medicine and Public Health* (4 a year), *The Journal: Journal of the Faculty of Arts* (2 a year), *Thai Journal of Phytopharmacy* (2 a year)

DEANS

Faculty of Dentistry: Assoc. Prof. THEERA-LAKSNA SUDDHASTHIRA

Faculty of Engineering: Asst Prof. RAWIN RAVIWONGSE

Faculty of Environmental and Resource Studies: Asst Prof. SITTIPONG DILOKWANICH

Faculty of Graduate Studies: Prof. BANCHONG MAHAISAVARIYA

Faculty of Information and Communication Technology: Assoc. Prof. JARERNSRI MITR-PANONT

Faculty of Liberal Arts: Prof. PRASIT WATA-NAPA (acting)

Faculty of Medical Technology: Prof. VIRA-PONG PRACHAYASITTIKUL

Faculty of Medicine, Ramathibodi Hospital: Prof. RAJATA RAJATANAVIN

Faculty of Medicine, Siriraj Hospital: Clinical Prof. TEERAWAT KULTHANAN

Faculty of Nursing: Assoc. Prof. FONGCUM TILOKSKULCHAI

Faculty of Pharmacy: Assoc. Prof. CHUTHA-MANEE SUTHISISANG (acting)

Faculty of Physical Therapy: Assoc. Prof. ROONGTIWA VACHALATHITI

Faculty of Public Health: Assoc. Prof. PHI-TAYA CHARUPOONPHOL

Faculty of Science: Prof. SKORN MONGKOLSUK

Faculty of Social Sciences and Humanities: Assoc. Prof. WARIYA CHINWANNO

Faculty of Tropical Medicine: Assoc. Prof. PRATAP SINGHASIVANON

Faculty of Veterinary Science: Assoc. Prof. PARNTEP RATANAKORN

NARESUAN UNIVERSITY

Phitsanulok 65000

Telephone: (55) 261-000

E-mail: international@nu.ac.th

Internet: www.nu.ac.th

Founded 1990

State control

Academic year: June to March

Library of 120,000 vols

Number of teachers: 867

Number of students: 21,435

Publication: *Naresuan University Journal*.

NATIONAL INSTITUTE OF DEVELOPMENT ADMINISTRATION

118 Seri Thai Rd, Klongchan, Bangkapi, Bangkok 10240

Telephone: (2) 377-7400

Fax: (2) 375-8798

E-mail: nisnida@nida.nida.ac.th

Internet: www.nida.ac.th

Founded 1966

State control

Languages of instruction: Thai, English

Academic year: June to May (3 semesters)

Pres.: Assoc. Prof. Dr PREECHA JARUNGIDANAN

Vice-Pres. for Academic Affairs: Assoc. Prof. Dr SAGOL JARIYAVIDYANONT

Vice-Pres. for Admin.: Assoc. Prof. CHAMAI-PORN KUNAKEMAKORN

Vice-Pres. for Planning: Prof. Dr CHARTCHAI NA CHIANGMAI

Library of 233,000 vols

Number of teachers: 155

Number of students: 10,391

Publications: *NIDA Bulletin* (6 a year), *Thai Journal of Development Administration* (4 a year)

DEANS

School of Applied Statistics: Assoc. Prof. Dr JIRAWAN JITHAVECH

School of Business Administration: Dr THA-KOL NUNTHIRAPAKORN

School of Development Economics: Asst Prof. Dr WISARN PUPPHAVESA

School of Language and Communication: Assoc. Prof. Dr PATCHAREE POKASAMRIT

School of Public Administration: Prof. Dr SOMBAT THAMRONGTHANYAWONG

School of Social Development: Asst Prof. Dr TONG-ON MUNJAITON

DIRECTORS

Graduate Development Centre: Assoc. Prof. Dr SAGOL JARIYAVIDYANONT (acting)

Graduate Programme in Human Resource Development: Asst Prof. Dr MANEEWAN CHAT-UTHAI (acting)

Library and Information Centre: SIRIPORN SUWANNA

Research Centre: Assoc. Prof. Dr SAGOL JARIYAVIDYANONT (acting)

Training Centre: Dr BOORAPA CHODCHOEY (acting)

PROFESSORS

School of Applied Statistics (tel. (2) 375-8944; fax (2) 374-4061; e-mail jirawan@nida.nida.ac.th):

SUWATTEE, P., Statistics

School of Business Administration (tel. (622) 375-8874; fax (662) 374-3282; e-mail thakol@nida.nida.ac.th):

CHAMNONG, V., Organizational Behaviour

School of Public Administration (tel. (662) 375-1296; fax (662) 375-1297; e-mail sombat@nida.nida.ac.th):

CHANGRIEN, P., Political Science
PERMANJIT, G., City and Regional Planning
THAMRONGTANYAWONG, S., Public Policy and Planning

School of Social Development (tel. (662) 375-9111; fax (662) 375-0941; e-mail tangon@nida.nida.ac.th):

BHANTHUMNAVIN, D., Social Psychology
NORANITPADUNGKARN, C., Social Sciences
SMUCKARN, S., Social Psychology

PAYAP UNIVERSITY

Amphur Muang, Chiang Mai 50000

Telephone: (53) 851-478

Fax: (53) 241-983

E-mail: intexch@payap.ac.th

Internet: www.payap.ac.th

Founded 1974

Private control

Languages of instruction: Thai, English

Academic year: June to March (Thai Programme),September to April (English Programme)

Pres.: Dr BOONTHONG POOCHAROEN

Vice-Pres. for Academic Affairs: Dr YUWALAK CHIVAKIDAKARN

Vice-Pres. for Finance: Dr RUX PROHMPALIT

Vice-Pres. for Int. Affairs: MARTHA G. BUTT

Vice-Pres. for Planning and Devt: Dr TAWEE-SAK SUPASA
Vice-Pres. for Religious Affairs: Dr ESTHER WAKEMAN
Librarian: SUNTREE RATAYA-ANANT
Library of 125,100 vols
Number of teachers: 390
Number of students: 9,000
Publication: *Payap Journal* (1 a year)

DEANS

Faculty of Accountancy, Finance and Banking: MANIT PABUT
Faculty of Business Administration: YUVA-LUCK CHIVAKIDAKARN
Faculty of Humanities: Dr NARONG PRACHA-KHESUWAT
Faculty of Law: Dr KHETTAI LANGKARPINT
Faculty of Nursing: KAMOLWAN DISABUT
Faculty of Science: DUANGDUEN POOCHAROEN
Faculty of Social Science: MONTHATHIP RUN-GRUANGSRI
Faculty of Theology: Rev. WILLIAM J. YODER
Graduate School: Dr RATANAPORN SETHAKUL
International College: Dr TAWAT BUNREUANG

PRINCE OF SONGKLA UNIVERSITY

71/1 Moo 5 Thanon Karnjanavanich Tambon Kor-Hong, POB Hat-Yai, Hat-Yai Dist., Songkla 90110
Telephone: (74) 282-000 (Hat-Yai Campus)
Fax: (74) 212-828 (Hat-Yai Campus)
E-mail: hatyai-pr@psu.ac.th
Internet: www.psu.ac.th
Founded 1967
State control
Languages of instruction: English, Thai
Academic year: June to March (2 semesters)
Pres.: Assoc. Prof. Dr SUNTHORN SOTTHI-BANDHU
Vice-Pres. for Academic Affairs (Hat-Yai Campus): Dr PAIRAT SA-NGUANSAI
Vice-Pres. for Academic Affairs (Pattani Campus): Asst Prof. Dr SUWIMON KIEW-KAEW
Vice-Pres. for Devt: Asst Prof. Dr SUJITRA JARAJIT
Vice-Pres. for Devt Affairs (Pattani Campus): PRAMOTE KRAMUT
Vice-Pres. for Hat-Yai Campus: Asst Prof. Dr METHI SUNBHANICH
Vice-Pres. for Pattani Campus: Asst Prof. PRAPAN WISETRATTAKAM
Vice-Pres. for Planning and Devt: Assoc. Prof. UDOM CHOMCHAN
Vice-Pres. for Research and Int. Relations: Assoc. Prof. Dr PRASERT CHITAPONG
Vice-Pres. for Spec. Affairs (Pattani Campus): PANN YAUNLAIE
Number of teachers: 1,428
Number of students: 13,048
Publication: *PSU Arts and Culture*

DEANS

College of Islamic Studies: Dr ISMA-AE ALEE (Dir)
Faculty of Agro-Industry (Hat-Yai Campus): Assoc. Prof. PAIBOON THAMMARATWASIK
Faculty of Dentistry (Hat-Yai Campus): KRASSANAI WONGRANGSIMAKUL
Faculty of Education (Pattani Campus): Asst Prof. Dr WIRAT THUMMARPORN
Faculty of Engineering (Hat-Yai Campus): PICHIT RERNGSANGVATANA
Faculty of Environmental Management Establishment Project (Hat-Yai Campus): Asst Prof. Dr CHADCHAI RATANACHAI
Faculty of Hospitality and Tourism: Assoc. Prof. MANAT CHAISAWAT (Dir)
Faculty of Humanities and Social Sciences (Pattani Campus): Asst Prof. PRAPAN WISE-TRATAKAN

Faculty of Management Science (Hat-Yai Campus): Asst Prof. Dr SOMPORN FUANG-CHAN
Faculty of Medicine (Hat-Yai Campus): Assoc. Prof. PUNTIPYA SANGUANCHUA
Faculty of Natural Resources (Hat-Yai Campus): Assoc. Prof. Dr SOMKIAT SAITANOO
Faculty of Nursing (Hat-Yai Campus): Asst Prof. Dr SUNUTTRA TABOONPONG
Faculty of Pharmaceutical Science (Hat-Yai Campus): Asst Prof. Dr PITI TRISDIKOON
Faculty of Science (Hat-Yai Campus): Prof. PUANGPEN SIRIRUGSA
Faculty of Science and Technology (Pattani Campus): Asst Prof. PREECHA PONGBHAI

RAMKHAMHAENG UNIVERSITY

Ramkhamhaeng Rd, Huamark, Bangkok 10240
Telephone: (2) 310-8118
Fax: (2) 310-8022
E-mail: admin@ram1.ru.ac.th
Internet: www.ru.ac.th
Founded 1971
State control
Languages of instruction: Thai, English
Academic year: June to March (two semesters)
Rector: Prof. RANGSAN SAENGSOOK
Vice-Rector for Academic Affairs and Research: Prof. Dr CHUTA THIANTHAI
Vice-Rector for Admin.: Assoc. Prof. PRASAT SANGASILP
Vice-Rector for Amnartcharoen Province Regional Campus: Asst Prof. CHALERMCHAI PIWRUANGNONT
Vice-Rector for Campus Affairs: Assoc. Prof. KIM CHAISANSOOK
Vice-Rector for Cultural Affairs: Dr WICHAI SUNGPRAPAI
Vice-Rector for Devt: Assoc. Prof. WIRAT SANGUANWONWAN
Vice-Rector for Educational Technology: Asst Prof. Dr PANYA SIRIROJ
Vice-Rector for Finance: Assoc. Prof. SOM-CHINTANA SIVALI
Vice-Rector for Gen. Affairs: Assoc. Prof. ARUNTAVADEE PHATNIBUL
Vice-Rector for Int. Affairs: Assoc. Prof. RAMPAI SIRIMANAKUL
Vice-Rector for Khon Kaen Province Regional Campus: Assoc. Prof. VICHAI THARANONT
Vice-Rector for Legal Affairs and Property: Prof. SURACHAI SUWANPREECHA
Vice-Rector for Nakhornpanom Province Regional Campus: Asst Prof. VIBOON TOVA-NABOOT
Vice-Rector for Nakhornratsrima Province Regional Campus: Assoc. Prof. VISIT TAWEESET
Vice-Rector for Nakhornsrithammarat Province Regional Campus: Assoc. Prof. Dr AROM CHANUANCHIT
Vice-Rector for Policy and Planning: Assoc. Prof. MANOP PRAMANACHOTE
Vice-Rector for Prachinburi Province Regional Campus: Asst Prof. CHAMNAN TEMMUANGPUK
Vice-Rector for Prae Province Regional Campus: Assoc. Prof. KULYANEE TARASUEB
Vice-Rector for Public Relations: Assoc. Prof. Dr WISANU SUWANA-PERM
Vice-Rector of the Rector's Office: Assoc. Prof. Dr KHOSIT INTAWONGSE
Vice-Rector for Sri Sa Ket Province Regional Campus: WICHIAN CHUENCHOB
Vice-Rector for Student Affairs: Assoc. Prof. SUMETH KAEWPRAG
Vice-Rector for Sukhothai Province Regional Campus: Asst Prof. SAMRAN SOMBOONPHOL
Vice-Rector for Trang Regional Campus: Assoc. Prof. PETJARAPORN JANTARASUT
Vice-Rector for Univ. Affairs: Assoc. Prof SITTIPAN BUDDHAHUN

Vice-Rector for Uthaithani Province Regional Campus: Asst Prof. ROENGRAK JAMPANGOEN
Vice-Rector for Welfare: Assoc. Prof. NOPPA-KUN KUNACHEVA
Number of teachers: 852
Number of students: 340,231 (329,599 undergraduate, 10,632 graduate)
Publication: *Ramkhamhaeng University Newsletter* (52 a year)

DEANS

Faculty of Business Administration: Prof. RANGSAN SAENGSOOK (acting)
Faculty of Economics: Assoc. Prof. VANCHAI RIMVITAGAYORN
Faculty of Education: Assoc. Prof. RAVIWAN SRIKRAMKRAN
Faculty of Engineering: Asst Prof. SUVAT SRIVITHAYARAKS
Faculty of Humanities: Assoc. Prof. Dr PIT SOMPONG
Faculty of Law: Assoc. Prof. JARAL LENGVIT-TAYA
Faculty of Political Science: Assoc. Prof. PRONCHAI DHEBPANYA
Faculty of Science: Assoc. Prof. SUPOTE CHAITIUMVONG

RANGSIT UNIVERSITY

52/347, Muang Ake, Phaholyothin Rd, Tambon-Lakhok, 12000 Pathum Thani
Telephone and fax (2) 997-2200
E-mail: info@rangsit.rsu.ac.th
Internet: www.rsu.ac.th
Founded 1985
Private control
Languages of instruction: English, Thai
Academic year: May to April
Pres.: Dr ARTHIT OURAIRAT
Vice-Pres. for Academic Affairs: Asst Prof. Dr NARES PANTARATORN
Vice-Pres. for Admin.: AUMNOUVUT SARASALIN
Vice-Pres. for Planning and Quality Devt: Dr ARTAWIT OURAIRAT
Vice-Pres. for Student Affairs: Dr PHONGPAT ANUMUTRATHCHAKIJ
Library Dir: Dr MALIRAN PRADITTEERA
Library of 106,895 vols
Number of teachers: 2,011
Number of students: 30,000

SIAM UNIVERSITY

235 Petchkasem Rd, Phasi-Charoen, Bangkok 10160
Telephone: (2) 867-8088
Fax: (2) 457-6657
E-mail: siam@siam.edu
Internet: www.siam.edu
Founded 1973
Private control
Academic year: June to March
Pres.: Dr PORNCHAI MONGKHONVANIT
Vice-Pres. for Academic Affairs: Prof. Dr NIMNUAN SRICHAD
Vice-Pres. for Planning and Devt: Dr PAYUNGSAK JANTRASURIN
Vice-Pres. for Public Affairs and Cooperative Education: THANAVADEE BOONLUE
Vice-Pres. for Research: Prof. Dr NIPONE SOOKPREEDEE
Registrar: SURADEJ PRUGSAMATZ
Librarian: JIRAPAT HARNNUSSORN
Library of 161,561 vols
Number of teachers: 530
Number of students: 14,299
Publications: *Cultural Approach* (2 a year), *Engineering Journal of Siam University* (2 a year), *Journal of Nursing, Siam University* (2 a year), *Siam Business Review* (3 a year), *Siam University Law Journal* (1 a year), *Siam University Review* (6 a year)

DEANS

Graduate School of Business: Dr VICHIT SUPINIT
Graduate School of Communication Arts: Assoc. Prof. Dr THANAVADEE BOONLUE
Graduate School of Education: Assoc. Prof. Dr AMORNCHAI TANTIMEDH
Graduate School of Engineering: Dr VANCHAI RIJIRAVANICH
Graduate School of Information Technology: Assoc. Prof. Dr WICHIAN PREMCHAISWADI
Graduate School of Public Administration: Assoc. Prof. Dr SURAPOL KANCHANACHITRA
School of Business Administration: Dr SUMRIT TIANDUM
School of Communication Arts: Assoc. Prof. Dr SIRICHAI SIRIKAYA
School of Engineering: Assoc. Prof. SARAVUTH VORASUMANTA
School of Law: Dr SOMMAI CHANRUANG
School of Liberal Arts: Dr SUBORDAS WARMSINGH
School of Nursing Science: Assoc. Prof. ORNTIPA SONGSIRI
School of Science: Dr KANJANA MAHATTANATAWEE

SILPAKORN UNIVERSITY

22 Boromrachachonnani Rd, Taling-Chan, Bangkok 10170
Telephone: (2) 880-7374
Fax: (2) 880-7372
E-mail: webmaster@su.ac.th
Internet: www.su.ac.th
Founded 1943
State control
Language of instruction: Thai
Academic year: June to March (2 semesters)
Pres.: Dr UTHAI DULYAKASEM
Vice-Pres. for Academic and Research Affairs: Assoc. Prof. Dr MANEE LUANGTANA-ANAN
Vice-Pres. for Admin. Affairs: Asst Prof. RAPEEPUN CHALONGSUK
Vice-Pres. for Art and Culture: Asst Prof. YANAWIT KUNCHAETHONG
Vice-Pres. for Planning and Devt: Assoc. Prof. CHARUNPAT PUVANANT
Vice-Pres. for Student Affairs: PORNSAWAN AMARANONTA
Vice-Pres. for Quality Assurance in Education: Asst Prof. Dr RENU VEJARATPIMOL
Registrar: SAICHON SAJJANIT
Librarian: KANCHANA SUKONTHAMANEE
Library of 552,330 vols
Number of teachers: 1,016
Number of students: 22,340

DEANS

Faculty of Music: THANATORN JIARAKUN
Graduate School: Assoc. Prof. Dr SIRICHAI CHINATANKUL
Silpakorn University International College (SUIC): Assoc. Prof. Dr SOMPID KATTIYAPIKUL (Dir)

CONSTITUENT CAMPUSES

Phetchaburi Information Technology Campus: 1 Moo 3, Cha-am, Pranburi Rd, Samphraya, Amphoe Cha Am, Phetchaburi 76120; tel. (3) 259-4043; fax (3) 259-4026

DEANS

Faculty of Animal Sciences and Agricultural Technology: Assoc. Prof. Dr KRIENGSAK POONSUK
Faculty of Information and Communication Technology: Asst Prof. CHAICHARN THAVARAVEJ
Faculty of Management Sciences: Asst Prof. Dr WANCHAO SUTANANTA

Sanamchand Palace Campus: 6 Rajamaka Nai Rd, Mueang Dist., Nakhon Pathom

73000; tel. (34) 253-910; fax (34) 255-099; Vice-Pres. Dr CHACORN VIPUSANAVANISH; Asst Pres. for Student Affairs Asst Prof. Dr BUSARAKORN MAHAYOTHEE; Librarian KANCHANA SUKONTHAMANEE

DEANS

Faculty of Arts: Asst Prof. Dr MANEEPIN PHROMSUTHIRAK
Faculty of Education: Assoc. Prof. Dr KANIT KHEOVICHAI
Faculty of Engineering and Industrial Technology: Asst Prof. Dr JESDAWAN WICHITWECHKARN
Faculty of Pharmacy: Assoc. Prof. Dr JURAIRAT NANTANIT
Faculty of Science: Asst Prof. Dr JARUNGSAENG LAKSANABOONSONG

Wang Thapra Palace Campus: 31 Na-Phra Lan Rd, Phra Nakhorn Dist., Bangkok 10200; tel. (2) 623-6115; fax (2) 225-7258; Vice-Pres. Asst Prof. SOMCHAI EKPANYAKUL; Asst Pres. for Student Affairs Assoc. Prof. TINNAKORN KASORNSUWAN

DEANS

Faculty of Archaeology: Assoc. Prof. SAYAN PRAICHARNJIT (acting)
Faculty of Architecture: Assoc. Prof. CHINASAK TANDIKUL
Faculty of Decorative Arts: Assoc. Prof. EAKACHART JONEURAIRATANA
Faculty of Painting, Sculpture and Graphic Arts: Assoc. Prof. PARINYA TANTISUK

SOUTH-EAST ASIA UNIVERSITY

19/1 Phetkasem Rd, Nona Khaem, Bangkok 10160
Telephone: (2) 807-4500
Fax: (2) 807-4528
E-mail: webmaster@sau.ac.th
Internet: www.sau.ac.th
Pres.: Assoc. Prof. Dr NARONG SINSAWASDI
Founded 1973 as South-East Asia College, univ. status 1992
Faculties of arts and sciences, business administration, engineering, law; graduate school; language institute
Library of 68,000 vols, 650 journals
Number of students: 5,191

SRINAKHARINWIROT UNIVERSITY

114 Sukhumvit 23, Bangkok 10110
Telephone: (2) 664-1000
Fax: (2) 258-4006
E-mail: ird@swu.ac.th
Internet: www.swu.ac.th
Founded 1954, univ. status 1974
State control
Language of instruction: Thai
Academic year: June to May
Pres.: Assoc. Prof. Dr SUMONTHA PROMBOON
Vice-Pres. for Academic Affairs: Assoc. Prof. Dr SAKCHAI NIRUNTHAWEE
Vice-Pres. for Admin. Affairs: Assoc. Prof. Dr PAISAL WANGPHANICH
Vice-Pres. for Arts and Culture: VINAI BHURAHONGSE
Vice-Pres. for Finance and Personnel: Assoc. Prof. Dr PINITI RATANANUKUL
Vice-Pres. for Int. Relations: Dr SUTASSI SMUTHKOCHORN
Vice-Pres. for Planning and Devt: Asst Prof. Dr CHAVANEE TONGROACH
Vice-Pres. for Research: Prof. Dr SERMSAK WISALAPORN
Vice-Pres. for Student Affairs: Asst Prof. MANEE THONGGOOM
Registrar: ORAPIN KAEWLAI
Dir of Central Library: Asst Prof. NONGNATH CHAIRAT

Library: see under Libraries and Archives
Number of teachers: 1,523
Number of students: 16,877
Publication: journals in humanities, nursing, pharmaceutical science, physical education and science, each 2 a year

DEANS

Faculty of Dentistry: Assoc. Prof. Dr TIPAPORN VONGSURASIT
Faculty of Education: Assoc. Prof. Dr KHOMPET CHATSUPAKUL
Faculty of Engineering: AREE HANSUEBSAI
Faculty of Fine Arts: Prof. Dr WIROON TUNGCHAROEN
Faculty of Health Science: Assoc. Prof. Dr WITTAYA TONSUWONNONT
Faculty of Humanities: Asst Prof. SUPA PANCHAROEN
Faculty of Medicine: Assoc. Prof. ARUNWONG THEPCHATRI
Faculty of Nursing: Assoc. Prof. Dr TASSANA BOONTHONG
Faculty of Pharmaceutical Sciences: Lt-Col Dr NOPDOL THONGNOPNUA
Faculty of Physical Education: Asst Prof. PHAN JIARANAI
Faculty of Science: Dr YUVADEE NAKAPADUNGRUT
Faculty of Social Sciences: Asst Prof. KAWEE WORRAKAWIN
Graduate School: Assoc. Prof. Dr NAPAPORN HAWANONDHA

SRIPATUM UNIVERSITY

Bangkhen Campus, 61 Phaholyotin Rd, Jatujak, Bangkok 10900
Telephone: (2) 579-1111
Fax: (2) 561-1721
E-mail: webspu@spu.ac.th
Internet: www.spu.ac.th
Founded 1970
Languages of instruction: Thai, English
Academic year: August to April
Pres.: RUTCHANEEPORN POOKAYAPORN PHUKKAMARN
Vice-Pres. for Academic Affairs: Asst Prof. Dr NIMNUAN SRICHAD
Vice-Pres. for Admin.: CHUA MAICHAROEN
Vice-Pres. for Student Affairs: SOPIT PANOMAI
Vice-Pres. for Technology: Assoc. Prof. Dr SUCHAI THANAWASTIEN
Library Dir: Asst Prof. Dr NAMTIP VIPAWIN
Library of 104,000 vols
Number of teachers: 493
Number of students: 16,442 (16,000 undergraduate, 442 postgraduate)

DEANS

Faculty of Accounting: KALAYAPORN BANMARUNG BURKE
Faculty of Architecture: Asst Prof. SUTHON VIRIYASOMBOON
Faculty of Business Administration: Dr KAMOL CHAIYAWAT
Faculty of Communication Arts: Assoc. Prof. ARUNEEPRAPA HOMSETHI
Faculty of Economics: SOMNUEK TANGEHAROEN
Faculty of Engineering: Assoc. Prof. NARONG U-THANOM
Faculty of Informatics: AMNUAY MUTHITAJAROEN
Faculty of Law: PARINYA PATHUMPONG
Faculty of Liberal Arts: Asst Prof. Dr GLORIA VIDHEECHAROEN
Graduate School: Dr NITINAI BUNNAG

SUKHOTHAI THAMMATHIRAT OPEN UNIVERSITY

Bangpood, Pakkred, Nonthaburi 11120
Telephone: (2) 503-2121

Fax: (2) 503-3607
E-mail: stou@samsorn.stou.ac.th
Internet: www.stou.ac.th
Founded 1978
State control
Language of instruction: Thai
Academic year: July to April (2 semesters)
Pres.: Prof. Dr IAM CHAYA-NGAM
Vice-Pres. for Academic Affairs: Assoc. Prof. Dr JUMPOL NIMPANICH
Vice-Pres. for Admin.: Assoc. Prof. NATEE KHLIBTONG
Vice-Pres. for Devt: Assoc. Prof. Dr CHOW ROJANASANG (acting)
Vice-Pres. for Operations: Assoc. Prof. CHUTIMA SACCHANAND
Vice-Pres. for Planning: Assoc. Prof. Dr CHOW ROJANASANG (acting)
Vice-Pres. for Services: Assoc. Prof. NATEE KHLIBTONG (acting)
Vice-Pres. for Spec. Affairs: Assoc. Prof. CHUTIMA SACCHANAND (acting)
Registrar: Assoc. Prof. Dr SOMSAK MEESAP-LAK

Library of 651,000 vols, 1,930 periodicals
Number of teachers: 393
Number of students: 221,269

DEANS

School of Agricultural Extension and Cooperatives: Asst Prof. Dr PONGPHAN THIENHIRUN
School of Communication Arts: Assoc. Prof. SUMON YUESIN
School of Economics: Asst Prof. Dr SOMCHIN SUNTAVARUK
School of Educational Studies: Assoc. Prof. Dr SOMPRASONG WITTAYAGIAT
School of Health Science: Asst Prof. Dr ADISAK SATTAM
School of Home Economics: Assoc. Prof. Dr JUMPOL NIMPANICH (acting)
School of Law: THIENCHAI NA NAKORN
School of Liberal Arts: Assoc. Prof. Dr PAITOON MIKUSOL
School of Management Science: Assoc. Prof. SUNA SITHILERTPRASIT
School of Political Science: Assoc. Prof. ROSALIN SIRIYAPHAN
School of Science and Technology: Assoc. Prof. Dr JUMPOL NIMPANICH

SURANAREE UNIVERSITY OF TECHNOLOGY

111 University Ave, Muang Dist., Nakhon Ratchasima 30000
Telephone: (44) 224-141
Fax: (44) 224-4140
E-mail: cenintaf@sut.ac.th
Internet: www.sut.ac.th
Founded 1990
State control
Languages of instruction: English, Thai
Academic year: May to April
Rector: Prof. Dr PRASART SUEBKA
Vice-Rector for Academic Affairs: Prof. Dr SUKIT LIMPIJUMNONG
Vice Rector for Admin. Affairs: Dr WUT DANKITTIKUL
Vice Rector for Devt: Assoc. Prof. Dr RANGSAN WONGSAN
Vice Rector for Gen. Affairs: Asst Prof. Dr ARAK TIRA-UMPHON
Vice Rector for Planning: Assoc. Prof. Dr SITTICHAI SEANGATITH
Vice-Rector for Student Affairs: Dr GUNTIMA SIRIJEERACHAI
Registrar: Asst Prof. Dr AIM-ORN TASSANA-SORN
Librarian: Assoc. Prof. Dr PRAPAVADEE SUEB-SONTHI

Library of 118,149 books, 415 periodicals
Number of teachers: 356

Number of students: 12,956 (11,257 undergraduate, 1,699 postgraduate)

DEANS

Institute of Agricultural Technology: Assoc. Prof. Dr SUWAYD NINGSANOND
Institute of Engineering: Asst Prof. Dr KONTORN CHAMNIPRASART
Institute of Medicine: Prof. Dr VANICH VANA-PRUKS
Institute of Nursing: SRIKIAT ANANSAWAS
Institute of Science: Assoc. Prof. Dr PRAPAN MANYUM
Institute of Social Technology: Dr PEERASAK SIRIYOTIN

THAKSIN UNIVERSITY

140 Moo 4 Tambon Khao Roop Chang, Muang Dist., Song Khla 90000
Telephone: (74) 311-885
Fax: (74) 324-440
E-mail: tsuinter@tsu.ac.th
Internet: www.tsu.ac.th
Founded 1996
Pres.: SOMBOON CHITPONG
Faculties of education, humanities and social sciences, science; institute of Southern Thai studies.

THAMMASAT UNIVERSITY

2 Prachand Rd, Bangkok 10200
Telephone: (2) 221-6111
Fax: (2) 224-8105
E-mail: inter@tu.ac.th
Internet: www.tu.ac.th
Founded 1934
State control
Languages of instruction: Thai, English
Academic year: June to February (2 semesters), summer sessionMarch to May
Rector: Prof. Dr SURAPON NITIKRAIPOT
Vice-Rector for Academic Affairs: Prof. Dr SIRILUCK ROTCHANAKITUMNUAI
Vice-Rector for Devt Planning and Technology: Asst Prof. Dr PRODPRAN SIRITHEERASAS
Vice-Rector for Financial Admin.: Asst Prof. SURASAK LIKASITWATANAKUL
Vice-Rector for Gen. Admin. (Lampang Center): Asst Prof. KAMONTHIP CHAMKRAJANG
Vice-Rector for Gen. Admin. (Rangsit Center): Assoc. Prof. GASINEE WITOONCHART
Vice-Rector for Gen. Admin. (Tha Prachan Center): Assoc. Prof. Dr UDOM RATHAMARIT
Vice-Rector for Int. Affairs: Assoc. Prof. Dr CHULACHEEP CHINWANNO
Vice-Rector for Personnel: Assoc. Prof. HARIRAK SUTABUTRA
Vice-Rector for Research Devt: Assoc. Prof. Dr PREECHA WANICHSETAKUL
Vice-Rector for Student Affairs: Asst Prof. Dr PARINYA THEWANARUEMITKUL
Registration Office Dir: Asst Prof. Dr VIRAVAT CHANTACHOTE
Librarian: SRICHAN CHANCHEEWA

Library: see under Libraries and Archives
Number of teachers: 1,623
Number of students: 32,507

Publications: *Faculty Bulletin, Journal of Business Administration, Journal of Political Science, Social Work Journal, Thammasat Law Journal, Thammasat University Journal*

DEANS

College of Innovative Education: Assoc. Prof. M. R. PONGSVAS SVASTI
College of Interdisciplinary Studies: Assoc. Prof. Dr NANTANA RONAKIAT
Faculty of Allied Health Science: Prof. Dr VITHOON VIYANANT
Faculty of Architecture and Planning: Prof. Dr SANTIRAK PRASERTSUK

Faculty of Commerce and Accountancy: Assoc. Prof. Dr KULPATRA SIRODOM
Faculty of Dentistry: YUVABOON CHANCHAM-CHAROON
Faculty of Economics: Assoc. Prof. Dr PATA-MAWADEE SUZUKI
Faculty of Engineering: Assoc. Prof. Dr URUYA WEESAKUL
Faculty of Fine and Applied Arts: SUTHIDA KALAYANAROOJ
Faculty of Journalism and Mass Communication: Asst Prof. Dr PORNCHIT SOMBUTPHA-NICH
Faculty of Law: Prof. Dr SOMKIT LERT-PAITHOON
Faculty of Liberal Arts: Assoc. Prof. Dr CHATCHAWADEE SARALAMBA
Faculty of Medicine: Assoc. Prof. CHITTINAD HAVANOND
Faculty of Nursing: Asst Prof. Dr SIRIPORN KHAMPALIKIT
Faculty of Political Science: Assoc. Prof. Dr SIRIPORN WAJJWALKU
Faculty of Public Health: Assoc. Prof. Dr NUNTAVARN VICHIT-VADAKAN
Faculty of Science and Technology: Assoc. Prof. SAITONG AMORNWICHET
Faculty of Social Administration: Asst Prof. Dr DECHA SUNGKAWAN
Faculty of Sociology and Anthropology: Asst Prof. PORNCHAI TRAKULWARANONT
Graduate School: Assoc. Prof. MANOON PAHIRAH
Pridi Banomyong International College: Assoc. Prof. Dr PIMPAN VESSAKOSOL
Sirindhon International Institute of Technology: Prof. Dr CHONGRAK POLPRASERT

UBON RATCHATHANI UNIVERSITY

85 Sathonlamark Rd, Warin Chamrap, Ubon Ratchathani 34190
Telephone: (45) 353-052
Fax: (45) 288-394
E-mail: intercoop@ubu.ac.th
Internet: www.ubu.ac.th
Founded 1987
State control
Languages of instruction: Englsih, Thai
Academic year: June to May
Pres.: Prof. Dr NONGNIT TEERAWATANASUK
Vice-Pres. for Academic Affairs: Dr UTITH INPRASIT
Vice-Pres. for Admin. and Community Relations: MANOON SRIVIRAT
Vice-Pres. for Facilities: NITISAK KAEWSENA
Vice President for Research and Innovations: Dr INTHIRA SAHEE
Vice-Pres. for Int. Relations: Prof. Dr PATAR-EEYA WISAIJORN
Vice-Pres. for Planning and Devt: Dr JUTHA-MAS JITCHAROEN
Vice-Pres. for Research and Academic Services: Asst. Prof. Dr KUNGWAN THUMMA-SAENG
Vice-Pres. for Student Devt: Dr NARINTORN BOONBRAHM
Vice-Pres. for Student Affairs: THAI SANGTH-EAN
Librarian: SUOACHAI HATHONGKHAM

Library of 221,483 vols of books, 53,618 periodicals, 17,561 audio visuals, 13 databases
Number of teachers: 646
Number of students: 13,712 (12,989 undergraduate, 610 masters, 113 doctoral)

DEANS

College of Medicine and Public Health: PUAN SUTHIPINITTHARM
Faculty of Agriculture: Assoc. Prof. Dr WATCHARAPONG WATTANAKUL
Faculty of Applied Arts and Design: Asst. Prof. Dr WANWALAI ATHIWASPONG (acting)

Faculty of Engineering: Prof. Dr NOTE SANG-TIAN

Faculty of Law: BUNLEU KONGCHAN

Faculty of Liberal Arts: Asst. Prof. Dr KANOKWAN MANOROM (acting)

Faculty of Management Science: Dr WIROTE MANOPIMOKE

Faculty of Nursing: Dr SUREE TRUMIKABORWORN

Faculty of Pharmaceutical Science: Assoc. Prof. CHUTINUN PRASITPURIPRECHA

Faculty of Political Science: Assoc. Prof. Dr CHAIYAN RATCHAKUL

Faculty of Science: Asst Prof. JANPEN INTARAPRASERT

UNIVERSITY OF THE THAI CHAMBER OF COMMERCE

126/1 Vibhavadi Rangsit Rd, Bangkok 10320

Telephone: (2) 276-1040

Fax: (2) 276-2126

E-mail: nitima@morakot.nectec.or.th

Internet: www.utcc.ac.th

Founded 1940 as College of Commerce; present name and status 1984

Pres.: CHIRADET OUSAWAT

Library of 100,000 vols, 6,000 periodicals.

WALAILAK UNIVERSITY

222 Thaiburi, Thasala Dist., Nakhon Si Thammarat 80160

Telephone: (75) 384-000

Fax: (75) 384-258

E-mail: wu@praduu.wu.ac.th

Internet: www.wu.ac.th

Pres.: Dr SUPAT POOPAKA

Founded 1992

State control

Institutes of agricultural technology, allied health sciences and public health, engineering and resources management, information science, liberal arts, management, nursing and science.

Colleges and Institutes

AGRICULTURE

Ayuthaya Agricultural College: Ayuthaya.

Bang Phra Agricultural College: Bang Phra, Cholburi; tel. (38) 777-503; fax (38) 341-808; e-mail bp_library@hotmail.com; internet www.bparg.rit.ac.th; f. 1957; teacher training, training in farming; library: 10,000 vols; 130 teachers; 1,600 students; Dir Dr SURAPHOL SANGUANSRI.

Rajamangola Institute of Technology, Surin Campus: Surin; tel. (44) 511-022; fax (44) 519-034; internet www.surin.rit.ac.th; f. 2001, fmrly Surin Agricultural College; 143 teachers; 2,289 students; Dir Asst Prof. Dr WIEHIEN OUNRUEN.

TECHNOLOGY

Northern Technical Institute: Huay Kaew Rd, Chiang Mai; f. 1957; library: 50,777 vols; 2–3-year diploma courses; Dir C. SUWATHEE.

Rajamangala Institute of Technology, Bangkok Technical Campus: 2 Nang Linchee Rd, Bangkok 10120; tel. 2863991; f. 1952; degree courses, 2- to 5-year certificate and diploma courses; library: 61,048 vols; 431 teachers; 6,111 students; Dir SKUL VEJAKORN.

Rajamangala Institute of Technology, Khon Kaen Campus: 150 Srichan Rd, Khon Kaen; tel. (43) 236-451; f. 1963 (fmrly Thai-German Technical Institute); specializes in industrial technology; 3-year vocational certificate course, 2-year higher vocational diploma, 2-year BS; library: 11,186 vols (mainly industrial education); Dir SUBHAN TUENGSOOK.

Southern Technical Institute: Songkla.

TIMOR-LESTE

The Higher Education System

Universidade Nasionál Timór Lorosa'e (formerly Universitas Timor Timur), which was founded in 2000, predates Timor-Leste (formerly East Timor)'s independence from Indonesia in 2002. It is Timor-Leste's principal institution of higher education. It was largely destroyed during civil unrest in 1999, but reopened in November 2000. In 2001 there were an estimated 6,349 students enrolled in tertiary education. Since 2000 there has been significant growth in the higher education sector with the number of institutions growing from six in 1999 to over 20 in 2007. In 2008/09 total enrolment within tertiary education stood at 16,727 students. The Ministry of Education, Culture, Youth and Sport is responsible for the provision of higher education. The National Commission for Academic Assessment and Accreditation was established in 2006 to take full responsibility for defining standards and criteria for academic accreditation and assessment and for accrediting higher education institutions and their programmes.

Regulatory Body

GOVERNMENT

Ministry of Education, Culture, Youth and Sport: Díli; e-mail education@gov .east-timor.org; Minister JOÃO CÂNCIO.

Research Institutes

LANGUAGE AND LITERATURE

Instituto Nacional de Linguística (National Institute of Linguistics): Liceu 'Dr Francisco Macado', Avda Cidade de Lisboa, Díli; tel. 3313-142; fax 3321-211; e-mail indldili@yahoo.com; internet www.shlrc.mq .edu.au/~leccles; f. 2001 to study, protect and foster the official languages of Timor-Leste, Tetum and Portuguese; official govt body with the charter of coordinating and overseeing all indigenous language research and development projects; attached to National University of East Timor; Dir-Gen. Prof. Dr BENJAMIM DE ARAÚJO E CORTE-REAL; Dir of Research and Publications Prof. Dr GEOF-

FREY HULL; publ. *Research Bulletin* (electronic, 2 a year).

NATURAL SCIENCES

Centro Nacional de Investigação Científica (National Centre of Scientific Research): Liceu Dr Francisco Machado, Avda Cidade de Lisboa, Díli; tel. 3332-705; e-mail cnic_timor@yahoo.com; internet www .cnictimor.org; f. 2001 to develop the economic, social and political welfare of Timor-Leste by means of scientific research; areas of research: agriculture, business and economics, education, political and social sciences, technology; Dir Prof. HELDER DA COSTA.

Libraries and Archives

Díli

National University of Timor Lorosa'e Library: Avda Cidade de Lisboa, Díli; fmrly library of Universitas Timor Timur; large part of its collection removed or destroyed during civil unrest in 1999; University Librarian VENCESLAO DO REGO.

Xanana Gusmão Reading Room: Rua Belarmina Lobo Lecidere, POB 3, Díli; tel. 3322-831; e-mail xgrroom@mail .timortelecom.tp; internet www.xgrroom.org; f. 2000; Dir KIRSTY SWORD GUSMÃO.

University

UNIVERSIDADE NASIONÁL TIMÓR LOROSA'E
(National University of East Timor)

Avda Cidade de Lisboa, Díli

Telephone: 3321-210
Fax: 3322-535
E-mail: bcorte_real@hotmail.com

Founded 2000, succeeded Universitas Timor Timur (f. 1986, under Indonesian control), which was largely destroyed during civil unrest in 1999

State control

Rector: Prof. Dr BENJAMIM DE ARAÚJO E CORTE-REAL

Univ. Librarian: VENCESLAU DO REGO

Number of students: 7,000

TOGO

The Higher Education System

The principal institution of higher education is the Université de Lomé (formerly University of Benin), which was founded in 1965 as the Institut Supérieur de Bénin (Advanced Institute of Benin) in conjunction with the neighbouring state of Benin. The Université de Lomé had about 14,000 students in the early 2000s, and scholarships to French universities are also available. A second university opened in Kara, in the north of Togo, in early 2004. In 2006/07 32,502 students were enrolled in tertiary education.

Higher education is the responsibility of the Ministry of Higher Education and Research. The funding of higher education is administered by the Grand Conseil des Universités (General Higher Education Council), which determines institutional budgets following consultation with the institutions. Students' tuition fees account for approximately 5% of income.

The secondary school Baccalauréat is the main requirement for admission to higher education. Applicants without the Baccalauréat are required to sit an entrance examination. A three-tier, credit-based Licence–Master–Doctorat (LMD) degree system was introduced in 2006, thus bringing Togo's system closer into line with the Bologna-style European model. The new system, which reduced the number of semesters in each academic year from three to two, begins with a three-year first cycle of undergraduate study leading to award of the Licence. Following the Licence, students may proceed to a two-year postgraduate Masters degree. The third and final cycle is the Doctorat, which requires a minimum of three years'

additional study. The LMD reform will lead to the eventual abolishment of the old university degree system, which was based on the old French system of three cycles. The first cycle typically lasted two years and led to the award of the undergraduate Diplôme Universitaire d'Études Générales, Diplôme Universitaire d'Études Littéraires, Diplôme Universitaire de Techniques Juridiques or Diplôme Universitaire d'Études Scientifiques, or, in professional fields, the Diplôme de Technicien Supérieur. The second cycle consisted of one year of study leading to the award of the Licence (Bachelors), followed by a further year leading to the award of the Maîtrise (Masters). Finally, the third cycle comprised firstly a one- to two-year period of study leading to the award of the Diplôme d'Études Supérieures Specialisées or Diplôme d'Études Approfondies, and secondly a two-year period of study culminating with the award of the Doctorat (Doctorate). Professional degrees lasting longer than four years were offered by faculties of the university and specialist schools, such as the Diplôme d'Ingénieur Agronome (five years), Diplôme d'Ingénieur de Conception (five years) and Doctorat de Médecine (seven years).

The technical and vocational education system has also been undergoing a period of reform. A Baccalauréat is required for entry to the Brevet de Technicien Supérieur, which requires three years of study and qualifies the holder to access professional training or to work in their chosen field of study. The introduction of a two-year Diplôme Universitaire de Technologie is under development.

Regulatory Bodies

GOVERNMENT

Ministry of Communication, Culture and Civic Training: BP 40, Lomé; tel. 221-29-30; fax 221-43-80; e-mail info@ republicoftogo.com; Minister CORNÉLIUS AÏDAM.

Ministry of Higher Education and Research: rue Colonel de Roux, BP 12175, Lomé; tel. 222-09-83; fax 222-07-83; Minister MESSAN ADIMADO ADUAYOM.

Learned Societies

BIBLIOGRAPHY, LIBRARY SCIENCE AND MUSEOLOGY

Association Togolaise pour le Développement de la Documentation, des Bibliothèques, Archives et Musées: c/o Bibliothèque de l'Université de Bénin, BP 1515, Lomé; f. 1959; promotes research in the field of documentation and library science; participates in the education of adults and young people; holds conferences, etc.; 60 mems; Pres. KOFFI ATTIGNON; Sec.-Gen. EKOUE AMAH.

LANGUAGE AND LITERATURE

Goethe-Institut: 25, Rue Kokéti, angle Rue de l'Eglise, BP 914, Lomé; tel. 2210894; fax 2220777; e-mail info@lome.goethe.org; internet www.goethe.de/lome; offers courses and exams in German language and culture and promotes cultural exchange with Germany; Dir TORSTEN OERTEL.

Research Institutes

GENERAL

Institut de Recherche pour le Développement (IRD): BP 375, Lomé; tel. 221-43-44; fax 221-03-43; e-mail ird_lome@netcom .tg; f. 1949; agronomy, geology, pedology, geography, sociology, hydrology, geophysics, library; Admin. Agent BERNADETTE NAKU; see main entry under France.

AGRICULTURE, FISHERIES AND VETERINARY SCIENCE

Institut de Recherches Agronomiques Tropicales et des Cultures Vivrières (IRAT): BP 1163, Lomé; tel. 221-21-48; Dir M. SARAGONI; see main entry under France.

Institut de Recherches du Café, du Cacao et Autres Plantes Stimulantes (IRCC): BP 90, Kpalimé; tel. 441-00-34; fax 441-00-60; f. 1967; research to improve quality and production of coffee, cocoa and other stimulants; experimental unit at Tové; Dir K. EDEM DJIEKPOR.

Institut Togolais de Recherche Agronomique/Centre de Recherche Agronomique de la Savane Humide: BP 01, Kolokopé Anié; tel. 444-30-00; fax 444-30-02; e-mail crash@laposte.tg; f. 1948; see main entry under France; Dir M. BONFOH BEDIBETE; publ. *Coton et Fibres Tropicales*.

NATURAL SCIENCES

General

Institut National de la Recherche Scientifique: BP 2240, Lomé; tel. 221-01-39; f. 1965; initiation of national scientific research; rural development research; 12

permanent staff; library of 5,000 vols; publ. *Etudes Togolaises* (2 a year).

TECHNOLOGY

Service des Mines du Togo: c/o Ministère des Mines, Ave de la Marina, Lomé; Dir-Gen. ANKOUM P. AREGBA.

Libraries and Archives

Lomé

Archives Nationales du Togo: POB 1002, Lomé; tel. 221-04-10; f. 1976; administered by the Nat. Ministry for Education and Scientific Research; 2,500 vols, specializing in colonial history, tropical agronomy, stock breeding, health; Curator SENGHOR MOUSSA.

Bibliothèque du Ministère de l'Intérieur: Rue Albert Sarraut, Lomé; Librarian KWAOVI GABRIEL JOHNSON.

Bibliothèque Nationale: BP 1002, Lomé; tel. 221-04-10; fax 222-19-67; e-mail dban@tg .refer.org; German and French archives; 18,050 vols, 400 periodicals (incl. 74 current); Dir WENMI-AGORE M. COULIBALEY.

Museum

Lomé

Direction du Musée National, des Sites et Monuments: BP 12156, Lomé; tel. 221-68-07; fax 221-43-80; f. 1974; Curator of the National Museum NAYONDJOUA DJANGUENANE.

Universities

UNIVERSITÉ DE KARA

BP 43, Kara
Telephone: 661-02-56
Fax: 660-12-74
Founded 2004
State Control
Pres.: AÏSSAH AGBÉTRA

Number of teachers: 30
Number of students: 1,477
Faculties of arts and humanities, economics and management, law and politics.

UNIVERSITÉ DE LOMÉ

BP 1515, Lomé
Telephone: 221-35-00
Fax: 221-85-95
E-mail: ngayiber@tg.refer.org
Internet: www.ub.tg
Founded 1965 as a Higher Institute; univ. status 1970; incl. all the instns of higher education in the country
State control
Language of instruction: French
Academic year: October to June (three terms)
Pres.: Prof. NICOUÉ L. GAYIBOR
Vice-Pres.: THIOU T. K. TCHAMIE

Sec.-Gen.: ABALO KODJO TABO
Librarian: A. B. F. GBIKPI-BENISSAN
Library of 70,000 vols
Number of teachers: 650
Number of students: 14,168

Publications: *Livret de l'Etudiant, Annales (Lettres, Sciences, Médecine, Droit-Economie), Actes des Journées Scientifiques, Annuaire statistique, Journal de la Recherche Scientifique, Campus Actualités*

DEANS AND DIRECTORS

Faculty of Economics and Business Management: K. AYASSOU
Faculty of Law: Prof. PEDRO AKUETE SANTOS
Faculty of Letters and Humanities: Prof. KOMLA M. F. NUBUKPO
Faculty of Medicine: Prof. KOFFI N'DAKENA
Faculty of Sciences: Prof. M. GBEASSOR
CIC-CAFMICRO (Computer Centre): TSATSOU FIADJOE
Distance Learning Centre: MARYSE A. QUASHIE
Higher School of Agriculture: K. AGBEKO
Higher Secretarial School: A. MAGNAN
Medical Training School: Prof. BATOMA SOSSOU
National Higher School of Engineering: E. K.-S. BEDJA
National Institute of Education: A. KOMLAN

University Technical Institute of Food and Biological Sciences: Prof. COMLAN A. DE SOUZA
University Technical Institute of Management: N. BIGOU-LARE

Colleges

Centre de Formation Professionnelle Agricole de Tove: BP 401, Kpalimé; f. 1901; 21 teachers; 230 students; library: 3,500 vols; Dir S. N. KANKARTI; Sec.-Gen. I. KUEVI.

Ecole Africaine des Métiers d'Architecture et d'Urbanisme: BP 2067, Lomé; tel. 221-62-53; fax 222-06-52; f. 1975; specialist courses in architecture and town planning; in-service courses for trained architects; library: 1,957 vols; 23 staff; 102 students; Dir AHMED ASKIA SIDI.

Ecole Nationale d'Administration: Ave de la Libération, Lomé; tel. 221-21-30; fax 221-35-29; f. 1958; provides training for Togolese civil servants; 100 teachers; 500 students; library: 1,000 vols; Dir DAGO YABRE; Sec.-Gen. KOMIKUMA DOGBEVI.

TONGA

The Higher Education System

Institutions of higher education pre-date the independence of Tonga from the United Kingdom in 1970, with the oldest being the 'Atenisi Institute, which was founded in 1966. In 1999 a total of 467 students attended technical and vocational colleges, of which there were four in 2001. There was one teacher-training college in 1999, with 288 students. In 1990 there were 230 Tongans studying overseas. The University of the South Pacific has a centre in Tonga. Some degree courses are also offered at the university division of the 'Atenisi Institute, although this is not recognized by the Tongan Government. A new establishment offering higher education, the 'Unuaki-'o-Tonga Royal Institute, opened in 2004.

Higher Education is overseen by the Tonga National Qualifications and Accreditation Board (TNQAB). The Board was created by the TNQAB Bill, which was approved in 2004 and enacted in 2007.

Among the qualifications required for admission to higher education are the Higher Leaving Certificate, New Zealand University Entrance Certificate and Pacific Secondary Certificate. There is also a one-year Foundation Programme for applicants to the University of the South Pacific. The Bachelors is the undergraduate degree and typically lasts three years, although some courses may last longer; the Bachelors in medicine at the Fiji School of Medicine, for example, is a four-year degree. Following completion of the Bachelors, graduates may study for the Masters, which is a one- or two-year course of study. The highest university degree is the Doctorate, requiring a minimum of a further two years' study following award of the Masters.

The Government provides over one-half of all facilities and training for post-secondary vocational and technical education. Institutions providing such education include the Community Development Training Centre, the Tonga Institute of Science and Technology, the Civil Service Training Centre and the Royal School of Science and Technology.

Regulatory Bodies

GOVERNMENT

Ministry of Education, Women's Affairs and Culture: POB 61, Vuna Rd, Kolofo'ou, Nuku'alofa; tel. 23511; fax 23596; e-mail moe@kalianet.to; internet www.tongaeducation.gov.to; Minister Dr ANA MAUI TAUFE'ULUNGAKI.

ACCREDITATION

Tonga National Qualifications and Accreditation Board: New City Bldg, Nuku'alofa; tel. 28124; f. 2007; attached to Min. of Education, Women's Affairs and Culture; reviews and approves qualifications for schools and public and private post-secondary education; informs learners, education providers, employers and others on the status and standard of awards provided; CEO Dr 'UHILA-MOE-LANGI FASI.

Learned Societies

BIBLIOGRAPHY, LIBRARY SCIENCE AND MUSEOLOGY

Tonga Library Association: c/o USP Tonga Centre, POB 278, Nuku'alofa; tel. 29055; fax 29249; e-mail taufui_l@usp.ac.fj; f. 1981; training courses and library-related activities; provides support for both govt and non-govt libraries incl. academic, schools and spec. libraries; 40 mems; Pres. LOSALINE TAUFU'I.

NATURAL SCIENCES

Tonga Wildlife Centre: PMB 52, Nuku'alofa; tel. and fax 29449; e-mail birdpark@kalianet.to; internet www.tongaturismo.info/twc.htm; protects rare and endangered birds; educates people; collects information on birds and their needs.

Libraries and Archives

Nuku'alofa

Ministry of Education, Women Affairs and Culture Library: POB 123, Nuku'alofa; tel. 21588; fax 24105; f. 1976; provides supplementary reading and text books for students; public library service; 12,432 vols; 1,515 vols of Pacific spec. colln; Librarian TU'ILOKAMANA TUITA.

University of the South Pacific, Tonga Campus Library: POB 278, Nuku'alofa; tel. 29240; fax 29249; 15,000 vols; Library Officer LOSALINE TAUFU'I.

Museum

Nuku'alofa

Tupou College Museum: POB 25, Nuku'alofa; tel. 32240; f. 1866; artefacts from Tonga's history; Prin. Rev. SIOSAIA PELE.

Universities

'ATENISI UNIVERSITY

POB 90, Nuku'alofa
Telephone and fax 24819
E-mail: thedean@atenisi.edu.to
Internet: www.atenisi.edu.to
Founded 1975; attached to 'Atenisi Institute
Private control
Academic year: February to December

Schools of arts, humanities, natural sciences, social sciences

Dean: Dr MICHAEL G. HOROWITZ
Assoc. Dean: FIRITIA VELT
Library Coordinator: ROBERT H. BECK.

'UNUAKI'-O-TONGA ROYAL INSTITUTE

POB 2936, Taufa'ahau Rd, Haveluloto, Nuku'alofa,
Telephone: 25663
Fax: 25664
Internet: www.utri.edu.to
Founded 2004
Chair.: HRH Princess SALOTE MAFILE'O PILOLEVU TUITA
Pres. and Vice-Chair.: Prof. 'ETUATE LAVULAVU
Vice-Pres. for Academic Affairs and Chief Exec. Dir: Prof. Dr MICHAEL FAIA

Exec. Vice-Pres.: SIONE TUALAU VIMAHI
Vice-Pres.: Prof. VINOD TRIVEDI
Dir for Admin. and Int. Relations: MELE LUPEHA'AMOA 'ILAIU
Dir for Admissions: KALOLAINE KOLUSE
Dir for Finance: MEHTA BHAVIK
Dir for Research and Deputy Dir of Admissions: SIONA TALANOA FIFITA
Dir for Student Services: TELESIA LAVULAVU
Dir for Technical and Vocational Training: PITA LIKILIKI PUA.

Colleges

'Atenisi Institute: POB 90, Nuku'alofa; tel. and fax 24819; e-mail director1@atenisi.edu.to; internet www.atenisi.edu.to; f. 1966; anthropology, astronomy, chemistry, economics, global history, languages, life science, literature, mathematics, music and art, philosophy, physics, politics, psychology, sociology; comprises univ. (q.v.) and performing arts centre; Private control; library: 5,000 vols; Dir SISI'UNO HELU; Library Coordinator ROBERT H. BECK.

Hango Agricultural College: POB 16, Ohonua, Eua; tel. 50044; fax 50128; f. 1968; attached to Free Wesleyan Church Education System; 1-year diploma course in para-veterinary studies, 1-year diploma course in horticulture/cropping, 2-year certificate course; library: 1,200 vols; 7 teachers; 55 students.

Tonga Institute of Science and Technology: POB 485, Nuku'alofa; tel. 22667; fax 24334; e-mail tist1uf@kalianet.to; f. 1985; offers training in maritime studies and technical trades; library: 300 vols; 20 teachers; 160 students; Prin. Dr 'UHILA-MOE-LANGI FASI.

University of the South Pacific, Tonga Centre: POB 278, Nuku'alofa; tel. 29055; fax 29249; f. 1971, present location 1987; extension centre with responsibilities for distance education, adult non-formal education; interests in village and community devt and technology; 2 centres: Vava'u and Ha'apai; library: see under Libraries and Archives; Dir Dr 'ANA HAU'ALOFA'IA KOLOTO.

TRINIDAD AND TOBAGO

The Higher Education System

The Trinidad campus of the University of the West Indies (UWI) at St Augustine offers undergraduate and postgraduate programmes. The UWI Institute of Business offers postgraduate courses, and develops programmes for local companies. Other institutions of higher education are the Eric Williams Medical Sciences complex, the Polytechnic Institute and the East Caribbean Farm Institute. The country has one teacher-training college and three government-controlled technical institutes and vocational centres, including the Trinidad and Tobago Hotel School. In the late 1990s the Government established the Trinidad and Tobago Institute of Technology and the College of Science, Technology and Applied Arts of Trinidad and Tobago. In March 2004 a steering committee was appointed to conduct a strategic review of tertiary education and distance and lifelong learning in an attempt to improve consistency within the tertiary sector, and in relation to the education system as a whole. A Tertiary Qualifications Framework has been drafted and was awaiting approval at 2011; upon approval, the Framework would formally implement a six-tier qualifications system, comprising Certificate, Diploma, Associate degree, Bachelor degree, Masters degree and Doctorate qualifications. In 2004/05 there were 16,920 students in three institutions of higher education.

The Ministry of Science, Technology and Tertiary Education is the national agency with overall responsibility for higher education in Trinidad and Tobago. The National Training Agency is the body responsible for coordinating, monitoring and evaluating technical and vocational education, while the Accreditation Council of Trinidad and Tobago is the governing body for the assurance of quality in post-secondary and tertiary education.

Applicants are required to have a minimum of two GCE A-Levels for admission to undergraduate courses, and either the Caribbean Examinations Council Secondary Education Certificate or GCE O-Levels for admission to preliminary science, evening or part-time courses. Undergraduate Certificate programmes typically last one year, while Diploma programmes generally require two years' study. Two-year Associate degrees are awarded by institutions such as the College of Nursing and the National Institute of Higher Education, and the undergraduate Bachelors degree is a three- or four-year programme of study at the University of the West Indies. The postgraduate degrees are the Masters, which lasts two years, and Doctorate programmes, which must be completed within five years and culminate in submission of a thesis.

Post-secondary technical and vocational education is administered according to a framework of national vocational qualifications (TTNVQs). There are five levels: Pre-Craft, Craft, Technician, Professional, and Chartered or Advanced Professional. TTNVQs are offered by a range of professional institutes and centres. However, there are plans to replace TTNVQs with Caribbean Vocational Qualifications (CVQs), a competency-based qualification intended to introduce greater portability of qualifications across the Caribbean region. As with TTNVQs, there are five levels of CVQs: Semi-Skilled Worker, Skilled or Independent Worker, Supervisor or Technician or Instructor, Manager or Entrepeneur and Executive Professional.

Regulatory and Representative Bodies

GOVERNMENT

Ministry of Education: 18 Alexandra St, St Clair; tel. 622-2181; fax 622-4892; e-mail mined@tstt.net.tt; internet www.moe.gov.tt; Min. Dr Tim Gopeesingh; Permanent Sec. Angela Jack.

Ministry of Science, Technology and Tertiary Education: The International Waterfront Centre, Levels 16–18, Tower C, 1A Wrightson Rd, Port-of-Spain; tel. 623-9922; fax 625-5428; e-mail stte@stte.gov.tt; internet www.stte.gov.tt; Min. Fazal Karim Kangaloo.

Ministry of the Arts and Multiculturalism: JOBCO Bldg, 51–55 Frederick St, Port-of-Spain; tel. 625-8519; fax 627-4991; e-mail culturedivision.tt@gmail.com; internet www .culture.gov.tt; Min. Winston Peters.

ACCREDITATION

Accreditation Council of Trinidad and Tobago (ACTT): Level 3, Bldg B, ALGICO Plaza, 91–93 St Vincent St, Port-of-Spain; tel. 623-2500; fax 624-5711; e-mail info@actt .org.tt; internet www.actt.org.tt; f. 2004; assures the quality and integrity of higher education through the recognition, registration and accreditation of instns and programmes; board of 10 mems; Chair. Dr Michael Dowlath; Exec. Dir Michael Bradshaw.

Learned Societies

AGRICULTURE, FISHERIES AND VETERINARY SCIENCE

Agricultural Society of Trinidad and Tobago: POB 256, 13A Pembroke St, Port-of-Spain; tel. 627-3087; fax 623-7797; e-mail agrisoc@tstt.net.tt; internet www.agriculture .gov.tt; f. 1894; 528 mems; Pres. Wendy Lee Yuen; publ. *Journal* (1 a year).

Sugar Manufacture Association of Trinidad and Tobago: 80 Abercromby St, POB 230, Port-of-Spain; tel. 623-6106; f. 1967; to promote information of interest to the sugar industry; 272 mems; Pres. T. N. Skinner; Sec. M. Y. Khan; publ. *Proceedings*.

Tobago District Agricultural Society: Main St, Scarborough; Pres. Capt. R. H. Harrower; Sec. S. A. Davies.

ARCHITECTURE AND TOWN PLANNING

Trinidad and Tobago Institute of Architects: POB 585, Port-of-Spain; tel. 624-8842; fax 624-5217; e-mail info@ttiarch.com; internet www.ttiarch.com; f. 1954, present name 1982; 90 mems (incl. overseas); Pres. Mark Raymond; Sec. Steve Jameson; publ. *Journal* (1 a year).

BIBLIOGRAPHY, LIBRARY SCIENCE AND MUSEOLOGY

Library Association of Trinidad and Tobago: POB 1275, Port-of-Spain; e-mail secretary@latt.org.tt; internet www.latt.org .tt; f. 1960; Pres. Dr Lillibeth Ackbarali; Exec. Sec. Sally Anne Montserin; publ. *Bulletin*.

ECONOMICS, LAW AND POLITICS

Law Association of Trinidad and Tobago: POB 534, Port-of-Spain; tel. 625-9350; fax 625-2478; e-mail lawassociationtt@ gmail.com; internet www.lawassociationtt .com; f. 1986; 750 mems; Pres. Martin G. Daly; Sec. Patricia Dindyal; publ. *The Lawyer* (2 a year).

FINE AND PERFORMING ARTS

Trinidad Music Association: Bishop Anstey High School, Abercromby St, Port-of-Spain; f. 1941; 102 mems; Pres. Robert Johnstone; Hon. Sec. Velma Jardine.

HISTORY, GEOGRAPHY AND ARCHAEOLOGY

Historical Society of Trinidad and Tobago: c/o POB 780, Port-of-Spain; f. 1932; 45 mems; Pres. Max B. Ifill; Hon. Sec. and Treas. Kent Villafana.

LANGUAGE AND LITERATURE

Alliance Française: 17 Alcazar St, Clair, POB 1288, Port-of-Spain; tel. 622-6726; fax 628-8226; e-mail info@alliancetnt.com; internet www.alliancetnt.com; offers courses and exams in French language and culture, and promotes cultural exchange with France.

British Council: c/o British High Commission, 19 St Clair Ave, St Clair, POB 778, Port-of-Spain; tel. 628-0565; fax 622-2853; e-mail information@britishcouncil.org.tt; internet www.britishcouncil.org/tt; offers courses and exams in English language and British culture, and promotes cultural exchange with the UK; Man. Harriet Massingberd.

MEDICINE

Pharmacy Board of Trinidad and Tobago: Professional Centre Building, Wrightson Rd Extension, Port-of-Spain; tel. 627-6731; fax 627-6731; e-mail pboftt@tstt .net.tt; f. 1899; 300 mems; Pres. ANDREW RAHAMAN; Hon. Sec. NORMA INNISS.

NATURAL SCIENCES

Physical Sciences

Geological Society of Trinidad and Tobago: POB 3524, La Romaine, Trinidad; tel. 679-6064; fax 679-6064; e-mail gstt@tstt .net.tt; internet www.gstt.org; f. 1976; 250 mems; library of 2,000 vols; Pres. Dr FAZAL HOSEIN; Pres. Elect CURTIS ARCHIE.

Research Institute

AGRICULTURE, FISHERIES AND VETERINARY SCIENCE

Caribbean Agricultural Research and Development Institute (CARDI): University Campus, St Augustine, Trinidad; tel. 645-1205; fax 645-1208; e-mail infocentre@ cardi.org; internet www.cardi.org; f. 1975; sites in 13 Caribbean countries; Exec. Dir FRANK B. LAUCKNER.

Libraries and Archives

Port-of-Spain

Central Library of Trinidad and Tobago: POB 547, corner Duke and Pembroke Sts, Port-of-Spain; tel. 624-3120; fax 625-5369; f. 1941; a division of the Office of the Prime Minister; 442,000 vols; public library; Heritage Library held jointly with Trinidad Public Library; 13 brs; Dir PAMELLA BENSON; publ. *Trinidad and Tobago National Bibliography.*

National Archives: The Government Archivist, POB 763, 105 St Vincent St, Port-of-Spain; tel. 626-2874; fax 625-2689; e-mail nattenquires@moi.gov.tt; internet www.natt .gov.tt; f. 1960; records from 1797; govt and private archives; microfilm copies of Trinidad and Tobago records in other countries; Govt Archivist SHERYL LEE KIM; publ. *Select Documents.*

National Library and Information System Authority: National Library of Trinidad and Tobago, corner Hart and Abercromby Sts, Port-of-Spain; tel. 624-4496; fax 625-6096; e-mail nalis@nalis.gov .tt; internet www2.nalis.gov.tt; f. 1998; 23 public libraries; heritage library; 124 school libraries; 29 spec. libraries; 24 br. libraries; colln of 729,715 items; Exec. Dir ANNETTE WALLACE.

St Augustine

University of the West Indies, Main Library: St Augustine; tel. 662-2002 ext. 2132; fax 662-9238; e-mail mainlib@sta.uwi .tt; internet www.mainlib.uwi.tt; f. 1960; 403,503 vols, 49,455 bound serials, 22,783 microfilms, 27,000 other non-book items, 1,418 maps, 4,054 multimedia items, 5,804 photographs, 10,721 vertical files, 816 video cassettes, 1,323 audio cassettes, 1,610 vinyl records; spec. collns: W Indiana, Oral and Pictorial Records Collns Index, journal articles on the W Indies or by W Indians; Campus Librarian JENNIFER JOSEPH.

San Fernando

San Fernando Carnegie Free Library: Harris Promenade, San Fernando; tel. 652-2921; fax 653-9645; internet www.nalis.gov .tt; f. 1919; lending and reference service for children and adults; 36,109 vols; special collection: West Indies, Carnival; Librarian REYNOLD BASSANT.

Museum and Art Gallery

Port-of-Spain

National Museum and Art Gallery of Trinidad & Tobago: 117 Frederick St, Port-of-Spain; tel. 623-5941; fax 624-7116; e-mail nationalmuseum117@gmail.com; internet www.nmag.gov.tt; f. 1892; archaeology, art, Carnival, history, natural history, petroleum technology; Curator NIMAH MUWAKIL-ZAKURI (acting).

Universities

UNIVERSITY OF THE WEST INDIES, ST AUGUSTINE CAMPUS

St Augustine, Trinidad
Telephone: 662-2002
Fax: 663-9684
Internet: www.sta.uwi.edu
Founded 1948 by the Govts of the Caribbean Commonwealth Territories with the cooperation of the British Govt
Autonomous
Language of instruction: English
Academic year: August to July
Serves Jamaica, Trinidad and Tobago, Barbados and the Commonwealth Territories in the Caribbean
Chancellor: Sir GEORGE ALLEYNE
Vice-Chancellor: Prof. E. NIGEL HARRIS
Pro-Vice-Chancellor and Campus Prin.: Prof. CLEMENT SANKAT
Deputy Prin.: Prof. RHODA REDDOCK
Registrar: JEREMY CALLAGHAN
Librarian: JENNIFER JOSEPH
Library of 403,503 vols, 49,455 bound serials, 10,047 periodicals, 22,783 microforms, 5,804 photographs, 1,418 maps, 1,323 CDs, 816 video cassettes, 811 audio cassettes
Number of teachers: 726
Number of students: 16,408
Publications: *Caribbean Agro Economic Society* (conf. proceedings), *Caribbean Dialogue* (policy bulletin of Caribbean affairs), *Caribbean Review of Gender Studies* (online), *Creating Language Links, History in Action* (online), *Journal of Business, Finance and Economics in Emerging Economies, Journal of Caribbean Curriculum, Journal of Caribbean History, Journal of Tropical Agriculture, Journal of West Indian Literature, St Augustine News, UWI Today Newspaper, West Indian Journal of Engineering*

DEANS

Faculty of Engineering: Prof. BRIAN COPELAND
Faculty of Humanities and Education: Dr FUNSO AIYEJINA
Faculty of Medical Sciences: Prof. SAMUEL RAMSEWAK
Faculty of Science and Agriculture: Prof. DYER NARINESINGH
Faculty of Social Sciences: Dr H. GHANY

PROFESSORS

ADESIYUN, A., Public Health
ADDAE, J., Physiology
ADOGWA, A., Anatomy
AGARD, J., Life Sciences
AGOZINO, O., Criminology
AIYEJINA, F., Literature
AKINGBALA, J., Chemical Engineering
ALI, Z., School of Medicine
BERTRAND, W., Chemical Engineering
BHATT, B., Mathematics and Computer Science
BISSESSAR, A., Public Management
BRATHWAITE, R., Food Production
CHADWICK, A., Civil Engineering
COOPER, J., Pathology
COPELAND, B., Electrical and Computer Engineering
DAISLEY, H., Anatomical Pathology
DAWE, R., Chemical Engineering
EKWUE, E., Mechanical Engineering
EZENWAKA, C., Para-Clinical Science
EZEOKOLI, C., Veterinary Surgery
GIFT, S., Electrical Engineering
GIRVAN, N., International Relations
HUTCHINSON, G., Clinical Medical Science
IMBERT, C., Mechanical Engineering
KOCHHAR, G., Mechanical Engineering
LALLA, B., Linguistics
LAWRENCE, A., Environmental Biology
LEWIS, T., Civil Engineering
LEWIS, W., Mechanical Engineering
MAHARAJH, H., Clinical Medical Science
MCRAE, A., Human Anatomy
MOHAMMED, P., Centre for Gender and Development Studies
MONTEIL, M., Para-Clinical Science
MURTI, P., Histopathology
NARAYNSINGH, V., Surgery
NARINESINGH, D., Chemistry
OPADEYI, J., Land and Surveying
PANTIN, D., Economics
PINTO PEREIRA, L., Basic Health Science
PITT-MILLER, P., Anaesthetics
POSTHOFF, C., Mathematics and Computer Science
PUN, K., Mechanical Engineering
RAMDATH, D., Basic Health Science
RAMNARINE, I., Life Sciences
RAMSARAN, R., International Relations
RAMSEWAK, S., Obstetrics and Gynaecology
REDDOCK, R., Gender, Social Change and Development
ROBERTSON, I., Linguistics
SAHAI, A., Math and Computer Science
SAUNDERS, R., Physics
SEEMUNGAL, T., School of Medicine
SHARMA, C., Electrical and Computer Engineering
SHAW, P., Food Production
SINGH, G., Chemistry
STEVENSON, A., Centre for Medical Science Education
SURYA RAO, D., Civil Engineering
SYAN, C., Mechanical Engineering
TEELUCKSINGH, S., School of Medicine
THEODORE, K., Economics
TYLER, B., Chemical Engineering
UMAHARAN, P., Life Sciences
YOUSSEF, V., Linguistics

UNIVERSITY OF TRINIDAD AND TOBAGO (UTT)

74–98 O'Meara Industrial Park, Arima
Telephone: 642-8888
Fax: 643-1617
E-mail: utt.marketing@utt.edu.tt
Internet: utt.edu.tt
Founded 2004
State control
Language of instruction: English
Academic year: September to July
Pres.: Prof. KENNETH RAMCHAND
Provost: Dr FAZAL ALI
Vice-Provost for Postgraduate Studies: Prof. ADEL SHARAF
Assoc. Provost for Humanities, Soc. Sciences and the Academies: JEANETTE MORRIS
Assoc. Provost for Science, Engineering and Technology: Prof. PRAKASH PERSAD
Vice-Pres. for Finance and Admin.: VISHWANATH MAHARAJH
Vice-Pres. for Quality Assurance and Institutional Effectiveness: Dr RUBY S. ALLEYNE

Asst Vice-Pres. for Human Resources: CEDRIC CONNOR

Asst Vice-Pres. for Student Support Services: STEPHEN SHEPPARD

Registrar and Corporate Sec.: DEBBIE SIRJU-SINGH

Chief Univ. Librarian: Dr MARTHA PREDDIE

Library of 60,103 vols, 677 print journals, 2,253 multimedia items

Number of teachers: 437

Number of students: 6,838

Publications: *Caribbean Journal of Criminology and Public Safety, Caribbean Journal of Teacher Education and Pedagogy, Talkaree*

PROFESSORS

AL-TAWEEL, A., Process Engineering
ATHRE, K., Mechanical Engineering
BLAIR, P., Sports and Leisure Studies
DEOSARAN, R., Criminology and Public Safety
EL-SAYED, M., Utilities Engineering
GAINHAM, K., Performing Arts
JOSEPH, A., Environmental Science and Management

KHAN, J., Biosciences, Agriculture and Food Technologies
LIVERPOOL, H., Carnival Studies Programmes
MORRIS, J., Cognition, Learning and Education
PERSAD, P., Undergraduate Studies, Design and Manufacturing
SHARAF, A., Research and Postgraduate Studies, Energy Systems
SMITH, M., Information, Computing and Telecommunications and Digital Media Studies
STEVENSON, C., Maritime Programmes
SUITE, W., Civil Engineering Programmes

TUNISIA

The Higher Education System

The University of Tunisia was founded in 1960, and divided in 1986 into three universities: Tunis, Centre and Sfax-South. In 1987 the university at Tunis was divided into four subject-based institutions, which in turn were later reorganized into multidisciplinary institutions. Several private universities have received accreditation since 2000. A distance-learning university, Université Virtuelle de Tunis, was established in 2002. In 2009/10 there were 346,079 full-time students at higher education institutions, which numbered 192 in 2008/09. Inadequacies within the higher education system and high youth unemployment levels, even among high-calibre university graduates, were among a number of grievances that gave forth to the outpouring of widespread popular discontent in December 2010 that ultimately led to the ousting of President Zine al-Abidine Ben Ali in January 2011; however, it remains to be seen whether the revolution will engender real opportunities for meaningful higher education reform in Tunisia.

Higher education is funded from the national budget. Institutions of higher education are accredited by the Ministry of Higher Education and Scientific Research. Private higher education institutions operate on the basis of a licence granted by the Ministry. This licence enables them to offer specific courses in specific fields. Licences are reviewed periodically in order to maintain standards of quality.

The secondary school Baccalauréat is the main requirement for admission to higher education. Tunisia has traditionally followed the French system of higher education but is currently undergoing reform. It aims to introduce a three-tier system of Licence–Master–Doctorat (LMD) and bring Tunisian education into line with the European Bologna Process. The implementation of the LMD started in 2006 with the aim of enrolling all students onto these new programmes by 2009; the system was thus to be fully implemented by 2012, following which traditional qualifications would still be available but only upon request. The traditional university degrees are divided into three cycles: the first cycle ends with the award of the Diplôme Universitaire d'Études Scientifiques or Diplôme Universitaire d'Études Littéraires; the second cycle comprises the Licence or a Maîtrise; and the third cycle the doctoral-level degrees, specifically Diplôme d'Études Approfondies and Doctorat d'État. The professional title Diplôme d'Ingénieur is a second-cycle degree awarded after three years and the Docteur en Médecine is awarded after seven years. The new LMD system comprises three awards. The Licence is an undergraduate degree awarded three years after the Baccalauréat de l'Enseignement Secondaire. There are two types of Licence available, namely the Licence Fondamentale and the Licence Appliquée. The Master is a postgraduate degree awarded two years after the Licence. There are two types of Masters available, namely the Master Recherché and the Master Professionnel. The first year is classroom based, the second year contains independent research or professional training, including project work. The Doctorat is a postgraduate research degree awarded three years after the Master degree. Studies are organized in credit points (60 credit points correspond to one year of study) similar to the European Credit Transfer System within the Bologna System.

Technical and vocational programmes are administered by the Ministry of Vocational Training and Employment . The leading qualification of post-secondary technical and vocational education is the Brevet de Technicien Supérieur (BTS), which requires the Baccalauréat or Brevet de Technicien Professionnel and comprises 65% practical training and 35% classroom-based learning. The BTS allows access to Tunisia's private, but not public, universities.

Regulatory Bodies

GOVERNMENT

Ministry of Culture: 8 rue 2 mars 1934, la Kasbah, 1006 Tunis; tel. (71) 56-30-06; fax (71) 56-38-16; e-mail minculture@email.ati .tn; internet www.culture.tn; Minister MEHDI MABROUK.

Ministry of Education: Blvd Bab Benat, 1030 Tunis; tel. (71) 56-87-68; e-mail ministere@minedu.edunet.tn; internet www .education.gov.tn; Minister ABDELLATIF ABID.

Ministry of Higher Education and Scientific Research: ave Ouled Haffouz, 1030 Tunis; tel. (71) 78-63-00; fax (71) 78-67-01; e-mail mes@mes.rnu.tn; internet www.mes .tn; Minister MONCEF BEN SALEM.

Learned Societies

GENERAL

Comité Culturel National: 105 ave de la Liberté, 1002 Tunis; tel. (71) 28-81-54; fax (71) 79-26-39; f. 1968; central body co-ordinating national and international cultural activities, sponsored by the Min. of Culture and by foreign embassies; regional and local cultural committees throughout the country; 16 mems; Pres. MOHAMED TALBI; Sec.-Gen. SAMIR BELHAJ YAHIA.

BIBLIOGRAPHY, LIBRARY SCIENCE AND MUSEOLOGY

Association Tunisienne des Bibliothé-caires, Documentalistes et Archivistes: BP 380, 1015 Tunis; f. 1965; information sciences; 250 mems; Pres. ABDELBAKI DALY; publ. *Rassid* (multilingual, 4 a year).

Comité National des Musées: Musée National du Bardo, Tunis; f. 1961; Pres. HABIB BEN YOUNES; publ. *Les musées de Tunisie.*

EDUCATION

Arab League Educational, Cultural and Scientific Organization (ALECSO) (Organisation Arabe pour l'Education, la Culture et la Science): POB 1120, ave Mohamed V, Tunis; tel. (71) 90-62-36; fax (71) 90-90-65; e-mail alecso@alecso.org.tn; internet www.alecso.org.tn; f. 1970; regional units: Arab Centre for Arabization, Translation, Authorship and Publication (Damascus, Syria), Institute of Arab Manuscripts (Cairo, Egypt), Institute of Arab Research and Studies (Cairo, Egypt), Khartoum International Institute for Arabic Language (Khartoum, Sudan), Arabization Coordination Bureau (Rabat, Morocco); promotes devt of education, culture and sciences in Arab countries; 22 Arab countries; library of 8,200 vols, 110 periodicals; Dir-Gen. MOHAMED EL AZIZ BEN ACHOUR; Deputy Dir-Gen. MOHAMED EL KADASI; publs *Arab Journal of Culture* (2 a year), *Arab Journal of Education* (2 a year), *Arab Journal of Sciences and Information* (2 a year), *Journal of Mass Education* (2 a year).

FINE AND PERFORMING ARTS

Union Nationale des Arts Plastiques: Musée du Belvédère, Tunis.

LANGUAGE AND LITERATURE

British Council: c/o British Embassy, 5 place de la Victoire, BP 229, 1015 Tunis; tel. (71) 25-90-53; fax (71) 35-34-11; e-mail info@ tn.britishcouncil.org; internet www .britishcouncil.org.tn; offers courses and exams in English language and British culture, and promotes cultural exchange with the UK; library of 8,000 vols; Dir WILL TODD (acting).

Teaching Centre:

Teaching Centre: 2nd/3rd Fl., 47 ave Habib Bourguiba, Tunis 1001; tel. (71) 35-35-68; fax (71) 35-39-85; Man. TANIA PUGLIESE (acting).

Goethe-Institut: 6 place d'Afrique, rue du Sénégal, 1002 Tunis-Belvédère; tel. (71) 84-82-66; fax (71) 84-17-51; internet www .goethe.de/wm/tun/deindex.htm; offers courses and examinations in German language and culture, and promotes cultural exchange with Germany; Dir ECKEHART VOGT.

Institut des Belles Lettres Arabes: 12 rue Jamâa al Haoua, 1008 Tunis Bab Menara;

tel. (71) 56-01-33; fax (71) 57-26-83; e-mail ibla@gnet.tn; internet www.iblatunis.org; f. 1930; cultural centre; library of 32,000 vols on Tunisian studies and Arabic literature; Dir Dr JEAN FONTAINE; publ. *IBLA* (2 a year).

Instituto Cervantes: 120 ave de la Liberté, 1002 Tunis Belvédère; tel. (71) 78-88-47; fax (71) 79-38-25; e-mail centun@cervantes.es; internet tunez.cervantes.es; offers courses and examinations in Spanish language and culture, and promotes cultural exchange with Spain and Spanish-speaking Latin and Central America; library of 16,000 vols; Dir FRANCISCO CORRAL SÁNCHEZ-CABEZUDO.

Union des Écrivains Tunisiens: 20 ave de Paris, 1000 Tunis; tel. (71) 25-78-07; fax (71) 34-42-65; e-mail uniondesecrivains@yahoo.fr; internet www.uet.c.la; f. 1970; 560 mems; Pres. D. SHAHEDDINNE BOUJAH; Sec.-Gen. SLAHEDDINNE LAHMADI; publ. *El Massar*.

Research Institutes
GENERAL

Centre d'Études Maghrébines à Tunis: 19 bis rue d'Angleterre, Impasse Menabrea, BP 404, 1049 Tunis-Hached; tel. (71) 32-62-19; fax (71) 32-83-78; e-mail cemat@planet .tn; internet www.la.utexas.edu/research/ mena/cemat; f. 1985; operated by American Institute for Maghreb Studies, Univ. of Arizona, Tucson; sponsors research by scholars of all nationalities and in all disciplines; gives research grants to Americans and Maghribis; facilitates liaison with North African scholars; holds annual research conf. and frequent lectures; library of 2,300 vols, 1,000 dissertations; Dir Dr LAURENCE MICHALAK.

Institut de Recherche pour le Développement (IRD): see main entry under France: 5 impasse Chahrazed, BP 434, 1004 Tunis El Menzah; tel. (71) 75-00-09; fax (71) 75-02-54; f. 1958; pedology, hydrology, microbiology, medical entomology, agricultural economics, archaeology, desertification, remote detection; library; Dir J. CLAUDE.

Institut National de Recherche Scientifique et Technique (INRST): BP 95, Hammam-Lif 2050; premises at: route Touristique, Borj-Cedria, Soliman; tel. (72) 43-02-15; fax (72) 43-09-34; f. 1969; applied physics, biology, chemistry, biotechnology, earth sciences, development of the use of domestic and industrial waste; library of 1,500 vols, 100 in spec. colln; Dir MOHAMED ENNABLT; Sec.-Gen. MESSAOUD CHAHTOUR.

AGRICULTURE, FISHERIES AND VETERINARY SCIENCE

Centre de Recherche du Génie Rural: BP 10, Ariana 2080; tel. (71) 71-80-55; f. 1959; agronomy, irrigation, etc.; Dir MOHAMED NEJIB REJEB; publ. *Cahier du CRGR*.

Institut de la Recherche Vétérinaire de Tunisie: rue Djebel Lakhdhar La Rabta, 1006 Tunis; tel. (71) 56-26-02; fax (71) 56-96-92; e-mail hammami.salah@iresa.agrinet.tn; f. 1887; veterinary research, laboratory disease diagnosis, food hygiene; library of 3,000 vols; Dir-Gen. Prof. Dr HAMMAMI SALAH; publ. *Bulletin of Epidemiology*.

Institut National de la Recherche Agronomique de Tunisie (INRAT): rue Hédi Karray 2049, Ariana; tel. (71) 23-00-24; fax (71) 75-28-97; e-mail netij.benmechlia@iresa .agrinet.tn; f. 1914; improvement of vegetable and livestock production through the use of appropriate agroecological and socioeconomic methods; 7 research laboratories, 2 research units, 13 regional experimental stations; library of 8,000 vols, 1,500 period-

icals; Dir Dr N. BEN MECHLIA; publ. *Annales* (1 a year).

Institut National de Recherches Forestières de Tunisie: BP 2-2080, Ariana; f. 1967 under present title; research in all aspects of forestry; library: Documentation Centre comprises 2,981 vols and 3,144 documents; Dir M. DAHMAN; publs *Bulletin d'Information* (2 or 3 a year), *Annales*, *Notes de Recherches*.

Institut National des Sciences et Technologies de la Mer: 28 rue 2 mars 1934, 2025 Salammbô; tel. (71) 73-04-20; fax (71) 73-26-22; e-mail messaoudi.saida@instm.rnrt .tn; internet www.instm.rnrt.tn; f. 1924; fisheries research, aquaculture, fishing technology, marine environment, toxicology, algology; marine museum; library of 40,000 vols; Dir-Gen. Prof. RIDHA MRABET; Librarian SAIDA MESSAOUDI; publs *Bulletin*, *INSTM* (1 a year), *Notes* (3 a year).

BIBLIOGRAPHY, LIBRARY SCIENCE AND MUSEOLOGY

Institut National du Patrimoine: 4 place du Château, 1008 Tunis; tel. (71) 26-16-22; f. 1957; archaeology, museography, ethnography, research, protection and evaluation of the national heritage; library of 25,000 vols; Dir ABDELAZIZ DAOULATLI; publ. *Africa*.

EDUCATION

Institut National des Sciences de l'Éducation: 17 rue d'Irak, 1002 Tunis-Belvédère; tel. (71) 28-77-22; fax (71) 79-54-23; f. 1969; conducts research, undertakes assessment of curricula, books, students and teaching techniques, develops the use of audiovisual aids in education, organizes seminars and conferences; library of 30,000 vols; Dir NEJIB AYED; publs *Bulletin pédagogique*, *Cahiers de l'INSE*, *Revue Tunisienne des Sciences de l'Education*.

MEDICINE

Institut Pasteur: BP 74, 13 place Pasteur, 1002 Tunis Belvédère; tel. (71) 78-96-08; fax (71) 79-18-33; f. 1893; research in health sciences; library of 4,500 vols, 200 periodicals; Dir Prof. K. DELLAGI; publ. *Archives* (4 a year).

TECHNOLOGY

Centre National de l'Informatique: 17 rue Belhassen Ben Chaâbane, El-Omrane, 1005 Tunis; tel. (71) 78-30-55; fax (71) 78-18-62; f. 1976; assistance, training, development of computer applications and software, management of processing centres; library of 4,000 vols; Dir MONGI MILED.

Office National des Mines: BP 215, 1080 Tunis Cedex; premises at: 24 rue 8601, La Charguia, 2035 Tunis; tel. (71) 78-88-42; fax (71) 79-40-16; f. 1962; geological research and map-making; bibliographic database on geology of Tunisia; library of 15,000 vols, 450 periodicals; Pres. and Dir-Gen. MOHAMED FADHEL ZERELLI; publs *Annales des Mines et de la Géologie*, *Notes du service géologique*.

Libraries and Archives
Tunis

Archives Nationales: Le Premier Ministère, La Casbah, 1020 Tunis; tel. (71) 56-05-56; fax (71) 56-91-75; f. 1874; 5,000 vols, MSS in Arabic, Turkish, French, Italian and English; Dir MONCEF FAKHFAKH; publ. *Inventaires des documents d'archives conservés*.

Bibliothèque Nationale: BP 42, 1000 Tunis; tel. (71) 57-27-06; fax (71) 57-28-87; e-mail bibliothequenationale@email.at.tn;

internet www.bnt.nat.tn; f. 1885; depository of books published in Tunisia (mostly in Arabic); documentation and information dept; 1.5m. vols in 12 languages; 15,000 periodicals; 40,000 Arabic and Oriental MSS; Curator SAMIA KAMARTI; publs *Catalogue général des manuscrits* (1 a year), *Le Livre Tunisien* (1 a year).

Bibliothèques Publiques: Head Office: 39 rue Asdrubal, Lafayette, 1002 Tunis; tel. (71) 78-25-52; fax (71) 79-77-52; f. 1965; 293 public libraries throughout the country, notably at Tunis, Béjà, Bizerte, Gabès, Gafsa, Jendouba, Kairouan, Kasserine, El Kef, Medenine, Monastir, Nabeul, Sfax, Sousse, Siliana, Mahdia, Ariana, Ben Arous, Zagnouan, Sidi Bouzid, Tozeur, Kébili and Tetaouine; 233 children's libraries, 266 local and community libraries and 27 mobile libraries; 2.75m. vols; Chief Curator ALI MARZOUKI; publs *Bulletin* (1 a year), *Répertoire*, *Statistics of Public Libraries*.

Centre de Documentation Nationale: blvd 7 Novembre, 1004 Tunis-El Menzah; tel. (71) 70-49-60; fax (71) 79-22-41; e-mail csi .cdn@email.ati.tn; f. 1966; 13,500 monographs, 2,400 periodicals, 210,000 press articles, 30,000 photographs; Dir-Gen. SAHRAOURI GAMAOUN.

Museums and Art Galleries
Carthage

Musée National de Carthage: BP 3, 2016 Carthage; tel. (71) 73-00-36; fax (71) 73-00-99; f. 1964; library of 5,000 vols on archaeology (special collection: antiquity); Dir ABDELMAJID ENNABLI.

El Jem

Musée Archéologique d'El Jem: El Jem; tel. (73) 630093; fax (73) 630969; e-mail ibenjerbania@yahoo.fr; Archaeologist in Charge of Research BEN JERBANIA IMED.

Kairouan

Musée d'Art Islamique: Kairouan.

Makthar

Musée Archéologique de Makthar: Makthar; Punic and Roman.

Monastir

Musée d'Art Islamique du Ribat: Monastir.

Sbeïtla

Musée de Sbeïtla: Sbeïtla; Roman antiquities.

Sfax

Musée Archéologique de Sfax: Sfax.

Sousse

Musée Archéologique de Sousse (Kasbah): Sousse.

Tunis

Maison des Arts: Parc du Belvédère, 1002 Tunis; tel. (71) 28-37-49; fax (71) 79-58-60; f. 1992; art exhibition, musical and cultural activities; library of 6,000 vols; Dir ALI LOUATI.

Musée National du Bardo: 2000 Le Bardo, Tunis; tel. (71) 51-36-50; fax (71) 51-40-50; f. 1888; contains prehistoric collections, relics of Punic, Greek and Roman art, and ancient and modern Islamic arts, largest collection in the world of Roman mosaics; library of 4,700 vols; Dir HABIB BEN YOUNES; publ. *Les Nécropoles Puniques de Tunisie*.

Universities

UNIVERSITÉ DU 7 NOVEMBRE À CARTHAGE

29 rue Asdrubal, 1002 Tunis
Telephone: (71) 78-75-02
Fax: (71) 78-87-68
E-mail: pu7nc@univ7nc.rnu.tn
Internet: www.univ7nc.rnu.tn/fr/indexfr.htm
Founded 1988 as Université de Droit, d'Économie et de Gestion; present name 2000
Pres.: Prof. TAÏEB HADHRI
Sec.-Gen.: MOHAMED AMEUR ISMAÏL
Number of teachers: 2,003
Number of students: 30,590

DEANS

Faculty of Economics and Management (Nabeul): EZZEDDINE ZOUARI
Faculty of Law, Political and Social Sciences (Tunis): (vacant)
Faculty of Sciences (Bizerte): CHAABANE CHEFI

UNIVERSITÉ DU CENTRE, SOUSSE

rue Khalifa El Karoui Sahloul, BP 526, 4002 Sousse
Telephone: (73) 36-81-25
Fax: (73) 36-81-26
E-mail: universite.centre@uc.rnu.tn
Internet: www.uc.rnu.tn
Founded 1986 as Université de Monastir pour le Centre; present name 1991
State control
Pres.: MOHAMED ALI HAMZA
Number of teachers: 2,585
Number of students: 51,490

DEANS

Faculty of Arts and Humanities, Khairouan: SAHBI ALLANI
Faculty of Arts and Humanities, Sousse: HÉDI JATLAOUI
Faculty of Dental Medicine, Monastir: KHALED BOURAOUI
Faculty of Economics and Management, Mahdia: ALI FRAJ
Faculty of Law, Economics and Political Science, Sousse: MONGI TARCHOUNA
Faculty of Medicine, Monastir: HABIB SABBAH
Faculty of Medicine, Sousse: BECHIR BEL HADJ ALI
Faculty of Pharmacy, Monastir: MOHAMED KALLEL
Faculty of Science, Monastir: MONGI BEN AMARA

UNIVERSITÉ EZZITOUNA

21 rue Sidi Jelizi, place Maakel Ezzaïm, 1008 Tunis
Telephone: (71) 57-55-14
Fax: (71) 57-61-51
Internet: www.uz.rnu.tn
Founded 1988 from existing faculties
State control
Pres.: SALEM BOUYAHIA
Faculties of theology and religious studies
Publications: *Al-Miskat* (1 a year), *Ettanwir* (1 a year).

UNIVERSITÉ DE LA MANOUBA

Campus Universitaire de la Manouba, la Manouba 2010
Telephone: (71) 60-14-99
Fax: (71) 60-22-11
E-mail: mail@uma.rnu.tn
Internet: www.uma.rnu.tn
Founded 2001
State control

Pres.: SLAHEDDINE GHERISSI
Vice-Pres.: MOHAMED EL KADHI
Sec.-Gen.: SAID GHRAB
Number of students: 30,557.

ATTACHED RESEARCH INSTITUTES

Faculty of Letters: tel. (71) 60-10-45; fax (71) 60-09-10; Dean CHOKRI MABKHOUT; Sec.-Gen. AHMED EL BOUKHARI CHETOUI.

Higher Institute for the Promotion of the Handicapped: IPH, 2 rue Jabrane Khalil Jabrane, la Manouba 2010; tel. (70) 60-40-91; fax (71) 60-40-71; e-mail directeur .iph@iph.org.tn; internet www.iph.nat.tn; Dir LOFTI BELLALEHOM; Sec.-Gen. MOUNIRA CHAABOUNI.

Higher Institute of Accounting and Business Administration: tel. (71) 60-18-90; fax (71) 60-24-04; Dir SAMIR EL GHAZOUANI; Sec.-Gen. LOTFI CHABBI.

Higher Institute of Documentation: tel. (71) 60-16-50; fax (71) 60-02-00; Dir KHALED MILED; Sec.-Gen. ABDERRAOUF BOUBAKAR.

Higher Institute of Multimedia Arts: ISAMM, Charguia 1; tel. (70) 83-72-06; fax (70) 83-76-03; Dir CHIRAZ LAATIRI.

Higher Institute of Sport and Physical Education: ISSEP, Kssar Essaid, la Manouba 2010; tel. (71) 54-84-32; fax (71) 65-42-82; e-mail crd@issep-ks.rnu.tn; internet www .issep-ks.rnu.tn; Dir MOURAD JALEL MAAOUI; Sec.-Gen. ALI NCIRI.

Higher Institute of the History of the National Movement: Dir MOHAMED LOFTI CHAIBI.

Higher School of Commerce: tel. (71) 60-27-60; fax (71) 60-13-11; internet www.esct .rnu.tn; Dir HAFEDH BEN ABDENNEBI; Sec.-Gen. HAMDA YAAKOUBI.

Higher School of Sciences and Design Technology: ESSTD, ave de l'Indépendance, Denden 2011; tel. (71) 61-07-00; fax (71) 61-07-50; Dir RAIF MALEK; Sec.-Gen. ADEL HENID.

Institute of Press and Communications Science (IPSI): tel. (71) 60-03-55; fax (71) 60-05-70; e-mail ipsi@ipsi.rnu.tn; internet www.ipsi.rnu.tn; Dir MOHAMED HAMDANE; Sec.-Gen. AHMED HADJI.

National School of Computer Sciences: tel. (71) 60-04-44; fax (71) 60-04-49; internet www.ensi.rnu.tn; Dir KHALID GHEDIRA.

School of e-Commerce: tel. (71) 60-29-19; fax (71) 60-26-62; Dir MALEK GHANIMA.

School of Veterinary Medicine: Dir MOHAMED HABIB JEMLI.

Sidi Thabet Higher Institute of Biotechnology: ISB, Sidi Thabet 2020; tel. (71) 52-05-88; fax (71) 52-12-67; Dir RAFIKA CHEKIR; Sec.-Gen. HAYET MANSOURI.

UNIVERSITÉ DE SFAX

route de l'Áeroport, 3029 Sfax
Telephone: (74) 24-09-86
Fax: (74) 24-09-13
E-mail: uss@uss.rnu.tn
Internet: www.mes.tn/uss
Founded 1986 from existing faculties; campus at Gafsa
State control
Languages of instruction: Arabic, French
Academic year: September to June
Pres.: EZZEDDINE BOUASSIDA
Sec.-Gen.: LOTFI SELLAMI
Number of teachers: 2,798
Number of students: 39,656

DEANS

Faculty of Arts and Humanities: MABROUK EL BEHI

Faculty of Economics and Administration: BORHEN TRIGUI
Faculty of Law: MOHAMED MAHFOUDH
Faculty of Medicine: KHALED ZGHAL
Faculty of Sciences: MAHER MNIF BEN SALAH

CONSTITUENT INSTITUTES

Higher Institute of Applied Humanities Studies, Gafsa: Dir IBRAHIM JADLA.

Higher Institute of Business Administration: Dir ABDELWAHEB REBAI.

Higher Institute of Business Administration, Gafsa: Dir MALEK OURIMI.

Higher Institute of Crafts and Technical Training: Dir NOURREDINE ELHENI.

Higher Institute of Electronics and Telecommunications Technology: Dir LOFTI KAMOUN.

Higher Institute of Industrial Management: Dir HABIB CHABCHOUB.

Higher Institute of Information Technology and Media Studies: Dir ABDELMAJID BEN HAMADOU.

Higher Institute of Management Training, Gafsa: Dir AMMAR AKRIMI.

Higher Institute of Music: Dir MOURAD SIALA.

Higher Institute of Sport and Physical Education: Dir JALEL MILADI.

Higher Institute of Technology, Gafsa: Dir JALEL KHDIRI.

Higher Institute of Technology, Sfax: Dir SLIMÈNE GABSI.

Institute of Advanced Business Studies: Dir FAIKA SCANDER CHARFI.

National School of Commerce: Dir ABDELKADER CHAABANE.

National School of Engineering: Dir BOUBAKER EL EUCH.

National School of Health Science and Technology: Dir MONGIA HACHICHA.

Olivier Institute: Dir TAÏ MILADI.

Preparatory Institute for Engineers: Dir FATHI LAADHAR.

RESEARCH CENTRE

Biotechnology Centre: Dir HAMADI AYADI.

UNIVERSITÉ DE SOUSSE

Ave Khelifa Karooui, Sahloul IV, Sousse
Telephone: (73) 36-81-29
Fax: (73) 36-81-26
E-mail: universite.centre@uc.rnu.tn
Internet: www.uc.rnu.tn
Founded 1986
State control
Languages of instruction: Arabic, French
Academic year: September to July
Pres.: Prof. FAYÇAL MANSOURI
Vice-Pres.: MOHAMED SAID
Library of 277,010 vols
Number of teachers: 2,100
Number of students: 33,500

DEANS

Faculty of Arts and Humanities: MONCEF BEN ABDELJALIL
Faculty of Economic Sciences and Management: Dr AMINE HAMMAS
Faculty of Law and Political Sciences: LOTFI TARCHOUNA
Faculty of Medicine: ALI MTIRAOUI
High School of Sciences and Technology of Hammam Sousse: NAJEH FARHAT
Institute of Agronomy of Chott Meriem: ABDELHAMID BOUJELBEN
Institute of Applied Sciences and Technology: NABIL BELKAHLA

Institute of Computer Sciences and Communication Techniques of Hammam Sousse: OUAJDI KORBAA

Institute of Finance and Fiscality: SANA MANSOURI

Institute of Fine Arts: MONGI SOYAD

Institute of Higher Commercial Studies: LASSAD LAKHAL

Institute of Management: JALELEDDINE BEN RAJEB

Institute of Music: MOHAMED GARFI

Institute of Nursing Sciences: SOUAD CHALBI

Institute of Science and Health Technics: MOHAMED BENDHIEB

Institute of Transport and Logistics: KHALIFA SELLIMI

National School of Engineers: ZOUBEIR TOURKI

UNIVERSITÉ DE TUNIS

92 blvd du 9 avril 1938, 1007 Tunis

Telephone: (71) 56-73-22

Fax: (71) 56-06-33

Founded 1988 as Université des Lettres, des Arts et des Sciences Humaines (Tunis I) from existing faculties, present name 2001

Pres.: ABDERRAOUF MAHBOULI

Sec.-Gen.: LAMJED MESSOUSSI

Library of 186,000 vols

Number of teachers: 1,280

Number of students: 32,000

Publications: Les Annales de l'Université (in Arabic), Les Cahiers de Tunisie (multilingual), La Revue des Langues (multilingual), La Revue Tunisienne des Sciences de la Communication, Revue Géographique (multilingual)

DEANS AND DIRECTORS

Centre for Economic and Social Studies and Research: HACHMI LABAÏED

Faculty of Humanities and Social Sciences: HABIB DLALA

Faculty of Law, Economics and Management: CHOKRI MAMOGHLI

Faculty of Letters: (vacant)

Higher Documentation Institute: HENDA HAJAMI BEN GHZALA

Higher Institute of Applied Studies in Humanities: JAMEL BEN TAHAR

Higher Institute of Cultural Studies and Heritage Professions of Tunis: HABIB BAKLOUTI

Higher Institute of Drama: MOHAMED MESSAOUD DRISS

Higher Institute of Education and Training: MALIKA TRABELSI

Higher Institute of Management: ABDELWAHED TRABELSI

Higher Institute of Music: MUSTAPHA ALOULOU

Higher Institute for Youth and Cultural Activity: MONCEF JAZZAR

Higher Teacher Training School: MABROUK EL MANNAÏ

National Institute of Heritage: BÉJI BEN MAMI

Preparatory Institute for Engineering Studies: MOHAMED ABEDELMANAF BEN ABDRABOU

Tunis College of Science and Technology: JILANI LAMLOUMI

Tunis Higher Institute of Fine Arts: MOHAMED BEN TAHER GUIGA

UNIVERSITÉ DE TUNIS EL MANAR

Campus Universitaire, Manar II, 2092 Tunis

Telephone: (71) 87-33-66

Fax: (71) 87-20-55

E-mail: unitumanar@tun2.rnu.tn

Founded 1988 as Université des Sciences, des Techniques et de Médecine de Tunis (Tunis II) from existing faculties, present name 2001

Pres.: Prof. YOUSSEF ALOUANE

Sec.-Gen.: ISMAIL KHALIL

Number of teachers: 2,733

Number of students: 23,488

Publication: Revue de l'Université (6 a year)

DEANS

Bourguiba Institute of Modern Languages: ABED EL MAJID EL BEDOUI

El Khawarizmi Computer Centre: HENDA HADJAMI BEN GHEZELA

El Manar Preparatory School of Engineering: MOHAMED EL ABAAD

Faculties of Economics and Management: MOHAMED HADDAR

Faculty of Mathematics, Physics and Natural Sciences: CHEDLI TOUBLI

Faculty of Medicine: RACHID MECHMECH

Faculty of Law and Political Science: CHAFIK SAÏED

Higher Institute of Computer Science: SAMIR BEN AHMED

Higher Institute of Humanities: MOHAMED MAHJOUB

Higher Institute of Medical Technology: FATMA SLIM EL HILA

Higher Institute for Sport and Physical Education: ABDELAZIZ SFAR

Higher School of Food Technology: ABDELKADER CHERIF

Higher School of Health Sciences and Technology: MOHAMED HABIB JAAFOURA

Higher School of Post and Telecommunication: NACEUR AMMAR

Higher School of Science and Technology: SLAHEDDINE EL-GHRISSI

Institute for the Advancement of Disabled People: RAOUF BEN AMMAR

Kef Higher School of Agriculture: BOUZID NASRAOUI

Kef Institute for Sport and Physical Education: YOUSSEF FEKIH

Mateur Higher School of Agriculture: HEDI ABDOULI

Mateur Preparatory School of Engineering: MOHAMED BEJAOUI

Medjez el Bab Higher School of Rural Engineering: ABDERRAZEK SUISSI

Mograne Higher School of Agriculture: TIJANI MAHOUACHI

Nabeul Preparatory Institute of Engineering: MONCEF HADDED

National Agricultural Research Institute: SALAH MEKNI

National Institute of Agronomy: MONCEF EL-HARRABI

National Research Institute of Rural Engineering for Water and Forests: NEJI RAJEB

National Research Institute of Sciences and Technology: MOHAMED NOBIL

National School of Computer Science: FAROUK KAMMOUN

National School of Engineering: KHALIFA MAÂLEL

National University Centre for Scientific and Technical Documentation: FATMA CHAMMAM BEN ABDALLAH

Pasteur Institute: KOUSSAI EDALAJI

Polytechnic Institute: TAIEB HADHRI

Preparatory Institute of Scientific Studies and Technology: FAOUZIA CHARFI

School of Civil Aviation and Meterorlogy: MOHAMED TOUIL

Sidi Thabet National School of Veterinary Medicine: ATEF MALEK

Tabarka Forestry School: HAMDA SAOUDI

Veterinary Research Institute: MALEK ZRELLI

Other Institutions of Higher Education

Centre Culturel International d'Hammamet: ave des Nations Unies, 8050 Hammamet; tel. (72) 28-04-10; fax (72) 28-07-22; f. 1962; theatrical techniques, history and sociology of the theatre and video; Dir TAOUFIK BESBÈS.

Conservatoire National de Musique, de Danse et d'Arts Populaires: 20 ave de Paris, Tunis.

École Nationale d'Administration: 24 ave du Docteur Calmette, Mutuelleville, Tunis; tel. (71) 28-83-00; f. 1964; library: 53,000 vols; 1,050 students; Dir MAHER KAMOUN; publ. Revue Tunisienne d'Administration Publique (3 a year).

École Nationale de la Statistique: BP 65, Tunis; f. 1969; 1- and 2-year diploma courses.

Institut d'Économie Quantitative: 27 rue de Liban, 1002 Tunis; tel. (71) 28-36-33; fax (71) 78-70-34; f. 1964; methodological research in planning and documentation in social and economic fields; library: 7,500 vols, 300 periodicals; Dir-Gen. GHORBEL HÉDI.

Institut National du Travail et des Études Sociales: Z. I. Charguia II, BP 692, 1080 Tunis; tel. (71) 70-62-07; fax (71) 70-34-64; e-mail intes@intes.rnu.tn; internet www.intes.rnu.tn; language of instruction: Arabic; library: 5,000 vols; 110 teachers (34 full-time, 76 part-time); 2,200 students; Dir Prof. MUSTAPHA NASRAOUI; publ. Travail et Développement (2 a year).

TURKEY

The Higher Education System

Institutions of higher education include universities, faculties, institutes, colleges, conservatories, vocational colleges and research centres. Turkey joined the Bologna Process in 2001; however, reforms to the degree structure were not required since the Turkish higher education system was already based on three cycles. The Lisbon Convention was signed in 2004 and came into force in 2007. In 2005/06 2,181,217 students attended 1,306 higher education institutes, including 69 universities of various types, although a large number of new institutes have been established in subsequent years. In 2005/06 there were 73,061 students enrolled at İstanbul Üniversitesi (founded 1453, reorganized 1933). Quality assurance remains based on internal institutional evaluation, with some degree programmes assessed by specialized agencies, but full implementation of a national quality assurance system is planned. The National Qualifications Framework was approved in January 2010 and pilot implementation commenced in June 2011, with full implementation scheduled to be effected by December 2012.

The Yükseköğretim Kurulu (YöK—Council of Higher Education), which operates within the provisions set forth in the Constitution (Articles 130 and 131) and the 1981 Higher Education Law (No. 2547), is a fully autonomous public body responsible for the planning, coordination, governance and supervision of higher education in Turkey, and sets institutional budgets and defines criteria for the award of degrees. In accordance with the Higher Education Law, the rectors of all the public universities are appointed jointly by the faculty, the YöK and the President of Turkey, although the Turkish Government has in recent years mooted proposals to eliminate the YöK and the system of political influence within the higher education system.

The main criteria for admission to higher education is the Ögrenci Secme Sinavi (ÖSS—State University Entrance Examination), administered by the Öğrenci Seçme ve Yerleştirme Sistemi (ÖSYS—Student Selection and Placement Centre). Universities set their own entrance requirements based on scores in the ÖSS. In mid-2009 the YöK voted to reform the admissions system in order to end discrimination against graduates of vocational high schools, including religious schools; under the new system, the value of the points achieved by graduates of vocational high schools would no longer be lowered if they sought to study new subjects, as had been the case under the old system. Since 2002 the two-year Ön Lisans Diplomasi (Associate Degree) has been broadened to encompass technical and vocational education. The Lisans Diplomasi (Bachelors) is mostly a four-year programme of study, although some disciplines require longer periods of study, such as dentistry, architecture, veterinary medicine (five years) and medicine (six years). The first postgraduate degree is the two-year Yüsek Lisans Diplomasi (Masters), admission to which is on the basis of a competitive examination administered by the ÖSYM. The final university degree is the Doctor of Philosophy (Doktora); again, admission, which is open to holders of a Masters degree, or equivalent qualification, is on the basis of a competitive examination administered by the ÖSYM, and students are required to complete a four-year period of study and research, culminating in submission of a thesis.

As determined by the Law on Apprenticeship and Vocational Training (1986), technical and vocational education is provided by one of the three following methods: formal vocational education, apprenticeship training, or vocational courses. Since 2002 students have been allowed to enter vocational higher education without taking an entrance examination. In terms of formal vocational training, the main institutions are specialist vocational schools attached to universities, in addition to two-year colleges of technology and commercial colleges. Students who successfully complete the course of study are awarded the Ön Lisans (followed by subject name) and title of Tekniker (Technician). Apprenticeship training is offered largely at the secondary level, while vocational courses (where the highest available qualification is the Usta Ögreticilik Belgesi—Master Trainer Certificate) are aimed at adults who have left formal education.

Regulatory and Representative Bodies

GOVERNMENT

Ministry of Culture and Tourism: Kültür ve Turizm Bakanlığı, Atatürk Bul. 29, 06050 Opera, Ankara; tel. (312) 309-08-50; fax (312) 312-43-59; e-mail info@kulturturizm.gov.tr; internet www.kultur.gov.tr; Minister ERTUĞRUL GÜNAY.

Ministry of National Education: Milli Eğitim Bakanlığı, Atatürk Bul., Bakanlıklar, Ankara; tel. (312) 419-14-10; fax (312) 417-70-27; e-mail meb@meb.gov.tr; internet www.meb.gov.tr; Minister ÖMER DİNÇER.

ACCREDITATION

ENIC/NARIC Turkey: European Union and Int. Relations Office, Yükseköğretim Kurulu Baskanligi (YÖK), 06539 Bilkent, Ankara; tel. (312) 298-72-43; fax (312) 266-47-44; e-mail naric@yok.gov.tr; Head DENIZ ATES.

NATIONAL BODIES

Türk Üniversite Rektörleri Komitesi (Turkish University Rectors' Committee): Yükseköğretim Kurulu, Bilkent, Ankara; tel. (312) 266-47-25; fax (312) 266-51-53; f. 1967; rectors of all Turkish univs, with 5 former rectors; advises the Higher Education Ccl and the Interuniversity Board on university affairs, promotes cooperation between univs; Pres. Prof. Dr KEMAL GÜRÜZ; Sec. Prof. Dr UĞUR BÜGET.

Yükseköğretim Kurulu (Council of Higher Education): 06539 Bilkent, Ankara; tel. (312) 298-70-00; fax (312) 266-47-59; e-mail webadmin@yok.gov.tr; internet www.yok.gov.tr; f. 1981; NGO responsible for the organization and governance of the higher education instns, and for the teaching and research carried out; 22 mems; Pres. Prof. Dr YUSUF ZİYA ÖZCAN; Gen. Sec. TURGUT KILIÇ.

Learned Societies

AGRICULTURE, FISHERIES AND VETERINARY SCIENCE

Türk Veteriner Hekimleri Birliği (Turkish Veterinary Medical Association): Ehlibeyt Mah. Ceyhun Atıf Kansu Cad. Aktas Apt. 1/2-3 Balgat/Cankaya, Ankara; tel. (312) 435-54-15; fax (312) 435-18-53; e-mail merkezkonseyi@tvhb.org.tr; internet www.tvhb.org.tr; f. 1954; 20,000 mems; Pres. MEHMET ALKAN; Vice-Pres. Dr NAHIT YAZICIOGLU; Gen-Sec. ALI KOÇ; publ. *Turkish Veterinary Medical Association/Turk Veteriner Hekimleri Birligi Dergisi* (irregular).

BIBLIOGRAPHY, LIBRARY SCIENCE AND MUSEOLOGY

Türk Kütüphaneciler Derneği (Turkish Librarians' Association): Necatibey Cad. Elgün Sok. 8/8, 06440 Kızılay, Ankara; tel. (312) 230-13-25; fax (312) 232-04-53; e-mail tkd.dernek@gmail.com; internet www.kutuphaneci.org.tr; f. 1949; 2,000 mems; Pres. ALI FUAT KARTAL; Sec.-Gen. EMRE HASAN AKBAYRAK; publ. *Türk Kütüphaneciliği* (4 a year).

ECONOMICS, LAW AND POLITICS

Türk Hukuk Kurumu (Turkish Law Association): 2 Cad. 55/6 Bahçelievler, Ankara; f. 1934; publs *La Turquie* (Vie Juridique des Peuples, Paris), *Türk Hukuk Lûgati* (Turkish Law Dictionary).

HISTORY, GEOGRAPHY AND ARCHAEOLOGY

Türk Tarih Kurumu (Turkish Historical Society): Kızılay Sok. 1, 06100 Sıhhıye Ankara; tel. (312) 310-23-68; fax (312) 310-

16-98; e-mail ttkinfo@ttk.org.tr; internet www.ttk.org.tr; f. 1931; 40 mems; library of 228,577 vols; Pres. Prof. Dr YUSUF HALAÇO-ĞLU; publs *Belgeler* (1 a year), *Belleten* (3 a year).

LANGUAGE AND LITERATURE

British Council: Posta Kutusu 34, Çankaya, Ankara; tel. (312) 455-36-00; fax (312) 455-36-36; internet www.britishcouncil.org/turkey; f. 1940; offers courses and exams in English language and British culture and promotes cultural exchange with the UK; attached offices in Istanbul (teaching centre) and Izmir; Dir of Operations, Turkey JEFF STREETER.

Goethe-Institut: Atatürk Bulvarı 131, Bakanlıklar, 06640 Ankara; tel. (312) 419-52-83; fax (312) 418-08-47; e-mail il@ankara .goethe.org; internet www.goethe.de/om/ank; offers courses and exams in German language and culture and promotes cultural exchange with Germany; attached centres in Istanbul and Izmir; library of 15,000 vols; Dir Dr THOMAS LIER.

Instituto Cervantes: Tarlabasi Bulvarı, Zambak Sokak 33, 80080 Istanbul; tel. (212) 292-65-36; fax (212) 292-65-37; e-mail cenest@cervantes.es; internet estambul .cervantes.es; offers courses and exams in Spanish language and culture and promotes cultural exchange with Spain and Spanish-speaking Latin and Central America; library of 7,500 vols; Dir PABLO MARTÍN ASUERO.

PEN Yazarlar Derneği (Turkish PEN Centre): Istiklal Cad., 225, Beyoglu is Merkezi, B Blok, Kat 2, 143, Beyoglu, Istanbul; e-mail pprtr@superonline.com; f. 1989; 200 mems; Pres. VECDI SAYAR; publ. *Turkish PEN Reader* (in English, 2 a year).

Türk Dil Kurumu (Turkish Language Institute): Atatürk Bulvarı 217, Kavaklıdere, 06680 Ankara; tel. (312) 428-61-00; fax (312) 468-07-83; e-mail bim@tdk.org.tr; internet www.tdk.org.tr; f. 1932; 40 mems; library of 35,000 vols on Turkish studies; Pres. Prof. Dr ŞÜKRÜ HALUK AKALIN; Sec.-Gen. ALI KARA-ÇALI; publs *Tercüme Yıllığı* (Yearbook of Translation), *Türk Dili Araştırmaları Yıllığı* (Yearbook of Turkic Studies), *Türk Dili Dergisi* (Journal of Turkish Language, 12 a year), *Türk Dünyası Dergisi* (Journal of Turkish World, 2 a year).

MEDICINE

Türk Cerrahi Derneği (Turkish Surgical Society): Koru Mah. Ihlamur Cad. 26, 06810 Çayyolu, Ankara; tel. (312) 241-99-90; fax (312) 241-99-91; e-mail turkcer@turkcer.org .tr; internet www.turkcer.org.tr; f. 1929.

Türk Mikrobiyoloji Cemiyeti (Turkish Microbiological Society): PK 57, 34492 Beyazit, Istanbul; tel. and fax (212) 531-70-89; e-mail tmc@tmc-online.org; internet www .tmc-online.org; f. 1931; 350 mems; Pres. Prof. Dr NEHAZAT GÜRLER; Sec.-Gen. Doc. Dr ORHAN CERN AKTEPE; publ. *Türk Mikrobiyoloji Cemiyeti Dergisi* (Journal, 4 a year).

Türk Nöropsikiyatri Derneği (Turkish Neuropsychiatric Society): Op. Dr. Raif Bey Sok. 31/2, 34360 Sisli, Istanbul; tel. (212) 219-97-77; fax (212) 343-00-95; f. 1914; 1,200 mems; meetings to discuss aspects of psychiatry and neurology; Pres. Prof. PEYKAN GÖKOLP; publ. *Nöropsikiyatri Arşivi* (Archives of Neuropsychiatry, 4 a year).

Türk Ortopedi ve Travmatoloji Birliği Derneği (Turkish Association of Orthopaedics and Traumatology): Bayraktar Mahallesi Ikizdere Sok. 21/12, Kat 2 GOP, Ankara; tel. (312) 436-11-40; fax (312) 436-27-16; internet www.totbid.org.tr; Pres. Prof. Dr BÜLEIT ALPARSLAN.

Türk Oto-Rino-Larengoloji Cemiyeti (Turkish Otorhinolaryngological and Head and Neck Surgery Society): Buyudere Cad. Tankaya 18/1 Kat 1, Şişli, 80260 Istanbul; tel. (212) 233-11-26; fax (212) 233-11-27; e-mail kbb@kbb.org.tr; internet www.kbb .org.tr; f. 1930; 2,500 mems; Pres. Prof. Dr ASIM KAYTAZ; Gen. Sec. Prof. Dr FERHAN ÖZ; publ. *Turkish Archives of Otolaryngology* (3 a year).

Türk Tabipleri Birliği (Turkish Medical Association): GMK Bul. Şehit Daniş Tunalı-gil Sok. 2 Kat 4, Maltepe, 06570 Ankara; tel. (312) 231-31-79; fax (312) 231-19-52; e-mail ttb@ttb.org.tr; internet www.ttb.org.tr; f. 1953; 98,500 mems; Pres. Dr ERIŞ BILALOĞLU; Gen. Sec. Dr FERIDE AKSU TANIK.

Türk Tibbi Elektro Radyografi Cemiyeti (Turkish Electro-Radiographical Society): Valikonagi Cad. 10, Harbiye, Istanbul; f. 1924.

Türk Tıp Tarihi Kurumu (Turkish Medical History Society): c/o Uludağ Üniversitesi, Tıp Fakültesi, Deontoloji ve Tıp Tarihi Anabilim Dalı, Bursa; tel. (532) 452-94-37; e-mail ademirer@yahoo.com; f. 1938; 120 mems; library of 70,000 vols; Pres. Prof. Dr AYŞEGÜL ERDEMIR DEMIRHAN.

Türk Tüberküloz ve Toraks Derneği (Turkish Association of Tuberculosis and Thorax): Ankara Üniversitesi, Tıp Fakültesi, Göğüs Hastalıkları Anabilim Dalı, 06100 Cebeci- Ankara; tel. (312) 319-00-27; fax (312) 319-00-46; e-mail akaya@medicine .ankara.edu.tr; internet www.tubtoraks.org; Dir Dr ÖZLEM ÖZDEMIR KUMBASAR; publ. *Journal* (4 a year).

Türk Üroloji Derneği (Turkish Urological Society): c/o Prof. Nurettin Öktem Sokak, Lale Palas Apt. 18/2, 34382 Şişli, Istanbul; tel. and fax (212) 232-46-89; e-mail uroturk@ uroturk.org.tr; internet www.uroturk.org.tr; f. 1933; 1,093 mems; Pres. Prof. VURAL SOLOK; publ. *Türk Üroloji Dergisi* (Turkish Journal of Urology, 4 a year).

NATURAL SCIENCES
Mathematical Sciences

Türkiye Matematik Derneği (Mathematical Society of Turkey): Sabancı Üniversitesi, Karaköy İletişim Merkezi, Bankalar Cad. 2, 80020 Karaköy, Istanbul; tel. (212) 292-49-39; e-mail emrah@su.sabanciuniv.edu; internet www.tmd.org.tr; f. 1948; development of mathematics among young people; 509 mems; Pres. Prof. Dr TOSUN TERZIOĞLU; Gen. Sec. Prof. Dr HÜLYA ŞENKON; publ. *Matematik Dünyası* (2 a year).

Physical Sciences

Türkiye Kimya Derneği (Chemical Society of Turkey): Halaskârgazi Cad. 53, D. 8 Uzay Apt, Harbiye, Istanbul; tel. (212) 240-73-31; e-mail tkd@turchemsoc.org; internet www .turchemsoc.org; f. 1919; 1,500 mems; Pres. Prof. Dr OSMAN YAVUZ ATAMAN'IN; publ. *Kimya ve Sanayi* (Chemistry and Industry).

PHILOSOPHY AND PSYCHOLOGY

Türkiye Felsefe Kurumu (Philosophical Society of Turkey): Ahmet Rasim Sok. 8/2, Çankaya, 06550 Ankara; tel. (312) 440-74-08; fax (312) 441-02-97; e-mail toc@tfk.org.tr; internet www.tfk.org.tr; f. 1974.; promotes philosophy and philosophical education in Turkey; encourages philosophical thinking in public life and secures int. cooperation through seminars, symposia and courses; 175 individual mems; Pres. IOANNA KUÇUR-ADI; Sec.-Gen. GULRIZ UYGUR; publ. *Bülten* (3 a year).

Yeni Felsefe Cemiyeti (New Philosophical Society): Işık Lisesi, Nişantaşı, Istanbul; f. 1943.

TECHNOLOGY

TMMOB Jeoloji Mühendisleri Odası (Chamber of Geological Engineers of Turkey): PK 464, Yenişehir, 06444 Ankara; tel. (312) 434-36-01; fax (312) 434-23-88; e-mail jmo@jmo.org.tr; internet www.jmo.org.tr; f. 1974; 9,780 mems; library of 17,000 vols; Pres. AYDÝN CELEBI; Sec.-Gen. BAHATTIN MURAT DEMIR; publs *Abstracts of the Geological Congress of Turkey* (1 a year), *Abstracts of Geological Research in Turkey* (1 a year), *Blue Planet* (2 a year), *Bulletin News* (4 a year), *Geological Bulletin of Turkey* (2 a year), *Journal of Geological Engineering* (2 a year).

Research Institutes
GENERAL

Research Centre for Islamic History, Art and Culture (IRCICA): POB 24, Beşiktaş, 80692 Istanbul; Yildiz Sarayi, Seyir Kosku Barbaros Bulvarı, Besiktas, 34349 Istanbul; tel. (212) 259-17-42; fax (212) 258-43-65; e-mail ircica@ircica.org; internet www.ircica .org; f. 1979; a subsidiary of the Organization of Islamic Cooperation; activities relating to research, publishing, documentation and information on subjects concerning Islamic civilisation and Muslim cultures incl. history of Muslim nations, history of science, archaeology, architecture and urbanism, fine arts and handicrafts, preservation of cultural heritage, and cultural devt issues; organization of conferences, symposia, exhibitions, workshops, training courses and competitions; publishes books in various languages, newsletter appears quarterly in English, French and Arabic; library of 720,000 vols, 1,764 periodicals, 70,000 historical photographs, 1,500 historical maps, 1,150 microfilms, 200 CDs and DVDs, 1,860 audio cassettes, 6,150 archive documents, 4,000 calligraphy plates; Dir-Gen. Dr HALIT EREN.

Türk Kültürünü Araştırma Enstitüsü (Turkish Cultural Research Institute): 17° Sok. 38, Bahçelievler, Ankara; tel. (312) 213-31-00; fax (312) 213-41-35; f. 1961; scholarly research into all aspects of Turkish culture; Dir Dr ŞÜKRÜ ELÇİN; publs *Cultura Turcica* (1 a year), *Türk Kültürü* (12 a year), *Türk Kültürü Araştırmaları* (1 a year).

Türkiye Bilimsel ve Teknik Araştırma Kurumu (Scientific and Technical Research Council of Turkey): Tunus Cad. 80, 06100 Kavaklıdere, Ankara; tel. (312) 468-53-00; fax (312) 427-74-89; e-mail www-adm@ tubitak.gov.tr; internet www.tubitak.gov.tr; f. 1963; govt body which carries out, sponsors, promotes and coordinates research activities in pure and applied sciences; library of 19,000 vols, 426 periodicals; Pres. Prof. Dr NÜKET YETIS; Sec.-Gen. IBRAHIM BERBEROGLU (acting); publs *Bilim ve Teknik* (Science and Technology, 12 a year), *Turkish Journal of Agriculture and Forestry Sciences* (6 a year), *Turkish Journal of Biology* (6 a year), *Turkish Journal of Botany* (6 a year), *Turkish Journal of Chemistry* (6 a year), *Turkish Journal of Earth Sciences* (6 a year), *Turkish Journal of Electrical Engineering and Computer Sciences* (3 a year), *Turkish Journal of Engineering and Environmental Sciences* (6 a year), *Turkish Journal of Mathematics* (6 a year), *Turkish Journal of Medical Sciences* (6 a year), *Turkish Journal of Physics* (6 a year), *Turkish Journal of Veterinary and Animal Sciences* (6 a year), *Turkish Journal of Zoology* (6 a year).

Attached Institutes:

Defence Research and Development Institute: PK 16 Mamak, 06261 Ankara; tel. (312) 399-03-38; fax (312) 212-37-49; Dir Prof. Dr ERES SÖYLEMEZ.

Marmara Araştırma Merkezi (Marmara Research Centre): PK 21, 41470 Gebze, Kocaeli; tel. (262) 677-20-00; fax (262) 641-23-09; e-mail info@mam.gov.tr; internet www.mam.gov.tr; f. 1972; materials science, optoelectronics, earth sciences, food science, nutrition, information technology, chemistry, chemical technology, environmental technology and energy; library of 30,000 vols, 90,000 bound periodicals; Dir (vacant).

TÜBİTAK Marmara Araştırma Merkezi Gen Mühendisliği ve Biyoteknoloji Araştırma Enstitüsü (TÜBİTAK Marmara Research Centre Genetic Engineering and Biotechnology Institute): Anibal Cad. Barış Mah., PK 21, 41470 Gebze, Kocaeli; tel. (262) 677-20-00; fax (262) 641-23-09; e-mail gmbe.web@mam.gov.tr; internet www.rigeb.gov.tr; f. 1983; Dir Asst Prof. AYNUR BASALP.

TÜBİTAK Uzay Teknolojileri Araştırma Enstitüsü (TUBITAK Space Technologies Research Institute): Middle East Technical Univ. (ODTÜ) Campus, 06531 Ankara; tel. (312) 210-13-10; fax (312) 210-13-15; e-mail info@uzay.tubitak.gov.tr; internet www.uzay.tubitak.gov.tr; f. 1985; research and devt in space technologies, electronics, software, power electronics, power distribution systems; Dir TAMER BEŞER.

Ulusal Elektronik ve Kriptoloji Araştırma Enstitüsü (National Electronics and Cryptology Research Institute): PK 74, 41470 Gebze, Kocaeli; tel. (262) 648-10-00; fax (262) 648-11-00; e-mail uekae@uekae.tubitak.gov.tr; internet www.uekae.tubitak.gov.tr; library of 2,700 vols, 70 periodicals; Dir Prof. Dr AYHAN TÜRELI.

AGRICULTURE, FISHERIES AND VETERINARY SCIENCE

Kavak ve Hızlı Gelişen Tür Orman Ağaçları Araştırma Müdürlüğü (Poplar and Fast-Growing Forest Trees Research Institute): PK 93, 41001 Izmit, Kocaeli; tel. (262) 311-69-64; fax (262) 311-69-72; e-mail kavak@kavak.gov.tr; internet www.kavak.gov.tr; f. 1962; attached to the Ministry of Forests; development of forest nursery and reafforestation techniques, introduction of new forest tree species, increase of wood production, research in poplar cultivation and management techniques; library of 3,700 vols; Dir Dr FARUK Ş. ÖZAY; publs *Annual Bulletin, Magazine, Technical Bulletin.*

Tarım ve Köyişleri Bakanlığı, Zirai Mücadele Araştırma Enstitüsü (Ministry of Agricultural and Rural Affairs, Plant Protection Research Institute): Yenimahalle, Gayret Mahallesi Fatih Sultan Mehmet Bulv. 66, 06172 Ankara; tel. (312) 344-74-30; fax (312) 315-15-31; internet www.zmmae.gov.tr; f. 1934; depts dealing with research into combating plant diseases, pests and weeds; engaged in phytopathology, entomology, insect taxonomy and toxicology, nematology; analyzes pesticides and crop pesticide residues; library of 5,000 vols; Dir Dr ALI TAMER; publ. *Bitki Koruma Bülteni* (Plant Protection Bulletin, English, French or German summary, irregular).

HISTORY, GEOGRAPHY AND ARCHAEOLOGY

British Institute at Ankara: Tahran Cad. 24, 06700 Kavaklıdere, Ankara; tel. (312) 428-03-30; fax (312) 428-03-31; e-mail library@biaatr.org; internet www.biaa.ac.uk *London Office:* c/o Claire McCafferty, British Institute at Ankara, British Academy, 10 Carlton House Terrace, London, SW1Y 5AH, UK; f. 1947; supports, promotes and publishes British research focused on Turkey and the Black Sea littoral, in all academic disciplines within the arts, humanities and social sciences; maintains centre of excellence in Ankara, focused on the archaeology and related subjects of Turkey; library of 50,000 vols; Dir Dr LUTGARDE VANDEPUT; Admin. CLAIRE MCCAFFERTY; publs *Anatolian Studies* (1 a year), *Heritage Turkey.*

Deutsches Archäologisches Institut İstanbul Şubesi (Deutsches Archäologisches Institut Istanbul Branch): 34437 Gümüşsuyu/İnönü Caddesi 10, Istanbul; tel. (212) 393-76-00; fax (212) 393-76-14; e-mail sekretariat@istanbul.dainst.org; internet www.dainst.de; f. 1929; research into archaeology and cultural history in Turkey from prehistory to the Ottoman period; library of 60,000 vols; Dir Prof. Dr F. PIRSON; publs *Byzas, Istanbuler Beihefte, Istanbuler Forschungen, Istanbuler Mitteilungen des DAI* (1 a year).

Hollanda Araştırma Enstitüsü (Netherlands Institute in Turkey): Istiklâl Caddesi 181, Beyoğlu, Istanbul; tel. (212) 293-92-83; fax (212) 251-38-46; e-mail nit@nit-istanbul.org; internet www.nit-istanbul.org; f. 1958; library of 15,000 vols; Dir Dr FOKKE GERRITSEN; Librarian GÜLTEN YILDIZ; publ. *Anatolica* (1 a year).

Institut Français d'Etudes Anatoliennes d'Istanbul (Fransız Anadolu Araştırmaları Enstitüsü/French Institute of Anatolian Studies, Istanbul): PK 54, Palais de France, Nuru Ziya Sok, 80072 Beyoğlu-Istanbul; tel. (212) 244-17-17; fax (212) 252-80-91; e-mail ifea@ifea-istanbul.net; internet www.ifea-istanbul.net; f. 1930; Anatolian studies from prehistory to contemporary period; 15 mems; library of 24,000 vols; Dir PIERRE CHUVIN; publs *Anatolia antiqua* (1 a year), *Anatolia moderna* (1 a year).

Orient-Institut Istanbul/Deutsche Gesellschaft Geisteswissenschaftlicher Institute im Ausland/Orient Enstitüsü, İstanbul (Orient Institute Istanbul): Susam Sokak 16, D.8, 34433 Cihangir, Istanbul; tel. (212) 293-60-67; fax (212) 249-63-59; e-mail oiist@oidmg.org; internet www.oidmg.org; f. 1987; Turkish, Ottoman and central Asian Studies; library of 40,000 vols, 1,388 periodicals; Dir Prof. Dr RAOUL MOTIKA; Asst Dir Dr RICHARD WITTMANN.

MEDICINE

Çocuk Sağlığıı Enstitüsü, Hacettepe Üniversitesi İhsan Doğramacı Çocuk Hastanesi (Institute of Child Health at Hacettepe University Children's Hospital): İhsan Doğramacı Çocuk Hastanesi 2, Blok 3, 06100 Yenisehir-Ankara; tel. (312) 324-42-91; fax (312) 324-32-84; e-mail tkutluk@hacettepe.edu.tr; internet www.cocuk.hacettepe.edu.tr; f. 1958; Masters and PhD training in paediatric sub-specialties; Dir Prof. Dr TEZER KUTLUK; publs *Çocuk Sağlıgı ve Hastalıkları Dergisi* (abstracts in English, 4 a year), *Turkish Journal of Paediatrics* (4 a year).

NATURAL SCIENCES

General

İstanbul Üniversitesi Deniz Bilimleri ve İşletmeciliği Enstitüsü (University of Istanbul Institute of Marine Sciences and Management): Müsküle Sok 1 Vefa, 34410 Istanbul; tel. (212) 528-25-39; fax (212) 526-84-33; e-mail kcguven@yahoo.com.tr; internet www.istanbul.edu.tr/enstituler/denizbilimleri/denizbilimleri.htm; f. 1993; marine sciences; library of 11,243 vols; Dir Prof. Dr KASIM CEMAL GUVEN; publ. *Turkish Journal of Marine Science* (3 a year).

Türk Bilim Tarihi Kurumu (Turkish Society for History of Science): POB 24, 34349 Beşiktaş, Istanbul; tel. (212) 259-17-42; fax (212) 258-43-65; e-mail ircica@superonline.com; f. 1989; research and publication on history of science with emphasis on Ottoman history of science; organization of symposia; Pres. Prof. Dr EKMELEDDIN İHSANOĞLU.

Physical Sciences

Maden Tetkik ve Arama Genel Müdürlüğü (MTA) (General Directorate of Mineral Research and Exploration): İsmet İnönü Bulvarı, Ankara; tel. (312) 287-34-30; fax (312) 287-91-88; e-mail mta@mta.gov.tr; internet www.mta.gov.tr; f. 1935; conducts the Geological Survey of Turkey and evaluates mineral resources; library: see Libraries and Archives; Dir-Gen. A. KEMAL ISIKER; publs *Bulletin of Mineral Research and Exploration* (2 a year, in English), annual reports and maps.

RELIGION, SOCIOLOGY AND ANTHROPOLOGY

Islâm Araþtýrmalarý Merkezi (Centre for Islamic Studies): Ycadiye Baðlarbaþý Caddesi, Number 40, 34660 Üsküdar, Istanbul; tel. (216) 474-08-50; fax (216) 474-08-74; e-mail isam@isam.org.tr; internet www.isam.org.tr; f. 1988; library of 225,000 vols, 3,300 periodical titles; Chair. Prof. Dr M. AKIF AYDIN; publ. *Turkish Journal of Islamic Studies.*

TECHNOLOGY

Afet İşleri Genel Müdürlüğü Deprem Araştırma Dairesi (General Directorate of Disaster Affairs Earthquake Research Department): Yüksel Cad. 7/B, Yenişehir, Ankara; tel. (312) 287-36-45; e-mail zemin@deprem.gov.tr; internet www.deprem.gov.tr; f. 1969; 78 staff; attached to the Ministry of Public Works and Resettlement; establishment, operation and maintenance of nationwide strong ground motion recorder network; earthquake prediction; preparation of codes and regulations for earthquake-resistant design and construction; research on earthquake hazard minimization; education and information for the public; comprises Earthquake Engineering, Seismology and Laboratory Divisions; Dir MUSTAFA TAYMAZ; publ. *Bulletin* (4 a year).

Araştırma Dairesi Başkanlığı (Demiryollar, Limanlar ve Hava Meydanları İnşaatı Genel Müdürlüğünün) (Department of Research and Materials (General Directorate of Railways, Harbour and Airport Construction)): Macun mah. Serpme Sok 3, 06338 Yenimahalle, Ankara; tel. (312) 397-33-50; fax (312) 397-38-11; e-mail dlharastirma1@ttnet.net.tr; internet www.dlh.gov.tr/arastirma; f. 1948; road materials testing, pavement design, soil and rock mechanics and geotechnical investigations; 60 staff; library of 2,467 vols; Dir YUSUF ZIYA BOYACI; publ. *Research Bulletin.*

Devlet Su İşleri, Teknik Araştırma ve Kalite Kontrol Dairesi (State Hydraulic

Works, Technical Research and Quality Control Department): Ismet Inonu Bul., 06100 Yücetepe, Ankara; tel. (312) 417-83-00; fax (312) 418-24-98; e-mail takk@dsi.gov.tr; internet www.dsi.gov.tr; f. 1958; research and laboratory work on hydraulic engineering, soil mechanics, construction materials and concrete, chemistry, isotopes for hydrology; *in situ* research on water works; library; Dir HAYDAR KOÇAKER; publ. *DSI Teknik Bülteni* (original papers, some in foreign languages).

Marmara Research Centre: POB 21, 41470 Gebze, Kocaeli; tel. (262) 641-23-00; fax (262) 641-23-09; e-mail bilgi@mam.gov.tr; internet www.mam.gov.tr; f. 1972; research on basic and applied sciences, and industrial research; library of 90,000 vols, 746 periodicals; Dir Prof. ÖMER KAYMAKÇALAN.

Sarayköy Nükleer Araştırma ve Eğitim Merkezi (Sarayköy Nuclear Research and Training Centre): Saray Mahallesi, Atom Caddesi, 27 Kazan, 06983 Ankara; tel. (312) 815-43-00; fax (312) 815-43-07; internet www.anaem.gov.tr; f. 1967; attached to the Turkish Atomic Energy Authority; applied research in radiation chemistry and physics, electronics, nuclear agriculture, materials sciences and plasma physics; library of periodicals and technical reports; Dir İ. TUKENMEZ; publ. *Turkish Journal of Nuclear Sciences* (2 a year).

Libraries and Archives

Afyon

Gedik Ahmed Paşa Library: Dumlupınar Mah. Şeyh Mehmet, Cad. 1, Afyon; tel. and fax (272) 213-54-33; f. 1785; 30,000 vols.

Ankara

Ankara Üniversitesi, Kütüphane ve Dokümantasyon Daire Başkanlığı (Ankara University Libraries and Documentation Centre): Sevket Aziz Kansu Bldg, İncitaşı Sok, Beşevler, Ankara; tel. (312) 223-57-61; fax (312) 213-95-32; e-mail atilgan@ankara.edu.tr; internet www.ankara.edu.tr; f. 1946; 722,309 vols, 33,000 e-books, 621 printed periodicals, 11,000 e-journals, 4,308 audiovisual materials, 17,872 MSS and 29,029 dissertations and theses; Library Dir Dr DOGAN ATILGAN; publs *Ankara Avrupa Çalışmaları Dergisi, Ankara Üniversitesi Dil ve Tarih-Coğrafya Fakültesi Dergisi, Ankara Üniversitesi Hukuk Fakültesi Dergisi, Ankara Üniversitesi Siyasal Bilgiler Fakültesi Dergisi, Ankara Üniversitesi Tıp Fakültesi Mecmuası, Ankara Üniversitesi Veteriner Fakültesi Dergisi, Ankara Üniversitesi Ziraat Fakültesi Tarım Bilimleri Dergisi.*

Library of National Defence: Ankara; f. 1877; 8,678 vols in Turkish, 5,820 vols in other languages; state-governed.

Maden Tetkik ve Arama Genel Müdürlüğü Kütüphanesi (General Directorate of Mineral Research and Exploration Library): İsmet İnönü Bulvarı, Ankara; f. 1935; 180,000 vols in various languages, 2,118 periodicals; Librarian ÜMİT ERKMEN; publ. *Bulletin* (in Turkish and English).

Middle East Technical University Library: Universiteler Mahallesi, Dumlupina Bulvarı Number 1, 06800 Ankara; tel. (312) 210-27-80; fax (312) 210-27-78; e-mail lib-hot-line@metu.edu.tr; internet www.lib.metu.edu.tr; f. 1956; maintains custody of the univ.'s recording, microfilm and projection equipment; 644,692 vols, 445,974 books, 180,468 bound periodicals, 1,385 journal subscriptions, 59,900 e-journals, 117,713 e-

books in 150 databases, 18,250 master and doctoral theses; Dir CEVAT GÜVEN.

Milli Kütüphane (National Library of Turkey): Bahçelievler, Ankara 06940; tel. (312) 222-38-12; fax (312) 223-04-51; e-mail info@mkutup.gov.tr; internet www.mkutup.gov.tr; f. 1946; 1,136,997 vols, 911,675 vols of periodicals, 35,024 MSS, 197,577 non-book items; Pres. TUNCEL ACAR; publs *Türkiye Bibliyografyası* (Turkish National Bibliography, 12 a year), *Türkiye Makaleler Bibliyografyası* (Bibliography of articles in Turkish periodicals, 12 a year).

Public Library: Ankara; f. 1922; 21,000 vols in Turkish, 10,200 vols in European languages, over 1,200 MSS in Arabic and Persian.

Türkiye Büyük Millet Meclisi Kütüphane ve Arşiv Hizmetleri Başkanlığı (Turkish Grand National Assembly Library and Archives Services Department): TBMM Kütüphane ve Arşiv Hizmetleri Başkanlığı, 06543 Bakanlıklar, Ankara; tel. (312) 420-68-35; fax (312) 420-75-48; e-mail kutuphane@tbmm.gov.tr; internet www.tbmm.gov.tr/kutuphane; f. 1920; 271,298 vols in social sciences incl. 243,606 in Turkish, 12,578 in Ottoman Turkish language, 34,349 in English, 17,090 in French, 1,000 in Arabic and Persian, 60 MSS, 59,134 vols of periodicals; Chair. MEHMET TOPRAK; publ. *Bilgi* (4 a year).

Antalya

Antalya Tekelioğlu İl Halk Kütüphanesi (Tekelioğlu Library): Ucgen Mah. 96. Sok. 54, Antalya; tel. (242) 344-51-37; f. 1924; 5,000 vols, nearly 2,000 MSS in Persian, Arabic and Turkish; Dir AYŞE D. SAVGUN.

Balıkeşir

Il Halk Kütüphanesi, Balıkeşir (Provincial Public Library, Balıkeşir): Bahçelievler Mah Kıralı Sok., Balıkeşir; tel. (266) 241-32-33; fax (266) 243-04-12; f. 1901; 1,286 MSS in Turkish, Arabic and Persian, 49,000 vols in Turkish, Arabic and English, 766 in other languages, 5,088 periodicals; Dir A. ERCAN TIĞ.

Darende

Mehmet Paşa Library: Darende; f. 1776; 4,000 vols, 800 MSS.

Edirne

Selimiye Library: Edirne; f. 1575; 36,113 vols (incl. 3,172 MSS and 3,894 vols in Arabic); Librarian Mrs OZLEM AĞIRGAN.

Isparta

Halil Hamit Paşa Library: Isparta; f. 1783; 20,200 vols, over 850 MSS; Dir MAHMUT KAYICI.

Istanbul

Atatürk Kitaplığı (Ataturk Library): Mete Caddesi 45, Taksim, Istanbul; tel. (212) 249-56-83; fax (212) 251-79-72; f. 1929; public library; 184,000 vols.

Beyazıt Devlet Kütüphanesi (Beyazit State Library): Turan Emeksiz Sok 6, 344450 Beyazıt, Istanbul; tel. (212) 522-31-67; f. 1882; legal deposit library; 500,000 vols in various languages, 11,120 MSS, 32,992 photographs, 21,616 periodicals; Dir YUSUF TAVACI.

Boğaziçi University Library: Bebek, 80815 Istanbul; tel. and fax (212) 257-50-16; e-mail bulib@boun.edu.tr; internet www.library.boun.edu.tr; f. 1863; 375,000 vols in English and other languages, incl. a special colln of over 30,332 vols on the Near East, 10,000 rare books and MSS; 220 periodicals, 2,500 records and 200 CDs; Librarian HATICE ÜN.

Ecumenical Patriarchate Library: İstanbul Rum Patrikliği, Sadrazam Ali Paşa Caddesi 35, 34220 Fener, Istanbul; internet www.patriarchate.org; foundation dates from beginning of Patriarchate, reorganization 1890; 25,000 vols in main library, and 1,500 MSS; 45,000 vols in branch library at Orthodox Seminary of Heybeliada; Dir Rev. PANAGHIOTIS THEODORIDIS (under the jurisdiction of the Holy Synod).

Institute of Turkology Library: Istanbul University, 34452 Beyazıt, Istanbul; f. 1924; 50,000 vols relating to Turkish language, literature, history and culture.

Istanbul Teknik Üniversitesi Kütüphane ve Dokümantasyon Daire (Istanbul Technical University Library and Documentation Division): Ayazağa Kampüsü, Maslak 34469, Istanbul; tel. (212) 285-35-96; fax (212) 285-33-02; e-mail kutuphane@itu.edu.tr; internet www.library.itu.edu.tr; f. 1795; six separate libraries on five university campuses; 372,000 vols; Dir of Libraries AYHAN KAYGUSUZ.

Istanbul University Library and Documentation Centre: University PTT 34452, Beyazıt, Istanbul; tel. (212) 455-57-83; fax (212) 455-57-84; e-mail uko@istanbul.edu.tr; internet www.kutuphane.istanbul.edu.tr; f. 1925; comprises the central university library and 17 faculty libraries; 500,000 vols, 18,606 MSS, 18,000 periodicals (3,100 current), 35,000 theses; Dir Doç. Dr ÜMIT KONYA.

Köprülü Yazma Eser Kütüphanesi (Köprülü Library): Divan Yolu Cad. 29, Cemberlitas-Eminonu, Istanbul; tel. (212) 516-83-13; f. 1677; 3,000 vols, 2,755 MSS, of which 193 are from early Ottoman presses, and 42 handwritten works from before the 10th century.

Millet Kütüphanesi (Public Library): Macar Kardeşler Cad. 85, 34260 Fatih, Istanbul; tel. (212) 631-36-07; f. 1916; 33,980 vols, 8,844 MSS.

Nuruosmaniye Library: Camii Avlusu, Cagaloglu, Istanbul; tel. (212) 527-20-04; f. 1755; 6,000 vols, 5,000 MSS.

Süleymaniye Kütüphanesi (Süleymaniye Library): Aysekadin Hamami Sok. 35, Beyazıt, Istanbul; tel. (212) 520-64-60; fax (212) 520-64-62; f. 1557; 113,068 vols and 66,117 MSS in Turkish, Uyghur, Arabic and Persian; 109 different collections incl. those from Ayasofya, Fatih and Husrev Pasha; MS restoration service; brs at Atif Efendi, Hacı Selim Ağa, Köprülü, Nuru-Osmaniye, Ragıppaşa; Dir Dr NEVZAT KAYA.

Women's Library and Information Center Foundation: Fener Mahallesi, Fener Vapur Iskelesi Karşısı, Fener Haliç, 34220 Istanbul; tel. (212) 534-95-50; fax (212) 523-74-08; 6,500 vols; Dir BEKIR KEMAL ATAMAN.

Izmir

National Library of Izmir: Milli Kütüphane Cad. 39, Konak- Izmir; f. 1912; 299,000 vols in Turkish, 40,000 vols in European languages, 19,000 vols in Oriental scripts, 4,000 MSS, 4,843 periodicals; Dir ALİ RIZA ATAY.

Konya

Public Library: Purcuklu Mah., Turbe Cad. 23, Karatoy, Konya; f. 1947; 20,000 vols, 6,000 MSS.

Nevşehir

Damat Ibrahim Paşa Library: Nevşehir; f. 1727; 5,500 vols, 600 MSS.

Museums and Art Galleries

Adana

Adana Bölge Müzesi (Adana Regional Museum): Adana; f. 1926; depts of archaeology and ethnography; conference hall, laboratories, library and administrative sections; more than 107,000 items from the Neolithic to Roman and Byzantine periods; unique statue of a god made from natural crystal dating from Hittite Empire.

Amasya

Amasya Müzesi: Atatürk Cad. 91 Amasya; tel. (358) 218-45-13; fax (358) 218-69-57; f. 1926, moved 1961 to the Gök Medrese Mosque; archaeological finds from the early Bronze Age to Ottoman period; includes mummies dating from the Imperial period.

Ankara

Anadolu Medeniyetleri Müzesi (Museum of Anatolian Civilizations): Samanpazarı, Ankara; tel. (312) 324-31-60; fax (312) 311-28-39; f. 1921; exhibits cover the Palaeolithic, Neolithic, Chalcolithic, Early Bronze Age, Hittite, Phrygian, Urartian and Classical periods; Hittite reliefs from Alaca, Carchemish, Sakcagözü and Aslantepe and Ankara regions; collections represent excavations at Karain, Çatal Hüyük, Hacılar, Can Hasan, Alacahöyük, Ahlatlıbel, Karaz, Alişar, Karaoğlan, Karayavşan, Oymaağaç, Merzifon, Beycesultan, Kültepe, Acemhöyük, İnandık, Boğazköy, Eskiyapar, Patnos, Adilcevaz, Uşak-İkiztepe, Pazarlı, Gordion (now Yassihoyuk), Altıntepe, with special sections for cuneiform tablets and coins; library of 6,567 vols; Dir İLHAN TEMİZSOY; publs *The Anatolian Civilizations Museum Periodical*, *Museum Annual*, *Museum Conference Annual*, *Museum Lectures* (1 a year), *Museum News* (2 a year).

Anıtkabir Atatürk Müzesi (Atatürk's Mausoleum and Museum): Anıt Caddesi, Tandoğan, Ankara; tel. (312) 231-79-75; fax (312) 231-53-80; internet www.tsk.mil.tr./anitkabir; f. 1953; official and civil possessions of Mustafa Kemal Atatürk (1881–1938), founder of the Turkish Republic and its first Pres.; colln incl. documents, medals, plaques and albums; panoramas and paintings of the most important battles of the founding of the Turkish republic; library of 3,123 vols from the private library of Atatürk; Museum Commander Lt-Col HALIM KURT.

Ethnographical Museum: Talatpasa Bulvarı, Ankara; tel. (312) 311-95-56; f. 1930; specimens of Turkish and Islamic art, archives and Islamic seals; library of 6,245 vols; Dir Mrs SEMA KOÇ.

Kurtuluş Savaşı ve Cumhuriyet Müzeleri (Museums of the Turkish Independence War and Turkish Republic): Cumhuriyet Bulvarı No. 14–22, Ulus, Ankara; f. 1961; located in former Grand National Assembly buildings; library of 60,000 vols and 20,000 documents; Dir MUSTAFA SÜEL.

Natural History Museum: MTA, Genel Müdürlüğü, Eskişehir Yolu Balgat, 06520 Ankara; tel. (312) 201-23-96; fax (312) 284-14-77; e-mail muze1@mta.gov.tr; internet www.mta.gov.tr; f. 1968; attached to General Directorate of Mineral Research and Exploration; Dir Dr GONCA NALCIOGLU.

Antakya

Hatay Museum: Gündüz Cad. 1, Antakya, Hatay; tel. (326) 214-61-68; fax (326) 213-33-86; f. 1934; collection of mosaics from Roman Antioch, also finds from Al-Mina, Atchana,

Çatal Hüyük, Judeidah and Tainat excavations; Dir MEHMET ERDEM.

Antalya

Antalya Müzesi (Antalya Museum): Konyaaltı Caddesi, Antalya; tel. (242) 238-56-88; fax (242) 238-56-87; f. 1922; prehistory, archaeology, numismatics, ethnography, children's section and garden exhibition; library of 7,500 vols; Dir SELAHATTIN EYÜP AKSU.

Aydın

Aydın Müzesi: Hasan Efendi Mahallesi, Kapalı Spor Salonu yanı Aydın; tel. (256) 225-22-59; fax (256) 213-35-91; f. 1959; archaeology, ethnography, historical coins.

Bergama

Pergamon Museum: Cumhurıyet Cadd. 10, 35700 Bergama-İzmir; tel. (232) 631-28-83; fax (232) 631-07-77; f. 1936; houses the historical relics discovered as the result of excavations conducted at Pergamon; Dir ADNAN SARIOĞLU.

Bodrum

Bodrum Sualtı Arkeoloji Müzesi (Bodrum Museum of Underwater Archaeology): 48000 Bodrum; tel. (252) 316-25-16; fax (252) 313-76-46; e-mail bodrum-museum@yahoo.com; internet www.bodrum-museum.com; f. 1964 in the castle of Bodrum (built 15th century, by the Knights of St John from Rhodes); finds from land and underwater, incl. ceramics, metal, stone, gold and glass, from the Mycenaean, Attic, Hellenic, Roman, Byzantine and Ottoman eras; remains of late Bronze age ship; Dir (vacant).

Bursa

Bursa Arkeoloji Müzesi: Kültürpark, Bursa; tel. (224) 234-49-18; fax (224) 234-49-19; f. 1902; archaeological finds from Bursa, Balıkesir and Bilecik; prehistoric, Roman and Byzantine finds, stone, ceramic, glass and metal objects, coins; library of 3,824 vols; Chief Officer SALİH KÜTÜK.

Bursa Türk ve Islâm Eserleri Müzesi (Bursa Turkish and Islamic Art Museum): Yeşil, Bursa; tel. (224) 327-75-39; f. 1975 in the Yeşil Medrese, built by the Ottoman Sultan Mehmet I Çelebi; items from 12th century to late Ottoman period; illuminated MSS, samples of calligraphy, woodwork, metalwork, embroidery, costumes, ceramics; open-air museum of gravestones.

Çanakkale

Truva Müzesi (Troy Museum): Çanakkale; at the entrance to the ruins of Troy in Çanakkale; small exhibitions of pottery, figurines, statues and glass objects.

Eskişehir

Eskişehir Arkeoloji Müzesi: Akarbaşı Mahallesi, Hasan Polatkan Bul. 64, Eskişehir; tel. (222) 230-13-71; fax (222) 230-17-49; e-mail muze2603@kultur.gov.tr; f. 1935; plant and animal fossils; prehistory (ceramics, idols, stone and bone objects); the walls are decorated with late Roman mosaics found in excavations at Doryleum; Museum Head M. DURSUN ÇAĞLAR.

Istanbul

Âsiyan Museum: Aşiyan Yokuşu, 80810 Bebek, Istanbul; tel. (212) 263-69-86; home of Turkish poet and artist T. Fikret (1867–1915).

Askeri Müze ve Kültür Sitesi Komutanlığı (Military Museum and Cultural Centre): Harbiye, Istanbul; tel. (212) 233-27-20; fax (212) 296-86-18; f. 1846; military uniforms, weapons, tents, trophies, flags and standards

from ancient times; library of 26,000 vols; Dir Col ZAFER KILIÇ.

Ayasofya (Hagia Sophia—Saint Sophia) Museum: Sultanahmet, Fatih, 34122 Istanbul; tel. (212) 522-09-89; fax (212) 512-54-74; e-mail ayasofyamuzesi@kultur.gov.tr; internet www.kultur.gov.tr; f. 1935; built as an East Roman Basilica by Justinian and dedicated in AD 537, it was a church until 1453, after which it became a mosque; in 1935 it was made a state museum; contains East Roman and Turkish antiquities; Pres. Assoc. Prof. A. HALUK DURSUN; Dir HAYRULLAH CENGIZ; publ. *The Annual of St Sophia*.

Istanbul Arkeoloji Müzeleri (Archaeological Museums of Istanbul): Gülhane, 34400 Istanbul; tel. (212) 520-77-40; fax (212) 527-43-00; f. 1891; includes Archaeological, Turkish Tiles and Ancient Orient museums, with Sumerian, Akkadian, Hittite, Assyrian, Egyptian, Urartu, Phrygian, Greek, Roman and Byzantine works of art; more than 1m. exhibits; library of 80,000 vols; Dir HALIL ÖZEKNLI.

İstanbul Deniz Müzesi (Istanbul Naval Museum): Deniz Müzesi Komutanlığı, Beşiktaş, Istanbul; tel. (212) 327-43-45; fax (212) 236-68-93; e-mail muze.istanbul.iletisim@dzkk.tsk.tr; internet www.denizmuzeleri.tsk.tr; f. 1897, present location 1961; colln of 20,000 objects incl. Atatürk's belongings, historical caiques, paintings, ship models, weapons, maps, ship riggings, escutcheons and coat-of-arms, tughras of sultans, figureheads, navigational instruments, lights, uniforms, orders (decorations) and medals, coins, stamps, seals, photographs, flags and ensigns, tombstones, stone inscription tablet, lithographic limestone, plates, bells, certificates, firmans, MSS, amphoras, clocks and furniture; library of 20,000 vols, 20m. documents, 15 catalogues, 863 maps, 41 atlases and photographs consisting of 30,000 pieces; Dir Capt. FATIH ERBAS.

Istanbul Resim ve Heykel Müzesi (Museum of Painting and Sculpture): Beşiktaş, Istanbul; tel. (212) 261-42-98; fax (212) 244-03-98; f. 1937; Turkish paintings and sculptures since 19th century; international art exhibitions; Dir Prof. KEMAL İSKENDER.

Sabancı Üniversitesi Sakıp Sabancı Müzesi (Sabancı University Sakıp Sabancı Museum): Sakıp Sabancı Cad. 42, Emirgan 34467, Istanbul; tel. (212) 277-22-00; fax (212) 229-49-14; e-mail muze@sabanciuniv.edu; internet muze.sabanciuniv.edu; f. 2002; permanent colln of calligraphic items since 15th century, paintings since 19th century; temporary exhibitions; Dir Dr NAZAN ÖLÇER.

Tanzimat Müzesi (Tanzimat Museum): Gülhane Parkı, 94400 Sirkeci, Istanbul; tel. (212) 512-63-04; f. 1952 in Ihlamur Pavilion, current site since 1983; operated by Istanbul Metropolitan Municipality; documents, paintings and objects pertaining to the Tanzimat period of reform 1839–76; Curator FADIME GELEŞ.

Topkapı Palace Museum: Sultanahmet 34400, Istanbul; tel. (212) 522-44-22; fax (212) 528-59-91; internet www.kultur.gov.tr; palace built by Mehmed II; collections of Turkish armour, cloth, embroidery, glass and porcelain, copper- and silver-ware, treasure, paintings, miniatures, illuminated manuscripts, royal coaches, collections of Sèvres and Bohemian crystal and porcelain, clocks, important collection of Chinese and Japanese porcelain amassed by the Sultans, collection of manuscripts, Ottoman tent; Audience Hall, Council Hall of Viziers, Baghdad and Revan Köşks, Harem; library of 18,000 MSS and 200,000 archive documents; Dir FILIZ ÇAĞMAN.

Türk ve Islam Eserleri Müzesi (Museum of Turkish and Islamic Art): Ibrahim Paşa Sarayı, At Meydani 46, Sultanahmet, Istanbul 34400; tel. (212) 518-18-05; fax (212) 518-18-07; internet www.tiem.org; f. 1914; Turkish and Islamic rugs, illuminated MSS, sculpture in stone and stucco, woodcarvings, metalwork and ceramics, traditional crafts and ethnographical material, all gathered from Turkish mosques and tombs; library: 4,142 MSS and 3,279 vols; Dir NAZAN ÖLCER.

Izmir

Izmir Arkeoloji Müzesi: Halit Rıfat Paşa Cad. 4, Konak, Izmir; tel. (232) 489-07-96; fax (232) 483-28-37; e-mail izmirmuze@ttnet.net .tr; f. 1927; works from the Archaic, Classical and Hellenistic periods of the Ionian civilization; Dir MEHMET TUNA.

Konya

Konya Museums: Il Kültür Müdürlüğü, Müze Müdürlüğü, Konya Valiliği; Dir of Museums Dr ERDOĞAN EROL.

Attached Museums:

Atatürk Museum:colln of documents and objects connected with Atatürk, also Konya clothing and other ethnographic exhibits.

Classical Museum:collns of Neolithic, early Bronze Age, Hittite, Phrygian, Greek, Roman and Byzantine monuments.

Mevlâna Museum: f. in Mevlâna Turbe; Seljuk, Ottoman and Turkish collections, clothing, carpets, coins, library.

Seljuk Museum: f. in Ince Minare; contains stone and wooden works of the Seljuk period.

Sirçali Medresseh:sarcophagus and inscription, collections of Seljuk and Ottoman period.

Turkish Ceramics Museum: f. in Karatay Medresseh; contains ceramics from 13th–18th centuries.

Polatlı

Gordion Museum: Polatlı, Ankara; tel. (312) 638-21-88; fax (312) 311-28-39; e-mail anmedmuz@marketweb.net.tr; f. 1965; built near the Great Tumulus believed to be that of the Phrygian king Midas; archaeological items found during excavations at Gordion (now Yassıhöyük); Dir ILHAN TEMIZSOY.

Selçuk

Efes Müzesi Müdürlügü (Ephesus Museum): Kusadasi Cad., 35920 Selçuk-Izmir; tel. (232) 892-60-10; fax (232) 892-70-02; f. 1929; art (mostly statues and reliefs) excavated from Ephesus; library of 3,200 vols; Dir SELAHATTIN ERDEMGIL; publ. *Efes Müzesi Yıllıgı* (1 a year).

Selimiye

Side Müzesi: Manavgat-Antalya, Side (Selimiye); tel. (242) 753-10-06; fax (242) 753-27-49; f. 1962; museum is located in a Late Roman bath; statues and busts of Roman gods, goddesses and emperors; library of 985 vols; Dir ORHAN ATVUR.

Van

Van Müzesi: Şerefiye Mahallesi, Hacıosman Sokak 9 Van; tel. (432) 216-11-39; fax (432) 214-25-10; f. 1947; archaeological finds from the Urartu Civilization.

Universities

ABANT IZZET BAYSAL ÜNİVERSİTESİ

Gölköy Kampüsü, 14280 Bolu
Telephone: (374) 254-10-00

Fax: (374) 253-45-06
Internet: www.ibu.edu.tr
Founded 1992
State control
Languages of instruction: Turkish, English
Academic year: September to June
Pres.: Prof. Dr HAYRI COSKUN
Vice-Pres.: Prof. Dr AKCAHAN GEPDIREMEN
Vice-Pres.: Prof. Dr MEHMET BAHAR
Vice-Rector: Prof. Dr RESUL ERYIGIT
Number of teachers: 927
Number of students: 17,449

DEANS

Faculty of Arts and Sciences: Prof. Dr AHMET VARILCI
Faculty of Dentistry: Prof. Dr ISMET DURAN
Faculty of Economics and Admin. Sciences: Prof. Dr RAMAZAN GOZEN
Faculty of Education: Prof. Dr CANAN CETIN-KANAT
Faculty of Engineering: Prof. Dr MAHMUT ACIMIS
Faculty of Fine Arts: Prof. Dr HAYRI COSKUN (acting)
Faculty of Medicine: Prof. Dr HASAN KOCO-GLU

ADNAN MENDERES ÜNİVERSİTESİ

Aytepe Mevkii, Merkez Kampus, 09010 Aydin
Telephone and fax (256) 218-20-37
E-mail: erasmus@adu.edu.tr
Internet: www.adu.edu.tr
Founded 1992
State control
Language of instruction: Turkish
Academic year: September to June
Rector: Prof. Dr MUSTAFA BIRINCIOĞLU
Vice-Rector: Dr ALI BELGE
Vice-Rector: Prof. Dr A. SEDA SARACALOĞLU
Vice-Rector: Prof. Dr CAVIT BIRCAN
Sec.-Gen.: YUSUF KÖK (acting)
Number of teachers: 1,238
Number of students: 28,128
Publications: *Bulletin* (4 a year), *Journal of Medical Faculty*

DEANS

Faculty of Agriculture: Prof. Dr ÖMER FARUK DURDU
Faculty of Economics and Administration: Prof. Dr MUSTAFA BIRINCIOĞLU
Faculty of Education: Prof. Dr A. SEDA SARACALOĞLU
Faculty of Medicine: Prof. Dr ABDULVAHIT YÜKSELEN
Faculty of Science and Letters: Prof. Dr ADNAN ERDAĞ
Faculty of Veterinary Science: Prof. Dr HASAN EREN

AFYON KOCATEPE ÜNİVERSİTESİ

Ahmet Necdet Sezer Kampüsü, Gazligol Yolu, 03200 Afyonkarahisar
Telephone: (272) 444-03-03
Fax: (272) 228-14-08
E-mail: rektor@aku.edu.tr
Internet: www.aku.edu.tr
Founded 1992
State control
Rector: Prof. Dr ALI ALTUNTAŞ
Vice-Rectors: Prof. Dr BELKIS ÖZKARA, Prof. Dr KEMALETTIN ÇONKAR, Prof. Dr NECAT İMİRZALIOĞLU
Gen. Sec.: İSMET DOĞAN
Librarian: ABDULLAH KÜNDEYİ
Library of 127,592 print vols and e-books, 840 periodicals
Number of teachers: 1,032

Number of students: 28,849 (27,339 undergraduate, 1,510 graduate)

DEANS

Faculty of Arts and Sciences: Prof. Dr BELKIS ÖZKARA
Faculty of Arts and Sciences (Uşak): Prof. Dr LÜTFI ÖZAV
Faculty of Economics and Administrative Sciences (Uşak): Prof. Dr H. HÜSEYIN BAYRAKLI
Faculty of Economics and Management Science: Prof. Dr KEMALETTIN ÇONKAR
Faculty of Education: Prof. Dr MUSTAFA ERGÜN
Faculty of Education (Uşak): Prof. Dr ADNAN ŞIŞMAN
Faculty of Engineering: Prof. Dr RAMAZAN ŞEVIK
Faculty of Engineering (Uşak): Prof. Dr FIKRI ŞENOL
Faculty of Fine Arts: Prof. Dr RIZA AŞIKOĞLU
Faculty of Medicine: Prof. Dr NECAT İMİRZA-LIĞOLU
Faculty of Technical Education: Prof. Dr GALIP SAİD
Faculty of Veterinary Medicine: Prof. Dr HIFZI OĞUZ SARIMEHMETOĞLU

Research Centres incl. Animal Breeding Research Centre, Atatürk and History of Revolution Research and Application Centre, Experimental Animal Research and Application Centre, Food Control Research and Application Centre, Kocatepe Great Attack Research Centre, Technology Application and Research Centre, Turkish Handicrafts Research and Application Centre, Turkish World Research Centre

AKDENİZ ÜNİVERSİTESİ

Dumlupınar Bulvarı Kampus, 07058 Antalya
Telephone: (242) 227-59-83
Fax: (242) 227-55-40
E-mail: international@akdeniz.edu.tr
Internet: www.akdeniz.edu.tr
Founded 1982; previously affiliated to Ankara Univ.
State control
Language of instruction: Turkish
Academic year: October to June
Rector: Prof. Dr MUSTAFA AKAYDIN
Vice-Rectors: Prof. Dr MEHMET RIFKI AKTE-KIN, Prof. Dr SADIK ÇAKMAKÇI, Prof. Dr MUSTAFA PEKMEZCI
Gen. Sec.: NUSRET ÇELIK
Librarian: NEVZAT ŞABAN
Number of teachers: 1,646
Number of students: 19,090
Publications: *Journal of the Faculty of Agriculture, Journal of the Faculty of Medicine* (4 a year), *University Bulletin*

DEANS

Faculty of Agribusiness: Prof. Dr AHMET AKTAŞ
Faculty of Agriculture: Prof. Dr HALIL İBRA-HIM UZUN
Faculty of Arts and Sciences: Prof. Dr MUSTAFA GÖKÇEOĞLU
Faculty of Communications: Prof. Dr ÜMIT ATABEK
Faculty of Economics and Administrative Sciences: Prof. Dr FULYA SARVAN
Faculty of Education: Prof. Dr MEHMET YALÇIN
Faculty of Engineering: Prof. Dr HIKMET RENDE
Faculty of Fine Arts: Prof. Dr ABDULLAH UZ
Faculty of Fisheries: Prof. Dr RAMAZAN İKIZ
Faculty of Law: Prof. Dr MERAL SAĞIR ÖZTOPRAK
Faculty of Medicine: Prof. Dr MUSTAFA MELIKOĞLU

Faculty of Veterinary Science: Prof. Dr BAYRAM ALI YUKARI

There are 4 Vocational Schools within Akdeniz University, 8 Vocational Schools in Antalya and 4 Graduate Schools.

ANADOLU ÜNİVERSİTESİ
(Anadolu University)

Yunus Emre Kampüsü, 26470 Eskişehir
Telephone: (222) 335-05-80
Fax: (222) 335-36-16
E-mail: gensek@anadolu.edu.tr
Internet: www.anadolu.edu.tr
Founded 1958
State control
Languages of instruction: Turkish, English
Academic year: September to June

Rector: Prof. Dr DAVUT AYDIN
Vice-Rector: Prof. Dr AYDIN ZIYA OZGUR
Vice-Rector: Prof. Dr MERYEM AKOGLAN KOZAK
Vice-Rector: Prof. Dr MUSTAFA CAVCAR
Vice-Rector: Prof. Dr ENDER SUVACI
Vice-Rector: Prof. Dr NACI GUNDOGAN
Registrar and Sec.-Gen.: CETIN KAYA
Librarian: ADNAN YILMAZ

Library of 200,000 vols
Number of teachers: 1,800
Number of students: 1,387,729 (incl. open-education students)

Publications: *Journal of Sciences and Technology* (2 a year), *Journal of Social Sciences* (2 a year), *Online International Journal of Communication Studies* (2 a year), *Turkish Online Journal of Distance Education* (2 a year)

DEANS

Faculty of Architecture and Design: Prof. Dr SEVIN AKSOYLU
Faculty of Communication Sciences: Prof. Dr E. NEZIH ORHON
Faculty of Economics: Prof. Dr SADIK RIDVAN KARLUK
Faculty of Economic and Administrative Sciences: Prof. Dr RECAI DONMAZ
Faculty of Education: Prof. Dr GUL DURMUSOGLU KOSE
Faculty of Engineering and Architecture: Prof. Dr TUNCAY DOGEROGLU
Faculty of Fine Arts: Prof. Dr BILGIHAN UZUNER
Faculty of Humanities: Prof. Dr MUHSIN MACIT
Faculty of Law: Prof. Dr UFUK AYDIN
Faculty of Management: Prof. Dr MELIH ERDOGAN
Faculty of Open Education: Prof. Dr KERIM BANAR
Faculty of Pharmacy: Prof. Dr YASEMIN YAZAN
Faculty of Science: Prof. ERTUGRUL YORUKOGULLARI

ATTACHED SCHOOLS

College for the Handicapped: Dir Prof. Dr AHMET KONROT.
School of Civil Aviation: Dir Prof. Dr MUSTAFA KARA.
School of Drama and Music: Dir NAZLI GÜLMEZ.
School of Foreign Languages: Dir Assoc. Prof. HANDAN YAVUZ.
School of Industrial Arts: Dir Prof. Dr YAŞAR HOŞCAN.
School of Physical Education and Sports: Dir Prof. Dr COŞKUN BAYRAK.
School of Tourism and Hotel Management: Dir Prof. Dr DENIZ BÜLER.

GRADUATE SCHOOLS

Graduate School of Health Sciences: Dir Prof. Dr YUSUF ÖZTÜRK.
Graduate School of Science: Dir Prof. Dr ORHAN ÖZER.
Graduate School of Social Sciences: Dir Prof. Dr ALTUĞ İFTAR.
Handicapped Research Institute: Dir Prof. Dr GÖNÜL SELVER KIRCAALÜ.
Institute of Communication Sciences: Dir (vacant).
Institute of Educational Sciences: Dir Prof. Dr İLKNUR KEÇİK.
Institute of Fine Arts: Dir Prof. Dr ATILLA ATAR.
Institute of Satellite and Space Sciences: Dir Assoc. Prof. Dr CAN AYDAY.
Institute of Transport Economics: Dir Prof. Dr NEZIH VARCAN.

ANKARA ÜNİVERSİTESİ

06100 Tandoğan, Ankara
Telephone: (312) 212-60-40
Fax: (312) 212-60-49
Internet: www.ankara.edu.tr
Founded 1946
State control
Language of instruction: Turkish
Academic year: October to June

Rector: Prof. Dr CEMAL TALUĞ
Vice-Rector: Prof. Dr NILGÜN HALLORAN
Vice-Rector: Prof. Dr N. YASEMIN YALIM
Vice-Rector: Prof. Dr ARGUN KARACABEY
Gen.–Sec.: SERPIL GÜNER
Registrar: Prof. Dr S. TUNA KARAHAN
Registrar: SINEM ÖZKARA
Librarian: Prof. Dr DOĞAN ATILGAN

Library of 800,000 vols and 7,984 periodicals
Number of teachers: 3,553
Number of students: 44,514

Publications: *Ankara Üniversitesi Yıllığı* (Annals of the University), *Turkish Journal of Geographical Sciences*, and faculty and research institute publications

DEANS

Çankırı Faculty of Forestry: Prof. Dr İLHAMİ KÖKSAL
Faculty of Agriculture: Prof. Dr AHMET ÇOLAK
Faculty of Communication: Prof. Dr ESER KÖKER
Faculty of Dentistry: Prof. Dr ADNAN ÖZTÜRK
Faculty of Divinity: Prof. Dr NESIMI YAZICI
Faculty of Education: Prof. Dr GÖNÜL AKÇAMETE
Faculty of Engineering: Prof. Dr ALI ULVI YILMAZER
Faculty of Health Education: Prof. Dr ŞENGÜL HABLEMITOĞLU
Faculty of Law: Prof. Dr MUSTAFA AKKAYA
Faculty of Humanities: Prof. Dr RAHMI ER
Faculty of Medicine: Prof. Dr İLKER ÖKTEN
Faculty of Natural and Applied Science: Prof. Dr MUAMMER CANEL
Faculty of Pharmacy: Prof. Dr MAKSUT COŞKUN
Faculty of Political Science: Prof. Dr CELAL GÖLE
Faculty of Veterinary Medicine: Prof. Dr İBRAHİM BURGU

DIRECTORS OF APPLIED RESEARCH CENTRES

Astronomy and Aerospace Sciences: Prof. Dr BERAHITDIN ALBAYRAK
Atatürk's Principles: Prof. Dr ÜNSAL YAVUZ
Autistic Children: Prof. Dr EFSER KERIMOĞLU
Biotechnology: Prof. Dr TUNCER ÖZDAMAR
Cardiology: Prof. Dr DERVİŞ ORAL
Children's Studies: Prof. Dr BEKIR ONUR
Communications: Prof. Dr ASKER KARTARI

Continuous Training: Prof. Dr NEJLA TURAL
Cyprus: Prof. Dr FÜSUN ARSAVA
Distance Learning: Doç. Dr NURETTIN ŞIMŞEK
Earthquake Science: Prof. Dr AHMET TUĞRUL BAŞOKUR
Education-Rehabilitation: Prof. Dr EFSER KERIMOĞLU
Environmental Problems: Prof. Dr NEVIN AKPINAR
European Communities: Prof. Dr M. NAIL ALKAN
Fishery Products: Prof. Dr GÜLTEN KÖKSAL
Foreign Language Teaching: Prof. Dr ERSIN ONULDURAN
Gastroenterology: Prof. Dr ALI ÖZDEN
Human Resource Management: Doç. Dr RECEP VARÇIN
Intellectual and Industrial Property: ARZU OĞUZ
International Agriculture: Prof. Dr NEŞET KILINÇER
Medical and Scented Plants: Prof. Dr SEMRA KURUNCU
Oncology: Prof. Dr FİKRİ İÇLİ
Ottoman History: Prof. Dr ESIN KAHYA
Pediatric Haemotology and Oncology: Prof. Dr ŞÜKRÜ CIN
Psychiatric Crisis: Prof. Dr IŞIK SAYIL
Public Finance and Politics: Prof. Dr AHMET KIRMAN
River, Lake and Sea Geology: Prof. Dr MUSTAFA ERGIN
Science and Technology: Prof. Dr TAMER BAYKARA
Strategic Research: Prof. Dr YAVUZ ERCAN
Turkish Geography: Doç. Dr ALI ÖZÇAĞLAR
Turkish Language Teaching Centre: Doç. Dr ENGIN UZUN
Women's Studies: SERPIL ÜŞÜR

ATTACHED INSTITUTES

Graduate Institute of Biotechnology: Dir Prof. Dr NEJAT AKAR.
Graduate Institute of Education: Dir Prof. Dr MERAL UYSAL.
Graduate Institute of Hepatology: Dir Prof. Dr S. CIHAN YURDAYDIN.
Graduate Institute of the History of the Turkish Revolution: Dir Prof. Dr YAVUZ ERCAN.
Graduate Institute of Medical Jurisprudence: Dir Prof. Dr HALIL GÜMÜŞ.
Graduate Institute of Medical Sciences: Dir Prof. Dr RIFAT VURAL.
Graduate Institute of Science: Dir Prof. Dr METIN OLGUN.
Graduate Institute of Social Sciences: Dir Prof. Dr CAN HAMAMCI.

ATTACHED SCHOOLS AND COLLEGES

Çankırı School of Health: Dir Prof. Dr MEHMET KIYAN.
School of Başkent: Dir Prof. Dr HANDE K. ERSOY.
School of Beypazarı: Dir Prof. Dr İLHAN KARAÇAL.
School of Çankırı: Dir Prof. Dr SABAHATTİN BALCI.
School of Cebeci Health Services: Dir Doç. Dr TÜLIN BEDÜK.
School of Dikimevi Health Services: Dir Prof. Dr AHMET DERYA AYSEV.
School of Foreign Languages: Dir Prof. Dr ERSIN ONULDURAN.
School of Home Economics (Faculty of Agriculture): Dir Prof. Dr EMINE GÖNEN.
School of Justice (Faculty of Law): Dir Doç. Dr HALUK KONURALP.
School of Kalecik: Dir Prof. Dr DOĞAN ERDOĞAN.

School of Kastamonu: Dir Prof. Dr BAHRİ GÖKÇEBAY.

School of Physical Education and Sports: Dir Prof. Dr EMIN ERGEN.

State Conservatory: Dir Prof. Dr NURHAN KARADAĞ.

ATATÜRK ÜNİVERSİTESİ

Rektörlüğü, 25240 Erzurum

Telephone: (442) 231-10-30

Fax: (442) 236-10-14

E-mail: ata@atauni.edu.tr

Internet: www.atauni.edu.tr

Founded 1957, reorganized 1982 following the Higher Education Reform

State control

Language of instruction: Turkish

Academic year: October to June

Pres.: HIKMET KOÇAK

Sec.-Gen.: USTUN OZEN

Head of Int. Affairs Office: FAHRI YAVUZ

Library of 300,000 vols

Number of teachers: 2,527 (incl. teaching assts)

Number of students: 40,191

Publications: *Atatürk Dergisi* (2 a year), *Atatürk Üniversitesi Diş Hekimliği Fakültesi Dergisi* (4 a year), *Atatürk Üniversitesi Erzincan Hukuk Fakültesi Dergisi* (2 a year), *Atatürk Üniversitesi İlahiyat Fakültesi Dergisi* (2 a year), *Atatürk Üniversitesi Tıp Dergisi* (4 a year), *Erzincan Eğitim Fakültesi Dergisi* (2 a year), *Güzel Sanatlar Enstitüsü Dergisi* (2 a year), *Güzel Sanatlar Fakültesi Sanat Dergisi* (2 a year), *İktisadi ve İdari Bilimler Dergisi* (2 a year), *Kazım Karabekir Eğitim Fakültesi Dergisi* (2 a year), *Sosyal Bilimler Dergisi* (2 a year), *Sosyal Bilimler Enstitüsü Dergisi* (2 a year), *Türkiyat Araştırmaları Enstitüsü Dergisi* (2 a year), *Ziraat Fakültesi Dergisi* (4 a year)

DEANS

Faculty of Agriculture: MUSTAFA YILDIRIM CANBOLAT

Faculty of Arts: Prof. Dr YILMAZ ÖZBEK

Faculty of Arts and Sciences (Erzincan): Prof. Dr MUHARREM GÜLERYÜZ

Faculty of Communication and Journalism: Prof. Dr ÖNDER BARLI

Faculty of Dentistry: Prof. Dr ABUBEKIR HARORLI

Faculty of Economics and Administrative Sciences: Prof. Dr SUPHI ORHAN

Faculty of Education: Prof. Dr SAMIH BAYRAKÇEKEN

Faculty of Education (Ağrı): Prof. Dr BILGE SEYİDOĞLU

Faculty of Education (Bayburt): Prof. Dr AHMET GÜRSES

Faculty of Education (Erzincan): Prof. Dr ERDOĞAN BÜYÜKKASAP

Faculty of Engineering: Prof. Dr CAFER ÇELİK

Faculty of Fine Arts: Prof. Dr KEMALETTIN YİĞİTER

Faculty of Law School (Erzincan): Prof. Dr AHMET NEZIH KÖK

Faculty of Medicine: Prof. Dr M. SELÇUK ATAMANALP

Faculty of Pharmacy: Prof. Dr FATIH AKÇAY

Faculty of Science: Ö. IRFAN KÜFREVİOĞLU

Faculty of Theology: Prof. Dr BAHATTIN KÖK

Faculty of Veterinary Sciences: Prof. Dr MUSTAFA ATASEVER

ATILIM ÜNİVERSİTESİ

Kızılcaşar Mah. Köyü, 06836 İncek Gölbası, Ankara

Telephone: (312) 586-80-00

Fax: (312) 586-80-91

E-mail: iro@atilim.edu.tr

Internet: www.atilim.edu.tr

Private control

President: Prof. Dr ABDURRAHIM ÖZGENOĞLU

Gen. Sec.: Prof. Dr ABDÜLAZIZ ŞEREN

Vice-Presidents: Prof. Dr İSMAIL BIRCAN, Prof. Dr İHSAN TARAKÇIOĞLU

DEANS

Faculty of Arts and Sciences: Prof. Dr OYA BATUM MENTEŞE

Faculty of Engineering: Prof. Dr KAMIL İBRAHIM AKMAN

Faculty of Law: Prof. Dr NAMI ÇAĞAN

Faculty of Management: Prof. Dr HALIL İBRAHIM ÜLKER

DIRECTORS

Graduate School of Natural and Applied Sciences: Prof. Dr SELÇUK SOYUPAK

Graduate School of Social Sciences: Prof. Dr ERTUĞRUL ÇETİNER

Preparatory School: AYTUNA KOCABIYIKOĞLU

BAHÇEŞEHIR ÜNİVERSİTESİ

34538 Bahçeşehir, Istanbul

Telephone: (212) 669-65-23

Fax: (212) 669-43-98

E-mail: info@bahcesehir.edu.tr

Internet: www.bahcesehir.edu.tr

Founded 1998

Rector: Prof. Dr SÜHEYL BATUM

Vice-Presidents: Prof. Dr NURBAY GÜLTEKIN, Prof. Dr ESER KARAKAŞ

Library of 43,095 vols, 22,000 e-books, 472 periodicals and 3,106 e-journals

Number of teachers: 150

Number of students: 1,207

DEANS

Faculty of Architecture: Prof. Dr ERHAN A. BALKAN

Faculty of Arts and Science: Prof. Dr ÖMER ASIM SAÇLI

Faculty of Engineering: Prof. Dr ŞENAY YALÇIN

Faculty of Law: Prof. Dr CUMHUR ÖZAKMAN

Faculty of Management: Prof. Dr İLKAY SUNAR

BALIKESIR ÜNİVERSİTESİ

Soma Cad., 10100 Balikesir

Telephone: (266) 245-96-50

Fax: (266) 245-96-63

E-mail: hacioglu@balikesir.edu.tr

Internet: www.balikesir.edu.tr

State control

Academic year: September to July

Rector: Prof. Dr NECDET HACIOĞLU

Gen. Sec.: Prof. Dr FAIZ TÜRKAN

Library of 14,520 vols, 294 periodical subscriptions, 17 databases

Number of teachers: 607

Number of students: 22,141 full-time, 9,108 evening

DEANS

Faculty of Arts and Sciences: OKTAY ARSLAN

Faculty of Economics and Administration: ADEM ÇABUK

Faculty of Education: BEDRIYE TUNÇSIPER

Faculty of Engineering and Architecture: ŞERIF SAYLAN

DIRECTORS

Geothermal Research Institute: OSMAN ÇENET

Olive Trade and Agribusiness Institute: SAKIN VURAL VARLI

BAŞKENT ÜNİVERSİTESİ

Baglica Kampusu Eskisehir Yolu 20 km, Baglica, 06530 Etimesgut, Ankara

Telephone: (312) 234-10-10

Fax: (312) 234-12-16

E-mail: webmaster@baskent.edu.tr

Internet: www.baskent.edu.tr

Founded 1993

Private control

Rector: Prof. Dr MEHMET HABERAL

Library of 117,044 vols, 1,041 periodicals

Number of teachers: 947

Number of students: 8,489 undergraduate, 858 postgraduate

DEANS

Faculty of Commercial Sciences: Prof. Dr DOĞAN YAŞAR AYHAN

Faculty of Communications: Prof. Dr AHMET NEDIM TULUNGÜÇ

Faculty of Dentistry: Prof. Dr KENAN ARAZ

Faculty of Economic and Administrative Sciences: Prof. Dr ABDULKADIR VAROĞLU

Faculty of Education: Prof. Dr ŞEREF MIRASYEDIOĞLU

Faculty of Engineering: Prof. Dr BERNA DENGIZ

Faculty of Fine Arts, Design and Architecture: Prof. Dr ADNAN TEPECIK

Faculty of Health Sciences: Prof. Dr KORKUT ERSOY

Faculty of Law: Prof. Dr KUDRET GÜVEN

Faculty of Medicine: Prof. Dr HALDUN MÜDERRISOĞLU

Faculty of Science and Letters: Prof. Dr RAHMI YAĞBASAN

BEYKENT ÜNİVERSİTESİ

34900 Beykent, Istanbul

Telephone: (212) 872-64-32

Fax: (212) 872-24-89

E-mail: info@beykent.edu.tr

Internet: www.beykent.edu.tr

Founded 1997

Language of instruction: English

Academic year: October to June

Rector: Prof. Dr MEHMET FIKRET GEZGIN

Vice-Rector: Prof. Dr MUSTAFA DELICAN, Prof. Dr ÜNSAL OSKAY

Gen. Sec.: Prof. Dr NURETTIN ERDEM

Library and Learning Centre Man.: UĞUR BULGAN

Library of 27,500 vols, 165 periodicals, 2,000 CDs, 850 audio tapes

Number of teachers: 200

Number of students: 2,500

DEANS

Faculty of Arts and Science: ZAFER ASLAN

Faculty of Economics and Administrative Sciences: Prof. Dr MEHMET ZELKA

Faculty of Engineering and Architecture: Prof. Dr ERTAN ÖZKAN

Faculty of Fine Arts: Prof. Dr ÜNSAL OSKAY

Preparatory School: MUSTAFA MELEK (Dir)

BILKENT ÜNİVERSİTESİ
(Bilkent University)

Bilkent, 06800 Ankara

Telephone: (312) 266-41-25

Fax: (312) 266-41-27

E-mail: contact@bilkent.edu.tr

Internet: www.bilkent.edu.tr

Founded 1984

Private control (educational foundation)

Language of instruction: English

Academic year: September to June

Pres., Bd of Trustees: Prof. ALI DOĞRAMACI

Rector: Prof. ABDULLAH ATALAR

Vice-Rector for Academic Affairs and Provost: Prof. METIN HEPER

Vice-Rector for Admin. and Financial Affairs and Gen. Sec.: Prof. KÜRŞAT AYDOĞAN
Vice-Rector for Student Affairs: Prof. ORHAN AYTÜR
Vice-Rector and Librarian: Dr PHYLLIS L. ERDOĞAN
Number of teachers: 1,100
Number of students: 12,000

DEANS

Faculty of Art, Design and Architecture: Prof. BÜLENT ÖZGÜÇ
Faculty of Business Administration: Prof. ERDAL EREL
Faculty of Economic, Administrative and Social Sciences: Prof. DILEK ÖNKAL
Faculty of Education: Prof. MEHMET BARAY
Faculty of Engineering: Prof. LEVENT ONURAL
Faculty of Humanities and Letters: Prof. TALAT HALMAN
Faculty of Law: Prof. OSMAN BERAT GÜRZU-MAR
Faculty of Music and Performing Arts: Assoc. Prof. IŞIN METIN
Faculty of Science: Prof. HASAN ERTEN
School of Applied Languages: TANJU İNAL
School of English Language: JOHN O'DWYER
Vocational School of Computer Technology and Office Management: KAMER RODOPLU
Vocational School of Tourism and Hotel Services: KAMER RODOPLU

BOĞAZIÇI ÜNİVERSİTESİ
(Boğaziçi University)

34342 Bebek, Istanbul
Telephone: (212) 358-15-00
Fax: (212) 265-63-57
E-mail: halkilis@boun.edu.tr
Internet: www.boun.edu.tr

Founded 1863; fmrly Robert College
State control
Languages of instruction: Turkish, English
Academic year: September to July

Rector: Dr AYSE SOYSAL
Vice-Rectors: Prof. Dr CEM BEHAR, Prof. Dr GULEN AKTAS GREENWOOD, Prof. Dr TURAN ÖZTURAN
Dean of Students: Prof. Dr ALI IZZET TEKCAN
Sec.-Gen.: MINE KALENDEROĞLU
Registrar: ZELIHA BALKAN
Librarian: HATICE ÜN
Number of teachers: 984
Number of students: 9,973

Publications: Boğaziçi University Journal (1 a year), Biomedical Engineering Bulletin (4 a year), Education Bulletin (2 a year)

DEANS

Faculty of Arts and Sciences: Prof. Dr OMER OGUZ
Faculty of Economics and Administrative Sciences: Prof. Dr ESER BORAK
Faculty of Education: Prof. Dr CEM ALPTEKIN
Faculty of Engineering: Prof. Dr ALI RIZA KAYLAN

ATTACHED SCHOOLS AND COLLEGES

School of Applied Disciplines: Dir Prof. Dr MELTEM ÖZTURAN.
School of Foreign Languages: Dir Prof. Dr ESER TAYLAN.
School of Vocational Education: Dir Prof. Dr MELTEM ÖZTURAN.

ÇAĞ ÜNİVERSİTESİ

Adana-Mersin, Karayolu üzeri, 33800 Yenice/Mersin
Telephone: (324) 651-48-00
Fax: (324) 651-48-11
E-mail: cag@cag.edu.tr
Internet: www.cag.edu.tr

Founded 1997
Private control
Languages of instruction: Turkish, English
Academic year: September to June

Rector: Prof. Dr H. ÇETIN BEDESTENCI
Vice-Rector: Prof. Dr MUSTAFA BAŞARAN
Librarian: ESRA İSCAN

Library of 100,000 vols
Number of teachers: 220
Number of students: 3,100

Publication: Journal of Social Sciences (2 a year)

DEANS

Faculty of Arts and Sciences Faculty: Prof. Dr M. EMIN ÖZEL
Faculty of Economics and Admin. Science: Prof. Dr SÜLEYMAN TÜRKEL
Faculty of Law: Prof. Dr YÜCEL ERTEKIN
Higher Vocational School: Prof. Dr MUSTAFA BAŞARAN
Institute of Social Sciences: Assoc. Prof. Dr HALUK KORKMAZYÜREK

ÇANAKKALE ONSEKIZ MART ÜNİVERSİTESİ

Terzioðlu Kampüsü, 17020 Çanakkale
Telephone: (286) 218-00-18
Fax: (286) 218-06-08
E-mail: comurek@comu.edu.tr
Internet: www.comu.edu.tr

Founded 1992
State control
Academic year: October to June

Rector: Prof. Dr RAMAZAN AYDIN
Asst Rectors: Prof. Dr SUZAN ERBAŞ, Prof. Dr ALI ÖZPINAR, Prof. Dr ALI OSMAN ÖZTÜRK
Number of teachers: 695
Number of students: 15,000

DEANS

Faculty of Agriculture: Prof. Dr KENAN KAYNAŞ
Faculty of Economics and Administrative Studies: Prof. Dr ALI AKDEMIR
Faculty of Education: Prof. Dr REMZI Y. KINCAL
Faculty of Engineering and Architecture: Prof. Dr SALIH ZEKI TUTKUN
Faculty of Fine Arts: Prof. Dr MUSTAFA APAYDIN
Faculty of Fisheries: Prof. Dr ŞÜKRAN CIRIK
Faculty of Sciences and Arts: Prof. Dr KAZIM KAYA
Faculty of Theology: Prof. Dr NASUHI ÜNAL KARAARSLAN

PROFESSORS

Faculty of Agriculture (Terzioðlu Kampüsü, 17020 Çanakkale):
ALTAY, H.
BAYTEKIN, H.
GÖKKUŞ, A.
KAPTAN, H.
KAYNAŞ, K.
KUMUK, T.
ÖZPINAR, A.
ŞENER, S.
SEREZ, M.

Faculty of Economics and Administrative Studies (Biga) (Biga, Çanakkale):
AKDEMIR, A.
ERDOĞAN, E.

Faculty of Education (Terzioðlu Kampüsü, 17020 Çanakkale):
ERBAŞ, S.
METE TUNÇOKU, A.
OSMAN ÖZTÜRK, A.
YILDIRIM, H.
Y KINCAL, R.
YÜCE, K.

Faculty of Engineering and Architecture (Terzioðlu Kampüsü, 17020 Çanakkale):
BILIŞLI, A.
GÜVEN, S.
YIÐITBAŞ, E.
ZEKI TUTKUN, S.

Faculty of Fine Arts (Terzioðlu Kampüsü, 17020 Çanakkale):
APAYDIN, M.
UYANIK, M.

Faculty of Fisheries (Terzioðlu Kampüsü, 17020 Çanakkale):
ALPASLAN, M.
CIRIK, S.
KARAFISTAN, A. İ.
TUNCER, S.

Faculty of Sciences and Arts (Terzioðlu Kampüsü, 17020 Çanakkale):
AYDIN, N.
AYDIN, R.
AYSEL, V.
BARAN, Y.
DEMIRCAN, O.
İBRAHIMOV, A.
KAYA, K.
ÖDEN, Z. G.
ÖZDEMIR, E.
ÖZEL, M. E.
TOK, V.
UÐUZMAN, T.
UYSAL, A. O.

Faculty of Theology (Terzioðlu Kampüsü, 17020 Çanakkale):
KARAARSLAN, N. Ü.

ATTACHED SCHOOLS AND INSTITUTES

Natural and Applied Sciences Institute: Terzioðlu Kampüsü, 17020 Çanakkale; Dir Prof. Dr MEHMET EMIN ÖZEL.

School of Health Services: Saglik Yuksekokulu, Onsekiz Mart Univs, 17100 Canakkale; tel. (286) 217-10-01; fax (286) 217-10-01; internet www.syo.comu.edu.tr; Dir Prof. GUNHAM ERDEM.

School of Tourism and Health Management: Terzioðlu Kampüsü, 17020 Çanakkale.

Social Studies Institute: Terzioðlu Kampüsü, 17020 Çanakkale; Dir Assoc. Prof. R. CENGIZ AKÇAY.

ÇANKAYA ÜNİVERSİTESİ

Öğretmenler Cad. 14, Yüzüncü Yil, 06530 Balgat, Ankara
Telephone: (312) 284-45-00
Fax: (312) 285-96-31
E-mail: webadmin@cankaya.edu.tr
Internet: www.cankaya.edu.tr

Founded 1997
Private control
Languages of instruction: Turkish, English
Academic year: September to June

President: SITKI ALP
Vice-Presidents: İSMAIL AKINALTUĞ, YUSUF GUNGOR
Rector: Prof. Dr ZIYA AKTAŞ
Vice-Rector: Prof. Dr KENAN TAS
Secretary-General: LÜTFI ÖNSOY
Director of Library: FATIH KUMSEL
Library of 9,278 vols, 140 periodicals
Number of teachers: 207
Number of students: 3,182 (2,977 undergraduate, 205 postgraduate)

DEANS

Faculty of Arts and Sciences: Prof. Dr EMEL DOGRAMACI
Faculty of Economics and Administrative Sciences: Prof. Dr AHMED YALNIZ
Faculty of Engineering and Architecture: Prof. Dr ZIYA AKTAŞ

Faculty of Law: Prof. Dr TURGUT ÖNEN

DIRECTORS

Graduate School of Natural and Applied Sciences: Prof. Dr YURDAHAN GÜLER
Graduate School of Social Sciences: Prof. Dr ÖZHAN ULUATAM
Preparatory School: Prof. Dr CENGIZ TOSUN
Vocational School: Asst Prof. Dr NÜZHET AKIN

CELAL BAYAR ÜNIVERSITESI

45000 Manisa
Telephone: (236) 237-28-86
Fax: (236) 237-24-42
E-mail: kutuphane@bayar.edu.tr
Internet: www.bayar.edu.tr
Founded 1992
State control
Rector: Prof. Dr CEMIL ÖZCAN
Vice-Rectors: Prof. Dr ÜLGEN OK, Prof. Dr CENGIZ YILMAZ
Number of teachers: 1,094
Number of students: 21,435
Publications: *Journal of Management and Economics* (2 a year), *Journal of Social Sciences* (2 a year)

DEANS

Faculty of Arts and Sciences: Prof. ŞULE AYCAN
Faculty of Economic and Administrative Sciences: Prof. SEMRA ÖNCÜ
Faculty of Education: Prof. NAZMI TOPÇU
Faculty of Engineering: Prof. ERGUN KÖSE
Faculty of Medicine: Prof. EROL ÖZMEN

ÇUKUROVA ÜNIVERSITESI

Balcalı Kampüsü, 01330 Balcalı, Adana
Telephone: (322) 338-60-84
Fax: (322) 338-64-11
E-mail: international@cu.edu.tr
Internet: www.cu.edu.tr
Founded 1973
State control
Language of instruction: Turkish
Academic year: September to July
Rector: Prof. Dr ALPER AKINOĞLU
Vice-Rector: Prof. Dr BANU İNANÇ
Vice-Rector: Prof. Dr M. RIFAT ULUSOY
Vice-Rector: Prof. Dr SÜLEYMAN GÜNGÖR
Sec.-Gen.: NAZAN KARATAŞ
Librarian: TURHAN YILMAZ
Library of 140,000 vols
Number of teachers: 1,899
Number of students: 36,050
Publications: *University Bulletin* (2 a year), faculty journals (all 3 a year)

DEANS

Faculty of Agriculture: Prof. Dr AYZIN B. KÜDEN
Faculty of Arts and Sciences: Prof. Dr SADULLAH SAKALLIOĞLU
Faculty of Communication: Prof. Dr VEDAT PEŞTEMALCI
Faculty of Dentistry: Prof. Dr İLTER UZEL
Faculty of Divinity: Prof. Dr ALI OSMAN ATEŞ
Faculty of Economics and Admin. Sciences: Prof. Dr MUAMMER TEKEOĞLU
Faculty of Education: Prof. Dr A. NECMI YAŞAR
Faculty of Engineering and Architecture: Prof. Dr BEŞIR ŞAHIN
Faculty of Fine Arts: Prof. Dr YUSUF GÜRÇINAR
Faculty of Fisheries: Prof. Dr OYA IŞIK
Faculty of Law: Prof. Dr ALPER AKINOĞLU
Faculty of Medicine: Prof. Dr BEHNAN ALPER

CUMHURIYET ÜNIVERSITESI
(Republic University)

58140 Campus-Sivas
Telephone: (346) 219-11-58
Fax: (346) 219-11-03
E-mail: rektor@cumhuriyet.edu.tr
Internet: www.cumhuriyet.edu.tr
Founded 1974, reorganized 1982
State control
Language of instruction: Turkish
Academic year: October to June
Rector: Prof. Dr FERIT KOÇOĞLU
Vice-Rectors: Prof. Dr ZAFER KARS, Prof. Dr HALDUN SÜMER, Prof. Dr ORHAN TATAR
Sec.-Gen.: Dr EROL ŞANLI
Librarian: AYGÜL ÜNAL
Number of teachers: 1,322
Number of students: 20,000

DEANS

Faculty of Arts and Sciences: Prof. Dr RAIF GÜLER
Faculty of Dentistry: Prof. Dr TIMUR ESENER
Faculty of Economic and Administrative Sciences: Prof. Dr M. ALI AKPINAR
Faculty of Education: Prof. Dr NEVZAT BATTAL
Faculty of Engineering: Prof. Dr ALI ÖZTÜRK
Faculty of Fine Arts: Prof. Dr KADIR KARKIN
Faculty of Medicine: Prof. Dr REYHAN EĞILMEZ
Faculty of Theological Studies: Prof. Dr N. YAŞAR AŞIKOĞLU YILMAZ

DIRECTORS OF INSTITUTES

Basic Sciences: Prof. Dr RAUF EMIROV
Medical Sciences: Prof. Dr ÖGE ÇETINKAYA
Social Sciences: Prof. Dr BAYRAM KAGMAZOĞLU

DICLE ÜNIVERSITESI
(Tigris University)

21280 Diyarbakır
Telephone: (412) 248-80-30
Fax: (412) 248-80-47
E-mail: fcan@dicle.edu.tr
Internet: www.dicle.edu.tr
Founded 1966 as branch of Ankara Univ., ind. 1973
State control
Academic year: October to June
Rector: Prof. Dr FIKRI CANORUÇ
Vice-Rectors: Prof. Dr ERALP ARIKAN, Prof. Dr ZÜLKÜF GÜLSÜN
Gen. Sec.: MEHMET TEKDÖŞ
Librarian: SEVGI EKMEKÇILER
Academic year: October to May
Library of 72,000 books, 6,000 periodicals, 1,350 theses and 3 CD databases
Number of teachers: 700
Number of students: 9,000
Publications: *Medical Faculty Journal*, *University Annual*

DEANS

Faculty of Agriculture: Prof. Dr DOĞAN ŞAKAR
Faculty of Dentistry: Prof. Dr FATMA ATAKUL
Faculty of Education: Prof. Dr ÖMER SAYA
Faculty of Education (Siirt): Assoc. Prof. YÜKSEL COŞKUN
Faculty of Engineering and Architecture: Assoc. Prof. FIKRI KAHRAMAN
Faculty of Law: Assoc. Prof. Dr FAZIL HÜSNÜ ERDEM
Faculty of Medicine: Assoc. Prof. Dr RECEP IŞIK
Faculty of Science and Letters: Prof. Dr HALIL HOŞGÖREN
Faculty of Technical Education (Batman): Prof. Dr O. ZEKI HEKIMOĞLU
Faculty of Theology: Assoc. Prof. ABDULKERIM ÜNALAN

Faculty of Veterinary Medicine: Prof. Dr SAVAŞ HATIPOĞLU

PROFESSORS

Faculty of Arts and Sciences:
BAŞARAN, D., Botany
BILGIN, F. H., Zoology
GÜLSÜN, Z., Atomic and Molecular Physics
GÜMGÜM, B., Inorganic Chemistry
GÜNIGÜNI, B., Inorganic Chemistry
TEZ, Z., Physical Chemistry
YILMAZ, A., General Physics
Faculty of Education:
ASLAN, E., Turkish Language and Literature
SÖNMEZ, A., Physics
Faculty of Medicine:
ARIKAN, E., Microbiology
AYDINOL, B., Biochemistry
BAHÇECI, M., Internal Diseases
BAYHAN, N., Anaesthesiology
BUDAK, T., Medical Biology
CANORUÇ, F., Internal Diseases
ÇELIK, S., Biophysics
DEĞERTEKIN, H., Internal Diseases
DERICI, M., Dermatology
ERDOĞAN, F., Physical Rehabilitation
GÜL, T., Gynaecology and Obstetrics
GÜRGEN, F., Psychiatry
İLÇIN, E., Public Health
IŞIKOĞLU, B., Internal Diseases
KELLE, A., Medical Biology
METE, Ö., Microbiology
MÜFTÜOĞLU, E., Internal Diseases
NERGIS, Y., Histology
ÖZAYDIN, M., Pathology
ÖZGEN, G., Cardiovascular and Thoracic Surgery
TAŞ, M. A., Public Health
TOPCU, I., Otorhinolaryngology
TOPRAK, N., Internal Diseases
YILMAZ, N., Gynaecology and Obstetrics

DOGUS UNIVERSITY

Acıbadem, Zeamet Sok 21, 34722 Kadıköy, Istanbul
Telephone: (216) 544-55-55
Fax: (216) 544-55-32
E-mail: info@dogus.edu.tr
Internet: www.dogus.edu.tr
Founded 1997
Private control
Languages of instruction: Turkish, English
Academic year: September to June
Rector: Prof. Dr MITAT UYSAL
Gen. Sec.: MINE KALENDEROGLU
Library and Documentation Centre: SÖNMEZ ÇELIK
Library of 107,200 vols, 300 print journals, 23,700 electronic journals
Number of teachers: 464
Number of students: 4,187 (3,940 undergraduate, 247 postgraduate)
Publication: *Dogus University Journal*

DEANS

Faculty of Arts and Sciences: Prof. Dr DILEK DOLTAŞ
Faculty of Economic and Administrative Sciences: Prof. Dr ERTAN OKTAY
Faculty of Engineering: Prof. Dr FÜSUN ÜLENGIN
Faculty of Fine Arts and Design: Prof. Dr RIFAT ÇELEBI
Faculty of Law: Prof. Dr HASAN FEHIM ÜÇIŞIK
Institute of Science and Technology: Prof. Dr AHMET NURI CERANOGLU
Institute of Social Sciences: Prof. Dr ELIF ÇEPNI
Vocational School: MEHMET EEMEK

DOKUZ EYLUL UNIVERSITY
(Ninth September University)

Cumhuriyet Bul. 144, 35210 Alsancak, Izmir
Telephone: (232) 412-1212
Fax: (232) 464-8135
E-mail: gen.sek@deu.edu.tr
Internet: www.deu.edu.tr

Founded 1982
State control
Languages of instruction: English, Turkish
Academic year: September to June

Rector: Prof. Dr MEHMET FUZUN
Vice-Rector: Prof. Dr ALP TIMUR
Vice-Rector: Prof. Dr HALIL KOSE
Vice-Rector: Prof. Dr İSMAIL HAKKI BAHAR
Sec.-Gen.: Prof. Dr CAN KARACA
Librarian: HALE BALTEPE

Library of 300,000 vols, 70 databases, 130,000 e-books, 26,000 e-periodicals
Number of teachers: 3,042
Number of students: 50,000

Publications: *Arpa Boyu Dergisi, Sosyal Bilimler Enstitüsü Dergisi* (Social Sciences Institute Review, 2 a year), *Tip Fakültesi Dergisi* (Faculty of Medicine Review), *Yedi Dergisi* (Faculty of Theology Review)

DEANS

Faculty of Architecture: Prof. Dr ORCAN GÜNDÜZ
Faculty of Arts and Sciences: Prof. Dr NİLGÜN MORALİ
Faculty of Business Administration: Prof. Dr ORHAN İAÖZ
Faculty of Economics and Administrative Sciences: Prof. Dr ŞENAY ÜÇDOĞRUK
Faculty of Education: Prof. Dr FERDA AYSAN
Faculty of Engineering: Prof. Dr CÜNEYT GÜZELIŞ
Faculty of Fine Arts: Prof. Dr SELÄHATTIN PARLADIR
Faculty of Law: Prof. Dr ŞEREF ERTAŞ
Faculty of Medicine: Prof. Dr ŞEBNEM ÖZKAN

DUMLUPINAR ÜNİVERSİTESİ

M. Kampüs Rektörlük Binası Tavşanlı, Yolu 10 km, 43100 Kütahya
Telephone: (274) 265-20-31
Fax: (274) 265-20-14
E-mail: ssevim@dumlupinar.edu.tr
Internet: www.dumlupinar.edu.tr

Founded 1992
State control
Academic year: November to July

Rector: Prof. Dr GÜNER ÖNCE
Vice-Rectors: Prof. Dr BAHRI ÖTEYAKA, Prof. Dr ALI SARIKOYUNCU
Sec.-Gen.: YALÇIN KALAY
Registrar: MIKTAT BEKTAŞ
Head of Library: İSMAIL BAYRAM

Library of 28,000 books, 168 periodicals
Number of teachers: 515
Number of students: 19,000

DEANS

Faculty of Arts and Sciences: Prof. ALI SARIKOYUNCU
Faculty of Economic and Administrative Sciences (Bilecik): Prof. BAHRI ÖTEYAKA
Faculty of Education: Prof. Dr AHMET YAMIK
Faculty of Engineering: Prof. Dr CEM ŞENSÖĞÜT
Faculty of Fine Arts: Prof. Dr ADNAN TEPECİK
Faculty of Technical Education (Simav): Prof. GÜNER ÖNCE
Graduate School of Science and Engineering: Assoc. Prof. İSKENDER IŞIK
Graduate School of Social Sciences: Prof. AHMET KARAASLAN

EGE ÜNİVERSİTESİ
(Aegean University)

Bornova, Izmir
Telephone: (232) 388-01-10
Fax: (232) 339-90-90
E-mail: ulkubay@med.ege.edu.tr
Internet: www.ege.edu.tr

Founded 1955
State control
Languages of instruction: Turkish and, in some departments, English
Academic year: October to June

Rector: Prof. Dr ÜLKÜ BAYINDIR
Vice-Rectors: Prof. Dr HALUK BAYLAS, Prof. Dr FIKRET İKIZ, Prof. Dr MUSTAFA METIN
Gen. Sec.: CIHANGIR SOYGÜL
Librarian: NURCAN ESLİK BAYKAL

Number of teachers and assistants: 992
Number of students: 30,887

Publications: *Aegean Medical Journal, Fen Dergisi, Tıp Fakültesi Mecmuası, Ziraat Fakültesi Dergisi*, and faculty publications

DEANS

Faculty of Agriculture: Prof. Dr SEMIH ERKAN
Faculty of Communications: Prof. Dr AHMET BÜLENT GÖKSEL
Faculty of Dentistry: Prof. Dr SELDA ERTÜRK
Faculty of Economics and Administrative Sciences: Prof. Dr REZAN TATLIDIL
Faculty of Education: Prof. Dr KADIR ASLAN
Faculty of Engineering: Prof. Dr MUSTAFA TÜRKSEVER
Faculty of Fisheries: Prof. Dr AHMET KOCATAŞ
Faculty of Medicine: Prof. Dr ATA ERDENER
Faculty of Pharmacy: Prof. Dr ERÇIN ERCIYAS
Faculty of Science: Prof. Dr BEKIR ÇETINKAYA
Faculty of Science and Letters: Prof. Dr KASIM EĞİT

DIRECTORS

Conservatory of Turkish Music: Prof. Dr REFET SAYGILI
Institute for Medical Sciences: Prof. Dr NECMETTİN ZEYBEK
Institute for Nuclear Sciences: Prof. Dr SELMAN KINACI
Institute for Science: Prof. Dr FERİDUN TOPALOĞLU
Institute for Solar Energy: Prof. Dr MEHMET AYDIN
Professional School: Prof. Dr MEHMET DOKUZOĞUZ
School of Nursing: Prof. Dr İNCI EREFE
School of Press and Publications: Prof. Dr ÖZCAN ÖZAL
School of Water Products: Prof. Dr ATİLLA ALPBAZ

RESEARCH CENTRES

Agricultural Research Center: Dir Prof. Dr TAYFUN ÖZKAYA.
Botanical Garden and Herbarium Research Center: Dir Prof. Dr ÖZCAN SEÇMEN.
Cancer Surveillance and Research Center: Dir Prof. Dr AYFER HAYDAROĞLU.
Centre for Strategic Studies.
Environmental Studies Research Center: Dir Prof. Dr ÜMIT ERDEM.
European Languages and Cultures Research Center (ADİKAM): Dir Prof. Dr GERTRUDE DURUSOY.
Family Planning and Infertility Research Center.
Genetic Disease Research Center: Dir Prof. Dr CIHANGIR ÖZKINAY.
Health Research Center (University Hospital).

Information and Communication Technologies Research Center: Dir Prof. Dr FAZIL APAYDIN.
Izmir Research Center: Dir Prof. Dr IŞIK TARAKÇIOĞLU.
Natural History Research Center (The Museum of Natural History): Dir Prof. Dr NIMET ÖKTEM.
Organ Transplantation Research Centre: Dir Prof. Dr ÖZDEMİR YARARBAŞ.
Poison Research Center.
Principles of Atatürk and Recent Turkish History Research Center: Dir Prof. Dr FAZILET VARDAR-SUKAN.
Science and Technology Research Center: Dir Prof. Dr S. ŞUHA SUKAN.
Seed Technology Research Center: Dir Prof. Dr BENIAN ESER.
Submarine Research Center.
Textile and Apparel Manufacturing Research Center: Dir Prof. Dr IŞIK TARAKÇIOGLU.
Women's Studies Research Center.

ERCİYES ÜNİVERSİTESİ

38039 Kayseri
Telephone: (352) 437-49-22
Fax: (352) 437-49-31
E-mail: info@erciyes.edu.tr
Internet: www.erciyes.edu.tr

Founded 1978
State control
Language of instruction: Turkish
Academic year: October to June

Rector: Prof. Dr FAHRETTIN KELEŞTEMUR
Vice-Rector: Prof. Dr METIN HÜLAGÜ
Vice-Rector: Prof. Dr MUSTAFA ÇETIN
Vice-Rector: Prof. Dr IBRAHIM UZMAY
Registrar: SEMA ASLAN
Librarian: GÜLNUR YAKAN

Library of 240,000 vols, 85,000 e-books, 40,650 e-journals, 79,000 journals
Number of teachers: 2,044
Number of students: 40,710

Publications: *Journal of the Faculty of Economics and Administrative Sciences, Journal of the Medical School, Journals of the Graduate School of Health Sciences, Journals of the Graduate School of Sciences, Journals of the Graduate School of Social Sciences, Journals of the Theology Faculty, Journals of the Veterinary Medicine Faculty*

DEANS

Faculty of Agriculture: Prof. Dr ALI İRFAN İLBAŞ SEVİĞ
Faculty of Architecture: Prof. Dr İBRAHIM UZMAY
Faculty of Arts: Prof. Dr ÜMIT TOKATLI
Faculty of Communication: Prof. Dr HAMZA ÇAKIR
Faculty of Dentistry: Prof. Dr ALPER ALKAN
Faculty of Economics and Administrative Sciences: Prof. Dr EKREM ERDEM
Faculty of Education: Prof. Dr ABDULLAH SAYDAM
Faculty of Engineering: Prof. Dr MUSTAFA ALÇI
Faculty of Fine Arts: Prof. Dr FAHRETTIN KELEŞTEMUR
Faculty of Health Science: Prof. Dr ÜMIT SEVİĞ
Faculty of Law: Doç. Dr İSMAIL KAYAR
Faculty of Medicine: Prof. Dr MUHAMMET GÜVEN
Faculty of Pharmacy: Prof. Dr MÜBERRA KOŞAR
Faculty of Science: Prof. Dr HÜSEYIN ALTINDIŞ
Faculty of Theology: Prof. Dr M. ZEKI DUMAN

Faculty of Veterinary Medicine: Prof. Dr
HALIT CANATAN

PROFESSORS

Faculty of Architecture (Erciyes University,
38039 Kayseri; tel. (352) 437-52-82; fax (352)
437-65-54; internet www.erciyes.edu.tr/
mimart.htm):

LÖKÇE, S.
ÖZCAN, Z.
YURTSEVER, H.

Faculty of Arts and Science (Erciyes University, 38039 Kayseri; tel. (352) 437-52-62; fax
(352) 437-49-33; internet www.matrix
.erciyes.edu.tr):

AKÇAMUR, Y.
AKKURT, M.
AKTAN, A.
ALTINDIŞ, H.
ALTURAL, B.
ARGUNŞAH, H.
ARGUNŞAH, M.
AYYILDIZ, E.
AYYILDIZ, N.
BARAN, M.
BAYRAKTAR, B.
BOR, H.
ÇOBAN, A.
GÖRKEM, İ.
GÜLENSOY, T.
GÜNDÜZ, M.
GÜZEL, Y.
HÜLAGÜ, M. M.
KARAÖRS, M. M.
KARTAL, Ş.
KESKİN, M.
KESKİN, M.
KÖK, T. R.
MANAŞLI, N.
MUCUK, O.
ÖNEM, Ş C.
ÖZDEMIR, M.
ÖZKAN, N.
ÖZSOY, S.
PATAT, Ş.
SARIPINAR, E.
SOYLAK, M.
TAŞDEMİRCİ, E.
TOKATLI, U.
TUNÇBILEK, A. Ş.
TÜRKMEN, K.
ÜLGEN, A.
YILDIRIM, İ.
YUVALI, A.

Faculty of Arts and Science (Yozgat) (Erciyes
University, Yozgat; tel. (354) 263-82-70; fax
(354) 263-82-71; internet www.yozgatfef
.erciyes.edu.tr):

AKÇAMUR, Y.

Faculty of Communication (Erciyes University, 38039 Kayseri; tel. and fax (352) 437-52-
61; internet iletsim.erciyes.edu.tr):

AKDOĞAN, Ş.
YERLIKAYA, İ.

Faculty of Dentistry (Erciyes University,
38039 Kayseri; tel. and fax (352) 437-49-01;
internet dent.erciyes.edu.tr):

KESIM, B.

Faculty of Economics and Administrative
Sciences (Erciyes University, 38039 Kayseri;
tel. (352) 437-49-13; fax (352) 437-52-39;
e-mail iibf@erciyes.edu.tr; internet www.iibf
.erciyes.edu.tr):

AKDOĞAN, A. A.
AKDOĞAN, M. Ş.
ANDAÇ, F.
ATALAY, M.
BİLGİNOĞLU, M. A.
ÇALIŞKAN, F.
DURA, C.
DURSUN, Y.
ERDEM, E.
NAKİP, M.

ÖZGÜVEN, C.
SAATÇI, M.
SÖNMEZ, İ. H.
UNUTULMAZ, O.
YILDIZ, R.

Faculty of Economics and Administrative
Sciences (Nevşehir) (Erciyes University,
Nevşehir; tel. (384) 215-20-07; fax (384)
215-20-10; internet www.iibf.eunev.edu.tr):

YILDIZ, R.

Faculty of Economics and Administrative
Sciences (Yozgat) (Erciyes University, Yozgat; tel. (354) 263-82-48; fax (354) 263-82-81;
internet yiibf.erciyes.edu.tr):

UNUTULMAZ, O.

Faculty of Education (Erciyes University,
38039 Kayseri; tel. and fax (352) 437-32-06;
internet egitim.erciyes.edu.tr):

TAŞDEMIRCI, E.

Faculty of Engineering (Erciyes University,
38039 Kayseri; tel. (352) 437-57-55; fax (352)
437-57-84; internet mf.erciyes.edu.tr):

ALÇI, M.
APALAK, M. K.
BILIŞIK, A.
DANIŞMAN, K.
GÜNEY, K.
HAKTANIR, T.
KARABOĞA, D.
KARAMIŞ, M. B.
KILIK, R.
TAŞPINAR, H.
UZMAY, İ.
YAPICI, H.
YETIM, H.

Faculty of Engineering and Architecture
(Yozgat) (Erciyes University, Yozgat; tel.
(354) 263-82-72; fax (354) 263-82-76;
internet ymmf.erciyes.edu.tr):

KILIK, R.

Faculty of Fine Arts (Erciyes University,
38039 Kayseri; tel. (352) 437-52-81; fax
(352) 437-36-52; internet guzelsanat.erciyes
.edu.tr):

YENER, S.

Faculty of Law (Erciyes University, 38039
Kayseri; tel. (352) 437-49-01; fax (352) 437-
49-31; internet hukuk.erciyes.edu.tr):

KAYAR, İ

Faculty of Medicine (Erciyes University,
38039 Kayseri; tel. (352) 437-49-10; fax
(352) 437-52-85; internet tip.erciyes.edu.tr):

AKÇALI, Y. F.
AKDEMİR, H.
AKTAS, E.
ALTUNBAŞ, M.
ALTUNTAŞ, H.
ARGUN, M.
ARITAŞ, Y.
ARMAN, F.
AŞCIOĞLU, M.
AŞCIOĞLU, Ö.
AYCAN, K.
AYDOĞAN, S.
AYGEN, B.
AYGEN, E. M.
AYKUT, M.
BAKTIR, A.
BALKANLI, S.
BAŞAR, E.
BAŞBUĞ, M.
BAŞTÜRK, M.
BAYRAM, F.
BOYACI, A.
CANER, Y.
ÇETIN, N.
ÇETIN, S.
ÇETİNKAYA, F.
ÇEYHAN, O.
ÇOKSEVIM, B.
DEMIR, R.
DEMIRTAŞ, H.

DOĞAN, H.
DOĞANAY, M.
DÜNDAR, M.
DÜNDAR, M.
DURAK, A. C.
DURSUN, N.
DÜŞÜNSEL, R.
EMİROĞULLARİ, O. N.
ERENMEMİŞOĞLU, A.
ERGIN, A.
ERKAN, M.
ERKILIÇ, K.
ERSOY, A. Ö.
ESMAOĞLU, A.
GÖLGELİ, A.
GÜLEÇ, M.
GÜLMEZ, İ.
GÜLMEZ, İ.
GÜNAY, G. K.
GÜNAY, O.
GÜNDÜZ, Z.
GÜNEY, E.
GÜVEN, K.
KAHRAMAN, H. C.
KARACAGİL, M.
KARAKÜÇÜK, M. S.
KELEŞTIMUR, H. F.
KENDIRCİ, M.
KİLİÇ, H.
KIRNAP, M.
KOÇ, A. N.
KOÇ, R. K.
KONTAŞ, O.
KÖSE, S. K.
KÜÇÜKAYDIN, M.
KÜLAHLİ, İ.
KUMANDAŞ, S.
KURTOĞLU, S.
MADENOĞLU, H.
MIRZA, G. E.
MIRZA, M.
MÜDERRIS, İ. İ.
MUHTAROĞLU, S.
NARIN, N.
OKTEN, T.
OKUR, H.
OYMAK, O.
ÖZBAKİR, Ö.
ÖZBAL, Y.
ÖZCAN, N.
ÖZDAMAR, M. A.
ÖZDEMIR, M. A.
ÖZESMİ, Ç.
ÖZESMİ, M.
ÖZKUL, Y.
ÖZTÜRK, F.
ÖZTÜRK, M. A.
ÖZTÜRK, M. K.
ÖZTÜRK, Y.
PATIROĞLU, T.
PATIROĞLU, T. E.
ŞAHİN, İ.
ŞAHİN, Y.
SELÇUKLU, A.
SOFUOĞLU, S.
SOYUER, A.
SÖZÜER, E. M.
SÜER, C.
SÜMERKAN, A. B.
TALASLIOĞLU, A.
TATLIŞEN, A.
TAYYAR, M.
TEKOL, Y.
TERCAN, E.
TURAN, C.
TÜRK, C. Y.
TUTUŞ, A.
UKŞAL, Ü.
ÜNAL, A.
ÜNLÜ, Y.
ÜSTDAL, K. M.
UTAŞ, C.
UTAŞ, S.
ÜZÜM, K.
YAKAN, B.
YIĞITBAŞI, , O. G.

YILMAZ, Z.
YÜCESOY, M.

Faculty of Pharmacy (Erciyes University, 38039 Kayseri; tel. (352) 437-49-01; fax (352) 437-49-31; internet pharmacy.erciyes .edu.tr):

BERÇIN, E.

Faculty of Theology (Erciyes University, 38039 Kayseri; tel. (352) 437-60-64; fax (352) 437-42-00; internet ilahiyat.erciyes .edu.tr):

APAYDIN, H. Y.
ATİK, M. K.
AYDİN, M. Ş.
BAĞCECİ, M.
COŞKUN, A.
DEMİRCİ, A.
DUMAN, M. Z.
GÜNAY, Ü.
GÜNGÖR, H.
KIRCA, C.
KOÇ, T.
PAZARBAŞI, E.
POLAT, S.
ŞAHİN, H.
ŞAMUR, S.
SEVERCAN, Ş.
TAŠTAN, A.
TOKSARI, A.
TUNÇ, C.
UĞUR, A.

Faculty of Veterinary Science (Erciyes University, 38039 Kayseri; tel. (352) 339-94-84; fax (352) 337-27-40; internet www.erciyes .edu.tr/veterinert.htm):

ATASEVER, A.
AYDIN, F.
BEKYÜREK, T.
İNCİ, A.
İŞCAN, K. M.
LIMAN, B. C.
LIMAN, N.
NUR, İ. H.

FATİH ÜNİVERSİTESİ

34500 Büyükçekmece, Istanbul
Telephone: (212) 866-33-00
Fax: (212) 866-33-37
E-mail: info@fatih.edu.tr
Internet: www.fatih.edu.tr
Founded 1996
Private control
Language of instruction: English(in faculties)
Language of instruction: Turkish (in Vocational Schools)
Academic year: September to June
Rector: Prof. Dr SERIF ALI TEKALAN
Vice-Rectors: Prof. Dr FAHRETTIN GUCIN, Prof. Dr AYHAN BOZKURT, Prof. Dr MUHAMMET RAMAZAN YIGITOGLU (acting)
Sec.-Gen.: ERTUGRUL MESCIOGLU
Dir of Financial Affairs: MUTTALIP YILMAZ
Dir of Int. Programs Office: FERHAT ARSLAN
Dir of Int. Students Office: ERDOGAN TUZEN
Dir of Library and Documentation: ERCUMENT DEMIRBOZAN
Dir of Student Affairs Office: CUNEYT UMUTLU
Librarian: ERCÜMENT DEMIRBOZAN
Library of 69,760 vols, 47,092 e-books, 7,651 journals, 979 theses, 70,000 e-theses, 40 periodicals, 882 CDs
Number of teachers: 344
Number of students: 11,808
Publications: *Civilacademy: Journal of Social Sciences* (3 a year), *EJEPS, European Journal of Economic and Political Studies, Fatih Bulletin, Genc Kariyer, Journal of Economic and Social Research* (2 a year), *Kariyer Penceresi, Peers (Student Journal)* (2 a year), *Politics, Reflec-tions (Student Journal)* (2 a year), *Text (Student Journal)* (3 a year)

DEANS

Ankara Vocational School: YUKSEL NIZAMOGLU
Ankara Vocational School of Medical Sciences: YUKSEL NIZAMOGLU
Faculty of Arts and Sciences: Prof. Dr CEVDET NERGIZ
Faculty of Economics and Admin. Sciences: Prof. Dr MURAT KARAGOZ
Faculty of Education: Prof. Dr FAHRETTIN GUCIN
Faculty of Engineering: Prof. Dr CEVDE MERIC
Faculty of Law: Prof. OSMAN KASIKCI
Faculty of Medicine: Prof. Dr MUHAMMET RAMAZAN YIGITOGLU (acting)
Faculty of Theology: Prof. Dr MUHIT MERT
Graduate School of Biomedical Engineering: Prof. SADIK KARA
Graduate School of Sciences and Engineering: Assoc. Prof. NURULLAH ARSLAN
Graduate School of Social Sciences: Assoc. Prof. MEHMET KARAKUYU
Istanbul Vocational School: Assoc. Prof. OSMAN NURI ARAS
School of Nursing: Prof. SENOL DANE
Vocational School of Justice: Prof. OSMAN KASIKCI

FİRAT ÜNİVERSİTESİ
(Euphrates University)

23119 Elaziğ
Telephone: (424) 212-85-10
Fax: (424) 212-27-10
E-mail: okalem@firat.edu.tr
Internet: www.firat.edu.tr
Founded 1975
Language of instruction: Turkish
Academic year: October to June
Rector: Prof. Dr MEHMET HAMDI MUZ
Vice-Rectors: Prof. Dr A. Y. ERKIN OĞUR, Prof. Dr HARUN ÖZER
Gen. Sec.: GAZI ÖZCAN
Librarian: Prof. Dr FAHRETTIN GÖKTAŞ
Number of teachers: 1,558
Number of students: 15,906
Publications: *Journal of Health Sciences* (2 a year), *Journal of Science and Engineering* (2 a year), *Journal of Social Sciences* (2 a year)

DEANS

Faculty of Agriculture (Bingöl): (vacant)
Faculty of Aquatic Sciences: Prof. Dr BÜLENT ŞEN
Faculty of Arts and Sciences: Prof. Dr İBRAHIM YILMAZÇELİK
Faculty of Communication: Prof. Dr ASAF VAROL
Faculty of Economic and Management Sciences (Tunceli): (vacant)
Faculty of Education: Prof. Dr MEHMET AYDOĞDU
Faculty of Education (Muş): (vacant)
Faculty of Engineering: Prof. Dr DURSUN PEHLIVAN
Faculty of Medicine: Prof. Dr ÖZGE ARDIÇOĞLU
Faculty of Technical Education: Prof. Dr ALI İNAN
Faculty of Theology: Doç. Dr MUSTAFA ÖZTÜRK
Faculty of Veterinary Medicine: Prof. Dr H. BASRI GÜLCÜ

ATTACHED SCHOOLS AND COLLEGES

College of Health Sciences: Dir Prof. Dr EMINE ÜNSALDI.

College of Health Sciences (Elazig): Dir Prof. Dr ZÜLAL AŞCI TORAMAN.

College of Physical and Sports Education (Elazig): Dir Prof. Dr MEHMET ÜLKER.

College of Social Sciences (Elazig): Dir Doç. Dr ORHAN KILIÇ.

College of Technical Sciences (Elazig): Dir Doç. Dr NECATI KULOĞLU.

College of Vocational Education (Bingöl): Dir Prof. Dr MÜKREMIN APAYDIN.

College of Vocational Education (Maden): Dir Doç. Dr ALI İNAN.

College of Vocational Education (Malazgirt): Dir Prof. Dr KADIR SERVI.

College of Vocational Education (Muş): Dir Doç. Dr KADIR SERVİ.

College of Vocational Education (Sivrice): Dir Prof. Dr HARUN ÖZER.

College of Vocational Education (Tunceli): Dir Prof. Dr SALIH ÖZÇELİK.

Fine Arts–Music: Dir Assoc. Prof. Dr GÜLDENIZ EKMEN AGİŞ.

Keban Sleyman Demırel College of Vocational Education: Dir Assoc. Prof. Dr HÜSAMETTIN KAYA.

Kemaliye Hacı Ali Akin College of Vocational Education: Dir Prof. Dr MEHMET CEBECI.

GALATASARAY ÜNİVERSİTESİ

Ciragan Cad. 36, 34357 Ortaköy, Istanbul
Telephone: (212) 227-44-80
E-mail: dyarsuvat@gsu.edu.tr
Internet: www.gsu.edu.tr
Founded 1992
Academic year: October to June
State control
Rector: Prof. Dr DUYGUN YARSUVAT
Vice-Rectors: Prof. Dr SEYFETTIN GÜRSEL, Prof. Dr PIERRE LE MIRE, Prof. Dr ETHEM TOLGA, Prof. Dr NECMI YÜZBAŞIOĞLU
Gen. Sec.: Prof. Dr İSMAIL ÖZTÜRK
Library of 42,000 vols
Number of teachers: 140
Number of students: 1,674

DEANS

Faculty of Communications: Prof. Dr E. ÖZDEN CANKAYA
Faculty of Engineering and Technology: Prof. Dr ETHEM TOLGA
Faculty of Law: Prof. Dr HAMDI YASAMAN
Faculty of Science and Letters: Prof. Dr KENAN GÜRSOY

GAZİ ÜNİVERSİTESİ

06500 Teknikokullar, Ankara
Telephone: (312) 202-22-22
Fax: (312) 221-32-02
E-mail: rektor@gazi.edu.tr
Internet: www.gazi.edu.tr
Founded 1982
State control
Language of instruction: Turkish
Academic year: September to June
Rector: Prof. Dr RIZA AYHAN
Vice-Rectors: Prof. Dr METIN AKTAS, Prof. Dr CUMHUR SAHIN, Prof. Dr DURAN ALTIPARMARK
Sec.-Gen.: Prof. Dr BAHTIYAR AKYILMAZ
Librarian: TÜNSEL CANATALI
Library of 308,723 vols
Number of teachers: 3,756
Number of students: 64,663 (55,068 undergraduate, 9,595 postgraduate)
Publication: *Gazi Üniversitesi Bülteni* (6 a year)

DEANS

Faculty of Architecture: Prof. Dr HÜSNU CAN

Faculty of Arts and Design: Prof. Dr FATMA ALI SINANOGLU

Faculty of Commerce and Tourism: Prof. Dr NEVZAT AYPEK

Faculty of Communication: Prof. Dr NACI BOSTANCI

Faculty of Dentistry: Prof. Dr DERVIS YILMAZ

Faculty of Economic and Administrative Sciences: Prof. Dr KADIR ARIKI

Faculty of Economics and Administrative Sciences (Çorum): Prof. Dr HASAN KAVAL

Faculty of Education (Gazi): Prof. Dr MUSTAFA SAFRAN

Faculty of Education (Kastamonu): Prof. Dr ALEMI YETIM

Faculty of Education (Kırşehir): Prof. Dr SELAHATTIN SALMAN

Faculty of Engineering (Çorum): Prof. Dr NAIL UNSAL

Faculty of Forestry (Kastamonu): Prof. Dr HASAN VURDU

Faculty of Fine Arts: Prof. Dr ALEV CAKMAOGLU KURU

Faculty of Health Sciences: Prof. Dr A. GULSAN TURKOZSUCAK

Faculty of Industrial Arts Education: Prof. Dr İRFAN SÜER

Faculty of Law: Prof. Dr IHSAN ERDOGAN

Faculty of Medicine: Prof. Dr PEYAM CINAZ

Faculty of Pharmacy: Prof. Dr TURHAN BAYKAL

Faculty of Sciences (Kırşehir): Prof. Dr İRFAN AKGÜN

Faculty of Technical Education: Prof. Dr CEMIL CETINKAYA

Faculty of Theology (Çorum): Prof. Dr HASAN ONAT

Faculty of Vocational Education: Prof. Dr FATMA ALI SINANOGLU

GRADUATE SCHOOLS

Graduate School of Accident Research and Prevention: Dir Prof. Dr ALI BUMIN.

Graduate School of Educational Sciences: Dir Prof. Dr SEMIH YALÇIN.

Graduate School of Health Sciences: Dir OKTAY ÜNER.

Graduate School of Natural Sciences: Maltepe, Ankara; Dir Prof. Dr AHMET BIGER.

Graduate School of Social Sciences: Kavaklıdere, Ankara; Dir Prof. Dr İHSON ERDOĞAN.

GAZİANTEP ÜNİVERSİTESİ

POB 300, 27310 Gaziantep
Telephone: (342) 360-10-10
Fax: (342) 360-10-13
E-mail: gensek@gantep.edu.tr
Internet: www.gantep.edu.tr
Founded 1987
Academic year: October to June
Rector: Prof. Dr ERHAN EKİNCİ
Number of teachers: 2,821
Number of students: 49,250
Publications: *Sosyal Bilimler Dergisi* (social sciences, 1 a year), *Tıp Fakültesi Dergisi* (medicine, 2 a year)

DEANS

Faculty of Arts and Science: IHSAN ÜNVER

Faculty of Arts and Science (Kilis): ÖMER BAKKALOGLU

Faculty of Economics and Business Administration: ISMAIL H. ÖZSABUNCUOĞLU

Faculty of Education: MUHSIN MACIT

Faculty of Education (Adiyaman): HACI DURAN

Faculty of Education (Kilis): ALI RIZA TEKIN

Faculty of Engineering: MUSTAFA ÖZAKÇA

Faculty of Medicine: ABDURAHMAN KADAYIFÇI

GAZİOSMANPAŞA ÜNİVERSİTESİ

60150 Tokat
Telephone: (356) 252-14-52
Fax: (356) 252-14-52
E-mail: tokat@gop.edu.tr
Internet: www.gop.edu.tr
Founded 1992
State control
Academic year: October to June
Rector: Prof. Dr ZEHRA SEYFIKLI
Vice-Rector: Prof. Dr MEHMET ARSLAN
Vice-Rector: Prof. Dr MEHMET TEKIN
Librarian: ERDAL ŞAHINI

Library of 60,063 vols, 1,425 theses, 375 periodicals, 48 musical notes, 40 diskettes, 295 CD-ROMs, 19 electronic databases
Number of teachers: 842
Number of students: 13,328 (12,520 undergraduate, 808 postgraduate)

DEANS

Faculty of Agriculture: Prof. Dr GÜNGÖR YILMAZ

Faculty of Arts and Sciences: Prof. Dr HANEFI VURAL

Faculty of Economic and Administrative Sciences: Prof. Dr OSMAN KARAKACIER

Faculty of Education: Prof. Dr MUSTAFA BALOĞLU

Faculty of Medicine: Prof. Dr MURAT FIRAT

Faculty of Natural Sciences and Engineering: (vacant)

GEBZE YÜKSEK TEKNOLOJİ ENSTİTÜSÜ

PK 141, 41400, Gebze Kocaeli
Telephone: (262) 605-15-01
Fax: (262) 653-84-90
E-mail: okalem@gyte.edu.tr
Internet: www.gyte.edu.tr
Founded 1992
Language of instruction: Turkish
State control
Academic year: September to June

Faculties of architecture, business and administration, engineering, science

Rector: Prof. Dr ORHAN ŞAHIN
Vice-Rector: Prof. Dr MUAMMER KALYON
Vice-Rector: Prof. Dr TAŞKIN KAVZOĞLU

Library of 14,000 vols, 49 e-databases, 60,000 online periodicals, 27 printed periodicals
Number of teachers: 468
Number of students: 3,688 (1,532 undergraduate 2,156 graduate)

HACETTEPE ÜNİVERSİTESİ

Hacettepe Üniversitesi, 06100 Ankara
Telephone: (312) 305-5000
Fax: (312) 310-5552
E-mail: information@hacettepe.edu.tr
Internet: www.hacettepe.edu.tr
Founded 1967
State control
Language of instruction: English, French, German, Turkish
Academic year: September to August

Rector: Prof. Dr UĞUR ERDENER
Vice-Rectors: Prof. Dr HASAN KAZDAĞLI, Prof. Dr HÜSEYIN SELÇUK GEÇIM, Prof. Dr SEVIL GÜRGAN
Sec.-Gen.: TURHAN MENTEŞ
Registrar: A. RIFKI GÖKMEN (Deputy Registrar)
Dir of Libraries: AYŞEN KÜYÜK (Deputy Director)

Library: Beytepe campus library of 185,554 vols, 34,940 journals, 1,216,181 theses, 1,996 CDs, 1,071 record albums
Number of teachers: 3,645
Number of students: 30,000

Publications: *Hacettepe Tıp/Cerrahi Bülteni* (4 a year), and several faculty bulletins

DEANS

Beytepe Campus:

Faculty of Communication: Prof. Dr SUAVI AYDIN

Faculty of Economics and Adminstrative Sciences: Prof. Dr AHMET BURÇIN YERELI

Faculty of Education: Prof. Dr BUKET AKKOYUNLU

Faculty of Engineering: Prof. Dr HAYRI YILMAZ KAPTAN

Faculty of Fine Arts: Prof. Dr UĞURCAN AKYÜZ

Faculty of Law: Prof. Dr SELMA ÇETINER

Faculty of Letters: Prof. Dr MUSA YAŞAR SAĞLAM

Faculty of Science: Prof. Dr MEHMET AŞKIN TÜMER

Hacettepe Campus:

Faculty of Dentistry: Prof. Dr CELAL TÜMER

Faculty of Health Sciences: Prof. Dr HALIT TANJU BESLER

Faculty of Medicine: Prof. Dr SARP SARAÇ

Faculty of Pharmacy: Prof. Dr A. AHMET BAŞARAN

Sihhiye Campus:

Faculty of Pharmacy: Prof. Dr LÜTFIYE ÖMÜR DEMIREZER

Kastamonu Faculty of Medicine: Prof. Dr SÜLEYMAN SIRRI KES

PROFESSORS

Faculty of Dentistry:

ALPARSLAN, M. G., Oral and Dental Therapeutics

ALTAY, A., Paediatric Dentistry

ANIL (GAZI), N., Prosthesis

ASLAN, Y., Prosthesis

AVCI, M., Prosthesis

BAŞEREN, N. M., Oral and Dental Therapeutics

BERKER, A. E., Periodontics

BOLAY (SARİOĞLU), Ş., Oral and Dental Therapeutics

CANAY (ÖLGUN), R. Ş., Prosthesis

ÇAĞLAYAN, F., Periodontics

ÇAĞLAYAN, G., Periodontics

ÇALT, T., Endodontics

CIĞER, S., Orthodontics

DAYANGAÇ, B., Oral and Dental Therapeutics

DAYANGAÇ, B., Prosthesis

DEMIREL (USLU), F., Prosthesis

DURMAZ, V., Oral and Dental Therapeutics

ERATALAY, Y. K., Periodontics

GÖKALP, S., Oral and Dental Therapeutics

GÖRDUYSUS, M., Endodontics

GÖRÜCÜ, J., Oral and Dental Therapeutics

GÜRGAN, S., Oral and Dental Therapeutics

HERSEK, N. E., Prosthesis

KANSU, A. Ö., Oral and Dental Therapeutics

KANSU, H., Oral and Dental Therapeutics

KEYF (HAMARAT), F., Prosthesis

KOCADERELI, İ., Orthodontics

KÖPRÜLÜ, H., Oral and Dental Therapeutics

KÖSEOĞLU, O. T., Dental Surgery

KURANER, T., Oral and Dental Therapeutics

NAZLIEL, H., Periodontics

NOHUTÇU, R. M., Periodontics

ÖKTEMER, M., Prosthesis

ÖLMEZ, M. S., Paediatric Dentistry

ÖNEN, A., Oral and Dental Therapeutics

ÖZÇELİK, B., Oral and Dental Therapeutics

ÖZGÜNALTAY, H. G., Oral and Dental Therapeutics

ŞAHIN, E., Prosthesis

ŞAHIN (SÖKMEN), S., Prosthesis

ŞAHMALI, S., Prosthesis

SAYGILI, G., Prosthesis

ŞENGÜN, F. D., Periodontics
ŞERPER, A., Endodontics
TAŞAR, F., Dental Surgery
TAŞMAN, F., Endodontics
TUNCER, M., Periodontics
URAN, N., Oral Surgery
YAMALIK, N., Periodontology
YENİGÜL, M., Prosthesis

Faculty of Economics and Administrative Sciences:

AKALIN, G., Public Finance
AKTAN, O. H., Economics
BİLİCİ, N., Public Finance
ÇAĞLAR, A., Public Administration
CAN, H., Economics
ERDOĞAN, M., Public Administration
İPÇİ, M. O., Accounting and Finance
KARAN, M., Business Administration
KAZDAĞLI, H., Economics
MORGİL, O., Economics
ŞAHİNÖZ, A., Economics
ŞİŞİK, Ü., Economics
TANYERİ, İ, Economics
TELATAR, M. E., Economics
TİMUR, H., Economics
TOKAT, M., Economics
UYGUN, H., Economics

Faculty of Education:

ABAK, M., Physics
ACAR, N., Counselling and Guidance
AKKOYUNLU, B., Computer Education and Instructional Technologies
AKMAN, B., Pre-School Teaching
AŞKAR, P., Computer Education and Instructional Technologies
BAŞAR, H., Education
BAŞKAN, A. G., Educational Administration, Supervision, Planning and Economics
BÜLBÜL, A., Mathematics Teaching
DEMİREL, O., Education
DEMİREZEN, M., Language Studies
ERATALAY, N., French
ERÇETİN, Ş. Ş., Educational Administration, Supervision, Planning and Economics
EREN, A., Physics
ERSEVER, O. G., Counselling and Guidance
ERTEM, C., Language and Literature
GENÇ, A., German Language Teaching
HAMAN, S., Physics Teaching
KAVAK, Y., Education
KESKİL, G., English Language Teaching
KIRAN, A., Language Studies
KİZİROĞLU, İ, Biology
MORGİL, I., Analytical Chemistry
ÖNALP, B., Biology
ÖNSOY, R., Education
ÖZ, H., English Language Teaching
PATİR, S., Chemistry
SAĞLAM, N., Biology
SALİHOĞLU, H., Language Studies
SENEMOĞLU, N., Education
SİPAHİLER, F., Biology
SÖNMEZ, V., Education
SORAN, H., Biology
TUĞRUL, B., Pre-School Teaching

Faculty of Engineering:

ACAR, J., Food
AKSU, Z., Process and Reactor Design
ALPER, E., Chemistry
APAYDIN, F., Physics
ARIKAN, A., Hydrogeology
AYDAR, E., Mineralogy, Petrography
AYTAÇ, S., Food Sciences
BAYARİ, S. C., Hydrogeology
BAYHAN, H., Geology
BEŞKARDEŞ, O., Chemistry
BİRGÜL, Ö., Nuclear Physics
BOZDEMİR, M. T., Unit Operations and Thermodynamics
ÇADIRCI, I., Electrical Engineering
ÇAĞLAR, A., Chemistry
CANKURTARAN, M., Physics

ÇELELBİ, S. S., Chemistry
ÇELİK, H., Physics
ÇELİK, S., Food Sciences
ÇELİK, T., Physics
ÇİNER, T. A., Geology
ÇOLAK, Ü., Nuclear Physics
DEMİRCİOĞLU, H., Electrical Engineering
DEMİREL, H., Mining Engineering
DURUBOY, H. Z., Physics
DURUSOY (DÖRTER), B. T., Mining Engineering
ERAY, A., Solid State Physics
ERCAN, B., Electrical Engineering
ERKAN, Y., Geology
FIRAT, T., Physics
GEÇİM, S., Electrical Engineering
GİRGİN, İ, Mining Engineering
GÜMÜŞDERELİOĞLU, M., Chemistry
GÜNDÜC, Y., Electrical Engineering
HÖKELEK, T., Physics
İDE, S., General Physics
İNAN, İ. D., Physics
KAPTAN, Y., Physics
KARAKAŞ, M. Ü., Computer Science Engineering
KARAYIĞIT, A., Mineral Deposits, Geochemistry
KASAPOĞLU, K. E., Geology
KAYHAN, S., Telecommunications
KENDİ, E., General Physics
KÖKSAL, A., Electromagnetic Waves and Microwaves
KÖKSEL, H., Food
KORKMAZ, M., Physics
KULAKSIZ, S., Mining and Mineral Processing
KUTSAL, T., Chemistry
MUTLU, M., Food
ÖKTÜ, Ö., General Physics
ÖNDER, M., Physics
ÖNER, M., Mining Engineering
ÖNER, M., Mining and Mineral Processing
ORAL, B., Physics
ÖZBAŞ, Y., Food Technology
ÖZBAY (DANACİ), S., General Physics
ÖZBEY, T., Physics
ÖZDURAL, A. R., Chemistry
ÖZTECİN, E., Physics
PİŞKİN, E., Chemistry
SAATÇI, A., Computer Science Engineering
ŞAFAK, M., Electrical Engineering
SAĞ, Y., Process and Reactor Design
SALDAMLI, İ., Food
SARAÇ, C., Mineral Deposits, Geochemistry
SAYDAM, A., Environmental Engineering
ŞENYUR, M. G., Mining and Mineral Processing
ŞİMŞEK, S., Hydrogeology
SUNGAR, R., General Physics
SÜNNETÇİOĞLU, M., Physics
TABAK, F., Physics
TANYOLAÇ, A., Chemistry
TEMEL, A., Mineral Deposits, Geochemistry
TEMİZ, A., Food
TERCAN, A., Mining and Mineral Processing
TOLUNAY, H., Solid State Physics
TOPAÇLI, C., Physics
TOPAÇLI(SUNGUR), A., Atomic and Molecular Physics
TÖRECİ, E., Computer Science Engineering
TUNCEL, S. A., Process and Reactor Design
TUNOĞLU, C., General Geology
ÜLKÜ, D., Physics
ULUSAY, R., Applied Geology
ÜNVER, B., Mining and Mineral Processing
US, F., Food
VURAL, H., Food Sciences
YARIMAĞAN, Ü., Computer Science Engineering
YAZGAN, E., Electrical Engineering

Faculty of Fine Arts:

AKYÜZ, U., Graphic Art
AYDINÖZ, A. A., Art
DAKAK, H., Painting

GENCAYDIN, Z., Fine Arts
KAYA, İ., Graphic Art
MİSMAN, H. A., Painting
PEKMEZCI, H., Painting
PEKTAŞ, H., Graphic Art
SAVAŞ, R., Sculpture

Faculty of Letters:

AKAN, A. V., Sociology
AKKOYUNLU, Z., Folklore Studies
AKSOY, B. M., English Translation and Interpretation
AKSOY, E., Western Language and Literature
ALTAY (AKANSEL), A., English Translation and Interpretation
ARIKAN (GÜRER), G., Sociology
AYDIN, O., Experimental Psychology
BAĞCİ, S., History of Art
BAYDUR, K. G., Librarianship
BAYKAN, F., Philosophy
BOZBEYOĞLU, S., French Language and Literature
BOZER, A. D., English Language and Literature
ÇAKIN, İ., Librarianship
ÇELİK, A., Librarianship
ÇELİK-ŞAVK, Ü., Turkish Language and Literature
DİKEÇLİĞİL, F. B., Sociometry
DOĞAN, Ş., German Language and Literature
ERCİLASUN, B., Literature
ERGAN, N., Sociology
ERKENAL, A., History of Art
ERLAT, J., French Studies
EROL, B., English Language and Literature
HORATA, O., Turkish Language and Literature
İÇLİ, T., Sociology
İNAL, T., French Studies
İZGİ, Ö., General Turkish History
KARAKAŞ, S., Experimental Psychology
KIRAN, Z., French Studies
KÖNİG, G., Linguistics
KULA, O., German Language and Literature
KURBANOĞLU, S. S., Librarianship
OCAK, A. Y., History
OCAK, F. T., History
OPPERMANN (TUNÇ), S., English Language and Literature
ÖTÜKEN, S. Y., Archaeology
ÖZ, M., History
ÖZBEK, M., Social Anthropology
ÖZGEN, E., Archaeology
ÖZMEN, K., French Studies
ÖZÖNDER, M. C., Sociology
ÖZYER, N., German Language and Literature
SAĞLAM, M. Y., German Language and Literature
TEPE, H., Philosophy
TONTA, Y., Librarianship
UMUNÇ, H., English Language and Literature
UNAN, F., History
YILDIRIM, D., Literature
YILDIZ, S., German Studies
YİMAZ, E., Turkish Language and Literature

Faculty of Medicine:

ABBASOĞLU, O., Internal Medicine
AÇAN, L., Biochemistry
ACAROĞLU, R.E., Orthopaedics
ADALAR, N., Internal Medicine
ADALIOĞLU, G., Paediatrics
AKALAN, N., Neurosurgery
AKALIN, N., Neurosurgery
AKAN, H. T., Dermatology
AKATA, D., Radiology
AKHAN, H. M. O., Radiology
AKIN, A., Community Health
AKINCI, F.A., Physical Therapy and Rehabilitation
AKOVA, M., Internal Medicine

AKŞİT, D., Anatomy
AKSÖYEK, S., Cardiology
AKSU, A. T., Obstetrics and Gynaecology
AKYOL, F. H., Oncology
AKYOL, Ö., Biochemistry
AKYOL, U. M., Otorhinolaryngology
AKYÜZ (CELEPOĞLU), C., Oncology
ALAÇAM, R., Microbiology
ALEHAN, D., Paediatrics
ALPAR, C., Biostatistics
ALPARSLAN, M., Orthopaedics
ANLAR, B. F., Paediatrics
ARAN, Ö., Surgery
ARAS (SULHUN), T., Nuclear Medicine
ARIKAN, S., Microbiology
ARIOĞLU, S., Internal Medicine
ARIYÜREK, O. M., Radiology
ARSLAN, S., Internal Medicine
AŞAN, E., Morphology
ATAHAN, İ. L., Oncology
ATAKAN, Z. N., Dermatology
AYAS, K., Ear, Nose and Throat Surgery
AYDIN, E., Medical Ethics and History
AYDINGÖZ, Ü., Radiology
AYHAN, A., Obstetrics and Gynaecology
AYPAR, Ü., Anaesthesiology
AYSUN, S., Paediatrics
AYTAR, Ş., Medical Biology
BAKKALOĞLU, A., Paediatrics
BAKKALOĞLU, A. M., Urology
BALCI, S., Paediatrics
BALKANCI, F., Radiology
BARIŞTA, İ., Internal Medicine
BAŞAR, R., Anatomy
BAŞGÖZE, O., Physical Therapy and Rehabilitation
BATMAN, F., Internal Medicine
BAYRAKTAR, M., Internal Medicine
BAYRAKTAR, Y., Internal Medicine
BEKSAÇ, S., Obstetrics and Gynaecology
BELGİN, E., Ear, Nose and Throat Surgery
BENLİ, K., Neurosurgery
BEŞBAŞ, N., Paediatrics
BESİM, A., Radiology
BİLGİÇ, S., Ophthalmology
BİLİR, N., Community Health
BÖKE, E., Cardiovascular and Thoracic Surgery
BOZKURT, A., Pharmacology
BÜLBÜL, F. F., Plastic and Reconstructive Surgery
BÜYÜKPAMUKÇU, M., Oncology
BÜYÜKPAMUKÇU, N., Paediatric Surgery
ÇAĞLAR, M., Nuclear Medicine
ÇAĞLAR, M., Paediatrics
ÇAKAR, A. N., Morphology
ÇAKMAK, F., Urology
ÇALGÜNERİ, M., Internal Medicine
CANER, B. E., Nuclear Medicine
ÇEKIRGE, H., Radiology
ÇEKIRGE, I. S., Radiology
ÇELEBİOĞLU, B., Anaesthesiology
ÇELIK, H. H., Anatomy
ÇELİKER, A., Paediatrics
ÇELİKER, A. R., Physical Therapy and Rehabilitation
ÇELİKER, V., Anaesthesiology and Reanimation
ÇETIN, M., Paediatrics
CEYHAN, M., Paediatrics
ÇIFTÇI, A., Paediatrics
CIĞER, A., Institute of Neurological Sciences
CILA, A., Radiodiagnostics
ÇOKUĞRAŞ, N. A., Biochemistry
ÇÖPLÜ, L., Thoracic Diseases
COSKUN, T., Paediatrics
ÇUHADAROĞLU, F., Psychiatry
CUMHUR, M., Morphology
DAĞDEVİREN, A., Histology and Embryology
DALKARA, N. E. T., Institute of Neurological Sciences
DEMİRCİN, M., Cardiovascular and Thoracic Surgery
DEMIRKAZİK, F., Radiology
DEMIRPENÇE (TANSEL), E., Biochemistry

DİNÇER, F., Physical Therapy and Rehabilitation
DİNÇER, P. R., Medical Biology
DOĞAN, P., Biochemistry
DOĞAN, R., Cardiovascular and Thoracic Surgery
DORAL, M. N., Orthopaedics
DUMAN, O., Physiology
DÜNDAR, S., Internal Medicine
DURUKAN, T., Obstetrics and Gynaecology
ELDEM, M. B., Ophthalmology
ELİBOL, B., Neurology
EMRE (DÖKMECI), S., Internal Medicine
ERBAŞ, A. T., Internal Medicine
ERBAŞ, B. H., Nuclear Medicine
ERDEM, Y., Internal Medicine
ERDENER, U., Ophthalmology
ERGEN, A., Urology
ERGÜVEN (DIKEL), S., Microbiology
ERK, Y., Plastic Surgery
ERKAN, İ., Urology
ERSOY, F. N., Paediatrics
ERSOY, Ü., Cardiovascular and Thoracic Surgery
ERTENLİ, A. İ., Internal Medicine
GEDİK, O., Internal Medicine
GEDİKOĞLU, G., Pathology
GÖKLER, B., Psychiatry
GÖKÖZ, A., Pathology
GÜÇ, D., Oncology
GÜÇ, M. O., Pharmacology
GÜLER, Ç., Community Health
GÜLER, E. N., Internal Medicine
GÜLLÜ, İ., Oncology
GÜMRÜK, F., Paediatrics
GÜNALP, G. S., Obstetrics and Gynaecology
GÜNGEN, Y. Y., Pathology
GÜR (AKMAN), D., Paediatrics
GÜRAKAN, H., Paediatrics
GÜRGAN, T., Obstetrics and Gynaecology
GÜRGEY, A., Paediatrics
GÜRKANYNAK, H. M., Oncology
GÜRLEK, Ö. A., Internal Medicine
GÜRSEL, B., Ear, Nose and Throat Surgery
HALILOĞLU, M., Radiology
HAMALOĞLU, E., General Surgery
HAŞÇELIK, A. G., Microbiology
HAŞÇELIK, H. Z., Physical Therapy and Rehabilitation
HAZNEDAROĞLU, C., Internal Medicine
HOŞAL, A., Otorhinology
ILGI, N. S., Morphology
İLHAN, M., Pharmacology
İRKEÇ, M., Ophthalmology
KABAKÇİ, M.G., Cardiology
KALAYCI, C., Paediatrics
KALE, G., Paediatrics
KALYONCU, A. F., Thoracic Diseases
KANBAK (SOYLU), M., Anaesthesiology and Reanimation
KANDEMIR, N., Paediatrics
KANSU, E., Oncology
KANSU, T., Institute of Neurological Sciences
KARAAĞAOĞLU, A. E., Medical Biology
KARABUDAK, R., Neurology
KARADUMAN, A., Dermatology
KARS, S. A., Internal Medicine
KART, A., Medical Biology
KAYA, S., Ear, Nose and Throat Surgery
KAYNAROLĞU, Z. V., Surgery
KEÇİK, A., Plastic Surgery
KENDİ, S., Urology
KES, S., Internal Medicine
KILINÇ, K., Biochemistry
KİPER, E. N., Childhood Health and Diseases
KIRATLI, H., Ophthalmology
KÖLEMEN, B., Dermatology
KÜÇÜKALİ, T., Pathology
KUŞ, M. S., Biochemistry
KUTLUK, M. T., Paediatrics
KUTSAL, F. Y., Physical Therapy and Rehabilitation
MAVİLİ, M. E., Plastic and Reconstructive Surgery

MOCAN, G., Pathology
MÜFTÜOĞLU, S., Histology and Embryology
MUŞDAL, Y., Orthopaedics and Traumatology
NAZLI, N., Internal Medicine, Cardiology
NURLU (ÖZGÜR), G., Neurology
OCAL, M. T., Anaesthesiology
ÖĞRETMENOĞLU, O., Otorhinology
OĞUŞ, İ. H., Biochemistry
ÖKTEM (BONCUK), F., Psychiatry
ONAT, D., Surgery
ÖNDEROĞLU, L. S., Obstetrics and Gynaecology
ÖNDEROĞLU, S., Anatomy
ÖNER, Z. N., Surgery
ÖNERCİ, T. M., Ear, Nose and Throat Surgery
ONUR, E. R., Pharmacology
ORAN, M. B., Radiology
ORER, H., Pharmacology
ORHAN, M., Ophthalmology
OTO, M. A., Internal Medicine
ÖVÜNÇ, K., Cardiology
ÖZCAN, E. O., Neurosurgery
ÖZCEBE, L. H., Community Health
ÖZCEBE, O. İ., Internal Medicine
ÖZÇELIK, H., Paediatrics
ÖZDEMİR, A., Surgery
ÖZDEN, A. K., Medical Biology
ÖZEN, H., Paediatrics
ÖZEN, H. A., Urology
ÖZEN, S., Paediatrics
ÖZENÇ, A. M., Surgery
ÖZER, E. S., Paediatrics
ÖZER, N., Biochemistry
ÖZGEN, T., Institute of Neurological Sciences
ÖZGEN (ULUPINAR), S., Anaesthesiology
ÖZGÜÇ, M., Medical Biology
ÖZGÜNEŞ, N., Biochemistry
ÖZIŞIK, Y. Y., Oncology
ÖZKAN, S., Ear, Nose and Throat Surgery
ÖZKARA (ŞAHİN), A., Biochemistry
ÖZKUTLU, H., Internal Medicine
ÖZKUTLU, S., Paediatrics
ÖZKUYUMCU, C., Microbiology
ÖZMEN, F., Internal Medicine
ÖZMEN, M. N., Radiology
ÖZMERT, E., Paediatrics
ÖZTEK, A. Z., Community Medicine
ÖZTÜRK, N., Biophysics
ÖZYAR, E., Radiation Oncology
ÖZYAZICI, A., Morphology
PALAOĞLU, Ö. S., Institute of Neurological Sciences
PEKCAN, H., Community Health
PURALİ, N., Biophysics
ŞAFAK, T., Plastic and Reconstructive Surgery
ŞAHİN, A., Urology
ŞAHİN, A. A., Internal Medicine
ŞAHİN, S., Dermatology
SANAÇ, A. Ş., Ophthalmology
SANAL, S. O., Paediatrics
SARGON, M. F., Anatomy
SAYEK, İ., Surgery
SAYGI (SÜTÇÜ), S., Neurology
SEÇMEER, G., Paediatrics
ŞEFTALIOĞLU, A., Histology
ŞEKEREL, B., Paediatrics
ŞELÇUK, Z., Chest Diseases
SELEKLER, K., Neurology
ŞENER, B., Microbiology
ŞENER, E. C., Ophthalmology
SENNAROĞLU, L., Ear Nose and Throat Surgery
ŞENOCAK, M. E., Paediatric Surgery
ŞİMŞEK, H., Internal Medicine
SİVRİ, B., Internal Medicine
SÖYLEMEZOĞLU, F., Pathology
SÖZEN, T., Internal Medicine
SÖZER, A. B., Ear, Nose and Throat Surgery
SUNGUR, A. A., Oncology
SURAT, A., Orthopaedics
TAN, M. E., Neurology

TANYEL, F. C., Paediatric Surgery
TASAR, C., Oncology
TATAR, G., Internal Medicine
TEKGÜL, S., Urology
TEKİNALP, G., Paediatrics
TEKUZMAN, G., Oncology
TEZCAN, F., Biochemistry
TEZCAN, F. İ., Paediatrics
TEZCAN, S., Community Medicine
TOKATLI, A., Paediatrics
TOKGÖZOĞLU, M., Orthopaedics and Traumatology
TOKGÖZOĞLU, S. L., Internal Medicine
TOPALOĞLU, H., Paediatrics
TOPALOĞLU, R., Paediatrics
TOPÇU, M., Institute of Neurological Sciences
TUNCEL, H. M., Anatomy
TUNÇBİLEK, E., Paediatrics
TUNCER, A., Paediatrics
TUNCER, A. M., Paediatrics
TUNCER, M., Pharmacology
TUNCER, Z. S., Obstetrics and Gynaecology
TUNÇKANAT, F. F., Microbiology
TURAN, E., Ear, Nose and Throat Surgery
TURGAN, Ç., Internal Medicine
UĞUR, O., Nuclear Medicine
ULUĞ, B., Psychiatry
ULUŞAHIN, N. A., Psychiatry
ÜNAL, M. F., Child Psychiatry
ÜNAL, S., Internal Medicine
UNGAN, P., Biophysics
ÜNSAL, M., Radiology
US (ERSÖZ), A. D., Microbiology
USMAN, A., Internal Medicine
USTAÇELEBİ, S., Microbiology
UZUN (ÖZMEN), Ö., Internal Medicine
VARLI, K., Neurology
YALÇIN, Ş., Internal Medicine
YALÇINRIDVANAĞAOĞLU, A., Physiology
YARALİ, H., Obstetrics and Gynaecology
YASAVUL, Ü., Internal Medicine
YAZICI, M., Orthopaedics
YAZICI, M. K., Psychiatry
YETKİN, S., Paediatrics
YİĞİT, Ş., Paediatrics
YILMAZ, E., Medical Biology
YORDAM, N., Paediatrics
YÖRÜKAN, S., Physiology
YÜCE, A., Childhood Health and Diseases
YÜCE, K., Obstetrics and Gynaecology
YURDAKÖK, K., Paediatrics
YURDAKÖK, M., Paediatrics
YURTER (ERDEM), H., Medical Biology
ZORLU, A. F., Radiation Oncology

Faculty of Pharmacy:
ALTINÖZ SARİSOY, S., Analytical Chemistry
BALKAN (TAYHAN), A., Pharmaceutical Chemistry
BAŞARAN, A. A., Pharmacognosy
BAŞARAN (GÜNDÜZ), N., Pharmaceutical Toxicology
BAŞÇI, N., Analytical Chemistry
BİLGİN, A., Pharmaceutical Chemistry
ÇALIŞ, İ., Pharmacognosy
ÇALIŞ, Ü., Pharmaceutical Chemistry
ÇALIŞ, Y. S., Pharmaceutical Technology
ÇAPAN, Y., Pharmaceutical Technology
DALKARA, S., Pharmaceutical Chemistry
DEMİRDAMAR, S. R., Pharmacy
DEMİREZEN, L.O., Pharmacognosy
DEMİREZER, L. Ö., Pharmacognosy
ELDEM (ER), T., Pharmaceutical Biotechnology
ERDEMLİ(ŞAHİN), İ., Pharmaceutical Toxicology
ERDOĞAN, H., Pharmaceutical Chemistry
ERSÖZ, T., Pharmacognosy
ERTAN, M., Pharmaceutical Chemistry
EZER, N., Pharmaceutical Botanics
HEKİMOĞLU (KONUR), S., Pharmaceutical Chemistry
HINCAL, A., Galenic Pharmacy
HINCAL, F., Pharmaceutical Toxicology
KIR (KOT), S., Analytical Chemistry

ÖNER, A. F., Pharmaceutical Chemistry
ÖNER, L., Pharmaceutical Chemistry
ÖZALTIN (LEBLEBİC), N., Analytical Chemistry
ÖZER, A. Y., Pharmaceutical Chemistry
ÖZER, İ., Biochemistry
ÖZGÜNES, H., Pharmaceutical Toxicology
PALASKA, E., Pharmaceutical Chemistry
PEKINER, C., Pharmacology
ŞAFAK, C., Pharmaceutical Toxicology
ŞAHIN, G., Pharmaceutical Toxicology
ŞAKAR, M. K., Pharmaceutical Chemistry
SARAÇ, S., Pharmaceutical Chemistry
SARAÇOĞLU, İ., Pharmacognosy
ŞENEL, S., Pharmaceutical Technology
SÜMER (İLKİZ), N. A., Biochemistry
ŞUMLU, M., Pharmaceutical Technology
TEMİZER, A., Analytical Chemistry
UMA, S., Pharmaceutical Toxicology
ÜNLÜ (KARABABA), N., Pharmaceutical Technology
YEŞİADA, A., Pharmacy

Faculty of Science:
AKAY, M. T., Zoology
AKGÜN, A., Molecular Biology
AKSÖZ, E., Molecular Biology
AKSÖZ, N., General Biology
BALCIOĞLU, N., Organic Chemistry
BARLAS (EMIR), N., Zoology
BEKTAŞ, F. S., Analytical Chemistry
BOŞGELMEZ, A., Zoology
BOZCUK, A. N., Biology
BOZCUK, S., Biology
BROWN, L. M., Mathematics
ÇAĞATAY, N., Zoology
ÇAĞLAR, P., Analytical Chemistry
CANSUNAR, E., General Biology
CIHANGIR, N., Biotechnology
ÇİNGİ, H., Statistics
ÇIRAKOĞLU, Ç., Molecular Biology
DEMİREZEN, Ş., General Biology
DEMİRSOY, A., Zoology
DENİZLİ, A., Biochemistry
DIRIL, N., Molecular Biology
DOĞAN, M., Analytical Chemistry
DURUSOY, M., Molecular Biology
DÜZ, S. F., Chemistry
EKMEKÇİ, F. G., Hydrobiology
ERIK, S., Botany
ERK, A. F., Hydrobiology
EŞ, A. H., Mathematics
ESENSOY, Ö., Statistics
GÖKOĞLU, E., Analytical Chemistry
GÜNAY, S., Statistics
GÜNDÜZ, E., Hydrobiology
GÜNER, A., Polymer and Theoretical Chemistry
GÜVEN, O., Physical Chemistry
HARMANCI, A., Mathematics
İMAMOĞLU, Y., Analytical Chemistry
İNAL, C., Statistics
KALAYCIOĞLU, A., Molecular Biology
KARAN (ZÜMREOĞLU), B., Inorganic Chemistry
KAZANCI, N., Hydrobiology
KESKIN (ELDEM), N., Applied Biology
KILBARER, A. G., Physical Chemistry
KIŞ, M., Physical Chemistry
KOLANKAYA, D., Zoology
KOLANKAYA, N., General Biology
OKAY, G., Organic Chemistry
ORAL (HOCAOĞLU), G., Statistics
ÖNER, C., Molecular Biology
ÖNER (ÖZDÖNMEZ), R., Biotechnology
ÖZÇAĞ, E., Mathematics
PEKMEZ, K., Analytical Chemistry
PEKMEZ (ÖZÇIÇEK), N., Analytical Chemistry
RZAYEV, Z. M. O., Chemistry
SALİH, B., Physical Chemistry
ŞENEL (UYANİK), S., Physical Chemistry
ŞOLTANOV, K. N., Mathematics
SORKUN, K., Applied Biology
SÖZER, T., Statistics
TATLIDİL, H., Statistics

TERCAN, A., Algebra and Theory of Numbers
TERZİOĞLU, S., Botany
TIRAŞ, Y., Algebra and Theory of Numbers
TOKTAMIŞ, Ö., Statistics
TÜMER, M. A., General Biology
TÜNOĞLU, N., Organic Chemistry
ÜNALEROĞLU, C., Organic Chemistry
ÜNLÜ, H., General Biology
YALVAÇ, T., Mathematics, Geometry and Topology
YERLİ, S. V., Hydrobiology
YILDIRIMLI, Ş., Botany
YILDIZ, A., Analytical Chemistry

HALİÇ ÜNİVERSİTESİ
(Haliç University)

Büyükdere Cad. 101, 34394 Mecidiyeköy, Istanbul

Telephone: (212) 275-20-20
Fax: (212) 274-81-22
E-mail: info@halic.edu.tr
Internet: www.halic.edu.tr

Founded 1998

Pres.: Prof. Dr GÜNDÜZ GEDİKOĞLU

Library of 11,000 vols
Number of teachers: 200
Number of students: 1,200

Faculties of arts and science, business administration, engineering and medicine.

HARRAN ÜNİVERSİTESİ

Sanlıurfa

Telephone: (414) 312-84-56
Fax: (414) 312-81-44
E-mail: rektor@harran.edu.tr
Internet: www.harran.edu.tr

Founded 1992
State control

President: Prof. Dr UGUR BUYUKBURC
Vice-Presidents: Prof. Dr URAL DINÇ, Prof. Dr I. HALIL MUTLU, Prof. Dr SELCUK YUCESAN

Number of teachers: 794
Number of students: 5,900

DEANS

Faculty of Agriculture: Prof. Dr MEHMET AKTAS
Faculty of Arts and Sciences: Prof. Dr GÖKSENIN ESELLER
Faculty of Economics: Prof. Dr MUSTAFA PIRILI
Faculty of Engineering: Prof. Dr BILGE ERDILLER
Faculty of Medicine: Prof. Dr SELCUK YUCESAN
Faculty of Theology: Prof. Dr IBRAHIM DUZEN
Faculty of Veterinary Sciences: Prof. Dr NAFIZ YURDAYDIN

DIRECTORS

Institute of Health Sciences: Prof. Dr A. ZIYA KARAKILCIK
Institute of Natural Sciences: Prof. Dr İBRAHIM BOLAT
Institute of Social Sciences: Prof. Dr ZUHAL KARAHAN KARA

İNÖNÜ ÜNİVERSİTESİ

Elazığ Yolu 15. km, 44280 Malatya

Telephone: (422) 341-00-28
Fax: (422) 341-00-34
E-mail: rektor@inonu.edu.tr
Internet: www.inonu.edu.tr

Founded 1975
State control
Language of instruction: Turkish (English in Faculty of Medicine)
Academic year: October to July

Rector: Prof. Dr FATIH HİLMİOĞLU

Vice-Rectors: Prof. Dr SADİK KELEŞ, Prof. Dr MUSTAFA KILIÇ, Prof. Dr HASAN KÜÇÜKBAY
Sec.-Gen.: REŞAT ÖZKAN
Librarian: NEZIHA ÜSTÜNER
Number of teachers: 2,112
Number of students: 19,137

DEANS

Adıyaman Faculty of Science and Literature: Prof. Dr ENGIN ŞENER
Faculty of Economics and Administrative Sciences: Prof. Dr MUSTAFA KILIÇ
Faculty of Education: Prof. Dr K. BÜLENT BIROL
Faculty of Engineering: Prof. Dr MUSA SARIKAYA
Faculty of Fine Arts: (vacant)
Faculty of Medicine: Prof. Dr ÖZCAN ERSOY
Faculty of Pharmacy: Prof. Dr ENGIN ŞARER
Faculty of Religious Studies: Prof. Dr ASLAN AKSOY
Faculty of Science and Literature: Prof. Dr ÖZFER YEŞILADA

DIRECTORS

Institute of Health Sciences: Asst Prof. Dr TAYFUN GÜLDÜR
Institute of Science: Asst Prof. Dr ALI ŞAHİN
Institute of Social Sciences: Prof. Dr KEMAL KARTAL

IŞIK ÜNİVERSİTESİ

Kumbaba Mevkii, 34980 Sile, Istanbul
Telephone: (216) 528-70-45
Fax: (216) 712-14-68
E-mail: isikun@isikun.edu.tr
Internet: www.isikun.edu.tr
Founded 1885, present status 1996
Private control
Academic year: October to June

Pres.: Prof. Dr NAFIYE GÜNEÇ KIYAK

DEANS

Faculty of Arts and Sciences: Prof. Dr SABRI ARIK
Faculty of Economics and Administrative Sciences: Prof. Dr MEHMET KAYTAZ
Faculty of Engineering: Prof. YORGO İSTEFANOPULOS
Institute of Science and Engineering: Prof. Dr MUSTAFA KARAMAN
Institute of Social Sciences: Prof. Dr MURAT FERMAN

İSTANBUL ÜNİVERSİTESİ

Beyazıt, 34052 Istanbul
Telephone: (212) 440-00-00
Fax: (212) 440-00-10
E-mail: postmaster@istanbul.edu.tr
Internet: www.istanbul.edu.tr
Founded 1453, reorganized 1933
State control
Languages of instruction: Turkish, English
Academic year: October to February, March to July

Rector: Prof. Dr MESUT PARLAK
Vice-Rectors: Prof. Dr TAYLAN AKKAYAN, Prof. Dr OSMAN ÖZDEMIR, Prof. Dr NUR SERTER
Admin. Officer: NURETTIN ERDEM

Number of teachers and assistants: 5,000
Number of students: 49,000

DEANS

Faculty of Communication: Prof. Dr SUAT GEZGIN
Faculty of Dentistry: Prof. Dr BETÜL TUNCELLI
Faculty of Economics: Prof. Dr MITHAT ZEKI DINÇER
Faculty of Engineering: Prof. Dr CUMA BAYAT
Faculty of Fisheries and Aquatic Science: Prof. Dr MEHMET SALIH ÇELIKKALE

Faculty of Forestry: Prof. Dr BÜLENT SEÇKIN
Faculty of Law: Prof. Dr TANKUT CENTEL
Faculty of Letters: Prof. Dr TANER TARHAN
Faculty of Management: Prof. Dr HAYRI ÜLGEN
Faculty of Medicine: Prof. Dr FARUK ERZENGIN
Faculty of Medicine (Cerrahpaşa): Prof. Dr FIKRET SIPAHIOĞLU
Faculty of Pharmacy: Prof. Dr AYSEL GÜRSOY
Faculty of Political Science: Prof. Dr FERYAL ORHON BASIK
Faculty of Science: Prof. Dr NURETTİN MERIÇ
Faculty of Theology: Prof. Dr EMRULLAH YÜKSEL
Faculty of Veterinary Science: Prof. Dr AHMET ALTINEL

İSTANBUL BİLGİ ÜNİVERSİTESİ
(Istanbul Bilgi University)

İnönü Cad. 28, Kuştepe, 34387 Şişli, Istanbul
Telephone: (212) 311-50-00
Fax: (212) 216-24-00
E-mail: bilgi@bilgi.edu.tr
Internet: www.bilgi.edu.tr
Founded 1994, as Istanbul School of International Studies; present name and status 1996
Private control
Language of instruction: English
Academic year: October to July

Rector: Prof. Dr HALIL GÜVEN
Vice-Rector: Prof. Dr REMZI SANVER
Sec.-Gen.: ÇAĞRI BAĞCIOĞLU
Registrar: MICHEL PAUS
Library of 68,000 vols
Number of teachers: 574
Number of students: 8,640
Publications: Bilgi Bellek, Foreign Policy (6 a year)

DEANS

European Institute: Prof. Dr AYHAN KAYA
Faculty of Architecture: Prof. Dr İHSAN BILGIN
Faculty of Arts and Sciences: Prof. Dr DIANE SUNAR
Faculty of Communication: Prof. Dr HALIL NALÇAOĞLU
Faculty of Economics and Administrative Sciences: Dr EGE YAZGAN
Faculty of Engineering: Prof. Dr LALE DURUIZ
Faculty of Law: Prof. Dr TURGUT TARHANLI
Institute of Natural and Applied Sciences (Graduate School): Prof. Dr DOĞAN GÜNEŞ
Social Science Institute (Graduate School): Dr GÖKSEL AŞAN

İSTANBUL KÜLTÜR ÜNİVERSİTESİ

E5 Karayolu Üzeri, 22 Ataköy Metro Istasyonu Karsısı, Sirinevler, 34510 Istanbul
Telephone: (212) 639-30-24
Fax: (212) 551-11-89
E-mail: kultur@iku.edu.tr
Internet: www.iku.edu.tr
Founded 1997
Private control
Languages of instruction: Turkish, English
Academic year: October to May

Rector: Prof. Dr DURSUN KOÇER
Vice-Rectors: Prof. Dr GETIN BOLCAL, Prof. Dr TAMER KOÇEL
Registrar: Asst Prof. Dr METIN BOLCAL
Library of 6,800 books
Number of teachers: 114
Number of students: 2,109 (2,064 undergraduate, 45 postgraduate)
Publication: Journal (4 a year)

DEANS

Faculty of Arts: Prof. Dr NÜKET GÜZ

Faculty of Business Administration: Prof. Dr TAMER KOÇEL
Faculty of Engineering and Architecture: Prof. Dr OKAY EROSKAY
Faculty of Law: Prof. Dr TAYFUN AKGÜNER
Faculty of Science and Letters: Prof. Dr LATIF TOPAKTAŞ
Vocational School: Prof. Dr TANER BULAT

İSTANBUL TEKNİK ÜNİVERSİTESİ

Ayazağa Kampüsü, 34469 Istanbul
Telephone: (212) 285-30-30
Fax: (212) 285-29-10
E-mail: karadogan@itu.edu.tr
Internet: www.itu.edu.tr
Founded 1773
State control
Languages of instruction: Turkish, English
Academic year: October to July (two semesters)

Rector: Prof. FARUK KARUDOGAN
Vice-Rectors: Prof. A. FUAT ANDAY, Prof. HALUK KARADOĞAN, Prof. S. ERKIN NASUF
Provost: NEVZAT ÖZKÖK
Librarian: AYHAN KAYGUSUZ
Library: see Libraries and Archives
Number of teachers: 1,861
Number of students: 17,500
Publications: ARI (physical and engineering sciences, 4 a year), Catalog (every 2 years), ITU'den Haberler (4 a year)

DEANS

Faculty of Aeronautics and Astronautics: Prof. FEVZI ÜNAL
Faculty of Architecture: Prof. CENGIZ GIRITLIOĞLU
Faculty of Chemical and Metallurgical Engineering: Prof. HASAN CAN OKUTAN
Faculty of Civil Engineering: Prof. DERIN ORHON
Faculty of Electrical and Electronic Engineering: Prof. HAKAN KUNTMAN
Faculty of Management: Prof. AHMET FAHRI ÖZOK
Faculty of Mechanical Engineering: Prof. TANER DERBENTLI
Faculty of Mines: Prof. MAHIR VARDAR
Faculty of Naval Architecture and Ocean Engineering: Prof. ÖMER GÖREN
Faculty of Science and Letters: Prof. FIGEN KADIRGAN (Deputy)
Faculty of Textile Technologies and Design: Prof. BÜLENT ÖZIPEK
Maritime Faculty: Prof. SAMI AYDIN ŞALCI
Turkish Music Conservatory: Prof. CAN ETILI ÖKTEM

ATTACHED CONSERVATORY AND DEPARTMENTS

Department of Fine Arts: Dir AYLA ÖDEKAN.

Department of Languages and History: Dir ÖNER GÜNÇAVDI.

Department of Physical Education and Sports: Dir EMIN TACER.

Turkish Music Conservatory: Dir CAN ETILI ÖKTEM.

ATTACHED GRADUATE INSTITUTES

Institute of Energy: Dir HASAN SAYGIN.

Institute of Eurasia Earth Sciences: Dir OKAN TÜYSÜZ.

Institute of Informatics: Dir NÜZHET DALFES.

Institute of Science and Technology: Dir MEHMET KARACA.

Institute of Social Sciences: Dir NURAN ZEREN GÜLERSOY.

İSTANBUL TİCARET ÜNİVERSİTESİ
(Istanbul Commerce University)

Ragıp Gümüşpala Cad. 84, 34378 Eminönü, Istanbul

Telephone: (212) 511-41-50
Fax: (212) 553-94-22
E-mail: rektorluk@iticu.edu.tr
Internet: www.iticu.edu.tr
Academic year: September to August

Pres.: Prof. Dr NAZIM EKREN
Library Dir: YASIN DEMIRBAŞ

Library of 40,000 vols
Number of teachers: 250
Number of students: 5,000

DEANS

Faculty of Commercial Science: Prof. Dr AHMET KARA
Faculty of Communications: Prof. Dr CUNEYT BINATLI
Faculty of Engineering: Prof. Dr OĞUZ BORAT
Faculty of Law: Prof. Dr MUSTAFA ERDOĞAN
Faculty of Science: Prof. Dr EKREM SAVAS

İZMİR EKONOMI ÜNİİVERSITESİ
(Izmir University of Economics)

Sakarya Caddesi 156, 35330 Balçova, İzmir

Telephone: (232) 279-25-25
Fax: (232) 279-26-26
E-mail: oia@ieu.edu.tr
Internet: www.ieu.edu.tr
Founded 2001
Private control
Language of instruction: English
Academic year: September to June

Rector: Prof. Dr ATTILA SEZGİN
Vice-Rector: Prof. Dr M. CEMALI DİNÇER
Vice-Rector: Prof. Dr OĞUZ ESEN
Vice-Rector: Prof. Dr TUNÇDAN BALTACIOĞLU
Provost: Prof. Dr M. CEMALI DİNÇER
Sec.-Gen: LEVENT GÖKÇEER
Dean of Students: MINE KAYICAN
Librarian: ALI TUTAL

Number of teachers: 440
Number of students: 6,206

DEANS

Faculty of Arts and Sciences: Prof. Dr İSMIHAN BAYRAMOĞLU
Faculty of Communication: Prof. Dr SEVDA ALANKUŞ
Faculty of Economics and Administrative Sciences: Prof. Dr ALEV KATRINLI
Faculty of Engineering and Computer Science: Prof. Dr TURHAN TUNALI
Faculty of Fine Arts and Design: Prof. Dr TEVFIK BALCIOĞLU

İZMİR YÜKSEK TEKNOLOJİ ENSTİTÜSÜ
(Izmir Institute of Technology)

Gülbahçe Köyü, 35430 Urla, İzmir

Telephone: (232) 750-60-01
Fax: (232) 750-60-15
E-mail: semraulku@iyte.edu.tr
Internet: www.iyte.edu.tr
Founded 1992
State control
Languages of instruction: Turkish, English
Academic year: October to June

Rector: Prof. Dr SEMRA ÜLKÜ
Vice-Rectors: Prof. Dr CEMAL ARKON, Prof. Dr RECAI ERDEM
Librarian: GULIZAR USLU

Library of 21,492 books, 96 periodicals, 6,443 online scientific periodicals
Number of teachers: 423
Number of students: 1,733 (1,203 undergraduate, 530 postgraduate)

DEANS

Faculty of Architecture: Prof. Dr CEMAL ARKON
Faculty of Engineering: Prof. Dr MUHSIN ÇIFTIÇOGLU
Faculty of Science: Prof. Dr SEMRA ÜLKÜ
Graduate School of Engineering and Sciences: Assoc. Prof. SEMAHAT ÖZDEMIR

KADİR HAS ÜNİVERSİTESİ

Cibali Merkez Kampüsü, Hisarattı Cad., 34230-01 Cibali-Fatih, Istanbul

Telephone: (212) 533-65-32
Fax: (212) 533-65-15
E-mail: info@khas.edu.tr
Internet: www.khas.edu.tr
Founded 1997
Private control
Languages of instruction: Turkish, English
Academic year: October to June

Pres.: Prof. Dr YÜCEL YILMAZ
Vice-Pres.: Prof. Dr NÜKHET TAN
Gen. Sec.: Dr AHMET B. SÖĞÜTLÜOĞLU
Registrar: SELMA DÖNMEZ
Head Librarian: ERTUĞRUL ÇIMEN

Library of 13,857 vols
Number of teachers: 142
Number of students: 1,500

DEANS

Faculty of Arts and Sciences: Prof. Dr KEMAL YELEKÇI
Faculty of Communications: Prof. Dr DENIZ BAYRAKDAR SEVGEN
Faculty of Economics and Business Administration: Prof. Dr EROL ÜÇDAL
Faculty of Engineering: Prof. Dr TUNCAY SAYDAM
Faculty of Fine Arts: Prof. Dr FATMA OYA BOYLA (acting)
Faculty of Law: Prof. Dr SELÇUK ÖZTEK

KAFKAS ÜNİVERSİTESİ

Rektörlüğü, Pasacayiri Mh., 36040 Kars

Telephone: (474) 242-68-00
Fax: (474) 242-68-47
E-mail: bidab@kafkas.edu.tr
Internet: www.kafkas.edu.tr
Founded 1992
State control

Rector: Prof. Dr NECATI KAYA

Number of teachers: 481
Number of students: 10,000

Publications: University Bulletin (1 a year), University Gazette (4 a year).

KAHRAMANMARAŞ SÜTÇÜ IMAM ÜNİVERSİTESİ

KSÜ Rektörlüğü, Avşar Kampüsü, 46100 Kahramanmaraş

Telephone: (344) 219-10-00
Fax: (344) 219-10-12
E-mail: baytorun@ksu.edu.tr
Internet: www.ksu.edu.tr
Founded 1992
State control
Academic year: October to June

Rector: Prof. Dr A. NAFI BAYTORUN
Vice-Rectors: Prof. Dr ORHAN DOĞAN, Prof. Dr CAFER MART, Prof. Dr CEMAL TUNCER
Sec.-Gen.: RÜŞTÜ ERTUĞRUL
Librarian: ŞEREF AKBEN

Library of 25,000 books and periodicals
Number of teachers: 700
Number of students: 11,000

DEANS

Faculty of Agriculture: Prof. Dr ERFAN EFE

Faculty of Economics and Administrative Sciences: Prof. Dr AHMET HAMDI AYDIN
Faculty of Education: Prof. Dr ADNAN KÜÇÜKÖNDER
Faculty of Engineering and Architecture: Prof. Dr MEHMET NURI BODUR
Faculty of Forestry: Prof. Dr ORHAN ERDAŞ
Faculty of Medicine: Prof. Dr İLHAMI TANER KALE
Faculty of Sciences and Literature: Prof. Dr ALI DOĞAN
Faculty of Theology: Prof. Dr M. KAMAL ATİK

KARADENİZ TEKNİK ÜNİVERSİTESİ
(Karadeniz Technical University)

61080 Trabzon

Telephone: (462) 377-30-00
Fax: (462) 325-32-05
E-mail: head@ktu.edu.tr
Internet: www.ktu.edu.tr
Founded 1955
State control
Languages of instruction: Turkish, English
Academic year: October to August

Rector: Prof. Dr İBRAHIM ÖZEN
Vice-Rectors: Prof. Dr SELAHATTIN KÖSE, Prof. Dr NECATI TÜYSÜZ, Prof. Dr ORHAN AYDIN
Gen. Sec.: Assoc. Prof. CÜNEYT ŞEN
Librarian: Prof. Dr MEHMET ARSLAN

Library of 220,000 vols
Number of teachers: 1,568
Number of students: 38,000

Publications: KTÜ Bu Hafta (univ. news bulletin, 48 a year), KTÜ Bülteni (bulletin, 2 a year), KTÜ Education Activities (1 a year)

DEANS

Faculty of Agriculture (Ordu): Prof. Dr Y. NURETTIN İSMAILÇELEBIOĞLU
Faculty of Architecture: Prof. Dr AYŞE SAĞSÖZ
Faculty of Arts and Sciences (Rize): Prof. Dr NAZMI TURAN OKUMUŞOĞLU
Faculty of Communication: Prof. Dr MUSTAFA EMIR
Faculty of Dentistry: Prof. Dr MEHMET TOSUN
Faculty of Economics and Administrative Sciences: Prof. Dr KAMIL YAZICI
Faculty of Economics and Administrative Sciences (Giresun): Prof. Dr METIN BERBER
Faculty of Education (Artvin): Prof. Dr OKTAY TORUL
Faculty of Education (Fatih): Prof. Dr ALIPAŞA AYAS
Faculty of Education (Giresun): Prof. Dr MEHMET TÜFEKÇI
Faculty of Education (Rize): Prof. Dr MEHMET AKBAŞ
Faculty of Engineering: Prof. Dr MUSTAFA AYTEKIN
Faculty of Engineering (Gümüşhane): Prof. Dr FIKRI BULUT
Faculty of Fine Arts: Prof. Dr MUSTAFA KANDİL
Faculty of Forestry: Prof. Dr ZAFER CEMAL ÖZKAN
Faculty of Law: Prof. Dr OSMAN PEHLIVAN
Faculty of Marine Sciences: Prof. Dr İBRAHIM OKUMUŞ
Faculty of Marine Sciences (Sürmene): Prof. Dr ERTUĞ DÜZGÜNEŞ
Faculty of Medicine: Prof. Dr SÜLEYMAN BAYKAL
Faculty of Pharmaceutical Sciences: Prof. Dr RASIN ÖZYAVUZ
Faculty of Science and Literature: Prof. Dr KENAN İNAN
Faculty of Science and Literature (Giresun): Prof. Dr ZIYA YAPAR
Faculty of Technology: Prof. Dr KENAN GELİŞİ

Faculty of Theology: Prof. Dr S. KEMAL SANDIKÇI

PROFESSORS

Faculty of Agriculture (Ordu) (Ordu; tel. (452) 225-05-77; fax (452) 225-12-61; e-mail ziraat@ktu.edu.tr):

İSMAİLÇELEBİOĞLU, Y. N., Soil Science
ŞILBIR, Y., Field Crops

Faculty of Architecture (Kanuni Kampüsü, 61080 Trabzon; tel. (462) 377-26-70; fax (462) 325-55-88):

ÇEVIK, S., Architecture
GÜR, Ş., Architecture
KANDIL, M., Architecture
PEHLEVAN, A., Architecture
SAĞSÖZ, A., Architecture
USTA, G., Architecture
YAŞAR, Y., Architecture

Faculty of Arts and Sciences (Giresun) (Gazi Cad. Kışla Hamam Sok., Giresun; tel. (454) 216-25-20; fax (454) 216-45-18):

YANMAZ, E., Physics

Faculty of Arts and Sciences (Rize) (Engindere Mah., Köy Hizmetleri Yanı, 53100 Rize; tel. (464) 223-53-75; fax (464) 223-53-76):

OKUMUŞOĞLU, N. T., Physics

Faculty of Economics and Administrative Sciences (Kanuni Kampüsü, 61080 Trabzon; tel. (462) 325-32-12; fax (462) 325-72-81; e-mail iibf@ktu.edu.tr):

ACUNER, T., Business Administration
AKSAR, Y., International Relations
AKTAŞ, H., International Relations
AKYAZI, H., Economics
ARAFAT, M., International Relations
BOCUTOĞLU, E., Economics
ÇELIK, K., Economics
ÇIFTÇI, O., Labour Economics and Industrial Relations
ÇIKRIKÇI, M., Management
DAĞLI, H., Business Administration
EMIR, M., Business Administration
KARAMUSTAFA, O., Business Administration
KESIM, A., Economics
KOÇER, G., International Relations
KÜÇÜKKALE, Y., Economics
ÖZYURT, H., Economics
SÜRMEN, Y., Business Administration
TANDOĞAN, A., Economics
TERZI, H., Economics
TÜREDİ, H., Management
YAMAK, N., Economics
YAZICI, K., Business Administration
YAZICI, K., Management
ZENGIN, H., Econometrics

Faculty of Economics and Administrative Sciences (Giresun) (Giresun):

BERBER, M., Economics

Faculty of Education (Artvin) (Artvin):

TORUL, O., Chemistry

Faculty of Education (Fatih) (Söğütlü, Trabzon; tel. (462) 248-23-05; fax (462) 248-73-44):

AKDENIZ, A., Secondary Science and Mathematics Education
AYAS, A., Secondary Science and Mathematics Education
BAĞIROV, N., Fine Arts Education
BAKI, A., Secondary Science and Mathematics Education
ÇAPA, M., Secondary Social Science Education
ÇEPNI, S., Primary Education
KARANIS, N., Turkish Education
ŞAHIN, B., Secondary Science and Mathematics Education
SESLI, E., Secondary Science and Mathematics Education

Faculty of Education (Giresun) (Giresun; tel. (454) 215-53-72; fax (464) 215-53-75; e-mail gef@ktu.edu.tr):

TÜFEKÇI, M., Chemistry

Faculty of Education (Rize) (Rize; tel. (464) 532-67-92; fax (464) 532-86-12; e-mail ktu .cayeli@superonline.com):

TORUL, O., Chemistry

Faculty of Engineering (Gümüşhane) (Gümüşhane; tel. (456) 233-74-27; fax (456) 233-74-27):

BULUT, F., Geology
DURMUŞ, A., Civil Engineering
UZMAN, Ü., Civil Engineering

Faculty of Engineering (Kanuni Kampüsü, 61080 Trabzon; tel. (462) 325-31-72; fax (462) 325-74-05):

AKÇAY, M., Geological Engineering
AKPINAR, A., Electrical and Electronics Engineering
AKYOL, N., Geomatics Engineering
ALTAŞ, İ., Electrical and Electronics Engineering
ARICI, M., Mechanical Engineering
ARSLAN, F., Metallurgical and Materials Engineering
ARSLAN, M., Geological Engineering
AYDIN, O., Mechanical Engineering
AYTEKIN, M., Civil Engineering
AYVAZ, Y., Civil Engineering
BAYDAR, E., Mechanical Engineering
BAYRAKTAR, A., Civil Engineering
BEKTAŞ, O., Geological Engineering
BERKÜN, M., Civil Engineering
BILGIN, A., Mechanical Engineering
BIYIK, C., Geomatics Engineering
BIYIKLIOĞLU, A., Mechanical Engineering
BULUT, F., Geological Engineering
ÇAKIROĞLU, A.O., Civil Engineering
ÇAPKINOĞLU, Ş., Geological Engineering
ÇELIK, F., Civil Engineering
ÇUHADAROĞLU, B., Mechanical Engineering
DALOĞLU, A., Civil Engineering
DALOĞLU, A., Mechanical Engineering
DILAVER, A., Geomatics Engineering
DOĞAN, M., Mechanical Engineering
DUMANOĞLU, A., Civil Engineering
DURGUN, O., Mechanical Engineering
DURMUŞ, A., Civil Engineering
ERDOĞDU, Ş., Civil Engineering
ERDÖL, R., Civil Engineering
ERTAŞ, B., Civil Engineering
GELIŞLI, K., Geophysical Engineering
GENÇ, S., Geological Engineering
GÖKALP, E., Geomatics Engineering
GÜRÜNLÜ, C., Electrical and Electronics Engineering
HÜSEM, M., Civil Engineering
KARADENIZ, S., Mechanical Engineering
KARALI, C., Geomatics Engineering
KAYA, A., Geomatics Engineering
KESIMAL, A., Mining Engineering
KORKMAZ, S., Geological Engineering
NABIYEV, V., Computer Engineering
ÖNSOY, H., Civil Engineering
SADIKLAR, M., Geological Engineering
SAVAŞKAN, T., Mechanical Engineering
ŞEN, K., Geomatics Engineering
SOFUOĞLU, H., Mechanical Engineering
TÜYSÜZ, N., Geological Engineering
ÜNAL, A., Mechanical Engineering
UZMAN, Ü., Civil Engineering
UZUNER, B., Civil Engineering
YAZICI, R., Computer Engineering
YILMAZ, C., Geological Engineering
YÜKSEK, Ö., Civil Engineering

Faculty of Fine Arts (İnönü Cad. 53, 61300 Akçaabat, Trabzon; tel. (462) 228-12-02; fax (462) 228-12-83):

ALESKEROV, A., Painting

Faculty of Forestry (Kanuni Kampüsü, 61080 Trabzon; tel. (462) 377-28-28; fax (462) 325-74-99):

ACAR, C., Landscape Architecture
ACAR, H., Foresty Engineering
ALTUN, L., Foresty Engineering

AY, N., Forest Industrial Engineering
BAŞKENT, E., Foresty Engineering
BILGILI, E., Foresty Engineering
ÇOLAKOĞLU, G., Forest Industrial Engineering
DEMIRCI, A., Foresty Engineering
DEMIREL, Ö., Landscape Architecture
DENIZ, İ., Forest Industrial Engineering
EROĞLU, M., Foresty Engineering
GERÇEK, Z., Foresty Engineering
GÜMÜŞ, C., Foresty Engineering
KALAYCIOĞLU, H., Forest Industrial Engineering
KIRCI, H., Forest Industrial Engineering
KÖSE, S., Foresty Engineering
NEMLI, G., Forest Industrial Engineering
ÖZBILEN, A., Landspace Architecture
ÖZKAN, Z., Foresty Engineering
TERZIOĞLU, S., Foresty Engineering
TÜRKER, M., Foresty Engineering
TURNA, İ., Foresty Engineering
ÜÇLER, A., Foresty Engineering
USTA, M., Forest Industrial Engineering
YAHYAOĞLU, Z., Foresty Engineering
YAVUZ, H., Foresty Engineering
YILDIZ, Ü., Forest Industrial Engineering

Faculty of Marine Sciences (Sürmene) (Çamburnu, Trabzon; tel. (462) 752-28-05; fax (462) 752-21-58):

BORAN, H., Fisheries Technology Engineering
DINÇER, H., Fisheries Technology Engineering
KÖSE, H., Naval Architecture & Marine Engineering
DÜZGÜNEŞ, E., Fisheries Technology Engineering
KARAÇAM, H., Fisheries Technology Engineering
SEYHAN, H., Fisheries Technology Engineering

Faculty of Medicine (Kanuni Kampüsü, 61080 Trabzon; tel. (462) 377-54-05; fax (462) 325-22-70):

AĞAOĞLU, N., General Surgery
AK, İ., Psychiatry
AKGÜN, A., Physiology
AKYOL, N., Ophtalmology
ALHAN, E., General Surgery
ALIOĞLU, Z., Neurology
ARSLAN, M., General Surgery
ARSLAN, M., Internal Medicine
ASLAN, Y., Paediatrics
AYAR, A., Physiology
AYDIN, F., Internal Medicine
AYNACI, O., Orthopedics and Traumatology
BAHADIR, S., Dermatology
BAKI, A., Paediatrics
BAKI, C., Orthopedics and Traumatology
BAYKAL, S., Neurosurgery
BOZKAYA, H., Obstetrics and Gynaecology
ÇAN, G., Public Health
ÇALIK, A., General Surgery
ÇIMŞIT, G., Dermatology
ÇINEL, A., General Surgery
CIVELEK, A., Cardiovascular Surgery
DEĞER, O., Biochemistry
DILBER, E., Paediatrics
DINÇ, H., Radiodiagnostic
ERCEYES, H., Anaesthesiology and Reanimation
ERDURAN, E., Paediatrics
EREM, C., Internal Medicine
ERSÖZ, H., Internal Medicine
ERTÜRK, M., Microbiology
GEDIK, Y., Paediatrics
GÖKÇE, M., Cardiology
GÖR, A., Urology
GÜLER, M., Physical Medicine and Rehabilitation
GÜMELE, H., Radiodiagnostic
İMAMOĞLU, H., Ophtalmology
İMAMOĞLU, M., Otorhinolaryngology
IŞIK, A., Otorhinolaryngology
KALAYCIOĞLU, A., Anatomy

KALKAN, A., Infectious Diseases
KALYONCU, N., Pharmacology
KANDIL, S., Paediatric Psychiatry
KARAGÜZEL, A., Medical Biology
KARAHAN, S., Biochemistry
KEHA, E., Biochemistry
KÖKSAL, İ., Infectious Diseases
KUTLU, M., Cardiology
KUZEYLI, K., Neurosurgery
ODACI, E., Histology and Embriology
ÖKTEN, A., Paediatrics
OMAY, S., Internal Medicine
ÖNCÜ, M., General Surgery
ÖNDER, Ç., Orthopedics and Traumatology
ÖNDER, E., Biochemistry
ÖREM, A., Biochemistry
ORHAN, F., Paediatrics
OVALI, E., Internal Medicine
ÖZCAN, F., Cardiovascular Surgery
ÖZEN, İ., Anaesthesiology and Reanimation
ÖZGÜR, G., Urology
ÖZGÜR, O., Internal Medicine
ÖZLÜ, T., Chest Disease
ÖZMENOĞLU, M., Neurology
ÖZORAN, Y., Pathology
ÖZTÜRK, M., Radiodiagnostic
ÖZYAVUZ, R., Urology
REIS, A., Pathology
SARI, A., Radiodiagnostic
SARI, R., Internal Medicine
SARIHAN, H., Paediatric Surgery
SÖNMEZ, F., Paediatrics
TESTERECI, H., Biochemistry
TOSUN, M., Physical Medicine and Rehabilitation
TURGUTALP, H., Pathology
TURHAN, A., Orthopedics and Traumatology
ULUSOY, Ş., Internal Medicine
UZUN, D., Internal Medicine
VELIOĞLU, S., Neurology
YANDI, M., General Surgery
YARIŞ, E., Pharmacology
YENILMEZ, E., Histology and Embryology
YILDIZ, K., Pathology
YILDIZ, M., Orthopedics and Traumatology

Faculty of Science and Literature (Kanuni Kampüsü, 61080 Trabzon; tel. (462) 325-31-41; fax (462) 325-31-95):

ABBASOV, R., Chemistry
AHMET AYAZ, F., Biology
AKBAŞ, M., Mathematics
ALAADDIN YALÇINKAYA, M., History
ALTUNBAŞ, M., Physics
AYAZ, S., Biology
BEYAZOĞLU, O., Biology
ÇAVUŞ, A., Mathematics
ÇELEBI, S., Physics
ÇELIK, A., Turkish Language and Literature
ÇEVIK, U., Physics
ÇIÇEK, K., History
COŞKUN, E., Mathematics
DEMIRBAĞLU, Z., Biology
DOĞAN, A., Turkish Language and Literature
HINTISTAN, S., Nursing
İHSAN KOBYA, A., Physics
İNAN, K., History
İSMAYILOV, Z., Mathematics
KADIOĞLU, A., Biology
KANTEKIN, H., Chemistry
KARABÖCEK, S., Chemistry
KARAL, H., Physics
KARSLIOĞLU, S., Chemistry
KAYGUSUZ, K., Chemistry
KEMAL KAYRA, O., Turkish Language and Literature
KHADJIEV, D., Mathematics
KÜÇÜKÖMEROĞLU, B., Physics
ÖKSÜZ, H., History
OSMAN BELDÜZ, A., Biology
ŞENTÜRK, H., Chemistry
SÖKMEN, A., Chemistry
SÖKMEN, M., Biology

TIRAŞOĞLU, E., Physics
TÜFEKÇI, M., Chemistry
ÜNVER, İ., Mathematics
YALÇINKAYA, M., History
YANMAZ, E., Physics
YAPAR, Z., Mathematics
YAYLI, N., Chemistry
YEREBAKAN, İ., English Language and Literature
YEŞILÇIÇEK ÇALIK, K., Midwifery
YILMAZ, S., Chemistry

Faculty of Theology (Rize) (Atatürk Cad., Piri Çelebi Mah., Rize; tel. (464) 214-11-20; fax (464) 214-11-24; e-mail ilahiyat@ktu.edu.tr):

SANDIKÇI, S. K., Islamic Education

Faculty of Water Resource Sciences (Rize) (İyidere, Rize; tel. (464) 223-52-39; fax (464) 223-41-18):

KADIOĞLU, A., Biology

GRADUATE SCHOOLS

Graduate School of Health Sciences: Dir Prof. Dr ORHAN DEĞER.
Graduate School of Natural and Applied Sciences: Dir Prof. Dr SALIH TERZIOĞLU.
Graduate School of Social Sciences: Dir Prof. Dr HAYDAR AKYAZI.

KIRIKKALE ÜNIVERSITESI

Ankara Karayolu 7 km, 71450 Kırıkkale
Telephone: (318) 357-36-44
Fax: (318) 357-36-94
E-mail: rektorluk@kku.edu.tr
Internet: www.kku.edu.tr
Founded 1992
State control
Academic year: October to July (two semesters)
Rector: Prof. Dr EKREM YILDIZ
Vice-Rector: Prof. Dr ADNAN KARAISMAILOGLU
Vice-Rector: Prof. Dr OSMAN CAGLAYAN
Librarian: AHMET ÖZKAN
Library of 63,000 vols, 87 periodicals
Number of teachers: 849
Number of students: 15,542

DEANS

Faculty of Dentistry: Prof. Dr ABDÜRRAHIM ŞENGÜN
Faculty of Economics and Administrative Sciences: Prof. Dr MUSTAFA ACAR
Faculty of Education: Prof. Dr MEHMET KUTLU
Faculty of Engineering: Prof. Dr VELI ÇELIK
Faculty of Fine Arts: Prof. Dr SALIH AKKAŞ
Faculty of Law: Prof. Dr ENVER BOZKURT
Faculty of Medicine: Prof. Dr MURAT KAÇMAZ
Faculty of Science and Letters: Prof. Dr MUSTAFA YIĞITOĞLU
Faculty of Veterinary Medicine: Prof. Dr ERTUĞUL ELMA
School of Physical Education and Sports: Asst Prof. Dr MEHMET ÖÇALAN

KOÇ UNIVERSITY

Rumelifeneri Yolu, 34450 Sarıyer, Istanbul
Telephone: (212) 338-10-00
E-mail: information@ku.edu.tr
Internet: www.ku.edu.tr
Founded 1993
Private control
Language of instruction: English
Academic year: September to June
Pres.: Prof. Dr UMRAN İNAN
Vice-Pres. for Academic Affairs: Prof. Dr SELÇUK KARABATI
Vice-Pres. for Research and Devt: Prof. Dr İRŞADI AKSUN
Gen. Sec.: MURAT HALIMOĞLU
Librarian: TUBA AKBAYTÜRK ÇANAK

Library of 211,779 vols
Number of teachers: 447
Number of students: 4,910

DEANS

College of Administrative Sciences and Economics: Prof. Dr BARIŞ TAN
College of Sciences: Prof. Dr ALPHAN SENNAROĞLU
College of Social Sciences and Humanities: Prof. Dr SAMI GÜLGÖZ
Law School: Prof. Dr BERTIL EMRAH ODER
School of Medicine: Prof. Dr ŞEVKET RUACAN

KOCAELI ÜNIVERSITESI

Umuttepe Yerleskesi, 41380 Umuttepe, Izmit/Kocaeli
Telephone: (262) 303-13-21
Fax: (262) 303-13-23
E-mail: kutuphane@kocaeli.edu.tr
Internet: www.kocaeli.edu.tr
Founded 1992
State control
Academic year: September to June
Rector: Prof. Dr SEZER SENER KOMSUOGLU
Vice-Rector for Academic Services: Prof. Dr AYSE SEVIM GOKALP
Vice-Rector for Admin. Services: Prof. Dr HASRET COMAK
Vice-Rector for Financial Services: Prof. Dr ARIF DEMIR
Chief Librarian: PERIHAN SEMERCI
Library of 80,000 vols incl. books, 100,627 e-books, 60 online databases, 39,816 e-journals
Number of teachers: 1,951
Number of students: 59,354
Publications: *Ilke Journal* (2 a year), *Journal of Applied Earth Sciences* (2 a year), *Journal of Social Sciences Institute* (2 a year), *Kocaeli University Communication Faculty Research Journal* (2 a year), *Kocaeli University Law Faculty Journal* (2 a year)

DEANS

Faculty of Architecture and Interior Design: Prof. Dr KAMURAN OZTEKIN
Faculty of Arts: Prof. Dr M. REŞAT BAŞAR
Faculty of Communication: Prof. Dr HASAN AKBULUT
Faculty of Dentistry: Prof. Dr ALI İHYA KARAMAN
Faculty of Economics: Prof. Dr ABDURRAHMAN FETTAHOGLU
Faculty of Education: Prof. Dr YUNUS KISHALI
Faculty of Engineering: Prof. ALPASLAN FIGLALI
Faculty of Law: Prof. Dr ZEHRA GONUL BALKIR
Faculty of Medicine: Prof. Dr ALI DEMIRCI
Faculty of Science: Prof. Dr HALIS AYGUN
Faculty of Technical Education: Prof. Dr MUSTAFA CANAKCI
Faculty of Technology: Prof. Dr MUSTAFA CANAKCI

MALTEPE ÜNIVERSITESI

Marmara Eğitim Köyü, 34857 Maltepe, Istanbul
Telephone: (216) 626-10-50
Fax: (216) 626-10-70
E-mail: maltepe@maltepe.edu.tr
Internet: www.maltepe.edu.tr
Founded 1997
State control
Languages of instruction: Turkish, English
Academic year: October to June
Rector: Prof. Dr MESUT RAZBONYAH
Librarians: NAZAN KARAKAŞ, BURCU ESENER, ARZU ACAR
Library of 17,230 vols, 531 periodicals
Number of teachers: 240

Number of students: 2,220

Publications: *Fen-Edebiyat Fakültesi Dergisi* (Science and Letters Faculty Journal, 2 a year), *Hukuk Fakültesi Dergisi* (Law Faculty Journal, 2 a year), *İktisadi ve İdari Bilimler Fakültesi Dergisi* (Economics and Business Administration Faculty Journal, 2 a year), *İletişim Fakültesi Dergisi* (Communication Faculty Journal, 2 a year)

DEANS

Faculty of Architecture: Prof. Dr ERKUT ÖZEL
Faculty of Communication: Prof. Dr SABRI ÖZAYDIN
Faculty of Economics and Business Administration: Prof. Dr ERTAN OKTAY
Faculty of Education: Prof. Dr İSA EŞME
Faculty of Engineering: Prof. Dr MESUT RAZBONYALI
Faculty of Law: Prof. Dr AYDIN AYBAY
Faculty of Medicine: Prof. Dr ŞEFİK GÜNEY
Faculty of Science and Letters: Prof. Dr MÜCELLA ULUĞ

MARMARA ÜNİVERSİTESİ

Göztepe Kampüsü Kadıköy, 34722 Istanbul
Telephone: (216) 414-05-45
Fax: (216) 346-20-96
Internet: www.marmara.edu.tr
Founded 1883, reorganized 1982
State control
Language of instruction: Arabic, English, French, German, Turkish
Academic year: September to July

Rector: Prof. Dr ZAFER GÜL
Deputy Rector: Prof.Dr HASAN SELÇUK
Deputy Rector: Prof. Dr HAMZA KANDUR
Deputy Rector: Prof. Dr M. EMIN ARAT
Sec.-Gen.: Dr MAHMUT DOĞAN
Librarian: SEVİNC KAZAZ

Library of 193,630 vols
Number of teachers: 2,775
Number of students: 68,213

Publications: *Argumentum, Din Eğitimi Araştırmaları Dergisi, Finansal Araştırmalar ve Çalışmalar Dergisi, İktisadi İdari bilimler Fakültesi Dergisi, Journal of Marmara University Dental Faculty, Marmara İletişim Dergisi, Marmara Medical Journal, Marmara'nın Sesi, Marmara Pharmaceutical Journal, Marmara sosyal Araştırmalar Dergisi, Marmara Üniversitesi Atatürk Eğitim Fakültesi Eğitim Bilimleri Dergisi, Marmara Üniversitesi Avrupa Topluluğu Enstitüsü Avrupa Araştırmaları Dergisi, Marmara Üniversitesi Bankacılık ve Sigortacılık Enstitüsü e-Dergisi, Marmara Üniversitesi Fen Bilimleri Dergisi, Marmara Üniversitesi Hukuk Fakültesi Hukuk Araştırmaları Dergisi, Marmara Üniversitesi İlahiyat Fakültesi Dergisi, Marmara Üniversitesi Sağlık bilimleri Enstitüsü Dergisi, Marmara Üniversitesi Tıp Fakültesi Dergisi, Öneri, Sanat-Tasarım Dergisi, Türklük Araştırmaları Dergisi*

DEANS

Atatürk Faculty of Education: Prof. Dr CEMIL ÖZTÜRK
Faculty of Arts and Sciences: Prof. Dr NIHAT ÖZTOPRAK
Faculty of Communication: Prof. Dr YUSUF DEVRAN
Faculty of Dentistry: Prof. Dr MAHIR GÜNDAY
Faculty of Economic and Administrative Sciences: Prof. Dr ERCAN GEGEZ
Faculty of Engineering: Prof. Dr ERTURUL TAÇGIN
Faculty of Fine Arts: Prof. Dr İNCİ DENIZ ILGIN
Faculty of Health Sciences: Prof. Dr GÜLDEN POLAT
Faculty of Law: Prof. Dr M. EMIN ARTUK

Faculty of Medicine: Prof. Dr HASAN FEVZI BATIREL
Faculty of Pharmacy: Prof. Dr GÜLDEN Z. OMURTAG
Faculty of Technical Education: Prof. Dr OSMAN KILIÇ
Faculty of Technology: Prof. Dr AHMET KORHAN BINARK
Faculty of Theology: Prof. Dr ALI KÖSE

MERSİN ÜNİVERSİTESİ

Çiftlik Köyü Kampüsü, 33343 Mersin
Telephone: (324) 361-00-22
Fax: (324) 361-00-15
E-mail: webadmin@mersin.edu.tr
Internet: www.mersin.edu.tr
Founded 1992
State control
Rector: Prof. Dr UĞUR ORAL
Librarian: HÜSEYIN GÖLALMIŞ
Number of teachers: 100
Number of students: 18,000

DEANS

Faculty of Architecture: Prof. Dr TAMER GÖK
Faculty of Communication: Prof. Dr SELIM AKSÖYEK
Faculty of Economics and Administrative Sciences: Prof. Dr TAYFUR ÖZŞEN
Faculty of Education: Prof. Dr ZAFER GÖKÇAKAN
Faculty of Engineering: Prof. Dr CEMIL CENGIZ ARCASOY
Faculty of Fine Arts: Prof. Dr E. BERIKA İPEKBAYRAK
Faculty of Fisheries: Prof. Dr GÜRKAN EKINGEN
Faculty of Medicine: Prof. Dr ESAT YILGÖR
Faculty of Pharmacy: Prof. Dr ATILLA YALÇIN
Faculty of Science and Letters: Prof. Dr AYHAN SEZER
Faculty of Technical Education (Tarsus): Prof. Dr ÖZDEN BAŞTÜRK

MİMAR SİNAN GÜZEL SANATLAR ÜNİVERSİTESİ
(Mimar Sinan Fine Arts University)

Fındıklı, 80040 Istanbul
Telephone: (212) 145-00-00
E-mail: ulik@msu.edu.tr
Internet: www.msu.edu.tr
Founded 1883, univ. status 1982
State control
Language of instruction: Turkish
Rector: Prof. Dr ÝSMET VILDAN ALPTEKIN
Chief Admin. Officer: ERDAL KÜPELI
Librarian: ASİYE ALAGÖZOĞLU

Library of 51,200 vols
Number of teachers: 420
Number of students: 3,509

DEANS

Faculty of Architecture: Prof. ÝLGI YÜCE AŞKÝN
Faculty of Fine Arts: Prof. RAHMI AKSUNGUR
Faculty of Sciences and Literature: Prof. Dr GÜLAY BAŞARÝR KÝROĞLU

MUĞLA ÜNİVERSİTESİ

48000 Mugla Üniversitesi Rektörlüğü, Kötekli Yerleşkesi, Muğla
Telephone: (252) 211-19-60
Fax: (252) 211-10-51
E-mail: intoffice@mu.edu.tr
Internet: www.mugla.edu.tr
Founded 1992; present status 2012
State control
Languages of instruction: English, Turkish
Academic year: September to June
Rector: Prof. Dr MANSUR HARMANDAR

Vice-Rector: Prof. Dr ALI OSMAN GÜNDOĞAN
Vice-Rector: MUSTAFA IŞILOĞLU
Vice-Rector: Prof. Dr YUSUF ZIYA ERDIL
Sec.-Gen.: Prof. Dr TUNCER ASUNAKUTLU

Library of 100,000 vols, 500 printed periodicals
Number of teachers: 1,034
Number of students: 26,405

DEANS

Faculty of Economics and Administrative Sciences: Prof. Dr TURGAY UZUN
Faculty of Education: Prof. Dr MUSTAFA VOLKAN COŞKUN
Faculty of Engineering: Prof. Dr TUĞRUL YILMAZ
Faculty of Fine Arts: Prof. Dr MUSTAFA VOLKAN COŞKUN (Deputy)
Faculty of Fisheries: Prof. Dr TAÇNUR BAYGAR
Faculty of Letters and Humanities: Prof. Dr PERVIN ÇAPAN
Faculty of Medicine: Prof. Dr İRFAN ALTUNTAŞ
Faculty of Science: Prof. Dr BEDRETTIN MERCIMEK
Faculty of Technical Education: Prof. Dr TUNCER ASUNAKUTLU
Faculty of Technology: Prof. Dr OSMAN GÖKTAŞ

MUSTAFA KEMAL UNIVERSITY

31040 Antakya, Hatay
Telephone and fax (326) 221-5815
E-mail: erasmus@mku.edu.tr
Internet: www.mku.edu.tr
Founded 1992
State control
Languages of instruction: English, Turkish
Academic year: September to July
Rector: Prof. Dr HÜSNÜ SALIH GÜDER
Vice-Rector: Prof. Dr ALI KOÇ
Vice-Rector: Prof. Dr MEHMET DALKIZ
Vice-Rector: Prof. Dr M. FATIH CAN

Number of teachers: 1,023
Number of students: 29,261

DEANS

Agriculture: Prof. Dr EMINE ÖZDEMIR
Economics and Administrative Sciences: Prof. Dr YAKUP BULUT
Engineering: Prof. Dr ERTUĞRUL BALTACIOĞLU
Fisheries: Prof. Dr AYŞE BAHAR YILMAZ
Veterinary Sciences: Prof. Dr SUAT ERDOĞAN

NİĞDE ÜNİVERSİTESİ

Niğde Üniversitesi Rektörlüğü, 51100 Niğde
Telephone: (388) 225-26-04
Fax: (388) 225-26-00
E-mail: ozelkalem@nigde.edu.tr
Internet: www.nigde.edu.tr
Founded 1992
State control
Academic year: September to June
Rector: Prof. Dr ADNAN GÖRÜR
Vice-Rectors: Prof. Dr MEHMET ŞENER
Vice-Rector: Prof. Dr MURAT ALP
Sec.-Gen.: Assoc. Prof. Dr MUSTAFA BAYRAK
Dir of the Library and Documentation Dept: MAZLUME VURAN

Library of 13,000 books, 100 periodicals
Number of teachers: 654
Number of students: 13,913 (13,136 undergraduate, 777 postgraduate)
Publications: *Natural Sciences, Social Sciences*

DEANS

Faculty of Arts and Science: MUSA ŞAŞMAZ
Faculty of Economics and Business Administration: ZEKI DOĞAN
Faculty of Education: MURAT ALP

Faculty of Engineering: SAIR KAHRAMAN
Faculty of Architecture: MEHMET ŞENER

OKAN ÜNİVERSİTESİ

Hasanpaşa Uzunçayır Cad. 6, Kadıköy, Istanbul
Telephone: (216) 325-48-18
Fax: (216) 339-61-36
E-mail: okan@okan.edu.tr
Internet: www.okan.edu.tr
Founded 2003
Rector: Prof. Dr SADIK KIRBAŞ
Vice-Rector: Prof. Dr CEVDET ÖĞÜT
Librarian: KENAN ÖZTOP
Number of students: 450

DEANS

Faculty of Arts and Sciences: Prof. Dr HASAN ÖZEKES
Faculty of Economics and Administrative Sciences: Prof. Dr SADIK KIRBAŞ
Faculty of Engineering: Asst Prof. Dr CEVDET ÖĞÜT

DIRECTORS

School of Computer Sciences and Tourism and Hotel Management: Prof. Dr ALI RIZA BÜYÜKUSLU
Social Institute: Asst Prof. Dr GONCA TELLI YAMAMOTO

ONDOKUZ MAYIS ÜNİVERSİTESİ
(Ondokuz Mayis University)

Kurupelit, 55139 Samsun
Telephone: (362) 312-19-19
Fax: (362) 457-60-91
E-mail: inter@omu.edu.tr
Internet: www.omu.edu.tr
Founded 1975
State control
Language of instruction: Turkish
Academic year: September to June
Rector: Prof. Dr HÜSEYIN AKAN
Vice-Rector: Prof. AHMET BULUT
Vice-Rector: FERŞAT KOLBAKIR
Vice-Rector: Prof. Dr SAIT BILGIÇ
Sec.-Gen.: Asst Prof. SELAHATTIN ÖZYURT
Registrar: NURİYE GÜRKANLI
Librarian: ÖMER BOZKURT

Number of teachers: 1,944
Number of students: 36,076

Publication: *Faculty Journals* (12 a year)

DEANS

Faculty of Aeronautics and Space Sciences: Prof. Dr ERDEM KOÇ
Faculty of Agriculture: Prof. Dr MEHMET KURAN
Faculty of Arts and Sciences: Prof. Dr ŞENOL EREN
Faculty of Communication: Prof. Dr ZEKERIYA ULUDAĞ
Faculty of Dentistry: Prof. Dr SELIM ARICI
Faculty of Economics and Administrative Sciences: Prof. Dr FATIH YÜKSEL
Faculty of Education: Prof. Dr CEVDET YIL-MAZ
Faculty of Engineering: Prof. Dr FEHMI YAZICI
Faculty of Law: Prof. Dr HAKAN HAKERI
Faculty of Medicine: Prof. Dr HAYDAR ŞAHI-NOĞLU
Faculty of Theology: Prof. Dr YAVUZ ÜNAL
Faculty of Veterinary Medicine: Prof. Dr MUSTAFA ALISARI

PROFESSORS

Faculty of Agriculture (Kurupelit 55139 Samsun; tel. (362) 457-60-86; fax (362) 457-60-34; e-mail iac-agric@omu.edu.tr; internet www.omu.edu.tr/a/en/academics/faculties/agriculture):

ACAR, Z., Agronomy
APAN, M., Agricultural Structures and Irrigation
BİLGENER, Ş., Horticulture
CİNEMRE, H. A., Agricultural Economics
DEMİR, Y., Agricultural Structures and Irrigation
ECEVİT, O., Plant Protection
ERENER, G., Feeds and Animal Nutrition
GÜLÜMSER, A., Agronomy
KEVSEROĞLU, K., Agronomy
KORKMAZ, A., Soil Science
KURAN, M., Agricultural Biotechnology
MEYDAN, M. A., Agricultural Machinery
MENNAN, H., Plant Protection
ODABAŞ, F., Horticulture
OKUMUS, A., Biometry-Genetics
ÖZCAN, M., Horticulture
ÖZDEMİR, N., Soil Science
ÖZTÜRK, T., Agricultural Structures and Irrigation
PINAR, Y., Agricultural Machinery
SARICA, M., Animal Science
SARIÇİÇEK, B. Z., Animal Science
TUNCER, C., Entomology
TUNALI, B., Phytopathology

Faculty of Arts and Sciences (Ordu) (Ordu Fen-Edebiyat Fakültesi, Perşembe, 52750 Ordu; tel. (452) 517-43-70; fax (452) 517-43-68; internet www.ome.edu.tr/akad/fklt/ordufen/index.html):

AKÇIN, Ö. E., Biology
EKİNCİ, İ., History
MAĞDEN, S., Mathematics
YAPAR, C., Mathematics

Faculty of Arts and Sciences (Samsun) (Kurupelit 55139 Samsun; tel. (362) 457-60-80; fax (362) 457-60-81; internet www.omu.edu.tr/a/en/academics/faculties/science-art):

AFŞIN, B., Chemistry
ALPASLAN, F., Statistics
BATI, B., Chemistry
BİÇER, ENDER, Physical Chemistry
BİLGENER, M., Biology
BÜYÜKGÜNGÖR, O., Physics
ÇALIŞKAN, M., Mathematics
ÇALIŞKAN, N., Physics
ÇELİK, F., Physics
DİNÇER, M., Physics
DEMİR, H., Applied Mathematics
EDİNSEL, K., Psychology
ERDÖNMEZ, A., Physics
EREN, Z., Biology
ERLER, M. Y., History
GÖNÜLOL, A., Biology
GÜLEL, A., Biology
GÜMRÜKÇÜOĞLU, İ. E., Chemistry
GÜMÜŞ, H., Physics
GÜRKANLI, A. T., Mathematics
İPEK, N., Born Modern
IŞILDAK, İ., Chemistry
KARACAN, T., Turkish
KARTAL, I., General Physics
KARTAL, V., Biology
KEFELİOĞLU, H., Biology
KILINÇ, M., Biology
KÖKSAL, F., Physics
KORKMAZ, H., Chemistry
KUTBAY, H. G., Biology
MENEK, N., Chemistry
NİŞANCI, A., Geography
OKUMUŞOĞLU, N. T., Physics
ÖLMEZ, H., Chemistry
ONAR, A. N., Chemistry
ÖZBALCI, M., Turkish
ÖZKANCA, R., Biology
ÖZKAPLAN, H., Physics
ÖZKOÇ, İ., Biology
PANCAR, A., Mathematics
POLAT, N., Biology
SAĞLIK, S., New Turkish Language
ŞENEL, G., Biology
ŞENEL, İ., Physics
TAPRAMAZ, R., Physics
TARAKÇI, C., Turkish

USTA, N., Sociology
UZUN, A., Physical Geography
YAVUZ, M., Physics
YILMAZ, M., Mathematics
YILMAZ, V. T., Chemistry
ZEYBEKOĞLU, Ü., Biology

Faculty of Arts and Sciences (Sinop) (Sinop Fen-Edebiyat Fakültesi, Sinop; tel. (368) 271-55-20; fax (368) 271-55-24; e-mail sinopfenedebiyat@yahoo.com; internet www.omu.edu.tr/akad/sinopfen):

ÇANKAYA, E., Statistics
DEMİRCİ, K., Mathematics
SIVACI, R., Biology

Faculty of Dentistry (Dişhekimliği Fakültesi, Kurupelit, 55139 Samsun; tel. (362) 457-60-30; fax (362) 457-60-32; e-mail dentistry@omu.edu.tr; internet www.omu.edu.tr/a/en/academics/faculties/dentistry/index.php):

AYDEMİR, H., Endodontics
AÇIKGÖZ, G., Periodontology
ALKAN, A., Oral and Maxillofacial Surgery
ÇELENK, P., Oral Diagnosis and Radiology
CEYLAN, G., Prosthodontics
KÖPRÜLÜ, H., Dental Diseases and Treatment
KOYUTÜRK, A. E., Pedodontics
TOLLER, M. Ö., Oral and Maxillofacial Surgery
TÜRK, T., Orthodontics

Faculty of Economics and Administrative Sciences (Samsun) (İktisadi ve İdari Bilimler Fakültesi, Kurupelit Kampüsü, 55139 Samsun; tel. (362) 312-19-19; fax (362) 457-60-17):

KÖKTAŞ, M. E., Political Science and Social Science
GÜZEL, H. A., Economics

Faculty of Economics and Administrative Sciences (Ünye) (Ünye İktisadi ve İdari Bilimler Fakültesi, Ünye; tel. (452) 323-86-96; fax (452) 323-82-56; e-mail gurolo@omu.edu.tr):

ÖZCÜRE, G., Economics

Faculty of Education (Amasya) (Amasya Eğitim Fakültesi, Amasya; tel. (358) 252-62-30; fax (358) 252-62-22; e-mail amasyaeg@omu.edu.tr; internet www.omu.edu.tr/akad/fklt/aegt/amsegtgiris.htm):

KARAMUSTAFAOĞLU, O., Computers and Teaching Technology
ORBAY, M., Primary Education
ÜSTÜN, A., Education
YİĞİT, M., Turkish
ZİYAGİL, M. A., Physical Education and Sport

Faculty of Education (Samsun) (Eğitim Fakültesi, Kurupelit, 55139 Samsun; tel. (362) 312 19 19; fax (362) 457 60 78; internet www.omu.edu.tr/a/en/academics/faculties/education):

AKBULUT, D. A., History
AYDIN, M., Turkish Language
BARUT, Y., Special Education
BAŞAR, E., Primary Education
BAYRAKTARKATAL, E., Music
BOLAT, H., Foreign Languages
ÇOLAK, M., Foreign Languages
ÇORUH, U., Computer Education and Educational Technology
DİNDAR, B., Education
ENGİN, A., Natural Sciences and Mathematics
ERSANLI, K., Education
KIRCI, M., Turkish
KOYUNCU, S., Fine Arts

Faculty of Education (Sinop) (Sinop Eğitim Fakültesi, Sinop; tel. (368) 271-55-35; fax (368) 271-55-30; e-mail sinopegit@omu.edu.tr; internet www.ome.edu.tr/akad/sinop-egt):

AYDIN, H., Computers and Teaching Technology
BAŞAR, E., Primary Education
BOSTANCI, B. A., Foreign Languages
MENTEŞE, S., Education
ÖZDEMIR, O., Primary Education

Faculty of Engineering (Kurupelit , 55139 Samsun; tel. (362) 457-60-36; fax (362) 457-60-35; e-mail onergun@omu.edu.tr; internet www.omu.edu.tr/a/en/academics/faculties/engineering):

BAYRAKLI, F., Environmental Engineering
BEKTAŞ, S., Geodesy and Photogrammetric Engineering
BÜYÜKGÜNGÖR, H., Environmental Engineering
ÇAKIRCIOĞLU, M., Civil Engineering
EFENDIYEV, Ç., Telecommunications
ELEVLI, B., Industrial Engineering
ERGUN, O. N., Environmental Engineering
HURŞIT, A., Food Engineering
KASIMZADE, A., Civil Engineering
KOCA, F., Food Engineering
ÖNBILGIN, G., Electrical and Electronic Engineering
TOPALOĞLU, B., Machine Engineering
ULUTAŞ, M., Computer Engineering

Faculty of Fisheries (Sinop) (Su Ürünleri Fakültesi, Akliman Kampüsü, 57000 Sinop; tel. (368) 287-62-62; fax (368) 287-62-55; internet www.omu.edu.tr/akad/fklt/ssu/anamenu.html):

BAT, L., Basic Fisheries Sciences
BIRCAN, R., Fish Breeding
BÜYÜKHATIPOĞLU, Ş., Fish Breeding
ERDEM, M., Fish Breeding
ERKOYUNCU, İ., Fishing and Fish Processing Technology
KALMA, M., Fish Breeding
SAMSUN, O., Fishing and Fish Processing Technology

Faculty of Medicine (Kurupelit 55139 Samsun; tel. (362) 457-60-70; fax (362) 457-60-41; internet www.omu.edu.tr/akad/fklt/tip/anamenu.htm):

ACAR, S., Paediatric Oncology
AĞAR, E., Physiology
AKAN, H., Radiodiagnostics
AKBAŞ, S., Child Psychiatry
AKPOLAT, İ., Pathology
AKPOLAT, M. T., Nephrology
ALBAYRAK, D., Paediatric Haematology
ALPER, T., Obstetrics and Gynaecology
ALVUR, M., Biochemistry
ANLAR, F. Y., Paediatrics
ARIK, A. C., Psychiatry
ARIK, N., Nephrology
ARITÜRK, E., Paediatric Surgery
AŞÇI, R., Urology
AYDIN, M., Paediatric Endocrinology
BAĞCI, H., Medical Biology
BAKIR, T., Gastroenterology
BARIŞ, S., Pathology
BAŞOĞLU, A., Thoracic Surgery
BAŞOĞLU, T., Nuclear Medicine
BAYSAL, M. K., Paediatrics
BEDIR, A., Biochemistry
BEK, Y., Bio-statistics
BERNAY, R. F., Paediatric Surgery
BILGIÇ, S., Anatomy
BIRINCI, , Ophthalmology
BÜYÜKALPELLI, R., Urology
CANTÜRK, F., Physical Medicine and Rehabilitation
CANTÜRK, T., Dermatology
ÇELIK, F., Neurosurgery
ÇELIK, S., Pharmacology
CENGIZ, K., Nephrology
ÇIFTÇI, N., Histology and Embryology
DABAK, N., Orthopaedics and Traumatology
DIKICI, M. F., Family Practice
DIREN, H. B., Radiodiagnostics
DURU, F., Paediatrics

DURUPINAR, B., Microbiology
ELBISTAN, M., Medical Biology
ERKAN, D., Ophthalmology
ERKAN, L., Thoracic Diseases
ERZURUMLU, K., General Surgery
GEPTIREMEN, A., Pharmacology
GÖKÇE, Ş. Ç., Radiation Oncology
GÜLDOĞUŞ, F., Anaesthesiology
GÜLMAN, B., Orthopaedics and Traumatology
GÜNAL, N., Paediatrics
GÜNAYDIN, M., Microbiology
GÜRMEN, N., Radiodiagnostics
GÜVEN, H., First Aid and Emergency Aid
İÇTEN, N., Anatomy
İNCESU, L., Radiodiagnostics
İŞLEK, İ., Paediatrics
İYIGÜN, Ö., Neurosurgery
KAHRAMAN, H., Endocrinology
KALAYCI, A. G., Paediatrics
KANDEMIR, B., Pathology
KAPLAN, S., Histology and Embryology
KARACALAR, A., Plastic and Reconstructive Surgery
KARAGÖZ, F., Pathology
KARAISMAILOĞLU, N., Orthopaedics and Traumatology
KEÇELIGIL, H. T., Cardiovascular Surgery
KESIM, M., General Surgery
KESIM, Y., Pharmacology
KOCAKAVAK, C., Cardiology
KÖKÇÜ, A., Obstetrics and Gynaecology
KOLBAKIR, F., Cardiovascular Surgery
KOPUZ, C., Anatomy
KORKMAZ, A., Histology and Embryology
KOYUNCU, M., Otorhinolaryngology
KÜÇÜKODÜK, Ş., Paediatrics
KURU, O., Physical Medicine and Rehabilitation
LEBLEBICIOĞLU, H., Clinical Bacteriology and Infectious Diseases
MALATYALIOĞLU, E., Obstetrics and Gynaecology
MALAZGIRT, Z., General Surgery
MARANGOZ, C., Physiology
ÖGE, İ., Ophthalmology
OĞUR, M. G., Paediatrics
ÖKTEN, G., Medical Biology
ONAR, M. K., Neurology
ÖZBENLI, T., Neurology
ÖZEN, N., General Surgery
ÖZKAN, K., General Surgery
ÖZTÜRK, F., Paediatrics
PEKŞEN, Y., Public Health
RAKUNT, C., Neurosurgery
RIZALAR, R., Paediatric Surgery
ŞAHIN, A. R., Psychiatry
ŞAHIN, M., Cardiology
ŞAHIN, M., Nuclear Medicine
ŞAHINOĞLU, H., Anaesthesiology
SANIÇ, A., Microbiology
SARIHASAN, B., Anaesthesiology and Reanimation
SARIKAYA, Ş., Urology
SELÇUK, M. B., Radiodiagnostics
ŞEŞEN, T., Otolaryngology
TANYERI, F., Internal Medicine (Endocrinology)
TANYERI, Y., Otorhinolaryngology
TAŞÇI, N., Physiology
TAŞDEMIR, H. A., Paediatrics
TEKAT, A., Otorhinolaryngology
TÜLEK, N., Clinical Bacteriology and Infectious Diseases
TUNALI, G., Neurology
TÜR, A., Anaesthesiology
TURANLI, A. Y., Dermatology
TÜRE, U., Neurosurgery
TURLA, A., Forensic Medicine
ULUSOY, A. N., General Surgery
ÜNAL, R., Otorhinolaryngology
ÜSTÜN, C., Obstetrics and Gynaecology
ÜSTÜN, F. E., Anaesthesiology
YEŞILDAĞ, O., Cardiology
YILMAZ, A. F., Urology
YILMAZ, Ö, Cardiology

YÜCEL, İ., Internal Medicine (Oncology)

Faculty of Theology (Kurupelit 55139 Samsun; tel. (362) 457-60-84; fax (362) 457-60-83; e-mail ilhdek@omu.edu.tr; internet www.omu.edu.tr/a/en/academics/faculties/divinity):

CAN, Y., Islamic History and Arts
DOĞAN, İ., Basic Islamic Sciences
GÜNER, O., Basic Islamic Sciences
KAYA, M., Teaching Ethics and Religious Culture in Primary Education
KOÇAK, M., Basic Islamic Sciences
KÖYLÜ, M., Philosophy and Religious Sciences
PEKER, H., Philosophy and Religion
TERZI, M. Z., Islamic History and Art
TURAN, A., Basic Islamic Sciences
YAZICI, İ., Basic Islamic Sciences
YETIK, E., Basic Islamic Sciences
ZÜMRÜT, O., Islamic History and Art

Faculty of Veterinary Medicine (Kurupelit, 55139 Samsun; tel. (362) (362) 312-19-19 ext. 2800; fax (362) (362) 4576922):

AKSOY, A., Pharmacology And Toxicology
ALISARLI, M., Food Hygiene and Technology
CELEBI, M., Reproduction And Artificial Insemination
FINDIK, M., Obstetrics And Gynecology
GULBAHAR, M. Y., Pathology
MUĞLALI, H., Animal Science and Animal Nutrition
UMUR, Ş., Parasitology
YURDUSEV, N., Microbiology

ORTA DOĞU TEKNIK ÜNIVERSITESI (Middle East Technical University)

İsmet İnönü Bulvarı, Ankara 06531
Telephone: (312) 210-20-00
Fax: (312) 210-11-05
E-mail: rektor@metu.edu.tr
Internet: www.metu.edu.tr

Founded 1956
State control
Languages of instruction: Turkish, English
Academic year: October to June (two semesters)

Pres.: Prof. Dr AHMET ACAR
Gen. Sec.: Prof. Dr TANJU MEHMETOĞLU (acting)
Registrar: NESRIN ÜNSAL
Librarian: CEVAT GÜVEN (acting)

Library: see Libraries and Archives
Number of teachers: 2,529
Number of students: 23,624

Publications: *METU Journal of Faculty of Architecture* (2 a year), *METU Journal of Human Sciences* (2 a year), *METU Studies in Development* (4 a year)

DEANS

Faculty of Architecture: Prof. Dr HALUK PAMIR
Faculty of Arts and Sciences: Prof. Dr CÜNEYT CAN
Faculty of Economic and Administrative Sciences: Prof. Dr YAŞAR EYÜP ÖZVEREN
Faculty of Education: Prof. Dr M. YAŞAR ÖZDEN
Faculty of Engineering: Prof. Dr ZAFER DURSUNKAYA

PROFESSORS

Faculty of Architecture (tel. (312) 210-22-01; fax (312) 210-11-08; e-mail facultyweb@arc.metu.edu.tr; internet www.arch.metu.edu.tr):

AKTÜRE, S., City and Regional Planning
BAKIRER, Ö., Architecture
BALAMIR, M., City and Regional Planning
ERAYDIN, A., City and Regional Planning
ERSOY, M., City and Regional Planning

ERZEN, J. A., Architecture
EVYAPAN, G., Architecture
GEDİK, A., City and Regional Planning
GÜVEN, S., Architecture
İMAMOĞLU, V., Architecture
PAMİR, H., Architecture
SALTIK, E., Architecture
TUNA, N., City and Regional Planning
TÜREL, A., City and Regional Planning
YAVUZ, A., Architecture
YAVUZ, Y., Architecture

Faculty of Arts and Sciences (tel. (312) 210-31-01; fax (312) 210-12-79; e-mail wwwfef@metu.edu.tr; internet www.fef.metu.edu.tr):

ADALI, O., Biology
AKBULUT, U., Chemistry
AKGÜN, S., History
AKINOĞLU, G. B., Physics
AKKAYA, E. U., Chemistry
AKKAYA, M., Chemistry
AKŞİT, B., Sociology
AKYILDIZ, E., Mathematics
ALPAY, Ş., Mathematics
ALYÜRÜK, K., Chemistry
ARAS, L., Chemistry
ARINÇ, E., Biology
ATAMAN, O. Y., Chemistry
AYATA, S., Sociology
AYDIN, R., Physics
AYGÜN, R. S., Chemistry
AYHAN, H. Ö., Statistics
AYTUNA, A., Mathematics
BALCI, M., Chemistry
BAYIN, S. Ş., Physics
BAYKAL, A., Physics
BAYRAMLI, E., Chemistry
BİLHAN, M., Mathematics
BİLİKMEN, K. S., Physics
CAN, C., Physics
ÇELEBİ, O., Mathematics
CEYLAN, Y., Philosophy
CİVELEK, F. R., Physics
DEMİR, A. S., Chemistry
DEMİRCİ, Ş., Chemistry
DOĞAN, M., Biology
ECEVİT, A., Physics
ECEVİT, M. C., Sociology
ECEVİT, Y., Sociology
ELLİALTIOĞLU, Ş., Physics
ERÇELEBİ, A. Ç., Physics
ERGÜDEN, A., Philosophy
ERKOÇ, Ş., Physics
ERTÜRK, Y., Sociology
GÖKALP, A., Physics
GÖKMEN, A., Chemistry
GÖKMEN, İ. G., Chemistry
GÖKTÜRK, E. H., Chemistry
GÜLEN, D., Physics
GÜNAL, İ., Physics
GÜNDÜZ, U., Biology
GÜRAY, T., Biology
HACALOĞLU, J., Chemistry
HASIRCI, N., Chemistry
HASIRCI, V. N., Biology
İLTAN, E. O., Physics
İMAMOĞLU, O., Psychology
İNAM, A., Philosophy
İSCAN, M., Biology
İŞÇİ, H., Chemistry
KARANCI, N. A., Psychology
KARASÖZEN, B., Mathematics
KARASU, A., Physics
KATIRCIOĞLU, B., Physics
KATIRCIOĞLU, Ş., Physics
KAYA, A., Mathematics
KAYA, Z., Biology
KAYRAN, H. C., Biology
KENCE, A., Biology
KILDIR, M., Chemistry
KIRBIYIK, H., Physics
KISAKÜREK, D., Chemistry
KIZILOĞLU, N., Physics
KIZILOĞLU, Ü., Physics
KOCABIYIK, S., Biology
KÜÇÜKYAVUZ, S., Chemistry

KÜÇÜKYAVUZ, Z., Chemistry
KUZUCUOĞLU, M., Mathematics
MUTLU, M. K., Sociology
MUTMAN, M., Sociology
NALBANTOĞLU, H. Ü., Sociology
NURLU, Z., Mathematics
ÖKTEM, H. A., Biology
ÖNAL, A. M., Chemistry
ÖNDER, T., Mathematics
ÖNSİPER, H., Mathematics
ÖZCENGİZ, G., Biology
ÖZDEMİR, S., Physics
ÖZKAN, H., Physics
ÖZKAN, İ., Chemistry
ÖZKAR, S., Chemistry
ÖZSAN, F. S., Physics
PAK, N. K., Physics
PEYNİRCİOĞLU, N. B., Chemistry
SAVCİ, M., Physics
SEVER, R., Physics
SEVERCAN, F., Biology
TALASLI, U., Psychology
TANYELİ, C., Chemistry
TARHAN, O., Chemistry
TAŞELİ, H., Mathematics
TATLI, A., Physics
TEZER, C., Mathematics
TEZER, M., Mathematics
TİNÇER, T., Chemistry
TOGAN, İ, Biology
TOGAN, İ, History
TOMAK, M., Physics
TOPPARE, L. K., Chemistry
TUNCEL, S., Chemistry
TURAN, G., Physics
TURAN, R., Physics
TÜRKER, L., Chemistry
ULA, A. T., Statistics
USANMAZ, A., Chemistry
UZUN, A., Statistics
VOLKAN, M., Chemistry
YILMAZ, O., Physics
YÜCEL, M., Biology
YURTSEVEN, H., Physics
ZAFER, A., Mathematics
ZEYREK, T. M., Physics

Faculty of Economic and Administrative Sciences (tel. (312) 210-11-07; fax (312) 210-11-07; e-mail feas@feas.metu.edu.tr; internet www.feas.metu.edu.tr):

ACAR, A., Management
ACAR, A. F., Political Sciences and Public Administration
AKDER, H., Economics
AKSOY, Ş., Political Sciences and Public Administration
AYATA, A., Political Sciences and Public Administration
BAĞCI, H., International Relations
BÖLÜKBAŞIOĞLU, S., International Relations
ÇAKMAK, E. H., Economics
DAĞI, D. İ., International Relations
ERALP, Y. A., International Relations
ERLAT, G., Economics
ERLAT, H., Economics
EROL, C., Management
GİTMEZ, A. S., Management
GÖKTAN, E., Management
KAYA, A. R., Political Sciences and Public Administration
MUĞAN, F. N. C., Management
ÖZUEREN, E., Economics
ŞENSES, F., Economics
TANSEL, A., Economics
TAYMAZ, E., Economics
TİLEYLİOĞLU, A., Management
TONAK, E., Economics

Faculty of Education (tel. (312) 210-40-01; fax (312) 210-11-12; e-mail top@metu.edu.tr; internet www.fedu.metu.edu.tr):

AKSU, M., Educational Sciences
ALPSAN, D., Science Education
AYDIN, A. G., Educational Sciences
BERBEROĞLU, G. H., Science Education

ÇİLELİ, M., Foreign Language Education
DEMİR, A. G., Educational Sciences
ENGİNARLAR, H., Foreign Language Education
ERTEPINAR, H., Science Education
GEBAN, Ö., Science Education
İÇÖZ, N., Foreign Language Education
KAŞ, A. D., Foreign Language Education
KÖNİG, W., Foreign Language Education
KORKUSUZ, F., Physical Education and Sports
ÖZDEN, Y., Computer Education and Instructional Technology
ŞİMŞEK, H., Educational Sciences
TEZER, E., Educational Sciences
YILDRIM, A., Educational Sciences
ZEYREK, D., Foreign Language Education

Faculty of Engineering (tel. (312) 210-25-01; fax (312) 210-11-10; e-mail engfac@eng.metu.edu.tr; internet www.eng.metu.edu.tr):

AKDENİZ, V., Metallurgical Engineering
AKGÖZ, Y. C., Engineering Sciences
AKGÜN, A. M., Aeronautical Engineering
AKIN, T., Electrical and Electronic Engineering
AKKÖK, M., Mechanical Engineering
AKMANDOR, İ. S., Aeronautical Engineering
AKSEL, H. M., Mechanical Engineering
AKYILMAZ, M. Ö., Civil Engineering
ALBAYRAK, K., Mechanical Engineering
ALEMDAROĞLU, N., Aeronautical Engineering
ALTINBİLEK, D. H., Civil Engineering
ALTINER, D., Geological Engineering
ANKARA, A., Metallurgical Engineering
ARIKAN, M. A. S., Mechanical Engineering
ARINÇ, F., Mechanical Engineering
AROL, A. İ., Mining Engineering
AŞKAR, M., Electrical and Electronic Engineering
ATALA, H., Metallurgical Engineering
ATALAY, Ü. M., Mining Engineering
ATIMTAY, A., Environmental Engineering
ATIMTAY, E., Civil Engineering
BAÇ, N., Chemical Engineering
BAĞCI, A. S., Petroleum and Natural Gas Engineering
BAKIR, U. B., Chemical Engineering
BALKAN, T., Mechanical Engineering
BAYINDIRLI, A., Food Engineering
BAYINDIRLI, L. A., Food Engineering
BAYKA, A. D., Mechanical Engineering
BAYKAL, A. D., Electrical and Electronic Engineering
BEŞİKÇI, C., Electrical and Electronic Engineering
BİLGEN, S., Electrical and Electronic Engineering
BİRAND, M. T., Electrical and Electronic Engineering
BİRLİK, G. A., Engineering Sciences
BOR, Ş., Metallurgical Engineering
BOZKURT, E., Geological Engineering
BOZOĞLU, F. T., Food Engineering
BOZŞAHIN, E. N. Ö., Industrial Engineering
BOZYİĞİT, M., Computer Engineering
BÖLÜKBAŞI, N., Mining Engineering
BÜYÜKDURA, O. M., Electrical and Electronic Engineering
ÇALIŞKAN, M., Mechanical Engineering
CANATAN, F., Electrical and Electronic Engineering
ÇELENLİGİL, M. C., Aeronautical Engineering
ÇİLİNGİR, F. C., Industrial Engineering
ÇOKÇA, E., Civil Engineering
ÇULFAZ, A., Chemical Engineering
DARENDELİLER, H., Mechanical Engineering
DEMİRAL, B., Petroleum and Natural Gas Engineering
DEMİRBAŞ, K., Electrical and Electronic Engineering
DEMİREKLER, M., Electrical and Electronic Engineering

DİLEK, F. B., Environmental Engineering
DOĞAÇ, A., Computer Engineering
DOĞU, T., Chemical Engineering
DOYUM, A. B., Mechanical Engineering
DOYURAN, V., Geological Engineering
DURSUNKAYA, Z., Mechanical Engineering
ERALP, O. C., Mechanical Engineering
ERGİN, A., Civil Engineering
ERGÜL, R., Electrical and Electronic Engineering
ERGÜN, M. U., Civil Engineering
ERKİP, N., Industrial Engineering
ERKMEN, A., Electrical and Electronic Engineering
ERKMEN, İ., Electrical and Electronic Engineering
ERMIŞ, M., Electrical and Electronic Engineering
EROĞLU, İ., Chemical Engineering
EROL, A. O., Civil Engineering
ERSAK, A., Electrical and Electronic Engineering
ERTAN, B. H., Electrical and Electronic Engineering
ERTAŞ, A., Electrical and Electronic Engineering
ESİN, A., Food Engineering
EYÜBOĞLU, B. M., Electrical and Electronic Engineering
GEÇİT, M. R., Engineering Sciences
GENÇ, F. P., Computer Engineering
GENÇER, G. N., Electrical and Electronic Engineering
GEVECİ, A., Metallurgical Engineering
GÖĞÜŞ, M., Civil Engineering
GÖKÇAY, C. F., Environmental Engineering
GÖKLER, M. İ., Mechanical Engineering
GÖNCÜOĞLU, C., Geological Engineering
GÜLEÇ, N., Geological Engineering
GÜLKAN, P., Civil Engineering
GÜMRAH, F., Petroleum and Natural Gas Engineering
GÜNALP, T. N., Electrical and Electronic Engineering
GÜNDÜZ, G., Chemical Engineering
GÜRAN, H., Electrical and Electronic Engineering
GÜRBUZ, R., Metallurgical Engineering
GÜRKAN, T., Chemical Engineering
GÜRÜZ, G., Chemical Engineering
GÜVEN, A. N., Electrical and Electronic Engineering
GÜVEN, Ç., Industrial Engineering
GÜYAGÜLER, T., Mining Engineering
HALICI, U., Electrical and Electronic Engineering
HAMAMCI, H., Food Engineering
HİÇYILMAZ, C., Mining Engineering
HIZAL, A., Electrical and Electronic Engineering
HIZAL, M., Electrical and Electronic Engineering
HOŞTEN, Ç., Mining Engineering
İDER, S. K., Mechanical Engineering
İNAL, A., Civil Engineering
KAFTANOĞLU, B., Mechanical Engineering
KALKANLI, A., Metallurgical Engineering
KARAHANOĞLU, N., Geological Engineering
KARAKAYA, İ., Metallurgical Engineering
KARPUZ, C., Mining Engineering
KAYALIGIL, S., Industrial Engineering
KILIÇ, E. S., Mechanical Engineering
KINCAL, N. S., Chemical Engineering
KİPER, A., Computer Engineering
KIRCA, Ö., Industrial Engineering
KISAKÜREK, B., Chemical Engineering
KOCAOĞLAN, E., Electrical and Electronic Engineering
KOÇYİĞİT, A., Geological Engineering
KÖK, M. V., Petroleum and Natural Gas Engineering
KÖKSALAN, M., Industrial Engineering
KUZUOĞLU, M., Electrical and Electronic Engineering
LEBLEBİCİOĞLU, K., Electrical and Electronic Engineering

MEHMETOĞLU, T., Petroleum and Natural Gas Engineering
ÖGEL, B., Metallurgical Engineering
ÖGEL, Z. B. S., Food Engineering
OKANDAN, E., Petroleum and Natural Gas Engineering
ÖNAL, I., Chemical Engineering
ÖNDER, H., Civil Engineering
ORAL, S., Mechanical Engineering
ORÇAN, Y., Engineering Sciences
OSKAY, R., Mechanical Engineering
ÖZAY, N., Electrical and Electronic Engineering
ÖZBAYOĞLU, G., Mining Engineering
ÖZBELGE, Ö., Chemical Engineering
ÖZBELGE, T., Chemical Engineering
ÖZCEBE, G., Civil Engineering
ÖZENBAŞ, M., Metallurgical Engineering
ÖZGEN, C., Chemical Engineering
ÖZGÖREN, K., Mechanical Engineering
ÖZGÜVEN, N., Mechanical Engineering
ÖZHAN, E., Civil Engineering
ÖZKAN, M. Y., Civil Engineering
ÖZTÜRK, A., Metallurgical Engineering
ÖZTÜRK, T., Metallurgical Engineering
PARLAKTUNA, M., Petroleum and Natural Gas Engineering
PARNAS, L., Mechanical Engineering
PAYKOÇ, E., Mechanical Engineering
PLATİN, B. E., Mechanical Engineering
POLAT, F., Computer Engineering
SAATÇİOĞLU, Ö., Industrial Engineering
SAKA, M. P., Engineering Sciences
SARIOĞLU, F., Metallurgical Engineering
SAYAN, G. T., Electrical and Electronic Engineering
SELÇUK, E., Metallurgical Engineering
SELÇUK, N., Chemical Engineering
ŞENDİL, U., Civil Engineering
ŞEVAIOĞLU, O., Electrical and Electronic Engineering
SEVERCAN, M., Electrical and Electronic Engineering
SEVİNÇ, N., Metallurgical Engineering
SEVÜK, A. S., Civil Engineering
ŞORMAN, A. Ü., Civil Engineering
SÖYLEMEZ, E., Mechanical Engineering
SOYLU, R., Mechanical Engineering
SUCUOĞLU, H., Civil Engineering
SÜRÜCÜ, G., Environmental Engineering
TANIK, Y., Electrical and Electronic Engineering
TANKUT, A. T., Civil Engineering
TEKİN, E., Metallurgical Engineering
TİMUÇIN, M., Metallurgical Engineering
TOKDEMİR, T., Engineering Sciences
TOKER, C., Electrical and Electronic Engineering
TOKYAY, M., Civil Engineering
TOPKAYA, Y., Metallurgical Engineering
TOPRAK, G. M. V., Geological Engineering
TOSUN, İ., Chemical Engineering
TULUNAY, E., Electrical and Electronic Engineering
TULUNAY, Y., Aeronautical Engineering
TÜMER, T. S., Mechanical Engineering
TUNCEL, G., Environmental Engineering
TUNCER, İ. H., Aeronautical Engineering
TURHAN, D., Engineering Science
TÜRKMENOĞLU, A. G., Geological Engineering
ÜÇTUĞ, Y., Electrical and Electronic Engineering
ÜNAL, E., Mining Engineering
ÜNER, D., Chemical Engineering
ÜNGAN, S., Food Engineering
ÜNLÜ, K., Environmental Engineering
ÜNLÜSOY, Y. S., Mechanical Engineering
ÜNVER, Z., Electrical and Electronic Engineering
UTKU, M., Civil Engineering
VURAL, F. T., Computer Engineering
VURAL, H., Mechanical Engineering
YALABIK, N., Computer Engineering
YAMAN, Y., Aeronautical Engineering
YANMAZ, M. A., Civil Engineering

YAZICI, A., Computer Engineering
YAZICIGİL, H., Geological Engineering
YEŞİN, A. O., Mechanical Engineering
YEŞİN, T., Mechanical Engineering
YETİŞ, U., Environmental Engineering
YILDIRIM, N., Electrical and Electronic Engineering
YILDIRIM, R. O., Mechanical Engineering
YILDIZ, F., Food Engineering
YILMAZ, Ç., Civil Engineering
YILMAZ, L., Chemical Engineering
YILMAZER, Ü., Chemical Engineering
YÜCEL, H., Chemical Engineering
YÜCEMEN, M. S., Civil Engineering
YÜKSEL, Y. Ö., Electrical and Electronic Engineering
YÜNCÜ, H., Mechanical Engineering

Graduate School of Marine Sciences (33731 Erdemli; tel. (324) 521-21-50; fax (324) 521-23-27; e-mail ilkay@imf.metu.edu.tr; internet www.ims.metu.edu.tr):

BİNGEL, F., Marine Sciences
KIDEYŞ, E. A., Marine Sciences
LATİF, M. A., Marine Sciences
OĞUZ, I. T., Marine Sciences
ÖZSOY, E., Marine Sciences
TUĞRUL, S., Marine Sciences
YILMAZ, A., Marine Sciences

OSMANGAZİ ÜNİVERSİTESI

Meşelik Kampüsü, 26480 Eskişehir

Telephone: (222) 239-49-37
Fax: (222) 229-14-18
E-mail: ogubim@ogu.edu.tr
Internet: www.ogu.edu.tr
Founded 1970
State control
Languages of instruction: Turkish, English
Academic year: October to September

Chancellor: (vacant)
Vice-Chancellor: (vacant)
Rector: Prof. Dr NECAT A. AKGUN
Vice-Rectors: Prof. Dr MACIT YAMAN, Prof. Dr ATİLLA YILDIRIM
Registrar: ESAT ÇELİK

Library of 33,883 books, 7,521 periodicals
Number of teachers: 866
Number of students: 8,790 (7,930 undergraduate, 860 postgraduate)

Publications: *Journal of the Faculty of Engineering and Architecture* (2 a year), *Journal of the Faculty of Medicine* (2 a year)

DEANS

Faculty of Agriculture: Prof. Dr YAŞAR PANCAR
Faculty of Arts and Sciences: Prof. Dr YALÇIN ŞAHİN
Faculty of Economic and Administrative Sciences: Prof. Dr FAZIL TEKİN
Faculty of Education: Prof. Dr NACI EKEM
Faculty of Engineering and Architecture: Prof. Dr ERCENGİZ YILDIRIM
Faculty of Medicine: Prof. Dr EROL GÖKTÜRK
Faculty of Theology: Prof. Dr MEHMET MAKSUDOĞLU

PAMUKKALE ÜNİVERSİTESI

Kinikli Campus, 20070 Denizli

Telephone: (258) 296-23-56
Fax: (258) 296-23-30
E-mail: internationaloffice@pau.edu.tr
Internet: pau.edu.tr/pau
State control
Languages of instruction: English, Turkish
Rector: Prof. Dr HUSEYIN BAGCI
Vice-Rector: Prof. Dr ALI KESKIN
Vice-Rector: Prof. Dr SEBAHATTIN NAS

Number of teachers: 698
Number of students: 31,581

DEANS

Faculty of Arts and Sciences: Prof. Dr HALIL CETISLI

Faculty of Economic and Administrative Sciences: Prof. Dr ALI İHSAN KARAALP

Faculty of Education: Prof. Dr SELAHITTIN OZCELIK

Faculty of Engineering: Prof. Dr MUZAFFER TOPCU

Faculty of Medicine: Prof. Dr MUSTAFA KILIC

Faculty of Technical Education: Prof. Dr RASIM KARABACAK

SABANCİ ÜNİVERSİTESİ

Orhanli, 34956 Tuzla, Istanbul

Telephone: (216) 483-90-00

Fax: (216) 483-90-05

E-mail: db@sabanciuniv.edu

Internet: www.sabanciuniv.edu

Founded 1994

Private control

Languages of instruction: English, Turkish

Academic year: October to July

Rector: Prof. TOSUN TERZIOĞLU

Gen. Sec.: HALUK BAL

Librarian: HILMI ÇELIK

Library of 60,000 vols, 56 databases

Number of teachers: 410

Number of students: 2,010

DEANS

Faculty of Arts and Social Sciences: Prof. AHMET ALKAN

Faculty of Engineering and Natural Sciences: Prof. KEMAL İNAN

Graduate School of Management: Prof. NAKIYE AVDAN BOYACIGILLER

SAKARYA ÜNİVERSİTESİ

Esentepe Kampüsü, 54187 Sakarya

Telephone: (264) 295-54-54

Fax: (264) 295-50-36

E-mail: basin@sakarya.edu.tr

Internet: www.sakarya.edu.tr

Founded 1992

State control

Languages of instruction: Turkish, English

Academic year: September to June

Rector: Prof. Dr MEHMET DURMAN

Vice-Rectors: Prof. Dr MUZAFFER ELMAS, Prof. Dr H. RIZA GÜVEN, Prof. Dr H. BINNAZ BAYTEKIN

Sec.-Gen.: Dr ZAFER DEMIR

Dir of Library: MUSTAFA ESMELI

Library of 100,008 vols

Number of teachers: 1,241

Number of students: 45,576

Publications: *Adapazarı Meslek Yüksekokulu Dergisi Akademik İncelemeler, Saü Bulletin, TOJET: The Turkish Online Journal of Educational Technology*

DEANS

Faculty of Arts and Humanities: Prof. Dr MURAT TUTUNCU

Faculty of Economic and Administrative Sciences: Prof. Dr ENGIN YILDIRIM

Faculty of Education: Prof. VAHDETTIN SEVINÇ

Faculty of Engineering: Prof. Dr MEHMET ALI YALÇIN

Faculty of Fine Arts: Prof. Dr NILGÜN BILGE

Faculty of Technical Education: Prof. Dr HÜSEYIN EKIZ

Faculty of Theology: Prof. Dr ALI ERBAŞI

School of Health Sciences: Prof. Dr SEVIN ALTINKAYNAK

School of Physical Education and Sports: Asst. Prof. Dr ERTUĞRUL GELEN

SELÇUK ÜNİVERSİTESİ

Vali Izzet Bey Cad., Karatay Müzesi Karşisi, 42151 Konya

Telephone: (332) 350-70-05

Fax: (332) 352-09-98

E-mail: mesaj@selcuk.edu.tr

Internet: www.selcuk.edu.tr

Founded 1975

State control

Language of instruction: Turkish

Academic year: October to May

Rector: Prof. Dr SÜLEYMAN OKUDAN

Vice-Rectors: Prof. Dr DINÇER BEDÜK, Prof. Dr ŞEFIK BILIR, Prof. Dr KÜRŞAT TURGUT

Librarian: Dr CENGIZI KORKMAZ

Number of teachers: 3,264

Number of students: 75,000

Publications: *Journal of Faculty of Engineering and Architecture* (2 a year), *Journal of the Faculty of Medicine* (4 a year), *Journal of Veterinary Science* (4 a year)

DEANS

Faculty of Agriculture: Prof. Dr MUSTAFA ONDER

Faculty of Communication: Prof. Dr HALUK HADI SUMER

Faculty of Dentistry: Prof. Dr TAMER ATAOGLU

Faculty of Economics and Administrative Sciences: Prof. Dr SERIF SIMSEK

Faculty of Economics and Administrative Sciences (Konya): Prof. Dr ORHAN GÖKÇE

Faculty of Education: Prof. Dr MUSA GURSEL

Faculty of Engineering and Architecture: Prof. Dr CEVAT INAL

Faculty of Fine Arts: Prof. Dr FEVZI GUNUC

Faculty of Law: Prof. Dr MEHMET AYAN

Faculty of Literature: Prof. Dr AHMET TIRPAN

Faculty of Medicine (Meram): Prof. Dr AHMET OZKAGNICI

Faculty of Medicine (Selcuklu): Prof. Dr KAGAN KARABULUT

Faculty of Science: Prof. Dr İSMET UCAN

Faculty of Technical Education: Prof. Dr ALI UNUVAR

Faculty of Theology: Prof. Dr AHMET ONKAL

Faculty of Veterinary Sciences: Prof. Dr ZAFER DURGUN

Faculty of Vocational Education: Prof. Dr KADIRCAN OZKAN

SÜLEYMAN DEMIREL ÜNİVERSİTESİ

Merkez Kampüs, Çünür, 32260 Isparta

Telephone: (246) 211-10-00

Fax: (246) 237-04-31

E-mail: ozelkalem@sdu.edu.tr

Internet: www.sdu.edu.tr

Founded 1992

State control

Languages of instruction: English, Turkish

Academic year: September to July

Rector: Prof. Dr HASAN İBICIOĞLU

Vice-Rector: Prof. Dr MEHMET NUMAN TAMER

Vice-Rector: Prof. Dr İSKENDER AKKURT

Vice-Rector: Prof. Dr HÜSEYIN AKYILDIZ

Gen. Sec.: AZIZ BAYRAK

Library Dir: UĞUR BULGAN

Library of 205,000 vols, 40,000 e-periodicals

Number of teachers: 3,200

Number of students: 50,000

Publications: *Cell Membranes and Free Radical Research* (1 a year, in English), *European Journal of Mineral Processing and Environmental Protection* (3 a year), *International Journal of Technological Sciences* (2 a year, in Turkish), *Journal of Engineering Science of Design* (2 a year, in Turkish), *Journal of Natural and Applied Sciences* (1 a year, in Turkish), *Journal of SDU Faculty of Dentistry* (2 a year, in Turkish), *Journal of Sleep Health* (2 a

year, in Turkish), *Journal of the Faculty of Administrative Sciences and Education* (2 a year, in Turkish), *Journal of the Faculty of Agriculture* (2 a year, in Turkish), *Journal of the Faculty of Forestry* (2 a year, in Turkish), *Medical Journal* (4 a year, in Turkish), *Medical Journal of Suleyman Demirel University* (4 a year, in Turkish), *SDÜ Art-e* (2 a year, in Turkish), *SDÜ Eğirdir Su Ürünleri Fakültesi Dergisi* (1 a year, in Turkish), *SDÜ Egzersiz Dergisi* (1 a year, in Turkish), *SDÜ Fen Bilimleri Enstitüsü Dergisi* (3 a year, in Turkish), *SDU Journal of Science* (2 a year, in Turkish), *SDÜ Sağlık Bilimleri Enstitüsü Dergisi* (2 a year, in Turkish), *SDÜ Teknik Bilimler Dergisi* (2 a year, in Turkish), *SDÜ Vizyoner Dergisi* (2 a year, in Turkish), *SDÜ Yaşam Dergisi* (2 a year, in Turkish), *SDÜ Yekarum Dergisi* (2 a year, in Turkish)

DEANS

Faculty of Agriculture: Prof. Dr ZEKERIYA AKMAN

Faculty of Arts and Sciences: Prof. Dr ALI KÖKCE

Faculty of Communication: Prof. Dr İLKER HÜSEYIN ÇARIKÇI

Faculty of Dentistry: Prof. Dr MUHAMMED HAKAN TÜRKKAHRAMAN

Faculty of Economic and Admin. Sciences: Prof. Dr ABDULLAH EROĞLU

Faculty of Education: Prof. Dr MENDERES COŞKUN

Faculty of Engineering and Architecture: Prof. Dr ERDOĞAN KÜÇÜKÖNER

Faculty of Fine Arts: Prof. Dr SERPIL SAVAŞ

Faculty of Fisheries: Prof. Dr ÖZNUR DILER

Faculty of Forestry: Prof. Dr CAHIT BALABANLI

Faculty of Health: Prof. Dr SÜLEYMAN KUTLUHAN

Faculty of Law: Prof. Dr FARUK TURHAN

Faculty of Medicine: Prof. Dr HÜSEYIN YORGANCIGIL

Faculty of Technical Education: Prof. Dr ALI KEMAL YAKUT

Faculty of Technology: Prof. Dr OSMAN İPEK

Faculty of Theology: Prof. Dr TALIP TÜRCAN

Graduate School of Fine Arts: Doç. Dr MEHMET ÖZHANLI

Graduate School of Health Sciences: Prof. Dr MEHMET FEHMI ÖZGÜNER

Graduate School of Natural and Applied Sciences: Prof. Dr MEHMET CENGIZ KAYACAN

Graduate School of Social Sciences: Prof. Dr SÜLEYMAN SEYDI

Graduate School of Water: Prof. Doç Dr İBRAHIM DILER

TRAKYA ÜNİVERSİTESİ

22050 Karaağaç, Edirne

Telephone: (284) 223-40-04

Fax: (284) 223-42-03

E-mail: rectorsoffice@trakya.edu.tr

Internet: www.trakya.edu.tr

Founded 1982 from existing faculties in Edirne

Academic year: October to June

Rector: Prof. Dr ENVER DURAN

Vice-Rectors: Prof. Dr BEYHAN KARAMANLIOGLU, Prof. Dr TIMUR KIRGIZ, Prof. Dr ALI KEMAL KUTLU

Librarian: ENDER BILAR

Number of teachers: 1,238

Number of students: 20,265

Publications: *Journal of the Faculty of Agriculture* (2 a year), *Journal of the Faculty of Medicine* (4 a year), *Medical Journal Of Trakya University* (3 a year), *Trakya Uni-*

versity Journal of Scientific Research (2 a year)

DEANS

Faculty of Arts and Sciences: Prof. Dr BÜNYAMIN ÖZGÜLTEKIN
Faculty of Economics and Administrative Sciences: Prof. Dr DERMAN KÜÇÜKALTAN
Faculty of Education: Prof. Dr HILMI İBAR
Faculty of Engineering and Architecture: Prof. Dr AHMET CAN
Faculty of Health Sciences: Prof. Dr FERDA ÖZDEMİR
Faculty of Medicine: Prof. Dr MURAT DİKMEN-GİL
Faculty of Science and Letters: Prof. Dr ŞEVKET EROL OKAN

UFUK ÜNİVERSİTESİ

Mevlana Bulvarı (Konya Yolu) 86-88, 06520 Balgat, Ankara
Telephone: (312) 284-77-77
Fax: (312) 287-23-90
E-mail: ufukuni@ufuk.edu.tr
Internet: www.ufuk.edu.tr
Founded 1972; present name and status 1999
Rector: Prof. Dr A. ERGÜN ERTUĞ
Gen. Sec.: İSMET ATIK
Number of teachers: 23
Number of students: 66
Faculties of arts and science, economics and administration, education, law and medicine.

ULUDAĞ ÜNİVERSİTESİ

Görükle Kampüsü, Rektörlük Uluslararası İlişkiler Ofisi, 16059 Bursa
Telephone: (224) 294-00-72
Fax: (224) 294-00-80
E-mail: intoffice@uludag.edu.tr
Internet: www.uludag.edu.tr
Founded 1975 as Bursa Üniversitesi; present name and structure 1982
State control
Language of instruction: Turkish
Academic year: September to June
Rector: Prof. Dr KAMIL DILEK
Vice-Rector: Prof. Dr A. SAIM KILAVUZ
Vice-Rector: Prof. Dr İRFAN KARAGÖZ
Vice-Rector: Prof. Dr MÜFIT PARLAK
Sec.-Gen.: ÖZGÜR AKGÜN KARABULUT
Head of Libraries and Documentation Centre: CANAN KORKMAZ
Library of 67,493 vols
Number of teachers: 2,102
Number of students: 41,057
Publications: *Agriculture* (1 a year), *Education* (1 a year), *Engineering* (1 a year), *Medicine* (1 a year), *Science and Literature* (1 a year), *Theology* (1 a year), *Veterinary Science* (1 a year)

DEANS

Faculty of Agriculture: Prof. Dr İSMAIL FILYA
Faculty of Economics and Administrative Sciences: Prof. Dr İSMAIL EFIL
Faculty of Education: Prof. Dr MURAT ALTUN
Faculty of Engineering and Architecture: Prof. Dr ABDULVAHAP YIĞIT
Faculty of Medicine: Prof. Dr MUSTAFA GÜLLÜLÜ
Faculty of Science and Letters: Prof. Dr İSMAIL NACI CANGÜL
Faculty of Theology: Prof. Dr YAŞAR AYDINLI
Faculty of Veterinary Medicine: Prof. Dr ENGIN KENNERMAN

YAŞAR ÜNİVERSİTESİ

Şehitler Cad. 1522, Sok 6, 35230 Alsancak, Izmir
Telephone: (232) 463-33-44

Fax: (232) 463-07-80
E-mail: info@yasar.edu.tr
Internet: www.yasar.edu.tr
Founded 1998; present status 2001
Rector: Prof. Dr NECATI SEN
Gen. Sec.: DIDEM ÖKTEM

DEANS

Faculty of Business Economics and Administration: Prof. Dr CENGIZ PINAR
Faculty of Communications: Prof. Dr CENGIZ PINAR (Deputy)
Faculty of Engineering and Architecture: Prof. Dr DEMIR ASLAN
Faculty of Law: Prof. Dr DEMIR ASLAN (Deputy)
Faculty of Science and Letters: Prof. Dr COŞKUN IŞÇI

DIRECTORS

School of Foreign Languages: Asst Prof. Dr SENA TULPAR
Vocational School: Prof. Dr HASAN HÜSNÜ ÇATALCA

YEDİTEPE ÜNİVERSİTESİ

26 Agustos Yerlesimi, Kayışdağı Caddesi, 34755 Ataşehir, Istanbul
Telephone: (216) 578-00-00
Fax: (216) 578-02-44
E-mail: halklailiskiler@yeditepe.edu.tr
Internet: www.yeditepe.edu.tr
Founded 1996
Private control
Rector: Prof. Dr NURCAN BAÇ
Vice-Rector: Prof. Dr MELIH BORAL
Vice-Rector: Prof. Dr NEDRET KURAN BURÇO-GLU
Sec.-Gen.: LEYLA YEŞILADA (acting)
Number of students: 17,380

DEANS

Faculty of Architecture and Engineering: Prof. Dr İBRAHIM FAHIR BORAK
Faculty of Arts and Sciences: Prof. Dr AHMET İNCE
Faculty of Commercial Sciences: Prof. Dr ÖMER GÖKAY
Faculty of Communication: Prof. Dr SUAT ANAR
Faculty of Dentistry: Prof. Dr TURKER SAN-DALLI
Faculty of Economics and Administrative Sciences: Prof. Dr KADIR AYKUT TOP
Faculty of Education: AYŞE SEMRA AKYEL
Faculty of Fine Arts: Prof. Dr BIKE KOCAOĞLU
Faculty of Law: Prof. Dr HALUK KABAALIOĞLU
Faculty of Medicine: Prof. Dr AYÇA VITRİNEL
Faculty of Pharmacy: Prof. Dr DILEK EROL

YILDIZ TEKNİK ÜNİVERSİTESİ

80750 Beşiktaş, Istanbul
Telephone: (212) 259-70-70
Fax: (212) 261-42-84
E-mail: uerden@yildiz.edu.tr
Internet: www.yildiz.edu.tr
Founded 1911; reorganized 1982 (fmrly State Acad. of Engineering and Architecture)
Academic year: October to July
Rector: Prof. Dr DURUL ÖREN
Vice-Rector for Admin.: Prof. Dr SALIH DURER
Vice-Rector for Education: Prof. Dr ZEKERIYA POLAT
Vice-Rector for Research and Planning: Prof. Dr GÖRÜN ARUN
Sec.-Gen.: ÜMIT ERDEN
Number of teachers: 1,111
Number of students: 17,000
Publication: *Periodical* (4 a year)

DEANS

Faculty of Architecture: Prof. Dr EMRE AYSU
Faculty of Art and Design: Prof. Dr TOMUR ATAGÖK
Faculty of Arts and Sciences: Prof. Dr DURUL OREN
Faculty of Chemical and Metallurgical Engineering: Prof. Dr SABRIYE PIŞKIN
Faculty of Civil Engineering: Prof. Dr YALÇIN YÜKSEL
Faculty of Economic and Administrative Sciences: Prof. Dr AYKUT POLATOĞLU
Faculty of Electrical and Electronic Engineering: Prof. Dr GALIP CANSEVER
Faculty of Mechanical Engineering: Prof. Dr HASAN HEPERKAN

ATTACHED COLLEGES

School of Foreign Languages: Dir Prof. Dr NÜKET ÖCAL.
School of Vocational Studies: Dir Assoc. Prof. Dr MUSTAFA SUNU.

YÜZÜNCÜ YIL ÜNİVERSİTESİ
(Centennial University)

65080 Van
Telephone: (432) 225-10-10
Fax: (432) 225-10-09
Internet: www.yyu.edu.tr
Founded 1982
State control
Language of instruction: Turkish
Academic year: October to July
Rector: Prof. Dr YÜCEL AŞKIN
Vice-Rectors: Prof. Dr HASAN CEYLAN, Prof. Dr ALI FUAT DOĞU, Prof. Dr AYŞE YÜKSEL
Gen. Sec.: Dr IŞIK TEPE
Librarian: (vacant)
Library of 31,000 vols
Number of teachers: 300
Number of students: 6,100
Publications: *Artos* (Universities and Colleges in Literature, 1 a year), *Eastern Journal of Physical Medicine and Rehabilitation* (12 a year), *Journal of Agricultural Sciences* (1 a year), *Journal of the Faculty of Arts and Sciences-Sciences* (irregular), *Journal of the Faculty of Education-Sciences* (12 a year), *Journal of the Faculty of Education-Social Sciences* (12 a year), *Journal of the Faculty of Theology* (12 a year), *Journal of the Faculty of Veterinary Science* (12 a year), *Journal of the Graduate School of Sciences* (irregular), *Journal of Health Sciences* (12 a year), *Journal of the Institute of Social Sciences* (irregular), *Rahva* (education, 12 a year), *University Bulletin* (12 a year), *Van Medical Journal* (12 a year), *Yeldegirmeni* (Arts, 12 a year)

DEANS

Faculty of Agriculture: Prof. Dr FIRAT CENGIZ
Faculty of Arts and Sciences: Prof. Dr ERKSIN GÜLEÇ
Faculty of Economic and Administrative Sciences: Prof. Dr BÜLENT KARAKAŞ
Faculty of Education: Prof. Dr RAUF YILDIZ
Faculty of Education (Hakkari): Prof. Dr RECAI KARAHAN
Faculty of Engineering: Prof. Dr A. ÜMIT TOLLUOĞLU
Faculty of Fine Arts: Prof. Dr ZÜHRE ŞENTÜRK
Faculty of Medicine: Prof. Dr MANSUR KAMACI
Faculty of Theology: Prof. Dr SELAHATTIN KIYICI
Faculty of Veterinary Science: Prof. Dr NIHAT MERT

PROFESSORS

Faculty of Agriculture:
AKYUZ, N.

ASKİN, Y.
COKSOYLER, N.
ŞEN, S. M.
YASAR, B.

Faculty of Arts and Science:
AMİRALİ, G.
CEYLAN, H.
KARAKAS, B.
ONLER, Z.
OZTURK, A.
RASİMGİL, R.
TİLEKLİOĞLU, B.
ULUCAM, A.
YİLMAZ, A.

Faculty of Education:
SAVAS, E.
TOZLU, N.

Faculty of Engineering:
ORCEN, S.
TOLLUOĞLU, A. U.

Faculty of Medicine:
AKSOY, H.
ATAY, G.
BURDURLU, Y.
CEYLAN, A.
DALKİLİC, A. E.
DEMİRORS, A. P.
GOKSOY, T.
KAMACİ, M.

ODABAS, D.
TURAN, F.
YAKUT, C.
YETKİN, Y.
YUKSEL, A.

Faculty of Veterinary Science:
AGAOĞLU, Z. T.
BOLAT, D.
BOYNUKARA, B.
KARADAG, H.
MERT, N.

ZONGULDAK KARAELMAS ÜNİVERSİTESİ

67100 Zonguldak
Telephone: (372) 257-41-30
Fax: (372) 257-21-40
Internet: www.karaelmas.edu.tr
Founded 1992
State control
Academic year: September to July
Rector: Prof. Dr BEKTAŞ AÇIKGÖZ
Vice-Rectors: Prof. Dr TURGAY ATALAY, Prof. Dr H. YILMAZ KAPTAN, Prof. Dr YADIGAR MÜFTÜOĞLU
Chief Librarian: FATMA CEYLAN
Library of 35,000 vols, 12,000 periodicals
Number of teachers: 1,194

Number of students: 10,194 full-time, 2,143 evening
Publications: *Journal of the Faculty of Engineering* (4 a year), *Journal of the Faculty of Forestry* (2 a year)

DEANS

Faculty of Arts and Science (Devrek): Prof. Dr TÜRKAN KOPAÇ
Faculty of Economics and Administration (Çaycuma): Prof. Dr GÜVEN MURAT
Faculty of Education (Ereğli): Prof. Dr BAKI HAZER
Faculty of Engineering: Prof. Dr H. YILMAZ KAPTAN
Faculty of Forestry (Bartın): Prof. Dr HÜDA-VERDI EROĞLU
Faculty of Medicine: Prof. Dr GAMZE MOÇAN KUZEY
Faculty of Technical Education (Karabük): Prof. Dr ETEM SAIT ÖZ

DIRECTORS

Graduate School of Health Sciences: Prof. Dr Z. NUR BANOĞLU
Graduate School of Natural and Applied Sciences: Prof. Dr ETEM KİŞİOĞLU
Graduate School of Social Sciences: Prof. Dr TURHAN KORKMAZ

TURKMENISTAN

The Higher Education System

Institutions of higher education pre-date the independence of Turkmenistan (formerly Turkmen SSR) from the USSR in 1991, with the oldest being the Turkmen State Medical Institute, which was founded in 1931. Following independence, a policy of bilim (education) was initiated, aimed at distancing Turkmenistan from its Soviet (and hence, Russian) past; a key element in this policy was the reformation of the Turkmen language, primarily through the substitution of the Latin for the Cyrillic alphabet. Free education at Turkmenistan's universities was reported to have been abolished in 2003, while it was reported that the number of places for students in educational establishments had been sharply reduced since the mid-1990s. In 2004 a presidential decree invalidating all higher education degrees received abroad came into effect; all teachers with such degrees were to be dismissed. In 2007 the new President, Gurbanguly Berdymuhamedov, extended the period of higher education from two to five years, effective from the beginning of the 2007/08 school year; in that academic year 13,800 students were enrolled at the country's 18 institutions of higher education. Students were no longer required to complete two years of practical work experience before applying to universities and recognition of foreign degrees was restored. In addition, postgraduate education was introduced for the first time, effective from the beginning of the 2008/09 academic year. President Berdymuhamedov also announced that the Academy of Sciences of Turkmenistan, which had been closed in 1993, was to reopen; a presidential decree re-establishing the Academy, which was to be fully funded by the state budget, was signed in June 2009.

Higher education, which is overseen by the Ministry of Education, is governed according to the Law on Education (2009). The implementation of the new law, inter alia, resurrected degrees for higher and professional education through evening and correspondence courses, which had b n abolished during the previous administration of the late President Gen. Saparmyrat Niyazov. Accreditation is the responsibility of the Council of Ministers.

The main requirements for admission to higher education are the Attestat o Srednem Obrazovanji (Certificate of General Secondary Education) and results in competitive entrance examinations, which comprise both written and oral tests. The main undergraduate qualification is the Specialist Diploma (equivalent to the Bachelors degree), which typically lasts five years, although some programmes, including medicine, take six years to complete. From 2008/09 postgraduate courses are available in academic and professional subjects and are open to holders of the Specialist Diploma who also have relevant work experience in their chosen field of study. For admission to doctoral studies, candidates are required to pass two entrance examinations, one testing knowledge of the chosen subject and the other testing proficiency in a foreign language; the doctoral cycle culminates with submission and public defence of a thesis and leads to award of the Doctorate of Science.

Post-secondary technical and vocational education consists of short-term courses of up to one-and-a-half years open to students who have completed nine years of sec ndary education. Qualifications studied for include Certificates and Diplomas, and are intended to prepare students for employment; they do not grant access to higher education.

Regulatory Bodies

GOVERNMENT

Ministry of Culture, Television and Radio Broadcasting: 744000 Ashgabat, ul. Pushkin 14; tel. (12) 35-41-05; fax (12) 35-35-60; Min. GULMURAT MURADOV.

Ministry of Education: 744000 Ashgabat, ul. Gurungan 2; tel. (12) 35-58-03; fax (12) 39-88-11; Min. GULSAT MAMMEDOWA.

Learned Society

GENERAL

Academy of Sciences of Turkmenistan: 744000 Ashgabat, ul. Gogolia 15; tel. (12) 25-44-74; fax (12) 25-53-67; internet science.gov .tm; f. 1951; ensures practical realization of scientific and technical policy; Pres. GURBANMYRAT MEZILOV; Deputy Pres. P. KOUWANDYK.

Research Institutes

GENERAL

National Institute of Deserts, Flora and Fauna: 744000 Ashgabat, Bitarap Turkmenistan str. 15; tel. (12) 39-54-27; fax (12) 35-37-16; e-mail desert@online.tm; internet science.gov.tm/en/organisations/desert_institute; f. 1962; attached to Min. of Nature Protection; fundamental and applied research on problems of biology, ecology, human environment; rational use of nature with regard to functional peculiarities of arid

ecosystem; Dir Prof. Dr PALTAMET ESENOV (acting); publ. *Problems of Desert Development* (4 a year).

AGRICULTURE, FISHERIES AND VETERINARY SCIENCE

Gara-Kala Experimental Station for Plant Genetic Resources: Balkan Province, Gara-Kala; tel. (48) 3-17-99; f. 1900; Dir ASHIRMUKHAMET SAPARMURADOV.

Research Institute of Cotton Growing of the MAWR: 746423 Maryiskiy velayat, Eloten Region, Institutskiy v.; tel. (560) 2-26-02; Dir Prof. SEITBARDY KURBANGELDIEV; Deputy Dir Dr AKMUKHAMMET CHAPAU.

Research Institute of Livestock and Veterinary Science: 744012 Ashgabat, ul. Gerogly 70; tel. (12) 34-82-97; fax (12) 34-97-98; Chair. NURMURAT ATAEV.

Scientific Research Institute of Farming: 744000 Ashgabat, ul. Ostrovskiy 30; tel. (12) 34-74-35; fax (12) 35-74-12; f. 1900; attached to Min. of Agriculture; Dir ORAZ SOUNOV.

Scientific Research Institute of Grain Crops: 744205 Akhal, Esnev Village, ul. O. Jumaev 1; tel. (13) 73-64-76; f. 1900; Head KHUDAYBERDI KADJIEV.

Turkmen Research Institute of Grain: 744012 Ashgabat, ul. Ostrovskiy 1; tel. (12) 34-74-35; fax (12) 34-74-72; Dir Dr AKMUKHAMMED DURDIEV.

ECONOMICS, LAW AND POLITICS

Institute of Economics: 744032 Ashgabat, Bikrova Sad Keshi 28; tel. (12) 24-02-52; Dir G. M. MURADOV.

Institute of Philosophy and ıw: 744000 Ashgabat, ul. Gogolia 15; tel. (12) 25-41-69; Dir O. MUSAYEV.

HISTORY, GEOGRAPHY AND ARCHAEOLOGY

Institute of History: 744000 Ashgabat, 2001 Azady St 61,; tel. (12) 35-31-38; fax (12) 39-86-87; e-mail history@online.tm; f. 1936, present name and status 2009; attached to Acad. of Sciences of Turkmenistan; research on the history of Turkmenistan and the Turkmen people from prehistory to present; Dir GULSHAT ORAZMUHAMMEDOWA.

Southern Turkmen Multidisciplinary Archaeological Expedition: 744000 Ashgabat, ul. Gogolia 15; tel. (12) 25-15-25; Man. KAKAMURAD KURBANSAKHATOV.

LANGUAGE AND LITERATURE

Bailyev Institute of Linguistics: 744000 Ashgabat, ul. Gogolia 15; tel. (12) 25-27-73; Dir M. SOYEGOV.

Magtymguly Institute of Literature: 744000 Ashgabat, ul. Bitarap 15; tel. (12) 35-35-09; e-mail diledeninstitut@rambler.ru; Dir GYZYLGUL HAKBERDYEVNA KYYASOVA.

MEDICINE

Scientific Clinical Centre of Cardiology: 744006 Ashgabat, ul. Gerogly 31; tel. (12) 39-

04-90; fax (12) 33-01-07; e-mail kykmh@mail.ru; attached to Min. of Health and Medical Industry.

Scientific Clinical Center of Eye Diseases: 744000 Ashgabat, ul. 1973 32; tel. and fax (12) 35-48-70; f. 1932; Dir A. SHAMURAT.

Turkmenistan Scientific-Clinical Centre of Oncology: 744020 Ashgabat, ul. Gorogly 53; tel. (12) 34-48-03; fax (12) 34-50-19; improves methods of medical treatment of cancer in Turkmenistan.

Turkmen Research Institute of Preventive and Clinical Medicine: 744006 Ashgabat, ul. 2009 31; tel. (12) 29-01-88; fax (12) 24-11-93; f. 1989; Dir Dr NINA KERIMI.

NATURAL SCIENCES

Biological Sciences

Institute of Botany: 744000 Ashgabat, ul. 2033 79; tel. (12) 25-37-58; Dir NURJAMAL ORAZOVNA ORAZMUHAMMEDOVA.

Institute of Physiology: 744000 Ashgabat, Magtymguly St 58; tel. (12) 35-71-44; f. 1959; Dir K. AMMANEPESOV.

Institute of Zoology: 744000 Ashgabat, ul. Engelsa 6; tel. (12) 25-37-91; Dir T. TOGKAYEV.

Physical Sciences

Institute of Chemistry: 744012 Ashgabat, Esgerler str. 92; tel. (12) 34-05-08; fax (12) 34-41-71; e-mail chem@online.tm; f. 1957, present status 2007; Dir GELDYEV OTUZBAY ANNABAEVICH.

Institute of Oil and Gas: Ashgabat, ul. Tehran 6; tel. and fax (12) 39-18-46; f. 1970 as Institute 'Turkmen Gas Technology', present name 1993; Dir Dr KHOSHGELDY BABAEV.

Research Institute of Geology: 744000 Ashgabat, Magtymguly Ave 81; tel. (12) 39-17-65; fax (12) 35-52-33; f. 1998; Dir ODEK A. ODEKOV.

Research Institute of Seismology: 744000 Ashgabat, ul. Acad T. Berdyev 20; tel. (12) 39-06-92; fax (12) 39-06-13; e-mail gaip@icctm.org; f. 1998; attached to Min. of Construction; Dir MYRAT MERETLIEVICH CHARYEV; publ. *Seismological Report* (2 a year).

Turkmensuvylymtaslama Institute: 744000 Ashgabat, ul. Beki Seytakov 1; tel. and fax (12) 35-18-35; e-mail tgvh@online.tm; water economy of Turkmenistan; Dir Dr MOSES SARKISOV; Deputy Dir USMAN SAPAROV.

TECHNOLOGY

Biotechnology Scientific Technological Centre: 744000, Ashgabat, ul. Bitarap 15; tel. and fax (3632) 35-14-39; attached to Acad. of Sciences; Head Dr TACHDURDY GEDEMOV.

Institute of Mathematics and Mechanics: 744000 Ashgabat, ul. Gogolia 15; tel. (12) 29-87-13; Dir M. B. ORAZOV.

Physical Engineering Institute: 744000 Ashgabat, ul. Gogolia 15; tel. (12) 25-42-85; Dir A. BERKELIYEV.

Libraries and Archives

Ashgabat

Central Scientific Library: 744007 Ashgabat, ul. 2002 15A; tel. (12) 35-65-71; internet library.science.gov.tm; f. 1941, present status 1957; attached to High Ccl for Science and Technology; colln of rare and valuable edns of valuable stock CSL Turkmen books with various graphics (Arabic, Latin, Cyrillic) for the period up to 1917 and subsequent years; publishes scientific support bibliographical

aids; received books on all brs of science from the Central Reservoir libraries of Russia (Moscow); 2.13m. vols; Dir A. B. YAZBERDIYEV.

Magtymguly Turkmen State University Library: 744005 Ashgabat, Sapamurat Turkmenbashi shayely 31; tel. (12) 5-39-22; f. 1950; provides scientific information; participates in educational process; promotes culture; 542,000 vols; Dir. A. T. VOROBEVA.

National Library of Turkmenistan: 744000 Ashgabat, pl. 2001, Berzengi, Nat. Cultural Centre; tel. (12) 35-74-89; fax (12) 25-38-43; f. 1895; 5,500,000 vols; Dir OGULGOZEL MUHAMMETGULYEVA.

Museums and Art Galleries

Ashgabat

Carpet Museum: 744000 Ashgabat, ul. Gorogly 5; f. 1994; colln of more than 8,000 Turkmen carpets from 17th to 20th century; museum workshop shows weaving of carpets; Dir TUVAKBIBI K. DURDYEVA.

Central Botanical Garden: 744012 Ashgabat, ul. Timiryazeva 17; tel. (12) 24-18-57; f. 1929; spec. collns of native flora, tropical and subtropical plants, Crataegus, Astragalus, Lonicera, Cotoneaster, Quercus, Juniperus, Pinus, Rosa, Allium; Dir B. B. KERBABAEV.

National Museum of Turkmenistan: 744000 Ashgabat, ul. Novofiruzinskoye 30; tel. (12) 51-90-20; fax (12) 51-90-22; e-mail vip@online.tm; f. 1998 by merger of Nat. Museum of History and Ethnography of Turkmenistan, State Museum of History of Turkmenistan and Turkmen State Museum of Fine Art; over 500,000 unique exhibits depicting history, ethnography, fine art; library of 8,830 vols; Dir OVEZMUHAMED MAMETNUROV.

Turkmen History Museum: Ashgabat, 1 Shevchenko St; tel. (12) 35-45-54; displays archeological finds, Ivory ritons; Dir AGABAI ATAGARRYEV.

Charjou

Charjou Historical and Ethnographical Museum: Charjou, 35 Shaidjanov St; tel. (422) 4-80-79; colln of artifacts from the Lebab velayat; Dir MAYA AKMAMEDOVA.

Universities

INTERNATIONAL TURKMEN–TURKISH UNIVERSITY

744012 Ashgabat, ul. Gyorogly 84

Telephone: (12) 90-84-26
Fax: (12) 95-85-38
E-mail: ikez@mail.ru
Internet: www.ittu.edu.tm

Founded 1994

Rector: GELDYEV REJEPMUHAMED
Vice-Chancellor: RAHMANKULOV FAYZULLA

Faculties of economics, education, engineering.

TURKMEN AGRICULTURAL UNIVERSITY NAMED AFTER S. A. NIYAZOV

744012 Ashgabat, Gyorogly str. 62

Telephone: (12) 34-26-52
Fax: (12) 34-68-80

Founded 1930
State control

Rector: MAMEDKULIEV GURBANDURDY

Depts of accounting, agrochemistry, animal husbandry, fruit and vegetable growing, mechanization, veterinary science, viticulture

Library of 136,000 vols
Number of teachers: 216
Number of students: 2,000

TURKMEN STATE UNIVERSITY NAMED AFTER MAGTYMGULY

744000 Ashgabat, Saparmurat Turkembashi shayoly 31

Telephone and fax (12) 35-11-59
E-mail: math3@online.tm

Founded 1931 as Ashgabat Pedagogical Institute, present status and name 1950
State control

Faculties of biology, chemistry, foreign languages, geography, history, humanities and social sciences, law and int. relations, management and int. trade, mathematics and applied maths, physics, Russian philology, theology, Turkmen philology

Rector: Prof. TUGIEV CHARYYAR
Pro-Rector: Prof. ATDAYEV SAPARGELDY ATDAYEVICH

Number of teachers: 544
Number of students: 11,000

Other Higher Educational Institutes

State Academy of Arts of Turkmenistan: 744012 Ashgabat, 90 A. Navoi St; tel. (12) 39-38-02; fax (12) 34-66-65; f. 1994; attached to Min. of Culture, Television and Radio Broadcasting; painting (graphic solution of cinema, machine drawing, theatrical-decorative); graphics; sculpture; architecture; design; national art (carpets, ceramics, jewellery); art criticism; Rector BEGMYRADOV GULNAZAR; Vice-Rector TADJYMOVA JEREN.

Turkmen Institute of National Economy: 744027 Ashgabat, Atamurad Nyyazov shayely 46; tel. (12) 41-90-36; fax (12) 46-98-05; faculties of accounting, economic planning, trade economics; Rector MAKHAMMETGELDI ANNAAMANOV.

Turkmen Medical Institute: 744001 Ashgabat, ul. 2028 58; tel. and fax (12) 35-19-53; e-mail medins@online.tm; f. 1931; attached to Acad. of Sciences of Turkmenistan; faculties of medical science, paediatrics, stomatology, pharmaceutical, medico-prophylactic; library: 191,000 vols; Rector GURBANGULY M. BERDYMUKHAMMEDOV (acting).

Turkmen National Institute of Sport and Tourism: 744001 Ashgabat, Atamyrad Nyyazov Shayoly 15A; tel. (12) 36-25-40; fax (12) 36-24-56; faculties of hotel business, tourism business, sport, physical training; Rector ATALYEV YALKAPBERDY.

Turkmen National Institute of World Languages named after D. Azadi: 744011 Ashgabat, ul. Ostrovskogo 47; tel. (12) 34-54-24; fax (12) 34-39-88; f. 1984; European languages: English, French, German, Russian language and literature; Eastern languages: Arabic, Persian, Turkish, Turkmen language and literature; 117 teachers; 805 students; Rector CHARYEV SAPARBERDY; Vice-Rector TAGANDURDYEV TAGANDURDY.

Turkmen Polytechnic Institute: 744025 Ashgabat, B. Annanova str. 62; tel. (12) 41-18-00; fax (12) 41-18-01; faculties of construction, oil and gas, chemical technology, energy, economics, computer technology and sanitation technology; managing of production; Rector YAZ MOVLYAMOV.

Turkmen State Institute of Culture: 744000 Ashgabat, Magtymguly Shayoly 4; tel. (12) 27-21-27; fax (12) 47-43-11; e-mail miras@cpart.org; theatrical art, production; archives; Rector SAPARMUHAMEDOV ANNAMURAD; Vice-Rector GOSHAYEV DADEBAY.

Turkmen State Institute of Energy: 745400 Mary, ul. Bayramali 62; tel. and fax (52) 26-04-12; electrical systems and networks; manual and automatic management of technical systems; production of electronics; work up and technology of metals and machines; apparatus of chemical industry; chemical technology of inorganic matters; Rector JUMAGYLYJOV ANNAGULY; Vice-Rector KAKABAYEV SAPAR.

Turkmen State Institute of Transport and Communications: 744028 Ashgabat, ul. Oguzhana 13; tel. (12) 27-26-79; fax (12) 42-55-83; e-mail durdyev@online.tm; Rector MERED ASHIRBAYEV.

Turkmen State Pedagogical Institute named after S.Seydi: 746100 Türkmenabat, ul. Shabende 7; tel. (42) 23-36-72; fax (42) 23-05-11; languages, teacher training; Chancellor G. MEZILOV; Rector YAZYLEV CHARY.

TUVALU

The Higher Education System

There was no higher education in Tuvalu before 1979. In that year the University of the South Pacific (Fiji) established an extension centre at Funafuti; the centre offers diploma and vocational courses and the first two years of degree courses (the latter requiring completion in Suva). The only other tertiary institution is the Tuvalu Maritime Training Institute at Amatuku on Funafuti, which was also founded in 1979 (as the Tuvalu Maritime School); about 60 people graduate from the school annually. A project to upgrade infrastructure and facilities at the Institute, in order to meet International Maritime Organization training standards, was undertaken during the 2000s; the project was funded by a US $2m. assistance package granted by the Asian Development Bank. Plans were under discussion for the establishment of a technical education centre that would offer training in a range of technical and vocational fields, including carpentry, engineering, plumbing and secretarial work. The Ministry of Education, Sports and Culture in Funafuti is responsible for higher education.

Regulatory Body

GOVERNMENT

Ministry of Education, Sports and Culture: POB 37, Vaiaku, Funafuti; tel. 20405; fax 20832; e-mail ses@tuvalu.tv; Minister Dr FALESA PITOI.

Libraries and Archives

Funafuti

National Library and Archives: POB 36, Funafuti; tel. 20711; fax 20832; depositary library for all govt documents; 19,500 vols, 150 periodicals; Nat. Librarian and Archivist MILA S. TULIMANU.

Parliamentary Library: Tuvalu Parliament, Vaiaku, Funafuti; tel. 20739; fax 20800; f. 1984; 600 vols; Librarian PAULSON PANAPA.

University

UNIVERSITY OF THE SOUTH PACIFIC, TUVALU CENTRE

POB 21, Funafuti
Telephone: 20811
Fax: 20704
E-mail: manuella_d@usp.ac.fj
Internet: www.usp.ac.fj/index.php?id=4502#tuvalu
Founded 1979
Dir: DAVID MANUELLA
Library Officer: TOGIOLA FUNAFUTI
Library of 3,000 vols.

UGANDA

The Higher Education System

Institutions of higher education predate Uganda's independence from the United Kingdom in 1962, the oldest being Makerere University in Kampala, which was founded in 1922 as a technical college for students from British East Africa. After 1949 it was affiliated to the University of London (United Kingdom), and in 1970 it was declared an independent university. There is also a university of science and technology at Mbarara, and a small Islamic university located in Mbale. Public institutions of higher education receive funding from the Ministry of Education and Sports and the Public Sector Commission. According to the Ministry of Education and Sports, the number of students enrolled at Uganda's higher education institutes totalled 155,082, of which 96,821 students were enrolled at one of the country's 23 universities (18 private, 5 public).

The National Council for Higher Education (NCHE) is responsible for accreditation and quality assurance, and institutions seeking to award degrees or other programmes of higher education must fulfil a number of requirements. Once an institution has been awarded a provisional licence by the Council it then has three years to apply for chartered status. In mid-2011 the NCHE announced a new tuition fees structure for public universities, which, if approved by the Government, would lead to an increase in fees of more than 300% for most study programmes.

Two passes in the Uganda Advanced Certificate of Education and five passes in the Uganda Certificate of Education are the main requirements for admission to undergraduate degrees. Sub-degree Certificate and Diploma courses lasting one or two years are offered in a range of subjects, often relating to professional fields of study. The principal undergraduate degree is the Bachelors, which requires completion of a final-year project and is usually a three-year programme of study, although degrees in agriculture, engineering, forestry, technology and veterinary science last four years, and degrees in architecture, medicine and pharmacy last five years. The Bachelors is required for admission to a Masters degree programme. Postgraduate Certificate and Diploma courses, which generally last one year, are open to holders of a Bachelors degree and are available primarily in professional disciplines such as education and medicine. Masters degrees last between 18 months and three years, although two years is increasingly becoming the norm. Following the Masters is the Doctorate, the highest university degree, which is awarded after a minimum of three years' study; depending on the subject, doctoral programmes may consist exclusively of research or may comprise a mixture of research and coursework. Higher Doctorates in arts and science are awarded on the basis of published work.

Post-secondary technical and vocational education is offered by a range of institutions, among them technical colleges, colleges of commerce, vocational training institutes and cooperative colleges. Awards are broadly classified as Craft, Technician or Higher Technician. The Uganda Vocational Qualifications Framework, which is intended to incorporate all nationally recognized vocational qualifications, was under development at 2011.

Regulatory and Representative Bodies

GOVERNMENT

Ministry of Education and Sports: Embassy House and Devt Bldg, Plot 9/11, Parliament Ave, POB 7063, Kampala; tel. (41) 4234451; fax (41) 42230437; e-mail akibenge@education.go.ug; internet www.education.go.ug; Min. NAMIREMBE BITAMAZIRE; Permanent Sec. F. X. K. LUBANGA.

ACCREDITATION

National Council for Higher Education: POB 7634, Cavers Crescent, Kyambogo, Kampala; tel. (31) 2262140; fax (31) 2262145; e-mail nche@infocom.co.ug; internet www.unche.or.ug; f. 2001; statutory agency regulating the management of higher education instns and the quality of higher education; accredits public and private tertiary instns and licenses private tertiary instns; Exec. Dir Prof. A. B. K. KASOZI.

NATIONAL BODIES

Association for Teacher Education in Africa: c/o Assoc. Prof. J. C. B. Bigala, Makerere University, POB 7062, Kampala; f. 1970; to develop and co-ordinate syllabuses and materials to be used in teacher education instns; 50 mem. instns in anglophone Africa; Pres. Prof. M. MOHAPELOA; Sec. Assoc. Prof. J. C. B. BIGALA; publs *Journal of West African Education, Education in Eastern Africa*.

Inter-University Council for East Africa: POB 7110, Kampala; tel. (41) 4256251; fax (41) 4342007; e-mail info@iucea.org; internet www.iucea.org; f. 1980 as a corporate body to succeed the Inter-University Committee for East Africa; aims to facilitate contact and cooperation between the universities of Kenya, Tanzania and Uganda, to provide a forum for discussion on academic matters, and to maintain comparable academic standards; also provides secretariat for the Asscn of Eastern and Southern African Universities (see under International); 36 mem. univs and colleges; Chair. Prof. F. I. B. KAYANJA (Vice-Chancellor, Mbarara University of Science and Technology); Exec. Sec. Prof. CHACHA NYAIGOTTI-CHACHA.

Learned Societies

GENERAL

Uganda Society: POB 4980, Kampala; e-mail ncid@infocom.co.ug; internet www.africa.upenn.edu/ugandasoc/ugandasociety.htm; f. 1923; present name 1933; premises in the Uganda Museum, Kira Rd, Kampala; membership open to persons of all nationalities and institutions, to promote interest in literary, historic, scientific and general cultural matters, discovering and recording facts about the country, arranging lectures and establishing contacts; library of 1,600 vols and periodicals; Pres. Prof. E. H. K. NSUBUGA; Sec. NANNY CARDER; publ. *The Uganda Journal* (2 a year).

BIBLIOGRAPHY, LIBRARY SCIENCE AND MUSEOLOGY

Uganda Library and Information Association: POB 40227, Kampala; tel. (41) 2495592; fax (41) 2540817; internet www.ou.edu/cas/slis/ula/ula_index.htm; f. 1972; 356 mems; Chair. MAGARA ELISAM; Sec. C. BATAMBUZE; publ. *Uganda Library and Information Science Journal* (2 a year).

LANGUAGE AND LITERATURE

Alliance Française: National Theatre, 1st Fl., POB 4314, Kampala; tel. (41) 2344490; fax (41) 2349812; e-mail afka@bushnet.net; offers courses and exams in French language and culture and promotes cultural exchange with France.

British Council: Rwenzori Courts, Plot 2 and 4A, Nakasero Rd, POB 7070, Kampala; tel. (41) 2234725; fax (41) 2254853; internet www.britishcouncil.org/uganda; offers courses and examinations in English language and British culture and promotes cultural exchange with the UK; library of 5,000 vols, 40 periodicals; Dir KATE EWART-BIGGS.

MEDICINE

Uganda Medical Association: Plot 8, 41–43 Circular Rd, POB 2243, Kampala; tel. (41) 2321795; fax (41) 2345597; e-mail myers28@hotmail.com; f. 1961; 1,500 mems; library of 700 vols; Pres. Dr MARGARET MUNGHERERA; Sec. Dr MYERS LUGEMWA; publ. *Uganda Medical Journal*.

Research Institutes

AGRICULTURE, FISHERIES AND VETERINARY SCIENCE

Animal Health Research Centre: POB 24, Entebbe; f. 1926; research and field work in animal diseases, husbandry and nutrition; herbarium; library of 13,950 vols; Dir Veterinary Research Services Prof. O. BWANGAMOI; Librarian H. R. KIBOOLE; publ. *Research Index* (irregular).

Kawanda Agricultural Research Institute: POB 7065, Kampala; tel. and fax (41) 2567649; e-mail karidir@imul.com; f. 1937; research on bananas and coffee, horticulture, post-harvest soil and soil fertility management, integrated pest management, biometrics, plant breeding, plant pathology; 9 research staff; library of 2,600 vols; plant herbarium; insect museum; Dir of Research Dr MATTHIAS MAGUNDA.

Nakawa Forestry Research Centre: POB 8668, Kampala; tel. (41) 2256261; fax (41) 2241682; f. 1952; logging, milling and building research; preservation and seasoning tests; small specialized library.

Namulonge Agricultural and Animal Production Research Institute: POB 7084, Kampala; tel. (41) 2573016; fax (41) 2726554; e-mail fopio@naro-ug.org; internet www.naro.go.ug/institute/namulonge; f. 1949; aims to increase efficiency and yield of crop and livestock production; specific objectives are genetic improvement of crops and livestock, pest and disease control, management of mandate crops, feed resource development and management for livestock; 127 scientific staff; library of 1,700 vols, 155 periodicals; Dir of Research Dr FINA OPIO.

ECONOMICS, LAW AND POLITICS

Centre for Basic Research: 15 Baskerville Ave, Kololo, POB 9863, Kampala; tel. (41) 2342987; fax (41) 2235413; internet www.cbr-ug.org; f. 1988; non-governmental organization active in social research; library of 14,000 vols; Exec. Dir Dr SIMON RUTABA-JUUKA.

Makerere University Institute of Social Research: POB 16022, Kampala; tel. (41) 2554582; fax (41) 2532821; e-mail misronlinetoday@gmail.com; internet misr.mak.ac.ug; f. 1948; conducts ind. research into economic, political and social problems of East Africa; 6 Research Fellows, University staff in depts of economics, environmental studies, political science, rural economy and extension, social administration, social work, sociology, women's studies; library of 10,000 vols, 70 current periodicals; Dir Prof. MAHMOOD MAMDANI; Dir Dr ADAM BRANCH; Librarian IRENE MBAWAKI; publs *East African Studies* (irregular), *East Africa Linguistic Studies* (irregular), *Mawazo Journal* (2 a year), *Policy Abstracts and Research Newsletter*, USSC Conference papers (1 a year), working papers.

MEDICINE

Uganda Virus Research Institute: Entebbe; tel. (41) 4321094; fax (41) 4321124; e-mail information@iavi.or.ug; f. 1936 as Yellow Fever Research Institute; East African Virus Research institute 1950; present name 1977; attached to Uganda National Health Research Organization, under Ministry of Health control; carries out scientific research concerning communicable diseases, especially viral diseases threatening to public health, and advises the govt on strategies for disease control and prevention; Communications Officer DAVID WALUGEMBE.

NATURAL SCIENCES
Physical Sciences

Geological Survey and Mines Department: POB 9, Entebbe; tel. (41) 2320559; fax (41) 2320364; e-mail muinda@energy.go.ug; internet www.energyandminerals.go.ug; f. 1919; library of 22,900 vols; Commissioner J. T. TUHUMWIRE.

Government Chemist Department: POB 2174, Kampala; tel. (41) 2250470; forensic chemical examination, bacteriological examination of foods and water, chemical analysis of water, food and drugs, pollution control, identification and assay of drugs, general chemical analysis of soils and ores, isolation and identification of active principles of medicinal plants; Dir GEOFFREY ONEN.

Libraries and Archives

Kampala

Cabinet Office Library: POB 7168, Kampala; tel. (41) 2254881; fax (41) 2235459; f. 1920; for government officials and for research workers; 10,000 vols; Librarian HERBERT R. KIBOOLE; publ. *Catalogue*.

Forestry Department Library: POB 7124, Kampala; tel. (41) 2347085; fax (41) 2347086; f. 1904; specialized library (open to students by special arrangement with the Commissioner for Forestry): literature on forestry and related sciences; 20,000 vols; Librarian W. M. BWIRUKA.

Makerere University, Albert Cook Library: Makerere Univ., College of Health Sciences, POB 7072, Kampala; tel. (41) 4534149; fax (41) 4530024; e-mail cooklib@chs.mak.ac.ug; internet mulib.mak.ac.ug/acooklib; f. 1946; 60,000 vols, 500 periodicals, covering all medical subjects, especially East African and tropical medicine, spec. collns: history of medicine, Mengo Notes, WHO publs, database of Ugandan health literature; Head and Sr Librarian RACHEL NAKALEMBE (acting); publ. *Uganda Health Information Digest* (3 a year).

Makerere University Library Service: POB 16002, Kampala; tel. (41) 2531041; fax (41) 2540374; e-mail info@mulib.mak.ac.ug; internet www.makerere.ac.ug/mulib; f. 1940; consists of a Main Library, functioning as National Reference Library, with seven sub-libraries: five located on the main campus: East African School of Library and Information Science Library, Education Library, Institute of Adult and Continuing Education Library, Makerere Institute of Social Research Library and the Veterinary Library; and two off-campus: Albert Cook Library at the Medical School, Mulago; and Makerere University Agricultural Research Institute Library at the Agricultural Institute, Kabayoro; 384,000 vols, 330 current periodicals, spec. colln on East Africa, Uganda legal deposit, and private archives; book-bank system of basic textbooks kept in departmental libraries, comprising 182,000 vols; Librarian Dr MARIA G. N. MUSOKE; publs *East African Studies, Makerere Law Journal, Makerere Political Review, Mawazo*.

National Library of Uganda: Buganda Rd, POB 4262, Kampala; tel. (41) 233633; fax (41) 348625; e-mail library@infocom.co.ug; internet www.nlu.go.ug; f. 1964 as Public Libraries Board; present name 2003; organizes the collection and management of the nation's documented heritage, for current and future use; assists local govts in the management of public libraries; provides bibliographic control and aims to promote a reading culture among Ugandans, through reading tents and book donations to schools; provides an information referral service on Uganda; 157,000 vols, 200 serial titles; Dir GERTRUDE KAYAGA MULINDWA; publ. *National Bibliography of Uganda*.

Museums and Art Galleries

Entebbe

Entebbe Botanical Gardens: Lugard Rd, POB 295, Entebbe; tel. (41) 2320638; fax (41) 2321070; e-mail curator@infocom.co.ug; f. 1898; conservation and devt of native and exotic plants, colln and planting of local medicinal plants; Curator JOHN MULUMBA-WASSWA; publ. *Index Seminum* (1 a year).

Game and Fisheries Museum, Aquarium and Library: Johnstone Rd, POB 4, Entebbe; collections of heads of game animals, reptiles, fish and butterflies, hunting and fishing implements and weapons; library of 1,100 vols; Commissioner for Fisheries CHRISTOPHER DHATEMWA; Commissioner for Wildlife MOSES OKUA.

Geological Survey Museum and Documentation Centre: POB 9, Entebbe; tel. (41) 2320559; fax (41) 2320364; e-mail minerals@infocom.co.ug; f. 1919; attached to Geological Survey and Mines Department; about 37,500 specimens of rocks and minerals; library of over 9,850 vols and 3,850 periodicals; Commissioner of the Geological Survey and Mines Department JOSHUA T. TUHUMWIRE.

Uganda Wildlife Education Centre: 56–57 Johnston St, POB 369, Entebbe; tel. (41) 4322169; fax (41) 4320073; e-mail info@uwec.ug; internet www.uweczoo.org; f. 1952, present name and status 1994; conservation, education, rescue and rehabilitation of orphaned, injured and/or confiscated wildlife; captive breeding of endangered wildlife species; Exec. Dir Dr JAMES MUSINGUZI.

Kampala

Uganda Museum: 5–7 Kira Rd, POB 365, Kampala; tel. (41) 2244060; fax (41) 2245580; f. 1908; natural history, geology, ethnology, archaeology, palaeontology; science and industry pavilion; special collection of African musical instruments; centre for archaeological research in Uganda; library of 4,000 vols; Curator Dr E. KAMUHANGIRE.

Universities

GULU UNIVERSITY

POB 166, Gulu
Telephone: (47) 1432095
Fax: (47) 1432094
Internet: www.gu.ac.ug
Founded 2002
State control
Language of instruction: English
Academic year: August to May
Rector: JACK H. PEN-MOGI NYOKI
Univ. Sec.: VINCENT M. OKOTH-OGOLA
Academic Registrar: GEOFFREY LAMTOO
Librarian: AREGU RAPHAEL
Library of 23,000 vols, 33 periodicals
Number of teachers: 188
Number of students: 3,831

DEANS

Faculty of Agriculture and Environment: Prof. CALLISTUS W. BALIDDAWA
Faculty of Business and Development Studies: UWONDA GILBERT

Faculty of Education and Humanities: OKUMU CHARLES
Faculty of Medicine: Prof. EMILIO OVUGA
Faculty of Science: Dr ANDOGAH GEOFFREY

ISLAMIC UNIVERSITY IN UGANDA

POB 2555, Mbale
Telephone: (35) 2512100
Fax: (35) 2280525
E-mail: info@iuiu.ac.ug
Internet: www.iuiu.ac.ug
Founded 1988
Private control
Languages of instruction: Arabic, English
Academic year: August to July

Rector: Dr AHMAD KAWESA SENGENDO
Vice-Rector for Academic Affairs: Dr MPEZA-MIHIGO MOUHAMAD
Vice-Rector for Finance and Admin.: Dr KAZIBA ABDUL MPAATA
Univ. Sec.: SSENTONGO ABUBAKAR
Academic Registrar: KASIITA MUSA
Librarian: Dr SESSANGA IDRIS
Library of 42,617 vols, 41,423 books, 1,490 serial titles, 570 online bibliographic items, 570 e-books, 170 reference books, 152 print journals, 3,205 research reports, theses and dissertations
Number of teachers: 358
Number of students: 6,738
Publications: Islamic University Journal (2 a year), IUIU Law Journal (1 a year)

DEANS

Faculty of Arts and Social Sciences: Dr MWANGA MOSES
Faculty of Education: Dr NIMULORA MAIMUNA
Faculty of Islamic Studies and Arabic Language: Dr HUSSEIN MUHAMMAD BOWA
Faculty of Law: SAIDAT NAKITTO
Faculty of Management Studies: KITAKULE MUBI HUSSEIN
Faculty of Science: ADAM ALI

KAMPALA UNIVERSITY

POB 25454, Kampala
Telephone: (41) 2258219
E-mail: kuniv@afsat.com
Private control
Vice-Chancellor: Prof. BADRU KATEREGA.

KYAMBOGO UNIVERSITY

POB 1, Kyambogo
Telephone: (41) 4285001
Fax: (41) 4220464
Internet: www.kyu.ac.ug
Founded 1954 as Uganda Polytechnic Kyambogo; univ. status 2001 following merger with Institute of Teacher Education Kyambogo and Uganda Nat. Institute for Special Education
State control
Chancellor: Dr ERIC TIYO SSEKEBUGA ADRIKO
Ccl Chair.: JAMES KALEBO
Vice-Chancellor: Prof. ISAIAH OMOLO NDIEGE
Univ. Sec.: PATRICK MADAYA (acting)
Dean of Students: CYRIACO KABAGAMBE
Registrar: ANDREW CULA (acting)
Librarian: JUSTINE KIYIMBA
Library of 150,000 vols, 12,000 periodicals
Number of students: 25,000

DEANS

Faculty of Arts and Social Sciences: Dr CYPRIAN ADUPA
Faculty of Education: Dr JOHN KAHEERU-KATIGO
Faculty of Engineering: DAUDI MUGISA
Faculty of Science: AARON WANYAMA

Faculty of Special Needs Education and Rehabilitation: Dr J. B. OKECH
Faculty of Vocational Studies: Dr WILLIAM EPEJU
School of Management and Entrepreneurship: JOCOB OYUGI

MAKERERE UNIVERSITY

POB 7062, Kampala
Telephone: (41) 2542803
Fax: (41) 2541068
E-mail: helpme@dicts.mak.ac.ug
Internet: mak.ac.ug
Founded 1922 as technical school; became Univ. College 1949, attained Univ. status 1970
State control
Language of instruction: English
Academic year: October to June

Chancellor: H. E. THE PRES. OF UGANDA
Vice-Chancellor: Prof. J. P. SEBUWUFU
Deputy Vice-Chancellor: Prof. J. EPELU-OPIO
Sec.: S. R. BYANAGWA
Academic Registrar: AMOS OLAL-ODUR
Librarian: J. MUGASHA
Number of teachers: 1,089
Number of students: 27,976
Publication: Mawazo

DEANS

Faculty of Agriculture: Assoc. Prof. E. N. SABIITI
Faculty of Arts: Dr O. NDOLERIIRE
Faculty of Commerce: WASWA-BALUNYWA
Faculty of Forestry and Nature Conservation: Dr J. KABOGGOZA
Faculty of Law: Assoc. Prof. J. OLOKA-ONYANGO
Faculty of Medicine: Assoc. Prof. N. SEWAN-KEMBO
Faculty of Science: Dr H. ORYEM-ORIGA
Faculty of Social Sciences: Dr JOY KWESIGA
Faculty of Technology: Dr B. M. KIGGUNDU
Faculty of Veterinary Medicine: Assoc. Prof. E. KATUNGA-RWAKISHAYA
Margaret Trowell School of Industrial and Fine Arts: J. MUKASA
School of Education: Dr C. MASEMBE-SSE-BUNGA

PROFESSORS

Faculty of Agriculture (tel. (41) 2542277; fax (41) 2531641; e-mail dean@foamak.ug.com; internet www.makerere.ac.ug):

BAREEBA, F. B., Animal Science
EKWAMU, A., Crop Science
KITUNGULU-ZAKE, Y. J., Soil Science
KIWUWA, G. H., Animal Science
OSIRU, D. O., Crop Science
RUBAIHAYO, P. R.
RUYOOKA, D., Forestry

Faculty of Arts (tel. (41) 2542241; fax (41) 2542265; e-mail faculty@arts.mak.ac.ug):

BYARUHANGA-AKIIKI, A. B. T., Religious Studies and Philosophy
DALFOVO, A. T., Philosophy
MUKAMA, R.
TIBENDERANA, P. K., History

Faculty of Law (tel. (41) 2542284; fax (41) 2543110; e-mail lawdean@muklaw.ac.ug):

BAKIBINGA, D. J., Commercial Law
KAKOOZA, J. M. N., Law and Jurisprudence

Faculty of Medicine (tel. (41) 2530020; fax (41) 2531091; e-mail sewankam@infocom.co.ug):

ANOKBONGGO, W. W., Pharmacology and Therapeutics
BULWA, F. M., Obstetrics and Gynaecology
MMIRO, F. A., Obstetrics and Gynaecology
MUGERWA, J. W., Pathology
MUNUBE, J., Microbiology

NDUGWA, C. M., Paediatrics and Child Health
ODOI-ADOME, R., Pharmacy
OTIM, M. A., Medicine
OWOR, R., Pathology
SWEANKAMBO, N. K., Medicine

Faculty of Science (tel. (41) 2541258; fax (41) 2531061; e-mail deansci@mak.ac.ug):

BANAGE, W. B., Zoology
BANDA, E. K. J., Physics
ILUKOR, J. O., Physics
KAHWA, Y., Physics
KAKONGE, E., Biochemistry
LUBOOBI, L. S., Mathematics
MUGAMBE, P. E., Physics
MUGAMBI, P. E., Mathematics
OKWAKOL, M. N., Zoology
OLWA-ODYEK, Chemistry
POMEROY, D. E., Zoology
SEKAALO, H., Chemistry
TALIGOOLA, H. K., Botany
TUKAHIRWA, E., Environmental Science

Faculty of Social Sciences (tel. (41) 2545040; fax (41) 2530815; e-mail deanfss@mak.ac.ug):

AKIIKI-MUJAJU, A. B., Political Science
GINGYERA-PINYCWA, A. C. G., Political Science
MWAKA, V. M.

Institute of Statistics and Applied Economics (tel. (41) 2534224):

NTOZI, S. P. N.
TULYA-MUHIKA

School of Education (tel. (41) 2540733; e-mail deaneduc@mak.ac.ug):

MUSAAZI, J. S., Higher Education
OCITTI, J., Geography
ODAET, C. F., Educational Foundations and Management
OPOLOT, J. A., Psychology

ATTACHED INSTITUTES

East African School of Librarianship: Kampala; f. 1963 to train librarians for all parts of East Africa; 3-year course leads to degree in Library and Information Science; Dir S. A. H. ABIDI.

Institute of Adult and Continuing Education: Kampala; f. 1953; three divisions: Adult Education and Communication Studies, Community Education and Extra-Mural Studies, Distance Education; one-year postsecondary school courses; shorter courses are also arranged both at the centre and in surrounding rural areas; Dir NUWA SENTONGO.

Institute of Statistics and Applied Economics: a joint enterprise of the Government of Uganda and the United Nations Development Programme; depts of Planning and Applied Statistics, Population Studies, and Statistical Methods; 3-year degree courses; Dir Dr X. R. MUGISHA.

Makerere Institute of Social Research: see under Research Institutes.

MBARARA UNIVERSITY OF SCIENCE AND TECHNOLOGY

POB 1410, Mbarara
Telephone: (48) 5221623
Fax: (48) 5220782
E-mail: vc@must.ac.ug
Internet: www.must.ac.ug
Founded 1989
State control
Language of instruction: English
Academic year: October to August

Chancellor: Prof. RAPHAEL OWOR
Vice-Chancellor: Prof. F. I. B. KAYANJA
Registrar: S. B. BAZIRAKE
Librarian: ANNE GAKIBAYO
Library of 22,100 vols

Number of teachers: 144
Number of students: 1,104
Publications: *Medical Journal* (1 a year),
Science Journal (1 a year)

DEANS

Faculty of Development Studies: Prof.
PAMELA MBABAZI
Faculty of Medicine: Prof. J. KABAKYENGA
Faculty of Science Education: Prof. J. BAR-
ANGA

PROFESSORS

BARANGA, J., Biology
BEGUMYA, Y. R., Physiology
JAEGER, B., Dermatology
KAYANJA, F. I. B., Histology
PEPPER, L., Medicine

ATTACHED INSTITUTE

**Institute of Tropical Forest Conserva-
tion:** POB 7487, Kampala; fax 245597; Dir
Dr A. MCNEILAGE.

NAMASAGALI UNIVERSITY

POB 241, Kamuli
Telephone: (77) 2861961
Founded 1975; present status 1998
Private control
Vice-Chancellor: SAMWIRI KIGWANA
Library of 5,000 vols
Number of teachers: 58
Number of students: 531

DEANS

Faculty of Education: PETER MUBIRU
Faculty of Management and Development
Studies: WILLIAM SAAZI

NDEJJE UNIVERSITY

POB 7088, Kampala
Telephone: (92) 730322
Fax: (77) 2610132
E-mail: vc@ndejjeuniversity.ac.ug
Founded 1992
Private control
Academic year: August to June
Schools of business administration and com-
puter science, education

Vice-Chancellor: Bishop Dr MICHAEL
SENYIMBA
Library of 47,083 vols
Number of teachers: 148
Number of students: 7,500

UGANDA CHRISTIAN UNIVERSITY

POB 4, Mukono
Telephone: (31) 2350800
Fax: (41) 4290800
E-mail: ucu@ucu.ac.ug
Internet: www.ucu.ac.ug
Founded 1913 as Bishop Tucker Theological
College, present name and status 1997
Private control
Language of instruction: English
Academic year: September to August
Chancellor: HENRY LUKE OROMBI
Vice-Chancellor: Dr JOHN MUSISI SENYONYI
Deputy Vice-Chancellor for Academic
Affairs: Dr ALEX KAGUME
Deputy Vice-Chancellor for Devt and Exter-
nal Relations: DOUG FOUNTAIN
Deputy Vice-Chancellor for Finance and
Admin.: Dr FLORENCE BAKIBINGA SAJJABI
Dir of Student Affairs: MILTON TWEHEYO
Univ. Librarian: Dr FREDRICK NATHANIEL
MUKUNGU
Library of 150,000 vols, 70 periodicals
Number of teachers: 175
Number of students: 11,000 (5 campuses)

DEANS

Bishop Barham Univ. College: Prof. MANUEL
MURANGA
Bishop Tucker School of Divinity and The-
ology: Dr OLIVIA NASSAKA BANJA
Faculty of Business and Admin.: VINCENT
KISENYI
Faculty of Education and Arts: Dr MEDARD
RUGYENDO
Faculty of Law: Dr PAMELA TIBIHIKIIRA-
KALYEGIRA
Faculty of Science and Technology: Dr
FABIAN NABUGOOMU
Faculty of Social Sciences: Dr ELIZABETH
BACWAYO KUKUNDA
School of Research and Post Graduate Stud-
ies: Prof. CHRISTOPHER BYARUHANGA
UCU Mbale Campus: Dr STEPHEN MUNGOMA

UGANDA MARTYRS UNIVERSITY

POB 5498, Kampala
Telephone: (38) 2410611
Fax: (38) 2410100
E-mail: umu@umu.ac.ug
Internet: www.fiuc.org/umu
Founded 1993
Private control
Academic year: August to September
Chancellor: Rt Rev. Bishop MATTHIAS SSEKA-
MANYA
Vice-Chancellor: Prof. Dr CHARLES OLWENY
Deputy Vice-Chancellor for Academic
Affairs: Asst Prof. Dr JOSEPH KISEKKA
Deputy Vice-Chancellor for Finance and
Admin.: Asst Prof. Dr SIMEON WANYAMA
Registrar: INNOCENT BYUMA
Librarian: JUDITH NANNOZI
Library of 38,435 vols
Number of teachers: 240
Number of students: 4,697

Publications: *Health Policy Journal*, *Journal
of Science*, *Mtafiti Mwafrika* (African
Researcher, 3 a year)

DEANS

Centre for Distance Learning: Dr GUDULA
NAIGA BASAZA
Centre for Extra-Mural Studies: Dr MARTIN
O'REILLY (Head)
Dept of Good Governance and Peace Studies:
Dr MAXIMIANO NGABIRANO (Head)
Dept of Information and Communications
Technology: CYPRIAN LWANGA (Head)
Dept of Information Systems: Prof. Dr PETER
KALEMA (Head)
East African School of Diplomacy, Govern-
ance and Int. Studies: SAMUEL BALIGIDDE
(Dir)
Faculty of Agriculture: Dr CHARLES KUDAMBA
Faculty of Built Environment: CONNIE NSHE-
MEREIRWE
Faculty of Business Administration and
Management: Dr ALEX IJO
Faculty of Education: Prof. BARNABAS OTAALA
Faculty of Health Sciences: Dr VINCENT
BWETE
Faculty of Sciences: HENRY KIWANUKA
Institute of Ethics and Development Studies:
Dr JUDE SSEBUWUFU (Dir)
School of Postgraduate Studies: Prof. Dr
PETER KANYANDAGO (Dir)

UKRAINE

The Higher Education System

Institutions of higher education predate Ukraine (formerly Ukrainian SSR)'s independence from the USSR in 1991, the oldest being National University of Kyiv-Mohyla Academy, which was founded in 1615. The next oldest institution is National University of Lviv 'Ivan Franko', which was founded in 1661. During the period of Soviet rule (1920–91) over 60 universities, academies and institutions of higher education were founded.

Since independence, the Law on Education (1991) is the defining legislation for all levels of the education system, and an accreditation system of licensing, assessment and certification of educational establishments has been in place since 1992. Ukraine has also become a member of the European Quality Assurance Register. Other than the Ministry of Education and Science, and Youth and Sport, institutions of higher education may also be attached to the relevant ministry. Ukraine signed up for the Bologna Process in 2005, the first phase of which was to adopt a credit-based system of comparable degrees with two main cycles (undergraduate and graduate). Since 2006/07 the European Credit Transfer and Accumulation System (ECTS) has been introduced for all programmes of the first and second cycles, directly corresponding with the national system of credits. Specialists in the fields of medicine and veterinary medicine, however, still follow a long integrated cycle. Higher education is classified into four levels, in ascending order: technical colleges (Level I), colleges (Level II), institutes (Level III) and universities, academies and institutes (Level IV). In 2010/11 there were 2,491,300 students enrolled in one of 854 higher education institutions. Proposals to reduce the number of institutions via closures and mergers in a bid to strengthen and consolidate the higher education system were under discussion in 2011. A draft national qualification framework was approved in October of that year and was awaiting approval by the Cabinet of Ministers.

The main requirements for admission to higher education are award of the Atestat pro Povnu Zagal'nu Sersdniu Osvitu (General Secondary Education Certificate) and satisfactory performance in the Independent External Examination, a standardized common university admissions examination introduced in 2008. In 1996 Ukraine introduced a two-tier Bachelors and Masters degree system. More recently, further reforms have been effected, including the introduction in 2006/07 of the ECTS, in accordance with the principles of the Bologna Process; however, the old-style degrees are still available. The Dyplom Bakalavra (Bachelors) is an undergraduate degree of four years, and is offered parallel to the Dyplom Spetsialista (Specialist Diploma), an integrated five-year programme of study mostly offered by institutes. The first postgraduate degree under the new system is the Dyplom Magistra (Masters), and it lasts for one or two years after the award of the Dyplom Bakalavra or Dyplom Spetsialista. Finally, doctoral-level studies consist of two awards, both lasting three years: the Dyplom pro Prysudzhenia Naukovogo Stupenia Kandydata Nauk (Diploma of Candidate of Sciences) and Dyplom pro Prysudzhenia Naukovogo Stupenia Doktora Nauk (Diploma of Doctor of Sciences).

Vocational education is provided by technical and vocational schools, which offer Qualification Certificates and Junior Specialist Diplomas.

Regulatory and Representative Bodies

GOVERNMENT

Ministry of Culture and Tourism: 01601 Kyiv, vul. Ivana Franka 19; tel. (44) 226-26-45; fax (44) 235-32-57; e-mail ministr@mincult.gov.ua; internet www.mincult.gov.ua; Min. VASYL V. VOVKUN.

Ministry of Education and Science, and Youth and Sport: 01601 Kyiv, blv T. Shevchenka 16; tel. (44) 226-26-61; fax (44) 274-10-49; e-mail press@mon.gov.ua; internet www.mon.gov.ua; Minister IVAN O. VAKARCHUK.

ACCREDITATION

ENIC/NARIC Ukraine: Dept for Licensing and Accreditation, Min. of Education and Science, and Youth and Sport, 10 Ave Pobedy, 01135 Kyiv; tel. and fax (44) 486-74-09; e-mail dlan@mon.gov.ua; internet www.mon.gov.ua; attached to Dept for Scientific Researches and Licensing, Min. of Education and Science, and Youth and Sport; recognizes academic foreign qualifications; verifies educational documents issued in Ukraine (apostille); int. academic mobility; Dir MICHAEL GONCHARENKO.

NATIONAL BODIES

Academy of Pedagogical Sciences of Ukraine: 04053 Kyiv, Artema vul. 52A; tel. (44) 211-94-01; fax (44) 226-31-80; e-mail info@apsu.org.ua; internet www.apsu.org.ua; f. 1992; Pres. Prof. VASYL H. KREMEN; publs *Biolohiya i Khimiya v Shkoli* (Biology and Chemistry at School, 4 a year), *Compyuter v Shkoli i Simyi* (Computer at School and at Home, 4 a year), *Defektolohiya* (Defectology, 4 a year), *Fizyka i Astronomiya v Shkoli* (Physics and Astronomy at School, 4 a year), *Heohrafiya i Osnovy Ekonomiky v Shkoli* (Geography and Fundamentals of Economics at School, 4 a year), *Istoriya v Shkolakh Ukrainy* (History in Ukrainian Schools, 4 a year), *Matemmatyka v Shkoli* (Mathematics at School, 4 a year), *Mystetstvo i Osvita* (Arts and Education, 4 a year), *Nauka i Osvita* (Science and Education, 2 a year), *Obdarovana Dytyna* (Gifted Child, 6 a year), *Pedahohichna Hazeta* (Pedagogical Newspaper, 12 a year), *Pedahohika i Psykholohiya* (Pedagogy and Psychology, 4 a year), *Praktychna Psykholohiya i Sotsialna Robota* (Applied Psychology and Social Work, 12 a year), *Profesiyno-Tekhnichna Osvita* (Vocational and Technical Education, 4 a year), *Shlyakh Osvity* (A Way of Education, 4 a year), *Ukrainska Literatura v Zahalnoosvitniy Shkoli* (Ukrainian Literature at Secondary School, 6 a year), *Ukrainska Mova i Literatura v Shkoli* (Ukrainian Language and Literature at School, 4 a year), *Vyshcha Osvita Ukrainy* (Higher Education in Ukraine, 4 a year), *Zarubizhna Literatura v Navchalnykh Zakladakh* (Foreign Literature at Educational Institutions, 12 a year).

Association of Non-State-Owned Educational Institutions of Ukraine: 252115 Kyiv, 16-v Vernadsky Ave; tel. (44) 452-76-55; fax (44) 444-05-44; e-mail assoc@ufimb.kiev.ua; internet www.ambernet.kiev.ua/~tlc/aeiunfp/index_e.htm; f. 1993; aims to improve the educational system in the Ukraine; 68 mem. instns; Head Prof. IVAN TIMOSCHENKO.

Council of Rectors of Ukrainian Institutions of Higher Education: 01017 Kyiv, Taras Shevchenko Kyiv Nat. Univ., vul. Volodymyrska 60; internet www.univ.kiev.ua; Pres. Prof. Dr VIKTOR V. SKOPENKO.

Learned Societies

GENERAL

National Academy of Sciences of Ukraine: 01601 Kyiv, Volodymyrska 54; tel. (44) 225-22-39; fax (44) 224-32-43; e-mail prez@nas.gov.ua; internet www.nas.gov.ua; f. 1918; sections of chemical and biological sciences, physical-technical and mathematical sciences, social sciences and humanities; depts of chemistry, earth sciences, economics, general biology, history, philosophy and law, informatics, literature, language and art criticism , mathematics, mechanics , molecular biology, biochemistry and experimental and clinical physiology, physical and technical problems of materials science, physical and technical problems of power engineering, physics and astronomy; attached research institutes: see under Research Institutes; 708 mems (207 full, 378 corresp., 123 foreign); library: see under Libraries and Archives; Pres. Acad. BORIS PATON; Vice-Pres. Acad. ANATOLIY SHPAK; Chief Scientific Sec. ANATOLIY ZAGORODNY; publs in Ukrainian and English: *Dopovidi NAN Ukrainy*, *Ekonomika Ukrainy* (Economy of Ukraine, 12 a year), *Kosmichna Nauka i Tekhnologiya* (Space Science and Engineering, 6 a year), *Kyivska Starovyna* (Kiev Antiquities, 6 a year), *Visnyk NAN Ukrainy* (Journal of the National Academy of Sciences of Ukraine,12 a year, in Ukrainian and English).

Shevchenko Scientific Society: 290013 Lviv, vul. Gen. Chuprynka 21; tel. (322) 34-51-63; fax (322) 76-04-97; e-mail ntsh@ipm .lviv.ua; f. 1873; broad range of arts and sciences; library of 30,000 vols; Pres. Prof. O. M. ROMANIV; Sec. O. A. KUPCHYNSKY; publ. *Memoires* (2 a year).

AGRICULTURE, FISHERIES AND VETERINARY SCIENCE

Ukrainian Academy of Agricultural Sciences: 01010 Kyiv, vul. Suvorova 9; tel. (44) 290-10-85; fax (44) 290-94-73; internet www .aginukraine.com/uaas; f. 1990; 4,900 mems; attached research institutes: see Research Institutes; publ. *Visnyk Agrarnoi Nauky* (Bulletin of Agricultural Science, 12 a year).

ARCHITECTURE AND TOWN PLANNING

National Union of Architects of Ukraine: 01001 Kyiv, vul. Hrychenka 7; tel. (44) 279-98-09; fax (44) 228-13-11; Pres. IHOR SHPARA.

BIBLIOGRAPHY, LIBRARY SCIENCE AND MUSEOLOGY

Association of Libraries of Ukraine: 03039 Kyiv, pr. Richchya Zhovtnya 3; tel. (44) 265-81-04; fax (44) 264-33-98; e-mail nlu@csl.freenet.kiev.ua; internet www.nbuv .gov.ua; Pres. OLEKSIY S. ONYSCHENKO.

ECONOMICS, LAW AND POLITICS

Academy of Legal Sciences of Ukraine: 61024 Kharkiv, vul. Pushkinska 70; tel. (57) 704-19-01; fax (57) 704-19-10; e-mail aprnu@ online.kharkiv.com; internet www.aprnu .kharkiv.org; f. 1993; Pres. Acad. VASIL YA. TATSIY.

FINE AND PERFORMING ARTS

National Artists' Union of Ukraine: 04053 Kyiv, vul. Sichovykh Striltsiv 1–5; tel. (44) 212-01-33; fax (44) 212-14-54; e-mail spilka@nbi.com.ua; internet www.nshu.org .ua; f. 1938; 33 regional constituent orgs; 4,330 mems; Head VOLODYMYR A. CHEPELNIK.

National Union of Cinematographers of Ukraine: 01033 Kyiv, vul. Saksahanskoho 6; tel. and fax (44) 287-75-57; e-mail ukrkino@ ln.ua; internet www.ukrkino.com.ua; f. 1958; 1,251 mems; Head BORIS I. SAVCHENKO.

National Writers' Union of Ukraine: 01024 Kyiv, vul. Bankova 2; tel. (44) 293-45-86; e-mail nspu@i.kiev.ua; internet www .nspu.kiev.ua; f. 1934 as part of the Writers' Union of the former USSR; 1,600 mems; Head VOLODYMYR O. YAVORIVSKY.

HISTORY, GEOGRAPHY AND ARCHAEOLOGY

Ukrainian Geographical Society: 03022 Kyiv, vul. Vasilkivska 90; fax (44) 266-54-17; e-mail vpsh@icchq.univ.kiev.ua; Head PETRO H. SHISHCHENKO.

LANGUAGE AND LITERATURE

British Council: 04070 Kyiv, 4/12 vul. Hryhoriya Skovorody; tel. (44) 490-56-00; fax (44) 490-56-05; e-mail enquiry@ britishcouncil.org.ua; internet www .britishcouncil.org/ukraine; teaching centre; offers courses and exams in English language and British culture and promotes cultural exchange with the UK; attached

offices in Donetsk, Kharkiv, Lviv and Odessa; training and professional development centre; Dir TERRY SANDELL; Teaching Centre Man. TONY HUBBARD.

Goethe-Institut: 04655 Kyiv, vul. Voloska, 12/4; tel. (44) 496-97-85; fax (44) 496-97-89; e-mail info@kiew.goethe.org; internet www .goethe.de/ukraine; f. 1994; offers courses and exams in German language and culture and promotes cultural exchange with Germany; Dir VERA BAGALIANTZ; Deputy Dir PETRA KÖPPEL MEYER.

Institut français d'Ukraine: 01054 Kiev, 84, rue Hontchara; tel. (44) 482-23-71; fax (44) 484-16-87; e-mail standard@ifu.kiev.ua; internet www.institutfrancais-ukraine.com; f. 1994; offers courses and exams in French language and culture; promotes cultural exchange with France; attached Institut français in Kharkiv; works in cooperation with the chain of Alliances Française in Ukraine: Dnepropetrovsk, Donetsk, Kharkiv, Lougansk, Lviv, Odessa, Rivne, Sebastopol, Simferopol and Zaporijjia.

MEDICINE

Gerontology and Geriatrics Society: Institute of Gerontology, 252655 Kyiv 114, Vyshgorodska vul. 67; tel. (44) 430-40-68; fax (44) 432-99-56; e-mail admin@geront.kiev .ua; f. 1963; 250 mems; library of 72,000 vols; Chair. V. V. BEZRUKOV; Chief Learned Sec. O. K. KULTCHITSKY; publ. *Problems of Ageing and Longevity* (4 a year).

National Academy of Medical Sciences of Ukraine: 04050 Kyiv, vul. Gertsena 12; tel. and fax (44) 483-34-11; e-mail drbut@ukr .net; internet www.amnu.kiev.ua; f. 1993; 132 mems (incl. 77 corresp. mems and 19 foreign mems); attached research institutes: see Research Institutes; Pres. ANDRII SERDYUK; Chief Scientific Sec. VOLODYMYR A. MIKHNOV; publ. *Journal* (4 a year).

Ukrainian Association of Radiologists: 03022 Kyiv, vul. Lomonsova 33/43; tel. and fax (44) 258-97-86; e-mail aru-kiev@ukr.net; internet www.aruk.org; f. 1992; 6,000 mems; Chair. Prof. VLADIMIR E. MEDVEDEV; publ. *Radiodiagnostics and Radiotherapy* (4 a year).

Ukrainian Physiological Society: 01024 Kyiv, vul. Bohomoltsya 4; tel. (44) 253-29-09; fax (44) 256-20-00; e-mail pkostyuk@biph .kiev.ua; internet uaphsoc.biph.kiev.ua; Head Acad. PLATON H. KOSTYUK; publ. *Fiziologichnyi Zhurnal* (Physiological Journal, 6 a year).

Ukrainian Scientific Society of Cardiologists: c/o Institute of Cardiology 'M. D. Strazhevska', 03151 Kyiv, vul. Narodnogo Opolcheniya 5; tel. (44) 449-70-03; internet www.ukrcardio.org; Pres. VOLODYMYR KOVALENKO.

Ukrainian Scientific Society of Hygienists: 02660 Kyiv, vul. Popudrenka 50; tel. and fax (44) 559-90-90; e-mail regina@usch .kiev.ua; f. 1953; Head ANDRIY M. SERDYUK.

Ukrainian Society of Allergology and Clinical Immunology: c/o Dept of Immunology and Allergy, National Medical University 'O. Bohomolets', 04053 Kyiv, vul. Kotsyubinskoho 9a; tel. (44) 216-54-03; fax (44) 216-24-02; Chair. Prof. H. DRANNIK.

Ukrainian Society of Ophthalmologists: c/o Institute of Eye Diseases and Tissue Therapy, 'V. P. Filatov', 65061 Odessa, bul. Frantsuzky 49/51; tel. (048) 60-34-46; fax (048) 68-48-51; e-mail iryna.ods@gmail.com; f. 1936; 1,200 mems.

NATURAL SCIENCES
General

Scientific and Technical Societies— National Headquarters: 252053 Kyiv, vul. Artema 21; tel. (44) 212-42-34.

Biological Sciences

Ukrainian Biochemical Society: c/o Palladin Institute of Biochemistry, 01601 Kyiv, vul. Leontovicha 9; tel. (44) 234-59-74; fax (44) 279-63-65; e-mail secretar@biochem.kiev .ua; internet www.biochemistry.org.ua; f. 1928; organizes congresses, seminars and confs; 680 mems; library of 86,000 vols; Chair. Prof. SERHIY V. KOMISARENKO; publs *Biotechnologia* (Biotechnology, 6 a year, in Ukrainian, English and Russian), *Ukrainskyi Biokhimichnyi Zhurnal* (Ukrainian Biochemical Journal, 6 a year, in Ukrainian, English and Russian).

Physical Sciences

Ukrainian Physical Society: 03680 Kyiv, pr. Glushkova 4; tel. and fax (44) 526-40-36; e-mail krav@univ.kiev.ua; internet www.ups .kiev.ua; f. 1990; 425 mems; Pres. Prof. VOLODYMYR G. LITOVCHENKO.

Ukrainian Society of Geodesy, Aerospace Surveying and Cartography: c/o Ministry of Environment and Natural Resources of Ukraine, 02094 Kyiv, vul. Popudrenka 54; tel. (44) 268-21-09; fax (44) 559-73-89; e-mail ssavchuk@polynet.lviv.ua; Pres. IHOR TREVOHO.

PHILOSOPHY AND PSYCHOLOGY

Ukranian Psychological Society: 01032 Kyiv, bul. T. Shevchenka 27A, Office 305; tel. and fax (44) 246-54-59; e-mail ucap@ukr.net; internet www.ucap.kiev.ua; Dir Dr VITALIY PANOK.

RELIGION, SOCIOLOGY AND ANTHROPOLOGY

Sociological Association of Ukraine: 01021 Kyiv, vul. Shovkovychna 12; tel. and fax (44) 291-52-46; e-mail sau@mail.kar.net; Dir Dr N. SHULGA.

TECHNOLOGY

Chornobyl Center for Nuclear Safety, Radioactive Waste and Radioecology: 07100 Kyiv, Slavutych, vul. Hvardeyskoi Divizii 77, 7/1; tel. (44) 792-30-16; fax (44) 792-81-44; e-mail center@chornobyl.net; internet www.chornobyl.net; f. 1996; Coordinating Dir Prof. YEVGEN V. GARIN.

Ukrainian Society of Mechanical Engineers: c/o Br. of Mechanics of the Nat. Acad. of Sciences of Ukraine, 49600 Dnipropetrovsk, vul. Leshko-Popelya 15; tel. (56) 745-12-38; fax (56) 247-34-13; e-mail itm@pvv.dp.ua; internet www.itm.dp.ua; Pres. Acad. VIKTOR PYLYPENKO.

Ukrainian Society for Non-Destructive Testing: 03680 Kyiv, vul. Bozhenko 11; tel. (44) 287-26-66; fax (44) 289-21-66; e-mail usndt@ukr.net; internet www.usndt.com.ua; f. 1990; 200 mems; Pres. Prof. VOLODYMYR TROITSKIY.

Ukrainian Society for Soil Mechanics, Geotechnics and Foundation Engineering: 03680 Kyiv, Ivana Klimenka 5/2; tel. and fax (44) 248-89-42; e-mail adm-inst@ ndibk.kiev.ua; f. 2001; promotes theory and practice of stabilization of weak soils in bases; interaction of upper structure and soil; devt of new technologies for bases preparation; other practical issues in the field of building; 138 mems; Pres. Prof. PETRO KRYVOSHEIEV; publ. *Geotechnic World*.

Research Institutes

AGRICULTURE, FISHERIES AND VETERINARY SCIENCE

Dairy and Meat Technology Institute: 02660 Kyiv, M. Raskovoi 4A; tel. (44) 517-17-37; fax (44) 517-02-28; e-mail verb@timm .kiev.ua; internet www.timm.kiev.ua; f. 1959; attached to Ukrainian Acad. of Agricultural Sciences; library of 27,000 vols; Dir G. A. ERESKO; publ. *Meat and Milk* (6 a year).

Institute of Agricultural Economics: 03680 Kyiv, vul. Geroev Oborony 10; tel. (44) 261-43-21; fax (44) 266-05-65; e-mail info@iae.com.ua; f. 1956; attached to Ukrainian Acad. of Agricultural Sciences; Dir PETRO SABLUK; publ. *Economics of AIC* (12 a year).

Institute of Agriculture: 08162 Kievska oblast, Kyevo-Svyatoshinsky raion, Chabani; tel. (44) 526-23-27; fax (44) 526-11-07; e-mail selectio@ukrpack.net; f. 1900; attached to Ukrainian Acad. of Agrarian Sciences; agriculture, crop-growing technologies, agricultural crops selection; library of 35,900 vols in scientific library; 100,000 in total; publs *Agriculture* (1 a year), *Proceedings of the International and All-Ukrainian Congresses*.

Institute of Beekeeping, P. I. Prokopovych: 03143 Kyiv, vul. Zabolotnogo 19; tel. (44) 266-67-98; fax (44) 266-31-89; e-mail prokopovych@ukr.net; f. 1989; attached to Ukrainian Acad. of Agrarian Sciences; library of 4,000 vols; Dir LEONID BODNARCHUK; publs *Apiary* (12 a year), *Beekeeping* (1 a year), *Ukrainian Beekeeper*.

Institute of Cereals: 49600 Dnipropetrovsk, vul. Dzerzhinskogo 14; tel. (56) 244-45-49; fax (56) 236-26-18; f. 1930; attached to Ukrainian Acad. of Agrarian Sciences; maize, winter wheat, other cereals and leguminous plants; library of 110,000 vols; Dir Dr YEVGEN LEBID; publ. *Bulletin* (2 a year).

Institute for Fisheries: 03164 Kyiv, vul. Obukhivska 165; tel. (44) 423-74-61; fax (44) 423-74-58; e-mail vitbekh@online.com.ua; attached to Ukrainian Acad. of Agrarian Sciences; research and devt into the exploitation of aquatic living resources in inland waters; fish genetics and selection; environmental safety; stock conservation and rehabilitation of rare and endangered species; and economic efficiency of Ukrainian fisheries; library of 50,000 vols; Dir OLEKSANDR TRETYAK; publ. *Rybne Gospodarstvo* (1 a year).

Institute for Mechanization of Animal Husbandry: 69097 Zaporizhzya, Island Khortitca; tel. and fax (612) 289-81-44; e-mail imtuaan@ukr.net; internet www.imt .zp.ua; f. 1930; attached to Nat. Acad. of Agrarian Sciences of Ukraine; research centre for electrification of agriculture; library of 45,000 vols; Dir Dr hab. IGOR ARKADIEVICH SHEVCHENKO; publ. *Mechanization, Ecology, Conversion of Bioresources in Animal Husbandry* (4 a year).

Institute of Plant Protection: 03022 Kyiv, 33 Vasilkovskaya; tel. (44) 257-11-24; fax (44) 257-21-85; e-mail plant_prot@ukr.net; internet ippuaan.by.ru; f. 1946; attached to Ukrainian Acad. of Agrarian Sciences; Dir Acad. Prof. Dr VITALIY FEDORENKO; publs *Karantyn i Zahyst Roslyn* (Plant Quarantine and Protection, 12 a year), *Ukrainian Entomological Journal* (2 a year), *Zahayst i Karantyn Roslyn* (Plant Protection and Quarantine, 2 a year).

Institute of Veterinary Research of the Ukrainian Academy of Agricultural Sciences: 03151 Kyiv, vul. Donetska 30; tel. and fax (44) 245-78-05; e-mail vet@ivm.kiev.ua; internet www.ivm.kiev.ua; attached to

Ukrainian Acad. of Agricultural Sciences; Dir ANATOLIY OBRAZHEV; publ. *Veterinary Biotechnology* (2 a year).

Land Use Research Institute: 03151 Kyiv, Narodnogo Opolcheniya 3; tel. (44) 275-73-88; f. 1961; attached to Ukrainian Acad. of Agrarian Sciences; Dir DMITRO S. DOBRYAK; publ. *Land-Use Systems* (4 a year).

Magarach Institute of the Vine and Wine: 334200 the Autonomous Republic of Crimea, Yalta, ul. Kirova 31; tel. (65) 432-55-91; fax (65) 423-06-08; e-mail magarach@ yalita.yalta.iuf.net; f. 1828; Dir A. M. AVIDZBA; publs *Magarach–Vinogradarstvo i Vinodelie* (in Russian, also English summaries, 4 a year), *Proceedings of the Magarach Institute for Vine and Wine* (in Russian, 2 a year), *Proceedings of the Scientific Centre of Viticulture and Oenology* (in Russian, 2 a year).

Pig Breeding Institute 'O. V. Kvasnitsky': 36006 Poltava, Shvedska Mogila 1; tel. (53) 252-74-19; fax (53) 222-27-53; e-mail slsvin@e-mail.pl.ua; internet web.poltava.ua/ firms/slsvin; f. 1930; library of 60,000 vols; Dir Prof. VALENTIN P. RYBALKO; publ. *Pig Breeding* (1 a year).

Plant Breeding and Genetics Institute: 65036 Odessa, Ovidiopolskaya doroga 3; tel. (482) 39-54-01; fax (482) 39-52-89; e-mail sgi-uaan@ukr.net; f. 1912; attached to National Acad. of Agricultural Sciences of Ukraine; devt of breeding and seed production theory, as well as new varieties and hybrids of winter wheat, spring and winter barley, triticale, maize, sunflower, soybean, alfalfa, Sudan grass, sorghum; operates 7 experimental farms for seed production; conferences and workshops on the problems of plant breeding; courses for agronomists and seed-growers; 3-year post-doctoral courses; assistance to agricultural research stations and institutes; organizes research, confs and workshops; library of 115,863 vols; Dir Dr VYACHESLAV SOKOLOV; publ. *Collected Scientific Papers* (2 a year).

Sugar Beet Research Institute: 03141 Kyiv, Klinichna vul. 25; tel. (44) 275-50-00; e-mail isb@isb.kiev.ua; internet www .sugarbeet.com.ua; f. 1922; attached to Ukrainian Acad. of Agrarian Sciences; library of 28,000 vols, 30,000 periodicals; Dir M. V. ROIK; publ. *Tsukrovi buryaky* (Sugar Beet, 6 a year).

Ukrainian Research Institute of Water Management and Ecological Problems: 252010 Kyiv, Inzhenerny prov. 4B; tel. and fax (44) 280-03-02; e-mail undiwep@ukrwecol .kiev.ua; internet www.nbuv.gov.ua/ undiwep; f. 1974; library of 10,000 vols; Dir Prof. A. V. YATSYK.

Ukrainian Scientific Research Institute of Ecological Problems: 61166 Kharkiv, vul. Bakulina 6; tel. and fax (57) 702-15-92; e-mail director@niiep.kharkov.ua; internet www.niiep.kharkov.ua; f. 1971 as the All-Union Scientific Research Institute for Protection of Water; Dir Dr GRIGORY D. KOVALENKO (acting).

'V. M. Remeslo' Mironovka Institute of Wheat: 08853 Kievska oblast, P/o Tsentralne Mironovka; tel. (45) 747-41-35; fax (45) 747-44-46; e-mail mwheats@ukr.net; f. 1911; attached to Nat. Acad. of Agrarian Sciences of Ukraine; wheat and barley breeding, seed production and plant growing; library of 40,000 vols; Dir V. S. KOCHMARSKYI; publ. *Annual Collected Papers*.

Zakarpatsky Institute of Agroindustrial Production: 90252 Zakarpatska oblast, Beregovo raion, Selo V. Bakhta; tel. and fax (3141) 2-34-04; e-mail insbakta@bereg.net .ua; f. 1989; 114 mems; library of 40,000

vols; Dir A. V. BAYLAN; publ. *Problems of Agroindustrial Complex of Karpaty* (every 2 years).

ARCHITECTURE AND TOWN PLANNING

Research Institute of Automated Systems in Construction: 03037 Kyiv, vul. M. Krivonosa 2A; tel. and fax (44) 249-72-30; e-mail office@ndiasb.kiev.ua; internet www .ndiasb.kiev.ua; Dir BORIS A. VOLOBOEV.

State Research Institute of Building Constructions: 03680 Kyiv, Ivan Klimenko 5/2; tel. (44) 249-72-34; fax (44) 248-89-09; e-mail adm-inst@ndibk.kiev.ua; internet www.niisk.com; f. 1943; bldg structures: modelling, designing, testing; 500 mems; library of 49,000 vols, 72,000 patents; Dir Dr GENNEDIY FARENYUK (acting); publs *Building Construction* (2 a year), *World of Geotechnics* (3 a year).

Ukrainian Zonal Scientific and Research Design Institute of Civil Engineering: 01133 Kyiv, bul. L. Ukrainki 26; tel. (44) 286-36-72; fax (44) 285-74-81; e-mail zniiep@adam.kiev.ua; internet www .zniiep.com.ua; f. 1963; library of 125,000 vols; Dir VLADIMIR B. SHEVELEV.

ECONOMICS, LAW AND POLITICS

Council for the Study of Productive Forces of Ukraine: 01032 Kyiv 32, bul. T. Shevchenka 60; tel. (44) 216-90-70; fax (44) 244-66-70; attached to Nat. Acad. of Sciences of Ukraine; 6 attached scientific schools; Dir A. N. ALYMOV.

Institute for Economic Research and Policy Consulting: 01034 Kyiv, Reytarska 8/5-A; tel. (44) 278-63-42; fax (44) 278-63-36; e-mail institute@ier.kiev.ua; internet www .ier.kiev.ua; Dir IGOR BURAKOVSKY.

Institute of Economics: 01011 Kyiv, vul. Panasa Mirnogo 26; tel. (44) 290-84-44; fax (44) 290-86-63; e-mail instecon@ln.ua; f. 1936; attached to Nat. Acad. of Sciences of Ukraine; Dir I. I. LUKINOV.

Institute of Industrial Economics: 83048 Donetsk, Universitetska vul. 77; tel. (62) 55-78-44; fax (62) 345-06-71; e-mail admin@iep .donetsk.ua; f. 1969; attached to Nat. Acad. of Sciences of Ukraine; Dir A. I. AMOSHA; publ. *Ekonomika Promyslovosti* (4 a year, Economics of Industry, in Ukrainian and Russian).

Institute of State and Law 'V. M. Koretsky': 01601 Kyiv, vul. Tryokhsviatitelskai 4; tel. (44) 278-51-55; fax (44) 278-54-74; e-mail jus@ukrpack.net; f. 1948; attached to Nat. Acad. of Sciences of Ukraine; research into the theory and practice of law and state-bldg; Dir YU. S. SHEMSHUCHENKO; publs *Lawful State* (1 a year), *Pravo Ukrainy* (Law of Ukraine, in Ukrainian and English, 12 a year).

Institute of World Economy and International Relations: 01030 Kyiv, vul. Leontovicha 5; tel. (44) 235-70-22; fax (44) 235-51-27; e-mail iweir_nas@iweir.org.ua; internet www.iweir.org.ua; f. 1992; attached to Nat. Acad. of Sciences of Ukraine; Dir Y. M. PAKHOMOV.

HISTORY, GEOGRAPHY AND ARCHAEOLOGY

Institute of Archaeology: 04210 Kyiv, Heroyiv Stalingrada 12; tel. (44) 418-27-75; fax (44) 418-33-06; e-mail sekretar@iananu .kiev.ua; internet www.iananu.kiev.ua; attached to Nat. Acad. of Sciences of Ukraine; Dir P. P. TOLOCHKO; publ. *Arkheologia* (Archaeology, 4 a year, in Ukrainian and English).

Krypiakevych, I., Institute of Ukrainian Studies: 79026 Lviv, Kozelnytska vul. 4; tel.

(32) 270-70-22; fax (32) 270-70-21; e-mail inukr@inst-ukr.lviv.ua; internet www .inst-ukr.lviv.ua; f. 1951; attached to Nat. Acad. of Sciences of Ukraine; archaeology, history, philology, political science; library of 10,000 vols; Dir YAROSLAV D. ISAIEVYCH; publs *Istorychni ta kulturolohichni studii* (4 a year), *Shashkevychiana* (1 a year), *Ukraina: kulturna spadshchyna, natsionalna svidomist, derzhavnist* (2 a year), *Ukrainska dialektna ta istorychna leksyka* (1 a year).

Ukrainian Institute of History: 01001 Kyiv, vul. Hrushevsky 4; tel. and fax (44) 229-63-62; e-mail institute@history.org.ua; internet www.history.org.ua; attached to Nat. Acad. of Sciences of Ukraine; Dir V. A. SMOLIY; publ. *Ukrainsky Istorychny Zhurnal* (Ukrainian Historical Journal, 6 a year, in Ukrainian and English).

LANGUAGE AND LITERATURE

Institute of Linguistics 'O. O. Potebni': 01001 Kyiv, vul. Hrushevsky 4; tel. (44) 229-02-92; fax (44) 228-43-83; attached to Nat. Acad. of Sciences of Ukraine; Dir V. H. SKLIARENKO; publ. *Movoznavstvo* (Linguistics, 6 a year, in Ukrainian and English).

Institute of Literature 'Shevchenko, T. G.': 01001 Kyiv 1, Hrushevskoho 4; tel. (44) 279-10-84; fax (44) 278-52-81; e-mail admin@ilnan.gov.ua; internet www.ilnan.gov.ua; f. 1926; attached to Nat. Acad. of Sciences of Ukraine; history of Ukrainian literature; source and textual researches of Ukrainian literature; Shevchenko studies; history of foreign literatures; theory of literature and methodology of literary researches; comparative literature; literature bibliography; library of 150,000 vols; Dir MYKOLA ZHU-LYNSKY; publ. *Slovo i Chas* (Word and Time, 12 a year, in Ukrainian).

MEDICINE

Donetsk Scientific Research Institute of Traumatology and Orthopaedics: 83048 Donetsk, vul. Artema 106; tel. (62) 311-05-08; fax (62) 335-14-61; e-mail info@dniito.org.ua; internet www.dniito.org.ua; f. 1953; Dir Prof. Dr VOLODYMYR KLYMOVYTSKYY; publ. *Trauma* (4 a year).

Filatov Institute for Eye Diseases and Tissue Therapy: 65061 Odessa, vul. Frantsi 49–51; tel. (48) 268-62-18; fax (48) 268-48-51; e-mail filatovorg@ukr.net; internet www .filatovinstitut.com.ua; f. 1936; library of 81,000 vols; Dir Prof. IVAN M. LOGAI; publ. *Ophthalmological Journal* (8 a year).

Grigoriev Institute for Medical Radiology: 61024 Kharkiv, vul. Pushkinska 82; tel. (57) 704-10-65; fax (57) 700-05-00; e-mail imr@ukr.net; internet www.medradiologia .kharkov.ua; f. 1920; attached to Nat. Academy of Medical Science of Ukraine; research, clinical and educational centre; 5 depts: cancer surgery, chemotherapy, nuclear medicine, radiation pathology, radiotherapy; investigates radiation lesions, radiation cytognetics and biodosimetry, immunology, endocrinology, radioprotectors, radiation hygiene and dosimetry; library of 70,000 vols; Dir Prof. Dr MYKOLA I. PYLYPENKO; publ. *Ukrainian Journal of Radiology* (4 a year).

Institute for Occupational Health: 01033 Kyiv, vul. Saksakanskogo 75; tel. (44) 284-34-27; fax (44) 289-66-77; e-mail yik@nanu .kiev.ua; f. 1928; attached to Ukraine Acad. of Medical Sciences; library of 50,000 vols; Dir Prof. Y. I. KUNDIEV; publ. *Ukrainian Journal of Occupational Health* (4 a year).

Institute for Problems of Cryobiology and Cryomedicine: 61015 Kharkiv, Per-

eyaslavskaya St 23; tel. (57) 373-41-43; fax (57) 373-30-84; e-mail cryo@online.kharkov .ua; internet www.cryo.org.ua; f. 1972; attached to Nat. Acad. of Sciences of Ukraine; library of 54,011 vols; Dir Acad. Prof. Dr ANATOLIY N. GOLTSEV (acting); publ. *Problemy Kriobiologii* (Problems of Cryobiology, 4 a year, in Ukrainian, Russian and English).

Institute of Cardiovascular Surgery, M. Amosov: 03110 Kiev, M. Amosova vul. 6; tel. and fax (44) 275-43-22; e-mail gvknyshov@ ukr.net; f. 1983; 980 mems; Dir Prof. GEN-NADY V. KNYSHOV; Deputy Dir Prof. VITALY B. MAKSYMENKO; publ. *Annual of Cardiovascular Surgery* (1 a year).

Institute of Clinical Radiology: 04075 Kyiv, Pushcha-Voditsa, vul. Gamarnikova 42; attached to Ukrainian Acad. of Medical Sciences; Dir VOLODYMYR BEBESHKO.

Institute of Dermatology and Venereology: 61057 Kharkiv, Chernyshevskogo vul. 7/9; tel. (57) 706-32-00; fax (57) 706-32-03; e-mail idvamnu@mail.ru; internet www .idvamnu.com.ua; f. 1924; attached to Acad. of Medical Sciences of Ukraine; library of 40,000 vols; Dir Prof. IVAN I. MAVROV; publ. *Journal of Dermatology and Venereology* (4 a year).

Institute of Epidemiology and Infectious Diseases 'L. V. Gromashevsky': 01601 Kyiv, vul. S. Razina 4; tel. (44) 277-37-11; Dir A. F. FROLOV.

Institute of Gerontology: 04114 Kyiv, Vyshgorodska vul. 67; tel. (44) 430-40-68; fax (44) 432-99-56; e-mail ig@geront.kiev.ua; internet www.geront.kiev.ua; f. 1958; attached to Ukrainian Acad. of Medical Sciences; Dir VLADISLAV V. BEZRUKOV; publ. *Problemy stareniya i dolgoletiya* (Problems of Ageing and Longevity, 4 a year).

Institute of Otolaryngology named after Prof. O. S. Kolomiychenko of National Academy of Medical Sciences of Ukraine: 03057 Kyiv, Zoologichna 3; tel. (44) 483-22-02; fax (44) 483-73-68; e-mail amtc@kndio.kiev.ua; internet iol.com.ua; f. 1960; diagnostics, conservative and surgical treatment of patients with ENT-diseases; library of 33,000 vols; Dir Prof. DMYTRO ZABOLOTNYI; publs *Journal of Ear, Nose and Throat Diseases* (6 a year), *Rhinology* (4 a year).

Institute of Pediatrics, Obstetrics and Gynaecology: 04050 Kyiv, Platona Maybor-ody 8; tel. (44) 483-80-67; fax (44) 483-80-26; e-mail ipag@ukr.net.

Institute of Surgery and Transplantology: 03680 Kyiv, vul. Geroev Sevastopolya 30; tel. (44) 488-13-74; fax (44) 488-19-09; e-mail surgery@i.com.ua; internet www .surgery.org.ua; f. 1972; library of 25,000 vols; Dir Prof. VALERY SAYENKO; publ. *Clinical Surgery* (12 a year).

Kyiv 'N. D. Strazhesko' Research Institute of Cardiology: 03151 Kyiv, vul. Narodnogo Opolchenia 5; tel. (44) 277-66-22; fax (44) 228-72-72; f. 1936; 650 mems; library of 65,000 vols; Dir Prof. V. A. BOBROV.

Kyiv Research Institute of Oncology: Kyiv, vul. Lomonosova 33/43; tel. (44) 266-75-67; f. 1920; library of 27,000 vols; Dir V. L. GANUL.

L. I. Medved's Institute of Ecohygiene and Toxicology: 03680 Kyiv, Heroiv Oborony St 6; tel. (44) 526-97-00; fax (44) 526-96-43; e-mail office@medved.kiev.ua; internet www.medved.kiev.ua; f. 1964; library of 42,000 vols; Dir Prof. Dr MYKOLA PRODAN-CHUK; publs *Modern Problems of Toxicology* (4 a year), *Preventive Medicine* (4 a year), *Problems of Nutrition* (4 a year).

Lviv Scientific Research Institute of Hereditary Pathology: 79000 Lviv, vul. Lysenko 31A; tel. (32) 276-54-99; fax (32) 275-38-44; f. 1940; library of 28,000 vols; Dir O. Z. HNATEIKO; publ. *Medychna Genetyka* (every 2 years, in Ukrainian with Russian and English abstracts).

National Research Centre for Radiation Medicine: 04050 Kyiv, 53, Melnikova str.; tel. (44) 451-82-94; fax (44) 409-29-55; e-mail bazyka@yahoo.com; f. 1986; attached to Nat. Academy of Medical Sciences of Ukraine; library of 32,000 vols; Gen. Dir Prof. DIMITRY BAZYKA; publ. *Problems of Radiation Medicine* (1 a year).

Phthisiology and Pulmonology Research Institute: vul. M. Amosova 10, 03680 Kyiv; tel. (44) 275-04-02; fax (44) 275-21-18; e-mail admin@ifp.kiev.ua; internet www.ifp.kiev.ua; f. 1922; Dir YURI I. FES-CHENKO; publs *Asthma and Allergy* (4 a year), *Ukrainian Chemotherapeutic Journal* (4 a year), *Ukrainian Journal of Pulmonology* (4 a year).

R. E. Kavetsky Institute of Experimental Pathology, Oncology and Radiobiology: 03022 Kyiv, Vasylkivska str. 45; tel. (44) 259-01-83; fax (44) 258-16-56; e-mail iepor@ onconet.kiev.ua; internet www.onconet.kiev .ua; f. 1960; attached to Nat. Acad. of Sciences of Ukraine; investigation of tumor cell biology and its microenvironment in devt of molecular and cellular mechanisms of oncogenesis; evaluation of molecular and cellular markers of initiation, promotion, progression and devt of methods for diagnostics of malignant tumours; determination of molecular aspects of pharmacological correction of carcinogenesis and drug resistance formation of malignant cell and epigenetic approaches; investigation of nanoparticles and nanocomposite's influence on normal and tumour cells' metabolism; devt of approaches to target therapy and sorption detoxification of organism; library of 67,352 vols, 21,450 books, 292 periodicals; Dir Prof. Acad. VASYL F. CHEKHUN; publs *Experimental Oncology* (4 a year, in English), *Oncologia* (4 a year, in Ukrainian and Russian).

Research Institute of Physical Methods of Treatment and Medical Climatology 'I. M. Sechenov': 98603 Yalta, Polikurovska vul. 25; tel. (65) 432-75-91; f. 1914; non-medical treatment and prophylaxis of lung diseases and diseases of the cardiovascular and nervous systems; Dir Prof. SERGEI SOL-DATCHENKO.

Research Institute of Psychology 'G. S. Kostyuk': 03037 Kyiv, vul. Pankivska 2; tel. (44) 224-19-63; attached to Nat. Acad. of Pedagogical Sciences of Ukraine.

Romodanov, A., Institute of Neurosurgery: 04050 Kyiv, vul. Mayborody 32; tel. and fax (44) 483-95-73; e-mail neuro.kiev@ gmail.com; internet www.neuro.kiev.ua; f. 1950; diagnosis, surgical and combined treatment of cerebral and spinal tumors, pathogenesis, diagnosis and treatment of CNS damage and its after-effects, surgical treatment of the most complex cerebrovascular pathologies, study of immune responses in patients with neurological CNS pathology; library of 78,000 vols; Dir Prof. YURIY ZOZULIA; publ. *Ukrainian Neurosurgical Journal* (4 a year).

State Scientific Centre of Drugs: Kharkiv 310085, Astronomicheska vul. 33; tel. (57) 744-10-33; fax (57) 744-11-18; e-mail samatov@phukr.kharkov.ua; internet farmacomua.narod.ru; f. 1920; production and devt of finished drugs and technologies for preparation of phytochemicals; library of 28,000 vols; Dir Prof. V. P. GEORGIEVSKY;

publ. *Pharmacom* (4 a year, in Ukrainian and Russian).

Sytenko Institute of Spine and Joint Pathology: 61024 Kharkiv, Pushkinska vul. 80; tel. (57) 715-75-06; e-mail post@sytenko .org.ua; internet www.sytenko.org.ua; f. 1907; attached to Acad. of Medical Sciences of Ukraine; library of 40,500 vols; Dir Prof. MYKOLA O. KORZH; publ. *Orthopaedics, Traumatology and Prosthetics* (4 a year).

Ukrainian Institute of Public Health: 01601 Kyiv, vul. Dymytrova 5, korp. 10A, 7th Fl.; tel. (44) 284-39-38; fax (44) 284-39-37; e-mail health@uiph.kiev.ua; internet www .uiph.kiev.ua; f. 1997; attached to Ukrainian Min. of Health; Dir Prof. V. M. PONOMARENKO; publ. *Bulletin of the Social Hygiene and Health Protection Organization of Ukraine* (4 a year).

Ukrainian Research Institute of Traumatology and Orthopaedics: 01601 Kyiv, vul. Vorovskogo 27; tel. (44) 216-42-49; fax (44) 216-44-62; e-mail travma@rql.net.ua; f. 1919; library of 57,000 vols; Dir G. V. GAIKO; publs *Statistical Data Report on Traumatological and Orthopaedic Aid to Ukrainians* (1 a year), *Vestnik Ortopedii, Travmatologii i Protezirovaniia* (Orthopaedics, Traumatology and Prosthesis, 4 a year).

Ukrainian Scientific Centre of Hygiene: 02094 Kyiv, vul. Popudrenko 50; tel. (44) 559-73-73; fax (44) 559-90-90; e-mail usch@ usch.kiev.ua; f. 1931; incl. Institute of General and Communal Hygiene, and Institute of Medical Genetics; library of 102,213 vols; Dir Dr ANDRIY SERDIUK; publ. *Environment and Health* (4 a year).

NATURAL SCIENCES

Biological Sciences

Institute of Biology of Southern Seas: Pr. Nakhimov 2, 99011 Sevastopol; tel. (69) 254-41-10; fax (69) 255-78-13; e-mail ibss@ ibss.iuf.net; internet www.ibss.iuf.net; f. 1871; attached to Nat. Acad. of Sciences of Ukraine; library of 150,000 vols; 350 mems; Dir Dr V. N. EREMEEV; publs *Ekologia Morya* (Ecology of the Sea, 4 a year), *Morskoj Ekologicheskij Zhurnal* (Marine Ecological Journal, 3 a year).

Institute of Botany 'M. G. Kholodny': 01601 Kyiv, Tereshchenkivska vul. 2; tel. (44) 224-40-41; fax (44) 224-10-64; e-mail inst@botan.kiev.ua; f. 1921; attached to Nat. Acad. of Sciences of Ukraine; library of 106,000 vols; Dir K. M. SYTNIK; publs *Algologiya* (Algology, 4 a year, in Ukrainian and English), *Ukrainsky Botanichny Zhurnal* (Ukrainian Botanical Journal, 6 a year, in Ukrainian and English).

Institute of Cellular Biology and Genetic Engineering: 03143 Kyiv, Vul. Zabolotnogo 148; tel. (44) 526-71-09; fax (44) 526-71-04; e-mail cytogen@iicb.kiev.ua; internet www.cytgen.com; f. 1967; attached to Nat. Acad. of Sciences of Ukraine; Dir YA. B. BLUME; Exec. Sec. MARY FEDYUK; publ. *Tsitologia i Genetika* (Cytology and Genetics, 6 a year, in Ukrainian and English).

Institute of Hydrobiology: 04210 Kyiv-210, pr. Geroyiv Stalingrada 12; tel. (44) 419-39-81; fax (44) 418-22-32; e-mail hydrobiol@ igb.ibc.com.ua; attached to Nat. Acad. of Sciences of Ukraine; Dir VIKTOR D. ROMANENKO; publ. *Gidrobiologichesky Zhurnal* (Hydrobiological Journal, 6 a year, in Ukrainian and English).

Institute of Molecular Biology and Genetics: 03680 Kyiv vul. Acad. Zabolotnoho 150; tel. (44) 526-11-69; fax (44) 526-07-59; e-mail inform@imbg.org.ua; internet www .imbg.org.ua; f. 1973; attached to Nat. Acad. of Sciences of Ukraine; central trends of

molecular biology, genetics and biotechnology: structural and functional genomics; proteomics and protein engineering; regulatory systems and signal transduction mechanisms; bioinformatics and computational modelling; gene and cell biotechnologies, gene therapy and diagnostics; library of 90,000 vols; Dir Prof. Dr ANNA V. EL'SKAYA; Scientific Sec. Dr YANINA R. MISHCHUK; publ. *Biopolymers and Cell* (6 a year, in Ukrainian and English).

Institute of Plant Physiology and Genetics: 03022 Kyiv, Vasylkivska vul. 31/17; tel. and fax (44) 257-51-50; e-mail plant@ifrg .kiev.ua; internet www.ifrg.kiev.ua; f. 1946; attached to Nat. Acad. of Sciences of Ukraine; plant physiology, genetics; Dir Dr VLADIMIR V. MORGUN; Scientific Sec. PAVLO MAJOR; publ. *Fiziologia i Biokhimia Kulturnykh Rastenii* (Physiology and Biochemistry of Cultivated Plants, 6 a year, in Ukrainian, Russian and English).

Institute for Sorption and Endoecology Problems: 03164 Kyiv, pr. Naumova 13; tel. (44) 452-93-28; fax (44) 452-93-27; e-mail ispe@ispe.kiev.ua; f. 1991; attached to Nat. Acad. of Sciences of Ukraine; Dir V. V. STRELKO.

Schmalhausen Institute of Zoology: 01601 Kyiv, vul. B. Khmelnytskoho 15; tel. (44) 235-10-70; fax (44) 234-15-69; e-mail iz@ izan.kiev.ua; internet www.izan.kiev.ua; f. 1930; attached to Nat. Acad. of Sciences of Ukraine; zoological collns; zoological scientific research; library of 161,947 vols; Dir Prof. IGOR A. AKIMOV; Scientific Dir Dr VITALIY KHARCHENKO; Scientific Dir Prof. IGOR DOVGAL; publ. *Vestnik Zoologii* (Zoological Journal, 6 a year, in Ukrainian and English, online).

'O. O. Bohomolets' Institute of Physiology: 01601 Kyiv, vul. Bohomoltsa 4; tel. (44) 293-20-13; fax (44) 253-64-58; e-mail pkostyuk@serv.biph.kiev.ua; attached to Nat. Acad. of Sciences of Ukraine; Dir P. H. KOSTYUK; publs *Fiziologichny Zhurnal* (Physiological Journal, 6 a year, in Ukrainian and English), *Neirofiziologia* (Neurophysiology, 6 a year, in Ukrainian and English).

Palladin Institute of Biochemistry: 01601 Kyiv 30, vul. Leontovicha 9; tel. (44) 234-59-74; fax (44) 279-63-65; e-mail secretar@biochem.kiev.ua; internet www .biochemistry.org.ua; f. 1925; attached to Nat. Acad. of Sciences of Ukraine; 360 mems; library of 82,000 vols; Dir Prof. SERHIY KOMISARENKO; publs *Biotechnologia* (Biotechnology, 6 a year, in Ukrainian, Russian and English), *Ukrainsky Biokhimichny Zhurnal* (Ukrainian Biochemical Journal, 6 a year, in Ukrainian, Russian and English).

Zabolotny Institute of Microbiology and Virology: 03143 Kyiv, vul. Akademika Zabolotnogo 154; tel. (44) 266-11-79; fax (44) 266-23-79; e-mail smirnov@imv.kiev.ua; internet www.imv.kiev.ua; f. 1928; attached to Nat. Acad. of Sciences of Ukraine; library of 121,000 vols; Dir V. V. SMIRNOV; publ. *Mikrobiolohichny Zhurnal* (Microbiology Journal, 6 a year, in Ukrainian, Russian and English).

Mathematical Sciences

Institute of Mathematics: 01601 Kyiv, vul. Repina 3; tel. (44) 234-53-16; fax (44) 235-20-10; e-mail institute@imath.kiev.ua; internet www.imath.kiev.ua; attached to Nat. Acad. of Sciences of Ukraine; Dir A. M. SAMOILENKO; publ. *Ukrainsky Matematychny Zhurnal* (Ukrainian Mathematical Journal, 12 a year, in Ukrainian and English).

Physical Sciences

A. V. Bogatsky Physico-Chemical Institute of the National Academy of Sciences of Ukraine: 65080 Odessa, Lustdorfskaya doroga 86; tel. (48) 766-20-44; fax (48) 765-96-02; e-mail medchem_department@ukr.net; internet physchemin-nas.od.ua/index.php; f. 1977; attached to Nat. Acad. of Sciences of Ukraine; 198 mems; Dir SERGEI ANDRONATI.

Bogolyubov Institute for Theoretical Physics: 03680 Kyiv, vul. Metrologichna 14B; tel. (44) 526-53-62; fax (44) 526-59-98; e-mail itp@bitp.kiev.ua; internet www.bitp .kiev.ua; f. 1966; attached to Nat. Acad. of Sciences of Ukraine; Dir Prof. A. G. ZAGORODNY; publ. *Ukrainian Journal of Physics* (12 a year).

Chuiko Institute of Surface Chemistry: 03164 Kyiv, vul. Naumova, 17; tel. (44) 422-96-04; fax (44) 424-35-67; e-mail info@isc.gov .ua; internet www.isc.gov.ua; f. 1986; attached to Nat. Acad. of Sciences of Ukraine; library of 20,000 vols; Dir Prof. M. T. KARTEL; publs *Chemistry, Physics and Technology of Surface* (4 a year), *Surface*.

Gas Institute: 03113 Kyiv, Degtiarivksa vul. 39; tel. (44) 456-44-71; fax (44) 456-88-30; e-mail ig-secr@i.com.ua; internet ingas .org.ua; f. 1949; attached to Nat. Acad. of Sciences of Ukraine; library of 110,000 vols; Dir Prof. B. I. BONDARENKO; publ. *Ekotekhnologia i Resursosberezheniye* (Energy Technologies and Resource Saving, 6 a year, in Russian with summary in Ukrainian and English).

G. V. Kurdyumov Institute for Metal Physics: 03680 Kyiv, Acad. Vernadsky blvd 36; tel. (44) 424-10-05; fax (44) 424-25-61; e-mail metall@imp.kiev.ua; internet www .imp.kiev.ua; f. 1945; attached to Nat. Acad. of Sciences of Ukraine; research and technologies based on the investigations of electronic structure, electrical, magnetic, optical, structural, thermal and mechanical properties of condensed matter; library of 129,000 vols; Dir Acad. OREST M. IVASISHIN; Deputy Dir Prof. VALENTYN A. TATARENKO; Deputy Dir Prof. VOLODYMYR M. NADUTOV; Academic Sec. Dr EUGENIA V. KOCHELAB; publs *Metallofizika i Noveishie Tekhnologii* (Metal Physics and Advanced Technology, 12 a year, in Ukrainian and English), *Nanosistemi, Nanomateriali, Nanotehnologii* (Nanosystems, Nanomaterials, Nanotechnologies, 4 a year, in English, Russian and Ukrainian), *Uspehi Fiziki Metallov* (Progress in Physics of Metals, 4 a year, in English, Russian and Ukrainian).

Institute of Bio-organic Chemistry and Petrochemistry: 02660 Kyiv, vul. Murmanska 1; tel. (44) 558-53-88; fax (44) 573-25-52; e-mail users@bpci.kiev.ua; f. 1987; attached to Nat. Acad. of Sciences of Ukraine; Dir Prof. V. P. KUKHAR; publ. *Katalys i Neftekhimiya* (Catalysis and Petrochemistry, 4 a year).

Institute of Colloid Chemistry and Water Chemistry 'A. V. Dumansky': 03680 Kyiv 142, Vernadsky pr. 42; tel. (44) 424-01-96; fax (44) 423-82-24; f. 1968; attached to Nat. Acad. of Sciences of Ukraine; Dir V. V. GONCHARUK; publ. *Khimiya i Tekhnologiya Vody* (Water Chemistry and Engineering, 6 a year, in Russian and English).

Institute of General and Inorganic Chemistry 'V. I. Vernadsky': 03680 Kyiv, pr. Akademika Palladina 32/34; tel. (44) 444-34-61; fax (44) 444-30-70; e-mail office@ionc .kiev.ua; internet www.ionc.kar.net; f. 1918; attached to Nat. Acad. of Sciences of Ukraine; fundamental and applied research in inorganic chemistry, coordination chemistry, chemistry of solids, nanochemistry, electrochemistry and physical chemistry of melts, aqueous and non-aqueous solutions, processing of original and recycled metal-containing materials; study of structure and properties of ionic melts, solid electrolytes, inorganic sorbents, coordination compounds of rare, rare-earth and other metals, liquid ionic crystals, membrane materials; research in priority directions of inorganic and physico-inorganic chemistry in the branches of high-temperature coordination chemistry in the melts, gas phases and plasma; synthesis and characterization of novel dielectric, semiconductive, optical, ultrapure oxide materials, superconductors and high-temperature ceramics; Dir Prof. Dr SERGIY V. VOLKOV; Dir Prof. Dr VASILY PEKHNYO; publ. *Ukrainsky Khimichesky Zhurnal* (Ukrainian Chemistry Journal, 12 a year, in Russian, Ukrainian and English).

Institute of Geochemistry, Mineralogy and Ore Formation: 03680 Kyiv-142, pr. Palladina 34; tel. (44) 424-01-05; fax (44) 424-12-70; e-mail pavlenko@igmr.relc.com; f. 1969; attached to Nat. Acad. of Sciences of Ukraine; library of 30,000 vols, 35 periodicals; Dir MYKOLA P. SHCHERBAK; publ. *Mineralogichesky Zhurnal* (Mineralogical Journal, 6 a year, in Ukrainian and English).

Institute of Geological Sciences: 01054 Kyiv, vul. Honchar 55B; tel. (44) 216-94-46; fax (44) 216-98-34; f. 1926; attached to Nat. Acad. of Sciences of Ukraine; Dir Prof. PETRO F. HOZHYK; publ. *Geolohichny Zhurnal* (Geological Journal, 4 a year, in Ukrainian and English).

Institute of Geology and Geochemistry of Combustible Minerals: 79060 Lviv, Naukova vul. 3A; tel. (32) 263-25-41; fax (32) 263-22-09; e-mail igggk@mail.lviv.ua; f. 1951; attached to Nat. Acad. of Sciences of Ukraine; Dir V. E. ZABIGAILO; publ. *Geologia i Geokhimia Horiuchykh Kopalyn* (Geology and Geochemistry of Mineral Fuels, 4 a year, in Ukrainian and English).

Institute of Geophysics: 03680 Kyiv, pr. Akademika Palladina 32; tel. (44) 424-01-12; fax (44) 450-25-20; e-mail earth@igph.kiev.ua; internet www.igph.kiev.ua; f. 1960; attached to Nat. Acad. of Sciences of Ukraine; Dir V. I. STAROSTENKO; publ. *Geofizichesky Zhurnal* (Geophysical Journal, 6 a year, in Russian, Ukrainian and English).

Institute of Ionosphere: 61002 Kharkiv, Krasnoznamennaya str. 16; tel. and fax (57) 706-22-87; e-mail iion@kpi.kharkov.ua; internet www.iion.org.ua; f. 1991; attached to Nat. Acad. of Sciences of Ukraine and Min. of Education and Science, Youth and Sport of Ukraine; incoherent scatter method, geophysics, geospace plasma, ionosphere, radio physics; Dir Prof. IGOR DOMNIN.

Institute of Nuclear Research: 03680 Kyiv, pr. Nauky 47; tel. (44) 265-23-49; fax (44) 265-44-63; e-mail interdep@kinr.kiev.ua; internet www.kinr.kiev.ua; f. 1970; attached to Nat. Acad. of Sciences of Ukraine; nuclear physics, atomic energy, radiation physics and radiation material science, physics of plasma, radiation ecology and biology; Dir IVAN M. VYSHNYEVSKYI; Deputy Dir VOLODYMYR OSTASHKO; publ. *Scientific Papers* (irregular).

Institute of Organic Chemistry: 02660 Kyiv, Murmanska vul. 5; tel. (44) 552-71-50; fax (44) 573-26-43; f. 1939; Dir MYRON O. LOZYNSKIY.

Institute of Physical-Organic Chemistry and Coal Chemistry 'L. M. Litvinenko': 83114 Donetsk, vul. R. Lyuksemburg 70; tel. and fax (62) 311-68-30; e-mail postmaster@infou.donetsk.ua; f. 1975; attached to Nat. Acad. of Sciences of Ukraine; coal and products of its processing; synthesis and investi-

gation of the structure and properties of heterocyclic compounds, incl. biologically active ones; library of 110,000 vols, 13 periodicals; Dir Acad. ANATOLY F. POPOV.

Institute of Physics: 03028 Kyiv, pr. Nauky 46; tel. (44) 525-12-20; fax (44) 525-15-89; e-mail fizyka@iop.kiev.ua; internet www.iop.kiev.ua; f. 1929; attached to Nat. Acad. of Sciences of Ukraine; Dir M. S. BRODYN; publ. *Ukrainsky Fizychny Zhurnal* (Ukrainian Physics Journal, 12 a year, in Ukrainian and English).

Institute of Radio Astronomy: 61002 Kharkiv, Chervonopraporna vul. 4; tel. (57) 706-14-10; fax (57) 706-14-15; e-mail rai@ri.kharkov.ua; internet www.ri.kharkov.ua; f. 1985; attached to Nat. Acad. of Sciences of Ukraine; Dir LEONID M. LYTVYNENKO; publ. *Radiofizyka i Radioastronomiya* (Radio Physics and Radio Astronomy, 4 a year, in Ukrainian, Russian and English).

Institute of Single Crystals: 61001 Kharkiv, pr. Lenina 60; tel. (57) 341-01-66; fax (57) 340-93-43; e-mail info@isc.kharkov.com; internet www.isc.kharkov.com; f. 1961; attached to Nat. Acad. of Sciences of Ukraine; Dir Dr VYACHESLAV M. PUZIKOV; publ. *Functional Materials* (4 a year, in English).

L. V. Pisarzhevsky Institute of Physical Chemistry: 03028 Kyiv, Pr. Nauki 31; tel. (44) 525-11-90; fax (44) 525-62-16; e-mail admini@inphyschem-nas.kiev.ua; internet www.inphyschem-nas.kiev.ua; f. 1927; attached to Nat. Acad. of Sciences of Ukraine; theory of chemical structure; kinetics and reactivity; catalysis; adsorption and adsorbents; chemistry of high energies; physico-inorganic chemistry; library of 135,000 vols (incl. books, brochures and periodic issues); Dir Acad. V. G. KOSHECHKO; publ. *Teoreticheskaya i Eksperimentalnaya Khimiya* (Theoretical and Experimental Chemistry, 6 a year, in Russian and English).

Main Astronomical Observatory: 03680 Kyiv, vul. Akademika Zabolotnogo 27; tel. (44) 526-31-10; fax (44) 526-21-47; e-mail director@mao.kiev.ua; internet www.mao.kiev.ua; f. 1944; attached to Nat. Acad. of Sciences of Ukraine; Dir YA. S. YATSKIV; publs *Kinematika i Fizika Nebesnykh Tel* (Kinematics and Physics of Celestial Bodies, 6 a year, in Ukrainian and English), *Space Science and Technology* (4 a year).

Marine Hydrophysical Institute: 99011 Sevastopol, vul. Kapitanska 2; tel. (69) 254-04-52; fax (69) 255-43-53; e-mail vaivanov@alpha.mhi.iuf.net; internet www.mhi.iuf.net; attached to Nat. Acad. of Sciences of Ukraine; Dir Prof. VITALY A. IVANOV; publs *Morskoy Gidrofizichesky Zhurnal* (Marine Hydrophysical Journal, in Ukrainian, Russian and English), *Physical Oceanography* (6 a year).

Research and Design Institute of Basic Chemistry: 61002 Kharkiv, Mironositska vul. 25; tel. (57) 700-01-23; fax (57) 700-48-25; e-mail office@niochim.kharkov.ua; internet www.niochim.kharkov.ua/niochim1.htm; f. 1923; library of 185,000 vols; Dir E. I. VELIEV.

Ukrainian State Geological Research Institute: 04114 Kyiv, vul. Avtozavodska 78; tel. (44) 430-70-24; fax (44) 430-41-76; e-mail ukrdgri@ukrdgri.gov.ua; internet www.ukrdgri.gov.ua; f. 1953; brs in Chirnigiv, Dnipropetrovsk, Lviv, Poltava and Simferopol; Dir MYKHAYLO D. KRASNOZHON.

V. Lashkaryov Institute of Semiconductor Physics: 03028 Kyiv, pr. Nauky 41; tel. (44) 525-40-20; fax (44) 525-83-42; e-mail info@isp.kiev.ua; internet www.isp.kiev.ua; f. 1960; attached to Nat. Acad. of Sciences of

Ukraine; scientific investigations; library of 172,689 vols, 23,846 books; Dir Acad. V. F. MACHULIN; Exec. Dir Prof. VASYL TOMASHYK; publs *Optoelektronika i Poluprovodnikovaya Tekhnika* (Optoelectronics and Semiconductor Technology, 1 a year), *Semiconductor Physics, Quantum Electronics and Optoelectronics* (4 a year, in English).

PHILOSOPHY AND PSYCHOLOGY

'H. S. Skovoroda' Institute of Philosophy: 01001 Kyiv, vul. Tryokhsviatytelska 4; tel. (44) 278-06-05; fax (44) 278-63-66; e-mail if-ukr@i.kiev.ua; internet www.filosof.com.ua; f. 1946; attached to Nat. Acad. of Sciences of Ukraine; research in different areas of philosophy; library of 65,000 vols; Dir Prof MYROSLAV POPOVYCH; publs *Filosofska Dumka* (Philosophical Thought, 6 a year, in Ukrainian), *Filosofski Obryi* (Philosophical Horizons, 2 a year, in Ukrainian), *Praktychna Filosofia* (Practical Philosophy, 4 as year), *Religiyna Panorama* (Religious Panorama, 12 a year).

RELIGION, SOCIOLOGY AND ANTHROPOLOGY

Institute of Art, Folklore Studies and Ethnography 'M. T. Rylsky': 01001 Kyiv, vul. Kirova 4; tel. (44) 266-20-08; e-mail etnolog@etnolog.kiev.ua; internet www.etnolog.kiev.ua; f. 1936; attached to Nat. Acad. of Sciences of Ukraine; Dir Prof. Dr H. A. SKRYPNYK; publ. *Folklore Studies*.

Institute of Sociology: 01021 Kyiv, Shovkovychna 12; tel. (44) 255-74-09; fax (44) 291-56-96; e-mail i-soc@i-soc.org.ua; internet www.i-soc.com.ua; f. 1990; attached to Nat. Acad. of Sciences of Ukraine; Dir Prof. VALERIY M. VORONA; publ. *Sotsiolohiya: Teoriya, Metody, Marketing* (Sociology: Theory, Methods, Marketing, 6 a year, in Ukrainian and English).

TECHNOLOGY

B. Verkin Institute of Low Temperature Physics and Engineering: 61103 Kharkiv, pr. Lenina 47; tel. (57) 340-22-23; fax (57) 340-33-70; e-mail ilt@ilt.kharkov.ua; internet www.ilt.kharkov.ua; f. 1960; attached to Nat. Acad. of Sciences of Ukraine; low and ultra low temperature physics; solid state physics; nanophysics and nanotechnologies, incl. nanobiophysics; mathematical physics, analysis and geometry; physical and engineering problems of materials science; library of 40,000 vols; Dir Prof. SERGEI LEONIDOVICH GNATCHENKO; Deputy Dir Dr NIKOLAY IVANOVICH GLUSHCHUK; Deputy Dir. Dr VLADIMIR NIKOLAEVICH SAMOVAROV; Science Sec. Dr ALEXANDER NIKOLAEVICH KALINENKO; publs *Fizika Nizkikh Temperatur* (Low-temperature Physics, 12 a year, in Ukrainian, Russian and English), *Matematicheskaya Fizika, Analiz, Geometria* (Mathematical Physics, Analysis, Geometry, 4 a year, in Ukrainian, Russian and English).

Donetsk Institute for Physics and Engineering 'O. O. Galkin': 83114 Donetsk, 72 R. Lyuksemburg St; tel. (62) 311-52-27; fax (62) 342-90-18; e-mail scsecr@scsecr.fti.dn.ua; internet www.fti.dn.ua; f. 1965; attached to Nat. Acad. of Sciences of Ukraine; 12 scientific depts, 3 scientific-auxiliary depts, 12 auxiliary subdiv., centre for collective use; electronic and kinetic properties of solids, physics of magnetic phenomena, phase transitions, spectroscopy of solids, physics of strength and plasticity, physical material science, pressure treatment of materials, physical process of mining, high-pressure equipment, experimental technique, production equipment; library of 160,000 vols; Dir Prof. Dr VIKTOR N. VARYU-

KHIN; Deputy Dir VIKTOR A. BELOSHENKO; Scientific Sec. IRINA YU. RESHIDOVA; publ. *Fizika i Tekhnika Vysokikh Davleniy* (Highpressure Physics and Technology, 4 a year, in Ukrainian and English).

Frantsevich, I. N., Institute of Problems of Materials Science: 03142 Kyiv, vul. Krzhizhanovskoho 3; tel. (44) 424-01-02; fax (44) 424-21-31; e-mail dir@materials.kiev.ua; f. 1952; attached to Nat. Acad. of Sciences of Ukraine; Dir V. V. SKOROHOD; publ. *Poroshkovaya Metallurgia* (Powder Metallurgy, 12 a year, in Ukrainian and English).

G. E. Pukhov Institute for Modelling in Energy Engineering: 03164 Kyiv vul. Generala Naumova 15; tel. (44) 424-10-63; fax (44) 424-05-86; e-mail em@ipme.kiev.ua; internet www.ipme.kiev.ua; f. 1981; attached to Nat. Acad. of Sciences of Ukraine; 150 mems; Dir V. F. EVDOKIMOV; publ. *Elektronnoe Modelirovanie* (Electronic Modelling, 6 a year, in Russian and English).

G. S. Pisarenko Institute for Problems of Strength: 01014 Kyiv, Timiryazevska vul. 2; tel. (44) 285-16-87; fax (44) 286-16-84; e-mail ips@ipp.kiev.ua; internet www.ipp.kiev.ua; f. 1966; attached to Nat. Acad. of Sciences of Ukraine; Dir V. T. TROSHCHENKO; publ. *Problemy Prochnosti* (Strength of Materials, 6 a year, in Russian and English).

Institute of Applied Mathematics and Mechanics: 83114 Donetsk, vul. R. Lyuksemburg 74; tel. (622) 55-23-94; fax (622) 55-22-65; e-mail math@iamm.ac.donetsk.ua; internet www.iamm.ac.donetsk.ua; f. 1965; attached to Nat. Acad. of Sciences of Ukraine; library of 89,415 vols; Dir ALEKSANDR M. KOVALEV; publs *Mekhanika Tverdogo Tela* (1 a year), *Nelineinye Granichnye Zadachi* (1 a year), *Trudy Instituta Prikladnoi Matematiki i Mehaniki NAN Ukrainy* (1 a year), *Ukrains'kyi Matematychnyi Visnyk* (Ukrainian Mathematical Bulletin, 4 issues in 1 vol, 1 a year).

Institute of Cybernetics 'V. M. Hlushkov': 03680 Kyiv MSP, Glushkova 20; tel. (44) 266-20-08; fax (44) 266-74-18; e-mail aik@public.icyb.kiev.ua; internet www.icyb .kiev.ua; attached to Nat. Acad. of Sciences of Ukraine; Dir I. K. SERHIENKO; publs *Kibernetika i Sistemny Analiz* (Cybernetics and Systems Analysis, 6 a year, in Ukrainian and English), *Problemy Upravlenia i Informatiki* (Problems of Control and Informatics, 6 a year, in Ukrainian and English), *Upravlyauschie Sistemy i Mashiny* (Control Systems and Computers, 6 a year, in Ukrainian and English).

Institute of Electrodynamics: 03680 Kyiv, Peremohy 56; tel. (44) 456-01-51; fax (44) 456-94-94; internet www.ied.org.ua; f. 1947; attached to Nat. Acad. of Sciences of Ukraine; Dir O. V. KYRYLENKO; publs *Tekhnichna Elektrodynamika* (Technical Electrodynamics, 6 a year, in Ukrainian, Russian and English), *Works of Institute of Electrodynamics* (3 a year, in Ukrainian and Russian).

Institute of Engineering Mechanics 'A. M. Pidhorny': 61046 Kharkiv, vul. Pozharskoho 2/10; tel. (57) 294-55-14; fax (57) 294-46-35; e-mail root@ipmach.kharkov.ua; internet www.ipmach.kharkov.ua; attached to Nat. Acad. of Sciences of Ukraine; Dir YURI M. MATSEVITIY; publ. *Problemy Mashinostroenia* (Problems of Mechanical Engineering, 4 a year, in Ukrainian and English).

Institute of Engineering Thermophysics: 03057 Kyiv, vul. Zhelyabova 2A, k. 102; tel. (44) 456-62-82; fax (44) 456-60-91; e-mail admin@ittf.kiev.ua; internet www.ittf .kiev.ua; attached to Nat. Acad. of Sciences of Ukraine; Dir ANATOLIY A. DOLINSKIY; publ. *Promyshlennaya Teplotekhnika* (Industrial Thermal Engineering, in Ukrainian and English, 6 a year).

Institute of Geotechnical Mechanics: 320095 Dnipropetrovsk, Simferopolska vul. 2A; tel. (56) 246-01-51; fax (56) 246-24-26; e-mail nanu@igtm.dp.ua; internet www.igtm .narod.ru; f. 1962; attached to Nat. Acad. of Sciences of Ukraine; library of 109,000 vols; Dir A. F. BULAT; publ. *Geotechnical Mechanics* (4 a year).

Institute of Hydromechanics: 03057 Kyiv, vul. Zhelyabova 8/4; tel. (44) 456-43-13; fax (44) 455-64-32; e-mail office@hydromech.com .ua; internet www.hydromech.kiev.ua; f. 1926; attached to Nat. Acad. of Sciences of Ukraine; library of 84,727 vols; Dir VIKTOR T. GRINCHENKO; publs *Acoustics Bulletin* (4 a year), *Applied Hydromechanics* (4 a year).

Institute for Information Recording: 03113 Kyiv, vul. Shpaka 2; tel. (44) 446-83-89; fax (44) 241-72-33; e-mail petrov@ipri .kiev.ua; internet www.ipri.kiev.ua; f. 1987; attached to Nat. Acad. of Sciences of Ukraine; optical storage, information-analytical systems, information security, digital transfer of Edison cylinders with audio-cultural heritage, expert decision-making support systems; 210 mems; Dir V. V. PETROV; publs *Reestracia Zberezenna i Obrobka Danih* (Data Recording, Storage and Processing, 4 a year, in Ukrainian, Russian and English), *Ukrainsky Referatyvny Zhurnal 'Dzherelo'* (Ukrainian Journal of Abstracts 'Dzherelo', 6 a year, in Ukrainian and English).

Institute of Mining and the Chemical Industry: 79026 Lviv, Striiska vul. 98; tel. (32) 297-13-77; fax (32) 234-40-61; e-mail ghp@ghp.lviv.ua; internet www.glrhimprom .narod.ru; f. 1956; Chair. I. I. ZOZULIA.

Institute of Pulse Research and Engineering: 54018 Mykolayiv, Zhovtnevy pr. 43A; tel. (51) 222-41-13; fax (51) 222-61-40; e-mail iipt@iipt.com.ua; internet www.iipt.com.ua; f. 1962; attached to Nat. Acad. of Sciences of Ukraine; library of 126,000 vols; Dir O. I. VOVCHENKO.

Institute for Superhard Materials: 04074 Kyiv, Avtozavodska vul. 2; tel. (44) 468-86-32; fax (44) 468-86-25; internet www.ism.ua; f. 1961; attached to Nat. Acad. of Sciences of Ukraine; Dir Prof. N. V. NOVIKOV; publs *Instumentalnyi Swit* (World of Tools, 6 a year), *Sverkhtviordye Materialy* (Superhard Materials, 6 a year, in Russian and English).

Iron and Steel Institute 'Z. I. Nekrasov': 49050 Dnipropetrovsk, pl. Akademika Starodubova 1; tel. (56) 776-53-15; fax (56) 776-59-24; e-mail isi-nasu@a-teleport.com; internet www.isi.dnepr.net; f. 1939; attached to Nat. Acad. of Sciences of Ukraine; Dir Prof. Dr VADIM I. BOLSHAKOV; publ. *Fundamental and Applied Problems of the Steel Industry* (proceedings, 1 a year).

Karpenko Physico–Mechanical Institute of the National Academy of Sciences of Ukraine: 79060 Lviv, Naukova str. 5; tel. (32) 263-30-88; fax (32) 264-94-27; e-mail pminasu@ipm.lviv.ua; internet www.ipm .lviv.ua; f. 1951; problems of modern materials science, physicochemical fracture mechanics of materials and strength of structures; library of 100,000 vols; Dir Acad. V. V. PANASYUK; Scientific Sec. DMYTRO DOSYN; publs *Fizyko-Khimichna Mekhanika Materialiv* (Physical and Chemical Mechanics of Materials, 6 a year, in Ukrainian and English), *Vidbir i Obrobka Informatsii* (Information Extraction and Processing, 2 a year, in Ukrainian).

Pidstryhach Institute of Applied Problems of Mechanics and Mathematics: 79060 Lviv, Naukova str. 3B; tel. (32) 263-83-77; fax (32) 263-62-70; e-mail adm@ iapmm.lviv.ua; internet www.iapmm.lviv.ua; f. 1973; attached to Nat. Acad. of Sciences of Ukraine; library of 15,000 vols; Dir Prof. ROMAN M. KUSHNIR; Deputy Dir VOLODYMYR PELYKH; publs *Applied Problems of Mechanics and Mathematics* (1 a year), *Mathematical Methods and Physicomechanical Fields* (4 a year).

Research and Development Institute of the Merchant Marine of Ukraine: 65026 Odessa, Lanzheronovska vul. 15A; tel. (48) 741-17-04; fax (48) 741-11-77; e-mail unii@ paco.net; internet www.unii.odessa.ua; f. 1947; Dir ALEXANDER LESNIK.

Research Institute of the Sewn Goods Industry: 03680 Kyiv, vul. P. Lyubchenko 15; tel. (44) 528-55-41; fax (44) 528-64-57; e-mail legprom@i.kiev.ua; internet www .iptelecom.net.ua/~legprom; f. 1961; library of 22,500 vols; Dir V. P. KRYSKO.

State Research and Design Institute of Chemical Engineering 'Khimtekhnologiya': 93400 Luhansk oblast, Severodonetsk, vul. Vilesova 1; tel. (64) 523-42-20; fax (64) 522-50-42; internet www.ixt.lg.ua; f. 1950; library of 130,000 vols; Dir PETR P. BORISOV; publ. *Collected Research Papers* (12 a year).

State Titanium Research and Design Institute: 69035 Zaporizhia, Lenina 180; tel. (61) 233-23-23; fax (61) 224-67-01; e-mail common@timag.org; internet www .timag.org; f. 1956; design and devt of nonferrous metallurgical processes, production of semiconductors and carbon-graphite materials; Dir-Gen. Dr IGOR V. ZABELIN.

Timoshenko, S. P., Institute of Mechanics: 03057 Kyiv, vul. Nesterova 3; tel. (44) 456-93-51; fax (44) 456-03-19; e-mail ang@ imech.freenet.kiev.ua; internet www.inmech .kiev.ua; library of 20,000 vols; f. 1918; mechanics of composite and inhomogenous materials; structural mechanics; mechanics of coupled fields in materials and structures; mechanics of fracture and fatigue; dynamics and stability of mechanical system motion; attached to Nat. Acad. of Sciences of Ukraine; Dir Prof. Dr ALEXANDER N. GUZ; publs *International Applied Mechanics* (12 a year, in English), *Prikladnaya Mekhanika* (12 a year, in Russian).

Ukrainian State Research and Design Institute of Mining Geology, Rock Mechanics and Mine Surveying (UkrNIMI): 83121 Donetsk, vul. Chelyuskintsev 291; tel. (62) 348-16-48; fax (62) 348-16-47; e-mail ukrnimi@ukrnimi.donetsk.ua; internet www .ukrnimi.donetsk.ua; f. 1929; attached to Nat. Acad. of Science of Ukraine; Dir Dr A. V. ANTSIFEROV.

Usikov Institute of Radiophysics and Electronics: 61085 Kharkiv, 12, Ac. Proskura St; tel. (57) 720-33-19; fax (57) 315-21-05; e-mail secretar@ire.kharkov.ua; internet www.ire.kharkov.ua; f. 1955; attached to Nat. Acad. of Sciences of Ukraine; interaction between electromagnetic waves and solids as well as biological objects; radio wave propagation in the environment; radiophysical sensing of man-made and natural objects; library of 135,000 vols; Dir Prof. VLADIMIR M. YAKOVENKO; Deputy Dir Dr ALEKSANDR KOGUT; Deputy Dir PETER MELEZHIK; publ. *Radiophysics and Electronics* (4 a year).

Vniichimprojekt Institute: 02002 Kyiv-2, vul. M. Raskovoi 11; tel. (44) 517-05-81; fax (44) 517-15-18; e-mail vniichim@nbi.com.ua; internet www.himpro.com.ua; f. 1970; develops synthetic detergents, personal care products and packaging materials; library of 38,800 vols; Pres. VALERY N. KRIVOSHEI; publs *Khimichna Promyslovist Ukrainy* (6 a year), *Upakovka* (6 a year).

Yuzhniigiprogaz Institute OJSC: 83121 Donetsk, vul. Artema 169G; tel. (62) 305-76-61; fax (62) 305-71-76; e-mail ex@yuzh-gaz .donetsk.ua; internet www.ungg.org; f. 1933; library of 38,000 vols; Dir V. D. BONDARTSOV.

Libraries and Archives
Chernivtsi
Scientific Library Yuriy Fedkovych Chernivtsi National University: 58000 Chernivtsi, vul. Lesi Ukrainki 23; tel. (37) 258-47-60; e-mail biblio@chnu.cv.ua; internet www.library.chnu.edu.ua; f. 1852; 2.6m. vols; Dir MYKHAILO B. ZUSHMAN.

Dnipropetrovsk
Dnipropetrovsk National University Library 'O. Gonchar': 49050 Dnipropetrovsk, vul. Kozakova 8; tel. (56) 246-61-95; e-mail librarydnu@gmail.com; internet www .dsu.dp.ua/lib.html; 1,417,000 vols; Dir S. V. KUBYSHKINA.

Donetsk
Scientific Library of Donetsk National University: 83055 Donetsk, Universitetska vul. 24; tel. (62) 299-23-78; fax (62) 292-71-12; e-mail bdongu@dongu.donetsk.ua; internet library.dongu.donetsk.ua; f. 1937; 1,052,763 vols; Dir N. A. KARYAGINA; Deputy Dir MAKHNO IRINA.

Kharkiv
Kharkiv V. N. Karazin National University Central Scientific Library: 61022 Kharkiv, pl. Svobody 4; tel. (57) 707-52-86; fax (57) 705-12-55; e-mail cnb@univer .kharkov.ua; internet www-library.univer .kharkov.ua; f. 1804; 3.4m. vols, incl. 50,000 rare editions, 19 incunabula, more than 1,000 manuscripts, books by classical writers and scholars published in their lifetimes; Dir IRINA K. ZHURAVLYOVA (acting).

Kyiv
Archives of Ukraine:
Attached Archives:
Central State Archive and Museum of Literature and Art of Ukraine: 01601 Kyiv, Volodymyrska vul. 22A; tel. and fax (44) 278-44-81; f. 1966; Dir LEONID SKRYPKA.
Central State Archive of Public Organizations of Ukraine: 01011 Kyiv, Kutuzova vul. 24; tel. (44) 295-55-32; e-mail cdago@online.com.ua.
Central State Archive of Supreme Bodies of Power and Government of Ukraine: tel. (44) 275-36-66; e-mail tsdavo@archives.gov.ua.
Central State CinePhotoFono Archive of Ukraine 'H. S. Pshenychniy': 03110 Kyiv, Solomyanska str., 24; tel. (44) 275-37-77; e-mail tsdkffa@archives.gov.ua; internet www.tsdkffa.archives.gov.ua; Dir NINA TOPISHKO.
Central State Historical Archive of Ukraine in Kyiv: 03110 Kyiv, Solomyanska vul. 24; tel. and fax (44) 275-30-02; e-mail mail@cdiak.archives.gov.ua; internet www.archives.gov.ua; f. 1852; Dir IVAN KISIL.
State Archive of Kyiv Oblast: 04119 Kyiv, Melnykova vul. 38; tel. (44) 213-75-72.
State Archive of the City of Kyiv: 04060 Kyiv, Oleny Telihy vul. 23; tel. (44) 440-54-16; e-mail archiv@archiv.kyiv-city.gov.ua.
State Committee on Archives of Ukraine: 03110 Kyiv, Solomyanska vul.

24; tel. (44) 275-27-77; fax (44) 275-36-55; e-mail mail@archives.gov.ua; internet www.archives.gov.ua; f. 1919; Dir-Gen. OLHA HINZBURH.
Kyiv National University 'Taras Shevchenko' Library: 01601 Kyiv, vul. Volodymyrska 58; tel. (44) 235-70-98; fax (44) 235-70-98; e-mail info@libcc.univ.kiev.ua; internet www.library.univ.kiev.ua; f. 1834; 3,559,000 vols; Dir VALENTINA G. NESTERENKO.
National Historical Library of Ukraine: 01601 Kyiv vul. Lavrska 9; tel. (44) 280-46-17; e-mail nibu.kiev@ukr.net; internet dibu .kiev.ua; f. 1939; Dir ALLA SKOROKHVATOVA.
National Parliamentary Library of Ukraine: 01001 Kyiv, vul. M. Hrushevskoho 1; tel. (44) 228-85-12; fax (44) 228-85-12; internet www.nplu.kiev.ua; f. 1866; 4,000,000 vols; Dir A. P. KORNIENKO; publ. *Kalendar znamennikh i pamyatnikh dat* (4 a year).
National Scientific Medical Library: 01033 Kyiv, vul. L. Tolstogo 7; tel. (44) 234-51-97; fax (44) 235-11-35; e-mail medlib@ library.gov.ua; internet www.library.gov.ua; f. 1930; 1.5m. vols; Gen. Dir RAISA I. PAVLENKO.
State Archival Service of Ukraine: 03110 Kyiv, Solomianska St 24; tel. (44) 275-27-77; fax (44) 275-36-55; e-mail mail@archives.gov .ua; internet www.archives.gov.ua; f. 1919; Head OLHA HINZBURH.
State Scientific Agricultural Library of Ukrainian Academy of Agricultural Sciences: 03680 Kyiv, vul. Heroyiv Oborony 10; tel. (44) 527-80-75; fax (44) 526-05-09; e-mail cnsgb@faust.kiev.ua; internet dnsgb.kiev.ua; f. 1921; 1,017,323 vols; Dir Dr VIKTOR A. VERGUNOV; publs *Agropromysloviy Complex Ukraiiny* (abstract journal, 4 a year), *Akademiky Ukrainskoi Akademii Agrarnykh Nauk* (bibliographic series, 6–7 a year), *Silskohospodarki Knyhy* (4 a year).
State Scientific and Technical Library of Ukraine: 03650 Kyiv, vul. Antonovicha 180; tel. (44) 528-21-85; fax (44) 529-34-91; e-mail alex@gntb.gov.ua; internet gntb.gov .ua; f. 1935; 20m. vols, incl. books, documents and patents related to science and technology; Dir V. H. DRYGAYLO.
Ukrainian Institute of Scientific-Technical and Economic Information: 03680 Kyiv, vul. Horkogo 180; tel. (44) 268-25-79; fax (44) 268-25-41; e-mail uintei@uintei.kiev .ua; Dir N. N. ERMOSHENKO.
Vernadsky National Library of Ukraine: 03039 Kyiv, pr. 40 Richja Zhovtnja 3; tel. (44) 265-81-04; fax (44) 264-33-98; e-mail nlu@csl .freenet.kiev.ua; internet www.nbuv.go.ua; f. 1919; over 14m. vols; colln incl. books, newspapers, magazines, serials, maps, music scores, fine arts materials, manuscripts, old and rare books, incunabula, documents; colln of Slavic writings; archives of outstanding Ukrainian and foreign scientists; archives of the National Academy of Sciences of Ukraine; 40 departments and centres of preservation and restoration, culture and education, computer technologies, and publishing; Dir-Gen. O. S. ONYSHCHENKO; publs *Bibliotechnyi Visnyk* (Library Journal, 6 a year, in Ukrainian and English), *Naukovi Pratsi* (Scientific Works, 2 or 3 a year).

Lviv
Lviv Ivan Franko State University Library: 290602 Lviv, vul. Dragomanova 5; tel. (32) 273-04-94; 2.5m. vols; Dir V. K. POTAICHUK.
Lviv National Stefanyk Scientific Library of Ukraine: 79000 Lviv, vul. Stefanyka 2; tel. (32) 274-43-72; fax (32)

2272-91-47; e-mail library@lsl.lviv.ua; internet www.lsl.lviv.ua; f. 1940; 6m. vols; Dir MIROSLAV. M. ROMANYUK.

Odessa
Scientific Library of the Odessa National I. I. Mechnikov University: 65082 Odessa, str. Preobrazhenskaya 24; tel. and fax (48) 726-04-01; e-mail library@ onu.edu.ua; internet www.lib.onu.edu.ua; f. 1817; 3,900,000 vols; Dir MARINA A. PODREZOVA; Deputy Dir and IT-Man. ZAYCHENKO ALLA; publ. *Odessa National University Herald. Series: Library studies, Bibliography studies, Bibliology*.

Simferopol
Taurida National University 'V. I. Vernadsky', Library: 95007 Simferopol, pr. Vernaskogo 4; tel. (65) 251-69-98; fax (65) 251-71-35; e-mail library@crimea.edu; 776,000 vols; Librarian V. I. SPIROVA.

Uzhgorod
Uzhgorod National University Library: Uzhgorod, Kapytulna vul. 9; tel. (31) 223-72-29; internet www.univ.uzhgorod.ua/~library; 1.5m. vols; Dir OLENA I. POCHEKUTOVA.

Museums and Art Galleries
Alupka
Alupka State Palace and Park Preserve: Alupka, Dvortsove shosse 10; tel. and fax (65) 472-29-51; f. 1921; Russian noble culture and way of life in 19th century; spec. colln of 17th century maps of Europe and America; library of 10,000 vols; Dir K. K. KASPEROVICH.

Alushta
Alushta Literary Memorial Museum of S. M. Sergeev-Tsensky: Alushta, vul. Sergeeva-Tsenskogo 15; tel. (65) 603-06-64; house where the author lived; Dir T. A. FEFYUZA.

Bakhchisarai
Bakhchisarai Historical and Cultural State Preserve: 98405 Crimea, Bakhchisarai, vul. Richna 133; tel. and fax (65) 544-28-81; e-mail hansaray@crimeastar.net; internet www.hansaray.org.ua; f. 1917; works of art, architectural monuments, the Khan Palace of Bakhchisarai (built 1532), cave towns; archeological sites; archeology and ethnographic collns; library of 12,000 vols; Dir-Gen. EUGENY PETROV; Deputy Dir OLEKSA HAIWORONSKI.

Chernihiv
Chernihiv Literary Museum 'Mikhailo Kotsyubinsky': 14000 Chernihiv, vul. Kotsyubinskogo 3; tel. (46) 224-04-59; f. 1934; life and work of Kotsyubinsky; library of 11,000 books; Dir IGOR KOTSYUBINSKY; publ. *Collections* (every 5 years).

Chernivtsi
Chernivtsi Memorial Museum 'Yu. A. Fedkovych': Chernivtsi, vul. Pushkina 17; tel. (37) 22-56-78; f. 1945; life and work of the writer A. Fedkovich; Dir D. FYLYPCHUK.

Dniprodzerzhynsk
Dniprodzerzhynsk Museum of Town History: 51931 Dniprodzerzhynsk; tel. (56) 923-11-10; f. 1931; library of 10,000 vols; Dir NATALIA BULANOVA.

Dnipropetrovsk
Dnipropetrovsk Historical Museum 'D. I. Yavornystkiy': Dnipropetrovsk, vul. K.

Marksa 16; tel. (56) 246-24-28; fax (56) 246-05-12; e-mail muzeum@a-teleport.com; internet www.museum.dp.ua; Dir NADEZHDA KAPUSTINA.

Dnipropetrovsk State Art Museum: 49044 Dnipropetrovsk, vul. Shevchenko 21; tel. (56) 247-32-65; e-mail info@globe.dp.ua; internet www.artmuseum.dp.ua; Dir VLADIMIR KULICHIKHIN.

Donetsk

Donetsk Art Museum: 83055 Donetsk, Pushkina 35; tel. (62) 304-83-03.

Donetsk Botanical Gardens: 83059 Donetsk, pr. Ilicha 110; tel. (62) 294-12-80; fax (62) 294-61-57; e-mail herb@herb.dn.ua; f. 1964; attached to Nat. Acad. of Sciences of Ukraine; Dir A. Z. GLUKHOV.

Kamyanets-Podilsky

Kamyanets-Podilsky State Historical Museum-Preserve: 32300 Khmelnitska oblast, Kamyanets-Podilsky, vul. Ioanno-Predtechenska 2; tel. (38) 492-37-84; f. 1890; Dir L. P. STANISLAVSKA.

Kerch

Kerch State Archaeological Museum: 98300 Crimea, Kerch, Sverdlova 7; tel. and fax (65) 2-04-75; e-mail museum@kerch.com.ua; f. 1826; library of 20,000 vols; Dir P. I. IVANENKO; publ. *Arkheologiya i istoriya Bospora* (irregular).

Kharkiv

Kharkiv State Art Museum: 61002 Kharkiv, Sovnarkomivska vul. 11; tel. and fax (57) 706-33-95; e-mail artmuseum_kharkiv@i.ua; internet artmuseum.kharkov.ua; f. 1920; Ukrainian, Russian and foreign art from 15th–21st centuries; 24,000 exhibits; library of 19,000 vols; Dir V. V. MYZGINA.

Kharkiv State Historical Museum: 61003 Kharkiv, Universitetska vul. 10; tel. and fax (57) 223-20-94; Dir N. A. VOEVODIN.

Khomutovo

Ukrainian Steppe Nature Reserve: 87620 Donetsk oblast, Novoazov raion, Khomutovo; tel. (62) 792-73-25; f. 1961; attached to Nat. Acad. of Sciences of Ukraine; Dir Dr ANATOLIY P. GENOV.

Kolomiya

Kolomiya State Museum of Folk Art: Ivano-Frankivska oblast, Kolomiya, Teatralna vul. 25; tel. and fax (34) 332-39-12; e-mail jatkachuk@hutsul.museum; internet hutsul.museum; f. 1926; exhibitions, confs, festivals, scientific work; 87 mems; library of 6,000 vols; Dir Y. TKACHUK; publ. *People's House* (6 a year).

Kyiv

Bohdan and Varvara Khanenko Museum of Arts: 01004 Kyiv, Tereshchenkivska 15–17; tel. (44) 235-02-25; fax (44) 235-02-06; e-mail khanenkomuseum@ukr.net; f. 1919; holds more than 20,000 items of western European, Oriental and ancient art; Dir VIRA VYNOHRADOVA; publ. *Khanenko Readings* (1 a year).

Kyiv Museum of Russian Art: 01004 Kyiv, Tereshchenkivska vul. 9; tel. (44) 451-40-27; fax (44) 234-61-07; e-mail museumru@ukr.net; f. 1922; library of 17,000 vols; Dir IURII VAKULENKO.

Kyiv State Literary Museum 'Lessya Ukrainka': 01032 Kyiv, vul. Saksaganskogo 97; tel. (44) 220-57-52; f. 1962; life and work of the Ukrainian poets and artists of the 19th and early 20th centuries; library of 5,000 vols; Dir IRINA L. VEREMEYEVA.

Museum of Theatrical, Musical and Cinematographic Art of Ukraine: 01015 Kyiv, str. Lavrska 9/24; tel. and fax (44) 280-16-22; e-mail tmf-museum@ukr.net; internet www.tmf-museum.kiev.ua; f. 1923; library of 30,000 vols; Dir IRYNA DROBOT.

National Art Museum of Ukraine: 01001 Kyiv, M. Hrushevskoho str. 6; tel. and fax (44) 278-13-57; e-mail pr@namu.kiev.ua; f. 1899; colln of Ukrainian figurative art; 40,000 exhibits, incl. masterpieces of Ukrainian painting, sculpture and graphics from Kyiv Rus age to present day; Dir A. I. MELNIK.

National Botanical Gardens 'M. M. Gryshko': 01014 Kyiv, Timiryazevska vul. 1; tel. (44) 285-41-05; fax (44) 285-26-49; e-mail nbg@nbg.kiev.ua; f. 1935; attached to Nat. Acad. of Sciences of Ukraine; library of 39,041 vols; Dir Prof. Dr N. V. ZAIMENKO.

National Kyiv-Pechersk Lavra Museum: 01015 Kyiv, vul. Sichnevogo Povstannya 25; tel. (44) 254-22-57; e-mail lavra@lavra.kiev.ua; internet www.lavra.kiev.ua; ancient monastery, icons.

National Museum of the History of Ukraine: 01034 Kyiv, vul. Volodymyrska 2; tel. (44) 228-65-45; fax (44) 228-43-23; e-mail mhistory@i.com.ua; f. 1899; history, archaeology, religion, ethnography, 600,000 exhibits; Dir SERHIY CHAIKOVSKYI.

National Taras Shevchenko Museum: 12 Taras Shevchenko bulv., 01004 Kyiv; tel. (44) 234-25-23; fax (44) 288-33-81; e-mail shevchenko-museum@ukr.net; life and work of the poet T. G. Shevchenko; f. 1940; Dir CHRISTINA KLIMENKO.

St Sophia of Kiev National Conservation Area: 01034 Kyiv, Volodymyrska vul. 24; tel. (44) 278-26-20; fax (44) 278-67-06; e-mail stsophia@i.kiev.ua; internet www.sophia.org.ua; f. 1934; comprises 11th-century St Sofia cathedral (with early frescoes and mosaics) and other, 18th-century bldgs; attached museums incl. St Cyril Church Museum, St Andrew Church Museum, Golden Gates Museum (11th-century town gatehouse) and, in the Crimea, 6th–15th-century Sudak fortress; Dir-Gen. NELYA M. KUKOVALSKA.

Ukrainian Museum of Folk and Decorative Art: 01015 Kyiv, vul. Sichnevoho Povstannya 21; tel. (44) 290-13-43; f. 1954; library of 3,180 vols; Dir V. G. NAGAI; publ. *Folk Creative Work and Ethnography.*

Lviv

Lviv Historical Museum: 79008 Lviv, pl. Rynok 4/6/24; tel. (322) 74-33-04; f. 1893; Dir BOGDAN CHAYKOVSKIY.

Lviv State Picture Gallery: 79000 Lviv, vul. Stefanika 3; tel. (32) 272-39-48; fax (32) 272-30-09; f. 1907; West European and Ukrainian contemporary art; library of 34,276 vols; Dir BORIS VOZNITSKY.

The Andrey Sheptytsky National Museum in Lviv: 79008 Lviv, Svobody 20; tel. (32) 2235-88-46; fax (32) 2235-88-49; e-mail nml_shept@ukr.net; f. 1905; colln of over 160,000 artworks; preservation, devt, study and promotion of 11th–21st century Ukrainian art; library of 30,000 scientific vols; Dir IHOR KOZHAN; Academic Sec. ANGELINA ZABYTIVSKA; publ. *Litopys* (Chronicle of the Andrey Sheptytsky National Museum in Lviv, 1 a year).

State Museum of Ethnography, Arts and Crafts: Lviv, pr. Svoboda 15; tel. (32) 2727012; f. 1873; attached to Nat. Acad. of Sciences of Ukraine.

State Natural History Museum: 79008 Lviv, Teatralna vul. 18; tel. and fax (32) 274-23-07; e-mail museum@museum.lviv.net; internet museum.lviv.net; f. 1870;

attached to Nat. Acad. of Sciences of Ukraine; library of 69,000 vols; Dir Prof. YURIY M. CHORNOBAY; publ. *Proceedings* (1 a year).

Odessa

Odessa Archaeological Museum: 65026 Odessa, vul. Lanzheronovska 4; tel. 722-01-71; e-mail archaeology@farlep.net; internet www.archaeology.farlep.odessa.ua; f. 1825; history of the Northern Black Sea Coast area; library of 28,000 vols; Dir V. P. VANCHUGOV; Librarian H. P. UKRAINSKA.

Odessa Fine Arts Museum: 65082 Odessa, Sofievska vul. 5A; tel. (48) 223-82-72; fax (48) 223-83-93; e-mail ofam@tm.odessa.ua; internet www.museum-finearts.odessa.ua; f. 1899; Ukrainian and Russian art since 15th century; library of 15,000 vols; Dir NATALYA S. POLISHCHUK.

Odessa Museum of Western and Eastern Art: 270026 Odessa, Pushkinska vul. 9; tel. and fax (482) 22-48-15; e-mail oweamuseum@hotbox.ru; internet www.oweamuseum.odessa.ua; f. 1920; library of 14,000 vols; Dir VICTOR S. NIKIFOROV.

Poltava

Poltava Art Museum: 314020 Poltava, Spaska 11; tel. (53) 227-27-11; f. 1919; library of 4,000 vols; Curator KIM SKALATSKY.

Poltava State Museum: Poltava, Lenina 2; life and work of the writers P. Mirnyi, J. Kotlyarevsky, V. G. Korolenko, N. V. Gogol; library of 80,000 vols; Dir GALINA P. BELOUS.

Sevastopol

National Preserve of Tauric Chersonesos: 99045 Crimea, Sevastopol, vul. Drevnyaya 1; tel. and fax (69) 255-02-78; e-mail info@chersonesos.org; internet www.chersonesos.org; f. 1892; archaeological park incorporating museum and ruins of Greek colony and Byzantine city of Tauric Chersonesos; library of 30,000 vols; Dir Dr LEONID V. MARCHENKO; publ. *Khersonesskyi Sbornik* (Chersonesos Collected Articles, 1 a year).

Shevchenkovo

Shevchenko, T. G., State Memorial Museum: Cherkasska oblast, Zvenigorodsky raion, Shevchenkovo; f. 1939; life and work of T. G. Shevchenko; library of 3,000 vols; Dir T. V. GULAK.

Sumy

Sumy Art Museum 'Nukanor Onatsky': 40030 Sumy, Krasnaya pl. 1; tel. (54) 222-04-81; internet www.city.sumy.ua/artgallery; f. 1920; Dir GALINA V. AREFEVA.

Yalta

Nikita Botanical Gardens: 98648 Crimea, Yalta, Nikita; tel. (65) 433-55-30; fax (65) 433-53-86; e-mail nbs1812@gmail.com; internet www.nbg.crimea.ua; f. 1812; attached to Ukrainian Acad. of Agrarian Sciences; library of 213,000 vols; 50,000 species and hybrids of flowers, fruits, and woody, subtropical, industrial, oil-bearing and medical plants; Dir Prof. Dr V. N. EZHOV; publs *Bulletin* (3 a year), *Collected Scientific Works* (3 a year).

Universities

AGRARIAN UNIVERSITIES

BILA TSERKVA STATE AGRARIAN UNIVERSITY

09117 Kyivska obl., Bila Tserkva, bul. 50-Richchya Perermoti 96

Telephone: (44) 633-11-01

E-mail: rector@btsau.kiev.ua
Internet: www.btsau.kiev.ua
Founded 1750, present name and status 1995
Faculties of agronomy, biotechnology, culture and art, economics, external studies, languages, law, physical education, qualification improvement, veterinary medicine
Rector: Dr MYKHAILO M. BARANOVSKIY
First Pro-Rector: Prof. Dr VITALIY P. NOVAK
Pro-Rector for Distance Studies: Prof. Dr SVETLANA I. TSEKHMISTRENKO
Pro-Rector for Finance: Dr TATYANA V. ARBUZOVA
Pro-Rector for Research: Prof. Dr IHOR L. YAKIMENKO
Pro-Rector for Studies: Prof. Dr LYLIYA V. BARANOVSKAYA
Publication: *Vestnik BSGAU* (Bila Tserkva State Agrarian University Bulletin).

CRIMEAN AGROTECHNOLOGICAL UNIVERSITY

95492 Simferopol, Agrarnoye
Telephone: (65) 226-33-52
Fax: (65) 222-39-66
E-mail: rectorat@csau.crimea-ua.com
Internet: www.csau.crimea-ua.com
Founded 1922
Public control
Languages of instruction: Russian, Ukrainian
Academic year: September to July
Dir: Prof. MYKHAYLO M. MELNIKOV
Library of 542,425 vols
Number of teachers: 380
Number of students: 4,047

DEANS

Faculty of Agronomy: Dr VALERIY F. VIL'CHINSKIY
Faculty of Economics and Management: Dr VITALIY M. DYATEL
Faculty of Land Planning and Geodesy: Dr VOLODYMYR M. GORBATYUK
Faculty of Mechanization of Producing and Technology of Processing of Agricultural Production: Dr YURI B. GERBER
Faculty of Veterinary Medicine: Dr VIKTOR I. SKRIPNIK

DNIPROPETROVS'K STATE AGRARIAN UNIVERSITY

49600 Dnipropetrovsk, vul. Voroshylov 25
Telephone: (56) 744-81-32
E-mail: interdsau@gmail.com
Internet: www.dsau.dp.ua
Founded 1922
Public control
Language of instruction: Ukraine
Academic year: September to June
Rector: Prof. ANATOLIY S. I. KOBETS
First Vice-Rector for Education: Prof. Dr DMYTRO M. ONOPRIYENKO
Vice-Rector for Research: Prof. YURIY I. GRYTSAN
Dir of Library: ANTONINA G. BRATCHYK
Library of 400,000 vols
Number of teachers: 488
Number of students: 6,314 (3,653 full-time, 2,661 external)
Publication: *Agrosvit* (2 a year)

DEANS

Faculty of Accounting and Finance: Prof. GALYNA Y. PAVLOVA
Faculty of Agricultural Mechanization: Prof. Dr PETRO M. KUKHARENKO
Faculty of Agronomy: Prof. Dr OLEXANDR O. MYTSYK
Faculty of Biotechnology: Prof. Dr STANISLAV G. PISHCHAN

Faculty of Ecology and Irrigation: Prof. Dr ANDRIY V. TKACHUK
Faculty of Marketing and Management: TAMARA M. SAMILYK
Faculty of Veterinary Medicine: Prof. Dr IVAN A. BIBEN

KHARKIV STATE AGRARIAN UNIVERSITY 'V. V. DOKUCHAYEV'

62483 Kharkiv, P/O 'Komunist-1', vul. Mazepy 10
Telephone: (57) 293-71-46
Fax: (57) 293-60-67
Internet: www.hgau.narod.ru
Founded 1816
Rector: Prof. MYKOLA D. YEVTUSHENKO
Library of 600,000 vols
Number of teachers: 258
Number of students: 5,195
Publications: *Agrochemistry, Common Agriculture, Forestry, Plant Growing and Vegetable Production, Series on Crop Production, Series on Economics and Natural Sciences, Series on Soil Science*

DEANS

Faculty of Agrochemistry and Soil Science: VASYL DEKHTYARYOV
Faculty of Agronomy: YEVGEN OGURTSOV
Faculty of Continuing Education: VOLODYMYR PUZIK
Faculty of Correspondence Studies: VOLODYMYR BILIUSKO
Faculty of Economics: OLEKSANDR ULYANCHENKO
Faculty of Forestry: ANATOLIY POLYVYANIY
Faculty of Land Management: VASYL BALAKYRSKY
Faculty of Plant Protection: VOLODYMYR TURENKO

LVIV NATIONAL AGRARIAN UNIVERSITY

80381 Lviv V. Velikogo Str., 1
Telephone: (32) 224-23-35
Fax: (32) 224-29-19
E-mail: lnau@mail.lviv.ua
Internet: www.lnau.lviv.ua
Founded 1856
State control
Academic year: September to June
Depts agronomy, architecture, ecology, economics, energetics, farm building, land surveying, mechanics
Rector: Prof. Dr VOLODYMYR V. SNITYNSKYY
Library of 600,000 vols
Number of teachers: 370
Number of students: 11,000
Publication: *Transactions*.

NATIONAL AGRICULTURAL UNIVERSITY OF UKRAINE

03041 Kyiv, vul. Heroyiv Oborony 15
Telephone: (44) 267-81-19
Fax: (44) 261-42-34
E-mail: inter@nauu.kiev.ua
Internet: www.nauu.kiev.ua
Founded 1898
Rector: DYMTRO O. MELNYCHUK
Library: 1m. vols
Number of teachers: 2,827
Number of students: 22,034
Brs in Berezhany, Boyarka, Irpin, Nemishayiv, Nizhyn, Zalishchiky
Publication: *For Agricultural Specialists* (6 a year)

DEANS

Faculty of Agricultural Biology: ANATOLIY V. BYKIN
Faculty of Agricultural Management: KOVTUN O. ANATOLIVNA
Faculty of Agricultural Mechanical Engineering: YAROSLAV M. MYKHAYLOVYCH
Faculty of Animal Health: VITALIY Y. LUBETSKIY
Faculty of Animal Husbandry, Output Production and Processing Technology: YURIY V. ZASUKHA
Faculty of Construction and Design: KONSTYANTYN H. LOPATKO
Faculty of Ecology and Biotechnology: NATALYA M. RIDEY
Faculty of Economics: SERHIY M. KVASHA
Faculty of Electrification and Automation of Agriculture: IVAN P. RADKO
Faculty of Forestry: SERHIY B. KOVALEVSKY
Faculty of Land Management: BOHDAN I. NOVAK
Faculty of Landscape Engineering: ANATOLIY I. KUSHNIR
Faculty of Law: VOLODYMYR I. KURILO
Faculty of Quality and Safety of Agricultural Production: OLGA M. YAKUBCHAK
Faculty of Small Animal Health: OLEG F. PETRENKO
Faculty of Social Pedagogy: PETRO H. LUZAN
Faculty of Water Resources and Aquaculture: PETRO H. SHEVCHENKO

STATE AGROECOLOGICAL UNIVERSITY

10008 Zhytomyr, Stary bul. 7
Telephone: (41) 237-49-31
Fax: (41) 222-14-02
Internet: www.academy.zt.ua
Founded 1922
Depts of agricultural ecology, agricultural engineering, animal husbandry, economics and agribusiness, veterinary medicine
Rector: V. P. SLAVOV
Library of 370,000 vols
Number of teachers: 276
Number of students: 2,859

UKRAINIAN NATIONAL FORESTRY UNIVERSITY

79057 Lviv, vul. Gen. Chuprynka 103
Telephone: (32) 237-80-94
Fax: (32) 237-89-05
E-mail: nltu@ukr.net
Rector: YURIY YU. TUNYTSYA
Vice-Rector: HRYHORIY T. KRYNYTSKYY
Library of 450,000 vols
Number of teachers: 310
Number of students: 3,600
Publications: *Naukovyy visnyk* (Scientific bulletin), *Ukrainski lis* (Ukrainian Forest)

DEANS

Extra Mural Faculty: Dr YAROSLAV LYKO
Faculty of Economy: Dr YAROSLAV KULCHYTSKYY
Faculty of Forest Mechanics: Prof. Dr MYKOLA KIRYK
Faculty of Forestry: Prof. Dr STEPAN MYKLUSH
Faculty of Technology: Prof. Dr VOLODYMYR MAKSYMIV
Institute of Ecological Economics: Dir: Dr LYUDMYLA MAKSYMIV

HUMANITIES AND SCIENCES UNIVERSITIES

CHERNIVTSI NATIONAL UNIVERSITY 'YURIY FEDKOVYCH'

58012 Chernivtsi, vul. Kotsyubinskoho 2
Telephone: (37) 222-62-35
Fax: (37) 255-29-14
E-mail: rector@chnu.cv.ua
Internet: www.chnu.cv.ua

Founded 1875
State control
Language of instruction: Ukrainian
Academic year: September to June

Rector: STEPAN V. MELNYCHUK
First Pro-Rector, Pro-Rector for Research: S. V. MELNYCHUK
Pro-Rector for Academic Affairs: ROMAN I. PETRYSHYN
Pro-Rector for Academic Devt: TAMARA V. MARUSYK
Librarian: OLEG I. SHLYUK
Library: see Libraries and Archives
Number of teachers: 786
Number of students: 14,103 (7,421 full-time, 6,682 part-time)
Publications: *Scientific University Annual, Universitetsky Visnyk* (12 a year)

DEANS

Faculty of Applied Mathematics: R. I. PETRYSHYN
Faculty of Biology: M. M. MARCHENKO
Faculty of Chemistry: O. S. LYAVYNETS
Faculty of Computer Science: (vacant)
Faculty of Economics: L. S. BILYK
Faculty of Engineering and Technology: Prof. O. V. ANGELSKIY
Faculty of Foreign Languages: R. V. VATSEBA
Faculty of Geography: V. P. RUDENKO
Faculty of History, Politology and International Relations: O. V. DOBRZHANSKIY
Faculty of Law: P. S. PATSURKIVSKIY
Faculty of Pedagogy: I. M. ZVARYCH
Faculty of Philology: B. I. BUNCHUK
Faculty of Philosophy and Theology: V. O. BALUKH
Faculty of Physics: I. V. GUTSUL

DNIPROPETROVSK NATIONAL UNIVERSITY

49050 Dnipropetrovsk, vul. Naukova 13
Telephone: (56) 246-00-95
Fax: (56) 776-58-33
E-mail: admin@dsu.dp.ua
Internet: www.dsu.dp.ua

Founded 1918
Languages of instruction: Ukrainian, Russian
Academic year: September to July

Pres.: MYKOLA POLYAKOV
Vice-Pres. and President's Deputy: O. O. KOCHUBEY
Vice-Pres. for Academic Affairs: V. G. MUSIYAKA
Vice-Pres. for Foreign Affairs: V. V. KOSTYRKO
Vice-Pres. for Research: M. M. DRON
Librarian: L. S. KUBISHKINA
Library: see Libraries and Archives
Number of teachers: 1,233
Number of students: 13,260
Publication: *Dnipropetrovsk University Newspaper* (12 a year)

DEANS

Faculty of Applied Mathematics: S. V. CHERNYSHENKO
Faculty of Biology and Ecology: O. Y. PAKHOMOV
Faculty of Chemistry: V. F. VARGALYUK

Faculty of Geology and Geography: V. V. BOGDANOVICH
Faculty of History: S. I. SVITLENKO
Faculty of International Economics: N. Y. BOYTSUN
Faculty of Law: P. I. GNATENKO
Faculty of Mass Media: V. D. DEMCHENKO
Faculty of Mechanics and Mathematics: V. O. SYASEV
Faculty of Medicine: J. S. SAPA
Faculty of Philology: O. V. RODNY
Faculty of Physics: R. S. TUTIK
Faculty of Psychology and Pedagogics: I. V. RASPOPOV
Faculty of Radio Physics: V. M. DOLGOV
Faculty of Ukrainian Philology and Art History: I. S. POPOVA
Institute of Economics: S. O. SMIRNOV
Institute of Physics and Technology: Y. A. DZUR

DONETSK NATIONAL UNIVERSITY

83001 Donetsk, vul. Universytetska St 24
Telephone: (62) 337-19-45
Fax: (62) 335-22-56
E-mail: postmaster@univ.donetsk.ua
Internet: www.donnu.edu.ua

Founded 1965, Donetsk State Univ. until 2000
State control
Languages of instruction: Russian, Ukrainian
Academic year: September to July

Rector: Prof. V. P. SHEVCHENKO
Deputy Rector: Prof. P. V. YEGOROV
Vice-Rector: Prof. N. P. IVANITSYN
Librarian: N. O. KORYAGINA
Library: see under Libraries and Archives
Number of teachers: 900 .
Number of students: 17,500

Publications: *Bulletin* (1 a year), *Donetsk Archaeological Bulletin* (1 a year), *Eastern Ukraine Linguistic Collected Articles* (2 a year), *Economical Cybernetics* (4 a year), *Finance, Accounting, Banks* (2 a year), *Historical and Political Studies* (4 a year), *Juridical Studies* (4 a year), *Management Models in Market Economy* (2 a year), *New Pages in the History of Donbass* (2 a year), *Philological Studies* (2 a year), *Theoretical and Applied Mechanics* (1 a year).

DONETSK NATIONAL UNIVERSITY OF ECONOMICS AND TRADE 'M. TUHAN-BARANOVSKIY'

83050 Donetsk, vul. Shchorsa 31
Telephone: (62) 335-10-29
Fax: (62) 304-83-16
E-mail: info@donduet.edu.ua
Internet: www.donduet.edu.ua

Founded 1920
State control
Academic year: September to June
Languages of instruction: English, Russian, Ukrainian

Rector: O. O. SHUBIN
First Vice-Rector: L. O. OMELYANOVYCH
Vice-Rector for Economic and Technical Provisions: A. B. ROMANOV
Vice-Rector for Scientific Affairs: A. A. SADEKOV
Vice-Rector for Scientific-Pedagogical Activity and Int. Relations: V. G. POGREBNYAK
Vice-Rector for Social and Educational Affairs: S. V. DROZHZHINA
Librarian: T. P. TKACHENKO
Library of 67,000 vols, 75,000 periodicals
Number of teachers: 450
Number of students: 14,876

DEANS

Institute of Accounting and Finance: V. A. ORLOVA
Institute of Economics and Management: L. V. FROLOVA
Institute of Foodstuff Industries: V. A. SUKMANOV
Faculty of Marketing, Trade and Customs Activity: Prof. I. KH. BASHYROV
Faculty of Restaurant and Hotel Business: Prof. T. V. NUZHNA
International Faculty of Foreign Specialist Training: V. E. VOYLOSHNIKOVA

KHARKIV NATIONAL UNIVERSITY OF ECONOMICS

61001 Kharkiv, 9A pr. Lenina
Telephone: (57) 702-03-04
Fax: (57) 702-07-17
E-mail: mail@hneu.edu.ua
Internet: www.hdeu.edu.ua

Founded 1930
State control
Languages of instruction: English, Russian, Ukrainian
Academic year: September to June

Rector: Prof. Dr VOLODYMYR PONOMARENKO
Vice-Rector for Int. Relations: Prof. VOLODYMYR YERMACHENKO
Librarian: NATALYA BOZHKO
Library of 864,329 vols, 13,679 periodicals, 2,070 copies of theses and thesis abstracts
Number of teachers: 712
Number of students: 14,000 (incl. 205 postgraduate and doctoral)
Publications: *Business Inform, Development Management, Economy of Development*

DEANS

Correspondence Faculty: Prof. Dr SERGIJ LUKASHOV
Faculty of Accounting and Audit: Prof. Dr GRIGORY AZARENKOV
Faculty of Economic Informatics: Prof. Dr VOLODYMYR GRACHOV
Faculty of Economy and Law: Prof. Dr TETYANA SERIKOVA
Faculty of Int. Economic Relations: Prof. Dr IVAN PIDDUBNY
Faculty of Management and Marketing: Prof. Dr OLEKSANDR TIMONIN
Finance Faculty: Prof. Dr PAVLO PRONOZA

KHMELNYTSKY STATE UNIVERSITY

29016 Khmelnytsky, vul. Instytutska 11
Telephone: (38) 272-80-76
Fax: (38) 222-32-65
E-mail: centr@mailhub.tub.km.ua
Internet: www.tup.km.ua

Founded 1962

Rector: MYKOLA SKYBA
Deputy Rector for Academic Work: SERGIY KOSTOGRYZ (Academic Work)
Deputy Rector for Academic Work: MYKHAYLO VOYNARENKO
Deputy Rector for Admin. Work: ANATOLIY FOMOV
Deputy Rector for Finance and Economic Activity: VIKTOR NYZHNYK
Deputy Rector for Int. Relations: MYKOLA YOKHNA
Deputy Rector for Scientific Work: VITALIY KAPLUN

Number of teachers: 637
Number of students: 12,976

Publications: *Measuring and Computing Devices in Technological Processes* (2 a year), *Problems of Trybology International Scientific Journal* (2 a year), *University Herald* (6 a year)

DEANS

Faculty of Applied Mathematics and Computer Technologies: SERGIY KOVALCHUK
Faculty of Business: LIDIYA TORGOVA
Faculty of Correspondence Studies 1: VITALIY KARAZEY
Faculty of Correspondence Studies 2: VIRA BEGNYAK
Faculty of Distance Studies: MYKOLA MAZUR
Faculty of Economics: MYKOLA BONDARENKO
Faculty of Engineering Mechanics: GEORGIY DRAPAK
Faculty of Humanities and Pedagogics: LYUDMYLA STANISLAVOVA
Faculty of International Relations: VITALIY TRETKO
Faculty of Management: LYUDMYLA LYUBOKHYNETS
Faculty of Pre-University and Post-University Training: MYKOLA BABYCH
Faculty of Radio Electronics and Computer Engineering: VOLODYMYR KOSENKOV
Faculty of Technology and Design: DOMBROVSKIY

KYIV NATIONAL LINGUISTIC UNIVERSITY

03680 Kyiv GSP 150, vul. Chervonoarmiyska 73

Telephone: (44) 227-33-72
Fax: (44) 227-67-88
E-mail: knlu@knlu.kiev.ua
Internet: www.knlu.kiev.ua

Founded 1948
Public control
Academic year: September to June

Rector: Dr ROMAN V. VASKO

Library: 1m. vols
Number of teachers: 605
Number of students: 6,230

Publications: *Methods in Foreign Language Teaching* (4 a year, in Ukrainian and other languages), *Philology of Foreign Languages* (4 a year, in Ukrainian and other languages)

DEANS

Faculty of Economics and Law: MYKOLA HAMZYUK
Faculty of German Philology: IRYNA MOYSEYENKO
Faculty of Oriental Studies: SERGUY SOROKIN
Faculty of Romance Philology: ANATOLIY CHERNUKHA
Faculty of Slavic Philology: ALLA KENDYUSHENKO
Faculty of Translation: OKSANA FRANKO

KYIV NATIONAL UNIVERSITY OF TRADE AND ECONOMICS

02156 Kyiv, vul. Kioto 19
Telephone: (44) 531-47-73
Fax: (44) 513-85-36
E-mail: rio@knteu.kiev.ua
Internet: www.knteu.kiev.ua

Rector: Prof. Dr ANATOLII A. MAZARAKI
Vice-Rector for Admin. and Economic Work: Prof. Dr LEONID G. SHAPOVAL
Vice-Rector for Scientific-Educational and Methodological Work: Prof. Dr NATALIA V. PRYTULSKA
Vice-Rector for Scientific and Pedagogical Work and Int. Relations: Prof. Dr VALERII M. SAI
Vice-Rector for Scientific-Pedagogic Work: Prof. Dr SVITLANA L. SHAPOVAL

Library of 2,000,000 vols
Number of students: 39,000

DEANS

Commodity Science Faculty: Prof. VICTOR OSYKA

Faculty of Accounting and Economics: Prof. Dr OLEKSANDR A. KHARCHENKO
Faculty of Economics, Management and Law: Dr NATALIYA M. HULYAYEVA
Faculty of Finance and Banking: Dr IGOR V. SMOLIN
Faculty of the Restaurant, Hotel and Tourist Industry: Prof. Dr MYKHAILO I. PERESICHNYY

NATIONAL UNIVERSITY OF KYIV-MOHYLA ACADEMY

04070 Kyiv, vul. Skovorody 2
Telephone: (44) 416-45-15
Fax: (44) 463-67-83
E-mail: rec@ukma.kiev.ua
Internet: www.ukma.kiev.ua

Founded 1615, closed 1817, re-established 1991, nat. univ. 1994
State control
Languages of instruction: Ukrainian, English
Academic year: September to June

Pres.: VYACHESLAV BRYUKHOVETSKY
First Vice-Pres. and Vice-Pres. for Research and Devt: MYKHAILO BRYK
Vice-Pres. for Academic Affairs: VADYM ZUBKO
Vice-Pres. for Devt: NATALYA SHUMKOVA
Vice-Pres. for Finance and Admin.: LYUDMYLA DYACHENKO
Vice-Pres. for Foreign Cooperation: VOLODYMYR PANCHENKO
Vice-Pres. for Graduate and Postgraduate Studies: LYUDMYLA DYACHENKO
Dean of Students: OLENA TRETYAKOVA
Registrar: NATALIA HRYBCHUK
Librarian: TETYANA YAROSHENKO

Library of 300,000 vols
Number of teachers: 157
Number of students: 2,300

Publications: *Magisterium* (4 a year), *Mandrivets* (Traveller, 6 a year), *Naukovi Zapysky* (Scientific Notes, 13 a year)

DEANS

Faculty of Computer Science: MYKOLA HLYBOVETS
Faculty of Economics: Prof. YURIY BAZHAL
Faculty of Humanities: Prof. VITALIY SCHERBAK
Faculty of Legal Sciences: Dr ANDRIY A. MELESHEVICH
Faculty of Natural Sciences: Dr IRYNA VYSHENSKA
Faculty of Social Sciences and Technology: Prof. SERHIY M. KVIT
Kyiv-Mohyla Business School: PAVLO M. SHEREMETA

NATIONAL UNIVERSITY OF LVIV 'IVAN FRANKO'

79000 Lviv, Universytetska vul. 1
Telephone: (32) 274-12-62
Fax: (32) 2297-16-68
E-mail: kyrylych@franko.lviv.ua
Internet: www.franko.lviv.ua

Founded 1661
Language of instruction: Ukrainian
Academic year: September to June

Rector: Prof. V. VYSOCHANSKY
Vice-Rector for Admin. Affairs: V. VLASEVYCH
Vice-Rector for Economic and Financial Affairs: M. LOZYNSKY
Vice-Rector for Int. Affairs: V. KYRYLYCH
Vice-Rector for Research: B. KOTUR
Vice-Rector for Student Affairs: ZVENISLAVA MAMCHUR
Vice-Rector for Teaching and Educational Affairs: M. ZUBRYTSKA
Provost: V. VYSOCHANSKY
Librarian: VASYL KMET

Library: see under Libraries and Archives
Number of teachers: 1,709
Number of students: 31,000

Publications: *Filolohiya* (Philology), *Inozemna Filologiya* (Foreign Philology), *Matematychni Studii* (Mathematical Studies), *Mineralogichniy Zbirnyk* (Proceedings on Mineralogy), *Paleontologichniy Zbirnyk* (Proceedings on Palaeontology), *Teoretychna Elektrotekhnika* (Theoretical Electrical Engineering), *Ukraina Moderna* (Modern Ukraine), *Ukrainske Literaturoznavstvo* (Ukrainian Literature Studies), *Zhurnal Fizychnykh Doslidzhen* (Journal of Physical Research)

DEANS

Dept of Life Safety: Prof. ZYNOVIY YAREMKO
Dept of Pedagogy: Prof. DMYTRO HERTSYUK
Dept of Physical Culture and Sport: Dr ROMANNA SIRENKO
Faculty of Applied Mathematics and Informatics: Prof. YAREMA G. SAVULA
Faculty of Biology: Assoc. Prof. SVITLANA HNATUSH
Faculty of Chemistry: Prof. MYKHAYLO KALYCHAK
Faculty of Economics: Prof. STEPAN PANCHYSHYN
Faculty of Electronics: Prof. IHOR POLOVINKO
Faculty of Foreign Languages: Assoc. Prof. VOLODYMYR SULYM
Faculty of Geography: Assoc. Prof. YAROSLAV KHOMYN
Faculty of Geology: Prof. MYKOLA PAVLUN
Faculty of History: Assoc. Prof. POMAN SHUST
Faculty of International Relations: MARKIAN MALSKY
Faculty of Journalism: Assoc. Prof. MYKHAYLO PRYSIAZHNY
Faculty of Law: Prof. ANDRIY BOYKO
Faculty of Mechanics and Mathematics: MYKAILO ZARICHNY
Faculty of Philosophy: VOLODYMYR MELNYK
Faculty of Physics: PETRO YAKYBCHUK
Faculty of Pre-University Training: Assoc. Prof. ROMAN O. KROKHMALNY

ODESSA NATIONAL UNIVERSITY 'I. I. MECHNIKOV'

65082 Odessa, vul. Dvoryanska 2
Telephone: (48) 723-52-54
Fax: (48) 723-35-15
E-mail: rector@onu.edu.ua
Internet: www.onu.edu.ua

Founded 1865
State control
Languages of instruction: Ukrainian, Russian
Academic year: September to July

Rector: Prof. Dr IGOR KOVAL
Pro-Rector for Academic Affairs: Assoc. Prof. ALEXANDR ZAPOROZHCENKO
Pro-Rector for Academic and Methodological Work: Prof. EVGENIY STRELTSOV
Pro-Rector for Administrative Work: VYACHESLAV IGNATENKO
Pro-Rector for Int. Relations: Assoc. Prof. SERGEY SKOROKHOD
Pro-Rector for Scientific Research: Prof. VLADIMIR IVANITSA
Librarian: MARINA PODREZOVA

Library: see under Libraries and Archives
Number of teachers: 1,700
Number of students: 13,000

Publications: *Fisika aerodispersnikh sistem* (1 a year), *Fotoelektronika* (1 a year), *Odessa State University Herald* (1 a year), *Studies in Literature* (1 a year)

DEANS

Faculty of Biology: Assoc. Prof. VENIAMIN ZAMOROV

Faculty of Chemistry: Assoc. Prof. VASILIY MENCHUK

Faculty of Economics and Law: Assoc. Prof. VYACHESLAV TRUBA

Faculty of Geology and Geography: Prof. EVGENIY CHERKEZ

Faculty of History: Assoc. Prof. VYACHESLAV KUSHNIR

Faculty of Philology: Prof. EVGENIY CHERNOI-VANENKO

Faculty of Philosophy: Assoc. Prof. ALEXANDR CHAYKOVSKY

Faculty of Physics: Prof. YURY VAKSMAN

Faculty of Romance and Germanic Philology: Assoc. Prof. LIDIYA GOLUBENKO

Illiychevsk Institute of ONU: Prof. GRIGORIY DRAGAN

Institute of Innovation and Postgraduate Education: Prof. L. DUNAEVA

Institute of Mathematics, Economics and Mechanics: Prof. VIKTOR KRUGLOV

Institute of Social Studies: Prof. VIKTOR GLEBOV

Pervomaysk Educational Centre of Science: Assoc. Prof. NATALIA MIKHAL'CHENKO

Preparatory Faculty: Assoc. Prof. NIKOLAY PASCHENKO

Preparatory Faculty for Foreign Citizens: Assoc. Prof. SERGEY FEDORKO

ODESSA STATE ECONOMIC UNIVERSITY

65082 Odessa, Preobrazhenska vul. 8

Telephone: (48) 723-61-58

Fax: (48) 232-04-46

E-mail: rector@oseu.edu.ua

Internet: www.oseu.edu.ua

Founded 1921

State control

Rector: M. I. ZVERYAKOV

Vice-Rector: GEORGE SHUBARTOVSKIY

Library of 423,000 vols

Number of teachers: 455

Number of students: 6,355

POLTAVA UNIVERSITY OF ECONOMICS AND TRADE

36014 Poltava, 3, Koval str.

Telephone: (532) 50-91-70

Fax: (532) 50-97-95

E-mail: rector@uccu.org.ua

Internet: www.pusku.edu.ua

Founded 1974, fmrly known as Poltava Univ. of Consumer Cooperatives in Ukraine, present name 2010

State control

Languages of instruction: Ukrainian, Russian, English

Academic year: September to June

Rector: Prof. OLEKSIY O. NESTULYA

Vice-Rector: Prof. MYKOLA G. ROGOZA

Vice-Rector for Research and Int. Relations: Prof. OLGA V. KARPENKO

Dir of Library: S. SADOVA

Library of 365,645 vols, 9,464 periodical titles

Number of teachers: 484

Number of students: 10,000

Publication: *PUET Scientific Bulletin*

DEANS

Dept of Economics and Management: P. VORONA

Dept of Finance and Accounting: N. PEDCHENKO

Dept of Food Technology, Hotel, Restaurant and Tourism Business: V. SHKARUPA

Dept of Merchandise and Commerce: N. TYAGUNOVA

Extramural Dept: U. STROCHIHIN

ATTACHED INSTITUTE

Institute of Continuing and Transition Education: courses in accounting and auditing, business, corporate economics, finance, marketing and international management.

PRECARPATHIAN NATIONAL UNIVERSITY 'VASYL STEFANYK'

76025 Ivano-Frankivsk, vul. Shevchenka 57

E-mail: inst@pu.if.ua

Internet: www.pu.if.ua

Founded 1940

Rector: Prof. Dr BOHDAN. K. OSTAFIYCHUK

First Pro-Rector: Prof. Dr BOHDAN. V. VASYLYSHYN.

'TARAS SHEVCHENKO' NATIONAL UNIVERSITY OF KYIV

01033 Kyiv, vul. Volodymyrska 64

Telephone: (44) 225-20-82

Fax: (44) 224-61-66

E-mail: stationery@univ.kiev.ua

Internet: www.univ.kiev.ua

Languages of instruction: Ukrainian, English

Founded 1834

State Control

Rector: Prof. Dr LEONID V. HUBERSKY

First Pro-Rector: Prof. Dr OLEG K. ZAKUSYLO

Pro-Rector for Int. Relations: Prof. Dr PETRO O. BEKH

Pro-Rector for Perspective Devt: Prof. Dr EUGENIY F. TOMIN

Pro-Rector for Research and Education: Prof. Dr OLEKSANDR A. NIKITUK

Pro-Rector for Science and Educational Work: Assoc. Prof. Dr VOLODYMYR P. BUGROV

Pro-Rector for Scientific Work: Prof. Dr VALERIY I. HRYHORUK

Librarian: VALENTYNA G. NESTERENKO

Library: see Libraries and Archives

Number of teachers: 2,175 ; 1,251 scientists

Number of students: 22,500

Publication: *Vestnik Kievskogo Universiteta*

DEANS

Faculty of Biology: Prof. Dr LYUDMYLA I. OSTAPCHENKO

Faculty of Chemistry: Prof. YULIAN M. VOLOVENKO

Faculty of Cybernetics: Prof. ANATOLIY V. ANISIMOV

Faculty of Economics: Prof. VIKTOR D. BAZYLEVICH

Faculty of Geography: Prof. YAROSLAV B. OLIYNYK

Faculty of Geology: Prof. SERHIY A. VYZHVA

Faculty of History: Prof. VIKTOR F. KOLESNYK

Faculty of Law: Prof. IVAN S. HRYTSENKO

Faculty of Mechanics and Mathematics: Prof. MYKHAILO F. HORODNIY

Faculty of Philosophy: Prof. ANATOLIY YE. KONVERSKYI

Faculty of Physics: Prof. MYKOLA V. MAKARETS

Faculty of Psychology: Prof. IRYNA P. MANOKHA

Faculty of Radiophysics: Prof. IHOR O. ANISIMOV

Faculty of Sociology: ANDRIY P. HORBACHYK

Preparatory Faculty: Prof. TETIANA V. TABENSKA

ATTACHED INSTITUTES

Astronomical Observatory: 01033 Kyiv, Observatorna St 3; tel. (44) 486-26-91; fax (44) 486-26-30; e-mail director@observ.univ .kiev.ua; internet www.observ.univ.kiev.ua/mainu.htm; Dir B. I. HNATYK.

Centre for Ukrainian Studies: 01033 Kyiv, Volodymyrska St 60, Rm 105; tel. (44) 239-31-84; e-mail uaznavstvo@mail.univ .kiev.ua; internet uaznavstvo.univ.kiev.ua; Dir Prof. MYKOLA I. OBUSHNYI.

Information and Computer Centre: 01033 Kyiv, Academician Glushkov Ave 2, Bldg 6; tel. and fax (44) 521-35-14; e-mail admin@univ.kiev.ua; internet www.icc.univ .kiev.ua; Dir Dr YURIY V. BOYKO.

Institute of International Relations: 01033 Kyiv, Melnykova St 36/1; tel. (44) 481-44-37; fax (44) 483-10-43; e-mail decanat_relat@univ.kiev.ua; internet www .iir.kiev.ua; Dir Prof. VALERIY V. KOPIYKA.

Institute of Journalism: 01033 Kyiv, Melnykova St 36/1; tel. (44) 481-44-01; fax (44) 483-09-81; e-mail inst@journ.univ.kiev.ua; internet www.journ.univ.kiev.ua; Dir Prof. VOLODYMYR V. RIZUN.

Institute of Management and Finance: 01033 Kyiv, Vasylkivska St 90A; tel. (44) 521-33-37; e-mail kiembi@econom.univ.kiev.ua; internet www.imf.kiev.ua; Dir DMYTRO M. CHERVANOV.

Institute of Philology: tel. (44) 239-33-02; fax (44) 239-31-13; e-mail philolog@univ.kiev .ua; internet www.philology.kiev.ua; Dir HRIHORIY F. SEMENIUK.

Institute of Postgraduate Education: 01033 Kyiv, Vasylkivska St 36; tel. (44) 521-35-60; fax (44) 257-71-32; e-mail ipe@ ipe.univ.kiev.ua; internet www.ipe.univ.kiev .ua; Dir Prof. VALERIY M. PERESEKIN.

Military Institute: 01033 Kyiv, Academician Glushkov Ave 2, Bldg 8; tel. and fax (44) 521-32-92; e-mail balabin@mil.univ.kiev.ua; internet www.mil.univ.kiev.ua; Dir Col VIKTOR V. BALABIN.

Scientific and Research Department: 01033 Kyiv, Lev Tolstoj St 14A, Rm 17; tel. (44) 289-85-80; fax (44) 239-32-40; internet science.univ.kiev.ua; Vice-Rector Prof. Dr VALERIY I. HRYHORUK.

Ukrainian Humanitarian Lyceum: 01033 Kyiv, Kozlovskyi Lane 3; tel. (44) 253-07-89; e-mail upgl@upgl.edu.ukrsat.com; internet www.uhl-edu.kiev.ua; Dir Prof. HALYNA S. SAZONENKO.

Ukrainian Physico–Mathematical Lyceum: 01033 Kyiv, Academician Glushkov Ave 6; tel. (44) 259-03-94; e-mail fizmat_dir@ukr.net; internet www.upml .univ.kiev.ua; Dir OLEH M. KHOMIAKOV.

TAURIDA NATIONAL 'V. I. VERNADSKY UNIVERSITY'

95007 Simferopol, pr. Vernadskoho 4

Telephone: (65) 251-64-98

Fax: (65) 251-71-35

E-mail: rector@tnu.crimea.ua

Internet: www.tnu.crimea.ua

Founded 1918, present name 1999

State control

Language of instruction: Russian

Academic year: September to July

Rector: NIKOLAY V. BAGROV

Vice-Rectors: ELENA N. CHUJAN, VIKTOR F. SHULGIN, ALEXANDER M. TIMOHIN

Registrar: NIKOLAY V. PRAVDIN

Librarian: VIKTORIA I. SPIROVA

Library: see Libraries and Archives

Number of teachers: 800

Number of students: 15,000

Publications: *Dynamic Systems* (1 a year), *Ecological Aspects of Nature Protection in the Crimea* (1 a year), *Ecological Study of the Mountainous Crimea* (1 a year), *Ecosystems of the Mountainous Crimea in Studies of Nature Protection* (1 a year), *Notes of Geologists, Pontida: Journal of The Association for the Support of Biological and Landscape Diversity* (1 a year),

Scientific Notes (1 a year), *The Black Sea Peoples' Culture* (1 a year)

DEANS

Faculty of Biology: SERGEY F. KOTOV
Faculty of Chemistry: VLADIMIR O. KURJANOV
Faculty of Crimean Tatar and Oriental Philology: AIDER M. MEMETOV
Faculty of Economics: SVETLANA V. KLIMCHUK
Faculty of Foreign Languages: ALEXANDER D. PETRENKO
Faculty of Geography: BORIS A. VAKHRUSHEV
Faculty of History: ALEXANDER G. GERTSEN
Faculty of Jurisprudence: LUDMILA D. DONSKAYA
Faculty of Management: VLADIMIR A. PODSOLONKO
Faculty of Mathematics: ALEXANDER I. RUDSKOY
Faculty of Philosophy: YURI A. KATUNIN
Faculty of Physical Training: VLADIMIR F. KROVYAKOV
Faculty of Physics: MARINA V. GLUMOVA
Faculty of Psychology: EVGENIY V. CHERNY
Faculty of Slavic Philology and Journalism: GALINA YU BOGDANOVICH
Faculty of Ukrainian Philology and Ukrainian Studies: YRIY F. PRADID

PROFESSORS

AKULOV, M. R., History of Ukraine
APATOVA, N. V., Information Systems in Economics
ARIFOV, L. YA, Theoretical Physics
BERESTOVSKAYA, D. S., History of World Culture
BERZHANSKY, V. N., Experimental Physics
BOKOV, V. A., Geography
BUROV, G. M., Ancient and Medieval History
CHEKHOV, V. N., Theoretical and Applied Mechanics
CHIRVA, V. YA, Organic and Analytical Chemistry
DEMENTIEV, N. E., History of Russia
DONSKOY, V. I., Informatics
EMIROVA, A. M., Russian Language
FEDORENKO, A. M., Chemistry
FILIMONOV, S. B., History of Ukraine
GABRIELYAN, O. A., Political Science and Sociology
GUBANOV, I. G., Geography
GUBAR, A. I., Ukrainian Language
KALIN, V. K., General Psychology, History of Psychology
KALNOY, I. I., Social Philosophy
KASHENKO, S. G., History of Russian Law
KAZARIN, V. P., Russian and General Literature
KIRICHENKO, A. A., Law
KOPACHEVSKY, N. D., Mathematical Analysis
KORENYUK, I. I., Human and Animal Physiology
KOZLOV, A. S., Greek Language
KRAMARENKO, V. I., Management
KRICHEK, P. M., Ukrainian Literature
KRYUCHKOV, I. V., Economics
KUDRYASHOV, A. P., Political Economy
KUZHEL, A. V., Theory of Functions and Functional Analysis
LAZAREV, F. V., Philosophy
LYSENKO, N. I., General Land Science
MANAKOV, M. K., Physiology of Plants
MARTYNYUK, YU. N., Philosophy
MEMETOV, A. A., Philosophy
MISHNEV, V. G., Botany
NAGORSKAYA, M. N., Management
NIKOLKO, V. N., Philosophy
NOVIKOVA, M. A., Russian and General Literature
OLIFEROV, A. N., Oceanology
OREKHOVA, L. A., Russian Literature
PERSIDSKY, S. K., Differential and Integral Equations
PETRENKO, A. D., German Language
PODSOLONKO, V. A., Economics
POMERANETS, V. N., Economics

POPOV, V. K., Law
REGUSHEVSKY, E. S., Linguistics
RUDYAKOV, A. N., Linguistics
SHARAPA, V. F., History
SHEVLYAKOV, YU. M., Applied Mathematics
SHULGIN, V. F., Chemistry
SIDYAKIN, V. G., Human and Animal Physiology
SOKOLOVSKAYA, ZH. P., Philology
STADNIK, I. P., Theoretical Physics
STASHKOV, A. M., Animal Biophysics
TEMURYANTS, N. A., Human and Animal Physiology
TEREZ, E. K., Astronomy and Teaching Methods of Physics
UNKOVSKAYA, T. E., Management
URSU, D. P., Modern and Contemporary History
VOLYAR, A. V., Physics
YENA, V. G., Geography
YEFIMENKO, A. M., Theoretical Foundations of Physical Culture
YURAKHNO, M. V., Zoology

TERNOPIL NATIONAL ECONOMIC UNIVERSITY

46020 Ternopil, vul. Lvivska 11
Telephone: (35) 247-50-51
Fax: (35) 247-61-33
E-mail: rector@tneu.edu.ua
Internet: www.tneu.edu.ua

Founded 1966
State control
Languages of instruction: English, German, Polish, Ukrainian
Academic year: September to July

Rector: Prof. Dr SERHIY I. YURIY
Vice-Rector for Educational Research and Int. Relations: Dr BOHDAN LUTSIV
Vice-Rector for Educational Research and Organizational Work: Prof. ANDRII KRYSOVATYI
Vice-Rector for Educational Research and Teaching: Dr MYKOLA SHYNKARYK
Vice-Rector for Educational Research and Territory, Distant Structural Subdivisons, Accreditation, Licensing: Prof. HRYHORII ZHURAVEL
Vice-Rector for Humanities and Extra-Curricular Activities: Dr BOHDAN ADAMYK
Vice-Rector for Research: Prof. ZENOVIY ZADOROZHNY
Vice-Rector for Social and Economic Devt: VASYL BULAVYNETS
Librarian: KAZYMYR VOZNIY

Library of 481,493 vols
Number of teachers: 986
Number of students: 18,184

Publications: *Computing, Economic Analysis, Journal of European Economy* (in English, Russian, Ukrainian), *Psycholohiya I Suspilstvo* (Psychology and Society), *Regional Aspects of The Development and Placement of Productive Forces in Ukraine, Svit Finaciv* (World of Finances), *TNEU Herald, Ukrainian Science: Past, Nowadays and Future* (collns of research papers), *Young Science*

DEANS

Faculty of Accounting and Audit: Prof. YAROSLAV D. KRUPKA
Faculty of Agrarian Economics and Management: Prof. ROMAN HEVKO
Faculty of the Banking Business: Dr VASYL TKACHUK
Faculty of Computer and Information Technologies: Prof. MYKOLA P. DYVAK
Faculty of Economics and Management: Prof. YEVHEN KACHAN
Faculty of Finances: Prof. IHOR HUTSAL
Faculty of International Business and Management: Prof. ANATOLIY M. TYBIN

Faculty of Law: Dr VOLODYMYR VOZNIY
Faculty of Pre-University, Postgraduate Education and Master Training: Prof. OLEH IVASHCHUK
Ukrainian-Dutch Faculty of Economics and Investment Management: Dr LYUDMILA GAVRILYUK-JENSEN
Ukrainian-German Economic Faculty: Dr YURIY HAIDA

UZHHOROD NATIONAL UNIVERSITY

88000 Uzhhorod, vul. Pidhirna 46
Telephone and fax (31) 223-33-41
E-mail: admin@univ.uzhgorod.ua
Internet: www.univ.uzhgorod.ua

Founded 1945
State control
Language of instruction: Ukrainian
Academic year: September to July

Rector: Prof. Dr MYKOLA M. VEHESH
Pro-Rector for Academic Affairs: OLEXANDR H. SLYVKA
Pro-Rector for Admin. and Economic Affairs: VOLODYMYR V. SHETELYA
Pro-Rector for Research: IHOR P. STUDENJAK
Pro-Rector for Social Devt and Capital Construction: YAROSLAV S. HUK
Registrar: ROSTISLAV V. ROMANYUK
Librarian: OLENA I. POCHEKUTOVA

Library: see under Libraries and Archives
Number of teachers: 600
Number of students: 8,000

Publication: *Bulletin* (series: Biology, Chemistry, Mathematics, Medicine, Philology, Physics, Romance and Germanic Philology, 1 a year)

DEANS

Faculty of Biology: Asst Prof. V. I. NIKOLAYCHUK
Faculty of Chemistry: Asst Prof. VASYL LENDYEL
Faculty of Economics: Prof. VASIL MIKLOVDA
Faculty of Engineering: Asst Prof. IVAN TURYANYTSYA
Faculty of History: Asst Prof. VOLODYMYR FENYCH
Faculty of International Relations: Prof. M. A. LENDYEL
Faculty of Law: Prof. VASIL YAREMA
Faculty of Mathematics: Asst Prof. MYKHAYLO PAHYRYA
Faculty of Medicine: Asst Prof. BOLDIZHAR BOLDIZHAR
Faculty of Philology: Asst Prof. IVAN SABADOSH
Faculty of Physical Education and Sport: Asst Prof. STEPAN LASUR
Faculty of Physics: Prof. Dr VOLODYMYR LASUR
Faculty of Postgraduate Studies: Prof. IVAN MIKHAYLOVYCH
Faculty of Romance and Germanic Philology: Asst Prof. STEPAN BOBYNETS

VADYM HETMAN KYIV NATIONAL ECONOMIC UNIVERSITY

03680 Kyiv, 54/1, pr. Peremogy
Telephone: (44) 371-61-12
Fax: (44) 226-25-73
E-mail: rector@kneu.kiev.ua
Internet: www.kneu.kiev.ua

Founded 1906
State control
Language of instruction: Ukrainian
Academic year: September to June

Rector: Prof. Dr ANATOLII PAVLENKO
Librarian: TETYANA KYRYLENKO

Library of 1,366,000 vols, 331 journals
Number of teachers: 1,512 (incl. full-time and part-time)
Number of students: 37,174

Publications: *International Economic Policy, Marketing in Ukraine*

DEANS

Faculty of Accounting: Prof. VASYL IEFIMENKO
Faculty of Crediting: Prof. Dr MYKHAILO DYBA
Faculty of Economics and Management: Prof. Dr ANATOLII NALYVAIKO
Faculty of Economy of Agroindustrial Complex: Prof. MYKHAILO KOTSUPATRYI
Faculty of Finance: Prof. VOLODYMYR KHLIVNYY
Faculty of Information Systems and Technologies: Prof. OLEKSANDR SHARAPOV
Faculty of International Economics and Management: Prof. Dr DMYTRO LUKYANENKO
Faculty of Law: Prof. Dr VITALII OPRYSHKO
Faculty of Personnel Management and Marketing: Prof. Dr OLEKSANDR SHAFALYUK

V. N. KARAZIN KHARKIV NATIONAL UNIVERSITY

61022 Kharkiv, pl. Svobody 4
Telephone: (57) 705-12-47
Fax: (57) 705-12-36
E-mail: postmaster@univer.kharkov.ua
Internet: www.univer.kharkov.ua
Founded 1804
Public control
Languages of instruction: Russian, Ukrainian
Academic year: September to June
Rector: Prof. V. S. BAKIROV
Vice-Rector: Asst Prof. A. M. UDOD
Vice-Rector: Prof. I. I. ZALYUBOVSKIY
Vice-Rector: Prof. M. O. AZARENKOV
Vice-Rector: V. M. RYSHKOV
Vice-Rector: Prof. V. V. ALEKSANDROV
Vice-Rector: Prof. YU. V. KHOLIN
Vice-Rector: Asst Prof. Z. F. NAZYROV
Librarian: I. K. ZHURAVLYOVA
Library: 3.5m. vols
Number of teachers: 1,500
Number of students: 16,500
Publication: *Visnyk*

DEANS

International Students Education Centre: (vacant)
School of Biology: Asst Prof. L. I. VOROBYOVA
School of Chemistry: Asst Prof. O. M. KALUGIN
School of Computer Science: Prof. V. T. LAZURYK
School of Ecology: Asst Prof. G. V. TITENKO
School of Economics: Asst Prof. O. I. DAVYDOV
School of Foreign Languages: Prof. V. G. PASYNOK
School of Further Education: Asst Prof. L. P. KRUPSKA
School of Geology and Geography: Prof. V. A. PERESADKO
School of History: Prof. S. I. POSOKHOV
School of International Economic Relations and Tourist Industry: Prof. V. I. SIDOROV
School of Law: Asst Prof. T. YE. KAGANOVSKA
School of Mathematics and Mechanical Engineering: Prof. G. M. ZHOLTKEVYCH
School of Medicine: Prof. V. M. SAVCHENKO
School of Philology: Prof. YU. M. BEZKHUTRIY
School of Philosophy: Prof. I. V. KARPENKO
School of Physics: Asst Prof. A. A. ZAVGORODNIY
School of Physics and Energy: Prof. K. E. NYEMCHENKO
School of Physics and Technology: Prof. I. O. GIRKA
School of Psychology: Prof. N. P. KREYDYN
School of Radiophysics: Prof. S. M. SHULGA
School of Sociology: Prof. V. M. NIKOLAYEVSKIY

VOLODYMYR DAHL EAST UKRAINIAN NATIONAL UNIVERSITY

91034 Luhansk, Kvartal Molodezhnyi 20A
Telephone: (64) 241-70-22
Fax: (64) 241-31-60
E-mail: uni@snu.edu.ua
Internet: www.snu.edu.ua
Founded 1920
Public control
Languages of instruction: English, Russian, Ukrainian
Academic year: September to June
Rector: Prof. Dr OLEKSANDR L. GOLUBENKO (acting)
First Vice-Rector: Prof. Dr MYKHAILO F. SMYRNY (acting)
Vice-Rector for International Affairs: Prof. Dr VALERIY DYADYCHEV (acting)
Library: 1m. vols
Number of teachers: 2,750
Number of students: 36,000
Publications: *Actual Issues of Law: Theory and Practice, Applied Ecology, Economics. Management. Enterpreneurship, Historical Notes: Collection of Scientific Papers, Information Security, Marketing: Theory and Practice, Materials and Investigation on Archeology of East of Ukraine, Philosophical Investigations, Political Science Notes, Project Management and Development of Production, Scientific Conducts of Dahl University* (online), *Scientific Media Notes, Scientific Works of Lugansk Branch of International Academy of Informatization, Spiritual Identity: Methodology, Theory and Practice, Theoretical and Practical Problems of Psychology, Visnyk of Volodymyr Dahl East Ukrainian National University on-Technic-Economics-History-Chemical-Physics and Mathematics*

DEANS

Economics Management Department: Prof. MARYNA A. MELNYK
Educational and Scientific Institute of Housing and Communal Services and Building: Prof. MYKOLA D. ANDIYCHUK
Faculty of Applied Mechanics and Material Science: Prof. VLADYMYR I. SOKOLOV
Faculty of Computer Sciences and Technologies: Prof. LARYSA O. GUBACHEVA
Faculty of Electrotechnical Systems: Prof. OLEKSANDR S. ZAKHARCHUK
Faculty of Financial Management: Asst Prof. OLEKSANDR M. ROZMYSLOV
Faculty of Foreign Citizens Training: Asst Prof. EVGEN I. KHARCHENKO
Faculty of Innovation Economics and Cybernetics: Prof. SULTAN K. RAMAZANOV
Faculty of Law: Prof. LIDIA I. LAZOR
Faculty of Management: Prof. VITALIY M. DANICH
Faculty of Mass Communications: Asst Prof. TETYANA A. MIRONOVA
Faculty of Mathematics And Informatics: Asst Prof. YURIY I. STATYVKO
Faculty of Nanoelectronics and Nanotechnologies: Prof. OLEKSANDR P. KRAVCHENKO
Faculty of Natural Sciences: Prof. SERGIY D. KRYVONOSOV
Faculty of Philology: Asst Prof. OLGA E. KRSEK
Faculty of Philosophy: Prof. VIKTORIA K. SUKHANTSEVA
Faculty of Rail Communications Systems: Prof. VALENTYN I. MOGYLA
Faculty of Transport Systems and Logistics: Prof. GRYGORIY I. NECHAEV

ZAPORIZHZHYA NATIONAL UNIVERSITY

69063 Zaporizhia, vul. Zhukovskoho 66
Telephone: (61) 264-45-46

Fax: (61) 262-71-61
E-mail: rektor@zsu.zp.ua
Internet: www.zsu.edu.ua
Founded 1985
State control
Languages of instruction: Russian, Ukrainian
Academic year: September to July
Rector: Prof. V. A. TOLOK
Pro-Rector for Admin.: I. G. YAKUSHEV
Pro-Rector for Curriculum: V. V. HIRZHON
Pro-Rector for Research and Int. Cooperation: V. Z. HRYSTCHAK
Pro-Rector for Social Devt: V. G. TKACHENKO
Registrar: S. A. EVSTAFENKO
Librarian: V. A. HERASYMOVA
Number of teachers: 541
Number of students: 8,200
Publications: *Antiquities of the Steppe, Black Sea Region and Crimea, Bulletin, Cultural Bulletin* (scientific-theoretical annual of the Lower Dnieper region), *New Paradigm, New Philology, Notes of the Scientific Research Laboratory of the Southern Ukraine, Problems of Bioindication, Renaissance Studies, Zaporizhzhya Legacy* (history of the Southern Ukraine in the 18th century)

DEANS

Faculty of Biology: Dr V. I. DOMNICH
Faculty of Economics: Prof. V. V. KIRICHEVSKIY
Faculty of Foreign Philology: Prof. V. I. SKIBINA
Faculty of History: Prof. F. G. TURCHENKO
Faculty of Law: Dr T. A. DENISOVA
Faculty of Management: Dr I. G. SHAVKUN
Faculty of Mathematics: Prof. N. G. TAMUROV
Faculty of Philology: Prof. O. D. TURGAN
Faculty of Physical Training: Dr V. N. ZAYTSEVA
Faculty of Physics: Dr A. Y. OSIPOV
Faculty of Postgraduate Education: Dr L. D. KRIVEGA
Faculty of Social Pedagogics: Prof. L. I. MISCHIK
Faculty of Sociology and Administration: Prof. V. P. BEKH

PROFESSORS

BAYKINA, N. G., Sports
BEKH, V. P., Politics and Theory of Administration
BESSONOVA, V. P., Biology
BOVT, V. D., Biology
BYLOUSENKO, P. I., Ukrainian Language
CHABANENKO, V. A., General Linguistics
FROLOV, A. K., Human Physiology
GRISTCHAK, V. Z., Applied Mathematics
IVANENKO, V. K., Methods of Teaching Philological Disciplines
KARAGODIN, A. I., History
KIRICHEVSKIY, V. V., Applied Mathematics
LYAKH, S. R., History of Ukraine
MISCHIK, L. I., Pedagogics and Psychology
MOROZOV, L. V., Finance and Credit
NAUMENKO, A. M., German Philology
NOVIKOV, Y. F., Theory and Practice of Management
PAKHOMOVA, T. A., Methods of Teaching Philological Disciplines
PROZOROVA, N. S., History and Theory of State and Law
PRYKHODKO, N. I., Problems of Administration and Social Pedagogics
PRYVARNIKOV, A. K., Algebra and Geometry
PSARYOV, V. I., Physics
SERGEYEV, A. V., Physics
TAMUROV, N. G., Applied Mathematics
TOLOK, V. A., Applied Mathematics
TURCHENKO, F. G., History of the Ukraine
TURGAN, O. D., Theory of Literature and Journalism
TYKHOMIROV, V. N., Foreign Literature

TYMCHENKO, S. M., History of the Ukraine
YESHENKO, V. A., Physiology and Civil
Defence
ZATSNIY, Y. A., Theory and Practice of Translation

MEDICAL UNIVERSITIES

BUKOVINIAN STATE MEDICAL UNIVERSITY

58000 Chernivtsi, Teatralna pl. 2
Telephone: (372) 55-37-54
Fax: (372) 55-37-54
E-mail: bma@bsmu.edu.ua
Internet: www.bsmu.edu.ua

Founded 1944 as Chernivtsi State Medical
Institute; as Bukovinian State Medical
Acad. 1997; present name and Univ. status
2005
State control
Academic year: September to June
Rector: VASIL P. PISHAK
First Vice-Rector: MIHAILO Y. KOLOMOETS
Vice-Rector for Int. Relations: YURIY M.
NECHYTAYLO
Library of 350,000 vols
Number of teachers: 435
Number of students: 3,100
Publications: *Bukovinian Medical Herald* (4
a year), *Clinical Anatomy and Operative
Surgery* (4 a year), *Clinical and Experimental Pathology* (4 a year)

DEANS

VOLODYMYR HLUBOCHENKO
OLEKSANDR POLISCHUK
VIKTOR POLYOVIY
TAMILA SOROKMAN

CRIMEAN STATE MEDICAL UNIVERSITY 'S. I. GEORGIEVSKY'

95006 Simferopol, bul. Lenina 5/7
Telephone: (65) 227-44-62
Fax: (65) 227-20-92
E-mail: office@crsmu.com
Internet: www.crsmu.com
Founded 1931
Rector: Prof. A. A. BABANIN
Library of 634,371 vols
Number of teachers: 629
Number of students: 4,556
Publications: *Bulletin of Physiotherapy and
Balneology* (4 a year), *Problems, Achievements and Perspectives of the Development
of Biomedical Sciences and Practical Public Health of Ukraine* (colln of scientific
works, 4 a year), *Tavrian Biomedical Bulletin* (4 a year), *Tavrian Journal of Psychiatry* (4 a year)

DEANS

First Medical Faculty: Prof. A. I. KRADINOV
Second Medical Faculty: Prof. S. N. KRUTIKOV
Faculty of Stomatology: Prof. L. I. AVDONINA
International Faculty: Prof. M. N. GRISHIN
Postgraduate Faculty: Prof. N. P. BUGLAK

I. HORBACHEVSKY TERNOPIL STATE MEDICAL UNIVERSITY

46001 Ternopil, Maydan Voli 1
Telephone: (35) 252-44-92
Fax: (35) 252-41-83
E-mail: university@tdmu.edu.te.ua
Internet: www.tdmu.edu.te.ua
Founded 1957
Public control
Languages of instruction: English, Russian,
Ukrainian
Academic year: September to July
Rector: Prof. LEONID Y. KOVALCHUK

Library of 500,000 vols
Number of teachers: 560
Number of students: 4,000
Publications: *Achievements of Clinical and
Experimental Medicine* (2 a year), *Hospital
Surgery* (4 a year), *Infectious Diseases* (4 a
year), *Medical Chemistry* (4 a year), *Medical Education* (4 a year), *Scientific
Research Newsletter* (4 a year)

DEANS

Faculty of Dentistry: Prof. YAROSLAV NAGIRNY
Faculty of Foreign Students: Prof. MYKHAYLO
KORDA
Faculty of Medicine: Prof. ARKADIY SHULGAY
Faculty of Pharmacy: Prof. LIUDMYLA SOKOLOVA
Faculty of Postgraduate Education: Prof.
MARYAN GREBENYK

KHARKIV NATIONAL MEDICAL UNIVERSITY

61022 Kharkiv, 4 Lenin Ave
Telephone: (57) 705-07-11
Fax: (57) 700-41-32
E-mail: meduniver@knmu.kharkov.ua
Internet: www.knmu.kharkov.ua
Founded 1805, present name and status 2007
State control
Languages of instruction: English, Russian,
Ukrainian
Academic year: September to June
Rector: Prof. VLADIMIR LESOVOY
First Vice-Rector for Research and Education: Prof. VALERY KAPUSTNYK
Vice-Rector for Research: Prof. VALERIY MYASOEDOV
Vice-Rector for Research and Education:
Prof. IVAN LETIK
Vice-Rector for Research and Education:
Prof. VLADIMIR MARKOVSKYI
Vice-Rector for Medical Research and Education: Assoc. Prof. YURI REZUNENKO
Librarian: IRINA KIRICHOK
Library of 1,016,000 vols, 237 periodicals
Number of teachers: 822
Number of students: 5,763
Publications: *Clinical Genetics, Experimental
Clinical Medicine* (4 a year), *Medicine
Today and Tomorrow* (2 a year), *Ultrasonic
Perinatal Diagnosis* (2 a year)

DEANS

Dentistry Stomatological Faculty: Asst Prof.
VIKTOR NIKONOV
Forensic Medicine Medical Faculty II: Prof.
VASYL OLKHOVSKIY
Human Anatomy Medical Faculty I: Prof.
ANATOLIY TERESCHENKO
Infectious Diseases Medical Faculty VI for
Training Foreign Students: DMYTRO KATSAPOV
Microbiology Medical Faculty IV: Prof.
VALERIY MINUKHIN
Ophthalmology Medical Faculty III: Prof.
MYKOLA PANCHENKO
Pediatric Surgery Academic and Research
Institute for Postgraduate Education: Asst
Prof. VALERIY VYUN
Physiology Medical Faculty V for Training
Foreign Students: Asst Prof. DMYTRO MARAKUSHYN

LUHANSK STATE MEDICAL UNIVERSITY

91045 Luhansk, Kvartal 50-richchya Oborony Luhanska 1
Telephone: (64) 254-84-03
Fax: (64) 253-20-36
E-mail: kanc@lsmu.edu.ua
Internet: www.lsmu.edu.ua
Founded 1956, present name and status 1994

Faculties of dentistry, health care, nursing,
paediatrics and pharmacy
Rector: Prof. VALERIY K. IVCHENKO
Library of 420,000 vols
Number of teachers: 394
Number of students: 2,815

LVIV NATIONAL MEDICAL UNIVERSITY 'DANYLO HALYTSKIY'

79010 Lviv, Pekarska Str. 69
Telephone: (32) 272-26-60
Fax: (32) 276-79-73
E-mail: zimenkovsky@meduniv.lviv.ua
Internet: www.meduniv.lviv.ua
Founded 1784
Rector: Prof. Dr BORYS ZIMENKOVSKY
Library of 520,000 vols
Number of teachers: 1,200
Number of students: 4,977

DEANS

External Faculty: ROMAN EU. DARMOGRAIY
Faculty of Dentistry: ROSTYSLAV M. STUPNYTSKYI
Faculty of Nursing: VIRA I. PIROGOVA
Faculty of Pharmacy: ROMAN B. LESYK
Faculty of Postgraduate Education: OREST
YE. SICHKORIZ
Faculty of Stomatology: IVAN M. HOT
First Medical Faculty: BOGDAN V. DYBAS
Second Medical Faculty: YURI YA. KRYVKO
International Faculty: EUGENE VARYVODA

NATIONAL O. BOHOMOLETS MEDICAL UNIVERSITY

01601 Kyiv, bul. T. Shevchenka 13
Telephone: (44) 234-40-62
Fax: (44) 234-92-76
E-mail: interdeptnmu@gmail.com
Internet: www.nmu.edu.ua
Founded 1841
Public control
Languages of instruction: English, Russian,
Ukrainian
Academic year: September to June
Rector: Prof. Dr VITALIY MOSKALENKO
Vice-Rector for Int. Affairs, Research and
Education: Prof. Dr OLESYA HULCHIY
Library of 750,000 vols
Number of teachers: 1,200
Number of students: 10,000
Publications: *East European Journal Of
Public Health, Health Care in Ukraine,
Scientific Journal of National O. Bohomolets Medical University*

DEANS

Faculty for Int. Students: Prof. ALEXANDER
SAVYCHUK
Medical Faculty I (General Medicine): Prof.
VICTOR CHERKASOV
Medical Faculty II (General Medicine): Prof.
VASYL NETYAZHENKO
Medical Faculty III (Paediatrics): Prof. VASYL
PETRENKO
Medical Faculty IV (Preventive Care): Prof.
SERHIY OMELCHUK
School for Continuing Education for Trainers: Prof. YURIY MARUSHKO
School of Dentistry: Prof. VALERIY
NESPRYADKO
School of Medical Engineering: Prof. VALENTYN YATSENKO
School of Medical Psychology: Prof. SERHIY
MAKSYMENKO
School of Military Medicine: Col OLEG VLASENKO
School of Pharmacy: Prof. IRYNA NIZHENKIVSKA

NATIONAL UNIVERSITY OF PHARMACY

61002 Kharkiv, str. Pushkinskaya 53

Telephone: (57) 706-35-81
Fax: (57) 706-15-03
E-mail: mail@ukrfa.kharkov.ua
Internet: www.pharm.kharkiv.edu

Founded 1805
Public control
Languages of instruction: English, Russian, Ukrainian
Academic year: September to June (10 semesters)

Rector: Prof. Dr VALENTIN P. CHERNYKH
Vice-Rector For Scientific, Educational Work and Int. Affairs: Prof. Dr SERGEY B. POPOV
Librarian: NATALIYA B. LISOVOL
Library: 1m. vols
Number of teachers: 830
Number of students: 17,500 (incl. 1,200 int. students)
Publications: *Clinical Pharmacy* (4 a year), *Fisiologichno-Aktivni Rechovini* (Physiologically Active Substances, 2 a year), *Klinichna Farmatsiya* (Clinical Pharmacy, 4 a year), *Organic and Pharmaceutical Chemistry* (4 a year), *Visnik Farmatsii* (Pharmacy Bulletin, 4 a year), *Zdorovya Cheloveky* (Health to Mankind, 4 a year)

DEANS

Faculty of Correspondence and Distance Learning: Assoc. Prof. SVETLANA G. KALAYCHEVA
Faculty of Economics and Management: Assoc. Prof. VOLODYMYR V. MALY
Faculty of Foreign Students' Training: Assoc. Prof. VLADIMIR D. GORYACHIY
Faculty of Industrial Pharmacy: Assoc. Prof. TATYANA KRUTSKIKH
Faculty of Medical Pharmacy: Assoc. Prof. OLGA I. NABOKA
Faculty of Pharmacy: Assoc. Prof. LILIYA I. VISHNEVSKAYA
Preparatory Faculty for Foreign Citizens: ZOYA I. KOVALENKO

NATIONAL UNIVERSITY OF PHYSICAL EDUCATION AND SPORTS OF UKRAINE

03680 Kyiv, vul. Fizkultury 1

Telephone: (44) 227-54-52
Fax: (44) 287-61-91
E-mail: rectorat@uni-sport.edu.ua
Internet: www.uni-sport.edu.ua

Founded 1930

Faculties of Olympic and professional sport, physical rehabilitation and sports medicine, physical education, recreation and health-related physical culture; faculty of external studies

Rector: Prof. Dr VOLODYMYR M. PLATONOV
First Pro-Rector for Education: Prof. Dr YURIY M. SHKREBTIY
Pro-Rector for Research: Dr TETYANA YU. KRUTSEVICH.

VINNITSA NATIONAL MEDICAL UNIVERSITY 'M. I. PYROHOV'

21018 Vinnytsya, pr. Lenina 9

Telephone: (432) 32-06-85
Fax: (432) 32-16-13
E-mail: admission@vsmu.vinnica.ua
Internet: www.vnmu.vn.ua

Founded 1921

Rector: Prof. Dr VASYL M. MOROZ

Library of 500,000 vols
Number of teachers: 554
Number of students: 3,600

PEDAGOGICAL UNIVERSITIES

KHARKIV NATIONAL PEDAGOGICAL UNIVERSITY 'H. S. SKOVORODA'

61168 Kharkiv, vul. Blyukhera 2

Telephone: (57) 700-69-09
E-mail: rector@pu.ac.kharkov.ua
Internet: pu.ac.kharkov.ua

Founded 1804

Rector: Prof. Dr IVAN F. PROKOPENKO

Library of 714,689 vols

DEANS

Faculty of Art and Design: Prof. Dr NADEZDA V. SHYLOVTSEVA
Faculty of Economics: Prof. Dr HANNA M. GUZENKO
Faculty of Elementary Education: Prof. Dr NATALIYA M. YAKUSHKO
Faculty of Foreign Languages: Dr NATALIYA V. TUCHYNA
Faculty of History: Assoc. Prof. SVETLANA V. BEREZNAYA
Faculty of Law: Prof. Dr VIKTOR O. PROTSEVSKYY
Faculty of Music Education: Assoc. Prof. TETYANA A. SMIRNOVA
Faculty of Natural Sciences: Prof. Dr IGOR IONOV
Faculty of Physical Education: Prof. Dr MYKOLA I. GORODYSKYY
Faculty of Physics and Mathematics: Prof. Dr OLEKSANDR I. GONCHAROV
Faculty of Pre-School Education: Prof. Dr TETYANA P. TANKO
Faculty of Psychology and Sociology: Prof. Dr OKSANA G. VOLKOVA
Faculty of Russian Language and World Literature: Prof. Dr TAMARA P. STAKANKOVA
Faculty of Ukrainian Language and Literature: Prof. Dr IRYNA V. TYMCHENKO
External Faculty: Assoc. Prof. VIKTORIYA M. TYKHONOVICH

DIRECTORS

Institute of Post-Diploma Education: Prof. Dr MYKOLA V. GADETSKYY
Institute of World Languages: Prof. Dr TAMARA P. STAKANKOVA

NATIONAL PEDAGOGICAL DRAGOMANOV UNIVERSITY

01601 Kyiv, vul. Pyrohova 9

Telephone and fax (44) 234-11-08
E-mail: shef-npu@ukr.net
Internet: www.npu.kiev.ua

Founded 1834 as Gorky Kiev Pedagogical Institute, present name and status 1997
State control
Languages of instruction: English, Russian, Ukrainian
Academic year: September to May

Rector: Acad. Prof. Dr VIKTOR ANDRUSHCHENKO
First Vice-Rector: Dr VOLODYMYR BEKH
Vice-Rector: Prof. Dr ANATOLYI AVDIEVSKIY
First Vice-Rector for Economics and Educational Work: Dr OLEG PADALKA
Vice-Rector for Distance Learning and Innovational Technologies of Learning: Prof. ANATOLYI P. KUDIN
Vice-Rector for Educational and Methodological Work of Humanitarian Institutes: Prof. BOGDAN ANDRUSYSHYN
Vice-Rector for Int. Relations: Dr VOLODYMYR LAVRYNENKO
Vice-Rector for Methodological Work: Prof. ROMAN VERNYDUB
Vice-Rector for Research Work: Prof. HRIHORIY VOLYNKA
Dir of Library: LYUDMYLA SAVENKOVA

Library of 1,233,252 vols, 863,673 books, 150,351 periodicals, 7,149 foreign edns, 125 magnetic tapes and discs, 2,563 theses and dissertations defended within the Univ.
Number of teachers: 1,500
Number of students: 30,000

DEANS

Institute of Foreign Philology: Prof. VOLODYMYR GONCHAROV
Institute of Philosophical Education and Science: Prof. IVAN DROBOT
Institute of Physical Education and Sport: Prof. OLEKSIY TYMOSHENKO
Institute of Physics and Mathematics: Prof. MYKOLA PRATSYOVYTYI
Institute of Sociology, Psychology and Management: Prof. VOLODYMYR YEVTUKH

TECHNICAL UNIVERSITIES

DNIPRODZERZHYNSK STATE TECHNICAL UNIVERSITY

51948 Dnipropetrovska oblast, Dniprodzerzhynsk, vul. Dniprobudivska

Telephone: (56) 955-13-89
Fax: (56) 955-13-07
E-mail: science@dstu.dp.ua
Internet: www.dstu.dp.ua

Founded 1920, present name and status 1994

Rector: Prof. IHOR O. PAVLYUCHENKOV
First Pro-Rector: Dr VITALIY M. HULYAYEV

DEANS

Faculty of Chemical Technology: Dr OLEH I. POLYANCHYKOV
Faculty of Economics and Management: Dr SERHIY H. DRONOV
Faculty of Electronics and Computer Technology: Prof. OLEKSANDR M. SYANOV
Faculty of Mechanical Engineering: Dr VOLODYMYR SOLOD
Faculty of Metallurgy: Dr OLEKSANDR V. HRESS
Faculty of Post-Diploma Education: Prof. I. V. HUBARYEV
Faculty of Power Engineering: Prof. ANATOLIY M. PAVLENKO
Faculty of Sociology and Philology: Prof. MYKOLA S. KONOKH
External Faculty: Prof. YEVHEN B. LEYKO

DNIPROPETROVSK NATIONAL TECHNICAL UNIVERSITY OF RAILWAY TRANSPORT 'V. LAZARYAN'

49700 Dnipropetrovsk-10, vul. Lazaryana 2

Telephone: (56) 776-59-47
Fax: (56) 247-18-66
E-mail: dnuzt@diit.edu.ua
Internet: www.diit.edu.ua

Founded 1930

Specialist faculties incl. bridges and tunnels, economics and management in transport, industrial and civil engineering, management of transport processes in railway transport, mechanics, organization of railway construction and track maintenance, technical cybernetics and military training

Rector: Prof. Dr ALEXANDER N. PSHINKO
First Pro-Rector for Education: Prof. Dr BORIS E. BODNAR
Pro-Rector for Research: Dr SERHEY MYAMLYN

Library of 800,000 vols
Number of students: 4,200

DONBASS STATE TECHNICAL UNIVERSITY

94204 Alchevsk, pr. Lenina 16

Telephone: (64) 422-31-23

Fax: (64) 422-68-87
E-mail: info@dmmi.edu.ua
Internet: www.dmmi.edu.ua
Public control
Languages of instruction: English, Russian, Ukrainian
Academic year: September to July
Rector: Prof. Dr NIKOLAY NTOSCHENKO
First Vice-Rector for Academic Affairs: Dr VASILIY N. OKALELOV
Vice-Rector for Research: Dr NIKOLAY N. ZABLODSKIY

Library of 700,000 vols
Number of teachers: 470
Number of students: 14,000

Publication: *Impulse* (52 a year)

DEANS

Civil Engineering Dept: Dr VLADIMIR BONDARCHUK
Mechanical Engineering Dept: Dr ANDREY ZINCHENKO
Metallurgy Dept: Prof. Dr ALEXANDER NOVOKHATSKIY
Mining Engineering Dept: Dr ALEXANDER MELEZHYK

DONETSK NATIONAL TECHNICAL UNIVERSITY

83000 Donetsk, Artema 58
Telephone: (62) 337-17-33
Fax: (62) 304-12-78
E-mail: info@dgtu.donetsk.ua
Internet: www.donntu.edu.ua
Founded 1921
Rector: Prof. Dr ALEKSANDR A. MINAEV
First Pro-Rector: Prof. Dr ALEKSANDR A. TROYANSKIY
Pro-Rector for Academic Affairs: Dr ALEKSANDR V. LEVSHOV
Pro-Rector for Admin.: HEORHIY A. ROMANKO
Pro-Rector for Internal Communications and Economic Affairs: ILYA P. NAVKA
Pro-Rector for Research: Prof. Dr EVGENIY A. BASHKOV
Librarian: ANNA A. PETROVA

Library: 1.5m. vols
Number of teachers: 1,500
Number of students: 23,000

Publications: *Development of Mining Minerals* (2 a year), *Problems of Ecology* (1 a year)

Campuses in Gorlovka and Krasnoarmeysk

DEANS

Faculty of Computing Technology and Information Science: Dr ALEKSANDR ANOPRIENKO
Faculty of Ecology and Chemical Technology: Dr ALEKSANDR S. PARFENYUK
Faculty of Economics and Management: Prof. VYACHESLAV V. DEMENTYEV
Faculty of Electrotechnical Engineering: Prof. NILOLAY GREBCHENKO
Faculty of Geotechnology and Management in Manufacturing: Prof. YURI F. BULGAKOV
Faculty of Information Technologies and Automation: Dr ALEKSANDR V. KHORKHORDIN
Faculty of Mechanical Engineering: Dr SERGEY A. SELIVRA
Faculty of Mining and Geology: Prof. OLEG I. KALINICHENKO
Faculty of Physics and Metallurgy: Prof. SERGEY SAFYANTS
Faculty of Power Mechanics and Automation: Dr SERGEY A. SELIVRA
Faculty of Radiotechnology: Prof. PAVEL V. STEFANENKO
English-Language Technical Faculty: Dr SERGEY A. KOVALEV
French-Language Faculty of Engineering: Prof. GENNADIY S. KLYAGIN

German-Language Technical Faculty: Dr VIKTOR I. KALASHNIKOV
Polish-Language Technical Faculty: Dr ALEKSANDR YU. MAKEYEV
Foreign Students: Dr SERGEY F. SUKOV

IVANO-FRANKIVSK NATIONAL TECHNICAL UNIVERSITY OF OIL AND GAS

76019 Ivano-Frankivsk, vul. Karpatska 15
Telephone: (34) 224-22-64
Fax: (34) 224-21-39
E-mail: admin@nung.edu.ua
Internet: www.ifdtung.if.ua
Founded 1967
Faculties of automation and electrification, economics and management, engineering ecology, gas and oil industry, gas and oil pipelines, geological prospecting, mechanical, mechanics and technology
Rector: Y. I. KRYZHANIVSKY

Library of 790,000 vols
Number of teachers: 413
Number of students: 4,453

KHARKIV NATIONAL AUTOMOBILE AND HIGHWAYS UNIVERSITY

61002 Kharkiv, vul. Petrovskoho 25
Telephone: (57) 700-38-65
Fax: (57) 700-38-66
E-mail: admin@khadi.kharkov.ua
Internet: www.khadi.kharkov.ua
Founded 1930
State control
Languages of instruction: Russian, Ukranian
Academic year: September to June
Rector: Prof. Dr ANATOLIY N. TURENKO
First Pro-Rector: Prof. Dr IVAN P. GLADKIY
Vice-Rector for Research and Pedagogy: Prof. SERGIY Y. KHODYREV
Vice-Rector for Research and Pedagogy and Int. Contacts: Prof. GEORGIY I. TOKHTAR
Vice-Rector for Scientific Research: Prof. Dr VIKTOR A. BOGOMOLOV
Vice-Rector for Social, Economic and Admin. Affairs: VICTOR V. BEZRODNY

Library of 450,000 vols
Number of teachers: 573
Number of students: 10,956 full-time, 7,042 external

DEANS

Automobile Faculty: NIKOLAY ALEKSA
Faculty for Foreign Citizens: VLADIMIR BONDARENKO
Faculty of Business and Management: ILYA DMITRIEV
Faculty of Mechatronics: ANDREY LEVTEROV
Faculty of Transport Systems: YURI BEKETOV
Mechanical Faculty: IGOR KIRICHENKO
Road-Construction Faculty: VLADIMIR PSYURNIK

KHARKIV NATIONAL UNIVERSITY OF RADIOELECTRONICS

61166 Kharkiv, pr. Lenina 14
Telephone: (57) 702-18-07
Fax: (57) 702-10-13
E-mail: info@kture.kharkov.ua
Internet: www.kture.kharkov.ua
Founded 1930
Rector: Prof. Dr MYKHAYLO F. BONDARENKO

Library of 750,000 vols
Number of students: 8,500

DEANS

Faculty of Applied Mathematics and Management: LEONID I. SHKLYAROV
Faculty of Computer Engineering and Management: GENNADIY F. KRIVULYA

Faculty of Computer Sciences: VLADIMIR P. MASHTALIR
Faculty of Electronic Devices: VLADIMIR A. STOROZHENKO
Faculty of Electronic Technology: YURI N. ALEKSANDROV
Faculty of Radiotechnology: SERGEY N. SAKALO
Faculty of Telecommunications and Electronics: IGOR N. PRESNYAKOV
Foreign Students' Preparatory Faculty: VLADIMIR P. NEMCHENKO
Postgraduate Faculty: ZOYA V. DUDAR

DIRECTORS OF INSTITUTES

Institute of Computing and Information Technologies: VIKTOR M. LEVYKIN
Institute of Radioengineering and Electronics: VLADIMIR M. SHOKALO
Institute of Telecommunications: VIKTOR M. LEVYKIN

KHARKIV STATE TECHNICAL UNIVERSITY OF CIVIL ENGINEERING AND ARCHITECTURE

61002 Kharkiv, Sumska vul. 40
Telephone: (57) 700-10-66
Fax: (57) 700-02-50
E-mail: office@kstuca.kharkov.ua
Internet: www.kstuca.kharkov.ua
Founded 1930
Rector: Prof. Dr YURIY SHKODOVSKIY

Library of 683,000 vols
Number of teachers: 590
Number of students: 6,500

DEANS

Faculty of Architecture: Prof. OLEKSANDR VASILENKO
Faculty of Construction: Dr YEVGEN YAKOVLEV
Faculty of Economics and Management: Dr OLEKSANDR SYROVATSKIY
Faculty of External Education: Dr OLEKSANDR F. PUGACHOV
Faculty of Mechanical-Technical Engineering: Dr YURIY ZHURAVLEV
Faculty of Postgraduate Education: Dr GENNADIY SUKHORUKOV
Faculty of Pre-University Preparation: Dr IGOR EMETS
Faculty of Sanitary Engineering: Dr VIKTOR SHYLIN

KHERSON NATIONAL TECHNICAL UNIVERSITY

73008 Kherson, Beryslavske shose 24
Telephone and fax (55) 255-40-11
E-mail: kstu@tlc.kherson.ua
Internet: www.kstu.edu.ua
Founded 1957
Rector: FRANTS B. ROHALSKIY

Library of 400,000 vols

Publication: *Proceedings* (2 a year)

DEANS

Faculty of Cybernetics: Prof. NADIYA A. SOKOLOVA
Faculty of Distance Education: Prof. N. A. PUSTOVAYA
Faculty of Economics: Prof. VOLODYMYR E. TURSH
Faculty of International Economics: Prof. V. V. KRYUCHOVSKIY
Faculty of Machine Building: Prof. HRIHORIY DYNEVICH
Faculty of Technology and Design: Prof. N. I. VALKO
Preparatory Faculty: Prof. N. S. MYKOLAYCHUK

KIROVOHRAD NATIONAL TECHNICAL UNIVERSITY

25006 Kirovohrad, Universitetska 8
Telephone: (52) 255-93-59
Fax: (52) 255-92-53
E-mail: relintern@kdtu.kr.ua
Internet: www.kdtu.kr.ua

Founded 1929

Rector: Prof. Dr MYKHAILO I. CHERNOVOL
Pro-Rector for Education: Prof. MYKOLA M. PETRENKO
Pro-Rector for Science and Research: Dr VOLODYMYR M. KROPIVNIY

Library of 406,000 vols
Number of teachers: 400
Number of students: 7,000

DEANS

Faculty of Agricultural Mechanics: Prof. VASYL M. SALO
Faculty of Automation, Power Engineering and Programming: Prof. LARISA H. VIKHROVA
Faculty of Economics: Prof. HRIHORIY M. DAVIDOV
Faculty of Machine Design and Development: Dr VOLODYMYR V. YATSUN
Faculty of Mechanics and Technology: Prof. BORIS YE. NADVORNIY
Preparatory and Specialists' Retraining Faculty: Prof. YEVGEN K. SOLOVYKH
Preparatory Faculty for Foreign Specialists: Prof. OLEKSANDR Y. MAZHEYKA

KYIV NATIONAL UNIVERSITY OF CONSTRUCTION AND ARCHITECTURE

03037 Kyiv, Vozdukhoflotskii pr. 31
Telephone: (44) 248-49-05
Fax: (44) 248-49-01
E-mail: knuba@knuba.edu.ua
Internet: www.knuba.edu.ua

Founded 1930
Academic year: September to July

Rector: A. M. TUGAY

Library of 1,213,000 vols
Number of teachers: 850
Number of students: 6,800

'KYIV POLYTECHNIC INSTITUTE' NATIONAL TECHNICAL UNIVERSITY OF UKRAINE

03056 Kyiv, pr. Peremohy 37
Telephone and fax (44) 236-69-13
E-mail: zgur@zgurov.kiev.ua
Internet: www.ntu-kpi.kiev.ua

Founded 1898
Languages of instruction: Ukrainian, Russian, English
Academic year: September to June

19 Educational depts, 10 educational research institutes, 13 research institutes and 17 other scientific subdivisions (incl. design bureaux, engineering centres)

Rector: Acad. MYKHAYLO Z. ZGUROVSKIY

Library: 3m. vols
Number of students: 40,000

Publications: Kyivsky Politekhnik (newspaper, 48 a year), Vesti (2 a year)

DEANS

Faculty of Aircraft and Space Systems: Prof. OLEKSANDR V. ZBRUTSKIY
Faculty of Applied Mathematics: Prof. OLEKSANDR A. MOLCHANOV
Faculty of Biotechnology and Bioengineering: Prof. OLEKSIY M. DUGAN
Faculty of Chemical Engineering: Prof. YEVGEN M. PANOV

Faculty of Chemical Technology: Prof. IHOR M. ASTRELIN
Faculty of Electric Power Engineering and Automation: Prof. OLEKSANDR S. YANDULSKIY
Faculty of Electronics: Prof. VALERIY YA. ZHUYKOV
Faculty of Heat Power Engineering: Prof. YEVGEN M. PISMENNIY
Faculty of Informatics and Computer Science: Prof. OLEKSANDR A. PAVLOV
Faculty of Instrument Design and Engineering: Prof. HRIHORIY S. TYMCHYK
Faculty of Law and Sociology: Prof. ANATOLIY P. TUZOV
Faculty of Linguistics: Prof. NATALYA S. SAYENKO
Faculty of Management and Marketing: Prof. VASYL H. HERASIMCHUK
Faculty of Physics and Engineering: Prof. PETRO I. LOBODA
Faculty of Physics and Mathematics: Acad. Prof. VIKTOR H. BARYAKHTER
Faculty of Radio Engineering: Prof. OLEKSANDR I. RYBIN
Faculty of Welding: Prof. SERHIY K. FOMICHOV
Intercollegiate Faculty of Medical Engineering: Prof. V. P. YATSENKO

'LVIV POLYTECHNIC' NATIONAL UNIVERSITY

79013 Lviv, vul. St Bandery 12
Telephone: (32) 272-47-33
E-mail: rudavsky@polynet.lviv.ua
Internet: www.lp.edu.ua

Founded 1844

Rector: Prof. Dr YURIY K. RUDAVSKIY
First Pro-Rector: Prof. Dr PETRO P. KOSTROBIY
Pro-Rector for Education and Foreign Affairs: Prof. Dr YURIY M. RASHKEVYCH
Pro-Rector for Research: Prof. Dr YURIY YA. BOBALO

Library: 3m. vols
Number of teachers: 2,000
Number of students: 17,000

Publication: Journal (1 a year, 15 series)

DIRECTORS

Institute of Applied Mathematics and Fundamental Sciences: Prof. PETRO I. KALENYUK
Institute of Architecture: Prof. BOGDAN S. CHERKES
Institute of Chemistry and Chemical Technologies: Prof. YOSYP Y. YATCHYSHYN
Institute of Civil and Environmental Engineering: Prof. MYROSLAV A. SANYTSKY
Institute of Computer Sciences and Information Technologies: Prof. VOLODYMYR V. HRYTSYK
Institute of Computer Technologies, Automation and Metrology: Prof. BOHDAN I. STADNYK
Institute of Distance Education: Prof. BORYS M. ROMANYSHYN
Institute of Economics and Management: Prof. OLEH Y. KUZMIN
Institute of Engineering Mechanics and Transport: Prof. ZINOVIY A. STOTSKO
Institute of Geodesy: Prof. PETRO M. ZAZULYAK
Institute of Liberal Arts: Prof. LEONTIY E. DESCHYNSKIY
Institute of Power Engineering and Control Systems: Prof. PETRO M. ZAZULYAK
Institute of Telecommunications, Radioelectronics and Electronic Engineering: Prof. BOHDAN A. MANDZIY

NATIONAL AEROSPACE UNIVERSITY KHARKIV AVIATION INSTITUTE

61070 Kharkiv, Chkalova vul. 17
Telephone: (57) 315-10-56
Fax: (57) 315-11-31
E-mail: khai@khai.edu
Internet: www.khai.edu

Founded 1930
State control
Languages of instruction: English, Russian
Academic year: September to June

Rector: Prof. VLADIMIR S. KRIVTSOV

Library: 1m. vols
Number of teachers: 850
Number of students: 9,500

DEANS

Faculty of Aircraft Control Systems: ANATOLIY S. KULIK
Faculty of Aircraft Design: VITALIY N. KOBRIN
Faculty of Aircraft Radio-Electronic Systems: VIKTOR I. ILYUSHKO
Faculty of Aviation Engine-Building and Power Systems: ANATOLIY I. DOLMATOV
Faculty of Distance Education: YAKOV V. SAFRONOV
Faculty of Economics and Management: IGOR V. CHUMACHENKO
Faculty of Humanities: VOLODYMYR A. KOPILOV
Faculty of International Education: SERGIY I. PLANKOVSKIY
Faculty of Pre-University Training and Professional Skills Improvement: VLADYSLAV F. DEMENKO
Faculty of Rocket Engineering: OLEKSIY G. NIKOLAEV

NATIONAL AVIATION UNIVERSITY

03680 Kyiv, pr. Kosmonavta Komarova 1
Telephone: (44) 406-72-08
Fax: (44) 497-33-85
E-mail: interdep@nau.edu.ua
Internet: www.nau.edu.ua

Founded 1933
State control
Languages of instruction: English, Russian, Ukrainian
Academic year: September to June

Rector: Prof. Dr MYKOLA KULYK
First Vice-Rector: Prof. Dr MAKSYM LUTSKVI
Vice-Rector for Admin.-Economic Work: MYKOLA MYKHALKO
Vice-Rector for Corporate Management: Prof. Dr RYNAT SALIMOV
Vice-Rector for Correspondence Courses and Distance Studies: PAVLO BORSUK
Vice-Rector for Educational Issues: Prof. Dr ANATOLIY POLUKHIN
Vice-Rector for Educational-Methodological Cooperation: Prof. Dr SERGIV IVANOV
Vice-Rector for Scientific-Research Work: Prof. Dr VOLODYMYR KHARCHENKO

Library: 3m. vols

Publications: Aviator, Biplan, Bulletin of Engineering Academy of Ukraine, Business and Management, Development Strategy of Ukraine: Sociology, Economics, Law, Science and Youth, Information Security Scientific and Technical Magazine, Economics, Electronics and Control Systems, Higher Institution Establishments, Humanities Education in Engineering, Information Bulletin of Ministries of Industrial Policy of Ukraine in Standardation, Juridical Bulletin: Air and Space Law, Metrology and quality management, National Aviation University Bulletin, Problems of Improving Effectiveness and Infrastructure, Problems of Informatization and Management, Problems of Systems Approach in Economics, Scientific

Bulletin of International Relation Institute, Security of Information

DEANS

Computer Science Faculty: NICKOLAI SIDOROV
Dept of Military Preparation: OLEKSANDER VODCHYTS
Faculty of Computer Systems: OLEKSANDR LITVINENKO
Foreign Students Faculty: ANDREY KRYZHANOVSKYI

NATIONAL MINING UNIVERSITY OF UKRAINE

49027 Dnipropetrovsk, pr. K. Marksa 19

Telephone: (56) 247-07-66
Fax: (56) 247-07-66
E-mail: dfr@nmuu.dp.ua
Internet: www.nmuu.dp.ua

Founded 1899

Faculties of construction electrical engineering, construction of mines, economics, engineering, geotechnology, law, mining and prospecting

Rector: Prof. GENNADIY PIVNYAK

Library: 1.3m. vols
Number of teachers: 708
Number of students: 10,897

Publications: *University Monthly, University Newspaper* (52 a year).

NATIONAL SHIPBUILDING UNIVERSITY 'ADMIRAL MAKAROV'

54025 Kyiv, Mikolaiv, pr. Heroiv Stalinhrada

Telephone: (51) 235-91-48
Fax: (51) 242-46-52
E-mail: vc@usmtu.edu.ua
Internet: www.usmtu.edu.ua

Founded 1929

Rector: Prof. Dr HEORHIY F. ROMANOVSKIY
First Pro-Rector: Prof. Dr OLEKSANDR M. DUBOVIY
Pro-Rector for Research: Prof. Dr VYACHESLAV F. KVASNITSKIY

DEANS

Faculty of Engineering Economics: Prof. OLEKSANDR YU. YEGANOV
Preparatory Faculty: Prof. V. I. KONDRATENKO

NATIONAL TECHNICAL UNIVERSITY 'KHARKIV POLYTECHNIC INSTITUTE'

61002 Kharkiv, Frunze Str. 21

Telephone: (57) 706-32-16
Fax: (57) 707-66-01
E-mail: omsroot@kpi.kharkov.ua
Internet: www.kpi.kharkov.ua

Founded 1885

Rector: LEONID L. TOVAZHNYANSKY
Pro-Rector for Education and Int. Relations: VALERIY O. KRAVETS
Pro-Rector for Research: ANDRIY P. MARCHENKO

Number of teachers: 1,700
Number of students: 26,000

DEANS

Centre of Distance and Pre-University Training: Dr MYKOLA M. SIRENKO
Centre of Extramural Courses: Prof. EDUARD I. ZAIKA
Faculty of Automation and Instrument Making: Prof. ANATOLIY I. HAPON
Faculty of Business Administration: Prof. VIKTOR YA. ZARUBA
Faculty of Business and Finance: Prof. OLEKSANDR M. HAVRIS

Faculty of Chemical Engineering: Dr OLEKSIY M. PASSOKHA
Faculty of Computing and Information Technologies: Prof. MYKOLA I. ZAPOLOVSKYI
Faculty of Economics: Prof. PETRO H. PERERVA
Faculty of Electrical Engineering: Prof. VOLODYMYR V. VOINOV
Faculty of Electric Power: Prof. OLEKSANDR P. LASURENKO
Faculty of Engineering: Dr MIKHAILO S. STEPANOV
Faculty of Engineering Physics: Dr DMITRO V. BRESKLAVSKIY
Faculty of Information Science and Management: Prof. IHOR P. GAMAJUN
Faculty of Inorganic Substances Technology: Prof. SERGIY A. LESHCHENKO
Faculty of Integrated Training: Prof. ANDRIY V. KIPENSKIY
Faculty of Mechanics and Technology: Dr MYKOLA POHRIBNIY
Faculty of Organic Substances Technology: Prof. OLEKSANDR P. NEKRASOV
Faculty of Physics and Technology: Prof. SERHIY M. KOSMACHOV
Faculty of Power Engineering: Prof. MYKOLA O. TARASENKO
Faculty of Transport Engineering: Dr VITALIY V. YEPIFANOV
German Technical Faculty: Dr VIRA M. SHAMARDINA

NATIONAL TRANSPORT UNIVERSITY

01010 Kyiv, vul. Suvorova 1

Telephone: (44) 280-82-03
Fax: (44) 290-82-03
E-mail: general@ntu.edu.ua
Internet: www.ntu.edu.ua

Founded 1944

Rector: Prof. Dr MYKOLA F. DMYTRYCHENKO
First Pro-Rector: Prof. Dr MYKOLA O. BILYAKOVYCH
Pro-Rector for Research: Prof. Dr MYKOLA M. DYMYTRIEV

Library of 440,000 vols
Number of teachers: 909
Number of students: 15,000

DEANS

Faculty of Economics, Management and Law: LYUDMILA KOZAK
Faculty of Motor Mechanics: YURIY HUTAREVICH
Faculty of Road Building: VYACHESLAV SAVENKO
Faculty of Transport and Information Technologies: Prof. VICTOR DANCHUK

NATIONAL UNIVERSITY OF FOOD TECHNOLOGIES

01601 Kyiv, Volodymyrska vul. 68

Telephone: (44) 220-95-55
Fax: (44) 220-01-02
E-mail: indepart@nuft.edu.ua
Internet: www.nuft.edu.ua

Founded 1930 as Kyiv Institute of Sugar Refinery Production, present name and status 2002
State control
Languages of instruction: Ukrainian, Russian
Academic year: September to June

Rector: Prof. SERGII IVANOV

Library of 1,163,050 vols, 120 periodicals
Number of teachers: 742
Number of students: 13,019

Publications: *Food Industry* (4 a year), *Latest Achievements in the Food Industry and Scientific Research, Research Papers of the National University of Food Technologies* (4 a year), *Scientific Works*

DEANS

Faculty of Accounting, Finance and Business: OLEG SHEREMET
Faculty of Automation and Computer Systems: LIUDMILA MANOHA
Faculty of Biotechnology and Food Products Examination: ANDRIY CHAGAIDA
Faculty of Economics and Management: TATIANA MOSTENSKA
Faculty of Fermentation and Baking Industry: PETRO SHIYAN
Faculty of Hotel-Restaurant Business and Tourism: GALINA SEMAKHINA
Faculty of Mechanical Engineering and Packing Technologies: SERGIY BLAZHENKO
Faculty of Power Engineering: MYKHAILO MASLIKOV
Faculty of Sugar, Meat and Dairy Products: OKSANA KOCHUBEY-LITVINENKO
Preparatory Dept: VALENTINA KUDINA

NATIONAL UNIVERSITY OF WATER MANAGEMENT AND NATURE RESOURCES USE

33028 Rivne, vul. Soborna 11

Telephone: (36) 222-10-86
Fax: (36) 222-21-97
Internet: www.nuwm.rv.ua

Founded 1922
State control

Rector: VASYL A. HURYN
Vice-Rector of Admin. and Social Affairs: VOLODYMYR M. YAKYMCHUK (acting)
Vice-Rector of Research: MYKOLA HIROL
Vice-Rector of Science and Academic Affairs: OLEKSANDR TKACHUK (acting)
Vice-Rector of Science and Int. Relations: HRYHORIY SAPSAY
Vice-Rector of Science and Teaching Methods: ANATOLIY BILESTSKIY

Library of 900,000 vols
Number of teachers: 715
Number of students: 14,000

Publications: *Bulletin* (4 a year), *Hydroamelioration and Hydrotechnical Engineering* (1 a year), *Resource Saving Materials, Construction, Buildings and Structures* (4 a year)

DEANS

Faculty of Applied Mathematics and Computer-Integrated Systems: ANATOLIY P. VLASIUK
Faculty of Building and Architecture: HRYHORIY H. MASIUK
Faculty of Ecology and Natural Resource Application: MYKOLA O. KLYMENKO
Faculty of Economy and Business: SVITLANA O. LEVYTSKA
Faculty of Hydrotechnical Engineering and Hydroenergetics: ANATOLIY M. MAKOVSKIY
Faculty of Land Management and Geoinformation: PETRO H. CHERNIAGA
Faculty of Management: VITALIY P. OKORSKIY
Faculty of Mechanical and Power Engineering: MYKOLA M. MARCHUK
Faculty of Water Management: VASYL TURCHENIUK

ODESSA NATIONAL POLYTECHNIC UNIVERSITY

65044 Odessa, pr. Shevchenko 1

Telephone: (48) 222-34-74
E-mail: ospu@ospu.odessa.ua
Internet: www.ospu.odessa.ua

Founded 1918

Faculties of automation and computer technology, automation and electrification of industry, chemical technology, engineering economics, mechanical technology, nuclear power, radio engineering, robot systems, thermal power

Rector: Prof. Dr VALERIY P. MALAKHOV
Pro-Rector for Studies and Education: Prof.
Dr YURIY S. YAMOLSKY
Pro-Rector for Studies and Research: Prof.
Dr VALERIY P. MALAKHOV
Library of 1,500,000 vols
Number of teachers: 4,000
Number of students: 20,000

ODESSA STATE ENVIRONMENTAL UNIVERSITY

65016 Odessa, vul. Lvivska 15
Telephone: (48) 263-62-09
Fax: (48) 242-77-67
E-mail: synop@ogmi.farlep.odessa.ua
Internet: www.odeku.edu.ua
Founded 1932
Academic year: September to June
Rector: Prof. SERHIY M. STEPANENKO
Vice-Rector: Dr MYKOLA H. SERBOV
Chief of Int. Dept: V. M. SYTOV
Dean of Continuing Education and Training:
L. M. POLETAEVA
Library of 273,000 vols
Number of teachers: 245
Number of students: 3,790
Publication: *Meteorology, Climatology and
Hydrology* (4 a year)

DEANS
Faculty of Computer Science and Manage-
ment: V. V. AUROV
Faculty of Environmental Studies: O. H.
VOLODYMYROVA
Faculty of Hydrology, Hydrometeorological
Institute: M. P. EKHNICH (Dir)
Faculty of Metrology: G. P. IVUS

PROFESSORS
Faculty of Computer Science and Manage-
ment:
KORBAN, V. KH.
KRUGLYAK, Y. M.
PREPELIZHA, G. P.
Faculty of Environmental Studies:
GERASIMOV, O. I.
LOEVA, I. D.
MINICHEVA, G. G.
SAFRANOV, T. A.
SOKOLOV, Y. M.
ZHYKALO, A. N.
Hydrometeorological Institute:
EFIMOV, V. A.
GOPCHENKO, E. D.
LOBODA, N. S.
MICHAYLOV, V. I.
MISCHENKO, Z. A.
POLEVOY, A. M.
SHKOLNY, E. P.
STEPANENKO, S. N.
TUCHKOVENKO, Y. S.

POLTAVA NATIONAL TECHNICAL UNIVERSITY 'YU. KONDRATYUKA'

36601 Poltava, Pershotravnevyy pr. 24
Telephone: (53) 222-28-50
Fax: (53) 227-38-02
E-mail: v57@pntu.edu.ua
Internet: www.pntu.edu.ua
Founded 1930, present name and status 2002
State control
Rector: Prof. Dr VOLODYMYR O. ONYSHCHENKO
First Vice-Rector: Dr BOGDAN O. KOROBKO
Vice-Rector for Academic Work: Dr BOGDAN
KOROBKO
Vice-Rector for Science and Innovations:
Prof. Dr hab. VICTOR PASHYNSKY
Vice-Rector for Corporative Management:
ANATOLIY MARTYNENKO

Vice-Rector for Social and Int. Affairs: YURI
BEREZA
Chief Librarian: VELENTINA SIDORENKO
Library of 500,000 vols, 116 periodicals
Number of teachers: 540
Number of students: 10,000

DEANS
External Faculty: Dr I. O. IVANYTSKA
Faculty of Architecture: Prof. Dr hab. VASYL
SHULYK
Faculty of Civil Engineering: Dr LEONID
SHCHERBININ
Faculty of Electro-Mechanical Engineering:
Dr MYKOLA SHPYLKA
Faculty of Finance and Economics: Dr RAYISA
V. SHYNKARENKO
Faculty of Information, Telecommunication
Technologies and Systems: Dr OLEG ODAR-
USHCHENKO
Faculty of Management and Business: Dr
VOLODYMYR PENTS
Faculty of Sanitary Engineering: Dr STANI-
SLAV POPOV
Postgraduate Study Centre: GENNADIY
GOLOVKO

SEVASTOPOL NATIONAL TECHNICAL UNIVERSITY

99053 Sevastopol, Streletsky Bay, Studgor-
odok, vul. Mazepy 10
Telephone: (69) 223-50-08
Founded 1963
Rector: M. Z. LAVRINENKO
Library of 1,200,000 vols, spec. collns on
machine-building and environmental
monitoring
Number of teachers: 550
Number of students: 7,000

UKRAINIAN STATE UNIVERSITY OF CHEMICAL TECHNOLOGY

49005 Dnipropetrovsk, Gagarin Ave. 8
Telephone: (56) 247-08-13
Fax: (56) 247-33-16
E-mail: ughtu@dicht.dp.ua
Internet: www.udhtu.com.ua
Founded 1930
Public control
Academic year: July to September
Languages of instruction: Russian, Ukrai-
nian
Rector: Prof. Dr MYKHAYLO V. BURMISTR
First Vice-Rector: Prof. Dr MYKOLA NIKO-
LENKO
Vice-Rector of Science: Prof. Dr OLEG GIRIN
Vice-Rector of Science and Education: Prof.
Dr VIKTOR GOLEUS
Library of 800,000 vols
Number of teachers: 484
Number of students: 7,813
Publications: *Chemistry and Chemical Tech-
nology Questions* (4 a year), *Scientific-
Technological Digest* (4 a year), *Voprosy
himii i himicheskoi tehnologii* (6 a year)

DEANS
Advanced Technologies: ANGELA VACULICH
Faculty of Economics: NATALIA CHUPRINA
Faculty of High-Molecular Compounds Tech-
nology: SVETLANA VOLKOVA
Faculty of Inorganic Technology: OLEXANDER
PIVOVAROV
Faculty of Mechanical: ILLYA NACHOVNYY
Faculty of Organic Technology: NATALYA
EVDOKIMENKO
Faculty of Silicate Technology: OLGA RYZ-
HOVA

VINNYTSIA NATIONAL TECHNICAL UNIVERSITY

21036 Vinnytsia, Khmelnitske shose 95
Telephone: (43) 232-57-18
Fax: (43) 246-57-72
E-mail: vstu@vstu.vinnica.ua
Internet: www.vstu.edu.ua
Founded 1960
Rector: Prof. BORIS I. MOKIN
First Pro-Rector for Research, Int. Relations
and Economic and Political Affairs: VOLO-
DYMYR V. HRABKO
Library of 820,000 vols
Number of teachers: 542
Number of students: 7,492
Publications: *Proceedings* (6 a year), *Univer-
sity News* (12 a year)

DIRECTORS
Institute of Civil Engineering and Gas Sup-
ply: HEORHIY S. RATUSHNYAK
Institute of Electronics and Computer Sys-
tems' Management: ANATOLIY S. VASYURA
Institute of Information Technologies and
Computer Engineering: OLEKSIY D. AZAROV
Institute of Machine Building and Transport:
YURIY A. BURYENNIKOV
Institute of Management: MYKOLA I. NEBAVA
Institute of Power Engineering, Ecology and
Electrical Mechanics: MYKOLA P. SVRYDOV
Institute of Radio engineering, Telecommu-
nications and Electronic Instrument
Engineering: VASYL M. KYCHAK

ZAPORIZHZHYA NATIONAL TECHNICAL UNIVERSITY

69063 Zaporizhzhya, vul. Zhukovskoho 64
Telephone: (61) 764-25-06
Fax: (61) 764-21-41
E-mail: rector@zntu.edu.ua
Internet: www.zntu.edu.ua
Founded 1900
State control
Languages of instruction: Russian, Ukrai-
nian
Academic year: September to June
Rector: Prof. SERHIY B. BYELIKOV
First Pro-Rector for Education: Dr VOLODY-
MYR G. PRUSHKIVSKY
Pro-Rector for Education: Dr SERHIY T.
YARYMBASH
Librarian: RAISA I. KUCHERUK
Library: 1m. vols
Number of teachers: 770
Number of students: 13,000
Publications: *Electrotechnics and Electroe-
nergetics* (2 a year), *New Materials and
Technology in Metallurgy and Machine
Construction* (2 a year), *Radio Electronics,
Radio Electronics, Computer Science and
Control* (2 a year), *Journal* (12 a year)

DIRECTORS
Institute of Continuous Training: Dr SERGIY
T. YARYMBASH
Institute of Economics and Humanities: Prof.
PETRO V. GUDZ
Institute of Information Science and Radio-
electronics: Prof. DMYTRO M. PIZA
Institute of Machine Building: Acad. Prof.
LEONID Y. IVSCHENKO
Institute of Management and Law: VALEN-
TYNA M. ZAYTSEVA
Institute of Physics and Technology: Acad.
Prof. VALENTYN V. LUNOV

Academies

**Dnipropetrovsk State Medical Acad-
emy:** 49044 Dnipropetrovsk, vul. Dzerzhins-

koho 9; tel. (56) 245-15-65; fax (56) 370-96-38; e-mail dsma@dsma.dp.ua; internet www .dsma.dp.ua; f. 1916; main specialities: clinical pharmacology, dentistry, general practice, paediatrics, sanitary hygiene; library: 656,600 vols; 598 teachers; 4,045 students; Rector Dr GEORGY V. DZYAK; publs *Dermatology, Cosmetics and Sexual Pathology* (4 a year), *Medical Perspectives* (4 a year), *Urology* (4 a year).

Donbass State Academy of Civil Engineering and Architecture: 86123 Donetsk obl., Makeyevka vul. Derzhavina 2; tel. (62) 290-29-38; fax (62) 222-06-16; e-mail mailbox@dgasa.dn.ua; internet www.dgasa .dn.ua; f. 1972; faculties: architecture, basic and general engineering training, civil engineering, economics, environmental engineering, mechanical engineering, marketing and management; extra-mural preparatory dept for foreign students, humanities; library: 400,000 vols; 399 teachers; 5,769 students; Rector YEVHEN V. HOROKHOV; publs *Academy News* (12 a year), *Bulletin* (6 a year), *Metal Construction* (4 a year).

Donbass State Engineering Academy: 84313 Kramatorsk, vul. Shkadinova 72; tel. (62) 641-67-94; fax (62) 641-63-15; e-mail postmaster@dgma.edu.donetsk.ua; faculties: automation, automation of metal-shaping processes, economics, engineering and economics, humanities, machine-building.

Ivano-Frankivsk State Medical Academy: 76000 Ivano-Frankivsk, Halytska 2; tel. and fax (34) 222-42-95; e-mail ma@ifdma .if.ua; internet www.ifdma.if.ua; f. 1945; library: 319,000 vols; 389 teachers; 4,994 students; Rector Dr YE. NEIKO.

Kharkiv State Academy of Railway Transport: 61003 Kharkiv, pl. Feierbakha 7; tel. (57) 732-20-67; fax (57) 220-60-19; e-mail info@kart.kharkov.com; internet www .kart.edu.ua; f. 1930; faculties: automation, construction, economics, mechanics, telemechanics and communication, traffic management; brs in Donetsk, Kyiv; library: 700,000 vols; Rector NIKOLAY I. DANKO.

Kharkiv State Academy of Zooveterinary Science: 62341 Kharkiv obl., Dergachevskiy raion, P/O Malaya Danilovka; tel. (57) 635-74-65; fax (57) 635-70-76; e-mail zoovet@zoovet.kharkov.ua; f. 1851; library: 250,000 vols; 190 teachers; 2,500 students; Rector VALERY GOLOVKO.

Kharkiv State Municipal Academy: 61002 Kharkiv, vul. Revolyutsii 12; tel. (57) 243-21-62; fax (57) 247-65-00; e-mail root@ ksma.kharkov.ua; f. 1930; faculties: accounting and auditing, architecture, economics of civil engineering enterprises, economics of municipal economy enterprises, electric and underground transport, engineering ecology, landscape architecture, management in hotel business and tourism, management of public services and municipal finances, retraining, technical maintenance of buildings, urban electric power supply and lighting, urban planning and development; Electromechanical College, Municipal Economy College; library: 890,000 vols; 1,000 teachers; 12,000 students; Rector Prof. L. N. SHUTENKO.

Lviv Academy of Veterinary Medicine: 79301 Lviv, vul. Pekarska 50; tel. (32) 275-67-84; fax (32) 279-32-31; e-mail vetacademy@hotmail.com; internet www .vetacad.lviv.ua; f. 1784; faculties: biology and technology, economics and management, extra-mural studies, food technology, veterinary medicine; 292 teachers; 4,500 students; library: 333,000 vols; Rector Prof. Dr R. J. KRAVTSIV.

Lviv Commercial Academy: 79005 Lviv, vul. Tuhan-Baranovskoho 10; tel. (32) 275-65-50; e-mail academy@lac.lviv.ua; internet

www.lac.lviv.ua; f. 1899; faculties: commodity science, commerce, economics, international economic relations, law, management; 300 teachers; 5,740 students; library: 600,000 vols; Rector YA. A. HONCHARUK.

National Metallurgical Academy of Ukraine: 49600 Dnipropetrovsk, pr. Gagarina 4; tel. (56) 245-31-56; fax (56) 247-44-61; e-mail dmeti@dmeti.dp.ua; internet dmeti.dp .ua; f. 1899; faculties: computing systems and automation, ecology and chemical technologies, economic cybernetics, economics, electrometallurgy, energy and electromechanics, humanities, management, materials sciences and metal forming, mechanics and machine building, metallurgy; library: 524,327 vols; 732 teachers; 12,199 students; Rector OLEKSANDR H. VELYCHKO; publ. *Theory and Practice of Metallurgy* (4 a year).

Odessa National Academy of Food Technologies: 65039 Odessa, vul. Kanatna 112; tel. (482) 29-11-40; fax (482) 25-32-84; e-mail fedosov@optima.com.ua; internet www.osaft .odessa.ua; f. 1902; State control; academic year September to June; faculties: automation of technological processes; economics, management and business; food preserving technology and winemaking; grain and grain products technology; meat and dairy products technology and ecology; mechanical engineering; technology of bread, confectionery and nutrition; 566 teachers (incl. 53 full professors); 10,400 students; library: 600,000 vols; Rector Prof. BOGDAN YEGOROV; publs *Collection of Scientific Works* (2 a year), *Grain Products and Mixed Fodders* (4 a year).

Odessa National Maritime Academy: 65029 Odessa, Didrikhson 8; tel. (48) 777-57-74; fax (48) 234-52-67; e-mail info@ma .odessa.ua; internet www.ma.odessa.ua; f. 1944; faculties: automation, electrical engineering, marine engineering, maritime law, navigation, radio electronics; brs in Mariupol, Izmail, correspondence depts and the maritime college of the technical fleet; library: 578,000 vols; 401 teachers; 7,134 students; Rector Prof. MYKHAYLO V. MIYUSOV; publs *Automization of Ship's Technical Devices* (2 a year), *Marine Transportation and Transport Complexes* (1 a year), *Navigation* (2 a year), *Sea Review* (4 a year), *Ship's Power Plants* (2 a year).

Odessa State Academy of Civil Engineering and Architecture: 65029 Odessa, Didrikhson 4; tel. (482) 20-41-82; fax (482) 23-35-10; e-mail rektorat@gs.org.ua; internet www.ogasa.odessa.ua; f. 1930; faculties: architecture, construction engineering, power engineering, industrial and civil construction, technical engineering, sanitary engineering; library: 600,000 vols; Rector Prof. VITALIY S. DOROFEEV.

Odessa State Academy of Refrigeration: 65026 Odessa, vul. Dvoryanska 1/3; tel. (48) 223-22-20; fax (48) 223-89-31; e-mail admin@ osar.odessa.ua; internet www.osar.odessa .ua; f. 1922; faculties: automation and robot engineering, cryogenic engineering, environmental protection and rational use of natural resources, heat technology, mechanical engineering, refrigeration engineering, systems of automatized projection, thermophysics; library: 487,173 vols; 288 teachers; 3,500 students; Rector V. V. PRITULA; publ. *Refrigeration Engineering and Technology* (2 a year).

Poltava State Agrarian Academy: 314003 Poltava, vul. Skovorody 1/3; tel. (5322) 2-26-10; fax (5322) 2-29-57; e-mail antonov@ agroak.poltava.ua; internet agroak.poltava .ua; f. 1920; depts: accounting and auditing, agronomy, economy of enterprises, farm

mechanization, finance, management of organizations, veterinary medicine, zoological engineering; library: 315,000 vols; 247 teachers; 7,000 students; Rector Dr V. N. PISARENKO; publ. *Poltava Agrarian News* (4 a year).

Prydniprovska State Academy of Civil Engineering and Architecture: 49600 Dnipropetrovsk, Chernyshevskeho 24A; tel. and fax (562) 47-16-88; e-mail dik@pgasa.dp .ua; internet www.pgasa.dp.ua; f. 1930; faculties: architecture, building technology, civil engineering, construction, correspondence, economics, mechanics; library: 662,000 vols; 467 teachers; 6,392 students; Rector Prof. V. I. BOLSHAKOV.

State Academy of Food Technology and Management: 61051 Kharkiv, Klochkivska 333; tel. (57) 236-89-79; fax (57) 237-85-35; e-mail hdatoh@kharkov.com; internet www .hdatoh.kharkov.com; f. 1967; faculties: accountancy and auditing, economics, food industry machines and equipment, food science and food trade, food technology, industrial management, marketing, services management; 350 teachers; 5,000 students; library: 380,000 vols; Rector A. I. CHEREVKO; publ. *Zbirnyk naukovykh prats* (1 a year).

Ukrainian Engineering Pedagogics Academy: 61003 Kharkiv, Department of Foreign Relations, vul. Universytetska 16; tel. (572) 731-28-62; fax (572) 731-32-36; e-mail docents@vl.kharkov.ua; f. 1958; faculties: electrical and technological, electromechanics and computer systems, machine-building, mechanical and technological, mining engineering, power engineering, radio-electronics, social-economical; training centres for foreign citizens and engineering educators; library: 1m. vols; 350 teachers; 11,000 students; Rector ELENA KOVALENKO.

Yaroslav Mudry National Law Academy of Ukraine: 61024 Kharkiv, Pushkinskaya ul. 77; tel. (57) 704-11-20; fax (57) 704-11-71; e-mail uracad@bestnet.kharkov.ua; internet www.uracad.kharkiv.edu; f. 1804; library: 1m. vols, 1,000 dissertations, 29,000 rare books and MSS; 600 teachers; 15,000 students; Rector VASYL YA. TATSIY.

Zaporizhzhya State Engineering Academy: 69006 Zaporizhia, pr. Lenina 226; tel. (612) 15-90-34; fax (612) 12-38-87; e-mail admin@zgia.zp.ua; internet www.zgia.zp.ua; f. 1959; faculties: building and water resources, economics of enterprises, electronics and electronic technologies, information technologies, management and finance, mechanics and technology, metallurgy, postgraduate studies, power engineering and energy-saving; library: 501,777 vols; 350 teachers; 10,000 students; Rector Dr V. I. POZHUEV.

Institutes of Higher Education

Donetsk Musical-Pedagogical Institute: 340086 Donetsk, vul. Artema 44; tel. (622) 93-81-22; depts: choral conducting, composition, folk instruments, musicology, orchestral instruments, piano, singing.

Institute of National Economy: 03057 Kyiv, pr. Pobedy 54/1; tel. (44) 446-50-55; fax (44) 226-25-73; f. 1912; depts: accounting and audit, agricultural management, economics and management, engineering economics, finance, international relations, marketing; br. in Krivoi Rog; 600 teachers; 11,000 students; library: 800,000 vols; Rector ANATOLY PAVLENKO.

Kamyanets-Podilsk Institute of Agriculture: 32300 Khmelnytska r-n, Kamyanets-Podilsk, vul. Shevchenko 13; tel. (3849) 2-52-18; fax (3849) 3-92-20; f. 1920; depts: agronomy, animal husbandry, economics, mechanization of agriculture, veterinary medicine; library: 600,000 vols; Rector M. I. SAMOKISH.

Kharkiv Institute of Agricultural Mechanization and Electrification: 61078 Kharkiv, vul. Artema 44; tel. (57) 222-37-86; f. 1929; library: 150,000 vols; Rector M. K. EVSEEV.

Kherson A. D. Tsuryupa Agricultural Institute: 325006 Kherson, vul. Rozy Lyuksemburga 23; tel. (55) 2-64-71; f. 1874; faculties of agricultural construction and hydromelioration, agronomy, animal husbandry, economics and agrobusiness jurisdiction; library: 300,000 vols; Rector V. A. USHKARENKO.

Kirovograd Higher Flying School of Civil Aviation: 316005 Kirovograd oblastnoi, vul. Dobrovolskogo 1; tel. (5222) 2-38-64; faculties: air navigation, air traffic control, flying.

Krivoi Rog Ore Mining Institute: 324027 Krivoi Rog, vul. 22 Partsezda 11; tel. (564) 23-22-30; fax (564) 74-84-12; f. 1922; faculties: construction, electrical engineering, engineering, geology and dressing, mine surveying and geodesy, open-cast mining, underground mining; geological museum; 4,500 students; library of 1.2m. vols; Rector V. F. BIZOV; publ. *Collection of Works* (2 a year).

Lugansk Agricultural Institute: 348008 Lugansk 8; tel. (642) 95-20-40; depts: accounting, agronomy, economics, mechanization.

Mariupol Metallurgical Institute: 87500 Mariupol, Republiki 7; tel. (62) 934-30-97; f. 1929; faculties: industrial energy, mechanical engineering, metallurgy, technology, welding; library: 580,000 vols; 444 teachers; 5,600 students; Rector I. V. ZHEZHELENKO.

Melitopol Institute of Agricultural Mechanization: 72300 Zaporizhia oblast, Melitopol, pr. B. Khmelnitskoho 18; tel. (61) 22-21-32; f. 1932; 315 teachers; 4,045 students; library: 330,000 vols; Rector N. L. KRIZHACHKOVSKII; publ. collns of scientific articles (4 a year).

Odessa Agricultural Institute: 270039 Odessa, vul. Sverdlova 99; tel. (48) 222-37-23; fax (48) 224-01-84; f. 1918; depts: accounting, agronomy, animal husbandry, economics and management, fruit and vegetable growing, land management, mechanization, veterinary medicine, viticulture; br. in Nikolaev; 1,000 teachers; 5,200 students; library: 280,000 vols; Rector YU. S. TSUKANOV.

Odessa N. I. Pirohov Medical Institute: 270100 Odessa, per. Nariman Narimanova 2; tel. (48) 223-35-67; library: 433,000 vols.

Poltava Medical Stomatological Institute: 314024 Poltava, vul. Shevchenko 23; tel. (53) 22-88-25; Rector N. S. SKRIPNIKOV.

Ukrainian Institute of Printing: 290020 Lviv, vul. Podholosko 19; tel. (32) 259-94-01; faculties: book illustration, economics, editorial, mechanics, technology; library: 384,000 vols; Rector Dr STEPAN HUNKO; publ. *Journal of Printing and Publishing*.

Zaporizhzhia Medical Institute: 330074 Zaporizhzhia, vul. Mayakovskoho 26; tel. (61) 233-01-49; f. 1965; Rector I. I. TOKARENKO.

Schools of Art and Music

Kharkiv Institute of Industrial and Applied Arts: 61002 Kharkiv, vul. Krasnoznamennaya 8; tel. (57) 243-28-73; fax (57) 243-28-73; e-mail root@design.kharkov.ua; f. 1927 and renamed 1963; faculties: industrial design, interior design; library: 88,000 vols; 154 teachers; 577 students; Rector V. DANYLENKO.

Kharkiv State Academy of Culture: 61003 Kharkiv, Bursatski Uzviz 4; tel. and fax (57) 712-81-05; e-mail sheiko@ic.ac.kharkov.ua; internet www.ic.ac.kharkov.ua; f. 1929; depts of library and information science, cultural studies, documentation and information work, art, music, theatre, cinema and television; library: 400,000 vols; 257 teachers; 3,393 students; Rector Prof. VASYL M. SHEYKO; publs *Journal* (1 a year), *Kultura Ukrainy* (12 a year).

Kharkiv State Institute of Arts: 310003 Kharkiv, pl. Sovetskoi Ukrainy 11/13; tel. (572) 22-56-28; acting (puppets), choral conducting, composition, directing (puppets), musicology, orchestral instruments, piano, singing, theatre studies; library: 100,000 vols.

Kyiv State Academy of Fine Arts and Architecture: 04053 Kyiv, vul. Smirnova-Lastochkina 20; tel. (44) 212-15-40; fax (44) 212-10-48; f. 1917; faculties: architecture, art history, arts management, graphic art, painting, restoration, sculpture, theatrical decorative art; 130 teachers; 800 students; library: 130,000 vols; Rector Prof. ANDREI V. CHEBYKIN.

Kyiv State Institute of Culture: 01133 Kyiv, vul. Shchorsa 36; tel. (44) 269-98-44; fax (44) 212-10-48; departments: folk culture, library science.

Lviv Academy of Arts: 79011 Lviv, vul. Kubiyovycha 38; tel. (32) 276-14-82; fax (32) 276-14-77; e-mail artacademy@mail.lviv.ua; internet www.artacademy.lviv.ua; f. 1946; faculties: decorative and applied arts, design, fine art and restoration, history and theory of art; library: 90,000 vols; 250 teachers; 1,000 students; Rector Prof. ANDRIY BOKOTEY; Vice-Rectors Prof. IGOR GOLOD, Prof. OREST HOLUBETZ; publ. *Scientific Messenger* (1 a year).

Odessa State Conservatoire 'A. V. Nezhdanova': 65021 Odessa, vul. Ostrovidova 63; tel. (48) 226-78-76; fax (48) 223-75-37; f. 1913; choral conducting, composition, musicology, orchestral and folk instruments, piano, singing; 140 teachers; 680 students; library: 100,000 vols; Rector OLEKSANDR V. SOKOL.

State Academy of Music 'Mykola Lysenko': 79005 Lviv, vul. Nyzhankivsky 5; tel. (32) 274-31-06; fax (32) 272-36-13; e-mail musinst@lviv.gu.net; internet musicacademy.lviv.ua; f. 1852; faculties: choral conducting, composition, folk instruments, musicology, operatic and symphonic conducting, orchestral instruments, piano, singing; library: 200,000 vols; 175 teachers; 550 students; Rector IHOR PYLATIUK.

Ukrainian National Academy of Music 'P. Tchaikovsky': 01001 Kyiv, Gorodetska vul. 1–3/11; tel. (44) 229-07-92; fax (44) 229-35-30; e-mail nmau@iptelecom.net.ua; f. 1913; faculties: choral conducting, composition, folk instruments, music production, music education, opera and symphony orchestra conducting, orchestral instruments, piano, singing, theory and history of music; 304 teachers; 1,156 students; library: 355,000 vols; Rector OLEG TIMOSHENKO; publ. *Ukrainian Musicology* (1 a year).

UNITED ARAB EMIRATES

The Higher Education System

The United Arab Emirates (UAE)'s universities include the United Arab Emirates University (founded 1976), Ajman University of Science and Technology (founded 1988), University of Sharjah (founded 1997), Zayed University (founded 1998 with two campuses in Abu Dhabi, two in Dubai) and Abu Dhabi University (founded 2003). A branch of the Sorbonne University, based in Paris, France, opened in Abu Dhabi in 2006, and American universities are in operation in Dubai, Ras al-Khaimah and Sharjah. In September 1988 four higher colleges of technology (two for male and two for female students) opened, admitting a total of 1,150 students in 1992/93, all of whom were citizens of the UAE. The total number of higher colleges of technology had increased to 13 by the end of the 2000s. In 2008/09 a total of 87,006 students were enrolled in university and other higher education institutions. Many other students receive higher education abroad.

The Ministry of Higher Education and Scientific Research, founded in 1992, is responsible for all post-secondary education. It is also responsible for the regulation of private institutions in higher education. The Commission for Academic Accreditation, a department within the Ministry, licenses institutions and accredits degree programmes. The Commission introduced new, more stringent accreditation standards at the beginning of the 2011/12 academic year in a bid to improve the quality of higher education in the UAE; the standards also require institutions to make their facilities and expertise available to the community at large.

Admission to higher education is on the basis of an average score of at least 70% in the Tawjihiyya examinations (although, as entrance is so competitive, an average of at least 80% is typically required); many institutions also require a score in excess of 150 in the Common Educational Proficiency Assessment (CEPA) English examination. Degrees are awarded on a credit basis. The undergraduate Bachelors degree is a four-year programme of study (medicine lasts seven years). The Masters degree is a one- or two-year course following the Bachelors degree; some programmes follow the US model and include both coursework and thesis, while others are based on the British, research-based model and include only a small number of taught modules. Doctoral programmes were introduced at the United Arab Emirates University from the beginning of the 2009/10 academic year and have subsequently become available at a number of the country's other higher education institutions; such programmes, which typically last between three and four years, follow the US model, comprising one year of coursework and between two and three years of research, culminating in submission of a thesis.

Post-secondary technical and vocational education is offered by higher colleges of technology and other colleges. Higher colleges of technology, which are funded by the Ministry of Finance, provide training for professional and technology careers in the public and private sectors. Admission is on the basis of a score of at least 60% in the Tawjihiyya and performance in the CEPA English examination, and most candidates undertake a one-year preparatory Foundation programme. Among the qualifications offered by the higher colleges of technology are Certificates (two years), Diplomas (one to three years) and Higher Diplomas (three years). Bachelors degree programmes are also available at some higher colleges of technology, in conjunction with other higher education institutions; such programmes require a minimum period of four weeks' work placement.

There are a number of foreign institutions, such as the Birla Institute of Technology and Science Pilani (India), that operate programmes not accredited by the UAE Commission for Academic Accreditation, but accredited by foreign governments and accreditation bodies.

Regulatory Bodies

GOVERNMENT

Ministry of Culture, Youth and Community Development: POB 17, Abu Dhabi; tel. (2) 4466145; fax (2) 4452504; e-mail info@ mcycd.gov.ae; internet www.mcycd.ae; Minister ABD AL-RAHMAN MUHAMMAD AL-OWAIS.

Ministry of Education: POB 3962, Abu Dhabi; tel. (2) 4089999; fax (2) 6351164; e-mail ccc.moe@moe.gov.ae; internet www .moe.gov.ae; Minister HUMAID MUHAMMAD OBAID AL-QATTAMI.

Ministry of Higher Education and Scientific Research: POB 45253, Abu Dhabi; tel. (2) 6428000; fax (2) 6428778; e-mail mohe@uae.gov.ae; internet www.mohesr.ae; Minister SHEIKH NAHYAN BIN MUBARAK AL-NAHYAN.

ACCREDITATION

Commission for Academic Accreditation: Ministry of Higher Education, Al Najdah St, POB 41533, Abu Dhabi; tel. (2) 6427772; fax (2) 6428488; e-mail badr .aboulela@mohesr.ae; internet www.caa.ae; f. 2000; 4 mems; Dir MOHAMED BADR ELDIN ABOUL-ELA.

Learned Societies

LANGUAGE AND LITERATURE

Alliance Française: POB 2646, Abu Dhabi; tel. (2) 6666232; fax (2) 6669044; e-mail alliancefrancaise@af-aboudabi.net; internet www.af-aboudabi.net; offers courses and exams in French language and culture and promotes cultural exchange with France; attached teaching centre in Dubai.

British Council: Villa no. 7, Al Nasr St, Khalidya, Abu Dhabi, POB 46523; tel. (2) 6659300; fax (2) 6664340; e-mail information@ae.britishcouncil.org; internet www.britishcouncil.org/uae; teaching centre; offers courses and exams in English language and British culture and promotes cultural exchange with the UK; attached teaching centres in Dubai and Sharjah; Dir, United Arab Emirates JO MAHER; Deputy Dir PAUL MASON.

Research Institutes

GENERAL

Centre for Documentation and Research: POB 5884, Abu Dhabi; tel. (2) 4183333; fax (2) 4445811; e-mail dg@cdr.gov .ae; internet www.cdr.gov.ae; f. 1968; attached to Ministry of Presidential Court; documents, books, maps and articles relating to the Arabian Gulf and the Arabian Peninsula; publishes specialized research studies; convenes nat., regional and int. seminars and conferences; organizes exhibitions relating to the UAE; library of 32,000 vols in many languages, 6,481 microfiches, 7m. documents; Pres. Sheik MANSOUR BIN ZAYED AL-NAHYAN.

AGRICULTURE, FISHERIES AND VETERINARY SCIENCE

Agricultural Information Centre: POB 176, Ras al-Khaimah; tel. (2) 4495100; fax (2) 4495150; e-mail info@moew.gov.ae; f. 1975 as a UNDP-FAO assisted project, present name 1984; run by Ministry of Environment and Water; conducts research into irrigation, plant protection, vegetable varieties, vegetables under plastic houses, soil fertility; c. 48 staff; library of 500 vols; Research Dir MOHAMMED HASSAN AL-SHAMSI.

Libraries and Archives

Abu Dhabi

National Archives: POB 2380, Abu Dhabi; tel. (2) 4447797; fax (2) 4445639; internet www.cultural.org.ae; f. 1985; attached to the Cultural Foundation, an independent government body; cares for current and historical public records; Dir Dr NASSIR ALI AL-HIMIRI.

National Library: POB 2380, Abu Dhabi; tel. (2) 6515411; fax (2) 6433127; e-mail national-library@adach.ae; internet www .adach.ae; f. 1981; UN Deposit Centre; brs: Emirates and Gulf Library, Batten Children's Library, Al Nahyan Public Library, Al Ain Mall Public Library, Mezayad Mall Public Library, Al Rahah Mall Public Library; 4,000,000 vols, 3,000 periodical titles, 12,000 audiovisual items; Dir JUMAA AL QUBAISI; publs *National Bibliography* (in Arabic and English), *Union Catalogue of Periodicals in the UAE* (in Arabic and English).

Dubai

Dubai Municipality Public Libraries: POB 67, Dubai; tel. (4) 2262788; fax (4) 2266226; e-mail libraries@dm.gov.ae; internet login.dm.gov.ae; f. 1963; 205,970 vols, 1,707 periodicals; spec. colln of Arab Islamic art books; Head MOHAMMAD JASSIM AL-ERIADI.

Museums and Art Galleries

Al-Ain

Al-Ain Museum: POB 15715, Al-Ain; tel. (3) 764559; fax (3) 764559; e-mail antigan@ emirates.net.ae; internet www.aam.gov.ae; f. 1971; archaeology and ethnography; library of 200 vols; archaeological sites at Al-Ain and Umm al-Nar island; Dirs SAIF BIN ALI AL-DARMAKI, Dr WALID YASIN.

Sharjah

Sharjah Museums: POB 39939, Sharjah; tel. (6) 5566002; fax (6) 5566003; e-mail info@ sharjahmuseums.ae; internet www .sharjahmuseums.ae; f. 1995; Dir SHIEKHA HOOR AL-QASIMI.

Universities

ABU DHABI UNIVERSITY

POB 59911, Abu Dhabi
Internet: www.adu.ac.ae
Founded 2003
Private control
Accredited by Ministry of Higher Education and Scientific Research
Chancellor: Prof. Dr NABIL IBRAHIM
Librarian: OMAR ABBAS
Number of students: 4,000

DEANS

College of Arts and Sciences: (vacant)
College of Business Administration: Dr MOHAMED KHALIFA
College of Engineering and Computer Science: Dr ALY S. NAZMY
University College: Dr JEHAN ZITAWI

AL-AIN UNIVERSITY OF SCIENCE AND TECHNOLOGY

POB 64141, Al-Ain
Telephone: (3) 7611185
Fax: (3) 7611198
Internet: alain-university.com
Founded 2005
Private control
Accredited by Ministry of Higher Education and Scientific Research
Pres.: Prof. FUAD SHEIKH SALEM
Colleges of business administration, education, engineering and IT, law, pharmacy.

AL-GHURAIR UNIVERSITY

POB 37374, Dubai
Telephone: (4) 4200223
Fax: (4) 4200224
E-mail: admissions@agu.ac.ae
Internet: www.agu.ae
Founded 1999
Private control
Accredited by Ministry of Higher Education and Scientific Research
Pres.: Dr ABDURAHEM MOHAMMED AL-AMEEN
Colleges of business studies, computing, engineering and applied sciences; school of design.

AL-HOSN UNIVERSITY

POB 38772, Abu Dhabi
Telephone: (2) 4070700
Fax: (2) 4070799
Internet: www.alhosnu.ae
Founded 2003
Private control
Accredited by Ministry of Higher Education and Scientific Research
Vice-Chancellor: Prof. ABDUL RAHIM SABOUNI
Provost: Dr HAMDI SHEIBANI
Library Dir: Dr ALHAJ SALIM MUSTAFA
Publication: *Journal of Engineering and Applied Sciences* (every 2 years)

DEANS

Faculty of Arts and Social Sciences: Prof. HASSAN MUSTAPHA
Faculty of Business: Prof. AHMAD ZOHDI
Faculty of Engineering and Applied Sciences: Dr HAMDI SHEIBANI

AJMAN UNIVERSITY OF SCIENCE AND TECHNOLOGY (AUST)

POB 346, Ajman
Telephone: (6) 7482222
Fax: (6) 7438888
E-mail: info@ajman.ac.ae
Internet: www.ajman.ac.ae
Founded 1988
Private control
Pres.: Dr SAEED ABDULLAH SALMAN
Vice-Pres. for Admin. and Financial Affairs: THAMER SAEED ABDULLA ALI SALMAN
Vice-Pres. for External Relations and Cultural Affairs: AHMED ANKIT

DEANS

Faculty of Business Administration: Dr YAHYA HADDAD
Faculty of Computer Science: Dr MAHMOUD ABO-NAAJ
Faculty of Dentistry: (vacant)
Faculty of Education and Basic Science: Dr SALEH AWADH OMAR ARAM
Faculty of Engineering: Prof. FAHAR HAYATI
Faculty of Foreign Languages: Dr THARWAT SAKRAN
Faculty of Information, Mass Communication and Public Relations: (vacant)
Faculty of Pharmacy and Health Sciences: Dr SAMIR ISSA BLOUKH

AMERICAN UNIVERSITY IN DUBAI

POB 28282, Dubai
Telephone: (4) 3999000
Fax: (4) 3998899
Internet: www.aud.edu
Founded 1995
Private control
Accredited by Ministry of Higher Education and Scientific Research
Pres.: Dr LANCE DE MASI

Exec. Vice-Pres.: ELIAS BOU SAAB
Provost: Dr JIHAD S. NADER
Library Dir: LIZ OESLEBY
Library of 77,334 vols, 345 periodicals

DEANS

School of Business and Administration: Dr DWAYNE A. BANKS
School of Communication and Information Studies: (vacant)
School of Engineering: Dr ALAA K. ASHMAWY

AMERICAN UNIVERSITY IN THE EMIRATES

Block 6, Dubai International Academic City, Dubai
Telephone: (4) 4291200
Fax: (4) 4291205
E-mail: info@aue.ae
Internet: www.aue.ae
Private control
Colleges of business admin., computer information technology, fine arts and design, media and mass communication.

AMERICAN UNIVERSITY OF SHARJAH

POB 26666, Sharjah
Telephone: (6) 5155555
Internet: www.aus.edu
Founded 1997
Private control
Accredited by Ministry of Higher Education and Scientific Research
Chancellor: Dr PETER HEATH

DEANS

College of Arts and Sciences: WILLIAM HEID-CAMP
College of Engineering: YOUSEF AL-ASSAF
School of Architecture and Design: FATIH RIFKI
School of Business and Management: R. MALCOLM RICHARDS

BRITISH UNIVERSITY IN DUBAI

POB 502216, Dubai
Telephone: (4) 3913626
Fax: (4) 3664698
E-mail: info@buid.ac.ae
Internet: www.buid.ac.ae
Founded 1997
Private control
Accredited by Ministry of Higher Education and Scientific Research
Vice-Chancellor: Dr ABDULLAH M. ALSHAMSI
Faculties of business, education, engineering, informatics.

CANADIAN UNIVERSITY OF DUBAI

POB 117781, Dubai
Telephone: (4) 3218866
Fax: (4) 3211991
E-mail: info@cud.ac.ae
Internet: www.cud.ac.ae
Founded 2006
Private control
Accredited by Ministry of Higher Education and Scientific Research
Pres.: ANN BULLER
Schools of applied science and technology, architectural studies and interior design, business, engineering, environment and health.

GULF MEDICAL UNIVERSITY

POB 4184, Ajman
Telephone: (4) 7431333
Fax: (4) 7431222
E-mail: gmcajman@emirates.net.ae
Internet: www.gmcajman.com

Founded 1998 as Gulf Medical College; univ. status 2008
Private control; Thumbay Group
Accredited by Ministry of Higher Education and Scientific Research
Dir: MOIDEEN THUMBAY

Bachelors and Masters degree programmes.

HAMDAN BIN MOHAMMED E-UNIVERSITY

POB 71400, Dubai
Telephone: (4) 4241111
Fax: (4) 4393939
E-mail: hbmeu@hbmeu.ac.ae
Internet: www.hbmeu.ac.ae

Fmrly Electronic Total Quality Management (E-TQM College)
Private control
Accredited by Ministry of Higher Education and Scientific Research
Chancellor: Dr MANSOOR MOHAMED AQIL AL-AWAR
Vice-Chancellor: Dr IBRAHIM MAHMOOD BIN ABDULRAHMAN

DEANS

e-School of Business and Quality Management: Dr KHALID HAFEEZ
e-School of Health and Environmental Studies: Prof. RACHID HADJ-HAMOU
School of e-Education: Prof. ALAIN R. SENTENI

ITTIHAD UNIVERSITY

POB 2286, Ras al-Khaimah
Telephone: (7) 2059999
Fax: (7) 2059982
E-mail: ittihadu@emirates.net.ae
Internet: www.ittihad.ac.ae
Founded 1999
Private control
Chancellor: Dr ABDUL SATTAR AL-ALUSI.

KHALIFA UNIVERSITY OF SCIENCE, TECHNOLOGY AND RESEARCH

POB 573, Sharjah
Telephone: (6) 5611333
E-mail: info@kustar.ac.ae
Internet: www.ku.ac.ae

Founded 2007 incorporating the former Etisalat Univ. College as the Sharjah branch campus
Abu Dhabi Campus is under devt
Private control
Accredited by Ministry of Higher Education and Scientific Research
Pres.: Dr ARIF SULTAN AL-HAMMADI

Undergraduate and postgraduate degrees in Engineering.

MIDDLESEX UNIVERSITY DUBAI

POB 500697, Dubai
Telephone: (4) 3678100
Fax: (4) 3672956
E-mail: info@mdx.ac
Internet: www.mdx.ac
Founded 2005
Private control; Middlesex University, London (UK)
Dir: Prof. RAED AWAMLEH

Schools of arts and education, business, engineering and information sciences, health and social science
Number of students: 1,200

NYU ABU DHABI

POB 113100, Abu Dhabi
Telephone: (2) 4069677
E-mail: nyuad@nyu.edu
Internet: nyuad.nyu.edu
Founded 2009
Private control; New York Univ. (USA)
Provost: MARIËT WESTERMANN.

PARIS-SORBONNE UNIVERSITY ABU DHABI

POB 38044, Abu Dhabi
Telephone: (2) 5090555
Fax: (2) 5090656
E-mail: admissions@psuad.ac.ae
Internet: www.paris-sorbonne-abudhabi.ae
Founded 2006
Private control.

RAS AL-KHAIMAH MEDICAL AND HEALTH SCIENCES UNIVERSITY

POB 11172, Ras al-Khaimah
Telephone: (7) 2269999
Fax: (7) 2269998
E-mail: admissions@rakmhsu.ae
Internet: www.rakmhsu.com
Founded 1993
Jointly controlled by Ras Al-Khaimah Govt, Al Ghurair Investments and ETA Ascon Group, Dubai
Accredited by Ministry of Higher Education and Scientific Research
Vice-Chancellor: Dr S. GURUMADHVA RAO

Colleges of dental sciences, medical sciences, nursing, pharmaceutical sciences.

UNITED ARAB EMIRATES UNIVERSITY

POB 15551, Al-Ain
Telephone: (3) 7555557
Fax: (3) 7545277
E-mail: vice_chancellor@uaeu.ac.ae
Internet: www.uaeu.ac.ae
Founded 1976
State control
Languages of instruction: Arabic, English
Academic year: September to June
Chancellor: HH Sheikh NAHAYAN MABARAK AL-NAHAYAN
Vice-Chancellor: Dr ABDULLA AL-KHANBASHI
Provost, Chief Academic Officer and CEO: Dr WYATT R. HUME
Sec.-Gen.: Dr FATIMA AL-SHAMSI
Assoc. Provost for Academic Affairs: Prof. DONALD E. BOWEN
Asst Provost and Dean of Students: Dr COURTNEY STRYKER
Asst Provost for IT and Chief Information Officer: NICK MITCHELL CHOBAN
Asst Provost for Research: Dr MAITHA S. AL-SHAMSI
Library of 439,651 vols, 929 periodicals
Number of teachers: 667
Number of students: 17,000
Publication: individual faculty journals published annually

DEANS

College of Education: Dr GARY M. INGERSOLL
College of Engineering: Prof. REYADH ALMEHAIDEB
College of Food and Agriculture: Prof. GHALEB ALHADRAMI

College of Humanities and Social Sciences: Prof. DONALD BAKER
College of Information Technology: Dr BOUMEDIENE BELKHOUCHE
College of Law: Prof. JASSIM ALI SALEM ALSHAMSI
College of Science: Prof. M. NAIM ANWAR
Faculty of Business and Economics: Prof. DAVID GRAF
Faculty of Medicine and Health Sciences: Prof. GEORGE CARRUTHERS

UNIVERSITY OF ATLANTA—GULF REGION

41st Fl., Jumeirah Emirates Tower, Dubai
E-mail: dubai@uofa.edu
Internet: www.uofa.edu
Private control
Dir: Dr STEVE HERMES.

UNIVERSITY OF DUBAI

POB 14143, Dubai
Telephone: (4) 2072600
Fax: (4) 2242151
E-mail: info@ud.ac.ae
Internet: www.ud.ac.ae

Founded 1997 as Dubai Univ. College; present status 2006
Accredited by UAE Ministry of Higher Education and Scientific Research; member of the Association to Advance Collegiate Schools of Business (AACSB), the Accrediting Board for Engineering and Technology (ABET) and the European Foundation for Management Development (EFMD)
Under the control of the state-funded Dubai Chamber of Commerce and Industry
Languages of instruction: Arabic, English
Pres.: M. OMAR HEFNI
Number of teachers: 48
Number of students: 630

DEANS

College of Business Administration: Assoc. Prof. ANANTH RAO
College of Information Technology: Dr FAOUZI KAMOUN

UNIVERSITY OF SHARJAH

POB 27272, Sharjah
Telephone: (6) 5585000
Fax: (6) 5585099
E-mail: info@sharjah.ac.ae
Internet: www.sharjah.ac.ae
Founded 1997
Private control
Chancellor: Prof. SAMY A. MAHMOUD
Vice-Chancellor for Academic Affairs: Prof. SALIM SABRI
Vice-Chancellor for Admin. and Financial Affairs: Dr MOHAMMED ISMAIL
Vice-Chancellor for Medical Colleges: Prof. MOHAMMED HUSAM AL-DIN HAMDI
Dir of Libraries: QASIM MUHAMMAD AL-KHALIDI

DEANS

College of Arts, Humanities and Social Sciences: Prof. HAMID M. AL-NAIMIY
College of Business Admin.: Prof. MAHENDRA RAJ
College of Communication: Prof. MUHAMMED KIRAT
College of Dentistry: Prof. RANI SHAMSUDIN
College of Engineering: Prof. BOUALEM BOASHASH
College of Fine Arts and Design: Dr HASSAN ABDALLA
College of Health Sciences: Prof. BASSAMAT OMAR
College of Law: Prof. ADNAN SIRHAN

College of Medicine: Prof. MOHAMMED HUSAM AL-DIN HAMDI

College of Pharmacy: Prof. MAZEN KHALIL AL-QATO

College of Shari'a and Islamic Studies: Prof. EL-GURASHI EL-BASHIR (acting)

College of Sciences: Prof. HAMID M. AL-NAIMIY

UNIVERSITY OF WOLLONGONG IN DUBAI

POB 20183, Dubai

Telephone: (4) 3672400

Fax: (4) 3672760

E-mail: info@uowdubai.ac.ae

Internet: www.uowdubai.ac.ae

Founded 1993

Private control

Accredited by Ministry of Higher Education and Scientific Research

Pres.: Prof. ROB WHELAN

Number of students: 3,500

Faculties of business and management, computer science and engineering, finance and accounting.

ZAYED UNIVERSITY

POB 19282, Dubai

Telephone: (4) 4021111

Fax: (4) 4021008

E-mail: info@zu.ac.ae

Internet: www.zu.ac.ae

Founded 1998

State control

Pres.: Sheikh NAHAYAN MABARAK AL-NAHA-YAN

Vice-Pres.: Dr SULAIMAN AL-JASSIM

Provost: DAN JOHNSON

Assoc. Provost for Academic and Int. Affairs: BOB CRYAN

Chief Admin. and Finance Officer: ANDRÉ RACETTE

Dean of Libraries: PATRICIA WAND

DEANS

College of Arts and Sciences: MICHAEL ALLEN

College of Business Sciences: MICHAEL OWEN

College of Communication and Media Sciences: MARILYN ROBERTS

College of Education: PEGGY BLACKWELL

College of Information Technology: LEON JOLOLIAN

Colleges

Al-Khawarizmi International College: POB 25669, Abu Dhabi; tel. (2) 6789700; fax (2) 6789300; e-mail ceo@khawarizmi.com; internet www.khawarizmi.com; f. 1985; private control; accredited by Ministry of Higher Education and Scientific Research; affiliated to Liverpool John Moores Univ., UK; campus in Al-Ain; BSc in Computer Technology; Pres. NAEEM RADI.

American College of Dubai: POB 12867, Dubai; tel. (4) 2829992; fax (4) 2828060; e-mail info@acd.ae; internet www.centamed .com; private control; accredited by Ministry of Higher Education and Scientific Research; business, IT, liberal arts; library: 30,000 vols; Pres. WILLIAM J. O'BRIEN; Provost Dr NIGEL THORPE; Dean of Academic and Faculty Affairs Dr POONAN SINGH; Dean of Business Dr ZAFAR QUERESHI; Dean of Student Affairs S. SHARMA; Registrar CHRISTINE MASCAREN-HAS; Librarian RANI MANI.

Birla Institute of Technology and Science, Pilani—Dubai: POB 345055, Dubai;

tel. (4) 4200700; fax (4) 4200555; internet www.bitsdubai.com; private control.

Boston University Institute for Dental Research and Education: POB 505097, Dubai; tel. (4) 4248787; fax (4) 4248687; e-mail info@budubai.ae; internet www .budubai.ae; private control; CEO Dr STEVEN MORGANO.

Computer College: Dubai; tel. (4) 2826880; fax (4) 2826902; e-mail sales@ computer-centre.ae; internet www.cc-uae .com; f. 1993; private control; accredited by Ministry of Higher Education and Scientific Research; business admin. and IT.

Dubai Aerospace Enterprise Flight Academy: POB 10227, Ras al-Khaimah; tel. (7) 2043524; fax (7) 2043600; e-mail admissions@daeflightacademy.com; internet www.daeflightacademy.com; f. 2006; private control; Man. Dir Capt RICHARD MORRIS.

Dubai Medical College for Girls: POB 20170, Dubai; tel. (4) 2646465; fax (4) 2646130; internet www.dmcg.edu; private control; accredited by Ministry of Higher Education and Scientific Research; BSc in medicine and surgery; Dean Prof. MOHAMMED GALAL EL-DIN.

Dubai Pharmacy College: POB 19099, Dubai; tel. (4) 2646968; fax (4) 2646740; internet www.dpc.edu; f. 1999; private control; accredited by Ministry of Higher Education and Scientific Research; Dean Dr SAEED AHMED KHAN.

Dubai Police Academy: POB 53900 Dubai; tel. (4) 3482255; fax (4) 3481144; e-mail college@dubaipolice.gov.ae; internet www .dubaipolice.gov.ae; f. 1989; accredited by Ministry of Higher Education and Scientific Research; Dean Dr MOHAMMED AHMED BIN FAHAD.

Dubai School of Government: POB 72229, Dubai; tel. (4) 3293290; fax (4) 3293291; e-mail info@dsg.ae; internet www.dsg.ae; f. 2005; private control; masters degrees in public admin., public policy; Dean TARIK YOUSEF.

Emirates Academy of Hospitality Management: POB 29662, Dubai; tel. (4) 3155555; fax (4) 3155556; e-mail info@ emiratesacademy.edu; internet www .jumeirah.com/en/jumeirah-group/the-emira-tes-academy; f. 2001; private control; Jumeirah Group; accredited by Ministry of Higher Education and Scientific Research; 400 students; Man. Dir RON HILVERT.

Emirates Aviation College – Aerospace and Academic Studies: POB 53044, Dubai; tel. (4) 2824000; fax (4) 2824222; internet www.emiratesaviationcollege.com; f. 1991 by Dept of Civil Aviation; private control; Emirate Group; accredited by Ministry of Higher Education, bachelors degrees in aeronautical engineering, business admin. (air transport management); Vice-Pres. Dr AHMED AL-ALI.

Emirates College for Management and Information Technology: POB 39292, Dubai; tel. (4) 2675016; fax (4) 2675048; e-mail admissions@ecmit.ac.ae; internet www.ecmit.ac.ae; f. 1998; private control; Emirate Group; accredited by Ministry of Higher Education and Scientific Research; British Accreditation Council for Independent Further and Higher Education; Assoc. Science degrees in Business and Information Technology; Pres. and CEO SUDHIR KARTHA; Librarian SEENA SHAHAN.

Emirates College of Advanced Education: POB 126662, Abu Dhabi; tel. (2) 6964300; fax (2) 6421641; e-mail info@ecae .ac.ae; internet www.ecae.ac.ae; private control; Vice-Chancellor IAN HASLAM.

Emirates College of Technology: POB 41009, Abu Dhabi; tel. (2) 6266010; fax (2)

6276664; e-mail ectuae@emirates.net.ae; internet www.ectuae.com; f. 1993 as Emirates Institute of Technology; private control; accredited by Ministry of Higher Education and Scientific Research; diplomas in accounting, banking and finance, business admin. and computer information systems, computer graphic design and animation, e-commerce and marketing, human resource management; Pres. MOHAMED AL-MAZROUI.

Emirates Institute for Banking and Financial Studies: POB 4166, Sharjah; tel. (6) 5728880; fax (6) 5728080; e-mail info@eibfs.com; internet www.eibfs.com; f. 1983; private control; Diploma and short courses; br. in Abu Dhabi; Chair. AHMAD HUMAID AL-TAYER; Gen. Man. JAMAL AL-JASSMI.

European University College Brussels: POB 500691, Dubai; tel. (4) 3672323; fax (4) 3672777; e-mail admissions@ehsal-dubai .net; internet www.ehsal-dubai.net; private control; f. 2003; Dir-Gen. Dr KIRK DE CEU-LAER.

Falcon College of Hotel Management and Tourism: POB 43319, Abu Dhabi; tel. (2) 4491450; fax (2) 4494594; e-mail fchmuae@emirates.net.ae; f. 2007; private control; accredited by Ministry of Higher Education and Scientific Research; affiliated to Cesar Ritz Colleges, Switzerland; Chair. ABDULLA ABDULJALIL AL-FAHIM; Dean Dr OSKAR R. SYKORA.

Fujairah College: POB 1207, Fujairah; tel. (2) 2244499; fax (2) 2244488; e-mail info@fc .ac.ae; internet www.fc.ac.ae; f. 2006; state control; accredited by Ministry of Higher Education and Scientific Research; Assoc. degrees in Business Admin. and Information Technology; Exec. Dir Prof. GHASSAN AL-QAIMIRI.

Heriot Watt University—Dubai: Dubai International Academic City, Dubai; tel. (4) 3616999; e-mail dubaienquiries@hw.ac.uk; internet www.hw.ac.uk/dubai; private control; undergraduate degrees in construction, engineering, management, quantity surveying, textiles and fashion design; masters programmes in construction, energy, information technology, management, petroleum engineering.

Higher Colleges of Technology: POB 32092, Abu Dhabi; tel. (2) 6815654; fax (2) 6812637; e-mail enquiries@hct.ac.ae; internet www.hct.ac.ae; f. 1988; divs of applied communications, business, education, engineering technology, general education, graduate studies, health sciences, information technology; campuses at Al-Ain, Dubai, Fujairah, Ras al-Khaimah, Sharjah; library: 160,000 vols; 950 teachers; 16,000 students; Chancellor H. E. Sheikh NAHAYAN MABARAK AL-NAHAYAN; Vice-Chancellor Dr TAYEB KAMALI.

Institute of Management Technology: POB 345006, Dubai; tel. (2) 3604844; fax (2) 3604838; e-mail info@imtdubai.ac.ae; internet imtdubai.ac.ae; f. 2006; private control; accredited by Ministry of Higher Education and Scientific Research; MBA programmes; Dir Dr FARHAD RAD-SERECHT.

Islamic and Arabic Studies College: Dubai; tel. (2) 3604844; fax (2) 3604838; e-mail iasc@emirates.net.ae; internet www .islamic-college.co.ae; f. 1986; Private Control; accredited by Ministry of Higher Education and Scientific Research; bachelors, masters and PhDs in Arabic language, Arabic literature, Islamic Fiqh, Islamic studies, Shariah; 3,489 students.

Mahatma Gandhi University Off Campus Centre: Block 3, Dubai Knowledge Village, Dubai; tel. (4) 3902981; fax (4)

3664661; e-mail contact@mgudxboc.com; internet www.mgudxboc.com; f. 2003; private control; BSc in computer science, bachelor in fashion technology, BTS in tourism studies; 700 students.

Manipal University, Dubai Campus: Block 7, Academic City, Dubai; tel. (4) 4291214; fax (4) 3694541; e-mail admissions@mahedubai.com; internet www.mahedubai.com; private control; programmes in civil engineering, electronics and communication engineering, instrumentation and control engineering, mechanical engineering, mechatronics engineering.

Masdar Institute of Science and Technology: POB 54115, Abu Dhabi; tel. (2) 6988133; fax (2) 6988123; e-mail rorfali@masdar.ae; internet www.mist.ac.ae; f. 2006; private control; masters and PhD programmes in science and engineering disciplines.

Michigan State University – Dubai: POB 345001, Dubai; tel. (4) 5015314; e-mail dubai@msu.edu; internet www.dubai.msu.edu; private control; bachelors and masters degrees.

Murdoch University International Study Center: POB 345005, Dubai; tel. (4) 4355700; fax (4) 4355704; e-mail info@murdochdubai.ac.ae; internet www.murdochdubai.com; private control; Dir Prof. JOHN GRAINGER.

Naval College: POB 800, Abu Dhabi; tel. (2) 6157600; fax (2) 6157692; f. 1997; state control; accredited by Ministry of Higher Education and Scientific Research; bachelors degree in naval studies.

New York Institute of Technology: POB 5464, Abu Dhabi; tel. (2) 4048611; fax (2) 4450830; internet www.nyit.edu/nyit_worldwide/united_arab_emirates; f. 2005; private control; New York Institute of Technology (USA); initial accreditation by the Ministry of Higher Education and Scientific Research for Bachelor of Fine Arts in Interior Design programme.

Petroleum Institute: POB 2533, Abu Dhabi; tel. (2) 6075100; fax (2) 6075200; e-mail enquiries@pi.ac.ae; internet www.pi.ac.ae; f. 2001; private control; accredited by Ministry of Higher Education and Scientific Research; BSc degrees in chemical engineering, electrical engineering, mechanical engineering, petroleum engineering, petroleum geosciences; Masters of engineering in chemical engineering, electrical engineering, mechanical engineering, petroleum engineering; Provost and Pres. Dr MICHAEL OHADI (acting).

Police College: POB 163, Abu Dhabi; tel. (2) 4447700; fax (2) 4449720; e-mail general-manager@policecollege.ac.ae; internet www.policecollege.ac.ae; f. 1985; state control, Ministry of the Interior; accredited by Ministry of Higher Education and Scientific Research; Bachelors degree in law and policing sciences; Dir-Gen. MUSTAFA SHIHAB AL-HASHMI.

Police Sciences Academy Sharjah: POB 1510, Sharjah; tel. (6) 5585888; fax (6) 5585588; e-mail info@psa.ac.ae; internet www.psa.ac.ae; f. 1995; state control; accredited by Ministry of Higher Education and Scientific Research; bachelor of police sciences.

Rochester Institute of Technology—Dubai: POB 341055, Dubai; tel. (4) 5015314; e-mail dubai@rit.edu; internet www.rit.edu/dubai; private control; graduate degrees in business admin., finance, electrical engineering, mechanical engineering, networking and systems admin., service leadership and innovation; Pres. Dr MUSTAFA ABUSHAGUR.

Royal College of Applied Science and Technology: POB 10141, Ras al-Khaima; tel. (7) 2359080; fax (7) 2359081; e-mail bitic-uae@rcast.org; internet www.rcast.org;

f. 2004; private control; Sudhir Gopi Holdings (India); 2-year MBA programmes in finance, human resource management, marketing and IT; Pres. Prof. Dr PRAVEEN DHYANI.

SAE Institute Dubai: POB 500648, Dubai; tel. (4) 3616173; fax (4) 3686800; e-mail infodubai@sae.edu; internet www.sae-dubai.com; private control.

Shaheed Zulfikar Ali Bhutto Institute of Science and Technology: POB 345004, Dubai; tel. (4) 3664601; fax (4) 3664607; e-mail szabist@szabist.ac.ae; internet www.szabist.ac.ae; private control.

Skyline University College: POB 1797, Sharjah; tel. (6) 5441155; fax (6) 5441166; e-mail admissions@skylineuniversity.com; internet www.skylinecollege.info; f. 1990; private control; accredited by Ministry of Higher Education and Scientific Research; bachelor and masters in business admin.; Pres. KAMAL PURI.

Syscoms College: POB 72574, Abu Dhabi; tel. (2) 6760800; fax (2) 6760890; e-mail info@syscomscollege.com; internet www.syscomscollege.com; f. 1990; private control, EMKE Group; accredited by Ministry of Higher Education and Scientific Research; assoc. of science degree in information technology.

Troy University ITS Sharjah Campus: POB 5398, Sharjah; tel. (6) 5313111; fax (6) 5314545; e-mail info@shjcollege.ac.ae; internet www.shjcollege.ac.ae; f. 1990; private control; Troy Univ. (USA); assoc. and bachelor degrees in business admin., computer science; Pres. Dr E. M. S. EDIRISINGHE.

Universal Empire Institute of Medical Sciences: POB 500332, Dubai; tel. (4) 4332773; fax (4) 4370305; e-mail administration@ueims.com; internet www.ueims.com; private control; Universal Empire Int.; Chair. and Man. Dir SUDHIR GOPI.

UNITED KINGDOM

The Higher Education System

Institutions of higher education date from the 13th century, with the oldest being the University of Oxford, the oldest college of which was founded in 1249; the next oldest university is the University of Cambridge, the oldest college of which was founded in 1284. The oldest Scottish universities are the University of St Andrews and the University of Aberdeen, which were both founded in the 15th century. The 19th century saw a great expansion of the higher education system, with the foundation of over 90 universities, colleges and institutes in the United Kingdom. In 2007/08 there were 120 universities (including the Open University) and 49 other higher education institutions, together with the privately funded University of Buckingham. In that year there were 1,053,300 full-time and 2,415,700 part-time students (including from overseas) taking higher education courses. Institutions of higher education include universities, university colleges, colleges of higher education and some further education colleges. The United Kingdom joined the Bologna Process in 1999. However, since the United Kingdom already had a three-cycle degree structure based on Bachelors, Masters and doctorate-level qualifications, no structural changes were necessary. Higher education institutions are autonomous bodies and so implementation of Bologna reforms such as the use of the European Credit Transfer and Accumulation System and the issuing of the Diploma Supplement remains at institutional discretion.

Notable legislation pertaining to higher education includes the Further and Higher Education Act 1992, which brought to an end the binary system by which universities and polytechnics were treated separately and enabled former polytechnics to achieve university status, and the Higher Education Act 2004, which brought in changes to the funding of higher education by introducing a scheme whereby students contributed towards their tuition. Institutions of higher education are established by a Royal Charter and most receive some funding from the Government. However, they are autonomous bodies in which admissions, staffing and teaching are administered independently of the Government. Until 2007 the Secretary of State for Education and Skills was responsible, in principle, for all sectors of education in England. In that year some of these responsibilities, as well as some of those from the Department of Trade and Industry, were transferred to a newly created Department for Innovation, Universities and Skills, subsequently reorganized as the Department for Business, Innovation and Skills. In practice the individual Local Education Authorities (LEAs) have substantial autonomy over the education system in their area. The Secretary of State for Wales is responsible for all non-university education in Wales and, since April 1993, for the University of Wales College, Newport. Government finance for publicly funded higher education institutions is distributed by the Higher Education Funding Council (HEFC) in England, the Scottish Funding Council in Scotland, the Department for Education, Culture and Welsh Language in Wales, and the Department for Employment and Learning in Northern Ireland. Student loans are the main form of support for assistance with living costs for higher education students. The amount of loan depends on where a student lives or studies, the length of the academic year, the course of study, the year of the course and the student's and their family's income. Since the academic year 2000/01 eligible full-time Scottish-domiciled or non-British EU students studying in Scotland no longer pay tuition fees. Publicly funded universities in England, Wales and Northern Ireland may charge domestic students tuition fees for undergraduate courses, subject to a state-imposed limit; for the 2010/11 academic year the cap was set at £3,290. In a highly controversial development that provoked violent popular protests in London, in December 2010 Parliament voted significantly to increase the cap on tuition fees, to £9,000 annually, effective from the 2012/13 academic year. Additional forms of student support include dependant's allowances, young and mature student bursaries, hardship funds, disabled students' allowance and care leavers' grant, and the Student Grant Scheme, which was introduced at the beginning of the 2011/12 academic year in place of the Higher Education Grants Scheme.

The Quality Assurance Agency for Higher Education (founded 1997) is an independent body responsible for the accreditation and quality assurance of higher education in the United Kingdom. The review process in Wales is slightly different from that in England and Northern Ireland, reflecting the new framework for quality assurance that is being developed by the Higher Education Funding Council for Wales.

Students in England, Wales and Northern Ireland enter university upon completion of 13 years of education. Universities set their own standards for admission, which are usually based on a student's performance in their A-Level examinations. However, other awards at level 3 on the National Qualifications Framework (NQF) may also be accepted—for example, the BTEC National Diploma. All undergraduate admissions in the UK (including Scotland) are dealt with by the University and College Admissions Service (UCAS). This organization does not set admission standards, which are established by each individual institution, but it oversees the process of university admission and provides information to students on entry requirements for specific courses. The principal undergraduate degrees are the Bachelor of Arts (BA Hons) and Bachelor of Science (BSc Hons). These are usually full-time, three-year courses but can also be taken as longer part-time courses and may be available through distance learning. In Scotland, where students usually start a year earlier, a full-time first degree generally takes four years for Honours and three years for the broad-based Ordinary degree. The Foundation degree is a new higher education qualification (since 2001) of one year, with a vocational focus. It aims to increase the number of people qualified at higher technician and associate professional level (e.g. legal executives, engineering technicians, personnel officers, laboratory technicians, teaching assistants). Both full- and part-time courses are offered in a variety of work-related subjects and offer progression to a full Honours degree. The Higher National Diploma (HND) or Diploma of Higher Education (Dip HE) are two-year, full-time programmes, and there is the option of turning them into an Honours degree by studying for a further year. Some students go on to do postgraduate studies, usually leading to a Masters degree, such as a Master of Arts (MA), or Master of Science (MSc), or to a Doctorate (PhD). A Masters degree usually lasts one year full-time or two years part-time. A PhD usually lasts three years full-time or six years part-time. Since 2003 a four-year PhD has been introduced.

The Learning and Skills Act 2000 integrated all planning and funding for post-compulsory learning below higher education, including that provided in schools, into one overarching sector under the auspices of the Learning and Skills Council (LSC), which consists of a network of 10 regional directors and local branches. From 1986 onwards the National Council for Vocational Qualifications (NCVQ) established a framework on National Vocational Qualifications (NVQs) in England, Wales and Northern Ireland. In 1997 the Council's work was taken over by the Qualifications and Curriculum Authority. The framework is based on five defined levels of achievement, ranging from Level 1, broadly equating to foundation skills in semi-skilled occupations, to Level 5, equating to professional/senior management occupations. The competence-based system has also been extended in Scotland through a system of Scottish Vocational Qualifications (SVQs) along similar lines to the NVQs. General National Vocational Qualifications (GNVQs), along with General Scottish Vocational Qualifications (GSVQs) have also been introduced. The work of the Qualifications, Curriculum and Assessment Authority for Wales has been taken over by the Welsh Assembly Government.

The principal vocational qualifications now awarded in England, Wales and Northern Ireland are Vocational A-levels, introduced in September 2000, and the new A-Levels in applied subjects. These were designed to replace the Advanced GNVQ, with the aim of improving the standing of vocational qualifications and increasing flexibility within the system. Since September 2002 the Vocational GCSE has also replaced the Foundation, Intermediate and Part One GNVQs. From September 2008 the new 14–19 Diploma has been offered to students aged 14–19 who wish to combine their studies within the national curriculum with applied learning and relevant

work experience. The LSC is responsible for funding the further education sector in England. It is also responsible for funding provision for non-prescribed higher education in further education sector colleges and further education provided by LEA-maintained and other institutions, referred to as 'external institutions'. In Wales, the Department for Education, Culture and Welsh Language funds further education provision made by further education institutions via a third party or sponsored arrangements. The Scottish Funding Council funds further education colleges in Scotland, while the Department for Employment and Learning funds further education colleges in Northern Ireland. Further and higher education may be pursued through vocational or academic courses, on a full-time, part-time or 'sandwich' basis.

Regulatory and Representative Bodies

In the following section entries whose activities cover the whole of the United Kingdom are listed under the General subheading. Those active in specific nations, for example devolved government departments, are then listed separately under the relevant subheadings which appear in alphabetical order.

GOVERNMENT

England

Department for Business, Innovation and Skills: 1 Victoria St, London, SW1H 0ET; Kingsgate House, 66–74 Victoria St, London, SW1E 6SW; tel. (20) 7215-5000; e-mail info@dius.gsi.gov.uk; internet www.bis.gov.uk; Sec. of State Dr VINCE CABLE; Min. of State for Univs and Science DAVID WILLETTS; Min. of State for Further Education, Skills and Lifelong Learning JOHN HAYES; Min. of State for Business and Enterprise MARK PRISK; Permanent Sec. MARTIN DONNELLY (acting); Parliamentary Sec. for Business, Innovation and Skills Baroness WILCOX.

Department for Culture, Media and Sport: 2–4 Cockspur St, London, SW1Y 5DH; tel. (20) 7211-6000; fax (20) 7211-6032; e-mail enquiries@culture.gov.uk; internet www.culture.gov.uk; Sec. of State for Culture, Olympics, Media and Sport JEREMY HUNT; Min. for Tourism and Heritage JOHN PENROSE; Min. for Sport and the Olympics HUGH ROBERTSON; Min. for Culture, Communications and Creative Industries ED VAIZEY; Permanent Sec. JONATHAN STEPHENS.

Department for Education: Castle View House, E Lane, Cheshire, WA7 2GJ; fax (1928) 738248; internet www.education.gov.uk; Sec. of State MICHAEL GOVE; Min. of State for Schools NICK GIBB; Min. of State for Children and Families SARAH TEATHER; Min. of State for Further Education, Skills and Lifelong Learning JOHN HAYES; Parliamentary Under-Sec. of State for Children and Families TIM LOUGHTON; Parliamentary Under-Sec. of State for Schools LORD HILL; Permanent Sec. DAVID BELL.

Northern Ireland

Department of Culture, Arts and Leisure: Causeway Exchange, 1–7 Bedford St, Belfast, BT2 7EG; tel. (28) 9025-8825; fax (28) 9025-3450; e-mail dcal@dcalni.gov.uk; internet www.dcalni.gov.uk; Min. NELSON MCCAUSLAND; Permanent Sec. ROSALIE FLANAGAN.

Department of Education: Rathgael House, Balloo Rd, Bangor, BT19 7PR; tel. (28) 9127-9279; fax (28) 9127-9100; e-mail mail@deni.gov.uk; internet www.deni.gov.uk; Min. CAITRÍONA RUANE; Permanent Sec. PAUL SWEENEY; Deputy Sec. JOHN MCGRATH; Chief Inspector of Education and Training Inspectorate STANLEY GOUDIE.

Department for Employment and Learning: Adelaide House, 39–49 Adelaide St, Belfast, BT2 8FD; tel. (28) 9025-7777; fax (28) 9025-7778; e-mail del@nics.gov.uk; internet www.delni.gov.uk; Min. DANNY KENNEDY; Permanent Sec. ALAN SHANNON.

Wales

Department for Children, Education, Lifelong Learning and Skills: Welsh Assembly Govt, Cathays Park, Cardiff, CF10 3NQ; e-mail dcells.enquiries@wales.gsi.gov.uk; internet new.wales.gov.uk; Dir-Gen. EMYR ROBERTS; Min. LEIGHTON ANDREWS; Permanent Sec. Dr DAME GILLIAN MORGAN.

ACCREDITATION

General

Accreditation Service for International Colleges (ASIC): 13 Yarm Rd, Stockton-on-Tees, TS18 3NJ; tel. (1740) 617-920; fax (1740) 617-929; e-mail info@asic.org.uk; internet www.asic.org.uk; CEO MAURICE DIMMOCK.

British Accreditation Council (BAC): Seventh Fl., 76 Shoe Lane, London, EC4A 3JB; tel. (30) 0330-1400; fax (30) 0330-1401; e-mail info@the-bac.org; internet www.the-bac.org; f. 1984; acts as nat. accrediting body for private post-16 education in the UK; ind., registered charity comprising Ccl and Accreditation Cttee; accreditation by BAC is recognized by the Home Office as a qualifying requirement for instns wishing to enrol visa students; works closely with Ofsted and other bodies to maintain and improve the quality and standard in FE and HE Education; maintains close relationship with the British Council's Accreditation Unit UK and the Open and Distance Learning Quality Ccl; Chair. of Council TIM COX; CEO Dr GINA HOBSON; Head of Inspection Services Prof. STEVE BRISTOW; Head of Professional Services SHIELA NEEDHAM; Head of Accreditation FRANCINE KOUBEL; Chair. of Accreditation Cttee DIANE BILLAM.

British Council Accreditation Unit: Bridgewater House, 58 Whitworth St, Manchester, M1 6BB; tel. (161) 957-7692; fax (161) 957-7074; e-mail accreditation.unit@britishcouncil.org; internet www.britishcouncil.org/accreditation.htm; develops, establishes and maintains quality standards for English language provision for int. students delivered by UK providers; accredits English language providers in the UK; provides an assurance of quality of English language provision accredited under

the Scheme to int. students and their advisors; Man. ELIZABETH MCLAREN.

ENIC/NARIC United Kingdom: UK NARIC, Oriel House, Oriel Rd, Cheltenham, GL50 1XP; tel. (1242) 258-621; fax (1242) 258-611; e-mail info@naric.org.uk; internet www.naric.org.uk; provides information and advice on int. education and training systems and overseas skills and qualifications; incl. vocational, academic and professional qualifications; Head Dr CLOUD BAI-YUN.

Open and Distance Learning Quality Council: 79 Barnfield Wood Rd, Beckenham, BR3 6ST; tel. (20) 8658-8337; e-mail info@odlqc.org.uk; internet www.odlqc.org.uk; f. 1969 as Ccl for the Accreditation of Correspondence Colleges, present name and status 1995; enhances quality in education and training; Chair. JOHN AINSWORTH; Chief Exec. and Sec. to Council Dr DAVID MORLEY; Admin. Man. JULIE FOX.

Qualifications and Curriculum Development Agency (QCDA): 53–55 Butts Rd, Earlsdon Park, Coventry, CV1 3BH; tel. (300) 303-3010; fax (300) 303-3014; e-mail info@qcda.gov.uk; internet www.qcda.gov.uk; f. 1997 by merger of the Nat. Council for Vocational Qualifications (f. 1986) and the School Curriculum and Assessment Authority (f. 1993); a public body, sponsored by the Dept for Children, Schools and Families; maintains and develops the nat. curriculum and associated assessments, tests and examinations; accredits and monitors qualifications in schools, colleges and the workplace; offices in London and Northern Ireland; Chair. CHRISTOPHER TRINICK; CEO LIN HINNIGAN (acting); Exec. Dir of Education MICK WALKER; Exec. Dir for Policy Implementation SYLVIA MCNAMARA.

Scotland

Scottish Qualifications Authority (SQA): The Optima Bldg, 58 Robertson St, Glasgow, G2 8DQ; tel. (303) 333-0330; e-mail customer@sqa.org.uk; internet www.sqa.org.uk; sponsored by the Scottish Exec. Education Dept; nat. body in Scotland responsible for the devt, accreditation, assessment and certification of qualifications other than degrees; SQA qualifications incl. Higher Nat. Certificates and Diplomas, and Scottish Vocational Qualifications; has offices in Glasgow and Dalkeith; Chair. GRAHAM HOUSTON; Chief Exec. Dr JANET BROWN.

FUNDING

General

Arts and Humanities Research Council (AHRC): Polaris House, North Star Ave, Swindon, SN2 1FL; tel. (1793) 416-000; fax (1793) 416-001; e-mail enquiries@ahrc.ac.uk; internet www.ahrc.ac.uk; f. 2005 as successor to the Arts and Humanities Research

Board (f. 1998); operates programmes throughout the UK to support the highest quality research and postgraduate training in the arts and humanities; divided into 8 subject panels (Panel 1: Classics, Ancient History and Archaeology; Panel 2: Visual Arts and Media: practice, history and theory; Panel 3: English Language and Literature; Panel 4: Medieval and Modern History; Panel 5: Modern Languages and Linguistics; Panel 6: Librarianship, Information and Museum Studies; Panel 7: Music and Performing Arts; Panel 8: Philosophy, Law and Religious Studies); has an annual budget of more than £75m.; makes c. 550–600 awards in 7 research schemes and c. 1,500 awards in 3 postgraduate schemes; manages c. £10m. on an agency basis for the HEFCE to fund museums, galleries and other collns in English higher education instns; Chair. Prof. Sir ALAN WILSON; CEO Prof. RICK RYLANCE.

Skills Funding Agency: Cheylesmore House, Quinton Rd, Coventry, CV1 2WT; e-mail info@skillsfundingagency.bis.gov.uk; internet skillsfundingagency.bis.gov.uk; funds and regulates adult further education and skills training in England; Chief Exec. GEOFF RUSSELL.

UK Commission for Employment and Skills: 3 Callflex Business Park, Golden Smithies Lane, Wath-upon-Dearne, S63 7ER; tel. (1709) 774-800; fax (1709) 774-801; e-mail info@ukces.org.uk; internet www.ukces.org.uk; f. 2008; non-departmental public body providing strategic leadership on skills and employment issues in the four nations of the UK; 22 commissioners; Chair. CHARLIE MAYFIELD; Chief Exec. MICHAEL DAVIS.

England

Higher Education Funding Council for England (HEFCE): Northavon House, Coldharbour Lane, Bristol, BS16 1QD; tel. (117) 931-7317; fax (117) 931-7203; e-mail hefce@hefce.ac.uk; internet www.hefce.ac .uk; f. 1992; promotes and funds teaching and research; meets the needs of students, economy and the soc.; Chair. TIM MELVILLE-ROSS; Chief Exec. Sir ALAN LANGLANDS.

Scotland

Scottish Funding Council: Donaldson House, 97 Haymarket Terrace, Edinburgh, EH12 5HD; tel. (131) 313-6500; fax (131) 313-6501; e-mail info@sfc.ac.uk; internet www.sfc .ac.uk; f. 2005; replaced the Scottish Further Education Funding Council and the Scottish Higher Education Funding Council; a Non-Departmental Public Body of the Scottish Exec.; allocates resources for teaching and learning, research and other activities in Scotland's colleges and univs; Chair. JOHN McCLELLAND; Chief Exec. MARK BATHO.

Wales

Higher Education Funding Council for Wales (HEFCW): Linden Court, Ilex Close, Llanishen, Cardiff, CF14 5DZ; tel. (29) 2076-1861; fax (29) 2076-3163; e-mail info@hefcw .ac.uk; internet www.hefcw.ac.uk; f. 1992; distribution of funds for education, research and related activities at higher education instns and courses at further education colleges in Wales; Chair. ROGER THOMAS; Chief Exec. Prof. PHILIP GUMMETT.

NATIONAL BODIES
General

Alliance of Sector Skills Councils (SSCs): Unit 50D, St Olav's Court, London, SE16 2XB; e-mail info@sscalliance.org; internet www.sscalliance.org; f. 2008; 25 mems; collective campaigning org. represent-

ing all of the licensed Sector Skills Councils in the UK; speaks for 90% of the UK's employers on skills issues in 1.7m. UK businesses; the 25 SSCs represent the skills and training interests of small to large business; has offices in London, Edinburgh, Cardiff and Belfast; CEO JOHN McNAMARA.

City & Guilds: 1 Giltspur St, London, EC1A 9DD; tel. (20) 7294-2800; fax (20) 7294-2400; e-mail enquiry@cityandguilds.com; internet www.cityandguilds.com; f. 1878; awards vocational qualifications at all levels in 500 subjects at 8,500 training centres globally; Chair. MICHAEL HOWELL; Dir-Gen. CHRIS JONES.

College of Teachers: Institute of Education, 20 Bedford Way, London, WC1H 0AL; tel. (20) 7911-5536; fax (20) 7631-4865; e-mail enquiries@cot.ac.uk; internet www .collegeofteachers.ac.uk; f. 1846, incorporated by Royal Charter 1849; offers membership to educationists, awards qualifications by examination to teachers and others working in the field of education at Certificate of Educational Studies, Diploma of Educational Studies, Associateship, Licentiateship (equivalent to univ. first degree), Advanced Diploma of Educational Studies and Fellowship levels; 1,630 mems; Patron HRH THE DUKE OF EDINBURGH; Pres. Dr RAPHAEL WILKINS; CEO and Registrar MATTHEW MARTIN; publ. *Education Today* (4 a year).

Council for the Curriculum, Examinations and Assessment: 29 Clarendon Rd, Clarendon Dock, Belfast, BT1 3BG; tel. (28) 9026-1200; fax (28) 9026-1234; e-mail info@ ccea.org.uk; internet www.ccea.org.uk; f. 1994; reports to the Dept of Education of the Northern Ireland Exec.; advises Govt on what should be taught in Northern Ireland's schools and colleges, ensures quality and standard in the qualifications and examinations offered by awarding bodies in Northern Ireland; awards qualifications incl. GCSEs and GCE A- and AS-levels; Chief Exec. GAVIN BOYD.

GuildHE: Woburn House, 20 Tavistock Sq., London, WC1H 9HB; tel. (20) 7387-7711; fax (20) 7387-7712; e-mail info@guildhe.ac.uk; internet www.guildhe.ac.uk; f. 1978 as SCOP (the Standing Conference of Principals Ltd); present name 2006; acts as the rep. org. for higher education colleges, specialist instns and some univs; promotes institutional diversity and distinctiveness within the UK higher education sector; Chair. Prof. RUTH FARWELL; Chief Exec. ANDY WESTWOOD.

Learning and Skills Improvement Service (LSIS): Friars House, Manor House Dr., Coventry, CV1 2TE; tel. and fax (24) 7662-7900; e-mail enquiries@lsis.org.uk; internet www.lsis.org.uk; f. 2008 by merger of the Quality Improvement Agency (QIA) and the Centre for Excellence (CEL); accelerates improvement in the performance of learning and skills sector; builds the sector's capacity for self-improvement; helps the sector respond to strategic reforms; leads the sector quality improvement strategy; Chair. DAME SILVER; Chief Exec. ROB WYE; Deputy Chief Exec. MARGARET BENNETT.

National Conference of University Professors: c/o School of Construction Management and Engineering, Univ. of Reading, POB 219, Whiteknights, Reading, RG6 6AW; tel. (118) 3786753; fax (118) 9313856; e-mail ncup@reading.ac.uk; internet www.reading .ac.uk/ncup; f. 1989; supports univ. profs in carrying out their responsibilities for the maintenance of academic standards; provides a forum for discussion and a corporate voice on matters of concern to the nation's univ. system; improves public understanding of the work of univs; acts as a means of

collecting and disseminating information relevant to univs; 640 univ. profs; Pres. Prof. UGUR TUZUN; Vice-Pres. Prof. JAWED SIDDIQI; Sec. HELEN SPENCE.

National Institute of Adult Continuing Education (England and Wales): Renaissance House, 20 Princess Rd W, Leicester, LE1 6TP; tel. (116) 204-4200; fax (116) 285-4514; e-mail enquiries@niace.org.uk; internet www.niace.org.uk; f. 1921 by incorporation of the British Institute of Adult Education and Nat. Foundation for Adult Education; promotes adult learning; 151 individual mems, 426 corporate mems; 45 hon. life mems; library of 20,000 vols; Pres. DAVID SHERLOCK; CEO ALAN TUCKETT; publs *Adults Learning* (12 a year), *CONCEPT—Journal of Contemporary Community Education Practice Theory* (3 a year), *Convergence* (4 a year), *Journal of Access Policy and Practice* (2 a year), *Journal of Adult and Continuing Education* (2 a year), *Studies in the Education of Adults* (2 a year).

National Society for Education in Art and Design: 3 Mason's Wharf, Corsham, SN13 9FY; tel. (1225) 810134; fax (1225) 812730; e-mail info@nsead.org; internet www .nsead.org; f. 1888; recognized professional body and trade union for prins, lecturers and teachers employed in colleges and schools of art and all specialist teachers of art, craft and design; promotes interests of art, craft and design education in the UK; 2,500 mems; Pres. ANDREW MUTTER; Gen. Sec. LESLEY BUTTERWORTH; publs *AD* (3 a year), *International Journal of Art and Design Education* (3 a year).

Nord Anglia Education: Nord House, Third Ave, Centrum 100, Burton-upon-Trent, DE14 2WD; tel. (1283) 496-500; e-mail enquiries@nordanglia.com; internet www.nordanglia.com; f. 1972; provider of education, training and childcare within the UK and overseas; aims to deliver quality learning experiences to people at every stage of their lives; comprises Int. Schools Div., Learning Services Div. and Leapfrog Day Nurseries; has offices in Burton-upon-Trent, Cheadle and London; CEO ANDREW FITZMAURICE.

Office for Fair Access: Northavon House Coldharbour Lane, Bristol, BS16 1QD; tel. (117) 931-7171; fax (117) 931-7083; e-mail enquiries@offa.org.uk; internet www.offa.org .uk; f. 2004; safeguards and promotes fair access to higher education; Dir Sir MARTIN HARRIS.

Office for Standards in Education, Children's Services and Skills (Ofsted): Royal Exchange Bldgs, St Ann's Sq., Manchester, M2 7LA; tel. (300) 123-4666; e-mail enquiries@ofsted.gov.uk; internet www .ofsted.gov.uk; f. 2007 by merger of the Office for Standards in Education (Ofsted) and the Adult Learning Inspectorate; inspects and regulates care for children and young people; inspects education and training for learners of all ages; reports directly to Parliament (and to the Lord Chancellor about children and family courts administration); has offices in Bristol, London, Manchester, and Nottingham; Chair. Baroness SALLY MORGAN; Chief Inspector CHRISTINE GILBERT; publ. *Ofsted News* (online).

Quality Assurance Agency for Higher Education: Southgate House, Southgate St, Gloucester, GL1 1UB; tel. (1452) 557-000; fax (1452) 557-070; e-mail comms@qaa.ac.uk; internet www.qaa.ac.uk; f. 1997; ind. body funded by subscriptions from univs and colleges of higher education, and through contracts with the main higher education funding bodies; safeguards public interest in sound standards of higher education qualifications, and encourages continuous improvement in the management of the quality of higher education; has offices in Gloucester and Glasgow; Chair. Sir RODNEY BROOKE; Chief Exec. ANTHONY MCCLARAN; publ. *QAA News* (24 a year, online).

UK Council for Graduate Education: Lichfield Centre, The Friary, Lichfield, WS13 6QG; tel. (1543) 308-602; fax (1543) 308-604; e-mail ukcge@ukcge.ac.uk; internet www.ukcge.ac.uk; f. 1994; promotes distinct identity for graduate education and research in higher education; 125 full institutional mems, 8 assoc. institutional mems, 9 individual mems; Chair Prof. MALCOLM MCCRAE; Principal Officer CAROLYN RAVEN.

Universities and Colleges Admissions Service (UCAS): POB 28, Cheltenham, GL52 3LZ; Rosehill, New Barn Lane, Cheltenham, GL52 3LZ; tel. (1242) 222444; e-mail enquiries@ucas.ac.uk; internet www.ucas.com; manages applications to higher education courses in the UK; Chair. Prof. Sir ROBERT BURGESS; Chief Exec. MARY CURNOCK COOK.

Universities UK: Woburn House, 20 Tavistock Sq., London, WC1H 9HQ; tel. (20) 7419-4111; fax (20) 7388-8649; e-mail info@universitiesuk.ac.uk; internet www.universitiesuk.ac.uk; f. 2000. fmrly Cttee of Vice-Chancellors and Principals of the Univs of the UK (CVCP, f. 1918); promotes, encourages and develops British univs, and promotes understanding of the role, achievements and objectives of univs; 132 exec. heads of British univs; Pres. Prof. ERIC THOMAS; Chief Exec. NICOLA DANDRIDGE.

University and College Union: Carlow St, London, NW1 7LH; tel. (20) 7756-2500; fax (20) 7756-2501; e-mail hq@ucu.org.uk; internet www.ucu.org.uk; f. 2006, merger of Asscn of Univ. Teachers (f. 1919) and Nat. Asscn for Teachers in Further and Higher Education (f. 1976); Pres. ALAN WHITAKER; Gen. Sec. SALLY HUNT; publs *Environmental news* (online, irregular), *Equality News* (6 a year), *FE news* (online), *HE news* (online), *Health and safety news* (online, 12 a year), *UC* (4 a year).

England

General Teaching Council for England: Victoria Sq. House, Victoria Sq., Birmingham, B2 4AJ; tel. (370) 001-0308; fax (121) 345-0100; e-mail info@gtce.org.uk; internet www.gtce.org.uk; f. 2000; ind. body that aims to help improve standards of teaching and the quality of learning; maintains a register of more than 500,000 qualified teachers in England and regulates the teaching profession in the public interest; the GTC is the awarding body for qualified teacher status (QTS) in England; has offices in Birmingham and London; Chief Exec. ALAN MEYRICK; publ. *Teaching* (3 a year).

Independent Schools Inspectorate: CAP House, 9–12 Long Lane, London, EC1A 9HA; tel. (20) 7600-0100; fax (20) 7776-8849; e-mail info@isi.net; internet www.isi.net; responsible under Statute for inspecting 1,200 ind. schools in England that are mems of the Ind. Schools Ccl; promotes and safeguards the welfare and education of children in these schools through inspections; inspects British curriculum schools worldwide; Chair. JUNE TAYLOR; Chief Inspector CHRISTINE RYAN.

Northern Ireland

Colleges Northern Ireland: Millennium Community Outreach Centre, Springfield Educational Village, 400 Springfield Rd, Belfast, BT12 7DU; tel. (28) 9090-0060; e-mail info@anic.ac.uk; internet www.anic.ac.uk; f. 1998 as Association of Northern Ireland's Colleges; liaison with Northern Ireland Assembly, govt depts.

Education and Training Inspectorate: Inspection Services Br., Dept of Education, Rathgael House, 43 Balloo Rd, Bangor, Co Down, BT19 7PR; tel. (28) 9127-9726; fax (28) 9127-9721; e-mail inspectionservices@deni.gov.uk; internet www.etini.gov.uk; provides inspection services for, and information about the quality of education in N Ireland to, the Dept of Education, Dept of Culture, Arts and Leisure, and Dept for Employment and Learning; promotes highest possible standards of learning, teaching and achievement throughout education, training and youth sectors; Chief Inspector STANLEY GOUDIE.

Scotland

Educational Institute of Scotland: 46 Moray Pl., Edinburgh, EH3 6BH; tel. (131) 225-6244; fax (131) 220-3151; e-mail enquiries@eis.org.uk; internet www.eis.org.uk; f. 1847; 60,110 mems; Pres. ALAN MUNRO; Gen. Sec. RONALD A. SMITH; publ. *Scottish Educational Journal.*

Her Majesty's Inspectorate of Education: Denholm House, Almondvale Business Park, Almondvale Way, Livingston EH54 6GA; tel. (1506) 600-200; e-mail enquiries@hmie.gov.uk; internet www.hmie.gov.uk; ind. agency accountable to the Scottish mins; promotes and contributes to sustainable improvements in standards, quality and achievements for all learners in a Scottish education system that is inclusive; Sr Chief Inspector BILL MAXWELL.

Scotland's Colleges: Argyll Court, Castle Business Park, Stirling, FK9 4TY; tel. (1786) 892-000; fax (1786) 892-001; e-mail info@scotcol.ac.uk; internet www.scotlandscolleges.ac.uk; f. 2009, merger of sector support functions; supports, represents and promotes the Scottish college sector; Chair. BRIAN KEEGAN; Chief Exec. JOHN HENDERSON.

Universities Scotland: 53 Hanover St, Edinburgh, EH2 2PJ; tel. (131) 226-1111; fax (131) 226-1100; e-mail info@universities-scotland.ac.uk; internet www.universities-scotland.ac.uk; 20 mem. univs and other instns; Convener Prof. Sir TIMOTHY O'SHEA (acting); Dir ALASTAIR SIM.

Wales

Estyn: Anchor Court, Keen Rd, Cardiff, CF24 5JW; tel. (29) 2044-6446; fax (29) 2044-6448; e-mail enquiries@estyn.gov.uk; internet www.estyn.gov.uk; office of Her Majesty's Inspectorate for Education and Training in Wales; Chief Inspector ANN KEANE.

Higher Education Wales: 2 Caspian Point, Caspian Way, Cardiff Bay, CF10 4DQ; tel. (29) 2044-8020; fax (29) 2048-9531; e-mail hew@hew.ac.uk; f. 1996; provides an expert resource on all aspects of higher education in Wales; Chair. Prof. NOEL LLOYD; Dir AMANDA WILKINSON; Deputy Dir GREG WALKER.

Learned Societies

GENERAL

Academy of Social Sciences: 30 Tabernacle St, London, EC2A 4UE; tel. (20) 7330-0898; e-mail administrator@acss.org.uk; internet www.acss.org.uk; f. 1999; composed of individual academicians and learned socs; responds to govt and other consultations on behalf of the social science community; organizes meetings and seminars; sponsors schemes to promote social sciences; 400 academicians, 40 mem. learned socs; Exec. Dir CAROLINE BUCKLOW; publs *21st Century Society* (3 a year), *eBulletin* (10 a year).

British Academy: 10–11 Carlton House Terrace, London, SW1Y 5AH; tel. (20) 7969-5200; fax (20) 7969-5300; e-mail chiefexec@britac.ac.uk; internet www.britac.ac.uk; f. 1902; sections of Classical Antiquity, of African and Oriental Studies, of Theology and Religious Studies, of Linguistics and Philology, of Early Modern Languages and Literature, of Modern Languages, Literature and Other Media, of Archaeology, of Medieval Studies: History and Literature, of Early Modern History to 1800, of Modern History from 1800, of History of Art and Music, of Philosophy, of Law, of Economics and Economic History, of Social Anthropology and Geography, of Sociology, Demography and Social Statistics, of Political Studies: Political Theory, Government and International Relations, of Psychology; 900 mems; Pres. Sir ADAM ROBERTS; Chief Exec. ROBIN JACKSON; publ. *Proceedings.*

British Council: 10 Spring Gardens, London, SW1A 2BN; tel. (20) 7930-8466; fax (20) 7389-6347; e-mail general.enquiries@britishcouncil.org; internet www.britishcouncil.org; f. 1934; promotes a wider knowledge of the United Kingdom and the English language abroad and develops closer cultural relations with other countries; operates in 109 countries; maintains English Teaching Centres in 53 countries, and 209 overseas libraries and information centres; arranges for the invigilation overseas of British examinations and, in collaboration with the University of Cambridge Local Examinations Syndicate, offers service to test English-language proficiency of foreign students seeking admission to British instns; grants scholarships and other awards to overseas scholars and research workers to enable them to pursue their studies in the United Kingdom, and is responsible for administering in the United Kingdom a number of Fellowships schemes on behalf of other bodies including the UN and the Foreign and Commonwealth Office; promotes liaison between scientists in the United Kingdom and abroad and provides information on British science, medicine and technology; promotes British writers, actors and other artists abroad; organizes overseas exhibitions of British books and periodicals; Chair. NEIL KINNOCK; Chief Exec. MARTIN DAVIDSON.

Commonwealth Institute: New Zealand House, 80 Haymarket, London, SW1Y 4TE; tel. (20) 7024-9822; fax (20) 7024-9833; e-mail information@commonwealth-institute.org; internet www.commonwealth.org.uk; aims to advance primary and secondary education across the Commonwealth; Company Sec. JUDY CURRY.

Attached Centre:

Centre for Commonwealth Education: jt venture between the Commonwealth Institute and the Faculty of Education at the University of Cambridge; Dir Prof. CHRISTOPHER COLCLOUGH.

English-Speaking Union (of the Commonwealth): Dartmouth House, 37 Charles St, Berkeley Sq., London, W1J 5ED; tel. (20) 7529-1550; fax (20) 7495-6108; e-mail esu@esu.org; internet www.esu.org; f. 1918; int. voluntary org., which through its educational programmes is devoted to the promotion of understanding and friendship; 35,000 mems worldwide; library of 3,000 vols; Pres. HRH PRINCE PHILIP, DUKE OF EDINBURGH; Chair. Lord HUNT OF WIRRAL; Dir-Gen. MICHAEL LAKE; publ. *Dialogue* (4 a year).

Northern Ireland Foundation: Carnegie Bldg, 121 Donegall Rd, Belfast, BT12 5JL; tel. (28) 9089-1799; e-mail info@nifoundation .net; internet nifoundation.net; f. 2008; private, charitable and ind. org.; addresses the legacy of conflict in Northern Ireland by developing leadership programmes and promoting relevant int. research; Chair. JAMES HOLMES; Dir ALLAN LEONARD; Sec. QUINTIN OLIVER.

Royal Society: 6–9 Carlton House Terrace, London, SW1Y 5AG; tel. (20) 7451-2500; fax (20) 7930-2170; e-mail info@royalsoc.ac.uk; internet www.royalsoc.ac.uk; f. 1660; science, technology and engineering; 1,410 mems (1,280 fellows, 130 foreign mems); library: see Libraries and Archives; Pres. Prof. MARTIN REES, LORD REES OF LUDLOW; Vice-Pres. Prof. MARTIN TAYLOR; Biological Sec. Prof. DAVID READ; Foreign Sec. Prof. Dame JULIA HIGGINS; Physical Sec. Prof. MARTIN TAYLOR; Exec. Sec. STEPHEN COX; publs *Biology Letters* (4 a year), *Journal of the Royal Society Interface* (4 a year), *Notes and Records*, *Philosophical Transactions*, *Proceedings*.

Royal Society for the Encouragement of Arts, Manufactures and Commerce (RSA): 8 John Adam St, London, WC2N 6EZ; tel. (20) 7930-5115; e-mail general@rsa .org.uk; internet www.thersa.org; f. 1754; promotes arts, manufactures and commerce; 27,000 fellows; library of 8,000 vols, 11,000 MSS; Pres. HRH Prince PHILIP, DUKE OF EDINBURGH; Chair. LUKE JOHNSON; Chief Exec. MATTHEW TAYLOR; publ. *Journal* (4 a year).

Royal Society of Edinburgh: 22–26 George St, Edinburgh, EH2 2PQ; tel. (131) 240-5000; fax (131) 240-5024; e-mail rse@ royalsoced.org.uk; internet www.royalsoced .org.uk; f. 1783; arts and sciences, business and enterprise research; enterprise fellowships; policy advice to govts, young people's programme, learned journals; 1,527 fellows (1,402 ordinary, 64 hon., 61 corresp.); Pres. Sir JOHN ARBUTHNOTT; Gen. Sec. Prof. ALICE BROWN; Chief Exec. Dr WILLIAM DUNCAN; publs *Earth and Environmental Science Transactions of the Royal Society of Edinburgh* (earth and environmental sciences, 4 a year), *Proceedings of the Royal Society of Edinburgh, Section A: Mathematics* (mathematics, 6 a year).

Saltire Society: 9 Fountain Close, 22 High St, Edinburgh, EH1 1TF; tel. (131) 556-1836; e-mail saltire@saltiresociety.org.uk; internet www.saltiresociety.org.uk; f. 1936; conserves and fosters Scottish way of life through arts and crafts, architecture, education, literature; brs throughout Scotland; 1,200 mems; Pres. Lord CULLEN OF WHITEKIRK; Exec. Dir JIM TOUGH.

Sport and Recreation Alliance: SRA, Burwood House, 14–16 Caxton St, London, SW1H 0QT; tel. (20) 7976-3900; fax (20) 7976-3901; e-mail info@sportandrecreation .org.uk; internet www.sportandrecreation .org.uk; f. 1935, fmrly Central Ccl of Recreative Physical Training; promotes, protects and provides for sport and recreation sector; 320 nat. governing and rep. bodies; Pres. HRH PRINCE EDWARD, EARL OF WESSEX; Chair., Bd of Dirs ANDY REED; Chief Exec. TIM LAMB; Treas. MIKE POWER.

AGRICULTURE, FISHERIES AND VETERINARY SCIENCE

Agricultural Economics Society: AES Secretariat, Tangley Mount, Tangley, Andover, SP11 0SH; tel. (1264) 730872; fax (1264) 730869; e-mail aesoc@btopenworld .com; internet www.aes.ac.uk; f. 1926 to promote the study and teaching of all disciplines relevant to agricultural economics as they apply to the agricultural, food and related industries; 500 mems; Pres. ALLAN BUCKWELL; publs *EuroChoices* (3 a year), *Journal of Agricultural Economics* (3 a year).

British Society of Animal Science: POB 3, Penicuik, EH26 0RZ; tel. (131) 445-4508; fax (131) 535-3103; e-mail bsas@sac.ac.uk; internet www.bsas.org.uk; f. 1944; UK mem. org. of the European Asscn for Animal Production; 1,000 mems; Pres. CHRIS WARKUP; Chief Exec. MIKE STEELE; publs *Advances in Animal Biosciences* (1 a year), *ANIMAL* (12 a year).

British Society of Soil Science: BSSS Administrative Centre, Bldg 53, Cranfield University, Cranfield MK43 0AL; tel. (1224) 752983; fax (1224) 752970; e-mail admin@ soils.org.uk; internet www.soils.org.uk; f. 1947; advances the study of the soil itself and its management in agriculture, forestry, environmental matters and other fields; promotes public engagement with soil science; disseminates information and encourages discussion of soil science in a variety of fora; provides support for potential soil scientists and those on the boundary of soil science at all stages of their career; promotes soil science as a professional discipline; promotes the adoption of appropriate professional standards in all work involving soil science through the the publication of professional competency statements for use by government and industry when conducting or contracting out soil science work; provides certification and accreditation of members and offers soil scientists a route to qualification as chartered scientists; 950 mems; Exec. Officer Dr KATHRYN ALLTON; publs *European Journal of Soil Science* (4 a year), *Soil Use and Management* (4 a year).

British Veterinary Association: 7 Mansfield St, London, W1G 9NQ; tel. (20) 7636-6541; fax (20) 7436-2970; e-mail bvahq@bva .co.uk; internet www.bva.co.uk; f. 1881; promotes and supports the interests of mems, and the animals under their care, and develops and maintains channels of communication not least with govt, parliamentarians and the media; 11,000 mems; Pres. Dr DAVID CATLOW; publs *In Practice* (10 a year), *Off The Record* (10 a year), *The Veterinary Record* (52 a year).

Institute of Chartered Foresters: 59 George St, Edinburgh, EH2 2JG; tel. (131) 240-1425; fax (131) 240-1424; e-mail icf@ charteredforesters.org; internet www .charteredforesters.org; f. 1925, Royal Charter 1982; maintains and improves the standards of practice and understanding of forestry; awards chartered forester status (MICFor and FICFor); 1,300 mems; Exec. Dir SHIREEN CHAMBERS; publs *Forestry* (5 a year), *The Chartered Forester* (members' magazine, 4 a year).

Institution of Agricultural Engineers (IAgrE): Bullock Bldg (Bldg 53), Univ. Way, Cranfield, Bedford, MK43 0GH; tel. (1234) 750876; fax (1234) 751319; e-mail secretary@iagre.org; internet www.iagre.org; f. 1938; professional body for all involved in land-based sectors incl. agriculture, horticulture, forestry, amenities and the environment; awards professional qualifications; administers the Land Based Technician Accreditation Scheme (LTA); 2,100 mems; Chief Exec. CHRISTOPHER R. WHETNALL; publs *Biosystems Engineering* (12 a year), *Landwards* (4 a year).

Royal Agricultural Society of England: Stoneleigh Park, CV8 2LZ; tel. (24) 7669-6969; fax (24) 7669-6900; e-mail info@rase .org.uk; internet www.rase.org.uk; f. 1838 (Royal Charter 1840); 11,000 mems; established Nat. Agricultural Centre at Stoneleigh in 1963 to promote advancements in British Agriculture and disseminate information; organizes the Royal Show; arranges regular courses, confs.; agricultural history library; Chief Exec. DAVID GARDNER; publ. *RASE Journal* (1 a year).

Royal College of Veterinary Surgeons: Belgravia House, 62–64 Horseferry Rd, London, SW1P 2AF; tel. (20) 7222-2001; fax (20) 7222-2004; e-mail admin@rcvs.org.uk; internet www.rcvs.org.uk; f. 1844; governing body of the veterinary profession in the United Kingdom; maintains the Statutory Registers and the discipline of the profession and has supervisory functions in relation to veterinary education in British univs; possesses the foremost veterinary library in the United Kingdom, open to veterinary surgeons and *bona fide* scientific workers; 22,000 mems; Pres. Prof. SANDY TREES; Registrar JANE C. HERN; publ. *Directory of Veterinary Practices* (1 a year).

Royal Forestry Society: 102 High St, Tring, Herts, HP23 4AF; tel. (1442) 822028; fax (1442) 890395; e-mail rfshq@rfs.org.uk; internet www.rfs.org.uk; f. 1882 as the English Arboricultural Soc. to advance the knowledge and practice of forestry and arboriculture, and to disseminate knowledge of the sciences on which they are based; 4,000 mems; library of 1,500 vols; Chief Exec. Dr J. E. JACKSON; publs *E-news* (electronic, fortnightly), *Quarterly Journal of Forestry*.

Royal Highland and Agricultural Society of Scotland: Royal Highland Centre, Ingliston, Edinburgh, EH28 8NF; tel. (131) 335-6200; fax (131) 333-5236; e-mail info@ rhass.org.uk; internet www.rhass.org.uk; f. 1784, inc. by Royal Charter 1787, for the promotion of agriculture and related industries and education; 14,000 mems; library of 6,000 vols; Chief Exec. STEPHEN HUTT; Sec. ADELE THOMSON.

Royal Horticultural Society: Exhibition Halls, Library and Offices, 80 Vincent Square, London, SW1P 2PE; tel. (20) 7834-4333; e-mail info@rhs.org.uk; internet www .rhs.org.uk; Gardens and School, Wisley, Woking, Surrey; Gardens at Rosemoor, Great Torrington, Devon, Hyde Hall, Chelmsford, Essex and Harlow Carr, Harrogate, North Yorkshire; f. 1804; 230,000 mems; library of 50,000 vols (Lindley Library); Pres. Sir RICHARD CARE POLE; Dir-Gen. Dr ANDREW COLQUHOUN; Sec. ANDREW SMITH; publs *The Garden* (12 a year), *The New Plantsman*, *Proceedings*, *Wisley Handbooks*, etc.

Royal Scottish Forestry Society: Potholm, Langholm, DG13 0NE; tel. and fax (1387) 383845; e-mail administrator@rsfs.org .uk; internet www.rsfs.org; f. 1854, fmrly known as The Royal Scottish Arboricultural Soc., present name 1930; meetings; seminars; forest visits; discussion groups; 1,400 mems; Pres. CHRISTOPHER BADENOCH; Dir RICHARD KAY; publ. *Scottish Forestry* (4 a year).

Royal Welsh Agricultural Society: Llanelwedd, Builth-Wells, Powys, LD2 3SY; tel. (1982) 553683; fax (1982) 553563; e-mail requests@rwas.co.uk; internet www.rwas.co .uk; f. 1904; organizes Royal Welsh Show, Royal Welsh Agricultural Winter Fair and Royal Welsh Smallholder and Garden Festival; promotes agriculture, horticulture, forestry and conservation, particularly in Wales; 16,500 mems; Chief Exec. D. WALTERS; publ. *Royal Welsh Journal* (1 a year).

Society of Dairy Technology: POB 12, Appleby in Westmorland, CA16 6YJ; tel. (1768) 354034; fax (1768) 352546; e-mail execdirector@sdt.org; internet www.sdt.org; f. 1943; supports advancement of dairy technology and encourages technical education and scientific enquiry in the dairy industry; organizes confs. and seminars; publishes multi-author technical series; 400 mems; Pres. Dr LIZ WHITLEY; Exec. Dir MAURICE WALTON; publ. *International Journal of Dairy Technology* (4 a year).

ARCHITECTURE AND TOWN PLANNING

Architectural Association (Inc.): 34–36 Bedford Sq., London, WC1B 3ES; tel. (20) 7887-4000; fax (20) 7414-0782; internet www .aaschool.ac.uk; f. 1847; serves the AA School of Architecture, offers facilities for architectural studies to undergraduates and graduates; professional courses; research programmes; 3,200 mems worldwide; library of 45,500 vols, 49,000 classified periodical articles, 150,000 slides; Pres. ERIC PARRY; Company Sec. KATHLEEN FORMOSA; publs *AA Files* (3 a year), *Projects Review* (1 a year).

Association of Building Engineers: Lutyens House, Billing Brook Rd, Northampton, NN3 8NW; tel. (1604) 404121; fax (1604) 784220; e-mail building.engineers@ abe.org.uk; internet www.abe.org.uk; f. 1925; trains, examines and qualifies professional body for those specializing in the technology of building; 7,000 mems; Chief Exec. Dr JOHN HOOPES; Deputy Chief Exec. KATE ILOTT; Hon. Sec. DAVID B. SMITH; publ. *Building Engineer* (12 a year).

Campaign to Protect Rural England (CPRE): 128 Southwark St, London, SE1 0SW; tel. (20) 7981-2800; fax (20) 7981-2899; e-mail info@cpre.org.uk; internet www.cpre .org.uk; f. 1926; nat. charity that helps people to protect and enhance their local countryside; 60,000 mems; Pres. Sir MAX HASTINGS; Dir KATE PARMINTER; publ. *Countryside Voice* (3 a year).

Church Buildings Council: Church House, Great Smith St, London, SW1P 3AZ; tel. (20) 7898-1863; fax (20) 7898-1881; e-mail enquiries.ccb@churchofengland.org; internet www.churchcare.co.uk; f. 1921; maintains highest standards in preservation, restoration and alteration of Anglican churches and their contents by making available sound artistic and technical advice; library of 12,000 vols; Chair. ANNE SLOMAN; Sec. JANET GOUGH.

Civic Society Initiative: Unit 101, 82 Wood St, The Tea Factory, Liverpool, L1 4DQ; tel. (151) 708-9920; e-mail admin@ civicsocietyinitiative.org.uk; internet www .civicsocietyinitiative.org.uk; f. 2009, following closure of the Civic Trust; ensures the civic society movement has a strong national voice and an effective support structure; registered charity; supports over 1,000 local amenity societies; Dir TONY BURTON; Coordinator IAN HARVEY; publ. *Own the Future*.

Landscape Institute: 33 Great Portland St, London, W1W 8QG; tel. (20) 7299-4500; fax (20) 7299-4501; e-mail mail@ landscapeinstitute.org; internet www .landscapeinstitute.org; f. 1929; objects: advancement of the art of landscape architecture, theory and practice of landscape design, promotion of research and education therein, maintenance of a high standard of professional qualification, promotion of the highest standard of professional service; the Institute is the chartered institute in the UK for landscape architects, incorporating designers, scientists and managers; 5,194 mems (comprising students, assocs, mems and fellows); library of 15,313 vols, journal articles and landscape drawings; visits to library and archive by non-members by appointment; Chief Exec. ALASTAIR McCAPRA; publs *Landscape* (4 a year), *Landscape Journal Online* (24 a year).

London Society: Mortimer Wheeler House, 46 Eagle Wharf Rd, London, N1 7ED; tel. (20) 7253-9400; e-mail info@londonsociety.org.uk; internet www.londonsociety.org.uk; f. 1912; encourages a wider concern for the beauty of the capital city and the preservation of its charms; library: colln of books and MSS incl. journals since 1912, now housed at Mortimer Wheeler House; 848 mems; Pres. HRH THE DUKE OF GLOUCESTER; Chair. Exec. Cttee FRANK KELSALL; Hon. Sec. PATRICK GASKELL-TAYLOR; Admin. JANE JEPHCOTE; publ. *Journal* (2 a year).

National Trust for Places of Historic Interest or Natural Beauty: 36 Queen Anne's Gate, London SW1H 9AS; tel. (20) 7222-9251; fax (20) 7222-5097; e-mail enquiries@thenationaltrust.org.uk; internet www.nationaltrust.org.uk; f. 1895 for the purpose of promoting the permanent preservation of, and public access to, land of natural beauty and buildings of historic interest; 2.3m. mems; Chair. Sir SIMON JENKINS; Dir-Gen. FIONA REYNOLDS; publ. *Members' and Visitors' Handbook*.

National Trust for Scotland: Wemyss House, 28 Charlotte Sq., Edinburgh, EH2 4ET; tel. (131) 243-9300; fax (131) 243-9301; e-mail information@nts.org.uk; internet www.nts.org.uk; f. 1931; promotes the preservation of places of historical or architectural interest or natural beauty in Scotland; 250,000 mems.

Open Spaces Society: 25A Bell St, Henley-on-Thames, RG9 2BA; tel. (1491) 573535; fax (1491) 573051; e-mail hq@oss.org.uk; internet www.oss.org.uk; f. 1865; campaigns to protect common land, village greens, open spaces and public paths, and people's right to enjoy them; 2,300 mems; Chair. TIM CROWTHER; Gen. Sec. KATE ASHBROOK; publ. *Open Space* (3 a year).

Oxford Preservation Trust: 10 Turn Again Lane, Oxford, OX1 1QL; tel. (1865) 242918; fax (1865) 246706; e-mail info@oxfordpreservation.org.uk; internet www.oxfordpreservation.org.uk; f. 1927; preserves and enhances benefit of public amenities of Oxford and its surroundings; takes an active role in local planning; runs an annual Award Scheme to acknowledge projects that contribute to the conservation or enhancement of the built or natural environment; land ownership; membership and education programmes; restoration projects; small grant making programmes; 1,000 mems; Chair. Prof. ROGER AINSWORTH; Dir DEBORAH DANCE.

ROOM—the National Council for Housing and Planning: 41 Botolph Lane, London, EC3R 8DL; tel. (20) 7929-9494; fax (20) 7929-9490; e-mail room@rtpi.org.uk; internet www.room.org.uk; f. 1900 as the National Housing Reform Council to secure the abolition of unhealthy and socially undesirable houses; a campaigning organization with mems in both public and private sectors, seeking to promote the best standards of housing and planning; and to disseminate information on housing, planning and regeneration; 600 mems; Chair. CATHERINE CHATER; publ. *Axis* (6 a year).

Royal Incorporation of Architects in Scotland: 15 Rutland Sq., Edinburgh, EH1 2BE; tel. (131) 229-7545; fax (131) 228-2188; e-mail info@rias.org.uk; internet www.rias .org.uk; f. 1916 as a professional org.; 4,000 mems; Pres. DAVID DUNBAR; Sec. and Treas. NEIL BAXTER; publ. *Practice Information* (4 a year).

Royal Institute of British Architects: 66 Portland Pl., London, W1B 1AD; tel. (20) 7580-5533; fax (20) 7255-1541; e-mail info@ riba.org; internet www.architecture.com; f.

1834; 28,000 chartered mems; library: see entry for British Architectural Library; Pres. ANGELA BRADY; Chief Exec. HARRY RICH; publs *Directory of Practices* (1 a year), *RIBA Journal* (12 a year).

Royal Institution of Chartered Surveyors: 12 Great George St, Parliament Sq., London, SW1P 3AD; tel. (20) 7033-1600; fax (20) 7334-3811; e-mail contactrics@rics.org; internet www.rics.org; f. 1868; 140,000 mems; library of 35,000 vols; Chief Exec. LOUIS ARMSTRONG; Chief Operating Officer SEAN TOMPKINS; publ. *RICS Business* (12 a year).

Royal Town Planning Institute: 41 Botolph Lane, London EC3R 8DL; tel. (20) 7929-9494; fax (20) 7929-9490; e-mail online@rtpi.org.uk; internet www.rtpi.org .uk; f. 1914 to further the science and art of town planning for the benefit of the public; 20,000 mems; library of 10,000 vols; Pres. JIM CLAYDON; Sec.-Gen. ROBERT UPTON; publs *Planning Theory and Practice* (4 a year), *RTPI News* (52 a year).

Society for the Protection of Ancient Buildings: 37 Spital Sq., London, E1 6DY; tel. (20) 7377-1644; fax (20) 7247-5296; e-mail info@spab.org.uk; internet www.spab .org.uk; f. 1877 by William Morris; prevents the destruction of old bldgs and advises on their conservative repair through courses, campaigns, etc.; c. 8,500 mems; Pres. THE DUKE OF GRAFTON; Dir MATTHEW SLOCOMBE.

Town and Country Planning Association: 17 Carlton House Terrace, London, SW1Y 5AS; tel. (20) 7930-8903; fax (20) 7930-3280; e-mail tcpa@tcpa.org.uk; internet www .tcpa.org.uk; f. 1899 to campaign for garden cities; now concerns itself with all aspects of planning and the environment; campaigns for improvement to the environment by effective planning, community participation and sustainable development; holds conferences and study tours; 1,000 mems; Chair. LEE SHOSTAK; Chief Exec. GIDEON AMOS; publ. *Town and Country Planning* (11 a year).

Victorian Society: 1 Priory Gardens, Bedford Park, London, W4 1TT; tel. (20) 8994-1019; fax (20) 8747-5899; e-mail admin@ victoriansociety.org.uk; internet www .victoriansociety.org.uk; f. 1958; promotes Victorian and Edwardian architecture; studies the art and built environment of the period; makes suggestions to the English heritage for bldgs to be added to the statutory list; judges applications for listed bldgs to be demolished or altered; represents at public inquiries on preservation of bldgs; 3,500 mems; Chair. Prof. HILARY GRAINGER; Dir Dr IAN DUNGAVELL; publs *Journal* (irregular), *The Victorian Magazine* (3 a year).

BIBLIOGRAPHY, LIBRARY SCIENCE AND MUSEOLOGY

Arlis UK and Ireland/Art Libraries Society of United Kingdom and Ireland: Nat. Art Library, Victoria and Albert Museum, Cromwell Rd, S Kensington, London, B60 2NE; tel. (207) 9422317; fax (1527) 579298; internet www.arlis.org.uk; f. 1969; aims to promote art librarianship particularly by acting as a forum for the interchange of information and materials; 500 mems (250 UK and Ireland, 250 overseas); Chair. JUDITH PREECE; Business Man. LORRAINE BLACKMAN; publs *Art Libraries Journal* (4 a year), *Directory* (1 a year), *News-sheet* (6 a year).

Aslib (The Association for Information Management): Howard House, Wagon Lane, Bingley, BD16 1WA; tel. (12) 7477-7700; fax (12) 7478-5201; e-mail support@ aslib.com; internet www.aslib.com; f. 1924; asscn of industrial and commercial firms, govt depts, research asscns and instns, univs and learned socs in the UK and 40 other countries; provides consultancy; in-house training, short courses on all aspects of information work; organizes nat. and int. confs and meetings; 600 corporate mems and subscriber orgs; library: see under Libraries and Archives; Man. Dir Dir JOHN PETERS; Dir REBECCA MARSH; publs *Aslib Book Guide* (12 a year), *Aslib Proceedings* (10 a year), *Current Awareness Abstracts* (10 a year), *Library Hi Tech News incorporating Online and CD Notes* (10 a year), *Managing Information* (10 a year, print and online), *Performance, Measurement and Metrics* (3 a year), *Program* (4 a year), *Records Management Journal* (12 a year), *The Journal of Documentation* (5 a year).

Association of Independent Libraries: c/o The Leeds Library, 18 Commercial St, Leeds, LS1 6AL; tel. (113) 245-3071; e-mail enquiries@theleedslibrary.org.uk; internet www.independentlibraries.co.uk; f. 1989; 30 mems; Pres. ROBERT ANDERSON.

Bibliographical Society: c/o Institute of English Studies, Univ. of London, Senate House, Malet St, London, WC1E 7HU; tel. (20) 7862-8679; fax (20) 7862-8720; e-mail secretary@bibsoc.org.uk; internet www.bibsoc.org; f. 1892; promotes study and research in the fields of historical, analytical, descriptive and textual bibliography and the history of printing, publishing, bookselling, bookbinding and collecting; holds meetings, at which papers are read and discussed; prints and publishes a journal and books concerned with bibliography; maintains bibliographical library; awards medals for services to bibliography, and grants and bursaries to support bibliographical research; 1,000 mems; Pres. Dr DAVID PEARSON; Hon. Sec. MARGARET L. FORD; publ. *The Library* (4 a year).

Booktrust: Book House, 45 East Hill, London, SW18 2QZ; tel. (20) 8516-2977; internet www.booktrust.org.uk; ind. educational charity; f. 1925 as The Nat. Book Council to extend the use and enjoyment of books of all kinds; provides book lists and a book information service; administers literary prizes, the Children's Laureate, Children's Book Week and Bookstart (books for babies); 1,000 mems; Pres. DORIS LESSING; Chief Exec. CHRIS MEADE.

Cambridge Bibliographical Society: Univ. Library, Cambridge, CB3 9DR; tel. (1223) 333123; fax (1223) 333160; f. 1949; historical bibliography and history of the book trade; lectures and visits; 450 mems; Hon. Sec. TIM EGGINGTON; Treas. JOHN HALL; publs *Monographs* (irregular), *Transactions* (1 a year).

Chartered Institute of Library and Information Professionals (CILIP): 7 Ridgmount St, London, WC1E 7AE; tel. (20) 7255-0500; fax (20) 7255-0501; e-mail info@cilip.org.uk; internet www.cilip.org.uk; f. 2002, merger of Library Asscn and Institute of Information Scientists; professional body for librarians, information specialists and knowledge managers; provides practical career support for mems; 18,000 mems; Pres. BRIAN HALL; publ. *CILIP Update with Gazette* (12 a year).

Chartered Institute of Library and Information Professionals Scotland (CILIPS): 1st Floor, Block C, Brandon Gate, Leechlee Rd, Hamilton, ML3 6AU; tel. (1698) 458888; fax (1698) 283170; e-mail cilips@slainte.org.uk; internet www.slainte.org.uk; f. 1908, frmrly Scottish Library Association; attached to CILIP; 2,200 mems; Pres. ALAN HASSON; Dir ELAINE FULTON;

publs *Information Scotland* (6 a year), *Scottish Library and Information Resources*.

Chartered Institute of Library and Information Professionals Wales (CILIP Wales): c/o The Executive Officer, Dept of Information Studies, Llanbadarn Fawr, Aberystwyth SY23 3AS; tel. (1970) 622174; fax (1970) 622190; e-mail cilip-wales@aber.ac.uk; internet www.cilip.org.uk/wales; f. 1931; a branch of the Chartered Institute of Library and Information Professionals; a professional body of librarians and information professionals in Wales concerned with all aspects of librarianship and related matters; 850 mems; Exec. Officer SUE MACE; publs *Wales Current Awareness* (e-mail bulletin every 2 weeks), *Y Ddolen* (3 a year).

Edinburgh Bibliographical Society: c/o National Library of Scotland, George IV Bridge, Edinburgh, EH1 1EW; tel. (131) 623-3894; fax (131) 623-3888; e-mail joseph.marshall@ed.ac.uk; internet mcs.qmuc.ac.uk/ebs; f. 1890; discusses and elucidates questions connected with books, printed or MSS, especially Scottish; promotes and encourages bibliographical studies, and printing of bibliographical works; 150 mems; Pres. IAN McGOWAN; Hon. Sec. HELEN VINCENT; publ. *Journal* (1 a year).

Friends of the National Libraries: c/o Dept of Manuscripts, The British Library, 96 Euston Rd, London, NW1 2DB; tel. (20) 7412-7559; e-mail secretary@fnlmail.org.uk; internet www.friendsofnationallibraries.org.uk; f. 1931; promotes the acquisition of printed books, MSS and archives of historical, literary or artistic significance for libraries and record offices; 800 mems; Chair. Lord EGREMONT; Hon. Sec. MICHAEL BORRIE; publ. *Friends of the National Libraries*.

Museums Association: 24 Calvin St, London, E1 6NW; tel. (20) 7426-6910; fax (20) 7426-6961; e-mail info@museumsassociation.org; internet www.museumsassociation.org; f. 1889; promotes and improves museums and galleries; trains museum staff; 6,011 mems; Exec. Dir MARK TAYLOR; publs *Museum Journal* (12 a year), *Museums and Galleries Yearbook*, *Museums Practice* (4 a year).

Museums, Libraries and Archives Council (MLA): Grosvenor House 14 Bennetts Hill, Birmingham, B2 5RS; tel. (121) 345-7300; fax (121) 345-7303; e-mail info@mla.gov.uk; internet www.mla.gov.uk Wellcome Wolfson Building, 165 Queen's Gate, London, SW7 5HD; tel. (20) 7273-1444; fax (20) 7273-1404; f. 2000; advises the Govt on museum, library and archive affairs; exec. functions: allocates grants to Regional Agencies and co-ordinates funding and monitoring of other sectoral agencies; 15 mems; Chair. Prof. ANDREW MOTION; Chief Exec. ROY CLARE.

Society of College, National and University Libraries (SCONUL): 94 Euston St, London, NW1 2HA; tel. (20) 7387-0317; fax (20) 7383-3197; e-mail info@sconul.ac.uk; internet www.sconul.ac.uk; f. 1950; promotes the work of the nat. and univ. libraries of the UK and Ireland; 178 mem. institutions; Exec. Dir A. H. ROSSITER; Sec. A. J. C. BAINTON; publs *SCONUL Annual Library Statistics*, *SCONUL Focus*.

ECONOMICS, LAW AND POLITICS

Association of Chartered Certified Accountants: 29 Lincoln's Inn Fields, London, WC2A 3EE; tel. (20) 7059-7000; fax (20) 7059-7070; e-mail info@accaglobal.com; internet www.accaglobal.com; f. 1904; inc. by Royal Charter; 105,000 mems; Pres. CHRISTOPHER FORSTER; Chief Exec. ALLEN BLEWITT; publs *Accounting and Business* (12 a year), *Accountants' Guide*, *Student*

Accountant (12 a year), *Teach Accounting* (4 a year).

British Academy of Forensic Sciences: Academic Haematology, Blizard Institute, Barts and the London, 4 Newark St, London, E1 2AT; tel. (20) 7882-2274; fax (20) 7882-2183; e-mail lesley@bafsadmin.org; internet www.bafs.org.uk; f. 1959; advances forensic science in all its aspects to the benefit of justice and the law; scientific and medico-legal meetings; publ. of articles for lawyers, doctors, scientists and law-enforcement officers; 400 mems; Sec.-Gen. Dr DENISE SYNDERCOMBE COURT; publ. *Medicine, Science and the Law* (4 a year).

British Institute of International and Comparative Law: Charles Clore House, 17 Russell Sq., London, WC1B 5JP; tel. (20) 7862-5151; fax (20) 7862-5152; e-mail info@biicl.org; internet www.biicl.org; f. 1958 by the amalgamation of the Grotius Society and the Society of Comparative Legislation and Int. Law; organizes the Commonwealth Legal Advisory Service and research in comparative law, int. law, and law of the European Communities; holds conferences, meetings and lectures in int. and comparative law; 800 mems; Chair. Lord BINGHAM OF CORNHILL; Dir Prof. ROBERT McCORQUODALE; publs *Bulletin of International Legal Developments* (26 a year), *International and Comparative Law Quarterly* (4 a year), and other monographs on int. and comparative law.

Chartered Banker Institute: Drumsheugh House, 38B Drumsheugh Gardens, Edinburgh, EH3 7SW; tel. (131) 473-7777; fax (131) 473-7788; e-mail info@charteredbanker.com; internet www.charteredbanker.com; f. 1875; develops and promotes professional standards for bankers and provides professional qualifications for the financial services sector both in the UK and overseas; improves the qualifications of those engaged in banking, and raises their status and influence; 10,000 mems; Chief Exec. Prof. SIMON THOMPSON; publ. *Chartered Banker* (6 a year).

Chartered Institute of Management Accountants (CIMA): 26 Chapter St, London, SW1P 4NP; tel. (20) 7663-5441; fax (20) 7663-5442; internet www.cimaglobal.com; f. 1919, Royal Charter granted 1975; professional examining and membership body for chartered management accountants throughout the world; membership is gained through examination and practical experience; 195,000 mems and students in 176 countries; Pres. H. BAIRD; CEO C. TILLEY; publs *CIMA Insight* (12 a year), *Excellence in Leadership* (4 a year), *Financial Management* (12 a year).

Chartered Institute of Public Finance and Accountancy: 3 Robert St, London, WC2N 6RL; tel. (20) 7543-5600; fax (20) 7543-5700; e-mail corporate@cipfa.org; internet www.cipfa.org.uk; f. 1885; professional accountancy body for public services; provides education and training in accountancy and financial management, and monitors professional standards; 13,500 mems; 3,000 students; CEO STEVE FREER; publs *PMPA* (4 a year), *Public Finance* (52 a year).

Chartered Insurance Institute: 42–48 High Rd, South Woodford, London, E18 2JP; tel. (20) 8989-8464; fax (20) 8530-3052; e-mail customer.serv@cii.co.uk; internet www.cii.co.uk; f. 1897; inc. by Royal Charter 1912 with the object of providing and maintaining a central organization for the promotion of professionalism and progress among insurance and financial services employees; primarily an educational and examining body; 70,000 mems; library of 15,000 vols;

Dir-Gen. D. E. BLAND; Librarian R. L. CUNNEW; publ. *Journal* (6 a year).

Confederation of British Industry (CBI): Centre Point, 103 New Oxford St, London, WC1A 1DU; tel. (20) 7379-7400; fax (20) 7240-1578; internet www.cbi.org.uk; f. 1965; represents the interests of private enterprise and industry and seeks to influence govt policymaking; Pres. Sir ROGER CARR; Dir-Gen. JOHN CRIDLAND; publs *Business Voice* (12 a year), *CBI Distributive Trades Survey* (12 a year), *Economic Situation Report* (12 a year), *Industrial Trends Survey* (4 a year).

David Davies Memorial Institute of International Studies: c/o Dept of International Politics, Aberystwyth Univ., Aberystwyth, SY23 3FE; e-mail ddmstaff@aber.ac.uk; tel. (1970) 621770; fax (1970) 622709; internet www.aber.ac.uk/ddmi; f. 1951 to commemorate and continue the work of Lord Davies (1880–1944), on the means of establishing a viable world order; aims to advance and promote the devt of int. relations in the political, economic, legal, social, educational, ecological and other fields, and to carry out and instigate research; works through ad hoc groups, seminars, confs, bringing together experts in the relevant fields and publishing its findings; 2,500 mems; Dir Prof. KEN BOOTH; Deputy Dir Dr GRANT DAWSON.

Economics, Business and Enterprise Association: The Forum, 277 London Rd, Burgess Hill, RH15 9QU; tel. (1444) 240150; fax (1444) 240101; e-mail office@ebea.org.uk; internet www.ebea.org.uk; f. 1948; promotes and extends the study of economics, business studies, enterprise and related subjects in schools and colleges; acts as rep. body for economics and business studies teachers in educational matters; promotes knowledge of and interest in economics and related subjects among the gen. public; annual conf.; 1,300 mems; Chief Exec. DUNCAN CULLIMORE; publ. *Teaching Business and Economics* (3 a year).

Electoral Reform Society: 6 Chancel St, Blackfriars, London, SE1 0UU; tel. (20) 7928-1622; fax (20) 7401-7789; e-mail ers@electoral-reform.org.uk; internet www.electoral-reform.org.uk; f. 1884 as Proportional Representation Society, to secure an effective vote for every parliamentary and local government elector, by the adoption of the single transferable vote form of proportional representation, at all elections of representative bodies, and similarly for elections in all voluntary organizations; comprehensive reference library and archive; Electoral Reform (Ballot Services) Ltd (tel. (20) 8365-8909, fax (20) 8365-8587) provides advice and electoral administration service for UK organizations; Electoral Reform (International Services) (tel. (20) 7620-3794, fax (20) 7401-7789) provides advice for overseas organizations; the McDougall Trust is a charitable organization whose principal objective is to advance the knowledge of elections, voting systems and representative democracy; 2,000 mems; Pres. Rt Rev. COLIN BUCHANAN; Chair. ANDREW D. BURNS; Chief Exec. KATIE GHOSE.

European Movement: Southbank House, Black Prince Rd, London, SE1 7SJ; tel. (20) 3176-0543; e-mail emoffice@euromove.org.uk; internet www.euromove.org.uk; f. 1948; promotes European integration and unity at nat. and int. level; Pres. CHARLES KENNEDY; Chair. PETER LUFF.

Fabian Society: 11 Dartmouth St, London, SW1H 9BN; tel. (20) 7227-4900; fax (20) 7976-7153; e-mail info@fabian-society.org.uk; internet www.fabians.org.uk; f. 1884; public policy think-tank and socialist soc.;

conducts research, organizes confs and seminars; 7,000 mems; Gen. Sec. ANDREW HARROP; publs *Fabian Pamphlets* (6 a year), *Fabian Review* (4 a year).

Institute and Faculty of Actuaries: MacLaurin House, 18 Dublin St, Edinburgh, EH1 3PP; tel. (131) 240-1300; fax (131) 240-1313; e-mail libraries@actuaries.org.uk; internet www.actuaries.org.uk; f. 1856, present name and status 2010; 1,220 (1,174 fellows, 11 hon. fellows, 35 affiliates); library of 6,000 vols, 1,300 vols of historical colln; Sec. RICHARD MACONACHIE; Librarian DAVID HOOD; publs *Annals of Actuarial Science*, *British Actuarial Journal* (4–5 a year).

Faculty of Advocates: Advocates Library, Parliament House, Edinburgh, EH1 1RF; tel. (131) 226-5071; fax (131) 225-3642; internet www.advocates.org.uk; f. 1532; the sole professional body for Advocates (Barristers) in Scotland; it maintains professional standards, examines Intrants and represents its mems; 739 mems; library: copyright library in respect of legal works of 100,000 law books associated with Nat. Library of Scotland; Dean RICHARD KEEN; Clerk CALUM S. WILSON; Keeper of the Library MUNGO BOVEY.

Federal Trust for Education and Research: 31 Jewry St, London, EC3N 2EY; tel. (20) 7320-3045; e-mail info@fedtrust.co.uk; internet www.fedtrust.co.uk; f. 1945; confs, study groups, publications; promotes and carries out research and education into federal solutions to nat., European and global problems, in particular the European Union; 500 mems; Dir BRENDAN DONNELLY.

General Council of the Bar: 289–293 High Holborn, London, WC1V 7HZ; tel. (20) 7242-0082; fax (20) 7831-9217; internet www.barcouncil.org.uk; f. 1894, present constitution 1987; governing body for the barristers' profession in England and Wales; Chief Exec. DAVID HOBART; publs *Code of Conduct*, *Counsel* (incorporating *Bar News*) (12 a year).

Hansard Society: 40–43 Chancery Lane, London, WC2A 1JA; tel. (20) 7438-1222; fax (20) 7438-1229; e-mail contact@hansardsociety.org.uk; internet www.hansardsociety.org.uk; f. 1944; promotes parliamentary democracy, political education, political research and informed discussion of all aspects of modern parliamentary govt; 400 mems; Co-Pres. SPEAKER OF THE HOUSE OF COMMONS AND LORD SPEAKER; Chief Exec. FIONA BOOTH; publ. *Parliamentary Affairs* (4 a year).

IFS School of Finance: IFS House, 4–9 Burgate Lane, Canterbury, CT1 2XJ; tel. (1227) 818609; fax (1227) 763788; e-mail customerservices@ifslearning.ac.uk; internet www.ifslearning.com; f. 1879; provides the educational foundation and qualifications for a career in banking, building societies or other financial services; publishes textbooks for the financial sector; 41,000 mems; library of 30,000 vols; Chair DONALD BRYDON; Prin. GAVIN SHREEVE; publs *Eclectic* (4 a year), *Financial World* (12 a year), *IFS News* (12 a year).

Institute for Fiscal Studies: 7 Ridgmount St, London, WC1E 7AE; tel. (20) 7291-4800; fax (20) 7323-4780; e-mail mailbox@ifs.org.uk; internet www.ifs.org.uk; f. 1969 to provide high-quality economic analysis of public policy; produces briefing notes and working papers and organizes conferences, seminars and briefings; c. 650 individual mems; 100 corporate and institutional mems; Dir PAUL JOHNSON; Research Dir RICHARD BLUNDELL; publ. *Fiscal Studies* (4 a year).

Institute of Actuaries: Staple Inn Hall, High Holborn, London, WC1V 7QJ; tel. (20) 7632-2100; fax (20) 7632-2111 Education

Service and Library, Napier House, 4 Worcester St, Oxford, OX1 2AW; tel. (1865) 268200; fax (1865) 268211; e-mail institute@actuaries.org.uk; internet www.actuaries.org.uk; f. 1848, Royal Charter 1884; develops the role and standing of the actuarial profession; enhances its reputation in serving the public interest; sets examinations, courses in continuing professional devt; professional codes and disciplinary standards, awards research grants; 18,142 mems; 8,492 fellows; library of 15,000 vols, colln of rare books and archives incl. Archive of Equitable Life Assurance Society (London); Pres. NIGEL B. MASTERS; Chief Exec., Actuarial Profession CAROLINE M. INSTANCE; Head of Learning Dr TREVOR WATKINS; publs *Annals of Actuarial Science* (with Faculty of Actuaries, 2 a year), *British Actuarial Journal* (with Faculty of Actuaries, 3 a year).

Institute of Chartered Accountants in England and Wales: Chartered Accountants' Hall, Moorgate Pl., London, EC2P 2BJ; tel. (20) 7920-8100; fax (20) 7920-0547; internet www.icaew.co.uk; f. 1880 by Royal Charter; special collection of early European books on book-keeping; internationally important research library on the British accounting and tax systems; 128,000 mems; library of 40,000 vols, 40,000 journal records; Chief Exec. MICHAEL IZZA; Head of Library and Information Services SUSAN MOORE; publ. *Accountancy* (12 a year).

Institute of Chartered Accountants of Scotland: CA House, 21 Haymarket Yards, Edinburgh, EH12 5BH; tel. (131) 347-0100; fax (131) 347-0105; e-mail enquiries@icas.org.uk; internet www.icas.org.uk; f. 1854; deals with professional matters concerning its mems and the public in matters of chartered accountancy; runs information service; library of 3,000 vols, 140 periodicals, online databases; 19,000 mems; Pres. IAIN McLAREN; Chief Exec. ANTON COLELLA; publ. *CA Magazine* (12 a year).

Institute of Chartered Secretaries and Administrators: 16 Park Crescent, London, W1B 1AH; tel. (20) 7580-4741; fax (20) 7323-1132; e-mail info@icsaglobal.com; internet www.icsaglobal.com; f. 1891; 47,000 mems and students; qualifying body for company secretaries; authority on corporate governance; Information Man. SHEILA DOYLE; publs *Chartered Secretary* (12 a year), *Company Secretarial Practice* (4 a year), *The Company Secretary* (12 a year).

Institute of Economic Affairs: 2 Lord North St, Westminster, London, SW1P 3LB; tel. (20) 7799-3745; fax (20) 7799-2137; e-mail iea@iea.org.uk; internet www.iea.org.uk; f. 1955; to improve understanding of economics and its application to business and public policy; Dir-Gen. JOHN BLUNDELL; publs *Hobart Papers*, *Research Monographs*, *IEA Readings*, *Occasional Papers*, *Current Controversies*, *Choice in Welfare*, *Economic Affairs*, *Journal* (4 a year).

Law Society: 113 Chancery Lane, London, WC2A 1PL; tel. (20) 7242-1222; fax (20) 7831-0344; e-mail info.services@lawsociety.org.uk; internet www.lawsociety.org.uk; f. 1825; regulator and representative body for solicitors in England and Wales; 93,000 mems; library: see Libraries and Archives; Chief Exec. JULIA PARASKEVA; publ. *Gazette* (weekly).

Political Studies Association of the United Kingdom: Dept of Politics, Newcastle Univ., Newcastle upon Tyne, NE1 7RU; tel. (191) 222-8021; fax (191) 222-3499; internet www.psa.ac.uk; f. 1950; promotes the devt of political studies; 1,600 mems; Chair. Prof. VICKEY RANDALL; Hon. Sec. Prof. PAUL CARMICHAEL; publs *British*

Royal Musical Association: tel. (161) 861-7542; fax (161) 861-7543; e-mail jeffrey .dean@stingrayoffice.com; internet www.rma .ac.uk; f. 1874, inc. 1904; promotes investigation and discussion of subjects connected with the art, science and history of music; annual conf., research students' conf., 4–6 annual regional study days; 1,000 mems; Pres. Prof. MARK EVERIST; Exec. Officer Dr JEFFREY DEAN; Hon. Treas. BARBARA EVANS; publs *Journal of the Royal Musical Association* (2 a year), *Royal Musical Association Monographs* (1 a year), *Royal Musical Association Research Chronicle* (1 a year).

Royal Photographic Society of Great Britain: Fenton House, 122 Wells Rd, Bath, BA2 3AH; tel. (1225) 325733; fax (1225) 448688; e-mail reception@rps.org; internet www.rps.org; f. 1853; promotes advancement of the science and art of photography; offers distinctions programme and Imaging Scientist qualification; workshops and courses on photography; exhibitions; 15 spec. interest groups and UK regional groups and overseas chapters; 10,800 mems; library of 20,000 vols and periodicals, permanent colln of 200,000 photographs and 8,000 items of photographic equipment; Dir-Gen. Dr MICHAEL PRITCHARD; publs *RPS Journal* (10 a year), *The Imaging Science Journal* (4 a year).

Royal Scottish Academy of Art and Architecture: The Mound, Edinburgh, EH2 2EL; tel. (131) 225-6671; fax (131) 220-6016; e-mail info@royalscottishacademy.org; internet www.royalscottishacademy.org; f. 1826; ind., privately funded instn led by eminent artists and architects whose sole purpose is to promote and support the creation, understanding and enjoyment of the visual arts through exhibitions and related educational events; 129 mems (98 Acads, 31 hon. Acads); Programme Dir COLIN R. GREENSLADE; Collns Curator Dr JOANNA SODEN; Marketing Man. ALISA LINDSAY.

Royal Watercolour Society: Bankside Gallery, 48 Hopton St, Blackfriars, London, SE1 9JH; tel. (20) 7928-7521; fax (20) 7928-2820; e-mail info@banksidegallery.com; internet www.banksidegallery.com; f. 1804; small archive and diploma collection; 83 mems; Pres. FRANCIS BOWYER; Sec. JUDY DIXEY; publ. *Bankside Bulletin* (4 a year).

Royal West of England Academy: Queen's Rd, Clifton, Bristol, BS8 1PX; tel. (117) 973-5129; fax (117) 923-7874; e-mail info@rwa .org.uk; internet www.rwa.org.uk; f. 1844; encourages, advances and promotes the appreciation of the fine arts by exhibitions and occasional lectures and meetings; 160 academicians; library: small library, mainly exhibition catalogues; Chair. of Trustees NORMAN BIDDLE.

Society for Theatre Research: c/o National Theatre Archive, 83–101 The Cut, London, SE1 8LL; e-mail contact@str.org.uk; internet www.str.org.uk; f. 1948; encourages research into the history and technique of the British theatre; holds monthly lectures in the winter season; distributes research grants annually and offers an annual theatre book prize and new scholars prize; 700 individual and corporate mems; Pres. TIMOTHY WEST; Treas. BARRY SHEPPARD; publ. *Theatre Notebook* (3 a year).

Society of Architectural Illustration: Rosemary Cottage, Bletchinglye Lane, Rotherfield, TN6 3NN; tel. (1892) 852578; fax (1892) 853578; e-mail info@sai.org.uk; internet www.sai.org.uk; f. 1975; has established a professional body and a recognized qualification for mems of the design professions who specialize in architectural illustration; confers SAI (Member), FSAI (Fellow), Hon. FSAI (Hon. Fellow); 359 mems; Pres. PHILIP CROWE; Admin. ERIC MONK.

Society of Scribes & Illuminators: c/o 6 Queen Sq., London, WC1N 3AT; tel. and fax (1524) 251534; e-mail honsec@ calligraphyonline.org; internet www .calligraphyonline.org; f. 1921; re-establishes and perpetuates the tradition of craftsmanship, calligraphy and fine lettering; advanced training scheme; reference library; 500 mems; Hon. Sec. GILLIAN HAZELDINE; publ. *The Scribe* (2 a year).

SPNM—Promoting New Music: St Margaret's House, 4th Floor, 18–20 Southwark St, London, SE1 1TJ; tel. (20) 7407-1640; fax (20) 7403-7652; e-mail spnm@spnm.org.uk; internet www.spnm.org.uk; f. 1943; 1,700 mems; concerts and workshop performances of new music; educational projects and collaborations with venues and ensembles in United Kingdom; professional development and training for emerging composers; Pres. Sir PETER MAXWELL DAVIES; Exec. Dir ABIGAIL POGSON; publ. *New Notes* (12 a year).

HISTORY, GEOGRAPHY AND ARCHAEOLOGY

Ancient Monuments Society: St Ann's Vestry Hall, 2 Church Entry, London, EC4V 5HB; tel. (20) 7236-3934; e-mail office@ ancientmonumentssociety.org.uk; internet www.ancientmonumentssociety.org.uk; f. 1924; studies and conserves ancient monuments, historic bldgs of all ages and types, fine old craftsmanship, in partnership with the Friends of Friendless Churches; 2,200 mems; Pres. Earl of Leicester EDWARD COKE; Chair. GILES QUARME; Sec. M. J. SAUNDERS; publ. *Transactions* (1 a year).

Archives and Records Association UK and Ireland: Prioryfield House, 20 Canon St, Taunton, TA1 1SW; tel. (1823) 327030; fax (1823) 271719; e-mail ara@archives.org .uk; internet www.archives.org.uk; f. 1947; 2,000 mems; Chair. MARTIN TAYLOR; Chief Exec. JOHN CHAMBERS; publs *ARC Magazine* (12 a year), *Journal* (2 a year).

Baptist Historical Society: Baptist House, POB 44, 129 Broadway, Didcot, OX11 8RT; internet www.baptisthistory.org.uk; f. 1908; promotes the study of and records the history of the Baptists; assists researchers, and gives advice to Churches on care and preservation of records; library administered jtly with Angus Library, Regent's Park College, Oxford; 550 mems; Pres. Prof. J. H. Y. BRIGGS; Sec. Rev. S. L. COPSON; publ. *The Baptist Quarterly*.

British Agricultural History Society: Dept of History, Univ. of Exeter, Amory Bldg, Rennes Dr., Exeter, EX4 4RJ; tel. (1392) 263284; fax (1392) 263305; e-mail bahs@exeter.ac.uk; internet www.bahs.org .uk; f. 1952; 800 mems; Chair. Dr JANE WHITTLE; Sec. Dr NICOLA VERDON; Treas. Dr H. CROWE; publ. *Agricultural History Review* (2 a year).

British Archaeological Association: c/o John McNeill, 18 Stanley Rd, Oxford, OX4 1QZ; internet www.britarch.ac.uk/baa; f. 1843; 700 mems; Hon. Pres. Prof. LINDY GRANT; Hon. Sec. JOHN MCNEILL; publs *Conference Transactions* (1 a year), *Journal* (1 a year).

British Cartographic Society: c/o Royal Geographic Soc., 1 Kensington Gore, London, SW7 2AR; tel. and fax (115) 9328684; e-mail admin@cartography.org.uk; internet www .cartography.org.uk; f. 1963; promotes art and science of map-making through cartography, history of cartography, map library curatorship, GIS, technical devts and automation in cartography, design and technol-ogy and education and careers in cartography; 700 mems; Pres. PETER JOLLY; Hon. Sec. Dr TIM RIDEOUT; publ. *Cartographic Journal* (4 a year).

British Numismatic Society: c/o Warburg Institute, Woburn Sq., London, WC1H 0AB; tel. (20) 7016-1802; e-mail secretary@ britnumsoc.org; internet www.britnumsoc .org; f. 1903; 620 mems; Pres. Dr ROGER BLAND; Sec. PETER J. PRESTON-MORLEY; publ. *British Numismatic Journal* (1 a year).

British Records Association: c/o Finsbury Library, 245 St John St, London, EC1V 4NB; tel. (20) 7833-0428; fax (20) 7833-0416; e-mail britrecassoc@hotmail.com; internet www.britishrecordsassociation.org.uk; f. 1932 for the preservation and use of records (archives), and for the coordination of the work of institutions and individuals interested in the subject; 1,000 mems; annual conference, training day; Pres. RT HON. THE MASTER OF THE ROLLS; Hon. Sec. KATHERINE TAYLOR; publ. *Archives* (2 a year).

Cambrian Archaeological Association: c/o Heather James, Braemar, Llangunnor Rd, Carmarthen, SA31 2PB; tel. (1267) 231793; internet www.orchardweb.co.uk/ cambrians; f. 1846; 544 mems incl. 132 corporate, 47 corresp. socs; Pres. Prof. GWYN MEIRION-JONES; Gen. Sec. HEATHER JAMES; publ. *Archaeologia Cambrensis* (1 a year).

Canterbury and York Society: c/o Borthwick Institute, Univ. of York, York, YO10 5DD; internet www.canterburyandyork.org; f. 1904; 249 mems; Pres. Dr P. ZUTSHI; Sec. Dr C. FONGE; publ. *Medieval Bishops' Registers and other Ecclesiastical Records*.

Catholic Record Society: c/o Hon. Sec., 12 Melbourne Pl., Wolsingham, DL13 3EH; tel. (1388) 527747; internet www.catholic-history .org.uk/crs; f. 1904; publishes documentary material on Catholic history in England and Wales since the Reformation; int. membership; Hon. Sec. Dr LEO GOOCH; publ. *Monographs* (irregular).

Council for British Archaeology: St Mary's House, 66 Bootham, York, YO30 7BZ; tel. (1904) 671417; fax (1904) 671384; e-mail info@britarch.ac.uk; internet www .britarch.ac.uk; f. 1944; promotes study and safeguarding of Britain's historic environment; provides a forum for archaeological opinion; improves public knowledge of Britain's past; 600 institutional mems, 5,600 individual mems; Pres. Dr K. PRETTY; Dir Dr M. HEYWORTH; publ. *British Archaeology* (6 a year).

Council of British Geography: c/o Royal Geographical Society (with the Institute of British Geographers), 1 Kensington Gore, London, SW7 2AR; tel. (20) 7591-3000; fax (20) 7591-3001; f. 1988; provides a formal org. linking all British geographical socs for the advancement of British geography; coordinates policies of mem. socs, and takes initiatives in educational, academic, research or policy matters; Chair. Prof. M. ROBERTS; Hon. Sec. Prof. P. WOOD.

Ecclesiastical History Society: Dr Sheridan Gilley, Dept of Theology and Religion, Univ. of Durham, Abbey House, Palace Green, Durham, DH1 3RS; e-mail sheridan .gilley@talktalk.net; internet www.history.ac .uk/ehsoc; f. 1961; furthers the study of ecclesiastical history and maintains relations between British ecclesiastical historians and scholars abroad; 960 mems; Pres. Dr SHERIDAN GILLEY; Sec. STELLA FLETCHER; publs *Studies in Church History* (1 a year), *Subsidia* (irregular).

Economic History Society: School of Social and Political Sciences, Univ. of Glasgow, Lilybank House, Bute Gardens, Glasgow, G12 8RT; tel. (141) 330-4662; fax (141) 330-4889; e-mail ehsocsec@arts.gla.ac.uk; internet www.ehs.org.uk; f. 1927; promotes the study of economic and social history; establishes closer relations between students and teachers of economic and social history; holds annual conf.; cooperates with other orgs having kindred purposes; provides fellowships; training course for postgraduate students; 1,400 mems; Pres. Prof. K. J. HUMPHRIES; Hon. Sec. Dr W. P. HOWLETT; publ. *Economic History Review* (4 a year).

Egypt Exploration Society: 3 Doughty Mews, London, WC1N 2PG; tel. (20) 7242-1880; fax (20) 7404-6118; e-mail contact@ees.ac.uk; internet www.ees.ac.uk; f. 1882; excavation in Egypt and publication of work, lectures and study days; 3,000 mems; library of 20,000 vols, journals and pamphlets; Dir CHRIS NAUNTON; Librarian and Archivist Dr JOANNA KYFFIN; publs *Archaeological Survey* (irregular), *Egyptian Archaeology* (2 a year), *Excavation Memoirs* (irregular), *Graeco-Roman Memoirs* (1 a year), *Journal of Egyptian Archaeology* (1 a year).

English Place-Name Society: School of English, Institute for Name-Studies, University of Nottingham, Nottingham, NG7 2RD; tel. (115) 951-5919; fax (115) 951-5924; e-mail name-studies@nottingham.ac.uk; internet www.nottingham.ac.uk/english/ins; f. 1923 for the publication of a yearly volume on the place-names of a county, or part of a county; 500 mems; Hon. Dir RICHARD COATES; publ. *Journal* (1 a year).

Friends Historical Society: c/o Friends House, Euston Rd, London, NW1 2BJ; f. 1903; 400 mems; Clerk of Exec. GIL SKIDMORE; publ. *Journal* (1 a year).

Geographical Association: 160 Solly St, Sheffield, S1 4BF; tel. (114) 296-0088; fax (114) 296-7176; e-mail info@geography.org.uk; internet www.geography.org.uk; f. 1893; guards interests of teachers of geography and the study and teaching of geography generally; 6,000 mems; CEO Prof. DAVID LAMBERT; publs *Geography* (3 a year), *Teaching Geography* (3 a year), *Primary Geographer* (3 a year).

Hakluyt Society: c/o Map Library, British Library, 96 Euston Rd, London, NW1 2DB; tel. (1428) 641850; fax (1428) 641933; e-mail office@hakluyt.com; internet www.hakluyt.com; f. 1846; publishes primary source material of early exploratory voyages, travel and other geographical records; 1,500 mems; Pres. MICHAEL K. BARRITT.

Harleian Society: c/o College of Arms, Queen Victoria St, London, EC4V 4BT; tel. (20) 7236-7728; fax (20) 7248-6448; e-mail info@harleian.org.uk; internet harleian.org.uk; f. 1869, inc. 1902; transcribes, prints and publishes Heraldic Visitations of Counties, Parish Registers and MSS relating to genealogy, family history and heraldry; 300 subscribers; Chair. T. WOODCOCK; Hon. Sec. and Treas. T. H. S. DUKE (Chester Herald of Arms).

Heraldry Society: POB 772, Guildford, GU3 3ZX; tel. (1483) 237373; internet www.theheraldrysociety.com; f. 1947; advances study of heraldry, armory, chivalry, genealogy and kindred subjects; 1,000 mems; Patron THE DUKE OF NORFOLK; publs *The Coat of Arms* (2 a year), *The Heraldry Gazette* (4 a year).

Historic Buildings and Monuments Commission for England (English Heritage): POB 569, Swindon, SN2 2YP; tel. (870) 333-1181; fax (1793) 414-926; e-mail customers@english-heritage.org.uk; internet www.english-heritage.org.uk; f. 1983; executive non-departmental public body sponsored by the Department for Culture, Media and Sport; responsible for all aspects of protecting and promoting historic buildings and landscapes throughout England; funded by the UK Govt and from revenue earned from its historic properties; Chair. Sir NEIL COSSONS; publs *Buildings at Risk Register* (1 a year), *Conservation Bulletin* (4 a year), *Register of Parks and Gardens*.

Attached Organizations:

Centre for Archaeology: Fort Cumberland, Fort Cumberland Rd, Eastney, Portsmouth, PO4 9LD; tel. (23) 9285-6700; e-mail cfa@english-heritage.org.uk.

National Monuments Record: Kemble Dr., Swindon, SN2 2GZ; tel. (1793) 414600; fax (1793) 414606; e-mail nmrinfo@english-heritage.org.uk; internet www.english-heritage.org.uk/nmr; over 1m. photographs, plans, drawings, reports, records and publs covering England's archaeology, architecture, social and local history; library of 60,000 vols, 400 current journals.

Historical Association: 59A Kennington Park Rd, London, SE11 4JH; tel. (20) 7735-3901; fax (20) 7582-4989; e-mail enquiry@history.org.uk; internet www.history.org.uk; f. 1906; advances the study and teaching of history at all levels, to increase public interest in all aspects of the subject and to develop it as an essential element in the education of all; colln of history textbooks; 60 brs nationally; 6,500 mems; Pres. JACKIE EALES; Chief Exec. REBECCA SULLIVAN; publs *The Historian* (4 a year), *History* (4 a year), *Primary History* (3 a year), *Teaching History* (4 a year).

Honourable Society of Cymmrodorion: POB 55178, London, N12 2A4; tel. (20) 7631-0502; e-mail membership@cymmrodorion.org; internet www.cymmrodorion.org; f. 1751, Royal Charter 1951; promotes the practice and devt of literature, the arts and sciences insofar as they are of spec. interest to Wales, the Welsh people and those interested in Wales; 900 mems; Patron HRH THE PRINCE OF WALES; Pres. Prof. PRYS MORGAN; Hon. Sec. PETER JEFFREYS; publs *Dictionary of Welsh Biography*, *Transactions* (1 a year).

Huguenot Society of Great Britain and Ireland: The Huguenot Library, UCL, Gower St, London, WC1E 6BT; tel. (20) 6795-199; e-mail library@huguenotsociety.org.uk; internet www.huguenotsociety.org.uk; f. 1885; 1,385 mems (9 hon. fellows, 1,376 ordinary fellows); promotes the publication and exchange of knowledge about the Huguenots in the UK and Ireland; aims to form a bond of fellowship among those who, whether or not of Huguenot descent, respect and admire the Huguenots and seek to perpetuate their memory; library of 5,500 vols, colln of MSS and rare books, genealogical material; Pres. MICHAEL COURAGE; Hon. Sec. ANNE NUGENT; Librarian LUCY GWYNN; publs *New Series* (irregular), *Proceedings* (1 a year), *Quarto Series* (irregular).

Institute of Heraldic and Genealogical Studies: 79–82 Northgate, Canterbury, Kent, CT1 1BA; tel. (1227) 768664; fax (1227) 765617; e-mail admin@ihgs.ac.uk; internet www.ihgs.ac.uk; f. 1961; provides courses in family history and related subjects using traditional classroom methods and a correspondence course available online or by post, leading to accredited qualifications; spec. collns; 250 mems; library of 35,000 vols, 20,000 case studies; Pres. Rt Hon. THE EARL OF LYTTON; Prin. C. R. HUMPHERY-SMITH; Reg. MICHELLE WEBBER; publs *Atlas and Index of Parishes*, *Family History* (4 a year), *Syllabus of Study*, *Teacher's Aids*.

Jewish Historical Society of England: 33 Seymour Place, London, W1H 5AP; tel. (20) 7723-5852; fax (20) 7723-5852; e-mail info@jhse.org; internet www.jhse.org; f. 1893; Jewish Studies Library, University College, London; 800 mems; Administrator DAVID FREEMAN; Hon. Sec. Dr GERRY BLACK; publ. *Transactions* (1 a year).

London and Middlesex Archaeological Society: c/o Museum of London, London Wall, London, EC2Y 5HN; tel. (20) 7814-5734; internet www.lamas.org.uk; f. 1855; promotes and publishes archaeological and historical research on the London area; 644 mems; Pres. Prof. MARTIN BIDDLE; Hon. Sec. JACKIE KEILY; publ. *Transactions* (1 a year).

London Record Society: POB 691, Exeter, EX1 9PH; e-mail londonrecordsoc@btinternet.com; internet www.londonrecordsociety.org.uk; f. 1964; publishes original sources for the history of London and encourages public interest in archives relating to London; 292 mems; Chair. Prof. CAROLINE BARRON; Hon. Membership Sec. Dr STEPHANIE HOVLAND; Hon. Sec. Dr HELEN BRADLEY; Hon. Treas. Dr DAVID LEWIS.

London Topographical Society: 10 Tremaine Rd, London, SE20 7TZ; tel. (20) 8659-2405; e-mail m.galinou@virgin.net; internet www.topsoc.org; f. 1880; 1,100 mems; publishes material to assist in the study and appreciation of London's history, growth and topography, incl. reproductions of historic maps and views of London; Patron HRH THE DUKE OF EDINBURGH; Hon. Sec. MIREILLE GALINOU; publs *London Topographical Record* (every 5 years), maps, views and books.

Manchester Geographical Society: Meadowbank, Ringley Rd, Radcliffe, Manchester, M26 1FW; tel. (161) 723-1433; e-mail secretary@mangeogsoc.org.uk; internet www.mangeogsoc.org.uk; f. 1884; promotes the study of all brs of geographical science; lecture programme, funding research, publishing; 100 mems; library of 4,500 vols (now on permanent loan to the Univ. of Manchester); Hon. Sec. Dr PAUL HINDLE; publ. *North West Geography* (2 a year, online).

Monumental Brass Society: c/o H. M. Stuchfield, Lowe Hill House, Stratford St Mary, CO7 6JX; e-mail martin.stuchfield@intercitygroup.co.uk; internet www.mbs-brasses.co.uk; f. 1887 to promote the study of and interest in, better preservation of monumental brasses, and to compile and publish a full and accurate list of all extant and lost brasses, English and foreign; Pres. Rev. Canon D. G. MEARA; Hon. Sec. H. M. STUCHFIELD; publs *Bulletin* (3 a year), *Portfolio* (irregular), *Transactions* (1 a year).

Palestine Exploration Fund: 2 Hinde Mews, Marylebone Lane, London, W1U 2AA; tel. (20) 7935-5379; fax (20) 7486-7438; e-mail execsec@pef.org.uk; internet www.pef.org.uk; f. 1865; 900 subscribers; promotes research into the archaeology and history, manners, customs and culture, topography, geology and natural sciences of biblical to early-modern Palestine and the Levant (modern-day Syria, Lebanon, Jordan and Israel); specialist library and archaeological collns (restricted to mems); library of 5,000 vols; Exec. and Curator FELICITY COBBING; Consultant Financial Administrator IVONA LLOYD-JONES; Librarian ANDREA ZERBINI; publ. *Palestine Exploration Quarterly* (3 a year).

Prehistoric Society: c/o Institute of Archaeology, University College London, 31–34 Gordon Sq., London, WC1H 0PY; internet www.ucl.ac.uk/prehistoric; f. 1908; furthers prehistoric archaeology; 2,000 mems; Pres. Prof. GRAEME BARKER; Hon. Sec. Dr ALEX GIBSON; publs *Past* (3 a year), *Proceedings* (1 a year).

Regional Studies Association: POB 2058, Seaford, BN25 4QU; tel. (1323) 899698; fax (1323) 899798; e-mail info@rsa-ls.ac.uk; internet www.regional-studies-assoc.ac.uk; f. 1965; an interdisciplinary group exclusively concerned with regional issues at sub-nat. level; provides a forum for the exchange of ideas and information on regional problems, publishes the results of regional research, and stimulates studies and research in regional planning and related fields; holds meetings, confs and seminars; organizes study groups; 6 branches; 7 int. sections and present in more than 40 countries; 850 individual, 200 corporate mems, including government depts, ministries, local authorities, educational institutions, etc.; Chair. DAVID BAILEY; Chief Exec. SALLY HARDY; Hon. Sec. GILLIAN BRISTOW; publs *Regional Insights* (1 a year), *Regional Studies* (10 a year), *Regions* (4 a year), *Special Economic Analysis* (4 a year).

Royal Geographical Society (with the Institute of British Geographers): 1 Kensington Gore, London, SW7 2AR; tel. (20) 7591-3000; fax (20) 7591-3001; e-mail info@rgs.org; internet www.rgs.org; f. 1830; furtherance of geographical research, teaching and expeditions; 14,000 mems; library of 150,000 books, 1m. maps and charts, 4,500 atlases, 500,000 mid-19th-century to contemporary pictures and photographs; Pres. MICHAEL PALIN; Dir and Sec. Dr RITA GARDNER; publs *Area* (4 a year), *Geographical* (12 a year), *Geographical Journal* (4 a year), *Transactions* (4 a year).

Royal Historical Society: Univ. College London, Gower St, London, WC1E 6BT; tel. (20) 7387-7532; fax (20) 7387-7532; e-mail royalhistsoc@ucl.ac.uk; internet www.royalhistoricalsociety.org; f. 1868; 3,000 mems; library of 3,000 vols; Pres. Prof. PETER MANDLER; Exec. Sec. SUSAN CARR; publs *Transactions* (1 a year), *Camden* (5th series, 2 vols a year).

Royal Numismatic Society: c/o Dept of Coins and Medals, British Museum, London, WC1B 3DG; tel. (20) 7323-8272; fax (20) 7323-8171; e-mail info@numismatics.org.uk; internet www.numismatics.org.uk; f. 1836; 1,000 mems; Pres. J. CRIBB; Secs V. S. CURTIS, S. MOORHEAD; publ. *Numismatic Chronicle* (1 a year).

Royal Philatelic Society London: 41 Devonshire Pl., London, W1G 6JY; tel. (20) 7486-1044; fax (20) 7486-0803; e-mail secretary@rpsl.org.uk; internet www.rpsl.org.uk; f. 1869; 1,800 mems; Pres. BRIAN TROTTER; Sec. CHRISTINE A. EARLE; publ. *The London Philatelist* (10 a year).

Royal Scottish Geographical Society: Lord John Murray House, 15–19 North Port, Blackfriars, Perth, PH1 5LU; tel. (1738) 455-050; e-mail enquiries@rsgs.org; internet www.rsgs.org; f. 1884 to further the science of geography in all its branches; symposia, illustrated talks and schools conferences; provides research grants and support to scientific expeditions; library of 20,000 vols, 30,000 maps, 200 current periodicals, special collection of early maps of Scotland; 2,200 mems; Pres. THE EARL OF LINDSAY; Chief Exec. MIKE ROBINSON; publ. *The Scottish Geographical Journal* (4 a year).

Scottish History Society: Dept of Scottish History, Univ. of St Andrews, St Katharine's Lodge, The Scores, St Andrews, KY16 9AL; e-mail katie.stevenson@st-andrews.ac.uk; internet www.scottishhistorysociety.org; f. 1886 for the printing of unpublished documents illustrating the history of Scotland; 800 mems; Pres. Dr IAIN HUTCHISON; Hon. Sec. Dr KATIE STEVENSON.

Society for Army Historical Research: c/o National Army Museum, Royal Hospital Rd, London, SW3 4HT; internet www.sahr.co.uk; f. 1921; army and regimental history; military antiquities and pictures, uniforms, badges and medals, arms and equipment, customs and traditions and the history of land warfare in general; 1,000 mems; Pres. Field Marshal Sir JOHN CHAPPLE; Hon. Sec. GEORGE EVELYN; publ. *Journal* (4 a year).

Society for Medieval Archaeology: c/o Dept of Archaeology, Univ. of Sheffield, Northgate House, W St, Sheffield, S1 4ET; tel. (114) 222-2920; fax (114) 272-2563; e-mail d.m.hadley@sheffield.ac.uk; internet www.medievalarchaeology.org; f. 1957; studies archaeology of the post-Roman period; organizes regular confs; offers funds for research; 1,500 mems; library of 54 vols; Pres. LESLIE WEBSTER; Hon. Sec. DAWN HADLEY; Hon. Treas. Prof. STEPHEN RIPPON; Hon. Editor Dr SALLY FOSTER; publs *Medieval Archaeology* (1 a year), *Monograph Series* (irregular).

Society for Nautical Research: c/o 6 Ashmeadow Rd, Arnside, via Carnforth, LA5 0AE; tel. (1524) 761616; e-mail honsecretary.snr@btinternet.com; internet www.snr.org.uk; f. 1910; annual public lecture; 1,500 mems; Pres. HRH THE DUKE OF YORK; Chair. Sir KENNETH EATON; Sec. PETER WINTERBOTTOM; publ. *The Mariners' Mirror* (4 a year).

Society for Post-Medieval Archaeology Ltd: c/o David Cranstone, 267 Kells Lane, Low Fell, Gateshead NE9 5HU; tel. (191) 482-1037; fax (191) 482-2343; e-mail cranconsult@btinternet.com; internet www.spma.org.uk; f. 1967; 400 mems; Pres. Dr DAVID GAIMSTER; Sec. DAVID CRANSTONE; publ. *Post-Medieval Archaeology* (2 a year).

Society for Renaissance Studies: c/o Michelle O'Malley, Centre for Research in the History of Art, University of Sussex, Falmer, Brighton, BN1 9RQ; e-mail m.o-malley@sussex.ac.uk; internet www.sas.ac.uk/srs/default.htm; f. 1967 to advance scholarship on the Renaissance, including literature, philosophy, science, art and music; 550 mems; Hon. Chair. Dr DAVID CHAMBERS; Hon. Sec. Dr MICHELLE O'MALLEY; publs *Bulletin* (2 a year), *Renaissance Studies* (4 a year).

Society of Antiquaries of London: Burlington House, Piccadilly, London, W1J 0BE; tel. (20) 7479-7080; fax (20) 7287-6967; e-mail admin@sal.org.uk; internet www.sal.org.uk; f. 1707; 2,800 mems; library: see Libraries and Archives; Pres. Prof. MAURICE HOWARD; Gen. Sec. and CEO Dr DAVID GAIMSTER; publs *Archaeologia* (1 a year), *The Antiquaries Journal* (1 a year).

Society of Antiquaries of Scotland: c/o National Museums Scotland, Chambers St, Edinburgh, EH1 1JF; tel. (131) 247-4133; fax (131) 247-4163; e-mail info@socantscot.org; internet www.socantscot.org; f. 1780; promotes research, understanding and conservation of archaeological and historic environment of Scotland; study of Scottish antiquities and history, particularly by archaeological research; grants and awards available for research relating to Scotland; 3,000 mems; Pres. ALAN SAVILLE; Dir Dr SIMON GILMOUR; publs *Proceedings of the Society of Antiquaries of Scotland* (1 a year), *Scottish Archaeological Internet Reports* (online).

Society of Genealogists: 14 Charterhouse Bldgs, Goswell Rd, London, EC1M 7BA; tel. (20) 7251-8799; fax (20) 7250-1800; e-mail librarian@sog.org.uk; internet www.sog.org.uk; f. 1911; promotes the study, science and knowledge of genealogy and family history, through education and library programmes and online resources; 11,000

mems; library of 134,000 vols (incl. MSS collns, microforms and digital media); Pres. PATRIC DICKINSON; Chief Exec. JUNE PERRIN; Head of Library Services TIM LAWRENCE; publ. *Genealogists' Magazine* (4 a year).

Ulster Archaeological Society: c/o School of Geography and Palaeoecology, Queens Univ., 42 Fitzwilliam St, Belfast, BT9 6AX; e-mail arcpal@qub.ac.uk; internet www.uas.society.qub.ac.uk; f. 1853; promotes education in archaeology and history of Ulster; organizes public lectures and field trips; has survey group; 300 mems; Pres. BARRIE HARTWELL; Vice-Pres. TOM HAYES; Vice-Pres. Dr HARRY WELSH; Vice-Pres. Dr CHRIS LYNN; Hon. Sec. KEN PULLIN; Hon. Treas. JOHN MOORE; publ. *Ulster Journal of Archaeology* (1 a year).

United Reformed Church History Society: Westminster College, Madingley Rd, Cambridge, CB3 0AA; tel. (1223) 741300; e-mail hw374@cam.ac.uk; f. 1972 to incorporate the Congregational Historical Soc. (f. 1899), the Presbyterian Historical Soc. of England (f. 1913) and the Churches of Christ Historical Soc. (f. 1981); 250 mems; library of 5,000 vols; Hon. Sec. Rev. ELIZABETH J. BROWN; publ. *Journal* (2 a year).

Wesley Historical Society: c/o Dr John A. Hargreaves, 7 Haugh Shaw Rd, Halifax, HX1 3AH; tel. (1422) 250780; e-mail johnahargreaves@blueyonder.co.uk; internet www.wesleyhistoricalsociety.org.uk; f. 1893; promotes study of history and literature of Methodism; annual lecture, supporting programme; residential event every 3 years; access to network of regional historical socs; 600 mems; library: library at Westminster Institute of Education, Oxford Brookes Univ., Harcourt Hill Campus, Oxford, OX2 9AT; Pres. Prof. EDWARD ROYLE; Gen. Sec. Dr JOHN A. HARGREAVES; publ. *Proceedings* (3 a year).

LANGUAGE AND LITERATURE

Academi Gymreig, Yr/Welsh Academy, The: Mount Stuart House, Third Fl., Mount Stuart Sq., Cardiff, CF10 5FQ; tel. (29) 2047-2266; fax (29) 2049-2930; e-mail post@literaturewales.org; internet www.literaturewales.org; f. 1959; promotes interests of writers and literatures of Wales; 730 mems (250 in Welsh-language section, 480 in English-language section); Pres. for English language DANNIE ABSE; Pres. for Welsh language BOBI JONES; Co-Chair Dr HARRI PRITCHARD-JONES; Co-Chair Dr JOHN PIKOULIS; Chief Exec. PETER FINCH; publ. *Taliesin* (3 a year, in Welsh).

Alliance Française: 1 Dorset Sq., London, NW1 6PU; tel. (20) 7723-6439; fax (20) 7224-9512; e-mail info@alliancefrancaise.org.uk; internet www.alliancefrancaise.org.uk; offers courses and exams in French language and culture and promotes cultural exchange with France; attached offices in Bath, Belfast, Bristol, Cambridge, Exeter, Glasgow, Jersey, Loughborough, Manchester, Milton Keynes, Oxford, Totnes, York; Dir CHRYSTEL HUG.

Alliance of Literary Societies: 59 Bryony Rd, Birmingham, B29 4BY; tel. (121) 475-1805; e-mail l.j.curry@bham.ac.uk; internet www.allianceofliterarysocieties.org.uk; f. 1973; provides a voice for literary and authors' socs in defence of sites and legacies of literary importance; annual general meeting; information resource for literary socs in the UK; 125 mem. socs; Chair. LINDA CURRY; Hon. Sec. ANITA FERNANDEZ-YOUNG; Hon. Treas. and Membership Sec. JULIE SHORLAND; publ. *ALSo* (1 a year).

Association for Language Learning: Univ. of Leicester, University Rd, Leicester, LE1 7RH; tel. (116) 229-7600; fax (116) 223-1488; e-mail info@all-languages.org.uk;

internet www.all-languages.org.uk; f. 1990; offers help, in-service training and support to language teachers; promotes the learning and use of foreign languages; 5,500 mems; Dir LINDA PARKER; publs *Deutsch: Lehren und Lernen* (2 a year), *Francophonie* (2 a year), *Language Learning Journal* (3 a year), *Languages Today* (3 a year), *Language World* (4 a year), *Rusistika* (1 a year), *Tuttitalia* (1 a year), *Vida Hispánica* (2 a year).

Association of British Science Writers: Wellcome Wolfson Bldg, 165 Queen's Gate, London, SW7 5HD; e-mail absw@absw.org.uk; internet www.absw.org.uk; f. 1947; study trips, briefings, workshops, lunches and social events; 600 mems; Chair. Dr NATASHA LODER; Admin. ANGELA NICOLAIDES; publ. *The Science Reporter* (4 a year and online).

British Association for Applied Linguistics: c/o Dovetail Management Consultancy, POB 6688, London, SE15 3WB; tel. (20) 7639-0090; fax (20) 7635-6014; e-mail admin@baal.org.uk; internet www.baal.org.uk; f. 1967; promotes study of language in use; fosters interdisciplinary collaboration, provides common forum for those engaged in theoretical study of language and those interested in its practical use; 750 individual mems, 30 mem. publishers and univ. depts; Chair. GUY COOK; Sec. CAROLINE COFFIN; publs *Applied Linguistics* (4 a year, in asscn with American Asscn for Applied Linguistics), *British Studies in Applied Linguistics* (Edited Proceedings of Annual Meetings).

British Association of Academic Phoneticians: Phonetics Laboratory, Dept of English Language, Univ. of Glasgow, G12 8QQ; tel. (141) 330-6340; fax (141) 330-3531; e-mail mike.macmahon@glasgow.ac.uk; internet www.baap.ac.uk; f. 1984; 150 mems; Sec. and Archivist Prof. MICHAEL K. C. MACMAHON.

Brontë Society: The Brontë Parsonage Museum, Haworth, BD22 8DR; tel. (1535) 642323; fax (1535) 647131; e-mail bronte@bronte.org.uk; internet www.bronte.org.uk; f. 1893, inc. 1902; collects and acts as guardian of Brontë letters, MSS and personal belongings that are housed in the Brontë Parsonage Museum, fmr home of the Brontës and now in the care of the soc.; 3,000 mems; Library and Information Officer Dr SARAH LAYCOCK; publ. *Brontë Studies* (3 a year).

Canadian Linguistic Association/Association Canadienne de Linguistique: Département d'Études Françaises, University of Western Ontario, London, N6A 3K7; fax (519) 661-3470; internet homes.chass.utoronto.ca/~cla-acl; f. 1954; advances study of linguistics and languages in Canada; 220 mems; Pres. FRANCE MARTINEAU; Sec. ILEANA PAUL; Treas. CARRIE DYCK; publ. *The Canadian Journal of Linguistics/La Revue Canadienne de Linguistique* (3 a year).

Charles Lamb Society: BM Elia, London, WC1N 3XX; f. 1935; to promote the study of the lives and works of Charles Lamb and his circle and to form a collection of Eliana; 300 mems; library: library housed in the Guildhall Library, Corporation of London; Pres. Prof. J. R. WATSON; Chair. NICHOLAS POWELL; publ. *The Charles Lamb Bulletin* (4 a year).

Chartered Institute of Linguists: Saxon House, 48 Southwark St, London, SE1 1UN; tel. (20) 7940-3100; fax (20) 7940-3101; e-mail info@iol.org.uk; internet www.iol.org.uk; f. 1910; promotes proficiency in modern languages worldwide amongst professional linguists, incl. translators, interpreters and educationalists; helps to ensure equal access for all to the public services (law, health, local govt) by providing interpreting qualifications in most of the languages spoken in

the United Kingdom; 6,500 mems; library of 6,000 vols; Chief Exec. JOHN HAMMOND; publ. *The Linguist* (6 a year).

Classical Association: c/o Claire Daveport, Senate House, Malet St, London, WC1E 7HU; tel. (20) 7862-8706; fax (20) 7255-2297; e-mail office@classicalassociation.org; internet www.classicalassociation.org; f. 1903; 3,500 mems; Sec. Dr EMMA STAFFORD; Sec. BARBARA FINNEY; publs *CA News* (2 a year), *Classical Quarterly* (2 a year), *Classical Review* (2 a year), *Greece and Rome* (2 a year).

Dickens Fellowship: Dickens House, 48 Doughty St, London, WC1N 2LF; tel. (20) 7405-2127; fax (20) 7831-5175; internet www.dickens.fellowship.btinternet.co.uk; f. 1902 to knit together in a common bond of friendship lovers of Charles Dickens, and to assist in the preservation and purchase of buildings and objects associated with Dickens or mentioned in his works; 7,000 mems; Pres. HENRY DICKENS HAWKSLEY; Hon. Gen. Secs THELMA GROVE, Dr TONY WILLIAMS; publs *The Dickensian* (3 a year), *Mr Dick's Kite* (3 a year).

Early English Text Society: Lady Margaret Hall, Oxford, OX2 6QA; internet www.eets.org.uk; f. 1864; texts published annually; 900 mems; Hon. Dir Prof. ANNE HUDSON; Exec. Sec. Prof. VINCENT A. GILLESPIE.

English Association: Univ. of Leicester, Leicester, LE1 7RH; tel. (116) 229-7622; fax (116) 229-7623; e-mail engassoc@le.ac.uk; internet www.le.ac.uk/engassoc; f. 1906; promotes knowledge and appreciation of the English language and its literature, through confs, lectures and publs; 1,500 mems; Pres. Prof. PETER KITSON; Chair. Prof. MAUREEN MORAN; Chief Exec. HELEN LUCAS; publs *English* (4 a year), *English 4–11* (3 a year), *Essays and Studies*, *The Use of English* (3 a year), *The Year's Work in Critical and Cultural Theory*, *The Year's Work in English Studies*.

English Centre of International PEN: 6–8 Amwell St, London, EC1R 1UQ; tel. (20) 7713-0023; fax (20) 7837-7838; e-mail enquiries@englishpen.org; internet www.englishpen.org; f. 1921; 990 mems; Pres. Dr ALISTAIR NIVEN; Dir SUSANNA NICKLIN.

English Speaking Board: 26A Princes St, Southport, Merseyside, PR8 1EQ; tel. (1704) 501730; fax (1704) 539637; e-mail admin@esbuk.org; internet www.esbuk.org; f. 1953; promotes and encourages all aspects of oral communication in English; brings together people from educational, professional and industrial spheres who are concerned with oral education as a means of communication; individual and corporate mems in 34 countries; arranges courses and examinations in spoken English at all levels, from primary to higher education; certificates and diplomas awarded to teachers, professional speakers; assessments for individuals studying English as an acquired language; 450 mems; Hon. Pres. JOCELYN BELL; Chair. RICHARD ELLIS (acting); publ. *Speaking English* (3 a year).

Francis Bacon Society Inc.: c/o G. N. Salway, Flat 1, Lee House, 75A Effra Rd, London, SW19 8PS; tel. (20) 8542-4689; internet www.baconsocietyinc.org; f. 1886; registered charity; studies the works and life of Francis Bacon, and investigates evidence suggesting Bacon's authorship of plays attributed to Shakespeare; library; Pres. PETER A. WELSFORD; Sec. GERALD N. SALWAY; publ. *Baconiana*.

Goethe-Institut: 50 Princes Gate, Exhibition Rd, London, SW7 2PH; tel. (20) 7596-4000; fax (20) 7594-0240; e-mail mail@london.goethe.org; internet www.goethe.de/london; offers courses and exams in German language and culture and promotes cultural

exchange with Germany; attached centres in Glasgow and Manchester; library of 17,000 vols; Dir Dr ROLAND GOLL.

Institute of Translation and Interpreting: Suite 165, Milton Keynes Business Centre, Foxhunter Dr., Linford Wood, Milton Keynes, MK14 6GD; tel. (1908) 325250; fax (1908) 325259; e-mail info@iti.org.uk; internet www.iti.org.uk; f. 1986; promotes high standards in translation and interpreting; provides information on these services to govt, industry, the media and the gen. public; offers guidance to those entering the profession and advice to those who offer language services and their customers; 3,000 mems; Chief Exec. PAUL WILSON; publ. *ITI Bulletin* (6 a year).

Instituto Cervantes: 102 Eaton Sq., London, SW1W 9AN; tel. (20) 7235-0353; fax (20) 7235-0329; e-mail cenlon@cervantes.es; internet londres.cervantes.es; f. 1991; offers courses and exams in Spanish language and culture and promotes cultural exchange with Spain and Spanish-speaking Latin and Central America; attached centre in Manchester; library of 20,000 vols; Dir ISABEL CLARA LORDA-VIDAL.

Joseph Conrad Society: c/o POSK, 238–246 King St, London, W6 0RF; e-mail theconradian@aol.com; internet www.josephconradsociety.org; f. 1973; provides a forum and resource for scholars of Conrad's work; 200 mems; library of 800 vols; Hon. Sec. HUGH EPSTEIN; publ. *The Conradian* (2 a year).

Kipling Society: 6 Clifton Rd, London, W9 1SS; tel. and fax (20) 7286-0194; e-mail jmkeskar@btinternet.com; internet www.kipling.org.uk; f. 1927; honours and extends the influence of Rudyard Kipling; organizes meeting and luncheon with guest speakers; 500 mems; Pres. Lt. Col. R.C. AYERS; Hon. Sec. JANE KESKAR; publ. *The Kipling Journal* (4 a year).

Linguistics Association of Great Britain: c/o Dr Andrew Hippisley, School of Electronics and Physical Sciences, University of Surrey, Guildford, Surrey, GU2 7XH; e-mail a.hippisley@surrey.ac.uk; internet www.lagb.org; f. 1959 to promote the study of linguistics and provide a forum for discussion and co-operation in the field; annual general meeting; 600 mems; Pres. Prof. APRIL MCMAHON; Hon. Sec. Dr AD NEELEMAN; publ. *Journal of Linguistics* (2 a year).

Malone Society: tel. (20) 7862-8679; e-mail canor.wyer@sas.ac.uk; internet ies.sas.ac.uk/malone; f. 1906; makes accessible materials for the study of English Renaissance drama up to 1642; publishes edns of 16th- and 17th-century plays from MSS, photographic facsimile edns of printed plays of the period, and edns of original documents relating to Renaissance theatre and drama; 170 vols published; back issues available; 670 mems; Chair. LEAH SCRAGG; Exec. Sec. Prof. KATHARINE CRAIK.

Philological Society: School of Oriental and African Studies, Univ. of London, Thornhaugh St, Russell Sq., London, WC1H 0XG; fax (20) 7898-4399; e-mail secretary@philsoc.org.uk; internet www.philsoc.org.uk; f. 1842, inc. 1879; investigates and promotes study and knowledge of the structure, affinities and history of languages; 832 mems; Pres. Prof. SYLVIA ADAMSON; Sec Dr MARTIN ORWIN; publ. *Transactions* (3 a year).

Poetry Society: 22 Betterton St, London, WC2H 9BX; tel. (20) 7240-9880; fax (20) 7240-4818; e-mail info@poetrysociety.org.uk; internet www.poetrysociety.org.uk; f. 1909; promotes study, appreciation and enjoyment of poetry; organises poetry reading, educational activities and the Nat. Poetry Competition; awards the Foyle Young Poets of Year prize; 4,000 mems; Dir JUDITH PALMER; publs *Poetry News* (4 a year), *Poetry Review* (4 a year).

Royal Society of Literature of the United Kingdom: Somerset House, Strand, London, WC2R 1LA; tel. (20) 7845-4676; fax (20) 7845-4679; e-mail info@rslit.org; internet www.rslit.org; f. 1820; lectures and literary discussions; awards 3 prizes annually; 1,350 mems; Pres. COLIN THUBRON; Chair. ANNE CHISHOLM; Dir MAGGIE FERGUSSON.

Society for the Promotion of Hellenic Studies: Senate House, Malet St, London, WC1E 7HU; tel. (20) 7862-8730; fax (20) 7862-8731; e-mail hellenic@sas.ac.uk; f. 1879; 3,000 mems; library: see entry for Joint Library of the Hellenic and Roman Societies; Pres. Prof. MALCOLM SCHOFIELD; Hon. Sec. Dr PANTELIS MICHELAKIS; Exec. Sec. RICHELLA DOYLE; publs *Journal of Hellenic Studies* (1 a year), *Archaeological Reports* (in conjunction with the British School at Athens, 1 a year).

Society for the Promotion of Roman Studies: Senate House, Malet St, London, WC1E 7HU; tel. (20) 7862-8727; fax (20) 7862-8728; e-mail office@romansociety.org; internet www.romansociety.org; f. 1910; 3,000 mems; library: see Libraries and Archives; Pres. Dr ANDREW BURNETT; Hon. Sec. SAM MOORHEAD; Sec. Dr FIONA HAARER; Hon. Treas. Dr PHILIP KAY; publs *Britannia* (1 a year), *Journal of Roman Studies* (1 a year).

Society for the Study of Medieval Languages and Literature: c/o Dr Corinne Saunders, Department of English Studies, University of Durham, Hallgarth House, 77 Hallgarth St, Durham, DH1 3AY; internet www.mod-langs.ox.ac.uk/ssmll; f. 1932; Editors Dr E. KENNEDY, Prof. N. PALMER, Dr C. SAUNDERS; publ. *Medium Ævum* (2 a year).

Society of Authors: 84 Drayton Gardens, London, SW10 9SB; tel. (20) 7373-6642; fax (20) 7373-5768; e-mail info@societyofauthors .org; internet www.societyofauthors.org; f. 1884; promotes and protects the rights of authors; 9,000 mems; Gen. Sec. NICOLA SOLOMON; publ. *The Author* (4 a year).

Wells, H. G., Society: c/o Paul Allen, 1 Nackington Rd, Canterbury, Kent, CT1 3NU; internet hgwellsusa.50megs.com; f. 1960; promotes an interest in and appreciation of the life, work and thought of H. G. Wells; organizes annual conf. (September); 200 mems; library of 300 vols (H. G. Wells Colln, Library, London Metropolitan Univ.–North London campus); Treas. PAUL ALLEN; publ. *The Wellsian* (1 a year).

MEDICINE

Academy of Medical Sciences: 41 Portland Pl., London, W1B 1QH; tel. (20) 3176-2150; fax (20) 7580-1052; e-mail info@ acmedsci.ac.uk; internet www.acmedsci.ac .uk; f. 1998; promotes medical science and its translation; influences policy to improve health and wealth; helps researchers; encourages public and professional dialogue about medical sciences; 1,017 mems; Pres. Prof. Sir JOHN TOOKE; Exec. Dir Dr HELEN MUNN.

Anatomical Society: Dept of Anatomy and Human Sciences, King's College (Guy's Campus), Room HB4.1N, Hodgkin Bldg, London, SE1 1UL; tel. (20) 7848-8234; fax (20) 7848-8234; internet www.anatsoc.org.uk; f. 1887; promotes, develops and advances anatomical and related sciences; research into the anatomical and related sciences; publishes research relevant to anatomical sciences; promotes and advances education in the anatomical sciences; 500 mems; Exec. Admin. MARY-ANNE PIGGOTT; Pres. Prof. D. CERI DAVIES; publs *Aging Cell* (12 a year), *Journal of Anatomy* (12 a year).

Apothecaries of London, Worshipful Society of: Apothecaries' Hall, Black Friars Lane, London, EC4V 6EJ; tel. (20) 7236-1180; fax (20) 7329-3177; e-mail examoffice@ apothecaries.org; internet www.apothecaries .org; f. 1617 by King James I; grants a registrable medical qualification (LMSSA Lond.), also the postgraduate diplomas in Medical Jurisprudence (DMJ), in Genitourinary Medicine (DipGUM), HIV Medicine (DipHIV), the History of Medicine (DHMSA), Philosophy of Medicine (DPMSA), Musculo Skeletal Medicine (DMSM), Medical Care of Catastrophes (DMCC), Clinical Pharmacology (DCPSA), Forensic Medical Sciences (DFMS), Forensic Human Identification (DFHID), Mastership in Medical Jurisprudence (MMJ); 1,600 mems; Master Sir WILLIAM SHAND; Clerk ANDREW WALLINGTON-SMITH; Registrar KIM EDMUNDS.

Association for the Study of Medical Education: 12 Queen St, Edinburgh, EH2 1JE; tel. (131) 225-9111; fax (131) 225-9444; e-mail info@asme.org.uk; internet www .asme.org.uk; f. 1957 to exchange information and promote research into medical education; 1,200 individual mems, 85 corporate mems; Pres. Prof. Sir KENNETH CALMAN; Chair Prof. GRAHAM BUCKLEY; Chief Exec. Prof. FRANK SMITH; publs *Bulletin* (6 a year), *Medical Education* (12 a year), *The Clinical Teacher* (2 a year).

Association of Anaesthetists of Great Britain and Ireland: 21 Portland Pl., London, W1B 1PY; tel. (20) 7631-8801; e-mail info@aagbi.org; internet www.aagbi .org; f. 1932; promotes devt and study of anaesthetics and their administration and maintains the high standard of this branch of medicine; 10,000 mems; Pres. Dr BIRKS GEMMELL; Hon. Sec. Dr ROBERT BUCKLAND; publs *Anaesthesia* (12 a year), *Anaesthesia News* (12 a year).

Association of British Neurologists: Ormand House, 4th Fl., 27 Boswell St, London, WC1N 3JZ; tel. (20) 7405-4060; fax (20) 7405-4070; e-mail info@theabn.org; internet www.theabn.org; f. 1933; supports neurologists and neurological trainees in their clinical practice and research; advances understanding of the nervous system and its disorders; 1,500 mems; Pres. Prof. MARTIN ROSSOR; Hon. Sec. Dr RALPH GREGORY.

Association of Surgeons of Great Britain and Ireland: c/o The Royal College of Surgeons, 35–43 Lincoln's Inn Fields, London, WC2A 3PN; tel. (20) 7973-0300; fax (20) 7430-9235; e-mail admin@asgbi.org.uk; internet www.asgbi.org.uk; f. 1920 for the advancement of the science and art of surgery; Pres. DENIS C. WILKINS; Hon. Sec. JONATHAN K. PYE.

British Association for Sexual Health and HIV: c/o Simon Croker, RSM, 1 Wimpole St, London, W1G 0AE; tel. (20) 7290-2968; fax (20) 7290-2989; f. 1922 as Medical Society for the Study of Venereal Diseases, to study sexually transmitted and allied diseases, incl., more recently, HIV/AIDS; 900 mems; Pres. Dr SIMON BARTON; Hon. Sec. Dr KEITH RADCLIFFE; publ. *Sexually Transmitted Infections* (6 a year).

British Association of Plastic, Reconstructive & Aesthetic Surgeons: c/o The Royal College of Surgeons, 35–43 Lincoln's Inn Fields, London, WC2A 3PE; tel. (20) 7831-5161; fax (20) 7831-4041; e-mail secretariat@baprass.co.uk; internet www .bapras.org.uk; f. 1946; protects and preserves public health by the promotion and development of plastic surgery; Pres. E. FREEDLANDER; Hon. Sec. D. J. COLEMAN; publs *British Journal of Plastic Surgery* (8 a year), *Journal of Plastic, Reconstructive and Aesthetic Surgery (JPRAS)*, *The Voice of Plastic Surgery*.

British Dental Association: 64 Wimpole St, London, W1G 8YS; tel. (20) 7935-0875; fax (20) 7487-5232; e-mail enquiries@bda .org; internet www.bda.org; f. 1880; acts as trade union for dental profession; 20,000 mems, 3,500 student mems; library of 10,000 vols; Chief Exec. Dr P. WARD; publs *BDA News* (12 a year), *British Dental Journal* (24 a year).

British Dietetic Association: 5th Fl., Charles House, 148–149 Great Charles St Queensway, Birmingham, B3 3HT; tel. (121) 200-8080; e-mail info@bda.uk.com; internet www.bda.uk.com; f. 1936; 5,000 mems; CEO ANDY BURMAN; Sec. LORETTA COX; publ. *Journal of Human Nutrition and Dietetics* (6 a year).

British Geriatrics Society: 31 St John's Square, London, EC1M 4DN; tel. (20) 7608-1369; fax (20) 7608-1041; e-mail info@bgs.org .uk; internet www.bgs.org.uk; f. 1947 to improve standards of medical care for elderly patients and to encourage research into the problems of old age; 2,000 mems; Chief Exec. ALEX MAIR; publ. *Age and Ageing*.

British Institute of Radiology: 36 Portland Place, London, W1B 1AT; tel. (20) 7307-1400; fax (20) 7307-1414; e-mail admin@bir .org.uk; internet www.bir.org.uk; f. 1897; a centre for consultation on the medical, physical and biological applications of radiology; current and historic radiological library; 1,700 mems; Pres. PETER SHARPE; Gen. Sec. TONY HUDSON; publs *The British Journal of Radiology* (12 a year), *Imaging* (4 a year).

British Medical Association: BMA House, Tavistock Square, London, WC1H 9JP; tel. (20) 7387-4499; fax (20) 7383-6400; e-mail info.web@bma.org.uk; internet www.bma.org .uk; f. 1832; voluntary professional association for doctors; scientific and educational body, publisher of the British Medical Journal and provides services for members; 137,000 mems; library: see Libraries and Archives; Pres. Prof. ANTHONY KUMAR; Chair. JAMES JOHNSON; publs *BMA News* (weekly), *British Medical Journal* (weekly), and numerous journals on specialized medical subjects.

British Nutrition Foundation: High Holborn House, 52–54 High Holborn, London, WC1V 6RQ; tel. (20) 7404-6504; fax (20) 7404-6747; e-mail postbox@nutrition.org.uk; internet www.nutrition.org.uk; f. 1967; Hon. Pres. Prof. DEREK BURKE; Dir-Gen. Prof. JUDITH L. BUTTRISS; Sec. THOMAS BARCLAY; publ. *Bulletin* (4 a year).

British Orthodontic Society: c/o Dr David Tidy, Hon. Sec., British Orthodontic Soc., 12 Bridewell Pl., London, EC4V 6AP; tel. (20) 7353-8680; fax (20) 7353-8682; e-mail hon .sec@bos.org.uk; internet www.bos.org.uk; f. 1994; Chair. Prof. NIGEL HUNT; Hon. Sec. Dr DAVID TIDY; publ. *Journal of Orthodontics* (4 a year).

British Orthopaedic Association: 35–43 Lincoln's Inn Fields, London, WC2A 3PE; tel. (20) 7405-6507; fax (20) 7831-2676; e-mail secretary@boa.ac.uk; internet www.boa.ac .uk; f. 1918; the advancement of the science and art of orthopaedic surgery; 3,486 mems; Pres. CLARE MARX; Hon. Sec. J. DIAS; Chief Exec. D. C. ADAMS; publ. *Journal of Bone and Joint Surgery*.

British Pharmacological Society: 16 Angel Gate, City Rd, London, EC1V 2PT; tel. (20) 7239-0171; fax (20) 7417-0114;

e-mail info@bps.ac.uk; internet www.bps.ac.uk; f. 1931; 3,000 mems; Chief Exec. K. BAILLIE; publs *British Journal of Clinical Pharmacology* (12 a year), *British Journal of Pharmacology* (24 a year).

British Psychoanalytical Society: Byron House, 112A Shirland Rd, Maida Vale, London, W9 2EQ; tel. (20) 7563-5000; fax (20) 7563-5001; e-mail ginette@goulston-lincoln.com; internet www.psychoanalysis.org.uk; f. 1913 as The London Psychoanalytical Society, present name 1919; training of psychoanalysts, devt of the theory and practice of psychoanalysis, advancement of psychoanalysis as a science; 400 mems; library of 22,000 vols, incl. 1,600 monographs, 300 journals; Pres. MICHAEL BREARLEY; Hon. Sec. C. POLMEAR; publ. *The International Journal of Psycho-Analysis* (6 a year).

British Society for Research on Ageing: c/o Dr Matthew Hardman, Faculty of Life Sciences, AV Hill Bldg, Univ. of Manchester, Manchester, M13 9PT; e-mail web@bsra.org.uk; internet www.bsra.org.uk; f. 1945; encourages gerontological research in Great Britain by acting as a forum for the report and discussion of new advances in ageing research; open to all who are engaged in experimental gerontology; Chair. Prof. ANNE MCARDLE; Sec. Dr MATTHEW HARDMAN; publs *e-Lifespan* (12 a year, online), *Lifespan* (2 a year), *Mechanisms of Ageing and Development.*

British Society for Rheumatology: Bride House, 18–20 Bride Lane, London, EC4Y 8EE; tel. (20) 7842-0900; fax (20) 7842-0901; e-mail bsr@rheumatology.org.uk; internet www.rheumatology.org.uk; f. 1984; promotes excellence in the treatment of people with arthritis and musculo-skeletal conditions and supports those delivering it; 1,500 mems; Pres. DEBORAH BAX; Exec. Sec. SAMANTHA PETERS; publs *Musculoskeletal Care, Rheumatology.*

British Society of Gastroenterology: 3 St Andrews Pl., Regent's Park, London, NW1 4LB; tel. (20) 7935-3150; fax (20) 7487-3734; e-mail enquiries@bsg.org.uk; internet www.bsg.org.uk; f. 1937; training programmes, research workshops and scientific and clinical confs; 3,400 mems; Pres. Prof. JONATHAN RHODES; Sec. Dr C. D. R. MURRAY; Sec. Dr CATHRYN EDWARDS; Chief Exec. Dr TOM SMITH; Treas. Dr M. DAKKAK; publs *Frontline Gastroenterology* (6 a year), *Gut* (12 a year).

Chartered Society of Physiotherapy: 14 Bedford Row, London, WC1R 4ED; tel. (20) 7306-6666; fax (20) 7306-6611; e-mail enquiries@csp.org.uk; internet www.csp.org.uk; f. 1894 as Society of Trained Masseuses, became Incorporated Society of Trained Masseuses 1900, granted a Royal Charter 1920, merged with Institute of Massage and Remedial Gymnastics, present name 1944; professional, educational and trade union body for chartered physiotherapists, support workers and physiotherapy students in the UK; 51,000 mems; Chair. Dr HELENA JOHNSON; Treas. SUE ENGLAND; Pres. Baroness ILORA FINLAY OF LLANDAFF; Chief Exec. PHIL GRAY; publs *Physiotherapy Frontline* (24 a year), *Physiotherapy Journal* (4 a year).

College of Optometrists: 42 Craven St, London, WC2N 5NG; tel. (20) 7839-6000; fax (20) 7839-6800; e-mail optometry@college-optometrists.org; internet www.college-optometrists.org; f. 1980 by The British Optical Asscn, The Scottish Asscn of Opticians and The Worshipful Co of Spectacle Makers; improves and conserves human vision; incl. a library and museum; 13,357 mems incl. over 9,000 practising UK mems and Fellows; library of 7,000 vols, incl.

optical books, pamphlets and audiovisual titles, journals, British Standards, govt publs, college publs, gen. reference materials, historical collns; Pres. Dr KAMLESH CHAUHAN; Chair. CINDY TROMANS; CEO BRYONY PAWINSKA; publs *Ophthalmic and Physiological Optics* (6 a year, online), *Optometry in Practice* (4 a year, print).

Diabetes UK: 10 Parkway, London, NW1 7AA; tel. (20) 7424-1000; fax (20) 7424-1001; e-mail info@diabetes.org.uk; internet www.diabetes.org.uk; f. 1934 to help all people with diabetes and those interested in diabetes, to promote greater public understanding of the condition and to support research into diabetes; 190,000 mems; Chair. of Board of Trustees Sir MICHAEL HIRST; Chief Exec. PAUL STREETS; publs *Balance for Beginners* (updated annually), *Balance Magazine* (6 a year), *Diabetic Medicine* (10 a year), *Diabetes Update* (4 a year).

Harveian Society of London: 11 Chandos St, London, W1G 9EB; tel. (20) 7580-1043; e-mail harveiansoclondon@btconnect.com; internet www.harveiansocietyoflondon.btck.co.uk; f. 1831; promotes the advancement of medical science; 250 mems; Pres. Prof. ROBERT DOUGLAS; Hon. Sec. Prof. JOHN WALKER-SMITH; Exec. Sec. Cmdr ROGER IRELAND; Exec. Sec. BETTY SMALLWOOD.

Institute of Biomedical Science: 12 Coldbath Sq., London, EC1R 5HL; tel. (20) 7713-0214; fax (20) 7837-9658; e-mail mail@ibms.org; internet www.ibms.org; f. 1912; promotes and develops role of biomedical science and its practitioners within healthcare; establishes and maintains professional standards; 20,000 mems; Chief Exec. JILL RODNEY; publs *British Journal of Biomedical Science* (4 a year), *The Biomedical Scientist* (12 a year).

Medical Society of London: Lettsom House, 11 Chandos St, London, W1G 9EB; tel. (20) 7580-1043; fax (20) 7631-4817; e-mail medicalsoclondon@btconnect.com; internet www.medsoclondon.org; f. 1773; 440 mems; library of 4,500 vols; Registrar Cmdr ROGER IRELAND; publ. *Transactions* (1 a year).

MIND: Granta House, 15–19 Broadway, London, E15 4BQ; tel. (20) 8519-2122; fax (20) 8522-1725; e-mail info@mind.org.uk; internet www.mind.org.uk; f. 1946; works to create a better life for people with experience of mental distress; produces information and publs; offers services incl. advocacy, counselling, crisis helplines, drop-in centres, employment and training schemes, supported housing; 1,600 mems, 200 local asscns, 7 regional offices; Chief Exec. PAUL FARMER.

Northern Ireland Association for Mental Health: Central Office, 80 University St, Belfast, BT7 1HE; tel. (28) 9032-8474; e-mail alisondeane@niamh.co.uk; internet www.niamh.co.uk; f. 1959 as Beacon House; counselling, training and consultancy for employers on mental health in the workplace; Chief Exec. Prof ALAN FERGUSON; Chair. Dr GRAEME MCDONALD.

Nutrition Society: 10 Cambridge Court, 210 Shepherds Bush Rd, London, W6 7NJ; tel. (20) 7602-0228; fax (20) 7602-1756; e-mail office@nutsoc.org.uk; internet www.nutritionsociety.org.uk; f. 1941 to advance the scientific study of nutrition and its application to the maintenance of human and animal health; over 2,200 mems; Pres. Prof. J. J. STRAIN; publs *British Journal of Nutrition* (12 a year), *Nutrition Research Reviews* (2 a year), *Proceedings* (6 a year), *Public Health Nutrition* (8 a year).

Pathological Society: 2 Carlton House Terrace, London, SW1Y 5AF; tel. (20) 7976-1260; fax (20) 7930-2981; e-mail admin@

pathsoc.org; internet www.pathsoc.org; f. 1906; 1,500 mems; Pres. Prof. A. H. WYLLIE; Meetings Sec. Prof. I. O. ELLIS; Gen.-Sec. Prof. C. SIMON HERRINGTON; Treas. Prof. ALASTAIR D. BURT; publ. *Journal of Pathology.*

Royal Association for Disability and Rehabilitation: 12 City Forum, 250 City Rd, London, EC1V 8AF; tel. (20) 7250-3222; fax (20) 7250-0212; e-mail radar@radar.org.uk; internet www.radar.org.uk; f. 1977; covers the whole field of disability; a coordinating organization concerned with the needs and rights of disabled people; Dir KATE NASH.

Royal College of Anaesthetists: Churchill House, 35 Red Lion Sq., London, WC1R 4SG; tel. (20) 7092-1500; fax (20) 7092-1730; e-mail info@rcoa.ac.uk; internet www.rcoa.ac.uk; f. 1948; responsible for the science of anaesthesia throughout the United Kingdom and for ensuring the quality of patient care through the maintenance of standards in anaesthesia, critical care and pain management; 14,000 fellows, mems and trainees; Pres. Dr JUDITH HULF; publs *British Journal of Anaesthesia* (12 a year), *Bulletin* (6 a year).

Royal College of General Practitioners: 14 Princes Gate, London, SW7 1PU; tel. (20) 7581-3232; fax (20) 7225-3047; internet www.rcgp.org.uk; f. 1952 to ensure the highest possible standards in general medical practice; 21,000 mems; Chair. Dr MAYUR LAKHANI; Hon. Sec. Dr MAUREEN BAKER; publ. *British Journal of General Practice* (12 a year).

Royal College of Nursing of the United Kingdom: 20 Cavendish Sq., London, W1M 0AB; tel. (20) 7409-3333; fax (20) 7355-1379; internet www.rcn.org.uk; f. 1916 to represent the interests of nurses and advance the provision of healthcare generally; library of 60,000 vols; Pres. SYLVIA DENTON; publ. *Nursing Standard* (weekly).

Royal College of Obstetricians and Gynaecologists: 27 Sussex Pl., Regent's Park, London, NW1 4RG; tel. (20) 7772-6200; fax (20) 7723-0575; e-mail info@rcog.org.uk; internet www.rcog.org.uk; f. 1929; 10,705 mems; library of 15,000 vols; Pres. Dr TONY FALCONER; Chief Exec. Dr IAN WYLIE; publs *British Journal of Obstetrics and Gynaecology* (12 a year), *The Obstetrician and Gynaecologist* (4 a year).

Royal College of Ophthalmologists: 17 Cornwall Terrace, London, NW1 4QW; tel. (20) 7935-0702; fax (20) 7935-9838; internet www.rcophth.ac.uk; f. 1988 for the cultivation and promotion of ophthalmology; 3,200 mems; Pres. ALLAN TEMPLETON; Hon. Sec. BRENDA BILLINGTON; publ. *Eye* (6 a year).

Royal College of Paediatrics and Child Health: 5–11 Theobalds Rd, London, WC1X 8SH; tel. (20) 7092-6000; fax (20) 7092-6001; e-mail enquiries@rcpch.ac.uk; internet www.rcpch.ac.uk; f. 1928 to advance, for the benefit of the public, education in paediatrics and to relieve sickness by promoting the improvement of paediatric practice; 7,800 mems; Pres. Prof. ALAN CRAFT; Registrar Dr SHEILA SHRIBMAN; publ. *Archives of Disease in Childhood* (12 a year, with British Medical Association).

Royal College of Pathologists: 2 Carlton House Terrace, London, SW1Y 5AF; tel. (20) 7451-6700; fax (20) 7451-6701; e-mail info@rcpath.org; internet www.rcpath.org; f. 1962; 8,474 fellows and mems; library of 2,100 vols (spec. colln); Pres. Prof. ADRIAN NEWLAND; Chief Exec. DANIEL ROSS; publ. *Bulletin* (4 a year).

Royal College of Physicians: 11 St Andrews Pl., London, NW1 4LE; tel. (20)

7224-1539; fax (20) 7487-5218; e-mail infocentre@rcplondon.ac.uk; internet www .rcplondon.ac.uk; f. 1518; aims to promote the values of the medical profession, improve standards of clinical practice, support physicians in their practice of medicine through education and training, communicate with govt, the public and the profession and provide leadership on health and healthcare issues; 22,000 mems (13,000 fellows, 9,000 collegiate mems); library: see Libraries and Archives; Pres. Prof. I. GILMORE; Registrar Prof. R. BURNHAM; Chief Exec. M. ELSE; publ. *Clinical Medicine* (6 a year).

Royal College of Physicians and Surgeons of Glasgow: 232–242 St Vincent St, Glasgow, G2 5RJ; tel. (141) 221-6072; fax (141) 221-1804; internet www.rcpsg.ac.uk; f. 1599; a medical licensing corporation; 9,039 fellows and mems in medicine, surgery, dentistry and travel medicine; library: see Libraries and Archives; Pres. I. ANDERSON; Hon. Sec. Dr J. TAYLOR.

Royal College of Physicians of Edinburgh: 9 Queen St, Edinburgh, EH2 1JQ; tel. (131) 225-7324; fax (131) 220-3939; internet www.rcpe.ac.uk; f. 1681; 7,000 mems; library: see Libraries and Archives; Pres. Prof. N. J. DOUGLAS; Sec. Dr J. COLLINS; publ. *Journal* (4 a year).

Royal College of Psychiatrists: 17 Belgrave Sq., London, SW1X 8PG; tel. (20) 7235-2351; fax (20) 7245-1231; e-mail rcpsych@ rcpsych.ac.uk; internet www.rcpsych.ac.uk; f. 1971 by Charter, previously Royal Medico-Psychological Asscn; 12,000 Fellows and mems; Pres. Prof. S. BAILEY; Registrar Dr L. MYNORS-WALLIS; Chief Exec. V. CAMERON; publs *Advances in Psychiatric Treatment* (6 a year), *British Journal of Psychiatry* (12 a year), *The Psychiatrist* (12 a year).

Royal College of Radiologists: 38 Portland Pl., London, W1B 1JQ; tel. (20) 7636-4432; fax (20) 7323-3100; e-mail enquiries@ rcr.ac.uk; internet www.rcr.ac.uk; f. 1939; practice of radiology and oncology; 6,600 mems; Chief Exec. ANDREW HALL; publs *Clinical Oncology* (8 a year), *Clinical Radiology* (12 a year).

Royal College of Surgeons of Edinburgh: Nicolson St, Edinburgh, EH8 9DW; tel. (131) 527-1600; fax (131) 557-6406; e-mail reception@rcsed.ac.uk; internet www .rcsed.ac.uk; f. 1505; postgraduate education and assessment in surgery; c. 20,000 mems; Pres. D. A. TOLLEY; Chief Exec. A. ROONEY; publs *Surgeon News* (4 a year), *The Surgeon* (6 a year).

Royal College of Surgeons of England: 35–43 Lincoln's Inn Fields, London, WC2A 3PE; tel. (20) 7405-3474; fax (20) 7831-9438; e-mail education@rcseng.ac.uk; internet www.rcseng.ac.uk; f. 1800; supervises training of surgeons in approved posts; provides educational and practical workshops for surgeons and other medical professionals; promotes surgical research; acts as an advisory body to the Dept of Health and other health authorities, trusts, hospitals; attached information centre for surgeons in the library and museums; 14,300 fellows and mems; library of 100,000 vols; Pres. JOHN BLACK; publs *Annals of the Royal College of Surgeons of England* (8 a year), *Bulletin* (10 year).

Royal Institute of Public Health: 28 Portland Pl., London, W1B 1DE; tel. (20) 7580-2731; fax (20) 7580-6157; e-mail info@ riphh.org.uk; internet www.riphh.org.uk; f. 1898; 3,000 mems; Chief Exec. NICHOLA WILKINS; publs *Health and Hygiene* (4 a year), *Public Health* (6 a year).

Royal Medical Society: Students' Centre, Bristo Sq., Edinburgh, EH8 9AL; tel. (131) 650-2672; e-mail enquiries@royalmedical.co

.uk; internet www.royalmedicalsociety.co .uk; f. 1737; 2,000 mems; library of 2,000 vols; Pres. KRISTINA LEE; Sec. ANDREW BROOKES; Permanent Sec. ELIZABETH SINGH; publ. *Res Medica* (2 a year).

Royal Pharmaceutical Society: 1 Lambeth High St, London, SE1 7JN; tel. (20) 7572-2300; e-mail library@rpharms.com; internet www.rpharms.com; f. 1841; professional body for pharmacists in England, Scotland and Wales; c. 30,000 mems; library of 80,000 vols, pamphlets and MSS, 300 journals, colln of pharmacopoeias and formularies; Pres. MARTIN ASTBURY; CEO HELEN GORDON; publs *Annual Register of Pharmaceutical Chemists*, *British National Formulary* (jtly with the British Medical Assocn), *Journal of Pharmacy and Pharmacology* (12 a year), *Martindale: The Extra Pharmacopoeia, Medicines and Ethics, Pharmaceutical Sciences* (12 a year), *The Clinical Pharmacist* (11 a year), *The International Journal of Pharmacy Practice* (4 a year), *The Pharmaceutical Journal* (52 a year).

Royal Society for Public Health: John Snow House, 59 Mansell St, London, E1 8AN; tel. (20) 7265-7334; fax (20) 7265-7301; e-mail info@rsph.org.uk; internet www.rsph .org.uk; f. 2008 by merger of Royal Soc. for the Promotion of Health and the Royal Institute of Public Health; promotes protection and preservation of human health and wellbeing; examining body for food hygiene; holds confs. and lectures; 5,700 mems; Patron HM THE QUEEN; Pres. LORD HUNT OF KING'S HEATH; Chair of Ccl Dr SELWYN HODGE; publs *Perspectives in Public Health* (6 a year), *Public Health* (12 a year).

Royal Society of Medicine: 1 Wimpole St, London, W1G 0AE; tel. (20) 7290-2900; fax (20) 7290-2992; e-mail membership@rsm.ac .uk; internet www.rsm.ac.uk; f. 1805, first Royal Charter 1834; undertakes over 400 meetings a year covering 58 Sections of medicine and surgery; publishes journals for other orgs and proceedings of sponsored meetings; 23,000 mems; Pres. Prof. PARVEEN KUMAR; Chief Exec. IAN BALMER; publs *Aids and Hepatitis Digest* (6 a year), *Annals of Clinical Biochemistry* (6 a year, online), *Clinical Governance Bulletin* (6 a year, also online), *Clinical Risk* (6 a year, online), *Effective Health Care* (6 a year, also online), *Handbook of Practice Management* (4 a year, online), *Health Information on the Internet* (6 a year, online), *Health Services Management Research* (4 a year, also online), *International Journal of STD and AIDS* (12 a year, also online), *Journal of Health Services Research and Policy* (4 a year, online), *Journal of Integrated Care Pathways* (3 a year), *Journal of Laryngology and Otology* (12 a year, also online), *Journal of Medical Biography* (4 a year), *Journal of Medical Screening* (4 a year, also online), *Journal of Telemedicine and Telecare* (6 a year, online), *Journal of the British Menopause Society* (4 a year, also online), *Journal of the Royal Society of Medicine* (12 a year, also online), *Laboratory Animals* (4 a year, online), *Phlebology* (4 a year, also online), *Tropical Doctor* (4 a year).

Royal Society of Tropical Medicine and Hygiene: 50 Bedford Sq., London, WC1B 3DP; tel. (20) 7580-2127; fax (20) 7436-1389; e-mail info@rstmh.org; internet www.rstmh .org; f. 1907 to promote and advance the study, control and prevention of disease in humankind and other animals in the tropics and warm climates, and to facilitate the discussion and exchange of information among those interested in tropical medicine and international health; 2,000 mems; Pres. Prof. HAZEL DOCKRELL; Hon. Secs Prof. M. J. NEWPORT, Dr J. R. STOTHARD; Chief Exec.

GERRI MCHUGH; publs *International Health* (4 a year), *Transactions* (12 a year).

Society for Endocrinology: 22 Apex Court, Woodlands, Bradley Stoke, Bristol, BS32 4JT; tel. (1454) 642200; fax (1454) 642222; e-mail info@endocrinology.org; internet www.endocrinology.org; f. 1939; promotes the advancement of endocrinology; 1,900 mems; Chair. J. BUCKINGHAM; publs *Endocrine-Related Cancer* (4 a year, online), *Journal of Endocrinology* (12 a year), *Journal of Molecular Endocrinology* (6 a year, print; 12 a year, online), *The Endocrinologist* (4 a year).

Society of British Neurological Surgeons: c/o Suzanne Murray, 35–43 Lincoln's Inn Fields, London, WC2A 3PE; tel. (20) 7869-6892; fax (20) 7869-6890; e-mail admin@sbns.org.uk; internet www.sbns.org .uk; f. 1926; promotes high standards of professional practice through the Soc.'s involvement in the education and the examination of neurosurgeons and through its meetings and associated activities in the continual professional devt of neurosurgeons; 384 mems; Pres. Prof. JOHN PICKARD; Pres. Elect PHILIP VAN HILLE; publ. *Proceedings* (in *British Journal of Neurosurgery*).

Society of Occupational Medicine: Hamilton House, Mabledon Pl., London, WC1H 7BB; tel. (20) 7554-8627; fax (20) 7554-8526; e-mail admin@som.org.uk; internet www.som.org.uk; f. 1935; concerned with the protection of the health of people at work and the prevention of occupational diseases and injuries; stimulates research and education in occupational medicine; 1,800 mems; Pres. Dr R. J. L. HERON; Hon. Sec. Dr E. D'SOUZA; publ. *Occupational Medicine* (8 a year).

St John's Dermatological Society: St John's Institute of Dermatology, St Thomas' Hospital, Lambeth Palace Rd, London, SE1 7EH; tel. (20) 7188-9352; e-mail nuala .odonoghue@imperial.nhs.uk; internet www .st-johns-society.co.uk; meeting at St John's Hospital for Diseases of the Skin; f. 1911 to promote the knowledge and study of dermatology by presentation and discussion of rare and interesting cases; 250 Fellows; Pres. Dr ANDREW PEMBROKE; Hon. Sec. Dr NUALA O'DONOGHUE; publ. *Clinical and Experimental Dermatology* (1 a year).

Stroke Association: 240 City Rd, London, EC1V 2PR; tel. (845) 303-3100; e-mail info@ stroke.org.uk; internet www.stroke.org.uk; f. 1899, fmrly The Chest, Heart and Stroke Asscn; provides practical support to people who have had strokes and to their families, through community services and welfare grants; prevents strokes through health education; Chair. of Council Sir CHARLES GEORGE; Chief Exec. JON BARRICK; publ. *Stroke News* (4 a year).

Tavistock Institute of Medical Psychology: The Tavistock Centre, 120 Belsize Lane, London, NW3 5BA; tel. (20) 7435-7111; fax (20) 7435-1080; e-mail timp@tccr.org.uk; internet www.tccr.org.uk; f. 1929; promotes the study and practice of psychotherapy and provides grants for related small research projects; administers the Tavistock Centre for Couple Relationships, which offers a professional service to couples experiencing difficulty in relationships and trains counsellors; and Relationship Counselling for London, which provides a counselling consultation service and trains counsellors; Chair. Dr A. OBHOLZER; Company Sec. D. OBADINA; publ. *In Brief* (1 a year).

NATURAL SCIENCES

General

Association for Science Education: College Lane, Hatfield AL10 9AA; tel. (1707) 283000; fax (1707) 266532; e-mail membership@ase.org.uk; internet www.ase.org.uk; f. 1901; organizes meetings and workshops locally and nationally; aims to improve science teaching and to provide a medium of expression for science teachers; 21,000 mems; Chief Exec. Dr D. S. MOORE; publs *Education in Science* (5 a year), *Primary Science Review* (5 a year), *School Science Review* (4 a year), *Science Teacher Education* (3 a year).

British Science Association: Wellcome Wolfson Bldg, 165 Queen's Gate, London, SW7 5HD; tel. (870) 770-7101; fax (20) 7581-6587; e-mail info@britishscienceassociation.org; internet www.britishscienceassociation.org; f. 1831; promotes and advances public understanding and awareness of science and technology and their effect on soc.; 5,670 mems; Chief Exec. ROLAND JACKSON; publ. *People & Science* (4 a year).

British Society for the History of Science: POB 3401, Norwich, NR7 7JF; tel. (1603) 516236; fax (1252) 641135; e-mail execsec@bshs.org.uk; internet www.bshs.org.uk; f. 1947; promotes and furthers the study of the history and philosophy of science, technology and medicine; organizes meetings and confs; 750 mems; Exec. Sec. L TETLOW; publs *British Journal for the History of Science* (4 a year), *Viewpoint* (newsletter, 3 a year).

Cambridge Philosophical Society: Central Science Library, Arts School, Bene't St, Cambridge, CB2 3PY; tel. (1223) 334743; e-mail philosoc@hermes.cam.ac.uk; internet www.cambridgephilosophicalsociety.org; f. 1819; promotes scientific enquiry and facilitates the communication of facts connected with the advancement of science; 1,900 mems; Exec. Sec. B. LARNER; publs *Biological Reviews* (4 a year), *Mathematical Proceedings* (6 a year).

Council for Environmental Education: c/o SEEd, 9–13 Kean Street, London, WC2B 4AY; tel. (118) 950-2550; fax (118) 959-1955; e-mail info@se-ed.org.uk; internet www.cee.org.uk; f. 1968; umbrella org. for national and associated orgs working in environmental and sustainable development education; increases the effectiveness of the environmental education movement by developing and influencing policy and supporting and encouraging good practice; library: reference library and resource centre; 84 mems; Dir LIBBY GRUNDY; publs *CEEmail* (3 a year), *CEEview* (4 a year), *Earthlines* (3 a year).

Environment Council: POB 66755, London, WC1A 9EA; tel. (20) 8144-9049; fax (20) 7242-1180; e-mail info@envcouncil.org.uk; internet www.the-environment-council.org.uk; f. 1969, fmrly Ccl for Environmental Conservation; works with business, industry, govt, non-governmental organizations and the community to find sustainable solutions to environmental problems; 2,000 mems; Chief Exec. NIGEL HOMER.

Field Studies Council: Preston Montford, Montford Bridge, Shrewsbury, SY4 1HW; tel. (1743) 852100; fax (1743) 852101; e-mail enquiries@field-studies-council.org; internet www.field-studies-council.org; f. 1943; operates 17 residential and day centres throughout the UK, offering a range of courses for schools and colleges; leisure learning and professional devt courses are offered in the UK and overseas; provides outreach education, training and consultancy; publishes a number of titles to support its work, incl.

identification guides; 4,000 mems; Pres. Prof. I. D. MERCER; Chair. Prof. T. P. BURT; Dir R. LUCAS.

Foundation for Science and Technology: 10 Carlton House Terrace, London, SW1Y 5AH; tel. (20) 7321-2220; fax (20) 7321-2221; e-mail office@foundation.org.uk; internet www.foundation.org.uk; f. 1977; debates science, engineering, technology and medical science policy; Chief Exec. Dr DOUGAL GOODMAN; publ. *FST Journal* (4 a year).

Institution of Environmental Sciences: 38 Ebury St, London, SW1W 0LU; tel. (20) 7730-5516; fax (20) 7730-5519; internet www.ies-uk.org.uk; f. 1971 for consultation in matters of an environmental nature; aims to promote interdisciplinary studies of the environment, to diffuse information relating to environmental sciences at nat. and int. levels, and to bring together into a corporate professional body all persons throughout the world possessing responsibilities for environmental affairs; 1,003 individual mems; Chair. CAROLYN ROBERTS; Hon. Sec. J. R. BLUMHOF; publ. *The Environmental Scientist* (3 a year).

Kindrogan Field Studies Centre: Kindrogan Field Centre, Enochdhu, Blairgowrie PH10 7PG; tel. (1250) 870150; fax (1250) 881433; e-mail enquiries.kd@field-studies-council.org; internet www.field-studies-council.org/centres/kindrogan.aspx; f. 1945; provides residential courses and a venue for fieldwork in biology and geography; centre for biodiversity and outdoor learning; 400 mems; Chair. MARTYN JAMIESON.

London Natural History Society: c/o The Secretary, 381B Whitton Ave, Greenford, UB6 0JU; tel. (20) 8426-6621; e-mail davidhowdon@virgin.net; internet www.lnhs.org.uk; f. 1858; field meetings, talks, training days, recording of species and habitats; reading circles distribute a wide range of journals; sections cater for spec. interests: botany, entomology and general ecology, ornithology; 1,000 individual mems, 25 corporate mems; library of 3,500 vols, 5,000 periodicals; Library at the Angela Marmont Centre for UK Biodiversity at the Natural History Museum, London; Pres. Prof. TED TUDDENHAM; Treas. MICHAEL WEST; Sec. DAVID HOWDON; publs *London Bird Report* (1 a year), *The London Naturalist* (1 a year).

Royal Institution of Great Britain: 21 Albemarle St, London, W1S 4BS; tel. (20) 7409-2992; fax (20) 7629-3569; e-mail ri@ri.ac.uk; internet www.rigb.org; f. 1799; promotes science to the public through lectures, demonstrations and discussions; Davy Faraday Research Laboratory conducts research into the chemistry and physics of materials; active heritage dept; 3,200 mems; library: see Libraries and Archives; museum: see Museums and Art Galleries; Pres. HRH THE DUKE OF KENT; Sec. Prof. ALAN MARIES; Chief Exec. CHRIS ROFFE; Dir of the Davy Faraday Research Laboratory Prof. QUENTIN PANKHURST.

United Kingdom Science Park Association: Chesterford Research Park, Little Chesterford, Cambridge, CB10 1XL; tel. (1799) 532050; fax (1799) 532049; e-mail admin@ukspa.prestel.co.uk; internet www.ukspa.org.uk; f. 1984 to act as a forum for those concerned with the planning and management of science parks, and to promote awareness of science parks and provide information on their objectives and achievements; mems: 65 science parks; Chair. JANE DAVIES; Sec. PAUL CARVER; publs *Directory*, *Innovation Into Success*, *The Development and Operation of Science Parks*.

Wildlife Trusts: The Kiln, Waterside, Mather Rd, Newark, NG24 1WT; tel. (1636) 677711; fax (1636) 670001; e-mail enquiry@wildlifetrusts.org; internet www.wildlifetrusts.org; f. 1912 as Royal Society for Nature Conservation; inc. by Royal Charter 1916 and 1976, to promote the conservation of nature for study and research and to educate the public in the understanding and appreciation of nature, the awareness of its value and the need for its conservation; acts as the nat. office for the 46 Wildlife Trusts, Urban Wildlife Groups and Wildlife Watch (junior br.); 800,000 mems; Pres. Prof. DAVID BELLAMY; publ. *Natural World* (3 a year).

Biological Sciences

Association for the Study of Animal Behaviour: c/o Prof. F. Huntingford, Graham Kerr Building, University of Glasgow, Glasgow, G12 8QQ; tel. (141) 330-6643; fax (141) 330-5971; e-mail gbza10@udcf.gla.ac.uk; internet www.societies.ncl.ac.uk/asab; f. 1936; 2,000 mems; Pres. Prof. F. HUNTINGFORD; Sec. Dr C. MAGNHAGEN; publ. *Animal Behaviour* (12 a year).

Association of Applied Biologists: Warwick Enterprise Park, Wellesbourne, Warwick, CV35 9EF; tel. (1789) 472020; fax (1789) 470234; internet www.aab.org.uk; f. 1904; promotes study and advancement of all brs of biology, with spec. reference to their applied aspects; 800 mems; Pres. Prof. TREVOR HOCKING; Gen. Sec. Dr ELIZABETH STOCKDALE; publ. *Annals of Applied Biology* (6 a year).

Biochemical Society: Charles Darwin House, 12 Roger St, London, WC1N 2JU; tel. (20) 7685-2400; e-mail genadmin@biochemistry.org; internet www.biochemistry.org; f. 1911; advancement of the science of biochemistry; 5,000 mems; Chair. Prof. COLIN KLEANTHOUS; Chief Exec. Dr C. J. KIRK; publs *Biochemical Journal* (24 a year), *Biochemical Society Transactions* (6 a year), *Clinical Science* (12 a year), *Essays in Biochemistry* (2 a year), *Symposia* (1 a year), *The Biochemist* (6 a year), *Biology of the Cell* (on behalf of the Société de Biologie Cellulaire de France and the Société Française des Microscopies, 12 a year), *Biotechnology and Applied Biochemistry* (on behalf of the International Union of Biochemistry and Molecular Biology, 6 a year).

Biosciences Federation: Peer House, 8–14 Verulam St, London, WC1X 8LZ; tel. (1223) 400181; e-mail info@bsf.ac.uk; internet www.bsf.ac.uk; f. 2002; 50 mem. socs; Pres. Prof. Dame NANCY ROTHWELL; CEO Dr RICHARD DYER.

Botanical Society of Scotland: c/o Royal Botanic Garden Edinburgh, 20A Inverleith Row, Edinburgh, EH3 5LR; tel. (131) 552-7171; internet www.botsocscot.org.uk; f. 1836 (fmrly Botanical Soc. of Edinburgh); incorporates the Cryptogamic Soc. of Scotland; 300 mems and fellows; Pres. Prof. C. E. JEFFREE; Hon. Gen. Sec. Dr B. A. HARVIE; publ. *Plant Ecology and Diversity* (2 a year).

Botanical Society of the British Isles: c/o Dept of Botany, Natural History Museum, Cromwell Rd, London, SW7 5BD; tel. (20) 7942-5002; e-mail coordinator@bsbi.org.uk; internet www.bsbi.org.uk; f. 1836; studies British native flowering plants and ferns; exhibitions, confs, field meetings; 2,800 mems; Hon. Gen. Sec. LYNNE FARRELL; publs *BSBI News* (3 a year), *Watsonia* (2 a year).

British Biophysical Society: c/o Prof. John Seddon, Dept of Chemistry, Imperial College, London SW7 2AZ; tel. (20) 7594-5797; e-mail j.seddon@imperial.ac.uk; internet www.britishbiophysics.org.uk; f. 1960; 450 mems; Sec. Prof. JOHN M. SEDDON.

British Ecological Society: Charles Darwin House, 12 Roger St, London, WC1N 2JU; tel. (20) 7685-2500; fax (20) 7685-2501; e-mail info@britishecologicalsociety.org; internet www.britishecologicalsociety.org; f. 1913; publ. of scientific literature, incl. five internationally renowned journals; funding of numerous grant schemes, education work and policy work; 4,000 mems; Exec. Dir Dr HAZEL J. NORMAN; publs *Symposium* (1 a year), *Journal of Ecology* (6 a year), *Journal of Animal Ecology* (6 a year), *Journal of Applied Ecology* (6 a year), *Functional Ecology* (6 a year).

British Mycological Society: The Wolfson Wing, Jodrell Laboratory, Royal Botanic Gardens, Kew, Richmond, Surrey, TW9 3AB; tel. (23) 9284-2024; fax (23) 9252-5902; e-mail admin@britmycolsoc.info; internet www.britmycolsoc.org.uk; f. 1896; promotes mycology through scientific meetings, publs and education; 1,206 mems and 644 assocs; Pres. Prof. LYNNE BODDY; Gen. Sec. Dr GEOFFREY D. ROBSON; publs *Field Mycology* (4 a year), *Mycological Research* (12 a year), *Mycologist* (4 a year).

British Ornithologists' Union: Dept of Zoology, University of Oxford, South Parks Rd, Oxford, OX1 3PS; tel. and fax (1865) 8281842; e-mail bou@bou.org.uk; internet www.bou.org.uk; f. 1858 for the advancement of the science of ornithology; 1,800 ordinary mems, plus hon. mems and corresp. mems; Pres. Prof. C. M. PERRINS; Hon. Sec. N. J. BUCKNELL; publ. *Ibis* (4 a year).

British Society for Plant Pathology: Marlborough House, Basingstoke Rd, Spencers Wood, Reading, RG7 1AG; e-mail secretary@bspp.org.uk; internet www.bspp.org.uk; f. 1981; 650 mems; Pres. Dr JAMES BROWN; Sec. Dr ROGER WILLIAMS; publs *BSPP News* (4 a year), *Molecular Plant Pathology* (6 a year), *New Disease Reports* (4 a year), *Plant Pathology* (6 a year).

British Trust for Ornithology: The Nunnery, Thetford, IP24 2PU; tel. (1842) 750050; fax (1842) 750030; e-mail info@bto.org; internet www.bto.org; f. 1933; promotes and encourages wider understanding, appreciation and conservation of birds through scientific studies using the combined skills and enthusiasm of its mems, other bird watchers and staff; projects incl. Nat. Bird Ringing Scheme, Nest Records Scheme, Wetland Bird Survey, Breeding Bird Survey, Garden Bird Watch, Bird Atlas; offers advisory services to ecologists, land use planners, conservationists, developers; 13,000 mems; Pres. Baroness YOUNG OF OLD SCONE; Dir Dr F. A. CLEMENTS; publs *Bird Study* (4 a year), *Bird Table* (4 a year), *BTO News* (6 a year), *Ringing and Migration* (2 a year).

Fauna & Flora International: 4th Fl., Jupiter House, Station Rd, Cambridge, CB1 2JD; tel. (1223) 571000; fax (1223) 461481; e-mail info@fauna-flora.org; internet www.fauna-flora.org; f. 1903; protects threatened species and ecosystems from extinction worldwide; chooses solutions that are sustainable, based on science and take account of human needs; improving the livelihoods of local people; 3,000 mems; CEO MARK ROSE; Chair. MARTIN FISHER; publ. *Oryx* (4 a year).

Freshwater Biological Association: The Ferry Landing, Ambleside, LA22 0LP; tel. (15394) 42468; fax (15394) 46914; e-mail info@fba.org.uk; internet www.fba.org.uk; f. 1929; promotes study and application of freshwater biology; encourages adoption of freshwater science as best way to understand, protect and manage water resources; ferry landing on shores of Windermere, Cumbria; River Laboratory, East Stoke, Wareham, Dorset sited on River Frome;

1,650 mems; library of 150,000 vols, 10,000 vols. of scientific periodicals; Pres. Prof. ALAN HILDREW; Chair. of Ccl Prof. CHRIS SPRAY; Sec. and Dir Dr MICHAEL DOBSON; publs *FBA News* (3 a year), *FBA Scientific Publications* (irregular), *Freshwater Forum* (irregular), *Freshwater Reviews* (2 a year, online), *Inland Waters* (4 a year, online).

Genetics Society: c/o Jayne Richards, Roslin Institute, Roslin, Midlothian, EH25 9PS; tel. (131) 200-6391; fax (131) 200-6401; e-mail mail@genetics.org.uk; internet www.genetics.org.uk; f. 1919; all aspects of genetics, pure and applied; 2,000 mems; Pres. Prof. JONATHAN HODGKIN; Hon. Sec. Dr JOHN ARMOUR; publs *Genes and Development* (every 2 weeks), *Genetics Society News* (12 a year), *Heredity* (12 a year).

Linnean Society of London: Burlington House, Piccadilly, London, W1J 0BF; tel. (20) 7434-4479; fax (20) 7287-9364; e-mail info@linnean.org; internet www.linnean.org; f. 1788; possesses the unique colln of Linnaeus's plants and animals and other collns; library and archive; holds scientific meetings; 2,100 Fellows, incl. 50 Foreign Mems and 20 Hon. Fellows; library: see Libraries and Archives; Exec. Sec. Dr RUTH TEMPLE; Pres. Dr VAUGHN SOUTHGATE; Sec. for Botany Dr SANDRA KNAPP; Sec. for Collections SUSAN GOVE; Sec. for Editorial Dr JOHN EDMONDON; Sec. for Zoology Dr MALCOLM SCOBLE; publs *Biological Journal* (12 a year), *Botanical Journal* (12 a year), *Pulse* (4 a year), *Symposium* (vols), *Synopses of the British Fauna* (irregular), *The Linnean Newsletter and Proceedings* (4 a year), *Zoological Journal* (12 a year).

Malacological Society of London: c/o Dr V. Flari, Central Science Laboratory, Sand Hutton, York, YO4 1LZ; tel. (1904) 462349; e-mail vasiliki@flari.fsnet.co.uk; internet www.malacsoc.org.uk; f. 1893 to promote all aspects of the study of Mollusca; library: Radley Library deposited at University College London; 300 mems; Hon. Sec. Dr VASILIKI FLARI; publs *Journal of Molluscan Studies* (4 a year), *The Malacologist* (bulletin of the Society, 3 a year).

Marine Biological Association of the United Kingdom: The Laboratory, Citadel Hill, Plymouth, PL1 2PB; tel. (1752) 633207; fax (1752) 633102; e-mail sec@mba.ac.uk; internet www.mba.ac.uk; f. 1884; promotes scientific research into all aspects of life in the sea; receives grants from univs, research charities and other public bodies; 1,250 mems; library: National Marine Biological Library; 60,000 vols; Pres. Sir GEOFFREY HOLLAND; Sec. and Dir Prof. COLIN BROWNLEE; publ. *Journal* (8 a year).

Physiological Society: Peer House, Verulam St, London, WC1X 8LZ; tel. (20) 7269-5710; fax (20) 7269-5720; e-mail admin@physoc.org; internet www.physoc.org; f. 1876; promotes the advancement of physiology and facilitates communication between physiologists at home and abroad; 2,900 mems; Chief Exec. MIKE COLLIS; publs *Experimental Physiology* (12 a year online, 6 a year in print), *The Journal of Physiology* (26 a year), *The Physiological Society Magazine* (4 a year).

Ray Society: c/o Natural History Museum, Cromwell Rd, London, SW7 5BD; tel. (20) 7942-5560; e-mail t.ferrero@nhm.ac.uk; f. 1844; publishes works primarily concerned with the natural history of the British Isles and north-west Europe; 270 mems; Pres. E. PLATTS; Hon. Sec. Dr T. J. FERRERO.

Royal Entomological Society: The Mansion House, Chiswell Green Lane, St Albans, AL2 3NS; tel. (1727) 899387; fax (1727) 894797; e-mail info@royensoc.co.uk; internet

www.royensoc.co.uk; f. 1833; 2,025 Fellows; library of 11,000 vols, 750 periodicals, 30,000 reprints; Pres. Prof. LIN FIELD; Registrar W. H. F. BLAKEMORE; publs *Agricultural and Forest Entomology* (4 a year), *Antenna* (4 a year), *Ecological Entomology* (4 a year), *Insect Molecular Biology* (4 a year), *Medical and Veterinary Entomology* (4 a year), *Physiological Entomology* (4 a year), *Systematic Entomology* (4 a year).

Royal Society for the Protection of Birds: The Lodge, Sandy, SG19 2DL; tel. (1767) 680551; fax (1767) 692365; internet www.rspb.org.uk; f. 1889, inc. 1904; protects wild birds and their natural habitat; 1m. mems; library of 9,000 vols; Chair. IAN DARLING; Chief Exec. Dr MIKE CLARKE; publs *Bird Life* (6 a year), *Birds* (4 a year), and occasional titles.

Royal Zoological Society of Scotland: Scottish National Zoological Park, Edinburgh, EH12 6TS; tel. (131) 334-9171; fax (131) 314-0382; e-mail info@rzss.org.uk; internet www.edinburghzoo.org.uk; f. 1909, inc. by Royal Charter 1913, to promote, through the presentation of the Soc.'s living collns, the conservation of animal species and wild places by captive breeding, environmental education and scientific research; 23,000 mems; Chief Exec. HUGH ROBERTS; publ. *Lifelinks* (4 a year).

Scottish Association for Marine Science: Dunstaffnage Marine Laboratory, Dunbeg, Oban, PA37 1QA; tel. (1631) 559000; fax (1631) 559001; internet www.sams.ac.uk; f. 1884 for research and education in marine science; 470 mems, 150 staff; Pres. Prof. Sir JOHN ARBUTHNOTT; Dir Prof. LAWERCE MEE.

Selborne Society Ltd: 89 Daryngton Dr., Greenford, UB6 8BH; tel. (78) 7859-4290; e-mail contact@selbornesociety.org.uk; internet www.selbornesociety.org.uk; f. 1885; perpetuates the memory of Gilbert White of Selborne and promotes the study of natural history, esp. among schoolchildren; colln of originals of 'The Natural History of Selborne' and MSS by Gilbert White; 1,024 mems; Hon. Sec. ANDREW PEDLEY.

Society for General Microbiology: Marlborough House, Basingstoke Rd, Spencers Wood, Reading, RG7 1AG; tel. (118) 988-1800; fax (118) 988-5656; e-mail admin@sgm.ac.uk; internet www.sgm.ac.uk; f. 1945; promotes the advancement of microbiology; provides a common meeting ground for those working in specialized fields incl. medical, veterinary, agricultural and economic microbiology; 5,300 individual mems, 550 schools; Pres. Prof. HILARY LAPPIN-SCOTT; Chief Exec. Dr R. S. S. FRASER; publs *International Journal of Systematic and Evolutionary Microbiology* (12 a year), *Journal of General Virology* (12 a year), *Journal of Medical Microbiology* (12 a year), *Microbiology* (12 a year), *Microbiology Today* (4 a year).

Society of Biology: Charles Darwin House, 12 Roger St, London, WC1N 2JU; tel. (20) 7685-2550; e-mail info@societyofbiology.org; internet www.societyofbiology.org; f. 2009 by merger of the Biosciences Federation and the Institute of Biology; to create a single unified voice for UK biology, representing the discipline and its practitioners; 80,000 mems; Pres. Prof. Dame NANCY ROTHWELL; Chief Exec. Dr MARK DOWNS; publ. *Journal of Biological Education*.

Systematics Association: c/o Botany Dept, Natural History Museum, Cromwell Rd, London, SW7 5BD; tel. (20) 7942-5910; fax (20) 7942-5529; e-mail j.brodie@nhm.ac.uk; internet www.systass.org; f. 1937; studies systematics in relation to biology and evolution; 400 mems; Pres. Prof. JULIET BRODIE; Sec. for Programmes Dr J. COTTON; Sec. Dr P.

WILKIE; Sec. for Grants and Awards Dr T. RICHARDS.

Zoological Society of London: Regent's Park, London, NW1 4RY; tel. (20) 7722-3333; fax (20) 7449-6411; internet www.zsl.org; f. 1826; consists of: ZSL London Zoo and ZSL Whipsnade Zoo; conservation programmes, Institute of Zoology, library and fellowship services; 40,000 mems; library of 180,000 vols, 1,300 periodicals; Pres. Prof. Sir PATRICK BATESON; Dir-Gen. RALPH ARMOND; publs *Animal Conservation* (6 a year), *Conservation Science and Practice Book Series* (2 a year), *International Zoo Yearbook* (1 a year), *Journal of Zoology* (12 a year), *Nomenclator Zoologicus* (9 vols).

Mathematical Sciences

British Society for the History of Mathematics: 20 Dunvegan Close, Exeter, Devon, EX4 4AF; internet www.bshm.org; f. 1971; provides a forum for all interested in the history and development of mathematics and related disciplines; organizes conferences, workshops, visits; 500 mems; Hon. Sec. TONY MANN; publ. *Bulletin* (3 a year).

Institute of Mathematics and its Applications: Catherine Richards House, 16 Nelson St, Southend-on-Sea, SS1 1EF; tel. (1702) 354020; fax (1702) 354111; e-mail post@ima.org.uk; internet www.ima.org.uk; f. 1964, inc. by Royal Charter 1990; extends and diffuses knowledge of mathematics and of the applications of mathematics in science, engineering, economics; promotes education in mathematics; 5,000 mems; Pres. Prof. ROBERT MACKAY; Exec. Dir DAVID YOUDAN; publs *IMA Journal of Applied Mathematics* (6 a year), *IMA Journal of Management Mathematics* (4 a year), *IMA Journal of Mathematical Control and Information* (4 a year), *IMA Journal of Numerical Analysis* (4 a year), *IMA Teaching Mathematics and its Applications* (int. journal, 4 a year), *Information and Inference: a Journal of the IMA*, *Mathematical Medicine and Biology* (4 a year).

London Mathematical Society: De Morgan House, 57–58 Russell Sq., London, WC1B 4HS; tel. (20) 7637-3686; fax (20) 7323-3655; e-mail lms@lms.ac.uk; internet www.lms.ac.uk; f. 1865; promotes and extends mathematical knowledge; 2,450 mems; Pres. Dr G. B. SEGAL; Hon. Sec. Prof. J. M. E. HYLAND; Exec. Sec. F. C. NIXON; publs *Bulletin* (6 a year), *Journal* (6 a year), *Nonlinearity* (6 a year), *Proceedings* (6 a year).

Physical Sciences

Association of Public Analysts: Burlington House, Piccadilly, London W1V 0BN; tel. (1224) 491648; fax (1224) 276873; e-mail nmichie@aberdeencity.gov.uk; internet www.the-apa.co.uk; f. 1953 as a body to support analysts engaged in the public protection enforcement service, where chemical analysis and related testing are undertaken, especially in relation to the composition of foodstuffs, fertilizers, animal feed and other areas of consumer protection; 120 mems and Associate mems; Pres. NORMAN MICHIE; Hon. Sec. RON ENNION; publ. *Journal of the Association of Public Analysts* (online).

British Astronomical Association: Burlington House, Piccadilly, London, W1J 0DU; tel. (20) 7734-4145; fax (20) 7439-4629; e-mail office@britastro.org; internet www.britastro.org; f. 1890; asscn of amateur astronomical observers; 3,000 mems; publs *Handbook* (1 a year), *Journal* (6 a year).

British Cryogenics Council: 7 Leverton Gdns, Wantage, OX12 9NY; tel. (1372) 376544; fax (1372) 376544; e-mail admin@

bcryo.org.uk; internet www.bcryo.org.uk; f. 1967; fosters and encourages devt and application of cryogenics in Britain by means of contacts, education and research; 100 mem. instns; Chair. Prof. HARRY JONES; Treas. JOHN VANDORE; publ. *Low Temperature News* (4 a year).

British Horological Institute: Upton Hall, Upton, Newark, NG23 5TE; tel. (1636) 813795; fax (1636) 812258; internet www.bhi.co.uk; f. 1858; promotes the science and practice of horology; 3,000 mems; Pres. Dr J. K. LLOYD JONES; Sec. M. TAYLOR; publ. *The Horological Journal* (12 a year).

British Interplanetary Society: 27/29 South Lambeth Rd, London, SW8 1SZ; tel. (20) 7735-3160; fax (20) 7587-5118; e-mail mail@bis-space.com; internet www.bis-space.com; f. 1933; promotes study and research in science, engineering and technology of astronautics; organizes evening lectures; symposia; confs; visits; 3,300 mems (1,800 fellows, 1,500 mems); Pres. ROBERT PARKINSON; Exec. Sec. SUSZANN PARRY; publs *Journal of the British Interplanetary Society (JBIS)* (12 a year), *Space Chronicle* (2 a year), *Spaceflight* (12 a year).

British Nuclear Energy Society: 1–7 Great George St, London, SW1P 3AA; tel. (20) 7665-2241; fax (20) 7799-1325; internet www.bnes.com; f. 1962 in succession to British Nuclear Energy Conference to provide a forum for discussion, and directed to the broader aspects of nuclear energy, covering engineering and scientific disciplines; 12 constituent institutions; 1,200 mems; Sec. ANDREW TILLBROOK; publs *Nuclear Energy* (6 a year), *Conference Proceedings* (irregular).

Challenger Society for Marine Science: c/o National Oceanography Centre Empress Dock, European Way, Southampton, SO14 3ZH; tel. (23) 8059-5106; fax (23) 8059-5107; e-mail jennifer.jones@noc.ac.uk; internet www.challenger-society.org.uk; f. 1903; promotes study of oceanography, marine sciences; 500 mems; Pres. Prof. HARRY BRYDEN; publ. *Ocean Challenge* (2 a year).

Geological Society of London: Burlington House, Piccadilly, London, W1J 0BG; tel. (20) 7434-9944; fax (20) 7439-8975; e-mail enquiries@geolsoc.org.uk; internet www.geolsoc.org.uk; f. 1807; investigates the mineral structure of the Earth; 10,000 mems; library: see Libraries and Archives; Pres. Dr BRYAN LOVELL; Exec. Sec. EDMUND NICKLESS; publs *Geochemistry, Exploration, Environment, Analysis* (4 a year), *Journal* (6 a year), *Petroleum Geoscience* (4 a year), *Quarterly Journal of Engineering Geology and Hydrogeology* (4 a year).

Geologists' Association: Burlington House, Piccadilly, London, W1J 0DU; tel. (20) 7434-9298; fax (20) 7287-0280; e-mail geol.assoc@btinternet.com; internet www.geologist.demon.co.uk; f. 1858 to foster the progress and diffusion of the science of geology and to encourage research and the development of new methods; 2,000 mems; Pres. Dr ROBIN COCKS; Exec. Sec. SARAH STAFFORD; publs *GA Magazine* (4 a year), *Proceedings* (4 a year).

Institute of Acoustics: Third Fl., St Peter's House, 45–49 Victoria St, St Albans, AL1 3WZ; tel. (1727) 848195; fax (1727) 850553; e-mail ioa@ioa.org.uk; internet www.ioa.org.uk; f. 1974; 3,000 mems; Pres. BRIDGET SHIELD; Chief Exec. KEVIN MACAN-LIND; publ. *Acoustics Bulletin* (6 a year).

Institute of Physics: 76 Portland Place, London, W1B 1NT; tel. (20) 7470-4800; fax (20) 7470-4848; e-mail physics@iop.org; internet www.iop.org; f. 1918, chartered 1970; professional body for physicists in the UK and Ireland; 34,500 mems; Pres. Sir

JOHN ENDERBY; Hon. Sec. Prof. JOHN BEEBY; Chief Exec. Dr ROBERT KIRBY-HARRIS; publs *Chinese Physics* (12 a year), *Chinese Physics Letters* (12 a year), *Combustion Theory and Modelling* (4 a year), *European Journal of Physics* (6 a year), *Inverse Problems* (6 a year), *Journal of Cosmology and Astroparticle Physics* (online only), *Journal of High Energy Physics* (online only), *Journal of Micromechanics and Microengineering* (12 a year), *Journal of Physics* (series A 50 a year, B 24 a year, CM 50 a year, D 24 a year and G 12 a year), *Journal of Radiological Protection* (4 a year), *Journal of Turbulence* (online only), *Measurement Science and Technology* (12 a year), *Metrologia* (6 a year), *Modelling and Simulation in Materials Science and Engineering* (8 a year), *Nanotechnology* (12 a year), *New Journal of Physics* (online only, at www.njp.org), *Nonlinearity* (6 a year), *Nuclear Fusion* (12 a year), *Physics Education* (6 a year), *Physics in Medicine and Biology* (24 a year), *Physiological Measurement* (6 a year), *Plasma Physics and Controlled Fusion* (12 a year), *Plasma Sources Science and Technology* (4 a year), *Reports on Progress in Physics* (12 a year), *Semiconductor Science and Technology* (12 a year), *Smart Materials and Structures* (6 a year), *Superconductor Science and Technology* (12 a year).

Mineralogical Society of Great Britain and Ireland: 12 Baylis Mews, Amyand Park Rd, Twickenham, Middx, TW1 3HQ; tel. (20) 8891-6600; fax (20) 8891-6599; e-mail info@minersoc.org; internet www.minersoc.org; f. 1876 by Joseph Henry Collins; scientific publishing and promotion of the mineral sciences through scientific meetings and special interest groups; 1,000 mems; Pres. Prof. BEN HARTE; Gen. Sec. Dr MARK HODSON; Exec. Sec. Dr ADRIAN LLOYD-LAWRENCE; publs *Clay Minerals* (4 a year), *Mineralogical Magazine* (6 a year).

Palaeontographical Society: c/o Dept of Palaeontology, Natural History Museum, Cromwell Rd, London, SW7 5BD; tel. (20) 7942-5195; fax (20) 7942-5546; e-mail s.long@nhm.ac.uk; internet www.nhm.ac.uk/hostedsites/palsoc; f. 1847; illustration and description of British fossils; 181 individual mems, 174 mem. orgs; Pres. Dr A. B. SMITH; Sec. Dr S. L. LONG; Sec. Dr P. M. BARRETT; publ. *Monograph of the Palaeontographical Society* (1 a year).

Quekett Microscopical Club: c/o Natural History Museum, Cromwell Rd, London, SW7 5BD; tel. (20) 7942-5213; e-mail secretary@quekett.org; internet www.quekett.org; f. 1865; encourages study of every br. of microscopical science; 500 mems; library of 1,000 vols; Pres. CHARLES HUSSEY; publ. *Quekett Journal of Microscopy* (2 a year).

Royal Astronomical Society: Burlington House, Piccadilly, London, W1J 0BQ; tel. (20) 7734-4582; fax (20) 7494-0166; e-mail info@ras.org.uk; internet www.ras.org.uk; f. 1820, granted Royal Charter in 1831; 3,200 mems; library: see Libraries and Archives; Pres. Prof. K. WHALER; Exec. Sec. D. ELLIOTT; publs *Astronomy and Geophysics* (6 a year), *Geophysical Journal International* (12 a year), *Monthly Notices of the Royal Astronomical Society* (every 10 days).

Royal Meteorological Society: 104 Oxford Rd, Reading, Berks, RG1 7LS; tel. (1734) 568500; fax (1734) 568571; e-mail execdir@rmets.org; internet www.rmets.org; f. 1850; 3,000 mems; Pres. Prof. C. G. COLLIER; Gen. Sec. Dr P. RYDER; publs *Quarterly Journal*, *International Journal of Climatology* (15 a year), *Weather* (12 a year), *Meteorological*

Applications (4 a year), *Atmospheric Science Letters* (online), *Weather Front* (12 a year).

Royal Microscopical Society: 37–38 St Clements, Oxford, OX4 1AJ; tel. (1865) 248768; fax (1865) 791237; e-mail info@rms .org.uk; internet www.rms.org.uk; f. 1839, granted Royal Charter in 1866; for the promotion of microscopical science and its applications in the academic and industrial fields; 1,400 mems; Pres. Prof. CHRIS HAWKS; Exec. Dir ROBERT FLAVIN; publs *Journal of Microscopy* (12 a year), *Proceedings* (4 a year).

Royal Society of Chemistry: Thomas Graham House, Science Park, Milton Rd, Cambridge, CB4 0WF; tel. (1223) 420066; fax (1223) 426017; e-mail sales@rsc.org; internet www.rsc.org; f. 1980 from unification of the Chemical Soc. (f. 1841) and the Royal Inst. of Chemistry (f. 1877); 46,000 fellows and mems (designated Chartered Chemists), assoc. mems and affiliates, incl. 4,000 students; library: see Libraries and Archives; Pres. Prof. JIM FEAST; Chief Exec. Dr RICHARD PIKE; publs *The Analyst* (12 a year), *Analytical Abstracts* (12 a year), *Catalysts and Catalysed Reactions* (12 a year), *Chemical Biology* (12 a year), *Chemical Communications* (52 a year), *Chemical Science* (12 a year), *Chemical Society Reviews* (12 a year), *Chemical Technology* (12 a year), *Chemistry World* (12 a year), *Chromatography Abstracts* (published in collaboration with the Chromatographic Soc., 12 a year), *CrystEngComm* (electronic only, 12 a year), *Dalton Transactions* (52 a year), *Education in Chemistry* (6 a year), *Faraday Discussions* (3 a year), *Green Chemistry* (12 a year), *Journal of Analytical Atomic Spectroscopy* (12 a year), *Journal of Environmental Monitoring* (12 a year), *Journal of Materials Chemistry* (52 a year), *Lab on a Chip* (12 a year), *Laboratory Hazards Bulletin* (12 a year), *Mass Spectrometry Bulletin* (12 a year), *Methods in Organic Synthesis* (12 a year), *Molecular BioSystems* (12 a year), *Natural Product Reports* (6 a year), *Natural Product Updates* (12 a year), *New Journal of Chemistry* (published on behalf of the CNRS, 12 a year), *Organic and Biomolecular Chemistry* (26 a year), *PCCP–Physical Chemistry Chemical Physics* (jtly owned by Royal Soc. of Chemistry, Deutsche Bunsen-Gesellschaft für Physikalische Chemie and the chemical societies of Denmark, Finland, Ireland, Israel, Italy, the Netherlands, Norway, Spain, Sweden, Switzerland and Turkey, weekly), *Photochemical and Photobiological Sciences* (published on behalf of European Soc. for Photobiology (ESP), European Photochemistry Asscn (EPA), the Asia and Oceania Soc. for Photobiology (AOSP) and the Korean Soc. of Photoscience (KSP), 12 a year), *Soft Matter* (12 a year).

SCI (Society of Chemical Industry): International Headquarters, 14/15 Belgrave Square, London, SW1X 8PS; tel. (20) 7598-1500; fax (20) 7598-1545; internet www.soci .org; f. 1881; interdisciplinary network connecting industry, research and consumer affairs at all levels throughout the world; provides opportunities for people working in the areas of process and materials technologies, energy, water, agriculture, food, pharmaceuticals, construction and environmental protection to exchange ideas and gain new perspectives on markets, technologies and strategies; 6,000 mems; Pres. THOMAS M. SWAN; Gen. Sec. RICHARD DENYER; publs *Chemistry & Industry* (2 a month), *Journal of Chemical Technology and Biotechnology* (12 a year), *Journal of the Science of Food and Agriculture* (15 a year), *Pest Management Science* (12 a year), *Polymer International* (12 a year), *SCI Bulletin* (12 a year).

Yorkshire Geological Society: c/o Paul Hildreth, Kimberley, Bigby Rd, Brigg, DN20 8BU; tel. ((1652) 655-784; e-mail pandahildreth@hotmail.com; internet www .yorksgeolsoc.org.uk; f. 1837; works in fields of geology and the wider earth sciences of N England; scientific and public lecture meetings monthly in different locations; coordinates the annual Yorkshire Geology Month each May; 600 mems; library of 5,000 vols; Pres. Dr NOEL WORLEY; Gen. Sec. PAUL HINDRETH; Hon. Treas. Prof. PATRICK BOYLAN; publ. *Proceedings of the Yorkshire Geological Society* (2 a year).

PHILOSOPHY AND PSYCHOLOGY

Aristotelian Society: Room 281, Stewart House, Russell Sq., London, WC1B 5DN; tel. (20) 7862-8685; e-mail mail@ aristoteliansociety.org.uk; internet www .aristoteliansociety.org.uk; f. 1880 for the systematic study of philosophy, its historic devt and its methods and problems; meets fortnightly in London, throughout the academic year, to hear and discuss philosophical papers; papers are drawn from an int. base of contributors and discuss issues across a broad range of philosophical traditions, incl. those that are of greatest current interest; meetings are open to the public and the papers are subsequently published in the Soc.'s Journal; also an annual conference held in conjunction with the Mind Asscn; papers given at the conference are published in a Supplementary Vol; 700 individual mems, 1,357 mem. libraries; Exec. Sec. R. E. CARTER; publs *Proceedings* (annual; online journal, 3 a year), *Supplementary Volume* (1 a year).

British Psychological Society: St Andrews House, 48 Princess Rd East, Leicester, LE1 7DR; tel. (116) 254-9568; fax (116) 247-0787; e-mail mail@bps.org.uk; internet www.bps.org.uk; f. 1901; 40,000 mems; Pres. Dr GERRY MULHERN; Hon. Gen. Sec. Prof. PAM MARAS; publs *British Journal of Clinical Psychology* (4 a year), *British Journal of Developmental Psychology* (4 a year), *British Journal of Educational Psychology* (4 a year), *British Journal of Health Psychology* (4 a year), *British Journal of Mathematical & Statistical Psychology* (4 a year), *British Journal of Psychology* (4 a year), *British Journal of Social Psychology* (4 a year), *Journal of Occupational & Organisational Psychology* (4 a year), *Legal and Criminological Psychology* (4 a year), *Psychology and Psychotherapy: Theory, Research and Practice* (4 a year), *Selection & Development Review* (4 a year), *The Psychologist* (12 a year).

British Society of Aesthetics: c/o Prof. Graham McFee, The Chelsea School, Univ. of Brighton, 1 Denton Rd, Eastbourne, BN20 7SP; e-mail kathleen@british-aesthetics.org; internet www.british-aesthetics.org; f. 1960 to promote study, research and discussion in aesthetics and the growth of artistic taste among the public, and to facilitate communications between scholars at an international and European level; Pres. RICHARD WOLLHEIM; Sec. KATHLEEN STOCK; publ. *British Journal of Aesthetics* (4 a year).

Experimental Psychology Society: Dept of Experimental Psychology, Univ. of Bristol, 12A Priory Rd, Bristol, BS8 1TU; internet www.eps.ac.uk; f. 1946; furthers scientific enquiry in the field of psychology; 756 mems; Pres. Prof. V. BRUCE; Hon. Sec. Prof. C. JARROLD; publ. *Quarterly Journal of Experimental Psychology*.

Leeds Philosophical and Literary Society Ltd: c/o Armley Mills Museum, Canal Rd, Leeds, LS12 2QF; internet www

.leedsphilandlit.org.uk; f. 1820 to promote the advancement of science, literature and the arts in the city of Leeds and elsewhere; organizes public lectures and visits; provides assistance for scholarly research and publication; 135 mems; Sec. Dr J. LYDON.

Manchester Literary and Philosophical Society: MMU Business School, Aytoun St, Manchester, M1 3GH; tel. (161) 247-6774; fax (161) 247-6773; e-mail admin@manlitphil .co.uk; internet www.manlitphil.co.uk; f. 1781; promotes advancement of education and encourages public interest in, and appreciation of, any form of literature, science, the arts and public affairs; varied lectures throughout the academic year; 500 mems; library of 4,000 vols; Administrator ALLAN JEFFERIS; Administrator MARGARET GALLAGHER; Hon. Sec. PETER BARNES; Hon. Sec. DEREK CALDWELL; publ. *Manchester Memoirs* (1 a year).

Mind Association: c/o Dr Miranda Fricker, Dept of Philosophy, Birkbeck College, Malet St, London, WC1E 7HX; tel. (20) 7631-6383; e-mail m.fricker@bbk.ac.uk; internet www .mindassociation.org; f. 1900; organizes annual confs jtly with the Aristotelian Soc.; 300 mems; Hon. Sec. Dr MIRANDA FRICKER; publ. *MIND* (4 a year).

Philosophical Society of England: 6 Craghall Dean Ave, Newcastle upon Tyne, NE3 1QR; tel. (191) 284-1223; fax (191) 284-1223; e-mail m.c.bavidge@ncl.ac.uk; internet www.philsoc.co.uk; f. 1913; spreads knowledge of philosophy among public; organizes lectures, confs and workshops; sponsors local philosophical groups; 150 mems; Pres. Prof. BRENDA ALMOND; Chair. MICHAEL BAVIDGE; publ. *The Philosopher* (2 a year).

Royal Institute of Philosophy: 14 Gordon Square, London, WC1H 0AR; tel. (20) 7387-4130; fax (20) 7387-4061; e-mail j.garvey@ royalinstitutephilosophy.org; internet www .royalinstitutephilosophy.org; f. 1925; 700 mems; Pres. Lord QUINTON; Chair. Lord SUTHERLAND OF HOUNDWOOD; Dir Prof. A. O'HEAR; Sec. Dr JAMES GARVEY; publs *Conference Proceedings* (1 a year), *Philosophy* (4 a year), *Think* (4 a year).

Royal Philosophical Society of Glasgow: D12, 160 Bothwell St, Glasgow, G2 7EL; tel. (141) 564-3841; e-mail info@royalphil.org; internet www.royalphil.org; f. 1802; organizes lectures and promotes philosophical debate; 900 mems; Pres. Prof. HAMISH SCOTT; Hon. Sec. JIM MEARNS; Hon. Treas. MERVYN LOVAT.

Victoria Institute, or Philosophical Society of Great Britain (operates as Faith and Thought): 96 Hadleigh Rd, Leigh on Sea, SS9 2LZ; tel. and fax (1702) 472-710; e-mail apkerry@aol.com; internet www .faithandthought.org.uk; f. 1865; Pres. Sir JOHN HOUGHTON; publs *Faith & Thought* (2 a year), *Science and Christian Belief* (jtly with Christians in Science, 2 a year).

William Morris Society: Kelmscott House, 26 Upper Mall, London, W6 9TA; tel. (20) 8741-3735; fax (20) 8748-5207; e-mail william .morris@care4free.net; internet www .morrissociety.org; f. 1955 to encourage wider appreciation and understanding of the life, work and influence of William Morris and his circle; 1,400 mems; library of 2,000 vols; Hon. Sec. PETER FAULKNER; publ. *Journal* (2 a year).

RELIGION, SOCIOLOGY AND ANTHROPOLOGY

African Studies Association of the United Kingdom: 36 Gordon Sq., London, WC1H 0PD; tel. (20) 3073-8335; fax (20) 3073-8340; e-mail asa@soas.ac.uk; f. 1963;

advances academic studies relating to Africa by providing facilities for the interchange of information and ideas; holds inter-disciplinary confs and symposia; 1,000 mems; Hon. Pres. Prof. WILLIAM BEINART; Hon. Sec. Dr JUNE BAM-HUTCHISON.

British Association for South Asian Studies: c/o Royal Asiatic Society, 14 Stephenson Way (Second Fl.), London, NW1 2HD; tel. (20) 7388-5490; e-mail basas@basas .org.uk; internet www.basas.org.uk; f. 1972 as the Soc. for S Asian Studies; merged with British Asscn for S Asian Studies 2007; supports research and training in the arts, humanities and social sciences of S Asia; 600 mems; Chair. Prof. KUNAL SEN; Sec. Dr LAWRENCE SAEZ; publs *Contemporary South Asia* (1 a year), *South Asian Studies* (1 a year).

British Association for the Study of Religions: c/o Dr James Cox, Univ. of Edinburgh, New College, Mound Place, Edinburgh, EH1 2LX; tel. (131) 650-8942; fax (131) 650-7952; e-mail j.cox@ed.ac.uk; internet basr.open.ac.uk; f. 1973; affiliated to Int. Association for the History of Religions; organizes an annual conference; 250 mems; Pres. and Chair Dr JAMES COX; Hon. Sec. Dr GRAHAM HARVEY; publ. *Bulletin* (3 a year).

British Society for Middle Eastern Studies: Institute for Middle Eastern and Islamic Studies, Univ. of Durham, Al-Qasimi Bldg, Elvet Hill Rd, Durham, DH1 3TU; tel. (191) 334-5179; fax (191) 334-5661; e-mail a.l .haysey@durham.ac.uk; internet www .brismes.ac.uk; f. 1973; promotes study of the Middle Eastern region from the end of classical antiquity and the rise of Islam; organizes discussion and debates; fosters cooperation with similar socs; 550 mems; Pres. ALASTAIR NEWTON; Exec. Dir Prof. JAMES DICKINS; publ. *British Journal of Middle Eastern Studies* (4 a year).

British Sociological Association: Bailey Suite, Palatine House, Belmont Business Park, Belmont, Durham, DH1 1TW; tel. (191) 383-0839; fax (191) 383-0782; e-mail enquiries@britsoc.org.uk; internet www .britsoc.co.uk; f. 1951; promotes interest in sociology; advances its study and application in the UK; encourages contacts between workers in all relevant fields of enquiry; holds confs, seminars and workshops; 2,500 mems; Pres. Prof. JOHN HOLMWOOD; Exec. Team Chair Dr JUDITH BURNETT; Chief Exec. JUDITH MUDD; publs *Cultural Sociology* (3 a year), *Network* (3 a year), *Sociology* (6 a year), *Work Employment and Society* (6 a year).

Ecclesiological Society: EcclSoc, 38 Rosebery Ave, New Malden, Surrey, KT3 4JS; tel. (20) 8942-2111; e-mail info@ecclsoc.org; internet www.ecclsoc.org; f. 1879 as St Paul's Ecclesiological Soc.; lectures, confs, visits, publs; 950 mems; Pres. Rt Rev. DAVID STANCLIFFE; Chair. TREVOR COOPER; publ. *Ecclesiology Today* (2 a year).

Folklore Society: c/o Warburg Inst., Woburn Sq., London, WC1H 0AB; tel. (20) 7862-8564; e-mail enquiries@folklore-society .com; internet www.folklore-society.com; f. 1878; c. 1,000 mems and subscribers; library of 11,000 vols; Pres. ROBERT MCDOWALL; Hon. Sec. Prof. JAMES H. GRAYSON; Librarian Dr CAROLINE OATES; publs *FLS News* (3 a year), *Folklore* (3 a year).

Galton Institute: 19 Northfields Prospect, London, SW18 1PE; tel. (20) 8874-7257; e-mail betty.nixon@talk21.com; internet www.galtoninstitute.org.uk; f. 1907; advances public knowledge and understanding of human genetics and population prob-

lems; 400 mems; Pres. Prof. Sir WALTER BODMER; Gen. Sec. BETTY NIXON.

Henry Bradshaw Society: Music Collections, The British Library, 96 Euston Rd, London, NW1 2DB; e-mail nicolas.bell@bl.uk; internet www.henrybradshawsociety.org; f. 1890; publishes facsimiles and editions of rare texts relating to the liturgy of the medieval Christian church; 134 institutional mems, 152 individual mems; Chair. Prof. MICHAEL LAPIDGE; Sec. NICOLAS BELL.

Institute of Race Relations: 2–6 Leeke St, King's Cross Rd, London, WC1X 9HS; tel. (20) 7837-0041; fax (20) 7278-0623; e-mail info@irr.org.uk; internet www.irr.org.uk; f. 1958 to promote scientific study and publication on race and racism, and to make information and proposals available on race relations; Dir A. SIVANANDAN; publ. *Race & Class* (4 a year).

Maghreb Studies Association: c/o The Maghreb Bookshop, 45 Burton St, London, WC1H 9AL; tel. and fax (20) 7388-1840; e-mail maghreb@ maghreb-studies-association.co.uk; internet www.maghreb-studies-association.co.uk; f. 1981; promotes study of the history, politics and environment of North Africa and the broader Middle East and Islamic world; 155 mems; Chair. Prof. HÉDI BOURAOUI; Vice-Chair. Prof. ALLAN CHRISTELOW; Exec. Sec. MOHAMED BEN-MADANI; publ. *Maghreb Review* (4 a year).

Modern Church: c/o Rev. Jonathan Clatworthy, 9 Westward View, Liverpool, L17 7EE; tel. (845) 345-1909; e-mail office@ modernchurch.org.uk; internet www .modernchchurch.org.uk; f. 1898; advancement of liberal religious thought; 650 mems; Pres. Prof. JOHN BARTON; Chair. Rev. JOHN PLANT; Gen. Sec. Rev. JONATHAN CLATWORTHY; Administrator CHRISTINE ALKER; publ. *Modern Believing* (4 a year).

National Society (Church of England) for Promoting Religious Education: Church House, Great Smith St, Westminster, SW1P 3AZ; tel. (20) 7898-1518; fax (20) 7898-1493; e-mail info.natsoc@ churchofengland.org; internet www .churchofengland.org/education/national-society; f. 1811; promotes religious education in accordance with the principles of the Church of England; Chair. THE BISHOP OF OXFORD; Gen. Sec. Rev. JANINA AINSWORTH.

Royal African Society: 36 Gordon Sq., London, WC1H 0PD; tel. (20) 3075-8335; fax (20) 3075-8340; e-mail ras@soas.ac.uk; internet www.royalafricansociety.org; f. 1901; hosts regular programme of lectures in London, Bristol and Edinburgh; 1,000 mems; Chair. Lord MALLOCH-BROWN; Sec. GEMMA HAXBY; publ. *African Affairs* (4 a year).

Royal Anthropological Institute of Great Britain and Ireland: 50 Fitzroy St, London, W1T 5BT; tel. (20) 7387-0455; fax (20) 7388-8817; e-mail admin@therai.org.uk; internet www.therai.org.uk; f. 1843; lectures and film festivals; manages various trust and scholarship funds; awards medals and prizes; raises funds for research; film-hire library; photographic archive; 1,600 mems; library: borrowing rights to 120,000 vols; Pres. Prof. CLIVE GAMBLE; Dir Dr DAVID SHANKLAND; Hon. Sec. Dr ERIC HIRSCH; publs *Anthropology Today* (6 a year), *Journal of the Royal Anthropological Institute* (incorporating *Man*, 5 a year).

Royal Asiatic Society of Great Britain and Ireland: 14 Stephenson Way, London, NW1 2HD; tel. (20) 7388-4539; fax (20) 7391-9429; e-mail info@royalasiaticsociety.org; internet www.royalasiaticsociety.org; f. 1823; studies the history, religions, instns,

customs, languages, literature and art of Asia; 600 subscribing libraries; brs in various Asian cities; 800 mems; library: see Libraries and Archives; Dir ALISON OHTA; Exec. Officer CAMILLA LARSEN; publ. *Journal* (4 a year).

Royal Commonwealth Society: 18 Northumberland Ave, London, WC2N 5BJ; tel. (20) 7930-6733; fax (20) 7930-9705; e-mail info@ rcsint.org; internet www.rcsint.org; f. 1868; 10,000 mems worldwide.

Royal Society for Asian Affairs: 2 Belgrave Sq., London, SW1X 8PJ; tel. (20) 7235-5122; fax (20) 7259-6771; e-mail info@rsaa .org.uk; internet www.rsaa.org.uk; f. 1901; promotes greater knowledge and understanding of Asia and countries from the Middle East to Japan; hosts lectures and encourages debate on topics, from literature and the arts, exploration and the environment, to cultural, military and political history and current affairs; organises mem. tour to a country in part of Asia or the Middle East; 1,080 mems with knowledge of, and interest in, Asia; library of 5,000 vols; Pres. Lord DENMAN; Chair. Sir DAVID JOHN; Sec. Col NEIL S. PORTER; publ. *Asian Affairs* (3 a year).

Swedenborg Society: 20–21 Bloomsbury Way, London, WC1A 2TH; tel. (20) 7405-7986; fax (20) 7831-5848; e-mail richard@ swedenborg.org.uk; internet www .swedenborg.org.uk; f. 1810; translates and publishes writings of Emanuel Swedenborg, Swedish scientist, philosopher and theologian; organizes lectures and meetings to further knowledge of Swedenborg's life, works and influence; also incl. publishing; library of 15,000 vols; works of Swedenborg in Latin and translated in modern languages; colln of collateral literature (mainly 19th century); periodicals dating back to 1790; c. 850 mems; Pres. Dr ANDERS HALLENGREN; Sec. RICHARD LINES; Librarian JAMES WILSON; publ. *Journal of the Swedenborg Society* (1 a year).

Young Foundation: 18 Victoria Park Sq., London, E2 9PF; tel. (20) 8980-6263; fax (20) 8981-6719; e-mail reception@ youngfoundation.org; internet www .youngfoundation.org; f. 1954, fmrly Institute of Community Studies; social research on poverty, deprivation and comparative social policy; housing, urban planning and community; education; Dir Dr GEOFF MULGAN.

TECHNOLOGY

British Computer Society: 1 Sanford St, Swindon, Wilts., SN1 1HJ; tel. (1793) 417417; fax (1793) 480270; e-mail bcshq@ bcs.org.uk; internet www.bcs.org.uk; f. 1957; industry body for Information Technology professionals; sets standards for education and training through the BCS Professional Examination and through the inspection and accreditation of university courses and company training schemes; awards the Chartered IT Professional (CITP) qualification; licensed by the Engineering Council and the Science Council to appoint chartered and incorporated engineers and chartered scientists; 45,000 mems; library: joint library with Instn of Electrical Engineers; Pres. DAVID MORRISS; Registrar MANDY BRYAR; publs *The Computer Journal* (6 a year), *IT Now* (6 a year), *IEE Proceedings —Software* (6 a year, in conjunction with IEE), *Interacting with Computers Journal* (4 a year), *Formal Aspects of Computing Journal* (6 a year).

British Society of Rheology: c/o Prof. Simon Cox, Institute of Mathematics and Physics, Aberystwyth Univ., Aberystwyth SY23 3BZ; tel. (1970) 622764; fax (1970) 622826; e-mail secretary@bsr.org.uk; internet www.bsr.org.uk; f. 1940; promotes rheology, the science of the deformation and flow of matter; library at Univ. of Wales, Aberystwyth; 400 mems; Pres. BILL FRITH; Sec. Prof. SIMON COX; publ. *Rheology Abstracts* (4 a year).

BSI Group (British Standards Institution): 389 Chiswick High Rd, London, W4 4AL; tel. (20) 8996-9000; fax (20) 8996-7400; e-mail cservices@bsi-global.com; f. 1901 as Engineering Standards Committee; inc. 1918 as British Engineering Standards Association, f. 1929 under Royal Charter and Supplemental Charter in 1931, when scope was extended; independent certification of management systems and products; product-testing services; operates BSI British Standards, the national standards body of the UK, which develops standards for industry and the population in general; 15,000 subscribing mems; CEO STEVAN BREEZE; Dir of Legal Affairs and Company Sec. RICHARD CATT; publs *British Standards*, *BSI Catalogue* (1 a year), *Business Standards* (4 a year), *Standards Update* (12 a year).

Chartered Institute of Building: Englemere, Kings Ride, Ascot, SL5 7TB; tel. (1344) 630700; fax (1344) 630777; e-mail reception@ciob.org.uk; internet www.ciob.org.uk; f. 1834, inc. by Royal Charter 1980; professional body for managers in the construction industry; 46,000 mems; library of 40,000 vols, 400 British Standards, 150 journals; Pres. ALAN CRANE; Chief Exec. CHRIS BLYTHE; publs *Construction Innovation and Development* (4 a year), *Construction Manager* (10 a year), *Icon* (4 a year).

Chartered Institute of Logistics and Transport: Earlstrees Court, Earlstrees Rd, Corby, NN17 4AX; tel. (20) 1536 740100; fax (20) 1536 740101; e-mail enquiry@ciltuk.org.uk; internet www.cilt-international.com; f. 1919, inc. by Royal Charter 1926 to promote, encourage, and coordinate the study and advancement of the science and art of transport in all its branches, and to provide a source of authoritative views on transport; brs in Argentina, Australia, Bangladesh, Canada, Cyprus, Ghana, Greece, Hong Kong, India, Ireland, Kenya, Malawi, Malaysia, Malta, Mauritius, Nepal, New Zealand, Nigeria, Pakistan, Singapore, South Africa, Spain, Sri Lanka, Thailand, Uganda, United Arab Emirates, USA, West Indies, Zambia, Zimbabwe and elsewhere; 32,000 mems; Pres. RICHARD HUNT; Dir-Gen. CYRIL BLEASDALE; publ. *CILT World* (newsletter, 3 a year).

Chartered Institute of Patent Attorneys: 95 Chancery Lane, London, WC2A 1DT; tel. (20) 7405-9450; fax (20) 7430-0471; e-mail mail@cipa.org.uk; internet www.cipa.org.uk; f. 1882, chartered 1891, present name 2006; professional and examining body for patent attorneys; 3,200 mems; Chief Exec. LEE DAVIES; publs *CIPA* (12 a year), *Register of Patent Attorneys* (1 a year).

Chartered Institution of Building Services Engineers: 222 Balham High Rd, London, SW12 9BS; tel. (20) 8675-5211; fax (20) 8675-5449; e-mail enquiries@cibse.org; internet www.cibse.org; promotes the science and practice of such engineering services as are associated with the built environment and industrial processes and the advancement of education and research in building services engineering; 15,000 mems; Chief Exec. and Sec. JULIAN AMEY; publs *Building Services Engineering Research and Technology* (4 a year), *Building Services Journal* (12 a year), *Lighting Research and Technology* (4 a year).

Chartered Institution of Water and Environmental Management: 15 John St, London, WC1N 2EB; tel. (20) 7831-3110;

fax (20) 7405-4967; e-mail admin@ciwem.org.uk; internet www.ciwem.org.uk; f. 1895; to advance the science and practice of water and environmental management for the public benefit and to promote education, training, study and research in those areas; 12,000 mems; Pres. PETER TREADGOLD; Exec. Dir NICK REEVES; publs *Journal* (4 a year), *Water and Environment Magazine* (12 a year).

Chartered Management Institute: 2 Savoy Court, Strand, London, WC2R 0EZ; and Management House, Cottingham Rd, Corby, Northants., NN17 1TT; tel. (1536) 204222; fax (1536) 201651; e-mail enquiries@managers.org.uk; internet www.managers.org.uk; f. 1947 as British Institute of Management, name changed 1992; granted Royal Charter 2002; encourages and supports the lifelong development of managers; influences policy-makers and opinion-formers on management issues; 84,000 individual mems, 600 company mems; library: 80,000 items, 200 periodicals; Dir-Gen. MARY M. CHAPMAN; Sec. VALERIE HAMILL; publ. *Professional Manager* (6 a year).

Chartered Society of Designers: 1 Cedar Court, Royal Oak Yard, Bermondsey St, London, SE1 3GA; tel. (20) 7357-8088; fax (20) 7407-9878; e-mail info@csd.org.uk; internet www.csd.org.uk; f. 1930, incorporated by Royal Charter 1976; professional body for designers practising in product design, fashion and textiles design, interiors and graphics, design management, education and professional development; 4,000 mems; Pres. ADRIANNE LEMAN; publ. *CSD Magazine* (4 a year).

Crafts Council: 44A Pentonville Rd, London, N1 9BY; tel. (20) 7278-7700; fax (20) 7837-6891; e-mail reference@craftscouncil.org.uk; internet www.craftscouncil.org.uk; f. 1971 as the Crafts Advisory Cttee, present name 1979; directly funded by Arts Council England; nat. org. for contemporary crafts in Great Britain, offering exhibition and education programmes; Nat. Register of Makers; research library; library of 7,200 vols, 190 periodicals; Chair. JOANNA FOSTER; Dir ROSY GREENLEES; publ. *Crafts* (6 a year).

Design Council: 34 Bow St, London, WC2E 7DL; tel. (20) 7420-5200; fax (20) 7420-5300; e-mail info@designcouncil.org.uk; internet www.designcouncil.org.uk; f. 1944 to inspire, in the world context, the best use of design by the UK to improve prosperity and well-being; Chair. of Council Sir MICHAEL BICHARD; Chief Exec. DAVID KESTER.

Energy Institute: 61 New Cavendish St, London, W1G 7AR; tel. (20) 7467-7100; fax (20) 7255-1472; e-mail info@energyinst.org; internet www.energyinst.org; f. 2003 by merger of the Institute of Petroleum (f. 1913) and Institute of Energy (f. 1927); promotes safe, environmentally responsible and efficient supply and use of energy; research into oil, gas and other primary fuels and renewable sources of energy; power generation, transmission and distribution, sustainable devt, demand-side management and energy efficiency; publishes codes of safe practice, measurement manuals, test methods, journals; organizes confs, training courses; participates in careers and education work and offers an extensive library and information service; 12,000 individual mems and 400 group mems; library of 17,000 vols, 200 periodicals; Pres. JOAN MACNAUGHTON; Chief Exec. LOUISE KINGHAM; Library and Information Service Man. CATHERINE COSGROVE; publs *Energy World* (11 a year), *Journal of the Energy Institute* (4 a year), *Petroleum Review* (12 a year).

Engineering Council UK: 246 High Holborn, London, WC1V 7EX; tel. (20) 3206-0500; fax (20) 3206-0501; e-mail info@engc.org.uk; internet www.engc.org.uk; f. 1981 by Royal Charter; advances the education and training of engineers and technologists; improves the supply of qualified engineers and technologists; sets up and maintains relevant professional, educational and training standards; Chair. Prof. KEL FIDLER; CEO ANDREW RAMSAY.

Ergonomics Society: The Elms, Elmsgrove, Loughborough, LE11 1RG; tel. (1509) 234904; fax (1509) 235666; e-mail ergsoc@ergonomics.org.uk; internet www.ergonomics.org.uk; f. 1949; promotes ergonomics and the work of ergonomists in solving problems that arise between people, their working environment and things that they use; organizes confs and one-day events about ergonomics applications, incl. patient safety, human and organizational factors in the oil, gas and chemical industries, and access and integration into schools; 1,400 mems; Pres. JOHN WILSON; Chief Exec. DAVID O'NEILL; publs *Applied Ergonomics*, *Behaviour and Information Technology*, *Ergonomics*, *Injury Control & Safety Promotion*, *Theoretical Issues in Ergonomic Science*, *Work and Stress*.

Faculty of Royal Designers for Industry: RSA, 8 John Adam St, London, WC2N 6EZ; tel. (20) 7930-5115; fax (20) 7839-5805; e-mail rdi@rsa.org.uk; internet www.thersa.org; f. 1936; furthers the devt of design and in particular its application to industrial purposes; number of holders of RDI limited to 200 (135 at present plus 54 Hon.); Chair. LUKE JOHNSON; Master DINAH CASSON; Sec. SOPHIE THOMAS.

Gemmological Association Great Britain: 27 Greville St, London, EC1N 8TN; tel. (20) 7404-3334; fax (20) 7404-8843; e-mail information@gem-a.com; internet www.gem-a.com; f. 1908; promotes study of gemmology and the scientific and industrial study of all materials and articles used or dealt in by persons interested in the science of gems; 3,000 mems; CEO Dr JACK OGDEN; publs *Gem and Jewellery* (4 a year), *Journal of Gemmology* (1 a year), *MailTalk*.

Heritage Crafts Association: 132 The Glade, Old Coulsdon CR5 1SP; e-mail info@heritagecrafts.org.uk; internet www.heritagecrafts.org.uk; f. 2009; supports and promotes UK's heritage crafts; researches status of heritage crafts, identifies those crafts in decline or in imminent danger of being lost and raises awareness to ensure their survival; organizes educational events to raise awareness among public; 300 mems; Chair. ROBIN WOOD; Vice-Chair. PATRICIA LOVETT; Treas. CATHERINE DYSON; Sec. BRIAN CROSSLEY.

Institute of Corrosion: Corrosion House, Vimy Court, Vimy Rd, Leighton Buzzard, Beds., LU7 1FG; tel. (1525) 851771; fax (1525) 376690; e-mail admin@icorr.demon.co.uk; internet www.icorr.org; f. 1975; 1,600 mems; Pres. DAVID DEACON; Hon. Sec. JIM BURNELL-GRAY; publs *Corrosion Management* (6 a year), *Corrosion Science* (12 a year).

Institute of Food Science and Technology: 5 Cambridge Court, 210 Shepherd's Bush Rd, London, W6 7NJ; tel. (20) 7603-6316; fax (20) 7602-9936; e-mail info@ifst.org; internet www.ifst.org; f. 1964 to promote the knowledge, devt and application of science and technology of food, and the provision of a professional body for food scientists and technologists; 2,000 mems; Pres. Prof. CAROL PHILLIPS; Hon. Sec. S. TOMLINSON; Chief Exec. H. G. WILD; publs *Food Science and Technology* (4 a year),

International Journal of Food Science and Technology (12 a year).

Institute of Management Services: Brooke House, 24 Dam St, Lichfield, Staffs., WS13 6AA; tel. (1543) 266909; fax (1543) 257848; e-mail admin@ims-stowe.fsnet.co.uk; internet www.ims-productivity.com; f. 1941; promotion, practice and devt of methodologies and techniques for the improvement of productivity and quality; 1,800 mems; Chair. D. BLANCHFLOWER; publ. *Management Services Journal* (4 a year).

Institute of Marine Engineering, Science and Technology (IMarEST): 80 Coleman St, London, EC2R 5BJ; tel. (20) 7382-2600; fax (20) 7382-2670; e-mail info@imarest.org; internet www.imarest.org; f. 1889 as Institute of Marine Engineers, present name 2002; professional society representing those involved in marine engineering, science and technology; 15,000 mems; library: library and Marine Information Centre; Sec. K. F. READ; publs *Marine Engineers' Review* (10 a year), *Journal of Offshore Technology* (6 a year), *The Marine Scientist* (4 a year), *Proceedings* (Parts A and B), *Maritime Electronics* (6 a year).

Institute of Materials, Minerals and Mining: 1 Carlton House Terrace, London, SW1Y 5DB; tel. (20) 7451-7300; fax (20) 7839-1702; e-mail admin@iom3.org; internet www.iom3.org; f. 2002, merger of Institute of Materials and Institution of Mining and Metallurgy; advances the science and practice of engineering; facilitates the acquisition and preservation of knowledge pertaining to the associated professions; establishes, upholds and advances the industry standards of education, training and competence; organizes meetings and confs worldwide; administers scholarships and fellowships; 22,000 mems; library of 65,000 vols, 1,000 periodicals; Pres. Dr BARRY LYE; Chief Exec. Dr B. A. RICKINSON; publs *Advances in Applied Ceramics* (4 a year), *British Corrosion Engineering, Science and Technology* (4 a year), *Clay Technology* (6 a year), *Energy Materials* (4 a year), *Historical Metallurgy* (2 a year), *Interdisciplinary Science Reviews* (4 a year), *International Heat Treatment and Surface Engineering* (6 a year), *International Materials Reviews* (6 a year), *International Wood Products Journal* (2 a year), *Ironmaking and Steelmaking* (8 a year), *Materials Science and Technology* (4 a year), *Materials World* (12 a year), *Plastics, Rubber and Composites* (10 a year), *Powder Metallurgy* (4 a year), *Science and Technology of Welding and Joining* (8 a year), *Steel World* (2 a year), *Surface Engineering* (4 a year), *The Packaging Professional* (6 a year), *Transactions* of the fmr Institute of Mining and Metallurgy (12 a year), *Tribology* (4 a year), *Wood Focus* (3 a year).

Institute of Measurement and Control: 87 Gower St, London, WC1E 6AF; tel. (20) 7387-4949; fax (20) 7388-8431; e-mail ceo@instmc.org.uk; internet www.instmc.org.uk; f. 1944, inc. by Royal Charter 1975; to promote the advancement and application of the science and practice of measurement and control; to co-ordinate and disseminate information and to conduct examinations; 4,100 mems; Chief Exec. PETER MARTINDALE; publs *Measurement and Control* (10 a year, incl. *Inst MC Interface*, of which 2 a year), *Transactions* (5 a year), *Instrument Engineer's Yearbook*.

Institute of Physics and Engineering in Medicine: Fairmount House, 230 Tadcaster Rd, York, YO24 1ES; tel. (1904) 610821; fax (1904) 612279; e-mail office@ipem.ac.uk; internet www.ipem.ac.uk; f. 1995; promotes advancement of physics and engineering applied to medicine and biology and advances public education in the field; 4,000 mems; Pres. Prof. P. JARRITT; Gen. Sec. ROBERT W. NEILSON; publs *Medical Engineering and Physics* (10 a year), *Physics in Medicine and Biology* (26 a year), *Physiological Measurement* (12 a year).

Institute of Quarrying: 7 Regent St, Nottingham, NG1 5BS; tel. (115) 945-3880; fax (115) 948-4035; e-mail mail@quarrying.org; internet www.quarrying.org; f. 1917; provides education and training to improve science and practice of quarrying and to provide a forum for technical discussion; 5,000 home and overseas mems; Exec. Dir J. W. BERRIDGE; Sec. L. BRYDEN; publ. *Quarry Management* (12 a year).

Institute of Refrigeration: Kelvin House, 76 Mill Lane, Carshalton, SM5 2JR; tel. (20) 8647-7033; fax (20) 8773-0165; e-mail ior@ior.org.uk; internet www.ior.org.uk; f. 1899 as the Cold Storage and Ice Asscn; promotes advancement of refrigeration in all its applications; 2,600 mems; Pres. A. B. PEARSON; Sec. M. RODWAY; publ. *Proceedings*.

Institute of Science and Technology: Kingfisher House, 90 Rockingham St, Sheffield, S1 4EB; tel. (114) 2763197; fax (114) 2726354; e-mail office@istonline.org.uk; internet www.istonline.org.uk; f. 1954 from the Science Technologists' Assoc. (f. 1948); present name 2008; professional and qualifying body for specialist, technical and managerial staff; provides training for vocational qualifications and continuing professional devt; provides awards and prizes; 1,000 mems; Pres. ROBERT HARDWICK; Chair. JOHN ROBINSON; Hon Sec. AMANDA TAYLOR; publ. *Science Technology Journal* (2 a year).

Institute of Scientific and Technical Communicators: Airport House, Purley Way, Croydon, CR0 0XZ; tel. (20) 8253-4506; fax (20) 8253-4510; e-mail istc@istc.org.uk; internet www.istc.org.uk; f. 1972; establishes and maintains professional codes of practice for people engaged in all brs of scientific and technical communication; 1,500 mems; Pres. PAUL BALLARD; Exec. Administrator ELAINE COLE; publ. *Communicator* (4 a year).

Institution of Chemical Engineers: 165–189 Railway Terrace, Rugby, CV21 3HQ; tel. (1788) 578214; fax (1788) 560833; e-mail tjevans@icheme.org.uk; internet www.icheme.org; f. 1922, incorporated by Royal Charter to promote the science and practice of chemical engineering, to improve the standards and methods of education therein, and to act as a qualifying body for chemical engineers, etc.; 25,000 mems; Chief Exec. Dr T. J. EVANS; publs *Chemical Engineering Research and Design* (12 a year), *Food and Bioproducts Processing* (4 a year), *Process Safety and Environmental Protection* (6 a year), *The Chemical Engineer* (12 a year).

Institution of Civil Engineers: 1 Great George St, Westminster, London, SW1P 3AA; tel. (20) 7222-7722; fax (20) 7222-7500; e-mail secretariat@ice.org.uk; internet www.ice.org.uk; f. 1818; inc. by Royal Charter in 1828 for the general advancement of mechanical science and more particularly for promoting the acquisition of knowledge which constitutes the profession of a Civil Engineer, namely the art of directing natural sources of power for the use and convenience of man; two principal roles: (i) qualifying body for all three levels of registration: Chartered Engineers, Incorporated Engineers and Engineering Technicians; (ii) learned society; as a qualifying body the Institution is concerned with academic and professional achievements and with continuing education, and as a learned society it is concerned with the acquisition and dissemination of knowledge; 80,000 corporate and non-corporate mems; library of 100,000 vols; Pres. Prof. PAUL JOWITT; Dir-Gen. and Sec. TOM FOULKES; publs *Advances in Cement Research*, *Geotechnique* (4 a year), *Ground Improvement*, *Magazine of Concrete Research*, *Nuclear Energy*, *Proceedings* (in 16 parts: *Civil Engineering*, *Geotechnical Engineering*, *Structures & Building*, *Municipal Engineer*, *Transport*, *Water*, *Maritime Engineering*, *Bridge Engineering*, *Construction Materials*, *Energy*, *Engineering History and Heritage*, *Engineering Sustainability*, *Engineering and Computational Mechanics*, *Management, Procurement and Law*, *Urban Design and Planning*, *Waste and Resource Management*, *Water Management*, all 4 a year except the last which is 6 a year).

Institution of Electronics: 12 Bentfield Close, Higher Bebington, Wirral, CH63 8NB; tel. (151) 608-4236; e-mail info@institutionofelectronics.ac.uk; internet www.institutionofelectronics.ac.uk; f. 1930, inc. 1935; furtherance of the science of electronics and other scientific subjects; over 2,500 mems; Chair. ALAN HOLLINSHEAD-JONES; Membership Officer TIM HATCH; publs *Electron* (online, 4 a year), *Proceedings* (online, 4 a year).

Institution of Engineering and Technology: Savoy Place, London, WC2R 0BL; tel. (20) 7240-1871; fax (20) 7240-7735; internet www.theiet.org; f. 1871 (and inc. by Royal Charter in 1921, inc. the Institution of Radio and Electronic Engineers 1988 and Institution of Manufacturing Engineers 1991, Society of Engineers inc. into the Institution of Incorporated Engineers in 2005 and both merged with IET in 2006); to promote the general advancement of science, engineering and technology, and to facilitate the exchange of information and ideas on those subjects; fmrly Institution of Electrical Engineers; 150,000 mems; library: see Libraries and Archives; Pres. Sir ROBIN SAXBY; CEO Dr A. ROBERTS; publs *Communications Engineer* (6 a year), *Computing and Control Engineering* (6 a year), *Electronics Education* (3 a year), *Electronics Letters* (every 2 weeks), *Electronics Systems and Software* (6 a year), *Engineering Management* (6 a year), *Engineering & Technology* (12 a year), *Flipside* (6 a year), *Information Professional* (6 a year), *Manufacturing Engineer* (6 a year), *Power Engineer* (6 a year), *Proceedings* (6 a year), *Systems Biology* (4 a year).

Institution of Engineering Designers: Courtleigh, Westbury Leigh, Westbury, Wilts., BA13 3TA; tel. (1373) 822801; fax (1373) 858085; e-mail staff@ied.org.uk; internet www.ied.org.uk; f. 1945 to advance education in engineering, particularly in engineering and product design and to constitute a body of members qualified to a recognized high standard; a nominated body of the Engineering Council; 5,300 mems; Sec. ELIZABETH BRODHURST; publ. *Engineering Designer* (6 a year).

Institution of Engineers and Shipbuilders in Scotland: Clydeport, 16 Robertson St, Glasgow, G2 8DS; tel. (141) 248-3721; fax (141) 221-2698; e-mail secretary@iesis.org; internet www.iesis.org; f. 1857 to facilitate the exchange of information and ideas amongst its mems, and to promote the advancement of the science and practice of engineering and shipbuilding; 800 mems; Chair. E. CHAMBERS; publs *Transactions* (1 a year), *Year Book and List of Members* (every 2 years).

Institution of Fire Engineers: London Rd, Moreton-in-Marsh, GL56 0RH; tel. (1608)

812580; fax (1608) 812581; e-mail info@ife .org.uk; internet www.ife.org.uk; f. 1918, and inc. 1924, to promote, encourage, and improve the science of fire engineering and technology; 11,000 home and overseas mems; CEO ELLEN JESSETT; publ. *Fire Prevention and Fire Engineers Journal* (monthly, online).

Institution of Gas Engineers and Managers: IGEM House, 28 High St, Kegworth, DE74 2DA; tel. (844) 375-4436; fax (1509) 283110; e-mail general@igem.org.uk; internet www.igem.org.uk; f. 1863; Royal Charter 1929, to promote by research, discussion and education the sciences necessary for the better production, distribution or utilization of gas and of the by-products of its production; 5,000 mems; library of 10,000 vols; Chief Exec. JOHN WILLIAMS; publ. *Journal*.

Institution of Highways and Transportation: 119 Britannia Walk, London, N1 7JE; tel. (20) 7336-1555; fax (20) 7336-1556; e-mail info@iht.org; internet www.iht.org; f. 1930 as the Institution of Highway Engineers, present name 1987; concerned with the design, construction, maintenance and operation of sustainable transport systems and infrastructure; serves as a representative body for the profession, to implement best practice and technical excellence, to bring fellow professionals and ideas together and to provide training and professional competence; 11,000 UK-based mems, several hundred overseas mems; 18 UK-based brs, several overseas brs incl. Republic of Ireland, Hong Kong and Malaysia; Chief Exec. MARY LEWIS; publ. *Transportation Professional* (10 a year).

Institution of Lighting Engineers: Regent House, Regent Place, Rugby, Warwicks., CV21 2PN; tel. (1788) 576492; fax (1788) 540145; e-mail info@ile.org.uk; internet www.ile.org.uk; f. 1924 to promote, encourage and improve the science and art of efficient lighting in all fields, and to facilitate the exchange of information and ideas on this subject; 1,900 mems; Pres. DEREK ROGERS; Chief Exec. RICHARD FROST; publ. *Lighting Journal* (6 a year).

Institution of Mechanical Engineers: 1 Birdcage Walk, London, SW1H 9JJ; tel. (20) 7222-7899; fax (20) 7222-4557; internet www .imeche.org.uk; f. 1847, inc. by Royal Charter 1930; principal organization for professional mechanical engineers in the UK, and qualifying body for chartered and incorporated mechanical engineers; 75,000 mems worldwide; library of 60,000 books and various other documents; Pres. WILLIAM EDGAR; Chief Exec. ANDREW IVES; publs *Automotive Engineer* (10 a year), *Environmental Engineering* (4 a year), *Institution of Diesel and Gas Turbine Engineers* (6 a year), *Journal of Strain Analysis*, *Professional Engineering* (22 a year).

Institution of Nuclear Engineers: Allan House, 1 Penerley Rd, London, SE6 2LQ; tel. (20) 8698-1500; fax (20) 8695-6409; e-mail inucewh@aol.com; internet www.inuce.org .uk; f. 1959 for the advancement of nuclear engineering technology and its related fields; 1,700 mems; Pres. Dr P. A. BEELEY; publ. *The Nuclear Engineer* (6 a year).

Institution of Structural Engineers: 11 Upper Belgrave St, London, SW1X 8BH; tel. (20) 7235-4535; fax (20) 7235-4294; e-mail mail@istructe.org; internet www.istructe .org; f. 1908 as the Concrete Inst., present name 1922; inc. by Royal Charter 1934, to promote the general advancement of the science and art of structural eng.; library of 15,000 vols; 21,000 mems; Pres. DAVID HAR-

VEY; Chief Exec. Dr KEITH J. EATON; publ. *The Structural Engineer* (2 a month).

National Society for Clean Air and Environmental Protection: 44 Grand Parade, Brighton, East Sussex, BN2 9QA; tel. (1273) 878770; fax (1273) 606626; e-mail admin@nsca.org.uk; internet www.nsca.org .uk; f. 1899 as Coal Smoke Abatement Soc. and merged with the Smoke Abatement League of Great Britain in 1929; air pollution, contaminated land and noise control, environmental protection; 1,500 mems, incl. learned socs, local authorities, industrial concerns, etc.; Pres. Lord JULIAN HUNT; Chief Exec. PHILIP MULLIGAN (acting); publs *NSCA Briefing* (12 a year), *NSCA Pollution Handbook* (overview of pollution control legislation, annual).

Newcomen Society for the Study of the History of Engineering and Technology: Science Museum, Exhibition Rd, S Kensington, London, SW7 2DD; tel. and fax (20) 7371-4445; e-mail office@newcomen.com; internet www.newcomen.com; f. 1920; encourages the study of the history of engineering and technology worldwide; regular evening meetings in London and other regional centres; visits to sites of engineering interest; annual summer meeting and other visits at home and abroad; 1,000 mems and subscribers; Exec. Sec. TIM CRICHTON; publs *Links* (Bulletin of the Newcomen Society, 4 a year), *Transactions of the Newcomen Society / The International Journal for the History of Engineering and Technology* (2 a year).

Oil and Colour Chemists' Association: Priory House, 967 Harrow Rd, Wembley, Middlesex, HA0 2SF; tel. (20) 8908-1086; fax (20) 8908-1219; e-mail enquiries@occa .org.uk; internet www.occa.org.uk; f. 1918 to promote by discussion and scientific investigation the technology of the paint, oil, printing ink, and allied industries; 2,400 mems; Pres. D. FOULGER; Gen. Sec. C. PACEY-DAY; publs *Surface Coatings International Part A* (10 a year), *Surface Coatings International Part B* (4 a year), *Surface Coating Reviews*, *Surface Coating Monographs*.

Radio Society of Great Britain: 3 Abbey Court, Fraser Rd, Priory Business Park, Bedford, MK44 3WH; tel. (1234) 832700; fax (1234) 831496; e-mail ar.dept@rsgb.org.uk; internet www.rsgb.org; f. 1913 to promote interest in the science of radio-communication by amateurs, and to safeguard the interests of those of its members who operate or aspire to operate amateur transmitting stations; 30,000 mems; Gen. Man. PETER A. KIRBY; publ. *Radio Communication* (12 a year).

Remote Sensing and Photogrammetry Society: c/o School of Geography, Univ. of Nottingham, Nottingham, NG7 2RD; tel. (115) 951-5435; fax (115) 951-5249; e-mail rspsoc@nottingham.ac.uk; internet www .rspsoc.org; f. 2001; theory, techniques, instrumentation, applications in surveying, engineering, mapping, geographic information; annual conference; 1,000 mems; library of 2,000 vols; Hon. Gen. Sec. Dr PHILIPPA MASON; Exec. Sec. KAREN LAUGHTON; publs *International Journal of Remote Sensing* (24 a year), *The Photogrammetric Record* (4 a year).

Royal Academy of Engineering: 3 Carlton House Terrace, London, SW1Y 5DG; tel. (20) 7766-0600; fax (20) 7930-1549; internet www .raeng.org.uk; f. 1976; conducts engineering and educational studies, sponsors links between industry and higher education, co-sponsors with industry academic posts at higher education instns; 1,390 mems (1,266 fellows, 90 foreign mems, 34 hon. fellows); Pres. Lord JOHN BROWNE OF MADINGLEY;

Chief Exec. PHILIP GREENISH; publ. *Ingenia* (4 a year).

Royal Aeronautical Society: 4 Hamilton Place, London, W1J 7BQ; tel. (20) 7499-3515; fax (20) 7499-6230; internet www.aerosociety .com; f. 1866; 18,500 mems; library of 27,000 books, 1,300 periodicals (of which 300 current), 20,000 technical reports, 100,000 photographs; Dir KEITH MANS; publs *Aerospace International* (12 a year), *Aerospace Professional* (12 a year), *The Aeronautical Journal* (12 a year).

Royal Institution of Naval Architects: 10 Upper Belgrave St, London, SW1X 8BQ; tel. (20) 7235-4622; fax (20) 7259-5912; e-mail hq@rina.org.uk; internet www.rina.org.uk; f. 1860; advances naval architecture and marine technology; 9,500 mems; Pres. PETER FRENCH; Chief Exec. TREVOR BLAKELEY; publs *Transactions Part A: International Journal of Maritime Engineering* (4 a year), *Transactions Part B: International Journal of Small Craft Technology* (2 a year), *The Naval Architect* (10 a year), *Ship and Boat International* (6 a year), *Ship Repair and Conversion Technology* (4 a year), *Significant Ships* (1 a year), *Significant Small Ships* (1 a year), *Warship Technology* (5 a year), *Offshore Marine Technology* (4 a year).

Royal Television Society: Kildare House, 3 Dorset Rise, London, EC4Y 8EN; tel. (20) 7822-2810; fax (20) 7822-2811; e-mail info@ rts.org.uk; internet www.rts.org.uk; f. 1927; advances the art of television; forum for discussion and debate on all aspects of the profession; annual awards; 14 regional centres; over 3,000 mems; Pres. Sir ROBERT PHILLIS; Chief Exec. SIMON ALBURY; publ. *Television* (10 a year).

SCI (Steel Construction Institute): Silwood Park, Ascot, SL5 7QN; tel. (1344) 636525; fax (1344) 636570; e-mail reception@steel-sci .com; internet www.steel-sci.com; f. 1986; develops and promotes the proper and effective use of steel as a construction material; 850 mems; library of 11,000 vols; Dir Dr G. H. COUCHMAN; publ. *New Steel Construction* (10 a year).

Society for Underwater Technology: 80 Coleman St, London, EC2R 5BJ; tel. (20) 7382-2601; fax (20) 7382-2684; e-mail info@ sut.org; internet www.sut.org.uk; f. 1966; to promote the further understanding of the underwater environment, and to advance the development of the techniques and tools needed to explore, study and exploit the oceans; provides sponsorship for undergraduate and 1-year postgraduate students studying in an appropriate subject area; 1,000 individual and 110 corporate mems; Exec. Sec. I. N. L. GALLETT; publ. *Underwater Technology* (4 a year).

Society of Consulting Marine Engineers and Ship Surveyors: 202 Lambeth Rd, London, SE1 7JW; tel. (20) 7261-0869; fax (20) 7261-0871; e-mail sec@scmshq.org; internet www.scmshq.org; f. 1920; provides a central org. for consulting marine engineers, naval architects and ship surveyors; promotes status and procure advancement of interests of the profession; Sec. P. R. OWEN.

Society of Designer Craftsmen: 24 Rivington St, London, EC2A 3DU; tel. and fax (20) 7739-3663; e-mail info@ societyofdesignercraftsmen.org.uk; internet www.societyofdesignercraftsmen.org.uk; f. 1887 as Arts and Crafts Exhibition Society; annual exhibitions for mems and invited guests; occasional regional exhibitions; active licentiate scheme to assist recently graduated designer-makers; 650 mems; Pres. Prof. CHRISTOPHER FRAYLING; Chair. CHRISTINE DOVE.

Society of Dyers and Colourists: Perkin House, POB 244, 82 Grattan Rd, Bradford, BD1 2JB; tel. (1274) 725138; fax (1274) 392888; e-mail info@sdc.org.uk; internet www.sdc.org.uk; f. 1884; promotes advancement of the science and technology of colour and coloration; awards chartered qualifications; colour experience; 2,500 mems; Pres. Dr SANJIV KAMAT; Chief Exec. Dr GRAHAM CLAYTON; publs *Colour Index, Coloration Technology* (6 a year), *The Colourist* (4 a year).

Society of Glass Technology: 9 Churchill Way, Chapeltown, Sheffield, S35 2PY; tel. (114) 263-4455; fax (114) 263-4411; e-mail info@sgt.org; internet www.sgt.org; f. 1916; promotes the assocn of persons interested in glass technology; publishes books, journals and conf. proceedings; hosts and organizes int. and local confs on glass; provides information and holds a library and archive on glass; supports students with travel bursaries and final year project prizes; British rep. on int. bodies such as the Int. Commission on Glass and European Soc. of Glass Science and Technology; 600 mems; library of 10,000 vols; located at Univ. of Sheffield Applied Science Library; Hon. Sec. JOHN HENDERSON; publs *Glass Technology: European Journal of Glass Science and Technology Part A* (6 a year), *Physics and Chemistry of Glasses: European Journal of Glass Science and Technology Part B* (6 a year).

Society of Operations Engineers: 22 Greencoat Pl., London, SWIP 1PR; tel. (20) 7630-1111; fax (20) 7630-6677; e-mail soe@soe.org.uk; internet www.soe.org.uk; f. 2000 by merger of Institute of Road Transport Engineers (IRTE) and Instn of Plant Engineers (IPlantE); represents mems of road transport, plant engineering and engineer surveying industries; 15,000 mems; Pres. GARRY GILBY; Chief Exec. NICK JONES; publs *Plant Engineer* (6 a year), *Transport Engineer* (12 a year).

South Wales Institute of Engineers Educational Trust: Suite Two, Bay Chambers, W Bute St, Cardiff, CF10 5BB; tel. (29) 2063-0561; fax (29) 2063-0666; e-mail sandra.chapman@swieet2007.org.uk; internet www.swieet2007.org.uk; f. 1857; encouragement and advancement of engineering science and practice; Chief Exec. and Sec. DENYS M. MORGAN.

Textile Institute: see under International Organizations (Engineering and Technology).

TWI: Granta Park, Great Abington, Cambridge, CB21 6AL; tel. (1223) 899000; fax (1223) 892588; e-mail twi@twi.co.uk; internet www.twi.co.uk; f. 1946; undertakes gen. and contract research; advances welding technology in all aspects; provides consultancy and laboratory services; improves professional status and qualification of mems; specialized information services on materials-joining technology; training courses in welding engineering, welding inspection, practical welding, non-destructive testing, structural integrity, microjoining; 10,500 mems (3,500 research, 7,000 professional); library of 10,000 vols; Chief Exec. Dr CHRISTOPH WIESNER; publ. *Connect* (6 a year).

Research Institutes
GENERAL

Asia Research Centre: Houghton St, London, WC2A 2AE; f. 1997; attached to London School of Economics and Political Science, Univ. of London; conducts social science research on Asia; Dir Dr C. HUGHES.

Bill Douglas Centre for History of Cinema and Popular Culture: Academic Services, Univ. of Exeter, The Old Library, Prince of Wales Rd, Exeter, EX4 4SB; tel. (1392) 724321; e-mail soe.pgoffice@exeter.ac.uk; internet www.billdouglas.org; f. 1994; attached to Univ. of Exeter; study of twentieth century's art form and its precursors; Academic Dir Prof. STEVE NEALE.

Cambridge Programme for Sustainability Leadership: 1 Trumpington St, Cambridge CB2 1QA; tel. (1223) 768850; fax (1223) 768831; e-mail info@cpsl.cam.ac.uk; internet www.cpsl.cam.ac.uk; attached to Univ. of Cambridge; Dir POLLY COURTICE.

Centre for Alcohol and Drug Studies: Paisley Campus, Paisley, PA1 2BE; tel. (141) 848-3788; fax (141) 848-3891; attached to Univ. of the West of Scotland; Dir K. BARRIE.

Centre for Business Research: The Judge Business School Bldg, Trumpington St, Cambridge, CB2 1AG; tel. (1223) 765320; fax (1223) 765338; e-mail enquiries@cbr.cam.ac.uk; internet www.cbr.cam.ac.uk; attached to Univ. of Cambridge; Dir Prof. ALAN HUGHES (Sidney Sussex College).

Centre for Civil Society: Houghton St, London, WC2A 2AE; f. 1999; attached to London School of Economics and Political Science, Univ. of London; conducts research on problems and issues in management of voluntary agencies and NGOs; Dir Prof. J. HOWELL.

Centre for Early Modern Studies: The Centre for the Early Modern History, History Dept, School of Humanities and Social Sciences, Armory Bldg, Rennes Dr., Exeter, EX4 4RJ; tel. (1392) 264297; fax (1392) 263305; e-mail histoff@ex.ac.uk; internet centres.exeter.ac.uk/cems; f. 2007; attached to Univ. of Exeter; rareas of research incl. religious culture, social and economic relations, political and intellectual thought, gender and sexuality, space, landscape and national identities, history of the book, theatre and performance for the period between 1500 and 1800; Dir Prof. ALEX WALSHAM; Asst Dir Prof. ANDREW MCRAE.

Centre for Enterprise and Regional Development: College Rd, Bangor, Gwynned, LL57 2DG; attached to Bangor Univ.; Dir S. JONES.

Centre for Gymnastics Research: Loughborough, LE11 3TU; e-mail m.r.yeadon@lboro.ac.uk; f. 2004; attached to Loughborough Univ.; Dir Prof. FRED YEADON.

Centre for International Studies: Houghton St, London, WC2A 2AE; f. 1967; attached to London School of Economics and Political Science, Univ. of London; promotes research in all aspects of int. studies; Chair. of Steering Cttee Dr JOHN KENT.

Centre for Leadership Studies: XFI Bldg, Rennes Dr., Exeter, EX4 4ST; tel. (1392) 262555; fax (1392) 262559; e-mail leadership@exeter.ac.uk; internet centres.exeter.ac.uk/cls; f. 1997; attached to Univ. of Exeter; research area ranges from applied evaluation of leadership devt processes to the philosophical underpinnings of modern leadership; Dir Prof. JONATHAN GOSLING.

Centre for Olympic Studies & Research: School of Sport, Exercise and Health Sciences, Loughborough Univ., Loughborough, LE11 3TU; e-mail cosar@lboro.ac.uk; f. 2004; attached to Loughborough Univ.; promotes, facilitates and conducts academic research into Olympism and Olympic movement; Dir Prof. IAN HENRY.

Centre for Research in Human Rights: tel. (20) 8392-3661; fax (20) 8392-3231; e-mail l.gearon@roehampton.ac.uk; attached to Roehampton Univ.; Dir Dr LIAM GEARON.

Centre For Service Research: Univ. of Exeter Business School, Streatham Court, Rennes Dr., Exeter, EX4 4PU; tel. (1392) 263458; fax (1392) 263242; e-mail cserv@exeter.ac.uk; internet centres.exeter.ac.uk/cserv; attached to Univ. of Exeter; research focuses on customer, process, people, environment working together towards the service experience; Dir of Service Pricing, Revenue Management, Customer Commitment and Relationships Prof. IRENE NG; Dir of Service Quality Management, Service Processes Prof. ROGER MAULL.

Centre for the Study of Human Rights: Houghton St, London, WC2A 2AE; tel. (20) 7955-6428; fax (20) 7955-6934; e-mail z.gillard@lse.ac.uk; internet www2.lse.ac.uk/humanrights; f. 1998; attached to London School of Economics and Political Science, Univ. of London; promotes study of human rights; Dir Prof. CHETAN BHATT; Man. ZOE GILLARD.

Centre for the Study of War, State and Society: History Dept, School of Humanities and Social Sciences, Armory Bldg, Rennes Dr., Exeter, EX4 4RJ; tel. (1392) 264297; fax (1392) 263305; e-mail histoff@ex.ac.uk; internet centres.ex.ac.uk/wss; f. 2005; attached to Univ. of Exeter; researches on effects of armed conflict on states, societies, cultures; explores themes of warfare and societal transformation; Dir Prof. RICHARD OVERY.

Centre of Commonwealth Studies: Stirling, FK9 4LA; tel. (1786) 467495; fax (1786) 466210; e-mail english@stir.ac.uk; internet www.english.stir.ac.uk/research/profile/ccws.php; f. 1985; attached to Univ. of Stirling; postgraduate and undergraduate work relating to Commonwealth countries, particularly in fields of African history, African and Caribbean culture and writing, African and Caribbean religion, Australian writing and painting, literature of India and of New Zealand, and post-colonial critical theory; Dir Prof. DAVID RICHARDS.

Communications Research Centre: Dept of Social Sciences, Loughborough Univ., Loughborough, LE11 3TU; tel. (1509) 223365; e-mail e.a.van-zoonen@lboro.ac.uk; internet www.lboro.ac.uk/departments/ss/research/crc; attached to Loughborough Univ.; communication studies, culture and media, discourse and social interaction; Dir LIESBAT VAN ZOONEN; Dir CHARLES ANTAKI.

David Livingstone Institute of Overseas Development Studies: McCance Bldg, 16 Richmond St, Glasgow, G1 1XQ; attached to Univ. of Strathclyde; Dir Prof. J. PICKETT.

Early Childhood Research Centre: Dept of Education, Univ. of Roehampton, Froebel College, London, SW15 5PJ; tel. (20) 8392-3689; fax (20) 8392-3322; e-mail k.brehony@roehampton.ac.uk; attached to Univ. of Roehampton; interdisciplinary research in early childhood history and policy, measures of quality in early years provision, professional devt; Dir Prof. KEVIN J. BREHONY.

European Construction Institute: Loughborough, LE11 3TU; tel. (1509) 222620; fax (1509) 260118; e-mail eci@lboro.ac.uk; internet www.eci-online.org; f. 1990; attached to Loughborough Univ.; Pres. MICHEL VIRLOGEUX; Chair. JOHN OLIVER.

European Institute: Houghton St, London, WC2A 2AE; f. 1991; attached to London School of Economics and Political Science, Univ. of London; coordinates and develops research and research training on European issues; Dir Prof. PAUL TAYLOR.

European Research Institute: Edgbaston, Birmingham, B15 2TT; tel. (121) 414-6346; e-mail p.a.carr@bham.ac.uk; internet www

.eri.bham.ac.uk; f. 2001; attached to Univ. of Birmingham; research in the fields of culture and society, economics, European politics, history, law; Chair. Dr TIM HAUGHTON.

Exeter Centre for Strategic Processes and Operations (XSPO): Univ. of Exeter Business School, Streatham Court, Rennes Dr, Exeter, EX4 4PU; tel. (1392) 262557; fax (1392) 263242; e-mail xspo@exeter.ac.uk; internet centres.exeter.ac.uk/xspo; attached to Univ. of Exeter; research focuses on business process management; Dir for Service Quality Management Prof. ROGER MAULL; Dir for Service Process Management Prof. ANDI SMART.

Exeter Interdisciplinary Institute (EII): Univ. of Exeter, Queen's Dr., Exeter, EX4 4QJ; tel. (1392) 269302; e-mail r .gagnier@exeter.ac.uk; internet centres .exeter.ac.uk/interdisciplinaryinstitute; attached to Univ. of Exeter; researches across Exeter's strengths in cultural, natural, built environments with needs and opportunities in public sphere; Dir Prof. REGENIA GAGNIER.

Institute for Retail Studies: Stirling, FK9 4LA; tel. (1786) 467386; fax (1786) 466290; e-mail irst1@stir.ac.uk; internet www .management.stir.ac.uk; attached to Univ. of Stirling; Dir Prof. PAUL FREATHY; Deputy Dir Prof. LEIGH SPARKS.

Institute of Creative Enterprises: Coventry Univ. Enterprises, Puma Way, Coventry, CV1 2TT; tel. (24) 7615-8300; e-mail c .hamilton@coventry.ac.uk; internet wwwm .coventry.ac.uk/researchnet/ice; attached to Coventry Univ.; applied research activities for arts practice, communication and cultural studies, media, performing arts; postgraduate courses in performance, media, digital art; Dir CHRISTINE HAMILTON.

Institute of Rehabilitation: 215 Anlaby Rd, Kingston upon Hull HU3 2PG; tel. (1482) 675602; fax (1482) 675636; e-mail d.m .sharp@hull.ac.uk; internet www2.hull.ac .uk/pgmi/cmr/rehabilitation.aspx; f. 1997; attached to Univ. of Hull; Dir Dr DONALD SHARP (acting).

Institute of Sport and Leisure Policy: Loughborough, LE11 3TU; tel. (1509) 226365; fax (1509) 226301; e-mail p .downward@lboro.ac.uk; f. 1990, present name 1997; attached to Loughborough Univ.; theoretical analysis of sport and leisure policy; Dir PAUL DOWNWARD.

Institute of Youth Sport: Loughborough, LE11 3TU; e-mail c.e.taylor@lboro.ac.uk; f. 1998; attached to Loughborough Univ.; Dir MARY NEVILL.

Interdisciplinary Institute of Management: Houghton St, London, WC2A 2AE; f. 1990; attached to London School of Economics and Political Science, Univ. of London; promotes interdisciplinary research into management; research is closely linked with Centre for Economic Performance; Dir Prof. DIANE REYNIERS.

Loughborough Design School: Loughborough, LE11 3TU; tel. (1509) 226900; e-mail dsoffice@lboro.ac.uk; internet www.lboro.ac .uk/departments/lds; f. 2010 by merger of Dept of Design and Technology, Dept of Human Sciences (Ergonomics) and the Ergonomics and Safety Research Institute (ESRI); attached to Loughborough Univ.; Dir TONY HODGSON (acting).

LSE Gender Institute: Houghton St, London, WC2A 2AE; f. 1993; attached to London School of Economics and Political Science, Univ. of London; multi-disciplinary centre; addresses major intellectual challenges posed by contemporary changes in gender relations; Dir Prof. ANNE PHILLIPS.

Paisley Enterprise Research Centre: Paisley, Renfrewshire, PA1 2BE; f. 1995; attached to Univ. of the West of Scotland; Dir Prof. DAVID DEAKINS.

Peter Harrison Centre for Disability Sport: School of Sport Exercise and Health Sciences, Loughborough Univ., Loughborough, LE11 3TU; tel. (1509) 226387; e-mail phc@lboro.ac.uk; internet www .peterharrisoncentre.org.uk; f. 2005; attached to Loughborough Univ.; promotes knowledge in disability sport through applied research; Dir Dr VICKY TOLFREY; publs *Health and Well-being*, *Sport Culture and Science*, *Sport Science*.

Professional and Management Development Centre: Sir Richard Morris Bldg, Loughborough Univ., Loughborough, LE11 3TU; tel. (1509) 223140; fax (1509) 223963; e-mail pmdc@lboro.ac.uk; internet www .lboro.ac.uk/departments/sbe/pmdc; attached to Loughborough Univ.; Dir J. WHITTAKER.

Research Centre Wales: Bangor, Gwynned, LL57 2DG; tel. (1248) 382220; fax (1248) 388081; e-mail cyc@bangor.ac.uk; f. 1985; attached to Bangor Univ.; Dir Prof. C. R. BAKER.

Social Science Research Unit, Institute of Education: 18 Woburn Sq., London, WC1H 0NR; tel. (20) 7612-6391; fax (20) 7612-6400; e-mail ssru@ioe.ac.uk; internet www.ioe.ac.uk/ssru; f. 1990; attached to Institute of Education, Univ. of London; Dir Prof. DAVID GOUGH; Deputy Dir SANDY OLIVER.

Stirling Centre for Scottish Studies: Stirling, FK9 4LA; tel. (1786) 467495; fax (1786) 466210; e-mail english@stir.ac.uk; internet www.english.stir.ac.uk/research/ profile/centerofscottishstudies.php; f. 1996; attached to Univ. of Stirling; promotes research, publ. and postgraduate recruitment in Scottish Studies, literature, art, music, history, media, philosophy, politics, social issues and cultural theory; Dir MICHAEL PENMAN.

Stirling Media Research Institute: Stirling, FK9 4LA; tel. (1786) 467520; fax (1786) 466855; e-mail stirling.media@stir.ac.uk; attached to Univ. of Stirling; Dir Dr RICHARD HAYNES; publ. *International Journal of Media and Cultural Politics*.

AGRICULTURE, FISHERIES AND VETERINARY SCIENCE

Agri-Food and Biosciences Institute: AFBI HQ, Newforge Lane, Belfast, BT9 5PX; tel. (28) 9025-5689; fax (28) 9025-5035; e-mail info@afbini.gov.uk; internet www .afbini.gov.uk; f. 2006, by merger of Dept of Agriculture and Rural Devt (DARD) Science Service and the Agricultural Research Institute of Northern Ireland (ARINI); conducts high technology research and devt, statutory, analytical and diagnostic testing functions; offers scientific capabilities in areas of agriculture, animal health, food, environment and biosciences; Chair. SEÁN HOGAN; CEO Dr S. KENNEDY.

Animal Health and Veterinary Laboratories Agency: Woodham Lane, Addlestone, Surrey, KT15 3NB; tel. (1932) 341111; fax (1932) 347046; internet www.ahvla.gov.uk; f. 1917; exec. agency of the Dept for Environment, Food and Rural Affairs; Dir CATHERINE BROWN.

Animal Health and Welfare: Dept of Agriculture and Rural Development, Dundonald House, Upper Newtownards Rd, Belfast, BT4 3SB; tel. (28) 9052-4999; fax (28) 9052-4420; e-mail dardhelpline@dardni.gov.uk; internet www.dardni.gov.uk; attached to Dept of Agriculture and Rural Devt; animal and

animal product imports and by-products, diseases, control and prevention, animal welfare, artificial reproduction, export certification; library of 11,000 vols.

Animal Health Trust: Lanwades Park, Kentford, Newmarket, Suffolk, CB8 7UU; tel. (8700) 502424; fax (8700) 502425; e-mail info@aht.org.uk; internet www.aht.org.uk; f. 1942; aims to advance veterinary science and provide specialist clinical services for all companion animals; Pres. HRH the PRINCESS ROYAL; CEO Dr PETER WEBBON.

Biotechnology and Biological Sciences Research Council: Polaris House, North Star Ave, Swindon, SN2 1UH; tel. (1793) 413200; fax (1793) 413201; internet www .bbsrc.ac.uk; f. 1994; supports fundamental and strategic multidisciplinary research, with emphasis on the biological sciences, biotechnology and engineering, in its institutes and univs; furthers scientific knowledge, promotes economic growth, wealth and job creation; improves quality of life in the UK and beyond; focuses on farming, food, industrial biotechnology and pharmaceuticals; Chair. Prof. TOM BLUNDELL; Chief Exec. Prof. DOUGLAS KELL.

Institutes and Units:

Babraham Institute: Babraham Hall, Babraham, Cambridge, CB2 4AT; tel. (1223) 496000; fax (1223) 496021; internet www.babraham.ac.uk; f. 1948; research to advance understanding of function in animal cells and systems, with emphasis on cell signalling, recognition mechanisms and mammalism devt; Dir Dr R. J. BICKNELL (acting).

Institute for Animal Health: Ash Rd, Pirbright, GU24 0NF; tel. (1635) 578411; fax (1635) 577237; e-mail iahweb@bbsrc.ac .uk; internet www.iah.ac.uk; f. 1986; undertakes basic, strategic and applied research required for the understanding of the aetiology, pathogenesis, epidemiology and diagnosis of diseases of farm animals, incl. those exotic diseases that could spread to the United Kingdom, the study of newly recognized diseases and the influence of disease control measures on food safety and quality; Institute Dir Prof. JOHN FAZAKERLEY; Dir of Research Prof. DAVID PATON.

Sites:

Institute for Animal Health—Compton Laboratory: Compton, Nr Newbury, RG20 7NN; tel. (1635) 578411; fax (1635) 577237; e-mail iah@iah.ac.uk; internet www.iah.ac.uk; f. 1924; fundamental and applied research on selected viral diseases of livestock and poultry; Librarian CHRISTINE GIBBONS.

Institute for Animal Health—Pirbright Laboratory: Ash Rd, Pirbright, Woking, GU24 0NF; tel. (1483) 232441; fax (1483) 232448; Head Dr A. I. DONALDSON.

Neuropathogenesis Unit: Ogston Bldg, West Mains Rd, Edinburgh, EH9 3JF; tel. (131) 667-5204; fax (131) 668-3872.

Institute of Food Research: Norwich Research Park, Colney Lane, Norwich, NR4 7UA; tel. (1603) 255-000; fax (1603) 507-723; internet www.ifr.ac.uk; research into harnessing food for health and preventing food-related diseases; centred around the characterisation of the gut as an integrated biological system; helping to ensure competitiveness of agri-food and allied industries; Dir Prof. DAVID BOXER; publ. *Science+Innovation*.

Institute of Biological, Environmental and Rural Sciences - IBERS, Aberystwyth University: Edward Llwyd Building,

Pengalis Campus, Aberystwyth, SY23 3DA; tel. (1970) 622-316; fax (1970) 622-350; e-mail ibers@aber.ac.uk; internet www.aber .ac.uk/en/ibers; f. 2008; basic and strategic research into grassland and environmental research related to non-arable agriculture; increases understanding of genetic and competitive processes in pastures and natural plant populations in response to grazing and climatic variables, to elucidate processes controlling intake, growth, body composition and lactation in ruminants; investigates consequences of climatic and management changes on grassland agriculture and the opportunities for alternative animals and crops and studies the fluxes of nutrients and utilization efficiencies of inputs with reference to losses and environmental pollution; Dir Prof. W. POWELL; publ. *IBERS Knowledge-Based Innovations* (1 a year).

Sites:

Institute of Biological, Environmental and Rural Sciences (IBERS) - Gogerddan Research Centre: Plas Gogerddan, Aberystwyth, SY23 3EB; tel. (1970) 823-000; fax (1970) 828-357; e-mail ibers@aber .ac.uk; internet www.aber.ac.uk/en/ibers; f. 2008; library of 300 vols, 250 journals; Dir Prof. WAYNE POWELL; publ. *IBERS Knowledge-Based Innovations* (1 a year).

Institute of Grassland and Environmental Research—Bronydd Mawr Research Centre: Trecastle, Brecon, Powys, LD3 8RD; tel. (1874) 636-480; fax (1874) 636-542; Officer in charge J. M. M. MUNRO.

John Innes Centre: Colney Lane, Norwich, NR4 7UH; tel. (1603) 450-000; fax (1603) 450-045; internet www.jic.ac.uk; carries out fundamental research on plants and bacteria; describes the basis of the control of plant and bacterial form, behaviour and metabolism so that genetically modified plants and bacteria may be improved or changed to offer new industrial potentialities; Dir Prof. DALE SANDERS.

Rothamsted Research, North Wyke: Okehampton, EX20 2SB; tel. (1837) 883-500; e-mail nwlibrary@rothamsted.ac.uk; Assoc. Head of Dept Dr PHIL MURRAY.

Roslin Institute (Edinburgh): Roslin, Midlothian, EH25 9PS; tel. (131) 527-4200; fax (131) 440-0434; internet www.roslin.ac .uk; f. 1945; basic and strategic research on farm animals; Dir Prof. DAVID HUME.

Rothamsted Research: Rothamsted, Harpenden, AL5 2JQ; tel. (1582) 763-133; fax (1582) 760-981; internet www.rothamsted.ac .uk; f. 1843; basic, strategic and applied research on soils and crop plants; Dir Prof. IAN R. CRUTE.

Attached Site:

Broom's Barn Research Centre: Higham, Bury St Edmunds, IP28 6NP; tel. (1284) 812-200; fax (1284) 811-191; e-mail brooms.barn@bbsrc.ac.uk; internet www.broomsbarn.ac.uk; research into sugar beet and other crops; Dir BILL CLARK.

Sustainable Bioenergy Centre: e-mail info.bsbec@bbsrc.ac.uk; internet bsbec.bbsrc .ac.uk; six dedicated programmes in bioenergy research; centres have offices at universities incl. Cambridge, Dundee, Nottingham and York.

Centre for Applied Marine Sciences: Menai Bridge Anglesey, Bangor, LL59 5AB; tel. (1248) 713808; e-mail enquiries@cams .bangor.ac.uk; f. 1977; attached to Bangor Univ.; Dir Prof. A. J. ELLIOTT.

Centre for Rural Policy Research: Dept of Politics, College of Social Sciences & Int. Studies, Armory Bldg, Rennes Dr., Exeter, EX4 4RJ; tel. (1392) 722438; e-mail crprmail@exeter.ac.uk; internet centres .exeter.ac.uk/crpr; f. 1960 as Agricultural Economics Unit, renamed as Centre for Rural Research, present name and location 2007; attached to Univ. of Exeter; researches into aspects of rural economy and society with focus on agricultural, environmental and bioenergy policy; sustainable land management; agro-food regulation; sustainable communities; social and economic devt of agriculture; impacts of climate change on farming and land use; Co-Dir Prof. MICHAEL WINTER; Co-Dir Dr MATT LOBLEY.

Centre for the Environment, Fisheries and Aquaculture Science (CEFAS): Pakefield Rd, Lowestoft, NR33 0HT; tel. (1502) 562244; fax (1502) 513865; e-mail lowlibrary@cefas.co.uk; internet www.cefas .co.uk; exec. agency of the Dept for the Environment, Food and Rural Affairs; provides contract research, consultancy and training services in environmental impact assessment, environmental research and monitoring, aquaculture health and hygiene, and fisheries science and management; extensive research library; br at Weymouth; Chief Exec. R. JUDGE; Library Man. S. CARTER.

Food and Environment Research Agency (FERA): Sand Hutton, York, YO41 1LZ; tel. (1904) 462000; fax (1904) 462111; e-mail info@fera.gsi.gov.uk; internet www .defra.gov.uk/fera; f. 2009; exec. agency of the Dept for Environment, Food and Rural Affairs; research and advice in the fields of: plant health; the authenticity, chemical and microbiological safety and nutritional value of the food supply; pesticide safety (incl. the monitoring of residues in food); veterinary drug residues; proficiency testing schemes; the control of pests and diseases of growing and stored crops; the impact of food production on the environment and the consumer; alternative crops and biotechnology; animal health and welfare; and conservation and wildlife management; response and recovery from unforeseen and emergency situations; Chief Exec. ADRIAN BELTON.

Forest Research: Alice Holt Lodge, Wrecclesham, Farnham, GU10 4LH; tel. (1420) 22255; fax (1420) 23653; e-mail research .info@forestry.gsi.gov.uk; internet www .forestry.gov.uk/forestresearch; f. 1997; attached to Forestry Commission, f. 1919; advances research and technology related to forestry; informs and supports forestry's contribution to UK governmental policies; provides the evidence base for UK forestry practices and supports innovation; provides a range of products and services to support the land management and environmental technologies sectors; comprises 2 research stations with centres for forest resources and management, forestry and climate change and human and ecological sciences; library of 20,000 vols, 100 current journals; Chief Exec. Dr JAMES PENDLEBURY; Research Dir Prof. PETER FREER-SMITH; Librarian CATHERINE OLDHAM; publs *Forest Research Corporate Publications*, *Scientific and technical publications*.

Research Stations:

Northern Research Station: Roslin, EH25 9SY; tel. (131) 445-2176; fax (131) 445-5124; e-mail nrs@forestry.gsi.gov.uk.

Henry Doubleday Research Association: Ryton Organic Gardens, Coventry, CV8 3LG; tel. (24) 7630-3517; fax (24) 7663-9229; e-mail enquiry@hdra.org.uk; internet www .hdra.org.uk; f. 1954; conducts research in organic agriculture, with focus on commercial organic horticulture in temperate regions and subsistence agriculture in developing countries; maintains vegetable seed colln; sets standards for organic amenity horticulture; services to the public incl. membership of the Asscn and access to organic display gardens; Dir of Research Dr MARGI LENNARTSSON.

National Institute of Agricultural Botany: Huntingdon Rd, Cambridge, CB3 0LE; tel. (1223) 342200; fax (1223) 277602; e-mail info@niab.com; internet www.niab.com; f. 1919; applied, basic and translational research in crops and agronomy, genetics and breeding, varieties and seeds; Chair. TONY PEXTON; CEO Dr TINA BARSBY.

NIAB: Huntingdon Rd, Cambridge, CB3 0LE; tel. (1223) 276381; fax (1223) 277602; e-mail info@niab.com; internet www.niab .com; f. 1919 to promote the improvement of existing varieties of seeds, plants and crops in the UK; incl. Official Seed Testing Station for England and Wales, and other depts that are particularly concerned with crop variety testing and description, seed certification and seed production techniques; library of 10,000 vols; Dir Prof. BRIAN J. LEGG; Sec. J. W. HALL; publs *Plant Genetic Resources Characterization and Utilization* (print and online), *Varieties of Cereals, Oilseeds, Pulses* (2 a year), *Grass and Herbage Legumes Variety Book* (1 a year), *Potato Variety Handbook*.

Oxford Forestry Institute: University of Oxford, Department of Plant Sciences, South Parks Rd, Oxford, OX1 3RB; tel. (1865) 275000; fax (1865) 275074; e-mail ofi@plants .ox.ac.uk; internet www.plants.ox.ac.uk/ofi; f. 1924 (as Imperial, later Commonwealth Forestry Inst.), now fully inc. into the Dept. of Plant Sciences; library of 200,000 vols, in conjunction with CAB International; research and higher studies in forestry; Dir Prof. J. BURLEY.

Science and Advice for Scottish Agriculture: Roddinglaw Rd, Edinburgh, EH12 9FJ; tel. (131) 244-8890; fax (131) 244-8940; e-mail info@sasa.gsi.gov.uk; internet www .sasa.gov.uk; f. 2008, fmrly the Scottish Agricultural Science Agency; attached to Scottish Govt Rural Payments and Inspections Directorate; carries out scientific exec. work, associated research and consultation on: seed testing, testing of candidate cultivators of crop plants for Nat. Listing and Plant Breeders' Rights, certification of seed and planting stock, production of disease-tested clonal stocks of potatoes, statutory aspects of pest and disease control, pesticide usage assessment, pesticide residues, ecology of mammals and birds of actual or potential pest status; Head of SASA Dr GORDON C. MACHRAY; Librarian and Information Man. JILL TIVEY.

Research Institutes:

Hannah Research Institute: Ayr, KA6 5HL; tel. (1292) 674000; fax (1292) 674003; internet www.hri.sari.ac.uk; f. 1928; researches into human health and nutrition; programme areas: metabolism; life and death of the cell; CHARIS (food science and technology research); Dir Prof. C. KNIGHT (acting).

Macaulay Land Use Research Institute: Craigiebuckler, Aberdeen, AB15 8QH; tel. (1224) 395000; fax (1224) 311556; e-mail enquries@macaulay.ac.uk; internet www.macaulay.ac.uk; f. 1930; interdisciplinary research across the environmental and social sciences; supports the protection of natural resources, creation of integrated land-use systems and the devt of sustainable rural communities; Chief Exec. Prof. RICHARD ASPINALL.

Moredun Research Institute: Pentlands Science Park, Bush Loan, Penicuik, EH26 0PZ; tel. (131) 445-5111; fax (131) 445-6111; e-mail info@moredun.ac.uk; internet www.moredun.ac.uk; f. 1920; researches on livestock diseases that undermine biological efficiency, impair welfare or threaten public health; Dir Prof. JULIE FITZPATRICK.

Rowett Research Institute: Greenbank Rd, Buckburn, Aberdeen, AB21 9SB; tel. (1224) 712751; fax (1224) 715349; internet www.rowett.ac.uk; f. 1913; researches into how nutrition can prevent disease, into improving health and into enhancing the quality of food production in agriculture; Dir Prof. PETER MORGAN.

James Hutton Institute: Invergowrie, Dundee, DD2 5DA; tel. (8449) 285428; fax (8449) 285429; e-mail info@hutton.ac.uk; internet www.hutton.ac.uk; f. 2011 by merger of Macaulay Land Use Research Institute and SCRI; researches on plants and their interactions with the environment, particularly in managed ecosystems; addresses the public goods of sustainability and high quality and healthy food; crops of potatoes, barley and soft fruit are of particular interest; Chief Exec. Prof. IAIN GORDON; Chief Operating Officer Dr KAREN SHAW.

University of Hull International Fisheries Institute: Cottingham Rd, Hull, HU6 7RX; f. 1989; attached to Univ. of Hull; Dir Prof. Dr IAN G. COWX.

Woburn Experimental Station (Lawes Agricultural Trust): Husborne Crawley, Bedford; f. 1876 for the investigation of manurial and other problems of British crops; run as outstation of Rothamsted Experimental Station; Dir L. FOWDEN.

ARCHITECTURE AND TOWN PLANNING

Built Environment Research Institute: Room 04F14, School of the Built Environment, Univ. of Ulster, Jordanstown campus, Shore Rd, Newtownabbey, BT37 0QB; tel. (28) 9036-6566; e-mail adbe@ulster.ac.uk; internet www.beri.ulster.ac.uk; attached research centres: Centre for Sustainable Technologies (CST), Centre for Research on Property and Planning (RPP), Fire Safety Engineering Research and Technology Centre (FireSERT), Hydrogen Safety Engineering and Research (HySAFER); conducts research that enhances the quality of the built environment and addresses the changing needs of society in a more sustainable manner; Dir STANLEY MCGREAL; Sec. SADIE MAGEE.

Cities Programme: Houghton St, London, WC2A 2AE; f. 1996; attached to London School of Economics and Political Science, Univ. of London; undertakes design-based teaching and research on social, technical and economic aspects of cities and urban systems; Dir R. BURDETT.

Housing Policy and Practice Unit: School of Applied Social Science, Colin Bell Bldg, Univ. of Stirling, Stirling, FK9 4LA; tel. (1786) 467719; fax (1786) 466323; e-mail hppu1@stir.ac.uk; internet www.dass.stir.ac .uk; attached to Univ. of Stirling; teaching and research in sociology, social policy, social work, housing, services to people with dementia and addictions; Dir Prof. ISOBEL ANDERSON.

Innovative Manufacturing and Construction Research Centre: Wolfson School of Mechanical and Manufacturing Engineering, Loughborough Univ., Loughborough, LE11 3TU; tel. (1509) 227598; fax (1509) 227501; e-mail a.n.baldwin@lboro.ac .uk; internet www.lboro.ac.uk/eng/research/ imcrc; f. 2001; attached to Loughborough Univ.; research in business and management, computer science, construction,

design, manufacturing, processes and materials, systems engineering; Dir Prof. ANDREW BALDWIN.

Land Value Information Unit: Paisley, Renfrewshire, PA1 2BE; attached to Univ. of the West of Scotland; statistical research on behaviour of Scottish property market; Dir D. MARTIN.

LSE Housing and Communities: Houghton St, London, WC2A 2AE; tel. (207) 955-6330; fax (207) 955-6571; e-mail lsehousingandcommunities@lse.ac.uk; f. 1989; attached to London School of Economics and Political Science, Univ. of London; centre for research, devt and consultancy work in areas of housing policy and management; residents' consultation and involvement, tenant involvement, inner-city problems, difficult estates, energy efficiency, local and community action on environmental sustainability, sustainable transport incl. public transport, cities and int. experience, mixed communities, marginal groups, race relations and community cohesion; European housing issues; Coordinator Prof. ANNE POWER.

Parallelism, Algorithms and Architectures Research Centre: Dept of Computer Science, Loughborough Univ., Loughborough, LE11 3TU; tel. (1509) 222692; fax (1509) 211586; e-mail h.e.bez@lboro.ac.uk; internet parc.lboro.ac.uk; attached to Loughborough Univ.; research areas incl. coding and signal processing, concurrency, fundamental theoretical research, future architectures of parallel computers, parallel algorithms, vision and visualisation; Co-Dir Dr HELMUT BEZ; Co-Dir Dr ONDREJ SYKORA.

Prince's Foundation for Building Community: 19–22 Charlotte Rd, London, EC2A 3SG; tel. (20) 7613-8500; fax (20) 7613-8599; e-mail enquiry@princes-foundation.org; internet www.princes-foundation.org; f. 1992; research into all areas of sustainable traditional architecture, urbanism, regeneration and building crafts; public lectures, seminars and exhibitions; educational courses and consultancy; library of 10,200 vols; Librarian CARLA MARCHESAN.

ECONOMICS, LAW AND POLITICS

Bedford Group for Lifecourse and Statistical Studies: 20 Bedford Way, London, WC1H 0AL; f. 2002; combines Centre for Longitudinal Studies, Centre for Multilevel Modelling, DfES Centre for the Economics of Education, DfES Centre for Research on the Wider Benefits of Learning, DfES Nat. Centre for Research and Devt in Adult Literacy and Numeracy and Int. Centre for Research on Assessment; attached to Institute of Education, Univ. of London; Dir Prof. JOHN BYNNER.

Centre for Comparative Criminology and Criminal Justice: College Rd, Bangor, Gwynned, LL57 2DG; f. 1992; attached to Bangor Univ.; Dir Dr J. WARDHAUGH.

Centre for Economic Performance: Houghton St, London, WC2A 2AE; f. 1990; attached to London School of Economics and Political Science, Univ. of London; conducts interdisciplinary research on economic performance, focusing particularly on performance of firms; Dir Prof. J. VAN REENEN; Dir Prof. RICHARD FREEMAN.

Centre for Elections, Media and Parties (CEMaP): c/o Univ. of Exeter, Queen's Dr., Exeter, Devon, EX4 4QJ; tel. (1392) 723183; e-mail j.karp@exeter.ac.uk; internet centres .exeter.ac.uk/cemap; f. 2008; attached to Univ. of Exeter; research on campaigns, elections, political parties from both a British

and comparative perspective; Dir Prof. JEFFREY KARP.

Centre for European Governance: Dept of Politics, Univ. of Exeter, Armory Bldg, Rennes Dr., Exeter, Devon, EX4 4RJ; tel. (1392) 264490; e-mail s.j.heeks@exeter.ac.uk; internet centres.exeter.ac.uk/ceg; f. 1979 as Centre for European Studies; merged with the Centre for Regulatory Governance; attached to Univ. of Exeter; provides training and conducts research in EU politics, regulatory governance, public opinion, constitutional politics, political economy of European integration; Dir Prof. CLAUDIO RADAELLI.

Centre for European Legal Studies: School of Law, Univ. of Exeter, Armory Bldg, Rennes Dr., Exeter, EX4 4RJ; tel. (1392) 263365; fax (1392) 263196; e-mail lawlib@exeter.ac.uk; internet socialsciences .exeter.ac.uk; f. 1972; attached to Univ. of Exeter; conducts research on European Union and comparative law; evaluates its effects in the United Kingdom and other mem. states; Dir Prof. LEONE NIGLIA.

Centre for Legal History Research: c/o Univ. of Exeter, Armory Bldg, Rennes Dr., Exeter, EX4 4RJ; f. 2009; attached to Univ. of Exeter; Dir Prof. CHANTAL STEBBINGS; Dir Prof. ANTHONY MUSSON.

Centre for Professional Legal Studies: Graham Hills Bldg, 50 George St, Glasgow, G1 1BA; tel. (141) 548-3738; internet www .strath.ac.uk/humanities/lawschool; attached to Univ. of Strathclyde; Dir Prof. ALAN PATERSON.

Centre for Research into Economics and Finance in Southern Africa: Houghton St, London, WC2A 2AE; f. 1990; attached to London School of Economics and Political Science, Univ. of London; undertakes research into management of int. finance, foreign-exchange policy and domestic financial policy in South Africa, and macroeconomic and financial issues in S African region; Dir Dr J. LEAPE.

Centre for Studies in Security and Diplomacy: Muirhead Tower, Univ. of Birmingham, Edgbaston, Birmingham, B15 2TT; tel. (121) 414-3344; fax (121) 414-2693; e-mail cssd-bham@bham.ac.uk; internet www.cssd .bham.ac.uk; attached to Univ. of Birmingham; Dir Sir FRANCIS RICHARDS; Deputy Dir JUDY BATT; Assoc. Dir DANIELLE BESWICK.

Centre for the Study of Public Policy: McCance Bldg, 16 Richmond St, Glasgow, G1 1XQ; internet www.cspp.strath.ac.uk; attached to Univ. of Strathclyde; Dir Prof. R. ROSE; Sec. OHNA ROBERTSON.

Development Studies Institute: Houghton St, London, WC2A 2AE; f. 1990; attached to London School of Economics and Political Science, Univ. of London; a multidisciplinary centre for teaching economic research and devt studies, covering problems from around globe, of third-world and Europe; Head Prof. JOHN HARRISS.

Economic Research Council: 55 Tufton St, London, SW1P 3QL; tel. (20) 7340-6016; e-mail info@ercouncil.org; internet www .ercouncil.org; f. 1943; non-profit-making research and educational org. in the field of economics and monetary practice; Pres. Lord LAMONT; Chair. DAMON DE LASZLO; Hon. Sec. JIM BOURLET; publ. *Britain and Overseas* (4 a year).

Economic Research Institute of Northern Ireland: Floral Bldgs, 2–14 East Bridge St, Belfast, BT1 3NQ; tel. (28) 9072-7350; fax (28) 9031-9003; e-mail contact@erini.ac.uk; internet www.erini.ac.uk; f. 2003, merger of Northern Ireland Economic Research Centre (NIERC) and the Northern Ireland Economic Council (NIEC) 2004; ind. economic research and analyses; public policy making; research consultancy; Dir VICTOR HEWITT; Head of Research Dr MICHAEL ANYADIKE-DANES; publs *ERINI Research Reports*, *ERINI Working Papers* (print and online, irregular), *NIEC Publications* (print and online, irregular), *NIERC Northern Ireland Studies* (print and online, irregular), *NIERC Reports* (print and online, irregular).

European Policies Research Centre: EAC Bldg, 141 St James' Rd, Glasgow, G4 0LT; attached to Univ. of Strathclyde; Dir Prof. D. M. YUILL; Dir Prof. K. J. ALLEN.

Exeter Centre for Ethno-Political Studies (EXCEPS): Institute of Arab and Islamic Studies, Stocker Rd, Univ. of Exeter, Exeter, EX4 4ND; tel. (1392) 269250; fax (1392) 264035; e-mail l.newberry@exeter.ac.uk; internet centres.exeter.ac.uk/exceps; f. 2007; attached to Univ. of Exeter; conducts interdisciplinary research covering culture, memory and conflict, dynamics and management of ethnic conflict, unrecognised states, migrations and diasporas, language, literature and culture, security and terrorism; Dir Prof. GARETH STANSFIELD; Deputy Dir Prof ILAN PAPPE; Deputy Dir Dr JONATHAN GITHENS-MAZER.

Financial Markets Group: Houghton St, London, WC2A 2AE; f. 1987; attached to London School of Economics and Political Science, Univ. of London; undertakes basic research into the nature and operation of financial markets; Dir Prof. C. POLK.

Fraser of Allander Institute for Research on the Scottish Economy: Curran Bldg, 131 St James' Rd, Glasgow, G4 0LS; attached to Univ. of Strathclyde; Dir B. K. ASHCROFT.

Greater London Group: Houghton St, London, WC2A 2AE; tel. (20) 79556522; e-mail lselondon@lse.ac.uk; f. 1958; attached to London School of Economics and Political Science, Univ. of London; undertakes research and issues publs on govt and economy of Greater London and SE region; Dir TONY TRAVERS; Dir Prof. CHRISTINE WHITE-HEAD.

Institute for Democracy and Conflict Resolution: Univ. of Essex, Wivenhoe Park, Colchester, CO4 3SQ; tel. (1206) 872129; fax (1206) 872129; e-mail info@idcr.org.uk; internet www.idcr.org.uk; attached to Univ. of Essex; research in areas of democracy, conflict, human rights, justice and governance; dissemination of knowledge to policy makers, think tanks, non-governmental orgs and private companies; Dir Prof. TODD LANDMAN.

Institute for Social and Economic Research: Wivenhoe Park, Colchester, CO4 3SQ; annual panel survey of 5,000 British households, examines income distribution, etc., labour market behaviour, household formation and dissolution; attached to Univ. of Essex; Dir Prof. J. I. GERSHUNY.

Institute of Development Studies: Univ. of Sussex, Falmer, Brighton, BN1 9RE; tel. (1273) 606261; f. 1966; attached to Univ. of Sussex; nat. centre concerned with Third World devt and relationships between rich and poor countries; offers teaching and supervision for univ. graduate degrees; official depository for UN publs; library of 200,000 vols; Dir KEITH BEZANSON; publ. *IDS Bulletin* (4 a year).

Institute of Economic Research: Bangor, Gwynned, LL57 2DG; f. 1969; attached to Bangor Univ.; research in regional economics, economics of developing countries, tourism and economics of ports, policy-making and planning; data analysis; Dir Prof. R. R. MACKAY.

Institute of European Finance: Bangor, Gwynned, LL57 2DG; tel. (1248) 382277; fax (1248) 364760; e-mail ief@bangor.ac.uk; f. 1973; attached to Bangor Univ.; Dir Prof. E. P. M. GARDENER.

Institute of European Law: Birmingham Law School, Univ. of Birmingham, Edgbaston, Birmingham, B15 2TT; tel. (121) 414-6312; fax (121) 414-3585; e-mail iel@contacts.bham.ac.uk; internet www.iel.bham.ac.uk; f. 1989; attached to Univ. of Birmingham; provides interdisciplinary centre for research on European law; Dir Prof. MARTIN TRYBUS; Deputy Dir Dr LUCA RUBINI.

Institute of European Public Law: Cottingham Rd, Hull, HU6 7RX; tel. (1482) 465-742; f. 1992; attached to Univ. of Hull; Dir Prof. P. BIRKINSHAW.

Institute of Judicial Administration: Birmingham Law School, Univ. of Birmingham, Edgbaston, Birmingham, B15 2TT; tel. (121) 414-3637; fax (121) 414-3585; e-mail law@bham.ac.uk; internet www.law.bham.ac.uk/research/ija.shtml; f. 1968; attached to Univ. of Birmingham; initiates, coordinates and develops teaching and research in all aspects of the admin. of justice in England and Wales; Dir Dr MARIANNE WADE.

International Institute for Strategic Studies: Arundel House, 13–15 Arundel St, London, WC2R 3DX; tel. (20) 73797676; fax (20) 78363108; e-mail iiss@iiss.org; internet www.iiss.org; f. 1958; aims to promote discussion and research on the problems of international security arising from all causes; international membership, Council, and staff; 2,141 mems (1,623 ordinary, 391 assoc., 127 student), 165 corporate mems; Chair. of the Council FRANÇOIS HEISBOURG; Dir Dr JOHN CHIPMAN; publs *Strategic Comments* (electronic publ., 10 a year), *Survival* (4 a year), *The Military Balance* (1 a year), *Strategic Survey* (1 a year), *Adelphi Papers* (8–10 a year).

Jill Dando Institute for Crime Science: Third Fl., 1 Old St, London, EC1V 9HL; tel. (20) 7324-3000; fax (20) 7324-3003; e-mail jdi@ucl.ac.uk; internet www.jdi.ucl.ac.uk; f. 2001; attached to Univ. College London; Dir Prof. RICHARD WORTLEY.

LSE London: Houghton St, London, WC2A 2AE; f. 1998; attached to London School of Economics and Political Science, Univ. of London; studies economic and social issues of London region, as well as problems and potential of other urban and metropolitan regions; Dir Prof. I. GORDON.

Mannheim Centre for Criminology and Criminal Justice: Houghton St, London, WC2A 2AE; f. 1990; attached to London School of Economics and Political Science, Univ. of London; coordinates research in field of criminology and criminal justice; Dir Prof. DAVID DOWNES.

Midlands Centre for Criminology and Criminal Justice: Brockington Bldg, Loughborough Univ., Loughborough, LE11 3TU; tel. (1509) 228369; e-mail g.farrell@lboro.ac.uk; attached to Loughborough Univ.; research areas incl. crime prevention, criminal justice system, drug policy, policing; Dir Prof. GRAHAM FARRELL.

National Institute of Economic and Social Research: 2 Dean Trench St, Smith Sq., London, SW1P 3HE; tel. (20) 7222-7665; fax (20) 7654-1900; e-mail enquiries@niesr.ac.uk; internet www.niesr.ac.uk; f. 1938; library of 10,000 vols, 300 periodicals; Pres. Lord BURNS; Dir JONATHAN PORTES; publ. *National Institute Economic Review* (4 a year).

Overseas Development Institute: 111 Westminster Bridge Rd, London, SE1 7JD; tel. (20) 7922-0300; fax (20) 7922-0399; e-mail odi@odi.org.uk; internet www.odi.org.uk; f. 1960 to act as an independent think-tank on international development and humanitarian issues; works to inspire and inform policy and practice that lead to the reduction of poverty, the alleviation of suffering and the achievement of sustainable livelihoods in developing countries; has 14 research and policy groups and programmes; works with partners in the public and private sectors, in both developing and developed countries; library of 20,000 vols; Chair. Baroness MARGARET JAY OF PADDINGTON; Dir SIMON MAXWELL; publs *Development Policy Review* (4 a year), *Disasters: The Journal of Disaster Studies and Management* (4 a year), research work in the form of books, opinions, briefing papers and working papers.

Policy Studies Institute: 50 Hanson St, London, W1W 6UP; tel. (20) 7911-7500; fax (20) 7911-7501; e-mail website@psi.org.uk; internet www.psi.org.uk; f. 1978; attached to Univ. of Westminster; undertakes and publishes research studies relevant to social, economic, industrial and environmental policy; Dir MALCOLM RIGG.

Royal United Services Institute for Defence and Security Studies: Whitehall, London, SW1A 2ET; tel. (20) 7930-5854; fax (20) 7321-0943; e-mail information@rusi.org; internet www.rusi.org; f. 1831; professional forum in the UK for those concerned with nat. and int. defence and security; research programmes, lectures, confs and seminars; individual, corporate and diplomatic mems; library: see Libraries and Archives; Dir Rear Admiral RICHARD COBBOLD; publs *Chinese Military Update* (12 a year), *Documents of British Foreign and Security Policy* (irregular, jointly with the Stationery Office), *Homeland Security and Resilience Monitor* (10 a year), *Journal* (6 a year), *Newsbrief* (12 a year), *World Defence Systems* (3 a year).

Scottish Economic Policy Network: Stirling, FK9 4LA; tel. (1786) 473171; fax (1786) 463000; attached to Univ. of Stirling; Dir Prof. D. BELL.

Suntory and Toyota International Centres for Economics and Related Disciplines: Houghton St, London, WC2A 2AE; f. 1978; attached to London School of Economics and Political Science, Univ. of London; promotes research into applied economics and related fields; incl. Centre for Analysis of Social Exclusion; Dir Prof. TIMOTHY BESLEY.

Tayside Economic Research Centre: Bell St, Dundee, DD1 1HG; attached to Univ. of Abertay Dundee; Dir NEIL C. MCGREGOR.

Transitional Justice Institute: Jordanstown Campus, Shore Rd, Newtownabbey, BT37 0QB; tel. (28) 9036-6202; fax (28) 9036-8962 Magee Campus, Northland Rd, Londonderry, BT48 7JL; tel. (28) 7137-5146; fax (28) 7137-5184; e-mail transitionaljustice@ulster.ac.uk; internet transitionaljustice.ulster.ac.uk; attached to Univ. of Ulster; promotes theoretical and practical understanding of 'transitional justice'; raises awareness of gender and other issues in the realization of peace and justice; Assoc. Dir Prof CHRISTINE BELL; Co-Dir Prof. COLM CAMPBELL; Co-Dir Prof. FIONNUALA NÍ AOLÁIN.

EDUCATION

Academic Innovation and Continuing Education: Stirling, FK9 4LA; tel. (1786) 473171; fax (1786) 463000; attached to Univ. of Stirling; Dir Prof. J. FIELD.

Centre for Applied Research in Educational Technologies (CARET): First Fl.,

16 Mill Lane, Cambridge CB2 1SB; tel. (1223) 765357; fax (1223) 765505; e-mail stephanie@caret.cam.ac.uk; internet www .caret.cam.ac.uk; attached to Univ. of Cambridge; Administrator STEPHANIE SAUNDERS.

Centre for Educational Research: Houghton St, London, WC2A 2AE; f. 1990; attached to London School of Economics and Political Science, Univ. of London; carries out research into current educational topics incl. choice of schools, schools' admissions, nat. curriculum, funding of education, and European and int. issues; Dir Dr A. WEST.

Centre for Educational Research and Development: Brayford Pool, Univ. of Lincoln, Lincoln, LN6 7TS; tel. (1522) 837017; fax (1522) 886023; e-mail jhubbard@lincoln .ac.uk; internet www.lincoln.ac.uk/cerd; attached to Univ. of Lincoln; Dir Prof. MIKE NEARY.

Centre for Educational Studies: Wilberforce Bldg, Univ. of Hull, Cottingham Rd, Hull, HU6 7RX; tel. (1482) 466216; fax (1482) 466137; e-mail facultyofeducation@hull.ac .uk; internet www.hull.ac.uk/education; attached to Faculty of Education, Univ. of Hull; undergraduate, postgraduate and professional teacher training programmes; Head ALLISON DUNHILL (acting).

Centre for International Education and Research: School of Education, Univ. of Birmingham, Edgbaston, Birmingham, B15 2TT; tel. (121) 414-4809; fax (121) 414-4865; e-mail m.schweisfurth@bham.ac.uk; internet www.education.bham.ac.uk/research/cier; attached to Univ. of Birmingham; promotes role of education in economic, social, political devt; Dir Dr MICHELE SCHWEISFURTH.

Centre for Learning Development: Cottingham Rd, Hull, HU6 7RX; e-mail cld@hull .ac.uk; attached to Univ. of Hull; Head Prof. G. CHAMBERS (acting).

Centre for Mediterranean Studies: Dept of Classics and Ancient history, Univ. of Exeter, Queen's Dr., Exeter, Devon, EX4 4QJ; tel. (1392) 264203; e-mail l.g.mitchell@ ex.ac.uk; internet centres.exeter.ac.uk/cms; f. 1992; attached to Univ. of Exeter; promotes interdisciplinary teaching and research into history, culture and people of Mediterranean; Dir Dr LYNETTE MITCHELL.

Centre for Research in the Arts, Social Sciences and Humanities: Seven W Rd, Cambridge, CB3 9DT; tel. (1223) 766886; fax (1223) 315794; e-mail crassh-admin@lists .cam.ac.uk; internet www.crassh.cam.ac.uk; attached to Univ. of Cambridge; Dir Prof. SIMON GOLDHILL (King's College).

Centre for Russian and East European Studies: Muirhead Tower, Sixth Fl., Univ. of Birmingham, Edgbaston, Birmingham, B15 2TT; tel. (121) 414-6346; fax (121) 414-3423; e-mail d.l.averre@bham.ac.uk; internet www .crees.bham.ac.uk; f. 1963; attached to Univ. of Birmingham; research programmes incl. studies of Russian, Ukrainian and Central European politics, society and culture, postsocialist economic transformation, history of Russia and the Soviet Union, security studies; library of 90,000 vols; Dir Dr DEREK AVERRE; Deputy Dir KATARYNA WOLCZUK.

Centre for the Economics of Education: Houghton St, London, WC2A 2AE; f. 2000; attached to London School of Economics and Political Science, Univ. of London; Dir Prof. S. MACHIN.

Centre of Advanced International Studies: c/o Politics Dept, Univ. of Exeter, Armory Bldg, Rennes Dr., Exeter, EX4 4RJ; tel. (1392) 263164; fax (1392) 263305; e-mail politics@exeter.ac.uk; internet centres.exeter .ac.uk/cais; f. 2000; attached to Univ. of Exeter; researches into aspects of global

social relations across political, economic, cultural realms; Dir Prof. MICK DUMPER; Assoc. Dir Dr BICE MAIGUASHCA; Assoc. Dir Dr JOHN HEATHERSHAW.

Centre of African Studies: Alison Richard Bldg, Seven W Rd, Cambridge, CB3 9DT; tel. (1223) 334396; fax (1223) 769329; e-mail centre@african.cam.ac.uk; internet www .african.cam.ac.uk; attached to Univ. of Cambridge; Dir Prof. MEGAN VAUGHAN (King's College).

Centre of Latin American Studies: Second Fl., 17 Mill Lane, Alison Richard Bldg, Seven W Rd, Cambridge, CB3 9DT; tel. (1223) 335390; fax (1223) 335397; e-mail jac46@cam.ac.uk; internet www .latin-american.cam.ac.uk; f. 1966; attached to Univ. of Cambridge; Dir Dr CHARLES A. JONES.

Centre of South Asian Studies: Laundress Lane, Cambridge, CB2 1SD; tel. (1223) 338094; fax (1223) 767094; e-mail webmaster@s-asian.cam.ac.uk; internet www.s-asian.cam.ac.uk; attached to Univ. of Cambridge; Dir Prof. C. A. BAYLY.

Institute for Advanced Studies in the Humanities: Hope Park Sq., Edinburgh, EH8 9NW; tel. (131) 650-4671; fax (131) 668-2252; e-mail iash@ed.ac.uk; internet www.iash.ed.ac.uk; f. 1969; attached to Univ. of Edinburgh; Dir SUSAN MANNING.

Institute for Cultural Research: POB 2227, London, NW2 3BW; tel. (20) 8452-0960; fax (20) 8438-0311; e-mail admin@i-c-r .org.uk; internet i-c-r.org.uk; f. 1966; promotes and conducts research, advances public education in man's heritage of knowledge; 200 mems; library of 56 monographs; Chair. of Ccl CLARE MAXWELL-HUDSON; Hon. Sec. PATTI SCHNEIDER; Hon. Treas. T. R. WILLS.

Institute of Continuing Education: Madingley Hall, Madingley, Cambridge, CB23 8AQ; tel. (1223) 746262; fax (1223) 746200; e-mail registration@ice.cam.ac.uk; internet www.ice.cam.ac.uk; f. 1873; attached to Univ. of Cambridge; offers Masters programmes; Dir Dr REBECCA LINGWOOD.

Library and Information Statistics Unit: Holywell Park, Loughborough Univ., Loughborough, LE11 3TU; tel. (1509) 635680; fax (1509) 635699; e-mail lisu@lboro.ac.uk; internet www.lboro.ac.uk/departments/ls/ lisu; f. 1987; attached to Loughborough Univ.; research and information centre for library and information services; collects, analyses, interprets, publishes statistical information for and about the library domain in the UK; Dir CLAIRE CREASER.

National Foundation for Educational Research: The Mere, Upton Park, Slough, SL1 2DQ; tel. (1753) 574123; fax (1753) 691632; e-mail enquiries@nfer.ac.uk; internet www.nfer.ac.uk; f. 1946; provides independent research, assessment and information services for education, training and children's services; improves the practice and understanding of those who work with and for learners; library of 20,000 vols, 300 journals; Pres. Sir JAMES ROSE; Chair. RICHARD BUNKER; Chief Exec. SUE ROSSITER; publs *Educational Research* (2 a year), *Impact: NFER's Research News for Schools* (2 a year), *Practical Research for Education* (2 a year).

SCRE Centre: St Andrew's Bldg, 11 Eldon St, Glasgow, G3 6NH; tel. (141) 330-3490; fax (141) 330-3491; e-mail scre.info@scre.ac.uk; internet www.scre.ac.uk; f. 1928 as Scottish Council for Research in Education; conducts educational research of the highest quality and supports the use of research outcomes through the dissemination of findings; Dir Prof. PAUL BRNA.

Society for Research into Higher Education Ltd: 76 Portland Pl., London, W1B 1NT; tel. (20) 7637-2766; fax (20) 7637-2781; e-mail srheoffice@srhe.ac.uk; internet www .srhe.ac.uk; f. 1964 to encourage research and development in higher education and collect and disseminate the results; 237 corporate mems; Pres. Prof. Sir DAVID WATSON; Dir HELEN PERKINS; publs *Research into Higher Education Abstracts* (3 a year), *Studies in Higher Education* (4 a year), *Higher Education Quarterly*, *Newsletter* (3 a year), *International Newsletter* (3 a year).

FINE AND PERFORMING ARTS

Art and Design Research Institute: Room 82E02, School of Art and Design, Univ. of Ulster, Belfast campus, Belfast, BT15 1ED; tel. (28) 9026-7267; e-mail adbe@ulster.ac.uk; internet www.adbe.ulster.ac.uk/research/ artdes_ri; attached to Univ. of Ulster; research, knowledge and technology exchange, teaching; research in fine and applied arts, fashion and textile design, 2-d and 3-d design, visual communication, history and theory of art and design; Dir Prof KAREN FLEMING.

Centre for Advanced Welsh Music Study: College Rd, Bangor, LL57 2DG; tel. (1248) 382181; fax (1248) 383895; attached to Bangor Univ.; Dir Dr SALLY HARPER.

Centre for Dance Research: Roehampton Univ., Roehampton Lane, London SW15 5PH; tel. (20) 8392-3379; e-mail a.grau@ roehampton.ac.uk; attached to Roehampton Univ.; research projects in historical, analytical, anthropological, cultural studies and professional choreography; Dir Prof. ANDRÉE GRAU.

Centre for Research in Film and Audiovisual Cultures: Queen's Bldg, Roehampton Univ., Roehampton Lane, London, SW15 5PH; tel. (20) 8392-3513; e-mail p .mcdonald@roehampton.ac.uk; attached to Roehampton Univ.; critical, historical, analytic and practical research relating to film and other audiovisual media; supports research on cinema, television, video/DVD, interactive platforms and online media; Dir Prof. MICHAEL CHANAN; Dir Dr HEATHER NUNN.

Sainsbury Institute for the Study of Japanese Arts and Culture: 8A The Close, Norwich, NR1 4DH; tel. (1603) 624349; fax (1603) 625011; e-mail sisjac@ sainsbury-institute.org; internet www .sainsbury-institute.org; f. 1999; attached to Univ. of East Anglia; Dir NICOLE COOLIDGE ROUSMANIERE.

HISTORY, GEOGRAPHY AND ARCHAEOLOGY

Business History Unit: Houghton St, London, WC2A 2AE; f. 1978, jtly with Imperial College London; attached to London School of Economics and Political Science, Univ. of London; promotes research into business history, incl. technological aspects; Dir Dr T. GOURVISH.

Centre for City and Regional Studies: Cottingham Rd, Hull, HU6 7RX; tel. (1482) 465330; fax (1482) 465006; attached to University of Hull; Dir Prof. DAVID GIBBS; Dir Prof. G. HAUGHTON.

Centre for Contemporary British History: Institute of Historical Research, Senate House, Malet St, London, WC1E 7HU; tel. (20) 7862-8740; fax (20) 7862-8812; e-mail ccbhinfo@sas.ac.uk; internet www.ccbh.ac .uk; f. 1986, fmrly Institute of Contemporary British History; manages research projects, incl. colln of oral testimony for present and future historians; Dir Dr RICHARD ROBERTS (acting); publs *Contemporary British History* (4 a year), *Modern History Review* (4 a year), *Twentieth Century British History* (4 a year).

Centre for Medieval Studies: Univ. of Exeter, The Queen's Dr., Exeter, Devon, EX4 4QJ; tel. (1392) 264364; e-mail y.m .plumley@exeter.ac.uk; internet centres .exeter.ac.uk/medievalstudies; attached to Univ. of Exeter; Dir Dr YOLANDA PLUMLEY.

Centre for Research in History and Theory: Roehampton Lane, London, SW15 5PH; tel. (20) 8392-5793; e-mail w.gallois@ roehampton.ac.uk; internet www .roehampton.ac.uk/researchcentres/chat/ index.html; f. 2006; attached to Roehampton Univ.; research in art history, classical civilisation, dance, and drama, history, philosophy, theology and religious studies; Dir Prof. WILLIAM GALLOIS.

Centre for Research in Polish History: Stirling, FK9 4LA; tel. (1786) 467580; fax (1786) 467581; e-mail historyandpolitics@stir .ac.uk; internet ww.historyandpolitics.stir.ac .uk; f. 2000; attached to Univ. of Stirling; Dir Dr PETER D. STACHURA.

Centre for Research in Renaissance Studies: tel. (20) 8392-3334; e-mail s .greenhalgh@roehampton.ac.uk; internet www.roehampton.ac.uk/researchcentres/ renaissance/index.html; attached to Roehampton Univ.; research in classics, drama, English, history and art history, particularly in the fields of Italian Renaissance history; 17th-century politics; Shakespearean after lives in literature, theatre, and the media; gender and performance; early modern court and domestic cultures; textual editing; and Renaissance visual cultures and mythographies; Dir SUSANNE GREENHALGH.

Centre for South-Western Historical Studies: c/o Devon and Exeter Institution, 7 The Close Exeter, EX1 1EZ; tel. (1392) 263292; fax (1392) 263305; e-mail r.burt@ exeter.ac.uk; internet people.exeter.ac.uk/ rburt/swhs; f. 1985; attached to Univ. of Exeter; promotes historical research into all aspects of counties of Cornwall, Devon, Dorset, Somerset; Dir Prof. ROGER BURT.

German Historical Institute: 17 Bloomsbury Sq., London, WC1A 2NJ; tel. (20) 7309-2050; e-mail ghil@ghil.ac.uk; internet www .ghil.ac.uk; f. 1976; research in medieval, modern and comparative British and German history; study of int., esp. Anglo-German relations and history of the British Empire and Commonwealth; European history; organizes international confs and workshop programmes; library of 78,000 vols, 200 periodicals; Dir Prof. Dr ANDREAS GESTRICH; Admin. Officer WOLFGANG HAACK.

Royal Archaeological Institute: c/o Society of Antiquaries of London, Burlington House, Piccadilly, London, W1J 0BE; tel. (7826) 755779; e-mail admin@royalarchinst .org; internet www.royalarchinst.org; f. 1844; monthly lecture programmes and weekend confs; holds meetings for mems; awards grants for archaeological research and excavations; undergraduate and masters dissertations; publishes reports and newsletter; 1,000 mems; library of 167 vols; Pres. Prof. DAVID BREEZE; Hon. Sec. Dr GILL HEY; Treas. Dr ANDREW WILLIAMS; publ. *Archaeological Journal* (1 a year).

Scott Polar Research Institute: Univ. of Cambridge, Lensfield Rd, Cambridge, CB2 1ER; tel. (1223) 336540; fax (1223) 336549; e-mail enquiries@spri.cam.ac.uk; internet www.spri.cam.ac.uk; f. 1920; research and information centre on the polar regions (glaciology, geophysics, oceanography, remote sensing, history, anthropology, socioeconomics); exhibits; also offers Bachelors, Masters, MPhil and PhD courses; library of

100,000 vols, 700 periodicals; archives; photographic library; Dir Prof. JULIAN A. DOWDESWELL; Librarian and Keeper of Collns HEATHER LANE; publs *Polar and Glaciological Abstracts* (3 a year), *Polar Record* (4 a year).

Wetland Archaeology and Environments Research Centre: Cottingham Rd, Hull, HU6 7RX; attached to Univ. of Hull; Dir Dr M. LILLIE.

LANGUAGE AND LITERATURE

Arts and Humanities Research Council: Whitefriars, Lewins Mead, Bristol, BS1 2AE; tel. (117) 987-6500; fax (117) 987-6600; e-mail enquiries@ahrc.ac.uk; internet www .ahrc.ac.uk; f. 2005 to provide financial and practical support for research and postgraduate training in the arts and humanities, as well as funding for museums and art galleries; Chief Exec. Prof. PHILIP ESLER; Chair. Prof. Sir ALAN WILSON; publ. *Arcady Newsletter* (irregular).

Centre for Advanced Research in English: Edgbaston, Birmingham, B15 2TT; e-mail m.c.m.devereux@bham.ac.uk; internet www.care.bham.ac.uk; attached to Univ. of Birmingham; Dir Dr M. KNOWLES; Admin. MICHELLE DEVEREUX.

Centre for English Language Studies: Westmere House, Univ. of Birmingham, Edgbaston, Birmingham, B15 2TT; tel. (121) 414-5695; fax (121) 414-3298; e-mail cels@ bham.ac.uk; internet www.cels.bham.ac.uk; attached to Univ. of Birmingham; Dir CHRIS J. KENNEDY.

Centre for Scottish Cultural Studies: Level 6, Livingstone Tower, 26 Richmond St, Glasgow, G1 1XH; attached to Univ. of Strathclyde; Dir Dr K. G. SIMPSON.

Centre for South West Writing: Univ. of Exeter, Queen's Dr., Exeter, Devon, EX4 4QJ; tel. (1392) 264343; e-mail t.kendall@ exeter.ac.uk; internet centres.exeter.ac.uk/ southwestwriting; attached to Univ. of Exeter; promotes the appreciation of the region's many important creative writers; Dir ANDY BROWN.

Centre for the Standardisation of Terminology: Bangor, Gwynned, LL57 2DG; f. 1996; attached to Bangor Univ.; develops standardized dictionaries and glossaries of contemporary technical terms in Welsh; Dir Dr LLION JONES.

CILT, the National Centre for Languages: 3rd Fl., 111 Westminster Bridge Rd, London, SE1 7HR; tel. (20) 7633-3300; fax (20) 7379-5082; e-mail info@cilt.org.uk; internet www.cilt.org.uk; f. 1966; independent, registered charity, supported by govt grants; nat. centre for information on learning and teaching languages and on languages for employment; has an enquiry service, specialized library and multimedia colln, training and conference programme; library of 14,000 titles; Chief Exec. ISABELLA MOORE.

Dictionary Research Centre: Edgbaston, Birmingham, B15 2TT; tel. (121) 414-3364; fax (121) 414-5668; e-mail english@bham.ac .uk; internet www.english.bham.ac.uk/drc .shtml; f. 2001; attached to Univ. of Birmingham; research activities incl. work on Johnson's A Dictionary of the English Language, sourcing of Johnson's citations; corpus-based lexicography; bilingual and multilingual lexicography; lexicographical description of collocation; language of definitions; perceptions of dictionaries; metaphor and dictionaries; Dir Dr ROSAMUND MOON.

Foreign Language Centre: Univ. of Exeter, 2nd Fl., Queen's Bldg, Queen's Dr., Exeter, Devon, EX4 4QH; tel. (1392) 724306; e-mail languages@exeter.ac.uk;

internet www.sall.ex.ac.uk/flc; attached to Univ. of Exeter; Dir JONATHAN LIPPMAN.

Hispanic Research Centre: tel. (20) 8392-3572; e-mail i.santaolalla@roehampton.ac .uk; attached to Roehampton Univ.; Dir Dr ISABEL SANTAOLALLA.

Institute for Advanced Research in Arts and Social Sciences: 91 Oakfield Rd, Selly Park, Birmingham, B29 7HL; attached to Univ. of Birmingham; Hon. Dir Prof. E. W. IVES.

Institute of Cornish Studies: Tremough Campus, Treliever Rd, Penryn, Cornwall, TR1 9EZ; Univ. of Exeter, Cornwall Campus, Penryn, Cornwall, TR104 9EZ; tel. (1326) 371811; internet www.exeter.ac.uk/cornwall/ academic_departments/huss/ics/icsresearch .shtml; f. 1970, present bldg 2004; attached to Univ. of Exeter; Dir Prof. PHILIP J. PAYTON; Asst Dir Dr GARRY TREGIDGA; publ. *Cornish Studies* (1 a year).

Leopardi Centre: Edgbaston, Birmingham, B15 2TT; tel. (121) 414-5996; e-mail f .dintino@bham.ac.uk; internet www.leopardi .bham.ac.uk; f. 1998; attached to Univ. of Birmingham; promotes study and knowledge of Leopardi and his European context at postdoctoral, postgraduate, undergraduate level; facilitates research on Leopardi and on related topics, incl. the European reception of Leopardi's work; acts as a UK focus for research into the cultures of 18th and 19th century Italy; organizes research seminars and colloquia with specialists in 18th and 19th century studies and related fields from Italy, the UK and other countries; maintains and enhances colln of publs relating to Leopardi in the European languages; collects relevant bibliographical material; Dir Dr FRANCO D'INTINO.

Modern Humanities Research Association: 1 Carlton House Terrace, London, SW1Y 5AF; e-mail mail@mhra.org.uk; internet www.mhra.org.uk; f. at Cambridge Univ. in 1918; encourages advanced studies in modern and medieval languages and literatures; publishes journals and monographs; provides funding assistance for academic publishing, research and confs; Hon. Sec. Dr BARBARA BURNS; publs *Annual Bibliography of English Language and Literature*, *Austrian Studies*, *Modern Language Review* (4 a year), *Portuguese Studies* (2 a year), *The Slavonic and East European Review* (4 a year), *Yearbook of English Studies* (2 a year), *The Year's Work in Modern Language Studies*.

National Centre for Research in Children's Literature: tel. (20) 8392-3346; e-mail k.reynolds@roehampton.ac.uk; internet www.ncrcl.ac.uk; attached to Roehampton Univ.; Dir Prof. KIM REYNOLDS.

R. S. Thomas Study Centre: Bangor, Gwynned, LL57 2DG; tel. (1248) 382113; internet rsthomas.bangor.ac.uk; f. 2000; attached to Bangor Univ.; Dir Dr JASON WALFORD DAVIES; Dir Prof. TONY BROWN.

Shakespeare Institute: Mason Croft, Stratford upon Avon, CV37 6HP; tel. (1789) 293138; e-mail shakespeare@bham.ac.uk; Dir Prof. KATE McLUSKIE.

MEDICINE

Arthritis Research UK: Copeman House, St Mary's Court, St Mary's Gate, Chesterfield, S41 7TD; tel. (1246) 558033; fax (1246) 558007; e-mail enquiries@ arthritisresearchuk.org; internet www .arthritisresearchuk.org; f. 1936 as the Arthritis and Rheumatism Ccl; raises funds to promote medical research into causes, treatment and cure of arthritis and related musculoskeletal conditions; educates medical students, doctors and allied healthcare professionals about arthritis; provides information to people affected by arthritis and to the general public; basic science and clinical research is carried out in medical schools and univs across the UK; Chief Exec. Dr LIAM O'TOOLE; publ. *Reports on Rheumatic Diseases* (3 a year).

Asthma UK: Summit House, 70 Wilson St, London, EC2A 2DB; tel. (20) 7786-4900; fax (20) 7256-6075; e-mail info@asthma.org.uk; internet www.asthma.org.uk; f. 1927; ind. UK charity; funds research into asthma and provides advice and information; works with asthma patients, health professionals and researchers; influences healthcare policies; 7,000 mems; Chair. Dr ROB WILSON; Chief Exec. NEIL CHURCHILL; publ. *Asthma Magazine* (4 a year).

Bone and Joint Research Unit: John Vane Bldg, Charterhouse Sq., London, EC1M 6BQ; e-mail y.chernajovsky@qmul.ac.uk; internet www.whri.qmul.ac.uk/research/boneandjoint.html; f. 1978; attached to Queen Mary's School, Univ. of London; Dir Prof. YUTI CHERNAJOVSKY.

British Heart Foundation National Centre for Physical Activity and Health: School of Sport, Exercise and Health Sciences, Loughborough Univ., Epinal Way, Loughborough, LE11 3TU; tel. (1509) 226421; fax (1509) 226420; e-mail bhfnc@lboro.ac.uk; internet www.bhfactive.org.uk; f. 2000; attached to Loughborough Univ.; promotes physical activity and health; Admin. ANJNA NAGAR.

Burden Neurological Institute: Frenchay Park Rd, Bristol, BS16 1JB; tel. (117) 918-6720; e-mail burdeninstitute@hotmail.com; internet www.bristol.ac.uk/neuroscience/clinical/bni; f. 1939 to conduct research in neurology, neurophysiology, neuropsychology and psychiatry; stem cell research into multiple sclerosis; library of 4,000 vols; Dir Prof. NEIL J. SCOLDING; Sec. RODNEY C. NORTH.

Cancer Research UK: 61 Lincoln's Inn Fields, London, WC2A 3PX; tel. (20) 7242-0200; fax (20) 7269-3101; internet www.cancerresearchuk.org; f. 2002, by merger of Imperial Cancer Research Fund (f. 1902) and Cancer Research Campaign (f. 1923); library of 4,000 vols, 300 periodicals; Chair. DAVID NEWBIGGING; Chief. Exec. ALEX MARKHAM; publ. *Scientific Report* (1 a year).

Cancer Research UK Beatson Institute for Cancer Research: Garscube Estate, Switchback Rd, Bearsden, Glasgow, G61 1BD; tel. (141) 330-3953; fax (141) 942-6521; e-mail beatson@gla.ac.uk; internet www.beatson.gla.ac.uk; f. 1990; incorporates Beatson Institute for Cancer Research and the Univ. of Glasgow depts of Medical Oncology and Radiation Oncology; research in molecular and cell biology of cancer and related diseases; library of 1,000 textbooks, 83 journals; Dir of the Beatson Institute for Cancer Research K. H. VOUSDEN; publ. *Scientific Report* (1 a year).

Centre for Child and Family Research: Dept of Social Sciences, Schofield Bldg, Loughborough Univ., Loughborough, LE11 3TU; tel. (1509) 228355; fax (1509) 223943; e-mail ccfr@lboro.ac.uk; internet www.lboro.ac.uk/research/ccfr; f. 2002; attached to Loughborough Univ.; Dir Prof. HARRIET WARD.

Centre for Mechanisms of Human Toxicity: Hodgkin Bldg, Univ. of Leicester, POB 138, Lancaster Rd, Leicester, LE1 9HN; tel. (116) 252-5544; fax (116) 252-5616; internet www.le.ac.uk/cmht; f. 1993; Dir Prof. ANNE WILLIS.

Centre for Medical History: Armory Bldg, Rennes Dr., Exeter, EX4 4RJ; tel. (1392) 263289; fax (1392) 263305; e-mail cfmhmail@exeter.ac.uk; internet centres.exeter.ac.uk/medhist; f. 1997; attached to Univ. of Exeter; researches within the field of medical history, social study of contemporary medical and health-related activities; Dir Dr KATE FISHER; Asst Dir Prof. JO MELLING.

Centre for Social Policy Research and Development: College Rd, Bangor, Gwynned, LL57 2DG; f. 1986; attached to Bangor Univ.; scientific research primarily in areas of human devt, health studies and social care provision; Dir V. BURHOLT.

Children's Health and Exercise Research Centre: Univ. of Exeter, St Luke's Campus, Exeter, EX1 2LU; tel. (1392) 262884; e-mail sshs-school-office@exeter.ac.uk; internet centres.exeter.ac.uk/cherc; f. 1987; attached to Univ. of Exeter; research in paediatric exercise science; Dir Prof. NEIL ARMSTRONG; Co-Dir Assoc. Prof. CRAIG WILLIAMS; Assoc. Dir Dr RICHARD WINSLEY.

Dementia Services Development Centre: Stirling, FK9 4LA; tel. (1786) 473171; fax (1786) 463000; attached to Univ. of Stirling; Dir Prof. JUNE ANDREWS.

Essex Biomedical Sciences Institute: University of Essex, Wivenhoe Park, Colchester, CO4 3SQ; tel. (1206) 872918; e-mail klenovae@essex.ac.uk; internet www.essex.ac.uk/bs/ebsi; attached to Univ. of Essex; promotes clinically-relevant, biomedical and health-related translational research; Dir Prof. ELENA KLENOVA; Assoc. Dir Dr TONY ELSTON.

Health and Rehabilitation Sciences Research Institute: Room 01B102, School of Health Sciences, Jordanstown Campus, Univ. of Ulster, Shore Rd, Newtownabbey, BT37 0QB; tel. (28) 9036-6851; internet www.science.ulster.ac.uk/hrsri; attached to Univ. of Ulster; research in physiotherapy, speech and language therapy, occupational therapy, radiography, podiatry and clinical physiology; Dir Prof STEPHANIE MCKEOWN; Sec. ANNA MOONEY.

School of Health and Human Sciences: Wivenhoe Park, Colchester, CO4 3SQ; tel. (20) 6872854; internet www.essex.ac.uk/hhs; attached to Univ. of Essex; applied teaching, training and research in health incl. nursing, occupational therapy, oral health, physiotherapy and speech and language therapy; Head of School Prof. JOANNA JACKSON.

Health Protection Agency: Porton Down, Salisbury, SP4 0JG; tel. (1980) 612100; fax (1980) 611096; e-mail business@hpa.org.uk; internet www.hpa.org.uk; f. 2003; attached to Dept of Health; protects the UK population against biological, chemical and radiological health threats.

History of Medicine Unit: 90 Vincent Dr., Edgbaston, Birmingham, B15 2TT; tel. (121) 415-8174; fax (121) 414-4036; e-mail f.l.worrall@bham.ac.uk; internet www.medicine.bham.ac.uk/histmed; f. 2000; attached to Univ. of Birmingham; supports and promotes teaching and research in the history of medicine; Dir Dr JONATHAN REINARZ; Sec. FRANCES WORRALL.

Institute for Ageing and Health: c/o Lynn Patterson, Wolfson Research Centre, Newcastle General Hospital, Newcastle upon Tyne, NE4 6BE; tel. (191) 256-3014; fax (191) 256-3011; internet www.ncl.ac.uk/iah; f. 1994 to undertake clinical research into gerontology and the health-related issues of the ageing process; 200 mems; small specialist library; Dir Prof. TOM KIRKWOOD.

Institute of Cancer Research: see under University of London.

Institute of Medical and Social Care Research: Bangor, Gwynned, LL57 2DG; tel. (1248) 388771; e-mail imscar@bangor.ac.uk; f. 1998; attached to Bangor Univ.; Dir Prof. I. T. RUSSELL.

Institute of Neurology: The Nat. Hospital, Queen Sq., London, WC1N 3BG; tel. (20) 7837-3611; fax (20) 7278-5069; internet www.ucl.ac.uk/ion; postgraduate institute of UCL; eight research depts doing clinical and basic research in themes: neurodegenerative disease; molecular neuroscience, clinical and experimental epilepsy; motor neuroscience and movement disorders; imaging neuroscience; brain repair and rehabilitation, neuroinflammation and clinical neurosciences; library of 16,000 vols; Dir Prof. A. THOMPSON; Sec. ROBERT WALKER.

Institute of Nursing Research: Room G 242, School of Nursing, Univ. of Ulster, Coleraine Campus Cromore Rd, Coleraine, BT52 1SA; tel. (28) 7012-4094; fax (28) 7012-4951; internet www.science.ulster.ac.uk/inr; attached to Univ. of Ulster; activities related to intellectual and developmental disabilities, managing chronic illness, maternal fetal and infant research; Dir Prof BRENDAN MCCORMACK; Sec. JULIE CUMMINS.

Liverpool School of Tropical Medicine: Pembroke Pl., Liverpool, L3 5QA; tel. (151) 705-3100; fax (151) 705-3370; e-mail ruth.pollard@liv.ac.uk; internet www.liv.ac.uk/lstm; f. 1898 and received its Charter of Incorporation 1905; affiliated to the Univ. of Liverpool; its objects are to train medical and paramedical personnel in all aspects of individual or community medicine in the tropics, to conduct original research into tropical diseases and their control, and to organize and conduct clinical and prophylactic measures against tropical diseases; also undertakes research and technical assistance work in other health sector areas; library of 50,000 vols and periodicals, incl. Ronald Ross collection; Dir Prof. JANET HEMINGWAY; publs *Annals of Tropical Medicine and Parasitology*, *Annals of Tropical Paediatrics*.

LSE Health and Social Care: Houghton St, London, WC2A 2AE; f. 2000; attached to London School of Economics and Political Science, Univ. of London; undertakes research, consultancy and training in int. comparative health policy; coordinates European Health Policy Research Network; Dir Dr E. MOSSIALOS; Dir Prof. MARTIN KNAPP.

Medical Research Council (MRC): 20 Park Crescent, London, W1B 1AL; tel. (20) 7636-5422; fax (20) 7436-6179; e-mail corporate@headoffice.mrc.ac.uk; internet www.mrc.ac.uk; f. 1913; promotes research for improvement of human health; undertakes research in molecular science and public health in a network of 64 research establishments complementing the research resources of univs and hospitals; supports research training by means of fellowships, studentships and grants to scientists; Chair. Sir JOHN CHISHOLM; Chief Exec. Prof. LESZEK BORYSIEWICZ; publs *Annual Review*, *Research Strategy* (1 a year).

Attached Research Establishments:

Centre for Brain Ageing and Vitality: Univ. of Newcastle Upon Tyne, Campus for Ageing and Vitality, Newcastle Upon Tyne, NE4 5PL; tel. (191) 248-1200; fax (191) 248-1101; e-mail hazel.glass@ncl.ac.uk; internet www.ncl.ac.uk/biomedicine/research/centres/cbav.htm; Dir Prof. DOUG TURNBULL.

Centre for Cognitive Ageing and Cognitive Epidemiology: Dept of Psychology, Univ. of Edinburgh, 7 George Sq., Edinburgh, EH8 9JZ; tel. (131) 650-8275; fax (131) 651-1771; e-mail ccace@ed.ac.uk; internet www.ccace.ed.ac.uk; Dir Prof. IAN J. DEARY.

Crucible Centre: Univ. College London, Gower St, London, WC1E 6BT; tel. (20) 7679-1597; e-mail r.thoreau@ucl.ac.uk; internet www.ucl.ac.uk/crucible; research on all aspects of ageing process from philosophy, biology, economics, clinical practice to design of the built environment; Dir Prof. NICK TYLER.

MRC Anatomical Neuropharmacology Unit: Mansfield Rd, Oxford, OX1 3TH; tel. (1865) 271865; fax (1865) 271647; e-mail mary.gilgunn-jones@pharm.ox.ac.uk; internet www.mrc.ox.ac.uk; f. 1984; Dir Prof. PETER SOMOGYI.

MRC Asthma UK Centre in Allergic Mechanisms of Asthma: King's College London, School of Medicine, 5th Floor, Thomas Guy House, Guy's Hospital, London, SE1 9RT; tel. (20) 7188-1943; fax (20) 7403-8640 Imperial College London, S Kensington Campus, Sir Alexander Fleming Bldg, London, SW7 2AZ; tel. (20) 7594-3159; internet www.asthma-allergy.ac.uk; Dir at KCL Prof. TAK LEE; Dir at ICL Prof. TIM WILLIAMS.

MRC Biomedical Nuclear Magnetic Resonance Centre: Nat. Institute for Medical Research, The Ridgeway, Mill Hill, London, NW7 1AA; tel. (20) 8816-2026; fax (20) 8906-4477; e-mail tom .frenkiel@nimr.mrc.ac.uk; internet www .nmrcentre.mrc.ac.uk; f. 1980; Head Dr TOM FRENKIEL.

MRC Biostatistics Unit: Institute of Public Health, Univ. Forvie Site, Robinson Way, Cambridge, CB2 0SR; tel. (1223) 330366; fax (1223) 330365; internet www .mrc-bsu.cam.ac.uk; f. 1970; Hon. Dir Prof. SIMON THOMPSON.

MRC Cambridge Centre for Brain Repair: E. D. Adrian Bldg, Forvie Site, Robinson Way, Cambridge, CB2 0PY; tel. (1223) 331160; fax (1223) 331174; e-mail pj214@cam.ac.uk; internet www.brc.cam .ac.uk; Chair. Prof. J. W. FAWCETT.

MRC Cancer Cell Unit: Hutchison/MRC Research Centre, Hills Rd, Cambridge, CB2 0XZ; tel. (1223) 763240; fax (1223) 763241; e-mail reception@hutchison-mrc .cam.ac.uk; internet www.hutchison-mrc .cam.ac.uk; f. 2002; Dir Prof. ASHOK VENKITARAMAN; Dir Prof. BRUCE PONDER; Dir Prof. RON LASKEY.

MRC/Cancer Research UK/BHF Clinical Trial Service Unit & Epidemiological Studies Unit (CTSU): Richard Doll Bldg, Old Rd Campus, Roosevelt Dr., Oxford, OX3 7LF; tel. (1865) 743743; fax (1865) 743985; e-mail secretary@ctsu.ox.ac .uk; internet www.ctsu.ox.ac.uk; Co-Dir Prof. RORY COLLINS; Co-Dir Prof. RICHARD PETO.

MRC Cell Biology Unit: MRC Laboratory for Molecular Cell Biology, Univ. College London, Gower St, London, WC1E 6BT; tel. (20) 7679-7806; fax (20) 7679-7805; internet www.ucl.ac.uk/lmcb; Dir Prof. MARK MARSH.

MRC Centre for Behavioural and Clinical Neuroscience Institute (BCNI): Dept of Experimental Psychology, Univ. of Cambridge, Downing Site, Cambridge, CB2 3EB; tel. (1223) 333558; fax (1223) 314547; internet www.psychol.cam.ac.uk; Dir Prof. TREVOR ROBBINS.

MRC Centre for Causal Analyses in Translational Epidemiology: Oakfield House, 15–23 Oakfield Grove, Clifton, BS8

2BN; tel. (117) 331-0098; fax (117) 331-0123; e-mail info-caite@bristol.ac.uk; internet www.bristol.ac.uk/caite; f. 2007; develops and applies novel methods that can be used to determine causes of health and disease in population; covers range of disease and health-related outcomes, incl cardiovascular disease, obesity, diabetes, cancer, mental ill-health, smoking, alcohol and physical activity; Dir Prof. GEORGE DAVEY SMITH; Deputy Dir Prof. DEBBIE LAWLOR; Deputy Dir Prof. IAN DAY.

MRC Centre for Developmental and Biomedical Genetics: Dept of Biomedical Science, Firth Court, Univ. of Sheffield, Western Bank, Sheffield, S10 2TN; tel. (114) 222-2710; fax (114) 276-5413; e-mail cdbg@sheffield.ac.uk; internet cdbg.shef.ac .uk; f. 1997 as Centre for Developmental Genetics, present status 2004; Dir Prof. MARYSIA PLACZEK.

MRC Centre for Developmental Neurobiology: King's College London, New Hunt's House, 4th Fl., Guy's Hospital Campus, London, SE1 1UL; tel. (20) 7848-8148; fax (20) 7848-6550; e-mail lauren.ryan@kcl.ac.uk; internet www.kcl .ac.uk; Dir Prof. ANDREW LUMSDEN.

MRC Centre for Drug Safety Science: School of Biomedical Sciences, Univ. of Liverpool, Liverpool, L69 3BX; tel. (151) 794-5852; fax (151) 794-5540; e-mail neil .french@liverpool.ac.uk; internet www.liv .ac.uk/drug-safety; Dir Prof. KEVIN PARK.

MRC Centre for Genomics and Global Health: Roosevelt Dr., Oxford, OX3 7BN; tel. (1865) 287500; fax (1865) 287501; e-mail victoria.cornelius@well.ox.ac.uk; internet www.cggh.ox.ac.uk; Dir Prof. DOMINIC KWIATKOWSKI.

MRC Centre, London: Stephenson House, 158–160 N Gower St, London, NW1 2ND; tel. (20) 7670-4600; fax (20) 7670-4690; e-mail enquiries@centre-london .mrc.ac.uk; internet www.centre-london .mrc.ac.uk; Head of Centre Dr IAN VINEY.

MRC Centre for Neurodegeneration Research: King's College London, Institute of Psychiatry, POB 55, De Crespigny Park, Denmark Hill, London, SE5 8AF; tel. (20) 7848-0611; fax (20) 7708-0017; internet cnr.iop.kcl.ac.uk; Dir Prof. CHRISTOPHER SHAW.

MRC Centre for Neuromuscular Diseases: POB 102, Nat. Hospital for Neurology and Neurosurgery, Queen Sq., London, WC1 3BG; tel. (845) 155-5000; fax (20) 7692-1208; e-mail admin-cnmd@ion.ucl.ac .uk; internet www.cnmd.ac.uk; Dir Prof. MIKE HANNA.

MRC Centre for Neuropsychiatric Genetics and Genomics: Institute of Psychological Medicine and Clinical Neuroscience, Cardiff Univ., Henry Wellcome Bldg, Heath Park, Cardiff, CF14 4XN; tel. (29) 2068-7065; e-mail psychmedadmin@cf .ac.uk; internet www.cardiff.ac.uk/cngg; Dir Prof. MICHAEL OWEN.

MRC Centre for Nutritional Epidemiology in Cancer Prevention and Survival (CNC): Dept of Public Health and Primary Care, Univ. of Cambridge, Cambridge, CB1 8RN; tel. (1223) 740151; fax (1223) 740147; internet www.srl.cam.ac .uk/cnc; Dir Prof. KAY TEE KHAW.

MRC Centre, Oxford: Old Rd Campus, Oxford Univ., Oxford, OX3 9DU; tel. (1865) 222580; fax (1865) 222549; Head Dr ANNE-MARIE CORIAT.

MRC Centre for Obesity and Related Metabolic Diseases: Univ. of Cambridge Metabolic Research Laboratories, Level 4, Institute of Metabolic Science, POB 289,

Addenbrooke's Hospital, Cambridge, CB2 0QQ; tel. (1223) 336792; internet www .mrc-cord.org; f. 2007; Dir Prof. STEVE O'RAHILLY.

MRC Centre for Outbreak Analysis and Modelling: Imperial College Faculty of Medicine, St Mary's Campus, Norfolk Pl., London, W2 1PG; tel. (20) 7594-3296; internet www1.imperial.ac.uk; Dir Prof. NEIL FERGUSON.

MRC Centre for Protein Engineering: Hills Rd, Cambridge, CB2 0QH; tel. (1223) 402136; fax (1223) 402140; e-mail murphyp@mrc-lmb.cam.ac.uk; internet www.mrc-cpe.cam.ac.uk; f. 1989; Dir Prof. Sir ALAN FERSHT.

MRC Centre for Regenerative Medicine: Scottish Centre for Regenerative Medicine, Five Little France Dr., Edinburgh, EH16 4UU; tel. (131) 651-9500; fax (131) 651-9501; internet www.scrm.ed.ac .uk; Dir Prof. CHARLES FFRENCH-CONSTANT.

MRC Centre for Stem Cell Biology and Regenerative Medicine: Cambridge Stem Cell Initiative, Univ. of Cambridge, Cambridge, CB2 2XY; tel. (1223) 763366; e-mail contact@stemcells.cam.ac.uk; internet www.stemcells.cam.ac.uk; Dir Prof. ROGER PEDERSON.

MRC Centre for Synaptic Plasticity: Dept of Anatomy, School of Medical Sciences, Univ. Walk, Bristol, BS8 1TD; tel. (117) 331-1905; internet www.bris.ac.uk/ synaptic; Dir Prof. G. L. COLLINGRIDGE.

MRC Centre for Transplantation: King's College London, 5th Fl. Tower Wing, Guy's Hospital, Great Maze Pond, London, SE1 9RT; tel. (20) 7188-8711; fax (20) 7188-5660; e-mail mrccentre@kcl.ac .uk; internet transplantation.kcl.ac.uk; Dir Prof. STEVE SACKS.

MRC Centre of Epidemiology for Child Health: Institute of Child Health, 30 Guilford St, London, WC1N 1EH; tel. (20) 7905-2602; fax (20) 7905-2381; internet www.ich.ucl.ac.uk; Dir Prof. CAROL DEZATEUX.

MRC Clinical Sciences Centre: Faculty of Medicine, Imperial College London, Hammersmith Hospital Campus, Du Cane Rd, London, W12 0NN; tel. (20) 8383-8249; fax (20) 8383-8337; internet www.csc.mrc.ac.uk; f. 1994; Dir Prof. AMANDA FISHER.

MRC Clinical Trials Units: 222 Euston Rd, London, NW1 2DA; tel. (20) 7670-4700; fax (20) 7670-4818; e-mail contact@ctu.mrc .ac.uk; internet www.ctu.mrc.ac.uk; f. 1998; Dir Prof. MAX PARMAR.

MRC Cognition and Brain Sciences Unit: 15 Chaucer Rd, Cambridge, CB2 7EF; tel. (1223) 355294; fax (1223) 359062; e-mail info@mrc-cbu.cam.ac.uk; internet www.mrc-cbu.cam.ac.uk; f. 1944; investigates fundamental human mental processes such as attention, emotion, memory and knowledge, speech and language; conducts behavioural experiments to probe the functional properties of psychological systems and build computer models of their operation; carries out neuropsychological and neuroimaging (PET, MRI, MEG, EEG) studies of the underlying neural mechanisms in the brain and explores the clinical implications of the research for patient therapy and rehabilitation; Dir Prof. SUSAN GATHERCOLE.

MRC Collaborative Centre for Human Nutrition Research: Elsie Widdowson Laboratory, Fulbourn Rd, Cambridge, CB1 9NL; tel. (1223) 426356; fax (1223)

437515; internet www.mrc-hnr.cam.ac.uk; f. 1998; Dir Dr ANN PRENTICE.

MRC Epidemiology Resource Centre: Southampton Gen. Hospital, Southampton, SO16 6YD; tel. (23) 8077-7624; fax (23) 8070-4021; e-mail postmaster@mrc .soton.ac.uk; internet www.mrc.soton.ac .uk; f. 1979 as Environmental Epidemiology Unit; present status 2003; Dir Dr CYRUS COOPER.

MRC Epidemiology Unit: Institute of Metabolic Science, POB 285, Addenbrooke's Hospital, Hills Rd, Cambridge, CB2 0QQ; tel. (1223) 330315; fax (1223) 330316; internet www.mrc-epid.cam.ac.uk; Dir Prof. NICK WAREHAM.

MRC Functional Genomics Unit: Univ. of Oxford, Dept of Physiology, Anatomy and Genetics, Le Gros Clark bldg, South Parks Rd, Oxford, OX1 3QX; tel. (1865) 285867; fax (1865) 282862; e-mail mrc .fgu@dpag.ox.ac.uk; internet www.mrcfgu .ox.ac.uk; Hon. Dir Prof. KAY DAVIES.

MRC Harwell: Harwell Science and Innovation Campus, Harwell, OX11 0RD; tel. (1235) 841000; fax (1235) 841172; internet www.mgu.har.mrc.ac.uk; Dir Prof. S. BROWN.

MRC Human Genetics Unit: Western Gen. Hospital, Crewe Rd, Edinburgh, EH4 2XU; tel. (131) 332-2471; fax (131) 467-8456; e-mail enquiries@hgu.mrc.ac.uk; internet www.hgu.mrc.ac.uk; f. 1967; Dir Prof. NICK D. HASTIE.

MRC Human Immunology Unit: Weatherall Institute of Molecular Medicine, Univ. of Oxford, John Radcliffe Hospital, Headington, Oxford, OX3 9DS; tel. (1865) 222443; fax (1865) 222737; internet www.imm.ox.ac.uk; Dir Prof. Sir ANDREW McMICHAEL.

MRC Human Reproductive Sciences Unit: Centre for Reproductive Biology, Queen's Medical Research Institute, 47 Little France Crescent, Edinburgh, EH16 4TJ; tel. (131) 242-9100; fax (131) 242-6197; e-mail enquiries@hrsu.mrc.ac.uk; internet www.hrsu.mrc.ac.uk; Dir Prof. R. P. MILLAR.

MRC Immunochemistry Unit: Dept of Biochemistry, South Parks Rd, Oxford, OX1 3QU; tel. (1865) 275354; fax (1865) 275729; internet www.bioch.ox.ac.uk/ immunoch; Dir Prof. K. B. M. REID.

MRC Institute of Hearing Research: Univ. of Nottingham, Nottingham, NG7 2RD; tel. (115) 922-3431; fax (115) 951-8503; e-mail enquiries@ihr.mrc.ac.uk; internet www.ihr.mrc.ac.uk; f. 1977; Dir Prof. DAVE MOORE.

MRC International Nutrition Group: Nutrition and Public Health Intervention Research Unit, London School of Hygiene & Tropical Medicine, Keppel St, London, WC1E 7HT; tel. (20) 7958-8140; Dir Prof. ANDREW PRENTICE.

MRC Laboratories, The Gambia: POB 273, Banjul, Gambia; tel. 4495442; fax 4495919; e-mail communications@mrc.gm; internet www.mrc.gm; f. 1947; researches into improvement of health care for developing countries; areas of speciality include virology, malaria, bacterial diseases and genetics; Dir and Chair. Prof. CORRAH TUMANI.

MRC Laboratory for Molecular Cell Biology: Univ. College London, Gower St, London, WC1E 6BT; tel. (20) 7679-7806; fax (20) 7679-7805; internet www.ucl.ac .uk/lmcb; Dir Prof. C. R. HOPKINS.

MRC Laboratory of Molecular Biology (LMB): Hills Rd, Cambridge, CB2 0QH;

tel. (1223) 248011; fax (1223) 213556; e-mail webmaster@mrc-lmb.cam.ac.uk; internet www2.mrc-lmb.cam.ac.uk; f. 1947, moved to present site in 1962; Dir HUGH PELHAM.

MRC Mitochondrial Biology Unit: Wellcome Trust/MRC Bldg, Hills Rd, Cambridge, CB2 0XY; tel. (1223) 252700; fax (1223) 252715; internet www.mrc-mbu .cam.ac.uk; Dir Prof. Sir JOHN WALKER.

MRC Molecular Haematology Unit: Weatherall Institute of Molecular Medicine, John Radcliffe Hospital, Headington, Oxford, OX3 9DS; tel. (1865) 222359; fax (1865) 222500; Hon. Dir Prof. DOUG HIGGS.

MRC Prion Unit: Institute of Neurology, Queen Sq., London, WC1N 3BG; tel. (20) 7837-4888; fax (20) 7676-8047; e-mail pacollinge@prion.ucl.ac.uk; internet www .prion.ucl.ac.uk; f. 1998; Dir Prof. JOHN COLLINGE.

MRC Protein Phosphorylation Unit: Sir James Black Centre, College of Life Sciences, Univ. of Dundee, Dundee, DD1 5EH; tel. (1382) 384238; fax (1382) 223778; internet www.ppu.mrc.ac.uk; f. 1990; Hon. Dir Prof. Sir PHILIP COHEN.

MRC Social and Public Health Sciences Unit: 4 Lilybank Gardens, Glasgow, G12 8RZ; tel. (141) 357-3949; fax (141) 357-2389; e-mail enquiries@sphsu.mrc.ac.uk; internet www.sphsu.mrc.ac.uk; f. 1998; Dir Prof. SALLY MACINTYRE.

MRC Social, Genetic and Developmental Psychiatry Centre: Institute of Psychiatry, De Crespigny Park, Denmark Hill, London, SE5 8AF; tel. (20) 7848-0873; fax (20) 7848-0866; internet www.iop.kcl .ac.uk; Dir Prof. ROBERT PLOMIN.

MRC Technology: 20 Park Crescent, London, W1B 1AL; tel. (20) 7291-5300; fax (20) 7291-5325; e-mail info@tech.mrc .ac.uk; internet www.mrctechnology.org; CEO Dr DAVID TAPOLCZAY.

MRC Toxicology Unit: Hodgkin Bldg, Univ. of Leicester, POB 138, Lancaster Rd, Leicester, LE1 9HN; tel. (116) 252-5544; fax (116) 252-5616; internet www.le.ac.uk/ mrctox; f. 1947; Dir Prof. G. COHEN (acting).

MRC Unit for Lifelong Health and Ageing: 33 Bedford Pl., London, WC1B 5JU; tel. (20) 7670-5700; fax (20) 7580-1501; internet www.nshd.mrc.ac.uk; includes MRC Nat. Survey of Health and Devt; Dir Prof. DI KUH.

MRC/University College London Centre for Medical Molecular Virology: Univ. College London, Windeyer Bldg, 46 Cleveland St, London, W1T 4JF; tel. (20) 7679-9119; Dir Prof. MARY COLLINS.

MRC/University of Birmingham Centre for Immune Regulation: Dept of Immunology, Univ. of Birmingham, Edgbaston, Birmingham, B15 2TT; tel. (121) 414-4068; fax (121) 414-3599; e-mail a.s.shakespeare@bham.ac.uk; internet www.mrcbcir.bham.ac.uk; Dir Prof. ERIC J. JENKINSON.

MRC/University of Edinburgh Centre for Inflammation Research: Queen's Medical Research Institute, 47 Little France Crescent, Edinburgh, EH16 4TJ; tel. (131) 242-9195; fax (131)242-6578; e-mail paula.saikko@ed.ac.uk; internet www.cir.med.ed.ac.uk; Dir Prof. JOHN IREDALE.

MRC/University of Sussex Centre in Genome Damage and Stability: Science Park Rd, Univ. of Sussex, Falmer, Brighton, BN1 9RQ; tel. (1273) 678123;

fax (1273) 678121; e-mail gdsc@sussex.ac .uk; internet www.sussex.ac.uk/gdsc; Dir Prof. ANTHONY CARR.

MRC/UVRI Uganda Research Unit on AIDS, Uganda: Uganda Virus Research Institute, POB 49, Entebbe, Uganda; tel. (417) 704000; fax (414) 321137; e-mail mrc@mrcuganda.org; internet www .mrcuganda.org; f. 1989; Dir Dr HEINER GROSSKURTH.

MRC Virology Unit: Institute of Virology, Church St, Glasgow, G11 5JR; tel. (141) 330-4017; fax (141) 337-2236; e-mail enquiries@mrcvu.gla.ac.uk; internet www .mrcvu.gla.ac.uk; Dir Prof. CHRIS M. PRESTON (acting).

National Institute for Medical Research: The Ridgeway, Mill Hill, London, NW7 1AA; tel. (20) 8959-3666; fax (20) 8906-4477; e-mail enquiries@nimr.mrc.ac .uk; internet www.nimr.mrc.ac.uk; f. 1914; Dir Prof. JIM SMITH; publ. *Mill Hill Essays* (1 a year).

Radiation Oncology and Biology Initiative: Radiobiology Research Institute, Churchill Hospital, Headington, Oxford, OX3 7LJ; tel. (1865) 857532; fax (1865) 857533; internet www.rob.ox.ac.uk; Dir Prof. GILLIES McKENNA.

Scottish Collaboration for Public Health Research and Policy: MRC Human Genetics Unit, W. Gen. Hospital, Crewe Rd, Edinburgh, EH4 2XU; tel. (131) 332-2471; Dir Prof. JOHN FRANK.

UK Human Genome Mapping Project Resource Centre: Hinxton Hall, Cambridge, CB10 1SB; tel. (1223) 496750; fax (1223) 496751; e-mail support@hgmp.mrc .ac.uk; internet www.hgmp.mrc.ac.uk; Dir Dr D. CAMPBELL.

Miles Dyslexia Centre: Bangor, LL57 2DG; tel. (1248) 382203; fax (1248) 383614; e-mail dyslex-admin@bangor.ac.uk; internet www .dyslexia.bangor.ac.uk; attached to Bangor Univ.; student support teaching service and training workplace assessment; Dir Dr MARKETA CARAVOLAS.

National Centre for Training and Education in Prosthetics and Orthotics: Curran Bldg, 131 St James' Rd, Glasgow G4 0LS; attached to University of Strathclyde; Dir Prof. J. HUGHES.

Paterson Institute for Cancer Research: Christie Hospital (NHS) Trust, Wilmslow Rd, Withington, Manchester, M20 9BX; tel. (161) 446-3000; fax (161) 446-3109; e-mail inquiries@picr.man.ac.uk; internet www .paterson.man.ac.uk; f. 1932; conducts basic and clinical cancer research; Dir NIC JONES.

Peninsula Magnetic Resonance Research Centre: Peninsula Medical School, Univ. of Exeter, St Lukes Campus, Magdalen Rd, Exeter, EX1 2LU; tel. (1392) 262982; fax (1392) 262926; e-mail a .benattayallah@exeter.ac.uk; internet centres.exeter.ac.uk/pmrrc; f. 2002; collaboration of the Univ. of Exeter, the Peninsula Medical School and the Univ. of Plymouth; jtly run by the Schools of Physics, Sports Science and Psychology at Exeter, the Institute of Neuroscience at Plymouth and the Peninsula Medical School; research projects incl. MRI, EEG, MEG, eyetracker; Dir IAN R. SUMMERS; Dir ADELMALEK BENATTAYALLAH.

Public Health Laboratory Service: 61 Colindale Ave, London, NW9 5HT; tel. (20) 8200-4400; fax (20) 8200-7874; internet www .phls.co.uk; f. 1946; library of 35,000 vols; Dir (vacant); publs *Communicable Disease and Public Health* (4 a year), *Communicable Disease Report* (52 a year), *PHLS Food and Environment Bulletin* (12 a year), *PHLS HIV Bulletin, PHLS Library Bulletin* (weekly).

Scottish Network for Chronic Pain Research: Stirling, FK9 4LA; tel. (1786) 473171; fax (1786) 463000; attached to Univ. of Stirling; Dir Dr E. BRODIE.

Strangeways Research Laboratory: Worts' Causeway, Cambridge, CB1 8RN; tel. (1223) 740145; fax (1223) 740147; internet www.srl.cam.ac.uk; f. 1912; research into cell biology, developmental biology, cancer; primary research into cancer genetics, epidemiology, cardiovascular disease and diabetes; Dirs Prof. J. DANESH, Prof. B. PONDER.

Strathclyde Institute for Drug Research: Royal College Bldg, 204 George St, Glasgow G1 1XW; attached to Univ. of Strathclyde; Dir Prof. A. L. HARVEY.

Thomas Coram Research Unit: 27–28 Woburn Sq., London, WC1H 0AA; f. 1973; multi-disciplinary designated research unit of the Dept of Health; research in health, education and devt of children; attached to Institute of Education, Univ. of London; Dir Prof. PETER AGGLETON.

Trafford Centre for Medical Research: University of Sussex, Falmer, Brighton, BN1 9RH; attached to Univ. of Sussex; Dir Prof. A. L. MOORE (acting).

Wellcome Trust/Cancer Research UK Gurdon Institute: Tennis Court Rd, Cambridge, CB2 1QN; tel. (1223) 334088; fax (1223) 334089; e-mail info@gurdon.cam.ac.uk; internet www.gurdon.cam.ac.uk; attached to Univ. of Cambridge; Dir Prof. DANIEL ST JOHNSTON.

NATURAL SCIENCES
General

Engineering and Physical Sciences Research Council: Polaris House, North Star Ave, Swindon, SN2 1ET; tel. (1793) 444100; fax (1793) 444005; e-mail infoline@epsrc.ac.uk; internet www.epsrc.ac.uk; f. 1994; supports basic, strategic and applied research and related postgraduate training in engineering and the physical sciences; funds engineers and physical scientists to conduct research; Chair. JOHN ARMITT; CEO Prof. DAVID DELPY; publs *Connect, Impact* (www.impactworld.org.uk), *Newsline, Pioneer, Spotlight.*

Natural Environment Research Council (NERC): Polaris House, North Star Ave, Swindon, SN2 1EU; tel. (1793) 411500; fax (1793) 411501; e-mail requests@nerc.ac.uk; internet www.nerc.ac.uk; f. 1965; funds centres and univs to carry out research and train and support environmental scientists; provides sustainable solutions to problems concerning biodiversity, environmental risks and hazards, global change, natural resource management, and pollution and waste; focuses on resilience to natural hazards, human health and pollution, climate change, biodiversity loss and ecosystem services, renewable energy and green economy; works in partnership with industry, policy makers and regulators; 6 environmental research centres: British Antarctic Survey, British Geological Survey, Centre for Ecology and Hydrology, Nat. Oceanography Centre, Nat. Centre for Atmospheric Science, Nat. Centre for Earth Observation; Chair. ED WALLIS; Chief Exec. Prof. DUNCAN WINGHAM; publ. *Planet Earth* (4 a year).

Component Institutes of the Council:

British Antarctic Survey: High Cross, Madingley Rd, Cambridge, CB3 0ET; tel. (1223) 221400; fax (1223) 362616; e-mail information@bas.ac.uk; internet www.antarctica.ac.uk; f. 1945 as Falkland Islands Dependencies Survey; present name 1962; operates 5 research stations, 2 Royal Research Ships and 5 aircraft in and around Antarctica; undertakes a programme of science in the Antarctic and related regions and aims to address key global and regional issues; undertakes jt research projects and over 120 nat. and int. collaborations; library of 8,500 vols, 350 periodicals; Dir Prof. C. RAPLEY, Prof. NICHOLAS OWENS.

British Geological Survey: Kingsley Dunham Centre, Nicker Hill, Keyworth, Nottingham, NG12 5GG; tel. (115) 936-3100; fax (115) 936-3200; e-mail enquiries@bgs.ac.uk; internet www.bgs.ac.uk; f. 1835; library: earth science reference library; Nat. Geoscience Data Centre; Exec. Dir Prof. JOHN LUDDEN; publ. *Earthwise* (2 a year).

Centre for Ecology & Hydrology: Maclean Bldg, Benson Lane, Crowmarsh Gifford, Wallingford, OX10 8BB; tel. (1491) 838800; fax (1491) 692424; e-mail enquiries@ceh.ac.uk; internet www.ceh.ac.uk; Dir Prof. PATRICIA NUTTALL.

Constituent Institutes:

CEH Bangor: Environment Centre Wales, Deinol Rd, Bangor, LL57 2UW; tel. (1248) 374500; fax (1248) 355363; internet www.ceh.ac.uk/sites/bangor.html; Head Prof. BRIDGET EMMETT.

CEH Edinburgh: Bush Estate, Penicuik, EH26 0QB; tel. (131) 445-4343; fax (131) 445-3943; internet www.ceh.ac.uk; Dir Prof. J. NEIL CAPE.

CEH Lancaster: Lancaster Environment Centre, Library Ave, Bailrigg, Lancaster, LA1 4AP; tel. (1524) 595800; fax (1524) 61536; e-mail lancaster@ceh.ac.uk; internet www.ceh.ac.uk/sites/lancaster.html; Head of Site Prof. RICHARD SHORE.

CEH Wallingford: Maclean Bldg, Benson Lane, Crowmarsh Gifford, Wallingford, OX10 8BB; tel. (1491) 838800; fax (1491) 629424; e-mail jsw@ceh.ac.uk; internet www.nwl.ac.uk; Dir Prof. JIM WALLACE.

Proudman Oceanographic Laboratory: 6 Brownlow St, Liverpool, L3 5DA; tel. (151) 795-4800; fax (151) 795-4801; e-mail polenquiries@pol.ac.uk; internet www.pol.ac.uk; Dir Dr ANDREW WILLMOTT.

Centre for Atmospheric Science: Dept of Chemistry, Univ. of Cambridge, Lensfield Rd, Cambridge, CB2 1EP; tel. (1223) 336473; fax (1223) 336473; internet www.atm.ch.cam.ac.uk/acmsu; Dir Dr J. A. PYLE.

Centre for Population Biology: Imperial College London, Silwood Park Campus, Ascot, SL5 7PY; tel. (20) 7594-2475; fax (1344) 873173; internet www.imperial.ac.uk/cpb; Dir Prof. GEORGIA MACE.

Environmental Systems Science Centre: Univ. of Reading, Harry Pitt Bldg, 3 Earley Gate, POB 238, Reading, RG6 6AL; tel. (118) 931-8741; fax (118) 931-6413; e-mail admin@mail.nerc-essc.ac.uk; internet www.nerc-essc.ac.uk; Head Prof. R. J. GURNEY.

National Centre for Atmospheric Science (NCAS): Dept of Meteorology, Univ. of Reading, Earley Gate, Reading, RG6 6BB; tel. (118) 378-8315; fax (118) 378-8316; e-mail n.d.bray@reading.ac.uk; internet climate.ncas.ac.uk; Dir for Climate Research Prof. ROWAN SUTTON.

National Oceanography Centre: Univ. of Southampton Waterfront Campus, European Way, Southampton, SO14 3ZH; tel. (23) 8059-6666; fax (23) 8059-6032; internet www.noc.soton.ac.uk; Dir Prof. ED HILL.

Plymouth Marine Laboratory: Prospect Pl., Plymouth, PL1 3DH; tel. (1752) 633100; fax (1752) 633101; e-mail forinf@pml.ac.uk; internet www.pml.ac.uk; f. 2002; CEO Prof. STEPHEN DE MORA.

Sea Mammal Research Unit: Gatty Marine Laboratory, Univ. of St Andrews, St Andrews, KY16 8LB; tel. (1334) 462630; fax (1334) 462632; e-mail smru.office@smru.st-and.ac.uk; internet smub.st-and.ac.uk; Dir Prof. P. HAMMOND.

Tyndall Centre for Climate Change Research: School of Environmental Sciences, Univ. of East Anglia, Norwich, NR4 7TJ; tel. (1603) 593900; fax (1603) 593901; internet www.tyndall.ac.uk; Dir Prof. KEVIN ANDERSON.

Biological Sciences

Biocomposites Centre: Deiniol Rd, Bangor, LL57 2UW; tel. (1248) 370588; fax (1248) 370594; e-mail bc@bangor.ac.uk; internet www.bc.bangor.ac.uk; f. 1991; attached to Bangor Univ.; conducts contract research on processing of wood and plant materials; Dir Dr PAUL FOWLER.

Biomedical Sciences Research Institute: tel. (28) 7032-3091; fax (28) 7032-4965; e-mail km.coyles@ulster.ac.uk; internet biomed.science.ulster.ac.uk/bmsri; f. 2004; attached to Univ. of Ulster; studies of biological mechanisms associated with degenerative diseases like cancer, diabetes, heart disease, osteoporosis and visual deterioration.

BIOS: Houghton St, London, WC2A 2AE; f. 2003; attached to London School of Economics and Political Science, Univ. of London; int. centre for research and policy on social aspects of life sciences and biomedicine; Dir Prof. NIKOLAS ROSE.

Biosciences Graduate Research School: Edgbaston, Birmingham, B15 2TT; tel. (121) 414-5560; fax (121) 414-5925; e-mail biosciences-phd@bham.ac.uk; internet www.biosciences.bham.ac.uk/study/graduate/research/phd.shtml; attached to Univ. of Birmingham; Dir Prof. C. M. THOMAS.

Bristol University Botanic Garden: Stoke Park Rd, Stoke Bishop, Bristol, BS9 1JG; tel. (117) 331-4906; fax (117) 331-4909; internet www.bris.ac.uk/depts/botanicgardens; f. 1882; advances public education and promotes teaching and research into botany and its related subjects; adult education programme, courses and tours; RHS centre; Curator NICHOLAS WRAY; publ. *Annual Seed List.*

Cambridge University Botanic Garden: Cory Lodge, Bateman St, Cambridge, CB2 1JF; tel. (1223) 336265; fax (1223) 336278; e-mail enquiries@botanic.cam.ac.uk; internet www.botanic.cam.ac.uk; f. 1762 (1846 on present site); teaching and research in botany and horticulture; library of 11,000 (incl. early vols of *Gardeners Chronicle* annotated by Charles Darwin); Dir Prof. J. S. PARKER; publ. *Seed List* (1 a year).

Chelsea Physic Garden: 66 Royal Hospital Rd, London, SW3 4HS; tel. (20) 7352-5646; fax (20) 7376-3910; e-mail enquiries@chelseaphysicgarden.co.uk; internet www.chelseaphysicgarden.co.uk; f. 1673; botanic garden and centre for research and education on plants, conservation of rare plants, and a public amenity; specializes in medicinal plants, tropical corridor glasshouse, cool fernery, listed pond rockery, beehives; adult learning programme of lectures and short courses; library: restricted-access library of 300 vols, incl. Society of Apothecaries Dale bequest; Curator C. BAILES; publ. *Index Seminum* (1 a year).

Economic and Social Research Council Centre for Genomics in Society (Egenis Centre): Univ. of Exeter, Byrne House, St

German's Rd, Exeter, Devon, EX4 4PJ; tel. (1392) 269140; fax (1392) 264676; e-mail egenis@ex.ac.uk; internet www .genomicsnetwork.ac.uk/egenis; f. 2002 as part of the ESRC Genomics Network; attached to Univ. of Exeter; conducts research on social impact of devts in genomic science; Dir Prof. JOHN DUPRÉ; Co-Dir Prof. S. BARRY BARNES; Deputy Dir Dr CHRISTINE HAUSKELLER.

Institute of Zoology: Zoological Society of London, Regent's Park, London, NW1 4RY; tel. (20) 7449-6610; fax (20) 7586-2870; e-mail enquiries@ioz.ac.uk; internet www .zoo.cam.ac.uk/ioz; f. 1977; studies aimed at the scientific advancement of conservation, breeding and management of animals in the wild and in captivity; research groups in reproductive biology (gamete biology, endocrinology, physiological ecology), genetics (population genetics, molecular genetics), veterinary science (incl. wildlife disease and comparative medicine), ecology (behavioural ecology and population dynamics); incorporates Nuffield Laboratories of Comparative Medicine and Wellcome Laboratories of Comparative Physiology; library and publs: see Zoological Society of London; Dir Prof. TIM BLACKBURN (acting); publ. *Science for Conservation* (1 a year).

Interdisciplinary Research Centre in Biomedical Materials: Queen, Mary, Univ. of London, Mile End Rd, London, E1 4NS; tel. (20) 7882-5151; f. 1991; attached to Queen Mary, University of London; funded by EPSRC as nat. centre; innovation of analogue biomaterials for tissue and joint replacement; second generation implants and prostheses for medical and dental applications; offers PhD, MD and MS degrees.

International Bee Research Association (IBRA): 16 North Rd, Cardiff, CF10 3DY; tel. (29) 2037-2409; fax (56) 0113-5640; e-mail mail@ibra.org.uk; internet www.ibra.org.uk; f. 1949; charity working to increase awareness of the vital role of bees in the environment and to encourage the use of bees as wealth creators; has a UK Council (8 mems) and an Int. Council (9 mems); library: transferred to the Nat. Library of Wales; Pres. Prof. OCTAAF VAN LAERE (Belgium); Chair. HANS KJAERSGAARD; Exec. Dir SARAH JONES; publs *Bee World* (4 a year), *Journal of Apicultural Research* (e-journal, 4 a year), *Journal of ApiProduct and ApiMedical Science* (e-journal, 4 a year).

National Institute for Biological Standards and Control—A Centre of the HPA: Blanche Lane, South Mimms, Potters Bar, Herts, EN6 3QG; tel. (1707) 641000; fax (1707) 641050; e-mail enquiries@nibsc.ac .uk; internet www.nibsc.ac.uk; f. 1976; the Nat. Biological Standards Board is responsible for control and standardization of biological substances used in human medicine, and its functions are executed through the Institute; biological substances inc. all vaccines such as poliomyelitis, measles, rubella and whooping cough, also blood products, certain hormones and a number of antibiotics; research and devt; designated a WHO Int. Laboratory for Biological Standards; library of 5,000 vols, 200 periodicals; Dir Dr S. INGLIS; publ. *Biological Reference Materials*.

Royal Botanic Garden, Edinburgh: 20A Inverleith Row, Edinburgh, EH3 5LR; tel. (131) 552-7171; fax (131) 248-2901; e-mail d&m@rbge.org.uk; internet www.rbge.org .uk; f. 1670; int. centre for the study of plant biodiversity and conservation; courses leading to HND in horticulture with plantsmanship; MSc course in biodiversity and plant taxonomy; Inverleith House Gallery with art

exhibitions inspired by nature; regional gardens—Benmore Botanic Garden, near Dunoon, Argyll; Logan Botanic Garden, Stranraer, Wigtownshire; Dawyck Botanic Garden, Stobo, Peeblesshire; Herbarium of 2,000,000 specimens; library: see Libraries and Archives; Regius Keeper Prof. STEPHEN BLACKMORE; publ. *Edinburgh Journal of Botany* (3 a year).

Royal Botanic Gardens, Kew: Richmond upon Thames, TW9 3AB; tel. (20) 8332-5000; fax (20) 8332-5197; e-mail info@kew.org; internet www.kew.org; f. 1759, became a public institution in 1841; taxonomic botany, horticulture, conservation, economic botany, biochemistry, genetics, mycology, propagation and seed storage; also gardens and facilities at Wakehust Place, W Sussex; library: see Libraries and Archives; Dir and CEO Prof. STEPHEN HOPPER; publs *Curtis's Botanical Magazine* (4 a year), *Kew Bulletin* (4 a year), *Kew Record of Taxonomic Literature* (4 a year).

Attached Institute:

> **Millennium Seed Bank Project:** Wakehurst Pl., Ardingly, Haywards Heath, RH17 6TN; tel. (1444) 894100; fax (1444) 894110; e-mail msbsci@kew.org; internet www.kew.org/science-conservation/conservation-climate-change/millennium-seed-bank; aims to save 25% of the world's plant species from extinction by 2020 through collection and conservation of seeds, incl. all UK native seed-bearing flora; undertakes British and int. programmes of seed collection; Convention to Combat Desertification est. to protect drylands flora species; Head of Seed Conservation PAUL SMITH.

University of Oxford Botanic Garden: Rose Lane, Oxford, OX1 4AZ; tel. (1865) 286690; fax (1865) 286693; e-mail postmaster@obg.ox.ac.uk; internet www .botanic.ox.ac.uk; f. 1621; 6,000 different plant species in glasshouses, walled garden, water garden, rock garden and seasonal borders; educational lectures and tours; Harcourt Arboretum south of Oxford; library of 1,000 vols on horticulture; Dir TIMOTHY WALKER; publ. *Guide*.

Wildfowl & Wetlands Trust: Slimbridge, GL2 7BT; tel. (1453) 891900; fax (1453) 890827; e-mail enquiries@wwt.org.uk; internet www.wwt.org.uk; f. 1946; concerned with all aspects of biology/ecology of wetlands and wildfowl, particularly those related to conservation, research, education and recreation; comparative colln of living wildfowl at Slimbridge; centres at Arundel, Sussex; Castle Espie, Co. Down; Martin Mere, Lancs.; Washington, Tyne and Wear; Welney, Norfolk; Llanelli, Dyfed; Caerlaverock, Dumfriesshire; Barnes, London; library: research library at Slimbridge; Chief Exec. MARTIN SPRAY; publs *Waterlife* (4 a year), *Wildfowl* (1 a year).

Mathematical Sciences

Centre for Applicable Mathematics: College Rd, Bangor, LL57 2DG; f. 1988; attached to Bangor Univ.; Dir Dr G. W. ROBERTS.

Hull Institute for Mathematical Science and Applications: Cottingham Rd, Hull, HU6 7RX; attached to Univ. of Hull; Dir Prof. V. VLADIMIROV.

Isaac Newton Institute for Mathematical Sciences: 20 Clarkson Rd, Cambridge, CB3 0EH; tel. (1223) 335999; fax (1223) 330508; e-mail info@newton.ac.uk; internet www.newton.ac.uk; attached to Univ. of Cambridge; Dir Prof. JOHN F. TOLAND.

Mathematics Education Centre: Schofield Bldg, Loughborough Univ., Loughborough, LE11 3TU; tel. (1509) 228250; fax

(1509) 228211; internet mec.lboro.ac.uk; f. 2002; attached to Loughborough Univ.; research in different fields of mathematics; curriculum devt projects; organizes courses and seminars; Dir Dr CAROL ROBINSON.

National Computing Centre: The Flint Glass Works, 64 Jersey St, Manchester, M4 6JW; tel. (845) 519-1055; fax (870) 134-0931; e-mail info@ncc.co.uk; internet www.ncc.co .uk; f. 1966; a membership organization run on a commercial basis to promote the effective use of information technology; acts as a focus for its mems and represents their views at nat. and int. level; provides consultancy and training services, software packages and other products; co-operates with other bodies to foster standards and best practices; Exec. Chair. MICHAEL GOUGH; Man. Dir STEFAN FOSTER.

Scottish Informatics, Mathematics, Biology and Statistics: Bell St, Dundee, DD1 1HG; attached to Univ. of Abertay Dundee; Dir Prof. JOHN W. PALFREYMAN.

XFi Centre for Finance and Investment: Univ. of Exeter Business School, Streatham Court, Rennes Dr., Exeter, EX4 4ST; tel. (1392) 263463; fax (1392) 262475; e-mail m.l .bishop@exeter.ac.uk; internet xfi.exeter.ac .uk; f. 2001; attached to Univ. of Exeter; financial market research; Dir Prof. ALAN GREGORY.

Physical Sciences

Astronomy Unit: School of Mathematical Sciences, Queen Mary, Univ. of London, London, E1 4NS; tel. (20) 7882-5514; fax (20) 7882-7684; e-mail w.white@qmul.ac.uk; internet www.maths.qmul.ac.uk/research/astronomy; attached to Queen Mary, Univ. of London; nat. centre conducting research in areas of astronomy; UK Cluster Science Centre is located in Unit.

Armagh Observatory: College Hill, Armagh, BT61 9DG; tel. (28) 3752-2928; fax (28) 3752-7174; e-mail info@arm.ac.uk; internet www.arm.ac.uk; f. 1789; study of astronomy, climate, stellar astrophysics and the solar system; library of 15,000 vols; Dir Prof. MARK E. BAILEY; Admin. JOE COPELAND.

Astrophysics Group, Cavendish Laboratory: JJ Thomson Ave, Cambridge, CB3 0HE; tel. (1223) 337294; fax (1223) 354599; e-mail k.scrivener@mrao.cam.ac.uk; internet www.mrao.cam.ac.uk; f. 1945; Head Dr PAUL ALEXANDER; publ. scientific papers.

Cambridge University Institute of Astronomy: Madingley Rd, Cambridge, CB3 0HA; tel. (1223) 337548; fax (1223) 337523; e-mail ioa@ast.cam.ac.uk; internet www.ast.cam.ac.uk; f. 1972 inc. fmr Observatory (f. 1823), Solar Physics Observatory (f. 1913) and Institute of Theoretical Astronomy (f. 1967); works on observational and theoretical astrophysics; library of 35,800 vols; Dir Prof. P. C. HEWETT.

Centre for Applicable Mathematics: College Rd, Bangor, LL57 2DG; f. 1988; attached to Bangor Univ.; Dir Dr G. W. ROBERTS.

Centre for Arid Zone Studies: College Rd, Bangor, LL57 2DG; f. 1984; attached to Bangor Univ.; specializes in natural resource management and rural devt in drought-prone areas; Dir Dr W. I. ROBINSON.

Centre for Electromagnetic Materials Research (CEMR): Harrison Bldg, N Park Rd, Exeter, EX4 4QF; tel. (1392) 263628; fax (1392) 217965 Physics Bldg, Stocker Rd, Exeter, EX4 4QL; tel. (1392) 264151; fax (1392) 264111; e-mail cemr@exeter.ac.uk; internet centres.exeter.ac.uk/cemr; attached to Univ. of Exeter; research areas include diffractive optics, photonic control of light-matter interactions, thin-film magnetics, magnetic, optical, probe data storage, microwave photonics and plasmonics, phasechange materials, photonics in biology, Terahertz photonics and plasmonics, liquid crystals; Dir Prof. KEN EVANS.

Centre for Energy and Environment: Room 303, Physics Bldg, Univ. of Exeter, Stocker Rd, Exeter, Devon, EX4 4QL; tel. (1392) 724144; fax (1392) 724111; e-mail g.s.j .hitchcock@exeter.ac.uk; internet emps .exeter.ac.uk/research/cee; f. 1975; attached to Univ. of Exeter; researches on issues surrounding sustainable bldgs, energy, transport; Dir Dr GUY HITCHCOCK.

Centre for Environmental Studies: Loughborough, LE11 3TU; tel. (1509) 222558; fax (1509) 223925; e-mail l.e.child@ lboro.ac.uk; internet www.lboro.ac.uk/ research/cens; f. 2000; attached to Loughborough Univ.; teaching and research in environmental topics; vocational training and education in environmental studies at postgraduate level; Coordinator Dr LOIS CHILD.

Centre for Hazard & Risk Management: Loughborough, LE11 3TU; tel. (1509) 222155; fax (1509) 223991; e-mail m.jost@ lboro.ac.uk; attached to Loughborough Univ.; applied research in environmental pollution control, human factors and safety culture, organisational health and safety management, risk and continuing professional devt; Dir CHARLES HANCOCK.

Centre for Maritime Historical Studies: College of Humanities, Armory Bldg, Rennes Dr., Exeter, EX4 4RJ; e-mail history@exeter .ac.uk; internet centres.exeter.ac.uk/cmhs; f. 1991; attached to Univ. of Exeter; promotes research into economic, social, political, naval, environmental aspects of British maritime with help from European and int. experience; Dir Dr MARIA FUSARO.

Centre for Philosophy of Natural and Social Science: Houghton St, London, WC2A 2AE; f. 1990; attached to London School of Economics and Political Science, Univ. of London; promotes study of philosophical and methodological issues; Dir Dr CARL HOEFER.

Centre for Renewable Energy Systems Technology: Dept of Electronic and Electrical Engineering, Loughborough Univ., Loughborough, LE11 3TU; internet www .lboro.ac.uk/departments/el/research/centres/ crest; f. 1993; attached to Loughborough Univ.; research and education in renewable energy technology; Dir Prof. PHIL EAMES.

Centre for Research in Ecology: Dept of Life Sciences, Whitelands College, Roehampton Univ., Holybourne Ave, London, SW15 4JD; tel. (20) 8392-3456; fax (20) 8392-3527; e-mail a.robertson@roehampton.ac.uk; internet www.roehampton.ac.uk/ researchcentres/cre; attached to Roehampton Univ.; research on aquatic, terrestrial and physiological ecology; Dir Dr ANNE ROBERTSON.

Centre for Research in Environmental History: Stirling, FK9 4LA; tel. (1786) 467-580; fax (1786) 467-581; f. 2002; attached to Univ. of Stirling; research on disciplinary backgrounds, incl. history, environmental science, philosophy and economics; Dir Dr RICHARD ORAM.

Centre for Sustainable Design: Falkner Rd, Farnham, Surrey, GU9 7DS; tel. (1252) 892772; fax (1252) 892747; e-mail cfsd@ ucreative.ac.uk; internet www.cfsd.org.uk; f. 1995; attached to Univ. for the Creative Arts; Dir MARTIN CHARTER; publ. *The Journal of Sustainable Product Design* (4 a year).

Centre for Water Systems (CWS): School of Engineering, Computing and Mathematics, Univ. of Exeter, N Park Rd, Exeter, EX4

4QF; tel. (1392) 263637; fax (1392) 217965; e-mail d.savic@exeter.ac.uk; internet centres .exeter.ac.uk/cws; f. 1994; attached to Univ. of Exeter; researches into water systems engineering focusing mainly on water supply and distribution systems, waste water and urban drainage systems, integrated modelling, risk and uncertainty, whole-life costing, water efficiency, catchment-based management, spatial water management; Head Prof. DAVID BUTLER; Head Prof. DRAGAN SAVIC.

Centre of Environmental and Waste Management: Paisley, PA1 2BE; tel. (141) 848-3146; e-mail cewm@uws.ac.uk; f. 1991; attached to Univ. of the West of Scotland; Dir Dr JENNIFER MCQUAID-COOK.

Environmental Sciences Research Institute: Room G157, School of Environmental Sciences, Univ. of Ulster, Coleraine, BT52 1SA; tel. (28) 7012-4242; e-mail science@ ulster.ac.uk; internet www.science.ulster.ac .uk/esri; attached to Univ. of Ulster; promotes understanding of the Earth systems for effective management of environment; Dir Prof. SANDY STEACY; Sec. LINDA ALLEN.

Exeter Biocatalysis Centre: Henry Wellcome Bldg for Biocatalysis, Stocker Rd, Exeter, Devon, EX4 4QD; tel. (1392) 263489; e-mail j.a.littlechild@exeter.ac.uk; internet centres.exeter.ac.uk/biocatalysis; f. 2003; attached to Univ. of Exeter; researches into aspects of biocatalysis incl. relationships between protein structure and function, protein engineering, molecular graphics, protein crystallography; Dir Prof. JENNIFER LITTLECHILD.

Graduate School of Environmental Studies: Level 7, Graham Hills Bldg, 50 Richmond St, Glasgow, G1; attached to Univ. of Strathclyde; Dir J. FORBES.

Hull Environment Research Institute (HERI): Cottingham Rd, Hull, HU6 7RX; internet www2.hull.ac.uk/science/heri.aspx; f. 2004; attached to Univ. of Hull; research across interdisciplinary span of environmental science; Dir Prof. L. FROSTICK.

Institute of Estuarine and Coastal Studies: Cottingham Rd, Hull, HU6 7RX; tel. (1482) 464120; fax (1482) 464130; e-mail iecs@hull.ac.uk; research on coastal environment ranging from biological and physical environments (topography, vegetation, ornithology, benthic and pelagic fauna) to coastal planning, environmental quality, marine law and environmental impact assessment; attached to Univ. of Hull; Dir Prof. M. ELLIOTT.

Jodrell Bank Observatory/University of Manchester: Macclesfield, Cheshire, SK11 9DL; tel. (1477) 571321; fax (1477) 571618; e-mail lisa.mcdermott@manchester.ac.uk; internet www.jb.man.ac.uk; f. 1945; the observatory uses 7 large steerable radio telescopes, including the Lovell (fmrly Mark 1A) 250-ft diameter radio telescope; these can be connected into MERLIN array which extends to Cambridge (base-line: 230 km) to study radio objects in any part of the sky; research on galactic and extra-galactic astrophysical continuum and spectral line radio emissions and cosmic microwave background; observations of radio emission from quasars, pulsars and stars; multi-telescope interferometry and very long base-line interferometry; Dir Prof. PHILIP DIAMOND.

Met Office: Fitzroy Rd, Exeter, EX1 3PB; tel. (1392) 885680; fax (1392) 885681; e-mail enquiries@metoffice.gov.uk; internet www .metoffice.gov.uk; f. 1854; provides a nat. meteorological service and is responsible for implementing the objectives of the World Meteorological Org. (see Int. Org.); provides comprehensive forecasting and consultative services; involved with major research into all aspects of meteorology, climatology and

atmospheric science, partly in cooperation with univs and other nat. and int. agencies; work on the physics and dynamics of the atmosphere ranges in scale from global numerical analyses and forecasts to the microphysics of clouds; library: see Libraries and Archives; Chief Exec. J. HIRST; publ. *Scientific and Technical Review.*

Attached Research Centre:

Met Office Hadley Centre: Fitzroy Rd, Exeter, EX1 3PB; tel. (870) 9000100; fax (870) 9005050; e-mail enquiries@metoffice .gov.uk; internet www.metoffice.gov.uk/ climate-change; f. 1990; monitors, understands and predicts global and regional climate variability and change; provides advocacy services to govt on climate change issues; Head Prof. STEPHEN BELCHER; publ. *COP Climate Change* (1 a year).

Oxford Institute for Energy Studies: 57 Woodstock Rd, Oxford, OX2 6FA; tel. (1865) 311377; fax (1865) 310527; e-mail information@oxfordenergy.org; internet www.oxfordenergy.org; f. 1982; attached to Univ. of Oxford; library of 12,500 vols; Dir CHRISTOPHER ALLSOP.

Science and Technology Facilities Council: Polaris House, N Star Ave, Swindon, SN2 1SZ; tel. (1793) 442000; fax (1793) 442002; internet www.stfc.ac.uk; f. 2007; granted Royal Charter in 2007; operates large-scale research facilities and provides strategic advice to British govt on their devt; manages int. research projects in support of a broad cross-section of the UK research community; directs, coordinates and funds research, education and training; Chair. Prof. MICHAEL STERLING; Chief Exec. Prof. JOHN WOMERSLEY; publ. *Fascination.*

Attached Centre:

UK Astronomy Technology Centre: Royal Observatory, Blackford Hill, Edinburgh, EH9 3HJ; tel. (131) 668-8313; fax (131) 668-8314; e-mail library@roe.ac.uk; internet www.roe.ac.uk; f. 1998; manages the 3.8-m infra-red telescope and the James Clerk Maxwell mm-wave telescope in Hawaii, USA; responsible for the optical telescope at La Palma Observatory, Canary Islands, Spain; houses the Dept of Astronomy of Edinburgh Univ.; has a Starlink data processing centre and a Super-COSMOS high-speed plate scanning machine; library of 75,000 vols; Dir Dr IAN ROBSON.

Scottish Institute for Wood Technology: Bell St, Dundee, DD1 1HG; attached to Univ. of Abertay Dundee; Sr Research Dir Prof. JOHN W. PALFREYMAN.

Strathclyde Fermentation Centre: Royal College Bldg, 204 George St, Glasgow, G1 1XW; attached to Univ. of Strathclyde; Dir Prof. B. KRISTIANSEN.

Tyndall Centre for Climate Change Research: School of Environmental Sciences, Norwich, NR4 7TJ; tel. (1603) 593900; fax (1603) 593901; e-mail tyndall@ uea.ac.uk; internet www.tyndall.ac.uk; attached to Univ. of East Anglia; Dir Prof. MIKE HULME.

Science and Technology Facilities Council: Chilton, Didcot, OX11 0QX; tel. (1235) 821900; fax (1235) 445808; e-mail enquiries@stcc.ac.uk; internet www.scitech .ac.uk; f. 1995; provides advanced and large-scale laboratory facilities, and expertise, to support univ. and industrial research; Chief Exec. Prof. KEITH MASON; publ. *Science and Technology* (3 a year).

Laboratories:

Daresbury Laboratory: Keckwick Lane, Daresbury Science and Innovation Campus, Warrington, WA4 4AD; tel. (1925) 603000; fax (1925) 603100; e-mail enquiries@stfc.ac.uk; internet www.stfc.ac .uk; f. 1958; operates synchrotron X-ray source; provides advanced surface science and other materials facilities, and computational support in a broad range of disciplines; Chief Exec. Prof. JOHN WOMERSLEY; Head Prof. SUSAN SMITH.

Rutherford Appleton Laboratory: Harwell Science and Innovation Campus, Didcot, OX11 0QX; tel. (1235) 445000; fax (1235) 445808; e-mail enquiries@stfc.ac.uk; internet www.stfc.ac.uk; f. 1957; operates pulsed source of neutrons and muons (ISIS), high-power lasers, microelectronic design and microengineering facilities, and space engineering and data centres; provides supercomputing, detector technology and particle physics support; Chief Exec. Prof. JOHN WOMERSLEY.

United Kingdom Atomic Energy Authority: Manor Court, Chilton, Didcot, Oxon., OX11 0RN; tel. (1235) 431810; fax (1235) 436899; internet www.ukaea.org.uk; f. 1954; has responsibility for the safe management and decommissioning of the nuclear reactors and other research and development facilities used to develop the UK's nuclear power programme, together with the safe disposal of the radioactive waste; implements the UK's contribution to the European fusion programme; sites at Dounreay (Caithness), Windscale (Cumbria), Risley (Cheshire), Culham (Oxfordshire), Harwell (Oxfordshire), Winfrith (Dorset); Chair. Sir KENNETH EATON; Chief Exec. Dr JOHN McKEOWN.

University of London Observatory: 553 Watford Way, Mill Hill Park, London, NW7 2QS; tel. (20) 8959-0421; fax (20) 8238-8872; e-mail vmp@star.ucl.ac.uk; internet www.ulo .ucl.ac.uk; f. 1929; part of Dept of Physics and Astronomy, University College, London; teaching and research in astronomy; specialized astronomical library; Dir Prof. I. D. HOWARTH; publ. *Communications* (irregular, online only).

PHILOSOPHY AND PSYCHOLOGY

Anna Freud Centre: 12 Maresfield Gdns, London, NW3 5SU; tel. (20) 7794-2313; fax (20) 7794-6506; e-mail info@annafreud.org; internet www.annafreud.org; f. 1947 by Anna Freud, daughter of Sigmund Freud, 1952–1982 as the Hampstead Child Therapy Course and Clinic, present name 1982; psychotherapeutic treatment of children and young people with emotional difficulties and family support; academic courses and training for professionals; research into child devt and psychotherapeutic techniques; library open only to those working or studying at the Centre; library of 3,500 vols; Chair. of Directorial Team LINDA MAYES; Chief Exec. PETER FONAGY; Professional Dir MARY TARGET.

Centre for Attention Perception and Motor Control: College Rd, Bangor, LL57 2DG; studies interaction between vision and movement and role of selective attention and memory in control of goal-directed behaviour; attached to Bangor Univ.; Dir Prof. S. TIPPER.

Centre for Experimental Consumer Psychology: College Rd, Bangor, LL57 2DG; tel. (1248) 382211; e-mail psychology@ bangor.ac.uk; f. 2000; attached to Bangor Univ.; undergraduate and postgraduate courses; research and consulting services; Dir Dr JAMES INTRILIGATOR.

Clinical and Health Psychology Research Centre: Department of Psychology, Whitelands College, Roehampton University, Holybourne Ave, London, SW15 4JD; tel. (20) 8392-3744; e-mail l.gibson@

roehampton.ac.uk; internet www .roehampton.ac.uk/researchcentres/chp; attached to Roehampton Univ.; investigates interaction of behavioural, biological environmental and sociocultural factors in the aetiology, maintenance and prevention of health problems, and in health promotion; developmental, food, neuropsychological and psychophysiological laboratories; Dir Dr LEIGH GIBSON.

Psychology Research Institute: Room G213, School of Psychology, Coleraine Campus, Cromore Rd, Coleraine, BT52 1SA; tel. (28) 7032-4656; internet www.science.ulster .ac.uk/psyri; attached to Univ. of Ulster; research groups: Behavioural Neuroscience, Peace and Conflict, Health Psychology, and Measurement and Statistical Modelling; Dir Prof. MAURICE STRINGER; Sec. FIONA HARKIN.

RELIGION, SOCIOLOGY AND ANTHROPOLOGY

Centre for Analysis of Social Exclusion Houghton St, London, WC2A 2AE; 5th Fl. Lionel Robbins Bldg, Portugal St 10, London WC2A 2HD; tel. (20) 7955-6679; fax (20 7955-6951; e-mail j.dickson@lse.ac.uk internet sticerd.lse.ac.uk/case; f. 1997 attached to London School of Economics and Political Science, Univ. of London research and consultancy on different dimensions of social disadvantage, particularly from longitudinal and neighbourhood perspectives, and examination of impact of public policy; organizes seminars and co-organizes monthly welfare policy and analysis seminar; Dir Prof. JOHN HILLS.

Centre for Biblical Studies: c/o Univ. of Exeter, Amory Bldg, Exeter, EX4 4RJ; tel. (1392) 724288; e-mail d.g.horrell@exeter.ac .uk; internet humanities.exeter.ac.uk/ theology/research/centres/cbs; f. 2008; attached to Dept of Theology and Religion, Univ. of Exeter; provides a forum for research in biblical studies; organizes seminars; Dir Prof. DAVID HORRELL.

Centre for Crime and Justice Studies (ISTD): Two Langley Lane, London, SW8 1GB; tel. (20) 7840-6110; fax (20) 7848-1689; e-mail info@crimeandjustice.org.uk; internet www.crimeandjustice.org.uk; f. 1931; ind. objective forum for all criminal justice professionals and those with a lay interest in crime; arranges confs, courses and visits; promotes understanding of social harm, the centrality of social justice and the limits of criminal justice; Chair. of Ccl ELIZABETH HILL; Dir RICHARD GARSIDE; publs *British Journal of Criminology* (4 a year), *Criminal Justice Matters* (4 a year).

Centre for Research in Evolutionary Anthropology: Department of Life Sciences, Whitelands College, Roehampton University, Holybourne Ave, London, SW15 4JD; tel. (20) 8392-3645; fax (20) 8392-3527; e-mail a.maclarnon@roehampton.ac.uk; internet www.roehampton.ac.uk/ researchcentres/crea; f. 2002; attached to Roehampton Univ.; research on fields in primatology, incl. socioecology, life history strategies, communication, welfare, reproductive endocrinology, comparative morphology and crop-raiding behaviour; Dir Prof. ANN MACLARNON.

Centre for Research in Social Policy: Loughborough, LE11 3TU; e-mail a.p .france@lboro.ac.uk; internet www.lboro.ac .uk/study/postgraduate/courses/departments/socialsci/research/centreforresearch-insocialpolicy; attached to Loughborough Univ.; research in field of social policy; provides information on which policy decisions are made; Dir Prof. ALAN FRANCE.

Centre for the Advanced Study of Religion in Wales: Bangor, LL57 2DG; tel. (1248) 382079; e-mail theology@bangor.ac .uk; f. 1998; attached to Bangor Univ.; Dir Prof. D. DENSIL MORGAN; Dir Dr ROBERT POPE.

Centre for the Study of Migration: Mile End Rd, London, E1 4NS; f. 1994; attached to Queen Mary, Univ. of London; acts as focal point for those engaged in study of migration locally, nationally and internationally.

Centre for the Study of the Christian Church: Dept of Theology, Univ. of Exeter, Exeter, Devon, EX4 4QH; tel. (1392) 264242; e-mail theology@exeter.ac.uk; internet centres.exeter.ac.uk/cscc; attached to Univ. of Exeter; promotes scholarly study of the Christian Church; Dir Rev. Dr PAUL AVIS; publ. *International Journal for the Study of the Christian Church* (2 a year).

Economic and Social Research Council: Polaris House, North Star Ave, Swindon, SN2 1UJ; tel. (1793) 413000; fax (1793) 413001; e-mail comms@esrc.ac.uk; internet www.esrc.ac.uk; f. 1965; ind. org. funded mainly by Govt; research and training agency; aims to provide research on issues of importance to business, public sector and govt; Chair. Dr ALAN GILLESPIE; Chief Exec. Prof. PAUL BOYLE; publs *Social Sciences* (3 a year), *The Edge* (3 a year).

European Muslim Research Centre: Armory Bldg, Rennes Dr., Exeter, EX4 4RJ; tel. (1392) 723367; e-mail emrc@exeter.ac.uk; internet centres.exeter.ac.uk/emrc; attached to Univ. of Exeter; researches on roles that Muslim communities play in European soc.; Co-Dir Dr JONATHAN GITHENS-MAZER; Co-Dir Dr ROBERT LAMBERT.

Exeter Centre for the Study of Esotericism (EXESESO): c/o Univ. of Exeter, Queen's Dr., Exeter, Devon, EX4 4QJ; tel. (1392) 723252; e-mail n.goodrick-clarke@ exeter.ac.uk; internet centres.exeter.ac.uk/ exeseso; f. 2005; attached to Univ. of Exeter; researches into historical and comparative aspects of esoteric traditions from Hellenistic period in late antiquity through Renaissance and early modern period to present; offers Masters programme and doctorate in Western Esotericism; library: 1m. vols of books and journals; Dir Prof. Dr NICHOLAS GOODRICK-CLARKE.

Exeter Turkish Studies: Armory Bldg, Rennes Dr., Exeter, EX4 4RJ; tel. (1392) 264195; fax (1392) 263305; e-mail exts@ exeter.ac.uk; internet centres.exeter.ac.uk/ exts; attached to Univ. of Exeter; researches on Turkish history and culture; Dir STEPHEN MITCHELL; Co-Dir GERALD MacLEAN.

Family Assessment and Support Unit: Cottingham Rd, Hull, HU6 7RX; attached to Univ. of Hull; Dir T. ALLCOTT.

Institute of Applied Social Studies: Muirhead Tower, Birmingham, B15 2TT; tel. (121) 414-2676; fax (121) 414-5726; internet www .iass.bham.ac.uk; attached to Univ. of Birmingham; research in social policy and social work; Dir DAVE MARSH.

Institute of Arab and Islamic Studies: Stocker Rd, Univ. of Exeter, Exeter, EX4 4ND; tel. (1392) 725250; fax (1392) 264035; e-mail iais-info@exeter.ac.uk; internet socialsciences.exeter.ac.uk/iais; f. present bldg 2001; attached to Univ. of Exeter; researches in areas within field of Arab, Middle Eastern, Islamic studies; Dir Prof. GARETH STANSFIELD; Deputy Dir Prof. IAN NETTON.

Institute of Ismaili Studies: 210 Euston Rd, London, NW1 2DA; tel. (20) 7756-2700; fax (20) 7756-2740; e-mail info@iis.ac.uk; internet www.iis.ac.uk; f. 1977 by the Aga

Khan; research into Islam, with emphasis on Shi'ism and Ismaili tariqah; library of 25,000 vols, MSS and audiovisual items; Dir Prof. AZIM NANJI.

London Middle East Institute: SOAS, Russell Sq., London, WC1H 0XG; tel. (20) 7898-4330; fax (20) 7898-4329; e-mail lmei@soas.ac.uk; internet www.lmei.soas.ac.uk; attached to the School of Oriental and African Studies (SOAS), Univ. of London; Dir Dr HASSAN HAKIMIAN; publ. *The Middle East in London* (12 a year).

Methodology Institute: Houghton St, London, WC2A 2AE; f. 1991, jtly with external research bodies; attached to London School of Economics and Political Science, Univ. of London; researches methodological aspects of social surveys; Dir Prof. G. GASKELL.

Muslim Institute: 109 Fulham Palace Rd, London, W6 8JA; tel. (20) 8563-1995; fax (20) 8563-1993; e-mail info@musliminstitute.com; internet www.musliminstitute.com; f. 1972; research in early history of Islam, Islamic economics, philosophy of science, international relations, global Islamic movement; teaching (short courses) in political thought, philosophy of science, Arabic language, journalism; monthly meetings of academics, writers and activists dealing with issues such as reform within Islam, Islamic identity and citizenship and the future of Islam in Europe; library of 600 vols; Dir Dr FARIDA OWAISI.

Network for Religion in Public Life: Armory Bldg, Rennes Dr., Devon, EX4 4RJ; Univ. of Exeter, Dept of Theology, Exeter, Devon, EX4 4RJ; tel. (1392) 264241; fax (1392) 264195; e-mail e.d.reed@exeter.ac.uk; internet centres.exeter.ac.uk/nrpl; f. 2007; attached to Univ. of Exeter; promotes understanding and cooperation between academics and religious communities; Dir Dr ESTHER D. REED.

Oxford Centre for Buddhist Studies: Linton Rd, Oxford, OX2 6UD; tel. (1865) 274098; e-mail info@ocbs.org; internet www.ocbs.org; attached to Univ. of Oxford; Exec. Dir GEOFFREY BAMFORD; Academic Dir Prof. RICHARD GOMBRICH.

Oxford Centre for Hebrew and Jewish Studies: Yarnton Manor, Yarnton, Kidlington, OX5 1PY; tel. (1865) 377946; fax (1865) 375079; e-mail enquiries@ochjs.ac.uk; internet www.ochjs.ac.uk; f. 1972; attached to Univ. of Oxford; Master of Studies (MSt) degree; library: Leopold Muller Memorial Library: Kressel colln of 30,000 vols and pamphlets and 400,000 newspaper cuttings, Elkoshi colln of 17,000 vols, Yizkor colln of 450 Holocaust memorial books; Pres. Dr DAVID ARIEL; publ. *the Journal of Jewish Studies*.

Oxford Centre for Hindu Studies: 13–15 Magdalen St, Oxford, OX1 3AE; tel. (1865) 304300; fax (1865) 304301; e-mail info@ochs.org.uk; internet www.ochs.org.uk; f. 1997; attached to Univ. of Oxford; ind. centre of Oxford Univ.; study of Hindu culture, soc., philosophies and languages in all parts of the world and of all periods; preserves India's cultural heritage and promotes understanding of it through education, publishing and research; library of 20,000 vols; Dir SHAUNAKA RISHI DAS; Academic Dir Prof. GAVIN FLOOD; publ. *Journal of Hindu Studies*.

Oxford Centre for Islamic Studies: George St, Oxford, OX1 2AR; tel. (1865) 278730; fax (1865) 248942; e-mail islamic.studies@oxcis.ac.uk; internet www.oxcis.ac.uk; attached to Univ. of Oxford; f. 1985; Dir FARHAN AHMAD NIZAMI (Magdalen College); publ. *The Journal of Islamic Studies* (3 a year).

Population Investigation Committee: POR.2.01, London School of Economics, Houghton St, London, WC2A 2AE; tel. (20) 7955-7666; e-mail pic@lse.ac.uk; internet www2.lse.ac.uk/socialpolicy/researchcentresandgroups/pic/home.aspx; f. 1936; attached to London School of Economics and Political Science, Univ. of London; promotes and undertakes research into population questions; promotes study of demography in both its qualitative and qualitative aspects; Chair. Prof. JOHN CLELAND; Gen. Sec. ANNE SHEPHERD; publ. *Population Studies: A Journal of Demography* (3 a year (www.popstudies.net)).

School of Theology and Ministry Studies: Brayford Pool, Lincoln, LN6 7TS; attached to Univ. of Lincoln; Head Rev. Dr MARK HOCKNULL.

Social Work Research Centre: Stirling, FK9 4LA; tel. (1786) 473171; fax (1786) 463000; attached to Univ. of Stirling; Dir Prof. G. MCIVOR.

Tavistock Institute: 30 Tabernacle St, London, EC2A 4UE; tel. (20) 7417-0407; fax (20) 7417-0566; e-mail central.admin@tavinstitute.org; internet www.tavistockinstitute.org; f. 1947; study of human relations in conditions of well-being, conflict or breakdown in the family, the work group, the community and the larger organization; disciplines range from social science to organizational development; Sec. DEBBIE SORKIN; publs *Evaluation* (4 a year), *Human Relations* (12 a year).

Welsh National Centre for Religious Education: Bangor, LL57 2DG; tel. (1248) 383594; e-mail ems023@bangor.ac.uk; internet wncre.bangor.ac.uk; f. 1979; attached to Bangor Univ.; promotes the devt of religious education in schools, colleges and churches of all types throughout Wales; Head VAUGHAN SALISBURY; Dir Prof. L. FRANCIS.

TECHNOLOGY

Advanced Virtual Reality Research Centre: Loughborough, LE11 3TU; tel. (1509) 635678; fax (1509) 211586; e-mail r.s.kalawsky@lboro.ac.uk; internet www.lboro.ac.uk/departments/el/research/centres/avrrc; attached to Loughborough Univ.; research and devt in advanced modelling, simulation and visualization techniques; Dir Prof. ROY KALAWSKY.

Animation Research Centre: Falkner Rd, Farnham, Surrey, GU9 7DS; f. 2000; attached to Univ. for the Creative Arts; Dir Dr SUZANNE BUCHAN.

BHR Group Ltd: Fluid Eng. Centre, Cranfield, Beds., MK43 0AJ; tel. (1234) 750422; fax (1234) 750074; e-mail solutions@bhrgroup.com; internet www.bhrgroup.com; f. 1947; provides research, devt and consultancy on all aspects of fluid eng. and process technology, for a wide range of industries; specializes in abrasive water-jet cutting, fluid power, hydraulics, mixing, pumping, process intensification, chemical reaction eng., micromaterials and nanomaterials technology, multiphase flow, pipe networks, sealing and containment, slurry transport; biodiesel; field studies; conferences and specialist training courses; technical information services; Chief Exec. J. A. R. MUIR.

BMT Group Ltd: Goodrich House, 1 Waldegrave Rd, Teddington, TW11 8LZ; tel. (20) 8943-5544; fax (20) 8943-5347; internet www.bmt.org; f. 1985; provides industry with high-level research and technical assistance; solutions to the problems of designers and operators of structures and vehicles on land, coastal terrain and at sea; 22 subsidiary and assoc. operating companies; Chair. Dr NEIL CROSS; Chief. Exec. PETER FRENCH; publs *BMT Abstracts* (12 a year), *Focus*.

British Textile Technology Group (BTTG): Wira House, West Park Ring Rd, Leeds, LS16 6QL; tel. (113) 259-1999; fax (161) 278-0306; e-mail info@bttg.co.uk; internet www.bttg.co.uk; f. 1918; engaged in research, devt, testing and evaluation for textile and related industries; undertakes product devt and testing, int. consulting work; Man. Dir STEPHEN DONNELLY.

Building Research Establishment (BRE): Bucknalls Lane, Garston, Watford, WD25 9XX; tel. (1923) 664000; fax (1923) 664010; e-mail enquiries@bre.co.uk; internet www.bre.co.uk; f. 1921; research and consultancy covering building, construction, energy efficiency and the prevention and control of fire; certification of building products, accreditation of product installers and energy assessors; environmental assessment of bldgs; Chief Exec. Dr PETER BONFIELD; Chief Exec. CAROL ATKINSON; publs *BRE Information Papers series* (10 a year), *BRE Digest series* (6 a year).

Centre for Automotive Management: Loughborough, LE11 3TU; tel. (1509) 223294; e-mail s.e.hollick@lboro.ac.uk; internet www.lboro.ac.uk/departments/sbe/pmdc/areas/automotive/index.html; f. 1997; attached to Loughborough Univ.; research within the automotive industry; specialist training and devt for practising dealer principals, managers, supervisors and team leaders; Dir Prof. JIM SACKER.

Centre for Computational Chemistry: College Rd, Bangor, LL57 2DG; develops industrial applications of modelling in materials science for natural and advanced materials; attached to Bangor Univ.; Dir Dr J. N. MACDONALD.

Centre for Electrical Power Engineering: Royal College Bldg, 204 George St, Glasgow, G1 1XW; attached to Univ. of Strathclyde; Dir Prof. O. FARISH.

Centre for Engineering and Design Education: Keith Green Bldg, Faculty of Engineering, Loughborough University, Loughborough, LE11 3TU; tel. (1509) 227191; fax (1509) 227181; e-mail cede@lboro.ac.uk; internet cede.lboro.ac.uk; f. 1997, present name 2011; attached to Loughborough Univ.; provides engineering and design education activities; Head MELANIE KING; Assoc. Dir FIONA LAMB.

Centre for Innovative and Collaborative Construction Engineering: Loughborough, LE11 3TU; tel. (1509) 228549; fax (1509) 223982; e-mail cice@lboro.ac.uk; internet www.lboro.ac.uk/cice; f. 1999; attached to Loughborough Univ.; training and research in engineering and management of the construction field; Dir Prof. DINO BOUCHLAGHEM.

Centre for Internet Computing: Cottingham Rd, Hull, HU6 7RX; attached to Univ. of Hull; Head Dr C. GASKELL.

Centre for Magnetic Resonance Investigations: Anlaby Rd, Hull, HU3 2JZ; tel. (1482) 674078; fax (1482) 320137; f. 1992; attached to Univ. of Hull; Dir Prof. L. W. TURNBULL.

Centre for Mobile Communications Research: Loughborough, LE11 3TU; tel. (1509) 227006; fax (1509) 227008; internet www.lboro.ac.uk/departments/el/research/centres/cmcr; f. 1998; attached to Loughborough Univ.; research in the design of antennas and associated components for mobility applications;encourages cross fertilization between physical, firm and soft aspects of communications technology; Dir YIANNIS VARDAXOGLOU.

Centre for Particle Characterization and Analysis: Paisley, PA1 2BE; tel. (141) 848-3241; e-mail cpca@uws.ac.uk; attached to Univ. of the West of Scotland; Man. Dr A. HURSTHOUSE.

CERAM Research Ltd: Queens Rd, Penkhull, Stoke-on-Trent, ST4 7LQ; tel. (1782) 764444; fax (1782) 412331; e-mail enquiries@ceram.com; internet www.ceram.com; f. 1948; researches into ceramics and materials processing, manufacture of ceramic components and the use of ceramic products for clients involved in metals, composites, construction and the environment; services incl. contract research and devt, manufacturing consultancy, testing and analysis; library of 13,000 vols and 60,000 pamphlets; Chair. DAVID DRY; Chief Exec. Dr NEIL SANDERSON; publ. *World Ceramics Abstracts* (online).

CIRIA: Classic House, 174–180 Old St, London, EC1V 9BP; tel. (20) 7549-3300; fax (20) 7253-0523; e-mail enquiries@ciria.org; internet www.ciria.org; f. 1960; improves the quality, efficiency, cost-effectiveness and safety in both the provision and operation of the modern built environment; 500 mem. orgs; Chief Exec. BILL HEALY; publ. *Evolution* (2 a year).

Computer Science Research Institute: Room D092, School of Computing and Information Engineering, Univ. of Ulster, Coleraine campus, Cromore Rd, Coleraine, BT52 1SA; tel. (28) 7032-4648; internet www.compeng.ulster.ac.uk/csri.php; f. 2004; attached to Univ. of Ulster; research in artificial intelligence and applications, information and communication engineering, intelligent systems and smart environments; attached research centres: Electronics Production and Innovation (EPI) Centre, Intelligent Systems Research Centre, Wireless Technology Research Centre; Dir Prof B. W. SCOTNEY.

Computer Security Research Centre: Houghton St, London, WC2A 2AE; f. 1991; attached to London School of Economics and Political Science, Univ. of London; studies computer security issues from organizational, management, social and technical perspectives; Dir Dr J. BACKHOUSE.

Defence Science and Technology Laboratory (DSTL): Porton Down, Salisbury, Wilts, SP4 0JQ; tel. (1980) 613121; fax (1980) 613085; e-mail central-enquiries@dstl.gov.uk; internet www.dstl.gov.uk; f. 2001 following re-organization of the former Defence Evaluation and Research Agency (DERA); part of the Ministry of Defence; locations: Alverstoke, Fort Halstead, Harwell, Porton Down, Portsdown West; library: MOD Scientific Reports Collection of 750,000 items from WWII to the present; publs *Defence Reports Abstracts* (monthly; available only to the MOD, its agencies and contractors), *Defence Technology Alerts* (monthly, information about technological developments in the defence community; available only to the MOD, its agencies and contractors).

Engineering Innovation Institute: Cottingham Rd, Hull, HU6 7RX; tel. (1482) 466470; attached to Univ. of Hull; Dir GAVIN CUTLER.

Hasselblad Centre for High Resolution Digital Imaging: Fort Pitt, Rochester, Kent, ME1 1DZ; attached to Univ. for the Creative Arts; Contact Prof. ORI GERSHT.

Health Design and Technology Institute: Coventry Univ. Technology Park, Puma Way, Coventry, CV1 2TT; tel. (24) 76158000; e-mail hdti.info@coventry.ac.uk; internet www.coventry.ac.uk/hdti; attached to Coventry Univ.; research in areas such as bldg and vehicle adaptations, walking aids and wheelchairs, consumer health products and healthcare technology for the elderly and people with disabilities; Dir SIMON FIELDEN.

Industrial Control Centre: Marland House, 40 George St, Glasgow, G1 1BA; attached to Univ. of Strathclyde; Dir Prof. M. GRIMBLE.

Infoterra Ltd: Delta House, Southwood Crescent, Southwood, Farnborough, Hants., GU14 0NL; tel. (1252) 362000; fax (1252) 375016; e-mail info@infoterra-global.com; internet www.infoterra-global.com; f. 1989 to commercialize the National Remote Sensing Centre and Earth Observation Centre; supplier of products and services based on information extracted from data acquired by Earth observation satellites and aerial photography; consultancy services; Marketing Dir ANTHONY DENNISS.

Institute of Bioelectronic and Molecular Microsystems: Dean St, Bangor, LL57 1UT; tel. (1248) 382010; fax (1248) 361429; e-mail info@ibmm-microtech.co.uk; internet www.eng.bangor.ac.uk; f. 1983; attached to Bangor Univ.; Dir Prof. D. M. TAYLOR.

Institute of Development Engineering: Loughborough, LE11 3TU; incl. Water, Engineering and Devt Centre (WEDC); research on infrastructure needs of underdeveloped countries for the British Govt's Dept for Int. Devt, int. orgns, foreign govts and agencies; attached to Loughborough Univ.; Dir I. SMOUT.

Interdisciplinary Research Centre in Materials Processing: Edgbaston, Birmingham, B15 2TT; tel. (121) 414-3446; fax (121) 414-3441; internet www.irc.bham.ac.uk; f. 1989, present name 2001; attached to Univ. of Birmingham; research on metals and ceramics, covering processing, property and microstructural studies; Head Dr S. BLACKBURN.

International Centre for Computer Games and Virtual Entertainment: Bell St, Dundee, DD1 1HG; f. 2001; attached to Univ. of Abertay Dundee; academic research and devt centre for computer games and digital entertainment industry; Head Prof. LACHLAN MACKINNON.

John Logie Baird Centre for Research in Television and Film: Livingstone Tower, 26 Richmond St, Glasgow G1 1XH; attached to University of Strathclyde; Dir Prof. S. W. FRITH.

National Physical Laboratory: Hampton Rd, Teddington, Middx, TW11 0LW; tel. (20) 8977-3222; fax (20) 8943-6458; e-mail enquiry@npl.co.uk; internet www.npl.co.uk; f. 1900; nat. standards laboratory; establishes measurement standards, and undertakes research into improved techniques, engineering materials and information technology; Dir Dr BRIAN BOWSHER.

Natural Resources Institute: Univ. of Greenwich, Central Ave, Chatham Maritime, ME4 4TB; tel. (1634) 880088; fax (1634) 880066; e-mail nri@greenwich.ac.uk; internet www.nri.org; f. 1987; became an institute of the Univ. of Greenwich 1996; supplier of research, consultancy and training services in the environment and natural resources sector to support devt assistance programmes, sustainable management of natural resources, environmental sciences, cost-effective and environmentally safe pest management, devt and transfer of technologies to improve food security, social, economic and institutional analysis to enhance the impact of devt projects and policies; training (some courses accredited for post-graduate qualifications); library of 300,000 vols and information service; Dir Dr ANDREW WESTBY; publ. *NRI Annual Review*.

Pera International: Nottingham Rd, Melton Mowbray, LE13 0PB; tel. (1664) 501501; fax (1664) 501554; e-mail innovation@pera.com; internet www.pera.com; f. 1946; a multi-disciplinary technology centre specializing in all aspects of manufacture, incl. materials, quality training, methods, computer applications, human resources and manufacturing integration; Non-Exec. Chair. ROGER WHYSALL; Chief Exec. JOHN HILL.

QinetiQ: Cody Technology Park, Ively Rd, Farnborough, GU14 0LX; tel. (8700) 100942; internet www.qinetiq.com; f. 2001 as government-owned UK PLC following reorganization of the former Defence Evaluation and Research Agency (DERA); researches and develops services and technologies in various fields: defence, maritime, aviation, security, energy and power, automative, finance, health, highways and traffic, public sector, rail, space, telecoms, media and electronics; locations: Aberporth, Bedford, Bincleaves, Bishopton, Boscombe Down, Bridgwater, Bristol, Buckingham Gate (London), Burntisland, BUTEC (Rosshire), Chertsey, Cobbett Hill, Defford, Eskmeals, Farnborough, Fort Halstead, Foulness, Fraser (Portsmouth), Funtington (Chichester), Haslar, Hebrides, Kirkcudbright, Larkhill, Llanbedr, Loch Goil, Malvern, Pendine, Pershore, Plymouth, Portland Bill, Portsdown, Portsdown West, Rona, Rosneath, Rosyth, Shoeburyness, Skipness, Sundridge, West Freugh, Weston-Super-Mare, Winfrith; CEO LEO QUINN.

Scottish Microelectronics Centre: The Kings Bldgs, W Mains Rd, Edinburgh, EH9 3JF; tel. (131) 650-7474; fax (131) 650-7475; internet www.scotmicrocentre.co.uk; attached to Univ. of the West of Scotland; research and devt in semiconductor sector; delivers services in four areas: incubation, analytical, processing and assembly; Chief Exec. IAIN HYSLOP; Dir Prof. ANTHONY J. WALTON.

Scottish Transputer Centre & DTI Centre for Parallel Signal Processing: Royal College Bldg, 204 George St, Glasgow, G1 1XW; attached to Univ. of Strathclyde; Dir Prof. T. DURRANI.

Scottish Universities Environmental Research Centre: Rankine Ave, Scottish Enterprise Technology Park, E Kilbride, Glasgow, G75 0QF; tel. (1355) 223332; fax (1355) 229898; e-mail maleana.provan@glasgow.ac.uk; internet www.glasgow.ac.uk/suerc; f. 1963; provides research and teaching facilities in radioactive and stable isotopes in the environment, ultratrace analysis, radiation mapping, nuclear waste disposal, thermoluminescence dating and dosimetry, food irradiation, radiochemistry, environmental studies, geochronology, isotope geology, stable isotope geochemistry, carbon dating and cosmogenic isotope analysis, including accelerator mass spectrometry; Dir Prof. ANGUS B. MACKENZIE; Dir of Research Prof. ROBERT M. ELLAM.

Smart Structures Research Institute: Royal College Bldg, 204 George St, Glasgow, G1 1XW; attached to Univ. of Strathclyde; Dir P. GARDINER.

Smith Institute: Surrey Technology Centre, Surrey Research Park, Guildford, GU2 7GG; tel. (1483) 579108; fax (1483) 568710; e-mail gillian@smithinst.co.uk; internet www.smithinst.co.uk; f. 1993; non-profit organization; mathematics and computing depts of univs throughout the UK; joint industry/academic institute for research in industrial mathematics and system engineering; training in energy, telecommunications and insurance sectors; Dir Dr ROBERT LEESE; Business Devt Dir Dr HEATHER TEWKESBURY.

Sports Technology Institute: Loughborough Park, Loughborough Univ., Loughborough, LE11 3TU; tel. (1509) 564819; fax (1509) 564820; e-mail k.e.brand@lboro.ac.uk; internet sti.lboro.ac.uk; attached to Loughborough Univ.; Dir Prof. MIKE CAINE.

Science and Technology Policy Research Unit: Freeman Centre, Univ. of Sussex, Falmer, Brighton, BN1 9QE; tel. (1273) 686758; fax (1273) 685865; e-mail spru@sussex.ac.uk; internet www.sussex.ac.uk/spru; attached to Univ. of Sussex; analysis of science, technology and innovation; research in the field of social sciences; Dir Prof. GORDON MACKERRON.

Systems Engineering Innovation Centre: Sir Denis Rooke Bldg, Holywell Park, Loughborough University, Loughborough, LE11 3TU; tel. (1509) 635200; fax (1509) 635231; e-mail seic@lboro.ac.uk; internet www.seic-loughborough.com; f. 2003; attached to Loughborough Univ.; promotes systems engineering as a strategic discipline; Technical Head Dr PHIL GREENWAY.

Thin Film Centre: High St, Paisley, PA1 2BE; tel. (141) 848-3610; fax (141) 848-3627; e-mail thinfilmcentre@uws.ac.uk; internet www.thinfilmcentre.co.uk; f. 2000; devt of deposition processes for thin films; design and fabrication of thin film products; characterisation of thin films and dissemination of information about applications of thin films; Dir Prof. FRANK PLACIDO.

TRL Ltd: Crowthorne House, Nine Mile Ride, Wokingham, RG40 3GA; tel. (1344) 773131; fax (1344) 770356; e-mail info@trl.co.uk; internet www.trl.co.uk; f. 1933; ind. research and devt and consultancy org. specializing in road materials and construction, structures, road safety and traffic, vehicle safety, environment, security, travel behaviours and attitudes, software; library of 200,000 vols, 250 current journals, int. roads and transport database; Chief Exec. Dr SUSAN SHARLAND; publ. *TRL Journal of Research* (3 or 4 a year).

Tun Abdul Razak Research Centre: Brickendonbury, Hertford, SG13 8NL; tel. (1992) 584966; fax (1992) 554837; f. 1938; research and devt on natural rubber; library of 3,000 books and 200 periodicals, information retrieval system containing 100,000 items; Dir of Research Dr A. J. TINKER.

TUV NEL Ltd: East Kilbride, Glasgow, G75 0QF; tel. (1355) 220222; fax (1355) 272999; internet www.tuvnel.com; f. 1947; applied engineering research, development; calibration, consultancy and prototype manufacture for private and public sectors; Gen. Man. Dr F. KINGHORN; publs *Conference Proceedings*, technical papers, reports.

Urban Water Technology Centre: Level 5, Kydd Bldg, Bell St, Dundee, DD1 1HG; tel. (1382) 308170; fax (1382) 308117; e-mail uwtc@abertay.ac.uk; internet www.uwtc.tay.ac.uk; f. 1993; attached to Univ. of Abertay Dundee; provides research, academic and consultancy services to the water industry (in the UK and overseas); Head Dr CHRIS JEFFERIES.

WRc PLC: Frankland Rd, Blagrove, Swindon, SN5 9YF; tel. (1793) 865000; fax (1793) 865001; e-mail solutions@wrcplc.co.uk; internet www.wrcplc.co.uk; f. 1927; ind. research and devt and consultancy org. specializing in water and environmental management; Chief Exec. RON CHAPMAN.

Libraries and Archives

Aberdeen

Aberdeen City Council Library and Information Services: Central Library, Rosemount Viaduct, Aberdeen, AB25 1GW; tel. (1224) 652500; fax (1224) 641985; internet www.aberdeencity.gov.uk/libraries; f. 1884; 17 brs; Central Library—Adult Lending Library, Children's Library, Media Centre, Internet access, Aberdeen College Learning Centre, information service, Local Studies, Community Contacts Directory; Careers Information Point, Scottish Parliament Partner Library, Nat. Library of Scotland Partner, Europe Direct Centre Enquiry and Research service, Migrant Communities Information Point, Enquire online nat. reference service; 500,000 vols; spec. collns incl. Scottish genealogy, local photographs, North Sea oil, British patent abstracts, 10,000 standard specifications, trade marks, business information; Library and Information Services Manager FIONA CLARK.

Robert Gordon University Library: Garthdee Rd, Aberdeen, AB10 7QE; tel. (1224) 263450; fax (1224) 263460; e-mail library@rgu.ac.uk; internet www.rgu.ac.uk/library; f. 1992; 205,470 vols; Dir of Library Services MICHELLE ANDERSON.

University of Aberdeen: Library Special Collections and Museums: Bedford Rd, Aberdeen, AB24 3AA; tel. (1224) 273600; fax (1224) 273596; e-mail library@abdn.ac.uk; internet www.abdn.ac.uk/library; f. 1495; consists of Queen Mother Library, Taylor Library and European Documentation Centre, Medical Library; Special Libraries and Archives on King's College Campus; 1,200,000 vols; McBean Jacobite colln, O'Dell railway colln, Biesenthal Hebrew colln, Taylor psalmody colln, G. W. Wilson photographic colln, Gregory, Melvin and other spec. collns; Librarian and Dir CHRIS BANKS.

Aberystwyth

Ceredigion County Library: Public Library, Corporation St, Aberystwyth, SY23 2BU; tel. (1970) 633703; fax (1970) 625059; e-mail llyfrgell.library@ceredigion.gov.uk; f. 1996; 290,000 vols; 7 brs, 6 mobile libraries; County Libraries Officer WILLIAM H. HOWELLS.

National Library of Wales: Aberystwyth, Ceredigion, SY23 3BU; tel. (1970) 632800; fax (1970) 615709; internet www.llgc.org.uk; f. 1907; legal deposit library; 5,000,000 printed books, 30,000 MSS, over 3,500,000 deeds and docs and 200,000 maps, prints and drawings, incl. the finest existing Welsh colln; diaries and correspondence of David Lloyd George; Librarian ANDREW M. W. GREEN; publ. *The National Library of Wales Journal* (2 a year).

University of Wales Aberystwyth, Hugh Owen Library: Penglais Campus, Aberystwyth, Ceredigion, SY23 3DZ; tel. (1970) 622391; fax (1970) 622404; e-mail libinfo@aber.ac.uk; internet www.aber.ac.uk; f. 1872; 730,000 vols, 3,647 periodicals; spec. collns in Hugh Owen Library incl. Celtic Colln (13,000 vols), Gregynog Press books and private press books since beginning of 20th century, George Powell Colln (19th-century English and French literature, fine art and music), James Camden Hotten Collection, Rudler Collection of geological pamphlets, Duff Colln of pamphlets (Classics), League of Nations and UN Documents, microforms incl. Early American Imprints 1639–1800, David De Lloyd Papers (Welsh folksongs), Lily Newton Papers (water pollution), Thomas Webster letters (19th-century geologist), British Soc.

of Rheology Library; spec. collns in Thomas Parry Library (incl. Welsh Institute of Rural Studies Library) incl. Horton Colln (early children's books), Appleton Colln (Victorian colour printing and binding); Dir of Information Services REBECCA DAVIES.

Aldershot

Prince Consort's Library: Knollys Rd, Aldershot, Hants., GU11 1PS; tel. (1252) 349381; fax (1252) 349382; e-mail alibs.detsa.co.uk; f. 1860; public access by written appointment only; military history library; 60,000 vols; Head of Library Services TIM WARD.

Amagh

Southern Education and Library Board: 3 Charlemont Pl., The Mall, Armagh, BT61 9AX; tel. (28) 3751-2200; e-mail selb.hq@selb.org; internet www.selb.org; f. 1973; 23 brs, 6 mobile libraries; serves the district council areas of Armagh, Banbridge, Cookstown, Craigavon, Dungannon and South Tyrone, Newry and Mourne; 1,450,000 vols; Chief Exec. TONY MURPHY.

Armagh Public Library: 43 Abbey St, Armagh, BT61 7DY; tel. (28) 3752-3142; fax (28) 3752-4177; e-mail admin@armaghpubliclibrary.co.uk; internet armaghpubliclibrary.arm.ac.uk; f. 1771, by Archbishop Richard Robinson, museum status 2001; 17th- and 18th-century books on theology, philosophy, classic and modern literature, voyages and travels, history, medicine and law; library colln incl. subjects on art, history, religion, Ireland, Armagh City and County, Jonathan Swift, St. Patrick, Church of Ireland, Rokeby Colln (prints), Beresford Colln (Irish artefacts); 45,000 ; Keeper Very Rev. GREGORY DUNSTAN.

Ashton under Lyne

Tameside Metropolitan Borough Council Libraries and Customer Services Department: Council Offices, Wellington Rd, Ashton under Lyne, OL6 6DL; tel. (161) 342-8355; fax (161) 342-3744; e-mail information.direct@tameside.gov.uk; internet www.tameside.gov.uk/libraries; f. 1974; 288,078 vols, 150 periodicals; spec. collns: local studies and archives, sound recordings, video cassettes, computer software; Head of Library Services MANDY KINDER.

Aylesbury

Buckinghamshire County Library: County Offices, Walton St, Aylesbury, HP20 1UU; tel. (845) 230-3232; e-mail library@buckscc.gov.uk; internet www.buckscc.gov.uk/libraries; f. 1918; 927,000 vols; 34 brs; Library Systems Man. HAZEL EDWARDS.

Ballymena

North Eastern Education and Library Board: County Hall, 182 Galgorm Rd, Ballymena, BT42 1HN; tel. (28) 2566-3333; fax (28) 2563-2038; e-mail foi@neelb.org.uk; internet www.neelb.org.uk; f. 1973; 28 brs, 8 mobile libraries; 2m. vols; Chief Exec. SHANE McCURDY.

Bangor

Library and Archives Service, Bangor University: Bangor, LL57 2DG; tel. (1248) 382981; fax (1248) 382979; e-mail library@bangor.ac.uk; internet www.bangor.ac.uk/library; f. 1884; Bangor Cathedral Library; local Estate archives; 6 brs; 500,000 vols; Librarian SUE HODGES.

Barry

Vale of Glamorgan Library and Information Service: Provincial House, Kendrick Rd, Barry, CF62 8UF; tel. (1446)

709381; fax (1446) 709448; internet www .valeofglamorgan.gov.uk/libraries; 10 brs; Chief Librarian SIAN E. JONES.

Bath

University of Bath Library: Bath, BA2 7AY; tel. (1225) 385000; fax (1225) 386229; e-mail library@bath.ac.uk; internet www .bath.ac.uk/library; 500,000 vols; incl. Sir Isaac Pitman's Library; Univ. Librarian H. D. NICHOLSON.

Bedford

Bedford Borough Libraries: Bedford Borough Council, Borough Hall, Cauldwell St, Bedford, MK42 9AP; tel. (1234) 267422; e-mail bedfordshirelibraries@bedford.gov.uk; internet www.bedford.gov.uk/ leisure_and_culture/libraries.aspx; 5 brs and 1 mobile library; Man. ANDY BAKER.

Central Bedfordshire Libraries: Central Bedfordshire Council, Priory House, Monks Walk, Chicksands, Shefford SG17 5TQ; tel. (300) 300-8000; 12 brs.

Belfast

Belfast Education & Library Board: 40 Academy St, Belfast, BT1 2NQ; tel. (28) 9056-4000; e-mail info@belb.co.uk; internet www.belb.org.uk; f. 1973; Central Library, 20 community libraries and 2 mobile libraries; Central Lending Library 57,000 vols; Central Reserve colln 100,000 vols; Humanities and Gen. Reference Library 120,000 vols; Irish Library 40,000 books, pamphlets and MSS on all aspects of Ireland, Ulster and Belfast; Fine Arts and Literature 74,000 vols; Music Library 12,000 vols, 24,000 scores, 24,000 records and cassettes; Business, Science and Technology Library 68,000 vols; other spec. collns: bibliographies, govt and agency publs, patents, rare books, microfilms; Chief Librarian KATHERINE McCLOSKEY.

Linen Hall Library: 17 Donegall Sq., North, Belfast, BT1 5GB; tel. (28) 9032-1707; fax (28) 9043-8586; e-mail info@ linenhall.com; internet www.linenhall.com; f. 1788 as Belfast Reading Soc., still known as Belfast Library and Soc. for Promoting Knowledge for legal purposes; 350,000 vols; spec. colln: 70,000 Irish colln incl. early Ulster printing and colln of political ephemera relating to civil conflict since 1968; 5,000 17th-century pamphlets, 18th- and 19th-century travel, biography; Pres. G. PRIESTLEY; Vice-Pres. A. DAVIES; Hon. Sec. H. CAMPBELL; Hon. Treas. C. HUNTER; Deputy Dir PATRICIA SAUNDERS; Librarian JOHN KILLEN; Deputy Librarian MONICA McERLANE.

Public Record Office of Northern Ireland: 2 Titanic Blvd, Belfast, BT3 9HQ; tel. (28) 9025-5905; fax (28) 9025-5999; e-mail proni@dcalni.gov.uk; internet www.proni.gov .uk; f. 1923; attached to Dept of Culture, Arts and Leisure for Northern Ireland; retains official and private records relating mainly to the history of Northern Ireland (dating from c. 1600 to the present day); Chair. and Chief Exec. AILEEN McCLINTOCK; Archivist LIAM O'REILLY.

Queen's University Library: Information Services, Queen's Univ., Belfast, BT7 1NN; tel. (28) 9097-6322; fax (28) 9032-3340; e-mail library@qub.ac.uk; internet www.qub .ac.uk/lib; f. 1849; 1.2m. vols, periodicals, pamphlets, MSS, theses and microforms; spec. collns: Hibernica Colln (incl. R. M. Henry Colln, O'Rahilly Colln; Antrim Presbytery Library, MacDouall Colln (Philology), Hamilton Harty Music Colln, Thomas Percy Library; Asst Dir for Library Services and Research Support ELIZABETH TRAYNOR; Asst Dir for Resources Management TREVOR LYTTLE; Sr Subject Librarian for Arts and Humanities DEIRDRE WILDY; Sr Subject Librarian for Medicine and Health Sciences ANGELA THOMPSON; Sr Subject Librarian for Science and Engineering DAN HOLDEN; Sr Subject Librarian for Social Sciences, Education and Law JOHN KNOWLES.

South Eastern Education and Library Board: Grahambridge Rd, Dundonald, Belfast, BT16 2HS; tel. (28) 9056-6200; fax (28) 9056-6366; e-mail info@seelb.org.uk; internet www.seelb.org.uk; f. 1973; 24 brs, 5 mobile libraries; 652,000 vols, 6,000 maps, 18,000 microforms, 22,000 CDs, 3,000 video recordings, 2,000 DVDs; Chief Exec. and Accounting Officer STANTON G. SLOAN.

Birmingham

Aston University Library and Information Services: Aston Triangle, Birmingham, B4 7ET; tel. (121) 204-4525; fax (121) 204-4530; e-mail library@aston.ac.uk; internet www.aston.ac.uk/lis; f. 1895; 237,000 vols, 88 print journal titles, 14,620 e-journal titles; Dir Dr N. R. SMITH.

Birmingham Library Services: Central Library, Chamberlain Sq., Birmingham, B3 3HQ; tel. (121) 303-4511; fax (121) 303-2861; e-mail libraries@birmingham.gov.uk; internet www.birmingham.gov.uk/libraries; f. 1861; 1,362,708 vols incl. 134 incunabula; 39 community libraries; reference library (f. 1866); depts: archives (incl. Diocesan Record Office and Boulton and Watt colln); arts, business information, language and literature (including John Ash Oberammergau Passion Play colln, King's Norton Parish Library, Sheldon Rector's Library, Parker colln of early children's books and games, Samuel Johnson, Milton, Cervantes, Baskerville and war poetry collns, early printed books, fine bindings and private press books, and Shakespeare Library—f. 1864, 45,000 vols in 90 languages), local studies and history (incl. Priestley colln, Sir Benjamin Stone colln of photographs, Marston Rudland colln of engraved portraits, Francis Frith negative archive, Bedford Photographic colln, and Warwickshire Photographic Survey), Music Library, Science and Technology, Social Sciences , Learning Centre; Head of Library and Archives Services LINDA BUTLER.

Orchard Learning Resources Centre (University of Birmingham): Hamilton Drive, Weoley Park Rd, Selly Oak, Birmingham, B29 6QW; tel. (121) 415-8454; fax (121) 415-8476; e-mail olrc@bham.ac.uk; internet www.olrc.bham.ac.uk; f. 1997; anthropology and world area studies, communications, development economics, Islamics, Christian theology and missiology, social studies, world religions, education, child and youth studies; 225,000 vols; Greek papyri; spec. collns incl. Harold W. Turner Colln on New Religious Movements; Mingana Collection of Arabic and Syriac MSS, archives relating to Christian mission and Christian education; Resource Centre Man. DOROTHY VUONG.

University of Birmingham Library: Edgbaston, Birmingham, B15 2TT; tel. (121) 414-5816; fax (121) 471-4691; internet www.is .bham.ac.uk; f. 1880 (as Mason Science College Library); 2,655,251 vols, 7,500 current periodicals, 3,000,000 MSS; special collections include: archives of Joseph, Austen and Neville Chamberlain, Anthony Eden, W. H. Dawson, Francis Brett Young, Harriet Martineau, Bishop E. W. Barnes, Sir Oliver Lodge, Church Missionary Society Archives (pre-1950), YMCA archives; St Mary's, Warwick and Bengeworth parish libraries, Wigan Library from Bewdley, Worcs, Baskerville collection; Birmingham and Midland Institute pamphlet collection; Librarian M. I. SHOEBRIDGE.

Blackburn

Blackburn with Darwen Library and Information Services: Central Library, Town Hall St, Blackburn, BB2 1AG; tel. (1254) 661221; fax (1254) 678898; e-mail library@blackburn.gov.uk; internet www .blackburn.gov.uk/libraries; f. 1998; unitary authority with 5 public libraries and mobile services; Head of Library and Information Services KATH SUTTON; Senior Librarian CATHERINE SNELLING.

Blackpool

Blackpool Library Service: Leisure, Culture and Community Learning, Progress House, Clifton Road, Blackpool, FY4 4US; tel. (1253) 478111; fax (1253) 478072; e-mail library.info@blackpool.gov.uk; 152,284 vols, 43 periodicals; Head of Libraries ANNE ELLIS.

Bournemouth

Bournemouth Libraries: 22 The Triangle, Bournemouth, BH2 5RQ; tel. (1202) 454848; fax (1202) 454840; e-mail bournemouth@ bournemouthlibraries.org.uk; 277,404 vols, 41,237 audiovisual items, 13,276 sheet music, 16,720 microforms, 2,339 maps, 532 newspapers and periodicals; Area Services and Arts Manager CAROLYN DATE.

Bracknell

Bracknell Forest Borough Library and Information Service: Bracknell Library, Town Sq., Bracknell, RG12 1BH; tel. (1344) 352400; fax (1344) 411392; e-mail bracknell .library@bracknell-forest.gov.uk; internet www.bracknell-forest.gov.uk/libraries; f. 1998; 9 brs; Head of Libraries, Arts and Heritage RUTH BURGESS.

Bradford

Bradford Libraries: Prince's Way, Bradford, BD1 1NN; tel. (1274) 753600; fax (1274) 395108; e-mail public.libraries@bradford.gov .uk; internet www.bradford.gov.uk; f. 1887; 1,000,000 vols; 32 libraries and 3 mobile libraries, provide general collections; Central Library specializes in: local history, business information, Asian languages, and audio and video services; Head of Service JOHN TRIFFITT.

University of Bradford Library: Bradford, BD7 1DP; tel. (1274) 233301; fax (1274) 233398; e-mail library@bradford.ac.uk; internet www.bradford.ac.uk/library; f. 1966; 580,000 vols; J. B. Priestley Library; Management Library; Commonweal Colln; spec. collns incl. J. B. Priestley Colln; Head of Library Services GRACE HUDSON; publ. occasional bibliographies and guides.

Bridgend

Bridgend County Borough Library and Information Service: Ravens' Court, Brewery Lane Bridgend, CF31 4AP; tel. (1656) 754800; fax (1656) 642431; e-mail blis@ bridgend.gov.uk; internet www.bridgend.gov .uk/libraries; 13 brs; Prin. Officer Libraries MARGARET GRIFFITHS.

Bridgwater

Somerset County Council, Library Service: Mount St, Bridgwater, TA6 3ES; tel. (1823) 336370; fax (1823) 272178; e-mail enquiry@somerset.gov.uk; internet www .somerset.gov.uk/libraries; f. 1919; 34 brs, 6 mobile libraries; 933,217 vols and sound recordings; Group Man., Heritage and Libraries TOM MAYBERRY; Sr Librarian MAGGIE HARRIS.

Brighton

Brighton and Hove City Libraries: Jubilee Library, Jubilee St, Brighton, BN1 1GE; tel. (1273) 290800; fax (1273) 296951; e-mail libraries@brighton-hove.gov.uk; internet www.citylibraries.info; Head of Libraries and Information Services SALLY MCMAHON.

Constituent Library:

Jubilee Library: Jubilee St, Brighton, BN1 1GE; tel. (1273) 290800; e-mail brightonlibrary@brighton-hove.gov.uk; internet www.citylibraries.info/jubilee/default.asp; f. 2005; holdings include 45,000 rare and historical books.

University of Sussex Library: Falmer, Brighton, BN1 9QL; tel. (1273) 678163; fax (1273) 678441; e-mail library@sussex.ac.uk; internet www.sussex.ac.uk/library; f. 1961; 750,000 vols; Librarian KITTY INGLIS.

Bristol

Bristol City Council: Central Library, College Green, Bristol, BS1 5TL; tel. (117) 903-7200; fax (117) 922-1081; e-mail refandinfo@bristol.gov.uk; f. 1613; 27 brs; reference library; learning centre; 876,332 vols; Head of Libraries KATE MURRAY.

University of Bristol Library: Tyndall Ave, Bristol, BS8 1TJ; tel. (117) 928-9000; fax (117) 925-5334; e-mail library-enquiries@bris.ac.uk; internet www.bris.ac.uk/is/library; f. 1909; 1,500,000 vols and pamphlets; spec. collns incl. the English novel to 1850, the Sir Allen Lane Penguin colln, business histories, early geology, medicine, mathematics, chemistry and physics, Pinney Papers (17th–19th century), Brunel workbooks and papers, British philosophers, landscape gardening, courtesy books, Gen. Election addresses (part of the Nat. Liberal Club Library), Wiglesworth Ornithological Library, EDC, Addington Symonds Papers, Papers of the Somerset Miners' Assoc.; Dir of Library Services CATHRYN GALLACHER.

Caernarfon

Gwynedd Library and Information Service: Gwynedd Council, Council Offices, Caernarfon, LL55 1SH; tel. (1286) 679504; fax (1286) 677347; e-mail library@gwynedd.gov.uk; internet www.gwynedd.gov.uk; f. 1996; 17 brs; 320,089 vols; Prin. Librarian HYWEL JAMES.

Cambridge

British and Foreign Bible Society's Library: Cambridge Univ. Library, West Rd, Cambridge, CB3 9DR; tel. (1223) 333000 ext. 33075; fax (1223) 333160; e-mail bslib@lib.cam.ac.uk; internet www.lib.cam.ac.uk; f. 1804; large colln of printed Bibles, over 40,000 vols of Scripture in more than 2,500 languages; archives of the Bible Society from 1804; Librarian P. M. MEADOWS.

Cambridge University Library: West Rd, Cambridge, CB3 9DR; tel. (1223) 333000; fax (1223) 333160; e-mail library@lib.cam.ac.uk; internet www.lib.cam.ac.uk; f. 1400; legal deposit library; 7,115,065 printed books and serial vols, numerous spec. collns, 157,186 MSS, large collns of papers and correspondence, 1,151,087 maps, 1,800,324 microforms; the collns have been accumulating since the beginning of the 15th century; Librarian ANNE JARVIS.

College Libraries:

Christ's College Library: Cambridge, CB2 3BU; tel. (1223) 334905; fax (1223) 334973; e-mail library@christs.cam.ac.uk; internet www.christs.cam.ac.uk; f. 1448, refounded 1505; 100,000 vols, incunabula, periodicals; spec. collns: works of John Milton, incl. items published before 1700, Charles Lesingham Smith colln of early mathematical and scientific books, William Robertson Smith Oriental Library, Sir Stephen Gaselee colln of Coptic studies, A. H. Wratislaw colln of Slavonic language

and literature, W. H. D. Rouse colln of Indian studies and 16th-century English books, D. Dickson colln of C.P. Snow, David Stanbury Darwin colln; College Librarian AMELIE ROPER; Fellow Librarian Dr GAVIN ALEXANDER.

Churchill College Library: Cambridge, CB3 0DS; tel. (1223) 336138; e-mail librarian@chu.cam.ac.uk; internet www.chu.cam.ac.uk; f. 1960; 53,750 vols; spec. collns incl. political, military and scientific archives mainly since late 19th century, Powys colln, Winston Churchill's books on Napoleon; Librarian MARY KENDALL.

Clare College Library: Memorial Court, Clare College, Cambridge, CB3 9AJ; tel. (1223) 333202; fax (1223) 765560; e-mail library@clare.cam.ac.uk; internet www.clare.cam.ac.uk/libraries; f. 1326; 38,000 vols; comprises Fellows' Library (8,000 vols); Forbes Mellon Library (30,000 vols); spec. collns: Cecil Sharp MSS, Geoffrey Elton papers, Duncan Forbes papers; Fellows' Librarian Dr FIONA EDMONDS; Forbes Mellon Librarian ANNE C. HUGHES.

Corpus Christi College: Parker Library: Trumpington St, Cambridge, CB2 1RH; tel. (1223) 338025; fax (1223) 339041; e-mail parker-library@corpus.cam.ac.uk; internet www.corpus.cam.ac.uk; f. 1352; spec. collns: Parker bequest of MSS and early printed books, Lewis colln of coins, gems and other antiquities (at present on loan to the Fitzwilliam Museum); Stokes colln on Jewish history; readers by appointment; 20,000 vols, 600 MSS; Fellow Librarian Dr C. DE HAMEL.

Downing College: The Maitland Robinson Library: Regent St, Cambridge, CB2 1DQ; tel. (1223) 334829; internet www.dow.cam.ac.uk; f. 1800, Maitland Robinson Library opened 1993; 50,000 vols; spec. collns of Bowtell MSS relating to the city and univ. of Cambridge; library of 500 vols of Naval history and navigation and large colln of law, Civil War and Interregnum newspapers; College Librarian KAREN LUBARR.

Emmanuel College Library: St Andrew's St, Cambridge, CB2 3AP; tel. (1223) 334233; e-mail library@emma.cam.ac.uk; internet www.emma.cam.ac.uk/teaching/library; f. 1584; 72,000 vols, rare book collns, incl. the Graham Watson Colln and library of William Sancroft, Archbishop of Canterbury; 400 MSS (readers by appointment only); Librarian Dr H. C. CARRON.

Fitzwilliam College Library: Cambridge, CB3 0DG; tel. (1223) 332042; fax (1223) 477976; e-mail library@fitz.cam.ac.uk; internet www.fitz.cam.ac.uk/library; f. 1963; 39,000 vols; Librarian CHRISTINE ROBERTSLEWIS.

Girton College Library: Huntingdon Rd, Cambridge, CB3 0JG; tel. (1223) 338970; fax (1223) 339890; e-mail library@girton.cam.ac.uk; internet www.girton.cam.ac.uk/library; f. 1869; spec. collns: Blackburn Colln of women's rights materials, Newall Colln of Scandinavian material, Frere Colln of Hebrew MSS, Crews Colln of Judeo-Spanish material, Somerville Colln of science and mathematics, Bibas Colln of 18th-century French works; College Archive covers the history of higher education for women via the College's institutional records and numerous collns of personal papers; 95,000 vols, 100 periodicals; Librarian and Curator FRANCES GANDY.

Gonville and Caius College Library: Cambridge, CB2 1TA; tel. (1223) 332419; e-mail library@cai.cam.ac.uk; internet www.cai.cam.ac.uk; f. 1348; 85,000 vols,

900 incunabula, 1,000 MSS related to medieval law and science; Librarian MARK STATHAM; Fellow Librarian Prof. D. S. H. ABULAFIA.

Jesus College Old Library: Jesus College, Cambridge, CB5 8BL; tel. (1223) 339405; fax (1223) 324910; f. 1500; spec. collns: Civil War tracts, military science, library of the Malthus family, large theological colln; 8,600 vols, 39 incunabula, 80 medieval MSS from north-country monasteries, 17 Oriental MSS; Keeper of the Old Library Prof. S. C. HEATH.

King's College Library: Cambridge, CB2 1ST; tel. (1223) 331232; fax (1223) 331891; e-mail library@kings.cam.ac.uk; internet www.kings.cam.ac.uk/library; f. 1441; spec. collns: MSS of Sir Isaac Newton (available on microfilm in the Univ. Library), 20th-century MSS, notably major collns of Rupert Brooke, E. M. Forster, T. S. Eliot, J. M. Keynes, Joan Robinson; incl. the Rowe Music Library; f. 1928; 25,000 vols; 125,000 vols; Librarian P. M. JONES.

Magdalene College Old Library: Cambridge, CB3 0AG; tel. (1223) 332125; e-mail library@magd.cam.ac.uk; MSS of works by Thomas Hardy, Rudyard Kipling, T. S. Eliot, I. A. Richards and 38 medieval MSS, incl. a 13th-century Apocalypse; papers of Ferrar family of Little Gidding; incunabula, foreign-printed books of 16th, 17th and 18th centuries, early theological works; Diaries of A. C. Benson, W. R. Inge and letters of George Mallory; access by appointment only (made in writing); 17,000 vols; Keeper Dr RICHARD LUCKETT.

Newnham College Library: Cambridge, CB3 9DF; tel. (1223) 335740; e-mail librarian@newn.cam.ac.uk; internet www.library.newn.cam.ac.uk; f. 1871; 9 medieval MSS, incunabula, early editions of poets, dramatists and chroniclers of 16th- and 17th-centuries; Skilliter Centre for Ottoman Studies holds 4,500 vols relating to Ottoman history; 90,000 vols; Librarian DEBORAH HODDER.

Pembroke College Library: Cambridge, CB2 1RF; tel. (1223) 338121; fax (1223) 338163; e-mail library@pem.cam.ac.uk; f. 1347; spec. collns: papers of Gray, William Mason, R. Storrs; 65,000 vols, 317 medieval MSS; Librarian PATRICIA ASKE.

Pepys Library (Magdalene College): Cambridge, CB3 0AG; tel. (1223) 332125; e-mail pepyslibrary@magd.cam.ac.uk; f. 1724 in its present location; Pepys's own colln (MSS, books, music, maps, prints and drawings), not added to since his death in 1703; Pepys's own catalogue; spec. collns: Pepys MSS (incl. Diary), medieval MSS, naval and historical MSS (mostly English, 16th- and 17th-century), colln of calligraphy, prints of London and Westminster, incunabula, broadside ballads, plays; 3,000 vols in original bookcases; Pepys Librarian Dr RICHARD LUCKETT.

Peterhouse (Perne) Library: Cambridge, CB2 1RD; tel. (1223) 338251; fax (1223) 337578; e-mail perne@pet.cam.ac.uk; internet www.pet.cam.ac.uk; f. 1594; 5,000 vols, 80 incunabula, 280 medieval MSS, 16th- and 17th-century musical MSS (on permanent deposit in Univ. Library); spec. collns incl. first editions of classics in science, 16th-century theological books; Librarian S. H. MANDELBROTE.

Queens' College Old Library: Cambridge, CB3 9ET; tel. (1223) 335549; fax (1223) 335522; e-mail librarian@queens.cam.ac.uk; internet www.queens.cam.ac.uk; f. 1448; colln incl. medieval MSS and incunabula; 28,000 vols; catalogue by Thomas Hartwell Horne (1827); Milner colln of works on history of Reformation and 18th-century science and mathematics; Thomas Smith colln of Renaissance humanist writings; College Librarian Dr T. EGGINGTON.

St Catharine's College Library: Cambridge, CB2 1RL; tel. (1223) 338343; fax (1223) 338340; e-mail librarian@caths.cam .ac.uk; internet www.caths.cam.ac.uk/ library; f. 1473; 69,000 vols (44,000 vols in undergraduate library; 25,000 vols in spec. collns: 17th-century political and religious tracts, 184 vols of 18th-century medical works (Addenbrooke colln), medieval Romance literature, Spanish books and MSS of 16th and 17th centuries (Chaytor colln); MSS, 30 incunabula); Librarian COLIN HIGGINS.

St John's College Library: Cambridge, CB2 1TP; tel. (1223) 338662; fax (1223) 337035; e-mail library@joh.cam.ac.uk; internet www.joh.cam.ac.uk/library; f. 1511; MSS; spec. collns: 15th-century books, Matthew Prior bequest, Sir Soulden Lawrence law colln, Thomas Baker's colln of printed books and MSS, Samuel Butler colln, Smith colln of Rabelais literature, Wordsworthiana, papers of Sir Cecil Beaton, mathematical works of historical interest from libraries of Adams, Todhunter and Pendlebury, Udny Yule colln of Thomas à Kempis edns, Hugh Gatty colln, Sparrow bequest of Samuel Parr books, papers of Sir Fred Hoyle; Librarian Dr MARK NICHOLLS.

Selwyn College Library: Grange Rd, Cambridge, CB3 9DQ; tel. (1223) 335880; e-mail lib@sel.cam.ac.uk; internet www.sel .cam.ac.uk/library; f. 1896; 40,000 vols, MSS, incunabula; spec. collns incl. diaries and papers of George Augustus Selwyn (1809–78) Primate of New Zealand and later Bishop of Lichfield, large colln of theological works incl. 19th-century sermons, 19th-century missionary colln with particular emphasis on Melanesia and New Zealand, and 3,000 19th-century English ecclesiastical pamphlets; Librarian SARAH STAMFORD.

Sidney Sussex College Library: Cambridge, CB2 3HU; tel. (1223) 338852; fax (1223) 338884; e-mail librarian@sid.cam.ac .uk; internet www.sid.cam.ac.uk/life/lib; f. 16th century; 38,000 vols, 70 periodicals; Muniment Room: 7,300 vols, 119 MSS, incunabula; spec. collns incl. 18th- and 19th-century mathematical books; Taylor Mathematical Library (separately administered); Librarian ALAN STEVENS.

Trinity College Library: Cambridge, CB2 1TQ; tel. (1223) 338488; fax (1223) 338532; e-mail trin-lib@lists.cam.ac.uk; internet www.trin.cam.ac.uk; f. 1546; 300,000 vols; spec. collns incl. medieval western and oriental MSS; literary MSS of Milton, Tennyson, Housman, Capell colln of Shakespeareana; Rothschild library of 18th-century English literature; Isaac Newton's library; papers of economists, philosophers, politicians since 19th century; Librarian Prof. D. McKITTERICK.

Trinity Hall Library: Cambridge, CB2 1TJ; tel. (1223) 332546; fax (1223) 332537; e-mail library@trinhall.cam.ac.uk; f. 1350; 25,000 vols, 31 MSS; spec. collns incl. early canon law, Larman Bequest of books and MSS relating to Reformation and Tudor periods, particularly heraldry, ecclesiastical history and theology; Dir of Library Services DOMINIQUE RUHLMANN; Deputy Librarian HELEN MURPHY.

Special Libraries:

Balfour and Newton Libraries: Univ. of Cambridge, Dept of Zoology, Downing St, Cambridge, CB2 3EJ; tel. (1223) 336648;

fax (1223) 336676; e-mail library@zoo.cam .ac.uk; internet www.zoo.cam.ac.uk/ library; Balfour Library f. 1883, Newton Library f. 1907; 155,000 vols, incl. 19,600 books, 22,600 periodicals and over 110,000 reprints; Librarian CLAIR M. CASTLE.

Churchill Archives Centre: Churchill College, Cambridge, CB3 0DS; tel. (1223) 336087; fax (1223) 336135; e-mail archives@chu.cam.ac.uk; internet www .chu.cam.ac.uk/archives; f. 1973; houses papers of Sir Winston Churchill, Lady Thatcher and many other senior political figures; Dir of the Archives ALLEN PACKWOOD.

Marshall Library of Economics: Sidgwick Ave, Cambridge, CB3 9DB; tel. (1223) 335217; fax (1223) 335475; e-mail marshlib@econ.cam.ac.uk; f. 1925; 97,000 vols; Librarian ROWLAND THOMAS.

Squire Law Library: 10 West Rd, Cambridge, CB3 9DZ; tel. (1223) 330077; fax (1223) 330048; f. 1904; 130,000 vols; spec. collns incl. Roman law, legal history, comparative law, conflict of laws, int. law, environmental law, intellectual property, political biographies; research library; Librarian D. F. WILLS.

Cambridgeshire Libraries, Archives and Information: 7 Lion Yard, Cambridge, CB2 3QD; tel. (345) 045-5225; fax (1223) 712011; e-mail your.library@cambridgeshire.gov.uk; internet www.cambridgeshire.gov.uk/ library; f. 1974; 32 brs, 4 mobile libraries; 1,155,000 vols; Library Man. IAN DOUGLAS; Head of Libraries, Archives and Information CHRISTINE MAY.

Needham Research Institute: E Asian History of Science Library, 8 Sylvester Rd, Cambridge, CB3 9AF; tel. (1223) 311545; fax (1223) 362703; e-mail admin@nri.org.uk; internet www.nri.org.uk; f. 1976; from collns assembled since 1942 by Dr Joseph Needham and Dr Lu Gwei-Djen, from sources in China and the West, primarily intended for the research on which is based the series 'Science and Civilization in China' (24 vols of which have so far been published); governed by the Needham Research Institute Trust (fmrly E Asian History of Science Trust, f. 1968), an educational charity; a unique colln specialized in works in the history of science, technology and medicine in E Asia and consisting of books, periodicals, off-prints, MSS in Asian and European languages, also archival and iconographic material (notes, photographs, maps, microfilms, etc.); open to research scholars by appointment, 30,000 monographs; Dir Dr CHRISTOPHER CULLEN; Librarian JOHN P. C. MOFFETT.

Tyndale House Library: 36 Selwyn Gardens, Cambridge, CB3 9BA; tel. (1223) 566604; fax (1223) 566608; e-mail librarian@tyndale.cam.ac.uk; internet www .tyndale.cam.ac.uk; f. 1944; a residential centre for biblical research; intended for postgraduate and post-doctoral study in biblically related fields, with a view to promoting evangelical scholarship; 46,000 vols; Librarian Dr ELIZABETH MAGBA; publ. *Tyndale Bulletin* (2 a year).

Canterbury

Canterbury Cathedral Archives and Library: The Precincts, Canterbury, CT1 2EH; tel. (1227) 865330 (Archives); tel. (1227) 865287 (Library); fax (1227) 865222; e-mail archives@canterbury-cathedral.org; internet www.canterbury-cathedral.org; f. c. 597; books and archives have been used and maintained here throughout the cathedral's existence; documents since 8th century; MSS of Christ Church Cathedral Priory and the Dean and Chapter of Canterbury; archives of

the Diocese of Canterbury; archives of Canterbury City and District Parish; records for parishes in the Archdeaconry of Canterbury (eastern Kent); 52,000 printed books: early printed books, Bibles, prayer books, Catholic and anti-Catholic writings, natural science, travel, theology, history, 17th–19th century pamphlets, material on the slave trade, music; 2 parish libraries (Elham and Preston-next-Wingham); Cannon Librarian CHRISTOPHER IRVINE; Sr Library Asst KAREN BRAYSHAW; Archivist CRESSIDA WILLIAMS.

University of Kent, The Templeman Library: Canterbury, CT2 7NU; tel. (1227) 764000; fax (1227) 823984; e-mail library-enquiry@kent.ac.uk; internet www .kent.ac.uk; f. 1964; 800,000 vols; special collections include Cartoon Centre (80,000 original political cartoons), Victorian and Edwardian Popular Theatre (Pettingell, Melville and Reading-Rayner MSS and printed plays, mainly 19th century), Maddison collection (history of science), C. P. Davies Wind and Watermill collection, the papers of Lord Weatherill; Dir of Information Services and Librarian MARGARET M. COUTTS.

Cardiff

Amgueddfa Cymru—National Museum Wales Library: Cathays Park, Cardiff, CF10 3NP; tel. (29) 2057-3202; fax (29) 2057-3321; e-mail library@museumwales.ac .uk; internet www.museumwales.ac.uk; 220,000 vols, books and periodicals relevant to the museum collns; spec. collns: Tomlin (conchology), Willoughby Gardner (early natural history), Vaynor (James) Colln (early works on astronomy); also houses libraries of Cardiff Naturalists' Soc. and Cambrian Archaeological Asscn; Librarian J. R. KENYON.

Cardiff Central Library: Central Library, The Hayes, Cardiff, CF10 1FL; tel. (29) 2038-2116; fax (29) 2078-0989; e-mail centrallibrary@cardiff.gov.uk; internet www .cardiff.gov.uk/libraries; f. 1862, present bldg 2009; main library incl. lending and reference books; music and sound recordings library; DVD colln; children's library; local studies library incl. maps, prints and MSS, large colln of Welsh history; facilities for disabled; 547,269 vols incl. 10,000 Welsh language and 10,000 community language items; Central Library Man. NIC RICHARDS; Operational Man. of Libraries ELSPETH MORRIS.

Cardiff University Library Service: Information Services Directorate, 40–41 Park Pl., Cardiff, CF10 3BB; tel. (29) 2087-4818; fax (29) 2087-4285; e-mail library@ cardiff.ac.uk; internet www.cardiff.ac.uk/ 1495; f. 1883; consists of 17 libraries: Aberconway (Business, Economics and Transport), Archie Cochrane (Medicine), Architecture, Arts and Social Studies, Biomedical Sciences, Brian Cooke Dental, Bute, Cancer Research Wales, Law, Legal Practice, Music, Nursing and Healthcare Studies, School of Nursing and Midwifery Studies, Science, Senghennydd (Mathematics and Lifelong Learning), Sir Herbert Duthie (Medicine), Trevithick (Engineering and Science); research collns: Ann Griffiths colln, Architecture Rare Books colln, Arts and Social Studies Special colln, Cochrane archive, Cudlipp colln, David Bainton archive, European Documentation Centre, First Edition archive, Historical Book colln (Healthcare), Osman archive (Photojournalism), Salisbury colln (Welsh History), UCAC (Undeb Cenedlaethanol Athrawon Cymru) archive; Dir of Libraries and Univ. Librarian JANET PETERS.

Carlisle

Cumbria Libraries: Arroyo Block, The Castle, Carlisle, CA3 8UR; tel. (1228) 227295; fax (1228) 607299; e-mail libraries@cumbriacc.gov.uk; internet www.cumbria.gov.uk/libraries.

Carmarthen

Carmarthenshire County Library: Public Library, St Peter's St, Carmarthen, SA31 1LN; tel. (1267) 224824; fax (1267) 221839; e-mail library@carmarthenshire.gov.uk; 660,000 vols; 17 brs, 5 mobile libraries; spec. collns: coal mine plans, Theodore Nichol Colln, the library of the Carmarthenshire Antiquarian Soc.; Library Services Man. MARK JEWELL; Library Services Man. MYRDDIN MORGAN; Library Services Man. WIL PHILLIPS.

Chelmsford

Anglia Ruskin University Library: Rivermead Campus, Bishop Hall Lane, Chelmsford, CM1 1SQ; tel. (1245) 493131; fax (1245) 490835; 250,000 vols; Librarian NICOLA KERSHAW.

Essex County Council Libraries: County Hall, Market Rd, Chelmsford, CM1 1LH; tel. (845) 603-7628; e-mail answers.direct@essex.gov.uk; internet www.essex.gov.uk/libraries; 73 brs, 10 mobile libraries; Dir of Libraries and Culture SUSAN CARRAGHER.

Chester

Cheshire Libraries: Cheshire County Council, Libraries and Culture, Room 286, County Hall, Chester, CH1 1SF; tel. (1244) 606034; fax (1244) 602767; e-mail webmaster@cheshire.gov.uk; internet www.cheshire.gov.uk/library/home.htm; f. 1922; 1,500,000 vols; 35 full-time, 6 part-time, 3 dual use brs, 6 mobile libraries and 1 research library; HQ special collections; Education Library Service; County Libraries Officer I. DUNN.

Chichester

West Sussex County Council Library and Information Service: Greyfriars, 61 N St, Chichester, West Sussex, PO19 1NB; tel. (1243) 382541; fax (1243) 382554; e-mail county.libraries@westsussex.gov.uk; internet www.westsussex.gov.uk/libraries; f. 1925; 1,117,000 vols; 36 brs, 3 mobile libraries; Service Man. Libraries LESLEY SIM.

Colchester

University of Essex, The Albert Sloman Library: Wivenhoe Park, Colchester, CO4 3SQ; tel. (1206) 873333; fax (1206) 872289; internet www.essex.ac.uk; f. 1964; 1m. vols and microforms, 9,904 current periodicals; spec. collns: Latin America, fmr USSR, Social Democratic Party (SDP) archives, SDP papers of Lord Rodgers of Quarrybank, Tawney Soc. archives, Nat. Viewers' and Listeners' Asscn archives, Boundary Comm. for England archives (1992–93 public enquiries), papers and pubs of the Cttee on Standards in Public Life (Nolan Cttee), Sigmund Freud and related collns (papers and pubs), papers of Lord Alport, Sir Vincent Evans colln, Paul Sieghart memorial archive, SCOPE-ENUWAR archive, papers of Lord Brimelow, Gaudier-Brzeska colln, Royal Statistical Soc. (historical) colln, Essex Soc. for Archaeology and History Library, John Hassall colln, Lord Hill of Wivenhoe papers, T. E. Lawrence letters, Samuel Harsnett Library (Archbishop of York, 1629–31), Ellis East European Elections colln, Windscale Inquiry (1977) papers, archives of the Talking Newspaper Asscn of the UK, Margery Allingham/Philip Youngman Carter colln, Bernie Hamilton (Human Rights) archive,

Georg Groddeck archive, papers of Sir Frederick Warner, Papers of Enid Balint (Psychoanalyst), Papers of Lord Brimelow (under-sec. of State, Foreign Office, 1969–73), Charter 88 Archives (1990–97), Colohester Medical Society Library (f. 1774), Levine/Sky Television Internet Video Archive, B. B. Zeitlyn Memorial Library (Psychology and Psychoanalysis); Librarian R. BUTLER.

Conwy

Conwy County Borough Council Library, Information and Culture Service: Bodlondeb, Conwy, LL32 8DU; tel. (1492) 576140; fax (1492) 592061; e-mail llyfr.lib.pencadlys.hq@conwy.gov.uk; f. 1996; 200,000 vols; 13 brs, 1 mobile library; special collections: local history, Welsh language and literature; Head of Service: Library, Information and Culture RONA ALDRICH.

Coventry

Coventry Libraries and Information Services: Central Library, Smithford Way, Coventry, CV1 1FY; tel. (24) 7683-2314; fax (24) 7683-2440; e-mail central.library@coventry.gov.uk; internet www.coventry.gov.uk/libraries; f. 1868; 480,000 vols; spec. collns on trade unions and industrial relations; 16 community libraries and 1 mobile library; Head of Libraries and Information Services CARMEL REED; Central Library Man. CAROL ROBINSON (acting).

University of Warwick Library: Gibbet Hill Rd, Coventry, CV4 7AL; tel. (24) 7652-3523; fax (24) 7652-4211; e-mail library@warwick.ac.uk; internet library.warwick.ac.uk; f. 1963; 1,000,000 vols; spec. collns: British and foreign statistical serials (trade, finance, production), current and retrospective, pre-1948 collections of Howard League for Penal Reform, Modern Records Centre (labour history, employers' records, industrial relations), Modern German Literature; Librarian ANNE BELL.

Cwmbran

Monmouthshire Libraries and Information Service: Chepstow Library, Manor Way, Chepstow, NP16 5HZ; tel. (1291) 635730; fax (1291) 635736; e-mail infocentre@monmouthshire.gov.uk; internet libraries.monmouthshire.gov.uk; 6 brs, 1 mobile library; 150,000 vols; Prin. Librarian ANN JONES.

Darlington

Darlington Libraries: Central Library, Crown St, Darlington, DL1 1ND; tel. (1325) 462034; fax (1325) 381556; e-mail crown.street.library@darlington.gov.uk; internet www.darlington.gov.uk/library; f. 1885; Libraries Man. LYNNE LITCHFIELD.

Derby

Derby City Libraries: Saxon House, Heritage Gate, Friary St, Derby, DE1 1AN; tel. (1332) 641723; fax (1332) 715549; e-mail libraries@derby.gov.uk; internet www.derby.gov.uk/libraries; f. 1997; Head of Library Services DAVID POTTON.

Dorchester

Dorset County Library: Colliton Park, Dorchester, DT1 1XJ; tel. (1305) 225000; fax (1305) 224344; e-mail dorsetlibraries@dorsetcc.gov.uk; internet www.dorsetcc.gov.uk; f. 1920, reorganized 1997; 34 brs; 5 mobile libraries; special collns: Dorset colln, Thomas Hardy colln, Powys colln; 625,000 vols; Head of Community Services P. LEIVERS.

Dundee

Central Library Leisure and Culture Dundee: The Wellgate, Dundee, DD1 1DB; tel. (1382) 431500; fax (1382) 431558; e-mail central.library@leisureandculturedundee.com; internet www.leisureandculturedundee.com/library; f. 1869; 13 brs, mobile library; spec. collns: local history and genealogy, commerce, music, Wighton Colln of National Music (620 vols), British Standards, audio and video library; Dir for Leisure and Culture Dundee STEWART MURDOCH.

University of Dundee Library and Learning Centre: Dundee, DD1 4HN; tel. (1382) 384087; fax (1382) 386228; e-mail library@dundee.ac.uk; internet www.dundee.ac.uk/library; f. 1881; 684,352 vols, 4,804 periodicals; Dir RICHARD PARSONS.

Durham

Durham Arts, Libraries and Museums Department: POB, County Hall, Durham, DH1 5TY; tel. (191) 383-3595; fax (191) 384-1336; e-mail enquiries@durhamcityarts.org.uk; f. 1923; 876,000 vols; 38 full-time brs, 2 trailers, 4 mobile and 3 travelling libraries, 1 bookbus for the elderly; Dir PATRICK CONWAY.

University of Durham Library: Main Univ. Library, Stockton Rd, Durham, DH1 3LY; tel. (191) 334-2968; fax (191) 334-2971; e-mail main.library@durham.ac.uk; internet www.dur.ac.uk/library; f. 1833; 1,500,000 printed items on 4 sites, incl. Middle East Documentation Unit; dept of Archives and Spec. Collns houses extensive spec. collns of early printed books, MSS, maps, prints, photographs; printed book spec. collns incl. those formed by Bishop Cosin, M. J. Routh, Bishop Maltby, Dr Winterbottom, and the Sharp Library from Bamburgh Castle; 200 incunabula, 2,200 STC, 10,000 Wing; collns of MSS and archives incl. medieval MSS, modern literary MSS (C. C. Abbott, Basil Bunting, William Plomer Collns), Earl Grey Papers, Malcolm MacDonald Papers, Durham Cathedral Archives, Durham diocesan and probate records, Howard of Naworth Papers and other collns of local family and estate records, Sudan Archive; Librarian JON PURCELL; publ. *Durham University Library Publications* (irregular).

Ebbw Vale

Blaenau Gwent Libraries: Facilities Section, Municipal Offices, Civic Centre, Ebbw Vale, NP23 6XB; tel. (1495) 355311; fax (1495) 355456; e-mail libraries@blaenau-gwent.gov.uk; 120,000 vols; 7 brs, 2 mobile libraries; County Borough Librarian MARY JONES.

Edinburgh

Edinburgh City Libraries and Information Services: Central Library, George IV Bridge, Edinburgh, EH1 1EG; tel. (131) 242-8000; fax (131) 242-8009; e-mail eclis@edinburgh.gov.uk; internet www.edinburgh.gov.uk/libraries; f. 1890; 1,365,000 items; 25 community libraries, 4 mobile libraries; Central Reference (incl. business information, British Standards, electronic information; 346,229 items); spec. colln: Edinburgh Room (contains information on life in Edinburgh and on Scott, Stevenson, Ballantyne; press cuttings; illustrations; playbills; 120,000 items; Scottish (especially genealogy, history and Scottish Parliament information; 97,000 items), Music and Audio (CDs, scores, Scottish music; 148,000 items), Fine Art (includes costume, fashion and photography; slides, Japanese prints, video cassettes, artists' books, press cuttings on Scottish art, architecture, design and photography; 90,000 items); City Librarian BILL WALLACE.

Edinburgh University Library, Museums and Galleries: George Square, Edinburgh, EH8 9LJ; tel. (131) 650-3384; fax (131) 650-3380; e-mail library@ed.ac.uk; internet www.lib.ed.ac.uk; f. 1580; 3,462,947 printed items, 279,814 microforms, 111,832 maps in sheets, 7,700 metres of MSS and archives, 33,808 theses, 6,826 audio-visual items, 4,417 electronic and 4,430 print current periodicals; Drummond (of Hawthornden) Collection; Laing Charters and MSS; Halliwell-Phillipps Collection; MSS on Scottish history and the Scottish literary renaissance; Arthur Koestler MSS and part library; Corson Sir Walter Scott Collection; New Zealand Studies Collection; MSS and printed books on early 20th-century English literature; Scottish Enlightenment; history of science and medicine; African, East Asian, Islamic and Middle Eastern studies; includes the Main Library, Law and Europa Library, Moray House Library (Education), New College Library (Divinity), Science Libraries and Royal (Dick) School of Veterinary Studies Libraries, Royal Infirmary Library, Reid Concert Hall Museum of Instruments (John Donaldson Collection), St Cecilia's Hall Museum of instruments (Raymond Russell Collection of Early Keyboard Instruments) and the Talbot Rice Gallery; Dir of Library Services SHEILA E. CANNELL.

Heriot-Watt University Library: Riccarton, Edinburgh, EH14 4AS; tel. (131) 451-3570; fax (131) 451-3164; e-mail libhelp@hw.ac.uk; internet www.hw.ac.uk/library; f. 1821; 164,800 vols, 20,000 print and e-journals; Librarian G. A. McDONALD (acting).

National Archives of Scotland: HM General Register House, Edinburgh, EH1 3YY; tel. (131) 535-1314; fax (131) 535-1360; e-mail enquiries@nas.gov.uk; internet www.nas.gov.uk; f. 1993 as an Executive Agency; local and church records; records of Scottish govt and law since 12th century; contains private and business collns; Keeper of the Records of Scotland GEORGE P. MACKENZIE.

National Library of Scotland: George IV Bridge, Edinburgh, EH1 1EW; tel. (131) 623-3700; fax (131) 623-3701; e-mail enquiries@nls.uk; internet www.nls.uk; f. 1680 as the Advocates' Library; legal deposit library; contains 13,000,000 vols and pamphlets and a large colln of MSS; Library's Inter-Library Services (33 Salisbury Pl., Edinburgh, EH9 1SL) maintain a stock (120,000 vols) of scarce books to supplement the reserves of Scottish public libraries, act as the headquarters for Scottish inter-library co-operation, and house Scottish Union Catalogue; Chair. of the Trustees Prof. MICHAEL ANDERSON; Nat. Librarian MARTYN WADE; publ. *Discover NLS* (4 a year).

Attached Library:

National Library of Scotland Map Library: 159 Causewayside, Edinburgh, EH9 1PH; tel. (131) 623-3970; fax (131) 623-3971; e-mail maps@nls.uk; internet maps.nls.uk; f. 1958; modern topographic and thematic map coverage of most parts of the world; particular interest in early/modern maps with Scottish association; Sr Map Curator CHRIS FLEET.

National Museums Scotland Library: Chambers St, Edinburgh, EH1 1JF; tel. (131) 247-4137; fax (131) 247-4311; e-mail library@nms.ac.uk; internet www.nms.ac.uk; f. 1854; 320,000 vols, esp. European decorative arts, N European archaeology and Scottish history; MS collns incl. Society of Antiquaries of Scotland, Harvie Brown (natural sciences), William Spiers Bruce (Antarctic exploration), Sir William Jardine (natural

sciences); Head of Information Services EVELYN SIMPSON.

Royal Botanic Garden Library: Edinburgh, EH3 5LR; 20A Inverleith Row, Edinburgh, EH3 5LR; tel. (131) 522-7171; fax (131) 248-2901; e-mail library@rbge.org.uk; internet www.rbge.ac.uk; f. 1670; incorporates the botanical libraries of the Plinian (1841), Wernerian (1858) and Botanical (1872) socs of Edinburgh, Dr John Hope (1899), Cleghorn Memorial Library (1941) and Mr Robert Scarlett (1975); compiles indexes to Monographs, Floras, Gardens, botanists, botanical expeditions, etc.; 100,000 vols, incl. pre-Linnean literature on botany, horticulture, agriculture and medicine; 100,000 pamphlets and separates; 4,000 (1,500 current) periodicals; extensive colln of botanical drawings and prints, photographs, cuttings, etc., correspondence, diaries, maps, plans, MSS, etc., relating to the early Regius Keepers and Curators and botanists and horticulturists in the UK and abroad; Head of Library Services JANE HUTCHEON; publs *Catalogue of Plants* (irregular), *Edinburgh Journal of Botany* (3 a year), *Sibbaldia: an occasional series of horticultural notes* (irregular).

Royal College of Physicians of Edinburgh Library: 9 Queen St, Edinburgh, EH2 1JQ; tel. (131) 225-7324; fax (131) 220-3939; e-mail library@rcpe.ac.uk; internet www.rcpe.ac.uk; f. 1681; 50,000 books, 1,000 vols of MSS; open to all *bona fide* enquirers; particularly rich in the early sources of medical knowledge; colln of periodicals; Librarian I. A. MILNE.

Royal College of Surgeons of Edinburgh Library and Archive: Nicolson St, Edinburgh, EH8 9DW; tel. (131) 527-1630; fax (131) 557-6406; e-mail library@rcsed.ac.uk; internet www.library.rcsed.ac.uk; f. 1505; 50,000 vols, 170 periodicals; historical and contemporary medical and surgical stock; images library; college archive since 1505; private library for Fellows and members (access to researchers by appointment); CEO ALISON ROONEY; publs *Surgeons' News*, *The Surgeon*.

Signet Library: Parliament Sq., Edinburgh, EH1 1RF; tel. (131) 225-4923; fax (131) 220-4016; e-mail library@wssociety.co.uk; internet www.signetlibrary.co.uk; f. 1594, but there were Writers to Her Majesty's Signet as early as 1460; library of a private soc.; Scots law and Scottish history and genealogy; 90,000 vols; Librarian FELICITY CROSS; publ. *Signet Magazine* (3 a year).

Eton

Eton College Library: Eton College, Windsor, SL4 6DB; tel. (1753) 671221; fax (1753) 801507; e-mail collections@etoncollege.org.uk; f. 1440; 85,000 items, incl. 200 medieval MSS, 200 incunabula; important collns of edns of classical writers and related material (16th–18th centuries), early science, Elizabethan, Jacobean and Restoration drama, large colln of Civil War and early 18th-century English pamphlets, 16th-century Italian books; bindings, English and Continental, since 12th century; Topham colln of drawings and engravings (c. 2,500 items); Etoniana colln (c. 5,000 printed books, drawings, prints, scrap-books, MSS); School Books colln; Parikian colln of Armenian printed books 1500–1900; Kessler colln of books on China and Russia; English literature since 19th century, incl. Elizabeth Barrett Browning, Anne Thackeray Ritchie, Thomas Hardy, Edward Gordon Craig, Moelwyn Merchant collections; mezzotint colln (1,000 items); Librarian M. C. MEREDITH; Archivist P. C. HATFIELD.

Exeter

Devon Libraries: Great Moor House, Bittern Rd, Sowton, Exeter, EX2 7NL; tel. (1392) 384315; fax (1392) 384316; e-mail devlibs@devon.gov.uk; internet www.devon.gov.uk/libraries; f. 1924; 50 brs, 8 mobile libraries; 1,169,987 vols; Head of Libraries CIARA EASTELL.

Exeter Cathedral Library and Archives: West Wing, The Palace, Palace Gate, Exeter, EX1 1HX; tel. (1392) 495954; fax (1392) 285986; e-mail library@exeter-cathedral.org.uk; internet www.exeter-cathedral.org.uk/admin/library.html; f. 11th century when Bishop Leofric gave 66 MS vols to the Cathedral Church; 20,000 vols; MS vols incl. Exeter Book of Old English Poetry and Exon Domesday Book; spec. collns incl. Cathedral MSS and archives, early printed books in medicine and science, Cook Colln (16th–19th century works, early linguistics), printed tracts (mainly English Civil War period), Harington Collection (16th–19th century theology, ecclesiastical history, history); archive of 50,000 items; Cathedral Librarian PETER W. THOMAS; Cathedral Archivist ELLIE JONES.

National Meteorological Library and Archive: Met Office, Fitzroy Rd, Exeter, EX1 3PB; tel. (1392) 884841; fax (1392) 885681; e-mail metlib@metoffice.gov.uk; internet www.metoffice.gov.uk/learning/library; f. 1870; nat. library and archive for meteorology, climatology; incl. comprehensive records of data published by British and foreign instns; early weather diaries; official weather records and charts; ships' weather log books; open to the public; separate record stores for Scotland (Edinburgh) and N Ireland (Belfast); 300,000 vols and 5,000 images.

University of Exeter Library: Stocker Rd, Exeter, EX4 4PT; tel. (1392) 263869; fax (1392) 263871; e-mail library@exeter.ac.uk; internet www.library.ex.ac.uk; f. 1937; 1,200,000 vols; administers Library of Devon and Exeter Institution (36,000 vols); Dir of Academic Services MICHELE SHOEBRIDGE.

Falkirk

Falkirk Council Library Services: Public and Schools Library Service, Victoria Bldgs, Queen St, Falkirk, FK2 7AF; tel. (1324) 506800; fax (1324) 506801; e-mail library.support@falkirk.gov.uk; internet www.falkirk.gov.uk; local history colln; Prin. Librarian SHONA HILL (acting); publ. *Current Awareness Bulletin* (48 a year).

Glasgow

Glasgow Caledonian University Library: The Saltire Centre, Glasgow Caledonian University, Cowcaddens Rd, Glasgow, G4 0BA; tel. (141) 273-1000; fax (141) 331-3005; e-mail library@gcu.ac.uk; internet www.gcu.ac.uk/library; f. 1993; 275,000 vols; 39,000 e-books and access to 35,000 journals online; Dir of Library Services ROBERT RUTHVEN; Sr Librarian and Resource Man. MARIAN MILLER.

Glasgow Libraries: 20 Trongate, Glasgow, G1 5ES; tel. (141) 287-4350; fax (141) 287-5151; e-mail info@glasgowlife.org.uk; internet www.glasgowlife.org.uk; 32 district libraries; spec. collns of foreign literature and local history; 2,145,000 vols; Head of Libraries and Community Facilities KAREN CUNNINGHAM.

Attached Library:

Mitchell Library: North St, Glasgow, G3 7DN; tel. (141) 287-2999; fax (141) 287-2815; e-mail archives@csglasgow.org; internet www.mitchelllibrary.org; f. 1874; 1,235,000 vols; special collns: on Glasgow

(20,000 vols), music (43,000 vols), Robert Burns (5,000 vols), Scottish poetry (12,000 vols) and Patent Depositary Library; business users' service; receives a copy of every publication issued by HMSO, and is also a Depository Library for the unrestricted publications of the UN, UNESCO and FAO; Librarian F. MacPHERSON.

Royal College of Physicians and Surgeons of Glasgow Library: 234 St Vincent St, Glasgow, G2 5RJ; tel. (141) 227-3234; fax (141) 221-1804; e-mail library@rcpsg.ac.uk; internet www.rcpsg.ac.uk; f. 1698; 35,000 vols; houses works on all aspects of medicine and surgery incl. very fine and early examples of medical texts from the 16th and 17th centuries; Glasgow Colln, books relating to the history of Glasgow and the West of Scotland; archives from 1602 until the present day.; Library and Heritage Man. CAROL PARRY.

University of Glasgow Library: Hillhead St, Glasgow, G12 8QE; tel. (141) 330-6704; fax (141) 330-4952; e-mail library@lib.gla.ac.uk; internet www.lib.gla.ac.uk; f. 15th century; 1.3m. books, 7,308 m of MSS, archives; 15,000 serial titles; incorporates Trinity College Glasgow Library (Church of Scotland); Hunterian Books and MSS, Euing Collns of the Bible and music, Farmer Music Colln, Laver, MacColl and Wright Papers on fine art, Hamilton Colln of philosophy, Ferguson Colln of the history of chemistry, Stirling Maxwell Colln of Emblem books, J. M. Whistler archive, David Murray regional history colln, Scottish Theatre Archive, Edwin Morgan Papers, Trotsky Colln; Univ. Librarian HELEN DURNDELL.

University of Strathclyde Library: 101 St James' Rd, Glasgow, G4 0NS; tel. (141) 548-4620; fax (141) 552-3304; e-mail library@strath.ac.uk; internet www.lib.strath.ac.uk; f. 1796; spec. collns incl. Anderson colln (founder's library), Young colln (alchemy and early chemistry), Laing colln (mathematics vols from the 18th and 19th centuries), Robertson colln (Scottish history and topography); 986,330 vols; Asst Dir STUART BROUGH.

Gloucester

Gloucestershire Libraries and Information HQ: Quayside House, Shire Hall, Gloucester, GL1 2HY; tel. (845) 230-5420; fax (1452) 425042; e-mail libraryhelp@gloucestershire.gov.uk; internet www.libraries.gloucestershire.gov.uk; spec. collns incl. Gloucestershire Colln; Library Services Man. for Strategy SUE LAURENCE; Library Services Man. for Operations JO HAND.

Grays

Thurrock Libraries: Grays Library, Orsett Rd, Grays, RM17 5DX; tel. (1375) 413973; e-mail grays.library@thurrock.gov.uk; internet www.thurrock.gov.uk/libraries; 9 brs, 1 mobile library; Head of Libraries ANN HALLIDAY.

Guildford

Surrey Libraries: Enquiries Direct, c/o Guildford Library, 77 N St, Guildford, GU1 4AL; tel. (1483) 543599; fax (1483) 543597; e-mail libraries@surreycc.gov.uk; internet www.surreycc.gov.uk; offers public library service to Surrey; 52 brs and an enquiries dept; 1,913,000 vols, 78,400 audiovisual items; Head of Libraries and Culture PETER MILTON.

University of Surrey Library: Guildford, GU2 7XH; tel. (1483) 683325; fax (1483) 689500; e-mail library-enquiries@surrey.ac.uk; internet www.surrey.ac.uk/library; f. 1894; 625,000 vols, 7,900 periodicals; spec. collns incl. National Resource Centre for

Dance, E. H. Shepard archive; Dir of Library and Learning Support Services J. SAVIDGE.

Hatfield

Hertfordshire Libraries Culture and Learning: New Barnfield, Travellers Lane, Hatfield, Herts., AL10 8XG; tel. (1438) 737333; fax (1438) 737334; e-mail hertsdirect@hertscc.gov.uk; internet www.hertsdirect.org; f. 1925; 1,373,048 vols, other media 119,852 items; 49 brs, 13 mobile libraries, 1 prison library; spec. collns: performing arts, local history, business information, official publs; Head of Libraries GLENDA WOOD.

Haverfordwest

Pembrokeshire County Library: Dew St, Haverfordwest, SA61 1SU; tel. (1437) 775244; fax (1437) 769218; e-mail gill.gilliland@pembrokeshire.gov.uk; internet www.pembrokeshire.gov.uk; reference library, incl. the Pembrokeshire Colln; local studies colln; 12 br. lending libraries; Principal Librarian for Devt ANITA THOMAS.

Hawarden

Gladstone's Library: Hawarden, Deeside, Flintshire, CH5 3DF; tel. (1244) 532350; fax (1244) 520643; e-mail enquiries@gladlib.org; internet www.gladstoneslibrary.org; f. 1894 by William Ewart Gladstone (1809–98); 200,000 vols, 50,000 pamphlets, and MSS material; theology, philosophy, history (esp. 19th century), classics, English literature, Gladstonian studies; accommodation for 40 residents; Warden Rev. PETER FRANCIS; Librarian PATRICIA WILLIAMS.

Hereford

Herefordshire Council Libraries: Shire Hall, Hereford, HR1 2HX; tel. (1432) 261644; fax (1432) 260127; e-mail libraries@herefordshire.gov.uk; internet www.herefordshire.gov.uk/leisure/libraries/1566.asp; f. 1998; 10 libraries, 1 volunteer-run service; 186,294 vols, 11,104 media items; Libraries Man. JON CHEDGZOY.

Huddersfield

Kirklees Culture and Leisure Services: Headquarters, Red Doles Lane, Huddersfield, W Yorks., HD2 1YF; tel. (1484) 226300; fax (1484) 226342; e-mail cultural.services@kirklees.gov.uk; f. 1974; 1,250,000 vols; Head of Culture and Leisure Services KIMIYO RICKETT.

University of Huddersfield Learning Centre: Queensgate, Huddersfield, Lw Yorks., HD1 3DH; tel. (1484) 473888; fax (1484) 517987; internet www.hud.ac.uk; f. 1841; 450,000 vols; Dir of Library Services PHIL SYKES.

Ipswich

Suffolk County Council—Libraries, Archives and Information: Endeavour House, Russell Rd, Ipswich, IP1 2BX; tel. (1473) 584263; fax (1473) 216847; e-mail help@suffolklibraries.co.uk; internet www.suffolklibraries.co.uk; f. 1974 by merger with fmr Suffolk library authorities; 1.2m. vols; Head of Service Delivery, Libraries, Archives and Information ROGER McMASTER.

Keele

University of Keele Library: Keele, ST5 5BG; tel. (1782) 733535; fax (1782) 734502; e-mail libhelp@lib.keele.ac.uk; internet www.keele.ac.uk/depts/li; f. 1949; 620,000 vols; Librarian P. R. REYNOLDS.

Keyworth

British Geological Survey Library: British Geological Survey, Keyworth, Notting-

ham, NG12 5GG; tel. (115) 936-3205; fax (115) 936-3200; e-mail libuser@bgs.ac.uk; internet www.bgs.ac.uk; f. 1837; regional office library at Edinburgh; information office in London; open access repository; 500,000 vols, 400 current periodicals, 200,000 maps, 20,000 archives, nat. collns of 100,000 photographs largely illustrating British scenery and geology; Head of Research Knowledge Services KEN HOLLYWOOD.

Kingston upon Hull

Kingston upon Hull City Libraries: Central Library, Albion St, Hull, HU1 3TF; tel. (1482) 223344; fax (1482) 616858; e-mail reference.library@hullcc.gov.uk; internet www.hullcc.gov.uk/libraries; f. 1903; public library, reference and information service; Asst Head of Service (Libraries and Information) MICHELLE ALFORD.

University of Hull, Library and Learning Innovation: Cottingham Rd, Hull, HU6 7RX; tel. (1482) 466581; fax (1482) 466205; e-mail libhelp@hull.ac.uk; internet www.hull.ac.uk/lib; f. 1929; 1,000,000 vols; spec. collns: SE Asia, India, British Labour history; Dir of Library and Learning Innovation and Univ. Librarian R. G. HESELTINE.

Kirkcaldy

Fife Council Libraries and Museums: East Fergus Pl., Kirkcaldy, KY1 1XT; tel. (1592) 583204; e-mail fife.libraries@fife.gov.uk; internet www.fifedirect.org.uk/libraries; 628,000 vols; Service Man. DOROTHY BROWSE.

Lampeter

University of Wales, Lampeter Campus Learning Resource Centre: Lampeter, Ceredigion, SA48 7ED; tel. (1570) 424798; fax (1570) 423875; e-mail lampeterlrc@tsd.ac.uk; internet www.trinitysaintdavid.ac.uk; 275,000 vols, incl. Tract colln of 11,000 items; Librarian EMMA HARVEY-WOODASON; publ. *Trivium*.

Lancaster

University of Lancaster Library: Bailrigg, Lancaster, LA1 4YH; tel. (1524) 592515; fax (1524) 63806; f. 1963; spec. collns: business history, Quaker, Redlich (music), Socialist, European Documentation Centre; 936,000 vols, pamphlets and other items, 3,000 current serials; Librarian JACQUELINE WHITESIDE; publ. *Report of the Librarian*.

Branch Library:

Ruskin Library and Research Centre: Univ. of Lancaster, Bailrigg, Lancaster, LA1 4YH; tel. (1524) 593587; fax (1524) 593580; e-mail ruskin.library@lancaster.ac.uk; internet www.lancs.ac.uk/depts/ruskinlib; Whitehouse colln of documents relating to the writer and thinker, John Ruskin (1819–1900), (incl. 1,700 works of art by Ruskin and his circle, Ruskin's exhaustive diaries, 8,000 of his letters, 200 MSS, 3,500 books and 1,000 original photographs); Dir and Curator Prof. STEPHEN WILDMAN; Sec. JEN SHEPHERD.

Leeds

Leeds Library and Information Services: Central Library, Calverley St, Leeds, LS1 3AB; tel. (113) 2478282; fax (113) 3951833; e-mail businessandresearch@leedslearning.net; internet www.leeds.gov.uk/libraries; f. 1884; 40 brs and 7 mobile libraries; central library incl. specialist central depts: business and patents, local and family history, art and music and the information centre housing special collns (porton colln of Judaica, Gott bequest of early gardening books and the gascoigne colln of militaria); Chief Officer, Libraries, Arts and Heritage CATHERINE BLANSHARD.

Leeds University Library: Leeds, LS2 9JT; tel. (113) 233-6388; fax (113) 233-5561; f. 1874; 2,500,000 vols, pamphlets and microforms including the Brotherton Collection which contains over 50,000 vols and pamphlets and a large number of MSS, deeds and letters; includes fmr Ripon Cathedral Library containing early MSS, Service Books, Books of Hours, MSS since the 13th century, important printed books from 15th–18th century; Liddle Collection of First World War archive materials; Librarian M. COUTTS; publs *Al-Masaq, Journal of Educational Administration and History, Leeds Studies in English, Leeds Texts and Monographs, Northern History, Proceedings of the Leeds Philosophical and Literary Society: literary and historical section, Proceedings of the Leeds Philosophical and Literary Society: scientific section, Proceedings of the Yorkshire Geological Society, Publications of the Thoresby Society, University of Leeds Review.*

Leicester

De Montfort University Library: Kimberlin Library, The Gateway, Leicester, LE1 9BH; tel. (116) 257-7042; fax (116) 257-7046; e-mail justask@dmu.ac.uk; internet www.library.dmu.ac.uk; Head of Library Services KATHRYN ARNOLD.

Leicester City Libraries: New Walk Centre, Welford Place, Leicester, LE1 6ZG; tel. (116) 252-6762; fax (116) 255-9257; e-mail libraries@leicester.gov.uk; internet www.leicester.gov.uk/libraries; Head of Library and Information Services ADRIAN WILLS.

Leicestershire Library Services: County Hall, Glenfield, Leicester, LE3 8SS; tel. (116) 305-6988; fax (116) 265-7370; e-mail libraries@leics.gov.uk; internet www.leics.gov.uk/libraries; f. 1974.

University of Leicester Library: POB 248, University Rd, Leicester, LE1 9QD; tel. (116) 252-2042; fax (116) 252-2066; e-mail library@le.ac.uk; internet www.le.ac.uk/library; f. 1921; 1,000,000 items; spec. collns of local history of England and Wales, papers of Joe Orton and of Sue Townsend; Dir of Library Services L. JONES.

Lewes

East Sussex Library and Information Service: C15G, County Hall, St Anne's Crescent, Lewes, BN7 1UE; tel. (1273) 481870; fax (1273) 481716; 750,000 vols; 24 full-time and part-time brs; Asst Dir: Libraries and Culture Dr IRENE CAMPBELL.

Lichfield

Dean Savage Library: 19A The Close, Lichfield, WS13 7LD; tel. (1543) 306175; e-mail library@lichfield-cathedral.org; f. 1924; books on theology and ecclesiastical history; 6,000 vols; Man. CLARE TOWNSEND.

Lincoln

Discover Stamford—Heritage at your library: High St, Lincoln, PE9 2BB; tel. (1522) 782010; e-mail stamford.library@lincolnshire.gov.uk; internet www.lincolnshire.gov.uk/stamfordlibrary; f. 2012; attached to Lincoln Heritage Services; stories of the town through objects, pictures, interactive trails.

Lincolnshire County Council Communities Directorate—Libraries: County Offices, Newland, Lincoln, LN1 1YL; tel. (1522) 552222; fax (1522) 552811; e-mail library.support@lincolnshire.gov.uk; internet www.lincolnshire.gov.uk; f. 1974 from 7 fmr Lincolnshire library authorities; 1,528,773 vols; 46 brs, 11 mobile libraries; spec. collns: Music, Drama, Lincolnshire

material, Alfred Lord Tennyson; Head of Libraries JONATHAN PLATT.

Liverpool

Liverpool Libraries and Information Services: Central Library, William Brown St, Liverpool, L3 8EW; tel. (151) 233-5835; fax (151) 233-5866; e-mail refbt.central.library@liverpool.gov.uk; f. 1852; 1,500,000 vols, pamphlets, MSS, etc.; reference services (incl. Hornby Library: rare books, fine bindings, MSS, prints, etc. and patents library), services to business, record office, family history service; EU depository library; Head of Service JOYCE LITTLE.

University of Liverpool Library: POB 123, Liverpool, L69 3DA; tel. (151) 794-2674; fax (151) 794-2681; e-mail libcontactelec@liverpool.ac.uk; internet www.liv.ac.uk/library; f. 1881; over 1,900,000 vols, 4,900 current periodicals; spec. collns incl. 254 incunabula, the T. G. Rylands collection (early cartography, Lancashire and Cheshire history), the William Blake colln, the Scott Macfie colln (gypsy studies), the William Noble colln (Kelmscott and other private presses), the Knowsley colln (17th- to 19th-century English pamphlets), the Peers colln (Spanish Civil War), the Fraser colln (c. 900 books and pamphlets on tobacco; also much material on positivism and secularism), the Robert Graves Colln, Merseyside poets; modern MS holdings incl. the Rathbone, Blanco White, Brunner and Glasier papers, Science Fiction Foundation Colln, Olaf Stapledon colln; the Education Library contains an important colln of children's books; Librarian P. SYKES; publ. *Guide to Special Collections.*

Llandrindod Wells

Powys Library and Archive Service: Cefnllys Lane, Llandrindod Wells, Powys, LD1 5LD; tel. (1597) 826860; fax (1597) 826872; f. 1974; 300,000 vols; 18 brs; special local history collections; County Librarian T. L. ADAMS.

Llangefni

Isle of Anglesey County Library: Llangefni Library, Lon-y-Felin, Llangefni, Anglesey, LL77 7RT; tel. (1248) 752092; fax (1248) 750197; e-mail jrtlh@ynysmon.gov.uk; internet www.ynysmon.gov.uk; Head of Services JOHN REES THOMAS.

London

Aslib-IMI Information and Library Service: Temple Chambers, 3–7 Temple Ave, London, EC4Y 0HP; tel. (20) 7583-8900; fax (20) 7583-8401; e-mail aslib@aslib.co.uk; internet www.aslib.com/info; 16,000 vols on information management, incl. documentation, information science, special libraries and related subjects, 370 current periodicals of the world and about 25,000 references to articles, reports, etc., on library and information science; publs *Aslib Book Guide* (12 a year), *Aslib Guide to Copyright* (3 a year), *Aslib Proceedings* (10 a year), *Current Awareness Abstracts* (10 a year), *Forthcoming International Scientific and Technical Conferences* (4 a year), *Journal of Documentation* (5 a year), *Managing Information* (10 a year), *Online and CD Notes* (10 a year), *Program: Electronic Library and Information Systems* (4 a year), *Records Management Journal* (3 a year).

Barking and Dagenham Libraries: Barking Library, 2 Town Sq., Barking, IG11 8DQ; tel. (20) 8724-8725; fax (20) 8724-8733; e-mail 3000direct@lbbd.gov.uk; internet www.lbbd.gov.uk/leisureartsandlibraries/libraries/pages; f. 1888; 600,000 vols; public library service in the London Borough of Barking and Dagenham; 10 brs throughout

the borough, mem. of the LLC (London Libraries Consortium); Group Man. Libraries ZOINUL ABIDIN.

Barnet Education—Libraries: Bldg 4, North London Business Park, Oakleigh Rd South, London, N11 1NP; internet www.barnet.gov.uk; f. 1965; 66,000 vols; special collection of Sociology; Head of Libraries, Museums and Local Studies P. A. LITTLE.

Bexley Library Service: Ground Floor, Footscray Offices, Maidstone Rd, Sidcup, DA14 5HS; tel. (20) 8303-7777; fax (20) 8309-4142; e-mail libraries@bexley.gov.uk; internet www.bexley.gov.uk; 600,000 vols; 12 brs; 3 mobile libraries, reference library; Local Studies and Archive Centre; Library Services Man. JUDITH MITLIN.

Brent Library Service: Brent Council, Town Hall, Forty Lane, Wembley, Middlesex, HA9 9HD; tel. (20) 8937-3144; fax (20) 8937-3023; e-mail libraryservice@brent.gov.uk; internet ww.brent.gov.uk/library.nsf; f. 1965; 580,000 vols; 12 brs, mobile library, housebound service, Grange Museum of Local History; Head of Library Service KAREN TYERMAN.

British Architectural Library: RIBA, 66 Portland Pl., London, W1B 1AD; tel. (20) 7580-5533; fax (20) 7631-1802; e-mail info@riba.org; internet www.architecture.com; f. 1834; 150,000 vols, 700 current serials, 1,400 dead runs, 1.5m. photographs, 300,000 negatives, 700 m of MSS, and a colln of 600,000 drawings (housed at the Henry Cole Wing, Victoria and Albert Museum, London); one of the most comprehensive architectural libraries in the world; Dir Dr IRENA MURRAY; Deputy Dir WENDY FISH; publs *APId: Architectural Publications Index* (on disc, 4 a year), *Architectural Periodicals Index and Books catalogued by the British Architectural Library* (4 a year), *RIBA List of Recommended Books* (1 a year).

BFI Collections: 21 Stephen St, London, W1T 1LN; tel. (20) 7255-1444; fax (20) 7436-0165; internet www.bfi.org.uk; f. 1935 as a division of the British Film Institute; 60,000 fiction films, over 120,000 non-fiction titles and 725,000 television programmes; 600 spec. collns, 30,000 unpublished scripts, 1m. stills, 15,000 posters and 3,000 set designs of artistic and historical value; incl. J. Paul Getty Jr Conservation Centre (in Berkhamsted), Nat. Film and Television Archive, and Library (in London); 65,000 vols, 45,000 books, 4,000 audio tapes, 5,000 serials, 2m. newspaper cuttings; Head of Collns and Information RUTH KELLY; Head Curator ROBIN BAKER; Head of Information GABRIELE POPP.

British Geological Survey London Information Office: Natural History Museum, Cromwell Rd, London, SW7 5BD; tel. (20) 7589-4090; fax (20) 7584-8270; e-mail bgslondon@bgs.ac.uk; internet www.bgs.ac.uk; f. 1986; information and advisory service; public reference colln of British Geological Survey; publs incl. geological maps, memoirs, reports, research reports and information illustrating the geology of the British Isles; online access to British Geological Survey databases; some overseas maps and textbooks; Man. CLARE M. TOMBLESON.

British Library: St Pancras, 96 Euston Rd, London, NW1 2DB; tel. (843) 208-1144; e-mail press-and-pr@bl.uk; internet www.bl.uk; f. 1973; legal deposit library; 150m. items in most known languages, incorporating books, newspapers, periodicals, manuscripts, maps, prints and drawings, music scores, patents and the National Sound Archive; document supply service at Boston Spa, Wetherby, West Yorks., LS23 7BQ; Chair. Sir COLIN LUCAS; Chief Exec. LYNNE

BRINDLEY; publ. *British Library Journal* (online only).

British Library of Political and Economic Science: London School of Economics, 10 Portugal St, London, WC2A 2HD; tel. (20) 7955-7229; fax (20) 7955-7454; e-mail library.enquiries@lse.ac.uk; internet www.lse.ac.uk/library; f. 1896 as The British Library of Political Science, present name 1925; colln incl. economics, political science, law (esp. int. law), sociology, history, geography; 4m. bibliographic items comprising journals, govt publs, other serial publs and 1.2m. monographs; Dir of Library Services ELIZABETH CHAPMAN; Deputy Dir of Library Services NICOLA WRIGHT; publ. *The International Bibliography of the Social Sciences* (1 a year, online).

British Medical Association Library: BMA House, Tavistock Sq., London, WC1H 9JP; tel. (20) 7383-6625; fax (20) 7388-2544; e-mail bma-library@bma.org.uk; internet www.bma.org.uk; f. 1887; provides expert medical information services to members and staff; specialises in current clinical practice, medical ethics and education; 30,000 vols, 2,000 periodicals, 3,500 films and video cassettes; Librarian JACKY BERRY; Sub-Librarian FIONA ROBERTSON; Sub-Librarian LINA COELHO; publ. *BMA Library Bulletin* (online only).

Bromley Libraries: Central Library, High St, Bromley, BR1 1EX; tel. (20) 8461-7155; fax (20) 8466-7860; e-mail informationservices@bromley.gov.uk; f. 1894; 51,945 audiovisual items, 676 multimedia items, 98,878 microtext items; spec. collns: Crystal Palace, Walter de la Mare, H. G. Wells; Head of Services JUDITH MITLIN.

Camden Leisure and Community Services (Libraries, Arts and Tourism): The Crowndale Centre, 218–220 Eversholt St, London, NW1 1BD; tel. (20) 7974-1647; fax (20) 7974-1615; 759,537 vols; Head of Libraries DAVID JONES.

Canning House Library: Canning House, 2 Belgrave Sq., London, SW1X 8PJ; tel. (20) 7235-2303 ext. 208; fax (20) 7838-9258; e-mail library@canninghouse.org; internet www.canninghouse.org; f. 1947; attached to Hispanic and Luso-Brazilian Council; collns on the Spanish- and Portuguese-speaking countries covering disciplines such as Social Sciences and Humanities; 70,000 vols on Latin America, Caribbean, Spain and Portugal; Library and Information Services Man. ALAN BIGGINS; publ. *British Bulletin of Publications on Latin America, the Caribbean, Portugal and Spain* (2 a year).

City of Westminster Libraries and Archives: Dept of Environment and Leisure, Westminster City Hall, Victoria St, London, SW1E 6QP; tel. (20) 7641-1300; fax (20) 7641-6594; internet www.westminster.gov.uk/services/libraries; 11 community libraries, total stock: 1,196,903 books and other materials; Dir DAVID RUSE; Head of Library Operations IONA CAIRNS.

Notable Constituent Libraries:

City of Westminster Archives Centre: 10 St Ann's St, London, SW1P 2DE; tel. (20) 7641-5180; e-mail archives@westminster.gov.uk; internet www.westminster.gov.uk/archives; collns document the socio-economic, cultural, admin. and community history; houses the archives of Jaeger, Liberty and Gillows; 200,000 books, pamphlets, directories, newspapers, journals, maps and plans, prints, drawings and photographs, local government records, electoral registers, census returns, parish registers and business archives; Archives Man. ADRIAN AUT-

TON; Local Studies Librarian JUDITH BOTTOMLEY.

Westminster Music Library: 160 Buckingham Palace Rd, London, SW1W 9UD; tel. (20) 7641-1300; fax (20) 7641-4281; e-mail musiclibrary@westminster.gov.uk; internet www.westminster.gov.uk/services/libraries/special/music; f. 1946; 62,400 items on music (not recordings).

Westminster Reference Library: 35 St Martin's St, London, WC2H 7HP; tel. (20) 7641-1300; fax (20) 7641-5232; e-mail referencelibrarywc2@westminster.gov.uk; internet www.westminster.gov.uk/libraries/findalibrary/westref.cfm; 432,000 vols; key collns incl. law and British official publs (Hansard, LexisNexis); performing arts (theatre, film, television, radio, dance); art and design (MLA designated colln of nat. importance); business information (market research reports, directories and online services); Gen. Reference Librarian EVELEEN ROONEY.

College of Arms: Queen Victoria St, London, EC4V 4BT; tel. (20) 7248-2762; fax (20) 7248-6448; e-mail enquiries@college-of-arms.gov.uk; internet www.college-of-arms.gov.uk; f. 1484; genealogical, heraldic, antiquarian collns; Arundel MSS, deeds and charters; 30,000 vols; Archivist MATTHEW JONES; Librarian PETER O'DONOGHUE.

Croydon Public Libraries: Katharine St, Croydon, CR9 1ET; tel. (20) 8726-6900; fax (20) 8253-1004; internet www.croydon.gov.uk; f. 1888; 695,017 vols, 23,592 audio items; Libraries Officer A. BATT.

Department for Children, Schools and Family Library: Sanctuary Bldgs, Great Smith St, London, SW1P 3BT; tel. (20) 7925-5040; fax (20) 7925-5085; e-mail enquiries.library@dcfs.gsi.gov.uk; internet www.dcfs.gov.uk; f. 1854; 210,000 vols; Chief Librarian GILL BAKER.

Department of Health Library: Skipton House, 80 London Rd, London, SE1 6LH; tel. (20) 7972-6541; fax (20) 7972-5976; e-mail library.skh@dh.gsi.gov.uk; internet www.dh.gov.uk; f. 1834; 200,000 vols and pamphlets, 650 print periodicals and various databases and electronic journals on public health, health services policy and management, medicine, hospitals, and social care; Head of Library and Information Services PEK LAN BOWER; Senior Librarian JAMES DENMEAD; publs *DH-Data* (online), *DH-Data Thesaurus* (print), *HMIC* (online and CD-ROM).

Associated Library:

Department of Health Knowledge Centre: Room 5E01, Quarry House, Quarry Hill, Leeds, LS2 7UE; tel. (113) 254-5080; fax (113) 254-5084; e-mail knowledgecentre-qh@dh.gsi.gov.uk; archive of Dept of Health (incl. predecessors) publs; producer of DH data; Sr Librarian NATALIE GUDGEON.

Dr Williams's Library: 14 Gordon Sq., London, WC1H 0AR; tel. (20) 7387-3727; e-mail enquiries@dwlib.co.uk; internet www.dwlib.co.uk; f. 1729; lending and reference library of theological, philosophical and historical works, relating in particular to religious Non-conformity and esp. to Congregational, English Presbyterian and Unitarian traditions; 300,000 vols; Dir Dr DAVID L. WYKES; Prin. Librarian ALICE FORD-SMITH; publ. *Lectures of Friends of Dr Williams's Library* (1 a year).

Attached Library:

Congregational Library: 14 Gordon Sq., London, WC1H 0AR; tel. (20) 7387-3727; e-mail enquiries@dwlib.co.uk; internet www.dwlib.co.uk; f. 1831; 70,000 vols, mainly relating to Church history, the

history and activities of the Nonconformists, theology, religious liberty and hymnology.

Ealing Libraries: Perceval House, ISW, 14/16 Uxbridge Rd, London, W5 2HL; tel. (208) 825-7261; f. 1965; 650,000 vols; Library Man. for Devt and Stock KATE GODDARD.

Enfield Libraries: Enfield Town Library, 66 Church St, Enfield, EN2 6AX; tel. (20) 8379-8393; fax (20) 8379-8331; e-mail enfield.town.library@enfield.gov.uk; internet www.enfield.gov.uk/library; f. 1965; 620,000 vols; 16 brs, 3 reference libraries, mobile library; spec. collns: linguistics, local history; mobile library; Head of Library Services JULIE GIBSON.

Geological Society of London, Library: Burlington House, Piccadilly, London, W1J 0BG; tel. (20) 7432-0999; fax (20) 7439-3470; e-mail library@geolsoc.org.uk; internet www.geolsoc.org.uk; f. 1807; 300,000 vols, 40,000 maps; lending restricted to the UK, via British Library Document Supply Centre; reference access by appointment; Chief Librarian SHEILA MEREDITH.

Gray's Inn Library: South Sq., Gray's Inn, London, WC1R 5ET; e-mail library.information@graysinn.org.uk; internet www.graysinn.org.uk; f. c. 1522; Legal Reference Library, for mems of Gray's Inn, others admitted on application; spec. collns: 12th–14th century MSS, Baconiana; 40,000 vols; Librarian T. L. THOM.

Greenwich Libraries: Library Support Services, Plumstead Library, 232 Plumstead High St, London, SE18 1JL; tel. (20) 8317-4466; internet www.greenwich.gov.uk/council/publicservices/libraries.htm; f. 1905; 750,833 vols, 85,213 sound recordings; Borough Librarian and Head of Community Services JULIA NEWTON.

Guardian News and Media Archive: Kings Pl., 90 York Way, London, N1 9GU; tel. (20) 3353-3304; fax (20) 7837-2114; e-mail archives@guardian.co.uk; internet www.guardian.co.uk/gnm-archive; f. 2002 as the Newsroom; archives of orgs and people associated with the Guardian and Observer newspapers; photographic libraries; microfilm, bound hard-copy and digital back-issues; permanent display details history of the two newspapers; Archivist MARIAM YAMIN.

Guildhall Library, City of London: Aldermanbury, London, EC2V 7HH; tel. (20) 7332-1868; fax (20) 7600-1098; e-mail guildhall.library@cityoflondon.gov.uk; internet www.cityoflondon.gov.uk/guildhalllibrary; f. c. 1425; MSS records of the city livery cos, stock exchange, St Paul's cathedral, Lloyd's of London and Christ's hospital; public reference library, particularly rich in books on all aspects of London history business history, maritime history, food and wine, clock making; Dir of Libraries and Guildhall Art Gallery DAVID PEARSON.

Branch Library:

City Business Library, City of London: Guildhall, Aldermanbury, London, EC2V 7HH; tel. (20) 7332-1812; fax (20) 7332-1847; e-mail cbl@cityoflondon.gov.uk; internet www.cityoflondon.gov.uk/cbl; f. 1970; finance, investment and banking; contains co-financial data, country information (incl. global markets) and market research information; Business Librarian GORETTI CONSIDINE.

Hackney Library Services: Hackney Central Library, 1 Reading Lane, London, E8 1GQ; e-mail reference.library@hackney.gov.uk; internet www.hackney.gov.uk/cl-libraries; f. 1965; 900,000 vols; 7 brs, ref. library; spec. collns: mechanic trades, woodwork and furniture, local history, John Dawson Colln; Head of Library Services, Archives and Information Services EDWARD ROGERS.

Hammersmith and Fulham Public Libraries: Hammersmith Library, Shepherds Bush Rd, London, W6 7AT; tel. (20) 8753-3813; fax (20) 8753-3815; internet www .lbhf.gov.uk; f. 1888; 550,000 vols, 48,000 audio items; special collections: law, politics, Christianity, HMSO publs since 1970, video and audio cassettes, DVDs, CDs; Head of Libraries DAVID HERBERT.

Haringey Libraries: Central Library, High Rd, Wood Green, London, N22 6XD; tel. (20) 8489-2781; e-mail library.service@haringey .gov.uk; internet www.haringey.gov.uk/data/ libraries; Head of Libraries DIANA EDMONDS.

Harrow Public Library Service: POB 4, Civic Centre, Station Rd, Harrow, HA1 2UU; tel. (20) 8424-1055; fax (20) 8424-1971; e-mail civiccentre.library@harrow.gov.uk; internet www.harrow.gov.uk; f. 1965; 412,000 vols; 38,000 audiovisual items; spec. collns: architecture and building; 11 brs; Library Services Man. TIM BRYAN.

Havering Library Service: Central Library, St Edward's Way, Romford, RM1 3AR; tel. (1708) 432389; fax (1708) 432391; e-mail central.library@havering.gov.uk; internet www.havering.gov.uk/libraries; f. 1964; 500,000 vols; 9 brs; Library Services Man. ANN RENNIE.

Hillingdon Libraries, London Borough of Hillingdon: Central Library, 14 High St, Uxbridge, Middx., UB8 1HD; tel. (1895) 250600; fax (1895) 239794; e-mail librarycontact@hillingdon.gov.uk; internet www.hillingdon.gov.uk/libraries; f. 1965; 843,105 vols; Dir (vacant).

Home Office Information Services Centre: Lower Ground, Seacole Bldg, 2 Marsham St, London, SW1P 4DF; tel. (20) 7035-6699; fax (20) 7035-4022; e-mail informationservicescentre@homeoffice.gsi .gov.uk; internet www.homeoffice.gov.uk; 42,000 vols, 100,000 microforms, 2,000 periodicals; social sciences, esp. official publs, criminal law and admin. of justice, criminology, police, immigration, nationality, probation and community relations; regular access for Home Office staff only; access for staff from other govt depts by appointment; Library and Information Services JACKIE KING; Customer Liaison Man. JANET COCKAYNE.

Hounslow Library Network: Hounslow Community Services, CentreSpace, Treaty Centre, High St, Hounslow, Middx, TW3 1ES; tel. and fax (845) 456-2800; e-mail hounslow-info@laing.com; internet www .hounslow.info; Dir of Culture and Heritage (vacant).

House of Commons Library: London, SW1A 0AA; tel. (20) 7219-4272; e-mail hcinfo@parliament.uk; f. 1818; research div. issues internal reference sheets and background papers on subjects of current interest to mems; library private to MPs; Information Office handles enquiries on Parliament from the gen. public; over 260,000 vols, plus Parliamentary Papers; reference library files contain more than 700 periodicals, 1,500 e-journals, 100 newspapers; Dir-Gen. of Information Services and Librarian JOHN PULLINGER; Head of Library Resources KATHARINE MARKE; publ. *POST Notes*.

House of Lords Library: London, SW1A 0PW; tel. (20) 7219-5242; fax (20) 7219-6396; e-mail hllibrary@parliament.uk; f. 1826; 120,000 vols, legal and Parliamentary history, gen. literature and reference; Dir of

Information Services and Librarian Dr ELIZABETH HALLAM SMITH.

Imperial College of London Libraries: South Kensington, London, SW7 2AZ; tel. (20) 7594-8820; fax (20) 7594-8876; e-mail library@imperial.ac.uk; internet www .imperial.ac.uk/library; central library and 5 departmental libraries on South Kensington campus; 5 Faculty of Medicine libraries at Charing Cross, Chelsea and Westminster, Royal Brompton, St Mary's and Wellcome Library, Hammersmith campuses; also Michael Way Library at Silwood Park and the Kempe Centre at Wye campus; 580,000 vols, 25,000 e-journal titles, 1,000 print titles; Dir of Library Services DEBORAH SHORELY.

Inner Temple Library: Inner Temple, London, EC4Y 7DA; tel. (20) 7797-8217; fax (20) 7583-6030; e-mail library@innertemple .org.uk; internet www.innertemplelibrary .org.uk; f. 1500; 80,000 vols, mostly legal and historical; contains, in addition to British law and legal history, an extensive colln of law relating to the Commonwealth; spec. colln of 10,000 MSS, including Petyt MSS, available to the public (by written application, access granted at Librarian's discretion) for historical research; Librarian MARGARET CLAY.

Institute of Advanced Legal Studies Library: Univ. of London, 17 Russell Sq., London, WC1B 5DR; tel. (20) 7862-5790; fax (20) 7862-5850; e-mail ials@sas.ac.uk; internet www.ials.sas.ac.uk; f. 1947; serves academic researchers nationally and internationally; 300,000 vols, 3,073 current serials; comprehensive colln of legal literature (except for Oriental laws and literature of East European law in East European languages), with spec. emphasis on the legal systems of the UK, the Commonwealth, the USA, Western Europe and Latin America; comparative law; int. law; incl. the Foreign and Commonwealth Office Commonwealth Law Library; the Records of Legal Education Archives; Dir of Institute Prof. AVROM SHERR; Librarian and Assoc. Dir of Institute JULES WINTERTON.

Institute of Historical Research Library: Univ. of London, Senate House, London, WC1E 7HU; tel. (20) 7862-8760; e-mail ihr.library@sas.ac.uk; internet www .history.ac.uk; f. 1921; colln of printed historical sources covering W Europe and its colonial history, from end of Roman period; 171,000 vols; Librarian JENNIFER HIGHAM.

Institution of Engineering and Technology Library and Archives: Savoy Place, London, WC2R 0BL; tel. (20) 7344-5461; fax (20) 7344-8467; e-mail libdesk@theiet.org; internet www.theiet.org/library; f. 1871; 75,000 books, 200,000 bound vols of periodicals, 850 current periodicals, 20,000 reports and pamphlets; spec. collns of historical electrical works; Sir Francis Ronalds Colln (6,000 vols and pamphlets), Sylvanus P. Thompson Library (4,500 vols and 8,000 pamphlets), Faraday MSS, and library, notebooks and MSS of Oliver Heaviside; holds library of British Computer Society; produces INSPEC database and provides specialized information services; Man. of Library and Archives Services JOHN W. COUPLAND; publs *Electronics Letters* (24 a year), *Engineering and Technology* (12 a year), *IET Proceedings* (6 a year), *IET Research Journals*.

Islington Library and Heritage Services: Central Library, 2 Fieldway Crescent, London, N5 1PF; tel. (20) 7527-6900; fax (20) 7527-6906; e-mail library.informationunit@ islington.gov.uk; internet www.islington.gov .uk/libraries; 10 libraries incl. the Central Reference Library, Lewis Carroll Children's Library, Islington Local History Centre, Islington museum, and two adult learning

centres: First Steps Learning Centre and Islington Computer Skills Centre; f. 1905; 544,357 vols; Head of Library and Heritage Service ROSEMARY DOYLE; Information and Learning Man. JOHN SMITH.

Joint Library of the Hellenic and Roman Societies: Senate House, Malet St, London, WC1E 7HU; tel. (20) 7862-8709; fax (20) 7862-8735; e-mail colin.annis@sas.ac.uk; internet icls.sas.ac.uk/library/home.htm; f. 1879, since 1953 run in asscn with Univ. of London's Institute of Classical Studies Library; classical archaeology, art, history, religion, philosophy, language and literature; 130,000 vols, 19,500 periodicals, 650 current periodicals; classified colln of 6,800 coloured slides, 200 CD-ROMs; Librarian COLIN ANNIS.

Kensington and Chelsea Library Service: Central Library, Phillimore Walk, London, W8 7RX; tel. (20) 7361-3010; e-mail libraries@rbkc.gov.uk; internet www.rbkc .gov.uk/leisureandlibraries; f. 1888; 620,000 vols; system incl.: Central Library, Phillimore Walk; Chelsea Library, Chelsea Old Town Hall, Kings Rd, London, SW3 5EZ; 4 brs; spec. collns: genealogy and heraldry, biography, languages, folklore, costume and local history; Head of Libraries JANE BATTYE.

King's College London Library: Chancery Lane, London, WC2A 1LR; tel. (20) 7848-2424; fax (20) 7848-1777; e-mail libraryenquiry@kcl.ac.uk; internet www.kcl .ac.uk/library; f. 1829; sites incl. Chancery Lane (humanities, law, science), Denmark Hill Campus (medicine, dentistry), Guy's Campus (medicine, dentistry, biomedical sciences), St Thomas's Campus (medicine) and Waterloo Campus (life sciences, nursing and midwifery, education, management); 1,200,000 vols; Dir of Library Services ROBERT HALL.

Kingston upon Thames Public Libraries: Fairfield Rd, Kingston upon Thames, KT1 2PS; tel. (20) 8547-6413; fax (20) 8547-6426; internet www.kingston.gov.uk/browse/ leisure/libraries.htm; f. 1882; 230,000 vols; Strategic Manager Library and Heritage Service GRACE MCELWEE.

Lambeth Libraries and Archives: 1st Fl., Blue Star House, 234–244 Stockwell Rd, Brixton, London, SW9 9QS; tel. (20) 7926-0750; fax (20) 7926-0751; e-mail libraries@ lambeth.gov.uk; internet www.lambeth.gov .uk; f. 1888; 9 brs; mobile library and home visit library service; archives and local history service; over 600,000 vols; Head of Service SANDRA GOODWIN.

Lambeth Palace Library: Lambeth Palace Rd, London, SE1 7JU; tel. (20) 7898-1400; fax (20) 7928-7932; e-mail archives@ churchofengland.org; internet www .lambethpalacelibrary.org; f. 1610; 200,000 printed items (esp. Church history) and 4,500 vols of 9th–20th century MSS; Sion College Library MSS and early printed books; archives; Librarian and Archivist GILES MANDELBROTE.

Law Society Library: 113 Chancery Lane, London, WC2A 1PL; tel. (20) 7320-5946; fax (20) 7831-1687; e-mail library@lawsociety .org.uk; internet www.lawsociety.org.uk/ library; f. 1828; private library for solicitors who are mems of the Law Society of England and Wales; 45,000 vols; Reader Services Librarian JANET HORSLEN.

Lewisham Library Service: Town Hall, Catford, London, SE6 4RU; tel. (20) 8314-6399; e-mail libraries@lewisham.gov.uk; internet www.lewisham.gov.uk/ leisureandculture/libraries; f. 1890; 700,000 vols; 12 brs, Central Reference Library, Local History Centre, Open Learning Centre; Head of Library and Information Services JOHN

HUGHES; publs *Looking Back at Lewisham*, local history publs.

Library of Anti-Slavery International: Thomas Clarkson House, The Stableyard, Broomgrove Rd, London, SW9 9TL; tel. (20) 7501-8939; fax (20) 7738-4110; e-mail library@antislavery.org; internet www .antislavery.org; f. 1839; literature, photographs and video cassettes on historical and contemporary slavery and human rights issues (modern issues incl. bonded labour, child labour, descent-based slavery, forced labour, indigenous peoples and trafficking; historical issues incl. the Transatlantic Slave Trade and colonialism); Librarian JEFF HOWARTH.

Library of the Religious Society of Friends in Britain: Friends House, Euston Rd, London, NW1 2BJ; tel. (20) 7663-1135; fax (20) 7663-1001; e-mail library@quaker .org.uk; internet www.quaker.org.uk/library; f. 1673; collects and preserves Quakers' historic and continuing recorded heritage; increases access to information about the Society of Friends; encourages study in Quaker and related activities incl. peace, prison reform, humanitarian assistance and the anti-slavery movement; studies Quaker history, faith, thought and practice; 80,000 vols of books and pamphlets, 3,000 vols of periodicals, 4,000 MSS, 40,000 prints and photographs; Head of Library and Archives DAVID BLAKE.

Lilian Storey Memorial Library Foundation for Theosophical Studies: 50 Gloucester Pl., London, W1U 8EA; tel. (20) 7563-9816; fax (20) 7935-9543; e-mail books@ theosoc.org.uk; internet www.theosoc.org.uk; f. 1875; visitors by appointment; organizes lectures, seminars and summer school; 14,000 vols; Librarian (vacant); publ. *Esoterica*.

Lincoln's Inn Library: Holborn, London, WC2A 3TN; tel. (20) 7242-4371; fax (20) 7404-1864; e-mail library@lincolnsinn.org .uk; internet www.lincolnsinn.org.uk; f. by 1475; 170,000 vols on law and 2,000 vols of MSS, incl. the Hale Colln; Librarian G. F. HOLBORN.

Linnean Society Library: Burlington House, Piccadilly, London, W1J 0BF; tel. (20) 7434-4479; fax (20) 7287-9364; e-mail library@linnean.org; internet www.linnean .org; f. 1788; books on natural history, incl. Linnaeus's own library; colln of MSS, engravings and portraits; 95,000 vols; Librarian LYNDA BROOKS; publs *Biological Journal of the Linnean Society of London*, *Botanical Journal of the Linnean Society of London*, *Pulse, Synopses of the British Fauna (New Series)*, *The Linnean*, *Zoological journal of the Linnean Society of London*.

London Library: 14 St James's Sq., London, SW1Y 4LG; tel. (20) 7930-7705; fax (20) 7766-4766; e-mail membership@ londonlibrary.co.uk; internet www .londonlibrary.co.uk; f. 1841; open to subscribing mems; an educational charity; 1,000,000 vols mainly in the arts, humanities and social sciences; Librarian INEZ T. P. A. LYNN.

London Oratory Library: The Oratory, Brompton Rd, South Kensington, London, SW7 2RP; tel. (20) 7808-0900; fax (20) 7584-1095; e-mail bromptonoratory@aol.com; internet www.bromptonoratory.com; f. 1854; contains 40,000 vols and 3,000 pamphlets on theology and Church history; separate library (4,000 vols) of David Lewis, Tractarian convert; Librarian and Archivist Father LIBRARIAN.

London School of Hygiene and Tropical Medicine Library: Keppel St, London, WC1E 7HT; tel. (20) 7927-2283; fax (20) 7927-2273; e-mail library@lshtm.ac.uk; internet www.lshtm.ac.uk/library; f. 1924; public health and tropical medicine in all aspects; many series of medical reports; archives incl. the papers of Sir Ronald Ross and many other eminent public health and tropical medicine professionals; Head of Library and Archives Service CAROLINE LLOYD.

Marx Memorial Library: Marx House, 37A Clerkenwell Green, London, EC1R 0DU; tel. (20) 7253-1485; fax (20) 7251-6039; e-mail info@marx-memorial-library.org; internet www.marx-memorial-library.org; f. 1933; 150,000 vols; pamphlets, files of Labour, Socialist and Communist periodicals; spec. collns: Peace Movement, Spanish Civil War, USA, and the Hunger Marches; James Klugmann colln of Chartist and early British working-class history; lectures and discussion confs; Dir of Archives and Librarian Dr JOHN CALLOW (acting); publ. *Bulletin* (2 a year).

Merton Libraries and Heritage Service: Merton Civic Centre, London Rd, Morden, SM4 5DX; tel. (20) 8545-3783; fax (20) 8545-3237; e-mail library.admin@merton.gov.uk; internet www.merton.gov.uk; f. 1887; 500,000 vols; spec. collns: William Morris, Nelson; Head of Library and Heritage Services INGRID LACKAJIS.

Middle Temple Library (The Hon. Society of the Middle Temple): Ashley Bldg, Middle Temple Lane, London, EC4Y 9BT; tel. (20) 7427-4830; fax (20) 7427-4831; e-mail library@middletemple.org.uk; internet www.middletemplelibrary.org.uk; f. 1641; private library for members of the Hon. Soc. of the Middle Temple; 125,000 vols of works on British, American, Public Int. and European Communities law; spec. collns: 80 incunabula, misc. tracts, mainly 17th-century, 83 vols from John Donne's library; Librarian V. HAYWARD.

Ministry of Defence, Information Services: Ministry of Defence Main Bldg, Whitehall, London, SW1A 2HB; tel. (20) 7218-4445; fax (20) 7218-5413; e-mail cio-svcslibrary-office@mod.uk; covers defence policy, defence forces, military, naval and aviation strategy and technology, int. relations, politics, management and computer science; 50,000 vols, 300 periodicals; Chief Librarian PATRICK RYAN.

National Archives: Ruskin Ave, Kew, Richmond upon Thames, TW9 4DU; tel. (20) 8876-3444; fax (20) 8878-8905; e-mail enquiry@nationalarchives.gov.uk; internet www.nationalarchives.gov.uk; f. 2003 following merger of the Public Record Office (f. 1838) and the Historical Manuscripts Commission (f. 1869); national archives for England and Wales and for the United Kingdom; holds the records of central government and the central courts of law since 11th century; central UK advisory body on archives and manuscripts relating to British history; Keeper of Public Records and Historical Manuscripts Commissioner SARAH TYACKE; publ. *National Register of Archives* (previously published by the Historical Manuscripts Commission and containing 43,000 indexed unpublished lists of MSS).

National Art Library: Victoria and Albert Museum, Cromwell Rd, London, SW7 2RL; tel. (20) 7942-2400; fax (20) 7942-2401; e-mail nal.enquiries@vam.ac.uk; internet www.vam.ac.uk/nal; f. 1837; attached to Victoria and Albert (V&A) Museums; reference library for the int. documentation of art and design; 1,000,000 vols on art and allied subjects; spec. collns: Dyce (1869) and Forster (1876) literary libraries, Clements Colln of armorial book-bindings, Piot Colln of festival literature, and many others; Keeper of the Word and Image Dept JULIUS BRYANT.

Attached Archive:

Archive of Art and Design: 23 Blythe Rd, Olympia, London, W14 0QX; tel. (20) 7603-1514, ext. 209; fax (20) 7602-0980; e-mail archive@vam.ac.uk; internet www .vam.ac.uk/resources/archives/aad; f. 1978; colln of principally 20th-century archives of designers, design asscns and cos involved in the design process; Keeper of the Word and Image Dept JULIUS BRYANT.

Natural History Museum, Library and Archives: Cromwell Rd, London, SW7 5BD; tel. (20) 7942-5460; fax (20) 7942-5559; e-mail library@nhm.ac.uk; internet www .nhm.ac.uk; f. 1881; print and e-resources covering botany, entomology, museum techniques, palaeontology, mineralogy, parasitology, physical anthropology, zoology and ornithology; 1,000,000 vols; spec. collns: Carl Linnaeus, Sir Joseph Banks, Alfred Russel Wallace; 1,800 MSS, 400,000 original works of art; Head of Library JANE SMITH; publs *Journal of Systematic Palaeontology* (4 a year), *Systematics and Biodiversity* (4 a year).

Newham Public Libraries: East Ham Library, High St South, London, E6 6EL; tel. (20) 8430-2000; fax (20) 8430-2412; e-mail customer.services@newham.gov.uk; internet www.newham.gov.uk/services/ libraryservices; f. 1965; 500,530 vols, 57,243 reference stock, 14,031 audio items; Chief Librarian (vacant).

Queen Mary, University of London, Library: Mile End Rd, London, E1 4NS; tel. (20) 7882-7379; e-mail library-acquisitions@qmul.ac.uk; internet www.library.qmul.ac.uk; f. 1887; 600,000 vols on the arts, sciences, engineering, medicine, social studies and law; European Documentation Centre; Dir of Library Services EMMA BULL.

Medical Libraries:

St Bartholomew's and the Royal London, Queen Mary's School of Medicine and Dentistry, Libraries: Turner St, London, E1 2AD; tel. (20) 7882-7112; fax (20) 7882-7113; internet www.library.qmul .ac.uk; incl. Whitechapel, W Smithfield, London Chest Hospital, Wolfson Institute of Preventive Medicine.

Richmond upon Thames Public Libraries: Central Lending Library, Little Green, Richmond upon Thames, TW9 1QL; Central Reference Library, Old Town Hall, Whittaker Ave, Richmond upon Thames, Surrey, TW9 1TP; tel. (20) 8734-3303 (CLL); tel. (20) 8734-3308 (CRL); fax (20) 8734-3330 (CLL); fax (20) 8940-6899 (CRL); f. 1880; incl. Borough Local Studies Colln; Head of Libraries and Culture IAN DODDS.

Royal Academy of Arts Library: Burlington House, London, W1J 0BD; tel. (20) 7300-5737; fax (20) 7300-5765; e-mail library@ royalacademy.org.uk; internet www .royalacademy.org.uk; f. 1768; 60,000 vols on the fine arts and standard reference books; original drawings, MSS, prints and photographs; Librarian ADAM WATERTON.

Royal Academy of Music Library: Marylebone Rd, London, NW1 5HT; tel. (20) 7873-7323; fax (20) 7873-7322; e-mail library@ram.ac.uk; internet www.ram.ac.uk; f. 1822; 150,000 vols, 5,500 sets of orchestral parts, sound recordings; special collns include MSS and early editions, Sir Henry Wood Library, Angelina Goetz Library, David Munrow Library, Sullivan Archive, Robert Spencer Colln, Foyle Menuhin Archive; Librarian KATHRYN ADAMSON.

Royal Asiatic Society Library: 14 Stephenson Way, London, NW1 2HD; tel. (20) 7388-4539; fax (20) 7391-9429; e-mail library@royalasiaticsociety.org; internet www.royalasiaticsociety.org; f. 1823; holds monthly lectures, organizes study days; 60,000 vols; collns incl. 1,500 Asian MSS, 2,000 paintings and drawings, 5,000 photographs; Dir ALISON OHTA; Librarian KATHY LAZENBATT; publ. *Journal* (4 a year).

Royal Astronomical Society Library and Archives: Burlington House, Piccadilly, London, W1J 0BQ; tel. (20) 7734-4582; fax (20) 7494-0166; e-mail info@ras.org.uk; internet www.ras.org.uk; f. 1820; 31,000 vols, plus archives, dealing with astronomy, history of astronomy and geophysics; Librarian P. D. HINGLEY.

Royal Botanic Gardens, Kew, Library, Art & Archives: Kew, Richmond upon Thames, TW9 3AE; tel. (20) 8332-5414; fax (20) 8332-5430; e-mail library@kew.org; internet www.kew.org; f. 1852; botany (esp. taxonomic, floristic and economic aspects), history of gardening, botanical art, conservation, biochemistry, anatomy, genetics, molecular systematics, propagation and seed science and storage; 300,000 vols, 170,000 monographs, 5,000 periodicals, 150,000 pamphlets, 200,000 botanical illustrations, 4,600 collns within archives consisting of 250,000 letters and MSS and registered files; Head of Library, Art and Archives CHRISTOPHER MILLS.

Royal College of Art Library: Kensington Gore, London, SW7 2EU; tel. (20) 7590-4224; fax (20) 7590-4217; e-mail library@rca.ac.uk; internet www.rca.ac.uk; f. 1953; 70,000 vols on the visual arts, history and philosophy of design, history and criticism of the arts; Colour Reference Library: comprehensive colln of books and articles on all aspects of colour; admittance by appointment only; Head of Information and Learning Services PETER HASSELL; Library Man. DARLENE MAXWELL.

Royal College of Music Library: Prince Consort Rd, South Kensington, London, SW7 2BS; tel. (20) 7591-4325; fax (20) 7591-4326; e-mail library@rcm.ac.uk; internet www.rcm.ac.uk/library; f. 1883; admission for reference only; more than 400,000 vols, incl. MSS and early printed music; Librarian PETER LINNITT.

Royal College of Physicians' Library Archive and Museum Services: 11 St Andrews Pl., Regent's Park, London, NW1 4LE; tel. (20) 3075-1539; fax (20) 7486-3729; e-mail infocentre@rcplondon.ac.uk; internet www.rcplondon.ac.uk; f. 1518; services incl. enquiry service, exhibitions, research facilities, tours; services for fellows and mems incl. loans, expert search and information retrieval; medical education resource centre; 60,000 vols (mostly related to history of medicine, but some on current medical issues), 100 incunabula, 200 linear m of MSS, 30,000 portrait photographs and other pictorial items; Man. JULIE BECKWITH; publs *Munk's Roll* (online (munksroll.rcplondon.ac.uk)), *The Royal College of Physicians and its Collections*.

Royal College of Surgeons of England Library and Lumley Study Centre: 35–43 Lincoln's Inn Fields, London, WC2A 3PE; tel. (20) 7869-6555; fax (20) 7405-4438; e-mail library@rcseng.ac.uk; internet www.rcseng.ac.uk; f. 1800; 150,000 vols on surgery and dentistry, 400 current periodicals; Librarian THALIA KNIGHT; publ. *Annals*.

Royal College of Veterinary Surgeons Trust Library: Belgravia House, 62–64 Horseferry Rd, London, SW1P 2AF; tel. (20) 7202-0752; fax (20) 7202-0751; e-mail library@rcvstrust.org.uk; internet www.rcvslibrary.org.uk; f. 1844; open to qualified veterinary surgeons and veterinary nurses; open to mems of the public by appointment; 30,000 vols; Librarian CLARE BOULTON.

Royal Geographical Society (with the Institute of British Geographers) Library: Kensington Gore, London, SW7 2AR; tel. (20) 7591-3044; fax (20) 7591-3001; e-mail enquiries@rgs.org; internet www.rgs.org; f. 1830; 250,000 books and bound periodicals; 500 current periodicals; map room contains 1m. maps and charts, 3,000 atlases, large selection of gazetteers and expedition reports; picture library of 500,000 images; archives; Prin. Librarian E. M. RAE; Map Curator D. McNEILL; publs *Area*, *Geographical Journal*, *Transactions*.

Royal Institute of International Affairs Library: Chatham House, 10 St James's Sq., London, SW1Y 4LE; tel. (20) 7957-5723; fax (20) 7957-5710; e-mail libenquire@chathamhouse.org.uk; internet www.chathamhouse.org.uk/library; f. 1920; Chatham House archives; private research library; 75,000 vols, 200 current periodicals; Library and Information Services Man. DAVID BATES; publs *International Affairs* (24 a year), *The World Today* (24 a year).

Royal Institution of Great Britain Archives: 21 Albemarle St, London, W1S 4BS; tel. (20) 7409-2992; fax (20) 7629-3569; e-mail archivist@ri.ac.uk; internet www.rigb.org; f. 1799; 25,000 vols on all brs of science, spec. collns: early scientific books and journals especially of 18th and 19th centuries, accessible through archive; Head of Collns and Heritage Prof. FRANK JAMES.

Royal National Institute for Deaf People (RNID) Library: 330–332 Gray's Inn Rd, London, WC1X 8EE; tel. (20) 7915-1553; f. 1911; 18,000 books and 200 current journals on all aspects of deafness and other communication disorders; Librarian MARY PLACKETT.

Royal Society Centre for History of Science: 6–9 Carlton House Terrace, London, SW1Y 5AG; tel. (20) 7451-2606; fax (20) 7930-2170; e-mail library@royalsociety.org; internet royalsociety.org; f. 1660; colln on history of science and scientists, science policy, science education, science and the public; 150,000 vols; Library Man. RUPERT BAKER; Head of Library and Information Services KEITH MOORE; publ. *Notes and Records of the Royal Society* (scholarly journal covering history of science activities, 4 a year).

Royal Society of Chemistry Library and Information Centre: Burlington House, Piccadilly, London, W1J 0BA; tel. (20) 7440-3373; fax (20) 7287-9798; e-mail library@rsc.org; internet www.rsc.org; f. 1841; 100,000 vols; Librarian NIGEL LEES.

Royal Society of Medicine Library: 1 Wimpole St, London, W1G 0AE; tel. (20) 7290-2940; fax (20) 7290-2939; e-mail library@rsm.ac.uk; internet www.rsm.ac.uk/library; f. 1805; 600,000 vols, 1,200 current periodicals, 10,000 back titles; lending restricted to mems; back-up library to British Library; worldwide mail order photocopy service; historical colln from 1474; medical portrait colln; Dir of Library Services WAYNE SIME; Librarian NICOLA WOOD.

Royal United Services Institute Library of Military History: 61 Whitehall, London, SW1A 2ET; tel. (20) 7930-5854; fax (20) 7747-2636; e-mail library@rusi.org; internet www.rusi.org/about/library; f. 1831; maintains 3 in-house research depts covering int. security studies, military science and nat. security and resilience; organizes lectures, seminars and conferences; 16,000 vols on military history incl. British regimental and unit histories; c. 4,000 biographies, memoirs and personal experiences (published works, the library does not keep MSS or similar documents); books lent to RUSI mems and to other libraries, mems of the public should apply to the librarian for reference access; Librarian JOHN MONTGOMERY; publs *Homeland Security and Resilience Monitor* (10 a year), *RUSI Defence Systems* (3 a year), *RUSI Journal* (6 a year), *Whitehall Papers* (2 a year), *Whitehall Reports* (irregular).

St Bride Library: Bride Lane, Fleet St, London, EC4Y 8EE; tel. (20) 7353-4660; e-mail nigel@sbf.org.uk; internet www.stbride.org; f. 1891, opened 1895; early technical literature, drawings, MSS, prospectuses, patents, printing, papermaking, bookbinding, illustration, graphic design, materials for printing and type founding; organizes exhibitions and lectures; 3 annual confs; printing workshop educational programme; 50,000 books and pamphlets, 3,500 periodical titles; Librarian NIGEL ROCHE; publs *Printing History News* (4 a year), *Ultrabold* (2 a year).

St Paul's Cathedral Library: London, EC4M 8AE; tel. (20) 7246-8342; fax (20) 7248-3104; e-mail library@stpaulscathedral.org.uk; internet www.stpauls.co.uk; f. 1707; 13,500 vols and 11,500 pamphlets; early printed books of theology and Greek and Latin classics, 20 medieval MSS; Librarian JO WISDOM.

School of Oriental and African Studies Library: Univ. of London, Thornhaugh St, Russell Square, London, WC1H 0XG; tel. (20) 7898-4160; fax (20) 7898-4159; internet www.soas.ac.uk; f. 1916; 859,000 vols and pamphlets, 4,500 periodicals, 2,700 MSS and archive collections dealing with Asian and African languages, literature, philosophy, religions, history, law, cultural anthropology, art and archaeology, social sciences; back-up library to the British Library for loans; Librarian ANNE POULSON.

Science Museum Library: Imperial College Rd, South Kensington, London, SW7 5NH; tel. (20) 7942-4242; fax (20) 7942-4243; e-mail smlinfo@sciencemuseum.org.uk; internet www.sciencemuseum.org.uk/library; f. 1883; printed and archive collns; provides access to academics, students, authors, general public and schools; access to Swindon collns by appointment; 500,000 vols; collns housed in London incl. history, biography and social context of all brs of science, technology and medicine, also 400 current journal titles; collns housed in Swindon incl. contemporary science technology and medicine books and journals, published in 15th–20th centuries, reports, directories, trade literature; also at Swindon the Archives colln containing original MSS, letters, company records, drawings, etc. on scientific, technical and medical subjects; Head of Library and Archives RUPERT WILLIAMS.

Senate House Library, University of London: Senate House, Malet St, London, WC1E 7HU; tel. (20) 7862-8500; fax (20) 7862-8480; e-mail shl.enquiries@london.ac.uk; internet www.shl.lon.ac.uk; f. 1838; research library principally in the arts, humanities and social sciences, for reference and loan, incl. special collns, e.g., Goldsmiths' Library of Economic Literature, Harry Price Colln, Sterling Library, Durning-Lawrence Library, Eliot-Phelips Colln, Bromhead Library, Carlton Shorthand Colln, Porteus Library, Malcolm Morley Theatre Colln and the Libraries of the Canadian and Australian High Commissions; 2,000,000 vols; Dir of Research Library Services CHRISTOPHER PRESSLER.

Sir John Soane's House and Museum Library: 13 Lincoln's Inn Fields, London, WC2A 3BP; tel. (20) 7440-4251; fax (20) 7831-3957; e-mail library@soane.org.uk; internet www.soane.org; f. 1837; contains Sir John Soane's colln of 8,000 vols on art, antiquities, architecture, classical and gen. literature, architectural drawings, personal and business archive; Librarian Dr STEPHANIE COANE.

Society of Antiquaries Library & Collections: Burlington House, Piccadilly, London, W1J 0BE; tel. (20) 7479-7084; fax (20) 7287-6967; e-mail library@sal.org.uk; internet www.sal.org.uk; f. 1707; 100,000 vols, 650 current periodicals on British and foreign archaeology and history, heraldry, genealogy, etc.; MSS, prints, drawings, early printed books, brass rubbings, paintings, museum objects, seal casts; Head of Library and Collns HEATHER ROWLAND; publ. *Antiquaries Journal* (1 a year).

Southwark Culture, Libraries, Learning and Leisure: 160 Tooley St, London, SE1 2QH; tel. (20) 7525-2000; fax (20) 7525-1586; e-mail southwark.libraries@southwark.gov.uk; internet www.southwark.gov.uk/libraries; 600,000 vols; 12 brs; 1 museum; Head of Culture, Libraries, Learning and Leisure ADRIAN WHITTLE.

Supreme Court Library: Royal Courts of Justice, Ministry of Justice, Strand, London, WC2A 2LL; tel. (20) 7947-6587; fax (20) 7947-6661; internet www.justice.gov.uk; f. 1970; 300,000 vols; spec. collns: Court of Appeal (Civil Div.) Transcripts 1950–; old edns of legal textbooks (in Supreme Court Library—Bar—f. 1883); Librarian J. ROBERTSON.

Sutton Library Service: Central Library, St Nicholas Way, Sutton, Surrey, SM1 1EA; tel. (20) 8770-4700; fax (20) 8770-4777; f. 1936; 9 libraries; 316,100 vols; 26,759 audio items, 9,067 visual items; spec. colln: genealogy and heraldry; Heads of Libraries and Heritage C. MCDONOUGH, A. FLETCHER.

Thames Valley University Learning Resource Centre: Walpole House, 18–22 Bond St, Ealing, London, W5 5AA; tel. (20) 8231-2246; fax (20) 8231-2631; internet lrs.tvu.ac.uk; f. 1992; 259,000 vols in 5 sites; Head of Learning Resources J. I. WOLSTENHOLME.

Tower Hamlets Idea Stores and Libraries: c/o Head of Idea Store, Gladstone Pl., 1 Ewart Pl., London, E3 5EQ; tel. (20) 7364-4332; e-mail ideastore@towerhamlets.gov.uk; internet www.ideastore.co.uk; f. 1965; local history library; colln of books, CDs and DVDs in Bengali, Chinese, Somali, Urdu and Vietnamese; 627,564 vols; Head of Idea Store JUDITH ST JOHN.

Treasury and Cabinet Office Library: Parliament St, London, SW1P 3AG; tel. (20) 7270-5290; fax (20) 7270-5681; 120,000 vols; 1,500 periodicals; covers economics, finance and public administration; Librarian JEAN CLAYTON.

UCL Library Services: Gower St, London, WC1E 6BT; tel. (20) 7679-7793; fax (20) 7679-7373; e-mail library@ucl.ac.uk; internet www.ucl.ac.uk/library; f. 1828; libraries incl.: main arts and humanities library, science library, Archway Healthcare library and UCL Bartlett Library, Cruciform library, UCL Institute of Archaeology Library, UCL Ear Institute and RNID libraries at the Royal Nat. Throat Nose and Ear Hospital, UCL Eastman Dental Institute Library, UCL Institute of Child Health Library, UCL Institute of Neurology, Queen Square Library, UCL Institute of Ophthalmology Library, Institute of Orthopaedics Library, UCL Language and Speech Science library, Royal free medical library, UCL School of Pharmacy Library, UCL School of Slavonic and East European Studies Library and information services; spec. collns: medieval period to present day; 2,000,000 vols, c. 30,000 journals printed and electronic format; Dir PAUL AYRIS.

University of Greenwich Information and Library Services: Old Royal Naval College, Greenwich, London, SE10 9LS; tel. (20) 8331-8196; fax (20) 8331-9084; internet www.gre.ac.uk/lib; Head of Learning Services ANN MURPHY.

Upper Norwood Joint Library: Westow Hill, London, SE19 1TJ; tel. (20) 8670-2551; fax (20) 8670-5468; e-mail info@uppernorwoodlibrary.org; internet www.uppernorwoodlibrary.org; f. 1900; 60,000 vols; collns on the Crystal Palace and its historical background, the Gerald Massey colln, the J. B. Wilson colln; Chief Librarian BRADLEY MILLINGTON.

Vaughan Williams Memorial Library: English Folk Dance and Song Soc., Cecil Sharp House, 2 Regents Park Rd, London, NW1 7AY; tel. (20) 7485-2206; fax (20) 7284-0523; e-mail library@efdss.org; internet www.efdss.org/library.htm; f. 1930; maintained by English Folk Dance and Song Soc. (*q.v.*); England's main source of information on traditional song, dance, customs and folk culture; 20,000 vols, MS collns, microfilms, press cuttings, broadsides, 10,000 audiovisual items, 15,000 photographic images; open to public for reference; Library Dir MALCOLM TAYLOR; publs *English Dance and Song (EDS)* (4 a year), *Folk Music Journal* (1 a year).

Victoria and Albert Museum, Library of the: see National Art Library.

Vision Redbridge Culture and Libraries: Central Library, Clements Rd, Ilford, IG1 1EA; tel. (20) 8708-2420; fax (20) 8708-2431; e-mail central.library@visionrcl.org.uk; internet www.redbridge.gov.uk; f. 1965; 633,104 vols; Information Heritage Librarian IAN DOWLING (acting).

Waltham Forest Public Libraries: Walthamstow Library, High St, Walthamstow, London, E17 7JN; tel. (20) 8496-5134; fax (20) 8509-9539; e-mail wf.libs@walthamforest.gov.uk; internet www.walthamforest.gov.uk; f. 1893; 448,427 vols; spec. collns: Cookery, Domestic Economy, Fiction Authors U, V; Librarian CAROLINE RAE.

Wandsworth Public Libraries: Town Hall, Wandsworth High St, London, SW18 2PU; tel. (20) 8871-8536; fax (20) 8871-7630; e-mail libraries@wandsworth.gov.uk; internet www.wandsworth.gov.uk/libraries; f. 1883; 721,101 vols; 12 brs; reference library, 2 music libraries, local history library, home delivery library service; special collns: architecture, town planning, European history, geography and travel, occult sciences, local history, early children's books, G. A. Henty; Head of Library and Heritage Service ANDREW GREEN.

Warburg Institute Library: Woburn Sq., London, WC1H 0AB; tel. (20) 7862-8949; fax (20) 7862-8939; e-mail warburg.library@sas.ac.uk; internet warburg.sas.ac.uk/library; f. 1922; cultural and intellectual history of Europe from Classical Antiquity to modern times, incl. history of art, literature, science, religion, humanism; houses libraries of the Royal and British Numismatic Socs; 350,000 vols, 1,100 current serials, 450,000 photographs; Librarian Prof. JILL KRAYE; publ. *Journal of the Warburg and Courtauld Institutes* (1 a year).

Wellcome Library: 183 Euston Rd, London, NW1 2BE; tel. (20) 7611-8722; fax (20) 7611-8369; e-mail library@wellcome.ac.uk; internet library.wellcome.ac.uk; f. 1890, opened to the public in 1949; records medicine and its role in society, past and present; includes popular science, biomedical ethics and the public understanding of science; 700,000 vols, ephemera, 55,000 pamphlets, 2,700 periodical titles, 9,000 Western MSS, 12,000 Oriental MSS in 43 languages, 200,000 prints, drawings, photographs, paintings, 700 collns of medical archives, 2,500 films, 700 incunabula; Head of Library Dr SIMON CHAPLIN.

Westminster Abbey Library and Muniment Room: E Cloister, London, SW1P 3PA; tel. (20) 7654-4830; fax (20) 7654-4827; e-mail library@westminster-abbey.org; internet www.westminster-abbey.org; f. 1623; 20,000 vols since the 16th century, predominantly theological but also general literature and music; Abbey records and other documents since the 11th century; Librarian and Head of Abbey Collns Dr TONY TROWLES; Keeper of Muniments Dr R. MORTIMER.

The Wiener Library Institute of Contemporary History: 4 Devonshire St, London, W1W 5BH; tel. (20) 7636-7247; fax (20) 7436-6428; e-mail info@wienerlibrary.co.uk; internet www.wienerlibrary.co.uk; f. in Amsterdam in 1933 by Dr Alfred Wiener, moved to London 1939; 65,000 vols incl. books and pamphlets; 3,000 periodicals; 900 catalogued documents on the Holocaust, anti-Semitism, the Third Reich, Fascism, Neo-Fascism, contemporary German-Jewish history and exile studies; Dir BEN BARKOW; Sr Librarian KATHARINA HÜBSCHMANN; publ. *Wiener Library News*.

Women's Library, London Metropolitan University: 25 Old Castle St, London, E1 7NT; tel. (20) 7320-2222; fax (20) 7320-2333; e-mail moreinfo@thewomenslibrary.ac.uk; internet www.thewomenslibrary.ac.uk; f. 1926 as London Society for Women's Service Library, present status 1977; attached to London Metropolitan Univ.; documents changing role of women in soc.: women's history and women's contemporary lives in the UK; suffrage collns; organizes exhibitions; 60,000 vols, 43,000 books, 3,500 periodicals, 17,000 pamphlets, 500 zines, 4,500 museum objects, 300 web archives, 500 personal and organisational archives; Collns Man. TERESA DOHERTY.

Zoological Society of London Library: Regent's Park, London, NW1 4RY; tel. (20) 7449-6293; fax (20) 7586-5743; e-mail library@zsl.org; internet www.zsl.org; f. 1826; photograph library; archives of Zoological Soc. of London; information about zoos; 180,000 vols, 1,300 current periodicals connected with zoology and animal conservation; Librarian ANN SYLPH; Archivist MICHAEL PALMER; publs *Animal Conservation, International Zoo Yearbook, Journal of Zoology*.

Loughborough

Loughborough University—Pilkington Library: Loughborough, LE11 3TU; tel. (1509) 222360; fax (1509) 223993; e-mail library@lboro.ac.uk; internet www.lboro.ac.uk; f. 1909; incl. the Univ. Archives; 550,000 vols, 4,000 periodicals; Univ. Librarian RUTH JENKINS.

Luton

Luton Cultural Services Trust: Luton Libraries, St George's Sq., Luton, LU1 2NG; tel. (1582) 547440; fax (1582) 547461; e-mail libraryinfo@lutonculture.com; internet www.lutonlibraries.co.uk; Luton Libraries is now part of Luton Cultural Services Trust; Dir of Libraries JEAN GEORGE.

Maidenhead

Royal Borough of Windsor and Maidenhead Libraries: Maidenhead Library, St Ives Rd, Maidenhead, SL6 1QU; tel. (1628) 796969; fax (1628) 766971; e-mail maidenhead.library@rbwm.gov.uk; Head of Library, Arts and Heritage MARK TAYLOR.

Maidstone

Kent Libraries, Registration and Archives: Kent History and Library Centre, James Whatman Way, Maidstone, ME14 1LQ; tel. (1622) 696438; fax (1622) 696445; e-mail libraries.informationservices@kent.gov.uk; internet www.kent.gov.uk/libraries; f. 1921; 70,000 vols; Head of Libraries and Archives CATH ANLEY.

Manchester

Chetham's Library: Long Millgate, Manchester, M3 1SB; tel. (161) 834-7961; fax (161) 839-5797; e-mail librarian@chethams.org.uk; internet www.chethams.org.uk; f. 1653 as a free public reference library; local history records; 100,000 vols, incl. many works from the 17th and 18th centuries; Librarian Dr MICHAEL POWELL.

John Rylands University Library, University of Manchester: Oxford Rd, Manchester, M13 9PP; tel. (161) 275-3751; fax (161) 273-7488; internet www.library.manchester.ac.uk; f. 2004 by merger of the John Rylands University Library of Manchester (f. 1972 by merger of John Rylands Library—f. 1900 with Manchester University Library—f. 1851) and the Library of UMIST (f. 1824); 4,500,000 printed books, 1,000,000 MSS or archival items, 800,000 titles on microform, 9,000 serials currently received; numerous spec. colln, several of international renown such as Althorp Library of 2nd Earl Spencer and manuscript portion of Bibliotheca Lindesiana, containing, *inter alia,* 220,000 books printed before 1801, among them 4,500 incunabula and 1,500 Aldines; Librarian and Dir WILLIAM G. SIMPSON; publ. *Bulletin* (3 a year).

Manchester Libraries and Theatres: Central Library, St Peter's Sq., Manchester, M2 5PD; tel. (161) 234-1900; fax (161) 234-1963; internet www.manchester.gov.uk/libraries; f. 1852; closed for renovation, will reopen in 2014; incl. regional local studies and archives centre, lending and reference libraries, business and information library, Henry Watson Music Library, exhibition spaces, computer facilities and performance space; spec. collns incl. the Newman Flower, Henry Watson, and Gaskell; 24 community libraries; prison library service; 2,430,000 vols, 54,000 audiovisual items; Head of Libraries and Archives NEIL MACINNES.

Manchester Metropolitan University Library: Sir Kenneth Green Library, All Saints, Manchester Metropolitan University, Manchester, M15 6BH; tel. (161) 247-6104; fax (161) 247-6349; internet www.mmu.ac.uk/library; f. 1970; 867,000 vols; Librarian GILL BARRY.

Matlock

Derbyshire County Council, Cultural and Community Services, Libraries and Heritage Division: County Hall, Matlock, DE4 3AG; tel. (845) 605-8058; fax (1629) 585995; e-mail derbyshire.libraries@derbyshire.gov.uk; internet www.derbyshire.gov.uk/leisure/libraries; f. 1923; 46 brs; 1,000,000 vols; Strategic Dir of Cultural and Community Services MARTIN MOLLOY.

Merthyr Tydfil

Merthyr Tydfil County Borough Library: Central Library, High St, Merthyr Tydfil, CF47 8AF; tel. (1685) 723057; fax (1685) 370690; e-mail library.services@merthyr.gov.uk; internet www.libraries.merthyr.gov.uk; f. 1935; Public Library Service with active collection and promotion of local history; 163,210 vols; 2 brs; Head of Libraries GERAINT H. JAMES.

Middlesbrough

Middlesbrough Libraries and Information: Central Library, Victoria Sq., Middlesbrough, TS1 2AY; tel. (1642) 729001; fax (1642) 729953; 400,000 vols; central library, 12 brs; Chief Librarian JEN BRITTAIN (acting).

Teesside University Library and Information Services: Library and Information Services, Borough Rd, Middlesbrough, TS1 3BA; tel. (1642) 342100; fax (1642) 342190; e-mail libraryhelp@tees.ac.uk; internet lis.tees.ac.uk; 290,000 vols; Dir LIZ JOLLY.

Milton Keynes

Milton Keynes Council Library Service: Milton Keynes Central Library, 555 Silbury Blvd, Central Milton Keynes, MK9 3HL; tel. (1908) 254050; fax (1908) 254088; internet www.mkweb.co.uk/library-services; f. 1981; Reference and Information Librarian AGGIE O'HARA.

Library Services The Open University: Walton Hall, Milton Keynes, MK7 6AA; tel. (1908) 659001; fax (1908) 653571; e-mail lib-help@open.ac.uk; internet www.open.ac.uk/library; f. 1969; 206,000 books, 450 current periodicals, 50,000 online journal titles; Dir of Library Services NICKY WHITSED.

Mold

Flintshire Library and Information Service: County Hall, Mold, CH7 6NW; tel. (1352) 704400; fax (1352) 753662; 16 libraries, 2 mobile libraries, 1 library for the housebound; spec. collns: Arthurian literature, local studies; Wales Euro Information Centre; Head of Libraries and Archives LAWRENCE RAWSTHORNE.

Morpeth

Northumberland County Library: Gas House Lane, Morpeth, NE61 1TA; tel. (1670) 500390; fax (1670) 534513; e-mail infohelp@northumberland.gov.uk; internet www.northumberland.gov.uk; f. 1924; 34 brs, 4 mobile libraries; 635,000 vols; spec. collns: local history, vocal scores, cinema, drama, Northern Poetry Library; Devt Man. for Libraries Registrars and Coroners JUDITH WALKER.

Newbury

West Berkshire Libraries: W Berkshire District Ccl, Market St, Newbury, RG14 5LD; tel. (1635) 519900; fax (1635) 519906; e-mail newburylibrary@westberks.gov.uk; internet www.westberks.gov.uk; f. 1998; public library; Library Services Man. CHRISTINE OWEN; Librarian FIONA DAVIES.

Newcastle upon Tyne

Newcastle Libraries and Information Service: Charles Avison Bldg, 33 New Bridge St W, Newcastle upon Tyne, NE1 8AX; tel. (191) 277-4100; fax (191) 277-4137; e-mail information@newcastle.gov.uk; internet www.newcastle.gov.uk/libraries; f. 1880; 600,000 vols, 50,000 audiovisual items; extensive local and family history resources; Thomas Bewick Colln (first edns, engravings, original woodblocks, Bewick's worktable and toolbox), Thomlinson Library (4,351 vols from the 16th, 17th and 18th centuries, mainly theological); City Library and 17 brs; Library and Information Officer NICK STOPFORTH.

Newcastle University The Robinson Library: Newcastle upon Tyne, NE1 7RU; tel. (191) 222-7662; fax (191) 222-6235; e-mail lib-readerservices@ncl.ac.uk; internet www.ncl.ac.uk/library; f. 1871 as Library of Durham College of Physical Science; spec. collns incl. Pybus (medical history), Robert White, Gertrude Bell, Runciman Papers, Trevelyan Papers, Catherine Cookson, Wallis, Butler, Booktrust (children's literature); 1.2m. vols, 10,000 periodicals (electronic and print); Librarian WAYNE CONNOLLY.

Newport (Gwent)

Newport Community Learning and Libraries: Central Library, John Frost Sq., Newport, NP20 1PA; tel. (1633) 656656; fax (1633) 222615; e-mail central.library@newport.gov.uk; internet www.newport.gov.uk/libraries; 12 brs; Community Learning and Libraries Man. GILL JOHN.

Newport (Isle of Wight)

Isle of Wight Council Library Services: 5 Mariners Way, Somerton Industrial Estate, Cowes, Isle of Wight, PO31 8PD; tel. (1983) 203880; fax (1983) 203899; e-mail libraries@iow.gov.uk; internet www.iwight.com/thelibrary; f. 1904; 11 brs; Head of Libraries and Information Services (vacant).

Newtownabbey

University of Ulster Learning Resource Centre: Shore Rd, Newtownabbey, BT37 0QB; tel. (28) 9036-6399; fax (28) 9036-6849; internet library.ulster.ac.uk; f. 1985; campus learning resource centres at Belfast, Coleraine, Jordanstown and Londonderry; 640,994 vols (all campuses); Asst Dir for Library COLETTE MCKENNA (acting).

Campus Libraries:

Belfast Campus Library: York St, Belfast, BT15 1ED; tel. (28) 9026-7268; fax (28) 9026-7278; e-mail illbfast@ulster.ac.uk; 68,226 vols, mostly arts-related: painting, history of art and architecture, sculpture, design, fashion, film and photography, museum studies, Irish language; Man. MARION KHORSHIDIAN.

Coleraine Campus Library: Cromore Rd, Coleraine, BT52 1SA; tel. (28) 7032-4345; fax (28) 7032-4928; e-mail illcol@ulster.ac.uk; 297,689 vols;spec. collns: First and Second World Wars, Henry Davis Gift of incunabula, Henry Morris Colln of Irish material, Stelfox natural history colln; Man. STEPHANIE MCLAUGHLIN.

Jordanstown Campus Library: Shore Rd, Newtownabbey, BT37 0QB; tel. (28) 9036-6399; fax (28) 9036-6849; e-mail illjord@ulster.ac.uk; 273,004 vols; American and women's studies; UK, US and Irish radical newspapers and periodicals on microfilm; Man. LAURA MILLS.

Magee Campus Library: Northland Rd, Londonderry, BT48 7JL; tel. (28) 7137-5264; fax (28) 7137-5626; e-mail illmagee@ulster.ac.uk; internet library.ulster.ac.uk/lib/maglib.htm; 82,000 vols; history, modern languages, music, drama, dance, American studies, informatics, law and social work; Irish Colln of 5,400 books and 800 pamphlets, rare books Colln. Derry & Raphoe Diocesan Library; Man. CIARAN CREGAN.

Northallerton

North Yorkshire County Library: County Library Headquarters, Grammar School Lane, Northallerton, North Yorks., DL6 1DF; tel. (1609) 767800; fax (1609) 780793; e-mail julie.blaisdale@northyorks.gov.uk; 1,059,000 vols; 45 brs; Head of Libraries, Archives and Arts JULIE BLAISDALE.

Northampton

Northamptonshire Libraries and Information Service: POB 216, John Dryden House, 8–10 The Lakes, Northampton, NN4 7DD; tel. (1604) 237955; fax (1604) 237937; e-mail nlis@northamptonshire.gov.uk; internet www3.northamptonshire.gov.uk/leisure/libraries; f. 1927; 1,224,000 vols; 107,000 sound recordings and video cassettes; 35 brs, 6 mobile libraries; Supervisor (Libraries) WENDY SMITH.

Norwich

Norfolk Library and Information Service: County Hall, Martineau Lane, Norwich, NR1 2UA; tel. (844) 800-8006; fax (1603) 222422; e-mail libraries@norfolk.gov.uk; internet www.norfolk.gov.uk; public; f. 1925, reorganized 1974; 1,153,295 vols; 47 libraries incl. Norfolk and Norwich Millennium Library, 14 mobiles, services to hospitals, prisons, residential settings, School Library Service, Home Library service; Dir of Cultural Services PAUL ADAMS.

Norwich Cathedral Library: 12 The Close, Norwich, NR1 4DH; tel. (1603) 218443; fax (1603) 766032; e-mail library@cathedral.org.uk; internet www.cathedral.org.uk/learning; medieval monastic (Benedictine) foundation; privately managed by Norwich Cathedral, for public use; 20,000 vols modern theology loan colln; 8,000 vols historic colln, some incunabula and MSS; houses 450 vols of the Swaffham Parochial Church Library and other parish books; Canon Librarian Dr P. DOLL; Librarian GUDRUN WARREN.

University of East Anglia Library: Norwich, NR4 7TJ; tel. (1603) 592425; fax (1603) 259490; e-mail library@uea.ac.uk; internet www.lib.uea.ac.uk; f. 1962; 725,000 vols; Dir of Library and Learning Resources JEAN STEWARD.

Nottingham

Nottingham City Libraries and Information Service: Central Library, Angel Row, Nottingham, NG1 6HP; tel. (115) 915-2828; fax (115) 915-2840; e-mail enquiryline@nottinghamcity.gov.uk; internet www.nottinghamcity.gov.uk/libraries; f. 1868; spec. collns incl. local history, D. H. Lawrence, Byron and Robin Hood; 480,000 vols, 33,000 sound recordings; Head of Service CHRISTINA DYER.

University of Nottingham Information Services: University Park, Nottingham, NG7 2RD; tel. (115) 951-4555; fax (115) 951-4558; internet www.nottingham.ac.uk/is; f. (University College) 1881; 1,000,000 vols and pamphlets, 5,450 current periodicals, 7,600 electronic journals; MSS and archives (Portland, Newcastle, Middleton, Manvers, etc.) 3m. items; spec. collns incl. D. H. Lawrence, early children's books, French Revolution, meteorology, ornithology; incl. Hallward Library (arts, social sciences and law), George Green Library of Science and Engineering, James Cameron Gifford Library of Agricultural and Food Sciences (Sutton Bonington), Greenfield Medical Library and Djanogly Learning Resources Centre (education, business and computer science); Chief Information Officer STEPHEN PINFIELD.

Oakham

Rutland Library Service: Oakham Library, Catmos St, Oakham, LE15 6HW; tel. (1572) 722918; fax (1572) 724906; e-mail libraries@rutland.gov.uk; internet www.rutland.gov.uk/libraries; f. 1997; 54,943 vols; Head of Culture and Leisure ROBERT CLAYTON; Prin. Librarian EMILY BARWELL.

Omagh

Western Education & Library Board: 1 Hospital Rd, Omagh, BT79 0AW; tel. (28) 8241-1411; fax (28) 8241-1400; e-mail info@welbni.org; internet www.welbni.org; provides library services in the council areas of Omagh, Fermanagh, Londonderry, Strabane and Limavady; Chair. Rev. R. HERRON; Vice-Chair. P. DUFFY; Chief Exec. B. MULHOLLAND.

Oxford

Bodleian Library: Oxford, OX1 3BG; tel. (1865) 277000; fax (1865) 277182; e-mail reader.services@bodleian.ox.ac.uk; internet www.bodleian.ox.ac.uk; f. 1602; legal deposit library; the principal library of Oxford Univ.; incl. the Old Library, the Radcliffe Camera, New Library and the following dependent libraries: Radcliffe Science Library, Hooke Library, Bodleian Law Library, Indian Institute Library, Bodleian Library for Commonwealth and African Studies (at Rhodes House), Vere Harmsworth Library (for the history of the United States), Bodleian Japanese Library, Philosophy Library, Oriental Institute Library and Institute for Chinese Studies Library; 9,000,000 vols; Librarian Dr SARAH E. THOMAS; publ. *The Bodleian Library Record* (2 a year).

Oxfordshire Libraries Headquarters: Customer Services Unit, Library Support Services, Holton, Oxford, OX33 1QQ; tel. (1865) 810240; e-mail librarycustomerservicesunit@oxfordshire.gov.uk; internet www.oxfordshire.gov.uk/libraries; 43 static libraries, 5 mobile libraries; 930,000 vols, 40,000 scores, 18,000 sound recordings, 38,000 DVDs; Library Service Man. JILLIAN SOUTHWELL; Prin. Librarian of Information Service KATHARINE SPACKMAN.

Sackler Library: St John St, Oxford, OX1 2LG; tel. (1865) 288190; fax (1865) 278098; e-mail enquiries@saclib.ox.ac.uk; internet www.saclib.ox.ac.uk; f. 2001, fmrly Ashmolean Library (since 1683); 270,000 vols; archaeology, ancient history and ancient Near Eastern studies, and Byzantine studies, numismatics, classical languages and literature, Western art and architecture. Special collections include Grenfell and Hunt Papyrological Library, Griffith Egyptological Library, Haverfield and Richmond Archives and original documentation of principal archaeological expeditions and explorations and classification of artefacts; Librarian-in-Charge Dr G. PIDDOCK.

Taylor Institution Library: Oxford Univ. Library Services, St Giles', Oxford, OX1 3NA; tel. (1865) 278158; fax (1865) 278165; e-mail enquiries@taylib.ox.ac.uk; internet www.taylib.ox.ac.uk; f. 1847; 600,000 vols; medieval and modern continental European (and related) languages and literature (esp. French, German, Italian, Spanish, Portuguese, incl. the languages and literature of Latin America, the literature of Canada, and North and sub-Saharan Africa); Dutch, Yiddish, Celtic, Afrikaans, Romanian; linguistics and philology; spec. collns incl.: Voltaire and the French Enlightenment; Dante and Futurist holdings; the G. B. Guarini colln; Golden Age literature; literature of the former German Democratic Republic; Luther *Flugschriften* and the Fiedler colln; letters and papers of Modern European writers; and the Strachan colln of *livres d'artistes*; Slavonic, East European and Modern Greek languages and literature housed separately at 47 Wellington Sq., Oxford, OX1 2JF; the Taylor Instn houses the Taylor Instn Modern Languages Faculty Library, as well as the Main Library; Librarian in Charge A. J. PETERS.

University of Oxford Libraries:.
Constituent Libraries:

Balliol College Library: Oxford, OX1 3BJ; tel. (1865) 277709; fax (1865) 277803; e-mail library@balliol.ox.ac.uk; internet www.balliol.ox.ac.uk; f. 1263; 120,000 vols; Librarian Dr P. A. BULLOCH.

Brasenose College Library: Oxford, OX1 4AJ; tel. (1865) 277827; e-mail library@bnc.ox.ac.uk; internet www.bnc.ox.ac.uk; f. 1509; 60,000 vols; Fellow Librarian Dr E. H. BISPHAM; College Librarian LIZ KAY.

Christ Church Library: Oxford, OX1 1DP; tel. (1865) 276169; e-mail library@chch.ox.ac.uk; internet www.chch.ox.ac.uk; f. 1546; 130,000 vols.

Codrington Library (All Souls College): Oxford, OX1 4AL; tel. (1865) 279318; fax (1865) 279299; e-mail codrington.library@all-souls.ox.ac.uk; internet www.all-souls.ox.ac.uk; f. 1710; 178,000 vols; spec. collns: medieval and modern history, military history, strategic studies and law; Librarian Prof. I. MACLEAN.

Corpus Christi College Library: Oxford, OX1 4JF; tel. (1865) 276744; fax (1865) 276767; e-mail library.staff@ccc.ox.ac.uk; internet www.ccc.ox.ac.uk/library-and-archives; f. 1517; 80,000 vols, MSS; spec. collns: incunabula, early English printed books, 17th- and 18th-century Italian books, English, French and German books on 19th-century philosophy; Fellow Librarian Dr. H. MOORE; Librarian JOANNA SNELLING.

Exeter College Library: Oxford, OX1 3DP; tel. (1865) 279600; fax (1865) 279630; e-mail library@exeter.ox.ac.uk; f. 1314; 41,000 vols on open shelves, 35,000 vols in spec. collns; Librarian J. BOWRING.

Green Templeton College Library: Oxford, OX2 6HG; tel. (1865) 274770; fax (1865) 274796; e-mail gill.edwards@gtc.ox.ac.uk; internet library.green.ox.ac.uk; f. 1979; 12,000 vols; Medicine and Social Science Librarian GILL EDWARDS; Business Studies Librarian DEBRA FARRELL.

Hertford College Library: Oxford, OX1 3BW; tel. (1865) 279409; e-mail susan.griffin@hertford.ox.ac.uk; internet www.hertford.ox.ac.uk; 50,000 vols; 17th-century colln from Magdalen Hall (forerunner of Hertford College); Fellow Librarian Dr T. C. BARNARD; Librarian S. M. GRIFFIN.

Jesus College Library: Oxford, OX1 3DW; tel. (1865) 279704; e-mail librarian@jesus.ox.ac.uk; internet www.jesus.ox.ac.uk/library; f. 1571; 65,000 vols, incl. periodicals; Celtic colln; Fellows' Library (f. 1571): 12,000 early printed books, 150 MSS; spec. collns: library of Lord Herbert of Cherbury, material relating to T. E. Lawrence (of Arabia); Meyricke Library (f. 1865): undergraduate library; college's archives are separately maintained; Fellow Librarian Prof. T. CHARLES-EDWARDS; College Librarian OWEN McKNIGHT; Archivist C. JEENS.

Keble College Library: Oxford, OX1 3PG; tel. (1865) 272797; e-mail library@keb.ox.ac.uk; f. 1876; 40,000 vols in working library; spec. collns: medieval MSS, incunabula and early printed books, Brooke colln, Millard colln, Hatchett-Jackson colln, Port-Royal, John Keble's own library, part of Henry Liddon's library, 19th-century archive material; Librarian M. M. SZURKO.

Lincoln College Library: Oxford, OX1 3DR; tel. (1865) 279831; e-mail library@lincoln.ox.ac.uk; f. 1427; 40,000 vols; Librarian F. M. PIDDOCK.

Magdalen College Library: Oxford, OX1 4AU; tel. (1865) 276045; fax (1865) 276057; e-mail library@magd.ox.ac.uk; internet www.magd.ox.ac.uk/college_life/libraries_and_archives.shtml; f. 1458; spec. collns: 16th- to 18th-century books, late medieval English history, late medieval MS books, early printed botanical books and medical books; 120,000 vols; Fellow Librarian Dr CHRISTINE Y. FERDINAND; Deputy Librarian HILARY PATTISON; Asst Librarian TABITHA TUCKETT.

Merton College Library: Oxford, OX1 4JD; tel. (1865) 276380; fax (1865) 276361; e-mail library@merton.ox.ac.uk; internet www.merton.ox.ac.uk/aboutmerton/library.shtml; f. 1264; 70,000 vols; Librarian Dr JULIA WALWORTH.

New College Library: Holywell St, Oxford, OX1 3BN; tel. (1865) 279580; fax (1865) 279590; e-mail naomi.vanloo@new.ox.ac.uk; internet www.new.ox.ac.uk/the_library; f. 1379; 100,000 vols; spec. collns: medieval MSS, incunabula, early archives, modern papers of Milner Colln (deposited in Bodleian Library); Librarian NAOMI VAN LOO; publ. *New College Notes*.

Nuffield College Library: Oxford, OX1 1NF; tel. (1865) 278550; fax (1865) 278621; e-mail librarian@nuffield.ox.ac.uk; internet www.nuffield.ox.ac.uk/library; f. 1937; postgraduate research library in the social sciences covering politics, int. relations, sociology and economics; spec. collns: modern political MSS, labour history, trade unions, political parties, William Cobbett, Daniel Defoe, William Morris, Lord Nuffield; 200,000 vols; Librarian ELIZABETH MARTIN.

Oriel College Library: Oxford, OX1 4EW; tel. (1865) 276558; e-mail library@oriel.ox.ac.uk; f. 1326; 100,000 vols; spec. colln of personages who attended Oriel College; Librarian MARJORY SZURKO.

Pembroke College, McGowin Library: Oxford, OX1 1DW; tel. (1865) 276409; fax (1865) 276418; e-mail library@pmb.ox.ac.uk; internet www.pmb.ox.ac.uk; f. 1624; 40,000 vols; Chandler colln of Aristotelia; Librarian LUCIE WALKER.

Queen's College Library: High St, Oxford, OX1 4AW; tel. (1865) 279130; fax (1865) 790819; e-mail library@queens.ox.ac.uk; internet www.queens.ox.ac.uk/library; f. 1341; 150,000 vols; Librarian A. J. SAVILLE.

St Edmund Hall Library: Queen's Lane, Oxford, OX1 4AR; tel. (1865) 279062; e-mail book.loans@seh.ox.ac.uk; internet www.seh.ox.ac.uk/index.cfm?do=library; f. 1970; 45,000 vols; spec. collns: Emden (naval and military history), Aularian (Hall members' publs), John Oldham, Thomas Hearne; Librarian BLANCA MARTIN.

St John's College Library: Oxford, OX1 3JP; tel. (1865) 277300; fax (1865) 277435; e-mail library@sjc.ox.ac.uk; internet www.sjc.ox.ac.uk/385/library-and-archives; f. c. 1598; 80,000 vols; spec. collns incl. 400 MSS (200 Medieval); 20,000 early printed books; archives of papers of Robert Graves, A.E. Housman & Spike Milligan; Librarian STEWART TILEY.

Trinity College Library: Oxford, OX1 3BH; tel. (1865) 279863; fax (1865) 279902; e-mail alison.felstead@trinity.ox.ac.uk; internet www.trinity.ox.ac.uk/college/library; Librarian ALISON FELSTEAD.

University College Library: Oxford, OX1 4BH; tel. (1865) 276621; fax (1865) 276987; e-mail library@university-college.ox.ac.uk; internet www.lib.ox.ac.uk/libraries/guides/uni.html; f. 1249; 50,000 vols; spec. collns, incl. the Attlee Papers, are deposited in the Bodleian Library (see above); Librarian C. M. RITCHIE.

Wadham College Library: Oxford, OX1 3PN; tel. (1865) 277914; e-mail library@wadh.ox.ac.uk; f. 1610; 55,000 vols; spec. collns: 16th-century theology, 17th-century science; Persian history and literature; Fellow Librarian Prof. R. W. FIDDIAN; Librarian TIM KIRTLEY.

Worcester College Library: Oxford, OX1 2HB; tel. (1865) 278354; fax (1865) 278387; internet www.worc.ox.ac.uk/library; f. 1714; 75,000 vols; spec. collns: Clarke Papers (Civil War and Commonwealth documents), architectural books and drawings (Inigo Jones, Hawksmoor), English poetry and drama from 1550–1750, Pottinger colln of 19th-century pamphlets, 17th- and 18th-century print colln; Librarian Dr JOANNA PARKER.

Paisley

Paisley Campus Library: High St, Paisley, PA1 2BE; tel. (141) 848-3758; fax (141) 848-3761; e-mail library@uws.ac.uk; internet www.uws.ac.uk/library; attached to Univ. of West of Scotland Library; 12,114 online journals; Univ. Librarian GORDON HUNT.

Renfrewshire Libraries: Abbey House, Paisley, Renfrewshire, PA1 1AJ; tel. (141) 840-3003; fax (141) 840-3004; e-mail libraries.els@renfrewshire.gov.uk; internet www.renfrewshire.gov.uk/libraries; 13 libraries, incl. Paisley Central Reference Library; toy library; 2 mobile libraries; 321,500 vols; 29,000 audiovisual items; Libraries Man. JENIFER McFARLANE (acting).

Peterborough

Peterborough Cathedral Library: c/o Chapter Office, Minster Precincts, Peterborough, PE1 1XS; tel. (1733) 562125; fax (1733) 552465; e-mail fiona.west@peterborough-cathedral.org.uk; f. c. 1670 by Dean Duport; 8,000 vols, some important medieval MSS and some early printed books (books and MSS printed before 1800 are now deposited in the Cambridge University Library, save those of local concern); Librarian Canon J. HIGHAM.

Peterborough City Libraries: Peterborough Central Library, Broadway, Peterborough, PE1 1RX; tel. (1733) 742700; fax (1733) 555277; e-mail libraryenquiries@peterborough.gov.uk; internet www.peterborough.gov.uk/page-37; f. 1892; 8 brs, 2 mobile libraries; Library Service Man. HEATHER WALTON.

Plymouth

City of Plymouth Libraries and Information Services: Central Library, Drake Circus, Plymouth, PL4 8AL; tel. (1752) 305923; fax (1752) 305929; e-mail library@plymouth.gov.uk; internet www.plymouth.gov.uk/libraries; 16 brs; City Librarian ALASDAIR MacNAUGHTAN.

Pontllanfraith

Caerphilly Library Service: Penallta House, Tredomen Park, Ystrad Mynach, Hengoed, CF82 7PG; tel. (1443) 864068; e-mail libraries@caerphilly.gov.uk; internet www.caerphilly.gov.uk; 19 brs, 1 mobile library; Sr Man. GARETH EVANS.

Pontypool

Torfaen Libraries: Torfaen Co Borough Ccl, Ty Blaen Torfaen, Panteg Way, New Inn, Pontypool Torfaen, NP4 0LS; tel. (1495) 628943; fax (1495) 766709; internet www.torfaen.gov.uk/leisureandculture/libraries/ home; 3 brs; 1 mobile service; 110,000 vols; Information Man. CHRISTINE GEORGE.

Poole

Borough of Poole Libraries: Poole Central Library, Dolphin Centre, Poole, BH15 1QE; tel. (1202) 262424; fax (1202) 262442; e-mail libraries@poole.gov.uk; internet www.boroughofpoole.com; public library service; 10 static libraries and 1 mobile library; 152,195 vols; Head of Service KEVIN McERLANE.

Port Talbot

Neath Port Talbot Library and Information Service: Reginald St, Velindre, Port Talbot, SA13 1YY; tel. (1639) 899829; fax (1639) 899152; e-mail npt.libhq@neath-porttalbot.gov.uk; internet www.neath-porttalbot.gov.uk; f. 1996; 17 brs, 2 mobile libraries; 391,000 vols; Co Librarian WAYNE JOHN.

Porth

Rhondda Cynon Taff County Borough Library Services: Ty Trevithick, Abercynon, Mountain Ash, CF45 4UQ; tel. (1443) 744029; fax (1443) 744023; internet www.rhondda-cynon-taff.gov.uk/libraries; 550,000 vols; 28 brs, 4 mobile libraries; Head of Libraries ROS WILLIAMS (acting).

Portsmouth

Portsmouth City Libraries: Central Library, Guildhall Square, Portsmouth, PO1 2DX; tel. (23) 9281-9311; fax (23) 9283-9855; e-mail library.admin@portsmouthcc.gov.uk; internet www.portsmouth.gov.uk/leisure/libraries; f. 1976; Library Services Man. COLIN BROWN (acting).

University of Portsmouth Library: Univ. of Portsmouth, Cambridge Rd, Portsmouth, PO1 2ST; tel. (23) 9284-3222; fax (23) 9284-3233; e-mail library@port.ac.uk; internet www.port.ac.uk/departments/studentsupport/library; 600,000 vols; Librarian ROISIN GWYER.

Preston

Lancashire County Library: Bowran St, Preston, PR1 2UX; tel. (1772) 534003; fax (1772) 534200; f. 1924; 3,018,000 vols; 84 brs, 12 mobile libraries, 2 trailer libraries; Admin. Officer LINDA WHITFIELD.

Reading

Reading Borough Libraries: Central Library, Abbey Sq., Reading, RG1 3BQ; tel. (118) 901-5950; e-mail info@readinglibraries.org.uk; internet www.readinglibraries.org.uk; f. 1883; 280,000 vols; 7 brs, 2 mobile libraries; Local Studies Library; Head of Cultural Services AMAR DAVE.

University of Reading Library: Whiteknights, POB 233, Reading, RG6 6AE; tel. (118) 378-8770; fax (118) 378-6636; e-mail library@reading.ac.uk; internet www.reading.ac.uk/library; f. 1892; 1.1m. catalogued items, 26,274 current periodical subscriptions, 24,000 e-periodicals; Univ. Museums and Spec. Collns Service, Redlands Rd, gives access to MLA Designated Collns of British Publishers' Archives and material by and about Samuel Beckett; also Overstone Library, Stenton Library on English history, Cole Library on early zoology, Finzi collns of music and English poetry, Turner Colln of French Revolution pamphlets, Stendhal Colln, agricultural history, children's books, papers of Lord and Lady Astor; Librarian JULIA MUNRO.

Rochester

Medway Council: Chatham Library, Gun Wharf, Dock Rd, Chatham, ME4 4TX; tel.

(1634) 337799; fax (1634) 337800; e-mail chatham.library@medway.gov.uk; internet www.medway.gov.uk/libraries; f. 1998; 16 brs, 2 mobile libraries, Medway Archives and Local Studies Centre; Head of Libraries SIMON SWIFT.

Runcorn

Halton Borough Libraries: Halton Borough Council, Municipal Building, Kingsway, Widnes, Cheshire, WA8 7QF; tel. (303) 333-4300; fax (1928) 790221; internet www2.halton.gov.uk; f. 1998; 4 brs, 1 mobile library; Head of Libraries PAULA RILEY-COOPER.

Ruthin

Denbighshire Library Service: Yr Hen Garchar, 46 Clwyd St, Ruthin, Denbighshire, LL15 1HP; tel. (1824) 708204; fax (1824) 708202; e-mail library.services@denbighshire.gov.uk; internet www.denbighshire.gov.uk; 8 libraries, 1 mobile library, 1 home library service; special collections: Welsh music, local history; 219,260 vols; Head of Libraries R. ARWYN JONES.

St Andrews

University of St Andrews Library: North St, St Andrews, KY16 9TR; tel. (1334) 462283; fax (1334) 462282; e-mail library@st-andrews.ac.uk; internet www.st-andrews.ac.uk/library; f. 1612; 1m. MSS, maps and numerous special collns, incl. Donaldson (Classics and Education), J. D. Forbes (Science), Von Hügel (Theology and Philosophy), 200,000 early and rare printed vols, MSS holdings and photographic colln, 33,900 e-journals; Univ. Librarian and Dir of Library Services JOHN MACCOLL.

Salford

HM Revenue and Customs Library: Ralli Quays, 3 Stanley St, Salford, M60 9LA; tel. (161) 827-0625; fax (161) 827-0491; f. 1991; also at Revenue and Customs Library; 5,000 vols; Chief Librarian LORNA BANKES.

University of Salford Information Services Division: Clifford Whitworth Bldg, Peel Park Campus, The Crescent, Salford, M5 4WT; tel. (161) 295-2444; fax (161) 295-5888; e-mail isd-servicedesk@salford.ac.uk; internet www.isl.salford.ac.uk; f. 1896; 675,000 items, 5,000 periodicals; Dir of Information Services TONY LEWIS.

Salisbury

Salisbury Cathedral Library: The Cathedral, Salisbury, SP1 2EN; f. 11th century; contains printed books and medieval MSS; open only to *bona fide* research students by appointment; an exhibition of books and documents incl. an original Magna Carta is on show in the Chapter House from March to December; Librarian SUZANNE EWARD.

Sheffield

Sheffield Hallam University Learning and Information Services: Adsetts Learning Centre, City Campus, Howard St, Sheffield, S1 1WB; tel. (114) 225-3333; fax (114) 225-3859; e-mail learning.centre@shu.ac.uk; internet www.shu.ac.uk/services/sls/learning; 550,000 vols, 16,000 subscribed journal titles, 38,000 e-journals; Dir NUALA DEVLIN.

Sheffield Libraries and Information Services: Central Library, Surrey St, Sheffield, S1 1XZ; tel. (114) 273-4712; fax (114) 273-5009; e-mail libraries@sheffield.gov.uk; internet www.sheffield.gov.uk; f. 1856; 28 community libraries, 1 mobile library; local spec. collns incl. 19th-century periodicals, botanical illustrations, climbing library, patents, standards and the World Metal Index; central library (incl. private press books, books printed in England 1765–79); business, science and technology standards, local studies, circulation services (incl. Whitworth Colln of organ books, Climbing colln, Alan Rowse colln), Sheffield Archives (incl. Strafford papers, Edmund Burke papers, Edward Carpenter papers, Fairbank map colln); 915,000 vols (excluding MSS); Head of Libraries, Archives and Information Services ANDREW MILROY (acting).

University of Sheffield Library: Western Bank, Sheffield, S10 2TN; tel. (114) 222-7200; fax (114) 222-7290; e-mail library@sheffield.ac.uk; internet www.shef.ac.uk/library; f. 1905; 1,400,000 vols; spec. collns: Sir Charles Firth's collection of 17th-century tracts and 19th-century broadside ballads, the Samuel Hartlib Papers, the papers of Sir Hans Krebs (FRS and Nobel Laureate), National Fairground Archive, Sir Thomas Beecham Music Library; Dir of Library Services and Univ. Librarian M. J. LEWIS.

Shrewsbury

Shropshire Libraries: Shirehall, Abbey Foregate, Shrewsbury, SY2 6ND; tel. (1743) 255000; fax (1743) 255050; e-mail libraries@shropshire.gov.uk; internet www.shropshire.gov.uk/library.nsf; f. 1925; 22 brs, 8 mobile libraries; 510,000 vols, audiovisual collns; Library Service Man. CLAIRE CARTLIDGE.

Slough

Slough Borough Council Libraries and Information Service: Slough Library, High St, Slough, SL1 1EA; tel. (1753) 535166; fax (1753) 825050; internet www.sloughlibrary.org.uk; 3 brs, 1 mobile library; Head of Libraries and Information YVONNE COPE.

Southampton

Southampton City Libraries: Central Library, Civic Centre, Southampton, SO14 7LW; tel. (23) 8091-7582; fax (23) 8033-6305; internet www.southampton.gov.uk/libraries; Libraries Man. DAVID BALDWIN; Central Librarian MARTIN PAVEY.

University of Southampton Library: Southampton, SO17 1BJ; tel. (23) 8059-2180; fax (23) 8059-3007; e-mail libenqs@soton.ac.uk; internet www.library.soton.ac.uk; f. 1862 as Hartley Institution; main and br. libraries; Health Services Library, Nat. Oceanographic Library, Winchester School of Art Library, Ford Colln of Parliamentary Papers (since 1801), Wellington Papers, Broadlands Archives (Palmerston, Shaftesbury, Mountbatten), Cope colln of Hampshire material, Perkins Agricultural Library, Parkes Library (relationship between Jewish and non-Jewish worlds), archive collns relating to Anglo-Jewry, Hampshire Field Club library; 2,400,000 vols, 22,000 current periodicals; Librarian Dr MARK BROWN; Deputy Librarian RICHARD WAKE.

Southend on Sea

Southend on Sea Borough Libraries Department: Southend Library, Victoria Ave, Southend on Sea, Essex, SS2 6EX; tel. (1702) 215011; fax (1702) 469241; e-mail library@southend.gov.uk; internet www.southend.gov.uk/libraries; 7 brs; Head of Service SIMON MAY.

Stafford

Staffordshire Library and Information Services: Tipping St, Stafford, ST16 2DH; tel. (1785) 278311; fax (1785) 278319; internet www.staffordshire.gov.uk; f. 1916; 1,067,000 vols, 38,000 CDs, 17,000 DVDs, 43 static libraries, 8 mobile libraries; Commissioner for Culture and Leisure JANENE COX; Libraries Man. CATHERINE MANN.

Stirling

Stirling Council Library Services: Borrowmeadow Rd, Stirling, FK7 7TN; tel. (1786) 432383; fax (1786) 432395; e-mail libraryheadquarters@stirling.gov.uk; internet www.stirling.gov.uk; 330,000 vols; Libraries and Archives Man. R. RUTHVEN.

University of Stirling Library: Stirling, FK9 4LA; tel. (1786) 467235; fax (1786) 466866; e-mail library@stir.ac.uk; internet www.is.stir.ac.uk; f. 1966; 450,000 vols, 4,000 periodicals; colln of works by Sir Walter Scott and contemporaries, John Grierson archive, Lindsay Anderson archive, Howietoun Fish Farm archive, labour history collection; facilities for online information retrieval; some spec. collns will be inaccessible due to redevelopment work between May 2009 and August 2010; Dir of Information Services MARK TOOLE.

Stockport

RNIB National Library Service: Far Cromwell Rd, Bredbury, Stockport, SK6 2SG; tel. (303) 123-9999; fax (161) 355-2098; e-mail library@rnib.org.uk; internet www.rnib.org.uk; f. 1882, present status 2008 by merger of the Nat. Library for the Blind and the Royal Nat. Institute of Blind People; 4,000,000 vols (incl. music, in Braille, giant print and audio incl. talking books); Head of Nat. Library Service HELEN BRAZIER; publs *New Books* (4 a year), *Read On* (2 a year).

Stoke on Trent

Staffordshire University Library: POB 664, College Rd, Stoke on Trent, ST4 2XS; tel. (1782) 294443; fax (1782) 295799; 300,000 vols; Librarian LIZ HART.

Stoke on Trent City Council Libraries and Archives: City Central Library, Bethesda St, Hanley, Stoke on Trent, ST1 3RS; tel. (1782) 238455; fax (1782) 238499; e-mail libraries.support@stoke.gov.uk; internet www.stoke.gov.uk/libraries; 352,000 vols; Solon ceramics colln; Strategic Man. JANET THURSFIELD; City Archivist CHRIS LATIMER.

Stratford upon Avon

Shakespeare Centre Library and Archive, Shakespeare Birthplace Trust: Henley St, Stratford upon Avon, CV37 6QW; tel. (1789) 204016; fax (1789) 296083; e-mail scla@shakespeare.org.uk; internet www.shakespeare.org.uk; f. 1864; Shakespeare Birthplace Trust (the Shakespeare collns-all aspects of Shakespeare's life, work and times; the local collns-history of Stratford-upon-Avon and surrounding area) and the Royal Shakespeare Company Archive (incl. its admin. and production archives, prompt books, photographs, programmes, press clippings, playbills and ephemera); 55,000 vols; Head of Collns Devt DELIA GARRATT; Collns Man. PAUL WEBB.

Swansea

City and County of Swansea Library and Information Service: Central Library, Civic Centre, Oystermouth Rd, Swansea, SA1 3SN; tel. (1792) 636464; fax (1792) 636235; e-mail libraryline@swansea.gov.uk; internet www.swansea.gov.uk/libraries; spec. collns: Dylan Thomas, Welsh and Local History; 986,546 vols; Head of Libraries STEVE HARDMAN.

Swansea University Library: Singleton Park, Swansea, SA2 8PP; tel. (1792) 295697; fax (1792) 295851; e-mail library@swansea.ac.uk; internet www.swan.ac.uk/lis/

index.asp; f. 1920; 800,000 vols; Dir of Information Services and Systems KEVIN DANIEL.

Swindon

Swindon Borough Libraries: Central Library, Regent Circus, Swindon, SN1 1QG; tel. (1793) 463238; e-mail central.library@ swindon.gov.uk; internet www.swindon.gov.uk/libraries; f. 1943; Librarian ROGER TRAY-HURN; Libraries Services Manager ALLYSON JORDAN; publs *Swindon Evening Advertiser*, *The Times (London)* and *Times Digitial*.

Telford

Telford and Wrekin Libraries: Telford Town Centre Library, St Quentin Gate, Telford, TF3 4JG; tel. (1952) 292151; fax (1952) 292078; e-mail telfordlibrary@hotmail.com; internet twlibraries.enta.net; 9 brs, 1 mobile library; Libraries and Heritage Services Man. PAT DAVIS.

Torquay

Torbay Libraries: Torquay Library, Lymington Rd, Torquay, TQ1 3DT; tel. (1803) 208300; fax (1803) 208311; e-mail libraries@torbay.gov.uk; internet www.torbay.gov.uk/libraries; f. 1907; 4 brs, 1 mobile library; local studies colln; 190,955 vols; Exec. Head of Residents and Visitors Services SUE CHERITON.

Trowbridge

Wiltshire Libraries and Heritage and Arts: Bythesea Rd, Trowbridge, BA14 8BS; tel. (300) 456-0100; fax (1225) 713993; internet www.wiltshire.gov.uk; f. 1919; 869,000 vols, cassettes, compact discs, video cassettes, etc.; 31 brs, 4 mobile libraries; special collections: Wiltshire, agriculture, life of Christ, anthropology and sociology of the family; public and private archives for Wiltshire and the Diocese of Salisbury; Assistant Dir, Libraries and Heritage PAULINE PALMER.

Truro

Cornwall Library Service: Unit 17, Threemilestone, Truro, Cornwall, TR4 9LD; tel. (1872) 324676; fax (1872) 223509; e-mail library@cornwall.gov.uk; internet www.cornwall.gov.uk/library; f. 1925; 835,000 vols; 29 brs; Asst Head of Shared Services ANNE MCSEVENEY.

Warrington

Warrington Borough Libraries: Warrington Library, Museum St, Warrington, WA1 1JB; tel. (1925) 442890; fax (1925) 411395; e-mail library@warrington.gov.uk; internet www.warrington.gov.uk/libraries; f. 1848; 11 brs; Head of Culture, Libraries and Heritage MARTIN GAW.

Warwick

Warwickshire Library and Information Service: Barrack St, Warwick, CV34 4TH; tel. (1926) 412657; fax (1926) 412471; e-mail librarieslearningandculture@warwickshire.gov.uk; internet www.warwickshire.gov.uk/libraries; f. 1920; 1,105,000 vols; 34 libraries; 5 mobile and community libraries; spec. collns: Warwickshire Colln, George Eliot Colln; Head of Libraries and Culture SIMON ROBSON; Head of Communities and Wellbeing RON WILLIAMSON.

West Bretton

National Arts Education Archive, Lawrence Batley Centre for: University of Leeds, Special Collections, Bretton Hall Campus, West Bretton, WF4 4LG; tel. (1924) 832020; fax (1924) 832077; e-mail s.kielty@leeds.ac.uk; internet naea.leeds.ac.uk; f. 1985; to establish an illustrated 'trace' of work in art and design education 1880 to date, to make this available to scholars and the general public, and to promote academic research and more informed teaching through its use; colln of works of art illustrating the development of the Child Art and Basic Design movements in art education; includes many thousands of original papers, letters, slides, films, video cassettes, tapes and books; Senior Library Asst SONJA KIELTY.

Winchester

Hampshire Library and Information Service: 5/6 Moorside Place, Moorside Rd, Winchester, SO23 7FZ; tel. (1962) 826600; fax (1962) 856615; e-mail library@hants.gov.uk; internet www3.hants.gov.uk/library/library-finder.htm; f. 1974; 2,840,000 vols; 53 brs; 9 mobile libraries; Head of Operations ALEC KENNEDY.

Worcester

Worcestershire Libraries and Learning Service: Culture and Community Services, Worcestershire County Council, County Hall, Spetchley Rd, Worcester, WR5 2NP; tel. (1905) 822819; fax (1905) 766930; e-mail librarieshq@worcestershire.gov.uk; internet www.worcestershire.gov.uk/libraries; f. 1998; 21 library brs, 5 mobile libraries; Strategic Libraries and Learning Man. KATHY KIRK.

Wrexham

Wrexham County Borough Council, Library and Information Service: 16 Lord St, Wrexham, LL11 1LG; tel. (1978) 298855; fax (1978) 292611; e-mail library@wrexham.gov.uk; internet www.wrexham.gov.uk/libraries; 12 libraries, 1 mobile library, 1 library for the housebound; special collns: business information centre, Europe Direct, BFI Mediatheque; 220,552 vols; Libraries Officer DYLAN HUGHES.

York

City of York Libraries: York Central Library, Museum St, York, YO1 7DS; tel. (1904) 655631; fax (1904) 552835; internet www.york.gov.uk/libraries; f. 1893; Head of Library Service FIONA WILLIAMS.

University of York Library and Archives: Heslington, York, YO10 5DD; tel. (1904) 433873; fax (1904) 433866; e-mail lib-enquiry@york.ac.uk; internet www.york.ac.uk/library; f. 1963; 1,000,000 vols; Dir STEPHEN TOWN.

York Minster Library: The Old Palace, Dean's Park, York, YO1 7JQ; fax (1904) 611119; e-mail library@yorkminster.org; internet www.yorkminster.org/learning/the-historic-collections/library; f. 7th–8th century; 125,000 vols, 115 incunabula, 101 medieval MSS, 200 music MSS; spec. collns incl. Civil War Tracts and Yorkshire local history (120,000 vols); Librarian SARAH GRIFFIN; Archivist PETER YOUNG.

Museums and Art Galleries

Aberdeen

Aberdeen Art Gallery and Museums: Schoolhill, Aberdeen, AB10 1FQ; tel. (1224) 523700; fax (1224) 632133; e-mail info@aagm.co.uk; internet www.aberdeencity.gov.uk; Art Gallery and Museums Man. CHRISTINE REW.

Selected Museums and Galleries:

Aberdeen Art Gallery: Schoolhill, Aberdeen, AB10 1FQ; tel. (1224) 523700; fax (1224) 632133; e-mail info@aagm.co.uk; internet www.aberdeencity.gov.uk; f. 1885; fine and decorative arts; major collns of British art since the 18th century; Art Gallery and Museums Man. CHRISTINE REW.

Aberdeen Maritime Museum: Shiprow, Aberdeen, AB11 5BY; tel. (1224) 337700; fax (1224) 213066; e-mail info@aagm.co.uk; internet www.aagm.co.uk; f. 1984; displays covering all aspects of Aberdeen and the North East of Scotland's maritime heritage; Lead Curator JUDITH STONES.

Alloway

Burns Cottage and Museum: Murdoch's Lone, Alloway, Ayr, Ayrshire, KA7 4PQ; tel. (1292) 443700; fax (1292) 441750; e-mail burns@nts.org.uk; internet www.burnsheritagepark.com; f. 1881; birthplace of the poet Robert Burns; MSS and correspondence; Visitor Services Supervisor JOHN MANSON.

Anstruther

Scottish Fisheries Museum: St Ayles, Harbourhead, Anstruther, KY10 3AB; tel. (1333) 310628; e-mail enquiries@scotfishmuseum.org; internet www.scotfishmuseum.org; f. 1969; visual historical record of every aspect of the Scottish fishing industry from prehistoric times to the present; touring boat; library: reference library and archive of 1,000 vols (open by appointment); photographic archive; Dir TOM SUNTER.

Bangor

Gwynedd Museum and Art Gallery, Bangor: Ffordd Gwynedd, Bangor, LL57 1DT; tel. (1248) 353368; fax (1248) 370149; e-mail gwyneddmuseum@gwynedd.gov.uk; internet www.gwynedd.gov.uk/museums; f. 1884; artefacts relating to social history of North Wales, incl. archaeology, furniture, costume and Welsh textiles, domestic items; exhibitions incl. painting, photography and sculpture by local and int. artists; Curator ESTHER ROBERTS.

Barnard Castle

Bowes Museum: Barnard Castle, DL12 8NP; tel. (1833) 690606; fax (1833) 637163; e-mail info@thebowesmuseum.org.uk; internet www.thebowesmuseum.org.uk; f. 1892; collns formed 1862–75 by John and Joséphine Bowes, mainly of all forms of European fine and decorative art, incl. works by Goya, El Greco and Canaletto; ceramics, furniture and textiles; ongoing programme of exhibitions; education work; Dir ADRIAN JENKINS.

Bath

American Museum in Britain: Claverton Manor, Bath, BA2 7BD; tel. (1225) 460503; fax (1225) 469160; e-mail info@americanmuseum.org; internet www.americanmuseum.org; f. 1961; illustrates the devt of American decorative arts from the 17th to the 19th century; textile colln; printed maps from the 15th and 16th centuries; Native American colln; library: reference library of 10,500 vols; Dir Dr RICHARD WENDORF; Curator LAURA BERESFORD; publ. *America in Britain* (1 a year).

Holburne Museum of Art: Great Pulteney St, Bath, BA2 4DB; tel. (1225) 466669; e-mail holburne@bath.ac.uk; internet www.bath.ac.uk/holburne; f. 1893; paintings, silver, sculpture, porcelain and furniture in an 18th-century building; Dir ALEXANDER STURGIS.

Beamish

Beamish Museum: Beamish, Co. Durham, DH9 0RG; tel. (191) 370-4000; fax (191) 370-4001; e-mail museum@beamish.org.uk; internet www.beamish.org.uk; f. 1970 to study, collect, preserve and exhibit buildings, machinery, objects and information illustrating the devt of industry, social history, agriculture and way of life in the N of England; the museum covers more than 300 acres and includes a colliery village, railway station, a working farm and The Town of around 1913; Pockerley Manor and horse yard illustrate yeoman farming lifestyle in early 19th century; working replica of George Stephenson's *Locomotion No. 1* railway engine, and *Steam Elephant* of 1815; library of 20,000 vols, 10,000 trade catalogues; photographic archive containing 250,000 photographs; oral history colln with 800 tape recordings; Dir (vacant).

Beaulieu

National Motor Museum: Beaulieu, Brockenhurst, SO42 7ZN; tel. (1590) 612345; fax (1590) 612624; e-mail nmmt@beaulieu.co.uk; internet www.nationalmotormuseum.org.uk; f. 1972; houses designated collns of 270 vehicles, 43,000 motor objects, motoring reference, film and video library; Caravan Club Colln; Shell Art Colln; library: reference library, film library, photograph library; CEO RUSSELL BOWMAN.

Belfast

National Museums Northern Ireland: Cultra, Holywood, BT18 0EU; tel. (845) 608-0000; fax (28) 9042-8728; e-mail info@nmni .com; internet www.nmni.com; Chair. DAN HARVEY; Vice-Chair. TOM SHAW; Chief Exec. TIM COOKE.
Constituent Museums:

Armagh County Museum: The Mall East, Armagh, BT61 9BE; tel. (28) 3752-3070; e-mail acm@nmni.com; internet www.nmni.com; f. 1935; collns in archaeology, art, domestic life, history, natural world, transport, textiles and costumes, social life and traditions; library: extensive reference library; Curator Dr GREER RAMSEY; Learning and Outreach Officer RACHEL MCCANCE.

Ulster American Folk Museum: 2 Mellon Rd, Castletown, Omagh, BT78 5QU; tel. (28) 8224-3292; internet www.folkpark .com; f. 1976; open-air museum illustrating history of emigration from Ulster to the USA during the 18th and 19th centuries; reconstructions of bldgs and activities; full-size reconstruction of 19th-century sailing ship; Curator Dr PHILIP MOUNT.

Ulster Folk and Transport Museum: Cultra, Holywood, BT18 0EU; tel. (28) 9042-8428; internet www.uftm.org.uk; f. 1964; nat. museum comprising open-air museum with authentic bldgs illustrating Ulster folk life, both rural and urban; separate transport museum; library of 18,000 vols; Chair. of Bd of Trustees M. ELLIOTT; Divisional Head JONATHAN BELL; publ. *Ulster Folklife* (1 a year).

Ulster Museum: Botanic Gardens, Belfast, BT9 5AB; tel. (845) 608-0000; internet www.ulstermuseum.org.uk; f. 1833; fine and applied arts, archaeology, ethnography, history, botany, geology, zoology; Chief Exec. TIM COOKE.

Birmingham

Birmingham Museums and Art Gallery: Chamberlain Sq., Birmingham, B3 3DH; tel. (121) 303-2834; fax (121) 303-1394; e-mail bmag_enquiries@birmingham.gov.uk; internet www.bmag.org.uk; f. 1867; Departments of Fine and Applied Art (foreign schools from Renaissance, English from the 17th century, early English watercolours and Pre-Raphaelite paintings and drawings, modern art, sculpture, silver, metalwork, costume, glass,

stained glass, ceramics and textile collections); Staffordshire Hoard, Archaeology, Ethnography and Local History (collections from Ancient Egypt, Ur, Nineveh, Jericho, Nimrud, Vinca, Jerusalem, Petra, Vounos (Cyprus), Mexico and Peru, Prehistoric, Roman and British Medieval antiquities, British 20th century); Pacific ethnography collection; British coin collection; restricted access to comprehensive collections of minerals, gemstones and molluscs, British birds, lepidoptera and coleoptera; Midlands flora; prints (access by appointment only); br. museums incl. Aston Hall, Blakesley Hall, Weoley Castle, Sarehole Mill, Soho House, Museum of the Jewellery Quarter; picture library; Head RITA MCLEAN; Head, Museum Operations SIMON CANE.

Thinktank, Birmingham Museum: Millennium Point, Curzon St, Birmingham, B4 7XG; tel. (121) 202-2222; e-mail findout@ thinktank.ac; internet www.thinktank.ac; consists of 10 galleries of interactive exhibits on science, technology, medicine, natural and local history; also planetarium; Chief Exec. NICK WINTERBOTHAM.

Bishop's Stortford

Bishop's Stortford Museum: South Rd, Bishop's Stortford, CM23 3JG; tel. (1279) 651746; fax (1279) 467171; e-mail museum@ rhodesbishopsstortford.org.uk; internet www .rhodesbishopsstortford.org.uk; f. 1938 as the Rhodes Memorial Museum, present name 2005; exhibits relating to the life and times of colonialist Cecil Rhodes (1853–1902); African art and culture; also incorporates local history museum; Curator SARAH TURNER.

Blackburn

Blackburn Museum and Art Gallery: Museum St, Blackburn, Lancs., BB1 7AJ; tel. (1254) 667130; fax (1254) 685541; e-mail info@blackburn.gov.uk; f. 1874; local history, Indian and Pakistani textiles and jewellery, military history, icons, coins, books, MSS, early printed books, fine and decorative arts, Japanese prints.

Bradford

National Media Museum: Bradford, West Yorks., BD1 1NQ; tel. (870) 701-0200; fax (1274) 723155; e-mail talk@ nationalmediamuseum.org.uk; internet www .nationalmediamuseum.org.uk; f. 1983 as part of the National Museum of Science and Industry; explores the history, art and science of photography, film and television, with interactive exhibits; photographic colln incorporates the Kodak Museum colln and colln of the Royal Photographic Society; cinematography colln focuses on film-making; also exhibits of books, posters, designs and ephemera; the Museum houses an IMAX projection system, with cinema screen and a Cinerama cinema; library: access to the Kraszna-Krausz personal library and to other relevant books, MSS and periodicals; Head COLIN PHILPOTT.

Brighton

Booth Museum of Natural History: 194 Dyke Rd, Brighton, BN1 5AA; tel. (1273) 292777; fax (1273) 292778; e-mail boothmuseum@brighton-hove.gov.uk; internet www.brighton-hove-rpml.org.uk/ museums/boothmuseum/pages; f. 1874; displays of British birds in recreated natural settings, and galleries of butterflies from all over the world and geology and vertebrate evolution; reference collections of eggs, insects, minerals, palaeontology, osteology, skins and herbaria; library of 15,000 vols; Keeper of Natural Sciences (vacant); Curator of Natural Sciences LEE ISMAIL.

Brighton Museum and Art Gallery: Royal Pavilion Gardens, Brighton, East Sussex, BN1 1EE; tel. (1273) 290900; fax (1273) 292871; e-mail museums@brighton-hove.gov .uk; internet www.brighton.virtualmuseum .info; f. 1873; collection of paintings since the 15th century, drawings and prints; English pottery and porcelain, including the Willett Collection; decorative art and furniture of Art Nouveau and Art Deco periods; fashion gallery; ethnography; local history; Assistant Dir of Heritage PAULINE SCOTT-GARRETT.

Royal Pavilion: Brighton, E Sussex, BN1 1EE; tel. (3000) 290900; fax (1273) 292871; e-mail visitor.services@brighton-hove.gov .uk; internet www.royalpavilion.org.uk; f. 1851; Regency seaside palace of King George IV with Mughal-style exterior and Chinese-style interiors; audioguides in English, French, German, Spanish, Italian, Cantonese, Mandarin; Head of Museums and Royal Pavilion JANITA BAGSHAWE.

Bristol

Bristol City Museums and Art Gallery: Queen's Rd, Bristol, BS8 1RL; tel. (117) 922-3571; fax (117) 922-2047; e-mail general_museum@bristol-city.gov.uk; internet www.bristol-city.gov.uk/museums; galleries incl. Old Masters, French School, British collection, Modern Art and Bristol School; decorative arts collection incl. Eastern Art, ceramics, silverware and glassware; minerals, fossils and natural history collections; archaeological collection; also 16th-century Red Lodge (Park Row), Georgian House (Gt George St), Blaise Castle House Museum (Henbury), Bristol Industrial Museum (Princes Wharf); Kingsweston Roman Villa; Dir KATE BRINDLEY; publ. *Events* (3 a year).

British Empire and Commonwealth Museum: Clock Tower Yard, Temple Meads, Bristol, BS1 6QH; tel. (117) 925-4980; fax (117) 954-4849; e-mail admin@ empiremuseum.co.uk; internet www .empiremuseum.co.uk; f. 2002; charts the history of the British empire and examines its legacy in contemporary Britain; holds over 1m. items incl. documents, photographs, film, paintings, prints, costumes, textiles, domestic and personal artefacts, books, music and an extensive oral history archive; Bristol site closed in 2008 to relocate to new premises in London in 2012; Dir Dr GARETH GRIFFITHS.

Burnley

Towneley Hall Art Gallery and Museums: Towneley Hall, Towneley Park, Burnley, BB11 3RQ; tel. (1282) 424213; fax (1282) 436138; e-mail towneleyhall@burnley .gov.uk; internet www.towneleyhall.org.uk; f. 1902; collections incl. natural history, Egyptology, local history, textiles, decorative art and furniture; art collection focuses on 19th-century British artists; Curator MIKE TAREND.

Cambridge

Fitzwilliam Museum: Trumpington St, Cambridge, CB2 1RB; tel. (1223) 332900; fax (1223) 332923; e-mail fitzmuseum-enquiries@lists.cam.ac.uk; internet www.fitzmuseum.cam.ac.uk; f. 1816; art collns of the Univ. of Cambridge; paintings, drawings, prints, sculpture; rare coins and medals; ceramics, glass, textiles, arms and armour, and other applied arts; Greek, Roman, Cypriot, western Asiatic and Egyptian antiquities; library of 250,000 vols and medieval, literary and music MSS, autograph letters, early printed books, illuminated medieval books of hours, autograph letters, printed music, books on history of art; Assis. Dir KATE CARRENO; publ. *Biennial Review*.

University Museum of Archaeology and Anthropology: Downing St, Cambridge, CB2 3DZ; tel. (1223) 333516; fax (1233) 333517; e-mail admin@maa.cam.ac.uk; internet maa.cam.ac.uk; f. 1884; anthropology and prehistoric archaeology of all parts of the world; also local archaeology of all periods; Dir and Curator Prof. N. J. THOMAS.

University Museum of Zoology: Downing St, Cambridge, CB2 3EJ; tel. (1223) 336650; fax (1223) 336679; e-mail umzc@zoo.cam.ac .uk; internet www.museum.zoo.cam.ac.uk; f. 1815; collns of recent and fossil zoological species; Collns Man. MATHEW LOWE.

Cardiff

Amgueddfa Cymru/National Museum Wales: Cathays Park, Cardiff, CF10 3NP; tel. (29) 2057-3951; fax (29) 2057-3321; internet www.museumwales.ac.uk; f. 1907; Pres. PAUL LOVELUCK; Dir-Gen. DAVID ANDERSON.

Associated Museums:

Big Pit: National Coal Museum: Blaenafon, Torfaen, NP4 9XP; tel. (1495) 790311; internet www.museumwales.ac .uk/en/bigpit; f. 1980; working coal mine and exhibits relating to Welsh mining history; Man. PETER WALKER.

National Museum Cardiff: Cathays Park, Cardiff, CF10 3NP; tel. (29) 2039-7951; internet www.museumwales.ac.uk/en/cardiff; f. 1907; houses the Welsh nat. colln of fine and applied art; also archaeological, numismatic, natural history and geological collns; library of 2,000,000 vols; also print and drawings study room open by appointment; Dir MICHAEL TOOBY.

National Roman Legion Museum: High St, Caerleon, NP18 1AE; tel. (1633) 423134; internet www.museumwales.ac .uk/en/roman; f. 1850; fmr Roman fortress, comprising ruins and relevant exhibits; open by appointment; Man. DAI PRICE.

National Slate Museum: Llanberis, Gwynedd, LL55 4TY; tel. (1286) 870630; fax (1286) 871906; internet www .museumwales.ac.uk/en/slate; f. 1972; machinery, relics and bldgs relating to the Wales slate industry; library: open by appointment; Keeper DAFYDD ROBERTS.

National Waterfront Museum: Oystermouth Rd, Maritime Quarter, Swansea, SA1 3RD; tel. (1792) 638950; fax (1792) 638956; e-mail waterfront@museumwales .ac.uk; internet www.museumwales.ac.uk/en/swansea; 15 themed display areas on the effect of the Industrial Revolution on Welsh life.

National Wool Museum: Dre-fach Felindre, near Newcastle Emlyn, Llandysul, Sir Gaerfyrddin, Carmarthenshire, SA44 5UP; tel. (1559) 370929; fax (1559) 370929; e-mail gwlan@amgueddfacymru .ac.uk; internet www.amgueddfacymru.ac .uk; f. 1976; displays of bldgs and artefacts relating to the Welsh woollen industry, incl. working historic textile machinery and textile gallery; Man. ANN WHITTALL.

St Fagans: National History Museum: St Fagans, Cardiff, CF5 6XB; tel. (29) 2057-3500; internet www.museumwales .ac.uk/en/stfagans; f. 1948; museum of Welsh social history, with over 40 original bldgs re-erected on site; library: library open by appointment; Dir BETHAN LEWIS.

Turner House Gallery: Plymouth Rd, Penarth, CF64 3DM; tel. (29) 2070-8870; e-mail post@nmgw.ac.uk; internet www .nmgw.ac.uk; f. 1921; art gallery; Dir MICHAEL TOOBY.

Carmarthen

Carmarthenshire County Museum: Abergwili, Carmarthen, SA31 2JG; tel. (1267) 228696; fax (1267) 223830; e-mail museums@carmarthenshire.gov.uk; internet www.carmarthenshire.gov.uk; f. 1978; local authority museum; geology, archaeology, social history, folk life, furniture, ceramics, art, costume; County Museums Man. A. DORSETT.

Chawton

Jane Austen's House: Chawton, Alton, Hampshire; tel. (1420) 83262; e-mail enquiries@jane-austens-house-museum.org .uk; internet www .jane-austens-house-museum.org.uk; f. 1949; portraits, documents, furniture and objects relating to Jane Austen and her family; Dir T. F. CARPENTER.

Cirencester

Corinium Museum: Park St, Cirencester, GL7 2BX; tel. (1285) 655611; e-mail coriniummuseum@cotswold.gov.uk; internet www.cotswold.gov.uk/go/museum; important colln of Roman material; mosaic pavements, sculpture, military and civil tombstones, household domestic utensils, personal ornaments, and Samian and coarse pottery, all giving ample evidence of the importance and wealth of Corinium, which was the second largest town in Roman Britain; regional museum for the Cotswolds; Museums Service Man. AMANDA HART.

Colchester

Colchester Museums: Museum Resource Centre, 14 Ryegate Rd, Colchester, Essex, CO1 1YG; tel. (1206) 282931; fax (1206) 282925; internet www.colchestermuseums .org.uk; f. 1860 from the collections of Essex Archaeological Society; local human and natural history; large collns in the Norman Castle, with extensive Roman section; 3 br. museums (covering Natural History, social history, Colchester Clocks); Head of Museums PETER BERRIDGE.

Devizes

Wiltshire Heritage Museum: 41 Long St, Devizes, SN10 1NS; tel. (1380) 727369; fax (1380) 722150; e-mail wanhs@ wiltshireheritage.org.uk; internet wiltshireheritage.org.uk; f. 1853; collects and preserves history of the county; archaeological and historical collns from Wiltshire, incl. Stonehenge, with emphasis on Bronze Age period; Wiltshire art colln; archives relating to Wiltshire; library of 8,000 vols; Chair. Dr NEGLEY HARTE; Dir DAVID DAWSON; Curator LISA BROWN; publ. *Wiltshire Archaeological and Natural History Magazine* (1 a year).

Doncaster

Doncaster Museum and Art Gallery: Chequer Rd, Doncaster, DN1 2AE; tel. (1302) 734293; fax (1302) 735409; e-mail museum@doncaster.gov.uk; internet www .doncaster.gov.uk/museums; f. 1909; regional natural history, geology, archaeology and local history collns; permanent art colln, paintings, ceramics and glass; Regimental colln of the King's Own Yorkshire Light Infantry; Man. C. DALTON; Assist Man. J. ADAMS.

Dorchester

Dorset County Museum and Dorset Natural History and Archaeological Society: High West St, Dorchester, Dorset, DT1 1XA; tel. (1305) 262735; fax (1305) 257180; e-mail dorsetcountymuseum@dor-mus .demon.co.uk; internet www .dorsetcountymuseum.org; f. 1846 (Museum), merged with Society (f. 1875) in 1928; natural history, palaeontology, archaeology, fine arts, geology, literature (incl. Thomas Hardy), and the local history of Dorset; lectures, conferences and seminars are held in the Museum during the first half of the calendar year; Pres. CAROLINE MONTAGU, COUNTESS OF SANDWICH; Dir of the Museum and Sec. to the Society JUDY LINDSAY; publ. *The Proceedings of the Dorset Natural History and Archaeological Society* (1 a year).

Dumfries

Dumfries Museums: The Observatory, Rotchell Rd, Dumfries, DG2 7SW; tel. (1387) 253374; fax (1387) 265081; e-mail dumfriesmuseum@dumgal.gov.uk; internet www.dumgal.gov.uk/museums; f. 1836 as an observatory and Camera Obscura; building erected as a windmill c. 1790; exhibits Roman relics, Stone and Bronze Age artefacts, natural and local history from Dumfries and Galloway; incorporates Dumfries Museum, Thornhill Museum, Langholm Museum and Myrseth Museum collns; MSS concerning Carlyle and Barrie; Camera Obscura; period rooms at Old Bridge House (1660) nearby; Robert Burns Centre in Dumfries Town Mill (1781): exhibitions on Burns and his life in South West Scotland; Burns House: period house occupied by Burns 1793–96 and where he died: exhibits incl. MSS, first editions, personal belongings; Sanquhar Museum in Adam-designed Town House (1735) covers local history and geology; Museum Officer SIOBHAN RATCHFORD.

Dundee

Leisure & Culture Dundee: McManus: Dundee's Art Gallery & Museum Albert Sq., Meadowside, Dundee, DD1 1DA; tel. (1382) 307200; fax (1382) 307207; e-mail themcmanus@leisureandculturedundee.com; internet www.leisureandculturedundee.com; f. 1873; operates 4 heritage sites open to the public: McManus: Dundee's Art Gallery & Museum (Victorian Scottish paintings, contemporary art and photography, decorative arts, local history displays from time of earliest settlers to modern era, costume gallery, natural history); Broughty Castle Museum (history of Broughty Ferry, natural history of the seashore, paintings from the Orchar Colln), Mills Observatory (10-inch Victorian telescope, modern 12-inch reflecting telescope with 'go to' technology, displays on the solar system and space exploration, displays of historic equipment and information of local importance; planetarium), McManus Collns Unit (city's History, Archaeology and Natural History Collns); Cultural Services Man. BILLY GARTLEY.

Durham

Durham University, Oriental Museum: Elvet Hill, off South Rd, Durham, DH1 3TH; tel. and fax (191) 334-5694; e-mail oriental .museum@durham.ac.uk; internet www.dur .ac.uk/oriental.museum; f. 1960; Duke of Northumberland's colln of Egyptian antiquities; MacDonald colln of Chinese ceramics; Charles Hardinge colln of Chinese jades; Henry de Laszlo colln of Chinese art and other examples of oriental art and archaeology covering Ancient Egypt and the Near East, the Indian subcontinent, Japan and SE Asia; Curator Dr CRAIG P. BARCLAY.

Killhope, the North of England Lead Mining Museum: nr Cowshill, Upper Weardale, Co. Durham, DL13 1AR; tel. (1388) 537505; fax (1388) 537617; e-mail info@ killhope.org.uk; internet www.killhope.org

.uk; f. 1984 as Killhope Lead Mining Centre; present name 2000; fully restored 19th-century lead mine; Man. IAN FORBES.

Edinburgh

Edinburgh City Museums and Art Galleries: City Art Centre, 2 Market St, Edinburgh, EH1 1DE; tel. (131) 529-2427; fax (131) 529-3977; e-mail museumsandgalleries@edinburgh.gov.uk; comprise Museum of Edinburgh, 142 Canongate (local history), People's Story, Canongate Tolbooth, 163 Canongate (life and work of Edinburgh's people), Museum of Childhood, 42 High St, Writers' Museum, Lawnmarket (collection of Scott, Burns and Stevenson), City Art Centre (museum headquarters), Market St (temporary exhibitions and artists since the 19th century), Lauriston Castle, Cramond Rd South (furniture collection in Edwardian interior), Queensferry Museum, South Queensferry (local history); Newhaven (local history), Brass Rubbing Centre, Chalmers Close, Royal Mile; Head of Museums and Arts LYNNE HALFPENNY.

National Galleries of Scotland: The Mound, Edinburgh, EH2 2EL; tel. (131) 624-6200; e-mail enquiries@nationalgalleries.org; internet www.nationalgalleries.org; f. 1859; collns of Western art ranging from the Middle Ages to the present day; Dir-Gen. JOHN LEIGHTON; publ. *eBulletin* (describing new acquisitions, exhibitions, events, public programme highlights of the 4 nat. galleries,12 a year).

Constituent Galleries:

Dean Gallery: 73 Belford Rd, Edinburgh, EH4 3DS; tel. (131) 624-6200; e-mail gmainfo@nationalgalleries.org; internet www.nationalgalleries.org; f. 1999; Paolozzi gift of sculpture and graphic art, Dada and Surrealist colln; library and archive; Dir Dr SIMON GROOM.

National Gallery of Scotland: The Mound, Edinburgh, EH2 2EL; tel. (131) 624-6200; fax (131) 220-0917; e-mail nginfo@nationalgalleries.org; internet www.nationalgalleries.org; f. 1859; European and Scottish paintings up to 1900; also drawings, prints and sculpture; Dir MICHAEL CLARKE.

Royal Scottish Academy of Art and Architecture: The Mound, Edinburgh, EH2 2EL; tel. (131) 225-6671; fax (131) 220-6016; e-mail info@royalscottishacademy.org; internet www.royalscottishacademy.org; f. 1826; collns of painting, sculpture and architecture from academicians since 1831; contemporary art; administers scholarships, awards and residencies; historic colln of Scottish artworks and archive; library: library of material on fine arts and architecture; open by appointment; Dir COLIN R. GREENSLADE.

Scottish National Gallery of Modern Art: 75 Belford Rd, Edinburgh, EH4 3DR; tel. (131) 624-6200; fax (131) 343-2802; e-mail gmainfo@nationalgalleries.org; internet www.nationalgalleries.org; f. 1960; displays Scottish and European paintings, drawings, prints and sculptures since beginning of 20th century; int. postwar works; library of 50,000 vols; Dir Dr SIMON GROOM.

Scottish National Portrait Gallery: 1 Queen St, Edinburgh, EH2 1JD; tel. (131) 624-6200; fax (131) 558-3691; e-mail pginfo@nationalgalleries.org; internet www.nationalgalleries.org; f. 1889; portraits of Scottish historical interest; an extensive reference section of engravings and photographs of portraits; the nat. photography colln; Dir NICOLA KALINSKY.

National Museums Scotland: Chambers St, Edinburgh, EH1 1JF; tel. (131) 225-7534; fax (131) 220-4819; e-mail info@nms.ac.uk; internet www.nms.ac.uk; f. 1985; Dir Dr GORDON RINTOUL.

Constituent Museums:

Museum of Flight: East Fortune Airfield, East Lothian, EH39 5LF; tel. (131) 247-4238; fax (131) 247-4442; e-mail info@nms.ac.uk; internet www.nms.ac.uk/flight; colln of aircraft, rockets and aeroengines displayed in the hangars of a former RAF wartime station; houses a decommissioned Concorde aircraft; archives, propellers, incl. reference library; Curator ALISTAIR DODDS.

Museum of Rural Life: Philipshill Rd, Wester Kittochside, East Kilbride, G76 9HR; tel. (131) 247-4369; fax (1355) 571290; e-mail info@nms.ac.uk; internet www.nms.ac.uk/our_museums/museum_of_rural_life.aspx; f. 2001, fmrly Museum of Scottish Country Life; includes Georgian farmhouse and a 1950s working farm; Gen. Man. DUNCAN DORNAN.

Museum of Scotland: Chambers St, Edinburgh, EH1 1JF; tel. (131) 225-7534; fax (131) 220-4819; e-mail info@nms.ac.uk; internet www.nms.ac.uk/scotland; f. 1998; history and geology of Scotland; Dir Dr GORDON RINTOUL.

National Museum of Costume: New Abbey, DG2 8HQ; tel. (131) 247-4030; fax (1387) 850461; e-mail info@nms.ac.uk; internet www.nms.ac.uk/costume; f. 1977; 19th-century country house; changing exhibitions of costume from the 1870s to the 1950s; Man. MARGARET ROBERTS.

National War Museum of Scotland: Edinburgh Castle, Edinburgh, EH1 2NG; tel. (131) 247-4413; fax (131) 225-3848; e-mail info@nms.ac.uk; internet www.nms.ac.uk/war; f. 1930; collns of the Scottish experience of war and military service since 1700; Curator ALLAN CARSWELL.

Royal Museum: Chambers St, Edinburgh, EH1 1JF; tel. (131) 247-4422; fax (131) 220-4819; e-mail info@nms.ac.uk; internet www.nms.ac.uk/royal; f. 1854; int. collns of decorative arts, archaeology, ethnography, natural history, geology, science and technology; Dir Dr GORDON RINTOUL.

Gateshead

BALTIC Centre for Contemporary Art: Gateshead Quays, South Shore Rd, Gateshead, NE8 3BA; tel. (191) 478-1810; fax (191) 478-1922; e-mail info@balticmill.com; internet www.balticmill.com; f. 2002; Dir GODFREY WORSDALE; Head of Learning and Engagement EMMA THOMAS.

Glasgow

Glasgow Museums: 200 Woodhead Rd, Nitshill Glasgow, G53 7NN; tel. (141) 276-9300; fax (141) 276-9305; e-mail museums@glasgowlife.org.uk; internet www.glasgowlife.org.uk/museums; colln displayed in 10 venues across the city of Glasgow;incl. Glasgow Museums Resource Centre; Museum Man. GARETH JAMES.

Constituent Museums:

Burrell Collection: Pollok Country Park, 2060 Pollokshaws Rd, Glasgow G43 1AT; tel. (141) 287-2550; fax (141) 287-2597; e-mail museums@glasgowlife.org.uk; internet www.glasgowlife.org.uk; f. 1983; colln of c. 8,000 objects bequeathed to City of Glasgow by Sir William Burrell 1944; antiquities from Iraq, Egypt, Greece and Italy; Oriental art, incl. Chinese ceramics, bronzes and jades, Japanese prints, Near

Eastern carpets, rugs, ceramics and metal work; European decorative arts of 14th–18th centuries including tapestries, stained glass, sculpture, furniture, glass, silver and ceramics; fine art, especially French 19th-century works by Degas, Boudin, Monet and Daumier; Sr Curator, Ancient Civilizations SIMON ECCLES.

Gallery of Modern Art (GOMA): Royal Exchange Sq., Glasgow, G1 3AH; tel. (141) 297-3040; fax (141) 297-3062; e-mail museums@glasgowlife.org.uk; internet www.glasgowmuseums.com; f. 1996; exhibits work by local, nat. and int. artists; aims to address contemporary social issues through major biennial projects; museum bldg combines old and new architecture and incorporates a number of artists' commissions; Man. VICTORIA HOLLOWS.

Glasgow Museums Resource Centre (GMRC): 200 Woodhead Rd, Nitshill, Glasgow, G53 7NN; tel. (141) 276-9300; fax (141) 276-9305; e-mail museums@glasgowlife.org.uk; internet www.glasgowlife.org.uk/museums; f. 2003; publicly accessible store of 200,000 items held by Glasgow's museum service; home of the Open Museum; formal and informal learning programmes; research facilities; Man. GARETH JAMES.

Kelvingrove Art Gallery and Museum: Argyle St, Glasgow, G3 8AG; tel. (141) 287-2699; fax (141) 287-2690; e-mail museums@csglasgow.org; internet www.glasgowmuseums.com; f. 1901; collns incl. Dutch and French Impressionist paintings, Scottish colourists, arms and armour, Charles Rennie Mackintosh and the Glasgow Style, natural history, technology, costume; discovery and study centres.

People's Palace and Winter Gardens: Glasgow Green, Glasgow, G40 1AT; tel. (141) 276-0789; fax (141) 276-0787; e-mail museums@csglasgow.org; internet www.glasgowmuseums.com; f. 1898; local and social history museum; story of the city of Glasgow and its inhabitants since 1750; the Winter Gardens houses exotic palms and plants; Curator FIONA HAYES.

Pollok House: Pollok Country Park, 2060 Pollokshaws Rd, Glasgow, G43 1AT; tel. (844) 493-2202; fax (844) 493-2203; e-mail pollokhouse@nts.org.uk; internet www.nts.org.uk; 18th-century Palladian house with Victorian additions, furnished c. 1750–1820 and with Stirling Maxwell colln of Spanish and European paintings; managed by the Nat. Trust of Scotland on behalf of Glasgow Museums; Property Man. IAN McGREEVY (acting); Admin. Asst ALISON SIMMS.

Provand's Lordship: 3 Castle St, Glasgow, G4 0RB; tel. (141) 276-1625; fax (141) 276-1626; e-mail museums@glasgowlife.org.uk; internet www.glasgowlife.org.uk/museums; built 1471, the oldest house in Glasgow, with period room displays; home to the St Nicholas Garden, a herb garden containing 15th-century medicinal plants, the Tontine Faces (colln of carved stone faces originally carved for the new Town Hall 1740); Man. SANDRA EWIRI.

Riverside Museum: 100 Pointhouse Pl., Glasgow, G3 8RS; tel. (141) 287-2720; fax (141) 287-2692; e-mail museums@glasgowlife.org.; internet www.glasgowmuseums.com; f. 1964; history of transport and technology; displays incl. Glasgow trams and buses, Scottish-built cars, commercial vehicles, cycles and motor cycles, railway locomotives, fire engines, horse-drawn vehicles, ship models; toy cars, prams, the oldest surviving pedal cycle in the world and a reproduction of a typical Glasgow street of 1938; Man. LAWRENCE FITZGERALD.

St Mungo Museum of Religious Life and Art: 2 Castle St, Glasgow, G4 0RH; tel. (141) 276-1625; fax (141) 276-1626; e-mail museums@glasgowlife.org.uk; internet www.glasgowlife.org.uk/museums; f. 1993; art objects associated with religious faiths; displays on religion in art, world faiths, religion in Scottish history; permanent Zen garden; Man. SANDRA EWIRI.

Scotland Street School Museum: 225 Scotland St, Glasgow, G5 8QB; tel. (141) 287-0504; fax (141) 287-0515; e-mail museums@glasgowlife.org.uk; internet www.glasgowmuseums.com; f. 1906; designed by Charles Rennie Mackintosh between 1903 and 1906; history of Scotland Street Public School, and devts in education in Scotland; reconstructed classrooms from the Victorian period, World War II, the 1950s and 1960s; colln of old school photographs; Curator for Decorative Arts ALISON BROWN; Curator for Social History ISOBEL MCDONALD.

Hunterian Museum and Art Gallery: University of Glasgow Main/Gilbert-Scott Bldg, University Ave, Glasgow, G12 8QQ; tel. (141) 330-4221; fax (141) 330-3617; e-mail hunter@museum.gla.ac.uk; internet www.hunterian.gla.ac.uk; f. 1807; based around the collns of the Surgeon Extraordinary to Queen Charlotte, William Hunter (1718–83); geological, prehistoric, Roman, ethnographical and coin collns, scientific instruments; zoological, anatomical and pathological collns in univ. depts of Zoology, Anatomy and Pathology; books and MSS in univ. library; Dir EWEN SMITH.

Attached Gallery:

Hunterian Art Gallery: University of Glasgow, 82 Hillhead St, Glasgow, G12 8QQ; tel. (141) 330-5431; fax (141) 330-3618; e-mail hunter@museum.gla.ac.uk; internet www.gla.ac.uk/museum; f. 1980; collns of C. R. Mackintosh and J. M. Whistler; works by Chardin, Stubbs and Reynolds; Scottish painting since the 18th century; Old Master and modern prints; Dir EWEN SMITH.

Gloucester

City Museum and Art Gallery: Brunswick Rd, Gloucester, GL1 1HP; tel. (1452) 396131; fax (1452) 410898; e-mail city.museum@gloucester.gov.uk; internet www.gloucester.gov.uk; f. 1859; natural history, archaeology (before AD 1500), fine and applied art; temporary art, science, archaeology, natural sciences and textile exhibitions; collns online at livinggloucester.co.uk.

Gloucester Folk Museum: 99–103 Westgate St, Gloucester, GL1 2PG; tel. (1452) 396868; fax (1452) 330495; e-mail folk .museum@gloucester.gov.uk; internet www .gloucester.gov.uk/folkmuseum; f. 1935; local history, crafts, trades and industries of City and County of Gloucester since 1500; housed in Tudor and Jacobean timber-framed buildings with new extensions; regular special exhibitions, activities and events; social history reference colln (access by appointment); Man. CHRIS MORRIS.

Grasmere

Dove Cottage and the Wordsworth Museum: Dove Cottage, Grasmere, Ambleside, LA22 9SH; tel. (1539) 435544; fax (1539) 435748; e-mail enquiries@wordsworth.org .uk; internet www.wordsworth.org.uk; f. 1890; fmr home of William and Dorothy Wordsworth and, later, of Thomas de Quincey; contains original furniture and personal

effects, and a museum containing MSS, books, paintings, diaries, letters, poetry books, manuscripts as well as personal items, clothing, pictures, sculptures, objects relating to the poet, and to Grasmere life of the period; library: major research library for the Romantic period, The Jerwood Centre; access by appointment; Dir MICHAEL MCGREGOR.

Grays

Thurrock Museum: Thameside Complex, Orsett Rd, Grays, RM17 5DX; tel. (1375) 413965; fax (1375) 392666; e-mail thurrock .museum@thurrock.gov.uk; internet www .thurrock.gov.uk/museum; f. 1956; archaeology and history of Thurrock with accent on the growth of technology in a Thameside landscape; Museum and Heritage Officer JONATHAN CATTON.

Haverfordwest

Pembrokeshire Museum Service: The County Library, Dew St, Haverfordwest, Pembs. SA61 1SU; tel. (1437) 779500; fax (1437) 779500; internet www.pembrokeshire .gov.uk; f. 1967; Museums Officer NICK SUFFOLK.

Attached Museums:

Penrhos Cottage: Pembrokeshire Museum Service, The County Library, Dew St, Haverfordwest, Pembs., SA61 1SU; Llanycefn, Clunderwen; tel. (1437) 779500; fax (1437) 779500; e-mail adam@ writegood.co.uk; f. 1971; traditional thatched Welsh cottage with original furniture; open by appointment only; Museums Officer NICK SUFFOLK.

Scolton Manor Museum: Spittal, Haverfordwest; tel. (1437) 731328; fax (1437) 779500; f. 1972; regional history of Pembrokeshire; includes period rooms in early Victorian manor, World War II exhibition, railway exhibits, geology, river fishing, coal mining, servant life, costume; history of the domestic iron; Museums Officer NICK SUFFOLK.

High Wycombe

National Trust, Hughenden Manor: Hughenden Manor, High Wycombe, Bucks., HP14 4LA; tel. (1494) 755573; fax (1494) 474284; e-mail hughenden@nationaltrust.org .uk; internet www.nationaltrust.org.uk/hughendenmanor; f. 1947; Disraeli's country estate; contains Disraeli's books, furniture, paintings and personal effects; property of the National Trust (*q.v.*); library of 4,000 vols; Gen Man. JIM FOY; Regional Curator LUCY PORTEN.

Huddersfield

Tolson Memorial Museum: Ravensknowle Park, Wakefield Rd, Huddersfield, HD5 8DJ; tel. (1484) 223830; fax (1484) 223843; e-mail tolson.museum@kirklees.gov.uk; f. 1922; illustrates natural and human history of the district; prehistory, folk-life, development of woollen industry; colln of costume and textiles, decorative and applied art, music, weapons and war, coins and medals, personalities, science and technology, vehicles.

Ironbridge

Ironbridge Gorge Museums: Coach Rd, Coalbrookdale, Shropshire, TF8 7DQ; tel. (1952) 884391; fax (1952) 435999; e-mail information@ironbridge.org.uk; internet www.ironbridge.org.uk; f. 1968; explains and interprets the industrial and social history of the East Shropshire Coalfield, regarded as the 'Birthplace of the Industrial Revolution'; 6-mile site on the River Severn comprising: Coalbrookdale Museum of Iron and Darby Furnace, Ironbridge with the Museum of the Gorge, the world's first Iron Bridge (built

1779), Blists Hill Victorian Town, Coalport China Museum, Jackfield Tile Museum, Ironbridge Institute at Coalbrookdale, Rosehill and Dale House (restored home of the Darby family), Tar Tunnel (200-year-old source of natural bitumen), Broseley Pipeworks, 'Enginuity' (engineering and technological exhibits); designated a World Heritage Site by UNESCO; library of 50,000 vols; Chief Exec. STEVE MILLER.

Kendal

Abbot Hall Art Gallery and Museum of Lakeland Life & Industry: Kendal, LA9 5AL; tel. (1539) 722464; e-mail info@ abbothall.org.uk; internet www.abbothall .org.uk; f. 1962 (gallery), 1971 (museum); gallery provides changing exhibitions of local and int. interest; houses permanent collns of 18th-century furniture, paintings, , modern paintings, sculpture and drawings; museum features the working and social life of the area; Chief Exec. GORDON WATSON; Dir EDWARD KING.

Attached Museum:

Blackwell, The Arts & Crafts House: Bowness-on-Windermere, Cumbria, LA23 3JT; tel. (1539) 446139; fax (1539) 488486; e-mail info@blackwell.org.uk; internet www.blackwell.org.uk; f. 2001; bldg designed by Baillie Scott and built 1898–1900; period house with Arts and Crafts interiors and exhibitions of historic and contemporary crafts; Chief Exec. GORDON WATSON.

Kendal Museum of Natural History and Archaeology: Station Rd, Kendal, Cumbria, LA9 6BT; tel. (1539) 815597; fax (1539) 737976; e-mail info@kendalmuseum.org.uk; internet www.kendalmuseum.org.uk; f. 1796; Westmorland Gallery of local history and archaeology, World Wildlife gallery, Natural History gallery of geology, flora and fauna of the district; Curator MORAG CLEMENT.

Kirkcaldy

Kirkcaldy Museum and Art Gallery: War Memorial Gardens, Kirkcaldy, Fife, KY1 1YG; tel. (1592) 583213; e-mail kirkcaldy .museum@fife.gov.uk; internet www .fifedirect.org.uk/museums; f. 1925; local history, archaeology, earth and natural sciences, industrial history, decorative arts, costume, ceramics; Scottish paintings since 19th century; Service Devt Man., Heritage and Art DALLAS MECHAN.

Leeds

Leeds Museums and Galleries: Carlisle Road, Hunslet, Leeds, LS10 1LB; tel. (113) 224-4370; e-mail museumsandgalleries@ leeds.gov.uk; internet www.leeds.gov.uk/museumsandgalleries; f. 1820; Dir TIM CORUM; publ. *Museums and Galleries Review* (1 a year).

Selected Museums and Galleries:

Abbey House Museum: Abbey Walk, Kirkstall, Leeds, LS5 3EH; tel. (113) 230-5492; fax (113) 230-5499; e-mail abbey .house@leeds.gov.uk; internet www.leeds .gov.uk/abbeyhouse; f. 1927; gatehouse of Kirkstall Abbey (www.leeds.gov.uk/kirkstallabbey), recreation of Victorian Leeds; Curator SAMANTHA FLAVIN.

Armley Mills (Leeds Industrial Museum): Canal Rd, Armley, Leeds, LS12 2QF; tel. (113) 263-7861; fax (113) 263-7861; e-mail armley.mills@leeds.gov .uk; internet www.leeds.gov.uk/armleymills; f. 1969; textiles, printing, cinematography, history of engine and locomotive manufacturing in Leeds; manager's and mill-workers' houses; Keeper NINA BAPTISTE.

Leeds Art Gallery: The Headrow, Leeds, LS1 3AA; tel. (113) 247-8256; e-mail city .art.gallery@leeds.gov.uk; internet www .leeds.gov.uk/artgallery; f. 1888; 19th-century English and European paintings; early English watercolours, incl. Kitson and Lupton collns; modern paintings and sculpture; library: Print Room and Art Library; linked with Henry Moore Institute Archive and Library supporting the study of sculpture; Curator, Contemporary Art NIGEL WALSH.

Lotherton Hall: Lotherton Lane, Aberford, Leeds, LS25 3EB; tel. (113) 281-3259; fax (113) 281-2100; e-mail museumsandgalleries@leeds.gov.uk; internet www.leeds.gov.uk/lothertonhall; f. 1969; country house dating from the 19th and 20th centuries; Gascoigne Colln of furniture, silver, ceramics, costume and paintings from the 17th to 19th centuries; modern crafts; oriental gallery; Curator ADAM WHITE.

Temple Newsam House: Temple Newsam Rd, off Selby Rd, Leeds LS15 0AE; tel. (113) 336-7461; e-mail temple .newsam.house@leeds.gov.uk; internet www.leeds.gov.uk/templenewsamhouse; f. 1923; Tudor-Stuart house, birthplace of Lord Darnley; contains extensive collns of old master and Ingram family paintings and the decorative arts; Curator POLLY PUTNAM.

Royal Armouries Museum: Armouries Dr., Leeds, LS10 1LT; tel. (113) 220-1999; fax (113) 220-1954; e-mail enquiries@armouries .org.uk; internet www.royalarmouries.org; f. 1996; nat. colln of arms and armour and artillery; Dir Gen. Dr JONATHON RILEY; Museum Dir PETER ARMSTRONG; publ. *Arms and Armour: Journal of the Royal Armouries.*

Leicester

Leicestershire Museums: Leicestershire County Council, Leicester Rd, Glenfield, Leicester, LE3 8TB; tel. (116) 305-6642; fax (116) 265-6844; e-mail museums@leics.gov .uk; internet www.leics.gov.uk/museums; f. 1849; local museums incl. Charnwood Museum, Donington-le-Heath Manor House, Harborough Museum, Melton Carnegie Museum, Snibston Discovery Park and the Record Office at Wigston Magna; Leicester 'Open Museum' comprises exhibits for hire within the county; museums concentrate on archaeology, natural life, cultural life, working life, Leicestershire history and education; Head Y. C. COURTNEY.

National Space Centre: Exploration Dr., Leicester, LE4 5NS; fax (116) 261-0261; e-mail info@spacecentre.co.uk; internet www.spacecentre.co.uk; f. 2001; displays about space and space exploration; incl. space science research unit; Chief Exec. CHAS BISHOP.

Lincoln

Lincolnshire Heritage Services: Cultural Services Branch, Lincolnshire County Council Offices, Newland, Lincoln, LN1 1YQ; tel. (1522) 552222; e-mail education@lincolnshire .gov.uk; internet www.lincolnshire.gov.uk; f. 1974; operates 7 museums (see below) and several other sites, incl. Lincoln Castle, Judge's Lodgings, Battle of Britain Memorial Flight Visitor Centre, Lincolnshire Archives, and windmills in Alford, Burgh le Marsh, Heckington and Lincoln; Head of Heritage and Regeneration HEATHER CUMMINS.

Attached Museums:

Church Farm Museum: Church Rd South, Skegness, PE25 2HF; tel. (1754)

766658; fax (1754) 898243; e-mail info@ churchfarmvillage.org.uk; f. 1976; a complex of 18th- and 19th-century farmhouse and agricultural bldgs with displays of agricultural equipment typical of the area; farmhouse furnished to period c. 1900; Chair. STEVE KIRK.

The Collection: Art and Archaeology in Lincolnshire: Danes Terrace, Lincoln, LN2 1LP; tel. (1522) 550990; fax (1522) 550991; e-mail thecollection@lincolnshire .gov.uk; internet www.thecollection.lincoln .museum; f. 1906 as City and County Museum, present status 2005; comprises exhibits from the former City and County Museum (artefacts since medieval era, incl. collns of coins, medals, arms and natural science) and the Usher Gallery (fine, decorative and contemporary arts); Collns Officer DAWN HEYWOOD; Collns Officer ANTONY LEE.

Gainsborough Old Hall: Parnell St, Gainsborough, DN21 2NB; tel. (1427) 612669; fax (1427) 612779; e-mail gainsboroughholdhall@lincolnshire.gov.uk; internet www.lincolnshire.gov.uk/ gainsboroughholdhall; f. 1974; 15th-century timber framed manor house with great hall, medieval kitchen; guided tours; events and exhibits; heritage education programme; Site Coordinator VICTORIA MASON.

Grantham Museum: St Peter's Hill, Grantham, NG31 6PY; tel. (1476) 568783; fax (1476) 592457; e-mail grantham .museum@lincolnshire.gov.uk; f. 1923; local prehistoric artefacts, Roman and Saxon archaeology, Grantham local history, trades and industries, display of Victorian dolls, and a colln devoted to notable figures born locally, incl. Sir Isaac Newton and Margaret Thatcher; District Man. NICOLA ROGERS.

Museum of Lincolnshire Life: Burton Rd, Lincoln, LN1 3LY; tel. (1522) 528448; fax (1522) 521264; e-mail lincolnshire_museum@lincolnshire.gov.uk; f. 1969; displays illustrating the social, agricultural and industrial history of Lincolnshire over the 17th–20th centuries; also contains Lincolnshire Regiment Museum; manages the Ellis Windmill; Dist. Man. N. ROGERS.

Usher Gallery: Lindum Rd, Lincoln, LN2 1NN; tel. (1522) 527980; fax (1522) 550991; e-mail usher.gallery@lincolnshire.gov.uk; internet www.thecollection.lincoln .museum; houses the Usher colln of watches, miniatures and decorative art, and a colln of fine art, sculpture and coins, incl. works by De Wint, Lowry, Turner and contemporary artists Grayson Perry and Terry Frost; attached to The Collection (county archaeological collns; see above); Area Service Man. JEREMY WEBSTER.

Liverpool

National Museums Liverpool: 127 Dale St, Liverpool,; tel. and fax (151) 207-0001; internet www.liverpoolmuseums.org.uk; f. 1986 as Nat. Museums and Galleries on Merseyside, present name 2003; groups the 7 museums of Liverpool, incl. the Museum of Liverpool; Dir DAVID FLEMING.

Constituent Museums and Galleries:

Conservation Centre: Midland Railway Bldg, 1 Peter St, Liverpool, L1 6BL; tel. (151) 478-41812; fax (151) 236-5105; e-mail val.ward@liverpoolmuseums.org.uk; internet www.liverpoolmuseums.org.uk; f. 1996; illustrates the arts and science of the conservation of museum exhibits; depts of ceramics, conservation science, frames, metals, organics, paintings, paper, sculp-

ture, shipkeeping, taxidermy and textiles; Head of Conservation SALLY ANN YATES.

Lady Lever Art Gallery: Port Sunlight Village, Wirral, CH62 5EQ; tel. (151) 478-4136; internet www.liverpoolmuseums.org .uk/ladylever; f. 1922; colln of British Pre-Raphaelite 18th- and 19th-century paintings, 18th-century furniture; colln of Wedgewood and Chinese porcelain.

Merseyside Maritime Museum: Albert Dock, Liverpool, L3 4AQ; tel. (151) 478-4499; fax (151) 478-4590; internet www .liverpoolmuseums.org.uk/maritime; f. 1980; set in Liverpool's docklands; displays and exhibits on the region's maritime past; gallery of maritime paintings; library: reference library of maritime material, incl. archives and records.

Seized! Border and Customs Uncovered: Merseyside Maritime Museum, Albert Dock, Liverpool, L3 4AQ; tel. (151) 478-4499; internet www .liverpoolmuseums.org.uk/maritime; f. 1994 fmrly HM Customs and Excise National Museum; exhibits relating to smuggling and revenue colln since 1700; holds nat. colln of Dept of Customs and Excise and UK Border Agency; displays of equipment, prints, paintings and photographs; Press Assist. ALISON CORNMELL.

Sudley House: Mossley Hill Rd, Liverpool; tel. (151) 724-3245; internet www .liverpoolmuseums.org.uk; f. 1986; fmr home of 19th-century shipowner; 18th-and 19th-century art incl. works by Gainsborough, Landseer and artists of the Pre-Raphaelite movement; Dir of Art Galleries REYAHN KING.

Walker Art Gallery: William Brown St, Liverpool L3 8EL; tel. (151) 478-4199; fax (151) 478-4190; internet www .liverpoolmuseums.org.uk/walker; collns of European art since 1300; sculpture gallery; Keeper JULIAN TREUHERZ.

World Museum Liverpool: William Brown St, Liverpool, L3 8EN; tel. (151) 478-4399; fax (151) 478-4390; internet www.liverpoolmuseums.org.uk/wml; f. 1851, rebuilt 1964–69, present name 2005; spec. collns incl. the Mayer-Fejérvàry Gothic ivories, the Bryan Fausset group of Anglo-Saxon antiquities, the Lord Derby and Tristram ornithological collns; bug house, aquarium, ethnology, time and space gallery, planetarium, Clore natural history centre, Weston discovery centre; Dir Dr STEVE JUDD.

London

Bank of England Museum: Threadneedle St, London, EC2R 8AH; tel. (20) 7601-5545; fax (20) 7601-5808; e-mail museum@ bankofengland.co.uk; internet www .bankofengland.co.uk/education/museum; f. 1694; illustrates the history of the Bank and its current work; collns incl. banknotes and coins, furniture, pictures and photographs, silver; Curator JOHN KEYWORTH.

British Museum: Great Russell St, London, WC1B 3DG; tel. (20) 7323-8000; e-mail information@thebritishmuseum.ac.uk; internet www.thebritishmuseum.ac.uk; f. 1753 in pursuance of the will of Sir Hans Sloane, and with the addition of the Cottonian and Harleian Libraries; opened 1759, present bldgs begun 1823, completed 1852; collns and exhibitions of prehistoric, Egyptian, Assyrian, medieval, oriental and other archaeological collns, ethnography, prints, drawings, ceramics, coins, medals and banknotes; many catalogues and reproductions are published; Chair. of Board of Trustees NIALL FITZGERALD; Dir NEIL MACGREGOR; Keepers of Depts JONATHAN KING (Africa, Oceania and the Americas), VIVIAN DAVIES (Ancient Egypt and Sudan), Dr JOHN CURTIS (Ancient Near East), JAN STUART (Asia), JOE CRIBB (Coins and Medals), DAVID SAUNDERS (Conservation, Documentation and Scientific Research), Dr DYFRI WILLIAMS (Greek and Roman Antiquities), JONATHAN WILLIAMS (Prehistory and Europe), ANTHONY GRIFFITHS (Prints and Drawings).

British Postal Museum & Archive: Freeling House, Phoenix Place, London, WC1X 0DL; tel. (20) 7239-2570; fax (20) 7239-2576; e-mail info@postalheritage.org.uk; internet www.postalheritage.org.uk; f. 1966; colln of stamps, essays, drawings and official documents dating back to Rowland Hill's proposals for Uniform Penny Postage in 1837–39; also the Post Office collection of stamps of the world and of British stamps since the early 20th century, and the philatelic archives (1855–1965) of Thomas De La Rue and Co., security printers, on microfilm; postboxes and other postal exhibits; Dir ADRIAN STEEL.

Carlyle's House: 24 Cheyne Row, Chelsea, London, SW3 5HL; tel. (20) 7352-7087; e-mail carlyleshouse@nationaltrust.org.uk; built 1708; occupied by the Victorian writer, Thomas Carlyle (1834–81) and his wife Jane; National Trust property; contains books, paintings, furniture, and personal relics.

Courtauld Gallery: Somerset House, Strand, London, WC2R 0RN; tel. (20) 7848-2526; fax (20) 7848-2589; e-mail galleryinfo@courtauld.ac.uk; internet www.courtauld.ac.uk/gallery; f. 1932; Old Master, Impressionist and Post-Impressionist paintings, prints and drawings, (incl. works by Botticelli, Cézanne, Goya, Manet, Michelangelo, Rembrandt, Renoir, Rubens, Tiepolo, Turner and Van Gogh); sculpture and applied arts; Head Dr ERNST VEGELIN.

Cuming Museum (Borough of Southwark): 151 Walworth Rd, London, SE17 1RS; tel. (20) 7525-2332; fax (20) 7525-2345; e-mail cuming.museum@southwark.gov.uk; internet www.southwark.gov.uk; f. 1906; worldwide collns of the Cuming family joined with the local history of Southwark, from Roman times to the present; Collns Man. DEYAN SUDJIC.

Design Museum: Butler's Wharf, 28 Shad Thames, London, SE1 2YD; tel. (20) 7403-6933; fax (20) 7378-6540; e-mail info@designmuseum.org; internet www.designmuseum.org; f. 1981; ind. museum set up by the Conran Foundation, to promote awareness of the importance of design in education, industry, commerce and culture; colln of mass-produced design; Chair. LUQMAN ARNOLD; Dir DEYAN SUDJIC.

Dulwich Picture Gallery: Gallery Rd, London, SE21 7AD; tel. (20) 8693-5254; fax (20) 8299-8700; e-mail enquiries@dulwichpicturegallery.org.uk; internet www.dulwichpicturegallery.org.uk; f. 1811; houses colln of Old Masters incl. Rembrandt, Rubens, Cuyp, Van Dyck, Teniers, Poussin, Claude, Watteau, Raphael, Tiepolo, Gainsborough, Murillo, etc.; schedule of temporary exhibitions and educational activities; Curator Dr. XAVIER BRAY; Dir IAN DEJARDIN.

Estorick Collection of Modern Italian Art: 39A Canonbury Sq., London, N1 2AN; tel. (20) 7704-9522; fax (20) 7704-9531; e-mail curator@estorickcollection.com; internet www.estorickcollection.com; f. 1998; 20th-century Italian art, especially Futurist; also sculpture; library of 2,000 vols, periodicals and catalogues; library open by appointment; Dir ROBERTA CREMONCINI.

Fashion and Textile Museum: 83 Bermondsey St, London, SE1 3XF; tel. (20) 7407-8664; fax (20) 7089-9416; e-mail info@ftmlondon.org; internet www.ftmlondon.org; f. 2003; British and world fashion and textile design; Head of Museum CELIA JOICEY; Curator DENNIS NOTHDRUFT.

Foundling Museum: 40 Brunswick Sq., London, WC1N 1AZ; tel. (20) 7841-3600; fax (20) 7841-3601; e-mail enquiries@foundlingmuseum.org.uk; internet www.foundlingmuseum.org.uk; f. 2004; documents history of the Foundling Hospital (f. 1739), London's first home for abandoned children, and of its founder, philanthropist Thomas Coram, artist William Hogarth and composer George Frideric Handel; collns of art, social history and music in a restored and refurbished bldg adjacent to the original site of the Hospital; collns of 18th century art, interiors, social history and music; Chair. ANDREW FANE; Pres. PATRICK WALKER; Dir CARO HOWELL.

Freud Museum: 20 Maresfield Gardens, London, NW3 5SX; tel. (20) 7435-2002; fax (20) 7431-5452; e-mail info@freud.org.uk; internet www.freud.org.uk; f. 1986; fmr London home of Sigmund Freud and his daughter Anna; incl. Sigmund Freud's colln of antiquities, including 1,500 Egyptian, Greek, Roman and Oriental antiquities; his psychoanalytical couch, library and furniture; also a psychoanalysis research centre; library of 1,600 vols from Sigmund Freud's colln; reference library relating to the history of psychoanalysis; archive containing Freud family documents and photographs; Dir CAROL SEIGEL; Librarian KEITH DAVIES.

Geffrye Museum: 136 Kingsland Rd, London, E2 8EA; tel. (20) 7739-9893; fax (20) 7729-5647; e-mail info@geffrye-museum.org.uk; internet www.geffrye-museum.org.uk; f. 1914; English furniture, textiles, domestic objects and paintings arranged in a series of period rooms from 1600–2000; herb and period gardens; library: reference library of books and periodicals on the arts and social history; Dir DAVID DEWING.

Hampton Court Palace: Surrey, KT8 9AU; tel. (844) 482-7777; e-mail hamptoncourt@hrp.org.uk; internet www.hrp.org.uk; home of Henry VIII, contains colln of paintings and tapestries, incl. Andrea Mantegna's 9 great tempera paintings of 'The Triumphs of Julius Caesar'; Palace Dir PAUL GRAY; Superintendent of the Royal Colln C. STEVENS.

Hayward Gallery: South Bank Centre, Belvedere Rd, London, SE1 8XZ; tel. (20) 7921-08138; fax (20) 7401-2664; e-mail hginfo@hayward.org.uk; internet www.hayward.org.uk; f. 1968; contemporary perspectives on art past and present, focusing on individual artists, historical themes and artistic movements, other cultures, and contemporary art; administers national touring exhibitions and the Arts Council Collection (7,500 items); Dir CAROLINE FELTON (acting).

Horniman Museum and Gardens: 100 London Rd, Forest Hill, London, SE23 3PQ; tel. (20) 8699-1872; fax (20) 8291-5506; e-mail enquiry@horniman.ac.uk; internet www.horniman.ac.uk; f. 1901; 3 major collns: ethnography, natural history and musical instruments (incl. archive documents); Aquarium; 16 acres of gardens; education activities with schools, community groups and gen. public; specialist research library; library of 30,000 vols, mainly on African history, entomology, botany, ethnography, natural history, musical instruments; Dir JANET VITMAYER.

Hunterian Museum at the Royal College of Surgeons: 35–43 Lincoln's Inn Fields, London, WC2A 3PE; tel. (20) 7869-6560; fax (20) 7869-6564; e-mail museums@rcseng.ac.uk; internet www.hunterianmuseum.org; f. 1813, built around the colln of anatomist and surgeon John Hunter (1728–93); collns of comparative anatomy and pathology specimens, skeletons, skulls and teeth, teaching models, historical surgical and dental instruments, paintings, drawings and sculpture; temporary exhibitions, lectures, family events and educational workshops; Dir of Museums and Archives Dr SAMUEL ALBERTI; Curator SARAH PEARSON; Head of Conservation Unit MARTYN COOKE.

Imperial War Museum: Lambeth Rd, London, SE1 6HZ; tel. (20) 7416-5320; fax (20) 7416-5374; e-mail mail@iwm.org.uk; internet www.iwm.org.uk; f. 1917, to illustrate and record the operations in which the Armed Forces of the British Commonwealth have been engaged since 1914; nat. museum and picture gallery; contains many exhibits on all aspects of war, incl. 19,000 works of art, 6m. photographs, 120m. ft of film and 46,000 hours of sound and video recordings; library of 270,000 items, incl. pamphlets, periodicals, maps and drawings; Chair. of the Board of Trustees Sir PETER SQUIRE; Dir-Gen. DIANE LEES; publ. *Imperial War Museum Review* (1 a year).

Branches:

Churchill Museum and Cabinet War Rooms: Clive Steps, King Charles St, London, SW1A 2AQ; tel. (20) 7766-0120; fax (20) 7839-5897; e-mail cwr@iwm.org.uk; internet cwr.iwm.org.uk; Churchill's underground headquarters; incorporates the Churchill Museum (churchillmuseum.iwm.org.uk), exploring the life of Winston Churchill (1874–1965); Dir P. REED.

HMS Belfast: Morgans Lane, Tooley St, London, SE1 2JH; tel. (20) 7940-6300; fax (20) 7403-0719; internet hmsbelfast.iwm.org.uk; Second World War cruiser moored in the Pool of London; Dir E. J. WENZEL.

Imperial War Museum Duxford: Duxford, Cambridgeshire, CB22 4QR; tel. (1223) 835000; fax (1223) 837267; e-mail duxford@iwm.org.uk; internet www.iwm.org.uk/duxford; f. 1977; airfield that featured in the Battle of Britain (1940), housing historic colln of aircraft, military vehicles, tanks and artillery; incl. American Air Museum (aam.iwm.org.uk); interactive exhibitions; Dir RICHARD ASHTON.

Imperial War Museum North: The Quays, Trafford Wharf Rd, Manchester, M17 1TZ; tel. (161) 836-4000; fax (161) 836-4090; e-mail iwmnorth@iwm.org.uk; internet www.iwm.org.uk/north; f. 2002; war and its impact on the 20th and 21st centuries, through exhibits, audiovisual shows and interactive exhibits and changing programme of events; Dir GRAHAM BOXER.

Iveagh Bequest: Kenwood, Hampstead Lane, London, NW3 7JR; tel. (20) 8348-1286; left to the nation by Edward Cecil Guinness, first Earl of Iveagh, in 1927; includes paintings of British, Dutch, Flemish and French Schools, housed in an 18th-century mansion (Kenwood House) designed by Robert Adam, containing an ornate library; exhibitions on aspects of 18th-century art; Admin. Trustee English Heritage (HBMC); Dir of E. H. London Region RICHARD FREELAND; publs catalogues.

London Transport Museum: 39 Wellington St, Covent Gdn, London, WC2E 7BB; tel. (20) 7379-6344; fax (20) 7565-7254; e-mail enquiry@ltmuseum.co.uk; internet www.ltmuseum.co.uk; f. 1961, present location 1980; 400,000 items; educational and heritage preservation charity; conserves and explains the history of London's transport; offers people an understanding of the Capital's past devt of transport and engages in the debate about its future; library of 13,200 vols incl. books, journals and spec. collns on the history and devt of Londons's transport from 1800 to the present day, incl. art, design and architecture, 500 journals; Man. Dir SAM MULLINS.

Museum of London: London Wall, London, EC2Y 5HN; tel. (20) 7001-9844; fax (20) 7600-1058; e-mail info@museumoflondon.org .uk; internet www.museumoflondon.org.uk; formed from amalgamation of London Museum and Guildhall Museum; social history of London from prehistory to 20th century; exhibits incl. the Lord Mayor's coach, 18th-century prison cell, Victorian shop fronts; Chair. of Board of Govs MICHAEL CASSIDY; Dir SHARON AMENT.

National Army Museum: Royal Hospital Rd, Chelsea, London, SW3 4HT; tel. (20) 7730-0717; fax (20) 7823-6573; e-mail info@ nam.ac.uk; internet www.nam.ac.uk; f. 1960; displays depicting the history of the British Army since 1066 until the present day, the Indian Army until Independence in 1947, and colonial land forces; reference collections of 43,000 books, 30,000 pamphlets, 1,000 ft of archives, 50,000 prints, drawings and watercolours, 5,000,000 photographs; 80,000 uniforms, 250,000 badges; 20,000 medals and weapons; personal equipment and a sound and film archive; Dir Dr ALAN J. GUY.

National Gallery: Trafalgar Sq., London, WC2N 5DN; tel. (20) 7747-2885; fax (20) 7747-2423; e-mail information@ng-london .org.uk; internet www.nationalgallery.org .uk; f. 1824; contains examples of all the principal schools of Western European painting from 1250 to 1900; a selection of British painters from Hogarth to Turner; guided tours and public lectures; picture library; Chair. MARK GETTY; Senior Curator DAVID JAFFÉ; Dir of Collections SUSAN FOISTER; Dir of Conservation LARRY KEITH; Dir of Scientific Research Dr ASHOK ROY.

National Maritime Museum: Park Row, Greenwich, London, SE10 9NF; tel. (20) 8858-6516; fax (20) 8312-6599; internet www.nmm.ac.uk; f. 1934; opened 1937; illustrates British maritime history; the collection includes portraits and sea pieces, models, ship's plans, instruments, maps and charts, weapons, medals, a library of books and MSS; photo library of 330,000 images and negatives; Queen's House: 17th-century royal apartments of Queen Henrietta Maria; also the Royal Observatory Greenwich, where the displays illustrate themes concerned with astronomy, time and navigation, the meridian line, and a planetarium; library of 20,000 vols on maritime history; Dir ROY CLARE; publ. *Journal for Maritime Research.*

National Portrait Gallery: St Martin's Pl., London, WC2H 0HE; tel. (20) 7306-0055; fax (20) 7306-0056; internet www.npg.org.uk; f. 1856; portraits of the most eminent people in British history; library of 40,000 vols; Dir SANDY NAIRNE; Chair. of Trustees Prof. DAVID CANNADINE.

Natural History Museum: Cromwell Rd, South Kensington, London, SW7 5BD; tel. (20) 7942-5000; internet www.nhm.ac.uk; originates from the Natural History Depts of the British Museum, and a br. comprising the Natural History Museum at Tring, Herts.; separate instn 1963; incorporates the Geological Museum; library: see Libraries and Archives; Chair. of the Board of Trustees OLIVER STOCKEN; Dir (vacant); Science Dir RICHARD PAUL LANE; Keeper of Botany Dr JOHANNES VOGEL; Keeper of Entomology Dr MALCOLM SCOBLE; Keeper of Mineralogy Dr ANDREW FLEET; Keeper of Palaeontology Prof. NORMAN MACLEOD; Keeper of Zoology Prof. PHIL RAINBOW.

Polish Institute and Sikorski Museum: 20 Princes Gate, London, SW7 1PT; tel. (20) 7589-9249; f. 1945; archives, museum, research centre and publishing house; includes the Sikorski Collection (personal belongings, memorabilia, wartime diary, etc. of Gen. Wladyslaw Sikorski, 1881–1943), militaria (over 10,000 items), maps, paintings and engravings, sculptures, porcelain, miniatures, coins and medals.

Royal Academy of Arts: Burlington House, Piccadilly, London, W1J 0BD; tel. (20) 7300-8000; internet www.royalacademy.org.uk; f. 1768; permanent colln incl. works by Turner, Gainsborough, Reynolds and Hockney; temporary exhibitions of works borrowed from major instns worldwide; Pres. Sir CHRISTOPHER LE BRUN.

Royal Air Force Museum London: Grahame Park Way, London, NW9 5LL; tel. (20) 8205-2266; fax (20) 8200-1751; e-mail london@rafmuseum.org; internet www .rafmuseum.org; f. 1963, opened 1972; grant-aided through the Ministry of Defence; exhibits 100 full-size British and foreign aircraft from 1909 to the present day, together with supporting material recording the history of the Royal Air Force and the development of aviation generally; activities cover many aspects of aviation, including military, civil, artistic, scientific, industrial and political; br. at Cosford (West Midlands); library of 100,000 vols, and archives and photographic collection; Dir-Gen. PETER DYE.

Royal Armouries: HM Tower of London, London, EC3N 4AB; tel. (20) 7480-6358; fax (20) 7481-2922; e-mail enquiries@armouries .org.uk; internet www.royalarmouries.org and Royal Armouries Museum, Armouries Drive, Leeds, W. Yorks., LS10 1LT; tel. (113) 220-1999; fax (113) 220-1995 and Artillery Collection, Fort Nelson, Down End Rd, Portsdown Hill, Fareham, PO17 6AN; tel. (1329) 233734; fax (1329) 822092; the nat. museum of arms and armour and museum of the Tower of London, originating from the working arsenal at the Tower and the collection of royal armours begun by Henry VIII; first open to the public c. 1660; the national and royal collections cover the development of arms and armour since c. AD 1000; Leeds-based picture library of 167,000 prints, transparencies and slides; archives relating to the history of the museum and the Royal Small Arms Factory; library: Leeds-based reference library of 40,000 vols; also libraries at the Tower of London and Fort Nelson; Chief Exec. PAUL EVANS; Chair. ANN GREEN; Museum Dir PETER ARMSTRONG; publ. *Arms and Armour* (2 a year).

Royal College of Music Museum of Instruments: Prince Consort Rd, South Kensington, London, SW7 2BS; tel. (20) 7591-4842; fax (20) 7589-7740; e-mail museum@rcm.ac.uk; internet www.cph.rcm .ac.uk; f. 1970; colln of instruments and accessories since 1480, incl. Donaldson, Tagore, Hipkins, Ridley, Hartley, Fleming, Walton and Steele-Perkins collns; Curator JENNY NEX.

Royal Institution of Great Britain Michael Faraday Museum: 21 Albemarle St, London, W1S 4BS; tel. (20) 7409-2992; fax (20) 7670-2920; e-mail archivist@ri.ac.uk; internet www.rigb.org; f. 1799; original apparatus made and used by Faraday and other key scientists such as Humphry Davy, John Tyndall and William and Lawrence Bragg; incl. Faraday's magnetic laboratory, restored to the form it was known to have in 1845 and containing much of his apparatus; library of 30,000 vols (works on physics and chemistry since the 1700s); Head of Collns and Heritage Prof FRANK JAMES.

Saatchi Gallery: Duke of York's HQ, King's Rd, Sloane Sq., Chelsea, London, SW3 4SQ; e-mail admin@saatchigallery.com; internet www.saatchi-gallery.co.uk; f. 1985; colln of mostly modern art from contemporary British artists (incl. Damien Hirst, Tracey Emin, Sarah Lucas, Jenny Saville, Chapman brothers), new art from China; also exhibits work of lesser-known int. artists; Dir PHILLY ADAMS.

Science Museum: South Kensington, London, SW7 2DD; tel. (870) 870-4771; fax (20) 7942-4302; internet www.sciencemuseum .org.uk; f. 1857; official title the National Museum of Science and Industry; collns: science, medicine, information and communications technologies, engineering technologies; library: see Libraries and Archives; Dir Prof. IAN BLATCHFORD.

Sir John Soane's House and Museum: 13 Lincoln's Inn Fields, London, WC2A 3BP; tel. (20) 7440-4251; fax (20) 7831-3957; e-mail library@soane.org.uk; internet www.soane .org; f. 1837 (built by Sir John Soane 1812, est. by Act of Parliament for the promotion of the study of architecture and allied arts 1833); colln incl. paintings by Hogarth, the Egyptian Sarcophagus of Seti I, Italian bronzes, paintings, antique sculpture, 18th-century English sculpture, models, 30,000 architectural drawings; library: library: see Libraries and Archives; Dir TIM KNOX.

South London Gallery: 65 Peckham Rd, London, SE5 8UH; tel. (20) 7703-6120; fax (20) 7252-4730; e-mail mail@ southlondongallery.org; internet www .southlondongallery.org; f. 1891; regular exhibitions of innovative contemporary art supported by a full programme of education events and workshops; Dir MARGOT HELLER; Programme Man. SIMON PARRIS.

Tate: Millbank, London, SW1P 4RG; tel. (20) 7887-8888; fax (20) 7887-8007; e-mail information@tate.org.uk; internet www.tate .org.uk; f. 1897; Dir Sir NICHOLAS SEROTA.

Constituent Museums:

> **Tate Britain:** Millbank, London, SW1P 4RG; tel. (20) 7887-8008; fax (20) 7887-8007; e-mail information@tate.org.uk; internet www.tate.org.uk; f. 1897 by Sir Henry Tate; nat. gallery of British art since 1500, incl. works by Hogarth, Blake, Constable and the Pre-Raphaelites, with the Turner Collection housed in the Clore Gallery; Dir STEPHEN DEUCHAR.

> Research Centre:

>> **Tate Library and Archive:** Hyman Kreitman Reading Rooms, Tate Britain, Millbank, London, SW1P 4RG; tel. (20) 7887-8838; fax (20) 7887-3952; e-mail reading.rooms@tate.org.uk; internet www.tate.org.uk/research/researchservices/readingrooms; f. 2002; covers British art from 1500 and int. art from 1900; Archive colln (700 individual archives) covers British art from 1900, incl. unpublished material on British artists, art world figures and orgs; Gallery Records colln; exhibition catalogues, monographs, artists' books, ephemera; library of 250,000 vols; Head of Library and Archive JANE BRAMWELL.

> **Tate Liverpool:** Albert Dock, Liverpool, L3 4BB; tel. (151) 702-7400; e-mail visiting .liverpool@tate.org.uk; internet www.tate .org.uk/liverpool; f. 1988; home of the Nat. Colln of Modern Art in the North; 4 floors displaying work selected from the Tate Colln and spec. exhibitions of artwork loaned from around the world; modern and contemporary art since 1900, incl. painting and sculpture, photography, video

installations; tours and lectures; Dir CHRISTOPH GRUNENBERG.

Tate Modern: Bankside, London, SE1 9TG; tel. (20) 7887-8888; fax (20) 7887-8007; e-mail visiting.modern@tate.org.uk; internet www.tate.org.uk; f. 2000; int. modern art since 1900; Dir VICENTE TODOLÍ.

Tate St Ives: Porthmeor Beach, St Ives, TR26 1TG; tel. (1736) 796226; e-mail tatestives@tate.org.uk; internet www.tate .org.uk; f. 1993; modern painting, sculpture and ceramics by artists associated with St Ives, as well as int. figures; incl. Barbara Hepworth Museum and Sculpture Garden; Dir SUSAN DANIEL-MCELROY

Victoria and Albert (V&A) Museums:.

Constituent Museums:

Victoria and Albert Museum (V&A): South Kensington, London, SW7 2RL; tel. (20) 7942-2000; e-mail vanda@vam.ac.uk; internet www.vam.ac.uk; f. 1852; all forms of art and design, with collns of ceramics, furniture, fashion, glass, jewellery, metalwork, sculpture, textiles and paintings; library: library: see entry for Nat. Art Library; Dir MARK JONES; Keepers BETH MCKILLOP (Asian Dept), C. WILK (Furniture, Textiles and Fashion Dept), JULIUS BRYANT (Prints, Drawings and Painting/Nat. Art Library Dept), Dr P. WILLIAMSON (Sculpture, Metalwork, Ceramics and Glass Dept).

V&A Department of Theatre and Performance—National Museum for the Performing Arts: Reading Room, Blythe House, 23 Blythe Rd, London, W14 0QX; tel. (20) 7942-2697; fax (20) 7471-9864; e-mail tmenquiries@vam.ac.uk; internet www.vam.ac.uk/page/t/theatre-and-performance; f. 1974, opened to the public 1987; nat. record of stage performance; history, craft and practice of the performing arts in Britain; library of 100,000 vols (incorporating British Theatre Asscn colln and library of the Soc. for Theatre Research); spec. archive collns incl. D'Oyly Carte Co, English Stage Co, Engish Shakespeare Co, Arts Council of Great Britain, Diaghilev's Ballets Russes and Edward Gordon Craig; spec. photographic archives incl. Houston Rogers, Gordon Anthony and Anthony Crickmay; Nat. Video Archive of Performance; Dir GEOFFREY MARSH.

V&A Museum of Childhood: Cambridge Heath Rd, London, E2 9PA; tel. (20) 8983-5200; fax (20) 8983-5225; e-mail moc@vam .ac.uk; internet www.museumofchildhood .org.uk; f. 1872; dolls' houses, toys, games, costume, nursery furniture; Chair. SAMIR SHAH; Dir RHIAN HARRIS.

Wallace Collection: Hertford House, Manchester Square, London, W1U 3BN; tel. (20) 7563-9500; fax (20) 7224-2155; e-mail enquiries@wallacecollection.org; internet www.wallacecollection.org; f. 1900; library of 15,000 vols; collns of 18th-century French pictures, furniture, Sèvres porcelain and sculpture, 17th-century paintings, armoury and objets d'art, bequeathed to the nation in 1897 by Lady Wallace; Dir ROSALIND SAVILL.

White Cube: 48 Hoxton Sq., London, N1 6PB; tel. (20) 7930-5373; fax (20) 7749-7480; e-mail enquiries@whitecube.com; internet www.whitecube.com; f. 2000; modern British art; Man. Dir JAY JOPLING.

Whitechapel Gallery: 77–82 Whitechapel High St, London, E1 7QX; tel. (20) 7522-7888; fax (20) 7377-1685; e-mail info@ whitechapelgallery.org; internet www .whitechapelgallery.org; f. 1901, reopened in 2009; temporary exhibitions, principally of modern or contemporary art; no permanent

colln; charitable trust supported by the Arts Council, local authorities, charitable bodies and the business community; Chair. of Trustees ROBERT TAYLOR; Dir IWONA BLAZWICK.

Manchester

Manchester City Galleries: Mosley St, Manchester, M2 3JL; tel. (161) 235-8888; fax (161) 235-8899; internet www .manchestergalleries.org; f. 1823; dept of Manchester City Ccl, operates 4 galleries in and around Manchester.

Constituent Galleries:

Gallery of Costume: Platt Hall, Rusholme, Manchester, M14 5LL; tel. (161) 245-7245; e-mail m.lambert@manchester.gov .uk; internet www.manchestergalleries .org; f. 1947; 18th-century fmr textile merchant's house; 20,000 items of clothing and fashion accessories from 17th century to the present; library of 20,000 vols, 25000 portrait photographs, fashion journals, tailoring and etiquette books, shop catalogues, paper patterns; Senior Man. Dr MILES LAMBERT.

Heaton Hall: Heaton Park, Prestwich, Manchester, M25 5SW; tel. (161) 773-2581; fax (161) 235-8805; e-mail galleryeducation@notes.manchester.gov .uk; internet www.manchestergalleries .org; Grade I listed, 18th-century neo-classical country house; interiors restored to illustrate life as it was in the late 18th and 19th centuries.

Manchester Art Gallery: Mosley St, Manchester, M2 3JL; tel. (161) 235-8888; fax (161) 235-8899; e-mail galleryeducation@notes.manchester.gov .uk; internet www.manchestergalleries .org; f. 2002 following re-organization of the fmr Manchester City Art Gallery; 25,000 items; fine art colln includes 2,000 oil paintings, 3,000 watercolours and drawings, 250 sculptures, 90 miniatures, 1,000 prints, notable works by the Pre-Raphaelites: Rossetti, Millais, Hunt, Burne-Jones; colln of decorative arts ranges from ancient Greek pottery to contemporary furniture; contemporary local art and design, incl. works by Lowry; gallery of craft and design.

Wythenshawe Hall: Wythenshawe Park, Northenden, Manchester, M23 0AB; tel. (161) 990-5083; fax (161) 235-8805; e-mail galleryeducation@notes.manchester.gov .uk; internet www.manchestergalleries .org; f. 1926; Tudor house.

Manchester Museum: Univ. of Manchester, Oxford Rd, Manchester, M13 9PL; tel. (161) 275-2634; fax (161) 275-2676; e-mail museum@manchester.ac.uk; internet www .manchester.ac.uk/museum; f. 1821; archaeology, Egyptology, ethnology, geology, botany, zoology, entomology, archery, numismatics; education and exhibition services; 15 galleries; public events for families and adults; Dir Dr NICHOLAS MERRIMAN.

Museum of Science and Industry in Manchester: Liverpool Rd, Castlefield, Manchester, M3 4FP; tel. (161) 832-2244; e-mail collections@msim.org.uk; internet www.msim.org.uk; f. 1983; housed in the world's oldest passenger railway station; explores the history, science and industry of Manchester, with displays focusing on textiles, communications, utilities, steam power and the railways, cameras, aircraft; Xperiment! (interactive science centre); Dir IAN GRIFFIN (acting).

Urbis: Cathedral Gardens, Manchester, M4 3BG; tel. (161) 605-8200; e-mail info@urbis .org.uk; internet www.urbis.org.uk; f. 2002; exhibits on social, historical and cultural

aspects of city life, with interactive galleries; Learning Admin. ALEXIA ANTHONY.

Newcastle upon Tyne

Tyne and Wear Museums: Discovery Museum, Blandford Sq., Newcastle upon Tyne, NE1 4JA; tel. (191) 232-6789; fax (191) 230-2614; internet www.twmuseums .org.uk; f. 1974; Dir ALEC COLES.

Selected Museums and Galleries:

Arbeia Roman Fort: Baring St, South Shields, NE33 2BB; tel. (191) 456-1369; fax (191) 427-6862; internet www.twmuseums .org.uk/arbeia; f. 1953; Roman coins, military equipment, pottery, jewellery; excavations and reconstructions; Curator ALEX CROOM.

Discovery Museum: Blandford Sq., Newcastle upon Tyne, NE1 4JA; tel. (191) 232-6789; fax (191) 230-2614; e-mail discovery@twmuseums.org.uk; internet www.twmuseums.org.uk/discovery; f. 1934; displays of fashion, military history, social history and maritime history, and ship *Turbinia*; Museum Man. HAZEL EDWARDS.

Great North Museum: Barras Bridge, Newcastle upon Tyne, NE2 4PT; tel. (191) 222-6765; fax (191) 261-7537; internet www.twmuseums.org.uk/greatnorthmuseum; f. 2009, incorporates collns from the Hancock Museum (f. 1829), Newcastle Univ.'s Museum of Antiquities (f. 1813), the Shefton Museum (f. 1956) and the Hatton Gallery; reserve natural science and archaeology collns comprising 500,000 items; large-scale, interactive model of Hadrian's Wall, displays of the animal and plant kingdoms, objects from ancient Greece, mummies from ancient Egypt, planetarium.

Laing Art Gallery: New Bridge St, Newcastle upon Tyne, NE1 8AG; tel. (191) 232-7734; e-mail infor@laingartgallery.org.uk; internet www.laingartgallery.org.uk; f. 1904; British oil paintings and watercolours since 1700 (incl. works by Reynolds, Gainsborough, Turner, Landseer, Burne-Jones, Holman Hunt, Spencer, etc.); silver, ceramics and glass (incl. display of enamelled glass by William Beilby); Curator JULIE MILNE.

Monkwearmouth Station Museum: North Bridge St, Sunderland, SR5 1AP; tel. (191) 567-7075; fax (191) 510-9415; e-mail info@ monkwearmouthstationmuseum.org.uk; internet www .monkwearmouthstationmuseum.org.uk; f. 1973; collns relating to transport, incl. rolling stock, printed material, photographs and models; Curator JULIET HORSLEY.

Segedunum Roman Fort, Baths and Museum: Buddle St, Wallsend, NE28 6HR; tel. (191) 236-9347; fax (191) 295-5858; internet www.twmuseums.org.uk/segedunum; f. 2000; Roman collection incl. defensive missiles from the fort; Industry Gallery has artefacts associated with coalmining and shipbuilding, incl. model of the ship *Carpathia*; Curator GEOFF WOODWARD.

Shipley Art Gallery: Prince Consort Rd, Gateshead, NE8 4JB; tel. (191) 477-1495; e-mail shipley@twmuseums.org.uk; internet www.twmuseums.org.uk/shipley; f. 1917; contemporary craft; design; decorative arts; British and European paintings; Curator AMY BARKER.

South Shields Museum and Art Gallery: Ocean Rd, South Shields, NE33 2JA; tel. (191) 456-8740; fax (191) 456-7850;

internet www.twmuseums.org.uk/southshields; local history in relation to South Tyneside; Catherine Cookson gallery; local art and crafts; Curator ALISDAIR WILSON.

Stephenson Railway Museum: Middle Engine Lane, North Shields, NE29 8DX; tel. and fax (191) 200-7146; internet www.twmuseums.org.uk/stephenson; colln of steam, diesel and electric locomotives, incl. the early locomotive *Billy*; social history relating to railways; Curator JOHN CLAYSON.

Sunderland Museum and Winter Gardens: Burdon Rd, Sunderlands SR1 1PP; tel. (191) 553-2323; fax (191) 553-7828; internet www.twmuseums.org.uk/sunderland; f. 1846; archaeology, local history, geology, glass, pottery, paintings (incl. by Lowry), natural history; ethnography; Curator JULIET HORSLEY.

Newport (Gwent)

Newport Museum and Art Gallery: John Frost Square, Newport, NP20 1PA; tel. (1633) 840064; e-mail museum@newport.gov.uk; internet www.newport.gov.uk; f. 1888; collns of Roman material from Caerleon and Caerwent; oils, early English watercolours and prints, and other paintings (incl. by Lowry); teapot displays; ceramics; natural and local history collections; Museums Officer (Collections) BRUCE CAMPBELL; Museums and Heritage Officer MIKE LEWIS.

Norwich

Norfolk Museums and Archaeology Service: The Shirehall, Market Ave, Norwich, NR1 3JQ; tel. (1603) 493625; fax (1603) 493623; e-mail museums@norfolk.gov.uk; internet www.museums.norfolk.gov.uk; Head of Museums VANESSA TREVELYAN.

Selected Museums:

Ancient House Museum: White Hart St, Thetford; tel. (1842) 752599; e-mail ancient.house.museum@norfolk.gov.uk; 15th-century timber-framed bldg; local history; Curator OLIVER BONE.

Bridewell Museum: Bridewell Alley, Norwich, NR2 1AQ; tel. (1603) 629127; fax (1603) 614018; e-mail hannah.maddox@norfolk.gov.uk; local industries and crafts in medieval house; Curator HANNAH MADDOX.

Cromer Museum: Cromer; tel. (1263) 513543; e-mail cromer.museum@norfolk.gov.uk; internet www.museums.norfolk.gov.uk; f. 1978; local history, archaeology, geology, natural history; Curator ALISTAIR MURPHY; Area Museum Officer JAMIE EVERITT.

Elizabethan House Museum: Great Yarmouth; tel. (1493) 745526; fax (1493) 745459; domestic life, toys, porcelain, glassware.

Gressenhall Farm and Workhouse: Gressenhall; tel. (1362) 860563; e-mail gressenhall.museum@norfolk.gov.uk; historic workhouse; social and rural history displays and collections; farm with rare breeds of animal.

Lynn Museum: Market St, King's Lynn, PE30 1NL; tel. (1553) 75001; e-mail lynn.museum@norfolk.gov.uk; social history, natural history, archaeology and geology of West Norfolk.

Norwich Castle Museum and Art Gallery: Castle Meadow, Norwich, NR1 3JN; tel. (1603) 493625; fax (1603) 493623; e-mail museums@norfolk.gov.uk; internet www.museums.norfolk.gov.uk; f. 1894; Norman keep; fine art, ceramics, social history, natural history, archaeology.

Royal Norfolk Regimental Museum: Market Ave, Norwich, NR1 3JQ; tel. (1603) 493650; e-mail museums@norfolk.gov.uk; social history of the county regiment since 1685.

Time and Tide: Great Yarmouth; tel. (1493) 743930; various aspects of East Anglian maritime history.

Tolhouse Museum: Great Yarmouth; tel. (1493) 745526; fax (1493) 745459; e-mail yarmouth.museums@norfolk.gov.uk; internet www.museums.norfolk.gov.uk; history of crime and punishment in Great Yarmouth.

Town House: 46 Queen St, King's Lynn, PE30 5DQ; tel. (1553) 773450; social history of King's Lynn.

Sainsbury Centre for Visual Arts: Univ. of East Anglia, Norwich, NR4 7TJ; tel. (1603) 593199; e-mail scva@uea.ac.uk; internet www.scva.ac.uk; f. 1978; modern European art and art, sculpture and design of other cultures and periods; library of 13,000 vols (mainly non-Western art and anthropology); Dir Prof. PAUL GREENHALGH.

Nottingham

Nottingham Castle Museum: Friar Lane, off Maid Marian Way, Nottingham, NG1 6EL; tel. (115) 915-3700; fax (115) 915-3653; e-mail castle@ncmg.org.uk; internet www.nottinghamcity.org.uk; f. 1878; archaeology and ethnography, fine and applied arts, military, social and local history; Dir MICHAEL WILLIAMS.

Nottingham Natural History Museum: Wollaton Hall, Nottingham, NG8 2AE; tel. (115) 915-3900; fax (115) 915-3940; internet www.nottinghamcity.gov.uk; f. 1867; collections of botanical, zoological, and geological material; extensive British and foreign herbaria, Crowfoot collection of exotic butterflies, Pearson collection of European butterflies, Fowler collection of British Coleoptera, Hollier collection of Wenlock Limestone fossils, Carrington series of Mountain Limestone fossils; library of 3,500 vols; Nottinghamshire environmental database; controlled by Nottingham City Council; Senior Keeper G. WALLEY.

Overton

National Coal Mining Museum for England: Caphouse Colliery, New Rd, Overton, Wakefield, WF4 4RH; tel. (1924) 848806; fax (1924) 840694; e-mail info@ncm.org.uk; internet www.ncm.org.uk; f. 1988; mine workings and mine exhibits; library of 20,000 vols, library of material on all aspects of coal-mining; Museum Dir Dr MARGARET FAULL; Librarian ANISHA CHRISTISON; Librarian JUDITH DENNIS.

Oxford

Ashmolean Museum, University of Oxford: Beaumont St, Oxford, OX1 2PH; tel. (1865) 278000; fax (1865) 278018; e-mail director@ashmus.ox.ac.uk; internet www.ashmolean.org; f. 1683; contains the art and archaeological collns of the Univ. of Oxford; British, European, Mediterranean, Egyptian and Near Eastern archaeology; Italian, Dutch, Flemish, French and English oil paintings; Old Master and modern drawings, watercolours and prints; miniatures; European ceramics; sculpture and bronzes; English silver; objects of applied art; Hope colln of engraved portraits; coins and medals of all countries and periods; Chinese and Japanese porcelain, paintings and lacquer; Chinese bronzes, Tibetan art; Indian sculpture and painting; Islamic pottery and metalwork; Dir Dr CHRISTOPHER BROWN.

Modern Art Oxford: 30 Pembroke St, Oxford, OX1 1BP; tel. (1865) 722733; fax (1865) 722573; e-mail info@modernartoxford.org; internet www.modernartoxford.org.uk; f. 1965; exhibits contemporary and 20th-century painting, sculpture, design, photography, architecture, film and video; Dir MICHAEL STANLEY.

Pitt Rivers Museum, University of Oxford: South Parks Rd, Oxford, OX1 3PP; tel. (1865) 270927; fax (1865) 270943; e-mail prm@prm.ox.ac.uk; internet www.prm.ox.ac.uk; f. 1884; attached to School of Anthropology and Museum of Ethnography; ethnographic, archaeological and related photographic and manuscript collns; library of 45,000 vols, 250 periodicals; spec. collns of historic photographs and MSS; Dir Dr MICHAEL O'HANLON.

Plymouth

Plymouth City Museum and Art Gallery: Drake Circus, Plymouth, PL4 8AJ; tel. (1752) 304774; fax (1752) 304775; e-mail museum@plymouth.gov.uk; internet www.plymouth.gov.uk; f. 1897; illustrates the arts and sciences of the West Country; comprises the Cottonian Colln of early printed and illuminated books, Old Master engravings and drawings, portraits by Sir Joshua Reynolds; gen. collns of Fine Art (since 16th century) and of Decorative Arts incl. Plymouth silver and William Cookworthy's Plymouth and Bristol porcelain; natural history, ethnography, archaeology and local history; the Merchant's House (f. 1977), 33 St Andrew's St (16th–17th centuries); the Elizabethan House (f. 1929), 32 New St (16th century) and Smeaton's Tower lighthouse, The Hoe; Curator NICOLA MOYLE.

Portsmouth

Portsmouth City Museum and Records Office: Museum Rd, Portsmouth, PO1 2LJ; tel. (23) 9282-7261; fax (23) 9287-5276; e-mail mvs@portsmouthcc.gov.uk; internet www.portsmouthmuseums.co.uk; f. 1972; local history, fine and decorative art; re-creation of domestic interiors from various periods; Arthur Conan Doyle Colln; Fine and Decorative Art Gallery; Records Office contains official records of the City of Portsmouth since 14th century; Museums and Records Services Man. Dr JANE MEE.

Branch Museums:

Charles Dickens Birthplace: 393 Old Commercial Rd, Portsmouth, PO1 4QL; tel. (23) 9282-7261; fax (23) 9287-5276; e-mail mvs@portsmouthcc.gov.uk; internet www.portsmouthmuseums.co.uk; f. 1904; built 1805; birthplace of Charles Dickens in 1812; a small terraced house restored, decorated and furnished in the Regency style; Museums and Records Services Man. Dr JANE MEE.

D-Day Museum and Overlord Embroidery: Clarence Esplanade, Southsea, PO5 3NT; tel. (23) 9282-7261; fax (23) 9287-5276; e-mail mvs@portsmouthcc.gov.uk; internet www.ddaymuseum.co.uk; f. 1984; houses the 'Overlord Embroidery', commemorating the D-Day Landings; displays of original archive material, vehicles, uniforms and artefacts; Museums and Records Services Man. Dr JANE MEE.

Southsea Castle: Clarence Esplanade, Southsea, PO5 3PA; tel. (23) 9282-7261; fax (23) 9287-5276; e-mail mvs@portsmouthcc.gov.uk; internet www.portsmouthmuseums.co.uk; f. 1967; built 1544 by Henry VIII to protect Portsmouth harbour; 'Life in the Castle' experience; history of the defences of Portsmouth; displays on the Tudors, the English Civil

War, 18th century and the Victorian period; audiovisual show and underground passages; Museums and Records Services Man. Dr JANE MEE.

Preston

Harris Museum and Art Gallery: Market Sq., Preston, Lancs., PR1 2PP; tel. (1772) 258248; fax (1772) 886764; e-mail harris .museum@preston.gov.uk; internet www .harrismuseum.org.uk; f. 1893; fine art, decorative art, costumes and textiles, archaeology, local history, photography; Head of Arts and Heritage Services ALEXANDRA WALKER.

Reading

Museum of English Rural Life: Univ. of Reading, Redlands Rd, Reading, RG1 5EX; tel. (118) 378-8660; fax (118) 378-5632; e-mail merl@reading.ac.uk; internet www .reading.ac.uk/merl; f. 1951; nat. colln of objects, photographs, archives, records and publs relating to English rural and agricultural history; 1m. photographic prints and negatives; library of 70,000 vols incl. large sections on agricultural sciences and technology and pre-1950 agricultural devt overseas; Dir KATE ARNOLD-FORSTER.

Museum of Reading: Blagrave St, Reading, Berks, RG1 1QH; tel. (118) 939-9800; fax (118) 939-9881; e-mail curator@ readingmuseum.org.uk; internet www .readingmuseum.org.uk; f. 1883; collns cover art, archaeology, local history, world history and natural history; over 400,000 objects of local, regional and nat. importance incl. archaeological finds from the Roman site at Silchester, British artworks from between the wars, Romanesque carvings from Reading Abbey and the Huntley and Palmers Colln relating to the famous Reading biscuit company; also offers Hands-on Learning programme for schools and community groups, incl. loan box service; Sr Curator MATTHEW WILLIAMS.

Salisbury

Salisbury and South Wiltshire Museum: The King's House, 65 The Close, Salisbury, Wilts., SP1 2EN; tel. (1722) 332151; fax (1722) 325611; e-mail museum@ salisburymuseum.org.uk; internet www .salisburymuseum.org.uk; f. 1860; archaeology, local history, ceramics, costume, Pitt Rivers colln, topographical pictures, numismatics; temporary exhibitions; Dir P. R. SAUNDERS.

Selborne

Gilbert White's House and Garden and the Oates Museum: The Wakes, High St, Selborne, Alton, Hants; tel. (1420) 511275; e-mail info@gilbertwhiteshouse.org.uk; f. 1954; private collections funded by the Oates Memorial Trust; furnished period rooms, original MSS about the natural history of Selborne; 18th-century plants grown in the garden; exploration in Africa by Frank Oates and in Antarctica by Capt. Lawrence Oates; Oates Memorial Library.

Sheffield

Kelham Island Museum: Alma St, Sheffield, S3 8RY; tel. (114) 272-2106; fax (114) 275-7847; e-mail postmaster@simt.co.uk; internet www.simt.co.uk/kelham; f. 1982; objects, pictures and archives relating to Sheffield's industrial heritage; Exec. Dir JOHN HAMSHERE.

Weston Park Museum: Western Bank, Sheffield, S10 2TP; tel. (114) 278-2600; e-mail info@sheffieldgalleries.co.uk; internet www.sheffieldgalleries.org.uk; f. 1875 as Sheffield City Museum and Mappin Art Gallery; collns of Sheffield cutlery, Old Sheffield Plate, British and European cutlery, coins and medals, ceramics, local archaeology, natural sciences, local geology, etc.; Victorian paintings, Old Masters; Dir NICK DODD.

Singleton

Weald and Downland Open Air Museum: Singleton, Chichester, PO18 0EU; tel. (1243) 811363; fax (1243) 811475; e-mail courses@ wealddown.co.uk; internet www.wealddown .co.uk; f. 1967 to save interesting examples of vernacular architecture from South-east England that have been threatened with demolition; more than 45 bldgs ranging from early medieval times to the 19th century have been re-erected on the site; working exhibits incl. a watermill and treadwheel; working farm with animals; continuing education courses for adults in building conservation, traditional building methods and traditional rural trades and crafts; diverse curriculum of subjects offered to schools, Masters degree course in building conservation and timber building conservation; library: research library and archive; Dir RICHARD HARRIS; Head of Learning DIANA ROWSELL.

Southampton

Southampton City Art Gallery: Civic Centre, Commercial Rd, Southampton, SO14 7LP; tel. (23) 8083-2277; fax (23) 8083-2153; e-mail art.gallery@southampton .gov.uk; internet www.southampton.gov.uk/ leisure/arts; f. 1916 by a bequest fund for purchase and display of works of art; opened 1939; collns incl. Old Masters, French 19th- and 20th-century Schools, British painting since the 18th century, with emphasis on the Camden Town School; large colln of British contemporary painting and sculpture; library of 1,500 vols; Curator of Art TIM CRAVEN.

Southport

Atkinson Art Gallery: Lord St, Southport, PR8 1DH; tel. (151) 934-2110; fax (151) 934-2109; internet www.seftonarts.co.uk; f. 1878 for the exhibition of the town's permanent colln; British oils and watercolours since the 18th century; contemporary sculpture, paintings and prints; closed for refurbishment until 2013; Arts and Cultural Services Man. (Museums and Galleries) JOANNA JONES.

Stoke on Trent

Chatterley Whitfield Mining Museum: Tunstall, Stoke on Trent, ST6 8UN; tel. (1782) 813337; f. 1979 at a former colliery; aims to demonstrate the realities of mining development; recreation of surface and underground conditions; reference library; mining artefacts, photographs, films, documents, maps and plans, and oral history recordings; Dir JAMES HUTCHINSON; publs *Chatterley Whitfield News*, *Primary Teachers' Pack*, *Schools Roadshow Pack*.

Stoke on Trent Museums: Bethesda St, Hanley, Stoke on Trent, ST1 3DW; tel. (1782) 232323; fax (1782) 232500; e-mail museums@ stoke.gov.uk; internet www.stokemuseums .org.uk; Head of Museums IAN LAWLEY.

Constituent Museums:

Etruria Industrial Museum: Lower Bedford St, Etruria, Stoke on Trent, ST4 7AF; tel. (1782) 233144; fax (1782) 233141; e-mail museums@stoke.gov.uk; internet www.stokemuseums.org.uk; steam-powered potter's mill.

Ford Green Hall: Ford Green Rd, Smallthorne, Stoke on Trent, ST6 1NG; tel. (1782) 233195; fax (1782) 233194; e-mail fordgreenhall.museum@gmail.com; internet www.stokemuseums.org.uk; 17th-century timber-framed bldg and period garden.

Gladstone Pottery Museum: Uttoxeter Rd, Longton, Stoke on Trent, ST3 1PQ; tel. (1782) 237777; fax (1782) 237076; e-mail gladstone@stoke.gov.uk; internet www .stokemuseums.org.uk; f. 1974; complete Victorian pottery factory; workshops demonstrating traditional skills; Visitor Services KERRY WALTERS, ALISON PORTER.

Potteries Museum and Art Gallery: Bethesda St, City Centre, Stoke on Trent, ST1 3DW; tel. (1782) 232323; fax (1782) 232500; e-mail museums@stoke.gov.uk; internet www.stokemuseums.org.uk; Staffordshire pottery and porcelain, art, natural history, archaeology, local history; Strategic Man. KEITH BLOOR.

Wakefield

Wakefield Metropolitan District Council Access and Culture—Libraries and Museums: Wakefield Art Gallery, Wentworth Terrace, Wakefield, WF1 3QW; tel. (1924) 305796; fax (1924) 305770; e-mail cmacdonald@wakefield.gov.uk; internet www.wakefield.gov.uk/culture; f. 1934; museums and sites incl. Wakefield Art Gallery, Wakefield Museum, Pontefract Museum, Castleford Museum Room, Pontefract Castle, Sandal Castle, Clarke Hall Educational Museum; Head of Libraries and Museums COLIN MACDONALD.

Weybridge

Brooklands Museum: Brooklands Rd, Weybridge, Surrey, KT13 0QN; tel. (1932) 857381; fax (1932) 855465; e-mail info@ brooklandsmuseum.com; internet www .brooklandsmuseum.com; f. 1991; cars, motorcycles, aircraft, historic Brooklands racetrack, interactive science gallery; Dir ALLAN WINN.

Widnes

Catalyst—Science Discovery Centre and Museum: Mersey Rd, Widnes, WA8 0DF; tel. (151) 420-1121; e-mail info@catalyst.org.uk; internet www.catalyst.org.uk; f. 1987; informs the public about the role of chemistry in society past and present, incl. its relationship to the environment; enthuses school pupils about science through workshops, science demonstrations and interactive galleries; colln of relevant artefacts; library: reference library on history of the chemical industry; archive of historical photographs, industry archives; Marketing Officer MERYL JAMESON.

Wolverhampton

Wolverhampton Art Gallery and Museums: Lichfield St, Wolverhampton, WV1 1DU; tel. (1902) 552055; fax (1902) 552053; e-mail artgallery@wolverhampton .gov.uk; internet www.wolverhamptonart .org.uk; f. 1884; collns of fine art since the 18th century and temporary exhibitions; br. museums: Bantock House (period house, enamels, japanned ware); Bilston Craft Gallery (contemporary craft and temporary exhibitions); Head of Arts and Museums CORINNE MILLER.

York

Jorvik Viking Centre: Coppergate, York, YO1 9WT; tel. (1904) 615505; fax (1904) 627097; e-mail jorvik@yorkat.co.uk; internet www.vikingjorvik.com; f. 1984; reconstruction of part of the Viking city of Jorvik, based on archaeological evidence; many artefacts from the York Archaeological Trust's excavation are on display in the Gallery; Dir of Attractions SARAH MALTBY.

National Railway Museum: Leeman Rd, York, YO26 4XJ; tel. (844) 815139; e-mail nrm@nrm.org.uk; internet www.nrm.org.uk; f. 1975; part of the Science Museum (*q.v.*); houses a large part of the National Railway Colln reflecting over 150 years of British railway heritage; full-size rolling stock of diesel, electric and steam locomotives, carriages and wagons, models, signalling equipment, railway relics, posters, prints, films, technical drawings, photographs and paintings; Institute of Railway Studies, based at the Museum, provides university-level teaching on history and heritage of rail and urban transport; library of 15,000 vols; Head STEVE DAVIES.

York Castle Museum: Eye of York, York, YO1 9RY; tel. (1904) 687687; e-mail castle.museum@ymt.org.uk; internet www.yorkcastlemuseum.org.uk; f. 1938; England's first major folk museum; Kirk collection illustrates English life since the 17th century, including reconstructed shops and streets; also costumes, arms and armour, craft workshops, 1960s exhibition and the 18th-century Castle Prison; Museums Man. IAN CARLISLE.

York City Art Gallery: Exhibition Sq., York, YO1 7EW; tel. (1904) 687687; fax (1904) 697966; e-mail art.gallery@ymt.org.uk; internet www.yorkartgallery.org.uk; f. 1879; paintings of the Italian, Dutch, Flemish, German, French, Spanish and British Schools; William Etty colln; large colln of 20th-century studio ceramics; library of 7,000 vols; Gallery Man. LORNA SERGEANT; Curator LAURA TURNER.

Yorkshire Museum: Museum Gardens, York, YO1 7FR; tel. (1904) 687687; e-mail yorkshire.museum@ymt.org.uk; internet www.yorkshiremuseum.org.uk; f. 1822; archaeology (Romans, Anglo-Saxon, Viking and medieval life); natural history and geology; Museums Man. IAN CARLISLE.

Universities in England

ANGLIA RUSKIN UNIVERSITY

Chelmsford Campus: Bishop Hall Lane, Chelmsford, CM1 1SQ
Cambridge Campus: East Rd, Cambridge, CB1 1PT
Telephone: (1245) 683757
Fax: (1245) 490835
E-mail: answers@apu.ac.uk
Internet: www.anglia.ac.uk
Founded 1858, present status 1992, present name 2005
Academic year: September to July
Chancellor: Lord ASHCROFT
Vice-Chancellor: Prof. MICHAEL THORNE
Deputy Vice-Chancellor: Prof. ALAN SIBBALD
Deputy Vice-Chancellor: Prof. HELEN VALENTINE
Deputy Vice-Chancellor: Prof. LESLEY DOBREE
Librarian: NICKY KERSHAW
Library of 152,885 vols, 73,000 e-books, 16,920 electronic and print journals
Number of teachers: 709
Number of students: 31,000

DEANS

Faculty of Arts, Law and Social Science: DERRIK FERNEY
Faculty of Health, Social Care and Education: Prof. DAVID HUMBER
Faculty of Science and Technology: Prof. EAMON STRAIN
Lord Ashcroft International Business School: Dr TREVOR BOLTON

ASTON UNIVERSITY

Aston Triangle, Birmingham, B4 7ET
Telephone: (121) 204-3000
Fax: (121) 204-3696
E-mail: prospectus@aston.ac.uk
Internet: www.aston.ac.uk
Founded 1895, present status 1966
Academic year: October to June
Chancellor: Sir MICHAEL BETT
Pro-Chancellor: Dr PAUL GOLBY
Vice-Chancellor: Prof. JULIA KING
Sr Pro-Vice-Chancellor: Prof. HELEN HIGSON
Pro-Vice-Chancellor for Learning and Teaching Innovation: Prof. ALISON HALSTEAD
Pro-Vice-Chancellor for Business Partnerships and Knowledge Transfer: Dr PHIL EXTANCE
Pro-Vice-Chancellor for Research: Prof. MARTIN GRIFFIN
Univ. Sec.: ADELE MACKINLAY
Dir of Library and Information Services: Dr NICK SMITH
Library: see under Libraries and Archives
Number of teachers: 343
Number of students: 6,623 (5,700 full-time, 923 part-time)

DEANS

Aston Business School: Prof. MIKE WEST
School of Engineering and Applied Science: Prof. ROBERT BERRY
School of Languages and Social Science: Prof. PAM MOORES
School of Life and Health Sciences: Prof. HELEN GRIFFITHS

PROFESSORS

ANDERSON, S., Clinical Neuroscience
BAILEY, C., Pharmacology
BARKER, P., Chemical Engineering
BENNET, D., Technology Management and Head of International Liaison, Aston Business School
BENNION, I., Opto Electronics
BHATTACHARYYA, G., Sociology
BLOW, K., Photonic Systems
BOOTH, R., Occupational Health and Safety
BRETT, P., Medical Engineering
BRIDGWATER, T., Engineering and Applied Science
BRIGNALL, S., Finance Accounting and Law, Aston Business School
BROOKES, J., Life and Health Sciences
BROWN, M., Pharmacy
CHELLEY-STEELEY, P., Finance Accounting and Law, Aston Business School
COLEMAN, M., Toxicology, Medicinal Chemistry
COULTHARD, M., Forensic Linguistics
FLOOD, J., Electronic Engineering
FURLONG, P., Clinical Neuroimaging
GAFFNEY, J., Languages and Social Sciences
GEOFFREY, G., Chemical Engineering
GEORGESON, M., Vision Sciences
GIBSON, J., Ophthalmology
GILMARTIN, B., Optometry
GREEN, S., Languages and Social Sciences
GRIFFIN, M., Biochemistry
HARDING, G., Life and Health Sciences
HART, M., Small Business and Entrepreneurship
HOMER, J., Chemistry
HORNUNG, A., Chemical Engineering
JARZABKOWSKI, P., Strategic Management, Aston Business School
JOSEPH, N., Finance Accounting and Law, Aston Business School
LOWE, A., Finance Accounting and Law, Aston Business School
LOWE, D., Informatics
MARRIOTT, J., Pharmacy Practice
NABNEY, T., Computer Science
PEARCE, G., Finance Accounting and Law, Aston Business School

PENNY, J., Engineering Systems and Management
POOLE, J., Commercial Law
PORTER, K., Chemical Engineering
REERSHEMIUS, G., German Linguistics
ROBERTS, B., Auditory Perception
ROGERS, M., Economics and Strategy, Aston Business School
ROPER, S., Business Innovation, Aston Business School
SAAD, D., Information Maths
SAUNDERS, J., Marketing, Aston Business School
SCHWALBE, C., Medicinal Chemistry
SCOTT, G., Chemical Engineering
SERI, S., Clinical Neurophysiology
SHAW, D., Operations and Information Management, Aston Business School
SILLINCE, J., Operations and Information Management, Aston Business School
STEELEY, J., Finance Accounting and Law, Aston Business School
STEVENS, A., European Studies
SULLIVAN, J., Surface Science
TANSLEY, G., Mechanical Engineering
THANASSOULIS, E., Operations and Information Management, Aston Business School
TIGHE, J., Polymer Chemistry
TISDALE, M., Cancer Biochemistry
TURITSYN, S., Electronic Engineering
ZHANG, L., Electronic Engineering

BATH SPA UNIVERSITY

Newton Park Campus: Newton St Loe, Bath, BA2 9BN
Telephone: (1225) 875875
Fax: (1225) 875444
Sion Hill Campus: Lansdown, Bath, BA1 5SF
Telephone: (1225) 875875
Fax: (1225) 875666
E-mail: enquiries@bathspa.ac.uk
Internet: www.bathspa.ac.uk
Founded 1898, granted taught degree-awarding powers 1992; present name and status 2005
Academic year: September to June
Vice-Chancellor: Prof. FRANK MORGAN
Deputy Vice-Chancellor: Dr ALUN THOMAS
Deputy Vice-Chancellor: Prof. NEIL SAMMELLS
Deputy Vice-Chancellor: JON BRADY
Registrar: CHRISTOPHER ELLICOTT
Head of Library and Information Services: Prof. ALISON BAUD
Number of teachers: 600
Number of students: 5,500

BIRMINGHAM CITY UNIVERSITY

Perry Barr, Birmingham, B42 2SU
Telephone: (121) 331-5000
Fax: (121) 331-7994
E-mail: choices@bcu.ac.uk
Internet: www.bcu.ac.uk
Founded 1971, as Birmingham Polytechnic, gained university status in 1992 and was renamed Univ. of Central England in Birmingham, present name 2007
Academic year: October to July
Chancellor: Lord Mayor of Birmingham, Cllr MICHAEL NANGLE
Vice-Chancellor: Prof. DAVID TIDMARSH
Pro-Vice-Chancellor: SALLY WESTNEY
Pro-Vice-Chancellor: Prof. MARY CARSWELL
Pro-Vice-Chancellor for Corporate Devt: Prof. DAVID MAGUIRE
Univ. Sec.: CHRISTINE ABBOTT
Library of 950,000 vols, 9,000 journals
Number of teachers: 700
Number of students: 25,000

DEANS

Birmingham City Business School: Prof. CHRISTOPHER PRINCE

Birmingham Institute of Art and Design: Prof. CHRIS O'NEIL

Faculty of Education, Law and Social Sciences: Prof. R. WOODS

Faculty of Health: Prof. IAN BLAIR

Faculty of Performance, Media and English: Prof. JOHN ROUSE

Faculty of Technology, Engineering and Environment: Prof. MELVYN LEES

BOURNEMOUTH UNIVERSITY

Fern Barrow, Poole, BH12 5BB

Telephone: (1202) 524111

Fax: (1202) 962736

E-mail: enquiries@bournemouth.ac.uk

Internet: www.bournemouth.ac.uk

Founded 1976, as Dorset Institute of Higher Education, became Bournemouth Polytechnic 1990, present name and status 1992

Academic year: September to July

Chancellor: Lord NICHOLAS PHILLIPS

Vice-Chancellor: Prof. JOHN VINNEY

Deputy Vice-Chancellor: DAVID WILLEY

Pro-Vice-Chancellor for Academic Affairs: Prof. PAUL LUKER

Pro-Vice-Chancellor for Corporate Development and Finance: DAVID WILLEY

Registrar: NOEL RICHARDSON

Librarian: DAVID BALL

Library of 150,000 vols

Number of teachers: 391

Number of students: 17,502 incl. full-time and part-time

DEANS

Business School: Prof. ANDROS GREGORIOU

Media School: STEPHEN JUKES

School of Applied Sciences: Prof. MATTHEW BENNETT

School of Design, Engineering and Computing: Prof. JIM ROACH

School of Health and Social Care: Dr B. GAIL THOMAS

School of Tourism: Dr KEITH WILKES

BRUNEL UNIVERSITY

Kingston Lane, Uxbridge, UB8 3PH

Telephone: (1895) 274000

Fax: (1895) 232806

E-mail: admissions@brunel.ac.uk

Internet: www.brunel.ac.uk

Founded 1966 as Brunel College of Technology, College of Advanced Technology 1962, Univ. Charter 1966, inc. W London Institute in the Univ. in 1995

State control

Academic year: September to June

Chancellor: Lord WAKEHAM

Pro-Chancellor: Lord LINGFIELD

Vice-Chancellor and Prin.: Prof. CHRIS JENKS

Vice-Prin.: Prof. MANSOOR SARHADI

Pro-Vice-Chancellor for Quality Affairs: Dr MARIANN RAND-WEAVER

Pro-Vice-Chancellor for Research: Prof. GEOFF RODGERS

Pro-Vice-Chancellor for Strategy, Devt and External Relations: Prof. DANY NOBUS

Pro-Vice-Chancellor for Student Experience and Staff Devt: Prof. IAN CAMPBELL

Library of 458,000 vols, 17,000 journals

Number of teachers: 1,057

Number of students: 15,201

PROFESSORS

ABASS, A., Law

AKEMANN, G., Mathematical Sciences

AL-RAWESHIDY, H., Electronic and Computer Engineering

ANDERSON, N., Business and Management

ANDREWS, B., Brunel Institute of Bioengineering

ANGELIDES, M., Mechanical Engineering

BAHAI, H., Mechanical Engineering

BALACHANDRAN, W., Electronic and Computer Engineering

BALMER, J. M. T., Business and Management

BANTEKAS, I., Law

BEASLEY, J., Mathematical Sciences

BENNETT, J., Economics and Finance

BERESFORD, P., Social Care

BIRRINGER, J., Drama

BRACKENRIDGE, C., Sport

BRAGANZA, A., Business and Management

BROADHURST, S., Drama

BUCKINGHAM, S., Social Care

BUNCE, D., Psychology

BUXTON, M., Health Economics Research Group

CAMPOS, N., Economics and Finance

CAPEL, S., School of Sport and Education

CAPORALE, G., Economics and Finance

CHENG, K., Mechanical Engineering

CHIGARA, B., Law

COSMAS, J., Electronic and Computer Engineering

DESOUZA, L., School Health Sciences and Social Care

DICKSON, K., Business and Management

ESAT, I., Mechanical Engineering

EVANS, R., Biological Sciences

FISHER, D., Brunel Institute of Bioengineering

FISHER, J., Politics and History

FITZGERALD, G., Information Systems

FOX, C., Music

FOX-RUSHBY, J., Health Economics Research Group

GAN, T., Electronic and Computer Engineering

GIACOMIN, J., Design

GILBERT, D., Information Systems

GILHOOLY, M., Health Studies and Community Health

GOBET, F., Psychology

GONZALEZ-ALONSO, J., Sport

GOODWIN, R., Psychology

HACKNEY, R., Business and Management

HARRISON, D., Design

HARWIN, J., Social Care

HIERONS, R., Information Systems

HOBSON, P., Electronic and Computer Engineering

IOSSA, E., Economics and Finance

IRANI, Z., Brunel Business School

IRVING, M., Electronic and Computer Engineering

JAFFEY, P., Law

JARVIS, R., Business and Management

KAIKOBAD, K., Law

KAPLUNOV, J., Mathematical Sciences

KARANASOS, M., Economics and Finance

KARAYIANNIS, T., Mechanical Engineering

KATHIRGAMANATHAN, P., Wolfson Centre

KHAN, A., Electronic and Computer Engineering

KING, G., Film and Television

KLEINBERG, J., Politics and History

KOLOKOTRONI, M., Electronic and Computer Engineering

KOSHY, V., Education

KRZYWINSKA, T., Film and Television

KULJIS, J., Mathematical Sciences

KUMAR RAY, A., Wolfson Centre

LEASK, M., Education

LEROY, S., Environmental Studies

LIU, G., Business and Management

LIU, X., Information Systems

LOUVIERIS, P., Information Systems

LUNT, P., Sociology and Communication

MACREDIE, R., Information Systems

MCCONNELL, A., Sport

MIKHAILOV, S., Mathematical Sciences

MORGAN, K., Politics and History

MOUSSY, F., Brunel Institute of Bioengineering

MUSHKAT, R., Law

MYERS, L., Psychology

NEOCLEOUS, M., Politics and History

NEWBOLD, R., Cancer, Genetics and Pharmaceuticals

NOBUS, D., School of Social Sciences

OLOWOFOYEKU, A., Brunel Law School

PETLEY, J., Film and Television

PIPER, C., Law

POLDEN, P., Law

RAWLINS, A., Mathematical Sciences

REHMAN, J., Law

RITA VICTOR, C., Health Studies and Community Health

RIVERS, I., Sport

ROJEK, C., Sociology and Communication

SADKA, A., Electronic and Computer Engineering

SCAMANS, G., BCAST

SHARIF, A., Business and Management

SHEPPERD, M., Information Systems

SIMPSON, R., Business and Management

SONG, J., Mechanical Engineering

STELARC, X., Performance Arts

STOLARSKI, T., Mechanical Engineering

STONHAM, T., Electronic and Computer Engineering

SUMPTER, J., Institute for the Environment

TASSOU, S., School of Engineering and Design

TEW, P., English Studies

VASEGHI, S., Electronic and Computer Engineering

WANG, Z., Mathematical Sciences

WARLEIGH-LACK, A., Politics and History

WATKIN, W., English Studies

WATTS, M., Education

WELDON, F., English Studies

WHITEMAN, J., Mathematical Sciences

WIEGOLD, P., Music

WITHNALL, R., Wolfson Centre

WOODS, A., Business and Management

WOOLRICH, J., Music

WRIGHT, D., Design

WRIGHT, M., Psychology

WROBEL, L., Mechanical Engineering

WYDELL, T., Sociology and Communication

YOUNG, T., Information Systems

ZHAO, H., Mechanical Engineering

BUCKINGHAMSHIRE NEW UNIVERSITY

Queen Alexandra Rd, High Wycombe, HP11 2JZ

Telephone: (1494) 522141

Fax: (1494) 524392

E-mail: advice@bucks.ac.uk

Internet: bucks.ac.uk

Founded 1893; present name and status 2007

Vice-Chancellor and CEO: Prof. RUTH FARWELL

Deputy Vice-Chancellor: Prof. DEREK GODFREY

Pro-Vice-Chancellor: Prof. CHRIS KEMP

Pro-Vice-Chancellor: Prof. DAVID SINES

Pro-Vice-Chancellor: Prof. TREVOR NICHOLLS

Dir for Business Planning: STEPHEN DEWHURST

Number of students: 9,017

DEANS

Faculty of Design, Media and Management: Prof. CHRIS KEMP

Faculty of Society and Health: Prof. DAVID SINES

School of Advanced and Continuing Practice: LAUREN GRIFFITHS (Head)

School of Applied Management and Law: Dr LORRAINE WATKINS-MATHYS (Head)

School of Applied Production and New Media: FRAZER MACKENZIE (Head)

CANTERBURY CHRIST CHURCH UNIVERSITY

North Holmes Rd, Canterbury, CT1 1QU
Telephone: (1227) 767700
Fax: (1227) 470442
E-mail: admissions@canterbury.ac.uk
Internet: www.canterbury.ac.uk

Founded 1962 as a Church of England Teacher Training College; University College 1995; present name and status 2005

Chancellor: Dr ROWAN WILLIAMS
Vice-Chancellor: Prof. ROBIN BAKER
Pro-Chancellor: Prof. PETER HERMITAGE
Deputy Pro-Chancellor: STEPHEN CLARK
Sr Pro-Vice-Chancellor: Prof. JANET DRUKER
Pro-Vice-Chancellor: Dr PAUL DALTON
Pro-Vice-Chancellor: Prof. TONY LAVENDER
Pro-Vice-Chancellor for Academics: Prof. SUE PIOTROWSKI
Pro-Vice-Chancellor for Learning and Quality: Dr KEITH GWILYM
Pro-Vice-Chancellor for Students: Prof. MARGARET ANDREWS
Strategic Dir: ANDREW IRONSIDE

Number of teachers: 1,334 (f.t.e.)
Number of students: 16,755

Publication: *Inspire*

DEANS

Faculty of Arts and Humanities: Dr PAUL DALTON
Faculty of Business and Management: Prof. GIOIA PESCETTO
Faculty of Education: Dr JOHN MOSS
Faculty of Health and Social Care: HAZEL COLYER
Faculty of Social and Applied Sciences: Prof. TONY LAVENDER

CITY UNIVERSITY

Northampton Sq., London, EC1V 0HB
Telephone: (20) 7040-5060
Fax: (20) 7040-5070
E-mail: registry@city.ac.uk
Internet: www.city.ac.uk

Founded 1894 as Northampton Institute, Northampton College of Advanced Technology 1957, Univ. Charter 1966
Academic year: September to July

Chancellor: THE LORD MAYOR OF LONDON
Vice-Chancellor: Prof. PAUL CURRAN
Deputy Vice-Chancellor: Prof. JULIUS WEINBERG
Deputy Vice-Chancellor for Education: Prof. DAVID BOLTON
Deputy Vice-Chancellor for Research and Int.: Prof. DINOS ARCOUMANIS
Pro-Vice-Chancellor for External Affairs: Prof. COSTAS GRAMMENOS
Univ. Sec.: FRANK TOOP
Librarian: B. M. CASEY

Library of 350,000 vols
Number of teachers: 1,842
Number of students: 21,727

Publication: *City*

DEANS

Cass Business School: Prof. COSTAS GRAMMENOS
City Law School: SUSAN NASH (Dir)
School of Arts: CHRISTINA SLADE (acting)
School of Community and Health Sciences: MARTIN CARAHER (acting)
School of Engineering and Mathematical Sciences: KEN GRATTAN
School of Informatics: KEN GRATTAN
School of Social Sciences: CHRISTINA SLADE

PROFESSORS

ATKINSON, J. H., Soil Mechanics
BADEN-FULLER, C., Business Strategy
BARBUR, J. L., Optics and Visual Science

BARONE-ADESI, G., Financial Engineering
BATCHELOR, R., Banking and Finance
BOOTH, P., Real Estate Finance
BOSWELL, L. F., Civil Engineering
BOWERS, L., Psychiatric Nursing
BOYLAN, P. J., Arts Policy and Management
BRADLEY, K., Management
BRYER, R.
BUCKLEY, R. J., Ocular Medicine
BURN, E. H., Law
BURRIDGE, P., Economics
BYNG, S., Communication Disability
CAPIE, F. H., Economic History
CARSON, E. R., Systems Science
COHEN, B., Computing
COLLINS, M. A., Marketing Research
CONNELL, T. J., Languages for the Professions
COYLE, A., Sociology
CRESSY, R., Accounting and Finance
CROMPTON, R., Sociology
CUBBIN, J., Economics
D'ANDREA, V., Educational Development
DANIELS, P. G., Applied Mathematics
DICKINSON, G. M., International Insurance
DINENIS, E., Investment and Risk Management
DOCKRAY, M. S., Law
DONE, G. T. S., Aeronautics
DOUGLAS, R. H., Visual Science
FAHLE, M., Optometry
FINKELSTEIN, L., Measurement and Instrumentation
GARDINER, J. M., Psychology
GEMMILL, G. T., Finance
GLEN, S., Nursing
GLYCOPANTIS, D., Economics
GOLOMBOK, J. M., Psychology
GRAMMENOS, C. TH., Shipping, Trade and Finance
GRANT, R. M., Management
GRATTAN, K. T. V., Measurement and Instrumentation
GREENSLADE, R., Journalism
HABERMAN, S., Actuarial Science
HAINES, C. R., Mathematics Education
HAMPTON, J., Psychology
HEFFERNAN, S. A., Banking and Finance
HENDRY, C., Organizational Behaviour
HEYMAN, B., Nursing
HINES, M., Psychology
HOLTHAM, C. W., Information Management
KARCANIAS, N., Control Theory and Design
LASSFER, M., Finance
LEVIS, M., Finance
LITTLEWOOD, B., Software Engineering
LOVELAND, I., Law
McGUIRE, A. J., Economics
MARKS, D., Psychology
MARTIN, P. P., Mathematical Physics
MATHON, J., Mathematical Physics
MENOU, M., Information Policy
MEYER, J., Adult Nursing
MINTZ, B., Engineering Materials
MOODY, E., Arts Policy and Management
NEWBY, J., Statistical Science
PALMER, A. W., Electrical Engineering
PARKIN, D., Health Economics
PEAKE, D. J., Aero and Fluid Dynamics
PHYLAKTIS, E., International Finance
PRICE, S., Economics
PURDUE, H. M., Law
RAHMAN, A., Photonic Devices
RAPER, J. F., Information Science
RATTANSI, A., Sociology
RYAN, C. L., Law
SALMON, M., Financial Markets
SAMUEL, R., Music
SANDALL, J., Midwifery
SELIM, G., Internal Auditing
SMALLEY, D., Music
SMITH, I. K., Applied Thermodynamics
STEPHENSON, H., Journalism
STOSIC, N., Positive Displacement Compressor Technology
STRIGINI, L., Systems Engineering
TAYLOR, R. N., Geotechnical Engineering

THOMAS, P.
THORLEY, A. R. D., Fluid Engineering
TUMBER, H., Sociology
TUNSTALL, C. J., Sociology
VERRALL, R., Actuarial Science and Statistics
VIRDI, K. S., Structural Engineering
WATTS, M., Psychology
WEINBERG, J.
WILLETTS, P., Global Politics
WILLIAMS, A. P. O., Organizational and Occupational Psychology
WOLL, B., Sign Language and Deaf Studies
WOOD, G., Economics
WOODIWISS, A., Sociology
WOODWARD, E. G., Optometry and Visual Science
WOOTTON, L. R., Engineering

COVENTRY UNIVERSITY

Priory St, Coventry, CV1 5FB
Telephone: (24) 7688-7688
Fax: (24) 7688-8638
E-mail: info.rao@coventry.ac.uk
Internet: www.coventry.ac.uk

Founded 1970, by merger of Coventry College of Art, Lanchester College of Technology and Rugby College of Engineering Technology, present name and status 1992
Academic year: September to June

Chancellor: Sir JOHN EGAN
Vice-Chancellor: Prof. MADELAINE ATKINS
Deputy Chancellor for Business Devt: JOHN LATHAM
Deputy Vice-Chancellor for Acad.: Prof. IAN MARSHALL
Deputy Vice-Chancellor for Planning and Resources: DAVID SOUTTER
Pro-Vice-Chancellor for Continuous Improvement: DONNA KENDALL
Pro-Vice-Chancellor for Int. Experience and Mobility Service: Dr DAVID PILSBURY
Pro-Vice-Chancellor for Student Empowerment: IAN DUNN
Registrar and Sec.: KATE QUANTRELL
Librarian: P. NOON

Library of 400,000 vols
Number of teachers: 600
Number of students: 18,000

Publications: *Biological Agriculture and Horticulture* (4 a year), *Coventry University Law Journal* (2 a year), *The Holocene*, *International Journal of Media and Cultural Politics*, *Ultrasonics – Sonochemistry*

DEANS

Faculty of Business, Environment and Society: Prof. DAVID NOON
Faculty of Engineering and Computing: Prof. PAUL IVEY
Faculty of Health and Life Sciences: Dr LINDA MERRIMAN
School of Art and Design: Prof. JILL JOURNEAUX
School of Lifelong Learning Staff: SUE RIVERS (acting)

PROFESSORS

Faculty of Business, Environment and Society:

BAKER, B., African Security
BARRETT, H., Development Geography
BEIDER, H., Community Cohesion
BRODERICK, A., Marketing/Advertising
CANTLE, E.
CHADWICK, S., Sport Management and Marketing
DONNELLY, T., Automotive Business
FARNELL, R., Neighbourhood Regeneration
FORBES, N., International History
HARRIS, P., Plant Design
HUNTER, A., Asian Studies
McINTOSH, M., Human Security

MITCHELL, B., Criminal Law and Criminal Justice
NESI, H., English Language
NOON, D., Economic Regeneration
RENWICK, N., Global Security
RIGBY, A., Peace Studies
SKINNER, D., Human Resource Management
WORRALL, L., Strategic Analysis

Faculty of Engineering and Computing:
BENJAMIN, S., Fluid Dynamics
BLUNDELL, M., Vehicle Dynamics and Impact
BURNHAM, K., Industrial Control Systems
CHAO, K., Computing
CLAISSE, P., Construction Materials
HOLDO, A., Energy and Environment
IVEY, P.
JAMES, A., Data Systems Architecture
LAWSON, D., Mathematics and Education
LEHANEY, B., Statistics and Operational Research Subject Group
MOLOKOV, S., Applied Mathematics
NAGUIB, R., Biomedical Computing
POPPLEWELL, K., Engineering Manufacture and Management
WHITE, P., Thermofluid Dynamics

Faculty of Health and Life Sciences:
BARLOW, J., Health Psychology
HARRISON, K., Physiotherapy and Dietetics
MASON, T., Chemistry
SAVIN-BADEN, M., Higher Education Research
TOFT, B., Patient Safety
WALLACE, L., Psychology and Health
WOOLLARD, M., Pre-Hospital and Emergency Care

School of Art and Design:
DUTTON, S., Creative Practice
HALL, G., Media and Performing Arts
JOURNEAUX, J., Fine Art Education
RICHARDS, C., Information Design
WHATLEY, S., Dance
WOODCOCK, A., Educational Ergonomics and Design

CRANFIELD UNIVERSITY

Cranfield campus: Cranfield, MK43 0AL
Telephone: (1234) 750111
Fax: (1234) 750875

Shrivenham campus: CDT, Shrivenham, Swindon, SN6 8LA
Telephone: (1793) 785810
Fax: (1793) 783878
E-mail: info@cranfield.ac.uk
Internet: www.cranfield.ac.uk

Founded 1946 as College of Aeronautics; became Cranfield Institute of Technology 1969; took responsibility for academic work at Royal Military College of Science, Shrivenham, 1984; present name 1993
Academic year: October to September

Chancellor: Baroness BARBARA YOUNG OF OLD SCONE
Pro-Chancellor: GORDON PAGE
Vice-Chancellor: Prof. Sir JOHN O'REILLY
Deputy Vice-Chancellor: Prof. CLIFFORD FRIEND
Pro-Vice-Chancellor: Prof. DAVID J. STEPHENSON
Sec. and Registrar: Prof. WILLIAM STEPHENS
Univ. Librarian: SIMON BEVAN (acting)

Library of 440,915 vols, 9,708 journals (electronic and print)
Number of students: 2,300 , 13,000 short-course delegates per annum

PROFESSORS
AKHAVAN, J., Explosive Chemistry
ALLEN, D., Microengineering
ASPINALL, R., Translational Medicine
BARR, H., Medicine and Biosciences
BOLTON, S., Creative Design

BOURNE, M., Business Performance
BRAITHWAITE, G., Air Transport
BRENNAN, F., Offshore
BUCHANAN, D., Organizational Behaviour
BURKE, A., Entrepreneurship
CARR, K., Human Systems
CHIVERS, H., Information Systems
CULLEN, D., Bioanalytical Technology
DRIKAKIS, D., Aerospace Sciences
EDWARDS, C., Management Information Systems
FRIEND, C.
GARRY, K., Aerodynamics Group
GELMAN, L., Vibro-Acoustic Monitoring
GOFFIN, K., Innovation and New Product Development
GRAYSON, D., Corporate Social Responsibility
GUENOV, M., Engineering Design
HARRIS, J., Environmental Technology
HIGSON, S., Bio- and Electroanalysis
HORSFALL, I., Armour Systems
HORWITZ, F., Management
IRVING, P., CAA Damage Tolerance
JENKINS, M., Business Strategy
JOHN, P., Dept of Systems Engineering and Human Factors
JUDD, S., Membrane Technology
KAKABADSE, A., Management Development
KIBBLEWHITE, M., Applied Soil Science
KIRK, G., Soil Systems
KNOWLES, K., Aeromechanical Systems
LUNEC, J., Health
MAGAN, N., Applied Mycology
MATTHEWS, R., Defence Economics
MURRAY, S., Ordnance Science and Technology
NEAL, D., Defence Strategic Change
NEELY, A., Research
NELLIS, J., International Management Economics
NICHOLLS, J., Coatings Technology
OAKEY, J., Energy Technology
ORMONDROYD, R., Communication Networks
PARTRIDGE, I., Polymer Composites
PATEL, M., Engineering
PEPPARD, J., Information Systems
PILETSKY, S., Bio-Organic Polymer Chemistry
PILIDIS, P., Power and Propulsion
POLLARD, S., Environmental Risk Management
POSHAKWALE, S., International Finance
REINMOELLER, P., Strategic Management
RICKSON, J., Soil Erosion and Conservation
RITZ, K., Soil Biology
ROGERS, K., Materials/Medical Science
ROY, R., Competitive Design
RYALS, L., Strategic Sales—Account Management
SAVILL, M., Computational Aerodynamics Design
SHORE, P., Ultra Precision Engineering
SMITH, H., Security and Resilience
STEPHENSON, T., Applied Sciences
TATAM, R., Engineering Photonics Group
TAYLOR, J., Land Resources Monitoring
THOMPSON, C., Applied Mathematics and Computing
TSOURDOS, A., Control Engineering
TURNBULL JAMES, K., Executive Learning
TURNER, A., Biotechnology
VAUGHAN, N., Automotive Engineering Group
VIGNJEVIC, R., Applied Mechanics
VINNICOMBE, S., Organizational Behaviour
WALLACE, I.
WANG, F., e-Science and Grid Computing
WARNER, P., Molecular Diagnostics
WEBB, P., Engineering
WHITE, S., Integrated Catchment Management
WILDING, R., Supply Chain Risk Management
WILLIAMS, S., Welding Science and Technology
WILSON, H., Strategic Marketing
WITTY, R., Information Systems Engineering
ZBIKOWSKI, R., Control Engineering

DE MONTFORT UNIVERSITY

The Gateway, Leicester, LE1 9BH
Telephone: (116) 255-1551
Fax: (116) 250-6204
E-mail: enquiry@dmu.ac.uk
Internet: www.dmu.ac.uk

Founded 1969, as Leicester Polytechnic, later became Leicester Polytechnic; present name and status 1992

Chancellor: Lord WAHEED ALLI
Pro-Chancellor: DAVID STEVENS
Vice-Chancellor: Prof. DOMINIC SHELLARD
Pro-Vice-Chancellor for Research: (vacant)
Pro-Vice-Chancellor for Teaching, Learning and Student Experience: Prof. HEIDI MACPHERSON
Acad. Registrar: EUGENE CRITCHLOW
Univ. Librarian: K. ARNOLD

Library of 479,135 vols, 16,490 periodicals
Number of teachers: 3,240
Number of students: 20,500

DEANS
Faculty of Art and Design: Dr GERARD MORAN
Faculty of Business and Law: Prof. DAVID WILSON
Faculty of Health and Life Sciences: Prof. BARRY MITCHELL
Faculty of Humanities: Prof. TIM O'SULLIVAN
Faculty of Technology: Prof. ADRIAN HOPGOOD

EDGE HILL UNIVERSITY

St Helens Rd, Ormskirk, L39 4QP
Telephone: (1695) 575171
Fax: (1695) 579997
Internet: www.edgehill.ac.uk

Founded 1885, present status 2008

Chancellor: Prof. TANYA BYRON
Pro-Chancellor: CHRIS TRINICK
Vice-Chancellor: Dr JOHN CATER
Pro-Vice-Chancellor for Academic Affairs: Prof. BILL BRUCE
Pro-Vice-Chancellor for Students and External Relations: Dr DAVID LAW
Pro-Vice-Chancellor for Resources: STEVE IGOE
Univ. Sec. and Clerk to Governors: LESLEY MUNRO
Academic Registrar: IAN JONES
Dean of Learning Services: ALISON MACKENZIE

Number of teachers: 4,000
Number of students: 24,000

DEANS
Faculty of Arts and Sciences: GEORGE TALBOT
Faculty of Education: ROBERT SMEDLEY
Faculty of Health: SETH CROFTS

KINGSTON UNIVERSITY

River House, 53–57 High St, Kingston upon Thames, KT1 1LQ
Telephone: (20) 8417-9000
Fax: (20) 8547-7980
E-mail: admissions-info@kingston.ac.uk
Internet: www.kingston.ac.uk

Founded 1899, as Kingston Technical Institute, present name and status 1992
Academic year: September to July

Chancellor: Sir PETER HALL
Vice-Chancellor: Dr DAVID MACKINTOSH (acting)
Deputy Vice-Chancellor: Dr DAVID MACKINTOSH
Pro-Vice Chancellor for Acad. Support and Student Services: Prof. MARTYN JONES
Pro-Vice Chancellor for Corporate Affairs and Univ. Sec.: NEIL LATHAM
Pro-Vice-Chancellor for Research and Enterprise: Prof. PENNY SPARKE

Acad. Registrar: Dr DAVID ASHTON
Head of Library Services: GRAHAM BULPITT
Library of 450,000 vols
Number of teachers: 661
Number of students: 22,782
Publication: *Kingston review*

DEANS

Faculty of Art, Design and Architecture: Dr SIMON OFIELD-KERR
Faculty of Arts and Social Sciences: Prof. MARTIN MC QUILLON
Faculty of Business and Law: Prof. JEAN-NOEL EZINGRARD
Faculty of Computing, Information Systems and Mathematics: Prof. TIMOTHY ELLIS
Faculty of Engineering: Prof. PETER MASON
Faculty of Health and Social Care Sciences: Prof. FIONA ROSS
Faculty of Science: Prof. ANDY AUGOUSTI

LEEDS METROPOLITAN UNIVERSITY

City Campus, Leeds, LS1 3HE
Telephone: (113) 812-0000
E-mail: helpzone@leedsmet.ac.uk
Internet: www.leedsmet.ac.uk
Founded 1970 as Leeds Polytechnic; present name and status 1992
Chancellor: BRENDAN FOSTER
Vice-Chancellor: Prof. SUSAN PRICE
Pro-Vice-Chancellor and Provost: SALLY BROWN
Deputy Vice-Chancellor for Research and Enterprise: Prof. ANDREW SLADE
Deputy Vice-Chancellor for Strategic Devt: Dr PAUL SMITH
Deputy Vice-Chancellor for Student Experience: Prof. SALLY GLEN
Sec. and Registrar: STEVE DENTON
Dir of Libraries and Learning Innovation: JO NORRY
Library of 330,000 vols, 22,000 periodicals
Number of teachers: 3,000
Number of students: 30,000

DEANS

Faculty of Arts, Environment & Technology: Prof. CHRISTOPHER BAILEY
Faculty of Business and Law: BARBARA COLLEDGE
Faculty of Health and Social Sciences: Prof. IEUAN ELLIS
Carnegie Faculty of Sports and Education: GARETH DAVIES

LIVERPOOL HOPE UNIVERSITY

Hope Park, Liverpool, L16 9JD
Telephone: (151) 291-3000
Fax: (151) 291-3100
E-mail: admission@hope.ac.uk
Internet: www.hope.ac.uk
Founded 1844; present name 1995, present status 2005
Academic year: September to July
Chancellor: Baroness CAROLINE COX
Vice-Chancellor and Rector: Prof. GERALD PILLAY
Pro-Vice-Chancellor for External Relations and Widening Participation: Prof. BILL CHAMBERS
Pro-Vice-Chancellor for Research and Acad. Devt: Prof. KENNETH NEWPORT
Pro-Vice-Chancellor for Resource Management and Planning: Dr IAN VANDEWALLE
Pro-Vice-Chancellor for Student Support and Well-being: Bishop IAN STUART
Univ. Sec.: GRAHAM DONELAN
Number of students: 7,000

DEANS

Arts and Humanities: Dr TERRY PHILIPS

Business and Computer Sciences: Dr JOHN BRINKMAN
Education: Prof. BART MCGETTRICK
Sciences and Social Sciences: Dr PENNY HAUGHAN

LIVERPOOL JOHN MOORES UNIVERSITY

Roscoe Court, 4 Rodney St, Liverpool, L1 2TZ
Telephone: (151) 231-5090
Fax: (151) 231-3194
Internet: www.livjm.ac.uk
Founded 1825, as Liverpool Mechanics' School of Arts, present name and status 1992
Academic year: September to May
Chancellor: Dr BRIAN MAY
Vice-Chancellor and Chief Exec.: Prof. MICHAEL BROWN
Pro-Vice-Chancellor for Admin. and Univ. Sec.: ALISON WILD
Pro-Vice-Chancellor for Acad. and Enhancement: Prof. DIANA BURTON
Pro-Vice-Chancellor for Student Experience: STEVE KENNY
Pro-Vice-Chancellor for Infrastructure: ALLAN BICKERSTAFFE
Dir of Learning and Information Services: MAXINE MELLING
Number of teachers: 2,800
Number of students: 24,000

DEANS

Faculty of Business and Law: Prof. ROGER WEBSTER
Faculty of Education, Community and Leisure: KATE JOHNSTON
Faculty of Health and Applied Social Sciences: Prof. GODFREY MAZHINDU
Faculty of Media, Arts and Social Science: Prof. ROGER WEBSTER
Faculty of Science: Prof. PETER WHEELER
Faculty of Technology and Environment: Prof. DIANE MEEHAN

LONDON METROPOLITAN UNIVERSITY

London City campus: 133 Whitechapel High St, London, E1 7QA
North London campus: 166–220 Holloway Rd, London, N7 8DB
Telephone: (20) 7423-0000
E-mail: admissions@londonmet.ac.uk
Internet: www.londonmet.ac.uk
Founded 2002, by merger of Univ. of North London and London Guildhall Univ.
Pres.: Sir RODERICK CASTLE FLOUD
Vice-Chancellor and Chief Exec.: Prof. MALCOLM GILLIES
Deputy Vice-Chancellor for Acad. Affairs: BOB AYLETT
Deputy Vice-Chancellor for Planning and Resources: MAX WEAVER
Deputy Vice-Chancellor for Research and Devt: Prof. PAUL LISTER
Acad. Registrar: JILL GRINSTEAD
Number of students: 33,000
Publication: *The Metropolitan* (1 a year).

LONDON SOUTH BANK UNIVERSITY

103 Borough Rd, London, SE1 0AA
Telephone: (20) 7928-8989
Fax: (20) 7815-8155
E-mail: lsbuinfo@lsbu.ac.uk
Internet: www.lsbu.ac.uk
Founded 1970 as South Bank Polytechnic, present name and status 1992
State control
Academic year: September to July
Chancellor: Sir TREVOR MCDONALD

Vice-Chancellor: Prof. MARTIN J EARWICKER
Pro-Vice-Chancellor for Academic Affairs: Prof. PHIL CARDEW
Pro-Vice-Chancellor for External Affairs: BEV JULLIEN
Univ. Sec.: JAMES STEVENSON
Registrar: R. PHILLIPS
Librarian: J. AKEROYD
Library of 280,000 vols
Number of teachers: 652
Number of students: 25,441

DEANS

Business School: JANE HOUZER
Faculty of Arts and Human Sciences: Prof. MIKE MOLAN
Faculty of Engineering, Science and Built Environment: Prof. RAO BHAMIDIMARRI
Faculty of Health and Social Care: Prof. JUDITH ELLIS

LOUGHBOROUGH UNIVERSITY

Loughborough, LE11 3TU
Telephone: (1509) 263171
Fax: (1509) 223901
E-mail: k.j.raine@lboro.ac.uk
Internet: www.lboro.ac.uk
Founded 1966, as univ.; fmrly Loughborough College of Advanced Technology, univ. charter 1966
Academic year: September to June
Chancellor: Sir NIGEL RUDD
Vice-Chancellor and Pres.: Prof. SHIRLEY PEARCE
Deputy Vice-Chancellor and Provost: Prof. CHRIS LINTON
Pro-Vice-Chancellor for Teaching: Prof. MORAG BELL
Pro-Vice-Chancellor for Research: Prof. KEN PARSONS
Pro-Vice-Chancellor for Enterprise: Prof. STEVE ROTHBERG
Dir for Finance: ANDY STEPHES
Librarian: RUTH JENKINS
Library of 500,000 vols, 19,000 e-journals
Number of teachers: 770
Number of students: 16,629

DEANS

Aeronautical, Automotive, Chemical and Materials Engineering: Prof. JON BINNER
Loughborough Design School: Dr TRACY BHAMRA
School of Business and Economics: Prof. ANGUS LAING
School of Civil and Building Engineering: Prof. TONY THORPE
School of Electronic, Electrical and Systems Engineering: Prof. YIANNIS VARDAXOGLOU
School of Science: Dr PAUL CHUNG
School of Social, Political and Geographical Sciences: Prof. JONATHAN POTTER
School of Sport, Exercise and Health Sciences: Prof. MYRA NIMMO
School of the Arts, English and Drama: Prof. TERRY KAVANAGH
Wolfson School of Mechanical and Manufacturing Engineering: Prof. ROB PARKIN

PROFESSORS

ACKERS, P., Industrial Relations and Labour History
ALEXANDROV, A., Theoretical Physics
ALLEN, D., European and International Politics
ANDERSON, J., Physical Geography
ANDREWS, J., Risk and Reliability Analysis
ANTAKI, C., Language and Psychology
ANUMBA, C., Construction Engineering and Informatics
ARNOLD, J., Organizational Behaviour
AUSTIN, S., Structural Engineering
BABITSKY, V., Dynamics

BACKHOUSE, C., Product Innovation
BAGILHOLE, B., Social Policy and Equal Opportunities
BAIRNER, A., Sport and Social Theory
BELL, M., Cultural Geography
BIDDLE, S., Exercise and Sport Psychology
BILLIG, M., Social Sciences
BOUCHLAGHEM, D., Architectural Engineering
BOWMAN, R., Organic Chemistry
BRISTOW, A., Transport Studies
BUCK, T., International Business
BURNS, N., Manufacturing Systems
CADOGAN, J., Marketing
CAINE, M., Sports Technology and Innovation
CALLOW, G., Industrial Professor
CAMERON, N., Human Biology
CARRILLO, P., Strategic Management in Construction
CASE, K., Computer aided Engineering
CHAMBERS, J., Communications and Signal Processing
CHUNG, P., Computer Science
COHEN, L., Organization Studies
CONWAY, P., Manufacturing Processes
COUPLAND, J., Applied Optics
CRAMER, D., Psychological Health
CREASER, C., Analytical Chemistry
DAINTY, A. R. J., Construction Sociology
DAMODARAN, L., Participative Design and Change Management
DANIELS, K., Organizational Psychology
DAVIDSON, I., Accounting and Finance
DICKENS, J., Engineering Education
DICKENS, P., Manufacturing Technology
DIXON, N., Geotechnical Engineering
DOBSON, P., Competition Economics
DOHERTY, N., Information Management
EBBATSON, R., English Studies
EDWARDS, D., Psychology
EVANS, J., Sociology of Education and Physical Education
FARRELL, G., Criminology
FAULKNER, R., Physical Metallurgy
FEATHER, J., Library and Information Studies
FITZGERALD, L., Management Accounting
FLETCHER, S., Physical Chemistry
FORBES, W., Accounting and Finance
GANE, M., Sociology
GARNER, C., Applied Thermodynamics
GERSTNER, E., Marketing and Retail
GIBB, A., Construction Engineering Management
GILBERT, M., Polymer Technology
GLEESON, M., Exercise Biochemistry
GOLDING, P., Sociology
GOODALL, R., Control Systems Engineering
GREEN, C., Banking and Finance
GRIFFITHS, J., Applied Mathematics
GRIMSHAW, R. H. J., Mathematical Sciences
GROVES, M., Mathematics
HAGUE, R., Innovative Manufacturing
HALL, M., Banking and Financial Regulation
HALLIWELL, N., Optical Engineering
HANKINSON, G., Safety Engineering
HANTRAI, L., European Social Policy
HARGRAVE, G., Optical Diagnostics
HASLAM, R., Health and Safety Ergonomics
HAVENITH, G., Environmental Physiology and Ergonomics
HENRY, I., Leisure Policy and Management
HENSHAW, M., Systems Engineering
HEWITT, C., Pharmaceutical Engineering
HOBBY, E., 17th-century Studies
HOCKING, B., International Relations
HOGERVORST, E., Psychology
HOLDICH, R., Chemical Engineering
HORNE, J., Psychophysiology
HOULIHAN, B., Sport Policy
HOWCROFT, B., Retail Banking
HUBBARD, P., Urban Social Geography
HUNTLEY, J., Applied Mechanics
ISON, S., Transport Policy
JONES, R., Organic and Biological Chemistry
JONES, S., Sports Technology
KALAWSKY, R., Human-Computer Integration
KAVANAGH, T., Design

KHOMSKII, D., Novel Material
KING, M., Management Sciences
KONG, M., Bioelectrics Engineering
KORCZYNSKI, M., Sociology of Work
KRYLOV, V., Acoustics and Vibration
KUSMARTSEV, F., Condensed Matter Theory
LINTON, C., Applied Mathematics
LISTER, R., Social Policy
LIU, J., Operations Management
LLEWELLYN, D., Money and Banking
LOUCOPOULOS, P., Information Systems
LOUGHLAN, J., Aerospace Structures
LOVEDAY, D., Building Physics
MCCAFFER, R., Construction Management
MCGUIGAN, J., Cultural Analysis
MCGUIRK, J., Aerodynamics
MCIVER, P., Applied Mathematics
MCKEE, V., Inorganic Chemistry
MCKNIGHT, C., Information Studies
MAGUIRE, J., Sociology of Sport
MATTHEWS, G., Information Management
MAUGHAN, R., Sport and Exercise Nutrition
MILLS, T., Applied Statistics and Econometrics
MORGAN, K., Gerontology
MORRIS, A., Information Science
MORTIMER, R., Physical Chemistry
NEISHTADT, A., Applied Mathematics
NIMMO, M., Exercise Physiology
OPPENHEIM, C., Information Science
OVERTON, W., Literature
PAGE, P., Organic Chemistry
PARISH, D., Communication Networks
PARKIN, R., Mechatronics
PARRY-JONES, R., Industrial Professor
PARSONS, K., Environmental Ergonomics
PENTECOST, E., Economics
PORTER, M., Design Ergonomics
POTTER, J., Discourse Analysis
POYAGO-THEOTOKY, J., Microeconomics
PRICE, A., Project Management
RADLEY, A., Social Psychology
RAHNEJAT, H., Dynamics
RAMAN, K., Marketing
RAOOF, M., Structural Engineering
RASTOGI, S., Polymer Technology
REID, I., Physical Geography
RENDELL, H., Physical Geography
RIELLY, C., Chemical Engineering
ROTHBERG, S., Vibration Engineering
SEAL, W., Accounting
SHAW, M., English
SHIONO, K., Environmental Hydrodynamics
SILBERSCHMIDT, V., Mechanics of Materials
SINGH, S., Autonomous Systems
SKELTON, T., Critical Geographies
SLATER, D., Human Geography
SMITH, D., Sociology
SMITH, I., Electrical Power Engineering
SMITH, M., European Politics
SMITH, R., Analytical Chemistry
SMITH, R., Mathematical Engineering
STAROV, V., Chemical Engineering
STOBART, R. K., Automotive Engineering
STURGES, P., Library Studies
SUMMERS, R., Information Science
TAYLOR, P., Geography
THOMAS, P., Analytical Chemistry
THOMSON, R., Materials Engineering
THORPE, A., Construction Information Technology
THRING, R., Fuel Cell Engineering
TIPPETT, M., Accounting and Finance
TIWARI, A., Renewable Energy Systems
VARDAXOGLOU, Y., Wireless Communications
VESELOV, A., Mathematics
WAKEMAN, R., Chemical Engineering
WARD, H., Child and Family Research
WARWICK, P., Environmental Radiochemistry
WELLS, P., Animation
WESTON, R., Flexible Automation
WEYMAN-JONES, T., Industrial Economics
WHEATLEY, A., Water Technology
WILKINSON, S., Feminisim and Health Studies
WILLIAMS, C., Sports Science

WILLIAMS, D., Healthcare Engineering
WILSON, J., Operational Research
WOLFREYS, J., Modern Literature and Culture
WOOD, N., Literature
WOODHEAD, M., Systems Engineering
WOODWARD, B., Underwater Acoustics
WRIGHT, J., Building Optimization
YANG, S., Networks and Control
YEADON, F., Computer Simulation in Sport
ZHAO, H., Mathematics
ZIEBECK, K., Physics

MANCHESTER METROPOLITAN UNIVERSITY

All Saints Bldg, Manchester, M15 6BH

Telephone: (161) 247-2000
Fax: (161) 247-6390
E-mail: enquiries@mmu.ac.uk
Internet: www.mmu.ac.uk

Founded 1970, as Manchester Polytechnic, present name and status 1992
Academic year: September to July

Chancellor: Dame JANET SMITH
Pro-Chancellor: ALAN BENZIE
Vice-Chancellor: Prof. JOHN BROOKS
Deputy Vice-Chancellor for Student Experience: Prof. KEVIN BONNETT
Deputy Vice-Chancellor for Strategic Planning: Prof. GERRY KELLEHER
Registrar: GWYN ARNOLD
Librarian: Prof. C. HARRIS

Library: see under Libraries and Archives
Number of teachers: 5,818
Number of students: 34,968

Publication: *Success*

DEANS

Business School: Prof. RUTH ASHFORD
Faculty Hollings: Prof. RICHARD MURRAY
Faculty of Art and Design: Prof. DAVID CROW
Faculty of Health, Psychology and Social Care: Prof. V. K. RAMPROGUS
Faculty of Humanities, Law and Social Science: Prof. J. BEER
Faculty of Science and Engineering: Prof. M. NEAL
Institute of Education: ANDY JONES
MMU Cheshire: DENNIS DUNN

MIDDLESEX UNIVERSITY

The Burroughs, London, NW4 4BT

Telephone: (20) 8411-5555
Fax: (20) 8411-5649
E-mail: intadmissions@mdx.ac.uk
Internet: www.mdx.ac.uk

Founded 1973, as Middlesex Polytechnic, present name and status 1992; comprises fmr Enfield and Hendon Colleges of Technology, Hornsey College of Art, New College of Speech and Drama, Trent Park College of Education, College of All Saints and North London College of Health Studies
Academic year: September to July

Chancellor: Lord SHEPPARD OF DIDGEMERE
Vice-Chancellor: Prof. MICHAEL DRISCOLL
Deputy Vice-Chancellor: STEVE KNIGHT
Deputy Vice-Chancellor: KATIE BELL
Deputy Vice-Chancellor for International Affairs: Dr TERRY BUTLAND
Deputy Vice-Chancellor for Academic: Prof. MARGARET HOUSE
Deputy Vice-Chancellor for Finance and External Relations: MELVYN KEEN
Deputy Vice-Chancellor for Research and Enterprise: Prof. WAQAR AHMAD

Library of 540,000 vols, 130,000 vols of periodicals
Number of teachers: 853
Number of students: 35,000

DEANS

School of Arts and Education: Prof. EDWARD J. ESCHE
School of Engineering and Information Sciences: Prof. MARTIN LOOMES
School of Health and Social Sciences: Prof. JAN WILLIAMS
Middlesex University Business School: ANNA KYPRIANOU

NEWCASTLE UNIVERSITY

Executive Office, King's Gate, Newcastle upon Tyne NE1 7RU
Telephone: (191) 222-6000
Fax: (191) 222-8685
E-mail: postmaster@ncl.ac.uk
Internet: www.ncl.ac.uk
Founded 1834, present status 1963
Academic year: September to June
Chancellor: Prof. Sir LIAM DONALDSON
Chair. of Ccl and Pro-Chancellor: MARK I'ANSON
Vice-Chancellor: Prof. CHRIS BRINK
Deputy Vice-Chancellor: Prof. ELLA RITCHIE
Dean for Int. Business Devt and Student Recruitment: Prof. GERARD CORSANE
Pro-Vice-Chancellor for Planning and Resources: Prof. TONY STEVENSON
Pro-Vice-Chancellor for Research and Innovation: Prof. NICK WRIGHT
Pro-Vice-Chancellor for Learning and Teaching: Prof. SUZANNE CHOLERTON
Registrar: Dr JOHN HOGAN
Librarian: WAYNE CONNOLLY
Library of 1,000,000 vols, 500,000 e-books, 10,500 periodicals
Number of teachers: 2,199
Number of students: 21,045

PRO-VICE-CHANCELLORS

Faculty of Humanities and Social Sciences: Prof. CHARLES HARVEY
Faculty of Medical Sciences: Prof. CHRIS DAY
Faculty of Science, Agriculture and Engineering: Prof. STEVE HOMANS

NORTHUMBRIA UNIVERSITY

Ellison Pl., Newcastle upon Tyne NE1 8ST
Telephone: (191) 232-6002
Fax: (191) 227-3903
E-mail: er.pressoffice@northumbria.ac.uk
Internet: www.northumbria.ac.uk
Founded 1969, as Newcastle upon Tyne Polytechnic, present name and status 1992
Academic year: September to July
Chancellor: Lord STEVENS OF KIRKWHELPINGTON
Chair and Pro-Chancellor: Sir LESLIE ELTON
Vice-Chancellor and Chief Exec.: Prof. ANDREW WATHEY
Deputy Vice-Chancellor and Finance Dir: DAVID CHESSER
Deputy Vice-Chancellor for Learning and Teaching: Prof. PAUL CRONEY
Deputy Vice-Chancellor for Region, Engagement and Partnerships: LUCY WINSKELL
Deputy Vice-Chancellor for Research and Innovation: Prof. PETER GOLDING
Deputy Vice-Chancellor for Strategic Planning: Prof. IAN POSTLETHWAITE
Academic Registrar: PAUL KELLY
Univ. Sec.: PHILIP BOOTH (acting)
Library of 550,000 vols with 2,500 titles available as e-books
Number of teachers: 924 (full-time)
Number of students: 34,018 (23,185 full-time and sandwich, 10,833 part-time)

DEANS

School of Arts and Social Sciences: Prof. LYNN DOBBS

School of Built and Natural Environment: STEPHEN HODGSON (acting)
School of Computing, Engineering and Information Science: Prof. ALISTAIR SAMBELL
School of Design: Prof. STEVEN KYFFIN
School of Health, Community and Education Studies: Prof. KATH MCCOURT (acting)
School of Life Sciences: Prof. PAM BRIGGS
Newcastle Business School: Prof. SHARON MAVIN (acting)
Northumbria Law School: Prof. PHILIP PLOWDEN

NOTTINGHAM TRENT UNIVERSITY

Burton St, Nottingham, NG1 4BU
Telephone: (115) 941-8418
Fax: (115) 848-4852
E-mail: cor.web@ntu.ac.uk
Internet: www.ntu.ac.uk
Founded 1843, as Nottingham Government School of Design, present name and status 1992
Academic year: September to July
Chancellor: Sir MICHAEL PARKINSON
Vice-Chancellor: Prof. NEIL T. GORMAN
Sr Pro-Vice-Chancellor: Prof. PETER JONES
Pro-Vice-Chancellor: Prof YVONNE BARNETT
Pro-Vice-Chancellor: Prof. NIGEL HASTINGS
Pro-Vice-Chancellor: ANN PRIEST
Registrar: D. W. SAMSON
Librarian: SUE MCKNIGHT
Library of 467,299 vols, 2,550 periodicals, 7,150 electronic journals, 261 databases
Number of teachers: 927 (767 full-time, 160 part-time)
Number of students: 24,000
Publications: *Collapsing Soil Communique* (2 a year), *Comparative American Studies* (4 a year), *Gearing and Transmissions Journal* (2 a year), *Interventions Journal* (3 a year), *John Clare Society Journal* (1 a year), *Journal of Construction Procurement* (2 a year), *Journal for Critical Realism* (3 a year), *Journal of Strategic Change* (8 a year), *Loess Letter* (2 a year), *Mercian Geologist* (1 a year), *Nottingham Law Journal* (2 a year), *Studies in Travel Writing* (2 a year)

DEANS

School of Animal, Rural and Environmental Sciences: Dr EUNICE SIMMONS
School of Architecture, Design and Built Environment: PETER WESTLAND
School of Art and Design: Prof. JUDITH MOTTRAM
School of Arts and Humanities: Prof. MURRAY PRATT
School of Education: Dr GILL SCOTT
School of Science and Technology: Prof. ROGER ECCLESTON
School of Social Sciences: CHRIS POLE
Nottingham Business School: Prof. BABACK YAZDANI
Nottingham Law School: ANDREA NOLLENT

OPEN UNIVERSITY

Walton Hall, Milton Keynes, MK7 6AA
POB 197, Milton Keynes, MK7 6BJ
Telephone: (1908) 274066
Fax: (1908) 653744
E-mail: general-enquiries@open.ac.uk
Internet: www.open.ac.uk
Founded 1969
Academic year: variable; teaching takes place over up to 9 months, depending on courses
Chancellor: Lord PUTTNAM
Pro-Chancellor: Baron HASKINS OF SHIDBY
Treas.: RICHARD DEL BRIDGE
Vice-Chancellor: MARTIN BEAN

Pro-Vice-Chancellor for Curriculum and Qualifications: Prof ALAN TAIT
Pro-Vice-Chancellor for Learning, Teaching and Quality: Prof DENISE KIRKPATRICK
Pro-Vice-Chancellor for Research and Staff: Prof. BRIGID HEYWOOD
Pro-Vice-Chancellor for Strategy and External Affairs: Prof. DAVID VINCENT
Pro-Vice-Chancellor for Students, Quality and Standards: Prof. ALAN COCHRANE
Univ. Sec.: FRASER WOODBURN
Finance Dir: HILES HEDGET
Dir, Students: WILLIAM SWANN
Dir of Library Services: NICKY WHITSED
Number of teachers: 8,200 incl. 7,000 tutors and 1,200 full-time
Number of students: 250,000
Publications: *Open Business School Brochure, PGCE Brochure, Research Degree Prospectus, Studying with the Open University, Taught Master's Degree Prospectuses*

DEANS

Faculty of Arts: Prof DAVID ROWLAND
Faculty of Education and Language Studies: Dr SHARON DING
Faculty of Health and Social Care: JEREMY ROCHE
Faculty of Mathematics, Computing, and Technology: Prof. ANNE DE ROECK
Faculty of Science: Prof PHILIP POTTS
Faculty of Social Sciences: Prof SIMON BROMLEY
Open University Business School: Prof. JAMES FLECK

DIRECTORS OF UNITS

Institute of Educational Technology: Prof. JOSIE TAYLOR
Knowledge Media Institute: Dr PETER SCOTT

REGIONAL DIRECTORS

East Midlands Region: G. LAMMIE
East of England Region: HELEN WILDMAN
Ireland: Dr R. HAMILTON
London Region: ROSEMARY MAYES
North Region: DAVID KNIGHT
North West Region: LYNDA BRADY
Scotland: PETER SYME
South East Region: LIZ GRAY
South Region: CELIA COHEN
South West Region: LINDA BRIGHTMAN
Wales: ROB HUMPHREYS
West Midlands Region: Dr MICHAEL ROOKES
Yorkshire Region: NICK BERRY

PROFESSORS

ALDGATE, P. J., Social Care
ALLEN, J. R., Social Science
APPLEBY, C., Business Development
ATKINSON, D., Learning Disability
BASSINDALE, A., Organometallic Chemistry
BENNETT, T., Sociology
BENTON, T. J., Art History
BERRY, F., Inorganic Chemistry
BISSELL, C. C., Telematics
BLOWERS, A. T., Social Sciences
BORNAT, J., Oral History
BRAITHWAITE, N., Engineering Physics
BRANNAN, D. A., Pure Mathematics
BROWN, S., Philosophy
BURROWS, D. J., Music
BURTON, K. W., Isotope Geochemistry
BUSH, P.
CANDLIN, C. N., Applied Linguistics
CHAMBERS, E.
CHATAWAY, J. C., Development Manager
CLARKE, J., Social Policy
COCHRANE, A., Public Policy
COCKELL, C. S., Geomicrobiology
COLEMAN, J. A., Languages
COLLINS, R. E., Media Studies
COOK, G., Education
CRITCHLEY, F., Statistics

CROSS, N. G., Design Studies (Technology)
DANIEL, E. M., Information Management
DAVIES, C., Health Care
DE ROECK, A. N., Computing
DOBSON, A. N. H., Politics
DU GAY, P. L. J., Sociology
EARL, C., Engineering Product Design
EDWARDS, L., Structural Integrity
EISENSTADT, M., Artificial Intelligence
ELLIOTT, D., Technology Policy
EMSLEY, C., Arts
ENGLANDER, R., History
FORRESTER-PATON, R., Social Enterprise
GARTHWAITE, P. H., Statistics
GELLATLY, A. R. H., Cognitive Psychology
GLATTER, R. G., Education
GOODMAN, D. C., History of Science and Technology
GOWER, J. C., Statistics
GRANNELL, M. J., Pure Mathematics
GRANT, J., Education in Medicine
GRAY, J. J., History of Mathematics
GRIGGS, T. S., Pure Mathematics
HALL, P. A. V., Computing
HALLIDAY, T. R., Evolutionary Biology
HAMMERSLEY, M., Educational and Social Research
HARDWICK, L. P., Classical Studies
HARRIS, N. B. W., Tectonics
HARRISON, C. T., Art History
HERBERT, T., Music
HIMMELWEIT, S. F., Economics
HOLLWAY, W., Psychology
INCE, D. C., Computing
ISON, R. L., Systems
JOHNSON, J., Complexity, Science and Design
JONES, B. W., Astronomy
JONES, M. C., Statistics
KAYE, G. R., Information Management
KING, C., Art History
LAING, A. W., Marketing
LAURENCE, E. A., History
LENTIN, A., History
LEWIS, V., Education
MCCORMICK, R., Learning Schools Programme
MCDONNELL, J. A., Planetary Space Science
MACKINTOSH, M., Economics
MALE, D., Immunology
MASON, J. H., Mathematics Education
MASON, N., Physics
MASON, R., Educational Technology
MASSEY, D. B., Geography
MERCER, N., Education
MONK, J. S., Digital Systems
MOON, R. E., Education
MUNCIE, J. P., Criminology
NAUGHTON, J., Public Understanding of Technology
NEWMAN, J. E., Social Policy
NUSEIBEH, B., Computing
O'DAY, R., History
OWENS, W. R., Art
PETERS, G., Systems Strategy
PHOENIX, A. A., Psychology
PILLINGER, C. T., Planetary Sciences
PLUMBRIDGE, W. J., Materials
POND-JANZEN, C. M., Biological Sciences
QUINTAS, P. R., Knowledge Management
RICHARDS, D., Applied Mathematics
RICHARDSON, J. T. E., Student Learning and Assessment
ROSE, S. P. R., Biology
ROY, R., Design and Environment
RUTTERFORD, J., Financial Management
SALAMAN, G., Organization Studies
SAWARD, M., Politics
SCANLON, E., Educational Technology
SEGAL-HORN, S., International Strategy
SELF, S., Volcanology
SHUKER, D. E. G., Organic Chemistry
SILVERTOWN, J. W., Ecology
SLAPPER, G., Law
SLATER, J. B.
SPICER, R. A., Earth Sciences
STEWART, D.

STEWART, M. G., Neuroscience
STOREY, J., Human Resource Management
SWITHENBY, S. J., Physics
THOMPSON, G. F., Political Economy
THORPE, M. S., Educational Technology
WALDER, D. J., Literature
WATSON, S., Sociology
WETHERELL, M., Business
WHATMORE, S. J., Geography
WIELD, D. V., Innovation and Development
WILKINSON, M., Applied Mathematics
WILSON, R. C. L., Earth Sciences
WOLFFE, J. R., Religious History
ZARNECKI, J., Space Sciences

OXFORD BROOKES UNIVERSITY

Gipsy Lane, Headington, Oxford, OX3 0BP
Telephone: (1865) 484848
Fax: (1865) 483073
E-mail: query@brookes.ac.uk
Internet: www.brookes.ac.uk
Founded 1865, as Oxford School of Art, became Oxford Polytechnic 1970, university status 1992
State control
Academic year: September to July
Chancellor: SHAMI CHAKRABARTI
Pro-Chancellor: DANBY BLOCH
Vice-Chancellor: Prof. JANET BEER
Pro-Vice-Chancellor for Research: Prof DIANA WOODHOUSE
Pro-Vice-Chancellor for Student Experience: Prof. JOHN RAFTERY
Registrar: PAUL LARGE (acting)
Library of 500,000 vols
Number of teachers: 750
Number of students: 18,167
Publication: *Observe*

DEANS

Faculty of Business: Prof. CHRIS COOPER
Faculty of Health and Life Sciences: JUNE GIRVIN
Faculty of Humanities and Social Sciences: DEREK ELSOM
Faculty of Technology, Design and Environment: MARS STREET

ROEHAMPTON UNIVERSITY

Erasmus House, Roehampton Lane, London, SW15 5PU
Telephone: (20) 8392-3232
Fax: (20) 8392-3470
E-mail: enquiries@roehampton.ac.uk
Internet: www.roehampton.ac.uk
Founded 1841, present status 2004
Chancellor: JOHN SIMPSON
Pro-Chancellor: WILLIAM MACINTYRE
Pro-Vice-Chancellor: ANDREW MASHETER
Vice-Chancellor: Prof. PAUL O'PREY
Deputy Vice-Chancellor and Provost: Prof. JANE BROADBENT
Pro-Vice-Chancellor: CHRIS COBB
Pro-Vice-Chancellor: ANDY MASHETER
Dir for Finance: REGGIE BLENNERHASSETT
Univ. Sec. and Registrar: ROBIN GELLER
Prin. of Digby Stuart College: PAUL HODGES
Prin. of Froebel College: SIMON DORMAN
Prin. of Southlands College: YVONNE GUERRIER
Prin. of Whitelands College: Rev. Prof. GEOFFREY WALKER

DEANS

School of Arts: LYNDIE BRIMSTONE
School of Business and Social Sciences: Prof. YVONNE GUERRIER
School of Education: Dr JEANNE KEAY
School of Human and Life Sciences: MICHAEL BARHAM
Business School: Prof. ELAINE HARRIS (Dir)

PROFESSORS

School of Arts:
FISHER, A., Art History
JORDAN, S., Dance
READ, A., Drama and Theatre Studies
School of Business and Social Sciences:
BALES, K., Sociology
EADE, J., Sociology and Anthropology
FENNELL, G., Sociology and Social Policy
GLOVER, J., Employment Studies
GUERRIER, Y., Organizational Studies
School of Education:
BREHONY, K. J., Early Childhood Studies
HARGREAVES, D., Child Development
MAHONY, P., Education
MASON, R., Art Education
WATTS, M., Education
School of English and Modern Languages:
COATES, J., English Languages and Linguistics
DOBSON, M., English Literature
HARTLEY, J., English Literature
HEADLAM-WELLS, R., English Literature
LEADER, Z., English Literature
PRIESTMAN, M., English Literature
School of Humanities and Cultural Studies:
DEAN, T., Medieval History
EDWARDS, P., History
GIBSON, A., Philosophy
TOSH, J., History
School of Initial Teacher Education:
BEST, R., Education
School of Human and Life Sciences:
MACLARNON, A., Evolutionary Anthropology
School of Psychology and Therapeutic Studies:
BEAUMONT, G., Neuropsychology
ESSAU, C., Developmental Psychopathology
REID, M., Nutritional Psychology
VOGELE, C., Clinical and Health Psychology

SHEFFIELD HALLAM UNIVERSITY

City Campus, Howard St, Sheffield, S1 1WB
Telephone: (114) 225-5555
Fax: (114) 225-4449
E-mail: admissions@shu.ac.uk
Internet: www.shu.ac.uk
Founded 1969, as Sheffield Polytechnic, later Sheffield City Polytechnic; present name and status 1992
Academic year: September to June
Chancellor: Lord WINSTON
Vice-Chancellor: PHILIP JONES
Deputy Vice-Chancellor: CLIFF ALLAN
Pro-Vice-Chancellor for Research: MIKE SMITH
Dir of Human Resources: PHILL DIXON
Sec. and Registrar: LIZ WINDERS
Academic Registrar: GWYN ARNOLD
Library of 540,000 vols
Number of teachers: 955
Number of students: 28,279 (20,993 undergraduate, 7,286 postgraduate)

DEANS

Faculty of Arts, Computing Engineering and Sciences: Prof. ALISTAIR SAMBELL
Faculty of Devt and Society: SYLVIA JOHNSON
Faculty of Health and Wellbeing: Prof. RHIANNON BILLINGLSEY
Sheffield Business School: CHRISTINE BOOTH

SOUTHAMPTON SOLENT UNIVERSITY

East Park Terrace, Southampton, SO14 0YN
Telephone: (23) 8031-9000
Fax: (23) 8033-4161

E-mail: ask@solent.ac.uk
Internet: www.solent.ac.uk
Founded 1855, as a school of art; present name and status 2005
Chancellor: Admiral Lord WEST OF SPITHEAD
Vice-Chancellor: Prof. VAN GORE
Deputy Vice-Chancellor: Dr RICHARD BLACK-WELL
Deputy Vice-Chancellor: Prof. JANE LONG-MORE
Deputy Vice-Chancellor: Dr MIKE WILKINSON
Number of students: 16,000
Publications: *headway*, *Issue*

DEANS

Faculty of Business, Sport and Enterprise: Prof. JENNY ANDERSON
Faculty of Media, Arts and Society: Prof. ROD PILLING
Faculty of Technology: Prof. JOHN REES
Warsash Maritime Academy: JOHN MILLICAN

STAFFORDSHIRE UNIVERSITY

College Rd, Stoke on Trent, ST4 2DE
Telephone: (1782) 294000
Fax: (1782) 292796
E-mail: international@staffs.ac.uk
Internet: www.staffs.ac.uk
Founded 1970 as North Staffordshire Polytechnic, became Staffordshire Polytechnic 1988; present name and status 1992
Academic year: September to July
Chancellor: Sir Lord BILL MORRIS
Vice-Chancellor and Chief Exec.: Prof. MICHAEL GUNN
Deputy Vice-Chancellor and Deputy Chief Exec.: PAUL RICHARDS
Univ. Sec.: KEN SPROSTON
Academic Registrar: FRANCESCA FRANCIS
Librarian: LIZ HART
Library of 300,000 vols, 2,000 periodicals
Number of teachers: 589
Number of students: 16,575 (10,991 full-time undergraduate, 1,972 postgraduate, 3,612 part-time)
Publications: *Horizon* (journal for former students; 3 a year), *Research Report* (1 a year), *Shine On* (1 a year)

DEANS

Business School: Prof. SUSAN FOREMAN
Faculty of Arts, Media and Design: Dr ASTRID HERHOFFER
Faculty of Computing, Engineering and Technology: Prof. MIKE GOODWIN
Faculty of Health: HILARY JONES
Faculty of Sciences: Prof. DAVID WHITE (acting)
Law School: ROSEMARY EVANS

TEESSIDE UNIVERSITY

Borough Rd, Middlesbrough, TS1 3BA
Telephone: (1642) 218121
Fax: (1642) 342067
E-mail: enquiries@tees.ac.uk
Internet: www.tees.ac.uk
Founded 1929 as Constantine College of Technology, became Teesside Polytechnic 1970, present name and status 1992
Academic year: September to June
Chancellor: Lord SAWYER OF DARLINGTON
Vice-Chancellor and Chief Exec.: Prof. GRAHAM HENDERSON
Deputy Vice-Chancellor for Learning and Student Experience: Prof. EILEEN MARTIN
Deputy Vice-Chancellor for Partnerships and Standards: Prof. CAROLINE MACDONALD
Deputy Vice-Chancellor for Research and Business Engagement: Prof. CLIFF HARDCASTLE
Univ. Sec. and Clerk to the Governors: J. MORGAN MCCLINTOCK

Academic Registrar: TIM COBBETT
Dir of Library and Information Services: LIZ JOLLY
Library of 369,641 vols
Number of teachers: 7,857 full-time
Number of students: 28,094

DEANS

Graduate Research School: Prof. ZULFI ALI
School of Arts and Media: Prof. GERDA ROPER
School of Computing: Dr SIMON STOBART
School of Health and Social Care: Prof. PAUL KEANE
School of Science and Engineering: Prof. SIMON HODGSON
School of Social Sciences and Law: Dr MARK SIMPSON
Teesside Univ. Business School: ALASTAIR THOMSON

THAMES VALLEY UNIVERSITY

St Mary's Rd, Ealing, London, W5 5RF
Telephone: (20) 8579-5000
Fax: (20) 8566-1353
E-mail: learning.advice@tvu.ac.uk
Internet: www.tvu.ac.ukWellington St, Slough, Berks, SL1 1YG
Telephone: (1753) 534585
Founded 1860, as Lady Byron School, present name and status 1992
Academic year: September to July
Chancellor: Lord BILIMORIA
Vice-Chancellor: Prof. PETER JOHN
Pro-Vice-Chancellor for Academic Affairs and Student Services: Prof. KATH MITCHELL
Deputy Vice-Chancellor for Enterprise and External Services: Dr IAN TUNBRIDGE
Univ. Sec. and Clerk to the Board: MAUREEN SKINNER
Head of Registry Services: (vacant)
Library of 270,000 vols, 1,300 print journals
Number of teachers: 638 (388 full-time, 250 part-time)
Number of students: 25,741 (9,004 full-time and sandwich, 16,737 part-time and distance learning)

DEANS

Faculty of Arts: ROSY CREHAN
Faculty of Health and Human Sciences: ANDREW MACCALLUM
Faculty of Professional Studies: Prof. DAVID JONES

UNIVERSITY FOR THE CREATIVE ARTS

Canterbury campus: New Dover Rd, Canterbury, Kent, CT1 3AN
Telephone: (1227) 817302
Fax: (1227) 817500
E-mail: admissionscanterbury@ucreative.ac.uk
Epsom campus: Ashley Rd, Epsom, Surrey, KT18 5BE
Telephone: (1372) 728811
Fax: (1372) 747050
E-mail: admissionsepsom@ucreative.ac.uk
Farnham campus: Falkner Rd, Farnham, Surrey, GU9 7DS
Telephone: (1252) 722441
Fax: (1252) 892616
E-mail: admissionsfarnham@ucreative.ac.uk
Maidstone campus: Oakwood Park, Maidstone, Kent, ME16 8AG
Telephone: (1622) 620000
Fax: (1622) 621100
E-mail: admissionsmaidstone@ucreative.ac.ukRochester campus: Fort Pitt, Rochester,

Kent, ME1 1DZ
Telephone: (1634) 888702
Fax: (1634) 820700
E-mail: admissionsrochester@ucreative.ac.uk
Internet: www.ucreative.ac.uk
Founded 2005, as Univ. College for Creative Arts by merger of Kent Inst. of Art and Design (f. 1987) and Surrey Inst. of Art and Design, University College (f. 1995); present name 2008
Academic year: September to May
Vice-Chancellor: Prof. ELAINE THOMAS
Deputy Vice-Chancellor: Prof. MARK HUNT
Pro-Vice-Chancellor for Corporate Resources: ALAN COOKE
Pro-Vice-Chancellor for Further Education and Widening Participation: Prof. DIANNE TAYLOR GEARING
Pro-Vice-Chancellor for Learning and Teaching: Prof. PAUL COYLE
Pro-Vice-Chancellor for Research and Devt: Dr SEYMOUR ROWORTH-STOKES
Sec.: MARION WILKS
Number of students: 6,500

UNIVERSITY OF BATH

Claverton Down, Bath, BA2 7AY
Telephone: (1225) 388388
Fax: (1225) 386559
E-mail: registry@bath.ac.uk
Internet: www.bath.ac.uk
Founded 1856, designated College of Advanced Technology 1960, independent instn with direct-grant status 1962, Univ. Charter 1966
Academic year: September to June
Chancellor: Lord TUGENDHAT OF WIDDINGTON
Vice-Chancellor: Prof. GLYNIS BREAKWELL
Deputy Vice-Chancellor: Prof. KEVIN EDGE
Pro-Vice-Chancellor for Learning and Teaching: Prof. BERNIE MORLEY
Pro-Vice-Chancellor for Research: Prof. JANE MILLAR
Sec.: MARK HUMPHRISS
Librarian: HOWARD NICHOLSON
Library: see Libraries and Archives
Number of teachers: 533
Number of students: 13,959

DEANS

Faculty of Engineering and Design: Prof. GARY HAWLEY
Faculty of Humanities and Social Sciences: Prof. ROGER EATWELL
Faculty of Science: Prof. DAVID BIRD
School of Management: Prof. RICHARD ELLIOTT

PROFESSORS

ACHARYA, K. R., Biology and Biochemistry
AGGARWAL, R. K., Electronic and Electrical Engineering
ALMOND, D. P., Materials Science
BENDING, S. J., Physics
BIRD, D. M., Physics
BLAKE, D. R., Medical Sciences
BRAMLEY, A. N., Engineering and Applied Sciences
BRITTON, N., Mathematical Sciences
BROOKS, S. W., European Studies and Modern Languages
BROWN, A. D., Management
BUDD, C. J., Applied Mathematics
BULL, A., European Studies and Modern Languages
BURSTALL, F. E., Mathematical Sciences
CARUSO, A., Architecture and Civil Engineering
CHARNLEY, A. K., Biology and Biochemistry
CHAUDHURI, J. B., Chemical Engineering
COLEMAN, P. G., Physics
CRITTENDEN, B. D., Chemical Engineering

CRONIN, N. J., Physics
DANIELS, H. R., Education
DANSON, M. J., Biochemistry
DAVENPORT, J. H., Information Technology
DAVIDSON, M. G., Chemistry
DAVIES, J. J., Physics
EATWELL, R., European Studies and Modern Languages
EDGE, K., Mechanical Engineering
EGGLESTONE, C., Psychology
EISENTHAL, R., Biology and Biochemistry
FFRENCH-CONSTANT, R., Biology and Biochemistry
FINEMAN, S., Management
FITCH, J. P., Software Engineering
FORD, I. D., Management
FRAENKEL, L. E., Mathematical Sciences
GALAKTIONOV, V. A., Mathematical Sciences
GARLAND, C. J., Pharmacy and Pharmacology
GILLESPIE, D., Russian
GOODING, D. C., Psychology
GOUGH, I. R., Social Sciences
GOULD, N., Social and Policy Sciences
GRAHAM, I. G., Mathematical Sciences
GREEN, R. H., Management
GURSUL, I., Mechanical Engineering
GUY, R., Pharmacy and Pharmacology
HAMMOND, G. P., Environmental Engineering
HARLAND, C. M., Management
HASTE, H. E., Psychology
HAWLEY, J. G., Mechanical Engineering
HOLMAN, G. D., Biochemistry
HOPE, V., Management
HORROCKS, M., School for Health
HUDSON, J. R., Economics and International Development
HUNT, G. W., Mechanical Engineering
HURST, L. D., Biology
IBELL, T. J., Architecture and Civil Engineering
IOANNIDIS, C., Management
JENNISON, C., Statistics
JOHNSON, P., Computer Science
JONES, P. R., Economics and International Development
KERWIN, D. G., Sport and Exercise Science
KNIGHT, J. C., Physics
KOLACZKOWSKI, S. T., Chemical Engineering
LAUDER, H., Education
LEWIS, A., Psychology
LEWIS, M. A., Management
LOGEMANN, H., Mathematical Sciences
MCKAY, A., Economics and International Development
MARKANDYA, A., Economics and International Development
MARSH, R. J., Modern Languages
MARSHALL, J., Management
MARTIN, B., Marketing
MAYER, M., Strategic Management
MEDLAND, A. J., Design Engineering
MILEHAM, A. R., Mechanical Engineering
MILES, A. W., Mechanical Engineering
MILLAR, J., Social Policy
MITCHELL, N., Electronic and Electrical Engineering
MOLLOY, K., Chemistry
MONRO, D. M., Electronics
MORTON, K. W., Mathematical Sciences
NANDEIBAM, S., Economics and International Development
NAUDE, P., Management
ORTON, P., School for Health
PACE, N. G., Physics
PARKER, S. C., Chemistry
PENROSE, M., Mathematical Sciences
PETER, L. M., Physical Chemistry
POTTER, B. V. L., Pharmacy
POWELL, P., Management
PURCELL, J., Management
PYM, D., Computer Science
RAITHBY, P. R., Chemistry
REASON, P., Management
REDFERN, P., School for Health
REYNOLDS, S. E., Biology
RICKELLS, P., Architecture

RODGER, D., Electronic and Electrical Engineering
ROOM, G. J., Social Sciences
RUSSELL, P. ST. J., Physics
RYAN, E. P., Mathematical Sciences
SCOTT, R. J., Biology and Biochemistry
SCOTT, W. A. H., Education
SKEVINGTON, S. M., Psychology
SLACK, J. M. W., Cell and Molecular Biology
SMITH, A. W., Pharmacy
SMYSHLYAEV, V., Mathematical Sciences
SPENCE, A., Numerical Analysis
STABLES, A. W., Education
STEVENS, R., Engineering and Applied Science
TATE, G. D., European Studies and Modern Languages
TAVERNOR, R. W., Architecture
TAYLOR, J. T., Electronic and Electrical Engineering
TOLAND, J. F., Mathematics
TURNBULL, D., Architecture and Civil Engineering
TYRELL, R. M., Pharmacy and Pharmacology
VASSILIEV, D. G., Mathematical Sciences
VIDGEN, R, Management
VINCENT, J. F. V., Mechanical Engineering
WALLACE, A. M., Education
WANG, W. N., Physics
WARD, S., Pharmacy and Pharmacology
WELHAM, M., Pharmacy and Pharmacology
WHITMAN, R., Politics
WILKINSON, B., Management
WILLIAMS, I., Chemistry
WILLIAMS, J. M. J., Chemistry
WILLIS, P. J., Mathematical Sciences
WONNACOTT, S. J., Biology and Biochemistry
WOOD, G. D., Economics and International Development

UNIVERSITY OF BEDFORDSHIRE

Park Sq., Luton, Bedfordshire, LU1 3JU
Telephone: (1582) 489286
Fax: (1582) 489323
E-mail: admission@beds.ac.uk
Internet: www.beds.ac.uk
Founded 2006, by merger of Univ. of Luton (f. 1993) and De Montfort Univ.'s Bedford campus
Academic year: September to September

Chancellor: ALISTAIR DARLING
Vice-Chancellor and Chief Exec.: Prof. LES EBDON
Deputy Vice-Chancellor for Acad. Affairs: Prof. MARY MALCOLM
Deputy Vice-Chancellor for Resources: DONALD HARLEY
Registrar: ALICE HYNES
Librarian: TIM STONE
Library of 250,000 vols
Number of teachers: 1,200
Number of students: 21,000

DEANS

Bedfordshire Business School: Prof. PAUL BURNS
Faculty of Creative Arts, Technologies and Science: Prof. JAMES CRABBE
Faculty of Education, Sport and Tourism: Prof. MARILYN LEASK
Faculty of Health and Social Sciences: Prof. MICHAEL PRESTON-SHOOT

UNIVERSITY OF BIRMINGHAM

Edgbaston, Birmingham, B15 2TT
Telephone: (121) 414-3344
Fax: (121) 414-3971
Internet: www.bham.ac.uk
Founded 1900
Academic year: September to June
Chancellor: Sir DOMINIC CADBURY

Vice-Chancellor and Prin.: Prof. DAVID EASTWOOD
Provost and Vice-Prin.: Prof. MICHAEL SHEPPARD
Pro-Vice-Chancellor for Estates and Infrastructure: Prof. JOHN HEATH
Pro-Vice-Chancellor for Research and Knowledge Transfer: (vacant)
Pro-Vice-Chancellor for Teaching, Learning and Quality: Prof. ADRIAN RANDALL
Registrar and Sec.: LEE SANDERS
Librarian: M. SHOEBRIDGE (acting)
Library: see Libraries and Archives
Number of teachers: 2,291
Number of students: 26,073

Publications: *Court Reporter* (1 a year), *Medlines* (2 a year), *The Birmingham Magazine* (1 a year)

PROFESSORS

ABELL, S., Functional Materials
ADAMS, D. H., Hepatology
AHMED, A., Reproductive Physiology
AL-RUBEAI, M., Biotechnology
ALCOCK, P., Social Policy and Administration
ALEXANDER, D., Accounting
ALLEMANN, R., Chemical Biology
AMANN, R., Soviet Politics
ARNULL, A. M., European Law
BACKHOUSE, R. E., History and Philosophy of Economics
BACON, P. A., Rheumatology
BALDWIN, A. J., Judicial Administration
BALE, J. S., Environmental Biology
BANFIELD, S. D., Music
BARBER, K., African Popular Culture
BARKER, A., Classics
BARNDEN, J., Artificial Intelligence
BARNETT, A. H., Diabetic Medicine
BATLEY, R. A., Development Administration
BEEVERS, D. G., Medicine
BELL, T., Metallurgy
BESRA, G., Biosciences
BIDDLESTONE, A. J., Chemical Engineering
BIRKETT, J., French Studies
BLACKBURN, S., Solids Processing
BLAKE, J. R., Applied Mathematics
BOOTH, D. A., Psychology
BOOTH, I. W., Paediatric Gastroenterology and Nutrition
BOWEN, P., Mechanical Metallurgy
BOWERY, N. G., Pharmacology
BRADBURY, A., Vascular Surgery
BREUILLY, J. J., Modern History
BROOKS, N. P., Medieval History
BROWN, N. L., Molecular Genetics and Microbiology
BROWNE, K., Forensic and Family Psychology
BRYAN, S., Health Economics
BUCKLEY, C., Rheumatology
BURKE, F., Primary Dental Care
BUSBY, S. J. W., Biochemistry
BUTLER, M. G., Modern German Literature
BUTLER, P. J., Comparative Physiology
CAESAR, M. P., Italian
CALLOW, J. A., Botany
CAMPBELL, J., Casting Technology
CARROLL, D., Applied Psychology
CHAPPLE, I., Periodontology
CHENG, K. K., Public Health and Epidemiology
CHILD, J., Commerce (International Management and Organization)
CHIPMAN, J., Cell Toxicology
CLARK, L. A., Structural Engineering
CLARKE, M., Public Policy
CLIFFORD, C. M., Nursing
COCHRANE, R., Psychology
COLE, J. A., Microbial Physiology and Biochemistry
COOPER, J. M., Russian Economic Studies
COOTE, J. H., Physiology
COULTHARD, R. M., English Language and Linguistics

Cox, A. W., Business Strategy and Procurement
Croft, S. J., International Relations
Crossley, E. C. D., 19th-century French Studies
Cruikshank, G. S., Neurosurgery
Cruise, A. M., Astrophysics and Space Research
Curtis, R., Combinatorial Algebra
Dadson, T. J., Hispanic Studies
Daniels, H. R. J., Special Education and Educational Psychology
Daniels, P. W., Geography
Davies, G., Engineering
Davies, L., English
Davies, M. L., International Education
Davis, A., Social Work
Dawe, D. J., Structural Mechanics
De Chernatony, L., Brand Marketing
Dean, T. A., Manufacturing Engineering
Deb, S., Neuropsychiatry and Intellectual Disability
Delecluse, H.-J., Molecular Pathology
Dent, N. J. H., Philosophy
Dickenson, D., Global Ethics
Doe, W., Medicine
Doling, J. F., Housing Studies
Dowden, K., Classics
Duda, J., Sports Psychology
Dutta, J., Economics
Edwards, A., Education
Edwards, P. P., Inorganic Chemistry
Ellis, E. D., Public Law
Ellis, S., English Literature
Enonchong, N., Law
Evans, H., Metallurgy and Materials
Faddy, M., Statistics
Feldman, D. J., Jurisprudence
Fender, J., Macroeconomics
Forgan, E. M., Condensed Matter Physics
Frame, J. W., Oral Surgery
Franklin, F., Plant Molecular Biology
Franklyn, J. A., Medicine
Freemantle, N., Clinical Epidemiology and Biostatistics
Fryer, P. J., Chemical Engineering
Gallimore, P. H., Cancer Studies
Garvey, J., Particle Physics
Gordon, J., Cellular Immunology
Gray, R., Medical Statistics
Greaves, C., Solid State Chemistry
Gunn, J. M. F., Theoretical Physics
Haldon, J. F., Byzantine Studies
Hall, P. S., Communications Engineering
Ham, C. J., Health Policy and Management
Harber, C., International Education
Harris, I. R., Materials Science
Harris, J., Law
Harris, K. D. M., Structural Chemistry
Harrison, R. M., Environmental Health
Hawkey, P., Immunology
Hay, C., Political Analysis
Heath, J. K., Biochemistry
Henderson, W., Continuing Education
Hicks, C., Health Care Psychology
Hobbs, F. D. R., Primary Care and General Practice
Hughes, A., 20th-century French Literature
Humphreys, G. W., Cognitive Psychology
Hunter, J. R., Ancient History and Archaeology
Hutton, P., Anaesthetics and Intensive Care
Jackson, J. B., Bioenergetics
Jefferies, R., Molecular Immunology
Jeffery, C., German Politics
Jefferys, J. G. R., Basic Neuroscience
Jenkinson, E. J., Experimental Immunology
Jennings, J., Political Theory
Johnson, P., Oncology and Translational Research
Jones, D. A., Sport and Exercise Sciences
Jones, E. L., Pathology
Jones, I. P., Physical Metallurgy
Jones, P. M., French History
Jones, R. H., Public Sector Accounting
Jung, A., Computer Science

Kaplan, J., Drama and Theatre Arts
Kearsey, M., Biometrical Genetics
Keighley, M. R. B., Surgery
Kelsey, D., Economic Theory
Kendall, K., Chemical Engineering
Kendall, M., Clinical Pharmacology
Kerali, R., Highway Engineering and Management
Kilby, M., Maternal and Foetal Medicine
Kinson, J. B., High Energy Physics
Klapper, J., Foreign Language Pedagogy
Knight, D., Water Engineering
Knott, J. F., Metallurgy and Materials
Knowles, P. J., Theoretical Chemistry
Kwiatkowska, M., Computer Science
Laird, W. R. E., Prosthetic Dentistry
Lancaster, M., Communications Engineering
Lawrance, A. J., Statistics
Le Sueur, A., Jurisprudence
Leather, P., Urban and Regional Studies
Lerner, I., Theoretical Physics
Lewis, A., Special Education and Educational Psychology
Lilford, R., Public Health and Epidemiology
Lloyd-Bostock, S., Law and Psychology
Logan, A., Molecular Neuroscience
Lote, C., Experimental Nephrology
Lucas, W., American Studies
Luesley, D. M., Gynaecology
Lyddiatt, A., Process Biotechnology
Macarthur, C., Maternal and Child Epidemiology
Macaskie, L., Applied Microbiology
McCaskie, T., Asante History
Mackay, R., Hydrogeology
MacLennan, I. C. M., Immunology
Madelin, K. B., Civil Engineering
Maher, E., Medical Genetics
Mallin, C., Business Finance
Marquis, P. M., Biomaterials
Marsh, D., Political Science and International Studies
Marshall, J. M., Cardiovascular Science
Martin, G. R., Avian Sensory Science
McLeod, D. H., Church History
Menon, A., European Studies
Michell, R. H., Biochemistry
Miller, C., English Law
Minnikin, D., Microbial Chemistry
Moayyedi, P., Primary Care and General Practice
Morrison, K., Neurology
Morton, D. B., Biomedical Science and Biomedical Ethics
Moss, P. A. H., Haematology
Mullineux, A. W., Global Finance
Murie, A., Urban and Regional Studies
Murinde, V., Developmental Finance
Murray, P. I., Ophthalmology
Nash, G., Cardiovascular Rheology
Neal-Sturgess, C. E., Automotive Engineering
Nelson, J. M., Nuclear Physics
Nielsen, J., Theology
Nienow, A. W., Biochemical Engineering
Noonan, H., Philosophy
Norton, J. P., Control Engineering
Oliver, C., Clinical Psychology
Orford, J. F., Clinical and Community Psychology
Paliwoda, S., Marketing
Pallen, M., Infection
Palmer, R. E., Experimental Physics
Parker, D., Textual Criticism and Palaeography
Parle, J., Primary Care
Parratt, J., Third-World Theologies
Paterson, W. E., German Studies
Peck, E., Health Services Management
Penn, C., Molecular Microbiology
Perrie, M., Russian History
Perry, J. G., Civil Engineering
Petts, G., Physical Geography
Petts, J., Environmental Risk Management
Piddock, L., Microbiology

Pilkington, H., Sociology and Russian Area Studies
Ponman, T., Astrophysics
Preston, P., Political Sociology
Prewett, P., Microsystems Manufacture
Raftery, J. P., Health Economics
Raine, J., Management in Criminal Justice
Rakodi, C., Public Policy
Randall, A. J., English Social History
Ranson, P. R. S., Education
Reddy, U., Computer Science
Redmond, J., European Studies
Richards, S., Public Management
Rickinson, A. B., Cancer Studies
Riddoch, M., Cognitive Neuropsychology
Robinson, G., Pure Mathematics
Rogers, C., Geotechnical Engineering
Russell, M., Electronic and Electrical Engineering
Salmon, M., Experimental Rheumatology
Samuels, J. M., Business Finance
Savage, C., Nephrology
Scase, W., Medieval English Literature
Schofield, A., Theoretical Physics
Scott, I. R., Law
Sen, S., Development Economics
Seville, J. P. K., Chemical Engineering
Sharples, M., Educational Technology
Sheppard, M. C., Medicine
Shute, S., Criminal Law and Criminal Justice
Siebert, W. S., Labour Economics
Simnett, G. M., High-Energy Astrophysics
Sinclair, P. J. N., Economics
Skelcher, C., Local Government Studies
Sloman, A., Artificial Intelligence and Cognitive Science
Small, I. C., English Literature
Smith, A., Oral Biology
Smith, M., Experimental Neurology
Sorahan, T., Occupational Epidemiology
Southwood, T., Paediatric Rheumatology
Speirs, R. C., German
Spencer, K. M., Local Policy
Spurgeon, P. C., Health Services Management
Stevens, A., Public Health
Stewart, P. M., Medicine
Strain, A., Biochemistry
Sugden, R., Commerce
Sugirtharajah, R., Biblical Hermeneutics
Swanson, R., Medieval Ecclesiastical History
Tann, J., Commerce
Taylor, A., Economics
Taylor, A. M. R., Cancer Genetics
Taylor, E. W., Animal Physiology
Taylor, M., World Faiths Development Dialogue
Tellam, J., Hydrogeology
Temple, J. G., Surgery
Teubert, W., English
Theobald, M. F., Accounting
Thomas, C. M., Molecular Genetics
Thomas, C. R., Biochemical Engineering
Thomas, H. R., Economics of Education
Timms, C. R., Music
Toolan, M., Applied English Linguistics
Trayer, I. P., Biochemistry
Turnbull, P., Marketing
Turner, B. M., Experimental Genetics
Tziovas, D. P., Modern Greek Studies
Ustorf, W., Mission
Verdi, R., Fine Art and Art History
Vinzent, M., Theology
Wakelam, M. J. O., Molecular Pharmacology
Walmsley, A., Dentistry
Walsh, M., English Literature
Walton, D., Mechanical Engineering
Webber, J., Theology
West, S., Art History
Westbrook, G. K., Geophysics
Westbury, D. R., Physiology
Wharton, C., Biochemistry
Wheatley, K., Medical Statistics
Whenham, E., Music History
Whitehand, J. W. R., Urban Geography

WHITTLE, M. J., Foetal Medicine
WICKHAM, C. J., Early Medieval History
WILSON, J. S., Pure Mathematics
WILSON, R., Group Theory
WING, A. M., Human Movement
WINTERBOTTOM, J., Chemical Reaction Engineering
WOOD, D. M., French Literature
WOODMAN, G., Comparative Law
WRIGHTSON, P., Physiotherapy
YAO, X., Computer Science
YOUNG, F. M., Theology
YOUNG, L. S., Cancer Biology

UNIVERSITY OF BOLTON

Deane Rd, Bolton, BL3 5AB

Telephone: (1204) 900600
Fax: (1204) 399074
E-mail: enquiries@bolton.ac.uk
Internet: www.bolton.ac.uk

Founded 1824, present status 2005
State control
Language of instruction: English
Academic year: September to July

Chancellor: Baroness MORRIS OF BOLTON
Vice-Chancellor: Dr GEORGE HOLMES
Pro-Vice-Chancellor: Prof. ROB CAMPBELL
Library Man.: TREVOR HODGSON

Library of 180,000 vols, 18,000 books, 8,000 e-books, 400 print journals, 15,000 e-journals
Number of teachers: 320
Number of students: 9,238 (7,445 undergraduate, 1,793 postgraduate)

Publication: *The Bolt* (4 a year)

DEANS

Faculty of Advanced Engineering and Sciences: ANDY GRAHAM
Faculty of Arts and Media Technologies: SAM JOHNSON
Faculty of Well Being and Social Sciences: Prof. CAROLE TRUMAN

UNIVERSITY OF BRADFORD

Richmond Rd, Bradford, BD7 1DP

Telephone: (1274) 232323
Fax: (1274) 236260
E-mail: enquiries@bradford.ac.uk
Internet: www.bradford.ac.uk

Founded 1882, as Bradford Technical College, Royal Charter 1966
Academic year: September to May to May (2 semesters)

Chancellor: IMRAN KHAN
Vice-Chancellor and Prin.: Prof. MARK CLEAREY
Pro-Chancellor and Chair.: PAUL JAGGER
Treas. and Pro-Chancellor: ROLAND CLARK
Pro-Chancellor: DIANA CHAMBERS
Sec.: MARY-ROSE MILLIN
Deputy Vice-Chancellor: S. KERSHAW
Deputy Vice-Chancellor for Academic Affairs: Prof. GEOFF LAYER
Dir of Learning Resources Unit: Dr S. J. HOUGHTON
Librarian: J. J. HORTON

Library: see Libraries and Archives
Number of teachers: 536
Number of students: 8,435

Publications: *News and Views*, *Vice-Chancellor's Research Report* (1 a year)

DEANS

Engineering, Design and Technology: Prof. A. S. WOOD
Health Studies: Prof. G. BRADSHAW
School of Computing, Informatics and Media: Dr I. J. PALMER
School of Life Sciences: Prof. D. COATES

School of Lifelong Education and Devt: N. MIRZA
School of Management: Prof. A. FRANCIS
School of Social and Int. Studies: Prof. J. CUSWORTH

PROFESSORS

ALDERSON, G., Medical Microbiology
ANDERSON, D., Biomedical Sciences
ASHLEY, R. M., Urban Water
ASHMORE, M. R., Environmental Science
BAILES, P. J., Process Engineering
BALMER, J. M. T., Corporate Identity
BARRY, B. W., Pharmaceutical Technology
BENKREIRA, H., Coating and Polymer Processing
BIBBY, M. C., Cancer Research
CHALMERS, M. G., International Politics
CHOUDHRY, T., Finance
CHRYSTYN, H., Clinical Pharmacy
CLARK, B. J., Pharmaceutical Technology
COATES, P. D., Polymer Engineering
COSTALL, B., Neuropharmacology
COWLING, P. I., Computing
CUSWORTH, J. W., International Development Management
DANDO, M. R., International Security
DAY, A. J., Quality Engineering
DOUBLE, J. A., Experimental Cancer Chemotherapy
DOWNS, M. G., Dementia Studies
DUNCAN, S. S., Comparative Social Policy
EARNSHAW, R. A., Electronic Imaging
EDWARDS, H. G. M., Molecular Spectroscopy
EXCELL, P. S., Applied Electromagnetics
FELL, A. F., Pharmaceutical Chemistry
FILOTOTCHEV, I. R., Strategic Management
FRANCIS, F. A. S., Management
GALLAGHER, T. G. P., Ethnic Conflict and Peace
GARDINER, J. G., Electronic Engineering
GARDNER, M. L. G., Physiological Biochemistry
GRAVES-MORRIS, P. R., Numerical Analysis
GREEN, J. N., Romance Linguistics
HOGARTH-SCOTT, S., Marketing and Entrepreneurship
HOPE, C. A., Service Quality
HUSBAND, C. H., Social Analysis
JAMES, A. L., Social Sciences
JAMES, P. W., Environmental Sciences
JENKINS, T. C., Drugs Design
JIANG, J., Electronic Imaging and Media Communications
JOBBER, D., Marketing
KOUVATSOS, D. D., Computer Systems Modelling
LAYER, G. M., Lifelong Learning
LUCAS, J., Learning and Teaching
McCOLM, I. J., Ceramic Materials
MELLORS, C., Political Science
MIRZA, H. R., International Business
MUHLEMANN, A. P., Operations Management
NAYLOR, R. J, Pharmacology
NEWELL, R. J., Nursing Research
O'HEAR, A., Philosophy
OSTELL, A. E., Organizational Health and Behaviour
PEARCE, J. V., Latin American Politics
PIKE, R. H., Finance and Accounting
POLLARD, A. M., Archaeological Sciences
PRICE, D. H. R., Operational Research
RADAELLI, C. M., Public Policy
RAMSBOTHAM, O. P., Peace Studies
RANDALL, V. A., Biomedical Sciences
ROGERS, P. F., Peace Studies
SCHALLREUTER, K. U., Clinical and Experimental Dermatology
SEAWARD, M. R. D., Environmental Biology
SHEPHERD, S. J., Cryptography and Computer Communications Security
SHERIFF, R. E., Mobile Communications
SMALL, N. A., Community and Primary Care
TAYLOR, W. A., Business Information Systems
TOROPOV, V. V., Computational Mechanics

VOURDAS, A., Computing
WALLS, J. R., Chemical Engineering
WEISS, J. A., Development Economics
WHALLEY, R., Mechanical Engineering
WHITAKER, D. J., Optometry
WILLIAMS, A. C., Contemporary German Studies
WINN, B., Optometry
WOOD, J. M., Medical Biochemistry
WOODHOUSE, T., Conflict Resolution
WOODWARD, M. E., Telecommunications
YORK, P., Physical Pharmaceutics
ZAIRI, M., Best Practice Management

UNIVERSITY OF BRIGHTON

Mithras House, Lewes Rd, Brighton, BN2 4AT

Telephone: (1273) 600900
Fax: (1273) 642607
E-mail: enquiries@brighton.ac.uk
Internet: www.brighton.ac.uk

Founded 1970 as Brighton Polytechnic, present name and status 1992
Academic year: September to June

Vice-Chancellor: Prof. JULIAN CRAMPTON
Deputy Vice-Chancellor: STUART LAING
Pro-Vice-Chancellor for Business and Marketing: COLIN MONK
Pro-Vice-Chancellor for Research: Prof. BRUCE BROWN
Registrar and Sec.: CAROL BURNS
Dir of Finance: SUE McHUGH
Dir of Information Services: MARK TOOLE

Library of 550,000 vols
Number of teachers: 1,122 (f.t.e.)
Number of students: 23,000

DEANS

Brighton and Sussex Medical School: Prof. JON COHEN
Faculty of Arts: Prof. BRUCE BROWN
Faculty of Education and Sport: PAUL GRIFFITHS
Faculty of Health and Social Science: Prof. DAVID TAYLOR
Faculty of Management and Information Sciences: Prof. DAVID ARNOLD
Faculty of Science and Engineering: Prof. ANDREW LLOYD

UNIVERSITY OF BRISTOL

Senate House, Tyndall Ave, Bristol, BS8 1TH

Telephone: (117) 928-9000
Fax: (117) 925-1424
Internet: www.bristol.ac.uk

Founded 1909, previously established as Univ. College, Bristol, 1876
Academic year: October to July

Chancellor: Baroness HALE OF RICHMOND
Vice-Chancellor: Prof. ERIC THOMAS
Deputy Vice-Chancellor: Prof. DAVID CLARKE
Pro-Vice-Chancellor for Education and Students: Prof. AVRIL WATERMAN-PEARSON
Pro-Vice-Chancellor for Enterprise: Prof. GUY ORPEN
Registrar: DEREK PRETTY

Library: see under Libraries and Archives
Number of teachers: 2,129
Number of students: 18,615

Publications: *re:search*, *Subtext*

DEANS

Faculty of Arts: Prof. CHARLES MARTINDALE
Faculty of Engineering: Prof. NICK LIEVEN
Faculty of Medical and Veterinary Sciences: Prof. CLIVE ORCHARD
Faculty of Medicine and Dentistry: Prof. PETER MATHIESON
Faculty of Science: Prof. JON KEATING
Faculty of Social Sciences and Law: Prof. JUDITH SQUIRES

PROFESSORS
(Some professors serve in more than one faculty)

Faculty of Arts (Senate House, Tyndall Ave, Bristol, BS8 1TH; tel. (117) 928-8897; internet www.bris.ac.uk/depts/artspgc/facart .htm):

BANFIELD, S. D., Music
BANN, S., History of Art
BENNETT, A. J., English
BIRD, A. J., Philosophy
BROOKSHAW, D. R., Luso-Brazilian Studies
BRYCE, J. H., Italian
BUXTON, R. G. A., Greek Language and Literature
CLARK, E. G., Ancient History
CORNWELL, N. J., Russian and Comparative Literature
DOYLE, W., History
FOWLER, R. L. H., Greek
FREEMAN, M. J., French Language and Literature
HARRISON, R. J., European Prehistory
HOOK, D., Hispanic Studies
HOPKINS, D. W., English Literature
HUTTON, R. E., History
KENNEDY, D. F., Latin Literature and Theory of Criticism
KERSHAW, B. R., Drama
KOSENINA, A., German
LOWE, R., Contemporary History
MARTINDALE, C. A., Latin
OFFORD, D. C., Russian Intellectual History
PARKIN, J., French Literary Studies
PARRY, M. M., Italian Linguistics
POOLE, G. R., Composition
PUNTER, D. G., English
SAMPSON, R. B. K., Romance Philology
STREET, S. C. J., Film
UNWIN, T. A., French
VINCENT, J. R., History
WEBB, E. T., English
WHITE, M. E., Theatre
WILLIAMS, P. M., Indian and Tibetan Philosophy

Faculty of Engineering (Queen's Building, University Walk, Bristol, BS8 1TR; tel. (117) 928-9760; internet www.fen.bris.ac.uk):

ADAMS, R. D., Applied Mechanics
BEACH, M. A., Radio Systems Engineering
BLOCKLEY, D. I., Civil Engineering
BOWES, S. R., Electrical and Electronic Engineering
BULL, D. R., Digital Systems Processing
CANAGARAJAH, C. N., Multimedia Signal Processing
CHALMERS, A. G., Computer Graphics
CHAMPNEYS, A. R., Applied Non-linear Mathematics
CLUCKIE, I. D., Worldwide Water Management
DAGLESS, E. L., Microelectronics
FLACH, P. A., Artificial Intelligence
FRISWELL, M. I., Aerospace Engineering
HOGAN, S. J., Mathematics
JOSZA, R. O., Computer Science
KRAUSKOPF, B., Applied Non-linear Mathematics
LIEVEN, N. A. J., Aerospace Dynamics
MAY, M. D., Computer Science
McGEEHAN, J. P., Communications Engineering
MELLOR, P. H., Electrical Engineering
MUIR WOOD, D., Civil Engineering
NIX, A. R., Wireless Communication Systems
PRADHAN, D. K., Computer Science
QUARINI, G. L., Process Engineering
RAILTON, C. J., Electrical and Electronic Engineering
RARITY, J. G., Optical Communications Systems
SMART, N. P., Cryptology

SMITH, D. J., Mechanical Engineering
STOTEN, D. P., Dynamics and Control
TAYLOR, C. A., Earthquake Engineering
WISNOM, M. R., Aerospace Structures

Faculty of Medical and Veterinary Sciences (University Walk, Bristol, BS8 1TD; tel. (117) 331-7484; internet www.bristol.ac.uk/fmvs/):

BANTING, G. S., Molecular Cell Biology
BASHIR, Z. I., Cellular Neuroscience
BENNETT, P. M., Bacterial Genetics
BRADY, R. L., Biochemistry
BROWN, M. W., Anatomy and Cognitive Neuroscience
CLARKE, A. R., Biochemistry
COLLINGRIDGE, G., Neuroscience in Anatomy
CULLEN, P. J., Biochemistry
DAY, M. J., Veterinary Pathology
DENTON, R. M., Biochemistry
DUFFUS, W. P. H., Veterinary Medicine
GRUFFYDD-JONES, T. J., Feline Medicine
HALESTRAP, A. P., Biochemistry
HALFORD, S. E., Biochemistry
HALL, E. J., Companion Animal Studies
HALL, L., Molecular Genetics
HASSAN, A. B., Adult Oncology
HEADLEY, P. M., Physiology
HENDERSON, G., Pharmacology
HENLEY, J. M., Molecular Neuroscience
HEYDERMAN, R. S., Infectious Diseases and International Health
HOLT, P. E., Veterinary Surgery
HUMPHREY, T. J., Veterinary Zoonotic Bacteriology
KUWABARA, P. E., Genomics
LAWSON, S. N., Physiology
LISNEY, S. J. W., Physiology
MacGOWAN, A. P., Clinical Microbiology and Antimicrobial Therapeutics
MARRION, N. V., Neuroscience
MARTIN, P. B., Cell Biology
MOLNAR, E., Anatomy
MULLER, R. L., Neuroscience
NICOL, C. J., Animal Welfare
ORCHARD, C. H., Physiology
PARASKEVA, M. M., Experimental Oncology
PATON, J. F. R., Physiology
PIGNATELLI, M., Histopathology
RIVETT, A. J., Biochemistry
ROBERTS, P. J., Neurochemical Pharmacology
RUTTER, G. A., Biochemistry and Cell Biology
SIDDELL, S. G., Virology
STOKES, C. R., Mucosal Immunology
TAVARE, J. M., Biochemistry
VAZQUEZ-BOLAND, J. A., Veterinary Molecular Biology
VIRJI, M., Molecular Microbiology
WATERMAN-PATERSON, A. E., Veterinary Anaesthesia
WILLIAMS, N. A., Immunology
WOOD, J. D., Food Animal Science
WRAITH, D. C., Pathological Sciences

Faculty of Medicine and Dentistry (Senate House, Tyndall Ave, Bristol, BS8 1TH; tel. (117) 928-9951; internet www.medici.bris.ac .uk/medf/):

ADDY, M., Periodontology
ALDERSON, D., Gastrointestinal Surgery
ANGELINI, G., Cardiac Surgery
ARMITAGE, W. J., Opthalmology
BINGLEY, P. J., Diabetes
CAMPBELL, A. V., Ethics in Medicine
COLLINGRIDGE, G., Neuroscience in Anatomy
COWPE, J. G., Oral Surgery
DAVEY SMITH, G., Clinical Epidemiology
DICK, A. D., Ophthalmology
DONOVAN, J. L., Social Medicine
EBRAHIM, S. B. J., Epidemiology of Ageing
EMOND, A. M., Community Child Health
EVESON, J. W., Head and Neck Pathology
FINN, A. H. R., Paediatrics

FLEMING, P. J., Infant Health and Developmental Psychology
FRANKEL, S. J., Epidemiology and Public Health Medicine
GALE, E. A. M., Diabetic Medicine
GOLDING, M. J., Paediatric and Perinatal Epidemiology
GUNNELL, D. J., Epidemiology
HANKS, G. W. C., Palliative Medicine
HARRISON, G. L., Mental Health
HOLLANDER, A. P., Rheumatology and Tissue Engineering
HOLLY, J. M. P., Clinical Sciences
JAGGER, D. C., Restorative Dentistry
JENKINSON, H. F., Oral Microbiology
KARSCH, K. R., Cardiology
KIRWAN, J. R., Rheumatic Diseases
LEARMONTH, I. D., Orthopaedic Surgery
LEWIS, G. H., Psychiatric Epidemiology
LIGHTMAN, S. L., Medicine
LOPEZ BERNAL, A., Human Reproductive Biology
LOVE, S., Neuropathology
MATHIESON, P. W., Renal Medicine
MURPHY, D., Experimental Medicine
NEWBY, A. C., Vascular Cell Biology
NUTT, D. J., Psychopharmacology
PETERS, T. J., Primary Health Care Services Research
PIGNATELLI, M. M., Histopathology
PRIME, S. S., Experimental Pathology
REES, M. R., Clinical Radiology
SALISBURY, C. J., Primary Health Care
SANDY, J. R., Orthodontics
SCOLDING, N. J., Clinical Neurosciences
SHARP, D. J., Primary Health Care
SOOTHILL, P. W., Maternal and Foetal Medicine
STEVENS, M. C. G., Paediatric Oncology
THORESEN, M., Neo-natal Neuroscience
UNEY, J. B., Molecular Neuroscience
WHITELAW, A. G. L., Neonatal Medicine
WILCOCK, G. K., Care of the Elderly
WILLIAMS, G., Medicine and Dentistry
WOLF, A. R., Anaesthesia
WYNICK, D., Molecular Medicine

Faculty of Science (Senate House, Tyndall Ave, Bristol, BS8 1TH; tel. (117) 928-9957; internet www.bris.ac.uk/depts/science/ sciweb.htm):

AGGARWAL, V. K., Synthetic Organic Chemistry
ALAM, M. A., Physics
ALLAN, N. L., Physical Chemistry
ALLEN, G. C., Materials Science
ANDERSON, M. G., Geography
ANNETT, J. F., Physics
ASHFOLD, M. N. R., Physical Chemistry
BALINT-KURTI, G. G., Theoretical Chemistry
BAMBER, J. L., Geography
BATES, P. D., Hydrology
BENTON, M. J., Vertebrate Palaeontology
Sir BERRY, MICHAEL, Physics
BIRKINSHAW, M., Cosmology and Astrophysics
BLUNDY, J. D., Petrology
BRERETON, R. G., Chemometrics
CHERNS, D., Physics
CLOKE, P. J., Geography
CONNELLY, N. G., Inorganic Chemistry
CONREY, J. B., Number Theory
COSGROVE, T., Physical Chemistry
CUTHILL, I. C., Behavioural Ecology
DAVIS, A. P., Supramolecular Chemistry
EASTOE, J. G., Chemistry
EDWARDS, K. J., Cereal Functional Genomics
EGGERS, J. G., Applied Mathematics
EVANS, D. V., Applied Mathematics
EVANS, R., Physics
EVERSHED, R. P., Chemistry
FOSTER, B., Physics
FRANKS, N. R., Animal Behaviour and Ecology

FREEMAN, N. H., Cognitive Development
GALLAGHER, T. C., Organic Chemistry
GIBSON, W. C., Protozoology
GOLDSTEIN, H., Statistics
GREEN, B. J., Pure Mathematics
GREEN, P. J., Statistics
HANNAY, J. H., Theoretical Physics
HARRIS, S., Environmental Sciences
HAWKESWORTH, C. J., Earth Sciences
HAYDEN, S. M., Physics
HAYES, P. K., Biology
HEATH, G. P., Physics
HELFRICH, G. R., Seismology
HENSHAW, D. L., Physics
HOOD, B. M., Development Psychology
HOUSTON, A. I., Theoretical Biology
JONES, G., Biological Sciences
JONES, K., Human Quantitative Geography
KEATING, J. P., Mathematical Physics
KEMPSON, H. E., Personal Finance and Social Policy Research
KENDALL, J.-M., Earth Sciences
LARNER, W. J., Human Geography and Sociology
LINDEN, N., Theoretical Physics
LISKEVICH, V., Mathematics
LLOYD-JONES, G. C., Chemistry
MANN, S., Chemistry
MCNAMARA, J. M., Mathematics and Biology
MANNERS, I., Inorganic Materials and Chemistry
MILES, M. J., Physics
NASON, G. P., Statistics
OBERAUER, K., Psychology
ORPEN, A. G., Structural Chemistry
ORR-EWING, A. J., Chemistry
PEREGRINE, D. H., Applied Mathematics
POPESCU, S., Physics
PRENTICE, I. C., Earth System Science
PRINGLE, P. G., Inorganic Chemistry
RAGNARSDOTTIR, K. V., Environmental Geochemistry
RICHARDSON, R. M., Physics
RICKARD, J. C., Mathematics
ROBERT, D., Bionanoscience
ROBERTS, A., Zoology
ROGERS, P. J., Biological Psychology
SCHOFIELD, A. H., Pure Mathematics
SHERMAN, D. M., Geochemistry
SIEGERT, M. J., Physical Geography
SIMPSON, T. J., Organic Chemistry
SMART, P. L., Geography
SPARKS, R. S. J., Geology
STEEDS, J. W., Physics
STOBART, A. K., Plant Biochemistry
TICKELL, A. T., Human Geography
TINSLEY, R. C., Zoology
TRANTER, M., Geography
TROSCIANKO, T. S., Psychology
VALDES, P. J., Physical Geography
VAN DEN BERG, M., Pure Mathematics
VINCENT, B., Physical Chemistry
VINEY, M. E., Biological Sciences
WALL, R. L., Zoology
WALSBY, A. E., Botany
WELCH, P. D., Mathematics
WIGGINS, S. R., Applied Mathematics
WILLIS, C. L., Organic Chemistry
WOOD, B. J., Earth Sciences
WORRALL, D. M., Physics

Faculty of Social Sciences and Law (Senate House, Tyndall Ave, Bristol, BS8 1TH; tel. (117) 928-7797; internet www.bris.ac.uk/depts/socsci):

ASHTON, D. J., Accountancy and Finance
ATTFIELD, C. L. F., Econometrics
BAILEY-HARRIS, R. J., Law
BRADLEY, H. K., Sociology
BREWER, A. A., History of Economics
BURGESS, S. M., Economics
CARVER, T. F., Political Theory
COWAN, D. S., Law and Policy
CROSSLEY, M. W., Comparative and International Education

DEEM, R., Education
DOYAL, L., Health and Social Care
DUGDALE, D., Management Accounting
FARMER, E. R. G., Child and Family Studies
FENTON, C. S., Sociology
FORREST, R. S., Urban Studies
FORSTER, A. W., Politics and International Relations
FOX, K. R., Exercise and Health Sciences
FRIEDMAN, A. L., Management and Economics
GORDON, D., Social Justice
GREGG, P. A., Economics
GROUT, P. A., Political Economy
HESTER, M., Gender, Violence and International Policy
HILL, J. D., Law
HUGHES, R. M., Education
JOHNSON, M. L., Health and Social Policy
KERRIDGE, J. R., Law
KYLE, J. G., Deaf Studies
LEVITAS, R., Sociology
LITTLE, R., International Politics
MCFARLANE, A. E., Education
MCLENNAN, G., Sociology
MCMEEL, G. P., Law
MODOOD, T., Sociology, Politics and Public Policy
MOK, K. J., East Asian Studies
OSBORN, M. J., Education
PARK, I.-U., Industrial Organization
PARTINGTON, T. M., Law
PRIDHAM, G. F. M., European Politics
PROPPER, C., Economics
PROSSER, J. A. W., Public Law
QUINTON, D. L., Psychosocial Development
REA-DICKINS, P. M., Applied Linguistics in Education
ROBERTSON, S. L., Education (Sociology)
ROSE, F. D., Commercial Law
SKULTANS SHELLEY, V., Social Anthropology
STANTON, K. M., Law
SUFRIN, B. E., Law
SUTHERLAND, R. J., Education
TEMPLE, J. R. W., Economics
WARD, L. M., Disability and Social Policy
WEBSTER, A., Educational Psychology

UNIVERSITY OF BUCKINGHAM

Hunter St, Buckingham, MK18 1EG
Telephone: (1280) 814080
Fax: (1280) 822245
E-mail: info@buckingham.ac.uk
Internet: www.buckingham.ac.uk
Founded 1976, Royal Charter 1983
Private control
Academic year: January to December (4 10-week terms)
Chancellor: Lord TANLAW
Chairman of Ccl: CHLOE WOODHEAD
Vice-Chancellor: Dr TERENCE KEALEY
Deputy Vice-Chancellor: Prof. ANDREW MILES
Registrar: Prof. LEN EVANS
Librarian: LOUISE HAMMOND
Number of teachers: 164 (93 full-time, 91 part-time)
Number of students: 1,000
Publication: *Denning Law Journal* (1 a year)

DEANS

School of Business: Dr JANE TAPSELL
School of Humanities: Prof. MARTIN RICKETTS
School of Law: Prof. SUSAN EDWARDS
School of Medicine: Prof. KAROL SIKORA (Dean-Elect)
School of Sciences: Prof. MIKE CAWTHORNE

PROFESSORS

ADAMS, C. J., Information Systems
ADAMSON, J., Modern History
ALCOCK, A., Corporate Law
ALDERMAN, G., Politics and Contemporary History

ARCH, J., Metabolic Research
CAWTHORNE, M. A., Metabolic Research
CLARKE, J. C., History
DURAND, A., European Law
EDWARDS, S., Law
FOSTER, N., European Law
GLEES, A., Security/Intelligence Studies
JASSIM, S., Mathematics
O'HEAR, A., Philosophy and Education
O'KEEFE, D., Education
RICKETTS, M., Economic Organisation
RIDLEY, J., History
SMITHERS, A., Education
WOOD, G., Economics
WOODHEAD, C., Education

UNIVERSITY OF CAMBRIDGE

Cambridge CB2 1TN
Telephone: (1223) 337733 (Central Switchboard); (1223) 332200 (Central Administration)
Fax: (1223) 339669
E-mail: communications@admin.cam.ac.uk
Internet: www.cam.ac.uk
Founded 13th century
Academic year: October to June
Chancellor: HRH PRINCE PHILIP, THE DUKE OF EDINBURGH
Vice-Chancellor: Prof. Sir LESZEK BORYSIEWICZ
Pro-Vice-Chancellor for Education: Prof. JOHN RALLISON
Pro-Vice-Chancellor for Int. Strategy: Dr JENNIFER BARNES
Pro-Vice-Chancellor for Institutional Affairs: Prof. IAN WHITE
Pro-Vice-Chancellor for Planning and Resources: Prof. STEVE YOUNG
Pro-Vice-Chancellor for Research: Prof. LYNN GLADDEN
High Steward: Dame BRIDGET OGILVIE
Registrary: Dr J. NICHOLLS
Librarian: P. K. FOX
Number of teachers: 1,500
Number of students: 15,821 (11,160 undergraduate, 4,661 postgraduate)

PROFESSORS

Faculty of Archaeology and Anthropology (Pembroke St, Cambridge, CB2 3QY; tel. (1223) 762846; fax (1223) 335460; e-mail archanth-enquiries@lists.cam.ac.uk; internet www.archanth.cam.ac.uk):

BARKER, G., Archaeology (St John's College)
CHAKRABARTI, D., McDonald Institute for Archaeological Research
FOLEY, R. A., Human Evolution (King's College)
HUMPHREY, C., Collaborative Anthropology (King's College)
JONES, M. K., Archaeological Science
KEMP, B., McDonald Institute for Archaeological Research
LEGGE, A. J., McDonald Institute for Archaeological Research
MASCIE-TAYLOR, C. G. N., Biological Anthropology (Churchill College)
MELLARS, P. A., Prehistory and Human Evolution (Corpus Christi College)
MILLETT, M. J., Classical Archaeology (Fitzwilliam College)
MOORE, H. L., Social Anthropology (Jesus College)
POSTGATE, N., Assyriology (Trinity College)
RAY, J., Egyptology (Selwyn College)
Lord RENFREW, Archaeology

Faculty of Architecture and History of Art (1–5 Scroope Terrace, Trumpington St, Cambridge, CB2 1PX; tel. (1223) 332950; fax (1223) 332960; e-mail enquiries@aha.cam.ac.uk; internet www.aha.cam.ac.uk):

BINSKI, P., History of Medieval Art (Gonville and Caius College)

ECHENIQUE, M. H., Land Use and Transport Studies (Churchill College)

HOWARD, D. J., Architectural History (St John's College)

JOANNIDES, P. E., Art History

MASSING, J. M., History of Art (King's College)

SHORT, A., Architecture (Clare Hall)

STEEMERS, K., Sustainable Design (Wolfson College)

Faculty of Asian and Middle Eastern Studies (Sidgwick Ave, Cambridge, CB3 9DA; tel. (1223) 335106; fax (1223) 335110; e-mail enquiries@ames.cam.ac.uk; internet www.ames.cam.ac.uk):

BOWRING, R., Japanese Studies (Downing College)

DE LANGE, N., Hebrew and Jewish Studies (Wolfson College)

GORDON, R., Hebrew (St Catharine's College)

KHAN, G., Semitic Philology

KORNICKI, P., East Asian Studies (Robinson College)

MELVILLE, C., Persian History (Pembroke College)

MONTGOMERY, J., Classical Arabic (Trinity Hall)

POSTGATE, N., Assyriology (Trinity College)

RAY, J., Egyptology (Selwyn College)

STERCKX, R., Chinese (Clare College)

SULEIMAN, Y., Modern Arabic Studies (King's College)

VAN DE VEN, H., Modern Chinese History

Faculty of Biology (School of the Biological Sciences, 17 Mill Lane, Cambridge, CB2 1RX; tel. (1223) 766894; fax (1223) 332355; e-mail mb422@admin.cam.ac.uk; internet www.bio.cam.ac.uk/index.html):

AFFARA, N. A., Pathology (Hughes Hall)

ASHBURNER, M., Genetics (Churchill College)

BARLOW, H. B., Physiology, Development and Neuroscience (Trinity College)

BATE, C. M., Developmental Biology (King's College)

BAULCOMBE, D. C., Plant Sciences

Sir BLUNDELL, TOM, Biochemistry (Sidney Sussex College)

BURROWS, M., Neurobiology (Wolfson College)

CLAYTON, N. S., Comparative Cognition (Clare College)

CLUTTON-BROCK, T. H., Animal Ecology (Magdalen College)

COLLINS, V. P., Histopathology

COOKE, A., Pathology (King's College)

CRAWFORD, A. C., Neurophysiology (Trinity College)

DAVIES, N. B., Behavioural Ecology (Pembroke College)

DICKINSON, A., Comparative Psychology (Hughes Hall)

ELLAR, D. J., Biochemistry (Gonville and Caius College)

ELLINGTON, C. P., Zoology (Downing College)

EVERITT, B. J., Behavioural Neuroscience (Downing College)

FIELD, M. C., Pathology

FITZSIMONS, J. T., Physiology, Development and Neuroscience (Gonville and Caius College)

FOWDEN, A. L., Biological Sciences (Girton College)

GILLIGAN, C. A., Mathematical Biology (King's College)

GLOVER, D. M., Genetics (Fitzwilliam College)

GRAY, J. C., Plant Molecular Biology (Robinson College)

GRIFFITHS, H., Plant Sciences (Clare College)

HARRIS, W. A., Physiology, Development and Neuroscience (Clare College)

HUANG, C. L.-H., Cell Physiology (Murray Edwards College)

HUGHES, C., Pathology (Trinity College)

IRVINE, R. F., Molecular Pharmacology (Corpus Christi College)

JACKSON, R. J., Biochemistry (Pembroke College)

JACKSON, S. P., Zoology (St John's College)

JOHNSON, M. H., Reproductive Sciences (Christ's College)

KEVERNE, E. B., Behavioural Neuroscience (King's College)

LASKEY, R. A., Animal Embryology (Darwin College)

LAUE, E. D., Biochemistry (St John's College)

LAUGHLIN, S. B., Zoology (Churchill College)

LEADLAY, P. F., Biochemistry (Clare College)

LOKE, Y. W., Reproductive Immunology (King's College)

MCNAUGHTON, P. A., Pharmacology (Christ's College)

METCALFE, J. C., Mammalian Cell Biochemistry (Darwin College)

MINSON, A. C., Virology (Wolfson College)

MOLLON, J. D., Visual Neuroscience (Gonville and Caius College)

MOORE, B. C. J., Auditory Perception (Wolfson College)

PARKER, J. S., Plant Cytogenetics (St Catharine's College)

PERHAM, R. N., Structural Biochemistry (St John's College)

ROBBINS, T. W., Cognitive Neuroscience (Downing College)

ROBERTS, A. C., Behavioural Neuroscience (Girton College)

RUDD, C. E, Pathology

SALMOND, G. P. C., Biochemistry (Wolfson College)

SCHULTZ, W., Neuroscience (Churchill College)

SMITH, A., Wellcome Trust Centre for Stem Cell Research

SMITH, J. C., Zoology (Christ's College)

STANLEY, M. A., Pathology (Christ's College)

SURANI, M. A. H., Physiology of Reproduction (King's College)

SUTHERLAND, W. J., Conservation Biology (Clare College)

TAYLOR, C. W., Pharmacology (Downing College)

TYLER, L. K., Cognitive Neuroscience (Clare College)

WARING, M. J., Pharmacology (Jesus College)

WATT, F. M., Molecular Genetics

WYLLIE, A. H., Pathology (St John's College)

Faculty of Classics (Sidgwick Site, Sidgwick Ave, Cambridge, CB3 9DA; tel. (1223) 335151; fax (1223) 335409; internet www.classics.cam.ac.uk):

BEARD, M., Classics (Newnham College)

CARTLEDGE, P. A., Greek History and Greek Culture (Clare College)

DIGGLE, J., Greek and Latin (Queens' College)

GOLDHILL, S., Greek Literature and Culture (King's College)

HENDERSON, J., Classics (King's College)

HOLTON, D. W., Modern Greek

HORROCKS, G. C., Comparative Philology (St John's College)

HUNTER, R. L., Greek (Trinity College)

MILLETT, M. J., Classical Archaeology (Fitzwilliam College)

OAKLEY, S. P., Latin (Emmanuel College)

OSBORNE, R., Ancient History (King's College)

SCHOFIELD, M., Ancient Philosophy (St John's College)

SEDLEY, D. N., Ancient Philosophy (Christ's College)

Faculty of Divinity (West Rd, Cambridge, CB3 9BS; tel. (1223) 763002; fax (1223) 763003; e-mail faculty-office@divinity.cam.ac.uk; internet www.divinity.cam.ac.uk):

COAKLEY, S., Divinity (Murray Edwards College)

DAVIES, G. I., Old Testament Studies (Fitzwilliam College)

DE LANGE, N. R. M., Hebrew and Jewish Studies (Wolfson College)

DUFFY, E., History of Christianity (Magdalene College)

FORD, D. F., Divinity (Selwyn College)

LIEU, J., Divinity (Robinson College)

LIPNER, J., Hinduism and Comparative Study of Religion (Clare Hall)

Faculty of Earth Sciences and Geography (Downing Place, Cambridge, CB2 3EN; tel. (1223) 333393; e-mail secretary@esg.cam.ac.uk; internet www.esg.cam.ac.uk):

ADAMS, B., Conservation and Development (Downing College)

ARTACHO, E., Mineral Sciences

BENNETT, R. J., Geography (St Catharine's College)

BICKLE, M. J., Tectonics, Basin and Crustal Development and Sedimentology (Queens' College)

CARPENTER, M. A., Mineralogy and Mineral Physics (Magdalene College)

CLIFF, A. D., Theoretical Geography (Christ's College)

CONWAY MORRIS, S., Evolutionary Palaeoecology (St John's College)

DOVE, M., Mineralogy and Mineral Physics (Jesus College)

DOWDESWELL, J. A., Physical Geography (Jesus College)

ELDERFIELD, H., Environmental Change and Marine Geochemistry (St Catharine's College)

HAINING, R. P., Human Geography (Fitzwilliam College)

HODELL, D. A., Climate Change and Earth-Ocean-Atmosphere Systems

HUPPERT, H., Geological Fluid Mechanics (King's College)

JACKSON, J., Geophysics, Geodynamics and Tectonics

LEADER-WILLIAMS, N., Conservation Leadership (Dir (Churchill College)

MCKENZIE, D. P., Geophysics, Geodynamics and Tectonics (King's College)

MARTIN, R. L., Economic Geography (St Catharine's College)

OWENS, S., Environment and Policy (Newnham College)

PRIESTLEY, K., Geophysics, Geodynamics and Tectonics

REDFERN, S., Mineral Sciences

RICHARDS, K. S., Geography (Emmanuel College)

SALJE, E. K. H., Mineralogy and Petrology (Darwin College)

SMITH, R., Historical Geography and Demography (Downing College)

WHITE, R. S., Geophysics, Geodynamics and Tectonics (St Edmund's College)

WOODS, A. W., Geophysics, Geodynamics and Tectonics (St John's College)

Faculty of Economics (Austin Robinson Bldg, Sidgwick Ave, Cambridge, CB3 9DD; tel. (1223) 335200; fax (1223) 335475; e-mail faculty@econ.cam.ac.uk; internet www.econ.cam.ac.uk):

BROWN, W. A., Industrial Relations (Darwin College)

Sir DASGUPTA, PARTHA, Economics (St John's College)

GOYAL, S., Economics (Christ's College)

HARRIS, C. J., Economics (King's College)

HARVEY, A. C., Econometrics (Corpus Christi College)
NEWBERY, D. M. G., Economics (Churchill College)
OGILVIE, S., Economic History
PESARAN, M. H., Economics (Trinity College)
RUSTICHINI, A., Political Economy
SABOURIAN, H., Economics and Game Theory (King's College)
SMITH, R. J., Economic Theory and Economic Statistics (Gonville and Caius College)

Faculty of Education (184 Hills Rd, Cambridge, CB2 8PQ; tel. (1223) 767600; fax (1223) 767602; e-mail reception@educ.cam.ac.uk; internet www.educ.cam.ac.uk):
ARNOT, M., Sociology of Education (Jesus College)
COLCLOUGH, C., Education and Development
GOSWAMI, U., Education (St John's College)
GRAY, J. M., Education
GRONN, P., Education (Hughes Hall)
HOWE, C., Education (Lucy Cavendish College)
MERCER, N., Education (Hughes Hall)
NIKOLAJEVA, M., Education
REAY, D., Education
RUTHVEN, K., Education (Hughes Hall)

Faculty of English (9 West Rd, Cambridge, CB3 9DP; tel. (1223) 335070; fax (1223) 335075; e-mail english-faculty@lists.cam.ac.uk; internet www.english.cam.ac.uk):
COLLINI, S. A., English
COOPER, H., English (Magdalene College)
DE BOLLA, P., English (King's College)
GLEN, H. J., English (Murray Edwards College)
HAWKINS, J., Research Centre for English and Applied Linguistics
HEATH, S., English (Jesus College)
JACOBUS, M. L., English (Churchill College)
JARVIS, S., English (Robinson College)
KERRIGAN, J. F., English (St John's College)
LEIGHTON, A., English (Trinity College)
POOLE, A., English (Trinity College)
TROTTER, D., English (Gonville and Caius College)
WINDEATT, B. A., English (Emmanuel College)

Faculty of History (West Rd, Cambridge, CB3 9EF; tel. (1223) 335340; fax (1223) 335968; e-mail gen.enq@hist.cam.ac.uk; internet www.hist.cam.ac.uk):
ABULAFIA, D. S. H., History of the Mediterranean Countries in the Middle Ages (Gonville and Caius College)
ANDREW, C. M., Modern and Contemporary History (Corpus Christi College)
BADGER, A. J., American History since 1930 (Clare College)
Sir BAYLY, CHRISTOPHER, Modern Indian History and the History of the Expansion of Europe (St Catharine's College)
CARPENTER, M. C., Medieval English History
CLARK, C., Modern Europe (St Catharine's College)
DAUNTON, M. J., Economic History (Trinity Hall)
DUFFY, E., Religious History (Magdalene College)
EVANS, R. J., Modern European History (Gonville and Caius College)
HASLAM, J., History of International Relations (Corpus Christi College)
HATCHER, M. J., Economic History (Corpus Christi College)
HILTON, B., British History (Trinity College)
MANDLER, P., British History since 1800 (Gonville and Caius College)

McKITTERICK, R. D., Medieval History (Sidney Sussex College)
MORRILL, J. S., British and Irish History (Selwyn College)
O'BRIEN, M., Modern Intellectual Culture (Jesus College)
PARRY, J. P., British Political and Constitutional History (Pembroke College)
REYNOLDS, D., International History (Christ's College)
SMITH, R., Historical Demography (Downing College)
STEDMAN-JONES, G., Modern European Political Thought (King's College)
THOMPSON, D., Church History (Fitzwilliam College)
TOMBS, R., Modern French and European History (St John's College)
VAUGHAN, M., African History (King's College)

Faculty of Law (10 West Rd, Cambridge, CB3 9DZ; tel. (1223) 330033; fax (1223) 330055; e-mail enquiries@law.cam.ac.uk; internet www.law.cam.ac.uk):
ALLAN, T. R. S., Public Law and Jurisprudence (Pembroke College)
Sir BAKER, JOHN H., Laws of England (St Catharine's College)
BARNARD, C., European Union Law (Trinity College)
BELL, J. S., Law (Pembroke College)
BENTLY, L. A. F., Intellectual Property (Emmanuel College)
Sir BOTTOMS, ANTHONY E., Criminology (Fitzwilliam College)
CHEFFINS, B. R., Corporate Law (Trinity Hall)
CLARKE, M. A., Commercial Contract Law (St John's College)
CORNISH, W. R., Intellectual Property Law (Magdalene College)
CRAWFORD, J. R., International Law (Jesus College)
DASHWOOD, A. A., European Law (Sidney Sussex College)
FARRINGTON, D. P., Psychological Criminology (Darwin College)
FELDMAN, D., English Law (Downing College)
FERRAN, E. V., Company and Securities Law (St Catharine's College)
FORSYTH, C. F., Public Law and Private International Law (Robinson College)
GRAY, C. D., International Law (St John's College)
GRAY, K. J., Law (Trinity College)
HOOLEY, R. J. A., Law (Fitzwilliam College)
IBBETSON, D. J., Civil Law (Corpus Christi College)
KOSKENNIEMI, M. A., Legal Science (Jesus College)
KRAMER, M. H., Legal and Political Philosophy (Churchill College)
LIEBLING, A., Criminology
LÖSEL, F., Institute of Criminology (Dir)
SHERMAN, L. W., Criminology
SIMESTER, A. P., Law (Wolfson College)
SPENCER, J. R., Law (Selwyn College)
TILEY, J., Law of Taxation (Queens' College)
VIRGO, G. J., English Private Law (Downing College)
WIKSTROM, P. O., Ecological and Developmental Criminology
YATES, A. D., Law (Robinson College)

Faculty of Mathematics (Centre for Mathematical Sciences, Wilberforce Rd, Cambridge, CB3 0WA; tel. (1223) 765000; fax (1223) 765900; e-mail reception@maths.cam.ac.uk; internet www.maths.cam.ac.uk):
BAKER, A., Pure Mathematics (Trinity College)
BARROW, J. D., Applied Mathematics (Clare Hall)

COATES, J. H., Pure Mathematics (Emmanuel College)
DAVIS, A.-C., Theoretical Physics
DAWID, A. P., Statistics
DOREY, N., Theoretical Physics
FOKAS, T., Nonlinear Mathematical Science
GIBBONS, G. W., Theoretical Physics (Clare College)
GOLDSTEIN, R. E., Complex Physical Systems
GOWERS, W. T., Mathematics (Trinity College)
GREEN, B. J., Pure Mathematics (Trinity College)
GREEN, M. B., Theoretical Physics (Clare Hall)
GRIMMETT, G. R., Mathematical Statistics (Churchill College)
GROJNOWSKI, I., Mathematics
HAWKING, S. W., Gravitational Physics
HAYNES, P. H., Applied Mathematics
HINCH, E. J., Fluid Mechanics (Trinity College)
HORGAN, R. R., Theoretical and Mathematical Physics
HUPPERT, H. E., Theoretical Geophysics (King's College)
HYLAND, J. M. E., Mathematical Logic (King's College)
ISERLES, A., Numerical Analysis of Differential Equations (King's College)
JOHNSTONE, P. T., Foundations of Mathematics (St John's College)
JOZSA, R., Applied Mathematics and Theoretical Geophysics
KELLY, F. P., Mathematics of Systems (Christ's College)
KÖRNER, T. W., Fourier Analysis (Trinity Hall)
LEADER, I. B., Pure Mathematics (Trinity College)
LISTER, J. R., Fluid Dynamics (Trinity College)
MANTON, N. S., Mathematical Physics (St John's College)
MARKOWICH, P. A., Applied Mathematics
NORRIS, J. R., Stochastic Analysis (Churchill College)
OSBORN, H., Mathematics
PATERNAIN, G. P., Mathematics (Trinity College)
PEAKE, N., Applied Mathematics (Emmanuel College)
PROCTOR, M. R. E., Astrophysical Fluid Dynamics (Trinity College)
QUEVEDO, F.
RALLISON, J. M., Fluid Dynamics (Trinity College)
ROGERS, L. C. G., Statistical Science (St John's College)
SAXL, J., Algebra (Gonville and Caius College)
SCHOLL, A. J., Number Theory and Algebra
SHELLARD, E. P.
SHEPHERD-BARRON, N. I., Algebraic Geometry (Trinity College)
SPIEGELHALTER, D. J., Public Understanding of Risk
SUHOV, Y. M., Applied Probability (St John's College)
TAVARÉ, S., Applied Mathematics and Theoretical Geophysics
THOMASON, A. G., Combinatorial Mathematics (Clare College)
TOTARO, B. J., Astronomy and Geometry
TOWNSEND, P. K., Theoretical Physics (Queens' College)
WADHAMS, P., Ocean Physics
WEBER, R. R., Mathematics for Operational Research (Queens' College)
WILSON, P. M. H., Algebraic Geometry (Trinity College)
WORSTER, M. G., Mathematics for Natural Sciences (Trinity College)

Faculty of Modern and Medieval Languages (Sidgwick Ave, Cambridge, CB3 9DA; tel. (1223) 335000; fax (1223) 335062; e-mail mml-faculty-office@lists.cam.ac.uk; internet www.mml.cam.ac.uk):

- BARANSKI, Z. G., Italian (Murray Edwards College)
- BAYLEY, P., French (Gonville and Caius College)
- BENNETT, W., French Philology and Linguistics (Murray Edwards College)
- BOYLE, N., German (Magdalene College)
- FINCH, A.
- FORD, P. J., French and Neo-Latin Literature (Clare College)
- FRANKLIN, S. C., Slavonic Studies (Clare College)
- HAWKINS, S., Phonetic Sciences (Clare Hall)
- HOLTON, D. W., Modern Greek (Selwyn College)
- HUOT, S., Medieval French Literature (Pembroke College)
- KIRKPATRICK, R., Italian and English (Robinson College)
- LISBOA, M. M., Portuguese Literature and Culture (St John's College)
- NOLAN, F. J., Phonetics (Fitzwilliam College)
- ROBERTS, I. G., Linguistics (Downing College)
- SINCLAIR, A., Modern Spanish Literature and Intellectual History (Clare College)
- SMITH, P. J., Spanish (Trinity Hall)

Faculty of Music (11 West Rd, Cambridge, CB3 9DP; tel. (1223) 763481; fax (1223) 335067; e-mail tkw23@cam.ac.uk; internet www.mus.cam.ac.uk):

- COOK, N. J., Music (Darwin College)
- FENLON, I. A., Historical Musicology (King's College)
- HOLLOWAY, R. G., Musical Composition (Gonville and Caius College)
- RANKIN, S. K., Medieval Music (Emmanuel College)
- RINK, J. S., Musical Performance Studies

Faculty of Philosophy (Sidgwick Ave, Cambridge, CB3 9DA; tel. (1223) 335090; fax (1223) 335091; e-mail phil-admin@lists.cam.ac.uk; internet www.phil.cam.ac.uk):

- BLACKBURN, S. W., Philosophy (Trinity College)
- CRANE, T., Philosophy (Peterhouse)
- GEUSS, R., Philosophy
- HEAL, B. J., Philosophy (St John's College)

Faculty of Physics and Chemistry (Institute of Astronomy, Madingley Rd, Cambridge, CB3 0HA; tel. (1223) 766644; fax (1223) 337523; e-mail smo@ast.cam.ac.uk; internet www.ast.cam.ac.uk/physchemfaculty):

- ABELL, C., Biological Chemistry (Christ's College)
- BALASUBRAMANIAN, S., Medicinal Chemistry (Trinity College)
- BAUMBERG, J. J., Nanophotonics (Jesus College)
- BEST, S. M., Materials Science
- BHADESHIA, H. K. D. H., Metallurgy (Darwin College)
- BLAMIRE, M. D., Device Materials
- BURSTEIN, G. T., Materials Chemistry and Corrosion (Selwyn College)
- CAMERON, R. E., Materials Science (Lucy Cavendish College)
- CHEETHAM, A. K., Materials Science (Downing College)
- CLARKE, C. J., Institute of Astronomy
- CLYNE, T. W., Mechanics of Materials (Downing College)
- COOPER, J. R. C., Quantum Matter (Darwin College)
- COOPER, N. R., Theoretical Physics (Pembroke College)

- DAVIES, P. B., Laser Spectroscopy (Corpus Christi College)
- DOBSON, C. M., Chemistry (St John's College)
- DONALD, A. M., Biological and Soft Systems (Robinson College)
- DONALD, A. M., Experimental Physics (Robinson College)
- DRISCOLL, J. L., Materials Science (Robinson College)
- EFSTATHIOU, G. P., Astrophysics (King's College)
- ELLIOTT, S. R., Chemistry (Trinity College)
- EVANS, W., Institute of Astronomy
- EVETTS, J. E., Device Materials (Pembroke College)
- FABIAN, A. C., Institute of Astronomy
- Sir FERSHT, ALAN, Organic Chemistry (Gonville and Caius College)
- FRENKEL, D., Chemistry (Trinity College)
- Sir FRIEND, RICHARD, Physics (St John's College)
- GIBSON, V., High Energy Physics (Trinity College)
- GILMORE, G. F., Institute of Astronomy (King's College)
- GLEN, R. C., Chemistry (Clare College)
- GREENHAM, N. C., Optoelectronics (Clare College)
- GREER, A. L., Materials Science
- GREY, C. P., Materials Chemistry
- GULL, S., Physics (St John's College)
- HANIFF, C. A., Astrophysics (Downing College)
- HANSEN, J.-P., Chemistry (Corpus Christi College)
- HEWETT, P. C., Institute of Astronomy
- HILLS, R. E., Physics (St Edmund's College)
- HUCK, W. T. S., Nanotechnology (Gonville and Caius College)
- HUMPHREYS, C. J., Materials Science (Selwyn College)
- JONES, R., Photochemistry (Queens' College)
- JONES, W., Materials Chemistry (Sidney Sussex College)
- KENNICUTT, R. C., Astronomy and Experimental Philosophy
- KHMELNITSKII, D. E., Theory of Condensed Matter (Trinity College)
- Sir KING, DAVID, Physical Chemistry (Downing College)
- KLENERMAN, D., Chemistry (Christ's College)
- KLINOWSKI, J., Chemistry (Peterhouse)
- LAMBERT, R. M., Chemistry (King's College)
- LASENBY, A. N., Astrophysics and Cosmology (Queens' College)
- LEY, S. V., Organic Chemistry (Trinity College)
- LITTLEWOOD, P. B., Theoretical Physics (Trinity College)
- LONZARICH, G. G., Theoretical Physics (Trinity College)
- MACKAY, C. D., Institute of Astronomy
- MACKAY, D., Natural Philosophy
- MIDGLEY, P. A., Materials Science
- NEEDS, R., Theoretical Physics (Robinson College)
- OSTRIKER, J., Astronomy (Clare College)
- PARKER, A., High Energy Physics (Peterhouse)
- PATERSON, I., Chemistry (Jesus College)
- PAYNE, M. C., Theory of Condensed Matter (Pembroke College)
- PETTINI, M., Institute of Astronomy
- PHILLIPS, R. T., Physics (Clare College)
- PRINGLE, J. E., Astronomy (Emmanuel College)
- PYLE, J. A., Atmospheric Chemistry (St Catharine's College)
- RITCHIE, D. A., Experimental Physics (Robinson College)
- SANDERS, J. K. M., Inorganic Chemistry (Selwyn College)

- SIMONS, B. D., Theoretical Physics (St John's College)
- SIRRINGHAUS, H., Electron Device Physics (Churchill College)
- SMITH, C. G., Semiconductor Physics (Clare Hall)
- SPRIK, M., Chemistry (Clare College)
- STEINER, U., Physics of Materials (St Edmund's College)
- STIRLING, J., Natural Philosophy (Peterhouse)
- TERENTJEV, E. M., Polymer Physics (Queen's College)
- THOMSON, E., Experimental Particle Physics (Emmanuel College)
- WALES, D., Chemistry (Emmanuel College)
- WARD, D. R., Particle Physics (Queen's College)
- WARNER, M., Theoretical Physics (Corpus Christi College)
- WEBBER, B. R., Theoretical High Energy Physics (Emmanuel College)
- WINDLE, A. H., Materials Science (Trinity College)
- WITHINGTON, S., Analytical Physics (Downing College)

Faculty of Politics, Psychology, Sociology and International Studies (Free School Lane, Cambridge, CB2 3RQ; tel. (1223) 334520; fax (1223) 334550; e-mail enquiries@ppsis.cam.ac.uk; internet www.ppsis.cam.ac.uk; merger of Faculty of Social and Political Sciences and Centre of International Studies (CIS) 2009):

- BORN, G. E. M., Sociology, Anthropology and Music
- DUNN, J. M., Political Theory (King's College)
- GAMBLE, A. M., British Political Economy
- GOLOMBOK, S., Family Research (Newnham College)
- HASLAM, J. G., History of International Relations (Corpus Christi College)
- HILL, C. J., International Relations (Sidney Sussex College)
- HINES, M., Psychology (Churchill College)
- LAMB, M., Social and Development Psychology
- MAYALL, J. B. L., International Relations (Sidney Sussex College)
- RUST, J., Psychometrics Centre (Dir)
- SCOTT, J. L., Empirical Sociology (Queens' College)
- SIMMS, B. P., History of International Relations
- THERBORN, G., Sociology
- THOMPSON, J. B., Sociology (Jesus College)

School of Clinical Medicine (Addenbrooke's Hospital, Box 111, Hills Rd, Cambridge, CB2 0SP; tel. (1223) 336700; fax (1223) 336709; e-mail school-enquiries@medschl.cam.ac.uk; internet www.medschl.cam.ac.uk):

- ALLAIN, J.-P., Transfusion Medicine (Corpus Christi College)
- BARON, J.-C., Stroke Medicine
- BENNETT, M. R., Cardiovascular Sciences
- BLACKWELL, J. M., Molecular Parasitology (Newnham College)
- BOBROW, M., Medical Genetics (Wolfson College)
- BRADLEY, J. A., Surgery
- BRAYNE, C. E. G., Public Health (Darwin College)
- BROWN, M. J., Clinical Pharmacology (Gonville and Caius College)
- BULLMORE, E. T., Psychiatry
- CALDAS, C., Cancer Medicine
- CARRELL, R. W., Haematology (Trinity College)
- CHATTERJEE, V. K. K., Endocrinology (Churchill College)
- CHILVERS, E. R., Respiratory Medicine (St Edmund's College)
- CLAYTON, D., Biostatistics

COMPSTON, D. A. S., Neurology (Jesus College)

COMPSTON, J. E., Bone Medicine

COX, T. M., Medicine (Sidney Sussex College)

DANESH, J., Public Health and Primary Care

DAY, N. E., Public Health and Primary Care (Hughes Hall)

DUNGER, D. B., Paediatrics

EDWARDS, A. W. F., Public Health and Primary Care (Gonville and Caius College)

FAWCETT, J. W., Medicine (King's College)

FEARON, D. T., Immunology (Trinity College)

FFRENCH-CONSTANT, C. K., Neurological Genetics (Pembroke College)

FLETCHER, P., Psychiatry

GASTON, J. S. H., Rheumatology (St Edmund's College)

GOODYER, I. M., Child and Adolescent Psychiatry (Wolfson College)

GREEN, A. R., Haematology

GRIFFITHS, G., Medicine

GRIFFITHS, J., Molecular Imaging

HODGES, J. R., Medicine (King's College)

HOLLAND, A. J., Learning Disability

HUGHES, I. A., Paediatrics (Clare Hall)

HUPPERT, F., Psychology (Darwin College)

JODRELL, D., Cancer Therapeutics

JONES, P. B., Psychiatry

KARET, F. E., Nephrology

KHAW, K.-T., Clinical Gerontology (Gonville and Caius College)

KINMONTH, A. L., General Practice (St John's College)

LEHNER, P. J., Medicine

LEVER, A. M. L., Infectious Diseases (Peterhouse)

LOMAS, D. A., Respiratory Medicine (Trinity College)

LOMAS, D. J., Radiology

LUZIO, J. P., Clinical Biochemistry (St Edmund's College)

MANT, J., Primary Care Research

MENON, D. K., Anaesthesia (Queens' College)

MORRELL, N. W., Cardiopulmonary Medicine

MURPHY, G., Oncology

NEAL, D. E., Surgery

O'RAHILLY, S., Clinical Biochemistry and Medicine (Churchill College)

OWEN, D., Clinical Biochemistry

PEDERSEN, R., Regenerative Medicine

PETERS, A. M., Nuclear Medicine (New Hall)

Sir PETERS, KEITH, Physic (Christ's College)

PICKARD, J. D., Neurosurgery (St Catharine's College)

PONDER, B. A. J., Clinical Oncology (Jesus College)

READ, R. J., Haematology

ROBINSON, M., Clinical Biochemistry

ROLAND, M., Health Services Research

ROSENGARD, B. R., Surgery

RUBINSZTEIN, D., Molecular Neurogenetics

RUDD, C., Pathology

RUSHTON, N., Orthopaedic Research

SAHAKIAN, B. J., Clinical Neuropsychology

ST GEORGE-HYSLOP, P., Clinical Neurosciences

SIDDLE, K., Clinical Biochemistry (Churchill College)

SINCLAIR, J. H., Infectious Diseases

SISSONS, J. G. P., Infectious Diseases (Darwin College)

SMITH, G. C. S., Obstetrics and Gynaecology

SMITH, K. G. C., Experimental Medicine

SUTTON, S. R., Behavioural Science

TAVARÉ, S., Bioinformatics

TODD, J. A., Medical Genetics (Gonville and Caius College)

TROWSDALE, J., Pathology

VENTIKARAMAN, A. R., Cancer Research (New Hall)

WAREHAM, N., Epidemiology

WEISSBERG, P. L., Cardiovascular Medicine (Wolfson College)

WICKER, L., Medical Genetics

Department of Chemical Engineering and Biotechnology (New Museums Site, Pembroke St, Cambridge, CB2 3RA; tel. (1223) 334777; fax (1223) 334796; e-mail webmaster@ceb.cam.ac.uk; internet www.ceb.cam.ac.uk):

CHASE, H., Biochemical Engineering (Magdalene College)

GLADDEN, L. F., Chemical Engineering (Trinity College)

HALL, E. A. H., Analytical Biotechnology (Queens' College)

KRAFT, M., Chemical Engineering (Churchill College)

LOWE, C., Biotechnology (Trinity College)

MACKLEY, M. R., Chemical Engineering (Robinson College)

SLATER, N. K. H., Chemical Engineering (Fitzwilliam College)

Department of Engineering (Trumpington St, Cambridge, CB2 1PZ; tel. (1223) 332600; fax (1223) 332662; e-mail reception@eng.cam.ac.uk; internet www.eng.cam.ac.uk):

AINGER, C., Engineering

AMARATUNGA, G. A. J., Electrical Engineering (Churchill College)

BOLTON, M. D., Soil Mechanics (Churchill College)

BRITTER, R. E., Engineering (Pembroke College)

CALLADINE, C., Engineering

CAMPBELL, A. M., Engineering (Christ's College)

CANT, R. S., Engineering (Selwyn College)

CARDWELL, D. A., Superconducting Engineering

CEBON, D., Mechanical Engineering (Queens' College)

CIPOLLA, R., Information Engineering (Jesus College)

CLARKSON, P. J., Engineering Design

COLES, H. J., Electrical Engineering (St Catharine's College)

COLLINGS, N., Engineering (Robinson College)

COLOURIS, G., Engineering

CONTI, R., Engineering

DAVIDSON, P., Fluid Mechanics

DAWES, W. N., Aeronautical Engineering (Churchill College)

Dame DOWLING, ANN, Mechanical Engineering (Sidney Sussex College)

EARL, C. F., Engineering

FITZGERALD, W. J., Applied Statistics and Signal Processing

FLECK, N. A., Mechanics of Materials (Pembroke College)

GHAHRAMANI, Z., Information Engineering

GLOVER, K., Information Engineering (Sidney Sussex College)

GODSILL, S. J., Statistical Signal Processing (Corpus Christi College)

GREGORY, M. J., Manufacturing Engineering (Churchill College)

GUTHRIE, P. M., Engineering (St Edmund's College)

HOCHGREB, S., Engineering

HODSON, H. P., Aerothermal Engineering (Girton College)

HOPPER, A., Communications (Corpus Christi College)

HUTCHINGS, I. M., Manufacturing Engineering (St John's College)

IWAI, Y., Engineering

KELLY, M. J., Technology (Trinity Hall)

KINGSBURY, N. G., Signal Processing

KITTELSON, D., Engineering

LANGLEY, R. S., Mechanical Engineering (Fitzwilliam College)

LIDDELL, W. I., Engineering

MCFARLANE, D., Service and Support Engineering

MACIEJOWSKI, J. M., Control Engineering

MAIR, R. J., Geotechnical Engineering (Jesus College)

MASTORAKOS, E., Energy Technologies (Fitzwilliam College)

MIGLIORATO, P., Electrical Engineering (Trinity College)

MILNE, W. I., Electrical Engineering (Churchill College)

NEELY, A., Institute for Manufacturing

NEWLAND, D. E., Engineering (Selwyn College)

PALMER, A. E., Engineering

PEAKE, N., Applied Mathematics

PELLEGRINO, S., Engineering (Corpus Christi College)

PENTY, R. V., Photonics

PRAGER, R. V., Medical Imaging (Queens' College)

ROBERTSON, J., Electrical Engineering (Churchill College)

SMITH, M. C., Control Engineering (Gonville and Caius College)

SOGA, K., Civil, Structural and Environmental Engineering

STRONGE, W. J., Applied Mechanics (Jesus College)

TUCKER, P. G., Engineering

UDREA, F., Electrical Engineering (Girton College)

WALLACE, K. M., Engineering (Selwyn College)

WELLAND, M. E., Nanotechnology (St John's College)

WHITE, I. H., Electrical Engineering (Jesus College)

WILLIAMS, J. A., Engineering Tribology

WOLPERT, D., Engineering (Trinity College)

WOODHOUSE, J., Engineering (Clare College)

WOODLAND, P., Information Engineering (Peterhouse)

XU, L., Turbomachinery (Downing College)

YOUNG, J. B., Applied Thermodynamics (King's College)

YOUNG, S. J., Information Engineering (Emmanuel College)

Department of History and Philosophy of Science (Free School Lane, Cambridge, CB2 3RH; tel. (1223) 334500; fax (1223) 334554; e-mail hps-admin@lists.cam.ac.uk; internet www.hps.cam.ac.uk):

FORRESTER, J. P., History and Philosophy of Psychoanalysis and Human Sciences (King's College)

JARDINE, N., History and Philosophy of the Sciences (Darwin College)

SCHAFFER, S., History of Physical Science

SECORD, J., Social History of Science

Department of Land Economy (19 Silver St, Cambridge, CB3 9EP; tel. (1223) 337147; fax (1223) 337130; e-mail landecon-ugadmissions@lists.cam.ac.uk; internet www.landecon.cam.ac.uk):

ALLMENDINGER, P., Land Economy

Department of Veterinary Medicine (Madingley Rd, Cambridge, CB3 0ES; tel. (1223) 337694; fax (1223) 337610; e-mail enquiries@vet.cam.ac.uk; internet www.vet.cam.ac.uk):

ALLEN, W. R., Equine Reproduction (Robinson College)

BLAKEMORE, W. F., Neuropathology (Wolfson College)

BROOM, D. M., Animal Welfare (St Catharine's College)

FRANKLIN, R., Neuroscience

HEENEY, J. L., Comparative Pathology

HERRTAGE, M. E., Animal Welfare

JEFFERY, N., Veterinary Clinical Studies

KAUFMAN, J., Pathology

McCONNELL, I., Veterinary Science (Clare Hall)

MASKELL, D. J., Farm Animal Health, Food Science and Food Safety (Wolfson College)

WOOD, J., Equine and Farm Animal Science

Judge Business School (Trumpington St, Cambridge, CB2 1AG; tel. (1223) 339700; fax (1223) 339701; e-mail enquiries@jbs.cam.ac.uk; internet www.jbs.cam.ac.uk; Judge Institute of Management Studies renamed to present 2005):

Dame DAWSON, SANDRA, Management (Sidney Sussex College)

Lord EATWELL, Financial Policy (Queens' College)

HUGHES, A., Enterprise Studies (Sidney Sussex College)

KILDUFF, M. J., Management Studies

MEEKS, G., Financial Accounting

NOLAN, P. H., Chinese Management (Jesus College)

PRABHU, J., Indian Business and Enterprise

RALPH, D., Operations Research

SCHOLTES, S., Health Management

WALSHAM, G., Management Studies

Computer Laboratory (William Gates Bldg, 15 J. J. Thomson Ave, Cambridge, CB3 0FD; tel. (1223) 763500; fax (1223) 334678; e-mail departmental-secretary@cl.cam.ac.uk; internet www.cl.cam.ac.uk):

ANDERSON, R. J., Security Engineering

BACON, J. M., Distributed Systems (Jesus College)

CROWCROFT, J. A., Communications Systems (Trinity College)

DAUGMAN, J. G., Computer Vision and Pattern Recognition

DAWAR, A., Logic and Algorithms (Robinson College)

GORDON, M. J. C., Computer Assisted Reasoning (King's College)

HOPPER, A., Computer Technology (Corpus Christi College)

LESLIE, I. M., Computer Science (Christ's College)

MYCROFT, A., Computing (Robinson College)

PAULSON, L., Computational Logic (Clare College)

PITTS, A. M., Theoretical Computer Science (Darwin College)

ROBINSON, P., Computer Technology (Gonville and Caius College)

WINSKEL, G., Computer Science (Emmanuel College)

WOMEN'S COLLEGES

Lucy Cavendish College: Lady Margaret Rd, Cambridge, CB3 0BU; tel. (1223) 332190; fax (1223) 332178; e-mail lcc-admin@lists.cam.ac.uk; internet www.lucy-cav.cam.ac.uk; f. 1965; library of 27,000 vols; Pres. Prof. JANET TODD.

Murray Edwards College: New Hall, University of Cambridge, Cambridge, CB3 0DF; tel. (1223) 762100; fax (1223) 763110; e-mail enquiries@murrayedwards.cam.ac.uk; internet www.newhall.cam.ac.uk; f. 1954; New Hall was re-named as present name 2008; Pres. Dr JENNIFER BARNES.

Newnham College: Sidgwick Ave, Cambridge, CB3 9DF; tel. (1223) 335700; fax (1223) 357898; internet www.newn.cam.ac.uk; f. 1871; library of 90,000 vols; Prin. Dame PATRICIA HODGSON.

MIXED COLLEGES

Christ's College: St Andrew's St, Cambridge, CB2 3BU; tel. (1223) 334900; fax (1223) 334973; e-mail library@christs.cam.ac.uk; internet www.christs.cam.ac.uk; f. 1505

for men; library of 80,000 vols; women admitted 1978; Master Prof. FRANK KELLY.

Churchill College: Storey's Way, Cambridge, CB3 0DS; tel. (1223) 336000; fax (1223) 336180; internet www.chu.cam.ac.uk; f. 1960 for men; women admitted 1972; Master Sir DAVID WALLACE.

Clare College: Trinity Lane, Cambridge, CB2 1TL; tel. (1223) 333200; fax (1223) 333219; internet www.clare.cam.ac.uk; f. 1326 for men; women admitted 1972; Master Prof. A. J. BADGER.

Corpus Christi College: Trumpington St, Cambridge, CB2 1RH; tel. (1223) 338000; fax (1223) 338061; internet www.corpus.cam.ac.uk; f. 1352 for men; women admitted 1983; Master STUART LAING.

Downing College: Regent St, Cambridge, CB2 1DQ; tel. (1223) 334800; fax (1223) 363852; e-mail college-office@dow.cam.ac.uk; internet www.dow.cam.ac.uk; f. 1800 for men; women admitted 1978; Master Prof. BARRY EVERITT.

Emmanuel College: St Andrew's St, Cambridge, CB2 3AP; tel. (1223) 334200; fax (1223) 334426; internet www.emma.cam.ac.uk; f. 1584 for men; women admitted 1978; Master Lord WILSON OF DINTON.

Fitzwilliam College: Storey's Way, Cambridge, CB3 0DG; tel. (1223) 332000; fax (1223) 464162; internet www.fitz.cam.ac.uk; f. 1966 for men; women admitted 1978; Master Prof. ROBERT LETHBRIDGE.

Girton College: Huntington Rd, Cambridge, CB3 0JG; tel. (1223) 338999; fax (1223) 338896; internet www.girton.cam.ac.uk; f. 1869 for women, men admitted 1977; Mistress Prof. SUSAN J. SMITH.

Gonville and Caius College: Trinity St, Cambridge, CB2 1TA; tel. (1223) 332400; fax (1223) 332456; internet www.cai.cam.ac.uk; f. 1348 for men; women admitted 1978; Master Prof. Sir ALAN FERSHT.

Homerton College: Hills Rd, Cambridge, CB2 8PH; tel. (1223) 747111; fax (1223) 747120; e-mail porters@homerton.cam.ac.uk; internet www.homerton.cam.ac.uk; f. 1824 as a Training College (Approved Society 1976); men re-admitted 1978; Prin. Dr KATE PRETTY.

Hughes Hall: Mortimer Rd, Cambridge, CB1 2EW; tel. (1223) 334898; fax (1223) 311179; internet www.hughes.cam.ac.uk; f. 1885 as the Cambridge Training College for Women (Approved Foundation 1968); Pres. SARAH SQUIRE.

Jesus College: Jesus Lane, Cambridge, CB5 8BL; tel. (1223) 339339; fax (1223) 339313; internet www.jesus.cam.ac.uk; f. 1497 for men; women admitted 1978; Master Prof. ROBERT MAIR.

King's College: King's Parade, Cambridge, CB2 1ST; tel. (1223) 331100; fax (1223) 331315; e-mail info@kings.cam.ac.uk; internet www.kings.cam.ac.uk; f. 1441 for men; women admitted 1972; library of 130,000 vols; Provost Prof. ROSS HARRISON.

Magdalene College: Magdalene St, Cambridge, CB3 0AG; tel. (1223) 332100; fax (1223) 363637; internet www.magd.cam.ac.uk; f. 1428 for men; women admitted 1987; Master DUNCAN ROBINSON.

Pembroke College: Trumpington St, Cambridge, CB2 1RF; tel. (1223) 338100; fax (1223) 338163; e-mail enquiries@pem.cam.ac.uk; internet www.pem.cam.ac.uk; f. 1347 for men; women admitted 1983; Master Sir ROGER TOMKYS.

Peterhouse: Trumpington St, Cambridge, CB2 1RD; tel. (1223) 338200; fax (1223) 337578; e-mail info@pet.cam.ac.uk; internet

www.pet.cam.ac.uk; f. 1284 for men; women admitted 1984; Master Prof. ADRIAN DIXON.

Queens' College: Silver St, Cambridge, CB3 9ET; tel. (1223) 335511; fax (1223) 335522; e-mail enquiries@quns.cam.ac.uk; internet www.quns.cam.ac.uk; f. 1448 for men; women admitted 1979; Pres. Prof. Lord EATWELL.

Robinson College: Grange Rd, Cambridge, CB3 9AN; tel. (1223) 339100; fax (1223) 351794; internet www.robinson.cam.ac.uk; f. 1979; Warden Prof. DAVID YATES; Dir of Studies MIA GRAY.

St Catharine's College: Trumpington St, Cambridge, CB2 1RL; tel. (1223) 338300; fax (1223) 338340; internet www.caths.cam.ac.uk; f. 1473 for men; women admitted 1978; Master Prof. Dame JEAN THOMAS.

St Edmund's College: Mount Pleasant, Cambridge, CB3 0BN; tel. (1223) 336250; fax (1223) 762822; e-mail reception@st-edmunds.cam.ac.uk; internet www.st-edmunds.cam.ac.uk; f. 1896 for men; (Approved Foundation 1975); women admitted 1978; Master Prof. J. PAUL LUZIO; Dean Rev. Dr JOHN PATRICK KENRICK.

St John's College: St John's St, Cambridge, CB2 1TP; tel. (1223) 338600; fax (1223) 337720; e-mail enquiries@joh.cam.ac.uk; internet www.joh.cam.ac.uk; f. 1511 for men; women admitted 1981; Master Prof. C. M. DOBSON.

Selwyn College: Grange Rd, Cambridge, CB3 9DQ; tel. (1223) 335846; fax (1223) 335837; internet www.sel.cam.ac.uk; f. 1882 for men; women admitted 1976; Master Prof. RICHARD BOWRING.

Sidney Sussex College: Sidney St, Cambridge, CB2 3HU; tel. (1223) 338800; fax (1223) 338884; e-mail enquiries@sid.cam.ac.uk; internet www.sid.cam.ac.uk; f. 1596 for men; women admitted 1976; Master Dr ANDREW WALLACE-HADRILL.

Trinity College: Trinity St, Cambridge, CB2 1TQ; tel. (1223) 338400; fax (1223) 338564; e-mail college.office@trin.cam.ac.uk; internet www.trin.cam.ac.uk; f. 1546 for men; women admitted 1977; library of 300,000 vols; Master Lord REES OF LUDLOW.

Trinity Hall: Trinity Lane, Cambridge, CB2 1TJ; tel. (1223) 332500; fax (1223) 332537; e-mail info@trinhall.cam.ac.uk; internet www.trinhall.cam.ac.uk; f. 1350 for men; women admitted 1977; Master Prof. MARTIN DAUNTON.

MIXED COLLEGES FOR GRADUATE STUDENTS

Clare Hall: Herschel Rd, Cambridge, CB3 9AL; tel. (1223) 332360; fax (1223) 332333; e-mail college.secretary@clarehall.cam.ac.uk; internet www.clarehall.cam.ac.uk; f. 1966 (Approved Foundation); Pres. Sir MARTIN HARRIS.

Darwin College: Silver St, Cambridge, CB3 9EU; tel. (1223) 335660; fax (1223) 335667; e-mail deanery@darwin.cam.ac.uk; internet www.dar.cam.ac.uk; f. 1964; Master Prof. WILLIAM A. BROWN; Dean Dr LEO HOWE.

Wolfson College: Barton Rd, Cambridge, CB3 9BB; tel. (1223) 335900; fax (1223) 335908; e-mail registrar@wolfson.cam.ac.uk; internet www.wolfson.cam.ac.uk; f. 1965; academic year October to September; Pres. Prof. RICHARD EVANS.

UNIVERSITY OF CENTRAL LANCASHIRE

Preston, PR1 2HE

Telephone: (1772) 201201

Fax: (1772) 892911

E-mail: cenquiries@uclan.ac.uk

Internet: www.uclan.ac.uk

Founded 1828, as Instn for the Diffusion of Knowledge, present name and status 1992
Academic year: September to July
Chancellor: Sir RICHARD EVANS
Vice-Chancellor: Dr MALCOLM MCVICAR
Deputy Vice-Chancellor for Academic Affairs: GRAHAM BALDWIN
Deputy Vice-Chancellor for Strategic Planning and Performance Management: DAVE PHOENIX
Pro-Vice-Chancellor for Student Experience: ROD DUBROW-MARSHALL
Pro-Vice-Chancellor for Research: (vacant)
Pro-Vice-Chancellor for International Affairs: ANGELA MURPHY
Librarian: KEVIN ELLARD
Number of teachers: 1,006
Number of students: 35,000

DEANS

Faculty of Arts, Humanities and Social Sciences: JOHN JOUGHIN
Faculty of Health: EILEEN MARTIN
Faculty of Management: DHARMA KOVVURI
Faculty of Science and Technology: DAVID PHOENIX
Lancashire Business School: DAVID HAMBLIN

UNIVERSITY OF CHESTER

Parkgate Rd, Chester, CH1 4BJ
Telephone: (1244) 511000
Fax: (1244) 511300
E-mail: enquiries@chester.ac.uk
Internet: www.chester.ac.uk
Founded 1839, present status 2005
Vice-Chancellor and Prin.: Prof. TIMOTHY WHEELER
Sr Pro-Vice-Chancellor for Resources and Quality: Dr MALCOLM RHODES
Pro-Vice-Chancellor: Prof. PETER HARROP
Pro-Vice-Chancellor for Student Experience and Corporate Performance: Dr CHRIS HASLAM
Pro-Vice-Chancellor for Acad. Sec.: ADRIAN LEE
Pro-Vice-Chancellor for Acad.: Prof. MIKE THOMAS
Univ. Sec.: DAVID STEVENS
Number of teachers: 413
Number of students: 14,000

DEANS

Applied Sciences: Prof. SARAH ANDREW
Arts and Media: BRENDAN O'SULLIVAN
Business, Enterprise and Lifelong Learning: Prof. PHIL HARRIS
Education and Children's Services: ANNA SUTTON
Health and Social Care: Prof. MICHAEL THOMAS
Humanities: Prof. ROB WARNER
Social Sciences: DAVID BALSAMO

UNIVERSITY OF CHICHESTER

Bishop Otter Campus, College Lane, Chichester, PO19 6PE
Telephone: (1243) 816000
Fax: (1243) 816080
E-mail: admissions@chi.ac.uk
Internet: www.chi.ac.uk
Founded 1839; became Univ. College Chichester 1999, present name and status 2005
Language of instruction: English
Academic year: September to July
Vice-Chancellor: Prof. CLIVE BEHAGG
Deputy Vice-Chancellor: IAN CHILD
Deputy Vice-Chancellor for Academic Affairs: Dr SARAH GILROY
Library of 220,000 vols and 1,651 periodical titles
Number of teachers: 188

Number of students: 5,343
Publications: *Humanitus, Other Memorial Papers*

DEANS

Arts, Business and Humanities: MARK MASON (Deputy Dean)
Education, Social Sciences and Sport: GILL BUTLER (Deputy Dean)

UNIVERSITY OF DERBY

Kedleston Rd, Derby, DE22 1GB
Telephone: (1332) 590500
Fax: (1332) 294861
E-mail: askadmissions@derby.ac.uk
Internet: www.derby.ac.uk
Founded 1851, present name and status 1993, merged with High Peak College 1998
Academic year: September to June
Chancellor: Duke Of Devonshire PEREGRINE CAVENDISH
Vice-Chancellor and Chief Exec.: Prof. JOHN COYNE
Pro-Vice-Chancellor: Prof. LIZ BARNES
Pro-Vice-Chancellor: Prof. PHILIP PLOWDEN
Librarian: PAT JOHNSON
Library of 370,000 vols
Number of teachers: 694
Number of students: 22,300

DEANS

Faculty of Arts, Design and Technology: Prof. HUW DAVIES
Faculty of Business, Computing and Law: Prof. KEITH HORTON
Faculty of Education, Health and Sciences: Prof. GUY DALY
University of Derby College, Buxton: Prof. PETER DEWHURST

UNIVERSITY OF DURHAM

University Office, Old Elvet, Durham, DH1 3HP
Telephone: (191) 334-2000
Fax: (191) 334-6250
E-mail: pro.directory@durham.ac.uk
Internet: www.dur.ac.uk
Founded 1832
Academic year: October to June (3 terms)
Chancellor: Sir THOMAS ALLAN
Vice-Chancellor and Warden: Prof. CHRISTOPHER HIGGINS
Deputy Warden: Prof. JOHN ASHWORTH
Pro-Vice-Chancellor for Education: Prof. ANTHONY FORSTER
Pro-Vice-Chancellor for Research: Prof. TOM MCLEISH
Pro-Vice-Chancellor for the Faculty of Arts and Humanities: Prof. SETH KUNIN
Pro-Vice-Chancellor for the Faculty of Science: Prof. ANDREW DEEKS
Pro-Vice-Chancellor for the Faculty of Social Sciences and Health: Prof. ROBIN CONINGHAM
Pro-Vice-Chancellor: Prof. RAY HUDSON
Registrar and Sec.: CAROLYN FOWLER
Treas.: PAULINA LUBACZ
Librarian: JON PURCELL
Library: see Libraries and Archives
Number of teachers: 1,449
Number of students: 15,768

PROFESSORS

Faculty of Arts and Humanities:
ARCHER, R. L. A., Spanish
BAGULEY, D., French
BARCLAY, J. M. G., Divinity
BARNES, G. L., Japanese
BROOKS, C. W., History
BROWN, D. W., Divinity
CLARK, T. J. A., English Studies

COOPER, D. E., Philosophy
COWLING, D. J., French
DAVIES, D. J., Study of Religion
DIBBLE, J. C., Music
HALL, E. M., Greek Cultural History
HARRIS, E., Classics and Ancient History
HARRIS, H. J., History
HAYWARD, C. T. R., Hebrew
LOUTH, A., Patristic and Byzantine Studies
LOWE, E. J., Philosophy
MANNING, P. D., Music
MICHIE, R. C., History
O'MEARA, P., Russian
O'NEILL, M. S. C., English Studies
PADDISON, M. H., Music
PRESTWICH, M. C., History
REGAN, S., English Studies
RHODES, P. J., Ancient History
ROLLASON, D. W., History
ROWE, C. J., Greek
SANDERS, A. L., English Studies
SAUL, N. D. B., German
STUCKENBRUCK, L. T., Biblical Studies
TAYLOR, J. H. M., French
WAUGH, P., English Studies
WILLIAMSON, P. A., History

Faculty of Science:
ABRAM, R. A., Physics
ABRASHKIN, V. A., Mathematics
ADAMS, C. S., Physics
APPLETON, E., Engineering
BADYAL, J. P., Chemistry
BENNETT, K. H., Engineering
BOWER, R. G., Physics
BROERSMA, H. J., Computer Science
BRYCE, M. R., Chemistry
CAMPBELL, A. C., Psychology
CHAMBERLAIN, J. M., Applied Physics
CROUCH, R., Engineering
DAVIDSON, J. P., Earth Sciences
DOREY, P. E., Mathematics
EDWARDS, R., Biological and Biomedical Sciences
FARBER, M. S., Pure Mathematics
FINDLAY, J. M., Psychology
FLOWER, D. R., Physics
FOULGER, G. R., Earth Sciences
FRENK, C. S., Fundamental Physics
GATHERCOLE, S. E., Psychology
GLOVER, E. W. N., Physics
GOLDSTEIN, M., Statistics
GOULTY, N. R., Earth Sciences
HATTON, P. D., Physics
HE, L., Engineering
HEYWOOD, C. A., Psychology
HOLDSWORTH, R. E., Earth Sciences
HOWARD, J. A. K., Chemistry
HUNTLEY, B., Biological and Biomedical Sciences
HUSSEY, P. J., Plant Molecular Cell Biology
HUTCHISON, C. J, Animal Cell Biology
HUTSON, J. M., Chemistry
LINDSAY, S. W., Biological and Biomedical Sciences
LINDSEY, K., Plant Molecular Biology
MANSFIELD, P., Mathematics
MARDER, T. B., Chemistry
MAROPOULOS, P., Engineering
MENSHIKOV, M. V., Statistics
MILNER, A. D., Cognitive Neuroscience
MONKMAN, A. P., Physics
MUNRO, M., Computer Science
NIU, Y., Earth Sciences
PARKER, D., Chemistry
PENNINGTON, M. R., Mathematical Sciences and Physics
PETTY, M. C., Engineering
PURVIS, A., Engineering
QUINLAN, R. A., Biomedical Sciences
SALOUS, S., Engineering
SEARLE, R. C., Geophysics
SHANKS, T., Physics
SHARPLES, R. M., Physics
SLABAS, A. R., Plant Sciences
STEWART, I. A., Computer Science

STIRLING, W. J., Mathematical Sciences and Physics
STRAUGHAN, B., Numerical Analysis
TANNER, B. K., Physics
TAVNER, P., Engineering
THOMPSON, R. N., Geology
TUCKER, M. E., Geological Sciences
UNSWORTH, A., Engineering
WALMSLEY, A. R., Infectious Diseases
WARD, M. J., Physics
WARD, R. S., Mathematics
ZAKRZEWSKI, W. J., Mathematics

Faculty of Social Sciences and Health:

ABHYANKAR, A., Finance
ALLEN, T., Law
ALLISON, R. J., Geography
AMIN, A., Geography
ANTONIOU, A., Business School
BAILEY, D., Applied Social Sciences
BAILIFF, I. K., Archaeology
BARR, D. G., Business School
BASU, P., Economics
BILSBOROUGH, A., Anthropology
BLACKMAN, T. J., Applied Social Sciences
BOHLANDER, M., Law
BOYNE, R. D., Sociology and Social Policy
BURT, T. P., Geography
BYRAM, M. S., Education
BYRNE, D. S., Applied Social Sciences
CAMPBELL, D., Cultural and Political Geography
CAMPBELL, I. D., Law
CARRITHERS, M. B., Anthropology
CLARK, T., Organizational Behaviour
COCKERILL, T. A. J., Business Management and Economics
COOPER, B., Education
DARNELL, A. C., Business School
DEGELING, P., Clinical Management Development
DIXON, R., Managerial Accounting
EHTESHAMI, A., Middle Eastern and Islamic Studies
ELLIOTT, J., Education
EVANS, H. M., Humanities in Medicine
FENWICK, H. M., Law
FERGUSON, R. I., Physical Geography
GLOVER, G. R., Public Mental Health
GOTT, R., Education
GRAHAM, S., Geography
GREAVES, R.-M., European Law
HAMILTON, J. D., Academic Director of Phase 1 Medicine
HOBBS, R. F., Law
HOLMES, P. R., Business School
HUDSON, R., Geography
HUNGIN, A. P. S., Health
HUNTER, D. J., Health Policy and Management
JOHNSON, P. S., Business School
KOUKRAKOS, P., Law
LAFFIN, M., Public Policy and Management
LANE, S., Geography
LAYTON, R. H., Anthropology
LEIGH, I. D., Law
LINSTEAD, S., Organizational Analysis
LONG, A. J., Geography
MASON, J., Health
McGLYNN, C. M. S., Law
McKENDRICK, D. G., Strategy
MEYER, J. H. F., Education
MOORE, G., Business School
NEWTON, L. D., Education
PAINTER, J. M., Geography
PALMER-COOPER, J. A., Education
PARKER, S. C., Entrepreneurship
PAUDYAL, K., Business School
POLOS, L., Business School
PRICE, A. J., Archaeology
READ, D., Business School
REDMAN, T., Business School
RIDGWAY, J. E., Education
RIGG, J. D., Geography
ROBERTS, C. A., Archaeology
SCOTT, S. J., Applied Social Sciences

SHENNAN, I., Geography
SHONE, R., Business School
SILLITOE, P., Anthropology
SMITH, R. D., Education
SMITH, S. J., Human Geography
SULLIVAN, G. R., Law
TOWNSEND, A. R., Regional Regeneration and Development Studies
TYMMS, P. B., Education
van WITTELOOSTUIJN, A., Strategy
WARBRICK, C. J., Law
WATSON, R., Financial Management
WILLIAMS, R. J., Politics
WILSON, R. J. A., Middle Eastern and Islamic Studies
WRIGHT, G., Management

COLLEGES

College of St Hild and St Bede: Durham, DH1 1SZ; tel. (191) 334-8300; fax (191) 334-8301; internet www.dur.ac.uk/hild-bede; f. 1975, by merger of College of the Venerable Bede (for men) and St Hild's College (for women); Prin. Prof. CHRIS HUTCHISON; Vice-Prin. LAURA WILSON.

Collingwood College: South Rd, Durham, DH1 3LT; tel. (191) 334-5000; fax (191) 334-5035; internet www.dur.ac.uk/collingwood; f. 1972; 1,100 students; Prin. Prof. EDWARD CORRIGAN.

Grey College: South Rd, Durham, DH1 3LG; tel. (191) 334-5900; fax (191) 334-5901; e-mail grey.college@durham.ac.uk; internet www.dur.ac.uk/grey.college; f. 1959; Master Prof. J. M. CHAMBERLAIN.

Hatfield College: North Bailey, Durham, DH1 3RQ; tel. (191) 334-2633; fax (191) 334-1541; e-mail hatfield.reception@durham.ac.uk; internet www.dur.ac.uk/hatfield.college; f. 1846; Master Prof. TIM BURT (acting).

John Snow College: Stockton-on-Tees, TS17 6BH; tel. (191) 334-0046; e-mail snow.college@durham.ac.uk; internet www.dur.ac.uk/johnsnow.college; f. 2001; Prin. Prof. CAROLYN SUMMERBELL.

Josephine Butler College: South Rd, Durham, DH1 3DF; tel. (191) 334-7260; fax (191) 334-7259; internet www.dur.ac.uk/butler.college; f. 2001; 800 students; Prin. ADRIAN SIMPSON.

Queen's Campus, Stockton: Thornaby, Stockton-on-Tees, TS17 6BH; tel. (191) 334-0022; fax (191) 334-0010; internet www.dur.ac.uk/queens-campus; f. 1992 as Univ. College Stockton; awards jt qualifications of Univs of Durham and Teesside; Dean Prof. JO PHOENIX.

St Aidan's College: Windmill Hill, Durham, DH1 3LJ; tel. (191) 334-5769; fax (191) 334-5770; internet www.dur.ac.uk/st-aidans.college; f. 1895, known as St Aidan's Society until 1961; Prin. J. S. ASHWORTH.

St Chad's College: 18 North Bailey, Durham, DH1 3RH; tel. (191) 334-3358; fax (191) 334-3371; e-mail chads@dur.ac.uk; internet www.dur.ac.uk/stchads; f. 1904; 500 students; Prin. Rev. Canon Dr J. P. M. CASSIDY.

St Cuthbert's Society: 12 South Bailey, Durham, DH1 3EE; tel. (191) 334-3400; fax (191) 334-3401; e-mail st-cuthberts.society@durham.ac.uk; internet www.dur.ac.uk/st-cuthberts.society; f. 1888, known as non-Collegiate until 1947; Prin. Prof. GRAHAM TOWL.

St John's College with Cranmer Hall: 3 South Bailey, Durham, DH1 3RJ; tel. (191) 334-3894; fax (191) 334-3501; e-mail enquiries@cranmerhall.co; internet www.dur.ac.uk/cranmerhall; f. 1909; Prin. Rev. Dr DAVID WILKINSON.

St Mary's College: Elvet Hill Rd, Durham, DH1 3LR; tel. (191) 334-5719; fax (191) 334-

5720; internet www.dur.ac.uk/st-marys.college; f. 1899; Prin. Prof. SIMON HACKETT.

Stephenson College: Stockton-on-Tees, TS17 6JZ; tel. (191) 334-0560; fax (191) 334-0054; e-mail stephenson@durham.ac.uk; internet www.dur.ac.uk/stephenson; f. 2001; Prin. Prof. A. C. DARNELL.

Trevelyan College: Elvet Hill Rd, Durham, DH1 3LN; tel. (191) 334-7000; fax (191) 334-5371; e-mail admissions.trevelyan@durham.ac.uk; internet www.dur.ac.uk/trevelyan.college; f. 1966; 600 students; Prin. Prof. H MARTYN EVANS.

University College: Durham Castle, Palace Green, Durham, DH1 3RW; tel. (191) 334-4099; fax (191) 334-3801; internet www.dur.ac.uk/university.college; f. 1832; Master Prof. M. E. TUCKER.

Ushaw College: Durham, DH7 9RH; tel. (191) 373-8517; e-mail courses@ushaw.ac.uk; internet www.ushaw.ac.uk; f. 1808; Rector Rev. T. P. DRAINEY.

Ustinov College: Howlands Farm, Durham, DH1 3DE; tel. (191) 334-7241; fax (191) 334-7231; e-mail ustinov.college@durham.ac.uk; internet www.dur.ac.uk/ustinov.college; f. 1965; Prin. Dr PENELOPE WILSON (acting).

Van Mildert College: Mill Hill Lane, Durham, DH1 3LH; tel. (191) 334-7100; e-mail vm.reception@durham.ac.uk; f. 1963; academic year October to June; 1,000 students; Prin. Prof. DAVID HARPER.

UNIVERSITY OF EAST ANGLIA

Norwich, NR4 7TJ

Telephone: (1603) 456161
Fax: (1603) 458553
Internet: www.uea.ac.uk

Founded 1963

Academic year: September to June

Chancellor: Sir BRANDON GOUGH
Vice-Chancellor: Prof. EDWARD ACTON
Pro-Vice-Chancellor for Academics: Prof. TOM WARD
Pro-Vice-Chancellor for Research, Enterprise and Engagement: Prof. TREVOR DAVIES
Registrar and Sec.y: BRIAN SUMMERS
Librarian: JEAN C. STEWARD
Library of 800,000 items (700,000 books, CDs and DVDs, 100,000 print periodicals)
Number of teachers: 1,000
Number of students: 14,313
Publications: *Pretext* (2 a year), *Reactions* (1 a year), *Scandinavica* (2 a year)

DEANS

Faculty of Arts and Humanities: Prof. DAVID PETERS CORBETT
Faculty of Health: Prof. IAN HARVEY
Faculty of Science: Prof. DAVID RICHARDSON
Faculty of Social Sciences: Prof. NEIL WARD

PROFESSORS

School of American Studies (tel. (1603) 592220; fax (1603) 507728; e-mail wwweas@uea.ac.uk; internet www.uea.ac.uk/eas):

BIGSBY, C. W. E.
CROCKATT, R.
HOMBERGER, E.

School of Biological Sciences (tel. (1603) 593503; fax (1603) 592250; e-mail diana.cook@uea.ac.uk; internet www.uea.ac.uk/bio):

DAWSON, A., Biology
DUNCAN, G., Biology
EDWARDS, D. R., Cancer Studies
HEWITT, G. M., Biology
JOHNSTON, A. W. B., Biology
REYNOLDS, J., Biology
RICHARDSON, D. J.
SUTHERLAND, W. J., Biology

WATKINSON, A. R., Ecology

School of Chemical Sciences and Pharmacy (tel. (1603) 593145; fax (1603) 592003; e-mail k.e.bezants@uea.ac.uk; internet www.uea.ac.uk/cap):

ANDREWS, D. L., Chemistry
BELTON, P., Chemistry
BOCHMANN, M., Chemistry
COOK, M. J., Chemistry
CRAIG, D., Pharmacy
FIELD, R., Chemistry
MOORE, G. R., Chemistry
ROBINSON, B. H., Chemistry
RUSSELL, D., Chemistry
THOMSON, A. J., Chemistry

School of Computing Sciences (tel. (1603) 592847; fax (1603) 593345; e-mail www-admin@uea.ac.uk; internet www.cmp.vea.uea.ac.uk):

BANGHAM, J. A., Electronic Systems Engineering
GLAUERT, J., Computing Science
FINLAYSON, G., Information Systems
FORREST, A. R., Computing Science
RAYWARD-SMITH, V. J., Computing Science
SLEEP, M. R., Computing Science

School of Developmental Studies (tel. (1603) 592807; fax (1603) 451999; e-mail dev.general@uea.ac.uk; internet www.uea.ac.uk/dev):

ELLIS, F. T., Development Studies
JENKINS, R., Development Studies
SEDDON, D., Development Studies
STOCKING, M. A., Development Studies

School of Economics (tel. (1603) 592070; fax (1603) 250434; e-mail m.watling@uea.ac.uk; internet www.uea.ac.uk/eco):

CUBITT, R., Economics
DAVIES, S. W., Economics
HARGREAVES HEAP, S. P., Economics
LAWSON, S., International Relations
LOOMES, G., Economics
LYONS, B. R., Economics
SUGDEN, R., Economics

School of Education and Lifelong Learning (tel. (1603) 591451; fax (1603) 593446; e-mail edv.reception@uea.ac.uk; internet www.uea.ac.uk/edu):

BRIDGES, D., Education
ELLIOTT, J., Education
NORRIS, N. F. J., Education
SCHOSTAK, J. F., Education
TICKLE, L., Education
WALKER, R., Education

School of Environmental Sciences (tel. (1603) 592542; fax (1603) 592327; e-mail env@uea.ac.uk; internet www.uea.ac.uk/env):

BATEMEN, I., Environmental Sciences
BENTHAM, C. G., Environmental Sciences
BRIMBLECOMBE, P., Environmental Sciences
HEY, R. D., Environmental Sciences
HULME, M., Environmental Sciences
JICKELLS, T. D., Environmental Sciences
LEEDER, M. R., Environmental Sciences
LISS, P. S., Environmental Sciences
O'RIORDAN, T., Environmental Sciences
PENKETT, S. A., Environmental Sciences
PIDGEON, N. F., Environmental Sciences
PLANE, J. M. C., Environmental Sciences
SCHELLNHUBER, J., Environmental Sciences
TURNER, R. K., Environmental Studies
VINCENT, C. E., Environmental Sciences
WATKINSON, A. R., Ecology
WIGLEY, T. M. C., Environmental Sciences

School of Film and Television Studies (tel. (1603) 593820; fax (1603) 507728; internet www.uea.ac.uk/eas):

BARR, C. J. A., Film Studies
HIGSON, A., Film Studies
JANCOVICH, M., Film Studies

TASKER, Y., Contemporary Popular Culture

School of History (tel. (1603) 593521; fax (1603) 593519; e-mail h.ashdown@uea.ac.uk; internet www.uea.ac.uk/his):

CHARMLEY, J. D., Modern British History
DAVIS, J. C., English History
HARPER-BILL, C., English History
HOWE, A. C., Modern History
RAWCLIFFE, C., English History
SANDERSON, M., Modern Social History
VINCENT, N., English and European History

School of Language, Linguistics and Translation Studies (tel. (1603) 592750; fax (1603) 250599; e-mail pg.llt@uea.ac.uk; internet www.uea.ac.uk/llt):

CHILTON, P., Linguistics

School of Law (tel. (1603) 593042; fax (1603) 250245; e-mail pglaw@uea.ac.uk; internet www.uea.ac.uk/law):

HVIID, M., Competition and Contract Law
MULLIS, A., International Commercial Law
PATTENDEN, R. D., Law
PRIME, T., Law
SMITH, I. T., Employment Law
WINSHIP, P., Law

School of Literature and Creative Writing (tel. (1603) 593820; fax (1603) 507728; e-mail k.durnford@uea.ac.uk; internet www.uea.ac.uk/eas):

DUNCKER, P., Creative Writing
HOLMES, R., Literature
ROBERTS, M., Creative Writing
ROBINSON, M., Scandinavian Studies
SAGE, V., Literature
SALES, R., English Literature
SCOTT, C., European Literature (French)
YARROW, R., Drama

School of Management (tel. (1603) 593029; fax (1603) 593343; e-mail pg.mgt@uea.ac.uk; internet www.mgt.uea.ac.uk):

DREW, S., Management
FLETCHER, K. P., Management
TZOKAS, N., Customer Relationship Management
WADDAMS, C., Management

School of Mathematics (tel. (1603) 592597; fax (1603) 593868; e-mail ann.barnes@uea.ac.uk; internet www.mth.uea.ac.uk):

EVEREST, G. R., Mathematics
JOHNSON, J. A., Mathematics
VANDER-BROECK, J. M., Applied Mathematics
WARD, T., Pure Mathematics
ZALESSKII, A., Pure Mathematics

School of Medicine (tel. (1603) 593061; fax (1603) 593752; e-mail m.newport@uea.ac.uk; internet www.med.uea.ac.uk):

BACHMANN, M., Healthcare Interfaces
BARRETT, A., Clinical Oncology
HARVEY, I., Epidemiology and Public Health
HOWE, A. C., Clinical Professor
HUNTER, P. R., Clinical Professor
MACGREGOR, A., Public Health
MUGFORD, M., Health Economics
REYNOLDS, S., Medicine

School of Music (tel. (1603) 592452; fax (1603) 250454; e-mail n.swan@uea.ac.uk; internet www.uea.ac.uk/mus):

CHADD, D., Music

School of Nursing and Midwifery (tel. (1603) 421422; fax (1603) 421505; e-mail nam.admissions@uea.ac.uk; internet www.uea.ac.uk/nam):

SALTER, B., Health Services Research

School of Philosophy (tel. (1603) 593717; fax (1603) 250434; e-mail m.watling@uea.ac.uk; internet www.uea.ac.uk/phi):

O'HAGAN, T., Philosophy

School of Political, Social and International Studies (tel. (1603) 593717; fax (1603) 250434; e-mail m.watling@uea.ac.uk; internet www.uea.ac.uk/psi):

GOODWIN, B., Politics
LAWSON, S., International Relations
STREET, J. R., Politics

School of Social Work and Psychosocial Sciences (tel. (1603) 592068; fax (1603) 593552; e-mail pgswk@uea.ac.uk; internet www.uea.ac.uk/swk):

HOWE, D. K., Social Work
THOBURN, J., Social Work

School of World Art Studies and Museology (tel. (1603) 592817; fax (1603) 593642; e-mail pgwam1@uea.ac.uk; internet www.uea.ac.uk/art):

HODGES, R. A., Visual Arts
JORDANOVA, L., Visual Arts
ONIANS, J. B., Visual Arts

UNIVERSITY OF EAST LONDON

University Way, Docklands, London, E16 2RD

Telephone: (20) 8223-3000
Fax: (20) 8223-4072
E-mail: study@uel.ac.uk
Internet: www.uel.ac.uk

Founded 1970, as North East London Polytechnic, later became Polytechnic of East London, present name and status 1992

Academic year: September to July

Chancellor: Lord RIX
Vice-Chancellor: Prof. PATRICK MCGHEE
Deputy Vice-Chancellor: Prof. JOHN JOUGHIN
Pro-Vice-Chancellor: NIRMAL BORKHATARIA
Pro-Vice-Chancellor for Learning, Teaching and Student Experience: GRAHAM CURTIS
Pro-Vice-Chancellor for Int.: JOHN SHAW
Pro-Vice-Chancellor for Strategic Planning and External Devt: SELENA BOLINGBROKE
Univ. Sec. and Registrar: JILL GRINSTEAD
Librarian: ANDREW MCDONALD

Library of 248,000 vols, 1,400 current periodicals
Number of teachers: 530 (485 full-time, 45 part-time)
Number of students: 23,000

DEANS

Cass School of Education: ANN SLATER
Royal Docks Business School: Prof. LEN SHACKLETON
School of Architecture and the Visual Arts: PETE COBB (acting)
School of Computing, Information Technology and Engineering: Prof. MOHAMMAD DASTBAZ
School of Health and Bioscience: Prof. NEVILLE PUNCHARD
School of Humanities and Social Sciences: STEVEN P. TREVILLION
School of Law: FIONA FAIRWEATHER
School of Psychology: Prof. MARK DAVIES

UNIVERSITY OF ESSEX

Wivenhoe Park, Colchester, CO4 3SQ

Telephone: (1206) 873333
Fax: (1206) 873598

East 15 (Loughton) Campus, Hatfields, Rectory Lane, Loughton, IG10 3RY

Telephone: (20) 8508-5983
Fax: (20) 8508-7521

Southend Campus, Elmer Approach, Southend-on-Sea, SS1 1LW

Telephone: (1702) 328200
Fax: (1702) 328201
E-mail: admit@essex.ac.uk
Internet: www.essex.ac.uk

Founded 1964

Academic year: October to July

Chancellor: Lord PHILLIPS OF SUDBURY
Vice-Chancellor: Prof. COLIN RIORDAN
Pro-Vice-Chancellor for Research and Enterprise: Prof. DAVID SANDERS
Pro-Vice-Chancellor for Academic and Regional Devt: Prof. NIGEL SOUTH
Pro-Vice Chancellor for Academic Standards: Prof. JANE WRIGHT
Pro-Vice Chancellor for Learning and Teaching: Prof. ANDY DOWNTOWN
Deputy Vice-Chancellor and Pro-Vice-Chancellor for Sustainability and Resources: Prof. JULES PRETTY
Dean, Univ. of Essex Southend: Prof. STUART MANSON
Dean, Academic Partnerships: Dr AULAY MACKENZIE
Registrar and Sec.: Dr TONY RICH
Librarian: ROBERT BUTLER
Library: see under Libraries and Archives
Number of teachers: 610
Number of students: 10,280

DEANS

Faculty of Health: Prof. JOHN CLIBBENS
Faculty of Humanities and Comparative Studies: Dr LEON BURNETT
Faculty of Law and Management: PETER LUTHER
Faculty of Science and Engineering: Dr DAVID PEVALIN
School of Social Sciences: Dr MIKE JONES
Graduate School: Prof. PAM COX

PROFESSORS

ADAMS, M., Computer Science And Electronic Engineering
ADES, D., Art History And Theory
BAKER, N., Biological Sciences
BALKAN, A., Computer Science And Electronic Engineering
BARRY, C., Psychology
BENEKE, R., Biological Sciences
BENTON, E., Sociology
BLACKBURN, R., Sociology
BOOTH, A., Economics
BORSLEY, R., Language And Linguistics
BOYLE, C., Law
BUSFIELD, N., Sociology
CALLAGHAN, V., Computer Science And Electronic Engineering
CHAMBERS, M., Economics
CLAHSEN, H., Language And Linguistics
CLIBBENS, J., Faculty Of Science And Engineering
COAKLEY, J., Ebs-Essex Business School
COLBECK, I., Biological Sciences
COLES, M., Economics
COOPER, C., Biological Sciences
COX, N., Art History And Theory
DEWS, P., Philosophy
DORUSSEN, H., Government
DOWNTON, A., Computer Sci And Electronic Engineering
ELSON, D., Sociology
ERMISCH, J., Iser
FERNANDEZ, N., Biological Sciences
FIGLIO, K., Centre For Psychoanalytic Studies
FOX, E., Psychology
FRANCESCONI, M., Economics
FRASER, V., Art History And Theory
GALEOTTI, A., Economics
GEIDER, R., Biological Sciences
GHANBARI, M., Computer Science And Electronic Engineering
GHIGLINO, C., Economics
GILBERT, G., Law
GILLIES, J., Literature, Film, And Theatre Studies
GLEDITSCH, K., Government
GLUCKSMANN, M., Sociology
GOBERT, J., Law

GRAY, R., Literature, Film, And Theatre Studies
GREEN, G., Health And Human Sciences
HADFIELD, B., Law
HAGRAS, H., Computer Science And Electronic Engineering
HAMILTON, C., Law
HAMPSON, F., Law
HANLEY, J., Psychology
HAN-PILE, B., Philosophy
HARVEY, M., Sociology
HATTON, T., Economics
HAWKINS, R., Language And Linguistics
HAWKSFORD, M., Computer Science And Electronic Engineering
HENNING, I., Computer Science And Electronic Engineering
HENSON, M., Computer Science And Electronic Engineering
HIGGINS, P., Mathematical Sciences
HIGGS, E., History
HINSHELWOOD, R., Centre For Psychoanalytic Studies
HOPFL, H., Ebs-Essex Business School
HU, H., Computer Science And Electronic Engineering
HULME, P., Literature, Film, And Theatre Studies
HUNT, P., Law
IVERSEN, M., Art History And Theory
JENKINS, S., Iser
KING, A., Government
LANDMAN, T., Government
LANDMAN, T., Inst For Democracy and Conflict Resolution
LEADER, S., Law
LUBBOCK, J., Art History And Theory
LUCAS, S., Computer Science And Electronic Engineering
LYNN, P., Iser
MANSON, S., Ebs-Essex Business School
MARKOSE-CHERIAN, S., Economics
MARTIN, W., Philosophy
MCDONALD-MAIER, K., Computer Science And Electronic Engineering
MEDDIS, R., Psychology
MILLARD, F., Government
MIRSHEKAR-SYAHKAL, D., Computer Science And Electronic Engineering
MITRA, J., Ebs-Essex Business School (Southend)
MORAWSKA, E., Sociology
MORRIS, L., Sociology
MUGASHA, A., Law
MULLINEAUX, P., Biological Sciences
NANKERVIS, J., Ebs-Essex Business School
NEDWELL, D., Biological Sciences
NORTON, J., Biological Sciences
ORBELL, S., Psychology
PACKER, F., Human Rights Centre
PAPADOPOULOS, R., Centre For Psychoanalytic Studies
PATRICK, P., Language And Linguistics
PEERS, S., Law
PLUMPER, T., Government
POLI, R., Computer Science And Electronic Engineering
PRETTY, J., Biological Sciences
PUDNEY, S., Iser
RADFORD, A., Language And Linguistics
RAINES, C., Biological Sciences
RANDALL, M., Government
RAVEN, J., History
REYNOLDS, C., Biological Sciences
ROBERSON, D., Psychology
RODLEY, N., Law
ROPER, M., Sociology
RUBIN, L., East 15 Acting School, Loughton Campus
RUSSO, R., Psychology
SACKER, A., Iser
SADLER, L., Language And Linguistics
SAMUELS, A., Centre For Psychoanalytic Studies
SANDERS, D., Government
SANTOS SILVA, J., Economics

SCHURER, K., Uk Data Archive
SHERER, M., Ebs-Essex Business School
SIKKA, P., Ebs-Essex Business School
SIMEONIDOU, D., Computer Science And Electronic Engineering
SMITH, E., Economics
SMITH, S., History
SOUTH, N., Sociology
SPENCER, A., Language And Linguistics
SQUINTANI, F., Economics
STANWAY, G., Biological Sciences
STONE, P., Law
STONES, R., Sociology
SUNKIN, M., Law
SUTHERLAND, H., Iser
TEMPLE, C., Psychology
TSANG, E., Computer Science And Electronic Engineering
TURNER, R., Computer Science And Electronic Engineering
UNDERWOOD, G., Biological Sciences
UPTON, G., Mathematical Sciences
VEGA-REDONDO, F., Economics
VERGO, P., Art History And Theory
WALKER, S., Computer Science And Electronic Engineering
WALTER, J., History
WARD, H., Government
WARD, G., Psychology
WARNER, M., Literature, Film, And Theatre Studies
WHITELEY, P., Government
WILKINS, A., Psychology
WILSON, M., Biological Sciences
WRIGHT, J., Law
ZHANG, Q., Computer Science And Electronic Engineering

UNIVERSITY OF EXETER

Northcote House Exeter, EX4 4QJ

Telephone: (1392) 661000
Fax: (1392) 723060
E-mail: ug-ad@exeter.ac.uk
Internet: www.exeter.ac.uk

Founded 1922, as University College, present status 1955
Academic year: October to July
Chancellor: Baroness FLOELLA BENJAMIN
Vice-Chancellor and Chief Exec.: Prof. STEVE SMITH
Deputy Vice-Chancellor for Education: Prof. JANICE KAY
Deputy Vice-Chancellor for Research and Knowledge Transfer: Prof. NICHOLAS J. TALBOT
Sr Deputy Vice-Chancellor: Prof. NEIL ARMSTRONG
Deputy Vice-Chancellor for External affairs: Prof. MARK OVERTON
Registrar and Deputy Chief Exec.: DAVID ALLEN
Asst Dir for Library Research and Support: Dr JESSICA GARDNER

Library: see under Libraries and Archives
Number of teachers: 3,025
Number of students: 17,210 (15,760 full-time, 1,450 part-time)

Publications: *Bracton Law Journal* (1 a year), *Cornish Studies* (1 a year), *FACT: focus on alternative and complementary therapies* (4 a year), *New Arabian Studies* (1 a year), *Studies in Theatre Production* (2 a year)

DEANS

Business School: Prof. ROBIN MASON
College of Engineering, Mathematics and Physical Sciences: Prof. KEN EVANS
College of Humanities: Prof. NICK KAYE
College of Life and Environmental Sciences: Prof. MARK GOODWIN

College of Social Sciences and International Studies: Prof. ROBERT VAN DE NOORT (acting)
University of Exeter Medical School: Prof. STEVE THORNTON

UNIVERSITY OF GLOUCESTERSHIRE

The Park, Cheltenham, GL50 2RH
Telephone: (1242) 714666
Fax: (1242) 714827
E-mail: admissions@glos.ac.uk
Internet: www.glos.ac.uk
Founded 1990 as Cheltenham and Gloucester College of Further Education through merger of existing colleges, present name and status 2001
State control
Chancellor: Lord CAREY OF CLIFTON
Vice-Chancellor and Chief Exec.: STEPHEN MARSTON
Deputy Vice-Chancellor: RICHARD O'DOCHERTY
Academic Registrar and Clerk to the Council: JULIE THACKRAY
Head of Library Services: LESLEY CARSTONS
Number of teachers: 388
Number of students: 9,412
Publications: *Business School Research Journal* (4 a year), *Contexts* (2 a year), *Journal of Learning and Teaching* (2 a year), *Landscape Issues* (2 a year)

DEANS

Media, Arts and Technology: Dr BEN CALVERT
Natural and Social Sciences: MIKE COGGER

UNIVERSITY OF GREENWICH

Telephone: (20) 8331-8590
Fax: (20) 8331-8145
E-mail: courseinfo@greenwich.ac.uk
Internet: www.greenwich.ac.uk
Founded 1890, later became Thames Polytechnic; present name and status 1992
Academic year: September to July
Chancellor: Lord HART OF CHILTON
Vice-Chancellor: Baroness TESSA BLACKSTONE
Deputy Vice-Chancellor for Academic Development: Prof. SIMON JARVIS
Deputy Vice-Chancellor for Resources: Prof. NEIL GARROD
Deputy Vice-Chancellor for Research and Enterprise: Prof. TOM BARNES
Registrar and Sec.: LINDA CORDING
Librarian: D. HEATHCOTE
Library of 610,000 vols
Number of teachers: 709
Number of students: 24,843
Publications: *Applied Mathematical Modelling* (12 a year), *Computational Fluid Dynamics News* (4 a year)

DEANS

Business School: Prof. BARRY CURNOW
Greenwich Maritime Institute: Prof. CHRIS BELLAMY (Dir)
Medway School of Pharmacy: Prof. IAIN CUMMING
Natural Resources Institute: Prof. ANDREW WESTBY (Dir)
School of Architecture and Construction: Prof. NEIL SPILLER
School of Computing and Mathematical Sciences: Dr LIZ BACON
School of Education: CHRIS PHILPOTT
School of Engineering: Prof. NDY EKERE
School of Health and Social Care: LIZ MEERABEAU
School of Humanities and Social Sciences: Prof. JOANNE FINKELSTEIN

School of Science: Prof. MARTIN SNOWDEN
Urban Renaissance Institute: LOUISE THOMAS (Dir)

UNIVERSITY OF HERTFORDSHIRE

College Lane, Hatfield, AL10 9AB
Telephone: (1707) 284800
Fax: (1707) 284870
E-mail: admissions@herts.ac.uk
Internet: www.herts.ac.uk
Founded 1952, as Hatfield Technical College, became Hatfield Polytechnic in 1969; present name and status 1992
Main campus in Hatfield and Law campus in St Albans
Academic year: October to June
Chancellor: Lord MACLAURIN OF KNEBWORTH
Vice-Chancellor: Prof. QUINTIN MCKELLAR
Deputy Vice-Chancellor: Prof. GRAHAM GALBRAITH
Pro-Vice-Chancellor for Int. Affairs: Prof. BARRY HUNT
Pro-Vice-Chancellor for Enterprise: JULIE NEWLAN
Pro-Vice-Chancellor for Research: Prof. JOHN SENIOR
Pro-Vice-Chancellor for Regional Affairs: Dr STEPHEN BOFFEY
Pro-Vice-Chancellor for Student Experience: Dr ANDREW CLUTTERBUCK
Sec. and Registrar: PHILIP E. WATERS
Librarian: D. MARTIN
Library of 600,000 vols
Number of teachers: 2,700
Number of students: 24,500

DEANS

Business School: JULIE NEWLAN
Faculty of Engineering and Information Sciences: Prof. JOHN SENIOR
Faculty of Health and Human Sciences: Prof. BARRY HUNT
Faculty of Humanities, Law and Education: Dr ANDREW CLUTTERBUCK
Faculty of Interdisciplinary Studies: Dr STEPHEN BOFFEY

UNIVERSITY OF HUDDERSFIELD

Queensgate, Huddersfield, HD1 3DH
Telephone: (1484) 422288
Fax: (1484) 516151
E-mail: admissions@hud.ac.uk
Internet: www.hud.ac.uk
Founded 1841, formerly Huddersfield College of Technology, became Polytechnic of Huddersfield in 1970, present name and status 1992
Academic year: September to June
Chancellor: Prof. Sir PATRICK STEWART
Vice-Chancellor: Prof. BOB CRYAN
Deputy Vice-Chancellor: Prof. PETER SLEE
Pro-Vice-Chancellor for Teaching and Learning: Prof. TIM THORNTON
Pro-Vice-Chancellor for Research and Enterprise: Prof. ANDREW BALL
Univ. Sec.: TONY MEARS
Acad. Registrar: KATHY SHERLOCK
Library of 416,000 vols
Number of teachers: 1,900
Number of students: 23,000

DEANS

Business School: Prof. CHRIS COWTON
School of Applied Sciences: Prof. BOB CYWINSKI
School of Art, Design and Architecture: EMMA HUNT
School of Computing and Engineering: Prof. STEVE DONNELLY
School of Education and Professional Devt: Prof. CHRISTINE JARVIS

School of Human and Health Sciences: SUE BERNHAUSER
School of Music, Humanities and Media: Prof. MIKE RUSS

UNIVERSITY OF HULL

Cottingham Rd, Hull, HU6 7RX
Telephone: (1482) 346311
Fax: (1482) 465936
Internet: www.hull.ac.uk
Founded 1928, as University College of Hull, Univ. Charter 1954
Academic year: September to June
Chancellor: Baroness BOTTOMLEY
Vice-Chancellor: Prof. CALIE PISTORIUS
Deputy Vice-Chancellor and Pro-Vice Chancellor for Acad. Affairs: Prof. J. W. BRUCE
Pro-Vice-Chancellor for Engagement: Prof. JOHN LEACH
Pro-Vice-Chancellor for Learning and Teaching: Prof. GLENN BURGESS
Pro-Vice-Chancellor for Research and Enterprise: Prof. BARRY WINN
Quality Dir, Univ. Registrar and Sec.: FRANCES OWEN
Librarian and Academic Services Dir: Dr R. G. HESELTINE
Library: see under Libraries and Archives
Number of teachers: 1,026
Number of students: 20,000

DEANS

Business School: Prof. M. JACKSON
Faculty of Arts and Social Sciences: Prof. VALERIE SANDERS (acting)
Faculty of Education: DINA LEWIS
Faculty of Health and Social Care: CHRISTINE ENGLISH
Faculty of Science: DEREK P. WILLS
Hull York Medical School: Prof. TONY KENDRICK
Postgraduate Medical Institute: Prof. NICHOLAS D. STAFFORD

PROFESSORS

ALEKSEEVSKY, D., Mathematics
ATTENBOROUGH, K., Engineering
BENNETT, J., Hull York Medical School
BINKS, B., Chemistry
BIRKINSHAW, P. J., Law
BOSCH, P., Mathematics
BOTTERY, M., Educational Studies
BROOKES, G. R., Computer Science
BURGESS, M., Politics
BURGESS, P., History
CAMPION, P. D., Public Health and Primary Care Medicine
CARVALHO, G., Biological Science
CHESTERS, G., IfL Office
CLELAND, J., Cardiology
COLQUHOUN, D., Educational Studies
CRAIG, G., Comparative and Applied Social Sciences
CROUCH, D., History
CUMMINGS, A., Engineering Design and Manufacture
CUTLAND, N. J., Pure Mathematics
DAVIES, K., International Leadership Centre
DYER, P. E., Physics
ELTIS, D., Economic Studies
FLETCHER, P. D., Chemistry
FROSTICK, L. E., Geography and Earth Resources
GIBBS, D. C., Geography and Earth Resources
GILBERT, P., Philosophy
GILLESPIE, W., Hull York Medical School
GOODBY, J. W., Chemistry
GRABBE, L. L., Theology
GREEN, R., Economics
GRIFFIN, G., Gender Studies
HARDISTY, J. H., Geography and Earth Resources
HARRIS, R. J., Politics

HASWELL, S., Chemistry
HAUGHTON, G., Geography
HAYWOOD, S., Engineering
HOPPEN, T., History
JACKSON, M., Business School
JESSHOPE, C., Computer Science
JOHNSTON, R., Psychology
KILLICK, S. R., Obstetrics and Gynaecology
KING, V. T., Politics
KITCHEN, P., Business School
LA TORRE, M., Law
LEIGHTON, A., English
LIND, M. J., Oncology
LLOYD, H. A., History
LOVEJOY, P., History
McCOLLUM, P. T., Surgery
McNAUGHTON, L., Sport Science
MAUNDERS, K. T., Accounting, Business and Finance
MONSON, J. R. T., Surgery
MORICE, A. H., Respiratory Medicine
MORTIMER, A., Psychiatry
Lord NORTON OF LOUTH, Politics
OKELY, J. M., Comparative and Applied Social Sciences
O'SULLIVAN, N. K., Politics
PATTON, R. J., Electronic Engineering
PHILLIPS, R., Computer Science
RATLEDGE, C., Biological Science
RICHARDSON, P. D., Economic Studies
RIGBY, B., English
SANDERS, V., English Literature
SCHLUDERMANN, B., Dutch Studies
SHNIRELMAN, A., Mathematics
SMITH, P. M., French
STAFFORD, N., Otolaryngology and Head and Neck Surgery
SWIFT, K. G., Engineering Design and Manufacture
TOWNSHEND, A., Chemistry
TURNBULL, L. W., Magnetic Resonance Investigation
TURNER, G., Biological Science
TURNER, M. E., Economic Studies
VLADIMIROV, V., Mathematics
WALKER, L., Rehabilitation
WATSON, R., Care of the Older Person
WILLIAMS, D., French

UNIVERSITY OF KEELE

Keele, ST5 5BG
Telephone: (1782) 732000
E-mail: international@mac.keele.ac.uk
Internet: www.keele.ac.uk

Founded 1949, as Univ. College of North Staffordshire, present name and status 1962
State control
Academic year: August to July

Chancellor: JONATHAN PORRITT
Vice-Chancellor: Prof. NICK FOSKETT
Deputy Vice-Chancellor: RAMA THIRUNAMA-CHANDRAN
Pro-Vice-Chancellor for Education and Student Experience: Prof. MARILYN ANDREWS
Pro-Vice-Chancellor for Community and Partnerships: KEVIN MATTINSON
Pro-Vice-Chancellor for Research: Prof. MARK ORMEROD
Librarian: PAUL REYNOLDS
Library: see under Libraries and Archives
Number of teachers: 604
Number of students: 8,371 (F.t.e.)

Publications: *British Journal for the History of Philosophy*, *Sociological Review*

DEANS

Faculty of Health: Prof. ANDY GARNER
Faculty of Humanities and Social Sciences: Prof. DAVID SHEPHERD
Faculty of Natural Sciences: Prof. PATRICK BAILEY

PROFESSORS

ALLAN, G., Sociology
ALLIN, S., Organic Chemistry
AMIGONI, D., Victorian Literature
ANDREW, J., Literature and Culture
ANDREWS, M., Professional Education in Health
BAILEY, P., Natural Sciences
BELL, I., American Literature
BERNARD, M., Social Gerontology
BLADEN-HOVELL, R., Economics
BLENKINSOPP, A., Practice of Pharmacy
BRADNEY, A., Law
BRUCE, S., English
CHAPMAN, C., Applied Mathematics
CHAPMAN, S., Prescribing Studies
COWNIE, F., Law
CROOK, M., French History
CROPPER, S., Management
DOBSON, A., Politics
DOBSON, J., Biophysics and Biomedical Engineering
DOYLE, T., Politics and International Relations
EGGLESTON, P., Molecular Entomology
EVANS, A., Astrophysics
FARRELL, W., Human Genomics
FISCHMAN STEREMBERG, R., Composition
FORSYTH, V., Biophysics
FOX, M., Law
FU, Y., Applied Mathematics
GARNER, A., Health Sciences
GIFFORD, L., Pharmacy Education
GODFREY, B., Criminology
GOKAY, B., International Relations
GREENHOUGH, T., Structural Biology
HALEY, M., Property Law
HARRIS, O., American Studies
HAYCOCK, P., Environmental Engineering
HELLIER, C., Astrophysics
HOLDSWORTH, C., Social Geography
HOOLE, D., Fish Diseases
HORTON, J., Political Philosophy
HOWELL, J., Organometallic Chemistry
HUGHES, A., Early Modern History
HUNT, K., British History
HURD, H., Parasitology
JACKSON, P., Medieval History
JESTER, R., Orthopaedic Nursing
JONES, P., Statistics
KELEMEN, M., Management Studies
KELLY, B., Musicology
KING, C., Earth Science Education
KITCHENHAM, B., Quantitative Software Engineering
KLAES, M., Commerce
LANOT, G., Economics
LAWRENCE, P., Development Economics
LIPPENS, R., Criminology
MAIN, C., Psychology (Pain Management)
MASLIN-PROTHERO, S., Nursing
MAXWELL, D., African History
McCABE, D., Organisational Analysis
McCRACKEN, M., English Literature
MILAS, C., Finance/Financial Relations
MURRAY, M., Psychology
NEWEY, G., Politics and International Relations
ONG, B., Health Services Research
ORMEROD, R., Inorganic Materials Chemistry
PATON, C., Public Policy
PHILLIPSON, C., Applied Social Studies and Social Gerontology
PUGH, R., Social Work
QUINNEY, D., Computer Assisted Learning in Mathematics
RAMSDEN, C., Organic Chemistry
RANGACHARI, P., Health Education
ROGERSON, G., Applied Mathematics
ROTENBERG, K., Psychology
SCHARF, T., Social Gerontology
SEMENOV, S., Imaging
SHARPE, A., Law
SHEPHERD, D., Humanities and Social Sciences

SHRIRA, V., Applied Mathematics
SIM, J., Health Care Research
SPANEL, P., Trace Gas Analysis
STENNING, P., Criminology
STRANGE, R., Clinical Biochemistry
STYLES, P., Applied and Environmental Geophysics
THOMSON, M., Law, Culture and Society
TOWNSHEND, C., International History
VAN DER WINDT, D., Primary Care Epidemiology
VAUGHAN, M., Humanities
WARD, R., Medical Entomology
WASIK, M., Criminal Justice
WASS, V., Medical Education
WEARDEN, J., Psychology
WENZELBURGER, J., Economics
WERBNER, P., Social Anthropology
WILKINSON, S., Bioethics
WILLIAMS, C., Social Justice
WILLIAMS, G., Structural Geology
WILLIAMS, G., Biochemistry
WILLIS, P., Cultural Theory and Qualitative Social Research

UNIVERSITY OF KENT

The Registry, Canterbury, CT2 7NZ
Telephone: (1227) 764000
E-mail: information@kent.ac.uk
Internet: www.kent.ac.uk

Founded 1965
State control
Academic year: September to June

Chancellor: Sir ROBERT WORCESTER
Vice-Chancellor: Prof. JULIA GOODFELLOW
Sr Deputy Vice-Chancellor: DAVID NIGHTINGALE
Deputy Vice-Chancellor: Prof. KEITH MANDER
Deputy Vice-Chancellor: DENISE EVERITT
Pro Vice-Chancellor: Prof. JOHN BALDOCK
Pro Vice-Chancellor: Prof. ALEX HUGHES
Sec. of Council: KAREN GOFFIN
Head of Library Services: CAROLE PICKAVER

Library: 1.3m. vols
Number of teachers: 630
Number of students: 17,000

DEANS

Faculty of Humanities: Prof. KARL LEYDECKER
Faculty of Sciences: Prof. MARK BURCHELL
Faculty of Social Sciences: Prof. JOHN WIGHTMAN

PROFESSORS

Faculty of Humanities (Marlowe Bldg, Univ. of Kent, Canterbury, CT2 7NR; tel. (1227) 764000; fax (1227) 827127):

ALLAIN, P., Theatre and Performance
ANDERSON, G., Classics
ANDREWS, M. Y., Victorian and Visual Studies
AYERS, D., Modernism and Critical Theory (English)
BEECH, A., Fine Art
CARRETTE, J., Religion and Culture
CONNELLY, M., Modern British History
COWIE, E., Film Studies
DITCHFIELD, G., Eigtheenth-Century History
FINCHAM, K., Early Modern History
FONTANA-GIUSTI, G., Regional Regeneration
GILL, R., Theology
GOLDSTEIN, L., Philosophy
GURNAH, A., English and Postcolonial Literatures
HOWIE, T., Contemporary Music
KLEIN, B., English Literature
LANDRY, D., English and American Literature
LEYDECKER, K., German and Comparative Literature

LYNCH, G., Modern Theology
MONTEFIORE, J., English and American Literature
NIKOLOPOULOU, M., Sustainable Architecture
PAVIS, P., Drama and Theatre Studies
READ, P. F., French
SCHMIDT, U., Modern History
SMITH, C. W., History of Science
SMITH, M., Film Studies
WELCH, D. A., Modern European History
WELLER, S., Comparative Literature
WILLIAMSON, J., Reasoning, Inference and Scientific Method

Faculty of Sciences (School of Mathematics, Statistics and Actuarial Science, Univ. of Kent Canterbury, CT2 7NR; tel. (1227) 764000; fax (1227) 827154):

BOWMAN, H., Cognition and Logic (Computing)
BROWN, D., Structural Biology
BROWN, M., Actuarial Science
BROWN, P., Medieval English Literature
BROWN, P. J., Medical Statistics
BURCHELL, M., Space Sciences
CARPENTER, I., Human Ageing
CHADWICK, A. V., Physical Chemistry
CHADWICK, D., Informations Systems Security
CLARKSON, P., Mathematics
COLCHESTER, A. C. F., Clinical Neuroscience and Medical Image Computing
FAIRHURST, M. C., Computer Vision
FARRELL, P., Digital Communications
FINCHER, S., Computing Education
FLEISCHMAN, P., Mathematics
GEEVES, M. A., Physical Biochemistry
GRIFFIN, D., Genetics
GRIFFITHS, R., Biological Conservation
GULLICK, W., Cancer Biology
HONE, A., Mathematics
HOWARD, P., Ethnobotany
JACKSON, D. A., Applied Optics
JEFFRIES, P., Mycology
JONES, R., Computer Systems
KOLLING, M., Computer Science
KRSKA, J., Clinical and Professional Practice (Pharmacy)
MATHIE, A., Pharmacology
MANDER, K., Computer Science
MANSFIELD, E., Mathematics
MICHAELIS, M., Cell Biology
MORGAN, B. J. T., Applied Statistics
NEWPORT, R., Materials Physics
PODOLEANU, A., Biomedical Optics
RIDOUT, M., Applied Statistics
STRANGE, P., Actuarial Science
SWEETING, P., Actuarial Science
SMALES, M., Mammalian Cell Biotechnology
SMITH, M., Astrophysics
SPURGEON, S., Control Engineering
THOMPSON, S., Logic and Computation
TUITE, M., Molecular Biology
USHKARYOV, Y., Biological Sciences
WALKER, S., Statistics
WANG, J., Telecommunications
WANG, F., Future Computing
WAYMAN, J., Biometric Information Technology
WARREN, M. J., Biochemistry
WELCH, P. H., Parallel Computing
WENT, M., Forensic Science and Chemistry
YAN, Y., Electronic Instrumentation
ZHANG, J., Statistics

Faculty of Social Sciences (Marlowe Bldg, University of Kent, Canterbury, CT2 7NR; tel. (1227) 764000; fax (1227) 823959):

ABRAMS, W. D. J., Social Psychology
BALDOCK, J., Social Policy
BEECHAM, J., Health and Social Care Economics
BURGESS, M., Federal Studies
CALNAN, M., Sociology of Health Studies
CARRUTH, A., Economics

CHADHA, J., Economics
CONAGHAN, J., Law
COOPER, D., Law
COULTON, S., Health Services Research
CRISP, R., Psychology
DAVIDOVA, S., European Agricultural Policy
ELLEN, R. F., Anthropology and Human Ecology
EVANS, M. S., Women's Studies
FISCHER, M., Anthropological Sciences
FITZPATRICK, J., Law
FRASER, R., Economics
FUNNELL, W., Accounting and Finance
FUREDI, F., Sociology
GRIEF, N., Law
HALE, C., Criminology
HARROP, S., Wildlife Management Law
HEADY, C., Economics
HERMAN, D., Law
HOUSTON, D., Psychology
HOWARTH, W., Environmental Law
HUBBARD, P., Urban Studies
HUNTER, R., Law
IRELAND, P., Law
JOHNSTON, R., Cognitive Psychology
KERR, N., Psychology
KROLZIG, H., Economics
LEON-LEDESMA, M., Economics
LUI, S. W., Management Science and Computational Mathematics
MACMILLAN, D., Conservation and Applied Resource Economics
MANSELL, W., Law
MAR, M., Management Science
MOHR, A., Strategy (Business)
MIALL, A., International Relations
MURPHY, G., Applied Psychology of Learning Disability
NETTEN, A., Social Welfare
PHILLIPS, P., Strategic Management
RAMSAY, I., Law
ROOTES, C., Environmental Politics and Political Sociology
RUTLAND, A., Developmental Psychology
RAY, L., Sociology
RUBIN, G., Law
SAKWA, R., Russian and European Politics
SALHI, S., Management Science
SAMUEL, G., Law
SAYERS, J., Psychoanalytic Psychology
SAYERS, S., Philosophy
SCHEPEL, H., Law
SHAUGHNESSY, R., Theatre
SHELDON, S., Law
SHILLING, C., Sociology
STEVENS, A., Criminal Justice
STEPHENSON, G., Social Psychology
TAYLOR-GOOBY, P., Social Policy
TUNARU, R., Quantitative Finance
THIRLWALL, A. P., Applied Economics
TWIGG, J., Social Policy and Sociology
UGLOW, S., Criminal Justice
VICKERSTAFF, S., Social Policy, Sociology, Social Research
VICKERMAN, R. W., Regional and Transport Economics
WHITMAN, R., Politics and International Relations
WILLIAMS, T., Law
YOUNG, J., Sociology

UNIVERSITY OF LANCASTER

Univ. House, Lancaster, LA1 4YW
Telephone: (1524) 65201
Fax: (1524) 843087
E-mail: ugadmissions@lancaster.ac.uk
Internet: www.lancs.ac.uk
Founded 1964
Academic year: October to July
Chancellor: Sir CHRISTIAN BONINGTON
Pro-Chancellor: BRYAN GRAY
Vice-Chancellor: Prof. PAUL WELLINGS

Deputy Vice-Chancellor: Prof. ROBERT MCKINLAY
Pro-Vice-Chancellor for Colleges and Student Experience: Prof. AMANDA CHETWYND
Pro-Vice-Chancellor for Research: Prof. TREVOR J. MCMILLAN
Univ. Sec.: FIONA AIKEN
Librarian: CLARE POWNE
Library: see under Libraries and Archives
Number of teachers: 800
Number of students: 16,500

DEANS

Faculty of Arts and Social Sciences: Prof. TONY MCENERY
Faculty of Science and Technology: Prof. MARY SMYTH
School of Health and Medicine: Prof. TONY GATRELL
Management School: Prof. SUE COX

PROFESSORS

ACKROYD, S. C., Organizational Behaviour
ALDERSON, J. C., Linguistics and English Language Education
ALLSOP, D., Neuroscience
ARAUJO, L., Industrial Marketing
ARCHARD, D., Philosophy
ASTON, E., Theatre Studies
BARDGETT, R. D., Ecology
BARTON, D., Language and Literacy
BELLANY, I., Politics
BEVEN, K. J., Environmental Science
BINLEY, A., Hydrogeophysics
BLACKLER, F. H. M., Behaviour in Organizations
BLAIR, G. S., Distributed Systems
BLINKHORN, R. M., History
BLOOMFIELD, B., Organizational Behaviour
BRADLEY, S., Economics
BRAY, R. W., Music
BREMNER, J. G., Developmental Psychology
BURGOYNE, J. G., Management Learning
BYGATE, M., Linguistics
CARTER, R. G., Electronic Engineering
CHADWICK, R., Philosophy
CHAPMAN, G. P., Geography
CHETWYND, A. G., Mathematics and Statistics
CLARK, D., Medical Sociology
CLARKE, I., Marketing
COLLINSON, D., Management Learning
COULSON, G., Distributed Systems
COX, S. J., Safety and Risk Management
CROUCHLEY, R., Applied Statistics
DAVIES, N.A. J., Computing
DAVIES, W. J., Environmental Physiology
DAVISON, W., Environmental Chemistry
DENVER, D. T., Politics
DIGGLE, P. J., Mathematics and Statistics
DILLON, G. M., Politics
DIX, A., Computing
DUFFIELD, M., Politics
EASTERBY-SMITH, M. P. V., Management Learning
EASTON, G., Marketing
EMERSON, E., Clinical Psychology
EVANS, E. J., Social History
FAIRCLOUGH, N. L., Linguistics
FALKO, V., Condensed Matter Theory
FIDDLER, A., German and Austrian Studies
FILDES, R. A., Management Science
FINDLAY, A., Renaissance Drama
FORDE, B., Plant Biotechnology
FOX, S., Social and Management Learning
FRANCIS, B. J., Social Statistics
FRANKLIN, S., Sociology
GATRELL, A. C., Health
GELLERSEN, H.-W., Computing
GRAHAM, H., Social Policy
HAMILTON, M. E., Adult Learning and Literacy
HANLEY, K. A., English Literature
HARMAN, P. M., History of Science
HATTON, C. R., Psychology, Health and Social Care

HEELAS, P. L. F., Religion and Modernity
HENDERSON, R., Biostatistics
HETHERINGTON, A. M., Plant Cell Physiology
HEWITT, C. N., Atmospheric Chemistry
HONARY, B., Communications Engineering
HONARY, F., Space Plasma and Radio Science
HOPKINS, J. B., Psychology
HUGHES, J. A., Sociological Analysis
HUTCHISON, D., Computing
INTRONA, L., Organization, Technology and Ethics
IVANIC, R., Linguistics and Education
JESSOP, R. D., Sociology
JOHNES, G., Economics
JOHNSON, K., Linguistics and Language Education
JONES, K. C., Environmental Chemistry and Ecotoxicology
KATAMBA, F. X., Linguistics
KIRBY, M. W., Economic History
KRIER, A., Semiconductor Physics
KUHN, A. F., Film Studies
LAMBERT, C. J., Theoretical Condensed Matter Physics
LAMBRECHT, B. M., Accounting and Finance
LAW, J., Sociology
LEA, P. J., Biological Sciences
LEWIS, C. N., Family and Developmental Psychology
LYTH, D., Astro-Particle Physics
MACDONALD, R., Environmental Science
MAHER, B., Geography
MAY-CHAHAL, C., Applied Social Science
McCLINTOCK, P. V. E., Physics
McENERY, A. M., English Language and Linguistics
McMILLAN, T. J., Cancer Biology
McNEILL, M., Women's Studies and Cultural Studies
MORRIS, P. E., Psychology
MULLETT, M. A. A., Cultural and Religious History
NIEDUSZYNSKI, I. A., Connective Tissue Biochemistry
O'HANLAN, J. F., Finance
O'NEILL, J. F., Philosophy
ORMEROD, T., Cognitive Psychology
OTLEY, D. T., Accounting and Finance
PAYNE, J. P., German Studies
PEARCE, L., Literary Theory and Women's Writing
PEASNELL, K. V., Accounting and Finance
PENN, R. D., Economic Sociology and Statistics
PERCY, K. A., Adult Continuing Education
PICCIOTTO, S., Law
PICKETT, G. R., Low Temperature Physics
PIDD, M., Management Science
PINKERTON, H., Physical Volcanology
POOLEY, C. G., Geography
POPAY, J., Social and Public Health
POPE, P. F., Accounting and Finance
POWER, S. C., Mathematics
RATOFF, P. N., Experimental Particle Physics
READER, I. J., Religious Studies
REYNOLDS, P. M., Management Learning
RICHARDS, J. M., Cultural History
RICHARDSON, A. M. D., Microsystems Engineering
ROBERTS, G., Mathematics
RODWELL, J. S., Plant Ecology
ROGERS, C. G., Educational Research
ROSE, M., Entrepreneurship
ROTHSCHILD, R., Economics
ROWE, P., Law
SAUNDERS, M. S., Evaluation in Education and Work
SAYER, R. A., Sociology
SEGAL, R., Theories of Religion
SEWARD, D. W., Engineering Design
SHAPIRO, D. Z., Sociology
SHORT, M. H., Linguistics
SIEWIERSKA, A. M., Linguistics
SMITH, D. B., Criminology
SMITH, L., Educational Research
SMYTH, M. M., Experimental Psychology

SOMMERVILLE, I. F., Computing
SOOTHILL, K. L., Social Research
STACEY, J., Women's Studies and Cultural Studies
STRINGER, K. J., Medieval British History
SUCHMAN, L., Sociology
SUGARMAN, D., Law
TAWN, J. A., Statistics
TAYLOR, J., Economics
TAYLOR, S. J., Finance
THORPE, D. H., Applied Social Science
TIHANOV, G., Comparative Literature
TROWLER, P., Higher Education
TUCKER, R. W., Mathematical Physics
TURVEY, G. J., Engineering Mechanics
URRY, J. R., Sociology
WEBER, C. L., Politics
WHITELEY, N. S., Visual Arts
WHITTAKER, J. B., Biological Sciences
WHITTON, D. W., French Theatre
WHYTE, I. D., Historical Geography
WIGMORE, J. K., Condensed Matter Physics
WILSON, L., Environmental Science
WILSON, R. F., Renaissance Studies
WISE, S., Social Justice
WYNNE, B. E., Science Studies
XYDEAS, C. S., Communications Engineering
YADAV, P. K., Accounting and Finance

UNIVERSITY OF LEEDS

Leeds, LS2 9JT
Telephone: (113) 243-1751
Fax: (113) 244-3923
E-mail: enquiry@leeds.ac.uk
Internet: www.leeds.ac.uk
Founded 1874 as Yorkshire College of Science, Univ. Charter 1904
Academic year: September to June
Chancellor: Lord BRAGG
Pro-Chancellor: LINDA POLLARD
Vice-Chancellor: Prof. MICHAEL ARTHUR
Deputy Vice-Chancellor: Prof. JOHN FISHER
Pro-Vice-Chancellor for Int. Partnerships: Prof. RICHARD WILLIAMS
Pro-Vice-Chancellor for Student Education: Prof. VIVIEN JONES
Pro-Vice-Chancellor for Research and Innovation: Prof. ANDREW THOMPSON
Pro-Vice-Chancellor for Staff: Prof. STEPHEN SCOTT
Sec: ROGER GAIR
Librarian and Keeper of Brotherton Colln: MARGARET COUTTS
Library: see under Libraries and Archives
Number of students: 32,500

DEANS

Faculty of Arts: Prof. FRANK FINLAY
Faculty of Biological Sciences: Prof. STEVE HOMANS
Faculty of Business: Prof. PETER MOIZER
Faculty of Education, Social Sciences and Law: Prof. JEREMY HIGHAM (acting)
Faculty of Engineering: Prof. PETER JIMACK
Faculty of Environment: Prof. JANE FRANCIS
Faculty of Mathematics and Physical Sciences: Prof. MICHAEL WILSON
Faculty of Medicine and Health: Prof. PETER McWILLIAM
Faculty of Performance, Visual Arts and Communications: Prof. DAVID COOPER

PROFESSORS

Faculty of Arts:

AGIUS, D. A., Arabic and Islamic Material Culture
ATACK, M. K., French
BLACK, R. D., Renaissance History
BROCK, R. W., Renaissance History
BUTLER, M., Renaissance Drama
CANTOR, G. N., History of Science
CHARTRES, J. A., Social and Economic History

CHILDS, J. C. R., Military History
DIXON, S. M., Modern History
ELLIOTT, J. K., New Testament Textual Criticism
FAIRER, D., 18th-century English Literature
FINLAY, F. J., German
FRENCH, S. R. D., Philosophy of Science
GARNER, P., Spanish
GIDLEY, CM., American Literature
GOOCH, J., International History
HAMMOND, P., 17th-century English Literature
HARTLEY, T., Translation Studies
HEATH, M. F., Greek Language and Literature
HILL, J., Visiting Professor
HOLMES, D., French
HUGGAN, G., Commonwealth and Postcolonial Literatures
JOHNSON, S., Linguistics
JONES, V., 18th-century Gender and Culture
KILLICK, R., Quebec Studies and 19th-century French Studies
KING, V. T., South-East Asian Studies
KNIGHT, R. A., Language Centre
KNOTT, K., Religious Studies
KOCIENSKI, P., Chemistry
LARRISSY, E., English Literature
LEVENE, D. S., Latin Language and Literature
LINDLEY, D., Renaissance Literature
LOOSELY, D. L., Contemporary French Culture
LOUD, G. A., Medieval Italian History
MALTBY, R., Latin Philology
McFADYEN, A. I., Theology and Religious Studies
MORRIS, R. H., Medieval Studies
NAGIB, L., Centenary Professor of World History
NELSON, M. T., Philosophy
NETTON, I. R., Arabic Studies
PLATTEN, D. P., French
POIDEVIN, R. Le, Metaphysics
RICHARDSON, B. F., Italian
SILVERMAN, M., Modern French Studies
SIMONS, P. M., Philosophy
SPIERS, E. M., Strategic Studies
SUTTON, J. F., Russian
TABERNER, S. J., German
TOLLIDAY, S. W., Economic History
WAWN, A., Anglo-Icelandic Studies
WILLIAMS, M. B., East Asian Studies
WILSON, K. M., International Politics
WOOD, I. N., Early Medieval History

Faculty of Biological Sciences:

ALEXANDER, R. M., Biology
ALTRINGHAM, J. D., Biomechanics
ATKINSON, H. J., Nematology
BALDWIN, S. A., Biochemistry
BAUMBERG, S., Bacterial Genetics
BEECH, D. J., Cellular and Molecular Physiology
BENTON, T. G., Population Ecology
BOOTH, A. G., Online Learning
BROWN, S. B., Biochemistry
BUCKLEY, N. J., Neuroscience
CARDING, S., Molecular Immunology
CHOPRA, I., Microbiology
FINDLAY, J. B. C., Biochemistry
FORBES, J. M., Agricultural Sciences
GILMARTIN, P. M., Plant Molecular Genetics
HANDYSIDE, A., Developmental Biology
HENDERSON, P. J. F., Biochemistry and Molecular Biology
HOLDEN, A. V., Computational Biology
HOLLAND, K. T., Microbiology
HOMANS, S. W., Structural Biology
HOOPER, N. M., Biochemistry
HUGHES, I. E., Pharmacology Education
INGHAM, E., Medical Immunology
ISAAC, R. E., Comparative Biochemistry

KILLINGTON, R. A., Virology Education

KRAUSE, J., Behavioural Ecology

MCPHERSON, M. J., Biochemistry and Molecular Biology

MEYER, P., Plant Genetics

ORCHARD, C. H., Physiology

PHILLIPS, S. E. V., Biophysics

RADFORD, S. E., Structural Molecular Biology

RAYNER, J. M. V., Zoology

ROBERTSON, B., Neurobiology

ROWLANDS, D. J., Molecular Virology

SHORROCKS, B., Population Biology

SMITH, J. E., Parasitology

STOCKLEY, P. G., Biological Chemistry

TRINICK, J. A., Animal Cell Biology

TURNER, A. J., Biochemistry

WARD, S. A., Sport and Exercises

WILCOX, M. H., Medical Microbiology

WITHINGTON, D. J., Auditory Neuroscience

WOOD, E. J., Biochemistry

WRAY, D. A., Pharmacology

YATES, M. S., Biomedical Sciences

Faculty of Earth and Environment:

ALEXANDER, R. M., Biology

BAILEY, A. J., Population Geography

BELL, M., Traffic and Environmental Pollution

BEST, J. L., Process Sedimentology

BONSALL, P. W., Transport Planning

CARSTEN, O., Transport Safety

CLARKE, G. P., Business Geography

CLARKE, M. C., Geographic Modelling

FAIRHEAD, J. D., Applied Geophysics

FORBES, R. D., Business Geography

FRANCIS, J. E., Paleoclimatology

GUBBINS, D., Geophysics

HAISEMAN, G. A., Geophysics

KNEALE, P. E., Applied Hydrology

KNIPE, R. J., Structural Geology

KROM, M. D., Marine and Environmental Geochemistry

LLOYD, J. J., Centenary Professor of Earth Science Systems

MCDONALD, A. T., Environmental Management

MACKIE, P. J., Transport Studies

MAY, A. D., Transport Engineering

MOBBS, S. D., Atmospheric Dynamics

NASH, C. A., Transport Economics

RAISWELL, R. W., Sedimentary Geochemistry

REES, P. H., Population Geography

SMITH, M. H., Atmospheric Physics

SMITH, N. J., Project and Transport Infrastructure Management (joint post with Faculty of Engineering)

STILLWELL, J. C. H., Migration and Regional Development

TZEDAKIS, P. C., Quarternary Earth System History

VALENTINE, G., Human Geography

WATLING, D., Centenary Professor of Transport Analysis

WILSON, B. M., Igneous Petrogenesis

YARDLEY, B. W. D., Metamorphic Geochemistry

Faculty of Education, Social Sciences and Law:

ACKERS, H. L., European Law

BAGGULEY, P., Sociology and Social Policy

BARNES, C., Disability Studies

BATES, I., Education and Work

BAYNHAM, M. J., TESOL

BELL, D. S., French Government and Politics

BLUTH, C., International Studies

CAMERON, L. J., Applied Linguistics

CHASE, M. S., Continuing Education

CRAWFORD, T. A., Criminology and Criminal Justice

DEACON, A. J., Social Policy

DONNELLY, J. F., Science Education

HALSON, D. R., Law

HODKINSON, P. M., Lifelong Learning

KEAY, A., Corporate and Commercial Law

KERR, A., Sociology

LEACH, J., Science Education

LODGE, J., European Studies

MCCARGO, D., Politics and International Studies

MCMULLEN, J., Labour Law

ORMEROD, D., Law

OSLER, A. H., Education

PEARSON, R., Development Studies

RADICE, H. K., International Political Economy

ROSENEIL, S., Sociology and Gender Studies

SCOTT, P., Science Education

SHORROCKS-TAYLOR, D., Assessment and Evaluation in Education

SUBEDI, S. P., International Law

SUGDEN, D. A., Special Needs in Education

THEAKSTON, K., British Government

VINCENT-JONES, P., Law

WALKER, C. P., Criminal Justice

WALL, D. S., Legal History

WILLIAMS, F., Social Policy

ZUKAS, M., Adult Education

Faculty of Engineering:

ANDREWS, G. E., Combustion Engineering

BARTON, D. C., Solid Mechanics

BELL, A. J., Electronic Materials

BERZINS, M., Scientific Computation

BIGGS, S. R., Particle Science and Technology

BONSALL, P. W., Transport Planning

BOYLE, R. D., Computing

BRADLEY, D., Mechanical Engineering

BRODLIE, K. W., Visualization

CHILDS, T. H. C., Manufacturing Engineering

COHN, A. G., Automated Reasoning

DAVIES, A. G., Electronic and Photonic Engineering

DE PENNINGTON, A., Computer-aided Engineering

DEW, P. M., Computer Science

DOWSON, D., Mechanical Engineering

DYER, M. E., Theoretical Computer Science

EDMONDS, D. V., Metallurgy

FAIRWEATHER, R. M., Thermofluids and Combustion

FISHER, J., Mechanical Engineering

GASKELL, P. H., Fluid Mechanics

GHADIRI, M., Chemical Engineering

HARRISON, P. H., Quantum Electronics

HOGG, D. C., Artificial Intelligence

HOWES, M. J., Electronic Engineering

HOYLE, B. S., Vision and Image Systems

HUNTER, I. C., Microwave Signal Processing

JHA, A., Applied Materials Science

JIMACK, P., Scientific Computing

JIN, Z. M., Computational Biomechanics/Bioengineering

LINFIELD, E., Terahertz Electronics

MARA, D. D., Civil Engineering

MARKARIAN, G., Communication Systems

MCINTOSH, A. C., Thermodynamics and Combustion Theory

MILES, R. E., Semiconductor Electronics

NEVILLE, A., Engineering Tribology

PAGE, C. L., Civil Engineering Materials

POLLARD, R. D., High-frequency Measurements

POURKASHANIAN, M., High Temperature Combustion Processes

PRIEST, M., Engineering Tribology

RAND, B., Ceramics

RHODES, J. D., Electronic and Electrical Engineering

ROBERTS, K. J., Chemical Engineering

ROBERTSON, I. D., Centenary Professor of Microwave and Millimetre Wave Circuits

SHEPPARD, C. G. W., Applied Thermodynamics and Combustion Science

SMITH, N. J., Project and Transport Infrastructure Management (joint position with Transport Studies)

VIRK, G. S., Robotics and Control

WILLIAMS, P. T., Environmental Engineering

WILLIAMS, R. A., Mineral and Process Engineering

XU, J., Computing

Faculty of Mathematics and Physical Sciences:

BATCHELDER, D. N., Physics

BEDDARD, G., Chemical Physics

BLOOR, M. I. G., Applied Mathematics

BODEN, N., Physical Chemistry

BRINDLEY, J., Applied Mathematics

COOPER, S. B., Pure Mathematics

CRAWLEY-BOEVEY, W. W., Pure Mathematics

CYWINSKI, R., Experimental Physics

DALES, H. G., Pure Mathematics

DICKINSON, E., Food Colloids

DYSON, J. E., Astronomy

EVANS, S. D., Molecular and Nanoscale Physics

FALLE, S. A. E. G., Astrophysical Fluid Dynamics

FORDY, A. P., Nonlinear Mathematics

GREIG, D., Physics

GRIFFITHS, J. F., Functional Dye Chemistry

GRIGG, R. E., Organic Chemistry

GUTHRIE, J. T., Polymer and Surface Coatings, Science and Technology

HAMLEY, I. W., Polymer Materials

HARTQUIST, T. W., Astrophysics

HEARD, D. E., Atmospheric Chemistry

HICKEY, B., Physics

HILLAS, A. M., Physics

HUGHES, D. W., Applied Mathematics

INGHAM, D. B., Applied Mathematics

JOHNSON, A. P., Computational Chemistry

KENNEDY, J. D., Inorganic Chemistry

KENT, J. T., Statistics

KOCIEŃSKI, P. J., Organic Chemistry

LANCE, E. C., Pure Mathematics

LAWRIE, I. D., Theoretical Physics

LEWIS, D. M., Colour Chemistry

LUO, M. R., Colour and Imaging Science

MACPHERSON, H. D., Pure Mathematics

MARDIA, K. V., Applied Statistics

MCLEISH, T. C. B., Polymer Physics

MERKIN, J. H., Applied Mathematics

MIKHAILOV, A. V., Mathematical Physics

MORGAN, G. J., Theoretical Physics

MORGAN, M. R., Food Biochemistry

NIJHOFF, F. W., Mathematical Physics

PARTINGTON, J. R., Pure Mathematics

PILLING, M. J., Physical Chemistry

POVEY, M. J. W., Food Physics

RATHJEN, M., Pure Mathematics

READ, C. J., Pure Mathematics

ROBINSON, D. S., Food Science

ROBSON, J. C., Pure Mathematics

SAVAGE, M. D., Thin Liquid Films and Coatings

SCOTT, S. K., Mathematical Chemistry

SLEEMAN, B. D., Applied Mathematics

TAYLOR, C. C., Statistics

TRUSS, J. K., Pure Mathematics

VEDRAL, V., Centenary Professor of Quantum Information Science

VERETENNIKOV, A. Y., Statistics

WAINER, S. S., Pure Mathematics

WARD, I. M., Physics

WATSON, A. A., Physics

WEDZICHA, B. L., Food Science

WHITAKER, B. J., Chemical Physics

WILSON, M. J., Applied Mathematics

WOOD, J. C., Pure Mathematics

Faculty of Medicine and Health:

ADAMS, C., Adult Psychiatry and Mental Health Services Research

ALIMO-METCALFE, B. M., Leadership Studies

BALL, S. G., Cardiology

BARKHAM, M., Clinical and Counselling Psychology
BIRD, H. A., Pharmacological Rheumatology
BISHOP, T., Genetic Epidemiology
BLUNDELL, J. E., Psychobiology
BONIFER, C., Experimental Haematology
BONTHRON, D. T., Molecular Medicine
BOYLSTON, A. W., Pathology
BRUNTON, P. A., Restorative Dentistry
CADE, J., Nutritional Epidemiology and Public Health
CHEATER, F., Public Health Nursing
CLEREHUGH, M. A., Periodontology
CLOSS, J., Nursing Research
COTTRELL, D. J., Child and Adolescent Psychiatry
CUCKLE, H. S., Reproductive Epidemiology
DICKSON, R. A., Orthopaedic Surgery
DRIFE, J. O., Obstetrics and Gynaecology
DUGGAL, M. S., Child Dental Health
EMERY, P., Rheumatology
FORMAN, D., Cancer Epidemiology
GIANNOUDIS, P. P., Orthopaedic Surgery
GRANT, P. J., Molecular Vascular Medicine
GREEN, A., International Health Planning
GUILLOU, P. J., Surgery
HALE, C., Clinical Nursing
HALL, A. S., Clinical Cardiology
HANBY, A. M., Breast Pathology
HAWARD, R., Cancer Studies
HAY, A., Environmental Toxicology
HEWISON, J., Healthcare Psychology
HEYWOOD, P. L., Primary Care
HILLHOUSE, E., Dean of the School of Medicine and Health
HOPKINS, P. M., Anaesthesia
HOUSE, A. O., Liaison Psychiatry
HOWDLE, P. D., Clinical Education
HULL, M. A., Molecular Gastroenterology
HUME, W. J., Oral Pathology
INGLEHEARN, C., Molecular Ophthalmology
KAPLAN, R. S., Clinical Cancer Studies
KEEN, J., Health Politics and Information Management
KELLETT, M., Restorative Dentistry
KIRKHAM, J., Oral Biology
KNOWLES, M., Experimental Cancer Research
LEVENE, M. I., Paediatrics and Child Health
LONG, A., Health Systems Research
MACLENNAN, K., Tumour Pathology
MARKHAM, A. F., Medicine
MARSH, P. D., Oral Microbiology
MCDERMOTT, M., Experimental Rheumatology
MCGONAGLE, D., Investigative Rheumatology
MCMAHON, M. J., Surgery
MCWILLIAM, P. N., Cardiovascular Physiology
MORLEY, S. J., Clinical Psychology
MURDOCH-EATON, D., Medical Education
PEERS, C. S., Cellular Physiology
QUIRKE, P., Pathology
RAYNOR, D. K., Pharmacy Practice, Medicine and their Users
ROBERTS, T. E., Medical Education
ROBINSON, C., Oral Biology
RODGERS, R. J., Behavioural Pharmacology
SANDLE, G. I., Clinical Science
SELBY, P. J., Cancer Medicine
SEYMOUR, M., Gastro-intestinal Medicine
TENNANT, A., Rehabilitation Studies
TWELVES, C. J., Clinical Pharmacology and Oncology
WALKER, J. J., Obstetrics and Gynaecology
WILD, C., Molecular Epidemiology
WILLIAMS, S. A., Oral Health Services Research
WISTOW, G., Health and Social Care
WOOD, D. J, Dental Materials
WOOD, E. J., Biochemistry

Faculty of Performance, Visual Arts and Communications:
BARBER, G. D., Performance Studies (Music)
BOON, R., Performance Studies
BROWN, C., Applied Musicology
BROWN, R. C. M., International Communications
BURKINSHAW, S. M., Textile Chemistry
CASSIDY, T., Design
COOPER, D. G., Music
DANIELS, S. M., Performance and Cultural Industries
GREEN, V., Fine Art, Film and Media
HANN, M. A., Design Theory
HAY, K. G., Contemporary Art Practice
HILL, D., Fine Art
LAWRENCE, C. A., Textile Engineering
MCQUILLAN, M., Fine Art, History of Art and Cultural Studies
MORRISON, D. E., Communications Research
ORTON, L. F., Art History and Theory
PALMER, R., Fine Art
POLLOCK, G. F. S., Social and Critical Histories of Art
RASTALL, G. R., Historical Musicology
TAYLOR, P. M., International Communications
WALLIS, M., Performance and Culture
WESTLAND, S., Colour Science and Technology

Leeds University Business School:
BUCKLEY, P. J., International Business
CLEGG, L. J., European Integration and International Business Management
COLLINS, M., Financial History
GERRARD, W. J., Sport Management and Finance
HAYES, J., Management Studies
HILLIER, D., Financial Markets
HODGKINSON, G. P., Organizational Behaviour and Strategic Management
KATSIKEAS, C. S., Marketing and International Management
KEASEY, K., Financial Services
LOCK, A. R., Marketing and Business Administration
MACKIE, P. J., Transport Studies
MAULE, A. J., Human Decisions
MCNULTY, T. H., Management and Governance
MICHELL, P. C. N., Marketing and Communications
MOIZER, P., Accounting
NASH, C. A., Transport Economics
NOLAN, P. J., Industrial Relations
OAKLAND, J. S., Business Excellence and Quality Management
PEARMAN, A. D., Management Decision Analysis
PÉROTIN, V., Economics
SAWYER, M. C., Economics
SCHENK-HOPPÉ, K. R., Renaissance History
SHIN, Y., Applied Econometrics
STUART, M., Human Resources Management and Employment Relations
THORPE, R., Management Development
WILSON, N., Credit Management

UNIVERSITY OF LEICESTER

University Rd, Leicester, LE1 7RH
Telephone: (116) 252-2522
Fax: (116) 252-2200
Internet: www.le.ac.uk

Founded 1918 as Univ. College, Charter 1950, Univ. Charter 1957
Academic year: September to June

Visitor: HER MAJESTY THE QUEEN
Chancellor: (vacant)
Pro-Chancellor: (vacant)
Pro-Chancellor: P. BATEMAN
Vice-Chancellor: Prof. Sir R. G. BURGESS

Sr Pro-Vice-Chancellor: Prof. M. P. THOMPSON
Pro-Vice-Chancellor: C. FYFE
Pro Vice-Chancellor: Prof. K. SCHÜRER
Registrar and Sec.: D. E. HALL
Head of Library Services: L. JONES
Library: see Libraries and Archives
Number of teachers: 751 full-time
Number of students: 23,000
Publications: Graduates' Review (1 a year), Insider, LE1 (2 a year)

PRO-VICE-CHANCELLORS AND HEADS OF COLLEGE
College of Arts, Humanities and Law: Prof. D. TALLACK
College of Medicine, Biological Sciences and Psychology: Prof. D. WYNFORD-THOMAS
College of Science and Engineering: Prof. M. BARSTOW
College of Social Sciences: Prof. E. MURPHY

PROFESSORS
College of Arts, Humanities and Law (tel. (116) 252-2679; fax (116) 252-5213; e-mail kxb@le.ac.uk; internet www2.le.ac.uk/colleges/artshumlaw):

FOXHALL, L., Ancient History
HOUSLEY, N. J., History
MATTINGLY, D. J., Roman Archaeology
SHIPLEY, D. G. J., Ancient History
STANNARD, M. J., Modern English Literature
WOOD, S., Modern Languages

College of Medicine, Biological Sciences and Psychology (tel. (116) 252-2969; fax (116) 252-3013; e-mail med-admis@le.ac.uk; internet www.le.ac.uk/medicine):

ABRAMS, K. R., Epidemiology and Public Health
ANDREW, P. W., Microbial Pathogenesis
BAKER, R. H., Quality in Health Care
BRUGHA, T. S., Psychiatry
BURTON, P. R., Genetic Epidemiology
COLMAN, A. M., Psychology
DAVIES, M., Diabetes Medicine
DYER, M. J. S., Pathology
EPERON, I. C., Biochemistry
FIELD, D. J., Neonatal Medicine
FORSYTHE, I. D., Neuroscience
GOTTLOB, I., Ophthalmology
HESLOP-HARRISON, J. S., Plant Cell Biology, Molecular Cytogenetics
HOLLIN, C. R., Criminological Psychology
Sir JEFFREYS, A., Genetics
JONES, D. R., Medical Statistics
KETLEY, J. M., Genetics
KYRIACOU, C. P., Behavioural Genetics
LONDON, N. J. M., Surgery
MELLON, J. K., Urology
NG, L. L., Medicine and Therapeutics
NICHOLSON, K. G., Infectious Diseases
NICHOLSON, M. L., Transplant Surgery
O'CALLAGHAN, C. L. P., Paediatrics
PANERAI, R. B., Physiological Measurement
PETERSEN, S. A., Medical Education
ROBERTS G. C. K., Biochemistry
ROWBOTHAM, D. J., Anaesthesia and Pain Management
RUTTY, G. N., Forensic Pathology
SAMANI, N. J., Cardiovascular Medicine
STEWARD, W. P., Oncology
THOMPSON, J. R., Ophthalmology
TWELL, D., Plant Biology
VOSTANIS, P., Child and Adolescent Psychiatry
WARDLAW, A. J., Respiratory Medicine
WILLIAMS, B., Medicine
WOODS, K. L., Therapeutics

College of Science and Engineering (tel. (116) 252-5012; fax (116) 252-2770; e-mail science@le.ac.uk; internet www.le.ac.uk/science):

BINNS, C., Physics and Astronomy
BRADSHAW, M. J., Human Geography
COWLEY, S. W. H., Solar-Planetary Physics

CULLIS, P. M., Organic Chemistry
FISHER, P. F., Geographical Information
FOTHERGILL, J. C., Engineering
FRASER, G. W., Detector Physics
HILLMAN, A. R., Physical Chemistry
HOPE, E. G., Inorganic Chemistry
KING, A. R., Astrophysics
LESTER, M., Physics and Astronomy
LOVELL, M. A., Petrophysics
NORRIS, C., Surface Physics
PAN, J., Mechanics and Materials
PARRISH, R. R., Isotope Geology
RAMAN, R., Computer Science
ROBINSON, T. R., Space Plasma Physics
SAUNDERS, A. D., Geochemistry
THOMAS, R. M., Mathematics and Computer Science
WARWICK, R. S., X-Ray Astronomy

College of Social Sciences (tel. (116) 252-2842; fax (116) 252-5073; e-mail socsci@le.ac.uk; internet www.le.ac.uk/socsci):

BURRELL, G., Organization Theory
CHAREMZA, W., Economics
DEMETRIADES, P. O., Financial Economics
FRASER, C. D., Economics
JACKSON, P. M., Economics; Public Sector Economics
SNELL, K. D. M., English Local History

School of Law (tel. (116) 252-2363; fax (116) 252-5023; e-mail law@le.ac.uk; internet www.le.ac.uk/law):

CLARKSON, C. M. V., Law
GRAHAM, C., Law
SHAW, M. N., International Law
SZYSZCZAK, E. M., Competition and Labour Law
WHITE, R. C. A., Law

UNIVERSITY OF LINCOLN

Brayford Pool, Lincoln, LN6 7TS
Telephone: (1522) 882000
Fax: (1522) 886041
E-mail: enquiries@lincoln.ac.uk
Internet: www.lincoln.ac.uk

Founded 1861 as School of Art and Design; as Humberside College of Higher Education 1978; Humberside Polytechnic 1990; University of Humberside 1992; University of Lincolnshire and Humberside 1996; incorporated Lincoln School of Art and Lincolnshire School of Agriculture 2001; present name and status 2001

Vice-Chancellor: Prof. MARY STUART
Sr Deputy Vice-Chancellor for Research, Innovation and Enterprise: Prof. ANDREW ATHERTON
Deputy Vice-Chancellor for Devt: Dr FRANCES MANNSAKER
Deputy Vice-Chancellor for Teaching Quality and Student Experience: Prof. SCOTT DAVIDSON
Registrar: EDMUND FITZPATRICK
Dir of Learning Support: MICHELLE ANDERSON

Library of 240,000 vols, 1,000 periodicals
Number of teachers: 573
Number of students: 10,682

Publications: *Institute of Communication Ethics* (4 a year), *Lincoln Magazine*

DEANS

Faculty of Agriculture, Food and Animal Sciences: VAL BRAYBROOKS
Faculty of Art, Architecture and Design: Prof. NORMAN CHERRY
Faculty of Business and Law: Prof. DAVID HEAD
Faculty of Health, Life and Social Science: Prof. SARA OWEN
Faculty of Media, Humanities and Technology: Prof. DAVID SLEIGHT

UNIVERSITY OF LIVERPOOL

Liverpool, L69 3BX
Telephone: (151) 794-2000
Fax: (151) 708-6502
Internet: www.liv.ac.uk

Founded 1882, as Univ. College, Royal Charter 1903

Chancellor: Prof. Sir DAVID KING
Pro-Chancellor: Prof. JAMES KEATON
Vice-Chancellor: Prof. Sir HOWARD NEWBY
Deputy Vice-Chancellor: Prof. JON SAUNDERS
Exec. Pro-Vice-Chancellor: Prof. ANDREW DERRINGTON
Exec. Pro-Vice-Chancellor: Prof. STEPHEN HOLLOWAY
Exec. Pro-Vice-Chancellor: Prof. IAN GREER
Pro-Vice-Chancellor for Int. Affairs: Prof. MICHAEL HOEY
Pro-Vice-Chancellor for Student Experience: Prof. KELVIN EVEREST
Registrar: M. D. CARR
Librarian: PHILIP SYKES

Library: see under Libraries and Archives
Number of teachers: 1,400
Number of students: 18,000

Publications: *Bulletin of Hispanic Studies* (4 a year), *Third World Planning Review* (4 a year), *Town Planning Review* (4 a year)

PROFESSORS

Faculty of Arts:

BATE, A. J., English Literature
BELCHEM, J. C., History
CLARK, S. R. L., Philosophy
DAVIES, J. K., Ancient History and Classical Archaeology
ELLIOTT, M., Irish Studies
EVEREST, K. D., Modern English
FISHER, J. R., Latin-American History
FORSDICK, C., French
GASKIN, R. M., Philosophy
GOWLETT, J. A. J., Archaeology, Classics and Oriental Studies
HIGGINS, J., Latin American Literature
HOEY, M. P., English Language
LEE, W. R., Economic and Social History
MEE, C., Archaeology, Classics and Oriental Studies
MILLARD, A. R., Hebrew and Ancient Semitic Languages
MILLS, A. D., English Language and Literature
SAUL, N. D. B., German
SEED, D., English
SEVERIN, D. S., Spanish
SHAW, J., Archaeology, Classics and Oriental Studies
SLATER, E. A., Archaeology
STAFFORD, P. A., History
TALBOT, M. O., Music
WRIGHT, R. H. P., Hispanic Studies

Faculty of Engineering:

BACON, D. J., Materials Science and Engineering
BUNGEY, J. H., Civil Engineering
BURROWS, R., Environmental Hydraulics
CANTWELL, W. J., Engineering
CHALKER, P. R., Engineering
ECCLESTON, W., Electronic Engineering
ESCUDIER, M. P., Mechanical Engineering
FANG, M. T. C., Applied Electromagnetism
GOODHEW, P. J., Materials Engineering
HALL, S., Electrical Engineering and Electronics
HON, K. K. B., Manufacturing Systems
JONES, G. R., Electrical Engineering and Electronics
JONES, N., Mechanical Engineering
LUCAS, J., Electrical Engineering and Electronics
MOTTERSHEAD, J. E., Applied Mechanics
NANDI, A. K., Electrical Engineering and Electronics

OWEN, I., Mechanical Engineering
PADFIELD, G. D., Engineering
POND, R. C., Materials Science and Engineering
TATLOCK, G. J., Engineering
WATKINS, K. G., Engineering
WU, Q. H., Electrical Engineering

Faculty of Medicine:

ASHFORD, R. W., Parasite and Vector Biology
BACK, D. J., Pharmacology and Therapeutics
BURGOYNE, R. D., Physiology
CALVERLEY, P. M. A., Rehabilitation Medicine
CAPEWELL, S. J., Public Health
CARTY, H. M. L., Paediatric Radiology
CAWLEY, J. C., Haematology
CHADWICK, D. W., Neurology
COOKE, R. W. I., Paediatric Medicine
DIMALINE, R., Physiology
DOCKRAY, G. J., Physiology
DOWRICK, C. F., Primary Care
EMBERY, G., Clinical Dental Sciences
FIELD, J. K., Molecular Oncology
FOSTER, C. S., Pathology
FRASER, W. D., Clinical Chemistry
FROSTICK, S. P., Orthopaedics
GALLAGHER, J. A., Human Anatomy and Cell Biology
GARNER, P. A., Tropical Medicine
GOSDEN, C. M., Medical Genetics
GOWERS, S. G., Adolescent Psychiatry
GRIERSON, I., Experimental Ophthalmology
GRIFFITHS, R. D., Medicine
HART, C. A., Medical Microbiology
HART, I., Medicine
HILL, J., Child and Development Psychiatry
HOMMEL, M., Tropical Medicine
HUNTER, J. M., Anaesthesia
JACKSON, M. J., Cellular Pathophysiology
JOHNSON, P. M., Immunology
KROEGER, A., International Community Health
LEUWER, M., Anaesthesia
LLOYD, D. A., Paediatric Surgery
MOLYNEUX, M. E., Tropical Medicine
MORRISS, R. K., Psychiatry
NEILSON, J. P., Obstetrics and Gynaecology
NEOPTOLEMOS, J. P., Surgery
NURMIKKO, T. J., Neurology
PARK, B. K., Pharmacology and Therapeutics
PETERSEN, O. H., Physiology
PINE, C. M., Clinical Dental Sciences
PIRMOHAMED, M., Pharmacology and Therapeutics
QUINN, J. P., Human Anatomy and Cell Biology
RHODES, J. M., Medicine
ROBERTS, J. N., Magnetic Resonance
SALMON, P., Clinical Psychology
SCOTT, J., Oral Diseases
SHENKIN, A., Clinical Chemistry
SMYTH, R. L., Child Health
STEWART, J. P., Medical Microbiology
TEPIKIN, A. V., Physiology
THEAKSTON, R. D. G., Tropical Medicine
TOWNSON, H., Medical Entomology
TRAYHURN, P., Medicine
TREES, A. J., Tropical Medicine
VARRO, A., Physiology
WALLEY, T. J., Clinical Pharmacology
WARD, S., Tropical Medicine
WARENIUS, H. M., Research Oncology
WARNKE, P. C., Neurology
WATSON, A. J. M., Medicine
WATTS, A., Restorative Dentistry
WEINDLING, A. M., Child Health
WHITEHEAD, M. M., Public Health
WILKINSON, D. G., Liaison Psychiatry
WILLIAMS, D. F., Clinical Engineering
WILLIAMS, G., Medicine
WILSON, K. C. M., Psychiatry of Old Age

WINSTANLEY, P. A., Pharmacology and Therapeutics
WRAY, S. C., Physiology

Faculty of Science:

ALLPORT, P., Physics
APPLEBY, P. G., Mathematical Sciences
BEGON, M. E., Biological Sciences
BHANSALI, R. J., Mathematical Sciences
BOWCOCK, T. J. V., Physics
BRUCE, J. W., Pure Mathematics
CANTER, D. V., Psychology
COOPER, S. J., Psychology
COSSINS, A. R., Biological Sciences
CRAMPTON, J. M., Molecular Biology
DAINTON, J. B., Physics
DEROUANE, E. G. J., Chemistry, Innovative Catalysis
DONALD, I., Psychology
DUNBAR, R. I. M., Psychology
EDWARDS, C., Biological Sciences
EDWARDS, S. W., Biological Sciences
ELLIOTT, T. J., Geology
FISHER, M. D., Computer Science
FLINT, S. S., Earth Sciences
GIBLIN, P., Mathematical Sciences
GORYUNOV, W., Mathematical Sciences
HEATON, B. T., Inorganic Chemistry
HETHERINGTON, M. M., Psychology
HOLLOWAY, S., Chemical Physics
IRVING, A. C., Mathematical Sciences
JONES, A. C., Chemistry
KEMP, S. J., Biological Sciences
KUSZNIR, N. J., Geophysics
MARRS, R. H., Applied Plant Biology
MAYES, A. R., Psychology
MCCARTHY, A. J., Biological Sciences
MCLENNAN, A. G., Biological Sciences
MICHAEL, C., Theoretical Physics
MORTON, H. R., Mathematical Sciences
MOSS, B., Botany
MOVCHAN, A., Mathematical Sciences
MUELLER, M. M., Psychology
NIKULIN, W., Mathematical Sciences
NORTON, T. A., Marine Biology
PARKER, G. A., Zoology
RAVAL, R., Chemistry
REES, H. H., Biological Sciences
REES, S. M., Mathematical Sciences
RITCHIE, D. A., Genetics
ROBERTS, S. M., Organic Chemistry
ROSSEINSKY, M. J., Chemistry
RUDLAND, P. S., Biochemistry
SAUNDERS, J. R., Genetics and Microbiology
SCHIFFRIN, D. J., Physical Chemistry
SHAW, J., Earth Sciences
STIRLING, W. G., Experimental Physics
TOMSETT, A. B., Biological Sciences
VAN DEN BERG, C. M. G., Earth Sciences
VAN DER HOEK, W., Computer Science
VEDRINE, J., Chemistry
WEIGHTMAN, P., Physics
WOOLDRIDGE, M. J., Computer Science

Faculty of Social and Environmental Studies:

ARORA, A., Law
BARON, J. S., Management
BATEY, P. W. J., Town and Regional Planning
CORNER, J., Politics and Communication Studies
DEARING, J. A., Geography
DELANTY, G., Sociology
DRUMMOND, H., Decision Sciences
DUNSTER, D., Architecture
ELLIOTT, D., Management
GIBBS, B. M., Acoustics
GILLESPIE, R., Politics
GOULD, W. T. S., Geography
HADRI, K., Economics and Accounting
HARVEY, A. M., Geography
HILL, J. J., Management
HOJMAN, D. E., Economics and Accounting
JONES, C., Social Policy and Social Work
JONES, M. A., Law
KAVANAGH, D. A., Politics and Communication Studies

KEHOE, D. F., Management
LYON, C. M., Common Law
MACLEOD, J. K., Law
MCCABE, B. P. M., Economics
MCGOLDRICK, D., Law
MUNCK, R. P., Sociology
NEUWAHL, N. A. E. M., European Law
OLDHAM, D. J., Building Engineering
PEPPER, S. M., Architecture and Building Engineering
ROBERTS, K., Sociology
RUSSELL, T., Centre for Research into Primary Science and Technology
SADLER, D., Geography
SAPSFORD, D. R., Economics and Accounting
SMITH, D., Management
SMITHERS, A. G., Education
TAYLOR, P. J., Economics and Accounting
WARBURTON, J., Law
WONG, Y. L. C., Civic Design
WOODS, R. I., Geography

Faculty of Veterinary Science:

BENNETT, M., Veterinary Pathology
BEYNON, R. J., Veterinary Pre-Clinical Science
CARTER, S. D., Veterinary Science
DOBSON, H., Veterinary Reproduction
EDWARDS, G. B., Equine Studies
GASKELL, C. J., Small Animal Studies
GASKELL, R. M., Veterinary Pathology
HURST, J. L., Animal Science
INNES, J. F., Veterinary Clinical Science and Animal Husbandry
MORGAN, K. L., Epidemiology
SHIRAZI-BEECHEY, S. P., Veterinary Pre-Clinical Science

UNIVERSITY OF LONDON

Senate House, Malet St, London, WC1E 7HU

Telephone: (20) 7862-8000
Fax: (20) 7862-8358
E-mail: enquiries@london.ac.uk
Internet: www.london.ac.uk

Founded 1836, as examining body, became also a teaching body in 1898

Chancellor: HRH THE PRINCESS ROYAL
Vice-Chancellor: Prof. GEOFFREY CROSSICK
Deputy Vice-Chancellor: Prof PAUL WEBLEY
Dir of Admin.: CATHERINE SWARBRICK
Academic Registrar: GILLIAN ROBERTS
Library: see under Libraries and Archives
Number of teachers: 7,881
Number of students: 170,000 incl. students of distance learning.

COLLEGES OF THE UNIVERSITY

Birkbeck, University of London

Malet St, London, WC1E 7HX

Telephone: (20) 7631-6000
Fax: (20) 7631-6270
Internet: www.bbk.ac.uk

Founded 1823, Charter of Incorporation 1926
State control
Academic year: September to July

Master: Prof. DAVID S. LATCHMAN
Vice-Master: Prof. PHILIP DEWE
Dean of College: Dr KATE MACKENZIE DAVEY
Sec.: KEITH HARRISON
Registrar: DEAN PATEMAN
Librarian: PHILIP PAYNE

Library of 364,102 vols
Number of teachers: 927 (incl. 575 part-time)
Number of students: 18,000

DEANS

School of Arts: Prof. HILARY FRASER
School of Business, Economics and Informatics: Prof. PHILIP POWELL
School of Law: Prof. PATRICIA TUITT
School of Science: Prof. NICHOLAS KEEP

School of Social Sciences, History and Philosophy: Prof. MIRIAM ZUKAS

PROFESSORS

ANNETTE, J., Citizenship and Lifelong Learning
ARCHIBUGI, D., Innovation, Governance and Public Policy
BARNES, J., Psychology
BARNES, P., Applied Crystallography
BELSKY, J., Psychology
BOURKE, J., History
BRAH, A., Sociology
BRAKE, L., Literature and Print Culture
BRINER, R., Organizational Psychology
BRUMMELHUIS, R., Mathematical Finance
CHRISTIE, I., Film and Media History
CLARK, S., Renaissance Literature
CONNOR, S., Modern Literature and Theory
COOLE, D., Political and Social Theory
COOMBES, A., Material and Visual Culture
DAVIES, D., Chemistry
DENCH, E., Ancient History
DEWE, P., Organizational Behaviour
DICKENSON, D., Medical Ethics and Humanities
DOUZINAS, C., Law
DOWNES, H., Geochemistry
DRIFFILL, J., Economics
EDWARDS, C., Ancient History and Culture
EIMER, M., Psychology
FIGES, O., History
FITZPATRICK, P., Law
FRASER, H., Nineteenth-century Studies
FROSH, S., Psychology
GOLDSWORTHY, G. J., Biology
HEALY, T., Renaissance Studies
HILEY, B., Physics
HORNSBY, J., Philosophy
HOUNSELL, E., Biological Chemistry
HOWELLS, R., French
HUNTER, M., History
JAMES, S., Philosophy
JENKINS, R., Political Science
JOHNSON, M. H., Psychology
JONES, R. C., Creative Writing
KELLY, J., Industrial Relations
LEVENE, M., Computer Science
LOVENDUSKI, J., Politics
MACMILLAN, F., Law
MAYBANK, S., Computer Science
MCAUSLAN, P., Law
MELHUISH, E., Psychology
MIRKIN, B., Computer Science
MORAN, L., Law
MOSS, D., Biomolecular Structure
MULCAHY, L., Law and Society
MÜLLER, H., Cognitive Psychology
MULVEY, L., Film Studies
NEAD, L., History of Art
OUGHTON, C., Management
PICK, D., History
POLLARD, P., French
POULOVASSILIS, A., Computer Science
PRICE, G. D., Mineral Physics
PSARADAKIS, Z., Econometrics
ROWE, W., Poetics
SAIBIL, H., Structural Biology
SEGAL, L., Psychology and Gender Studies
SHEPHERD, J., Geography
SIBERT, A., Economics
SINGH, R., Politics
SMITH, R., Applied Economics
SNOWER, D. J., Economics
SOLA, M., Economics
THOMPSON, W., Political Economy
USHER, M., Psychology
WAKSMAN, G., Structural Molecular Biology
WALLACE, B., Crystallography
WELLS, D. A., German

Courtauld Institute of Art

Somerset House, Strand, London, WC2R 0RN

Telephone: (20) 7848-2777

Fax: (20) 7848-2410
E-mail: ugadmissions@courtauld.ac.uk
Internet: www.courtauld.ac.uk
Founded 1932, became an ind. college of the
Univ. of London 2002
Academic year: September to July
Dir: Dr DEBORAH SWALLOW
Dean and Deputy Dir: Prof. DAVID SOLKIN
Sec. and Registrar: MICHAEL ARTHUR
Academic Registrar: Dr GARETH MORGAN
Number of teachers: 29
Number of students: 381 (329 full-time, 52
part-time)
Publication: *Journal of the Warburg and
Courtauld Institutes* (1 a year)

PROFESSORS

CORMACK, R., History of Art
CROSSLEY, P., History of Art
CUNO, J., History of Art
GREEN, C., History of Art
HOUSE, J., History of Art
LOWDEN, J., History of Art
RIBEIRO, A., History of Dress
RUBIN, P., History of Art
SOLKIN, D., History of Art

Goldsmiths, University of London

New Cross, London, SE14 6NW
Telephone: (20) 7919-7171
Fax: (20) 7919-7975
E-mail: ext-comms@gold.ac.uk
Internet: www.gold.ac.uk
Founded 1891
Academic year: September to June
Warden: PATRICK LOUGHREY
Deputy Warden for Academic Devt: Prof.
SIMON MCVEIGH
Pro-Warden for Research and Enterprise:
Prof. JANE POWELL
Pro-Warden of Students and Learning Devt
(vacant)
Registrar and Sec.: LIZ BROMLEY
Library of 221,000 vols
Number of teachers: 396 and 319 visiting
tutors and 169 assoc. tutors
Number of students: 9,609 (7,823 full-time,
1,786 part-time)
Publications: *African Affairs* (historical and
cultural studies), *African Identities, Death
and Dying* (sociological), *Economy and
Society* (4 a year), *Goldsmiths Journal of
Education* (2 a year), *History Workshop
Journal* (4 a year), *Journal of Buddhist
Ethics* (historical and cultural studies),
Scriblerian (English language and litera-
ture, 2 a year), *Social Identities, Street
Signs* (urban and community research, 2 a
year), *Third Text* (historical and cultural
studies)

PROFESSORS

ADKINS, L., Sociology
AHMED, S., Media and Communications
ALEXANDER, S., History
ATKINSON, D., Educational Studies
BACK, L., Sociology
BALDICK, C., English and Comparative Lit-
erature
BELL, V., Sociology
BERRY, C., Media and Communications
BESSON, J., Anthropology
BLAMIRES, A., English and Comparative Lit-
erature
BOND, F., Psychology
BOWERS, J., Design
CAPLAN, P., Anthropology
CARR, H., English and Comparative Litera-
ture
CASSIDY, R., Anthropology
CAYGILL, H., History
CHITTY, C., Educational Studies

COHEN, J., English and Comparative Litera-
ture
COULDRY, N., Media and Communications
CURRAN, J. P. P., Media and Communications
DAVIDOFF, J., Psychology
DAY, S., Anthropology
DE VILLE, N., Visual Arts
D'INVERNO, M., Computing
DOWNIE, A., English and Comparative Lit-
erature
DRYDEN, W., Professional and Community
Education
DUNWOODIE, P., English and Comparative
Literature
DUTTMAN, A., Visual Cultures
DUTTON, M., Politics
FLETCHER, C., Psychology
FOL LEYMARIE, F., Computing
FRENCH, C., Psychology
GAVER, B., Design
GEORGE, R., Educational Studies
GORDON, R., Drama
GREGORY, E., Educational Studies
GRUZELIER, J., Psychology
HEMSWORTH, G., Art
HEWITT, R., Sociology
HUTNYK, J., Cultural Studies
IVASHKIN, A., Music
JEFFERIES, J., Computing
JONES, K., Educational Studies
KEOWN, D., History
KIMBELL, R. A., Design
KNOWLES, C., Sociology
LASH, S., Cultural Studies
LATHAM, W., Computing
LOMAX, Y., Art
LURY, C., Sociology
MARGOLIES, D., English and Comparative
Studies
MAYO, M., Professional and Community Edu-
cation
MCDONALD, R., English and Comparative
Literature
MCROBBIE, A., Media and Communications
MCVEIGH, S., Music
MICHAEL, M., Sociology
MOORE-GILBERT, B., English and Compara-
tive Literature
MORLEY, D., Media and Communications
MORRIS, B., Anthropology
MORRISON, B., English and Comparative Lit-
erature
NEGUS, K., Music
NEWMAN, M., Art
NUGENT, S., Anthropology
OHTANI, N., Design
PAECHTER, C., Educational Studies
PEARSON, G., Professional and Community
Education
PICKERING, A., Psychology
PLATT, L., Professional and Community Edu-
cation
POWELL, J., Psychology
PRING, L., Psychology
PROPHET, J. A., Computing
RIFKIN, A., Art
ROBINS, K., Media and Communications
ROGOFF, I., Visual Cultures
SEIDLER, V., Sociology
SETH, S., Politics
SHEVTSOVA, M., Drama
SHOBEN, A., Computing
SIMONE, A. M., Sociology
SKEGGS, B., Sociology
SMITH, P. K., Psychology
STABLES, K., Design
STIEGLER, B., Cultural Studies
VALENTINE, T., Psychology
VELMANS, M., Psychology
VERGES, F, Cultural Studies
WALLER, D., Professional and Community
Education
WIGGINS, G., Computing
WOOD, J., Design
ZIMMER, R., Computing

Heythrop College

Univ. of London, Kensington Sq., London,
W8 5HN
Telephone: (20) 7795-6600
Fax: (20) 7795-4200
E-mail: enquiries@heythrop.ac.uk
Internet: www.heythrop.ac.uk
Founded 1614, became part of Univ. of
London 1970
Academic year: September to June
Specialist courses in theology and philoso-
phy; receives HEFCE grant
Prin.: Rev. Dr JOHN MCDADE SJ
Academic Registrar: ANNABEL CLARKSON
Asst Registrar: ANTONY CHARLES
Library of 180,000 vols
Number of teachers: 42
Number of students: 920

Publications: *Heythrop Journal* (4 a year),
*Heythrop Studies in Contemporary Phil-
osophy, Religion and Theology* (2 a year).

Imperial College London

South Kensington Campus, London, SW7
2AZ
Telephone: (20) 7589-5111
Fax: (20) 7584-7596
E-mail: info@imperial.ac.uk
Internet: www.imperial.ac.uk
Founded 1907 by fed. of Royal College of
Science, Royal School of Mines, and City
and Guilds College, (1988) St Mary's Hos-
pital Medical School, (1995) National
Heart and Lung Institute, (1997) Charing
Cross and Westminster Medical School and
Royal Postgraduate Medical School, and
(2000) Wye College
Academic year: October to June
Rector: Sir KEITH O'NIONS
Deputy Rector: Prof. STEPHEN RICHARDSON
Pro-Rector for Education and Academic Ser-
vices: Prof. JULIA BUCKINGHAM
Pro-Rector for Enterprise: EDWARD ASTLE
Pro-Rector for Research: Prof. DONAL BRAD-
LEY
Pro-Rector for Int. Affairs: Prof. SIMON
BUCKLE
College Sec.: Dr RODNEY EASTWOOD
Academic Registrar: NIGEL WHEATLEY
Dir of Library Services: DEBORAH SHORLEY
Number of teachers: 1,240
Number of students: 13,964

PRINCIPALS

Business School: Prof. DAVID BEGG
Faculty of Engineering: Prof. JEFF MAGEE
Faculty of Medicine: Prof. ANTHONY NEWMAN
TAYLOR
Faculty of Natural Sciences: MAGGIE DALL-
MAN
Graduate School: Prof. ANDREW GEORGE (Dir)

PROFESSORS

ADCOCK, I. M., Respiratory Cell and Molecu-
lar Biology
ALBANESE, C., Mathematical Finance
ALBERTI, J. G. M. M., Metabolic Medicine
ALIABADI, F. M. H., Aerostructures
ALLDAY, M. J., Virology
ALLEN-MERSH, T. G., Gastrointestinal Sur-
gery
ALTON, E. W. F. W., Gene Therapy
AMIS, A. A., Orthopaedic Biomechanics
ANAND, P., Clinical Neurology
ANDERSON, R. M., Infectious Disease Epide-
mology
APSIMON, H. M., Air Pollution Studies
ARMSTRONG, A., Organic Chemistry
ARST, H. N., Microbial Genetics
ATKINSON, A., Materials Chemistry
ATKINSON, C., Applied Mathematics
BALDING, D. J., Statistical Genetics
BALOGH, A., Space Physics

BANGHAM, C., Immunology
BARBER, J., Biochemistry
BARLOW, J. G., Technology and Innovation Management
BARNES, P. J., Thoracic Medicine
BARNES, T. R. E., Clinical Psychiatry
BARNHAM, K. W. J., Physics
BARRETT, A. G. M., Organic Chemistry
BARRETT, J. W., Numerical Analysis
BEDDINGTON, J. R., Applied Population Biology
BEGG, D. K. H., Economics
BELL, A. R., Plasma Physics
BELL, J. N. B., Environmental Pollution
BELL, M. G. H., Transport Operations
BELVISI, M., Respiratory Pharmacology
BENNETT, P. R., Obstetrics and Gynaecology
BLACKMOND, D. G., Catalysis
BLANE, D., Medical Sociology
BLOMLEY, M. J., Radiology
BLOOM, S. R., Metabolic Medicine
BLUNT, M. J., Petroleum Engineering
BOOBIS, A. R., Biochemical Pharmacology
BOSANQUET, N. F. G., Health Policy
BOTTO, M., Rheumatology
BRADLEY, D. D. C., Experimental Solid State Physics
BRANDON, N. P., Sustainable Development in Energy
BRENNAN, F. M., Immunopathology
BRIDSON, M. R., Pure Mathematics
BRIGGS, D. J., Public Health
BRINSON, C. E. J., German Studies
BRISCOE, B. J., Interface Engineering
BRONSTEIN, A. M., Clinical Neurology
BROOKS, D. J., Neurology
BROSENS, J. J., Reproductive Sciences
BUCHANAN, D. L., Mining Geology
BUCK, K. W., Plant and Fungal Virology
BUCK, M., Molecular Microbiology
BUCKINGHAM, J. C., Pharmacology
BUENFELD, N. R., Concrete Structures
BULPITT, C. J., Geriatric Medicine
BUSH, A., Paediatric Respirology
BUTLER, D., Water Engineering
CALLAN, M. F. C., Immunology and Rheumatology
CARGILL, P. J., Physics
CASH, J. R., Numerical Analysis
CASS, A. E. G., Chemical Biology
CAWLEY, P., Mechanical Engineering
CHADWICK, D., Applied Catalysis
CHATURVEDI, N., General Practice
CHEN, Y., Mathematical Physics
CHEUNG, P., Digital Systems
CHRISTOFIDES, N., Operational Research
CHUNG, K. F., Respiratory Medicine
CLARK, K. L., Computational Logic
COLLINS, P., Clinical Cardiology
CONNERADE, J.-P., Atomic and Molecular Physics
CONSTANTINIDES, A. G., Signal Processing
CONWAY, G. R., Int. Devt
COOK, H. T., Renal Pathology
COOKSON, W. O. C., Respiratory Genetics
COOMBES, R. C. D. S., Medical Oncology
COUCHMAN, J. R., Cell Biology
COUTELLE, C. C., Gene Therapy
COWBURN, R. P., Nanotechnology
COWIE, M. R., Cardiology
COWLEY, S. R., Plasma Physics
CRAIG, D. D. C., Organic Synthesis
CRASTER, R. V., Applied Mathematics
CRAWLEY, M. J., Community Ecology
CRISANTI, A., Molecular Parasitology
CROWDER, M. J., Stochastic Modelling
CUMPSTY, N. A., Mechanical Engineering
CUTHBERTSON, K., Finance
DAINTY, J. C., Applied Optics
DALLMAN, M. J., Immunology
DAMZEN, M. J., Experimental Laser Physics
DARLINGTON, J., Programming Methodology
DARZI, A., Minimal Access Surgery
DAVIS, M. H. A., Mathematics
DE BELLEROCHE, J. S., Neurochemistry
DE MELLO, A. J., Chemical Nanosciences

DELL, A., Carbohydrate Biochemistry
DERWENT, R. G., Atmospheric Chemistry
DJAMGOZ, M. B. A., Neurobiology
DOKAL, I. S., Haematology
DONALDSON, S. K., Pure Mathematics
DONNELLY, C., Statistical Epidemiology
DORNAN, P. J., Experimental Particle Physics
DOUGHERTY, M. K., Space Physics
DREW, J. E., Astrophysics
DRIVER, C., Economics
DUGWELL, D. R., Chemical Engineering
DURHAM, S. R., Allergy and Clinical Immunology
DURUCAN, S., Mining and Environmental Engineering
EDALAT, A., Computer Science and Mathematics
EDGERTON, D. E. H., History of Science, Technology and Medicine
EDWARDS, A. D., Neonatology
ELGIN, J. N., Applied Mathematics
ELLAWAY, P. H., Physiology
ELLIOTT, P., Epidemiology and Public Health Medicine
EVANS, A. W., Risk Management
EVANS, J., Tropical Forestry
EWINS, D. J., Vibration Engineering
FARRELL, P. J., Tumour Virology
FELDMAN, M., Cellular Immunology
FENNER, R. T., Engineering Computation
FENWICK, A., Tropical Parasitology
FERENCZI, M. J., Physiological Sciences
FERGUSON, N. M., Mathematical Biology
FIRMIN, D., Biomedical Imaging
FIRTH, J. A., Anatomy
FISK, D. J., Engineering for Sustainable Development
FISK, N. M., Obstetrics and Gynaecology
FOSTER, R. G., Molecular Neurology
FOULKES, W. M. C., Physics
FOXWELL, B. M., Immune Cell Signalling
FRANKEL, G., Molecular Pathenogenesis
FRANKS, N. P., Biophysics
FRANKS, S., Reproductive Endocrinology
FRASER, R. W., Agricultural Economics
FREEMONT, P. S., Structural Biology
FRENCH, P. M. W., Physics
FRIEDLAND, J. S., Infectious Diseases and Microbiology
FROGUEL, P., Genomic Medicine
GABRA, H., Medical Oncology
GABRIEL, J., Organizational Theory
GANN, D. M., Technology and Innovation Management, Built Environment
GARNETT, G., Microparasite Epidemiology
GARRALDA HUALDE, M. E., Child and Adolescent Psychiatry
GAUNTLETT, J. P., Theoretical Physics
GELENBE, S. E., Computer and Communication Networks
GEORGE, A., Molecular Immunology
GHATEI, M., Peptide Endocrinology
GHOSH, S., Gastroenterology
GIBBON, J. D., Applied Mathematics
GIBSON, S. E., Chemistry
GIBSON, V. C., Organic Chemistry
GILKS, C. F., International Health
GILLON, R., Medical Ethics
GLAISTER, S., Transport and Infrastructure
GLOVER, V. A., Perinatal Psychobiology
GODFRAY, H. C. J., Evolutionary Biology
GOGOLIN, A. O., Mathematical Physics
GORDON, M. Y. A., Experimental Haematology
GOSMAN, A. D., Computational Fluid Dynamics
GOTCH, F. M., Immunology
GRAEBER, M., Neuroscience
GRAHAM, J. M. R., Unsteady Aerodynamics
GRAHAM, N. J. D., Environmental Engineering
GRASBY, P. M., Psychiatry
GREENHALGH, R. M., Surgery
GRIFFITHS, D. S., Human Resource Management
GRIGORYAN, A., Pure Mathematics

GRIMES, R. W., Materials Science
GRIMM, S. W., Toxicology
GRINGARTEN, A., Petroleum Engineering
GRUZELIER, J. G., Psychology
GUO, Y., Computing Science
HABIB, N. A., Hepto-biliary Surgery
HAIGH, J. D., Atmospheric Physics
HAJNAL, J. V., Imaging Science
HALL, G., Physics
HALL, P., Applied Mathematics
HALL, S. G. F., Economics
HALLIWELL, J. J., Theoretical Physics
HAND, D. J., Statistics
HANKINS, M. W., Visual Neuroscience
HARDIE, R. J., Insect Physiology
HARDING, S., Cardiac Pharmacology
HARRIES, J. E., Earth Observation
HARRISON, N., Chemistry
HARRISON, P. G., Computing Science
HASKARD, D. O., Cardiovascular Medicine
HASSELL, M. P., Insect Ecology
HENCH, L. L., Ceramic Materials
HENRY, J. A., Accident and Emergency Medicine
HIGGINS, C. F., Clinical Sciences
HIGGINS, J. S., Polymer Science
HILL, B., Policy Analysis
HILLIER, R., Compressible Flow
HINDS, E. A., Quantum Optics
HODKINSON, I., Logic and Computation
HODSON, M. E., Respiratory Medicine
HOLDEN, D. W., Molecular Microbiology
HOLM, D. D., Applied Mathematics
HOLMES, A. B., Organic and Polymer Chemistry
HOPKINS, C. R., Biochemistry
HUDSON, J. A., Rock Mechanics
HUGHES, A. D., Clinical Pharmacology
HUGHES, S. F. R., Orthopaedic Surgery
HUHTANIEMI, I. T., Reproductive Biology
HULL, C., Theoretical Physics
IMREGUN, M., Computational Engineering Dynamics
ISHAM, C. J., Theoretical Physics
IVANOV, A. A., Pure Mathematics
IWATA, C. J., Biochemistry
JACKSON, G., Chemical Physics
JAMES, G. D., Pure Mathematics
JARDINE, R. J., Geomechanics
JARVELIN, M., Lifecourse Epidemiology
JEGER, M., Agroecology
JENSEN, H. J., Mathematics
JOHNSON, H. D., Petroleum Geology
JOHNSTON, D. G., Clinical Endocrinology
JOHNSTON, S. L., Respiratory Medicine
JONES, T. S., Physical Chemistry
JONES, W. G., High Energy Physics
JONES, W. P., Combustion
KANDIYOTI, R., Chemical Engineering
KELSALL, G. H., Electrochemical Engineering
KENNARD, C., Clinical Neurology
KILNER, J. A., Materials Science
KING, P. R., Petroleum Engineering
KINLOCH, A. J., Adhesion
KITNEY, R. I., Biomedical Systems Engineering
KLUG, D., Chemical Biophysics
KLUMPES, P. J. M., Accounting
KNIGHT, P. L., Quantum Optics
KORNYSHEV, A. A., Chemical Physics
KRAMER, J., Distributed Computing
KRUSHELNICK, K. M., Plasma Physics
KYDD, J., Agricultural Economics and Business Management
LALANI, E. M. A., Molecular and Cell Pathology
LANE, D. A., Molecular Haematology
LAWRENCE, C., Fluid Mechanics
LAYCOCK, J. F., Endocrine Physiology
LEATHERBARROW, R., Chemical Biology
LESCHZINER, R., Computational Aerodynamics
LESTER, J. N., Water Technology
LEUNG, K. K., Internet Technology
LEVER, M. J., Physiological Mechanics
LEVIN, M., Paediatrics

LIEBECK, M. W., Pure Mathematics
LIMEBEER, D. J. N., Control Engineering
LINDSTEDT, R. P., Thermofluids
LIVINGSTON, A. G., Chemical Engineering
LLOYD SMITH, D., Structural Mechanics
LOMAX, M. A., Animal Sciences
LONG, K. R., Experimental Particle Physics
LUCKHAM, P. F., Particle Technology
LUK, W. W.-C., Computer Engineering
MACCHIETTO, S., Process Systems Engineering
MACCULLOCH, R. J., Economics
MACDERMOT, J., Clinical Pharmacology
MACKINNON, A., Theoretical Solid State Physics
MADEN, A., Psychiatry
MAGEE, A. I., Membrane Biology
MAGEE, J. N., Computing Science
Sir MAINI, R. N., Rheumatology
MAJEED, F. A., Primary Healthcare and General Practice
MAMDANI, E. H., Telecommunications Strategy and Services
MANSFIELD, J., Biology
MARANGOS, J. J., Laser Physics
MAROS, I., Computational Methods of Operations Research
MARSTON, S. B., Cardiovascular Biochemistry
MATHIAS, C. J., Neurovascular Medicine
MATTHEWS, S. J., Chemical and Structural Biology
MAXWELL, P. H., Nephrology
MAZE, M., Anaesthetics
MCCLURE, M. O., Retrovirology
MEADE, N., Quantitative Finance
MEIKLE, W. P. S., Astrophysics
MILLER, A., Organic Chemistry and Structural Biology
MITCHELL, J., Pharmacology in Critical Care
MOORE, G. E., Molecular Genetics
MUGGLETON, S. H., Bioinformatics
MUMFORD, J., Natural Resource Management
MUNTONI, F., Paediatric Neurology
NAGASE, H., Rheumatology
NETHERCOT, D. A., Civil Engineering
NEW, G. H. C., Non-linear Optics
NICHOLSON, J. K., Biological Chemistry
NORTHOVER, J. M. A., Intestinal Surgery
OPENSHAW, P. J. M., Experimental Medicine
OWENS, I., Evolutionary Ecology
PANTELIDES, C. C., Chemical Engineering
PARKER, K. H., Physiological Fluid
PARKER, M. G., Obstetrics and Gynaecology
PARRY, A. O., Statistical Physics
PARRY, G., Applied Physics
PARRY, S., Radiochemistry
PARTRIDGE, M. R., Respiratory Medicine
PASVOL, G., Infection and Tropical Medicine
PAVLOVIC, M., Structural Engineering and Mechanics
PENDRY, J. B., Theoretical Solid-state Physics
PENNELL, D. J., Cardiology
PEPPER, J., Cardiothoracic Surgery
PERRAUDIN, W. R. M., Finance
PETERS, N. S., Cardiac Electrophysiology
PHILLIPS, C. C., Experimental Solid-state Physics
PHILLIPS, D., Physical Chemistry
PISTIKOPOULOS, E. N., Chemical Engineering
PLANT, J. A., Applied Geochemistry
PLAYFORD, R., Gastroenterology
PLENIO, M. B., Quantum Physics
POLAK, J. M., Endocrine Pathology
POTTS, D. M., Analytical Soil Mechanics
POULTER, N. R., Preventative Cardiovascular Medicine
PRABHU, J. C., Marketing
PUSEY, C. D., Renal Medicine
QUIRKE, N., Physical Chemistry
RAWLINGS, R. D., Materials Science
REED, M. J., Steroid Biochemistry
REGAN, L., Obstetrics and Gynaecology
REYNOLDS, R., Cellular Neurobiology
RICHARDS, B., Computing Science
RICHARDSON, S., Public Health
RICHARDSON, S. M., Chemical Engineering

RITTER, M. A., Immunology
RIVERS, R. J., Theoretical Physics
ROBB, M. A., Chemistry
ROBERTS, I., Paediatrics Haematology
ROSE, M. L., Transport Immunology
ROWAN-ROBINSON, G. M., Astrophysics
RUDD, C. E., Haematology
RUSSELL, N. J., Biology
RUSTEM, B., Computational Methods in Operations
RZEPA, H. S., Computational Fluid Dynamics
SAKLATVALA, J., Experimental Pathology
SANDERSON, D. J., Geology
SCHROTER, R. C., Biological Mechanics
SCHWARTZ, S. J., Space Physics
SCOTT, J., Medicine
SCREATON, G. R., Medicine
SEABRA, M. C., Molecular Genetics
SECKL, M., Molecular Cancer Medicine
SEDDON, J. M., Physical Chemistry
SEFTON, J. A., Economics
SELKIRK, M. E., Biochemical Parasitology
SENSKY, J., Applied Mathematics
SERGOT, M. J., Computational Logic
SEVER, P. S., Clinical Pharmacology and Therapeutics
SEVERS, N. J., Cell Biology
SHAH, N., Process Systems Engineering
SHAUNAK, S., Infectious Diseases
SHAW, R. J., Thoracic Medicine
SHERIDAN, D. J., Clinical Cardiology
SINDEN, R. E., Parasite Cell Biology
SKOROBOGATOV, A. N., Pure Mathematics
SLOMAN, M. S., Distributed Systems Management
SMITH, G. L., Experimental Pathology
SMITH, R. A., Mechanical Engineering
SMITH, R. W., Physics
SOBEY, R. J., Fluid Mechanics
SOUTHWOOD, D. J., Physics
SPIKES, H. A., Lubrication
SPRATT, B. G., Molecular Microbiology
SQUIRE, J. M., Structural Biophysics
STAMP, G. W. M., Histopathology
STARK, J., Applied Mathematics
STEER, P. J., Obstetrics and Gynaecology
STELLE, K. S., Physics
STERNBERG, M. J. E., Structural Bioinformatics
STUCKEY, D. C., Biochemical Engineering
SUGDEN, P. H., Cellular Biochemistry
SUMMERFIELD, J. A., Experimental Medicine
SUMNER, T. J., Experimental Astrophysics
SUTTON, A. P., Nanotechnology
SWAN, C., Hydrodynamics
SYMS, R. R., Microsystems
SZYMANSKI, S. A., Economics
TAYLOR, A., Neurophysiology
TAYLOR, A. M. K. P., Thermofluids
TAYLOR, J. R., Ultrafast Physics and Technology
TAYLOR, K. M., Cardiac Surgery
TEMPLER, R., Biophysical Chemistry
THIRTLE, C. G., Agricultural Economics
THOMAS, H. C., Medicine
THOMPSON, R. C., Experimental Physics
TOUMAZOU, C., Analogue Circuit Design
TRUSLER, J. P. M., Thermophysics
TSEYTLIN, A., Theoretical Physics
TYRER, P. J., Community Psychiatry
UNDERWOOD, S. R., Cardiac Imaging
van HEEL, M., Structural Biology
VASSILICOS, C., Fluid Mechanics
VAZ DE MELO, J., Molecular Haematology
VENABLES, P. J., Viral Immunorheumatology
VINEIS, P., Environmental Epidemiology
VINTER, R. B., Control Theory
VIRDEE, T. S., Physics
VVEDENSKY, D., Theoretical Solid-State Physics
WAAGE, J. K., Applied Ecology
WALDEN, A. T., Statistics
WANG, Y., Reservoir Geophysics
WARK, D. L., High Energy Physics
WARNER, M. R., Geophysics
WARWICK, A. C., History of Science

WAXMAN, J., Medical Oncology
WEBER, J. N., Genito-urinary Medicine and Communicable Diseases
WEBSDALE, D. M., Physics
WEBSTER, J. P. G., Agricultural Business Management
WHEATER, H. S., Hydrology
WILKINS, M. R., Clinical Pharmacology
WILLIAMS, A. J., Membrane Biophysics
WILLIAMS, T. J., Applied Pharmacology
WINSTON, R. M., Fertility Studies
WISE, C. M., Civil Engineering Design
WISE, R. J. S., Neurology
WOOD, D. A., Clinical Epidemiology
WOODS, J. D., Oceanography
WRIGHT, D. J., Pest Management
YANG, G. Z., Medical Image Computing
YOUNG, D. B., Medical Microbiology
ZEGARLINSKI, B., Pure Mathematics

Institute of Education

20 Bedford Way, London, WC1H 0AL
Telephone: (20) 7612-6000
Fax: (20) 7612-6126
E-mail: info@ioe.ac.uk
Internet: www.ioe.ac.uk

Founded 1902 as London Day Training College, transferred to control of Univ. of London in 1932, became School of Univ. in 1987

Academic year: September to June

Dir: Prof. CHRIS HUSBANDS
Sec: BRYN MORRIS
Academic Registrar: Dr LORETO LOUGHRAN
Librarian: ANNE PETERS

Library of 270,000 vols, 1,160 periodicals
Number of teachers: 176
Number of students: 4,424 (1,372 full-time, 3,052 part-time)

Publication: *London Review of Education* (3 a year)

PROFESSORS

AGGLETON, P., Education
ALDERSON, P., Childhood Studies
ALDRICH, R., History of Education
BALL, S., Sociology of Education
BARNETT, R., Higher Education
BARTON, L., Inclusive Education
BLATCHFORD, P., Education and Psychology
BRANNEN, J., Sociology of the Family
BRIGHOUSE, H., Philosophy of Education
BUCKINGHAM, D., Education
BYNNER, J., Education
CAMERON, D., Languages
DAVID, N., Educational Technology
DOCKRELL, J., Psychology and Special Needs
DOLTON, P., Education
ELBOURNE, D., Evidence-informed Policy and Practice
EVANS, K., Education (Lifelong Learning)
GILLBORN, D., Education
GOLDSTEIN, H., Statistical Methods
GORDON, P., History of Education
GREEN, A., Education
GUNDARA, J., Education
HALPIN, D., Education
HIRST, P., Education
HOYLES, C. M., Mathematics Education
JOSHI, H., Education
KENT, A., Geography Education
KRESS, G., English
LAWTON, D., Education
LEONARD, D., Sociology of Education and Gender
LEVACIC, R., Economics and Finance of Education
LITTLE, A., Education with spec. reference to Developing Countries
LUNT, I., Educational Psychology
MACGILCHRIST, B., Education
MAYALL, B., Childhood Studies
MOSS, P., Early Childhood Provision
NOSS, R., Mathematics Education

OAKLEY, A. R., Sociology and Social Policy
POWER, S., Education
REISS, M., Science Education
ST JAMES ROBERTS, I., Child Development
SAMMONS, P., Education
SHATTOCK, M., Higher Education Management
SIRAJ-BLATCHFORD, I., Early Childhood Education
WELCH, G., Music Education
WHITE, J., Philosophy of Education
WHITTY, G. J., Sociology of Education
WOLF, A., Education

King's College London

Strand, London, WC2R 2LS

Telephone: (20) 7836-5454

Denmark Hill campus: 10 Cutcombe Rd, London, SE5 9RJ

Guy's campus: New Hunts House, London, SE1 1UL

Telephone: (20) 7848-6004

St Thomas' campus: Westminster Bridge Rd, London, SE1 7EH

Telephone: (20) 7188-7188

Waterloo campus: James Clerk Maxwell Bldg, 57 Waterloo Rd, London, SE1 8WA

E-mail: ceu@kcl.ac.uk

Internet: www.kcl.ac.uk

Founded 1829 by merger of Queen Elizabeth College and Chelsea College 1985, the Institute of Psychiatry 1997, and United Medical and Dental Schools of Guy's and St Thomas' Hospitals 1998

Academic year: September to June

Prin. and Pres.: Prof. RICK TRAINOR (acting)

Vice-Prin. for Arts and Sciences: Prof. KEITH HOGGART

Vice-Prin. for Education: Prof. EEVA LEINO-NEN

Vice-Prin. for Health: Prof. ROBERT LECHLER

Vice-Prin. for Research and Innovation: CHRIS MOTTERSHEAD

Vice-Prin. for Strategy and Devt: Prof. Sir LAWRENCE FREEDMAN

Head of Admin. and College Sec.: IAN CREAGH

Chief Information Officer and College Librarian: KAREN STANTON

Library: see Libraries and Archives

Number of teachers: 1,535

Number of students: 23,000 (incl. School of Medicine and Dentistry)

Publications: *Dispatches* (3 a year), *King's College Law Journal* (2 a year)

PROFESSORS

Guy's, King's and St Thomas' School of Biomedical Sciences (1st Fl., Henrietta Raphael House, London, SE1 1UL; tel. (20) 7848-6400; fax (20) 7848-6399; e-mail biomed.admin@kcl.ac.uk):

BERRY, M., Anatomy
BRAIN, S. D., Pharmacology
BUCKLAND-WRIGHT, J. C., Radiological Anatomy
CICLITIRA, P. J., Gastroenterology
FILE, S. E., Psychopharmacology
FRASER, L. R., Reproductive Biology
GOULD, H. G., Biophysics
HALLIWELL, B., Biochemistry
HEARSE, D. J., Cardiovascular Biochemistry
HOLDER, N. H., Anatomy
HOWELL, S. L., Physiology
JENNER, P. G., Pharmacology
JONES, G. E., Cell Biology
LITTLETON, J. M., Pharmacology
LUMSDEN, A. G. S., Developmental Neurobiology
MADEN, M., Developmental Biology
MANN, G. E., Vascular Physiology
MARSHALL, J., Ophthalmology
MCMAHON, S. B., Physiology

MCNAUGHTON, P. A., Physiology
NAFTALIN, R. J., Physiology
NEAL, M. J., Pharmacology
PAGE, C. P., Pharmacology
PATIENT, R. K., Molecular Genetics
PEARSON, J. D., Physiology
PRICE, R. G., Biochemistry
QUINN, P. J., Biochemistry
RICE-EVANS, C., Biochemistry
RITTER, J. M., Clinical Pharmacology
RUTTER, M., Psychopathology
SIMMONS, R., Biophysics
STANDRING, S. M., Applied Neurobiology
THURSTON, C. F., Microbiology
TIMBRELL, J. A., Biochemical Toxicology
WEBSTER, K., Anatomy
WILLIAMS, W. P., Environmental Science

Guy's, King's and St Thomas' School of Dentistry (Guy's Tower, Guy's Hospital, London, SE1 9RT; tel. (20) 7188-7188; fax (20) 7188-1159):

BEIGHTON, D., Oral Microbiology
CHALLACOMBE, S. J., Oral Medicine
ELEY, B. M., Periodontology
GELBIER, S., Dental Public Health
GIBBONS, D. E., Oral Health Services Research
JOHNSON, N., Dental Sciences
KIDD, E. A., Cariology
LANGDON, J., Oral and Maxillofacial Surgery
LINDEN, R., Craniofacial Biology
MCGURK, M., Oral and Maxillofacial Surgery
MEIKLE, M. C., Orthodontics
MEREDITH SMITH, M., Evolutionary Dentoskeletal Biology
PALMER, R. M., Implant Dentistry and Periodontology
PITT-FORD, T. R., Endodontology
SHARPE, P. T., Craniofacial Biology
SMITH, B. G. N., Conservative Dental Surgery
SMITH, N. J. D., Dentistry
WADE, W. G., Oral Microbiology
WATSON, R., Prosthetic Dentistry

School of Education (Franklin-Wilkins Bldg (WBW), Waterloo Rd, London, SE1 9NN; tel. (20) 7848-3183; fax (20) 7848-3182):

BROWN, M. L., Education
COX, M. J., Information Technology in Education
DUSCHL, R., Science Education
JOHNSON, D. C., Education
STREET, B. U., Language in Education
WILLIAM, D. A. P. R., Educational Assessment

School of Health and Life Sciences (Franklin-Williams Bldg, 150 Stamford St, London, SE1 9NN; e-mail health-life@kcl.ac.uk):

CAMMACK, R., Health and Life Siences
COWAN, D. A., Pharmaceutical Toxicology
COWLEY, S. A., Community Practice Development
EBRINGER, A. M. A., Immunology
FRANK, L. S., Children's Nursing Research
GEISSLER, C. A., Nutrition
HALL, D. O., Health and Life Sciences
HIDER, R. C., Pharmacy
MARRIOTT, C., Pharmacy
REDFERN, S. J., Nursing Studies
ROSS MURPHY, S. B., Life Sciences
SANDERS, T. A., Nutrition
STAINES, N. A., Immunology
TINKER, A. M., Gerontology
WHILE, A. E., Nursing Studies
WILSON-BARNETT, J., Nursing Studies

School of Humanities (Strand, London, WC2R 2LS; tel. (20) 7848-2374; fax (20) 7848-2415; e-mail humanities@kcl.ac.uk):

ADLER, J. D., German
BANNER, M. C., Moral and Social Theology
BEATON, R. M., Modern Greek
BIRTWISTLE, H., Musical Composition

BOND, B. J., War Studies
BRIDGE, C., Australian Studies
BUSH, C., American Literature
BUTT, J. W., Modern Hispanic Studies
CHABAL, P. E., Lusophone-African Studies
CLARKE, M., Defence Studies
CLARKE, P. B., History and Sociology of Religion
DANDEKER, C., Military Sociology
DEATHRIDGE, J. W., King Edward Chair of Music
DOCKRILL, M. L., Diplomatic History
DREYFUS, L., Music
FREEDMAN, L. D., War Studies
GANZ, D., Palaeography
GARNETT, J., Defence Studies
GAUNT, S. B., French Language and Literature
GILLIES, D. A., Philosophy of Science and Mathematics
GRIFFITHS, R. M., French Studies
HAMNETT, C., Human Geography
HEATH, M. J., French Literature
HELM, P., Theology and Religious Studies
HERRIN, J. E., Late Antique and Byzantine Studies
HOGGART, K., Geography
HOOK, D., Spanish Medieval Studies
IFE, B. W., Spanish and Spanish-American Studies
JORDANOVA, L., Modern History
KARSH, E., Mediterranean Studies
KNIBB, M. A., Old Testament Studies
LAPPIN, S., Linguistics
LIEU, J., New Testament Studies
MCCABE, M. M. A., Ancient Philosophy
MACEDO, H. M., Portuguese and Brazilian Studies
MACHOVER, M., Philosophy
MAYER, R. G. M., Classics
NELSON, J. L., Medieval History
NEWITT, M. D. D., History
NEWSON, L. A., Geography
NOKES, D. L., English Literature
ORMOND, L., Victorian Studies
OVERY, R. J., Modern History
PAPINEAU, D. C., Philosophy
PORTER, A. N., History
PROUDFOOT, G. R., English
ROBERTS, J. A., English Language and Medieval Literature
ROSEVEARE, H. G., History
RUSSELL, C. S. R., History
SABIN, P. A. G., Strategic Studies
SAINSBURY, R. M., Philosophy
SAVILE, A. B., Philosophy
SCHIESARO, A., Latin Language and Literature
SILK, M. S., Latin Language and Literature
SORABJI, R. R. K., Philosophy
STOKES, J., English Literature
THORNES, J. B., Geography
WAYWELL, G. B., Classics
WHITE, J. J., German

School of Law (Strand, London, WC2R 2LS; tel. (20) 7836-5454; e-mail gen.genlaw@kcl.ac.uk):

BLACKBURN, R., Law
EECKHOUT, P. O. V., Law
EWING, K. D., Law
GEARTY, C. A., Human Rights Law
GLOVER, J. C. B., Ethics (Dir)
GUEST, A. G., Law
HAYTON, D. J., Law
LOMNICKA, E. Z., Law
MARTIN, J. E., Law
MORSE, C. G., Law
MULLERSON, R., International Law
NORRIE, A. W., Criminal Law and Criminal Justice
PHILLIPS, J. C., Law
WHISH, R., Law

Guy's, King's and St Thomas' School of Medicine (1st Fl., Hodgkin Bldg, London, SE1 9RT; tel. (20) 7848-6971; fax (20) 7848-6969):

ADAM, A., Interventional Radiology
ADAMS, A. P., Anaesthetics
AMIEL, S., Diabetic Medicine
BANATVALA, J. E., Clinical Virology
BATES, G. P., Neurogenetics
BENJAMIN, I., Surgery
BOURAS, N., Psychiatry of Learning Difficulties
BRAUDE, P. R., Obstetrics and Gynaecology
BURNAND, K. G., Vascular Surgery
BURNEY, P. G. J., Public Health Medicine
COLLINS, W. P., Obstetrics and Gynaecology
CRAIG, T. K., Community Psychiatry
DAVID, A., Cognitive Neuropsychiatry
DAVIS, H. M., Child Health Psychology
DOHERTY, P., Cell Biology
EADY, R. A., Experimental Dermatopathology
EASTERBROOK, P. J., Medicine
EYKYN, S. J., Clinical Microbiology
FABRE, J., Clinical Sciences
FARZANEH, F., Molecular Medicine
FENTIMAN, I. S., Surgical Oncology
FOGELMAN, I., Nuclear Medicine
FORSLING, M. L., Neuroendocrinology
FRENCH, G. L., Medical Microbiology
GARETY, P. A., Clinical Psychology
GIANNELLI, F. B., Molecular Genetics
GLEESON, M. J., Otolaryngology
GREAVES, M. W., Dermatology
GREENOUGH, A., Clinical Respiratory Physiology
HART, I. R., Cancer Research
HAWK, J. L. M., Dermatological Photobiology
HAWKES, D. J., Computational Imaging
HAY, R. J., Cutaneous Medicine
HAYCOCK, G. B., Paediatrics
HAYDAY, A. C., Immunobiology
HEATLEY, F. W., Orthopaedic Surgery
HENDRY, B., Renal Medicine
HIGGINSON, I., Palliative Care
HIGGS, R., General Practice
HUGHES, R. A. C., Neurology
JACKSON, S., Clinical Gerontology
JONES, R. H., General Practice
KALRA, L., Stroke Medicine
KEMENY, D. M., Immunology
KOPELMAN, M. D., Neuropsychiatry
LEE, T. H., Allergy and Respiratory Medicine
LEHNER, T., Basic and Applied Immunology
LOWY, C., Endocrinology
LUCAS, S. B., Clinical Histopathology
MACDONALD, A. J. D., Old-Age Psychiatry
MAISEY, M. N., Radiological Sciences
MARTEAU, T. M., Health Psychology
MATHEW, C. G. P., Molecular Genetics
MCGREGOR, A., Medicine
MILLS, K. R., Clinical Neurophysiology
MILNER, A. D., Neonatology
MUFTI, G., Haematological Oncology
NICOLAIDES, K., Obstetrics and Gynaecology
PANAYI, G. S., Rheumatology
PEARSON, T. C., Haematology
PETERS, T. J., Clinical Biochemistry
POLKEY, C., Neurosurgery of Epilepsy
POSTON, L., Foetal Health
RAMIREZ, A. J., Liaison Psychiatry
RICHARDS, M. A., Palliative Medicine
ROBERTS, V. C., Clinical Prof.
ROBINSON, R. O., Paediatric Neurology
ROSS, E., Community Paediatrics
RUBENS, R. D., Clinical Oncology
SACKS, S. H., Nephrology
SAVIDGE, G. F., Coagulation Medicine
SCOTT, D. L., Clinical Rheumatology
SELLER, M. J., Developmental Genetics

SHEPHERD, G. W., Mental Health Rehabilitation
SIMONOFF, E. A., Child and Adolescent Psychiatry
SOLOMON, E., Human Genetics
SONKSEN, P. H., Endocrinology
SWAMINATHAN, R., Clinical Biochemistry
SWIFT, C., Health Care of the Elderly
TYNAN, M. J., Paediatric Cardiology
VIBERTI, G., Diabetes and Metabolic Medicine
WATSON, J. P., Psychiatry
WEINMAN, J. A., Psychology Applied to Medicine
WESSELEY, S., Liaison Psychiatry
WILLIAMS, D. G., Medicine

Florence Nightingale School of Nursing and Midwifery (James Clerk Maxwell Bldg, 57 Waterloo Rd, London, SE1 8WA; tel. (20) 7848-4698; e-mail nightingale@kcl.ac.uk; internet www.kcl.ac.uk/nursing):

COWLEY, S.
FRANCK, L.
HUMPHREY, C.
NORMAN, I.
RICHARDSON, A.
SANDALL, J.
WHILE, A.

School of Physical Sciences and Engineering (Strand, London, WC2R 2LS; tel. (20) 7848-2267; fax (20) 7848-2766; e-mail pse.schooloffice@kcl.ac.uk):

AGHVAMI, A. H., Telecommunications Engineering
BUSHNELL, C. J., Mathematics
CLARKSON, T. G., Electrical Engineering
COLLINS, A. T., Physics
DAVIES, A. C., Electrical Engineering
DAVIES, E. B., Mathematics
DAVIES, G., Physics
GABBAY, D. M., Logic
GAUNT, D. S., Physics
GIBSON, S. E., Chemistry
GOSPEL, H. F., Management
HALL, T. J., Optoelectronics
HEATH, C. C., Work and Orgs
HIBBERT, F., Chemistry
HOLWILL, M. E. J., Biological Physics
HOWE, P. S., Applied Mathematics
HUGHES, M. N., Chemistry
LAUGHLIN, R., Physical and Engineering Sciences
PIKE, E. R., Physical and Engineering Sciences
PRESSLEY, A. N., Mathematics
ROBB, M. A., Chemistry
ROBINSON, D. C., Mathematics
ROGERS, A. J., Electrical Engineering
SAFAROV, Y., Mathematics
SANDLER, M. B., Signal Processing
SARKAR, S., Theoretical Physics
SAUNDERS, P. T., Mathematics
STREATER, R. F., Mathematics
SWANSON, J. G., Electrical Engineering
TURNER, C. W., Electrical Engineering
UFF, J., Engineering Law
WEST, P. C., Mathematics
WINDER, R., Computer Science
YIANNESKIS, M., Fluid Mechanics

Institute of Psychiatry (De Crespigny Park, London, SE5 8AF; tel. (20) 7836-5454; e-mail spjgams@iop.kcl.ac.uk; internet www.iop.kcl.ac.uk):

ANDERTON, B. H., Neuroscience
BANERJEE, S. S., Mental Health and Ageing
BARKER, G. J., Magnetic Resonance Physics
BOLTON, D., Philosophy and Psychopathology
CHALDER, T., Psychological Medicine
CRAIG, T. K. J., Psychological Medicine
GOODMAN, R., Child and Adolescent Psychiatry
HEMSLEY, D. R., Psychology
HOTOPF, M., General Hospital Psychiatry

HUXLEY, P. J., Social Work
JONES, E., History of Medicine and Psychiatry
KNAPP, M. R. J., Health Economics
MACDONALD, A. J. D., Psychological Medicine
McGUFFIN, P., Social, Genetic and Developmental Psychiatry
MORRIS, R. G., Neuropsychology
SALKOVSKIS, P. M., Psychology
STOLERMAN, I., Behavioural Pharmacology
STRANG, J., Addiction Research
WESSELY, S., Epidemiological and Liaison Psychiatry

ATTACHED CENTRE

Centre for Defence Studies: King's College London, Strand, London, WC2R 2LS; tel. (20) 7848-2338; fax (20) 7848-2748; e-mail cds@kcl.ac.uk; internet www.kcl.ac.uk/depsta/rel/cds; f. 1990; Dir Dr JOHN GEARSON; publ. *Conflict, Security and Development* (3 a year).

London Business School

Regent's Park, London, NW1 4SA
Telephone: (20) 7000-7000
Fax: (20) 7000-7001
E-mail: webenquiries@london.edu
Internet: www.london.edu
Founded 1965
Academic year: August to July
Dean: Sir ANDREW LIKIERMAN
Deputy Dean for Programmes: Prof. ANDREW SCOTT
Deputy Dean for Faculty: Prof. STEPHEN SCHAEFER
Number of teachers: 158
Number of students: 1,700 (postgraduate); over 8,000 exec. education participants

PROFESSORS

BIRKINSHAW, J., Strategic and International Management
BUNN, D. W., Decision Science
CORNELLI, F., Finance
DEGRAEVE, Z., Decision Sciences
DIMSON, E., Finance
FRANKS, J. R., Finance
GOFFEE, R. E., Organizational Behaviour
GRATTON, L., Organizational Behaviour
HENNESSY, C., Finance
LIKIERMAN, A., Accounting (Dean)
MARKIDES, C., Strategic and International Management
NAIK, N., Finance
NICHOLSON, N., Organizational Behaviour
PETERSON, R., Organizational Behaviour
PILLUTLA, M., Organizational Behaviour
PORTES, R., Economics
RAMDAS, K., Management Science and Operations
REY, H., Economics
SCOTT, A., Economics
SHIVAKUMAR, L., Accounting
TALMOR, E., Accounting
WARREN, K., Management Science and Operations
WEBER, B., Management Science and Operations

ATTACHED RESEARCH INSTITUTES

Aditya Birla India Centre: e-mail indiacentre@london.edu; Co-Dir NIRMALYA KUMAR; Co-Dir PHANISH PURANAM.

Centre for Corporate Governance: e-mail vfarnell@london.edu; Academic Dir JULIAN FRANKS.

Coller Institute of Private Equity: e-mail peinstitute@london.edu; Founder and Chair. Prof. ELI TALMOR.

Foundation and Endowment Asset Management: e-mail sacharya@london.edu; Academic Dir ELROY DIMSON.

Hedge Fund Centre: e-mail hedgefunds@london.edu; Dir NARAYAN NAIK.

Management Lab: e-mail jbirkinshaw@london.edu; Co-founder and Research Dir JULIAN BIRKINSHAW.

London School of Economics and Political Science

Houghton St, London, WC2A 2AE

Telephone: (20) 7405-7686

Fax: (20) 7955-6001

E-mail: stu.rec@lse.ac.uk

Internet: www.lse.ac.uk

Founded 1895

Academic year: October to July

Dir (vacant)

Pro-Dir for Planning and Resources: Prof. GEORGE GASKELL

Pro-Dir for Teaching and Learning: Prof. JANET HARTLEY

Pro-Dir: Prof. S CORBRIDGE

Sec. and Dir of Admin.: ADRIAN HALL

Library: see Libraries and Archives

Number of teachers: 579 (full-time)

Number of students: 9,500 (8,700 full-time, 800 part-time)

Publications: *BioSocieties* (4 a year), *British Journal of Industrial Relations* (4 a year), *Economica* (4 a year journal of economics, economic history and statistics), *Journal of Global History* (3 a year), *Journal of Transport Economics and Policy* (3 a year), *Population Studies* (3 a year), *The British Journal of Sociology* (4 a year), *The International Bibliography of the Social Sciences* (4 vols, 1 a year)

PROFESSORS

ALPERN, S. R., Mathematics
ANDERSON, R. W., Accounting and Finance
ANGELL, I. O., Information Systems
BALDWIN, R., Law
BALFOUR, S., Govt
BARKER, E. V., Sociology
BARKER, R. S., Govt
BARR, N. A., European Institute
BEAN, C. R., Economics/CEP
BESLEY, T. J., Economics
BHATTACHARYA, S., Accounting and Finance
BIGGS, N. L., Mathematics
BLOCH, M. E. F., Anthropology
BRIGHTWELL, G. R., Mathematics
BROMWICH, M., Accounting and Finance
BROWN, C. J., International Relations
BUZAN, B. G., International Relations
CARTWRIGHT, N. L. D., Philosophy
CHANT, S. H., Geography and Environment
CHARVET, J. C. R., Govt
CHESHIRE, P. C., Geography and Environment
CHINKIN, C. M., Law
CIBORRA, C., Information Systems
COHEN, S., Sociology
COLEMAN, J., Govt
COLLEY, L. J., European Institute
COLLINS, H. G., Law
CONNOR, G., Accounting and Finance
CORBRIDGE, S. E., Geography and Environment
COWELL, F. A., Economics
COX, M., International Relations
CRAFTS, N. F. R., Economic History/CEP
DAVIES, P. L., Law
DESAI, LORD, Economics
DOWDING, K. M., Govt
DOWNES, D. M., Social Policy
DUNLEAVY, P., Govt
DYSON, T. P., Population Studies
EPSTEIN, S. R., Economic History
FEATHERSTONE, K., European Institute
FELLI, L., Economics

FREEMAN, R. B., CEP
FULLER, C. J., Anthropology
GALLIERS, R., Information Systems
GASKELL, G. D., Social Psychology
GEARTY, C. A., Sociology
GORDON, I. R., Geography and Environment
GRAY, J. N., Govt
GREENWOOD, C. J., Law
HALLIDAY, F., International Relations
HARDMAN MOORE, J., Economics
HARRISS, J. C., Development Studies Institute
HARTLEY, T. C., Law
HELD, D., Govt
HEMMER, T., Accounting and Finance
HIDALGO, F. J., Economics
HILL, C. J., International Relations
HILLS, J. R., STICERD
HOBCRAFT, J. N., Population Studies, Social Policy
HOWSON, C., Philosophy
HUMPHREY, N. K., Centre for Philosophy of Natural and Social Science
HUMPHREY, P. C., Social Psychology
HUTTER, B. M., Centre for Analysis of Risk and Regulation
HYMAN, R., Industrial Relations
JACKMAN, R. A., Economics
JOHNSON, P. A., Economic History
JONES, D. K. C., Geography and Environment
JONES, G. W., Govt
KALDOR, M. H., Centre for the Study of Global Governance
KELLY, J. E., Industrial Relations
KIERNAN, K. E., Social Policy
KIYOTAKI, N., Economics
KNAPP, M. R. J., Social Policy
KNOX, B. M., International History
LACEY, N. M., Law
LAYARD, P. R. G., Economics/CEP
LE GRAND, J., Social Policy
LIEVEN, D. C. B., Govt
LIGHT, M. M., International Relations
LINTON, O., Economics
LIVINGSTONE, S. M., Social Psychology
LOUGHLIN, M., Law
MACVE, R. H., Accounting and Finance
MANNING, A. P., Economics
MANSELL, R. E., Sociology
MARSDEN, D. W., Industrial Relations
McGUIRE, A. J., Social Policy
METCALF, D. H., Industrial Relations/CEP
MILLER, P. B., Accounting and Finance
MOORE, H. L., Anthropology
MORGAN, M. S., Economic History
MOUZELIS, N. P., Sociology
MURPHY, M. J., Population Studies
MURPHY, T., Law
NEWBURN, W. H. T., Social Policy
NICKELL, S. J., Economics
NORBERG, R., Statistics
O'LEARY, B., Govt
PAGE, E. C., Govt
PARRY, J. P., Anthropology
PHILIP, G. D. E., Govt
PHILLIPS, A. M., Gender Institute
PIACHAUD, D. F. J., Social Policy
PICCIONE, M., Economics
PISCHKE, J. S., Economics
PISSARIDES, C. A., Economics
POWER, A. E., Social Policy
POWER, M. K., Accounting and Finance
PRESTON, P., International History
QUAH, D., Economics
RAWLINGS, R., Law
REES, J. A., Geography and Environment
REINER, R., Law
REYNIERS, D. J., Interdisciplinary Institute of Management
ROBERTS, S. A., Law
ROBINSON, P. M., Economics
ROCK, P. E., Sociology
RODRIGUEZ-SALGADO, M., International History
ROSE, N. S., Sociology
ROSENHEAD, J. V., Operational Research

RYDIN, Y. J., Geography and Environment
SAITH, A., Development Studies Institute
SASSEN, S., Geography and Environment
SENNETT, R., Sociology
SHIN, H. S., Accounting and Finance
SMITH, A. D. S., Govt
STERN, N. H., Economics
STEVENSON, D., International History
SUTTON, J., Economics
TAYLOR, P. G., International Relations
TEUBNER, G., Law
TIMMERMANN, A. G., Accounting and Finance
TONG, H., Statistics
VENABLES, A. J., Economics
WADE, R., Development Studies Institute
WALLACE, W., International Relations
WEBB, D. C., Accounting and Finance
WHITEHEAD, C. M. E., Economics
WILLIAMS, H. P., Operational Research
WORRALL, J., Philosophy
YAHUDA, M. B., International Relations
YAO, Q., Statistics

London School of Hygiene and Tropical Medicine

Keppel St, London, WC1E 7HT

Telephone: (20) 7636-8636

Fax: (20) 7436-5389

E-mail: registry@lshtm.ac.uk

Internet: www.lshtm.ac.uk

Founded 1899

Academic year: September to September

Dir: PETER PIOT

Sec. and Registrar: WENDY SURRIDGE

Library: see Libraries and Archives

Number of teachers: 432 (incl. research staff)

Number of students: 1,800

Publications: *Health Policy and Planning*, *Journal of Tropical Medicine and Hygiene*

PROFESSORS

ACKERS, J., Postgraduate Education in Public Health
BERRIDGE, V., History
BLACK, N. A., Health Services Research
CAIRNCROSS, A. M., Environmental Health
CAIRNS, J., Health Economics
CLELAND, J., Medical Demography
COLEMAN, M. P., Epidemiology and Vital Statistics
COUSENS, S. N., Epidemiology and Medical Statistics
CROFT, S. L., Parasitology
CURTIS, C., Medical Entomology
DOCKRELL, H., Immunology
DOWIE, J., Health Impact Analysis
ELBOURNE, D., Health Care Evaluation
FINE, P. E. M., Communicable Disease Epidemiology
FLETCHER, A., Epidemiology and Ageing
FOSTER, A., International Eye Health
GREENWOOD, B. M., Communicable Diseases
GRUNDY, E., Demographic Gerontology
HALL, A. J., Infectious Disease Epidemiology
HAYES, R. J., Epidemiology and International Health
HILL, A. A., Community Nutrition
KAYE, P. M., Cellular Immunology
KELLY, J. M., Molecular Biology
KENWARD, M. G., Biostatistics
KIRKWOOD, B. R., Epidemiology and International Health
LEON, D., Epidemiology
MABEY, D., Communicable Diseases
McADAM, K. P. W., Clinical Tropical Medicine
McKEE, C. M., European Public Health
MILES, M. A., Medical Protozoology
MILLS, A. J., Health Economics and Policy
MULHOLLAND, K., Infectious Disease Epidemiology
NOAH, N. D., Public Health
PETO, J., Cancer Epidemiology
POCOCK, S. J., Medical Statistics

PRENTICE, A., International Nutrition
RILEY, E. M., Infectious Disease Immunology
ROBERTS, I., Epidemiology and Public Health
RODRIGUES, L., Infectious Disease Epidemiology
ROY, P., Virology
SMITH, P. G., Tropical Epidemiology
TAYLOR, M. G., Medical Helminthology
UAUY, R., Public Health Nutrition
WALT, G., International Health Policy
WELLINGS, K., Sexual and Reproductive Health
WHITWORTH, J. A., International Public Health
WREN, B. W., Microbial Pathogenesis

Queen Mary, University of London

Mile End Rd, London, E1 4NS

Telephone: (20) 7882-5315
Fax: (20) 7882-5556
E-mail: international-office@qmul.ac.uk
Internet: www.qmul.ac.uk

Founded 1989 as Queen Mary and Westfield College, following merger of Queen Mary College (f. 1934) and Westfield College (f. 1882); present name 2000
Academic year: September to June

Prin.: Prof. SIMON GASKELL
Sr Vice-Prin.: Prof. PHILIP OGDEN
Vice-Prin. for External Relations: Prof. RAY PLAYFORD
Vice-Prin. for Humanities and Social Sciences: Prof. MORAG SHIACH
Vice-Prin. for Science and Engineering: Prof. JEREMY KILBURN (acting)
Vice-Prin. for Research and Int. Affairs: Prof. EVELYN WELCH
Vice-Prin. for Teaching and Learning: Prof. SUSAN DILLY
Vice-Prin. and Warden, Barts and the London School of Medicine and Dentistry: Prof. RICHARD TREMBATH
Chief Admin. Officer: DEAN CURTIS
Sec. to Council and Academic Registrar: WENDY APPLEBY
Dir of Library Services: E. J. BULL

Library: see Libraries and Archives
Number of teachers: 1,000
Number of students: 16,500

PROFESSORS

Faculty of Arts:

ADAMOWICZ, E., French
ADGER, D. J., Linguistics
BOFFEY, J., English
CHESHIRE, J. L., Linguistics
DADSON, T. J., Hispanic Studies
DELGADO, M. M., Drama and Theatre Arts
DEYERMOND, A. D., Spanish
EDWARDS, M. J., Classics
ELLIS, M., English Literary History
EVANS, P. W., Film Studies
GOERNER, R., German
GUSSENHOVEN, C., Linguistics
HAMILTON, P. W. A., English
HENNESSY, P. J., Contemporary History
HOBSON JEANNERET, M. E., French Language and Literature
JACKSON, J., History
JANOWITZ, A., English
JARDINE, L. A., English and Drama
MILLER, J. L., History
MORIARTY, M. M., French Literature and Thought
OLSCHNER, L. M., German
PARSONS, D. W., Public Policy
PENNY, R. J., Romance Philology
RAMSDEN, J. A., Modern History
RANAWAKE, S. A., German
RAYFIELD, D., Russian
REES, G. C., English
ROSE, J., English
RUBIN, M., History
SASSOON, D., History

SHIACH, M., Cultural History

Faculty of Engineering and Mathematical Sciences:

ALIABADI, M. H., Engineering
ANDREWS, E. H., Materials
ARROWSMITH, D. K., Mathematics
ASHBY, D., Mathematics
BADER, D. L., Engineering
BAILEY, R. A., Statistics
BULLET, S. R., Mathematics
CAMERON, P. J., Mathematics
CARR, B. J., Mathematics and Astronomy
CLARRICOATS, P., Electrical Engineering
CROOKES, R., Combustion Engineering
CUTHBERT, L. G., Electronic Engineering
DAVIES, K. L., Materials
DONKIN, S., Pure Mathematics
DRIKAKIS, D., Engineering
EDIRISINGHE, M., Materials
EVANS, J., Materials
GASTER, M., Experimental Aerodynamics
GOLDSHEID, I., Probability Theory
GUO, Z. X., Materials
HODGES, W. A., Mathematics
HOGG, P., Materials
LAUGHTON, M. A., Electrical and Electronic Engineering
LAWN, C. J., Thermo-fluids Engineering
LEEDHAM-GREEN, C. R., Pure Mathematics
LESCHZINER, M. A., Engineering
LINDSAY, P., Electrical Engineering
MACCALLUM, M. A. H., Applied Mathematics
MURRAY, C. D., Mathematics and Astronomy
O'HEARN, P., Computer Science
OLVER, A. D., Electrical and Electronic Engineering
PAKER, Y., Parallel Computing
PAPALOIZOU, J. C. B., Mathematics and Astronomy
PARINI, C., Antenna Engineering
ROBINSON, E., Computer Science
ROSE, J. W., Mechanical Engineering
ROXBURGH, I. W., Mathematics and Astronomy
SCHWARTZ, S. J., Space Plasma Physics
STARK, J. P. W., Aeronautical Engineering
TANNER, K., Materials
WEHRFRITZ, B. A. F., Pure Mathematics
WILLIAMS, I. P., Mathematics and Astronomy

Faculty of Law and Social Sciences:

ADAMS, J., Property Law
ATKINSON, B. W., Geography
BAILLIE, R. T., Economics
BLAKENEY, M., Intellectual Property Law
COTTERRELL, R. B. M., Legal Theory
CURTIS, S., Geography
FITZPATRICK, P., Law
FLETCHER, I. F., Commercial Law
GHIGLINO, C., Economics
HASKEL, J., Economics
LAHORE, J. C., Intellectual Property Law
LEE, R., Geography
MALGOSIA, F.
MCCONVILLE, S. D. M., Criminal Justice
NORTON, J. J., Banking Law
O'DONOVAN, K., Law
OGDEN, P. E., Geography
REED, C., Electronic Commerce Law
RICHARDSON, G. M., Public Law
SMITH, D. M., Geography
SORGER, G., Economics
SPENCE, N. A., Human Geography
THOMAS, G., Equity and Property Law
TZAVALIS, E., Economics
VAN BUEREN, G., International Human Rights Law
YELLAND, J. L., Law

Faculty of Natural Sciences:

ADE, P. A. R., Experimental Astrophysics
AYLETT, B. J., Chemistry
BONNETT, R., Research Chemistry

BRADLEY, D. C., Chemistry
BUGG, D. V., Nuclear Physics
CARTER, A. A., Particle Physics
CHARAP, J. M., Theoretical Physics
CLEGG, P. E., Astrophysics
COVNEY, P. V., Physical Chemistry
DUCKETT, J. G., Botany
DUNSTAN, D. J., Experimental Physics
EDGINGTON, J. A., Physics
EMERSON, J., Physics
GRIFFITHS, D. V., Organic Chemistry
HILDREW, A. G., Ecology
KALMUS, P., Physics
LICHTENSTEIN, C. P., Molecular Biology
MARTIN, D., Physics
PERCIVAL, I. C., Physics
PYE, J. D., Biological Sciences
RANDALL, E. W., Research Chemistry
SEWELL, G., Physics
SULLIVAN, A., Inorganic Chemistry
THOMPSON, G., Physics
THORPE, A., Biology
UTLEY, J. H. P., Organic Chemistry
VLCEK, A., Inorganic Chemistry
WARREN, M. J., Biological Sciences
WHITE, G. J., Physics and Astronomy
WILSON, E. G., Physics

Barts and the London School of Medicine and Dentistry (Turner St, London, E1 2AD; tel. (20) 7377-7611; fax (20) 7377-7612; e-mail medicaladmissions@qmul.ac.uk; internet www.mds.qmul.ac.uk):

ANSEAU, M. R., Institute of Dentistry
ARMSTRONG, P., Haematology, Oncology and Imaging
ARMSTRONG-JAMES, M. A., Biomedical Sciences
ASHBY, D., Wolfson Institute of Preventive Medicine
BENJAMIN, N., Pharmacology
BERRY, C. L., Molecular Pathology, Infection and Immunity
BESSER, G. M., Metabolism
BRADLEY, P. F., Institute of Dentistry
BRITTON, K. E., Haematology, Oncology and Imaging
BROCKLEHURST, K., Biomedical Sciences
BURRIN, J., Metabolism
CARTER, Y. H., Community Sciences
CHARD, T., Haematology, Oncology and Imaging
CLARK, A. J. L., Metabolism
COHEN, R. D., Metabolism
COID, J. W., Community Sciences
COSTELOE, K., Metabolism
CURTIS, M., Oral Microbiology
DAVIES, R. J., Molecular Pathology, Infection and Immunity
DOYAL, L., Metabolism
ELLIOTT, J. C., Institute of Dentistry
FELDMAN, R. A., Surgery, Clinical Neuroscience and Intensive Care
FLOWER, R. J., Pharmacology
GALTON, D., Metabolism
GOODE, A. W., Surgery, Clinical Neuroscience and Intensive Care
GOWLAND, G., Pharmacology
GROSSMAN, A., Metabolism
GRUDZINSKAS, J. G., Community Sciences
HAJ, M., Metabolism
HAJEK, P., Clinical Psychology
HARDIE, J. M., Institute of Dentistry
HEATH, M., Institute of Dentistry
HILLIER, S. M., Community Sciences
HITMAN, G. A., Metabolism
HUGHES, F., Periodontology
ILES, R. A., Metabolism
JACOBS, I., Gynaecological Oncology
JEFFRIES, R. A., Molecular Pathology, Infection and Immunity
KOPELMAN, P. G., Metabolism
KUMAR, P., Clinical Medical Education
LEIGH, I. M., Haematology, Oncology and Imaging
LESLIE, R. D. G., Metabolism

LILLEYMAN, J. S., Metabolism
LISTER, T. A., Haematology, Oncology and Imaging
LOWE, D. G., Molecular Pathology, Infection and Immunity
LUMLEY, J. S., Surgery, Clinical Neurosurgery and Intensive Care
MACDONALD, T. T., Metabolism
MARTIN, J. E., Molecular Pathology, Infection and Immunity
MILLER, G., Epidemiology
MILLER, N. E., Metabolism
MONSON, J., Clinical Endocrinology
NEWLAND, A. C., Haematology, Oncology and Imaging
OLIVER, R. T. D., Haematology, Oncology and Imaging
OXFORD, J., Molecular Pathology, Infection and Immunity
PERRETT, D., Metabolism
PHILLIPS, I. R., Biomedical Sciences
PINCHING, A. J., Molecular Pathology, Infection and Immunity
PRICE, C. P., Metabolism
PRIEBE, S., Community Sciences
PRIESTLEY, J. V., Biomedical Sciences
REES, L. H., Metabolism
REZNEK, R., Haematology, Oncology and Imaging
SANDERSON, I. R., Metabolism
SAVAGE, M., Metabolism
STRUNIN, L., Surgery, Clinical Neuroscience and Intensive Care
SUGDEN, M. C., Biomedical Sciences
SWAIN, C., Gastrointestinal Endoscopy
SWASH, M., Surgery, Clinical Neuroscience and Intensive Care
TABAQCHALI, S., Molecular Pathology, Infection and Immunity
THIEMERMANN, C., Pharmacology
TOMLINSON, D. R., Biomedical Sciences
TROTT, K. R., Haematology, Oncology and Imaging
VINSON, G. P., Biomedical Sciences
WALD, N. J., Wolfson Institute of Preventive Medicine
WHITTLE, B. J., Pharmacology
WILLIAMS, D. M., Institute of Dentistry
WILLIAMS, N. S., Surgery, Clinical Neuroscience and Intensive Care
WILLOUGHBY, D. A., Pharmacology
WINGATE, D. L., Metabolism

Royal Academy of Music
Marylebone Rd, London, NW1 5HT
Telephone: (20) 7873-7373
Fax: (20) 7873-7374
E-mail: go@ram.ac.uk
Internet: www.ram.ac.uk
Founded 1822, inc. by Royal Charter 1830
State control
Pres.: HRH THE DUCHESS OF GLOUCESTER
Prin.: Prof. JONATHAN FREEMAN-ATTWOOD
Deputy Prin.: MARK RACZ
Deputy Prin. for Programmes and Research: TIMOTHY JONES
Academic Registrar: PHILIP WHITE
Library of 125,000 vols, incl. colln of early sheet music and MSS
Number of teachers: 155
Number of students: 700
Publication: *RAM Magazine* (2 a year).

Royal Holloway, University of London
Egham Hill, Egham, TW20 0EX
Telephone: (1784) 434455
Fax: (1784) 437520
E-mail: admissions@rhul.ac.uk
Internet: www.rhul.ac.uk
Founded 1886 as Royal Holloway College, present status 1985
Prin.: Prof. PAUL LAYZELL
Deputy Prin.: Prof. ROB KEMP

Dir of Library Services: JOHN TUCK
Library of 600,000 vols, 17,000 e-journals
Number of teachers: 1,525
Number of students: 8,500

DEANS
Faculty of Arts: Prof. KATIE NORMINGTON
Faculty of History and Social Sciences: Prof. ROSEMARY DEEM
Faculty of Science: Prof. PHILIP BEESLEY

PROFESSORS
Faculty of Arts:
  ALSTON, R., Classics
  ARMSTRONG, T. D., English Literature
  BOEHMER, E. D., English
  BOWIE, A., German
  BRADBY, D. H., Drama and Theatre Studies
  BRATTON, J. S., Theatre and Cultural History
  BRUZZI, S., Film Studies
  CARROLL, J. F. M., Philosophy and German
  CAVE, R. A., Drama and Theatre Studies
  CHARLTON, D. P., Music
  COOK, N. J., Music
  DZELAINIS, M. M., Early Modern Literature and Thought
  ELLIS, J. C. P., Media Arts
  EVERSON, J. E., Italian Literature
  GARNETT, A., Media Arts
  GIBSON, A. W., Modern Literature and Theory
  GOULD, W. L., English Literature
  GUNDLE, S., Italian
  HAMPSON, R. G., Modern Literature
  HILL, W. J., Media Arts
  HUGHES, E. J., Modern French Literature
  HUGHES, J., German and Comparative Literature
  KAHANE, A., Classics
  LEE SIX, A. E., Hispanic Studies
  LONGERICH, P., German History
  MERCK, A. J., Media Arts
  MOTION, A., Creative Writing
  O'BRIEN, J. P., French Renaissance Literature
  PIKE, L., Music
  POWELL, J. G. F., Classics
  RINK, J., Music
  ROBERTSON, E., French
  RYAN, K. J. P., English Language and Literature
  SAMSON, J., Music
  SCHAFER, E. J., Drama
  TOSI, A., Italian Studies
  VILAIN, R. L., German and Comparative Literature
  VILASECA, D., Spanish
  WATHEY, A., Music History
  WHITE, I. A., German
  WILES, D., Theatre
  WILLIAMS, J., French Literature and Film
Faculty of History and Social Sciences:
  ANSARI, K. H., Islam and Culture
  BARN, R., Health and Social Care
  BARRON, C. M., History of London
  BROADBENT, P. J., Management
  CESARANI, D., History
  CHAMPION, J. A. I., Early Modern Ideas
  CLAEYS, G. R., History of Political Thought
  CORFIELD, P. J., History
  CROFT, J. P., Early Modern History
  DENNEY, D., Applied Social Studies
  DREWRY, G., Public Admin.
  EDWARDS, J. R., Social Policy
  FAULKNER, D. O., Management
  FERLIE, E. B., Management
  FRANK, J. L., Economics
  GRAHAM, H. E., History
  HACKLEY, C. E., Marketing
  HEYES, A., Economics
  LEE, R. M., Social Research Methods
  McSWEENEY, L. B., Management
  MANDLER, M., Economics
  MATTEN, D., Management

  McCONVILLE, S. D. M., Criminal Justice
  NEWELL, S. M., Management
  NORMAN, H., Economics
  PILBEAM, P., Modern European History
  ROBINSON, F. C. R., History of Southeast Asia
  ROSENBERG, D., Information and Communication Management
  SAUL, N. E., Medieval History
  SELZER, A., Economics
  SMITH, C. D., Organization Studies
  SPAGAT, M., Economics
  STONE, D., Modern History

Faculty of Science:
  ANDREWS, B. D., Abnormal Psychology
  BLACKBURN, S., Mathematics
  BLAIR, G. A., Physics
  BOLWELL, G. P., Plant Biochemistry
  BOWYER, J. R., Plant Biochemistry
  BRADLEY, C., Health Psychology
  BRAMLEY, P. M., Biochemistry
  BRYSBAERT, M. M. C., Psychology
  CASTIELLO, U., Psychology
  CATCHPOLE, C. K., Animal Behaviour
  CHERVONENKIS, A. Y., Computer Science
  COHEN, D. A., Computer Science
  COLLINSON, M. E., Plant Palaeobiology
  COWAN, B. P., Physics
  CRANG, P. A., Geography
  DAVIES, E. R., Machine Vision
  DICKSON, J. G., Molecular Cell Biology
  DRIVER, F. F., Human Geography
  DUDEN, R., Biological Sciences
  EBINGER, C. J., Tectonics
  EYSENCK, M. W., Psychology
  FOWLER, C. M. R., Geography
  FUNNELL, E., Neuropsychology
  GAMBLE, C. S., Geography
  GAMMERMAN, A., Computer Science
  GREEN, M. G., Particle Physics
  GUTIN, Z., Computer Science
  HALL, R., Geology
  HARMAN, G., Mathematics
  HARRIS, M., Psychology
  IMRIE, R. F., Human Geography
  JANSEN, V., Mathematical Biology
  KEMP, R. A., Physical Geography
  LEA, M. J., Physics
  LOEWENTHAL, C., Psychology
  LOWE, J. J., Geography
  LUO, Z., Computer Science
  MACLEOD, A. K., Psychology
  McCLAY, K. R., Structural Geology
  MENZIES, M. A., Geochemistry
  MITCHELL, C. J., Information Security
  MOORE, A. M., Crystallography
  MURPHY, S. P., Mathematics
  MURTAGH, F., Computer Science
  NISBET, E. G., Geology
  O'MAHONY, P. F., Applied Mathematics
  PATERSON, K. G., Mathematics
  PETRASHOV, V. T., Physics
  ROSE, J., Geography
  SAUNDERS, J., Low Temperature Physics
  SCHACK, R., Mathematics
  SCOTT, A. C., Applied Palaeobotany
  SIMON, D., Development Geography
  SMITH, A. T., Psychology
  SOLOVYEV, W., Computer Science
  STRONG, J. A., Experimental Physics
  THIRLWALL, M. F., Isotope Geochemistry
  UNWIN, P. T., Geography
  VAPNIK, V., Computer Science
  VOVK, V. G., Computer Science
  WILD, P. R., Mathematics
  ZANKER, J. M., Neuroscience

Royal Veterinary College
Royal College St, London, NW1 0TU
Telephone: (20) 7468-5000
Fax: (20) 7388-2342
E-mail: registry@rvc.ac.uk
Internet: www.rvc.ac.uk
Founded 1791

Academic year: September to July
Prin.: Prof. STUART REID
Asst Prin. and Sec.: ELAINE ACASTER
Librarian: SIMON JACKSON
Number of teachers: 109
Number of students: 1,058

PROFESSORS

BROWNLIE, J., Veterinary Pathology
CHANTLER, P. D., Veterinary Molecular and Cellular Biology
CHURCH, D. B., Small Animal Studies
ELLIOTT, J., Pharmacology
GOODSHIP, A. E., Orthopaedic Sciences
GREGORY, N. G., Animal Welfare Physiology
HOWARD, C. R., Veterinary Microbiology and Parasitology
JACOBS, D. E., Veterinary Parasitology
JOHNSTON, A. M., Veterinary Public Health
LANYON, L., Veterinary Anatomy
LEES, P., Veterinary Pharmacology
LLOYD, D. H., Veterinary Dermatology
MAY, S. A., Equine Medicine and Surgery
McGOWAN, M., Farm-Animal Medicine and Surgery
PFEIFFER, D. U., Veterinary Epidemiology
SCARAMUZZI, R. J., Veterinary Physiology
SKERRY, T. M., Developmental Biology
SMITH, R., Equine Orthopaedics
STICKLAND, N. C., Veterinary Anatomy
STOKER, N. G., Molecular Bacteriology
WATHES, D. C., Veterinary Reproduction
WATSON, P. F., Reproductive Biology
WILLIAMS, A. E., Veterinary Pathology

St George's Hospital Medical School

Cranmer Terrace, London, SW17 0RE

Telephone: (20) 8672-9944
Fax: (20) 8725-3426
E-mail: webmaster@stgeorges.nhs.uk
Internet: www.sghms.ac.uk

Founded 1751
Academic year: September to August
Prin.: Prof. PETER KOPELMAN
Deputy Prin.: Prof. SEAN HILTON
Academic Registrar and Sec.: SOPHIE BOWEN
Library of 150,000 vols
Number of teachers: 400
Number of students: 6,068

PROFESSORS

ANDERSON, H. R., Epidemiology and Public Health
AUSTEN, B. M., Protein Science
BELL, B. A., Neurosurgery
BENNETT, D. C., Anatomy
BENNETT, E. D., Anaesthesia
BLAND, J. M., Medical Statistics
BOLTON, T. B., Pharmacology
BROWN, N., Anatomy and Developmental Biology
BURNS, T. P., Community Psychiatry
CAMM, A. J., Clinical Cardiology
CAMPBELL, S., Obstetrics and Gynaecology
CAPPUCCIO, F., General Practice and Primary Care
CARTER, N. D., Developmental Biochemistry
CHALMERS, R. A., Paediatric Metabolism
CHAMBERS, T. J., Tissue Pathology
CLEMENS, M. J., Biochemistry
COATES, A. R. M., Medical Microbiology
COLLIER, J. G., Clinical Pharmacology
COOK, D., Epidemiology
DALGLEISH, A. G., Oncology
DUFF, M. J. B., Physiological Medicine
EASTMAN, N. L. G., Psychiatry
FISHER, L. M., Biochemistry
GHODSE, A. H., Psychiatry of Addictive Behaviour
GILLBERG, C., Psychiatry
GORDON-SMITH, E. C., Haematology
GRIFFIN, G. E., Infectious Diseases and Medicine
GRIFFITHS, J. R., Medical Biochemistry

HALL, G. M., Anaesthesia
HAY, F. C., Immunology
HERMON-TAYLOR, J., Surgery
HILTON, S. R., General Practice and Primary Care
HOLLINS, S. C., Psychiatry of Learning Disability
HORTON, R., Clinical Pharmacology
HOWLIN, P. A., Clinical Psychology
JOHNSTONE, A. P., Molecular Immunology
JONES, I., Sociology of Health and Illness
JONES, P. W., Medicine
KASKI, J. C., Cardiological Sciences
KRISHNA, S., Infectious Diseases
LACEY, J. H., Psychiatry
LARGE, W. A., Pharmacology
LEVICK, J. R., Physiology
MacGREGOR, G. A., Cardiovascular Medicine
MALIK, M., Cardiology
MARKUS, H., Clinical Neuroscience
McKENNA, W. J., Cardiac Medicine
McLAREN, S., Nursing
MORTIMER, P. S., Physiological Medicine
OLIVEIRA, D. B. G., Renal Medicine
PATTON, M., Medical Genetics
ROSS, F., Nursing Primary Care
SEYMOUR, C. A., Clinical Biochemistry and Metabolism
STRACHAN, D. P., Public Health
VICTOR, C. R., Public Health Sciences
WALLER, G., Psychiatry
WALTERS, D. V., Child Health
WEST, R. J., Psychology
WHINCUP, P. H., Public Health Sciences
WHIPP, B. J., Physiology
XU, Q., Cardiological Sciences

School of Oriental and African Studies

Thornhaugh St, Russell Sq., London, WC1H 0XG

Telephone: (20) 7637-2388
Fax: (20) 7436-3844
E-mail: study@soas.ac.uk
Internet: www.soas.ac.uk

Founded 1916
Academic year: September to June
Dir and Prin.: Prof. PAUL WEBLEY
Pro-Dir for Learning and Teaching: Prof. NIRMALA RAO
Pro-Dir for Research and Enterprise: Prof. GRAHAM FURNISS
Vice-Prin. for External Relations: Prof. ELISABETH CROLL
Registrar and Sec.: DONALD BEATON
Library: see under Libraries and Archives
Number of teachers: 200
Number of students: 4,700
Publications: *Journal of African Law, The China Quarterly*

DEANS

Faculty of Arts and Humanities: Prof. GURHARPAL SINGH
Faculty of Languages and Cultures: Prof. ANNE PAUWELS
Faculty of Law and Social Sciences: Prof. STEPHEN CHAN

PROFESSORS

ABDEL-HALEEM, M. A. S., Islamic Studies
ABU-DEEB, K. M., Arabic
ACHCAR, G., Development Studies and International Relations
AL-ANI, N., Gender Studies
ASH, R. F., Taiwan Studies
ASHIAGBOR, D., Law
BADERIN, M., Law
BANDA, F., Law
BARRETT, T. H., East Asian History
BEHRENS-ABOUSEIF, D., Islamic Art and Archaeology
BERNSTEIN, H., Development Studies
BOOTH, A. E., Economics (Asia)
BRAMALL, C., Economics (Asia Pacific)

BRAGINSKY, V. I., South East Asian Languages and Literatures
BROWN, I., Economic History (South East Asia)
CLARENCE-SMITH, W. G., Economic History (Asia and Africa)
CRAMER, C., Development Studies
CRAVEN, M., Law
CULLET, P., Law
DORWARD, A., Development Economics
DRIVER, C., Financial Economics
DWYER, R., South Asia Indian Cultures and Cinema
FARDON, R., Anthropology (West Africa)
FATTOUH, B., Finance and Management (Middle East)
FINE, B., Economics
FUEHRER, B., Sinology
FURNISS, G., African Languages, Literature and Popular Culture
GEORGE, A., Babylonian
GERSTLE, C. A., Japanese Studies
HARDING, A., Law
HARRIS, L., Economics
HAWKINS, J. D., Ancient Anatolian Languages
HAWTING, G., History (Near and Middle East)
HEWITT, B. G., Caucasian Languages
HEZSER, C., Jewish Studies
HOBART, M., Critical Media and Cultural Studies (South East Asia)
HOCKX, M., Chinese
HOWARD, K., Music
HOWE, C., Chinese Business and Management
HUTT, M., Nepali and Himalayan Studies
INGHAM, B., Arabic Linguistic Studies
ISMAIL, S., Comparative and International Politics (Middle East)
KABEER, N., Development Studies
KARSHENAS, M., Economics (Middle East)
KENNEDY, H., Arabic
KHAN, M., Economics
KRATZ, U., Indonesian and Malay
LAPAVITSAS, C., Economics (Japan)
MARCHAND, T., Social Anthropology
McKINLEY, T., Development, Policy and Research
MENSKI, W., Law
MOSSE, D., Social Anthropology
MUCHLINSKI, P., Law
NISSANKE, M., Economics
OUGHTON, C., Managerial Economics
PALMER, M., Law
PAUWELS, A., Sociolinguistics
PEEL, J. D. Y., Anthropology and Sociology (Africa)
PERRY-KESSARIS, A., Economic Law
PICTON, J., African Art
POTTIER, J., Anthropology (Africa)
RATHBONE, R. J. A. R., Modern African History
ROBB, P. G., History of India
SAAD-FILHO, A., Political Economics
SACHDEV, I., Linguistics
SCARAMOZZINO, P., Economics
SCOBBIE, I., Law, Peace Building, Human Rights
SHACKLE, C., Modern Languages of South Asia
SHANKAR, B., Development, Environment and Policy
SIMS-WILLIAMS, N., Iranian and Central Asian Studies
SREBERNY, A., Global Media and Communications
SRIRAM, C., Law
SUN, L., Business and Management (China)
TAPPER, R. L., Anthropology (Middle East)
TOPOROWSKI, J., Economics and Finance
TRIPP, C., Politics (Middle East)
WEEKS, J., Development Economics
WELCHMAN, L., Law
WEST, H., Anthropology
WIDDESS, R., Music
WRIGHT, O., Musicology of the Middle East

School of Pharmacy

29–39 Brunswick Sq., London, WC1N 1AX
Telephone: (20) 7753-5800
Fax: (20) 7753-5829
E-mail: registry@pharmacy.ac.uk
Internet: www.pharmacy.ac.uk

Founded 1842, Royal Charter of Incorporation 1952
Academic year: October to June

Dean and Prin.: Prof. ANTHONY W. SMITH
Chief Operating Officer: MAUREEN BOYLAN
Head of Registry: JOHN PECK
Head of Library and Information Services:
  MICHELLE WAKE

Number of teachers: 53
Number of students: 1,200

PROFESSORS

ALPAR, O., Drug Delivery Research
BARBER, N., Practice and Policy
BATES, I., Pharmacy Education
BEEZER, A., Biophysical Chemistry
BROCCHINI, S., Chemical Pharmaceuticals
BUCKTON, G., Pharmaceutics
HADGRAFT, J., Biophysical Pharmaceutics
HEINRICH, M., Pharmacognosy and Phytotherapy
HORNE, R., Behavioural Medicine
MOFFAT, A. C., Pharmaceutical Analysis
NEIDLE, S., Chemical Biology
SMITH, F., Pharmacy Practice
STEPHENSON, F. A., Molecular Neuroscience
TAYLOR, D., Pharmaceutical and Public Health Policy
TAYLOR, K., Clinical Pharmaceutics
TAYLOR, P., Microbiology
THOMSON, A. M., Pharmacology
THURSTON, D., Pharmaceutical and Biological Chemistry
UCHEGBU, I., Pharmaceutical Nanoscience
WONG, I., Paediatric Pharmacy

University College London

Gower St, London, WC1E 6BT
Telephone: (20) 7679-2000
Fax: (20) 7387-8057
E-mail: international@ucl.ac.uk
Internet: www.ucl.ac.uk

Founded 1826, merged with Royal Free Hospital School of Medicine 1998

Pres. and Provost: Prof. MALCOLM GRANT
Vice-Provost for Academic and Int. Affairs: Prof. MICHAEL WORTON
Vice-Provost for Enterprise: Prof. STEPHEN CADDICK
Vice-Provost for Health: Prof. Sir JOHN TOOKE
Vice-Provost for Operations: REX KNIGHT
Vice-Provost for Research: Prof. G. DAVID PRICE
Registrar: CHRISTOPHER HALLAS
Library: see Libraries and Archives
Number of teachers: 4,078
Number of students: 21,126
Publications: *The World of UCL, UCL Universe*

DEANS

Faculty of Arts and Humanities: Prof. HENRY WOUDHUYSEN
Faculty of Biomedical Sciences: Prof. IAN JACOBS
Faculty of the Built Environment: Prof. ALAN PENN
Faculty of Engineering Sciences: Prof. ANTHONY C W FINKELSTEIN
Faculty of Laws: Prof. Dame HAZEL GENN
Faculty of Life Sciences: Prof. MARY K. L. COLLINS
Faculty of Mathematical and Physical Sciences: Prof. RICHARD CATLOW
Faculty of Social and Historical Sciences: Prof. STEPHEN R. SMITH

PROFESSORS

ADLER, M. W., Sexually Transmitted Diseases
AEPPLI, G., Physics
AGHION, P., Economics of Public Policy
AIELLO, L. C., Biological Anthropology
AIKEN, J., Fine Art
AKBAR, A. N., Immunology
ALLSOP, R. E., Transport Studies
ANDERSON, J. E., Organic Chemistry
ANDERSON, J. M., Mathematics
ANDERSON, P. N., Experimental Neuroscience
ANDERSON, R. H., Paediatric Cardiac Morphology
ANDREWS, D. J., Engineering Design
ARRIDGE, S. R., Image Processing
ASHMORE, J. F., Biophysics
ASHTON, R. D., English Language and Literature
ATKINSON, J., Psychology
ATTANASIO, O. P., Economics
ATTWELL, D. I., Physiology
AYAZI SHAMLOU, P., Biochemical Engineering
AYNSLEY-GREEN, A., Child Health
BABIKER, A. G., Medical Statistics and Epidemiology
BALL, K. M., Mathematics
BANISTER, D. J., Transport Planning
BARENDT, E. M., Law of Media of Communication and Expression
BARKER, J. A., Hydrogeology
BARLOW, M. J., Astrophysics
BARNES, M. P., Scandinavian Studies
BARTLETT, R. P., Russian History
BARTLEY, M., Medical Sociology
BATE, S. P., Health Services Management
BATTERBEE, R. W., Environmental Change
BATTY, J. M., Spatial Analysis and Planning
BAYVEL, P., Optical Communications and Networks
BEBBINGTON, P. E., Social and Community Psychiatry
BEGENT, R. H. J., Oncology
BERGER, M. A., Mathematics
BETTERIDGE, D. J., Endocrinology and Metabolism
BEVAN, S. J., Pharmacology
BEVERLEY, P. C. L., Tumour Immunology
BHATTACHARYA, S. S., Experimental Ophthalmology
BINDMAN, D., History of Art
BIRD, A. C., Clinical Ophthalmology
BISHOP, S. R., Non-linear Dynamics
BLUNDELL, R., Economics
BLUNN, G. W., Biomedical Engineering
BOGLE, I. D. L., Chemical Engineering
BOLSOVER, S. R., Cell Physiology
BORDEN, I. M., Architecture and Urban Culture
BORGERS, T., Economics
BOSHOFF, C. H., Cancer Medicine
BOSTOCK, H., Neurophysiology
BOULOS, P. B., Surgery
BOWLING, A., Health Services Research
BOWMAKER, J., Visual Research
BOWN, S. G., Laser Medicine and Surgery
BOYD, I. W., Electronic Materials
BRAMWELL, S. T., Physical Chemistry
BREWIN, C. R., Clinical Psychology
BRIDGE, M. G., Commercial Law
BROCKES, J. P., Cell Biology
BRODY, M. B., Linguistics
BROWN, D. A., Pharmacology
BROWN, M. M., Stroke Medicine
BROWN, R. A., Tissue Engineering
BROWN, S. N., Mathematics
BROWNE, E. J., History of Medicine
BRUCKDORFER, K. R., Biochemistry
BRYSON, W. N., History and Theory of Art
BURGESS, J. A., Geography
BURK, K. M., Modern and Contemporary History
BURNHAM, P. C., Social Anthropology
BURNSTOCK, G., Anatomy
BURROUGHS, A. K., Hepatology

BUTLER, W. E., Comparative Law
BUTTERWORTH, B. L., Cognitive Neuropsychology
BUXTON, B. F., Information Processing
BYNUM, W. F., History of Medicine
CALLARD, R., Immunology
CAMPBELL, J. A., Computer Science
CAMPBELL, R., Communication Disorders
CARLIN, W. J., Economics
CATLOW, C. R. A., Chemistry
CHAIN, B. M., Immunology
CHARLES, I. G., Molecular Biology
CHESHER, A. D., Economics
CLARK, J. B., Neurochemistry
CLARK, R. J. H., Chemistry
CLARKE, P. E. L., Physics
CLAYTON, P. T., Paediatric Metabolic Disease and Hepatology
CLOUT, H. D., Geography
COCKCROFT, S., Cell Physiology
COLHOUN, H. M., Clinical Epidemiology
COLLINGE, J., Neurodegenerative Disease
COLLINS, M. K. L., Immunology
COLQUHOUN, D., Pharmacology
CONWAY, S. R., History
COOK, P. F. C., Architecture
COOTER, R. J.
COPP, A. J., Developmental Neurobiology
COVENEY, P. V., Physical Chemistry
CRAGGS, M. D., Applied Neurophysiology
CRAIG, G., Paediatric Genetics
CRANE, T. M., Philosophy
CRAWFORD, M. H., Ancient History
CROLL, J. G. A., Civil and Environmental Engineering
CROSS, P. A., Geomatic Engineering
CULHANE, J, L., Physics
CULL-CANDY, S. G., Pharmacology
CURRAN, H. V., Psychopharmacology
CUZNER, M. L., Neurochemistry
D'AVRAY, D. L., History
DACRE, J. E., Medical Education
DANPURE, C. J., Molecular Cell Biology
DARBYSHIRE, J. H., Epidemiology
DAVIDSON, B. R., Surgery
DAVIES, S. W., Experimental Neuropathology
DAVIES, W. E., History
DAWID, A. P., Statistics
DAYAN, P., Computational Neuroscience
DEAN, M. C., Anatomy
DEEMING, A. J., Chemistry
DELETANT, D. J., Romanian Studies
DELHANTY, J. D. A., Human Genetics
DELPY, D. T., Medical Photonics
DENNIS, I. H., English Law
DEZATEUX, C. A., Paediatric Epidemiology
DHILLON, A. P., Histopathology
DICKENSON, A. H., Neuropharmacology
DIMITRIOU, H., Planning Studies
DOLAN, R., Neuropsychiatry
DOLPHIN, A., Pharmacology
DOWD, P. M., Dermatology
DOWMAN, I. J., Photogrammetry and Remote Sensing
DUCHEN, M. R., Physiology
DUNCAN, J. S., Clinical Neurology
DUNNILL, P., Biochemical Engineering
DUSHEIKO, G. M., Medicine
DWORKIN, R. M., Jurisprudence
EDWARDS, J. C. W., Connective-tissue Medicine
EDWARDS, Y. H., Human Genetics
EKINS, R. P., Biophysics
ELL, P. J., Nuclear Medicine
ELTON, L., Higher Education
EMERY, V. C., Virology
EVANS, A. W., Transport Safety
EVANS, M. C. W., Plant Chemistry
FEARN, T., Applied Statistics
FERGUSSON-PELL, M., Neuromuscular Restoration and Rehabilitation
FINE, L. G., Medicine
FINKELSTEIN, A. C. W., Software Systems Engineering
FINNEY, J. L., Physics

FISH, D. R., Clinical Neurophysiology and Epilepsy
FISHER, A. J., Physics
FISHER, E. M. C., Neurogenetics
FITZGERALD, M., Developmental Neurobiology
FITZKE, F. W., Visual Optics
FLETCHER, I. F., International Commercial Law
FONAGY, P., Psychoanalysis
FOOT, M. M., Library and Archive Studies
FOREMAN, J. C., Immunopharmacology
FORGACS, D. A., Italian
FORGE, A., Auditory Cell Biology
FORTY, J. A., History of Architecture
FOURNIER, C. L., Architecture and Urban Planning
FOWLER, C. J., Uro-neurology
FRACKOWIAK, R. S. J., Cognitive Neurology
FRANCK, L. S., Children's Nursing Research Studies
FREEMAN, M. D. A., English Law
FRENCH, D. W., History
FRISTON, K. J., Imaging Neuroscience
FRITH, C. D., Neuropsychology
FRITH, U., Cognitive Development
FRY, C. H., Cellular Physiology
FULBROOK, M. J. A., German History
FULLER, J. H., Clinical Epidemiology
FURNHAM, A. F., Psychology
GABELLA, G., Histology and Cytology
GAGE, S. A., Innovative Technology in Architecture
GALLIVAN, S., Mathematics
GARB, T., History of Art
GARDINER, R. M., Paediatrics
GARDNER-MEDWIN, A. R., Physiology
GARTHWAITE, J., Experimental Neuroscience
GELLER, M. J., Jewish Studies
GENN, H. G., Socio-Legal Studies
GILBERT, A. G., Geography
GILLAN, M. J., Physics
GILLESPIE, S. H., Medical Microbiology
GOADSBY, P. J., Clinical Neurology
GODOVAC-ZIMMERMANN, J., Protein Biochemistry
GOLDSPINK, G., Anatomy
GOLDSTEIN, D. B., Evolutionary and Population Genetics
GOLDSTONE, A. H., Haematology
GOODSHIP, A. E., Orthopaedic Sciences
GOODWIN, P. B., Transport Policy
GOSWAMI, U., Cognitive Developmental Psychology
GRAFFY, J. J., Russian Literature and Cinema
GRANTHAM-MCGREGOR, S. M., Child Health and Nutrition
GRASS, A. J., Fluid Mechanics
GREEN, C. J., Surgery
GREENHALGH, P. M., Primary Care Development
GREENWOOD, J., Biomedical Research
GREGORY, J., Water Chemistry
GRIFFITHS, H. D., Electronics
GRIFFITHS, P. D., Virology
GUERRINI, R., Paediatric Neurology
GUEST, J. E., Planetary Science
GUEST, S. F. D., Legal Philosophy
GURLING, H. M., Molecular Psychiatry
HALE, K. J., Chemistry
HALL, A., Molecular Biology
HALL, C., Modern British Social and Cultural History
HALL, C. M., Paediatric Radiology
HALL, P. G., Planning Studies
HAMILTON-MILLER, J. M. T., Medical Microbiology
HAMMOND, P., Dental and Medical Informatics
HANN, I., Paediatric Haematology and Oncology
HANSON, J. M., House Form and Culture
HARRIS, J. M., Linguistics
HARRIS, R., Geography
HARRISON, C. M., Geography
HARRISON, M. J. G., Clinical Neurology

HART, S. M., Hispanic Studies
HARTLEY, J. A., Cancer Studies
HARVEY, N. J. W., Judgement and Decision Research
HASSAN, F. A., Archaeology
HATCH, D. J., Paediatric Anaesthesia
HAUSSER, M. A., Neuroscience
HAWKINS, P. N., Medicine
HAWLEY, C., Architectural Studies
HAWORTH, S. G., Developmental Cardiology
HAZELL, R. J. D., Govt and the Constitution
HEBDEN, J. C., Biomedical Optics
HERMANS, T. J., Dutch and Comparative Literature
HERTZMAN, C., Paediatric Radiology
HEYDECKER, B. G., Transport Studies
HEYES, C. M., Psychology
HILLIARD, J., Fine Art Media
HILLIER, W. R. G., Architectural and Urban Morphology
HILLSON, S. W., Bioarchaeology
HITCHINGS, R. A., Glaucoma and Allied Studies
HOARE, M., Biochemical Engineering
HOBKIRK, J. A., Dental Prosthetics
HOBSON, R. P., Developmental Psychopathology
HOCKEY, S. M., Library and Information Studies
HODGSON, H., Medicine
HOMEWOOD, K. M., Human Ecology
HOPPIT, J., British History
HORNBLOWER, N. S. R., Classics and Ancient History
HORNE, F. P., English Language and Literature
HORTON, M. A., Bone Biology and Mineral Metabolism
HOSKING, G. A., Russian History
HOWARTH, I. D., Astronomy
HOWELL, P., Experimental Psychology
HUDSON, R. A., Linguistics
HUGHES, L. A. J., Russian History
HUMBERSTON, J. W., Physics
HUMPHRIES, S. E., Cardiovascular Genetics
HUNT, D. M., Molecular Genetics
HUNT, J. C. R., Climate Modelling
HUNT, N. P., Orthodontics
HUNT, S. P., Molecular Neurobiology
HYAMS, J. S., Cell Biology
ICHIMURA, H., Economics
INGRAM, D., Health Informatics
ISENBERG, D. A., Rheumatology
ISHAM, V. S., Probability and Statistics
JANOSSY, G., Immunology
JARVIS, M. J., Health Psychology
JAUNIAUX, E. R. M., Obstetrics and Fetal Medicine
JAYNE, J. E., Mathematics
JEHIEL, P., Economics
JESSEN, K. R., Developmental Neurobiology
JOHNSON, A. M., Primary Care and Population Sciences
JOHNSON, E. R., Mathematics
JOHNSON, F. E. A., Mathematics
JOHNSTON, A., Psychology
JONES, A. G., Chemical Engineering
JONES, D. T., Bioinformatics
JONES, J. S., Human Genetics
JONES, T. W., Physics
JORDAN, D., Physiology
JOWELL, J. L., Public Law
KAPLAN, B. J., Dutch History
KARLIN, D. R., English
KATONA, C. L. E., Psychiatry of the Elderly
KATZ, D. R., Immunopathology
KEMP, D. T., Auditory Biophysics
KHAW, P. T., Glaucoma Studies and Wound Healing
KING, M., Primary Care Psychiatry
KINNON, C., Molecular Immunology
KIRBY, D. G., Modern History
KIRSTEIN, P. T., Computer Systems
KLIER, J. D., Modern Jewish History
KOERNER, J. L., History of Art
KOLANKIEWICZ, J. M., Sociology

KUHRT, A. T. L., Ancient Near Eastern History
KULLMANN, D. M., Neurology
LARMAN, D. G., Mathematics
LAST, D. M., Anthropology
LATCHMAN, D. S., Human Genetics
LAURENT, G. J., Pulmonary Biochemistry
LAWRENCE, C. J., History of Medicine
LAYCOCK, G. K., Crime Science
LEES, A. J., Clinical Neurology
LEES, W. R., Medical Imaging
LEMON, R. N., Neurophysiology
LEONARD, J. V., Paediatric Metabolic Disease
LEWIS, A. D. E., Comparative Legal History
LIEBERMAN, A. R., Anatomy
LIGHTMAN, S. L., Clinical Ophthalmology
LIM, L., Neurochemistry
LINCH, D. C., Clinical Haematology
LINDON, J. M. A., Italian Studies
LITTLEWOOD, R., Anthropological Psychiatry
LLOYD, M. H., General Practice
LONDEI, M., Autoimmunity
LONGLEY, P. A., Geographic Information
LUMLEY, R., Italian Cultural History
LUND, V. J., Rhinology
LUTHERT, P. J., Pathology
LUXON, L. M., Audiological Medicine
LYDYARD, P. M., Immunology
MACHIN, S. J., Economics
MACHIN, S. J., Haematology
MACKETT, R. L., Transport Studies
MACLEAN, A. B., Obstetrics and Gynaecology
MACRORY, R. B., Environmental Law
MAJEED, F. A., Primary Care and Public Health
MALLET, J., Biological Diversity
MALONE-LEE, J. G., Geriatric Medicine
MARGETTS, H. Z., Political Science
MARKESINIS, B., Common Law and Civil Law
MARMOT, M. G., Epidemiology and Public Health
MARTIN, B. R. C., Physics
MARTIN, J. F., Cardiovascular Medicine
MARTIN, M. G. F., Philosophy
MARTIN, P., Tissue Repair
MASON, K. O., Astronomy
MASTERS, J. R. W., Experimental Pathology
MATHEWS, T. P., French
MATHIAS, C. J., Neurovascular Medicine
MCARTHUR, J. M., Geochemistry
MCCARTHY, M., Public Health
MCDOWELL, L. M., Economic Geography
MCEWEN, K. A., Physics
MCGUIRE, W. J., Geological Hazards
MCLEAN, P., Fine Art
MCMANUS, I. C., Psychology and Medical Education
MCMILLAN, P. F., Solid State Chemistry
MCMILLIN, A. B., Russian Literature
MCMULLEN, P., Mathematics
MEGHIR, C. H. D., Economics
MEREDITH, P. G., Rock Physics
MIDWINTER, J. E., Electrical Engineering
MILLA, P. J., Paediatric Gastroenterology
MILLER, A. I., History and Philosophy of Science
MILLER, D. H., Clinical Neurology
MILLER, D. J., Physics
MILLER, D. M. S., Anthropology
MIRSKY, R., Developmental Neurobiology
MOBBS, P. G., Physiology
MONCADA, S., Experimental Biology and Therapeutics
MONK, M., Molecular Embryology
MOORE, A. T., Ophthalmology
MORRIS, P. W. G., Construction and Project Management
MOSS, S. E., Biomedical Research
MOSS, S. J., Molecular Pharmacology and Cell Biology
MOTHERWELL, W. B., Chemistry
MULLER, J.-P. A. L., Image Understanding and Remote Sensing
MUNDY, A. R., Urology
MUNTON, R. J. C., Geography
MYTHEN, M. G., Paediatric Anaesthesia

NAZARETH, I. D., Primary Care and Population Science
NEILD, G. H., Nephrology
NEVILLE, B., Paediatric Neurology
NEWELL, M. L., Paediatric Epidemiology
NEWELL, W. R., Physics
NEWMAN, A. F., Economics
NEWMAN, S. P., Health Psychology
NORTH, J. A., History
NUGENT, J. H. A., Plant Biochemistry
NUTT, B. B., Facility and Environment Management
NUTTON, V., History of Medicine
O'DALY, G. J. P., Latin
O'HARE, M. J., Cell Biology
O'HIGGINS, P., Anatomy
O'KEEFE, J., Cognitive Neuroscience
O'KEEFFE, D., European Law
O'NEILL, M. E., Mathematics
O'REILLY, J. J., Telecommunications
ODA, H., Japanese Law
OLIVER, A. D. H., Constitutional Law
OLSEN, I., Cell Biology and Tissue Engineering
ONO, S. J., Ocular Immunology
ORDIDGE, R. J., Medical Physics
ORENGO, C. A., Bioinformatics
ORESZCZYN, T., Energy and Environment
ORTON, C. R., Quantitative Archaeology
OWEN, J. S., Molecular Medicine
PALMER, N. E., Law of Art and Cultural Property
PARKIN, I. P., Chemistry
PARMAR, M. K. B., Medical Statistics and Epidemiology
PARNAVELAS, J. G., Neuroanatomy
PARTRIDGE, L., Biometry
PATTISON, J. R., Medical Microbiology
PEARCE, D. W., Economics
PEARCE, F. L., Biological Chemistry
PECKHAM, C., Paediatric Epidemiology
PEPYS, M., Medicine
PERKINS, R. M., Norse Studies
PERKINS, S. J., Structural Biochemistry
PETTET, B. G., Company and Capital Markets Law
PHILLIPS, A., Epidemiology and Biostatistics
PICKERING, K. T., Sedimentology and Stratigraphy
PIERRO, A., Paediatric Surgery
PIPER, P. W., Molecular Microbiology
PITT, C. W., Electrical Engineering
PLATT, J. P., Geology
PLOTKIN, H. C., Psychobiology
POLLOCK, A. M., Health Services Policy
POMIANKOWSKI, A., Genetics
PORTER, J. B., Haematology
PORTER, S. R., Oral Medicine
POULTER, L. W., Immunology
POUNDER, R. E., Medicine
POVEY, M. S., Human Somatic Cell Genetics
POWER, C., Epidemiology and Public Health
POWIS, S. H., Renal Medicine
PRASHER, D. K., Audiology
PREECE, M., Child Health and Growth
PREISS, D., Pure Mathematics
PRICE, C. A., Archaeological Conservation
PRICE, G. D., Mineral Physics
PRICE, S. D., Chemical Physics
PRICE, S. L., Chemistry
PROWSE, P., Theatre Design
PYNSENT, R. B., Czech and Slovak Literature
QUINN, N. P., Clinical Neurology
RADEMACHER, T. W., Molecular Medicine
RAWSON, P. F., Geology
REHREN, T. H. H., Archaeological Materials and Technologies
REVELL, P. A., Histopathology
RICH, P. R., Bioenergetics
RICHARDS, C. D., Experimental Physiology
RICHARDS, P., Anthropology
RICHARDSON, W. D., Biology
ROBERTS, B. P., Chemistry
ROBERTS, G. J., Children's Dentistry
ROBERTSON, M. M., Neuropsychiatry
RODECK, C. H., Obstetrics and Gynaecology

ROEMER, C. E., Papyrology
RON, M. A., Neuropsychiatry
ROOK, G. A. W., Medical Microbiology
ROSEN, F. R., History of Political Thought
ROSEN, S., Speech and Hearing Sciences
ROTHWELL, J. C., Human Neurophysiology
ROWLAND, S. C. W., Higher Education
ROWLANDS, M. J. J., Material Culture
RUBIN, G. S., Visual Function and Rehabilitation
RUSSELL, M. A., Addiction
RYAN, J. M., Post-Conflict Recovery
SAGGERSON, E. D., Biochemistry
SALT, J., Geography
SALT, T. E., Visual Science
SALVERDA, R., Dutch Language and Literature
SAMMONDS, P. R., Geophysics
SANDER, J. W. A., Epilepsy
SANDS, P. J., Law
SAUNDERS, M. I., Oncology
SCAMBLER, G. N., Medical Sociology
SCAMBLER, P. J., Molecular Medicine
SCARAVILLI, F., Neuropathology
SCHAPIRA, A. H. V., Neurology
SCHOFIELD, T. P., History of Legal and Political Thought
SCULLY, C. M., Special Needs Dentistry
SEEDS, A. J., Opto-electronics
SEGAL, A. W., Medicine
SENN, S. J., Pharmaceutical and Health Statistics
SEYMOUR, R. M., Mathematics
SHALLICE, T., Psychology
SHANKS, D. R., Experimental Psychology
SHARPLES, R. W., Classics
SHEIHAM, A., Dental Public Health
SHENNAN, S. J., Theoretical Archaeology
SHEPHARD, E. A., Molecular Biology
SHEPHERD, P. R., Cellular Signalling
SHERR, L., Clinical and Health Psychology
SHORVON, S. D., Clinical Neurology
SILLITO, A. M., Visual Science
SIMONS, S. J. R., Chemical Engineering
SINDET-PEDERSEN, S., Oral Implantology
SINGER, A., Gynaecological Research
SINGER, M., Intensive Care Medicine
SLATER, M., Virtual Environments
SMART, T. G., Pharmacology
SMITH, A., Detector Physics
SMITH, A. H., Political Economy
SMITH, F. T., Mathematics
SMITH, N. V., Linguistics
SMITH, S. R., Economics
SNOWDON, P. F.
SOMMER, V., Evolutionary Anthropology
SOUTHGATE, L. J., Primary Care and Education
SPEIGHT, P. M., Oral Pathology
SPELLER, R. D., Medical Physics
SPIRO, S. G., Respiratory Medicine
SPOOR, C. F., Evolutionary Anatomy
SPYER, K. M., Physiology
STANFORD, J. L., Medical Microbiology
STEADMAN, J. P., Urban and Built Form Studies
STEPHENS, J. A., Physiology
STEPTOE, A. P. A., Psychology
STOCKMAN, A., Investigative Eye Research
STOCKS, J., Respiratory Medicine
STONEHAM, A. M., Physics
STOREY, P. J., Physics
STROBEL, S., Paediatrics and Clinical Immunology
SURTEES, R. A. H., Paediatric Neurology
SUTHERLAND, J. A., Modern English Literature
SUTTON, S. R., Social and Health Psychology
SWALES, M. W., German
SWALLOW, D. M., Biology
SWANN, P. F., Molecular Oncology
SWANSON, T. M., Law and Economics
TAIT, W. J., Egyptology
TAYLOR, B., Community Child Health
TAYLOR, I., Surgery
TEDDER, R. S., Medical Virology

TENNYSON, J., Physics
THIMBLEBY, H. W., Human Interaction with Systems
THOMAS, D. G. T., Neurological Surgery
THOMAS, K. D., Human Palaeoecology
THOMPSON, A. J., Clinical Neurology and Neurorehabilitation
THOMPSON, E. J., Neurochemistry
THORNTON, J. M., Biomolecular Structure
THRASHER, A. J., Paediatric Immunology
TILLEY, C. Y., Anthropology and Archaeology
TITCHENER-HOOKER, N. J., Biochemical Engineering
TOBIAS, J. S., Cancer Medicine
TODD, C. J., Network Science
TODD-POKROPEK, A. E., Medical Physics
TOFTS, P. S., Medical Physics
TOMKINS, A. M., International Child Health
TONETTI, M., Periodontology
TOOK, J. F., Dante Studies
TRELEAVEN, P. C., Computer Science
TRIMBLE, M. R., Behavioural Neurology
TURNER, M. W., Molecular Immunology
TURNER, R., Anthropology
TWINING, W. L., Jurisprudence
TYLER, N. A., Communities and Transport
UCKO, P. J., Comparative Archaeology
UNWIN, R., Nephrology and Physiology
VALLANCE, P., Clinical Pharmacology
VAN DER LELY, H. K. J., Developmental Language Disorders and Cognitive Neuroscience
VAN GRIETHUYSEN, W. J., Naval Architecture
VAN REENEN, J. M., Economics
VARGHA-KHADEM, F., Developmental Cognitive Neuroscience
VERGANI, D., Immunopathology
WAKELY, P. I., Urban Development
WALTON, S. J., Norwegian
WARDLE, F. J., Clinical Psychology
WARNER, A. E., Developmental Biology
WASHBROOK, J., Computer Science
WATERFIELD, M. D., Biochemistry
WEIS, R. J., English
WEISS, R. A., Viral Oncology
WELLER, I. V. D., Sexually Transmitted Diseases
WELLS, J. C., Phonetics
WESTON, H. D., History of Art
WHITEHOUSE, R. D., Archaeology
WIGZELL, F. C. M., Russian Literature and Culture
WILBUR, S. R., Distributed Systems
WILKIN, C., Physics
WILLIAMS, G. H., Histopathology
WILLIAMS, R. S., Hepatology
WILLIS, A. J., Astronomy
WILSON, D. S. M., Linguistics
WILSON, E. J., Latin American Literature
WILSON, M., Microbiology
WILSON, S. W., Developmental Genetics
WINCHESTER, B. G., Biochemistry
WINGHAM, D. J., Climate Physics
WINSLET, M. C., Surgery
WINTER, R. M., Clinical Genetics
WOLEDGE, R. C., Experimental Physiology
WOLFF, J., Philosophy
WOLPERT, D. M., Motor Neuroscience
WOLPERT, L., Biology as applied to Medicine
WOO, P. M. M., Paediatric Rheumatology
WOOD, N. W., Clinical Neurogenetics
WOOD, P. A., Geography
WOOLF, A. S., Nephrology
WORTON, M. J., French Language and Literature
WOTTON, R. S., Biology
WOUDHUYSEN, H. R., English Language and Literature
WRIGHT, A., Otorhinolaryngology
WU, G., Computational Fluid Dynamics
WYATT, J. S., Neonatal Paediatrics
YANG, Z., Statistical Genetics
YATES, J. G., Chemical Engineering
YELLON, D. M., Cellular Cardiology
YIP, M. J., Linguistics
YOUSRY, T. A., Neuroradiology

YUDKIN, J. S., Medicine
ZEKI, S., Neurobiology
ZUMLA, A., Infectious Diseases and International Health

SCHOOL OF THE COLLEGE

UCL School of Slavonic and East European Studies: Univ. of London, London, WC1E 7HU; tel. (20) 7636-8000; f. 1915, merged with Univ. College London 1999; library of 400,000 vols; 60 teachers; 500 students (460 full-time, 40 part-time); Dir Dr ROBIN P. AIZLEWOOD; Academic Registrar CAROL PEARCE; publ. *The Slavonic and East European Review* (4 a year).

UNIVERSITY INSTITUTES

University of London Institute in Paris

9–11 rue de Constantine, 75340 Paris Cedex 07, France
Telephone: (1) 44-11-73-73
Fax: (1) 45-50-31-55
E-mail: french@ulip.lon.ac.uk
Internet: www.ulip.lon.ac.uk
Founded 1894 as 'Guilde Franco-Anglaise', attached to Univ. of Paris 1927, now a central institute of Univ. of London, partner of Queen Mary and Royal Holloway, Univ. of London
Languages of instruction: French, English
Academic year: September to July
Dean: Prof. ANDREW HUSSEY
Project Man.: ANNA GRAY
Office Man.: COLLETTE BROWN
Librarian: ERICA BURNHAM
Library of 10,000 vols, 25 journals and electronic subscriptions
Number of teachers: 13
Number of students: 160 f.t.e.
Publication: *Francosphères*

PROFESSORS
HUSSEY, A., French Studies

University Marine Biological Station Millport

Millport, Isle of Cumbrae, Scotland, KA28 0EG
Telephone: (1475) 530581
Fax: (1475) 530601
E-mail: tracy.price@millport.gla.ac.uk
Internet: www.gla.ac.uk/marinestation
Founded 1970 in asscn with Univ. of Glasgow
Teaches and researches in marine biology
Library of 5,000 vols
Dir: Prof. JIM ATKINSON (acting)
Deputy Dir: FIONA HANNAH
Sec.: TRACY E. PRICE

PROFESSORS
ATKINSON, R. J. A., Marine Biology
MOORE, P. G., Marine Biology.

CONSTITUENT INSTITUTES OF THE SCHOOL OF ADVANCED STUDY

Dean of the School of Advanced Study: Prof. C. N. J. MANN

School of Advanced Studies

17 Russell Sq., London, WC1B 5DR
Telephone: (20) 7862-5800
Fax: (20) 7862-5850
E-mail: ials@sas.ac.uk
Internet: www.ials.sas.ac.uk
Academic year: October to December
Founded 1947
Man.: MARGARET R. WILSON
Assoc. Dir and Librarian: JULES WINTERTON
Library: see Libraries and Archives
Publication: *Amicus Curiae*

PROFESSORS
DAINTITH, T. C., Constitutional and Admin. Law, Economic Law
RIDER, B. A. K., Company Law, Commercial Criminal Law
SHERR, A. H., Legal Education, the Legal Profession, Legal Services

Institute of Classical Studies

Senate House, Malet St, London, WC1E 7HU
Telephone: (20) 7862-8700
Fax: (20) 7862-8722
E-mail: admin.icls@sas.ac.uk
Internet: www.icls.sas.ac.uk
Founded 1953
Library of basic research books complemented by library of Hellenic and Roman Socs (jt library of 100,000 vols); seminars and lectures for students
Dir: Prof. JOHN NORTH
Sec.: Dr OLGA KRZYSZKOWSKA
Publications: *Bulletin* (3 a year), *Bulletin Supplements*.

Institute of Commonwealth Studies

Second Fl., S Block, Senate House, Malet St, London, WC1E 7HU
Telephone: (20) 7262-8844
Fax: (20) 7262-8813
E-mail: ics@sas.ac.uk
Internet: commonwealth.sas.ac.uk
Founded 1949
Academic year: September to June
Dir: Prof. PHILIP MURPHY
Admin. Man.: ALISON STEWART
Information Resources Man.: DAVID CLOVER
Library of 190,000 vols, 9,000 periodical and serial publs, 230 archival collns
Number of teachers: 5 (full-time)
Number of students: 80
Publication: *Journal of Imperial and Commonwealth History* (4 a year)

PROFESSORS
HOLLAND, R., Imperial and Commonwealth History
MANOR, J., Emeka Anyaoku prof. of Commonwealth Studies
MURPHY, P., British and Commonwealth History

ATTACHED INSTITUTE

Commonwealth Policy Studies Unit (CPSU): internet www.cpsu.org.uk; Head Dr VICTORIA TE VELDE; Asst Dir Dr LEO ZEILIG.

Institute of English Studies

School of Advanced Study, Senate House, Malet St, London, WC1E 7HU
Telephone: (20) 7862-8675
Fax: (20) 7862-8720
E-mail: ies@sas.ac.uk
Internet: ies.sas.ac.uk
Founded 1991 as Centre for English Studies; present name 1999
State control
Academic year: September to June
Dir: Prof. WARWICK GOULD
Number of teachers: 35
Number of students: 28

Institute of Germanic and Romance Studies

Senate House, Malet St, London, WC1E 7HU
Telephone: (20) 7862-8677
Fax: (20) 7862-8672
E-mail: igrs@sas.ac.ukGermanic Studies

Library: 29 Russell Sq., London, WC1B 5DP
Telephone: (20) 7862-8967
Fax: (20) 7862-8970
E-mail: igslib@sas.ac.uk
Internet: igrs.sas.ac.uk
Founded 2004, by merger of Institute of Germanic Studies (f. 1950) and Institute of Romance Studies (f. 1989)
Academic year: October to June
Dir: Prof. NAOMI SEGAL
Admin. Sec.: ROSEMARY LAMBETH
Librarian: WILLIAM ABBEY; 1,320 mems
Library of 100,000 vols
Number of teachers: 6
Number of students: 25
Publications: *Journal of Romance Studies* (3 a year), *London German Studies* (irregular).

Institute of Historical Research

Senate House, Malet St., London, WC1E 7HU
Telephone: (20) 7862-8740
Fax: (20) 7862-8745
E-mail: ihr@sas.ac.uk
Internet: www.history.ac.uk
Founded 1921
Academic year: October to August
Dir: Prof. MILES TAYLOR
Institute Administrator: ELAINE WALTERS
Librarian: ALISON GAGE
Library: see Libraries and Archives
Number of teachers: 8
Number of students: 57
Publications: *Historical Research* (4 a year), *Past and Future, Teachers of History* (1 a year), *Theses in Progress and Theses Completed* (1 a year)

PROFESSORS
ROBERTS, R., Contemporary British History
TAYLOR, M., Modern History
THANE, P., Contemporary British History

Institute of Musical Research

Senate House, Malet St, London, WC1E 7HU
Telephone: (20) 7664-4865
Fax: (20) 7664-4867
E-mail: music@sas.ac.uk
Internet: music.sas.ac.uk
Founded 2005, began operating 2006
Funded by HEFCE; fosters collaborative research; hosts visiting scholars; organizes confs and other events; provides research training support for postgraduate students
Dir: Dr PAUL ARCHBOLD
Administrator: VALERIE JAMES.

Institute of Philosophy

Senate House, Malet St, London, WC1E 7HU
Telephone: (20) 7862-8683
Fax: (20) 7862-8639
E-mail: philosophy@sas.ac.uk
Internet: www.philosophy.sas.ac.uk
Founded 2005
Promotes and disseminates research in philosophy
Dir: Prof. BARRY C. SMITH
Administrator: Dr SHAHRAR ALI.

Institute for the Study of the Americas

Senate House, Malet St, London, WC1H 7HU
Telephone: (20) 7862-8870
Fax: (20) 7862-8886
E-mail: americas@sas.ac.uk
Internet: www.americas.sas.ac.uk
Founded 2004 by merger of Institute of Latin American Studies (f. 1964) and Institute of United States Studies (f. 1965)

Academic year: October to July
Dir: Prof. MAXINE MOLYNEUX
Admin. Man.: PAUL SULLIVAN
Librarian: CHRISTINE ANDERSON
Number of teachers: 9
Number of students: 80
Publication: *Journal of Latin American Studies* (4 a year)

PROFESSORS

MIDDLEBROOK, K., Politics
MOLYNEUX, M., Sociology
MORGAN, I., United States Studies

Warburg Institute

Woburn Sq., London, WC1H 0AB
Telephone: (20) 7862-8949
Fax: (20) 7862-8955
E-mail: warburg@sas.ac.uk
Internet: www.warburg.sas.ac.uk
Founded 1921
Academic year: October to September
Dir: Prof. P. W. MACK
Librarian: Prof. JILL KRAYE
Library: see under Libraries and Archives
Number of teachers: 5
Number of students: 15
Publications: *Journal of the Warburg and Courtauld Institutes* (1 a year), *Warburg Institute Colloquia* (1 a year), *Warburg Studies and Texts* (irregular)

PROFESSORS

BURNETT, C. S. F., History of Islamic Influences in Europe
KRAYE, J. A., History of Renaissance Philosophy.

ASSOCIATE INSTITUTION

The following institution has recognized teachers of the University of London on its staff and offers courses leading to degrees of the University.
Institute of Cancer Research: 123 Old Brompton Rd, London, SW7 3RP; tel. (20) 7352-8133; fax (20) 7370-5261; internet www .icr.ac.uk; f. 1909; library of 25,000 vols; Chief Exec. Prof. ALAN ASHWORTH; Sec. CATHY SCIVIER; Academic Dean Prof. ALAN HORWICH.

UNIVERSITY OF MANCHESTER

Oxford Rd, Manchester, M13 9PL
Telephone: (161) 306-6000
E-mail: ug-admissions@manchester.ac.uk
Internet: www.manchester.ac.uk
Founded 2004 following merger of Univ. of Manchester (f. 1851) and UMIST (f. 1824)
Academic year: September to June
Chancellor: TOM BLOXHAM
Pres. and Vice-Chancellor: Prof. Dame NANCY J. ROTHWELL
Deputy Pres. and Deputy Vice-Chancellor: Prof. ROD COOMBS
Pro-Chancellor: NORMAN ASKEW (Chair. of the Board of Governors)
Pro-Chancellor: Sir JOHN KERR
Registrar and Sec.: ALBERT MCMENEMY
Vice-Pres.: Prof. COLIN BAILEY
Vice-Pres.: Prof. KEITH BROWN
Vice-Pres.: Prof. MARTIN HUMPHRIES
Vice-Pres.: Prof. ALAN NORTH
Vice-Pres. for Research and Innovation: Prof. LUKE GEORGHIOU
Vice-Pres. for Teaching and Learning: Prof. COLIN STIRLING
Univ. Librarian: JAN WILKINSON
Library: See John Rylands Univ. Library of Manchester
Number of teachers: 3,972
Number of students: 37,021

DEANS

Faculty of Engineering and Physical Sciences: Prof. COLIN BAILEY
Faculty of Humanities: Prof. KEITH BROWN
Faculty of Life Sciences: Prof. MARTIN HUMPHRIES
Faculty of Medical and Human Sciences: Prof. ALAN NORTH

PROFESSORS

Faculty of Engineering and Physical Sciences
School of Chemical Engineering and Analytical Science:
ALDER, J. F.
CILLIERS, J.
DAVEY, R.
DEWHURST, R.
DYAKOWSKI, T.
FIELDEN, P.
GODDARD, N.
GRIFFITHS, R.
HEGGS, P.
MANN, R.
MAVITUNA, F.
MCCARTHY, J.
PERSAUD, K.
ROBERTS, S.
SHARRATT, P.
SMITH, R.
SNOOK, R.
TIDDY, G.
VICKERMAN, J.
WEBB, C.

School of Chemistry:
ANDERSON, N. W.
BAILEY, P. D.
CLARKE, J. H. R.
CLAYDEN, J. P.
CONNOR, J. N. L.
GASKELL, S. J.
HELLIWELL, J. R.
HILLIER, I. H.
KELL, D. B.
LIVENS, F. R.
MORRIS, G. A.
MUNN, R. W.
O'BRIEN, P.
STOODLEY, R. J.
SUTHERLAND, J.
TAIT, P. J. T.
THOMAS, E. J.
TURNER, M.
VICKERMAN, J. C.
WAUGH, K. C.
WINPENNY, R.
WOODPENNY, L. V.

School of Computer Science:
ACZEL, P.
BARRINGER, H.
BARTON, S.
BREE, D.
FURBER, S.
GOBLE, C.
GURD, J.
HORROCKS, I.
HUBBOLD, R.
KAHN, H.
MIDDLETON, B.
PATON, N.
RECTOR, A.
TAYLOR, C.
VORONKOV, A.
WARBOYS, B.
WATSON, I.

School of Earth, Atmospheric and Environmental Sciences:
CHOULARTON, T. W., Atmospheric Physics
CURTIS, C., Geochemistry
GAWTHORPE, R., Sedimentation and Tectonics
HENDERSON, M., Petrology
JONAS, P. R., Atmospheric Physics
PATTRICK, R., Earth Sciences

RUTTER, E., Earth Sciences
SELDEN, P., Earth Sciences
TURNER, G., Earth Sciences
VAUGHAN, D., Mineralogy
VAUGHAN, G., Atmospheric Sciences
ZUSSMAN, Z., Earth Sciences

School of Electrical and Electronic Engineering:
ALLINSON, N. M.
BROWN, A. K.
DAVIS, L. E.
GOTT, G. F.
HICKS, P. J.
JENKINS, N.
KIRSCHEN, D.
MCCANN, H.
MISSOUS, M.
MUNRO, N.
PEAKER, A. R.
REZAZADEH, A.
STRBAC, G.
WANG, H.
WILLIAMSON, S.
YORK, T. A.

School of Materials:
DERBY, B., Materials Science
FREER, R., Materials Science
HUMPHREYS, F. J., Materials Science
LORIMER, G., Materials Science
LOVELL, P., Polymer Science
O'BRIEN, P., Inorganic Materials, Chemistry
ROBERTS, J., Textiles and Paper
SALE, F., Chemical Metallurgy and Materials Science
SHERRY, A., Corrosion and Protection
STANFORD, J., Polymer Materials Science
STOTT, H., Corrosion and Protection
THOMPSON, G., Corrosion and Protection
WITHERS, P., Materials Science
YOUNG, R., Polymer Science and Technology

School of Mathematics:
ABRAHAMS, I. D., Applied Mathematics
ACZEL, P. H., Mathematical Logic and Computing Science
BOROVIK, A., Pure Mathematics
BROOMHEAD, D., Applied Mathematics
BRYANT, R., Pure Mathematics
DODSON, K., Geometry
DOLD, J., Applied Mathematics
DONEY, R. A., Probability Theory
DUCK, P. W., Applied Mathematics
GLENDINNING, P., Applied Mathematics
HIGHAM, N. J., Applied Mathematics
PARIS, J. B., Pure Mathematics
PLYMEN, R. J., Pure Mathematics
PREMET, A. A., Algebra
PREST, M., Pure Mathematics
RAY, N., Pure Mathematics
ROWLEY, P., Mathematics
RUBAN, A., Computational Fluid Dynamics
SILVESTER, D., Applied Mathematics
SUBBA RAO, T., Statistics
TAYLOR, M. J., Pure Mathematics
WOOD, R. M. W., Algebra

School of Mechanical, Aerospace and Civil Engineering:
AL-HASSANI, S. T. S., Mechanical Engineering
BAILEY, C., Structural Engineering
BALL, A. D., Maintenance Engineering
COOPER, J. E., Engineering
DAVIES, M., Structural Engineering
HAYHURST, D. R., Design, Manufacture and Materials
HINDUJA, S., Mechanical Engineering
JACKSON, J. D., Mechanical and Nuclear Engineering
LAUNDER, B. E., Mechanical Engineering
LAURENCE, D., Computational Fluid Dynamics
LEUNG, A., Engineering
LEVERMORE, G., Built Environment

LI, L., Laser Engineering
MARSDEN, B., Nuclear Graphite Technology
REID, S. R., Mechanical Engineering
SANDOZ, D. J., Control Engineering
SMITH, I., Geotechnics
STANSBY, P., Hydrodynamics
THOMPSON, G., Mechanical Engineering
TURAN, A., Mechanical Engineering
VARLOW, B. R., Industrial Liaison
WINCH, G., Construction Project Management
WOOD, N., Aerospace Engineering
WRIGHT, J. R., Mechanical Engineering

School of Physics and Astronomy:

BARLOW, S. J., Particle Physics
BISHOP, R. F., Theoretical Physics
BRAY, A. J., Theoretical Physics
DIAMOND, P. D., Astronomy and Astrophysics
DURELL, J. L., Nuclear Physics
FLAVELL, W. R., Photon Physics
FORSHAW, J. R., Particle Physics
GEIM, A. K., Condensed Matter Physics
GLEESON, H. F., Nonlinear and Liquid Crystal Physics
KING, G. C., Photon Physics
KING, T. A., Photon Physics
LAFFERTY, G. D., Particle Physics
LU, J., Biological Physics
LYNE, A. G., Astronomy and Astrophysics
MARSHALL, R., Particle Physics
MILLAR, T. J., Astronomy and Astrophysics
MOORE, M. A., Theoretical Physics
MULLIN, T., Nonlinear and Liquid Crystal Physics
WALET, N. R., Theoretical Physics
WILKINSON, P. N., Astronomy and Astrophysics
WYATT, T. R., Particle Physics
ZIJLSTRA, A. A., Astronomy and Astrophysics

Faculty of Humanities

School of Arts, Histories and Culture:

ADAMSON, S., Linguistics and Literary History
ALEXANDER, P., Post-Biblical Jewish Studies
BERGIN, J., Modern History
BROOKE, G. J., Biblical Studies
CASKEN, J., Music
CAUSEY, A., Modern Art History
COOPER, B., Music
CORNELL, T., Ancient History
CROWLEY, T., Modern English Literature
DENISON, D., English Linguistics
EAGLETON, T., Cultural Theory
FALLOWS, D., Music
FANNING, D., Music
FOURACRE, P., History
GARDNER, V., Theatre Studies
GATRELL, P., Modern History
GRAHAM, E. L., Social and Pastoral Theology
GRANGE, P., Music
HAMMOND, G., English Literature
HOGG, R. M., English Language and Medieval English Literature
JACKSON, B. S., Modern Jewish Studies
JANTZEN, G. M., Philosophy of Religion
JONES, A., History of Art
JOYCE, P., Modern History
LANGSLOW, D., Classics
LING, R., Archaeology
MILLWARD, R., Economic History
PARKIN, T., Ancient History
PEARSON, J., English Literature
PITTOCK, M., Scottish and Romantic Literature
SCRAGG, D., Anglo-Saxon Studies
SHARROCK, A., Classics
SUMMERFIELD, P., Modern History
THOMAS, J., Archaeology
WARD, B., American Studies

WARD, G., Contextual Theology
WOOLFORD, J., 19th-century Literature and Culture

School of Education:

AINSCOW, M., Education
BAMFORD, J., Audiology and Deaf Education
CONTI-RAMSDEN, G., Specific Language Impairment
DAVIES, A., Education
DYSON, A., Education
FARRELL, P., Educational Psychology
THOMPSON, L., Language and Literacy Studies
WEST, M., Educational Leadership
WILLIAMS, J. S., Mathematics Education

School of Environment and Development:

AGNEW, C., Geography
ALLOTT, T., Geography
BEBBINGTON, A., Management in International Development
BRADFORD, M., Geography
CASTREE, N., Geography
COOK, P., Economics and Development Policy
DOUGLAS, I., Geography
HANDLEY, J., Land Restoration and Management
HEBBERT, M., Town Planning
HENDERSON, J., International Economic Sociology
HULME, D., Development Studies
KIRKPATRICK, C., Development Economics
MACDOUGALL, G., Architecture and Advanced Technology
ROBSON, B., Geography
STONEHOUSE, R., Architecture
THOMAS, R., Geography
WILLIAMS, G., Urban Planning and Development
WOOD, C., Environmental Planning

School of Informatics:

BLENKHORN, P., Interactive Systems Design
KEANE, J., Data and Decision Engineering
LOUCOPOULOS, P., Information Systems
MACAULAY, L., System Design
RAMSAY, A., Data and Decision Engineering
SUTCLIFFE, A., Interactive Systems Design
WASTELL, D., Information Systems
WOOD, J., Information Systems
WOOD-HARPER, A., Information Systems

School of Languages, Linguistics and Cultures:

ALEXANDER, P. S., Middle Eastern Studies
BERGER, S., Modern German and Comparative European History
DURRELL, M., German
GÜNSBERG, M., Italian
LAWRANCE, J., Spanish
PARKER, S., German
PERRIAM, C., Hispanic Studies
SMITH, G. R., Middle Eastern Studies
TOLZ, V., Russian

School of Law:

BRAZIER, M., Law
BRAZIER, R., Law
DOBASH, R., Law
DUXBURY, N., Law
GIBBONS, T., Law
HARRIS, J., Law
HARRIS, N., Law
HÄYRY, M., Law
JACONELLI, J., Law
MCCORMACK, G., Law
MCGEE, A., Law
MILLMAN, D., Law
OGUS, A., Law
QURESHI, A., Law
SANDERS, A., Law
SHAW, J., Law
TSUJII, J., Text Mining

Manchester Business School:

BARRAR, P., Operations Management
BOWE, M., International Finance
BRUCE, M., Design Management and Retailing
CHITTENDEN, F., Small Business Finance
CONYON, M., Corporate Governance
COOMBS, R., Technology Management
DAVIDSON, M., Managerial Psychology
DAVIES, G., Corporate Reputation
EASINGWOOD, C., Marketing
EDWARDS, P., Accountancy
FRENCH, S., Information and Decision Sciences
GARRETT, I., Accounting and Finance
GEORGHIOU, L., Technology and Entrepreneurship Management and Policy
GHAURI, P., International Business
GREEN, K., Technology and Entrepreneurship Management and Policy
HASSARD, J., Organizational Analysis
HIGGINS, J., Health Policy
HOWELLS, J., Innovation and Competition
HUMPHREY, C., Accounting
JACKSON, P., Corporate Communications
KANG, J., Marketing
LEWIS, B., Marketing
LITTLER, D., Strategic Management
MARCHINGTON, M., Human Resource Management
MCGOLDRICK, P., Retailing
MILES, I., Technology and Entrepreneurship Management and Policy
NAUDÉ, P., Marketing
NEWMAN, M., Management Accounting and Information Systems
OAKEY, R., Business Development
OGDEN, S., Accounting and Finance
O'LEARY, T., Accounting
PAXSON, D., Finance
POON, S.-H., Finance
RICKARDS, T., Creativity and Organizational Change
ROBSON, K., Accounting
RUBERY, J., Comparative Employment Systems
SANGHAVI, N., Retail Marketing and Strategy
SCAPENS, R., Management Accounting and Information Systems
SPARROW, P., International Human Resource Management
STAPLETON, R., Finance
STARK, A., Accounting
STEPHEN, F., Regulation
STRONG, N., Finance
TURLEY, S., Accounting
WADDINGTON, J., Human Resource Management
WALKER, M., Finance and Accounting
WALSH, V., Innovation Management
WALSHE, K., Health Policy and Management
WILLIAMS, K., Accounting and Political Economy
YANG, J.-B., Decision Sciences and Operations Management

School of Social Sciences:

AGÉNOR, P.-R., Economics
BLACKBURN, K., Economics
CALLAHAN, W., International Politics
COLMAN, D., Economics
EVSTIGNEEV, I., Economics
GLEDHILL, J., Social Anthropology
HARVEY, P., Social Anthropology
HENLEY, P., Social Anthropology
MADDEN, P., Economics
MASON, J., Sociology
METCALFE, S., Economics
NIXSON, F., Economics
OSBORN, D., Economics
SMART, C., Sociology
WADE, P., Social Anthropology
WERBNER, R., Social Anthropology
YOUNG, T., Economics

Faculty of Life Sciences:
ABADI, R.
ATTWOOD, T.
BALMENT, R.
BARNES, G.
BRASS, A.
BROWN, T. A.
BULLEID, N.
CASE, M.
CHARMAN, W.
CRONLY-DILLON, J.
CROSSMAN, A.
DAVID, R.
DIXON, M.
DUNNE, M.
EDDY, A.
EFRON, N.
FERGUSON, M.
FOSTER, D.
GARROD, D.
GRANT, R.
GRENCIS, R.
HARDINGHAM, T.
HIGH, S.
HUMPHRIES, M.
HUTCHINSON, I.
HYDE, J. E.
ITZHAKI, R.
KADLER, K.
KAUPPINEN, R.
KIELTY, C.
KULIKOWSKI, J.
LIAN, L. Y.
LOUDON, A.
MCCARTHY, J. E. G.
MOORE, A.
NORTH, R. A.
OLIVER, S.
PICKSTONE, J.
POLLER, L.
ROBERTS, I.
ROTHWELL, N.
SHARROCKS, A.
SIBLEY, C.
STERN, P.
STIRLING, C.
STREULI, C.
TERENGHI, G.
TOMLINSON, D.
TRINCI, A.
TURNER, S.
VERKHRATSKY, A.
WESTON, A.
WHETTON, A. D.
WHITE, A.
WORBOYS, M.

Faculty of Medical and Human Sciences
School of Dentistry:
BLINKHORN, A. S., Oral Health
DIXON, M. J., Dental Genetics
FERGUSON, M. W. J., Basic Dental Sciences
O'BRIEN, K. D., Orthodontics
SHAW, W. C., Orthodontics and Dentofacial Development
SLOAN, P., Experimental Oral Pathology
THORNHILL, M. H., Medicine in Dentistry
WILSON, N. H. F., Restorative Dentistry
School of Medicine:
ADAMS, J. E., Diagnostic Radiology
AGIUS, R., Occupational and Environmental Medicine
BIRCH, J. M., Cancer Research Campaign, Paediatric and Familial Cancer Research Group
BOULTON, A. J. M., Medicine
BURNIE, J. P., Medical Microbiology
CASE, R. M., Physiology
CHERRY, N. M., Occupational and Environmental Medicine
CROSSMAN, A. R., Anatomy
DAVID, T. J., Child Health and Paediatrics
DAVIS, J. R. E., Medicine
DUNN, G., Biomedical Statistics
DURRINGTON, P. N., Medicine

EDEN, O. B., Paediatric Oncology
EISNER, D., Cardiac Physiology
FREEMONT, A. J., Tissue Pathology
GALASKO, C. S. B., Orthopaedic Surgery
GALLAGHER, S. T., Oncology
GARROD, D. R., Developmental Biology
GORDON, D., Medicine
GRANT, M. E., Medical Biochemistry
GREEN, R., Physiology
GRENCIS, R. K., Immunology
GRIFFITHS, C. E. M., Dermatology
HAWKINS, R. E., Medical Oncology
HEAGERTY, A., Medicine
HELLER, R., Public Health
HERHOLZ, K., Clinical Neurosciences
HICKMAN, J., Molecular Pharmacology
HORAN, M. A., Geriatric Medicine (South)
HOWELL, A., Medical Oncology
HUTCHINSON, I. V., Immunology
IRVING, M. H., Surgery
JACKSON, A., Neuroradiology
KIERNAN, C. C., Behavioural Studies in Mental Handicap
KIRKWOOD, T. B. L., Biological Gerontology
KITCHENER, H. C., Gynaecological Oncology
LOWENSTEIN, P. R., Molecular Medicine and Gene Therapy
MALLICK, N. P., Renal Medicine
MAWER, E. B., Bone and Mineral Metabolism
MAYES, A., Cognitive Neuroscience
MCALLISTER, I., Medicine
MCCLURE, J., Pathology
MCCOLLUM, C. N., Surgery
MCCORD, J. F., Restorative Care of the Elderly
MCLEOD, D., Ophthalmology
MÜLLER, R., Pharmaceutics, Biopharmaceutics and Biotechnology
O'BRIEN, K. D., Orthodontics
OLLIER, W. E. R., Immunogenetics
POLLARD, B. J., Anaesthesia
PRICE, P., Radiation Oncology
READ, A. P., Human Genetics
RECTOR, A. L., Medical Informatics
ROLAND, M. O., General Practice
SCARFFE, J. H., Oncology
SEYMOUR, L., Gene Therapy
SIBBALD, B. S., Health Services Research
SIBLEY, C. P., Child Health and Physiology
SILMAN, A. J., Rheumatic Diseases Epidemiology
STANLEY, J. K., Hand Surgery
TALLIS, R. C., Geriatric Medicine (Salford)
TAYLOR, C. J., Medical Biophysics
THATCHER, N., Oncology
THOMPSON, D. G., Gastroenterology
VADGAMA, P., Clinical Biochemistry
WHITE, A., Endocrine Sciences
WHITEHOUSE, C. R., Teaching Medicine in the Community
WILKIN, D., Health Services Research
WOODMAN, C. B. J., Cancer Epidemiology and Public Health
YATES, D. W., Accident and Emergency Surgery
School of Nursing, Midwifery and Social Work:
CARLISLE, E., Education in Nursing and Midwifery
LUKER, K., Nursing and Midwifery
THOMSON, A., Midwifery
TODD, C., Primary Care and Community Health
WATERMAN, H., Nursing and Midwifery
School of Pharmacy and Pharmaceutical Sciences:
ATTWOOD, D.
CANTRILL, J.
CLARKE, D.
COLLETT, J.
DIVE, C.
DOUGLAS, K.
GIFFORD, L.
GILBERT, P.

HOUSTON, J. B.
NOYCE, P.
ROWLAND, M.
STRATFORD, I.
School of Psychological Sciences:
BAMFORD, J.
BARROWCLOUGH, C.
BEATTIE, G.
BENTALL, R.
CONTI-RAMSEN, G.
DAVIS, A.
LAMBON-RALPH, M.
LIEVEN, E.
MEUDELL, P.
PARKER, D.
TARRIER, N.
WEARDEN, J. H.

UNIVERSITY OF NORTHAMPTON

Park Campus, Boughton Green Rd, Northampton, NN2 7AL
Ave Campus, St George's Ave, Northampton, NN2 6JD
Telephone: (1604) 735500
Fax: (1604) 720636
E-mail: study@northampton.ac.uk
Internet: www.northampton.ac.uk
Founded 1975 by merger of College of Education, College of Technology and College of Art, present name and status 2005
Academic year: September to July
Chancellor: Baroness FALKNER OF MARGRAVINE
Vice-Chancellor: ANN TATE
Vice-Chancellor: Prof. NICK PETFORD
Pro-Vice-Chancellor for Acad.: Prof. PETER BUSH
Pro-Vice-Chancellor for Research and Devt: Dr FRANK BURDETT
Pro-Vice-Chancellor for Strategic Planning and Resources: JOHN HOSKINSON
Library of 375,000 vols, 15,000 journals
Number of teachers: 465
Number of students: 10,000

DEANS

School of Education: Prof. ANN SHELTON MAYES
School of Health: Dr SUE ALLEN
School of Science and Technology: Prof. KAMAL BECHKOUM
School of Social Sciences: CHRIS MOORE
School of the Arts: PAUL MIDDLETON
Northampton Business School: Dr IAN BROOKS

UNIVERSITY OF NOTTINGHAM

University Park, Nottingham, NG7 2RD
Telephone: (115) 951-5151
Fax: (115) 951-3666
Internet: www.nottingham.ac.uk
Founded 1881, Univ. Charter 1948
Academic year: September to August
Chancellor: Prof. YANG FUJIA
Vice-Chancellor: Prof. Sir DAVID GREENAWAY
Pro-Vice-Chancellor for Environment, Infrastructure and Information Services: Prof. ALAN DODSON
Pro-Vice-Chancellor for Human Resources, Access and Community Relations: Prof. KAREN COX
Pro-Vice-Chancellor for Internationalization: Prof. CHRISTINE ENNEW
Pro-Vice-Chancellor for Knowledge Transfer, Business Engagement, Devt and Alumni Relations Office: Prof. CHRIS RUDD
Pro-Vice-Chancellor for Research and Graduate School: Prof. BOB WEBB
Pro-Vice-Chancellor for Teaching and Learning: Prof. SAUL TENDLER
Registrar: Dr PAUL GREATRIX

Library: see Libraries and Archives
Number of teachers: 2,700
Number of students: 32,044
Publications: *Exchange Magazine, Gazette, Global Review*

DEANS

Faculty of Arts: Prof. ALAN FORD
Faculty of Engineering: Prof. HAI-SUI YU
Faculty of Medicine and Health Sciences: Prof. IAN HALL
Faculty of Science: Prof. EDMUND BURKE
Faculty of Social Sciences: Prof. SARAH O'HARA
Graduate School: Prof. CLAIRE O'MALLEY

PROFESSORS

AITKENHEAD, A., Anaesthesia and Intensive Care
ALDRICH, R. J., Politics
ARCHER, D. B., Microbiology
ARMOUR, E. A. G., Mathematical Physics
ARROWSMITH, S. L., Law
ASHER, G. M., Electrical and Electronic Engineering
ASHWORTH, J., American and Canadian Studies
AZZOPARDI, B. J., Chemical, Environmental and Mining Engineering
BACKHOUSE, R. C., Computer Science and Information Technology
BAILEY, S. H., Law
BALL, F. G., Statistics
BARNARD, C. J., Animal Behaviour and Ecology
BATES, C., Physics and Astronomy
BATH, P., Stroke Medicine
BECKER, A. A., Mechanical Engineering
BECKETT, J. V., History
BEHNKE, J. M., Infections and Immunity
BELAVKIN, V., Mathematical Physics
BENFORD, S. D., Computer Science and Information Technology
BENNETT, M. J., Plant Science
BENNETT, T., Biomedical Sciences
BENSON, T. M., Electrical and Electronic Engineering
BERRY, R. H., Accounting and Finance
BETON, P. H., Physics and Astronomy
BINKS, M. R., Institute for Enterprise and Innovation
BIRCH, D. J., Law
BLACK, C. R., Plant Science
BLEANEY, M. F., Economics
BOWLEY, R. M., Physics and Astronomy
BOWTELL, R. W., Physics and Astronomy
BRADLEY, J. E., Infections and Immunity
BRADSHAW, C. M., Psychiatry
BRAILSFORD, D. F., Computer Science and Information Technology
BRIGGS, D., Pharmaceutical Sciences
BRINCAT, M. P., Nurture Unit
BRITTON, J., Respiratory Medicine
BROOK, J. D., Genetics
BROUGHTON-PIPKIN, F., Obstetrics and Gynaecology
BROWN, A. D., Business School
BROWN, S. F., Civil Engineering
BRUCE, A. C., Economics and Insurance
BURKE, E. K., Computer Science and Information Technology
BURKHARDT, H., Education
BUTTERY, P. J., Nutritional Biochemistry
BYCROFT, B. W., Pharmaceutical Sciences
CALLEN, A. E., Art History
CAMPBELL, K. H., Animal Physiology
CARDWELL, R. A., Hispanic and Latin American Studies
CARTER, R. A., English Studies
CASEY, P. M., Theology
CHALLIS, R. E., Electrical and Electronic Engineering
CHESTERS, M. A., Physical Chemistry
CHOI, K.-S., Fluid Mechanics
CHOONARA, I., Human Devt

CHRISTOPOULOS, C., Electrical and Electronic Engineering
CLARK, J. S., Organic Chemistry
CLARKE, B., Genetics
CLARKE, D. D., Psychology
COLES, P., Physics and Astronomy
COLLIS, J., Atmospheric Environment
CONNERTON, I., Food Sciences
COOKE, M., Music
COX, K., Nursing
COX, T. R., Institute of Work, Health and Orgs
CREMONA, J. E., Mathematical Sciences
CURRIE, G., Business School
CURRIE, G., Philosophy
DANCHEV, A., Int. Relations
DANIELS, S., Geography
DAVIES, M. C., Pharmaceutical Sciences
DAVIS, S. S., Pharmaceutical Sciences
DAVIS, T., Orthopaedic and Accident Surgery
DAY, C., Education
DENBY, B., Chemical, Environmental and Mining Engineering
DERRINGTON, A. M., Psychology
DEVLIN, J., Marketing
DIACON, S. R., Business School
DINGWALL, R. W. J., Institute for the Study of Genetics, Biorisks and Society
DISNEY, R. F., Economics
DODSON, A. H., Civil Engineering
DONNELLY, R., Vascular Medicine
DOWD, K., Centre for Risk Insurance Studies
DRYDEN, I. L., Statistics
DUNCAN, A. S., Economics
EAVES, L., Physics and Astronomy
ELLIMAN, D. G., Computer Science and Information Technology
ENNEW, C. T., Business School
EVETTS, J. A., Sociology and Social Policy
FALVEY, R. E., Economics
FAWCETT, A. P., Architecture
FAWCETT, J. J., Law
FENN, P. T., Business School
FESENKO, I., Pure Mathematics
FINCH, R., Microbiology and Infectious Diseases
FLINT, A. P. F., Animal Physiology
FORBES, I., Politics
FORD, G. A., Theology
FORD, P. H., Computer Science and Information Technology
FOXON, C. T. B., Physics and Astronomy
FRANCIS, R. A., French
FRASER, D., Midwifery
GARDINER, S. M., Biomedical Sciences
GARNER, C. D., Inorganic Chemistry
GARVEY, S. D., Mechanical Engineering
GEARY, R. J., History
GILL, P. M. W., Physical Chemistry
GILLIES, P. A., Public Health Sciences
GINDY, N. N. Z., Manufacturing Engineering and Operations Management
GLASS, R. E., Genetics
GOW, I. T., Business School
GRAVELLS, N. P., Law
GREENAWAY, D., Economics
GREENHAFF, P. L., Biomedical Sciences
GRIERSON, D., Plant Science
GRIFFITHS, A., Institute of Work, Health and Orgs
HALL, I., Therapeutics
HAMMOND, B. S., English Studies
HARDING, S. E., Food Sciences
HARGREAVES, A., Education
HARRIS, D. J., Law
HARRISON, C., Education
HASLAM, C., Institute of Work, Health and Orgs
HEFFERNAN, M. J., Geography
HENDERSON, J., Archaeology
HEPTINSTALL, S., Cardiovascular Medicine
HERVEY, T. K., Law
HEWITT, N., French
HEYWOOD, P. M., Politics
HILL, S. J., Biomedical Sciences
HOLLIS, C., Psychiatry

HOPKINSON, B., Vascular Surgery
HOWDLE, S. M., Inorganic Chemistry
HYDE, T. H., Mechanical Engineering
IRVING, W., Microbiology and Infectious Diseases
JACKSON, S., Psychology
JAKEMAN, E., Electrical and Electronic Engineering
JAKEMAN, E., Theoretical Mechanics
JAMES, R., Microbiology and Infectious Diseases
JAMES, V. C., Nursing
JENSEN, O. E., Theoretical Mechanics
JESCH, J., English Studies
JOHNSON, C. M., French
JOHNSON, I. R., Human Devt
JONES, R. G., Physical Chemistry
JORDAN, T. R., Psychology
KENDALL, D. A., Biomedical Sciences
KENNER, J., European Law
KING, J. R., Theoretical Mechanics
KING, R. H., American and Canadian Studies
KNIGHT, D. M., French
LANGLEY-EVANS, S., Human Nutrition
LARKINS, E., Electrical and Electronic Engineering
LAYBOURN-PARRY, J., Life and Environmental Sciences
LEDGEWAY, T., Vision Research
LEICESTER, M., Continuing Education
LEYBOURNE, S. J., Economics
LEYSHON, A., Geography
LINCOLN, N. B., Psychology
LLOYD, R. G., Genetics
McCARTNEY, D. G., Materials Engineering and Materials Design
McCORQUODALE, R. G., Law
McCOUSTRA, M., Chemical Physics
MACDONALD, I. A., Biomedical Sciences
McGUIRK, B. J., Hispanic and Latin American Studies
McRAE, J., English Studies
MADELEY, R., Community Health Sciences
MAHAJAN, R., Anaesthesia and Intensive Care
MANNING, N. P., Sociology and Social Policy
MARLOW, N., Human Devt
MARSDEN, C. A., Biomedical Sciences
MATHER, P. M., Geography
MAYER, R. J., Biomedical Sciences
MAYHEW, T. M., Biomedical Sciences
MELLER, H. E., History
MEPHAM, B., Biosciences
MERRIFIELD, M. R., Physics and Astronomy
MESSENT, P. B., American and Canadian Studies
MILES, N. J., Chemical, Environmental and Mining Engineering
MILLINGTON, M. I., Hispanic and Latin American Studies
MILNE, L. M., Russian and Slavonic Studies
MILNER, C. R., Economics
MITCHELL, J. R., Food Sciences
MITCHELL, P., Psychology
MITHEN, R. F., Agricultural Sciences
MONTEITH, S., American Studies
MOON, J., Int. Centre for Corporate Social Responsibility
MOORE, T., Engineering Surveying and Space Geodesy
MORGAN, W. J., Continuing Education
MORRIS, P. G., Physics and Astronomy
MORSE, G. K., Law
MURPHY, R. J. L., Education
MURPHY, S., Biomedical Sciences
NEWBOLD, P., Economics
NEWMAN, J. A., American and Canadian Studies
O'BRIEN, C., Manufacturing Engineering and Operations Management
O'CONNELL-DAVIDSON, J., Sociology and Social Policy
O'SHEA, P. S., Biomedical Sciences
OC, T., Built Environment
PARKER, S., Continuing Education

PASHBY, I. R., Manufacturing Engineering and Operations Management
PATIENT, R. K., Genetics
PATTENDEN, G., Chemistry
PEBERDY, J. F., Institute for Enterprise and Innovation
PERKINS, A., Human Devt
PIERSON, C., Politics
POLIAKOFF, M., Inorganic Chemistry
POWER, H., Mechanical Engineering
PRINGLE, M., General Practice
PRITCHARD, D. I., Pharmaceutical Sciences
RAY, D., Biomedical Sciences
REES, W., Int. Security
REEVE, D. E., Civil Engineering
RIFFAT, S. B., Built Environment
RILEY, D. S., Theoretical Mechanics
ROBERTS, J. A., Plant Science
RODDEN, T. A., Computer Science and Information Technology
ROSSLYN, W., Russian and Slavonic Studies
ROWLANDS, B. J., Gastrointestinal Surgery
RUDD, C. D., Mechanical Engineering
RUSSELL, N., Haematology
SABLITZKY, F., Genetics
SARRE, P. J., Physical Chemistry
SCHOLEFIELD, J., Surgery
SCHRODER, M., Inorganic Chemistry
SEABROOK, M. F., Agricultural Sciences
SEDDON, A. B., Materials Engineering and Materials Design
SHAKESHEFF, K., Pharmaceutical Sciences
SHARP, P. M., Genetics
SHAW, P. E., Biomedical Sciences
SHAW, R., Obstetrics and Gynaecology
SHAYLER, P. J., Mechanical Engineering
SIMESTER, A. P., Law
SIMPKINS, N. S., Organic Chemistry
SINCLAIR, M. T., Business School
SNAPE, C. E., Chemical, Environmental and Mining Engineering
SOCKET, E., Bacterial Genetics
SOMEKH, M. G., Electrical and Electronic Engineering
SOMMERSTEIN, A. H., Classics
SPIESS, M. K., Pure Mathematics
STARKEY, K. P., Business School
STARMER, C. V., Economics
STEPHENSON, T., Child Health
STEVENS, M. F. G., Pharmaceutical Sciences
STILL, J. M., French
TALLACK, D. G., American and Canadian Studies
TATTERSFIELD, A., Respiratory Medicine
TAYLOR, A. J., Food Sciences
TENDLER, S. J. B., Pharmaceutical Sciences
THORNE, C. R., Geography
THORNTON, J., Obstetrics and Gynaecology
TOMS, J. S., Business School
TUCK, B., Electrical and Electronic Engineering
TUCKER, G. A., Nutritional Biochemistry
TURVILLE-PETRE, T. F. S., English Studies
TYNAN, A. C., Business School
UNDERWOOD, G., Psychology
VAN ZYL SMIT, D., Law
WAITES, W. M., Food Sciences
WALKER, R. L., Sociology and Social Policy
WALLACE, W. A., Orthopaedic and Accident Surgery
WARD, C., Rehabilitation and Ageing
WEBB, R., Agricultural Sciences
WESTHEAD, P., Business School
WHITE, N. D., Law
WHYNES, D. K., Economics
WILCOX, R. G., Cardiovascular Medicine
WILKINSON, R., Epidemiology and Public Health Sciences
WILLIAMS, H., Medical and Surgical Sciences
WILLIAMS, P., Institute of Infections and Immunity
WILLIAMS, P., Pharmaceutical Sciences
WILSON, J., Business School
WILSON, J. R., Manufacturing Engineering and Operations Management
WILSON, R. J. A., Archaeology

WINGFIELD, J., Pharmaceutical Sciences
WOOD, A. T., Statistics
WOOD, D. J., Psychology
WOOD, J. V., Materials Engineering and Materials Design
WOODS, R. A. M., German
WORTHEN, J., English Studies
WRIGHT, D. M., Business School
WRIGHT, N., Environmental Fluid Mechanics
WRIGLEY, C. J., History
YOUNG, J. W., History
YOUNG, L., Molecular Embryology
YU, H., Civil Engineering

UNIVERSITY OF OXFORD

Univ. Offices, Wellington Sq., Oxford, OX1 2JD

Telephone: (1865) 270000
Fax: (1865) 270708
E-mail: information.officer@admin.ox.ac.uk
Internet: www.ox.ac.uk

Founded 12th century

Academic year: October to June

Chancellor: Rt Hon. the Lord PATTEN OF BARNES
High Steward: Rt Hon. the Lord RODGER OF EARLSFERRY
Vice-Chancellor: Dr ANDREW HAMILTON
Pro-Vice-Chancellor for Devt and External Relation: Prof. NICK RAWLINS (acting)
Pro-Vice-Chancellor for Education: Dr SALLY MAPSTONE
Pro-Vice-Chancellor for Personnel and Equality: Dr STEPHEN GOSS
Pro-Vice-Chancellor for Planning and Resources: Prof. WILLIAM JAMES
Pro-Vice-Chancellor for Research, Academic Services and Univ. Collns: Prof. IAN WALMSLEY
Registrar: Prof. EWAN MCKENDRICK
Academic Registrar and Sec. of Faculties: MICHAEL SIBLY
Bodley's Librarian and Dir, Library Services: Dr SARAH THOMAS

Library: the Bodleian Libraries comprise some 40 libraries, excl. college libraries, and holds over 9m. vols
Number of teachers: 1,600 f.t.e.
Number of students: 21,535 (incl. 19,803 full-time and 1,732 part-time)

PROFESSORS

Note: Faculties, Schools, Depts, etc. are grouped by Div. (each div. has a full-time head and an elected board who are responsible for day-to-day operations incl. finance and planning) as follows: *Humanities Div.*(Rothermere American Institute, Faculty of Classics, Faculty of English Language and Literature, Faculty of Linguistics, Philology and Phonetics, Faculty of Medieval and Modern European Languages, Faculty of History, Faculty of Music, Faculty of Oriental Studies, Faculty of Philosophy, Ruskin School of Drawing and Fine Art, Faculty of Theology); *Mathematical, Physical and Physical Sciences Div.*(Dept of Chemistry, Dept of Computer Science, Dept of Earth Sciences, Dept of Engineering Science, Dept of Materials, Mathematical Institute, Dept of Physics, Dept of Plant Sciences, Dept of Statistics, Dept of Zoology, e-Research Centre); *Medical Sciences Div.*(Clinical Depts: Nuffield Dept of Anaesthetics, Dept of Cardiovascular Medicine, Nuffield Dept of Clinical Laboratory Sciences, Nuffield Dept of Clinical Medicine, Dept of Clinical Neurology, Dept of Clinical Pharmacology, Medical Oncology, Weatherall Institute of Molecular Medicine, Nuffield Dept of Obstetrics and Gynaecology, Nuffield Laboratory of Ophthalmology, Nuffield Dept of Orthopaedics, Rheumatology and Musculoskeletal Science, Dept of Paediatrics, Dept of Primary Health Care, Dept of Psychiatry,

Dept of Public Health, Nuffield Dept of Surgical Sciences. Non-Clinical Depts: Dept of Biochemistry, Dept of Experimental Psychology, Sir William Dunn School of Pathology, Dept of Pharmacology, Dept of Physiology, Anatomy and Genetics); *Social Sciences Div.*(School of Anthropology and Museum Ethnography, School of Archaeology, Interdisciplinary Area Studies, Dept of Economics, Dept of Education, School of Geography and the Environment, Oxford Internet Institute, Faculty of Law, Faculty of Management (Saïd Business School), Dept of Politics and International Relations, Dept of International Development, Dept of Social Policy and Intervention, Dept of Sociology). *Dept for Continuing Education* is not part of a Div.

Nuffield Department of Anaesthetics (John Radcliffe Hospital, Headley Way, Headington, Oxford, OX3 9DU; tel. (1865) 231515; fax (1865) 234844; e-mail anaesthetics@nda.ox .ac.uk; internet www.nda.ox.ac.uk):

TRACEY, I. M. C., Anaesthetic Science (Pembroke College)

Rothermere American Institute (1A South Parks Rd, Oxford, OX1 3UB; tel. (1865) 282710; fax (1865) 282720; e-mail enquiries@rai.ox.ac.uk; internet www.rai.ox .ac.uk):

WOLFE, A., American Government (Balliol College)

School of Anthropology and Museum Ethnography (51 Banbury Rd, Oxford, OX2 6PE; tel. (1865) 274624; fax (1865) 274630; e-mail info@anthro.ox.ac.uk; internet www .anthropology.ox.ac.uk):

BANKS, M. J., Visual Anthropology (Wolfson College)
BARNES, R. H., Social Anthropology (St Antony's College)
DUNBAR, R. I. M., Evolutionary Anthropology (Magdalen College)
GELLNER, D. N., Social Anthropology (All Souls College)
KEITH, M., Personal Professorship (Merton College)
ULIJASZEK, S. J., Human Ecology (St Cross College)
VERTOVEC, S., Transnational Anthropology (Linacre College)
WHITEHOUSE, H., Social Anthropology (Magdalen College)

School of Archaeology (34–36 Beaumont St, Oxford, OX1 2PG; tel. (1865) 278240; fax (1865) 278254; e-mail administrator@arch.ox .ac.uk; internet www.arch.ox.ac.uk):

BARTON, R. N. E., Palaeolithic Archaeology (Hertford College)
GOSDEN, C. H., European Archaeology (Keble College)
HAMEROW, H. F., Archaeology (St Cross College)
LEE-THORP, J., Scientific Archaeology (St Cross College)
MITCHELL, P. J., African Archaeology (St Hugh's College)
POLLARD, A. M., Archaeological Science (Linacre College)
RAMSEY, C. B., Archaeological Science
ROBINSON, M. A., Environmental Archaeology (St John's College)

Department of Biochemistry (South Parks Rd, Oxford, OX1 3QU; tel. (1865) 613200; fax (1865) 613201; e-mail admin@bioch.ox.ac.uk; internet www.bioch.ox.ac.uk):

ARMITAGE, J. P., Biochemistry (Merton College)
BROCKDORFF, N., Biochemistry
DAVIS, I., Cell Biology (Jesus College)
ENDICOTT, J. A., Structural Biology (St Cross College)

FERGUSON, S. J., Biochemistry (St Edmund Hall)

GARMAN, E. F., Molecular Biophysics (Brasenose College)

HANDFORD, P. A., Biochemistry (St Catherine's College)

HODGKIN, J. A., Genetics (Keble College)

MAHADEVAN, L. C., Biochemistry (Trinity College)

MELLOR, E. J. C., Biochemistry (The Queen's College)

NASMYTH, K., Biochemistry (Trinity College)

NOBLE, M. E. M., Structural Biology (Somerville College)

NOVÁK, B., Integrative Systems Biology (Merton College)

SANSOM, M. S. P., Molecular Biophysics (Corpus Christi College)

WATTS, A., Biochemistry (St Hugh's College)

WHITBY, M. C., Molecular Genetics

Department of Cardiovascular Medicine (Level 6, West Wing, John Radcliffe Hospital, Headington, Oxford, OX3 9DU; tel. (1865) 234657; fax (1865) 234658; e-mail enquiries@cardiov.ox.ac.uk; internet www.cardiov.ox.ac.uk):

BHATTACHARYA, S., Cardiovascular Medicine (Green Templeton College)

CASADEI, B., Cardiovascular Medicine

CHANNON, K. M., Cardiovascular Medicine (Lady Margaret Hall)

FARRALL, M., Cardiovascular Genetics (Keble College)

NEUBAUER, S., Cardiovascular Medicine (Christ Church)

WATKINS, H. C., Cardiovascular Medicine (Exeter College)

Department of Chemistry (Chemistry Research Laboratory, 12 Mansfield Rd, Oxford, OX1 3TA; tel. (1865) 285000; fax (1865) 275633; internet www.chem.ox.ac.uk):

ANDERSON, H. L., Chemistry (Keble College)

ARMSTRONG, F. A., Chemistry (St John's College)

BATTLE, P. D., Chemistry (St Catherine's College)

BAYLEY, J. H. P., Chemical Biology (Hertford College)

BEER, P. D., Chemistry (Wadham College)

BROUARD, M., Chemistry (Jesus College)

CLARY, D. C., Chemistry (Magdalen College)

COMPTON, R. G., Chemistry (St John's College)

DAVIES, S. G., Chemistry (Magdalen College)

DAVIS, B. G., Chemistry (Pembroke College)

DIXON, D. J., Chemistry (Wadham College)

DONOHOE, T. J., Chemistry (Magdalen College)

EDWARDS, P. P., Inorganic Chemistry (St Catherine's College)

EGDELL, R. G., Inorganic Chemistry (Trinity College)

FAULKNER, S., Chemistry (Keble College)

FLEET, G. W. J., Chemistry (St John's College)

FOORD, J. S., Chemistry (St Catherine's College)

GOUVERNEUR, V., Chemistry (Merton College)

HANCOCK, G., Chemistry (Trinity College)

HODGSON, D. M., Chemistry (Oriel College)

HORE, P. J., Physical Chemistry (Corpus Christi College)

HOWARD, B. J., Chemistry (Pembroke College)

LOGAN, D. E., Theoretical Chemistry (University College)

MANOLOPOULOS, D. E., Theoretical Chemistry (St Edmund Hall)

McGRADY, J., Computational Inorganic Chemistry (New College)

MOUNTFORD, P., Chemistry (St Edmund Hall)

O'HARE, D. M., Chemistry (Balliol College)

ROBINSON, C. V., Chemistry (Exeter College)

SCHOFIELD, C. J., Chemistry (Hertford College)

SOFTLEY, T. P., Chemical Physics (Merton College)

TSANG, S. C. E., Chemistry (University College)

WELLER, A. S., Chemistry (Magdalen College)

Faculty of Classics (Ioannou Centre for Classical and Byzantine Studies, 66 St Giles, Oxford, OX1 3UL; tel. (1865) 288391; fax (1865) 288386; e-mail enquiries@classics.ox.ac.uk; internet www.classics.ox.ac.uk):

HARRISON, S. J., Classical Languages and Literature (Corpus Christi College)

HOWGEGO, C. J., Greek and Roman Numismatics (Wolfson College)

HUTCHINSON, G. O., Greek and Latin Languages and Literature (Exeter College)

JENKYNS, R. H. A., The Classical Tradition (Lady Margaret Hall)

KURTZ, D. C., Classical Art (Wolfson College)

LEIGH, M. G. L., Classical Languages and Literature (St Anne's College)

LEMOS, I. S., Classical Archaeology (Merton College)

PARKER, R. C. T., Ancient History (New College)

PELLING, C. B. R., Greek (Regius) (Christ Church)

PURCELL, N., Ancient History (Brasenose College)

REINHARDT, T., Latin Language and Literature (Corpus Christi College)

SMITH, R. R. R., Classical Archaeology and Art (Lincoln College)

WILLI, A., Comparative Philology (Worcester College)

WILSON, A. I., Archaeology of the Roman Empire (All Souls College)

Nuffield Department of Clinical Laboratory Sciences (Level 4, Academic Block, John Radcliffe Hospital, Headington, Oxford, OX3 9DU; tel. (1865) 221166; fax (1865) 220524; e-mail enquiries@ndcls.ox.ac.uk; internet www.ndcls.ox.ac.uk):

BELL, J. I., Medicine (Regius) (Christ Church)

BRUNNER, T., Translational Clinical Oncology

FERGUSON, D. J. P., Ultrastructural Morphology

GATTER, K. C., Pathology (St John's College)

HELLEDAY, T., Cancer Therapeutics

HIGGS, D. R., Haematology (Brasenose College)

JACOBSEN, S. E. W., Developmental and Stem Cell Biology (St Cross College)

McKENNA, W. G., Radiation Oncology and Biology (Wolfson College)

MUSCHEL, R. J., Molecular Pathology (St Hilda's College)

PEZZELLA, F., Tumour Pathology

ROBERTS, D. J., Haematology (Trinity College)

VOJNOVIC, B., Biophysics

WAINSCOAT, J. S., Haematology

WATT, S. M., Haematology

WILKIE, A. O. M., Pathology (Merton College)

Nuffield Department of Clinical Medicine (John Radcliffe Hospital, Headington, Oxford, OX3 9DU; tel. (1865) 221325; fax (1865) 222901; e-mail enquiries@ndm.ox.ac.uk; internet www.ndm.ox.ac.uk):

ARMITAGE, J. M., Clinical Trials and Epidemiology

BAIGENT, C., Epidemiology

BERAL, V., Epidemiology (Green Templeton College)

BUCHAN, A. M., Clinical Geratology (Green Templeton College)

CERUNDOLO, V., Immunology (Merton College)

CHAPEL, H., Clinical Immunology

CHEN, Z., Epidemiology (Green Templeton College)

COLLINS, R. E., Medicine and Epidemiology

CORNALL, R. J., Immunology

CROOK, D. W. M., Microbiology

DARBY, S. C., Medical Statistics (Green Templeton College)

DAVIS, S. J., Molecular Immunology

DAY, N. P. J., Tropical Medicine

ENVER, T., Molecular Haematology

FARRAR, J., Tropical Medicine

FRAYN, K. N., Human Metabolism (Green Templeton College)

GAUGUIER, D., Mammalian Genetics

HARPER, S., Gerontology (Nuffield College)

HILL, A. V. S., Human Genetics (Magdalen College)

HOLMAN, R. R., Diabetic Medicine

JONES, E. Y., Protein Crystallography (Jesus College)

KLENERMAN, P., Immunology (Brasenose College)

KNAPP, S., Structural Biology

LU, X., Cancer Medicine

MARSH, K., Tropical Medicine

McCARTHY, M., Diabetic Medicine (Green Templeton College)

McMICHAEL, A. J., Molecular Medicine (Corpus Christi College)

MOTT, R., Bioinformatics and Statistical Genetics

NEWBOLD, C. I., Tropical Medicine (Green Templeton College)

NOSTEN, F., Tropical Medicine

Sir PETO, RICHARD, Medical Statistics and Epidemiology (Green Templeton College)

PETO, T. E. A., Medicine

PHILLIPS, R. E., Clinical Medicine

POWRIE, F. M., Gastroenterology (Green Templeton College)

PUGH, C. W., Renal Medicine (Kellogg College)

RATCLIFFE, P. J., Clinical Medicine (Magdalen College)

RORSMAN, P., Diabetic Medicine (Harris Manchester College)

ROWLAND-JONES, S. L., Immunology (Christ Church)

SNOW, R. W., Tropical Public Health

STRADLING, J. R., Respiratory Medicine

STUART, D. I., Biochemistry (Hertford College)

THAKKER, R. V., Medicine (Somerville College)

TOMLINSON, I., Molecular and Population Genetics (The Queen's College)

WASS, J. A. H., Endocrinology (Green Templeton College)

WHITE, N. J., Tropical Medicine (St John's College)

Department of Clinical Neurology (Level 6, West Wing, John Radcliffe Hospital, Headley Way, Headington, Oxford, OX3 9DU; tel. (1865) 231909; fax (1865) 231914; internet www.clneuro.ox.ac.uk):

BEESON, D. M. W., Neurosciences

EBERS, G. C., Clinical Neurology (St Edmund Hall)

FUGGER, L., Clinical Neuroimmunology (Oriel College)

JEZZARD, P., Neuroimaging

KENNARD, C., Clinical Neurology (Green Templeton College)

ROTHWELL, P. M., Clinical Neurology

SMITH, S. M., Biomedical Engineering

Department of Clinical Pharmacology (Old Rd Campus Research Bldg, Old Rd Campus, Roosevelt Dr., Oxford, OX3 7DQ; tel. (1865) 617024; fax (1865) 617100; e-mail admin@ clinpharm.ox.ac.uk; internet www.clinpharm .ox.ac.uk):

LA THANGUE, N. B., Cancer Biology (Linacre College)
SEYMOUR, L. W., Genetic Therapy (Wolfson College)

Department of Computer Science (Wolfson Bldg, Parks Rd, Oxford, OX1 3QD; tel. (1865) 273838; fax (1865) 273839; e-mail enquiries@ cs.ox.ac.uk; internet www.cs.ox.ac.uk):

ABRAMSKY, S., Computing (Wolfson College)
BENEDIKT, M., Computing Science (University College)
BURRAGE, K., Computational and Systems Biology (New College)
DAVIES, J. W. M., Software Engineering (Kellogg College)
DE MOOR, O., Computing Science (Magdalen College)
GAVAGHAN, D. J., Computational Biology (New College)
GILES, M., Scientific Computing (St Hugh's College)
GOTTLOB, G., Computing Science (St Anne's College)
HORROCKS, I. R., Computing Science (Oriel College)
JEAVONS, P. G., Computer Science (St Anne's College)
KWIATKOWSKA, M. Z., Computing Systems (Trinity College)
LOWE, G., Computer Science (St Catherine's College)
MELHAM, T. F., Computing Science (Balliol College)
ONG, C. H. L., Computing Science (Merton College)
PULMAN, S. G., Computational Linguistics (Somerville College)
ROSCOE, A. W., Computing Science (University College)
SMITH, N. P., Computational Biology (St John's College)

Continuing Education (1 Wellington Sq., Oxford, OX1 2JA; tel. (1865) 270360; fax (1865) 270309; e-mail enquiries@conted.ox.ac .uk; internet www.conted.ox.ac.uk):

DU SAUTOY, M. P. F., Public Understanding of Science (New College)
MICHIE, J., Innovation & Knowledge Exchange (Kellogg College)

Ruskin School of Drawing and Fine Art (74 High St, Oxford, OX1 4BG; tel. (1865) 276940; fax (1865) 276949; e-mail info@ ruskin-sch.ox.ac.uk; internet www .ruskin-sch.ox.ac.uk):

CATLING, B. D., Fine Art (Linacre College)
CHEVSKA, M., Fine Art (Brasenose College)

Department of Earth Sciences (South Parks Rd, Oxford, OX1 3AN; tel. (1865) 272000; fax (1865) 272072; e-mail enquiries@earth.ox.ac .uk; internet www.earth.ox.ac.uk):

BRASIER, M. D., Palaeobiology (St Edmund Hall)
BURTON, K. W., Earth Sciences
ENGLAND, P. C., Geology (University College)
FRASER, D. G., Earth Sciences (Worcester College)
HALLIDAY, A. N., Geochemistry (St Hugh's College)
HENDERSON, G. M., Earth Sciences (University College)
HESSELBO, S. P., Stratigraphy (St Peter's College)
PARSONS, B. E., Geodesy and Geophysics (St Cross College)

PYLE, D. M., Earth Sciences (St Anne's College)
SEARLE, M. P., Earth Sciences (Worcester College)
SIVETER, D. J., Earth Sciences (St Cross College)
WATTS, A. B., Marine Geology and Geophysics (Wolfson College)
WOOD, B., Earth Sciences (Wolfson College)
WOODHOUSE, J. H., Geophysics (Worcester College)

Department of Economics (Manor Rd Bldg, Manor Rd, Oxford, OX1 3UQ; tel. (1865) 271089; fax (1865) 271094; e-mail reception@ economics.ox.ac.uk; internet www.economics .ox.ac.uk):

ALLEN, R. C., Recent Social and Economic History (Nuffield College)
ANAND, S., Quantitative Economic Analysis (St Catherine's College)
BROWNING, M. J., Economics (Nuffield College)
COLLIER, P., Economics (St Antony's College)
CRAWFORD, V. P., Political Economy (All Souls College)
ELLISON, M., Economics (Exeter College)
FAFCHAMPS, M., Development Economics (Mansfield College)
HENDRY, D. F., Economics (Nuffield College)
KELLER, R. G., Microeconomic Theory
KLEMPERER, P. D., Economics (Nuffield College)
MALCOMSON, J. M., Economics (All Souls College)
MUELLBAUER, J. N. J., Economics (Nuffield College)
MUKERJI, S., Economics (University College)
NEARY, J. P., Economics (Merton College)
NOCKE, V., Industrial Economics (Jesus College)
OFFER, A., Economic History (All Souls College)
QUAH, J. K.-H., Economic Theory (St Hugh's College)
ROBERTS, K. S. W., Economics (Nuffield College)
SHEPHARD, N., Economics (Nuffield College)
STEVENS, M. J., Economics (Lincoln College)
VENABLES, A. J., Economics (New College)
VINES, D. A., Economics (Balliol College)
WALLACE, C. C., Economics (Economic Theory) (Trinity College)
WREN-LEWIS, S., Economics (Merton College)
YOUNG, H. P., Economics (Nuffield College)

Department of Education (15 Norham Gardens, Oxford, OX2 6PY; tel. (1865) 274024; fax (1865) 274027; e-mail general.enquiries@ education.ox.ac.uk; internet www.education .ox.ac.uk):

BAIRD, J. A., Educational Assessment (St Anne's College)
FURLONG, J., Educational Studies (Green Templeton College)
MACARO, E., Applied Linguistics and Second Language Acquisition (Worcester College)
MARSH, H. W., Educational Studies (St Cross College)
NUNES, T., Educational Studies (Harris Manchester College)
OZGA, J., Sociology of Education (Green Templeton College)
PHILLIPS, D., Comparative Education (St Edmund Hall)
WATSON, A., Mathematics Education (Linacre College)

Department of Engineering Science (17 Parks Rd, Oxford, OX1 3PJ; tel. (1865) 273000; fax (1865) 273010; e-mail enquiries@eng.ox.ac.uk; internet www.eng .ox.ac.uk):

BHATTACHARYA, A., Engineering Science
BLAKEBOROUGH, A., Engineering Science (Worcester College)
BORTHWICK, A. G. L., Engineering Science (St Edmund Hall)
BUCKLEY, C. P., Engineering Science (Balliol College)
COCKS, A. C. F., Materials Engineering (St Anne's College)
COUSSIOS, C. C., Biomedical Engineering (Magdalen College)
CUI, Z. F., Chemical Engineering (Hertford College)
DANIEL, R. W., Engineering Science (Brasenose College)
DARTON, R. C., Engineering Science (Keble College)
DUNCAN, S. R., Engineering Science (St Hugh's College)
DUNNE, F. P. E., Engineering Science (Hertford College)
EDWARDS, D. J., Engineering Science (Wadham College)
ELSTON, S. J., Engineering Science (St John's College)
FOX, J. P., Engineering Science
HILLS, D. A., Engineering Science (Lincoln College)
HOULSBY, G. T., Civil Engineering (Brasenose College)
IRELAND, P. T., Turbomachinery (St Catherine's College)
KORSUNSKY, A. M., Engineering Science (Trinity College)
KOUVARITAKIS, B., Engineering Science (St Edmund Hall)
LIMEBEER, D. J. N., Control Engineering (New College)
MURRAY, D. W., Engineering Science (St Anne's College)
NOBLE, J. A., Biomedical Engineering (St Hilda's College)
NOWELL, D., Engineering Science (Christ Church)
ROBERTS, S. J., Engineering Science (Somerville College)
STONE, C. R., Engineering Science (Somerville College)
TARASSENKO, L., Electrical and Electronic Engineering (St John's College)
TAYLOR, P. H., Engineering Science (Keble College)
THOMPSON, I. P., Engineering Science
WILLIAMS, M. S., Engineering Science (New College)
WILSON, T., Engineering Science (Hertford College)
ZISSERMAN, A. P., Computer Vision Engineering

Faculty of English Language and Literature (St Cross Bldg, Manor Rd, Oxford, OX1 3UL; tel. (1865) 271055; fax (1865) 271054; e-mail english.office@ell.ox.ac.uk; internet www .english.ox.ac.uk):

BALLASTER, R. M., Eighteenth-century Studies (Mansfield College)
BOEHMER, E. D., World Literatures in English (Wolfson College)
BREWER, C. D., English Language and Literature (Hertford College)
BUSH, R. L., American Literature (St John's College)
CAMERON, D. J., Language and Communication (Worcester College)
CUNNINGHAM, V. D., English Language and Literature (Corpus Christi College)
GILLESPIE, V. A., English Language and Literature (Lady Margaret Hall)
GODDEN, M. R., Anglo-Saxon (Pembroke College)

HANNA, R., Palaeography (Keble College)

HILL, G. W., Poetry (Keble College)

MAGUIRE, L. E., English Literature (Magdalen College)

MARCUS, L., English Literature (New College)

McCABE, R. A., English Language and Literature (Merton College)

MUGGLESTONE, L. C., History of English (Pembroke College)

NEWLYN, L. A., English Language and Literature (St Edmund Hall)

NORBROOK, D. G. E., English Literature (Merton College)

ROMAINE, S., English Language (Merton College)

STAFFORD, F. J., English Language and Literature (Somerville College)

SUTHERLAND, K., Bibliography and Textual Criticism (St Anne's College)

WOMERSELY, D. J., English Literature (St Catherine's College)

WU, S., English Language and Literature (St Catherine's College)

Oxford e-Research Centre (7 Keble Rd, Oxford, OX1 3QG; tel. (1865) 610600; fax (1865) 610624; e-mail info@oerc.ox.ac.uk; internet www.oerc.ox.ac.uk):

CHEN, M., Scientific Visualisation (Pembroke College)

TREFETHEN, A. E., Scientific Computing (Keble College)

Department of Experimental Psychology (9 South Parks Rd, Oxford, OX1 3UD; tel. (1865) 271444; fax (1865) 310447; e-mail general@psy.ox.ac.uk; internet www.psych .ox.ac.uk):

BISHOP, D. V. M., Developmental Neuropsychology (St John's College)

FLINT, J., Neuroscience (Merton College)

GAFFAN, D., Behavioural Neuroscience

HEYES, C. M., Psychology (All Souls College)

HEWSTONE, M. R. C., Social Psychology (New College)

MARTIN, R. M. A., Abnormal Psychology (St Edmund Hall)

NATION, K., Experimental Psychology (St John's College)

NOBRÉ, A. C. DE O., Cognitive Neuroscience (New College)

PLUNKETT, K. R., Cognitive Neuroscience (St Hugh's College)

RAWLINS, J. N. P., Psychology (Wolfson College)

ROGERS, B. J., Experimental Psychology (Pembroke College)

RUSHWORTH, M. F. S., Cognitive Neuroscience

SPENCE, C. J., Experimental Psychology (Somerville College)

School of Geography and the Environment (Dyson Perrins Bldg, South Parks Rd, Oxford, OX1 3QY; tel. (1865) 285070; fax (1865) 275885; e-mail enquiries@ouce.ox.ac .uk; internet www.ouce.ox.ac.uk):

ALLEN, M. R. (Linacre College)

BANISTER, D., Transport Studies (St Anne's College)

CLARK, G. L., Geography (St Peter's College)

LIVERMAN, D. M., Environmental Policy and Development (Linacre College)

MALHI, Y. S., Terrestrial Ecology (Oriel College)

McDOWELL, L. M., Human Geography (St John's College)

PALLOT, J., Human Geography of Russia (Christ Church)

THOMAS, D. S. G., Geography (Hertford College)

VILES, H. A., Biogeomorphology and Heritage Conservation (Worcester College)

WHATMORE, S. J., Environment and Public Policy (Linacre College)

WHITTAKER, R. J., Biogeography (St Edmund Hall)

Faculty of History (Old Boys' School, George St, Oxford, OX1 2RL; tel. (1865) 615000; fax (1865) 250704; internet www.history.ox.ac .uk):

BLAIR, W. J., Medieval History and Archaeololgy (Queen's College)

BROCKLISS, L. W. B., Early Modern French History (Magdalen College)

BROWN, J. M., History of the British Commonwealth (Balliol College)

CAPLAN, J., Modern European History (St Antony's College)

CLUNAS, C., History of Art (Trinity College)

CORSI, P., History of Science (Linacre College)

FOSTER, R. F., Irish History (Hertford College)

GILDEA, R. N., Modern History (Worcester College)

HAMEROW, H. F., Archaeology (St Cross College)

HARRISON, M., History of Medicine (Green Templeton College)

HOTSON, H. B., Early Modern Intellectual History (St Anne's College)

HUMPHRIES, K. J., Economic History (All Souls College)

KNIGHT, A. S., History of Latin America (St Antony's College)

LANGFORD, P., Modern History (Lincoln College)

MACLEAN, I. W. F., Renaissance Studies (All Souls College)

MITTER, R. S. R., History and Politics of Modern China (St Cross College)

O'ROURKE, K. H., Economic History (All Souls College)

ROPER, L. A., Modern History (Regius) (Oriel College)

SERVICE, R. J., Russian History (St Antony's College)

SHARPE, R., Diplomatic (Wadham College)

STRACHAN, H. F. A., History of War (All Souls College)

TYRRELL, I., American History (Queen's College)

WICKHAM, C. J., Medieval History (All Souls College)

School of Interdisciplinary Area Studies (12 Bevington Rd, Oxford, OX2 6LH; tel. (1865) 284996; fax (1865) 284992; e-mail enquiries@ area.ox.ac.uk; internet www.area-studies.ox .ac.uk):

ANDERSON, D. MCBEATH, African Politics (St Cross College)

BEINART, W., Race Relations (St Antony's College)

FOWERAKER, J. W., Latin American Politics (St Antony's College)

GOODMAN, R. J., Modern Japanese Studies (St Antony's College)

HARRISS-WHITE, B., Development Studies (Wolfson College)

KARIYA, T., Sociology of Japanese Society (St Antony's College)

NEARY, I. J., Politics of Japan (St Antony's College)

PAYNE, L. A, Sociology (Latin American Societies) (St Antony's College)

SHUE, V., Contemporary China (St Antony's College)

Department of International Development (3 Mansfield Rd, Oxford, OX1 3TB; tel. (1865) 281800; fax (1865) 281801; e-mail qeh@qeh .ox.ac.uk; internet www.qeh.ox.ac.uk):

ALEXANDER, J., Development Studies (Linacre College)

DERCON, S., Development Economics (Wolfson College)

FITZGERALD, E. V. K., International Development (St Antony's College)

HARRISS-WHITE, B., Development Studies (Wolfson College)

WOOD, A., International Development (Wolfson College)

ZETTER, R., Refugee Studies (Green Templeton College)

Oxford Internet Institute (1 St Giles, Oxford, OX1 3JS; tel. (1865) 287210; fax (1865) 287211; e-mail enquiries@oii.ox.ac.uk; internet www.oii.ox.ac.uk):

DUTTON, W. H., Internet Studies (Balliol College)

MARGETTS, H., Society and the Internet (Mansfield College)

MAYER-SCHÖNBERGER, V., Internet Governance and Regulation (Keble College)

Faculty of Law (St Cross Bldg, St Cross Rd, Oxford, OX1 3UL; tel. (1865) 271491; fax (1865) 271493; e-mail lawfac@law.ox.ac.uk; internet www.law.ox.ac.uk):

ARMOUR, J. H., Law and Finance (Oriel College)

ASHWORTH, A. J., English Law (All Souls College)

BRIGGS, A., Private International Law (St Edmund Hall)

BRIGHT, S. L., Land Law (New College)

CARTWRIGHT, J., Law of Contract (Christ Church)

CRAIG, P. P., English Law (St John's College)

DAVIES, P. L., Corporate Law (Jesus College)

DINWOODIE, G. B., Intellectual Property and Information Technology Law (St Peter's College)

DOUGLAS-SCOTT, S., European and Human Rights Law (Lady Margaret Hall)

EDELMAN, J. J., Law of Obligations (Keble College)

ENDICOTT, T. A. O., Legal Philosophy (Balliol College)

FREDMAN, S. D., Law (Exeter College)

FREEDLAND, M. R., Employment Law (St John's College)

FREEDMAN, J. A., Taxation Law (Worcester College)

GALLIGAN, D. J., Socio-legal Studies (Wolfson College)

GARDNER, J. B., Jurisprudence (University College)

GREEN, L., Philosophy of Law (Balliol College)

LOADER, I., Criminology (All Souls College)

LOWE, A. V., Public International Law (All Souls College)

McCRUDDEN, J. C., Human Rights Law (Lincoln College)

McKENDRICK, E. G., English Private Law (Lady Margaret Hall)

ROBERTS, J. V., Criminology (Worcester College)

SAROOSHI, D., Public International Law (Queen's College)

SIRKS, A. J. B., Civil Law (Regius) (All Souls College)

VOGENAUER, S., Comparative Law (Brasenose College)

WEATHERILL, S. R., European Community Law (Somerville College)

WHITTAKER, S. J., European Comparative Law (St John's College)

ZEDNER, L. H., Criminal Justice (Corpus Christi College)

ZUCKERMAN, A. A. S., Civil Procedure (University College)

Centre for Linguistics and Philology (Clarendon Institute, Walton St, Oxford, OX1 2HG; tel. (1865) 280400; fax (1865) 280412; e-mail enquiries@ling-phil.ox.ac.uk; internet www.ling-phil.ox.ac.uk):

COLEMAN, J. S., Phonetics (Wolfson College)

DALRYMPLE, M. E., Linguistics (Linacre College)

LAHIRI, A., Linguistics (Somerville College)

WILLI, A., Comparative Philology (Worcester College)

Faculty of Management (Saïd Business School, Park End St, Oxford, OX1 1HP; tel. (1865) 288800; fax (1865) 288805; e-mail reception@sbs.ox.ac.uk; internet www.sbs.ox.ac.uk):

BARNETT, M., Strategy (St Anne's College)

DENRELL, J., Strategy and Organisation (Keble College)

DEVEREUX, M., Business Taxation (Oriel College)

DOPSON, S., Organisational Behaviour (Green Templeton College)

FLYVBJERG, B., Major Programme Management (St Anne's College)

FUEST, C., Business Taxation

HOLT, D. B., Marketing (Worcester College)

JENKINSON, T. J., Finance (Keble College)

MAYER, C. P., Management Studies (St Edmund Hall)

MORRIS, T. J., Management Studies (Green Templeton College)

MORRISON, A. D., Finance (Merton College)

NOE, T. H., Management Studies (Balliol College)

PETTIGREW, A. M., Strategy and Organisation (Brasenose College)

POWELL, T. C., Strategy (St Hugh's College)

RAYNER, S., Science and Civilisation (Keble College)

SAKO, M., Management Studies (Green Templeton College)

SCOTT, L., Entrepreneurship and Innovation (Green Templeton College)

TAYLOR, J. W., Decision Science (St Cross College)

UPTON, D. M., Operations Management (Christ Church)

WESTBROOK, R. K., Operations Management (St Hugh's College)

WHITTINGTON, R. C., Strategic Management (New College)

WOOLGAR, S. W., Marketing (Green Templeton College)

Department of Materials (16 Parks Rd, Oxford, OX1 3PH; tel. (1865) 273700; fax (1865) 273789; e-mail enquiries@materials.ox.ac.uk; internet www.materials.ox.ac.uk):

BRIGGS, G. A. D., Nanomaterials (St Anne's College)

GRANT, P. S., Materials Science (St Catherine's College)

GROVENOR, C. R. M., Materials (St Anne's College)

KIRKLAND, A. J., Materials (Linacre College)

MARROW, T. J., Energy Materials (Mansfield College)

MARZARI, N., Materials Modelling (St Anne's College)

ROBERTS, S. G., Materials (St Edmund Hall)

Mathematical Institute (24–29 St Giles, Oxford, OX1 3LB; tel. (1865) 273525; fax (1865) 273583; e-mail enquiries@maths.ox.ac.uk; internet www.maths.ox.ac.uk):

Sir BALL, J. M., Natural Philosophy (The Queen's College)

BATTY, C. J. K., Analysis (St John's College)

BRESSLOFF, P., Applied Mathematics (Jesus College)

BRIDSON, M. R., Pure Mathematics (Magdalen College)

CANDELAS, P., Mathematics (Wadham College)

CHAPMAN, S. J., Mathematics and its Applications (Mansfield College)

COLLINS, M. J., Mathematics (University College)

DRUTU BADEA, C., Mathematics (Exeter College)

DU SAUTOY, M. P. F., Public Understanding of Science (New College)

EKERT, A., Quantum Information (Merton College)

ETHERIDGE, A. M., Probability (Magdalen College)

FLYNN, E. V., Mathematics (New College)

GILES, M. B., Scientific Computing (St Hugh's College)

GORIELY, A., Mathematical Modelling (St Catherine's College)

GOULD, N. M., Numerical Optimization (Exeter College)

GUI-QIANG, G. C., Analysis of Partial Differential Equations (Keble College)

HAYDON, R. G., Mathematics (Brasenose College)

HEATH-BROWN, D. R., Pure Mathematics (Worcester College)

HITCHIN, N. J., Geometry (New College)

HOWISON, S. D., Applied Mathematics (Christ Church)

JOYCE, D. D., Mathematics (Lincoln College)

KIRCHHEIM, B., Mathematics (Trinity College)

KIRWAN, F. C., Mathematics (Balliol College)

KRAMKOV, D., Mathematical Finance

LACKENBY, M., Mathematics (St Catherine's College)

LENNOX, J. C., Mathematics (Green Templeton College)

LYONS, T. J., Mathematics (St Anne's College)

MAINI, P. K., Mathematical Biology (Brasenose College)

MASON, L., Mathematics (St Peter's College)

NIETHAMMER, B., Applied Mathematics (St Edmund Hall)

PRIESTLEY, H. A., Mathematics (St Anne's College)

RIORDAN, O., Discrete Mathematics (St Edmund Hall)

ROUQUIER, R., Pure Mathematics (Magdalen College)

SCOTT, A. D., Mathematics (Merton College)

SEGAL, D., Mathematics (All Souls College)

SEREGIN, G. A., Pure Mathematics (St Hilda's College)

SÜLI, E., Numerical Analysis (Worcester College)

TILLMANN, U. L., Mathematics (Merton College)

TOD, K. P., Mathematical Physics (St John's College)

TREFETHEN, L. N., Numerical Analysis (Balliol College)

VASSEUR, A. F., Mathematics (Lincoln College)

WENDLAND, H., Numerical Analysis (Exeter College)

WOODHOUSE, N. M. J., Mathematics (Wadham College)

ZHOU, X., Mathematical Finance (St Hugh's College)

ZILBER, B., Mathematical Logic (Merton College)

Department of Medical Oncology (Churchill Hospital, Oxford, OX3 7LJ; tel. (1865) 235310; fax (1865) 235986):

ELLIOTT, T. J., Immunology (Balliol College)

GODING, C. R., Oncology

HARRIS, A. L., Medical Oncology (St Hugh's College)

MIDDLETON, M. R., Experimental Cancer Medicine

Faculty of Medieval and Modern European Languages (47 Wellington Sq., Oxford, OX1 2JF; tel. (1865) 270570; fax (1865) 270757; e-mail reception@mod-langs.ox.ac.uk; internet www.mod-langs.ox.ac.uk):

BETHEA, D. M., Russian Studies (Wadham College)

CHARLES-EDWARDS, T. M. O., Celtic (Jesus College)

COOPER, R. A., French (Brasenose College)

CRONK, N. E., French Literature (St Edmund Hall)

EARLE, T. F., Portuguese Studies (St Peter's College)

FIDDIAN, R. W., Spanish (Wadham College)

HOWELLS, C. M., French (Wadham College)

JEFFERSON, A. M., French Literature (New College)

KELLY, C. H. M., Russian (New College)

KOHL, K. M., German Literature (Jesus College)

LAUXTERMANN, M. D., Modern Greek Language and Literature (Exeter College)

LEEDER, K. J., Modern German Literature (New College)

MAIDEN, M. D., Romance Languages (Trinity College)

McGUINNESS, P. R. A., French and Comparative Literature (St Anne's College)

McLAUGHLIN, M. L., Italian Studies (Magdalen College)

PALMER, N. F., German Medieval and Linguistic Studies (St Edmund Hall)

PARISH, R. J., French (St Catherine's College)

PEARSON, R. A. G., French (Queen's College)

PHELAN, A., German Romantic Literature (Keble College)

ROBERTSON, R. N. N., German Language and Literature (The Queen's College)

SHERINGHAM, M. H. T., French Literature (All Souls College)

VIALA, A., French Literature (Lady Margaret Hall)

VOLFING, A. M., Medieval German Studies (Oriel College)

WATANABE-O'KELLY, H., German Literature (Exeter College)

WILLIAMSON, E. H., Spanish Studies (Exeter College)

ZORIN, A. L., Russian (New College)

Weatherall Institute of Molecular Medicine (John Radcliffe Hospital, Headington, Oxford, OX3 9DS; tel. (1865) 222443; fax (1865) 222737; internet www.imm.ox.ac.uk):

BEESON, D., Neuroscience

CERUNDOLO, V., Immunology (Merton College)

DAVIS, S.

ENVER, T., Stem Cell Biology

FUGGER, L., Clinical Neuroimmunology (Oriel College)

HARRIS, A. L., Clinical Oncology (Oriel College)

HASSAN, B., Medical Oncology (Lincoln College)

HICKSON, I., Molecular Oncology

HIGGS, D. R., Heamatology (Brasenose College)

JACKSON, D., Human Immunology

JACOBSEN, S. E. W., Developmental and Stem Cell Biology (St Cross College)

Sir McMICHAEL, A. J., Molecular Medicine (Corpus Christi College)

NEWBOLD, C. I., Tropical Medicine (Green Templeton College)

PATIENT, R., Developmental Haemopoiesis

ROWLAND-JONES, S., Immunology (Christ Church)

TOWNSEND, A. R. M., Molecular Immunology (New College)

WILKIE, A. O. M., Pathology

WOOD, W. G., Haematology

Faculty of Music (St Aldate's, Oxford, OX1 1DB; tel. (1865) 276125; fax (1865) 276128; e-mail office@music.ox.ac.uk; internet www .music.ox.ac.uk):

CLARKE, E. F., Music (Wadham College)
CROSS, J. G. E., Musicology (Christ Church)
DREYFUS, L., Music (Magdalen College)
FRANKLIN, P. R., Music (St Catherine's College)
HIGGINBOTTOM, E., Choral Music (New College)
SAXTON, R. L. A., Composition (Worcester College)

Nuffield Department of Obstetrics and Gynaecology (John Radcliffe Hospital, Oxford, OX3 9DU; tel. (1865) 221004; fax (1865) 769141; e-mail enquiries@obs-gyn.ox .ac.uk; internet www.obs-gyn.ox.ac.uk):

MARDON, H. J., Reproductive Science (St Catherine's College)
POULTON, J., Mitochondrial Genetics (Lady Margaret Hall)
SARGENT, I. L., Reproductive Science (Mansfield College)

Nuffield Laboratory of Ophthalmology (Level 5, West Wing, John Radcliffe Hospital, Headington, Oxford, OX3 9DU; tel. (1865) 234782; fax (1865) 234795; e-mail enquiries@eye.ox .ac.uk; internet www.eye.ox.ac.uk):

FOSTER, R. G., Circadian Neuroscience (Brasenose College)
HANKINS, M. W., Visual Neuroscience
MACLAREN, R., Ophthalmology (Merton College)

Faculty of Oriental Studies (Oriental Institute, Pusey Lane, Oxford, OX1 2LE; tel. (1865) 278200; fax (1865) 278190; e-mail orient@orinst.ox.ac.uk; internet www.orinst .ox.ac.uk):

ALLAN, J. W., Eastern Art (St Cross College)
BAINES, J. R., Egyptology (The Queen's College)
FLOOD, G. D., Hindu Studies
FRELLESVIG, B., Japanese Linguistics (Hertford College)
GOODMAN, M. D., Jewish Studies (Wolfson College)
HERZIG, E., Persian Studies (Wadham College)
HOLES, C. D., Contemporary Arab World (Magdalen College)
JOHNS, J., Art and Archaeology of the Islamic Mediterranean (Wolfson College)
MINKOWSKI, C. Z., Sanskrit (Balliol College)
O'HANLON, R., Indian History and Culture (St Cross College)
RAMADAN, T., Contemporary Islamic Studies (St Antony's College)
SANDERSON, A. G. J. S., Eastern Religions and Ethics (All Souls College)
SMITH, M. J., Egyptology (University College)
VAN GELDER, G. J. H., Arabic (St John's College)
VAN LINT, T. M., Armenian Studies (Pembroke College)
WALLACE, V. A., Buddhist Studies (Balliol College)
WATSON, O. J., Islamic Art and Architecture (Wolfson College)
WILLIAMSON, H. G. M., Hebrew (Regius) (Christ Church)

Nuffield Department of Orthopaedics, Rheumatology and Musculoskeletal Sciences (Nuffield Orthopaedic Centre, Windmill Rd, Headington, Oxford, OX3 7LD; tel. (1865) 227374; fax (1865) 737640; internet www .ndos.ox.ac.uk):

ARDEN, N. K., Rheumatology and Musculoskeletal Sciences (Lady Margaret Hall)

ATHANASOU, N. A., Osteoarticular Pathology (Wadham College)
BULSTRODE, C. J. K., Orthopaedic Surgery (Green Templeton College)
CARR, A. J., Orthopaedic Surgery (Worcester College)
COOPER, C., Musculoskeletal Sciences (St Peter's College)
FAIRBANK, J. C. T., Spinal Surgery
LAMB, S. E., Trauma Rehabilitation (Wadham College)
MURRAY, D., Orthopaedic Surgery
OPPERMANN, U. C. T., Musculoskeletal Sciences (St Catherine's College)
WILLETT, K. M., Orthopaedic Trauma Surgery (Wolfson College)
WORDSWORTH, B. P., Rheumatology (Green Templeton College)

Department of Paediatrics (Level 2, Children's Hospital (John Radcliffe), Headington, Oxford, OX3 9DU; tel. (1865) 234239; fax (1865) 234242; e-mail enquiries@paediatrics .ox.ac.uk; internet www.paediatrics.ox.ac .uk):

GOULDER, P. J. R., Immunology (Brasenose College)
HOLLANDER, G. A. P., Paediatrics (Jesus College)
KWIATKOWSKI, D. P., Tropical Paediatrics (St John's College)
POLLARD, A. J., Paediatric Infection and Immunity (St Cross College)
WILKINSON, A. W., Paediatrics (All Souls College)

Sir William Dunn School of Pathology (South Parks Rd, Oxford, OX1 3RE; tel. (1865) 275500; fax (1865) 275515; e-mail enquiries@path.ox.ac.uk; internet www.path .ox.ac.uk):

ACUTO, O., Molecular Cell Signalling (Lincoln College)
BARCLAY, A. N., Chemical Pathology (Lincoln College)
BELL, S. D., Microbiology (Wadham College)
COOK, P. R., Cell Biology (Lincoln College)
HALE, G., Therapeutic Immunology
JAMES, W. S., Virology (Brasenose College)
LEA, S., Chemical Pathology (Brasenose College)
PROUDFOOT, N. J., Molecular Biology (Brasenose College)
SATTENTAU, Q. J., Immunology (Magdalen College)
VAN DER MERWE, P. A., Molecular Immunology (Brasenose College)
WALDMANN, H., Pathology (Lincoln College)

Department of Pharmacology (Mansfield Rd, Oxford, OX1 3QT; tel. (1865) 271850; fax (1865) 271853; e-mail info@pharm.ox.ac.uk; internet www.pharm.ox.ac.uk):

GALIONE, A. G., Pharmacology (Lady Margaret Hall)
GARLAND, C. J., Vascular Pharmacology (Magdalen College)
Baroness GREENFIELD, S., Pharmacology (Lincoln College)
PLATT, F. M., Biochemistry and Pharmacology (Merton College)
SIM, E., Pharmacology (St Peter's College)
TERRAR, D. A., Cardiac Electrophysiology (Worcester College)

Faculty of Philosophy (10 Merton St, Oxford, OX1 4JJ; tel. (1865) 276926; fax (1865) 276932; e-mail enquiries@philosophy.ox.ac .uk; internet www.philosophy.ox.ac.uk):

ARNTZENIUS, F., Philosophy (University College)
BOSTROM, N. R. L., Applied Ethics (St Cross College)
BROOME, J. R., Moral Philosophy (Corpus Christi College)
BROWN, H. R., Physics (Wolfson College)

CHARLES, D. O. M., Philosophy (Oriel College)
COOPE, U. C., Ancient Philosophy (Corpus Christi)
CRISP, R. S., Moral Philosophy (St Anne's College)
DAVIES, M. K., Mental Philosophy (Corpus Christi College)
HAWTHORNE, J., Metaphysical Philosophy (Magdalen College)
HYMAN, J., Aesthetics (The Queen's College)
IRWIN, T. H., Ancient Philosophy (Keble College)
MOORE, A. W., Philosophy (St Hugh's College)
MULHALL, S. J., Philosophy (New College)
RODRIGUEZ-PEREYRA, G., Metaphysics (Oriel College)
SAUNDERS, S. W., Philosophy of Physics (Linacre College)
SAVULESCU, J., Practical Ethics (St Cross College)
SHIELDS, C. J., Classical Philosophy (Lady Margaret Hall)
TRIFOGLI, C., Medieval Philosophy (All Souls College)
WEDGWOOD, R., Philosophy (Merton College)
WILLIAMSON, T., Logic (New College)

Department of Physics (Clarendon Laboratory, Parks Rd, Oxford, OX1 3PU; tel. (1865) 272200; fax (1865) 272400; e-mail enquiries@ physics.ox.ac.uk; internet www.physics.ox.ac .uk):

ABRAHAM, D. B., Statistical Mechanics (Wolfson College)
ANDREWS, D. G., Physics (Lady Margaret Hall)
BILLER, S. D., Particle Physics (Mansfield College)
BINNEY, J. J., Physics (Merton College)
BLUNDELL, K. M., Astrophysics (St John's College)
BLUNDELL, S. J., Physics (Mansfield College)
BOOTHROYD, A. T., Physics (Oriel College)
BURROWS, P. N., Accelerator Physics (Jesus College)
CAVALLERI, A., Physics (Merton College)
CHALKER, J. T., Physics (St Hugh's College)
CLOSE, F., Theoretical Physics (Exeter College)
COOPER, S., Experimental Physics (St Catherine's College)
COOPER-SARKAR, A. M., Particle Physics (St Hilda's College)
DAVIES, R. L., Astrophysics (Christ Church)
DEVENISH, R. C. E., Physics (Hertford College)
DIMOPOULOS, S., Physics (New College)
ESSLER, F. H. L., Physics (Worcester College)
EWART, P., Physics (Worcester College)
FERREIRA, P. G., Astrophysics (Oriel College)
FOOT, C. J., Physics (St Peter's College)
FOSTER, B., Experimental Physics (Balliol College)
GLAZER, A. M., Physics (Jesus College)
GREGG, J. F., Physics (Magdalen College)
HARNEW, N., Physics (St Anne's College)
HOOK, I. M., Astrophysics (Christ Church)
HOOKER, S. M., Atomic and Laser Physics (Merton College)
JELLEY, N. A., Physics (Lincoln College)
JONES, H., Condensed Matter Physics
JONES, J. A., Physics (Brasenose College)
JONES, M. E., Experimental Cosmology
KRAUS, H. A. P., Physics (Corpus Christi College)
LUKAS, A., Theoretical Physics (Balliol College)
MARCH-RUSSELL, J., Physics (New College)

MARSHALL, D. P., Physical Oceanography (St Hugh's College)

NICHOLAS, R. J., Physics (University College)

PALMER, T. N., Physics (Jesus College)

PEACH, K., Physics (Wolfson College)

PODSIADLOWSKI, P., Physics (St Edmund Hall)

RADAELLI, P., Experimental Philosophy (Wadham College)

RAWLINGS, S. G., Physics (St Peter's College)

READ, P. L., Physics (Trinity College)

RENTON, P. B., Physics

ROCHE, P. F., Physics (Hertford College)

ROSS, G. G., Theoretical Physics (Wadham College)

RYAN, J. F., Physics (Christ Church)

SARKAR, S., Physics (Linacre College)

SERYI, A., Accelerator Physics

SILVER, J. D., Physics (New College)

STEANE, A. M., Physics (Exeter College)

TAYLOR, F. W., Physics (Jesus College)

TAYLOR, R., Condensed Matter Physics (The Queen's College)

THATTE, N., Astrophysics (Keble College)

TURBERFIELD, A. J., Physics (Magdalen College)

VEDRAL, V., Quantum Information Science (Wolfson College)

WALMSLEY, I. A., Experimental Physics (St Hugh's College)

WARK, J. S., Physics (Trinity College)

YASSIN, G., Astrophysics

YEOMANS, J. M., Physics (St Hilda's College)

Department of Physiology, Anatomy and Genetics (Le Gros Clark Bldg, South Parks Rd, Oxford, OX1 3QX; tel. (1865) 272169; fax (1865) 272420; e-mail enquiries@dpag.ox.ac.uk; internet www.dpag.ox.ac.uk):

ASHCROFT, F. M., Physiology (Trinity College)

BLAKEMORE, C. B., Physiology (Magdalen College)

CLARKE, K., Physiological Biochemistry (Merton College)

Dame DAVIES, K. E., Anatomy (Hertford College)

KING, A. J., Neurophysiology (Lincoln College)

MCVEAN, G. A. T., Statistical Genetics (Linacre College)

MIESENBÖCK, G., Physiology (Magdalen College)

PAREKH, A. K., Physiology (Keble College)

PARKER, A. J., Physiology (St John's College)

PATERSON, D. J., Cardiovascular Physiology (Merton College)

PONTING, C. P., Genomics

RILEY, P. R., Development and Reproduction (Jesus College)

ROBBINS, P. A., Physiology (Queen's College)

SATTELLE, D. B., Molecular Neurobiology

VAUGHAN-JONES, R. D., Cellular Physiology (Exeter College)

Department of Plant Sciences (South Parks Rd, Oxford, OX1 3RB; tel. (1865) 275000; fax (1865) 275074; e-mail reception@plants.ox.ac.uk; internet www.plants.ox.ac.uk):

DOLAN, L., Botany (Magdalen College)

GURR, S. J., Molecular Plant Pathology (Somerville College)

HARBERD, N. P., Plant Sciences (St John's College)

LANGDALE, J. A., Plant Development (Queen's College)

RATCLIFFE, R. G., Plant Sciences (New College)

SMITH, J. A. C., Plant Sciences (Magdalen College)

TSIANTIS, M. S., Plant Developmental Genetics (Wadham College)

Department of Politics and International Relations (Manor Rd, Oxford, OX1 3UQ; tel. (1865) 278700; fax (1865) 278725; e-mail enquiries@politics.ox.ac.uk; internet www.politics.ox.ac.uk):

BERMEO, N., Comparative Politics (Nuffield College)

CANEY, S., Political Theory (Magdalen College)

CAPLAN, R. D., International Relations (Linacre College)

CAPOCCIA, G., Comparative Government (Corpus Christi College)

CEADEL, M. E., Politics (New College)

DEIGHTON, A. F., European International Politics (Wolfson College)

DUCH, R., Quantitative Political Science (Nuffield College)

EVANS, G., Sociology of Politics (Nuffield College)

FOOT, R. J., International Relations (St Antony's College)

FOWERAKER, J. W., Latin American Politics (St Antony's College)

FREEDEN, M. S., Politics (Mansfield College)

HOOD, C. C., Government (All Souls College)

HURRELL, A. J., International Relations (Balliol College)

KHONG, Y. F., International Relations (Nuffield College)

KING, D. S., American Government (Nuffield College)

MACFARLANE, S. N., International Relations (St Anne's College)

MATTLI, W., International Political Economy (St John's College)

MCBEATH ANDERSON, D., African Politics (St Antony's College)

MCNAY, L., Theory of Politics (Somerville College)

NEARY, I. J., Politics of Japan (St Antony's College)

NICOLAÏDIS, K. A., International Relations (St Antony's College)

ROBERTSON, D. B., Politics (St Hugh's College)

RUEDA, D., Comparative Politics (Merton College)

SHLAIM, A., International Relations (St Antony's College)

SKACH, C., Comparative Government

SNIDAL, D. J., International Relations (Nuffield College)

SNIJDERS, T. A. B., Statistics in the Social Sciences (Nuffield College)

SOSKICE, D., Comparative Political Economy (Nuffield College)

WALDRON, J. J., Social and Political Theory (All Souls College)

WARE, A. J., Politics (Worcester College)

WELSH, J. M., International Relations (Somerville College)

WHITEFIELD, S. D., Comparative Russian and East European Politics and Society (Pembroke College)

WOODS, N. T., International Political Economy (University College)

ZIELONKA, J., European Politics (St Antony's College)

Department of Primary Health Care (23-38 Hythe Bridge St, Oxford, OX1 2ET; tel. (1865) 289288; fax (1865) 289287; internet www.primarycare.ox.ac.uk):

FARMER, A. J., General Practice (Exeter College)

GLASZIOU, P. P., Evidence-based Medicine (Kellogg College)

HOBBS, F. D. R., General Practice (Harris Manchester College)

NEIL, H. A. W., Clinical Epidemiology (Wolfson College)

Department of Psychiatry (Warneford Hospital, Oxford, OX3 7JX; tel. (1865) 223635;

fax (1865) 793101; e-mail information@psych.ox.ac.uk; internet www.psych.ox.ac.uk):

BURNS, T. P., Social Psychiatry (Kellogg College)

COWEN, P. J., Psychopharmacology

EBMEIER, K. P., Old Age Psychiatry (Linacre College)

FAIRBURN, C. J. A. G., Psychiatry (Merton College)

FLINT, J., Molecular Psychiatry (Merton College)

GEDDES, J., Epidemiological Psychiatry

GOODWIN, G. M., Psychiatry (Merton College)

HARRISON, P. J., Psychiatry (Wolfson College)

HAWTON, K. E., Psychiatry (Green Templeton College)

LLEWELYN, S. P., Clinical Psychology (Harris Manchester College)

ROGERS, R. D., Cognitive Neuroscience (Jesus College)

STEIN, A. J., Child and Adult Psychiatry (Linacre College)

Department of Public Health (Old Rd, Headington, Oxford, OX3 7LF; tel. (1865) 289200; fax (1865) 289260; internet www.dphpc.ox.ac.uk):

BROCKLEHURST, P., Perinatal Epidemiology

FITZPATRICK, R. M., Public Health and Primary Health Care (Nuffield College)

GOLDACRE, M. J., Public Health (Magdalen College)

GRAY, A. M., Health Economics

HOPE, R. A., Medical Ethics (St Cross College)

JAFFE, H. W., Public Health (St Cross College)

JENKINSON, C. P., Health Services Research (Harris Manchester College)

PARKER, M. J., Bioethics (St Cross College)

Department of Social Policy and Intervention (Barnett House, 32 Wellington Sq., Oxford, OX1 2ER; tel. (1865) 270325; fax (1865) 270324; internet www.spi.ox.ac.uk):

COLEMAN, D. A., Demography

GARDNER, F. E. M., Child and Family Psychology (Wolfson College)

KEMP, P. A., Social Policy (St Cross College)

NOBLE, M. W. J., Social Policy (Green Templeton College)

RINGEN, S., Sociology and Social Policy (Green Templeton College)

WALKER, R. L., Social Policy (Green Templeton College)

Department of Sociology (Manor Rd, Oxford, OX1 3UQ; tel. (1865) 281740; fax (1865) 286171; e-mail enquiries@sociology.oxford.ac.uk; internet www.sociology.ox.ac.uk):

DE GRAAF, N. D., Sociology (Nuffield College)

GAMBETTA, D., Sociology (Nuffield College)

GERSHUNY, J., Sociology (St Hugh's College)

HARPER, S., Gerontology (Nuffield College)

HESTROM, P., Sociology (Nuffield College)

KARIYA, T., Sociology of Japanese Society (St Antony's College)

PAYNE, L. A., Sociology (Latin American Societies) (St Antony's College)

VARESE, F., Criminology (Linacre College)

Department of Statistics (1 South Parks Rd, Oxford, OX1 3TG; tel. (1865) 272860; fax (1865) 272595; e-mail info@stats.ox.ac.uk; internet www.stats.ox.ac.uk):

DONNELLY, P. J., Statistical Science (St Anne's College)

ETHERIDGE, A. M., Mathematics (Magdalen College)

GRIFFITHS, R. C., Mathematical Genetics (Lady Margaret Hall)

HEIN, J. J., Bioinformatics (University College)
HOLMES, C., Biostatistics (Lincoln College)
LAURITZEN, S. L., Statistics (Jesus College)
MCDIARMID, C. J. H., Combinatronics (Corpus Christi College)
MCVEAN, G. A. T., Statistical Genetics (Linacre College)
REINERT, G., Statistics (Keble College)
RIPLEY, B. D., Applied Statistics (St Peter's College)
SILVERMAN, B. W., Statistics (Green Templeton College)
SNIJDERS, T. A. B., Statistics in the Social Sciences (Nuffield College)

Nuffield Department of Surgical Sciences (John Radcliffe Hospital, Headington, Oxford, OX3 9DU; tel. (1865) 220532; fax (1865) 768876; e-mail enquiries@nds.ox.ac.uk; internet www.nds.ox.ac.uk):

AUSTYN, J. M., Immunobiology (Wolfson College)
AZIZ, T. Z., Neurosurgery
BYRNE, J. V., Neuroradiology
FRIEND, P. J., Transplantation (Green Templeton College)
HAMDY, F. C., Surgery (Balliol College)
JOHNSON, P. R. V., Paediatric Surgery (St Edmund Hall)
TAGGART, D. P., Cardiothoracic Surgery
WOOD, K. J., Immunology (Green Templeton College)

Faculty of Theology (Theology Faculty Centre, 41 St Giles, Oxford, OX1 3LW; tel. (1865) 270790; fax (1865) 270795; internet www.theology.ox.ac.uk):

Rev. BARTON, J., Interpretation of Holy Scripture (Oriel College)
BIGGAR, N. J., Moral and Pastoral Theology (Regius) (Christ Church)
BOCKMUEHL, M., Biblical and Early Christian Studies (Keble College)
DAY, J., Old Testament Theology (Lady Margaret Hall)
FIDDES, P. S., Systematic Theology (Regent's Park College)
FOOT, S. R. I., Ecclesiastical History (Regius) (Christ Church)
HARRISON, P., Science and Religion (Harris Manchester College)
LEFTOW, B., Philosophy of the Christian Religion (Oriel College)
MACCULLOCH, D. N. J., History of the Church (St Cross College)
PATTISON, G. L., Divinity (Christ Church)
ROWLAND, C. C., Exegesis of Holy Scripture (Queen's College)
STROUMSA, G. G., Study of the Abrahamic Religions (Lady Margaret Hall)
TUCKETT, C. M., New Testament Studies (Wolfson College)

Department of Zoology (South Parks Rd, Oxford, OX1 3PS; tel. (1865) 271234; fax (1865) 310447; internet www.zoo.ox.ac.uk):

GODFRAY, H. C. J., Zoology (Entomology) (Jesus College)
GRAFEN, A., Theoretical Biology (St John's College)
GUILFORD, T. C., Animal Behaviour (Merton College)
GUPTA, S., Epidemiology of Infectious Diseases (Linacre College)
HARVEY, P., Zoology (Jesus College)
HOLLAND, P. W. H., Zoology (Merton College)
KACELNIK, A., Behavioural Ecology (Pembroke College)
Lord KREBS, Zoology (Jesus College)
MACDONALD, D. W., Wildlife Conservation (Lady Margaret Hall)
MAIDEN, M. C. J., Molecular Epidemiology (Hertford College)
Lord MAY, Zoology (Merton College)

MCLEAN, A. R., Mathematical Biology (St Catherine's College)
RANDOLPH, S. E., Parasite Ecology (Oriel College)
ROGERS, D. J., Ecology (Green Templeton College)
SHELDON, B. C., Field Ornithology (Wolfson College)
THOMAS, A. L. R., Biomechanics (Lady Margaret Hall)
THOMAS, J. A., Ecology (New College)
WEST, S. A., Evolutionary Biology
WILLIS, K. J., Biodiversity (Merton College)

DIRECTORS AND HEADS OF UNIVERSITY INSTITUTIONS AND DEPARTMENTS

Institute of Archaeology (34–36 Beaumont St, Oxford, OX1 2PG; tel. (1865) 278240; fax (1865) 278254; e-mail administrator@arch.ox.ac.uk; internet www.archinst.ox.ac.uk):

A. I. WILSON, Archaeology of the Roman Empire (All Souls College)

Institute for Chinese Studies (Clarendon Institute Bldg, Walton St, Oxford, OX1 2HG; tel. (1865) 280387; fax (1865) 280435; e-mail enquiries@chinese.ox.ac.uk; internet www.orinst.ox.ac.uk/ea/chinese):

Chinese Studies: (vacant)

Institute of European and Comparative Law (St Cross Bldg, St Cross Rd, Oxford, OX1 3UL; tel. (1865) 281610; fax (1865) 281611; e-mail enquiries@iecl.ox.ac.uk; internet www.iecl.ox.ac.uk):

S. VOGENAUER, Comparative Law (Brasenose College)

Institute of Social and Cultural Anthropology (51 Banbury Rd, Oxford, OX2 6PF; tel. (1865) 274624; fax (1865) 274630; e-mail info@anthro.ox.ac.uk; internet www.isca.ox.ac.uk):

M. J. BANKS, Visual Anthropology (Wolfson College)

Centre for Criminology (Manor Rd, Oxford, OX1 3UQ; tel. (1865) 274444; fax (1865) 281924; e-mail ccr@crim.ox.ac.uk; internet www.crim.ox.ac.uk):

Dir I. LOADER, Criminology (All Souls College)

Centre for Linguistics and Philology (Walton St, Oxford, OX1 2HG; tel. (1865) 280400; fax (1865) 280412; e-mail enquiries@ling-phil.ox.ac.uk; internet www.ling-phil.ox.ac.uk):

Curator A. LAHIRI, Linguistics (Somerville College)

Centre for Socio-Legal Studies (Manor Rd, Oxford, OX1 3UQ; tel. (1865) 284220; fax (1865) 284221; internet www.csls.ox.ac.uk):

Dir Dr F. PIRIE, Socio-Legal Studies (St Cross College)

Environmental Change Institute (Oxford University Centre for the Environment, South Parks Rd, Oxford, OX1 3QY; tel. (1865) 275848; fax (1865) 275850; e-mail enquiries@eci.ox.ac.uk; internet www.eci.ox.ac.uk):

Dir J. HALL, Climate and Environmental Risks (Linacre College)

Nissan Institute of Japanese Studies (27 Winchester Rd, Oxford, OX2 6NA; tel. (1865) 274570; fax (1865) 274574; e-mail secretary@nissan.ox.ac.uk; internet www.nissan.ox.ac.uk):

Dir I. J. NEARY, Politics of Japan (St Antony's College)

Oriental Institute (Pusey Lane, Oxford, OX1 2LE; tel. (1865) 278200; fax (1865) 278190; e-mail orient@orinst.ox.ac.uk; internet www.orinst.ox.ac.uk):

Chair. of the Faculty Prof. E. HERZIG, Persian Studies (Wadham College)

Oxford Learning Institute (Littlegate House, 16/17 St Ebbe's St, Oxford, OX1 1PT; tel. (1865) 286808; fax (1865) 286801; e-mail services@learning.ox.ac.uk; internet www.learning.ox.ac.uk):

S. GOSS, Teaching and Learning in Higher Education (Wadham College)

Language Centre (12 Woodstock Rd, Oxford, OX2 6HT; tel. (1865) 283360; fax (1865) 283366; e-mail admin@lang.ox.ac.uk; internet www.lang.ox.ac.uk):

Dir R. N. VANDERPLANK (Kellogg College)

Latin American Centre (St Antony's College, Oxford, OX2 6JF; tel. (1865) 274486; fax (1865) 274489; e-mail enquiries@lac.ox.ac.uk; internet www.lac.ox.ac.uk):

T. J. POWER, Latin American Politics (St Cross College)

Philosophy Centre (10 Merton St, Oxford, OX1 4JJ; tel. (1865) 276926; fax (1865) 276932; e-mail enquiries@philosophy.ox.ac.uk; internet www.philosophy.ox.ac.uk):

Chair. of the Faculty Dr M. K. DAVIES, Mental Philosophy (Corpus Christi College)

Department of the History of Art and Centre for Visual Studies (Littlegate House, St Ebbes, Oxford, OX1 1PT; tel. (1865) 286830; fax (1865) 286831; e-mail admin@hoa.ox.ac.uk; internet www.hoa.ox.ac.uk):

Head A. C. CLUNAS, History of Art (Trinity College)

Ruskin School of Drawing and Fine Art (74 High St, Oxford, OX1 4BG; tel. (1865) 276940; fax (1865) 276949; internet www.ruskin-sch.ox.ac.uk):

Head J. GAIGER, Fine Art

Inorganic Chemistry Laboratory (South Parks Rd, Oxford, OX1 3QR; tel. (1865) 272600; fax (1865) 272690; internet www.chem.ox.ac.uk/icl):

Head P. P. EDWARDS, Inorganic Chemistry (St Catherine's College)

Organic Chemistry Laboratory (Chemistry Research Laboratory, 12 Mansfield Rd, Oxford, OX1 3TA; tel. (1865) 285000; fax (1865) 275632; internet www.chem.ox.ac.uk/oc):

Head T. J. DONOHOE, Organic Chemistry (Magdalen College)

Phonetics Laboratory (41 Wellington Sq., Oxford, OX1 2JF; tel. (1865) 270444; fax (1865) 270445; e-mail enquiries@phon.ox.ac.uk; internet www.phon.ox.ac.uk):

Dir J. S. COLEMAN, Phonetics (Wolfson College)

Physical and Theoretical Chemistry Laboratory (South Parks Rd, Oxford, OX1 3QZ; tel. (1865) 275400; fax (1865) 275410; internet www.chem.ox.ac.uk/ptcl):

Head G. HANCOCK, Chemistry (Trinity College)

Research Laboratory for Archaeology and the History of Art (Dyson Perrins Bldg, South Parks Rd, Oxford, OX1 3QY; tel. (1865) 285222; fax (1865) 285220; internet www.rlaha.ox.ac.uk):

A. M. POLLARD, Archaeological Science (Linacre College)

University Archives (Bodleian Library, Broad St, Oxford, OX1 3BG; tel. (1865) 277145; fax (1865) 277187; e-mail enquiries@oua.ox.ac.uk; internet www.oua.ox.ac.uk):

Keeper S. BAILEY (Linacre College)

Ashmolean Museum of Art and Archaeology (Beaumont St, Oxford, OX1 2PH; tel. (1865) 278002; fax (1865) 278018; internet www.ashmolean.org):

C. P. H. BROWN (Worcester College)

Museum of the History of Science (Old Ashmolean Bldg, Broad St, Oxford, OX1 3AZ; tel. (1865) 277280; fax (1865) 277288; internet www.mhs.ox.ac.uk):

Dir J. A. BENNETT (Linacre College)

Pitt Rivers Museum (South Parks Rd, Oxford, OX1 3PP; tel. (1865) 270927; fax (1865) 270943; e-mail prm@prm.ox.ac.uk; internet www.prm.ox.ac.uk):

Dir M. O'HANLON (Linacre College)

University Museum of Natural History (Parks Rd, Oxford, OX1 3PW; tel. (1865) 272950; fax (1865) 272970; e-mail info@oum .ox.ac.uk; internet www.oum.ox.ac.uk):

Natural History: (vacant)

Bodleian Library (Broad St, Oxford, OX1 3BG; tel. (1865) 277000; fax (1865) 277182; e-mail enquiries@bodley.ox.ac.uk; internet www.ouls.ox.ac.uk/bodley):

Bodley's Librarian and Dir of Univ. Library Services S. E. THOMAS (Balliol College)

Botanic Garden (Rose Lane, Oxford, OX1 4AZ; tel. (1865) 286690; fax (1865) 286693; e-mail postmaster@obg.ox.ac.uk; internet www.botanic-garden.ox.ac.uk):

Dir T. WALKER (University College)

National Perinatal Epidemiology Unit (Old Rd Campus, Headington, Oxford, OX3 7LF; tel. (1865) 289700; fax (1865) 289701; e-mail general@npeu.ox.ac.uk; internet www.npeu .ox.ac.uk):

Dir P. BROCKLEHURST

Transport Studies Unit (Oxford University Centre for the Environment, South Parks Rd, Oxford, OX1 3QY; tel. (1865) 285070; fax (1865) 275885; internet www.tsu.ox.ac.uk):

Dir D. BANISTER, Transport Studies (St Anne's College)

Wellcome Unit for the History of Medicine (45–47 Banbury Rd, Oxford, OX2 6PE; tel. (1865) 274600; fax (1865) 274605; e-mail wuhmo@wuhmo.ox.ac.uk; internet www .wuhmo.ox.ac.uk):

Dir M. HARRISON, History of Medicine (Green Templeton College)

COLLEGES

All Souls College: High St, Oxford, OX1 4AL; tel. (1865) 279379; internet www .all-souls.ox.ac.uk; f. 1438; for Fellows only; Warden Prof. Sir JOHN VICKERS.

Balliol College: Broad St, Oxford, OX1 3BJ; tel. (1865) 277777; fax (1865) 277803; e-mail academic.registrar@balliol.ox.ac.uk; internet www.balliol.ox.ac.uk; f. 1263; Master ANDREW GRAHAM; publ. *Floreat Domus* (1 a year).

Brasenose College: Radcliffe Sq., Oxford, OX1 4AJ; tel. (1865) 277830; fax (1865) 277822; e-mail college.office@bnc.ox.ac.uk; internet www.bnc.ox.ac.uk; f. 1509; Prin. Prof. ROGER CASHMORE; Prin. Prof. ALAN K. BOWMAN (acting).

Christ Church: St Aldates, Oxford, OX1 1DP; tel. (1865) 276150; fax (1865) 286588; internet www.chch.ox.ac.uk; f. 1546; Dean The Very Rev. CHRISTOPHER LEWIS.

Corpus Christi College: Merton St, Oxford, OX1 4JF; tel. (1865) 276700; fax (1865) 276767; e-mail college.office@ccc.ox.ac .uk; internet www.ccc.ox.ac.uk; f. 1517; Pres. Prof. RICHARD CARWARDINE.

Exeter College: Turl St, Oxford, OX1 3DP; tel. (1865) 279600; fax (1865) 279645; e-mail academic.administrator@exeter.ox.ac.uk; internet www.exeter.ox.ac.uk; f. 1314; Rector FRANCES CAIRNCROSS.

Green Templeton College: Woodstock Rd, Oxford, OX2 6HG; tel. (1865) 274770; fax (1865) 274796; internet www.gtc.ox.ac.uk; f. 2008; Prin. Sir DAVID WATSON.

Harris Manchester College: Mansfield Rd, Oxford, OX1 3TD; tel. (1865) 271006; fax (1865) 271012; e-mail enquiries@hmc.ox.ac .uk; internet www.hmc.ox.ac.uk; f. 1786 for mature students; Prin. The Rev. Dr RALPH WALLER.

Hertford College: Catte St, Oxford, OX1 3BW; tel. (1865) 279400; fax (1865) 279437; internet www.hertford.ox.ac.uk; f. 1740; Prin. Dr JOHN LANDERS.

Jesus College: Turl St, Oxford, OX1 3DW; tel. (1865) 279700; fax (1865) 279687; e-mail lodge@jesus.ox.ac.uk; internet www.jesus.ox .ac.uk; f. 1571; Prin. Lord KREBS.

Keble College: Parks Rd, Oxford, OX1 3PG; tel. (1865) 272727; fax (1865) 272705; e-mail enquiries@keble.ox.ac.uk; internet www .keble.ox.ac.uk; f. 1870; Warden Sir JONATHAN PHILLIPS.

Kellogg College: Banbury Rd, Oxford, OX2 6PN; tel. (1865) 612000; fax (1865) 612001; e-mail college.office@kellogg.ox.ac.uk; internet www.kellogg.ox.ac.uk; f. 1990 for adult, part-time and professional devt students; Pres. Prof. Dr JONATHAN MICHIE.

Lady Margaret Hall: Norham Gardens, Oxford, OX2 6QA; tel. (1865) 274300; fax (1865) 274313; e-mail lodge@lmh.ox.ac.uk; internet www.lmh.ox.ac.uk; f. 1878; Prin. Dr FRANCES LANNON.

Linacre College: St Cross Rd, Oxford, OX1 3JA; tel. (1865) 271650; fax (1865) 271668; e-mail college.secretary@linacre.ox.ac.uk; internet www.linacre.ox.ac.uk; f. 1962, as Linacre House for graduates; Prin. Dr NICK BROWN.

Lincoln College: Turl St, Oxford, OX1 3DR; tel. (1865) 279800; fax (1865) 279802; e-mail info@lincoln.ac.uk; internet www.linc.ox.ac .uk; f. 1427; Rector Prof. PAUL LANGFORD.

Magdalen College: High St, Oxford, OX1 4AU; tel. (1865) 276000; fax (1865) 276030; internet www.magd.ox.ac.uk; f. 1458; Pres. Prof. DAVID CLARY.

Mansfield College: Mansfield Rd, Oxford, OX1 3TF; tel. (1865) 270999; fax (1865) 270970; e-mail admissions@ox.ac.uk; internet www.mansfield.ox.ac.uk; f. 1886; Prin. Dr DIANA WALFORD.

Merton College: Merton St, Oxford, OX1 4JD; tel. (1865) 276310; fax (1865) 276361; internet www.merton.ox.ac.uk; f. 1264; Warden Prof. Sir MARTIN TAYLOR.

New College: Holywell St, Oxford, OX1 3BN; tel. (1865) 279555; fax (1865) 289189; internet www.new.ox.ac.uk; f. 1379; Warden Sir CURTIS PRICE.

Nuffield College: New Rd, Oxford, OX1 1NF; tel. (1865) 278500; fax (1865) 278621; e-mail lodge@nuffield.ox.ac.uk; internet www.nuff.ox.ac.uk; f. 1958; Warden Prof. STEPHEN NICKELL.

Oriel College: Oriel Sq., Oxford, OX1 4EW; tel. (1865) 276555; fax (1865) 791823; e-mail lodge@oriel.ox.ac.uk; internet www.oriel.ox .ac.uk; f. 1326; Provost Sir DEREK MORRIS.

Pembroke College: St Aldate's, Oxford, OX1 1DW; tel. (1865) 276444; fax (1865) 276418; internet www.pmb.ox.ac.uk; f. 1624; Master GILES HENDERSON.

Queen's College, The: High St, Oxford, OX1 4AW; tel. (1865) 279120; fax (1865) 790819; internet www.queens.ox.ac.uk; f. 1341; Provost Prof. PAUL MADDEN.

St Anne's College: Woodstock Rd, Oxford, OX2 6HS; tel. (1865) 274800; fax (1865) 274899; e-mail enquiries@st-annes.ox.ac.uk;

internet www.st-annes.ox.ac.uk; f. 1878 as Society of Oxford Home Students; Prin. TIM GARDAM.

St Antony's College: Woodstock Rd, Oxford, OX2 6JF; tel. (1865) 284700; fax (1865) 274526; internet www.sant.ox.ac.uk; f. 1953; Warden Prof. MARGARET MACMILLAN.

St Catherine's College: Manor Rd, Oxford, OX1 3UJ; tel. (1865) 271700; fax (1865) 271685; e-mail college.office@stcatz.ox.ac.uk; internet www.stcatz.ox.ac.uk; f. 1868, reconstituted as a full College 1963; Master Prof. ROGER W. AINSWORTH.

St Cross College: St Giles, Oxford, OX1 3LZ; tel. (1865) 278490; fax (1865) 278484; internet www.stx.ox.ac.uk; f. 1965; Master Sir MARK JONES.

St Edmund Hall: Queen's Lane, Oxford, OX1 4AR; tel. (1865) 279000; fax (1865) 279090; e-mail college.secretary@seh.ox.ac .uk; internet www.seh.ox.ac.uk; f. c. 1278; Prin. Prof. KEITH GULL.

St Hilda's College: Cowley Pl., Oxford, OX4 1DY; tel. (1865) 276884; fax (1865) 276816; e-mail outreach@st-hildas.ox.ac.uk; internet www.st-hildas.ox.ac.uk; f. 1893; Prin. SHEILA FORBES.

St Hugh's College: St Margaret's Rd, Oxford, OX2 6LE; tel. (1865) 274900; fax (1865) 274912; e-mail academic .administrator@st-hughs.ox.ac.uk; internet www.st-hughs.ox.ac.uk; f. 1886; Prin. ANDREW DILNOT.

St John's College: St Giles', Oxford, OX1 3JP; tel. (1865) 277300; fax (1865) 277435; e-mail college.office@sjc.ox.ac.uk; internet www.sjc.ox.ac.uk; f. 1555; Pres. Sir MICHAEL SCHOLAR.

St Peter's College: New Inn Hall St, Oxford, OX1 2DL; tel. (1865) 278900; fax (1865) 278855; internet www.spc.ox.ac.uk; f. 1929 as St Peter's Hall; Master MARK DAMAZER (acting); Dean Dr ROGER ALLEN.

Somerville College: Woodstock Rd, Oxford, OX2 6HD; tel. (1865) 270600; fax (1865) 270601; e-mail secretariat@some.ox.ac.uk; internet www.some.ox.ac.uk; f. 1879; Prin. Dr ALICE PROCHASKA.

Trinity College: Broad St, Oxford, OX1 3BH; tel. (1865) 279900; fax (1865) 279902; internet www.trinity.ox.ac.uk; f. 1555; Pres. Sir IVOR ROBERTS.

University College: High St, Oxford, OX1 4BH; tel. (1865) 276602; internet www.univ .ox.ac.uk; f. 1249; Master Sir IVOR CREWE.

Wadham College: Parks Rd, Oxford, OX1 3PN; tel. (1865) 277900; fax (1865) 277937; internet www.wadham.ox.ac.uk; f. 1610; Warden Sir NEIL CHALMERS.

Wolfson College: Linton Rd, Oxford, OX2 6UD; tel. (1865) 274100; fax (1865) 274125; internet www.wolfson.ox.ac.uk; f. 1965 for graduates; Pres. Prof. HERMIONE LEE (acting).

Worcester College: Walton St, Oxford, OX1 2HB; tel. (1865) 278300; fax (1865) 278369; internet www.wor.ox.ac.uk; f. 1714; Provost RICHARD G. SMETHURST.

PERMANENT PRIVATE HALLS

Blackfriars: 64 St Giles', Oxford, OX1 3LY; tel. (1865) 278400; e-mail secretary@bfriars .ox.ac.uk; internet www.bfriars.ox.ac.uk; f. 1221; Regent Very Revd Dr RICHARD FINN.

Campion Hall: Brewer St, Oxford, OX1 1QS; tel. (1865) 286100; fax (1865) 286148; e-mail enquiries@campion.ox.ac.uk; internet www.campion.ox.ac.uk; f. 1896; Master Rev. BRENDAN CALLAGHAN.

Regent's Park College: Pusey St, Oxford, OX1 2LB; tel. (1865) 288120; fax (1865) 288121; e-mail enquiries@regents.ox.ac.uk;

internet www.rpc.ox.ac.uk; f. 1810; Prin. Rev. Dr ROBERT ELLIS.

St Benet's Hall: 38 St Giles, Oxford, OX1 3LN; tel. (1865) 280556; fax (1865) 280792; e-mail enquiries@stb.ox.ac.uk; internet www .st-benets.ox.ac.uk; f. 1897; Master Father FELIX STEPHENS.

St Stephen's House: 16 Marston St, Oxford, OX4 1JX; tel. (1865) 613500; fax (1865) 613513; e-mail enquiries@ssho.ox.ac .uk; internet www.ssho.ox.ac.uk; f. 1876; Prin. Rev. Canon Dr ROBIN WARD.

Wycliffe Hall: 52–54 Banbury Rd, Oxford, OX2 6PW; tel. (1865) 274200; fax (1865) 274215; e-mail enquiries@wycliffe.ox.ac.uk; internet www.wycliffe.ox.ac.uk; f. 1877; Prin. Rev. Dr RICHARD TURNBULL.

UNIVERSITY OF PLYMOUTH

Drake Circus, Plymouth, PL4 8AA

Telephone: (1752) 600600

Fax: (1752) 232293

E-mail: publicrelations@plymouth.ac.uk

Internet: www.plymouth.ac.uk

Founded 1970 as Plymouth Polytechnic, name changed to Polytechnic South West in 1989, present name and status 1992

Academic year: September to June

Vice-Chancellor and Chief Exec.: Prof. WENDY PURCELL

Deputy Vice-Chancellor: Prof. MARY WATKINS

Pro-Vice-Chancellor for Research: Prof. JOHN SCOTT

Pro-Vice-Chancellor: Prof. JULIAN BEER

Pro-Vice-Chancellor: Prof. RICHARD STEPHENSON

Pro-Vice-Chancellor: DAVID COSLETT

Pro-Vice-Chancellor: Prof. DAVID WHEELER

Dean of Students: Dr ANITA JELLINGS

Univ. Sec. and Acad. Registrar: JANE HOPKINSON

Dir for Information Learning Services: PENNY HOLLAND (acting)

Dir for Marketing and Communications: JANE CHAFER

Dir for Human Resources: ROLAND BUCKLEY

Dir for Research and Enterprise: Prof. JULIAN BEER

Library of 450,000 vols, 14,000 journal titles

Number of teachers: 2,942

Number of students: 32,933

Publication: *Research Report*

DEANS

Faculty of Arts: DAVID COSLETT

Faculty of Education: WILL MCBURNIE (acting)

Faculty of Health and Social Work: Prof. JOHN CLIBBENS (acting)

Faculty of Science and Technology: Prof. RICHARD GIBB

Faculty of Social Science and Business: Prof. Dr JOAN CHANDLER

Faculty of Technology: Prof. NEIL JAMES

Peninsula College of Medicine and Dentistry: Prof. STEVE THORNTON

Plymouth Business School: Prof. DAVID WHEELER

University of Plymouth Colleges: Dr COLIN WILLIAMS

UNIVERSITY OF PORTSMOUTH

University House, Winston Churchill Ave, Portsmouth, PO1 2UP

Telephone: (23) 9284-8484

Fax: (23) 9284-3082

E-mail: info.centre@port.ac.uk

Internet: www.port.ac.uk

Founded 1869, as Portsmouth School of Science and Art, became Portsmouth Polytechnic in 1969; present name and status 1992

Academic year: September to June

Chancellor: Lord PALUMBO

Vice-Chancellor: Prof. JOHN CRAVEN

Deputy Vice-Chancellor: REBECCA BUNTING

Pro-Vice-Chancellor: Dr DAVID ARRELL

Pro-Vice-Chancellor: Prof. JOHN TURNER

Acad. Registrar: A. REES

Univ. Librarian: ROISIN GWYER

Library of 600,000 vols

Number of teachers: 1,200

Number of students: 19,000

DEANS

Faculty of Creative and Cultural Industries: Dr SIMON CLARIDGE

Faculty of Humanities and Social Sciences: DAVE RUSSELL

Faculty of Science: Prof. PAUL HAYES

Faculty of Technology: Prof. DJAMEL AIT-BOUDAOUD

Portsmouth Business School: ANN RIDLEY

UNIVERSITY OF READING

Whiteknights, POB 217, Reading, RG6 6AH

Telephone: (118) 987-5123

Fax: (118) 931-4404

E-mail: communications@reading.ac.uk

Internet: www.reading.ac.uk

Founded 1892, as Univ. Extension College, univ. status 1926

Academic year: October to July

Chancellor: Sir JOHN MADEJSKI

Vice-Chancellor: Prof. GORDON MARSHALL

Deputy Vice-Chancellor: Prof. TONY DOWNES

Pro-Vice-Chancellor for Int. and External Engagement: Prof. STEVEN MITHEN

Pro-Vice-Chancellor for Research and Innovation: Prof. CHRISTINE WILLIAMS

Pro-Vice-Chancellor for Teaching and Learning: Prof. ROB ROBSON

Dir of Student Services: JENNIFER GHANDHI

Treas.: Dr PETER WARRY

Librarian: JULIA MUNRO

Library: see Libraries and Archives

Number of teachers: 2,005

Number of students: 17,500

Publication: *Research Review* (2 a year)

DEANS

Faculty of Arts and Humanities: Prof. SUE WALKER

Henley Business School: Prof. CHRIS BONES

Faculty of Life Sciences: Prof. RICHARD ELLIS

Faculty of Science: Prof. GAVIN BROOKS

Faculty of Social Sciences: Prof. DIANNE BERRY

PROFESSORS

(Some professors serve in more than one faculty)

Faculty of Arts and Humanities (Whiteknights, POB 218, Reading, RG6 6AA; tel. (118) 931-8063; fax (118) 931-0748):

ARNOLD, B. C. B., History

BARANSKI, Z., Italian Studies

BARBER, M. C., History

BIDDISS, M. D., History

BROWN, C. C., English and American Literary Studies

BUCKLEY, S., Arts and Communication Design

BULL, J., Arts and Communication Design

BULLEN, J. B., English and American Literary Studies

COOK, G.W. D., Linguistics and Applied Language Studies

COOPER, P. J., Psychology

COTTINGHAM, J. G., Humanities

CURRY, A. E., History

DANCY, J. P., Humanities

DUNSBY, J. M., Arts and Communication Design

ELIOT, S. J., Arts and Communication Design; English and American Literary Studies

EVANS, A. W., Environmental Economics

GARMAN, M. A. G., Linguistics and Applied Language Studies

GILCHRIST, R., Archaeology

HOOKER, B., Humanities

HOULBROOKE, R.A., History

HOWELLS, C. A., English and American Literary Studies

JAMES, E. F., History

LUNA, P., Arts and Communication Design

NOBLE, P. S., Modern Languages

PARRINDER, J. P., English and American Literary Studies

PILLING, J., English and American Literary Studies

POTTS, A., Humanities

ROACH, P. J., Lingustic and Applied Language Studies

ROBEY, D. J. B., Modern Languages

RUTHERFORD, I. C., Humanities

SANDFORD, J. E., Modern Languages

SEGAL, N., Modern Languages

STRAWSON, G. J., Humanities

TUCKER, G. H., Modern Languages

WALLACE-HADRILL, A. F., Humanities

WARBURTON, I. P., Linguistic Science

WILKINS, D. A., Linguistics and Applied Language Studies

WOODWARD, P. R., Politics

Faculty of Economic and Social Sciences (Whiteknights, POB 218, Reading, RG6 6AA; tel. (118) 931-8183; fax (118) 931-6658; e-mail fasug@reading.ac.uk):

BELLAMY, R., Politics and Sociology

BREHENY, M. J., Business

BUCKLEY, R. A., Law

BUSH, A. W., Education

CANTWELL, J. A., Business

CASSON, M. C., Business

CROLL, P., Education

CROSBY, F. N., Business

DAVIES, J. C. H., Politics and Sociology

DOWNES, T. A., Law

EDWARDS, V. K., Education

EVANS, A. W., Business

FIDLER, F. B., Education

FRANZONI, R., Politics and Sociology

GHANDI, P. R., Law

GILBERT, J. K., Education

GRAY, C. S., Politics and Sociology

JONES, G. G., Business

KEENE, J., Health and Social Care

LIZIERI, C. M., Business

MALVERN, D. D., Education

MURDOCH, J. R., Law

NOBES, C. W., Business

PATTERSON, K. D., Business

PEMBERTON, J., Business

POPE, M. L., Education

RICHARDS, B. J., Education

SCOTT-QUINN, B., Business

SOUTHWORTH, G. W., Education

STYCHIN, C., Law

UTTON, M. A., Business

WADDINGTON, P. A. J., Politics and Sociology

WARD, C. W., Business

WOODWARD, P. R., Politics and Sociology

Faculty of Life Sciences (Whiteknights, POB 200, Reading, RG6 6AF; tel. (118) 931-8342; fax (118) 931-5509; e-mail sciug@reading.ac .uk):

BARNETT, J. R., Plant Sciences

BEEVER, D. E., Agriculture, Policy and Development

BISBY, F. A., Plant Sciences

BROWN, V. K., Agriculture, Policy and Development

CALIGARI, P. D. S., Plant Sciences

COLLINS, M. D., Food Biosciences

CRABBE, M. J. C., Animal and Microbial Sciences

DUNWELL, J. M., Plant Sciences

ELLIS, R. H., Agriculture, Policy and Development

FRANCE, J., Agriculture, Policy and Development

GARFORTH, C. J., Agriculture, Policy and Development

GIBSON, G. R., Food Biosciences

HADLEY, P., Plant Sciences

HOLLAND, P. W. H., Animal and Microbial Sciences

JOHN, P., Plant Sciences

JONES, I. M., Animal and Microbial Sciences

KNIGHT, P. G., Animal and Microbial Sciences

LEDWARD, D. A., Food Biosciences

LOWRY, P. J., Animal and Microbial Sciences

MOTTRAM, D. V., Food Biosciences

OWEN, E., Agriculture, Policy and Development

PAGEL, M., Animal and Microbial Sciences

PAYNE, C. C., Plant Sciences

PYLE, D. L., Food Biosciences

ROBSON, R. L., Animal and Microbial Sciences

SCHOFIELD, J. D., Food Biosciences

SIBLY, R. M., Animal and Microbial Sciences

STRANGE, P., Animal and Microbial Sciences

SWINBANK, A., Agriculture, Policy and Development

TRAILL, B., Agriculture, Policy and Development

WHITEHEAD, J. R., Applied Statistics

WILLIAMS, C. M., Food Biosciences

Faculty of Science (Whiteknights, POB 200, Reading, RG6 6AF; tel. (118) 931-8342; fax (118) 975-5509; e-mail sciug@reading.ac.uk):

ALLOWAY, B. J., Human and Environmental Sciences

ANDREWS, B., Computer Science, Cybernetics and Electronic Engineering

ASTILL, G. G., Human and Environmental Sciences

ATKINS, A. G., Construction Management and Engineering

BAKER, K. D., Computer Science, Cybernetics and Electronic Engineering

BASSETT, D. C., Mathematics, Meteorology and Physics

BERRY, D. C., Psychology

BON, R., Construction Management and Engineering

BOWKER, M., Chemistry

BRADLEY, R. J., Human and Environmental Sciences

BROWNING, K. A., Mathematics, Meteorology and Physics

CARDIN, D. J., Chemistry

CHAPLIN, C. R., Construction Management and Engineering

CHAPMAN, R. W., Human and Environmental Sciences

CLEMENTS-CROOME, T. D. J., Construction Management and Engineering

CODLING, K., Mathematics, Meteorology and Physics

COLEMAN, M. L., Human and Environmental Sciences

COLQUHOUN, H. M., Chemistry

COOPER, P. J., Psychology

DREW, M. G. B., Chemistry

FISHER, G. N., Construction Management and Engineering

FLANAGAN, R., Construction Management and Engineering

FULFORD, M. G., Human and Environmental Sciences

GILBERT, A., Chemistry

GILCHRIST, R., Human and Environmental Sciences

GREGORY, P. J., Human and Environmental Sciences

GURNEY, R., Mathematics, Meteorology and Physics

HAINES, K., Mathematics, Meteorology and Physics

HARRISON, R., Computer Science, Cybernetics and Electronic Engineering

HARWOOD, L. M., Chemistry

HILTON, A. J. W., Mathematics, Meteorology and Physics

HOSKINS, B. J., Mathematics, Meteorology and Physics

JERONIMIDIS, G., Construction Management and Engineering

MCKENNA, F. P., Psychology

MEGSON, G. M., Computer Science, Cybernetics and Electronic Engineering

MITCHELL, G. R., Mathematics, Meteorology and Physics

MITHEN, S. J., Human and Environmental Sciences

MURRAY, L., Psychology

NEEDHAM, D. J., Mathematics, Meteorology and Physics

NICHOLS, N. K., Mathematics, Meteorology and Physics

O'NEILL, A., Mathematics, Meteorology and Physics

PORTER, D., Mathematics, Meteorology and Physics

RICE, D. A., Chemistry

SELLWOOD, B. W., Human Sciences

SHARKEY, P. M., Computer Science, Cybernetics and Electronic Engineering

SHINE, K. P., Mathematics, Meteorology and Physics

SLINGO, G. M., Mathematics, Meteorology and Physics

SMITH, P. T., Psychology

THORPE, A. J., Mathematics, Meteorology and Physics

VALDES, P. J., Mathematics, Meteorology and Physics

WADGE, G. M., Mathematics, Meteorology and Physics

WALSH, R., Chemistry

WANN, J. P., Psychology

WARBURTON, D. M., Psychology

WARWICK, K., Computer Science, Cybernetics and Electronic Engineering

WHITEHEAD, P. G., Human and Environmental Sciences

WRIGHT, A. C., Mathematics, Meteorology and Physics

WRIGHT, J. D. M., Mathematics, Meteorology and Physics

Rural History Centre (Whiteknights, POB 229, Reading, RG6 6AG; tel. (118) 931-8342; fax (118) 931-5509; e-mail rhc@reading.ac.uk):

HOYLE, R. W.

UNIVERSITY OF SALFORD

Salford, Greater Manchester, M5 4WT

Telephone: (161) 295-5000

Fax: (161) 295-5999

E-mail: office-exrel@salford.ac.uk

Internet: www.salford.ac.uk

Founded 1896, as the Royal Technical Institute, later Royal College of Advanced Technology, Univ. Charter granted 1967

Academic year: October to July

Chancellor: Dr IRENE KHAN

Vice-Chancellor: Prof. MARTIN HALL

Deputy Vice-Chancellor and Registrar and Sec.: Dr ADRIAN GRAVES

Pro-Vice-Chancellor for Academic: Prof. HUW MORRIS

Pro-Vice-Chancellor for International Affairs: Prof. CYNTHIA PINE

Pro-Vice-Chancellor for Research and Innovation: Prof. GHASSAN AOUAD

Pro-Vice-Chancellor for Strategic Partnerships: KEITH BARNES

Dir of Academic Information Services and Librarian: TONY LEWIS

Number of teachers: 800

Number of students: 18,000

DEANS

Arts and Social Sciences: Prof. HUW MORRIS

Health and Social Care: Prof. CYNTHIA PINE

Science and Technology: Prof. GHASSAN AOUAD

PROFESSORS

ALEXANDER, K., Construction and Property Management

ALSHAWI, M., Surveying

AOUAD, G., Surveying

ARMOUR, D. G., Physics

ARNELL, R. D., Aeronautical, Mechanical and Manufacturing Engineering

AVIS, N., Information Technology Institute

AYLETT, R., Information Systems Institute

BAKER, R. D., Accounting, Economics and Management Service

BARIC, L. F., Information Technology Institute

BARRETT, P. S., Surveying

BETTS, M. P., Surveying

BLAKEMORE, D. L., Modern Languages

BOARDMAN, A. D., Physics

BOOTH, J. G., Physics

BOTHAM, D., Management

BOWKER, P., Rehabilitation

BRANDON, P. S., Surveying

BROWN, G. R., Surveying

BRYANT, C. G. A., Sociology

BULL, M. J., Politics and Contemporary History

CALDWELL, D., Electronic and Electrical Engineering

CARTER, G., Physics

CHADWICK, D. W., Information System Institute

CHRISTER, A. H., Computer and Mathematics Science

COLLIER, C. G., Civil and Environmental Engineering

COLLIGON, J. S., Electronic and Electrical Engineering

COLLINS, D. N., Geography

COLQUHOUN, H. M., Chemistry and Applied Chemistry

COOK, R., Media and Performance

COOPER, G., Information Technology

COOPER, I., Centre for Regional Development and Sustainability

COOPER, R., Art and Design Technology

CRAIG, P. S., Biological Sciences

CROSSLEY, T. R., Aeronautical, Mechanical and Manufacturing Engineering

DANGERFIELD, B. C., Accounting, Economics and Management Science

DANSON, F. M., Environment and Life Sciences

DAVIES-COOPER, R., Art and Design Technology

DONNELLY, S. E., Physics

EASSON, A. W., English

EDGELL, S. R., Sociology

EDWARDS, J., Rehabilitation

EKERE, N. N., Aeronautical, Mechanical and Manufacturing Engineering

FERNANDO, T. P., Information Systems Institute

FLYNN, R., Sociology

GARSIDE, P. L., European Studies Research Institute

GERBER, R., Physics

GLEAVE, M. B., Geography

GOLDSMITH, M. J. F., Politics and Contemporary History

GRAY, J. O., Electronic and Electrical Engineering
GRUNDY, P. J., Physics
HARDING, A., Regional Development and Urban Politics
HARRIS, G. T., Modern Languages
HICKEY, L. D., Modern Languages
HILL, R., Computer and Mathematical Sciences
HORNER, A., English
HUGHES, R., Chemistry and Applied Chemistry
KAY, S., Health and Social Care
KEIGER, J. F. V., Modern Languages
KOBBACY, K. A. H., Accounting, Economics and Management Science
LAM, Y. W., Acoustics and Electronic Engineering
LARMOUTH, J., Information Technology Institute
LAWSON, R., Biological Sciences
LEONARD, J., Sciences
LINGE, N., Electronic and Electrical Engineering
LONG, A. F., Health Care Practice
LONGHURST, B. J., English, Sociology, Politics and Contemporary History
LORD, D., Physics
MARVIN, S., Centre for Regional Development and Sustainability
MASON, R. S., Business Studies
MAY, T., Sociology
MELBOURNE, C., Civil and Environmental Engineering
MORGAN, C. G., Biological Sciences
NAGY, F. L. N., Information Technology
NEAL, F., European Studies
PEMBLE, M. E., Chemistry and Applied Chemistry
POPAY, J., Public Health Research and Resource Centre
POWELL, J. A., Information Technology
PROCTER, G., Chemistry and Applied Chemistry
RAYNES, N., Health and Social Care
REZGUI, Y., Information Systems Institute
RICHARDS, J., Science
ROSS, D. K., Physics
SAMPSON, A. A., Economics
SANGER, D. J., Aeronautical, Mechanical and Manufacturing Engineering
SARSHAR, M., Construction and Property Management
SCOTT, D. B., Music
SHARDLOW, S. M., Social Work
SIMMONS, C., Accounting, Economics and Management Science
STEELE, A., Environment and Life Sciences
STOREY, D. M., Biological Sciences
TAYLOR, I. R., Sociology
TOLZ, V., English, Sociology, Politics and Contemporary History
TOMLINSON, P., Languages
TONGE, J., English, Sociology, Politics and Contemporary History
TOWELL, R. J., Modern Languages
VADERA, S., Sciences
WALKDEN, F., Computer and Mathematics Science
WEBSTER, P. J., Civil and Environmental Engineering
WHITEHEAD, C., Physics
WHITELEY, S., Media, Music and Performance
WHITELOCK, J., Management
WOOD, J. R. G., Computer and Mathematical Sciences, Information and Educational and Materials Development
WOOD, L., Business and Informatics
WOOD-HARPER, A. T., Computer and Mathematics Science
WRIGHT, F., Surveying
WYN JONES, E., Chemistry and Applied Chemistry

UNIVERSITY OF SHEFFIELD

Firth Court, Western Bank, Sheffield, S10 2TN

Telephone: (114) 222-2000
Fax: (114) 279-8603
E-mail: externalrelations@sheffield.ac.uk
Internet: www.sheffield.ac.uk
Founded 1879 as Univ. College, Royal Charter 1905
Academic year: September to June
Chancellor: Lord DAINTON
Pro-Chancellor: K. E. RIDDLE
Pro-Chancellor: P. FIRTH
Pro-Chancellor: ANTHONY PAUL PEDDER
Vice-Chancellor: Prof. KEITH BURNETT
Pro-Vice-Chancellor for Learning and Teaching: Prof. PAUL WHITE
Pro-Vice-Chancellor for Research and Innovation: Prof. RICHARD JONES
Pro-Vice-Chancellor for Internaional Affairs: Prof. REBECCA HUGHES
Pro-Vice-Chancellor for the Faculty of Arts and Humanities: Prof. MICHAEL BRADDICK (acting)
Pro-Vice-Chancellor for the Faculty of Engineering: Prof. MICHAEL HOUNSLOW
Pro-Vice-Chancellor for the Faculty of Medicine, Dentistry and Health: Prof. ANTHONY WEETMAN
Pro-Vice-Chancellor for the Faculty of Science: Prof. ANTHONY RYAN
Pro-Vice-Chancellor for the Faculty of Social Sciences: Prof. ANTHONY PAYNE
Registrar and Sec.: P. HARVEY
Librarian: MARTIN LEWIS

Library: see Libraries and Archives
Number of teachers: 1,500
Number of students: 24,916

PROFESSORS
(Some staff serve in more than one faculty)

Faculty of Architectural Studies:
BLUNDELL JONES, P. M., Architecture
CAMPBELL, H., Town and Regional Planning
CROOK, A. D. H., Town and Regional Planning
HENNEBERRY, J., Town and Regional Planning
KANG, J., Architecture
LAWSON, B. R., Architecture
PLANK, R. J., Architecture
SWANWICK, C. A., Landscape
TILL, J., Architecture
TREGENZA, P. R., Architecture

Faculty of Arts:
AINSWORTH, P. F., French
Canon ALEXANDER, L. C. A., Biblical Studies
BARRETT, J. C., Archaeology
BELL, D. A., Philosophy
BENNET, J., Archaeology
BRADDICK, M. J., History
BRANIGAN, K., Archaeology
BROOKSBANK JONES, A., Hispanic Studies
CLARKE, E. F., Music
CLINES, D. J. A., Biblical Studies
COLLIS, J. R., Archaeology and Prehistory
COOK, R. J., History
CROSS, M. F., French
DENNELL, R. W., Archaeology
DIVERS, J., Philosophy
DUFFIELD, N. G., English Language and Linguistics
ENGLAND, J. P., Hispanic Studies
EXUM, J. C., Biblical Studies
GREENGRASS, M., History
HAFFENDEN, J., English Literature
HATTAWAY, M., English Literature
HILL, P. H. A. W., French
HOOKWAY, C. J., Philosophy
HOPKINS, R., Philosophy
JONES, G. E. M., Archaeology

Sir KERSHAW, I., Modern History
KING, E. J., History
LEATHERBARROW, W. J., Russian and Slavonic Studies
LINN, A. R., English Language and Linguistics
MCMAHON, A. M. S., English Language and Linguistics
OWENS, D. J., Philosophy
PERRAUDIN, M. F., Germanic Studies
PHIMISTER, I. P., International History
ROBERTS, N. J., English Literature
RUSSELL, R., Russian and Slavonic Studies
SAUL, J. M., Philosophy
SHELLARD, D. M., English Literature
SHEPHERD, D. G., Russian and Slavonic Studies
SHOEMAKER, R. B., History
SHUTTLEWORTH, S. A., English Literature
SIMEONE, N. A., Music
STAUB, M. H., History
STERN, R. A., Philosophy
STOCK, J. P. J., Music
SWANSON, P., Hispanic Studies
WALKER, D. H., French
WHITELAM, K. W., Biblical Studies
ZVELEBIL, M., Archaeology

Faculty of Engineering:
ALLEN, R. W. K., Chemical and Process Engineering
ALLERTON, D. J., Automatic Control and Systems Engineering
ALLINSON, N. M., Electronic and Electrical Engineering
ANDERSON, W. F., Civil and Structural Engineering
ASHLEY, R. M., Civil and Structural Engineering
ASKES, H., Civil and Structural Engineering
BANKS, S. P., Automatic Control and Systems Engineering
BANWART, S. A., Civil and Structural Engineering
BEYNON, J. H., Metallurgy
BILLINGS, S. A., Control Engineering
BOLLER, C., Mechanical Engineering
BROWN, M. W., Mechanical Engineering
BURGESS, I. W., Civil and Structural Engineering
CHAMBERS, B., Electronic and Electrical Engineering
CULLIS, A. G., Electronic and Electrical Engineering
DALEY, S., Automatic Control and Systems Engineering
DAVID, J. P. R., Electronic and Electrical Engineering
DAVIES, H. A., Engineering Materials
FLEMING, P. J., Automatic Control and Systems Engineering
GIBBS, M. R. J., Engineering Materials
HARDING, J., Engineering Materials
HOUNSLOW, M. J., Chemical and Process Engineering
HOUSTON, P. A., Electronic and Electrical Engineering
HOWARD, I. C., Mechanical Engineering
HOWE, D., Electrical Engineering
JAMES, P. F., Engineering Materials
JOHNSON, C. M., Electronic and Electrical Engineering
JONES, F. R., Engineering Materials
JONES, H., Engineering Materials
LEE, W. E., Engineering Materials
LERNER, D. N., Civil Engineering
MACNEIL, S., Tissue Engineering
MATTHEWS, A., Engineering Materials
OWENS, D. H., Automatic Control and Systems Engineering
PAVIC, A., Civil and Structural Engineering
PILAKOUTAS, K., Civil and Structural Engineering
QIN, N., Mechanical Engineering
RAINFORTH, W. M., Engineering Materials

REES, G. J., Electronic and Electrical Engineering
RIDGWAY, K., Mechanical Engineering
SAUL, A. J., Civil and Structural Engineering
SHARIFI, V. N., Chemical and Process Engineering
SHORT, R. D., Engineering Materials
SOUTIS, C., Aerospace Engineering
SWITHENBANK, J., Chemical and Process Engineering
TOMLINSON, G. R., Engineering Dynamics
UNGAR, G., Engineering Materials
WALDRON, P., Civil and Structural Engineering
WEST, A. R., Engineering Materials
WILSON, C. W., Mechanical Engineering
WORDEN, K., Mechanical Engineering
WRIGHT, P. C., Chemical and Process Engineering
WRIGHT, P. V., Engineering Materials
YATES, J. R., Mechanical Engineering
ZHU, Z. Q., Electronic and Electrical Engineering

Faculty of Law (fax (114) 222-6832):

ADAMS, J. N., Intellectual Property
BEYLEVELD, D., Law
BIRDS, J. R., Commercial Law
BRADGATE, J. R., Commercial Law
BRADNEY, T. A., Law
DIGNAN, J., Criminology and Restorative Justice
DITTON, J., Criminology
HARDEN, I., Law
HOLDAWAY, S. D., Sociology
KINDERLERER, J., Biotechnical Law
LEWIS, N. D., Constitutional Law, Sociology of Law
LUXTON, P., Property Law
MERRILLS, J. E. G., International Law
SHAPLAND, J. M., Criminal Justice

Faculty of Medicine (Beech Hill Rd, Sheffield, S10 2RX; fax (114) 271-3960):

AHMEDZAI, S., Palliative Medicine
AKEHURST, R. L., Health Economics
BARBER, D. C., Medical Imaging and Medical Physics
BAX, N. D. S., Medical Education
BISHOP, N. J., Paediatric Bone Disease
BOISSONADE, F. M., Oral and Maxillofacial Surgery
BRAZIER, J. E., Health Economics
BROOK, A. H., Oral Health and Development
BROOK, I. M., Oral and Maxillofacial Surgery
BROOKER, C. G. D., Mental Health
BROWN, B. H., Medical Physics
BROWN, B. L., Cell Signalling and Endocrinology
BROWN, N. J., Surgical Sciences
CAMPBELL, M. J., Medical Statistics
CANNINGS, C., Mathematics and Informatics
COLEMAN, R., Medical Oncology
CROSSMAN, D. C., Cardiology
CROUCHER, P. I., Bone Biology
DOLAN, P. H. R., Health Economics
DOWER, S. K., Molecular Immunology
DUFF, G. W., Molecular Medicine
EASTELL, R., Bone Metabolism
EL-NAHAS, A. M., Nephrology
ENDERBY, P. M., Community Rehabilitation
FORREST, A. R. W., Clinical Chemistry
GERRISH, K., Nursing Practice Development
GRANT, G. W. B., Cognitive Disability
GRIFFITHS, P. D., Academic Radiology
Sir HALL, D. M. B., Community Paediatrics
HAMDY, F., Urology
HANCOCK, B. W., Clinical Oncology
HATTON, P. V., Adult Dental Care
HELLEWELL, P. G., Vascular Biology
HENDERSON, I. W., Functional Genomics

HUTCHINSON, A., Public Health Medicine
INCE, P., Neuropathology
KERSHAW, B., Nursing and Midwifery
KIRKHAM, M. J., Midwifery
LEDGER, W. L., Obstetrics and Gynaecology
LENNON, M. A., Oral Health and Development
LEWIS, C. E., Molecular and Cellular Pathology
MACNEIL, S., Tissue Engineering
MATHERS, N., General Practice
MEUTH, M., Cellular Genetics
MILROY, C. M., Forensic Pathology
MOORE, H. D. M., Reproductive Biology
NICHOLL, J. P., Medical Care Research Centre
NICOLSON, P., Health Psychology
NOLAN, M. R., Gerontological Nursing
PALEY, M. N. J., Magnetic Resonance Physics
PARKER, S. G., Health Care for Elderly People
PARRY, G. D., Applied Psychological Therapies
PAYNE, S., Palliative Care Nursing
PEAKE, I. R., Molecular Medicine
PERKINS, M. R., Human Communications Science
PHILP, I., Health Care for Elderly People
POCKLEY, A. G., Immunobiology
POWERS, H. J., Nutritional Biochemistry
QWARNSTRÖM, E. E., Cell Biology
READ, R. C., Infectious Diseases
READ, S. M., Acute and Critical Care Nursing
REED, M. W. R., Surgical Oncology
REILLY, C. S., Anaesthesia
RENNIE, I. G., Ophthalmology
ROBINSON, P. G., Oral Health and Development
ROBINSON, P. P., Oral and Maxillofacial Surgery
ROLF, C. G., Sports Medicine
ROSS, R. J. M., Endocrinology
SAYERS, J. R., Functional Genomics
SHAW, P. J., Neurology
SPEIGHT, P. M., Oral Pathology
STACKHOUSE, R. J., Human Communication Science
TANNER, M. S., Paediatrics
TANTAM, D. J. H., Psychotherapy
TAYLOR, C. J., Paediatric Gastroenterology
THOMPSON, D. R., Acute and Critical Care
TUCKER, G. T., Molecular Pharmacology and Pharmacogenetics
UNDERWOOD, J. C. E., Pathology
van NOORT, R., Adult Dental Care
WALSH, T. F., Adult Dental Care
WARNES, A. M., Social Gerontology
WEETMAN, A. P., Medicine
WELLS, M., Gynaecological Pathology
WELLS, W. B., Human Communication Science
WHYTE, M. K. B., Respiratory Medicine
WOLL, P. J., Medical Oncology
WOODRUFF, P. W. R., Academic Clinical Psychiatry

Faculty of Pure Science:

ANDERSON, C. W., Mathematics and Statistics
ANDREWS, P. W., Biomedical Science
ARMS, S. P., Chemistry
ARMSTRONG, H. W., Geography
ARTYMIUK, P. J., Molecular Biology and Biotechnology
ATKIN, R. J., Applied Mathematics
BAILEY, G. J., Applied Mathematics
BEERLING, D. J., Palaeoclimatology
BIGG, G. R., Geography
BIGGINS, J. D., Probability and Statistics
BINGHAM, N. H., Probability and Statistics
BIRKHEAD, T. R., Zoology
BLACKSTOCK, W., Molecular Biology and Biotechnology

BULLOUGH, P. A., Molecular Biology and Biotechnology
BURKE, T. A., Molecular Ecology
BUTLIN, R. K., Evolutionary Biology
CALLAGHAN, T. V., Arctic Ecology
CALOW, P., Zoology
CARSWELL, D. A., Geology
CHATWIN, P. C., Applied and Computational Mathematics
CIRAVEGNA, F., Computer Science
COOKE, M. P., Computer Science
DEAN, P., Psychology
DERRICK, J., Computer Science
DORLING, D. F. L., Geography
EBDON, J. R., Chemistry
EISER, C., Psychology
EISER, J. R., Psychology
FLEMING, A. J., Plant Sciences
FOSTER, S. J., Molecular Biology and Biotechnology
FRISBY, J. P., Psychology
GAIZAUSKAS, R., Computer Science
GASTON, K. J., Biodiversity and Conservation
GEHRING, G. A., Solid State Physics
GREEN, J., Molecular Biology and Biotechnology
GREEN, P. D., Computer Science
GREENLEES, J. P. C., Probability and Statistics
GREGSON, N., Geography
GRUNDY, D., Biomedical Science
HARDY, G., Clinical Psychology
HEATHWAITE, A. L., Geography
HIGGINS, J. A., Molecular Biology and Biotechnology
HOCKEY, G. R. J., Psychology
HOLCOMBE, W. M. L., Computer Science
HOLLEY, M. J., Biomedical Science
HORTON, P., Molecular Biology and Biotechnology
HUGHES, D. W., Physics and Astronomy
HUNTER, C. A., Chemistry
HUNTER, C. N., Molecular Biology and Biotechnology
INGHAM, P. W., Biomedical Science
JACKSON, P. A., Human Geography
JACKSON, R. F. W., Synthetic Chemistry
JONES, R. A. L., Physics
JORDAN, D. A., Pure Mathematics
KELLY, D. J., Molecular Biology and Biotechnology
LEE, J. A., Environmental Biology
LEEGOOD, R. C., Plant Biochemistry
LEGGETT, G. J., Nanoscale Analytical Science
MALTBY, L., Environmental Biology
MANN, B. E., Chemistry
MAYHEW, J. E. W., Psychology
MCLEOD, C. W. M., Chemistry
MOERDIJK, I., Pure Mathematics
MOORE, H. D. M., Reproductive Biology
MOORE, R., Computer Science
NICOLSON, R. I., Psychology
NIRANJAN, M., Computer Science
O'HAGAN, A., Probability and Statistics
OUTHWAITE, C. W., Mathematics and Statistics
PARSONS, L. M., Psychology
PATTIE, C. J., Geography
PICKUP, B. T., Chemistry
PIPER, P., Molecular Biology and Biotechnology
PLACZEK, M., Biomedical Science
POOLE, R. K., Molecular Biology and Biotechnology
PRESS, M. C., Physiological Ecology
QUEGAN, S., Applied and Computational Mathematics
QUICK, W. P., Plant Physiology
RATNIEKS, F. L. W., Apiculture
READ, D. J., Plant Sciences
REDGRAVE, P., Psychology
REES, M., Plant Ecology
RICE, D. W., Molecular Biology and Biotechnology

ROSZKOWSKI, L., Physics and Astronomy
RUDERMAN, M. S., Applied Mathematics
RYAN, A. J., Chemistry
SCHOLES, J. D., Plant and Microbial Science
SHARKEY, N. E., Computer Science
SHARP, R. Y., Pure Mathematics
SHEERAN, P., Psychology
SIEGAL, M., Psychology
SKOLNICK, M. S., Experimental Condensed Matter
SLADE, P., Clinical Psychology
SMALLWOOD, R., Computer Science
SMYTHE, C., Biomedical Science
SMYTHE, E., Biomedical Science
SNAITH, V. P., Pure Mathematics
SPENCER, C. P., Psychology
SPOONER, N. J. C., Physics
STRICKLAND, N. P., Pure Mathematics
SURPRENANT, A., Biomedical Science
TADHUNTER, C. N., Physics and Astronomy
THOMPSON, M.J., Applied Mathematics
TURNER, G., Genetics
TURPIN, G., Clinical Psychology
VALENTINE, G., Geography
VON FÁY-SIEBENBÜRGEN, R., Applied Mathematics
WALL, T. D., Psychology
WALKER, M., Computer Science
WALTHO, J. P., Molecular Biology and Biotechnology
WARD, M. D., Chemistry
WHITE, P. E., Geography
WILKS, Y., Computer Science
WILLIAMSON, M. P., Molecular Biology and Biotechnology
WOODWARD, F. I., Plant Ecology
WYATT, L. R., Applied Mathematics
ZINOBER, A. S. I., Applied Mathematics

Faculty of Social Sciences:
ADCOCK, C. J., Financial Econometrics
ARMSTRONG, D., Education
BEAULIEU, M., Management
BOOTH, T. A., Social Policy
BROOKES, R. G., Education
CARR, W., Education
CASSELL, C. M., Management
CHAPPELL, D., Mathematical Economics
CLEGG, C. W., Work Psychology
COLE, P., Journalism
CORRALL, S., Librarianship and Information Management
FORD, N. J., Information Studies
FRANKLIN, R., Media Communications
GAMBLE, A. M., Politics
GEDDES, A. P., Politics
GRAYSON, J. H., East Asian Studies
GRUGEL, J. B., Politics
GUNTER, B., Journalism
HANNON, P. W., Education
HEALD, D. E. A, Management
HOCKEY, J. L., Sociological Studies
HOOK, G. D., Japanese Studies
HOOPER, B. J., East Asian Studies
JAMES, A., Sociological Studies
JENKINS, R., Sociology
KENNEDY-PIPE, C., International Relations, Politics
MACDONALD, S., Management
MALTBY, J. A., Management
MARSH, P., Child and Family Welfare
MCCONNELL, D., Education
MOSLEY, P., Economics
NIXON, J. D., Education
NORRIS, C. A., Sociology
PARRY, G., Education
PAYNE, A. J., Politics
REDMAN, T. A., Management
SMITH, M. J., Politics
STANDISH, P., Education
TAYLOR, A. J., Politics
TAYLOR, P. D., Leisure Management
TYLECOTE, A. B., Economics and Management of Technological Change
USHERWOOD, R. C., Information Studies

VINCENT, A. W., Politics
WALKER, A. C., Social Policy
WEBB, S. C., Institute of Lifelong Learning
WELLINGTON, J. J., Education
WHITTAKER, S. J., Information Studies
WILLETT, P., Information Studies
WOOD, S. J., Work Psychology
WRIGHT, T., East Asian Studies

ATTACHED SCHOOLS
School of Health and Related Research: Dean Prof. R. L. AKEHURST.

School of Management: Dir Prof. M. BEAULIEU.

UNIVERSITY OF SOUTHAMPTON

University Rd, Southampton, SO17 1BJ
Telephone: (23) 8059-5000
Fax: (23) 8059-3131
E-mail: admissns@soton.ac.uk
Internet: www.soton.ac.uk
Founded 1952; opened as the Hartley Institution 1862; incorporated as the Hartley Univ. College 1902
Academic year: October to July
Vice-Chancellor: Prof. DON NUTBEAM
Provost and Deputy Vice-Chancellor: Prof. ADAM WHEELER
Pro-Vice-Chancellor: Prof. PHILIP NELSON
Pro-Vice-Chancellor: MARK SPEARING
Pro-Vice-Chancellor for Education: Prof. DEBRA HUMPHRIS
Chief Operating Officer: MALCOLM ACE
Registrar: TESSA HARRISON
Head Student Information and Records: GILLIAM HOLF
Librarian: Dr MARK BROWN
Library: see Libraries and Archives
Number of teachers: 2,280
Number of students: 22,834 (20,869 full-time and 1,965 part-time)

DEANS
Faculty of Business and Law: Prof. JEREMY HOWELLS
Faculty of Engineering and the Environment: Prof. WILLIAM POWRIE
Faculty of Health Sciences: Prof. JESSICA CORNER
Faculty of Humanities: Prof. ANNE CURRY
Faculty of Medicine: Prof. IAIN CAMERON
Faculty of Natural and Environmental Sciences: Prof. STEPHEN HAWKINS
Faculty of Physical and Applied Sciences: Prof. Dame WENDY HALL
Faculty of Social and Human Sciences: Prof. JUDITH PETTS

UNIVERSITY OF SUNDERLAND

Edinburgh Bldg, City Campus, Chester Rd Sunderland, SR1 3SD
Telephone: (191) 515-2000
Fax: (191) 515-2960
E-mail: student-helpline@sunderland.ac.uk
Internet: www.sunderland.ac.uk
Founded 1969 as Sunderland Polytechnic; present name and status 1992
Academic year: September to June
Chancellor: STEVE CRAM
Vice-Chancellor and Chief Exec.: Prof. PETER FIDLER
Deputy Vice-Chancellor for Resources: SHIRLEY ATKINSON
Deputy Vice-Chancellor for Academic: Prof. PETER STRIKE
Deputy Vice-Chancellor for Academic: Prof. JULIE MENNELL
Sec. and Clerk to the Board: J. D. PACEY
Dir of Information Services: Prof. ANDREW MACDONALD
Library of 280,000 vols
Number of teachers: 1,302

Number of students: 18,944

DEANS
Faculty of Applied Sciences: Prof. JOHN MACINTYRE
Faculty of Arts, Design and Media: GRAEME THOMPSON
Faculty of Business and Law: VIVIAN KINNAIRD
Faculty of Education and Society: Prof. G. SHIELD

PROFESSORS
ALABASTER, T., Environmental Informatics
ARTHUR, W. W., Population Biology
BAINBRIDGE, E., Fine Art
BRAYNE, H., Law
CHILTON, P., Politics and Peace Studies
COCKTON, G., Computer Software Engineering
COX, C. S., Control Engineering
CRISELL, A. P., Broadcasting Studies
CROZIER, G., Education
DARBY, J., Humanities
EDWARDS, H. M., Computer Software Engineering
ELLIOTT, J., Education
ELLIS, P., Performance Arts
FLETCHER, E. J., Applied Computing
GROUNDWATER, P. W., Organic Chemistry
HANMER, J., Humanities
HARVEY, B. P., Humanities
HEPBURN, A., Modern Irish History
HESTER, M., Social Studies
HARRISON, R., Renewable Energy
ITZIN, C., Health and Community Studies
LEES, G., Neurophysiology and Neuropharmacology
LILLEY, T. H., Physical Chemistry
MACINTYRE, J., Computer Software Engineering
MALIN, N. A., Health Services Research
MOSCARDINI, A. O., Mathematical Modelling
O'BRIEN, M., Librarian, Communication and Media Studies
OVER, D. E., Philosophical Logic
PALOVA, Z., Design and Creative Arts
PETROVA, S., Glass
PODCZECK, G. F., Pharmaceutics
PRENTICE, R. C., Tourism
PRINGLE, K., Comparative Social Policy
REED, M. A., Criminal and Private International Law
RICHARDS, D. S., International Business and Cross-Cultural Management
SIM, S. D., Critical Theory
SINGH, G., Pharmacy
STOREY, J. C., Librarian, Communication and Media Studies
TAIT, J. I., Computer Software Engineering
THOMPSON, B., Design and Creative Arts
THORNHAM, S., Librarian, Communication and Media Studies
TINDLE, J., Computer Software Engineering
VAN LEEUWEN, C. C., Psychology
VAN ZON, H., Social Studies
WALDRON, P., Modern European History
WERMTER, S., Information Systems
WILSON, P. H., Early Modern History

UNIVERSITY OF SURREY

Guildford, GU2 5XH
Telephone: (1483) 300800
Fax: (1483) 683948
Internet: www.surrey.ac.uk
Founded 1891 as Battersea Polytechnic Institute, designated a College of Advanced Technology 1956, University Charter 1966
Academic year: October to June
Chancellor: HRH THE DUKE OF KENT
Vice-Chancellor and Chief Exec.: Prof. CHRISTOPHER M. SNOWDEN
Sr Deputy Vice-Chancellor: Prof. NIGEL SEATON

Deputy Vice-Chancellor for Academic Devt: Prof. GILLIAN NICHOLLS
Deputy Vice-Chancellor for Research and Innovation: Prof. STEPHEN WILLIAMSON
Pro-Vice-Chancellor for Int. Relations: Prof. COLIN GRANT
Univ. Registrar: CAROLINE JOHNSON (acting)
Dir of Corporate Services: GREG MELLY
Dir of Finance: DAVID SHARKEY
Dir of Information Services and University Librarian: T. J. A. CRAWSHAW
Number of teachers: 997 (incl. 350 part-time associate lecturers)
Number of students: 15,187
Publication: Surrey Matters

DEANS

Faculty of Arts and Human Sciences: Prof. PHILLIP POWRIE
Faculty of Engineering and Physical Sciences: Prof. MICHAEL KEARNEY
Faculty of Health and Medical Sciences: Prof. JOHN HAY
Faculty of Management and Law: Prof. DAVID ALLEN

PROFESSORS

School of Arts:
ANDERMAN, G. M., Translation Studies
BARTA, P., Russian and Cultural Studies
CORBETT, G. G., Linguistics and Russian Language
EADE, J.
FLOCKTON, C. H., European Economic Studies
FLOOD, C. G., European Studies
FORBES, S.
GRANT, C. B., Communication Studies
HOLFORD, J. A. K.
HUTCHINGS, S. C., Russian
JARVIS, P., Continuing Education
JUDGE, A., French
LANSDALE, J. H., Dance Studies
LUTZEIER, P. R., German
MCNAIR, S., Education
MIDDLEHURST, R. M., Higher Education
MOORE, A., Music
UPEX, R. V., Law

School of Biomedical and Life Sciences:
ADAMS, M. R., Food Microbiology
BUSHELL, M. E., Microbial Physiology
CLIFFORD, M. N., Food Safety
DALE, J. W., Molecular Microbiology
DANIL DE NAMOR, A., Chemistry
FERNS, G. A. A., Metabolic and Molecular Medicine
GIBSON, G. G., Molecular Toxicology
GOLDFARB, P. S. G., Molecular Biology
HAY, J. N., Materials Chemistry
HEYES, D. M., Chemistry
HINDMARCH, I., Human Psychopharmacology
HOURANI, S. M. O., Pharmacology
HOWELL, N. K., Food Science
KITCHEN, I., Neuropharmacology
LYNCH, J. M., Life Sciences
MCFADDEN, J., Molecular Genetics
MILLWARD, D. J., Nutrition
ROBERTSON, W. R.
SERMON, P., Physical Chemistry
SKENE, D. J., Neuroendocrinology
SLADE, R. C. T., Inorganic Chemistry
SMITH, C., Functional Genomics

School of Electronics and Physical Sciences:
ADAMS, A. R.
AHMAD, KH., Artificial Intelligence
ALLAM, J., Ultra-fast Optoelectronics
BRIDGES, T. J., Mathematics
CLOUGH, A. S.
COWERN, N. E. B., Nanoscale Materials Processing
EVANS, B. G., Information Systems
GELLETLY, W.

HESS, O., Computational Quantum Electronics
HOMEWOOD, K. P., Semiconductor Optoelectronics
ILLINGWORTH, J., Machine Vision
KEARNEY, M. J., Electronic Device Engineering
KITTLER, J. V., Machine Intelligence
KONDOZ, A. M., Multimedia Communication Systems
KRAUSE, P. J., Software Engineering
MCDONALD, P. J.
MELBOURNE, I., Mathematics
PAVLOU, G., Communication and Information Systems
PETROU, M., Image Analysis
REED, G. T., Optoelectronics
ROBERTS, R. M., Mathematics
ROGERS, A. J.
SANDSTEDE, B., Mathematical Sciences
SCHNEIDER, S. A., Computing
SEALY, B. J., Solid State Devices and Ion Beam Technology
SILVA, S. R. P., Solid State Electronics
SPYROU, N. M.
Sir SWEETING, MARTIN, Satellite Engineering
TAFAZOLLI, R., Mobile Communications
THOMPSON, I. J.
TOSTEVIN, J. A.
WALKER, P. M.
WEBB, R. P., Ion Beam Physics
WEISS, B. L., Microelectronics

School of Engineering:
AZAPAGIC, A., Sustainable Engineering
CHEW, J. W., Mechanical Engineering
CHRYSSANTHOPOULOS, M. K., Structural Systems
CLIFT, R., Environmental Technology
CROCOMBE, A. D., Structural Mechanics
GILLAN, M. A., Aerospace Engineering
GORINGE, M. J., Materials
HOLLAWAY, L. C., Composite Structures
JACKSON, T., Sustainable Development
JEFFERIS, S., Civil Engineering
KOKOSSIS, A. C., Process Systems Engineering Optimization
LAWSON, M., Construction Systems
LLOYD, B. J., Environmental Health Engineering
NOOSHIN, H., Space Structures
PARKE, C. A. R., Structural Engineering
PARKER, G. A., Mechanical Engineering
ROBINS, A. G., Environmental Fluid Mechanics
SMITH, P. A., Composite Materials
THORPE, R., Multiphase Engineering
TOY, N., Fluid Mechanics
TSAKIROPOULOS, P., Metallurgy
TÜZÜN, U., Process Engineering
WATTS, J. F., Materials Science

School of Human Sciences:
ARBER, S. L., Sociology
BAG, P., Economics
BARRETT, M. D., Psychology
BIRD, G. R., Economics
BROWN, J. M., Forensic Psychology
BULMER, M. I. A., Sociology
CRAWFORD, I., Economics
DAVIES, I. R. L., Psychology
EMLER, N., Social Psychology
FIELDING, N. G., Sociology
GILBERT, G. N., Sociology
GROEGER, J. A., Cognitive Psychology
HAMPSON, S. E., Psychology and Health
HUNT, L. C., Economics
LEVINE, P., Economics
OGDEN, J., Health Psychology
RICKMAN, N. J., Economics
SHEPHERD, R., Psychology
STERR, A., Cognitive Neuroscience and Neuropsychology
TARLING, R., Sociology
UZZELL, D. L., Environmental Psychology

ZIJLSTRA, F., Occupational and Organizational Psychology
School of Management:
AIREY, D. W., Tourism Management
ARCHER, G. S. H., Financial Management
BUTLER, R. W., Tourism
DESOMBRE, T., Health Care Management
GILBERT, D., Marketing
HALES, C., Organizational Behaviour
JONES, P. L. M., Productions and Operations Management
KIRBY, D., Entrepreneurship
LIU, X., International Business
LOCKWOOD, A. J., Hospitality Management
LOWE, M., Retail Management
O'KEEFE, R. M., Information Management
PHILLIPS, P. A., Hotel Management
RILEY, M. J., Organizational Behaviour
SADLER-SMITH, E., Management Development and Organizational Behaviour
European Institute of Health and Medical Sciences:
BRYAN, K., Clinical Practice
BUCKLE, P., Health Ergonomics
HUNT, G.
POPE, R., Nurse Education
ROBBINS, I., Mental Health Practice
SMITH, P. A., Nurse Education
STUBBS, D. A., Ergonomics
Postgraduate Medical School:
FARMER, R. D. T., Epidemiology
THOMAS, H., Oncology

UNIVERSITY OF SUSSEX

Sussex House, Brighton, BN1 9RH
Telephone: (1273) 606755
Fax: (1273) 678335
E-mail: information@sussex.ac.uk
Internet: www.sussex.ac.uk
Founded 1961
Academic year: October to June
Chancellor: SANJEEV BHASKAR
Vice-Chancellor: Prof. MICHAEL FARTHING
Deputy Vice-Chancellor and Pro Vice-Chancellor for Research: Prof. BOB ALLISON
Pro Vice-Chancellor for Int. Affairs: Prof. CHRIS MARLIN
Pro Vice-Chancellor for Teaching and Learning: Prof. CLARE MACKIE
Registrar and Sec.: JOHN DUFFY
Librarian: KITTY INGLIS
Library: see Libraries and Archives
Number of teachers: 552
Number of students: 11,478

PROFESSORS

ABBS, P. F., Creative Writing
ABRAHAM, J. W., Sociology
ABRAHAM, S. C. S., Psychology
ARMES, S. P., Chemistry
BACON, J. P., Neuroscience
BAILIN, D., Theoretical Physics
BEEBEE, J. J. C., Molecular Ecology
BENJAMIN, P. R., Neuroscience
BILLINGHAM, N. C., Chemistry
BLISS, J. F., Education
BODEN, M. A., Philosophy and Psychology
BUXTON, H., Visual Intelligence
CAWSON, A., Digital Media
CHATWIN, C. R., Manufacturing Systems
CHERRY, D., History of Art
CLARK, A. J., Philosophy
CLARK, T. D., Physical Electronics
CLOKE, F. G. N., Chemistry
CLUNAS, A. C., History of Art
COATES, R. A., Linguistics
COLCLOUGH, C. L., Development Studies
COLLETT, T. S., Neurobiology
COPELAND, E. J., Theoretical Physics
DARWIN, C. J., Experimental Psychology
DAVEY, G. C. L., Psychology
DEARLOVE, J. N., Politics

DOMBEY, N. D., Theoretical Physics
DU BOULAY, J. B. H., Artificial Intelligence
DUNFORD, M. F., Economic Geography
DYHOUSE, C. A., History
ERAUT, M. R., Education
FAIRHEAD, J., Social Anthropology
FALLOWFIELD, L. J., Psycho-Oncology
FENDER, S. A., American Studies
FIELDING, A. J., Human Geography
FLOWERS, T. J., Plant Physiology
GANN, D. M., Science and Technology Policy Research
GARDINER, J. M., Psychology
GARNHAM, A., Experimental Psychology
GAZDAR, G. J. M., Computational Linguistics
GOLDIE, C. M., Statistics
GOUGH, M. P., Space Science
GRAY, F. G., Continuing Education
GRIFFITH-JONES, S., Development Studies
GRILLO, R. D., Social Anthropology
GRIMSDALE, R. L., Electronic Engineering
HANSON, J. R., Chemistry
HART, V. M., American Studies
HENNESSY, M., Computer Science
HINDS, E. A., Experimental Physics
HIRSCHFELD, J. W. P., Mathematics
HOBDAY, M. G., Science and Technology Policy Research
HOLMWOOD, J. M., Sociology
HOWKINS, A. J., Social History
HUMPHREY, C. J., Development Studies
HUTCHINGS, M. J., Ecology
JAYAWANT, B. V., Electrical and Systems Engineering
KAPLINSKY, R. M., Development Studies
KEDWARD, H. R., History
KING, R. L., Geography
Sir KROTO, H. W., Chemistry
LAND, M. F., Neurobiology
LEACH, M. A., Development Studies
LEHMANN, A. R., Molecular Genetics
LEWIN, K. M., Education
LIDDLE, A. R., Astrophysics
LISTER, P. F., Electronics
LLEWELLYN, N. G., History of Art
MANOR, J. G., Development Studies
MARTIN, B. R., Science and Technology Policy Research
MATHER, G. W., Experimental Psychology
McCAFFERY, A. J., Chemistry
MELLOR, D. A., History of Art
MILNER-GULLAND, R. R., Russian
MITTER, P., History of Art
MOORE, A. L., Biochemistry
MOORE, M. P., Development Studies
MURPHY, R. J., German, Comparative Literature and Film
NICHOLLS, P. A., English and American Literature
NIXON, J. F., Chemistry
O'SHEA, M. R., Neuroscience
OAKHILL, J. V., Experimental Psychology
OSMOND-SMITH, D., Music
OUTHWAITE, R. W., Sociology
PAIN, V. M., Biochemistry
PARSONS, P. J., Organic Chemistry
PAVITT, K. L. R., Science and Technology Policy Studies
PENDLEBURY, J. M., Experimental Physics
PERRY-ROBINSON, J. P., Science and Technology Policy Research
PLATT, J. A., Sociology
POWNER, E. T., Electronic Engineering
PRASSIDES, K., Chemistry
RAJAK, H. H., Law
RICHARDS, R. L., Chemistry
RÖHL, J. C. G., History
ROLLO, J. M. C., European Economic Integration
ROPER, T. J., Biology
ROSS, M. G., European Law
ROYLE, N. W. O., English
RUSSELL, I. J., Neurobiology
RYAN, C. J., Italian
SAMPSON, G. R., Natural Language Computing

SCHMITZ, H., Development Studies
SHAW, M., International Relations and Politics
SHORT, B. M., Geography
SINFIELD, A. J., English
SKELDON, R., Geography
SMITH, L. J., English
SMITH, P. B., Social Psychology
SMITH, P. H., Media Studies
SOBOLEV, A. V., Mathematics
STACE, A. J., Chemistry
STEINMUELLER, W. E., Science and Technology Policy Research
STEPHENS, D. N., Experimental Psychology
STOBART, R. K., Automotive Engineering
SUMNER, M. T., Economics
TAPPER, E. R., Politics
TAYLOR, I. J., Social Care and Social Work
TEMKIN, J., Law
TIDD, J., Science and Technology Policy Research
TIMMS, E. F., German Studies
TORRANCE, H., Education
TOWNSEND, P. D., Experimental Physics
TROSCIANKO, T., Psychology
TURNER, A. B., Mechanical Engineering
VAN DER PIJL, K., International Relations
VAN GELDEREN, M. A. J., Intellectual History
VANCE, R. N. C., English
VINCENT, R., Medical Science
VON TUNZELMANN, G., Economics of Science and Technology
WAGSTAFF, R. A. S., Economics
WALLIS, M., Biochemistry
WARK, D. L., Physics
WATTS, C. T., English
WEBB, P. D., Politics
WILKINSON, R. G., Trafford Centre for Graduate Medical Education and Research
WINTERS, L. A., Economics
WORDEN, A. B., Early Modern History
YOUNG, D. W., Chemistry
ZHANG, K., Pure Mathematics

UNIVERSITY OF THE ARTS LONDON

272 High Holborn, London, WC1V 7EY
Telephone: (20) 7514-6000
Fax: (20) 7514-6131
E-mail: info@arts.ac.uk
Internet: www.arts.ac.uk

Founded 2004

Rector: Sir NIGEL CARRINGTON
Deputy Rector of Academic Devt and Quality: ELIZABETH ROUSE
Deputy Rector of Planning and Operations: WILLIAM BRIDGE
Dir of Information Services: PAT CHRISTIE
Library of 400,000 vols, 3,500 magazines and periodicals, 10,000 video cassettes and other media, 130 databases, 170 electronic resources and 12,000 e-journals
Number of teachers: 1,228
Number of students: 22,051.

COLLEGES OF THE UNIVERSITY

Camberwell College of Arts

Peckham Rd, London, SE5 8UF
Telephone: (20) 7514-6302
Fax: (20) 7514-6310
E-mail: info@camberwell.arts.ac.uk
Internet: www.camberwell.arts.ac.uk

Founded 1898

Main subject areas: ceramics, design products, conservation, drawing, graphic design, illustration, painting, photography, sculpture; another campus at Wilson Rd
Head: CHRIS WAINWRIGHT
Dean: NATALIE BRETT

Number of teachers: 150
Number of students: 1,746

Central Saint Martins College of Art and Design

Southampton Row, London, WC1B 4AP
Telephone: (20) 7514-7022
Fax: (20) 7514-7254
E-mail: info@csm.arts.ac.uk
Internet: www.csm.arts.ac.uk

Founded 1989 by merger of Central School of Arts and Crafts (f. 1896) and St Martin's School of Art (f. 1854), incorporated Drama Centre London (f. 1962) 1999 and London Studio Centre 2003

Incl. Drama Centre London and the Cochrane Theatre; three schools: school of art, school of graphic and industrial design, school of fashion and textiles

Head: JANE RAPLEY

Library of 80,000 vols
Number of students: 4,883 students

Chelsea College of Art and Design

Millbank, London, SW1P 4JU
Telephone: (20) 7541-7751
Fax: (20) 7514-7778
E-mail: enquiries@chelsea.arts.ac.uk
Internet: www.chelsea.arts.ac.uk

Founded 1895

Main subject areas: fine art, communication design, interior and spatial design, textile design, history and theory of visual and multimedia cultures
Dean: Prof. DAVID GRACIA
Head: Prof. CHRIS WAINWRIGHT

Number of teachers: 80
Number of students: 1,751

London College of Communication

Elephant and Castle, London, SE1 6SB
Telephone: (20) 7514-6500
Fax: (20) 7514-6476
E-mail: info@lcc.arts.ac.uk
Internet: www.lcc.arts.ac.uk

Founded 1894, fmrly London College of Printing, present name 2004

Main subject areas: animation, graphic design, graphic communication, journalism, media, photography
Head: Prof. SANDRA KEMP
Number of students: 5,432 .

London College of Fashion

20 John Princes St, London, W1G 0BJ
Telephone: (20) 7514-7400
Fax: (20) 7514-7484
E-mail: enquiries@fashion.arts.ac.uk
Internet: www.fashion.arts.ac.uk

Founded 1906, as Shoreditch Technical Institute Girls School

Head of College: FRANCES CORNER
Number of students: 5,113

Publication: *Pigeons and Peacocks*.

Wimbledon College of Art

Merton Hall Rd, London, SW19 3QA
Telephone: (20) 7514-9641
Fax: (20) 7514-9642
E-mail: info@wimbledon.ac.uk
Internet: www.wimbledon.arts.ac.uk

Founded 1890, as an Art Class in the Rutlish School for Boys, present name and status 2006

Schools of specialist art and design
Head: CHRIS WAINWRIGHT
Dean: Prof. GEORGE BLACKLOCK

Library of 28,000 vols
Number of teachers: 47
Number of students: 1,124

UNIVERSITY OF THE WEST OF ENGLAND (UWE)

Frenchay Campus, Coldharbour Lane, Bristol, BS16 1QY

Telephone: (117) 965-6261

Fax: (117) 328-2810

E-mail: admissions@uwe.ac.uk

Internet: www.uwe.ac.uk

Founded 1969 as Bristol Polytechnic, present name and status 1992

Language of instruction: English

Academic year: September to June

Chancellor: Sir IAN CARRUTHERS

Vice-Chancellor: Prof. STEVEN WEST

Deputy Vice-Chancellor For Academic Affairs: Prof. PAUL GOUGH

Deputy Vice-Chancellor For Resources, Planning and Infrastructure: JOHN RUSHFORTH

Academic Registrar: ANDREA CHESHIRE

Librarian: CATHY REX

Library of 561,219 vols, 516,105 books and e-books, 45,114 journals

Number of teachers: 1,185

Number of students: 27,502 (21,170 full-time and 6,332 part-time)

DEANS

Faculty of Arts, Creative Industries and Education: ALEX GILKISON

Faculty of Business and Law: Dr JANE HARRINGTON (acting)

Faculty of Environment and Technology: Prof. PAUL OLOMOLAIYE

Faculty of Health and Life Sciences: Prof. HELEN LANGTON

UNIVERSITY OF WARWICK

Coventry CV4 7AL

Telephone: (24) 7652-3523

Fax: (24) 7646-1606

Internet: www2.warwick.ac.uk

Founded 1965

Academic year: September to July

Chancellor: Sir RICHARD LAMBERT

Vice-Chancellor: Prof. NIGEL THRIFT

Deputy Vice-Chancellor: Prof. KOEN LAMBERTS

Pro-Vice-Chancellor: Prof. CHRISTINA HUGHES

Pro-Vice-Chancellor for Access, Widening Participation and Devt: Prof. MARGOT FINN

Pro-Vice-Chancellor for Research (Faculties of Arts and Social Studies): Prof. STUART CROFT

Pro-Vice-Chancellor for Knowledge Transfer, Business Engagement and Research (Faculties of Science and Medicine): Prof. TIM JONES

Pro-Vice-Chancellor for Education and Student Experience: Prof. ANN CAESAR

Registrar: KEN SLOAN

Librarian: (vacant)

Library: 1m. vols

Number of teachers: 932

Number of students: 23,420

DEANS

School of Engineering: Prof. NIGEL STOCKS

Warwick Business School: Prof. MARK TAYLOR

Warwick Medical School: Prof. PETER WINSTANLEY

PROFESSORS

Faculty of Arts (internet www2.warwick.ac.uk/fac/arts):

BASSNETT, S. E., Centre for Translation and Comparative Cultural Studies

BATE, J., English and Comparative Literary Studies

BEACHAM, R. C., Theatre Studies

BELL, M., English

BENNETT, O., Theatre Studies

BERG, M. L., History

BRUNSDON, C. M., Film and Television Studies

BURNS, R. A., German Studies

CAESAR, A., Italian

CAPP, B. S., History

CLARK, C. F., History

DABYDEEN, D., Caribbean Studies

DAVIS, C. J., French Studies

DAVIS, J., Theatre Studies

DOCHERTY, T., English and Comparative Literary Studies

DYER, R. W., Film and Television Studies

GARDNER, J., History of Art

HEUMAN, G. J., Caribbean Studies, History

HILL, L. J., French Studies

HINDLE, S., History

HINTON, J. S., History

HUGHES, D. W., English

JONES, C. D. H., History

KING, J. P., History

LAZARUS, N., English

MACK, P. W. D., English

McFARLANE, A. J., History

MULRYNE, J. R., English

NYE, D., History

O'BRIEN, K., English and Comparative Literary Studies

PATERSON, L. M., French Studies

READ, C. J., History

ROSENTHAL, M. J., History of Art

RUTTER, C. C., English and Comparative Literary Studies

SHARPE, K., English

STEEDMAN, C. K., Social History

SWAIN, S. C. R., Classics

TREGLOWN, J. D., English

VINCENDEAU, G. O. R., Film and Television Studies

WHITBY, L. M., Classics

Faculty of Medicine, Warwick Medical School (internet www2.warwick.ac.uk/fac/med):

CARTER, Y., Dean, Warwick Medical School

DALE, J., Division of Health in the Community

FULFORD, K. W. N., Philosophy and Mental Health

GRIFFIN, D., Orthopaedics and Trauma

HUNDT, G. A., School of Health and Social Studies

KUMAR, S., Medicine, Diabetes and Metabolism

LAMB, S., Physiotherapy and Rehabilitation

LEHNERT, H., Medicine

PEILE, E., Medical Education

SINGER, D., Clinical Pharmacology

SPANSWICK, D., Molecular Neurosciences

STANFIELD, P. R., Dept of Biological Sciences

STEWART-BROWN, S., Public Health

THORNTON, S., Biological Sciences

THOROGOOD, M., Epidemiology

WEICH, S., Psychiatry

Faculty of Science (internet www2.warwick.ac.uk/fac/sci; some members also serve in the Faculty of Medicine):

ANDERSON, D., Civil and Mechanical Engineering

BALL, R. C., Theoretical Physics

BARKLEY, D., Mathematics

BHATTACHARYYA, S. K., Manufacturing Systems

BRIGHT, S.

BROWN, G. D. A., Psychology

BRYANSTON-CROSS, P. J., Civil and Mechanical Engineering

BUGG, T. D. H., Biological Chemistry

BURNS, I.

CAMPBELL-KELLY, M., Computer Science

CARPENTER, P. W., Mechanical Engineering

CHAPMAN, S. C., Physics

CHATER, N., Psychology

CHETWYND, D. G., Civil and Mechanical Engineering

COOPER, M. J., Physics

COPAS, J. B., Statistics

CRITOPH, R. E., Civil and Mechanical Engineering

DALE, N., Biological Sciences

DALTON, H., Biological Sciences

DAVEY, J., Biological Sciences

DERRICK, P. J., Chemistry

DIMMOCK, N. J., Biological Sciences

DOWSETT, M. G., Physics

DOWSON, C. G., Biological Sciences

DUPREE, R., Physics

EASTON, A. J., Biological Sciences

ELWORTHY, K. D., Mathematics

FIRTH, D., Statistics

FLOWER, J. O., Engineering

FREEDMAN, R. B., Biological Sciences

FRIESECKE, G., Mathematics

FULFORD, K. W. M., Philosophy and Mental Health

FULOP, V., Biological Sciences

GARDNER, J. W., Electronic Engineering

GODFREY, K. R., Electrical and Electronic Engineering

GREEN, R. J., Electronic Communication Systems

HADDLETON, D. M., Chemistry

HARRISON, P. F., Physics

HOLT, D. F., Mathematics

HUANG, T., Civil and Mechanical Engineering

HUTCHINS, D. A., Electrical and Electronic Engineering

HUTTON, J. L., Statistics

JONES, G. V., Psychology

JONES, J. D. S., Mathematics

KEMP, T. J., Chemistry

KENDALL, W. S., Statistics

KERR, R., Mathematics

KERR, R. M., Civil and Mechanical Engineering

LAMBERTS, K., Psychology

LAWRENCE, A. J., Statistics

LEWIS, M. H., Physics

LORD, J. M., Biological Sciences

MacKAY, R., Mathematics

MANN, N. H., Biological Sciences

MARSH, T., Physics

MAYOR, E. A., Psychology

McCONVILLE, C. F., Physics

McCRAE, M. A., Biological Sciences

MEDLEY, G. F. H., Biological Sciences

MILLAR, A. J., Biological Sciences

MILLS, P.

MOND, D. M. Q., Mathematics

MOORE, P., Chemistry

MURRELL, J. C., Biological Sciences

NUDD, G. R., Computer Science

PARKER, E. H. C., Semiconductor Physics

PATERSON, M. S., Computer Science

PAUL, D. McK., Physics

PELED, D., Computer Science

POLLICOTT, M., Mathematics

RAND, D. A., Mathematics

RAWNSLEY, J. H., Mathematics

REID, M. A., Mathematics

ROBERTS, L. M., Biological Sciences

ROBINSON, C., Biological Sciences

RODGER, P. M.

ROURKE, C. P., Mathematics

SCOTT, P., Chemistry

SERIES, C. M., Mathematics

SHIPMAN, M., Chemistry

SMITH, J. Q., Statistics

SMITH, M. E., Physics

STANFIELD, P. R., Biological Sciences

STAUNTON, J. B., Physics

STEEL, M. F., Statistics

STEWART, I. N., Mathematics

STRIEN, S. VAN, Mathematics

STUART, A., Mathematics

TAYLOR, P. R., Chemistry

THOMAS, B.

THORNTON, S., Obstetrics and Gynaecology

UNWIN, P. R., Chemistry

WALTERS, P., Mathematics

WELLINGTON, E. M. H., Biological Sciences
WHALL, T. E., Physics
WHIPPS, J.
WILLS, M., Chemistry
WILSON, A. J., Medical Physics
WILSON, R. G., Computer Science
WILSON, T. M. A., Biological Sciences
WOODLAND, H. R., Biological Sciences
WOODRUFF, D. P., Physics

Faculty of Social Studies (internet www2
.warwick.ac.uk/fac/soc; some members also
serve in the Faculty of Medicine):
ALI, S. S., Law
ANSELL-PEARSON, K., Philosophy
ANWAR, M., Ethnic Relations
ARCHER, M. S, Sociology
ARULAMPALAM, S. W., Economics
AUBREY, C., Institute of Education
BAXI, U., Law
BEALE, H. G., Law
BECKFORD, J. A., Sociology
BENINGTON, J., Business Studies
BLACKORBY, A. B., Economics
BRESLIN, S., Politics and International Studies
BREWER, B., Philosophy
BRIDGES, L. T., Law
BROADBERRY, S. N., Economics
BRYER, R. A., Accounting and Finance
BURNELL, P. J., Politics and International Studies
BURNHAM, P., Politics and International Studies
BURRIDGE, R. H. M., Law
CAMPBELL, R. J., Institute of Education
CARNALL, C., Business Studies
CAVE, M., Centre for Management under Regulation
CHARLES, N., Sociology
CLARKE, S. R. C., Sociology
CLUBB, C., Accounting and Finance
COHEN, R., Sociology
COWLING, K. G., Industrial Economics
CROUCH, C., Governance and Public Management
CURRIE, W., Information Systems
DALE, J., Primary Care
DAVIES, R., Business Studies
DEVEREUX, M. P., Economics and Business Studies
DICKENS, L. J., Business Studies
DUTTA, B., Economics
DYSON, R. G., Business Studies
EDWARDS, P. K., Business Studies
EILAN, N. H., Philosophy
ELIAS, D. P. B., Employment Research
ELLIOTT, R., Business Studies
FAUNDEZ, J., Law
FINE, R. D., Sociology
FULFORD, K. W. M., Philosophy and Mental Health
FULLER, S., Sociology
GEMMILL, G., Accounting and Finance
GHOSAL, S., Economics
GLEESON, D., Institute of Education
GRANT, W. P., Politics and International Studies
HARRIS, A., Institute of Education
HARRIS, J., Health and Social Studies
HARRISON, R. M., Economics
HARTLEY, J., Local Government Centre
HIGGOTT, R. A., Politics and International Studies
HODGES, S. D., Financial Management
HOSKIN, K. W., Business Studies
HOULGATE, S., Philosophy
HUDDLESTON, P. J., Institute of Education
HURLEY, S., Politics and International Studies
IRELAND, N. J., Economics
JACKSON, R. M. D., Institute of Education
JOHNSTON, R., Business Studies
JOLY, D., Centre for Research in Ethnic Relations

LAYTON-HENRY, Z. A., Politics and International Studies
LEGGE, K., Business Studies
LEWANDO-HUNDT, G., Social Sciences and Health
LINDLEY, R. M., Employment Research
LINDSAY, G. A., Special Educational Needs
LOCKWOOD, B., Economics
LOVELL, T. A., Women and Gender
LUNTLEY, M., Philosophy
MARGINSON, P., Industrial Relations
MASSON, J. M., Law
MAWSON, J., Local Government Centre
McCONVILLE, M. J., Law
McELDOWNEY, J. F., Law
McGEE, J., Marketing and Strategic Management
MILLER, M. H., Economics
MITCHELL, C., Centre for Management under Regulation
MORGAN, G., Industrial Relations
MULLENDER, A., Social Work
NAYLOR, R. A., Economics
NEAL, A., Law
NEUBERGER, A., Accounting and Finance
OSWALD, A. J., Economics
PALIWALA, A., Law
PERRONI, C., Economics
PHIZACKLEA, A. M., Sociology
PIERCY, N., Marketing and Strategic Management
POGANY, S. I., Law
RAI, S. M., Politics and International Studies
RANKIN, N., Economics
RATCLIFFE, P. B., Sociology
REEVE, A. W., Politics and International Studies
SALMON, M., Accounting and Finance
SARNO, L., Business Studies
SCARBOROUGH, H., Business Studies
SCHOLTE, J. A., Politics and International Studies
SKIDELSKY, R., Political Economy
SLACK, N. D. C., Manufacturing and Strategy Policy
SLADE, M., Economics
SMITH, H., Politics and International Studies
SMITH, R. J., Economics
SPENCER, N. J., Community Paediatrics
STEWART, M. B., Economics
STONEMAN, P., Business Studies
STOREY, D. J., Business Studies
STURDY, A., Industrial Relations and Organizational Behaviour
SWAN, J. A., Organizational Behaviour
SZCZEPURA, A., Business Studies
TALL, D. O., Institute of Education
TAYLOR, M. P., Economics
TERRY, M. A., Business Studies
THOMAS, H., Business Studies
TRIGG, R. H., Philosophy
TSOUKOS, H., Industrial Relations and Organizational Behaviour
WAGNER, P., Sociology
WALKER, I., Economics
WARHURST, A., Corporate Citizenship Unit
WATERSON, M. J., Economics
WENSLEY, J. R. C., Marketing and Strategic Management
WHALLEY, J., Development Economics
WHITE, B., Politics and International Studies
WHITESIDE, N., Sociology
WILLCOCKS, L., Information Management and e-Business
WILSON, D. C., Strategic Management
WOODERS, M., Economics
WRAY, D., Institute of Education

UNIVERSITY OF WESTMINSTER

309 Regent St, London W1B 2UW
Telephone: (20) 7911-5000

Fax: (20) 7911-5858
E-mail: course-enquiries@westminster.ac.uk
Internet: www.westminster.ac.uk
Founded 1838 as Polytechnic Institution; became Royal Polytechnic Institution 1839 and Polytechnic of Central London 1970; present name and status 1992
Academic year: September to August
Vice-Chancellor and Rector: Prof. GEOFFREY PETTS
Deputy Vice-Chancellor and Pro-Vice-Chancellor: Prof. RIKKI MORGAN-TAMOSUNAS
Pro-Vice-Chancellor: Dr MYSZKA GUZKOWSKA
Registrar and Sec.: CAROLE MAINSTONE
Dir for Finance: MICHAEL WEBB
Director for Information Systems and Library Services: SUZANNE ENRIGHT
Library of 420,000 vols
Number of teachers: 1,204
Number of students: 23,000

DEANS

School of Architecture and Built Environment: Prof. JEREMY TILL
School of Life sciences: Prof. JANE LEWIS
School of Electronics and Computer Science: Prof. GRAHAM MEGSON
School of Law: Prof. ANDREW BOON
School of Media, Arts and Design: SALLY FELDMAN
School of Social Sciences, Humanities and Languages: Dr JEREMY COLWILL
Westminster Business School: Prof. BARBARA ALLAN

UNIVERSITY OF WINCHESTER

Sparkford Rd, Winchester, SO22 4NR
Telephone: (1962) 841515
Fax: (1962) 842280
E-mail: course.enquiries@winchester.ac.uk
Internet: www.winchester.ac.uk
Founded 1840, present name and status 2005
Chancellor: MARY FAGAN
Vice-Chancellor: Prof. JOY CARTER
Univ. Librarian: DAVID FARLEY
Deputy Vice-Chancellor: TOMMY GEDDES
Pro-Vice-Chancellor: Prof. ELIZABETH STUART
Pro-Vice-Chancellor: NEIL MARRIOTT
Dir for Finance and Strategy: SIMON COWHIG
Library of 250,000 vols
Number of teachers: 650 (f.t.e.)
Number of students: 5,906

DEANS

Faculty of Arts: Prof. ANTHONY DEAN
Faculty of Business, Law and Sport: Prof. NEIL MARRIOTT
Faculty of Education, Health and Social Care: Prof. JOYCE GOODMAN
Faculty of Humanities and Social Sciences: Prof. KRISTYAN SPELMAN MILLER

UNIVERSITY OF WOLVERHAMPTON

Molineux St, Wolverhampton, WV1 1SB
Telephone: (1902) 321000
Fax: (1902) 322680
E-mail: enquiries@wlv.ac.uk
Internet: www.wlv.ac.uk
Founded 1969 as Wolverhampton Polytechnic; present name and status 1992
Constituent Colleges: City of Wolverhampton College, Dudley College, Rodbaston College, Sandwell College, South Birmingham College, Telford College of Arts and Technology, Walsall College of Arts and Technology
Chancellor: Lord PAUL OF MARYLEBONE
Vice-Chancellor: Prof. CAROLINE GIPPS
Deputy Vice-Chancellor: Prof. GEOFF HAMPTON
Deputy Vice-Chancellor and Dir of Finance: GARRY SPROSTON

Pro-Vice-Chancellor for Academic Affairs: Prof. SALLY GLEN
Pro-Vice-Chancellor and Dir for Corporate Services: HELEN LLOYD WILDMAN
Pro-Vice-Chancellor for Student Affairs: JANE NELSON
Pro-Vice-Chancellor for Research and Enterprise: Prof. IAN OAKES
Registrar: PAUL TRAVILL
Dir for Learning and Information Services: FIONA PARSONS
Dean for Students: JON ELSMORE
Univ. Sec.: A. W. (TONY) LEE

Library of 363,471 vols
Number of teachers: 978
Number of students: 23,084

DEANS

Applied Sciences: Prof. JOHN DARLING
Art and Design: Dr BRYONY CONWAY
Education: Prof. KIT FIELD
Health and Wellbeing: Prof. LINDA LANG
Institute for Learning Enhancement: Dr GLYNIS COUSIN
Law, Social Sciences and Communications: Dr JUDITH BURNETT
Sport, Performing Arts and Leisure: JOHN PYMM
Technology: Prof. ROBERT MORETON
University of Wolverhampton Business School: Prof. KIT FIELD (acting)

UNIVERSITY OF WORCESTER

Henwick Grove, Worcester, WR2 6AJ
Telephone: (1905) 855000
E-mail: admissions@worc.ac.uk
Internet: www.worc.ac.uk

Founded 1946 as Emergency Teacher Training College, present name and status 2005
Academic year: September to May

Chancellor: HRH PRINCE RICHARD, THE DUKE OF GLOUCESTER
Vice-Chancellor and Chief Exec.: Prof. DAVID GREEN
Deputy Vice-Chancellor: Prof. ROSALIND FOSKETT
Pro-Vice-Chancellor for Resources: Dr MARTIN DOUGHTY
Registrar and Univ. Sec.: JOHN RYAN

Library of 130,000 vols, 400 print periodicals, 12,000 e-periodicals
Number of teachers: 700
Number of students: 10,095

UNIVERSITY OF YORK

Heslington, York, YO10 5DD
Telephone: (1904) 320000
Fax: (1904) 323433
E-mail: admissions@york.ac.uk
Internet: www.york.ac.uk

Founded 1963
Academic year: October to June (three terms)

Chancellor: GREG DYKE
Pro-Chancellor: Sir CHRISTOPHER O'DONNELL
Pro-Chancellor: LESLEY WILD
Pro-Chancellor: Dr ROBERT BRECH
Vice-Chancellor: Prof. BRIAN CANTOR
Deputy Vice-Chancellor: Prof. TREVOR SHELDON
Pro-Vice-Chancellor: Prof. COLIN MELLORS
Pro-Vice-Chancellor: ELIZABETH HEAPS
Pro-Vice-Chancellor: Dr JANE GRENVILLE
Pro-Vice-Chancellor: Prof. JOHN LOCAL
Registrar and Sec.: Dr DAVID DUNCAN
Dir for Corporate Planning: DAVID MUCKERSIE
Dir for Estates and Campus Services: JON MEACOCK
Dir for External Relations: JOAN CONCANNON
Dir for Finance: GRAHAM GILBERT
Dir for Human Resources: PAT LOFTHOUSE

Dir for Information and Univ. Librarian: STEPHEN TOWN
Dir for Research and Enterprise: MARK MORTIMER
Library: see under Libraries and Archives
Number of teachers: 770
Number of students: 13,000
Publication: *University of York Magazine* (6 a year)

PROFESSORS

ABADIR, K., Economics, Mathematics
AFSHAR, H., Politics
ANDREWS, R., Educational Studies
ARTHURS, A. M., Mathematics
ATTRIDGE, D., English
BABIKER, M., Physics
BALDWIN, T. R., Philosophy
BARRELL, J. C., English
BEHRINGER, W., History
BERTHOUD, J. A., English
BESSEL, R., History
BILLER, P., History
BOWLBY, R., English
BOWLES, D. J., Biology
BRADSHAW, J. R., Social Policy
BRAUNSTEIN, S., Quantum Computing
BURNS, A., Computer Science
BURR, A., Electronics
CALLINICOS, A., Politics
CAMPBELL, C., Sociology
CARR-HILL, R., Health Economics
CARVER, M. O., Archaeology
CLARK, J. H., Chemistry
CORRIGAN, E., Mathematics
CRESSER, M., Environment
CULYER, A. J., Economics
DE FRAJA, G., Economics
DITCH, J. S., Social Policy and Social Work
DIVALL, C., Railway Studies
DIXON, H. D., Economics
DODSON, E., Chemistry
DODSON, G. G., Chemistry
DODSON, M., Mathematics
DOLLIMORE, J., English
DRUMMOND, M. F., Health Economics
EL-GOMATI, M. M., Electronics
ELLIS, A. W., Psychology
FITTER, A. H., Biology
FORD, J. R., Housing Policy
FORREST, A. I., History
FOUNTAIN, J., Mathematics
GILBERT, B. C., Chemistry
GODBY, R., Physics
GODFREY, C., Centre for Health Economics, Health Services
GODFREY, L. G., Social and Economic Statistics
GRAHAM, I., Biology
GRAVELLE, H. S. E., Economics
GUEST, H., English
HALL, G., Psychology
HARRISON, M. D., Computer Science
HARTLEY, K., Economics
HEY, J. D., Social and Economic Statistics
HITCH, G., Psychology
HOLMAN, J., Chemistry
HOWARD, D., Electronics
HOWELL, D., Politics
HUBBARD, R., Chemistry
HULME, C., Psychology
HUTTON, J. P., Economics and Econometrics
INESON, P., Biology
JACKSON, S. F., Women's Studies
JONES, A., Economics
KEMP, P., Social Policy Research Unit
KITZINGER, C., Sociology
KLEIJNEN, J. E., Centre for Reviews and Dissemination
LAMARQUE, P., Philosophy
LAMBERT, P., Economics
LE FANU, N., Music
LEESE, H. J., Biology
LEWIN, R. J., Health Studies
LINDSAY SMITH, J., Chemistry

LOCAL, J. K., Linguistics
MACPHAIL, E., Psychology
MAITLAND, N. J., Biology
MARKS, R., History of Art
MARSH, R., Music
MARVIN, A. C., Electronics
MATTHEW, J. A. D., Physics
MAYNARD, A. K., Health Studies
MAYNARD, M. A., Social Policy and Social Work
MAYSTON, D. J., Public Sector Economics
MCDERMID, J. A., Computer Science
MCDOUGALL, C., Criminal Justice
MCQUEEN-MASON, S., Biology
MENDUS, S., Politics
MILLAR, R., Educational Studies
MILNER, A. J., Biology
MINNIS, A. J., Medieval Literature
MONK, A., Psychology
MULKAY, M., Sociology
MULLER-DETHLEFS, K., Chemistry
O'CONNOR, T., Archaeology
O'GRADY, K., Physics
ORMROD, M., History
PARRY, G., English
PERRINGS, C., Environment
PERT, G. J., Computational Physics
PERUTZ, R. N., Chemistry
PHILLIPS, P., Economics
POSNETT, J., York Health Economics Consortium
PRUTTON, M., Physics
QURESHI, H., Social Policy and Social Work
RAFFAELLI, D., Environment
RAINEY, L. S., English
RIDDY, F J., English
ROBARDS, A. W., Biology
ROBINSON, J., Electronics
ROYLE, E., History
RUNCIMAN, C., Computer Science
RUSSELL, I. T., Health Sciences
SANDERS, D., Biology
SHARPE, J. A., History
SHAW, I., Social Work
SHELDON, T., Health Sciences
SIMMONS, P. J., Economics
SINCLAIR, I. A. C., Social Work
SLOPER, P., Social Policy Research Unit
SMITH, D. M., Borthwick Institute
SMITH, P. C., Economics
SNOWLING, M. S., Psychology
SOUTHGATE, J., Biology
SPARROW, J., Biology
STEIN, M., Social Work
SUDBERY, A., Mathematics
TAYLOR, R. J. K., Chemistry
THOMPSON, D. R., Health Studies
TYRRELL, A. M., Electronics
VULLIAMY, G., Educational Studies
WALTON, P., Chemistry
WALVIN, J., History
WAND, I. C., Computer Science
WARD, N. A.-M. F., English
WARNER, A. R., Language
WATT, I. S., Health Studies
WEBSTER, A., Sociology
WELLINGS, A. J., Computer Science
WICKENS, M. R., Economics
WILKINSON, A. J., Chemistry
WILLIAMS, A. H., Economics
WILSON, K., Chemistry
WILSON, R. A., Biology
WOOLHOUSE, R., Philosophy
YEARLEY, S., Sociology
YOUNG, A. W., Psychology
YOUNG, J. P. W., Biology

YORK ST JOHN UNIVERSITY

Lord Mayor's Walk, York, YO31 7EX
Telephone: (1904) 624624
Fax: (1904) 612512
Internet: w3.yorksj.ac.uk

Founded 1841, as York Diocesan Training School, present name and status 2006

Chancellor: Archbishop of York, Dr JOHN SENTAMU
Vice-Chancellor: Prof. DAVID FLEMING
Deputy Vice-Chancellor: Prof. DAVID MAUGHAN BROWN
Registrar: PAULINE ALDOUS
Number of teachers: 235
Number of students: 5,627
Publication: *The White Rose* (1 a year)

DEANS
Faculty of Arts: Prof. STEVE PURCELL
Faculty of Education and Theology: Prof. JULIAN STERN
Faculty of Health and Life Sciences: Prof. PAMELA DAWSON
York St John Business School: JACKIE MATHERS

University Colleges in England

University Colleges have taught degree awarding powers only and do not carry out research.

Arts University College at Bournemouth: Wallisdown, Poole, BH12 5HH; tel. (1202) 363-233; fax (1202) 363-378; e-mail general@aucb.ac.uk; internet www.aucb.ac.uk; f. 1885; specialist instn; diploma, undergraduate, postgraduate degree courses in art, design and creative media; library: 45,000 vols, 40,000 e-books, 300 specialist journals; 3,000 students.

Bishop Grosseteste University College: Lincoln, LN1 3DY; tel. (1522) 527347; fax (1522) 530243; e-mail info@bishopg.ac.uk; internet www.bishopg.ac.uk; f. 1862; undergraduate, postgraduate and work-based programmes in education, arts and humanities and cultural industries; Provost Dame JUDITH MAYHEW JONAS; Prin. Prof. MURIEL ROBINSON; Head of Library Services EMMA SANSBY.

BPP University College: Aldine House, Aldine Place, 142–144 Uxbridge Rd, London, W12 8AW; tel. (20) 7633-4410; fax (2074) 041389; e-mail admissions@bpp.com; internet www.bppuc.com; f. 1992; consists of business school and law school; undergraduate, postgraduate and professional programmes; campuses in Birmingham, Bristol, Leeds, Manchester and in 3 centres in London; acquired by Apollo Global, Inc.; library: 6,200 vols; 64 teachers; 600 full-time postgraduate students; Prin. CARL LYGO.

College of Law: Braboeuf Manor, Portsmouth Rd, St Catherines, Guildford, GU3 1HA; tel. (1483) 216-000; fax (1483) 460-305; internet www.college-of-law.co.uk; f. 1967, degree awarding powers 2006; postgraduate courses; brs in Birmingham, Bristol, Chester, London, Manchester and York; Chief Exec. Prof. NIGEL SAVAGE; Chair. DAVID YATES; Deputy Chair. JONATHAN HAW; Deputy Chair. GUY BERINGER.

Greenwich School of Management: Meridian House, Royal Hill, Greenwich, London SE10 8RD; tel. (20) 8516-7800; fax (20) 8516-7801; e-mail admissions@greenwich-college.ac.uk; internet www.greenwich-college.ac.uk; f. 1973 incorporates the Greenwich School of Law; provides univ. MBA, MSc, EMBA, BSc, LLB, BBA PhD, DBA, CIPS, undergraduate, postgraduate, doctoral programmes and professional courses; Prin. Dr WILLIAM HUNT.

Henley Business School: Whiteknights, Reading, RG6 6UD; tel. (118) 378-5044; fax (118) 378-4029; e-mail helpdesk@henley.com; internet www.henley.reading.ac.uk; f. 1945;

attached to Univ. of Reading; has campus in Greenland; courses in accountancy, business, management, finance, real estate, planning, informatics, and coaching; 7,000 students; Dean Prof. JOHN BOARD; Deputy Dean Prof. GINNY GIBSON.

ifs School of Finance: 36 Monument St, London, EC3R 8LJ; tel. (20) 7444-7111; fax (20) 7444-7115; e-mail customerservices@ifslearning.ac.uk; internet www.ifslearning.ac.uk; f. 1879 as Institute of Bankers, present name 2006, acquisition of taught degree-awarding powers 2010; courses in banking and financial management; Chair. BRUCE CARNEGIE-BROWN; Prin. GAVIN SHREEVE; Treas. ROY RANSLEY.

Leeds Trinity University College: International Office, Brownberrie Lane, Horsforth, Leeds, LS18 5HD; tel. (1132) 837178; fax (1132) 837200; e-mail international@leedstrinity.ac.uk; internet www.leedstrinity.ac.uk; f. 1980 by merger of Leeds Trinity and All Saints College, power to award taught degrees and became univ. college 2009; undergraduate and postgraduate courses in media, business and marketing, arts and social sciences, forensic psychology, sports psychology; accredited by Leeds Univ.; 3,000 students; Prin. and Chief Exec. Dr FREDA BRIDGE; Deputy Prin. MARK SHIELDS; Vice-Prin. and Registrar JENNY SHARE.

Newman University College: Genners Lane, Bartley Green, Birmingham, B32 3NT; tel. (121) 476-1181; fax (121) 476-1196; e-mail admissions@newman.ac.uk; internet www.newman.ac.uk; f. 1968; offers foundation degrees, BA (Hons), professional graduate certificate of education, teacher training courses; postgraduate research students awarded by Univ. of Leicester; library: 90,000 books, 500 periodicals; Prin. and CEO Prof. PETER LUTZEIER; Vice-Prin. KATHRYN SOUTHWORTH; Registrar and Univ. College Sec. HEATHER SOMERFIELD.

Norwich University College of the Arts: 3–7 Redwell St, Norwich, NR2 4SN; tel. (1603) 610561; fax (1603) 615728; e-mail info@nuca.ac.uk; internet www.nuca.ac.uk; f. 1845, as Norwich School of Design, present name and status 2008; library: 30,000 vols, 2,500 DVDs, 100 journals; 1,500 students; Prin. Prof. JOHN LAST.

Royal Agricultural College: Stroud Rd, Cirencester, GL7 6JS; tel. (1285) 652-531; fax (1285) 650-219; e-mail admissions@rac.ac.uk; internet www.rac.ac.uk; f. 1842 royal charter in 1845; education, research and consultancy; undergraduate and postgraduate courses in agricultural, land, business management, food, equine, property industries; library: 40,000 vols, 1,000 journal subscriptions, 50,000 e-books; 49 full-time teachers; 25 visiting professors; 650 full-time students; Prin. Prof. CHRIS GASKELL.

St Mary's University College: Strawberry Hill, Twickenham, London TW1 4SX; tel. (20) 8240-4000; fax (20) 8240-4255; internet www.smuc.ac.uk; f. 1850, present status 2006; library: 11,500 vols, 13,500 journals; 100 teachers; Prin. Prof. PHILIP ESLER; Vice-Prin. Prof. MICHAEL HAYES; Vice-Prin. DAVID LEEN.

University College Birmingham: Summer Row, Birmingham, B3 1JB; tel. (121) 604-1000; internet www.ucb.ac.uk; f. 1918, present name and status 2007; library: 75,000 vols, 1,000 journals; 7,500 students; Prin. Prof. RAY LINFORTH.

University College Falmouth: Woodlane, Falmouth, TR11 4RH; tel. (1326) 211077; fax (1326) 213880; e-mail admissions@falmouth.ac.uk; internet www.falmouth.ac.uk; f. 1902, merged with Dartington college of arts in 2008, aims to become specialist arts univ. by

2012; college of arts;campuses at Woodlane in Falmouth and Tremough in Penryn; library: 100,000 vols; 80 teachers; 1,700 students; Rector and CEO Prof. ANNE CARLISLE.

University College Plymouth St Mark and St John: Derriford Rd, Plymouth, PL6 8BH; tel. (1752) 636700; fax (1752) 636819; e-mail info@ucpmarjon.ac.uk; internet www.marjon.ac.uk; f. 1926, by merger of St John's College and St Mark's College, present name and status 2007; library: 120,000 vols; 3,500 students; Prin. Prof. MARGARET NOBLE; Vice-Prin. for Academic Dr GEOFF STOAKES; Vice-Prin. for Resources KAREN COOK.

Colleges in England

These institutions are not able to award their own degrees, but offer courses leading to a degree from a recognized body.

GENERAL

Abingdon and Witney College: Wootton Rd, Abingdon, OX14 1GG; tel. (1235) 555585; fax (1235) 553168; e-mail enquiry@abingdon-witney.ac.uk; internet www.abingdon-witney.ac.uk; f. 2001 by merger of Abingdon College and West Oxfordshire College; five campuses; foundation courses, diploma, full-time, part-time academic and vocational degree courses; Prin. TERESA KELLY.

Accrington and Rossendale College: Broad Oak Rd, Accrington, BB5 2AW; tel. (1254) 389933; fax (1254) 354001; e-mail info@accross.ac.uk; internet www.accross.ac.uk; 3 campuses; degree courses in health, sports, technology; Prin. STEPHEN CARLISLE.

Alpha Meridian College: Meridian House, Greenwich High Rd, Greenwich, London, SE10 8TL; tel. (20) 8853-4111; fax (20) 8858-5553; e-mail info@alphameridian.co.uk; internet www.alphameridian.co.uk; f. 1994; private independent educational instn; graduate, postgraduate and diploma courses in computing, IT, accounting, business administration and management, travel, tourism, hospitality and English language.

Alton College: Old Odiham Rd, Alton, GU34 2LX; tel. (1420) 592200; fax (1420) 592253; e-mail admissions@altoncollege.ac.uk; internet www.altoncollege.ac.uk; Level 1–4 courses; subsidiary and extended diploma, Ofsted grade 1 ratings; library: 30,000 vols; Prin. JANE MACHELL; publ. *The Alternative* (student online magazine).

American InterContinental University London: 110 Marylebone High St, London, W1U 4RY; tel. (2074) 675640; e-mail aiuadministration@aiuniv.edu; internet www.aiuniv.edu/london; f. 1970; Bachelors and Masters in business, fashion, design, education and IT; 22 teachers; CEO and Pres. STEPHEN J. TOBER.

Ashton Sixth Form College: Darnton Rd, Ashton-under-Lyne, OL6 9RL; tel. (1613) 302330; fax (1613) 391772; e-mail contact@asfc.ac.uk; internet www.asfc.ac.uk; foundation degrees, BA (Hons) degrees; library: 10,000 printed resources and multimedia materials; Prin. Dr JANET NEVIN.

Aylesbury College: Oxford Rd, Aylesbury, HP21 8PD; tel. (1296) 588588; e-mail customerservices@aylesbury.ac.uk; internet www.aylesbury.ac.uk; f. 1962 as Aylesbury College of Further Education; vocational courses including hospitality and catering, construction, care, hair and beauty and sport; 5,500 (4500 part-time, 1000 full-time); Prin. and Chief Exec. PAULINE ODU-LINSKI.

Barking and Dagenham College: Rush Green Campus, Dagenham Rd, Romford, RM7 0XU; tel. (20) 8090-3020; fax (20) 8090-3021; internet www.barkingcollege.ac.uk; f. 1993; higher education courses incl. animation and creative video, business studies, computing, construction, fine art, graphic design, management, performing arts, photography, teacher training; Prin. and CEO CATHY WALSH.

Barnet College: Wood St., Barnet, EN5 4AZ; tel. (20) 8200-8300; fax (20) 8205-7177; e-mail info@barnet.ac.uk; internet www.barnet.ac.uk; campus at Grahame Park, two learning centres; offers 2,000 academic, professional, vocational and general interest courses; Prin. MARILYN HAWKINS.

Basingstoke College of Technology: Worting Rd, Basingstoke, RG21 8TN; tel. (1256) 354141; fax (1256) 306444; e-mail information@bcot.ac.uk; internet www.bcot.ac.uk; two sites and three outreach centres; higher education diploma in art and design, health, primary education; foundation degree in childhood studies, management; BA (Hons) in Textiles for Fashion, full time courses in business and sports; library: 24,000 vols, 100 journals; 7,000 (2000 full-time, 5,000 part-time); Prin. JUDITH ARMSTRONG.

Bedford College: Cauldwell St, Bedford, MK42 9AH; tel. (1234) 291000; fax (1234) 342674; e-mail info@bedford.ac.uk; internet www.bedford.ac.uk; higher education, professional and part-time courses; partnership with Univ. of Bedfordshire; library: 40,000 items, 8000 e-journals; Prin. and Chief Exec. IAN PRYCE.

Bishop Burton College: York Rd, Bishop Burton, Beverley, HU17 8QG; tel. (1964) 553000; fax (1964) 553101; e-mail enquiries@bishopburton.ac.uk; internet www.bishopburton.ac.uk; f. 1954; land-based college; degrees validated by Univ. of Hull, Leeds Metropolitan Univ.; library: 46,000 items; 370 journal and magazine subscriptions; Prin JEANETTE DAWSON.

Blackpool and The Fylde College: Ashfield Rd, Bispham, Blackpool, FY2 0HB; tel. (1253) 352-352; fax (1253) 356-127; e-mail visitors@blackpool.ac.uk; internet www.blackpool.ac.uk; attached to Lancaster Univ.; offers undergraduate, professional and vocational courses; 30,000 students; Prin. and Chief Exec. PAULINE WATERHOUSE.

Bradford College: Great Horton Rd, Bradford, BD7 1AY; tel. (1274) 433348; fax (1274) 741060; e-mail international@bradfordcollege.ac.uk; internet www.bradfordcollege.ac.uk; f. 1832; provides undergraduate, postgraduate and professional courses; consists of law school, business school and school of teaching, health and care; 23,000 students; Prin. MICHELE SUTTON.

Bromley College of Further and Higher Education: Rookery Lane, Bromley, BR2 8HE; tel. (20) 8295-7001; fax (20) 8295-7099; e-mail info@bromley.ac.uk; internet www.bromley.ac.uk; Bachelors degrees, foundation degrees and HNDs in vocational subjects; validated by Univ. of Greenwich; 600 teachers; 8,000 students; Prin. SAM PARRETT.

Burnley College: Princess Way, Burnley, BB12 0AN; tel. (1282) 733373; internet www.burnley.ac.uk; sixth form, university and adult education with a campus at the Univ. of Central Lancashire; Prin. HUGH BRAMWELL.

Castle College Nottingham: The People's Campus, Maid Marian Way, Nottingham,

NG1 6AB; tel. (1158) 842218; e-mail international@castlecollege.ac.uk; internet www.castlecollege.ac.uk/castle; f. 2006 by merger of Broxtowe College and The People's College; 11 sites; associate college of De Montfort Univ., Nottingham Trent Univ., Univ. of Bedfordshire, Univ. of Northampton and Univ. of Derby; HNC, HND, foundation degrees and vocational courses; Interim Prin. MALCOLM COWGILL.

Cavendish College: 35–37 Alfred Place, London, WC1E 7DP; tel. (20) 7580-4074; fax (20) 7255-1591; e-mail learn@cavendish.ac.uk; internet www.cavendish.ac.uk; full-time and part-time, diploma, certificate; foundation, undergraduate and postgraduate degrees in management, hospitality, digital media, designing and English language.

Chesterfield College: Infirmary Rd, Chesterfield, S41 7NG; tel. (1246) 500500; fax (1246) 500587; e-mail advice@chesterfield.ac.uk; internet www.chesterfield.ac.uk; f. 1841; 3 campuses; provides foundation courses, A-levels, vocational and professional qualifications, diplomas and degrees; library: 340,000 books, journals, magazines and DVDs; Prin. JUDITH McARTHUR.

City College Brighton and Hove: Pelham St, Brighton, BN1 4FA; tel. (1273) 667788; fax (1273) 667703; e-mail info@ccb.ac.uk; internet www.ccb.ac.uk; has campuses at Preston Rd and Wilson Ave; vocational courses in digital design, business and finance, catering and hospitality, tourism, heritage engineering, instrumentation, automation and control engineering; library: 40,000 vols, 300 periodicals, 2,500 video cassettes and DVDs; 9,000 students; Prin. and Chief Exec. PHIL FRIER; Vice-Prin. for Curriculum and Planning STEVE LEWIS; Vice-Prin. for Learning and Quality JAMES METTYEAR; Vice-Prin. for Student and Learning Support REBECCA FOREMAN.

City College Norwich: Ipswich Rd, Norwich, NR2 2LJ; tel. (1603) 773-483; fax (1603) 773-301; e-mail cfitzger@ccn.ac.uk; internet www.ccn.ac.uk; in conjunction with Univ. of East Anglia; higher national certificates and diplomas, foundation degrees, undergraduate degrees, postgraduate degrees, English language qualification; library: 80,000 books, 700 periodicals; Prin. DICK PALMER.

City of Bath College: Avon St, Bath, BA1 1UP; tel. (1225) 312-191; fax (1225) 444-213; e-mail enquiries@citybathcoll.ac.uk; internet www.citybathcoll.ac.uk; 6 local centres; undergraduate, part-time, full-time courses in arts, crafts and design, business and management, computing and information technology, construction and engineering, early years, music and performing arts, sports and fitness, teacher training; library: 35,000 print resources; 100 journals; Prin. MATT ATKINSON.

City of London College: 80 Backchurch Lane, London, E1 1LX; tel. (20) 7553-0430; fax (20) 7553-0431; e-mail info@clc-london.ac.uk; internet www.clc-london.ac.uk; f. 1979; courses validated by Birmingham City Univ., Univ. of Greenwich, Unv. of London, Univ. of Wales, Trinity Univ. College; courses in accounting and finance, business and management, economics, social sciences, computing, hospitality management, travel and tourism management, health and social care, English language; library: 2,500 vols, 2,000 students; Man. Dir Dr S. YOUSUF; Prin. DAVID J. NIXON.

City of Sunderland College: Durham Rd, Sunderland, SR3 4AH; tel. (191) 511-6000; e-mail informationservices@citysun.ac.uk; internet www.citysun.ac.uk; HE degrees by Univ. of Sunderland; Prin. ANGELA O'DONOGHUE.

Colchester Institute: Colchester Campus, Sheepen Rd, Colchester Essex, CO3 3LL; tel. (1206) 712000; fax (1206) 712800; internet www.colchester.ac.uk; 6 campuses, vocational colleges, part-time, full-time courses, foundation, higher national certificate, diploma, undergraduate and postgraduate courses; validated by Univ. of Essex; Prin. DANNY CLOUGH.

College of West Anglia: King's Lynn campus, Tennyson Ave, King's Lynn, PE30 2QW; tel. (1553) 761144; fax (1553) 815555; e-mail enquiries@col-westanglia.ac.uk; internet www.cwa.ac.uk; f. 1894 as King's Lynn Technical School; four campuses; offers degrees, foundation degrees and higher national diplomas; partnership with Anglia Ruskin Univ.; Prin. DAVID POMFRET.

Cornwall College: Cornwall College Camborne, Trevenson Rd, Pool, Redruth, TR15 3RD; tel. (1209) 611-611; fax (1209) 611-612; e-mail enquiries@cornwall.ac.uk; internet www.cornwall.ac.uk; f. 1929; 7 campuses; higher and further education college; 2,800 staff; 45,000 students (4,500 full-time, 40,500 part-time); Prin. and CEO DAVE LINNELL.

Craven College: High St, Skipton, BD23 1JY; tel. (1756) 708-008; fax (1756) 794-872; e-mail international@craven-college.ac.uk; internet www.craven-college.ac.uk; 2 campuses, 2 centres, 2 academies; foundation degrees, BA Hons, higher national diplomas and certificates; Prin. ALAN BLACKWELL.

Croydon College: College Rd, Croydon, CR9 1DX; tel. (20) 8760-5914; fax (20) 8760-5880; e-mail internationaloffice@croydon.ac.uk; internet www.croydon.ac.uk; 3 campuses; entry level courses, BTECs, A-levels, Access courses and NVQs, univ. level courses; more than 350 qualifications; validation by Univ. of Sussex; library: 80,000 books, 400 newspaper and magazine titles; 13,000 students; Prin. and Chief Exec. FRANCES WADSWORTH.

Doncaster College: High Melton, DN5 7SZ; tel. (1302) 553-592; fax (1302) 553-591; e-mail international@don.ac.uk; internet www.don.ac.uk; 2 campuses, 539 courses at all levels; degrees validated by the Univ. of Hull; 1,072 teachers; 19,813 students; Prin. and Chief Exec. GEORGE TROW.

East Riding College: Beverley campus, Gallows Lane, Beverly, HU17 7DT; e-mail info@eastridingcollege.ac.uk; internet www.eastridingcollege.ac.uk; 3 campuses; part-time and full-time courses, A-level, nat. vocational qualifications, diploma courses, foundation degrees and Bachelors degree courses; Prin. and Chief Exec. DEREK BRANTON.

EThames Graduate School: 197 Marsh Wall, Docklands, London, E14 9SG; tel. (20) 7531-7320; fax (20) 7987-0762; internet etgs.org.uk; centre in Essex; 7 depts: business, finance, computing, health and social care, hospitality and tourism, English, corporate training; Prin. SUSAN J HINDLEY.

Exeter College: Hele Rd Centre, Hele Rd, Exeter, EX4 4JS; tel. (8451) 116-000; fax (1392) 205-842; e-mail info@exe-coll.ac.uk; internet www.exe-coll.ac.uk; f. 1970; 5 centres; higher national diploma/certificate, foundation degree Bachelors degree, postgraduate certificate in education, English language courses; 12,250 students (4,250 full-time, 8,000 part-time); Prin. RICHARD ATKINS.

Furness College: Channelside, Barrow-in-Furness, LA14 2PJ; tel. (1229) 825-017; e-mail info@furness.ac.uk; internet www.furness.ac.uk; full-time, part-time courses at school leaving, univ. education level; partnership with Univ. of Central Lancashire,

Univ. of Cumbria and Lancaster Univ.; 5,000 students; Prin. ANNE ATTWOOD.

Gateshead College: Baltic Campus, Quarryfield Rd, Baltic Business Quarter, Gateshead, NE8 3BE; tel. (1914) 902-246; internet www.gateshead.ac.uk; 4 campuses; partnership with Northumbria Univ., Univ. of Sunderland, Univ. of Teesside; provides foundation degrees and Bachelors degree courses; 700 teachers; 13,000 students; Prin. and CEO RICHARD THOROLD.

Grimsby Institute of Further and Higher Education: Nuns Corner, Grimsby, DN34 5BQ; tel. and fax (1472) 311-238; e-mail international@grimsby.ac.uk; internet www.grimsby.ac.uk; 3 campuses; English teaching, International Foundation in Business, further education, higher national certificates/diplomas, foundation degrees, undergraduate, postgraduate degree programmes; 1,350 staff; Prin. and Chief Exec. SUE MIDDLEHURST.

Guildford College: Stoke Rd, Guildford, GU1 1EZ; tel. (1483) 448-688; fax (1483) 448-689; e-mail international@guildford.ac.uk; internet www.guildford.ac.uk; f. 1939; 3 campuses; English teaching, international A-level, univ. access, undergraduate and other college courses; library: 50,000 books, magazines, videos and DVDs; 10,000 students; Prin. and CEO CLIVE COOKE.

Harlow College: Velizy Ave, Harlow, CM20 3LH; tel. (1279) 868000; e-mail reception@harlow-college.ac.uk; internet www.harlow-college.ac.uk; Anglia Ruskin Univ.'s Centre and courses; Chair. PAUL TAYLOR; Prin. COLIN HINDMARCH.

Havering College of Further and Higher Education: International Devt Unit, Ardleigh Green Rd Campus, Ardleigh Green Rd, Hornchurch, RM11 2LL; tel. (1708) 462-793; fax (1708) 462-736; e-mail international@havering-college.ac.uk; internet www.havering-college.ac.uk; 2 main campuses, 5 learning centres; 35 higher education programmes from higher national certificates/diplomas to foundation degrees, undergraduate degrees and postgraduate programmes in vocational and academic subjects; Prin. and Chief Exec. NOEL OTLEY.

Hertford Regional College: Broxbourne Campus, Turnford, Broxbourne, SG12 9JF; tel. (1992) 411-400; e-mail info@hrc.ac.uk; internet www.hrc.ac.uk; 2 campuses; partnership with Hertfordshire Univ. and Univ. of Greenwich; apprenticeship, vocational courses, adult and community learning courses, foundation degrees and degree level courses; 3,900 students; Prin. ANDY FORBES.

Holborn College: Woolwich Rd, London, SE7 8LN; tel. (20) 7403-8080; fax (20) 8317-6001; e-mail international@kaplan.co.uk; internet www.holborncollege.ac.uk; f. 1969; undergraduate, postgraduate law and business degrees validated by Univ. of Wales, Univ. of London, Liverpool John Moores Univ.; library: 10,000 vols; Dean TIM HARRIS.

Holy Cross College: Manchester Rd, Bury, BL9 9BB; tel. (1617) 624-500; fax (1617) 624-501; e-mail information@holycross.ac.uk; internet www.holycross.ac.uk; univ. centre and sixth form college; partnership with Liverpool Hope, Edge Hill, Surrey and Leeds Metropolitan Univ.; library: 20,000 vols; Prin. DAVID FROST.

Hull College: Queen's Gardens, Chesters Bldg, Hull, HU1 3DG; tel. (1482) 381-921; fax (1482) 598-733; e-mail info@hull-college.ac.uk; internet www.hull-college.ac.uk; English language courses; more than 1,000 courses from foundation level to BA (Hons) degrees; Prin. and Chief Exec. Dr ELAINE MCMAHON.

K College: Brook St, Tonbridge, TN9 2PW; tel. (845) 207-8220; e-mail info@kcollege.ac.uk; internet www.kcollege.ac.uk; f. 2010, by merger of South Kent College and West Kent College; 5 campuses in Ashford, Dover, Folkestone, Tonbridge and Tunbridge Wells; 20,000 students; Prin. and Chief Exec. BILL FEARON; Deputy Prin. ALISON MONK.

Kaplan International Colleges: Shepherds Bldg, Charecroft Way, London, W14 0EE; tel. (20) 8727-3515; fax (20) 8727-3566; e-mail ukireland@kaplaninternational.com; internet www.kaplaninternational.com; f. 1938, present name and status 2009; schools in UK, Ireland, USA, Canada, Australia and New Zealand; English language courses and degree programmes.

Manchester College: International Office, Nicholls House, Hyde Rd, Ardwick, Manchester, M12 6BA; tel. (1614) 552-434; fax (1619) 532-955; e-mail international@themanchestercollege.ac.uk; internet www.themanchestercollege.ac.uk; f. 2008 by merger of Manchester College of Arts and Technology and City College Manchester; partnership with Univ. of Salford; full-time and part-time higher national diplomas/certificates, foundation degrees and Bachelors degree courses; Prin. PETER TAVERNOR.

Middlesbrough College: Dock St, Middlesbrough, TS2 1AD; tel. (1642) 333-700; e-mail courseinfo@mbro.ac.uk; internet www.mbro.ac.uk; f. 2002 by merger of Middlesbrough College and Teesside Tertiary College; courses leading to foundation degrees, higher national diplomas/certificates, BA (Hons), BSc (Hons), univ. certificates, professional qualifications; degrees awarded by Teesside Univ.; library: 45,000 vols, 6,000 online newspapers, journals; Prin. MIKE HOPKINS.

Ming-Ai (London) Institute: 1 Cline Rd, London, N11 2LX; tel. (20) 8361-7161; fax (20) 8361-4207; e-mail enquiry@ming-ai.org.uk; internet www.ming-ai.org.uk; f. 1993, asscn with Middlesex Univ. 1995; attached to Middlesex Univ.; promotes social, cultural, educational and economic exchanges among people of Hong Kong, China and Britain; courses in languages, catering and hospitality, business and ICT skills, arts and leisure; Dir Dr W. H. SHAK.

New College Durham: Framwellgate Moor Campus, Durham, DH1 5ES; tel. (1913) 754-000; fax (1913) 754-222; e-mail help@newdur.ac.uk; internet www.newcollegedurham.ac.uk; f. 1977 by merger of Neville's Cross College and Durham Technical College; higher national diplomas/certificates, foundation degrees, degrees and professional qualifications in part time and full time courses in variety of subjects; library: 65,000 vols, 300 periodicals; Prin. and Chief Exec. JOHN WIDDOWSON.

New College Nottingham: International Office, The Adams Bldg, Stoney St Lace Market, Nottingham, NG1 1NG; tel. (1159) 104-615; e-mail internat5@ncn.ac.uk; internet www.ncn.ac.uk; 7 centres; English language, vocational, higher national certificate, foundation degree and undergraduate courses; 22,000 students; Prin. and Chief Exec. GEOFF HALL.

Newbold College of Higher Education: St Marks Rd, Binfield, Bracknell, RG42 4AN; tel. (1344) 407-407; fax (1344) 407-406; e-mail info@newbold.ac.uk; internet www.newbold.ac.uk; higher education courses in management, arts, theology, accredited by Open Univ. Validation Services, Univ. of Wales Lampeter; 36 teachers (28 full-time, 8 part-time); 300 students; Prin. Dr SVEIN MYKLEBUST.

Newham College: East Ham Campus, High St South, London, E6 6ER; tel. (20) 8257-4446; e-mail international@newham.ac.uk; internet www.newham.ac.uk; f. 1985 by merger of East Ham and West Ham technical colleges; 2 main campuses; courses offered in business, management, combined studies, counselling, professional devt; assoc. college of London Metropolitan Univ.; 20,000 students; Prin. and Chief Exec. DENISE BROWN-SACKEY.

North Hertfordshire College: Stevenage Centre, Monkswood Way, Stevenage, SG1 1LA; tel. (1462) 424-242; e-mail enquiries@nhc.ac.uk; internet www.nhc.ac.uk; 5 main centres, foundation degrees, BA Hons degree in computer science, business admin. and science; assoc. college of Univ. of Hertfordshire; library: 20,000 books, 100 journals; 15,000 students; Prin. FINTAN DONOHUE.

North Lindsey College: Kingsway, Scunthorpe, DN17 1AJ; tel. (1724) 281-111; fax (1724) 294-020; e-mail info@northlindsey.ac.uk; internet www.northlindsey.ac.uk; assoc. college of Univ. of Lincoln; wide range of foundation degrees, Bachelors degrees in education and training, business studies, English and history and social science; programmes validated by Univ. of Hull, Univ. of Huddersfield; Prin. Prof. ROGER BENNETT.

North West Kent College: Dartford Campus, Oakfield Lane, Dartford, DA1 2JT; tel. (1322) 629-400; fax (1322) 629-468; e-mail course.enquiries@nwkcollege.ac.uk; internet www.nwkcollege.ac.uk; 2 campuses; partnership with Univ. of Greenwich; BA (Hons), foundation degrees, higher national diplomas and certificates in art, design photography and multimedia, business studies, media studies, performing and technical arts, professional care, travel and tourism and management studies, construction and building services, engineering, hotel and catering, motor vehicle, professional care, refrigeration; Prin. DAVID GLEED.

Prince's School of Traditional Arts: 19–22 Charlotte Rd, London, EC2A 3SG; tel. (20) 7613-8532; fax (20) 7613-8599; e-mail enquiry@psta.org.uk; internet www.psta.org.uk; f. 2004; research and postgraduate degrees validated by Univ. of Wales; courses in arts and philosophy; Chair. Sir DAVID GREEN; Dir Dr KHALED AZZAM.

Redbridge College: Barley Lane, Romford, RM6 4XT; tel. (20) 8548-7400; e-mail info@redbridge-college.ac.uk; internet www.redbridge-college.ac.uk; Chair. LEE ROGERS; Prin. and Chief Exec. THERESA DROWLEY.

South Cheshire College: Dane Bank Ave, Cheshire, Crewe, CW2 8AB; tel. (1270) 654654; fax (1270) 651515; e-mail info@s-cheshire.ac.uk; internet www.s-cheshire.ac.uk; Chair. KEN LEA; Prin. and Chief Exec. PETER SWIFT.

South Essex College: Luker Rd, Southend-on-Sea, SS1 1ND; tel. (1702) 220-571; fax (1702) 432-320; e-mail learning@southessex.ac.uk; internet www.southessex.ac.uk; f. 2010, by merger of Thurrock and Basildon College and South East Essex College; degrees validated by Univ. of Essex, Univ. of East London, or Anglia Ruskin Univ.; campuses in Basildon and Thurrock; Prin. and Chief Exec. JAN HODGES.

South Nottingham College: 1 Station St, Nottingham, Bingham, NG13 8AP; tel. (1949) 838901; e-mail enquiries@snc.ac.uk; internet www.snc.ac.uk; centres in West Bridgford, Clifton; 7 schools: business, IT, and humanities, foundation learning, health and lifestyle, lifelong learning, sport, leisure, travel and tourism, visual arts and digital media, automotive training; Chair. KEITH BEAUMONT; Prin. MALCOM COWGILL; Deputy Prin. for Corporate Services JOHN SNOW.

South Thames College: Wandsworth High St, London, SW18 2PP; tel. (20) 8918-7777; internet www.south-thames.ac.uk; f. 1895, as Wandsworth Technical Institute; attached to Kingston Univ.; degrees validated by Kingston Univ., London South Bank Univ., Christ Church Canterbury Univ; 21,000 students; Prin. SUE RIMMER.

South Tyneside College: St. George's Ave, South Shields, NE34 6ET; tel. (191) 427-3500; e-mail info@stc.ac.uk; internet www.stc.ac.uk; degrees validated by Univ. of Sunderland, Northumbrian Univ., Univ. of Huddersfield; 17,000 students; Prin. and chief Exec. LINDSEY WHITEROD.

Spurgeon's College: South Norwood Hill, London, SE25 6DJ; tel. (20) 8653-0850; fax (20) 8771-0959; e-mail enquiries@spurgeons.ac.uk; internet www.spurgeons.ac.uk; degrees validated by Univ. of Wales; library: 60,000 vols; Chair. ROBERT AMESS; Prin. Dr NIGEL WRIGHT.

St-Patrick's International College: 24 Great Chapel St, London, W1F 8FS; tel. (20) 7287-6664; fax (20) 7287-6282; e-mail registrar@st-patricks.ac.uk; internet www.st-patricks.ac.uk; f. 1803, as St. Patrick's School; courses in accounting, business management, technology, healthcare management, hospitality management, and law; Prin. and Chief Exec. GIRISH CHANDRA.

St Helens College: Water St, St Helens, WA10 1PP; tel. (1744) 733766; fax (1744) 623913; internet www.sthelens.ac.uk; degree courses validated by Univ. of Central Lancashire, Edge Hill Univ., Liverpool John Moores Univ., Univ. of Salford, Sheffield Hallam Univ.; library: 60,000 vols, 200 periodicals; Prin. PAT BACON.

St John's College: Chilwell Lane, Nottingham, NG9 3DS; tel. (115) 925-1114; fax (115) 943-6438; e-mail enquiries@stjohns-nottm.ac.uk; internet www.stjohns-nottm.ac.uk; undergraduate and postgraduate courses in theology for ministry and theology validated by Univ. of Chester; Prin. Dr CHRISTINA BAXTER.

St Mary's College: Shear Brow, Blackburn, BB1 8DX; tel. (1254) 580464; fax (1254) 665991; e-mail reception@stmarysblackburn.ac.uk; internet www.stmarysblackburn.ac.uk; honours degree validated by Liverpool Hope Univ.; courses in English, education and society, sport and health studies, management of information and enterprise; 1,500 students; Dir of Devt S. FLANAGAN; Librarian ZANIB MALIK.

Stanmore College: Elm Park, London, Stanmore, HA7 4BQ; tel. (20) 8420-7780; fax (20) 8385-7269; internet www.stanmore.ac.uk; library: 20,000 vols; Prin. JACQUI MACE.

Stroud College: Stratford Rd, Stroud, GL5 4AH; tel. (1453) 763424; e-mail enquire@stroudcol.ac.uk; internet www.stroud.ac.uk; courses in art, design, media and music, construction and engineering, computing and information technology; library: 14,000 vols; Prin. BERI HARE; Deputy Prin. and Dir of Finance ANDREW CLARE; Vice-Prin. for Quality, Planning and Innovation PETER CLEGG.

Swindon College: North Star Ave, Swindon, SN2 1DY; tel. (1793) 491591; internet www.swindon-college.ac.uk; degrees validated by Oxford Brookes Univ. and Univ. of Bath; library: 32,000 vols; 9,500 students; Prin. ANDREW MILLER; Deputy Prin. for Finance and Resources NICK LETCHET; Vice-Prin. for Curriculum and Quality JOHN EVANS.

Trafford College: Talbot Rd, Manchester, Stretford, M32 0XH; tel. (161) 886-7000; fax (161) 872-7921; e-mail enquiries@trafford.ac.uk; internet www.trafford.ac.uk; centres in Cheshire; 4 centres in Manchester; 11,000 students; Chair. GRAHAM LUCCOCK; Prin. Sir BILL MOORCROFT.

Tresham College of Further and Higher Education: George St, Corby, NN17 1QA; tel. (845) 658-8990; fax (1536) 413357; e-mail info@tresham.ac.uk; internet www.tresham.ac.uk; f. 1978 by merger of 2 technical colleges in Kettering and Corby, present name and status 1992 by merger of Wellingborough College and Tresham College; degree courses validated by Univ. of Northampton and Univ. of Bedfordshire; courses in engineering, business and management, sport, computing, art and design, accounting, 10,000 students; Chair. E. R. BAINES; Prin. and Chief Exec. MARK SILVERMAN.

Tyne Metropolitan College: Battle Hill Dr., Wallsend, NE28 9NL; tel. (191) 229-5000; e-mail enquiries@tynemet.ac.uk; internet www.tynemet.ac.uk; has campus in North Shields; courses in art and design, computing, health and social care, business, floristry and horticulture, first aid, sport, retail, engineering and technology, catering and hospitality, pharmacy and laboratory services; Prin. and CEO JON VINCENT; Deputy Prin. for Finance and Corporate Devt ANN-MARIE CROZIER; Deputy Prin. for Curriculum and Business Devt AUDREY KINGHAM.

University Campus Suffolk: Neptune Quay, Ipswich, IP4 1QJ; tel. (1473) 338000; e-mail info@ucs.ac.uk; internet www.ucs.ac.uk; f. 2007; centres in Bury St Edmunds, Great Yarmouth, Lowestoft and Otley; degrees jtly validated by Univ. of East Anglia and Univ. of Essex; Provost and CEO Prof. MIKE SAKS; Head of Learning Resources STEVE PHILIPS.

University Centre Yeovil: 91 Preston Rd, Yeovil, BA20 2DN; tel. (1935) 845454; fax (1935) 415483; e-mail ucy@yeovil.ac.uk; internet www.ucy.ac.uk; courses validated by Bournemouth Univ., Univ. of the West of England and Exeter Univ.; courses in heritage and horticulture, engineering, forensic science, health and care, education, design and media, business and computing.

Uxbridge College: Park Rd, Uxbridge, UB8 1NQ; tel. (1895) 853333; fax (1895) 853377; e-mail enquiries@uxbridgecollege.ac.uk; internet www.uxbridge.ac.uk; f. 1965; courses validated by Thames Valley Univ. and Univ. of Greenwich; Prin. LARAINE SMITH.

Wakefield College: Margaret St, Wakefield, WF1 2DH; tel. (1924) 789789; fax (1924) 789340; e-mail info@wakefield.ac.uk; internet www.wakefield.ac.uk; f. 1868; foundation and bachelors degrees validated by univs; 13,000 full-time and part-time students; Prin. SUE GRIFFITHS; Deputy Prin. JOHN FOSTER; Deputy Prin. KAYE FISHER.

Wesley College, Bristol: Henbury Rd, Bristol, BS10 7QD; tel. (117) 959-1200; e-mail admin@wesley-college-bristol.ac.uk; internet www.wesley-college-bristol.ac.uk; f. 1945, present name and status 1967; BA (Hons) and MA programmes validated by Univ. of Bristol; foundation degree validated by St Mary's Univ. College; Prin. Rev. Dr JONATHAN PYE; Librarian MIKE BREALEY.

West Cheshire College: Eaton Rd, Chester, CH4 7ER; tel. (1244) 677677; e-mail info@west-cheshire.ac.uk; internet www.west-cheshire.ac.uk; has campus at Ellesmere Port and technology campus at Chester; Prin. SARA MOGEL.

West London College: 35 North Row, Mayfair, London, W1K 6DB; tel. (20) 7491-1841; fax (20) 7499-5853; internet www.w-l-c.co.uk; courses in business admin., finance and accounting, information technology, tourism management, fashion design; 1,000 students; Prin. PAUL SMITH; Deputy Prin. NEIL TETHER; Librarian NICOLE JOURDAN.

West Thames College: London Rd, Isleworth, TW7 4HS; tel. (20) 8326-2000; e-mail info@west-thames.ac.uk; internet www.west-thames.ac.uk; foundation Degrees accredited by Kingston Univ., TVU and St Mary's Univ. College; 6,500 students; Chair. J. ROBERTS; Prin. M. SEMPLE.

Wiltshire College: Cocklebury Rd, Chippenham, SN15 3QD; tel. (1249) 464644; fax (1249) 465326; e-mail info@wiltshire.ac.uk; internet www.wiltshire.ac.uk; f. 2000, merger with Salisbury College 2008; courses in computing, social work, applied arts, engineering, animal science and management, degrees validated; campuses in Corsham, Devizes, Lackham, Salisbury, Warminster, Trowbridge; 9,300 students incl. part-time and full-time; Prin. DIANE DALE.

AGRICULTURE

Askham Bryan College: Askham Bryan, York, YO23 3FR; tel. (1904) 772277; fax (1904) 772288; e-mail enquiries@askham-bryan.ac.uk; internet www.askham-bryan.ac.uk; f. 1948, as Yorkshire Institute of Agriculture; degrees validated by Harper Adams Univ. College, Univ. of Leeds and York St John Univ.; courses in agriculture; animal management; arboriculture, business; 4,000 students; Prin. and Chief Exec. LIZ PHILIP.

Brooksby Melton College: Melton Campus, Asfordby Rd, Melton Mowbray, LE13 0HJ; tel. (1664) 855444; internet www.brooksbymelton.ac.uk; 4 campuses; independent college specializing in animal care and agriculture, also leading performing arts college; associate college for Univ. of Lincoln, Leicester De Montfort Univ.; Prin. CHRIS BALL.

Hadlow College: Hadlow Campus, Hadlow, Tonbridge, TN11 0AL; fax (1732) 853-207; e-mail enquiries@hadlow.ac.uk; internet www.hadlow.ac.uk; f. 1969 by merging Sittingbourne Farm Institute and Swanley Horticultural Institute; 3 campuses; higher national diploma and degree courses in agriculture and sustainability, animal management, conservation and wildlife, equestrian studies and outdoor activities, fisheries management, horticulture, landscape and design; library: 18,000 specialist resources; Prin. and Chief Exec. PAUL HANNAN.

Moulton College: West St, Moulton, NN3 7RR; tel. (1604) 491-131; fax (1604) 491-127; e-mail enquiries@moulton.ac.uk; internet www.moulton.ac.uk; foundation degrees, diplomas, undergraduate, postgraduate courses in land based, construction and furniture disciplines; 400 part time courses in 15 disciplines; links with Univ. of Northampton; Prin. CHRIS MOODY.

Reaseheath College: Nantwich, CW5 6DF; tel. (1270) 625131; e-mail enquiries@reaseheath.ac.uk; internet www.reaseheath.ac.uk; f. 1921, as Cheshire School of Agriculture; attached to Harper Adams Univ. College and Univ. of Chester; Bachelors degrees in veterinary, ecology, agricultural engineering, equine science, food industry, landscape design and management; 500 teachers; 6,250 students; Prin. MEREDYDD DAVID.

Writtle College: Chelmsford, CM1 3RR; tel. (1245) 424200; fax (1245) 420456; e-mail info@writtle.ac.uk; internet www.writtle.ac.uk; f. 1893; specialist college providing undergraduate and postgraduate courses focused on business and green industries; degrees validated by Univ. of Essex; library: 40,000 vols, 300 periodical titles; 2,600 students; Prin. DAVID BUTCHER.

ART AND DESIGN

Christie's Education London: 153 Great Titchfield St, London, W1W 5BD; tel. (20) 7665-4350; fax (20) 7665-4351; e-mail education@christies.com; internet www.christieseducation.com; degrees validated by Univ. of Glasgow; courses in art, style and design of Europe, modern and contemporary art; centre in New York; 160 students; Academic Dir Dr M. A. MICHAEL.

City and Guilds of London Art School: 124 Kennington Park Rd, London, SE11 4DJ; tel. (20) 7735-2306; fax (20) 7582-5361; e-mail info@cityandguildsartschool.ac.uk; internet www.cityandguildsartschool.ac.uk; f. 1879; BA (Hons) degree courses in painting, sculpture, fine arts; diploma courses in wood-carving and gilding, stone carving; library: 5,500 vols, 750 films and cinema titles, 1400 slides, 30 journal subscriptions; 60 part-time teachers; 200 students; Prin. TONY CARTER.

Cleveland College of Art and Design: Green Lane, Linthorpe, Middlesbrough, TS5 7RJ; tel. (1642) 288-000; fax (1642) 288-828; internet www.ccad.ac.uk; 2 campuses; specialist art and design education; partnership with Univ. of Teeside; library: 25,000 books, 100 magazines and journals, 1,600 DVDs and videocassettes; Prin. MARTIN RABY.

Courtauld Institute of Art: part of University of London (see entry).

Hereford College of Arts: Folly Lane, Hereford, HR1 1LT; tel. (1432) 273-359; fax (1432) 341-099; e-mail enquiries@hca.ac.uk; internet www.hca.ac.uk; f. 1851; specialist art, design and performing arts college, courses from entry level through to foundation and undergraduate degrees; library: 24,000 books, 80 specialist journals; 37 teachers; 850 students; Prin. RICHARD HEATLY.

Inchbald School of Design: 7 Eaton Gate, London, SW1W 9BA; tel. (20) 7730-5508; e-mail interiors@inchbald.co.uk; internet www.inchbald.co.uk; f. 1960; 2 campuses; independent school of design offering Masters degree, diploma and certificate courses in architectural interior design, interior decoration and garden design, short courses in computer aided design; Prin. JACQUELINE DUNCAN.

Leeds College of Art: Blenheim Walk, Leeds, LS2 9AQ; tel. (113) 202-8000; fax (113) 202-8001; e-mail info@leeds-art.ac.uk; internet www.leeds-art.ac.uk; f. 1842, as Leeds School of Art; graduate degrees validated by Open Univ.; courses in creative arts and design; library: 30,000 vols, 140 nat. and int. magazines; Chair. PETER YENDELL; Prin. SIMONE WONNACOTT.

Norwich School of Art and Design: Francis House, 3–7 Redwell St, Norwich, NR2 4SN; tel. (1603) 610-561; fax (1603) 615-728; e-mail info@nuca.ac.uk; internet www.nuca.ac.uk; f. 1846 became Norwich University College of the Arts in 2008; undergraduate, postgraduate and doctoral courses in arts, design and media disciplines; library: 30,000 vols, 80,000 photographs, 2,500 DVDs, 100 journals; 1,500 students; Prin. JOHN LAST.

Plymouth College of Art: Tavistock Pl., Plymouth, PL4 8AT; tel. (1752) 203434; fax (1752) 203444; e-mail enquiries@plymouthart.ac.uk; internet www.plymouthart.ac.uk; f. 1856, as Plymouth School of Art; graduate and postgraduate

degrees validated by Open Univ.; courses in design and fine arts; library: 20,000 vols, 130 journals, magazines and newspapers; Prin. Prof. ANDREW BREWERTON.

Ravensbourne College of Design and Communication: Ravensbourne, 6 Penrose Way, London, SE10 0EW; tel. (20) 3040-3500; fax (20) 8325-8320; e-mail info@rave.ac.uk; internet www.rave.ac.uk; f. 1962; degree courses in broadcast engineering and communication and technology, fashion design, furniture design, graphic design, interaction design, interior design, moving image design, product design, professional broadcasting; BTEC HNDs in broadcast operations, engineering and production; BTEC HNCs in broadcast post production, and digital technology for the creative industries; BTEC NC in broadcast engineering; foundation course in art design and media; MA in Interactive Digital Media; 137 teachers incl. 200 part-time; 1,500 students; Dir Prof. ROBIN BAKER.

Royal Academy Schools: Burlington House, Piccadilly, London, W1J 0BD; tel. (20) 7300-8000; fax (20) 7300-5856; internet www.royalacademy.org.uk; f. 1768; offers three-year, full-time postgraduate fine arts course; Pres. Sir NICHOLAS GRIMSHAW.

Royal College of Art: Kensington Gore, London, SW7 2EU; tel. (20) 7590-4444; fax (20) 7590-4500; e-mail admissions@rca.ac.uk; internet www.rca.ac.uk; f. 1837, awarded Charter 1967 empowering it to grant its own degrees; postgraduate instn receiving direct grant from HEFCE; library: 70,000 vols, 200 periodicals; 800 students; Visitor HRH The DUKE OF EDINBURGH; Provost Sir TERENCE CONRAN; Rector and Vice-Provost Prof. Sir CHRISTOPHER FRAYLING; Registrar ALAN SELBY.

School of Architecture, Architectural Association: 34–36 Bedford Square, London, WC1B 3ES; tel. (20) 7887-4000; fax (20) 7414-0782; e-mail info@aaschool.ac.uk; internet www.aaschool.ac.uk; f. 1847; 1-year foundation course; 5-year course leading to AA Dipl.; postgraduate courses and research in architecture, building conservation, conservation (landscape and gardens), emergent technologies and design, environment and energy, histories and theories of architecture, housing and urbanism, landscape urbanism; campus at Hooke Park; library: 46,000 vols, 2,000 architectural drawings, paintings, 150,000 slides; 120 teachers; 580 students; Dir BRETT STEELE; publ. *AA Files* (2 a year).

School of Design London: 1–15 Bradley Close, White Lion St, London, N1 9PN; tel. (20) 7713-1991; fax (20) 7713-1997; e-mail design.london@northumbria.ac.uk; internet www.northumbria.ac.uk/sd/academic/scd/london; attached to Northumbria Univ.; MA in fashion management and entrepreneurship; MA in design innovation management and entrepreneurship; MA in design craftsmanship and entrepreneurship; Dean STEVEN KYFFIN.

Slade School of Fine Art: University College London, Gower St, London, WC1E 6BT; tel. (20) 7679-2313; fax (20) 7679-7801; e-mail slade.enquiries@ucl.ac.uk; internet www.ucl.ac.uk/slade; f. 1871; attached to University College London; BA (Hons) degree course in Fine Art (painting, sculpture or fine art media); MA in Fine Art; MFA in Fine Art; MPhil/PhD in Fine Art; short, non-degree courses in drawing and painting; 38 teachers; 260 students; Dir and Slade Prof. Prof. JOHN AIKEN.

Somerset College: Wellington Rd, Somerset, TA1 5AX; tel. (1823) 366331; fax (1823) 366418; e-mail enquiries@somerset.ac.uk; internet www.somerset.ac.uk; f. 1856, as

School of Art and Science; attached to Univ. of Plymouth; undergraduate courses in design, fine art and business admin.; Prin. and Chief Exec. RACHEL DAVIES.

Sotheby's Institute of Art: 30 Bedford Sq., London, WC1B 3EE; tel. (20) 7462-3232; fax (20) 7580-8160; e-mail info@sothebysinstitute.com; internet www.sothebysinstitute.com; campuses in New York and Singapore; postgraduate courses in art business, contemporary art, photography, fine and decorative art, east Asian art and contemporary design; library: 15,000 vols; Dir JOS HACKFORTH-JONES; Academic Dir MEGAN ALDRICH.

BUSINESS AND COMMERCE

Ashridge Business School: Berkhamsted, HP4 1NS; tel. (1442) 843-491; fax (1442) 841-209; e-mail contact@ashridge.org.uk; internet www.ashridge.org.uk; f. 1959 as Ashridge Management College, present status 2008; MBA, MSc, doctorate, diploma and executive devt programmes; 90 full-time teachers; 6,000 students; library: 8,000 vols, spec. colln incl. Ashridge learning guides; CEO KAI PETERS; Library and Information Services Man. LORRAINE OLIVER; publs *360°*, *the Ashridge Journal* (2 a year), *Converse* (1 a year), *Network, the Ashridge Magazine*.

Chartered Management Institute: 2 Savoy Court, Strand, London, WC2R 0EZ; tel. (20) 7497-0580; fax (20)74 97-0463; e-mail enquiries@managers.org.uk; internet www.managers.org.uk; awards Chartered Manager qualification; Chief Exec. RUTH SPELLMAN; publ. *Professional Manager*.

City Banking College: 7–13 Melior St, London, SE1 3QP; tel. (20) 7403-3770; fax (20) 7403-8355; e-mail admin@citybankingcollege.co.uk; internet www.citybankingcollege.co.uk; course provider in banking, finance and management; undergraduate and postgraduate courses in association with Roehampton University; 9 teachers; Prin. MOHAMED KHAN.

College of Estate Management: Whiteknights, Reading, RG6 6AW; tel. (1189) 214-696; fax (1189) 214-620; e-mail courses@cem.ac.uk; internet www.cem.ac.uk; f. 1919, Royal Charter 1922; undergraduate and professional distance learning courses in real estate; 270 teachers (245 external, 25 internal); 4,000 students.

European Business School London: Regent's College, Inner Circle, Regent's Park, London, NW1 4NS; tel. (20) 7487-5505; fax (20) 7487-7425; e-mail ebsl@regents.ac.uk; internet www.ebslondon.ac.uk; f. 1979 in UK, centres also in Germany, France, Italy, Japan, Russia, Spain and USA; BA (Hons) degree in European Business Administration, and other degrees with business and language mix; summer courses; library: 25,500 vols; 750 full-time students; Dir Prof. MICHAEL SCRIVEN.

European College of Business and Management: 69–71 Great Eastern St, London, EC2A 3HU; tel. (20) 7749-5930; fax (20) 7729-6264; e-mail info@eurocollege.org.uk; internet www.eurocollege.org.uk; f. 1988 as British–German School for Vocational Training, present name 2000; Bachelors and Masters courses in business and management; centre in Germany; Dir RICHARD BILLS; Treas. PHIL SAMPSON.

European School of Economics: 8–9 Grosvenor Pl., London, SW1X 7SH; tel. (20) 7245-6148; fax (20) 7245-6164; e-mail info@eselondon.ac.uk; internet www.eselondon.ac.uk; private college of higher education in international business; Bachelors, Masters,

MBA, and certificate programmes; validated by Univ. of Buckingham; Pres. ELIO D'ANNA.

Henley Business School: Greenlands, Henley-on-Thames, RG9 3AU; tel. (1491) 571-454; fax (1491) 571-635; e-mail helpdesk@henley.com; internet www.henley.reading.ac.uk; f. 1945 as the Administrative Staff College; attached to Univ. of Reading; undergraduate and postgraduate degrees in accountancy, business, management, finance, real estate, planning, informatics, and coaching; campus at Whiteknights, Reading; 113 teachers (53 full-time, 60 associate); 7,000 students; library: 18,000 vols; Dean Prof. JOHN BOARD; publ. *Journal of General Management*.

Kensington College of Business: Wesley House, 4 Wild Court, London, WC2B 4AU; tel. (20) 7404-6330; fax (20) 7404-6330; e-mail kcb@kensingtoncoll.ac.uk; internet www.kensingtoncoll.ac.uk; f. 1982; courses at undergraduate and postgraduate levels; Prin. IAN PIRIE.

London College of Accountancy: 19 Charter House St, London, EC1N 6RA; tel. (20) 7400-6789; fax (20) 7400-6799; internet www.londoncollege.org; accountancy and management courses; undergraduate and postgraduate programmes from Anglia Ruskin Univ.; 5,000 students; Man. Dir RAVI GILL.

London College of Business: 129 Oxford St, London, W1D 2UH; tel. (20) 7287-3040; fax (20) 7284-1166; e-mail info@lcbuk.org; internet www.lcbuk.org; centre in Birmingham and Essex; courses in sectors of business and information technology validated by Univ. of Wales; Pres. ZENON ADAMEK.

London College of Management and IT (LCMIT): Winchester House Campus, 80 Backchurch Lane, London, E1 1LX; tel. (20) 7553-0434; fax (20) 7553-0435; e-mail info@lcmit.com; internet lcmit.com; undergraduate, postgraduate, professional courses in accounting, management, computing and English language; library: 2,500 vols; Prin. DAVID NIXON.

London School of Accountancy and Management: 12–20 Camomile St, London, EC3A 7PT; tel. (20) 7623-8777; fax (20) 7623-8778; e-mail training@londonsam.ac; internet www.londonsam.org.uk; degrees validated by Staffordshire Univ. and Univ. of Wales; centres in Asia; Prin. Dr DAK PATEL.

London School of Commerce: Chaucer House, White Hart Yard, London, SE1 1NX; tel. (20) 7357-0077; fax (20) 7403-1163; e-mail info@lsclondon.co.uk; internet www.lsclondon.co.uk; degree, postgraduate and MBA courses in finance, management and business; associate college of Univ. of Wales Institute, Cardiff.

Manchester Business School: Booth St West, Manchester, M15 6PB; tel. (161) 275-6333; internet www.mbs.ac.uk; f. 2004, by merger of Institute of Innovation Research (IoIR), Victoria Univ. of Manchester's School of Accounting and Finance, UMIST's Manchester School of Management and Manchester Business School; courses in accounting and finance, business systems, marketing, int. business and strategy and management; 200 teachers; 2,000 students; Dir Prof. MICHAEL LUGER.

Oxford Business College: 65 George St, Oxford, OX1 2BQ; tel. (1865) 791908; fax (1865) 245059; e-mail enquiries@oxfordbusinesscollege.co.uk; internet www.oxfordbusinesscollege.net; courses in business management and accounting and travel and tourism; Vice-Prin. PRISCILLA CLARK-CHRISTOPHER.

Oxford House College: 30 Oxford St, London, W1D 1AU; tel. (20) 7436-4872; fax (20) 7323-4582; internet www.oxfordhousecollege.co.uk; f. 1974; degrees validated by Univ. of Sunderland; courses in business admin, int. tourism and hospitality management; Prin. TIM MATTHEW.

Rayat London College: 32–42 New Heston Rd, Heston, TW5 0LJ; tel. (20) 8754-3330; fax (20) 8754-3331; e-mail info@rayatlondoncollege.co.uk; internet www.rayatlondoncollege.co.uk; f. 2004; centre in New Delhi, India; validated by Univ. of Wales; courses in business, professional accounting, admin. management; Chair. NIRMAL SINGH RAYAT; Prin. Prof. C. MICHAEL WILKINSON.

Regent's Business School London: Inner Circle, Regent's Park, London, NW1 4NS; tel. (20) 7487-7505; fax (20) 7487-7425; e-mail rbsl@regents.ac.uk; internet www.rbslondon.ac.uk; f. 1997; foundation courses, undergraduate and postgraduate degrees in business, finance and management; 60 teachers; 430 students; Academic Dir Dr RICHARD GREGSON.

Resource Development International: 1A Brandon Lane, Coventry, CV3 3RD; tel. (24) 7651-5700; fax (24) 7651-5701; e-mail info@rdi.co.uk; internet www.rdi.co.uk; f. 1990; distance learning, undergraduate, postgraduate and vocational course; provides on campus degrees through Institute of Business and Management; 3,000 students; CEO Dr PHILIP HALLAM.

School of Technology and Management: Hannibal House, London, SE1 6TE; tel. (20) 7378-9061; fax (20) 7403-1163; e-mail info@stmlondon.co.uk; internet www.stmlondon.co.uk; attached to Univ. of East London; postgraduate courses in business and information technology.

TASMAC London School of Business: 1–3 Valley Dr., Kingsbury, NW9 9NG; tel. (20) 8206-0066; fax (20) 8206-1999; e-mail info@tasmac.org.uk; internet www.tasmac.org.uk; has campuses at Wembley, London and Pune, India; undergraduate and postgraduate business degree programmes accredited by Univ. of Wales and open and distance learning BA and MBA programmes from IGNOU; Head Prof. MARSHALL G. HALL.

Williams College: 5 Holborn Circus, Holborn, London, EC1N 2HB; tel. (20) 7583-9222; fax (20) 7583-9095; internet www.williamscollege.co.uk; f. 2002; MBA and BA or BSc degrees in various business related subjects incl. accounting, banking, finance, int. business, management, management information systems and marketing; Prin. Dr JOHN POMEROY.

MEDICINE, THERAPY, COUNSELLING AND HEALTHCARE

Anglo–European College of Chiropractic: 13–15 Parkwood Rd, Bournemouth, BH5 2DF; tel. (1202) 436200; fax (1202) 436312; e-mail admissions@aecc.ac.uk; internet www.aecc.ac.uk; f. 1965; chiropractic education and research at undergraduate and postgraduate level; assoc. college of Bournemouth Univ.; library: 10,000 vols, 100 current periodicals; Prin. Dr KENNETH VALL.

College of Integrated Chinese Medicine: 19–21 Castle St, Reading, RG1 7SB; tel. (1189) 508-880; fax (1189) 508-890; e-mail admin@cicm.org.uk; internet www.acupuncturecollege.org.uk; f. 1993; BSc (Hons) Acupuncture, MSc Chinese Medicine, Licentiate in Acupuncture validated by Kingston Univ.; 40 teachers; Dean PETER MOLE.

College of Medical and Dental Sciences: Edgbaston, Birmingham, B15 2TT; tel. (121) 414-3858; e-mail mdsenquiries@contacts.bham.ac.uk; internet www.medicine.bham.ac.uk; f. 2008; attached to Univ. of Birmingham; courses in medicine, medical sciences, dentistry, nursing and physiotherapy; 1,000 teachers; 750 students; Head Prof. LAWRENCE YOUNG.

College of Osteopaths: 13 Furzehill Rd, Borehamwood, WD6 2DG; tel. (20) 8905-1937; fax (20) 8953-6140; e-mail admin@collegeofosteopaths.ac.uk; internet www.collegeofosteopaths.ac.uk; f. 1948; foundation to masters courses in osteopathy; in collaboration with Keele Univ. and Middlesex Univ.; Prin. PAT HAMILTON.

European School of Osteopathy: Boxley House, The Street, Boxley, Maidstone, ME14 3DZ; tel. (1622) 671-558; fax (1622) 662-165; e-mail info@eso.ac.uk; internet www.eso.ac.uk; f. 1965; undergraduate and postgraduate courses; validated by Univ. of Greenwich; Prin. ADRIAN BARNES.

Hull York Medical School: John Hughlings Jackson Bldg, University of York, Heslington York, YO10 5DD; Hertford Bldg, Univ. of Hull, Hull HU6 7RX; tel. (1482) 463-074; fax (1482) 464-705; internet www.hyms.ac.uk/home.aspx; f. 2003; partnership between Univ. of Hull and Univ. of York; medical school with undergraduate, postgraduate courses; library: 2m. books, 20,000 journal titles; Dean Prof. TONY KENDRICK.

International College of Oriental Medicine: Green Hedges House, Green Hedges Ave, East Grinstead, RH19 1DZ; tel. (1342) 313-106; fax (1342) 335-104; e-mail info@orientalmed.ac.uk; internet www.orientalmed.ac.uk; f. 1972; accredited by the British Acupuncture Accreditation Board; BSc (Hons) Acupuncture validated by Univ. of Greenwich; 17 teachers; Joint Prin. PENNY KHARROUBI; Joint Prin. CRAIG MINTO.

Matrix College of Counselling and Psychotherapy: 18–20 Queen's Rd, Hethersett, NR9 3DB; tel. (1603) 812479; e-mail sue@matrix-training.org; internet www.matrix-training.org; f. 2001 as Matrix Integrative Training; programmes in integrative counselling validated by Middlesex Univ.; Dir Dr SUSIE JONES.

McTimoney College of Chiropractic: Kimber House, 1 Kimber Rd, Abingdon, OX14 1BZ; tel. (1235) 523-336; fax (1235) 523-576; e-mail courseoffice@mctimoney-college.ac.uk; internet www.mctimoney-college.ac.uk; f. 1972 as Oxfordshire School of Chiropractic; undergraduate, postgraduate courses in chiropractic; validated by Univ. of Wales; Prin. CHRISTINA CUNLIFFE.

Metanoia Institute: 13 North Common Rd, Ealing, London, W5 2QB; tel. (20) 8579-2505; fax (20) 8832-3070; e-mail info@metanoia.ac.uk; internet www.metanoia.ac.uk; professional training of counsellors, psychotherapists, counselling psychologists, coaching, organisational devt; courses validated by Middlesex Univ.; CEO SHEILA OWEN-JONES.

National Institute of Conductive Education: Cannon Hill House, 14 Russell Rd, Moseley, Birmingham, B13 8RD; tel. (1214) 491-569; e-mail mmccann@conductive-education.org.uk; internet www.conductive-education.org.uk; f. 1986; degree-level conductor training for handling children and adults with cerebral palsy; BA (Hons) Conductive Education from Univ. of Wolverhampton.

National Institute of Medical Herbalists: 54 Mary Arches St, Exeter, EX4 3BA; tel. (1392) 426022; fax (1392) 498963; e-mail info@nimh.org.uk; internet www.nimh.org.uk; f. 1864, as Nat. Asscn of Medical Herbalists; sets profession's educational standards and runs accreditation system for training establishments, maintains mandatory programmes of professional devt; publ. *European Journal of Herbal Medicine*.

School of Psychotherapy and Counselling Psychology: Regent's Park, London, NW1 4NS; tel. (20) 7487-7505; fax (20) 7487-7446; e-mail spc@regents.ac.uk; internet www.spc.ac.uk; f. 1990; attached to Regent's College; validation by Univ. of Wales; Head Dr JOHN NUTTALL (acting).

Sherwood Psychotherapy Training Institute: Thiskney House, 2 St James Terrace, Nottingham, NG1 6FW; tel. (115) 844-7904; fax (115) 924-2738; e-mail enquiries@spti.net; internet www.spti.net; f. 1987; full time and part time courses in psychotherapy and counselling; 200 students; Dir ROSEMARY LANGFORD-BELLABY.

MUSIC, DANCE AND DRAMA

Academy of Contemporary Music: Rodboro Bldgs, Bridge St, Guildford, GU1 4SB; tel. (1483) 500800; e-mail enquiries@acm.ac.uk; internet www.acm.ac.uk; music industry education; degree courses in music; other courses in music production; Founding Dir PHIL BROOKES.

Academy of Live and Recorded Arts: John Archer Way, London, SW18 3SX; tel. (20) 8870-6475; fax (20) 8875-0789; e-mail info@alra.co.uk; internet www.alra.co.uk; f. 1979; courses accredited by Nat. Council for Drama Training; centre in Wigan; course in acting, stage management; Chair. HARRY COWD; Co-Dir CLIVE DUNCAN; Co-Dir ADRIAN HALL.

Arts Educational Schools London: Cone Ripman House, 14 Bath Rd, Chiswick, London, W4 1LY; tel. (20) 8987-6666; fax (20) 8987-6699; internet www.artsed.co.uk; f. 1939 as the Cone Ripman School; undergraduate, postgraduate courses in acting, theatre and screenwriting; Prin. JANE HARRISON.

Bird College—Dance, Music and Theatre Performance: The Centre, 27 Station Rd, Sidcup, DA15 7EB; tel. (20) 8300-6004; fax (20) 8308-1370; e-mail luis.deabreu@birdcollege.co.uk; internet www.birdcollege.co.uk; f. 1946; performing arts college; offers degrees, foundation courses and diplomas validated by Univ. of Greenwich, Trinity College London; Prin. and Chief Exec. SHIRLEY COEN.

Birmingham School of Acting: International Office, Birmingham City Univ., Perry Barr, Birmingham, B42 2SU; tel. (1213) 316714; e-mail bcuinternational@enquiries.uk.com; internet www.bcu.ac.uk/pme/school-of-acting; f. 1936; attached to Faculty of Performance, Media and English at Birmingham City Univ.; specialist institution offering full-time higher education courses at undergraduate and postgraduate level; owned and operated by the Birmingham School of Speech and Drama Training Trust; 30 teachers; Dir STEPHEN SIMMS.

Brighton Institute of Modern Music: BIMM West, 38–42 Brunswick St, Hove, BN3 1EL; tel. (1273) 626666; e-mail info@bimm.co.uk; internet www.bimm.co.uk; 4 centres in Brighton and Bristol, 10 core courses in various areas; degree, diploma and certificate; validated by Univ. of Sussex; Prin. VASEEMA HAMILTON.

Bristol Old Vic Theatre School: 1–2 Downside Rd, Bristol, BS8 2XF; tel. (1179) 733-535; fax (1179) 809-258; e-mail enquiries@oldvic.ac.uk; internet www.oldvic.ac.uk; f. 1946; undergraduate and postgraduate courses in acting, stage management, theatre design, wardrobe and technical aspects of the theatre; Prin. PAUL RUMMER.

Central School of Speech and Drama: Embassy Theatre, 64 Eton Ave, London, NW3 3HY; tel. (20) 7722-8183; fax (20) 7722-4132; e-mail enquiries@csdd.ac.uk; internet www.cssd.ac.uk; f. 1906; attached to Univ. of London; undergraduate, postgraduate, PhD and research courses in art, design and the performing arts, in education and in therapy; 90 staff; 750 students; Prin. GARY HENDERSON.

Guildford School of Acting: Stag Hill Campus, Guildford, GU2 7XH; tel. (1483) 560-701; fax (1483) 684-070; e-mail gsaenquiries@gsa.surrey.ac.uk; internet www.conservatoire.org; f. 1964; subsidiary company of Univ. of Surrey; vocational training in acting, musical theatre, stage management; courses ranging from national diplomas and foundation degrees to postgraduate qualifications; 29 teachers; Dir. PETER BARLOW.

Guildhall School of Music and Drama: Silk St, Barbican, London, EC2Y 8DT; tel. (20) 7628-2571; fax (20) 7256-9438; e-mail info@gsmd.ac.uk; internet www.gsmd.ac.uk; f. 1880 by the Corpn of London; offers teaching in music, acting, technical theatre, professional devt and music therapy; 300 teachers; 800 students; Prin. BARRY IFE.

Italia Conti Academy of Theatre Arts: Italia Conti House, 23 Goswell Rd, London, EC1M 7AJ; tel. (20) 7608-0047; fax (20) 7253-1430; e-mail admin@italiaconti.com; internet www.italiaconti.com; f. 1911; offer full-time courses in theatre arts at secondary, further and higher education levels; Prin. A. M. SHEWARD.

Leeds College of Music: 3 Quarry Hill, Leeds, LS2 7PD; tel. (1132) 223-416; fax (1132) 438-798; e-mail enquiries@lcm.ac.uk; internet www.lcm.ac.uk; f. 1965 as Leeds Music Centre; offers higher and further education courses in jazz, classical and popular music, music production; 2,500 students (1,000 full-time, 1,500 part-time); Prin. PHILIP MEADEN.

Liverpool Institute for the Performing Arts: Mount St, Liverpool, L1 9HF; tel. (151) 330-3000; fax (151) 330-3131; e-mail reception@lipa.ac.uk; internet www.lipa.ac.uk; f. 1996; performing arts higher education instn; degrees administered by Liverpool John Moores Univ.; 80 teachers; 650 students; Chief Exec. and Prin. MARK FEATHERSTONE-WITTY.

London Academy of Music and Dramatic Art: 155 Talgarth Rd, London, W14 9DA; tel. (20) 8834-0500; fax (20) 8834-0501; e-mail enquiries@lamda.org.uk; internet www.lamda.org.uk; f. 1861; professional theatrical training, acting and stage management; Prin. JOANNA READ.

London Contemporary Dance School: The Place, 17 Duke's Rd, London, WC1H 9PY; tel. (20) 7121-1020; fax (20) 7121-1144; e-mail info@theplace.org.uk; internet www.theplace.org.uk/lcds; f. 1966; dance conservatoire; BA (Hons), postgraduate diploma, MA in contemporary dance; undergraduate course validated by Univ. of Kent; 27 teachers; Dir VERONICA LEWIS.

London Studio Centre: 42–50 York Way, London, N1 9AB; tel. (20) 7837-7741; fax (20) 7837-3248; internet www.london-studio-centre.co.uk; f. 1978; Bachelors courses in classical ballet, contemporary dance, jazz theatre dance, music theatre validated by Univ. of the Arts London; Dir NIC ESPINOSA; Librarian FIONA COMPTON.

Mountview Academy of Theatre Arts: Ralph Richardson Memorial Studios, Clarendon Rd, Wood Green, London, N22; tel. (20) 8881-2201; fax (20) 8829-0034; e-mail enquiries@mountview.org.uk; internet www.mountview.org.uk; undergraduate, postgraduate diploma, degree courses in acting, musical theatre and production arts; national qualifications in professional acting, musical theatre, and production skills validated by Trinity College London.

Northern School of Contemporary Dance: 98 Chapeltown Rd, Leeds, LS7 4BH; tel. (113) 219-3000; fax (113) 219-3030; e-mail info@nscd.ac.uk; internet www.nscd.ac.uk; f. 1985; training programme and bachelor in performing arts: contemporary dance and choreography; Prin. GURMIT HUKAM; Vice-Prin. RUSSELL TRIGG (acting); Vice-Prin. DEBORA JOHNSON (acting).

Rose Bruford College of Theatre and Performance: Lamorbey Park, Burnt Oak Lane, Sidcup, DA15 9DF; tel. (20) 8308-2600; e-mail enquiries@bruford.ac.uk; internet www.bruford.ac.uk; f. 1951, as Rose Bruford Training College for Speech and Drama; MPhil and PhD research degrees validated by Univ. of London; honours degree in professional acting and theatre practice validated by Univ. of Manchester; Prin. and CEO Prof. MICHAEL EARLEY.

Royal Academy of Dance: 36 Battersea Sq., London, SW11 3RA; tel. (20) 7326-8000; e-mail info@rad.org.uk; internet www.rad.org.uk; f. 1920; undergraduate and postgraduate courses in dance validated by Univ. of Surrey; centres in Wales and Scotland; Chief Exec. LUKE RITTNER; publs *Dance Gazette*, *UK & Ireland diary* (3 a year).

Royal Academy of Dramatic Art (RADA): 62–64 Gower St, London, WC1E 6ED; tel. (20) 7636-7076; fax (20) 7323-3865; e-mail enquiries@rada.ac.uk; internet www.rada.ac.uk; f. 1904; vocational training for actors, stage managers, directors, designers and technical stage craft specialists; library: 30,000 vols, 1,000 videocassettes, 500 DVDs; Dir EDWARD KEMP.

Royal Academy of Music: see University of London.

Royal College of Music: Prince Consort Rd, South Kensington, London, SW7 2BS; tel. (20) 7589-3643; fax (20) 7589-7740; e-mail info@rcm.ac.uk; internet www.rcm.ac.uk; f. 1882; BMus (Hons) degree, BSc in Physics with musical performance; Masters and Doctorate in music; 610 students; library: see under Libraries and Archives; Dir Prof. COLIN LAWSON.

Royal Northern College of Music: 124 Oxford Rd, Manchester, M13 9RD; tel. (161) 907-5200; fax (161) 273-7611; e-mail info@rncm.ac.uk; internet www.rncm.ac.uk; f. 1973; four-year BMus Hons in association with Univ. of Manchester; two-year foundation degree in popular music practice course; the Graduate School in Music; library: library contains extensive collection of MSS, reference works, gramophone records, tape cassettes, CDs, video cassettes, periodicals, and important archive material incl. an historical instrument collection; 150 teachers; 600 students; Prin. Prof. JONTY STOCKDALE.

Trinity Laban Conservatoire of Music and Dance: Trinity, King Charles Court, Old Royal Naval College, Greenwich, London, SE10 9JF; tel. (20) 8305-4444; fax (20) 8305-9444; e-mail info@tcm.ac.uk; internet www.trinitylaban.ac.uk; f. 2005 by merger of Trinity College of Music and Laban; undergraduate, postgraduate and one-year course programmes; 323 teachers; 570 students (500 full-time, 70 part-time); Prin. ANTHONY BOWNE; publ. *Dance Theatre Journal* (4 a year).

SCIENCE AND TECHNOLOGY

British Institute of Technology and E-Commerce: Avicenna House, 258–262 Romford Rd, London, E7 9HZ; tel. (20) 8552-3071; fax (20) 8552-3546; e-mail admissions@bite.ac.uk; internet bite.ac.uk; f. 2000; MBA, MA, MSc qualifications, LLM, BSc (Technology), BA (e-commerce), professional qualification, NVQs; degrees conferred by Univ. of East London, Coventry Univ. and Univ. of Wales; Prin. and Chief Exec. Dr MUHAMMAD FARMER; publ. *e-Britain*.

Camborne School of Mines: Cornwall Campus, Penryn, TR10 9EZ; tel. (1326) 371-800; fax (1326) 370-450; e-mail cornwall@exeter.ac.uk; internet www.ex.ac.uk/csm; f. 1888; attached to College of Engineering, Mathematics and Physical Sciences, Univ. of Exeter; undergraduate, postgraduate and research degree programmes in geology, mining, minerals processing and renewable energy; library: 30,000 vols; 25 teachers; 300 students; Head Prof. FRANCES WALL.

CECOS London College: 59 Compton Rd, Islington, London, N1 2YT; tel. (20) 7359-3316; fax (20) 7288-1599; e-mail info@cecos.co.uk; internet www.cecos.co.uk; f. 1998; courses in information technology, business admin., computer sciences; Dir Dr KEITH SHARP.

College of Technology London: 153–159 Bow Rd, London, E3 2SE; tel. (20) 8980-7888; fax (20) 8983-4911; e-mail info@ctlondon.ac.uk; internet www.ctlondon.ac.uk; 3 academic depts: business, information technology and academic English; library: 5,000 vols.

Farnborough College of Technology: Farnborough Campus, Boundary Rd, Farnborough, GU14 6SB; tel. (1252) 407-028; fax (1252) 407-041; e-mail admissions@farn-ct.ac.uk; internet www.farn-ct.ac.uk; f. 1957; 2 campuses, degrees by Univ. of Surrey; full-time, part-time and short courses in health, education, construction, education, engineering, business and media; Prin. CHRISTINE SLAYMAKER.

Herefordshire College of Technology: Hereford Campus, Folly Lane, Hereford, HR1 1LS; tel. (1432) 352-235; fax (1432) 353-449; e-mail enquiries@hct.ac.uk; internet www.hct.ac.uk; f. 1949; 2 campuses, 90 full-time vocational courses, courses available from foundation studies to Bachelors degree level; apprenticeships; library: 20,000 vols; 600 teachers; 7,000 students; Prin. and Chief Exec. IAN PEAKE.

National Computing Centre Education: Wilmslow Rd, Manchester, M20 2EZ; tel. (161) 438-6200; fax (161) 438-6240; e-mail customer.service@nccedu.com; internet www.nccedu.com; f. 1966; courses in business studies, business admin., computing and information systems; degrees validated by Univ. of Wales, Univ. of Greenwich and Univ. of Hertfordshire; centres in Asia (incl. Hong Kong), Africa, Middle East; Man. Dir Prof. FELIX STRAVENS.

National Film and Television School: Beaconsfield Studios, Station Rd, Beaconsfield, HP9 1LG; tel. (1494) 731-425; fax (1494) 674-042; e-mail info@nfts.co.uk; internet www.nftsfilm-tv.ac.uk; f. 1970 as National Film School; postgraduate and professional training for film and television production; 30 teachers; other visiting lecturers and tutors; 220 full-time students; 1,024 part-time; library: research and information library; Dir NIK POWELL.

Regents Theological College: West Malvern Rd, West Malvern, WR14 4AY; tel. (845) 302-6750; fax (845) 302-6752; e-mail info@regents-tc.ac.uk; internet www

.regentstheologicalcollege.org.uk; graduate and postgraduate degrees validated by Univ. of Wales and Univ. of Bangor; library: 36,000 vols; Gen. Man. ANDREW CAVE; Academic Registrar JOHN OWEN.

SAE London: 1412 High Rd, London, N20 9BH; tel. (20) 7923-9159; fax (20) 7691-7653; e-mail london@sae.edu; internet london.sae.edu; f. 1985; degrees validated by Middlesex Univ.; courses in audio production, digital film making, media practice; campuses in Oxford, Liverpool, Glasgow; Man. LUCA BARASSI.

Telford College of Arts and Technology: Haybridge Rd, Wellington, TF1 2NP; tel. (1952) 642-200; fax (1952) 642-293; internet www.tcat.ac.uk; 800 teachers; 17,000 students; Chair. MIKE LOWE; Prin. JANET ELLIS.

THEOLOGY AND RELIGIOUS STUDIES

All Nations Christian College: Easneye, Ware, SG12 8LX; tel. (1920) 443500; fax (1920) 462997; internet www.allnations.ac.uk; f. 1971 by merger of three missionary colleges; certificate, diploma and graduate degree course in biblical and inter-cultural studies; library: 50,000 books, papers, maps and audiovisual items; 12 full-time, 12 visiting; Exec. Dir MIKE WALL.

Cambridge Theological Federation: Jesus Lane, Cambridge, CB5 8BQ; tel. (1223) 741055; e-mail general-enquiries@theofed.cam.ac.uk; internet www.theofed.cam.ac.uk; f. 1972; courses validated by Anglia Ruskin Univ. and Cambridge Univ.; courses in Christian theology and pastoral theology; Prin. CHRISTINE AMJAD-ALI.

Centre for Youth Ministry: Trinity Business Centre, Stonehill Green, Swindon, SN5 7DG; tel. (1793) 418336; e-mail enquiries@centreforyouthministry.ac.uk; internet www.centreforyouthministry.ac.uk; courses validated by Staffordshire Univ., Univ. of Gloucestershire; centres in Wales and Ireland; courses in schools, youth and community work and practical theology, reflective practice and applied theology; Asst Centre Dir ROBIN BARDEN.

Cliff College: Calver, Hope Valley, S32 3XG; tel. (1246) 584-200; e-mail ilc@cliffcollege.ac.uk; internet www.cliffcollege.ac.uk; full-time, part-time courses in theology and mission at undergraduate and postgraduate level and research degrees; accredited by Univ. of Manchester; library: 30,000 items; 9 teachers; Prin. Rev. Dr CHRIS BLAKE; publ. *Cliff Today* (3 a year).

College of the Resurrection: Stocksbank Rd, Mirfield, WF14 0BW; tel. (1924) 490441; fax (1924) 492738; e-mail hscott@mirfield.org.uk; internet college.mirfield.org.uk; graduate, postgraduate and research degrees validated by Univ. of Sheffield; library: 2,600,000 vols, 9,000 periodicals; Prin. Rev. Dr JOE KENNEDY.

Islamic College for Advanced Studies: The Islamic College, 133 High Rd, Willesden, London, NW10 2SW; tel. (20) 8451-9993; fax (20) 8451-9994; e-mail info@islamic-college.ac.uk; internet www.islamic-college.ac.uk; f. 1998; partnership with Middlesex Univ.; A-level, certificate, diploma, undergraduate, postgraduate courses in Islamic studies, culture and theology; 24 teachers; Prin. M. S. BAHMANPOUR; publ. *Journal of Shi'a Islamic Studies*.

Leo Baeck College: The Sternberg Centre, 80 East End Rd, London, N3 2SY; tel. (20) 8349-5600; fax (20) 8349-5619; internet www.lbc.ac.uk; f. 1956 as Jewish Theological College; five year rabbinic programme, MA in Jewish education, advanced diploma in professional devt for Jewish education, foun-

dation courses for religion school teachers; Prin. Rabbi Prof. MARC SAPERSTEIN; publ. *European Judaism*.

Markfield Institute of Higher Education: Ratby Lane, Markfield, LE67 9SY; tel. (1530) 244-922; fax (1530) 243-102; e-mail info@mihe.org.uk; internet mihe.org.uk; f. 2000; study of Islam in an Islamic instn; postgraduate courses validated by Loughborough Univ.; library: 30,000 vols, 420 serials with 85 current journals; Dir Dr ATAULLAH SIDDIQUI.

Maryvale Institute: Maryvale House, Old Oscott Hill, Birmingham, B44 9AG; tel. (1213) 608-118; fax (1213) 666-786; internet www.maryvale.ac.uk; f. 1980; int. catholic distance-learning college for theology and religious education at undergraduate and postgraduate levels; courses validated by Open University; library: 15,000 vols; 21 teachers.

Oxford Centre for Mission Studies: Woodstock Rd, Oxford, OX2 6HR; tel. (1865) 556-071; fax (1865) 517-722; e-mail ocms@ocms.ac.uk; internet www.ocms.ac.uk; research degrees validated by Univ. of Wales and; library: 13,000 vols; Exec. Dir Dr WONSUK MA; Librarian RALPH BATES; publ. *Transformation*.

Queen's Foundation: Somerset Rd, Birmingham, B15 2QH; tel. (121) 454-1527; fax (121) 454-8171; e-mail enquire@queens.ac.uk; internet www.queens.ac.uk; f. 1828; research degrees validate by Univ. of Birmingham; graduate and postgraduate courses; library: 50,000 vols, 80 journals; Prin. Rev. Dr DAVID HEWLETT.

Redcliffe College: Horton Rd, Gloucester, GL1 3PT; tel. (1452) 308097; internet www.redcliffe.org; f. 1892; degrees validated by Univ. of Gloucestershire; courses in Asian studies, Bible and mission, global issues in contemporary mission, global leadership; Prin. ROB HAY.

Wesley Study Centre: 3 South Bailey, Durham, DH1 3RJ; tel. (191) 334-3850; fax (191) 334-3501; e-mail p.a.bissell@durham.ac.uk; internet www.dur.ac.uk/wsc.online; attached to Univ. of Durham; graduate and postgraduate theology and ministry courses validated by Univ. of Durham; Dir Rev. Dr CALVIN SAMUEL.

YMCA George Williams College: 199 Freemasons Rd, London, E16 3PY; tel. (20) 7540-4900; fax (20) 7511-4900; e-mail registry@ymca.ac.uk; internet www.ymca.ac.uk; f. 1970; undergraduate courses in youth and community work validated by Canterbury Christ Church Univ.; library: 25,000 vols; 1,000 students; Prin. MARY WOLFE; Librarian SAMANTHA MAKWANA.

Universities in Northern Ireland

QUEEN'S UNIVERSITY BELFAST

University Rd, Belfast, BT7 1NN
Telephone: (28) 9024-5133
Fax: (28) 9024-7895
E-mail: vc.office@qub.ac.uk
Internet: www.qub.ac.uk

Founded 1845, as Queen's College, original Univ. Charter 1908, present Charter 1982
State control
Language of instruction: English
Academic year: September to September

Chancellor: KAMALESH SHARMA
Pro-Chancellor: Sir DAVID FELL
Pro-Chancellor: ROTHA JOHNSTON

Pres. and Vice-Chancellor: Prof. PETER GREGSON

Pro-Vice-Chancellor for Education and Students: Prof. ELLEN DOUGLAS-COWIE

Pro-Vice-Chancellor for Academic Planning and External Relations: Prof. TONY GALLAGHER

Pro-Vice-Chancellor for Research and Postgraduates: Prof. JAMES MCELNAY

Registrar: JAMES O'KANE

Library Systems Man.: ELIZABETH TRAYNOR

Library: see under Libraries and Archives

Number of teachers: 1,600 full-time

Number of students: 17,500 (full-time and part-time); 10,000 part-time students enrolled at Institute of Lifelong Learning

DEANS

Faculty of Arts, Humanities and Social Sciences: Prof. SHANE O'NEILL

Faculty of Engineering and Physical Sciences: Prof. TOM MILLAR

Faculty of Medicine, Health and Life Sciences: Prof. SEAN GORMAN

PROFESSORS

Faculty of Arts, Humanities and Social Sciences (73 University Rd, Belfast, BT7 1NN; tel. (28) 9097-5347; fax (28) 9024-9864; e-mail deansofficeahss@qub.ac.uk; internet www.qub.ac.uk/fhum):

ALCORN, M., Music and Sonic Arts
ANDREW, M., English
BALES, R., Languages, Literatures and (Performing) Arts
BELL, D., Languages, Literatures and (Performing) Arts
BEW, P., Politics, International Studies and Philosophy
BOWLER, P., History and Anthropology
BURNETT, M., English
CAMPBELL, J., History and Anthropology
CARAHER, B., English
CAREY, M., Management and Economics
CARSON, C., English
CLOUGH, P., Education
CONNOLLY, P., Education
CONNOLLY, S., History and Anthropology
CULLEN, B., Politics, International Studies and Philosophy
DALY, M., Sociology, Social Policy and Social Work
DAVIES, S., Languages, Literatures and (Performing) Arts
DAWSON, N., Law
DEMIRAG, S., Management and Economics
DICKSON, B., Law
DONNAN, H., History and Anthropology
DOUGLAS COWIE, E., Arts, Humanities and Social Sciences
ELWOOD, J., Education
ENGLISH, R., Politics, International Studies and Philosophy
EVANS, J., Politics, International Studies and Philosophy
FORKER, J., Management and Economics
GALLAGHER, A., Education
GARDNER, J., Arts, Humanities and Social Sciences
GEOGHEGAN, V., Politics, International Studies and Philosophy
GORMAN, J., Politics, International Studies and Philosophy
GRAY, P., History and Anthropology
GREEN, I., History and Anthropology
GUELKE, A., Politics, International Studies and Philosophy
HARVEY, C., Law
HAYTON, D., History and Anthropology
HELLAWELL, P., Music and Sonic Arts
HILLYARD, P., Sociology, Social Policy and Social Work
HYNDMAN, N., Management and Economics
JACKSON, J., Law
JEFFCUTT, P., Management and Economics

JEFFERY, K., History and Anthropology
JOHNSTON, D., Languages, Literatures and (Performing) Arts
KENNEDY, L., History and Anthropology
LEITH, P., Law
MACDONALD, C., Politics, International Studies and Philosophy
MAGENNIS, H., English
MANN, M., Sociology, Social Policy and Social Work
MCEVOY, J., Politics, International Studies and Philosophy
MCEVOY, K., Law
MCKILLOP, D., Management and Economics
MCLAUGHLIN, E., Sociology, Social Policy and Social Work
MILTON, K., History and Anthropology
MOORE, M., Management and Economics
MORISON, J., Law
MULLETT, M., History and Anthropology
O'DOWD, L., Sociology, Social Policy and Social Work
O'DOWD, M., History and Anthropology
O'HEARN, D., Sociology, Social Policy and Social Work
O'NEILL, S., Politics, International Studies and Philosophy
PHILIP, G., Management and Economics
PINKERTON, J., Sociology, Social Policy and Social Work
PRIOR, L., Sociology, Social Policy and Social Work
SCRATON, P., Law
SHEEHAN, E., English
SIMPSON, P., English
SMACZNY, J., Music and Sonic Arts
TEAGUE, P., Management and Economics
THOMPSON, J., English
TURNER, J., Management and Economics
TURNER, S., Law
WALKER, B., Politics, International Studies and Philosophy
WALKER, G., Politics, International Studies and Philosophy
WHEELER, S., Law
WHITEHEAD, D., History and Anthropology
WHITEHOUSE, H., History and Anthropology
WIENER, A., Politics, International Studies and Philosophy
WILFORD, R., Politics, International Studies and Philosophy
WILLIAMS, F., Arts, Humanities and Social Sciences
WOODFIELD, I., Music and Sonic Arts

Faculty of Engineering and Physical Sciences (NI Technology Centre, Cloreen Park, Belfast, BT9 5HN; tel. (28) 9097-5443; fax (28) 9097-4536; e-mail deaneps@qub.ac.uk; internet www.qub.ac.uk/feng):

ALLEN, S. J., Chemical Engineering
ARMITAGE, D. H., Pure Mathematics
ARMSTRONG, C. G., Mechanical and Manufacturing Engineering
ARMSTRONG, G. A., Electrical and Electronic Engineering
ATKINSON, R., Physics and Astronomy
BASHEER, P. A. M., Civil Engineering
BELL, D. A., Computer Science
BELL, K. L., Applied Mathematics and Theoretical Physics
BLAIR, G. P., Mechanical and Aerospace Engineering
BOYD, D. R., Chemistry
BURCH, R., Chemistry
CAMPBELL, B., Geography
CLELAND, D. J., Civil Engineering
CLINT, M., Computer Science
COWAN, C. F. N., Electrical and Electronic Engineering
COWIE, R., Psychology
CRAWFORD, R., Mechanical and Aerospace Engineering
CROOKES, D., Computer Engineering

CROSSLEY, P., Electrical and Electronic Engineering
CROTHERS, D. S. F., Applied Mathematics and Theoretical Physics
DE SILVA, A. P., Chemistry
DOUGLAS, R., Mechanical and Manufacturing Engineering
DUFTON, P. L., Physics and Astronomy
FEE, A. J., Mechanical and Manufacturing Engineering
FINNIS, M. W., Physics and Astronomy
FLECK, R., Mechanical and Manufacturing Engineering
FUSCO, V. F., Electrical and Electronic Engineering
GAMBLE, H. S., Electrical and Electronic Engineering
GRAHAM, W. G., Physics and Astronomy
HALL, V., Archaeology and Palaeoecology
HARDACRE, C., Chemistry
HARKIN-JONES, E. M. A., Mechanical and Manufacturing Engineering
HEPPER, P., Psychology
HIBBERT, A., Applied Mathematics and Theoretical Physics
HOWE, J., Environmental Planning
HU, P., Chemistry
IRWIN, G. W., Electrical and Electronic Engineering
KALIN, R. M., Civil Engineering
KEENAN, F. P., Applied Mathematics and Theoretical Physics
LATIMER, C. J., Physics and Astronomy
LEWIS, C. L. S., Physics and Astronomy
LIVINGSTONE, D. N., Mechanical and Aerospace Engineering
MAGEE, T. R. A., Chemical Engineering
MALLORY, J., Archaeology and Palaeoecology
MANN, J., Chemistry
MARSHALL, A. J., Electrical and Electronic Engineering
MCCANNY, J. V., Electrical and Electronic Engineering
MCCORMAC, G., Archaeology and Palaeoecology
MCELDOWNEY, J. M., Environmental Planning
MCGARVEY, J. J., Chemistry
MCGUINNESS, C., Psychology
ORFORD, J. D., Geography
ORR, J. F., Mechanical and Manufacturing Engineering
PERROTT, R. H., Computer Science
RAGHUNATHAN, S. R., Aeronautical Engineering
SCOTT, N. S., Computer Science
SEDDON, K. R., Chemistry
SHEEHY, N., Psychology
SMITH, B., Geography
SMYTH, A., Environmental Planning
TAYLOR, K. T. A., Applied Mathematics and Theoretical Physics
WALMSLEY, D. G., Physics and Astronomy
WALTERS, H. R. J., Applied Mathematics and Theoretical Physics
WHALLEY, W. B., Geography
WHITAKER, M. A. B., Physics and Astronomy
WICKSTEAD, A. W., Pure Mathematics
WILLIAMS, I., Physics and Astronomy
WOODS, R., Electrical and Electronic Engineering
WOOLLEY, T. A., Architecture

Faculty of Medicine, Health and Life Sciences (Whitla Medical Bldg, 97 Lisburn Rd, Belfast, BT9 7BL; tel. (28) 9097-5177; e-mail dean-mhls@qub.ac.uk; internet www.qub.ac.uk/fmhs):

AMES, J., Biological and Food Sciences
CAMPBELL, F., Biomedical Sciences
CHAKRAVARTHY, U., Biomedical Sciences
COSBY, S., Biomedical Sciences
DAVIES, R., Biological and Food Sciences
DRING, M., Biological and Food Sciences

ELBORN, J., Medicine and Dentistry
ELWOOD, R., Biological and Food Sciences
ENNIS, M., Medicine and Dentistry
EVANS, A., Medicine and Dentistry
FEE, J., Medicine and Dentistry
FREEMAN, R., Medicine and Dentistry
GORMAN, S., Pharmacy
HALL, P., Medicine and Dentistry
HAMILTON, P., Biomedical Sciences
HARKIN, D., Biomedical Sciences
HAY, R., Medicine and Dentistry
HIRST, D., Pharmacy
HUGHES, A., Medicine and Dentistry
HUGHES, C., Pharmacy
HUTCHINSON, G., Biological and Food Sciences
JOHNSTON, G., Medicine and Dentistry
JOHNSTON, J., Biomedical Sciences
JOHNSTON, P., Biomedical Sciences
JONES, D., Pharmacy
KEE, F., Medicine and Dentistry
LAMEY, P., Medicine and Dentistry
LAPPIN, T., Biomedical Sciences
LARKIN, M., Biological and Food Sciences
LEWIS, S., Medicine and Dentistry
LINDEN, G., Medicine and Dentistry
LYNCH, E., Medicine and Dentistry
MAGGS, C., Biological and Food Sciences
MAULE, A., Biological and Food Sciences
MAXWELL, A., Medicine and Dentistry
MCCLURE, N., Medicine and Dentistry
MCDERMOTT, B., Medicine and Dentistry
MCELNAY, J., Medicine, Health and Life Sciences
MCVEIGH, G., Biomedical Sciences
MIRAKHUR, R., Medicine and Dentistry
MONTGOMERY, W., Biological and Food Sciences
ORR, J., Nursing and Midwifery
PORTER, S., Nursing and Midwifery
REILLY, P., Medicine and Dentistry
REYNOLDS, G., Medicine and Dentistry
RIMA, B., Biomedical Sciences
SAVAGE, J., Medicine and Dentistry
SHAW, C., Pharmacy
SHIELDS, M., Medicine and Dentistry
STITT, A., Biomedical Sciences
STOUT, R., Medicine and Dentistry
TRIMBLE, E., Medicine and Dentistry
VANDENBROECK, K., Pharmacy
WALKER, B., Pharmacy
WOOLFSON, D., Pharmacy
YOUNG, I., Medicine and Dentistry

UNIVERSITY OF ULSTER

Coleraine Campus, Cromore Rd, Coleraine, BT52 1SA
Jordanstown Campus, Shore Rd, Newtownabbey, BT37 0QB
Belfast Campus, York St, Belfast, BT15 1ED
Magee Campus, Northland Rd, Londonderry, BT48 7JL

Telephone: (28) 7012-3456
E-mail: online@ulster.ac.uk
Internet: www.ulster.ac.uk

Founded 1984 by Royal Charter following merger of New Univ. of Ulster and Ulster Polytechnic
State control
Academic year: September to May
Chancellor: Sir RICHARD NICHOLS
Pro-Chancellor: Prof. ROSEMARY PETER-GALLAGHER
Pro-Chancellor: Dr JEREMY HARBINSON
Pro-Chancellor: GERRY MALLON
Vice-Chancellor: Prof. RICHARD BARNETT (acting)
Pro-Vice-Chancellor for Communication and External Affairs: Prof. ALASTAIR ADAIR
Pro-Vice-Chancellor for Sport and Student Services: Prof. JIM ALLEN
Pro-Vice-Chancellor for Research and Innovation: Prof. NORMAN BLACK

Pro-Vice-Chancellor for Teaching and Learning: Prof. DENISE MCALISTER
Dean for Academic Planning and Magee: Prof. DEIRDRE HEENAN
Dean for Campus Devt, Coleraine Campus and Provost: Prof. ROBERT HUTCHINSON

Number of teachers: 1,092
Number of students: 25,339 (17,075 full time and 8,264 part time)

DEANS

Faculty of Arts: Prof. PÓL O'DOCHARTAIGH
Faculty of Art, Design and the Built Environment: Prof. IAN MONTGOMERY
Faculty of Computing and Engineering: Prof. RICHARD MILLAR (acting)
Faculty of Life and Health Sciences: Prof. HUGH MCKENNA
Faculty of Social Sciences: Prof. PAUL CARMICHAEL
Ulster Business School: Prof. MARIE MCHUGH

PROFESSORS

Faculty of Arts (Univ. of Ulster Coleraine Campus, Cromore Rd, Coleraine, BT52 1SA; tel. (28) 7032-4517; fax (28) 7032-4925; e-mail arts@ulster.ac.uk; internet www.arts.ulster.ac.uk):

BRADFORD, R. W., Literary History and Theory
GILLESPIE, J., French
JEDRZEJEWSKI, J., Comparative Literature
JONES, G. J., Social and Intellectual History
KENNEDY-ANDREWS, E., English
KOCKEL, U., Ethnology and Folk Life
LARRES, K., History and International Affairs
MACMATHÚNA, S., Irish Studies
McLOONE, M., Film Studies
McMINN, J. M., Anglo-Irish Literature
NIC CRAITH, M., Irish Culture and Language
O'CORRAIN, A. P., Modern Irish Studies
O'DOCHARTAIGH, P., German
TONER, G., Irish Languages and Literature
UPTON, C., Drama
MOORE, P., Creative Technologies
THATCHER, I., History

Faculty of Art, Design and the Built Environment (Univ. of Ulster, Belfast Campus, York St, Belfast, BT15 1ED; tel. (28) 9036-6310; fax (28) 9036-6816; e-mail jai.montgomery@ulster.ac.uk; internet www.adbe.ulster.ac.uk):

ALI, F., Building Services Engineering
BERRY, J. N., Urban Planning and Property Development
DELICHATSIOS, M., Fire Safety and Engineering
DOHERTY, W. J., Video Art
FLEMING, K., Textile Art
GRAY, P., Housing
HEANEY, G., Construction
HEWITT, N., Energy
HINE, J. P., Transport
KELLY, W., Irish Visual Culture
LLOYD, G. M., Urban Planning
MACLENNAN, M., Fine Art
MCCLELLAND, B., Design
MCGREAL, W. S., Property Research
MOLKOV, V., Hydrogen Fire Safety Science
MONTGOMERY, I., Design
NADJAI, A., Fire Structural Engineering
NOVOZHILOV, V., Fire Dynamics
PARSA, A. G., Urban Planning and Business Development
SEAWRIGHT, P., Photography
WOODSIDE, A. R., Highways Engineering
WRIGHT, T., Visual Arts
YOHANIS, Y., Building Services Engineering

Faculty of Computing and Engineering (Univ. of Ulster, Jordanstown Campus, Shore Rd, Newtownabbey, BT37 0QB; tel. (28) 9036-6855; fax (28) 9036-6803; e-mail engineering@ulster.ac.uk; internet www.compeng.ulster.ac.uk):

ANDERSON, J. M. C. C., Biomedical Engineering
ANDERSON, T. J., Interactive Computing
BROWN, N. M. D., Chemistry (Surface Science)
BUSTARD, D. W., Computing Science
CLARKE, R. B., Mechanical Engineering
DAVIS, J., Biomedical Sensors
ESCALONA, O. J., Cardiovascular Research
FARAHMAND, K., Mathematics
HULL, M. E. C., Computing Science
MAGUIRE, L. P., Computational Intelligence
MAGUIRE, P. D., Plasmas and Nanofabrication
McCLEAN, S. I., Mathematics
MCGINNITY, T. M., Intelligent Systems Engineering
MCKEAG, D., Product Development
MCKEVITT, P., Digital Multimedia
MCLAUGHLIN, J. A., Advanced Functional Materials
MCTEAR, M., Knowledge Engineering
MEENAN, B. J., Biomedical Materials
MILLAR, R. J., Computer Science
MULVENNA, M. D., Computer Science
NUGENT, C. D., Biomedical Engineering
PAPKONSTANTINOU, P., Advanced Materials
PARR, G. P., Telecommunications
SCOTNEY, B. W., Informatics

Faculty of Life and Health Sciences (Univ. of Ulster, Coleraine Campus, Cromore Rd, Coleraine, BT52 1SA; tel. (28) 7032-4491; fax (28) 7032-4596; e-mail science@ulster.ac.uk; internet www.science.ulster.ac.uk):

ANDERSON, R. S., Vision Science
BANAT, I., Microbiology
BJOURSON, A. J., Genomics
BROWN, J., Primary Health Care—General Practice
BUNTING, B. P., Psychology
CAIRNS, S. E., Psychology
COATES, V., Nursing Research
COOK, T.,
COOPER, J. A. G., Coastal Studies
DAY, K. R., Environmental Sciences
DOBBS, F., Primary Care
DOLK, H. M., Epidemiology and Health Services Research
DOOLEY, J. S. G., Microbiology
DOWNES, C. S., Cancer Biology
DUBITZKY, W., Bioinformatics
EASTWOOD, D. A., Environmental Studies
FLATT, P. R., Biological and Biomedical Sciences
GILLAN, U., International Primary Health Care
HANNIGAN, B. M., Biomedical Sciences
HARRISON, S. J., Social Anthropology
HOWARD, V., Bioimaging
JACKSON, D., Coastal Geomorphology
KERNOHAN, W. G., Health Research
LESLIE, J., Psychology
LIDDELL, C., Psychology
LIVINGSTONE, M. B. E., Nutrition
MARCHANT, R., Microbial Biotechnology
McCANCE, T., Nursing Research and Development
McCARRON, P., Pharmaceutics
McCLENAGHAN, N., Bio-Innovation and Enterprise
McCLOSKEY, J., Geophysics
McCONKEY, R. A., Developmental Disabilities
McCORMACK, B., Nursing Research
McDONOUGH, S. M., Health and Rehabilitation
McDOWELL, D. A., Food Studies
McHALE, A. P., Medical Biotechnology

McKELVEY-MARTIN, V., Molecular Biosciences
McKENNA, H. P., Nursing
McKEOWN, S. R., Cancer Biology
McMULLAN, G., Microbiology
McNULTY, H. M., Nutritional Science
MURPHY, M., Sports and Exercise
O'HARTE, F. P. M, Endocrinology and Metabolism
PARAHOO, K. A., Nursing and Health Research
PIERSCIONEK, K., Vision Science
POULTON, B. C., Community Health Nursing
RAE, G., Psychology
RIPPEY, B., Environmental Science
RUSHTON, B. S., Botany
SAKMANN, B., Biomedical Sciences
SINCLAIR, M., Midwifery Research
SOTO, A., Cancer Development
SMYTH, W. F., Bio-analytical Chemistry
STEACEY, S., Earthquake Physics
STRAIN, J. J., Human Nutrition
STRINGER, M., Psychology
WALLACE, E., Sports Biomechanics
WALSH, D. M., Rehabilitation Research
WELSH, R., Food Science and Nutrition
WILSON, R., Psychology

Faculty of Social Sciences (Univ. of Ulster, Jordanstown Campus, Shore Rd, Newtownabbey, BT37 0QB; tel. (28) 9036-6157; fax (28) 9036-6806; e-mail socsci@ulster.ac.uk; internet www.socsci.ulster.ac.uk):

AUGHEY, A. H., Politics
BELL, C. M., Public International Law
BIRRELL, W. D., Social Administration and Policy
BOROOAH, V. K., Applied Economics
CAMPBELL, C., Law
CARMICHAEL, P., Public Policy/Government
ERRIDGE, A. F., Public Policy and Management
GEARY, F., Economic History
HAMBER, B., Incore
HARGIE, O. D. W., Communication
HEENAN, D. A., Social Policy
HENRY, A. M., Linguistics
HUME, J., Incore
KNOX, C. G., Comparative Public Policy
McALEAVY, G. J., Further and Higher Education
McALISTER, D. A., Health Policy
McWILLIAMS, M. M., Women's Studies
MORAN, A., Education
NI AOLAIN, F., Law
O'CONNOR, J. S., Social Policy
OFFER, J. W., Social Theory and Policy
OSBORNE, R. D., Applied Policy Studies
OSMANI, S. R., Applied Economics
PATTERSON, H. H., Politics
ROBINSON, G., Social Research
ROLSTON, W. J., Sociology
SMITH, A., Education
THAIN, C., Politics
TRIDIMAS, G., Political Economy
WILSON, J., Communication

Ulster Business School (Univ. of Ulster, Coleraine Campus, Cromore Rd, Coleraine, BT52 1SA; tel. (28) 9036-6351; fax (28) 9036-6805; e-mail business@ulster.ac.uk; internet www.business.ulster.ac.uk):

BALLANTINE, J., Accounting
BOYD, S., Tourism
BROWN, S., Marketing Research
CARSON, D., Marketing
GILMORE, A. J., Services Marketing
GLASS, J. C., Applied Financial Economics
GREENAN, K., Management Education
HAMILL, P., Finance and Investment
HUMPHREYS, P. K., Operations Management
KIRK, R. J., Accounting and Finance
McADAM, R., Innovation Management
McCOY, J., Management Decvelopment

McGOWAN, P., Entrepreneurship and Business Development
McHUGH, M. L., Organizational Behaviour
McIVOR, R., Operations Management
MURRAY, A. E., Hospitality Management
O'REILLY, M. D., International Business Strategy
QUINN, B., Retail Accounting
WARD, A. M., Accounting
WARD, J. D., Taxation

Colleges in Northern Ireland

These institutions are not able to award their own degrees, but offer courses leading to a degree from a recognized body.

Belfast Bible College: Glenburn Rd South, Belfast, Dunmurry, BT17 9JP; tel. (28) 9030-1551; e-mail info@belfastbiblecollege.com; internet www.belfastbiblecollege.com; f. 1943, as Belfast Bible School and Missionary Training Home; attached to Queen's Univ. Belfast; courses in youth and community work and practical theology; undergraduate and postgraduate programmes in conjunction with Queen's Univ. Belfast and Univ. of Cumbria; library: 16,000 vols, 87 journals; 200 students; Prin. IAN DICKSON (acting); Librarian DOROTHY ANDERSON.

Belfast Metropolitan College: The Directorate, Gerald Moag Campus, Bldg 1, Level 2, Room 9, 125–153 Millfield, Belfast, BT1 1HS; tel. (28) 9026-5459; fax (28) 9026-5401; e-mail central_admissions@belfastmet.ac.uk; internet www.belfastmet.ac.uk; f. 1991, from College of Technology (f. 1901), College of Business Studies and Rupert Stanley College; full-time courses conducted at Brunswick St, Castlereagh, College Sq., Millfield, Tower St, Whiterock Campus bldgs; acad. depts of business and management, community education and training, computing and admin. studies, continuing education, creative and health studies, general education, hospitality, leisure and tourism, technology; 1,000 teachers; 53,000 students; Chair. RICHARD O'RAWE; Dir and Chief Exec. MAIRE-THÉRÈSE McGIVERN.

College of Agriculture, Food and Rural Enterprise: Greenmount Campus, 45 Tirgracy Rd, Antrim, BT41 4PS; tel. (28) 9052-4420; e-mail enquiries@cafre.ac.uk; internet www.cafre.ac.uk; higher national certificate, diploma and degree courses in agriculture and animal care; campuses in Antrim, Enniskillen, Loughry.

Irish Baptist College: 19 Hillsborough Rd, Moira, BT67 0HG; tel. (28) 9261-9267; internet www.irishbaptistcollege.co.uk; f. 1892; undergraduate and postgraduate courses, validated by the University of Chester, in theology, ministry and philosophy; 50 students; Prin. EDWIN EWART; Registrar VALERIE HAMILTON.

North West Regional College: Londonderry Campus, Strand Rd, Londonderry, BT48 7AL; tel. (28) 7127-6000; fax (28) 7126-0520; internet www.nwrc.ac.uk; f. 2007, by merger of Limavady College and North West Institute; campuses in Limavady, Londonderry and Strabane; smaller centres situated throughout North West; 24,000 students; Prin. and Chief Exec. S MURPHY; Library Man. JONATHAN MOOR.

Northern Regional College: Antrim Campus, Fountain St, Antrim, BT41 4AL; tel. (28) 9446-3916; fax (28) 9446-5132; internet www.nrc.ac.uk; campuses in Antrim, Ballymena, Ballymoney, Coleriane, Larne, Magherafelt and Newtownabbey; faculties of access, built

environment and design, business, community, engineering, hair and beauty therapies, hospitality and catering, IT, media and performing arts, science, social care and early years, sport and essential skills, travel and tourism; library: 35,000 vols, 3,000 ebooks, 70 journal titles; Dir T. NEILANDS; Sec. JIM HUNTER.

Saint Mary's University College: 191 Falls Rd, Belfast, BT12 6FE; tel. (28) 9032-7678; fax (28) 9033-3719; internet www.stmarys-belfast.ac.uk; f. 1900, as St Mary's Training College, present name and status 1985; attached to Queen's Univ. Belfast; faculties of education, liberal arts; library: 90,000 vols, 100 periodicals and newspapers; Chair. Rev. NOEL TREANOR; Vice-Chair. Rev. DONAL McKEOWN; Prin. Prof. PETER B. FINN; Librarian FELICITY JONES.

South Eastern Regional College: Lisburn Campus, 39 Castle St, Lisburn, BT27 4SU; tel. (28) 9267-7225; fax (28) 9267-7291; e-mail info@serc.ac.uk; internet www.serc.ac.uk; f. 1914; main campuses in Bangor, Downpatrick, Lisburn and Newtownards, Newcastle and Ballynahinch; Chair. BRIAN ACHESON; Prin. and Chief Exec. KEN WEBB.

South West College: Enniskillen Campus, Fairview, 1 Dublin Rd, Enniskillen, BT74 6AE; tel. (845) 603-1881; fax (28) 6632-6357; e-mail enquiries@swc.ac.uk; internet www.swc.ac.uk; campuses in Cookstown, Dungannon, Enniskillen and Omagh; 500 teachers; 18,500 students; Chair. JOSEPH MARTIN (acting).

Southern Regional College: The Directorate, SRC Newry Campus, Patrick St, Newry, BT35 8DN; tel. (28) 3026-1071; fax (28) 3025-9679; e-mail info@src.ac.uk; internet www.src.ac.uk; offers over 600 courses; campuses in Armagh, Banbridge, Newry, Portadown, Kikeel and Lurgan; 1,100 teachers; 45,000 students; Chief Exec. BRIAN DORAN; Chair. ANDREW SAUNDERS; Vice-Chair. ANGELA COFFEY.

Stranmillis University College: Stranmillis Rd, Belfast, BT9 5DY; tel. (28) 9038-1271; fax (28) 9066-4423; e-mail info@stran.ac.uk; internet www.stran.ac.uk; f. 1922; attached to Queen's Univ. Belfast; depts of initial teacher education, early childhood education, health and physical education; Chair. S. COSTELLO; Vice-Chair. S. E. D. BELL; Prin. and Chief Exec. Dr ANNE HEASLETT.

Union Theological College: 108 Botanic Ave, Belfast, BT7 1JT; tel. (28) 9020-5080; fax (28) 9020-5099; e-mail admin@union.ac.uk; internet www.union.ac.uk; f. 1978, by merger of Assembly's College (f. 1853) and Magee College (f. 1865); attached to Institute of Theology, Queen's University Belfast; 3 depts: biblical studies; systematic theology and church history; practical theology and min.; library: 60,000 vols, 20,000 pamphlets, 100 journals and periodicals; Registrar and Admin. SANDRA McKINNEY; Librarian DAVID KERRY.

Universities in Scotland

EDINBURGH NAPIER UNIVERSITY

Merchiston Campus, 10 Colinton Rd, Edinburgh, EH14 1DJ

Telephone: (131) 455-3555
Fax: (131) 455-6464
E-mail: info@napier.ac.uk
Internet: www.napier.ac.uk

Founded 1964 as Napier Technical College, present name and status 2012
Academic year: August to May

Chancellor: TIM WATERSTONE

Prin. and Vice-Chancellor: Prof. Dame JOAN STRINGER
Vice-Prin.: Prof. JOHN DUFFIELD
Vice-Prin.: Dr JENNY REES
Univ. Sec.: Dr GERRY WEBBER
Dir of Learning Information Services: CHRIS PINDER

Library of 210,000 vols
Number of teachers: 879
Number of students: 17,605

DEANS

Business School: Prof. GEORGE STONEHOUSE
Faculty of Engineering, Computing and Creative Industries: Dr SANDRA CAIRNCROSS
Faculty of Health, Life and Social Sciences: IAIN MCINTOSH

GLASGOW CALEDONIAN UNIVERSITY

Cowcaddens Rd, Glasgow, G4 0BA

Telephone: (141) 331-3000
Fax: (141) 331-3005
E-mail: helpline@gcal.ac.uk
Internet: www.caledonian.ac.uk

Founded 1971 as Glasgow Polytechnic; merged with The Queen's College; present name and status 1993
State control
Academic year: September to June

Chancellor: Prof. Dr MUHAMMAD YUNUS
Prin. and Vice-Chancellor: Prof. PAMELA GILLIES
Vice-Prin. and Pro-Vice-Chancellor for External Relations: Prof. KAREN STANTON
Vice-Prin. and Pro-Vice-Chancellor for Learning and Teaching: Prof. MIKE MANNION
Pro-Vice-Chancellor for Strategy: Prof. MIKE SMITH
Vice-Prin. and Exec. Dir of Finance: DAVID BEEBY
Vice-Prin. and Univ. Sec.: JAN HULME
Chief Information Officer: JEFF MURRAY (acting)

Number of students: 17,000

DEANS

Caledonian Business School: Prof. ŽELJKO ŠEVIĆ
School of Built and Natural Environment: Prof. PETER KENNEDY
School of Engineering and Computing: Prof. MALCOLM ALLAN (acting)
School of Health: Prof. FRANK CROSSAN
School of Law and Social Sciences: Prof. BILL HUGHES (acting)
School of Life Sciences: Prof. KEVAN M. A. GARTLAND

HERIOT-WATT UNIVERSITY

Edinburgh Campus: Edinburgh, EH14 4AS
Scottish Borders Campus: Netherdale, Galashiels, TD1 3HF

Telephone: (131) 449-5111 (Edinburgh); (1896) 753351 (Scottish Borders)
Fax: (131) 449-5153 (Edinburgh); (1896) 758965 (Scottish Borders)
E-mail: enquiries@hw.ac.uk
Internet: www.hw.ac.uk

Founded 1821 as Edinburgh School of Arts; became Heriot-Watt College 1885; present name and status 1966
Academic year: September to August

Chancellor: Baroness SUSAN GREENFIELD
Prin. and Vice-Chancellor: Prof. STEVE CHAPMAN
Vice-Prin.: Prof. JULIAN D. C. JONES
Sr. Deputy Prin.: Prof. ANDY C. WALKER
Deputy Prin. for Learning and Teaching: Prof. ROBERT J. M. CRAIK

Deputy Prin. for Research and Knowledge Transfer: Prof. ALAN MILLER
Sec.: ANN MARIE DALTON
Librarian: GILL A. MCDONALD (acting)
Number of teachers: 450
Number of students: 23,000

HEADS OF SCHOOLS

Edinburgh Business School: Prof. KEITH G. LUMSDEN (Dir)
Institute of Petroleum Engineering: Prof. S. STEWART
School of Built Environment: Prof. GARRY PENDER
School of Engineering and Physical Sciences: (vacant)
School of Life Sciences: Prof. D. HOPKINS
School of Management and Languages: Prof. G. HOGG
School of Mathematical and Computer Sciences: Prof. PHILIP DE WILDE
School of Textiles and Design: Prof. ALISON J. HARLEY (acting)

PROFESSORS

School of the Built Environment (tel. (131) 451-4644; fax (131) 451-4617; e-mail a.j.ormston@hw.ac.uk):

ASPINALL, P., Building Engineering and Surveying
BANFILL, P., Construction Materials
BRAMLEY, G., Urban Studies
CAO, Z., Civil Engineering
CHRISP, T., Civil Engineering
CRAIK, R., Acoustics, Deputy Principal (Teaching and Learning)
DHILLON, B., Building Engineering and Surveying
HULL, A., Spatial Planning
JENKINS, P., Architecture and Human Settlements
JONES, C., Estate Management
JOWITT, P., Sustainable Technology
KAKA, A., Construction Economics and Management and William Watson Chair, Dubai Campus
MAY, I., Civil Engineering
MCCARTER, W., Civil Engineering Materials
OGUNLANA, S., Construction Project Management
PAWSON, H., Housing Policy
PENDER, G., Civil Engineering
PRIOR, A., Planning and Housing
ROAF, S., Architectural Engineering
ROBERTSON, B., School of the Built Environment
SWAFFIELD, J., Building Services Engineering
WANG, Y., Urban Studies

School of Engineering and Physical Sciences (tel. (131) 451-3082; fax (131) 451-3136; e-mail l.bruce@hw.ac.uk):

ADAMS, D., Chemistry
BAKER, H., Physics
BULLER, G., Physics
CLOSE, A., Electrical Engineering
DESMULLIEZ, M., Electrical Engineering
GALBRAITH, I., Physics
GREENAWAY, A., Physics
GREENHALGH, D., Physics
GUTOWSKI, M., Chemistry
HALL, D., Physics
HAND, D., Physics
HARVEY, A., Electrical Engineering
JOHN, P., Chemistry
JONSON, M., Physics
JONES, J., Physics
KAR, A., Physics
KEANE, M., Chemical Engineering
LANE, D., Electrical Engineering
MACGREGOR, S., Chemistry
MARKX, G., Chemical Engineering
MCCOUSTRA, M., Chemical Physics
MCKENDRICK, K., Chemistry

MOORE, A., Mechanical Engineering
NI, X., Chemical Engineering
OCONE, R., Chemical Engineering
PETILLOT, Y., Electrical Engineering
POWELL, A., Chemistry
REAY, D., Electrical Engineering
REID, D., Physics
REUBEN, R., Mechanical Engineering
RICHARDS, B., Mechanical Engineering
RITCHIE, J., Mechanical Engineering
TAGHIZADEH, M., Physics
WALKER, A., Physics
WALLACE, A., Electrical and Electronic Engineering
WELCH, A., Chemistry
WHERRETT, B., Theoretical Physics
WILSON, J., Physics

School of Life Sciences (tel. (131) 451-3456; fax (131) 451-3009; e-mail j.e.j.lodder@hw.ac.uk):

GREEN, P., Psychology
HUGHES, P., Brewing and Distilling
MAIR, J., Marine Biology
NORTH, A., Psychology
QUAIN, D., Brewing
SCHWEIZER, H., Biological Sciences
WILKINSON, M., Marine Biology

School of Management and Languages (tel. (131) 451-8143; fax (131) 451-3498; e-mail enquiries@sml.hw.ac.uk):

BOSER, U., Languages and Intercultural Studies
COBHAM, D., Economics
CRAIG, V., Employment Law
FERNIE, J., Retail Marketing
HARE, P., Economics
JAMASB, T., Economics
MARSTON, C., Accountancy
MASON, I., Languages
MCKINNON, A., Logistics
MELITZ, J., Economics
PEREZ, I., Languages
ROSLENDER, R., Accounting
SAWKINS, J., Economics
SCHAFFER, M., Economics
SHARWOOD SMITH, M., Languages
TOWERS, N., Business Management
TURNER, G., Translation, Languages

School of Mathematical and Computer Sciences (tel. (131) 451-3420; fax (131) 451-3327; e-mail enquiries@macs.hw.ac.uk):

AYLETT, R., Computer Science
CAIRNS, A., Actuarial Mathematics and Statistics
CARR, J., Mathematics
CHANTLER, M., Computer Science
CORNE, D., Computer Science
DE WILDE, P., Computer Science
DUNCAN, D., Mathematics
EILBECK, J., Mathematics
FOSS, S., Actuarial Mathematics and Statistics
GIBSON, G., Statistics
HOWIE, J., Mathematics
JOHNSTON, D., Mathematics
KAMAREDDINE, F., Computer Science
KONSTANTOPOULOS, P., Actuarial Mathematics
KUKSIN, S., Mathematics
LACEY, A., Mathematics
LORD, G., Mathematics
MACDONALD, A., Actuarial Mathematics
MCNEIL, A., Actuarial Mathematics
MICHAELSON, G., Computer Science
RYNNE, B., Mathematics
SHERRATT, J., Mathematics
SZABO, R., Mathematics
TAYLOR, N., Computer Science
TRINDER, P., Computer Science
WATERS, H., Actuarial Mathematics and Statistics
WILKIE, A., Actuarial Mathematics and Statistics
WILLIAMS, M., Computer Science

Institute of Petroleum Engineering (tel. (131)
451-3567; fax (131) 451-3127; e-mail jane
.wells@pet.hw.ac.uk):

CHRISTIE, M., Reservoir Engineering
CORBETT, P., Geoengineering
COUPLES, G., Petroleum Engineering
DAVIES, D., Petroleum Engineering
FORD, J., Petroleum Engineering
MACBETH, C., Reservoir Geophysics; Time-
lapse and Multi Components
SIDE, J., Civil Engineering
SMART, B., Petroleum Engineering
SORBIE, K., Petroleum Engineering
STEWART, S., Petroleum Engineering
STOW, D., Petroleum Engineering
TODD, A., Petroleum Engineering
TOHIDI KALORAZI, B., Petroleum Engineer-
ing

School of Textiles and Design (tel. (1896)
753351; fax (1896) 758965; e-mail l.a
.lindsay@hw.ac.uk):

CHRISTIE, R., Colour Chemistry
HARLEY, A., Textiles and Design
SHENK, P., Textile Design
STYLIOS, G., Textiles
WARDMAN, R., Textiles

Edinburgh Business School (tel. (131) 451-
3090; fax (131) 451-3002; e-mail enquiries@
ebs.hw.ac.uk):

KAY, N., Economics
LOTHIAN, N., Accounting
LUMSDEN, K., Economics
O'FARRELL, P., Consultant
POOLEY, R., Computer Science
SCOTT, A., Economics
SIMMONS, J., Mechanical Engineering

QUEEN MARGARET UNIVERSITY

Musselburgh, Edinburgh, EH21 6UU
Telephone: (131) 474-0000
Internet: www.qmu.ac.uk
Founded 1875, present name and status 2007
Chancellor: Sir TOM FARMER
Prin. and Vice-Chancellor: Prof. PETRA WEND
Vice-Prin. for Resources and Devt and Univ.
Sec.: ROSALYN MARSHALL
Vice-Prin. for Academics: Prof. ALAN GIL-
LORAN
Dir for Campus Services: STEVE SCOTT
Dir for Finance: MALCOLM CUTT
Dir for Human Resources: DEE DENHOLM
Dir for Registry and Secretariat: IRENE HYND
Library of 67,423 vols and 112,251 e-titles,
142 printed journals, 19,744 e-journals
Number of teachers: 461
Number of students: 6,333

DEANS

School of Arts and Social Sciences: Dr
CHRISTINE BOVIS-CNOSSEN
School of Health Sciences: Dr FIONA COUTTS

ROBERT GORDON UNIVERSITY

Schoolhill, Aberdeen, AB10 1FR
Telephone: (1224) 262000
Fax: (1224) 263000
Internet: www.rgu.ac.uk
Founded 1750, present name and status 1992
Academic year: September to July
Chancellor: Sir IAN WOOD
Prin. and Vice-Chancellor: Prof. FERDINAND
VON PRONDZYNSKI
Sec.: Dr ADRIAN GRAVES
Acad. Registrar: HILARY DOUGLAS
Chief Librarian: ELAINE DUNPHY
Library of 250,946 vols, 1,901 periodicals,
4,939 online journals
Number of teachers: 702 (full-time)
Number of students: 15,000

DEANS

Aberdeen Business School: Prof. RITA MAR-
CELLA
Faculty of Design and Technology: Prof.
JOHN WATSON
Faculty of Health and Social Care: Prof.
VALERIE MAEHLE

HEADS OF SCHOOLS

Aberdeen Business School (Garthdee Rd,
Aberdeen, AB10 7QE; tel. (1224) 263550;
fax (1224) 263838; e-mail j.dey@rgu.ac.uk):

Accounting and Finance: ELIZABETH GAM-
MIE
Business and Management: MORAG HAMIL-
TON
Information and Media: IAN M. JOHNSON
Public Administration and Law: VERONICA
STRACHAN

Faculty of Design and Technology (Scott
Sutherland School, Garthdee Rd, Aberdeen,
AB10 7QB; tel. (1224) 263750; fax (1224)
263757; e-mail c.black@rgu.ac.uk):

School of Computing: Prof. SUSAN CRAW
School of Engineering: Prof. JOHN WATSON
Gray's School of Art: Prof. MIKE PRESS
Scott Sutherland School: Prof. ROBERT W.
POLLOCK

Faculty of Health and Social Care (Garthdee
Rd, Aberdeen, AB10 7QG; tel. (1224) 263050;
fax (1224) 263053; e-mail s.barnett@rgu.ac
.uk):

Applied Social Studies: Prof. JOYCE LISH-
MAN
Health Sciences: ELIZABETH HANCOCK
Life Sciences: Prof. MAUREEN MELVIN
Nursing and Midwifery: JENNIE PARRY
Pharmacy: Prof. TERENCE M. HEALEY

ROYAL CONSERVATOIRE OF SCOTLAND

100 Renfrew St, Glasgow, G2 3DB
Telephone: (141) 332-4101
Fax: (141) 332-8901
E-mail: principal@rcs.ac.uk
Internet: www.rcs.ac.uk
Founded 1847 as The Glasgow Athenaeum,
became The Scottish Nat. Acad. of Music
1928, The Royal Scottish Acad. of Music
1944, present status 1993, present name
2011
Academic year: September to June
Patron: HRH Prince CHARLES
Pres.: Sir CAMERON MACKINTOSH
Chair.: Lord VALLANCE OF TUMMEL
Prin.: Prof. JOHN WALLACE
Vice-Prin.: Prof. MAGGIE KINLOCH
Library of 80,120 music vols, 13,750 books,
7,570 sound recordings
Number of students: 836

DEANS

School of Drama and Dance: HUGH HODGART
School of Music: HAVILLAND WILLSHIRE

UHI MILLENNIUM INSTITUTE

12B Ness Walk, Inverness, IV3 5SQ
Telephone: (1463) 279-000
Fax: (1463) 279-001
E-mail: info@uhi.ac.uk
Internet: www.uhi.ac.uk
Founded 1993, present status 2008
Private control
Rector: GARRY COUTTS
Prin.: JAMES FRASER
Vice-Prin. for Research and Enterprise: Dr
JEFF HOWARTH
Vice-Prin. for Acad.: Dr CRICHTON LANG
Sec.: FIONA LARG
Librarian: GILLIAN ANDERSON
Number of students: 8,156

DEANS

Faculty of Arts, Humanities and Business:
Dr NEIL SIMCO
Faculty of Science, Health and Education:
IAN LESLIE

UNIVERSITY OF ABERDEEN

Telephone: (1224) 272000
Fax: (1224) 276054
E-mail: pubrel@abdn.ac.uk
Internet: www.abdn.ac.uk
Founded 1495
Chancellor: Lord WILSON OF TILLYORN
Prin. and Vice-Chancellor: Prof. IAN DIAMOND
Rector: STEPHEN ROBERTSON
Sec.: STEVE CANNON
Sr Vice-Prin.: Prof. STEPHEN LOGAN
Vice-Prin. for Culture and Communities:
Prof. CHRIS GANE
Vice-Prin. for Curriculum Reform: Prof.
BRYAN MACGREGOR
Vice-Prin. for Research and Commercializa-
tion: Prof. DOMINIC HOULIHAN
Vice-Prin. for Learning and Teaching: Prof.
PETER MCGEORGE
Acad. Registrar: Dr GILLIAN MACKINTOSH
Librarian: CHRIS BANKS
Library: see Libraries and Archives
Number of teachers: 1,400
Number of students: 16,000
Publications: Aberdeen University Review,
Gaudeamus (1 a year)

PROFESSORS

College of Arts and Social Sciences (Univ. of
Aberdeen, King's College, Aberdeen, AB24
3FX; tel. (1224) 272084; fax (1224) 272082;
e-mail adf076@abdn.ac.uk):

ADAMS, C. D., Land Economy
ARTER, D., Politics and Int. Relations
BEAUMONT, P. R., Law
BEBBINGTON, K. J., Accountancy
BLAIKIE, J. A. D., Sociology and Anthropol-
ogy
BRIDGES, R. C., History and Economic
History
BRITTON, C. M., French
BRUCE, C., Sociology
BRYDEN, J. M., Geography
BUCKLAND, R., Accountancy
BURGESS, G. J., German
CAMERON, J. R., Philosophy
CAREY-MILLER, D. L., Law
CHAPMAN, K., Geography
CLARK, B., Geography
DAWSON, P. M., Management Studies
DEVINE, T. M., Research Institute of Irish
and Scottish Studies
DUFF, P. R., Law
DUKES, P., History and Economic History
DUNKLEY, J., French
EDWARDS, K. J., Geography
ELLIOTT, R. F., Economics
EVANS-JONES, R., Law
FERGUSSON, D. A. S., Divinity with Reli-
gious Studies
FORTE, A. D. M., Law
FRASER, P., Accountancy
GANE, C. H. W., Law
GRAHAM, L. G., Philosophy
HARRIS, D. R., Hispanic Studies
HARRISON, R. T., Management Studies
HEALD, D. A., Accountancy
HENDERSHOTT, P. H., Land Economy
HENDRY, L. B., Centre for Educational
Research
HEWITT, D. S., English
HOESLI, M. E. R., Accountancy
HOTSON, H., Early Modern History
INGOLD, T., Sociology and Anthropology
JOHNSTONE, W., Divinity with Religious
Studies

JORDAN, A. G., Politics and Int. Relations
KEATING, M. J., Politics and Int. Relations
KEMP, A. G., Economics
KIDD, M., Economics
LEBOUTTE, R. F. M. P., History
LEE, C. H., Economics
LYALL, F., Law
MACDONALD, I. R., Hispanic Studies
MACGREGOR, B. D., Land Economy
MACINNES, A. I., History
MANNINGS, D., History of Art
MATHER, A. S., Geography
MATTHEWS, E. H., Philosophy
McKEE, L., Management Studies
MEEK, D. E., Celtic
MILLER, D., Law
MURRAY, I., English
O'BOYLE, C. J. M., Celtic
OHLMEYER, J., History
PAYNE, P. L., History and Economic History
PORTER, J. W., English (Elphinstone Institute)
ROBERTS, C., Accountancy
ROBERTSON, R., Sociology
ROWAN-ROBINSON, J. R., Law
SALMON, T. C., Politics and Int. Relations
SAUNDERS, A. M., French
SEWEL, J. B., Politics and Int. Relations
SHEEHAN, M. J., Politics and Int. Relations
SHUCKSMITH, D. M., Land Economy
SOULSBY, C., Geography
SWANSON, P., Hispanic Studies
THEODOSSIOU, I., Economics
THOMANECK, J. K. A., German
TORRANCE, I. R., Divinity with Religious Studies
URWIN, D. W., Politics and Int. Relations
VAN DER MERWE, C. G., Law
WALKER, N. C., Law
WALKER, S., Geography
WATSON, F. B., Divinity with Religious Studies
WATSON, G. J. B., English

College of Life Sciences and Medicine (Univ. of Aberdeen, Polworth Bldg, Foresterhill, Aberdeen, AB25 2ZD; tel. (1224) 552504; fax (1224) 840708; internet w3.abdn.ac.uk/medicine):

ALEXANDER, D. A., Mental Health
ASHFORD, M. L. J., Biomedical Sciences
BOOTH, I. R., Microbiology
BROWN, A. J. P., Molecular and Cell Biology
CASSIDY, J., Medicine and Therapeutics (Oncology)
CATTO, G. R. D., Medicine and Therapeutics
DOCHERTY, K., Molecular and Cell Biology (Biochemistry)
EL-OMAR, E. M., Medicine and Therapeutics
FORRESTER, J. V., Ophthalmology
FOTHERGILL, J. E., Molecular and Cell Biology (Biochemistry)
GILBERT, F. J., Radiology
GODDEN, D. J., Highlands and Islands Health Research Institute
GOLDEN, M. H. N., Medicine and Therapeutics
GOODAY, G. W., Molecular and Cell Biology
GOW, N. A. R., Molecular and Cell Biology
GRANT, A. M., Public Health
GREAVES, M., Medicine and Therapeutics (Haematology)
HAITES, N. E., Medicine and Therapeutics, and Molecular and Cell Biology
HAMILTON, W. A., Medical Microbiology
HANNAFORD, P., Primary Care
HARRIS, W. J., Molecular and Cell Biology (Genetics)
HAWKSWORTH, G. M., Biomedical Sciences, and Medicine and Therapeutics
HELMS, P. J. B., Child Health
HUHTANIEMI, I. T., Obstetrics and Gynaecology

HUKINS, D. W. L., Biomedical Physics and Bioengineering
HUTCHISON, J. D., Surgery (Orthopaedics)
KIDD, C., Biomedical Sciences (Physiology)
LITTLE, J., Medicine and Therapeutics (Epidemiology)
LOGAN, S. D., Biomedical Sciences (Neuroscience)
MACLEOD, A. M., Medicine and Therapeutics
MAUGHAN, R. J., Environmental and Occupational Medicine
MCCAIG, C. D., Biomedical Sciences
NEEDHAM, G., Medical Faculty
NORMAN, J. N., General Practice and Primary Care
ODDS, F. C., Molecular and Cell Biology
PENNINGTON, T. H., Medical Microbiology
PERTWEE, R. G., Biomedical Sciences
POPE, M. H., Medicine and Therapeutics
PRICE, D. B., General Practice and Primary Care
PROSSER, J. I., Molecular and Cell Biology
RALSTON, S. H., Medicine and Therapeutics
REES, A. J., Medicine and Therapeutics
REID, D. M., Medicine and Therapeutics
RITCHIE, L. D., General Practice and Primary Care
RUSSELL, E. M., Public Health
SEATON, A., Environmental and Occupational Medicine
SEYMOUR, D. G., Medicine and Therapeutics, and General Practice and Primary Care
SHARP, P. F., Biomedical Physics and Bioengineering
SHAW, D. J., Molecular and Cell Biology
SMITH, W. C. S., Public Health
TEMPLETON, A. A., Obstetrics and Gynaecology
VAN DER MOLEN, T., General Practice and Primary Care
WALKER, F., Pathology
WEBSTER, N. R., Medicine and Therapeutics (Anaesthesia and Intensive Care)
WHALLEY, L. J., Mental Health
WISCHIK, C. M., Mental Health

College of Physical Sciences (Univ. of Aberdeen, King's College, Aberdeen, AB24 3FX; tel. (1224) 272081; fax (1224) 272082; e-mail adf073@abdn.ac.uk):

ALEXANDER, I. J., Plant and Soil Sciences
ARCHBOLD, R. J., Mathematical Sciences
BAKER, M. J., Engineering
BOYLE, P. R., Zoology
CHANDLER, H. W., Engineering
CRAWFORD, J. E., Psychology
DELLA SALA, S. F., Psychology
DEREGOWSKI, J. B., Psychology
DUFFY, J. A., Chemistry
ENGLISH, P. R., Agriculture
FLIN, R., Psychology
FORRESTER, A. R., Chemistry
FREESTON, M. W., Computing Science
GLASSER, F. P., Chemistry
GORMAN, D. G., Engineering
GRAY, P. M. D., Computing Science
HALL, G. S., Mathematical Sciences
HOULIHAN, D. F. J., Zoology
HOWE, R. F., Chemistry
HUBBUCK, J. R., Mathematical Sciences
HUNTER, J., Computing Science
HURST, A., Geology and Petroleum Geology
INGRAM, M. D., Chemistry
JOLLIFFE, I. T., Mathematical Sciences
KILLHAM, K. S., Plant and Soil Sciences
LOGIE, R. H., Psychology
LOMAX, M. A., Agriculture
MACDONALD, D. I. M., Geology and Petroleum Geology
MEHARG, A. A., Plant and Soil Sciences
MILLER, H. G., Agriculture and Forestry
MITCHELL, C. P., Agriculture and Forestry
MORDUE, W., Zoology
NAYLOR, R. E. L., Agriculture

PENMAN, J., Engineering
PLAYER, M. A., Engineering
PRIEDE, I. G., Zoology
RACEY, P. A., Zoology
ROBINSON, D., Plant and Soil Sciences
RODGER, A. A., Engineering
SECOMBES, C. J., Zoology
SLEEMAN, D. H., Computing Science
SPEAKMAN, J. R., Zoology
SPRACKLEN, C. T., Engineering
THOMSON, K. J., Agriculture
VAS, P., Engineering
WIERCIGROCH, M., Engineering
WILLETTS, B. B., Engineering

UNIVERSITY OF ABERTAY DUNDEE

Bell St, Dundee, DD1 1HG
Telephone: (1382) 308000
Fax: (1382) 308877
E-mail: sro@abertay.ac.uk
Internet: www.abertay.ac.uk
Founded 1888 as Dundee Technical Institute, present name and status 1994
Academic year: October to June

Chancellor: Lord DOUGLAS CULLEN
Vice-Chancellor and Prin.: Prof. BERNARD KING
Vice-Prin. and Deputy Vice-Chancellor: Prof. NICHOLAS TERRY
Pro-Vice-Chancellor for Acad. Devt: Prof. STEVE OLIVIER
Pro-Vice-Chancellor for Recruitment and Student Experience: Prof. ROSITSA BATESON
Head of Information Services: MICHAEL TURPIE

Library of 120,000 vols, 400 journals
Number of teachers: 380 (230 full-time, 150 part-time)
Number of students: 5,084

HEADS OF SCHOOL

Dundee Business School: Prof. HEATHER TARBERT
School of Computing and Engineering Systems: Dr COLIN MILLER
School of Contemporary Sciences: Prof. JOHN W. PALFREYMAN
School of Social and Health Sciences: RAY LLOYD

UNIVERSITY OF DUNDEE

Dundee, DD1 4HN
Telephone: (1382) 383000
Fax: (1382) 385505
E-mail: university@dundee.ac.uk
Internet: www.dundee.ac.uk
Founded 1881 as Univ. College, Dundee, Royal Charter 1967
Academic year: September to August

Chancellor: Lord NAREN PATEL
Rector: BRIAN COX
Prin. and Vice-Chancellor: Prof. C. PETER DOWNES
Vice-Prin.: Prof. DOREEN CANTRELL (acting)
Vice-Prin.: Prof. J. CALDERHEAD
Vice-Prin.: Prof. CHRISTOPHER WHATLEY
Vice-Prin.: Prof. Dr IRENE LEIGH
Deputy Prin.: Prof. GEORGINA FOLLETT
Sec.: Dr J. MCGEORGE
Librarian: Dr RICHARD PARSONS
Library: see under Libraries and Archives
Number of teachers: 3,000
Number of students: 17,000

DEANS

College of Art, Science and Engineering: Prof. ANNE ANDERSON
College of Arts and Social Sciences: Prof. CHRISTOPHER WHATLEY
College of Life Sciences: Prof. M. A. J. FERGUSON

College of Medicine, Dentistry and Nursing:
Prof. IRENE LEIGH

PROFESSORS

College of Arts and Social Sciences (Tower Bldng, Dundee, DD1 4HN; tel. (1382) 384935; e-mail cassoffice@dundee.ac.uk; internet www.dundee.ac.uk/cass):

ANDREWS-SPEED, C., Energy Policy
BELCHER, C., Law
BENNETT, R., Developmental Biology
BONELL, M., Catchment Science
BROWN, C., Religious and Cultural History
CAMERON, P., International Energy Law and Policy
CHALKLEY, M. J., Economics
CHATTERJI, M., Applied Economics
CHURCHILL, R., Law
COLLISON, D., Accounting and Society
DAY, A., English Literature
DEWHURST, J. H. L., Economic, Social and Regional Statistics
DOBSON, A. P., Politics
FERGUSON, Scots Law
FINDLAY, A. M., Geography
FISCHER, M., Psychology
FYFE, N., Human Geography
GUNN, K., Creative Writing
HARRIS, R., Social Care
HASLAM, J., Business Finance
HOBER, K., International Law
HUDSON, B., Education
KELLY, T., Social Work
KITSON, P., English Literature
MCELEAVY, P., Law
MCKEAN, C., Scottish Architectural History
MCLEAN, J., Law
MOLANA, H., Economics
MONTAGNA, ., Economic Studies
POWER, D., Business Finance
RAITT, F., Law
REID, C., Environmental Law
RODRIGUES, S., Science Education
SPRAY, C., Water Science
TOMLINSON, J., Bonar Modern History
WERRITTY, A., Physical Geography
WILLIAMS, J., European Philosophy
WILLSON, P., History
WOUTERS, P., International Water Law and Policy

College of Art, Science and Engineering (Queen Mother Bldg, Dundee, DD1 4HN; tel. (1382) 386610; e-mail case@dundee.ac.uk; internet www.dundee.ac.uk/case/index.htm):

ABEL, E. W., Biomedical Engineering
ARNOTT, J. L., Communication Systems
CHAPLAIN, M. A., Mathematical Biology
COLVIN, C. M., Fine Art Photography
DAVIES, P. A., Fluid Dynamics
DONG, P., Coastal Engineering
FISHER, G. R.,
GILLESPIE, , Sculpture
HANSON, V. L., Inclusive Technologies
INNS, T. G., Design
JENG, D., Civil Engineering
JOHNSON, N. M., Numerical Analysis/Computational Mathematics
LIN, P., Numerical Analysis/Computational Mathematics
MACDONALD, M J S., History Of Scottish Art
MARTIN, T., Animal Conservation
MCKENNA, S. J., Computer Vision
MELZER, A., Foundation Director Of Imsat
MUIR WOOD, D., Geotechnical Engineering
PARTRIDGE, S., Media Art
PRESS, M., Design Policy
REED, C. A., Art And Policy
RENWICK, G. T., Assistive Systems And Healthcare Computing
RICKETTS, I. W.
ROSE, M. J., Physical Electronics
SHEMILT, T. E., Fine Art Printmaking
TRUCCO, E., Inclusive Technologies

Faculty of Education, Social Work and Community Education (Gardyne Rd, Dundee, DD5 1NY; tel. (1382) 464000; fax (1382) 464900; e-mail edusocwk@dundee.ac.uk; internet www.dundee.ac.uk/facedusoc):

BALDWIN, N., Child Care and Protection
DANIEL, D. M., Child Care and Protection
HARTLEY, J. D., Educational Theory and Policy
TOPPING, K. J., Educational and Social Research

Faculty of Engineering and Physical Sciences (Carnegie Bldg, Dundee, DD1 4HN; tel. (1382) 344190; fax (1382) 344389; e-mail engineering@dundee.ac.uk; internet www.dundee.ac.uk/facengphys):

ABEL, E. W., Biomedical Engineering
ARNOTT, J. L., Communications Systems
CHAPLAIN, M. A., Mathematical Biology
DAVIES, M. C. R., Civil Engineering
DAVIES, P. A., Fluid Dynamics
DHIR, R. K., Concrete Technology
FITZGERALD, A. G., Physics
FLETCHER, R., Mathematics
GOODMAN, T. N. T., Applied Analysis
HORNER, R. M. W., Engineering Management
NEWELL, A. F., Electronics and Microcomputer Systems
PANFILOV, A., Mathematical Biology
RICKETTS, I. W., Assistive Systems and Healthcare Computing
VARDY, A. E., Civil Engineering
WATSON, G. A., Numerical Analysis

Faculty of Law (Scrymgeour Bldg, Dundee, DD1 4HN; tel. (1382) 344185; fax (1382) 345094; e-mail lawandaccy@dundee.ac.uk; internet www.dundee.ac.uk/faclawacc):

BELCHER, C. A., Law
BISSETT-JOHNSON, A., Private Law
CAMERON, P. D., International Energy Law and Policy
FERGUSON, P. R., Scots Law
GRINYER, J. R., Accountancy
HELLIER, C. V., Accountancy and Business Finance
NIXON, W. A. J., Accountancy
PAGE, A. C., Public Law
PALMER, K. F., Mineral Policy
POUNDER, D. J., Forensic Medicine
POWER, D. M., Business Finance
REID, C. T., Environmental Law
STEVENS, P., Petroleum Policy and Economics
WALDE, T. W., International Economic, Energy and Natural Resources Law

College of Life Sciences (MSI/WTB/JBC Complex, Dow St, Dundee, DD1 4HN; tel. (1382) 385136; fax (1382) 345519; e-mail d.a.hill@dundee.ac.uk; internet www.lifesci.dundee.ac.uk):

BARTON, G. J., Bioinformatics
BIRCH, P. R. J., Plant Pathology
BLACK, S. M., Anatomy and Forensic Anthropology
BLOW, J. J., Chromosome Maintenance
BROWN, J. W. S., Molecular Plant Sciences
CODD, G. A, Microbiology
FAIRLAMB, A. H., Wellcome Trust Building
FLAVELL, A. J., Plant Genomics
GADD, G. M., Microbiology
GILBERT, I. H., Medicinal Chemistry
HALPIN, C., Plant Biology And Biotechnology
HARDIE, D. G., Cellular Signalling
HAY, R. T., Molecular Biology
HOPKINS, A. L., Medicinal Informatics
HUNDAL, H. S., Molecular Physiology
HUNTER, W. N., Structural Biology
LAMOND, A. I., Biochemistry
LILLEY, D. M. J., Molecular Biology
NATHKE, I. S., Epithelial Biology
OWEN-HUGHES, T. A., Chromatin Structure And Dynamics

PALMER, T., Molecular Microbiology
SARGENT, F., Bacterial Physiology
SCHAAP, P., Developmental Signalling
SOAMES, M., Anatomy
STARK, M. J. R., Yeast Molecular Biology
SWEDLOW, J. R., Quantitative Cell Biology
VAN AALTEN, D. M. F., Biological Chemistry
WATTS, C., Immunobiology
WEIJER, C. J., Developmental Physiology
WILLIAMS, J. A., Developmental Biology
WYATT, P. G., Drug Discovery

College of Medicine, Dentistry and Nursing (Ninewells Hospital and Medical School, Dundee, DD1 9SY; tel. (1382) 232763; fax (1382) 644267; e-mail cmdn-office@dundee.ac.uk; internet www.dundee.ac.uk/cmdn):

ABBOUD, R. J., Education in Biomechanics
ANDERSON, A. S., Food Choice
ASHFORD, M. L. J., Neuroscience
BALFOUR, D. J. K., Behavioural Pharmacology
BARBOUR, R., Health and Social Care
BARRATT, C., Reproductive Medicine
BEARN, D., Orthodontics
BELCH, J. J. F., Vascular Medicine
CADDEN, S. W., Oral Biology
CLARKE, P. R., Cancer Cell Biology
CLARKSON, J. E., Clinical Effectiveness
COLHOUN, H., Public Health
CROMBIE, I. K., Public Health
DAVEY, P. G., Pharmacoeconomics
DONNAN, P. T., Epidemiology And Biostatistics
ENTWISTLE, V. A., Values In Health Care
EVANS, A., Breast Imaging
FLEMING, S., Cellular and Molecular Pathology
FREEMAN, R. E., Dental Public Health Research
GUTHRIE, B., Primary Care Medicine
HALES, T. G., Anaesthesia
HAYES, J. D., Molecular Carcinogenesis
HIOM, K., Biomedical Research Institute
HOUSTON, S., Imaging
HUME, R., Developmental Medicine
JOVANOVIC, A., Experimental Medicine
KEARNEY, N., Nursing and Midwifery
LAMBERT, J. J., Neuropharmacology
LANG, C. C., Cardiology
LIPWORTH, B. J., Allergy and Respiratory Medicine
MACDONALD, T. M., Clinical Pharmacology and Pharmacoepidemiology
MACFARLAINE, G. T., Bacteriology
MCLEAN, W. H. I., Human Genetics
MCMURDO, M. E. T., Ageing and Health
MIRES, G. J., Perinatal Health And Education
MORRIS, A. D., Diabetic Medicine
MOSSEY, P. A., Craniofacial Dev And Dentofacial Orthopaedics
MUNRO, A. J., Radiation Oncology
OGDEN, G. R., Oral and Maxillofacial Surgery
PALMER, C. N. A., Pharmacogenomics
PARKIN, I. G., Applied Clinical Anatomy
PETERS, J. A., Pharmacolog
PITTS, N. B., Dental Health
RANKIN, E. M., Cancer Medicine
REES, C., Education Research
RICKETTS, D. N. J., Cariology And Conservative Dentistry
SCHWEIGER, S., Molecular Medicine
STEELE, J. D., Neuro-Imaging
STEELE, R. J., Surgery
STONEBRIDGE, P. A., Vascular Surgery
STRUTHERS, A. D., Cardiovascular Medicine and Therapeutics
SULLIVAN, F. M., General Practice and Primary Care
TAYLOR, J. S., Family Health
THOMPSON, A. M., Surgical Oncology
WOLF, C. R., Molecular Pharmacology
WRIGHT, E. G., Experimental Haematology
WYATT, J., Health Informatics

Faculty of Duncan of Jordanstone College (Perth Rd, Dundee, DD1 4HT; tel. (1382) 345213; fax (1382) 227304; internet www .dundee.ac.uk/facdjcad):

COLVIN, C., Fine Art Photography
FISHER, G. R., Sculpture
FOLLETT, G. L. P., Design
INNS, T. G., Design
PARTRIDGE, S., Media Art
ROBB, A., Fine Art
UNWIN, S. D. A., Architecture

UNIVERSITY OF EDINBURGH

Old College, South Bridge, Edinburgh EH8 9YL

Telephone: (131) 650-1000
Fax: (131) 650-2147
E-mail: communications.office@ed.ac.uk
Internet: www.ed.ac.uk
Founded 1583
Academic year: September to June

Chancellor: HRH THE PRINCESS ROYAL
Prin.: Prof. Sir TIMOTHY O'SHEA
Rector: PETER MCCOLL
Sec.: Dr KIM WALDRON
Hon. Vice-Prin.: Prof. CHRIS BREWARD
Vice-Prin. for Academic Enhancement: Prof. DAI HOUNSELL
Vice-Prin. for Devt: YOUNG DAWKINS
Vice-Prin. for Equality and Diversity: Prof. LORRAINE WATERHOUSE
Vice-Prin.l for High Performance Computing: Prof. RICHARD KENWAY
Vice-Prin. for Int. Affairs: Prof. STEVE HILLIER
Vice-Prin. for Knowledge Management and Chief Information Officer: Prof. JEFF HAYWOOD
Vice-Prin. for Planning, Resources and Research Policy: Prof. APRIL MCMAHON
Vice-Prin. for Research Training and Community Relations: Prof. MARY BOWNES
Dir of Registry: RIO WATT
Dir of Finance: JON GORRINGE
Dir of Int. Office: ALAN MACKAY
CEO of Edinburgh Research and Innovation: DEREK WADDELL
Librarian: Prof. JEFF HAYWOOD
Library: see Libraries and Archives
Number of teachers: 2,730
Number of students: 26,951

Publications: *EDIT Magazine* (2 a year), *Scottish Affairs* (4 a year), *Scottish Studies* (1 a year), *The University of Edinburgh Journal* (2 a year)

HEADS OF COLLEGES

Edinburgh College of Art: Prof. IAN HOWARD (Prin.)
College of Humanities and Social Science: Prof. DOROTHY MIELL
College of Medicine and Veterinary Medicine: Prof. Sir JOHN SAVILL
College of Science and Engineering: Prof. NIGEL BROWN

PROFESSORS

College of Humanities and Social Science (Administration Office, 55–56 George Sq., Edinburgh, EH8 9JU; tel. (131) 650-4646; fax (131) 650-6512; internet www.hss.ed.ac .uk):

ABHYONKAR, A., Financial Markets
ADLER, M. E., Socio-Legal Studies
ALTHAUS-REID, M., Contextual Theology
ANDERSON, R. D., Modern History
ANGOLD, M. J., Byzantine History
ANSELL, J. I., Risk Management
ARCHIBALD, T. W., Business Modelling
BAILEY, P., Modern Chinese History
BANKOWSKI, Z., Legal Theory
BANNER, M. C., Ethics and Public Policy in Life Sciences

BARKER, A. W., Austrian Studies
BARNARD, A. J., Anthropology of Southern Africa
BARRINGER, J. M., Greek Art and Archaeology
BARSTAD, H. M., Hebrew and Old Testament Studies
BLOOR, D., Sociology of Science
BLOXHAM, D., Modern History
BOYLE, A. E., Public International Law
BRAY, F., Social Anthropology
BRODIE, D., Employment Law
BROWN, S. J., Ecclesiastical History
BRUCE, V., Psychology
CAIRNS, D. L., Classics
CAIRNS, J. W., Legal History
CAMPBELL, I., Scottish and Victorian Literature
CARR, C. H., Corporate Strategy
CARR, D., Philosophy of Education
CARSTEN, J. F., Social and Cultural Anthropology
CASTLES, F. G., Social and Public Policy
CLARK, A., Logic and Metaphysics
CLARK, C., Social Work Ethics
CLASON, J., Comparative Social Policy
COGLIANO, F. D., American History
COLEBROOK, C. M., Literary Theory
COLVIN, S., German
COWLING, E. G., 20th-century European Art
COX, J. L., Religious Studies
COYNE, A. R., Architectural Computing
CREE, V. E., Social Work Studies
CROOK, J. N., Business Economics
CURRIE, C., Child and Adolescent Health
DAVIDSON, R., Social History
DAWSON, J., Reformation History
DAYAN, P., French
DEARY, I. J., Differential Psychology
DELLA SALA, S., Human Cognitive Neuroscience
DEVINE, T. M., Scottish History and Palaeography
DUFFY, J. H., French
ERSKINE, A., Ancient History
FABRE, C., Political Theory
FERGUSSON, D., Divinity
FERREIRA, F., Language and Cognition
FRANSMAN, M., Economics
FROTH, S., Music
GENTZ, N., Chinese
GIEGERICH, H. J., English Linguistics
GILLIES, W., Celtic Languages, Literature, History and Antiquities
GILMORE, W. C., Int. Criminal Law
GOODE, A., Social Anthropology in Practice
GREASLEY, D. G., Economic History
GREEN, J., Medieval History
GRETTON, G. L., Law
GRIFFITHS, A., Anthropology of Law
GRIFFITHS, M., Classroom Learning
HARDING, D. W., Archaeology
HARDMAN MOORE, J. H., Political Economy
HAYWARD, T., Environmental Political Theory
HAYWOOD, J., Education and Technology
HENDERSON, J., Visual Cognition and Cognitive Neuroscience
HENLEY, J. S., Int. Management
HEYCOCK, C., Syntax
HIGGINS, P., Outdoor and Environmental Education
HILLENBRAND, C., Islamic History
HILLENBRAND, R., Islamic Art
HIMSWORTH, C. M. G., Admin. Law
HOPKINS, E. H. K., Economics
HOUNSELL, D., Higher Education
HURFORD, J. R., General Linguistics
HURTADO, L. W., New Testament Language, Literature and Theology
JACKSON, A., History
JAMIESON, L. H. A., Sociology of Families and Relationships
JEFFERY, C., Politics
JEFFERY, P. M., Sociology

JEFFERY, R., Sociology of South Asia
JEFFREYS-JONES, R., American History
JOSEPH, J. E., Applied Linguistics
KREBER, C., Teaching and Learning in Higher Education
LADD, D. R., Linguistics
LAPSLEY, I. McL., Accountancy
LAURIE, G. T., Medical Jurisprudence
LIM, T. M., Hebrew Bible and Second Temple Judaism
LINGARD, R., Education
LOGIE, R. H., Human Cognitive Neuroscience
MACDONALD, A. J., Architectural Studies
MACINNES, J., Sociology
MACKENZIE, D. A., Sociology
MACQUEEN, H. L., Private Law
MAHER, G., Criminal Law
MAIN, B. G. M., Business Economics
MANNING, S., English Literature
MARDER, R., Midwifery
MARSHALL, D. W., Marketing and Consumer Behaviour
MCCRONE, D., Sociology
MCDOUGALL, B. S., Chinese
MCMAHON, A., English Language
MCMILLAN, J. F., History
MEEK, D. E., Scottish and Gaelic Studies
MELIA, K. M., Nursing Studies
MEYERHOFF, M., Sociolinguistics
MITCHELL, F., Management Accounting
MOLINA, A. H., Technology Strategy
MUNN, P., Curriculum Research
MUNRO, C. R., Constitutional Law
MYERS, A., Organology
NELSON, P., Music and Technology
NICHOLSON, C. E., 18th-century and Modern Literature
NORTHCOTT, M. S., Ethics
NUGENT, P., Comparative African History
NUTLEY, S., Public Management
O'DONOVAN, O., Christian Ethics and Practical Theology
OLIVER, N., Management
OSBORNE, N., Music
OSBORNE, S., Int. Public Management
OZGA, J., Educational Research
PATERSON, L., Educational Policy
PEDRESCHI, R., Architectural Technology
PELTENBURG, E. J., Archaeology
PETERSON, J., Int. Politics
PICKERING, M., Psychology of Language and Communication
POLLOCK, A., Health Policy
POWER, M. J., Clinical Psychology
PRITCHARD, D., Philosophy
PULLUM, G., General Linguistics
RAAB, C. D., Govt
RAFFE, D., Sociology of Education
RALSTON, I., Prehistoric European Archaeology
REID, K. G. C., Property Law
RIDDELL, S., Inclusion and Diversity
RIDGE, M. R., Moral Philosophy
ROBBINS, J. M. W., Hispanic Studies
RODGER, R., Economic and Social History
ROSA, P., Entrepreneurship and Family Business
SAKOVICS, J., Economic Theory
SANDERS, R., Sport Science
SCALTSAS, T., Ancient Philosophy
SCHOFIELD, J., Healthcare Management
SCOTT, A. G., European Union Studies
SHAW, J., European Institutions
SNELL, A. J., Economics and Econometrics
SORACE, A., Developmental Linguistics
SPARKS, R., Criminology
SPENCER, J., Anthropology of South Asia
STANLEY, E., Sociology
STEPHENSON, A. J. R., Modern German History
STEVENSON, R., 20th-century Literature
TAFFER, R., Finance and Investment
TETT, L., Community Education and Lifelong Learning
THOMAS, J. P., Economics

THOMSON, R., Fine Art
USHER, J., Italian
WASOFF, F., Family Policies
WATERHOUSE, L. A. M., Social Work
WEBB, J., Sociology of Organizations
WHYTE, I. B., Architectural History
WHYTE, W. J., Social Work
WILLIAMS, R., Social Research on Technology
WISHART, J. G., Developmental Disabilities in Childhood
YEARLEY, S., Sociology of Scientific Knowledge

College of Medicine and Veterinary Medicine (The Queen's Medical Research Institute, 47 Little France Crescent, Edinburgh, EH16 4TJ; tel. (131) 242-9300; fax (131) 242-9301; e-mail mvm@ed.ac.uk; internet www.mvm.ed.ac.uk):

AMOS, A., Health Promotion
AMYES, S. G. B., Microbial Chemotherapy
ANDERSON, R., Clinical Reproductive Science
ARGYLE, D., Veterinary Clinical Studies
BACKETH-MILLBURN, K. C., Sociology of Families and Health
BALL, K., Biochemistry and Cell Signalling
BARD, J., Bio-informatics and Devt
BATEMAN, D. N., Clinical Toxicology
BELL, J. E., Neuropathology
BEST, J. J. K., Medical Radiology
BHOPAL, R., Public Health
BLACKWOOD, D., Psychiatric Genetics
BOYD, K. M., Medical Ethics
BROPHY, P. J., Veterinary Anatomy and Cell Biology
CALDER, A. A., Obstetrics and Gynaecology
CAMPBELL, H., Genetic Epidemiology and Public Health
CLUTTON, E., Veterinary Anaesthesiology
CORCORAN, B. M., Veterinary Cardiopulmonary Medicine
CRAWFORD, D. H., Bacteriology
CRITCHLEY, H., Reproductive Medicine
CUMMING, A. D., Medical Education
CUNNINGHAM-BURLEY, S. J., Medical and Family Sociology
DAVIES, J., Experimental Anatomy
DENNIS, M. S., Stroke Medicine
DEWHURST, D., Student Learning (e-Learning)
DIXON, P. M., Equine Surgery
DONALDSON, K., Respiratory Toxicology
DOUGLAS, N. J., Respiratory and Sleep Medicine
DROUSFIELD, I., Leukocyte and Lung Cell Biology
DUNLOP, M. G., Coloproctology
EBMEIER, K. P., Psychiatry
ELSE, R. W., Diagnostic Veterinary Pathology
FALLON, M. T., Palliative Medicine
FAZAKERLEY, J., Virology
FEARON, K. C. H., Surgical Oncology
FFRENCH-CONSTANT, C., Multiple Sclerosis
FLEETWOOD-WALKER, S. M., Sensory Neuroscience
FORBES, S. J., Transplantation and Regenerative Medicine
FOWKES, F. G. R., Epidemiology
FOX, K. A. A., Cardiology
GALLY, D. L., Microbial Genetics
GARDEN, O. J., Clinical Surgery
GHAZAL, P., Molecular Genetics and Biomedicine
GOVAN, J. R. W., Microbial Pathogenecity
GRANT, S. G. N., Molecular Neuroscience
GREENING, A. P., Pulmonary Disease
GREGORY, C. D., Inflammatory Cell Biology
GUNN-MOORE, D., Feline Medicine
HARKISS, G. D., Veterinary Immunopathology
HARMAR, A. J., Molecular Pharmacology
HARRISON, D. J., Pathology
HASLETT, C., Respiratory Medicine

HAYES, P. C., Hepatology
HECK, M., Cell Biology and Genetics
HILLIER, S. G., Reproductive Endocrinology
HOOPER, M. L., Molecular Pathology
HOPKINS, J., Veterinary Immunology
HOWIE, S. E. M., Immunopathology
HUPP, E., Cancer Research
IBBETSON, R. J., Dental Primary Care
IREDALE, J., Medicine
IRONSIDE, J. W., Clinical Neuropathology
JARMAN, A. P., Developmental Cell Biology
JODRELL, D., Cancer Therapeutics
JOHNSTONE, E. C., Psychiatry
KAUFMAN, M. H., Anatomy
LAMB, J. R., Veterinary Clinical Immunology
LAWRIE, S. M., Psychiatric Imaging
LENG, G., Experimental Physiology
LINCOLN, Q. A., Biological Tuning
LUDWIG, M., Neurophysiology
MACNEE, W., Respiratory and Environmental Medicine
MACPHERSON, S. G., Postgraduate Medical Education
MARSHALL, I., Magnetic Resonance Physics
MASON, J. I., Clinical Biochemistry
McCULLOCH, J., Neuropharmacology
McDICKEN, W. N., Medical Physics and Medical Engineering
McGORUM, B. C., Equine Medicine
McINTOSH, N., Child Life and Health
McQUEEN, D. S., Sensory Pharmacology
McKEEVER, D., Veterinary Clinical Science
MELTON, D. W., Somatic Cell Genetics
MIMS, R. A., Paediatric Neurology
MORRIS, R. G. M., Neuroscience
MURRAY, G. D., Medical Statistics
MURRAY, S. A., Primary Palliative Care
NASH, A. A., Veterinary Pathology
NEWBY, D., Cardiology
OWENS, D. G. C., Clinical Psychiatry
PETTIGREW, G. W., Bioenergetics
PORTEOUS, D. J., Human Molecular Genetics and Medicine
POWER, I., Anaesthetics, Critical Care and Pain
POXTON, I. R., Microbial Infection and Immunity
PRESCOTT, R. J., Health Technology Assessment
PRICE, D. J., Developmental Neurobiology
RALSTON, S. H., Rheumatology
REES, J. L., Dermatology
RHIND, S. M., Veterinary Medical Education
ROCHESTER, R. R., Cellular Neuroscience
ROSS, J. A., Liver Cell Biology
ROSSI, A., Respiratory and Inflammation Pharmacology
RUSSELL, J. A., Neuroendocrinology
SALLER, D. M., Osteoarticular Pathology
SANDERCOCK, P., Medical Neurology
SATSANGI, J., Gastroenterology
SAVILL, J. S., Experimental Medicine
SECKL, J. R., Molecular Medicine
SETHI, T. J., Respiratory and Lung Cancer Biology
SHARPE, M., Psychological Medicine and Symptoms Research
SHEIKH, A., Primary Care Research and Devt
SHIPSTON, M. J., Physiology
SIMMONDS, P., Virology
SIMPSON, A. H. R. W., Orthopaedic Surgery
SIMPSON, J. W., Canine Medecine
SMYTH, J. F., Medical Oncology
TAYLOR, D. W., Tropical Animal Health
THODAY, K. L., Veterinary Dermatology
TURNER, A. N., Nephrology
TURNER, M., Cellular Therapy
VAN HEYNINGEN, S., Learning and Teaching
WALKER, B. R., Endocrinology
WARDLAW, J. M., Applied Neuroimaging
WARLOW, C. P., Medical Neurology
WATSON, E. D., Veterinary Reproduction
WEBB, D. J., Clinical Pharmacology

WELBURN, S., Medical and Veterinary Molecular Epidemiology
WELLER, D., General Practice
WHITTLE, I. R., Surgical Neurology
WILL, R. G., Clinical Neurology
WILMUT, I., Reproductive Science
WOOLHOUSE, M. E. J., Veterinary Public Health and Quantitative Epidemiology

College of Science and Engineering (Weir Bldg, King's Bldgs, West Mains Rd, Edinburgh, EH9 3JY; tel. (131) 650-5759; fax (131) 650-5738; e-mail sciengmail@ed.ac.uk; internet www.scieng.ed.ac.uk):

ACKLAND, G. J., Computer Simulation
AITKEN, A., Protein Biochemistry
AITKEN, C. G. G., Forensic Statistics
ALLEN, J. E., Immunology
ALLSHIRE, R., Chromosome Biology
ANDERTON, X., Therapeutic Immunology
ARSLAN, T., Integrated Electronic Systems
ATKINSON, M. P., e-Science
ATTFIELD, J. P., Materials Science at Extreme Conditions
BALL, R. D., Mathematical Physics
BARLOW, P. N., Structural Biology
BARTHOLEMIE, R. J., Renewable Energy
BARTON, N. H., Evolutionary Genetics
BAXTER, R. L., Chemical Biology
BEGGS, J. D., Molecular Biology
BIALEK, J. W., Electrical Engineering
BIRD, A. P., Genetics
BISHOP, C. M., Computer Science
BLAXTER, M. L., Evolutionary Genomics
BONDI, E., Social Geography
BOULTON, G. S., Geology
BOWNES, M., Developmental Biology
BRADEN, H. W., Integrable Systems
BRADLEY, M., Chemical Biology
BRAND, P. W. J. L., Astrophysics
BRANDONI, S., Chemical Engineering
BRANFORD, D., Photonuclear Physics
BRUCE, A. D., Statistical Physics
BRYDON, I. G., Renewable Energy
BULFIELD, G., Animal Genetics
BUNDY, A. R., Automated Reasoning
BUNEMAN, P., Database Systems
CAMPBELL, D. M., Musical Acoustics
CARBERY, A., Mathematics
CATES, M., Natural Philosophy
CHAPMAN, S. K., Biological Inorganic Chemistry
CHEUNG, R., Nanoelectronics
CLARKE, P., e-Science
COOPER, J. M., Micro- and Nanosystems
CRAIN, J., Applied Physics
CROWLEY, T., Earth Systems Science
DAVIE, A. M., Mathematical Analysis
DAVIES, M., Signal Processing
DAVIS, I., Cell Biology
DONOVAN, R. J., Chemistry
DUGMORE, A. J., Geosciences
DUNLOP, J. S., Extragalactic Astronomy
EASSON, W. J., Fluid Mechanics
FAN, W., Web Data Management
FARMER, J. G., Environmental Geochemistry
FIGUEROA-O'FARRILL, J., Geometric Physics
FINNEGAN, D. J., Molecular Genetics
FISHER, R. B., Computer Vision
FITTON, J. G., Igneous Petrology
FORDE, M. C., Civil Engineering Construction
FOURMAN, M. P., Computer Systems
FRY, S. C., Plant Biochemistry
GILLESPIE, T. A., Mathematical Analysis
GONDZIS, J., Optimization
GORDON, I., Mathematics
GORYANIN, I., Systems Biology
GRACE, J., Environmental Biology
GRAHAM, C. M., Experimental Geochemistry
GRANT, P. M., Electronic Signal Processing
GRAY, D., Immunology
GYÖNGY, I. J., Probability
HALL, C., Materials

HALLIDAY, I., Physics
HARLEY, S. L., Lower Crustal Processes
HARRISON, A., Solid-State Chemistry
HARTE, B., Metaphorism
HASZELDINE, S., Sedimentary Geology
HEAVENS, A. F., Theoretical Astrophysics
HEGGIE, D. C., Mathematical Astronomy
HILLSTON, J., Quantitative Modelling
HUDSON, A. D., Developmental Genetics
HUXLEY, A., Physics, Quantum Ordering at Extreme Positions
ILLIUS, A. W., Animal Ecology
JACK, M. A., Electronic Systems
JACOBS, J. M., Cultural Geography
JERRUM, M. R., Algorithms and Complexity
KEIGHTLEY, P. D., Evolutionary Genetics
KENNEDY, A. D., Computational Science
KENWAY, R. D., Mathematical Physics
KLEIN, E., Cognitive Systems
KROON, D., Geology
LAWRENCE, A., Astronomy
LEACH, D. R. F., Molecular Genetics
LEIGH, D. A., Organic Chemistry
LEIGH BROWN, A. J., Evolutionary Genetics
LEIM-KUHLER, B., Applied Mathematics
LENAGAN, T. H., Non-commutative Algebra
LIBKIN, L., Foundations of Data Management
LOAKE, G. J., Molecular Plant Sciences
LU, Y., Structural Mechanics
MADDON, P., Physical Chemistry
MAIN, I. G., Seismology and Rock Physics
MAIZELS, R. M., Zoology
MATTHEWS, K., Parasite Biology
McKINNON, K. I. M., Operational Research
McLAUGHLIN, S., Electronic Communications Systems
McMAHON, M., High Pressure Physics
McNABB, H., Heterocyclic Chemistry
MEDVINSKY, A., Haematopoietic Stem Cell Biology
METCALFE, S. E., Environmental Change
MILLER, A. J., Systems Biology
MONCRIEFF, J., Micrometeorology
MOORE, J. D., Artificial Intelligence
MULGREW, B., Signals and Systems
MULHEIM, F., Particle Physics
MURRAY, A. F., Neural Electronics
NEE, S., Social Evolution
NELMES, R. J., Physical Crystallography
O'BOYLE, M., Computer Science
OBERLANDER, J., Epistemics
OOI, J., Particulate Solid Mechanics
OPARKA, K. J., Plant Science
PARKER, D. F., Applied Mathematics
PARSONS, S., Crystallography
PEACOCK, J. A., Cosmology
PEMBERTON, J. M., Molecular Ecology
PLAYFER, S. M., Experimental Particle Physics
PLOTKIN, G. D., Computation Theory
PONTON, J. W., Chemical and Process Systems Engineering
POON, W. C. K., Condensed Matter Physics
PUSEY, P. N., Physics
RANICKI, A. A., Algebraic Surgery
RANKIN, D. W. H., Structural Chemistry
READ, A. F., Natural History
REID, G. A., Molecular Microbiology
RENALS, S., Speech Technology
RESBOL, N. D., Fungal Cell Biology
ROBERTSON, A. H. F., Geology
ROTTER, J. M., Civil Engineering
ROUNSEVELL, M., Rural Economy and Environmental Sustainability
SANNELLA, D. T., Computer Science
SAWYER, L., Biomolecular Structure
SCHÄFER, A., Environmental Engineering
SEATON, N. A., Interfacial Engineering
SHEIKHDESLAMI, R., Chemical Process Engineering
SHOTTER, A. C., Experimental Physics
SIEGERT, M. J., Geoscience
SINGER, M., Geometry
SMOKTURNOWICZ, A., Algebra
STAEHELI, L., Geography

STEEDMAN, M., Cognitive Science
STENNING, K., Human Communications
STIRLING, C., Computation Theory
SUGDEN, D. E., Geography
SUMMERFIELD, M. A., Geomorphology
TASKER, P. A., Industrial Chemistry
TATE, A., Knowledge-based Systems
TELEMAN, C., Mathematics
TETT, S. F. B., Earth Systems Dynamics
THOMPSON, R., Environmental Geophysics
TOPHAM, N. P., Computer Systems
TORERO, J. L., Fire Safety Engineering
TREW, A. S., Computational Science
TUDHOPE, A. W., Climate Science
TYER, S. M. D., Systems Biology
UNDERHILL, J. R., Seismic Stratigraphy
UNDERWOOD, I., Electronic Displays
USAMI, A. S., Structural Engineering and Computational Mechanics
VOLBERG, A., Mathematical Sciences
WALDER, P., Theoretical Computer Science
WALKINSHAW, M. D., Structural Biochemistry
WALLACE, A. R., Renewable Energy Systems
WALTON, A. J., Microelectronic Manufacturing
WEBBER, B., Intelligent Systems
WEST, S. A., Evolutionary Ecology
WHALER, K. A., Geophysics
WHITTEMORE, C. T., Agriculture and Rural Economy
WILLIAMS, C. K. I., Machine Learning
WILLIAMS, W., Mineral Physics
WILLSHAW, D., Computational Neurobiology
WITHERS, C. W. J., Geography
WOODS, P. J., Nuclear Physics
WRIGHT, J., Mathematical Analysis
YELLOWLEES, L. J., Inorganic Electrochemistry
ZIOLKOWSKI, A. M., Petroleum Geoscience

CONSTITUENT COLLEGE

New College: Mound Pl., Edinburgh, EH1 2LX; f. 1846; Prin. Rev. Prof. A. G. AULD.

UNIVERSITY OF GLASGOW

Glasgow, G12 8QQ
Telephone: (141) 330-2000
Fax: (141) 330-4808
E-mail: media@gla.ac.uk
Internet: www.gla.ac.uk
Founded 1451, reconstituted 1577
Academic year: October to June
Chancellor: Prof. Sir KENNETH CALMAN
Prin. and Vice-Chancellor: Prof. ANTON MUSCATELLI
Pro-Vice-Prin.: Prof. JOHN COGGINS
Sr Vice-Prin. and Deputy Vice-Chancellor: ANDREA NOLAN
Vice-Prin. for Learning and Teaching: Prof. FRANK COTON
Vice-Prin. for Life Sciences and Medicine: Prof. JOHN COGGINS
Vice-Prin. for Research and Enterprise: Prof. STEVE P. BEAUMONT
Vice-Prin. for Strategy and Resources: Prof. NEAL JUSTER
Clerk of Senate: Prof. GRAHAM CAIE
Rector: CHARLES KENNEDY
Sec. of Court: DAVID NEWALL
Librarian: HELEN DURNDELL
Library: see Libraries and Archives
Number of teachers: 2,607
Number of students: 21,954
Publications: *Avenue* (2 a year), *News Review* (2 a year)

HEADS OF COLLEGES AND SCHOOLS

Arts Lab: Prof. JOHN CAUGHIE (Dir)
Business School: Prof. FARHAD NOORBAKHSH
College of Arts: Prof. MURRAY PITTOCK

College of Medical, Veterinary and Life Sciences: Prof. ANNA DOMINICZAK
College of Science and Engineering: Prof. JOHN CHAPMAN
College of Social Sciences: Prof. ANNE ANDERSON
School of Chemistry: Prof. STEPHEN CLARK
School of Computing Science: Prof. JOSEPH S. SVENTEK
School of Critical Studies: Prof. NIGEL J. LEASK
School of Culture and Creative Arts: Prof. NICHOLAS J. PEARCE
School of Education: Prof. ROBERT A. DAVIS
School of Engineering: Prof. JOHN H. MARSH
School of Geographical and Earth Sciences: Prof. TREVOR HOEY
School of Humanities/Sgoil nan Daonnachdan: Prof. SIMON J. BALL
School of Interdisciplinary Studies: Prof. DAVID CLARK (Dir)
School of Law: Prof. ROSA GREAVES
School of Life Sciences: Dr ROBERT AITKEN
School of Mathematics and Statistics: Prof. NICHOLAS A. HILL
School of Medicine: Prof. DAVID H. BARLOW
School of Modern Languages and Cultures: Prof. JOHN MACKLIN
School of Physics and Astronomy: Prof. ANDREW R. LONG
School of Psychology: Prof. ANTHONY M. BURTON
School of Social and Political Sciences: Prof. MICHAEL J. FRENCH
School of Veterinary Medicine: Prof. STUART W. REID

PROFESSORS

Faculty of Arts (6 University Gardens, Glasgow, G12 8QQ; tel. (141) 330-6319; fax (141) 330-4537; e-mail dean@arts.gla.ac.uk; internet www.arts.gla.ac.uk):
ABRAMS, L. C., Gender History
ADAMS, A. R., Emblem Studies
BISHOP, P. C., German
BLACK, C. F., Italian History
BROADIE, A., Logic and Rhetoric
BUTT, J. A., Music (Gardiner Chair)
CAIE, G. D., English Language
CARTER, A. B., Moral Philosophy
CASTILLO, S., American Literature (John Nichol Chair)
CAUGHIE, J. M., Film and Television Studies
CLANCY, T. O., Celtic
COHN, S. K., Medieval History
COWAN, E. J., Scottish History
CRONIN, R., English Literature
GERAGHTY, C., Film and TV Studies
GEYER-KORDESCH, J. M., European Natural History and Medicine
GIFFORD, D. G., Scottish Literature
GONZALEZ, M. A., Latin American Studies
GRANT, R. A., Cultural and Political Thought
GREEN, R. P., Humanity
HAIR, G. B., Music
HANSON, W. S., Roman Archaeology
HAZLETT, W. I., Ecclesiastical History
HOPKINS, D., Art History
JASPER, D., Literature and Theology
KAY, C. J., English Language
KIDD, C., Modern History (Chair)
KIRK, J., Scottish History
KNAPP, A. B., Mediterranean Archaeology
KNOWLES, D. R., Political Philosophy
LEASK, N., English Language and Literature (Regius Chair)
LEONARD, T. A., Creative Writing
MACKENZIE, A. L., Spanish (Ivy McClelland Research Chair)
MacMAHON, M. K. C., Phonetics
MALEY, W. T., Renaissance Studies
MARSHALL, W. J., Modern French Studies
MAWDSLEY, E., International History

McDONALD, J. B., Drama (James Arnott Chair)
McLEOD, M. D., African Studies
MOIGNARD, E. A., Classical Art and Archaeology
MORRIS, C. D., Archaeology
MOSS, M. S., Archival Studies
NEWLANDS, G. M., Divinity
NEWMAN, S. P., American Studies (Sir Denis Brogan Chair)
O'MAOLALAIGH, R., Celtic
O'DOCHARTAIGH, C. N. O., Celtic
PEACOCK, N. A., French (Marshall Chair)
READER, K. A., Modern French Studies
RIACH, A. S., Scottish Literature
ROBERTSON, P. B., Mackintosh Studies
ROSS, S., Humanities Informatics and Digital Curation
RYCROFT, M. E., Music
SCHMIDT-LEUKEL, P. H., World Religions for Peace
SMITH, J. J., English Philology
STALLEY, R. F., Ancient Philosophy
STEPHENSON, R. H., German Language and Literature; Modern Languages (William Jacks Chair)
TAYLOR, R. C., Social Policy and Social Work
THORP, N. R., History of Art
TODD, J., English Literature (Francis Hutcheson Chair)
WARD, M. G., German Language and Literature
YARRINGTON, A. W., Fine Art (Richmond Chair)

Faculty of Biomedical and Life Sciences (Room 237, West Medical Bldg, Glasgow, G12 8QQ; tel. (141) 339-8855; fax (141) 330-4758; e-mail ilbs-acstaff@bio.gla.ac.uk; internet www.gla.ac.uk/ibls/faculty/html):

BIRKBECK, T. H., Marine Microbiology
BLATT, M. R., Botany (Regius Chair)
CAMPBELL, A. M., Biochemical Immunology
CLEMENTS, J. A., Virology
COGDELL, R. J., Botany (Hooker Chair)
COGGINS, J. R., Molecular Enzymology
COOMBS, G. H., Biochemical Parasitology
CROZIER, A., Plant Biochemistry and Human Nutrition
CUSHLEY, W., Molecular Immunology
DAVIES, R. W., Biotechnology (Robertson Chair)
DOW, J. A. T., Molecular and Integrative Physiology
ELLIOTT, R. M., Molecular Virology
EVANS, D. J., Virology
FERRELL, W. R., Clinical Physiology
FURNESS, R. W., Seabird and Fishing Interactions
GILLESPIE, D. A. F., Molecular and Cell Biology
GOULD, G. W., Membrane Biology
HAGAN, P., Parasitology
HOUSLAY, M. D., Biochemistry (Gardiner Chair)
HOUSTON, D. C., Zoology
HUNTINGFORD, F. A., Functional Ecology
JENKINS, G. I., Plant Cell and Molecular Biology
KENNEDY, M. W., Infection Biology
KOLCH, W., Molecular and Cellular Biology
LA THANGUE, N. B., Biochemistry (Cathcart Chair)
LINDSAY, J. G., Medical Biochemistry
MacLEAN, M. R., Pulmonary Pharmacology
MARTIN, W., Cardiovascular Pharmacology
MAXWELL, D. J., Neuroanatomy
McGRATH, J. C., Physiology (Regius Chair)
METCALFE, N. B., Behavioural Ecology
MILLIGAN, G., Molecular Pharmacology
MILNER-WHITE, E.J., Structural Bioinformatics
MITCHELL, T. J., Microbiology
MONAGHAN, P., Animal Ecology
MONCKTON, D. G., Human Genetics

MORRIS, B. J., Molecular Neurobiology
MUTRIE, N., Physical Activity and Health Science
NIMMO, H. G., Plant Biochemistry
PAGE, R. D., Taxonomy
PAYNE, A. P., Anatomy
PHILLIPS, R. S., Parasitology
PRICE, N. C., Protein Science
RUXTON, G. D., Theoretical Ecology
SMITH, G. L., Cardiovascular Physiology
STARK, W. M., Molecular Genetics
STONE, T. W., Pharmacology
TAYLOR, A. C., Physiological Ecology
TODD, A. J., Neuroscience
TURNER, C. M. R., Parasitology
WHITE, R. J., Gene Transcription

Faculty of Education (St Andrew's Bldg, Glasgow, G12 8QQ; tel. (141) 330-3700; fax (141) 330-3005; e-mail faculty@educ.gla.ac.uk; internet www.gla.ac.uk/faculties/education):

BARON, S., Urban Education
BARR, J. L., Adult and Continuing Education
CONROY, J. C., Religious and Philosophical Education
McGETTRICK, B. J., Educational Studies
McGONIGAL, J., English in Education
MENTER, I. J., Teacher Education
PETERS, M. A., Education
PREECE, J., Adult and Lifelong Education
WHITEHEAD, R. R., Theoretical Physics
WILKINSON, J. E., Education

Faculty of Engineering (James Watt South Bldg, Glasgow, G12 8QQ; tel. (141) 330-3733; fax (141) 330-4722; internet www.eng.gla.ac.uk):

ACHA, E., Electrical Power Systems
AITCHISON, J. S., Photonics
ARNOLD, J. M., Applied Electromagnetics
ASENOV, A. M., Device Modelling
BARKER, J. R., Electronics
BARLTROP, N. D. P., Naval Architecture and Ocean Engineering (John Elder Chair)
BICANIC, N. J. D., Civil Engineering (Regius Chair)
CARTMELL, M. P., Mechanical Engineering
COOPER, J. M., Bioelectronics and Bioengineering
COTON, F. N., Low Speed Aerodynamics
COWLING, M. J., Marine Technology
CUMMING, D., Microelectronics
DAS, P. K., Marine Structures
DAVIES, J. H., Physical Electronics
DE LA RUE, R. M., Optoelectronics
ERVINE, D. A., Water Engineering
GALBRAITH, R. A. M., Engineering (Shoda Chair)
HANCOCK, J. W., Mechanical Engineering
HUNT, K. J., Mechanical Engineering (Wylie Chair)
HUTCHINGS, D., Optical and Quantum Electronics
IRONSIDE, C. N., Quantum Electronics
MARSH, J. H., Optoelectronic Systems
McINNES, C. R., Space Systems Engineering
MILLER, T. J. E., Electrical Engineering
MURRAY-SMITH, D. J., Engineering Systems and Control
O'REILLY, J., Control Engineering
SEWELL, J. I., Electronic Systems
STANLEY, C. R., Semiconductor Materials
THAYNE, I., Ultrafast Systems
VASSALOS, D., Naval Architecture
WEAVER, J. M. R., Applied Nanofabrication
WHEELER, S. J., Civil Engineering (Cormack Chair)
WILKINSON, C. D. W., Electrical Engineering (James Watt Chair)

Faculty of Information and Mathematical Sciences (Room 311, Boyd Orr Bldg, Glasgow, G12 8QQ; tel. (141) 330-4269; fax (141)

330-2359; e-mail gs@fims.gla.ac.uk; internet www.gla.ac.uk/faculties/ims):

ANDERSON, A. H., Psychology
ATKINSON, M. P., Computing Science
BOWMAN, A. W., Statistics
BREWSTER, S. A., Human Computer Interaction
BROWN, K. A., Mathematics
BURTON, A. M., Psychology
CALDER, M., Formal Methods
COHEN, S. D., Number Theory
FEARN, D. R., Applied Mathematics
FORD, I., Biostatistics
GARROD, S. C., Cognitive Psychology
GILBERT, D. R., Biomedical Informatics
HILL, N. A., Mathematics (Simson Chair)
JOHNSON, C. W., Computing Science
JONES, B. T., Psychology
KROPHOLLER, P. H., Mathematics
O'DONNELL, P.
OGDEN, R. W., Mathematics (George Sinclair Chair)
PRIDE, S. J., Mathematics
SANFORD, A. J., Psychology
SCHWEINBERGER, S. R., Psychology
SCHYNS, P. G., Visual Cognition
SCOTT, E. M., Environmental Statistics
SENN, K.S. J., Statistics
SMITH, P. F., Mathematics
SVENTEK, J., Communications Systems
TITTERINGTON, D. M., Statistics
VAN RIJSBERGEN, K.J., Computing Science
WATT, D. A., Computing Science
WEBB, J. R. L., Mathematics
WELLAND, R. C., Software Engineering

Faculty of Law and Financial Studies (5–9 Stair Bldg, The Square, Univ. of Glasgow, Glasgow, G12 8QQ; tel. (141) 330-6075; fax (141) 330-4900; e-mail faculty@law.gla.ac.uk; internet www.gla.ac.uk/faculties/law):

BEATTIE, V. A., Accounting
BURROWS, N., European Law
CRERAR, L. D., Banking Law
DANBOLT, J., Finance
DAVIDSON, F. P., Law, Commercial Law (Alexander Stone Chair)
EMMANUEL, C. R., Accountancy
FARMER, L. A., Law
GRAY, R. H., Accounting
HOLLAND, J. B., Accountancy
KINNON, D. H., Accounting (Johnstone Smith Chair)
McLEAN, S. A., Law and Ethics in Medicine (International Bar Assoc Chair)
McPHAIL, K., Social and Ethical Accounting
MULLEN, T. J., Law
MURDOCH, J. L., Public Law
OPONG, K. K., Finance and Accounting
ORUCU, E., Comparative Law
REES, W., Accountancy
RENNIE, R., Conveyancing
SHACKLETON, J. K., Accounting History
THOMSON, J. M., Law (Regius Chair)
TOMKINS, A., Public Law (John Millar Chair)
WOOLFSON, C. A., Labour Studies

Faculty of Medicine (Wolfson Medical Bldg, University Ave, Univ. of Glasgow, Glasgow, G12 8QQ; tel. (141) 330-5921; fax (141) 330-3360; e-mail postmaster@student.gla.ac.uk; internet www.gla.ac.uk/faculties/medicine):

AYOUB, A. F., Oral Surgery
BAGG, J., Clinical Microbiology
BAKER, A. H., Molecular Medicine
BARLOW, D. H., Reproductive Medicine
BROWN, R., Cancer Therapeutics
CASSIDY, J., Oncology
COBBE, S. M., Medical Cardiology (Walton Chair)
CONNELL, J. M. C., Endocrinology
CONNOR, J. M., Medical Genetics (Burton Chair)
COOKE, T. G., Surgery (St Mungo Chair)

COOPER, S. A., Learning Disabilities
DOMINICZAK, A. F., Cardiovascular Medicine
ELLIOTT, A. T., Clinical Physics
ESPIE, C. A., Clinical Psychology
EVANS, J. J., Applied Neuropsychology
EVANS, T. J., Molecular Microbiology
FRANKLIN, I. M., Transfusion Medicine
GARSIDE, P., Immunobiology
GEMMELL, C. G., Bacterial Infection and Epidemiology
GEORGE, W. D., Surgery (Regius Chair)
GRAHAM, G. J., Molecular and Structural Immunology
GREER, I. A., Obstetrics and Gynaecology (Muirhead Chair)
GUSTERSON, B. A., Pathology
HANLON, P. W., Public Health
HARNETT, M. M., Immune Signalling
HILLAN, E. M., Midwifery
HILLIS, W. S., Cardiovascular and Exercise Medicine
HOLE, D. J., Epidemiology and Biostatistics
HOLYOAKE, T., Experimental Haematology
JUDGE, K. F., Health Promotion Policy (HEBS Chair)
KEITH, W. N., Molecular Oncology
KENNEDY, P. G. E., Neurology (Burton Chair)
KENNY, G. N. C., Anaesthesia
LANGHORNE, P., Stroke Care
LEAN, M. E. J., Human Nutrition (Rank Chair)
LEES, K. R., Cerebrovascular Medicine
LIEW, F. Y., Immunology (Gardiner Chair)
LOWE, G. D. O., Vascular Medicine
LUMSDEN, M. A., Medical Education and Gynaecology
LYALL, F., Maternal and Fetal Health
MacDONALD, D. G., Oral Pathology
MacFARLANE, P. W., Electrocardiology
MACRAE, I. M., Neuroscience
McCOLL, K. E. L., Gastroenterology
McINNES, G. T., Clinical Pharmacology
McINNES, I. B., Experimental Medicine
McKILLOP, J. H., Medicine (Muirhead Chair)
McMILLAN, T., Clinical Neuropsychology
McMURRAY, J. I. V., Medical Cardiology
MILLAR, K., Behavioural Science
MORRISON, J. M., General Practice
MOWAT, A. M., Mucosal Immunology
MURRAY, T. S., General Practice
O'DWYER, P. J., Gastrointestinal Surgery
OLIVER, J. S., Forensic Toxicology
RAMPLING, R. P., Neuro-oncology
REID, J. L., Materia Medica, Medicine and Therapeutics (Regius Chair)
REID, M., Professor of Women's Health
SATTAR, N. A., Metabolic Medicine
SHEPHERD, J., Pathological Biochemistry
SMITH, L. N., Nursing Studies
STONE, D. H., Paediatric Epidemiology
STOTT, D. J., Geriatric Medicine (David Cargill Chair)
STURROCK, R. D., Rheumatology (McLeod/Arthritis and Rheumatism Council Chair)
THOMSON, N. C., Respiratory Medicine
WATT, G. C. M., General Practice (Norrie-Miller Chair)
WEAVER, L. T., Child Health (Samson Gemmell Chair)
WELBURY, R. R., Paediatric Dentistry
WELSH, J., Palliative Medicine (Dr Olav Kerr Chair)
WHEATLEY, D. J., Cardiac Surgery
WILLISON, H. J., Neurology
WRAY, D., Oral Medicine

Faculty of Physical Sciences (Room 234, Kelvin Bldg, Univ. of Glasgow, Glasgow, G12 8QQ; tel. (141) 330-4374; fax (141) 330-4371; e-mail physci@gla.ac.uk; internet www.facps.gla.ac.uk):

BARRON, L. D., Physical Chemistry (Gardiner Chair)
BISHOP, P. M., Geography
BRIGGS, J. A., Geography
BROWN, J. C., Astrophysics, Astronomy (Regius Chair)
BROWN, R. W., Earth Sciences
CHAPMAN, J. N., Physics
COOPER, A., Biophysical Chemistry
CRAVEN, A. J., Physics
DAVIES, C. T., Physics
DOYLE, A. T., Physics
FALLICK, A. E., Isotope Geosciences
FROGGATT, C. D., Physics
GILMORE, C. J., Crystallography
HOEY, T., Numerical Geoscience
HOUGH, J., Physics
ISAACS, N. W., Protein Crystallography (Joseph Black Chair)
JACKSON, S. D., Catalysis Science
KOCOVSKY, P., Chemistry (Ramsay Chair)
LEAKE, R. E., Endocrine Oncology
LONG, A. R., Physics
PADDISON, R., Geography
PADGETT, M. J., Physics
PHILO, C., Geography
ROBERTSON, N. A., Experimental Physics
ROBINS, D. J., Bio-organic Chemistry
ROSNER, G., Natural Philosophy (Cargill Chair)
RUSSELL, M. J., Applied Geology (Dixon Chair)
SAXON, D. H., Physics (Kelvin Chair)
STRAIN, K. A., Physics
WILSON, C., Chemistry (Regius Chair)
WINFIELD, J. M., Inorganic Chemistry

Faculty of Social Sciences (Adam Smith Bldg, 40 Bute Gardens, Glasgow, G12 8RT; tel. (141) 330-0347; fax (141) 330-3547; e-mail enquiries@socsci.gla.ac.uk; internet www.gla.ac.uk/faculties/socialsciences):

ADAMS, C. D., Ian Mactaggart Chair of Property and Urban Studies
BEAUMONT, P. B., Employee Relations
BERRY, C. J., Political Theory
BURMAN, M., Criminology
CORRIN, C. A., Feminist Politics
CROWTHER, M. A., Social History
FERGUSON, H., Sociology
FRENCH, M. J., Economic History
FRISBY, D. P., Sociology
FURLONG, A., Sociology
GIRVIN, B., Comparative Politics
GOODLAD, R., Housing and Urban Studies
GORDON, E. J., Gender and Social History
HARRIS, R., Cairncross Professor of Applied Economics
HILL, M., Study of the Child (St Kentigern Chair)
KEARNS, A. J., Urban Studies
LAING, A. W., Business and Management
MACBETH, D. K., Supply Chain Management
MacDONALD, R., Bonar-Macfie Chair of Economics
MACLENNAN, D., Urban Studies, Economics and Finance (Mactaggart Chair of Urban Studies)
MALLEY, J., Economics
McGREGOR, A. M., Housing and Urban Studies
McKEGANEY, N. P., Drug Misuse Research
MILLER, W. L., Politics (Edward Caird Chair)
MOUTINHO, L. A., Marketing
MUSCATELLI, A., Economics (Daniel Jack Chair)
NOORBAKHSH, F., Development Economics
ORME, J. E., Social Work
PARR, J. B., Regional and Urban Economics
PATON, R. A., Management
PETCH, A. J., Nuffield Trust Professor of Community Care
PETERSON, J. C., European Politics (Jean Monnet Chair)

PHILO, G., Communications and Social Change
SCHENK, C., International Economic History
STOKES, R. G., International Industrial History
TUROK, I. N., Urban Economic Development
VIRDEE, S., Sociology
WATSON, N., Disability Studies
WEAVER, R., Entrepreneurship
WHITE, J. D., Russian and East European History
WHITE, S. L., Government
WILSON, F. M., Organizational Behaviour

Faculty of Veterinary Medicine (464 Bearsden Rd, Glasgow, G61 1QH; tel. (141) 330-5700; fax (141) 942-7215; internet www.gla.ac.uk/faculties/vet):

BARRY, J. D., Molecular Parasitology
BENNETT, D., Small Animal Clinical Studies
CAMERON, E. R., Molecular and Cellular Oncology
CAMPO, M. S., Viral Oncology
CARMICHAEL, S., Veterinary Clinical Studies
DEVANEY, E., Parasite Immunobiology
ECKERSALL, P. D., Veterinary Biochemistry
FITZPATRICK, J. L., Farm Animal Medicine
GRIFFITHS, I., Comparative Neurology
HOLMES, P. H., Veterinary Physiology
JARRETT, R. F., Molecular Pathology
LOVE, S., Equine Clinical Studies
MOTTRAM, J. C., Molecular and Cellular Parasitology
NASH, A. S., Small Animal Medicine
NEIL, J. C., Virology and Molecular Oncology
NOLAN, A., Veterinary Pharmacology
ONIONS, D. E., Veterinary Pathology
O'SHAUGHNESSY, P. J., Reproductive Biology
PALMARINI, M., Molecular Pathogenesis
PARKINS, J. J., Animal Health
REID, J., Veterinary Anaesthesia
REID, S. W. J., Veterinary Informatics and Epidemiology
ROBERTS, M., Molecular Bacteriology
STEAR, M. J., Veterinary Medicine
SULLIVAN, M., Veterinary Surgery and Diagnostic Imaging
TAIT, A., Veterinary Parasitology
TAYLOR, D. J., Veterinary Bacteriology and Public Health

Hunterian Museum and Art Gallery: (see Museums and Art Galleries)

UNIVERSITY OF ST ANDREWS

St Andrews KY16 9AJ
Telephone: (1334) 476161
Internet: www.st-and.ac.uk
Founded 1413
Chancellor: Sir MENZIES CAMPBELL
Prin. and Vice-Chancellor: Prof. Dr LOUISE RICHARDSON
Deputy Prin. and Vice-Prin. for Research: Prof. CHRISTOPHER HAWKESWORTH
Vice-Prin. for External Relations: STEPHEN MAGEE
Vice-Prin. for Governance and Planning: Prof. RONALD PIPER
Vice-Prin. for Learning and Teaching: Prof. PAT WILLMER
Rector: KEVIN DUNION
Master of the United College: Prof. NEVILLE V. RICHARDSON
Proctor: Prof. PETER CLARK
Quaestor and Factor: DEREK WATSON
Dir of Library Services: JEREMY UPTON (acting)

Library: see Libraries and Archives
Number of teachers: 935

Number of students: 7,730

DEANS

Faculty of Arts: Prof. ROY DILLEY
Faculty of Divinity: Prof. IVOR DAVIDSON
Faculty of Medicine: Prof. HUGH MacDOU-
GALL
Faculty of Science: Prof. ALYSON TOBIN

PROFESSORS

Faculty of Arts:

BARTLETT, R. J., Medieval History
BEATH, J. A., Economics and Finance
BEBBINGTON, J., Management
BENTLEY, M. J., Modern History
BROADIE, S., Moral Philosophy
BROWN, K. M., Scottish History
CARRADICE, I. A., Art History
CHAMBERS, H. E., German
CRAWFORD, R., English
DAVIES, H. T. O., Management
DE GROOT, G. J., Modern History
DENNIS, N., Spanish
DUNN, D. E., English
FERGUSON, R., French
FITZROY, F. R., Economics and Finance
GIVEN-WILSON, C. J., Medieval History
GOW, P., Philosophical and Anthropological
Studies
GRATWICK, A., Classical Philology
GRAY, R. H., Management
HALDANE, J. J., Moral Philosophy
HALLIWELL, F. S., Greek
HARRIES, J. D., Ancient History
HINNEBUSCH, R., International Relations
HOUSTON, R. A., Modern History
HUDSON, J., History
HUGHES-HALLETT, A., Economics and
Finance
HUMFREY, P., Art History
LITTLER, C., Management Centre for Busi-
ness Education
MAGDALINO, P., Medieval History
McKIERNAN, P., Management
McKINLAY, A., Management
NOLAN, C., Economics and Finance
PETTEGREE, A. D. M., Modern History
POLLMANN, K., Classics
PRIEST, G., Philosophy
RAPPORT, N. J., Social Anthropology
REID, G. C., Economics and Finance
RENGGER, N. J., International Relations
RHODES, N., English
ROE, N. H., English
SCOTT, H. M., Modern History
SELLERS, S. C., English
SKORUPSKI, J., Moral Philosophy
SMITH, C. J., Classics
SUTHERLAND, A. J., Economics and Finance
WALKER, W. B., International Relations
WOOLF, G. D., Classics
WRIGHT, C. J. G., Logic and Metaphysics

Faculty of Divinity:

ESLER, P. F., Divinity
HART, T. A., Divinity
PIPER, R. A., Divinity
TORRANCE, A. J., Divinity

Faculty of Medicine:

HERRINGTON, S., Medicine
HUMPHRIS, G., Medicine
MacDOUGALL, R. H., Medicine
RICHES, A., Medicine

Faculty of Science:

BALLANTYNE, C. K., Geography and Geos-
ciences
BOYD, I., Biology
BOYLE, P. J., Geography and Geosciences
BROWN, V., Psychology
BRUCE, P. G., Chemistry
BUCKLAND, S. T., Mathematics and Statis-
tics
BYRNE, R. W., Psychology
CAIRNS, R. A., Applied Mathematics
CAMERON, A. C., Physics and Astronomy

COLE-HAMILTON, D. J., Chemistry
DEARLE, A., Computer Science
DHOLAKIA, K., Physics and Astronomy
DRITSCHEL, D. G., Mathematics
DUNN, M. H., Photonics
FALCONER, K. J., Mathematics and Statis-
tics
FLOWERDEW, R., Geography and Geos-
ciences
HARWOOD, J., Biology
HOOD, A. W., Mathematics
HORNE, K. D., Physics and Astronomy
IRVINE, J. T. S., Chemistry
JOHNSTON, I. A., Comparative Physiology
KRAUSS, T. F., Physics and Astronomy
LEE, S., Physics and Astronomy
LEONHARDT, U., Physics and Astronomy
MACKENZIE, A., Physics and Astronomy
MacLEOD, M., Psychology
MAGURRAN, A. E., Biology
MEAGHER, T. R., Biology
MORRIS, R., Chemistry
NAISMITH, J. H., Chemistry
O'HAGAN, D., Chemistry
PATERSON, D. M., Biology
PERRETT, D. I., Psychology
PRIEST, E. R., Theoretical Solar Physics
RANDALL, R. E., Biology
REICHER, S., Psychology
RICHARDSON, N. V., Chemistry
RITCHIE, M. G., Biology
ROBERTS, B., Mathematics
SAMUEL, I., Physics and Astronomy
SIBBETT, W., Natural Philosophy
SILLAR, K. T., Biology
TAYLOR, G. L., Biology
TODD, C. D., Biology
WALTON, J. C., Chemistry
WHITEN, D. A., Psychology
WILLMER, P. G., Biology
WINN, P., Psychology
WOOLLINS, J. D., Chemistry

UNIVERSITY OF STIRLING

Stirling, FK9 4LA
Telephone: (1786) 473171
Fax: (1786) 463000
Internet: www.stir.ac.uk
Founded 1967
Public control
Academic year: September to May (two
semesters)
Chancellor: Dr JAMES NAUGHTIE
Prin. and Vice-Chancellor: Prof. GERRY
McCORMAC
Sr Deputy Prin.: Prof. STEVE BURT
Sr Deputy Prin.: Prof. EDMUND BURKE
Deputy Prin.: Prof. GRANT JARVIE
Deputy Prin.: Prof. IAN SIMPSON
Univ. Sec.: KEVIN CLARKE
Deputy Sec.: Dr EILEEN SCHOFIELD
Library: see Libraries and Archives
Number of teachers: 1,400
Number of students: 12,300

Publication: *Stirling Minds*.

UNIVERSITY OF STRATHCLYDE

16 Richmond St, Glasgow, G1 1XQ
Telephone: (141) 552-4400
Fax: (141) 552-0775
E-mail: rkes@strath.ac.uk
Internet: www.strath.ac.uk
Founded 1796 as Anderson's Institution,
present status 1964
Academic year: September to June
Chancellor: Lord HOPE OF CRAIGHEAD
Prin. and Vice-Chancellor: Prof. JIM McDO-
NALD
Vice-Prin.: Prof. KENNETH MILLER
Deputy Prin.: Prof. DAVID GANI
Chief Operating Officer: HUGH HALL
Chief Financial Officer: Prof. DAVID COYLE

Number of teachers: 841
Number of students: 14,800

DEANS

Faculty of Education: IAIN SMITH
Faculty of Engineering: Prof. SCOTT MACGRE-
GOR
Faculty of Humanities and Social Sciences:
Prof. TONY McGREW
Faculty of Science: Prof. IAIN HUNTER
Strathclyde Business School: Prof. SUSAN
HART

PROFESSORS

ACKERMANN, F., Management Science
AINSWORTH, M., Mathematics
ALEXANDER, J., Immunology
ANDERSON, J., Bioscience
ANDONOVIC, I., Electronic and Electrical
Engineering
ASHCROFT, B. K., Economics
BACHTLER, J., European Policy
BALENDRA, R., Design, Manufacture and
Engineering Management
BANKS, W. M., Advanced Materials
BARNETT, S., Quantum Optics
BARON, S., Education
BATES, T., Law
BATH, M., English
BAUM, T. G., Hospitality Management
BEDFORD, T., Management Science
BELTON, V., Management Science
BINGHAM, R., Physics
BIRCH, D. J. S., Photophysics
BITITCI, U., Design, Manufacture and Engin-
eering Management
BLACKIE, J. W. G., Scots Law
BOYD, B., Language Education
BOYLE, J. T., Mechanics of Materials
BRIDGES, A., Architecture
BROWN, C., History
BRYCE, T. G. K, Education
CARTER, S., Marketing
CHAKRABARTI, M., Social Work
CLARK, N., Environmental Studies
CLARKE, J. A., Energy Systems
COMMON, M., Environmental Studies
CONNOLLY, P., Bioengineering
CONNOR, R., Computer and Information Sci-
ences
COOPER, C., Accounting and Finance
CORCORAN, M., Architecture
COURTNEY, J. M., Bioengineering
CRESTANI, F., Computer and Information
Sciences
CROSS, R. B., Economics
CULSHAW, B., Optoelectronics
CURTICE, J., Government
DAVIES, J. B., Psychology
DONALDSON, G. B., Applied Physics
DUNLOP, J., Communications Engineering
DURRANI, T., Signal Processing
DUXBURY, G., Chemical Physics
EDEN, C., Graduate School of Business
ELPHINSTONE, M., Writing
FABB, N., English
FAIRLEY, J., Environmental Planning
FARRELL, J., Modern Languages
FERGUSON, A. I., Photonics
FINN, G., Educational Studies
FIRTH, W. J., Experimental Physics
FISCHER, C., History
FOOT, H. C., Psychology
FRASER, W. H., History
GENNARD, J., Human Resource Management
GETTINBY, G. C., Statistics
GIBB, F., Computer and Information Sciences
GORDON, G., Academic Practice
GORMAN, D., Mechanical Engineering
GRANT, C. D., Chemical Engineering
GRANT, M., Bioengineering
GRAY, T. G. F., Fracture Mechanics
GRIMBLE, M. J., Industrial Systems
GURNEY, A., Pharmacology
GURNEY, W. S. C., Mathematical Ecology
HALL, P., Chemical Engineering

HALLIDAY, J., Educational Studies
HALLING, P. J., Biocatalyst Science
HARNETT, W., Immunology
HART, S., Marketing
HARVEY, A. L., Pharmacology
HASTINGS, G., Marketing
HAYWARD, G., Signal Processing
HENDRY, A., Metallurgy and Engineering Materials
HIGHAM, D., Mathematics
HILLIER, D., Accounting and Finance
HOGWOOD, B. W., Politics
HOOD, N., Business Policy
HOWE, C., Psychology
HUDSON, S., Pharmaceutical Care
HUMES, W., Educational Studies
HUNTER, I., Molecular Microbiology
HUTTON, N., Law
HUXHAM, C., Management Science
JACKSON, M., Environmental Health
JACOBS, N., Training and Education in Prosthetics
JAROSZYNSKI, D., Physics
JOHNSON, G., Strategic Management
JOHNSON, M., Electronic and Electrical Engineering
JUDGE, D., Politics
JUSTER, N., Design and Manufacture
KANE, K., Physiology and Pharmacology
KARTVEDT, P., Architecture
KAY, N. M., Business Economics
KENDRICK, A., Childcare Initiative
KERR, W., Pure and Applied Chemistry
LANGFORD, D. A., Construction
LAW, D., Computer and Information Sciences
LEDINGHAM, K., Physics
LEITHEAD, W., Electronic and Electrical Engineering
LITTLEJOHN, D., Analytical Chemistry
LLOYD, I. J., Law
LO, K. L., Power Engineering
LOVE, J., Economics
MACDONALD, J., Power Engineering
MACDONALD, R., International Finance
MACFARLANE, C. J., Subsea Engineering
MACGREGOR, S., Electronic and Electrical Engineering
MACKAY, G., Educational Support and Guidance
MANGAN, J. A., Cultural Studies in Education
MAO, X., Statistics
MARSHALL, A., Accounting and Finance
MASON, C., Entrepreneurship
MAVER, T. W., Computer-aided Design
MCBRIDE, A., Mathematics
MCCALL, J., Education
MCGETTRICK, A. D., Computer and Information Sciences
MCGOWN, A., Civil Engineering
MCGREGOR, P., Economics
MCKEE, S., Mathematics
MCNAB, A., Electronic and Electrical Engineering
MCNICOLL, I. H., Applied Economics
MEARNS, D., Counselling Unit
MILBURN, R., Community Education
MILLAN, C. G., French Studies
MILLER, K., Employment Law
MILLS, A., Pure and Applied Chemistry
MITCHELL, J., Government
MULVEY, R. E., Inorganic Chemistry
MURDOCH, A., Mathematics
MURPHY, J., Preparative Chemistry
NICOL, A., Bioengineering
NICOLSON, D., Law
NIMMO, M., Exercise Physiology
NIXON, P., Computer and Information Sciences
NORRIE, K., Law
O'DONNELL, K., Physics
OPPO, G.-L., Physics
OSIPOV, M., Mathematics
PACIONE, M., Geography
PADGETT, S., Government
PATERSON, A. A., Law
PETHRICK, R. A., Physical Chemistry

PHELPS, A., Plasma Physics
PLEVIN, R., Physiology and Pharmacology
PYNE, N., Physiology and Pharmacology
REID, S., Veterinary Informatics
RENSHAW, E., Statistics and Modelling Science
RHODES, J., Mechanics of Materials
ROBERTSON, B., Physiology and Pharmacology
ROBERTSON, C., Statistics
ROBSON, P., Law
RODGER, B., Law
SAREN, M., Marketing
SAWDAY, J., English
SCULLION, H., Human Resource Management
SHAW, S. A., Marketing
SHERRINGTON, D. C., Polymer Chemistry
SLOAN, D. McP., Numerical Analysis
SMITH, W. E., Inorganic Chemistry
SPIER, S., Architecture
STACK, M., Mechanical Engineering
STEPHEN, F. H., Economics
STEVENS, H., Pharmaceutical Sciences
STIMSON, W. H., Immunology
SUCKLING, C. J., Chemistry
SUMMERS, H. P., Theoretical Atomic Physics
SUPPLE, J., French
SWALES, J., Economics
THOMPSON, P., Human Resource Management
THOMSON, J., Psychology
UCHEGBU, I., Pharmaceutical Sciences
UTTAMCHANDANI, D., Electronic and Electrical Engineering
VASSALOS, D., Naval Architecture and Marine Engineering
WADSWORTH, R., Physiology and Pharmacology
WAIGH, R. D., Pharmacy
WALLS, L., Management Science
WATSON, J., Biochemistry
WEETMAN, P., Accounting and Finance
WEIR, A. D., Education
WHITTY, N., Law
WILLIAMS, H., Management Science
WILLIAMS, T., Management Science
WILSON, C. G., Pharmacy
WILSON, S., Mathematics
WOOD, R. C., Hospitality Management
WRIGHT, G., Business Administration
WRIGHT, H. D., Structural Engineering
WRIGHT, R., Business
YADAV, P. K., Accounting and Finance
YEO, E., History
YOUNG, S., Marketing
YUILL, D., European Policies

UNIVERSITY OF THE WEST OF SCOTLAND

Paisley, PA1 2BE

Telephone: (141) 848-3000
Fax: (141) 887-0812
E-mail: uni-direct@paisley.ac.uk
Internet: www.paisley.ac.uk

Founded 1897 as Paisley College of Technology, present name and status 2007
Academic year: October to June

Chancellor: Sir ROBERT SMITH
Prin. and Vice-Chancellor: Prof. SEAMUS MCDAID (acting)
Vice-Prin.: PAUL MARTIN
Deputy Prin. and Vice-Prin. for Strategy: GILL TROUP (acting)
Vice-Prin. for Teaching And Learning: Prof. MALCOLM FOLEY
Vice-Prin. for Research and Commercialisation: Prof. RODDY WILLIAMSON
Sec.: KENNETH ALEXANDER
Librarian: STUART JAMES

Number of teachers: 2,000
Number of students: 20,000

DEANS

School of Education: IAN SMITH

School of Engineering and Science: Prof. ROGER MCLEAN
School of Health, Nursing and Midwifery: Prof. JACK RAE
School of Information Communication Technologies: Dr CHRIS HALSALL
School of Media: ALEX GILKISON
School of Social Sciences: Dr TONY CLARKE
Paisley Business School: ALAN GODFREY

Colleges in Scotland

These institutions are not able to award their own degrees, but offer courses leading to a degree from a recognized body.

Aberdeen College: Gallowgate Centre, Gallowgate, Aberdeen, AB25 1BN; tel. (1224) 612-000; fax (1224) 612-001; e-mail enquiry@abcol.ac.uk; internet www.abcol.ac.uk; f. 1959; courses include English as a foreign language, EX training (electrical work in hazardous environments), interpreter/translator, agriculture, art and design, business studies, communication, electrical and electronic engineering, hospitality, journalism, mechanical engineering, offshore industries, systems analysis and design, sports coaching and development, social studies; 266 full-time teachers; 6,000 full-time, 18,000 part-time students; library: 25,000 vols; Prin. and Chief Exec. ROB WALLEN (acting).

Adam Smith College: St Brycedale Ave, Kirkcaldy, KY1 1EX; tel. (1592) 223400; fax (1592) 223402; e-mail enquiries@adamsmith.ac.uk; internet www.adamsmithcollege.ac.uk; f. 2005 by merger of Glenrothes College and Fife College; 5 campuses; offers degrees and professional devt awards in courses incl. built environment, business and management, care and social sciences, computing, creative industries, hair and beafuty, languages and ESOL, sport and fitness, tourism and hospitality, engineering and renewables, science, skills for life and work; 900 staff; 35,000 teachers; Prin. Dr CRAIG THOMSON.

Al-Maktoum Institute for Arabic and Islamic Studies: 124 Blackness Rd, Dundee, DD1 5PE; tel. (1382) 908070; fax (1382) 908077; e-mail info@almi.abdn.ac.uk; internet www.almi.abdn.ac.uk; research and masters programmes in Islamic subjects; courses validated by Univ. of Aberdeen; library: 17,000 vols; Prin. Prof MALORY NYE.

Carnegie College: Halbeath Campus, Pittsburgh Rd, Dunfermline, KY11 8DY; tel. (1383) 845-010; e-mail info@carnegiecollege.ac.uk; internet www.carnegiecollege.ac.uk; f. 1899 as Lauder College; 4 campuses; courses to degree level; library: 27,000 books, DVDs, newspapers, journals; 10,000 srudents; Prin. and Chief Exec. GEOFF FENLON.

City of Glasgow College: 300 Cathedral St, Glasgow, G1 2TA; tel. (1412) 716-500; fax (1412) 716-511; e-mail info@newcampusglasgow.ac.uk; internet www.cityofglasgowcollege.ac.uk; f. 2010 by merger of Central College Glasgow, Glasgow Metropolitan College and Glasgow College of Nautical Studies; courses in accounting, advertising, art and design, business studies, computing, distribution, hairdressing and beauty therapy, librarianship, marketing, office studies, sports therapy; 1,200 teachers; 40,000 students; Prin. PAUL G. K. LITTLE.

Edinburgh College of Art: Lauriston Place, Edinburgh, EH3 9DF; tel. (131) 221-6000; fax (131) 221-6028; e-mail marketing@eca.ac.uk; internet www.eca.ac.uk; f. 1907; art, design, architecture and landscape architecture programmes at undergraduate, postgraduate and research degree level; degrees validated by Univ. of Edinburgh;

library: 85,000 vols, 350 periodicals; 350 academic staff; 1,700 students; Prin. Prof. IAN HOWARD.

Free Church of Scotland College: The Mound, Edinburgh, EH1 2LS; tel. (131) 226-5286; fax (131) 220-0669; e-mail secretary@freescotcoll.ac.uk; internet www.freescotcoll.ac.uk; f. 1843; undergraduate, postgraduate and part-time courses in biblical studies, Christian theology and related disciplines; 8 teachers; Prin. JOHN L. MACKAY.

Glasgow School of Art: 167 Renfrew St, Glasgow, G3 6RQ; tel. (141) 353-4500; fax (141) 353-4746; e-mail registry@gsa.ac.uk; internet www.gsa.ac.uk; f. 1845; BA, MA and MPhil courses in Architecture, Fine Art and Design; all degree courses validated by Univ. of Glasgow; library: 80,000 vols, 59,000 slides, 250 periodicals of art, design, craft and architecture; 400 teachers; 1,900 students; Dir Prof. SEONA REID.

International Christian College: 110 St James Rd, Glasgow, G4 0PS; tel. (1415) 524-040; fax (1415) 520-808; e-mail college@icc.ac.uk; internet www.icc.ac.uk; f. 1998 by merger of Glasgow Bible College and Northumbria Bible College; undergraduate, postgraduate, certificate courses and doctoral research in Christian studies and theology; library: 45,000 vols, 180 periodical titles, 40 CD-ROMs; 20 teachers; Prin. Rev. RICHARD TIPLADY.

International Correspondence Schools Ltd: 45 Finnieston St, Glasgow, G3 8JU; tel. (141) 302-5487; internet www.icslearn.co.uk; f. 1890; distance learning courses in law, psychology, English and history, fashion textile, health and social care, business, educational studies; degrees in asscn with Univ. of East London, Anglia Ruskin Univ. and Edinburgh Napier Univ.; 36,000 students; Man. Dir SALLY PULVERTAFT.

James Watt College: Finnart Campus, Finnart St, Greenock, PA16 8HF; tel. (1475) 724433; fax (1475) 888079; e-mail enquiries@jameswatt.ac; internet www.jameswatt.ac.uk; f. 1908 as James Watt Memorial College; 4 campuses; vocational courses in full-time and part-time, evening classes and open learning; Prin. and Chief Exec. SUE PINDER.

Scottish Agricultural College: Ayr Campus, Auchincruive Estate, Ayr, KA6 5HW; tel. (131) 535-4391; fax (131) 667-2601; e-mail recruitment@sac.ac.uk; internet www.sac.ac.uk/learning; f. 1900; campuses at Ayr, Aberdeen and Edinburgh (associated with Univ. of Edinburgh); undergraduate, postgraduate courses in agriculture and land based studies; library: 50,000 vols, 670 current journal titles; 250 teachers; 1,200 students; Prin. and Chief Exec. Prof. WILLIAM McKELVEY.

Scottish Baptist College: K202, Univ. of the West of Scotland, High St., Paisley, PA1 2BE; tel. (141) 848-3988; fax (141) 848-3989; e-mail scottishbaptistcollege@uws.ac.uk; internet www.scottishbaptistcollege.org; f. 1894 as Baptist Theological College of Scotland; attached to Univ. of West of Scotland; certificate, diploma and Bachelors courses in Christian theology; Prin. Rev. Dr JIM GORDON.

Scottish Institute of Human Relations: Park Business Centre, 5 La Belle Place, Glasgow, G3 7LH; tel. (141) 332-0011; fax (141) 332-3999; e-mail info@sihr.org.uk; internet www.sihr.org.uk; f. 1971; postgraduate programmes and services for psychoanalytic, psychodynamic and systemic thinking; validated by Univ. of Strathclyde; Exec. Dir AMANDA CORNISH.

Universities in Wales

ABERYSTWYTH UNIVERSITY

Old College, King St, Aberystwyth, Ceredigion, SY23 2AX

Telephone: (1970) 623111
Fax: (1970) 611446
E-mail: dym@aber.ac.uk
Internet: www.aber.ac.uk

Founded 1872, present status 2007
Languages of instruction: English, Welsh
Academic year: September to June
Pres.: Sir EMYR JONES PARRY
Vice-Pres.: ELIZABETH FRANCE
Vice-Pres.: WINSTON RODDICK
Vice-Chancellor: Prof. NOEL G. LLOYD
Pro-Vice-Chancellor: Prof. ALED JONES
Pro-Vice-Chancellor: Dr JOHN HARRIES
Pro-Vice-Chancellor: Prof. MARTIN JONES
Registrar and Sec.: Dr CATRIN HUGHES
Library: see entry for Univ. of Wales Aberystwyth, Hugh Owen Library
Number of teachers: 813
Number of students: 10,210
Publication: *Prom* (1 a year)

DEANS

Faculty of Arts: Prof. TIM S. WOODS
Faculty of Postgraduate Studies: Prof. COLIN J. MCINNES
Faculty of Science: Prof. JOHN P. GRATTAN
Faculty of Social Sciences: Prof. LEN V. SCOTT

PROFESSORS

ALEXANDER, M. S., International Politics
ALEXANDER, N. S., School of Management and Business
BARKER, M. J., Theatre, Film and Television Studies
BARNES, D., Computer Science
BARRY, P., English and Creative Writing
BOOTH, K., International Politics
BORSAY, P., History and Welsh History
BROPHY, P., Biological, Environmental and Rural Sciences
CLARK, I., International Politics
CLARKE, A., Law and Criminology
CRAIG, H., Biological, Environmental and Rural Sciences
DRAPER, J., Biological, Environmental and Rural Sciences
DULLER, G. A. T., Geography and Earth Sciences
EDKINS, J. A., International Politics
ELLIS, D., Information Studies
ERSKINE, T. A., International Politics
EVANS, D., Mathematical and Physical Sciences
FOLEY, M., International Politics
GLASSER, N. F., Geography and Earth Sciences
GOUGH, J., Mathematical and Physical Sciences
GOUGH, R., Theatre, Film and Television Studies
GRANDE, M., Mathematical and Physical Sciences
GREAVES, G. N., Mathematics and Physical Siences
HAMBREY, M. J., Geography and Earth Sciences
HANNAH, M. G., Geography and Earth Sciences
HARDING, C., Law and Criminology
HARESIGN, W., Biological, Environmental and Rural Sciences
HARVEY, J., Art
HAYCOCK, M., Welsh Language and Literature
HUTTON, S., English and Creative Writing
KAY, D., Geography and Earth Sciences
KEAR, A., Theatre, Film and Television Studies
KING, R. D., Computer Science

LAVALLEE, D. E., Sport and Exercise Science
LEE, M. H., Computer Science
LINKLATER, A., International Politics
LUCAS, R. M., Geography and Earth Sciences
MACKLIN, M. G., Geography and Earth Sciences
MALTMAN, A. J., Geography and Earth Sciences
MAVRON, V., Mathematical and Physical Sciences
McGUIRE, S. M., School of Management and Business
MIDMORE, P. R., School of Management and Business
MISHURIS, G., Mathematical and Physical Sciences
NEWBOLD, C. J., Biological, Environmental and Rural Sciences
O'MALLEY, T. P., Theatre, Film and Television Studies
PEARSON, M. J., Theatre, Film and Television Studies
PIOTROWICZ, R. W., Law and Criminology
POSTER, J. P., English and Creative Writing
POWELL, W., Biological, Environmental and Rural Sciences
PRICE, C. J., Computer Science
PRICE, R. D., History and Welsh History
PYKETT, L., English and Creative Writing
RABEY, D. I., Theatre, Film and Television Studies
ROWLAND, D., Law and Criminology
RUBINSTEIN, W. D., History and Welsh History
SCHOFIELD, P. R., History and Welsh History
SCULLY, R., International Politics
SHEN, Q., Computer Science
SIMS-WILLIAMS, P., Welsh Language
STEPHENS, E. C., Theatre, Film and Television Studies
SUGANAMI, H., International Politics
THOMAS, C., Biological, Environmental and Rural Sciences
TROTTER, D., European Languages
WATT, P. D., English and Creative Writing
WHEELER, N. J., International Politics
WILKINSON, M., Biological, Environmental and Rural Sciences
WILLIAMS, G. A., Law and Criminology
WILLIAMS, H. L., International Politics
WOODS, T. S., Geography and Earth Sciences
YOUNG, N., Biological, Environmental and Rural Sciences
ZWIGGELAAR, R., Computer Science

BANGOR UNIVERSITY

Bangor LL57 2DG
Telephone: (1248) 351151
Fax: (1248) 370451
Internet: www.bangor.ac.uk

Founded 1884
Academic year: September to June
Pres.: Lord ELIS-THOMAS OF NANT CONWY
Vice-Chancellor: Prof. JOHN HUGHES
Deputy Vice-Chancellor: Prof. C. FERGUS LOWE
Pro-Vice-Chancellor: Prof. W. THOMAS
Pro-Vice-Chancellor for Teaching and Learning: Prof. COLIN BAKER
Pro-Vice-Chancellor for Research and Enterprise: Prof. DAVID SHEPHERD
Academic Registrar: DAVID FORDHAM (acting)
Dir of Information and Library Services: DAVID LEARMONT
Library: see entry for Univ. of Wales, Bangor, Information Services
Number of teachers: 692
Number of students: 13,600

DEANS

College of Arts and Humanities: Prof. A. M. CLAYDON
College of Business, Social Sciences and Law: Prof. PHIL MOLYNEUX (acting)

College of Education and Lifelong Learning: Prof. J. PRITCHARD
College of Health and Behavioural Sciences: Prof. OLIVER TURNBULL (acting)
College of Natural Sciences: Prof. COLIN JAGO (acting)
College of Physical and Applied Sciences: Prof. PAUL SPENCER (acting)

PROFESSORS

College of Arts and Humanities:
BROWN, A. D., English
BUSHELL, A., Modern Languages
CORNS, T. N., English
DEUCHAR, M., Linguistics and English Language
EDWARDS, J., English
FRANCIS, L., Theology and Religious Studies
HARPER, G., Creative Industries
LEWIS, A.P., Music
LYNCH, P., Welsh
MORGAN, D. D., Theology and Religious Studies
PRYCE, A. H., History and Welsh History
SCHMIDT-BESTE, T. C., Music
TANNER, D. M., History and Welsh History
THOMAS, J. A., Linguistics and English Language
WILCOX, H., English
WILLIAMS, G., Welsh

College of Business, Social Sciences and Law:
CAIN, M., Management Science
CHAKRAVARTY, S. P., Economics
DAVIS, H., Social Sciences
GARDENER, E. P. M., Banking
GODDARD, J., Financial Economics
HESTER, S., Social Sciences
JOHNSON, H., Law
McLEAY, S. J., Treasury
MOLYNEUX, P., Banking and Finance
ROWLEY, J., Marketing and Information Management

College of Education and Lifelong Learning:
BAKER, C. R., Education
ROBERTS, H. G. FF., Education

College of Health and Behavioural Sciences:
COX, W. M., Psychology of Addictive Behaviours
GATHERCOLE, V. M., Psychology
HARDY, L., Sport, Health and Exercise Sciences
HASTINGS, R. P., Psychology
LOWE, C. F., Psychology
MADDISON, P., Sport, Health and Exercise Sciences
NOYES, J., Nursing
RAFAL, R. D., Psychology of Neuroscience and Neuropsychology
RAYMOND, J., Experimental Consumer Psychology
REES, M. R., Vascular Studies
RUSSELL, I. T., Public Health
SHAPIRO, K. L., Cognitive Neuroscience
STUART, N. S. A., Cancer Studies
TIPPER, S. P., Cognitive Science
VIHMAN, M. M., Developmental Psychology
WOODS, R. T., Clinical Psychology of the Elderly

College of Natural Sciences:
CARVALHO, G. R., Biological Sciences
DANDO, P. R., Marine Biology
DAVIES, A. G., Physical Oceanography
EDWARDS-JONES, G., Environment and Natural Resources
ELLIOTT, A. J., Ocean Sciences
FARRAR, J. F., Biological Sciences
FREEMAN, C., Biological Sciences
GODBOLD, D. L., Environment and Natural Resources
HUGHES, R. N., Biological Sciences
JONES, D. L., Environment and Natural Resources

KAISER, M. J., Ocean Sciences
PRICE, C., Environment and Natural Resources
SCOURSE, J. D., Ocean Sciences
SEED, R., Marine Ecology
SIMPSON, J. H., Ocean Sciences
STUART, N. S. A., Biological Sciences
THOMAS, D. N., Ocean Sciences
THORPE, R. S., Biological Sciences
TOMOS, A. D., Biological Sciences
WILLIAMS, P. A., Biological Sciences

College of Physical and Applied Sciences:
ASHWELL, G. J., Chemistry
BAIRD, M. S., Chemistry
HOPE, S., Computer Science
IRVINE, S. J. C., Chemistry
JOHN, N. W., Computing
KALAJI, M., Chemistry
PETHIG, R., Electronic Engineering
SHORE, K. A., Electronic Engineering
SPENCER, P. S., Electronic Engineering
TAYLOR, D. M., Electronic Engineering

CARDIFF UNIVERSITY

Cardiff, CF10 3XQ
Telephone: (29) 2087-4000
E-mail: prospectus@cardiff.ac.uk
Internet: www.cardiff.ac.uk
Founded 2004 by merger of Cardiff University (f. 1883) and University of Wales College of Medicine (f. 1931)
Academic year: September to June
Pres.: Prof. Sir MARTIN EVANS
Vice-Chancellor: Dr DAVID GRANT
Deputy Vice-Chancellor: Prof. ELIZABETH TREASURE
Pro-Vice-Chancellor for Engagement and Int.: Prof. HYWEL THOMAS
Pro-Vice-Chancellor for Education and Students: Prof. JONATHAN OSMOND
Pro-Vice-Chancellor for Estates: Prof. TIM WESS
Pro-Vice-Chancellor for Research: Prof. GRAHAM HUTCHINGS
Pro-Vice-Chancellor for Staff and Diversity: Prof. TERRY THREADGOLD
Dean of Strategic Futures and Interdisciplinary Studies: Prof. PETER HALLIGAN
Library: see entry for Cardiff University Libraries
Number of teachers: 2,922
Number of students: 28,000

HEADS OF SCHOOLS

College of Humanities and Sciences:
Architecture: Prof. PHIL JONES
Business School: Prof. GEORGE BOYNE
Chemistry: Prof. PETER KNOWLES
City and Regional Planning: Prof. CHRISTOPHER WEBSTER
Computer Science: Dr. ROGER WHITAKER
Earth and Ocean Sciences: Prof. JOHN PARKES
Engineering: Prof. HYWEL THOMAS
English, Communication and Philosophy: Prof. MARTIN KAYMAN
European Studies: Prof. DAVID BOUCHER
History, Archaeology and Religion: Prof. PETER COSS
Journalism, Media and Cultural Studies: Prof. JUSTIN LEWIS
Law School: Prof. NIGEL LOWE
Lifelong Learning: Dr RICHARD EVANS
Mathematics: Prof. A RUSSELL DAVIES
Music: Prof. DAVID WYN JONES
Physics and Astronomy: Prof. WALTER GEAR
Social Sciences: Prof. MALCOLM WILLIAMS
Welsh: Prof. SIONED DAVIES

Wales College of Medicine, Biology, Life and Health Sciences:
Biosciences: Prof. OLE PETERSEN

Dentistry: Prof. ELIZABETH TREASURE
Healthcare Studies: Prof. PATRICIA PRICE
Medicine: Prof. PAUL MORGAN
Nursing and Midwifery Studies: Prof. SHEILA HUNT
Optometry and Vision Sciences: Prof. TIM WESS
Pharmacy: Prof. GARY BAXTER
Postgraduate Medical and Dental Education: Prof. DEREK GALLEN
Psychology: Prof. DYLAN JONES

PROFESSORS

College of Humanities and Sciences
Architecture:
WESTON, R.

Business School:
BLYTON, P. R.
BOYNE, G. A.
CHANDLER, R. A.
CLARKE, R.
COLLIE, D. R.
COPELAND, L.
DAVIES, A. J.
DELBRIDGE, R. I.
EDWARDS, J. R.
EZZAMEL, M. A.
FOREMAN-PECK, J.
FOSH, P.
FOXALL, G. R.
HARRIS, L. C.
HEERY, E. J.
HINES, P. A.
HUGHES HALLET, A.
JONES, D. T.
JONES, M. J.
KNOTT, J. H.
MAKEPEACE, G. H.
MARTIN, S. J.
MATTHEWS, K. G. P.
McNABB, R.
MELLETT, H. J.
MINFORD, A. P. L.
MORRIS, J. L.
NAIRN, M. M.
OGBONNA, E.
PEATTIE, K. J.
PEEL, M. J.
PENDLEBURY, M. W.
POOLE, M. J. F.
REED, M. I.
RHYS, D. G.
SILVER, M. S.
TOWILL, D. R.
TURNBULL, P. J.
WALKER, S. P.
WHITFIELD, K. L.
XU, X.

Chemistry:
ATTARD, G. A.
BOWKER, M.
CAVELL, K. J.
EDWARDS, P. G.
HARRIS, K. D. M.
HEWLINS, M. J. E.
JONES, C.
KNIGHT, D. W.
KNOWLES, P. J.
McKEOWN, N. B.
ROBERTS, M. W.
WELLS, P. B.
WILLIAMS, D. R.
WIRTH, T.

City and Regional Planning:
ALDEN, J. D.
CLAPHAM, D. F.
COOKE, P. N.
GUY, C. M.
HOOPER, A. J.
LOVERING, J.
MORGAN, K. J.
MURDOCH, J. L.
PUNTER, J. V.
WEBSTER, C. J.

WILLIAMS, H. C. W. L.

Computer Science:
AVIS, N. J.
BATCHELOR, B. G.
BROWN, B. M.
GRAY, W. A.
JONES, A. J.
JONES, C. B.
MARTIN, R. R.
WALKER, D. W.

Earth and Ocean Sciences:
BOWEN, D. Q.
CARTWRIGHT, J. A.
EDWARDS, D.
HARRIS, C.
LISLE, R. J.
O'HARA, M. J.
PARKES, R. J.
PEARCE, J. A.
PEARSON, P. N.
RICKARD, D. T.
SCHULTZ, A.
WRIGHT, V. P.
ZAHN, R.

Engineering:
BARR, B. I. G.
BARROW, D. A.
BORODICH, F. M.
CHAMBERS, J. A.
EVANS, H. P.
DIMOV, S. S.
FALCONER, R. A.
HUGHES, T. G.
KARIHALOO, B. L.
LEVER, K. V.
MILES, J. C.
MORGAN, D. V.
MOSES, A. J.
PHAM, D. T.
POOLEY, F. D.
ROWE, D. M.
SNIDLE, R. W.
SYRED, N.
TASKER, P. J.
WATTON, J.
WILLIAMS, F. W.

English, Communication and Philosophy:
ATTFIELD, R.
BELSEY, C.
COUPLAND, N. J. R.
KAYMAN, M. A.
KNIGHT, S. T.
NORRIS, C. C.
SARANGI, S. K.
SKILTON, D. J.
VAN LEEUWEN, T.
WEEDON, C. M.

European Studies:
BERENDSE, G.-J.
BOUCHER, D.
BRYDEN, K. M.
COLE, A. M.
DYSON, K. H. F.
HADDOCK, B. A.
HANLEY, D. L.
JACKSON, D. A.
LOUGHLIN, J. P.

History and Archaeology:
BENTON, G.
COSS, P. R.
EDBURY, P. W.
FREESTONE, I. C.
FISHER, N. R. E.
HINES, J.
HUDSON, P.
PRINGLE, R. D.
WHITTLE, A. W. R.

Journalism, Media and Cultural Studies:
HARGREAVES, I. R.
KITZINGER, J.
LEWIS, J. W.
MILLER, B. T. A.

TAIT, R.

Law School:
CAMPBELL, I. D.
CHURCHILL, R. R.
DOE, C. N.
DOUGLAS, G. F.
FENNELL, P. W. H.
HARPWOOD, V.
HOLM, S.
LEE, R. G.
LEWIS, R. K.
LOWE, N. V.
MIERS, D. R.
MORGAN, D. M.
MURCH, M.
NELKEN, D.
SMITH, K. J. M.
THOMAS, P. A.
WELLS, C. K.
WYLIE, J. C. W.

Mathematics:
BOURENKOV, K.
EVANS, D. E.
EVANS, W. D.
HOOLEY, C.
HUXLEY, M. N.
PHILLIPS, T. N.
WICKRAMASINGHE, N. C.
ZHIGLJAVSKY, A. A.

Music:
THOMAS, A. T.
TYRELL, J.
WALSH, S.

Physics and Astronomy:
ADE, P. A. R.
BLOOD, P.
DISNEY, M. J.
GEAR, W. K.
GRIFFIN, M. J.
GRISHCHUK, L.
INGLESFIELD, J. E.
IVANOV, A. L.
SATHYAPRAKASH, B. S.
WHITWORTH, A. P.

Religious and Theological Studies:
SAMUEL, G. B.
TREVETT, C.

Social Sciences:
ADAM, B. E.
ATKINSON, P.
BROWN, P.
COLLINS, H. M.
CROZIER, W. R.
DAVIES, W. B.
DRAKEFORD, M.
EPSTEIN, D. A.
FAIRBROTHER, P.
FEVRE, R. W.
FITZ, J.
GLASNER, P. E.
LAWN, M.
LEVI, M.
MAGUIRE, E. M. W.
MOORE, L. A. R.
NICHOLS, W. A. T.
POWER, S. A. R.
PRIOR, L. F.
REES, G. M.
REES, T. L.
WALKERDINE, V.
WALTERS, D.
WILLIAMS, G. H.

Welsh:
JONES, R. O.
THOMAS, P. W.
WILLIAMS, C. H.

Wales College of Medicine, Biology, Life and Health Sciences

Biosciences:
ARCHER, C. W.
BENJAMIN, M.

BODDY, L.
BOWEN, I. D.
BRUFORD, M. W.
BUCHMAN, V.
CATERSON, B.
CLARKE, A. R.
COAKLEY, W. T.
CRUNELLI, V.
DALE, T. C.
DAVIES, A. M.
DUANCE, V. C.
DUNNETT, S. B.
ECCLES, R.
EHRMANN, M.
FOX, K. D.
FRY, J. C.
HARWOOD, A. J.
HARWOOD, J. L.
JACOB, T. J. C.
JOHN, R. A.
KAY, J.
MOXHAM, B. J.
ORMEROD, S. J.

Dentistry:
DUMMER, P. M. H., Adult Dental Health
GLANTZ, P.-O. J., Adult Dental Health
JONES, M. L., Dental Health and Development
LEWIS, M. A. O., Oral Medicine
MACKENZIE, I. C., Adult Dental Health
RICHMOND, S., Dental Health and Development
SHEPHERD, J. R., Oral Surgery and Pathology
TREASURE, E. T., Dental Public Health
WHITTAKER, D. K., Basic Dental Science
WILTON, J. M. A., Adult Dental Health

Healthcare Studies:
PALASTANGA, N.

Medicine:
BURNETT, A. K., Haematology
CAMPBELL, A. K., Medical Biochemistry
CLARKE, A. J., Medical Genetics
COOPER, D. N., Human Molecular Genetics
DAVIES, D. P., Child Health
DUERDEN, B. I., Medical Microbiology
EVANS, W. H., Medical Biochemistry
FELCE, D., Mental Handicap Research
FIANDER, A., Obstetrics and Gynaecology
FINLAY, A. Y., Dermatology
FINLAY, I. G., Palliative Care
FRENNEAUX, N. P., Cardiology
GRIFFITH, T. M., Medical Imaging
HARDING, K. G., Rehabilitation Medicine
HARMER, M., Anaesthetics and Intensive Care Medicine
HARPER, P. S., Medical Genetics
HOUSTON, H. L. A., General Practice
KRAWCZAK, M., Mathematical Genetics
LAI, F. A., Cell Signalling
LEWIS, M. J., Cardiovascular Pharmacology
MANSEL, R. E., Surgery
MASON, M., Clinical Oncology
MORGAN, B. P., Medical Biochemistry
O'DONOVAN, M. C., Psychological Medicine
OWEN, M. J., Neuropsychiatric Genetics
OWENS, D. R., Diabetes
PALMER, S. R., Epidemiology, Statistics and Public Health
PILL, R., General Practice
ROUTLEDGE, P., Clinical Pharmacology
ROWE, M., Cell Biology
SAMPSON, J. R., Medical Genetics
SCANLON, M. F., Endocrinology
SHALE, D. J., Respiratory and Communicable Diseases
SIBERT, J. R., Community Child Health
SMITH, P. J., Cancer Biology
STEPHENS, S. D. G., Audiology
THAPAR, A., Child and Adolescent Psychiatry
WHEELER, M. H., Surgery
WILES, C. M., Neurology

WILKINSON, C., General Practice
WILLIAMS, B. D., Rheumatology
WILLIAMS, G. T., Pathology
WILLIAMS, J. D., Nephrology
WOODCOCK, J. P., Bioengineering
WOODHOUSE, K. W., Geriatric Medicine
WORWOOD, M., Haematology
WYNFORD-THOMAS, D., Pathology

Nursing and Midwifery Studies:

BURNARD, P., Nursing and Midwifery Education
LYNE, P. A., Nursing Research
TUCKER, A., Nursing and Midwifery

Optometry and Vision Sciences:

MEEK, K. M. A.
ROVAMO, J. M.
WESS, T. J.
WILD, J.

Pharmacy:

AKHTAR, S.
BROADLEY, K. J.
DUNCAN, R.
LUSCOMBE, D. K.
McGUIGAN, C.
MRSNY, R. J.
NICHOLSON, R. I.
RUSSELL, A. D.
WALKER, R. D.

Psychology:

AGGLETON, J. P.
ELLIS, H. D.
HALLIGAN, P.
HAY, D. F.
HONEY, R. C.
MANSTEAD, A. S. R.
OAKSFORD, M. R.
PAYNE, S. J.
PEARCE, J. M.
PIDGEON, N.
SMITH, A. P.
SNOWDEN, R. J.
SPEARS, R.
WRIGHT, P.

SWANSEA UNIVERSITY

Singleton Park, Swansea, SA2 8PP
Telephone: (1792) 205678
Fax: (1792) 295157
Internet: www.swan.ac.uk
Founded 1920
Academic year: September to June
Vice-Chancellor: Prof. RICHARD B. DAVIES
Pro-Vice-Chancellor for Acad. Devt: Prof. NOEL THOMPSON
Pro-Vice-Chancellor for Internationalization: Prof. IWAN DAVIES
Pro-Vice-Chancellor for Science and Engineering: Prof. IAN CLUCKIE
Pro-Vice-Chancellor for Student Experience and Acad. Quality Enhancement: Prof. ALAN SPEIGHT
Library: see Libraries and Archives
Number of teachers: 800
Number of students: 12,500

HEADS OF DEPARTMENTS

College of Arts and Humanities: Prof. JOHN SPURR
College of Engineering: Prof. JAVIER BONET
College of Human and Health Sciences: Prof. MELANIE JASPER
College of Medicine: Prof. GARETH MORGAN
College of Science: Prof. STEVE WILKS
Department of Adult Continuing Education: Prof. COLIN TROTMAN
School of Business and Economics: Prof. STEVEN COOK (acting)
School of Law: Prof. NOEL THOMPSON (acting)

UNIVERSITY OF GLAMORGAN

Pontypridd, CF37 1DL
Telephone: (1443) 480480
Fax: (1443) 654050
E-mail: enquiries@glam.ac.uk
Internet: www.glam.ac.uk
Founded 1913 as South Wales and Monmouthshire School of Mines, present name and status 1992
Academic year: September to July
Chancellor: Rt Hon Lord MORRIS OF ABERAVON
Vice-Chancellor: Prof. JULIE LYDON
Deputy Vice-Chancellor for Academic and Business Devt: HELEN MARSHALL
Deputy Vice-Chancellor for Research and Student Experience: Prof. CLIVE MULLHOLLAND
Deputy Vice-Chancellor for Strategic Resources: Dr HUW WILLIAMS
Academic Registrar: WILLIAM CALLAWAY
Library of 245,000 vols, 1,600 current periodicals
Number of teachers: 616
Number of students: 23,990

DEANS

Cardiff School of Creative and Cultural Industries: Prof. PETER ROBERTSON
Faculty of Advanced Technology: VASSILIS KONSTANTINOU
Faculty of Business and Society: Dr MONICA GIBSON-SWEET
Faculty of Health, Sport and Science: Prof. DONNA MEAD

UNIVERSITY OF WALES

University Registry, King Edward VII Ave, Cathays Park, Cardiff, CF10 3NS
Telephone: (29) 2037-6999
Fax: (29) 2037-6980
E-mail: uniwales@wales.ac.uk
Internet: www.wales.ac.uk
Founded 1893
Languages of instruction: English, Welsh
Chancellor: HRH Prince CHARLES, PRINCE OF WALES
Pro-Chancellor: The Most Revd Dr BARRY MORGAN, ARCHBISHOP OF WALES
Vice-Chancellor and Chief Exec.: Prof. MARC CLEMENT
Pro-Vice-Chancellor: Prof. NIGEL PALASTANGA
Sec.-Gen.: Dr LYNN E. WILLIAMS
Number of students: 80,000
Publication: Campus.

INSTITUTIONS AWARDING UNIVERSITY OF WALES DEGREES

Glyndŵr University

Mold Rd, Wrexham, LL11 2AW
Telephone: (1978) 290666
Fax: (1978) 290008
Internet: www.glyndwr.ac.uk
Founded 1887, present name and status 2008
Languages of instruction: English, Welsh
Academic year: September to June
Vice-Chancellor and Chief Exec.: Prof. MICHAEL SCOTT
Pro-Vice-Chancellor for Operations: Dr ALLAN HOWELLS
Pro-Vice-Chancellor for Academic Affairs: Prof. GRAEME WILKINSON
Library of 120,000 vols, DVDs, 6,000 e-journals
Number of students: 6,000

Swansea Metropolitan University

Mount Pleasant, Swansea, SA1 6ED
Telephone: (1792) 481000
Fax: (1792) 481085

E-mail: enquiry@smu.ac.uk
Internet: www.smu.ac.uk
Founded 1976 by merger of Swansea College of Art (f. 1853); Swansea College of Education (f. 1872) and Swansea Technical College (f. 1897), present name and status 2008
Languages of instruction: English, Welsh
Vice-Chancellor: Prof. DAVID WARNER
Chair.: Dr GERALD LEWIS
Library of 200,000 vols
Number of teachers: 322
Number of students: 7,000

University of Wales, Newport

Caerleon Campus, Lodge Rd, Caerleon, Newport, NP18 3QT
Telephone: (1633) 432432
Fax: (1633) 432046
E-mail: uic@newport.ac.uk
Internet: www.newport.ac.uk
Founded 1841, present name and status 1996
Vice-Chancellor: Dr PETER NOYES
Deputy Vice-Chancellor: GRAHAM ROGERS
Deputy Vice-Chancellor for Academic: Prof. STEPHEN HAGEN
Pro-Vice-Chancellor for Regional and International Development: CHRIS O'MALLEY
Pro-Vice-Chancellor for Resource Planning and Dir of Finance: DENIS JONES
Pro-Vice-Chancellor for Human Resources: BETHAN EDWARDS
Sec.: PAUL FOLAN
Number of teachers: 244
Number of students: 3,967

DEANS

School of Art, Media and Design: DEREK LAWTHER (acting)
School of Business: Dr TIM MCINTYRE-BHATTY
School of Education: Dr CARL PETERS
School of Health and Social Science: AMELIA LYONS
School of Int. Affairs: GRAHAM WOOD

University of Wales Trinity Saint David

Carmarthen, Carmarthenshire, SA31 3EP
Telephone: (300) 5001822
Fax: (1570) 423423
E-mail: vacancies@tsd.ac.uk
Internet: www.trinitysaintdavid.ac.uk
Founded 1822, inc. as constituent college of Univ. of Wales 1971 and as constituent institution 1987, present name and status by merger of Trinity University College and Univ. of Wales Lampeter
Academic year: October to June
Vice-Chancellor: Prof. MEDWIN HUGHES
Pro-Vice-Chancellor for Acad.: Dr CARTIN THOMAS
Pro-Vice-Chancellor for Finance and Resources: GWYNDAF TOBIAS
Library: see under Libraries and Archives
Number of teachers: 100
Number of students: 3,000
Publication: Trivium

DEANS

Faculty of Arts and Social Studies: ROGER MAIDMENT
Faculty of Education and Training: GWILYM DYFRI JONES
Faculty of Humanities: Dr MIRJAM PLANTINGA

PROFESSORS

AUSTIN, D., Archaeology
BADHAM, P., Theology and Religious Studies
BURNHAM, B. C., Archaeology
BURTON, J., History
COCKBURN, D., Philosophy
COHN-SHERBOK, D., Jewish Studies
DAVIES, D. P., Theology

EATOUGH, G., Classics
ELDRIDGE, C. C., History
FLEMING, A., Archaeology
O'LOUGHLIN, T., Theology
PRESCOTT, A., Library
ROFFE, I. M., Centre for Enterprise, Entrepreneurial and European Studies
WALKER, M. J. C., Archaeology

University of Wales Institute, Cardiff

Llandaff Campus, Western Ave, Cardiff, CF5 2SG

Telephone: (29) 2041-6070
Fax: (29) 2041-6286
E-mail: uwicinfo@uwic.ac.uk
Internet: www.uwic.ac.uk

Founded 1976, present name and status 1996
Academic year: October to July

Vice-Chancellor and Prin.: Prof. ANTHONY J. CHAPMAN
Pro-Vice-Chancellor: Prof. ROBERT BROWN
Deputy Vice-Chancellor: JACQUI HARE
Number of students: 11,000

DEANS

Cardiff School of Art and Design: Prof. GAYNOR KAVANAGH
Cardiff School of Education: PAUL THOMAS
Cardiff School of Health Sciences: Prof. ADRIAN PETERS
Cardiff School of Management: DAVID PRITCHARD
Cardiff School of Sports: DAVE COBNER

Colleges in Wales

These institutions are not able to award their own degrees, but offer courses leading to a degree from a recognized body.

Barry College: Colcot Rd, Barry, CF62 8YJ; tel. (1446) 725000; e-mail enquiries@barry.ac.uk; internet www.barry.ac.uk; 5 centres, 800 courses including construction, aircraft engineering, travel and tourism, computing, art and design; 500 staff; 10,000 students; Prin. and Chief Exec. KAY MARTIN.

Bridgend College of Further Education: Cowbridge Rd, Bridgend, CF31 3DF; tel. (1656) 302302; e-mail enquiries@bridgend.ac.uk; internet www.bridgend.ac.uk; f. 1928 as Bridgend Mining and Technical Institute; 400 courses in 20 vocational areas across 4 campuses; 15,000 students; Prin. M. JONES.

Coleg Gwent: The Rhadyr, Usk, NP15 1XJ; tel. (1495) 333333; fax (1495) 333526; e-mail info@coleggwent.ac.uk; internet www.coleggwent.ac.uk; 5 campuses; provides higher education and professional qualifications courses; Prin. and Chief Exec. JIM BENNETT.

Coleg Llandrillo Cymru: Rhos, Llandudno Rd, Rhos-on-Sea, LL28 4HZ; tel. (1492) 546-666; fax (1492) 543-052; e-mail admissions@llandrillo.ac.uk; internet www.llandrillo.ac.uk; merged with Coleg Meirion-Dwyfor; 10 main campuses, 200 learning venues; 3,000 full and part-time courses; library: 40,000 vols; 1,400 teachers; 20,000 students; Prin. HUW EVANS.

Coleg Menai: Ffriddoedd Rd, Bangor, LL57 2TP; tel. (1248) 370125; fax (1248) 370052; e-mail learner.services@menai.ac.uk; internet www.menai.ac.uk; 7 learning centres; 120 programmes; partnership with Bangor Univ.; 600 teachers; 9,000 students.

Coleg Morgannwg: Cwmdare Rd, Aberdare, CF44 8ST; tel. (1685) 887500; fax (1685) 876635; e-mail college@morgannwg.ac.uk; internet www.morgannwg.ac.uk; 4 main campuses, 80 outreach centres; courses in higher national certificates, diplomas, foundation, honours degrees, postgraduate, professional qualifications; partnership with Univ. of Glamorgan, Univ. of Wales; Prin. JUDITH EVANS.

Coleg Sir Gâr (Carmarthenshire College): Graig Campus, Sandy Rd, Pwll, SA15 4DN; tel. (1554) 748-000; fax (1554) 748-170; e-mail admissions@colegsirgar.ac.uk; internet www.colegsirgar.ac.uk; 5 campuses; courses include A-levels, NVQs, national diplomas, higher national certificates, foundation degrees, graduate and postgraduate programmes; 850 staff; 12,000 students; Prin. and Chief Exec. BARRY LILES.

Gower College Swansea: Tycoch Rd, Swansea, SA2 9EB; tel. (1792) 284000; fax (1792) 284074; e-mail enquiries@gowercollegeswansea.ac.uk; internet www.swancoll.ac.uk; f. 2010 by merger of Swansea College and Gorseinon College; 5 campuses; part-time and full-time degree and HND courses; all courses approved by Univ. of Glamorgan, Univ. of Wales; Prin. and Chief Exec. NICK BENNETT.

Harper Adams University College: Newport, TF10 8NB; tel. (1952) 820-280; fax (1952) 814-783; e-mail admissions@harper-adams.ac.uk; internet www.harper-adams.ac.uk; f. 1901; higher education for rural, land, animal and food-based studies; library: 50,000 books, 900 journal titles; 83 teachers; 4,000 students; Prin. Dr DAVID LLEWELLYN.

Neath Port Talbot College: Neath Campus, Dwr-y-Felin Rd, Neath, SA10 7RF; tel. (1639) 648000; fax (1639) 648009; e-mail admissions@nptc.ac.uk; internet www.nptc.ac.uk; f. 1999 by merger of Neath and Afan colleges; 8 campuses, 70 outreach centres; HNC, HND, foundation and Bachelors degree courses; library: 40,000 items; 14,000 students; Prin. and Chief Exec. MARK DACEY.

Pembrokeshire College: Haverfordwest, SA61 1SZ; tel. (1437) 753000; fax (1437) 753001; e-mail international.info@pembrokeshire.ac.uk; internet www.pembrokeshire.ac.uk; provides undergraduate and postgraduate degrees, HNDs and HNCs validated by Univ. of Glamorgan; accredited college of the univ.; 550 teachers; 8,500 students (2,000 full-time, 6,500 part-time); Prin. GLYN JONES.

Royal Welsh College of Music and Drama: Castle Grounds, Cathays Park, Cardiff, CF1 3ER; tel. (29) 2039-2854; fax (29) 2039-1301; e-mail admissions@rwcmd.ac.uk; internet www.rwcmd.ac.uk; f. 1949; national conservatoire of Wales; full- and part-time courses for performers, and degree and diploma courses validated by the Univ. of Wales; library: 50,000 books, play scripts, journals, performance scores, orchestral sets, audiovisual material and newspapers; 632 students; Prin. HILARY BOULDING.

Institute of Biological, Environmental and Rural Sciences: Aberystwyth Univ., Penglais, Aberystwyth, Ceredigion, SY23 3DA; tel. (1970) 622316; fax (1970) 622350; e-mail ibers@aber.ac.uk; internet www.aber.ac.uk/en/ibers; f. by merger of Institutes of Rural Sciences and Biological Sciences at Aberystwyth Univ.; undergraduate and postgraduate courses and research in biological, environmental and rural sciences; campuses in Gogerddan and Llanbadarn; library: 53,000 vols; 366 teachers; Dir Prof. WAYNE POWELL.

Ystrad Mynach College: Twyn Rd, Ystrad Mynach, Hengoed, CF82 7XR; tel. (1443) 816888; fax (1443) 816973; e-mail enquiries@ystrad-mynach.ac.uk; internet www.ystrad-mynach.ac.uk; f. 1959; 7 campuses; HNC/D, foundation degree, undergraduate degrees; franchised from Univ. of Wales Institute Cardiff, Univ. of Wales, Newport; 10,000 students; Prin. MALCOLM SAINSBURY.

BERMUDA

The Higher Education System

There is only one institution of post-secondary education on Bermuda—Bermuda College (founded in 1974), which offers technical and vocational courses, as well as programmes of a more academic nature for those wishing to pursue tertiary education overseas. Many Bermudan students apply to higher education institutions in the USA, the West Indies or the United Kingdom. In 2008/09 enrolment at Bermuda College totalled 1,366 students.

Admission to the College requires students to hold the Bermuda School Certificate, awarded upon successful completion of secondary school, and to sit the Computerized Placement Test, which is used to assess entry-level skills in mathematics, English and writing, as well as external tests such as SATs. Associate degree programmes, which last two years, grant direct access into employment or can be used to transfer to foreign universities at the discretion of the individual institution. The College also offers Certificate and Diploma programmes, which typically require between one and three years' study.

Regulatory Bodies
GOVERNMENT

Ministry of Culture and Social Rehabilitation: POB HM 788, Hamilton HM CX; Suite 304, Melbourne House, 11 Parliament St, Hamilton HM 12; tel. 296-1574; fax 295-2066; e-mail premier@gov.bm; internet www.gov.bm; Minister DALE D. BUTLER.

Ministry of Education: Dundonald Pl., 14 Dundonald St, Hamilton HM 09; tel. 278-3300; fax 278-3348; internet www.moed.bm; Minister ELVIN JAMES.

Learned Societies
GENERAL

Bermuda National Trust: POB HM 61, Hamilton HM AX; Waterville, 2 Pomander Rd, Paget PG 05; tel. 236-6483; fax 236-0617; e-mail palmetto@bnt.bm; internet www.bnt.bm; f. 1970; promotes preservation and appreciation of lands, buildings and artefacts of natural or historic interest; 4,000 mems; Pres. BILL HOLMES; Deputy Pres. SIMON VAN DE WEG; Exec. Dir JENNIFER GRAY; Curator ANDREW BAYLAY; publ. *Architectural Heritage–Bermuda* (irregular).

FINE AND PERFORMING ARTS

Bermuda Professional Photographic Association: POB 182, Southampton SN BX; tel. 238-4387; fax 295-4724; e-mail info@bermudaphotographers.com; internet www.bermudaphotographers.com; f. 1956; promotes professional photojournalism and creative photography; 26 mems.

Bermuda Society of Arts: POB HM 1202, Hamilton HM FX; The City Hall Arts Centre, 17 Church St, Hamilton; tel. 292-3824; fax 296-0699; e-mail bsoa@ibl.bm; internet www.bsoa.bm; f. c. 1950 as Society of Artists in Bermuda, present name 1956; exhibition space with 4 galleries showcasing Bermudan art and artists; 700 mems; Pres. DUNCAN HALL; Gallery Dir JULIE HASTINGS.

HISTORY, GEOGRAPHY AND ARCHAEOLOGY

Bermuda Historical Society: 13 Queen St, Hamilton HM 11; tel. 295-2487; f. 1895; promotes interest in history of Bermuda; attached museum; holds portraits, miniatures, antique furnishings, colln of early Bermuda coins and silver; attached library; 130 mems; Pres. ANDREW BERMINGHAM; Museum Curator COLIN BENBOW.

St George's Foundation: POB GE 58, St George's GE BX; Admiral's Walk, 16 Water St, St George's GE 05; tel. 297-8043; fax 297-2479; e-mail director@stgeorgesfoundation.org; internet www.stgeorgesfoundation.org; f. 1995; ind. not for profit org.; operates the St George's Historical Soc. Museum and Mitchell House (built c. 1830 purchased by St George's Historical Society 1922); contains antique furniture, paintings, porcelain and textiles; open Mondays to Thursdays and Saturdays, April–November, closed December, open Wednesdays only January–March; 150 mems; Chair. Dr KENNETH SNAITH; Pres. VIRGINIA OLANDER; Exec. Dir SHARON JACOBS; Dir of Education LEONDRA BURCHALL; Treas. HARRY WILKEN; Sec. ALISON OUTEBRIDGE.

MEDICINE

Bermuda Dental Association: POB 3059, Hamilton HM NX; tel. 236-9337; fax 236-1325; e-mail bdadental@gmail.com; internet www.bermudadental.bm; f. 1964; encourages the study of dentistry and allied sciences; promotes and maintains honour and dignity of the dental profession in Bermuda; Pres. Dr RONDA JAMES.

Bermuda Medical Society: POB HM 1023, Hamilton HM DX; King Edward VII Memorial Hospital, 7 Point Finger Rd, Paget DV 04; tel. 236-2345; fax 239-6324; f. 1970; asscn of medical doctors in practice in Bermuda; 70 mems; Pres. Dr JOHN GAUGAIN; Sec. Dr GERHARD BOONSTRA.

Bermuda Pharmaceutical Association: tel. 297-8427; e-mail admin@bpa.bm; internet www.bpa.bm; professional org; supports local pharmacists; Pres. KIRAN SHAH; Sec. (vacant); Treas. CAROLINE DICKINSON.

NATURAL SCIENCES
Biological Sciences

Bermuda Audubon Society: POB HM 1328, Hamilton HM FX; tel. 238-8628; e-mail info@audubon.bm; internet www.audubon.bm; f. 1954; environmental protection and education; 300 mems; Pres. ANDREW DOBSON; Exec. Sec. KAREN BORDER; Treas. PETER HOLMES; publ. *Newsletter* (2 a year).

Physical Sciences

Astronomical Society of Bermuda: POB HM 1046, Hamilton HM EX; tel. 236-3780; e-mail eddimac@ibl.bm; f. 1962; mem. meetings; educational activities; information provided to the media; promotes astronomy in Bermuda; 10 mems; Pres. EDDIE McGONAGLE; Sec. and Treas. CATHIE McGONAGLE.

Research Institutes
AGRICULTURE, FISHERIES AND VETERINARY SCIENCE

Department of Environmental Protection: POB HM 834, Hamilton HM CX; Botanical Gardens, 169 South Rd, Paget DV 04; tel. 236-4201; fax 236-7582; e-mail animals@gov.bm; internet www.gov.bm; f. 1898; management and devt of horticulture, environmental protection and Bermudan natural history; conducts research and monitors environment quality; Dir FREDERICK MING; Librarian ALISON GREEN; publ. *Envirotalk* (4 a year).

NATURAL SCIENCES
Biological Sciences

Bermuda Institute of Ocean Sciences: 17 Biological Station, Ferry Reach, St George's GE 01; tel. 297-1880; fax 297-8143; e-mail info@bios.edu; internet www.bios.edu; f. 1903 as Bermuda Biological Station for Research, present name 2006; ind. not-for-profit research instn; research in most aspects of marine sciences and oceanography and environmental sciences; courses organized during long vacation in marine invertebrates, ecology, pollution; high school and college facilities for instruction in marine sciences; attached research centres: Center for Integrated Ocean Observations (CINTOO), Int. Center for Ocean and Human Health (ICOHH); library of 20,000 vols; Chair. BRIAN DUPERREAULT; Pres. and Dir ANTHONY H. KNAP; publ. *Currents* (2 a year, print and online).

Libraries and Archives
Hamilton

Bermuda Archives: 30 Parliament St, Hamilton HM 12; tel. 295-5151; fax 295-8751; e-mail archives@gov.bm; internet www.gov.bm; f. 1974; repository for official, non-governmental records, private papers relating to Bermuda from 1615 to present; Dir JOANNE BRANGMAN (acting).

Bermuda National Library: Par-la-Ville, 13 Queen St, Hamilton HM 11; Bermuda Youth Library, 74 Church St, Hamilton HM 12; tel. 295-2905; fax 292-8443; e-mail bdanatlib@gov.bm; internet www.bnl.bm; f. 1839, present bldg (Adult Library) 1916; attached to Min. of Economy, Trade and Industry; spec. colln of Bermudiana materials; extensive talking book and large print collns; 117,655 vols (incl. 12,700 vols at the Youth Library); Head Librarian C. JOANNE BRANGMAN; Librarian for Adult Services JULIE BEAN; Librarian for Youth Services MARLA SMITH; Librarian for Colln Management PATRICE CARVELL; publ. *Bermuda National Bibliography* (4 a year; print and online).

Museums and Art Galleries
Flatts

Bermuda Aquarium, Museum & Zoo: POB FL 145, Flatts FL BX; 40 North Shore Rd, Flatts FL 04; tel. 293-2727; fax 293-4014; e-mail info.bzs@gov.bm; internet www.bamz.org; f. 1926; live zoological colln; aquarium with large reef tank; local natural history and other exhibits; library of 3,000 vols; Prin. Curator Dr IAN WALKER; publ. *Wild* (4 a year).

Hamilton

Bermuda National Gallery: Suite 191, 48 Par-la-Ville Rd, Hamilton HM 11; City Hall Arts Centre, Church St, Hamilton; tel. 295-9428; fax 295-2055; e-mail director@bng.bm; internet www.bng.bm; f. 1992; attached to Bermuda Fine Art Trust; nat. art colln; Watlington Colln: spec. colln of historic European paintings; educational and social events; Chair., Bermuda Fine Art Trust GARY L. PHILLIPS; Dir LISA HOWIE; Curator SOPHIE CRESSALL.

Bermuda National Trust Museum at the Globe Hotel: POB HM 61, Hamilton HM AX; 32 York St, St George's; tel. 297-1423; fax 236-0617; e-mail palmetto@bnt.bm; internet www.bnt.bm; f. 1970, housed at the Globe Hotel built c. 1700; attached to Bermuda Nat. Trust; displays depict Bermuda's role in the American Civil War; colln of antique furniture; Dir AMANDA OUTERBRIDGE; Curator ANDREW.

Masterworks Museum of Bermuda Art: POB HM 1929, Hamilton HM HX; The Botanical Gardens 183, South Rd, Paget DV 04; tel. 236-2950; fax 236-4402; e-mail mworks@logic.bm; internet www.bermudamasterworks.com; f. 2008; not-for-profit org.; art storage facilities; classroom, main gallery and a smaller gallery dedicated to local artists; Founder and Creative Dir TOM BUTTERFIELD; Chair. MICHAEL HAMER; Treas. JUDITH HOWE-TUCKER.

Tucker House Museum: POB HM 61, Hamilton HM AX; 5 Water St, St George's; tel. 297-0545; fax 236-0617; e-mail palmetto@bnt.bm; internet www.bnt.bm; f. 1970, bldg 1750; attached to Bermuda Nat. Trust; 18th-century house with colln of Tucker family silver, china, crystal, English mahogany and Bermuda cedar furniture; Dir AMANDA OUTERBRIDGE; Curator ANDREW.

Verdmont Museum: POB HM 61, Hamilton HM AX; 6 Verdmont Lane, off Collector's Hill, Smith's Parish; tel. 236-7639; fax 236-0617; e-mail palmetto@bnt.bm; internet www.bnt.bm; f. built c. 1710, sold to the Bermuda Nat. Trust 1951; attached to Bermuda Nat. Trust; 18th-century house with period furniture; early Georgian architecture; Exec. Dir JENNIFER GRAY.

Sandys

Bermuda Arts Centre at Dockyard: POB MA 66, Mangrove Bay MA BX; tel. 234-2809; fax 234-0540; e-mail artcentre@ibl.bm; internet www.artbermuda.bm; f. 1984; not-for-profit org.; forum for local artists; art workshops; display and sale of local art work.

Bermuda Maritime Museum: POB MA 133, Sandys, MA BX; tel. 234-1333; fax 234-1735; e-mail info@bmm.bm; internet www.bmm.bm; f. 1975; area incl. fortress of Bermuda Dockyard and exhibits represent Bermuda maritime history; Exec. Dir Dr EDWARD C. HARRIS; Curator ELENA STRONG; publs *Bermuda Journal of Archaeology and Maritime History* (1 a year), *MARITimes* (members' magazine).

College

Bermuda College: POB PG 297, Paget PG BX; Stonington Ave, South Rd, Paget PG 04; tel. 236-9000; fax 239-4008; e-mail info@college.bm; internet www.college.bm; f. 1974, by merger of Bermuda Technical Institute (est. 1956), Bermuda Hotel and Catering College (est. 1965) and Academic Sixth Form Centre (est. 1967); divs of applied science and technology, business and hospitality, liberal arts, professional and career education; 52 teachers; 1,366 students; library: 30,000 vols; Pres. Dr DURANDA GREENE; Head Librarian JAMES AGEE.

CAYMAN ISLANDS

The Higher Education System

The Government administers the University College Cayman Islands (founded in 1985; present status and name adopted in 1987 and 2004, respectively) and the Cayman Islands Law School (founded in 1982, and affiliated to the United Kingdom's University of Liverpool). The Cayman Islands are also home to the International College of the Cayman Islands (founded in 1970), which offers Associate, Bachelors and Masters degrees; St Matthew's University (founded in 1997), which operates a medical school and a veterinary medicine school; and the Institute for Theological and Leadership Development (a constituent institute of the International University of the Caribbean, founded in 2005 by the United Church in Jamaica and the Cayman Islands), which offers Certificate, Diploma, Bachelors and Masters programmes in a limited number of theological fields. Distance-learning programmes are available from the University of the West Indies, in conjunction with the University College Cayman Islands.

Regulatory and Representative Bodies

GOVERNMENT

Ministry of Education, Training and Employment: Royal Pl., 3rd Fl., George Town, Grand Cayman; tel. 244-2417; fax 949-9343; e-mail education@gov.ky; internet www.education.gov.ky; Min. Hon. ROLSTON M ANGLIN.

Ministry of Health, Environment, Youth, Sports and Culture: Govt Admin. Bldg, 3rd Fl., George Town, Grand Cayman; tel. 244-2318; fax 949-1790; internet www.ministryofhealth.gov.ky; Min. Hon. MARK SCOTLAND.

ACCREDITATION

Accreditation Commission on Colleges of Medicine (ACCM): see under Ireland.

Learned Societies

GENERAL

Cayman National Cultural Foundation: F. J. Harquail Cultural Centre, Harquail Dr. 17, POB 30201, Grand Cayman, KY1-1201; tel. 949-5477; fax 949-4519; e-mail admincncf@candw.ky; internet www.artscayman.org; f. 1984; facilitates and preserves cultural and artistic expression, particularly preservation and exploration of Caymanian performing, visual and literary arts; Chair. MARTYN C. W. BOULD.

National Trust for the Cayman Islands: POB 31116, Grand Cayman, KY1-1205; South Church St 558, Grand Cayman; tel. 749-1121; fax 749-1135; e-mail info@nationaltrust.org.ky; internet www.nationaltrust.org.ky; f. 1990; preserves natural environments and places of historic significance; Pres. CARLA REID; Sec. LOIS BLUMENTHAL; publ. *The Preserver* (4 a year).

FINE AND PERFORMING ARTS

Visual Arts Society of the Cayman Islands: POB 31060, Grand Cayman, KY1-1205; tel. 327-0751; internet www.visualartcayman.com; f. 1978; art appreciation, enhancement and learning; 75 mems; Chair. IVAN BURGES; Sec. SHIRLEY SCOTT.

Research Institutes

NATURAL SCIENCES

Biological Sciences

Central Caribbean Marine Institute: POB 37, Little Cayman KY3-2501; tel. 948-1094; fax 948-0092; e-mail info@reefresearch.org; internet www.reefresearch.org; f. 1998; sustains marine biodiversity through research, education, outreach and conservation programmes; Little Cayman research centre; Pres. Dr CARRIE MANFRINO; Sec. CHRISTOPHER HUMPHRIES; publ. *Green Guides*.

Queen Elizabeth II Botanic Park: POB 203, Grand Cayman, KY1-1701; tel. 947-3558; e-mail ma@botanic-park.ky; internet www.botanic-park.ky; f. 1994; preserves natural environments; incl. floral garden, heritage garden, lake and wetland area, nursery, woodland trail; Gen. Man. JOHN LAWRUS.

Libraries and Archives

George Town

Cayman Islands National Archive: POB 10160, KY1-1002; Archive Lane 37, George Town, Grand Cayman; tel. 949-9809; fax 949-9727; e-mail cina@gov.ky; internet www.cina.gov.ky; f. 2007; archive and records preservation, records policy unit and reprographics unit; Dir J. KIMLON LAWRENCE.

Cayman Islands Public Library Service: POB 1172, Grand Cayman, KY1-1102; Edward St 68, George Town, Grand Cayman; tel. 949-5159; fax 949-5015; e-mail foi.lib@gov.ky; internet www.cipl.gov.ky; f. 1920; 5 br. libraries and learning centre; local history reference colln; 64,025 vols; Dir JULIET LAWSON (acting).

Museums and Art Galleries

Cayman Brac

Cayman Brac Museum: POB 240, Cayman Brac, KY2-2101; tel. 948-2222; fax 948-2506; e-mail naturecayman@gov.ky; internet www.naturecayman.com; flora and fauna of the island; conserves natural environments; items of Cayman Brackers seafaring days.

George Town

Cayman Islands National Museum: POB 2189, George Town, KY1-1105; tel. 949-8368; fax 949-9309; internet www.museum.ky; f. 1990; preservation, research and dissemination of Caymanian heritage; over 8,000 items, incl. natural history specimens and rare documents; Dir DEBRA BARNES-TABORA (acting).

National Gallery of the Cayman Islands: POB 10197, Harbour Pl., Grand Cayman, KY1-1002; tel. 945-8111; fax 945-7103; internet www.nationalgallery.org.ky; f. 1997; promotes and encourages appreciation and practice of visuals arts; reference library with books and DVDs on history of art, design, and arts education and production; Chair. HENRY HARFORD; Dir NATALIE URQUHART; publ. *The Viewer* (4 a year).

Universities

ST MATTHEW'S UNIVERSITY

POB 32330, Grand Cayman, KY1-1209
Telephone: 945-3199
Fax: 945-3130

E-mail: admissions@stmatthews.edu
Internet: www.stmatthews.edu
Founded 1997
Academic year: September to August (3 semesters)
Chancellor: JOHN MARVIN
Library of 3,000 vols, 200 periodicals
Number of teachers: 280 (incl. 40 full-time)
Number of students: 1,000

DEANS

Faculty of Basic Sciences: Dr SENTHIL KUMAR
Faculty of Clinical Sciences: Dr JOHN RANDALL
Faculty of Veterinary Medicine: Dr WILLIAM WAGNER

UNIVERSITY COLLEGE CAYMAN ISLANDS

Olympic Way 168, POB 702, George Town, Grand Cayman, KY1-1107
Telephone: 623-8224
Fax: 949-6781
E-mail: suggestions@ucci.edu.ky
Internet: www.ucci.edu.ky
Founded 1985, present status 1987, present name 2004

State control
Academic year: September to July
Pres.: ROY BODDEN
Registrar: JOHN FREDERICK
Librarian: LUCILLE KONG
Library of 18,000 vols, 50 journals
Publication: *The Pipeline*.

Colleges

Cayman Islands Law School: POB 1568, Grand Cayman, KY1-1110; Old CIBC Bldg, 2nd–3rd Fl., George Town, Grand Cayman; tel. 945-0077; fax 946-1845; e-mail lovisa .vernon@gov.ky; internet www.lawschool.gov .ky; f. 1982; degree accredited by Univ. of Liverpool (UK); Dir MITCHELL DAVIES; Asst Dir D. BARKER.

International College of the Cayman Islands: Hirst Rd 595, POB 136, Grand Cayman, KY1-1501; tel. 947-1100; fax 947-1210; e-mail info@myicci.com; internet www .icci.edu.ky; f. 1970; Private control; undergraduate and postgraduate courses in science and business admin.; Dean SCOTT CUMMINGS.

GIBRALTAR

The Higher Education System

There are no higher education institutions offering degree programmes in Gibraltar. Students wishing to pursue higher education generally apply to institutions located within the United Kingdom; the Government of Gibraltar operates a scholarship and grant system, which allocates funding for students studying in the United Kingdom. The Gibraltar College of Further Education, which is administered by the Government, offers professional programmes of study leading to British vocational awards such as Business and Technology Education Council (BTEC), Royal Society of Arts (RSA) and City & Guilds qualifications. In 2010 there were approximately 400 full-time students enrolled at the College.

Regulatory Bodies

GOVERNMENT

H. M. Government of Gibraltar Ministry of Education: 23 Queensway; tel. 20077486; fax 20071564; e-mail education@gibraltar .gov.gi; internet www.gibraltar.gov.gi/ education-a-training; Minister of Education GILBERT LICUDI; Dir of Education Dr JOSEPH BRITTO.

Ministry of Culture, Heritage, Sport and Leisure: 310 Main St; tel. 20047592; fax 20052589; e-mail minculture@gibtelecom .net; internet www.gibraltar.gov.gi/culture; Min. EDWIN J. REYES; Dir of Culture YVETTE ZARB.

Learned Society

NATURAL SCIENCES

Biological Sciences

Gibraltar Ornithological & Natural History Society: Field Centre, Jews' Gate, Upper Rock Nature Reserve, POB 843; tel. 20072639; fax 20074022; e-mail info@gonhs .org; internet www.gonhs.org; f. 1976; attached to Strait of Gibraltar Bird Observatory; research and conservation of nature in Gibraltar; environmental and biological education; 450 mems; Gen. Sec. CHARLES PEREZ; publs *Alectoris* (1 a year), *Gibraltar Bird Report* (1 a year), *Gibraltar Nature News* (2 a year), *Iberis* (scientific journal).

Libraries and Archives

Gibraltar

Gibraltar Archives: 6 Convent Pl.; tel. and fax 20079461; e-mail archives@gibraltar.gov .gi; internet www.gibraltar.gov.gi/ gibraltar-archives; f. 1969; attached to Min. of Culture, Heritage, Sport and Leisure; colln and preservation of public and historical records from 18th to 20th centuries; research services; liaison with schools and other instns; Archivist T. J. FINLAYSON.

Gibraltar Garrison Library: Governor's Parade; tel. 20077418; fax 20079927; e-mail gibgarlib@gibconnect.net; internet gibraltargarrisonlibrary.info; f. 1793; culture and travel; lithographs and art prints; local history colln; colln of books published in 18th and 19th centuries; 45,000 books, incl. rare vols; Trust Sec. FRED TIBBO.

John Mackintosh Hall Library: 308 Main St, POB 939; tel. 20075669; fax 20040843; e-mail gfjmh@gibraltar.gi; f. 1964; attached to European Documentation Centre; 3 exhibition galleries, theatre, reference library, information office and conf. rooms; 33,000 vols; Dir Dr GERALDINE FINLAYSON.

Museum

Gibraltar

Gibraltar Museum: 18/20 Bomb House Lane, POB 939; tel. 20074289; fax 20079158; e-mail enquiries@museum.gib.gi; internet www.gib.gi/museum; f. 1930; colln of local natural history, archaeology and palaeontology (especially Palaeolithic, Neolithic and Phoenician) and military history; displays incl. Evelegh colln (colln of miniature ordnance 1779–83), artefacts from Gibraltar's Islamic past (711–1464), medieval baths built in 1333; Dir, Heritage Div. Dr CLIVE FINLAYSON; Dir, Institute for Gibraltarian Studies GERALDINE FINLAYSON; Deputy Dir DARREN FA; publ. *Gibraltar Heritage Magazine* (2 a year).

GUERNSEY

The Higher Education System

There are no universities on Guernsey, and consequently students wishing to pursue degree-level education must do so abroad, many choosing to apply to institutions in the United Kingdom. Students enrolled in British universities receive state financial support towards maintenance and tuition fees. Recent proposals to introduce student loans for those from middle- and upper-income households, as part of austerity measures intended to address an increasingly large public deficit, have met with staunch opposition and the issue remained unresolved at late 2011. Vocational programmes of study are available at the Guernsey College of Further Education (founded in 1969 as the Technical Training Centre; present name adopted in 1971). In 2010/11 more than 3,000 students were enrolled at the College, of whom around 400 were enrolled on a full-time basis. The GTA University Centre (founded in 1996), which is affiliated to the United Kingdom's University of Bournemouth, provides a range of professional and postgraduate programmes, and, from 2012, a Bachelors (Honours) degree programme in Business and Management was to be introduced. Additionally, professional training courses, primarily aimed at those in the finance and support industries, are provided by a number of private companies.

Regulatory Bodies

GOVERNMENT

Culture and Leisure Department: Information Centre, North Esplanade, St Peter Port, GY1 2LQ; tel. (1481) 713888; e-mail enquiries@cultureleisure.gov.gg; internet www.gov.gg/ccm/navigation/culture—leisure; Min. MIKE O'HARA.

Education Department: POB 32, Grange Rd, St Peter Port, GY1 3AU; tel. (1481) 710821; fax (1481) 714475; e-mail office@education.gov.gg; internet www.education.gg; Min. CAROL STEERE.

Learned Societies

GENERAL

Alderney Society: The Alderney Society Museum, High St, St Anne, GY9 3TG; tel. (1481) 823222; e-mail info@alderneysociety.org; internet www.alderneysociety.org; f. 1966; promotes awareness and encourages historical, environmental, scientific activities relating to the Island of Alderney; 600 mems; Pres. LOUIS JEAN; publ. *Bulletin* (1 a year).

La Société Guernesiaise: Candie Gardens, St Peter Port, GY1 1UG; tel. (1481) 725093; fax (1481) 726248; e-mail societe@cwgsy.net; internet www.societe.org.gg; f. 1882; activities incl. archaeology, astronomy, botany, entomology, family history, geology, historic buildings, history and philology, marine biology, nature conservation, ornithology; also manages island's nature reserves; 2,000 mems; Pres. RODNEY COLLENETTE; Vice-Pres. (vacant); Sec. KATE LEE; Hon. Treas. PETER BUDWIN; publs *Communiqué* (3 a year), *Transactions* (1 a year).

HISTORY, GEOGRAPHY AND ARCHAEOLOGY

Alderney Maritime Trust: POB 1, St Anne, GY9 3AA; tel. (1481) 822249; e-mail hugo@alderneywreck.com; internet www.alderneywreck.com; f. 1996 by the States of Alderney; preserves, protects and manages the historic Elizabethan shipwreck off the coast of Alderney and its contents; artefacts from the wreck are either stored or on display at the Alderney Soc. Museum; Chair. STUART TROUGHT; Excavation Dir MENSUN BOUND; Treas. DICKIN DREW.

Libraries and Archives

St Peter Port

Guille Allès Library: Market St, St Peter Port, GY1 1HB; tel. (1481) 720392; fax (1481) 712425; e-mail ga@library.gg; internet www.library.gg; f. 1882; admin. by the Guille Allès Trust to provide free library services for the community; Chief Librarian MAGGIE FALLA; Deputy Chief Librarian LAURA MILLIGAN.

Priaulx Library: Candie Rd, St Peter Port, GY1 1UG; tel. (1481) 721998; fax (1481) 713804; e-mail info@priaulxlibrary.co.uk; internet www.priaulxlibrary.co.uk; f. 1889; based on personal colln of Osmond de Beauvoir Priaulx; also incl. archives of local newspapers on microfilm, civil and ecclesiastical records, family history files and military colln; rare vols and incunabula; local studies in French and English; 30,000 vols; Chief Librarian AMANDA BENNETT; Deputy Chief Librarian SUE LAKER.

Museums and Art Galleries

St Anne

Alderney Society Museum: The Museum, High St, St Anne, GY9 3TG; tel. (1481) 823222; fax (1481) 824979; e-mail info@alderneymuseum.org; internet www.alderneysociety.org/museum.html; f. 1966, registered in 1993; attached to The Alderney Society; colln of 12,000 items incl. artefacts, documents, photographs; Admin. DON OAKDEN.

St Peter Port

Guernsey Museums & Galleries: Candie Gardens, St Peter Port, GY1 1UG; tel. (1481) 726518; fax (1481) 715177; internet www.museums.gov.gg; f. 1907, present status 2004; attached to Culture and Leisure Dept; history of Guernsey and its people; art gallery displays pictures of Guernsey by Guernsey painters; associated maritime and military museums at Fort Grey and Castle Cornet; Guernsey Telephone Museum; Dir Dr JASON MONAGHAN; Sr Curator ALAN HOWELL.

ISLE OF MAN

The Higher Education System

The Isle of Man College (founded in 1947 as the School of Technology, Arts and Crafts; present name adopted 1991) is the principal institution of higher education on the Isle of Man, and is affiliated to the United Kingdom's University of Chester, University of Liverpool and Liverpool Hope University. Distance-learning degree and other programmes are available through the Open University. In 2009/10 1,429 students were enrolled within higher education on the island. The Department of Education and Children provides financial support for those students enrolled within higher education institutions either on the Isle of Man or within the United Kingdom; at 2011 the Department paid such student's tuition fees in their entirety. Approximately 1,100 undergraduate and 120 post-graduate Isle of Man students enrolled within universities in the United Kingdom are supported by the Department each year, while a further 250 are supported at the Isle of Man College and the Isle of Man International Business School (founded in 1999). Means-tested maintenance grants are also available, subject to household income. Higher education programmes for employees within the Department of Health are provided by the Government and include the three-year Bachelor of Science (Honours) in Nursing, awarded by the University of Chester. Four new nursing degree programmes, including Bachelor of Science (Honours) and Master of Science degrees in specialist community public health nursing, were introduced by the Department at the beginning of the 2011/12 academic year.

Regulatory Body

GOVERNMENT

Department of Education and Children: St George's Court, Upper Church St, Douglas, IM1 2SG; tel. (1624) 685820; fax (1624) 685834; e-mail admin@doe.gov.im; internet www.gov.im/education; Minister EDDIE TEARE; Dir J. CAIN.

Learned Societies

HISTORY, GEOGRAPHY AND ARCHAEOLOGY

Isle of Man Family History Society: Derby Lodge, Derby Rd, Peel, IM5 1HH; tel. (1624) 843105; e-mail iomfhs@manx.net; internet www.iomfhs.im; f. 1979; local genealogy and family history; attached library; Chair. ERNEST CLEATOR; Sec. PAT NICHOLSON; Treas. DAVID CHRISTIAN; publ. *Fraueyn as Banglaneyn* (Roots and Branches, 4 a year).

Isle of Man Natural History and Antiquarian Society: Ballacrye Stream Cottage, Ballaugh, IM7 5EB; tel. (1624) 897306; internet www.manxantiquarians.com; f. 1879; archaeology, geography, geology, history, literature and natural history; 500 mems; Pres. Dr FIONA GELL; Hon. Sec. C. J. BRYAN; Hon. Treas. IAN WRENCH; Hon. Librarian SUSAN CHAMBERS; publ. *Proceedings* (every 2 years).

Research Institutes

HISTORY, GEOGRAPHY AND ARCHAEOLOGY

Centre for Manx Studies: Stable Bldg, Univ. Centre, Old Castletown Rd, Douglas, IM2 1QB; tel. (1624) 695777; fax (1624) 695783; e-mail cms@liv.ac.uk; internet www.liv.ac.uk/manxstudies; f. 1992; attached to Archaeology, Classics and Egyptology, School of Histories, Languages and Cultures, Univ. of Liverpool; research in history, archaeology, culture and environment of the Isle of Man; Dir Dr HAROLD MYTUM; Admin. GILL WILSON; publ. *Studeyrys Manninagh* (Journal of Manx Studies, online).

NATURAL SCIENCES

Biological Sciences

Port Erin Marine Laboratory: Port Erin, IM9 6JA; tel. (1624) 831000; fax (1624) 831001; e-mail peml@liv.ac.uk; internet www.liv.ac.uk/www/peml/; f. 1892; attached to University of Liverpool, School of Biological Sciences; research on fish population dynamics; Dir Prof. T. A. NORTON.

Libraries and Archives

Douglas

Manx National Heritage–National Library and Archives Service: Douglas, IM1 3LY; tel. (1624) 648040; fax (1624) 648069; e-mail library@mnh.gov.im; internet www.gov.im/mnh/heritage/library/nationallibrary.xml; f. 1923; nat. library and archives of the Isle of Man; covers all aspects of Manx heritage and acts as a place of deposit for public and diocesan records; Library and Archive Services Officer PAUL WEATHERALL.

Tynwald Library: Legislative Bldgs, Finch Rd, Douglas, IM1 3PW; tel. (1624) 685520; fax (1624) 685522; e-mail library@tynwald.org.im; internet www.tynwald.org.im; f. 1975; 5,000 vols, documents issued by the Isle of Man legislature (Tynwald) and govt; Head of Information Service J. CORKISH.

Museums and Art Galleries

Castletown

Nautical Museum: Bridge St, Castletown, IM9 1AX; internet www.gov.im/mnh/heritage/museums/nauticalmuseum.xml; f. 1951, museum originates from the discovery of the 18th-century armed yacht the 'Peggy' in 1935; attached to Manx Nat. Heritage (Eiraght Ashoonagh Vannin); considered of maritime importance on the Nat. Historic Ships Register.

Cregneash

National Folk Museum at Cregneash: Cregneash Rd, Cregneash, IM9 5PX; internet www.gov.im/mnh/heritage/museums/cregneashvillage.xml; f. 1938; attached to Manx Nat. Heritage (Eiraght Ashoonagh Vannin); provides a living, working illustration of life in a typical 19th- and early 20th-century Manx upland crofting community.

Douglas

Manx Museum: Kingswood Grove, Douglas, IM1 3LY; tel. (1624) 648000; fax (1624) 648001; e-mail enquiries@mnh.gov.im; internet www.gov.im/mnh/heritage/museums/manxmuseum.xml; f. 1922; attached to Manx Nat. Heritage (Eiraght Ashoonagh Vannin); Manx history and archaeology; art and map galleries; Dir, Manx Nat. Heritage E. SOUTHWORTH.

Colleges

Isle of Man College/Colleish Ellan Vannin: Homefield Rd, Douglas, IM2 6RB; tel. (1624) 648200; fax (1624) 648201; internet www.iomcollege.ac.im; f. 1971; publicly funded instn; affiliated to Univ. of Liverpool, Liverpool Hope Univ. and Univ. of Chester, offering joint degree courses in addition to gen. further education studies; courses in adult community education, art, design and media, business, management and professional studies, computing and information technology, construction, education, training and staff devt, engineering, gen. education, hair and beauty, health and social care, heritage and Manx studies, hospitality and catering, learning services, office technology, staff devt; library: 29,000 vols; Prin. RAY SMITH; Chair. A. C. COLLISTER; Dir Prof. R. CAREY.

Isle of Man International Business School: University Centre, Old Castletown Rd, Douglas, IM2 1QB; tel. (1624) 693700; fax (1624) 665095; e-mail enquiries@ibs.ac.im; internet www.ibs.ac.im; f. 1999; attached to Dept of Education & Children; MSc courses in financial regulation and compliance management, and in international banking and finance, BA (Hons) in business studies, MBA in business management; Dir of MBA Programmes Prof. AUGUSTINE OKAN-LAWON.

JERSEY

The Higher Education System

There are no universities on Jersey, and most students wishing to pursue degree-level education do so at universities in the United Kingdom; for such students, tuition fees are generally higher than for United Kingdom residents but not as high as for foreign students. There is no student loan system in place; however, limited means-tested student grants and bursaries are available. Highlands College (founded in 1881; present name and status adopted 1972), which is administered by the Department of Education, Sport and Culture, offers a limited number of degree courses at its University Centre, which was opened in 2009: Foundation degree programmes, which are offered in a number of professional fields, require two years' study, while the Bachelor of Science (Honours) degree, which is currently only available in the field of social sciences, is a three-year course. The College also provides a range of vocational training and adult education programmes.

Regulatory Body

GOVERNMENT

Department for Education, Sport and Culture: POB 142, Highlands Campus, St Helier, JE4 8QJ; tel. (1534) 445504; fax (1534) 445524; e-mail esc@gov.je; internet www.gov.je/esc; Minister for Education, Sport and Culture PATRICK RYAN.

Learned Societies

GENERAL

Société Jersiaise: 7 Pier Rd, St Helier, JE2 4XW; tel. (1534) 758314; fax (1534) 888262; e-mail societe@societe-jersiaise.org; internet www.societe-jersiaise.org; f. 1873; promotes the study of the history, archaeology, natural history, language and other fields relative to Jersey; library: Lord Coutanche Library contains books, newspapers, maps, prints, parish records and other material concerning the Channel Islands, Normandy, Brittany and southern England; 75,000 images in photographic archive; Pres. ROWLAND ANTHONY; Exec. Dir PAULINE SYVRET; publ. *Library and Photographic Archive* (online).

AGRICULTURE, FISHERIES AND VETERINARY SCIENCE

Royal Jersey Agricultural & Horticultural Society: Royal Jersey Showground, La Route de la Trinité, Trinity, JE3 5JP; tel. (1534) 866555; fax (1534) 865619; e-mail society@royaljersey.co.uk; internet www.royaljersey.co.uk; f. 1833; agricultural dept: provides a range of services to support the modern dairy industry; responsible for the management of the Jersey breed in the island; horticulture dept: promotes horticulture through talks, shows, garden competitions and general advice; Royal Jersey Showground: holds indoor and outdoor events; conference and exhibition facilities.

ECONOMICS, LAW AND POLITICS

Law Society of Jersey: POB 493, St Helier, JE4 5SZ; tel. (1534) 613920; fax (1534) 613928; e-mail ceolawsoc@gmail.com; internet www.jerseylawsociety.je; governing body of lawyers practising as advocates and solicitors of the Royal Court of Jersey; operates a fee complaints procedure; Pres. C. M. B. THACKER; Sec. S. E. FITZ; Hon. Treas. M. H. RICHARDSON; Hon. Librarian C. G. PARSLOW.

HISTORY, GEOGRAPHY AND ARCHAEOLOGY

Channel Islands Family History Society: POB 507, St Helier, JE4 5TN; e-mail cifhs@localdial.com; internet www.jerseyfamilyhistory.org; f. 1978; research colln held at Jersey Archive; Pres. JOHN NOEL; Sec. PAT NEALE; Treas. HARRY BAUDAINS; publ. *Journal* (4 a year).

Jersey Heritage: The Weighbridge, St Helier, JE2 3NF; tel. (1534) 633300; e-mail info@jerseyheritagetrust.org; internet www.jerseyheritagetrust.org; f. 1981; ind. org. funded by States of Jersey; promotes and preserves Jersey's heritage; main collns of archaeology, art, archives and social history; Chair. C. JONES; Vice-Chair. P. LE BROCQ; Dir JONATHAN CARTER.

Research Institute

MEDICINE

Cancer Research UK Jersey: Woodlands Court, La Route des Cotils, Grouville, JE3 9AP; tel. (1534) 500420; fax (1534) 858185; e-mail jersey@cancer.org.uk; internet www.cancerresearchukjersey.org; f. 1953 as Jersey Committee; fund-raising and research into the causes of cancer, means of treating cancer more effectively and ways of reducing the incidence of cancer; Chair. ROBERT CHRISTENSEN; Treas. CAROL RAFFERTY.

Libraries and Archives

St Helier

Jersey Archive: Clarence Rd, St Helier, JE2 4JY; tel. (1534) 833135; fax (1534) 833101; e-mail archives@jerseyheritage.org; internet www.jerseyheritage.org/research-centre/jersey-archive; f. 1993; attached to Jersey Heritage; preserves records of the States of Jersey, State cttees and depts, Royal Court, Lt-Governor, parishes, churches, businesses, societies and individuals; Head of Archives and Collns LINDA ROMERIL.

Jersey Library: Halkett Pl., St Helier, JE2 4WH; tel. (1534) 448700; fax (1534) 448730; e-mail je.library@gov.je; internet www.gov.je/library; gen. lending colln, local and British newspapers and periodicals since the 18th century; Chief Librarian PAT DAVIS.

Museums and Art Galleries

Grouville

La Hougue Bie Museum: La Route de la Hougue Bie, Grouville, JE2 7UA; internet www.jerseyheritage.org; attached to Jersey Heritage; passage graves; life and history of Jersey's neolithic community.

St Helier

Jersey Museum and Art Gallery: The Weighbridge, St Helier, JE2 3NG; tel. (1534) 633300; e-mail info@jerseyheritage.org; internet www.jerseyheritage.org; attached to Jersey Heritage; history of neolithic to modern day Jersey; spec. items on display incl. Bronze Age gold torque and Millais' portrait of Lillie Langtry; works of Claude Cahun; Victorian Merchant town house with traditional gas lamps and period furniture.

Maritime Museum: New North Quay, St Helier, JE2 3ND; tel. (1534) 633372; fax (1534) 874099; e-mail info@jerseyheritagetrust.org; internet www.jerseyheritage.org; f. 1997; attached to Jersey Heritage; seafaring and navigation; displays selected objects from maritime collector and Jersey resident Tony Titterington's collns incl. a torpedo, propeller and shaft, a restored 88-mm deck gun and sonar from a German armed trawler; ship bells, bronze cannon from HMS *Determinée*, a British man-of-war wrecked off Noirmont in 1803.

Occupation Tapestry Gallery: New North Quay, St Helier, JE2 3ND; tel. (1534) 633372; e-mail info@jerseyheritage.org; internet www.jerseyheritage.org; attached to Jersey Heritage; displays 12 panels of tapestry depicting life in Jersey during the Second World War.

St Lawrence

Hamptonne Country Life Museum: La Rue de la Patente, St Lawrence, JE3 1HS; tel. (1534) 633300; e-mail info@jerseyheritage.org; internet www.jerseyheritage.org; attached to Jersey Heritage; farm bldgs and meadows; cluster of restored farmhouses and outbuildings displaying 17th-century rural life in Jersey.

Jersey War Tunnels: Les Charrières Malorey, St Lawrence, JE3 1FU; tel. (1534) 860808; fax (1534) 860886; e-mail info@jerseywartunnels.com; internet www.jerseywartunnels.com; tunnel complex fmrly known as Höhlgangsanlage 8 (Ho8); hosts a series of galleries detailing the Occupation of Jersey during the Second World War.

College

Highlands College: POB 1000, St Saviour, JE4 9QA; tel. (1534) 608608; e-mail hcwebsite@highlands.ac.uk; internet www .highlands.ac.uk; f. 1881 as naval training college, present name and status 1972; attached to Dept for Education, Sport and Culture; vocational and leisure courses; adult education service; partnership with Plymouth and London South Bank Univs; attached Univ. Centre for undergraduate and graduate study; 6,000 students; Prin. and Chief Exec. Prof. EDWARD SALLIS; Deputy Prin. Dr GARY JONES; Vice-Prin. PETER WADE (acting).

UNITED STATES OF AMERICA

he Higher Education System

Institutions of higher education predate the USA's independence from the United Kingdom in 1776, the oldest being Harvard University, which was founded in 1636. Over 500 universities and colleges were founded during the 19th century, particularly following the Morrill Land-Grants Acts of 1862 and 1890, which gave over federal lands to the States for the purpose of establishing and funding educational institutions; the so-called 'A&M' (agricultural and mechanical) universities are among the most prominent of these institutions. There is no federal system of higher education, which is primarily provided by state governments and private institutions. However, the federal Department of Education is responsible for promoting education at all levels, dispensing federal aid and enforcing civil rights statutes. The Bill of Rights of the US Constitution guarantees academic freedom at all levels. Higher education is offered by universities and two-year, four-year and community colleges. In 2009 there were 4,409 degree-granting universities and colleges. Projected total enrolment within higher education institutions in 2010 was estimated at 20.6m. students, of whom 14.9m. attended public institutions and 5.7m. private institutions.

Admission to higher education is often on the basis of the High School Graduation Diploma and results in Scholastic Aptitude Tests (SATs), with institutions also applying their own criteria. Two-year Associate degrees are offered by both four-year institutions and two-year junior, technical and community colleges (junior colleges are usually privately run institutions and community colleges are funded by State or local governments). Students who have been awarded Associate degrees may transfer into four-year universities and colleges to complete full degrees. The Bachelors is the main undergraduate degree and typically lasts four years, consisting of two years of general education and then two years of study in a 'major' subject. However, Bachelors degrees in specialist or technical fields last five years. Most degrees are awarded on a 'credit-semester' basis, under which the student is required to accumulate a specified number of credits each semester in order to graduate. The minimum number of credits required for the award of the Bachelors degree is 120.

Postgraduate education in US institutions is referred to as 'graduate school' because degrees at this level are administered by university graduate schools. Admission to graduate school requires the Bachelors and an application supported by transcripts, statements of purpose and letters of recommendation. Applicants will also be required to achieve good scores in at least one of several standardized tests, depending on the subject area. Among these tests are Graduate Record Examinations, Miller Analogies Test, Graduate Management Admissions Test, Law School Admissions Test and the Medical College Admission Test. Masters degrees last between one and three years and are available on a taught or research basis, the difference being that taught degrees prepare students for professional entry and research degrees prepare students for further postgraduate studies. The PhD is the most common doctoral-level degree, and lasts between five to 10 years following the award of the Bachelors, depending on the subject and on whether the student has first undertaken a Masters or professional postgraduate degree; programmes in the humanities and professional fields generally take longer to complete than those in the physical sciences and engineering. The PhD consists of a period of intensive study leading to examinations before the student undertakes research for a doctoral dissertation, which is presented and defended before a panel.

There is no established federal framework of post-secondary technical and vocational qualifications. Occupational training takes place in the workplace, and educational certificates, diplomas and degrees consist of both classroom-based learning and practical experience.

Accreditation of universities and colleges is administered by the six main regional accrediting bodies, which are recognized by the Department of Education and are members of the Council for Higher Education Accreditation. They are: Middle States Association of Colleges and Schools (MSA) , Northwest Commission on Colleges and Universities (NWCCU), North Central Association of Colleges and Schools (NCA), New England Association of Schools and Colleges, Inc./Commission on Institutions of Higher Education (NEASC–CIHE), Southern Association of Colleges and Schools/Commission on Colleges (SACS–CC) and Western Association of Schools and Colleges/Accrediting Commission for Senior Colleges and Universities (WASC–Sr). There are also professional bodies and single-subject agencies that accredit specialist schools and individual programmes.

In 2009 President Barack Obama enacted legislation to make college more affordable by making working families eligible for a tax credit to help offset the cost of tuition and by expanding the Perkins Loan Programme. In March 2010 Obama enacted the Student Aid and Fiscal Responsibility Act, which provided for the investment of more than US $36,000m. into the Pell Grants programme over a 10-year period, and raised the maximum Pell Grant amount for the 2010/11 academic year to $5,500. Owing to a shortfall in funding, Congress voted in mid-2011 to reduce the average amount of aid available to students via the Pell Grant for 2011/12, although the maximum payment was to remain unchanged at $5,500. Obama also had plans to reform the nation's student loan system by decreasing the role of private lenders and placing the responsibility on the federal Government.

Regulatory and Representative Bodies

GOVERNMENT

Department of Education: 400 Maryland Ave, SW, Washington, DC 20202; tel. (202) 401-2000; fax (202) 401-0596; internet www.ed.gov; f. 1980; fed. govt agency; establishes policy; administers and coordinates most fed. assistance to education; provides grant, loan and work-study assistance to post-secondary students; collects data on America's schools and disseminates research; focuses nat. attention on key educational issues; prohibits discrimination and ensures equal access to education; Sec. of Education ARNE DUNCAN.

ACCREDITATION

ABET: 111 Market Pl., Suite 1050, Baltimore, MD 21202-4012; tel. (410) 347-7700; fax (410) 625-2238; e-mail comms@abet.org; internet www.abet.org; f. 1932 as Engineers Council for Professional Devt, present location 1996, present name 2005; advances quality education in applied science, computing, engineering and technology; manages operations and resources; consults and assists in devt and advancement of education in a financially self-sustaining manner; accredits over 3,100 programmes at more than 660 colleges and univs in 23 countries; 31 mem. socs; Exec. Dir Dr MICHAEL K. J. MILLIGAN; Pres. LARRY A. KAYE; Sec. JEFFREY J. SHROLA.

Accreditation Council for Business Schools & Programs: 11520 West 119th St, Overland Park, KS 66213; tel. (913) 339-9356; fax (913) 339-6226; e-mail info@acbsp.org; internet www.acbsp.org; f. 1988; promotes continuous improvement and recognizes excellence in accreditation of business education programmes around the world; Exec. Dir DOUGLAS VIEHLAND.

Accrediting Commission of Career Schools and Colleges (ACCSC): 2101

Wilson Blvd, Suite 302, Arlington, VA 22201; tel. (703) 247-4212; fax (703) 247-4533; internet www.accsc.org; f. 1965 as Accrediting Comm. of the Nat. Asscn of Trade and Technical Schools, present name and status 2009; serves as reliable authority on educational quality; promotes enhanced opportunities for students by establishing, sustaining and enforcing standards and practices contributing to devt of highly-trained and competitive workforce through quality career-oriented education; 800 mems; Exec. Dir and CEO Dr MICHALE S. McCOMIS.

Accrediting Council for Independent Colleges and Schools (ACICS): 750 First St, NE, Suite 980, Washington, DC 20002-4223; tel. (202) 336-6780; fax (202) 842-2593; e-mail info@acics.org; internet www.acics.org; f. 1912; not-for-profit org.; advances educational excellence at ind., non-public career schools, colleges and orgs in the USA and other countries; accredits more than 900 instns throughout the USA; Exec. Dir and CEO Dr ALBERT C. GRAY.

American Association of Colleges of Nursing: 1 Dupont Circle, NW, Suite 530, Washington, DC 20036; tel. (202) 463-6930; fax (202) 785-8320; internet www.aacn.nche.edu; f. 1969; autonomous accrediting agency; works to establish quality standards for nursing education; 690 mems; Exec. Dir JENNIFER BUTLIN.

American Bar Association: see under Learned Societies.

Association for Biblical Higher Education: 5850 T. G. Lee Blvd, Suite 130, Orlando, FL 32822; tel. (407) 207-0808; fax (407) 207-0840; internet www.abhe.org; f. 1947 as Accrediting Asscn of Bible Institutes and Bible Colleges, present name 2004; nat., faith-based accrediting agency; specializes in biblical ministry formation and professional leadership education; Pres. Dr RALPH E. ENLOW, JR.

Association of Theological Schools—Commission on Accrediting: 10 Summit Park Dr., Pittsburgh, PA 15275-1110; tel. (412) 788-6505; fax (412) 788-6510; e-mail communications@ats.edu; internet www.ats.edu; f. 1918 as conf. of theological schools, present status 2005; conducts post-baccalaureate professional and academic degree programmes to educate persons for practice of ministry and teaching and research in theological disciplines; 261 mems (222 USA, 39 Canada); Pres. RICHARD MOUW; Sec. PATRICIA SCHOELLES; Exec. Dir DANIEL O. ALESHIRE.

Council for Higher Education Accreditation: One Dupont Circle, NW, Suite 510, Washington, DC 20036-1135; tel. (202) 955-6126; fax (202) 955-6129; e-mail chea@chea.org; internet www.chea.org; f. 1966; nat. advocate and institutional voice for self-regulation of academic quality through accreditation; recognizes 60 institutional and programmatic accrediting orgs; 3,000 mems (degree-granting colleges and univs); Pres. Dr JUDITH S. EATON.

Council for Interior Design Accreditation (CIDA): 206 Grandville Ave, Suite 350, Grand Rapids, MI 49503-4014; tel. (616) 458-0400; fax (616) 458-0460; e-mail info@accredit-id.org; internet accredit-id.org; f. 1970 as Foundation for Interior Design Education Research, present name 2006; establishes and periodically updates standards for interior design education; evaluates and accredits interior design programmes of colleges and univs; facilitates outreach and

collaboration with stakeholders in interior design community; Exec. Dir HOLLY MATTSON; Dir of Accreditation MEGAN SCANLAN.

Distance Education and Training Council (DETC): 1601 18th St, NW, Suite 2, Washington, DC 20009; tel. (202) 234-5100; fax (202) 332-1386; internet www.detc.org; f. 1926 as Nat. Home Study Council, present status 1955, present name 1994; defines, maintains and promotes educational excellence in distance education instns; focuses on quality assurance, protection of rights of students and institutional self-improvement through voluntary accreditation via peer evaluation; 100 mems; Chair. TIMOTHY MOTT; Exec. Dir MICHAEL P. LAMBERT.

ENIC/NARIC United States of America: 5209 Sangamore Rd, Bethesda, MD 20816; tel. (301) 320-3842; internet www.enic-naric.net.

Middle States Commission on Higher Education: 3624 Market St, Second Fl., W, Philadelphia, PA 19104-2680; tel. (267) 284-5000; fax (215) 662-5501; e-mail info@msche.org; internet www.msche.org; f. 1919; attached to Middle States Asscn of Colleges and Schools; voluntary, non-governmental, membership asscn that defines, maintains and promotes educational excellence across instns with diverse missions, student populations and resources; accredits degree-granting instns incl. colleges, military academics, religious seminaries and univs in Middle States region, which inc. DE, DC, FL, MD, NJ, NY, PA, Puerto Rico, the US Virgin Islands and several locations internationally; Pres. Dr ELIZABETH H. SIBOLSKI.

National Association of Schools of Art and Design (NASAD): 11250 Roger Bacon Dr., Suite 21, Reston, VA 20190-5248; tel. (703) 437-0700; fax (703) 437-6312; e-mail info@arts-accredit.org; internet nasad.arts-accredit.org; f. 1944; produces statistical research, provides professional devt for leaders of art and design schools and engages in policy analysis; 309 mems; Exec. Dir SAMUEL HOPE.

National Association of Schools of Music: 11250 Roger Bacon Dr., Suite 21, Reston, VA 20190-5248; tel. (703) 437-0700; fax (703) 437-6312; e-mail info@arts-accredit.org; internet nasm.arts-accredit.org; f. 1924; aims at better understanding among instns of higher education engaged in work in music; establishes a more uniform method of granting credit; develops and maintains basic, threshold standards for the granting of degrees and other credentials; 636 mems; Exec. Dir SAMUEL HOPE.

National Association of Schools of Public Affairs and Administration (NASPAA): 1029 Vermont Ave, NW, Suite 1100, Washington, DC 20005-3517; tel. (202) 628-8965; fax (202) 626-4978; e-mail naspaa@naspaa.org; internet www.naspaa.org; f. 1970; promotes excellence in public service education; 280 mems; Exec. Dir LAUREL McFARLAND.

National Council for Accreditation of Teacher Education (NCATE): 2010 Massachusetts Ave, NW, Suite 500, Washington, DC 20036; tel. (202) 466-7496; fax (202) 296-6620; e-mail ncate@ncate.org; internet www.ncate.org; f. 1954; works to make a difference in the quality of teaching, teachers, school specialists and administrators; Chair. DENNIS VAN ROEKEL.

New England Association of Schools and Colleges: Commission on Institutions of Higher Education (NEASC—CIHE): New England Asscn of Schools and

Colleges, 209 Burlington Rd, Suite 201, Bedford, MA 01730-1433; tel. (781) 271-0022; fax (781) 271-0950; e-mail cihe@neasc.org; internet cihe.neasc.org; f. 1885; regional accreditation agency for over 234 colleges and univs in 6 New England states: CT, ME, MA, NH, RI and VT; 2 instns in Greece, 3 in Switzerland and 1 in Bulgaria, Bermuda and Lebanon, respectively, are also affiliated with CIHE; 242 mems; Pres. and Dir of Comm. Dr BARBARA E. BRITTINGHAM.

Higher Learning Commission: 230 S LaSalle St, Suite 7-500, Chicago, IL 60604-1411; tel. (312) 263-0456; fax (312) 263-7462; e-mail info@hlcommission.org; internet www.ncahlc.org; f. 1895; attached to North Central Asscn of Colleges and Schools; ind. corpn that accredits degree-granting post-secondary educational instns in N Central region: AR, AZ, CO, IA, IL, IN, KS, MI, MN, MO, ND, NE, OH, OK, NM, SD, WI, WV and WY; Pres. Dr SYLVIA MANNING.

Northwest Commission on Colleges and Universities: 8060 165th Ave, NE, Suite 100, Redmond, WA 98052; tel. (425) 558-4224; fax (425) 376-0596; internet www.nwccu.org; f. 1917, fmrly Commission on Colleges and Univs, present status 1952; ind., non-profit membership org.; recognized as regional authority on educational quality and institutional effectiveness of higher education instns in 7-state NW region of AK, ID, MT, NV, OR, UT and WA; establishes accreditation criteria and evaluation procedures by which the region's 162 instns are reviewed; Pres. Dr SANDRA E. ELMAN.

Southern Association of Colleges and Schools: Commission on Colleges: 1866 Southern Lane, Decatur, GA 30033; tel. (404) 679-4500; fax (404) 679-4558; e-mail questions@sacscoc.org; internet www.sacscoc.org; f. 1895; recognized regional accrediting body in 11 US Southern states (AL, FL, GA, KY, LA, MS, NC, SC, TN, TX and VA) and in Latin America for those instns of higher education that award Associate, Bachelors, Masters or doctoral degrees; Pres. of Comm. Dr BELLE S. WHEELAN.

Teachers Standards and Practices Commission: 250 Div. St, NE, Salem, OR 97301-1012; tel. (503) 378-3586; fax (503) 378-4448; e-mail contact.tspc@state.or.us; internet www.oregon.gov/tspc; establishes, upholds and enforces professional standards of excellence, and communicates those standards to the public and educators for benefit of Oregon's students; Exec. Dir VICTORIA CHAMBERLAIN.

Western Association of Schools and Colleges: Accrediting Commission for Senior Colleges and Universities: 985 Atlantic Ave, Suite 100, Alameda, CA 94501; tel. (510) 748-9001; fax (510) 748-9797; e-mail wascsr@wascsenior.org; internet www.wascsenior.org; f. 1962; promotes welfare, interests and devt of education in the W region; accredits 161 instns in CA, HI and the Pacific Basin; Chair. LINDA JOHNSRUD; Pres. and Exec. Dir RALPH A. WOLFF.

FUNDING

Alfred P. Sloan Foundation: 630 Fifth Ave, Suite 2550, New York, NY 10111; tel. (212) 649-1649; fax (212) 757-5117; e-mail officeofthepresident@sloan.org; internet www.sloan.org; f. 1934; makes grants for research and broad-based education related to science and technology, standard of living and economic performance, and education and careers in science and technology; Chair. STEPHEN L. BROWN; Pres. PAUL L. JOSKOW.

Bureau of Educational and Cultural Affairs (ECA): US Dept of State, SA-5,

2200 C St, NW, Washington, DC 20522-0500; tel. (202) 632-6445; fax (202) 632-2701; e-mail educationusa@state.gov; internet exchanges.state.gov; f. 1959; attached to US Dept of State; advances US foreign policy objectives through educational and cultural programmes that enhance mutual understanding between the USA and other nations; reflects diversity of the USA and global soc., its programmes, funding and other activities encouraging involvement of American and int. participants incl. women, racial and ethnic minorities and people with disabilities; Prin. Deputy Asst Sec. of State for Educational and Cultural Affairs J. ADAM ERELI.

Foundation Center: 79 Fifth Ave, 16th St, New York, NY 10003-3076; tel. (212) 620-4230; fax (212) 807-3677; e-mail communications@foundationcenter.org; internet foundationcenter.org; f. 1956; offices in Washington, DC, San Francisco, CA, Cleveland, OH, and Atlanta, GA; makes available information about philanthropic foundations; maintains colln of foundation reports; library of 2,500 vols, 3,250 pamphlets and articles, 500 foundation reports, computer files of foundation grants, aperture card system containing foundation IRS returns; Chair. M. CHRISTINE DEVITA; Pres. BRADFORD K. SMITH; publs *Foundation Directory* (online and 1 a year), *Foundation Grants to Individuals* (every 2 years), *Grant Guides in 30 Subjects* (1 a year), *Guide to Funding for International and Foreign Programs*, *National Directory of Corporate Giving* (1 a year).

Institute of Museum and Library Services: 1800 M St NW, Ninth Fl., Washington, DC 20036-5802; tel. (202) 653-4657; fax (202) 653-4600; internet www.imls.gov; f. 1996; inspires libraries and museums to advance innovation, learning and cultural and civic engagement through research, policy devt and grants; Dir SUSAN HILDRETH.

National Science Foundation: 4201 Wilson Blvd, Arlington, VA 22230; tel. (703) 292-5111; fax (703) 292-9232; e-mail info@nsf .gov; internet www.nsf.gov; f. 1950; funds research and education in fields of science and engineering; accounts for 20 per cent of fed. support to academic instns for basic research by US colleges and univs; supports nat. research centres, user facilities, certain oceanographic vessels, Antarctic research stations and cooperative research between univs and industry; Dir Dr SUBRA SURESH.

Rockefeller Foundation: 420 Fifth Ave, New York, NY 10018; tel. (212) 869-8500; fax (212) 764-3468; internet www.rockfound.org; f. 1913; makes grants in the fields of agriculture, health, population sciences, global environment, African initiatives; organized under Int. Programme to Support Science-Based Devt; arts and humanities; equal opportunity; school reform; offices in San Francisco, CA, Italy, Kenya and Thailand; Man. Dir CLAUDIA JUECH; Pres. JUDITH RODIN.

US Department of Energy—Office of Science: US Dept of Energy, 1000 Independence Ave, SW, Washington, DC 20585; tel. (202) 586-5430; fax (202) 586-4403; e-mail the.secretary@hq.doe.gov; internet science.energy.gov; f. 1977 as Office of Energy Research, present name 1998; funds researchers in univs and dept of energy nat. laboratories; devt of individual research programmes of outstanding scientists early in their careers; funds advanced scientific computing research, biological and environmental research, basic energy sciences, fusion energy sciences, high energy physics and

nuclear physics; Dir Dr WILLIAM F. BRINKMAN; Sec. Dr STEVEN CHU.

Woodrow Wilson International Center for Scholars: 1 Woodrow Wilson Plaza, 1300 Pennsylvania Ave, NW, Washington, DC 20004-3027; tel. (202) 691-4000; fax (202) 691-4001; e-mail wwics@wilsoncenter.org; internet www.wilsoncenter.org; f. 1968; non-partisan instn supported by public and private funds; fosters research, study, discussion and collaboration among a full spectrum of individuals concerned with policy and scholarship in nat. and world affairs; library of 20,000 vols, 250 periodicals; Chair. JOSEPH B. GILDENHORN; Pres., CEO and Dir JANE HARMAN; publ. *Wilson Quarterly*.

NATIONAL BODIES

American Association of Collegiate Registrars and Admissions Officers (AACRAO): One Dupont Circle, NW, Suite 520, Washington, DC 20036; tel. (202) 293-9161; fax (202) 872-8857; e-mail oies@aacrao .org; internet www.aacrao.org; f. 1910; provides professional devt, guidelines and voluntary standards to be used by higher education officials regarding the best practices in records management, admissions, enrolment management, admin. information technology and student services; 10,000 mems in 40 countries; Pres. NORA McLAUGHLIN; Exec. Dir (vacant); publ. *College & University* (4 a year).

American Association of State Colleges and Universities (AASCU): 1307 New York Ave, NW, Fifth Fl., Washington, DC 20005-4701; tel. (202) 293-7070; fax (202) 296-5819; internet www.aascu.org; f. 1961; improves higher education within its mem. instns through cooperative planning, studies, research on common educational problems and devt of a more unified programme of action; 420 mems; Chair. MICKEY BURNIM; Pres. Dr MURIEL A. HOWARD; publ. *Public Purpose*.

American Association of University Professors: 1133 19th St, NW, Suite 200, Washington, DC 20036-3655; tel. (202) 737-5900; fax (202) 737-5526; e-mail aaup@aaup .org; internet www.aaup.org; f. 1915; advances academic freedom and shared governance; defines fundamental professional values and standards for higher education; ensures higher education's contribution to common good; 47,000 mems; Pres. CARY NELSON; Sec. and Treas. HOWARD BUNSIS; publs *AAUP Journal of Academic Freedom* (online), *Academe: Magazine of the AAUP* (6 a year).

American Council on Education: One Dupont Circle, NW, Washington, DC 20036-1193; tel. (202) 939-9300; fax (202) 833-4760; e-mail comments@ace.nche.edu; internet www.acenet.edu; f. 1918; represents press and chancellors of US accredited, degree-granting instns: community colleges and four-year instns, private and public univs and non-profit and for-profit colleges; advocates on behalf of key higher education issues; ensures higher education has diverse, skilled and ample leadership; 1,859 mems; Chair. EDUARDO J. PADRÓN; Pres. MOLLY CORBETT BROAD; publ. *The Presidency* (3 a year).

American Federation of Teachers (AFT): AFL-CIO, 555 New Jersey Ave, NW, Washington, DC 20001; tel. (202) 879-4400; internet www.aft.org; f. 1916; represents economic, social and professional interests of classroom teachers; 1.5m. mems; Pres. RANDI WEINGARTEN; Sec. and Treas. ANTONIA CORTESE; publs *AFT On Campus*, *American Academic* (irregular), *American Educator* (4 a year), *American Teacher* (6 a year),

Healthwire (6 a year), *PSRP Reporter*, *Public Employee Advocate* (6 a year).

Association for Career and Technical Education (ACTE): 1410 King St, Alexandria, VA 22314; tel. (703) 683-3111; fax (703) 683-7424; e-mail acte@acteonline.org; internet www.acteonline.org; f. 1926; assures growth in local, state and fed. funding for career and technical programmes by communicating and working with legislators and govt leaders; increases public awareness and appreciation for career and technical programmes; 27,000 mems; Pres. JAMES W. COMER; Exec. Dir JAN BRAY; publ. *Techniques* (8 a year).

Association for Institutional Research (AIR): 1435 E Piedmont Dr., Suite 211, Tallahassee, FL 32308; tel. (850) 385-4155; fax (850) 385-5180; e-mail air@airweb.org; internet www.airweb.org; f. 1965; supports its mems in facilitating quality, data-informed decisions for enhancement of higher education; 4,000 mems and 160 int. mems; Exec. Dir Dr RANDY SWING; Pres. JENNIFER A. BROWN; Sec. ELIZABETH C. STANLEY; publs *AIR Professional File* (online), *IR Applications* (online), *Research in Higher Education*.

Association of American Colleges and Universities: 1818 R St, NW, Washington, DC 20009; tel. (202) 387-3760; fax (202) 265-9532; e-mail pub_desk@aacu.org; internet www.aacu.org; f. 1915 as Asscn of American Colleges, present name 1995; reinforces collective commitment to liberal education at nat. and local levels and helps individual instns keep the quality of student learning at the core of their work; 1,200 mems; Chair. HELEN F. GILES-GEE; Pres. Dr CAROL GEARY SCHNEIDER; publs *Diversity & Democracy* (3 a year), *Liberal Education* (4 a year), *Peer Review* (4 a year).

Association of American Universities: 1200 New York Ave, NW, Suite 550, Washington, DC 20005; tel. (202) 408-7500; fax (202) 408-8184; internet www.aau.edu; f. 1900; advances int. understanding of US research univs; focuses on issues related to research-intensive univs, such as funding for research, research policy issues and graduate and undergraduate education; 61 mems (59 US, 2 Canada); Chair. MARY SUE COLEMAN; Pres. HUNTER R. RAWLINGS, III; publ. *AAU Weekly Wrap-ups*.

Association of Community College Trustees: 1233 20th St, NW, Suite 301, Washington, DC 20036; tel. (202) 775-4667; fax (202) 223-1297; e-mail acctinfo@acct.org; internet www.acct.org; promotes effective board governance through advocacy and education; governs community, technical and junior colleges in the USA and beyond; 1,200 mems; Chair. ROBERTO URANGA; Pres. and CEO J. NOAH BROWN; Sec. and Treas. LEROY W. MITCHELL; publ. *Trustee Quarterly* (4 a year).

Association of Governing Boards of Universities and Colleges: 1133 20th St, NW, Suite 300, Washington, DC 20036; tel. (202) 296-8400; fax (202) 223-7053; e-mail info@ agb.org; internet www.agb.org; f. 1921; strengthens and protects the country's unique form of institutional governance through its research, services and advocacy; 1,200 mems; Chair. JAMES M. WEAVER; Pres. RICHARD D. LEGON; Sec. YVONNE R. JACKSON; publ. *Trusteeship* (6 a year).

Association of Public and Land-Grant Universities: 1307 New York Ave, NW, Suite 400, Washington, DC 20005-4722; tel. (202) 478-6040; fax (202) 478-6046; internet www.aplu.org; f. 1887 as American Association of Agricultural Colleges and Experiment Stations, merger of American Asscn of

Land-Grant Colleges and Univs with Nat. Asscn of State Univs 1963, present name 2009; research and advocacy org. of public research univs, land-grant instns and state univ. systems with mem. campuses in 50 states, US territories and District of Columbia; 217 mem. instns, incl. 74 US land-grant instns; Chair. GENE D. BLOCK; Pres. M. PETER MCPHERSON.

Center for Quality Assurance in International Education: 2001 Mayfair McLean Court, Falls Church, VA 22043; tel. (703) 534-6384; fax (703) 534-6383; e-mail cqaie@cqaie.org; internet www.cqaie.org; f. 1991; facilitates comparative study of nat. quality and competency assurance mechanisms to improve efforts within countries and promote mobility among nat. systems; assists countries in devt or enhancement of quality assurance systems for higher education; promotes globalization of professions; monitors issues of quality in transnational movement of higher education; offices in Washington, DC, Hanoi, Viet Nam, Abu Dhabi, United Arab Emirates; Chair. CAROL BOBBY; Pres. Dr BETHANY S. JONES.

College Board: 45 Columbus Ave, New York, NY 10023-6917; tel. (212) 713-8000; e-mail apexams@info.collegeboard.org; internet www.collegeboard.com; f. 1900 as College Entrance Examination Board; not-for-profit membership asscn; connects students to college success and opportunity; offices in New York, Washington, DC, Albany, NY, Reston, VA, Bala Cynwyd, PA, Chicago, IL, Waltham, MA, Duluth, GA, Tallahassee, FL, Austin, TX, San Jose, CA, Sacramento, CA and San Juan, PR; 5,900 mem. schools, colleges, univs and other educational orgs; Pres. GASTON CAPERTON.

Council on International Educational Exchange: 300 Fore St, Portland, ME 04101; tel. (207) 553-4000; fax (207) 553-4299; e-mail contact@ciee.org; internet ciee.org; f. 1947 as Council on Student Travel, present name 1967; non-profit, non-governmental int. exchange org.; creates and administers programmes that allow high school and univ. students and educators to study and teach abroad; office Boston, MA; Chair. ROBERT E. FALLON; Pres. and CEO Dr JAMES P. PELLOW; Sec. KENTON KEITH.

Education Commission of the States: 700 Broadway, Suite 810, Denver, CO 80203-3442; tel. (303) 299-3600; fax (303) 296-8332; e-mail ecs@ecs.org; internet www.ecs.org; f. 1967; helps states develop effective policy and practice for public education by providing data, research, analysis and leadership; 49 mem. states; Chair. JOHN HICKENLOOPER; Pres. ROGER SAMPSON; publ. *The Progress of Education Reform* (6 a year).

Institute of International Education: 809 United Nations Pl., New York, NY 10017; tel. (212) 883-8200; fax (212) 984-5401; e-mail development@iie.org; internet www.iie.org; f. 1919; ind. non-profit org.; promotes closer educational relations between the people of the USA and other countries; strengthens and link instns of higher learning globally; rescues threatened scholars and advances academic freedom; builds leadership skills and enhances capacity of individuals and orgs to address local and global challenges; 18 offices in the USA, Europe, Middle East and North Africa, Sub-Saharan Africa, South and Central Asia and East Asia and the Pacific; 1,100 mems; Chair. THOMAS S. JOHNSON; Pres. and CEO Dr ALLAN E. GOODMAN; publ. *Open Doors*.

NAFSA: Association of International Educators: 1307 New York Ave, NW, Eighth Fl., Washington, DC 20005-4701; tel. (202) 737-3699; fax (202) 737-3657;

e-mail inbox@nafsa.org; internet www.nafsa.org; f. 1948 as Nat. Asscn of Foreign Student Advisers, present name 1990; promotes int. education and provides professional devt opportunities; sets and upholds standards of good practice, and provides training opportunities; 10,000 mems; Pres. and Chair. of Board Dr MEREDITH M. McQUAID; Sec. Dr CHARLES A. S. BANKART; publs *International Educator* (6 a year), *Journal of Studies in International Education* (5 a year), *Policy Brief* (electronic, irregular).

National Academy of Education: 500 Fifth St, NW, Washington, DC 20001; tel. (202) 334-2341; fax (202) 334-2350; e-mail info@naeducation.org; internet www.naeducation.org; f. 1965; promotes the highest quality educational research and its use in policy formulation and practice; 165 mems, 46 foreign assocs; Exec. Dir GREGORY WHITE; Pres. Dr SUSAN FUHRMAN; Sec. and Treas. SUSAN MOORE JOHNSON.

National Association for Equal Opportunity in Higher Education: 209 Third St, SE, Washington, DC 20003; tel. and fax (202) 552-3300; internet www.nafeo.org; f. 1969; not-for-profit org. of Historically Black Colleges and Univs (HBCU) and Predominantly Black Institutions (PBI); advocates policies, programmes and practices designed to preserve and enhance HBCUs and PBIs; builds capacity of HBCUs; Pres. and CEO LEZLI BASKERVILLE.

National Association of State Boards of Education: 2121 Crystal Dr., Suite 350, Arlington, VA 22202; tel. (703) 684-4000; fax (703) 836-2313; e-mail boards@nasbe.org; internet www.nasbe.org; f. 1958; works to strengthen state leadership in educational policy-making, promote excellence in education of all students, advocate equality of access to educational opportunity and assure continued citizen support for public education; Exec. Dir JIM KOHLMOOS; Pres. GAYLE MANCHIN; Sec. and Treas. ROB HOVIS; publs *Headline Review* (52 a year), *State Education Standard*.

National Association of State Directors of Career Technical Education Consortium: 8484 Georgia Ave, Suite 320, Silver Spring, MD 20910; tel. (301) 588-9630; fax (301) 588-9631; internet www.careertech.org; f. 1920; provides leadership for career technical education's role in education, workforce preparation and economic devt; 200 mems; Exec. Dir KIMBERLY A. GREEN; Pres. Dr PATRICK AINSWORTH; Sec. and Treas. MARK WILLIAMS.

National Association of State Directors of Teacher Education and Certification: 1629 K St, NW, Suite 300, Washington, DC 20006; tel. (202) 204-2208; fax (202) 204-2210; e-mail philrogers@nasdtec.com; internet www.nasdtec.org; f. 1928; represents professional standards boards and comms and state depts of education in all 50 states, DC, the Dept of Defense Education Activity, the US Territories, AB, BC and ON that are responsible for the preparation, licensure, and discipline of educational personnel; promotes high standards for educators, teacher mobility across state lines, comprehensive personnel screening and a database on teacher discipline; Pres. BRIAN DEVINE; Exec. Dir Dr PHILIP ROGERS; publs *NASDTEC KnowledgeBase* (irregular, online), *The Communicator* (4 a year, online).

National Education Association: 1201 16th St, NW, Washington, DC 20036-3290; tel. (202) 833-4000; fax (202) 822-7974; internet www.nea.org; f. 1857; advocates for education professionals; focuses on improving quality of teaching, increasing student achievements and making schools safer;

3.2m. mems; Exec. Dir JOHN C. STOCKS; Pres. DENNIS VAN ROEKEL; Sec. and Treas. REBECCA S. PRINGLE; publs *Almanac* (1 a year), *NEA Today* (4 a year), *This Active Life* (6 a year), *Thought & Action* (1 a year), *Tomorrow's Teachers* (1 a year).

State Higher Education Executive Officers: 3035 Center Green Dr., Suite 100, Boulder, CO 80301-2205; tel. (303) 541-1600; fax (303) 541-1639; e-mail sheeo@sheeo.org; internet www.sheeo.org; f. 1954; works to develop and sustain excellent systems of higher education; emphasizes importance of state planning and coordination for higher education by promoting effective strategic planning and statewide coordination and governance; speaks as nat. org. in public and private forums, promoting interests of states in effectively planning and financing higher education; Chair. GEORGE PERNSTEINER; Pres. Dr PAUL E. LINGENFELTER.

United States Network for Education Information: US Dept of Education, 400 Maryland Ave, SW, Room 6W108, Washington, DC 20202; tel. (202) 401-0430; fax (202) 401-2508; internet www.ed.gov/about/offices/list/ous/international/usnei/edlite-index.html; f. 1996; information centre under Lisbon Convention on the Recognition of Qualifications Concerning Higher Education in the European Region, 1 of 6 UNESCO regional recognition conventions; provides guide to American and foreign systems of education to facilitate int. educational mobility; Man. Dr E. STEPHEN HUNT.

Learned Societies

GENERAL

American Academy of Arts and Letters: 633 W 155th St, New York, NY 10032-1799; tel. (212) 368-5900; fax (212) 491-4615; e-mail academy@artsandletters.org; internet www.artsandletters.org; f. 1904, merger with Nat. Institute of Arts and Letters (f. 1898) 1976; fosters and sustains interest in literature, music and fine arts; identifies and encourages individual artists by administering awards and prizes, exhibiting art and MSS, funding stage readings and performances of new works and purchasing works of art to be donated to museums; 250 mems; library of 25,000 vols; Pres. J. D. McCLATCHY; Exec. Dir VIRGINIA DAJANI; Sec. ROSANNA WARREN; Treas. CHARLES WUORINEN; publ. *Proceedings* (1 a year).

American Academy of Arts & Sciences: 136 Irving St, Cambridge, MA 02138; tel. (617) 576-5000; fax (617) 576-5050; e-mail aaas@amacad.org; internet www.amacad.org; f. 1780; ind. policy research centre; focuses on science and technology policy, global security, social policy, the humanities and culture, and education; 4,600 mems (4,000 American fellows, 600 foreign hon. mems); Chair. LOUIS W. CABOT; Pres. LESLIE C. BERLOWITZ; Sec. JERROLD MEINWALD; Treas. JOHN S. REED; publs *Bulletin* (4 a year), *Daedalus* (4 a year), *Occasional Papers*.

American Council of Learned Societies: 633 Third Ave, Eighth Fl., 40th & 41st Sts, New York, NY 10017-6795; tel. (212) 697-1505; fax (212) 949-8058; e-mail grants@acls.org; internet www.acls.org; f. 1919; supports humanities research through fellowships and grants awarded to individuals, groups and institutions; represents humanities scholars and promotes the scholarly humanities in the USA and int. public and policy arenas; provides a forum for learned socs to discuss and suggest improvements in scholarship, education and communication among humanities scholars; 71 mem. socs; Pres. PAULINE YU; Sec. JAMES J. O'DONNELL; Treas. NANCY J. VICKERS; publ. *Occasional Paper series*.

American Philosophical Society: 104 S Fifth St, Philadelphia, PA 19106-3387; tel. (215) 440-3400; fax (215) 440-3436; internet www.amphilsoc.org; f. 1743; promotes useful knowledge in sciences and humanities through excellence in scholarly research, professional meetings, publs, library resources and community outreach; mems from various fields: mathematical and physical sciences, biological sciences, social sciences, humanities, and the professions, arts and affairs; conducts symposia, lectures and presents awards (incl. the Magellanic Premium, the oldest American scientific award); offers grants for research; museum and exhibition programme; 1,004 mems (834 US citizens, 170 foreign); library of 350,000 vols, 11m. MSS, 250,000 images; Pres. BARUCH S. BLOMBERG; Exec. Officer MARY PATTERSON MCPHERSON; publs *Biographical Memoirs of Members of the American Philosophical Society*, *Proceedings* (4 a year), *Transactions* (1 a year), *Year Book*.

Asia Foundation: POB 193223, San Francisco, CA 94119-3223 (Main Office); 465 California St, Ninth Fl., San Francisco, CA 94104; tel. (415) 982-4640; fax (415) 392-8863; e-mail info@asiafound.org; internet www.asiafoundation.org; f. 1954; offices in Washington, DC, and 18 Asian and Pacific island countries; assists Asian economic and social devt through private American support to Asian instns, orgs and individuals working towards constructive social change, stable political devt and equitable economic growth within their socs; provides grants; Books for Asia Program distributes books and journals to libraries and instns in Asia; library of 3,370 vols on current Asian and world affairs; Pres. DAVID D. ARNOLD; publ. *Occasional Papers*.

Connecticut Academy of Arts and Sciences: POB 208211, New Haven, CT 06520-8211; tel. (203) 432-3113; fax (203) 432-5712; e-mail caas@yale.edu; internet www.yale.edu/caas; f. 1799; disseminates scholarly information through lectures and extensive publs; library merged with Yale Univ. Library; 400 mems; Pres. ERNEST I. KOHORN; Sec. MARGOT L. KOHORN; Treas. JANETTE MURDOCK; publs *A Manual of the Writings in Middle English* (irregular), *Memoirs* (irregular), *Transactions* (irregular).

English-Speaking Union of the United States: 144 E 39th St, New York, NY 10016; tel. (212) 818-1200; fax (212) 867-4177; e-mail info@esuus.org; internet www.esuus.org; f. 1920; non-profit org.; promotes communication and understanding among people of all nationalities through the medium of the English language; initiates and implements innovative educational programmes; 10,000 mems; library of 6,000 vols; Chair. PATRICIA S. SCHROEDER; Pres. and Exec. Dir ALICE BOYNE; Sec. MATILDE JONES; Treas. HOLLISTER STURGES; publ. *E-SU Today*.

Hispanic Society of America: 613 W 155th St, New York, NY 10032; tel. (212) 926-2234; fax (212) 690-0743; e-mail info@hispanicsociety.org; internet www.hispanicsociety.org/hispanic/society.htm; f. 1904; professional research staff; reference library and museum; 400 mems; library of 250,000 vols, 15,000 rare books; Dir MITCHELL A. CODDING.

National Academies: 500 Fifth St, NW, Washington, DC 20001; tel. (202) 334-2000; internet national-academies.org; f. 1863; est. by Congressional charter; linked group of

instns, coordinating their advice to Fed. Govt; publs *ILAR Journal* (4 a year), *The National Academies In Focus*.

Individual Institutions:

Institute of Medicine: 500 Fifth St, NW, Washington, DC 20001; tel. (202) 334-2352; fax (202) 334-1412; e-mail iomwww@nas.edu; internet www.iom.edu; f. 1970; 1,700 mems; Pres. HARVEY V. FINEBERG; Exec. Officer JUDITH A. STALERNO; publs *Informing the Future*, *IOM News* (4 a year).

National Academy of Engineering: 500 Fifth St, NW, Washington, DC 20001; tel. (202) 334-3200; fax (202) 334-2290; internet www.nae.edu; f. 1964; promotes technological welfare of the nation by marshalling expertise and insights of eminent mems of engineering profession; 2,000 mems; Pres. CHARLES M. VEST; Home Sec. THOMAS F. BUDINGER; Foreign Sec. VENKATESH (VENKY) NARAYANAMURTI; Exec. Officer LANCE A. DAVIS; publ. *The Bridge* (4 a year).

National Academy of Sciences: 500 Fifth St, NW, Washington, DC 20001; tel. (202) 334-2000; internet www.nas.edu; f. 1863; sections: anthropology, applied mathematical sciences, applied microbial sciences, applied physical sciences, computer and information sciences, astronomy, biochemistry, biophysics and computational biology, chemistry, cellular and developmental biology, cellular and molecular neuroscience, economic sciences, engineering sciences, evolutionary, biology, environmental, sciences and ecology, genetics, geology, geophysics, haematology and oncology, human environmental sciences, immunology, psychology, mathematics, medical genetics, microbial biology, nutritional and plant, soil and microbial sciences, physics, physiology and metabolism, physiology and pharmacology, plant biology, social and political sciences and systems neuroscience; 2,200 mems and 400 assocs; Pres. RALPH J. CICERONE; Home Sec. SUSAN WESSLER; Foreign Sec. MICHAEL T. CLEGG; publs *Issues in Science and Technology*, *Proceedings of the National Academy of Sciences* (52 a year).

National Research Council: 500 Fifth St, NW, Washington, DC 20001; internet www.national-academies.org/nrc; f. 1916; improves govt decision making and public policy; increases public understanding; promotes acquisition and dissemination of knowledge in matters involving science, engineering, technology and health; Chair., National Research Council RALPH J. CICERONE; Vice-Chair. CHARLES M. VEST.

National Foundation on the Arts and the Humanities: Washington, DC 20506; f. 1965; an ind. agency in the Exec. Br. of Govt; develops and promotes a broadly conceived nat. policy of support for the humanities and the arts in the United States.

Constituent Institutions:

Federal Council on the Arts and the Humanities: Washington, DC 20506; f. 1965; coordinates activities of the two Endowments with related fed. agencies and carries out fed. indemnity programme; mems incl. Chairmen of two Endowments; Secs of Depts of Education, Interior, State, Commerce, Transportation, Housing and Urban Devt and Labor; Commissioners of Fine Arts Comm., Admin. on Aging, and Public Bldgs Service; Administrators of Veterans' Admin. and Gen. Services Admin.; Dirs of Nat. Science Foundation, and Institute of Museum and Library Services; Librarian of Congress; Archivist

of the US; Chair. of Nat. Museum Services Board; mems who do not vote on indemnity incl. Dir, Nat. Gallery of Art; Sec. of Senate; Sec., Smithsonian Institution; Mem., House of Representatives.

National Council on the Arts: Washington, DC 20506; tel. (202) 682-5433; fax (202) 682-5538; f. 1964; advises Chair. of Nat. Endowment for the Arts on policies, programmes and procedures and reviews applications for financial assistance; Chair. of Council is Chair. of the Arts Endowment; 20 mems (14 private citizens appointed by Pres. for a 6-year term, 6 *ex-officio* from Congress).

National Council on the Humanities: Washington, DC 20506; f. 1965; advises the Chair. of the Nat. Endowment for the Humanities on policies, programmes and procedures and reviews applications for financial assistance; 26 private citizen mems appointed by the Pres. for 6-year terms (approx. one-third of the appointments expire every 2 years); Chair. of Council is Chair. of the Humanities Endowment.

National Endowment for the Arts: 1100 Pennsylvania Ave, NW, Washington, DC 20506; tel. (202) 682-5400; e-mail webmgr@arts.endow.gov; internet arts.endow.gov; f. 1965; establishes and carries out a programme of grants-in-aid to non-profit groups, individuals of exceptional talent and state art agencies, which promote progress in the arts; Chair. ROCCO LANDESMAN (acting); publ. *NEA Arts Magazine* (4 a year).

National Endowment for the Humanities: 1100 Pennsylvania Ave, NW, Washington, DC 20506-0001; e-mail webmgr@arts.endow.gov; tel. (202) 606-8400; internet www.neh.gov; f. 1965; carries out a programme supporting projects of research, education and public activity in the humanities; Chair. JIM LEACH; publ. *Humanities* (6 a year).

New York Academy of Sciences: 7 World Trade Center, 250 Greenwich St, 40th Fl., New York, NY 10007-2157; tel. (212) 298-8600; fax (212) 298-3650; e-mail nyas@nyas.org; internet www.nyas.org; f. 1817; sections of anthropology, atmospheric sciences and geology, biochemical pharmacology, chemical biology, computational biology and bioinformatics, emerging infectious diseases, environmental sciences, genome integrity, genomic medicine, history and philosophy of science, Imaging, microbiology, nanobiotechnology, neurogenerative diseases, neuroimmunology, psychology, RNAi, science education, systems biology, vision research, women investigators' network, women in science; 24,000 mems; Pres and CEO ELLIS RUBINSTEIN; Chair. NANCY ZIMPHER; Treas. ROBERT CATELL; Sec. LARRY SMITH; publs *eBriefings* (online), *The Annals of the New York Academy of Sciences* (irregular), *The New York Academy of Sciences Magazine* (3 a year).

North American Spanish Language Academy/Academia Norteamericana de la Lengua Española: POB 349, New York, NY 10116; tel. and fax (718) 761-0556; e-mail info@anle.us; internet www.anle.us; f. 1973; mem. of Asociación de Academias de la Lengua Española; corresp. of Real Academia, Spain; 36 tenured mems, and 150 corresponding mems; Dir D. GERARDO PIÑA-ROSALES; Sec. D. JORGE I. COVARRUBIAS; Treas. D. EMILIO BERNAL LABRADA; publs *Boletín de la Academia Norteamericana* (every 2 years), *Glosas* (4 a year).

Smithsonian Institution: POB 37012, SI Bldg, Rm 153, MRC 010, Washington, DC

20013-7012; 1000 Jefferson Dr., Washington, DC 20560-033; tel. (202) 633-1000; e-mail info@si.edu; internet www.si.edu; f. 1846; a museum, education and research complex for the 'increase and diffusion of knowledge' by bequest of English scientist James Smithson; 137m. artifacts, works of art and specimens; 17 mems of the Board of Regents, incl. the Chief Justice of the USA and the Vice-Pres. of the USA, 3 mems of the Senate and of the House of Representatives, and 9 citizen mems; library: 1.8m. vols; Sec. G. WAYNE CLOUGH; Chancellor THE CHIEF JUSTICE OF THE UNITED STATES; Deputy Sec. SHEILA BURKE; publs *American Art Journal, Archives of American Art Journal, Smithsonian Contributions to Anthropology, Smithsonian Contributions to Astrophysics, Smithsonian Contributions to Botany, Smithsonian Contributions to the Earth Sciences, Smithsonian Contributions to the Marine Sciences, Smithsonian Contributions to Paleobiology, Smithsonian Contributions to Zoology, Smithsonian Studies in Air and Space, Smithsonian Studies in History and Technology.*

Constituent libraries and archives; (unless indicated otherwise, each institution listed below has a separate entry in the USA chapter):

Air and Space Museum Archives: see entry for National Air and Space Museum.

American History Museum Archives Center: see entry for National Museum of American History.

Archives of American Art.

Archives of American Gardens: see entry for Smithsonian Horticulture Services Division.

Eliot Elisofon Photographic Archives: see entry for National Museum of African Art, Smithsonian Institution.

Juley Photographic Archive: see entry for Smithsonian American Art Museum and its Renwick Gallery.

National Anthropological Archives and Human Studies Film Archives: see entry for National Museum of Natural History.

Ralph Rinzler Folklife Archives and Collections: see entry for Center for Folklife and Cultural Heritage.

Smithsonian Institution Archives.

Smithsonian Institution Libraries: 22-branch library system: for details of individual libraries, see under entries for Smithsonian instns. For general details of the system, see main Smithsonian libraries entry.

Constituent museums and art galleries; (unless indicated otherwise, each institution listed below has a separate entry in the USA chapter):

Anacostia Museum and Center for African American History and Culture.

Arts and Industries Building.

Cooper-Hewitt, National Design Museums.

Freer Gallery of Art and Arthur M. Sackler Gallery.

Hirshhorn Museum and Sculpture Garden.

National Air and Space Museums.

National Museum of African Art.

National Museum of American History, Behring Center.

National Museum of the American Indian.

National Museum of Natural History.

National Portrait Gallery.

National Postal Museum.

National Zoological Park.

Smithsonian American Art Museum and the Renwick Gallery.

Smithsonian Institution Building—the Castle: see main Smithsonian entry for address and contact details.

Constituent science centres; (unless indicated otherwise, each institution listed below has a separate entry in the USA chapter):

Astrophysical Observatory (SAO): see entry for Harvard-Smithsonian Center for Astrophysics.

Carrie-Bow Marine Field Station—Caribbean Coral Reef Ecosystems (CCRE): see entry in Belize chapter.

Center for Earth and Planetary Studies.

Conservation and Research Center: see entry for Smithsonian National Zoological Park.

Environmental Research Center (SERC).

Marine Science: network of Smithsonian instns—see entries for Environmental Research Center (SERC), Marine Station at Fort Pierce, CCRE, Tropical Research Institute, National Museum of Natural History, and National Zoological Park.

Migratory Bird Center: see entry for Smithsonian National Zoological Park.

Natural History Museum Research and Collections: see entry for National Museum of Natural History.

Tropical Research Institute (STRI): see entry in Panama chapter.

Conservation research units; (unless indicated otherwise, each institution listed below has a separate entry in the USA chapter):

African Art Museum Conservation Research Department: see entry for National Museum of African Art.

Center for Materials Research and Education.

Freer and Sackler Galleries Department of Conservation and Scientific Research: see entries for Freer Gallery of Art and Arthur M. Sackler Gallery.

Cultural and scholarly programmes; (unless indicated otherwise, each institution listed below has a separate entry in the USA chapter):

Asian Pacific American Program: f. 1997 to provide leadership and support for all Asian Pacific America (APA) activities at the Smithsonian; Dir FRANKLIN ODO.

Center for Education and Museum Studies.

Center for Folklife and Cultural Heritage.

Jerome and Dorothy Lemelson Center for the Study of Invention and Innovation.

Latino Initiatives: see entry for Smithsonian Center for Latino Initiatives.

National Science Resources Center:.

AGRICULTURE, FISHERIES AND VETERINARY SCIENCE

Agricultural History Society: Dept of History, Mississippi State Univ., POB H, Mississippi State, MS 39762; tel. (662) 268-2247; internet www.aghistorysociety.org; f. 1919; inc. 1924 as a non-profit org.; encourages interest in, promotes study of and facilitates research and publ. on history of agriculture; 1,400 mems; Pres. BRIAN CANNON; Exec. Sec. JAMES C. GIESEN; Treas. ALAN

I. MARCUS; publ. *Agricultural History* (4 a year).

American Dairy Science Association: 2441 Village Green Place, Champaign, IL 61812; tel. (217) 356-5146; fax (217) 398-4119; e-mail adsa@adsa.org; internet www.adsa.org; f. 1906 as Nat. Asscn of Dairy Instructors and Investigators, present name 1916; int. org. of educators, scientists and industry representatives committed to advancing dairy industry; serves as an open forum where a full range of views on critical scientific questions may be addressed; publishes original research, reviews and timely information; 4,500 mems; Pres. ROBERT F. ROBERTS; Exec. Dir PETER STUDNEY; Treas. ALOIS G. KERTZ; publ. *Journal of Dairy Science* (12 a year).

American Forests: POB 2000, Washington, DC 20013; 734 15th St, NW, Suite 800, Washington, DC 20005; tel. (202) 737-1944; e-mail info@americanforests.org; internet www.americanforests.org; f. 1875 as American Forestry Asscn, present name 1990; non-profit conservation org.; provides information about forest ecosystems, habitat preservation and forest protection; 35,000 mems; Chair. LYNDA WEBSTER; CEO SCOTT STEEN; publ. *American Forests.*

American Society for Horticultural Science: 1018 Duke St, Alexandria, VA 22314-2851; tel. (703) 836-4606; fax (703) 836-2024; internet www.ashs.org; f. 1903; promotes and encourages scientific research and education in all brs of horticulture; 5,000 mems; Chair. FRED T. DAVIES; Pres. DEWAYNE INGRAM; Treas. CURT R. ROM; Exec. Dir MICHAEL W. NEFF; publs *HortScience* (12 a year), *HortTechnology* (6 a year), *Journal* (6 a year).

American Society of Agricultural and Biological Engineers: 2950 Niles Rd, St Joseph, MI 49085; tel. (269) 429-0300; fax (269) 429-3852; e-mail hq@asabe.org; internet www.asabe.org; f. 1907; develops efficient and environmentally sensitive methods of producing food, fiber, timber and renewable energy sources for an ever-increasing world population; 9,000 mems; Pres. SONIA M. MAASSEL JACOBSEN; Treas. STEPHEN W. SEARCY; Exec. Dir DARRIN J. DROLLINGER; publs *Applied Engineering in Agriculture* (6 a year), *Biological Engineering Transactions* (4 a year), *Journal of Agricultural Safety and Health* (4 a year), *Resource Magazine: Engineering & Technology for a Sustainable World* (6 a year), *Transactions of the ASABE* (6 a year).

American Society of Agronomy: 5585 Guilford Rd, Madison, WI 53711-5801; tel. (608) 273-8080; fax (608) 273-2021; e-mail headquarters@sciencesocieties.org; internet www.agronomy.org; f. 1907; conserves and wisely uses natural resources to produce food, feed and fiber crops while maintaining and improving the environment; 12,600 mems; Pres. NEWELL KITCHEN; Exec. Vice-Pres. Dr ELLEN BERGFELD; CEO ELLEN G. M. BERGFELD; publs *Agronomy Journal* (6 a year), *Crop Science* (6 a year), *Journal of Environmental Quality* (6 a year), *Journal of Plant Registrations* (3 a year), *Journal of Natural Resources and Life Sciences Education* (1 a year), *Soil Science Society of America* (6 a year), *Soil Survey Horizons* (4 a year), *The Plant Genome, Vadose Zone* (4 a year).

American Society of Animal Science: 2441 Village Green Pl., Champaign, IL 61822; tel. (217) 356-9050; fax (217) 398-4119; e-mail asas@assochq.org; internet www.asas.org; f. 1908; promotes devt of sciences beneficial to animal production; 6,500 mems; Pres. Dr MARGARET E. BENSON;

Exec. Dir Dr MEGHAN WULSTER-RADCLIFFE; publ. *Journal of Animal Science* (12 a year).

American Veterinary Medical Association: 1931 N Meacham Rd, Suite 100, Schaumburg, IL 60173-4360; tel. (800) 248-2862; fax (847) 925-1329; e-mail avmainfo@avma.org; internet www.avma.org; f. 1863; helps to improve animal and human health and advances veterinary medical profession; 81,500 mems; Pres. Dr RENÉ A. CARLSON; Treas. BARBARA SCHMIDT; Exec. Vice-Pres. Dr W. RON DEHAVEN; library of 5,000 vols, 400 periodicals; publs *American Journal of Veterinary Research* (12 a year), *Journal of the AVMA* (26 a year).

Association for International Agricultural and Extension Education: c/o Mark Erbaugh, 113 Ag. Admin. Bldg., 2120 Fyffe Rd, Columbus, OH 43210; tel. (353) 392-0502; fax (353) 392-9585; internet www.aiaee.org; f. 1984; a professional network of agricultural educators; improves and strengthens developing countries through agricultural education programmes and institutions; 200 mems; Pres. JAMES LINDNER; Sec. T. GRADY ROBERTS; Treas. J. MARK ERBAUGH; publ. *Journal of International Agricultural and Extension Education* (4 a year).

Council for Agricultural Science and Technology: 4420 W Lincoln Way, Ames, IA 50014-3447; tel. (515) 292-2125; fax (515) 292-4512; e-mail cast@cast-science.org; internet www.cast-science.org; f. 1972; non-profit consortium of scientific socs, orgs, cos, scientists and citizens interested in public policy and science of food and agriculture; compiles scientific information for Congress, the public, journalists and educators; 3,000 mems; Pres. NATHANIEL TABLANTE; Exec. Vice-Pres. and CEO Dr JOHN M. BONNER; Treas. TURNER SUTTON; publs *CAST Commentaries* (4 a year), *Issue Paper*, scientific publs.

Poultry Science Association Inc.: 1800 S Oak St, Suite 100, Champaign, IL 61820; tel. (217) 356-5285; fax (217) 398-4119; e-mail psa@assochq.org; internet www.poultryscience.org; f. 1908; stimulates discovery, application and dissemination of knowledge; creates forum for exchange of information among various segments of the poultry industry; publishes original research, reviews and timely information; recognizes outstanding personal achievement; 1,300 mems; Pres. Dr MICHAEL J. WINELAND; Sec. and Treas. R. MICHAEL HULET; Exec. Dir Dr STEPHEN E. KOENIG; publs *Journal of Applied Poultry Research* (4 a year), *Poultry Science* (12 a year).

Society of American Foresters: 5400 Grosvenor Lane, Bethesda, MD 20814-2198; tel. (301) 897-8720; fax (301) 897-3690; e-mail safweb@safnet.org; internet www.safnet.org; f. 1900; provides access to information and networking opportunities to prepare mems for challenges and changes that face natural resource professionals; 18,000 mems; Pres. MICHAEL B. LESTER; Exec. Vice-Pres. and CEO MICHAEL T. GOERGEN, JR; publs *Forest Science* (6 a year), *Journal of Forestry* (8 a year), *Northern Journal of Applied Forestry* (4 a year), *Southern Journal of Applied Forestry* (4 a year), *The E-Forester*, *The Forestry Source* (12 a year), *Western Journal of Applied Forestry* (4 a year).

Soil Science Society of America: 5585 Guilford Rd, Madison, WI 53711-5801; tel. (608) 273-8080; fax (608) 273-2021; e-mail headquarters@soils.org; internet www.soils.org; f. 1936; provides information about soils in relation to crop production, environmental quality, ecosystem sustainability, bioreme-

diation, waste management, recycling and wise land use; works closely with American Soc. of Agronomy and Crop Science Soc. of America; 6,000 mems; Pres. CHARLES RICE; CEO Dr ELLEN BERGFELD; publs *Journal of Environmental Quality* (6 a year), *Soil Science Society of America Journal* (6 a year), *Soil Survey Horizons* (irregular), *Vadose Zone Journal* (4 a year, online).

ARCHITECTURE AND TOWN PLANNING

American Institute of Architects: 1735 New York Ave, NW, Washington, DC 20006-5292; tel. (202) 626-7300; fax (202) 626-7547; e-mail infocentral@aia.org; internet www.aia.org; f. 1857; sponsors continuing education experiences to help architects maintain their licensure; sets industry standard in contract documents used in design and construction industry; provides web-based resources for emerging architecture professionals; conducts market research and provides analysis of economic factors that affect business of architecture; serves as an advocate of architecture profession; promotes design excellence and outstanding professional achievement through an awards programme; 74,000 mems; library of 30,400 vols; Pres. MICKEY JACOB; publs *Forward*, *Practice Management Digest*, *The Academy Journal* (1 a year).

American Planning Association: 205 N Michigan Ave, Suite 1200, Chicago, IL 60601; tel. (312) 431-9100; fax (312) 786-6700; internet www.planning.org; f. 1978 by merger of American Institute of Planners (f. 1917) with American Soc. of Planning Officials (f. 1939); non-profit research, educational and professional org. for city planners and others involved in land use and community devt; incl. American Institute of Certified Planners (AICP); 40,000 mems; library of 4,500 vols; Pres. MITCHELL J. SILVER; Exec. Dir and CEO PAUL FARMER; publs *APA Journal* (4 a year), *Journal of the American Planning Association* (4 a year), *PAS Memo*, *Planning* (12 a year), *Planning and Environmental Law* (12 a year), *Practicing Planner* (4 a year, online), *The Commissioner* (4 a year), *Zoning Practice* (12 a year).

National Trust for Historic Preservation: 1785 Massachusetts Ave, NW, Washington, DC 20036-2117; tel. (202) 588-6000; fax (202) 588-6038; e-mail info@nthp.org; internet www.preservationnation.org; f. 1949; encourages preservation of bldgs, sites and objects significant in American history and culture; 200,000 mems; library: (at Architecture School, Univ. of Maryland, College Park) of 14,000 vols, 400 periodicals; Pres. and CEO STEPHANIE MEEKS; Exec. Vice-Pres. and Chief Preservation Officer DAVID J. BROWN; publs *Forum*, *Preservation* (6 a year), *Preservation Law Reporter*.

Society of Architectural Historians: 1365 N Astor St, Chicago, IL 60610-2144; tel. (312) 573-1365; fax (312) 573-1141; e-mail info@sah.org; internet www.sah.org; f. 1940; preserves and promotes the study of important structures, landscapes and bldgs; mems incl. architects, architectural historians, preservationists, professionals and students; 3,500 mems; Pres. Prof. DIANNE HARRIS; Sec. Prof. GAIL FENSKE; Treas. HENRY KUEHN; publ. *Journal of the Society of Architectural Historians* (4 a year).

BIBLIOGRAPHY, LIBRARY SCIENCE AND MUSEOLOGY

American Association of Law Libraries: 105 W Adams St, Suite 3300, Chicago, IL 60603-6225; tel. (312) 939-4764; fax (312) 431-1097; internet www.aallnet.org; f. 1906; promotes and enhances value of law libraries

to legal and public communities; fosters profession of law librarianship; provides leadership in the field of legal information; 5,000 mems; Pres. DARCY KIRK; Sec. DEBORAH RUSIN; Treas. SUSAN LEWIS; Exec. Dir KATE HAGAN; publs *AALL Spectrum* (9 a year), *Index to Foreign Legal Periodicals* (4 a year), *Law Library Journal* (4 a year).

American Association of Museums: 1575 Eye St, NW, Suite 400, Washington, DC 20005; tel. (202) 289-1818; fax (202) 289-6578; e-mail infocenter@aam-us.org; internet www.aam-us.org; f. 1906; strengthens museums through leadership, advocacy, collaboration and service; programmes incl. accreditation, museum assessment, technical information service, continuing education, govt Affairs, int. programmes and AAM/ICOM; 21,000 mems (incl. 18,000 individuals and 3,000 institutions); Pres. FORD BELL; Chair. DOUGLAS G. MYERS; publs *Museum* (6 a year), *The Official Museum Directory* (1 a year).

American Library Association: 50 E Huron, Chicago, IL 60611; tel. (312) 944-6780; fax (312) 440-9374; e-mail ala@ala.org; internet www.ala.org; f. 1876; promotes effective library and information services and public access to information; offers professional services and publs to mems and non-mems; 62,000 mems; library of 12,000 vols; Pres. MOLLY RAPHAEL; Treas. JAMES (JIM) NEAL; Exec. Dir KEITH MICHAEL FIELS; Librarian KAREN MULLER; publs *American Libraries* (6 a year), *ANSS Currents* (2 a year), *base line* (6 a year), *Biblio-Notes* (2 a year, online), *Book Links: Connecting Books, Libraries, and Classrooms* (4 a year), *Booklist* (22 a year), *Children and Libraries: The Journal of the Association for Library Service to Children (ALSC)* (3 a year), *Children's Programming Monthly* (13 a year), *CHOICE: Current Reviews for Academic Libraries* (12 a year), *College and Research Libraries* (6 a year), *Documents to the People (DttP)* (4 a year), *Information Technology and Libraries (ITAL)* (4 a year), *Interface* (4 a year), *Knowledge Quest (KQ)* (5 a year), *Library Leadership & Management (LL&M)* (4 a year), *Library Resources and Technical Services (LRTS)* (4 a year), *Library Technology Reports* (6 a year), *Library Worklife: HR E-News for Today's Leaders* (12 a year), *Public Libraries* (6 a year), *RBM: A Journal of Rare Books, Manuscripts, and Cultural Heritage* (2 a year), *Reference & User Services Quarterly (RUSQ)* (4 a year), *School Library Media Research*, *Young Adult Library Services (YALS)* (4 a year).

American Society for Information Science and Technology (ASIS&T): 1320 Fenwick Lane, Suite 510, Silver Spring, MD 20910; tel. (301) 495-0900; fax (301) 495-0810; e-mail asis@asis.org; internet www.asis.org; f. 1937 as American Documentation Institute, present name 2000; concerned with devt of advanced methodologies and techniques; acts as a bridge between research and devt and requirements of diverse types of information systems; 4,000 mems; Pres. DIANE SONNENWALD; Treas. VICKI GREGORY; Exec. Dir RICHARD HILL; publs *Annual Proceedings* (1 a year), *Bulletin of the American Society for Information Science and Technology* (6 a year), *Journal of the American Society for Information Science and Technology (JASIST)* (12 a year).

American Theological Library Association: 300 S Wacker Dr., Suite 2100, Chicago, IL 60606-6701; tel. (312) 454-5100; fax (312) 454-5505; e-mail atla@atla.com; internet www.atla.com; f. 1946; professional asscn; fosters study of theology and religion by enhancing devt of theological and religious studies libraries and librarianship;

1,000 mems; library of 30,000 monologue titles preserved on microfiche and microfilm, 2,000 microfilm serial titles; Pres. JOHN B. WEAVER; Sec. CARRIE M. HACKNEY; Exec. Dir BRENDA BAILEY-HAINER; publs *Summary of Proceedings* (1 a year), *Theology Cataloging Bulletin* (4 a year).

Art Libraries Society of North America (ARLIS/NA): c/o Technical Enterprises, Inc., 7044 S 13th St, Oak Creek, WI 53154, Canada; tel. (414) 768-8000; fax (414) 768-8001; e-mail arlisna@igs.net; internet www.arlisna.org; f. 1972; sponsors confs and workshops; distributes publs; grants awards for art book publ. and student essays on visual librarianship; affiliated with ARLIS (UK), ARLIS (Australia—New Zealand), ARLIS (Norge), ARLIS (Norden), American Library Asscn, Visual Resources Asscn and College Art Asscn; 1,000 mems; Pres. JON EVANS; Sec. ALAN MICHELSON; Treas. TOM RIEDEL; publs *Art Documentation* (2 a year), *ARLIS/NA Update* (6 a year), *Handbook and List of Members* (1 a year), *Occasional Papers* (irregular), *Topical Papers* (irregular).

Association for Library and Information Science Education: 65 E Wacker Pl., Suite 1900, Chicago, IL 60601-7246; tel. (312) 795-0996; fax (312) 419-8950; e-mail contact@alise.org; internet www.alise.org; f. 1915 as The Asscn of American Library Schools, present name 1983; non-proft org.; promotes excellence in research, teaching, and service; provides understanding of values and ethos of library and information science; 500 individual mems, 60 institutional mems; Pres. Prof. LYNN HOWARTH; Sec. and Treas. JEAN PREER; Exec. Dir KATHLEEN COMBS; publs *Journal of Education for Library and Information Science* (4 a year), *Library and Information Science Education Statistical Report* (1 a year).

Association of Academic Health Sciences Libraries: 2150 N 107th St, Suite 205, Seattle, WA 98133; tel. (206) 367-8704; fax (206) 367-8777; e-mail aahsl@sbims.com; internet www.aahsl.org; f. 1978; supports academic health sciences libraries and dirs in advancing patient care, research, education and community service missions of academic health centers through visionary exec. leadership and expertise in health information, scholarly communication and knowledge management; 149 mems; Pres. PATRICIA THIBODEAU; Exec. Dir LOUISE MILLER; Sec. and Treas. JETT MCCANN; publ. *Annual Statistics of Medical School Libraries in the United States and Canada* (1 a year).

Association of Art Museum Directors: 120 E 56th St, Suite 520, New York, NY 10022; tel. (212) 754-8084; fax (212) 754-8087; internet www.aamd.org; f. 1916; promotes devt of scholarly and creative role for art museums and their dirs; applies its mems' knowledge and experience in the field of art to promote public good; encourages communication among art museums and their dirs; 199 mems; Pres. DAN MONROE; Sec. MICHAEL E. SHAPIRO; Treas. SARALYN REECE HARDY; Exec. Dir CHRISTINE ANAGNOS.

Association of Research Libraries: 21 Dupont Circle, NW, Suite 800, Washington, DC 20036; tel. (202) 296-2296; fax (202) 872-0884; e-mail arlhq@arl.org; internet www.arl.org; f. 1932; advances goals of its mem research libraries; provides leadership in public and information policy to scholarly and higher education communities; fosters exchange of ideas and expertise; facilitates emergence of new roles for research libraries; shapes future environment that leverages its interests with those of allied orgs; 126 institutional mems; Pres. WINSTON TABB; Exec. Dir CHARLES B. LOWRY; publs *ARL Annual*

Salary Survey (1 a year), *ARL Statistics* (1 a year), *Research Library Issues: A Bimonthly Report from ARL, CNI, and SPARC* (6 a year, online), *SPEC Kits* (6 a year).

Association of Vision Science Librarians: c/o Gale Oren, Kellogg Eye Center, Univ. of Michigan, 1000 Wall St, Ann Arbor, MI 48105; tel. (734) 763-9468; internet www.avsl.org; f. 1968; fosters collective and individual acquisition and dissemination of visual science information; improves services to those seeking such information; develops libraries' standards; 100 individual mems and 75 institutions; Chair. GALE OREN; Chair.-Elect and Sec. D. J. MATTHEWS; Treas. ELAINE WELLS; publs *Opening Day Book List* (every 2 years), *Standards for Vision Science Libraries*, *Vision Union List of Serials* (every 3 years).

Bibliographical Society of America: POB 1537, Lenox Hill Station, New York, NY 10021; tel. and fax (212) 452-2710; e-mail bsa@bibsocamer.org; internet www.bibsocamer.org; f. 1904, inc. 1927; dedicated to the study of books and MSS as physical objects; promotes bibliographical research and issues bibliographical publs; 1,000 mems; Pres. JOHN NEAL HOOVER; Sec. CAROLINE DUROSELLE-MELISH; Treas. G. SCOTT CLEMONS; Exec. Sec. MICHÈLE E. RANDALL; publ. *Papers of the Bibliographical Society of America* (4 a year).

Bibliographical Society of the University of Virginia: POB 400152, Alderman Library, Charlottesville, VA 22904-4152; tel. (434) 924-7013; e-mail ar3g@virginia.edu; internet www.bsuva.org; f. 1947; promotes study of books, MSS, printing and the graphic arts, bibliography and textual criticism; 650 mems; Pres. G. THOMAS TANSELLE; Sec. and Treas. ANNE G. RIBBLE; publs *Secretary's News Sheet* (1 a year), *Studies in Bibliography* (1 a year).

California Library Association: 2471 Flores St, San Mateo, CA 94403; tel. (650) 376-0886; fax (650) 539-2341; e-mail info@cla-net.org; internet www.cla-net.org; f. 1895 as Library Asscn of Central California, present name 1906; non-profit charitable org.; 2,400 mems; Pres. WAYNE DISHER; Treas. JACKIE GRIFFIN; Exec. Dir CAROL SIMMONS; publ. *California Libraries* (12 a year).

California School Library Association: 950 Glenn Dr., Suite 150, Folsom, CA 95630; tel. (916) 447-2684; fax (916) 447-2695; e-mail info@csla.net; internet www.csla.net; f. 1977; advocates, educates and collaborates, ensuring that all California students and educators are effective users of ideas and information; Pres. DIANE ALEXANDER; Exec. Dir DEIDRE BRYANT; publ. *CSLA Journal* (2 a year).

Catholic Library Association: 205 W Monroe St, Suite 314, Chicago, IL 60606-5061; tel. (312) 739-1776; fax (312) 739-1778; e-mail cla2@cathla.org; internet www.cathla.org; f. 1921, present status 1931; initiates, fosters and encourages activities and library programmes that promote literature and libraries, not only of a Catholic nature but also of an ecumenical spirit; 1,000 mems; Pres. MALACHY R MCCARTHY; Exec. Dir JEAN R. BOSTLEY; publs *Catholic Library World* (4 a year), *Catholic Periodical and Literature Index* (4 a year).

Council on Library and Information Resources: 1752 N St, NW, Suite 800, Washington, DC 20036; tel. (202) 939-4750; fax (202) 939-4765; internet www.clir.org; f. 1997 by merger of Council on Library Resources (f. 1956) with Comm. on Preservation and Access (f. 1986); fosters new approaches to management of digital and nondigital information resources so that they

will be available in the future; expands leadership capacity in the information professions; analyzes changes in information landscape and helps practitioners prepare for them; Pres. CHARLES HENRY; Chair. STEPHEN NICHOLS; publs *CLIR Issues* (6 a year), *Reports* (irregular).

Medical Library Association: 65 E Wacker Pl., Suite 1900, Chicago, IL 60601-7246; tel. (312) 419-9094; fax (312) 419-8950; e-mail info@mlahq.org; internet www.mlanet.org; f. 1898; non-profit educational org.; provides information for delivery of health care, education of health professionals, conduct of research and public's understanding of health; 4,700 mems (incl. 3,600 individuals and 1,100 institutions); Pres. GERALD (JERRY) PERRY; Sec. CYNTHIA L. HENDERSON; Treas. MARIANNE COMEGYS; Exec. Dir CARLA J. FUNK; publ. *Journal of the Medical Library Association* (4 a year).

Minnesota State Library Services: 1500 Highway 36W, Roseville, MN 55113-4266; tel. (651) 582-8791; fax (651) 582-8752; e-mail mde.lst@state.mn.us; internet education.state.mn.us/mde/stusuc/lib/statelibserv; f. 1899; attached to Minnesota Dept of Education; resource and information center serving state and local govt, libraries and library support groups; administers state library programmes and federal LSTA grant programme; State Librarian and Dir NANCY WALTON (acting); publ. *Minnesota Libraries*.

Music Library Association: 8551 Research Way, Suite 180, Middleton, WI 53562; tel. (608) 836-5825; fax (608) 831-8200; e-mail mla@areditions.com; internet www.musiclibraryassoc.org; f. 1931; professional forum for librarians, archivists and those who support the world's musical heritage; 2,900 mems; Pres. JERRY L. MCBRIDE; publs *Index and Bibliography Series* (irregular), *Music Cataloging Bulletin* (12 a year), *Notes: Quarterly Journal of the Music Library Association* (4 a year), *Technical Reports—Information for Music Media Specialists* (irregular).

Society of American Archivists: 17 N State St, Suite 1425, Chicago, IL 60602-4061; tel. (312) 606-0722; fax (312) 606-0728; e-mail servicecenter@archivists.org; internet www2.archivists.org; f. 1936; a professional asscn for archivists and institutions interested in the preservation and use of archives, MSS and current records; 5,500 individual and institutional mems; Exec. Dir NANCY PERKIN BEAUMONT; publ. *The American Archivist* (2 a year).

Special Libraries Association: 331 S Patrick St, Alexandria, VA 22314-3501; tel. (703) 647-4900; fax (703) 647-4901; e-mail sla@sla.org; internet www.sla.org; f. 1909; activities: professional devt, résumé referral service, employment clearing-house and career advisory service, chapters and div. services, book publishing, govt relations, public relations; Information Resources Center provides telephone reference service; research; 9,000 mems; library of 3,000 vols; Pres. CINDY ROMAINE; Treas. DAN TREFETHEN; Dir MARILYN BROMLEY; CEO JANICE R. LACHANCE; publ. *Information Outlook* (12 a year, online).

Theatre Library Association: c/o New York Public Library for the Performing Arts, 40 Lincoln Center Plaza, New York, NY 10023; e-mail info@tla-online.org; internet www.tla-online.org; f. 1937; supports librarians and archivists affiliated with theatre, dance, performance studies, popular entertainment, motion picture and broadcasting collns; promotes professional best practices in acquisition, org., access and preservation of performing arts resources in libraries, archives, museums, private collns and the digital environment; 327 mems; Pres. KENNETH SCHLESINGER; Vice-Pres. NANCY FRIEDLAND; Exec. Sec. DAVID NOCHIMSON; Treas. COLLEEN REILLY; publ. *Performing Arts Resources* (irregular).

ECONOMICS, LAW AND POLITICS

Academy of Political Science: 475 Riverside Dr., Suite 1274, New York, NY 10115-1274; tel. (212) 870-2500; fax (212) 870-2202; e-mail aps@psqonline.org; internet www .psqonline.org; f. 1880; promotes objective, scholarly analyses of political, social, and economic issues; 8,000 mems; Chair. PETER J. GOULANDRIS; Pres. DEMETRIOS JAMES CARALEY; publ. *Political Science Quarterly* (4 a year).

American Academy of Political and Social Science: Annenberg Public Policy Center, 202 S 36th St, Philadelphia, PA 19104-3806; tel. (215) 746-6500; fax (215) 573-2667; internet www.aapss.org; f. 1889; brings together public officials and scholars from across disciplines to tackle issues ranging from racial inequality and intractable poverty to threat of nuclear terrorism; conducts confs and symposia; 5,000 mems; Chair. HEIDI HARTMANN; Pres. DOUGLAS S. MASSEY; Exec. Dir Dr PHYLLIS KANISS; publ. *The Annals of the American Academy of Political and Social Science* (6 a year).

American Accounting Association: 5717 Bessie Dr., Sarasota, FL 34233-2399; tel. (941) 921-7747; fax (941) 923-4093; e-mail info@aaahq.org; internet aaahq.org; f. 1916 as American Asscn of Univ. Instructors in Accounting, present name 1936; professional soc. for educators, practitioners and students of accounting; promotes worldwide excellence in accounting education, research and practice; 13,000 mems; Pres. GREG WAYMIRE; Exec. Dir TRACEY SUTHERLAND; publs *Accounting Horizons* (4 a year), *Issues in Accounting Education* (4 a year), *The Accounting Review* (6 a year).

American Arbitration Association: 1633 Broadway, 10th Fl., New York, NY 10019; tel. (212) 716-5800; fax (212) 716-5905; e-mail websitemail@adr.org; internet www .adr.org; f. 1926; non-profit org. that offers broad range of dispute resolution services to business executives, attorneys, individual employees, trade asscns, unions, management, consumers, families, communities and all levels of govt; conducts seminars, confs, etc.; 5,400 mems, over 50,000 arbitrators on nat. panel; library of 23,500 vols, 244 periodical titles; Pres. WILLIAM K. SLATE, II; publs *AAA Yearbook, Arbitration in the Schools, Arbitration Journal, Arbitration Times, Dispute Resolution Journal, Forum New York, Labor Arbitration in Government, Lawyers' Arbitration Letter* (4 a year), *New York No-Fault Arbitration Reports* (12 a year), *Summary of Labor Arbitration Awards, The Claims Forum.*

American Bar Association: 321 N Clark St, Chicago, IL 60654; tel. (312) 988-5000; internet www.americanbar.org; f. 1878; provides law school accreditation, continuing legal education, information about the law, programmes to assist lawyers and judges in their work and initiatives to improve legal system for public; 400,000 mems; library of 50,000 vols; Pres. W. T. (BILL) ROBINSON, III; publs *ABAJournal* (12 a year), *ABA Journal of Labor & Employment Law* (3 a year), *Antitrust Law Journal* (3 a year), *Criminal Justice* (4 a year), *Family Law Quarterly* (4 a year), *Franchise Law Journal* (4 a year), *GPSolo* (8 a year), *Human Rights* (4 a year), *Judges' Journal* (4 a year), *Litigation* (4 a year), *Natural Resources & Environment* (4 a year), *Probate & Property* (6 a year), *Reports*

(1 a year), *Student Lawyer* (12 ayear), *The International Lawyer* (4 a year), *The Professional Lawyer* (4 a year), *The Urban Lawyer* (4 a year).

American Economic Association: 2014 Broadway, Suite 305, Nashville, TN 37203-2418; tel. (615) 322-2595; fax (615) 343-7590; e-mail aeainfo@vanderbilt.edu; internet www.aeaweb.org; f. 1885; encourages economic discussion, research and publs on economic subjects; c. 18,000 mems; Pres. ORLEY ASHENFELTER; Sec. and Treas. JOHN J. SIEGFRIED; publs *American Economic Review, American Economic Journal: Applied Economics, American Economic Journal: Economic Policy, American Economic Journal: Macroeconomics, American Economic Journal: Microeconomics, Journal of Economic Literature* (4 a year), *Journal of Economic Perspectives* (4 a year).

American Finance Association: Haas School of Business, Univ. of California Berkeley, 545 Student Services Bldg, Berkeley, CA 94720-1900; tel. (781) 388-8599; fax (781) 388-8232; internet www.afajof.org; f. 1940; makes available knowledge on current devts in the field of finance; 11,000 mems; Pres. RAGHURAM RAJAN; Exec. Sec. and Treas. Prof. DAVID PYLE; publ. *Journal of Finance* (6 a year).

American Judicature Society: The Opperman Center at Drake Univ., 2700 University Ave, Des Moines, IA 50311; tel. (515) 271-2281; fax (515) 279-3090; internet www.ajs.org; f. 1913; ind., non-partisan, membership org.; promotes effective admin. of justice; 6,000 mems; Pres. PETER D. WEBSTER; Chair. MARTIN H. BELSKY; Sec. Hon. JON B. COMSTOCK; Treas. THOMAS C. LEIGHTON; publ. *Judicature* (6 a year).

American Law Institute: 4025 Chestnut St, Philadelphia, PA 19104; tel. (215) 243-1600; fax (215) 243-1636; e-mail ali@ali.org; internet www.ali.org; f. 1923; promotes clarification and simplification of law; research work; 4,000 mems; library of 5,000 vols; Pres. ROBERTA COOPER RAMO; Sec. SUSAN FRELICH APPLETON; Treas. CAROLYN DINEEN KING; Dir LANCE LIEBMAN; publs *Model and Uniform Codifications, Proceedings of ALI Annual Meetings* (1 a year), *Restatements of the Law.*

American Law Institute-American Bar Association: Continuing Professional Education, 4025 Chestnut St, Philadelphia, PA 19104; tel. (215) 243-1600; fax (215) 243-1664; internet www.ali-aba.org; f. 1947; post-admission legal education; organizes, develops and carries out a nat. programme of continuing education of the bar; library of 5,000 vols; Pres. MAURY B. POSCOVER; Exec. Dir JULENE FRANKI; publs *ALI-ABA Estate Planning Course Materials Journal* (6 a year), *The Practical Lawyer* (6 a year), *The Practical Real Estate Lawyer* (6 a year), *The Practical Tax Lawyer* (4 a year).

American Peace Society: 1319 18th St, NW, Washington, DC 20036-1802; f. 1828; Pres. Dr EVRON M. KIRKPATRICK; Sec. L. EUGENE HEDBERG; publ. *World Affairs* (4 a year).

American Political Science Association: 1527 New Hampshire Ave, NW, Washington, DC 20036-2106; tel. (202) 483-2512; fax (202) 483-2657; e-mail apsa@apsanet.org; internet www.apsanet.org; f. 1903; promotes scholarly research and communication, domestically and internationally; 15,000 mems; Pres. G. BINGHAM POWELL; Sec. LISA L. MARTIN; Treas. JONATHAN BENJAMIN-ALVARADO; Exec. Dir MICHAEL A. BRINTNALL; publs *American Political Science Review* (4 a year), *Perspectives on Politics* (4 a year), *PS: Political Science & Politics* (4 a year).

American Society for Public Administration: 1301 Pennsylvania Ave, NW, Suite 700, Washington, DC 20004; tel. (202) 393-7878; fax (202) 638-4952; e-mail info@aspanet.org; internet www.aspanet.org; f. 1939; advances the art, science, teaching and practice of public and non-profit admin.; promotes value of joining and elevating public service profession; builds bridges among all who pursue public purposes nationally and internationally; provides networking and professional devt opportunities to those committed to public service values; achieves innovative solutions to the challenges of governance; nat. and regional confs, management institutes; 80 local chapters; 11,000 mems; Exec. Dir ANTOINETTE SAMUEL; publs *Public Administration Review* (6 a year), *Public Integrity.*

American Society of International Law: 2223 Massachusetts Ave, NW, Washington, DC 20008; tel. (202) 939-6000; fax (202) 797-7133; internet www.asil.org; f. 1906, inc. 1950; fosters study of int. law and promotes establishment and maintenance of int. relations on the basis of law and justice; 4,000 mems; library of 22,000 vols; Pres.-Elect DONALD FRANCIS DONOVAN; Sec. JAMES NAFIZGER; Treas. NANCY L. PERKINS; Exec. Dir ELIZABETH ANDERSEN; publs *Academic Bulletin* (3 a year), *American Journal of International Law* (4 a year), *Cultural Heritage and the Arts Review* (2 a year), *Proceedings of the Annual Meeting* (1 a year), *IL.post, International Law In Brief* (24 a year), *International Legal Materials* (6 a year), *Law of the Sea Reports* (online).

American Statistical Association: 732 N Washington St, Alexandria, VA 22314-1943; tel. (703) 684-1221; fax (703) 684-2037; e-mail asainfo@amstat.org; internet www .amstat.org; f. 1839; promotes inclusion of statistics in policymaking and funding of statistics research; sponsors educational programmes and meetings to enrich statistical knowledge; acknowledges and recognizes mems who have made outstanding contributions to statistics or asscn by sponsoring awards, honors, scholarships and fellowships; 18,000 mems; Pres. NANCY L. GELLER; Sec. and Exec. Dir RONALD L. WASSERSTEIN; publs *CHANCE* (4 a year), *Journal of Agricultural, Biological and Environmental Statistics* (4 a year), *Journal of Business & Economic Statistics* (4 a year), *Journal of Computational and Graphical Statistics* (4 a year), *Journal of Educational and Behavioral Statistics* (4 a year), *Journal of Statistics Education, Journal of Statistical Software, Journal of the American Statistical Association* (4 a year), *Significance, Statistics in Biopharmaceutical Research, Statistical Analysis and Data Mining, Statistics Survey, Technometrics* (4 a year), *The American Statistician* (4 a year).

Association of American Law Schools: 1201 Connecticut Ave, NW, Suite 800, Washington, DC 20036-2717; tel. (202) 296-8851; fax (202) 296-8869; e-mail aals@aals .org; internet www.aals.org; f. 1900; promotes improvement of legal profession through legal education; 172 institutional mems; Exec. Dir and CEO SUSAN WESTERBERG PRAGER; Pres. MICHAEL A. OLIVAS; publs *Clinical Law Review* (2 a year), *Directory of Law Teachers* (1 a year), *Journal of Legal Education* (4 a year), *Placement Bulletin* (4 a year), *Proceedings* (1 a year).

Atlantic Council of the United States: 1101 15th St, NW, 11th Fl., Washington, DC 20005; tel. (202) 463-7226; fax (202) 463-7241; e-mail info@acus.org; internet www .acus.org; f. 1961; non-partisan instn that promotes transatlantic cooperation and int. security; 130 board mems, 200 councillors,

400 acad. assocs; Chair. CHUCK HAGEL; Pres. and CEO FREDERICK KEMPE; Sec. WALTER B. SLOCOMBE; publs *Bulletin* (irregular), *Occasional Papers* (irregular), *Policy Papers* (irregular).

Carnegie Endowment for International Peace: 1779 Massachusetts Ave, NW, Washington, DC 20036-2103; tel. (202) 483-7600; fax (202) 483-1840; e-mail info@carnegieendowment.org; internet www.carnegieendowment.org; f. 1910; private, non-profit and non-partisan org. dedicated to advancing cooperation between nations and promoting active int. engagement by the USA; offices also in Moscow, Beijing, Beirut and Brussels; 130 mems; library of 8,000 vols; Pres. JESSICA T. MATHEWS; Chair. RICHARD GIORDANO; publs *Foreign Policy* (6 a year), *International Economic Bulletin* (52 a year), *Pro et Contra* (4 a year), *Sada* (online).

Century Foundation: 41 E 70th St, New York, NY 10021; tel. (212) 535-4441; fax (212) 879-9197; e-mail info@tcf.org; internet www.tcf.org; f. 1919; non-partisan foundation for public policy research on major economic, political and soc. insts and issues; Chair. ALAN BRINKLEY; Pres. JANICE NITTOLI; Treas. LEWIS B. KADEN; Sec. ALICIA H. MUNNELL.

Council for European Studies at Colombia University: 420 W 118th St, MC 3307 Int. Affairs Bldg, Room 1209, New York, NY 10027; tel. (212) 854-4172; fax (212) 854-8808; e-mail ces@columbia.edu; internet www.ces.columbia.edu; f. 1970; attached to Columbia Univ.; European studies programmes at over 80 univs in the USA, Canada and Europe; encourages greater scholarly interest in Europe; emphasizes commonality of problems that face nations of Europe and N America; sponsors research, information services, graduate student training; holds biennial conf. in Chicago; 800 mem. orgs; Chair. JOHN BOWEN; Dir SIOVAHN A. WALKER; publ. *Perspectives on Europe* (2 a year).

Council of State Governments: 2760 Research Park Dr., POB 11910, Lexington, KY 40578-1910; tel. (859) 244-8000; fax (859) 244-8001; e-mail membership@csg.org; internet www.csg.org; f. 1933; offices in Washington, DC, New York, Atlanta, GA, Chicago, IL, and San Francisco, CA; a non-partisan org. est. by the USA for service to the USA; region-based forum that fosters exchange of insights and ideas to help state officials shape public policy; Chair. BOB GODFREY; Pres. BRIAN SCHWEITZER; Exec. Dir DAVID ADKINS; publs *Book of the States* (2 a year), *CSG State Directories* (1 a year), *Spectrum* (4 a year), *State Government News* (12 a year), *Suggested State Legislation* (12 a year).

Council on Foreign Relations, Inc.: The Harold Pratt House, 58 E 68th St, New York, NY 10065; tel. (212) 434-9400; fax (212) 434-9800; e-mail corporate@cfr.org; internet www.cfr.org; f. 1921; ind., non-partisan membership org.; promotes understanding of foreign policy and America's role in the world; 4,500 mems; library: Foreign Relations library of 18,000 vols, 300 periodicals, clippings files; Co-Chair. CARLA A. HILLS; Co-Chair. ROBERT E. RUBIN; Pres. RICHARD N. HAASS; publ. *Foreign Affairs* (6 a year).

Counterpart International: 2345 Crystal Dr., Suite 301, Arlington, VA 22202; tel. (703) 236-1200; fax (703) 412-5035; e-mail communications@counterpart.org; internet www.counterpart.org; f. 1965 as Foundation for the South Pacific (FSP), present name 1992; empowers people and communities to implement innovative and enduring solutions to social, economic and environmental

challenges; attached offices in New York and Los Angeles, CA; operates programmes in Armenia, Azerbaijan, Belarus, Bosnia and Herzegovina, Bulgaria, Fiji, Georgia, Guatemala, India, Iraq, Kazakhstan, Kiribati, Kyrgyzstan, Moldova, Papua New Guinea, Russia, Samoa, Senegal, Solomon Islands, Tajikistan, Tonga, Turkmenistan, Tuvalu, Ukraine, Uzbekistan, Vanuatu and Viet Nam; Chair. JEFFREY T. LaRICHE; Pres. and CEO JOAN C. PARKER.

Economic History Association: Dept of Economics, 500 El Camino Real, Santa Clara Univ., Santa Clara, CA 95053-0385; tel. (408) 554-4348; fax (408) 554-2331; internet www.eh.net/eha; f. 1940; promotes teaching, research and publ. in all fields of economic history; 1,200 individual mems and 2,210 library mems; Pres. JEREMY ATACK; Exec. Dir ALEXANDER J. FIELD; publ. *Journal of Economic History* (4 a year).

Federal Bar Association: 1220 N Fillmore St, Suite 444, Arlington, VA 22201; tel. (571) 481-9100; fax (571) 481-9090; e-mail fba@fedbar.org; internet www.fedbar.org; f. 1920; works to promote admin. of justice and independence of judiciary; provides scholarships and opportunities for judges and lawyers to professionally and socially interact; 15,000 mems, 99 Chapters,20 sections in fields of federal law; Exec. Dir JACK D. LOCKRIDGE; Pres. FERN C. BOMCHILL; Treas. Hon. GUSTAVO GELPI; publ. *The Federal Lawyer* (10 a year).

Foreign Policy Association: 470 Park Ave S, New York, NY 10016; tel. (212) 481-8100; fax (212) 481-9275; e-mail info@fpa.org; internet www.fpa.org; f. 1918; non-profit org.; promotes citizen education in world affairs; assists orgs, communities and educational instns; develops programmes for citizen understanding and constructive participation in world affairs; advances public understanding of foreign policy problems through nat. programmes and publs of a non-partisan character based upon the principles of freedom, justice and democracy; Chair. GONZALO DE LAS HERAS; Pres. and CEO NOEL V. LATEEF; publs *Great Decisions* (2 a year), *Headline Series* (4 a year).

History of Economics Society: c/o Tim Leonard, Dept of Economics, Princeton Univ., Fisher Hall, Princeton, NJ 08544; internet historyofeconomics.org; f. 1974; non-profit corpn; promotes interest and inquiry into the history of economics and related parts of intellectual history; 300 mems; Pres. PHILLIP MIROWSKI; Sec. THOMAS LEONARD; Treas. NEIL B. NIMAN; publs *ERN History of Economics Journal*, *Journal of the History of Economic Thought* (4 a year).

Institute for Mediterranean Affairs, Inc.: Nat. Press Bldg, Suite 984, 14th and F Sts, NW, Washington, DC 120045; tel. (202) 662-7655; fax (202) 662-7656; e-mail medquarterly@aol.com; internet www.mediterraneanquarterly.com; est. under charter of the Univ. of the State of New York to evolve a better understanding of the historical background and contemporary political and socio-economic problems of the nations and regions that border on the Mediterranean Sea; to analyse the various tensions in the Eastern Mediterranean and to investigate the basic problems of the area; special attention is given to the Israeli–Arab conflict; 250 Academic Advisory mems; Man. Dir J. YAMPOLSKY; publ. *Mediterranean Quarterly: A Journal of Global Issues* (4 a year).

Institute for Operations Research and the Management Sciences: 7240 Parkway Dr., Suite 300, Hanover, MD 21076; tel. (443) 757-3500; fax (443) 757-3515; e-mail

informs@informs.org; internet www.informs.org; f. 1995 by merger of Operations Research Soc. of America (f. 1952) and Institute for Management Sciences (f. 1953); serves scientific and professional needs of operations research educators, investigators, scientists, students, managers and consultants; nat. and int. confs for academics and professionals; 10,200 mems; Pres. RINA R. SCHNEUR; Sec. ANTON KLEYWEGT; Treas. NICHOLAS G. HALL; Exec. Dir MELISSA MOORE; publs *Decision Analysis* (4 a year), *Information Systems Research* (4 a year), *INFORMS Journal on Computing* (4 a year), *INFORMS Transactions on Education* (3 a year), *Interfaces* (6 a year), *Management Science* (12 a year), *Manufacturing & Service Operations Management* (4 a year), *Marketing Science* (6 a year), *Mathematics of Operations Research* (4 a year), *Operations Research* (6 a year), *Organization Science* (6 a year), *Transportation Science* (4 a year).

Society of Actuaries: 475 N Martingale Rd, Suite 600, Schaumburg, IL 60173-2226; tel. (847) 706-3500; fax (847) 706-3599; e-mail feedback@soa.org; internet www.soa.org; f. 1949; educational, research and professional membership soc. for actuaries in life and health insurance and pension planning; spec. collns, reports and transactions from US, Canadian and int. actuarial orgs; 22,000 mems; library of 3,900 vols; Pres. DONALD J. SEGAL; Exec. Dir GREG HEIDRICH; publs *The Actuary Magazine* (6 a year), *The North American Actuarial Journal* (4 a year).

World Peace Foundation: 169 Holland St, Somerville, MA 02144; tel. (617) 627-2255; fax (617) 491-8588; e-mail worldpeace1910@gmail.com; internet www.worldpeacefoundation.org; f. 1910; an operating foundation that does not give outside grants; policy-orientated studies in world affairs; research concerning causes of state failure, and how to reinvigorate and manage resuscitation of wounded states; Exec. Dir ALEX DE WAAL; Chair. PHILIP S. KHOURY; Pres. ROBERT I. ROTBERG; Treas. THOMAS M. O'REILLY; publ. sponsors *International Organization* (4 a year).

EDUCATION

Carnegie Corporation of New York: 437 Madison Ave, New York, NY 10022; tel. (212) 371-3200; fax (212) 754-4073; internet www.carnegie.org; f. 1911; primary interests: education, int. affairs, democracy; promotes advancement and diffusion of knowledge and understanding among peoples of the USA and, with subsequent amendment of the charter, of some of the current or fmr British overseas Commonwealth; Pres. VARTAN GREGORIAN; Chair. THOMAS H. KEAN; publs *Carnegie Quarterly* (4 a year), *Carnegie Reporter* (2 a year), *Carnegie Results*, *Carnegie Review*.

International Montessori Society: 9525 Georgia Ave, Suite 200, Silver Spring, MD 20910; tel. (301) 589-1127; fax (301) 920-0764; internet www.imsmontessori.org; f. 1979; supports effective application of Montessori scientific educational principles; provides teacher education through correspondence; organizes workshops, mail-order book sales, audio CD and study guide; library; 400 mems; Dir LEE HAVIS.

Philosophy of Education Society: c/o Cris Mayo, PES Exec. Dir, Education Policy, Organization and Leadership, 1310 S Sixth St, Univ. of Illinois at Urbana Champaign, Champaign, IL 61820; tel. (217) 333-3673; internet philosophyofeducation.org; f. 1941; promotes fundamental philosophic treatment of problems of education; promotes clarification of agreements and differences among several philosophies of education through opportunities for discussion afforded by annual meetings; advances and improves teaching in philosophy of education both in schools for education of teachers and in other educational institutions; cultivate fruitful relationships between workers in general philosophy and workers in philosophy of education and between scholars in philosophy of education and those in other areas of education; encourages promising students in the field of philosophy of education; 550 mems; Pres. GERT BIESTA; Exec. Dir CRIS MAYO; publs *Contemporary Pragmatism*, *Education and Culture* (2 a year), *Educational Philosophy and Theory*, *Educational Theory* (4 a year), *Journal of Educational Controversy*, *Journal of Philosophy of Education*, *Studies in Philosophy and Education*, *Yearbook* (1 a year).

FINE AND PERFORMING ARTS

American Federation of Arts: 305 E 47th St, 10th Fl., New York, NY 10017; tel. (212) 988-7700; fax (212) 861-2487; e-mail pubinfo@afaweb.org; internet www.afaweb.org; f. 1909; works to strengthen ability of museums to enrich public's experience and understanding of art; organizes nat. and int. travelling art exhibitions and develops educational programmes in cooperation with museum community; Chair. TOM L. FREUDENHEIM; Pres. JASON N. R. HERRICK; Sec. RICHARD S. LANE; Treas. SCOTT A. DAHNKE; Dir GEORGE G. KIN; publ. *Memo to Members* (4 a year).

American Musicological Society: 6010 College Station, Brunswick, ME 04011-8451; tel. (207) 798-4243; fax (207) 789-4254; e-mail ams@ams-net.org; internet www.ams-net.org; f. 1934; research in the various fields of music as a br. of learning and scholarship; 3,300 individual mems, 1,200 institutional mems; Pres. CHRISTOPHER REYNOLDS; Sec. PAMELA F. STARR; Treas. JAMES LADEWIG; Exec. Dir ROBERT JUDD; publs *Abstracts of Papers read at the Annual Meeting* (1 a year), *Journal of the American Musicological Society* (3 a year).

Americans for the Arts: 1 E 53rd St, Second Fl., New York, NY 10022; tel. (212) 223-2787; fax (212) 980-4857; internet www.artsusa.org; f. 1960; provides extensive arts-industry research and professional devt opportunities for community arts leaders via specialized programmes and services; 150,000 organizational and individual mems; library of 5,000 vols; Pres. and CEO ROBERT L. LYNCH; Chair. C. KENDRIC FERGESON; Sec. MICHAEL SPRING; Treas. JULIE MURACO.

American Society for Aesthetics: POB 915, Pooler, GA 31322-0915; tel. (912) 748-9524; e-mail secretary-treasurer@aesthetics-online.org; internet www.aesthetics-online.org; f. 1942; research and publ. in aesthetics, criticism and theory of the arts; sponsors confs; 1,000 mems; Pres. Prof. PAUL GUYER; Sec. and Treasurer Dr DABNEY TOWNSEND; publs *ASAGE* (ASA Graduate e-journal), *Journal of Aesthetics and Art Criticism* (4 a year).

American Society for Theatre Research: POB 1798, Boulder, CO 80306-1798; tel. (303) 530-1838; fax (303) 530-1839; e-mail info@astr.org; internet www.astr.org; f. 1956; serves needs of theatre and performance studies historians and fosters knowledge of theatre in the USA and overseas; 706 mems; Pres. Prof. RHONDA BLAIR; Sec. Prof. MARLA CARLSON; Treas. TOBIN NELLHAUS; publ. *Theatre Survey* (2 a year).

American Society of Composers, Authors and Publishers (ASCAP): 1 Lincoln Plaza, New York, NY 10023; tel. (212) 621-6000; fax (212) 595-3342; e-mail info@ascap.com; internet www.ascap.com; f. 1914; a non-profit asscn of composers, songwriters, lyricists, and music publishers of every kind of music; issues licences for public performance of mems' copyright works; 420,000 mems; Pres. PAUL WILLIAMS; Treas. JAMES M. KENDRICK; publs *ASCAP Biographical Dictionary*, *ASCAP Playback* (4 a year).

College Art Association: 50 Broadway, 21st Fl., New York, NY 10004; tel. (212) 691-1051; fax (212) 627-2381; e-mail nyoffice@collegeart.org; internet www.collegeart.org; f. 1911; furthers scholarship and excellence in the teaching and practice of art and art history; 12,000 individual mems, 2,000 institutional mems; Pres. BARBARA NESIN; Sec. DEWITT GODFREY; Treas. JOHN HYLAND, JR; Exec. Dir LINDA DOWNS; publs *Art Bulletin* (4 a year), *Art Journal* (4 a year), *caa.reviews*.

Printing Industries of America: 200 Deer Run Rd, Sewickley, PA 15143-2600; tel. (412) 741-6860; fax (412) 741-2311; e-mail printing@printing.org; internet www.printing.org; f. 1887, merged with GATF 1999; non-profit scientific research and technical education org. serving int. graphic communications community; conducts technical workshops, in-plant assessments, seminars worldwide on various aspects of graphic communications; 14,000 mems in 60 countries; library: over 6,000 vols and periodicals; Chair. MICHAEL R. KEENE; Pres. and CEO MICHAEL MAKIN; Treas. HAL SLAGER; publs *Learning Modules*, *Second Sight* (technical reports), *The Magazine* (6 a year).

National Academy: Five E 89th St, New York, NY 10128; tel. (212) 996-1908; fax (212) 426-1711; e-mail info@nationalacademy.org; internet www.nationalacademy.org; f. 1825; membership exclusively of artists; sections: painting, sculpture, watercolour, graphic arts, architecture; attached art museum, art library and art school; 450 mems; Chair. DAVID KAPP; Pres. BRUCE FOWLE; Sec. DAWN HANDLER HARBART; Treas. STEPHEN VOGEL; Dir CARMINE BRANAGAN; publ. *Bulletin* (2 a year).

National Sculpture Society: c/o ANS, 75 Varick St, 11th Fl., New York, NY 10013; tel. (212) 764-5645; fax (212) 764-5651; e-mail news@nationalsculpture.org; internet www.nationalsculpture.org; f. 1893, inc. 1896; disseminates knowledge of American sculpture; promotes excellence in sculpture inspired by the natural world; 3,000 mems (incl. 320 professional mems); library of 400 vols; Pres. DAN OSTERMILLER; Sec. ANTHONY ANTONIOS; Exec. Dir GWEN PIER; publs *Sculpture Review* (4 a year), *The Bulletin* (24 a year).

Society for Ethnomusicology: Morrison Hall 005, 1165 E Third St, Bloomington, IN 47405-3700; tel. (812) 855-6672; fax (812) 855-6673; e-mail sem@indiana.edu; internet www.ethnomusicology.org; f. 1955; dedicated to the study of all forms of music from diverse humanistic and social scientific perspectives; examines music as central to human experience throughout space and time, and explores its profound relationship to cognition, emotion, language, dance, visual arts, spiritual belief, social org., collective identity, politics, conflict and peace, economics, physical body and mental health; 1,800 mems; Exec. Dir STEVE STUEMPFLE; Pres. GAGE AVERILL; Sec. JENNIFER C. POST; Treas. GREGORY BARZ; publ. *Ethnomusicology* (3 a year).

American Antiquarian Society: 185 Salisbury St, Worcester, MA 01609-1634; tel. (508) 755-5221; fax (508) 753-3311; e-mail library@americanantiquarian.org; internet www.americanantiquarian.org; f. 1812; focuses on American history before 1877; sponsors research, education, publs, lectures and concerts; library of 680,000 vols, 2m. MSS collns, 2m. newspaper issues, 200,300 items of graphic art; 950 mems; Chair. SIDNEY LAPIDUS; Pres. ELLEN S. DUNLAP.

American Association for State and Local History: 1717 Church St, Nashville, TN 37203-2991; tel. (615) 320-3203; fax (615) 327-9013; e-mail membership@aaslh.org; internet www.aaslh.org; f. 1904 as Conf. of State and Local Historical Socs, present name and status 1940; exchanges information on local and regional history and historical socs; dissemination knowledge through scholarly and popular publs of professional material and interpretative articles; 5,900 mems; Chair. D. STEPHEN ELLIOTT; Pres. and CEO TERRY DAVIS; publs *History News* (4 a year, professional news), *History News Dispatch* (12 a year).

American Catholic Historical Association: Dealy Hall, Room 637, 441 E Fordham Rd, Bronx, NY 10458; tel. (718) 817-3830; fax (718) 817-5690; e-mail acha@fordham.edu; internet www.achahistory.org; f. 1919; promotes interest in the history of the Catholic Church broadly considered; research work; 890 mems; Pres. LARISSA JULIET TAYLOR; Exec. Sec. and Treas. R. BENTLEY ANDERSON S.J.; publ. *The Catholic Historical Review* (4 a year).

American Historical Association: 400 A St, SE, Washington, DC 20003-3889; tel. (202) 544-2422; fax (202) 544-8307; e-mail aha@historians.org; internet www.historians.org; f. 1884; promotes historical studies; collects and preserves historical documents and artefacts; disseminates historical research; 16,000 mems; Pres. Prof. WILLIAM CRONON; Exec. Dir JAMES R. GROSSMAN; Controller RANDY NORELL; publs *American Historical Review* (5 a year), *Perspectives* (9 a year), *Program of the Annual Meeting* (1 a year).

American Irish Historical Society: 991 Fifth Ave, New York, NY 10028; tel. (212) 288-2263; fax (212) 628-7927; e-mail aihs@aihs.org; internet aihs.org; f. 1897; offers use of library and archives to researchers, writers and scholars; research in the history of the Irish in America; 800 mems; library of 10,000 vols; Dir WILLIAM COBERT; Chair. DONALD R. KEOUGH; Librarian Rev. JOSEPH A. O'HARE; publ. *The Recorder* (2 a year).

American Jewish Historical Society: 15 W 16th St, New York, NY 10011; tel. (212) 294-6160; fax (212) 294-6161; e-mail publicservices@cjh.org; internet www.ajhs.org; f. 1892; nat. ethnic historical org.; collects and publishes material bearing upon the history of Jews in America; promotes the study of American-Jewish history; contains many rare and valuable MSS from the 16th century; American-Jewish periodicals from the 18th century; 3,200 mems; library of 50,000 vols, and 2m. MSS; Pres. PAUL B. WARHIT; Sec. JOSHUA H. LANDES; Treas. STEVEN D. OPPENHEIM; Exec. Dir JONATHAN KARP; publ. *American Jewish History* (4 a year).

American Numismatic Society: 75 Varick St, 11th Fl., New York, NY 10013; tel. (212) 571-4470; fax (212) 571-4479; e-mail membership@numismatics.org; internet www.numismatics.org; f. 1858; non-profit org.; dedicated to the study of coins, currency, medals and tokens; 2,000 mems; library of 100,000 vols (incl. periodicals, MSS, photographs, pamphlets, auction catalogues and microforms); Chair. KENNETH L. EDLOW; Pres. ROGER S. SIBONI; Sec. and Exec. Dir UTE WARTENBERG KAGAN; Treas. SYDNEY F. MARTIN; publs *American Journal of Numismatics* (1 a year), *Ancient Coins in the North American Collections* (irregular), *ANS Magazine* (4 a year), *Numismatic Literature* (1 a year), *Numismatic Notes and Monographs* (irregular), *Numismatic Studies* (irregular), *Proceedings of the Coinage of the Americas Conference* (irregular), *Sylloge Nummorum Graecorum* (irregular), *The Collection of the American Numismatic Society* (irregular).

American Society for Eighteenth-Century Studies: POB 7867, Wake Forest Univ., Winston-Salem, NC 27109; tel. (336) 727-4694; fax (336) 727-4697; e-mail asecs@wfu.edu; internet asecs.press.jhu.edu; f. 1969, inc. 1970; ind. soc.; works through publs and meetings to foster interest and encourage interdisciplinary investigation in achievements of the 18th century in America and Europe; 2,500 mems, 50 instns and 1,077 libraries; Pres. Prof. LAURA BROWN; Treas. WILLIAM EDMISTON; Exec. Dir BYRON R. WELLS; publs *Eighteenth-Century Studies* (4 a year), *Studies in Eighteenth-Century Culture* (1 a year).

American Society of Church History: POB 2793, Santa Rosa, CA 95405-2793; tel. (707) 538-6005; fax (707) 538-2166; e-mail asch@churchhistory.org; internet www.churchhistory.org; f. 1888, reorganized 1906; scholarly study of history of Christianity and its relationship to surrounding cultures in all periods, locations and contexts; encourages study of Christian church and faith, its figures and movements, in institutional and non-institutional settings; 1,500 mems; Pres. BARBARA NEWMAN; Exec. Sec. KEITH FRANCIS; publ. *Church History: Studies in Christianity and Culture* (4 a year).

Archaeological Institute of America: Boston Univ., 656 Beacon St, Sixth Fl., Boston, MA 02215-2006; tel. (617) 353-9361; fax (617) 353-6550; e-mail aia@aia.bu.edu; internet www.archaeological.org; f. 1879; non-profit org.; promotes vivid and informed public interest in cultures and civilizations of the past; supports archaeological research, fosters sound professional practice of archaeology; advocates preservation of world's archaeological heritage; represents the discipline in the wider world; 200,000 mems; CEO PETER HERDRICH; Exec. Dir BONNIE R. CLENDENNING; Pres. ELIZABETH BARTMAN; Treas. BRIAN J. HEIDTKE; publs *American Journal of Archaeology* (4 a year), *Archaeological Field Work Opportunities Bulletin*, *Archaeology* (6 a year, illustrated).

Arizona Archaeological and Historical Society: Arizona State Museum, POB 210026, Univ. of Arizona, Tucson, AZ 85721-0026; internet www.az-arch-and-hist.org; f. 1916; attached to Arizona State Museum; non-profit, educational org.; encourages scholarly pursuits in history and anthropology of the SW USA and N Mexico; encourages preservation of archaeological and historical sites; publishes results of archaeological, historical and ethnographic investigations; organizes lectures, field trips and other activities; 1,150 mems; Pres. SCOTT O'MACK; Sec. JUDITH BILLINGS; Treas. GEORGE HARDING; publ. *Kiva* (4 a year).

Association of American Geographers: 1710 16th St, NW, Washington, DC 20009-3198; tel. (202) 234-1450; fax (202) 234-2744; e-mail gaia@aag.org; internet www.aag.org;

f. 1904; non-profit scientific and educational soc.; conducts educational and research projects that advance geographic understanding, geographic literacy and geographic learning; 10,700 mems; Exec. Dir DOUGLAS RICHARDSON; Pres. ERIC S. SHEPPARD; Sec. JENNY ZORN; Treas. AMY GLASMEIER; publs *Annals of the Association of American Geographers* (4 a year), *The Professional Geographer* (4 a year).

Brooklyn Historical Society: 128 Pierrepont St, Brooklyn, NY 11201; tel. (718) 222-4111; fax (718) 222-3794; e-mail membership@brooklynhistory.org; internet www.brooklynhistory.org; f. 1863 as Long Island Historical Soc.; preserves and encourages study of Brooklyn's extraordinary 400-year history; 1,250 mems; library of 155,000 bound vols, 100,000 graphic images, 2,000 ft of MSS, 2,000 maps and atlases; Chair. JAMES ROSSMAN; Pres. DEBORAH SCHWARTZ.

California Historical Society: 678 Mission St, San Francisco, CA 94105; tel. (415) 357-1848; fax (415) 357-1850; e-mail info@calhist.org; internet www.californiahistoricalsociety.org; f. 1871; holds primary and secondary materials on social, cultural, economic and political devt of California; 4,500 mems; library of 55,000 vols, rare MSS, pamphlets and maps, 500,000 historic photographs; Exec. Dir ANTHEA HARTIG; Pres. THOMAS R. OWENS; Sec. LARRY GOTLIEB; Treas. JOHN BROWN; publ. *California History* (4 a year).

Dallas Historical Society: POB 150038, Dallas, TX 75315-0038; The Hall of State at Fair Park, 3939 Grand Ave., Dallas, TX 75210; tel. (214) 421-4500; fax (214) 421-7500; internet www.dallashistory.org; f. 1922; encourages historical enquiry; collects, preserves and exhibits historical materials; custodian of the Hall of State (see under Museums and Galleries), which it operates as a museum and archive of Texas and Dallas history; 2,000 mems; library of 10,000 vols, 3,000,000 archival items, 10,000 museum artefacts and 30,000 photographs; Exec. Dir JACK BUNNING; publ. *Legacies* (2 a year, published jtly with other orgs).

Historical Society of Pennsylvania: 1300 Locust St, Philadelphia, PA 19107; tel. (215) 732-6200; fax (215) 732-2680; e-mail hsppr@hsp.org; internet www.hsp.org; f. 1824; historical and genealogical collns; 2,300 mems; library of 600,000 vols and pamphlets, 20m. MSS, 300,000 graphics; Pres. and CEO KIM SAJET; Chair. BRUCE K. FENTON; publs *Pennsylvania Legacies* (2 a year), *The Pennsylvania Magazine of History and Biography* (4 a year).

Kansas Historical Society: 6425 SW Sixth Ave, Topeka, KS 66615-1099; tel. (913) 272-8681; fax (913) 272-8682; e-mail reference@kshs.org; internet www.kshs.org; f. 1875; preserves and shares Kansas history by collecting, preserving, and interpreting materials and information pertaining to state govt and history for enhancing govt accountability, providing economic devt assistance and educating people of Kansas; state archives, newspapers and census, archaeology; manuscript, photograph and maps dept, museum, folk arts dept, education dept; library of 440,459 vols, 11,128 cubic ft MSS, 79,629 microfilm reels, 511,856 photographs and audio-visual items, 59,487 cubic ft state records, 42,646 cubic ft State Archives materials, 32,279 maps and architectural drawings; Exec. Dir JENNIE A. CHINN; Pres. PAUL M. BUCHANAN; Sec. DEBORAH BARKER; Treas. JAMES MAAG; publs *Kansas History: A Journal of the Central Plains* (4 a year), *Reflections*.

Maryland Historical Society: 201 W Monument St, Baltimore, MD 21201-4647; tel. (410) 685-3750; fax (410) 385-2105; internet www.mdhs.org; f. 1844; preserves remnants of Maryland's past; museum, library, press, and educational programmes; see Museums and Art Galleries; 5,000 mems; library: 7m. vols, incl. documents on Maryland's history; Pres. BURT KUMMEROW; Dir ROBERT R. NEALL; Sec. JAMES W. CONSTABLE; Treas. CECIL E. FLAMER; publ. *Maryland Magazine of Genealogy* (2 a year).

Massachusetts Historical Society: 1154 Boylston St, Boston, MA 02215-3695; tel. (617) 536-1608; fax (617) 859-0074; internet www.masshist.org; f. 1791; collects, preserves, makes accessible and communicates MSS that promotes study of Massachusetts and the nation; ind. research library and MSS repository; holds documents and artefacts vital to study of American history; library: see Libraries and Archives; Dir WILLIAM M. FOWLER; Pres. DENNIS A. FIORI; Chair. WILLIAM C. CLENDANIEL; Sec. JOHN F. MOFFITT; Treas. WILLIAM R. COTTER; publ. *The Massachusetts Historical Review* (1 a year).

Medieval Academy of America: 104 Mount Auburn St, 5th Fl., Cambridge, MA 02138; tel. (617) 491-1622; fax (617) 492-3303; e-mail info@themedievalacademy.org; internet www.medievalacademy.org; f. 1925; promotes research, publ. and instruction in medieval archaeology, art, history, languages, literature, life, philosophy, records, science and all other aspects of medieval civilization; 4,100 mems; Pres. ALICE-MARY TALBOT; Treas. EUGENE W. LYMAN; Exec. Dir EILEEN GARDINER; Exec. Dir RONALD G. MUSTO; publ. *Speculum: A Journal of Medieval Studies* (4 a year).

Minnesota Historical Society: 345 W Kellogg Blvd, St Paul, MN 55102-1906; tel. (651) 259-3000; fax (612) 297-3343; e-mail reference@mnhs.org; internet www.mnhs.org; f. 1849; history museum; state historic preservation office; state archives; colln of artefacts; archaeology; newspaper and audiovisual library; 78,000 cu ft of MSS; 26 historic sites and museums; 8,000 mems; library of 500,000 vols; Pres. WILLIAM R. STOERI; Dir and Sec. D. STEPHEN ELLIOTT; Treas. MISSY STAPLES THOMPSON; publ. *Minnesota History* (4 a year).

National Geographic Society: 1145 17th St, NW, Washington, DC 20036-4688; tel. (202) 912-6500; fax (202) 775-6141; e-mail askngs@nationalgeographic.com; internet www.nationalgeographic.com; f. 1888; non-profit scientific and educational instn; promotes environmental and historical conservation; 8,000,000 mems; library: see under Libraries and Archives; Pres. and CEO JOHN M. FAHEY Jr; publs *National Geographic* (12 a year), *National Geographic Adventure* (10 a year), *National Geographic Explorer* (6 a year, classroom magazine available only in USA), *National Geographic Kids* (12 a year), *National Geographic Traveler* (8 a year).

New York Historical Society: 170 Central Park W, New York, NY 10024-5194; tel. (212) 873-3400; fax (212) 595-5707; e-mail info@nyhistory.org; internet www.nyhistory.org; f. 1804; museum of 17th–19th-century American art, antiques and history, incl. portraits, landscapes and genre paintings; 3,300 mems; library of 350,000 vols, 10,000 newspaper titles, 10,000 published maps and atlases, 15,000 pieces of sheet music; Pres. and CEO Dr LOUISE MIRRER; Chair. ROGER HERTOG.

Omohundro Institute of Early American History and Culture: POB 8781, Williamsburg, VA 23187-8781; 400 Landrum Dr., Williamsburg, VA 23185; tel. (757) 221-

1114; fax (757) 221-1047; e-mail ieahc1@wm .edu; internet oieahc.wm.edu; f. 1943 as Institute of Early American History and Culture, present name 1996; annually awards post-doctoral fellowships, sponsors confs and publishes books; sponsored jtly by the College of William and Mary and the Colonial Williamsburg Foundation; 800 assoc. mems; library of 7,000 vols, 880 periodicals, 2,000 microfilms; Dir Prof. RONALD HOFFMAN; Chair. ROBERT C. RITCHIE; publ. *William and Mary Quarterly* (4 a year).

Oregon Historical Society: 1200 SW Park Ave, Portland, OR 97205-2483; tel. (503) 222-1741; fax (503) 221-2035; e-mail orhist@ohs .org; internet www.ohs.org; f. 1898; educates and informs through collecting, preserving and interpreting Oregon's past; 85,000 museum artefacts from Neolithic period to discovery, settlement of Oregon Country, Pacific NW; 6,500 mems; library of 30,000 vols, 25,000 maps, 8.5m. ft of film and video cassettes, 16,000 rolls of microfilm, and 12,000 linear ft of documents, 2.5m. photographic archives; Exec. Dir KERRY TYMCHUK; Pres. Dr JERRY HUDSON; Sec. Dr LESLEY HALLICK; Treas. PAT RITZ; publ. *Oregon Historical Quarterly* (4 a year).

Organization of American Historians: 112 N Bryan Ave, Bloomington, IN 47408-4141; tel. (812) 855-7311; fax (812) 855-0696; e-mail help@oah.org; internet www.oah.org; f. 1907; promotes historical study of American history; 9,300 indiv. mems, 2,400 institutional mems; Pres. ALICE KESSLER-HARRIS; Exec. Dir KATHERINE M. FINLEY; publs *Journal of American History* (4 a year), *OAH Magazine of History*.

Pilgrim Society: 75 Court St, Plymouth, MA 02360; tel. (508) 746-1620; fax (508) 746-3396; e-mail director@pilgrimhall.org; internet www.pilgrimhall.org; f. 1820; maintains pilgrim Hall Museum, the oldest public museum in N America; collns of pilgrim decorative arts, furnishings, prehistoric Native American collns; 600 mems; library of 12,000 vols and rare MSS collns dealing with the Plymouth Colony; Dir ANN BERRY.

Presbyterian Historical Society: 425 Lombard St, Philadelphia, PA 19147-1516; tel. (215) 627-1852; fax (215) 627-0509; e-mail refdesk@history.pcusa.org; internet www.history.pcusa.org; f. 1852; nat. archives of the Presbyterian Church (USA); serves church's nat. agencies, mid-councils and local congregations as well as scholars and gen. public; 700 mems; library of 250,000 vols (incl. monographs, serials and rare books), 30,000 cu ft archive material; Exec. Dir FREDERICK J. HEUSER, JR; Chair. PAUL G. WATERMULDER ; publ. *The Journal of Presbyterian History* (2 a year).

Renaissance Society of America: The Graduate School and Univ. Center, The City Univ. of New York, 365 Fifth Ave, Room 5400, New York, NY 10016; tel. (212) 817-2130; fax (212) 817-1544; e-mail rsa@rsa .org; internet www.rsa.org; f. 1954; interdisciplinary study of the period 1300–1650 in USA; 2,400 individual mems, 1,100 library mems; Pres. ELIZABETH CROPPER; Exec. Dir ANN E. MOYER; publ. *Renaissance Quarterly* (4 a year).

Rhode Island Historical Society: 110 Benevolent St, Providence, RI 02906; tel. (401) 331-8575; fax (401) 351-0127; internet www.rihs.org; f. 1822; collects, preserves and shares Rhode Island's history; 1,700 mems; library of 100,000 vols, 400,000 photographs and maps, 5,000 MSS; Pres. BARRY G. HITTNER; Sec. LAURIE WHITE; Treas. JAMES P. LORING; Exec. Dir Dr C. MORGAN GREFE; publ. *Rhode Island History* (2 a year).

Society of American Historians: Columbia Univ., 603 Fayerweather, MC 2538, New York, NY 10027; tel. (212) 854-6495; e-mail amhistsociety@columbia.edu; internet www .sah.columbia.edu; f. 1939; promotes historical studies and interests; awards prizes; 250 authors, 14 publishers; Pres. PAULINE MAIER; Exec. Sec. ANDIE TUCHER.

Vermont Historical Society: 60 Washington St, Barre, VT 05641-4209; tel. (802) 479-8500; fax (802) 479-8510; e-mail vhs-info@ state.vt.us; internet www.vermonthistory .org; f. 1838; objects: educational work in Vermont and American history; colln of books, documents and MSS relating to Vermont; publ. of historical magazines and books; maintenance of State Museum; 2,500 mems; library of 40,000 vols, early Vermont imprints; Pres. LAURA WARREN; Exec. Dir MARK HUDSON; publs *In Context* (4 a year), *Vermont History* (2 a year).

Western Reserve Historical Society: 10825 E Blvd, Cleveland, OH 44106; tel. (216) 721-5722; fax (216) 721-0645; e-mail info@wrhs.org; internet www.wrhs.org; f. 1867; preserves and presents history of people of NE Ohio; maintains a historical museum, family and regional history library, auto-aviation museum, five historical sites; 6,400 mems; library of 235,000 vols, 25,000 vols of newspapers, 30,500 rolls of microfilm, 1m. prints and photos, 6m. MSS; Pres. and CEO GAINOR B. DAVIS; Chair. DONALD J. DAILEY; Sec. GREGORY M. JELINEK; Treas. MARK W. BICHÉ.

Wisconsin Historical Society: 816 State St, Madison, WI 53706-1417; tel. (608) 264-6400; fax (608) 264-6404; internet www .wisconsinhistory.org; f. 1846; collects, preserves and shares stories; 7,200 mems; library of 1,085,000 vols (incl. pamphlets and govt documents), 1,888,000 microforms, 39,000 cu ft MSS, 49,000 cu ft public records, 25,000 maps and atlases, 1,000,000 pictures and negatives, 14,000 cinema and television films from major Hollywood studios, 2,000,000 motion picture and theatre promotional graphics; Dir GEORGE VOGT; Pres. ELLEN D. LANGILL; Sec. ELLSWORTH H. BROWN; Treas. SID BREMER; publs *Columns* (6 a year), *Wisconsin Magazine of History* (4 a year), *Wisconsin Public Documents* (6 a year).

LANGUAGE AND LITERATURE

Alliance Française: 618 SW 8th St, Miami, FL 33130; tel. (305) 859-8760; fax (305) 856-9398; e-mail dgo@alliance-us.org; internet www.alliance-us.org; offers courses and examinations in French language and culture and promotes cultural exchange with France; attached teaching offices in Albuquerque (NM), Atlanta (GA), Austin (TX), Berkeley (CA), Beverly Hills (CA), Bloomfield Hills (MI), Bonita Springs (FL), Boston (MA), Buffalo (NY), Chicago (IL), Cincinnati (OH), Denver (CO), Doylestown (PA), Earlysville (VA), Evanston (IL), Fort Lauderdale (FL), Fresno, (CA), Greenwich (CT), Hartford (CT), Hawaii (HI), Houston (TX), Jackson (MS), Jacksonville (FL), Kansas City (MO), Louisville (KY), Lynchburg (VA), Madison (WI), Miami (FL), Milwaukee (WI), Minneapolis-St Paul (MI), Missoula (MT), Napa (CA), Naperville (TN), New Haven (CT), New Orleans (LA), New York (NY), Newport Beach (CA), Norfolk (VA), Orlando (FL), Pasadena (CA), Philadelphia (PA), Phoenix (AZ), Pittsburg (PA), Portland (OR), Providence (RI), Sacramento (CA), Saint-Louis (MO), Salt Lake City (UT), San Antonio (TX), San Diego (CA), San Francsico (CA), San Rafael (CA), Santa Clara Valley (CA), Santa Cruz County (CA), Sarasota (FL), Saratoga (CA), Seattle (WA),

Toledo (OH), Tulsa (OK), Washington, DC, White Plains (NY), Wilmington (DE), Woodbury (CT); Dir of Operations, USA PIERRE HUDELOT; Chair. MARGARET GANONG.

American Center of PEN: 588 Broadway, Suite 303, New York, NY 10012; tel. (212) 334-1660; fax (212) 334-2181; e-mail pen@ pen.org; internet www.pen.org; f. 1922; promotes friendship and intellectual cooperation among writers, exchange of ideas and freedom of expression; confs, workshops, emergency fund for writers, translation prize; administers PEN/Nabokov Award and other literary awards; programme for inmate-writers in American prisons; 3,400 mems; library of 1,000 vols; Exec. Dir STEVEN L. ISENBERG; Pres. Prof. KWAME ANTHONY APPIAH; Sec. ROXANA ROBINSON; Treas. MARIA CAMPBELL; publs *Grants and Awards Available to American Writers* (every 2 years), *PEN America* (2 a year).

American Classical League: Miami Univ., 422 Wells Mill Dr., Oxford, OH 45056; tel. (513) 529-7741; fax (513) 529-7742; e-mail info@aclclassics.org; internet www .aclclassics.org; f. 1919; promotes study of classical languages in the USA and Canada; 3,400 mems; Pres. PETER HOWARD; Sec. CATHERINE STURGILL; Treas. DEB HEATON; publ. *The Classical Outlook* (4 a year).

American Comparative Literature Association: Univ. of South Carolina, Dept of Languages, Literatures and Cultures, 1620 College St, Room 813A, Columbia, SC 29208; tel. (803) 777-3021; fax (803) 777-3041; e-mail info@acla.org; internet www.acla.org; f. 1960; promotes study of intercultural relations that cross nat. boundaries, multi-cultural relations within a particular soc. and interactions between literature and other forms of human activity, incl. arts, sciences, philosophy and cultural artefacts of all kinds; 2,000 mems; Pres. LOIS PARKINSON ZAMORA; Sec. and Treas. ALEXANDER BEECROFT; publ. *Comparative Literature* (4 a year).

American Dialect Society: c/o Allan Metcalf, Dept of English, MacMurray College, Jacksonville, IL 62650; tel. (217) 479-7014; fax (217) 479-7013; e-mail americandialect@ mac.edu; internet www.americandialect.org; f. 1889; study of English language in N America, together with other languages or dialects of other languages influencing it or being influenced by it; sponsor of *Dictionary of American Regional English*; 350 mems; Pres. LUANNE VONNE SCHNEIDEMESSER; Exec. Sec. ALLAN METCALF; publ. *American Speech* (4 a year, with annual supplement).

American Philological Association: Univ. of Pennsylvania, 220S, 40th St, Suite 201E, Philadelphia, PA 19104-3512; tel. (215) 898-4975; fax (215) 573-7874; e-mail apaclassics@sas.upenn.edu; internet www .apaclassics.org; f. 1869; study of classical languages, literatures and history; 3,200 mems; Pres. KATHLEEN M. COLEMAN; Exec. Dir ADAM D. BLISTEIN; publs *Amphora* (2 a year), *Transactions of the American Philological Association (TAPA)* (2 a year).

British Council: c/o British Embassy, 3100 Massachusetts Ave, NW, Washington, DC 20008-3600; e-mail info-us@britishcouncil .org; internet www.britishcouncil.org/usa; offers courses and examinations in English language and British culture, and promotes cultural exchange with the UK; Dir SHARON MEMIS.

Goethe-Institut: 72 Spring St, 11th Fl., New York, NY 10012; tel. (212) 439-8700; fax (212) 439-8705; e-mail info@newyork .goethe.org; internet www.goethe.de/ newyork; offers courses and examinations in German language and culture, and promotes cultural exchange with Germany; attached centres in Boston (MA), Chicago (IL), Los Angeles (CA), San Francisco (CA) and Washington, DC; library of 12,000 vols, 150 periodicals; Exec. Dir Dr CHRISTOPH BART-MANN.

Instituto Cervantes: 211 E 49th St, New York, NY 10017; tel. (212) 308-7720; fax (212) 308-7721; e-mail cenny@cervantes.es; internet nyork.cervantes.es; offers courses and examinations in Spanish language and culture, and promotes cultural exchange with Spain and Spanish-speaking Latin and Central America; attached centres in Albuquerque (NM) and Chicago (IL); library of 85,000 vols (incl. books, magazines, DVDs, CDs and electronic resources); Exec. Dir ANTONIO MUÑOZ MOLINA.

Linguistic Society of America: 1325 18th St, NW, Suite 211, Washington, DC 20036-6501; tel. (202) 835-1714; fax (202) 835-1717; e-mail lsa@lsadc.org; internet www.lsadc .org; f. 1924; linguistic institute; annual meeting; web-based resources; cttees; fellowships; awards; 5,000 mems (incl individual and instns); Pres. KEREN RICE; Sec. and Treas. PAUL CHAPIN; Exec. Dir ALYSON W. REED; publs eLanguage, Language (4 a year).

Modern Language Association: 26 Broadway, Third Fl., New York, NY 10004-1789; tel. (646) 576-5000; fax (646) 458-0030; e-mail info@mla.org; internet www.mla.org; f. 1883; provides opportunities for its mems to share their scholarly findings and teaching experiences with colleagues and to discuss trends in the acad.; 30,000 mems; Pres. RUSSELL BERMAN; Exec. Dir Prof. ROSEMARY G. FEAL; publs ADE Bulletin (online), ADFL Bulletin (3 a year), MLA International Bibliography of Books and Articles on the Modern Languages and Literatures (1 a year), PMLA (4 a year), Profession (1 a year).

National Communication Association: 1765 N St, NW, Washington, DC 20036; tel. (202) 464-4622; fax (202) 464-4600; e-mail inbox@natcom.org; internet www.natcom .org; f. 1914; promotes widespread appreciation of the importance of communication in public and private life, application of competent communication to improve quality of human life and relationships and use of knowledge about communication to solve human problems; 7,500 mems; Pres. Dr LYNN H. TURNER; Exec. Dir Dr NANCY KIDD; publs Communication and Critical/Cultural Studies (4 a year), Communication Education (4 a year), Communication Monographs (4 a year), Communication Teacher (4 a year), Critical Studies in Media Communication (5 a year), Journal of Applied Communication Research (4 a year), Journal of International and Intercultural Communication (4 a year), Quarterly Journal of Speech (4 a year), Review of Communication (4 a year, online), Text and Performance Quarterly (4 a year).

Poetry Society of America: 15 Gramercy Park, New York, NY 10003; tel. (212) 254-9628; fax (212) 673-2352; internet www .poetrysociety.org; f. 1910; service org. for poets and readers of poetry; sponsors readings, lectures, workshops and annual prize-giving; 2,000 mems; library of 8,000 vols of American poetry; Exec. Dir ALICE QUINN; Pres. RUTH KAPLAN; Sec. GEORGE MINKOFF; Treas. ELLEN RACHLIN; publ. Journal (2 a year).

Society of Biblical Literature: POB 133158, Atlanta, GA 30333; The Luce Center, 825 Houston Mill Rd, Atlanta, GA 30329; tel. (404) 727-3100; fax (404) 727-3101; e-mail sblexec@sbl-site.org; internet www.sbl-site .org; f. 1880; study of biblical and related literature, language, history, religions; 8,500 mems; Chair. BRUCE C. BIRCH; Pres. CAROL

NEWSOM; Sec. CHRISTINE M. THOMAS; Treas. and Exec. Dir JOHN F. KUTSKO; publs International Voices in Biblical Studies, Journal of Biblical Literature (4 a year), TC: A Journal of Biblical Textual Criticism.

MEDICINE

Aerospace Medical Association: 320 S Henry St, Alexandria, VA 22314-3579; tel. (703) 739-2240; fax (703) 739-9652; e-mail inquiries@asma.org; internet www.asma.org; f. 1929; advancement of aerospace medicine, life sciences, bio-astronautics and environmental medicine; annual awards; 3,500 mems; Exec. Dir JEFFREY C. SVENTEK; Pres. Dr FANANCY L. ANZALONE; Sec. Dr ESTRELLA FORSTER; Treas. Dr HERNANDO ORTEGA; publ. Aviation, Space and Environmental Medicine (12 a year).

American Academy of Allergy, Asthma & Immunology: 555 E Wells St, Suite 1100, Milwaukee, WI 53202-3823; tel. (414) 272-6071; e-mail info@aaaai.org; internet www .aaaai.org; f. 1943 as American Acad. of Allergy, merger of Soc. for the Study of Asthma and Allied Conditions (on the East Coast) with American Assen for the Study of Allergy (on the West Coast); for the advancement of the knowledge and practice of allergy, asthma and immunology for optimal patient care; 6,500 mems; Pres. Dr DENNIS K. LEDFORD; Sec. and Treas. Dr LINDA COX; publs AAAAI Impact (4 a year), The Journal of Allergy and Clinical Immunology (12 a year).

American Academy of Family Physicians: POB 11210, Shawnee Mission, KS 66207-1210; 11400 Tomahawk Creek Parkway, Leawood, KS 66211-2680; tel. (913) 906-6000; fax (913) 906-6075; e-mail contactcenter@aafp.org; internet www.aafp .org; f. 1947 as American Acad. of General Practice, present name 1971; promotes and maintains high standards in the gen./family practice of medicine; 100,300 mems; Pres. Dr GLEN R. STREAM; Chair. ROLAND A. GOERTZ; publs American Family Physician (24 a year), Annals of Family Medicine (6 a year), Family Practice Management (10 a year).

American Academy of Ophthalmology: 655 Beach St, POB 7424, San Francisco, CA 94120-7424; 655 Beach St, San Franciso, CA 94109; tel. (415) 561-8500; fax (415) 561-8533; e-mail aaoe@aao.org; internet www .aao.org; f. 1896, inc. 1979; advances lifelong learning and professional interests of ophthalmologists to ensure that public can obtain best possible eye care; 20,777 mems; Chair. ALBERT CASTILLO; Dir TIM D. COUCH; publs EyeNet, Ophthalmology.

American Academy of Otolaryngology—Head and Neck Surgery: 1650 Diagonal Rd, Alexandria, VA 22314-2857; tel. (703) 836-4444; fax (703) 688-5100; e-mail info@ entnet.org; internet www.entnet.org; f. 1896; representing specialists who treat ear, nose, throat and related structures of head and neck; offers more than 500 continuing medical educational courses at annual meetings and through correspondence courses throughout the USA and abroad; 12,000 US and non-US fellows, scientific and assoc. mems; Pres. Dr RODNEY P. LUSK; Sec. and Treas. Dr JOHN W. HOUSE; Exec. Vice-Pres. and CEO Dr DAVID R. NIELSEN; publs The Bulletin (12 a year), Otolaryngology—Head and Neck Surgery (12 a year, peer-reviewed scientific journal).

American Academy of Pediatrics: 141 NW Point Blvd, Elk Grove Village, IL 60007-1098; tel. (847) 434-4000; fax (847) 434-8000; e-mail kidsdocs@aap.org; internet www.aap.org; f. 1930; works for physical, mental and social health, and well-being for

all infants, children, adolescents and young adults; 60,000 mems; Pres. Dr ROBERT W. BLOCK; Exec. Dir Dr ERROL R. ALDEN; publs AAP Grand Rounds (12 a year, online), Neoreviews (12 a year, online), Pediatrics (12 a year, online), Pediatrics in Review (12 a year, online), PREP Audio (audio journal).

American Academy of Periodontology: 737 N Michigan Ave, Suite 800, Chicago, IL 60611-6660; tel. (312) 787-5518; fax (312) 787-3670; internet www.perio.org; f. 1914 as American Acad. of Oral Prophylaxis and Periodontology, present name 1919; advances periodontal and gen. health of public and promotes excellence in the practice of periodontics; 8,000 mems; Pres. PAMELA K. MCCLAIN; Sec. and Treas. JOAN OTOMO-CORGE; Exec. Dir GERALD M. BOWERS; publs Annals of Periodontology (1 a year), Clinical Advances in Periodontics (4 a year, online), Journal of Periodontology (12 a year).

American Association of Anatomists: 9650 Rockville Pike, Bethesda, MA 20814-3998; tel. (301) 634-7910; fax (301) 634-7965; e-mail exec@anatomy.org; internet www .anatomy.org; f. 1888; serves as professional home for an int. community of biomedical researchers and educators focusing on anatomical form and function; researches and conducts professional devt activities; 2,753 mems; Exec. Dir ANDREA PENDLETON; Pres. Dr JEFFREY LAITMAN; Sec. and Treas. Dr RICHARD L. DRAKE; publs AAA Proceedings (1 a year), Anatomical Record (12 a year), Anatomical Sciences Education (6 a year), Developmental Dynamics (12 a year).

American Association of Immunologists: 9650 Rockville Pike, Bethesda, MD 20814; tel. (301) 634-7178; fax (301) 634-7887; e-mail infoaai@aai.org; internet www.aai .org; f. 1913; ind. body for exchange of information and advancement of knowledge in immunology and related fields; 7,400 mems; Chair. Dr BETTY DIAMOND; Exec. Dir Dr M. MICHELE HOGAN; Pres. Dr LESLIE J. BERG; Sec. and Treas. Dr MITCHELL KRONENBERG; publ. Journal of Immunology (24 a year).

American Cancer Society: 250 Williams St NW, Atlanta, GA 30303; tel. (866) 228-4327; internet www.cancer.org; f. 1913 as American Soc. for the Control of Cancer, present name 1945; voluntary health agency; strives to eliminate cancer as a major health problem by preventing cancer, saving lives and diminishing suffering from cancer, through research, education, advocacy and service; library of 16,000 vols; Chair. STEPHEN L. SWANSON; Pres. Dr EDWARD E. PARTRIDGE; Sec. LILA R. JOHNSON; Treas. DANIEL P. HEIST; publs Ca-A (6 a year, cancer journal for clinicians), Cancer (24 a year), Cancer Cytopathology (6 a year).

American College of Obstetricians and Gynecologists: POB 96920, Washington, DC 20090-6920; tel. (202) 638-5577; e-mail resources@acog.org; internet www.acog.org; f. 1951; advocates for quality health care for women; maintains highest standards of clinical practice and continuing education for its mems; promotes patient education and stimulates patient understanding of and involvement in medical care; increases awareness among its mems and public of changing issues facing women's health care; 55,000 mems; Exec. Dir Dr RALPH HALE; publ. Obstetrics and Gynecology (12 a year).

American College of Physicians: 190 N Independence Mall W, Philadelphia, PA 19106-1572; tel. (215) 351-2400; internet www.acponline.org; f. 1915, merger with American Soc. of Internal Medicine (f. 1956) 1998; enhances quality and effectiveness of health care by fostering excellence and professionalism in practice of medicine; 132,000 mems; Pres. Dr VIRGINIA L. HOOD; Chair., Board of Regents Dr YUL D. EJNES; Treas. Dr DENNIS SCHABERG; publs *ACP Hospitalist* (52 a year), *Annals of Internal Medicine* (26 a year).

American College of Rheumatology: 2200 Lake Blvd NE, Atlanta, GA 30319; tel. (404) 633-3777; fax (404) 633-1870; e-mail acr@rheumatology.org; internet www .rheumatology.org; education, research, advocacy and practice support; 4,000 mems; Pres. Dr DAVID BORENSTEIN; Sec. Dr JOSEPH FLOOD; Treas. Dr AUDREY UKNIS; publs *Arthritis & Rheumatism* (12 a year), *Arthritis Care & Research* (12 a year), *Hotline*.

American College of Surgeons: 633 N St Clair St, Chicago, IL 60611-3211; tel. (312) 202-5000; fax (312) 202-5001; e-mail postmaster@facs.org; internet www.facs.org; f. 1913; monitors and analyzes socioeconomic, legislative and regulatory issues affecting field of surgery; works to improve the care of injured and critically ill patients; provides gen. information to public about surgeons and surgical care; improves quality of care for surgical patient by setting high standards for surgical education and practice; 77,000 mems, incl. 4,000 fellows in other countries; Exec. Dir Dr DAVID B. HOYT; Pres. PATRICIA J. NUMANN; Sec. COURTNEY M. TOWNSEND JR.; Treas. ANDREW L. WARSHAW; publ. *Journal of the American College of Surgeons* (12 a year).

American Dental Association: 211 E Chicago Ave, Chicago, IL 60611-2678; tel. (312) 440-2500; fax (312) 440-3526; e-mail membership@ada.org; internet www.ada.org; f. 1859; nat. dental soc.; provides oral health-related information for dentists and their patients; 156,000 mems; library of 50,000 vols; Exec. Dir Dr JAMES BRAMSON; publs *American Dental Directory* (1 a year), *The Journal of the American Dental Association* (12 a year, online).

American Dietetic Association: 120 S Riverside Plaza, Chicago, IL 60606-6995; tel. (312) 899-0040; fax (312) 899-0008; e-mail membrshp@eatright.org; internet www.eatright.org; f. 1917; advances science of dietetics; promotes education in these and allied fields; strives to improve nutrition of human beings; 70,000 mems; library of 1,000 vols; CEO PATRICIA M. BABJAK; Pres. SYLVIA A. ESCOTT-STUMP; Treas. MARY K. RUSSELL; publ. *Journal* (12 a year, online).

American Geriatrics Society: 40 Fulton St, 18th Fl., New York, NY 10038; tel. (212) 308-1414; fax (212) 832-8646; e-mail info .amger@americangeriatrics.org; internet www.americangeriatrics.org; f. 1942; works towards the improvement of the health, independence and quality of life of all older people; provides leadership to health care professionals, policy makers and public by implementing and advocating for programmes in patient care, research, professional and public education and public policy; 6,000 mems; Chair. Dr SHARON A. BRANGMAN; Pres. Dr BARBARA RESNICK; Sec. Dr KEELA ANN HERR; Treas. Dr CATHY ALESSI ; publs *Annals of Long-term Care* (12 a year), *Clinical Geriatrics* (12 a year), *Journal of the American Geriatrics Society* (12 a year), *The American Journal of Geriatric Pharmacotherapy*.

American Gynecological and Obstetrical Society: 230 W Monroe, Suite 710, Chicago, IL 60606; tel. (312) 676-3920; fax (312) 235-4059; e-mail agos@agosonline.org; internet www.agosonline.org; f. 1982 by merger of American Gynecological Soc. with American Asscn Obstetricians and Gynecolo-

gists; advances health of women by providing dedicated leadership and promoting excellence in research, education and medical practice; 200 fellows, 92 life fellows, 43 hon. fellows; Exec. Dir JENNA CUMMINS; Pres. Dr MARY E. D'ALTON; Sec. Dr LARRY J. COPELAND; Treas. DONALD R. COUSTAN.

American Heart Association: Nat. Center, 7272 Greenville Ave, Dallas, TX 75231; tel. (214) 570-5978; fax (214) 706-1341; e-mail sessionsadmin@heart.org; internet www .americanheart.org; f. 1924; dedicated to the reduction of disability and death from cardiovascular diseases and stroke; supports cardiovascular research and brings its benefits to the public through professional education and community service programmes; coordinates efforts of all medical and lay groups in combating cardiovascular diseases; informs public of progress in cardiovascular field; 27,000 mems; CEO NANCY BROWN; Pres. GORDON F. TOMASELLI; Chair. BILL ROACH; publs *Arteriosclerosis, Thrombosis, and Vascular Biology* (12 a year), *Circulation* (52 a year), *Circulation: Arrhythmia and Electrophysiology* (6 a year), *Circulation: Cardiovascular Genetics* (6 a year), *Circulation: Cardiovascular Imaging* (6 a year), *Circulation: Cardiovascular Interventions* (6 a year), *Circulation: Cardiovascular Quality and Outcomes* (6 a year), *Circulation: Heart Failure* (6 a year), *Circulation Research* (24 a year), *Hypertension* (12 a year), *Stroke* (12 a year).

American Hospital Association: 155 N Wacker Dr., Chicago, IL 60606; tel. (312) 422-3000; internet www.aha.org; f. 1898; leads, represents and serves hospitals, health systems and other related orgs that are accountable to the community and committed to health improvement; advances health of individuals and communities; 40,000 individual mems, 5,000 institutional mems; library of 63,000 vols; Chair. JOHN W. BLUFORD, III; Pres. and CEO RICHARD UMBDENSTOCK; Senior Vice-Pres. LISA ALLEN; publs *H&HN Daily*, *Health Facilities Management*, *Hospitals & Health Networks* (12 a year), *Trustee* (12 a year).

American Institute of the History of Pharmacy: 777 Highland Ave, Madison, WI 53705-2222; tel. (608) 262-5378; e-mail aihp@aihp.org; internet www.pharmacy.wisc .edu/aihp; f. 1941; attached to School of Pharmacy, Univ. of Wisconsin-Madison; documents and preserves pharmaceutical heritage; 1,000 mems; Exec. Dir Dr GREGORY J. HIGBY; publ. *Pharmacy in History* (4 a year).

American Laryngological, Rhinological and Otological Society, Inc (Triological Society): 13930 Gold Circle, Suite 103, Omaha, NE 68144; tel. (402) 346-5500; fax (402) 346-5300; e-mail info@triological.org; internet www.triological.org; f. 1895; disseminates scientific information by presenting latest basic science and clinical information at scientific meetings and through publs; promotes research into the causes of and treatments for otolaryngic diseases; 1,200 mems; Pres. Dr ROBERT H. OSSOFF; Exec. Sec. Dr PATRICK E. BROOKHOUSER; Treas. Dr MYLES L. PENSAK; publ. *The Laryngoscope* (12 a year).

American Lung Association (ALA): 1301 Pennsylvania Ave, NW, Suite 800, Washington, DC 20004; tel. (202) 785-3355; fax (202) 452-1805; e-mail info@lungusa.org; internet www.lungusa.org; f. 1904; 115 affiliated asscns nationally; works to improve lung health and prevent lung disease; 11,000 mems; Chair. Dr ALBERT A. RIZZO; Pres. and CEO CHARLES DEAN. CONNOR; Sec. and Treas. CHRISTINE L. BRYANT.

American Medical Association: 515 N State St, Chicago, IL 60654; tel. (800) 621-8335; e-mail mediarelations@jama-archives .org; internet www.ama-assn.org; f. 1847; promotes art and science of medicine and betterment of public health; 296,000 mems; CEO and Exec. Vice-Pres. Dr JAMES L. MADARA; publs *Archives of Dermatology* (12 a year), *Archives of General Psychiatry* (12 a year), *Archives of Internal Medicine* (24 a year), *Archives of Otolaryngology—Head & Neck Surgery* (12 a year), *Archives of Surgery* (12 a year), *Archives of Neurology* (12 a year), *Archives of Ophthalmology* (12 a year), *Archives of Pediatrics & Adolescent Medicine*, *Archives of Facial Plastic Surgery* (6 a year), *JAMA* (48 a year).

American Medical Technologists: 10700 W Higgins, Suite 150, Rosemont, IL 60018; tel. (847) 823-5169; fax (847) 823-0458; e-mail amtmail@aol.com; internet www .americanmedtech.org; f. 1939; nationally and internationally recognized certification agency and membership soc. for allied health professionals; 29,000 mems; Exec. Dir CHRISTOPHER A. DAMON; Pres. ROXANN CLIFTON; Sec. SUSANNA HANCOCK; Treas. EVERETT BLOODWORTH; publs *AMT Events* (4 a year), *Journal of Continuing Education Topics & Issues* (3 a year).

American Neurological Association: 5841 Cedar Lake Rd, Suite 204, Minneapolis, MN 55416; tel. (952) 545-6284; fax (952) 545-6073; e-mail ana@llmsi.com; internet www .aneuroa.org; f. 1875; trains and educates neurologists and other physicians in neurologic sciences; expands understanding of diseases of nervous system and ability to treat them; 1,000 mems; Exec. Dir LINDA SCHER; Pres. Dr EVA L. FELDMAN; Treas. STEVEN P. RINGEL; publ. *Annals of Neurology* (1 a year).

American Occupational Therapy Association, Inc: 4720 Montgomery Lane, POB 31220, Bethesda, MD 20824-1220; tel. (301) 652-2682; fax (301) 652-7711; e-mail ajotsis@ aota.org; internet www.aota.org; f. 1917; assures quality of occupational therapy services; improves consumer access to health care services; promotes professional devt of mems; 42,000 mems; library of 4,000 vols; Pres. Dr FLORENCE CLARK; Sec. PAUL A. FONTANA; publs *American Journal of Occupational Therapy* (7 a year, incl. 1 online supplement), *OT Practice* (22 a year).

American Optometric Association, Inc: 243 N Lindbergh Blvd, St Louis, MO 63141; tel. (314) 991-4100; fax (314) 991-4101; internet www.aoa.org; f. 1898; promotes art and science of optometry; improves vision care and health of public; sets professional standards, helping its mems conduct patient care efficiently and effectively; lobbies with govt and other orgs; provides research and education leadership; 36,000 mems; Pres. Dr DORI M. CARLSON; Sec. and Treas. Dr DAVID A. COCKRELL; publ. *Optometry* (12 a year).

American Pediatric Society/Society for Pediatric Research: 3400 Research Forest Dr., Suite B7, The Woodlands, TX 77381; tel. (281) 419-0052; fax (281) 419-0082; e-mail info@aps-spr.org; internet www.aps-spr.org; f. 1888; 855 active mems; Exec. Dir DEBBIE ANAGNOSTELIS; Pres. Dr F. BRUDER. STAPLETON; Sec. and Treas. Dr JUDY L. ASCHNER; publ. *Pediatric Research* (12 a year).

American Physical Therapy Association: 1111 N Fairfax St, Alexandria, VA 22314-1488; tel. (703) 684-2782; fax (703) 706-8536; e-mail public-relations@apta.org; internet www.apta.org; f. 1921 as American Women's Physical Therapeutic Asscn, inc. 1930; develops art and science of physical therapy; represents and promotes the profession; 77,000 mems; library of 3,000 colln focus: physical rehabilitation, available to researchers by appointment only; CEO JOHN D. BARNES; Pres. Dr R. SCOTT WARD; Sec. LAURITA M. HACK; Treas. ELMER PLATZ; publs *Perspective Magazine* (3 a year), *Physical Therapy* (12 a year), *PT in Motion Magazine* (11 a year).

American Physiological Society: 9650 Rockville Pike, Bethesda, MD 20814-3991; tel. (301) 634-7164; fax (301) 634-7241; e-mail info@the-aps.org; internet www .the-aps.org; f. 1887; non-profit org.; fosters education, scientific research and dissemin- ation of information in the physiological sciences; 10,500 mems; Pres. Dr JOE P. GRANGER; Exec. Dir Dr MARTIN FRANK; publs *Advances in Physiology Education* (4 a year, online), *American Journal of Physiology— Consolidated* (24 a year), *American Journal of Physiology—Cell Physiology* (12 a year, online), *American Journal of Physiology— Endocrinology and Metabolism* (12 a year, online), *American Journal of Physiology— Gastrointestinal and Liver Physiology* (12 a year, online), *American Journal of Physi- ology—Heart and Circulatory Physiology* (12 a year, online), *American Journal of Physi- ology—Lung Cellular and Molecular Physi- ology* (12 a year, online), *American Journal of Physiology—Regulatory, Integrative and Comparative Physiology* (12 a year, online), *American Journal of Physiology—Renal Physiology* (12 a year, online), *APS Journal Legacy Content* (online), *Comprehensive Physiology* (4 a year), *Journal of Applied Physiology* (12 a year, online), *Journal of Neurophysiology* (12 a year, online), *Physio- logical Genomics* (24 a year, online), *Physio- logical Reviews* (4 a year), *Physiology* (6 a year, online), *The Physiologist* (6 a year, online).

American Psychiatric Association: 1000 Wilson Blvd, Suite 1825, Arlington, VA 22209-3901; tel. (703) 907-7300; e-mail apa@psych.org; internet www.psych.org; f. 1844; ensures humane care and effective treatment for all persons with mental dis- orders, incl. intellectual developmental dis- orders and substance use disorders; 36,000 mems; library of 10,000 vols; Pres. JOHN OLDHAM; publs *Academic Psychiatry* (6 a year), *FOCUS: The Journal of Lifelong Learning in Psychiatry* (4 a year), *The American Journal of Psychiatry* (12 a year), *The Journal of Neuropsychiatry and Clinical Neurosciences* (4 a year), *Psychiatric Services* (12 a year).

American Public Health Association: 800 I St, NW, Washington, DC 20001-3710; tel. (202) 777-2742; fax (202) 777-2534; e-mail comments@apha.org; internet www .apha.org; f. 1872; interests incl. environ- ment, personal health services, social factors, manpower and training in public health, global and int. health; 50,000 mems; Exec. Dir Dr J. ALAN BAKER; Pres. Dr MELVIN D. SHIPP; Treas. Dr RICHARD J. COHEN; publ. *American Journal of Public Health* (12 a year).

American Roentgen Ray Society: 44211 Slatestone Court, Leesburg, VA 20176-5109; tel. (703) 729-3353; fax (703) 729-4839; e-mail info@arrs.org; internet www.arrs.org; f. 1900; int. org. of physicians and scientists working in radiology and related fields; 20,000 mems; Exec. Dir SUSAN BROWN CAPPI- TELLI; Pres. Dr JAMES A. BRINK; Sec. and Treas. Dr MELISSA ROSADO DE CHRISTENSO; publs *American Journal of Roentgenology* (12 a year), *InPractice* (4 a year).

American Society for Clinical Labora- tory Science: 2025 M St, NW, Suite 800, Washington, DC 20036; tel. (202) 367-1174;

fax (301) 657-2909; e-mail ascls@ascls.org; internet www.ascls.org; f. 1933 as American Soc. of Clinical Laboratory Technicians, inc. 1936, present name 1993; local, state and regional socs; activities incl. education, edu- cation and research funding, professional affairs and membership services; 13,000 mems; Pres. CATHY OTTO; Sec. and Treas. GILMA RONCANCIO-WEEMER; publ. *Clinical Laboratory Science* (4 a year).

American Society for Clinical Path- ology: 33 W Monroe St, Suite 1600, Chicago, IL 60603; tel. (312) 541-4999; fax (312) 541- 4998; e-mail info@ascp.org; internet www .ascp.org; f. 1922; a non-profit medical soc. for promotion of pathology and laboratory medi- cine; 100,000 memss; library of 25,500 vols; Pres. Dr C. BRUCE ALEXANDER; Sec. Dr WILLIAM G. FINN Jr; Treas. Dr KENNETH EMANCIPATOR; publs *American Journal of Clinical Pathology* (12 a year), *LABMEDI- CINE* (12 a year).

American Society for Investigative Pathology: 9650 Rockville Pike, Suite E133, Bethesda, MD 20814-3993; tel. (301) 634-7130; fax (301) 634-7990; e-mail asip@ asip.org; internet www.asip.org; f. 1976; investigates mechanisms of disease; advo- cates for practice of investigative pathology and fosters professional career devt and education of its mems; 2,500 mems; Pres. Dr MARTHA FURIE; Sec. and Treas. Dr WILLIAM B. COLEMAN; Exec. Officer Dr MARK E. SOBEL; publs *American Journal of Path- ology* (12 a year), *The Journal of Molecular Diagnostics* (6 a year).

American Society for Microbiology: 1752 N St, NW, Washington, DC 20036-2904; tel. (202) 737-3600; fax (202) 942-9367; internet www.asm.org; f. 1899, present name 1961; supports programmes of education, training and public information; publishes journals and books; convenes meetings, workshops and colloquia; promotes contributions and promise of microbiological sciences; recog- nizes achievement and distinction among its practitioners; 39,000 mems; Exec. Dir MICHAEL I. GOLDBERG; Pres. Dr DAVID C. HOO- PER; Sec. JOSEPH M. CAMPOS; publs *Antimi- crobial Agents and Chemotherapy* (12 a year), *Applied and Environmental Microbiol- ogy* (24 a year), *Clinical and Diagnostic Laboratory Immunology* (12 a year), *Clinical and Vaccine Immunology (CVI)* (12 a year), *Clinical Microbiology Reviews* (4 a year), *Eukaryotic Cell* (12 a year), *Infection and Immunity* (12 a year), *Journal of Bacteri- ology* (24 a year), *Journal of Clinical Micro- biology* (12 a year), *Journal of Microbiology & Biology Education* (2 a year), *Journal of Virology* (24 a year), *Microbiology and Molecular Biology Reviews* (4 a year), *Molecular and Cellular Biology* (24 a year).

American Society for Nutritional Sci- ences: 9650 Rockville Pike, Bethesda, MD 20814; tel. (301) 634-7050; fax (301) 634- 7892; e-mail info@nutrition.org; internet www.nutrition.org; f. 1928; develops and extends knowledge of nutrition and facili- tates personal contact between investigators in nutrition and related fields of interest; 3,100 mems; Exec. Officer Dr JOHN E. COURTNEY; Pres. Dr SHARON DONOVAN; Sec. Dr MARIAN L. NEUHOUSER; Treas. Dr CHERYL ROCK; publs *Advances in Nutrition* (6 a year), *The American Journal of Clinical Nutrition* (12 a year), *The Journal of Nutrition* (12 a year).

American Society for Pharmacology and Experimental Therapeutics: 9650 Rockville Pike, Bethesda, MD 20814-3995; tel. (301) 634-7060; fax (301) 634-7061; e-mail info@aspet.org; internet www.aspet .org; f. 1908; basic and clinical pharmaco-

logical research in academia, industry and govt; helps develop new medicines and thera- peutic agents to fight existing and emerging diseases; 4,800 mems; Pres. Dr LYNN WECKER; Sec. and Treas. Dr MARY E. VORE; Exec. Officer Dr CHRISTINE K. CARRICO; publs *Drug Metabolism and Disposition* (12 a year), *Journal of Pharmacology and Experi- mental Therapeutics* (12 a year), *Molecular Pharmacology* (12 a year), *Pharmacological Reviews* (4 a year).

American Society of Clinical Hypnosis: 140 N Bloomingdale Rd, Bloomingdale, IL 60108-1017; tel. (630) 980-4740; fax (630) 351-8490; e-mail info@asch.net; internet www.asch.net; f. 1957; ind. org. of profes- sional people in medicine, dentistry, and psychology who share scientific and clinical interests in hypnosis; provides educational programmes to further understanding and acceptance of hypnosis as important tool of ethical clinical medicine and scientific research; 2,400 mems; Pres. Dr ELGAN L. BAKER; Exec. Dir for Governance and Policy MICHAEL WHITE; Sec. Dr ASSEN ALLADIN; publ. *The American Journal of Clinical Hypnosis* (4 a year).

American Society of Tropical Medicine and Hygiene: 111 Deer Lake Rd, Suite 100, Deerfield, IL 60015; tel. (847) 480-9592; fax (847) 480-9282; e-mail info@astmh.org; internet www.astmh.org; f. 1951 by merger of American Soc. of Tropical Medicine (f. 1903) with Nat. Malaria Soc. (f. 1940); pro- motes global health through prevention and control of infectious and other diseases that disproportionately afflict global poor; 3,000 mems; Exec. Dir BRIAN MADDOX; Pres. Dr PETER J. HOTEZ; Sec. and Treas. Dr JOSH D. BERMAN; publ. *American Journal of Tropical Medicine and Hygiene* (12 a year).

American Speech-Language-Hearing Association: 2200 Research Blvd, Rockville, MD 20850-3289; tel. (301) 296-5700; fax (301) 296-8580; e-mail actioncenter@asha.org; internet www.asha.org; f. 1925, fmrly Ameri- can Acad. of Speech Correction, present name 1978; advocates on behalf of persons with communication and related disorders; advances communication science; promotes effective human communication; 145,000 mems; Pres. PAUL R. RAO; Exec. Dir ARLENE A. PIETRANTON; publs *American Journal of Audiology* (2 a year, online), *American Jour- nal of Speech-Language Pathology* (4 a year, online), *Journal of Speech, Language, and Hearing Research* (4 a year, online), *Lan- guage Speech and Hearing Services in Schools* (4 a year, online).

American Surgical Association: 900 Cummings Center, Suite 221-U, Beverly, MA 01915; tel. (978) 927-8330; fax (978) 524-8890; e-mail asa@prri.com; internet www.americansurgical.info; f. 1880; org. for surgical science and scholarship; provides a nat. forum for presenting developing state of gen. and sub-speciality surgery; 1,000 mems; Pres. Dr TIMOTHY J EBERLEIN; Sec. Dr E. CHRISTOPHER ELLISON; Treas. Dr RUSSELL G. POSTIER; publ. *Annals of Surgery* (12 a year).

American Urological Association: 1000 Corporate Blvd, Linthicum, MD 21090; tel. (410) 689-3700; fax (410) 689-3800; e-mail aua@auanet.org; internet www.auanet.org; f. 1902; helps in advancement of urologic patient care through education, research and in the formulation of health care policy; 17,000 mems; Pres. Dr SUSHIL S. LACY; Sec. Dr GOPAL H. BADLANI; Treas. RICHARD A. MEMO; publs *Health Policy Brief* (12 a year), *The Journal of Urology* (12 a year).

Armed Forces Institute of Pathology: 6900 Georgia Ave, NW, Washington, DC 20306-6000; tel. (202) 782-2100; internet www.nlm.nih.gov/hmd/medtour/afip.html; f. 1862 as Army Medical Museum, present name 1949; central laboratory of pathology for the Dept of Defense serving both military and civilian sectors in education, consultation and research in medical, dental and veterinary sciences; research into leprosy, malaria, HIV/AIDS, sickle cell disease, radiation injury, trauma, drug toxicity and aerospace pathology; organized into: Center for Advanced Pathology, Center for Clinical Laboratory Medicine, Center for Admin. Services, Center for Education, Repository and Research Services, Office of the Armed Forces Medical Examiner and Nat. Museum of Health and Medicine; Dir Dr FLORABEL MULLICK.

Association of American Medical Colleges: 2450 N St, NW, Washington, DC 20037-1126; tel. (202) 828-0400; fax (202) 828-1125; e-mail amcas@aamc.org; internet www.aamc.org; f. 1876; works for betterment of medical care by supporting education, research and patient care activities; 136 US and 17 Canadian medical schools; more than 400 teaching hospitals and 93 academic and professional socs; 313,000 mems (incl. faculty mems, medical students and resident physicians); Pres. and CEO Dr DARRELL G. KIRCH; Chair. Dr MARK R. LARET; publs *AAMC Curriculum Directory* (1 a year), *AAMC Directory of Medical Education* (1 a year), *Academic Medicine* (12 a year), *Medical School Admission Requirements* (1 a year).

Association of American Physicians: 45685 Harmony Lane, Belleville, MI 48111; tel. (734) 699-1217; fax (617) 731-1541; e-mail admin@aap-online.org; internet www.aap-online.org; f. 1885; pursues medical knowledge; makes advancement through experimentation and discovery of basic and clinical science and their application to clinical medicine; 1,750 mems; Exec. Dir LORI ENNIS; Pres. DAVID BRENNER; Sec. RICHARD LIFTON; Treas. TIMOTHY LEY.

Center for the Study of Aging and Human Development: POB 3003, Duke Univ. Medical Center, Room 3502 Busse Bldg, Blue Zone, Duke S, Durham, NC 27710; tel. (919) 660-7500; fax (919) 668-0453; internet www.geri.duke.edu; f. 1955; attached to Duke Univ.; research incl. studies of age-related functional decline and dysmobility, genomic, proteonic and metabolomic biomarkers of aging, exercise, osteoporosis, Alzheimer's disease, cancer and aging, viral diseases of aging, depression in later life, caregiver stress and religion/spirituality and health; Dir Dr HARVEY JAY COHEN.

College of Physicians of Philadelphia: 19 S 22nd St, Philadelphia, PA 19103-3097; tel. (215) 563-3737; fax (215) 575-3499; e-mail info@collphyphil.org; internet www.collphyphil.org; f. 1787; increases understanding between health professions and gen. public; incl. Historical Medical Library, Mutter Museum (pathology and anatomy) and Francis C. Wood Institute for the History of Medicine; 1,500 fellows; library of 340,000 vols; CEO MARK HOCHBERG; Pres. Dr BENNETT LORBER; Sec. Dr ROGER J. PORTER; Treas. Dr MARJORIE A. BOWMAN; College Librarian ANNEMARIE BROGAN.

Commonwealth Fund: 1 E 75th St, New York, NY 10021; tel. (212) 606-3800; fax (212) 606-3500; e-mail cmwf@cmwf.org; internet www.commonwealthfund.org; f. 1918; helps Americans live healthy and productive lives; helps young people realize their potential through mentoring and educational enhancement programmes; improves health care services; promotes healthier life styles and betters health care of minorities; awards

Harkness Fellowships to study social issues in the USA; Chair. of Board JAMES R. TALLON; Pres. Dr KAREN DAVIS.

Gerontological Society of America: 1220 L St, NW, Suite 901, Washington, DC 20005; tel. (202) 842-1275; fax (202) 842-1150; e-mail geron@geron.org; internet www.geron.org; f. 1945; multidisciplinary sciences org., incl. an educational unit, AGHE (Asscn for Gerontology in Higher Education) and a policy institute, NAAS (Nat. Acad. on an Aging Soc.); 5,400 mems; Exec. Dir JAMES APPLEBY; Pres. TERRY T. FULMER; publs *Journals of Gerontology* (Series A: Biological Sciences and Medical Sciences; Series B: Psychological Sciences and Social Sciences), *Gerontology & Geriatrics Education* (4 a year), *Public Policy and Aging Report* (4 a year), *The Gerontologist* (6 a year).

Industrial Health Foundation, Inc: 34 Penn Circle W, Pittsburgh, PA 15206-3612; tel. (412) 363-6600; fax (412) 363-6605; e-mail admin@ihfincorp.com; f. 1935; a non-profit org. for advancement of healthy working conditions in industry; 120 mem cos and asscns; library of 2,000 vols; publs *Industrial Hygiene Digest* (12 a year), spec. technical bulletins.

John A. Hartford Foundation: 55 E 59th St, 16th Fl., New York, NY 10022-1713; tel. (212) 832-7788; fax (212) 593-4913; e-mail mail@jhartfound.org; internet www.jhartfound.org; f. 1929; ageing and health programme; health care training, research and service innovations that ensures well-being and vitality of older adults; Chair. of the Board NORMAN H. VOLK; Pres. KATHRYN D. WRISTON; Sec. WILLIAM T. COMFORT; Exec. Dir and Treas. CORINNE H. RIEDER.

Medical Society of the State of New York: 865 Merrick Ave, Westbury, New York, NY 11590; tel. (516) 488-6100; fax (516) 488-1267; e-mail mssny@mssny.org; internet www.mssny.org; f. 1807; non-profit org.; advocates health related rights, responsibilities and issues; 30,000 mems; library of 45,000 vols; Pres. Dr PAUL A. HAMLIN; Sec. MALCOLM D. REID; Treas. ANDREW Y. KLEINMAN; Exec. Dir WILLIAM R. ABRAMS; publ. *Medical Directory of New York State* (every 2 years).

Mental Health America: 2000 N Beauregard St, 6th Fl., Alexandria, VA 22311; tel. (703) 684-7722; fax (703) 684-5968; e-mail infoctr@mentalhealthamerica.net; internet www.mentalhealthamerica.net; f. 1909 as Nat. Mental Health Asscn; 320 affiliates nationally; educates public about ways to preserve and strengthen its mental health; fights for access to effective care and an end to discrimination against people with mental and addictive disorders; fosters innovation in research, practice, services and policy; provides support to individuals and families living with mental health and substance use problems; Pres. and CEO DAVID L. SHERN; Chair. PENDER MCELROY; Sec. and Treas. JEANNE ROHNER.

National Association for Biomedical Research: 818 Connecticut Ave, Suite 900, Washington, DC 20006; tel. (202) 857-0540; fax (202) 659-1902; e-mail info@nabr.org; internet www.nabr.org; f. 1979; advocates sound public policy that recognizes vital role of humane animal use in biomedical research, higher education and product safety testing; stands for scientific community on legislative, regulatory and legal mat-

ters affecting laboratory animal research; 300 institutional mems; Pres. FRANKIE L. TRULL; publs *NABR Alert* (26 a year), *NABR Update* (26 a year), *State Laws*.

New York Academy of Medicine: 1216 Fifth Ave, 103rd St, New York, NY 10029; tel. (212) 822-7200; fax (212) 876-6620; internet www.nyam.org; f. 1847; ind. org. that addresses health challenges facing world's urban population through interdisciplinary approaches to policy leadership, innovative research, evaluation, education and community engagement; 2,000 mems; library of 550,000 vols; see Libraries and Archives; Pres. Dr JO IVEY BOUFFORD; Chair. Dr THOMAS Q. MORRIS; Sec. KENNETH L. DAVIS; Treas. BRUCE L. BOOTH.

Radiological Society of North America: 820 Jorie Blvd, Oak Brook, IL 60523-2251; tel. (630) 571-2670; fax (630) 571-7837; e-mail membership@rsna.org; internet www.rsna.org; f. 1915; continuing medical education in radiology; 48,000 mems; Chair. Dr SARAH S. DONALDSON; Pres. Dr BURTON P. DRAYER; Sec. and Treas. GEORGE S. BISSET, III; publs *Index to Imaging Literature* (online index of 38 journals), *RadioGraphics* (6 a year), *Radiology* (12 a year), *Radiology Legacy Collection*.

Society of Medical Jurisprudence: POB 20678, New York, NY 10021-0073; f. 1883; investigation, study and advancement of science of medical jurisprudence, and attainment of a higher standard of medical testimony; mems incl. physicians, lawyers, chemists, forensic odontologists, health professionals and teachers in approved law or medical schools; 250 mems; publ. *Proceedings* (9 a year).

NATURAL SCIENCES
General

Academy of Natural Sciences of Drexel University: 1900 Benjamin Franklin Parkway, Philadelphia, PA 19103-1195; tel. (215) 299-1000; fax (215) 299-1028; e-mail presidentsoffice@ansp.org; internet www.ansp.org; f. 1812 as Acad. of Natural Sciences of Philadelphia; natural history museum; research in systematics and evolutionary biology, ecology, limnology and geology, and environmental monitoring; 24m. specimen collns of plants, animals and fossils of worldwide scope; teaching at all levels; innovative exhibits, publs and educational programmes; 200,000 mems; library: see Libraries and Archives; Pres. and CEO GEORGE W. GEPHART, JR (acting); Chair. CYNTHIA HECKSCHER; Sec. JUDITH E. SOLTZ; Treas. DAVID P. LAZAR, SR; publs *Notulae Naturae, Proceedings of the Academy of Natural Sciences, Special Publications*.

American Association for the Advancement of Science: 1200 New York Ave, NW, Washington, DC 20005; tel. (202) 326-6400; fax (202) 789-0455; e-mail media@aaas.org; internet www.aaas.org; f. 1848; int. non-profit org.; aims to advance science and serve soc. through initiatives in science policy; int. programmes; science education; 128,000 mems, 262 affiliates; Chair. Dr ALICE S. HUANG; Pres. Dr NINA V. FEDOROFF; CEO Dr ALAN I. LESHNER; publs *Science* (52 a year), *Science Signaling* (52 a year), *Science Translational Medicine* (52 a year).

American Society of Limnology and Oceanography: 5400 Bosque Blvd, Suite

680, Waco, TX 76710-4446; tel. (979) 845-5706; fax (979) 845-6331; e-mail secretary@aslo.org; internet aslo.org; f. 1936 as Limnological Soc. of America, present name 1948; creates, integrates and communicates knowledge across the full spectrum of aquatic sciences, advances public awareness and education about aquatic resources and research; promotes scientific stewardship of aquatic resources; 3,800 mems; Pres. DEBORAH BRONK; Sec. LISA CAMPBELL; Treas. PATRICIA MATRAI; publs *Limnology and Oceanography* (6 a year), *Limnology and Oceanography Bulletin* (4 a year), *Limnology and Oceanography: Fluids and Environments* (online), *Limnology and Oceanography: Methods* (1 a year).

Buffalo Society of Natural Sciences: c/o Buffalo Museum of Science, 1020 Humboldt Parkway, Buffalo, NY 14211; tel. (716) 896-5200; fax (716) 897-6723; internet www.sciencebuff.org; f. 1861; administers the Buffalo Museum of Science and Tifft Nature Preserve; samples of natural life in the USA; cultures from other eras to the present; Whem Ankh: The Cycle of Life in Ancient Egypt; Dinosaurs and Company; research in anthropology, botany, entomology, geology, mycology, ornithology, palaeontology, vertebrate zoology, with collns in these fields; 11,000 mems; library of 40,000 vols; Chair. RANDALL E. BURKARD; Sec. LAURIE DANN; publ. *Bulletin* (irregular).

California Academy of Sciences: 55 Music Concourse Dr., Golden Gate Park, San Francisco, CA 94118; tel. (415) 379-8000; e-mail info@calacademy.org; internet www.calacademy.org; f. 1853; promotes advancement of natural sciences through public education and research; inc. under the laws of the State of California 1871; 20,000 mems, incl. 300 fellows; Pres. Dr JOHN HAFERNIK; Exec. Dir Dr GREGORY C. FARRINGTON; publs *California Wild, Memoirs, Occasional Papers, Pacific Discovery* (4 a year), *Proceedings of the California Academy of Sciences.*

Chicago Academy of Sciences: c/o Peggy Notebaert Nature Museum2430 N Cannon Dr., Chicago, IL 60614; tel. (773) 755-5100; e-mail membership@naturemuseum.org; internet www.chias.org; f. 1857; research colln of plants, animals, fossils and minerals; also maintains Peggy Notebaert Nature Museum, with interactive displays treating the relationship between people and nature; 2,200 mems; library of 3,000 vols, 2,000 periodicals; Chair. STEPHEN R. FERRARA; Sec. JIM MURRAY; publs *Bulletin, Natural History Miscellanea.*

Cranbrook Institute of Science: POB 801, 39221 N Woodward Ave, Bloomfield Hills, MI 48303-0801; tel. (248) 645-3200; fax (248) 645-3050; internet science.cranbrook.edu; f. 1904; non-profit org. with exhibits and educational programmes in astronomy, mineralogy, geology, botany, zoology, ecology, anthropology, mathematics and physics; 4,000 mems; library of 18,000 vols; Dir Dr MICHAEL D. STAFFORD; Chair. LLOYD E. REUSS; Sec. CAROL A. WALTERS; Treas. FREDERICK M. ADAMS, JR; publ. *Homes for Wildlife.*

Franklin Institute: 222 N 20th St, Philadelphia, PA 19103; tel. (215) 448-1200; e-mail guestservices@fi.edu; internet www2.fi.edu; f. 1824 as The Franklin Institute of the State of Pennsylvania for the Promotion of the Mechanic Arts; non-profit science centre dedicated to public science education and to advancing knowledge in the physical sciences; its cttee on science and arts awards several medals, incl. Franklin Medal, for contributions to science and technology; also administers Bower Awards for science and business; incorporates Franklin Institute Science Museum (*q.v.*), Fels Planetarium, The Tuttleman Omniverse Theater and Musser Choices Forum, and houses Benjamin Franklin Nat. Memorial; observatory open to public; Pres. and CEO Dr DENNIS M. WINT; publ. *Journal.*

History of Science Society: 440 Geddes Hall, Univ. of Notre Dame, Notre Dame, IN 46556; tel. (574) 631-1194; fax (574) 631-1533; e-mail info@hssonline.org; internet www.hssonline.org; f. 1924; understands science, technology, medicine and their interactions with soc. in historical context; 3,500 mems; Exec. Dir ROBERT JAY MALONE; Pres. Prof. LYNN K. NYHART; Sec. MARSHA RICHMOND; Treas. ADAM APT; publs *Isis* (4 a year), *Isis Current Bibliography* (1 a year), *Osiris* (1 a year).

Mellon Institute: see Carnegie Mellon University under Universities and Colleges—Pennsylvania.

National Science Teachers Association: 1840 Wilson Blvd, Arlington, VA 22201-3000; tel. (703) 243-7100; fax (703) 243-7177; e-mail pubinfo@nsta.org; internet www.nsta.org; f. 1944; advances science teaching and science education at elementary, secondary and college levels; 60,000 mems; Pres. Dr PATRICIA SIMMONS; Exec. Dir and Sec. Dr FRANCIS Q. EBERLE; Treas. LeROY LEE; publs *Journal of College Science Teaching, Science & Children* (4 a year), *Science Scope* (4 a year), *The Science Teacher.*

Ohio Academy of Science: 1500 W Third Ave, Suite 223, Columbus, OH 43212-2817; tel. (614) 488-2228; fax (614) 488-7629; e-mail oas@iwaynet.net; internet www.ohiosci.org; f. 1891; fosters curiosity, discovery, understanding, dissemination and practice of education, science, mathematics, engineering, technology or their applications; 2,000 mems; CEO LYNN E. ELFNER; Pres. and Chair. HORTON H. HOBBS, III; Sec. DON R. GRUBBS; Treas. MICHAEL S. HERSCHLER; publs *Legislative Bulletin, The Ohio Journal of Science* (4 a year).

Sigma Xi, the Scientific Research Society: POB 13975, 3106 E NC Highway 54, Research Triangle Park, NC 27709; tel. (919) 549-4691; fax (919) 549-0090; e-mail memberinfo@sigmaxi.org; internet www.sigmaxi.org; f. 1886; encourages scientific research; publishes new scientific discoveries; 65,000 mems; Pres. MICHAEL CROSBY; Exec. Dir Dr JEROME F. BAKER; publ. *American Scientist* (6 a year).

Southern California Academy of Sciences: 900 Exposition Blvd, Los Angeles, CA 90007; tel. (909) 607-2836; fax (909) 621-8588; internet scas.jsd.claremont.edu; f. 1891, inc. 1907; promotes fellowship among scientists and those interested in science; contributes to scientific literature through publ. of pertinent MSS; encourages and promotes scholarship among young scientists; provides information to mems, public and public agencies on such matters as may be of joint interest to the sciences and to soc.; 400 mems; Pres. JON ROBERTS; Sec. EDITH REED; Treas. Dr DANIEL GUTHRIE; publ. *Bulletin of the Southern California Academy of Science* (3 a year).

World Future Society: 7910 Woodmont Ave, Suite 450, Bethesda, MD 20814; tel. (301) 656-8274; fax (301) 951-0394; e-mail info@wfs.org; internet www.wfs.org; f. 1966; private, non-profit org. promoting free discussion and study of alternative futures esp. on technological and social themes; 30,000 mems; Pres. TIMOTHY C. MACK; Sec. KENNETH W. HARRIS; Treas. KENNETH W. HUNTER; publs *Future Survey* (12 a year), *Outlook* (1 a year), *The Futurist* (10 a year), *World Future Review* (4 a year).

Biological Sciences

American Genetic Association: 2030 SE Marine Science Dr., Newport, OR 97365; tel. (541) 867-0334; e-mail agajoh@oregonstate.edu; internet www.theaga.org; f. 1903, fmrly American Breeders Asscn, present name 1914; publishes journals of plant and animal genetics; organizes and supports annual symposium and workshops; 300 mems; Pres. Dr SCOTT V. EDWARDS; Sec. Dr LINDA STRAUSBAUGH; Treas. Dr. NORMAN F. WEEDEN; publ. *Journal of Heredity* (6 a year).

American Institute of Biological Sciences: 1900 Campus Commons Dr., Suite 200, Reston, VA 20191; tel. (703) 674-2500; fax (703) 674-2509; e-mail admin@aibs.org; internet www.aibs.org; f. 1947; advances biological research and education; 250,000 mems; Pres. JAMES P. COLLINS; Sec. JUDITH SKOG; Treas. LOUIS GROSS; Exec. Dir Dr RICHARD O'GRADY; publ. *BioScience* (11 a year).

American Malacological Society: Dept of Zoology, Univ. of Rhode Island, Kingston, RI 02881; internet www.malacological.org; f. 1931, fmrly American Malacological Union; study of phylum mollusca–systematics, ecology, functional morphology, evolution; medical, neotological and palaeontological aspects; 750 mems; Pres. GARY ROSENBERG; Sec. AMANDA LAWLESS; Treas. DAWN DITTMAN; publ. *American Malacological Bulletin* (2 a year).

American Ornithologists Union: 5400 Bosque Blvd, Suite 680, Waco, TX 76710; tel. (505) 326-1579; fax (703) 790-2672; e-mail aou@aou.org; internet www.aou.org; f. 1883; scientific study of birds; 3,000 mems; Exec. Dir SCOTT W. GILLIHAN; Pres. JOHN R. FAABORG; Sec. SARA R. MORRIS; Treas. JAMES HERKERT; publs *AOU Check-List of North American Birds* (irregular), *Birds of North America, The Auk* (4 a year).

American Phytopathological Society: 3340 Pilot Knob Rd, St Paul, MN 55121; tel. (651) 454-7250; fax (651) 454-0766; e-mail aps@scisoc.org; internet www.apsnet.org; f. 1908; provides credible and beneficial information related to plant health; advocates and participates in exchange of knowledge with public, policy makers and larger scientific community; promotes and provides opportunities for scientific communication, career preparation and professional devt for its mems; plant health management; plant management network; 5,000 mems; Pres. CAROL A. ISHIMARU; publs *Molecular Plant-Microbe Interactions* (12 a year), *Phytopathology* (12 a year), *Plant Disease* (12 a year), *Plant Health Progress.*

American Society for Photobiology: POB 1897, Lawrence, KS 66044; tel. (785) 843-1235; fax (785) 843-1274; e-mail phot@allenpress.com; internet www.photobiology.org; f. 1972; promotes research in photobiology, integration of different photobiology disciplines, dissemination of photobiology knowledge; provides information on photobiological aspects of nat. and int. issues; 1,600 mems; Pres. TAYYABA HASAN; Sec.

DON FORBES; Treas. JOHN STREICHER; publ. *Photochemistry and Photobiology* (6 a year).

American Society of Human Genetics: 9650 Rockville Pike, Bethesda, MD 20814-3998; tel. (301) 634-7300; fax (301) 634-7079; e-mail society@ashg.org; internet www.ashg .org; f. 1948; serves research scientists, health professionals and public by providing forums; 8,000 mems; Pres. MARY-CLAIRE KING; Sec. Dr BRENDAN LEE; Treas. DANIEL L. VAN DYKE; Exec. Dir ELAINE STRASS; publ. *American Journal of Human Genetics* (12 a year).

American Society of Ichthyologists and Herpetologists: c/o Maureen A. Donnelly, Florida Int. Univ., Dept of Biological Sciences, 11200 SW 8th St, Miami, FL 33199; tel. (305) 348-1235; fax (305) 348-4172; e-mail asih@fiu.edu; internet www.asih.org; f. 1913; scientific study of fishes, amphibians and reptiles; publs, confs and symposia; 2,400 mems; Pres. MICHAEL E. DOUGLAS; Sec. MAUREEN A. DONNELLY; Treas. MARGARET A. NEIGHBORS; publ. *Copeia* (4 a year).

American Society of Mammalogists: 810 E 10th St, POB 1897, Lawrence, KS 66044-8897; tel. (785) 843-1235; fax (785) 843-1274; e-mail asm@allenpress.com; internet www .mammalsociety.org; f. 1919, inc. 1920; promotes interest in mammalogy by holding meetings, issuing serial or other publs and aiding research; 4,500 mems; Pres. MICHAEL A. MARES; Sec. and Treas. RONALD A. VAN DEN BUSSCHE; publs *Journal of Mammalogy* (4 a year), *Mammalian Species* (irregular).

American Society of Naturalists: 4328 Storer Hall, Univ. of California, Davis, CA 95616-8755; tel. (530) 752-1114; internet www.asnamnat.org; f. 1883; study of ecology, evolution and behaviour; 1,835 mems; Pres. Dr ROBERT E. RICKLEFS; Sec. Dr DANIEL I. BOLNICK; Treas. KATHLEEN DONOHUE; publ. *The American Naturalist* (12 a year).

American Society of Parasitologists: c/o Dennis J. Minchella, Dept of Biological Sciences, Purdue Univ., West Lafayette, IN 47907-2054; tel. (765) 494-8188; fax (765) 494-0876; internet asp.unl.edu; f. 1924; contributes to devt of parasitology as a discipline, and also to primary research in systematics, medicine, molecular biology, immunology, physiology, ecology, biochemistry and behaviour; 1,500 mems; Sec. and Treas. Dr DENNIS J. MINCHELLA; publ. *The Journal of Parasitology* (6 a year).

Biophysical Society: 11400 Rockville Pike, Suite 800, Rockville, MD 20852; tel. (240) 290-5600; fax (240) 290-5555; e-mail society@ biophysics.org; internet www.biophysics.org; f. 1957; dissemination of knowledge in biophysics through meetings, publs and cttee outreach activities; 9,000 mems; Pres. RICHARD ALDRICH; Sec. LUKAS TAMM; Treas. LINDA KENNEY; Exec. Dir ROSALBA KAMPMAN; publ. *Biophysical Journal* (24 a year).

Botanical Society of America: POB 299, St Louis, MO 63166-0299; tel. (314) 577-9566; fax (314) 577-9515; e-mail bsa-manager@botany.org; internet www .botany.org; f. 1893, fmrly Botanical Club of the American Ascn; studies of plants and allied organisms, and functions as an umbrella org. covering all specialties; 3,000 mems; Pres. STEPHEN G. WELLER; Sec. PAMELA DIGGLE; Treas. AMY LITT; Exec. Dir BILL DAHL; publs *American Journal of Botany* (12 a year), *Botany for the Next Millennium*, *Plant Science Bulletin* (4 a year).

Ecological Society of America: 1900 M St, NW, Suite 700, Washington, DC 20036; tel. (202) 833-8773; fax (202) 833-8775; e-mail esahq@esa.org; internet www.esa.org; f. 1915; promotes ecological science by improving communication among ecologists; raises public's level of awareness of importance of ecological science; increases resources available for conduct of ecological science; ensures appropriate use of ecological science in environmental decision making by enhancing communication between the ecological community and policy-makers; 10,000 mems; Exec. Dir KATHERINE S. McCARTER; Pres. STEWARD A. PICKETT; Sec. CHARLES D. CANHAM; publs *Bulletin* (4 a year), *Ecological Applications* (8 a year), *Ecological Monographs* (4 a year), *Ecology* (12 a year), *Ecosphere* (12 a year, online), *Frontiers in Ecology and the Environment* (10 a year).

Entomological Society of America: 10001 Derekwood Lane, Suite 100, Lanham, MD 20706-4876; tel. (301) 731-4535; fax (301) 731-4538; e-mail esa@entsoc.org; internet www.entsoc.org; f. 1889; professional and scientific needs of entomologists and people in related disciplines; 6,000 mems; Pres. Dr ERNEST S. DELFOSSE; Exec. Dir DAVID GAMMEL; publs *American Entomologist* (4 a year), *Annals of the Entomological Society of America* (6 a year), *Anthropod Management Tests* (1 a year), *Environmental Entomology* (6 a year), *Journal of Economic Entomology* (6 a year), *Journal of Integrated Pest Management* (4 a year, online), *Journal of Medical Entomology* (6 a year).

Environmental Mutagen Society: 1821 Michael Faraday Dr., Suite 300, Reston, VA 20190; tel. (703) 438-8220; fax (703) 438-3113; e-mail emshq@ems-us.org; internet www.ems-us.org; f. 1969; scientific research into causes and consequences of damage to genome and epigenome; promotes basic and applied studies of mutagenesis; informs and supports nat. and int. efforts to ensure a healthy, sustainable environment; 600 mems; Exec. Dir TONIA MASSON; Pres. CATHERINE B. KLEIN; Sec. SUZANNE M. MORRIS; Treas. BARBARA S. SHANE; publ. *Environmental and Molecular Mutagenesis* (8 a year).

Federation of American Societies for Experimental Biology: 9650 Rockville Pike, Bethesda, MD 20814; tel. (301) 634-7000; fax (301) 634-7001; e-mail info@faseb .org; internet www.faseb.org; f. 1912; promotes progress and education in biological and biomedical sciences; policy devt related to biomedical science and engineering for legislators, fed. agencies and media; 100,000 mems and 24 scientific socs.; library of 2,500 vols; Pres. Dr JOSEPH C. LaMANNA; Sec. and Exec. Dir Dr GUY FOGLEMAN; Treas. Dr FRED D. FINKELMAN; publ. *The FASEB Journal* (12 a year).

Genetics Society of America: 9650 Rockville Pike, Bethesda, MD 20814-3998; tel. (301) 634-7300; fax (301) 634-7079; internet www.genetics-gsa.org; f. 1931 by merger of Joint Genetics Sections of American Soc. of Zoologists and Botanical Soc. of America; works towards a unified science of genetics and to maximize its intellectual and practical impact; 4,200 mems; Pres. Dr ADAM P. FAGEN; Pres. Dr PAUL W. STERNBERG; Sec. Dr MARIANA F. WOLFNER; Treas. Dr CAROL S. NEWLON; publs *Genetics* (12 a year), *G3: Genes, Genomes, Genetics*.

Mycological Society of America: c/o Dr Jessie A. Glaeser, USFS Northern Research Station, 1 Gifford Pinchot Dr., Madison, WI 53726; tel. (608) 231-9215; fax (608) 231-9592; e-mail msasec1@yahoo.com; internet msafungi.org; f. 1937; study of fungi of all kinds incl. mushrooms, molds, truffles, yeasts, lichens, plant pathogens and medically important fungi; 1,300 mems; Pres. Dr DAVID S. HIBBETT; Sec. Dr JESSIE A. GLAESER; Treas. Dr MARC CUBETA; publ. *Mycologia* (6 a year, online).

National Audubon Society: 225 Varick St, 7th Fl., New York, NY 10014; tel. (212) 979-3000; fax (212) 979-3188; e-mail join@ audubon.org; internet www.audubon.org; f. 1905; works to conserve and restore natural ecosystems; focuses on birds, other wildlife, and their habitats for the benefit of humanity and the earth's biodiversity; 518 local chapters; 550,000 mems; Pres. and CEO DAVID YARNOLD; publs *Audubon* (6 a year), *Audubon Field Notes* (4 a year).

National Wildlife Federation: 11100 Wildlife Center Dr., Reston, VA 20190-5362; tel. (703) 438-6000; fax (703) 790-4075; internet www.nwf.org; f. 1936; conservation org.; protects and restores wildlife habitat, confronts global warming and connects with nature; 47 state affiliates; 4 m. mems; Pres. and CEO LARRY J. SCHWEIGER; Chair. STEPHEN K. ALLINGER; publs *Conservation Directory*, *International Wildlife Magazine*, *National Wildlife Magazine* (6 a year), *Ranger Rick* (10 a year), *Wild Animal Baby* (10 a year), *Your Big Backyard* (10 a year).

Nature Conservancy: Suite 100, 4245 N Fairfax Dr., Arlington, VA 22203-1606; tel. (703) 841-5300; e-mail member@tnc.org; internet nature.org; f. 1951; int. non-profit org. committed to preserving biological diversity by protecting lands and waters; 1m. mems; Pres. and CEO MARK R. TERCEK; Sec. FRANK E. LOY; Treas. MUNEER A. SATTER; publ. *Nature Conservancy* (6 a year).

Society for Developmental Biology: 9650 Rockville Pike, Bethesda, MD 20814-3998; tel. (301) 634-7815; fax (301) 634-7825; e-mail sdb@sdbonline.org; internet www .sdbonline.org; f. 1939; furthers study of devt in all organisms and at all levels; represents and promotes communication among students of devt; promotes field of developmental biology; 2,100 mems; Pres. MIKE LEVINE; Sec. MARY C. MULLINS; Treas. SALLY MOODY; publ. *Developmental Biology* (26 a year).

Society for Economic Botany: POB 299, St Louis, MO 63166-0299; tel. (314) 882-3038; e-mail seb@econbot.org; internet www .econbot.org; f. 1959; encourages scientific research, education and related activities on past, present and future uses of plants; relationship between plants and people, and to make results of such research available to scientific community; 1,000 mems; Pres. RAINER BUSSMANN; Sec. HEATHER McMILLEN; Treas. SY SOHMER; publ. *Economic Botany* (4 a year).

Society for Experimental Biology and Medicine: 130 W Pleasant Ave, Suite 334, Maywood, NJ 07607-1727; tel. (201) 962-3519; fax (201) 962-3522; e-mail sebm@inch .com; internet www.sebm.org; f. 1903; promotes investigation in biomedical sciences; 1,500 mems, 1,300 subscribers; Pres. Dr MICHAEL J. FRIEDLANDER; Exec. Dir FELICE O'GRADY; publ. *Experimental Biology and Medicine* (12 a year).

Society of Vertebrate Paleontology: 111 Deer Lake Rd, Suite 100, Deerfield, IL 60015; tel. (847) 480-9095; fax (847) 480-9282; e-mail svp@vertpaleo.org; internet www .vertpaleo.org; f. 1940; advances science of vertebrate paleontology; serves common interests and facilitates cooperation of all persons concerned with history, evolution, comparative anatomy and taxonomy of vertebrate animals; as well as field occurrence, colln and study of fossil vertebrates and the stratigraphy of the beds in which they are found; conservation and preservation of fossil sites; 2,300 mems; Exec. Dir DEBBIE TRUEBLOOD; Pres. PHILIP J. CURRIE; Sec. CHRISTOPHER J. BELL; Treas. TED J. VLAMIS; publs *Bibliography of Fossil Vertebrates* (online), *Journal of Vertebrate Paleontology* (6 a year),

Palaeontologia Electronica (2 a year, online), *SVP Memoir Series* (1 a year).

Wildlife Conservation Society: 2300 S Blvd, Bronx, NY 10460; tel. (718) 220-5100; fax (718) 220-2685; e-mail membership@wcs.org; internet www.wcs.org; f. 1895; saves wildlife and wild places worldwide through science, global conservation, education and management of world's largest system of urban wildlife parks; operates the Bronx Zoo, New York Aquarium, Central Park Zoo, Queens Zoo, Prospect Park Zoo, and c. 500 conservation field projects in over 60 nations; education programmes developed at the Bronx Zoo are in 50 states and 16 countries from K-12 grade with professional devt components; 100,000 mems; library of 6,000 vols; Chair. WARD W. WOODS; Pres. and CEO Dr STEVEN E. SANDERSON; Sec. ANDREW H. TISCH; Treas. BRIAN J. HEIDTKE; publ. *Wildlife Conservation* (6 a year).

Wildlife Management Institute: 1440 Upper Bermudian Rd, Gardners, PA 17324; tel. (717) 677-4480; internet www.wildlifemanagementinstitute.org; f. 1911; scientific and educational org. dedicated to conservation, enhancement and professional management of N America's wildlife and other natural resources; Pres. STEVEN A. WILLIAMS; publs *North American Wildlife and Natural Resources Conference Transactions* (1 a year), *Outdoor News Bulletin* (12 a year).

Wildlife Society: 5410 Grosvenor Lane, Suite 200, Bethesda, MD 20814-2144; tel. (301) 897-9770; fax (301) 530-2471; e-mail tws@wildlife.org; internet joomla.wildlife.org; f. 1937; develops and promotes sound stewardship of wildlife resources and of environments upon which wildlife and humans depend; undertakes active role in preventing human-induced environmental degradation; increases awareness and appreciation of wildlife values; seeks highest standards in all activities of wildlife profession; 9,100 mems; Exec. Dir and CEO MICHAEL HUTCHINS; publs *Journal of Wildlife Management* (8 a year), *The Wildlife Professional, The Wildlifer, Wildlife Monographs* (irregular), *Wildlife Society Bulletin* (4 a year).

Mathematical Sciences

American Mathematical Society: 201 Charles St, Providence, RI 02904-2294; tel. (401) 455-4000; fax (401) 455-4046; e-mail ams@ams.org; internet www.ams.org; f. 1888; sponsors meetings, symposia, seminars and institutes; provides employment services in the mathematical sciences; 32,000 mems; Exec. Dir Dr DONALD McCLURE; Pres. Prof. ERIC M. FRIEDLANDER; Sec. Prof. ROBERT J. DAVERMAN; Treas. JANE M. HAWKINS; publs *Abstracts of Papers Presented to the American Mathematical Society* (4 a year), *Bulletin of the American Mathematical Society* (4 a year), *Conformal Geometry and Dynamics* (electronic only), *Current Mathematical Publications* (17–18 a year), *Employment Information in the Mathematical Sciences* (5 a year), *Journal of the American Mathematical Society* (4 a year), *Mathematical Reviews* (12 a year), *Mathematics of Computation* (4 a year), *Memoirs of the American Mathematical Society* (6 a year), *Notices of the American Mathematical Society* (11 a year), *Proceedings of the American Mathematical Society* (12 a year), *Representation Theory* (electronic only), *St Petersburg Mathematical Journal* (6 a year), *Sugaku Expositions* (2 a year), *Theory of Probability and Mathematical Statistics* (2 a year), *Transactions of the American Mathematical Society* (12 a year), *Transactions of the Moscow Mathematical Society* (1 a year).

Dozenal Society of America: 5106 Hampton Ave Suite 205, St Louis, MO 63109-3115; tel. (631) 351-7456; e-mail contact@dozenal.org; internet www.dozenal.org; f. 1944 as the Duodecimal Soc. of America; educational corpn organized to conduct research and educate public in the use of base 12 in calculations, mathematics, weights and measures, and other brs of pure and applied science; 144 mems; library of 120 vols; Chair. Prof. JAY SCHIFFMAN; Pres. MICHAEL DE VLIEGER; publ. *Duodecimal Bulletin* (2 a year).

Mathematical Association of America: 1529 18th St, NW, Washington, DC 20036-1358; tel. (202) 387-5200; fax (202) 265-2384; e-mail maahq@maa.org; internet www.maa.org; f. 1915; non-profit, ind. org.; advances mathematical sciences, esp. at collegiate level; 21,000 mems; Exec. Dir TINA H. STRALEY; Pres. PAUL ZORN; Sec. BARBARA T. FAIRES; Treas. JIM DANIEL; publs *Mathematics Magazine* (5 a year), *Math Horizons* (4 a year), *The American Mathematical Monthly* (10 a year), *The College Mathematics Journal* (5 a year).

Society for Industrial and Applied Mathematics Society: 3600 Market St., 6th Fl., Philadelphia, PA 19104-2688; tel. (215) 382-9800; fax (215) 386-7999; e-mail service@siam.org; internet www.siam.org; f. 1951; promotes a better understanding of how mathematics may be used in the solution of complex problems in industry; 13,000 individual mems, 500 institutional mems; Pres. LLOYD TREFETHEN; Sec. L. PAMELA COOK; Treas. SAMUEL GUBINS; publs *SIAM review* (4 a year), 12 specialist journals, mainly 4 a year.

Physical Sciences

Acoustical Society of America: 2 Huntington Quadrangle, Suite 1N01, Melville, NY 11747-4502; tel. (516) 576-2360; fax (516) 576-2377; e-mail asa@aip.org; internet asa.aip.org; f. 1929; dedicated to increasing and diffusing knowledge of acoustics and its practical applications; 7,500 mems; Pres. MARDI C. HASTINGS; Exec. Dir CHARLES E. SCHMID; publs *Acoustics Today, Journal of the Acoustical Society of America* (12 a year), *Proceedings of Meetings on Acoustics* (online).

American Association of Petroleum Geologists: POB 979, Tulsa, OK 74101-0979; 1444 S Boulder, Tulsa, OK 74119; tel. (918) 584-2555; fax (918) 560-2665; e-mail bulletin@aapg.org; internet www.aapg.org; f. 1917; int. geological, professional geoscience org.; 31,995 mems; Exec. Dir DAVID CURTISS; Pres. PAUL WEIMER; Sec. DENISE M. COX; Treas. JAMES S. McGHAY; publs *AAPG Bulletin* (12 a year), *AAPG Explorer* (12 a year), *Environmental Geosciences* (12 a year).

American Astronomical Society: 2000 Florida Ave, NW, Suite 400, Washington, DC 20009-1231; tel. (202) 328-2010; fax (202) 234-2560; e-mail aas@aas.org; internet www.aas.org; f. 1899, inc. 1928; promotes interest in astronomy; disseminates and archives results of astronomical research; facilitates and strengthens interactions among mems through professional meetings; supports mem. divs representing specialized research and astronomical interests; represents goals of mems to the nation and the world; trains, mentors and supports next generation of astronomers; promotes increased participation of historically under-represented groups in astronomy; assists mems to develop skills in fields of education and public outreach; 7,000 mems; Exec. Officer Dr KEVIN MARVEL; Pres. DEBRA M. ELMEGREEN; publs *Astronomy Education Review* (online), *Bulletin of the American Astronomical Society, The Astro-nomical Journal* (12 a year), *The Astrophysical Journal* (36 a year).

American Chemical Society: 1155 16th St, NW, Washington, DC 20036; tel. (202) 872-4600; fax (202) 872-4615; e-mail help@acs.org; internet www.chemistry.org; f. 1876; publishes numerous scientific journals and databases, convenes major research confs and provides educational, science policy and career programmes in chemistry; 163,000 mems; Pres. NANCY B. JACKSON; Exec. Dir and CEO Dr MADELEINE JACOBS; publs *Accounts of Chemical Research, Advances in Chemistry, Analytical Chemistry, Biochemistry, Bioconjugate Chemistry, Biomacromolecules, Biotechnology Progress, Chemical Research in Toxicology, Chemical Reviews, Chemistry of Materials, Crystal Growth & Design, Energy & Fuels, Environmental Science & Technology, Industrial & Engineering Chemistry Research, Inorganic Chemistry, Journal of the American Chemical Society* (52 a year), *Journal of Agricultural and Food Chemistry, Journal of Chemical & Engineering Data, Journal of Chemical Education, Journal of Chemical Information and Modeling* (12 a year), *Journal of Chemical Theory and Computation, Journal of Medicinal Chemistry, Journal of Natural Products, Journal of Proteome Research, Langmuir, Macromolecules, Molecular Pharmaceutics, Nano Letters, Organic Letters, Organic Process Research & Development, Organometallics, The Journal of Organic Chemistry, The Journal of Physical Chemistry A, The Journal of Physical Chemistry B, The Journal of Physical Chemistry Letters.*

American Crystallographic Association, Inc.: POB 96, Ellicott Station, Buffalo, NY 14205-0096; tel. (716) 898-8690; fax (716) 898-8695; e-mail aca@hwi.buffalo.edu; internet www.amercrystalassn.org; f. 1949 by merger of American Soc. for X-Ray and Electron Diffraction with Crystallographic Soc. of America; promotes interactions among scientists who study structure of matter at atomic (or near atomic) resolution; 2,200 mems; Pres. THOMAS KOETZLE; Sec. CARRIE WILMOT; CEO WILLIAM L. DUAX; publs *Program and Abstracts* (1 a year), *Transactions* (1 a year).

American Geophysical Union: 2000 Florida Ave, NW, Washington, DC 20009-1277; tel. (202) 462-6900; fax (202) 328-0566; e-mail service@agu.org; internet www.agu.org; f. 1919; publishes journals and books; sponsors scientific meetings and a variety of other educational and scientific activities; 60,000 mems; Pres. MIKE McPHADEN; Exec. Dir and CEO CHRISTINE W. McENTEE, JR; publs *Earth Interactions* (electronic journal), *Geochemistry, Geophysics, Geosystems* (online), *Geophysical Research Letters* (26 a year), *Global Biogeochemical Cycles* (4 a year), *Journal of Advances in Modeling Earth Systems* (irregular), *Journal of Geophysical Research* (7 sections, 12 a year), *Nonlinear Processes in Geophysics* (4 a year), *Paleoceanography* (6 a year), *Radio Science* (6 a year), *Reviews of Geophysics* (4 a year), *Space Weather* (4 a year), *Tectonics* (6 a year), *Water Resources Research* (12 a year).

American Geosciences Institute: 4220 King St, Alexandria, VA 22302-1502; tel. (703) 379-2480; fax (703) 379-7563; e-mail agi@agiweb.org; internet www.agiweb.org; f. 1948; provides information services; plays a major role in strengthening geoscience education; strives to increase public understanding of the vital role the geosciences play in society's use of resources, resilience to natural hazards and interaction with environment; 49 mem. socs; Exec. Dir P. PATRICK LEAHY; Pres. Dr WAYNE D. PENNINGTON; Sec.

Dr BERRY H. TEW, JR; Treas. MICHAEL D. LAWLESS; publ. *EARTH* (12 a year).

American Institute of Chemists: 315 Chestnut St, Philadelphia, PA 19106-2702; tel. (215) 873-8224; fax (215) 629-5224; e-mail info@theaic.org; internet www.theaic .org; f. 1923; professional aspects of chemical practice, incl. nat. certification programme, involvement in governmental activities, awards, and sponsorship, through the AIC Foundation; honours top college chemistry seniors; 6,000 mems; Exec. Dir SHARON DOBSON; Pres. Dr DAVID M. MANUTA; Sec. Dr E. GERRY MEYER; Treas. Dr J. STEPHEN DUERR; publ. *The Chemist* (online).

American Institute of Physics: One Physics Ellipse, College Park, MD 20740-3843; tel. (301) 209-3100; fax (301) 209-0843; e-mail aipinfo@aip.org; internet www.aip .org; f. 1931; advances science of physics; tracks employment and education trends; Fosters connections between science and industry; promotes science in public realm; 550 student chapters; Niels Bohr Library; 95,000 mems, 18 affiliated socs, 94 corporate assocs; Chair. LOUIS J. LANZEROTTI; Exec. Dir and CEO H. FREDERICK DYLLA; publ. 46 publs, incl. *Physics Today*, journals, bulletins, translated Russian and Chinese journals, and secondary information services.

American Meteorological Society: 45 Beacon St, Boston, MA 02108-3693; tel. (617) 227-2425; fax (617) 742-8718; e-mail amsinfo@ametsoc.org; internet www.ametsoc .org; f. 1919, inc. 1920; promotes devt and dissemination of information and education on atmospheric and related oceanic and hydrologic sciences; 14,000 mems; Exec. Dir KEITH L. SEITTER; Pres. JON MALAY; Sec. and Treas. RICHARD D. ROSEN; publs *Bulletin of the American Meteorological Society* (12 a year), *Earth Interactions*, *Journal of Applied Meteorology and Climatology* (12 a year), *Journal of Atmospheric and Oceanic Technology* (12 a year), *Journal of Climate* (24 a year), *Journal of Hydrometeorology* (12 a year), *Journal of Physical Oceanography* (12 a year), *Journal of the Atmospheric Sciences* (12 a year), *Monthly Weather Review* (12 a year), *Weather and Forecasting* (6 a year), *Weather, Climate, and Society* (4 a year).

American Microscopical Society: c/o Dr John Zardus, The Citadel, 171 Moultrie St, Dept of Biology, Washington College, Chestertown, Charleston, SC 29407; tel. (843) 953-7511; fax (843) 953-7264; internet www .amicros.org; f. 1878; publishes reports of research on invertebrate biology; conducts annual meetings on research using microscopy; organizes workshops on techniques of microscopy and biology of organisms studied by microscopy; 695 mems; Pres. Dr KATHRYN A. COATES; Sec. Dr JOHN ZARDUS; Treas. Dr DAVID BRUCE CONN; publ. *Invertebrate Biology* (4 a year).

American Nuclear Society: 555 N Kensington Ave, La Grange Park, IL 60526; tel. (708) 352-6611; fax (708) 352-0499; e-mail nucleus@ans.org; internet www.ans.org; f. 1954; 17 professional divs: fusion energy, education and training, environmental sciences, isotopes and radiation, materials science and technology, mathematics and computation, nuclear criticality safety, suel cycle and waste management, human factors, nuclear reactor safety, radiation protection and shielding, power and operations, reactor physics, robotics and remote systems technology, thermal hydraulics, biology and medicine, decommissioning, decontamination and reutilization, accelerator applications; 52 local sections, 8 overseas local sections (Japan, South Korea, Latin America, Austria, Switzerland, Italy, France, Taiwan);

51 student brs; 11,000 mems; Pres. ERIC P. LOEWEN; Exec. Dir ROGER W. TILBROOK; publs *Fusion Science and Technology* (8 a year), *Nuclear Science and Engineering* (9 a year), *Nuclear Technology* (12 a year), nuclear standards.

American Pharmacists Association: 2215 Constitution Ave,NW, Washington, DC 20037; tel. (202) 628-4410; fax (202) 783-2351; e-mail infocenter@aphanet.org; internet www.pharmacist.com; f. 1852 as American Pharmaceutical Asscn; provides a forum for discussion, consensus building and policy setting for the profession of pharmacy; 60,000 mems; library of 6,000 vols; Exec. Vice-Pres. and CEO THOMAS E. MENIGHAN; Pres. MARIALICE S. BENNETT; publs *APhA Drug Infoline* (12 a year), *Journal of Pharmaceutical Sciences* (12 a year), *Journal of the American Pharmacists Association* (6 a year), *Student Pharmacist* (6 a year), *Pharmacy Today* (12 a year).

American Physical Society: 1 Physics Ellipse, College Park, MD 20740-3844; tel. (301) 209-3200; fax (301) 209-0865; e-mail exoffice@aps.org; internet www.aps.org; f. 1899; advances and diffuses knowledge of physics through research journals, scientific meetings, and education, outreach, advocacy and int. activities; 48,000 mems; Pres. BARRY C. BARISH; Exec. Officer Dr KATE P. KIRBY; publs *Physical Review A-E*, *Physical Review* (in 6 series), *Physical Review Letters* (52 a year), *Physical Review Special Topics–Accelerators and Beams* (12 a year), *Physical Review Special Topics–Physics Education Research*, *Physics* (online), *Reviews of Modern Physics* (4 a year).

American Society for Biochemistry and Molecular Biology: 11200 Rockville Pike, Suite 302, Rockville, MD 20852-3110; tel. (240) 283-6600; fax (301) 881-2080; e-mail asbmb@asbmb.org; internet www.asbmb.org; f. 1906 as American Soc. of Biological Chemists; advances science of biochemistry and molecular biology through publ. of scientific and educational journals; 12,000 mems; Exec. Dir BARBARA A. GORDON; Pres. SUZANNE R. PFEFFER; Sec. MARK A. LEMMON; Treas. MERLE S. OLSON; publs *Journal of Biological Chemistry* (52 a year), *Journal of Lipid Research* (12 a year), *Molecular and Cellular Proteomics* (12 a year).

Electrochemical Society: 65 S Main St, Bldg D, Pennington, NJ 08534-2839; tel. (609) 737-1902; fax (609) 737-2743; e-mail ecs@electrochem.org; internet www .electrochem.org; f. 1902; advances theory and practice of electrochemistry, solid-state science, and allied subjects; encourages research and dissemination of knowledge in these fields; assures availability of adequate training and education of fundamental and applied scientists and engineers in these fields; 8,000 individual mems, 100 corporate mems; Exec. Dir ROQUE J. CALVO; Pres. ESTHER TAKEUCHI; Sec. JOHNA LEDDY; Treas. CHRISTINA BOCK; publs *ECS Transactions* (online), *Electrochemical and Solid-State Letters* (12 a year, print and online), *Interface* (4 a year, print and online), *Journal of the Electrochemical Society* (12 a year, print and online).

Geochemical Society: Dept of Earth and Planetary Sciences, Washington Univ., 1 Brookings Dr., CB 1169, St Louis, MO 63130-4899; tel. (314) 935-4131; fax (314) 935-4121; e-mail gsoffice@geochemsoc.org; internet www.geochemsoc.org; f. 1955; encourages application of chemistry to solve geological and cosmological problems; 1,800 mems; Pres. SAMUEL MUKASA; Sec. EDWIN SCHAUBLE; Treas. SAM SAVIN; publs *Elements* (6 a year), *Geochemistry, Geophysics, Geosys-*

tems (online), *Geochimica et Cosmochimica Acta* (24 a year).

Geological Society of America: POB 9140, Boulder, CO 80301-9140; 3300 Penrose Place, Boulder, CO 80301-1806; tel. (303) 357-1000; fax (303) 357-1070; e-mail gsaservice@geosociety.org; internet www .geosociety.org; f. 1888; provides access to elements that are essential to the growth of earth scientists at all levels of expertise and from all sectors: academic, govt, business and industry; 24,000 mems; Pres. JOHN W. GEISSMAN; Exec. Dir and Sec. JOHN W. HESS; Treas. JONATHAN G. PRICE; publs *Environmental & Engineering Geoscience* (4 a year, online), *Geology* (12 a year), *Geosphere* (6 a year, online), *GSA Bulletin* (6 a year), *Lithosphere* (6 a year), *Memoirs* (1–2 a year).

Microscopy Society of America: 12100 Sunset Hills Rd, Suite 130, Reston, VA 20190; tel. (703) 234-4115; fax (703) 435-4390; e-mail associationmanagement@ microscopy.org; internet www.microscopy .org; f. 1942; annual meeting, presenting technical papers and exhibits; increases and diffuses knowledge of microscopy and related instruments and results obtained through their use; 2,300 mems; Pres. JANET WOODWARD; Sec. IAN ANDERSON; Treas. JOAN HUDSON; Man. Dir PETER DOHERTY; publs *Microscopy & Microanalysis* (6 a year), *Microscopy Today* (6 a year).

Mineralogical Society of America: 3635 Concorde Pkwy Suite 500, Chantilly, 20151-1110; tel. (703) 652-9950; fax (703) 652-9951; e-mail business@minsocam.org; internet www.minsocam.org; f. 1919; encourages fundamental research about natural materials; supports teaching of mineralogical concepts and procedures; encourages preservation of mineral collns, displays, mineral localities, type minerals and scientific data; 2,700 mems; Exec. Dir Dr J. ALEX SPEER; Pres. Dr MICHAEL F. HOCHELLA, JR; Sec. ANDREA M. KOZIOL; Treas. DARRELL J. HENRY; publs *Elements* (6 a year), *Reviews in Mineralogy and Geochemistry* (3–6 a year), *The American Mineralogist* (8 a year).

Oak Ridge Associated Universities: POB 117, MC100-44, Oak Ridge, TN 37831-0117; tel. (865) 576-3146; fax (865) 241-2923; e-mail communications@orau.org; internet www.orau.org; f. 1946; promotes collaborative partnerships with univs, fed. laboratories and industry; manages the Oak Ridge Institute for Science and Education for the US Dept of Energy; carries out research and devt, training and education, technical assistance activities for DOE and other fed. and private orgs; concentrates on the following major areas: science/engineering education, worldwide emergency response and training, workforce health and safety research and training, technical training systems and environmental monitoring; manages educational programmes for undergraduate, graduate and postdoctoral students and academic staff; develops training processes that encompass design, delivery and evaluation of training networks; performs radiological site investigations and verification surveys; manages Univ. Radioactive Ion Beam (UNIRIB) user facility; maintains medical, training and energy/ environment library; 101 mem univs; Pres. and CEO ANDY PAGE.

OSA—The Optical Society: 2010 Massachusetts Ave, NW, Washington, DC 20036; tel. (202) 223-8130; fax (202) 223-1096; e-mail info@osa.org; internet www.osa.org; f. 1916, present name 2008; devoted to the advancement of optics and the service of all who are interested in any aspect of that science; 16,000 mems; Pres. Prof. CHRISTO-

PHER DAINTY; CEO ELIZABETH ROGAN; publs *Advances in Optics & Photonics* (4 a year), *Applied Optics* (36 a year), *Biomedical Optics Express* (12 a year), *Journal of the Optical Society of America A* (12 a year), *Journal of the Optical Society of America B* (12 a year), *Optics Express* (26 a year), *Optics Letters* (24 a year), *Optical Materials Express* (12 a year).

Palaeontological Society: POB 9044, Boulder, CO 80301; tel. (855) 357-1032; fax (303) 357-1070; e-mail paleosoc@geosociety .org; internet www.paleosoc.org; f. 1908; publishes and disseminates palaeontological research; 550 institutional subscribers; 1,500 mems; Pres. SANDRA CARLSON; Sec. MARK A. WILSON; Treas. PETER HARRIES; publs *Journal of Paleontology* (6 a year), *Memoirs of the Paleontological Society* (irregular), *Paleobiology* (4 a year), *Palaeontologica Electronica*, *Paleontological Society Papers* (irregular), *Short Course Notes* (1 a year).

Seismological Society of America: 201 El Cerrito Plaza Professional Bldg, El Cerrito, CA 94530-4003; tel. (510) 525-5474; fax (510) 525-7204; e-mail info@seismosoc.org; internet www.seismosoc.org; f. 1906; seismology, earthquake engineering, earthquake geology; 1,900 mems; Exec. Dir SUSAN B. NEWMAN; Pres. CHRISTA VON HILLEBRANDT-ANDRADE; Sec. KEITH KNUDSEN; Treas. MITCH WITHERS; publs *Bulletin of the Seismological Society of America* (6 a year), *Seismological Research Letters* (6 a year).

SEPM Society for Sedimentary Geology: 4111 S Darlington, Suite 100, Tulsa, OK 74135-6373; tel. (918) 610-3361; fax (918) 621-1685; internet www.sepm.org; f. 1926; disseminates scientific information on sedimentology, stratigraphy, paleontology, environmental sciences, marine geology, hydrogeology and many additional related specialties; 5,000 mems; Pres. CHRIS R. FIELDING; Sec. and Treas. DIANE KAMOLA; Exec. Dir Dr HOWARD HARPER; publs *Journal of Sedimentary Research* (6 a year), *PALAIOS* (6 a year), *The Sedimentary Record* (4 a year).

Society of Economic Geologists: 7811 Shaffer Parkway, Littleton, CO 80127-3732; tel. (720) 981-7882; fax (720) 981-7874; e-mail seg@segweb.org; internet www .segweb.org; f. 1919; advances science of geology through scientific investigation of mineral deposits and mineral resources; 5,000 mems; Pres. M. STEPHENS ENDERS; Exec. Dir BRIAN G. HOAL; publ. *Economic Geology* (8 a year).

PHILOSOPHY AND PSYCHOLOGY

American Philosophical Association: Univ. of Delaware, 31 Amstel Ave, Newark, DE 19716-4797; tel. (302) 831-1112; fax (302) 831-8690; e-mail apaonline@udel.edu; internet www.apaonline.org; f. 1900; promotes exchange of ideas among philosophers; encourages creative and scholarly activity in philosophy and facilitates professional work of teachers of philosophy; 11,400 mems; Chair. MICHAEL BRATMAN; Exec. Dir DAVID SCHRADER; publ. *Proceedings and Addresses* (5 a year).

American Psychological Association: 750 First St, NE, Washington, DC 20002-4242; tel. (202) 336-5500; e-mail public .affairs@apa.org; internet www.apa.org; f. 1892; advances psychology as a science, a profession, and as a means of promoting health, education and human welfare; 154,000 mems; library of 2,500 vols; Pres. Dr DONALD BERSOFF; Exec. Vice-Pres. and CEO Dr NORMAN B. ANDERSON; publs *American Psychologist*, *Journal of Experimental Psychology: General* (4 a year), *Neuropsychology* (24 a year), and 65 others.

Metaphysical Society of America: c/o Brian Martine, Dept of Philosophy, Univ. of Alabama, Huntsville, AL 35899; tel. (205) 895-6555; fax (205) 895-6949; internet web02 .gonzaga.edu/faculty/henning/metaphysical_society/index.htm; f. 1950; studies of metaphysical problems without regard to sectarian divisions; 700 mems; Pres. EDWARD HALPER; Sec. and Treas. BRIAN MARTINE.

Philosophy of Science Association: Dept of Philosophy, Bloomsburg Univ., Bloomsburg, PA 17815; tel. (570) 389-4174; internet www.philsci.org; f. 1934; promotes research, teaching and free discussion of issues in philosophy of science from diverse standpoints; 1,000 mems; Pres. JAMES WOODWARD; Exec. Sec. and Treas. GARY HARDCASTLE; publ. *Philosophy of Science* (4 a year).

Psychometric Society: c/o Terry Ackerman, 207 Curry Bldg, POB 26171, Univ. of North Carolina at Greensboro, Greensboro, NC 27402-6170; tel. (336) 334-3474; e-mail taackerm@uncg.edu; internet www .psychometricsociety.org; f. 1935; advancement of quantitative measurement practices in psychology, education and social sciences; 800 mems; Pres. MARK WILSON; Sec. TERRY ACKERMAN; Treas. LUZ BAY; publ. *Psychometrika* (4 a year).

RELIGION, SOCIOLOGY AND ANTHROPOLOGY

African Studies Association: Rutgers Univ., Livingston Campus, 54 Joyce Kilmer Ave, Piscataway, NJ 08854-8045; tel. (848) 445-8173; fax (732) 445-1366; e-mail asapub@rci.rutgers.edu; internet www .africanstudies.org; f. 1957; encourages research and collects and disseminates information on Africa; 1,700 mems; Pres. AILI TRIPP; Exec. Dir KAREN JENKINS; publs *African Studies Review* (3 a year), *History in Africa: A Journal of Method* (1 a year).

American Academy of Religion: 825 Houston Mill Rd, NE, Suite 300, Atlanta, GA 30329-4205; tel. (404) 727-3049; fax (404) 727-7959; e-mail adminasst@aarweb.org; internet www.aarweb.org; f. 1909; inn. learned soc. and professional asscn of teachers and research scholars in the field of religion and religious studies; 10,000 mems; Exec. Dir. JOHN R. FITZMIER; Pres. KWOK PUI LAN; Sec. MICHEL DESJARDINS; Treas. DONNA BOWMAN; publ. *Journal of the American Academy of Religion (JAAR)* (4 a year).

American Anthropological Association: 2200 Wilson Blvd, Suite 600, Arlington, VA 22201-3357; tel. (703) 528-1902; fax (703) 528-3546; e-mail members@aaanet.org; internet www.aaanet.org; f. 1902; fosters and supports devt of spec. anthropological socs organized on regional or functional basis; publishes and promotes publ. of anthropological monographs and journals; encourages anthropological research; maintains effective liaison with related sciences and their orgs; 11,000 mems; Pres. VIRGINIA R. DOMINGUEZ; Sec. DEB MARTIN; Exec. Dir BILL DAVIS; publs *American Anthropologist* (4 a year), *American Ethnologist* (4 a year), *Annals of Anthropological Practice* (2 a year), *Anthropology and Education Quarterly* (4 a year), *Anthropology and Humanism* (2 a year), *Anthropology of Consciousness* (2 a year), *Anthropology of Work Review* (2 a year), *Archeological Papers of the AAA* (1 a year), *City and Society* (3 a year), *Cultural Anthropology* (4 a year), *Culture, Agriculture, Food and Environment* (2 a year), *Ethos* (4 a year), *General Anthropology* (2 a year), *Journal of Latin American and Caribbean Anthropology* (2 a year), *Journal of Linguis-tic Anthropology* (2 a year), *Medical Anthropology Quarterly* (4 a year), *Museum Anthropology* (2 a year), *North American Dialogue* (2 a year), *PoLAR: Political and Legal Anthropology Review* (2 a year), *Transforming Anthropology* (2 a year), *Visual Anthropology Review* (2 a year).

American Counseling Association: 5999 Stevenson Ave, Alexandria, VA 22304; tel. (703) 823-9800; fax (703) 823-0252; e-mail membership@counseling.org; internet www .counseling.org; f. 1952; counselling, guidance and student personnel services; divs: American College Counseling Asscn, Asscn for Counselor Education and Supervision, Nat. Career Devt Asscn, Counseling Asscn for Humanistic Education and Devet, American School Counselor Asscn, American Rehabilitation Counseling Asscn, Asscn for Assessment in Counseling, Nati. Employment Counseling Asscn, Asscn for Multicultural Counseling and Devt, Asscn for Spiritual, Ethical and Religious Values in Counseling, Int. Assocn of Addictions and Offender Counselors, American Mental Health Counselors Assocn, Assocn for Counselors and Educators in Govt, Assocn for Adult Devt and Aging, Assocn for Gay, Lesbian and Bisexual Issues in Counseling, Int. Assocn of Marriage and Family Counselors; Assocn for Creativity in Counseling; Assocn for Specialists in Group Work; Counselors for Social Justice; 50,427 mems; Pres. Dr DON W. LOCKE; Exec. Dir RICHARD YEP; publs *Counseling Outcome Research and Evaluation*, *Journal for Social Action in Counseling and Psychology*, *Journal for Specialists in Group Work*, *Journal of Creativity in Mental Health*, *Journal of LGBT Issues in Counseling*, *Journal of Mental Health Counseling*, *Measurement and Evaluation in Counseling and Development*, *Professional School Counseling*, *Rehabilitation Counseling Bulletin*, *The Family Journal*.

American Folklore Society: Mershon Center, Ohio State Univ., 1501 Neil Ave, Columbus, OH 43201-2602; tel. (614) 292-3375; fax (614) 292-2407; internet www.afsnet.org; f. 1888; asscn of people who study and communicate knowledge about folklore throughout the world; 2,200 mems; Pres. C. KURT DEWHURST; Exec. Dir TIMOTHY LLOYD; publ. *Journal of American Folklore* (4 a year).

American Oriental Society: Hatcher Graduate Library, Univ. of Michigan, Ann Arbor, MI 48109-1190; internet www.umich .edu/~aos; f. 1842; encourages basic research in the languages and literatures of Asia incl. archaeology, biography, epigraphy, linguistics, literary criticism, paleography, philology, textual criticism, and the history of the intellectual and imaginative aspects of Oriental civilizations, esp. of art and folklore, philosophy and religion; 1,350 mems; library of 22,000 vols; Pres. ROBERT JOE. CUTTER; Sec. and Treas. JONATHAN RODGERS; publ. *Journal of American Oriental Society* (4 a year).

American Society for Ethnohistory: Dept of Anthropology, McGraw Hall, Cornell Univ., Ithaca, NY 14853; tel. (607) 277-0109; internet www.ethnohistory.org; f. 1954 as Ohio Valley Historic Indian Conf., present 1966; scholarly org. that studies histories of cultures and socs in all areas of the world; 1,200 mems; Pres. KEVIN TERRACIANO; Sec. LARRY NESPER; Treas. CHARLOTTE GRADIE; publ. *Ethnohistory* (4 a year).

American Sociological Association: 1430 K St, NW, Suite 600, Washington, DC 20005; tel. (202) 383-9005; fax (202) 638-0882; e-mail executive.office@asanet.org; internet www.asanet.org; f. 1905; non-profit asscn; articulates policy and implement programmes likely to have broadest possible impact for sociology now and in future; 14,000 mems; Pres. ERIK OLIN WRIGHT; Sec. CATHERINE BERHEIDE; Exec. Officer SALLY T. HILLSMAN; publs *American Sociological Review* (6 a year), *City and Community* (4 a year), *Contemporary Sociology* (6 a year), *Contexts* (4 a year), *Journal of Health and Social Behavior* (4 a year), *Social Psychology Quarterly*, *Sociological Methodology* (1 a year), *Sociological Theory* (4 a year), *Sociology of Education* (4 a year), *Teaching Sociology* (4 a year).

Association for Asian Studies, Inc.: 825 Victors Way, Suite 310, Ann Arbor, MI 48108; tel. (734) 665-2490; fax (734) 665-3801; e-mail postmaster@aasianst.org; internet www.aasianst.org; f. 1941; scholarly, non-political, non-profit professional asscn open to all persons interested in Asia; 8,000 mems; Pres. GAIL HERSHATTER; Exec. Dir MICHAEL PASCHAL; publs *Bibliography of Asian Studies Online* (4 a year, electronic database), *Education about Asia* (3 a year), *Journal of Asian Studies* (4 a year).

Association for the Study of African American Life and History: Howard Center, 2225 Georgia Ave, NW, Suite 331, Washington, DC 20059; tel. (202) 238-5910; fax (202) 986-1506; e-mail info@asalh.net; internet www.asalh.org; f. 1915; promotes research, preservation, interpretation and dissemination of information about Black life, history and culture to global community; 2,200 mems; Pres. Dr JAMES STEWART; Sec. ZENDE CLARK; Treas. TROY THORNTON; Exec. Dir SYLVIA Y. CYRUS; publs *Black History Bulletin* (2 a year), *Fire!!! The Multimedia Journal of Black Studies*, *Journal of African American History* (4 a year), *The Woodson Review* (1 a year).

National Institute of Social Sciences: 161 E 91st St, New York, NY 10128-2018; tel. (212) 831-0560; f. 1899; 850 mems; Pres. J. SINCLAIR ARMSTRONG; Sec. BRUCE E. BALDING.

Pacific Sociological Association: Dept of Sociology, San Diego State Univ., 5500 Campanile Dr., San Diego, CA 92182-4423; tel. (619) 594-5522; fax (619) 594-1325; e-mail pacificsoc@csus.edu; internet www.pacificsoc.org; f. 1929 as Pacific Southwest Sociological Soc.; advances scholarly research on all social processes and areas of social life; promotes high quality teaching of sociological knowledge; mentors next generation of sociologists; 1,200 mems; Exec. Dir DEAN S. DORN; publ. *Sociological Perspectives* (4 a year).

Population Association of America: 8630 Fenton St, Suite 722, Silver Spring, MD 20910-3812; tel. (301) 565-6710; fax (301) 565-7850; e-mail membersvc@popassoc.org; internet www.populationassociation.org; f. 1930, fmrly American Nat. Cttee of the Int. Union for the Scientific Study of Population (f. 1927); non-profit, scientific, professional org. that promotes research on population issues; 3,000 mems; Exec. Dir STEPHANIE DUDLEY; Pres. DAVID A. LAM; Sec. and Treas. ANN E. BIDDLECOM; publ. *Demography* (4 a year).

Population Council: 1 Dag Hammarskjold Plaza, Ninth Fl., New York, NY 10017; tel. (212) 339-0500; fax (212) 755-6052; e-mail pubinfo@popcouncil.org; internet www.popcouncil.org; f. 1952; seeking to improve the well-being and reproductive health of current and future generations around the world and to help achieve a humane, equitable and sustainable balance between people and resources; conducts research worldwide to improve policies, programmes and products in 3 areas (HIV/AIDS; poverty, gender and youth; reproductive health); conducts

fundamental biomedical research in reproduction; develops contraceptives and other products for improvement of reproductive health; conducts studies to improve the quality and outreach of services related to family planning, HIV/AIDS and reproductive health; carries out research on reproductive health and behaviour, family structure and function, causes and consequences of population growth; works to strengthen professional resources in developing countries through collaborative research, awards, fellowships and training; Pres. Dr PETER J. DONALDSON; Exec. Dir BABATUNDE OSOTIMEHIN; Chief Financial Officer and Treas. SCOTT NEWMAN; Gen. Counsel and Sec. PATRICIA C. VAUGHAN; publs *Population and Development Review* (4 a year), *Studies in Family Planning* (4 a year).

Religious Research Association: 618 SW 2nd Ave, Galva, IL 61434-1912; tel. (309) 932-2727; fax (309) 932-2282; e-mail william_swatos@baylor.edu; internet rra.hartsem.edu; f. 1951 as Religious Research Fellowship; increases understanding of the function of religion in persons and soc. through application of social scientific and other scholarly methods; promotes religious research; cooperates with other socs interested in study of religion; meets annually in conjunction with the Soc. for the Scientific Study of Religion; 325 mems; Pres. Dr JOHN A. BARTKOWSKI; Sec. MARJORIE ROYLE; Treas. DAVID ROOZEN; Exec. Officer Dr WILLIAM H. SWATOS, JR; publ. *Review of Religious Research* (4 a year).

Russell Sage Foundation: 112 E 64th St, New York, NY 10065; tel. (212) 750-6000; fax (212) 371-4761; e-mail info@rsage.org; internet www.russellsage.org; f. 1907; promotes improvement of social and living conditions in the USA; supports projects on the future of work, immigration and the social psychology of cultural contact; library of 2,000 vols; Chair. ROBERT E. DENHAM; Pres. ERIC WANNER; Sec. PATRICIA WOODFORD; Treas. SHELLEY E. TAYLOR.

Society for Applied Anthropology: POB 2436, Oklahoma City, OK 73101-2436; tel. (405) 843-5113; fax (405) 843-8553; e-mail info@sfaa.net; internet www.sfaa.net; f. 1941; application of the social and behavioural sciences to contemporary problems; 3,000 mems; Exec. Dir Dr JUDE THOMAS MAY; Pres. MERRILL EISENBERG; Sec. SUSAN CHARNLEY; Treas. SHARON D. MORRISON; publs *Human Organization* (4 a year), *Practicing Anthropology* (4 a year).

Society for the Scientific Study of Religion: c/o Dr Arthur E. Farnsley, II, Indiana Univ.—Purdue Univ. Indianapolis: Center for the Study of Religion and American Culture, Cavanaugh Hall 417, 425 Univ. Blvd, Indianapolis, IN 46202-5140; tel. (317) 278-6491; fax (607) 871-2085; e-mail sssr@iupui.edu; internet www.sssrweb.org; f. 1949; dedicated to research and scholarly publs relating to religious phenomena; examining consequences of religious beliefs on individual and social behaviour, impact of religious orgs on other instns and problems of continuity and change within religious groups; c. 1,500 mems; Pres. JAMES BECKFORD; Sec. KORIE EDWARDS; Treas. JAMES CAVENDISH; Exec. Officer ARTHUR FARNSLEY; publ. *Journal for the Scientific Study of Religion* (4 a year).

Society for the Study of Evolution: c/o Judy Stone, Dept of Biology, Colby College, Waterville, ME 04901; tel. (207) 859-5736; fax (207) 859-5705; internet www.evolutionsociety.org; f. 1946; promotes study of organic evolution and integration of various fields of science concerned with evolu-

tion; 3,000 mems; Pres. Prof. JERRY COYNE; publ. *Evolution* (12 a year).

TECHNOLOGY

American Ceramic Society: POB 6136, Westerville, OH 43086-6136; 600 N Cleveland Ave., Suite 210, Westerville, Ohio 43082; tel. (866) 721-3322; fax (240) 396-5637; e-mail customerservice@ceramics.org; internet www.ceramics.org; f. 1898; advances study, understanding and use of ceramics and related materials; 9,500 mems; library of 11,000 vols; Pres. GEORGE G. WICKS; Exec. Dir CHARLIE SPAHR; publs *Bulletin* (12 a year), *Ceramic Engineering and Science Proceedings* (5 a year), *Ceramic Source* (1 a year), *International Journal of Applied Ceramic Technology* (6 a year), *International Journal of Applied Glass Science* (4 a year), *Journal of the American Ceramic Society* (12 a year).

American Council of Engineering Companies: 1015 15th St, NW, 8 Fl., Washington, DC 20005-2605; tel. (202) 347-7474; fax (202) 898-0068; e-mail acec@acec.org; internet www.acec.org; f. 1909, fmrly as American Institute of Consulting Engineers; represents engineering industries of USA; 5,800 mems; Chair. TERRY F. NEIMEYER; Pres. and CEO DAVID A. RAYMOND; publs *American Consulting Engineer*, *Directory*, *Engineering Inc.*

American Institute of Aeronautics and Astronautics: 1801 Alexander Bell Dr., Suite 500, Reston, VA 20191-4344; tel. (703) 264-7500; fax (703) 264-7551; internet www.aiaa.org; f. 1963 by merger of American Rocket Soc. (f. 1930) with Institute of Aerospace Science (f. 1932); fenables global movement of people and goods; leads global acquisition and dissemination of information and data; advances nat. security interests; provides source of scientific progress and inspiration by pushing the boundaries of exploration and innovation; 31,000 mems; Pres. Dr BRIAN DAILEY; Exec. Dir ROBERT DICKMAN; publs *AIAA Journal* (12 a year), *AIAA Student Journal* (4 a year, online), *Journal of Aerospace Computing, Information and Communication* (12 a year, online only), *Journal of Aircraft* (24 a year), *Journal of Guidance, Control and Dynamics* (24 a year), *Journal of Propulsion and Power* (24 a year), *Journal of Spacecraft and Rockets* (24 a year), *Journal of Thermophysics and Heat Transfer* (4 a year).

American Institute of Chemical Engineers: 3 Park Ave, New York, NY 10016-5991; tel. (203) 702-7660; fax (203) 775-5177; e-mail xpress@aiche.org; internet www.aiche.org; f. 1908; org. for chemical engineering professionals; provides access to information on recognized and promising chemical engineering processes and methods; 40,000 mems; Exec. Dir JUNE WISPELWEY; Pres. MARIA K. BURKA; Sec. KIMBERLY L. OGDEN; Treas. ANDRE R. DA COSTA; publs *AIChE Journal* (12 a year), *Biotechnology Progress* (6 a year), *Chemical Engineering Faculty Directory* (1 a year), *Chemical Engineering Progress* (12 a year), *Environmental Progress & Sustainable Energy* (4 a year), *Process Safety Progress* (4 a year).

American Institute of Mining, Metallurgical and Petroleum Engineers: 12999 E Adam Aircraft Circle, Englewood, CO 80112; tel. (303) 325-5185; fax (888) 702-0049; e-mail aime@aimehq.org; internet www.aimehq.org; f. 1871; has 4 mem socs; 130,000 mems; library of 550 vols; Pres. Dr BRAJENDRA MISHRA; Exec. Dir L. MICHELE LAWRIE-MUNRO.

American Iron and Steel Institute: 1140 Connecticut Ave, NW, Suite 705, Washington, DC 20036; tel. (202) 452-7100; internet www.steel.org; f. 1855, fmrly American Iron Asscn, present status 1908, present location 1974; advocates for public policies that support a competitive environment for domestic manufacturing; provides high-quality, value-added products to a wide array of customers; leads the world in innovation and technology in production of steel; produces steel in safe and environmentally friendly manner; increases market for North American steel in both traditional and innovative applications; 31 corporate mems; Chair. JOHN SURMA; Pres. and CEO THOMAS J. GIBSON.

American National Standards Institute: 25 W 43rd St, Fourth Fl., New York, NY 10036; tel. (212) 642-4900; fax (212) 398-0023; e-mail membership@ansi.org; internet www.ansi.org; f. 1918; coordinates devt of voluntary nat. standards; approves American Nat. Standards, and represents US interests in the ISO and the IEC; 125,000 mem companies; Chair. Dr ARTHUR E. COTE; Pres. and CEO S. JOE BHATIA; publs *Standards Action* (52 a year), *The ANSI Reporter* (4 a year).

American Society for Engineering Education: 1818 N St, NW, Suite 600, Washington, DC 20036-2479; tel. (202) 331-3500; fax (202) 265-8504; e-mail aseeexec@asee.org; internet www.asee.org; f. 1893; promotes improvement of higher and continuing education for engineers and engineering technologists, incl. teaching, counselling, research, ethics, etc.; 12,000 individual mems, 500 institutional mems; Exec. Dir and Sec. NORMAN FORTENBERRY; Pres. DON P. GIDDENS; publs *Advances in Engineering Education* (1 a year), *Chemical Engineering Education Journal* (4 a year), *Computers in Education Journal* (4 a year), *Engineering Design Graphics Journal* (1 a year, online), *Journal of Engineering Education* (4 a year), *Journal of Engineering Technology* (2 a year), *Prism* (12 a year), *Profiles of Engineering and Engineering Technology Colleges* (1 a year), *The Engineering Economist* (4 a year).

American Society for Photogrammetry and Remote Sensing: 5410 Grosvenor Lane, Suite 210, Bethesda, MD 20814-2160; tel. (301) 493-0290; fax (301) 493-0208; e-mail asprs@asprs.org; internet www.asprs.org; f. 1934; aerial photography, photogrammetry, photo-interpretation, remote sensing, geographic information systems (GIS), surveying, mapping, cartography; 6,000 mems; Pres. GARY R. FLORENCE; Exec. Dir and Sec. JAMES R. PLASKER; Treas. Dr DONALD T. LAUER; publ. *Photogrammetric Engineering and Remote Sensing* (12 a year, in print and online).

American Society of Civil Engineers: 1801 Alexander Bell Dr., Reston, VA 20191-4400; tel. (703) 295-6300; fax (703) 295-6222; internet www.asce.org; f. 1852; works for advancement of technology to enhance quality, knowledge, competitiveness, sustainability and environmental stewardship; 140,000 mems; Pres. ANDREW W. HERRMANN; Exec. Dir and Sec. PATRICK J. NATALE; Treas. MICHAEL H. WENNING; publs *ASCE* (12 a year), *Journal of Aerospace Engineering* (4 a year), *Journal of Architectural Engineering* (4 a year), *Journal of Energy Engineering* (3 a year), *International Journal of Geomechanics* (4 a year), and 28 online journals, *Publications Information* (6 a year).

American Society of Heating, Refrigerating and Air-Conditioning Engineers: 1791 Tullie Circle, NE, Atlanta, GA 30329; tel. (404) 636-8400; fax (404) 321-5478; e-mail ashrae@ashrae.org; internet www.ashrae.org; f. 1894 by merger of American

Soc. of Heating and Ventilating Engineers with American Soc. of Refrigerating Engineers; advances arts and sciences of heating, ventilation, air conditioning and refrigeration to serve humanity and promote a sustainable world through research, standards writing, publishing and continuing education; 51,000 mems; Pres. RONALD JARNAGIN; Exec. Vice-Pres. JEFF H. LITTLETON; Treas. WILLIAM BAHNFLETH; publs *ASHRAE Journal* (12 a year), *ASHRAE Handbook* (1 a year), *ASHRAE Transactions* (2 a year), *High Performing Buildings* (4 a year), *HVAC&R Research* (6 a year).

American Society of Mechanical Engineers: 3 Park Ave, New York, NY 10016-5990; tel. (973) 882-1170; fax (973) 882-1717; e-mail infocentral@asme.org; internet www.asme.org; f. 1880; enables collaboration, knowledge sharing and skill devt across all engineering disciplines; 120,000 mems; Exec. Dir THOMAS G. LOUGHLIN; Pres. VICTORIA ROCKWELL; Sec. and Treas. WILBUR J. MARNER; publs *Applied Mechanics Reviews* (12 a year), *Journal of Nanotechnology in Engineering and Medicine* (4 a year), *Mechanical Engineering* (12 a year), *Transactions* (divided into 17 periodicals, each published 4 times a year): *Biomechanical Engineering, Dynamic Systems, Engineering for Industry, Electronic Packaging, Energy Resources Technology, Engineering for Gas Turbines and Power, Engineering Materials and Technology, Fluids Engineering, Heat Transfer Mechanisms, Journal of Applied Mechanics, Manufacturing Review Measurement and Control, Pressure Vessel Technology, Solar Energy Engineering, Tribology, Transmissions and Automationin Design, Turbomachinery, Vibration and Acoustics.*

American Society of Naval Engineers: 1452 Duke St, Alexandria, VA 22314-3458; tel. (703) 836-6727; fax (703) 836-7491; e-mail asnehq@navalengineers.org; internet www.navalengineers.org; f. 1888; conceives, designs, develops, tests, constructs, outfits, operates and maintains complex naval and maritime ships, submarines and aircraft and their associated systems and subsystems; 5,000 mems; Pres. RONALD K. KISS; Exec. Dir, Sec. and Treas. Capt. (Retd) DENNIS K. KRUSE; publ. *Naval Engineers Journal* (4 a year).

American Welding Society: 550 NW Le Jeune Rd, Miami, FL 33126; tel. (305) 443-9353; fax (305) 443-7559; e-mail education@aws.org; internet www.aws.org; f. 1919, present location 1971; welding education seminars and confs, qualification and certification, annual int. exposition; 66,000 mems; Pres. JOHN L. MENDOZA; Exec. Dir R. W. SHOCK; publs *Inspection Trends* (4 a year), *Welding Journal* (12 a year), *Welding Handbook* (every 3 years).

ASM International: 9639 Kinsman Rd, Materials Park, OH 44073-0002; tel. (440) 338-5151; fax (440) 338-4634; e-mail memberservicecenter@asminternational.org; internet www.asminternational.org; f. 1913 as The Steel Treaters Club; technical soc. concerned with advanced materials technology; 36,000 mems; Pres. Prof. Dr CHRISTOPHER BERNDT; Man. Dir STANLEY C. THEOBALD; Treas. ROBERT FULTON; publs *Advanced Materials and Processes* (12 a year), *Alloy Digest* (12 a year), *Electronic Device Failure Analysis, International Materials Reviews* (6 a year, with Institute of Materials), *Journal of Failure Analysis and Prevention, Journal of Materials Engineering and Performance* (6 a year), *Journal of Phase Equilibria and Diffusion* (6 a year), *Journal of Thermal Spray Technology* (4 a year), *Metallography, Microstructure, and*

Analysis, Metallurgical Transactions A and B (6 a year) (with TMS–AIME) (12 a year).

Association for Iron and Steel Technology: 186 Thorn Hill Rd, Warrendale, PA 15086-7528; tel. (724) 814-3000; fax (724) 814-3001; e-mail memberservices@aist.org; internet www.aistech.org; attached to American Institute of Mining Metallurgical and Petroleum Engineers; holds int. confs, expositions and technical presentations concerning steel-related technologies; 11,268 mems; Exec. Dir RONALD E. ASHBURN; publ. *Iron and Steel maker* (12 a year).

Association of Consulting Chemists and Chemical Engineers: POB 902, Murray Hill, NJ 07974-0902; tel. and fax (908) 464-3182; e-mail accce@chemconsult.org; internet www.chemconsult.org; f. 1928; non-profit membership corpn; consultants serving chemical and related industries with expertise based on a wide variety of technical and business knowledge; 160 mems; Pres. Dr JOSPEH V. PORCELLI; Exec. Dir Dr JOHN BONACCI; publ. *Consulting Services Directory.*

ASTM International: 100 Barr Harbor Dr., POB C700, W Conshohocken, PA 19428-2959; tel. (610) 832-9500; fax (610) 832-9555; e-mail service@astm.org; internet www.astm.org; f. 1898 as American Section of the Int. Asscn for Testing and Materials, fmrly American Soc. for Testing and Materials, present name 2001; non-profit org. providing a global forum for the devt and publ. of voluntary consensus standards for materials, products, systems and services; 30,000 mems; Chair. CATHERINE H. PILARZ; Pres. JAMES A. THOMAS; publs *Cement, Concrete and Aggregates, Geotechnical Testing Journal, Journal of ASTM International, Journal of Composites, Technology and Research, Journal of Forensic Sciences, Journal of Testing and Evaluation.*

Edison Electric Institute: 701 Pennsylvania Ave, NW, Washington, DC 20004-2696; tel. (202) 508-5000; fax (202) 508-5360; e-mail news@eei.org; internet www.eei.org; f. 1933; provides public policy leadership, critical industry data, market opportunities, strategic business intelligence, one-of-a-kind confs and forums; 390 mems; Chair. THOMAS F. FARRELL, II; Exec. Dir RICHARD S. TEMPCHIN; Pres. THOMAS R. KUHN; Corporate Sec. EDWARD H. COMER; Treas. JOHN S. SCHLENKER; publ. *Electric Perspectives* (6 a year).

Illuminating Engineering Society: 120 Wall St, 17th Fl., New York, NY 10005-4001; tel. (212) 248-5000; fax (212) 248-5017; e-mail ies@ies.org; internet www.ies.org; f. 1906; dedicated to promoting the art and science of quality lighting to its mems, allied professional orgs and public; 8,000 mems; Pres. DENIS LAVOIE; publs *LEUKOS* (4 a year, online, 1 a year, printed compilation), *LD+A* (12 a year).

Industrial Designers Society of America: 45195 Business Court, Suite 250, Dulles, VA 20166-6717; tel. (703) 707-6000; fax (703) 787-8501; e-mail idsa@idsa.org; internet www.idsa.org; f. 1965; advances profession of industrial design through education, information, community and advocacy; organizes confs; 3,300 mems; Chair. GEORGE MCCAIN; Sec. and Treas. PETER BRESSLER; CEO CLIVE ROUX; Exec. Dir BOB SCHWARTZ; publ. *Innovation* (4 a year).

Institute of Electrical and Electronics Engineers: 3 Park Ave, 17th Fl., New York, NY 10016-5997; tel. (212) 419-7900; fax (212) 752-4929; e-mail society-info@ieee.org; internet www.ieee.org; f. 1884; serves professionals involved in all aspects of electrical, electronic and computing fields and related areas of science and technology that underlie modern civilization; 395,000 mems; Pres. and

CEO Dr MOSHE KAM; Sec. Prof. ROGER D. POLLARD; Treas. HAROLD L. FLESCHER; Exec. Dir Dr E. JAMES PRENDERGAST; publs *IEEE Journal of Selected Topics in Quantum Electronics* (1 a year), *IEEE Potentials* (12 a year), *Journal of Selected Topics in Signal Processing (J-STSP)*, *Proceedings* (12 a year), *Society and Council Transactions*.

Institute of Food Technologists: 525 W Van Buren, Suite 1000, Chicago, IL 60607; tel. (312) 782-8424; fax (312) 782-8348; e-mail info@ift.org; internet www.ift.org; f. 1939; wadvocates for food science and acts as catalyst for change around the world; educates media and policy makers and works with govts to shape regulations; 26,000 mems; Pres. ROGER CLEMENS; publs *Comprehensive Reviews in Food Science and Food Safety* (6 a year), *Food Technology* (12 a year), *Journal of Food Science* (12 a year, online), *Journal of Food Science Education* (4 a year).

Institute of Industrial Engineers: 3577 Parkway Lane, Suite 200, Norcross, GA 30092; tel. (770) 449-0460; fax (770) 441-3295; internet www.iienet.org; f. 1948 as American Institute of Industrial Engineers, present name 1981; provides leadership for application, education, training, research and development of industrial engineering; 30,000 mems; Pres. G. DON TAYLOR; Sec. JESSICA O. MATSON; Treas. DOUGLAS R. RABENECK; CEO and Exec. Dir DON H. GREENE; publs *IIE Transactions* (12 a year), *IIE Transactions on Healthcare Systems Engineering* (4 a year), *IIE Transactions on Occupational Ergonomics and Human Factors* (4 a year), *Industrial Engineer* (12 a year), *Industrial Management* (6 a year), *Journal of Enterprise Transformation* (4 a year), *The Engineering Economist* (4 a year).

International Communication Association: 1500 21st St, NW, Washington, DC 20036; tel. (202) 955-1444; fax (202) 955-1448; e-mail icahdq@icahdq.org; internet www.icahdq.org; f. 1950 as Nat. Soc. for the Study of Communication; brings together academics and professionals concerned with research and application of human communication theory; officially associated with the United Nations as a non-governmental asscn (NGO); 4,300 mems; Pres. LARRY GROSS; Exec. Dir MICHAEL L. HALEY; publs *Communication, Culture, & Critique*, *Communication Theory* (4 a year), *Human Communication Research* (4 a year), *Journal of Communication* (4 a year), *Journal of Computer-Mediated Communication*, *The Communication Yearbook* (1 a year).

International Society of Automation (ISA): POB 12277, 67 Alexander Dr., Research Triangle Park, NC 27709; tel. (919) 549-8411; fax (919) 549-8288; e-mail info@isa.org; internet www.isa.org; f. 1945 as Instrument Soc. of America; develops standards; certifies industry professionals; provides education and training; publishes books and technical articles; hosts confs and exhibitions for automation professionals; 30,000 mems; CEO ROB RENNER; Exec. Dir PATRICK GOUHIN; Pres. KIM MILLER DUNN; publs *InTech* (12 a year), *ISA Directory of Automation* (1 a year), *ISA Transactions* (4 a year).

Markle Foundation: 10 Rockefeller Pl., 16th Fl., New York, NY 10020-1903; tel. (212) 713-7600; fax (212) 765-9690; e-mail info@markle.org; internet www.markle.org; f. 1927; seeks to improve mass media and realize the potential of communications technology; addresses critical public needs, particularly in the areas of health and nat. security; collaborates with innovators and thought leaders from the public and private

sectors whose expertise lies in the areas of information technology, privacy, civil liberties; 25 mems; Chair. LEWIS B. KADEN; Pres. ZOË BAIRD BUDINGER; Man. Dir and Chief Financial Officer KAREN D. BYERS.

Minerals, Metals & Materials Society: 184 Thorn Hill Rd, Warrendale, PA 15086-7514; tel. (724) 776-9000; fax (724) 776-3770; e-mail tmsgeneral@tms.org; internet www.tms.org; attached to American Institute of Mining, Metallurgical and Petroleum Engineers; professional org. dealing with minerals processing and primary metals production; basic research and advanced applications of different materials; 10,000 mems; Pres. GARRY W. WARREN; Sec. and Exec. Dir Dr WARREN HUNT, JR; publs *Journal of Electronic Materials* (12 a year), *Journal of Metals* (12 a year), *Metallurgical and Materials Transactions A* (12 a year), *Metallurgical and Materials Transactions B* (12 a year).

National Society of Professional Engineers: 1420 King St, Alexandria, VA 22314-2794; tel. (703) 684-2800; fax (703) 836-4875; e-mail memserv@nspe.org; internet www.nspe.org; f. 1934; professional aspects of engineering; administers licensure and licensure preparation; operates a Board of Ethical Review; 45,000 mems; Pres. CHRISTOPHER M. STONE; Exec. Dir and Sec. LAWRENCE A. JACOBSON; Treas. LEANNE H. PANDURE; publ. *Engineering Times* (12 a year).

Society for Mining, Metallurgy & Exploration: tel. (303) 948-4200; fax (303) 973-3845; e-mail sme@smenet.org; internet www.smenet.org; attached to American Institute of Mining, Metallurgical and Petroleum Engineers; int. soc. of professionals in minerals industry; 8 divs: coal and energy, environmental, industrial minerals and aggregates, mineral and metallurgical processing, mining and exploration, Underground Construction Asscn (UCA), Int. Marine Minerals Soc. (IMMS) and woman's auxiliary to the AIME (WAAIME); 14,000 mems; Pres. JOHN N. MURPHY; Exec. Dir DAVID L. KANAGY; publs *Minerals & Metallurgical Processing* (4 a year), *Mining Engineering* (12 a year), *Transactions* (1 a year), *Tunneling and Underground Construction (T&UC)* (4 a year).

Society for the History of Technology: c/o Dept of Science, Technology & Soc., Univ. of Virginia, POB 400744, Charlottesville, VA 22904-4744; tel. (434) 987-6230; fax (434) 975-2190; e-mail shot@virginia.edu; internet www.historyoftechnology.org; f. 1958; concerned with history of technological devices and processes, relations of technology with science, politics, social change, the arts and humanities, and economics; affiliated to the American Asscn for the Advancement of Science, the American Council of Learned Socs; 1,500 mems; Pres. RON KLINE; Sec. BERNIE CARLSON; Treas. HUGH GORMAN; publ. *Technology and Culture* (4 a year).

Society of Automotive Engineers: 400 Commonwealth Dr., Warrendale, PA 15096-0001; tel. (724) 776-4841; fax (724) 776-0790; e-mail magazines@sae.org; internet www.sae.org; f. 1905; global body of scientists, engineers, and practitioners that advances self-propelled vehicle and system knowledge in a neutral forum for the benefit of soc.; 128,000 mems; Pres. RICHARD E. KLEINE; Sec. Dr DAVID L. SCHUTT; Treas. CAROL STORY; publs *Aerospace Engineering* (12 a year), *Automotive Engineering International* (12 a year), *Off-Highway Engineering* (6 a year), *SAE Handbook* (1 a year), *SAE Transactions* (1 a year), *SAE Update* (12 a year), *Vehicle Electrification*.

Society of Manufacturing Engineers: POB 930, Dearborn, MI 48121-0930; 1 SME

Dr., Dearborn, MI 48128; tel. (313) 425-3000; fax (313) 425-3400; e-mail communications@sme.org; internet www.sme.org; f. 1932 as Soc. of Tool Engineers, present name 1969; advances scientific knowledge in the field of manufacturing and applies its resources to research, writing, publishing and disseminating information; 25,000 mems; library of 7,000 vols; Pres. LaROUX GILLESPIE; Sec. and Treas. MICHAEL F. MOLNAR; Exec. Dir and Gen. Man. MARK C. TOMLINSON; publs *Composites in Manufacturing* (4 a year), *Electronics Manufacturing Engineering* (4 a year), *Finishing Line* (4 a year), *Forming and Fabricating* (12 a year), *Integrated Design and Manufacturing* (12 a year), *Journal of Manufacturing Processes* (4 a year), *Journal of Manufacturing Systems* (4 a year), *Machining Technology* (4 a year), *Plastics Insights* (4 a year), *Rapid Prototyping* (4 a year), *Robotics Today* (4 a year), *Transactions*, *Vision* (4 a year).

Society of Naval Architects & Marine Engineers: 601 Pavonia Ave, Suite 400, Jersey City, NJ 07306; tel. (201) 798-4800; fax (201) 798-4975; internet www.sname.org; f. 1893; encourages exchange and recording of information; sponsors applied research; offers career guidance; supports education; enhances professional status and integrity of its membership; 10,000 mems; Pres. EDWARD N. COMSTOCK; Exec. Dir ERIK W. SEITHER; publs *Journal of Ship Production and Design* (4 a year), *Journal of Ship Research* (4 a year), *Marine Technology* (4 a year).

Society of Petroleum Engineers: 222 Palisades Creek Dr., Richardson, TX 75080-2040; tel. (972) 952-9393; fax (972) 952-9435; e-mail spedal@spe.org; internet www.spe.org; f. 1957, inc. 1985; collects, disseminates and exchanges technical knowledge concerning exploration, devt and production of oil and gas resources and related technologies; 97,191 mems; Pres. GANESH C. THAKUR; Exec. Dir MARK A. RUBIN; publs *Journal of Canadian Petroleum Technology* (12 a year), *Oil and Gas Facilities* (6 a year), *SPE Drilling & Completion* (4 a year, online), *SPE Economics & Management* (4 a year, online), *SPE Journal* (4 a year), *SPE Production & Operations* (4 a year), *SPE Projects, Facilities & Construction* (4 a year), *SPE Reservoir Evaluation & Engineering* (6 a year).

Society of Rheology: c/o A. Jeffrey Giacomin, Rheology Research Center, Univ. of Wisconsin, Madison, WI 53706; tel. (608) 262-7473; fax (608) 265-2316; internet www.rheology.org; f. 1929; study of those properties of materials which determine their response to mechanical force; 1,700 mems; Pres. A. JEFFREY GIACOMIN; Sec. ALBERT CO; publs *Journal of Rheology* (6 a year), *Rheology Bulletin* (2 a year).

Research Institutes
GENERAL

Albert Schweitzer Institute: 275 Mount Carmel Ave, Hamden, CT 06518; tel. (203) 582-3144; fax (203) 582-8478; e-mail schweitzer@quinnipiac.edu; internet www.quinnipiac.edu/institutes-and-centers/albert-schweitzer-institute; f. 1984 as Albert Schweitzer Memorial Foundation, present status 2002; attached to Quinnipiac Univ.; focuses on health, humanitarian and peace efforts; supports health care devt in underserved areas; Exec. Dir DAVID T. IVES.

Getty Research Institute: Suite 1100, 1200 Getty Center Dr., Los Angeles, CA 90049-1688; tel. (310) 440-7335; fax (310) 440-7778; e-mail reference@getty.edu;

internet www.getty.edu/research; f. 1983; operating programme of the J. Paul Getty Trust; furthers knowledge and advances understanding of the visual arts through its expertise, its active collecting programme, public programmes, institutional collaborations, exhibitions, publs, digital services and residential scholars programme; library of 1,000,000 vols, incl. reference rare materials, serials and auction catalogues; Dir Prof. THOMAS W. GAEHTGENS; Deputy Dir ANDREW PERCHUK; Assoc. Dir GAIL FEIGENBAUM; Asst Dir DAVID FARNETH; Asst Dir KATHLEEN SALOMON; publ. *Getty Research Journal*.

Institute for the Arts and Humanities: Ihlseng Cottage, University Park, PA 16802; tel. (814) 865-0495; fax (814) 863-8349; e-mail arts-humanities@psu.edu; internet www.research.psu.edu/iah; f. 1966; attached to Pennsylvania State Univ.; sareas of research incl: philosophy, music, history, dance, comparative literature, landscape architecture; Dir Dr MICHAEL BÉRUBÉ.

National Humanities Centre: POB 12256, 7 Alexander Dr., Research Triangle Park, NC 27709-2256; tel. (919) 549-0661; fax (919) 990-8535; e-mail gharpham@nationalhumanitiescenter.org; internet nationalhumanitiescenter.org; f. 1977; encourages scholarship in the humanities and enhances the usefulness and influence of the humanities in the USA; awards fellowships (40 a year) to pursue advanced postdoctoral research and writing at the Centre; organizes seminars, lectures, confs; library: reference works, bibliographical aids, microfilm catalogue comprises 4 small collns; Chair. ALAN BRINKLEY; Pres. and Dir GEOFFREY GALT HARPHAN; Sec. JOHN F. ADAMS; Treas. MERRIL M. HALPERN.

RAND Corporation: 1776 Main St, POB 2138, Santa Monica, CA 90407-2138; tel. (310) 393-0411; fax (310) 393-4818; e-mail iao_katagiri@rand.org; internet www.rand.org; f. 1948, fmrly part of Douglas Aircraft Co; brs in Arlington, VA, Boston, MA, Jackson, MS, New Orleans, LA, Pittsburgh, PA, Cambridge (UK), Brussels (Belgium), Abu Dhabi (United Arab Emirates) and Doha (Qatar); rep. office in Mexico; research on matters affecting the public interest; education, civil and criminal justice, health sciences, int. affairs, labour and population, science and technology, national security, information processing systems; non-profit instn receiving funds from fed., state and local govt, foundations and the private sector; 718 research professionals; Pres. and CEO Dr JAMES A. THOMSON; Exec. Vice-Pres. MICHAEL D. RICH; publs *RAND Journal of Economics* (4 a year, online), *RAND Review* (3 a year).

Research Institute for Telecommunications Marketing (RITM): College of Business Admin., Ballentine Hall, Univ. of Rhode Island, Seven Lippitt Rd, Kingston, RI 02881-0802; tel. (401) 874-5065; fax (401) 874-4312; e-mail ritim@etal.uri.edu; internet ritim.cba.uri.edu; f. 1989; attached to College of Business Admin., Univ. of Rhode Island; focuses on marketing, behavioural, organizational and strategic aspects of telecommunications and information technology industries; Dir Dr RUBY ROY DHOLAKIA; Assoc. Dir Dr NIK DHOLAKIA.

Sierra Nevada Research Institute (SNRI): 5200 N Lake Rd, Merced, CA 95343; tel. (209) 228-4400; e-mail snri@ucmerced.edu; internet snri.ucmerced.edu; attached to Univ. of California, Merced; conducts basic and applied research in natural resources, physical and biological diversity; promotes social well being in the San Joaquin Valley and Sierra Nevada regions of

California; operates 2 facilities in the Great Valley and Sierra Nevada region: Environmental Analytical Laboratory and Yosemite Field Station at Wawona; Dir Dr ROGER BALES; Exec. Dir DAVID HOSLEY.

AGRICULTURE, FISHERIES AND VETERINARY SCIENCE

Agricultural Research Institute: 236 Massachusetts Ave, NE, Suite 401, Washington, DC 20002; tel. (202) 544-5534; fax (202) 544-5749; f. 1951; forum for agricultural research administrators to discuss agricultural research programmes and needs; Exec. Dir RICHARD A. HERRETT; publ. *Proceedings* (1 a year).

Forest Products Society: 2801 Marshall Court, Madison, WI 53705-2295; tel. (608) 231-1361; fax (608) 231-2152; internet www.forestprod.org; f. 1947; technology transfer concerning all areas of the forest products industry; Pres. PAUL MERRICK; Pres.-Elect PATRICE TARDIF; Vice-Pres. TIMOTHY M. YOUNG; Exec. Vice-Pres. STEFAN BERGMANN; publs *Forest Products Journal* (10 a year), *International Journal of Forest Engineering* (2 a year), *Journal of Forest Products Business Research* (online), *Wood Design Focus* (4 a year).

Louisiana State University Agricultural Center: POB 25203, Baton Rouge, LA 70894; 101 Efferson Hall, Baton Rouge, LA 70803; tel. (225) 578-4161; fax (225) 578-4143; e-mail web@agcenter.lsu.edu; internet www.lsuagcenter.com; attached to Louisiana State Univ. System; focus areas incl. alternative fuels, crop adaptability, coastal restoration, functional foods, childhood obesity, sustainable housing and rural initiatives; Chancellor WILLIAM B. RICHARDSON; Vice-Chancellor and Dir for Louisiana Agricultural Experiment Station JOHN RUSSIN; Vice-Chancellor and Dir for Louisiana Cooperative Extension Service PAUL COREIL; publ. *Louisiana Agriculture* (4 a year).

Ohio Agricultural Research and Development Center: 209 Research Services, 1680 Madison Ave, Wooster, OH 44691-4096; tel. (330) 263-3701; fax (330) 263-3688; e-mail oardc@osu.edu; internet www.oardc.ohio-state.edu; f. 1882 as Ohio Agricultural Experiment Station (OAES), present name 1965; attached to College of Food, Agricultural, and Environmental Sciences, Ohio State Univ.; research on better food and fiber production, environmental and water quality issues for both rural and urban population; emphasizes on new, improved and safer products for use in the agricultural endeavours of both the state of Ohio and the world community; Dir STEVEN A. SLACK; Librarian CONSTANCE J. BRITTON.

Rhode Island Agricultural Experiment Station: Woodward Hall, 9 E Alumni Ave, Kingston, RI 02881-0804; tel. (401) 874-5493; fax (401) 874-4017; internet riaes.cels.uri.edu; f. 1888; attached to Univ. of Rhode Island; conducts research dedicated to addressing challenges in agriculture, food production and processing, nutrition, natural resource policy and natural resource management, and renewable energy and climate change; Dir Dr RICHARD C. RHODES, III.

BIBLIOGRAPHY, LIBRARY SCIENCE AND MUSEOLOGY

Getty Conservation Institute: 1200 Getty Center Dr., Suite 700, Los Angeles, CA 90049-1684; tel. (310) 440-7325; fax (310) 440-7702; e-mail gciweb@getty.edu; internet www.getty.edu/conservation; f. 1985; programme of the J. Paul Getty Trust; works for the preservation of the world's cultural heritage; library of 60,000 vols; Dir TIMOTHY

P. WHALEN; Assoc. Dir for Admin. KATHLEEN GAINES; Assoc. Dir for Programmes JEANNE MARIE TEUTONICO; publs *Art and Archaeology Technical Abstracts* (online (aata.getty.edu/nps)), *GCI e-Bulletin* (6 a year).

National Federation of Advanced Information Services (NFAIS): 1518 Walnut St, Suite 1004, Philadelphia, PA 19102-3403; tel. (215) 893-1561; fax (215) 893-1564; e-mail nfais@nfais.org; internet www.nfais.org; f. 1958, present location 1965; a global non-profit org.; aims to serve the world's information community through education, research, and publ.; Pres. KEITH MACGREGOR; Exec. Dir BONNIE LAWLOR; Pres.-Elect BARBARA DOBBS MACKENZIE; Sec. MARK GAUTHIER; Treas. SUZANNE BEDELL.

Smithsonian Center for Education and Museum Studies: POB 37012, SI Bldg, Room 153, MRC 010, Washington, DC 20013-7012; tel. (202) 633-1000; e-mail educate@si.edu; internet museumstudies.si.edu; enhances quality of museum-studies teaching and learning; library: merged library of collns from the Museum Reference Center and Central Reference and Loan Services br. libraries; part of the Smithsonian Instn Libraries system; Exec. Dir STEPHANIE NORBY.

Smithsonian Museum Conservation Institute: Museum Support Center, 4210 Silver Hill Rd, Suitland, MD 20746; tel. (301) 238-1240; fax (301) 238-3709; e-mail mciweb@si.edu; internet www.si.edu/mci; f. 1963 as Conservation Research Laboratory; research in the fields of conservation and the scientific study of colln materials; conducts technical research studies and interpretation of anthropological, artistic, biological and historical objects; Dir Dr ROBERT J. KOESTLER; Deputy Dir PAULA T. DEPRIEST.

ECONOMICS, LAW AND POLITICS

Brookings: 1775 Massachusetts Ave, NW, Washington, DC 20036; tel. (202) 797-6000; fax (202) 797-6004; e-mail communications@brookings.edu; internet www.brook.edu; f. 1916; research, education, and publishing in the fields of economics, government and foreign policy; library of 75,000 vols, 700 periodical titles; not open to public; Pres. STROBE TALBOTT; Chair. JOHN L. THORNTON; Man. Dir WILLIAM ANTHOLIS; publs *Brookings Papers on Economic Activity* (2 a year), *Brookings Papers on Education Policy*, *Brookings Trade Forum* (1 a year), *Brookings—Wharton Papers on Financial Services*, *Brookings—Wharton Papers on Urban Affairs* (1 a year), *Economia* (2 a year).

Center for Strategic & International Studies (CSIS): 1800 K St, NW, Washington, DC 20006; tel. (202) 887-0200; fax (202) 775-3199; internet www.csis.org; f. 1962; research into new challenges to nat. and int. peace and security; helps to develop new methods of governance for the global age through programmes in technology and public policy, energy, and int. trade and finance; Chair. SAM NUNN; Pres. and CEO JOHN J. HAMRE; publ. *The Washington Quarterly*.

Center for the Study of Democratic Institutions: 10951 West Pico Blvd, Suite 300, Los Angeles, CA 90064; tel. (310) 474-0011; fax (310) 474-8061; e-mail nfo@npq.org; internet www.digitalnpq.org; f. 1959, fmrly Robert Maynard Hutchins Center for the Study of Democratic Institutions; Exec. Dir (vacant); publ. *New Perspectives Quarterly*.

East-West Center: 1601 East-West Rd, Honolulu, HI 96848-1601; tel. (808) 944-7111; fax (808) 944-7376; e-mail ewcinfo@eastwestcenter.org; internet www.eastwestcenter.org; f. 1960; a public, non-profit educational instn with an int. board of governors; research fellows, graduate students, and professionals in govt, academia and business each year work with the Center's int. staff in cooperative study, training, and research; they examine major issues related to int. relations, population, resources, economic devt and the environment in Asia, the Pacific and the USA; library of 50,000 vols, unpublished documents, periodicals and electronic resources; Pres. Dr CHARLES E. MORRISON; Chair. PUONGPUN SANANIKONE; Treas. RICKY KUBOTA; publs *Asia Pacific Issues Paper* (irregular), *Observer* (4 a year).

Institute for the Study of International Aspects of Competition: Dept of Economics, Univ. of Rhode Islands, 806 Chafee Hall, 10 Chafee Rd, Kingston, RI 02881-0808; tel. (401) 874-9195; fax (401) 874-2858; internet www.uri.edu/research/isiac; attached to Dept of Economics, Univ. of Rhode Island; areas of research incl. industrial org. and int. economics; Exec. Dir Dr JOHN P. BURKETT; Research Dir Dr MENG-JIEU CHEN.

Institute of International Business: J. Mack Robinson College of Business, Georgia State Univ., 14th Fl., Suite 1437, 35 Broad St, Atlanta, GA 30303; tel. (404) 413-7275; fax (404) 413-7276; e-mail iib@gsu.edu; internet robinson.gsu.edu/iib; attached to J. Mack Robinson College of Business, Georgia State Univ.; focuses on cross-border activities and studies political, cultural and commercial environment within which cross-border trade and investment activities take place; Dir Dr DANIEL BELLO.

International Center for Economic Growth: University of the Pacific, 3601 Pacific Ave, Stockton, CA 95211; tel. (209) 946-3265; fax (209) 496-2650; f. 1985; attached to School of Int. Studies, Univ. of the Pacific; promotes economic growth and human devt in developing and post-socialist countries, by strengthening the capacity of local research institutes to provide project leadership; operates in conjunction with 370 mem. institutes globally; sponsors confs and seminars; CEO ROBERT HODAM.

International Marketing Institute: c/o Carroll School of Management, Boston College, Fulton Hall 510, 140 Commonwealth Ave, Chestnut Hill, MA 02467; tel. (617) 552-8420; fax (617) 552-8738; f. 1960; supported by Carroll School of Management, Boston College; int. executive devt and management training programmes in management education, with marketing as the primary focus; Exec. Dir JOSEPH B. GANNON.

Marketing Science Institute: 1000 Massachusetts Ave, Cambridge, MA 02138-5396; tel. (617) 491-2060; fax (617) 491-2065; e-mail msi@msi.org; internet www.msi.org; f. 1961; non-profit marketing consortium that stimulates, supports and reports research in order to advance marketing knowledge and practice; sponsors and publishes academic research on all areas of marketing; 71 mem. companies; Chair. GORDON A. WYNER; Chief Operating Officer MARNI ZEA CLIPPINGER; Exec. Dir JOHN A. DEIGHTON; publs *Fast Forward Series*, *MSI Reports* (4 a year).

National Bureau of Economic Research: 1050 Massachusetts Ave, Cambridge, MA 02138; tel. (617) 868-3900; fax (617) 868-2742; e-mail info@nber.org; internet www.nber.org; f. 1920; fundamental qualitative analysis of the US economy; 50 dirs; br. in NY; Chair. JOHN CLARKESON; Pres. and CEO

JAMES POTERBA; Treas. ROBERT MEDNICK; publs *Bulletin on Aging and Health*, *Digest* (12 a year), *NBER Reporter* (4 a year).

Nelson A. Rockefeller Center at Dartmouth College: 6082 Rockefeller Hall, Hanover, NH 03755; tel. (603) 646-3874; e-mail rockefeller.center@dartmouth.edu; internet rockefeller.dartmouth.edu; f. 1983; supports high quality research on policy-related topics; Dir ANDREW A. SAMWICK; Deputy Dir SADHANA HALL; publ. *Direct Line* (4 a year).

Scripps Gerontology Center: Scripps Gerontology Center, 396 Upham Hall, Oxford, OH 45056; tel. (513) 529-2914; fax (513) 529-1476; e-mail scripps@muohio.edu; internet www.scripps.muohio.edu; f. 1922 as Scripps Foundation for Research in Population Problems, present status 1972; attached to Miami Univ.; research incl. health, disability, and longevity; long-term care policy, systems, and services; workforce issues and older workers; income security; racial and ethnic diversity and aging; translational health; quality improvement; supports undergraduate and graduate gerontology education at the univ.; promotes public awareness of aging issues; specializes in evaluation research and provides high quality applied research to legislators, public administrators, planners, service providers, gerontology students, academicians, other researchers and gen. public; library of 4,000 vols; Dir Dr SUZANNE R. KUNKEL.

EDUCATION

American Educational Research Association: 1430 K St, NW, Suite 1200, Washington, DC 20005; tel. (202) 238-3200; fax (202) 238-3250; e-mail pubs@aera.net; internet www.aera.net; f. 1916; improves educational process by encouraging scholarly inquiry related to education and evaluation and by promoting the dissemination and practical application of research results; Pres. ARNETHA F. BALL; Pres.-Elect WILLIAM G. TIERNEY; Exec. Dir Dr FELICE J. LEVINE; publs *American Educational Research Journal*, *Educational Evaluation and Policy Analysis*, *Educational Researcher* (9 a year), *Journal of Educational and Behavioral Statistics*, *Review of Educational Research*, *Review of Research in Education* (1 a year).

Center for the Study of Higher Education: 400 Rackley Bldg, University Park, PA 16802; tel. (814) 865-6346; fax (814) 865-3638; e-mail cshe@psu.edu; internet www.ed.psu.edu/cshe; f. 1969; attached to College of Education, Pennsylvania State Univ.; conducts theory-based research to improve higher education practice and policy; provides high-quality data and analysis to institutional, state, and fed policymakers; supports graduate training for students in higher education programmes; Dir Dr ROBERT M. HENDRICKSON.

Cohn-Haddow Center for Judaic Studies: Wayne State Univ., 2311 Faculty Admin. Bldg, 656 W Kirby, Detroit, MI 48202; tel. (313) 577-2679; fax (313) 577-8136; e-mail cohnhaddowcenter@wayne.edu; internet www.judaicstudies.wayne.edu; f. 1988; attached to Wayne State Univ.; serves as a resource to the Univ. and to the larger community in Jewish studies and related areas; conducts biannual int. confs, symposia and lectures; Dir Dr DAVID WEINBERG; Chair. CHARLES SOBERMAN.

Institute of Education Sciences (IES): 555 New Jersey Ave, NW, Washington, DC

20208; tel. (202) 219-1385; e-mail contact .ies@ed.gov; internet ies.ed.gov; f. 2002, fmrly the Office of Educational Research and Improvement (f. 1980), present name and status 2002; attached to US Dept of Education; funds research studies on ways to improve academic achievement, conducts large-scale evaluations of federal education programmes and reports a wide array of statistics on the condition of education, disseminates information through 10 regional education laboratories and 10 nat. research and devt centres; Dir JOHN Q. EASTON; publ. *National Assessment of Educational Progress*.

National Science Resources Center: 901 D St, SW, Suite 704B, Washington, DC 20024-0952; tel. (202) 633-2978; fax (202) 287-2070; internet www.nsrconline.org; f. 1985; formed by the Smithsonian Instn, Nat. Acad. of Sciences, Nat. Acad. of Engineering and Institute of Medicine to improve the teaching of science in schools; builds awareness for science education among leaders; helps develop science education leadership among groups from school districts and states; conducts programmes to support the professional growth of teachers; develops and disseminates information about exemplary science instructional materials; Exec. Dir SALLY GOETZ SHULER.

FINE AND PERFORMING ARTS

Institute of Contemporary Art: Porteous Bldg, 522 Congress St, Portland, ME 04101; tel. (207) 699-5040; e-mail ica@meca.edu; internet www.meca.edu/meca-life/campus-resources/ica; f. 1997; attached to Maine College of Art; research and devt of exhibitions; Dir DANIEL FULLER.

HISTORY, GEOGRAPHY AND ARCHAEOLOGY

Center for Reformation Research: Concordia Seminary, 801 Seminary Pl., St Louis, MO 63105; tel. (314) 505-7134; internet www.csl.edu/library/the-center-for-reformation--resources-collection; f. 1957 as Foundation for Reformation Research, present name 1974; attached to Concordia Seminary; microfilm library of original MSS and printed materials of the 15th and 16th centuries; reference library; library of 3,000 vols; Dir Prof. ROBERT ROSIN.

Leo Baeck Institute: Center for Jewish History, 15 W 16th St, New York, NY 10011; tel. (212) 744-6400; fax (212) 988-1305; e-mail lbaeck@lbi.cjh.org; internet www.lbi .org; f. 1955; research and documentation on German Jewish history; exhibitions and lectures; library of 80,000 vols in German, English and Hebrew, archives of family papers, community histories, business and public records, 2,000 personal memoirs, 35,000 photographs, 10,000 archival records (access to archive and library materials is available only through reading room of the Center for Jewish History); art colln; Pres. BERNARD BLUM; Vice-Pres. MICHAEL A. BAMBERGER; Exec. Dir CAROL KAHN STRAUSS; Head Librarian RENATE EVERS; Treas. LAWRENCE RAMER; publs *Jüdischer Almanach des LBI* (in German), *LBI News*, *Leo Baeck Yearbook*, *Overview*, *Stammbaum*.

Office of Geology: POB 2279, Jackson, MS 39225; 700 N State St, Jackson, MS 39202; tel. (601) 961-5500; fax (601) 961-5521; internet www.deq.state.ms.us/mdeq.nsf/page/geology_home; f. 1850; attached to Dept of Environmental Quality; research into geology and mineral resources of the state; regulates permitting of mines and reclamation of surface-mined land; administers Mississippi Digital Earth Model; library of 60,000 vols; Dir MICHAEL B. E. BOGRAD; publs *Environmental Geology*, *Mississippi Geology*, bulletins, geologic maps.

Paleontological Research Institution: 1259 Trumansburg Rd, Ithaca, NY 14850; tel. (607) 273-6623; fax (607) 273-6620; internet www.museumoftheearth.org; f. 1932; focuses on fossil and modern mollusks from the SE USA, Caribbean, and Latin America; also works on abundant Devonian marine invertebrates and Pleistocene mastodons of New York State and general fields of evolutionary paleobiology and macroevolution; colln of 3m. specimens; library of 50,000 vols; Dir Dr WARREN D. ALLMON; Assoc. Dir for Science Dr PAULA M. MIKKELSEN; publs *American Paleontologist* (4 a year), *Bulletins of American Paleontology* (2 a year), *Palaeontographica Americana* (irregular).

School for Advanced Research: POB 2188, Santa Fe, NM 87504-2188; 660 Garcia St, Santa Fe, NM 87505; tel. (505) 954-7200; fax (505) 989-9809; e-mail info@sarsf.org; internet www.sarweb.org; f. 1907 as School of American Archaeology; centre for advanced studies in anthropology and the humanities; grants to 6 resident scholars, incl. 1 native American, annually; native artist fellows; advanced seminars in anthropology; anthropological publs; extensive collns in SW American Indian art; library of 8,600 books and MSS; Pres. and CEO JAMES F. BROOKS; Chair. STEVE BOHLIN; Sec. DIANE STANLEY VENNEMA; Treas. JASON BRADY; publ. *Annual Review: Creativity and Research at SAR*.

LANGUAGE AND LITERATURE

Harry Ransom Center, The University of Texas at Austin: POB 7219, Austin, TX 78713-7219; 300 W 21st St, Austin, TX 78712; tel. (512) 471-8944; fax (512) 471-9646; internet www.hrc.utexas.edu; f. 1957 as Humanities Research Center at The Univ. of Texas at Austin, present location 1972, present name 1983; specializes in American, British and French literature and art since 19th century; library of 800,000 vols, 40,000,000 MSS, 5,000,000 photographs; Dir THOMAS F. STALEY.

H. H. Meeter Center for Calvin Studies: Hekman Library, 1855 Knollcrest Circle, SE, Grand Rapids, MI 49546-4402; tel. (616) 526-7081; fax (616) 526-7687; e-mail meeter@calvin.edu; internet www.calvin.edu/meeter; f. 1981; attached to Calvin College; specializes in John Calvin, Calvinism, reformation and early modern studies; library of 700,000 vols; Dir Dr KARIN MAAG; Curator PAUL FIELDS; publ. *John Calvin Bibliography*.

MEDICINE

American Association for Cancer Research: c/o Dr Margaret Foti, 615 Chestnut St, 17th Fl., Philadelphia, PA 19106-4404; tel. (215) 440-9300; fax (215) 440-9313; e-mail aacr@aacr.org; internet www.aacr.org; f. 1907; facilitates communication and dissemination of knowledge among scientists and others dedicated to cancer research; Pres. Dr JUDY E. GARBER; Pres.-Elect Dr FRANK MCCORMICK; CEO Dr MARGARET FOTI; Treas. Dr WILLIAM N. HAIT; publs *Cancer Epidemiology, Biomarkers & Prevention* (12

a year), *Cancer Discovery*, *Cancer Prevention Research* (12 a year), *Cancer Research* (24 a year), *Clinical Cancer Research* (12 a year), *Molecular Cancer Research* (12 a year), *Molecular Cancer Therapeutics* (12 a year).

American Federation for Medical Research: 500 Cummings Center, Suite 4550, Beverly, MA 01915; tel. (978) 927-8330; fax (978) 524-8890; e-mail afmr@prri.com; internet www.afmr.org; f. 1940 as American Federation for Clinical Research, present name 1996; asscn of scientists engaged in all areas of biomedical investigation-patient-oriented and basic research; fosters research in the medical sciences; provides leadership in articulating and publicizing the aims and goals of scientific research; disseminates the knowledge medical research generates; Pres. Dr SHARMA S. PRABHAKAR; Sec. and Treas. Dr ROBERT J. FREISHTAT; publ. *Journal of Investigative Medicine* (24 a year).

American Pediatric Society/Society for Pediatric Research: 3400 Research Forest Dr., Suite B-7, The Woodlands, TX 77381; tel. (281) 419-0052; fax (281) 419-0082; e-mail info@aps-spr.org; internet www.aps-spr.org; f. 1929; Exec. Dir DEBBIE ANAGNOSTELIS; Pres. Dr F. BRUDER STAPLETON; Vice-Pres. Dr BARBARA J. STOLL; Sec and Treas. Dr JUDY L. ASCHNER.

Association for Research in Nervous and Mental Disease: Weill Medical College of Cornell Univ., Dept of Psychiatry, 1300 York Ave, POB 171, Room F-1231, New York, NY 10065; tel. (212) 746-3770; fax (212) 746-8546; e-mail daw2026@med.cornell.edu; internet www.arnmd.org; f. 1920; brings together scientists from the fields of psychiatry, neurology and neuroscience to advance the scientific knowledge and understanding of neuropsychiatry at all levels; promotes dissemination of information about nature of scientific discovery and results and implications of latest neuropsychiatric research; provide annual conf. that presents groundbreaking research in a topical area encouraging the participation and attendance of physicians and trainees in these fields; Chair. JACK D. BARCHAS; Exec. Dir ANNLOUISE GOODERMUTH; Sec. and Treas. FRANCIS LEE; publ. *Clinical Neuroscience Research* (6 a year).

Association for Research in Vision and Ophthalmology: 1801 Rockville Pike, Suite 400, Rockville, MD 20852; tel. (240) 221-2900; fax (240) 221-0370; e-mail arvo@arvo.org; internet www.arvo.org; f. 1928 as Association for Research in Ophthalmology in Washington, DC, present name 1970, present location 2001; encourages and assists research, training, publication, and dissemination of knowledge in vision and ophthalmology; Pres. Dr JEFFREY. H. BOATRIGHT; Pres.-Elect Dr PENG T. KHAW; Exec. Dir Dr JOANNE G. ANGLE; Vice-Pres. Dr PAUL MITCHELL; Vice-Pres. Dr ROBERT FRANCIS MILLER; publs *Investigative Ophthalmology and Visual Science* (online at www.iovs.org), *Journal of Vision* (irregular, online at www.journalofvision.org).

Barbara Ann Karmanos Cancer Institute: 4100 John R., Detroit, MI 48201; fax (248) 304-2901; e-mail info@karmanos.org; internet www.karmanos.org; f. 1943 as Detroit Institute for Cancer Research, present name 1995; attached to Wayne State Univ.; focuses on prevention, early detection, treatment and eradication of cancer; conducts basic, behavioural, clinical, epidemiological and translational research; Pres. and

CEO Dr GEROLD BEPLER; publ. *Karmanos Hope* (4 a year).

Bioengineering Center: 818 W Hancock, Detroit, MI 48201; tel. (313) 577-0252; fax (313) 577-8333; internet www.bioengineeringcenter.org; f. 1939; attached to Biomedical Engineering Dept, College of Engineering, Wayne State Univ.; conducts research in areas of impact trauma, low back pain and orthopaedic biomechanics; Dir Prof. Dr KING H. YANG.

California Pacific Medical Center Research Institute: POB 7999, San Francisco, CA 94120; tel. (415) 600-1600; fax (415) 600-1725; internet www.cpmc.org/professionals/research; f. 1993 by merger of Medical Research Institute of San Francisco with California Pacific Medical Center; nonprofit research div. of medical centre conducting patient-orientated research in arthritis, HIV/AIDS, cancer, incl. leukemia and monoclonal antibodies, heart disease, immunology and infectious diseases, artificial heart research, organ transplantation and preservation, neurology, maternal foetal medicine, child health and human devt; CEO WARREN S. BROWNER; Scientific Dir Dr MICHAEL C. ROWBOTHAM; publ. *Currents* (1 a year).

Center for Molecular Medicine and Genetics: 3127 Scott Hall, 540 E Canfield, Detroit, MI 48201; tel. (313) 577-5323; fax (313) 577-5218; e-mail newgradapp@wayne.edu; internet cmmg.biosci.wayne.edu; f. 1986; attached to School of Medicine, Wayne State Univ.; focuses on molecular biology, molecular medicine, and genetics to increase understanding, diagnosis, treatment and prevention of human disease; library of 3,000 vols; Dir Prof. Dr LAWRENCE I. GROSSMAN.

Center to Advance Palliative-Care Excellence: 4201 St Antoine, Suite 5C-UHC, Detroit, MI 48201; tel. (313) 577-5751; fax (313) 745-4710; internet capewayne.med.wayne.edu; attached to School of Medicine, Wayne State Univ.; interdisciplinary community of scholars, educators, researchers and clinicians dedicated to improving lives of people suffering from mortal illness; Dir Dr ROBERT J. ZALENSKI.

Developmental Disabilities Institute: Wayne State Univ., 4809 Woodward Ave, Suite 268, Dettroit, MI 48202; tel. (313) 577-2654; fax (313) 577-3770; e-mail ddi@wayne.edu; internet ddi.wayne.edu; attached to Wayne State Univ.; works towards devt of inclusive communities, enhancement of quality of life of people with disabilities; enriches the field of disability research and service; Dir Dr BARBARA LEROY.

Eppley Institute for Research in Cancer and Allied Diseases: 985950 Nebraska Medical Center, Omaha, NE 68198-5950; tel. (402) 559-4090; e-mail info@eppleyits.com; internet www.unmc.edu/eppley; f. 1960; attached to Univ. of Nebraska Medical Center; understands causes of cancer; researches to improve methods for diagnosis of cancer and treatment and prevention of cancer and similar disorders; offers undergraduate, graduate and postdoctoral students; Dir Dr KENNETH H. COWAN.

Fox Chase Cancer Center: 333 Cottman Ave, Philadelphia, PA 19111-2497; tel. (215) 728-7784; fax (215) 728-3655; internet www.fccc.edu/research; f. 1904 as American Oncologic Hospital; researches on new technologies and cancer treatment, incl. fundamental mechanisms of biomolecular reactions and treatment; library of 23,000 vols, incl. 5,000 books and 450 scientific journals; Chair. DAVID G. MARSHALL; Pres. and CEO Dr

MICHAEL V. SEIDEN; Chief Scientific Officer JONATHAN CHERNOFF.

Gallaudet Research Institute: Dawes House, 800 Florida Ave, NE, Washington, DC 20002-3695; tel. (202) 651-5575; fax (202) 651-5746; internet www.gallaudet.edu/gallaudet_research_institute; attached to Gallaudet Univ.; conducts studies of language and learning processes in American Sign Language and English among deaf people from diverse cultural and educational backgrounds; Dir CAROL J. ERTING; publ. *Deaf Studies Digital Journal.*

Gerontology Institute: POB 3984, Atlanta, GA 30302-3984; tel. (404) 413-5210; fax (404) 413-5219; e-mail gerontology@gsu.edu; internet www.gsu.edu/gerontology; attached to College of Arts and Sciences, Georgia State Univ.; develops and coordinates research, instruction and service in gerontology; research areas incl. long-term care of older persons with disabilities and ethnicity and ageing; Dir Prof. ELISABETH O. BURGESS.

Huntington Medical Research Institutes: 734 Fairmount Ave, Pasadena, CA 91105-3104; tel. (626) 397-5805; fax (626) 397-5808; internet www.hmri.org; f. 1952; oncology, cell biology, differentiated cell culture, cancer genetics, prostatic cancer, immunotherapy, biomedical magnetic resonance spectroscopy, cardiology, devt of neural prosthetic devices; Pres. Dr WILLIAM OPEL.

Institute of Gerontology: Wayne State Uinv., 87 E Ferry St, 226 Knapp Bldg, Detroit, MI 48202; tel. (313) 664-2600; fax (313) 664-2667; e-mail ioginfo@wayne.edu; internet www.iog.wayne.edu; attached to Wayne State Uinv.; researches in social and behavioural sciences, cognitive neuroscience and issues related to aging and urban health; offers pre-doctoral, graduate certificate and continuing education programmes in gerontology; Dir Dr PETER LICHTENBERG; Deputy Dir Dr CATHY LYSACK.

Institute of Public Health: Georgia State Univ., POB 3995, Atlanta, GA 30302-3995; Urban Life Bldg, 140 Decatur St, Suite 848, Atlanta, GA 30303; tel. (404) 413-1130; e-mail publichealth@gsu.edu; internet publichealth.gsu.edu; f. 2004; attached to Georgia State Univ.; focuses on finding solutions to pressing urban health issues; offers doctor of philosophy in public health and Master's in public health with spec. emphasis in prevention sciences, health promotion and behaviour or health policy and management; Dir Prof. Dr MICHAEL ERIKSON.

Jackson Laboratory: 600 Main St, Bar Harbor, ME 04609-1500; tel. (207) 288-6000; fax (207) 288-6079; e-mail pubinfo@jax.org; internet www.jax.org; f. 1929; research in molecular genetics, cell biology, biochemistry, immunology and physiological genetics; library of 4,000 vols, 5,000 electronic journals, 80 print journals, over 5,000 photographs; Assoc. Dir and Chair. of Research Dr ROBERT BRAUN; publs *Inside the Jackson Laboratory* (4 a year), *Search, Scientific Report* (1 a year), *Training for Research* (1 a year).

Lovelace Respiratory Research Institute: 2425 Ridgecrest Dr., SE, Albuquerque, NM 87108-5127; tel. (505) 348-9400; fax (505) 348-8567; e-mail info@lrri.org; internet www.lrri.org; f. 1947; researches on prevention, treatment, and cure of respiratory diseases; areas of research incl. asthma, emphysema, lung cancer, inhalation toxicology, aerosol science, inhalation drug delivery, bronchitis, allergies, science service contracting, pulmonary fibrosis, pulmonary hypertension, infectious disease, radiation studies, chemical exposure research and clinical trials; library of 10,000 vols, 25,000 bound journals,

116 current journals; Pres. and CEO ROBERT RUBIN; publs *Advances, Breathe.*

Mayo Clinic: 200 First St SW, Rochester, MN 55905; tel. (507) 284-2511; fax (507) 284-0161; internet www.mayoresearch.mayo.edu/mayo/research/departments-mcr.cfm; f. 1919; clinical medicine, medical research, graduate and undergraduate education; also located at Scottsdale, AZ, and Jacksonville, FL; library of 275,000 vols and 3,500 periodicals; Chair. MARILYN CARLSON NELSON; Pres. and CEO JOHN H. NOSEWORTHY; Dir for Research Dr ROBERT A. RIZZA; publs *Discovery's Edge* (2 a year, online), *Forefront* (1 a year), *Mayo Clinic Magazine* (2 a year), *Mayo Clinic Proceedings* (12 a year), *Sharing Mayo Clinic* (4 a year).

Memorial Sloan-Kettering Cancer Center: 1275 York Ave, New York, NY 10065; tel. (212) 639-2000; e-mail publicaffairs@mskcc.org; internet www.mskcc.org; f. 1884 as New York Cancer Hospital, present location 1939, present status and name 1960; research in physical and biological sciences contributing to devt of new and better therapies for treatment of cancer; postdoctoral research training in laboratory investigations with scientific staff; graduate instruction with Cornell Univ.; Chair. DOUGLAS A. WARNER, III; Pres. and CEO Dr CRAIG B. THOMSON; Sec. NORMAN C. SELBY; Treas. CLIFTON S. ROBBINS.

Menninger: 2801 Gessner Dr., Houston, TX 77280-9045; tel. (713) 333-3320; fax (713) 333-3390; e-mail developmentoffice@menninger.edu; internet www.menningerclinic.com; f. 1925, present location 2003; attached to Baylor College of Medicine and Methodist Hospital; non-profit mental health centre for inpatient and outpatient treatment of mental illness through preventive psychiatry, clinical treatment, research and professional education; library of 50,000 vols; Pres. and CEO IAN AITKEN; publs *Bulletin of the Menninger Clinic* (4 a year), *Menninger Perspective* (4 a year).

Munroe-Meyer Institute: 985450 Nebraska Medical Center, Omaha, NE 68198-5450; tel. (402) 559-6430; fax (402) 559-5737; e-mail munroemeyer@unmc.edu; internet www.unmc.edu/mmi; f. 1968; attached to Univ. of Nebraska Medical Center; conducts basic investigations in developmental neurosciences like genetics of autism and other neurodevelopmental disorders to applied studies of treatments for disorders of movement, severe behaviour, feeding, communication, sleep, paediatric pain and learning; Dir Dr J. MICHAEL LEIBOWITZ.

National Institutes of Health: 9000 Rockville Pike, Bethesda, MD 20892; tel. (301) 496-4000; fax (301) 496-0019; e-mail nihinfo@od.nih.gov; internet www.nih.gov; f. 1887; attached to US Dept of Health and Human Services; biomedical research, research training, and biomedical communications; Nat. Library of Medicine: see Libraries and Archives; Dir Dr FRANCIS S. COLLINS.

Constituent Institutes:

Eunice Kennedy Shriver National Institute of Child Health and Human Development: Bldg 31, Room 2A32, MSC 2425, 31 Center Dr., Bethesda, MD 20892-2425; tel. (301) 496-5133; fax (301) 496-7101; e-mail nichdinformationresourcecenter@mail.nih.gov; internet www.nichd.nih.gov; f. 1962; supports, fosters and coordinates research and training in areas of maternal health, child health and human devt, focusing on the continuing process of growth and devt, biological and behavioural; also supports research in the population sciences, incl. contraceptive devt and evaluation, repro-

ductive health, behavioural and demographic research, and medical rehabilitation; Dir Dr ALLAN GUTTMACHER.

National Cancer Institute: Office of Communications and Education, Public Inquiries Office, 6116 Executive Blvd, Suite 300 Bethesda, MD 20892-8322; tel. (301) 496-5615; fax (301) 402-0338; e-mail cancergovstaff@mail.nih.gov; internet www.nci.nih.gov; f. 1937; prin. fed. govt agency for cancer research; supports research into the causes, prevention, early detection and treatment of cancer, and into supportive care; cooperates with state and local health agencies and voluntary bodies; Dir Dr HAROLD VARMUS; publ. *CCR Connections* (2 a year).

National Eye Institute: Information Office, 31 Center Dr., MSC 2510, Bethesda, MD 20892-2510; tel. (301) 496-5248; fax (301) 496-9970; e-mail 2020@nei.nih.gov; internet www.nei.nih.gov; f. 1968; conducts and supports research, training, health information dissemination, and other programmes relating to blinding eye diseases, visual disorders, mechanisms of visual function, preservation of sight; special health problems and requirements of the blind; research performed in Institute's own laboratories and through contracts; supports training, and directs Nat. Eye Health Education Program; Dir Dr PAUL A. SIEVING; publ. *Eye on NEI* (12 a year, online).

National Heart, Lung and Blood Institute: POB 30105, Bethesda, MD 20824-0105; Bldg 31, Room 5A52, 31 Center Dr., MSC 2486, Bethesda, MD 20892; tel. (301) 592-8573; fax (240) 629-3246; e-mail nhlbiinfo@nhlbi.nih.gov; internet www.nhlbi.nih.gov; f. 1948 as Nat. Heart Institute, redesignated 1969 and 1976; performs and supports research in diseases of the heart, blood vessels, lungs (exclusive of pulmonary malignancies) and blood; Dir Dr SUSAN B. SHURIN (acting).

National Human Genome Research Institute (NHGRI): Bldg 31, Room 4B09, 31 Center Dr., MSC 2152, 9000 Rockville Pike Bethesda, MD 20892-2152; tel. (301) 402-0911; fax (301) 402-2218; internet www.genome.gov; f. 1989 as National Center for Human Genome Research; directs and supports work on the sequencing of the human genome; funds research on the genome's structure, function and role in health and disease; supports studies on the ethical, legal and social implications (ELSI) of genome research; Dir Dr ERIC D. GREEN.

National Institute for Biomedical Imaging and Bioengineering (NIBIB): Clinical Center Office of Communications, 10 Cloister Court, Bldg 61, Room 100, Bethesda, MD 20892; tel. (301) 496-2563; e-mail info@nibib.nih.gov; internet www.nibib.nih.gov; f. 2000; accelerates pace of discovery and speeds devt of biomedical technologies that prevent illnesses or treat them when they strike; Dir Dr RODERIC I. PETTIGREW.

National Institute of Allergy and Infectious Diseases: 6610 Rockledge Dr., MSC 6612, Bethesda, MD 20892-6612; tel. (301) 496-5717; fax (301) 402-3573; e-mail ocpostoffice@niaid.nih.gov; internet www.niaid.nih.gov; f. 1887, present name 1955; supports basic and translational research to prevent, diagnose and treat infectious diseases such as HIV/AIDS and other sexually transmitted infections, influenza, tuberculosis, malaria and illness from potential agents of bioterrorism; supports research on transplantation and immune-related illnesses, incl. autoimmune disorders, asthma and allergies; Dir Dr ANTHONY S. FAUCI.

National Institute of Arthritis and Musculoskeletal and Skin Diseases: Bldg 31, Room 4C02, 31 Center Dr., MSC 2350, Bethesda, MD 20892-2350; tel. (301) 496-8190; fax (301) 480-2814; e-mail niamsinfo@mail.nih.gov; internet www .niams.nih.gov; f. 1986; research into the causes, treatment and prevention of arthritis and musculoskeletal and skin diseases; training of basic and clinical scientists to carry out this research; dissemination of information on progress in research; Dir Dr STEPHEN I. KATZ; Deputy Dir ROBERT H. CARTER; publs *NIAMS Update* (12 a year), *Multicultural Outreach News* (4 a year).

National Institute of Dental and Craniofacial Research: Nat. Institutes of Health, 31 Center Dr., MSC 2290, Bethesda, MD 20892-2190; tel. (866) 232-4528; fax (301) 480-4098; e-mail nidcrinfo@ mail.nih.gov; internet www.nidcr.nih.gov; f. 1948; conducts and supports research and training with the aim of preventing, diagnosing and treating dental, oral and craniofacial diseases and conditions; Dir Dr MARTHA J. SOMERMAN.

National Institute of Diabetes and Digestive and Kidney Diseases: Office of Communications and Public Liaison, Bldg 31, Rm 9A06 31 Center Dr., MSC 2560, Bethesda, MD 20892-2560; tel. (301) 496-3583; fax (301) 496-7422; e-mail niddk_inquiries@nih.gov; internet www .niddk.nih.gov; f. 1950 as Nat. Institute of Arthritis and Metabolic Diseases, present name 1986; conducts and supports research into diabetes, endocrinology, metabolic diseases, digestive diseases, nutrition, kidney and urologic diseases and haematology; information and education activities; Dir Dr GRIFFIN P. RODGERS.

National Institute of Environmental Health Sciences: POB 12233, MD K3-16 Research Triangle Park, NC 27709-2233; tel. (919) 541-3345; fax (919) 541-4395; internet www.niehs.nih.gov; f. 1969; conducts, fosters and coordinates research on the biological effects of chemical, physical and biological substances present in or introduced into the environment; Dir Dr LINDA S. BIRNBAUM; publ. *Environmental Health Perspectives* (12 a year).

National Institute of General Medical Sciences: 45 Center Dr., MSC 6200, Bethesda, MD 20892-6200; tel. (301) 496-7301; fax (301) 402-0156; e-mail info@ nigms.nih.gov; internet www.nigms.nih .gov; f. 1962; supports a programme of research and training in the basic medical sciences; Dir Dr JUDITH H. GREENBERG (acting); publ. *Findings* (2 a year).

National Institute of Mental Health (NIMH): Science Writing, Press, and Dissemination Br., 6001 Exec. Blvd, Room 8184, MSC 9663, Bethesda, MD 20892-9663; tel. (301) 443-4513; fax (301) 443-4279; e-mail nimhinfo@nih.gov; internet www.nimh.nih.gov; f. 1946; improves mental health through biomedical research on the mind, brain and behaviour; Dir Dr THOMAS R. INSEL.

National Institute of Neurological Disorders and Stroke: POB 5801, Bethesda, MD 20284; tel. (301) 496-5751; fax (301) 402-2186; e-mail braininfo@ninds.nih.gov; internet www.ninds.nih.gov; f. 1950; conducts, supports, fosters and coordinates research on the causes, prevention, diagnosis and treatment of disorders of the

brain and nervous system; Dir Dr STORY C. LANDIS.

National Institute of Nursing Research: c/o Nat. Institutes of Health, 31 Center Dr., Room 5B10, Bethesda, MD 20892-2178; tel. (301) 496-0207; fax (301) 480-8845; internet www.ninr.nih.gov; f. 1985, present status 1993; supports and conducts scientific research and research training to strengthen nursing practice and health care for prevention and amelioration of disease and disability; Dir Dr PATRICIA A. GRADY.

National Institute on Aging: Bldg 31, Room 5C27, 31 Center Dr., MSC 2292, Bethesda, MD 20892; tel. (301) 496-1752; fax (301) 496-1072; e-mail nianews3@mail .nih.gov; internet www.nia.nih.gov; f. 1974; conducts and supports biomedical, social and behavioural research and training related to the ageing process and diseases, and other special problems and needs of the aged; Dir Dr RICHARD J. HODES.

National Institute on Alcohol Abuse and Alcoholism (NIAAA): 5635 Fishers Lane, MSC 9304, Bethesda, MD 20892-9304; tel. (301) 443-3860; internet www .niaaa.nih.gov; f. 1970; conducts and supports research in a wide range of scientific areas, incl. genetics, neuroscience, epidemiology, health risks and benefits of alcohol consumption, prevention and treatment; Dir Dr KENNETH R. WARREN; publs *Alcohol Alert* (4 a year), *Alcohol Research & Health* (4 a year).

National Institute on Deafness and Other Communication Disorders: 31 Center Dr., MSC 2320, Bethesda, MD 20892-2320; tel. (301) 496-7243; fax (301) 402-0018; e-mail nidcdinfo@nidcd.nih.gov; internet www.nidcd.nih.gov; f. 1988; supports and conducts research on the normal processes and diseases of human communication, incl. hearing, balance, smell, taste, voice, speech and language; fosters training and disseminates science-based health information; Dir Dr JAMES F. BATTEY, JR.

National Institute on Drug Abuse (NIDA): 6001 Executive Blvd, Room 5213, Bethesda, MD 20892-9561; tel. (301) 443-1124; e-mail information@nida .nih.gov; internet www.nida.nih.gov; f. 1974; provides strategic support and conducts research on improving prevention and treatment on drug abuse and addiction; Dir Dr NORA D. VOLKOW.

National Institute on Minority Health and Health Disparities: 6707 Democracy Blvd, Suite 800, Bethesda, MD 20892-5465; tel. (301) 402-1366; fax (301) 480-4049; e-mail ncmhdinfo@od.nih.gov; internet www.ncmhd.nih.gov; f. 1993; promotes, assists and supports research capacity building activities in the minority and medically under-served communities; Dir Dr JOHN RUFFIN.

Naval Aerospace Medical Institute: 340 Hulse Rd, Pensacola, FL 32508-104; tel. (850) 452-2933; e-mail nomi-info@med.navy.mil; internet www.med.navy.mil/sites/ navmedmpte/nomi/nami; f. 1939; provides expert aeromedical consultation; develops services and application of aeromedical standards; trains aeromedical personnel for operational assignments; library of 20,000 vols; Officer in Charge Capt. CHARLES A. CICCONE.

Schepens Eye Research Institute—Massachusetts Eye and Ear Foundation: 20 Staniford St, Boston, MA 02114; tel. (617) 912-0100; fax (617) 912-0101; internet www .theschepens.org; f. 1950 as Retina Founda-

tion, present status and name 2011; basic and clinical research on causes, prevention and treatment of eye diseases, devt of diagnostic and therapeutic devices, instruments and techniques for ophthalmology, study of the processes of vision; library of 200 vols, 100 journals; Chair. KENNETH F. BURNES; Pres. JOHN FERNANDEZ; publ. *Sundial.*

Texas Biomedical Research Institute: POB 760549, San Antonio, TX 78425-0549; 7620 NW Loop 410, San Antonio, TX 78227-5301; tel. (210) 258-9400; internet www.sfbr .org; f. 1941, fmrly Southwest Foundation for Research and Education; basic research in biomedical sciences; designated in 1999 one of the regional primate research centres (Southwest Regional Primate Research Center); library of 50,000 journal vols; 6,700 books; Chair. JOHN R. HURD; Pres. KENNETH P. TREVETT; Chief Scientific Officer Dr JOHN L. VANDEBERG; publ. *Progress in Biomedical Research* (irregular).

Wistar Institute of Anatomy and Biology: 3601 Spruce St, Philadelphia, PA 19104; tel. (215) 898-3700; fax (215) 573-2097; internet www.wistar.org; f. 1892, present status 1972; ind. research centre, cellular and subcellular research in human diseases; library of 10,000 vols; Pres. and CEO Dr RUSSEL E. KAUFMAN; publ. *Focus* (2 a year).

Worcester Foundation for Biomedical Research: 222 Maple Ave, Shrewsbury, MA 01545; tel. (508) 842-8921; fax (508) 842-9632; f. 1944, present name 1995, present status 1997; attached to Univ. of Massachusetts Medical School; supports biomedical research at the Univ. of Massachusetts Medical School, ind. biomedical research centre; emphasis on cell biology, molecular biology, neurobiology and developmental-reproductive biology; conducts joint PhD programme with Clark Univ., Worcester Polytechnic Inst. and Univ. of Massachusetts Medical School; library of 25,000 vols; spec. colln: cellular/molecular biology, developmental biology, neurobiology, endocrine/ reproductive biology; Chair. MORTON H. SIGEL; Sec. WARNER S. FLETCHER; publs *Research Reporter* (4 a year), *Scientific Report.*

NATURAL SCIENCES
General

Bioanthropology Research Institute: 275 Mount Carmel Ave, Hamden, CT 06518-1908; tel. (203) 582-8200; internet www.quinnipiac.edu/x1978.xml; f. 1998; attached to School of Health Sciences, Quinnipiac Univ.; research areas incl. biology, archaeology, anthropology and palaeopathology through diagnostic imaging, video endoscopy and laboratory analysis; Co-Exec. Dir RONALD BECKETT; Co-Exec. Dir Prof. GERALD CONLOGUE.

Carnegie Institution for Science: 1530 P St, NW, Washington, DC 20005; tel. (202) 387-6400; fax (202) 387-8092; internet www .carnegiescience.edu; f. 1902; research and education in astronomy, developmental biology, Earth and planetary sciences, global ecology and plant biology; Chair. Board of Trustees MICHAEL GELLERT; Pres. Dr RICHARD A. MESERVE; publs *Carnegie Science* (3 a year), *Yearbook.*

Attached Departments:

Department of Embryology: 3520 San Martin Dr., Baltimore, MD 21218; tel. (410) 246-3001; internet www.ciwemb .edu; f. 1913; cellular, developmental and genetic biology; Dir ALLAN C. SPRADLING.

Department of Global Ecology: 260 Panama St, Stanford, CA 94305; tel. (650)

462-1047; fax (650) 462-5968; internet dge .stanford.edu; f. 2002; located in Stanford Univ.; conducts basic research on the interactions among the earth's ecosystems, land, atmosphere and oceans; Dir CHRISTO-PHER B. FIELD; publ. *Science Literature*.

Department of Plant Biology: 260 Panama St, Stanford, CA 94305; tel. (650) 325-1521; fax (650) 325-6857; internet dpb .carnegiescience.edu; f. 1903 as Desert Laboratory; basic problems of how plants function and grow; Dir WOLF B. FROMMER.

Department of Terrestrial Magnetism: 5241 Broad Branch Rd, NW, Washington, DC 20015-1305; tel. (202) 478-8820; fax (202) 478-8821; internet www.dtm.ciw .edu; f. 1904; maps the geomagnetic field of the Earth; discovers planets outside the solar system; determines age and structure of universe; studies causes of earthquakes and volcanoes; Dir SEAN C. SOLOMON.

Geophysical Laboratory: 5251 Broad Branch Rd, NW, Washington, DC 20015; tel. (202) 478-8900; fax (202) 478-8901; internet www.gl.ciw.edu; f. 1905, present location 1990; understands processes that control composition and structure of the Earth; researches also biology of the Earth, chemistry and physics; Dir RUSSELL J HEMLEY.

Observatories of the Carnegie Institution: 813 Santa Barbara St, Pasadena, CA 91101; tel. (626) 577-1122; fax (626) 795-8136; e-mail questions@obs .carnegiescience.edu; internet www.obs .carnegiescience.edu; f. 1904 as Mount Wilson Solar Observatory; basic research in astronomy; studies early universe, milky way, galaxies; Dir WENDY FREEDMAN.

Institute for Advanced Study: Einstein Dr., Princeton, NJ 08540; tel. (609) 734-8000; fax (609) 924-8399; e-mail contactus@ias.edu; internet www.ias.edu; f. 1930; encourages and supports fundamental research in the sciences and humanities—the original, often speculative, thinking that produces advances in knowledge that change the way we understand the world; Dir PETER GODDARD.

MRI Global: 425 Volker Blvd, Kansas City, MO 64110-2241; tel. (816) 753-7600; fax (816) 753-8420; e-mail info@mriresearch.org; internet www.mriresearch.org; f. 1944 as Midwest Research Institute, present name 2011; non-profit org.; conducts programmes in life sciences, agriculture and food safety, energy and environment, engineering and infrastructure, and nat. security and defence; Pres. and CEO Dr MICHAEL F. HELMSTETTER; Exec. Vice-Pres. Dr DAN E. ARVIZU; Vice-Pres. and Chief Information Officer LYLA PERRODIN; Sr Vice-Pres. and Chief Financial Officer R. THOMAS FLEENER; Sr Vice-Pres. and Dir for Technical Operations Dr THOMAS M. SACK.

Southern Research: 2000 Ninth Ave. S, POB 55305, Birmingham, AL 35205-5305; tel. (205) 581-2000; fax (205) 581-2726; internet www.southernresearch.org; f. 1941; attached to Univ. of Alabama, Birmingham; contract scientific research in the areas of advanced engineering, environmental protection, drug discovery and preclinical drug devt; library of 40,000 vols; Pres. and CEO Dr JOHN A. SECRIST, III; Chair. Dr CAROL GARRISON; Sec. Dr SHIRLEY SALLOWAY KAHN; Treas. RICHARD MARGISON.

World Resources Institute: 10 G St NE, Suite 800, Washington, DC 20002; tel. (202) 729-7600; fax (202) 729-7610; e-mail front@ wri.org; internet www.wri.org; f. 1982; provides information about global resources and environmental conditions, analysis of emerging issues, and devt of creative yet workable policy responses; seeks to deepen public

understanding by publishing a variety of reports and papers, undertaking briefings, seminars and confs, and offering material for use in the press and on the air; br. in Beijing, China; library of 10,000 vols, 200 journals; Pres. and Exec Vice-Pres. and Man.Dir MANISH BAPNA.

Biological Sciences

Boyce Thompson Institute for Plant Research: 533 Tower Rd, Ithaca, NY 14853-1801; tel. (607) 254-1234; fax (607) 254-1242; e-mail bmr6@cornell.edu; internet bti.cornell.edu; f. 1924; non-profit ind. affiliate of Cornell Univ.; research on plants and human health, incl. air and water pollution, biochemistry, entomology, molecular biology, plant pathology, plant physiology; library of 4,700 vols; Chair. EZRA CORNELL; CEO and Pres. Dr DAVID B. STERN; Vice-Pres. for Research Dr ERIC RICHARDS; Sec. DONNA L. CLAES; Treas. SOPHIA DARLING; publ. *Transcript* (4 a year).

Center for Bioethics & Human Dignity: 2065 Half Day Rd, Deerfield, IL 60015; tel. (847) 317-8180; fax (847) 317-8101; e-mail info@cbhd.org; internet www.cbhd.org; f. 1994, present status 2007; attached to Trinity Int. Univ.; explores relation between biomedicine, biotechnology and humanity; Exec. Dir Dr PAIGE C. CUNNINGHAM; Man. Dir Dr MICHAEL J. SLEASMAN; Dir for Devt JOEL DILLON.

Coastal Institute: Narragansett Bay Campus, Rm 124, Univ. of Rhode Island, Narragansett, RI 02882; tel. (401) 874-6513; fax (401) 874-6869; e-mail ci@edc.uri.edu; internet www.ci.uri.edu; attached to Univ. of Rhode Island; advances knowledge and develops solutions to environmental problems in coastal ecosystem; Dir JUDITH SWIFT.

Cold Spring Harbor Laboratory: 1 Bungtown Rd, Cold Spring Harbor, NY 11724; tel. (516) 367-8800; fax (516) 367-8496; e-mail pubaff@cshl.edu; internet www.cshl.org; f. 1890, present status 1962, present name 1970; non-profit instn; research on bioinformatics and genomics, cancer biology, molecular neuroscience, plant genetics, professional education, structural biology and DNA literacy; library of 30,000 vols, special collns on history of science and genetics; Chair. JAMIE C. NICHOLLS; Pres Dr BRUCE W. STILLMAN; Chief Operating Officer W. DILLAWAY AYRES, JR; Sec. EDWARD TRAVAGLIANTI; Treas. LEO A. GUTHART; publs *Cold Spring Harbor Perspectives in Biology* (12 a year, online (www.cshperspectives.cshlp.org)), *Cold Spring Harbor Protocols* (12 a year), *Genes & Development* (6 a year), *Genome Research* (12 a year), *Learning & Memory* (6 a year), *RNA* (12 a year, online (www.rnajournal.cshlp.org)).

Desert Research Institute: 2215 Raggio Parkway, Reno, NV 89512; tel. (775) 673-7300; fax (775) 673-7421; internet www.dri .edu; f. 1959, present status 1969; attached to Nevada System of Higher Education; conducts research in air, land and life and water quality across Nevada, the USA and on every continent; campuses in Reno and Las Vegas; Pres. Dr STEPHEN G. WELLS; Exec. Vice-Pres. for Research Dr TERRENCE SURLES; Sr Vice-Pres. for Finance and Admin. and Chief Operations Officer ELLEN OPPENHEIM; Vice-Pres. for Devt RUSSEL KOST; Library Dir MELANIE SCOTT.

Institute of Arctic Studies: 6048 Haldeman Center, Dartmouth College, Hanover, NH 03755; tel. (603) 646-2023; e-mail dickey .center@dartmouth.edu; internet www .dartmouth.edu/~arctic; f. 1989; attached to The John Sloan Dickey Center for Int. Understanding, Dartmouth College; focuses

on environmental, cultural and political dimensions of the N and impact of climate change; Dir ROSS VIRGINIA.

Institute for Energy & the Environment: New Mexico State Univ., POB 3000, Las Cruces, NM 88003-8001; tel. (575) 646-2038; e-mail iee@nmsu.edu; internet iee.nmsu.edu; attached to New Mexco State Univ.; centers on devt, transfer, promotion and commercialization of renewable energy technologies through advancing education, training, outreach and research on areas related to the environment, energy, water and food safety; meets increased global energy and energy-related needs; envisions advanced electric power delivery, public policy, alternative resources, materials sciences, and environmental surety; Dir Prof. ABBAS GHASSEMI.

Institute of Environmental Health Science: Eugene Applebaum College of Pharmacy and Health Sciences, Wayne State Univ., 259 Mack Ave, Rm 5137, Detroit, MI 48201; tel. (313) 577-0100; fax (313) 577-0082; e-mail iehs_info@wayne.edu; internet www.iehs.wayne.edu; attached to Eugene Applebaum College of Pharmacy and Health Sciences, Wayne State Univ.; engages in basic mechanistic studies using animal and cellular models and human investigations to determine the complex role of environmental exposure in disease devt; Dir Dr MELISSA RUNGE-MORRIS.

Lincoln Park Zoological Gardens: 2001 N Clark St, Chicago, IL 60614; tel. (312) 742-2000; fax (312) 742-2137; e-mail guestservices@lpzoo.org; internet www.lpzoo .org; f. 1868; specimens of mammals, birds, reptiles, and amphibians; farm; specialities: great apes, primates, perching birds, snakes, big cats; spec. programmes: Farm in the Zoo, Travelling Zoo and Endangered Species educational programmes; scientific studies incl. nutrition, behaviour, reproductive biology, physiology, African, Asian and South American field work; research centres: Alexander Center for Applied Population Biology, Davee Center for Epidemiology and Endocrinology and Lester E. Fisher Center for the Study and Conservation of Apes; library of 2,000 vols; Chair. JOHN ALEXANDER; Pres. and CEO KEVIN J. BELL; publ. *Lincoln Park Zoo Magazine* (3 a year).

MBL: 7 MBL St, Woods Hole, MA 02543; tel. (508) 289-7423; fax (508) 540-6902; e-mail comm@mbl.edu; internet www.mbl.edu; f. 1888 as Marine Biological Laboratory; research and teaching instn; offers courses and seminars on ecology, behaviour, developmental biology, microbiology, neurobiology, parasitology, cell and molecular biology and biological techniques, global infectious diseases; library of 150,000 vols, 3,000 periodicals; Chair. JOHN W. ROWE; Dir and CEO GARY G. BORISY; publs *Catalyst* (2 a year), *MBL Guide to Research and Education* (1 a year), *The Biological Bulletin* (6 a year).

Missouri Botanical Garden: 4344 Shaw Blvd., St Louis, MO 63110; tel. (314) 577-5100; fax (314) 577-9595; e-mail tourism@ mobot.org; internet www.mobot.org; f. 1859; botanical research, exploration, education and display, with emphases on monographic and floristic studies in N America, tropical Latin America and Africa; archives and non-book materials, herbarium colln (5.8m. vascular plants and 300,000 bryophytes); library of 160,300 vols, 2,000 current periodicals, 3,000 reference works, 40,000 microfiche, 500 images (incl. glass plate negatives, hand-tinted prints, stereographs, postcards and MSS); spec. collns: Art (7,000 items), Ewan (11,000 vols), Linnaean (900 vols), Niederlander (600 vols), Sturtevant Pre-Linnaean (1,000 vols), Steere (3, 000, vols incl. titles on bryology and pamphlets); also incl. rare book colln (3,000 vols), folio colln (1,000 vols), maps and atlas colln (7,000 items); Chair. ARNOLD W. DONALD; Pres. Dr PETER WYSE JACKSON; publs *Annals of the Missouri Botanical Garden* (4 a year), *Bulletin* (7 a year), *Novon* (4 a year).

Moss Landing Marine Laboratories: 8272 Moss Landing Rd, Moss Landing, CA 95039; tel. (831) 771-4400; fax (831) 632-4403; e-mail frontdesk@mlml.calstate.edu; internet www.mlml.calstate.edu; f. 1966; research, undergraduate and postgraduate education in the marine sciences; library of 10,000 vols; Dir Dr JAMES T. HARVEY.

Mote Marine Laboratory: 1600 Ken Thompson Parkway, Sarasota, FL 34236-1096; tel. (941) 388-4441; fax (941) 388-4312; e-mail info@mote.org; internet www.mote.org; f. 1955; ind., non-profit marine research org.; 7 centers for marine research; research incl. aquaculture, biology and behaviour of fishes, biomedical research, environmental assessment, estuarine and coastal ecology, marine chemistry, marine mammals, sea turtles and biomedical research toxicology; aquarium and environmental education programmes; library of 28,000 vols, 16,000 books and documents, 400 journal titles, 3,500 reprints, 1,500 Mote Technical Reports; Chair. ROBERT E. CARTER; Pres. and CEO Dr KUMAR MAHADEVAN; Vice-Chair. EUGENE BECKSTEIN; Sec. MICKEY CALLANEN; Treas. LT GEN. HOWARD G. CROWELL; publs *Collected Papers* (every 3 years), *Mote Magazine* (1 a year), *Mote Technical Reports* (irregular).

New England Aquarium: Central Wharf, Boston, MA 02110-3399; tel. (617) 973-5200; e-mail comments@neaq.org; internet www.neaq.org; f. 1969; public aquarium, conservation and research programmes, incl. bycatch and aquaculture, climate change and the oceans, endangered species and habitats and sustainable fisheries; library of 3,000 vols; Pres. and CEO BUD RIS; Exec. Vice-Pres., Chief Operating Officer and Treas. WALTER J. FLAHERTY; Sr Vice-Pres. Dr GREGORY STONE; publ. *Blue* (4 a year).

New Mexico Water Resources Research Institute: New Mexico State Univ., MSC 3167, POB 30001, Las Cruces, NM 88003-8001; Stucky Hall, 3170 S Espina St, Las Cruces, NM 88003-8001; tel. (575) 646-4337; fax (575) 646-6418; e-mail nmwrri@wrri.nmsu.edu; internet wrri.nmsu.edu; f. 1963; attached to New Mexico State Univ.; develops and disseminates knowledge that will assist the state and nation in solving water problems; funds research conducted by faculty and students from univs across the state to address water problems critical to NM and SW; mem. of Nat. Institutes for Water Resources and Powell Consortium; Dir SAM FERNALD; publ. *Journal of Transboundary Water Resources*.

New York Botanical Garden: 2900 S Blvd, Bronx, NY 10458-5126; tel. (718) 817-8700; fax (718) 220-6405; internet www.nybg.org; f. 1891; conducts basic research in plant biology and studies all species of plants and fungi; William and Lynda Steere Herbarium houses 7.3m. specimens; library: over 1m. items, incl. 196,000 vols; CEO GREGORY LONG; Chair. MAUREEN CHILTON; Sec. and Treas. THOMAS J. HUBBARD; publs *Botanical Review* (4 a year), *Brittonia* (4 a year), *Economic Botany* (4 a year).

Pennington Biomedical Research Center: 6400 Perkins Rd, Baton Rouge, LA 70808-4124; tel. (225) 763-2500; fax (225) 763-2525; internet www.pbrc.edu; f. 1988; attached to Louisiana State Univ.; houses 53 laboratories; research areas incl. epidemi-ology and prevention, physical activity and health, cancer, diabetes, obesity, neurodegeneration, genomics and molecular genetics, stem cell and devt biology, neurobiology and nutrient sensing and signalling; Exec. Dir Dr STEVEN B. HEYMSFIELD.

Rhode Island Sea Grant: 220 S Ferry Rd, Narragansett, RI 02882; tel. (401) 874-6800; fax (401) 789-8340; internet seagrant.gso.uri.edu; attached to Graduate School of Oceanography, Univ. of Rhode Island; supports research, extension, legal, and education programmes that address issues in the thematic areas of sustainable coastal devt, healthy coastal ecosystems, and safe and sustainable seafood; Dir Prof. BARRY A. COSTA-PIERCE; publ. *41°N*.

Salk Institute for Biological Studies: POB 85800, San Diego, CA 92186-5800; 10010 N Torrey Pines Rd, La Jolla, CA 92037; tel. (858) 453-4100; fax (858) 552-8285; e-mail communications@salk.edu; internet www.salk.edu; f. 1960; advanced biological research into HIV/AIDS, cell biology, chemistry and proteomics, computational and theoretical biology, metabolic research, molecular biology and genetics; neurosciences, plant biology, regulatory biology and stem cell biology; has 9 research centres; library of 15,000 vols; Chair. IRWIN MARK JACOBS; Pres. Dr WILLIAM R. BRODY; Exec. Vice-Pres. Dr MARSHA A. CHANDLER; publs *From the Bench*, *InsideSalk*, *Stories of Discovery*.

Smithsonian Environmental Research Center (SERC): POB 28, 647 Contees Wharf Rd, Edgewater, MD 21037-0028; tel. (443) 482-2200; fax (443) 482-2380; internet www.serc.si.edu; f. 1965 as Chesapeake Center for Field Biology, present name 1985; attached to Smithsonian Institution; multidisciplinary instn dedicated to increasing knowledge of the biological and physical processes that sustain life on earth; scientific programmes: animal–plant interactions, biogeochemistry, chemical ecology, ecological modelling, estuarine zoology, forest ecology, invasion studies, micro–zooplankton, phytoplankton, plant ecophysiology, plant ecology, plant physiology, solar radiation, terrestrial animal ecology; part of the Smithsonian Marine Science Network; library: br. library of the Smithsonian Instn Libraries system: 12,500 books and bound journals, 120 current journals, colln of *Chesapeakiana*; Dir TUCK HINES; Librarian ANGELA N. HAGGINS.

Smithsonian Gardens: POB 37012, Capital Gallery, Suite 3300, MRC 506, Washington, DC 20013-7012; tel. (202) 633-2220; fax (202) 633-5697; e-mail gardens@si.edu; internet gardens.si.edu; f. 1972; research and educational programmes; manages grounds of the Smithsonian Instn museums and creates horticultural exhibitions; Smithsonian Orchid colln (10,000 plants); library: Archives of American Gardens: 80,000 photographic images, records of historic and contemporary American gardens; special collns: Garden Club of America (40,000 images), J. Horace McFarland (glass lantern slides and photographs), Thomas Warren Sears (glass negatives).

Smithsonian Marine Station at Fort Pierce: 701 Seaway Dr., Fort Pierce, FL 34949; tel. (772) 462-6220; fax (772) 461-8154; internet www.sms.si.edu; f. 1969 as Fort Pierce Bureau, present name 1998; attached to Nat. Museum of Natural History, Smithsonian Instn; research into marine biodiversity and ecosystems of Florida; Head Scientist Dr VALERIE PAUL.

Smithsonian National Zoological Park: National Zoo Information, DEVS, POB 37012, MRC 5516, Washington, DC 20013-7012; 3001 Connecticut Ave, NW, Washington, DC 20008; tel. (202) 633-4888; e-mail nationalzoo@nzp.si.edu; internet nationalzoo.si.edu; f. 1889; attached to Smithsonian Instn; scientific research in behaviour, biodiversity monitoring, conservation ecology and nutrition, population management, reproductive biology and veterinary medicine; animal colln of 2,800 specimens from 435 species; Chair. JOHN W. MARRIOTT, III; Dir DENNIS W. KELLY; publ. *Smithsonian Zoogoer* (6 a year).

Attached Research Institutes:

Smithsonian Conservation Biology Institute: 1500 Remount Rd, Front Royal, Front Royal, VA 22630; tel. (202) 633-3055; internet nationalzoo.si.edu/scbi; f. 2010 fmrly Conservation and Research Center; veterinary and reproductive research; 6 centers of excellence: Center for Animal Care Sciences, Center for Conservation Ecology, Center for Conservation & Evolutionary Genetics, Center for Species Survival, Migratory Bird Center, Center for Conservation Education and Sustainability.

Stone Laboratory: 1314 Kinnear Rd, Area 100, Columbus, OH 43212-1156; tel. (614) 292-8949; fax (614) 292-4364; e-mail stonelab@osu.edu; internet www.stonelab.osu.edu; f. 1895; attached to Ohio State Univ.; freshwater biological field station; addresses problems facing the Great Lakes; Dir Dr JEFFERY M. REUTTER.

University of Maryland Center for Environmental Science: POB 775, Cambridge, MD 21613; tel. (410) 228-9250; fax (410) 228-3843; e-mail info@umces.edu; internet www.ca.umces.edu; research, education, service instn; focuses on science of coastal environments and their watersheds; incl. 4 laboratories; Pres. Prof. Dr DONALD F. BOESCH.

Physical Sciences

Argonne National Laboratory: 9700 S Cass Ave, Argonne, IL 60439; tel. (630) 252-2000; e-mail media@anl.gov; internet www.anl.gov; f. 1942 as Metallurgical Laboratory, present name 1946; attached to Univ. of Chicago; U.S. Dept of Energy's nat. laboratory for science and engineering research; primary focus on basic research in the physical, life and environmental sciences, and on technology-directed research in fission, fossil and fusion energy as well as conservation and renewable energy; library of 65,000 books, 550,000 technical reports, 4,000 journals and numerous standards, media, maps, translations and patents; Chair. R. J. ZIMMER; CEO D. H. LEVY; Dir Dr ERIC ISAACS; publ. *Argonne Now* (2 a year).

Association of Universities for Research in Astronomy (AURA): 1212 New York Ave NW, Suite 450, Washington, DC 20005; tel. (202) 483-2101; fax (202) 483-2106; e-mail dnarcisso@aura-astronomy.org; internet www.aura-astronomy.org; f. 1957; consortium of univs; operates the Space Telescope Science Institute, Baltimore, MD, and the Nat. Optical Astronomy Observatories, Tucson, AZ, which consist of the Kitt Peak Nat. Observatory, AZ, the Nat. Solar Observatory, AZ and NM, and Cerro Tololo Inter-American Observatory, Chile; manages the Int. Gemini Project, Tucson, AZ; library of 30,000 vols; Chair. Dr DAN CLEMENS; Pres. WILLIAM S. SMITH; Exec. Vice-Pres. HEIDI B. HAMMEL; Vice-Pres. for Admin. DEBORAH NARCISSO.

Byrd Polar Research Center at the Ohio State University: Scott Hall, Room 108, 1090 Carmack Rd, Ohio State Un., Columbus, OH 43210-1002; tel. (614) 292-6531; fax (614) 292-4697; internet bprc.osu.edu; f.

1960; research focuses on the role of cold regions in the Earth's overall climate system, and encompasses geological sciences, geochemistry, glaciology, paleoclimatology, meteorology, remote sensing, ocean dynamics and the history of polar exploration; library of 12,000 vols, 1,000 maps, also holds papers and memorabilia of Richard E. Byrd, Sir Hubert Wilkins and other polar explorers; Dir Dr ELLEN MOSLEY-THOMPSON; publs *Report* (irregular), *Technical Report* (irregular).

Case Western Reserve University Astronomy: 10900 Euclid Ave, Cleveland, OH 44106-7164; tel. (216) 368-3728; fax (216) 368-5203; e-mail dept@astronomy.case.edu; internet astronomy.case.edu; f. 1881; attached to Dept of Astronomy; astronomical research and education in galaxy formation and evolution, stellar chemical abundances, and telescope instrumentation and design; uses a $9\frac{1}{2}$" telescope on the Cleveland campus; owns and operates Burrell Schmidt Telescope; library of 3,000 vols, 4,000 bound periodicals, 480 linear ft of observatory publs; Dept Chair Dr CHRIS MIHOS.

Center for Earth and Planetary Studies (CEPS): Smithsonian Institution, POB 37012, Nat. Air and Space Museum, MRC 315, Washington, DC 20013-7012; tel. (202) 633-2470; internet www.nasm.si.edu/ceps; f. 1974; attached to Smithsonian Nat. Air and Space Museum; research into planetary and terrestrial geology and geophysics; application of remote sensing data from Earth-orbiting satellites and space missions; designated Regional Planetary Image Facility (RPIF); colln of Space Shuttle photographs; responsible for museum galleries 'Exploring the Planets' and 'Looking at Earth'; Chair. Dr JOHN GRANT; Programme Man. PRISCILLA STRAIN.

Fermilab: POB 500, Batavia, IL 60510-5011; Wilson and Kirk Rds, Batavia, IL 60510-5011; tel. (630) 840-3000; fax (630) 840-4343; e-mail fermilab@fnal.gov; internet www.fnal.gov; f. 1967 as Nat. Accelerator Laboratory, present name 1974; attached to US Dept of Energy; research in high energy physics; library of 15,000 vols, 250 periodicals; Dir PIERMARIA J. ODDONE; Deputy Dir YOUNG-KEE KIM; publs *International Science Grid This Week* (54 a year, online (www.isgtw.org)), *Symmetry* (12 a year).

Harvard–Smithsonian Center for Astrophysics (CfA): 60 Garden St, Cambridge, MA 02138; tel. (617) 495-7463; fax (617) 495-7468; internet sao-www.harvard.edu; f. 1973 by merger of Harvard College Observatory (f. 1839) with Smithsonian Astrophysical Observatory (f. 1890); scientific divs: atomic and molecular physics, high energy astrophysics, optical and infrared astronomy, radio and geoastronomy, solar, stellar and planetary sciences, theoretical astrophysics, science education; library: John G. Wolbach Library and Information Resource Center (combines libraries of the SAO and HCO) of 75,000 vols, 40,000 astronomic photographic plates; Dir CHARLES ALCOCK; Deputy Dir ROGER BRISSENDEN.

Lamont-Doherty Earth Observatory: POB 1000, 61 Route 9W, Palisades, NY 10964-1000; tel. (845) 359-2900; fax (845) 365-8101; e-mail director@ldeo.columbia.edu; internet www.ldeo.columbia.edu; f. 1949 as Lamont Geological Observatory, present name 1993; attached to Earth Institute, Columbia Univ.; research in atmospheric processes, climate, ecology and ecosystems, earth and ocean sciences, polar science, solid earth dynaimcs and surface and environmental processes; library of 30,000 vols, 500

journals; Dir ART LERNER-LAM; publs *List of Scientific Publications, Year Book.*

Lick Observatory: POB 85, Mount Hamilton, CA 95140; tel. (831) 459-5933; fax (831) 459-5244; e-mail giftshop@ucolick.org; internet mthamilton.ucolick.org; f. 1888; attached to Univ. of California Observatories; optical and near-infrared astronomy and astrophysics; library of 2,000 vols, 150,000 plates, 450 linear ft archival material; Dir M. BOLTE; Deputy Dir JOHN WAREHAM.

Liquid Crystal Institute: POB 5190, 1425 Univ. Esplanade, Kent, OH 44242-0001; tel. (330) 672-2654; fax (330) 672-2796; internet www.lcinet.kent.edu; f. 1965 as Glenn H. Brown Liquid Crystal Institute; attached to Kent State Univ.; addresses entire range of multidisciplinary topics associated with the science and technology of liquid crystals and related self-organized materials and devices; Dir and CEO Dr HIROSHI YOKOYAMA.

Lowell Observatory: 1400 W Mars Hill Rd, Flagstaff, AZ 86001; tel. (928) 774-3358; fax (928) 774-6296; e-mail info@lowell.edu; internet www.lowell.edu; f. 1894; non-profit research instn; conducts research on a range of solar system and astrophysical topics using ground-based, airborne and space-based telescopes; library: astronomical research library of 12,000 vols; Dir JEFFREY HALL; Librarian LAUREN AMUNDSON; publ. *The Lowell Observer.*

Lunar and Planetary Institute: 3600 Bay Area Blvd, Houston, TX 77058; tel. (281) 486-2100; fax (281) 486-2127; e-mail info@lpi.usra.edu; internet www.lpi.usra.edu; f. 1968 as Lunar Science Institute; attached to Univs Space Research Asscn (USRA); provides support services to NASA and planetary science community; centre for lunar and planetary science; conducts research on formation, evolution and current state of the Moon, planets, comets, asteroids, planetary satellites, cosmic dust and solar system; library of 60,000 vols (incl. books, documents, maps and globes, videos), 100 periodicals, also photographic and cartographic data from planetary spacecraft missions; Dir Dr STEPHEN MACKWELL.

Maria Mitchell Association: 4 Vestal St, Nantucket, MA 02554; tel. (508) 228-9198; fax (508) 228-1031; e-mail info@mmo.org; internet www.mmo.org; f. 1902; astronomical research, research training, public lectures and viewings; manages Hinchman House Natural Science Museum, Loines Observatory, Maria Mitchell Observatory, Mitchell House (birthplace of Maria Mitchell), Science Library, Aquarium; library of 8,000 vols of rare and out-of-print natural science, astronomy, and Nantucket books; Exec. Dir Dr JANET E. SCHULTE; Dir of Natural Sciences and Education and Programmes ANDREW MCKENNA-FOSTER; Dir of Astronomy Dr VLADIMIR STRELNITSKI.

Materials Research Institute: N-317 Millennium Science Complex, Pollock Rd, University Park, PA 16802-7003; tel. (814) 863-8407; fax (814) 863-8561; e-mail mri-info@research.psu.edu; internet www.mri.psu.edu; f. 1992; attached to Pennsylvania State Univ.; vertically integrates discovery of new substances with scientific understanding and engineering devt of their properties, and in parallel, link them with the materials integration and systems performance required to solve problems; materials for research incl. biomedical materials and devices, electronic materials and devices, materials, processes and tools, nanomaterials, nanostructures and nanofabrication and polymeric systems; Dir Prof. CARLO PANTANO; publ. *Focus On Materials.*

Mount Graham International Observatory (MGIO): 1480 W Swift Trail, Safford, AZ 85546; tel. (928) 428-2739; fax (928) 428-2854; e-mail mgiomail@as.arizona.edu; internet mgpc3.as.arizona.edu; attached to Steward Observatory, Dept of Astronomy, Univ. of Arizona; operates and maintains facilities in the Pinaleño Mountains in SE Arizona; Dir BUDDY E. POWELL.

Constituent Centres:

Arizona Radio Observatory (ARO): Univ. of Arizona, 933 N Cherry Ave, Tucson, AZ 85721; tel. (520) 621-5290; fax (520) 621-5554; e-mail opersmt@as.arizona.edu; internet aro.as.arizona.edu; operates the Heinrich Hertz Submillimeter Telescope (HHSMT); Dir Dr LUCY ZIURYS.

Large Binocular Telescope Observatory (LBTO): Univ. of Arizona, 933 N Cherry Ave, Room 552, Tucson, AZ 85721-0065; tel. (520) 626-5231; fax (520) 626-9333; internet www.lbto.org; f. 1988, operational 2007; the world's most powerful optical telescope; consists of 2 8.4-m mirrors on a common mount; a collaboration between the Italian astronomical community (represented by the Istituto Nazionale di Astrofisica—*q.v.*—the Univ. of Arizona, Arizona State Univ., Northern Arizona Univ., the LBT Beteiligungsgesellschaft in Germany, the Ohio State Univ., Research Corpn in Tucson and the Univ. of Notre Dame; Dir RICHARD F. GREEN.

Vatican Observatory Research Group (VORG): Steward Observatory, Univ. of Arizona, Tucson, AZ 85721; tel. (520) 621-3225; fax (520) 621-1532; e-mail ccorbally@as.arizona.edu; internet vaticanobservatory.org; f. 1981; attached to Vatican Observatory, Vatican City; operates the 1.8-m Alice P. Lennon Telescope with its Thomas J. Bannan Astrophysics Facility, known together as the Vatican Advanced Technology Telescope (VATT), on Mount Graham, Arizona; Vice-Dir for the Vatican Observatory for VORG Dr CHRISTOPHER J. CORBALLY.

NASA Goddard Institute for Space Studies: 2880 Broadway, New York, NY 10025; tel. (212) 678-5500; fax (212) 678-5552; internet www.giss.nasa.gov; f. 1961; attached to Earth Sciences Div., Goddard Space Flight Center; global climate, biogeochemical cycles, cloud studies, planetary atmospheres, global habitality; library of 15,000 vols; Dir Dr JAMES HANSEN.

National Center for Atmospheric Research (NCAR): POB 3000, Boulder, CO 80307-3000; 3090 Center Green Dr., Boulder, CO 80301; tel. (303) 497-2525; fax (303) 497-1194; internet www.ncar.ucar.edu; f. 1960; sponsored by Nat. Science Foundation; operated by the Univ. Corpn for Atmospheric Research (UCAR); research in weather prediction, causes of climatic trends, solar processes and influences of the sun on weather and climate, convective storms and global air quality; library of 100,000 items, 900 current journals; Dir Dr ROGER WAKIMOTO; Deputy Dir Dr MAURA HAGAN; publs *Highlights* (every 2 years), *NCAR Scientific Report, UCAR* (4 a year).

National Radio Astronomy Observatory: 520 Edgemont Rd, Charlottesville, VA 22903-2475; tel. (434) 296-0211; fax (434) 296-0278; e-mail hwinter@nrao.edu; internet www.nrao.edu; f. 1956; funded by the Nat. Science Foundation, operated under co-operative agreement by Assoc. Univs, Inc.; research in radio astronomy, radio astronomy electronics, design of radio telescopes; observing radio telescopes, incl. a 27-element array of 82-ft radio telescopes in New Mexico (Very Large Array); a 10-element array of 82-ft radio telescopes located in 7 states and the US Virgin Islands (Very Long Baseline Array) dedicated to very long baseline interferometry; and a 100-m fully steerable telescope in West Virginia (Robert C. Byrd Green Bank Telescope); library of 27,000 vols; Dir FRED K. Y. LO; Deputy Dir PHIL JEWELL.

National Solar Observatory: NSO Sacramento Peak, 3010 Coronal Loop, Sunspot, NM 88349; tel. (575) 434-7000; internet www .nso.edu; f. 1952; operated by AURA (q.v.); national centre for solar research; offers telescope use to astronomical community; conducts solar research; 50 staff, incl. 11 astrophysicists; library of 8,000 vols; Dir STEPHEN L. KEIL.

Physical Science Laboratory: POB 30002, Las Cruces, NM 88003-8002; Anderson Hall, Corner of Stewart and Espina, Las Cruces, NM 88003; tel. (575) 646-9200; fax (575) 646-9389; e-mail director@psl.nmsu.edu; internet www.psl.nmsu.edu; f. 1946; attached to New Mexico State Univ.; areas of research incl: sub-orbital platforms, information modeling for predictive decision making, specialized intelligence community support, advanced NASA scientific exploration and experimentation, homeland security sensing and detection technologies, and advanced weapons and countermeasures devt and testing; Dir Dr JAY JORDAN.

Radiation Research Society: POB 7050, Lawrence, KS 66044-8897; 810 E 10th St, Lawrence, KS 66044-8897; fax (785) 843-6153; e-mail info@radres.org; internet www .radres.org; f. 1952; facilitates inter-disciplinary cooperative research between biology, chemistry, medicine and physics in the study of the properties and effects of radiation; promotes dissemination of knowledge in these and related fields through publications, meetings and educational symposia; Pres. Dr JACQUELINE P. WILLIAMS; Pres.-Elect Dr TOM K. HEI; Exec. Dir. KATHY VOTAW; Sec. and Treas. Dr ELEANOR A. BLAKELY; publ. *Radiation Research* (12 a year).

Scripps Institution of Oceanography: 8622 Kennel Way, La Jolla, CA 92093-0210; tel. (858) 534-3624; fax (858) 534-5306; e-mail scrippsnews@ucsd.edu; internet www .scripps.ucsd.edu; f. 1903, present status 1912; attached to Univ. of California, San Diego; ocean and earth science research; education and public service; main depts: associated Univ. of California institutes: institute of geophysics and planetary physics, California space institute, center for atmospheric sciences, center for coastal studies, center for marine biotechnology and biomedicine, climate research, geosciences research, marine biology research, marine physical laboratory, marine research, marine life research group, physical oceanography, Scripps graduate dept; spec. facilities incl. hydraulics laboratory; operates 4 research vessels and 1 platform; public aquarium (Birch Aquarium) and museum; geological and biological collns; library of 227,000 vols, 700 print periodicals, more than 100,000 vols digitized; Dir Dr TONY HAYMET; publs *Explorations Now* (irregular), *Scripps Wide*.

Sproul Observatory: Computer Science Dept, Swarthmore College, 500 College Ave, Swarthmore, PA 19081-1397; tel. (610) 328-8272; fax (610) 328-8606; e-mail info@cs .swarthmore.edu; internet www.cs .swarthmore.edu/program/history/sproul .html; f. 1906; attached to Swarthmore College; hosts occasional physics and astronomy observing sessions; 61-cm reflector and echelle spectrometer; astrometry and stellar spectroscopy; library of 9,000 vols.

United States Naval Observatory: 3450 Massachusetts Ave, NW, Washington, DC 20392-5420; tel. (202) 762-1467; fax (202) 762-1489; e-mail usno_pao@navy.mil; internet www.usno.navy.mil/usno; f. 1830 as Depot of Charts and Instruments, present location 1893; provides astronomical data and products; serves as official source of time for the US Dept of Defense and standard of time for the USA; substation at Flagstaff, AZ; library of 75,000 vols; Superintendent Capt. R. SCOTT STEADLEY; Scientific Dir Dr KENNETH JOHNSTON; publs *Air Almanac, Astronomical Almanac, Astronomical Papers, Astronomical Phenomena, Multiyear Interactive Computer Almanac, Nautical Almanac, NavObs Circulars, Time Service Bulletins,* star catalogs.

Vanderbilt Dyer Observatory: 1000 Oman Dr., Brentwood, TN 37027; tel. (615) 373-4897; fax (615) 371-3904; e-mail lynn.d .mcdonald@vanderbilt.edu; internet www .dyer.vanderbilt.edu; f. 1953; attached to Vanderbilt Univ.; specializes in research on local structure of the Milky Way, photoelectric photometry of eclipsing binaries and variable stars, pre-planetary discs around young stars; equipped with combination 60-cm reflecting and Baker-Schmidt telescope, 40-cm computer-controlled automatic telescope, 30-cm and 40-cm Cassegrain reflecting telescopes and 15-cm refracting telescope; library of 12,000 vols; Dir ROCKY ALVEY; publ. *IAPPP Communications* (4 a year).

Woods Hole Oceanographic Institution: 266 Woods Hole Rd, Woods Hole, MA 02543-1050; tel. (508) 289-2252; fax (508) 457-2034; e-mail information@whoi.edu; internet www .whoi.edu; f. 1930; research in physical, chemical and biological oceanography, marine geology and marine geophysics, ocean acoustics, ocean engineering and marine policy; 4 ocean institutes: Coastal Oceans Institute, Deep Ocean Exploration Institute, Ocean & Climate Change Institute, and Ocean Life Institute; conducts jt PhD programme with Massachusetts Institute of Technology, postdoctoral fellowship programme and summer student fellowship programme; library of 150,000 vols, 5,000 periodicals, jt library with Marine Biological Laboratory; Pres. and Dir SUSAN K. AVERY; Dir of Research Dr LAURENCE P. MADIN; publs *Oceanus* (3 a year), *Woods Hole Currents* (irregular).

Yale Southern Observatory, Inc: Dept of Astronomy, Yale Univ., POB 208101, New Haven, CT 06520-8101; J. W. Gibbs Laboratory, Second Fl., 260 Whitney Ave, Yale Univ., New Haven, CT 06511; tel. (203) 432-3000; fax (203) 432-5048; internet www .astro.yale.edu/astrom/yso.html; f. 1962 as Yale-Columbia Southern Observatory, Inc., present status and name 1975; attached to Dept of Astronomy, Yale Univ.; non-profit corpn; provides framework for Yale faculty mems to perform astronomical research in the Southern Hemisphere; holds Double Astrograph telescope consisting of 2 lenses, each 20-inches in diameter: one designed for blue light and the other for visual light; publs *Bright Star Catalogue* (and supplement), *General Catalogue of Trigonometric Stellar Parallaxes, Transactions.*

Yerkes Observatory: 373 W Geneva St, Williams Bay, WI 53191; tel. (262) 245-5555; fax (262) 245-9805; internet astro.uchicago .edu/yerkes; f. 1897; attached to Dept of Astronomy and Astrophysics, Univ. of Chicago; provides laboratory space and access to telescopes for research and instruction; library of 25,000 books and journals; Dir Dr KYLE M. CUDWORTH.

PHILOSOPHY AND PSYCHOLOGY

American Society for Psychical Research, Inc.: 5 W 73rd St, New York, NY 10023; tel. (212) 799-5050; fax (212) 496-2497; e-mail aspr@aspr.com; internet www .aspr.com; f. 1885; study of paranormal phenomena such as telepathy, clairvoyance, precognition, psychokinesis, etc.; library of 15,000 vols, over 300 periodicals; Exec. Dir PATRICE KEANE; Librarian JEFF TWINE; publ. *Journal* (2 a year).

RELIGION, SOCIOLOGY AND ANTHROPOLOGY

Africana Studies and Research Center: 310 Triphammer Rd, Ithaca, NY 14850; tel. (607) 255-4625; fax (607) 255-0784; e-mail africana@cornell.edu; internet www.asrc .cornell.edu; attached to Cornell Univ.; studies African people, global migrations and reconstruction of African peoples, as well as patterns of linkages to the African continent; library of 17,000 vols; Dir ELIZABETH ADKINS-REGAN.

American Institutes for Research: 1000 Thomas Jefferson St, NW, Washington, DC 20007; tel. (202) 403-5000; fax (202) 403-5454; e-mail inquiry@air.org; internet www .air.org; f. 1946; independent, non-profit org. conducting research, devt, analysis and evaluation studies in the behavioural and social sciences and quality of education, health care, and workplace for clients in govt and the private sector; brs in San Mateo and Sacramento, CA, Atlanta GA, Honolulu, HI, Chicago IL, Baltimore, Frederick and Silver Spring MD, Boston Area MA, New York, NY, Chapel Hill, NC, Columbus, OH, Portland, OR; int. offices in Egypt, Ethiopia, Georgia, Haiti, Honduras, Kenya, Liberia, Malawi, Nicaragua, Pakistan, South Africa and Zambia; Chair. PATRICIA B. GURIN; Pres. and CEO DAVID MYERS.

American Research Center in Egypt (ARCE): 8700 Crownhill Blvd, Suite 507, San Antonio, TX 78209-1130; tel. (210) 821-7000; fax (210) 821-7007; e-mail info@arce .org; internet www.arce.org Cairo Office: 2 Midan Simón Bolívar, Garden City, Cairo, 11461, Egypt; tel. (2) 796-4681; fax (2) 794-8622; e-mail arce@internetegypt.com; f. 1948; ind., non-profit-making; promotes research on Egypt and the Middle East in the fields of archaeology, art, architecture, history, culture, social sciences; library: (in Cairo) of 25,000 vols, 300 journal titles; Pres. Dr EMILY TEETER; Vice-Pres. SAMEH ISKANDER; Treas. CHARLES FROHLICH; Asst Dir for US Operations RACHEL MAULDIN; Cairo Dir GERRY DEE SCOTT, III; publs *Bulletin of the American Research Center in Egypt* (2 a year), *Journal of the American Research Center in Egypt (JARCE)* (1 a year).

American Schools of Oriental Research: Boston Univ., 656 Beacon St, 5th Fl., Boston, MA 02215-2010; tel. (617) 353-6570; fax (617) 353-6575; e-mail asor@bu.edu; internet www .asor.org; f. 1900; promotes research into the cultures of the Near E and supports activities of ind. archaeological instns abroad: Albright Institute of Archaeological Research (Jerusalem, Israel), American Center of Oriental Research (Amman, Jordan), and Cyprus American Archaeological Research Institute (Nicosia, Cyprus); Pres. TIMOTHY P. HARRISON; Exec. Dir Dr ANDREW G. VAUGHN; publs *Bulletin of the American Schools of Oriental Research* (4 a year), *Journal of Cuneiform Studies* (1 a year), *Near Eastern Archaeology* (4 a year).

Arctic Studies Center: POB 37012, Dept of Anthropology, MRC 112, Washington, DC 20013-7012; tel. (202) 633-1887; fax (202) 357-2684; e-mail arctics@si.edu; internet www.mnh.si.edu/arctic; f. 1988; attached to Dept of Anthropology of the Smithsonian Instn's Nat. Museum of Natural History; research into peoples, history, archaeology and social change in the circumpolar regions; Dir WILLIAM W. FITZHUGH.

Regional Office:

Alaska Office: 625C St, Anchorage, AK 99501; tel. (907) 929-9207; fax (907) 929-9232; e-mail crowella@si.edu; publs *Contributions to Circumpolar Anthropology*, *Field Reports* (1 a year).

Calvin Center for Christian Scholarship: 3201 Burton St, SE, Grand Rapids, MI 49546; 2041 Raybrook, Suite 201G Grand Rapids, MI 49546; tel. (616) 526-7162; fax (616) 526-6681; e-mail info@calvin.edu; internet www.calvin.edu/admin/cccs; f. 1976; attached to Calvin College; coordinates and provides leadership for the project of advancing and improving intentional Christian scholarship at Calvin College; Dir Prof. Dr SUSAN M. FELCH.

Center for Advanced Study in the Behavioral Sciences: 75 Alta Rd, Stanford, CA 94305-8090; tel. (650) 736-0100; fax (650) 736-0221; e-mail info@casbs.info@casbs.stanford.edu; internet www.casbs.org; f. 1954; attached to Stanford Univ.; basic understanding of the social, psychological, historical, biological and cultural foundations of behaviour and soc.; library of 1,700 vols, colln of Ralph W. Tyler; Dir STEPHEN M. KOSSLYN; publ. *Reports*.

Center for Social Research: Calvin College, Raybrook Bldg 2041, Suite 103, 3201 Burton, SE, Grand Rapids, MI 49546; tel. (616) 526-7799; fax (616) 526-7683; e-mail csr@calvin.edu; internet www.calvin.edu/admin/csr; f. 1970; attached to Dept of Sociology, Calvin College; serves as a catalyst for scholarly research in social science; organizes grant-funded scholarly research projects; Dir Dr NEIL CARLSON.

Center for the Study of Citizenship: 656 W Kirby, Faculty Admin. Bldg, Detroit, MI 48202; tel. (313) 577-2593; fax (313) 577-6987; internet www.clas.wayne.edu/citizenship; attached to College of Liberal Arts and Sciences, Wayne State Univ.; promotes interdisciplinary research and exchange about citizenship within a global community of scholars, students, political community and business leaders and gen. public; Dir Dr MARC W. KRUMAN.

Center for Urban Studies: 5700 Cass, 2207 A/AB, Detroit, MI 48202; tel. (313) 577-2208; fax (313) 577-1274; e-mail cusinfo@wayne.edu; internet www.cus.wayne.edu; f. 1967; attached to Wayne State Univ.; conducts research and provides support to scholars, community organizations, businesses, municipalities, foundations, non-profits and others throughout SE Michigan; involved in education and policy analysis, geographic information systems and mapping, data colln, sampling, grants and data analysis; Dir Dr LYKE THOMPSON; Man. Dir CHARO HULLEZA.

Justice System Training & Research Institute: School of Justice Studies, 1 Old Ferry Rd, Bristol, RI 02809-2921; tel. (401) 254-3731; fax (401) 254-3351; internet www.rwu.edu/academics/schools/sjs/jstri; attached to School of Justice Studies, Roger Williams Univ.; trains public safety personnel; provides information for criminal justice community; acts as applied research resource; Dir Dr ROBERT MCKENNA.

Labor Studies Center—Labor@Wayne: 656 W Kirby St, 3178 Faculty Admin. Bldg, Detroit, MI 48201; tel. 313) 577-2191; fax (313) 577-7726; e-mail ac6644@wayne.edu;

internet www.clas.wayne.edu/lsc; attached to College of Liberal Arts and Sciences, Wayne State Univ.; labour education centre; strengthens capacity of organized labour to represent needs and interests of workers; conducts research and teaching on labour and workplace issues; Dir GAYLE HAMILTON.

Lewis Center for Church Leadership: 4500 Massachusetts Ave, NW, Washington, DC 20016; tel. (202) 885-8757; fax (202) 885-8683; e-mail lewiscenter@wesleyseminary.edu; internet www.churchleadership.com; f. 2003; attached to Wesley Theological Seminary; seeks holistic understanding of leadership that brings together theology and management, scholarship and practice, research and application; Chair. C. RANDALL NUCKOLLS; Dir Dr LOVETT H. WEEMS, JR.

Middle American Research Institute: Tulane Univ., Dinwiddie Hall, 3rd Fl., 6823 St, Charles Ave, New Orleans, LA 70118-5698; tel. (504) 865-5110; fax (504) 862-8778; e-mail mari@tulane.edu; internet www.tulane.edu/~mari; f. 1924 as Dept of Middle American Research; attached to Tulane Univ.; research, education and publs related to Mexico and Central America; supports publ., archaeological excavation and research in humanities and social sciences; small museum gallery; anthropological collns; engages in exhibitions, workshops, and symposia; Dir MARCELLO A. CANUTO; publ. *Bulletin* (2 a year).

Middle East Institute: 1761 N St, NW, Washington, DC 20036-2882; tel. (202) 785-1141; fax (202) 331-8861; e-mail information@mei.edu; internet www.mideasti.org; f. 1946; a non-profit, non-advocating resource centre; promotes American understanding of the Middle East, North Africa, the Caucasus and Central Asia; coordinates cultural presentations; library of 25,000 vols; Chair. ANTHONY ZINNI; Pres. WENDY J. CHAMBERLIN; Vice-Pres. KATE SEELYE; publs *Middle East Journal* (4 a year), *Encounters* (online), *Policy Briefs* (online), *Policy Insights* (online), *Viewpoints* (online).

Oak Institute for the Study of International Human Rights: Colby College, 5319 Mayflower Hill, Waterville, Maine 04901; tel. (207) 859-5319; fax (207) 859-5229; e-mail oakhr@colby.edu; internet www.colby.edu/oak; f. 1998; attached to Colby College; sponsors Oak Human Rights Fellow to teach and conduct research while residing at the College; organizes lectures and other events; Dir WALTER HATCH.

Population Research Institute: 601 Oswald Tower, University Park, PA 16802-6211; tel. (814) 865-0486; fax (814) 863-8342; e-mail info@pop.psu.edu; internet www.pop.psu.edu; f. 1972; attached to Pennsylvania State Univ.; encourages, organizes and supports innovative research and training in population sciences; Dir Dr JENNIFER VAN HOOK.

Reformed Church Center: New Brunswick Campus, 17 Seminary Pl., New Brunswick, NJ 08901; tel. (732) 247-5241; fax (732) 249-5412; e-mail helpdesk@nbts.edu; internet www.nbts.edu/newsite/rcc.cfm; attached to New Brunswick Theological Seminary; offers programmes and research opportunities to scholars interested in reformed tradition; 2 scholarships for research students: Albert A. Smith Fellowship and Alvin J. Poppen and John R. Young; Dir Rev. BARBARA FILLETTE.

Smithsonian Center for Folklife and Cultural Heritage: POB 37012, MRC 520, Washington, DC 20013-7012; Capital Gallery Bldg, 600 Maryland Ave, SW, Suite 2001, MRC 520, Washington, DC 20024; tel. (202) 633-6440; fax (202) 633-6474; e-mail

folklife-info@si.edu; internet www.folklife.si.edu; promotes the understanding and continuity of contemporary grassroots cultures in the USA and abroad; runs Smithsonian Folklife Festival, Smithsonian Folkways recordings, exhibitions, documentary films, symposia; library: Ralph Rinzler Folklife Archives and Collns: 17,300 commercial discs, 4,000 acetate discs, 45,000 audiotapes, 2,000 CDs, 1,000,000 stills, 2,500 video casettes, 500,000 ft of motion picture film; Moses and Frances Asch colln, consisting of recordings and material relating to Folkways Records; records and archives of the center; Dir DANIEL SHEEY; publ. *Folkways Magazine*.

Smithsonian Latino Center: Capital Gallery, 600 Maryland Ave, SW, Suite 7042, MRC 512, Washington, DC 20024; tel. (202) 633-1240; fax (202) 633-1132; internet latino.si.edu; f. 1997; coordinates all Smithsonian-related Latino exhibitions, initiatives, research and educational programmes; library: archive of papers of Latino and Latin American artists; Chair. PATRICIA Q. STONESIFER; Exec. Dir EDUARDO DIAZ (acting).

Social Science Research Council (SSRC): 1 Pierrepont Plaza, 15th Fl., 300 Cadmon Plaza W, Brooklyn, NY 11021; tel. (212) 377-2700; fax (212) 377-2727; e-mail info@ssrc.org; internet www.ssrc.org; f. 1923; ind., non-profit int. org.; plans for critical areas of social research; improves research training through training institutes and fellowship programmes; supports individual research through postdoctoral grants; sponsors interdisciplinary and int. research confs; Chair. MICHAEL KENNEDY; Pres. CRAIG CALHOUN; publ. *Items* (4 a year).

Wenner-Gren Foundation: 470 Park Ave S, 8th Fl., New York, NY 10016; tel. (212) 683-5000; fax (212) 683-9151; e-mail inquiries@wennergren.org; internet www.wennergren.org; f. 1941 as the Viking Fund; supports research in all brs of anthropology and closely related disciplines concerned with human origins, devt and variation; grants to aid individual research, incl. dissertation research, fellowships and post-PhD research grants; Conf. Grants Program; Historical Archives Program; Professional Devt Int. Fellowships and Int. Collaborative Research Grants; Chair. SETH MASTERS; Vice-Chair. Dr JOHN IMMERWAHR; Pres. Dr LESLIE C. AIELLO; Treas. WILLIAM COBB; publ. *Current Anthropology* (5 a year).

TECHNOLOGY

Applied Research Laboratory (ARL): POB 30, State College, PA 16804; N Atherton St, State College, PA 16801; tel. (814) 865-6343; internet www.arl.psu.edu; f. 1945; attached to Pennsylvania State Univ.; champions transfer of advanced technologies and manufacturing processes, in partnership with industry and Navy research devt centres, to acquisition programmes and fleet operations, as well as to other govt agencies and private sector; performs basic and applied research, exploratory and advanced devt and manufacturing technology in support of the Navy technology base; Dir Dr EDWARD G. LISZKA.

Battelle Memorial Institute: 505 King Ave, Columbus, OH 43201-2696; tel. (614) 424-6424; e-mail solutions@battelle.org; internet www.battelle.org; f. 1929; serves industry and govt in the generation, application and commercialization of technology; supports research and devt activities of clients in 30 countries; major areas of activity are community and education, energy, health and life sciences, nat. security and defense, and laboratory management; research operations in the USA and Europe; 130 offices worldwide; library: more than 150,000 vols; Pres. and CEO CARL E. KOHRT; Library Man. KEMBERLY LANG.

Board on Infrastructure and the Constructed Environment: The National Academies, 500, Fifth St, NW, Washington, DC 20001; tel. (202) 334-3505; fax (202) 334-3718; e-mail bice@nas.edu; internet www.nas .edu/bice; f. 1946 as Bldg Research Advisory Board unit of Div. on Engineering and Physical Sciences of the Nat. Research Council (NRC); advises exec. and legislative brs of govt and private sector on technology, science and public policy; develops strategic plans and oversees cttee activities involving studies, briefings, workshops, symposia, information dissemination activities; Chair. DAVID NASH; Dir DENNIS CHAMOT (acting).

Brookhaven National Laboratory: POB 5000, Upton, Long Island, NY 11973-5000; tel. (631) 344-8000; internet www.bnl.gov; f. 1947; operated by Brookhaven Science Assocs, under contract with the US Dept of Energy; basic and applied research by staff and visiting scientists in the fields of applied sciences, biology, chemistry, energy, environment, mathematics, medicine, particle accelerators, and physics , incl. the design, devt, acquisition and operation of large-scale facilities; training of scientists and engineers; dissemination of scientific and technical knowledge; library of 82,000 vols; Dir SAMUEL ARONSON; publs *Brookhaven Bulletin* (56 a year), *Discover Brookhaven*.

Center for Innovative Materials Research (CIMR): College of Engineering, Lawrence Technological Univ., 21000 W Ten Mile Rd, Southfield, MI 48075-1058; tel. (248) 204-2556; fax (248) 204-2568; internet www.ltu.edu/cimr; attached to College of Engineering, Lawrence Technological Univ.; f. 2005; researches and tests carbon fibre composite materials for defence applications; Dir Dr NABIL F. GRACE.

Combustion Institute: 5001 Baum Blvd, Suite 635, Pittsburgh, PA 15213-1851; tel. (412) 687-1366; fax (412) 687-0340; e-mail office@combustioninstitute.org; internet www.combustioninstitute.org; f. 1954; non-profit educational scientific soc.; promotes and disseminates research in combustion science; offices in 34 countries; Pres. Dr CHARLES K. WESTBROOK; Vice-Pres.and Pres.-Elect Prof. KATHARINA KOHSE-HOIN-GHAUS; Sec. Prof. DEREK DUNN-RANKIN; Treas. JAMES M. EKMANN; publs *Combustion and Flame* (12 a year), *Combustion Science and Technology* (12 a year), *Combustion Theory and Modelling* (6 a year), *The Proceedings of The Combustion Institute* (every 2 years).

HERTY Advanced Materials Development Center: 110 Brampton Rd, Savannah, GA 31408; tel. (912) 963-2600; fax (912) 963-2614; e-mail info@herty.com; internet www .herty.com; f. 1938; non-profit contractual research and devt of wood, non-wood and synthetic fibres; Chair. EUGENE CARTLEDGE; Pres. and CEO Dr WILLIAM G. BRUNDAGE.

Industrial Research Institute: 2200 Clarendon Blvd, Suite 1102, Arlington, VA 22201-3331; tel. (703) 647-2580; fax (703) 647-2581; internet www.iriweb.org; f. 1938; offers services to research and devt, and innovation to professionals in the US and China; Chair. ROBERT J. KUMPF; Pres. EDWARD BERNSTEIN; publ. *Research-Technology Management* (6 a year).

Institute for Security, Technology, and Society: Dartmouth College, 6211 Sudikoff Laboratory, Hanover, NH 03755; tel. (603) 646-0700; fax (603) 646-1672; e-mail info@ ists.dartmouth.edu; internet www.ists .dartmouth.edu; f. 2000; attached to Dart-

mouth College; engages in interdisciplinary research, education and outreach programmes that focus on information technology (IT) and its role in soc.; nurtures leaders and scholars, educates students and the community, and collaborates with its partners to develop and deploy IT, and to better understand how IT relates to socio-economic forces, cultural values and political influences; Dir DENISE ANTHONY.

Institute of Textile Technology: North Carolina State Univ., College of Textiles, 2401 Research Dr., POB 8301, Raleigh, NC 27695-8301; tel. (919) 513-7704; fax (919) 882-9410; internet www.itt.edu; f. 1944; research, graduate education and open funding of applied textile research; Pres. and CEO Dr W. GILBERT O'NEAL; Dir for Research Dr HENRY BOYTER.

Lemelson Center for the Study of Invention & Innovation: Nat. Museum of American History, Smithsonian Instn, Room 334, MRC 604, 14th St and Constitution Ave, NW, POB 37012, Washington, DC 20013-7012; tel. (202) 633-3450; fax (202) 357-4517; e-mail lemcen@si.edu; internet invention .smithsonian.org; f. 1995; attached to Smithsonian Instn's Nat. Museum of American History; documents, interprets and disseminates information about invention and innovation; encourages inventive creativity in young people; Dir ARTHUR MOLELLA; Deputy Dir JOYCE BEDI.

National Aeronautics and Space Administration (NASA): Suite 5K 39, Washington, DC 20546-0001; tel. (202) 358-0001; fax (202) 358-4338; e-mail public-inquiries@hq.nasa .gov; internet www.nasa.gov; f. 1958, fmrly Nat. Advisory Cttee for Aeronautics (f. 1915); conducts space and scientific research through 3 prin. org., aeronautics, human explorations and operations and science; Administrator CHARLES F. BOLDER, JR.

Main Research Centres:

Ames Research Center: NASA, Moffett Field, CA 94035; tel. (650) 604-5000; internet www.nasa.gov/centers/ames; f. 1939; supercomputing, networking and intelligent systems, aerospace and thermal protection systems, astrobiology, biotechnology, fundamental space biology, human factors and nanotechnology; Dir Dr SIMON P. WORDEN; Deputy Dir LEWIS S. G. BRAXTON, III.

Dryden Flight Research Center: POB 273, Edwards, CA 93523-0273; tel. (661) 276-3311; e-mail drydenpao@nasa.gov; internet www.nasa.gov/centers/dryden; f. 1946; research in aeronautics and space technology; Dir DAVID D. McBRIDE.

George C. Marshall Space Flight Center: Nat. Aeronautics and Space Admin., Huntsville, AL 35812; tel. (256) 544-1382; e-mail marshallpublicinquiries@msfc.nasa .gov; internet www.nasa.gov/centers/ marshall; f. 1960; develops and operates space systems America needs to journey into low Earth orbit and beyond; Dir ROBERT M. LIGHTFOOT, JR.

Glenn Research Center: NASA, 21000 Brookpark Rd, Cleveland, OH 44135; tel. (216) 433-4000; internet www.nasa.gov/ centers/glenn; f. 1941 as Aircraft Engine Research Laboratory, present name 1999; researches, designs, develops and tests innovative technology for aeronautics and spaceflight; Dir RAMON LUGO, III.

Goddard Space Flight Center: NASA, Public Inquiries, Mail Code 130, Greenbelt, MD 20771; tel. (301) 286-2000; fax (301) 286-1707; internet www1.nasa.gov/ centers/goddard; f. 1959; builds spacecraft, instruments and new technology to study

Earth, sun, solar system and the universe; library of 57,000 vols, 35,000 periodicals; Dir ROB STRAIN.

Jet Propulsion Laboratory: 4800 Oak Grove Dr., Pasadena, CA 91109; tel. (818) 354-4321; internet www.nasa.gov/centers/ jpl; centre for robotic exploration of the solar system; operated by California Institute of Technology; Dir Dr CHARLES ELA-CHI.

John F. Kennedy Space Center: NASA, FL 32899; tel. (321) 867-5000; e-mail ksc-public-inquiries@mail.nasa.gov; internet www1.nasa.gov/centers/kennedy; f. 1962 as Launch Operations Center, present name 1963; previously Launch Operations Center; space vehicle launch facility; library of 32,000 vols, 106,000 documents and reports, 589 periodicals; Dir ROBERT D. CABANA.

Langley Research Center: NASA, Hampton, VA 23681-2199; tel. (757) 864-3293; internet www1.nasa.gov/centers/ langley; f. 1917, present name 1958; research areas incl. aeronautics, atmospheric sciences and exploration; Dir LESA B. ROSE; publ. *Researcher News* (online).

Lyndon B. Johnson Space Center: 2101 NASA Parkway, Houston, TX 77058; tel. (281) 483-0123; internet /www.nasa.gov/ centers/johnson/home/index.html; f. 1961; responsible for the design, devtt and testing of manned spacecraft and associated systems, for the selection and training of astronauts and for the operation of manned space flights; operates White Sands Test Facility at Las Cruces, NM; library: Johnson Space Center Technical library of 49,000 vols, 550,000 technical reports, 600 periodicals; Dir MIKE COATS.

Stennis Space Center: Office of Public Affairs, MS, 39529; tel. (228) 688-2211; e-mail public-inquiries@ssc.nasa.gov; internet www.nasa.gov/centers/stennis; f. 1961 as Mississippi Test Operations, present name 1988; Dir PATRICK SCHEUER-MANN.

National Institute of Standards and Technology: 100 Bureau Dr., Stop 1070, Gaithersburg, MD 20899-1070; tel. (301) 975-6478; fax (301) 926-1630; e-mail inquiries@ nist.gov; internet www.nist.gov; f. 1901; attached to US Dept of Commerce; works with industry to develop and apply technology, measurements and standards; laboratory research focused on infrastructural technologies; operates research org JILA in CO with the Univ. of Colorado, Institute for Bioscience and Biotechnology Research (IBBR) (fmrly CARB), Rockville, MD, with Univ. of Maryland Biotechnology Institute, Joint Quantum Institute (JQI), MD with Univ. of Maryland and Hollings Marine Laboratory, Charleston, SC with 5 other univ. partners; Dir Dr PATRICK D. GALLAGHER; publs *Building Science, Journal of Research, National Standard Reference Database.*

National Renewable Energy Laboratory: 1617 Cole Blvd, Golden, CO 80401-3305; tel. (303) 275-3000; fax (303) 275-4091; internet www.nrel.gov; f. 1977 as Solar Energy Research Institute, present name and status 1991; attached to US Dept of Energy, Office of Energy Efficiency and Renewable Energy; fed. laboratory for long-range high-risk renewable energy research and devt; library of 105,000 books and reports, 350 journals; Dir Dr DAN E. ARVIZU; publ. *Continuum Magazine* (4 a year).

New Mexico Bureau of Geology and Mineral Resources: New Mexico Institute of Mining and Technology, 801 Leroy Pl., Socorro, NM 87801-4796; tel. (575) 835-5420;

fax (575) 835-6333; internet www.geoinfo
.nmt.edu; f. 1927 as New Mexico Bureau of
Mines & Mineral Resources, present name
2001; attached to New Mexico Institute of
Mining and Technology; conducts research
and interacts with State and Fed. agencies;
serves as the geological survey for State of
New Mexico; provides information to scientists, decision makers, and the New Mexico
people on the state's geologic infrastructure,
mineral and energy resources and geohydrology; provides timely information on potential
geologic hazards, incl. earthquakes, volcanic
events, soils-and subsidence-related problems, and flooding; provides public education
and outreach through college teaching and
advising; offices in Albuquerque and Carlsbad; incl. Geologic Information Center and a
mineralogical museum; library of 5,000 vols,
5,000 maps, 2,000 photographs, 1,200 theses
and dissertations; Dir L. GREER PRICE;
Librarian Dr MAUREEN WILKS; publs *Lite
Geology* (4 a year), *New Mexico Geology* (4 a
year).

New Mexico Space Grant Consortium:
POB 3001, MSC SG, Las Cruces, NM 88003;
tel. (505) 646-6414; fax (505) 646-7791;
e-mail nmsgc@nmsu.edu; internet
spacegrant.nmsu.edu; f. 1989; attached to
New Mexico State Univ.; mem. of Nat. Space
Grant College and fellowship programme of
NASA; encourages interdisciplinary training, research and public service programmes
on aerospace; encourages cooperative programmes among univs, aerospace industry
and fed., state and local govts; establishes
and maintains a nat. network of univs with
interests and capabilities in aeronautics,
space and related fields; recruits and trains
US citizens in aerospace science and technology; Dir Dr PAT HYNES.

Southwest Research Institute: POB
28510, 6220 Culebra Rd, San Antonio, TX
78228-0510; 9503 W Commerce, San Antonio, TX 78227-1301; tel. (210) 522-2122; fax
(210) 522-3496; internet www.swri.edu; f.
1947; ind. non-profit org. conducting
research and devt in the engineering and
physical sciences for govt, business and
industry around the world; library of 50,000
vols; Pres. J. DAN BATES; publ. *Technology
Today* (3 a year).

**Southwest Technology Development
Institute:** POB 3001, MSC 3SOLAR, Las
Cruces, NM 88003-8001; tel. (575) 646-6105;
fax (575) 646-3841; e-mail tdi@nmsu.edu;
internet www.nmsu.edu/~tdi; f. 1977 as
New Mexico Solar Energy Institute; attached
to College of Engineering, New Mexico State
Univ.; focuses on the devt, transfer, promotion and commercialization of renewable
energy technologies; areas incl: solar and
wind energy systems, geothermal research,
energy systems simulation, resource assessment and environmental analysis.; Dir
ANDREW L. ROSENTHAL.

SRI International: 333 Ravenswood Ave,
Menlo Park, CA 94025-3453; tel. (650) 859-
2000; e-mail info@sp.sri.com; internet www
.sri.com; f. 1946 as Stanford Research Institute, present status 1970, present name
1977; non-profit-making; centres for diversified research for industry and govt in pure
and applied science and engineering; br. in
Washington, DC, and other locations; overseas offices in Tokyo, Japan, Hong Kong,
China, Greenland, Sharjah and UAE; Chair.
VERN E. CLARK; Pres. and CEO CURTIS R.
CARLSON.

TRI Princeton: 601 Prospect Ave, POB 625,
Princeton, NJ 08542; tel. (609) 430-4820; fax
(609) 683-7836; e-mail info@triprinceton.org;
internet www.triprinceton.com; f. 1930; fundamental and applied research and continuing education in the physical and
engineering sciences relating to fibrous
materials, films, polymers, human hair, and
porous and nanoporous materials; library of
5,000 vols; Chair. ROBERT J. BIANCHINI; Pres.
Dr MICHAEL A. DRZEWINSKI; Sec. and Treas.
ELEANOR LEHMAN.

Libraries and Archives
Alabama

**Alabama Department of Archives and
History:** POB 300100, Montgomery, AL
36130; 624 Washington Ave, Montgomery,
AL 36130; tel. (334) 242-4435; fax (334) 240-
3433; e-mail reference@archives.alabama
.gov; internet www.archives.alabama.gov; f.
1901; records and artefacts of historical
value; Dir ED BRIDGES.

Autauga-Prattville Public Library: 254
Doster St, Prattville, AL 36067-3900; tel.
(334) 365-3396; fax (334) 365-3397; internet
www.appl.info; Alabama Room: spec. colln of
local history and genealogy materials; Dir
JAN EARNEST; Chair. WILLIS BRADFORD.

B. B. Comer Memorial Library: 314 N
Broadway Ave, Sylacauga, AL 35150-2528;
tel. (256) 249-0961; fax (256) 401-2492;
e-mail bbclibrary@sylacauga.net; internet
www.sylacauga.net/library; f. 1936 as Sylacauga Public Library; Dir SHIRLEY SPEARS.

Bessemer Public Library: 400 19th St N,
Bessemer, AL 35020-4819; tel. (205) 428-
7882; fax (205) 428-7885; e-mail
bessemerlibrary@gmail.com; internet www
.bessemerlibrary.org; f. 1907 as Bessemer
Carnegie Library, present name 1967;
research database incl. encyclopaedias, biographies, genealogy, literature, social sciences, health, science, magazines and
newspapers; Dir DONNA SCHREMSER; Pres.
DORIS LEWIS.

Birmingham Public Library: 2100 Park
Pl., Birmingham, AL 35203; tel. (205) 226-
3600; e-mail bpldirector@bham.lib.al.us;
internet www.bplonline.org; f. 1886; spec.
collns: Agee Cartographical Colln (incl.
Joseph H. Woodward Colln), Catherine Collins Colln of Dance, Scruggs Philately Colln,
Tutwiler Colln of Southern History and
Literature, govt documents, archives, MSS,
musical recordings, film and video; DIALOG
Online Computer Reference Service, Books
by Mail Service; 19 brs; 900,000 vols, 1m.
pieces of microfilm, 30,000,000 archival documents, 400,000 photographs; Dir RENEE BLA-
LOCK.

Boaz Public Library: 404 Thomas Ave,
Boaz, AL 35957; tel. (256) 593-3000; fax (256)
593-8153; e-mail library@cityofboaz.org;
internet www.boazpubliclibrary.org; f. 1973;
newspapers on microfilm from 1893 to 1983;
colln on ancestry of Abraham Lincoln; 60,000
vols; Librarian LYNN BURGESS.

Cheaha Regional Library: 935 Colleman
St, Heflin, AL 36264-1313; tel. (256) 463-
7125; fax (256) 463-7128; e-mail info@
cheaharegionallibrary.org; internet www
.cheaharegionallibrary.org; f. 1976, fmrly
Public Library of Anniston, present location
1989; multi-county library system; incl. 8
mem. libraries across 5 counties; 1 bookmobile; Dir EVI JONES.

Cullman County Public Library System:
200 Clark St NE, Cullman, AL 35055; tel.
(256) 734-1068; fax (256) 734-6902; internet
www.ccpls.com; f. 1890; photographic collns
of Beyer-Karter, Herfurth and Johnson documenting history of Cullman County till the
1970s; artefacts incl. archaeological relics
from Battle of Hog Mountain (1863); genealogical and historical periodicals; brs. incl.
Cullman (HQ), Fairview, Garden City, Han-
ceville and Tom Bevill Library-Colony;
150,000 vols (incl. print and electronic); Dir
MAX HAND; Chair. RON HOGUE; County
Librarian and CEO JOHN PAUL MYRICK.

Daphne Public Library: POB 1225, 2607
US Highway 98, Daphne, AL 36526-1225; tel.
(251) 621-2818; fax (251) 621-3086; e-mail
daphlib3@bellsouth.net; internet www
.daphneal.com/residents/library; f. 1969;
spec. colln incl. state and local folk life,
digitized photographs and articles; 68,000
vols; Dir TONJA YOUNG.

Demopolis Public Library: 211 E
Washington St, Demopolis, AL 36732; tel.
(334) 289-1595; fax (334) 289-8260; e-mail
demopolis.public.library@demopolisal.com;
internet www.demopolislibrary.info; f. 1922;
spec. colln on history of Alabama, Marengo
Co and Demopolis; Luther Franklin Bragg,
Jr, colln: genealogical and local history
records focusing on Alabama and other areas
of that co; 25,000 vols; Dir MORGAN GRIMES;
Chair. BETTY MCCANTS.

Enterprise Public Library: 101 E Grubbs
St, Enterprise, AL 36330-2531; tel. (334) 347-
2636; fax (334) 393-6477; e-mail epl@sanman
.net; internet www.enterpriselibrary.org; f.
1923; colln of audio cassettes and CDs for the
visually impaired and physically disabled;
53,000 vols; Dir DENISE UNRUH-KITCH; Chair.
BRUCE KEEL; Sec. CATHERINE ROTH; Treas.
MARY PENNY.

Fairhope Public Library: 501 Fairhope
Ave, Fairhope, AL 36532; tel. (251) 928-7483;
fax (251) 928-9717; e-mail director@
fairhopelibrary.org; internet www
.fairhopelibrary.org; f. 1900; Dir TAMARA
DEAN; Chair. MARTIN LANAUX.

Florence-Lauderdale Public Library:
350 N Wood Ave, Florence, AL 35630-4709;
tel. (256) 764-6564; fax (256) 764-6629;
e-mail events@flpl.org; internet www.flpl
.org; f. 1885 as The Ladies' Library, present
location 2002; colln of records on local
Lauderdale; Colbert (original part of Franklin) and Franklin co histories incl. Lauderdale County Probate Court record books on
microfilm from 1820 to 1927 as well as local
newspapers from 1824 to the present; colln of
records on several New England, Southern
and Mid-Western states; 100,000 vols; Exec.
Dir NANCY SANFORD; Chair. PATRICIA BULLS
BUTLER.

**Gardendale Martha Moore Public
Library:** 995 Mount Olive Rd, Gardendale,
AL 35071-4654; tel. (205) 631-6639; fax (205)
631-0146; internet gardendale.lib.al.us; f.
1959; database incl. magazine and newspaper index; a health reference centre;
55,200 vols; Dir CONNIE SMITH.

Shelby County Public Library System:
Harrison Library—System HQs, 50 Lester
St, Columbiana, AL 35051; tel. (205) 669-
3910; fax (205) 669-3940; e-mail info@
shelbycounty-al.org; internet www
.shelbycounty-al.org; f. 1940; 14 libraries:
Harrison Regional Library (HQ), 11 mem.
libraries, 2 brs and 1 mem.-br. library; Dir
BARBARA ROBERTS.

Hoover Public Library: 200 Municipal Dr.,
Hoover, AL 35216-5510; tel. (205) 444-7800;
fax (205) 444-7878; internet www
.hooverlibrary.org; f. 1983; colln: literature,
directories, encyclopedias, magazines and
newspapers; 240,578 vols; Dir LINDA R.
ANDREWS.

Horseshoe Bend Regional Library: 20
NW St, Dadeville, AL 36853-1355; tel. (256)
825-9232; fax (256) 825-4314; e-mail
horseshoebend@bellsouth.net; internet www
.horseshoebendlibrary.org; 8 public libraries

in Coosa, Elmore, Lee and Tallapoosa counties; Dir SUSIE ANDERSON.

Luverne Public Library: 148 E Third St, Luverne, AL 36049; tel. (334) 335-5326; fax (334) 335-6402; e-mail library@luverne.org; internet library.luverne.org; local history colln; Dir KATHRYN TOMLIN.

Montgomery City-County Public Library: 2885-B E South Blvd, Montgomery, AL 36116-2513; tel. (334) 240-4842; fax (334) 240-4980; internet www.mccpl.lib.al.us; f. 1899, present status 1974; 11 brs; comprehensive colln of books and data; 600,000 vols; Dir JAUNITA OWES.

State Law Library: 300 Dexter Ave, Montgomery, AL 36104; tel. 334 229-0578; e-mail reference@alalinc.net; internet www.alalinc .net/library; f. 1828; US govt depository; colln incl. reported decisions of the state and fed. appellate courts in the USA; statutes of all 50 states and the District of Columbia; 200,000 vols; Dir and State Law Librarian TIMOTHY A. LEWIS.

Tuscaloosa Public Library: 1801 Jack Warner Parkway, Tuscaloosa, AL 35401-1099; tel. (205) 345-5820; fax (205) 758-1735; e-mail info@tuscaloosa-library.org; internet www.tuscaloosa-library.org; f. 1879; genealogy and local history colln with microforms; Brown br. and Weaver Bolden br.; 2 bookmobiles; Exec. Dir MARY ELIZABETH HARPER; Chair. SHERIE GILES; Sec. Dr SAMORY PRUITT; Treas. J. BRAD SPRINGER.

University of Alabama Library: POB 870266, Tuscaloosa, AL 35487-0266; tel. (205) 348-6047; internet www.lib.ua.edu; f. 1831; regional depository for fed. documents; deptl libraries for business, education, engineering, sciences; spec. collns on Alabama and Southern history and literature; 2m.vols, 1m. govt documents, 3.5m. microform units and 2.75m maps; Dean of Libraries LOUIS A. PITSCHMANN.

Washington County Public Library: POB 1057, Chatom, AL 36518; 14102 St Stephens Ave, Chatom, AL 36518; tel. (251) 847-2097; fax (251) 847-2098; internet www.wcpls.org; f. 1956; main library in Chatom and a br. in McIntosh; Dir JESSICA M. ROSS; Chair. ASHLI PAGE.

Alaska

Alaska Resources Library and Information Services: Library Bldg, Suite 111, 3211 Providence Dr., Anchorage, AK 99508; tel. (907) 272-7547; fax (907) 786-7652; e-mail reference@arlis.org; internet www.arlis.org; provides access to natural and cultural resources information; 10,117 vols.

Alaska State Library: POB 110571, Juneau, AK 99811-0571; 333 Willoughby Ave, 8th Fl., State Office Bldg, Juneau, AK; tel. (907) 465-2910; fax (907) 465-2665; e-mail asl@alaska.gov; internet library .alaska.gov; f. 1900; 158,166 vols: information services 73,648 vols, historical collns 79,969 vols, incl. 859 MSS and 526 photographic collns; 3,164 vols in Anchorage office; information service, incl. service to Alaska govt and the gen. public; historical collns; library devt; talking book centre; State Librarian and Div. Dir LINDA THIBODEAU.

Delta Community Library: 2291 Deborah St, Delta Junction, AK 99737-0229; tel. (907) 895-4102; internet www.ci.delta-junction.ak .us; f. 1960.

Elmer E. Rasmuson and BioSciences Libraries: POB 756800, 310 Tanana Loop, Fairbanks, AK 99775-6800; tel. (907) 474-7481; fax (907) 474-6841; e-mail fyref@uaf .edu; internet www.library.uaf.edu; f. 1922; attached to Univ. of Alaska Fairbanks (UAF);

1.75m. vols; Dean of Libraries Dr BELLA KARR GERLICH.

Haines Borough Public Library: POB 1089, 111 Third Ave, Haines, AK 99827; tel. (907) 766-2545; fax (907) 766-2551; e-mail director@haineslibrary.org; internet www .haineslibrary.org; f. 1958; Dir PATRICIA BROWN.

Homer Public Library: 500 Hazel Ave, Homer, AK 99603; tel. (907) 235-3180; e-mail library@ci.homer.ak.us; internet www .cityofhomer-ak.gov/library; f. 1940; a department of the City of Homer and the library's basic operations are funded through the City's General Fund; 45,000 vols; Library Dir ANN DIXON.

Joyce K. Carver Soldotna Public Library: 235 N Binkley St, Soldotna, AK 99669; tel. (907) 262-4227; fax (907) 262-6856; e-mail kmcleod@ci.soldotna.ak.us; internet www.ci.soldotna.ak.us/library.html; Librarian TERRI BURDICK.

Juneau Public Libraries: 292 Marine Way, Juneau, AK 99801; tel. (907) 586-5249; fax (907) 586-5383; internet www .juneau.org/library; 3 brs; 124,000 vols; Library Dir BARBARA BERG.

Kegoayah Kozga Library: POB 1168, 223 Front St, Nome, AK 99762; tel. (907) 443-6628; fax (907) 443-3762; e-mail library@ nomealaska.org; internet www.nomealaska .org; Library Dir MARGUERITE LA RIVIERE.

Keith B. Mather Library: Geophysical Institute, Int. Arctic Research Center, 930 Koyukuk Dr., POB 757355, Fairbanks, AK 99775-7355; tel. (907) 474-7503; fax (907) 474-6846; e-mail gilibrary@gi.alaska.edu; internet www2.gi.alaska.edu/services/ library; f. 1946; attached to Geophysical Institute, Univ. of Alaska, Fairbanks; colln incl. atmospheric sciences, glaciology, global change, ice snow, permafrost, remote sensing, seismology, space physics and volcanology; US Patent and Trademark depository library; Librarian FLORA GRABOWSKA.

Ketchikan Campus Library: Ziegler Bldg, 2600 Seventh Ave, Ketchikan, AK 99901; tel. (907) 228-4567; fax (907) 228-4520; e-mail libket@uas.alaska.edu; internet www.ketch .alaska.edu/library; attached to Univ. of Alaska, SE; Librarian KATHLEEN WIECHEL-MAN.

Ketchikan Public Library: 629 Dock St, Ketchikan, AK 99901; tel. (907) 225-3331; e-mail library@firstcitylibraries.org; internet www.firstcitylibraries.org; f. 1901, present bldg 1969.

Petersburg Public Library: POB 549, 12 Nordic Dr., Petersburg, AK 99833; tel. (907) 772-3349; e-mail library@ci.petersburg.ak .us; internet www.psglib.org; f. 1932, present bldg 1960; City Librarian TARA ALCOCK.

Seward Community Library: POB 2389, 238 Fifth Ave, Seward, AK 99664; tel. (907) 224-4082; fax (907) 224-3521; e-mail tmorrow@cityofseward.net; internet www .cityofseward.net/library; Library Dir PATRI-CIA LINVILLE.

Tuzzy Consortium Library: POB 2130, Barrow, AK 99723; tel. (907) 852-4050; fax (907) 852-1729; e-mail tuzzy@tuzzy.org; internet www.tuzzy.org; Tuzzy Consortium Library is a mem. of OCLC (Online Computer Library Center); Library Dir DAVID ONGLEY.

Valdez Consortium Library: POB 609, Valdez, AK 99686; tel. (907) 835-4632; fax (907) 835-4876; e-mail vnvl@uaa.alaska.edu; internet www.ci.valdez.ak.us/library; combined public and college library; Head Librarian MOLLIE GOOD.

Wasilla Meta-Rose Public Library: 391 N Main St, Wasilla, AK 99654; tel. (907) 376-5913; fax (907) 376-2347; e-mail library@ci .wasilla.ak.us; internet www.cityofwasilla .com; f. 1917; Librarian K. J. MARTIN-ALB-RIGHT.

Z. J. Loussac Public Library: 3600 Denali St, Anchorage, AK 99503; tel. (907) 343-2975; internet www.muni.org/departments/library; 4 brs; Dir NANCY TILESTON.

Arizona

Apache County Library District: POB 2760, 30 S Second W, St. Johns, AZ 85936; tel. (928) 337-4923; internet www .apachecountylibraries.com; operates 7 public libraries located in Alpine, Concho, Greer, Round Valley, Sanders, St. Johns, and Vernon communities; Dir JUDITH PEPPLE.

Arizona Historical Society Library and Archives: 949 E Second St, Tucson, AZ 85719; tel. (520) 628-5774; fax (520) 629-8966; e-mail ahsref@azhs.gov; internet www .arizonahistoricalsociety.org/library_an-d_archives; 4 regional repositories in Flagstaff, Tempe, Tucson and Yuma; MSS, maps, personal papers, photographs, films, oral histories, books on history of Arizona, W and N Mexico; non-circulating libraries; colln of 500,000 prints, slides and original negatives showcases visual record of Arizona from the 1870s to present; Exec. Dir ANNE I. WOOSLEY.

Arizona State Library, Archives and Public Records: Suite 200, 1700 W Washington, Phoenix, AZ 85007; tel. (602) 926-4035; fax (602) 256-7983; e-mail services@lib.az.us; internet www.lib.az.us; f. 1864; attached to Sec. of State; historical MSS, govt records, books and photographs of Arizona and its peoples, genealogy, fed. and state documents; library extension assistance to public libraries, archives of historical records, library for the blind and physically handicapped, museums, public records; Carnegie Center; 1,127,196 vols; State Librarian JANET FISHER (acting).

Arizona State University Libraries: POB 871006, Arizona State Univ., Tempe, AZ 85287; 113 Hayden Library, Tempe, AZ 85287-1006; tel. (480) 965-6164; fax (480) 965-9169; e-mail askalib@asu.edu; internet lib.asu.edu; Univ. Archives; 8 brs on 4 campuses: Downtown Phoenix Campus, Polytechnic Campus, Tempe Campus, West Campus;repository of govt and fed. documents; Labriola Nat. American Indian Data Center; 2.5m. vols, 200,000 maps; spec. colln: 45,000 books, 2,000 linear ft of MSS and photographs, sound and video recordings; Univ. Librarian SHERRIE SCHMIDT.

Flagstaff City-Coconino County Public Library: Main Library, 300 W Aspen Ave, Flagstaff, AZ 86001; tel. (928) 779-7673; internet www.flagstaffpubliclibrary.org; f. 1884, present status 1927; incl. East Flagstaff Community Library; 4 brs; 4 affiliated public libraries; bookmobile services; Dir HEIDI HOLLAND.

Glendale Public Library: 5959 W Brown St, Glendale, AZ 85302; tel. (623) 939-0532; internet www.glendaleaz.com/library; f. 1890; 1 main library and 2 brs; Dir SUE KOMERNICKY; Library Man. KATHLEEN HAMEL.

Maricopa County Library District: 2700 N Central Ave, Suite 700, Phoenix, AZ 85004; tel. (602) 652-3000; internet www.mcldaz .org; 17 brs; 7 affiliated libraries; Dir CINDY KOLACZYNSKI.

Parker Public Library: 1001 Navajo Ave, Parker, AZ 85344; tel. (928) 669-2622; fax (928) 669-8668; internet www

.parkerpubliclibraryaz.org; f. 1956; Library Man. RUTHIE DAVIS.

Phoenix Public Library: 1221 N Central Ave, Phoenix, AZ 85004; tel. (602) 262-4636; fax (602) 495-5841; internet www .phoenixpubliclibrary.org; f. 1898; 15 brs; audiovisual material; Arizona and SW materials; art gallery and exhibitions; 1,735,924 vols, 4,315 periodical titles; Chair. JEAN KILKER; City Librarian TONI GARVEY.

Pima County Public Library: 101 N Stone Ave, Tucson, AZ 85701; tel. (520) 791-4010; fax (520) 594-5621; internet www.library .pima.gov; f. 1883 as Carnegie Free Library, present name and status 2006; HQ and colln at Joel D. Valdez Main Library; local, state, and fed. govt documents; holds records from Postal History Foundation Library and Tucson Museum of Art Research Library; 25 brs and bookmobile service; affiliate library: Oro Valley Public Library; Dir NANCY LEDEBOER; Pres. OBDÚLIA GONZÁLEZ.

Prescott Valley Public Library: 7401 E Civic Circle, Prescott Valley, AZ 86314; tel. (928) 759-3040; internet www.pvlib.net; part of Yavapai Library Network; 65,000 vols; Dir STUART MATTSON; Pres. DONNA MORGAN; Sec. KARYL COLOZZE.

Sedona Public Library: 3250 White Bear Rd, Sedona, AZ 86336; tel. (928) 282-7714; fax (928) 282-5789; internet www .sedonalibrary.org; f. 1958, present location 1994; mem. of Yavapai County Library Network; village service centre at Oak Creek; Dir VIRGINIA VOLKMAN; Pres. ANNE URUBURU; Sec. SANDRA IMMERSO; Treas. ROGER SHLONSKY.

Superior Court Law Library: East Court Bldg, 101 W Jefferson St, Phoenix, AZ 85003; tel. (602) 506-3461; fax (602) 506-3677; e-mail services@scll.maricopa.gov; internet www.superiorcourt.maricopa.gov/lawlibrary; f. 1913; provides legal research assistance in Maricopa co; colln incl. Arizona's legal materials, court admin. documents, fed. legal materials, foreign and int. legal treaties and monographs, books on legal topics, session laws and state and local bar asscn journals; 150,000 vols; Dir MARCUS REINKENSMEYER; publ. *The Court Informer* (6 a year).

University of Arizona Library: Main Library A349, POB 210055, Tucson, AZ 85721-0055; 1510 E University Blvd, Tucson, AZ 85721-0055; tel. (520) 621-2101; fax (520) 621-9733; internet www.library.arizona.edu; f. 1891; spec. collns: history of science, South-Western Americana and borderlands history, fine and theatre arts, British and American literature, rare books, MSS collns, photographs and other materials; 5,266,051 vols, 645,463 e-books, 54,464 e-journals; Dean of Univ. Libraries CARLA STOFFLE.

Arkansas

Arkansas History Commission Library: One Capitol Mall, Little Rock, AR 72201; tel. (501) 682-6900; e-mail state.archives@ arkansas.gov; internet www.ark-ives.com; f. 1905; attached to Arkansas Dept of Parks and Tourism; official state archives; copy and edit official records and other historical material; encourages historical work and research; 2 brs: NE Arkansas Regional Archives (NEARA) and Southwest Arkansas Regional Archives (SARA); Dir Dr WENDY RICHTER; Librarian SHEILA BEVILL.

Arkansas State Library: Suite 100, 900 W Capitol, Little Rock, AR 72201; tel. (501) 682-2053; fax (501) 682-1899; internet www .library.arkansas.gov; f. 1979; genealogy; state and fed. records; US patent and trademark depository; State Librarian CAROLYN ASHCRAFT.

Arkansas Supreme Court Library: Justice Bldg, 625 Marshall St, Suite 1500, Little Rock, AR 72201; tel. (501) 682-2147; fax (501) 682-6877; internet courts.arkansas.gov/ library; f. 1851, present bldg 1958; serves justices and staff of Arkansas Supreme Court, judges and staff of Arkansas Court of Appeals and judicial agencies; state and fed. depository library; maintains 13 satellite libraries; 100,000 vols; Dir AVA M. HICKS; Librarian JACQUELINE S. WRIGHT.

Boone County Library: 221 W Stephenson, Harrison, AR 72601; tel. (870) 741-5913; internet www.boonecountylibrary.org; 84,000 vols; Dir and Librarian LAVOYCE EWING.

Columbia County Library: POB 668, 2057 N Jackson St, Magnolia, AR 71754; tel. (870) 234-1991; fax (870) 234-5077; e-mail library@ colcnty.lib.ar.us; internet www2.youseemore .com/columbia; f. 1929 as Magnolia City Library, present name 1942; incl. Lafayette Co Library, Stamps Public Library and Taylor Public Library; Dir LAURA CLEVELAND.

Conway County Library: 101 W Church St, Morrilton, AR 72110; tel. (501) 354-5204; fax (501) 354-5206; internet www2 .youseemore.com/conwaycl; f. 1916; 35,000 vols; Chair. JANNA VIRDEN; Dir JAY CARTER.

Crawford County Library: 1409 Main St, Van Buren, AR 72956; tel. (479) 471-3226; fax (479) 471-3227; e-mail ccls@ crawfordcountylib.org; internet www2 .youseemore.com/crawfordcl; f. 1999; brs at Alma, Cedarville, Mountainburg and Mulberry; Van Buren Public Library (HQ); 143,351 vols; Dir EVA WHITE.

Craighead County Jonesboro Public Library: 315 W Oak Avenue, Jonesboro, AR 72401-3594; tel. (870) 935-5133; fax (870) 935-7987; e-mail reference@ libraryinjonesboro.org; internet www .libraryinjonesboro.org; f. 1917; 7 brs; 145,000 vols, 13,776 books on cassettes, DVDs,videos and CDs; Chair. MICHAEL JOHNSON.

Donald W. Reynolds Library: 300 Library Hill, Mountain Home, AR 72653; tel. (870) 580-0987; internet www.baxtercountylibrary .org; f. 2010; attached to Baxter County Library; br. at Gassville; 75,000 vols; Chair. JOHN AHRENS; Dir GWEN KHAYAT.

Fayetteville Public Library: 401 W Mountain St, Fayetteville, AR 72701; tel. (479) 856-7000; fax (479) 571-0222; e-mail questions@faylib.org; internet www.faylib .org; f. 1916; 245,000 vols (incl. books, CDs, DVDs, videos, audio cassettes, e-books and parenting kits); Exec. Dir DAVID JOHNSON; Pres. SUZANNE CLARK; Sec. KIM AGEE; Treas. MAYLON RICE.

Fort Smith Public Library: 3201 Rogers Ave, Fort Smith, AR 72903; tel. (479) 783-0229; fax (479) 782-8571; e-mail reference@ fortsmithlibrary.org; internet www .fortsmithlibrary.org; f. 1891; 3 brs; genealogy dept in main library; Pres. TRACY LONG; Sec. BRIAN DeLUNG; Treas. ROBERT KELLY.

Marion County Library: 308 Old Main, Yellville, AR 72687; tel. and fax (870) 449-6015; e-mail librarian@marcolib.org; internet marcolib.org; f. 1944; Dir ANITA PAULSON.

Springdale Public Library: 405 S Pleasant St, Springdale, AR 72764; tel. (479) 750-8180; fax (479) 750-8182; e-mail askus@ springdalelibrary.org; internet www .springdalelibrary.org; f. 1927; newspaper on microfilm from May 1887 to the present; cemetery indexes for Washington and Benton counties; mem. of Washington County Library System; Dir MARCIA RANSOM; Pres. JASON ENGLAND.

University of Arkansas Libraries: 365 N McIlroy Ave, Fayetteville, AR 72701-4002; tel. (479) 575-4104; fax (479) 575-6656; e-mail refer@uark.edu; internet ibinfo.uark .edu; David W. Mullins Library (main research facility), Robert A. and Vivian Young Law Library, Fine Arts Library, Chemistry and Biochemistry Library, Physics Library, Performing Arts and Media Library; spec. collns: local politics, Civil War, women's records, maps; 1.9m. vols, 5.5m. microforms, 100,000 pictures and photographs; Dean of Libraries CAROLYN HENDERSON ALLEN.

William F. Laman Public Library System: 2801 Orange St, North Little Rock, AR 72114; tel. (501) 758-1720; e-mail library .information@lamanlibrary.org; internet www.lamanlibrary.org; f. 1947; 1 br; 175,000 vols, 8,000 CDs and audiobooks, 3,000 DVDs; Dir JEFFREY L. BASKIN; Chair. RON OLIVER.

William J. Clinton Presidential Library & Museum: 1200 President Clinton Ave, Little Rock, AR 72201; tel. (501) 374-4242; fax (501) 244-2883; e-mail clinton.library@ nara.gov; internet www.clintonlibrary.gov; f. 2004; 10,000 vols (incl. Head of State gifts and non-Head of State gifts), 78m. pages of official records, 20m. email records, 2m. photographs, 5,900 audio cassettes and 12,500 video cassettes; Dir TERRI GARNER.

California

Alameda County Law Library: 125 12th St, Oakland, CA 94607-4912; tel. (510) 208-4800; fax (510) 208-3907; internet www .acgov.org/law; f. 1891; provides free access to the judiciary, state and county officials, members of the bar and residents of the county; colln incl. legal research materials; 196,941 vols, 105,000 vols in hard copy and 91,941 vols in microform; publ. *Recent Acquisitions List* (12 a year); Law Library Dir MARK E. ESTES.

Belvedere-Tiburon Library: 1501 Tiburon Blvd Tiburon, CA 94920; tel. (415) 789-2665; fax (415) 789-2650; e-mail refdesk@bel-tib-lib .org; internet www.bel-tib-lib.org; f. 1997; 71,339 35,223 adult colln, 3,389 reference colln,400 periodicals; Library Dir DEBORAH MAZZOLINI.

California State Library: POB 942837, Sacramento, CA 94237-0001; tel. (916) 654-0266; fax (916) 654-00641; e-mail cslinfo@ library.ca.gov; internet www.library.ca.gov; f. 1850; library service to state govt; preservation of CA materials; govt document depository; law library; books for the blind, and physically handicapped service; administrator of the state and fed. aid to public libraries; 696,000 vols, 3,011,835 govt publs; State Librarian STACEY A. ALDRICH; publs *California Library Directory* (1 a year), *California Library Laws* (1 a year), *California Library Statistics* (1 a year), *California State Publications* (12 a year).

County of Los Angeles Public Library: A C Bilbrew Library, 150 E El Segundo Blvd, Los Angeles, CA 90061; tel. (310) 538-3350; e-mail lacountylibrary@gmail.com; internet www.colapublib.org; f. 1912; 84 regional and community libraries; 1 institutional library; 4 bookmobiles; 5,488,446 vols, 789,237 titles, 6,742 periodicals, 59,352 govt publs, 298,033 audio materials, 600,095 videos, 2,118 CDs; County Librarian MARGARET DONNELLAN TODD.

Dr Martin Luther King Jr Library: 150 E San Fernando St, San Jose, CA 95112; tel. (408) 808-2000; internet www.sjlibrary.org; f. 1997; also known as King Library; spec. colln: materials related to Dr Martin Luther King, Jr, and the Civil Rights movement; 1.5m. vols.

Hoover Institution on War, Revolution and Peace: 434 Galvez Mall, Stanford, CA 94305-6010; tel. (650) 723-1754; fax (650) 723-1687; internet www.hoover.org; f. 1919; attached to Stanford Univ.; centre of documentation and research on int. and domestic political, social and economic change since beginning of the 20th century; 60m. documents, 100,000 political posters; 4,772 archival units on the causes and consequences of war and revolutionary movements, and on efforts to achieve peace; with emphasis on int. rivalries and global cooperation; research programme on political, economic and social problems in the USA; ind., within the framework of Stanford Univ.; Dir. RICHARD SOUSA; publs *China Leadership Monitor* (4 a year), *Education Next* (4 a year), *Hoover's Digest* (4 a year), *Policy Review* (6 a year).

Huntington Library, Art Collections and Botanical Gardens: 1151 Oxford Rd, San Marino, CA 91108; tel. (626) 405-2100; fax (626) 449-5703; e-mail publicinformation@huntington.org; internet www.huntington.org; f. 1919; collns incl. 375,000 rare books, 6,000,000 MSS, working reference library of 500,000 vols and 600,000 photographs; available to scholars and others engaged in research work on application to the Registrar; collns concentrate on British and American history, literature and art; particular strengths incl. English medieval and Renaissance, British drama, American colonial, American Civil War, American frontier, MSS since 19th century, early science; separate reference libraries located in the Botanical Div., the latter incl. 300,000 photographs, paintings and 6,000 British drawings; public programmes, lectures, exhibitions; See also Museums and Art Galleries; 6m. vols, incl. books, MSS and photographs; Pres. STEVEN KOBLIK; Avery Dir of the Library DAVID S. ZEIDBERG; publ. *Huntington Frontiers* (2 a year).

Kern County Library: 701 Truxtun Ave, Bakersfield, CA. 93301; tel. (661) 868-0700; fax (661) 868-0799; internet www .kerncountylibrary.org; 25 brs, 1 main library, 2 bookmobiles; 1,097,438 vols (incl. 16,172 govt documents, 14,358 microforms, 191 periodicals subscriptions, and 65,003 audio-visual items; Dir of Libraries SHERRY GOMEZ.

LA Law Library (Los Angeles County Law Library): 301 W First St, Los Angeles, CA 90012-3100; tel. (213) 785-2529; fax (213) 613-1329; e-mail reference@lalawlibrary.org; internet www.lalawlibrary.org; f. 1891 as Los Angeles County Law Library; br collns in courthouses in Long Beach, Norwalk, Pomona, Santa Monica and Torrance; spec. colln 7,500 vols on Roman, canon, civil, English law; public library partnerships: Pasadena, Compton, Lancaster; self-help colln for self-represented litigants; programme for mems of the California State Bar MCLE; collns of the US and int. legal materials; 1,000,000 vols (incl. print, media, microfilm and microfiche); Exec. Dir MARCIA J. KOSLOV; Sr Dir JAYE NELSON.

Los Angeles Public Library: 630 W Fifth St, Los Angeles, CA 90071; tel. (213) 228-7272; fax (213) 228-7369; e-mail asklapl@ hotmail.com; internet www.lapl.org; f. 1872; 70 brs; California, children's literature, cookery, genealogy, North American Indians, modern languages, orchestral scores, US patents, standards and specifications, English language, theatre, congressional documents and hearings, business and finance, corporate annual reports, video cassettes, DVDs, CDs, audiobooks, telephone and trade directories; 6m. vols; Dir Central Library GIOVANNA MANNINO (acting); Dir Br. Librar-

ies CHERYL COLLINS (acting); City Librarian MARTÍN GÓMEZ.

Nixon Presidential Library and Museum: 18001 Yorba Linda Blvd, Yorba Linda, CA 92886; tel. (714) 983-9120; e-mail nixon@nara.gov; internet www.nixonlibrary .gov; f. 2007; 4,000 of 'off air' video recordings; nearly 4,469 audio recordings; 30,000 gifts from foreign heads of states, American citizens, and others; 500,000 still photographs; 2m. ft of film; 46m. pages of documents; 3,700 hours of recorded presidential conversations.

Oakland Public Library: 125 14th St, Oakland, CA 94612; tel. (510) 238-3134; e-mail tdowns@oaklandlibrary.org; internet www.oaklandlibrary.org; f. 1878 as Oakland Free Library; 15 brs; 1 main library; 1 bookmobile; Dir of Library Services CARMEN L. MARTINEZ.

OC Public Libraries: Aliso Viejo Library, One Journey, Aliso Viejo, CA 92656; tel. (949) 360-1730; e-mail libraryadmin@occr.ocgov .com; internet www.ocpl.org; 33 brs; County Librarian HELEN FRIED.

Pasadena Public Library: 285 E Walnut St, Pasadena, CA 91101; tel. (626) 744-4066; internet www.ci.pasadena.ca.us; 1 main library; 9 brs; 775,469 vols,; Dir JAN SANDER.

Placer County Library: 350 Nevada St, Auburn, CA 95603; tel. (530) 886-4550; fax (530) 886-4555; e-mail library@placerlibrary .org; internet www.placer.ca.gov; 11 brs; 1 bookmobile; Dir of Library Services MARY GEORGE.

Plumas County Library: 445 Jackson St, Quincy, CA 95971; tel. (530) 283-6310; fax (530) 283-3242; internet www .countyofplumas.com; f. 1905; 1 main library, 3 brs; County Librarian DORA MITCHELL.

Ronald Reagan Presidential Library: 40 Presidential Dr. Simi Valley, CA 93065; tel. (805) 577-4000; fax (805) 577-4074; e-mail reagan.library@nara.gov; internet www .reagan.utexas.edu; f. 1991; repository of presidential records for Pres. Reagan's admin; 50m. pages of presidential documents, 1.6m. photographs, 500,000 ft of motion picture film.

Roseville Public Library: Downtown Library, 225 Taylor St, Roseville, CA 95678; tel. (916) 774-5221; e-mail library@roseville .ca.us; internet www.roseville.ca.us; 3 brs; contains a large history colln, and other research materials such as books, magazinesand online databases for all spheres of knowledge; 190,360 vols; City Librarian NATASHA CASTEEL.

Sacramento Public Library: 828 I St, Sacramento, CA 95814; tel. (916) 264-2700; fax (916) 264-2755; e-mail contact@saclibrary .org; internet www.saclibrary.org; f. 1879; spec. collns: Sacramento current and historical information, California colln, business colln, printing history, Sacramento area authors, art and music colln; central library, 26 brs; 2m. vols; Chair. SANDY SHEEDY; Dir RIVKAH K. SASS.

San Diego County Public Law Library: 1168 Union St, San Diego, CA 92101-3904; tel. (619) 531-3900; fax (619) 238-7716; e-mail refdesk@sdcpll.org; internet www .sdcpll.org; f. 1891; colln of California and US legal materials, such as statutes and codes, administrative regulations, case law; secondary legal resources, incl. federal, microform, reference, archival, electronic and self-help collections; main library under construction; 250,000 vols; Pres. JULIA C. KELETY; Dir JOHN ADKINS.

San Diego Public Library: 820 E St, San Diego, CA 92101-6416; tel. (619) 236-5800; fax (619) 236-5878; e-mail librarydirector@

sandiego.gov; internet www.sandiego.gov/ public-library; f. 1882; 1 central library and 35 brs; adult literacy program office (READ/ San Diego); 4.2m. books, incl. e-books, 3,888 periodicals, 1.6m. govt. documents, 291,000 books in 25 languages other than English; Dir DEBORAH BARROW.

San Francisco Law Library: 401 Van Ness Ave, Room 400, San Francisco, CA 94102; tel. (415) 554-6821; fax (415) 554-6820; e-mail sflawlibrary@sfgov.org; internet www .sflawlibrary.org; f. 1870; colln of materials relevant to legal research with an emphasis on California law; 3 brs; open to public; 246,000 vols (main library), 30,367 vols (br. libraries); Dir MARCIA R. BELL; Pres. KURT W. MELCHOIR; Treas. KATHLEEN V. FISHER.

San Francisco Public Library: 100 Larkin St, San Francisco, CA 94102-4733; tel. (415) 557-4400; fax (415) 557-4239; e-mail citylibrarian@sfpl.org; internet www.sfpl .org; 7,051,190 vols; City Librarian LUIS HERRERA.

Santa Cruz County Law Library: 701 Ocean St, Room 070, Santa Cruz, CA 95060; tel. (831) 420-2205; fax (831) 457-2255; e-mail scclawlib@yahoo.com; internet www .lawlibrary.org; f. 1896; 16,000 vols; Pres. JOHN GALLAGHER.

St Helena Public Library: 1492 Library Lane, St. Helena, CA 94574; tel. 963-5244; fax 963-5264; e-mail director@shpl.org; internet www.shpl.org; f. 1875, present bldg 1979; 96,000 vols; Library Dir JENNIFER BAKER.

Stanford University Libraries & Academic Information Resources (SULAIR): Cecil H. Green Library, East Wing, First Fl., Stanford, CA 94305; tel. (650) 725-1064; e-mail infocenter@stanford.edu; internet www-sul.stanford.edu; f. 1885; 16 libraries; 7.7m. vols, incl. the Green Library (2,837,863 vols), Hoover Institution on War, Revolution and Peace (1,257,466 vols) and 45 departmental and school libraries, of which the major ones are: Lane Medical Library (371,725 vols), Robert Crown Law Library (437,896 vols), Cubberley Education Library (175,849 vols), Branner Earth Sciences Library (132,446 vols), J. Hugh Jackson Business Library (548,639 vols), Linear Accelerator Center Library (8,840 vols), Falconer Biology Library (105,106 vols), Hopkins Marine Station Library (38,478 vols), Mathematical and Computer Sciences Library (127,396 vols), Swain Chemistry Library (55,529 vols), Art and Architecture (180,933 vols), Music (108,443 vols), Archive of Recorded Sound (6,382 items), Physics (59,401 vols), Eng. (114,039 vols); spec. collns: transportation, music, British and American Literature, history of science, book arts and history of the book, children's literature, Judaica and Hebraica; Univ. Librarian and Dir of Academic Information Resources MICHAEL A. KELLER.

University of Southern California Libraries: 3550 Trousdale Parkway, DML 335, Los Angeles, CA 90089-0183; tel. (213) 740-2543; fax (213) 749-1221; e-mail library@ usc.edu; internet www.usc.edu/isd/libraries; f. 1880; spec. collns: Cervantes, Lewis Carroll, Max Reinhardt; American literature; cinema and television, European philosophy; German exile literature; gerontology; int. relations; Korean studies, Latin American studies, natural history, Southern California history, Univ. Archives; 4,180,515 vols, 109,352 serial titles, 3,192,549 visual materials, 161,720 maps and cartographic materials, 6,472,630 microfilm units, 37,032 audio recordings, 37,980 film and video recordings, 49,251 linear ft MSS and archives, 399,112 e-books, 76,399 e-journals, 255,935 digital archive items; Dean of Libraries CATHERINE QUINLAN.

Colorado

Arapahoe Library District: 12855 E Adam Aircraft Circle, Englewood, CO 80112; tel. (303) 542-7279; fax (303) 798-2485; internet arapahoelibraries.org; f. 1966; serves Byers and Deer Trail, cities of Bow Mar, Centennial, Cherry Hills Village, Columbine, Glendale, Greenwood Village and Sheridan, and unincorporated areas of Arapahoe co; 8 br. libraries and 1 bookmobile; Man. ELOISE MAY.

Auraria Library: 1100 Lawrence St, Denver, CO 80204; tel. (303) 556-2740; fax (303) 556-3528; internet library.auraria.edu; archives and spec. colln; serves downtown Denver campus of Univ. of Colorado Denver, Auraria Higher Education Center, Metropolitan State College of Denver and Community College of Denver; Dir MARY M. SOMERVILLE.

Berthoud Community Library District: POB 1259, 236 Welch Ave, Berthoud, CO 80513-2259; tel. (970) 532-2757; fax (970) 532-4372; e-mail director.bpl@gmail.com; internet berthoud.colibraries.org; f. 1931; Dir SARA WRIGHT; Pres. KATHRYN CHURCHILL; Sec. LAURI WEAVER; Treas. PEG OBENHAUS.

Cardinal Stafford Library: 1300 S Steele St, Denver, CO 80210; tel. (303) 715-3146; fax (303) 282-3453; e-mail infosjv@archden.org; internet www.sjvdenver.edu/library; f. 1910; attached to St John Vianney Theological Seminary; colln on Catholic theology, church history, biblical studies, liturgy, canon law, religious art, philosophy and literature; spec. collns: over 500 rare books dating back to early 16th century and periodicals dating back to the 1800s; 150,000 vols, 300 print periodicals; E. M. Womack Colln: 10,000 vols; Dir STEPHEN SWEENEY.

Clear Creek County District Library: POB 666, Georgetown, CO 80444; 614 Taos St, Georgetown, CO 80444; tel. (303) 569-2403; fax (303) 569-2330; e-mail director@clearcreeklibrary.org; internet www2.youseemore.com/clearcreeklibrary; incl. John Tomay Memorial Library and Idaho Springs Public Library; Dir SUE LATHROP; Pres. MARIANNE LORITZ; Sec. SUSAN SERPA; Treas. VICTORIA COLLE.

Colorado State Archives: 1313 Sherman, Room 1B20 Denver, CO 80203; tel. (303) 866-2358; fax (303) 866-2257; internet www.colorado.gov/dpa/doit/archives; f. 1953; attached to Colorado Dept of Personnel and Admin.; preserves Colorado's legal and historical records and promotes their use by public; 1,000,000 archival entries; State Archivist TERRY KETELSEN.

Colorado State Library: 201 E Colfax Ave, Room 309, Denver, CO 80203; tel. (303) 866-6900; fax (303) 866-6940; internet www.cde.state.co.us/cdelib; f. 1959; attached to Colorado Dept of Education; access to information produced by state govt; free recorded, Braille and large-print library materials; Asst Commr EUGENE HAINER.

Colorado State University Libraries: Morgan Library, Colorado State Univ., 501 University Ave, 1019 Campus Delivery, Fort Collins, CO 80523-1019; tel. (970) 491-1841; fax (970) 491-1195; internet lib.colostate.edu; f. 1880; br. library in Veterinary Medical Center; fed. depository; 2,073,333 vols, 31,372 current serials (incl. magazines, journals and periodicals), 1 mile of archival materials, 24,106 e-journals; Dean of Libraries PATRICK BURNS.

Colorado Supreme Court Library: 101 W Colfax Ave, Suite A, Denver, CO 80202; tel. (303) 837-3720; fax (303) 864-4510; e-mail library@judicial.state.co.us; internet cscl.colibraries.org; colln for research of judiciary and mems of the bar; open to public; colln on primary law from fed. and state govts, treatise colln and other practice-oriented materials incl. form books, Colorado Continuing Legal Education materials and practice manuals; 80,000 vols, 12,000 titles.

Denver Public Library: 10 W 14th Ave, Pkwy, Denver, CO 80204-2731; tel. (720) 865-1111; fax (303) 640-6374; internet denverlibrary.org; f. 1889; 22 brs; specializes in Western US history, conservation of natural resources, energy and the environment, genealogy, fine printing, folk music, US 10th Mountain Div. soldiers; 2,288,842 vols; City Librarian SHIRLEY AMORE.

DOC Boulder Laboratories Library: 325 Broadway MC-5, Boulder, CO 80305; tel. (303) 497-3271; fax (303) 497-3890; e-mail boulderlabs.main.library@noaa.gov; internet library.bldrdoc.gov; f. 1954; attached to US Dept of Commerce; 45,000 vols, 350 current journals, 38,000 bound journal vols, 1,000 e-journals; Dir DOTTIE ANDERSON.

Douglas County Libraries: 100 S Wilcox St, Castle Rock, CO 80104; tel. (303) 791-7323; internet douglascountylibraries.org; f. 1929; libraries in Highlands Ranch, Lone Tree, Louviers, Parker, Castle Rock, Littleton; 713,448 vols; Dir JAMIE LARUE; Pres. AMY HUNT; Sec. DAVID STARCK; Treas. BOB McLAUGHLIN.

Garfield County Libraries: POB 832, Rifle, CO 81650; 207 E Ave, Rifle, CO 81650; tel. (970) 625-4270; fax (970) 625-4472; internet www.garfieldlibraries.org; f. 1938; 6 brs; Ancestry Library Edn with 4 billion records in census data, vital records, directories and photos from N America, Europe and Australia; 182,655 vols; Exec. Dir AMELIA SHELLEY; Pres. NELLA BARKER.

Grand County Library District: POB 1050, Granby, CO 80446; 225 E Jasper Ave, Granby, CO 80446; tel. (970) 887-9411; fax (970) 887-3227; e-mail adminoffice@gcld.org; internet www.gcld.org; f. 1995; provides sources and advisory to create new libraries; 5 brs; Exec. Dir MARY ANNE HANSON-WILCOX; Pres. JOHN KACIK; Sec. DEDE FAY; Treas. KIM JENSEN.

HealthONE Denver Medical Library: 1719 E 19th Ave, Denver, CO 80218; tel. (303) 839-6670; fax (303) 869-1643; e-mail info@denvermedlib.org; internet www.denvermedlib.org; f. 1893 as Colorado Medical Library Assn; open only to mems; Man. SHARON MARTIN.

Mesa County Libraries: 443 N Sixth St, Grand Junction, CO 81501; tel. (970) 243-4442; fax (970) 243-4744; internet www.mcpld.org; 7 brs; Dir EVE TALLMAN; Pres. LINDA DAVIDSON; Sec. LAURIE TASHIRO.

Pikes Peak Library District: POB 1579, Colorado Springs, CO 80901; tel. (719) 531-6333; internet library.ppld.org; f. 1903; incl. Community Breast Cancer Resource Center; bookmobile services; 13 brs; Exec. Dir PAULA J. MILLER.

University of Colorado at Boulder Libraries: 184 UCB, 1720 Pleasant St, Boulder, CO 80309-0184; tel. (303) 492-8705; fax (303) 492-1881; e-mail reflib@colorado.edu; internet ucblibraries.colorado.edu; f. 1877 as Teller Library; 5 brs; spec. collns: mountaineering, photobooks, peace and justice, western Americana; 3,928,431 vols, 6,993,960 microforms, 963,779 govt documents, 38,518 linear ft MSS and archives, 69,010 audio cassettes, 16,697 films and video cassettes; Dean of Libraries JAMES F. WILLIAMS.

Connecticut

Acton Public Library: 60 Old Boston Post Rd, Old Saybrook, CT 06475; tel. (860) 395-3184; fax (860) 395-2462; e-mail actonpubliclibrary@gmail.com; f. 1854; offers information in all areas incl. municipal, medical and career field; 75,000 vols; Dir MICHELE VAN EPPS.

Ansonia Library: 53 S Cliff St, Ansonia, CT 06401; tel. (203) 734-6275; fax (203) 732-4551; e-mail ansonialibrary@biblio.org; internet www.ansonialibrary.org; f. 1892; Dir JOYCE CECCARELLI; Chair. MARGARET SULLIVAN; Treas. VIOLET O'DONNELL.

Avon Free Public Library: 281 Country Club Rd, Avon, CT 06001; tel. (860) 673-9712; fax (860) 675-6364; e-mail avonref@avonctlibrary.info; internet www.avonctlibrary.info; f. 1798; Marian Hunter History Room that incl. photographs, postcards, scrapbooks, maps, deeds and other pieces of memorabilia; 100,403 vols; Dir VIRGINIA VOCELLI; Pres. MARY LaBELLE SUTER; Sec. RUTH TIMME; Treas. THOMAS IEZZI.

Bakerville Library: 6 Maple Hollow Rd, New Hartford, CT 06057; tel. (860) 482-8806; internet www.bakervillelibrary.org; f. 1949; colln of audio books, popular fiction and reference material; 14,000 vols; Librarian JULIE LaSATA; Chair. DIANNE LITCHFIELD.

Bethlehem Public Library: 32 Main St S, Bethlehem, CT 06751; tel. (203) 266-7792; internet www.ci.bethlehem.ct.us/library.htm; f. 1857, present name and status 1900; 23,000 vols; Dir ANNE SMALL.

Bill Memorial Library: 240 Monument St, Groton, CT 06340; tel. (860) 445-0392; fax (860) 449-8971; e-mail info@billmemorial.org; internet www.billmemorial.org; f. 1888; genealogy or local history room for research; colln incl. bestsellers, current non-fiction, classics and large print books; 21,000 vols.

Bridgeport Library: 925 Broad St, Bridgeport, CT 06604; tel. (203) 576-7777; fax (203) 333-0253; internet www.bportlibrary.org; f. 1881; brs: Burroughs and Saden, Black Rock, Newfield, North and Old Mill Green; City Librarian SCOTT HUGHES; Pres. JIM O'DONNELL; Sec. and Treas. TOM ERRICHETTI.

Cheshire Public Library: 104 Main St, Cheshire, CT 06410-2406; tel. (203) 272-2245; fax (203) 272-7714; e-mail cheshire@cheshirelibrary.org; internet www.cheshirelib.org; f. 1892; local history and genealogy, large print books and audio books for visually impaired; Dir RAMONA BURKEY; Chair. CAROL DiPIETRO.

Connecticut State Library: 231 Capitol Ave, Hartford, CT 06106; tel. (860) 757-6500; fax (860) 757-6503; e-mail isref@cslib.org; internet www.cslib.org; f. 1854, present bldg 1910; Connecticut newspapers, genealogy, history, law, legislative reference, public policy, Connecticut and US govt publs; 2.5m. vols; Chair. MOLLIE KELLER; State Librarian KENDALL F. WIGGIN.

Cora J. Belden and Library: 33 Church St, Rocky Hill, CT 06067; tel. (860) 258-7623; internet www.rockyhilllibrary.info/index.htm; f. 1794, present name and status 1950; Dir MARY HOGAN; Chair. CATHY PUGLISI CARONE; Sec. W. MURRAY LICHTNER.

Cragin Memorial Library: 8 Linwood Ave, Route 16, Colchester, CT 06415; tel. (860) 537-5752; fax (860) 537-4559; e-mail library@colchesterct.gov; internet www.colchesterct.gov; f. 1905; 63,000 vols; Dir KATE BYROADE.

East Hartford Public Library System: 840 Main St, East Hartford, CT 06108; tel. (860) 289-6429; fax (860) 291-9166; internet www.ehtfdlib.info; brs: Raymond Library and Wickham Library; 200,000 vols, 10,000 CDs, audio and video cassettes, and DVDs; Dir PAT JONES.

East Lyme Public Library: 39 Society Rd, Niantic, CT 06357-1100; tel. (860) 739-6926; fax (860) 691-0020; e-mail elpl@ely.lioninc .org; internet www.ely.lioninc.org; f. 1888 as Niantic Library and Reading Room Asscn, present location 1990; 147,000 vols.

Granby Public Library: 15 N Granby Rd, Granby, CT 06035; tel. (860) 844-5275; internet www.granby-ct.gov/ public_documents/granbyct_library/index; f. 1982; 2 brs: Granby Public Library and Frederick H. Cossitt Library; reference colln incl. 1,500 items; 63,000 vols; Dir for Library Services JOAN M. FOX.

Greenwich Library: 101 W Putnam Ave, Greenwich, CT 06830-5387; tel. (203) 622-7900; fax (203) 625-6556; internet www .greenwichlibrary.org; f. 1805; brs: Byram Shubert, Cos Cob and Perrot Memorial Library; Dir CAROL MAHONEY; Pres. JENNIFER BALDOCK; Sec. MARY JACOBSON; Treas. SUZANNE PEISCH.

Hamden Public Library: 2901 Dixwell Ave, Hamden, CT 06518; tel. (203) 287-2680; fax (203) 287-2685; e-mail info@ hamdenlibrary.org; internet www .hamdenlibrary.org; f. 1950; brs: Miller Memorial Central Library, Whitneyville Branch Library and Brundage Community Branch Library; colln incl. 21,101 videos and audio cassettes, spec. colln of books, MSS and photographs on the history of Hamden; 191,264 vols (incl. books, paperbacks and magazines); Dir BOB GUALTIERI.

Harwinton Public Library: 80 Bentley Dr., Harwinton, CT 06791; tel. (860) 485-9113; e-mail staff@harwintonpl.org; internet www2.youseemore.com/harwinton; 35,297 vols, 43 periodicals, 4,370 audio recordings and 1,942 videos; Dir STASIA MOTUZICK.

Hotchkiss Library of Sharon: POB 277, Sharon, CT 06069; 10 Upper Main St, Sharon, CT 06069; tel. (860) 364-5041; fax (860) 364-6060; internet www .hotchkisslibrary.org; f. 1893; historical colln of books and archives dating back to the Revolutionary War; 14,000 vols; Dir LOUISE MANTEUFFEL.

Levi E. Coe Library: 414 Main St, POB 458, Middlefield, CT 06455; tel. (860) 349-3857; fax (860) 349-2131; e-mail staff@ leviecoe.com; internet www.leviecoe.com; f. 1893; 10,000 works of fiction; colln incl. educational, cultural and recreational resources; 25,000 vols; Dir LOREN WEBBER.

Russell Library: 123 Broad St, Middletown, CT 06457; tel. (860) 347-2528; fax (860) 347-4048; e-mail infodept@russell.lioninc.org; internet www.russelllibrary.org; f. 1875; local history colln; microfilm archives incl. Mellili church records and discontinued Middletown newspapers; Dir ARTHUR MEYERS; Pres. RICHARD B. KAMINS; Sec. ANDREW E. BECKER; Treas. MARVIN FARBMAN.

Russell Library: 123 Broad St, Middletown, CT 06457; tel. (860) 347-2528; fax (860) 347-4048; e-mail infodept@russell.lioninc.org; internet www.russelllibrary.org; f. 1875; local history colln; microfilm archives incl. Mellili church records and discontinued Middletown newspapers; Dir ARTHUR MEYERS; Pres. RICHARD B. KAMINS; Sec. ANDREW E. BECKER; Treas. MARVIN FARBMAN.

Henry Carter Hull Library: 10 Killingworth Turnpike, Clinton, CT 06413; tel. (860) 669-2342; fax (860) 669-8318; internet www .hchlibrary.org; f. 1910; Lincoln colln: 250 books on Civil War and Abraham Lincoln; rare books and pamphlets about history of

Connecticut; 85,000 vols; Dir MARIBETH BREEN; Pres. RICH SANTANELLI.

University of Connecticut Library: 369 Fairfield Way, Storrs, CT 06269-2005; tel. (860) 486-2518; fax (860) 486-5636; e-mail elibrary@uconn.edu; internet www.lib.uconn .edu; f. 1881; largest public research colln in the state; 2.5m. vols, 9,000 current print periodicals, 25,000 electronic journals, 2.8m. microforms, 35,500 reference sources, 180,000 maps and a large repository of electronic information resources; Vice-Provost for Univ. Libraries BRINLEY FRANKLIN.

Yale University Library: POB 208240, 130 Wall St, New Haven, CT 06520-8240; 130 Wall St, New Haven, CT 06511; tel. (203) 432-1810; fax (203) 432-1294; e-mail smlref@ yale.edu; internet www.library.yale.edu; f. 1701; each of the 12 undergraduate colleges has its own library; 13m.vols; Univ. Librarian SUSAN GIBBONS.

Delaware

Corbit-Calloway Memorial Library: POB 128, 115 High St, Odessa, DE 19730; tel. (302) 378-8838; fax (302) 378-7803; internet corbitlibrary.org; f. 1847; colln incl. books, pamphlets, magazines and newspapers, photographs and postcards, posters and prints; 9,000 vols (Delmarva Colln); Pres. MARGARET RYAN; Treas. VIRGINIA BRICCOTTO; Sec. JANET BUTLER.

Delaware Division of Libraries: 121 Duke of York St, Dover, DE 19901; tel. (302) 739-4748; fax (302) 739-6787; internet www.state .lib.de.us; f. 1901; attached to Delaware Dept of State; spec. collns: US govt documents, talking books; Dir Dr ANNE E. C. NORMAN; Deputy Dir BETH-ANN RYAN; Sr Librarian MARIE CUNNINGHAM; Sr Librarian STEVE NEWTON.

Delaware Public Archives: 121 Duke of York St, Dover, DE 19901; tel. (302) 744-5000; e-mail aarchives@state.de.us; internet www.archives.delaware.gov; f. 1905, present location 2000; attached to Dept of State; 95,000 cubic ft of govt records and historical documents, incl. records of the exec., legislative and judicial brs of Delaware's state govt and holdings of county and municipal records from the late 17th century to the present (incl. 800,000 historical photographs); 500 rolls of microfilm holdings; MSS; reference library; Dir STEPHEN M. MARZ.

Dover Public Library: 45 S State St, Dover, DE 19901; tel. (302) 736-5025; fax (302) 736-5087; internet www.cityofdover .com/home-library; Library Dir MARGERY CYR.

Jewish Historical Society of Delaware Archives: 505 Market St Mall, Wilmington, DE 19801; tel. (302) 655-6232; e-mail jhsdel@ yahoo.com; internet www.hsd.org/jhsd.htm; f. 1974; audiovisual materials, artefacts, documents, memorabilia newspapers, oral histories, private papers and photographs that record and document the organizational, cultural, religious, educational, business and family activities of the Jewish Community in Delaware; 350 linear ft of archival space; records from the Jewish Community Center of Wilmington, Jewish Federation of Delaware, Adas Kodesch Shel Emeth Congregation and Vaad Hakashruth; holocaust-related materials.

John Eugene Derrickson Memorial Library: Delaware Technical & Community College, Wilmington Campus, W Bldg, First Fl., 333 Shipley St, Wilmington, DE 19801; tel. (302) 573-5422; internet www.library .dtcc.edu/wilmlib; attached to Delaware Technical & Community College; 2 sections: main library and audiovisual library and education centre; 50,000 vols (incl. colln of

Stanton Campus), 500 periodicals; Librarian KARENE CHESTER.

Lewes Historical Society Library: 110 Shipcarpenter St, Lewes, DE 19958; tel. (302) 645-7670; fax (302) 645-2375; e-mail research@historiclewes.org; internet www .historiclewes.org/research/library.html; history of Delaware, Delmarva history, natural and maritime history, some gen. American history works, family bibles, genealogy, spec. collns, 19th century medical texts, 19th- and early 20th-century school texts, and texts dealing with aspects of the Soc.'s museum collns; comprises libraries of John Farrace, Alice Watts and Joseph Enos; 4,000 vols; Pres. FRAN RICHMANN; Sec. H. EDWARD MAULL, JR; Treas. SUSAN McELLIGOTT-McKAY.

Stanton Campus Library: Room D 201, Delaware Technical and Community College, Stanton Campus, 400 Stanton-Christiana Rd, Newark, DE 19713; tel. (302) 453-3716; fax (302) 453-3079; internet www.library .dtcc.edu/stantlib; attached to Delaware Technical & Community College; colln supports the technologies taught at the campus; 29,000 vols, 1,500 audiovisual items, 270 periodical titles; Librarian JANET CHIN.

Stephen J. Betze Library: Seashore Hwy, POB 630, Georgetown, DE 19947; tel. (302) 856-9033; fax (302) 858-5462; internet www .library.dtcc.edu/owenslib; attached to Delaware Technical & Community College, Owens Campus; fiction and paperback colln; spec. collns incl. Quarto (oversized books), historical Delaware resource materials and pamphlets; also holds fed. govt documents; Dir Dr SHIRIN JAMASB.

Terry Campus Library: 100, Campus Dr., Dover, DE 19904; tel. (302) 857-1060; fax (302) 857-1099; internet www.dtcc.edu/terry/ library; attached to Delaware Technical & Community College; serves students in Terry campus' educational programmes, Delaware Tech credit courses, Univ. of Delaware assoc. in arts courses, and corporate and community programmes and training programmes; Head Librarian Dr MARGARET PROUSE.

University of Delaware Library: 181 S College Ave, Newark, DE 19717-5267; tel. (302) 831-2965; internet www.lib.udel.edu; incl. Hugh M. Morris Library and 3 br. libraries in Newark (agriculture library, chemistry library and physics library) and 1 br. library in Lewes (Marine Studies Library); Mark Samuels Lasner Colln: British literature and art from 1850 to 1900, with an emphasis on the Pre-Raphaelites and writers and illustrators of the 1890s; 7,500 first and other edns (incl. signed and asscn copies), MSS, letters, works on paper and ephemera; 2,800,000 vols, 330,000 e-books, 32,000 e-journals, 3,400,000 microforms, 510,000 DVDs and maps, 6,700 linear ft of MSS and archives, 25,000 film and video programmes; Librarian, Vice-Provost and May Morris Dir of Libraries SUSAN BRYNTESON.

William C. Jason Library: 1200 N DuPont Highway, Dover, DE 19901-2277; tel. (302) 857-6191; fax (302) 857-6177; internet www .desu.edu/library; attached to Delaware State Univ.; African-American Colln; Claude E. Phillips Herbarium Library; 800 vols of local, state and regional research materials; 1,000 titles of history of the univ.; yearbooks and books written by Delaware State Univ. profs and alumni; 475,033 vols; Dean of Univ. Libraries Dr R. BATSON.

District of Columbia

Archives of American Art: Smithsonian Instn, POB 37012, Victor Bldg, Suite 2200, MRC, 937, Washington, DC 20013-7012; 750 Ninth St, NW, Victor Bldg, Suite 2200,

Washington, DC 20001; tel. (202) 633-7940; fax (202) 633-7994; internet www.aaa.si.edu; f. 1954; attached to Smithsonian Instn; research centre; collects, preserves and provides access to primary sources that document history of visual arts in America; colln incl. letters, diaries and scrapbooks of artists, dealers, and collectors; MSS of critics and scholars; business and financial records of museums, galleries, schools and asscns; photographs of art, world figures and events; sketches and sketchbooks; rare printed material; film, audio and video recordings; 16m. items; Dir LIZA KIRWIN (acting); publ. *Journal* (2 a year).

Commerce Departmental Library: 1401 Constitution Ave, NW, Washington, DC 20230; tel. (202) 482-1154; fax (202) 482-0221; e-mail lawlibrary@doc.gov; internet www.library.doc.gov; f. 1913; attached to US Dept of Commerce; colln incl. legislative histories, Congressional hearings, reports, prints and documents, Code of Fed. Regulations, Fed. Register, treaties and journals; current legal material that supports the work of the Office of the Gen. Counsel; 50,000 vols, 2,000 vols microform; Dir JANE SESSA.

Department of the Treasury Library: Main Treasury Bldg, 1500 Pennsylvania Ave, NW, Washington, DC 20220; tel. (202) 622-2000; fax (202) 622-6415; e-mail ofe@treasury.gov; internet www.treasury.gov; f. c.1817; spec. collns: taxation, public finance, int. economic affairs, Treasury history; 74,000 vols, 495,000 microfiches and 7,800 reels of microfilm.

Department of Veterans Affairs, Headquarters Library: 810 Vermont Ave, NW, Washington, DC 20420; tel. (202) 461-5669; fax (202) 273-9125; internet www.va.gov; planning, policy, devt, training, centralized support services for the VA Library Network (VALNET); comprises 176 library services at 172 VA facilities; combined library holdings 1,398,000 vols, 145,000 audiovisual items, 75,655 journal subscriptions; Chief of VALNET GINNY DUPONT; Chief of Library CARYI KAZEN.

District of Columbia Public Library: 901 G St, NW, Washington, DC 20001; tel. (202) 727-0321; fax (202) 727-1129; e-mail boardoflibrarytrustees@dc.gov; internet www.dclibrary.org; f. 1896; Martin Luther King, Jr, Memorial Library (central library); 25 brs; Library for the Blind and the Physically Handicapped; spec. collns: Washingtoniana, Washington Star Colln, Black Studies, Musical Scores; 2,672,488 vols; Chief Librarian GINNIE COOPER; Pres. JOHN W. HILL, JR.

Dumbarton Oaks Research Library and Collection: 1703 32nd St, NW, Washington, DC 20007; tel. (202) 339-6401; fax (202) 339-6419; e-mail dumbartonoaks@doaks.org; internet www.doaks.org; f. 1940; attached to Harvard Univ.; collns of early Christian and Byzantine art and of Pre-Columbian art of Mexico; Central and S America; research programmes in Byzantine and Pre-Columbian studies, and studies in landscape architecture; incl. museum with collns of Byzantine and Pre-Columbian art and European masterpieces; 200,000 vols, 10,000 vols of rare book colln and 500,000 images; Dir of Library SHEILA KLOS; publs *Colloquium Papers*, *Conference Proceedings* (irregular), *Dumbarton Oaks Papers* (1 a year), *Dumbarton Oaks Texts* (irregular), *Studies in Pre-Columbian Art and Archaeology* (irregular).

EPA National Library Network: POB 3404T, 1200 Pennsylvania Ave, NW, Washington, DC 20460; tel. (202) 566-0556; e-mail epalibrarynetwork@epa.gov; internet www.epa.gov/natlibra; attached to US Environmental Protection Agency; provides access to information about environment and related scientific, technical, management and policy information.

Folger Shakespeare Library: 201 E Capitol St, SE, Washington, DC 20003; tel. (202) 544-4600; fax (202) 544-4623; e-mail reference@folger.edu; internet www.folger.edu; f. 1932; collns incl. original edns and reprints of Shakespeare; English Renaissance books 1475–1700; 16th- and 17th-century Continental European books incl. German Reformation, festival books and Italian drama; 17th- and 18th-century Strozzi MSS; Dryden colln; 16th-, 17th- and 18th-century English plays; 55,000 MSS since 16th century relating to early modern Britain, and the history of theatre and Shakespearean scholarship; 50,000 literary and theatrical prints and engravings; fellowships; Folger Institute; public and educational programmes; theatre; lectures; poetry readings; concerts; exhibitions; 256,000 vols, 60,000 MSS; 250,000 playbills; 200 oil paintings, 50,000 drawings, watercolours, prints and photographs; Chair. PAUL RUXIN; Dir Dr MICHAEL WHITMORE; Librarian Dr STEPHEN ENNISS; publs *Folger Magazine* (3 a year), *Shakespeare Quarterly* (4 a year).

George Washington University Libraries: Estelle and Melvin Gelman Library, 2130H St, NW, Washington, DC 20052; tel. (202) 994-6558; internet www.gelman.gwu.edu; Gelman Library System consists of Melvin Gelman Library at the Foggy Bottom campus, Eckles Library at the Mount Vernon Campus (both in Washington, DC) and Virginia Science and Technology Campus Library in Ashburn, Virginia; 2m. vols; 60,000 vols in Eckles Library; Univ. Librarian JACK A. SIGGINS.

Georgetown University Library: 37th and O St, NW, Washington, DC 20057-1174; tel. (202) 687-7425; fax (202) 687-7501; e-mail reference@georgetown.edu; internet www.library.georgetown.edu; f. 1796; incl. Joseph Mark Lauinger Memorial Library, Blommer Science Library, Woodstock Theological Center Library, Bioethics Research Library, Dahlgren Memorial Library, Riggs Memorial Library, Edward Bennett Williams Law Library, John Wolff Int. and Comparative Law Library and Maternal and Child Health Library; library in Qatar, Doha; 2.4m. vols, 400,000 e-books, 1.3m. microforms, 100,000 rare books, 700 MSS colln, 300,000 photographs and slides, 10,000 films, audio cassettes, video cassettes and phonograph recordings; Univ. Librarian ARTEMIS KIRK.

House of Representatives Library: c/o Office of the Clerk, US Capitol, Room H154, Washington, DC 20515-6601; tel. (202) 225-7000; e-mail info.clerkweb@mail.house.gov; internet library.clerk.house.gov; f. 1792; div. of the Legislative Resource Center; spec. bound collns of all House of Representatives publs since c. 1800; 125,000 vols; Librarian RAE ELLEN BEST.

Howard University Library System: 500 Howard Pl., NW, Washington, DC 20059; tel. (202) 806-7252; internet www.howard.edu/library; consists of a central library group (comprised of the Founders Library/Undergraduate Library and 4 br. libraries in professional schools—Architecture, Business, Divinity, and Social Work); Moorland-Spingarn Research Center; Louis Stokes Health Sciences Library; Law Library; Ralph J. Bunche Int. Affairs Center Library and Afro-American Studies Resource Center; 2.5m. vols, 16,600 current journal subscriptions, 4.2m. microforms, 18,000 MSS and thousands of audiovisual items; Dir Dr ARTHUREE R. WRIGHT.

Library of Congress: 101 Independence Ave, SE, Washington, DC 20540; tel. (202) 707-5000; internet www.loc.gov; f. 1800; provides services to other libraries; incl. the devt of scientific schemes of classification (Library of Congress and Dewey Decimal); a centralized acquisition and cataloguing programme; a 755-vol. *National Union Catalog: Pre-1956 Imprints*; an inter-library loan system; registers creative work for copyright; 144m. items (incl. 33m. books and other print material in 460 languages, 63m. MSS); Librarian of Congress JAMES H. BILLINGTON.

Moorland-Spingarn Research Center: 500 Howard Place, NW, Washington, DC 20059; tel. (202) 806-7240; fax (202) 806-6405; internet www.howard.edu/msrc; f. 1914; attached to Howard Univ.; documents the history and culture of people of African descent in the Americas, Africa and Europe; rare works dating from the 16th century; 200,000 vols, 650 MSS and archival collns, 700 oral histories, 150,000 photographs and other images and 3,000 pieces of sheet music; Dir Dr HOWARD DODSON.

National Geographic Society Library: 1145 17th St, NW, Washington, DC 20036-4688; tel. (202) 857-7783; fax (202) 429-5731; e-mail library@ngs.org; internet www.ngslis.org; f. 1903; reference reading room open to the public since 1920 for research by appointment; spec. collns: polar, natural history, exploration and discovery, soc. publs; 30,000 vols; Dir for Libraries and Information Services BARBARA PENFOLD FERRY; Sr Librarian KRISTA MANTSCH; publs *National Geographic Explorer*, *National Geographic Kids*, *National Geographic Magazine*, *National Geographic Traveller*.

National Library of Education: 400 Maryland Ave, SW, Washington, DC 20202; tel. (202) 205-5015; fax (202) 401-0547; e-mail library@ed.gov; internet ies.ed.gov/ncee/projects/nat_ed_library.asp; f. 1870 as Bureau of Education library, present name 1994; attached to US Dept of Education; fed. govt's primary resource centre for education information providing collns and information services to public, education community and other govt agencies on current and historical programmes, activities and publs of the US Dept of Education; fed. education policy and education research and statistics; complete ERIC (Education Resources Information Center) microfiche colln, archives of official print and electronic documents published by Dept of Education and histories and documentation of education legislation passed by the Congress; depositary library; 60,000 vols, 800 periodicals; Dir CHRISTINA DUNN.

Navy Department Library: 805 Kidder Breese St, SE, Washington, DC 20374-5060; tel. (202) 433-4132; fax (202) 433-9553; e-mail navylibrary@navy.mil; internet www.history.navy.mil/library/index.htm; f. 1800; attached to US Dept of Navy; periodicals and govt documents on naval, military and nautical history; incl. foreign navies; colln of historical literature on the US Navy; serves as fed. depository; 201,000 vols; Dir GLENN E. HELM.

Pentagon Library: Washington HQ Services, 1155 Defense Pentagon, Washington, DC 20301-1155; tel. (703) 695-1997; fax (703) 695-3999; internet www.whs.mil/library; f. 1944; 100 databases that helps to access to full text articles, abstracts, financial data, govt documents and reports; an e-journal management system; newsletters, magazines and newspapers; 4,000 digital versions of print books; 100,000 vols, 1,800 periodicals and 1m. documents; Acquisitions Librarian RICHARD C. MAY.

Ralph J. Bunche Library of the Department of State: US Dept of State, Room 3239, 2201 C St, NW, Washington, DC 20520-2442; tel. (202) 647-1099; fax (202) 647-2971; e-mail library@state.gov; internet www.state.gov/m/a/ls; f. 1789, present name 1997; materials relate primarily to economic, political and social conditions in foreign areas; treaties and agreements; int. relations and diplomatic history; 400,000 vols; Chief Librarian HUGH HOWARD.

Smithsonian Institution Archives: POB 37012, MRC 507, Washington, DC 20013-7012; Capital Gallery Bldg, Suite 3000, 600 Maryland Ave, SW, Washington, DC 20024-2520; tel. (202) 633-5870; fax (202) 633-5927; e-mail osiaref@osia.si.edu; internet www.si .edu/archives; f. 1970; repository for the official records of the Instn since its foundation in 1846, and official repository for numerous other orgs; personal papers of noted Smithsonian staff, artists, researchers and museum founders; 35,000 cubic ft of materials; 17,273 finding aids, digitized images, documents and publs; Dir ANNE VAN CAMP.

Smithsonian Institution Libraries: Office of the Dir, POB 37012, MRC 154, Washington, DC 20013-7012; Nat. Museum of Natural History Bldg, Room 22, Washington, DC 20560; tel. (202) 633-2240; fax (202) 786-2866; e-mail libmail@si.edu; internet www.sil .si.edu; f. 1846; exhibition gallery and annual colln-based curated exhibition; displays in Nat. Museum of American History, Nat. Air and Space Museum and Nat. Museum of Natural History; active exhibition loan programme; 20 brs; 1,571,114 vols (incl. spec. colln of 40,000 rare books), 2,109 linear ft of MSS, 190,207 microfilms, 5,534 journal subscriptions and 2,667 e-journals; Dir Dr NANCY E. GWINN.

United States Senate Library: Russell Senate Office Bldg, Washington, DC 20510; tel. (202) 224-7106; fax (202) 224-0879; f. 1871; research and reference for the use of the Senate and its cttees; services incl. legislative and gen. reference, automated information retrieval, Micrographics Center and photoduplication facilities; 250,000 vols, incl. spec. colln of legislative proceedings and documents from 1774; Senate Librarian LEONA I. FAUST; Head of Reference and Information Services ZOE DAVIS.

US Department of Justice Library System: Main Library, Robert F. Kennedy Justice Bldg, 950 Pennsylvania Ave, NW, Washington, DC 20530-0001; tel. (202) 514-3775; fax (202) 514-3546; e-mail askdoj@ usdoj.gov; internet www.justice.gov/jmd/ls; f. 1831; open to the public by appointment only; research facility with legal and non-legal holdings; service is provided mainly to the offices, boards and divs of the Dept of Justice; 11 br. libraries support the litigating divs and maintain specialised collns; 300,000 vols, 1m. items of microfiche and microfilm; Library Dir BLANE K. DESSY.

US Department of the Interior Library: 1849C St, NW, MS 1151, Washington, DC 20240; tel. (202) 208-5815; fax (202) 208-6773; e-mail library@nbc.gov; internet library.doi.gov; f. 1850; consists of 8 libraries; 1m. vols, incl. 15,000 serials and 2,500 periodicals; Dir GEORGE FRANCHOIS; publ. *Bibliographies.*

Wirtz Labor Library: US Dept of Labor, 200 Constitution Ave, NW, Room N-2445, Washington, DC 20210; tel. (202) 693-6600; fax (202) 693-6642; e-mail library@dol.gov; internet www.dol.gov/oasam/library; f. 1917; attached to US Dept of Labor; access to both

public and employees of the US Dept of Labor; colln incl. history of labour, labour unions and the growth and devt of the labour; consolidation of the libraries of the fmr Children's Bureau and the Bureau of Labor Statistics; spec. colln: James Taylor Colln, Trade Union Periodicals, Folio Colln and Portrait Colln; incl. Labor Law Library; 140,000 vols, 5,000 electronic and print periodical titles, 3,000 journals; Library Dir JAMES IGOE.

Florida
Boynton Beach City Library: 208 S Seacrest Blvd, Boynton Beach, FL 33435; tel. (561) 742-6395; fax (561) 742-6381; e-mail reference@boyntonlibrary.org; internet www.boyntonlibrary.org; spec. colln of books dealing with Florida history; 100,000 vols; Dir CRAIG CLARK.

Brockway Library: 10021 N E Second Ave, Miami Shores, FL 33138; tel. (305) 758-8107; internet www.brockwaylibrary.org; f. 1949; colln of books, magazines, newspapers, audio-books and large print books; 64,147 vols (incl. 1,892 large print books, 1,871 audio books and books on CD, 3,563 recreational and educational videos and DVDs, 115 current magazines and newspapers); Chair. CHERYL GOWING; Dir ELIZABETH ESPER.

Broward County Division of Libraries: 100 South Andrews Ave, Fort Lauderdale, FL 33301; tel. (954) 357-7444; internet www .broward.org/library; f. 1974; consists of a flagship main library, the African-American Research Library and Cultural Center, the Alvin-Sherman Library, Research, and Information Technology Center at Nova Southeastern Univ., 5 regional libraries, 37 br. libraries and 2 reading centres; spec. collns: black heritage, Spanish language, Floridiana; main library is a depository for govt documents; 3m.vols; Dir ROBERT E. CANNON.

Clearwater Public Library System: 100 N Osceola Ave, Clearwater, FL 33755-4083; tel. (727) 562-4970; internet www .myclearwater.com/cpl; f. 1916; brs: Beach Library, Countryside Library, East Library and North Greenwood Library; 600,000 vols; Chair. JAN REGULSKI; Dir BARBARA PICKELL.

Delray Beach Public Library: 100 W Atlantic Ave, Delray Beach, FL 33444; tel. (561) 266-0194; fax (561) 266-9757; e-mail info.delraylibrary@gmail.com; internet www .delraylibrary.org; f. 1913; book and media colln incl. audio and large print books, foreign language materials and videos; 250,000 vols; Dir ALAN KORNBLAU.

Eustis Memorial Library: 120 N Center St, Eustis, FL 32726; tel. (352) 357-5686; e-mail contactus@eustismemoriallibrary.org; internet www.eustismemoriallibrary.org; f. 2002; 117,000 vols, current and back issues of 200 periodicals and newspapers, 5,600 video cassettes and 2,400 audio cassettes.

Flagler County Public Library System: 2500 Palm Coast Parkway. NW, Palm Coast, FL 32137; tel. (386) 446-6763; internet www .flaglercounty.org; f. 1987; 2 brs: main and Bunnell; depository of genealogical information; books for visually impaired; Dir HOLLY ALBANESE.

Florida State University Libraries: 116 Honors Way, Tallahassee, FL 32306-2047; tel. (850) 644-5211; fax (850) 644-5016; internet www.lib.fsu.edu; f. 1851; incl. 8 libraries: Strozier Library, Dirac Science Library, Claude Pepper Library, College of Music Allen Music Library, School of Library and Information Studies Goldstein Library, College of Law Research Center, College of Medicine Maguire Medical Library, FAMU/ FSU Engineering Reading Room/Library; 3m. vols (incl. 549,000 e-books, 78,000 peri-

odicals); Dean of Univ. Libraries JULIA ZIMMERMAN.

Jacksonville Public Library: 303 N Laura St, Jacksonville, FL 32202; tel. (904) 630-2665; internet www.jaxpubliclibrary.org; f. 1878; 20 brs and the Main Library downtown; spec. collns: African-American Colln, Delius Colln, Digital Library Colln, Florida Colln, Genealogy Colln, Govt Documents Colln, Holocaust Colln, Lewis Ansbacher Map Colln; 3,023,307 vols; Chair. JIM SELZER; Dir BARBARA A. B. GUBBIN.

Lake Worth Public Library: 15 N M St, Lake Worth, FL 33460; tel. (561) 533-7354; fax (561) 586-1651; e-mail lwreference@ lakeworth.org; internet www.lakeworth .govoffice.com; f. 1912; Library Services Man. VICKIE JOSLIN.

LeRoy Collins Leon County Public Library: 200 W Park Ave, Tallahassee, FL 32301; tel. (850) 606-2665; internet www .leoncountyfl.gov/library; f. 1955; brs: Dr B. L. Perry, Jr Br. Library, Fort Braden Br. Library, Lake Jackson Br. Library, NE Br. Library and Parkway Br. Library; Dir CAY HOHMEISTER.

Lynn Haven Library: 901 Ohio Ave, Lynn Haven, FL 32444; tel. (850) 265-2781; fax (850) 265-7311; internet www2.youseemore .com/lynnhaven; f. 1911, present name and status in 1990; 25,000 vols.

Maitland Public Library: 501 S Maitland Ave, Maitland, FL 32751; tel. (407) 647-7700; e-mail board@maitlandpubliclibrary.org; internet www.maitlandpubliclibrary.org; f. 1896; 85,000 vols; Chair. SARAH CHAPMAN; Pres. WILLIAM WHITACRE; Sec. JOANNE MULINARE; Treas. BEN AYCRIGG.

Miami-Dade Public Library System: 101 West Flagler St, Miami, FL 33130-1523; tel. (305) 375-2665; fax (305) 375-3048; internet www.mdpls.org; f. 1971; main library, 49 brs, 4 mobile libraries; 3,878,771 vols, spec. collns incl. Florida history, Spanish books, urban affairs, genealogy; Dir RAYMOND SANTIAGO.

Orlando Public Library: 101 E Central Blvd, Orlando, FL 32801; tel. (407) 835-7323; fax (407) 835-7649; e-mail comments@ocls .info; internet www.ocls.lib.fl.us; f. 1920; acts as HQ and resource centre for the Orange Co Library System; 1.5m. vols; Dir and CEO MARY ANNE HODEL; Pres. RICHARD MALADECKI.

Osceola Library System: 211 E Dakin Ave, Kissimmee, FL 34741; tel. (407) 742-8888; e-mail thelibrary@osceola.org; internet www .osceolalibrary.org; f. 1989; brs: Hart Memorial Central Library, Poinciana Br. Library, Veterans Memorial Library-St Cloud, Buenaventura Lakes Br. Library, West Osceola Br. Library and Kenansville Br. Library; colln incl. resources related to Florida and Federal laws; 70,000 vols; Chair. JEFFEREY (SCOTT) MOUSSEAU.

Palm Beach County Library System: 3650 Summit Bold, West Palm Beach, FL 33406; tel. (561) 233-2600; fax (561) 233-2627; internet www.pbclibrary.org; f. 1967; main library, 15 brs and a bookmobile; 1.7m. vols; Dir JOHN J. CALLAHAN III.

Palm Harbor Library: 2330 Nebraska Ave, Palm Harbor, FL 34683; tel. (727) 784-3332; fax (727) 785-6534; internet www .palmharborlibrary.org; f. 1978; 126,916 vols; Dir GENE P. COPPOLA.

Sanibel Public Library: 770 Dunlop Rd, Sanibel, FL 33957; tel. (239) 472-2483; fax (239) 472-9524; internet www.sanlib.org; f. 1994; local history colln; 60,000 vols, 10,000 audio-visual items; Dir MARGARET MOHUNDRO.

Seminole County Public Library: 215 N Oxford Rd, Casselberry, FL 32707; tel. (407)

665-1500; fax (407) 665-1510; internet www .seminolecountyfl.gov; f. 1978; 5 brs: East Br. Library, Nortwest Br. Library, Jean Rhein Central Br. Library, North Br. Library and West Br. Library; 500,000 vols; Library Services Man. CHRISTINE PATTEN.

St. Lucie County Library System: 180 SW Prima Vista Blvd, Port St Lucie, FL 34983; tel. (772) 462-1615; fax (772) 462-2750; internet www.stlucieco.gov; f. 1903, present status 1954; attached to Dept of Housing and Community Services; 6 brs: Fort Pierce, Lakewood Park, Morning-Side, Port St Lucie, St Lucie W and Z. N. Hurston; Library Man. SUSAN JACOB.

State Library of Florida: R. A. Gray Bldg, 500 S Bronough St, Tallahassee, FL 32399-0250; tel. (850) 245-6600; fax (850) 245-6651; e-mail info@dos.state.fl.us; internet dlis.dos .state.fl.us/library; attached to Florida Dept of State, Div. of Library & Information Services; provides information resource to Florida Legislature and all state agencies; coordinates and helps to fund activities of public libraries; framework for library initiatives in the state; archival and records management services of published and unpublished documentary history of the state; 312,000 vols; 350,000 microforms; 60,000 books, MSS, maps, memorabilia and periodicals; 140,000 state documents; 150,000 federal publs from 1789 to present; Dir JUDITH RING.

George A. Smathers Libraries: Univ. of Florida, POB 117000, Gainesville, FL 32611-7000; tel. (352) 392-0342; fax (352) 392-7251; internet www.uflib.ufl.edu; f. 1853 as East Florida Seminary; present name in 1991; attached to Univ. of Florida; spec. collns: children's literature in English before 1900, contemporary American and British poetry, contemporary American creative writing, Floridiana, history of printing and book arts, Judaica, Latin Americana, New England literature before 1900, performing arts, United States Borderlands (Florida), Irish literature; 4m. vols; Dean of Univ. Libraries JUDITH RUSSELL.

Wilderness Coast Public Libraries: 1180 W Washington St, Monticello, FL 32344; tel. (850) 997-7400; fax (850) 997-7403; e-mail cturner@wildernesscoast.org; internet www .wild.lib.fl.us; f. 1992; admin. office for cooperative multi-county library system for Wakulla, Jefferson and Franklin counties; 100,000 vols; Chair. CORA RUSS; Sec. MARILYN LEWIS; Central Administrator CHERYL TURNER.

Georgia

Atlanta-Fulton Public Library System: One Margaret Mitchell Sq., Atlanta, GA 30303; tel. (404) 730-1700; e-mail librarycomments@fultoncountyga.gov; internet www.afpls.org/home; f. 1902; 34 brs; 2,437,444 vols (incl. books, magazines, periodicals and video cassettes); Dir JOHN F. SZABO.

Bartow County Library System: 429 W Main St, Cartersville, GA 30120; tel. (770) 382-4203; e-mail info@bartowlibrary.org; internet www.bartowlibraryonline.org; f. 1980; brs: Cartersville Public Library, Emmie Nelson Public Library and Adairsville Public Library; 137,521 vols; Dir CARMEN SIMS; Chair. KEN MILLER; Sec. JO TAYLOR; Treas. BRYAN CANTY.

Chattahoochee Valley Libraries: 3000 Macon Rd, Columbus, GA 31906; tel. (706) 243-2669; e-mail contact@cvrls.net; internet www.thecolumbuslibrary.org; serves counties of Muscogee, Chattahoochee, Marion and Stewart; research materials on local history, biographical and historical

resources, newspapers and maps; 7 brs; Dir CLAUDYA MULLER; Chair. ABBIE]DILLARD.

Chestatee Regional Library System: 342 Allen St, Dawsonville, GA 30534; tel. (706) 344-3690; internet www.chestateelibrary .org; f. 1953; 2 brs: Dawson Co Library and Lumpkin Co Library; history of Lumpkin and Dawson Counties; 115,124 vols; Dir CLAUDIA GIBSON; Chair. SUSANNE NEIL.

Clayton County Library System: 865 Battle Creek Rd, Jonesboro, GA 30236; tel. (770) 473-3850; internet www.claytonpl.org; f. 1941; 6 brs; 475,740 vols, 8,730 audio cassettes and CDs, 4,766 video cassettes and DVDs, 539 journals; Dir CAROL STEWART.

Cobb County Public Library System: Central Library, 266 Roswell St, Marietta, GA 30060; tel. (770) 528-2320; e-mail contactus@cobbcat.org; internet www .cobbcat.org; f. 1959; 17 br. libraries of Marietta and Cobb Co; Chair. CHARLES D. SWITZER; Sec. CHERRIE COLEMAN-GRAFFREAD.

Conyers-Rockdale Library System: Nancy Guinn Memorial Library, 864 Green St, Conyers, GA 30012; tel. (770) 388-5041; fax (770) 388-5043; internet www .conyersrockdalelibrary.org; f. 1920; 100,000 books, audio books, video cassettes, CDs and other materials in Nancy Guinn Memorial Library; Chair. MIKE KESSLER; Treas. JEANNE TALLEY.

DeKalb County Public Library: 215 Sycamore St, Decatur, GA 30030; tel. (404) 370-8450; fax (404) 370-8469; internet www .dekalb.public.lib.ga.us; f. 1925 fmrly Decatur Library; 1 central library and 21 brs; spec. colln incl. items related to Georgia history and genealogy; early local, state and area newspapers on microfilm; 808,682 vols, 46,612 audio cassettes and CDs, 46,633 video cassettes and DVDs; Dir ALISON WEISSINGER; Chair. DEBORAH TORBUSH.

East Central Georgia Regional Library: Augusta Library, 823 Telfair St, Augusta, GA 30901; tel. (706) 821-2600; fax (706) 724-6762; internet www.ecgrl.public.lib.ga.us; 15 libraries in 5 counties; Talking Book Center; 500,000 vols; Dir TERESA COLE.

Forsyth County Public Library: 585 Dahlonega Rd, Cumming, GA 30040; tel. (770) 781-9840; internet www.forsythpl.org; f. 1938; 3 brs: Cumming, Hampton Park and Sharon Forks; 300,000 vols; Dir JON McDANIEL.

Hall County Library System: 127 Main St NW, Gainesville, GA 30501; tel. (770) 532-3311; fax (770) 532-4305; e-mail info@ hallcountylibrary.org; internet www .hallcountylibrary.org; f. 1937; 4 brs: Gainesville (HQ), Blackshear Place, Murrayville, Spout Springs; Dir ADRIAN MIXSON; Chair. KILLIAN EDWARDS.

Henry County Library System: McDonough Public Library, 1001 Florence McGarity Blvd, McDonough, GA 30252; tel. (770) 954-2806; fax (770) 954-2808; e-mail md-reference@mail.henry.public.lib.ga.us; internet www.henry.public.lib.ga.us; f. 1959; brs: McDonough, Fairview, Locust Grove, Fortson and Cochran; 737,338 vols; Dir CAROLYN T. FULLER.

Jimmy Carter Library & Museum: 441 Freedom Parkway, Atlanta, GA 30307-1498; tel. (404) 865-7100; fax (404) 865-7102; internet www.jimmycarterlibrary.gov; f. 1980; attached to Nat. Archives and Records Admin.; 50,000 photographs and hundreds of hours film, audio and video cassettes; 27m. pages of Jimmy Carter's White House material, papers of admin. associates, incl. documents, memoranda and correspondence; Dir JAY HAKES.

Live Oak Public Libraries: 2002 Bull St, Savannah, GA 31401; tel. (912) 652-3600; fax (912) 652-3638; internet www.liveoakpl.org; f. 1903 as Savannah Public Library, present name 2002; 18 brs serving Chatham, Effingham and Liberty counties; 1 bookmobile; Dir CHRISTIAN KRUSE; Chair. Dr ALLEN BERGER.

Middle Georgia Regional Library System: Washington Memorial Library, 1180 Washington Ave, Macon, GA 31201-1790; tel. (478) 744-0800; fax (478) 742-3161; internet www.co.bibb.ga.us/library; f. 1836, present name 1939; serving Bibb, Crawford, Jones, Macon, Twiggs and Wilkinson counties; Genealogical and Historical Room colln incl. 32,000 vols and 24,000 microforms; MSS and archival records of historical significance for Middle Georgia; Dir THOMAS JONES.

Mountain Regional Library System: 698 Miller St, POB 159, Young Harris, GA 30582; tel. (706) 379-3732; fax (706) 379-2047; e-mail mountain@mountainregionallibrary .org; internet www.mountainregionallibrary .org; f. 1946, present name and status 1957; attached to Univ. System of Georgia; incl. HQ library and 3 brs: Towns Co Public Library, Union Co Public Library and Fannin Co Public Library; 105,948 vols; Dir DONNA W. HOWELL.

Newton County Library System: Covington Br. Library, 7116 Floyd St, Covington, GA 30014; tel. (770) 787-3231; fax (770) 784-2092; e-mail library@newtonlibrary.org; internet www.newtonlibrary.org; f. 1916, present name and status 1998; local history and genealogy colln; garden colln; Dir LACE KEATON.

Pine Mountain Regional Library System: POB 709, Manchester GA 31816; 218 Perry St, Manchester, GA 31816; tel. (706) 846-2186; fax (706) 846-8455; e-mail libraryh@pinemtnlibrary.org; internet www .pinemtnlibrary.org; f. 1938, present name 1958; 7 brs in Meriwether, Upson, Talbot and Taylor Counties; Dir CHARLES B. GEE.

Roddenbery Memorial Library: 320 N Broad St, Cairo, GA 39828; tel. (229) 377-3632; fax (229) 377-7204; e-mail rml@ rmlibrary.org; internet www.rmlibrary.org; f. 1939 as Cairo Public Library, present location 1964; co histories; The Cairo Messenger, newspaper, on microfilm and print from 1904 to present; Dir PAM GRIGG.

Statesboro Regional Public Libraries: 124 S Main St, Statesboro, GA 30458-5246; tel. (912) 764-1341; fax (912) 764-1349; internet www.strl.info; brs: Claxton, Metter, Richmond Hill, Pembroke, Swainsboro and Statesboro; 182,000 vols; Dir SHARON C. ROWE.

Twin Lakes Library System: Mary Vinson Memorial Library, 151 S Jefferson St SE, Milledgeville, GA 31061-3419; tel. (478) 452-0677; fax (478) 452-0680; internet twinlakeslibrarysystem.org; f. 1938; genealogy and local history colln;large print books; Dir BARRY REESE; Chair. DOROTHY BROWN.

Hawaii

Bishop Museum's Library and Archives: 1525 Bernice St, Honolulu, HI 96817; tel. (808) 848-4148; fax (808) 847-8241; e-mail library@bishopmuseum.org; internet www .bishopmuseum.org/research/library/libarch .html; 50,000 vols, 1,000 periodicals, and historical photographs, films, works of art, audio recordings and MSS.

Edwin H. Mookini Library: Univ. of Hawai'i at Hilo, 200 W Kawili St, Hilo, HI 96720-4091; tel. (808) 974-7344; fax (808) 974-7329; e-mail mookini@hawaii.edu; internet library.uhh.hawaii.edu; f. 1981; attached to Univ. of Hawaii at Hilo; 260,000 vols, 1,100 periodicals, 350,000 US state documents; Univ. Librarian Dr LINDA GOLIAN-LUI.

Hamilton and Sinclair Libraries: 2550 McCarthy Mall, Honolulu, HI 96822; tel. (808) 956-7214; e-mail emailref@hawaii.edu; internet library.manoa.hawaii.edu; f. 1920; attached to Univ. of Hawaii at Manoa; 3.4m. vols, 15,000 MSS and archives, 50,000 serial and journal titles, 73,000 audiovisual items, 95,000 maps and aerial photographs; Univ. Librarian PAULA MOCHIDA.

Hawaiian Historical Society Library: 560 Kawaiahao St, Honolulu, HI 96813; tel. (808) 537-6271; internet www .hawaiianhistory.org/lib/libmain.html; Hawaiian history resources; language books; newspapers published in Hawai'i; 19th- and early 20th-century maps of Honolulu, the Hawaiian Islands, and the Pacific Ocean; 300 broadsides published in Hawai'i from 1829 to the early 1900s; 12,000 vols, 35 linear ft of MSS, 10,000 photographs; Admin. Dir and Librarian BARBARA DUNN.

Hawaii Legislative Reference Bureau: Hawaii State Capitol, Room 005, Honolulu, HI 96813; tel. (808) 587-0690; fax (808) 587-0699; e-mail lrb@capitol.hawaii.gov; internet www.state.hi.us/lrb; f. 1943 as dept of Univ. of Hawaii, present status 1996; provides services to legislators, legislative cttee, and in some cases, mems of the public; legislative studies and exec. agency reports from Hawaii and across the country; Hawaii statutes, journals, court cases and county codes; statutes from 12 other states; fed. statutes and US Supreme Court cases; Dir CHARLOTTE CARTER-YAMAUCHI (acting).

Hawaii State Law Library System: Supreme Court Law Library, Ali'iolani Hale, Room 115, 417 S King St, Honolulu, HI 96813; tel. (808) 539-4964; fax (808) 539-4974; e-mail lawlibrary@courts.hawaii.gov; internet www.state.hi.us/jud/library; f. 1966; legal reference library; contains materials on laws for all federal and state jurisdictions, and practice materials for all major areas of law; 5 brs: Supreme Court Law Library in Oahu, Second Circuit Court Law Library in Maui, Third Circuit Court Law Libraries in Hilo and Kona, and a Fifth Circuit Court Law Library in Kauai; collns incl. print, microfilm, microfiche, audio, video and CD-ROM formats; a depository for materials published by the State Justice Institute.

Honolulu Community College Library: 874 Dillingham Blvd, Honolulu, HI 96817; tel. (808) 845-9199; e-mail library@hcc .hawaii.edu; internet www2.honolulu.hawaii .edu/library; Head Librarian IRENE MESINA.

Leeward Community College Library: 96-045 Ala Ike, Pearl City, HI 96782; tel. (808) 455-0210; e-mail lccref@hawaii.edu; internet www.leeward.hawaii.edu/lib; Head Librarian CHRIS MATZ.

Municipal Reference Center: 558 S King St, City Hall Annex, Honolulu, HI 96813-3006; tel. (808) 768-3765; fax (808) 768-3769; e-mail csdaccess@honolulu.gov; internet www1.honolulu.gov/csd/lrmb; f. 1929; permanent records and artefacts of depts and agencies of the City and County of Honolulu.

Sullivan Family Library: Chaminade Univ. of Honolulu, 3140 Waialae Ave, Honolulu, HI 96816; tel. (808) 735-4725; fax (808) 735-4891; e-mail library@chaminade.edu; internet www.chaminade.edu/library; f. 1957, present name 2008; attached to Chaminade Univ. of Honolulu; 70,000 vols, 239 journals subscriptions, 40,000 e-books, 19,000 e-journal subscriptions, 1,500 DVDs and CDs; Librarian PUANANI AKAKA.

University of Hawaii Maui College Library: 310 W Ka'ahumanu Ave, Kahului, HI 96732; tel. (808) 984-3233; e-mail mcclib@ hawaii.edu; internet maui.hawaii.edu/ library; 155,291 vols, 274 print periodicals, 5,429 video cassettes, DVDs and audio CDs; Public Services Librarian ELLEN PETERSON.

William S. Richardson School of Law Library: Univ. of Hawaii at Mānoa, 2525 Dole St, Honolulu, HI 96822-2328; tel. (808) 956-5581; e-mail lawcirc@hawaii.edu; internet www.law.hawaii.edu/library; f. 1983; attached to Univ. of Hawaii at Mānoa; Dir VICTORIA SZYMCZAK.

Idaho

Ada Community Library: 10664 W Victory Rd, Boise, ID 83709; tel. (208) 362-0181; fax (208) 362-0303; e-mail mdewalt@adalib.org; internet www.adalib.org; f. 1989; 4 brs; 160,000 vols (incl. 1,000 journals); Dir MARY DEWALT.

Boise Public Library: 715 S Capitol Blvd, Boise, ID 83702; tel. (208) 384-4076; fax (208) 384-4450; e-mail askalibrarian@cityofboise .org; internet www.boisepubliclibrary.org; f. 1895; 3 brs; Dir KEVIN BOOE.

Coeur d'Alene Public Library: 702 E Front Ave, Coeur d'Alene, ID 83814; tel. (208) 769-2315; fax (208) 769-2381; e-mail info@cdalibrary.org; internet www .cdalibrary.org; f. 1905; 500,000 vols; Library Dir BETTE AMMON.

Eagle Public Library: 100 N Stierman Way, Eagle, ID 83616; tel. (208) 939-6814; fax (208) 939-1359; internet www .eaglepubliclibrary.org; f. 1963; S Idaho's regional library consortium; 98,000 vols; Library Dir JANICE CAMPBELL.

Idaho Falls Public Library: 457 W Broadway, Idaho Falls, ID 83402; tel. (208) 612-8460; fax (208) 612-8467; e-mail director@ifpl .org; internet www.ifpl.org; f. 1884; microfilm copies of the Post Register and its predecessors dating back to 1880; 180 magazines and 26 newspaper subscription; Chair. HAL PETERSON.

Idaho State Law Library: 322 E Front St, Suite 560, Boise, ID 83702; tel. (208) 364-4555; fax (208) 334-2467; e-mail lawlibrary@ idcourts.net; internet www.isll.idaho.gov; f. 1869; primarily a research library; holds state and fed. law, as well as legal periodicals, digests, citators, encyclopedias and treatises of law; 192,000 vols.

Marshall Public Library: 113 S Garfield Ave, Pocatello, ID 83204; tel. (208) 232-1263; fax (208) 232-9266; e-mail admin@marshallpl .org; internet www.marshallpl.org; f. 1907; 160,000 vols; Dir ERIC SUESS.

Mountain Home Public Library: 790 N 10th E, Mountain Home, ID 83647; tel. (208) 587-4716; fax (208) 587-6645; internet mountainhome.lili.org; f. 1903; Dir LUISE HOUSE.

Nampa Public Library: 101-11th Ave S, Nampa, ID 83651; tel. (208) 468-5803; internet www.nampalibrary.org; f. 1900; Library Dir MARK ROSE.

Oneida County Library: 31 N 100, POB 185, Malad, ID 83252; tel. and fax (208) 766-2229; e-mail oclib@atcnet.net; internet www .maladidaho.org/library; f. 1977; 26,000 vols; Dir KAY CALDWELL.

Illinois

Abraham Lincoln Presidential Library and Museum: *Library*: 112 North 6th St, Springfield, IL; *Museum*: 212 North 6th St, Springfield, IL; tel. (217) 558-8844; fax (217) 558-8878; internet www.alplm.org; f. 2002; fmr Illinois State Historical Library (f. 1889) of 12m. items; spec. colln: Henry Horner

Lincoln Colln of 46,000 items incl. 1,500 signed MSS, 10,000 books and pamphlets, 1,000 posters, 1,000 prints and photographs, Gettysburg Address, Second Inaugural Address, Anti-Slavery Statement; Exec. Dir RICK BEARD.

Chicago Public Library: 400 S State St, Chicago, IL 60605-1203; tel. (312) 747-4300; e-mail info@chipublib.org; internet www .chipublib.org; f. 1873; 4,764,000 vols; Pres. JAYNE CARR THOMPSON; Vice-Pres. CHERRYL T. THOMAS; Sec. CHRISTOPHER P. VALENTI.

Cook County Law Library: 2900 Daley Center, 50 W Washington St, 29th Fl., Chicago, IL 60602; tel. (312) 603-5423; fax (312) 603-4716; internet www.cookcountygov .com/portal/server.pt/community/law_li brary/305; f. 1966; provides services at 7 brs; collns of law books, statutes, case law and digests for all 50 states amd numerous Illinois practice manuals; 350,000 vols; Dir and Exec. Law Librarian BENNIE E. MARTIN.

Illinois Institute of Technology Libraries: 35 W 33rd St, Chicago, IL 60616; tel. (312) 567-3616; fax (312) 567-5318; e-mail library@iit.edu; internet www.iit.edu/ libraries; 6 br. libraries at different campuses; 1.8m. vols (incl. 30,000 print and online journals, magazines and newspapers); Dean of Libraries KRISTIN STANDAERT.

Illinois State Archives: Margaret Cross Norton Bldg, Capitol Complex, Springfield, IL 62756; tel. (217) 782-4682; fax (217) 524-3930; internet www.cyberdriveillinois.com/ departments/archives/archives.html; f. 1921; depository of public records of Illinois state and local govt agencies of permanent admin., legal and historical research values documents; admin. of Illinois Regional Archives Depositories (IRAD); 53,000 cubic ft of state governmental records; State Archivist JESSE WHITE; Dir DAVID A. JOENS.

Illinois State Library: Gwendolyn Brooks Bldg, 300 S Second St, Springfield, IL 62701-1796; tel. (217) 785-5600; fax (217) 785-4326; e-mail islinfo@ilsos.net; internet www .cyberdriveillinois.com/departments/library/ home.html; f. 1839; permanent colln of 33 works of visual art by contemporary Illinois artists; 5m. items and documents; State Librarian JESSE WHITE; Dir ANNE CRAIG; publ. *Illinois Literacy* (4 a year).

Illinois Supreme Court Library: Supreme Court Bldg, 200 E Capitol Ave, Springfield, IL 62701; tel. (217) 782-2424; fax (217) 782-5287; internet www.state.il.us/court/ supremecourt/library.asp; f. 1842, present location 1908; serves state, fed. and local govts, the bar and gen. public; 100,000 vols, 350 legal periodicals; Librarian BRENDA LARISON.

John Crerar Library of the University of Chicago: 5730 South Ellis Ave, Chicago, IL 60637; tel. (773) 702-7715; fax (773) 702-3317; e-mail crerar-reference@lib.uchicago .edu; internet www.lib.uchicago.edu/e/ crerar; f. 1984 by merger of John Crerar Library (f. 1892) and Univ. of Chicago; organizes Kathleen A. Zar symposium and science exhibits and lectures; 1.4m. vols on biological, medical, physical sciences, general science and the philosophy and history of science, medicine, technology; Dir BARBARA KERN; Dir ANDREA TWISS-BROOKS.

Newberry Library: 60 W Walton St, Chicago, IL 60610-7324; tel. (312) 943-9090; fax (312) 255-3509; e-mail research@newberry .org; internet www.newberry.org; f. 1887; ind. research libary; maintains research and educational programmes in its Center for the History of Cartography, Center for the History of the American Indian, Center for Renaissance Studies, and Family and Community History Center; spec. collns on the American Indians, history of printing and book arts, music, American and English history and literature, exploration and early cartography, Portugal, the Renaissance in England and Europe, European history from the Renaissance to 1815, the Philippine Islands, colonial Latin America; 1.5m. vols in the humanities, 5m. MSS pages; Pres. and Librarian DAVID SPADAFORA; Chair. VICTORIA J. HERGET; Sec. PAUL J. MILLER; Treas. NORMAN BOBINS.

Northwestern University Libraries: 1970 Campus Dr., Evanston, IL 60208-2300; tel. (847) 491-7658; fax (847) 491-8306; e-mail library@northwestern.edu; internet www.library.northwestern.edu; f. 1856; Northwestern Univ. Library (humanities and social sciences, with spec. collns on Africa: comprehensive historically on sub-Sahara, francophone West Africa and South Africa; extensive holdings in Art Nouveau, dada, surrealism, futurism and expressionism, Samuel Johnson, siege and commune of Paris 1870–71, women's liberation movement; libraries for music and transportation); brs for science-eng., geology and mathematics; professional libraries (dentistry, law, medicine) and the Schaffner Library in Chicago; 4,930,613 vols, 4,603,214 microforms, 18,069 linear ft of archives and MSS, 208,757 maps, 601,153 graphic images, 66,977 audio files, 33,882 film and video cassettes, 98,844 journals; Dean of Libraries SARAH M. PRITCHARD.

Rockford Public Library: 215 N Wyman St, Rockford, IL 61101; tel. (815) 965-7606; fax (815) 965-0866; internet www.rockfordpubliclibrary.org; f. 1872; 5 brs; Andrew M. Potter Colln: 300 vols of 19th-century memoirs, regimental histories, histories of campaigns and materials dealing with accounts of Civil War; Rockford area music colln; 494,261 vols, 5,615 audiobook CDs, 4,996 video cassettes, 39,734 DVDs, 22,799 CDs, 1,274 CD-ROMs; Exec. Dir FRANK NOVAK; Pres. PAUL A. LOGLI; Sec. and Treas. EDWARD J. GEESER.

Ryerson & Burnham Libraries: 111 S Michigan Ave, Chicago, IL 60603-6404; tel. (312) 443-7279; e-mail reference@artic.edu; internet www.artic.edu/aic/libraries; f. 1957 by merger of Ryerson Library with Burnham Library of Architecture; attached to Art Institute of Chicago; art and architecture research colln; architecture of the 18th through 20th centuries and 19th-century painting, prints, drawings, and decorative arts; spec. colln incl. Percier and Fontaine Colln of 17th–19th century architectural books, Mary Reynolds Colln on Dada and Surrealism, George R. Collns Archive of Catalan Art and Architecture and Mrs. James Ward Thorne Colln of illustrated books; incl. archives; 400,000 vols, 1,200 current serial subscriptions; Exec. Dir JACK BROWN.

University of Chicago Library: 1100 E 57th St, Chicago, IL 60637-1502; tel. (773) 702-8740; fax (773) 702-6623; e-mail info@lib.uchicago.edu; internet www.lib.uchicago.edu; f. 1892; comprises Regenstein (humanities, business and social sciences), Crerar (science, medicine, technology), Harper (college), D'Angelo Law (nat. and int. law), Joe and Rika Mansueto, Eckhart (mathematics, statistics and computer science) and Social Services Admin. (social welfare and social work); Spec. Collns Research Center, incl. rare books, MSS, the Chicago Jazz Archive, Univ. Archives; E Asia, S Asia, Middle E, Slavic and E European area studies; 9,837,021 vols (incl. print and e-holdings); Dir and Univ. Librarian JUDITH NADLER.

University of Illinois (Urbana-Champaign) Library: 1408 W Gregory Dr., Urbana, IL 61801; tel. (217) 333-2290; fax (217) 244-4358; e-mail writeus@library.illinois.edu; internet www.library.illinois.edu; f. 1867; 40 deptl libraries; spec. collns in classical literature and history, English literature, incl. Milton and Shakespeare, Western US history, Lincolniana, Italian history, music, architecture, science and technology; 12m. vols, 9m. microforms, 90,000 periodicals and journals, 148,000 audio-recordings, over 930,000 audiovisual materials, over 280,000 e-books, 12,000 films, 650,000 maps; Dean of Libraries and Univ. Librarian PAULA T. KAUFMAN.

Indiana

Alexandrian Public Library: 115 W Fifth St, Mount Vernon, IN 47620; tel. (812) 838-3286; fax (812) 838-9639; e-mail alexpl@evansville.net; internet www.apl.lib.in.us; f. 1895; serves city of Mount Vernon and communities of Black, Marrs, Robinson, Lynn and Point townships; 92,383 vols, 4,554 video cassettes, 5,848 audio materials; Dir MARISSA PRIDDIS.

Allen County Public Library: 900 Library Pl., Fort Wayne, IN 46802; tel. (260) 421-1252; fax (260) 421-1386; e-mail ask@acpl.info; internet www.acpl.lib.in.us; f. 1895 as Fort Wayne Public Library; Fred J. Reynolds Historical Genealogy Colln; 13 brs; 3.7m. vols; Pres. JOHN GERNI; Vice-Pres. GENE G. HOEMIG; Dir JEFFREY R. KRULL.

Delphi Public Library: 222 E Main St, Delphi, IN 46923; tel. (765) 564-2929; fax (765) 564-4746; e-mail dplibrar@carrollnet.org; internet www.carrollnet.org/dpl; f. 1904; NW Carroll Br. Library at Yeoman; 61,063 vols, 5,777 video cassettes and DVDs, 3,456 audiobooks and CDs, 209 magazines and newspapers; Dir KELLY CURRIE; Pres. ANGIE MURRAY; Sec. KATHY ZINK; Treas. ROBERTA BLUE.

Fulton County Public Library: POB 307, 514 State Road 25, Fulton, IN 46931; tel. (574) 857-3895; fax (574) 857-2215; e-mail fulton@fulco.lib.in.us; internet www.fulco.lib.in.us; 3 brs; local genealogy colln; Dir BECKY WILLIAMS; Pres. GEORGE HAPNER; Sec. ROSA METZGER; Treas. BOB UHRICH.

Hancock County Public Library: 900 W McKenzie Rd, Greenfield, IN 46140-1741; tel. (317) 462-5141; fax (317) 462-5711; e-mail reference@hcplibrary.org; internet www.hcplibrary.org; f. 1878; colln in local hisory of Indiana and genealogy; br. in New Palestine; Dir and CEO DIANNE OSBORNE; Pres. PEGGY PRITZKE; Sec. JANE PFAFF; Treas. DEBBI BARNHART.

Harrison County Public Library: 105 N Capitol Ave, Corydon, IN 47112; tel. (812) 738-4110; fax (812) 738-5408; e-mail hcpl@hcpl.lib.in.us; internet www.hcpl.lib.in.us; f. 1914 as Corydon Public Library, present name 1998; 3 brs; Frederick Porter Griffin Center for Local History and Genealogy; Dir VI ECKART.

Hesburgh Libraries University of Notre Dame: 221 Hesburgh Library, Notre Dame, IN 46556; tel. (574) 631-6258; fax (574) 631-6772; internet www.library.nd.edu; f. 1873; spec. collns: Ambrosiana, American Catholic Studies, O'Neill Irish Music, Joyce Sports Research, medieval education, Descartes, Jacques Maritain, Dante, orchids, historical botany, Irish maps and sea charts, Irish Rebellion of 1798, Irish postage stamps; 2.5m. vols, 800,000 govt documents, 2,400 current journals, 125,000 vols of rare books; Univ. Librarian DIANE P. WALKER.

Indiana State Archives: 6440 E 30th St, Indianapolis, IN 46219; tel. (317) 591-5222;

fax (317) 591-5324; e-mail arc@icpr.in.gov; internet www.in.gov/icpr/2358.htm; records of the executive, legislative, and judicial brs of govt from the 1790s through the present; military records incl. holdings from the War of 1812, Black Hawk War, Mexican War, Civil War, Spanish-American War and veterans' enrollments from 1886, 1890 and 1894; 100,000 aerial photographs incl. colln from the Dept of Natural Resources and State Fair Comm; 25,000 cubic ft of records; Dir and State Archivist JIM CORRIDAN.

Indiana State Library: 315 W Ohio St, Indianapolis, IN 46202; tel. (317) 232-3675; fax (317) 232-3728; e-mail ldo@library.in.gov; internet www.library.in.gov; provides library service to state govt, advice and counsel to the libraries and librarians of the state, reference service and materials for local school, public, spec., and academic libraries; genealogy and spec. research collns; Indiana history colln; service to the blind and physically handicapped; library for Indiana Acad. of Science; 70,000 vols incl. histories, biographies, directories, magazines and newsletters, atlases, state documents, and works of fiction by Indiana authors, 50,000 pamphlets, 3m. MSS, 40,000 genealogy colln; State Librarian ROBERTA L. BROOKER; publs Focus on Indiana Libraries (12 a year), Indiana Libraries (4 a year).

Indiana Supreme Court Law Library: State House 316, 200 W Washington St, Indianapolis, IN 46204; tel. (317) 232-2557; fax (317) 233-8693; internet www.in.gov/judiciary/supreme; f. 1867; primary law library for state agencies, Office of Gov., the legislature, mems of private bar and gen. public; repository for publs produced under grants from State Justice Institute; 70,000 vols; Head Librarian TERRI LEA ROSS.

Indiana University Bloomington Libraries: 1320 E 10th St, Bloomington, IN 47405; tel. (812) 855-1673; fax (812) 855-3072; e-mail libtechs@indiana.edu; internet www.libraries.iub.edu; f. 1829; 8,908,159 vols, 40,557 linear ft MSS, 252,763 music scores, 350,058 slides, 301,850 maps and charts, 311,751 audio recordings, 116,604 serial titles (print and electronic) serials, 3,106,419 graphic materials (incl. photos), 1.1m. govt publs; Dean of Libraries BRENDA JOHNSON.

Indianapolis-Marion County Public Library: POB 211, Indianapolis, IN 46206-0211; One Library Sq., 40 E St, Clair St, Indianapolis, IN 46204; tel. (317) 275-4100; fax (317) 269-1768; internet www.imcpl.org; f. 1873; 22 brs; 3 bookmobiles; 2.1m. vols; CEO JACKIE NYTES.

Lawrenceburg Public Library District: 150 Mary St, Lawrenceburg, IN 47025; tel. (812) 537-2775; fax (812) 537-2810; e-mail lawplib@lpld.lib.in.us; internet www.lpld.lib.in.us; North Dearborn Br. Library at West Harrison; Dir SALLY STEGNER; Pres. PATRICIA RITZMANN; Sec. MARITA CIZEK.

Purdue University Libraries: 504 W State St, West Lafayette, IN 47907-2058; tel. (765) 494-2900; fax (765) 494-0156; e-mail libinfo@purdue.edu; internet www.lib.purdue.edu; f. 1869; divs of Archives and Special Collns (ASC), Health and Life Sciences (HLS), Humanities, Social Sciences, Education, and Business (HSSEB) and Physical Sciences, Engineering and Technology (PSET); 14 brs; 2,586,297 vols, 3,074,243 microform units, 483,072 govt documents, 59,268 serials; Dean of Libraries Prof. Dr JAMES L. MULLINS.

Iowa

Carnegie-Stout Public Library: 360 W 11th St, Dubuque, IA 52001; tel. (563) 589-4225; fax (563) 589-4217; internet www

.dubuque.lib.ia.us; f. 1902, present bldg 1981; spec. colln: obituary file dating to the late 1850s and a newspaper index to the Telegraph Herald and other local newspapers; Grant Wood art colln; 270,000 vols, 600 periodical and newspaper subscriptions; Dir SUSAN HENRICKS; Pres. JONITA GRABOW.

Cedar Falls Public Library: 524 Main St, Cedar Falls, IA 50613; tel. (319) 273-8643; fax (319) 273-8648; e-mail cedarfallslibrary@gmail.com; internet www.cedar-falls.lib.ia.us; f. 1878; 140,195 vols; Dir SHERYL McGOVERN; Pres. LYNN BLAIR-BROEKER; Sec. ELAINE PFALZGRAF .

Des Moines Public Library: 1000 Grand, Des Moines, IA 50309; tel. (515) 283-4152; e-mail trustees@dmpl.org; internet www.pldminfo.org; f. 1866 as Des Moines Library Asscn; selective fed. depository library for govt documents; colln on history of Iowa, esp. city of Des Moines; Shoah Visual History Colln: testimonies by Holocaust survivors and witnesses; 1 Central Library and 5 brs; Dir GREG HEID; Pres. KEVIN W. TECHAU.

Fayette Community Library: POB 107, 104 W State St, Fayette, IA 52142; tel. and fax (563) 425-3344; e-mail director@fayettelibrary.lib.ia.us; internet www.fayettelibrary.lib.ia.us; f. 1934; Dir LINDA K. ADAMS.

Herbert Hoover Presidential Library—Museum: 210 Parkside Dr., West Branch, IA 52358; tel. (319) 643-5301; fax (319) 643-6045; e-mail hoover.library@nara.gov; internet hoover.archives.gov; f. 1962; administered by the Nat. Archives and Records Admin.; official and personal papers of 31st Pres. of USA; 300 MSS collns; 20,000 vols, 8,247,000 MSS, 39,500 photographs, 420 hours sound recordings and 153,000 ft of film, 2,770 rolls of microfilm, 443 oral history transcripts covering history since beginning of the 20th century, econ. and political science; Dir Dr THOMAS SCHWARTZ; publ. *Historical Materials in the Herbert Hoover Presidential Library.*

Iowa City Public Library: 123 S Linn St, Iowa City, IA 52240; tel. (319) 356-5200; fax (319) 356-5494; internet www.icpl.org; f. 1896; 230,597 vols (incl. 182,993 books and e-books, 40,824 non-print materials, 6,340 print and e-reference, 440 periodicals and newspapers); Dir SUSAN CRAIG; Pres. THOMAS S. MARTIN; Sec. MEREDITH RICH-CHAPPELL.

Iowa State University Library: cnr of Osborn Dr. and Morrill Rd, Ames, IA 50011-2140; tel. (515) 294-3642; fax (515) 294-5525; e-mail spclref@iastate.edu; internet www.lib.iastate.edu; f. 1868; fed. depository; also comprises Archives of American Agriculture, Archives of American Veterinary Medicine, American Archives of the Factual Film, Women in Science and Eng. Archives, Univ. Archives; 2,626,074 vols, 3,527,542 microform units, 936,687 photographs and slides, 18,051 audio materials, 18,409 linear ft of MSS and archives, 85,655 e-journals, 33,769 films and videos, 99,209 aerial photographs and maps; Dean OLIVIA M. A. MADISON.

Mason City Public Library: 225 Second St SE, Mason City, IA 50401; tel. (641) 421-3670; fax (641) 423-2615; e-mail admin@masoncity.lib.ia.us; internet www.mcpl.org; f. 1940; Lee P. Loomis Archive: historical documents and photos, city directories, artefacts and Autograph Colln; colln of genealogical materials; Dir MARY MARKWALTER; Pres. DAVE GROOTERS.

Ossian Public Library: POB 120, 123 Main St, Ossian, IA 52161; tel. and fax (563) 532-9461; e-mail director@ossian.lib.ia.us; internet www.ossian.lib.ia.us; f. 1956; Dir

JUDE ZWEIBOHMER; Pres. KAY ELSBERND; Sec. ERICA DAVIS.

Scott County Library System: 200 N Sixth Ave, Eldridge, IA 52748; tel. (563) 285-4794; fax (563) 285-4743; internet www.scottcountylibrary.org; 5 brs; bookmobile services; Dir PAUL SEELAU; Pres. LINDA TUBBS; Sec. JENI CRISWELL.

Sioux City Public Library: 529 Pierce St, Sioux City, IA 51101; tel. (712) 255-2933; internet www.siouxcitylibrary.org; 1 main library and 2 brs; 238,500 vols; Dir BETSY THOMPSON; Pres. JAY E. DENNE; Sec. LISA M. KROGER.

State Historical Society of Iowa State Archives & Records Program: 600 E Locust, Des Moines, IW 50319-0290; tel. (515) 281-5111; fax (515) 282-0502; internet www.iowahistory.org/archives; br. in Iowa City; colln of genealogical material, records of functions and responsibilities of Office of Gov. and Lt Gov., military records of Iowa regiments fought in the Mexican War, Civil War and Spanish-American War, newspaper, MSS, audio-visual and map collns; spec. colln of photographs incl. old specimens of daguerreotype to digital; State Archivist JEROME THOMPSON; publ. *Iowa Heritage Illustrated* (4 a year); publ. *The Annals of Iowa* (4 a year).

State Library of Iowa: Miller Bldg, 1112 E Grand Ave, Des Moines, IA 50319; tel. (515) 281-4105; fax (515) 281-6191; internet www.statelibraryofiowa.org; f. 1838 as territorial library, present name and status 1846; attached to Iowa Dept of Education; focuses on improving library services and delivers specialized information services to state govt and public; law library; State Librarian MARY WEGNER.

University of Iowa Libraries: 100 Main Library (LIB), Iowa City, IA 52242-1420; tel. (319) 335-5299; fax (319) 335-5900; e-mail lib-ref@uiowa.edu; internet www.lib.uiowa.edu; f. 1847; 11 deptl libraries; depository for fed., State of Iowa, UN, and EU information; rare books from 15th century to present; Map Colln; Iowa Women's Archives; 5m. vols, 200,000 rare books, 800 MSS; Univ. Librarian NANCY L. BAKER.

Urbandale Public Library: 3520 86th St, Urbandale, IW 50322; tel. (515) 278-3945; fax (515) 278-3918; e-mail reference@urbandale.org; internet www.urbandalelibrary.org; f. 1961; Dir JULIE WELLS; Pres. JULIE KROLL; Sec. THOMAS P. GRAVES.

Waterloo Public Library: 415 Commercial St, Waterloo, IA 50701; tel. (319) 291-4480; fax (319) 291-6736; e-mail infowiz.wpl@gmail.com; internet www.waterloo.lib.ia.us; f. 1896; 172,580 vols; Dir SHERYL McGOVERN; Pres. SUE SMITH; Sec. TROYCE VICH.

Kansas

Arkansas City Public Library: 120 E Fifth Ave, Arkansas City, KS 67005; tel. (620) 442-1280; fax (620) 442-4277; e-mail arkcitypl@acpl.org; internet www.arkcity.org; f. 1892; 46,900 vols (incl. books, audio cassettes, audio CDs, video cassettes, DVDs, music CDs, microfilm and magazines); Dir DALENE McDONALD.

Bonner Springs City Library: 201 N Nettleton Ave, Bonner Springs, KS 66012; tel. (913) 441-2665; fax (913) 441-2660; internet www.bonnerlibrary.org; f. 1964; 50,000 vols; Dir KIMBERLY BEETS; Pres. VICKY WHEELER; Sec. JANE RINK; Treas. TED STOLFUS.

Dwight D. Eisenhower Presidential Library and Museum: POB 339, 200 SE Fourth St, Abilene, KS 67410; tel. (785) 263-6700; fax (785) 263-6715; e-mail eisenhower

.library@nara.gov; internet www.eisenhower.archives.gov; f. 1962; documents related to fmr Pres. Eisenhower, and MSS of important persons in Eisenhower's admin. and military career; museum with 65,000 artefacts; 28,500 vols, 26m. MSS pages, 31,850 pages oral history transcripts, 334,500 still photographs, 767,700 ft of motion picture film; Dir KARL WEISSENBACH; publ. *Overview* (4 a year).

Hays Public Library: 1205 Main St, Hays, KS 67601; tel. (785) 625-9014; fax (785) 625-8683; internet www.hayspublib.org; f. 1895 as Saturday Afternoon Club; mem. of Central Kansas Library System; Chair. DAVID DUNN; Dir ERIC NORRIS; Sec. KERRI SUNLEY; Treas. AVRY ST PETER.

Johnson County Kansas Law Library: 100 N Kansas Ave, First Fl., Olathe, KS 66061; tel. (913) 715-4154; fax (913) 715-4152; e-mail lawlib@jocogov.org; internet lawlibrary.jocogov.org; collns incl. statutes and case law, fed. statutes and case law, case law of other states, Missouri statutes and case law, practice handbooks covering Kansas and Missouri law in many areas, legal encyclopedias, treatises, recent legal periodicals.

Kansas Supreme Court Law Library: Kansas Judicial Center, 301 SW 10th Ave, First Fl., Topeka, KS 66612-1507; tel. (785) 296-3257; fax (785) 296-1863; e-mail lawlibrary@kscourts.org; internet www.kscourts.org/kansas-courts/law-library; colln incl. statutory and case law for all 50 states, treatises on various legal subjects, fed. documents, briefs of Kansas appellate level cases and court-related materials; fed. depository; 185,000 vols, 600 periodical titles; Dir (vacant).

K-State Libraries: 137 Hale Library, 1100 Mid-Campus Dr., Manhattan, KS 66506; tel. (785) 532-3014; e-mail library@k-state.edu; internet www.lib.k-state.edu; f. 1863; attached to Kansas State Univ.; research collns incl. cookery, the consumer movement, military history, biosecurity and food safety, grain science and milling, prairie studies, and children's literature; 5 brs (veterinary medical, engineering, maths and physics, architecture and technology and aviation); Consumer Movement Archives; 2.6m. vols; Dean of Libraries LORI A. GOETSCH; publs *KSU Library Cassette Series on Library Technology* (irregular), *Library Bibliography Series* (irregular).

Leavenworth Public Library: 417 Spruce St, Leavenworth, KS 66048; tel. (913) 682-5666; fax (913) 682-1248; internet www.leavenworthpubliclibrary.org; f. 1860, fmrly Leavenworth Mercantile Library, present location 1987; Dir KIM BAKER; Pres. PAULINE GRAEBER; Sec. JUSTIN STEWART; Treas. JENNIFER BRENNEMAN TOBEY.

Macksville City Library: 333 N Main St, Macksville, KS; tel. and fax (620) 348-3555; e-mail macksvillecitylibrary@hotmail.com; internet macksville.mykansaslibrary.org; f. 1935; mem. of S Central Kansas Library System; Dir JODY SUITER; Pres. JON ZWINK; Sec. AUDREY AUSTIN; Treas. KAREN SPENCER.

Manhattan Public Library: 629 Poyntz Ave, Manhattan, KS 66502; tel. (785) 776-4741; fax (785) 776-1545; e-mail refstaff@manhattan.lib.ks.us; internet www.manhattan.lib.ks.us; f. 1856; resource centre for N Central Kansas Libraries System; Dir LINDA KNUPP; Pres. TODD SIMON.

Marysville Public Library: 1009 Broadway, Marysville, KS 66508; tel. (785) 562-2491; fax (785) 562-4086; e-mail maryslb@bluevalley.net; internet marysville.mykansaslibrary.org; f. 1935; 36,000 vols;

Dir JAMIE KELLEY; Pres. AMY HEIMAN; Sec. STACY WULLSCHLEGER; Treas. DANA PIESCHL.

Rossville Community Library: POB 618, Rossville, KS 66533; 407 N Main, Rossville, KS 66533; tel. and fax (785) 584-6454; e-mail director@rossvillelibrary.org; internet www .rossvillelibrary.org; f. 1950; 11,614 ; Dir ADRIENNE OLEJNIK; Pres. ANDREW FOSTER; Sec. SEAN BIRD; Treas. ALICIA VANATTA.

Salina Public Library: 301 W Elm St, Salina, KS 67401; tel. (785) 825-4624; fax (785) 823-0706; e-mail ask4info@salpublib .org; internet www.salinapubliclibrary.org; f. 1868; Dir JOE MCKENZIE; Pres. SANDIE JOHNSON; Sec. and Treas. BRIAN SCHMIDT.

State Library of Kansas: Capitol Bldg, Room 169-W, 300 SW 10th Ave, Topeka, KS 66612-1593; tel. (785) 296-3296; fax (785) 368-7291; e-mail infodesk@library.ks.gov; internet www.kslib.info; f. 1855; provides information services for state and local govts, for local libraries and their users; collects and shares resources and govt information; educates librarians and trustees; advocates for open and equitable access, intellectual freedom and excellence in library services and support; depository for fed. documents since 1900; newspaper clippings dating back to 1913; 40,000 state govt documents dating back to 1856; State Librarian JO BUDLER.

Topeka and Shawnee County Public Library: 1515 SW 10th Ave, Topeka, KS 66604-1374; tel. (785) 580-4400; fax (785) 233-2055; internet www.tscpl.org; f. 1870 as Ladies Library Asscn, present name and status 1992; incl. Alice C. Sabatini Gallery; bookmobile services; genealogy and local history colln; spec. colln of handmade artist's books and book objects, miniature books, fore-edge books, pop-up books, first edns; Moses Colln of scholarly fine arts books; 500,000 vols; CEO GINA MILLSAP; Chair. DAN GUENTHER; Sec. MELISSA MASONER; Treas. ROBERT HARDER.

KU Libraries University of Kansas: Suite 502, 1425 Jayhawk Blvd, Lawrence, KS 66045-7544; tel. (785) 864-8983; fax (785) 864-5311; internet www.lib.ku.edu; f. 1866; 3.8m. vols, 322,000 maps, 3,370,000 microforms, 3m. graphics (mostly photographs), 30,000 sound recordings, 691,000 govt documents, 15,000 linear ft MSS, spec. colln: 250,000 vols printed since the mid-15th century and 500,000 MSS from Antiquity to present; Dean of Libraries LORRAINE J. HARICOMBE.

Kentucky

Allen County Public Library: 106 W Public Sq., Scottsville, KY 42164; tel. (270) 237-3861; fax (270) 237-4095; internet www2 .youseemore.com/allen; f. 1954; 35,000 vols; Dir SHELIA STOVALL.

Boyd County Public Library: 1740 Central Ave, Ashland, KY 41101; tel. (606) 329-0518; fax (606) 329-0578; e-mail reference@ thebookplace.org; internet www .thebookplace.org; f. 1981; spec. colln incl. Arnold Hanners Tri-State photograph colln, Boyd Co historical records colln, Hilton colln and KY vital records (1911–95); microfilm colln incl. KY Federal Census and regional census materials; genealogy and local history; 2 brs; 150,000 vols (incl. books, large print, movies, audio books, downloadable movies, downloadable audio books, iPods, and newspaper and magazine colln); Dir DEBBIE COSPER.

Clark County Public Library: 370 S Burns Ave, Winchester, KY 40391-1876; tel. (859) 744-5661; e-mail clarkbooks@gmail .com; internet www.clarkpublib.org; 1 bookmobile; Dir JULIE MARUSKIN; Pres. EDDIE

WILLIAMS; Sec. CINDY DARLING CODELL; Treas. BRENDA ROYSE.

Daviess County Public Library: 2020 Frederica St, Owensboro, KY 42301; tel. (270) 684-0211; fax (270) 684-0218; e-mail daviess@dcplibrary.org; internet www .dcplibrary.org; f. 1913 as Carnegie Free Public Library, present location 1968, present name and status 1995; 170,000 vols, 10,000 movies and audio cassettes, 42 newspapers, 14 CD-ROM programmes; Pres. POLLY REYNOLDS.

Grant County Public Library: 201 Barnes Rd, Williamstown, KY 41097; tel. (859) 824-2080; fax (859) 824-2083; e-mail grantcountypubliclibrary@fuse.net; internet www.grantlib.org; f. 1954; local history colln; 21,000 vols, 1,900 movies on DVD and VHS, 600 audio books on CD or audio cassettes, 950 music CDs, 100 newspaper and magazine subscriptions; Dir SUSAN NIMERSHEIM; Public Services Librarian WYNITA WORLEY.

Graves County Public Library: 601 N 17th St, Mayfield, KY 42066; tel. (270) 247-2911; fax (270) 247-2990; e-mail dianegcpl@ bellsouth.net; internet www.gcpl.org; f. 1940; 50,000 vols; Dir DIANE BENNETT; Pres. MARTHA BABB; Sec. KATHY O'NAN; Treas. PETE GALLOWAY.

Grayson County Public Library: 130 E Market St, Leitchfield, KY 42754; tel. (270) 259-5455; fax (270) 259-4552; e-mail jones@ graysoncountylibrary.org; internet www2 .youseemore.com/grayson; co and state histories, family records, News-Gazette on microfilm from 1940s to present; 40,000 vols, 60 periodicals, 1,000 videos and 400 audio books; Dir LISA JONES.

Henderson County Public Library: 101 S Main St, Henderson, KY 42420; tel. (270) 826-3712; fax (270) 827-4226; internet www .hcpl.org; f. 1904; large print books, genealogy and local history photo colln; 112,000 vols (incl. books, newspapers, magazines, audiovisual materials, microfilms); Pres. KEN CHRISTOPHER; Sec. LINDA A. MIODUSZEWSKI; Treas. STEPHEN W. MARTIN.

Jessamine County Public Library: 600 S Main St, Nicholasville, KY 40356-1839; tel. (859) 885-3523; fax (859) 885-5164; e-mail jcplcirculation@jesspublib.org; internet www .jesspublib.org; f. 1975 as Withers Memorial Public Library, present name and status 2001; Dir Dr RON CRITCHFIELD; Pres. BILLIE GOODWILL; Sec. TERRY MORGAN; Treas. ROB AMBURGEY.

Kenton County Public Library: 2171 Chamber Center Dr., Fort Mitchell, KY 41017; tel. (859) 341-3200; internet www .kenton.lib.ky.us; f. 1901; brs: Mary Ann Mongan Library Covington, Erlanger Br., William E. Durr Br.; 584,938 vols; Dir DAVE SCHROEDER.

Kentucky Department for Libraries and Archives: POB 537 Frankfort, KY 40602-0537; 300 Coffee Tree Rd, Frankfort, KY 40601; tel. (502) 564-8300; fax (502) 564-5773; internet www.kdla.ky.gov; 18,600 vols, 3,189 audiovisual items, 5,797 audio books, 33,502 govt documents, 149,133 e-books, 18,771 journals; State Librarian and Commissioner WAYNE ONKST.

Laurel County Public Library: 120 College Park Dr., London, KY 40741; tel. (606) 864-5759; internet www.laurellibrary.org; f. 1916; 120,000 vols and 10,000 audio-visual colln; Dist. Dir LORI ACTON.

Lexington Public Library: 140 E Main St, Lexington, KY 40507; tel. (859) 231-5500; internet www.lexpublib.org; f. 1795; brs: Beaumont, Eagle Creek, Northside, Tates Creek and Village; 623,186 vols; Exec. Dir

ANN HAMMOND; Dir of Library Services SUSIE LAWRENCE.

Logan County Public Library: 201 W Sixth St, Russellville, KY 42276; tel. (270) 726-6129; fax (270) 726-6127; internet www .loganlibrary.org; 3 brs: Central Library, Adairville br. and Auburn br; Dir LINDA KOMPANIK; Pres. OBIE VAN CLEAVE; Sec. NORARGENTINA LACAYO; Treas. MARTHA DAVENPORT.

Louisville Free Public Library: 301 York St, Louisville, KY 40203; tel. (502) 574-1611; fax (502) 574-1666; internet www.lfpl.org; f. 1908; attached to Louisville/Jefferson County Metro Govt; 36,000 phono-discs, 70,000 programmes on electronic tape, operates 2 FM radio stations for music and educational programmes; 18 brs, 1 bookmobile; spec. Kentucky History Colln; houses a 'Louisville Art Gallery'; Talking Book Library for the blind and physically handicapped; 1,172,236 vols; Chair. TAD THOMAS; Dir CRAIG BUTHOD; publ. *Library News*.

Mt. Sterling—Montgomery County Library: 241 W Locust St, Mt. Sterling, KY 40353; tel. (859) 498-2404; fax (859) 498-7477; e-mail askmtsterlinglibrary@yahoo .com; internet www.youseemore.com/ mtsterling; f. 1878; Dir MELISSA SMATHERS-BARNES; Chair. JOHN WENZ; Sec. KIM TONNING.

Nelson County Public Library: 201 Cathedral Manor, Bardstown, KY 40004; tel. (502) 348-3714; fax (502) 348-5578; e-mail nelsoncopublib@hotmail.com; internet www .nelsoncopublib.org; f. 1946, present name and status 1968; 2 brs: Bloomfield Br. and New Haven Br.; 1 bookmobile; Dir SHARON SHANKS; Pres. VAL DOWNS; Sec. BARBARA HEADDY; Treas. JEFF DICKERSON.

Nicholas County Public Library: 223 N Broadway, Carlisle, KY 40311; tel. (859) 289-5595; fax (859) 289-4340; internet www .nicholascountylibrary.com; f. 1947, present location 1967; 1 bookmobile; 26,000 vols; Dir BECKY REID.

Rowan County Public Library: 175 Beacon Hill Dr., Morehead, KY 40351; tel. (606) 784-7137; fax (606) 784-2130; e-mail email@ rowancountylibrary.org; internet www .youseemore.com/rowan; 140 vols (incl. newspapers and magazine subscriptions); Dir HELEN WILLIAMS; Pres. HELEN NORTHCUTT; Sec. KAY FREELAND; Treas. RYAN NEFF.

Spencer County Library: 168 Taylorsville Rd, Taylorsville, KY 40071; tel. (502) 477-8137; e-mail scpl@insightbb.com; internet members.iglou.com/scpl; f. 1979; spec. colln incl. genealogy items; Dir DEBRA LAWSON.

University of Kentucky Libraries: Lexington, KY 40506-0456; tel. (859) 257-0500; fax (859) 257-8379; e-mail refdesk@uky.edu; internet libraries.uky.edu; f. 1909; 15 br. and collegiate libraries; regional depository for govt publs and a depository for EU and Canadian publs, British parliamentary papers, Kentucky govt publs, and technical reports from US fed. agencies; King Library Press; univ. and audiovisual archives; large colln of Kentuckiana, spec. collns of 19th-century British literature, French and Spanish drama from 1600 to 1900, modern political manuscript collns, broadsides, ballads and chapbooks, Cortot colln of music theory, typography, history of books, Appalachian Regional Commission archives, oral history colln; Center for Digital Programs creates digital content for the Kentuckiana Digital Library, incl. electronic texts, digitized photographs, images and archival finding aids; 3,719,548 vols; 73,251 current serials, incl. 45,450 electronic journals, 406,014 electronic books, 415 commercial databases and 26,780 linear ft of MSS and archives; 417

licensed networked electronic resources, 260,702 maps, 1,102,510 govt documents, 2,097,143 photographs and graphic materials, 92,600 audio cassettes, film and video cassettes, 6,433,748 microforms; Dean of Libraries TERRY BIRDWHISTELL.

Woodford County Library: 115 N Main St, Versailles, KY 40383; tel. (859) 873-5191; fax (859) 873-1542; internet woodfordcountylibrary.org; 2 brs: Main Br. and Midway Br. (opened 2009); 1 bookmobile; 70,000 vols; Dir KAREN KASACAVAGE; Pres. CHARLANN WOMBLES; Sec. TIM MIDDLETON; Treas. Dr MICHAEL R. NICHOLS.

Louisiana

Allen Parish Libraries: 320 S Sixth St, Oberlin, LA 70655; tel. (337) 639-4315; fax (337) 639-2654; e-mail jsmith2@state.lib.la .us; internet www.allen.lib.la.us; f. 1957; Oberlin (HQ) and brs at Oakdale and Kinder; Dir GERALDINE HARRIS.

Ascension Parish Library: 708 S Irma Blvd, Gonzales, LA 70737; tel. (225) 647-8924; internet www.myapl.org; f. 1960; Donaldsonville (HQ); brs: Dutchtown, Gonzales and Galvez; 324,151 vols; Dir ANGELLE DESHAUTELLES.

Beauregard Parish Public Library: 205 S Washington Ave, DeRidder, LA 70634; tel. (337) 463-6217; fax (337) 462-5434; e-mail admin@beau.org; internet www.beau.lib.la .us/lib; f. 1947; brs: East Beauregard, Fields, Merryville, South Beauregard and Singer; local history colln has information on people, places and events; adult new readers colln incl. reading materials for literacy activities; 61,498 vols.

Bienville Parish Library: 2768 Maple St, Arcadia, LA 71001; tel. (318) 263-7410; fax (318) 263-7428; internet www .bienvillelibrary.org; f. 1964; Arcadia (HQ); brs: Ringgold, Saline and Castor; Dir PEGGY WALLS.

East Baton Rouge Parish Library: 7711 Goodwood Blvd, Baton Rouge, LA 70806; tel. (225) 231-3700; e-mail eref@ebrpl.com; internet www.ebrpl.com; f. 1939; brs: main library and 12 brs; 2 bookmobiles; 2m. vols; Dir DAVID FARRAR; Pres. KIZZY A. PAYTON; Treas. LAURENCE LAMBERT.

Iberia Parish Library System: 445 E Main St, New Iberia, LA 70560; tel. (337) 364-7024; fax (337) 364-7042; e-mail newiberialib@yahoo.com; internet www .iberia.lib.la.us; f. 1947; spec. colln: I.A. and Carroll Martin Photo Colln and the Bunk Johnson Colln; 7 brs; 210,000 vols; Dir KATHLEEN MILES.

Jefferson Davis Parish Library: 4747 W Napoleon Ave, Metairie, LA 70001; tel. (504) 838-1100; fax (504) 838-1110; internet www .jefferson-davis.lib.la.us; f. 1949; Jennings HQ; 4 brs and 1 bookmobile; Dir LON DICKERSON; Pres. JANICE ESTHAY; Treas. LEAVON LADNER.

Lafayette Public Library System: 301 W Congress St, Lafayette, LA 70501; tel. (337) 261-5775; internet www .lafayettepubliclibrary.org; f. 1897; brs: Broussard, Butler Memorial, Chenier, Duson, Jefferson St, Milton, North Regional, Scott, South Regional and Youngsville; main library closed for renovation; Dir SONA J. DOMBOURIAN; Pres. ANDREW DUHON.

LaSalle Parish Library: 3108 N First St, Jena, LA 71342; tel. (318) 992-5675; fax (318) 992-7374; internet www.lasalle.lib.la.br; f. 1963; main library and Olla br.; spec. colln incl. genealogy colln and microfilm; Dir ANDREA BOOK (acting); Pres. SAMMY FRANKLIN.

Law Library of Louisiana: 400 Royal St, Second Fl., New Orleans, LA 70130-2104; tel. (504) 310-2400; e-mail library@lasc.org; internet www.lasc.org/law_library/ library_information.asp; f. 1855; colln incl. complete chronology of both statutes and court reports for all states and fed. govt; 230,000 vols.

Livingston Parish Library: POB 397, Livingston, LA 70734; 13986 Florida Blvd, Livingston, LA 70734; tel. (225) 686-2436; internet www.main.mylpl.info; f. 1946; Livingston (HQ); brs: Albany-Springfield, Denham Springs-Walker, S and Watson; Dir GIOVANNI TAIROV.

Louisiana State University Libraries: Baton Rouge, LA 70803; tel. (225) 578-5652; fax (225) 578-9432; internet www.lib.lsu.edu; f. 1860; UN, fed. and state depositories; spec. collns incl. E. A. McIlhenny Natural History Colln, Louisiana Colln, sugar technology, Southern history, agriculture, plant pathology, petroleum, bibliography colln, aquaculture, incl. crawfish, wetlands research and marine biology; archives on Lower Mississippi Valley; 3m. vols, 5,375,405 microforms and 12m. MSS, databases, e-books and e-journals; Dean JENNIFER CARGILL; publ. *Library Lectures.*

New Orleans Public Library: 219 Loyola Ave, New Orleans, LA 70112; tel. (504) 596-2570; fax (504) 596-2609; internet nutrias .org; f. 1843; 12 brs; spec. collns: city archives colln, civil and criminal courts colln, carnivals, maps, photographs, rare books, early sheet music, early jazz recordings and MSS; incl. African American Resource Center and Business and Science Div.; 1,043,471 vols; Chair. LEE C. REID; Head of Main Public Services LINDA MARSHALL HILL.

Ouachita Parish Public Library: 1800 Stubbs Ave, Monroe, LA 71201; tel. (318) 327-1490; fax (318) 329-4057; internet www .ouachita.lib.la.us; f. 1884; main library and brs: Anna Meyer, Carver Br., Louise Williams, Ollie Burns, Ouachita Valley, Cptl J R Searcy, Sterlington Memorial, W Monroe and W Ouachita; Dir ROBIN TOMS; Pres. DARRIS WAREN.

Rapides Parish Library: 430 St James St, Alexandria, LA 71301; tel. (318) 445-6436; fax (318) 445-6196; internet www.rpl.org; f. 1942; brs: Westside Regional Library, Boyce, Gunter, Hineston, J. W. McDonald Memorial, Johnson, King, Martin and Robertson; main library and 1 bookmobile; Dir STEVE ROGGE; Pres. SUSIE C. SMITH.

Sabine Parish Library: 705 Main St, Many, LA 71449; tel. (318) 256-4150; internet www.sabine.lib.la.us; f. 1933; Sabine Parish (HQ); brs: Toledo, Converse, Pleasant Hill and Zwolle; Dir REBECCA MORRIS; Pres. LORENE JONES.

South St Landry Community Library: 235 Marie St, Sunset, LA 70584; tel. (337) 662-3442; fax (337) 662-3475; internet www .southstlandrylibrary.com; f. 1989; present name and status 1991; 34,000 vols; Dir BARBARA A. MALBRUE; Chair. ARMAND BRINKHAUS; Sec. ANDY DAKIN.

St. Tammany Parish Library: 310 W 21st Ave, Covington, LA 70433; tel. (985) 871-1219; fax (985) 871-1224; e-mail covington@ stpl.us; internet www.sttammany.lib.la.us; f. 1946; spec. colln incl. selected documents issued by state governmental agencies; census on microfilm; family histories and a local newspaper archive in geneology colln; Dir DONALD WESTMORELAND; Pres. Dr. ARGIRO MORGAN; Sec. and Treas. MARY RENEAU.

State Library of Louisiana: POB 131, Baton Rouge, LA 70821-0131; 701 N Fourth St, Baton Rouge, LA 70802-5345; tel. (225)

342-4923; fax (225) 219-4804; e-mail admin@ state.lib.la.us; internet www.state.lib.la.us; f. 1920, fmrly Louisiana Library Comm.; colln supplements Louisiana public libraries and meets research needs of state govt employees; 11m. vols; State Librarian REBECCA HAMILTON; publ. *Hotlines* (4 a year).

Terrebonne Parish Library System: 151 Library Dr., Houma, LA 70360; tel. (985) 876-5861; fax (985) 876-5864; internet www .mytpl.org; f. 1927; main br.; brs: Bourg, Chauvin, Dularge, E Houma, Gibson, Grand Caillou, Montegut and North Terrebonne; Dir MARY COSPER LEBOEUF.

Tulane University Libraries: 7001 Freret St, New Orleans, LA 70118; tel. (504) 865-5605; fax (504) 865-6773; e-mail libref@ tulane.edu; internet library.tulane.edu; f. 1834; spec. collns on New Orleans, Louisiana and Southern US history; Latin America, architecture and jazz; 16 libraries; 3.6m. vols (incl. law, medicine and 6 other collns); Dean of the Library LANCE QUERY.

Union Parish Library: 202 W Jackson St, Farmerville, LA 71241; tel. (318) 368-9226; internet www.youseemore.com/unionparish; f. 1955; 62,000 vols; Dir STEPHANIE ANTLEY HERRMANN; publ. *Beacon Bulletin* (12 a year).

Vermilion Parish Library: POB 640, Abbeville, LA 70510; 405 E St Victor St, Abbeville, LA 70510; tel. (337) 893-2674; fax (337) 898-0526; e-mail abbeville@vermilion .lib.la.us; internet www.vermilion.lib.la.us; f. 1942; brs: Abbeville, Delcambre, Erath, Gueydan, Kaplan and Maurice; Dir CHARLOTTE TROSCLAIR; Pres. RICKY LUQUETTE.

Maine

Auburn Public Library: 49 Spring St, Auburn, ME 04210; tel. (207) 333-6640; fax (207) 333-6644; e-mail email@ auburnpubliclibrary.org; internet www .auburn.lib.me.us; f. 1890; Dir LYNN LOCKWOOD; Pres. RICHARD L. TRAFTON.

Bangor Public Library: 145 Harlow St, Bangor, ME 04401; tel. (207) 947-8336; fax (207) 945-6694; e-mail bplill@bpl.lib.me.us; internet www.bpl.lib.me.us; f. 1830; spec. colln incl. co histories, local history resources and State and Fed. Census state resources like Maine Register Town Histories; Dir BARBARA McDADE; Pres. NORMAN MINSKY.

Boothbay Harbor Memorial Library: 4 Oak St, Boothbay Harbor, ME 04538; tel. 207-633-3112; e-mail bbhlibrary@bmpl.lib .me.us; internet www.bmpl.lib.me.us; f. 1924; 22,000 vols; Exec. Dir BETTY HUGHES; Pres. TOM CHURCHILL; Sec. JANE GARDNER; Treas. JOYCE ARMENDARIS.

Cary Library: 107 Main St, Houlton, ME 04730; tel. (207) 532-1302; fax (207) 532-4350; internet www.cary.lib.me.us; spec. colln incl. historical genealogical information from Houlton, Maine and its surrounding communities in the S Aroostook Co area; 55,000 vols (incl. 800 large print titles, 1,400 audio cassettes and CDs), 1,700 video cassettes and DVDs and 90 periodicals; Dir LINDA FAUCHER.

Curtis Memorial Library: 23 Pleasant St, Brunswick, ME 04011; tel. (207) 725-5242; e-mail director@curtislibrary.com; internet www.curtislibrary.com; f. 1883; 146,625 vols; Dir ELISABETH DOUCETT; Pres. CHRISTOPER GOODWIN; Sec. and Treas. LESTER HODGDON.

Falmouth Memorial Library: 5 Lunt Rd, Falmouth, ME 04105; tel. (207) 781-2351; internet www.falmouth.lib.me.us; f. 1944; 47,392 vols, 2,560 video cassettes and DVDs, 1,871 music CDs, 1,806 audio books and 107 periodicals; Dir LYNDA L. SUDLOW; Pres. JULIE RABINOWITZ.

Farmington Public Library: 117 Academy St, Farmington, ME 04938; tel. (207) 778-4312; internet www.farmington.lib.me.us; f. 1890; colln of Maine authors; local and town history; genealogy reference library; 30,000 vols; Librarian MELANIE COOMBS.

Gardiner Public Library: 152 Water St, Gardiner, ME 04345-2195; tel. (207) 582-3312; internet www.gpl.lib.me.us; f. 1796; Community Archives Room incl. colln on genealogy, state, county and local histories; Dir ANNE ESTRADA DAVIS.

Lithgow Public Library: 45 Winthrop St, Augusta, ME 04330; tel. (207) 626-2415; internet www.lithgow.lib.me.us; f. 1894; 65,000 vols; Dir ELIZABETH POHL.

Maine State Archives: 84 State House Station, Augusta, ME 04333; 230 State St, Augusta, ME 04333; tel. (207) 287-5790; fax (207) 287-6035; internet www.state.me.us/sos/arc; attached to Dept of State; colln incl. bills introduced in Legislature; Governor's Exec. Council reports; deeds to and from Maine; maps; fed. census records up to 1930; co court records dating back to 1639; 95m. pages of official State records; State Archivist DAVE CHEEVER.

Maine State Library: 64 State House Station, Augusta, ME 04333-0064; 230 State St, Augusta, ME 04333-0064; tel. (207) 287-5600; fax (207) 287-5624; e-mail reference.desk@maine.gov; internet www.maine.gov/msl; f. 1836; 350,615 vols, 703 periodicals, 848 audio cassettes, 650 video cassettes, 250,888 govt docs; State Librarian LINDA H. LORD.

Mark & Emily Turner Memorial Library: 39 Second St, Presque Isle, ME 04769; tel. (207) 764-2571; fax (207) 768-5756; internet www.presqueislelibrary.org; f. 1874; colln incl. genealogy resources and historical texts and memorabilia of Presque Isle and surrounding area; Dir SONJA PLUMMER-MORGAN; Chair. KEVIN SIPE; Sec. PAUL HAMLIN; Treas. ELAINE SIPE.

McArthur Public Library: 270 Main St, Biddeford, ME; tel. (207) 284-4181; e-mail reference@mcarthur.lib.me.us; internet www.mcarthurpubliclibrary.org; f. 1902; colln of antique photographs of the city and surrounding areas; 65,000 vols, 170 magazine subscriptions, 1,500 music cassettes or CDs, 2,000 video cassettes or DVDs, 1,500 audiobooks; Dir JEFF CABRAL.

Portland Public Library: 5 Monument Sq. Portland, ME 04101; tel. (207) 871-1700; fax (207) 871-1703; e-mail reference@portland.lib.me.us; internet www.portlandlibrary.com; f. 1867; 1 main library; 3 brs: Burbank, Peaks Island and Riverton; Exec. Dir STEPHEN J. PODGAJNY; Pres. NATHAN H. SMITH.

Rumford Public Library: 56 Rumford Ave, Rumford, ME 04276; tel. (207) 364-3661; fax (207) 364-7296; internet www.rumford.lib.me.us; f. 1903; Dir LUKE SORENSEN; Chair. CAROLYN KENNARD.

Scarborough Public Library: 48 Gorham Rd, Scarborough, ME 04074; tel. (207) 883-4723; fax (207) 883-9728; e-mail askspl@scarborough.lib.me.us; internet www.library.scarborough.me.us; f. 1899; 62,703 vols, 5,503 video cassettes, 4,334 audio books colln; Dir NANCY E. CROWELL.

South Berwick Public Library: 37 Portland St, South Berwick, ME 03908; tel. and fax (207) 384-3308; e-mail sbpl@south-berwick.lib.me.us; internet www.south-berwick.lib.me.us; f. 1971; colln incl. South Berwick History Colln, Sarah Orne Jewett Colln and large print books.

Thomaston Public Library: 60 Main St, Thomaston, ME 04861; tel. (207) 354-2453; e-mail tpl@thomaston.lib.me.us; internet www.thomaston.lib.me.us; f. 1898; 26,000 vols (incl. 23,800 books, 2,080 movies); Dir BRIAN SYLVESTER; Chair. JANET BOSWORTH; Sec. SHEILAGH GUYER; Treas. WILLIAM DASHIELL.

Wells Public Library: POB 699, Wells, ME 04090; 1434 Post Rd, Wells, ME 04090; tel. (207) 646-8181; fax (207) 646-5636; e-mail libstaff@wellstown.org; internet www.wells.lib.me.us; f. 1978; colln of large print books for visually impaired; Dir CINDY SCHILLING; Chair. AMY ANDERSON.

William Fogg Public Library: POB 359, 116 Old Rd, Eliot, ME 03903; tel. (207) 439-9437; e-mail front-desk@william-fogg.lib.me.us; internet www.william-fogg.lib.me.us; f. 1907; Fogg antiquarian book colln; American regional history, which incl. state histories, westward expansion, Revolutionary, Civil War, and Indian War materials; Dir and Head of Adult Services SUSAN SINNOTT.

Windham Public Library: 217 Windham Center Rd, Windham, ME 04062; tel. (207) 892-1908; fax (207) 892-1915; internet www.windham.lib.me.us; f. 1971; spec. colln on genealogy and books that deal with the state of Maine; 42,000 vols, 3,300 movies, 1,500 audio recordings, 850 music recordings, 80 periodicals and newspapers; Chair. ROBERT A. ROSBOROUGH.

Maryland

Allegany County Library System: 31 Washington St, Cumberland, MD 21502; tel. (301) 777-1200; fax (301) 777-7299; e-mail washingtonstlibrary@allconet.org; internet www.home.alleganycountylibrary.info; f. 1960; incl. 6 libraries and 1 bookmobile; spec. colln incl. Maryland Room colln of print materials of interest for local history and genealogy, incl. histories of Maryland and Allegany Co and nearby cities, towns, churches and businesses; Dir JOHN TAUBE.

Baltimore County Circuit Court Law Library: County Courts Bldg, 401 Bosley Ave, Towson, MD 21204; tel. (410) 887-3086; fax (410) 887-4807; internet www.baltimorecountymd.gov/agencies/circuit/library; provides legal information and information services to judges, attorneys, paralegals, govt officials and citizens representing themselves in legal matters who reside or practice in Baltimore Co, Maryland; colln incl. laws and cases of all 50 states and the Fed. govt; spec. emphasis on Maryland law and subject specific treatises; collns incl. Co codes, Court of Appeals briefs on microfiche, all currently available MICPELs, over 50 law reviews and extensive tax and labour collns; Dir STEPHANIE LEVASSEUR.

Caroline County Public Library: 100 Market St, Denton, MD 21629; tel. (410) 479-1343; fax (410) 479-1443; e-mail info@carolib.org; internet www.caro.lib.md.us; f. 1961; 3 brs and 1 bookmobile; colln incl. Maryland history geographic and economic studies; works by local authors; Caroline Co information; Spanish language colln; Pres. GALE P. NASHOLD; Sec. DEBORAH MANDYCZ; Treas. DAVID R. JONES.

Enoch Pratt Free Library: 400 Cathedral St, Baltimore, MD 21201-4484; tel. (410) 396-5430; fax (410) 837-5837; e-mail slrc@prattlibrary.org; internet www.pratt.lib.md.us; f. 1882; spec. collns: H. L. Mencken colln, Maryland history colln; 2,290,042 vols, 91,000 maps, 5,000 films, 19,094 video cassettes, 38,450 slides, 486 filmstrips, 34,802 recordings; CEO CARLA D. HAYDEN; publ. *Menckeniana* (4 a year).

Johns Hopkins University Libraries: Baltimore, MD 21218; tel. (410) 516-8335; internet webapps.jhu.edu/jhuniverse/libraries; f. 1876; incl. the Milton S. Eisenhower Library, 1 of the Sheridan libraries and the main research library of the univ.; spec. collns in medicine, int. affairs, music and earth and space science; 2,961,160 vols; Dean of Univ. Libraries WINSTON TABB.

Maryland State Archives: Dr Edward C. Papenfuse State Archives Bldg, 350 Rowe Blvd, Annapolis, MD 21401; tel. (410) 260-6400; fax (410) 974-2525; e-mail archives@mdsa.net; internet www.msa.md.gov; f. 1935, fmrly Hall of Records, present name 1984; central depository for government records; holdings date from Maryland's founding in 1634, and incl. colonial and state exec., legislative, and judicial records; co probate, land and court records; church records; business records; state publs and reports; spec. collns of private papers, maps, photographs and newspapers; State Archivist Dr EDWARD C. PAPENFUSE.

Maryland State Law Library: Robert C. Murphy Courts of Appeal Bldg, 361 Rowe Blvd, Annapolis, MD 21401; tel. (410) 260-1430; fax (410) 260-1572; e-mail lawlibrary@mdcourts.gov; internet www.lawlib.state.md.us; f. 1826 as State Library, present location 1972, present name 1978; legal and govt information resources; spec. colln: Anglo-American legal collns; Maryland legislative task force and comm. reports; Maryland govt pubs in the State and Code of Fed. Regulations; Dir STEVEN P. ANDERSON.

National Agricultural Library: Abraham Lincoln Bldg, 10301 Baltimore Ave, Beltsville, MD 20705-2351; tel. (301) 504-5755; fax (301) 504-5472; e-mail agref@ars.usda.gov; internet www.nal.usda.gov; f. 1862; attached to US Dept of Agriculture; agriculture and related sciences; spec. collns: Layne R. Beaty Papers (farm radio and television broadcasting); foreign and domestic nursery seed trade catalogues; flock, herd and stud books; audiovisual colln on food and nutrition; apiculture; Forest Service and USDA Photo colln on optical laser discs; M. Truman Fossum Colln (floriculture); James M. Gwin Colln (poultry); Charles E. North Colln (milk sanitation); Pomology Colln (original pomological art); Charles Valentine Riley Colln (entomology); plant exploration photograph colln; food and nutrition micro-computer software; MAPP colln of family life education materials; computer database (AGRICOLA) of 3m. records for books and journal articles in agriculture; information centres on agricultural trade and marketing, alternative farming systems, animal welfare, aquaculture, biotechnology, food and nutrition, plant genome, rural information, technology transfer, water quality and youth devt; 3.5m. vols; Dir Dr SIMON Y. LIU; publs *Agriculture Libraries Information Notes* (12 a year), *Quick Bibliography* (irregular).

National Archives and Records Administration: 8601 Adelphi Rd, College Park, MD 20740-6001; tel. (301) 837-2000; fax (301) 837-0483; internet www.archives.gov; f. 1934; ensures, for citizens and federal officials, ready access to essential evidence that documents the rights of American citizens, the actions of federal officials, and the nat. experience; establishes policies and procedures for managing US Govt records and assists federal agencies in documenting their activities, administering record management programmes, scheduling records, and retiring non-current records; obtains, arranges, describes, preserves and provides access to the essential documentation of the 3 brs of govt; manages the presidential libraries system, and publishes the laws, regulations, and presidential and other public documents; assists the Information Security Oversight Office, which manages federal classification and declassification policies, and the Nat.

Historical Publs and records Comm., which makes grants nationwide to help non-profit orgs identify, preserve, and provide access to materials that document American history; consists of 33 facilities nationwide, incl. 18 regional records services facilities and 10 presidential Libraries; on permanent display in the Exhibition Hall are the Declaration of Independence, the Constitution of the United States, and the Bill of Rights; 9 billion pages of textual records; 7.2m. maps, charts and architectural drawings; over 20m. still photographs; billions of machine-readable data sets; over 365,000 reels of film and 110,000 video cassettes; Archivist of the United States DAVID S. FERRIERO; publ. *Prologue* (4 a year).

National Institute of Standards and Technology Research Library: 100 Bureau Dr., Stop 2500, Gaithersburg, MD 20899-2500; tel. (301) 975-3052; fax (301) 975-6793; e-mail library@nist.gov; internet www.nist.gov; f. 1912; spec. collns: science, engineering and technology; archives colln incl. catalogued documents, artefacts, photographs, films, videos, oral histories, biographical files, subject files and other material; not open to the public; 300,000 vols, 1,000 journals; Dir Dr PATRICK D. GALLAGHER; Chief Information Officer DELWIN BROCKETT; publ. *Journal of Research of the National Institute of Standards and Technology*.

National Institutes of Health Library: Bldg 10, Room 1L25, 10 Center Dr., MSC 1150, Bethesda, MD 20892-1150; tel. (301) 496-5612; fax (301) 402-0254; internet nihlibrary.nih.gov; f. 1903; biomedical research library: biology, medicine, health sciences, chemistry, physiology, physics; 70,000 books, 160,000 periodicals, 9,000 journal subscriptions, 2,898 microforms; Library Dir SUZANNE GREFSHEIM; Librarian JEAN WEISS.

National Oceanic and Atmospheric Administration Central Library: 1315 EW Highway, SSMC3, Second Fl., Silver Spring, MD 20910; tel. (301) 713-2600; fax (301) 713-4598; e-mail library.reference@noaa.gov; internet www.lib.noaa.gov; f. 1807; attached to US Dept of Commerce; 35 libraries and information centres; networks with 30 NOAA libraries; disciplines incl. aeronomy, cartography, coastal studies, ecosystems, geodesy, marine ecology, marine resources, mathematics, oceanography, ocean engineering, nautical charting statistics and weather and atmospheric sciences; 1m. vols; Dir NEAL KASKE.

Nimitz Library: 589 McNair Rd, Annapolis, MD 21402-5029; tel. (410) 293-2420; internet www.usna.edu/library; f. 1973; attached to United States Naval Acad. (USNA); open for midshipmen and faculty; services also provided to USNA military and civilian staff and their family members and personnel attached to the other activities of the Annapolis Area Naval Complex; local retired faculty members and retired military personnel; 30,000 vols, 40,000 photographs and 400 MSS colln; Dir JAMES RETTIG.

Prince George's County Memorial Library System: 6532 Adelphi Rd, Hyattsville, MD 20782; tel. (301) 699-3500; internet www.pgcmls.info; 18 Community Libraries; Co Correctional Center Library; 1,906,457 vols (incl. 1,613,086 books, 76,630 serials, 120,328 audio recordings, 89,425 videos, 246,662 journals); Dir KATHLEEN TEAZE; Pres. MARK POLK.

Ruth Enlow Library of Garrett County: 6 N Second St, Oakland, MD 21550; tel. (301) 334-3996; fax (301) 334-4152; internet www.relib.net; f. 1915 as Oakland Free Public Library, present bldg 1950; print, non-print and e-resources; 1 main library (Oakland) and 4 brs in Accident, Friendsville, Grantsville and Kitzmiller; Dir CATHY ASHBY; Pres. SHERRY GEORG; Treas. KATHY HELBIG.

Somerset County Library System: 11767 Beechwood St, Princess Anne, MD 21853; tel. (410) 651-0852; fax (410) 651-1388; internet www.some.lib.md.us; f. 1967, present location 1988; Princess Anne Public Library; Corbin Memorial Library in Crisfield; Elwell School library in Smith Island; Dir JENNIFER RANCK.

University of Maryland Libraries: College Park, MD 20742-7011; tel. (301) 405-0800; internet www.lib.umd.edu; f. 1856; 8 campus libraries: McKeldin Library, Hornbake Library, Art Library, Architecture Library, Eng. and Physical Sciences Library, Michelle Smith Performing Arts Library, Shady Grove Library and Media Center, White Memorial (Chemistry) Library; 3,930,013 vols, 68,514 current serial titles; Dean PATRICIA A. STEELE.

US Census Bureau Library: 4600 Silver Hill Rd, Suitland, MD 20746; tel. (301) 763-2511; fax (301) 763-4407; e-mail library@census.gov; internet www.census.gov/prod/www/abs/library/databases.html; f. 1952; attached to US Dept of Commerce; collects, preserves and provides access to information resources produced by the Census Bureau to its employees, govt agencies and public; 250,000 vols, spec. int. colln 115,000 vols; Dir ROBERT M. GROVES.

US National Library of Medicine: 8600 Rockville Pike, Bethesda, MD 20894; tel. (301) 594-5983; fax (301) 402-1384; e-mail custserv@nlm.nih.gov; internet www.nlm.nih.gov; f. 1836; houses old and rare medical works; materials, information and research services in all areas of biomedicine and healthcare; 13m. vols; Dir Dr DONALD A. B. LINDBERG; publ. *Index Medicus* (12 a year).

Wicomico Public Library: 122 S Div. St, Salisbury, MD 21801; tel. (410) 749-3612; fax (410) 548-2968; e-mail askus@wicomico.org; internet www.wicomicolibrary.org; f. 1869; main library, centre br., Bivalve Station and Pittsville br.; 1 bookmobile; Dir TOM HEHMAN; Chair. VALERIE MURPHY; Sec. SUSAN BOUNDS; Treas. WINNIE STOKES.

Massachusetts

Abbot Library: 235 Pleasant St, Marblehead, MA 01945; tel. (781) 631-1481; fax (781) 639-0558; e-mail mar@noblenet.org; internet www.abbotlibrary.org; f. 1878; Dir PATRICIA J. ROGERS.

Amherst Center for Russian Culture: POB 2268, Amherst College, Amherst, MA 01002-5000; tel. (413) 542-8204; fax (413) 542-2798; internet www.amherst.edu; f. 1991; attached to Amherst College; rare Russian books, MSS, newspapers and periodicals; 15,000 vols; Dir Prof. STANLEY J. RABINOWITZ.

Amherst Libraries: 43 Amity St, Amherst, MA 01002; tel. (413) 259-3090; fax (413) 256-4096; e-mail info@joneslibrary.org; internet www.joneslibrary.org; Jones Library (HQ); brs: Munson Memorial Library and N Amherst Library; spec. colln: local and regional history, genealogy and Amherst authors; 210,845 vols and 25,516 audio and video materials; Dir SHARON SHARRY.

Athol Public Library: 568 Main St, Athol, MA 01331; tel. (978) 249-9515; fax (978) 249-7636; e-mail info@athollibrary.org; internet www.athollibrary.org; f. 1878; 50,000 vols (incl. books, magazines, periodicals, books on tape, videos, CDs); Dir DEBRA BLANCHARD; Chair. MARGARET YOUNG.

Bedford Free Public Library: 7 Mudge Way, Bedford, MA 01730; tel. (781) 275-9440; fax (781) 275-3590; e-mail bedford@minlib.net; internet www.bedfordlibrary.net; f. 1876; spec. colln incl. MSS, pamphlets and audiovisual materials focusing on Bedford history and culture; Nickerson Colln on learning and developmental disabilities; Chinese Language Colln: books in Chinese, Chinese music CDs, Chinese-language periodicals, and Chinese movies and TV series on DVD and VCD; Andrew Zuckerman Memorial Colln: global poverty, Southeast Asia (languages, music, books, histories, travel, memoirs, etc.), Eastern religions, Native American beliefs, sustainable agriculture, volunteering and social action, ecology and environment, medicinal plants and herbs, wildlife conservation; 119,287 vols; Dir RICHARD CALLAGHAN.

Belmont Public Library: 336 Concord Ave, POB 125, Belmont, MA 02478; tel. (617) 489-2000; e-mail belmont@minlib.net; internet www.belmont.lib.ma.us; f. 1868; Claflin Room: colln incl. 2 murals of old Belmont, original art, town reports, books by Belmont authors, materials relating to the town and historical artefacts; Dir MAUREEN CONNERS.

Boston Athenaeum: 10½ Beacon St, Boston, MA 02108-3777; tel. (617) 227-0270; fax (617) 227-5266; internet www.bostonathenaeum.org; f. 1807, present location 1849; ind. research library; 1.5m. vols, 600,000 books; history, biography, English and American literature, fine and decorative arts; spec. collns incl. confederate states imprints, books from libraries of George Washington, Gen. Henry Knox and the Adams Family, the King's Chapel Colln (1698), Gypsy literature, private press publs, 19th-century tracts, early US govt documents, maps, charts and atlases, and the Charles E. Mason print colln; Bartlett Hayes poster colln; 19th-century photographs; Dir and Librarian PAULA MATTHEWS; Pres. DEBORAH H. BORNHEIMER; Sec. ALEXANDER ALTSCHULLER; Treas. GILBERT M. RODDY, JR.

Boston Public Library: 700 Boylston St, Boston, MA 02116; tel. (617) 536-5400; fax (617) 236-4306; e-mail ask@bpl.org; internet www.bpl.org; f. 1848, present location 1895; the oldest free municipal library supported by public taxation in the world; 26 brs; 20m. vols; Chair. JEFFREY B. RUDMAN; Pres. AMY E. RYAN.

Boston University Libraries: 771 Commonwealth Ave, Boston, MA 02215; tel. (617) 353-2700; e-mail ask@bu.edu; internet www.bu.edu/library; f. 1839; 5 major libraries: Mugar Memorial Library (6 brs humanities and social sciences), Howard Gotlieb Archival Research Center (rare books and MSS), Pappas Law Library (fed. and state primary legal materials; major serials, treatises and other secondary materials; legal documents and reports and int. law materials), Medical Library, School of Theology Library (theology, Bible, church history, min., and historic Judaism); 2.4m. vols, 45,264 serials titles, 77,000 media titles and 28,000 periodicals; Univ. Librarian ROBERT HUDSON.

Burlington Public Library: 22 Sears St, Burlington, MA 01803; tel. (781) 270-1738; fax (781) 229-0406; internet www.burlingtonpubliclibrary.org; f. 1857; 91,681 vols; Dir LORI HODGSON.

Cambridge Public Library: 449 Broadway, Cambridge, 02138; tel. (617) 349-4041; fax (617) 349-9385; internet www.cambridgema.gov/cpl.aspx; f. 1849; 6 brs: Boudreau, Central Square, Collins, O'Connell, O'Neill and Valente; Dir SUSAN FLANNERY.

Chelmsford Public Library: 25 Boston Rd, Chelmsford, MA 01824; tel. (978) 256-5521; fax (978) 256-8511; e-mail askus@mvlc.org; internet www.chelmsfordlibrary.org; f. 1894; main library and Anna C. MacKay Br. Library; 140,000 vols (incl. books, periodicals, audio books, CDs, DVDs, videos and newspapers); Dir BECKY HERRMANN.

Countway Library of Medicine: 10 Shattuck St, Boston, MA 02115; tel. (617) 432-2136; fax (617) 432-4739; e-mail countadm@hms.harvard.edu; internet www.countway.harvard.edu; f. 1965; serves the Harvard Medical School, Harvard School of Public Health, Harvard School of Dental Medicine, Boston Medical Library and the Massachusetts Medical Soc.; 630,000 vols, 3,500 journals, 10,000 non-current biomedical journals; Dir Dr ISAAC KOHANE; Dir of Center for the History of Medicine SCOTT PODOLSKY.

East Longmeadow Public Library: 60 Center Sq., East Longmeadow, MA 01028; tel. (413) 525-5400; e-mail steale@cwmars.org; internet www.eastlongmeadow.org/library; f. 2004; colln in Local History Room incl. books, documents, photographs and maps related to the town's history; 80,606 vols; Chair. ARTHUR McGUIRE; Sec. AMIE SINGH; Dir SUSAN M. PETERSON.

Edgartown Public Library: 58 N Water St, POB 5249, Edgartown, MA 02539; tel. (508) 627-4221; fax (508) 627-9534; e-mail director@edgartownlibrary.org; internet www.edgartownlibrary.org; f. 1903; 40,725 vols (incl. 30,083 books, 1,787 audio CDs, 4,954 video DVD and VHS, 411 microfilms, 215 journals); Chair. PAT ROSE; Dir FELICIA CHENEY; Sec. HERBERT FOSTER.

Falmouth Public Library: 300 Main St, Falmouth, MA 02540; tel. (508) 457-2555; fax (508) 457-2559; e-mail info@falmouthpubliclibrary.org; internet www.falmouthpubliclibrary.org; f. 1876; brs: East Falmouth Br. and North Falmouth Br.; spec. colln on genealogy, local history (from 1876 to the present day) and rep. colln of work of Katharine Lee Bates; Chair. OTIS PORTER, JR; Dir LESLIE A. MORRISSEY; Sec. SYLVIA SZULKIN; Treas. JEROME FANGER.

Hamilton-Wenham Public Library: 14 Union St, South Hamilton, MA 01982; tel. (978) 468-5577; fax (978) 468-5535; internet www.hwlibrary.org; f. 2001 by merger of Wenham Town Library (f. 1885) with Hamilton Public Library (f. 1891); 105,993 vols, 464 print periodicals, newspapers and other print serials, 7,748 audio materials and 8,472 video materials; Dir JAN DEMPSEY.

Harvard University Library: Office of the Dir, Wadsworth House-1341, Massachusetts Ave, Cambridge, MA 02138; tel. (617) 495-3650; fax (617) 495-0370; e-mail administration@hulmail.harvard.edu; internet hul.harvard.edu; f. 1638; oldest library in the USA; central collns are housed in Widener, Houghton, Pusey, Lamont, Hilles, Cabot Science, Harvard-Yenching, Littauer, Loeb Music, Tozzer, Fine Arts and Geological Sciences Libraries; important collns in nearly every field of learning and 4,000 vols printed before 1501; 17m. vols; Exec. Dir HELEN SHENTON; Univ. Librarian ROBERT DARNTON; publ. *Harvard Library Bulletin*.

Jacob Edwards Library: 236 Main St, Southbridge, MA 01550; tel. (508) 764-5426; fax (508) 764-5428; e-mail refjel@cwmars.org; internet www.jacobedwardslibrary.org; f. 1870; colln about local history; books, photographs, maps, directories and memorabilia; local newspaper colln on microfilm; digital colln: agricultural and industrial history of Central and Western Massachusetts; Holmes Ammidown Colln: 18th century library that belonged to a prominent early

citizen of Southbridge; 73,493 vols; Chair. JOAN MENARD; Dir MARGARET MORRISSEY; Treas. PAULA DACOLES.

John F. Kennedy Presidential Library and Museum: Columbia Point, Boston, MA 02125; tel. (617) 514-1541; e-mail kennedy.library@nara.gov; internet www.jfklibrary.org; f. 1963; colln of textual documents, audiovisual items and museum artefacts of John F. Kennedy, Robert F. Kennedy, Joseph P. Kennedy and Rose Kennedy; 600 other colln incl. Kennedy family mems, authors, politicians and individuals; Ernest Hemingway Colln:MSS materials; 48m. items; Dir THOMAS J. PUTNAM; Museum Curator STACEY BREDHOFF.

Marlborough Public Library: 35 W Main St, Marlborough, MA 01752; tel. (508) 624-6900; e-mail mcardello@marlborough-ma.gov; internet www.marlborough-ma.gov/gen/marlboroughma_publibrary/index; f. 1871; 115,819 vols; Dir SALVATORE GENOVESE.

Massachusetts Historical Society Library: 1154 Boylston St, Boston, MA 02215-3695; tel. (617) 536-1608; fax (617) 859-0074; e-mail library@masshist.org; internet www.masshist.org/library; f. 1791; MSS: letters, diaries, and other personal papers of individuals and families who lived in Massachusetts; many famous documents such as Paul Revere's own account of his famous ride , MSS copies of the Declaration of Independence by both Thomas Jefferson and John Adams; 250,000 vols, 3,600 MSS collns; Chair. WILLIAM C. CLENDANIEL; Librarian PETER DRUMMEY; Librarian STEPHEN T. RILEY; Sec. JOHN F. MOFFITT; Treas. WILLIAM R. COTTER; publs *Proceedings* (1 a year), *The Massachusetts Historical Review* (1 a year).

Massachusetts Institute of Technology Libraries: 14S-216, 77 Massachusetts Ave, Cambridge, MA 02139-4307; tel. (617) 253-5655; fax (617) 253-8894; e-mail diroff-lib@mit.edu; internet libraries.mit.edu; f. 1861; 5 major subject libraries: architecture and planning, engineering, humanities, science, management and social science, as well as 5 specialized libraries and the Institute archives; 3m. vols and pamphlets, 17,000 current journals, 55,000 databases and electronic journals; Dir of Libraries ANN J. WOLPERT.

Salisbury Public Library: 17 Elm St, Salisbury, MA 01952; tel. (978) 465-5071; e-mail librarian@salisburyma.gov; internet www.salisburylibrary.org; f. 1885; provides access to holdings at more than 40 local libraries as well as libraries outside the region; Dir TERRY KYRIOS; Asst Librarian JOAN BOMBA.

Sargent Memorial Library: 427 Massachusetts Ave, Boxborough, MA 01719; tel. (978) 263-4680; fax (978) 263-1275; internet www.boxlib.org; f. 1891, present location 2005; 35,000 vols (incl. books, periodicals, VHS videos, DVDs, music and books on audio cassettes and CDs); Dir MAUREEN STRAPKO.

Springfield City Library: 220 State St, Springfield, MA 01103; tel. (413) 263-6828; fax (413) 263-6817; e-mail askalibrarian@springfieldlibrary.org; internet www.springfieldlibrary.org; f. 1857, present bldg 1912; has 6 brs; 668,856 vols, 32,490 audio recordings, 20,804 video cassettes, 3,933 CD-ROMs, 296 periodicals; Dir EMILY BADER.

State Library of Massachusetts: 24 Beacon St, State House, Room 341, Boston, MA 02133; tel. (617) 727-2590; fax (617) 727-9730; e-mail library.director@state.ma.us; internet www.mass.gov/lib; f. 1826; govt and public affairs library serving information and research needs of the exec. and legislative brs of Massachusetts state govt; depository for printed documents of the same and

for selected fed. documents; collns esp. strong in public law, public affairs, state and local history; 822,083 vols; State Librarian ELVERNOY JOHNSON; publ. *Commonwealth of Massachusetts Publications Received by the State Library* (4 a year).

Waltham Public Library: 735 Main St, Waltham, MA 02451; tel. (781) 314-3425; e-mail waltham@minlib.net; internet www.waltham.lib.ma.us; f. 1865; spec. colln of materials relating to the Waltham Watch Factory and other watch cos; 155,000 vols, 400 magazines or newspapers, 22,000 CDs and 18,000 videos and DVDs; Dir KATE TRANQUADA.

Westfield Athenaeum Library: 6 Elm St, Westfield, MA 01085; tel. (413) 568-7833; fax (413) 568-0988; e-mail cpennington@westath.org; internet www.westath.org; f. 1830; 500 linear ft of maps, drawings, papers, MSS, stereoscopes, Mayoral papers, diaries, business ledgers and emphera giving insight into life in Westfield; Dir CHRISTOPHER LINDQUIST.

Worcester Public Library: 3 Salem Sq., Worcester, MA 01608; tel. (508) 799-1655; internet www.worcpublib.org; f. 1859; 3 sites: main library at Salem Sq., Frances Perkins Library at Greendale and Great Brook Valley Br. Library; largest selective depository of fed. documents in central Massachusetts; 634,000 vols, 14,500 audio cassettes, 15,500 video cassettes and 120,700 microforms; Head Librarian MARK CONTOIS; Pres. KEVIN DOWD; Sec. JYOTI DATTA; Treas. DONNA J. McGRATH.

Michigan

Adams-Pratt Oakland County Law Library: 1200 N Telegraph Rd, Bldg 14E, Pontiac, MI, 48341-0481; tel. (248) 858-0012; fax (248) 858-1536; e-mail lawlib@oakgov.com; internet www.oakgov.com/lawlib; f. 1904, present name 1976; colln incl. Michigan and fed. statutes, digests, reports, Shepard's citators, treatises, law reviews, statutes and case law for all states; Chair. ROBERT GAYLOR; Sec. ROBERT TERA.

Alcona County Library: POB 348, 312 W Main, Harrisville, MI 48740; tel. (989) 724-6796; fax (989) 724-6173; internet library.alcona.lib.mi.us; brs in Harrisville (HQ), Lincoln, Caledonia and Mikado; Dir CAROL LUCK; Chair. PAM KERSTEN.

Ann Arbor District Library System: 343 S Fifth Ave, Ann Arbor, MI 48104; tel. (734) 327-4200; internet www.aadl.org; Downtown library and 4 brs: Malletts Creek, Traverwood, West and Pittsfield; 581,250 vols (incl. books, DVDs, CDs, magazines, CD-Roms, audio books, art prints, pamphlets and maps, language materials); Dir JOSIE PARKER; Pres. MARGARET LEARY; Sec. JAN BARNEY NEWMAN; Treas. BARBARA MURPHY.

Bay County Library System: 500 Center Ave. Bay City, MI 48708; tel. (989) 894-2837; fax (989) 894-2021; e-mail tbirch@baycountylibrary.org; internet www.baycountylibrary.org; 3 br. libraries, 1 main library and a bookmobile; incl. business resource centre and core reference colln; local history and genealogy colln; Dir TOM BIRCH; Chair. MARK KAPLENSKI; Sec. and Treas. ROBERT LA CHANCE.

Brighton District Library: 100 Library Dr., Brighton, MI 48116; tel. (810) 229-6571; internet brightonlibrary.info; serves Brighton, Genoa and Green Oak Townships; Dir Dr NANCY B. JOHNSON; Pres. JEANNETTE HILL; Sec. SALLY McKEE; Treas. JANE PETRIE.

Chelsea District Library: 221 S Main St, Chelsea, MI 48118; tel. (734) 475-8732; fax (734) 475-6190; internet www.chelsea.lib.mi.us; f. 1931, present name and status 2006; serves City of Chelsea, Dexter, Lima, Lyndon and Sylvan townships; 66,142 vols (incl. 54,757 print and 11,088 media materials); Dir WILLIAM H. HARMER; Pres. GARY ZENZ; Sec. DAWN CAPLIS; Treas. MARY BUDZINSKI.

Chippewa River District Library System: 301 S University, Mount Pleasant, MI 48858; tel. (989) 773-3242; fax (989) 772-3280; internet www2.youseemore.com/chippewa; f. 1998; brs incl. Veterans Memorial Library in Mount Pleasant and Faith Johnston Memorial Library in Rosebush; Dir LISE MITCHELL.

Detroit Public Library: 5201 Woodward Ave, Detroit, MI 48202; tel. (313) 481-1300; internet www.detroitpubliclibrary.org; f. 1865, present location 1921; main library and 23 brs and a bookmobile service; spec. collns: Burton Historical Colln (Michigan, Great Lakes and Old North-west Territory), Labor History Colln, Hackley Colln, Nat. Automotive History Colln; 2,655,156 vols, 163,158 maps, 754,397 microforms, 788,464 pictures, 20,000 video cassettes; Dir UZO ONYEMAECHI; Exec. Dir JO ANNE MONDOWNEY; Deputy Dir JULIET MACHIE.

Gerald R. Ford Presidential Library & Museum: 1000 Beal Ave, Ann Arbor, MI 48109; tel. (734) 205-0555; fax (734) 205-0571; e-mail ford.library@nara.gov; internet www.fordlibrarymuseum.gov; f. 1981; presidential papers of Gerald Ford and his White House staff; pre- and post-presidential papers of Gerald Ford; papers of Betty Ford; fed. records; archival materials on US domestic issues, foreign relations, and political affairs during the Cold War era; 25m. pages of memos, letters, meeting notes, reports and historical documents, 450,000 photographs, 787,000 ft motion picture film; Dir ELAINE DIDIER.

Jackson District Library: 244 W Michigan Ave, Jackson, MI 49201; tel. (517) 788-4087; internet www.myjdl.com; f. 1901; 13 brs; 417,200 vols, 25,000 audio CDs, 16,000 video cassettes and DVDs, 700 magazines and newspapers; Dir ISHWAR LAXMINARAYAN; Pres. DEBORAH A. HERBERT; Sec. and Treas. JAMES E. BEST.

Library of Michigan: POB 30007, 702 W Kalamazoo St, Lansing, MI 48909-7507; tel. (517) 373-1580; fax (517) 373-4480; e-mail librarian@michigan.gov; internet www.michigan.gov/libraryofmichigan; f. 1828; attached to Michigan Dept of Education; operates main and law library; specializes in MI history, current information, public policy issues, genealogy, state and fed. govt document depositories; 2.7m. vols; State Librarian NANCY R. ROBERTSON; publs *Directory of Michigan Libraries* (online), *District Library Law*, *Michigan Library Statistics*, *Michigan Public Libraries Data Digest* (1 a year, online).

Michigan State University Libraries: Main Library, 100 Library, East Lansing, MI 48824-1048; tel. (517) 353-8700; fax (517) 432-3532; internet www.lib.msu.edu; f. 1855; br. libraries within main bldg incl. Africana, Digital and Multimedia Center, Fine Arts, Govt Documents, Map Library, Spec. Collns (incl. Chicano and Boricua), Turfgrass Information Center, Vincent Voice Library; br. libraries outside main bldg incl. William C. Gast Business Library (incl. Human Resources and Labor Relations Library), Dubai Library, Engineering Library, Gull Lake Library, Law College Library, Mathematics Library, Veterinary Medical Center Library; Africana Colln, Cesar E. Chavez Colln; 4.5m. vols, 2,600 books, 4,000 current periodicals, 10,000 multimedia items, 3m. govt documents, 119,000 reels of microfilm, 1.1m. microfiche and microcards, 200,000

sheet maps, 4,000 atlases, gazetteers and other reference aids; Dir CLIFFORD H. HAKA.

MLibrary University of Michigan: 818 Hatcher S, Ann Arbor, MI 48109-1190; tel. (734) 764-9356; fax (734) 763-5080; internet www.lib.umich.edu; f. 1817; 20 brs; spec. colln: Dean C. Worcester Philippine History Colln, MSS from the Middle Ages and the Renaissance, works by Copernicus, Kepler, Euclid and Galileo, English and American literature, French historical pamphlets (16th–17th century), Joseph A. Labadie Colln, music and musicology (17th–19th century); 11,357,224 vols, 136,810 current serials, 70,143 audio cassettes, 64,235 film and video material, 348,107 maps, 5,077 linear ft MSS and archives; Univ. Librarian and Dean of Libraries PAUL N. COURANT.

Monroe County Library System: Mary K. Daume Library Service Center, 840 S Roessler St, Monroe, MI 48161; tel. (734) 241-5770; fax (734) 241-4722; internet monroe.lib.mi.us; f. 1934; 16 brs; genealogy colln; depository for fed., state, local and nuclear documents; George Armstrong Custer Colln; Dir NANCY BELLAIRE; Chair. MARYANNE BOURQUE; Sec. ELIZABETH TAYLOR.

Northville District Library: 212 W Cady St, Northville, MI 48167-1560; tel. (248) 349-3020; fax (248) 349-8250; internet www.northville.lib.mi.us; f. 1889, present name and status 1996; Dir JULIE HERRIN; Chair. JOSEPH CORRIVEAU; Sec. MIKE DeFRANCESCO; Treas. JEAN HANSEN.

Salem-South Lyon District Library: 9800 Pontiac Trail, South Lyon, MI 48178; tel. (248) 437-6431; fax (248) 437-6593; internet www.south-lyon.lib.mi.us; f. 1939; 65,546 vols, 1,525 magazines, 6,306 DVDs, 3,422 music CDs, 2,419 audiobooks; Dir DOREEN HANNON; Pres. KEN KNEISEL; Sec. ROBIN WHITE FANNING; Treas. W. DAVID McNEILL.

Wayne State University Libraries: 5150 Anthony Wayne Dr., Detroit, MI 48202; tel. (313) 577-4023; fax (313) 577-5525; e-mail acquisitions@wayne.edu; internet www.lib.wayne.edu; Shiffman Medical Library, Arthur Neef Law Library; spec. colln: Arthur L. Johnson African-American History Colln, Curriculum Guide Colln, Florence Nightingale Colln, Jeheskel (Hezy) Shoshani Library Endowed Colln, Trybom Memorial Colln, Juvenile Colln, Leonard Simons Colln of Rare Michigan History, Kasle Colln, Merrill-Palmer Institute Colln, Mildred Jeffrey Colln of Peace and Conflict Resolution, Millicent A. Wills Colln of Urban Ethnic Materials, Purdy/Kresge Microform Colln, Ramsey Colln of Literature for Young People, William Alfred Boyce Storytelling Colln; 3,665,805 vols, 360,223 e-books, 3,899,273 microforms, 56,346 maps and other cartographic materials, 50,109 audio recordings, 30,604 films and video recordings; Dean of Library Services Dr SANDRA G. YEE.

Minnesota

Duluth Public Library: 520 W Superior St, Duluth, MN 55802; tel. (218) 730-4200; fax (218) 723-3822; e-mail webmail@duluth.lib.mn.us; internet www.duluth.lib.mn.us; 2 brs; 620,101 vols, incl. 414,007 books and bound serials; Pres. DANIEL D'ALLAIRD; Library Man. CARLA POWERS.

East Central Regional Library: 244 S Birch St, Cambridge, MN 55008; tel. (763) 689-7390; fax (763) 689-7389; e-mail ecregion@ecrl.lib.mn.us; internet ecrl.lib.mn.us; 14 brs; bookmobile services; 396,800 ; Dir BARBARA MISSELT; Pres. WAYNE ZAUDTKE; Sec. JAMES RAISANEN; Treas. CHARLOTTE KRAMERS-MEIER.

Gilbert Public Library: POB 758, 17 N Broadway, Gilbert, MN 55741; tel. (218) 748-

2230; fax (218) 748-2229; e-mail illgil@arrowhead.lib.mn.us; internet www.gilbert.lib.mn.us; mem. of Arrowhead Library System; Chair. ROCCO LEONI; Dir NICK PRIEVE; Sec. JUDY THORSON.

Great River Regional Library: 1300 W Saint Germain St, St Cloud, MN 56301; tel. (320) 650-2500; internet www.griver.org; f. 1969; 32 brs; 955,483 vols; Dir KIRSTY SMITH; Pres. GERALD RUDA; Sec. LOUISE KUESTER; Treas. SPENCER BUERKLE.

Hennepin County Library: 12601 Ridgedale Dr., Minnetonka, MN 55305-1909; tel. (612) 543-8500; internet www.hclib.org; f. 1922, merged with Minneapolis Public Library (f. 1885) 2008; 41 brs; 5m. vols, CDs, DVDs, electronic resources; Dir LOIS LANGER THOMPSON.

James Jerome Hill Reference Library: 80 W Fourth St, Saint Paul, MN 55102; tel. (651) 265-5500; e-mail info@jjhill.org; internet www.jjhill.org; f. 1921; applied business and commerce; 240,000 vols (incl. business books, magazines, industry reports); Chair. GREG HEINEMANN; Dir of Library Services NIKKI MARCHAND.

Lake Agassiz Regional Library: POB 900, Moorhead, MN 56561-0900; 118 Fifth St S, Moorhead, MN 56560-2756; tel. (218) 233-3757; fax (218) 233-7556; internet larl.org; f. 1961; 13 brs; 300,000 vols; Regional Library Dir KATHY FREDETTE.

Marshall-Lyon County Public Library: 201 C St, Marshall, MN 56258; tel. (507) 537-7003; e-mail library@marshalllyonlibrary.org; internet www.marshalllyonlibrary.org; 2 brs; Dir HOLLY MARTIN HUFFMAN; Pres. PAM SUKALSKI; Treas. MARK GOODENOW.

Minnesota Historical Society Library: 345 Kellogg Blvd, W, Saint Paul, MN 55102-1906; tel. (651) 259-3300; fax (651) 297-7436; e-mail reference@mnhs.org; internet www.mnhs.org/library; f. 1849; N American history particularly relating to Minnesota and the Upper Midwest (esp. travel accounts, fur trade, Scandinavian and other immigration, labour, political and church history, railway records, local history and genealogy); 500,000 vols, 95m. MSS pages, 4,000 govt documents, 950,000 artefacts of archeology, 6,000 paintings, prints and drawings; Dir for Library and Collns JENNIFER JONES.

Minnesota State Archives: c/o Minnesota Historical Soc., 345 W Kellogg Blvd, St. Paul, MN 55102-1906; tel. (651) 259-3260; fax (651) 296-9961; internet www.mnhs.org/preserve/records; f. 1913; attached to Minnesota Historical Soc.; identifies, collects and preserves historically valuable records of 4,000 units of state and local govt; colln from exec. br. of state, legislative and judicial brs and local govt; local history colln; State Archivist SHAWN ROUNDS.

Minnesota State Law Library: Room G25, Minnesota Judicial Center, 25 Rev Dr Martin Luther King Jr, Blvd, St Paul, MN 55155; tel. (651) 296-2775; fax (651) 296-6740; e-mail askalibrarian@courts.state.mn.us; internet www.lawlibrary.state.mn.us; f. 1849; incl. 16 co law libraries; Marvin R. Anderson Spec. Collns Room: trials of American and British, France, Germany and fmr Soviet Union and series British notable trials; 400,000 vols; State Law Librarian JUDY REHAK (acting).

Minnesota State University Library: POB 8419, Mankato, MN 56002-8419; tel. (507) 389-5952; fax (507) 389-5155; internet lib.mnsu.edu; depository for state documents, nat. govt documents, US geological survey maps; univ. archives and Southern Minnesota Historical Center; Marilyn J. Lass Center for Minnesota Studies; 1.2m. vols,

55,000 periodicals (incl. print and electronic); Dean of Library Services JOAN ROCA.

Rochester Public Library: 101 Second St, SE, Rochester, MN 55904; tel. (507) 328-2310; internet www.rochesterpubliclibrary .org; f. 1865; 437,815 vols; Dir AUDREY S. BETCHER; Pres. DIANE MOENCH; Sec. JANICE M. ENGBERG.

Saint Paul Public Library: 90 W Fourth St, Saint Paul, MN 55102; tel. (651) 266-7000; fax (651) 266-7060; e-mail spplweb@ci .stpaul.mn.us; internet www.sppl.org; f. 1856; central library, 12 brs and a book-mobile; fed. depository; 1,131,578 vols; Dir KIT HADLEY.

Two Harbors Public Library: 320 Water-front Dr., Two Harbors, MN 55616; tel. (218) 834-3148; e-mail thpl@arrowhead.lib.mn.us; internet www.two-harbors.lib.mn.us; f. 1896, fmrly Carnegie Library; Archive Room holds scrapbooks, history and local newspapers dating back to the late 1890s; mem. of Arrowhead Library System; 30,000 vols; Pres. TONY LOCKHART; Sec. PATRICIA TOFTE.

University of Minnesota Libraries: 499 Wilson Library, 309 19th Ave S, Minneapolis, MN 55455; tel. (612) 626-2227; fax (612) 626-9353; e-mail infopoint@umn.edu; internet www.lib.umn.edu; f. 1851; gen. and 14 departmental libraries; spec. collns: law, immigration history, social welfare history, data processing, medicine, children's literature, horticulture, literary MSS; 7,111,311 vols, 109,681 serial subscriptions; Univ. Librarian Prof. WENDY PRADT LOUGEE; publ. *continuum* (1 a year).

Washington County Law Library: Washington County Courthouse, 14949 62nd St N, Room 1005, Stillwater, MN 55082; tel. (651) 430-6330; fax (651) 430-6331; e-mail lawlibrary@co.washington.mn .us; internet www.co.washington.mn.us/ info_for_residents/law_library; f. 1956; primary sources of Minnesota state law, fed. law, Wisconsin statutes annotated, Wisconsin rules of court, Wisconsin practice materials, Treatises, CLEs, form books, practice manuals, jury instructions and periodicals; Law Librarian BRIAN R. HUFFMAN; Law Librarian PATRICIA DOLAN.

Mississippi

Bolivar County Library System: 104 S Leflore Ave, Cleveland, MS 38732; tel. (662) 843-2774; fax (662) 843-4701; internet www .bolivar.lib.ms.us; f. 1958; brs: Robinson-Carpenter Memorial Library (HQ), Dr Robert T. Hollingsworth Public Library, Mound Bayou Public Library, Thelma Rayner Memorial Library, Rosedale Public Library, Gunnison Public Library, Benoit Public Library and Field Memorial Library; Dir LYNN F. SHURDEN.

Central Mississippi Regional Library System: POB 1749, Brandon, MS 39043; 100 Tamberline St, Brandon, MS 39042; tel. (601) 825-0100; fax (601) 825-0199; e-mail custsvc@cmrls.lib.ms.us; internet www.cmrls .lib.ms.us; 20 br. libraries in Rankin, Scott, Simpson and Smith counties; Dir KAILEEN THIELING.

Dixie Regional Library System: 111 N Main St, Pontotoc, MS 38863; tel. (662) 489-3960; fax 662) 489-7777; e-mail jmcneece@ dixie.lib.ms.us; internet www.dixie.lib.ms.us; library services in Pontotoc, Calhoun and Chickasaw counties; Dir JUDY McNEECE.

Hancock County Library System: 312 Highway 90, Bay St Louis, MS 39520; tel. (228) 467-5282; e-mail info@hancocklibraries .info; internet www.hancock.lib.ms.us; f. 1934, present status 1965; brs: Bay St Louis-Hancock County Library, Kiln Public Library, Pearlington Public Library and

Waveland Public Library; Chair. DOLLY LUNNDBERG; Exec. Dir PATTY FURR.

Jackson/Hinds Library System: 300 N State St, Jackson, MS 39201; tel. (601) 968-5811; fax (601) 968-5817; e-mail reference@ jhlibrary.com; internet www.jhlibrary.com; f. 1986; 14 brs and a main library; Margaret Walker Alexander Library incl. spec. colln of African-American history; 639,253 vols (incl. books, video cassettes, audio cassettes, CDs and multimedia kits); Exec. Dir CAROLYN McCALLUM; Chair. LOUIS WRIGHT; Sec. ROSA-LYN SYLVESTER; Treas. MARIA L. BROWN.

Laurel-Jones County Library System, Inc.: 530 Commerce St, Laurel, MS 39440-3998; tel. (601) 428-4313; fax (601) 428-0597; internet www.laurel.lib.ms.us; f. 1919 as Laurel Library Asscn, present location 1979; Laurel Jones Co Library (HQ) and Ellisville Public Library br.; Dir MARY LOUISE BRELAND.

Madison County Library System: 102 Priestly St, Canton, MS 39046; tel. (601) 859-3202; fax (601) 859-2728; e-mail feedback@mcls.ms; internet www.mcls.ms; brs: Canton, Camden, Flora, Madison and Ridgeland; Dir SANDRA SANDERS.

Meridian Lauderdale County Public Library: 2517 Seventh St, Meridian, MS 39301; tel. (601) 693-6771; fax (601) 486-2260; e-mail library@meridian.lib.ms.us; internet www.meridian.lib.ms.us; f. 1913; 192 magazine subscriptions and 31 local, state and nat. newspapers; microfilm edns of periodicals, incl. the *Meridian Star* dating 1898; Chair. J. D. WATSON.

Noxubee County Public Library: 103 E King St, Macon, MS 39341; tel. (662) 726-5461; internet www.noxubee.lib.ms.us; f. 1984; brs: Macon, Brooksville and Shuqualak; Harold Gibson Brown Research colln; Dir SHAMEKA CONNER.

Pearl River County Library System: 900 Goodyear Blvd, Picayune, MS 39466; tel. (601) 798-5081; fax (601) 798-5082; internet www.pearlriver.lib.ms.us; f. 1974; Margaret Reed Crosby Memorial Library & Cultural Center (HQ) and Poplarville Public Library; Dir LINDA TUFARO.

Starkville-Oktibbeha County Library System: 326 Univ. Dr, Starkville, MS 39759; tel. (662) 323-2766; fax (662) 323-9140; internet www.starkville.lib.ms.us; brs: Maben and Sturgis; Dir VIRGINIA HOLTCAMP.

Warren County-Vicksburg Public Library: 700 Veto St, Vicksburg, MS 39180; tel. (601) 636-6411; internet www .warren.lib.ms.us; f. 1916, present status 1986; incl. genealogy items, newspapers and local history materials; Dir DEB MITCHELL.

Washington County Library System: 341 Main St, Greenville, MS 38701; tel. (662) 335-2331; fax (662) 390-4758; e-mail wash-ref@washington.lib.ms.us; internet www.washington.lib.ms.us; f. 1967; brs: Greenville (HQ), Arcola, Avon, Glen Allan, Hollandale, Metcalfe and Leland; Dir K. CLANTON; Chair. JAMES SCOTT; Sec. MARGIE JOHNSON.

Waynesboro-Wayne County Library System: 1103A Mississippi Dr., Waynesboro, MS 39367-2415; tel. (866) 735-2268; fax (601) 735-6407; e-mail wlib@wwcls.lib.ms.us; internet www.wwcls.lib.ms.us; f. 1934; genealogy colln incl. books, periodicals and family histories; 3,508 video/DVD colln, 880 audio titles; Dir PATSY C. BREWER; Pres. BECKY RHINEHART.

Missouri

Adair County Public Library: One Library Lane, Kirksville, MO 63501; tel. (660) 665-6038; fax (660) 627-0028; e-mail

acpl@adairco.org; internet www2 .youseemore.com/adaircpl; f. 1986; Dir GLENDA HUNT; Pres. RON BRAND; Sec. SANDRA FLEAK; Treas. MARK LAUGHLIN.

Barry-Lawrence Regional Library: 213 Sixth St, Monett, MO 65708; tel. (417) 235-6646; fax (417) 235-6799; e-mail monett@ blrlibrary.org; internet www2.youseemore .com/blrl; 10 br. libraries in Barry and Lawrence counties; HQ at Monett Br. Library; Dir GINA MILBURN; Pres. ANN HALL; Sec. and Treas. FELICITY NESBITT.

Boonslick Regional Library: 219 W Third St, Sedalia, MO 65301; tel. (660) 827-7111; fax (660) 827-4668; internet brl.lib.mo.us; brs at Benton, Cooper and Pettis counties; bookmobile services; Dir LINDA ALLCORN.

Daniel Boone Regional Library: POB 1267, 100 W Broadway, Columbia, MO 65205-1267; tel. (573) 443-3161; fax (573) 443-3281; internet www.dbrl.org; f. 1959; Columbia Public Library (HQ); incl. Callaway County Public Library and Southern Boone County Public Library; bookmobile services; 549,502 vols; Dir MELISSA CARR; Pres. SUSAN DALY; Sec. JESSICA ROBINSON.

Dunklin County Library: 209 N Main, Kennett, MO 63857; tel. (573) 888-3561; fax (573) 888-6393; internet dunklin-co.lib.mo .us; 8 brs; genealogy colln; 140,000 vols; Dir JONELL MINTON; Pres. Dr LEWIS E. AUKES; Sec. LEON GODLEY; Treas. BILL BRIGANCE.

Harry S. Truman Library and Museum: 500 W US Highway 24, Independence, MO 64050-798; tel. (816) 268-8200; fax (816) 268-8295; e-mail truman.library@nara.gov; internet www.trumanlibrary.org; f. 1957; administered by the Nat. Archives and Records Admin.; 30,000 objects in museum related to Truman and his family; 15m. pages of MSS, 6,500,000 White House files, 112,000 photographs, 1,000 hours of audio disc and tape recordings, 400 motion pictures, 75 hours of video cassette recordings, 30,000 books, 10,000 serials, 1,400 microfilm copies of printed materials; Dir Dr MICHAEL J. DEVINE.

Jefferson County Library: 5678 State Rd PP, High Ridge, MO 63049; tel. (636) 677-8689; fax (636) 677-1769; e-mail info@ jeffersoncountylibrary.org; internet www .jeffersoncountylibrary.org; f. 1983; 3 brs; Dir PAM KLIPSCH; Pres. RETTA TUGGLE; Sec. BILL BUOL; Treas. SHARON REINERI.

Kansas City Public Library: 14 W 10th St, Kansas City, MO 64105; tel. (816) 701-3400; fax (816) 701-3401; internet www.kclibrary .org; f. 1873 as Public School Library of Kansas City; a central library and 9 brs; spec. historical collns incl. the Missouri Valley Colln (local history), Ramos Colln (African American history) and Western expansion materials; 2,326,922 vols; Exec. Dir R. CROSBY KEMPER, III; Deputy Exec. Dir CHEP-TOO KOSITANY-BUCKNER.

Linda Hall Library: 5109 Cherry St, Kansas City, MO 64110-2498; tel. (816) 363-4600; fax (816) 926-8790; e-mail library@ lindahall.org; internet www.lindahall.org; f. 1946; ind., non-profit, public access science, engineering and technology library, specializing in periodicals and scientific and technical research materials; document supplier; fee-based literature search services; 1m. vols, 12,330 current periodicals, 47,425 total serial titles, 528,000 monographs, 1,550,000 govt-contracted technical reports, incl. 70,000 maps, 170,000 standards and specifications, History of Science Colln (10,000 vols), US patent and trademark colln; Pres. LISA BROWAR.

Livingston County Library: 450 Locust St, Chillicothe, MO 64601; tel. (660) 646-

0547; fax (660) 646-5504; e-mail librarian@ livingstoncountylibrary.org; internet www .livingstoncountylibrary.org; f. 1920; 50,000 vols; Dir ROBIN WESTPHAL; Pres. MARION HARTER; Sec. MARGARET VANCE; Treas. LINDY CHAPMAN.

Missouri State Archives: POB 1747, 600 West Main St, Jefferson City, MO 65102; tel. (573) 751-3280; fax (573) 526-7333; e-mail archref@sos.mo.gov; internet www.sos.mo .gov/archives; f. 1965; official repository for state records of permanent and historical value; holdings date from 1770 and incl. exec., legislative and judicial records, records of state depts and agencies, land records, military records, state publ, photographic collns, co and municipal records on microfilm and MSS and reference collns; 336m. pages of paper, 400,000 photographs, 9,000 maps, 61,000 reels of microfilm, 560 cubic ft of published state documents and 1,000 audio-video items; State Archivist JOHN DOUGAN.

Missouri State Library: POB 387, 600 W Main St, Jefferson City, MO 65101; tel. (573) 751-0586; fax (573) 751-3612; e-mail mostlib@sos.mo.gov; internet www.sos.mo .gov/library; f. 1945; provides service in support of exec. and legislative brs of Missouri state govt; 80,000 vols, 495 periodicals, Wolfner Library of 360,000 vols and 70 periodicals; spec. colln: Missouri state documents; State Librarian MARGARET M. CON-ROY; publ. *Show Me Express* (52 a year).

MU Libraries University of Missouri: 104 Ellis Library, Columbia, MO 65201-5149; tel. (573) 882-4701; fax (573) 882-8044; internet mulibraries.missouri.edu; f. 1839; 6 brs; spec. collns of Western historical MSS and Missouriana; 3,152,151 vols, 33,000 periodicals, 7,518,745 microform units, 1,685,351 govt documents, 12,609 MSS and archives, 26,656 audio cassettes, 5,782 film and video materials; Dir of Libraries JAMES COGSWELL.

Riverside Regional Library: POB 389, 1997 E Jackson Blvd, Jackson, MO 63755; tel. (573) 243-8141; fax (573) 243-8142; e-mail librarylady98@gmail.com; internet www.riversideregionallibrary.org; 5 brs; Dir NANCY HOWLAND.

St Charles City-County Library District: POB 529, 77 Boone Hills Dr., St Peters, MO 63376; tel. (636) 441-2300; fax (636) 441-3132; internet www.youranswerplace.org; f. 1973 by merger of Kathryn Linnemann Library of St Charles with St Charles Co Library Dist.; 3 regional brs incl. larger collns and subject specialists; 4 gen. purpose brs; 2 Library Express; 3 mini brs in remote areas; spec. colln of local history and genealogy, business and public management, consumer health and govt documents; 1,079,783 vols (incl. 839,234 books, 64,070 DVDs, 64,112 CDs, 44,966 magazines, 4,907 govt documents, 26,522 e-documents, 9,356 e-books); Dir JIM BROWN; Pres. MYRA CROOK; Sec. MARY REESE; Treas. JOHN THOELKE.

St Louis County Library: 1640 S Lindbergh Blvd, St Louis, MO 63131-3598; tel. (314) 994-3300; e-mail reference@slcl.org; internet www.slcl.org; f. 1946; 20 brs and 19 bookmobiles; 1,986,576 vols, (incl. 1367736 books, 216,946 audiovisual materials, 141,098 govt documents, 33,731 periodicals, 214,887 microform units); Dir CHARLES PACE; Pres. LYNN BECKWITH, JR; Sec. Dr CHINGLING TAI; Treas. KENNETH STRICKER; publ. *PastPorts* (12 a year, online).

St Louis Public Library: 1301 Olive St, St Louis, MO 63103-2389; tel. (314) 241-2288; fax (314) 539-0393; e-mail webref@slpl.org; internet www.slpl.org; f. 1865 as Public School Library Soc. of St. Louis; 15 brs; Fed. Documents Depository since 1866; spec.

collns incl. the Julia Davis Colln (African American history and culture), genealogical sources dating from 1902, Steedman Colln (architecture); 4,702,299 vols; Exec. Dir WALLER McGUIRE; Pres. JACQUE LAND; publ. *Missouri Union List of Serial Publications*.

Saint Louis University Library: 3650 Lindell Blvd, St Louis, MO 63108; tel. (314) 977-3087; fax (314) 977-3108; e-mail piusref@ slu.edu; internet libraries.slu.edu; f. 1818; Omer Poos Law Library, Pius XII Memorial Library, Medical Center Library; Knights of Columbus Vatican Film Library (microfilm colln of medieval and renaissance MSS studies), univ. archives; spec. colln: MSS (Walter J. Ong colln, Tristan da Cunha colln), rare books (16th–19th century theology, church history, patristics, Jesuitica); 1,849,584 vols, 105,559 maps; Asst Vice-Pres. for Univ. Libraries Dr GAIL M. STAINES; publ. *Manuscripta* (2 a year).

Springfield-Greene County Library District: POB 760, 4653 S Campbell Ave, Springfield, MO 65801-0760; tel. (417) 883-5366; fax (417) 889-2547; e-mail humanresources@thelibrary.org; internet thelibrary.org; f. 1971 by merger of Greene Co Library (f. 1945) with Springfield Public Library (f. 1905); 10 br. libraries; bookmobile services; 550,000 vols; Exec. Dir REGINA GREER COOPER; Pres. LESLIE CARRIER; Sec. MARTHA CRISE; Treas. KIM KOLLMEYER.

Montana

Belgrade Community Library: 106 N Broadway, Belgrade, MT 59714; tel. (406)388-4346; fax (406)388-6586; internet www.belgradelibrary.org; f. 1932; 35,000 vols; Dir GALE BACON.

Bozeman Public Library: 626 E Main St, Bozeman, MT 59715; tel. (406) 582-2400; fax (406) 582-2424; internet www .bozemanlibrary.org; 133,055 vols; Dir SUSAN GREGORY.

Kohrs Memorial Library: 501 Missouri Ave, Deer Lodge, MT 59722-1152; tel. (406) 846-2622; e-mail wkkohrs@mtlib.org; internet kohrslibrary.org; Library Dir KATHY MORA.

Lewis & Clark Library: 120 S Last Chance Gulch, Helena, MT 59601; tel. (406) 447-1690; fax (406) 447-1687; internet www .lewisandclarklibrary.org; f. 1868; 3 brs; 115,000 vols; Dir JUDY HART.

Missoula Public Library: 301 E Main, Missoula, MT 59802; tel. (406) 721-2665; fax (406) 728-5900; e-mail mslaplib@missoula.lib .mt.us; internet missoulalibrary.com; f. 1894; 5 brs and 1 bookmobile; also provides Web on Wheels Bus services; Dir HONORE BRAY.

Montana State Library: POB 201800, 1515 E Sixth Ave, Helena MT 59620-1800; tel. (406) 444-3115; fax (406) 444-0266; e-mail msl@mt.gov; internet msl.mt.gov; State Librarian JENNIE STAPP.

Parmly Billings Library: 510 N Broadway, Billings, MT 59101; tel. (406) 657-8258; e-mail circdesk@ci.billings.mt.us; internet ci .billings.mt.us; f. 1901; Library Dir BILL COCHRAN.

Nebraska

Kilgore Memorial Library: 520 Nebraska Ave, York, NE 68467-3035; tel. (402) 363-2620; internet yorklib.org; f. 1885, present name and status 1986; 75,000 vols; Dir STAN SCHULZ; Pres. LEONARD HOSKINS.

Lincoln City Libraries: 136 S, 14th St, Third Fl., Lincoln, NE 68508-1899; tel. (402) 441-8500; e-mail library@lincolnlibraries .org; internet www.lincolnlibraries.org; 7 brs and 1 bookmobile; 903,992 vols; Dir PAT LEACH; Pres. MAJA HARRIS.

Link Library: Concordia Univ., 800 N Columbia Ave, Seward, NE 68434; tel. (402) 643-7254; e-mail library@cune.edu; internet www.cune.edu/academics/library; f. 1960; attached to Concordia Univ.; 230,000 vols; Dir of Library Services PHILIP HENDRICKSON.

Morton-James Public Library: 923 First Corso, Nebraska City, NE 68410; tel. (402) 873-5609; e-mail mlibrary@neb.rr.com; internet www.morton-jamespubliclibrary .com; f. 1867; 64,760 vols; Dir BARBARA HEGR; Pres. CAROL BOYCE.

Nebraska State Historical Society Library and Archives: POB 82554, 1500 R St, Lincoln, NE 68501; tel. (402) 471-4751; fax (402) 471-3100; e-mail nshs.libarch@ nebraska.gov; internet www.nebraskahistory .org/lib-arch; incl. Dept of Public Instruction Reports, govt and prison records, State Newspaper Project; newspapers dating back to 1854; archival collns incl. state and local govt records, incl. those of most Nebraska governors; photographs incl. sod house images taken by Solomon D. Butcher; private MSS collns incl. famous Nebraskans (Willa Cather, John Falter); 80,000 vols, 3,000 maps and atlases, 2,500 MSS, 500,000 photographs; Assoc. Dir ANDREA FALING.

Nebraska State Library: POB 98931, State Capitol Bldg, 15th and K Sts, Room 325, Third Fl., Lincoln, NE 68509-8931; tel. (402) 471-3189; fax (402) 471-1011; e-mail nsc .lawlibrary@nebraska.gov; internet supremecourt.ne.gov/state-library; f. 1855; attached to Nebraska Supreme Court; reference and research library serving Nebraska Supreme Court, Nebraska Court of Appeals, attorneys within the State of Nebraska, mems of Nebraska Legislature, mems of other state agencies, prose litigants and gen. public; 130,000 vols.

Newman Grove Public Library: POB 430, 615 Hale Ave, Newman Grove, NE 68758; tel. (402) 447-2331; e-mail ngpl@megavision.com; internet www.megavision.net/ngpl; f. 1923; 14,000 vols; Dir ARDIS VON SEGGERN; Pres. BRUCE BACKHAUS; Sec. MARY ROBERG.

North Platte Public Library: 120 W Fourth St, North Platte, NE 69101; tel. (308) 535-8036; fax (308) 535-8296; e-mail library@ci.north-platte.ne.us; internet www .ci.north-platte.ne.us/library; Dir CECELIA LAWRENCE.

Omaha Public Library: 215 S. 15th St, Omaha, NE 68102; tel. (402) 444-4833; internet www.omahapubliclibrary.org; 11 brs; HQ in W. Dale Clark Main Library; Dir GARY WASDIN; Pres. STUART CHITTENDEN; Sec. MARY A. HOLLAND.

University of Nebraska Libraries: POB 884100, 318 Love Library, Univ. of Nebraska-Lincoln, Lincoln, NE 68588-4100; tel. (402) 472-2526; internet libraries.unl .edu; 6 brs; spec. colln of MSS, univ. records and rare book collns; 3,500,601 vols, 39,000 serial subscriptions; Dean of Libraries Prof. Dr JOAN R. GIESECKE.

Wayne Public Library: 410 Pearl St, Wayne, NE 68787; tel. (402) 375-3135; fax (402) 375-5772; internet www.cityofwayne .org; f. 1902, present status 1910; Dir LAURAN LOFGREN; Pres. JOEL ANKENY; Sec. MOLLIE SPIEKER.

Nevada

Boulder City Library: 701 Adams Blvd, Boulder City, NV 89005; tel. (702) 293-1281; fax (702) 293-0239; internet bclibrary.org; Chair. AMY CARVALHO; Dir LYNN.

Elizabeth Sturm Library: Truckee Meadows Community College, 7000 Dandini Blvd, SIER LIB, Reno, NV 89512-3999; tel. (775) 674-7600; fax (775) 673-8231; internet www.tmcc.edu/library; f. 1971, present name 1988; attached to Truckee Meadows Community College; 20,000 vols; Library Dir MICHELLE NOEL.

Elko-Lander-Eureka County Library System: 720 Court St, Elko, NV 89801; tel. (775) 738-3066; fax (775) 738-8262; internet www.elkocountylibrary.org; 11 brs; Library Dir JEANETTE HAMMONS.

Great Basin College Library: McMullen Hall, 1500 College Parkway, Elko, NV 89801; tel. (775) 753-2222; internet www.gbcnv.edu/library; depository for govt documents; Library Dir DAVID ELLEFSEN.

Las Vegas-Clark County Library District: 7060 W Windmill Lane, Las Vegas, NV 89113; tel. (702) 734-7323; fax (702) 507-6187; e-mail administration@lvccld.org; internet www.lvccld.org; 25 brs; 2.7m. vols; Exec. Dir JEANNE GOODRICH.

Pahrump Community Library: 701 E St, Pahrump, NV 89048; tel. (775) 727-5930; fax (775) 727-6209; e-mail director@pahrumplibrary.com; internet www.pahrumplibrary.com; f. 1978 as Doris, Shirky Community Library.

Washoe County Law Library: Second Judicial District Court, 75 Court St, Room 101, Reno, NV 89501; tel. (775) 328-3250; internet www.co.washoe.nv.us; partial selective depository for US govt documents.

Washoe County Library: 301 S Center St, Reno, NV 89501; tel. (775) 327-8341; fax (775) 327-8393; e-mail libraryboard@washoecounty.us; internet www.washoecounty.us; f. 1904; Dir ARNIE MAURINS.

New Hampshire

Amherst Town Library: 14 Main St, Amherst, NH 03031; tel. (603) 673-2288; fax (603) 672-6063; e-mail library@amherst.lib.nh.us; internet www.amherst.lib.nh.us; f. 1892; Archives Room colln incl. historical items on Amherst and New Hampshire; 70,000 vols; Dir AMY LAPOINTE; Chair. DONALD HOLDEN; Sec. HELEN ROWE; Treas. RICHARD MARTINI.

Bedford Public Library: Three Meetinghouse Rd, Bedford, NH 03110; tel. (603) 472-2300; fax (603) 472-2978; internet www.bedford.lib.nh.us; Dir MARY ANN SENATRO; Chair. EDWARD MORAN; Treas. ANTHONY FREDERICK.

Derry Public Library: 64 E Broadway, Derry, NH 03038; tel. (603) 432-6140; fax (603) 432-6128; e-mail derrylib@derrypl.org; internet www.derry.lib.nh.us; f. 1905; Dir CHERYL LYNCH; Chair. ELIZABETH IVES; Sec. JOAN CRIMLISK; Treas. JACK ROBILLARD.

Dover Public Library: 73 Locust St, Dover, NH 03820-3753; tel. (603) 516-6050; fax (603) 516-6053; e-mail libraryquestions@dover.nh.gov; internet www.dover.lib.nh.us; f. 1883; historical photographs colln of Dover; Dir CATHLEEN BEAUDOIN.

Durham Public Library: Seven Mill Rd Unit H, Durham, NH 03824; tel. (603) 868-6699; fax (603) 868-9944; e-mail durhampl@gmail.com; internet www.durhampubliclibrary.org; f. 1900; Dir THOMAS MADDEN; Chair. DOUGLAS BENCKS; Sec. SIBYLLE CARLSON; Treas. ROBIN BALDUCCI.

Hollis Social Library: POB 659, Hollis, NH 03049-0659; Two Monument Sq., Hollis, NH 03049-0659; tel. (603) 465-7721; fax (603) 465-3507; e-mail helpdesk@hollislibrary.org; internet www.hollislibrary.org; f. 1799; colln. incl. reference section on genealogy; maps and history of Hollis and New Hampshire; Dir LUCINDA MAZZA; Chair. ROBERT BARTIS; Sec. JONE LABOMBARD; Treas. MARCIA BECKETT.

Hooksett Public Library: 31 Mount St Marys Way, Hooksett, NH 03106; tel. (603) 485-6092; fax (603) 485-6193; e-mail hplbooks@hooksettlibrary.org; internet www.hooksett.lib.nh.us; Dir HEATHER SHUMWAY; Chair. MARY FARWELL; Sec. TAMMY HOOKER; Treas. BARBARA DAVIS.

Howe Library: 13 S St, Hanover, NH 03755; tel. (603) 640-3267; e-mail reference@thehowe.org; internet www.thehowe.org; f. 1900; 73,000 vols; Dir MARY WHITE.

Keene Public Library: 60 Winter St, Keene, NH 03431; tel. (603) 352-0157; internet www.keenepubliclibrary.org; f. 1801; colln incl. large print books and New Hampshire town histories; Keene Sentinel microfilm from 1799 to present; full text of the New York Times from 1851 to present (online); 130,000 vols; Dir NANCY VINCENT; Pres. DON WILMETH; Sec. JOE DUMOND; Treas. HOPE THERRIEN.

Kelley Library: 234 Main St, Salem, NH 03079; tel. (603) 898-7064; e-mail kelleylb@kelleylibrary.org; internet www.kelleylibrary.org; f. 1894; colln incl. local histories, town reports, and local and state govt documents; 112,391 vols, 297 magazines and newspapers, 4,105 music CDs and other electronic media, 2,838 audio books, 7,038 video cassettes and DVDs; Dir ALISON BAKER; Chair. MARTHA BREEN; Treas. KATE NORTON.

Lane Memorial Library: Two Academy Ave, Hampton, NH 03842; tel. (603) 926-3368; fax (603) 926-1348; e-mail library@hampton.lib.nh.us; internet www.hampton.lib.nh.us; f. 1881; local history colln; Dir AMANDA REYNOLDS COOPER; Chair. LINDA SADLOCK; Sec. ROBERT LAMOTHE; Treas. MARY LOU HERAN.

Manchester City Library: 405 Pine St, Manchester, NH 03104; tel. (603) 624-6550; internet www.manchesternh.gov; f. 1854; Manchester City Library (HQ) and W Community Br. Library; 350,000 vols; Dir DENISE VAN ZANTEN; Chair. JOANNE BARRETT; Sec. KAREN SHEEHAN LORD; Treas. JEFF HICKOK.

Merrimack Public Library: 470 Daniel Webster Highway, Merrimack, NH 03054; tel. (603) 424-5021; e-mail mmkpl@merrimack.lib.nh.us; internet www.merrimack.lib.nh.us; f. 1892; colln incl. rare New Hampshire books, town histories and local archives; 85,326 vols; Dir JANET ANGUS.

New Hampshire Law Library: Supreme Court Bldg, One Charles Doe Dr., Concord, NH 03301; tel. (603) 271-3777; fax (603) 513-5450; e-mail lawlibrary@courts.state.nh.us; internet www.courts.state.nh.us/lawlibrary/index.htm; f. 1816, present name and status 1994; depository for US govt documents; legal information and related services to judicial, legislative and exec. brs of govt; 94,000 vols; Dir MARY S. SEARLES.

New Hampshire State Library: 20 Park St, Concord, NH 03301-6314; tel. (603) 271-2392; fax (603) 271-6826; internet www.nh.gov/nhsl; f. 1717, present building 1895; spec. collns of historical children's books, New Hampshire govt, town records and history; 600,000 vols; State Librarian MICHAEL C. YORK.

Pelham Public Library: 24 Village Green, Pelham, NH 03076-3172; tel. (603) 635-7581; e-mail librarydirector@pelhamweb.com; internet pelhampubliclibrary.org; f. 1893; 30,000 vols; Dir ROBERT (BOB) RICE JR; Chair. FRANCIS (FRAN) GARBOSKI; Sec. DIANE CHUBB; Treas. SUSAN SNIDE.

Portsmouth Public Library: 175 Parrott Ave, Portsmouth, NH 03801; tel. (603) 427-1540; fax (603) 433-0981; e-mail info@lib.cityofportsmouth.com; internet www.cityofportsmouth.com/library; f. 1881; Dir MARY ANN LIST; Chair. JODY RECORD; Sec. GRACE LESSNER; Treas. JOHN O'LEARY.

Richards Free Library: 58 N Main St, Newport, NH 03773; tel. (603) 863-3430; e-mail rfl@newport.lib.nh.us; internet www.newport.lib.nh.us; f. 1888; Dir ANDREA THORPE.

Rye Public Library: 581 Washington Rd, Rye, NH 03870; tel. (603) 964-8401; fax (603) 964-7065; e-mail contact@ryepubliclibrary.org; internet www.ryepubliclibrary.org; f. 1911; Dir ANDREW RICHMOND; Chair. KAREN W. OLIVER; Sec. BILL MCDADE; Treas. GARRY LAYMAN.

Seabrook Library: 25 Liberty Lane, Seabrook, NH 03874; tel. (603) 474-2044; fax (603) 474-1835; e-mail ocean@sealib.org; internet www.sealib.org; 47,000 vols; Dir ANN ROBINSON.

Wadleigh Memorial Library: 49 Nashua St, Milford, NH 03055; tel. (603) 673-2408; fax (603) 672-6064; e-mail wadleigh@wadleighlibrary.org; internet www.wadleighlibrary.org; 70,000 vols and 200 magazines and newspapers, 2,000 CDs, 3,000 video cassettes and DVDs; Dir MICHELLE SAMPSON; Chair. MARY BURDETT.

New Jersey

Atlantic City Free Public Library: One N Tennessee Ave, Atlantic City, NJ 08401; tel. (609) 345-2269; e-mail reflib@acfpl.org; internet www.acfpl.org; f. 1901; magazines, newspapers, journals, audio books, e-books on health, education, business, languages and immigration and naturalization; Alfred M. Heston Colln; 135,000 vols, 7,615 DVDs, 7,519 CDs and 28,357 books; Dir MAUREEN SHERR FRANK; Pres. WILLIAM K. CHEATHAM.

Atlantic County Library System: 40 Farragut Ave, Mays Landing, NJ 08330; tel. (609) 625-2776; fax (609) 625-8143; e-mail contactus@aclsys.org; internet www.atlanticlibrary.org; 10 brs, 1 community reading centre and 1 bookmobile; 507,671 vols; Dir KAREN L. GEORGE; Chief Librarian GAIR HELFRICH.

Belleville Public Library and Information Center: 221 Washington Ave, Belleville, NJ 07109-3189; tel. (973) 450-3434; fax (973) 450-9518; internet www.bellepl.org; spec. collns incl. Spanish language materials, business, New Jersey history, Italian-American History and local history; Dir JOAN TAUB; Sec. FLORENCE PENTOL; Treas. LOUIS J. MESSANO, JR.

Bergen County Cooperative Library System: 810 Main St, Hackensack, NJ 07601; tel. (201) 489-1904; fax (201) 489-4215; e-mail bccls@bccls.org; internet www.bccls.org; f. 1979; 74 public libraries in Bergen, Essex, Hudson and Passaic Counties; 5,481,163 vols; Exec. Dir ROBERT WHITE; Dir ARLENE SAHRAIE.

Berkeley Heights Public Library: 290 Plainfield Ave, Berkeley Heights, NJ 07922; tel. (908) 464-9333; fax (908) 464-7098; internet www.bhplnj.org; f. 1946; collns incl. encyclopedias, foreign language learning databases, literature and audio books; Dir STEPHANIE BAKOS; Pres. HOPE DANZIS; Sec. LESLIE KALTENBACH; Treas. SHEILA BUTHE.

Bernadsville Public Library: One Anderson Hill Rd, Bernardsville, NJ 07924; tel. (908) 766-0118; fax (908) 766-2464; e-mail librarian@bernardsvillelibrary.org; internet www.bernardsvillelibrary.org; f. 1840; books on local history; e-books; audio books; Exec. Dir KAREN BRODSKY; Pres. DONALD BURSET; Sec. TERRY THOMPSON; Treas. JOHN LA DUC.

Butler Public Library: One Ace Rd, Butler, NJ 07405; tel. (973) 838-3262; internet www.butlerlibrary.org; f. 1928; colln incl. databases of newspaper and magazine articles; business; helath and well-being and reference directories; Dir ROCHELLE LEVIN; Treas. MARIE PRA.

Camden County Library System: Vogelson Br., 203 Laurel Rd, Voorhees, NJ 08043; tel. (856) 772-1636; fax (856) 772-6105; internet www.camden.lib.nj.us; f. 1921; 7 brs; Dir LINDA DEVLIN.

Cherry Hill Public Library: 1100 Kings Highway N, Cherry Hill, NJ 08034-1911; tel. (856) 667-0300; fax (856) 667-9503; e-mail info@chplnj.org; internet www.chplnj.org; incl. research section; Dir MANUEL PAREDES.

Free Public Library & Cultural Center of Bayonne: 697 Avenue C, Corner of 31st St, Bayonne, NJ 07002; tel. (201) 858-6970; e-mail library@bayonnelibrary.org; internet www.bayonnelibrary.org; f. 1890 as Bayonne Public Library, present bldg 1904, present name 1989; art and music colln; audio books, catalogued in the 700s; reference section incl. traditional and e-books, newspapers, journals, maps, military history and oral history of Bayonne veterans; archives of Bayonne Public Library; Dir SNEH BAINS; Pres. CARMINE BORZELLI; Sec. BERNARD P. JABLONSKI; Treas. MARY-ANN D. ROWLAND.

Mercer County Library System: Lawrence HQ Br., 2751 Brunswick Pike, Lawrenceville, NJ 08648; tel. (609) 882-9246; fax (609) 538-9238; e-mail director@mcl.org; internet webserver.mcl.org; 9 brs incl Lawrence HQ br; Dir ELLEN BROWN.

New Jersey State Library: POB 520, Trenton, NJ 08625-0520; 185 W State St, Trenton, NJ 08625-0520; tel. (609) 278-2640; fax (609) 278-2647; e-mail refdesk@njstatelib.org; internet www.njstatelib.org; f. 1796; affiliate of Thomas Edison State College; databases, online journals and e-books; 2m. vols and documents, 800 current periodicals, 750,000 items on microfiche and microfilm; State Librarian NORMA E. BLAKE.

Newark Public Library: POB 630, Five Washington St, Newark, NJ 07101-0630; tel. (973) 733-7784; fax (973) 733-5648; e-mail reference@npl.org; internet www.npl.org; f. 1888; collns: art, music, science, technology, business histories, US patent specifications and drawings 1790 to present, US govt documents regional depository, New Jersey documents, New Jersey history, fine printing, black studies, Newark Evening News Morgue; 8 brs; 1,180,492 vols, 924,814 catalogued non-book items, 1,696,441 uncatalogued items, 411,531 periodicals, 1,015,095 prints, pictures and art slides; Library Dir WILMA J. GREY; Prin. Librarian JANE SEIDEN.

Ocean City Free Public Library: 1735 Simpson Ave, Suite 4, Ocean City, NJ 08226-3071; tel. (609) 399-2434; fax (609) 398-0751; internet home.oceancitylibrary.org; Dir CHRIS MALONEY.

Princeton Library: 65 Witherspoon St, Princeton, NJ 08542; tel. (609) 924-9529; e-mail comments@princetonlibrary.org; internet www.princeton.lib.nj.us; f. 1910; African-American history; genealogy; health and medicine; history and social sciences; languages; spec. colln public art; Dir LESLIE BURGER; Pres. KATHERINE McGAVERN.

Princeton University Library: One Washington Rd, Princeton, NJ 08544; tel. (609) 258-1470; fax (609) 258-0441; e-mail libhr@princeton.edu; internet libweb .princeton.edu; f. 1746; spec. collns incl. 450 medieval and Renaissance codices, 10,000 Islamic MSS, cuneiform tablets, stone seals and papyri, pre-Columbian indigenous materials (especially Mayan), George Cruikshank and Aubrey Beardsley, American

theatre (incl. papers of Max Gordon and Otto Kahn), archives of American publishers, especially Charles Scribner's Sons, the Morris L. Parrish Colln of Victorian Novelists, early American family papers, especially Edward Livingston and Blair-Lee, public policy papers since early 20th century, especially John Foster Dulles, Adlai Stevenson and the American Civil Liberties Union, 'Boom' period Latin American writers (incl. Mario Vargas Llosa); 6.9m. vols, 6m. microforms, 35,000 linear ft of MSS; Univ. Librarian KARIN A. TRAINER; publ. *Princeton University Library Chronicle*.

Ramsey Free Public Library: 30 Wyckoff Ave, Ramsey, NJ 07446; tel. (201) 327-1445; fax (201) 327-3687; e-mail ramscirc@bccls .org; internet www.ramseylibrary.org; f. 1907; open borrowing library with M.A.I.N., PALS, LMxAC and SWELL BCCLS' patrons; Dir WENDY B. BLOOM; Pres. EMILY J. RENNIE; Sec. MARIE O'NEILL; Treas. FRANK HURLEY.

Rutgers University Libraries: 169 College Ave, CAC, New Brunswick, NJ 08901-1163; tel. (732) 932-7505; fax (732) 932-7637; internet www.libraries.rutgers.edu; f. 1766; 26 libraries on Rutgers campuses in Camden, Newark and New Brunswick; spec. collns in medicine, physics, chemistry, mathematics, microbiology, art, alcohol studies, labour and management relations, urban research, law and music; 3m. vols; Univ. Librarian MARIANNE GAUNT.

Sussex County Library System: 125 Morris Turnpike, Newton, NJ 07860; tel. (973) 948-3660; fax (973) 948-2071; internet www .sussexcountylibrary.org; f. 1942 as bookmobile; main library in Frankford and 5 brs in Newton, Sussex, Franklin, Hopatcong and Vernon; fed. depository; Dir STAN POLLAKOFF; Chief Librarian ELLEN CALLANAN.

University Libraries: George F. Smith Library of the Health Sciences, 30 12th Ave, POB 1709, Newark, NJ 07101-1709; tel. (973) 972-4580; fax (973) 972-7474; e-mail libcwis@umdnj.edu; internet libraries .umdnj.edu; attached to Univ. of Medicine and Dentistry of New Jersey; George F. Smith Library of the Health Sciences, Newark campus; Robert Wood Johnson Library of the Health Sciences, NB/Piscataway Campus; Health Sciences Library at Stratford; Reuben L. Sharp Health Science Library, Camden Campus; Coriell Library, study annex campus; 92,802 vols, 703 e-books, 173,951 journals, 158 print journal subscriptions, 4,610 e-journal subscriptions and 84 database subscriptions; Univ. Librarian JUDY COHN.

Warren and Reba Lummis Library: 981 Ye Greate St, POB 16, Greenwich, NJ 08323; tel. (856) 455-8580; fax (856) 455-9333; e-mail cchistsoc@verizon.net; internet www .cchistsoc.org/lummis; attached to Cumberland Co Historical Soc.; holdings incl. genealogical and historical files, directories, maps, newspapers, deeds and indentures and microfilms on the USA and New Jersey census; 815 vols; Dir WARREN Q. ADAMS; Librarian CONSTANCE C. SCHUCHARD.

New Mexico

Albuquerque/Bernalillo County Library System: 501 Copper Ave, NW, Albuquerque, NM 87102; tel. (505) 768-5170; e-mail library@cabq.gov; internet www.cabq.gov/library; 17 brs; Dir DEAN P. SMITH.

Capitan Public Library: POB 1169, 101 E Second St, Capitan, NM 88316; tel. (575) 354-3035; fax (575) 354-3223; e-mail capitanlibrary@gmail.com; internet www .capitanlibrary.org; f. 1996; Dir PAT GARRETT; Pres. GEORGE HINCH; Sec. ANN CURTIS; Treas. SADIE MANN.

Clovis-Carver Public Library: 701 N Main St, Clovis, NM; tel. (575) 769-7840; fax (575) 769-7842; e-mail library@ cityofclovis.org; internet www.library .cityofclovis.org; f. 1949, present location 1991; 117,688 vols, 2,038 audio cassettes, 2,591 DVDs.

El Rito Library: POB 5, 182 Placitas Rd, El Rito, NM 87530; tel. (575) 581-4608; fax (575) 581-9591; e-mail elritopubliclibrary@yahoo .com; internet www.elritolibrary.org; f. 1986; spec. collns: arts, crafts and culture; Spanish language (books, videos, audio books); gardening and nature; 11,245 vols, 1,723 DVDs and video cassettes, 711 audio books and audio cassettes; Dir CHRISTINE TRUJILLO; Librarian RITA LARROW; Librarian TOM FORTSON.

Española Public Library: Richard Lucero Center, 313 N Paseo de Oñate, Española, NM 87532; tel. (505) 747-6087; fax (505) 753-5543; internet www2.youseemore.com/ espanola; f. 1925; depository for New Mexico State documents; 41,000 vols; Dir TEDDIE RIEHL.

Los Alamos County Library System: 133 Longview Dr., Los Alamos, NM 87544; tel. (505) 662-8253; e-mail libweb@lacnm.us; internet www.losalamosnm.us/library; incl. Rock Br. Library and Mesa Public Library; 182,050 vols, 152,692 books and magazines, 8,126 sound recordings, 130 framed art prints, 9,810 video recordings, 4,025 e-books and 1,879 audio books; Chair. LINDA ANDERMAN; Library Man. BERNADINE GOLDMAN (acting).

Los Alamos National Laboratory Research Library: POB 1663, MS-P362, Los Alamos, NM 87545-1362; tel. (505) 667-5809; fax (505) 665-4408; e-mail library@lanl .gov; internet library.lanl.gov; books, journals, databases, patents and technical reports; offers literature searching, training and outreach services; 150,000 vols, 100,000 print titles of books, 50,000 e-books, 10,000 journals, 8,500 e-journals, 150,000 bound journals, 1.5m. print and microfiche reports, 790 video and audio cassettes; Dir MIRIAM BLAKE; publs *1663–Los Alamos Science and Technology Magazine, National Security Science, Why* (employee magazine).

New Mexico Archives and Historical Services Division: New Mexico Library, Archives and Records Center Bldg, 1205 Camino Carlos Rey, Santa Fe, NM 87507; tel. (505) 476-7948; fax (505) 476-7909; e-mail archives@state.nm.us; internet www .nmcpr.state.nm.us/archives/archives_hm .htm; attached to Nat. Archives and Records Admin.; colln of govt records from 1621 to present, co records from 1850 to 1912, nongovt MSS, film and video colln, genealogy materials (Catholic church records, census, published family histories), private papers: letters, diaries, wills, maps and photographs related to New Mexico or SW; Dir MELISSA SALAZAR.

New Mexico State Library: 1209 Camino Carlos Rey, Santa Fe, NM 87507-5166; tel. (505) 476-9783; fax (505) 476-9701; internet www.nmstatelibrary.org; f. 1929; attached to Dept of Cultural Affairs (State Govt); 110 brs statewide; 3 bookmobiles for rural region; provides state agencies with library resources and services, and serves as a primary reference source for libraries in the state; spec. collns: Southwest Resources (books, journals and newspapers on the history of the southwestern area of the USA), New Mexico Documents (publs of the various depts, agencies, commissions comprising the state govt), Fed. Documents (selective depository focus on New Mexico federal agency publs); 2m. vols; State Librarian Benjamin T. Wakashige; publ. *Directory of New Mexico Libraries.*

Santa Fe Public Library: 145 Washington St, Santa Fe, NM 87501; tel. (505) 955-6789; fax (505) 955-6676; e-mail library@ santafenm.gov; internet www.santafelibrary .org; f. 1896; 2 brs; 230,166 vols, 10,795 video cassettes and DVDs, 6,505 audiobooks on cassettes and CDs, 4,787 music CDs, 388,003 other items; Pres. Jennifer Jaramillo.

University of New Mexico Libraries: MSC05 3020, One Univ. of New Mexico, Albuquerque, NM 87131-0001; tel. (505) 277-9100; fax (505) 277-7196; internet elibrary.unm.edu; f. 1892; brs: Centennial Science and Engineering library, Parish Memorial Library for Business and Economics, Fine Arts and Design Library and Zimmerman Library; regional depository for fed. documents since 1968; spec. collns: Center for Southwest Research and Spec. Collns, Chicano/Hispano/Latino Research Program, Div. of Iberian and Latin American Resources and Services, Indigenous Nations Library Program; 3m. vols, 60,000 journal subscriptions, 663,000 govt documents, 348,149 e-books, 14,728 linear ft MSS and archives, 235,000 maps and cartographic images, 3.8m. microform units, 37,000 audio materials, 9300 film and video materials; Dean of Univ. Libraries Martha Bedard.

New York

Association of the Bar of the City of New York Library: 42 W 44th St, New York, NY 10036; tel. (212) 382-6666; fax (212) 382-6790; e-mail library@nycbar.org; internet www.nycbar.org/index.php/library/overvie-w-hours; f. 1870; colln of current and early edn treatises; current and superseded statutes for Fed. and all state jurisdictions; case reporters; law reviews and int. law material; colln of US and New York State appellate court briefs and records on appeal; 600,000 vols; Dir Richard Tuske.

Brooklyn Public Library: 10 Grand Army Plaza, Brooklyn, NY 11238; tel. (718) 230-2100; internet www.brooklynpubliclibrary .org; f. 1892; 58 brs; spec. collns incl. Brooklyn history; business library; 7,189,998 items; Pres. and CEO Linda E. Johnson; Chair. Anthony W. Crowell; Sec. Antonia Yuille Williams; Treas. Peter Aschkenasy.

Buffalo and Erie County Public Library System: 1 Lafayette Sq., Buffalo, NY 14203; tel. (716) 858-8900; fax (716) 858-6211; internet www.buffalolib.org; f. 1886; 37 brs (incl. 8 city br. libraries); 3,639,922 vols; Dir Mary Jean Jakubowski.

Center for Inquiry Libraries: POB 741, Amherst, NY 14226-0741; 3965 Rensch Rd, Amherst, NY 14228; tel. (716) 636-4869; fax (716) 636-1733; internet www.cfilibraries .org; incl.: John and Mary Frantz Skeptics' Library, James Hervey Johnson Freethought and Humanist Library, Jo Ann Boydston Library of American Philosophical Naturalism, Humanist Institute colln (incl. the Joseph Blau colln), Arnold B. Levy colln of Literary, Artistic and Scientific Hoaxes in Honor of Steve Allen, Hal Verb Little Blue Book colln, Rare Book Room, Prometheus Repository; incl. microforms, microfiche, reference colln; Dir Timothy Binga.

Center for Jewish History: 15 W 16th St, New York, NY 10011; tel. (212) 294-8301; fax (212) 294-8302; e-mail inquiries@cjh.org; internet www.cjh.org; f. 2000; 5 partner orgs: American Jewish Historical Soc. American Seephardi Fed., Leo Baeck Institute, Yeshiva Univ. Museum, YIVO Institute for Jewish Research; artwork, textiles and ritual objects, music, films and photographs cover-

ing 600 years of Jewish history; 500,000 vols, 100m. archival documents; Co-Chair. Joseph S. Steinberg; Co-Chair. William A. Ackman; Dir for Archive and Library Services Laura E. Leone; Sec. Theodore N. Mirvis; Treas. Sidney Lapidus.

Chancellor Robert R Livingston Masonic Library: 71 W 23rd St, 14th Fl., New York, NY 10010-4171; tel. (212) 337-6620; e-mail info@nymasoniclibrary.org; internet www.nymasoniclibrary.org; f. 1850 as Masonic Library of the Grand Lodge, present status 1983, present location 1996; books on Masonic history, origins, philosophy, symbolism, current events, esoterica and occultism; Masonic periodicals from all over the US and the world from the 1700s to the present day; collns of Masonic memorabilia, ritual artefacts, jewellery, aprons and other textile artefacts, artwork, engravings, paintings and collns by Past Grand Masters of New York; 60,000 vols; Dir Thomas M. Savini; Pres. Barry Mallah; Sec. Richard C. Mills; Treas. Aldo Ghirarduzzi.

Clinton Essex Franklin Library System: 33 Oak St, Plattsburgh, NY 12901-2810; tel. (518) 563-5190; fax (518) 563-0421; e-mail info2@cefls.org; internet www.cefls.org; f. 1954; 30 public libraries, 1 bookmobile and 3 reading centres; Dir Ewa Jankowska; Pres. Chris de Grandpré; Sec. Lisa Minnich; Treas. Dr Nancy Church.

Columbia University Libraries: 535 W 114th St, New York, NY 10027; tel. (212) 854-7309; fax (212) 854-9099; e-mail lio@ columbia.edu; internet www.library .columbia.edu; f. 1754; 22 libraries at Columbia Univ. and its affiliated instns; collns in architecture, business, humanities, history, law, medicine, engineering, sciences and social sciences; 10.4m. vols; 144,787 current serial subscriptions; 6,379,196 microforms; 26m. MSS and 979,096 rare books; 156,717 videos, DVDs, CDs, sound recordings; 174,032 govt documents; Vice-Pres. for Information Services and Univ. Librarian James G. Neal.

Cornell University Library: 201 Olin Library, Ithaca, NY 14853; tel. (607) 255-3393; fax (607) 255-6788; e-mail libadmin@ cornell.edu; internet www.library.cornell .edu; f. 1868; collns in SE Asia studies, industrial relations, viticulture, Old Norse and Icelandic materials, agriculture, astronomy, chemistry, classics, French history and literature, human devt, mathematics, medieval studies, microbiology, N European language and literature, physics, and W European social sciences; 8m. vols, 8.5m. microforms, 71,000 cubic ft of MSS; Univ. Librarian Anne R. Kenney.

Department of Records and Information Services: Surrogate's Court Bldg, 31 Chambers St, New York, NY 10007; tel. (212) 788-8602; fax (212) 788-8614; internet www.nyc .gov/html/records; f. 1977; comprises Municipal Archives of the City of New York, City Hall Library and Municipal Records Management Div; 250,000 vols, 160,000 items in records div., 1m. photographs; Deputy Commr Eileen M. Flannely.

Finger Lakes Library System: 119 E Green St, Ithaca, NY 14850; tel. (607) 273-4074; fax (607) 273-3618; internet www.flls .org; f. 1958; 33 mem. libraries; central library Tompkins Co Public Library; serves the public libraries in Cayuga, Cortland, Seneca, Tioga, and Tompkins counties; Exec. Dir Kimberly A. Iraci; Pres. Christine Griffin; Sec. Grace Miller; Treas. Debora Kelsey.

Franklin D. Roosevelt Presidential Library and Museum: 4079 Albany Post Rd, Hyde Park, NY 12538; tel. (845) 486-

1142; fax (845) 486-1147; e-mail roosevelt .library@nara.gov; internet www.fdrlibrary .marist.edu; f. 1941; attached to Nat. Archives and Records Admin.; MSS, photographs, printed and museum materials concerning life and times of Franklin and Eleanor Roosevelt, incl. 4,700 lin. ft of Rossevelt's and his contemporaries papers; museum with 34,000 items; 72,000 vols, 17m. MSS pages, 130,000 photographs; Dir Lynn A. Bassanese.

Frick Art Reference Library: 10 E 71st St, New York, NY 10021; tel. (212) 547-0641; fax (212) 879-2091; e-mail library@frick.org; internet www.frick.org/library; f. 1920; repository for archives and spec. collns documenting the history of art and collecting in America; public and private collns date back to the 18th century; research databases and e-journals related to the study of art and art history; 285,000 vols, 80,000 auction catalogues and more than 1m. photographs; Dir Anne L. Poulet; Chair. Margot Bogert; Sec. John P. Birkelund; Treas. Franklin W. Hobbs.

Hispanic Society of America Library: 613 W 155 St, New York, NY 10032; Audubon Terrace, Broadway, 155 and 156 Sts, New York, NY; tel. (212) 926-2234; fax (212) 690-0743; e-mail library@ hispanicsociety.org; internet www .hispanicsociety.org/hispanic/library.htm; f. 1904; art, history and literature of Spain, Portugal and Hispanic America; 300,000 MSS; 15,000 books printed before 1701, incl. 250 incunabula; 250,000 later books; Curator of Modern Books Edwin X. Rolon; Curator of MSS and Rare Books John O'Neill.

Jewish Theological Seminary Library: 3080 Broadway, New York, NY 10027; tel. (212) 678-8082; fax (212) 678-8998; e-mail library@jtsa.edu; internet www.jtsa.edu/ library.xml; f. 1893; Louis Ginzberg Microfilm library (foreign collns of Hebrew MSS); incunabula; Bible, Rabbinics, Jewish history, liturgy, theology, early Yiddish, Hebrew literature, history of science and medicine; Haggadahs; Megillot (Esther scrolls); Ketuboth (marriage contracts); prints and photographs; musical scores; microfilms; video cassettes; sound recordings; e-resources; 400,000 vols, 11,000 MSS, 35,000 leaves of Cairo Genizah, Archives; Librarian David Kraemer; publ. *Quntres* (1 a year, online).

Library of Agudas Chassidei Chabad—Ohel Yosef Yitzchak—Lubavitch (Central Chabad Lubavitch Library and Archive Center): 770 E Parkway, Brooklyn, NY 11213; tel. (718) 493-1537; fax (718) 756-2919; e-mail library@chabad.org; internet www .chabadlibrary.org; f. 1941; Lubavitch Colln, Colln of Rabbi Yosef Yitzchak and the Colln of Lubavitcher Rebbe Menachem M. Schneerson; Judaic library; several thousand MSS on Chabad Chasidic philosophy; archive of correspondence and writings relating to Chabad philosophy and movement; colln of photographs of Chasidim and Chabad activities sent to Rabbi Yosef Yitzchak and his successor Rabbi Menachem M. Schneerson; incl. Chabad research centre; 250,000 vols (incl. 200,000 in Hebrew and Yiddish and 50,000 in other languages).

Medical Research Library of Brooklyn: 450 Clarkson Ave, POB 14, Brooklyn, NY 11203; tel. (718) 270-7410; fax (718) 270-7413; internet library.downstate.edu; f. 1962 as the jt library of the Acad. of Medicine of Brooklyn, Inc. (f. 1845) and the State Univ. of New York Downstate Medical Center (f. 1860); provides service to College of Medicine, College of Nursing, College of Health-Related Professions, School of Graduate

Studies, School of Public Health, Univ. Hospital and Graduate Medical Education of SUNY Downstate Medical Center; 67,078 vols, 388,320 printed journals, 4000 e-journals and 356 e-books; Dir of Libraries Dr RICHARD M. WINANT.

Middletown Thrall Library: 11–19 Depot St, Middletown, NY 10940; tel. (845) 341-5454; e-mail thrall7@warwick.net; internet www.thrall.org; f. 1901; literature, law, encyclopedias, science and technology, local history, language and health; incl. govt information centre; 321,042 vols; Dir MATTHEW PFISTERER; Pres. CARL S. BERKOWITZ; Sec. LOIS RUCKERT; Treas. BARBARA KAY.

Monroe County Library System: Central Library of Rochester and Monroe Co, 115 S Ave, Rochester, NY 14604-1896; tel. (585) 428-7300; internet www.libraryweb.org/central; f. 1912; fed. of 20 ind. public libraries in Monroe Co; 1,344,621 vols; Dir PATRICIA UTTARO; publ. *Rochester History* (2 a year).

Morgan Library & Museum: 225 Madison Ave, New York, NY 10016; tel. (212) 685-0008; fax (212) 481-3484; e-mail visitorservices@themorgan.org; internet www.morganlibrary.org; f. 1924; public museum and research library; collns formed by Pierpont Morgan and his son; incl. Medieval and Renaissance MSS from the 5th to the 16th century; colln of 10,000 drawings by artists since the 15th century; colln of Rembrandt prints; Pierre Matisse Gallery Archives; major monuments in the history of printing and typography, from Gutenberg and Caxton to modern times; comprehensive group of fine bindings; literary and historical MSS, incl. Dickens, Ruskin, the Brontës, Austen, Thoreau and Steinbeck; Carter Burden Colln of American Literature; colln of autograph scores, incl. works by Beethoven, Mahler, Mozart and Stravinsky; extensive Gilbert and Sullivan archive; regular public lectures and exhibitions; Dir WILLIAM M. GRISWOLD.

New York Academy of Medicine Library: 1216 Fifth Ave, New York, NY 10029; tel. (212) 822-7200; fax (212) 423-0275; e-mail library@nyam.org; internet www.nyam.org/library; f. 1847; spec. collns incl. medical Americana, history of medicine, medical biography, rare medical books and incunabula; Malloch Rare Book Room; 550,000 vols, 182,910 catalogued pamphlets, 275,788 catalogued illustrations and portraits, 2,700 serials; Pres. Dr JO IVEY BOUFFORD; publ. *Grey Literature Report* (6 a year).

New York Law Institute Library: 120 Broadway, Suite 932, New York, NY 10271-0043; tel. (212) 732-8720; fax (212) 406-1204; e-mail library@nyli.org; internet www.nyli.org; f. 1828; law library for practising attorneys; spec. collns and edns incl. George Washington's copy of the Code de Louis XIII: the Plantation Laws of Virginia, autographed by Richard Henry Lee; 300,000 vols, 1,450 reels of microfilm, 16,300 microfiches; Exec. Dir RALPH MONACO.

New York Public Library: Stephen A. Schwarzman Bldg, Fifth Ave and 42nd St, New York, NY 10018; tel. (917) 275-6975; fax (212) 930-9299; e-mail nyplweb@nypl.org; internet www.nypl.org; f. 1895 by merger of Astor, Tilden and Lenox Libraries; scholarly research collns; incl. Gutenberg Bible and Jefferson's MSS copy of the Declaration of Independence, Berg colln of English and American literature, Arents colln of books on tobacco and books in parts and Spencer colln of illustrated books; focuses on humanities and social sciences; performing arts; black history and culture; and business and industry; network of neighbourhood libraries throughout Bronx, Manhattan and Staten

Island; 90 local brs and 4 research centres; 65m. vols; Pres. and CEO Dr ANTHONY W. MARX; publs *Bookmark* (3 a year), *NOW* (3 a year), *Roar! UpRoar* (4 a year).

New York State Archives: New York State Education Dept, Cultural Education Center, Albany, NY 12230; tel. (518) 474-6926; e-mail dhs@mail.nysed.gov; internet www.archives.nysed.gov; f. 1971; archives and records of New York from the 17th century to the present; 200m. documents; Pres. ROBERT E. BULLOCK; Chief of Archival Services MARIA HOLDEN; publ. *New York Archives* (4 a year).

New York State Library: Cultural Education Center, 222 Madison Ave, Albany, NY 12230; tel. (518) 474-5355; fax (518) 474-5786; e-mail circ@mail.nysed.gov; internet www.nysl.nysed.gov; f. 1818; attached to Office of Cultural Education, New York State Education Dept; serves Research Library, Talking Book and Braille Library and Div. of Library Devt; American and New York State history, law, medicine, education, technology and genealogy; MSS and spec. collns; US govt depository; digital collns incl. 18th- and 19th-century historical materials from the Revolutionary War, the Civil War, Native American materials, New York State laws and natural history; 20m. items; spec. colln of 19m. items in Talking Book and Braille Library; State Librarian BERNARD A. MARGOLIS.

New York University Libraries: The Elmer Holmes Bobst Library, New York Univ., 70 Washington Square S, New York, NY 10012; tel. (212) 998-2500; fax (212) 995-4070; e-mail libweb@nyu.edu; internet www.nyu.edu/library; f. 1835; 9 brs; Bobst Library has 3 specialized research centres (digital projects, arts, labour history); Courant Institute of Mathematical Sciences focuses on research-level material in mathematics, computer science and related fields; Stephen Chan Library of Fine Arts houses collns in art history and archaeology; Jack Brause Real Estate Library; Frederick L. Ehrman Medical Library; the Dental Center's Waldman Memorial Library, Jack Brause Library; Institute for the Study of the Ancient World and the Law Library; 5.1m. vols; Dean of Div. of Libraries CAROL MANDEL.

Queens Library: 89–11 Merrick Blvd, Jamaica, NY 11432; tel. (718) 990-0700; fax (718) 291-8936; e-mail foundation@queenslibrary.org; internet queenslibrary.org; f. 1858, inc. 1907; books on literature and languages, social sciences, business, science and technology; spec. collns incl. Carter G. Woodson and Augusta Baker collns of African-American materials; 61 community libraries; 9.7m. vols, 1,250,000 books, 2,100 periodical subscriptions in print, 90,000 govt documents, 20,000 videos, DVDs and VCDs, 517 16mm film titles, 42,000 music scores, 500 libretti, 23,000 music CDs, 3,500 music cassettes, 700 CD-ROMs, 500 titles of language study materials on cassettes and CDs and 2,000 phonorecords; Pres. and CEO THOMAS W. GALANTE; publs *Enrich Your Life* (6 a year), *The Guide* (12 a year).

Research Library: Department of Library Services, American Museum of Natural History, Central Park W, 79th St, New York, NY 10024-5192; tel. (212) 769-5400; fax (212) 769-5009; e-mail libref@amnh.org; internet library.amnh.org; f. 1869; attached to American Museum of Natural History; subject areas incl. anthropology, astronomy, geology, palaeontology, zoology, exploration and travel, history of science, and museology; incl. astronomy colln transferred from Hayden Planetarium; 487,000 vols, 21,000 periodicals, 1m. photographs, 3,000 films, 13,000

rare vols; Dir TOM BAIONE; publs *Anthropological Papers of the American Museum of Natural History*, *Bulletin of the American Museum of Natural History*, *Memoirs of the American Museum of Natural History*, *Novitates* (irregular).

Stephen B. Luce Library: Maritime College, SUNY, Six Pennyfield Ave, Fort Schuyler, Throgs Neck, NY 10465; tel. (718) 409-7231; fax (718) 409-7256; e-mail library@sunymaritime.edu; internet www.sunymaritime.edu/stephenbluecelibrary; attached to Maritime College, SUNY; marine engineering, naval architecture, marine transportation, oceanography, transportation economics and management and meteorology; 80,000 vols, 374 magazines and journals subscriptions, 7,000 microfilms; Dir CONSTANTIA CONSTANTINOU.

Syracuse University Library: E. S. Bird Library, 222 Waverly Ave, Syracuse, NY 13244-5040; tel. (315) 443-2093; fax (315) 443-2060; e-mail libref@syr.edu; internet libwww.syr.edu; f. 1870; divs incl. Science and Technology Library, Spec. Collns Research Center and Belfer Audio Archive; 2,992,795 vols, 22,000 e-journals, 1.9m. e-books, 270,000 maps, 5,000 atlases, and 80,000 historical air photographs, 300,000 print and electronic fed., state and int. documents, 200,000 rare books and printed materials, 340,000 sound recordings of music, 300 sets of architectural drawings; Dean and Univ. Librarian SUZANNE E. THORIN (acting).

Burke Theological Library: 3041 Broadway, New York, NY 10027; tel. (212) 851-5606; fax (212) 851-5613; e-mail burke@libraries.cul.columbia.edu; internet www.library.columbia.edu/indiv/burke; f. 1836; attached to Columbia Univ. Libraries; colln incl. theological disciplines; periodicals, pamphlets, reports, MSS, microforms, digital resources and archival material; spec. colln: Americana colln, Auburn colln, Bonhoeffer colln, Christian Science colln, Gillett colln of American History and Theology, MSS colln, McAlpin colln of British History and Theology, Missionary Research colln, Reformation Tracts colln, Sacred Music colln, Thompson colln and Van Ess colln; 700,000 vols; spec. colln 12,000 vols from Auburn Theological Seminary; Library Dir ALYSSE JORDAN.

United Nations Dag Hammarskjöld Library: Room DN-2425, 220 E 42nd St, New York, NY 10017; tel. (212) 963-7412; fax (212) 963-2388; e-mail unreference@un.org; internet www.un.org/depts/dhl; f. 1949, present name 1961; colln of UN documents; specialized agencies and the League of Nations; activities and history of the UN; int. affairs since 1918; 600,000 vols, 10,000 serials, 6.5m. documents, 80,000 maps, 9,800 periodical titles; spec. colln of 8,600 vols of League documents and 6,500 related books and pamphlets; Head Librarian LORRAINE WAITMAN; publ. *Indices to Proceedings of the General Assembly, Security Council, Economic and Social Council and Trusteeship Council*.

United States Military Academy Library: Jefferson Hall, 758 Cullum Rd, West Point, NY 10996-1711; tel. (845) 938-8301; fax (845) 938-4000; e-mail 8lib@usma.edu; internet www.library.usma.edu; f. 1802; military-historical records (from 1802 through present), academic, govt documents, rare books; 50,000 vols, 1,500 linear ft MSS; Librarian and Assoc. Dean CHRISTOPHER BARTH.

University at Buffalo Libraries: 433 Capen Hall, Buffalo, NY 14260-1625; tel. (716) 645-2965; e-mail library@buffalo.edu;

internet library.buffalo.edu/libraries; Architecture and Planning Library, Health Sciences Library, Law Library, Libraries Annex, Lockwood Memorial Library, Music Library and Oscar A. Silverman Library; spec. colln comprises poetry, rare books and univ. archives; digital colln consists of 3-D objects, photographs, slides, video and audio; 3.6m. vols, 350 research databases and more than 10,000 e-journals; Vice-Provost for Univ. Libraries H. AUSTIN BOOTH.

University of Rochester Libraries: River Campus Libraries, 755 Library Rd, POB 270055, Rochester, NY 14627-0055; tel. (585) 275-4471; fax (585) 273-5309; internet www.rochester.edu/libraries; f. 1850; River Campus Libraries, Sibley Music Library; Miner Library; Allen Library; 3.5m. vols.

Vassar College Libraries: POB 20, 124 Raymond Ave, Poughkeepsie, NY 12604-0020; tel. (845) 437-5760; e-mail libfacil@vassar.edu; internet library.vassar.edu; f. 1865; incl. art library, music library, visual resources library; spec. colln incl. Virginia B. Smith Memorial MSS colln; 1m. vols, 50,000 serial titles, 612,000 microforms; Dir SABRINA PAPE.

Waterford Public Library: 117 Third St, Waterford, NY 12188; tel. (518) 237-0891; e-mail watpublibrary@gmail.com; internet www.waterfordlibrary.net; full-text magazine and newspaper articles; current health and business information; 24,500 vols, 1,000 DVDs, 400 music CDs, 1,000 books on audio cassettes and CDs; Dir TIMOTHY MCDONOUGH; Pres. MICHAEL MARCHESE; Sec. ANNE-MARIE MORRISSEY; Treas. JOANNE MCLEOD.

Westchester Library System: 540 White Plains Rd, Suite 200, Tarrytown, NY 10591; tel. (914) 674-3600; internet www.westchesterlibraries.org; f. 1958; collaborates with 38 libraries in Westchester Co; spec. colln incl. fed. govt documents, Helen Whitman Colln of Herbs, Horticulture and Gdns, John C. Jutkowitz Memorial Theatre Arts Colln, New York Govt Documents and Mills Law Colln; Exec. Dir TERRY L. KIRCHNER; Pres. PATRICIA N. DOHRENWEND; Sec. NASEEM JAMALI; Treas. DAVE DONELSON.

Yonkers Public Library: Riverfront Library, 1 Larkin Center, Yonkers, NY 10701; tel. (914) 337-1500; internet www.ypl.org; f. 1893; 3 brs: Riverfront, Grinton I. Will and Crestwood; business, technical and govt information sources in printed and e-formats; fine arts dept in Grinton I. Will br. houses visual and performing arts, sound recordings and musical scores; Dir STEPHEN E. FORCE; Pres. WILLIAM E. SHEERIN.

North Carolina

Alamance County Public Libraries: 342 S Spring St, Burlington, NC 27215; tel. (336) 229-3588; fax (336) 229-3592; e-mail reference.staff@alamancelibraries.org; internet www.alamancelibraries.org; May Memorial Library (HQ); brs: Graham Public Library, Mebane Public Library, N Park Library and S Annex Library; 250,000 vols; Dir M. J. GOODRUM.

Burke County Public Library: 204 S King St, Morganton, NC 28655; tel. (828) 437-5638; fax (828) 433-1914; e-mail admin@bcpls.org; internet www.bcpls.org; f. 1923; brs: Valdese Public Library, Morganton Public Library and C. B. Hildebrand Public Library; Chair. BAKHTIAR ALAM; Sec. ANNA WILSON.

Charlotte Mecklenburg Library: 310 N Tryon St, Charlotte, NC 28202; tel. (704) 416-0100; fax (704) 416-0677; internet www.plcmc.org; f. 1903; fmr name Public Library of Charlotte & Mecklenburg County, present name 2009; colln of foreign-language publs, local history and genealogy; 23 br. libraries;

1.5m. vols; Dir of Libraries CHARLES M. BROWN; Man. JONITA EDMONDS.

Chatham County Public Libraries: 197 NC Highway 87N, Pittsboro, NC 27312; tel. (919) 545-8084; fax (919) 545-8080; e-mail mail@chathamlibraries.org; internet www.chathamnc.org; Chatham Community Library (HQ); brs: Goldston Library and Wren Memorial Library; 90,000 vols; Dir LINDA CLARKE.

Cumberland County Public Library & Information Center: 300 Maiden Lane, Fayetteville, NC 28301-5000; tel. (910) 483-7727; e-mail library@cumberland.lib.nc.us; internet www.cumberland.lib.nc.us; f. 1932, present name 1945; brs: HQ, Cliffdale Regional, E Regional, N Regional, W Regional, Bordeaux, Hope Mills, Spring Lake, Law Library; 5,000,000 vols (incl. 33,000 foreign language books); Dir JODY RISACHER; Chair. OLE SORENSEN.

Duke University Library: POB 90193, Durham, NC 27708-0193; tel. (919) 660-5800; fax (919) 660-5923; e-mail asklib@duke.edu; internet library.duke.edu; f. 1838; British history and literature of 17th–19th centuries; gen. European history since 1870; French Revolution; church history of Reformation; E Asia; advertising history; American and Latin American history; S Americana; women's history; history of economic thought; labour history; French, English, Italian, German Baroque and American literature; int. law; 6 br. libraries and 4 professional school libraries: Law (Ford Library), medicine, business and divinity; 6,172,205 vols, 51,827 linear ft of MSS and archives; Univ. Librarian and Vice-Provost for Library Affairs Dr DEBORAH JAKUBS; publ. *Duke University Libraries* (3 a year).

Forsyth County Public Library: 660 W Fifth St, Winston-Salem, NC 27101; tel. (336) 703-2665; fax (336) 727-2549; internet www.forsyth.cc/library; Central Library (HQ); brs: Carver School Rd, Clemmons, Kernersville, Kernersville, Malloy/Jordan E Winston, Reynolda Manor, Rural Hall, Southside and Walkertown; fed. depository; Dir SYLVIA SPRINKLE-HAMLIN; Chair. DONNA L. STALEY.

Gaston-Lincoln Regional Library: 1555 E Garrison Blvd, Gastonia, NC 28054-5156; tel. (704) 868-2164; fax (704) 853-0609; e-mail celler@co.gaston.nc.us; internet www.glrl.lib.nc.us; Dir CINDY W. MOOSE; Chair. RALPH S. ROBINSON, JR.

Haywood County Public Library: 678 S Haywood St, Waynesville, NC 28786; tel. (828) 452-5169; fax (828) 452-6746; internet www.haywoodlibrary.org; f. 1891 as Waynesville Library; attached to Haywood County Govt; Waynesville (HQ); brs: Canton, Maggie Valley and Fines Creek; 158,000 vols, 11,500 audio cassettes, 9,000 videos, 545 journals; Dir SHARON WOODROW; Chair. BETTE SPRECHER; Sec. JOAN ROUTH.

Henderson County Public Library: 301 N Washington St, Hendersonville, NC 28739; tel. (828) 697-4725; internet www.henderson.lib.nc.us; f. 1914; brs: HQ, Fletcher, Edneyville, Etowah, Green River and Mills River; Chair. MORTON LAZARUS; Sec. STAN SHELLEY.

Hickory Public Library: 375 Third St NE, Hickory, NC 28601; tel. (828) 304-0500; fax (828) 304-0023; internet www.ci.hickory.nc.us/library; f. 1893; Patrick Beaver Memorial Library (HQ) and Ridgeview Br.; genealogy colln incl. Catawba and surrounding counties; 115,396 vols, 272 video cassettes, 6,946 audio recordings, 377 periodicals; Dir LOUISE HUMPHREY.

McDowell County Public Library: 90 W Court St, Marion, NC 28752; tel. (828) 652-3858; fax (828) 652-2098; e-mail

mcdowellcountypubliclibrary@yahoo.com; internet www.mcdowellpubliclibrary.org; f. 1920; McDowell Co Public Library (HQ); brs: Marion Davis Memorial Br. and McDowell Co Law Library; Dir ELIZABETH HOUSE.

Rockingham County Public Library: 527 Boone Rd, Eden, NC 27288; tel. (336) 627-1106; fax (336) 623-1258; e-mail reference@rcpl.org; internet www.rcpl.org; brs: Eden, Madison, Mayodan, Reidsville and Stoneville; colln of genealogy and local history materials; Dir MICHAEL P. ROCHE; Chair. MICHAEL ROSE.

Rowan Public Library: 201 W Fisher St, Salisbury, NC 28144; tel. (704) 216-8228; fax (704) 216-8237; e-mail info@rowancountync.gov; internet www.rowancountync.gov/government/departments/publiclibrary/tabid/145/default.aspx; f. 1911; Salisbury (HQ); brs: S Rowan Regional and East Br., Rockwell; Dir JEFF HALL.

Town of Chapel Hill Public Library: University Mall, 201 S. Estes Dr., Chapel Hill, NC 27514; tel. (919) 968-2780; e-mail library@townofchapelhill.org; internet www.chapelhillpubliclibrary.org; f. 1958; Dir KATHLEEN THOMPSON; Chair. MARTHA DIEFENDORF; Sec. PAUL JONES.

Transylvania County Library: 212 S Gaston St, Brevard, NC 28712; tel. (828) 884-3151; internet library.transylvaniacounty.org; f. 1912, present location 2006; Rowell Bosse North Carolina Room incl. colln of reference book titles, unpublished family histories, co heritage vols and church histories; Dir ANNA YOUNT; Chair. MICHAEL H. SHELLEY.

University of North Carolina Library: Chapel Hill, NC 27514-8890; tel. (919) 962-1301; fax (919) 843-8936; e-mail reference@unc.edu; internet www.lib.unc.edu; f. 1795; spec. collns on North Carolina, S Americana, the history of the book, incunabula, 16th-century books, incl. large colln of Estienne imprints, *crónicas* of the discovery and conquest of the New World, also Johnson, Boswell, Dickens, Shaw and selected contemporary authors, Napoleon and the French Revolution, World War I and World War II materials, early Americana, Confederate imprints, Spanish, Catalan and Portuguese drama, John Murray and Smith, Elder and Co imprints, Afro-American materials, fed. and state documents, Latin America, Mazarinades, music and historical MSS; 10 departmental libraries in scientific and other fields; Institute of Govt Library; separate libraries in Law, Health Sciences, Population and a Data Library; 6,526,824 vols; Univ. Librarian and Assoc. Provost for Univ. Libraries SARAH C. MICHALAK.

Wake County Public Libraries: 4020 Carya Dr., Raleigh, NC 27610; tel. (919) 250-1200; internet www.wakegov.com/libraries; f. 1901; 6 regional libraries and 14 community libraries; genealogy and local history library; 1 bookmobile; Dir MICHAEL J. WASILICK.

North Dakota

Adams County Library: Hettinger, ND 58639; tel. and fax (701) 567-2741; internet adamscountylibrary.org; f. 1913; Dir PAT ANDERSON.

Cavalier County Library: 600 Fifth Ave, Langdon, ND 58249; tel. (701) 256-5353; fax (701) 256-5163; internet ccl.utma.com; f. 1897, present name and status 1986, present bldg 1988; 27,500 vols, 1,000 videos and DVDs; Librarian SHANNON NUELLE.

Dickinson Area Public Library: 139 Third St, West Dickinson, ND, 58601; tel. (701) 456-7700; fax (701) 456-7702; e-mail dickinson.library@sendit.nodak.edu; internet www.dickinsonlibrary.com; f. 1908; 90,000 vols; Dir RENEE PAASCH.

Grand Forks Public Library: 2110 Library Circle, Grand Forks, ND 58201; tel. (701) 772-8116; fax (701) 772-1379; e-mail gfplreference@hotmail.com; internet www .gflibrary.com; f. 1892, present bldg 1972; 314,310 vols (incl. 25,108 audio items, 21,054 DVDs and videos), 341 journals, 6,000 e-books; Dir WENDY WENDT; Chair. BRIAN SCHILL.

Lake Region Public Library: 423 Seventh St, NE, Devils Lake, ND 58301; tel. (701) 662-2220; fax (701) 662-2281; e-mail lakeregion.pl@sendit.nodak.edu; internet www.ci.devils-lake.nd.us/departments/ library.html; f. 2003; spec. colln: Scandinavian Section, George Johnson Genealogical Section and microfilm; 42,500 vols; Dir JAMES CHATTIN; Pres. MONTE ENGEL.

North Dakota State Library: 604 E Blvd Ave, Bismarck, ND 58505-0800; tel. (701) 328-4622; fax (701) 328-2040; e-mail statelib@nd.gov; internet www.library.nd .gov; f. 1907 as Public Library Comm., present name 1979; State Librarian HULEN E. BIVINS.

North Dakota State University Libraries: POB 6050, NDSU Dept 2080, Fargo, ND 58108-6050; tel. (701) 231-8753; fax (701) 231-6128; e-mail ndsu-library-librarians@ listserv.nodak.edu; internet library.ndsu .edu; f. 1891; incl. Main Library, Architecture Library, Barry Library (Business), Chemistry Library, Health Sciences Library, Institute for Regional Studies and Univ. Archives, Germans for Russia Heritage Colln; 922,470 vols, 10,829 periodicals, 530,000 govt documents; Dean of Libraries MICHELE M. REID.

State Historical Society of North Dakota State Archives: 612 E Boulevard Ave, Bismarck, ND 58505; tel. (701) 328-2091; fax (701) 328-2650; e-mail archives@nd.gov; internet history.nd.gov; f. 1905; historic records of state and local govt in North Dakota; genealogical resources; State Archivist ANN B. JENKS.

University of North Dakota Libraries: 3051 University Ave, Grand Forks, ND 58202-9000; tel. (701) 777-2189; fax (701) 777-3319; internet www.library.und.edu; f. 1883; incl. Chester Fritz Library (US Patent and Trademark and govt publs depository), Energy and Environmental Research Center Library, F. D. Holland Geology Library, Gordon Erickson Music Library, Harley E. French Library of the Health Sciences and Thormodsgard Law Library; 3m. vols, access to 30,000 e-journals; Dir for Libraries WILBUR STOLT.

West Fargo Public Library: 109 Third St E, West Fargo, ND 58078; tel. (701) 433-5460; fax (701) 433-5479; internet www .westfargolibrary.org; 58,409 vols; Dir SANDRA HANNAHS; Pres. LEIGHAN AKER-MONSON.

Ohio

Akron Law Library: 209 S High St, Fourth Fl., Akron, OH 44308-1675; tel. (330) 643-2804; fax (330) 643-7457; internet akronlawlib.summitoh.net; f. 1888; colln on legal issues and Ohio-specific colln; 81,500 vols; Dir ALAN CANFORA.

Akron-Summit County Public Library: 60 S High St, Akron, OH 44326; tel. (330) 643-9000; internet ascpl.lib.oh.us; f. 1874; also has 2 bookmobiles; a mobile service van; 17 brs in Summit County; 2m. vols (incl. books, CDs, DVDs); Dir DAVID JENNINGS; Deputy Dir PAM HICKSON-STEVENSON.

Butler County Law Library: 10 Journal Sq., Suite 200, Hamilton, OH 45011; tel. (513) 887-3455; fax (513) 887-3696; internet

www.bclawlib.org; f. 1889; provides materials used for regular legal research: legal education materials from the Ohio State Bar Asscn and selected law reviews, legal periodicals and newspapers, incl. bar publs; colln of fed. practice and procedure materials, form books and legal encyclopedic works in print and electronic format; state codes, administrative codes and state court opinions; legal encyclopedia and legal dictionary; legal forms set; pleading and practice forms set; American Law Institute Restatements; uniform laws annotated; Dir JOE HODNICKI.

Case Western Reserve University Libraries: 11055 Euclid Ave, Cleveland, OH 44106-7151; tel. (216) 368-3506; fax (216) 368-6950; internet www.case.edu/dir/ libraries.html; f. 1826; Kelvin Smith Library is the main Univ. Library; other libraries are Astronomy Library, Cleveland Health Sciences Library, Allen Memorial Medical Library, Health Centre Library, Kulas Music Library, Law School Library and Technology Resources, Lillian F. and Milford J. Harris Library; spec. collns: early American children's books, German literature and philology, history of medicine, history of printing, history of science and technology, environmental sciences, natural history, public housing and urban devt; Kelvin Smith Library: 1.7m. vols (incl. books, journals, microfilm, scripts, electronic content, media, theses and dissertations—electronic and in print, digital collns); Astronomy Library: 3,000 books, 4,000 bound periodical vols, 480 linear ft of observatory publs; Cleveland Health Sciences Library: 380,000 vols and 1,700 journal; Kulas Music Library: 42,000 items, incl. music scores, books on music, sound recordings, microforms and music periodicals; Kulas Music Library: 42,000 items, incl. music scores, books on music, sound recordings, microforms, music periodicals; Law School Library and Technology Resources: 410,000 books of fed. and state law, law reviews, current law services, an extensive British and Commonwealth colln, and spec. collns in taxation, labor law, foreign investments, int. law, environmental law; Lillian F. and Milford J. Harris Library: 40,000 books and pamphlets, 325 journals, 700 media items; Univ. Librarian ARNOLD HIRSHON; Deputy Dir TIMOTHY ROBSON.

Clermont County Law Library Association: Clermont County Court House, 270 E Main St, Batavia, OH 45103; tel. (513) 732-7109; fax (513) 732-0974; e-mail cclaw@cclla .org; internet www.cclla.org; f. 1937; Dir CAROL SUHRE; Chair. GARY OSTENDARP.

Cleveland Law Library: 1 W Lakeside Ave, Fourth Fl., Cleveland, OH 44113-1023; tel. (216) 861-5070; fax (216) 861-1606; e-mail lawlib@clelaw.lib.oh.us; internet clelaw.lib.oh.us; f. 1869 as Cleveland Law Library Asscn; Dir and Librarian KATHLEEN M. SASALA; Pres. JOSEPH N. GROSS.

Cleveland Public Library: 325 Superior Ave, NE, Cleveland, OH 44114-1271; tel. (216) 623-2800; fax (216) 623-7015; e-mail info@cpl.org; internet www.cpl.org; f. 1869; 28 brs; services to hospitals, the homebound, the physically handicapped and the blind; telephone reference service; fee-based research service; spec. colln: Schweinfurth Colln (rare architectural publs), Chess and Checkers Collns, Folklore, Gypsies and Orientalia, Miniature Books, Tobacco Colln; 3,723,666 vols, 45,000 edns classical music and jazz in Naxos Music Library, 900 linear ft archives; Dir FELTON THOMAS, Jr; Deputy Dir CINDY LOMBARDO (acting); Pres. THOMAS D. CORRIGAN; Sec. ALAN SEIFULLAH.

Columbus Metropolitan Library: 96 South Grant Ave, Columbus, OH 43215; tel.

(614) 645-2275; fax (614) 645-2050; internet www.columbuslibrary.org; f. 1873; 20 brs; also jtly operates Northwest Library in cooperation with Worthington Libraries; 3m. vols; Exec. Dir PATRICK A. LOSINSKI; Chief Operating Officer CHRIS TAYLOR; Treas. DEWITT HARRELL.

Dayton Metro Library: 215 E Third St, Dayton, OH 45402; tel. (937) 463-2665; fax (937) 496-4300; internet www .daytonmetrolibrary.org; f. 1847; 20 brs; bookmobile service; service to homebound, elderly and blind; circulating colln of 16-mm films, records and cassettes; 1,509,623 vols; Exec. Dir TIM KAMBITSCH.

Hamilton County Law Library: 1000 Main St, Room 601, Hamilton County Courthouse, Cincinnati, OH 45202; tel. (513) 946-5300; fax (513) 946-5252; e-mail reference@ cms.hamilton-co.org; internet www .hamilton-co.org/cinlawlib; f. 1834, present name and status 2010; 150,000 vols; Dir and Law Librarian MARY JENKINS; Chair. JAMES T. O'REILLY.

Lake County Law Library: Lake County Courthouse, 47 N Park Pl., Painesville, OH 44077; tel. (440) 350-2638; fax (440) 350-2780; e-mail lawlibrary@lakecountyohio.org; internet www.lakecountyohio.org/lawlibrary; 3 brs in Municipal Courts of Mentor, Painesville and Willoughby; materials related to fed., state, tax, family, probate, real estate and labour law; Dir and Law Librarian ANGELA A. BALDREE; Chair. KENNETH R. GAUNTNER, JR.

Lorain County Law Library: Lorain County Admin. Bldg, First Fl., 226 Middle Ave, Elyria, OH; tel. (440) 329-5567; fax (440) 322-1724; internet lorainlawlib.org/ information.htm; 22,000 vols, 35,000 microfiche, 500 audio cassettes, 200 video cassettes and 70 CD-ROMs; Dir MARY KOVACS; Chair. JAMES TAYLOR.

Mahoning Law Library Association: Fourth Fl., Courthouse, 120 Market St, Youngstown, OH 44503-1752; tel. (330) 740-2295; fax (330) 744-1406; e-mail mlladir@ mahoninglawlibrary.org; internet www .mahoninglawlibrary.org; f. 1906; local court rules and ordinances, case law, treatises, legal periodicals, legal reference material, fed. and state statutes; 32,000 vols; Librarian ANNA PACZELT; Pres. ALAN R. KRETZER; Sec. and Treas. CHRISTOPHER J. SCHIAVONE.

Mansfield/Richland County Public Library: 43 W Third St, Mansfield, OH 44902; tel. (419) 521-3100; internet www .mrcpl.org; f. 1887; 8 brs; Dir JOSEPH C. PALMER; Pres. VIN BLACK; Sec. JACK WELSH.

Medina County District Library: 210 South Broadway, Medina, OH 44256; tel. (330) 725-0588; fax (330) 725-2053; internet www.medina.lib.oh.us; f. 1877, present name and status 1982; 1 main library and 5 brs; bookmobile services; Dir CAROLE KOWELL; Pres. ADRIENNE APPLEBY-BURES; Sec. PATRICIA BOYLE.

Montgomery County Law Library: 505 Montgomery County Courts Bldg, 41 N Perry St, POB 972, Dayton, OH 45422; tel. (937) 225-4496; fax (937) 225-5056; internet www .mcohio.org/government/law_library; f. 1868, fmrly Dayton Law Library Asscn, present name and status 2010; Law Librarian JOANNE R. BEAL.

Ohio Historical Society Archives and Library: Ohio History Center, 800E, 17th Ave, Columbus, OH 43211; tel. (614) 297-2510; fax (614) 297-2358; e-mail reference@ ohiohistory.org; internet www.ohiohistory .org/resource/archlib; colln of documents related to operation of state and local govts; incl. State Archives; 82,500 vols, 10,700 cubic ft MSS, 13,500 cubic ft local govt records, 15,000 maps, 85,000 rolls microfilm, 12,000 sheets microfiche, 4,500 newspapers, 1m. photographs, 20,000 cubic ft State Archives; State Archivist FRED PREVITS.

Ohio State University Libraries: 1858 Neil Ave Mall, Columbus, OH 43210-1286; tel. (614) 292-6785; fax (614) 292-7859; e-mail library@osu.edu; internet www.lib .ohio-state.edu; f. 1873; Main (Thompson) Library and 26 deptl and affiliated libraries; 6,161,657 vols, 108,051 monographs, 6,147,566 microforms, 90,965 serials incl. periodicals, 16,328 govt documents, 36,829 linear ft MSS and archives, 87,485 audio and video materials; spec. collns incl. American fiction, theatre, cartoons and cartooning, medieval Slavic MSS on microfilm; Dir of Libraries CAROL PITTS DIEDRICHS.

Public Library of Cincinnati and Hamilton County: 800 Vine St, Cincinnati, OH 45202-2009; tel. (513) 369-6900; fax (513) 369-6993; internet www.cincinnatilibrary .org; f. 1853; US Documents Depository; 41 brs; regional library for the blind and physically handicapped; spec. collns incl. local history, genealogy, theology, art, music, theatre, US patents and trademarks, Inland Rivers Library, Bibles, English-language dictionaries, Cincinnatiana, first edns of English and American authors, Edgar Rice Burroughs Colln, Theodore Langstroth Colln, Lafcadio Hearn Colln, Loeb Colln; 4,887,372 books, 150,000 maps; Exec. Dir KIMBER L. FENDER; Pres. WILLIAM J. MORAN; Sec. ROSS A. WRIGHT.

Rutherford B. Hayes Presidential Center Library: Spiegel Grove, Fremont, OH 43420-2796; tel. (419) 332-2081; fax (419) 332-4952; e-mail hayeslib@rbhayes.org; internet www.rbhayes.org/hayes/library; f. 1916, present name 1981; 12,000 vol of personal library and archival material from Pres. Hayes's military and political career (1877–81); colln areas incl. Rutherford B. Hayes and the Hayes family, Gilded Age, local history and local govt, The Great Lakes and the Erie Islands and spec. collns; 70,000 vols; Head Librarian BECKY HILL.

Stark County Law Library: 110 Central Plaza, S Suite 401, Canton, OH 44702; tel. (330) 451-7380; fax (330) 451-7381; e-mail inform@starklawlibrary.org; internet www .starklawlibrary.org; f. 1889; colln of revised code, gen. code, admin. code, reported and unreported cases, form books, legislative history materials, law journals, atty gen. opinions, local court rules for co courts, local municipal and township ordinances; 62,000 vols; Dir ANN CAPOZZI.

State Library of Ohio: 274 East First Ave, Columbus, OH 43201; tel. (614) 644-7061; fax (614) 466-3584; internet winslo.state.oh.us; f. 1817; 1.4m. vols; a spec. library for state govt, incl. periodicals, documents, pamphlets, services and microforms; spec. colln of management, genealogy, local history, education and health; State Librarian JO BUDLER.

Toledo-Lucas County Public Library: 325 Michigan St, Toledo, OH 43604; tel. (419) 259-5200; fax (419) 255-1332; internet www.toledolibrary.org; f. 1970; 18 brs; 1 outreach service; 1.9m. vols; Dir CLYDE S. SCOLES.

University of Cincinnati Libraries: POB 210033, Cincinnati, OH 45221-0033; tel. (513) 556-1424; fax (513) 556-0325; internet www.libraries.uc.edu; f. 1819; incl. Walter C. Langsam Library, Archives and Rare Books Library, Donald C. Harrison Health Sciences Library and 8 college and dept libraries; spec. colln: Archives and Rare Books Library (German-Americana Colln), Artists' Books, CCM Library Spec. Collns, Cohen Colln,

Elliston Poetry Room, Emile Male Colln, Geology Guidebook Colln, Historic K-12 Textbook Colln, Oesper Collns in the History of Chemistry, Henry R. Winkler Center for the History of the Health Professions; 3,123,318 vols; Dean and Univ. Librarian Dr VICTORIA A. MONTAVON.

Warren-Trumbull County Public Library: 444 Mahoning Ave NW, Warren, Ohio 44483; tel. (330) 399-8807; internet www.wtcpl.lib.oh.us; f. 1890; 5 brs and a bookmobile; Dir JAMES A. WILKINS; Pres. LILLIE JOHNSON; Sec. JAMES McFARLAND.

Oklahoma

Anadarko Community Library: 215 West Broadway, Anadarko, OK 73005; tel. (405) 247-7351; fax (405) 247-2024; internet www .anadarkopl.okpls.org; f. 1903, present name and status 1990; Dir CHRISTINA OWEN.

Bartlesville Public Library: 600 S Johnstone, Bartlesville, OK 74003; tel. (918) 338-4161; fax (918) 337-5338; e-mail bpl@ bartlesville.lib.ok.us; internet www .bartlesville.lib.ok.us; f. 1898; Dir JOAN SINGLETON.

Chickasaw Regional (Public) Library System: 601 Railway Express, Ardmore, OK 73401; tel. (580) 223-3164; fax (580) 223-3280; e-mail reference@crlsok.org; internet www.crlsok.org; brs in Atoka, Davis, Healdton, Tishomingo, Marietta, Sulphur and Wilson; provides free public library service to S-Central Oklahoma; Dir LYNN McINTOSH.

Duncan Public Library: 2211 N Highway 81, Duncan, OK 73533; tel. (580) 255-0636; fax (580) 255-6136; internet www2 .youseemore.com/duncan; f. 1921; Dir JAN COLE; Pres. RICK RODGERS; Sec. CAROL EUBANKS (acting).

Jay C. Byers Memorial Library: 215 E Wichita Ave, Cleveland, OK 74020; tel. (918) 358-2676; fax (918) 358-5606; e-mail info@ jcbyers.lib.ok.us; internet www .jcbyerslibrary.okpls.org; f. 1936, present name 2002; Chair. L. RUSTIN FERGUSON; Dir MICHELLE MILLER; Sec. JAN STEPHENS.

Mabel C. Fry Public Library: 1200 Lakeshore Dr., Yukon, OK 73099; tel. (405) 354-8232; fax (405) 350-7928; internet www .cityofyukonok.gov/city-departments/ mabel-c-fry-public-library; f. 1905, present location 1997; Chair. DONELDA WHEATLEY; Sec. JOYCE ROMAN; Head Librarian SARA SCHIEMAN.

Margaret Carder Library: 201 W Lincoln, Mangum, OK 73554; tel. (580) 782-3185; fax (580) 782-5308; e-mail mangumlib@mangum .lib.ok.us; internet www.mangum.okpls.org; f. 1922 as Mangum Public Library, present name 1995; 4,000 vols; Librarian MARTHA YOUNG; Pres. PAULA BANISTER; Sec. BRENDA SCOTT.

Miami Public Library: 200 N Main St, Miami, OK 74354-5918; tel. (918) 541-2292; fax (918) 542-9363; internet www.miami.lib .ok.us; Dir MARCIA JOHNSON; Head Librarian GAY FAIRCHILD; Chair. RON GILBERT; Sec. MICHELLE BASHORE.

Oklahoma Department of Libraries: 200 NE 18th St, Oklahoma City, OK 73105-3298; tel. (405) 521-2502; fax (405) 525-7804; internet www.odl.state.ok.us; f. 1967; state archives, state and federal govt depository; incl. Jan Eric Cartwright Memorial Library, State Records Center, Allen Wright Memorial Library; Dir SUSAN C. McVEY; Chair. HANNIBAL JOHNSON.

Oklahoma State University Libraries: 216 Library, Oklahoma State Univ., Stillwater, OK 74078-1071; tel. (405) 744-9775; e-mail okstatelibrary@hotmail.com; internet

www.library.okstate.edu; f. 1953; 3 brs: Mary L. Williams Curriculum Materials Library, John Rex Cunningham Architecture Library and Veterinary Medicine Library; North Boomer Annex; 3,468,428 vols, 198,512 govt documents, 70,030 print and e-serials, 4,567,900 microforms, 321,418 maps, 799,332 e-books; Dean of Libraries SHEILA GRANT JOHNSON.

Okmulgee Public Library: 218 S Okmulgee, Okmulgee, OK 74447; tel. (918) 756-1448; fax (918) 758-1148; e-mail library@ okmcity.net; internet www.okmulgeelibrary .org; bookmobile and inter-library services; genealogical colln; Dir KRISTIN CUNNINGHAM.

Ponca City Library: POB 1450, Ponca City, OK 74602; 516 E Grand, Ponca City, OK 74601; tel. (580) 767-0339; e-mail library@ poncacityok.gov; internet www .poncacitylibrary.com; f. 1904; Matzene Art Colln of artwork from Oriental and Western art; Richard Gordon Matzene colln incl. oils, charcoals, and water colours and three-dimensional bronze and pottery pieces; 80,000 vols; Dir HOLLY LaBOSSIERE.

Public Library of Enid and Garfield County: 120 W Maine, Enid, OK 73701; tel. (580) 234-6313; fax (580) 249-9280; e-mail publiclibrary@enid.org; internet www .enid.org/index.aspx?page=62; f. 1959 by merger of Enid Public Library with Garfield County Library; Dir MICHELLE R. MEARS.

Stillwater Public Library: 1107 S Duck, Stillwater, OK 74074; tel. (405) 372-3633; e-mail askalibrarian@stillwater.org; internet library.stillwater.org; f. 1922; spec. collns: multi-language, graphic novels, genealogy, and local govt and historical documents; 90,000 vols; Chair. SUSAN SIMMONS; Dir LYNDA REYNOLDS.

Tulsa City-County Library: 400 Civic Center, Tulsa, OK 74103; tel. (918) 549-7323; fax (918) 549-7434; internet www .tulsalibrary.org; 25 br. libraries; incl. Ruth G. Hardman Adult Literacy Services; 1,740,123 vols, 68,224 maps, 185,273 microforms, 524,669 govt documents; CEO GARY SHAFFER.

University of Oklahoma Libraries: 401 W Brooks St, Norman, OK 73019; tel. (405) 325-4142; fax (405) 325-7550; internet libraries .ou.edu; f. 1892; depository for fed. govt documents since 1893; 5 brs; spec. collns: Western history, John & Mary Nichols Rare Books and Spec. Collns, Bass Business History Colln, History of Science Collns; 5m. vols, 63,000 serials subscriptions, 17,000 linear ft of MSS and archives, 1.6m. photographs, 1.5m. maps, 70 incunabula; Dean of Univ. Libraries SUL H. LEE.

Oregon

Cedar Mill Community Library: 12505 NW Cornell Rd, Suite 13, Portland, OR 97229; tel. (503) 644-0043; fax (503) 644-3964; e-mail askuscml@wccls.org; internet library.cedarmill.org; f. 1974; 2 brs; 284,000 vols.

Chetco Community Public Library: 405 Alder St, Brookings, OR 97415; tel. (541) 469-7738; fax (541) 469-6746; internet www .chetcolibrary.org; f. 1927; 70,000 vols (incl. books, DVDs, videos, audiobooks, magazines and pamphlets); Chair. VIOLET LOVEJOY.

Eugene Public Library: 100 W 10th Ave, Eugene, OR 97401; tel. (541) 682-5450; e-mail libraryaskus@ci.eugene.or.us; internet www.eugene-or.gov; 400,000 vols (incl. CDs, DVDs, audio books, large print books, magazines and newspapers).

Jefferson County Library: 241 SE Seventh St, Madras, OR 97741; tel. (541) 475-3351; fax (541) 475-7434; e-mail library@jcld

.org; internet www.jcld.org; f. 1916; Library Dir DeRese Hall.

Multnomah County Library: 801 SW 10th Ave, Portland, OR 97205; tel. (503) 988-5402; fax (503) 998-5441; internet www.multcolib .org; f. 1864; 19 brs; 2m. vols; Dir Vailey Oehlke.

Oregon State Library: 250 Winter St, NE, Salem, OR 97301-3950; tel. (503) 378-4243; fax (503) 585-8059; e-mail library.help@state .or.us; internet www.oregon.gov/osl; f. 1905; provides service to state agencies and print-disabled persons; develops local library services; special collns: Oregon and Oregon authors; 1,140,680 vols.

Springfield Public Library: 225 Fifth St, Springfield, OR 97477-4636; tel. (541) 726-3766; e-mail library@ci.springfield.or.us; internet www.ci.springfield.or.us/library; f. 1908; Dir Rob Everett.

University of Oregon Libraries: 1299 Univ. of Oregon, Eugene, OR 97403-1299; tel. (541) 346-3053; fax (541) 346-3485; internet libweb.uoregon.edu; f. 1876; 3.1m. vols, 481,414 govt documents, 783,154 maps, 4.2m. microfilm units; 420,557 computer files; Dean of Libraries Deborah A. Carver; Head of Licensing, Grants and Collns Analysis Assoc. Prof. David C. Fowler.

Wilsonville Public Library: 8200 SW Wilsonville Rd, Wilsonville, OR 97070; tel. (503) 682-2744; fax (503)-682-8685; e-mail reference@wilsonvillelibrary.org; internet www.wilsonville.lib.or.us; access to over 1.5m. items from the Library Information Network of Clackamas County; 120,000 vols; Library Dir Patrick Duke.

Pennsylvania

Adams County Library System: 140 Baltimore St, Gettysburg, PA 17325; tel. (717) 334-5716; fax (717) 334-7992; internet www .adamslibrary.org; incl. 6 libraries and 1 bookmobile; main br. Gettysburg.

American Philosophical Society Library: 105 S Fifth St, Philadelphia, PA 19106-3386; tel. (215) 440-3400; fax (215) 440-3423; internet www.amphilsoc.org; f. 1743; nat. centre for research in the history of the sciences, medicine and technology; MSS collns range from 18th-century natural history, American Indian linguistics and culture, to nuclear physics, computer devt and medical science spec. collns on Benjamin Franklin, Thomas Paine, history of science, genetics, quantum physics, Darwinism; 350,000 vols, 11m. MSS, 250,000 images; Librarian Martin Levitt; publ. *Bulletin* (2 a year).

Athenaeum of Philadelphia: 219 S Sixth St, Philadelphia, PA 19106; tel. (215) 925-2688; fax (215) 925-3755; internet www .philaathenaeum.org; f. 1814; colln incl. history and antiquities of America and useful arts; resources incl. for the period of 1800–1945; Exec. Dir Dr Sandra L. Tatman.

Beaver County Library System: 109 Pleasant Dr., Suite 101, Aliquippa, PA 15001; tel. (724) 378-6227; e-mail foundationcenter@beaverlibraries.org; internet www.beaverlibraries.org; f. 1971; 11 public libraries and 1 Bookmobile.

Carnegie Library of Pittsburgh: 4400 Forbes Ave, Pittsburgh, PA 15213-4080; tel. (412) 622-3114; fax (412) 622-6278; e-mail info@carnegielibrary.org; internet www .carnegielibrary.org; f. 1895; 19 local brs; incl. main library and library for the blind and physically handicapped; 5,267,012 vols; Pres. and Dir Mary Frances Cooper.

Chester County Library System: 450 Exton Sq. Parkway, Exton, PA 19341; tel. (610) 280-2600; fax (610) 280-2694; internet

www.ccls.org; f. 1965; Dist. Center Library and 17 mem. libraries; Exec. Dir Joseph L. Sherwood; Pres. Richard Hankin; Sec. Buck Jones; Treas. Jo Ann Weinberger.

Dauphin County Library System: 101 Walnut St, Harrisburg, PA 17101; tel. (717) 234-4961; fax (717) 234-7479; e-mail exec-dir@dcls.org; internet www.dcls.org; incl. 8 libraries; 351,234 vols; Exec. Dir Rich Bowra; Pres. Bruce Senft; Sec. Christine Mummert; Treas. Dr Thomas Carey.

David Library of the American Revolution: POB 748, Washington Crossing, PA 18977; 1201 River Rd, Washington Crossing, PA 18977; tel. (215) 493-6776; fax (215) 493-9276; e-mail librarian@dlar.org; internet www.dlar.org; f. 1959, present bldg 1974; specialized research library for the study of American history c. 1750–1800; spec. colln incl. materials on women, families, African Americans and Native Americans, the French and Indian War and early nat. periods; 40,000 vols, 10,000 reels of microfilm; Chief Operating Officer Meg McSweeney; Librarian Katherine A. Ludwig; Treas. Barbara B. Faherty.

Delaware County Library System: 340 N Middletown Rd, Fair Acres Bldg 19, Media, PA 19063; tel. (610) 891-8622; fax (610) 891-8641; e-mail support@delcolibraries.org; internet www.delcolibraries.org; 26 libraries; 1.2m. vols; Exec. Dir David Belanger; Pres. L. James Bading; Sec. David Gallo; Treas. Victoria Gerstenfeld.

Donald F. and Mildred Topp Othmer Library of Chemical History: c/o Chemical Heritage Foundation, 315 Chestnut St, Philadelphia, PA 19106; tel. (215) 873-8269; e-mail reference@chemheritage.org; internet www.chemheritage.org/visit/library; f. 1988; attached to Chemical Heritage Foundation; rare books, oral histories, photographs about history of chemistry and related sciences and industries; spec. colln incl. alchemy, industries, gen. science, physics, physiology, medicine, toxicology, pathology, pharmacology, pharmacy and material medica, technology, engineering, environmental topics, mining and chemical manufacturers; 5,000 linear shelf ft; Dir Elsa Atson.

Ewell Sale Stewart Library and Archives of the Academy of Natural Sciences: 1900 Benjamin Franklin Parkway, Philadelphia, PA 19103-1195; tel. (215) 299-1040; fax (215) 299-1144; e-mail library@ansp.org; internet www.ansp.org/library; f. 1812; attached to Drexel Univ.; works published in the 1500s to current serials and monographs from all over the world; expedition literature, incl. works of scientists such as Lewis and Clark and published journals of amateur naturalists; illustrated works in natural sciences, from the pre-Linnaean classics of Gesner, Aldrovandi and Catesby (published before 1750) to the great bird books of Gould, Audubon, Elliot and Wilson, and the flora of Redouté, Sowerby and the Bauers, to the modern masters of wildlife art, F. L. Jaques, L. A. Fuertes and Terence Shortt; 200,000 vols, 2,500 current periodicals, 250,000 MSS, 1m. archival items; Pres. and CEO George W. Gephart, Jr; Sec. Judith E. Soltz; Treas. David P. Lazar, Sr.

Free Library of Philadelphia: Central Library, 1901 Vine St, Philadelphia, PA 19103-1189; tel. (215) 686-5322; internet www.library.phila.gov; f. 1891; 54 brs city-wide, incl. 3 larger regional libraries and Library for the Blind and Physically Handicapped; spec. collns incl.: Fleisher orchestral music; Carson history of common law; Widener incunabula; Drinker Choral Library; Lewis Illuminated MSS, European and Oriental; History of the Automobile; Elkins

Americana, Dickens, Goldsmith, Gimbel Poe; Lewis cuneiform tablets; theatre colln; map colln (over 130,000 single-sheet maps and atlases); 6m. items; Pres. and Dir Siobhan A. Reardon; Sec. Darwin Beauvais; Treas. Melissa Grimm.

Jenkins Law Library: 833 Chestnut St, Suite 1220, Philadelphia, PA 19107-4429; tel. (215) 574-7900; fax (215) 574-7920; e-mail circulation@jenkinslaw.org; internet www .jenkinslaw.org; f. 1802 as Law Library Company of the City of Philadelphia; legal and non-legal resources, incl. fed. and state cases, statutes, regulations, court records and briefs and treatises; rare and out-of-print materials; 600,000 vols; Pres. Alexander Kerr; Exec. Dir and Sec. Regina L. Smith; Treas. Harold Cramer.

Joseph P. Horner Memorial Library: German Soc. of Pennsylvania, 611 Spring Garden St, Philadelphia, PA 19123; tel. (215) 627-2332; fax (215) 627-5297; e-mail librarian@germansociety.org; internet www .germansociety.org/library; f. 1783; attached to German Soc. of Pennsylvania; books in German language; lbooks published after 1917; German-American Archive (10,000 books and pamphlets, 75 linear ft of MSS collns); 60,000 vols; Librarian Violet Lutz.

Library Company of Philadelphia: 1314 Locust St, Philadelphia, PA 19107; tel. (215) 546-3181; fax 215) 546-5167; e-mail cking@ librarycompany.org; internet www .librarycompany.org; f. 1731; American history and culture from the 17th through the 19th centuries; colln incl. rare books, MSS, broadsides, ephemera, prints, photographs and works of art; spec. colln incl. Afro-Americana; German-Americana; history of printing and publishing; American Judaica; printmaking, mapmaking, and photography in Philadelphia; libraries of James Logan and Benjamin Franklin; 500,000 vols; Dir Dr John C. Van Horne; Librarian James N. Green.

Pennsylvania Horticultural Society's McLean Library: 100 N 20th St, Philadelphia, PA 19103-1495; tel. (215) 988-8772; fax (215) 988-8810; e-mail mcleanlibrary@ pennhort.org; internet www .pennsylvaniahorticulturalsociety.org/garden/libraryhome.html; books and DVDs on gardening and plant care, botany, urban greening; rare gardening books; vintage seed catalogue colln and archives of the Soc. incl. Philadelphia Flower Show archives; 15,000 vols; Pres. Drew Becher; publ. *Green Scene* (6 a year).

Pennsylvania State University Libraries: 510 Paterno Library, University Park, PA 16802-1812; tel. (814) 865-6368; fax (814) 865-3665; e-mail s2w@psulias.psu.edu; internet www.libraries.psu.edu; f. 1859; 36 libraries at 24 locations throughout the Commonwealth of Pennsylvania; 5,441,121 vols, 430,694 maps, 3,553,455 microforms, 127,834 film and video materials, 47,000 online full-text journals and 125,000 e-books; Dean of Libraries Barbara I. Dewey.

State Library of Pennsylvania: Pennsylvania Dept of Education, Office of Commonwealth Libraries, Bureau of State Library, 333 Market St, Harrisburg, PA 17126-0333; 607 S Dr., Harrisburg, PA 17120-0600; tel. (717) 783-5950; fax (717) 772-8268; e-mail ra-reference@state.pa.us; internet www .statelibrary.state.pa.us; f. 1745; attached to Pennsylvania Dept of Education; colln incl. American history, education, political science, sociology, library science, law and genealogy, Pennsylvania history; newspapers, maps; spec. colln original Pennsylvania Assembly colln; 3,000 vols, 100,000 microfilms; Dir Alice Lubrecht.

Union County Library System: 255 Reitz Blvd, Lewisburg, PA 17837; tel. (570) 523-1172; internet www .unioncountylibrarysystem.com; f. 1998; Public Library for Union Co, Lewisburg; Herr Memorial Library, Mifflinburg; West End Library, Laurelton; Pres. SUSAN JORDAN; Sec. and Treas. KAREN SHIPTON.

University of Pennsylvania Library: 3420 Walnut St, Philadelphia, PA 19104-6206; tel. (215) 898-7555; fax (215) 898-0559; e-mail library@pobox.upenn.edu; internet www.library.upenn.edu; f. 1750; central library and 14 deptl and affiliated libraries; incl. books on archaeology, anthropology, Leibniz, Descartes, history of philosophy and science, Lithuanian history and literature, history of chemistry, criminology, French Revolution, Judaica, Modern Jewish history, modern Hebrew literature, Aristotelianism, Occam, Medieval history, medieval Church history, Inquisition, Middle East and Islamic studies, Italian Renaissance literature, Spanish literature of the Golden Age, Shakespeareana (Furness Library), Restoration drama, 18th- and early 19th-century English fiction, American drama, fiction, and poetry; 6,096,588 vols; Vice-Provost and Dir of Libraries H. CARTON ROGERS.

University of Pittsburgh Libraries: Pittsburgh, PA 15260; tel. (412) 648-7747; fax (412) 648-7887; internet www.pitt.edu/libraries.html; f. 1873; 22 separate libraries on or near main campus and 4 regional campus libraries in Bradford, Greensburg, Johnstown and Titusville; academic research library; 6.1m. vols, 5.4m. microforms, over 87,000 current serials, 5,500 e-journals, 200,000 e-books; Dir RUSH MILLER.

US Army War College Library: 122 Forbes Ave, Carlisle, PA 17013-5220; tel. (717) 245-3660; fax (717) 245-3720; e-mail usawc .libraryr@us.army.mil; internet www.carlisle .army.mil/library/index.htm; military strategy and operations, int. relations, foreign policy, regional studies, management and economics; 165,400 vols, 450 e-journals, 600 print journal subscriptions.

Rhode Island

Brown University Library: Providence, RI 02912; tel. (401) 863-2165; fax (401) 863-1272; e-mail libweb@brown.edu; internet dl .lib.brown.edu/libweb; f. 1764; incl. John D. Rockefeller, Jr. Library (research library for humanities, social sciences, fine arts), Sciences Library, Owing Music Library, John Hay Library (spec. collns, rare books, MSS archives), Art Slide Library; 6.8m. vols; Univ. Librarian HARRIETTE HEMMASI.

George Hail Free Library: 530 Main St, Warren, RI 02885; tel. (401) 245-7686; e-mail epatricrn@yahoo.com; internet www .georgehail.org; f. 1871; Pres. JOHN MILLARD; Dir PATRICIA REDFEARN.

Jamestown Philomenian Library: 26 N Rd, Jamestown, RI 02835; tel. (401) 423-7280; e-mail library@jamestownri.com; internet www.jamestownri.com/library; f. 1874; Pres. HEIDI KELLER MOON; Sec. CRAIG WATSON; Treas. DELIA KLINGBEIL; Dir DONNA FOGARTY.

John Carter Brown Library: Brown Univ., POB 1894, Providence, RI 02912; Brown Univ., 94 George St Providence, RI 02906; tel. (401) 863-2725; fax (401) 863-3477; e-mail jcbl_information@brown.edu; internet www.jcbl.org; f. 1846, present location 1901; independently funded and administered centre for advanced research in history and the humanities at Brown Univ.; contains primary historical sources pertaining to the colonial period of the Americas 1492–1825; offers fellowships, sponsors lectures and confs; regularly mounts exhibitions and publishes catalogues, bibliographies, and other works that interpret its holdings; 50,000 rare books, 16,000 reference books; Dir Dr EDWARD L. WIDMER; publ. *RBM: A Journal of Rare Books, Manuscripts, and Cultural Heritage.*

North Kingstown Free Library: 100 Boone St, North Kingstown, RI 02852; tel. (401) 294-3306; internet www.nklibrary.org; f. 1898; 129,000 vols; Chair. PATRICIA CARLSON; Dir CYNDI DESROCHERS.

North Scituate Public Library: 606 W Greenville Rd, North Scituate, RI 02857; tel. (401) 647-5133; fax (401) 934-1051; e-mail reference@scituatelibrary.org; internet scituatelibrary.org; f. 1906; Pres. JEFFREY AMYLON; Sec. TARA ANDERSON; Treas. PATIA BERTRAM; Dir LESLIE B. MCDONOUGH.

Providence Public Library: 150 Empire St, Providence, RI 02903; tel. (401) 455-8000; e-mail pplref@provlib.org; internet www .provlib.org; f. 1875; colln represents 4,000 years of human history and culture; Genealogy Coll: city directories, house directories, family biographies, Arnold's Vital Records and regimental histories of the Civil War; Rhode Island Colln: 10,000 books, 7,000 photographs of people, places and bldgs (print and online), historic and current maps pertaining to Rhode Island cities and towns, clippings, pamphlets, selected documents from the State of Rhode Island and the City of Providence; 40,000 vols (incl. books, MSS, pamphlets, ephemera, newspapers, maps, broadsides, art and artefacts), 15,000 scores and song books; Chair. WILLIAM S. SIMMONS; Sec. JULIUS KOLAWOLE; Treas. ELLEN K. HAYES; Dir DALE THOMPSON.

Providence Public Library: 150 Empire St, Providence, RI 02903; tel. (401) 455-8000; fax (401) 455-8080; e-mail pplref@provlib .org; internet www.provlib.org; f. 1876; 1m. vols (incl. 40,000 books, MSS, pamphlets, ephemera, newspapers, maps, broadsides, art and artefacts representing over 4,000 years of human history and culture); Chair. WILLIAM S. SIMMONS; Dir M. DALE THOMPSON; publ. *Occasional Nuggets* (4 a year).

Tiverton Public Library: 238 Highland Rd, Tiverton, RI 02878; tel. (401) 625-6796; internet www.tivertonlibrary.org; brs: Essex Public Library and Union Br. Library; Chair. BARBARA DONNELLY; Dir ANN GREALISH-RUST.

South Carolina

Anderson County Library System: 300 N McDuffie St, POB 4047, Anderson, SC 29621; tel. (864) 260-4500; e-mail administration@ andersonlibrary.org; internet www .andersonlibrary.org; f. 1840; brs: Belton, Honea Path, Iva, Pendleton, Piedmont, Piedmont, Westside and Williamston, 1 main library and a bookmobile; 300,000 vols; an expanded video and audio book colln; music CD colln: 4,000 titles in classical, jazz, rock, blues, country, R&B, gospel, and bluegrass music, as well as Broadway shows and movie themes; Dir FAITH LINE.

Berkeley County Library System: 1003 Highway 52, Moncks Corner, SC 29461; tel. (843) 719-4223; fax (843) 719-4226; e-mail bcls@berkeley.lib.sc.us; internet www.bcls.sc .gov; f. 1934; brs: Daniel Island, Sangaree, Goose Creek, Hanahan and St Stephen; Moncks Corner (HQ); Dir DONNA OSBORNE.

Charleston County Public Library: 68 Calhoun St, Charleston, SC 29401; tel. (843) 805-6930; fax (843) 727-3741; internet www .ccpl.org; f. 1930; 16 brs; 1 bookmobile; Jerry and Anita Zucker Holocaust Colln: books and CDs on Nazi persecution and destruction of European Jewry and other minorities; Shoah Visual History Colln; Exec. Dir DOUGLAS HENDERSON; Chair. JANET SEGAL; Sec. MAYA HOLLINSHEAD; Treas. STEVEN E. CLEM.

Darlington County Library System: 204 N Main St, Darlington, SC 29532; tel. (843) 398-4940; fax (843) 398-4942; internet www .darlington-lib.org; f. 1968; Darlington (HQ), Hartsville, Lamar and Society Hill; Chair. JENELLE DAVIS; Sec. and Treas. ANNE BALDWIN; Dir NANCY RAY.

Florence County Library System: 509 S Dargan St, Florence, SC 29506; tel. (843) 662-8424; fax (843) 661-7544; e-mail reference@florencelibrary.org; internet www .florencelibrary.org; f. 1903; 1 main library (Florence), 5 brs (Johnsonville, Lake City, Olanta, Pamplico and Timmonsville), 1 bookmobile; Chair. CHARLES HOWLE; Sec. and Treas. ANGELA LORENZ.

Greenville County Library System: 25 Heritage Green Pl., Greenville, SC 29601; tel. (864) 242-5000; fax (864) 235-8375; e-mail maincirc@greenvillelibrary.org; internet www.greenvillelibrary.org; f. 1921; 11 brs and 1 bookmobile; colln of materials that assist researchers interested in historical and genealogical research; 737,547 vols, 170,532 audio and visual items; Chair. DOUGLAS A. CHURDAR; Sec. SUSAN BARRY; Treas. S. ALLAN HILL; Exec. Dir BEVERLY JAMES.

Horry County Memorial Library: 1008 Fifth Ave, Conway, SC 29526; tel. (843) 248-1544; fax (843) 248-1443; internet www .horry.lib.sc.us; f. 1949; brs: Conway (HQ), Aynor, Bucksport, Green Sea/Floyds, Little River, Loris, North Myrtle Beach, Socastee and Surfside Beach; bookmobile; Dir CLIFTON BOYER.

Marion County Library: 101 E Court St, Marion, SC 29571; tel. (843) 423-8300; fax (843) 423-8302; e-mail marionlibr@spiritcom .net; internet www.marioncountylibrary.org; f. 1898; brs: Marion (HQ), Mullins and Nichols; 1 bookmobile; 86,534 ; Chair. H. PAUL DOVE, JR.; Sec. ESTHER W. ROGERS; Treas. VIOLA D. EDWARDS.

Oconee County Public Library: 501 W S Broad St, Walhalla, SC 29691-2105; tel. (864) 638-4133; fax (864) 638-4132; internet www .youseemore.com/oconee; f. 1948; brs: Walhalla (HQ), Salem, Seneca and Westminster; 1 mobile library; South Carolina history and local genealogy colln; family histories, historical maps, cemetery listings and indexes, biographies of noted South Carolinians and local newspapers on microfilm; Dir SUE BALDWIN.

Orangeburg County Library: 510 Louis St, Orangeburg, SC 29115; tel. (803) 531-4636; fax (803) 533-5860; e-mail oclnotify@ orangeburgcounty.org; internet www .orangeburgcounty.org/ocl; f. 1936; incl. libraries in Orangeburg, North, Holly Hill, Elloree, Santee and Springfield; Dir ROBERTA R. BIBBINS.

Richland County Public Library: 1431 Assembly St, Columbia, SC 29201; tel. (803) 799-9084; internet www.richland.lib.sc.us; f. 1896; incl. Main Library and 10 brs; 1.1m. books; 900 magazine titles in print; 15,000 online magazine titles; 150 newspaper titles; 90,000 videos, DVDs and CDs; 80 electronic databases; Exec. Dir MELANIE HUGGINS.

South Carolina State Library: POB 11469, Columbia, SC 29211; tel. (803) 734-8026; fax (803) 734-8676; e-mail reference@ statelibrary.sc.gov; internet www .statelibrary.sc.gov; f. 1929, present name and status 1969; fed. depository library since 1970; colln of publs on governance, management and admin., applied technology, history and social sciences; 303,681 vols, 264,144 federal documents, 94,564 state documents and 651,842 microforms, 2,088 periodicals, 4,553 audio-visual; Dir DAVID GOBLE; Chair. DAN B. MACKEY.

York County Library: 138 E Black St, Rock Hill, SC 29730; tel. (803) 981-5858; internet www.yclibrary.org; f. 1966; brs: Rock Hill (HQ), Clover, Fort Mill, Lake Wylie and York; books, periodicals, audio books, DVDs and video cassettes; book mobile: 3,000 vols; Dir COLLEEN KAPHENGST.

South Dakota

Brookings Public Library: 515 Third St, Brookings, SD 57006; tel. (605) 692-9407; fax (605) 692-9386; internet www .brookingslibrary.org; f. 1911; Dir ELVITA LANDAU.

Deadwood Public Library: 435 Williams St, Deadwood, SD 57732-2821; tel. (605) 578-2821; e-mail dwd@sdln.net; internet dwdlib .sdln.net; f. 1876; Dir JEANETTE CHANEY-MOODIE; Librarian CAROL HAUCK.

Grant County Public Library: 207 E Park Ave, Milbank, SD 57252; tel. (605) 432-6543; e-mail gclibrary21@hotmail.com; internet grantcountylibrary.com; f. 1979; 1 main library and 4 brs; Dir ROBIN SCHRUPP; Pres. MARJORIE BOHN.

Rapid City Public Libraries: 610 Quincy St, Rapid City, SD 57701-3630; tel. (605) 394-6139; fax (605) 566-7176; internet www.rcgov .org/library; f. 1879; 2 brs; Dir GRETA CHAP-MAN.

South Dakota State Archives: 900 Governors Dr., Pierre, SD 57501; tel. (605) 773-3804; fax (605) 773-6041; e-mail archref@ state.sd.us; internet history.sd.gov/archives; f. 1975; attached to South Dakota State Historical Soc.; collects, appraises, accessions, describes, organizes, preserves, determines significance, and makes available MSS collns, South Dakota state, county, and town govt records, photographs, maps and other archival materials which have permanent historical and research value; 12,000 cubic ft of records documenting South Dakota's history and heritage; State Archivist CHELLE SOMSEN; Govt Archivist VIRGINIA HANSON; Govt Archivist SARA CASPER.

South Dakota State Library: MacKay Bldg, 800 Governors Dr., Pierre, SD 57501; tel. (605) 773-3131; fax (605) 773-6962; e-mail library@state.sd.us; internet library .sd.gov; State govt publ. depository; 3,403,015 vols; State Librarian DAN SIEBERSMA; Pres. JUDY TRZYNKA.

South Dakota State University Library: POB 2115, Brookings, SD 57007; Briggs Library, SDSU, 1300 N Campus Dr., Brookings, SD 57007; tel. (605) 688-5107; fax (605) 688-6133; internet www.sdstate.edu/library; incl. archives and spec. colln of MSS and archival materials, books, serials, audiovisual materials, artefacts and photographs related to South Dakota history and life; Chief Univ. Librarian Prof. Dr KRISTI TORNQUIST.

University of South Dakota Libraries: 414 E Clark St, Vermillion, SD 57069; tel. (605) 677-5373; fax (605) 677-5488; e-mail library@usd.edu; internet www.usd.edu/ library; incl. archives and spec. colln; pre-1900 US govt publs and resources; genealogy colln; spec. collns: Chilson Colln (materials related to local histories, South Dakota history and Native American cultures), Mahoney Music Colln (violin and violin family instruments), Richardson Colln (MSS collns focusing on South Dakota's cultural, political and economic history), USD Photograph Colln; 488,000 vols; Dean of Univ. Libraries Dr ANNE COOPER MOORE.

Watertown Regional Library: POB 250, Watertown, SD 57201-0250; 160 Sixth St, NE, Watertown, SD 57201-0250; tel. (605) 882-6220; fax (605) 882-6221; e-mail adminwat@sdln.net; internet watweb.sdln .net; f. 1899; Pres. JUDY TRZYNKA.

Yankton Community Library: 515 Walnut St, Yankton, SD 57078; tel. (605) 668-5275; fax (605) 668-5277; e-mail ycllibrary@ sdln.net; internet www.cityofyankton.org/ yankton/library; f. 1868, present location 1974; 70,000 vols, 150 magazine and newspaper subscriptions; Dir KATHY JACOBS; Pres. ALICIA CORNEMANN.

Tennessee

C. E. Weldon Public Library: 100 Main St., Martin, TN 38237; tel. (731) 587-3148; fax (731) 587-4674; e-mail cew@ ceweldonlibrary.org; internet www .ceweldonlibrary.org; f. 1925 as Woman's Club Library, present name and status 1984; colln incl. genealogical files, large print books, videos, CDs, DVDs, audio books and microfilms; 40,000 vols; Dir ROBERTA PEA-COCK.

Clarksville Montgomery County Public Library: 350 Pageant Lane, Suite 501, Clarksville, TN 37040; tel. (931) 648-8826; fax (931) 648-8831; e-mail librarydirector@ clarksville.org; internet cmc-websvr .clarksville.org; f. 1894, present name and status 1959; colln incl. genealogy, periodicals, audio books; Dir MARTHA HENDRICKS.

Jean and Alexander Heard Library: 419 21st Ave S, Nashville, TN 37203-2427; tel. (615) 322-7100; fax (615) 343-8279; internet www.library.vanderbilt.edu; f. 1873; attached to Vanderbilt Univ.; housed in central, science—engineering, biomedical, divinity, education, law, management and music libraries; 3.5m. vols, 3.1m. microform, 1.2m. digital colln, 266,061 govt publs and 55,260 periodicals; Dean of Libraries CONNIE VINITA DOWELL; Dir for Collns JARED INGER-SOLL (acting).

Johnson City Public Library: 100 W Millard St, Johnson City, TN 37604; tel. (423) 434-4450; e-mail info@jcpl.net; internet www.jcpl.net; f. 1895; 125,000 vols; Pres. POLLY PETERSON; Sec. MICHAEL CLARK; Dir BOB SWANAY.

Knox County Public Library: 500 W Church Ave, Knoxville, TN 37902; tel. (865) 215-8750; e-mail reference@knoxlib.org; internet knoxrooms.sirsi.net; f. 1873; 20 facilities; local history and genealogy colln; 1m. books, periodicals, CDs, films and audio books; Dir MYRETTA BLACK.

Lawrence County Public Library: 519 E Gaines St, Lawrenceburg, TN 38464; tel. (931)-762-4627; fax (931)-766-1597; e-mail librarian@co.lawrence.tn.us; internet www .lawcopubliclibrary.com; f. 1941; colln incl. items on genealogy; Dir TERESA NEWTON.

Memphis Public Library & Information Center: 3030 Poplar Ave, Memphis, TN 38111-3527; tel. (901) 415-2749; fax (901) 725-8883; internet www.memphislibrary.org; f. 1893; 18 brs; CATV and colour videotaping studio; information and referral service (LINC-Library Information Center); 4.5m. vols; Dir KEENON MCCLOY; publ. *Kaleidoscope* (12 a year).

Nashville Public Library: 615 Church St, Nashville, TN 37219; tel. (615) 862-5800; internet www.library.nashville.org; f. 1903; 21 brs; audiobooks on audio cassettes and CDs; govt documents colln; spec. colln: historic colln of non-book materials, from newspaper photographs and recordings made by civil rights-era leaders, to an 1857 map of Nashville drawn by bookseller William A. Eichbaum and a hand-blocked poster pro-

moting Helen Hayes' appearance at the Ryman Auditorium in the 1930s; Wilson Limited Editions Colln: 800 books dating from 1929 to the present; Chair. MARGARET ANN ROBINSON; Dir DONNA NICELY.

Tennessee State Library and Archives: 403 Seventh Ave N, Nashville, TN 37243-1102; tel. (615) 741-2764; fax (615) 532-2472; e-mail reference.tsla@tn.gov; internet www .tennessee.gov/tsla; colln incl. county records and MSS, bibliographies; photographs depicting Tennessee; records dating back to 1763; 50,000 vols, 70 magazines; State Librarian and Archivist CHARLES A. SHER-RILL.

University of Tennessee, Knoxville Libraries: 607 John C. Hodges Library, 1015 Volunteer Blvd, Knoxville, TN 37996-1000; tel. (865) 974-6600; fax (865) 974-4259; e-mail eref@utk.edu; internet www.lib.utk .edu; f. 1794; spec. collns incl. Tennesseana, North American Indians; 3.5m. vols; Dean STEVE SMITH.

Watauga Regional Library: 2700 S Roan St, Suite 435, Johnson City, TN 37601; tel. (423) 926-2951; fax (423) 926-2956; e-mail nrenfro@wrlibrary.org; internet www .wrlibrary.org; consortium of libraries in Carter, Greene, Johnson, Sullivan, Unicoi and Washington counties; not open to the public; Dir NANCY RENFRO.

Texas

Amarillo Public Library: 413 E Fourth, Amarillo, TX 79101; tel. (806) 378-3054; fax (806) 378-9326; e-mail reference@ amarillolibrary.org; internet www .amarillolibrary.org; Downtown (central library); brs: SW, E, N and NW; 800,000 vols (incl. books, magazines and media materials).

Austin Public Library: POB 2287, Austin, TX 78768-2287; tel. (512) 974-7400; fax (512) 974-7475; internet www.ci.austin.tx.us/ library; f. 1926; 20 brs; system maintains a comprehensive colln of books, magazines, newspapers, recordings, audio cassettes and video cassettes; Austin History Center contains materials on history of Austin and Travis County; 4,316,785 vols; Dir BRENDA BRANCH.

Bastrop Public Library: 1100 Church St, Bastrop, TX 78602; tel. (512) 321-5441; e-mail genealogy@bastroplibrary.org; internet www.bastroplibrary.org; f. 1852, closed 1927, reopened 1971; 48,500 vols; Pres. MARY JO JENKINS; Dir MICKEY DUVALL.

Bedford Public Library: 2424 Forest Ridge Dr., Bedford, TX 76021; tel. (817) 952-2330; fax (817) 952-2396; internet lib .bedford.tx.us; f. 1964; 100,000 vols; Man. MARIA REDBURN.

Brazoria County Library System: 451 N Velasco, Suite 250, Angleton, TX 77515; tel. (979) 864-1505; fax (979) 864-1298; e-mail bcls@bcls.lib.tx.us; internet www.bcls.lib.tx .us; 11 libraries; Pres. MATINA BONNEN; Sec. STEWART COFFMAN; Librarian CATHERINE H. THREADGILL.

Brownsville Public Library System: 2600 Central Bld, Brownsville, TX 78521; tel. (956) 548-1055; fax (956) 548-0684; e-mail ask@brownsville.lib.tx.us; internet www2.youseemore.com/brownsville; f. 1906; brs: Central and Southmost; 200,000 vols.

Central Texas Library System, Inc.: 1005 W 41st St, Suite 100, Austin, TX 78756; tel. (512) 583-0704; fax (512) 583-0709; e-mail pat.tuohy@ctls.net; internet www.ctls.net; f. 1969; 79 mem. libraries; Chair. PEGGY GIB-SON; Sec. LYLE THORMANN; Treas. EILEEN ALTMILLER; Exec. Dir PATRICIA TUOHY.

Dallas Public Library: 1515 Young St, Dallas, TX 75201-5415; tel. (214) 670-1760; e-mail askalibrarian@dallaslibrary.org; internet www.dallaslibrary.org; f. 1901, present bldg 1954; 6,143,644 vols; Dir CORRINE HILL.

Fort Bend County Libraries: 1001 Golfview, Richmond, TX 77469; tel. (281) 342-4455; fax (281) 341-2688; e-mail genref@fortbend.lib.tx.us; internet www.fortbend.lib.tx.us; f. 1948; 9 brs; George Memorial Library (HQ); microfilm newspaper colln incl, Herald Coaster (1920s to present); foreign language colln; Dir CLARA RUSSELL.

Fort Worth Public Library: 500 W Third St, Fort Worth, TX 76102-7305; tel. (817) 392-7705; fax (817) 871-7734; e-mail librarywebmail@fortworthlibrary.org; internet www.fortworthlibrary.org; f. 1901; 15 brs; spec. collns: genealogy, local history, sheet music, postcards, bookplates; US and Texas govt depository; 2,066,000 vols; Dir Dr GLENIECE A. ROBINSON.

George Bush Presidential Library and Museum: 1000 George Bush Dr. West, College Station, TX 77845; tel. (979) 691-4000; fax (979) 691-4050; e-mail library.bush@nara.gov; internet bushlibrary.tamu.edu; f. 1997; museum of 100,000 artefacts relating to the life and career of President George Bush (1989–93); 44m. pages of official and personal papers, 2m. photographs, 2,500 hrs of video cassettes; Dir Dr WARREN FINCH.

Harris County Public Library: 8080 El Rio St, Houston, TX 77054; tel. (713) 749-9000; internet www.hcpl.net; 26 brs; 2,312,482 vols (incl. traditional printed books, magazines, newspapers, video cassettes, CDs and DVDs; Dir RHODA GOLDBERG; Man. for Br. Services BRUCE FARRAR.

Houston Area Library System: 500 McKinney St, Suite 400, Houston, TX 77002-5000; tel. (832) 393-1397; fax (832) 393-1474; e-mail elizabeth.swan@houstontx.gov; internet www.hals.lib.tx.us; mem. libraries across 28 counties in SE Texas; Library Chief and Coordinator ELIZABETH SWAN.

Houston Public Library: 500 McKinney St, Houston, TX 77002; tel. (832) 393-1300; fax (832) 393-1266; e-mail website@hpl.lib.tx.us; internet www.houstonlibrary.org; f. 1854 as Houston Lyceum, present status 1904; 35 brs; spec. collns: Bibles, Civil War, Salvation Army posters, early Houston photographs, early printing and illuminated MSS, juvenile literature, petroleum, sheet music, Texana, US and Texas depository; specializes in genealogy, art, architecture, business, management; jazz, Afro-American and Hispanic archives; 3.6m. items; Dir of Libraries RHEA BROWN LAWSON.

Jacksonville Public Library: 502 S Jackson St, Jacksonville, TX 75766; tel. (903) 586-7664; internet www.jacksonvillelibrary.com; f. 1913; colln on geneology; 65,000 vols; Dir BARBARA CROSSMAN.

Lyndon Baines Johnson Library & Museum: 2313 Red River St, Austin, TX 78705; tel. (512) 721-0200; e-mail johnson.library@nara.gov; internet www.lbjlibrary.org; f. 1971; administered by Nat. Archives and Records Admin.; audio-visual colln documenting Lyndon B. Johnson's life, career and presidency; spec. colln incl. vols on American politics and history; 45m. pages of historical documents; Dir MARK K. UPDEGROVE.

Midland County Public Library: 301 W Missouri, Midland, TX 79701; tel. (432) 688-4320; fax (432) 688-4939; e-mail circulation@co.midland.tx.us; internet www.co.midland.tx.us/lib; f. 1928; Downtown Library, Cen-

tennial Library (HQ) and Law Library; Dir JOHN TRISCHITTI.

Port Arthur Public Library: 4615 Ninth Ave, Port Arthur, TX 77642-5818; tel. (409) 985-2238; fax (409) 985-5969; internet www.pap.lib.tx.us; spec. colln of historic photographs on Port Arthur history; 140,000 vols (incl. 15,000 books on genealogy), 3,500 DVDs and VHS, 2,000 CDs; Dir JOSE MARTINEZ.

Quitman Public Library: POB 1677, Quitman, TX 75783-1677; 202 E Goode St, Quitman, TX 75783; tel. (903) 763-4191; fax (903) 763-2532; e-mail quitmanlibrarian@gmail.com; internet www.quitmanlibrary.org; genealogy colln; 30,000 vols; Dir DELENE H. ALLEN.

Seguin-Guadalupe County Public Library: 707 E College St, Seguin, TX 78155; tel. (830) 401-2422; fax (830) 401-2477; e-mail library@seguintexas.gov; internet www.seguin.lib.tx.us; local history and genealogy research materials; historic photographs and microfilmed copies of local newspapers dating back to 1847; 60,000 vols; Chair. MICHELLE JOHNSON; Dir JACKI GROSS.

Sevier County Public Library System: 408 High St, Sevierville, TX 37862; tel. (865) 453-3532; fax (865) 365-1665; e-mail dvess@sevierlibrary.org; internet www.sevierlibrary.org; f. 1968; brs: King Family, Kodak and Seymourn; Chair. DAVID SARTEN; Treas. JUDY GODFREY; Dir ROBIN COGDILL.

University of Texas Libraries: University of Texas at Austin, POB P, Austin, TX 78713-8916; tel. (512) 495-4350; fax (512) 495-4397; e-mail libs-hr@lib.utexas.edu; internet www.lib.utexas.edu; f. 1883; 8m. vols, also Arlington: 893,155 vols, El Paso: 746,308 vols, Permian Basin: 215,945 vols, San Antonio: 367,583 vols, Health Science Center, Houston: 54,000 vols, Health Science Center, Dallas: 224,732 vols, Health Science Center, Dallas: 224,732 vols, Health Science Center, San Antonio: 173,143 vols, Medical Br., Galveston: 291,326; Vice-Provost and Dir Dr FRED HEATH.

Weatherford Public Library: 1014 Charles St, Weatherford, TX 76086; tel. (817) 598-4150; fax (817) 598-4161; e-mail libinfo@ci.weatherford.tx.us; internet www.wpltx.com; spec. genealogy colln on Weatherford, Parker co and Texas; fed. census for Texas from 1850 to 1930; microfilm of local newspapers from 1901 to present; 90,000 vols; Dir DALE FLEEGER.

William T. Cozby Public Library: 177 N Heartz Rd, Coppell, TX 75019; tel. (972) 304-3655; e-mail library@coppelltx.gov; internet www.ci.coppell.tx.us/library-main; f. 1974; 93,000 vols, 170 periodicals and newspapers; Chair. THOMAS DWYER; Sec. SAUL FRIEDMAN; Dir VICTORIA CHIAVETTA.

Utah

Brigham City Carnegie Library: 26 E Forest St, Brigham City, UT 84302; tel. (435) 723-5850; e-mail brighamlibrary@gmail.com; internet bcpl.lib.ut.us; f. 1898; Dir SUE HILL.

City Library: 210 E 400S, Salt Lake City, UT 84111; tel. (801) 524-8200; internet www.slcpl.lib.ut.us; f. 1851; 5 brs; 1m. vols; Dir LINDA HAMILTON (acting).

Family History Library of the Church of Jesus Christ of Latter-day Saints: 35 N West Temple St, Salt Lake City, UT 84150-3400; tel. (866) 406-1830; fax (801) 240-3718; e-mail fhl@ldschurch.org; internet www.familysearch.org; f. 1894; 356,000 bound vols, 2.4m. reels of microfilm, 727,000 microfiches, 4,500 periodicals and 3,725 e-resources; Dir DON ANDERSON.

Giovale Library: 1840 S 1300E, Salt Lake City, UT 84105; tel. (801) 832-2250; fax (801) 832-3109; internet www.westminstercollege.edu/library; attached to Westminster College; Dir DIANE VANDERPOL.

J. Willard Marriott Library: 295 S 1500E, Salt Lake City, UT 84112-0860; tel. (801) 581-8558; fax (801) 581-3464; internet www.lib.utah.edu; f. 1850, present name 1969; attached to Univ. of Utah; spec. collns: archives, Middle East, MSS, rare books, W Americana, oral history; US state and UN documents depository; 3,159,576 vols, 86,266 serials; Dean and Univ. Librarian (vacant) JOYCE L. OGBURN.

Orem Public Library: 58 N State St, Orem, UT 84057; tel. (801) 229-7050; internet lib.orem.org; 285,000 vols, 13,000 videos, 20,000 DVDs, 31,000 CDs.

Park City Library: 1255 Park Ave, Park City, UT 84060; tel. (435) 615-5600; internet www.parkcitylibrary.org; f. 1888, present location 1993; 71,164 vols; Library Dir LINDA TILLSON.

President Millard Fillmore Library: 25 S 100W, Fillmore, UT 84631; tel. (435) 743-5314; e-mail info@fillmorelibrary.org; internet www.fillmorelibrary.org; f. 1925; Dir STEPHANIE ALEMAN.

Utah State Library Division: 250 N, 1950W, Suite A, Salt Lake City, UT 84116-7901; tel. (801) 715-6777; fax (801) 715-6767; internet library.utah.gov; f. 1957; Library Dir DONNA JONES MORRIS.

Vermont

Bennington Free Library: 101 Silver St, Bennington, VT 05201; tel. (802) 442-9051; e-mail reference@bfli.org; internet www.benningtonfreelibrary.org; f. 1865; colln on history of Bennington and Vermont; 57,000 vols (incl. books, periodicals and research materials); Dir LYNNE FONTENEAU McCANN.

John G. McCullough Free Library: 2 Main St, POB 339, North Bennington, VT 05257; tel. (802) 447-7121; e-mail mclibrary@comcast.net; internet www.mccullough.lib.vt.us; f. 1921; colln incl. periodicals and newspapers, biography and reference books, CDs (music and audio books), books on audio cassettes, DVDs and video cassettes, large print books; 20,000 vols; Chair. PRESTON McADOO; Sec. VIRGINIA SANDY; Treas. RACHEL SCHUMACHER; Dir SUSANNE WARREN.

Kellogg-Hubbard Library: 135 Main St, Montpelier, VT 05602; tel. and fax (802) 223-3338; e-mail info@kellogghubbard.org; internet www.kellogghubbard.org; f. 1885; remnants of Ancient Greece and Renaissance Italy; Pres. JOHN PAGE; Sec. JESSICA TURNER; Treas. TANYA MOREHOUSE; Dir ROBIN SALES.

Pierson Library: 5376 Shelburne Rd, Shelburne, VT 05482; tel. (802) 985-5124; fax (802) 985-5129; e-mail pierson@vals.state.vt.us; internet www.piersonlibrary.org; f. 1888, present name 1922, present bldg 2001; 27,000 vols and 104 periodicals; Chair. CAROLYN SICCAMA; Treas. MARLEEN MOORE; Dir KIP ROBERSON.

St. Albans Free Library: 11 Maiden Lane, Saint Albans, VT 05478; tel. (802) 524-1507; e-mail stalbans@vals.state.vt.us; internet www.stalbans.lib.vt.us; f. 1855 as Vermont Central Railroad Library Asscn, present bldg 1902; colln incl. Vermont town histories; US Census on microfilm (1810–1910) and information for family researchers; Chair. D. JOE DAVISON; Sec. DONNA HOWARD; Treas. LINDA LANG.

Stowe Free Library: 90 Pond St, Stowe, VT 05672; tel. (802) 253-6145; fax (802) 253-4808; internet www.stowelibrary.org; f. 1866; 25,000 vols, 2,000 film titles, 1,400 audio books on CDs, 200 music CDs, 100 magazine, journal and newspaper subscriptions; Chair. DAVID BRYAN; Sec. PHYLLIS THIBAULT; Treas. DICK JOHANNESEN; Dir REBEKKA MATEYK.

University of Vermont Libraries: 538 Main St, Burlington, VT 05405-0036; tel. (802) 656-2023; fax (802) 656-4038; internet library.uvm.edu; Bailey/Howe Library houses spec. collns of Vermont materials, rare books, govt documents and maps, and univ. archives; Cook Chemistry/Physics Library; Dana Medical Library; Library Reseach Annex; 1,523,977 vols, 1,123,993 govt documents, 2,037,527 microforms, 220,637 graphic materials,; Dean of Libraries and Information Services MAURA SAULE.

Howard and Alba Leahy Library: 60 Washington St, Barre, VT 05641-4209; tel. (802) 479-8500; fax (802) 479-8510; e-mail vhs-info@state.vt.us; internet www .vermonthistory.org; f. 2002 as Vermont Historical Society Library, present name 2007; collns of books and pamphlets dating from 1770; large genealogical colln; Librarian PAUL CARNAHAN; publ. *Vermont History* (1 a year).

Vermont State Archives and Records Administration Vermont Office of the Secretary of State: 1078 Route 2, Middlesex, Montpelier, VT 05633-7701; tel. (802) 828-3700; fax (802) 828-3710; e-mail archives@sec.state.vt.us; internet vermont-archives.org; f. 2008 by merger of Vermont State Archives and Div. of Public Records, Dept of Bldgs and Gen. Services; Sec. of State JAMES C. CONDOS; State Archivist GREGORY SANFORD; publ. *Records and Information Management Update* (4 a year).

Westford Public Library: 1717 Vermont Route 128, POB 86, Westford, VT 05494; tel. (802) 878-5639; e-mail westford_pl@vals .state.vt.us; internet www.westford.lib.vt.us; f. 1895, present bldg 1974; colln on Westford, Chittenden co and Vermont history; large print books and magazines; Chair. LINELL VILASECA; Sec. PETER JONES; Treas. ANDREA LETORNEY; Librarian VICTORIA TIBBITS.

Virginia

Alexandria Library: 5005 Duke St, Alexandria, VA 22304-2903; tel. (703) 746-1702; fax (703) 746-1763; internet www.alexandria .lib.va.us; f. 1794; 4 brs; spec. colln incl. historical materials related to Alexandria and Northern Virginia; historical photographs; govt. documents on Civil War; microfilm of local newspapers; rare books colln of Alexandria Library Company and journals on history, genealogy and historic preservation; 300,000 vols, 3,000 audio-visual materials (Charles E. Beatley Jr. Central Library); 110,000 vols (Kate Waller Barrett Br.); 18,000 books and audio-visual materials (Ellen Coolidge Burke Br.); 75,000 books and audio-visual materials (James M. Duncan Br.); Chair. DOROTHY KOOPMAN; Sec. GWENDOLYN DAY-FULLER; Treas. ANNE PAUL; Dir of Libraries ROSE T. DAWSON.

Fairfax County Public Library: 12000 Government Center Parkway, Suite 324, Fairfax, VA 22035-0012; tel. (703) 324-3100; e-mail www@fairfaxcounty.gov; internet www.co.fairfax.va.us/library; f. 1939; 21 brs; also CD-ROMs, microfilm, audio and video cassettes, periodicals, recorded and talking books, CATV hook-up; 3m. vols; Dir EDWIN S. CLAY, III.

Fauquier County Public Library: Old Town Warrenton, 11 Winchester St, Warrenton, VA 20186; tel. (540) 422-8500; fax (540) 422-8520; internet www.fauquiercounty.gov/ government/departments/library; f. 1969; brs: Warrenton, Bealeton, John Marshall and New Baltimore; 206,233 vols; Chair.

BARBARA SEVERIN; Sec. and Treas. JACK WHITING.

Hampton Public Library: 4207 Victoria Blvd, Hampton, VA 23669; tel. (757) 727-1154; internet www.hamptonpubliclibrary .org; f. 1926; colln on Virginia and Hampton history; local newspapers on microfilm; current City of Hampton documents; brs: Main, Northampton, Phoebus,Willow Oaks and George Wythe Law; 1 bookmobile; 316,828 vols; Dir ROBERT CARPENTER.

Jefferson-Madison Regional Library: 201 E Market St, Charlottesville, VA 22902; tel. (434) 979-7151; fax (434) 971-7035; e-mail reference@jmrl.org; internet www .jmrl.org; f. 1972; spec. colln incl. Roland E. Beauford Sr. African-American colln by or about African-Americans; periodicals, photographs, MSS and maps on community history; newspapers and magazines on microfilm; 9 brs and 1 bookmobile; 500,000 vols; Pres. TIMOTHY F. JOST TOLSON; Dir JOHN HALLIDAY.

Jones Memorial Library: 2311 Memorial Ave, Lynchburg, VA 24501; tel. (434) 846-0501; fax (434) 846-1572; e-mail refdesk@ jmlibrary.org; internet www.jmlibrary.org; f. 1908; specializes in genealogy and local history; Lynchburg newspapers on microfilms; co histories and court records, family histories and genealogies; 300 MSS.

Library of Virginia: 800 E Broad St, Richmond, VA 23219-8000; tel. (804) 692-3500; internet www.lva.virginia.gov; f. 1823, present location 1997; Virginia, Southern US history, Civil War, genealogy; NewsBank's America's Newspapers which offers current and archived edns of more than 600 local, regional, and nat. newspapers; archive colln of 55,000 cu ft; 700,000 vols, 834 current periodicals; Librarian SANDRA GIOIA TREADWAY; publ. *Virginia Cavalcade*.

Mariners' Museum Library: 100 Museum Dr., Newport News, VA 23606-3759; tel. (757) 591-7782; fax (757) 591-7310; e-mail library@marinersmuseum.org; internet www .mariner.org/library; f. 1933; library of materials related to human interaction with the world's waterways; spec. collns: Edwin Levick Colln of photographs of passenger ships, yachts, and America's Cup Races; A. Aubrey Bodine Colln of images of life on the Chesapeake Bay; Chris-Craft Colln documenting the construction of boats by one of America's most important pleasure boat builders; 1,750,000 vols (incl. books, magazines, rare books, MSS, maps and charts, vessel plans, newspaper articles, photographs, Chris-Craft archives, and The Mariners' Museum's archives); Dir SUSAN BERG.

Norfolk Public Library: 1155 Pineridge Rd, Norfolk, VA 23502; tel. (757) 664-7328; fax (757) 441-1114; e-mail npl.comments@ norfolk.gov; internet www.npl.lib.va.us; f. 1904; ltd Fed. Govt Depository; brs: Norfolk Main, Sargeant Memorial Room, Barron F. Black, Blyden, Horace C. Downing, Janaf, Jordan-Newby, Lafayette, Larchmont, Little Creek, Park Place, Mary D. Pretlow Anchor and Van Wyck; bookmobile; colln incl. classic and popular items from the late 19th century to today; Dir NORMAN L. MAAS.

Patent and Trademark Office Scientific and Technical Information Center: Remsen Bldg, Lobby Level, Room 1D58, 400 Dulany St, Alexandria, VA; tel. (571) 272-2520; e-mail usptoinfo@uspto.gov; internet www.uspto.gov; f. 1836; foreign patent documents in electronic, print, and micro formats since 1617 from 73 countries; 200,000 vols; Dir of the US Patent and Trademark Office DAVID KAPPOS; Commissioner for Patents ROBERT L. STOLL; Commissioner for Trademarks DEBORAH COHN.

Richmond Public Library: 101 E Franklin St, Richmond, VA 23219; tel. (804) 646-4256; fax (804) 646-7685; internet www .richmondpubliclibrary.org; f. 1924; 1 main library and 8 brs; 810,066 vols; Chair. CLARE OSDENE SCHAPIRO; Dir HARRIET HENDERSON COALTER.

University of Virginia Library: POB 400113, Charlottesville, VA 22904-4113; tel. (804) 924-3021; fax (804) 924-1431; e-mail library@virginia.edu; internet www.lib .virginia.edu; f. 1819; 5.1m. vols, 53,015 journals, 150,362 maps, 447,020 slides and photographs, 87,642 video and audio recordings, 70,000 CDs, 16m. MSS and archives; spec. collns incl. American history and literature, incl. McGregor Library of American History and the Barrett Library of American Literature, Massey-Faulkner colln, Streeter colln on Southeastern railways, optics, evolution, Thomas Jefferson, Scott Sporting Colln, Victorian fiction, Greek and Latin literature, music, int. law, history of printing, Gothic novels, Matthew Arnold, Jorge Luis Borges coln, Gordon colln of French books, Tibetan colln, Paul Mellon colln of Americana and Virginiana; Librarian KARIN WITTENBORG.

US Geological Survey Libraries Program: Room 1D 100, 12201 Sunrise Valley Dr., MS 950, Reston, VA 20192; tel. (703) 648-4301; fax (703) 648-6373; e-mail library@ usgs.gov; internet library.usgs.gov; f. 1879; incl. 4 central libraries at Denver, CO, Flagstaff, AZ, Menlo Prak, CA and Reston, VA; part of Core Science Systems within USGS; 1.7m. vols, 700,000 maps, 370,000 microforms, 270,000 pamphlets, 260,000 black and white photographs, 60,000 colour transparencies, 15,000 field record notebooks, 250 video cassettes; Dir RICHARD HUFFINE.

Virginia Beach Public Library: 4100 Virginia Beach Blvd, Virginia Beach, VA 23452; tel. (757) 385-4321; e-mail library@ vbgov.com; internet www.vbgov.com; 10 brs; a bookmobile; colln of old newspapers and magazines; 875,169 vols, 11,000 books; Dir MARCY SIMS.

Washington County Public Library System: 205 Oak Hill St, Abingdon, VA 24210; tel. (276) 676-6222; e-mail charlotte@wcpl .net; internet www.wcpl.net; f. 1954; Abingdon (HQ); brs: Damascus, Glade Spring, Hayters Gap and Mendota; local history and genealogy colln; 30,000 e-books; Chair. KENNY SHUMAN; Dir CHARLOTTE LEWIS PARSONS.

Williamsburg Regional Library: 7770 Croaker Rd, Williamsburg, VA 23188; tel. (757) 259-4050; fax (757) 259-4079; internet www.wrl.org; f. 1909, present location 1973; brs: Williamsburg Library and James City County Library; serves Williamsburg, James City Co and York Co; colln on periodicals and news content from New York Times since 1995; mobile library services; 345,000 vols; Chair. MICHAEL J. FOX; Dir JOHN A. MOORMAN.

Washington

Enumclaw Public Library: 1700 First St, Enumclaw, WA 98022; tel. (360) 825-2938; fax (360) 825-0825; e-mail library@ci .enumclaw.wa.us; internet www.enumclaw .lib.wa.us; f. 1923; photography colln; colln documents social, industrial, commercial and agricultural heritage in Enumclaw and surrounding region; 50,000 vols; Chair. FRED FLEISCHMANN.

Everett Public Library: 2702 Hoyt Ave, Everett, WA 98201; tel. (425) 257-8022; e-mail libref@ci.everett.wa.us; internet www .epls.org; f. 1894 as Everett Woman's Book Club; 2 brs; 236,359 vols, 805 magazine and newspaper titles, 3,972 vols govt documents, 11,694 DVDs, 5,712 videos; Dir EILEEN SIMMONS.

Fort Vancouver Regional Library District: 1007 E Mill Plain Blvd, Vancouver, WA 98663; tel. (360) 695-1561; e-mail contact@fvrl.org; internet www.fvrl.org; f. 1950; 13 libraries, 3 bookmobiles and a Vancouver operations centre; 721,000 books, magazines, video cassettes, DVDs, and audio book CDs, cassettes; Exec. Dir PATTY DUITMAN.

Longview Public Library: 1600 Louisiana St, Longview, WA 98632; tel. (360) 442-5300; internet www.longviewlibrary.org; f. 1922; Dir CHRIS SKAUGSET.

North Olympic Library System (NOLS): 2210 S Peabody St, Port Angeles, WA 98362; tel. (360) 417-8525; fax (360) 457-4469; e-mail director@nols.org; internet www.nols.org; 4 brs; 260,000 vols; Dir PAULA BARNES.

Pierce County Library System: Processing and Administrative Center, 3005 112th St, E, Tacoma, WA 98446; tel. (253) 548-3300; fax (253) 537-4600; e-mail director@piercecountylibrary.org; internet www.piercecountylibrary.org; f. 1946; 18 brs and 3 bookmobiles; 1.3m. books, CDs, DVDs and audiobooks; Exec. Dir NEEL PARIKH.

Puyallup Public Library: 324 S Meridian, Puyallup, WA 98371; tel. (253) 841-5454; fax (253) 841-5483; e-mail puylib@ci.puyallup.wa.us; internet www.cityofpuyallup.org; f. 1877; Library Dir MARY JO TORGESON.

Roslyn Public Library: 109 S First St, POB 451, Roslyn, WA 98941; tel. (509) 649-3420; e-mail rpl@inlandnet.com; internet www.roslynlibrary.org; f. 1898; 10,000 vols, 5,000 e-books and e-audiobooks; Librarian ERIN KRAKE.

Seattle Public Library: 1000 Fourth Ave, Seattle, WA 98104-1109; tel. (206) 386-4636; e-mail city.librarian@spl.org; internet www.spl.org; f. 1891; spec. collns: Aeronautics, Pacific NW Americana; 23 brs; 2m. vols, 20,000 int. and nat. newspapers and magazines; Pres. MARIE MCCAFFREY; City Librarian MARCELLUS TURNER.

Tacoma Public Library: 1102 Tacoma Ave S, Tacoma, WA 98402; tel. (253) 292-2001; internet www.tacomapubliclibrary.org; 1 main library; 7 brs; Library Dir SUSAN ODENCRANTZ.

University of Washington Libraries: POB 352900, Seattle, WA 98195-2900; tel. (206) 543-0242; fax (206) 685-8727; e-mail libquest@u.washington.edu; internet www.lib.washington.edu; f. 1862; incl. Law Library (separately administered; Librarian PENNY HAZELTON), Health Sciences Library, Odegaard Undergraduate Library, East Asia Library, Spec. Collns Div. and 9 br. libraries; 7,203,156 vols, 63,221 current serials, 8,006,596 microforms; Dir and Dean, Univ. of Washington Libraries LIZABETH A. WILSON.

Washington State Library: POB 42460, Olympia, WA 98504-2460; tel. (360) 704-5200; fax (360) 586-7575; e-mail askalibrarian@sos.wa.gov; internet www.sos.wa.gov/library; f. 1853; spec. collns: Washington authors, Pacific NW, Washington state documents, Washington state newspapers, transportation, labor and industries, utilities; 167,094 vols, 1,241,503 fed. and state documents, 198,142 microfiche, 49,183 microfilms, 8,914 films, 456,320 audio and video cassettes; State Librarian Dr RAND SIMMONS (acting).

West Virginia

Cabell County Public Library: 455 Ninth St Plaza, Huntington, WV 25701; tel. (304) 528-5700; fax (304) 528-5701; e-mail cabelllibrary@cabell.lib.wv.us; internet cabell.lib.wv.us; f. 1897, present bldg 1980; 7 brs and 1 main library; also serves libraries located in Logan, Mason, Mingo, Putnam and Wayne counties; Dir JUDY K. RULE; Pres. ROBERT JACKSON.

Greenbrier County Public Library: 152 Robert W McCormick Dr., Lewisburg, WV 24901; tel. (304) 647-7568; fax (304) 647-7569; e-mail greenbrier.library@mail.mln.lib.wv.us; internet greenbrier.lib.wv.us; f. 1941; genealogical material; local history room with colln of books related to local history.

Hampshire County Public Library: 153 W Main St, Romney, WV 26757; tel. (304) 822-3185; fax (304) 822-3955; internet www.hampshirecopubliclib.com; f. 1935; Dir AMANDA SNYDER; Head Librarian NORMA CZERNICKI; Pres. JOHN ZEILOR; Sec. KATHEE ROGERS; Treas. STEVE MORELAND.

Jackson County Public Library: 208 N Church St, Ripley, WV 25271; tel. (304) 372-5343; fax (304) 372-7935; internet jackson.park.lib.wv.us; f. 1949; HQ in Ripley and br. in Ravenswood; 50,000 vols; Pres. TERESA EVANS.

Kanawha County Public Library: 123 Capitol St, Charleston, WV 25301; tel. (304) 343-4646; internet www.kanawhalibrary.org; f. 1908 as Charleston Public Library, present name 1934; 1 main library, 9 brs and 1 mobile library; affiliation with Nitro Public Library and shares resources with libraries in Kanawha Co schools system; 600,000 vols; Dir ALAN ENGELBERT; Pres. MICHAEL ALBERT.

Marion County Public Library: 321 Monroe St, Fairmont, WV 26554; tel. (304) 366-1210; fax (304) 366-4831; internet www.marioncountypubliclibrary.org; f. 1892, present name and status 1939; HQ in Fairmont; 2 brs; bookmobile services; Dir ERIKA REED.

Monroe County Public Library: 103 South St, Union, WV 24983; tel. (304) 772-3038; fax (304) 772-4052; internet monroe.lib.wv.us; f. 1947; 30,000 vols; Dir DORIS MCCURDY; Pres. ELIZABETH MCLAY IRONS; Sec. CATHY ABERNATHY; Treas. JANE PEIRICK.

Ohio County Public Library: 52 16th St, Wheeling, WV 26003; tel. (304) 232-0244; e-mail ocplweb@weirton.lib.wv.us; internet wheeling.weirton.lib.wv.us; f. 1882; Chair. MICHAEL BAKER; Sec. and Treas. JIMMIE MCCAMIC.

Parkersburg and Wood County Public Library: 3100 Emerson Ave, Parkersburg, WV 26104-2414; tel. (304) 420-4587; fax (304) 420-4589; internet parkersburg.lib.wv.us; 3 brs; Dir BRIAN E. RAITZ.

Pocahontas County Free Libraries: 500 Eigth St, Marlinton, WV 24954; tel. (304) 799-6000; fax (304) 799-3988; e-mail info@pocahontaslibrary.org; internet www.pocahontaslibrary.org; br. libraries in Green Bank, Marlinton, Hillsboro, Durbin and Slatyfork; spec. collns: Pearl S. Buck E Pluribus Unum Colln, West Virginia/Appalachian Colln, Railroad and Logging Colln; Heritage Colln; Pres. SUE ANN HEATHERLY; Sec. DENISE MCNEEL; Treas. ELIZABETH LITTLE.

Putnam County Libraries: 4219 State Route 34, Hurricane, WV 25526; tel. (304) 757-7308; fax (304) 757-7384; internet putnam.lib.wv.us; f. 1961; 4 brs and 1 main library; Pres. SAM SENTELLE.

Raleigh County Public Library: 221 N Kanawha St, Beckley, WV 25801; tel. (304) 255-0511; fax (304) 255-9161; e-mail referen@raleigh.lib.wv.us; internet rcpl.lib.wv.us; 1 main library, 3 brs and bookmobile services; edns of Beckley Register Herald dating back to 1907; select edns of Charles-ton Gazette and New York Times on microfilm; Pres. CAROLYN LUCAS; Dir AMY LILLY.

Roane County Library: 110 Parking Plaza, Spencer, WV 25276; tel. (304) 927-1130; fax (304) 927-1196; internet roanecountylibrary.org; f. 1951; 2 brs; Dir MARY FURY.

State Law Library: State Capitol Bldg, Room E-404, 1900 Kanawha Blvd, E, Charleston, WV 25305; tel. (304) 558-2607; fax (304) 558-3673; internet www.state.wv.us/wvsca/library/menu.htm; attached to Supreme Court of Appeals West Virginia; 28 circuit court libraries; congressionally designated depository for US govt documents; State Law Librarian KAYE L. MAERZ.

Taylor County Public Library: 200 Beech St, Grafton, WV 26354; tel. (304) 265-6121; fax (304) 265-6122; e-mail taylib@clark.lib.wv.us; internet taylor.clark.lib.wv.us; f. 1981; 20,000 vols; Pres. PAUL ELDER; Sec. NANCY ELLEN JUDY; Treas. JULIE GREGORY.

West Virginia State Archives: c/o Archives and History Library, The Culture Center, 1900 Kanawha Blvd, E, Charleston, WV 25305-0300; tel. (304) 558-0230; internet www.wvculture.org/history/wvsamenu.html; f. 1905 as Bureau of Archives and History; attached to West Virginia Div. of Culture and History; genealogical colln related to West Virginia counties; colln of maps, MSS, periodicals, photographs, newspapers, state publs, state govt records, yearbooks, co court records on microfilm units; State Historian and Archivist JOSEPH N. GEIGER JR.

West Virginia University Libraries: POB 6069, Morgantown, WV 26506-6069; 1549 University Ave, Morgantown, WV 26506-6069; tel. (304) 293-4040; fax (304) 293-6638; e-mail ask_a_librarian@mail.wvu.edu; internet www.libraries.wvu.edu; f. 1867; incl. Downtown Campus Library, Evansdale Library, Health Sciences Library, Law Library, WVU Charleston Health Sciences Library; spec. collns: W Virginia historical art, Appalachian, Myers, rare books; 1.6m. vols, 2.3m. microforms, 24,000 e-journals; Dean FRANCES O'BRIEN.

Wisconsin

American Geographical Society Library: Univ. of Wisconsin-Milwaukee, POB 399, Milwaukee, WI 53201; UWM Libraries, Third Fl., E Wing, 2311 E Hartford Ave, Milwaukee, WI 53211; tel. (414) 229-6282; fax (414) 229-3624; e-mail agsl@uwm.edu; internet www.uwm.edu/libraries/agsl; f. 1851, present status 1978; attached to Univ. of Wisconsin-Milwaukee Libraries; specialized academic research library with emphasis on discovery and exploration, history of cartography, history of geographical thought, historical geography and geographical themes with a significant historical component; 2 research fellowship programmes available to support visiting scholars; sponsors various lecture series; home of the Map Soc. of Wisconsin; 222,000 vols, 512,000 maps, 10,700 atlases, 114 globes, 33,676 pamphlets, 450,000 photographs and slides, 2,450 CD-ROMs, 800 gigabytes of data storage; Curator Emeritus Dr CHRISTOPHER BARUTH; publ. Current Geographical Publications – Contents (online).

Antigo Public Library: 617 Clermont St, Antigo, WI 54409; tel. (715) 623-3724; fax (715) 627-2317; internet www.antigopl.org; 3 brs; Dir CYNTHIA TAYLOR; Pres. NANCY BUGNI; Treas. SHARON KIND.

Dwight Foster Public Library: 209 Merchants Ave, Fort Atkinson, WI 53538; tel. (920) 563-7790; fax (920) 563-7774; e-mail connect@fortlibrary.org; internet www.fortlibrary.org; f. 1892; 90,000 vols; Dir

CONNIE MEYER; Pres. ANN ENGELMAN; Sec. RITA GRAY.

Edgerton Public Library: 101 Albion St, Edgerton, WI 53534; tel. (608) 884-4511; fax (608) 884-7575; internet als.lib.wi.us/epl; f. 1907; mem. of Arrowhead Library System; 32,000 vols (incl. books, magazines, video recordings, audio recordings and historical materials); Dir SHERRY MACHONES; Pres. Dr WALT DIEDRICK; Sec. KATHY KLEIN; Treas. Dr MARK IRGENS.

Frank L. Weyenberg Library of Mequon—Thiensville: 11345 N Cedarburg Rd, Mequon, WI 53092; tel. (262) 242-2593; fax (262) 478-3200; e-mail admin@flwlib.org; internet www.flwlib.org; f. 1953, present location 1971; 130,000 vols; Dir LINDA A. BENDIX; Pres. DAVID J. HASE; Sec. MIMI ROSING; Treas. DREW WALLACH.

Greendale Public Library: 5647 Broad St, Greendale, WI 53129; tel. (414) 423-2136; fax (414) 423-2139; e-mail grnd.ref@mcfls.org; internet www.greendalepubliclibrary.org; f. 1972; mem. of Milwaukee County Federated Library System; 75,908 vols; Dir GARY WARREN NIEBUHR; Pres. STEPHANIE MARES.

Kenosha Public Library: POB 1414, 812 56th St, Kenosha, WI 53141-1414; tel. (262) 564-6100; internet www.mykpl.info; f. 1872, present name 1978; resource library for Kenosha County Library System; 4 brs; bookmobile services; 403,476 vols; Dir DOUGLAS BAKER; Pres. DIANE KASTELIC; Treas. GORDON WYLLIE.

Lake Geneva Public Library: 918 W Main St, Lake Geneva, WI 53147; tel. (262) 249-5299; fax (262) 249-5284; e-mail lakegene@ lakegeneva.lib.wi.us; internet www .lakegeneva.lib.wi.us; f. 1898; Dir ANDREA W. PETERSON; Pres. DUANNE LAFRENZ; Sec. DIANE JONES.

Madison Public Library: 201 W Mifflin St, Madison, WI 53703; tel. (608) 266-6300; e-mail libraryadministration@cityofmadison .com; internet www.madisonpubliclibrary .org; f. 1875 as Madison Free Library, present name 1958; spec. collns: Art of the Picture Book Colln, Audiobooks Colln, Comics and Anime Colln, Education, Employment and Housing Colln, Film and Film History Colln; mem. of S Central Library System; 9 brs; Dir BARBARA DIMICK; Pres. TRIPP WIDDER, III; Sec. and Treas. LAWRENCE PALM.

Menominee Tribal/County Library: POB 1090, W2760 Chief Little Wave Rd, Keshena, WI 54135; tel. (715) 799-5212; fax (715) 799-6516; internet www.nfls.lib.wi.us/kes; mem. of Nicolet Federated Library System; 9,000 vols; Chair. MABEL BROWN; Dir MICHAEL WILBER.

Milwaukee Public Library: 814 W Wisconsin Ave, Milwaukee, WI 53233; tel. (414) 286-3000; fax (414) 286-2794; internet www .mpl.org; f. 1878; spec. collns incl. Great Lakes marine colln, Milwaukee Road archives, Omar Khayyam colln, Arkham House colln, Philosopher Press colln, cookbooks, H. G. Wells, definitive edns of collected works of British and American authors, Charles King colln, Harry Franck colln, genealogy; depository for US fed. documents, US Geologic Survey, US Defense Mapping Agency maps and US Patent Office; 12 br. libraries, Wisconsin Regional Library for the Blind and Physically Handicapped headquarters; 1 mobile library, 2 library vans; 3,170,711 vols; Pres. ALDERMAN ASHANTI HAMILTON; Dir PAULA A. KIELY.

Park Falls Public Library: 121 N Fourth Ave, Park Falls, WI 54552; tel. (715) 762-3121; fax (715) 762-2286; e-mail pfpl@ifls.lib .wi.us; internet www.parkfallslibrary.org;

46,000 vols; Dir GARY OLSON; Pres. DOROTHY HARRIS; Sec. LUCY ROSS.

Pewaukee Public Library: 210 Main St, Pewaukee, WI 53072; tel. (262) 691-5670; fax (262) 691-5673; e-mail pwlib@pewaukee.lib .wi.us; internet www.pewaukeelibrary.org; jt library of the City and village of Pewaukee; incl. Harken Observatory; Dir JENNIE J. STOLTZ; Pres. DALE NOLL; Sec. LISA JANSEN; Treas. LAURA MUCHOWSKI.

University of Wisconsin-Madison Library: 728 State St, Madison, WI 53706; tel. (608) 262-3193; fax (608) 265-2754; e-mail userview-l@library.wisc.edu; internet www.library.wisc.edu; f. 1848; 59 campus libraries; Chester H. Thordarson Colln incl. rare books, MSS and archives, printed ephemera, pictorial materials, English and American literature, history of science, history of the book, European collns, and philosophy and theology; 7.3m. vols, 55,000 serial titles, 6.2m. microforms, 160 linear ft of MSS, 7m. govt documents, maps, musical scores, 20,000 e-journals; Dir-Gen. for Library System KENNETH FRAZIER.

Waukesha Public Library: 321 Wisconsin Ave, Waukesha, WI 53186; tel. (262) 524-3680; e-mail refemail@waukesha.lib.wi.us; internet www.waukesha.lib.wi.us; 326,459 vols; Dir JANE AMEEL; Pres. PAUL KASPROWICZ; Sec. JEFF FOWLE.

Waupaca Area Public Library: 107 S Main St, Waupaca, WI 54981; tel. (715) 258-4414; e-mail wau@mail.owls.lib.wi.us; internet www.waupacalibrary.org; mem. of Outagamie Waupaca Library System; 75,230 vols, 12,867 ebooks, 6,476 audio materials, 8,127 video materials; Dir PEG BURINGTON; Pres. MARY TRICE; Sec. and Treas. CONNIE ANDRASCHKO.

Winchester Public Library: 2117 Lake St, Winchester, WI 54557-9104; tel. and fax (715) 686-2926; internet winchester.wislib .org; f. 1985; mem. of Northern Waters Library Service; Dir CELA MCGINNIS; Pres. BILL HORNER; Sec. JUDY HABERMAN; Treas. FELICIA GORMAN.

Wisconsin State Law Library: POB 7881, Madison, WI 53707; 120 Martin Luther King Jr Blvd, Madison, WI 53703; tel. (608) 267-9696; fax (608) 267-2319; e-mail wsll.ref@ wicourts.gov; internet wilawlibrary.gov; f. 1836 as Wisconsin State Library, present name and status 1876; colln of primary law for all fed. and state jurisdictions and practice materials for all major areas of law; spec. collns incl. Appendices and Briefs for the Wisconsin Supreme Court and Court of Appeals and the Judicial Council colln; 140,000 vols; State Law Librarian JULIE TESSMER.

Wyoming

Albany County Public Library: 310 S Eighth St, Laramie, WY 82070-3969; tel. (307) 721-2580; fax (307) 721-2584; e-mail info@albanycountylibrary.org; internet www .albanycountylibrary.org; Rock River Br. Library and Centennial Valley Br. Library; Chair. ANTONIO BENDEZU; Sec. and Treas. REBECCA ROBERTS; Co Librarian SUSAN SIMPSON.

Big Horn County Library: POB 231, Basin, WY 82410-0231; 430 W C St, Basin, WY 82410-0231; tel. (307) 568-2388; fax (307) 568-2011; e-mail director@bhclibrary.org; internet www.bhclibrary.org; 5 brs; Dir JULIA KELSO; Pres. JUDY MORRIS; Sec. JO DEE FOSS; Treas. EDIE CROSBY; Librarian VICKI WALLACE.

Campbell County Public Library System: 2101 S 4J Rd, Gillette, WY 82718-5205; tel. (307) 687-0009; fax (307) 686-4009; internet ccpls.org; incl. Wright Br. Library;

Exec. Dir PATTY MYERS; Chair. KEVIN ANDERS; Treas. MATT SORENSON.

Carbon County Library System: 215 W Buffalo St, Rawlins, WY 82301; tel. (307) 328-2618; fax (307) 328-2617; internet carbonlibraries.org; f. 1925; 8 brs; 119,806 vols (incl. 104,588 print vols, 95 magazines, 11,005 audio cassettes, 7,025 video cassettes, 94 e-databases); Dir KRISTIN E. HERR; Chair. LARRY MOORE; Sec. JULIE EVANS; Treas. PATTI HAYS.

Converse County Library: 300 Walnut St, Douglas, WY 82633; tel. (307) 358-3644; fax (307) 358-6743; e-mail glenrockbranchlibrary@conversecountyli- brary.org; internet www .conversecountylibrary.org; f. 1905 as Douglas library, present bldg 1968; br. at Glenrock; 60,828 vols; Dir KAREN HOPKINS; Pres. SCOTT BARBER; Sec. and Treas. JEREMY MATTER.

Crook County Public Library System: POB 910, 414 Main St, Sundance, WY 82729-0910; tel. and fax (307) 283-1006; e-mail crookcountylib@rangeweb.net; internet www-wsl.state.wy.us/crook; incl. Moorcroft Br. Library and Hulett Br. Library; main br. at Sundance; Dir JILL MACKEY; Chair. DEE MCGIRR; Sec. JOANN BOHMONT; Treas. SHARON MILLAY.

Johnson County Library System: 171 N Adams Ave, Buffalo, WY 82834; tel. (307) 684-5546; fax (307) 684-7888; internet www .jclwyo.org; 1 main library and 2 brs; Dir CYNTHIA TWING; Chair. KATHY URRUTY; Sec. JENNIFER LOMPE; Treas. HELEN JONES.

Laramie County Library: 2200 Pioneer Ave, Cheyenne, WY 82001; tel. (307) 634-3561; internet www.lclsonline.org; f. 1886; 2 brs; bookmobile services; genealogy colln; 337,000 vols; Co Librarian LUCIE OSBORN; Chair. BARB COOK; Sec. BETH HOWARD; Treas. JEFF WHITE.

Lincoln County Library System: 519 Emerald St, Kemmerer, WY 83101; tel. (307) 877-6961; fax (307) 877-4147; internet www.linclib.org; 5 brs; Dir BRENDA MCGINNIS; Chair. ROSALIE TRATNIK; Treas. SUSAN PARK.

Natrona County Public Library: 307 E Second St, Casper, WY 82601; tel. (307) 237-4935; fax (307) 266-3734; e-mail reference@ natronacountylibrary.org; internet www .natronacountylibrary.org; f. 1902, present name and status 1909; 2 brs and 1 bookmobile; 200,166 vols; Dir BILL NELSON; Pres. RANDY BUFFINGTON; Sec. BOB HOPKINS; Treas. SHAWN HOUCK.

Platte County Public Library System: 904 Ninth St, Wheatland, WY 82201; tel. (307) 322-2689; fax (307) 322-3450; e-mail pcpl@plattecountylibrary.org; internet will .state.wy.us/platte; 1 main library and 3 brs; Dir JULIE HENION; Pres. PATSY PARKIN; Sec. JANE WILLIS; Treas. JEANNIE MITCHELL.

Sheridan County Public Library System: 335 W Alger St, Sheridan, WY 82801; tel. (307) 674-8585; e-mail diverson@will .state.wy.us; internet www .sheridanwyolibrary.org; 4 brs; 152,147 vols (incl. 134,231 print vols, 4,661 audio cassettes, 9,445 video cassettes, 3,810 magazines, 78 e-databases); Dir CAMERON DUFF; Chair. CHASE MCFADDEN; Sec. TONY WENDTLAND; Treas. LINDA THOMPSON.

University of Wyoming Libraries: Dept 3334, 1000 E University Ave, Laramie, WY 82071; tel. (307) 766-3279; fax (307) 766-2510; e-mail ncyrus@uwyo.edu; internet www-lib.uwyo.edu; br. libraries incl. American Heritage Center, Coe Library, Geology-Brinkerhoff Geology Library, Law Library, Learning Resource Center, Rocky Mountain

Herbarium, Univ. of Wyoming-National Park Service Research Centre, Library Annex; 1,552,501 vols, 838,395 e-books, 13,878 periodicals and serials, 75,150 e-journals, 1,912,170 microforms, 170,313 maps, 1,498,819 govt documents; Dean of Libraries MAGGIE FARRELL.

Wyoming State Archives: Barrett Bldg, 2301 Central Ave, Cheyenne, WY 82002; tel. (307) 777-7826; fax (307) 777-7044; e-mail wyarchive@state.wy.us; internet wyoarchives.state.wy.us; f. 1895; sponsors and participates in workshops and confs related to Wyoming history and preservation and management of records; Archives and Historical Research Supervisor CURTIS GREUBEL.

Wyoming State Law Library: Supreme Court Bldg, 2301 Capitol Ave, Cheyenne, WY 82002; tel. (307) 777-7509; fax (307) 777-7240; e-mail library@courts.state.wy.us; internet www.courts.state.wy.us/lawlibrary; colln of reported cases of American courts, fed. and state laws and statutes, fed. admin. regulations and decisions, US and Wyoming atty gen. opinions, legal treatises, legal periodicals and newspapers, selected US govt publs; Dir KATHY CARLSON.

Wyoming State Library: 2800 Central Ave, Cheyenne, WY 82002; tel. (307) 777-6333; fax (307) 777-6289; internet will.state.wy.us; State Librarian LESLEY BOUGHTON; publ. *Wyoming Library Roundup* (4 a year).

Museums and Art Galleries

Alabama

Alabama Museum of Natural History, University of Alabama: POB 870340, Tuscaloosa, AL 35487-0340; tel. (205) 348-7550; fax (205) 348-9292; e-mail museum.programs@ua.edu; internet amnh.ua.edu; f. 1907; exhibits and collns incl. the Hodges meteorite, the only meteorite known to have struck a human being, fossils, minerals and palaeontology; Dir Dr RANDY MECREDY; publ. *Nature South: The Magazine of the Alabama Museum of Natural History.*

Aliceville Museum: 104 Broad St, Aliceville, AL 35442; tel. (205) 373-2363; e-mail museum@nctv.com; internet www.cityofaliceville.com; f. 1995; camp artefacts of Camp Aliceville (Second World War German prisoner of war camp dating from 1942 to 1945); colln incl. wooden objects, weapons, photographs, uniforms, books, sculptures and other artefacts made by German prisoners of war; Exec. Dir MARY BESS PALUZZI.

Birmingham Civil Rights Institute: 520 16th St N, Birmingham, AL 35203; tel. (205) 328-9696; e-mail bcri@bcri.org; internet www.bcri.org; f. 1992; colln on American Civil Rights Movement, struggle of African-American citizens in Birmingham to be part of city's govt and business community; Pres. and CEO Dr LAWRENCE J. PIJEAUX, JR; Chair. ROBERT HOLMES, JR; Sec. PEGGIE F. MYLES; Treas. WALTER HOWLETT, JR.

Birmingham Museum of Art: 2000 Rev. Abraham Woods, Jr Blvd, Birmingham, AL 35203-2278; tel. (205) 254-2565; fax (205) 254-2714; internet www.artsbma.org; f. 1951; 24,000 paintings, sculptures, prints and drawings dating from ancient to modern times; holdings of Asian, European, American, African and native American art; library of 35,000 vols; Chair. RALPH COOK; Sec. DANNETTA K. THORNTON OWENS; Dir GAIL ANDREWS; Chief Curator JEANNINE A. O'GRODY.

Gadsden Museum of Art: 515 Broad St, Gadsden, AL 35901; tel. and fax (256) 546-7365; internet www.gadsdenmuseum.com; f. 1963; colln of paintings, sculptures, artefacts and items of historical significance depicting local history of Gadsden and Etowah Co; Dir STEVE TEMPLE.

Huntsville Museum of Art: 300 Church St, Huntsville, AL 35801; tel. (256) 535-4350; fax (256) 532-1743; internet www.hsvmuseum.org; f. 1970; 3,000 objects of 19th- and 20th-century American art focusing on SE; 200 prints in S photography; 400 paintings, drawings and sculptures in Sellars colln of art dating from 1850 to 1940; Chair. SARAH GESSLER; Sec. RICHARD CRUNKLETON; Treas. PATSY HAWS; Exec. Dir CHRISTOPHER MADKOUR.

Jule Collins Smith Museum of Fine Art: Auburn Univ., 901 S College St, Auburn, AL 36849; tel. (334) 844-1484; fax (334) 844-1463; e-mail jcsm@auburn.edu; internet jcsm.auburn.edu; f. 1948; attached to Auburn Univ.; Louise Hauss and David Brent Miller Audubon colln comprises 100 prints of Audubon; late 19th- and 20th-century European modernism work by Pierre-Auguste Renoir, Henri Matisse, Pablo Picasso, Joan Miró, Salvador Dalí and Marc Chagall; Dir MARILYN LAUFER.

Karl C. Harrison Museum of George Washington: 50 Lester St, Columbiana, AL 35051; tel. (205) 669-8767; e-mail info@washingtonmuseum.com; internet www.washingtonmuseum.com; f. 1982; 1,000 art and artefacts dating from colonial period to 1865; original 1787 Samuel Vaughn sketch of Mount Vernon grounds and writing instruments and tools from George Washington's survey case; Curator BONNIE ATCHISON.

Montgomery Museum of Fine Arts: POB 230819, Montgomery, AL 36123-0819; One Museum Dr., Montgomery, AL 36117; tel. (334) 240-4333; fax (334) 240-4384; e-mail museuminfo@mmfa.org; internet www.mmfa.org; f. 1930; 4,000 objects dating from Colonial period portraiture to 20th century: American art, old master prints, S regional and decorative arts; library of 5,000 vols, 17 periodicals; Dir MARK M. JOHNSON; Sr Curator MARGARET LYNNE AUSFELD.

Museum of Mobile: 111 S Royal St, POB 2068, Mobile, AL 36602; tel. (251) 208-7569; fax (251) 208-7686; e-mail museum@cityofmobile.org; internet www.museumofmobile.com; f. 1831; 80,000 artefacts incl. furniture and antique silver depicting local history; library of 5,000 vols; Dir DAVID ALSOBROOK.

National African American Archives & Museum: 564 Dr Martin Luther King, Jr Ave, Mobile, AL 36603; tel. (251) 433-8511; e-mail dnaaamus@aol.com; internet nationalafricanamericanarchives.org; f. 1932 as Davis Avenue Br. of the Mobile Public Library; colln on African-American history; colln incl. portraits, biographies, African carvings, family histories and other memorabilia; Pres. and Exec. Dir DELORES S. DEES.

Southern Museum of Flight: 4343 73rd St N, Birmingham, AL 35206-3642; tel. (205) 833-8226; fax (205) 836-2439; e-mail southernmuseumofflight@yahoo.com; internet www.southernmuseumofflight.org; colln incl. 75 aircrafts, engines, artefacts, photographs and paintings; Alabama Aviation Hall of Fame: 65 biographical plaques presenting Alabama aviation history through collective biography; Dir JAMES T. GRIFFIN.

United States Army Aviation Museum: POB 620610-0610, Fort Rucker, AL 36362; tel. (334) 598-2508; internet www.armyavnmuseum.org; f. 1956; colln incl. 160 military aircrafts and helicopters; 3,000

items in historical property colln; library: 1,600 technical and field manuals, 95,000 photographs.

Alaska

Alaska Museum of Natural History: 201 N Bragaw, Anchorage, AK 99508; tel. (907) 274-2400; e-mail education@alaskamuseum.org; internet www.alaskamuseum.org; f. 1994; holds 10,000 objects of Alaskan anthropological, biological, geological, historical, artistic, and educational significance; Exec. Dir KATCH BACHELLER; Education Dir KERRI JACKSON; Museum Man. BRONWYN JONES; Collns Man. PHYLLIS CALLINA.

Alaska Native Heritage Center Museum: 8800 Heritage Center Dr., Anchorage, AK 99504; tel. (907) 330-8000; fax (907) 330-8030; internet www.alaskanative.net; f. 1989; workshops, demonstrations and guided tours of indoor exhibits and outdoor village sites showcasing native traditions and customs; Board Chair. GAIL R. SCHUBERT; Pres. and CEO ANNETTE EVANS SMITH.

Alaska State Museum: 395 Whittier St, Juneau, AK 99801-1718; tel. (907) 465-2901; fax (907) 465-2976; e-mail bob.banghart@alaska.gov; internet www.museums.state.ak.us; f. 1900, opened to the public 1920; 27,000 objects; Alaskan history, Alaska's native people, Russian America, art, natural history and ethnographic materials; state-wide assistance to museums in Alaska; Alaska State Chief Curator BOB BANGHART; Dir for Libraries, Archives and Museums LINDA THIBODEAU.

Attached Museum:

> **Sheldon Jackson Museum:** 104 College Dr., Sitka, AK 99835; tel. (907) 747-8981; fax (907) 747-3004; internet www.museums.state.ak.us; f. 1888; 6,000 objects; Alaska Native artefacts; Chief Curator NADIA JACKINSKY-HORRELL (acting).

Alutiiq Museum Archaeological Repository: 215 Mission Rd Suite 101, Kodiak, AK 99615-7326; tel. (907) 486-7004; internet www.alutiiqmuseum.org; f. 1995; holds 250,000 items related to culture and history of the Alutiiq people, incl. archaeological materials, photographs, ethnographic objects, archival items, film and audio recordings, and natural history specimens; library of 1,700 vols, 1,400 journals, articles, catalogues, conf. papers, maps, newsletters, speeches, pamphlets, presentations, recordings, technical reports, transcripts and unpublished MSS (both original and copied); Exec. Dir Dr SVEN D. HAAKANSON.

Anchorage Museum: Rasmuson Center, 625 C St Anchorage, AK 99501; tel. (907) 929-9201; fax (907) 929-9290; e-mail museum@anchoragemuseum.org; internet www.anchoragemuseum.org; f. 1968; collects, preserves, exhibits and interprets art, history, anthropology and science of Arkansas and its relationship to the Circumpolar N; 17,500 objects and an additional education colln of 2,000 artefacts; 350,000 historical photographs; Dir and CEO JAMES PEPPER HENRY; Chair. GLORIA O'NEILL; Chair. KAREN COMPTON; Treas. SUSAN KNOWLES.

Baranov Museum: Kodiak Historical Soc., 101 Marine Way, Kodiak, AK 99615; tel. (907) 486-5920; fax (907) 486-3166; e-mail baranov@ak.net; internet www.baranovmuseum.org; f. 1954 incorporated by the Kodiak Historical Society; located within Kodiak's 200-year-old Nat. Historic Landmark bldg known as the Russian American Magazin or the Erskine House; colln of 2,000 objects dating from several thousand years ago to the present; comprehensive colln of 18th- and 19th-century Alutiiq and Aleut

(Alaska Native) material culture that incl. items from daily life as well as ceremonial objects; Exec. Dir KATIE OLIVER; Curator of Collns ANJULI GRANTHAM; Pres. NANCY KEMP; Sec. JANE VAN ATTA; Treas. LYNDA ROSS.

Clausen Museum: POB 708, Petersburg, AK 99833; 203 Fram St, Petersburg, AK 99833; tel. (907) 772-3598; fax (907) 772-2698; e-mail clausenmuseum@aptalaska.net; internet www.clausenmuseum.net; f. 1968; colln of 5,000 artefacts (fishing industry related items), 45,000 photographs and negatives; 200 archival colln; Dir SUE McCALLUM; Pres. BEV SIERCKS; Sec. SUZANNE PETERSON.

Fairbanks Community Museum: 410 Cushman St, Fairbanks, AK 99701; tel. (907) 457-3669; internet www.fairbankshistorymuseum.com; f. 1996; exhibits of the history and culture of the Fairbanks area; Exec. Dir BOB ELEY.

Hammer Museum: POB 702, 108 Main St, Haines, AK 99827; tel. (907) 766-2374; internet www.hammermuseum.org; f. 2002; 1,500 hammers ranging from ancient times to the present.

Iñupiat Heritage Center: POB 749, Barrow, AK 99723; 5421 N Star St, Barrow, AK 99723; tel. (907) 852-4594; fax (907) 852-4224; internet www.co.north-slope.ak.us/departments/planning/ihc.php; Iñupiaq culture, history and language through exhibits, classes, performances and educational activities; Facility Dir BEVERLY HUGO; Museum and Cultural Affairs Coordinator QAIYAAN HARCHAREK (acting).

Museum of the Aleutians: POB 648, Unalaska, AK, 99685; 314 Salmon Way, Unalaska, AK 99685; tel. (907) 581-5150; fax (907) 581-6682; e-mail museum@akwisp.com; internet www.aleutians.org; f. 1999; unique artefacts, quotes and historic photographs depicting the purchase of Alaska Territory by the USA in 1867; artefacts from World War period; Chair. SHARON-SVARNY-LIVINGSTON; Exec. Dir ZOYA JOHNSON; Sec. and Treas. DONNA DETWEILER.

Palmer Museum of History & Art: 723 S Valley Way, Palmer, AK 99645; tel. (907) 746-7668; fax (907) 745-7882; internet www.palmermuseum.org; colln incl. items that depict the history of the Palmer region, such as the region's art history, exploration, settlement, agriculture, and trade, cultural and social devt; Exec. Dir MELISSA JENSKI.

Pratt Museum: 3779 Bartlett St, Homer, AK 99603; tel. (907) 235-8635; fax (907) 235-2764; e-mail director@prattmuseum.org; internet www.prattmuseum.org; f. 1968; natural history museum with 24,000 objects; focuses on art, natural history, native cultures, homesteading, fishing, marine ecology and the Exxon Valdez oil spill, Alaskan wildlife dioramas and the salt-water aquaria; library of 1,500 vols; Museum Dir DIANE CONVERSE; Curator HOLLY CUSACK-McVEIGH; Pres. MILLI MARTIN; Sec. SARA JACKINSKY; Treas. JULIA CLYMER.

Sheldon Museum & Cultural Center: POB 269, Haines, AK 99827; tel. (907) 766-2366; fax (907) 766-2368; e-mail director@sheldonmuseum.net; internet www.sheldonmuseum.org; a cultural and historical centre for the Chilkat Valley; photographs from 1880 to the present; Dir JERRIE CLARKE; Pres. FRANKIE PERRY; Sec. BOB ADKINS; Treas. DIANA PYLE.

Sitka Historical Society and Museum: 330 Harbor Dr. Sitka, AK 99835; tel. (907) 747-6455; fax (907) 747-6588; e-mail sitka.history@yahoo.com; internet www.sitkahistory.org; f. 1967; exhibits, photographs, artefacts and archives related to Sitka's Tlingit, Russian and American history; particularly, period surrounding and following Alaska's 1867 transfer from Russia; Dir BOB MEDINGER.

Tongass Historical Museum: 629 Dock St, Ketchikan, AK 99901; tel. (907) 225-5600; fax (907) 225-5602; collects, preserves and interprets history, art and culture of Ketchikan and Southeast Alaska; Dir MICHAEL NAAB.

Totem Heritage Center: 629 Dock St Ketchikan, AK 99901; 601 Deermount St Ketchikan AK 99901; tel. (907) 225-5900; fax (907) 225-5901; f. 1976; preserves endangered 19th-century totem poles retrieved from uninhabited Tlingit and Haida village sites near Ketchikan; also preserves the traditional arts and crafts of Tlingit, Haida and Tsimshian cultures; Dir MICHAEL NAAB.

University of Alaska Museum of the North: POB 756960, 907 Yukon Dr., Fairbanks, AK 99775; tel. (907) 474-7505; e-mail museum@uaf.edu; internet www.uaf.edu/museum/; f. 1926; 1.4m. artefacts and specimens incl. archaeology, birds, documentary film, earth sciences, ethnology/history, fine arts, fishes/marine invertebrates, insects, mammals and plants; Museum Dir Dr CAROL DIEBEL.

Valdez Museum & Historical Archive: POB 8, Valdez, AK 99686; tel. (907) 835-2764; fax (907) 835-5800; e-mail info@valdezmuseum.org; internet www.valdezmuseum.org; f. 1901; textiles, photographs and documents that trace the community's history from its founding to modern times; Mary Whalen Colln; Owen Meals Colln; All-America City Colln; Pipeline Contruction Colln; Marine Colln; library of 2,000 vols; 35,000 photographs, MSS, documents; 510 maps; 5,500 edns of newspapers; Exec. Dir PATRICIA RELAY; Pres. DANNY SPARRELL; Sec. CAROL HARRIS; Treas. SPIKE GILSON.

Arizona

Arizona-Sonora Desert Museum: 2021 N Kinney Rd, Tucson, AZ 85743; tel. (520) 883-1380; fax (520) 883-2500; e-mail info@desertmuseum.org; internet www.desertmuseum.org; f. 1952; zoo, natural history museum and botanical garden; exhibits 300 animal species and 1,200 kinds of plants; 14,095 catalogued specimens of gem, mineral and fossils; vertebrate paleontology colln; art institute; library of 6,000 vols and 83 periodical subscriptions; Dir CRAIG S. IVANYI.

Arizona State Museum: POB 210026, Univ. of Arizona, Tucson, AZ 85721-0026; 1013 E University Blvd, Tucson, AZ 85721-0026; tel. (520) 621-6302; fax (520) 621-2976; e-mail dfl@email.arizona.edu; internet www.statemuseum.arizona.edu; f. 1893; attached to Univ. of Arizona; archaeology, anthropology and ethnology of Arizona and surrounding regions; research colln incl. Hohokam, Mogollon and other archaeological material, osteological remains, vertebrate zoo-archaeological and herbarial specimens, 1,500 linear ft of archive material and 250,000 photographs; collns of Southwest Indian basketry, 175,000 archaeological and ethnographic artefacts, 350,000 photographic negatives and original prints, Navajo textiles colln, Casas Grandes pottery colln, 500 Mexican folk masks from Cordry Colln; temporary exhibitions; 25,000 woven pieces of rare and outstanding baskets, sandals, cradle boards, mats, cordage, and preserved fibers; library of 70,000 vols, incl. rare titles, 1,500 periodicals, 6,000 maps, 1,500 linear ft of paper documents, 800 original sound recordings; Dir Dr BETH GRINDELL.

Arizona State University Art Museum: 10th St and Mill Ave, POB 872911, Tempe, AZ 85287-2911; tel. (480) 965-2787; internet asuartmuseum.asu.edu; f. 1950; attached to ASU Herberger Institute of Design and the Arts, Arizona State Univ.; 12,000 artefacts; contemporary art of new media and innovative methods of presentation; American ceramics; historic and contemporary prints; American and European paintings; SW art of Latino artists; historic American and modernist and contemporary Latin American works; Dir GORDON KNOX.

Center for Creative Photography: Univ. of Arizona, 1030 N Olive Rd, POB 210103, Tucson, AZ 85721-0103; tel. (520) 621-7970; fax (520) 621-9444; e-mail oncenter@ccp.library.arizona.edu; internet www.creativephotography.org; attached to Univ. of Arizona; art colln of 80,000 works by 2,000 photographers; archives incl. photographs, negatives, albums, work prints, MSS, audio-visual material, contact sheets, correspondence and memorabilia; Dir KATHARINE MARTINEZ.

Heard Museum: 2301 N Central Ave, Phoenix, AZ 85004; tel. (602) 252-8848; e-mail contact@heard.org; internet www.heard.org; f. 1929; art from ancestral artefacts to contemporary paintings and jewellery; colln of American Indian fine art, paintings, drawings, prints, photography and sculpture; resource colln on 25,000 American Indian artists, 300,000 historic and contemporary photographs; Scott L. Libby, Jr Amphitheater; library: 300 linear ft of MSS, personal collns and cultural materials, incl. 150 linear ft of institutional records; Dir Dr LETITIA CHAMBERS.

International Wildlife Museum: 4800 W Gates Pass Rd, Tucson, AZ 85745; tel. (520) 629-0100; fax (520) 618-3561; internet www.thewildlifemuseum.org; f. 1988; exhibits natural history; 400 species of insects, mammals and birds; dioramas depicting wild animals in their natural settings, videos, interactive computers, and hands-on exhibits; promotes wildlife appreciation and conservation; wildlife theatre; Dir RICHARD WHITE.

Jewish History Museum: POB 889, Tucson, AZ 85702; 564 S Stone Ave, Tucson, AZ 85701; tel. (520) 670-9073; fax (520) 670-9078; e-mail jhmtucson@gmail.com; internet www.jewishhistorymuseum.org; f. 1910; collects, preserves and teaches history, culture and traditions of Jewish people, from SW Pioneers to Jews of contemporary times; Pres. BARRY A. FRIEDMAN; Exec. Dir EILEEN WARSHAW.

Museum of Northern Arizona: 3101 N Ft. Valley Rd, Flagstaff, AZ 86001; tel. (928) 774-5213; fax (928) 774-1229; e-mail info@mna.mus.az.us; internet www.musnaz.org; f. 1928; collects, studies, interprets and preserves Colorado Plateau's natural and cultural heritage; 600,000 artefacts of anthropology, biology, geology and fine arts; fed. and tribal research collns; library of 50,000 vols, 25,000 separates, 300 MSS and 250,000 photographic images; Dir Dr ROBERT G. BREUNIG; Chair. DAVID CONNELL; Sec. MARGARET TAYLOR; Treas. BRAD RYAN; publ. *Plateau: Land and People of the Colorado Plateau* (2 a year).

Northern Arizona University Art Museum: POB 6021, Flagstaff, AZ 86011-6021; tel. (928) 523-3471; fax (928) 523-1424; e-mail art.museum@nau.edu; internet www4.nau.edu/art_museum; attached to College of Art & Letters, Norther Arizona Univ.; 448 framed pieces of lithographs, paintings and etchings; 300 pieces of ceramic, sculpture and textiles; colln dates from early 1700s to the present; Dir Dr GEORGE V. SPEER.

Phippen Museum: 4701 Highway 89N, Prescott, AZ 86301; tel. (928) 778-1385; fax (928) 778-4524; e-mail phippen@

phippenartmuseum.org; internet www .phippenartmuseum.org; f. 1984; colln of paintings, etchings, drawings, bronze sculptures, photography, American Indian artefacts and jewellery from late 19th century to early 21st century; library of 580 vols and 60 professional videos; Exec. Dir KIM VILLALPANDO; Chair. DICK CORNWELL; Treas. MAUREEN SHAFFER.

Phoenix Art Museum: McDowell Rd and Central Ave, 1625 N Central Ave, Phoenix, AZ 85004-1685; tel. (602) 257-1880; fax (602) 257-2127; e-mail info@phxart.org; internet www.phxart.org; f. 1959; 18,000 works of American, Asian, European, Latin American, W American, modern and contemporary art and fashion design; organizes festivals, live performances, ind. art films and educational programmes; library of 40,000 vols.

Pima Air & Space Museum: 6000 E Valencia Rd, Tucson, AZ 85756; tel. (520) 574-0462; internet www.pimaair.org; f. 1976; 300 aircraft and spacecraft from all over the world; 125,000 artefacts; Exec. Dir YVONNE MORRIS.

Pueblo Grande Museum: 4619 E Washington St, Phoenix, AZ 85034; tel. (602) 495-0901; fax (602) 495-5645; e-mail pueblo .grande.museum.pks@phoenix.gov; internet phoenix.gov/recreation/arts/museums/pueblo; f. 1929; attached to City of Phoenix Parks and Recreation Dept; archaeological site museum; repository for professionally excavated archaeological project collns from Phoenix metropolitan area; collects historic and contemporary Native American art objects, esp. from cultures with long standing ties to the Salt River Valley, such as the Akimel O'odham (Pima) and Piipash (Maricopa); cultural materials from site of Pueblo Grande and Greater SW; Dir ROGER LIDMAN.

Smoki Museum: 147 N Arizona Ave, POB 10224, Prescott, AZ 86304-0224; tel. (928) 445-1230; e-mail director@smokimuseum .org; internet www.smokimuseum.org; American Indian art and culture; Man. Dir CINDY GRESSER; Pres. JIM CHRISTOPHER; Sec. LINDA YOUNG; Treas. KENT ROBINSON.

Tucson Museum of Art and Historic Block: 140 N Main Ave, Tucson, AZ 85701; tel. (520) 624-2333; fax (520) 624-7202; e-mail info@tucsonmuseumofart.org; internet www.tucsonmuseumofart.org; f. 1924 as Tucson Fine Arts Asscn, present name and status 1975; art of Latin America, art of the American W, modern and contemporary art and Asian art, MSS and rare books; J. Knox Corbett House, La Casa Cordova, Edward Nye Fish House, Romero House and Stevens/Duffield House; library of 13,000 vols; Pres. ANNE LYMAN; CEO ROBERT E. KNIGHT; Sec. JEAN S. COOPER; Treas. HARRY GEORGE.

University of Arizona Museum of Art: POB 210002, Tucson, AZ 85721-0002; tel. (520) 621-7567; fax (520) 621-8770; e-mail vca@email.arizona.edu; internet artmuseum .arizona.edu; 5,000 paintings, sculptures, prints and drawings with emphasis on European and American fine art from Renaissance to present; Exec. Dir CHARLES A. GUERIN.

West Valley Art Museum: POB 6377, Peoria, AZ 85385; tel. (623) 972-0635; e-mail info@wvam.org; internet www.wvam .org; 1,651 items from 75 countries and 1,000 pieces of ethnic dress and textiles; 300 fine art prints; 19th-century historic Japanese woodcut prints; ethnographic artefacts incl. Chinese snuff bottles, calligraphy tools, ethnographic sculptures, Japanese fans, chopsticks and scrolls; Pres. Dr G. WILLIAM BENZ; Sec. and Treas. W. MCMILLIN.

Arkansas

Arkansas Air Museum: 4290 S School Ave, Fayetteville, AR 72701-8008; tel. (479) 521-4947; internet www.arkairmuseum.org; f. 1986; colln of classic aircraft in flight service condition from the 1920s and 1930s; modern planes from the post Second World War era; static displays of key military aircraft from the Vietnam era; still-flying aircraft on loan from private owners.

Arkansas Arts Center: POB 2137, Little Rock, AR 72203-2137; 501 E Ninth St, Little Rock, AR 72202; tel. (501) 372-4000; fax (501) 375-8053; e-mail info@arkarts.com; internet www.arkarts.com; f. 1960; colln of sheets by Cézanne, Van Gogh, Jackson Pollock, Georgia O'Keeffe, Alison Saar, Rembrandt and Rubens; 135 drawings and watercolours by Paul Signac, 100 Post-Minimalist drawings, Arthur Dove's Sketchbook 'E' and 80 works by Will Barnet; paintings by Diego Rivera, Odilon Redon and Francesco Bassano; sculpture by Henry Moore, Louise Nevelson and Roy Lichtenstein; prints by Rembrandt, Whistler and Dürer; contemporary objects in craft media, incl. teapots by contemporary artists, contemporary baskets, turned wood objects, studio glass, ceramics, metalwork and jewellery; library of 5,000 vols (incl. dictionaries, indexes, monographs, catalogues raisonnés and exhibition catalogues); Exec. Dir TODD HERMAN.

Arkansas Inland Maritime Museum: 120 Riverfront Park Dr., North Little Rock, AR 72114; tel. (501) 371-8320; fax (501) 244-9794; e-mail events@aimm.museum; internet www.aimm.museum; f. 2005; exhibition of historic naval vessels with emphasis on the era of Second World War through the present; artefacts incl. plaques, scrapbooks, brochures, patrol reports and photographs; incl. theatre; outdoor exhibits, incl. the Snook Memorial; library of 2,500 vols.

Arkansas State University Museum: POB 490, State Univ., Jonesboro, AR 72467; tel. (870) 972-2074; fax (870) 972-2793; e-mail museum@astate.edu; internet www .astate.edu/a/museum; f. 1985; 70,000 objects of natural history, archaeology and history of state; archives and photographic colln; library of 7,000 vols; Dir Dr MARTI L. ALLEN.

Arts & Science Center: 701 Main St, Pine Bluff, AR 71601; tel. (870) 536-3375; fax (870) 536-3380; e-mail info@artssciencecenter.org; internet www.artssciencecenter.org; f. 1968; 1,000 art works incl. paintings, sculptures, photography, drawings and prints by African-American artists, Arkansas artists and artists of S region of USA; organizes art exhibitions, performing arts, education and science exhibits; Exec. Dir LENORE SHOULTS; Chair. ADAM ROBINSON; Sec. LEIGH PHILIPPI; Treas. CAROL F. JONES.

Crystal Bridges Museum of American Art: 600 Museum Way, Bentonville, AR 72712; tel. (479) 418-5700; e-mail info@ crystalbridges.org; internet www .crystalbridges.org; f. 2011; American art works from colonial era to present incl. iconic images Rosie the Riveter by Norman Rockwell, Asher B. Durand's Kindred Spirits and Maxfield Parrish's The Lantern Bearers; library of 50,000 vols; Chair. ALICE WALTON; Exec. Dir DON BACIGALUPI.

Fort Smith Regional Art Museum: POB 1257, Fort Smith, AR 72902; 701 Rogers Ave, Fort Smith, AR 72901; tel. (479) 784-2787; fax (479) 784-9071; e-mail info@fsram.org; internet www.fsram.org; f. 1948; paintings, sculpture, lithographs, drawings, photographs and mixed media by int., regional and local artists; travelling exhibitions and works by regional artists; Exec. Dir LEE

ORTEGA; Pres. MARTA JONES; Sec. SUZZANNE SALSBURY; Treas. SHAREN REEDER.

Historic Arkansas Museum: 200 E Third St, Little Rock, AR 72201; tel. (501) 324-9351; fax (501) 324-9345; e-mail info@ historicarkansas.org; internet www .historicarkansas.org; f. 1973; 5 pre-Civil War houses; collns of art and paintings, furniture, guns, hunting horns, jewellery, knives, photographs, pottery, pottery of Caddo, quilts and silver; Dir BILL WORTHEN.

Museum of Discovery: Suite 150, 500 President Clinton Ave, Little Rock, AR 72201; tel. (501) 396-7050; fax (501) 396-7054; e-mail info@museumofdiscovery.org; internet museumofdiscovery.org; f. 1927 as Museum of Natural History and Antiquities, present name 1998; operates mobile science museum; sponsors educational programs; exhibits at partner museums and educational venues; exhibition related to media and science; colln of dinosaur fossils; Exec. Dir NAN SELZ.

Old State House Museum: 300 W Markham, Little Rock, AR 72201; tel. (501) 324-9685; fax (501) 324-9688; e-mail info@ oldstatehouse.org; internet www .oldstatehouse.com; f. 1947; state police colln of 72 years of Arkansas criminal justice history and memorabilia; colln of Arkansas's First Ladies' Gowns; quilts made by mems of Arkansas's black community from 1880 to present; Dir PAUL GREENBURG.

Shiloh Museum of Ozark History: 118 W Johnson Ave, Springdale, AR 72764; tel. (479) 750-8165; e-mail shiloh@springdalear .gov; internet www.shilohmuseum.org; f. 1965; Guy Howard Colln of Native American prehistoric and historic artefacts; Lockwood and Annabel Searcy Colln; Mooney-Barker Drugstore Colln; Morris Family Colln of First World War items; Jeanne Hoffer-Tucker Colln of paintings; Ada Lee Shook Colln; Lucy Cartmell Leming Colln; Robert G. Winn Colln; McGarrah-Reed Colln; 500,000 photographs; Dir ALLYN LORD; Pres. MYRON ENG; Sec. CAROLYN BAYLEY; Treas. Dr MARSHA JONES.

California

Asian Art Museum: Chong-Moon Lee Center for Asian Art and Culture, 200 Larkin St, San Francisco, CA 94102; tel. (415) 581-3500; fax (415) 581-4700; e-mail pr@asianart.org; internet www.asianart.org; f. 1969, present name 1994; museum and centre of research on outstanding collns of Chinese, Japanese, Korean, Indian, South-east Asian, Himalayan and Islamic art; colln of 17,000 artworks spanning 6,000 years of history; library of 40,000 vols; Chair. ANTHONY SUN; Sec. JANE CHANG TOM; Treas. TIMOTHY F. KAHN.

Autry: 4700 Western Heritage Way, Los Angeles, CA 90027-1462; tel. (323) 667-2000; fax (323) 660-5721; e-mail rroom@ theautry.org; internet www.theautry.org; f. 2003, by merger of Autry Museum of Western Heritage with Southwest Museum of the American Indian and Women of the West Museum; colln of 500,000 pieces of art and artefacts; 2 research libraries: Braun Research Library and Autry Library; library of 21,000 vols (incl. books, MSS, diaries and visual materials in the Rosenstock Colln of Western Americana) and 1,200 scripts; Pres and CEO DANIEL M. FINLEY; publ. Convergence (irregular).

California African American Museum: 600 State Dr., Exposition Park, Los Angeles, CA 90037; tel. (213) 744-7432; internet www .caamuseum.org; f. 1981; historic and contemporary colln of art, books, photographs and written materials about African Americans in California and the USA; library of

20,000 vols, incl. books, periodicals and records; Exec. Dir CHARMAINE JEFFERSON.

California Palace of the Legion of Honor: Lincoln Park, 34th Ave and Clement St, San Francisco, CA 94121; tel. (415) 750-3600; fax (415) 750-7686; internet contact@famsf.org; internet legionofhonor.famsf.org; f. 1924; attached to Fine Arts Museums of San Francisco; European decorative arts and paintings; ancient art; sculpture by Auguste Rodin; Achenbach Foundation for Graphic Arts has largest colln of prints and drawings in the Western USA (see also de Young Museum); Dir JOHN E. BUCHANAN, JR; Pres. DIANE B. WILSEY; publ. *Fine Arts Magazine* (3 or 4 a year).

Chinese American Museum: 125 Paseo de la Plaza, Suite 300, Los Angeles, CA 90012; 425 N Los Angeles St, Los Angeles, CA 90012; tel. (213) 485-8567; fax (213) 473-4224; e-mail pr@camla.org; internet www.camla.org; f. 2003, fmrly Museum of Chinese American History; arts, documents, images, and artefacts depicting history of Chinese immigrants in the US that began over 150 years ago; Exec. Dir PAULINE WONG; Pres. ALFRED H. SOO-HOO; Sec. JOE L. QUAN; Treas. DOROTHY HALL TAMASHIRO; Curator STEVE Y. WONG.

Craft and Folk Art Museum: 5814 Wilshire Blvd, Los Angeles, CA 90036; tel. (323) 937-4230; fax (323) 937-5576; e-mail info@cafam.org; internet www.cafam.org; f. 1965 as The Egg and The Eye, present name and status 1973; displays folk art and contemporary craft; Chair. WALLY MARKS, III; Exec. Dir SUZANNE ISKEN.

Drum Barracks Civil War Museum: 1052 Banning Blvd, Wilmington, CA 90744; tel. (310) 548-7509; fax (310) 548-2946; e-mail susan.ogle@lacity.org; internet www.drumbarracks.org; f. 1987; preservation of memorabilia concerning the Civil War and California's contribution towards it; library of 259 vols; Dir SUSAN OGLE; publs *American Heritage* (irregular), *Civil War Illustrated* (irregular).

de Young Museum: 50 Hagiwara Tea Garden Dr., Golden Gate Park, San Francisco, CA 94118; tel. (415) 750-3600; fax (415) 750-7692; e-mail contact@famsf.org; internet www.deyoungmuseum.org; f. 1894 as Fine Arts Bldg, reopened 2005; attached to Fine Arts Museums of San Francisco; collns of American art from the 17th to the 21st century; art of the native Americas, Africa and the Pacific (see also California Palace of the Legion of Honor); Dir JOHN E. BUCHANAN, JR; Pres. DIANE B. WILSEY; publ. *Fine Arts Magazine* (4 a year).

FIDM Museum & Galleries: 919 S Grand Ave, Suite 250, Los Angeles, CA 90015; tel. (213) 623-5821; e-mail info@fidmmuseum .org; internet www.fidmmuseum.org; f. 1978; colln of 15,000 objects covering more than 200 years of fashion history: 1800 to the present; haute couture and ready-to-wear, non-Western dress, film costumes, textiles, jewellery and fragrance; Dir BARBARA BUNDY; Curator KEVIN JONES.

Fort MacArthur Museum–Battery Osgood-Farley Historic Site: 3601 S Gaffey St, San Pedro, CA 90731; tel. (310) 548-2631; fax (310) 241-0847; e-mail director@ftmac.org; internet www.ftmac.org; f. 19851985; preserves and interprets history of Fort MacArthur; US Army post which guarded the Los Angeles harbour from 1914 to 1974; Museum Dir and Curator STEPHEN NELSON.

Fowler Museum at UCLA: POB 951549, Los Angeles, CA 90095-1549; 308 Charles E Young Dr. N, Los Angeles, CA 90095; tel. (310) 825-4361; fax (310) 206-7007; e-mail fowlerws@arts.ucla.edu; internet www.fowler.ucla.edu; f. 1963, present name 2006; colln of 150,000 art and ethnographic and 600,000 archaeological objects representing ancient, traditional and contemporary cultures of Africa, Native and Latin America, and Asia and the Pacific; Dir and Exhibition Curator MARLA C. BERNS.

Getty Villa: 17985 Pacific Coast Highway, Pacific Palisades, CA 90272; tel. (310) 440-7300; e-mail visitorservices@getty.edu; internet www.getty.edu/museum/home .html; f. 1953, reopened in 2006 after major renovations; educational centre and museum dedicated to the study of the arts and cultures of ancient Greece, Rome and Etruria, incl. re-creation of a Roman seaside villa, the Villa dei Papiri, which was destroyed by the eruption of Vesuvius in AD 79; houses permanent colln of 44,000 Greek, Roman and Etruscan antiquities, 1,200 of which are on public display; a library and other facilities for scholars supports research and study programmes; Dir (vacant).

Grammy Museum: 800 W Olympic Blvd, Suite A245, Los Angeles, CA 90015; tel. (213)765-6800; e-mail grammyinfo@grammymuseum.org; internet www.grammymuseum.org; f. 2008; keeps records of and explores all forms of music and musical legends in Grammy history; Exec. Dir BOB SANTELLI; Asst Curator TORY MILLIMAKI.

Griffith Observatory: 2800 E Observatory Rd, Los Angeles, CA 90027; tel. (213) 473-0800; fax (213) 473-0816; internet www.griffithobservatory.org; f. 1935; 3 main divs: the Observatory, with Zeiss twin 12-inch and 9-inch refracting telescopes and 3 solar telescopes; more than 100 exhibits; the Samuel Oschin Planetarium, with its Zeiss star projector and laser video all-dome animation; Dir Dr E. C. KRUPP; publ. *The Griffith Observer* (12 a year, illustrated).

Hammer Museum: 10899 Wilshire Blvd, Los Angeles, CA 90024; tel. (310) 443-7000; e-mail info@hammer.ucla.edu; internet www.hammer.ucla.edu; f. 1990; contemporary and historical work in all media of visual arts; paintings, garden sculptures and videos; Chair. and Pres. JOHN V. TUNNEY; Dir ANN PHILBIN; Treas. STEVEN A. OLSEN.

Hollywood Heritage Museum: POB 2586, Hollywood, CA 90078; Lasky-DeMille Barn, 2100 N Highland Ave, Hollywood, CA; tel. (323) 874-4005; e-mail museum@hollywoodheritage.org; internet www.hollywoodheritage.org; f. 1985; located within the restored Lasky-DeMille Barn; photographs from the silent movie days of motion picture production, movie props, historic documents and other movie related memorabilia; Pres. RICHARD ADKINS; Sec. ALAN SIMON; Treas. RANDY HABERKAMP.

Hollywood Museum: 1660 N Highland Ave, Hollywood Blvd, Hollywood, CA 90028; tel. (323) 464-7776; internet www.thehollywoodmuseum.com; colln of props, photographs, costumes and other memorabilia belonging to Hollywood history; Pres. DONELLE DADIGAN.

Huntington Library, Art Collections and Botanical Gardens: 1151 Oxford Rd, San Marino, CA 91108; tel. (626) 405-2100; fax (626) 449-5720; e-mail publicinformation@huntington.org; internet www.huntington.org; f. 1919; British and French paintings from 18th to 19th centuries (incl. full-length portraits by Reynolds, Gainsborough and Lawrence); 18th-century French sculpture, furniture and porcelain; European decorative arts from 16th to 18th centuries; American painting, furniture and decorative arts from 1730 to 1930; botanical gardens of 120 acres with 15,000 plant species; see under Libraries and Archives; library of 500,000 rare books, 500,000 ref. books, 6m. MSS, prints, 600,000 photographs and maps; Chair. STEWART R. SMITH; Pres. STEVEN S. KOBLIK; Dir Art Collns JOHN MURDOCH; publ. *Huntington Frontiers* (2 a year).

J. Paul Getty Museum: 1200 Getty Center Dr., Los Angeles, CA 90049-1687; tel. (310) 440-7330; fax (310) 440-7751; e-mail gettymuseum@getty.edu; internet www.getty.edu; f. 1954; Greek, Roman and Etruscan antiquities, European paintings; drawings, manuscripts, decorative arts; European and American photographs, modern and contemporary European and American outdoor sculpture; conservation work and symposia; Dir DAVID BOMFORD (acting).

Japanese American National Museum: 369 E First St, Los Angeles, CA 90012; tel. (213) 625-0414; fax (213) 625-1770; e-mail hr@janm.org; internet www.janm.org; f. 1985; colln of Japanese American objects, images and documents which provide insight into the ancestry of Japanese American people in the USA; Co-Exec. Dir NANCY ARAKI; Co-Exec. Dir MIYOKO OSHIMA.

Korean American Museum: 3727 W Sixth St, Suite 400, Los Angeles, CA 90020; tel. (213) 388-4229; fax (213) 381-1288; e-mail info@kamuseum.org; internet www.kamuseum.org; f. 1991; works towards the interpretation and preservation of the Korean American community and its history; Chair. KI SUH PARK; Programme Coordinator Dr CHANGMII BAE; publs *The Korea Central Daily (Joong-ang-ilbo)*, *The Korea Times (Han-kook-ilbo)*.

Korean Cultural Centre Los Angeles: 5505 Wilshire Blvd, Los Angeles, CA 90036; tel. (323) 936-7141; fax (323) 936-5712; internet www.kccla.org; colln of historical and contemporary Korean artefacts along with a variety of replicas of historical pieces from Korea's dynastic kingdoms such as Three Kingdoms Period and Joseon Dynasty (1329–1910); library of 26,000 vols; Dir JAEWON KIM.

LACMA–Los Angeles County Museum of Art: 5905 Wilshire Blvd, Los Angeles, CA 90036; tel. (323) 857-6000; fax (323) 857-6213; e-mail publicinfo@lacma.org; internet www.lacma.org; f. 1910, fmrly Los Angeles Museum of History, Science and Art, present name and status 1961; 100,000 objects dating from ancient times to the present; colln incl. Asian, Japanese, Latin American, Islamic, pre-Columbian art and modern art; CEO and Dir MICHAEL GOVAN.

Los Angeles Municipal Art Gallery (LAMAG): 4800 Hollywood Blvd, Los Angeles, CA 90027; tel. (323) 644-6269; fax (323) 644-6271; e-mail info@lamag.org; internet www.lamag.org; f. 1954; attached to City of Los Angeles Dept of Cultural Affairs; colln focusing on the artists and art of S California; colln incl. painting, sculpture, photography, architecture, design, video, sound, electronic, performance and installation works; Curator and Dir SCOTT CANTY.

Los Angeles Museum of the Holocaust: 100 S The Grove Dr., Los Angeles, CA 90036; tel. (323) 651-3704; fax (323) 651-3706; e-mail info@lamoth.org; internet www.lamoth.org; f. 1961; created by Holocaust survivors; colln of memorabilia: relics and other primary source materials from the Holocaust period (1933–45); Exec. Dir MARK A. ROTHMAN; Dir of Archive, Library and Historical Curatorship Dr VLADIMIR MELAMED.

Los Angeles Police Historical Society: 6045 York Blvd, Los Angeles, CA 90042; tel.

(323) 344-9445; fax (323) 344-9516; e-mail info@laphs.org; internet www.laphs.org; colln of memorabilia concerning the Los Angeles Police Dept history; Exec. Dir GLYNN MARTIN; Chair. TERRY HARA; Sec. TRACEY SCHUSTER; Treas. DAVE BROOKS.

Martial Arts History Museum: 2319 W Magnolia Blvd, Burbank, CA 91506; tel. (818) 478-1722; e-mail info@mamuseum .com; internet www.martialartsmuseum .com; f. 1999; Pres. MICHAEL MATSUDA.

Museum of Neon Art: POB 631, Glendale, CA 91209; tel. (213) 489-9918; e-mail info@ neonmona.org; internet www.neonmona.org; f. 1981; preserves, collects and interprets neon art; Exec. Dir KIM KOGA.

Museum of Tolerance: Simon Wiesenthal Plaza 9786, W Pico Blvd, Los Angeles, CA 90035; tel. (310) 553-8403; e-mail info@ museumoftolerance.com; internet www .museumoftolerance.com; f. 1993; attached to Simon Wiesenthal Center Museum; works towards educating people concerning prejudices, The Holocaust, civil rights, and to prevent hatred and genocide.

Natural History Museum of Los Angeles County: 900 Exposition Blvd, Los Angeles, CA 90007; tel. (213) 763-3466; e-mail info@ nhm.org; internet www.nhm.org; f. 1910; Western USA and American History, New World ethnology and archaeology, palaeontology, geology, mineralogy, botany, ichthyology, mammalogy, entomology, herpetology, invertebrate zoology, ornithology; active research centre in areas of living and fossil invertebrates, vertebrates, mineralogy, anthropology (Native American, pre-Columbian and Pacific) and history (California and Southwestern); incl. Page Museum at La Brea Tar Pits and William S. Hart Museum; library of 100,000 vols; Pres. Dr JANE G. PISANO; Dir JAMES L. POWELL; publs *Contributions in Science* (irregular), *Naturalist*, *Science Series* (irregular), *Terra* (6 a year).

San Diego Museum of Art: POB 122107, San Diego, CA 92112-2107; 1450 El Prado, Balboa Park, San Diego, CA; tel. (619) 232-7931; fax (619) 232-9367; e-mail information@sdmart.org; internet www .sdmart.org; f. 1925; Renaissance and Baroque paintings of Spanish, Italian, Dutch, Flemish and French schools; major works by El Greco, Zurbarán, Goya, Crivelli, Tiepolo, Guardi, Rubens, Rembrandt, Ruysdael, Hals, Matisse, Braque; early and contemporary American artists; Asiatic arts and sculpture, graphics and decorative arts from many countries; Latin American art; lectures, concerts and classes; library of 30,000 vols, 15,000 bound vols of art periodicals and 18,000 auction catalogues; Exec. Dir ROXANA VELASQUEZ; Pres. TOM GILDRED; Sec. CHARLES HELLERICH; Treas. KEN WILLIAMS.

San Diego Natural History Museum: POB 121390, San Diego, CA 92112-1390; 1788 El Prado, San Diego, CA 92101; tel. (619) 232-3821; fax (619) 232-0248; e-mail collections@sdnhm.org; internet www.sdnhm .org; f. 1917; depts of botany, herpetology, birds and mammals, entomology, palaeontology and marine invertebrates; Laurence Klauber Herpetology Colln; library of 56,000 vols (incl. standard and obscure references, journals, rare books and maps); Chair. VIRGINIA CROCKETT; Pres. Dr MICHAEL W. HAGER; Sec. WALT DAVIS; Treas. JEFF WITT; Library Dir MARGARET DYKENS; publs *Proceedings* (irregular), *Transactions* (irregular).

San Francisco Museum of Modern Art: 151 Third St, San Francisco, CA 94103; tel. (415) 357-4000; fax (415) 357-4037; e-mail collections@sfmoma.org; internet www .sfmoma.org; f. 1935; 27,000 artworks, photo-graphs and design objects; contemporary art; permanent colln: early Modernism, Analytical Cubism, Abstract Expressionism and other major schools since the beginning of the 20th century; also German Expressionism, Modernist Mexican painting, figurative art of the San Francisco Bay area; important photography dept with colln of images since the 1840s; dept of architecture and design focusing on works by architects and designers of the Pacific region; dept of media arts incl. multimedia, videotape, film and other works created in moving-image or image-reproduction media; library of 60,000 vols, incl. 1,890 periodicals, 45,000 artists files, 1,100 vols of Sydney Tillim colln, 700 CDs from Skowhegan Lecture Archive; Chair. CHARLES R. SCHWAB; Dir NEAL BENEZRA; Sec. and Treas. DENNIS J. WONG.

University of California, Berkeley Art Museum & Pacific Film Archive: 2625 Durant Ave, Berkeley, CA 94720-2250; tel. (510) 642-0808; fax (510) 642-4889; e-mail bampfa@berkeley.edu; internet www.bampfa .berkeley.edu; f. 1970; 10 exhibition galleries, sculpture garden; permanent colln of Asian and Western art; Hans Hofmann colln; 16,000 objects and 14,000 films and videos; serves the univ. and San Francisco Bay Area community with exhibitions, study collns, etc.; organizes and receives travelling exhibitions from major museums internationally; screens 550–600 films annually; library of 8,000 vols; 150 journal titles; 7,500 posters; 35,000 stills; 1,500 audio cassettes; 95,000 documentation files containing film reviews, press kits, and articles on filmmakers, performers, nat. cinemas, genres and other topics; Chair. BARCLAY SIMPSON; Dir LAWRENCE. RINDER; Chief Curator and Dir of Programmes and Colln LUCINDA BARNES.

Colorado

Clyfford Still Museum: 1250 Bannock St, Denver, CO 80204; tel. (720) 354-4880; e-mail info@clyffordstillmuseum.org; internet www .clyffordstillmuseum.org; f. 2004; 2,400 works of Clyfford; artist's archives of letters, sketchbooks, MSS, photograph albums and personal effects; 825 paintings and 1,575 works on paper; Dir DEAN SOBEL.

Colorado Springs Fine Arts Center: 30 W Dale St, Colorado Springs, CO 80903; tel. (719) 634-5581; fax (719) 634-0570; e-mail info@csfineartscenter.org; internet www .csfineartscenter.org; f. 1936; permanent colln of masterworks by American artists Richard Diebenkorn, Georgia O'Keeffe, Walt Kuhn, John Singer Sargent and artists associated with the Broadmoor Art Acad.; collns of Hispanic and American Indian art; 9 permanent colln galleries, 2 travelling exhibition galleries and Tactile Gallery; Chair. MARTHA MARZOLF; Pres. and CEO SAM GAPP-MAYER; Sec. DAN O'REAR; Treas. KIMBERLEY SHERWOOD; publ. *ArtsFocus*.

Colorado Springs Pioneers Museum: 215 S Tejon St, Colorado Springs, CO 80903; tel. (719) 385-5990; fax (719) 385-5645; e-mail cosmuseum@springsgov.com; internet www .springsgov.com; f. 1903; 60,000 objects incl. nationally significant collns of quilts, Van Briggle art pottery and regional art colln; native American colln of items rep. of the Ute, Cheyenne and Arapaho cultures; reconstruction of author Helen Hunt Jackson's house; collns related to founding of the City, area's mining and agricultural history, its early prominence as a health resort and its recent significance as centre for military training and operations; incl. Starsmore Centre for Local History, archives and research library; Dir MATT MAYBERRY.

CU Art Museum: Univ. of Colorado at Boulder, 318 UCB, Boulder, CO 80309; 1085 18th St., Boulder, CO 80309; tel. (303) 492-8300; fax (303) 735-4197; internet cuartmuseum.colorado.edu; f. 1939; attached to Univ. of Colorado at Boulder; 6,000 works of art; colln of ancient Greek ceramics, Pop Art paintings, Old Master works on paper, SW American and S American santos, SE Asian and Iranian pottery, African sculpture, 18th-century British engraving, 19th-century photography, Japanese ukiyo-e, American prints of 1930s and 1940s, minimalist works on paper and contemporary sculpture, prints, photographs and paintings; Dir LISA TAMIRIS BECKER; Chair. WALTER DIETRICH; Sec. KELLY FEENEY.

Denver Art Museum: 100 W 14th Ave Parkway, Denver, CO 80204-2788; tel. (720) 865-5000; fax (720) 913-0001; e-mail info@ denverartmuseum.org; internet www .denverartmuseum.org; f. 1893 as Artists' Club of Denver, present location 1949; exhibitions and art education programmes for children and adults; permanent collns incl. architecture, design and graphics, Asian; modern and contemporary; native art (incl. American Indian, African and Oceanic artworks); New World (incl. pre-Columbian and Spanish Colonial); painting and sculpture (incl. American and European); photography; Western American art; textile art; temporary exhibitions; Dir Dr CHRISTOPH HEINRICH; Pres. CATHEY FINLON; Chief Curator MARGARET YOUNG-SÁNCHEZ; publs *On & Off the Wall* (24 a year, mems magazine), *Western Passages* (1 a year).

Denver Museum of Nature and Science: 2001 Colorado Blvd, Denver, CO 80205-5978; tel. (303) 370-6000; fax (303) 331-6492; e-mail feedback@dmns.org; internet www .dmns.org; f. 1900; depts of anthropology and archaeology, archives, photographic archives, earth sciences, zoology, conservation, exhibitions, youth programmes, adult programmes; gates Planetarium, Hall of Life, IMAX theatre, auditorium; permanent exhibition: Egyptian mummies, expedition health, gems and minerals, North American Indian cultural artefacts, wildlife exhibits, space odyssey, prehistoric dinosaurs skeletons and fossils; library of 53,000 vols, incl. 2,000 children's books, 2,500 rare books and 9,000 vols of scientific periodicals, 700,000 photographs; Chair. JAMES H. CROCKER; Chief Curator Dr KIRK R. JOHNSON; Pres. and CEO GEORGE W. SPARKS; publ. *Denver Museum of Nature & Science Annals.*

Kirkland Museum of Fine & Decorative Art: 1311 Pearl St, Denver, CO 80203; tel. (303) 832-8576; e-mail info@ kirklandmuseum.org; internet www .kirklandmuseum.org; f. 1910; 3,300 works of 20th-century decorative arts on view of arts and crafts, art Nouveau, Glasgow style, Wiener Werkstätte, De Stijl, Bauhaus, art deco, modern and pop art; retrospective of painter Vance Kirkland; incl. historic studio of Vance Kirkland; Dir and Curator HUGH A. GRANT.

Koshare Indian Museum: POB 580, La Junta, CO 81050; 115 W 18th St, La Junta, CO 81050; tel. (719) 384-4411; e-mail kiva_clerk@ojc.edu; internet www .kosharehistory.org; f. 1949; Joseph Imhof colln (Imhof works of art by Taos founders, artists from Taos and Sante Fe, and Native American artists); sculptures and paintings byErnesto Zepeda; Andy Anderson woodcarving and caricature carving figures; letter colln of Daniel Kills Alive; colln of guns and W items dating Civil War; colln of pottery, kachinas, basketry, beadwork, tools, dolls, quill work, jewellery and handicraft artwork; Dir and Curator JEREMY MANYIK.

Leanin' Tree Museum and Sculpture Garden of Western Art: 6055 Longbow Dr., Boulder, CO 80301; e-mail mediadirector@leanintree.com; internet www.leanintreemuseum.com; f. 1949; fine art paintings and bronzes of W America created after 1930, incl. cowboys, Indians, wildlife and landscapes; 250 paintings and 150 bronze sculptures by 100 artists; Chair. ED TRUMBLE.

Littleton Museum: 6028 S Gallup St, Littleton, CO 80120; tel. (303) 795-3950; fax (303) 730-9818; e-mail mutn@littletongov .org; internet www.littletongov.org/museum; 40,000 historically significant artefacts; Dir TIM NIMZ.

Longmont Museum & Cultural Center: 400 Quail Rd, Longmont, CO 80501; tel. (303) 651-8374; fax (303) 651-0483; internet www .ci.longmont.co.us/museum; f. 1936, present status 1970; exhibits history and culture of Longmont and the St Vrain River Valley; colln incl. Lyons, Colorado, artist Kathy Bradford's sandblasted glass wall Hidden Paths, Unseen Trails; 3 pieces of public art; incl. archives; Dir WESLEY JESSUP.

Museo de las Americas: 861 Santa Fe Dr., Denver, CO 80204; tel. (303) 571-4401; e-mail info@museo.org; internet www.museo.org; 4,000 artefacts on ancient art of the Americas and Latin America; Exec. Dir MARUCA SALAZAR; Pres. GEORGE S. MARTINEZ; Treas. MARIA MONTOYA.

Museum of Western Colorado: POB 20000, Grand Junction, CO 81502-5020; tel. (970) 242-0971; e-mail info@westcomuseum .org; internet www.museumofwesternco .com; incl. Museum of the West, Dinosaur Journey Museum, Cross Orchards Historic Site, Loyd Files Research Library and Whitman Educational Centre; Exec. Dir MIKE PERRY; Pres. DALE TOOKER; Sec. RICK ADLEMAN; Treas. WILLIAM VOSS.

University Art Museum: 1778 Campus Delivery, Fort Collins, CO 80523-1778; tel. (970) 491-1989; fax (970) 492-4027; internet www.artmuseum.colostate.edu; attached to Colorado State Univ.; 3,000 art works incl. prints, photographs, paintings, sculpture, textiles and ceramics; modern and contemporary works on paper, incl. Soviet era photography and 250 prints by 19th-century lithographer and social critic, Honoré-Victorin Daumier; 200 19th-century and early 20th-century Japanese prints and African objects and textiles; Dir LINNY FRICKMAN.

University of Colorado Museum of Natural History: Henderson Bldg, 15th and Broadway, Boulder, CO 80309; tel. (303) 492-6892; fax (303) 492-4195; e-mail cumuseum@ colorado.edu; internet cumuseum.colorado .edu; f. 1909; colln of 4m. objects in anthropology, botany, entomology, paleontology and zoology; Dir PATRICK KOCIOLEK.

Connecticut

Bruce Museum: 1 Museum Dr., Greenwich, CT 06830-7157; tel. (203) 869-6786; fax (203) 869-0963; e-mail info@brucemuseum.org; internet brucemuseum.org; f. 1908; 15,000 objects of fine and decorative art, natural history and anthropology; local repository for archaeological sites and artefacts in Greenwich and Fairfield co; Exec. Dir and CEO PETER C. SUTTON; Co-Chair. NATHANIEL B. DAY; Co-Chair. TAMARA HOLLIDAY; Sec. MARTHA R. ZOUBEK; Treas. LAURENCE B. SIMON.

Connecticut State Museum of Natural History and Archaeology Center: 2019 Hillside Rd, Unit 1023, Storrs, CT 06269-1023; tel. (860) 486-4460; fax (860) 486-0827; e-mail csmnhinfo@uconn.edu; internet www .cac.uconn.edu; attached to College of Liberal Arts and Sciences, Univ. of Connecticut; 500,000 archaeological and ethnographic items primarily of Native North and South American origin, incl. 19th-century Plains Indian shirts and Palaeolithic stone tools dating from over 250,000 years ago; repository for artefacts from more than 400 archaeological sites from Connecticut, representing every town within the State; State Archaeologist Dr NICHOLAS BELLANTONI; Dir LEANNE KENNEDY HARTY.

Connecticut Trolley Museum: POB 360, East Windsor, CT 06088; tel. (860) 627-6540; fax (860) 627-6510; e-mail office@ceraweb .org; internet ceraonline.org; f. 1940; 70 pieces of rail equipment dating back to 1869; colln incl. elevated railway cars, locomotives (diesel and electric) and passenger and freight railroad cars; Chair. FRED STOINEY; Pres. GALEN SEMPREBON; Sec. TIM LESNIAK; Treas. STEPHEN TAYLOR.

Custom House Maritime Museum: 150 Bank St, New London, CT 06320; tel. (860) 447-2501; fax (860) 447-8086; e-mail nlmaritimedirector@gmail.com; internet www.nlmaritimesociety.org; f. 1983; colln promotes and interprets maritime life and history of port of New London and surrounding regions; library of 2,000 vols; Pres. and Chair. GEORGE SPRECACE; Sec. GWENDOLYN BOSCO; Treas. JOHN DESJARDINS; Dir SUSAN TAMULEVICH.

Danbury Railway Museum: POB 90, 120 White St, Danbury, CT 06813-0090; tel. (203) 778-8337; fax (203) 778-1836; internet www .danbury.org/drm; f. 1994; 70 pieces of historic railroad equipment and artefacts; colln incl. Boston and Maine 1455 steam engine; Pres. WADE ROESE; Sec. STEVE GOULD; Treas. PATTY OSMER.

Discovery Museum and Planetarium: 4450 Park Ave, Bridgeport, CT 06604; tel. (203) 372-3521; fax (203) 374-1929; e-mail info@discoverymuseum.org; internet www .discoverymuseum.org; f. 1958 as The Museum of Art Science and Industry; incl. Henry B. duPont Planetarium, Challenger Learning Center, interactive science galleries and educational programmes; Chair. DANIEL J. DONOVAN; Exec. Dir JEFFREY BISHOP; Dir for Finance and Admin. LAUREL ANDERSON; Treas. JOSEPH P. CARDONE.

Fairfield Museum and History Center: 370 Beach Rd, Fairfield, CT 06824; tel. (203) 259-1598; fax (203) 255-2716; e-mail info@ fairfieldhs.org; internet www.fairfieldhistory .org; f. 2007; colln on 375 years of Fairfield history; early 19th-century store items, genealogy records and resources, arms and weapons from mid-18th century to First World War and civil defence items from Second World War and Cold War era; repository for town records incl. real estate tax records dating back to 1890; Exec. Dir MICHAEL A. JEHLE; Pres. WILLIAM J. VOGEL; Sec. MISSY PALMISANO; Treas. STEVE WAGENBACH.

Florence Griswold Museum: 96 Lyme St, Old Lyme, CT 06371; tel. (860) 434-5542; fax (860) 434-9778; internet www.flogris.org; f. 1936; paintings and sculptures by artists in Connecticut dating from late Colonial period to early 20th century; library of 1,000 vols; Dir JEFF ANDERSEN; Curator AMY KURTZ LANSING.

Hill-Stead Museum: 35 Mountain Rd, Farmington, CT 06032; tel. (860) 677-4787; fax (860) 677-0174; internet www.hillstead .org; f. 1947; 250 prints and photographs, 290 ceramics, 400 pieces of furniture and 16,000 archival documents; French Impressionist paintings; library of 3,300 vols; Dir and CEO SUE STURTEVANT; Pres. PAUL H. EDDY; Sec. and Treas. JAMES W. FANELLI.

Keeler Tavern Museum & Garden House: POB 204, 132 Main St, Ridgefield, CT 06877; tel. (203) 438-5485; fax (203) 438-9953; e-mail info@keelertavernmuseum.org; internet keelertavernmuseum.org; f. 1966; paintings, prints, samplers and sculpture from early 19th century to mid-20th century; original engraving of Battle of Ridgefield published 1780; hand-carved decorative urns in gardens recreated in Italy from original blueprints; Pres. CHERYL CROWL; Sec. MARY KALETTA; Treas. GEORGE STUECK.

Lyman Allyn Art Museum: 625 Williams St, New London, CT 06320; tel. (860) 443-2545; e-mail info@lymanallyn.org; internet www.lymanallyn.org; f. 1932; 10,000 paintings, drawings, prints, sculptures, furniture and decorative arts focusing on American art dating from 16th to 20th century; Dir and Curator NANCY STULA.

Mark Twain House & Museum: 351 Farmington Ave, Hartford, CT 06105; tel. (860) 247-0998; e-mail info@marktwainhouse .org; internet www.marktwainhouse.org; f. 2003; home of author Samuel L. Clemens or Mark Twain and his family from 1874 to 1891; 16,000 artefacts incl. period decorative and fine arts pieces and 12-vols set of Twain's works in Russian; library of 6,000 vols and 5,280 photographs; Pres. GREGORY BOYKO; Sec. RICHARD F. AHLES; Treas. GREGORY SERVODIDIO; Exec. Dir JEFFREY L. NICHOLS.

New Britain Museum of American Art: 56 Lexington St, New Britain, CT 06052-1412; tel. (860) 229-0257; fax (860) 229-3445; e-mail nbmaa@nbmaa.org; internet www .nbmaa.org; f. 1953 as New Britain Institute, present name and status 1957; 10,236 works of American art incl. 1,133 oils and acrylics, 2,710 drawings, 1,518 graphics, 202 sculptures, 216 photographs and 1,782 illustrations; colonial and federal portraits, impressionist colln and mural series; Chair. KATHRYN COX; Sec. LINDA TOMASSO; Treas. HENRY R. MARTIN; Dir DOUGLAS HYLAND.

Railroad Museum of New England: POB 400, Thomaston, CT 06787-0400; tel. and fax (860) 283-7245; internet www.rmne.org; f. 1968; focus on historically significant examples of railroad equipments of New England; colln incl. steam and diesel locomotives, passenger cars and freight cars spanning over eras.

Wadsworth Atheneum Museum of Art: 600 Main St, Hartford, CT 06103; tel. (860) 278-2670; fax (860) 527-0803; e-mail info@ wadsworthatheneum.org; internet www .wadsworthatheneum.org; f. 1842; early American furniture, Hudson River School landscapes, Renaissance and Baroque paintings, African-American art; Meissen and Sèvres porcelains; costume and textiles; 19th-century French and Impressionist paintings; modernist and surrealist masterpieces; MATRIX Gallery for Contemporary Art; colln of 50,000 works of art spanning 5,000 years; library: Auerbach library of 40,000 vols; Dir and CEO SUSAN TALBOT; Chief Curator LINDA ROTH; Pres. SUSAN A. ROTTNER; Sec. HY J. SCHWARTZ; Treas. HENRY R. MARTIN.

Yale Peabody Museum of Natural History: Yale Univ., POB 208118, New Haven, CT 06520-8118; Yale Univ., 170–210 Whitney Ave, New Haven, CT 06511; tel. (203) 432-3752; fax (203) 432-9816; e-mail peabody .director@yale.edu; internet www.peabody .yale.edu; f. 1866; attached to Yale Univ.; extensive collns in the fields of anthropology, meteorites, botany, palaeobotany, invertebrate palaeontology, mineralogy, vertebrate palaeontology, invertebrate zoology and vertebrate zoology, historic scientific instruments, each with its own curator; also Yale

Peabody Museum Field Station; Dir DEREK E. G. BRIGGS; publs *Bulletin*, *Discovery*, *Postilla*.

Yale University Art Gallery: POB 208271, New Haven, CT 06520-8271; tel. (203) 432-0600; fax (203) 432-9274; e-mail artgalleryinfo@yale.edu; internet artgallery.yale.edu; f. 1750; colln of 185,000 works of African art, American paintings and sculpture dating from colonial America to mid-20th century; European art: paintings and sculpture from early Renaissance Tuscany to 19th-century France; coins, medals and paper money from 7th century BC to present; modern and contemporary art; Asian art; Ancient art; Dir JOCK REYNOLDS.

Delaware

Biggs Museum of American Art: POB 711, Dover, DE 19903; 406 Federal St, Dover, DE 19901; tel. (302) 674-2111; fax (302) 674-5133; e-mail admin@biggsmuseum.org; internet biggsmuseum.org; f. 1993; representational American paintings colln on the Delmarva Peninsula with highlights by the Peale family, Albert Bierstadt, Gilbert Stuart and Childe Hassam; sculptures by Hiram Powers and images by Brandywine School illustrator, Frank E. Schoonover; colln of regional silver; Dir LINDA A. K. DANKO; Curator RYAN GROVER.

Delaware Agricultural Museum & Village: 866 N DuPont Highway, Dover, DE 19901; tel. (302) 734-1618; fax (302) 734-0457; e-mail damv@verizon.net; internet www.agriculturalmuseum.org; f. 1980; non-profit org.; depicts technological growth and change in Delaware and Delmarva agricultural history; displays 10,000 artefacts: from butter churns to threshers, from an 18th-century log house to the first broiler chicken house; library of 442 vols, incl. 1,458 images, also houses archival material, oral histories and artefacts pertaining to Delaware agriculture; Pres. CHESTER DICKERSON, JR; Treas. ROBIN TALLEY; Sec. FRANCES WEST.

Delaware Art Museum: 2301 Kentmere Parkway, Wilmington, DE 19806; tel. (302) 571-9590; fax (302) 571-0220; e-mail info@delart.org; internet www.delart.org; f. 1938 as Delaware Art Center, present name and status 1972; colln of American art from the 19th century to the present day; pre-Raphaelite collns of Samuel Bancroft, Jr; paintings of Howard Pyle; artworks by John Sloan; library of 30,000 vols (incl. exhibition catalogues, monographs, periodicals, reference works and vertical files relating to individual artists); Exec. Dir DANIELLE RICE; Chief Curator MARGARETTA S. FREDERICK; Librarian RACHAEL DIELEUTERIO.

Delaware History Museum: 504 Market St, Wilmington, DE 19801; tel. (302) 656-0637; e-mail hsd@hsd.org; internet www.hsd.org/dhm.htm; attached to Delaware Historical Soc.; 3 galleries of changing interactive exhibits on Delaware history; displays rare items of everyday life, costumes, children's toys, regional decorative arts and paintings; library: 2m. MSS, 12,000 references, maps, prints and photographs, 700 rare book titles, 110 rare pamphlets and periodicals, 83 almanacs and 300 Delaware imprints; CEO SCOTT W. LOEHR; publ. *Delaware History* (2 a year).

Delaware Museum of Natural History: 4840 Kennett Pike, POB 3937, Wilmington, DE 19807-0937; tel. (302) 658-9111; fax (302) 658-2610; internet www.delmnh.org; f. 1972; 117,000 bird specimens and 220,000 lots of mollusks (shells); library of 10,000 vols (incl. works on mollusks, recent monographs, reprints and journals); Exec. Dir HALSEY SPRUANCE; publ. *Nemouria: Occasional*

Papers of the Delaware Museum of Natural History.

Delaware State Police Museum: 1425 N DuPont Highway, POB 430, Dover, DE 19903-0430; tel. (302) 739-7700; internet www.delawaretrooper.com/museum; f. 1998; showcases history of Delaware State Police; displays vehicles used by Delaware police and their uniform from the time of its inception to the present; Pres. ROBERT M. GOUGE; Treas. PAUL R. KANÉ; Curator JOHN ALSTADT.

DiscoverSea Shipwreck Museum: 708 Coastal Highway, Fenwick Island, DE 19944; tel. (302) 539-9366; fax (302) 539-1285; e-mail dsmuseum@aol.com; internet www.discoversea.com; f. 1995; preserves Delmarva's maritime heritage; displays 10,000 artefacts: both regional and worldwide shipwreck and recovered artefacts; Dir DALE W. CLIFTON, JR.

Hagley Museum and Library: POB 3630, Wilmington, DE 19807-0630; 298 Buck Rd E, Wilmington, DE 19807-0630; tel. (302) 658-2400; fax (302) 658-0568; e-mail info@hagley.org; internet www.hagley.org; f. 1972; non-profit org.; collects, preserves and interprets the unfolding history of American enterprise; incl. restored mills, workers' community and ancestral home and gardens of the du Pont family; library of 280,000 vols, 34,000 linear ft in the MSS and Archives Dept, 2m. visual items; Exec. Dir GEOFF HALFPENNY; Dir Museum Services JOAN HOGE-NORTH; Curator of Collns and Exhibits DEBRA HUGHES.

Historic Odessa Foundation: POB 697, Odessa, DE 19730; tel. (302) 378-4119; fax (302) 378-4050; e-mail info@historicodessa.org; internet www.historicodessa.org; f. 2005; 18th- and early 19th-century bldgs, incl. Corbit-Sharp House (c. 1774); Wilson-Warner House (c. 1769), Collins-Sharp House (c. 1700), Brick Hotel (c. 1822) and Odessa Bank (c. 1853); 4,000 objects spannig an interpretive period in regional decorative arts from 1760 to 1850; colln of regional paintings, prints, textiles, silver, pewter and other metals; Exec. Dir DEBORAH BUCKSON; Pres. ELIZABETH A SHARP; Treas. WILLIAM GOTWALS.

Milford Museum: 121 S Walnut St, Milford, DE 19963; tel. (302) 424-1080; internet www.milforddemuseum.org; f. 1983; displays local historic events from the 1700s to the present; historic doll colln; Victorian silverware colln; early Milford baseball; Exec. Dir CLAUDIA FURNISH LEISTER; Pres. DAVID KENTON; Sec. JOAN LOFLAND; Treas. DONALD ABRUTYN.

Milton Historical Society: POB 112, Milton, DE 19968; tel. (302) 684-1010; e-mail info@historicmilton.org; internet www.historicmilton.org; collects, preserves, and interprets stories, artefacts and documents related to Milton and the Broadkill Hundred for study and education; exhibits highlight Milton's heyday as a shipbuilding centre and offers a snapshot of Milton from the Civil War through the 1960s; Exec. Dir MELINDA LINDERER HUFF; Pres. DENNIS HUGHES; Treas. DAVID CAREY; Sec. BONNIE HUDSON.

Museum of Business History and Technology: 1200 Philadelphia Pike, Wilmington, DE 19809; tel. (302) 798-2100; internet www.mbht.com; f. 2001; 2,000 artefacts showcasing evolution of business technology; collns incl. machines of American manufactures between 1873 and 1940, such as automatic typewriters, calculating machines, copying machines, dictating machines, paging and calling systems, postage machines and word processing machines; James Watt's 1795 copier and Thomas Decolmar's 1820 calculator.

New Castle Historical Society: 2 E Fourth St, New Castle, DE 19720; tel. (302) 322-2794; fax (302) 322-8923; e-mail nchistorical@aol.com; internet www.newcastlehistory.org; f. 1934; 3 museums: Amstel House, Dutch House and Old Library Museum; collns of New Castle Library Company; also holds books, ceramics, documents, furniture, MSS, metals, photographs, textiles and works-on-paper preserving 300 years of local and nat. history; Exec. Dir MICHAEL CONNOLLY.

Seaford Museum: 203 High St, Seaford, DE 19973; tel. (302) 628-9828; fax (302) 628-2984; e-mail info@seafordhistoricalsociety.com; internet www.seafordhistoricalsociety.com/index.cfm?ref=89265; f. 2003; attached to Seaford Historical Soc.; holds artefacts on early agriculture, shipbuilding, canning, chicken industry and railroads.

University Museums: Univ. of Delaware, 208 Mechanical Hall, Newark, DE 19716; tel. (302) 831-8037; e-mail universitymuseums@udel.edu; internet www.udel.edu/museums; f. 1979 as Univ. Gallery; attached to Univ. of Delaware; 20th- and 21st-century American art (Brandywine School); African American art, photography, minerals and pre-Columbian ceramics; displays 10,000 objects; 3 museums: Mechanical Hall, Mineralogical Museum and Old College Gallery; Dir Dr JANIS A TOMLINSON; Curator of Collns JAN BROSKE.

Winterthur Museum, Garden & Library: 5105 Kennett Pike, Wilmington, DE 19735; tel. (302) 888-4600; fax (302) 888-4700; e-mail tourinfo@winterthur.org; internet www.winterthur.org; f. 1951; 90,000 American antiquities from 1630 to 1860 (colln incl. ceramics, glass, furniture, metalwork, paintings and prints, and textiles and needlework); MA programme in early American culture and MS programme in art conservation, both in conjunction with Univ. of Delaware; colln of over; library of 100,000 vols, 500,000 MSS, 20,000 rare American and European imprints, 110,000 photographs; Exec. Dir DAVE ROSELLE; publ. *Winterthur Portfolio* (4 a year).

Zwaanendael Museum: 102 Kings Highway, Lewes, DE 19958; tel. (302) 645-1148; internet history.delaware.gov/museums/zm/zm_main.shtml; f. 1931; showcases history of Sussex County, Lewes area maritime, military and social history; 11,000 years of Lewes culture through 5 thematic sections; artefacts, maps, sketches, lithographs and photographs of period bldgs.

District of Columbia

Anacostia Community Museum: 1901 Fort Pl., SE, Washington, DC 20020; tel. (202) 633-4820; fax (202) 287-3183; e-mail aminfo@si.edu; internet www.anacostia.si.edu; f. 1967; attached to Smithsonian Instn; artefacts, photographs, archival documents, media and art objects that document family and community locally, regionally, nationally and internationally; Griffith Family Colln; Lillian Evans-Tibbs Colln; Lorenzo Dow Turner Colln; library of 3,500 vols, 100 periodicals; Dir CAMILLE GIRAUD AKEJU (acting); Chair. JAMES LARRY FRAZIER.

Arthur M. Sackler Gallery: Smithsonian Instn, 1050 Independence Ave, SW, POB 37012, MRC 707, Washington, DC 20013-7012; tel. (202) 633-1000; fax (202) 357-4911; e-mail publicaffairsasia@si.edu; internet www.asia.si.edu; f. 1987; attached to Smithsonian Instn; colln incl. ancient Chinese jades and bronzes in the world and contemporary art from Asia as well as int. loan exhibitions; interlinked with Freer Gallery whose colln incl. 19th-century American art;

jt Sackler and Freer scientific and research dept; library of 80,000 vols; Dir JULIAN RABY; publs *Ars Orientalis* (1 a year), *Occasional Papers Series* (irregular).

Art Museum of the Americas: Org. of American States, 1889 F St, NW, Washington, DC 20006; 201 18th St, NW, Washington, DC 20006; tel. (202) 458-6016; fax (202) 458-6021; e-mail artmus@oas.org; internet www.museum.oas.org; f. 1976; attached to Org. of American States; 2,000 objects incl. painting, sculpture, installations, prints, drawings and photographs of America; contemporary Latin American and Caribbean art; works incl. early 20th-century American paintings and art; Dir LYDIA BENDERSKY.

Arts and Industries Building: 900 Jefferson Dr., SW, Washington, DC; tel. (202) 633-1000; e-mail info@si.edu; internet www.si.edu/museums/arts-and-industries-building; f. 1881; attached to Smithsonian Instn; exhibitions of Smithsonian Instn and other museums; art, history, natural history, history of technology, portraiture, air and space history, African-American and Native American history.

Corcoran Gallery of Art: Corcoran College of Art and Design, 500 17th St, NW, Washington, DC 20006-4840; tel. (202) 639-1700; fax (202) 639-1768; e-mail provostoffice@corcoran.org; internet www.corcoran.org; f. 1869; 16,000 items from 19th and 20th centuries; American and European painting, sculpture and photography, incl. works by Cuyp, Degas, Delacroix, Hopper, Elsworth Kelly, Monet, Picasso, Man Ray, Renoir, Rodin, Sargent, Warhol, Whistler; also houses the Corcoran College of Art and Design; Dir and Pres. KRISTIN GUITER; Man. of Curatorial Affairs LISA STRONG; Chair. HARRY F. HOPPER, III; Sec. SARAH E. CHAPOTON; Treas. FREDERICK W. KNOPS, III.

DAR Museum: c/o Nat. Soc. Daughters of the American Revolution, 1776D St, NW, Washington, DC 20006-5303; tel. (202) 628-1776; e-mail historian@dar.org; internet www.dar.org/museum; f. 1890; attached to Nat. Soc. Daughters of the American Revolution; comprises 31 period rooms and 2 galleries; 30,000 decorative and fine arts objects spanning the 18th and 19th centuries, incl. furniture, glass, ceramics, textiles and silver; spec. colln: folk art and Americana, artefacts of the abolitionist movement; library of 180,000 vols; Dir DIANE DUNKLEY; publ. *American Spirit.*

Fondo Del Sol Visual Arts Center: 2112R St, NW, Washington, DC 2008; tel. (202) 483-2777; e-mail info@fondodelsol.org; internet www.fondodelsol.org; f. 1973; colln of 800 paintings, prints and drawings; 500 photographic images; pre-Columbian, Santero and 20th-century Latino and Carribean art; film and video archive of over 200 works; Chair., Dir and Chief Curator MARC ZUVER; Treas. BRUCE TOONE.

Hillwood Estate, Museum & Gardens: 4155 Linnean Ave, NW, Washington, DC 20008; tel. (202) 686-8500; internet www.hillwoodmuseum.org; 16,000 works of art; colln of imperial Russian and 18th-century French decorative arts; library of 30,000 vols; Exec. Dir KATE MARKERT; Chief Curator LIANA PAREDES; Pres. ELLEN M. CHARLES; Sec. MICHAEL CANTACUZÈNE; Treas. RILEY K. TEMPLE.

Hirshhorn Museum and Sculpture Garden: Smithsonian Instn, POB 37012, MRC Code 350, Washington, DC 20013-7012; Independence Ave, Seventh St, SW, Washington, DC 20560; tel. (202) 633-4674; fax (202) 633-8796; e-mail hmsginquiries@si.edu; internet hirshhorn.si.edu; f. 1960; attached to Smithsonian Instn; modern and contemporary int.

art; sculpture of major artists of the 20th and 21st centuries; library of 62,000 vols, 50 serials, 980 non-colln photograph files, 13,000 slides from 900 contemporary artists; Chair. J. TOMILSON HILL; Sec. DANIEL SALLICK; Treas. PAUL C. SCHORR, III.

International Spy Museum: 800 F St, NW, Washington, DC 20004; tel. (202) 393-7798; fax (202) 654-0977; e-mail other@spymuseum.org; internet www.spymuseum.org; f. 2002; history and contemporary role of espionage from a global perspective; colln of int. espionage artefacts; Exec. Dir PETER EARNEST; Chair. MILTON MALTZ.

Kreeger Museum: 2401 Foxhall Rd, NW, Washington, DC 20007; tel. (202) 337-3050; fax (202) 337-3051; e-mail visitorservices@kreegermuseum.org; internet www.kreegermuseum.org; f. 1959; colln incl. works from the 1850s to the present; paintings of Pablo Picasso's life and career and that by 20th-century European artists as well as traditional African and Asian art; Dir JUDY A. GREENBERG.

National Air and Space Museum: Independence Ave, Sixth St, SW, Washington, DC 20560; tel. (202) 633-1000; fax (202) 633-8174; e-mail info@si.edu; internet www.nasm.si.edu; f. 1946 as Nat. Air Museum; attached to Smithsonian Instn; records the nat. devt of aeronautics and astronautics; collects, preserves and displays aeronautical and astronautical equipment of historical interest and significance: 38,200 aviation artefacts, 14,900 space related artefacts and 4,400 works of art; provides educational material for the historical study of aeronautics and astronautics; colln contains original full-size aircraft, spacecraft, recovered space exploration vehicles, engines, instruments, flight clothing, accessories of technical, historical, and biographical interest, photographs, scale models and extensive reference data; Paul E. Garber Preservation, Restoration and Storage Facility and Steven F. Udvar-Hazy Center; incl. Center for Earth and Planetary Studies (*q.v.*); library of 40,000 vols, archives: 14,000 cubic ft of materials, 2m. photographs, 20,000 motion picture and video items, 16,000 reels of microfilm, 2m. technical drawings; Dir Gen. JOHN R. DAILEY.

National Building Museum: 401 F St, NW, Washington, DC 20001; tel. (202) 272-2448; internet www.nbm.org; f. 1985; 75,000 photographic images; 68,000 architectural prints and drawings; 100 linear ft of documents and 4,500 objects; material samples, architectural fragments and bldg toys; spec. collns: S. H. Kress and Co Colln, Wurts Brothers Photography Colln and NW Terra Cotta Colln; Exec. Dir CHASE W. RYND; Sr Vice-Pres. and Curator G. MARTIN MOELLER, JR; Chair. MICHAEL J. GLOSSERMAN; Sec. EDWARD J. NEWBERRY; Treas. ROBERT W. HOLLEYMAN, II.

National Gallery of Art: 2000B South Club Dr., Landover, MD 20785; Nat. Mall, Third and Ninth St, Constitution Ave, Washington, DC 20565; tel. (202) 737-4215; fax (202) 789-2681; e-mail pressinfo@nga.gov; internet www.nga.gov; f. 1937; European and American paintings, sculpture and graphic arts since 12th century; photographic archives; slide colln; library of 365,000 vols, 2,321 periodicals; Pres. VICTORIA P. SANT; Dir EARL A. POWELL, III; publ. *Studies in the History of Art.*

National Museum of African Art: POB 37012, MRC 708, Washington, DC 20013-7012; 950 Independence Ave, SW, Washington, DC 20560; tel. (202) 633-4600; fax (202) 357-4879; e-mail nmafaweb@nmafa.si.edu; internet africa.si.edu; f. 1964; attached to Smithsonian Instn; 8,000 items from Africa,

incl. traditional and contemporary art; library of 25,000 vols, the Eliot Elisofon Photographic Archives: 300,000 photographic prints and transparencies, 120,000 ft of motion picture film and video cassettes; Dir Dr JOHNNETTA B. COLE; Chair. STUART BOHART.

National Museum of American History: Kenneth E. Behring Center, Dept of Education for Interpretation and Visitor Experience, POB 37012, MRC 603, Washington, DC 20013-7012; The Nat. Mall, 14th St and Constitution Ave, NW, Washington, DC 20560; tel. (202) 633-1000; e-mail info@si.edu; internet americanhistory.si.edu; f. 1964 as the Nat. Museum of History and Technology, present name 1980; attached to Smithsonian Instn; 3m. artefacts incl. gowns and locomotives; Archives Center with 1,200 documents, photographs and other works; lectures and concerts; Dir MARC PACHTER; Curator, Archives Center VANESSA BROUSSARD SIMMONS.

Attached Research Institute:

> **Jerome and Dorothy Lemelson Center for the Study of Invention and Innovation:** see separate entry.

National Museum of American Jewish Military History: 1811R St, NW, Washington, DC 20009; tel. (202) 265-6280; fax (202) 462-3192; e-mail nmajmh@nmajmh.org; internet www.nmajmh.org; f. 1958; 5,000 artefacts, incl. objects from every American military conflict, with spec. emphasis on Second World War; incl. archival colln of American Jewish military history from the Civil War to the present; Dir HERB ROSENBLEETH; Pres. NORMAN ROSENSHEIN; publ. *Hall of Heroes.*

National Museum of Natural History: POB 37012, Smithsonian Instn, Washington, DC 20013-7012; tel. (202) 357-2661; fax (202) 357-4779; e-mail naturalexperience@si.edu; internet www.mnh.si.edu; f. 1910; attached to Smithsonian Instn; 126m. natural science specimens and cultural artefacts; items incl. fossilized pollen, bones of Tyrannosaurus rex, algal samples, slab of a giant sequoia tree, tiny crustaceans, giant squid, DNA samples of whale skulls, ancient spear points, Chinese shoes, Hope Diamond and Moon rocks; 30m. insects; 7m. fish in liquid-filled jars; 2m. cultural artefacts; 400,000 photographs housed in the Nat. Anthropological Archives; 20,000 works of native art, 1,200 aluminium discs by J. P. Harrington; human studies film archives: 8m. ft of film and video; Chair. KATHRYN S. FULLER; Dir Dr CRISTIÁN SAMPER (acting); publ. *Smithsonian Contributions* (separate series for Anthropology, Botany, Earth Sciences, Palaeobiology, Zoology and Marine Sciences).

Attached Research Institutes:

> **Arctic Research Centre:** see separate entry.

> **Carrie-Bow Marine Field Station— Caribbean Coral Reef Ecosystems (CCRE):** see separate entry in Belize chapter.

> **Marine Station at Fort Pierce:** see separate entry.

National Museum of the US Navy: Washington Navy Yard, 805 Kidder Breese St, SE, Washington, DC 20374-5060; tel. (202) 433-4882; fax (202) 433-8200; e-mail navymuseum@navy.mil; internet www.history.navy.mil/branches/org8-1.htm; f. 1961; attached to Naval History and Heritage Command; naval artefacts, models, documents and fine art depicting the history of the US Navy from the American Revolution to the present conflicts; interactive exhibits of Navy's wartime heroes and battles as well as peacetime contributions in exploration, diplomacy, navigation and humanitarian service; Dir Rear Admiral JAY A. DeLOACH.

National Museum of Women in the Arts: 1250 New York Ave, NW, Washington, DC 20005-3970; tel. (202) 783-5000; internet www.nmwa.org; f. 1981; more than 3,000 works of art by women from the 16th century to the present; Renaissance paintings of Elisabetta Sirani, modern photographs by Barbara Morgan and Louise Nevelson's contemporary sculptures; archives on women artists: colln of research files of personal and biographic information of 18,000 women artists; library of 18,500 vols; Dir SUSAN FISHER STERLING; Chief Curator JORDANA POMEROY; Chair. WILHELMINA COLE HOLLADAY; Sec. CHARLOTTE CLAY BUXTON; Treas. SHEILA SHAFFER; publ. *Women in the Arts* (4 a year).

National Portrait Gallery: POB 37012, Victor Bldg, Suite 8300, MRC 973, Washington, DC 20013-7012; Eighth and F St, NW, Washington, DC 20001; tel. (202) 633-1000; fax (202) 633-8243; e-mail npgnews@si.edu; internet npg.si.edu; f. 1962; attached to Smithsonian Instn; portraits of persons who have made significant contributions to the history, devt or culture of the people of the USA; library of 180,000 vols; Dir MARTIN E. SULLIVAN; publ. *PROFILE* (4 a year).

National Postal Museum: POB 37012, MRC 570, Washington, DC 20013-7012; 2 Massachussetts Ave, NE, Washington, DC 20002; tel. (202) 633-5555; fax (202) 633-9393; internet www.postalmuseum.si.edu; f. 1886 as Nat. Philatelic Colln, present name and location 1993; attached to Smithsonian Instn; Nat. Philatelic Colln of 6m. items; incl. delivery vehicles, mailboxes and mailbags, uniforms and equipment and other items of postal history; library of 13,000 vols; Dir ALLEN R. KANE; Chief Curator of Philately CHERYL GANZ.

Phillips Collection: 1600 21st St, NW, Washington, DC 20009; tel. (202) 387-2151; fax (202) 387-2436; e-mail director@ phillipscollection.org; internet www .phillipscollection.org; f. 1918; 3,000 works by American and European artists; Center for the Study of Modern Art; library of 9,500 vols; Dir DOROTHY KOSINSKI; Chair. GEORGE VRADENBURG; Sec. BRIAN D. DAILEY; Treas. THOMAS D. RUTHERFOORD, JR.; Chief Curator ELIZA RATHBONE.

Sewall-Belmont House & Museum: 144 Constitution Ave, NE, Washington, DC 20002-5608; tel. (202) 546-1210; e-mail info@sewallbelmont.org; internet www .sewallbelmont.org; colln incl. 800 suffrage banners, archives, capes, sashes and ribbons used by the NWP for parades; artefacts of the suffrage movement and the campaign for Equal Rights Amendment (ERA); books, scrapbooks, political cartoons, textiles, photographs, organizational records, fine arts and decorative arts; library of 10,000 vols (incl. early women's magazines and suffrage journals written by and about women from 1880 to present day); Exec. Dir PAGE HARRINGTON; Pres. DIANNE CHASEN LIPSEY; Sec. SALLY PATTERSON; Treas. ALICIA DALY.

Smithsonian American Art Museum and the Renwick Gallery: POB 37012, MRC 970, Washington, DC 20013-7012; 750 Ninth St, NW, Washington, DC 20001; tel. (202) 633-7970; fax (202) 275-1424; e-mail americanartinfo@si.edu; internet americanart.si.edu; f. 1829; largest colln of American art in the world; 41,000 artworks since 18th century; incl. Lunder Conservation Center (permanent displays of the museum's preservation work) and provides information on conservation science and

techniques; other centres incl. Luce Foundation Center for American Art (art storage and study centre): 3,300 objects on display, incl. a discussion of each artwork, artist biographies, audio interviews, video-clips and still images; specialized art research databases of 500,000 records, incl. Inventory of American Paintings and Sculpture; pre-1877 Art Exhibition Catalogue Index and findings from the Save Outdoor Sculpture programme; photographic archives: 250,000 photographs, negatives and slides; Peter A. Juley and Son colln (127,000 images documenting the work of 11,000 American artists from the 1890s to 1975); and the Walter Rosenblum colln (7,500 black-and-white photographs documenting the New York art scene from 1945 to 1970); Graphic Arts Study Center (28,000 works on paper, including prints, drawings, watercolours and photographs) and the Joseph Cornell Study Center; Renwick Gallery of craft work; now part of the Donald W. Reynolds Center; library of 180,000 vols; Dir ELIZABETH BROUN; publ. *American Art* (3 a year).

Textile Museum: 2320 S St, NW, Washington, DC 20008-4088; tel. (202) 667-0441; fax (202) 483-0994; e-mail info@textilemuseum .org; internet www.textilemuseum.org; f. 1925; 9,000 objects spanning 5,000 years dating from 3,000 BC to the present; colln incl. 15th-century Mamluk rugs from Egypt, Spanish carpets and classical Indian carpet fragments; also incl. pre-Columbian Peruvian textiles; library of 20,000 vols; Dir MARYCLAIRE RAMSEY; Pres. BRUCE P. BAGANZ; publ. *Members' Magazine* (4 a year).

United States Holocaust Memorial Museum: 100 Raoul Wallenberg Pl., SW, Washington, DC 20024-2126; tel. (202) 488-0400; e-mail curator@ushmm.org; internet www.ushmm.org; f. 1993; collects and preserves historical record of the Holocaust; colln incl. original documents, photographs and artefacts related to Holocaust; 10,000 art and artefacts; 12,500 oral history testimonies and access to 52,000 oral histories from the USC Shoah Foundation Institute; 2 theatres; interactive computer learning centre; classrooms and a memorial space; library of 92,025 vols; Dir SARA J. BLOOMFIELD.

United States National Arboretum: 3501 New York Ave, NE, Washington, DC 20002-1958; tel. (202) 245-2726; fax (202) 245-4575; internet www.usna.usda.gov; f. 1927; attached to Beltsville Agricultural Research Center, Agricultural Research Service, US Dept of Agriculture; aquatic plants; Asian collns; Fern Valley Native Plant collns; Flowering Tree colln; Flowering Tree Walk; Friendship gdn; Gotelli Dwarf and Slow-Growing Conifer colln; Introduction gdn; Nat. Bonsai and Penjing Museum; Nat. Capitol Columns; Nat. Grove of State Trees; Nat. Herb Gdn; library of 11,000 vols, 100 journals; Dir Dr COLIEN HEFFERAN.

Florida

Appleton Museum of Art: College of Central Florida, 4333 E Silver Springs Blvd, Ocala, FL 34470-5001; tel. (352) 291-4455; fax (352) 291-4460; e-mail ormej@cf.edu; internet www.appletonmuseum.org; f. 1982, present status 2004; attached to College of Central Florida; 16,000 objects of European, American, Asian, African, Contemporary and pre-Columbian art and artefacts from 17th to 19th century; library of 2,000 vols; Dir Dr JOHN Z. LOFGREN; Chief Curator RUTH GRIM.

Bass Museum of Art: 2100 Collins Ave, Miami Beach, FL 33139; tel. (305) 673-7530; fax (305) 673-7062; e-mail info@bassmuseum .org; internet www.bassmuseum.org; f. 1963; 3,000 art works incl. European paintings and sculptures dating from 15th century to pre-

sent; textiles, tapestries and artefacts dating from 7th to 20th century; 20th- and 21st-century N American, Latin American, Asian and Caribbean art, photographs, prints and drawings; Exec. Dir and Chief Curator SILVIA KARMAN CUBIÑÁ; Pres. GEORGE LINDEMANN; Sec. LIDA RODRIGUEZ-TASEFF; Treas. ALAN RANDOLPH.

Boca Raton Museum of Art: 501 Plaza Real, Mizner Park, Boca Raton, FL 33432; tel. (561) 392-2500; fax (561) 391-6410; e-mail info@bocamuseum.org; internet www .bocamuseum.org; f. 1962, present name 1985; colln incl. European paintings and sculptures dating from 1775 to 1945; modern and contemporary art works dating from 1960s to present; 300 objects of African arts and artefacts; 800 European and American prints and drawings from 19th century; Dir STEVEN MAKLANSKY; Pres. PAUL W. CARMAN; Sec. ANDREA KLINE; Treas. JOSEPH BORROW.

Cornell Fine Arts Museum: 1000 Holt Ave, Winter Park, FL 32789-4499; tel. (407) 646-2526; fax (407) 646-2524; internet www .rollins.edu/cfam; f. 1941 as Morse Gallery of Art, present name 1978; attached to Rollins College; 5,000 objects from antiquity to contemporary, Middle E artefacts, religious iconography and fine paintings; works of Albert Bierstadt, Alex Katz, John Frederick Kensett, Henri Matisse, Thomas Moran and Pablo Picasso; Dir and Curator Dr JONATHAN F. WALZ.

Cummer Museum of Art & Gardens: 829 Riverside Ave, Jacksonville, FL 32204; tel. (904) 356-6857; fax (904) 353-4101; internet www.cummer.org; f. 1958; 6,000 art works spanning 2100BC through 21st century; colln incl. Wark colln of early Meissen porcelain, Dennis C. Hayes colln of Japanese woodblock prints and Eugène Louis Charvot colln of 19th-century prints and paintings; library of 10,000 vols; Chair. RUSSELL B. NEWTON, III; Sec. LINDA R. ALEXANDER; Treas. BARRY L. ALLRED; Dir HOPE McMATH; Curator HOLLY KERIS.

Dalí Museum: One Dali Blvd, St Petersburg, FL 33701; tel. (727) 823-3767; fax (727) 894-6068; e-mail info@thedali.org; internet thedali.org; f. 1982; colln of 1,300 graphics, sculptures and photographs; oil paintings dating from 1917 to 1970; Dir HANK HINE.

Harn Museum of Art: POB 112700, Gainesville, FL 32611-2700; SW 34th St and Hull Rd, Gainesville, FL 32611-2700; tel. (352) 392-9826; fax (352) 392-3892; e-mail info@harn.ufl.edu; internet www.harn.ufl .edu; f. 1990; attached to Univ. of Florida; 8,000 objects from Mesoamerica, Central America and Central Andes; 2,000 objects from Neolithic period to contemporary art; modern colln incl. 1,000 art works dating from 19th to 20th century; Dir Dr REBECCA M. NAGY.

John and Mable Ringling Museum of Art: 5401 Bay Shore Rd, Sarasota, FL 34243; tel. (941) 359-5700; fax (941) 359-7704; e-mail info@ringling.org; internet www .ringling.org; f. 1927; attached to Florida State Univ.; comprises Museum of Art (European, American and Non-Western art), 2 Circus Museums incl. the Tibbals Learning Center, home of the world's largest miniature circus, Cà d'Zan Mansion (former Ringling winter residence), Historic Asolo Theater (18th-century Venetian theatre from Asolo, Italy), 66-acre waterfront estate; 14,000 objects of European, American and Asian art; Koger Colln of Chinese ceramic; library of 80,000 vols and exhibition catalogues, 100 periodicals; Chair. PATRICK J. HENNIGAN; Sec. MICHÉLE D. REDWINE; Treas. MICHAEL E. URETTE; Exec. Dir Dr JOHN WETENHALL.

Lowe Art Museum: 1301 Stanford Dr., Coral Gables, FL 33124-6310; tel. (305) 284-3535; fax (305) 284-2024; internet www6 .miami.edu/lowe; f. 1950; attached to Univ. of Miami; 1,000 African objects; 3,000 N and S American art; Asian colln of 4,000 objects from E Asia; 1,500 paintings, sculptures and works on paper from antiquity through 19th century; Dir BRIAN DURSUM.

Mennello Museum of American Art: 900 E Princeton St, Orlando, FL 32803; tel. (407) 246-4278; fax (407) 246-4329; internet www .mennellomuseum.com; colln of paintings by Earl Cunningham (1893–1977) and other American Artists; Exec. Dir FRANK HOLT.

Miami Art Museum: 101 W Flagler St, Miami, FL 33130; tel. (305) 375-3000; fax (305) 375-1725; e-mail curatorial@ miamiartmuseum.org; internet www .miamiartmuseum.org; f. 1996, fmrly Center for the Fine Arts; 800 art works with focus on int. art of 20th and 21st centuries; Chair. AARON PODHURST; Pres. GAIL S. MEYERS; Sec. M. THÉRÈSE VENTO; Treas. JEFF KRINSKY.

Museum of Art – Fort Lauderdale: 1 E Las Olas Blvd, Andrews Ave, Fort Lauderdale, FL 33301; tel. (954) 525-5500; e-mail info@moafl.org; internet www.moafl.org; f. 1958 as Fort Lauderdale Art Center, present name 1963; attached to Nova Southeastern Univ.; 6,000 art works reflecting cultures of S Florida and Caribbean; Chair. DAVID HORVITZ; Sec. STANLEY GOODMAN; Exec. Dir IRVIN LIPPMAN; Curator JORGE HILKER SANTIS.

Museum of Arts & Sciences: 352 S Nova Rd, Daytona Beach, FL 32114; tel. (386) 255-0285; e-mail groupinfo@moas.org; internet www.moas.org; f. 1955; 30,000 objects of Cuban and Florida art, American fine and decorative arts, European fine and decorative arts, pre-Columbian and African artefacts, Pleistocene fossils, Florida history and regional natural history; Anderson C. Bouchelle Center for Decorative Arts: Russian enamels, French gilt bronze, and American Brilliant Period Glass; Abraham and Dorothy Frischer Sculpture Garden; planetarium; Pres. BARBARA COLEMAN; Sec. MELINDA DAWSON; Treas. MICHAEL SLICK; Exec. Dir DEBORAH B. ALLEN; Chief Curator CYNTHIA DUVAL; publ. *Arts & Sciences* (4 a year).

Museum of Contemporary Art: Joan Lehman Bldg, 770 NE 125th St, North Miami, FL 33161; tel. (305) 893-6211; fax (305) 891-1472; e-mail info@mocanomi.org; internet mocanomi.org; f. 1996, fmrly Center of Contemporary Art (f. 1981); 600 works of contemporary art; Pres. RAY ELLEN YARKIN; Chair. MICHAEL COLLINS; Sec. FRANCINE BIRBRAGHER-ROZENCWAIG; Treas. CARLOS J. ARRIZURIETA; Exec. Dir and Chief Curator BONNIE CLEARWATER.

Museum of Fine Arts: 255 Beach Dr., NE, St Petersburg, FL 33701-3498; tel. (727) 896-2667; fax (727) 894-4638; internet www .fine-arts.org; f. 1965; colln of 14,000 objects from antiquity to present day (spanning 4,500 years); European Art Colln: 17th to 19th century; American Art Colln: 18th and 19th centuries; Greek and Roman Antiquities and Pre-Columbian and Asian art; Dir Dr KENT LYDECKER; Chief Curator Dr JENNIFER HARDIN; publ. *MOSAIC* (4 a year).

Museum of Fine Arts: Florida State Univ., 250 Fine Arts Bldg, Tallahassee, FL 32306-1140; tel. (850) 644-6836; fax (850) 644-7229; internet www.mofa.fsu.edu; f. 1950; attached to College of Visual Arts, Theatre and Dance, Florida State Univ.; 5,000 objects from pre-Columbian pottery to contemporary art; Dir ALLYS PALLADINO-CRAIG.

Museum of Florida History: 500 S Bronough, Tallahassee, FL 32399; tel. (850) 245-6400; fax (850) 245-6433; internet www .museumoffloridahistory.com; f. 1977; attached to Florida Dept of State; 45,300 artefacts on Florida history dating from prehistoric era to mid-19th century; military artefacts from the 1830s to present; Florida's Second World War Living Memorial; Chair. BILL HERRLE; Dir JEANA BRUNSON; Curator CLINT FOUNTAIN.

Norton Museum of Art: 1451 S Olive Ave, West Palm Beach, FL 33401; tel. (561) 832-5196; fax (561) 659-4689; e-mail museum@ norton.org; internet www.norton.org; f. 1941; 7,000 works of 19th- to 20th-century American art; jades produced for emperor of China in mid-1700s; European art comprises paintings, sculpture, prints and drawings dating from 1450 to 1950; 2,200 photographs from 19th century to present; Chair. KEMP C. STICKNEY; Dir and CEO HOPE ALSWANG; Chief Curator ROGER WARD.

Patricia & Phillip Frost Art Museum: Florida Int. Univ., University Park, 10975 SW 17th St, Miami, FL 33199; tel. (305) 348-2890; fax (305) 348-2762; e-mail artinfo@fiu .edu; internet thefrost.fiu.edu; f. 1977, fmrly The Art Museum at FIU, present name 2003; attached to Florida Int. Univ.; represent American printmaking from the 1960s and 1970s; 2,300 objects incl. sculptures, photographs and paintings of 20th century, Japanese Netsukes and ancient bronzes from Asian and African cultures; pre-Columbian objects dating from AD 200–500; Dir Dr CAROL DAMIAN; publ. *Frost on View* (2 a year).

Pensacola Museum of Art: 407 S Jefferson St, Pensacola, FL 32502; tel. (850) 432-6247; fax (850) 469-1532; e-mail info@ pensacolamuseumofart.org; internet www .pensacolamuseumofart.org; f. 1954 as Pensacola Art Asscn, present name 1982; colln incl. 20th- and 21st-century art works representing modern and contemporary styles and periods, incl. Cubism, Realism, Pop art, Nonobjective art, Folk art and Illustration; decorative arts colln of European and American glass and African tribal art; Exec. Dir SONYA DAVIS.

Polk Museum of Art: 800 E Palmetto St, Lakeland, FL 33801; tel. (863) 688-7743; fax (863) 688-2611; e-mail info@ polkmuseumofart.org; internet polkmuseumofart.org; f. 1966 as Imperial Youth Museum, present name 1983; colln on modern and contemporary art, Asian art, European and American decorative arts and pre-Columbian art; artistic works ranging from 2,500 year old vessels made by the Chavin culture (now Peru) to contemporary artworks; Curator of Art ADAM JUSTICE.

Tampa Museum of Art: 120 W Gasparilla Plaza, Tampa, FL 33602; tel. (813) 274-8130; fax (813) 274-8732; internet www .tampamuseum.org; f. 1979; colln of material culture of Mediterranean region from Bronze Age to Roman Imperial period; 2,149 photographs incl. 19th-century photographs related to Greece and Rome and photography created after 1970; Chair. PETER M. HEPNER; Sec. EDWARD M. WALLER; Treas. JOHN T. WATTS; Exec. Dir TODD D. SMITH.

University of South Florida Contemporary Art Museum: 3821 Holly Dr., Tampa, Fl 33620-7360; tel. (813) 974-4133; fax (813) 974-5130; e-mail caminfo@arts.usf.edu; internet ira.usf.edu; f. 1968; attached to Institute for Research in Art, Univ. of South Florida; 5,000 art works incl. contemporary photography and African art; graphics and sculptures by int. artists; Dir MARGARET A. MILLER; Curator JANE SIMON.

Wolfsonian—Florida International University: 1001 Washington Ave, Second Fl., Miami Beach, FL 33139; tel. (305) 531-1001; fax (305) 531-2133; e-mail info@thewolf.fiu .edu; internet www.wolfsonian.org; f. 1986, present status 1997; 150,000 artefacts, rare books, ephemeral items, and archives of N American and European origin dating from 1885 to 1945; library of 45,000 vols; Dir CATHY LEFF; Curator SARAH SCHLEUNING.

Georgia

Albany Museum of Art: 311 Meadowlark Dr., Albany, GA 31707; tel. (229) 439-8400; fax (229) 439-1332; e-mail info@ albanymuseum.com; internet www .albanymuseum.com; f. 1964, present name and status 1983; colln incl. 2,100 works of art comprising 19th and 20th century American and European paintings, sculptures, prints, photographs and traditional African art in SE; Pres. BANKS MARGESON; Treas. RYAN SAVILLE; Sec. DACIA BERRY; Exec. Dir NICK NELSON.

Atlanta History Center: 130 W Paces Ferry Rd, NW, Atlanta, GA 30305-1366; tel. (404) 814-4000; fax (404) 814-2041; internet www.atlantahistorycenter.com; f. 1926, present name and status 1990; Decorative Arts and Material Culture Colln: 7,000 artefacts from 19th and 20th century, incl. furniture, fine art and glass work; Textiles and Social History Colln: 10,000 objects of clothing, accessories and household textiles; Civil War and Military Colln: 12,000 historical artefacts; Centennial Olympic Games Colln; Urban History Colln; houses Atlanta History Museum, Centennial Olympic Games Museum, Swan House, Smith Family Farm, 6 historic gardens and Kenan Research Center; Pres. and CEO SAL CILELLA; Chair. BILL SHEARER; Sec. BRAND MORGAN; Treas. LAURA MILES.

Augusta Museum of History: 560 Reynolds St, Augusta, GA 30907; tel. (706) 722-8454; fax (706) 724-5192; e-mail amh@ augustamuseum.org; internet www .augustamuseum.org; f. 1937; colln incl. objects on 12,000 years of local history; 1900 farm wagon and 1917 steam locomotive; Exec. Dir NANCY J. GLASER; Pres. PERRY M. SMITH; Treas. JEFFERSON B. A. KNOX, SR.

Booth Western Art Museum: POB 3070, Cartersville, GA 30120; 501 Museum Dr., Cartersville, GA 30120; tel. (770) 387-1300; e-mail director@boothmuseum.org; internet www.boothmuseum.org; f. 2003; colln incl. Western art, Civil War art, Presidential letters and portraits.

Columbus Museum: 1251 Wynnton Rd, Colombus, GA 31906; tel. (706) 748-2562; fax (706) 748-2570; e-mail information@ columbusmuseum.com; internet www .columbusmuseum.com; f. 1953; drawings, paintings, sculptures and decorative arts spanning over 300 years; 18th- and 19th-century American art colln; library of 4,000 vols; Dir CHARLES T. BUTLER.

Fernbank Museum of Natural History: 767 Clifton Rd NE, Atlanta, GA 30307; tel. (404) 929-6300; internet www .fernbankmuseum.org; f. 1989; documentation of prehistoric human activity on island dating 5,000 years back; Dorothy Methvin McClatchey colln: objects from Central and SE Asia, N America, Africa and Europe; Chair. DOROTHY SMITH HINES; Pres. and CEO SUSAN E. NUEGENT; Sec. KRISTINE PETERSON RUDOLPH; Treas. RONALD B. BOBO.

Georgia Museum of Art: 90 Carlton St, Univ. of Georgia, Athens, GA 30602-6719; tel. (706) 542.4662; fax (706) 542-1051; internet www.georgiamuseum.org; f. 1945; attached to Univ. of Georgia; 8,000 object colln incl. 19th- and 20th-century American paintings, S decorative arts and Asian art; American, European and Asian works on paper; Samuel H. Kress Study colln of Italian Renaissance paintings; library of 5,000 vols; Dir WILLIAM U. EILAND; Chief Curator PAUL MANOGUERRA.

Hammonds House Museum: 503 Peeples St, SW, Atlanta, GA 30310; tel. (404) 612-0500; fax (404) 752-8733; internet www .hammondshouse.org; f. 1988; Haitian paintings and 350 art works by African American artists from mid-19th century; Exec. Dir MYRNA ANDERSON-FULLER; Curator KEVIN SIPP; Pres. Dr JEFF HINES; Sec. DENIECE ACOSTA GRIFFIN; Treas. ISAAC WASHINGTON.

High Museum of Art: 1280 Peachtree St, NE, Atlanta, GA 30309; tel. (404) 733-4400; internet www.high.org; colln incl. 12,000 art works comprising anthology of 19th- and 20th-century American art; European paintings, decorative art, African American art and modern and contemporary art; Chair. LOUISE SAMS.

Michael C. Carlos Museum: 571 S Kilgo Circle, Atlanta, GA 30322; tel. (404) 727-4282; fax (404) 727-4292; e-mail mburell@ emory.edu; internet www.carlos.emory.edu; f. 1876; attached to Emory Univ.; 19th-century Asian materials by Methodist missionaries; colln on paper dating from Renaissance to present; colln of art objects from collections of art objects from ancient Egypt, Nubia, Greece, Rome, Africa and Asia; Dir BONNIE SPEED.

Morris Museum of Art: 1 10th St, Augusta, GA 30901-0100; tel. (706) 724-7501; fax (706) 724-7612; internet themorris.org; f. 1985; 5,000 paintings, works on paper, photographs and sculptures dating from the late-eighteenth century to the present; Civil War painting dating from 1861 to 1865; colln on late 20th century and contemporary art; library of 13,000 vols; Dir and Curator KEVIN GROGAN.

Museum of Aviation: POB 2469, Warner Robins, GA 31099; tel. (478) 926-6870; internet www.museumofaviation.org; f. 1984; colln incl. 6,000 historical artefacts, 100 aircrafts, missiles and cockpits dating from replica of early 1896 glider to modern-era aircraft such as B-1B bomber, SR-71 Blackbird, U-2 Dragon Lady and F-15 Eagle; Dir Col (Retd) KENNETH R. EMERY, II; Curator MIKE ROWLAND.

Museum of Contemporary Art of Georgia: 75 Bennett St, Suite A2, Atlanta, GA 30309; tel. (404) 367-8700; fax (404) 367-1477; e-mail info@mocaga.org; internet www .mocaga.org; f. 2000; colln incl. 750 works of contemporary art by 200 Georgia artists from the mid-1940s to present in various media (from painting to digital works) and styles (from folk to minimalism); Pres., CEO and Dir ANNETTE CONE-SKELTON.

National Infantry Museum & Soldier Center: 1775 Legacy Way, Colombus, GA 31903; tel. (706) 685-5800; internet www .nationalinfantrymuseum.com; 70,000 artefacts depicting 236 years of American history; Exec. Dir Lt Gen. CARMEN CAVEZZA.

Robert C. Williams Paper Museum: POB 0620, Institute of Paper Science and Technology, Georgia Tech, 500 10th St, NW, Atlanta, GA 30332-0620; tel. (404) 894-7840; fax (404) 894-4778; internet www.ipst .gatech.edu/amp; f. 1939, present name and status 1954; 10,000 watermarks, papers, tools, machines and MSS; library of 2,000 vols; Dir TERI WILLIAMS.

Roosevelt's Little White House: 401 Little White House Rd, Warm Springs, GA 31830; tel. (706) 655-5870; fax (706) 655-5872; internet www.fdr-littlewhitehouse.org; f. 1932; under direction of Georgia Dept of Natural Resources; remains as it was when Pres. Franklin Delano Roosevelt died here in 1945; exhibits and film of Roosevelt in Georgia; Franklin Delano Roosevelt Memorial Museum opened in April 2004 with expanded and updated exhibits and films; Superintendent (vacant); Volunteer Coordinator LYNN BARFIELD.

Telfair Museums: 121 Barnard St, Savannah, GA 31401; tel. (912) 790-8800; internet telfair.org; f. 1883; colln incl. 4,500 objects from America, Europe and Asia dating from 18th to 20th centuries; colln of visual art by Lebanese writer Kahlil Gibran; Chair. T. MILLS FLEMING; Dir CATHY SOLOMONS.

William Breman Jewish Heritage & Holocaust Museum: 1440 Spring St NW, Atlanta, GA 30309; tel. (678) 222-3700; internet www.thebreman.org; f. 1984; colln on history of the Holocaust and Jewish life in Georgia; Exec. Dir JANE D. LEAVEY; Pres. JOYCE SHLESINGER; Pres. SPRING ASHER; Sec. MARGIE STERN; Treas. MICHAEL WOOCHER.

Hawai'i

Bailey House Museum: 2375-A Main St, Wailuku, HI 96793; tel. (808) 244-3326; fax (808) 244-3920; e-mail baileyhousemuseum@ clearwire.net; internet www.mauimuseum .org; f. 1957; attached to Maui Historical Soc.; colln of Hawai'ian artefacts, paintings and furnishings from 19th century; Exec. Dir NICOLE MCMULLEN; Pres. LUISE BRAUN; Sec. MELISSA KIRKENDALL; Treas. GEORGE ANDRADE.

Bishop Museum: 1525 Bernice St, Honolulu, HI 96817; tel. (808) 847-3511; fax (808) 848-4147; e-mail library@bishopmuseum.org; internet www.bishopmuseum.org; f. 1889; 25m. works of art, plant and animal specimens; cultural artefacts representing Native Hawaiian, Pacific Island and Hawai'i immigrant life; 23m. specimens of plant and animal life; library of 115,000 vols and 1m. historic photographs, films, works of art, audio recordings and MSS; Pres. and CEO BLAIR D. COLLIS; publ. *Ka'Elele* (12 a year).

Attached Institute:

Amy B. H. Greenwell Ethnobotanical Garden: POB 1053, Captain Cook, HI 96704; tel. (808) 323-3318; fax (808) 323-2394; e-mail agg@bishopmuseum.org; internet www.bishopmuseum.org/ greenwell; f. 1974; 200 species of endemic, indigenous and Polynesian introduced plants; insect house; archaeological site; Man. PETER VAN DYKE.

Hawai'i State Art Museum: 1 Capitol Dist. Bldg, 250 S. Hotel St, Second Fl., Honolulu, HI 96813; tel. (808) 586-0300; fax (808) 586-0308; internet www.state.hi.us/sfca; f. 1965; attached to Hawaii State Foundation on Culture and the Arts; collns reflect culture, arts and history of Hawai'i; Exec. Dir RONALD K. YAMAKAWA.

Honolulu Academy of Arts: 900 South Beretania St, Honolulu, HI 96814-1495; tel. (808) 532-8700; fax (808) 532-8787; e-mail info@honoluluacademy.org; internet www .honoluluacademy.org; f. 1927; 60,000 works spanning 5,000 years (incl. 20,000 works of Asian art, 10,000 Japanese ukiyo-e woodblock prints, 15,000 works on paper); American and European painting and decorative arts, 19th- and 20th-century art, Asian textiles, and traditional works from Africa, Oceania, and the Americas; museum and art school; educational programmes for adults and young people; Doris Duke Theatre with frequent films, lectures, concerts and performances; outdoor gardens; arts festivals; guided tours/gallery talks; art classes and educational programmes for children and adults; spec. exhibitions; Robert Allerton Art Research Library; library of 45,000 vols; Dir STEPHAN JOST; Chair. LYNNE JOHNSON; publ. *Calendar News* (bulletin for members, 6 a year).

Hui No'eau Visual Arts Center: 2841 Baldwin Ave, Makawao, HI 96768; tel. (808) 572-6560; e-mail info@huinoeau.com; internet www.huinoeau.com; f. 1934, present status 1976; works of art and sculptures; Exec. Dir CAROLINE KILLHOUR; Pres. SHANNON HOEKSTRA; Sec. ROBIN FERRIER; Treas. SARAH BREDHOFF.

Isaacs Art Center Museum and Gallery: 65–1692 Kohala Mountain Rd, Kamuela, HI 96743; 65–1268 Kawaihae Rd, Kamuela, HI 96743; tel. (808) 885-5884; fax (808) 885-2714; e-mail isaacsartcenter@hpa.edu; internet www.isaacsartcenter.hpa.edu; f. 2002; attached to Hawai'i Preparatory Acad.; works of art, paintings, books, furniture, jewellery and photographs; Dir GAYLORD DILLINGHAM.

John Young Museum of Art: Outreach College, Univ. of Hawai'i at Mānoa, Krauss Hall, 2500 Dole St, Honolulu, HI 96822; tel. (808) 956-3634; internet www.outreach .hawaii.edu/jymuseum; f. 1999; attached to Univ. of Hawai'i at Mānoa Outreach College; objects incl. Neolithic pottery jars that date as far back as 3000–2000 BC, Han Dynasty tomb figures (206 BC–220 CE), early Ming Dynasty (14th century); several pieces from the Korean Three Kingdoms (5th–6th centuries) and early Goryeo (10th–11th centuries); Curator L. B. NERIO.

Kaua'i Museum: 4428 Rice St, Lihu'e, HI 96766; tel. (808) 245-6931; e-mail director@ kauaimuseum.org; internet www .kauaimuseum.org; f. 1954; colln incl. exhibit on early sugar plantation life, Missionary era furniture, pottery, photographs, books, artwork, quilts, saddles, and Second World War memorabilia; Dir JANE KAMAHAOKALANI GRAY; Collns Curator CHRIS FAYE; Pres. HOLBROOK GOODALE; Sec. STEVE C. TODD; Treas. KEITH HOLDEMAN.

Koa Art Gallery: 4303 Diamond Head Rd, Honolulu, HI 96816; tel. (808) 734-9374; fax (808) 734-9151; e-mail koaglry@hawaii.edu; internet koagallery.kcc.hawaii.edu; f. 1980; Dir and Curator DAVID BEHLKE.

DELETE Maui Arts & Cultural Center: One Cameron Way, Kahului, HI 96732; tel. (808) 242-2787; fax (808) 242-4665; e-mail info@mauiarts.org; internet www.mauiarts .org; f. 1994; art exhibitions and shows; Pres. and CEO ART VENTO.

Shangri La: 4055 Papu Circle, Honolulu, HI 96816; tel. (808) 734-1941; fax (808) 732-4361; internet www.shangrilahawaii.org; f. 1935; attached to the Doris Duke Foundation for Islamic Art; 3,500 items of Islamic art and craft: architectural features, furniture, ceramics, textiles and paintings; library of 1,500 vols; Exec. Dir DEBORAH POPE; Curator Dr KEELAN OVERTON.

Idaho

Basque Museum and Cultural Center: 611 Grove St, Boise, ID 83702; tel. (208) 343-2671; e-mail info@basquemuseum.com; internet www.basquemuseum.com; f. 1985; Juanita Uberuaga Hormachea Colln.

Boise Art Museum: 670 Julia Davis Dr., Boise, ID 83702; tel. (208) 345-8330; internet www.boiseartmuseum.org; f. 1931 as the Boise Art Asscn, present name 1937; permanent colln of 2,300 works of 20th-century American art with emphasis on artists of the Pacific NW; American Realism and ceramics; education programme; Exec. Dir MELANIE FALES; Pres. JIM BRANDSTETTER; Sec. MICHAEL SPINK.

Clearwater Historical Museum: POB 1454, 315 College Ave, Orofino, ID 83544-1454; tel. (208) 476-5033; e-mail info@clearwatermuseum.org; internet www.clearwatermuseum.org; 4,500 historical photographs, Nez Perce Indian history and artefacts; old mining history and logging pictures; Orofino newspapers from 1899; Chinese artefacts.

Discovery Center of Idaho: 131 Myrtle St, Boise, ID 83702; tel. (208) 343-9895; e-mail dcifilter@gmail.com; internet www.scidaho.org; photograph exhibits, artefacts and other material concerning devt and progress of engineering, math, technology and science; Exec. Dir JANINE BOIRE; Pres. BRUCE SCHREPPLE; Sec. HILARY SOLTMAN; Treas. STEVE SIMPSON.

Idaho Black History Museum: 508 Julia Davis Dr., Boise, ID 83702-7694; tel. (208) 433-0017; e-mail info@ibhm.org; internet www.ibhm.org; f. 1995; exhibits; educational and community outreach programmes incl. lectures, films, workshops, literacy programmes and musical performances.

Idaho Museum of Natural History: 921 S Eight Ave, Stop 8096, Pocatello, ID 83209; tel. (208) 282-3168; fax (208) 282-5893; internet imnh.isu.edu; f. 1934 as Historical Museum at the Southern Br. of the Univ. of Idaho, present name 1977; attached to Idaho State Univ.; collns of Anthropology, Earth Sciences, and Life Sciences; 500,000 specimens which document the natural history of Idaho and the Intermountain W; Dir. and Research Curator Dr HERBERT MASCHNER.

Idaho State Historical Museum: 610 N Julia Davis Dr., Boise, ID 83702; tel. (208) 334-2120; fax (208) 334-4059; internet history.idaho.gov/idaho-state-historical-museum; f. 1893; attached to Idaho State Historical Soc.; 250,000 artefacts incl. arms, agricultural items, clothing and textile artefacts, tools and transportation artefacts depicting the history of Idaho.

Museum of Idaho: 200 N E Ave, Idaho Falls, ID 83402; tel. (208) 522-1400; internet www.museumofidaho.org; f. 1982; Eagle Rock USA exhibit: representative of the architecture and furnishings of the time; Race for Atomic Power Exhibit.

Museum of North Idaho: POB 812, Coeur d'Alene, ID 83816-0812; tel. (208) 664-3448; e-mail museum@museumni.org; internet www.museumni.org; f. 1973; attached to North Idaho College; 20,000 images as well as archive material relating to the history of the Coeur dâAlene region; 3-D artefacts; Dir DOROTHY DAHLGREN.

Nez Perce National Historical Park: 39063 US Highway 95, Spalding, ID 83540-9715; tel. (208) 843-7020; fax (208) 843-7003; e-mail nepe_visitor_information@nps.gov; internet www.nps.gov/nepe; attached to Nat. Park Service, US Dept of the Interior; Nez Perce (Nimiipuu) history and culture; 38 sites marking important events related to war of 1877; incl. White Bird Battlefield, Big Hole National Battlefield and Bear Paw Battlefield.

Priest Lake Museum: POB 44, Coolin, ID 83821-0044; 38 Priest Lake Museum Rd, Priest Lake, ID 83856; tel. (208) 443-2676; e-mail priestlakemuseum@gmail.com; internet plmuseum.org; f. 1979; photos and artefacts depicting history of the Priest Lake region, incl. the natural and cultural characteristics.

Wallace District Mining Museum: POB 469, 509 Bank St, Wallace, ID 83873; tel. (208) 556-1592; e-mail info@wallaceminingmuseum.org; internet wallaceminingmuseum.org; mining history

with artefacts and exhibits depicting the hardships, toil and home life of the period.

Illinois

Adler Planetarium: 1300 S Lake Shore Dr., Chicago, IL 60605-2403; tel. (312) 922-7827; fax (312) 322-2257; internet www.adlerplanetarium.org; f. 1930; collns incl. astronomical artifacts, world's oldest known window sundial (dated 1529) and telescope made by William Herschel; 2,000 items of Scientific Instrument Colln incl. models from 12th to 20th century, celestial globes and gores; interactive virtual environments; sky shows, classes in astronomy, navigation and telescope making; public observation sessions, demonstrations, lectures, films; library of 5,000 vols, 3,000 vols of rare book colln; Chair. JOHN W. ESTEY; Pres. Dr PAUL H. KNAPPENBERGER, Jr; Sec. IRENE SIRAGUSA PHELPS; Treas. THOMAS A. NARDI.

Art Institute of Chicago: 111 South Michigan Ave, Chicago, IL 60603-6404; tel. (312) 443-3600; internet www.artic.edu; f. 1879, present location 1893; American painting and sculpture; European painting since 13th century, medieval and Renaissance art; prints and drawings; sculpture; Asian arts (of 5,000 years); African and Amerindian art; textiles; decorative arts; photography; architecture; Thorne Miniature Rooms (European interiors from late 13th century to 1930s and American furnishings from 17th century to 1930s); School of Art; Ryerson Library (f. 1901); Burnham Library of Architecture (f. 1912); Kraft Education Centre; library of 400,000 vols, 100,000 auction catalogs, 1,200 serial subscriptions and 340,000 slides on art and architecture; Chair. THOMAS J. PRITZKER; Dir JAMES CUNO; Pres. DOUGLAS DRUICK; Treas. FREDERICK H. WADDELL; publ. *Member Magazine* (6 a year).

Art Museum: 116 Altgeld Hall, Northern Illinois Univ., DeKalb, IL 60115; tel. (815) 753-1936; fax (815) 753-7897; internet www.niu.edu/artmuseum; f. 1960 present name and status 1990; attached to College of Visual & Performing Arts, Northern Illinois Univ.; incl. 1,000 art objects of 20th-century works of art on paper (prints, drawings and photographs) and contemporary paintings and sculpture; organizes art exhibitions along with written educational material, gallery talks, artist lectures, panel discussions and symposia; Dir JO BURKE.

Cedarhurst Center for the Arts: 2600 Richview Rd, POB 923, Mt Vernon, IL 62864; tel. (618) 242-1236; fax (618) 242-9530; e-mail vonda@cedarhurst.org; internet www.cedarhurst.org; f. 1973 as Mitchell Museum; 400 art works and decorative objects incl. works by Thomas Eakins, Robert Henri, William Glackens, George Luks, John Sloan, Arthur B. Davies and Maurice Prendergast, mems of The Eight, Childe Hassam and J. Alden Weir, mems of The Ten and Mary Cassatt and John Singer Sargent; 60 large-scale sculptures by Dennis Oppenheim, Alexander Liberman, Fletcher Benton and Chakaia Booker; Exec. Dir SHARON BRADHAM.

Field Museum: 1400 S Lake Shore Dr., Chicago, IL 60605-2496; tel. (312) 922-9410; fax (312) 427-7269; e-mail media@fieldmuseum.org; internet www.fieldmuseum.org; f. 1893 as Columbian Museum of Chicago, present location 1921; depts of anthropology, botany, geology, zoology (birds, fishes, insects, invertebrates, mammals, reptiles and amphibians); more than 20m. specimens; large colln of books on China, incl. several thousand in Chinese; Ornithological Section incl. many rare and illustrated vols; library of 275,000 vols, 300,000 photographs; Chair. JOHN A. CANNING, Jr; Pres. and CEO JOHN W. MCCARTER,

Jr; publs *Fieldiana* (peer-reviewed publs in anthropology, botany, geology and zoology; in two series: *Fieldiana Anthropology* and *Fieldiana Life and Earth Sciences*), *In The Field*.

Freeport Art Museum: 121 N Harlem Ave, Freeport, IL 61032; tel. (815) 235-9755; fax (815) 235-6015; e-mail info@freeportartmuseum.org; internet www.freeportartscenter.org; f. 1975; 4,000 artefacts, incl. antiquities, ethnographic objects from SE Asia, and Papua New Guinea, Pre-Columbian and Native American artefacts, 15th- to 19th-century European paintings, prints and sculpture, textiles from around the world and contemporary American prints, paintings and sculpture; Dir JENNIFER KIRKER PRIEST; Pres. VANESSA HUGHES; Sec. HEATHER MCPHERSON; Treas. GERALD POLLEY.

Illinois State Museum: 502 South Spring St, Springfield, IL 62706-5000; tel. (217) 782-7386; fax (217) 782-1254; e-mail info@museum.state.il.us; internet www.museum.state.il.us; f. 1877; natural history and anthropology (recreations of American Indian villages and natural habitats); 'At Home in the Heartland' exhibition of decorative arts in Illinois since 1750; historic and contemporary works by Illinois artists are exhibited in the fine and applied arts galleries; research laboratories and a Technology Learning Center; colln incl. 8m. archaeological specimens and ethnographic objects, 14,000 aesthetic and historical objects in fine and decorative arts colln, 111,000 botanical specimens, 200,000 specimens in geology collns, 140,000 specimens in zoology colln; library of 15,000 vols of monographs, 800 serials; Dir BONNIE W. STYLES; publs *Events and Activities* (4 a year), *Impressions* (4 a year), *The Living Museum* (4 a year).

Attached Museums and Galleries:

Dickson Mounds Museum: 10956 N Dickson Mounds Rd, Lewistown, IL 61542; tel. (309) 547-3721; fax (309) 547-3189; internet www.museum.state.il.us/ismsites/dickson; on-site archaeological museum covering 12,000 years of Illinois history; Nat. Historic Site; Dir Dr MICHAEL WIANT.

Illinois State Museum Lockport Gallery: 201 West 10th St, Lockport, IL 60441; tel. (815) 838-7400; fax (815) 838-7448; e-mail jzimmer@museum.state.il.us; internet www.museum.state.il.us/ismsites/lockport; f. 1987; exhibitions of art by past and contemporary Illinois artists and artisans; Dir JIM ZIMMER; Curator JENNIFER JASKOWIAK.

ISM Chicago Gallery: James R. Thompson Center, 100 W Randolph, Suite 2-100, Chicago, IL 60601-3219; tel. (312) 814-5322; fax (312) 814-3471; e-mail jstevens@museum.state.il.us; internet www.museum.state.il.us/ismsites/chicago/exhibitions.html; f. 1985; exhibitions of art by contemporary and historical Illinois artists; Dir of Art KENT SMITH.

Southern Illinois Art and Artisans Center: 14967 Gun Creek Trail, Whittington, IL 62897-1000; tel. (618) 629-2220; houses Southern Illinois Art Gallery: fine art, decorative art, and ethnographic collns of the Illinois State Museum to southern Illinois; Dir MARYLOU GALLOWAY.

John G. Shedd Aquarium: 1200 S Lake Shore Dr., Chicago, IL 60605; tel. (312) 939-2438; fax (312) 939-8069; e-mail contactus@sheddaquarium.org; internet www.sheddaquarium.org; f. 1930; exhibits both fresh-water and salt-water species; oceanarium re-creates a Pacific Northwest Coast environment and a Falkland Islands habitat; 90,000-gallon Coral Reef exhibit; Wild Reef re-creates a coral reef in the Philippines and offers a diverse shark habitat and garden eels; Pres. and CEO TED A. BEATTIE.

Lakeview Museum of Arts & Sciences: 1125 W Lake Ave, Peoria, IL 61614-5985; tel. (309) 686-7000; fax (309) 686-0280; e-mail development@lakeview-museum.org; internet www.lakeview-museum.org; f. 1954; 16,000 works and items of fine arts (paintings, sculptures, works on paper), decorative arts (furniture, ceramics, metal, glass, textiles), folk art (paintings, sculptures, graphics, decorative arts), ethnographic arts (Native American, African, Oceanic, Asian) and natural sciences (mineralogy, geology, entomology, conchology); planetarium, Illinois Folk Art Gallery, Discovery Center; Pres. and CEO JIM RICHERSON.

Mary and Leigh Block Museum of Art: 40 Arts Circle Dr., Evanston, IL 60208-2410; tel. (847) 491-4000; fax (847) 491-2261; e-mail block-museum@northwestern.edu; internet www.blockmuseum.northwestern.edu; f. 1980; attached to Northwestern Univ.; 4,000 works of art; historical and contemporary prints; Griffin architectural drawings and photographs; bronze sculptures; organizes lectures, symposia and workshops with artists and scholars; screens classic and contemporary films; Chair. CHRISTINE O. ROBB; Dir DAVID ALAN ROBERTSON.

Museum of Contemporary Art Chicago: 220 E Chicago Ave, Chicago, IL 60611; tel. (312) 280-2660; fax (312) 397-4095; e-mail jwolski@mcachicago.org; internet mcachicago.org; f. 1967; colln of visual art from 1945 to present with focus on surrealism, minimalism, conceptual photography and work by Chicago-based artists; 2,500 objects (painting, sculpture, and photography, installation and video); library of 15,000 vols; Dir MADELEINE GRYNSZTEJN; Chair. MARY ITTELSON; Sec. STEFAN EDLIS; Treas. MICHAEL CANMANN.

Museum of Contemporary Photography: c/o Columbia College Chicago, 600 S Michigan, Chicago, IL 60605; tel. (312) 663-5554; fax (312) 369-8067; e-mail mocp@colum.edu; internet www.mocp.org; f. 1984, fmrly Chicago Center for Contemporary Photography (f. 1976); attached to Columbia College Chicago; 9,000 photographs and photographically related objects produced since 1936; Dir NATASHA EGAN; Curator and Assoc. Dir KAREN IRVINE.

Museum of Science and Industry: 57th St and Lake Shore Dr., Chicago, IL 60637; tel. (773) 684-1414; fax (773) 684-7141; e-mail contact@msichicago.org; internet www .msichicago.org; f. 1933; 35000 artefacts, incl. metals, power, physics, chemistry, electronics, transportation, petroleum, food, space eng., communications and medical sciences; over 2,000 exhibit units incl. re-creation of a coal mine, German submarine, walk-through model of human heart, Colleen Moore's Fairy Castle, 'Yesterday's Main Street', actual Apollo 8 spacecraft, Henry Crown Space Center, 'Omnimax' theatre, and exhibits on space exploration and energy research; archival images of exhibits from past and photographs relating to *U-505 Submarine*, Pioneer Zephyr train, Chicago World's Fairs; Chair. DAVID B. SPEER; Pres. and CEO DAVID R. MOSENA; Sec. EILEEN M. CABRERA; Treas. DAVID J. VITALE.

National Veterans Art Museum: 1801 S Indiana Ave, Chicago, IL 60616; tel. (312) 326-0270; fax (312) 326-9767; e-mail info@ nvam.org; internet www.nvam.org; f. 1981, present status 1996, present name 2010; 2,000 works of art, incl. paintings, photography, sculpture, poetry and music by 255 artists; Exec. Dir LEVI MOORE; Chair. MIKE

HELBING; Sec. JIM MOORE; Treas. CAROL SHERMAN.

Oriental Institute Museum: 1155 E 58th St, Chicago, IL 60637; tel. (773) 702-9514; fax (773) 702-9853; e-mail oi-museum@uchicago .edu; internet oi.uchicago.edu/museum; f. 1919; attached to Univ. of Chicago; holds 202,000 registered objects from Egypt, Iran, Iraq, Israel, Jordan, Palestinian Autonomous Areas, Sudan, Syria and Turkey; research arm supports archaeological excavations in Egypt, Iran, Sudan, Syria and Turkey; has dictionary projects in Demotic Egyptian, Sumerian, Akkadian and Hittite; divs of collections: Museum Registration, Tablet Colln, Archives, Conservation, and Research Library; temporary exhibitions; library of 60,000 vols; Dir GIL STEIN; Chief Curator JACK GREEN; publ. *Journal of Near Eastern Studies* (2 a year).

Rockford Art Museum: 711 N Main St, Rockford, IL 61103; tel. (815) 968-2787; fax (815) 316-2179; internet www .rockfordartmuseum.org; f. 1888 as Rockford Sketch Club, present name 1913; 1,600 works of modern and contemporary American art; American masters from 1830 to 1940; photography, contemporary glass and outsider art; Exec. Dir LINDA DENNIS; Pres. JANE SMITH; Sec. SUSAN CARLIN; Treas. MIKE ABRAHAMS.

Smart Museum of Art: Univ. of Chicago, 5550 S Greenwood Ave, Chicago, IL 60637; tel. (773) 702-0200; fax (773) 702-3121; e-mail smart-museum@uchicago.edu; internet smartmuseum.uchicago.edu; f. 1974; attached to Univ. of Chicago; central repository for Univ.'s fine arts colln spanning 5,000 years of artistic creation; Asian art, European art, contemporary art, modern art and design; Chair. ROBERT FEITLER; Vice-Chair. and Treas. LORNA C. FERGUSON; Sr Curator RICHARD A. BORN.

Tarble Arts Center: Eastern Illinois Univ., 600 Lincoln Ave, Charleston IL 61920-3099; tel. (217) 581-2787; fax (217) 581-7138; e-mail tarble@eiu.edu; internet www.eiu .edu/tarble; f. 1982; attached to College of Arts and Humanities, Eastern Illinois Univ.; 20th-century Illinois folk arts with archive of audio and video cassettes; photographs and interviews of musicians, artists and crafts persons; prints, drawings and watercolours by contemporary Midwestern artists; American Scene or Regionalists prints and watercolours c. 1930s and 1940s; contemporary art in other media and art from other cultures and historical periods in various media; organizes education and outreach programmes, lectures and demonstrations by artists, Chamber music concerts and other performing arts; Dir MICHAEL WATTS.

Terra Foundation for American Art: 980 N Michigan Ave, Suite 1315, Chicago, IL 60611; tel. (312) 664-3939; fax (312) 664-2052; e-mail contact@terraamericanart.org; internet www.terraamericanart.org; f. 1978; colln of American art from 1740 to 1945; 725 paintings, prints, drawings, photographs and sculptures; resource centre in Paris; library of 9,000 vols; Chair. GERHARD CASPER; Pres. and CEO ELIZABETH GLASSMAN.

Ukrainian Institute of Modern Art: 2320 W Chicago Ave, Chicago, IL 60622; tel. (773) 227-5522; internet www.uima-chicago.org; f. 1971; collns of Ukrainian and Ukrainian-American abstract and minimalist works from the 1950s, 1960s and 1970s; Pres. PAUL NADZIKEWYCH; Sec. KALYNA POMIRKO; Treas. LUBOMYR KLYMKOWYCH; Curator STANISLAV GREZDO.

University Museum: 1000 Faner Dr., POB 4508, Southern Illinois Univ., Carbondale, IL 62901; 2469 Faner Hall, Southern Illinois

Univ., Carbondale, IL 62901; tel. (618) 453-5388; fax (618) 453-7409; e-mail museum@ siu.edu; internet www.museum.siu.edu; f. 1874; attached to Southern Illinois Univ. Carbondale; encyclopedic museum; 2,500 objects in fine and decorative arts; paintings, prints and drawings, sculpture, photography; ethnic arts collns of 20th-century regional, nat. and int. artists; science colln with 26,000 geological specimens; humanities colln of 22,000 artefacts reflecting history, world cultures and archaeological past; organizes workshops and art festivals; Dir Dr DONA R. BACHMAN.

Indiana

Art Museum of Greater Lafayette: 102 S Tenth St, Lafayette, IN 47905; tel. (765) 742-1128; internet artlafayette.org; f. 1909, present name 2000; 900 works of 19th- and 20th-century American art, with focus on Indiana artists; spec. colln of work of Laura Ann Fry; Exec. Dir KENDALL SMITH II; Pres. ELIZABETH LOCKREY; Curator MICHAEL ATWELL.

Ball State University Museum of Art: 2021 W Riverside Ave, Ball State Univ., Muncie, IN 47306; tel. (765) 285-5242; fax (765) 285-4003; e-mail artmuseum@bsu.edu; internet cms.bsu.edu/web/museumofart .aspx; f. 1892 as Art Students' League, present bldg 1935, present name 1991; 11,000 artwork of ancient, medieval, Renaissance, 17th century, 18th century, 19th century, modern, Asian, Africa, Oceania, the Americas; European and American decorative arts and furniture and works on paper, incl. drawings, prints and photographs; Dir PETER F. BLUME.

Brauer Museum of Art: Center for the Arts, Valparaiso Univ., 1709 Chapel Dr., Valparaiso, IN 46383-6493; tel. (219) 464-5365; fax (219) 464-5244; internet www.valpo .edu/artmuseum; attached to Valparaiso Univ.; 19th-, 20th- and 21st-century American art (works of Frederic Edwin Church, Asher B. Durand, Childe Hassam, Georgia O'Keeffe, and Ed Paschke); world religious art and Midwestern regional art (incl. paintings, sculpture, drawings, prints and photographs); spec. colln of works by Junius R. Sloan; Dir and Curator GREGG HERTZLIEB.

Conner Prairie: 13400 Allisonville Rd, Fishers, IN 46038; tel. (317) 776-6006; e-mail info@connerprairie.org; internet www.connerprairie.org; f. 1934; 5 themed historic areas—1863 Civil War Journey: Raid on Indiana, Prairietown, Animal Encounters Barn, Loom House at Conner Homestead, Lenape Indian Camp incl. Indian trading post about Lenape or Delaware Indians, 1859 Balloon Voyage in tethered helium-filled balloon; Chair. J. CHRISTOPHER COOKE; Pres. and CEO ELLEN M. ROSENTHAL; Sec. Dr MARY E. BUSCH; Treas. DAVID T. FRONEK.

Eiteljorg Museum of American Indians and Western Art: White River State Park, 500 W Washington St, Indianapolis, IN 46204; tel. (317) 636-9378; e-mail president@eiteljorg.com; internet www .eiteljorg.org; f. 1989; showcases Western and Native American art; contemporary works of art incl. paintings, photography, prints, drawings and sculpture and installations, incl. artists T. C. Cannon, N. C. Wyeth, Andy Warhol, Georgia O'Keeffe, Allan Houser, Frederic Remington, Charles Russell and Kay WalkingStick; library of 5,000 vols; Pres. and CEO JOHN VANAUSDALL; Chair. BETSY HARVEY; Chief Curatorial Officer JAMES NOTTAGE.

Evansville Museum of Arts, History & Science: 411 SE Riverside Dr., Evansville, IN 47713; tel. (812) 425-2406; fax (812) 421-

7509; e-mail info@emuseum.org; internet www.emuseum.org; f. 1906, present name and status 1938; collns in areas of art, history, anthropology and science; paintings and graphic works from 16th century to the present; anthropology colln on North and South American native life from 13,000 BC to the present; Science Center, Koch Planetarium; Exec. Dir JOHN STREETMAN; Pres. STEVE KROHN; Sec. ELAINE MCCARTHY; Treas. SARA ABU-HUSSEIN; publ. *COPIA*.

Fort Wayne Museum of Art: 311 E Main St, Fort Wayne, IN 46802; tel. (260) 422-6467; fax (260) 422-1374; e-mail mail@fwmoa.org; internet www.fwmoa.org; f. 1921, present status 1977; 1,400 American paintings, sculpture, drawings, prints and photographs; colln incl. paintings by Janet Fish, William Forsyth, George Inness, Thomas Moran and Larry Rivers; sculpture by Mark di Suvero and George Rickey; colln of 56 Indiana Amish quilts; Exec. Dir CHARLES A. SHEPARD III; Pres. BEN EISBART; Sec. JUDY PURSLEY; Treas. CINDY GOODMAN.

Indianapolis Museum of Art: 4000 Michigan Rd, Indianapolis, IN 46208-3326; tel. (317) 923-1331; fax (317) 931-1978; e-mail ima@imamuseum.org; internet www.imamuseum.org; f. 1883 as Art Asscn of Indianapolis, present name 1969; collns of African art, American painting and sculpture up to 1945; ancient art of the Americas (incl. Mesoamerican cultures, Olmec and civilizations of the Gulf Coast of Mexico, the Colima, and the Maya); ancient art of Mediterranean (displays objects from Italy, Cyprus, Iran, Greece, and Egypt); 400 works of art showing 4,000 years of Asian art from China, Japan, Korea, India, Tibet, and West and Southeast Asia; contemporary works of art; South Pacific art from Melanesia, Polynesia, Micronesia and Indonesia; textile and fashion arts in Irish embroidery, prints, drawings and photographs of famous artists; incl. Virginia B. Fairbanks Art and Nature Park and Oldfields—Lilly House and Gardens; library of 2,000 vols, 1,000 linear ft museum records, MSS, personal papers, ephemera, scrapbooks, photographs, video cassettes; Dir and CEO MAXWELL L. ANDERSON; Chair. STEPHEN RUSSELL; Sec. THOMAS HIATT; Treas. DANIEL CANTOR.

Indiana State Museum: 650 W Washington St, Indianapolis, IN 46204; tel. (317) 232-1637; e-mail museumcommunication@indianamuseum.org; internet www.indianamuseum.org; f. 1862, present location 2002; 542,000 cultural and natural history items ranging from prehistoric fossils to current popular culture items; also holds 25,000 items from Lincoln Financial Foundation Colln; Pres. and CEO THOMAS A. KING.

Indiana University Art Museum: 1133 E Seventh St, Bloomington, IN 47405-7509; tel. (812) 855-5445; e-mail iuam@indiana.edu; internet www.iub.edu/~iuam; f. 1941; 40,000 objects incl. ancient gold jewellery, African masks and paintings by Claude Monet and Pablo Picasso; Dir ADELHEID GEALT.

Purdue University Galleries: 552 W Wood St, West Lafayette, IN 47907-2002; tel. (765) 496-7899; e-mail galleries@purdue.edu; internet www.purdue.edu/galleries; organizes visual art exhibitions and lectures; serve as cultural resource for the Greater Lafayette; Stewart Center Gallery, Robert L. Ringel Gallery, Patti and Rusty Rueff Galleries; Dir CRAIG MARTIN.

Richmond Art Museum: 350 Hub Etchison Parkway, Richmond, IN 47375-0816; tel. (765) 966-0256; fax (765) 973-3738; internet www.richmondartmuseum.org; f. 1898; colln of American Impressionists, Taos School,

Hoosier Group, Richmond School and regional artists; local ceramic artists incl. works by potters of Arts and Craft Movement, Overbeck Sisters and Bethel Pike potters; organizes workshops and art classes; Exec. Dir SHAUN DINGWERTH.

Snite Museum of Art: POB 368, Moose Krause Circle, Univ. of Notre Dame, Notre Dame, IN 46556-0368; tel. (574) 631-5466; fax (574) 631-8501; e-mail sniteart@nd.edu; internet sniteartmuseum.nd.edu; attached to Univ. of Notre Dame; 24,000 works of art; Jack and Alfrieda Feddersen colln of Rembrandt etchings; the Noah L. and Muriel Butkin colln of 19th-century French art; John D. Reilly colln of Old Master and 19th-century drawings; Janos Scholz colln of 19th-century European photographs and the Mr and Mrs Russell G. Ashbaugh, Jr., colln of Mestrovic sculpture and drawings; Olmec and Preclassic Mesoamerican art; 20th-century art, North Native American art, decorative and design arts and 2 kinetic sculptures by George Rickey; Dir CHARLES R. LOVING; publs *Events* (2 a year), *Notre Dame magazine* (4 a year).

Swope Art Museum: 25 S Seventh St, Terre Haute, IN 47807; tel. (812) 238-1676; fax (812) 238-1677; e-mail info@swope.org; internet www.swope.org; f. 1942; 2,000 works of American art incl. 19th- and 20th-century paintings, sculptures and works on paper; paintings from 'American Regionalist' group incl. works by Thomas Hart Benton, Charles Burchfield, Edward Hopper, Reginald Marsh and Grant Wood; art from latter half of 20th century incl. works of Alexander Calder, Moses and Raphael Soyer, Robert Motherwell, Eva Hess, Robert Rauschenberg and Leonard Baskin; screenprints from Robert Indiana (Decade Portfolio) and Andy Warhol (Marilyn); art works by women artists; Exec. Dir MARIANNE RICHTER; Pres. RICHARD SHAGLEY; Sec. KATHY BRENTLINGER; Treas. TOM FRANCIS.

University Art Gallery: Dept of Art, FA108, Indiana State Univ., Terre Haute, IN 47809; tel. (812) 237-3720; fax (812) 237-4359; internet www.indstate.edu/artgallery; f. 1985 as Turman Gallery; attached to Indiana State Univ.; collects, preserves and exhibits modern and contemporary art; organizes exhibitions, workshops, gallery talks and lectures; promotes understanding and appreciation for visual arts; encourages visual art work scholarship; Dir MELISSA VANDENBERG; Univ. Curator BARBARA RACKER.

Iowa

Blanden Art Museum: 920 Third Ave S, Fort Dodge, IA 50501; tel. (515) 573-2316; fax (515) 573-2317; internet www.blanden.org; visual art works related to World Wars; Pres. KENNETH ADAMS; Dir MARGARET SKOVE.

Cedar Rapids Museum of Art: 410 Third Ave SE, Cedar Rapids, IA 52401; tel. (319) 366-7503; e-mail info@crma.org; internet www.crma.org; f. 1905; 7,200 works of art dating from Roman antiquity to the present; colln incl. works of art by Grant Wood, Roman portrait busts and print colln from 15th century; Exec. Dir TERENCE PITTS; Pres. BONNIE SCHMIDT; Sec. TOM DEBOOM; Treas. BRIAN COLLER.

Des Moines Art Center: 4700 Grand Ave, Des Moines, IA 50312-2099; tel. (515) 277-4405; internet www.desmoinesartcenter.org; f. 1948; Irma and Julian Brody colln, John C. Huseby Print colln, Louise Noun Colln of Art by Women, Paul and Anastasia Polydoran colln and Nathan Emory Coffin colln; Pres. WOODWARD G. BRENTON; Vice-Pres. and Treas. JAMES HUBBELL, III; Sec. PATRICIA

MCFARLAND; Dir JEFF FLEMING; Sr Curator GILBERT VICARIO.

Dubuque Museum of Art: 701 Locust St, Dubuque, IA 52001; tel. (563) 557-1851; e-mail info@dbqart.com; internet www.dbqart.com; f. 1874; 20th-century American art emphasizing on American Regionalism; 2,100 works of art, incl. works by Iowa Regionalist Grant Wood, Edward S. Curtis, N American Indian photogravures and texts, nat. artists incl. John Steuart Curry, Adrian Dornbush and Mauricio Lasansky, local artists incl. Francesco Licciardi, Louise Halliburton, Joseph Walter and Dorothy Rossiter and 900 etchings by artist and author Arthur Geisert; also organizes art classes and workshops; Exec. Dir MARK WAHLERT.

Figge Art Museum: 225 W Second St, Davenport, IA 52801; tel. (563) 326-7804; fax (563) 326-7876; internet figgeart.org; f. 1925 as Davenport Municipal Art Gallery, present name and location 2003; 3,500 paintings, sculptures and works on paper from 16th century to present; American colln of works from Colonial period to 1945, incl. 19th-century landscape traditions of the Hudson River School artists Asher B. Durand, John Kensett and Albert Bierstadt; Midwest Regionalist colln focuses on works of Grant Wood, Thomas Hart Benton, John Steuart Curry and Mid W artists who defined style in 1930s and 1940s; Mexican Colonial colln on growth of painting in New Spain in 17th and 18th centuries; Haitian colln on artistic tradition in Haiti since 1940s; Pres. ANDREW J. BUTLER; Sec. TARA BARNEY; Treas. KEN KOUPAL.

Iowa Museum Association: 1116 Washington St, Cedar Falls, IA 50613; tel. (319) 239-2236; e-mail imasweet@cfu.net; internet www.iowamuseums.org; f. 1976; provides training and devt to Iowa museum professionals and volunteers; provides education, communication, networking opportunities and advocacy for Iowa's museums; art centres and museums, botanical gardens, children's museums, historic sites, historical socs, living history sites, nature centres, natural history museums, planetariums, science and technology centres and zoos; Pres. LINDA WILLEKE; Exec. Dir CYNTHIA SWEET; Sec. SHALLA WILSON; Treas. ELAINE RALEIGH.

Iowa State University Museums: 290 Scheman Bldg, Ames, IA 50011-1110; tel. (515) 294-3342; fax (515) 294-7070; e-mail dwitter@iastate.edu; internet www.museums.iastate.edu; f. 1961; incl. Anderson Sculpture Garden, Art on Campus Colln, Brunnier Art Museum, Christian Petersen Art Museum and Farm House Museum; 30,000 objects of art dating from ancient to modern art; Dir and Chief Curator LYNETTE POHLMAN.

MacNider Art Museum: 303 Second St SE, Mason City, IA 50401; tel. (641) 421-3666; fax (641) 422-9612; e-mail macnider@macniderart.org; internet www.macniderart.org; f. 1966; paintings, prints, drawings, photographs, sculptures, ceramics and puppets on American art; Dir EDITH BLANCHARD.

National Mississippi River Museum & Aquarium: 350 E Third St, Port of Dubuque, IA 52001; tel. (563) 557-9545; e-mail info@rivermuseum.com; internet www.rivermuseum.com; attached to Dubuque Co Historical Soc.; archives of 20,000 items for river research incl. lithographs, glass plate negatives, boat blueprints, original contract and correspondence documents; artefact colln of small boats of 19th and 20th century; 1,200 steamboating artefacts; natural history specimens, Native American artefacts, minerals, fossils and early Dubuque history dating to 1870; fine art colln of furnishings about life in Dubuque in mid-19th century incl. china, parlour furniture and paintings; colln of large vessels; National Rivers Hall of Fame honouring people related to America's rivers and river industries, William Woodward Discovery Center and Fred W. Woodward Riverboat Museum; library of 4,000 vols; Exec. Dir JERRY ENZLER; Curator CRISTIN WATERBURY.

Sioux City Art Center: 225 Nebraska St, Sioux City, IA 51101-1712; tel. (712) 279-6272; fax (712) 255-2921; internet www .siouxcityartcenter.org; f. 1938; 1,000 works from Midwest, nat. and int. artists; organizes art classes; Chair. DOUG PALMER; Dir AL HARRIS-FERNANDEZ.

University of Iowa Museum of Art: 1375 Highway 1W, 1840 Studio Arts Bldg, Iowa City, IA 52242; tel. (319) 335-1727; fax (319) 335-3677; e-mail uima@uiowa.edu; internet uima.uiowa.edu; f. 1969; European and American art; colln of traditional African arts; European and American prints; drawings and photographs: 1900–70; artefacts of ancient Americas and native America; ceramics and metal work; Iowa gallery (digital art collns); temporary exhibitions; Provost WALLACE LOH; Exec. Dir SEAN O'HARROW; Sec. BETTY BREAZEALE; Chief Curator KATHLEEN EDWARDS; publ. *UIMA Magazine*.

University of Iowa Museum of Natural History: 10 Macbride Hall, Iowa City, IA 52242; tel. (319) 335-0480; fax (319) 335-0653; e-mail mus-nat-hist@uiowa.edu; internet www.uiowa.edu/~nathist; f. 1858; spec. collns incl. geology, ecology and native cultures; giant Ice Age sloth; North American birds; Mammal Hall incl. a skeleton of an Atlantic Right Whale; Dir JOHN LOGSDON; Curator TRINA ROBERTS.

Waterloo Center for the Arts: 225 Commercial St, Waterloo, IA 50701-1313; tel. (319) 291-4490; fax (319) 291-4270; e-mail museum@waterloo-ia.org; internet www .waterloocenterforthearts.org; f. 1962; Mid W regionalist art (incl. works by Grant Wood and Thomas Hart Benton), Haitian/Caribbean folk art, American decorative arts, int. folk art, murals and mosaics spread across city of Waterloo; organizes lectures, symposia, films and performances; Dir CAMMIE SCULLY; Curator KENT SHANKLE.

Kansas

Birger Sandzén Memorial Gallery: 401 N First St, POB 348, Lindsborg, KS 67456-0348; tel. (785) 227-2220; e-mail fineart@ sandzen.org; internet www.sandzen.org; f. 1957; colln of Birger Sandzén's paintings, prints, drawings and watercolours; colln of works of Henry Varnum Poor, Doel Reed, Carl Milles, Marsden Hartley, B. J. O. Nordfelt, John Bashor, Lester Raymer, Raymond Jonson and John Stuart Curry; colln of prints from European to American regionalist printmakers and Asia; organizes temporary exhibitions, gallery talks, chamber music concerts and docent tours; incl. archives; closed for renovation till March 2012.

Coutts Memorial Museum of Art: 110 N Main, El Dorado, KS 67042-0001; tel. (316) 321-1212; e-mail coutts@coutts.kscoxmail .com; internet www.skyways.org/museums/ coutts; f. 1970; colln of 1,000 objects of art, incl. paintings, sculptures, prints and drawings from Russia, China, France, Holland, England and S America; contemporary work of Prairie Printmakers incl. Seward, Foltz, Capps, Hotvedt, N. B. Hall, A. W. Hall, Thomas Hart Benton, Birger Sandzen, Americo, Eva Makk and son A. B. and Kansas artists Robert Carver, Charles Sanderson, Frederic James, J. R. Hamil, Charles Rogers and James Fallier; Dir ROD SEEL; Pres.

CONNIE WALTON; Sec. JEREMY SUNDGREN; Treas. TED FARMER.

Kansas African American Museum: 601 N Water, Wichita, KS 67203; tel. (316) 262-7651; fax (316) 265-6953; e-mail info@ tkaamuseum.net; internet www .tkaamuseum.org; f. 1917 as Calvary Baptist Church, present name and status 1997; permanent colln of African artefacts, incl. tribal masks, headdresses and statues, photographs from Kansas native Gordon Parks, artwork from Dr Samella Lewis, Elizabeth Catlett and Jacob Lawrence and jazz and blues photographs from area performers; temporary exhibitions related to stories of the African American experience in Kansas; Exec. Dir PRISCA BARNES; Pres. GWYNNE BIRZER; Sec. TEKETA HARDING.

Kansas Aviation Museum: 3350 S George Washington Blvd, Wichita, KS 67210; tel. (316) 683-9242; fax (316) 683-0573; e-mail ksaviation@kansasaviationmuseum.org; internet kansasaviationmuseum.org; f. 1991; 40 historically significant aircrafts; engines from earliest aircraft power plants to jet turbines; incl. Kansas Aviation Hall of Fame honouring people related to aviation by state, nat. or worldwide; library of 10,000 vols, 250,000 photographs, negatives and slides of rare aircraft, 15,000 journals, periodicals and printed matter; Exec. Dir LON SMITH; Pres. TIM BONNELL, SR; Sec. CHERYL KASTNER; Treas. JAMES WIEBE.

Kansas Museum of History: 6425 SW Sixth Ave, Topeka, KS 66615-1099; tel. (785) 272-8681; fax (785) 272-8682; e-mail reference@kshs.org; internet www.kshs.org/ portal_museum; f. 1875; colln of African American, American Indian artefacts, archaeology, ceramic, furniture, clothing, photographs, quilts, toys and railroads related to history of Kansas; Dir BOB KECKEISEN; Curator LAUREL FRITZSCH; Curator BLAIR TARR.

Marianna Kistler Beach Museum of Art: Kansas State Univ., 14th and Anderson, 701 Beach Lane, Manhattan, KS 66506; tel. (785) 532-7718; fax (785) 532-7498; e-mail beachart@ksu.edu; internet beach.k-state .edu; f. 1996; attached to Kansas State Univ.; 7,000 objects of art; colln of historical through contemporary art in all media; also promotes research and teaching mission of Kansas State Univ.; Dir LINDA DUKE; Chair. JACKIE HARTMAN; Sec. KATHY BORCK; Sr Curator BILL NORTH.

Mulvane Art Museum: 1700 SW Jewell Ave, Washburn Univ., Topeka, KS 66621; tel. (785) 670-1124; e-mail mulvane.info@ washburn.edu; internet www.washburn.edu/ main/mulvane; f. 1922, present name 1981; attached to Washburn Univ.; colln of 4,000 pieces of fine art from around the world incl. paintings, prints, drawings, sculptures, photographs and decorative art with focus on artists from Kansas and the MidWest and American art of 20th century; Dir CINDI MORRISON; Pres. MARK BORANYAK; Treas. CHRIS SCHULTZ.

Natural History Museum, University of Kansas: 1345 Jayhawk Blvd, Lawrence, KS 66045-7593; tel. (785) 864-4450; fax (785) 864-5335; e-mail naturalhistory@ku.edu; internet naturalhistory.ku.edu; f. 1903; attached to Univ. of Kansas Biodiversity Institute; covers 50,000 sq ft; exhibits and dioramas of the animals and plants of N America; 8m. specimens of plants and animals, from prehistoric to living species and from every continent and ocean, 1.2m. archeological artefacts; collns: botany, entomology, herpetology, ichthyology, ichthyology tissue, invertebrate palaeontology, invertebrate zoology, mammalogy, ornithology, palaeobo-

tany, vertebrate palaeontology; Dir LEONARD KRISHTALKA; Curator MARY ADAIR.

Nerman Museum of Contemporary Art: c/o Johnson Co Community College, 12345 College Blvd, Overland Park, KS 66210; tel. (913) 469-3000; fax (913) 469-2348; e-mail foundation.dept@jccc.edu; internet www .nermanmuseum.org; f. 2007; attached to Johnson Co Community College; colln of outdoor sculpture and paintings, ceramics, photography and works on paper; Dir BRUCE HARTMAN; Chair. JON STEWART; Sec. MELODY RAYL; Treas. LYNN MITCHELSON.

Prairie Museum of Art and History: 1905 S Franklin, Colby, KS 67701; tel. (785) 460-4590; fax (785) 460-4592; e-mail prairiem@ st-tel.net; internet www.prairiemuseum.org; colln of 40,000 artefacts, incl. 28,000 works of art from Kuska Colln of glass, furniture, ceramics, toys, dolls, stamps, clocks, coins, silver and jewellery; incl. sod house, one-room school, country church and 1930s farmstead; Dir SUE TAYLOR.

Spencer Museum of Art, University of Kansas: 1301 Mississippi St, Lawrence, KS 66045-7500; tel. (785) 864-4710; fax (785) 864-3112; e-mail spencerart@ku.edu; internet www.spencerart.ku.edu; f. 1928; 7 galleries; 37,000 artworks and artefacts in all media; incl. European and American art from ancient to contemporary; significant holdings of E Asian art; recently reopened 20/21 Gallery of modern and contemporary objects; spec. collns incl. medieval art; European and American paintings, sculpture and prints; photography; Japanese Edo-period painting and prints; 20th-century Chinese painting; Kansas Univ.'s ethnographic colln: incl. 10,000 Native American, African, Latin American and Australian works; runs public programmes, programmes for school children, Kansas Univ. students; objects not on view in the galleries are available by appointment; works on paper are accessible for viewing in the Print Room every Friday; organizes exhibitions of local, regional, national and int. interest; also houses Kress Foundation Dept of Art History and the Murphy Library of Art and Architecture; library of 165,000 vols in Murphy Library of Art and Architecture; 17,700 images in Digital Library Colln; Dir SARALYN REECE HARDY; publs *Register* (1 a year), *The Franklin D. Murphy Lecture* (1 a year).

Ulrich Museum of Art: Wichita State Univ., 1845 Fairmount St, Wichita, KS 67260-0046; tel. (316) 978-3664; fax (316) 978-3898; e-mail ulrich@wichita.edu; internet ulrich.wichita.edu; f. 1974; attached to Wichita State Univ.; colln of 6,300 works of 20th and 21st centuries; colln of works by Robert Henri, Milton Avery, Joan Miro, Alexander Calder, Robert Motherwell, Jacob Lawrence, Joan Mitchell, Claus Oldenburg, Luis Jiménez Jr., Zhang Huan, Andy Goldsworthy and Jules de Balincourt; photography colln by Berenice Abbott, Margaret Bourke-White, Edward Weston, Gordon Parks, W. Eugene Smith, Diane Arbus and Nikki Lee; outdoor sculpture colln; Chair. KELLY CALLEN; Dir Dr PATRICIA McDONNELL.

Wichita Art Museum: 1400 W Museum Blvd, Wichita, KS 67203-3296; tel. (316) 268-4921; fax (316) 268-4980; e-mail info@ wichitaartmuseum.org; internet wichitaartmuseum.org; f. 1935; permanent colln of 7,000 works of American art, spanning 3 centuries of painting, sculpture, glasses, works on paper and decorative arts, incl. Mary Cassatt, Winslow Homer, Horace Pippin, Edward Hopper and Charles M. Russell; library of 10,000 vols and 2,000 artist files; Dir CHARLES K. STEINER; Chief Curator STEPHEN GLEISSNER.

Kentucky

African American Heritage Center, Inc: POB 353, Franklin, KY 42135-0353; tel. (270) 598-9986; fax (270) 586-5719; e-mail africanamericanh@bellsouth.net; internet www.aahconline.org; f. 1994; academic research of African American achievements; highlights early account of foodways, burial customs, traditions, religion, education, social life, vital statistics, genealogy and employment.

Art Museum at the University of Kentucky: 405 Rose St, Lexington, KY 40506-0241; tel. (859) 257-5716; fax (859) 323-1994; e-mail artmuseum@email.uky.edu; internet www.uky.edu/artmuseum; 4,500 objects of American and European paintings, drawings, photographs, prints and sculptures; art of Africa and Asia; Dir KATHY WALSH-PIPER; Curator JANIE WELKER.

Behringer—Crawford Museum: 1600 Montague Rd, Devou Park, Covington, KY 41011; tel. (859) 491-4003; e-mail info@bcmuseum.org; internet www.bcmuseum.org; f. 1950 as William Behringer Memorial Museum, present name 1980; regional cultural history, minerals, fossils, and American Indian artefacts, transportation objects, art collns of Harlan Hubbard, Dr Wolfgang Ritschel and Mary Bruce Sharon; Exec. Dir LAURIE RISCH; Pres. JOHN BOH; Treas. MARK NEIKIRK.

Frazier History Museum: 829 W Main St, Louisville, KY 40202; tel. (502) 753-5663; e-mail info@fraziermuseum.org; internet www.fraziermuseum.org; f. 2004 as Frazier Historical Arms Museum; 5,000 artefacts spanning over 1,000 years of American and international artefacts and British Royal Armouries; Chair. OWSLEY BROWN FRAZIER; Sec. A. BETH REID; Exec. Dir Dr MADELEINE BURNSIDE.

Headley-Whitney Museum: 4435 Old Frankfort Pike, Lexington, KY 40510; tel. (859) 255-6653; fax (859) 255-8375; e-mail hwm@headley-whitney.org; internet www.headley-whitney.org; f. 1968; George Headley's colln of jewellery, bibelots and mounted semi-precious stones; library of 1,500 vols; Exec. Dir (vacant).

Kentucky Historical Society: 100 W Broadway, Frankfort, KY 40601; tel. (502) 564-1792; fax (502) 696-3846; e-mail refdesk@ky.gov; internet history.ky.gov; f. 1836; more than 12,000 artefacts; incl. a 'Historymobile' and 'Museums to go'; library of 90,000 vols, 16,000 reels of microfilm, 200,000 historic photographs, 1,900 cubic ft of MSS and 2,000 maps; Exec. Dir KENT WHITWORTH.

Museums:

Kentucky Military History Museum: 125 E Main St, Frankfort, KY 40601; the Old State Arsenal, a 2-storey brick Gothic-Revival 'castle' standing on a cliff overlooking the Kentucky River and the downtown area, built in 1850, houses the weapons and equipment of the Kentucky Militia, State Guard, and other volunteer military orgs, from the Revolution to the Gulf War; collns of firearms, edged weapons, artillery, uniforms, flags, photographs, personal items.

Old State Capitol: 300 W Broadway, Frankfort, KY 40601; f. 1830; nat. historical landmark introduced Greek-Revival architecture to the USA west of the Appalachian Mountains; bldg served as capitol of the Commonwealth of Kentucky from 1830 to 1910; site of the assassination of William Goebel, the only Governor in US history to die in office as a result of

assassination; re-creation of State Law Library.

Thomas D. Clark Center for Kentucky History: 100 W Broadway, Frankfort, KY 40601; prehistoric times to the present: First Kentuckians (10,000 BC to AD 1750), The Kentucky Frontier (1750–1800), The Antebellum Age (1800–60), War and Aftermath (1860–75), Continuity and Change (1875–1900), The New Century (1900–30), Depression and War (1930–50), and Many Sides of Kentucky (1950 to present); Pure Kentucky highlights the lives and contributions of famous Kentuckians through artefacts.

Kentucky Museum: Western Kentucky Univ., 1444 Kentucky St, Bowling Green, KY 42101; tel. (270) 745-2592; e-mail kymus@wku.edu; internet www.wku.edu/library/museum; f. 1939; attached to Western Kentucky Univ.; archaeology colln: 70,000 items incl. axes, mortars and scrapers; art colln: 1000 art works; clothing and textiles colln: 7,000 items of 19th- and 20th-century textiles; Julius Rather colln: 10,000 items of political memorabilia; glassware and ceramics colln: 1,300 items; Man. DEBORAH COLE.

Lincoln Museum: 66 Lincoln Sq., Hodgenville, KY 42748; tel. (270) 358-3163; e-mail abe@lincolnmuseum-ky.org; internet lincolnmuseum-ky.org; f. 1991; exhibits depicting life of Abraham Lincoln; paintings, drawings and other art works related to Lincoln era.

Locust Grove: 561 Blankenbaker Lane, Louisville, KY 40207; tel. (502) 897-9845; fax (502) 897-0103; e-mail lghh@locustgrove.org; internet www.locustgrove.org; f. 1964; nat. historic landmark; colln incl. late 18th- and early 19th-century furniture, ceramics, metals, prints, paintings, textiles, books, firearms, tools and domestic objects; Exec. Dir CAROL ELY.

Portland Museum: 2308 Portland Ave, Louisville, KY 40212; tel. (502) 776-7678; fax (502) 776-9874; e-mail pmuse@iglou.com; internet www.goportland.org; f. 1978; colln on history and material culture of Portland incl. photographs, documents, artefacts, costumes, paintings, drawings, oral histories and vernacular objects; Pres. BOB ARMSTRONG; Sec. BRYAN WARREN; Treas. MIKE LALLY; Exec. Dir NATHALIE TAFT ANDREWS.

Speed Art Museum: 2035 S Third St, Louisville, KY 40208; tel. (502) 634-2700; e-mail info@speedmuseum.org; internet www.speedmuseum.org; f. 1925 as J. B. Speed Memorial Museum; colln incl. Ancient, African, American, Contemporary, European and native American art; Dir and CEO Dr CHARLES L. VENABLE; Chief Curator RUTH CLOUDMAN.

Louisiana

Alexandria Museum of Art: POB 1028, Alexandria, LA 71309-1028; 933 Second St, Alexandria, LA 71309-1028; tel. (318) 443-3458; fax (318) 443-0545; internet www.themuseum.org; f. 1977; colln of contemporary Louisiana art and N Louisiana folk art; Chair. JOE LIPSEY; Exec. Dir CATHERINE M. PEARS; Curator SARA FUHRER.

DeQuincy Railroad Museum: 400 Lake Charles Ave, DeQuincy, LA 70633; tel. (337) 786-2823; e-mail dqgary@aol.com; internet www.dequincyrailroadmuseum.com; f. 1974; colln of railroad memorabilia incl. restored 1913 steam locomotive, 1947 passenger coach and 2 vintage cabooses; Pres. GARY W. COOPER; Sec. JOLENE CONSTANCE; Treas. EVALIN HESTER.

Historic New Orleans Collection: 533 Royal St, New Orleans, LA 70130; tel. (504) 523-4662; fax (504) 598-7108; e-mail wrc@

hnoc.org; internet www.hnoc.org; f. 1966; museum, research centre and publisher for study and preservation of history and culture of New Orleans and Gulf S region; library of 35,000 vols, 3,50,000 photographs, prints and drawings; Exec. Dir PRISCILLA LAWRENCE.

Louisiana Military Hall of Fame & Museum: POB 61930, Lafayette, LA 70596; 911 Revis Sirmon Loop, Abbeville, LA 70510; tel. (337) 898-9645; internet walshwebworks.net/lamilitary; f. 1991; colln incl. memorabilia, facts of First World War, Second World War, Korean conflict, Viet Nam War, Gulf War and Iraq War; Pres. Gen. BOB LEBLANC; Sec. N. R. BUBBA BROUSSARD, JR; Treas. JOEY LEROUGE.

Louisiana State Museum: POB 2448, New Orleans, LA 70176; tel. (504) 568-6968; internet www.crt.state.la.us/museum; f. 1906; decorative arts colln on Louisiana-related artefacts from 1790 to 1890; costumes and textiles colln dating from late 18th century to present; early Louisiana portraiture dating from 1780s to 1890s; 2,000 paintings and 14,000 works of art on paper; museum incl. Cabildo, Presbytere, 1850 House, old US mint, Madame John's Legacy, Patterson, Baton Rouge and E. D. White historic site in Thibodaux; Chair. ROSEMARY EWING; Sec. DARRYL GISSEL; Treas. RALPH LUPIN; Dir ROBERT WHEAT.

Louisiana State University Museum of Art: Shaw Center for the Arts, 100 Lafayette St, Baton Rouge, LA 70801; tel. (225) 389-7200; internet www.lsumoa.com; f. 2005; 5,000 art work colln incl. American and British portraiture and decorative arts, pre-Civil War silver, American arts and crafts, Chinese jade, modern and contemporary paintings, sculptures and photography; Exec. Dir THOMAS A. LIVESAY; Curator NATALIE MAULT.

Meadows Museum of Art: 2911 Centenary Blvd, Shreveport, LA 71104; tel. (318) 869-5169; fax (318) 869-5730; internet www.centenary.edu/meadows; f. 1967; attached to Centenary College of Louisiana; Indochina Colln of Jean Despujols; 1,500 objects incl. art works by George Grosz, Emilio Amero, Mary Cassatt and Alfred Maurer; Dir DIANE DUFILHO.

New Orleans Museum of Art: POB 19123, New Orleans, LA 70179; 1 Collins Diboll Circle, City Park, New Orleans, LA 70124; tel. (504) 658-4100; fax (504) 658-4199; e-mail education@noma.org; internet www.noma.org; f. 1911; paintings, sculpture, prints, drawings, photographs and decorative arts; spec. collns incl. history of glass; 150-year colln of photographs; Japanese paintings of the Edo Period; Chinese pottery and stone sculpture; 17th to 20th-century French paintings; Italian and Spanish paintings from Renaissance and Baroque periods; 16th- to 18th-century Low Countries paintings; tribal arts of sub-Saharan Africa; 18th-and 19th-century French porcelain; 20th-century American art and pottery; Spanish colonial Latin American paintings and sculpture; English and Continental portrait miniatures; P. C. Fabergé jewelled objects; 18th-to 20th-century American and English silver; arts of pre-Columbian Mexico, and of Central and South America; North American Indian arts; Sculpture Garden containing 50 works by Henry Moore, Fernando Botero, Elisabeth Frink, Barbara Hepworth and others; library of 20,000 vols, 70 periodicals; Dir SUSAN M. TAYLOR; publ. *Arts Quarterly*.

R. W. Norton Art Gallery: 4747 Creswell Ave, Shreveport, LA 71106-1899; tel. (318) 865-4201; fax (318) 869-0435; e-mail gallery@rwnaf.org; internet www.rwnaf.org; f. 1966; colln of 4,000 art work incl. 400 paintings by

100 artists dating from Renaissance old masters to modernist iconoclasts and contemporary neo-realists; 6 tapestries dating from 16th century; colln of American and European paintings, sculptures and decorative arts spanning over 4 centuries; library of 10,000 vols.

West Baton Rouge Museum: 845 N Jefferson Ave, Port Allen, LA 70767; tel. (225) 336-2422; fax (225) 336-2448; e-mail contact_us@wbrmuseum.org; internet www.westbatonrougemuseum.com; colln of photos, documents and arts on history and culture of West Baton Rouge Parish dating from late 18th century to present; Aillet House (c. 1830); Allendale Plantation Cabin (c. 1850); Reed Shotgun House (c. 1938); Dir JULIA ROSE.

Maine

Abbe Museum: POB 286, Bar Harbor, ME 04609; 26 Mount Desert St, Bar Harbor, ME 04609; tel. (207) 288-3519; e-mail info@abbemuseum.org; internet www.abbemuseum.org; f. 1926; colln of 50,000 objects on 10,000 years of native American culture and history; repository for cultural resource management archaeology colln in Maine; CEO CINNAMON CATLIN-LEGUTKO; Pres. Dr SANDRA K. WILCOX; Sec. Dr WILLIAM HAVILAND; Treas. JEFF DALRYMPLE.

Bowdoin College Museum of Art: 9400 College Station, Brunswick, ME 04011-8494; tel. (207) 725-3275; e-mail artmuseum@bowdoin.edu; internet www.bowdoin.edu/art-museum; f. 1894; colln incl. 18,500 objects of decorative arts, paintings, sculptures and works on paper; Dir KEVIN SALATINO; Curator JOACHIM HOMANN.

Brick Store Museum: 117 Main St, Kennebunk, ME 04043; tel. (207) 985-4802; fax (207) 985-6887; e-mail info@brickstoremuseum.org; internet www.brickstoremuseum.org; f. 1936; colln on history of the Kennebunks; colln of 70,000 items incl. artefacts and papers on maritime heritage of Kennebunks and paintings by Thomas Badger, John Brewster, Jr and Abbott Fuller Graves; Exec. Dir BRIAN COLLINS; Pres. STEPHEN P. SPOFFORD; Sec. MICHAEL I. MONTEMBEAU; Treas. DAVID N. MORAVICK.

Colby College Museum of Art: 5600 Mayflower Hill Dr., Waterville, ME 04901-8840; tel. (207) 859-5600; fax (207) 859-5606; e-mail museum@colby.edu; internet www.colby.edu/museum; f. 1959; 6,000 works dating from 18th- to 21st-century American art; Dir and Chief Curator SHARON CORWIN.

Davistown Museum: POB 144, Hulls Cove, ME 04644; tel. (207) 288-5126; fax (207) 288-2725; e-mail curator@davistownmuseum.org; internet www.davistownmuseum.org; f. 1999; incl. regional history, tools (18th- and 19th-century hand tools) and art museum; Curator H. G. SKIP BRACK.

Farnsworth Art Museum: 16 Museum St, Rockland, ME 04841; tel. (207) 596-6457; fax (207) 596-0509; e-mail writeus@farnsworthmuseum.org; internet www.farnsworthmuseum.org; f. 1948 as William A. Farnsworth Library and Art Museum; colln of 10,000 art works related to Maine; works by sculptor Louise Nevelso; Wyeth Center; library of 10,000 vols; Exec. Dir CHRISTOPHER BROWNAWELL; Pres. RICHARD ARONEAU; Sec. MARY BALDWIN COLLINS; Treas. JOHN W. ROSENBLUM.

Hudson Museum: Univ. of Maine, Collins Center for Arts, Orono, ME 04469-5746; tel. (207) 581-1901; fax (207) 581-1950; e-mail hudsonmuseum@umit.maine.edu; internet www.umaine.edu/hudsonmuseum; f. 1986; attached to Univ. of Maine; 8,000 ethnographic and archaeological objects, incl.

2,828 pre-Columbian ceramics, lithics and gold work dating from 2000BC to Spanish conquest; Dir GRETCHEN F. FAULKNER.

Maine Archives and Museums: POB 46, Cumberland Center, ME 04021; tel. (207) 400-6965; e-mail info@mainemuseums.org; internet www.mainemuseums.org; directory of 201 museums in Maine; Pres. JAY ADAMS; Dir LEIGH HALLETT; Curator CANDACE KANES; Sec. PATRICIA BURDICK; Treas. PATRICIA HENNER.

Maine Maritime Museum: 243 Washington St, Bath, ME 04530; tel. (207) 443-1316; fax (207) 443-1665; e-mail curator@maritimeme.org; internet www.mainemaritimemuseum.org; f. 1962 as Maine Research Soc. of Bath, present name 1975; 20,000 objects incl. shipbuilding tools, 550 ship models, 475 maritime paintings, more than 140 historic Maine watercraft of nat. significance, ceramics, engines, furniture, fishing and boat gear, jewellery, textiles and navigational equipment; library of 17,000 vols, 53,000 periodicals, 130,000 historical photographs, 42,000 sheets of ship plans, 2,000 linear ft MSS, 1,000 maps and charts, 482 video cassettes; Chair. WILLIAM A. ROGERS, JR; Sec. JACKSON PARKER; Treas. JEFFREY W. PETERS; Exec. Dir AMY LENT.

Maine State Museum: 83 State House Station, Augusta, ME 04333-0083; 230 State St, Augusta, ME 04330; tel. 207-287-2301; e-mail maine.museum@maine.gov; internet mainestatemuseum.org; f. 1965; colln of 500,000 artefacts on prehistory, history and natural science of Maine; 24,000 historic images; geological colln dates from 1830s; Dir JOSEPH R. PHILLIPS.

Matthews Museum of Maine Heritage: POB 582, Union, ME 04862; tel. (207) 542-2379; e-mail matthewsmuseum@gmail.com; internet www.matthewsmuseum.org; agricultural museum with colln of 10,000 exhibits incl. agricultural tools and equipment, carriages and musical instruments; Sec. MARTHA HOOPER.

Museum of African Culture: 13 Brown St, Portland, ME 04101; tel. (207) 871-7188; e-mail africart@museumafricanculture.org; internet www.museumafricanculture.org; f. 1998; colln of 1,500 objects incl. carved wooden masks, textiles, ceramic, bone, ivory and composite objects; 1,000 years old bronzes figures; 2,000 years old ivory flutes and clay vessels; Exec. Dir OSCAR O. MOKEME; Sec. LORRAINE KARDASH.

Ogunquit Museum of American Art: POB 815, Ogunquit, ME 03907; tel. (207) 646-4909; internet www.ogunquitmuseum.org; f. 1953; colln of 1,600 art works incl. paintings, sculptures, photography and graphics on American Art; Pres. TIMOTHY B. ELLIS; Sec. CAROLE J. AARON; Treas. MARK CONNOLLY; Exec. Dir RONALD L. CRUSAN.

Peary-MacMillan Arctic Museum & Arctic Studies Center: Bowdoin College, 9500 College Station, Brunswick, ME 04011-8495; tel. (207) 725-3416; e-mail ahawkes@bowdoin.edu; internet www.bowdoin.edu/arctic-museum; f. 1985; attached to Bowdoin College; colln incl. material donated by Donald B. MacMillan collected during his career as arctic explorer and researcher; colln incl. 20,000 images from E N American Arctic (1908–54); Dir SUSAN A. KAPLAN; Curator GENEVIEVE LEMOINE.

Portland Museum of Art: Seven Congress Sq., Portland, ME 04101; tel. (207) 775-6148; fax (207) 773-7324; e-mail info@portlandmuseum.org; internet www.portlandmuseum.org; f. 1882 as Portland Soc. of Art; 17,000 fine and decorative arts from 18th century to the present housed in 3 bldgs of architectural note: Charles Shipman

Payson Bldg, L. D. M. Sweat Memorial Galleries, McLellan House; Maine artists such as Winslow Homer, Marsden Hartley, Rockwell Kent, Louise Nevelson; European collns incl. works by Cassatt, Degas, Magritte, Monet, Munch, Picasso, Rodin; Chair. HANS UNDERDAHL; Dir MARK BESSIRE; Sec. JAMES A. HOULE; Treas. ROBERT S. NANOVIC.

Saco Museum: 371 Main St, Saco, ME 04072; tel. (207) 283-3861; fax (207) 283-0754; e-mail museum@sacomuseum.org; internet www.sacomuseum.org; f. 1866 as York Institute, present name 2000; colln of 10,000 fine, decorative and historic artefacts incl. documented local furniture, clocks, decorative arts such as silver, ceramics, textiles and costumes; Dir JESSICA SKWIRE ROUTHIER.

Maryland

Allegany Museum: 3 Pershing St, Cumberland, MD 21502; tel. (301) 777-7200; e-mail alleganymuseum1@verizon.net; internet www.alleganymuseum.org; f. 1999 as Allegany County Museum, present name 2008, present location 2010; colln of over 50,000 items; spec. colln incl. King James Bible, artefacts of Kelly-Springfield Tire Co, glassware, models showcasing Maryland's transportation history, canon boat models and photo display of Cumberland; Pres. GARY BARTIK; Sec. JERRY ROBINETTE; Treas. MIKE FETCHERO.

Annapolis Maritime Museum: POB 3088, Annapolis, MD 21403; 723 Second St, Annapolis, MD 21403; tel. (410) 295-0104; e-mail office@amaritime.org; internet www.amaritime.org; preserves and commemorates maritime heritage of Annapolis and neighbouring waters of Chesapeake Bay; Dir JEFF HOLLAND.

B & O Railroad Museum: 901 W Pratt St, Baltimore, MD 21223; tel. (410) 752-2490; fax (410) 752-2499; e-mail info@borail.org; internet www.borail.org; f. 1953; attached to Smithsonian Instn; collects, preserves and interprets artefacts (incl. locomotives and rolling stock, historic bldgs and small objects) related to early American railroading focusing on continuum of railroad technology history from 1830 through the present day, particularly the Baltimore and Ohio, Chesapeake and Ohio, W Maryland, and other mid-Atlantic railroads; also located at Ellicott City; Exec. Dir COURTNEY B. WILSON; Chief Curator DAVID SHACKELFORD; Chair. FRANCIS X. SMYTH; Sec. ROBERT F. SCHOLZ; Treas. GREGORY A. FARNO.

Baltimore Museum of Art: 10 Art Museum Dr., Baltimore, MD 21218-3898; tel. (443) 573-1700; fax (443) 573-1582; internet www.artbma.org; f. 1914; total colln of 90,000 items; Cone Colln of post-impressionist and modern art (incl. 500 works by Matisse, and examples by Picasso, Cézanne and Van Gogh); West Wing for Contemporary Art housing 16 galleries of art since 1960s; Old Master and 19th-century European paintings and sculpture; prints, drawings and photographs since 15th century; American paintings, sculpture and decorative arts from the 17th to the 19th century; Maryland period rooms; African, Asian, Native American, and Oceanic art; 3-acre sculpture garden; library of 71,000 vols; Chair. STILES TUTTLE COLWILL; Dir and Sec. DOREEN BOLGER; Treas. FREDERICK SINGLEY KOONTZ; publ. *BMA Today* (4 a year).

Baltimore Museum of Industry: 1415 Key Highway, Baltimore, MD 21230; tel. (410) 727-4808; e-mail info@thebmi.org; internet www.thebmi.org; colln of 100,000 objects; spec. colln incl. historic 1850s shipyard bell, early wooden gas pipe, rare 1820s Acorn printing press, 1922 Linotype machine, antique sewing machines and the entire colln from the Mount Vernon Museum of Incandescent Lighting; 250,000 photographs and negatives; Schneidereith Print Colln; incl. Maryland Center for Career and Technology Education Studies and Downtown Sailing Center; Exec. Dir ROLAND H. WOODWARD; Chair. STUART FITZGIBBON; Sec. C. WILLIAM SCHNEIDEREITH, JR; Treas. CHERYL GRAVEEN.

Banneker-Douglass Museum: 84 Franklin St, Annapolis, MD 21401; tel. (410) 216-6180; fax (410) 974-2553; e-mail bdmprograms@goci.state.md.us; internet www.bdmuseum.com; f. 1984; state's official repository of African American material culture; African permanent exhibit incl. American history in Maryland from 1633 through present day; incl. Sylvia Gaither Garrison Library; Pres. Dr JONI JONES; Curator of Collns TABITHA PRYOR.

Evergreen Museum & Library: Johns Hopkins Univ., 4545 N Charles St, Baltimore, MD 21210; tel. (410) 516-0341; e-mail evergreenmuseum@jhu.edu; internet www.museums.jhu.edu/evergreen.php; attached to Johns Hopkins Univ.; 50,0000 objects incl. architecture, paintings, decorative arts, rare books, philanthropy, Baltimore's railroad history; Garret family holdings; European paintings by Edgar Degas, Amedeo Modigliani and Ignacio Zuloaga; library of 30,000 vols; Dir and Curator JAMES ARCHER ABBOTT.

F. Brooke Whiting House & Museum: 632 Washington St, Cumberland, MD 21502; tel. (301) 777-7782; e-mail info@thewhitinghouse.org; internet www.thewhitinghouse.org; f. 1998; colln of art from Brooke Whiting's travels around the world: Asian Works of Art and American, British and European decorative arts; arts from America, Great Britain, Netherlands, France, Spain, Portugal, Italy, Greece, Egypt, Lebanon, Iran, India, China, Thailand, Viet Nam, Korea, Japan, Russia and Mexico; library of 1,500 vols, incl. photographic materials and ephemera from his travels.

Glenn L. Martin Maryland Aviation Museum: POB 5024, Baltimore, MD 21220; 701 Wilson Point Rd, Hangar Five, Suite 531, Baltimore, MD 21220; tel. (410) 682-6122; e-mail other@marylandaviationmuseum.org; internet www.marylandaviationmuseum.org; f. 1990; preserves and documents aviation and space history in Maryland; contributions of Glenn L. Martin and his Co; 13 historic aircraft; thousands of original motion picture films, plans, documents, research models, aircraft tools, and components; 200,000 aviation and Co's photographs; Exec. Dir ROBERT BYRNES.

Homewood Museum: The Johns Hopkins Univ., 3400 N Charles St, Baltimore, MD 21218; tel. (410) 516-5589; fax (410) 516-7859; e-mail homewoodmuseum@jhu.edu; internet www.museums.jhu.edu/homewood.php; attached to Johns Hopkins Univ.; colln incl. architecture (palladian and fed.), silver, Baltimore furniture, American history; Carroll family's fine and decorative arts objects; English ceramics, silver and furniture and items of Chinese and French manufacture; Dir and Curator CATHERINE ROGERS ARTHUR.

Jefferson Patterson Park and Museum, State Museum of Archaeology: 10515 Mackall Rd, St Leonard, MD 20685; tel. (410) 586-8501; fax (410) 586-0080; e-mail jppm@mdp.state.md.us; internet www.jefpat.org; f. 1983; Maryland Archaeological Conservation Laboratory (MAC Lab); over 8m. artefacts; library of 12,000 vols; Exec. Dir MARK THOMPSON.

Johns Hopkins Archaeological Museum: 150 Gilman Hall, 3400 N Charles St, Balti-more, MD 21218; tel. (410) 516-0383; fax (410) 516-5218; e-mail archmuseum@jhu.edu; internet www.archaeologicalmuseum.jhu.edu; f. 1882; attached to Johns Hopkins Univ.; 700 archaeological objects from ancient Greece, Rome, Egypt, the Near E and ancient Americas; Dir Dr BETSY M. BRYAN; Curator SANCHITA BALACHANDRAN.

Maryland Historical Society Museum and Library: 201 W Monument St, Baltimore, MD 21201-4674; tel. (410) 685-3750; fax (410) 385-2105; e-mail reference@mdhs.org; internet www.mdhs.org; f. 1844; exhibits Francis Scott Key's original MSS of The Star-Spangled Banner and the war of 1812; 350,000 objects, incl. paintings and miniatures, pieces of furniture, sculpture, drawings, silver, ceramics, jewellery, textiles, examples of porcelain and pottery, works on paper, misc. household, office and agricultural equipment, toys, dolls, games, silver holloware and flatware, maritime objects; MSS room incl. Calvert Papers, papers of Benjamin Henry Latrobe, over 1,300 letters and documents of the Lords Baltimore and their families, genealogical colln and many hundreds of prints and drawings; maritime colln emphasizing crafts of Chesapeake Bay; library: 7m. vols; Pres. BURT KUMMEROW; Chief Curator ALEXANDRA DEUTSCH; publ. *Maryland Historical Magazine* (4 a year).

Maryland Science Center: 601 Light St, Baltimore, MD 21230; tel. (410) 685-2370; e-mail observatory@marylandsciencecenter.org; internet www.mdsci.org; f. 1797 as Maryland Acad. of Sciences; exhibits incl. travelling, earth science, life science, physical science and space science; Davis Planetarium and IMAX theatre; educational instn focusing on science, technology engineering and mathematics; Pres. and CEO VAN R. REINER; Sec. PHYLLIS S. CLEMENTS; Treas. RICHARD M. HESSE.

National Cryptologic Museum: Fort George G., Meade, MD; tel. (301) 688-5849; fax (301) 688-5847; e-mail crypto_museum@nsa.gov; internet www.nsa.gov/about/cryptologic_heritage/museum; f. 1993; attached to Nat. Security Agency; colln of artefacts preserving the history of the cryptologic profession; Dir of Nat. Security Agency Gen. KEITH B. ALEXANDER.

Reginald F. Lewis Museum of Maryland African American History & Culture: 830 E Pratt St, Baltimore, MD 21202; tel. (443) 263-1800; fax (410) 333-1138; e-mail emailus@maamc.org; internet www.africanamericanculture.org; attached to Smithsonina Instn; colln incl. art, artefacts, textiles, material culture, photographs, rare books and other items; African American military experience, early American jazz recordings and Maryland community history; Exec. Dir Dr A. SKIPP SANDERS; Chair. Dr LESLIE KING-HAMMOND; Sec. KATHLEEN PONTONE; Treas. CARLA HAYDEN.

Richardson Maritime Museum: POB 1198, 401 High St, Cambridge, MD 21613; tel. (410) 221-1871; fax (410) 228-5471; e-mail info@richardsonmuseum.org; internet www.richardsonmuseum.org; more than 50 Chesapeake Bay wooden boat models; boatbuilding tools; watermen's equipment and gear; spec. colln incl. skipjack Nathan of Dorchester, the last skipjack built in the 20th century and life and work of James B; Chair. VICTOR H. MACSORLEY; Curator MELVIN HICKMAN.

Thrasher Carriage Museum: 19 Depot St, Frostburg, MD 21532; tel. (301) 689-3380; e-mail info@thethrashercarriagemuseum.com; internet www.thethrashercarriagemuseum.com; f. 1975; collns of horse-drawn vehicles, pleasure vehicles, funeral wagons, sleighs, carts; vehicles representing every walk of life; spec. collns: Extension Front Brougham, Queen Body Phaeton and Governess Cart.

United States Naval Academy Museum: Preble Hall, 118 Maryland Ave, Annapolis, MD; tel. (410) 293-2108; internet www.usna.edu/museum; f. 1845 as Naval School Lyceum, present location 1939; colln incl. ship models, paintings, prints, flags, uniforms, swords, firearms, medals, sculptures, manuscripts, rare books, photographs, ship instruments and gear and personal memorabilia; spec. colln incl. 6,000 prints of Beverley R. Robinson, United States Navy Trophy Flag and Malcolm Storer Naval Medals colln; Dir Dr J. SCOTT HARMON; Sr Curator JAMES CHEEVERS.

Walters Art Museum: 600 N Charles St, Baltimore, MD 21201; tel. (410) 547-9000; fax (410) 783-7969; e-mail info@thewalters.org; internet www.thewalters.org; f. 1931; 35,000 objects; collns range from predynastic Egypt to 20th-century Europe; Chinese, Japanese and Indian art; ancient Egyptian, Greek and Roman art; Byzantine art; Romanesque, early Gothic art; later Gothic art; Renaissance sculpture and decorative arts; MSS illumination; incunabula, arms and armour; old master paintings; 19th-century paintings, decorative arts; spec. colln incl. ancient Egyptian mummy masks and medieval armour and 19th-century French Impressionism; library of 120,000 vols; Chair. ANDREA B. LAPORTE; Dir and Sec. GARY VIKAN; Treas. FRANK K. TURNER, JR; Sr Curator WILLIAM R. JOHNSTON; publs *Journal* (1 a year), *The Walters Magazine* (4 a year).

Washington County Museum of Fine Arts: POB 423, 401 Museum Dr., Hagerstown, MD 21741; tel. (301) 739-5727; fax (301) 745-3747; e-mail info@wcmfa.org; internet www.wcmfa.org; f. 1929; 6,000 objects from Old Masters to 20th-century paintings, sculpture and decorative arts; conducts research on all works of art in its colln; art library.

Massachusetts

Adams National Historical Park: 135 Adams St, Quincy, MA 02169-1749; tel. (617) 773-1177; fax (617) 472-7562; e-mail adam_visitor_center@nps.gov; internet www.nps.gov/adam; f. 1946; attached to Nat. Park Service; donated to the USA in December 1946 by the Adams Memorial Soc.; designated a nat. historic site under the admin. of the Nat. Park Service of the Dept of the Interior; built in 1731 by Major Leonard Vassall of Boston; bought by John Adams in 1787; at the end of his term, he lived in the house until his death in 1826; the house then passed to his son, John Quincy Adams, in the middle of his term as sixth Pres.; the Adams family continued to live there until 1927; the house, contents, and garden are as the Adams family left them; the separate stone library, standing in the garden, was built in 1870 by Charles Francis Adams—comprises most of the libraries of John Quincy Adams and Charles Francis Adams, and some of the libraries of John Adams, Henry and Brooks Adams; library of 12,000 vols; Dir JONATHAN B. JARVIS; Superintendent MARIANNE PEAK.

Addison Gallery of American Art: Phillips Acad., 180 Main St, Andover, MA 01810-4161; tel. (978) 749-4015; fax (978) 749-4025; e-mail addison@andover.edu; internet www.andover.edu/museums/addison; f. 1931; 17,000 objects in media-painting, sculpture, photography, drawings, prints and decorative arts dating from the 18th century to present; Dir BRIAN T. ALLEN; Curator ALLISON N. KEMMERER.

Art Complex Museum: 189 Alden St, POB 2814, Duxbury, MA 02331; tel. (781) 934-6634; e-mail director@artcomplex.org; internet www.artcomplex.org; f. 1971; 8,000 objects on American paintings, prints, Shaker furniture and Asian art; library of 6,000 vols; Dir CHARLES WEYERHAEUSER; Librarian CHERYL O'NEILL.

Beneski Museum of Natural History: POB 5000, Amherst College, Amherst, MA 01002-5000; 11 Barrett Hill Rd, Amherst College, Amherst, MA 01002-5000; tel. (413) 542-2165; internet www.amherst.edu/museums/naturalhistory; f. 1821, present name and status 2011; attached to Amherst College; natural history colln of 200,000 objects; archaeology colln incl. 15,000 items made by Americans from New England and New York; rep. sample of 18 original meteorites; Dir PETER CROWLEY.

Berkshire Museum: 39 S St, Route 7, Pittsfield, MA 01201; tel. (413) 443-7171; internet www.berkshiremuseum.org; f. 1903; 19th- and 20th-century sculptures by American and European artists; artefacts of ancient history and natural science incl. fossil colln and 143-lb meteorite; neoclassical marble sculptures dating from 19th century; Exec. Dir VAN W. SHIELDS.

Cahoon Museum of American Art: POB 1853, 4676 Falmouth Rd, Cotuit, MA 02635; tel. (508) 428-7581; fax (508) 420-3709; internet www.cahoonmuseum.org; f. 1984; colln incl. folk paintings of Cahoon and 19th- and 20th-century contemporary American art; Dir RICHARD WATERHOUSE.

Concord Museum: POB 146, 200 Lexington Rd, Concord, MA 01742-0146; tel. (978) 369-9763; fax (978) 369-9660; e-mail cm1@concordmuseum.org; internet www.concordmuseum.org; f. 1886; history and decorative arts museum with 16 period rooms and galleries, with artefacts from Concord area; museum rooms chronicle life in Concord from Native American habitation to present; spec. collns incl. relics from the battle at N Bridge, the largest colln of Thoreau artefacts from his stay at Walden Pond, and the contents of Emerson's study; over 35,000 objects; Exec. Dir PEGGY BURKE.

Danforth Museum of Art: 123 Union Ave, Framingham, MA 01702-8291; tel. (508) 620-0050; fax (508) 872-5542; internet www.danforthmuseum.org; f. 1975; 3,500 works of art with focus on American art from 18th century to present; spec. colln incl. 19th- and 20th-century American art by artists like Gilbert Stuart, Faith Ringgold and Albert Bierstadt; Exec. Dir KATHERINE FRENCH.

Davis Museum and Cultural Center: Wellesley College, 106 Central St, Wellesley, MA 02481-8203; tel. (781) 283-2051; fax (781) 283-2064; internet www.davismuseum.wellesley.edu; f. 1889; attached to Wellesley College; colln incl. paintings, sculptures, works on paper, photographs and decorative objects dating from antiquity to present; Dir LISA FISCHMAN.

DeCordova Sculpture Park and Museum: 51 Sandy Pond Rd, Lincoln, MA 01773-2600; tel. (781) 259-8355; fax (781) 259-3650; e-mail info@decordova.org; internet www.decordova.org; f. 1950 as deCordova Museum and Sculpture Park, present name 2009; 3,400 works of modern and contemporary art in photography, prints, painting, drawing and sculpture; Pres. FAITH PARKER; Treas. ANNE COLUMBIA; Exec. Dir DENNIS KOIS; Curator DINA DEITSCH.

Emily Dickinson Museum: 280 Main St, Amherst, MA 01002; tel. (413) 542-8161; e-mail info@emilydickinsonmuseum.org; internet www.emilydickinsonmuseum.org; f. 2003; attached to Amherst College; colln of 8,000 objects incl. furniture, artwork and personal items of Emily Dickinson; Exec. Dir JANE WALD; Chair. KENT W. FAERBER; Sec. JAMES C. FRASER.

Fitchburg Art Museum: 25 Merriam Parkway, Fitchburg, MA 01420; tel. (978) 345-4207; fax (978) 345-2319; e-mail info@fitchburgartmuseum.org; internet www.fitchburgartmuseum.org; f. 1925; American and European paintings, prints, drawings, ceramics and decorative arts as well as Greek, Roman, Asian and pre-Columbian antiquities in 14 galleries; Dir PETER TIMMS.

Harvard Art Museums: 32 Quincy St, Cambridge, MA 02138; tel. (617) 495-9400; internet www.harvardartmuseums.org; f. 1891; incorporates the Fogg Museum (Western art from the Middle Ages to the present), Busch-Reisinger Museum (art of German-speaking countries), Arthur M. Sackler Museum (ancient, Asian, Islamic and later Indian art, reinstalled with works representing the collns of all 3 museums until 2013), Straus Center for Conservation, Center for the Technical Study of Modern Art, Harvard Art Museum Archives, and the US HQ for the Archaeological Exploration of Sardis; library of 3,000 vols of conservation-related books in the Straus Centre, 3,000 linear ft of historical records and artists papers in the archives (1895–present); Dir THOMAS W. LENTZ; Deputy Dir MAUREEN DONOVAN; Chief Curator DEBORAH MARTIN KAO; publ. *Next* (3 a year).

Higgins Armory Museum: 100 Barber Ave, Worcester, MA 01606-2444; tel. (508) 853-6015; fax (508) 852-7697; e-mail higgins@higgins.org; internet www.higgins.org; f. 1931 as John Woodman Higgins Armory; 4,500 artefacts on arms and armours from medieval and Renaissance Europe, Feudal Japan and ancient Greece and Rome; European colln incl. 3,000 armours and components, 1,000 weapons and accessories, 500 swords and daggers and 100 firearms; 1,000 African, Islamic, Indian and Japanese arms; Exec. Dir SUZANNE MAAS.

Isabella Stewart Gardner Museum: 280 The Fenway, Boston, MA 02115; tel. (617) 566-1401; fax (617) 566-7653; e-mail information@isgm.org; internet www.gardnermuseum.org; f. 1903; 2,500 objects incl. paintings, sculptures, textiles, drawings, silver, ceramics, illuminated MSS, rare books, photographs and letters from ancient Rome, medieval Europe, Renaissance Italy, Asia, Islamic world and 19th-century France and America; Dir ANNE HAWLEY.

Mead Art Museum: POB 5000, Amherst College, Amherst, MA 01002-5000; tel. (413) 542-2335; fax (413) 542-2117; e-mail mead@amherst.edu; internet www.amherst.edu/museums/mead; f. 1949; attached to Amherst College; colln incl. 16,000 works of art from America, Europe, Mexico, Asia, Africa and Russia; Dir and Chief Curator Dr ELIZABETH E. BARKER.

Milton Art Museum: 900 Randolph St, Canton, MA 02021; tel. (781) 821-2222; e-mail miltonmuseum@hotmail.com; internet miltonartmuseum.org; f. 1986; colln incl. fine art, limited prints, sculpture, photography and Asian art; Remington and Russell cast bronzes; American and European etchings and lithographs from 18th to 20th century; 17th-century oil painting by Dutch painter Cornelius Bisschop; Chair. and Interim Treas. ELLYN MOLLER; Sec. DAVID EHRMANN.

Museum of Fine Arts Boston: Ave of the Arts, 465 Huntington Ave, Boston, MA 02115-5523; tel. (617) 267-9300; fax (617) 267-0280; internet www.mfa.org; f. 1876, present location 1909; 450,000 objects; rare and important works incl. masters of American painting, Impressionist art, Asian scrolls and Egyptian mummies; library of 350,000 vols and catalogues; Dir MALCOLM ROGERS.

Museum of Science: 1 Science Park, Boston, MA 02114; tel. (617) 723-2500; fax (617) 589-0454; e-mail information@mos.org; internet www.mos.org; f. 1830 as Boston Soc. of Natural History; exhibits on astronomy, natural history, physical science, technology, medicine, etc.; educational programmes with more than 550 interactive exhibits; houses the Charles Hayden Planetarium, the Mugar Omni Theater and the Lyman Library; library of 40,000 vols and journals; Chair. HOWARD MESSING; Pres. and Dir IOANNIS N. MIAOULIS; publ. *Magazine* (2 a year).

National Heritage Museum: 33 Marrett Rd, Lexington, MA 02421; tel. (781) 861-6559; fax (781) 861-9846; internet www.nationalheritagemuseum.org; colln on history of American Freemasonry and fraternalism; colln incl. decorative arts, documents, photographs and fine art on American history; focus on material related to Lexington during American Revolution; library of 45,000 vols; Exec. Dir RICHARD V. TRAVIS.

Norman Rockwell Museum: Nine Route 183, Stockbridge, MA 01262; tel. (413) 298-4100; internet www.nrm.org; f. 1969; museum houses American painter and illustrator Norman Rockwell's 574 original paintings and drawings; more than 100,000 items, incl. working photographs, letters, personal calendars, fan mail and business documents; Chair. THOMAS L. PULLING.

Peabody Essex Museum: East India Sq., 161 Essex St, Salem, MA 01970-3738; tel. (978) 745-9500; fax (978) 744-6776; internet www.pem.org; f. 1799; 1m. works; maritime art and history, Asian, Oceanic, Indian, African and Native American art; American art and architecture; incl. Phillips Library; library of 400,000 vols, a mile in linear ft of MSS, colln of ephemera, broadsides, pamphlets, and periodicals; Exec. Dir and CEO DAN L. MONROE; Pres. ROBERT N. SHAPIRO; Sec. CARLA B. HERWITZ; Treas. C. RICHARD CARLSON; publs *American Neptune* (4 a year), *Quarterly Review of Archaeology*.

Peabody Museum of Archaeology and Ethnology: Harvard Univ., 11 Divinity Ave, Cambridge, MA 02138; tel. (617) 496-1027; fax (617) 495-7535; e-mail peapub@fas.harvard.edu; internet www.peabody.harvard.edu; f. 1866; works in close cooperation with the Dept of Anthropology of Harvard, and much of the research is jtly determined; since its founding more than 800 expeditions have been sent to every continent, resulting, with the addition of important gifts and purchases, in the building up of one of the most comprehensive collns of ethnology, archaeology and physical anthropology in the USA; the first scientific studies of Maya archaeology were made under its direction, and its collns from this area, and from Middle America generally, are extremely important; there are also collns of Old World archaeology; in ethnology, the material from the Pacific Islands is important, and the Museum is also rich in material representing the native tribes of Africa, of South America, and of the Plains and North-west Coast Indians of N America, where some of the objects date from the Lewis and Clark expedition of 1806; the archaeology of the south-western USA, incl. the Pueblo Indian area, is also strongly represented; the Tozzer Library covers the entire field of anthropology; library of 250,000 vols and pamphlets; Dir Prof. DAVID PILBEAM; publs *RES: Anthropology and Aesthetics, Symbols* (1 a year).

Smith College Museum of Art: Elm Street at Bedford Terrace, Northampton, MA 01063; tel. (413) 585-2760; fax (413) 585-2782; e-mail artmuseum@smith.edu; internet www.smith.edu/artmuseum; f. 1879, present bldg 2003; collns incl. examples from most periods and cultures with spec. emphasis on European and American paintings, sculpture, drawings, prints and photographs since 17th century; Cunningham Center houses over 1,600 drawings, 5,700 photographs and over 8,000 prints by artists from Dürer to contemporary print makers; Dir and Chief Curator JESSICA NICOLL; Assoc. Dir DAVID DEMPSEY.

Spellman Museum of Stamps & Postal History: 235 Wellesley St, Regis College, Weston, MA 02493; tel. (781) 768-8367; fax (781) 768-7332; e-mail info@spellman.org; internet www.spellman.org; f. 1960 as Cardinal Spellman Philatelic Museum; 2,000,000 items incl. those from Pres. Dwight David Eisenhower, violinist Jascha Heifetz and Gen. Matthew Ridgway; library of 4,800 vols; Pres. and Chair. MARK GALLAGHER; Sec. Sr ANN MARIE GRADY; Treas. LYNNE LINNEHAN.

Sterling and Francine Clark Art Institute: 225 S St, Williamstown, MA 01267; tel. (413) 458-2303; internet www.clarkart.edu; f. 1950; colln of European and American painting, sculpture, works on paper and decorative art dating from Renaissance to early 20th century; 19th-century European and American paintings; Dir MICHAEL CONFORTI.

USS Constitution Museum: POB 291812, Boston, MA 02129-0215; Charlestown Navy Yard, Bldg 22, Charlestown, MA 02129; tel. (617) 426-1812; fax (617) 242-0496; e-mail museumadmin@ussconstitutionmuseum.org; internet www.ussconstitutionmuseum.org; f. 1972; colln related to duty naval vessel USS Constitution; art and artefact colln incl. swords, pistols and muskets from 18th and 19th century; 7,500 items in MSS colln; library of 2,000 vols; Chair. JAMES C. STOKES; Sec. PAUL F. McDONOUGH, JR; Treas. WILLIAM WHITE.

Williams College Museum of Art: 15 Lawrence Hall Dr., Suite 2, Williamstown, MA 01267-3248; tel. (413) 597-2429; fax (413) 597-5000; internet wcma.williams.edu; f. 1926; attached to Williams College; 13,000 objects incl. Assyrian reliefs to contemporary photography; colln of American art from late 18th century to present; Dir KATY KLINE.

Worcester Art Museum: 55 Salisbury St, Worcester, MA 01609; tel. (508) 799-4406; fax (508) 799-4767; e-mail information@worcesterart.org; internet www.worcesterart.org; f. 1898; 40,000-piece colln of paintings, sculptures, decorative arts, photographs, prints, drawings and new media illustrating the evolution of art from early Egyptian civilization to modern times; esp. notable are ancient Egyptian, Greek, Roman, Asian and medieval sculpture; mosaics from Antioch; a French Romanesque Chapter House; Italian and other European schools of painting from 13th century to present; American collns from 17th century to the present; pre-Columbian art; Japanese and Western prints; offers a year-round studio art and art appreciation programme; library of 45,000 vols; Dir MATTHIAS WASCHEK.

Michigan

Cranbrook Art Museum: 39221 Woodward Ave, POB 801, Bloomfield Hills, MI 48303-0801; fax (248) 645-3324; e-mail artmuseum@cranbrook.edu; internet www.cranbrookart.edu/museum; f. 1930; attached to Cranbrook Academy of Art; 6,000 works of art, architecture and design from the Arts and Crafts Movement to the present; colln incl. sculpture, paintings, models and drawings, ceramics, glass, furniture, textiles and metalwork, decorative, applied and fine arts; Dir GREGORY WITTKOPP.

Dennos Museum Center: 1701 E Front St, Traverse City, MI 49686; tel. (231) 995-1055; e-mail dmc@nmc.edu; internet www.dennosmuseum.org; f. 1991; 2,000 works of art incl. Inuit prints, painting, sculpture and photography and sculptures; contemporary works by Michigan artists, 19th- and 20th-century American and European graphic art, 18th- and 19th-century Japanese prints, and 20th-century Great Lakes Indian and Canadian Indian art; incl. 3 exhibit galleries, sculpture court, Discovery Gallery, Inuit Art Gallery and Milliken auditorium; Exec. Dir EUGENE JENNEMAN.

Detroit Institute of Arts: 5200 Woodward Ave, Detroit, MI 48202; tel. (313) 833-7900; fax (313) 833-2357; e-mail operator@dia.org; internet www.dia.org; f. 1885 as Detroit Museum of Art, present name and location 1927; comprehensive fine arts colln from prehistoric to contemporary times; colln of American, Dutch, Flemish, French, Italian and German Expressionist painting; Ancient, African, Oceanic and New World cultures; Asian, Native American and Islamic art since the beginning of the 20th century; graphic arts; American and European decorative arts since the beginning of the 20th century; theatre arts colln; 100 galleries, art reference library and state-of-the-art conservation services laboratory; library of 190,000 vols; Dir, Pres. and CEO GRAHAM W. J. BEAL; Chief Curator KENNETH J. MYERS; publs *Bulletin of the Detroit Institute of Arts* (1 a year), *Your DIA* (12 a year).

Ella Sharp Museum of Art and History: 3225 Fourth St, Jackson, MI 49203; tel. (517) 787-2320; fax (517) 787-2933; e-mail info@ellasharp.org; internet www.ellasharp.org; f. 1965; Andrews Gallery of Wildlife Art, Jackson History Gallery and 3 galleries of temporary exhibitions; outdoor sculpture colln; historic sites of Ella Sharp's 19th-century Hillside Farmhouse, Dibble One-Room Schoolhouse, Eli Stilson's Log House and Merriman-Sharp Tower Barn.

Flint Institute of Arts: 1120 E Kearsley St, Flint, MI 48503; tel. (810) 234-1695; fax (810) 234-1692; internet www.flintarts.org/museum/museum.html; f. 1928 as Enos and Sarah DeWaters Art Center; 8,000 American, European, Native American, African, and Asian art incl. paintings, sculptures, prints, drawings, and decorative arts; colln incl. 15th- to 18th-century English, French and Italian decorative arts, panel by Peter Paul Rubens, 17th-century French tapestries, 18th- and 19th-century paperweights and European glass, American and French Impressionist and Post-Impressionist paintings, Hudson River School paintings, Regional and Great Lakes paintings, Modernist and Abstract Expressionist and Photorealist paintings; Dir JOHN HENRY; Pres. SAMUEL M. HARRIS; Sec. MARILYN KOPP; Treas. DIANE LINDHOLM; publ. *fia* magazine.

Grand Rapids Art Museum: 101 Monroe Center, Grand Rapids, MI 49503; tel. (616) 831-1000; fax (616) 831-1001; internet www.artmuseumgr.org; f. 1910, present name 1963; 19th and 20th centuries art, design and modern craft, prints, drawings and photographs; library of 8,000 vols; Dir and CEO DANA FRIIS-HANSEN; Pres. SCOTT WIERDA; Sec. and Treas. TONY S. LAWRENCE.

Grand Rapids Public Museum: 272 Pearl St NW, Grand Rapids, MI 49504; tel. (616) 929-1700; e-mail info@grmuseum.org; internet www.grmuseum.org; f. 1854; Roger B. Chaffee planetarium; museum sites: Voigt House, Community Archives, Calkins Law Office, Veen Observatory, Norton Mounds, 54 Jefferson and Van Andel Museum Center; colln of 250,000 artefacts and specimens incl. ethnographic cultural materials, historically significant fine art, bldgs and architectural fragments, archeological materials, fossils, rocks and minerals, clothing and textiles, decorative arts; archival colln of paper records, publs, photographs, art work, letters and diaries; Pres. and CEO DALE ROBERTSON; Chair. DANNY GAYDOU; Sec. and Treas. RICH NOREEN.

Holland Museum: 31 W 10th St, Holland, MI 49423; tel. (616) 796-3321; e-mail hollandmuseum@hollandmuseum.org; internet www.hollandmuseum.org; f. 1897, present name and status 1992; colln of works of art of Netherlands, Indonesia, local history, Hispanic and SE Asian, Native American, Cappon House, 1867 Settlers House; Archives incl. 1,585 linear ft of material; temporary exhibitions; Dir STEVEN W. ROSEN; Chair. HOWARD VENEKLASEN; Sec. SUSAN WOLFE; Treas. BILL BORGMAN.

Kalamazoo Institute of Arts: 314 S Park St, Kalamazoo, MI 49007; tel. (269) 349-7775; fax (269) 349-9313; e-mail museum@kiarts.org; internet www.kiarts.org; f. 1924; American paintings, sculpture and ceramics, American and European works on paper from 16th century and later, photography, oceanic objects, Pre-Columbian gold and ceramics, African art and E Asian art; library of 11,000 vols, 350 DVDs and video cassettes, 40 art-related periodicals; Exec. Dir JAMES BRIDENSTINE; Pres. COURTENAY VANDERMOLEN; Sec. LINDA DUNN; Treas. BRIAN HUDSON.

Kelsey Museum of Archaeology: 434 S State St, Ann Arbor, MI 48109-1390; tel. (734) 764-9304; e-mail kelseymuse@umich.edu; internet www.lsa.umich.edu/kelsey; f. 1928, present name and status 1953; attached to Univ. of Michigan; colln of 100,000 Greek, Near E and Roman artefacts (painted Egyptian mummy coffin, magical amulets from the ancient Near E, array of glass vessels, Greek pottery, Roman sculptures, and large-scale watercolour representation of Villa of the Mysteries murals from ancient Pompeii); excavation records and archive of 25,000 archaeological and fine arts photographs; library of 20,000 vols; Dir SHARON HERBERT.

Michigan State University Museum: W Circle Dr., East Lansing, MI 48824; tel. (517) 355-2370; fax (517) 432-2846; e-mail pr@museum.msu.edu; internet www.museum.msu.edu; f. 1857; colln of 1m. archaeological items, 25,000 ethnographic artefacts, 63,000 historical and cultural artefacts, 300 quilts and 5,000 files on Michigan quilts and quilters, cultural and folk art, 38,500 natural science specimens, 100,000 historical 3-D objects, archive of documents and photographs; temporary exhibitions; Dir GARY MORGAN.

Muskegon Museum of Art: 296 W Webster Ave, Muskegon, MI 49440; tel. (231) 720-2570; fax (231) 720-2585; internet www.muskegonartmuseum.org; f. 1912, present name 1980; Exec. Dir JUDITH HAYNER; Chair. LARRY HINES; Treas. TRIP JOHNSON; Sec. STACIE BEHLER; Sr Curator E. JANE CONNELL.

Saginaw Art Museum: 1126 N Michigan Ave, Saginaw, MI 48602-4763; tel. (989) 754-2491; fax (989) 754-9387; e-mail staff@saginawartmuseum.org; internet www.saginawartmuseum.org; f. 1948, present name 1967; colln of 2,500 art and artefacts spanning 4,500 years of art history; American and European artworks incl. decorative arts, drawings, MSS, paintings, prints, sculpture and textiles from 15th to 20th centuries; Asian art colln of decorative art, paintings, sculpture, textiles and woodcuts from China, India, Japan and Korea; modern and contemporary art holdings incl. prints, drawings and photographs by Robert Estes, Jasper Johns, and Claes Oldenburg and regional artists; library of 1,200 vols (incl. books, catalogues and periodicals); Deputy Dir and Curator RYAN KALTENBACH; Pres. CLARENCE RIVETTE; Sec. CHRISTINE HOFFMAN; Treas. LINDY MORLEY.

The Henry Ford: 20900 Oakwood Blvd, Dearborn, MI 48124-5029; tel. (313) 982-6001; internet www.thehenryford.org; f. 1929; indoor and outdoor museum of US history from European settlement to the present; domestic life, agriculture and industry, leisure and entertainment, transportation and communication; historic structures; incl. Henry Ford Museum, Greenfield Village, Ford Rouge Factory Tour, IMAX Theatre and Benson Ford Research Center; library: 37,600 books, 146,000 periodicals, 18,500 trade catalogues, 9,000 linear ft of archival material incl. records of the Ford Motor Co, 1m. photographic images and 50,000 graphic items; Chair. S. EVAN WEINER; Pres. and Sec. PATRICIA E. MOORADIAN; Treas. RALPH J. GERSON.

University of Michigan Museum of Art: 525 S State St, Ann Arbor, MI 48109-1354; tel. (734) 764-0395; fax (734) 764-3731; e-mail umma-press@umich.edu; internet www.umma.umich.edu; f. 1856; colln of 18,000 art works of African, American, Asian, European, Middle E, modern and contemporary, prints, drawings and photographs; 18 galleries; Dir JOSEPH ROSA; Chair. ROBERT BOHLEN; publ. *UMMA magazine* (6 a year).

Minnesota

American Museum of Asmat Art at the University of St. Thomas: c/o Dept of Art History, Univ. of St Thomas, 2115 Summit Ave, St Paul, MN 55105; tel. (651) 962-5512; fax (651) 962-5861; internet www.stthomas .edu/arthistory/asmat; Chair. GERALD D. BRENNAN; Dir Dr JULIE RISSER.

Minneapolis Institute of Arts: 2400 Third Ave S, Minneapolis, MN 55404; tel. (612) 870-3131; fax (612) 870-3004; internet www .artsmia.org; f. 1883 as Minneapolis Soc. of Fine Arts; 7 divs of colln: arts of Africa and Americas; contemporary art; decorative arts, textiles and sculpture; Asian art; paintings; photography and new media; prints and drawings; textiles; library of 60,000 vols mainly on world's history of art; Dir and Pres. KAYWIN FELDMAN.

Minnesota Lakes Maritime Museum: POB 1216, 205 Third Ave W, Alexandria, MN 56308; tel. (320) 759-1114; fax (320) 759-1101; e-mail boat@mnlakesmaritime.org; internet www.mnlakesmaritime.org; Pete and Mado Pederson Gallery: local resort hotel industry history on Lake Minnetonka; Mahan-Zimmerman Gallery: 3 historic launches—The Dungeness, Frieda and Stella and colln of toy boats; Mammel Foundation Exhibit Hall: classic wood boats; M. M. "Bud" Peterson Gallery: restored Larson boats from Mikkelson Colln in Willmar; Summer Porch-Minnesouri Club Exhibit; Fishing Gallery: antique tackle, fish mounts, guide stories and fishing memorabilia; New North Hall-History of Chris-Craft: chronological display of Chris-Craft co history and boat builder and racer Gar Wood Exhibit; Dir BRUCE OLSON.

Minnesota Museum of American Art: Historic Hamm Bldg, 408 St Peter St, Suite 419, St Paul, MN 55102; tel. (651) 797-4057; fax (651) 797-4748; e-mail info@mmaa.org;

internet www.mmaa.org; 3,800 works of art incl. American art from the 19th century to present, with spec. emphasis on paintings of School of the Eight, mid-century studio craft, modern drawings and artists from Minnesota and region; Exec. Dir Dr KRISTIN MAKHOLM; Chair. A. DAVID KELLY; Sec. ANN M. HEIDER; Treas. MATTHEW BELLIN.

Rourke Art Museum: 521 Main Ave, Moorhead, MN 56560; tel. (218) 236-8861; e-mail museum@rourkeart.org; internet www.wix .com/therourke/rourke; f. 1975 as Plains Art Museum, present status 1996; 3,000 contemporary paintings, prints, drawings, sculptures, photographs, African, Native American, Pre-Columbian and Hispanic works of art; Rourke Gallery.

Science Museum of Minnesota: 120 W Kellogg Blvd, St Paul, MN 55102; tel. (651) 221-9444; fax (651) 221-4777; e-mail info@ smm.org; internet www.smm.org; f. 1907; collns and research in anthropology, biology, palaeontology, ethnology, zoology, archaeology, geology and geography; outdoor research centre; a 300-seat omnitheatre; nature centre and public science education centre; Pres. ERIC J. JOLLY; Chair. JOHN M. STANOCH; Sec. RUSS NELSON; Treas. RICHARD O. LUND.

Thunder Bay National Marine Sanctuary: 500 W Fletcher, Alpena, MI 49707; tel. (989) 356-8805; fax (989) 354-0144; e-mail thunderbay@noaa.gov; internet thunderbay .noaa.gov; f. 2000; attached to Nat. Oceanic and Atmospheric Admin. and State of Michigan; protects nationally significant collns of shipwrecks and related maritime heritage resources; historic and archaeological features incl. stations, lighthouses, historic boats and ships, commercial fishing camps, docks and working ports; conducts, supports, promotes, and coordinates geological and archaeological research into prehistoric sites; Chair. STEVE KROLL.

Tweed Museum of Art: Univ. of Minnesota Duluth, 1201 Ordean Court, Duluth, MN 55812-2496; tel. (218) 726-7823; fax (218) 726-8503; e-mail tweed@d.umn.edu; internet www.d.umn.edu/tma; f. 1958; attached to Univ. of Minnesota Duluth; 6,000 art objects on major themes: Stories in Art, People and Places (art works from USA, Italy, Holland, Japan, W Africa and Cuba), Art and Environment and the Language of Art (paintings, sculptures, prints and photographs); 374 images of the Royal Canadian Mounted Police Force; Dir KEN BLOOM; Curator PETER SPOONER.

Walker Art Center: 1750 Hennepin, Minneapolis, MN 55403; tel. (612) 375-7600; fax (612) 375-7618; e-mail info@walkerart.org; internet www.walkerart.org; f. 1927; modern paintings, drawings, prints, sculpture, photography; extensive music, dance, film and video, theatre and education programmes; incl. Minneapolis Sculpture Garden; 800 holdings in Ruben Bentson Film and Video Study Colln; library of 35,000 vols; Dir OLGA VISO.

Weisman Art Museum: 333 E River Rd, Minneapolis, MN 55455; tel. (612) 625-9494; e-mail wamdir@umn.edu; internet weisman .umn.edu; f. 1934, present bldg 1993; attached to Univ. of Minnesota; colln of 1,700 works of art incl. 20th-century American artists, incl. Georgia O'Keeffe and Marsden Hartley, ceramics, Korean furniture and contemporary art; Dir LYNDEL KING; Curator DIANE MULLIN.

Mississippi

DeSoto County Museum: 111 E Commerce St, Hernando, MS 38632; tel. and fax (662) 429-8852; e-mail info@desotomuseum.org;

internet www.desotomuseum.org; artefacts and exhibits featuring history and devt of DeSoto Co dating from 1541 to present; Dir BRIAN HICKS.

Dunn-Seiler Geology Museum: Mississippi State Univ., Dept of Geosciences, 108 Hilbun Hall, POB 5448, Mississippi, MS 39762-5448; tel. (662) 325-3915; fax (662) 325-9423; internet www.geosciences.msstate .edu/museum.htm; f. 1946 as Franklin Seiler Museum, present name 1962; attached to Dept of Geosciences, Mississippi State Univ.; colln incl. mineral, rock, meteorites and fossils; Dir RENEE CLARY; Curator AMY MOE HOFFMAN.

Jacqueline House African American Museum: 1325 Main St, Vicksburg, MS 39183; tel. (601) 636-0941; internet www .stmaryvicksburg.org/jh; f. 1995; 20,000 items incl. photographs, books and MSS on history and culture of people of African descent in Vicksburg-Warren Co; Curator TILLMAN WHITLEY.

Lauren Rogers Museum of Art: POB 1108, Laurel, MS 39441-1108; 565 N Fifth Ave, Laurel, MS 39440; tel. (601) 649-6374; fax (601) 649-6379; e-mail info@lrma.org; internet lrma.org; f. 1923; colln incl. 19th- and 20th-century European and American art, Native American baskets, British Georgian silver and Japanese woodblock prints; library of 10,000 vols; Dir GEORGE BASSI; Curator JILL CHANCEY.

Meridian Museum of Art: 628 25th Ave, Meridian, MS 39301-4917; tel. 601-693-1501; e-mail meridianmuseum@bellsouth.net; internet www.meridianmuseum.org; focus on collecting and displaying work of renowned regional and Mississippi artists; Exec. Dir KATE CHERRY.

Mississippi Armed Forces Museum: Bldg 850, Camp Shelby, MS 39407; tel. (601) 558-2757; internet www.armedforcesmuseum.us; military history museum; exhibits of War of 1812, Mexican War, American Civil War, Spanish-American War, First and Second World War, Korean War, Viet Nam Conflict; Dir CHAD DANIELS.

Mississippi Museum of Art: 380 S Lamar St, Jackson, MS 39201; tel. (601) 960-1515; fax (601) 960-1505; internet www .msmuseumart.org; f. 1911, fmrly Mississippi Art Asscn, present name and status 1979; permanent colln of 3,800 pieces with an emphasis on mid-19th and 20th-century American art; incl. paintings, sculptures, prints, drawings and photographs by Albert Bierstadt, Arthur B. Davies, Robert Henri, George Inness, Georgia O'Keeffe, Thomas Sully, J. A. M. Whistler; photographs and works on paper incl. works by Thomas Hart Benton, Alexander Calder, William Eggleston, Walker Evans, Andy Warhol, Eudora Welty; Annie Laurie Swaim Hearin Memorial Exhibition Series hosts world-class exhibitions every 2 years; Chair. ROY D. CAMPBELL; Dir BETSY BRADLEY; Sec. MAYO FLYNT; Treas. DAVID FOWLER.

Mississippi Museum of Natural Science: 2148 Riverside Dr., Jackson, MS 39202-1353; tel. (601)576-6000; fax (601) 354-7227; e-mail rebeccag@mmns.state.ms.us; internet www .msnaturalscience.org; f. 1932; an aquarium system with over 200 living species of native fish, reptiles, amphibians and aquatic invertebrates; 1,700-sq. ft greenhouse called 'The Swamp' with another 20,000-gallon aquarium, provides a home for alligators, turtles, fish and a lush native plant garden; 200-seat auditorium, library, biological archives; 870,000 specimens; Chair. BRYAN JONES; Exec. Dir Dr SAM POLLES; Museum Dir LIBBY HARTFIELD.

University of Mississippi Museum: POB 1848, Oxford, MS 38677; tel. (662) 915-7073; fax (662) 915-7035; internet museum.olemiss .edu; f. 1939 as Mary Buie Museum, present status 1974; colln incl. S folk art, Greek and Roman antiquities and American fine art; 500 19th-century scientific instruments; 200 art works by Theora Hamblett; Dir WILLIAM PITTMAN ANDREWS.

Walter Anderson Museum of Art: 510 Washington Ave, Ocean Springs, MS 39564-4632; tel. (228) 872-3164; fax (228) 875-4494; e-mail wama@walterandersonmuseum.org; internet www.walterandersonmuseum.org; f. 1991; watercolors, drawings, oils, block prints, ceramics and carvings by the 3 Anderson brothers; Exec. Dir LINDA BLOOM; Pres. MORRIS STRICKLAND; Sec. LORI CARTER; Treas. Dr LARRY SHOEMAKER.

Missouri

Albrecht-Kemper Museum of Art: 2818 Frederick Ave, St Joseph, MO 64506; tel. (816) 233-7003; fax (816) 233-3413; e-mail frontdesk@albrecht-kemper.org; internet albrecht-kemper.org; f. 1913, present name and status 1991; collns of 18th-, 19th- and 20th-century American art in the Mid W region, incl. colonial portraits, American landscape paintings and American Impressionism; Dir TERRY OLDHAM.

Daum Museum of Contemporary Art: 3201 W 16th St, Sedalia, MO 65301; tel. (660) 530-5888; fax (660) 530-5890; e-mail info@daummuseum.org; internet www .daummuseum.org; f. 2002; attached to State Fair Community College in Sedalia; 1,000 objects of modern and contemporary works of art and design, incl. abstract paintings, drawings, prints, works in clay and sculpture created since mid-20th century; Dir THOMAS PICHÉ, JR.

Kansas City Museum: 3218 Gladstone Blvd, Kansas City, MO 64123-1199; tel. (816) 483-8300; internet kansascitymuseum .org; f. 1940; incl. Corinthian Hall, Beaux Arts limestone residence, Carriage House, StoryTarium in the fmr Conservatory; administered by Kansas City Museum Asscn; features films, lectures and other history-related programming on Kansas City's local and regional history; Dir CHRISTOPHER LEITCH.

Kemper Museum of Contemporary Art: 4420 Warwick Blvd, Kansas City, MO 64111; tel. (816) 753-5784; fax (816) 753-5806; e-mail visitorservices@kemperart.org; internet www.kemperart.org; f. 1994; colln of 1,000 works, incl. painting, sculpture, installations, prints and works on paper, photography and time-based media; works by Louise Bourgeois, Christian Boltanski, Manuel Neri, Jasper Johns, Helen Frankenthaler, Frank Stella, Joan Mitchell, Jackson Pollock, Robert Rauschenberg, Hung Liu, Robert Motherwell, Deborah Butterfield, Fairfield Porter, Wayne Thiebaud, Grace Hartigan, William Wegman, Red Grooms, Georgia O'Keeffe, Christopher Brown, Willem de Kooning, and Robert Mapplethorpe; 3 museum locations; Chair. CROSBY KEMPER; Dir and CEO RACHAEL BLACKBURN COZAD.

Mildred Lane Kemper Art Museum: c/o Washington Univ., 1 Brookings Dr., POB 1214, St Louis, MO 63130; tel. (314) 935-5490; fax (314) 935-7282; e-mail kemperartmuseum@wustl.edu; internet

wustl.edu/community/visitors/tour/danforth/ kemper-art-museum.html; f. 1881 as St Louis School and Museum of Fine Arts, present name 2006; attached to Washington Univ.; 19th-, 20th- and 21st-century European and American paintings, sculptures, prints, installations and photographs; colln also incl. some Egyptian and Greek antiquities and more than 100 Old Master prints; Dir and Chief Curator Dr SABINE ECKMANN.

Museum of Art and Archaeology: 1 Pickard Hall, Columbia, MO 65211-1420; tel. (573) 882-3591; fax (573) 884-4039; e-mail museumuser@missouri.edu; internet maa .missouri.edu; f. 1957 as Study Collns for Art History and Archaeology, present name 1961; attached to Univ. of Missouri; colln of art works and artefacts of Greek, Roman and Near Eastern, ancient Egypt and Byzantium, European and American art from 15th century to the present, incl. Samuel H. Kress Study Colln of European paintings, Asian, African, Ancient Americas and Oceanic cultures; incl. archives; Dir ALEX BARKER; publ. *MVSE* (1 a year).

National World War I Museum at Liberty Memorial: 100 W 26th St, Kansas City, MO 64108; tel. (816) 784-1918; e-mail info@ theworldwar.org; internet www.theworldwar .org; f. 1921 as Liberty Memorial, present status 2004; colln of 55,000 items in museum, library and archives; exhibits weapons, tanks, soldiers' uniforms, series of trenches, chronology walls giving data about the war; incl. memory hall; promotes research on First World War; 60,000 archival documents; library of 6,000 vols; Pres. and CEO BRIAN ALEXANDER; Chair. JAMES H. BERNARD, JR; Sec. JEANNETTE NICHOLS.

Nelson-Atkins Museum of Art: 4525 Oak St, Kansas City, MO 64111; tel. (816) 751-1278; fax (816) 561-4011; e-mail press@ nelson-atkins.org; internet www .nelson-atkins.org; f. 1933; depts of Asian art, prints, photography, modern and contemporary art, American art, American Indian art, European art, decorative arts, ancient art, African art, Chinese art, Japanese art, S and SE Asian art, Kansas City Sculpture Park (incl. monumental bronzes by Henry Moore); works by Thomas Hart Benton; library of 180,000 vols, 650 current periodicals; Dir and CEO JULIÁN ZUGAZAGOITIA.

Saint Louis Art Museum: 1 Fine Arts Dr., Forest Park, St Louis, MO 63110-1380; tel. (314) 721-0072; fax (314) 721-6172; e-mail publicrelations@slam.org; internet www .slam.org; f. 1879; publicly owned colln of about 35,000 art objects; important collns of Oceanic art, pre-Columbian and American art, ancient Chinese bronzes, and European and American art of the late 19th and 20th centuries, with particular strength in 20th-century German painting, Asian art, decorative arts and design, contemporary and modern art, Islamic art, African art, photographs, prints and drawings; temporary exhibitions; library of 100,000 vols, 425 periodicals; Chair. BARBARA W. ROBERTS; Dir BRENT R. BENJAMIN; Sec. CHERI J. FROMM; Treas. JOAN O'NEILL; publ. *Magazine*.

Springfield Art Museum: 1111 E Brookside Dr., Springfield, MO 65807; tel. (417) 837-5700; e-mail artmuseum@springfieldmo .gov; internet www.springfieldmo.gov/art; f. 1928, present status 1958; colln of 8,895 art objects incl. 19th-, 20th- and 21st-century American paintings, watercolour sculpture

and prints; Dir JERRY A. BERGER; Pres. JOAN MENCHETTI; Sec. NANCY DAILEY.

State Historical Society of Missouri: 1020 Lowry St, Columbia, MO 65201; tel. (573) 882-7083; e-mail shsofmo@umsystem .edu; internet shs.umsystem.edu/art; colln of paintings, engravings and lithographs by George Caleb Bingham and Thomas Hart Benton; editorial cartoon colln incl. drawings by Daniel Fitzpatrick, S. J. Ray, Bill Mauldin, Don Hesse and Tom Engelhardt; library of 460,000 vols, 500,000 MSS, 800 reels of microfilmed MSS, 150,000 state archival records and 2,900 maps; Exec. Dir, Sec. and Librarian GARY KREMER; Curator JOAN STACK; Pres. STEPHEN N. LIMBAUGH, JR; Treas. SABRINA MCDONNELL.

Montana

Blaine County Museum: 501 Indiana St, Chinook, MT 59523; tel. (406) 357-2590; e-mail blmuseum@mtintouch.net; internet www.blainecountymuseum.com; artefacts, photographs and documents depicting history of Blaine county; Exec. Dir JUDE SHEPPARD.

C. M. Russell Museum: 400 13th St N, Great Fall, MT 59401; tel. (406) 727-8787; internet cmrussell.org; artwork concerning the culture of the W during the late 1800s and early 1900s, incl. many works by Russell; Exec. Dir DARRELL BEAUCHAMP; Chief Curator SARAH BURT; Chair. JOE MASTERSON.

Holter Museum of Art: 12E, Lawrence, Helena, MT 59601; tel. (406) 442-6400; internet www.holtermuseum.org; f. 1987; visual arts exhibition programme that incl. all media; Exec. Dir KAREN BOHLINGER; Co-Pres. TERESA OLCOTT COHEA; Co-Pres. KATHERINE ORR; Sec. SIDNEY ARMSTRONG; Treas. DAVE HUNTER.

Huntley Project Museum of Irrigated Agriculture: POB 353, 770 Railroad Highway, Huntley, MT 59037; tel. (406) 348-2533; e-mail curator@huntleyprojectmuseum.org; internet www.huntleyprojectmuseum.org; history of the homesteading era; records and photographs of the Huntley Project Communities; Curator and Dir MELISSA KOCH; Pres. JAMES KNAPP; Sec. MARY KNAPP; Treas. MARVIN HAMMERSMARK.

Montana Cowboy Hall of Fame: 218 Third Ave, So - Suite C, Wolf Point, MT 59201; tel. (406) 653-3800; internet www .montanacowboyfame.com; f. 1991; collns concerning W culture and heritage; Exec. Dir CHRISTY STENSLAND; Pres. DuWAYNE WILSON; Sec. KATHY MCLANE; Treas. MICHAEL NEUTGENS.

Montana Historical Society Museum: POB 201201, 225 N Roberts, Helena, MT 59620-1201; tel. (406) 444-2694; e-mail mhslibrary@mt.gov; internet mhs.mt.gov/ museum; f. 1865; 50,000 fine art, historical, archaeological and ethnological artefacts that pertain to Montana and its adjoining geographic region; Native American Colln of 6,000 objects; incl. original Governor's Mansion and Moss Mansion historic house; Pres. STEVE LOZAR; Dir BRUCE WHITTENBERG; State Historic Preservation Officer Dr MARK BAUMLER; Sr Curator JENNIFER BOTTOMLY-O'LOONEY; publ. *Montana The Magazine of Western History* (4 a year).

Museum of the Rockies: 600 W Kagy Blvd, Bozeman, MT 59717; tel. (406) 994-2251; e-mail museum@montana.edu; internet museumoftherockies.org; f. 1957 as McGill Museum, present name 1965; attached to Montana State Univ.; cultural and natural history; palaeontology colln; on-site 19th-century farm; incl. planetarium, dinosaur complex and tyrannosaurus rex; fed. repository for fossils; Dean and Exec. Dir SHELDON MCKAMEY; Pres. PAT DOWNEY.

Paris Gibson Square Museum of Art: 1400 First Ave N, Great Falls, MT 59401,; tel. (406) 727-8255; fax (406) 727-8256; e-mail info@the-square.org; internet www.the-square.org; f. 1977; 611 pieces, incl. NW regional contemporary art, American Indian contemporary art and American self-taught art; Exec. Dir KATHY LEAR; Curator of Art COREY GROSS; Pres. REBECCA BOGDEN-RICHARDS; Sec. JULIE EASTON; Treas. MICHELLE KLUNDT.

Rocky Mountain Museum of Military History: c/o Tate Jones, POB 7263, Missoula, MT 59807; tel. (406) 549-5346; e-mail info@fortmissoula.org; internet www.fortmissoula.org; f. 1936; commemoration and study of the US armed services: from the Frontier Period to the war on terrorism; Exec. Dir TATE JONES; Pres. GARY R. LANCASTER; Treas. BO FOSTER.

Ursuline Centre: 2300 Central Ave, Great Falls, MT 59401; tel. (406) 452-8585; fax (406) 452-8586; e-mail ursuline@in-tch.com; internet www.ursulinecentre.com; f. 1912; Indian relics, antique furnishings, musical instruments and other artefacts; colln of over 100 years of history of the Ursuline Sisters, their lives and how they helped shape the history of Montana; Dir HARRY THOLEN.

World Museum of Mining: POB 33, 155 Museum Way, Butte, MT 59703; tel. 406-723-7211; e-mail info@miningmuseum.org; internet www.miningmuseum.org; f. 1963; 7,000 catalogued photos; company day books, maps, diaries, engineering diagrams, journals, log books and payroll records; Exec. Dir TINA DAVIS; Pres. BOB MCCARTHY; Sec. COURTNEY MCKEE; Treas. LINDA ROSIN.

Yellowstone Art Museum: 401 N 27th St, Billings, MT 59101; tel. (406) 256-6804; e-mail artinfo@artmuseum.org; internet yellowstone.artmuseum.org; f. 1964 as Yellowstone Arts Center, present name 1998; contemporary and historic art; Montana Colln of 1,925 regional artefacts; Virginia Snook Colln incl. illustrations from Will James, paintings and drawings from Joseph Henry Sharp, Charles M. Russell; Exec. Dir and Acting Curator ROBYN G. PETERSON; Pres. LINDA SHELHAMER; Sec. GLADYS PHELPS; Treas. SUSAN SULLIVAN.

Nebraska

Bone Creek Museum of Agrarian Art: 575 E St, David City, NE 68632; tel. (402) 367-4488; internet www.bonecreek.org; f. 2007; colln of art works of Agrarian Artists Winslow Homer, Harvey Dunn, John Steuart Curry, Thomas Hart Benton, Robert Gwathmey, Birger Sandzen, Augustus Dunbier, Peter Helck, Robert Wesley Amick, Gary Ernest Smith, Robert Bateman, Mark L. Moseman, Charles Banks Wilson, Jane Scott, Raymond Knaub, Jim Hamil, Hal Holoun, Robert Sudlow and John Roush; organizes artist talks and workshops; Pres. ANNA NOLAN; Vice-Pres. and Chief Curator MARK L. MOSEMAN; Sec. ALLEN COVAULT; Treas. MICHAEL MORAVEC.

Great Plains Art Museum: c/o Univ. of Nebraska-Lincoln, 1155 Q St, Hewit Place, POB 880250, Lincoln, NE 68588-0250; tel. (402) 472-6220; fax (402) 472-0463; e-mail gpac@unl.edu; internet www.unl.edu/plains/gallery/gallery.shtml; f. 1981; attached to Center for Great Plain Studies, Univ. of Nebraska-Lincoln; colln of bronze sculptures, paintings and drawings, other works on paper, photographs; artwork by Albert Bierstadt, William de la Montagne Cary, Robert F. Gilder, William Henry Jackson, Frederic Remington, Charles M. Russell and Olaf

Wieghorst; 20th Native American paintings from Patricia J. and Stanley H. Broder; Richard Lane colln of Western fiction and history; Regina Colln of Canadian Plains literature, yman Byxbe, Ray Ellis, John Falter, Michael Forsberg, Charles Guildner, Veryl Goodnight, Cliff Hollestelle, Laurie Houseman-Whitehawk, Keith Jacobshagen, Ted Long, Herb Mignery, Andrew Peters, Martha and Del Pettigrew, Jackson Pollock, Norman Rockwell, and Grant Wood; library of 7,500 vols; Museum Administrator and Curator AMBER MOHR.

Hastings Museum of Natural and Cultural History: POB 1286, Hastings, NE 68902; 1330 N Burlington Ave, Hastings, NE 68900; tel. (402) 461-4629; e-mail museum@hastingsmuseum.org; internet www.hastingsmuseum.org; f. 1927; incl. J. M. McDonald Planetarium, Groundwater Discovery Adventure and theatre; colln of species of animals set in their natural habitats incl. Whooping cranes; colln tells history of the early inhabitants of the Nebraska; Dir REBECCA MATTICKS.

Joslyn Art Museum: 2200 Dodge St, Omaha, NE 68102-1292; tel. (402) 342-3300; fax (402) 342-2376; internet www.joslyn.org; f. 1931; colln of ancient, European, American, American Indian, art of the American W, Latin American, Asian, modern and contemporary works of art; Peter Kiewit Foundation Sculpture Garden; Exec. Dir and CEO Dr JACK F. BECKER; Chair. JOHN P. NELSON; Sec. BRYAN E. SLONE; Treas. KIRK L. KELLNER; Chief Curator TOBY JUROVICS.

Lester F. Larsen Tractor Museum: POB 830833, Lincoln, NE 68583; tel. (402) 472-8389; fax (402) 472-8367; e-mail tractormuseum2@unl.edu; internet tractormuseum.unl.edu; f. 1998; attached to Univ. of Nebraska-Lincoln; collects, preserves, researches and interprets the traditions and technologies of agriculture; Curator Prof. LOUIS I. LEVITICUS.

Museum of Nebraska Art: 2401 Central Ave, Kearney, NE 68847; tel. (308) 865-8559; fax (308) 865-8104; e-mail mona@unk.edu; internet monet.unk.edu/mona; f. 1976 as Nebraska Art Colln, present name and status 1986; 5,000 works by George Catlin, early Nebraskans Robert Henri and J. Laurie Wallace, modern era artists Grant Reynard and John Falter, Nebraska wildlife artwork by John James Audubon; Cliff Hillegass Sculpture Garden; Dir AUDREY S. KAUDERS; Pres. SUE TALLMAN; Sec. DEANNA BOSSELMAN; Treas. TAMI HELLMAN; Curator TELIZA V. RODRIGUEZ.

Nebraska State Historical Society: POB 82554, Lincoln, NE 68501-2554; 1500 R St, Lincoln, NE 68501; tel. (402) 471-4754; fax (402) 471-3100; e-mail nshs.museum@nebraska.gov; internet www.nebraskahistory.org/museum; f. 1878; state-wide network of historical sites and museums; incl. Chimney Rock Nat. Historic Site, Fort Robinson Museums, Gerald R. Ford Conservation Center, John G. Neihardt State Historic Site, K St Govt Records Facility, Nebraska History Museum, Neligh Mill State Historic Site, Senator George W. Norris State Historic Site, Thomas P. Kennard House Nebraska Statehood Memorial, Willa Cather State Historic Site; documentation of bldg first transcontinental railroad through Union Pacific Railroad colln; 300,000 photographs, incl. colln of sod house photographs taken by Solomon D. Butcher; library of 80,000 vols, 12,000 film and video reels, 35,000 reels of microfilm with state newspapers dating from 1854 to present; Dir and CEO MICHAEL J. SMITH; Sr Curator LAURA MOONEY; publs *Nebraska*

History News (4 a year), *Nebraska History* (4 a year).

Sheldon Museum of Art: POB 880300, Lincoln, NE 68588-0300; 12 and R Sts, Lincoln, NE 68588-0300; tel. (402) 472-2461; fax (402) 472-4258; internet www.sheldonartmuseum.org; f. 1888; houses collns of Sheldon Art Asscn (f. 1888) and Univ. of Nebraska (f. 1929); 12,000 works of art in all media, incl. 19th century landscape and still life, American Impressionism, early Modernism, geometric abstraction, Abstract Expressionism, pop, minimalism and contemporary art; 30 monumental sculptures by Gaston Lachaise, Jacques Lipchitz, Claes Oldenburg and Coosje van Bruggen, David Smith, William Tucker, Bryan Hunt, Mark di Suvero, Michael Heizer and Richard Serra; library of 10,000 vols; Dir Dr JORGE DANIEL VENECIANO.

Strategic Air & Space Museum: 28210 W Park Highway, Ashland, NE 68003; tel. (402) 944-3100; fax (402) 944-3160; e-mail llessmann@strategicairandspace.com; internet www.sasmuseum.com; f. 1959; exhibits photographs, letters and personal mementos left at Vietnam Memorial Wall in Washington, DC; artefacts incl. flight suits, flown shuttle tire and cameras used by Gemini astronaut, Wally Schirra; Linebacker II display outlines men and machines of the US Seventh Air Force and US Navy Task Force 77 that took part in bombing missions on Haiphong and Hanoi, North Vietnam on December 1972; commemorates the Martin Bomber Plant; Doolittle's Tokyo Raiders; equipments of the 9th Air Force; Exec. Dir SCOTT TARRY; Chair. W. DAVID SCOTT; Sec. NICK BAXTER.

Stuhr Museum of the Prairie Pioneer: 3133 W Highway 34, Grand Island, NE 68801; tel. (308) 385-5316; e-mail info@stuhrmuseum.org; internet www.stuhrmuseum.org; f. 1961; colln of historical objects and information relating to life in Nebraska's prairie communities from the 1840s through 1920; 150,000 historical artefacts, incl. 60 historic bldgs and railroad equipment; archives and research library; Exec. Dir JOE BLACK; Pres. DENSEL RASMUSSEN; Exec. Sec. SHARON MANKIN; Treas. MARK HOCK.

University of Nebraska State Museum: 307 Morrill Hall, Univ. of Nebraska-Lincoln, Lincoln, NE 68588-0338; tel. (402) 472-2642; e-mail afox1@unl.edu; internet www.museum.unl.edu; incl. Mueller Planetarium; educational programming; collns and research in following: anthropology, botany, entomology, invertebrate palaeontology, parasitology, vertebrate palaeontology, zoology; Dir PRISCILLA C. GREW.

Affiliated Museums:

Ashfall Fossil Beds State Historical Park: 6930 517th Ave, Royal, NE 68773; tel. (402) 893-2000; e-mail ashfall2@unl.edu; internet ashfall.unl.edu; fossil site of int. significance left intact for public viewing; Superintendent RICK OTTO.

Trailside Museum of Natural History: Fort Robinson State Park, Crawford, NE 69339; tel. (308) 665-2929; internet trailside.unl.edu; f. 1961; geological and natural history; publ. *The Mammoth* (4 a year).

Nevada

Fleischmann Planetarium & Science Center: POB 272, 1650 N Virginia St, Univ. of Nevada, Reno, Reno, NV 89557; tel. (775) 784-4812; fax (775) 784-4822; internet planetarium.unr.nevada.edu; f. 1964 as Fleischmann Atmospherium-Planetarium; attached to Univ. of Nevada, Reno;

public star shows and large-format films; Spitz SciDome digital projector; Dir and Assoc. Vice-Provost for Extended Studies Dr DEE HENDERSON.

Hispanic Museum of Nevada: 3680 S Maryland Parkway, Suite 140, Las Vegas, NV 89169; tel. (702) 773-2203; e-mail hispanicmuseumnv@hotmail.com; internet www.hispanicmuseumnv.com; f. 1991; education and resources of the diverse Hispanic cultures and traditions to enhance intercultural understanding among community mems; Founder and Exec. Dir LYNNETTE SAWYER; Sec. and Treas. FELICIA ALAVA.

International Scouting Museum: Suite 2, Krolak Center, 2915 W Charleston Blvd, Las Vegas, NV 89102; tel. (702) 878-7268; internet www.worldscoutingmuseum.org; f. 1996; colln of Scouting memorabilia; Exec. Dir R. LYNN HORNE; Pres. GWEN KROGEN; Treas. JACQUES BEHAR; Sec. DEBORAH MARTZ.

Marjorie Barrick Museum: Univ. of Nevada, Las Vegas, POB 4009 4505 S Maryland Parkway, Las Vegas, NV 89154-4009; tel. (702) 895-3381; fax (702) 895-5737; e-mail barrick.museum@unlv.edu; internet barrickmuseum.unlv.edu; f. 1969, present name 1989; attached to Univ. of Nevada, Las Vegas; cultural objects concerning the American SW, Mesoamerica and their environs; Pre-Columbian Colln: objects from nearly every culture of Pre-Columbian Latin America as well as Mexican dance masks and retablos; Guatemalan, Bolivian, and Navajo textiles; Paiute and Hopi basketry; Navajo jewellery; Programme Dir AURORE GIGUET; Sec. TORI KLEIN.

National Atomic Testing Museum: 755 E Flamingo Rd, Las Vegas, NV 89119; tel. (702) 794-5151; e-mail atm@atomictestingmuseum .org; internet www.atomictestingmuseum .org; Exec. Dir ALLAN PALMER; Curator KAREN GREEN.

Nevada Museum of Art: 160 W Liberty St, Reno, NV 89501; tel. (775) 329-3333; fax (775) 329-1541; e-mail art@nevadaart.org; internet www.nevadaart.org; f. 1931 as Nevada Art Gallery, present name 1988; altered landscape incl. 600 pieces of contemporary landscape photography; contemporary colln focuses on w coast and Nevada-based artists; Sierra Nevada/Great Basin colln surveys artists' impressions of the landscape over 150 years; historical colln incl. paintings and sculptures; work-ethic themed E. L. Wiegand Colln; Curator of Exhibitions and Collns ANN M. WOLFE; Exec. Dir and CEO DAVID B. WALKER; Chair. JOHN WORTHINGTON; Sec. JENNIFER L. PATTERSON; Treas. RON ZIDECK.

Nevada State Museum and Historical Society: 309 S Valley View Blvd, Las Vegas, NV 89107; tel. (702) 486-5205; fax (702) 486-5172; biological sciences, earth sciences, regional history; Dir DAVID MILLMAN.

Walker African American Museum: 705 W Van Buren, Las Vegas, NV 89106; tel. (702) 399-8016; e-mail walkeraamuseum1@ yahoo.com; internet www .churchesinlasvegas.com/walkermuseum; books, magazines, dolls, stamps, postcards, trade cards, figurines, statues, sports and political items, newspapers and clippings, signs, church histories, biographies, prints, posters, painting, etc. about the history of people of African descent belonging to Nevada.

W. M. Keck Earth Science and Mineral Engineering Museum: Mackay School of Earth Sciences and Engineering, Univ. of Nevada, Reno, 1664 N Virginia St, Reno, NV 89557; tel. (775) 784-4528; fax (775) 784-1766; internet www.mines.unr.edu/museum; f. 1908, present name 1988; colln of fossils, minerals, ores and photographs related to mining; emphasis on early NV mining history; Mackay Silver Colln; Dir RUSS FIELDS.

New Hampshire

American Independence Museum: 1 Governors Lane, Exeter, NH 03833; tel. (603) 772-2622; fax (603) 772-0861; e-mail info@ independencemuseum.org; internet www .independencemuseum.org; f. 1991; focus on study, research, education and interpretation of American Revolution; colln incl. 2 rare drafts of the US Constitution, American furnishings, ceramics, silver, textiles and military ephemera; museum comprises 18th-century Ladd-Gilman House and Folsom Tavern; Exec. Dir GAIL NESSELL COLGLAZIER; Curator WENDY BERGERON.

Currier Museum of Art: 150 Ash St, Manchester, NH 03104-4393; tel. (603) 669-6144; fax (603) 669-7194; e-mail visitor@ currier.org; internet www.currier.org; f. 1929; 12,000 American and European works of art featuring decorative arts, photographs and sculptures; permanent colln incl. works by Picasso, Matisse, Monet, O'Keeffe, Calder and Wyeth; owns Frank Lloyd Wright's 1950 Zimmerman House; year-round exhibitions, tours and classical music performances; library of 15,000 vols; Dir and CEO SUSAN STRICKLER; Pres. DAVID A. JENSEN.

Exeter Historical Society: POB 924, 47 Front St, Exeter, NH 03833; tel. (603) 778-2335; e-mail info@exeterhistory.org; internet www.exeterhistory.org; f. 1931; colln on local history; Native American artefacts and 1740 English Common Press; Chair. LIONEL INGRAM; Curator BARBARA RIMKUNAS.

Hood Museum of Art: Dartmouth College, Hanover, NH 03755; tel. (603) 646-2808; fax (603) 646-1400; e-mail hood.museum@ dartmouth.edu; internet hoodmuseum .dartmouth.edu; f. 1985; attached to Dartmouth College; 65,000 works of art and artifacts of different cultures and historical periods; Dir MICHAEL TAYLOR.

Laconia Historical & Museum Society: POB 1126, Laconia, NH 03247; 695 Main St, Laconia, NH 03246; tel. (603) 527-1278; fax (603) 527-1277; e-mail lhmslpl@metrocast .net; internet www.laconiahistorical.org; f. 1998 by merger of Laconia Historical Soc. (f. 1951) with Laconia Museum Soc. (f. 1994); Jewett colln: 10,000 objects incl. photographs, MSS, etc. spanning 200 years; Pres. DEBBIE FRAWLEY DRAKE; Exec. Dir BRENDA M. POLIDORO; Curator LINDSAY BURKE.

Mariposa Museum & World Culture Center: 26 Main St, Peterborough, NH 03458; tel. (603) 924-4555; fax (603) 924-7893; e-mail admin@mariposamuseum.org; internet www.mariposamuseum.org; f. 2001; colln of folkart, textiles, costumes, art, puppets and instruments from 6 continents; Chair. S. MARTIN; Exec. Dir (vacant).

Millyard Museum: 200 Bedford St, Manchester, NH 03101; tel. (603) 622-7531; e-mail history@manchesterhistoric.org; internet www.manchesterhistoric.org/mill .htm; f. 1896; attached to Manchester Historic Asscn; colln incl. 600,000 documents and artefacts on local history.

Museum of Art: Univ. of New Hampshire, Paul Creative Arts Center, 30 Academic Way, Durham, NH 03824-3538; tel. (603) 862-3712; fax (603) 862-2191; e-mail museum .of.art@unh.edu; internet www.unh.edu/moa; f. 1960; attached to Univ. of New Hampshire; 1,600 historical and modern works by American, European and other artists; colln of 19th- and 20th-century prints and drawings; 200 Japanese wood block prints; Dir KRISTINA L. DUROCHER.

University of New Hampshire Museum: Room 103, Dimond Library, 18 Library Way, Durham, NH 03824; tel. (603) 862-1081; internet www.izaak.unh.edu/museum; f. 1966; colln incl. over 1,000 univ. memorabilia and historic artefacts dating from 1940s to present; Curator DALE VALENA.

Woodman Institute Museum: POB 1916, Dover, NH 03821; 182 Central Ave, Dover, NH 03820-4058; tel. (603) 742-1038; e-mail contact@woodmaninstitutemuseum.org; internet woodmaninstitutemuseum.org; f. 1916; 4 historic bldgs: colonial garrison house (1675), Hale House (1813), Keefe House (1825) and Woodman House (1818); colln incl. 800 items of area history, 1,300 specimens of minerals, Civil War artefacts and memorabilia.

Wright Museum of WWII History: POB 1212, 77 Center St, Wolfeboro, NH 03894; tel. (603) 569-1212; fax (603) 569-6326; e-mail info@wrightmuseum.org; internet www .wrightmuseum.org; f. 1983; artefacts of Second World War incl. vintage military vehicles and Army Air Corps mission map; Exec. Dir NORMAN STEVENS.

New Jersey

African Art Museum: 23 Bliss Ave, Tenafly, NJ 07670; tel. (201) 894-8611; e-mail museum@smafathers.org; internet smafathers.org/museum; f. 1980; attached to Soc. of African Missions; sub-Saharan sculpture and painting, costumes, textiles and decorative arts, religion and folklore; Dir BOB KOENIG.

Atlantic City Art Center: POB 1061, Atlantic City, NJ 08401; New Jersey Ave and Boardwalk, Atlantic City, NJ 08401; tel. (609) 347-5837; fax (609) 347-5844; e-mail acartcenter@aol.com; internet www .acartcenter.org; f. 1908; features artwork by contemporary artists and artisans of nat., regional and local level; Exe. Dir KALEEM SHABAZZ.

Belskie Museum of Art & Science: 280 High St, Closter, NJ 07624; tel. (201) 768-0286; fax (201) 768-4220; e-mail contact@ belskiemuseum.com; internet www .belskiemuseum.com; f. 1993; preserves, houses and exhibits works of Abram Belskie, a sculptor and medical illustrator.

Camp Olden Civil War Round Table & Museum, Inc.: POB 10565, Hamilton, NJ 08690; 2202 Kuser Rd, Hamilton, NJ; e-mail president@campolden.org; internet www .campolden.org; f. 1992; exhibits incl. uniforms, weapons, equipment and material relating to the experience of the common soldier in the Civil War; Pres. BRUCE SIRAK; Sec. MARY ANN SIRAK; Treas. CONNIE DAVIS; Curator BRUCE SMITH.

Franklin Mineral Museum: 32 Evans St, Franklin, NJ 07416; tel. (973) 827-3481; e-mail fmm1954@earthlink.net; internet www.franklinmineralmuseum.com; f. 1964; archaeological, geological, historical, mineralogical themes; 4,000 mineral specimens on display; a life size mine replica.

Hiram Blauvelt Art Museum: 705 Kinderkamack Rd, Oradell, NJ 07649; tel. (201) 261-0012; e-mail info@blauveltartmuseum.com; internet www.blauveltartmuseum.com; f. 1957; f. as a natural history museum; art of contemporary wildlife artists; Dir MARIJANE SINGER.

Hunterdon Art Museum: Seven Lower Center St, Clinton, NJ 08809-1303; tel. (908) 735-8415; fax (908) 735-8416; internet www.hunterdonartmuseum.org; f. 1952; contemporary art and design, incl. works on paper from the 1930s to the present; spec. colln: Anne Steele Marsh Colln; Dir of Exhibitions JONATHAN GREENE.

Jane Voorhees Zimmerli Art Museum: Rutgers, The State Univ. of New Jersey, 71 Hamilton St, New Brunswick, NJ 08901-1248; tel. (732) 932-7237; fax (732) 932-8201; internet www.zimmerlimuseum.rutgers.edu; attached to Rutgers, The State Univ. of New Jersey; 60,000 works of art, incl. Russian and Soviet art, French 19th-century art and American 19th- and 20th-century art; library of 4,000 vols; Dir SUZANNE DELEHANTY.

Macculloch Hall Historical Museum: 45 Macculloch Ave, Morristown, NJ 07960; tel. (973) 538-2404; fax (973) 538-9428; e-mail info@macullochhall.org; internet www .macullochhall.org; f. 1949; Thomas Nast's original works in the US; 50 specimens of French, German, English and Chinese export porcelain dating from 750 to 1850; presidential colln incl. silver, porcelain, letters, images, documents, and a Thanksgiving proclamation; Exec. Dir CARRIE FELLOWS; Curator RYAN HYMAN; Pres. JO ANN BURK; Sec. EUNICE LYNCH; Treas. SHARON CROSS.

Monmouth County Historical Association Museum & Library: 70 Court St, Freehold, NJ 07728; tel. (732) 462-1466; fax (732) 462-8346; internet www .monmouthhistory.org; f. 1898; 30,000 objects, incl. 1,550 paintings, drawings, watercolours, prints and miniatures of American art from the mid-18th to the mid-20th centuries; 900 pieces of furniture, incl. 1695 wainscot chair made by Scottish immigrant Robert Rhea; artefacts and objects related to the Battle of Monmouth; items related to Monmouth Co steamboat industry; kitchen and household equipment from the early 18th century to the present day; over 300 pieces of folk art, incl. local retail signs and carving; 3,500 pieces of historic clothing and textiles colln; Dir Dr LEE ELLEN GRIFFITH; Curator BERNADETTE ROGOFF; Pres. CLAIRE KNOPF; Sec. NANCY STEWART; Treas. GEORGE J. DITTMAR, III.

Montclair Art Museum: Three S Mountain Ave, Montclair, NJ 07042-1747; tel. (973) 746-5555; fax (973) 746-9118; internet www .montclairartmuseum.org; f. 1914; 12,000 works; 18th- and 19th-century American art; traditional and contemporary American Indian art and artefacts showcasing the cultural achievements in weaving, pottery, wood carving, jewellery, and textiles of indigenous Americans from 7 major regions—NW Coast, California, SW, Plains, Woodlands, SE and the Arctic; Yard School of Art; library of 44,000 vols; Dir LORA S. URBANELLI; Chief Curator GAIL STAVITSKY; Pres. NEWTON B. SCHOTT, JR; Sec. LYNN GLASSER; Treas. IRA A. WAGNER.

Montclair State University Art Gallery: Montclair State Univ., Normal Ave, Montclair, NJ 07043; tel. (973) 655-3382; fax (973) 655-7665; e-mail artgalleries@mail .montclair.edu; internet www.montclair.edu/ arts/galleries; 16th- to 19th-century European paintings; incl. George Segal Gallery: colln of modern and contemporary art; Cosla Colln and MFA Gallery; Wingert Colln of traditional African and Oceanic masks and sculptures; Dir M. TERESA LAPID RODRIGUEZ.

Morris Museum: Six Normandy Heights Rd, Morristown, NJ 07960; tel. (973) 971-3700; fax (973) 538-0154; e-mail info@ morrismuseum.org; internet www .morrismuseum.org; colln of 48,700 objects, incl. costumes and textiles, fine art, decorative art, dolls and toys, natural science, geology and paleontology and anthropology; Exec. Dir LINDA S. MOORE; Curator DAVID NALVEN (acting); Chair. PAUL J. LAUD; Sec. RICHARD A. WATSON; Treas. JOHN S. HEMMENDINGER.

Museum of Early Trades & Crafts: 9 Main St, Madison, NJ 07940; tel. (973) 377-2982; fax (973) 377-7358; e-mail info@metc .org; internet www.metc.org; f. 1970; preserves and interprets the tools used before the rise of industrialization in the USA; 8,800 artefacts related to 21 different trades; research library; Exec. Dir VIVIAN C. R. JAMES; Chair. ALLEN BLACK; Sec. ASTRI BAILLIE; Treas. IRENE MARONEY.

New Jersey Maritime Museum: 528 Dock Rd, Beach Haven, NJ 08008; tel. (609) 492-0202; fax (609) 492-7575; e-mail curator@ njmaritimemuseum.org; internet www .museumofnjmh.com; US life saving service exhibit; rare post-card colln of New Jersey towns, USLSS stations, lighthouses and other maritime-related fields; shipwreck artefacts recovered from various wreck sites off the New Jersey coast; china plates, platters, pitchers and other artefacts recovered from the 1827 wreck of the Aurora off Sandy Hook; Pres. DEBORAH WHITCRAFT; Sec. BEVERLY TROMM; Treas. ROBERT CUNNINGHAM.

New Jersey State Museum: POB 530, New Jersey Dept of State, 205 W State St, Trenton, NJ 08625; tel. (609) 292-6464; e-mail feedback@sos.state.nj.us; internet www.state.nj.us/state/museum; f. 1895; archaeology and ethnology colln of 2m. prehistoric and historic specimens from nearly 100 years of excavation and over 2,000 ethnographic objects; fine art colln incl. paintings, prints, drawings, sculpture and photographs since 1965; cultural history colln of 13,000 artefacts showcasing New Jersey's cultural, economic, military, political and social history; natural history colln; Planetarium; Exec. Dir ANTHONY GARDNER; Pres. STEVEN M. RICHMAN.

Newark Museum: 49 Washington St, Newark, NJ 07102; tel. (973) 596-6550; e-mail director@newarkmuseum.org; internet www .newarkmuseum.org; f. 1909; 80 galleries of collns incl. American, Asian, African and Classical; Natural Science Galleries feature 83,000 specimens; Alice and Leonard Dreyfuss Planetarium; library: 2,500 linear ft of paper records, 26,000 documentary photographs and 200 published articles; Dir and CEO MARY SUE SWEENEY PRICE; Sr Curator ULYSSES GRANT DIETZ; Chair. ARLENE LIEBERMAN.

Paul Robeson Galleries: Rutgers Univ., 350 Dr Martin Luther King Jr Blvd, Newark, NJ 07102; tel. (973) 353-1610; fax (973) 353-5912; e-mail galleryr@andromeda.rutgers .edu; internet andromeda.rutgers.edu/ artgallery; attached to Rutgers Univ.; dedicated to Paul Robeson; artistic and cultural centre of Rutgers Univ.; holds educational and public programmes; arts and visual cultural exhibitions; Dir and Curator ANONDA BELL.

Trenton City Museum: Ellarslie Mansion in Cadwalader Park, Trenton, NJ; tel. (609) 989-3632; fax (609) 989-3624; e-mail collections@ellarslie.org; internet www .ellarslie.org; f. 1978; colln of fine and decorative arts, cultural history and industrial artefacts; 19th- and 20th-centuries colln of tableware, sanitary ware and art ware.

New Mexico

Albuquerque Museum of Art and History: 2000 Mountain Rd NW, Albuquerque, NM 87104; tel. (505) 243-7255; fax (505) 764-6546; e-mail albuquerquemuseum@cabq.gov; internet albuquerquemuseum.org; f. 1967; colln of 7,000 works of art incl. Native American jewellery and ceramics, Hispanic religious and domestic folk arts, documentary sketches and paintings from Territorial-era exploration, late 19th- and early 20th-

century Taos and Santa Fe artists Ernest Blumenschein, John Sloan and Georgia O'Keeffe, contemporary reflections on land, landscape and regional cultures; outdoor Sculpture Garden; photoarchives; Casa San Ysidro: The Gutiérrez/Minge House; Dir CATHY L. WRIGHT; Chair. CHRISTINE S. GLIDDEN; Sec. and Treas. JACOBO DE LA SERNA; publ. *abqmuseum* (4 a year).

Anderson Museum of Contemporary Art: 409 E College Blvd, Roswell, NM 88201; tel. (575) 623-5600; e-mail email@ roswellamoca.org; internet www .roswellamoca.org; f. 1994; 300 works of art; fiberglass sculptures; paintings; ceramic sculpture and golf bag sharks; new media pieces; colln of photographs.

Georgia O'Keeffe Museum: 217 Johnson St, Santa Fe, NM 87501; tel. (505) 946-1000; internet www.okeeffemuseum.org; f. 1997; colln of 2,989 works incl. 1,149 O'Keeffe paintings, drawings and sculptures dating from 1901 to 1984 and 1,840 by other artists; Research Center; Dir ROBERT A. KRET; Chair. ANNE W. MARION; Pres. SAUL COHEN; Sec. BARRY G. KING, JR; publ. *O'Keeffe* (3 a year).

Harwood Museum of Art: 238 Ledoux St, Taos, NM 87571; tel. (575) 758-9826; fax (575) 758-1475; e-mail info@ harwoodmuseum.org; internet harwoodmuseum.org; f. 1916; 3,000 works of art and photographic archive of 17,000 images dating from 19th century to present; colln incl. Hispanic works, prints, drawings and photographs, works by Taos Soc. of Artists, contemporary art, Taos moderns; Dir SUSAN LONGHENRY; Chair. LINDA WARNING; Sec. MARCIA WINTER; Treas. WYNN GOERING.

Indian Pueblo Cultural Center: 2401 12th St NW, Albuquerque, NM 87104; tel. (505) 724-3564; internet indianpueblo.org; f. 1976; 2,000 colln of contemporary and historic forms of pottery; colln of jewellery, textiles, baskets, photographs, prints, paintings and murals to archaeological objects from each of the 19 Pueblos and other tribes of the greater SW; incl. archives and library and Institute for Pueblo Indian Studies; Museum Dir MARTH BECKTELL.

Maxwell Museum of Anthropology: 1 Univ. of New Mexico, Albuquerque, NM 87131-0001; tel. (505) 277-4405; fax (505) 277-1547; e-mail maxwell@unm.edu; internet www.unm.edu/~maxwell; f. 1932 as Museum of Anthropology of the Univ. of New Mexico, present name 1972; attached to Univ. of New Mexico; anthropological collns from North, South and Central America, Africa, Asia, Australia and the Pacific Islands; assoc. research institutes: Office of Contract Archaeology, Alfonso Ortiz Center for Intercultural Studies and Maxwell Center for Anthropological Research; Dir E. JAMES DIXON.

Millicent Rogers Museum: POB 1210, Taos, NM 87571; 1504 Millicent Rogers Rd, Taos, NM 87571; tel. (575) 758-2462; fax (575) 758-5751; e-mail mrm@millicentrogers .org; internet www.millicentrogers.org; f. 1956; colln of Native American, Hispanic arts, pottery, contemporary arts and designs from all cultures in Northern New Mexico, 1,000 pieces of Native American jewellery; Exec. Dir PAUL FIGUEROA; Pres. PHILIP PERALTA-RAMOS; Sec. YALE I. JONES; Treas. DOUG CLARK.

Museum of Contemporary Native Arts: 108 Cathedral Pl., Santa Fe, NM 87501; tel. (505) 983-8900; fax (505) 983-1222; internet www.iaia.edu/museum; f. 1972; attached to Institute of American Indian Arts; colln of 7,500 artworks incl. paintings, works on paper, sculpture, ceramics, jewellery, photography, contemporary apparel, textiles, cultural arts, new media and installations; Dir PATSY PHILLIPS; Chief Curator RYAN RICE.

Museum of New Mexico: POB 2087, Santa Fé, NM 87504-2087; internet www .museumofnewmexico.org; f. 1909; state agency, under Bd of Regents appointed by Governor, divs in anthropology, history, fine arts, int. folk art, Indian arts and culture, state monuments located in separate bldgs; library of 50,000 vols; Dir THOMAS A. LIVESAY; publ. *El Palacio* (4 a year).

Constituent Museums:

Museum of Indian Arts and Culture: 710 Camino Lejo, Santa Fe, NM 87505; tel. (505) 476-1250; fax (505) 476-1330; e-mail miac.info@state.nm.us; internet www .indianartsandculture.org; f. 1987; Native art and material culture; incl. Laboratory of Anthropology; archives with institutional and ethnographic records incl. 8,000 historic and contemporary images, MSS archives documenting early Laboratory of Anthropology staff projects, papers and correspondence relating to history of anthropology in the SW; Dir SHELBY TISDALE.

Museum of International Folk Art: 706 Camino Lejo, Santa Fe, NM 87505; tel. (505) 476-1200; fax (505) 476-1300; e-mail internationalfolkart@gmail.com; internet www.internationalfolkart.org; f. 1953; 135,000 artefacts in 4 divs: Bartlett, Girard, Hispanic Heritage and Neutrogena; Dir MARSHA C. BOL.

New Mexico Museum of Art: 107 W Palace Ave, Santa Fe, NM 87501; tel. (505) 476-5072; fax (505) 476-5076; internet www.mfasantafe.org; f. 1917 as Art Gallery for the Museum of New Mexico; 23,000 objects, focusing on the areas of photography and works on paper; paintings, sculpture and furniture since the beginning of the 20th century; Dir MARY KERSHAW.

New Mexico State Monuments: 725 Camino Lejo, Santa Fe, NM 87504; tel. (505) 476-1150; fax (505) 476-1220; internet www.nmmonuments.org; f. 1931; incl. Coronado State Monument (where Francisco Vásquez de Coronado—with 300 soldiers and 800 Indian allies from New Spain—entered the valley while looking for the fabled Seven Cities of Gold); Fort Seldon State Monument (est. in 1865 in an effort to bring peace to the south central region of present day New Mexico); Jemez State Monument (incl. stone ruins of a 500-year-old Indian village and the San José de los Jemez church dating to 1610); Lincoln State Monument (incl. 7 structures and outbuildings from 1870 and 1880s); El Camino Real International Heritage Center (commemorates El Camino Real de Tierra Adentro, the historic trade route and its impact on New Mexico); Bosque Redondo Memorial at Fort Sumner State Monument (inc. story of how the US Army forcibly moved the Navajo and Mescalero Apache people from their traditional homelands to the land surrounding this lonely outpost); Dir RUDY ACOSTA.

Palace of the Governors: 105 W Palace Ave, Santa Fe, NM 87501; tel. (505) 476-5100; fax (505) 476-5104; internet www .palaceofthegovernors.org; constructed in the early 17th century as Spain's seat of govt in what is today the American South-West; chronicles the history of Santa Fe, as well as New Mexico and the wider region; photo archives of 800,000 items incl. historic photographic prints, cased photographs, glass plate negatives, film negatives, stereographs, photo postcards,

panoramas, colour transparencies and lantern slides; Fray Angélico Chávez History Library; Dir FRANCES LEVINE.

Museum of Spanish Colonial Art: 750 Camino Lejo, Santa Fe, NM 87505; tel. (505) 982-2226; fax (505) 982-4585; e-mail museum@spanishcolonial.org; internet www .spanishcolonial.org; f. 1930; attached to Spanish Colonial Arts Soc.; art of the Hispanic SW; colln of 3,700 works of art, incl. historically significant and contemporary works; Pueblo Revival-style bldg; Curator ROBIN FARWELL GAVIN.

New Mexico Museum of Natural History and Science: 1801 Mountain Rd NW, Albuquerque, NM 87104; tel. (505) 841-2800; fax (505) 841-2831; internet www .nmnaturalhistory.org; exhibits dinosaurs cast in bronze, Tyrannosaurus rex, tyrannosaur, space exhibition, beginnings of life on Earth; Bioscience Colln of plants, mammals, birds, reptiles and amphibians, insects and mollusks; fossil and mineralogical collns; planetarium and Sandia Mountain Natural History Center; Dir CHARLIE WALTER.

New Mexico State University Museum: Kent Hall, MSC 3564, POB 30001, Las Cruces, NM 88003-88001; tel. (575) 646-5161; fax (575) 646-1419; e-mail museum@ nmsu.edu; internet www.nmsu.edu/museum/; f. 1959; 170,000 archaeological items; 5,000 ethnographic items; 10,000 historical items; Dir Dr MONTE MCCROSSIN; Curator Dr JENNIFER ROBLES.

Roswell Museum and Art Center: 100 W 11th St, Roswell, NM 88201; tel. (575) 624-6744; fax (575) 624-6765; internet www .roswellmuseum.org; f. 1935; fine art and historical materials that chronicle specific areas of cultural change in the SW, incl. 71 watercolour sketches from the 1880s, modernist works from Santa Fe and Taos art colonies, public colln of regionalists, contemporary fine arts, int. print colln dating from 16th century to present, hand-crafted furniture and decorative objects; planetarium; library of 8,000 vols; Dir LAURIE J. RUFE; Pres. ROBERT PHILLIPS; Sec. and Treas. ELINOR MULKEY.

Silver City Museum: 312 W Broadway, Silver City, NM 88061; tel. (575) 538-5921; e-mail info@silvercitymuseum.org; internet www.silvercitymuseum.org; f. 1967; colln of 20,000 objects; archival material incl. 5,000 household and personal objects dating from late 19th through early 20th centuries; artefacts rep. of Anglo and Hispanic settlers incl. clothing and accessories, furnishings and firearms; Native American artefacts of pieces of pottery and lithic material from the Mimbres, Mogollon and Casas Grandes peoples and ancient cultures; mining exhibits incl. the Tyrone Room; 50 ranching artefacts; H. B. Ailman House 1881 Mansard/Italianate structure; 17,000 photographs; Dir TRACY SPIKES; Pres. SANDRA HICKS; Sec. LUCY WHITMARSH.

Taos Art Museum: 227 Paseo del Pueblo Norte, POB 1848, Taos, NM 87571; tel. (575) 758-2690; fax (575) 758-7320; e-mail museum@taosartmuseum.org; internet www .taosartmuseum.org; f. 1994; colln of approx. 300 paintings, drawings and prints by Taos founders; art of early 20th-century Taos; colln of paintings by the masters of the Taos Soc. of Artists; Exec. Dir ERION SIMPSON.

University of New Mexico Art Museum: 1 Univ. of New Mexico, Albuquerque, NM 87131-0001; tel. (505) 277-4001; fax (505) 277-7325; e-mail artmuse@unm.edu; internet unmartmuseum.unm.edu; colln of 30,000 objects incl. photographs, prints and old master paintings; Dir E. LUANNE MCKINNON.

Wheelwright Museum of the American Indian: POB 5153, 704 Camino Lejo, Santa Fe, NM 87502; tel. (505) 982-4636; fax (505) 989-7386; e-mail info@wheelwright.org; internet www.wheelwright.org; f. 1937; access by appointment; houses collns of artefacts, archives, sound recordings and photographs, documenting Native American (esp. Navajo) culture, both historic and contemporary; contemporary and traditional American Indian art; Dir JONATHAN BATKIN; Curator CHERI FALKENSTIEN-DOYLE.

New York

Albright-Knox Art Gallery: 1285 Elmwood Ave, Buffalo, NY 14222-1096; tel. (716) 882-8700; fax (716) 882-1958; e-mail info@ albrightknox.org; internet www .albrightknox.org; f. 1862 as Buffalo Fine Arts Acad., present name 1962; colln of paintings since the 18th century; post-war American and European art; abstract expressionism; pop art and art from the 1970s; library of 45,000 vols; Dir LOUIS GRACHOS; Chief Curator Dr DOUGLAS DREISHPOON; Pres. LESLIE H. ZEMSKY; Sec. FREDERICK G. PIERCE, II; Treas. JOHN R. SANDERSON.

American Folk Art Museum: 2 Lincoln Sq., Columbus Ave, 66th St, New York, NY 10023-6214; tel. (212) 595-9533; fax (212) 595-6759; internet www.folkartmuseum.org; f. 1961 as Museum of Early American Folk Arts, present name 2001; holdings of 18th- and 19th-century artworks and objects from New England and the Mid-Atlantic states; works of folk art symbolising utility, community, individuality and symbolism; Contemporary Center; Henry Darger Study Center for multidisciplinary research;; library of 10,000 vols; Dir LINDA DUNNE (acting); Chair. LAURA PARSONS.

American Museum of Natural History: Central Park W, 79th St, New York, NY 10024-5192; tel. (212) 769-5100; fax (212) 769-5688; internet www.amnh.org; f. 1869; divs of anthropology, invertebrate zoology, paleontology, physical sciences, vertebrate zoology; Center for Biodiversity and Conservation; Sackler Institute for Comparative Genomics; SW Research Station; Hayden Planetarium; library: see Libraries and Archives; Chair. LEWIS W. BERNARD; Pres. ELLEN V. FUTTER; Sec. SIBYL R. GOLDEN; Treas. CHARLES H. MOTT; publs *American Museum Novitates, Anthropological Papers of the American Museum of Natural History, Bulletin of the American Museum of Natural History.*

Asia Society Museum: 725 Park Ave, 70th St, New York, NY 10021; tel. (212) 288-6400; fax (212) 517-8315; e-mail info@asiasociety .org; internet asiasociety.org/arts/ asia-society-museum; f. 1956; exhibitions of both traditional and contemporary Asian and Asian American art; objects from cultures across Asia that date from the 11th century BC to the 19th century; spec. colln: Rockefeller colln of Asian art in the USA; Dir MELISSA CHIU.

Binghamton University Art Museum: POB 6000, Binghamton, NY 13902-6000; Fine Arts Bldg, Rooms 179 and 213, 4400 Vestal Parkway E, Binghamton, NY 13902; tel. (607) 777-2000; e-mail info@binghamton .edu; internet www2.binghamton.edu/ art-museum; Italian Baroque painting, Asian art, African art prints and decorative arts, sculpture, prints, photographs, drawings, glass, ceramic, metalwork, MSS pages and textiles from Egypt, Greece, Asia, Africa, Europe, N America and pre-Columbian cultures; 3,000 objects from all major periods of art history and most parts of the world; Assistant Dir JACKIE HOGAN.

Bronx Museum: 1040 Grand Concourse, Bronx, NY 10456-3999; tel. (718) 681-6000; fax (718) 681-6181; e-mail info@bronxmuseum.org; internet www.bronxmuseum.org; f. 1971; 20th- and 21st-century works by artists of African, Asian and Latin American ancestry; Exec. Dir HOLLY BLOCK; Chair. R. DOUGLASS RICE; Sec. ALESSANDRA DiGIUSTO.

Brooklyn Botanic Garden: 1000 Washington Ave, Brooklyn, NY 11225; tel. (718) 623-7200; fax (718) 622-7839; e-mail feedback@bbg.org; internet www.bbg.org; f. 1910; living colln of 12,000 species and varieties; herbarium with 250,000 specimens; education programmes; plant information service; library of 30,000 vols, 150 current serials; Chair. FREDERICK BLAND; Sec. ELIZABETH GILE; Treas. SUZANNE T. MARQUARD; Curator KERRY BARRINGER; publ. *Urban Habitats* (online (www.urbanhabitats.org)).

Brooklyn Museum: 200 E Parkway, Brooklyn, NY 11238-6052; tel. (718) 638-5000; fax (718) 501-6136; e-mail information@brooklynmuseum.org; internet www.brooklynmuseum.org; f. 1823; Native American art; Peruvian textiles; pre-Columbian gold; Costa Rican sculpture; collns from Africa, Melanesia and Polynesia; collns from China, Korea, South-east Asia, Japan, India and Persia; Colonial South American art; American period rooms; sculpture garden; American and European paintings; prints and drawings; ancient art of the Near East, Egypt, Greece and Rome; American and European costumes; American glass, pewter and silver; contemporary paintings and sculpture; Elizabeth A. Sackler Center for Feminist Art, art reference library and Egyptological library; library of 170,000 vols, 11,710 glass lantern slides; Dir ARNOLD L. LEHMAN; Chief Curator KEVIN STAYTON; Dir ARNOLD L. LEHMAN; Chair. JOHN S. TAMAGNI; Sec. CONSTANCE L. CHRISTENSEN; Treas. RICHARD M. CASHIN.

Buffalo Museum of Science: 1020 Humboldt Parkway, Buffalo, NY 14211; tel. (716) 896-5200; fax (716) 897-6723; internet www.sciencebuff.org; f. 1929; attached to Buffalo Soc. of Natural Sciences; exhibition halls feature insects, dinosaurs and other fossils, birds, wild flowers and fungi, vertebrates, minerals, flora and fauna of the Niagara Frontier, life in ancient Egypt, solar system and space exploration, geology; solar and lunar observatory; loan collns, lectures, day and evening classes, etc.; operates Tifft Nature Preserve, S Buffalo; library of 45,000 vols, 400 journals; Pres. and CEO MARK MORTENSON; Curator of Collns KATHRYN LEACOCK; Chair. RANDALL E. BURKARD; Sec. LAURIE DANN; Treas. CHRISTOPHER HOGAN; publ. *Bulletin of the Buffalo Society of Natural Sciences*.

Cooper-Hewitt, National Design Museum: 2 E 91st St, New York, NY 10128; tel. (212) 849-8400; fax (212) 849-8401; e-mail redesignch@si.edu; internet www.cooperhewitt.org; f. 1897, present status 1967; attached to Smithsonian Instn; 250,000 items, incl. collns of original drawings and designs for architecture and the decorative arts; prints since 15th century; textiles, lace, woodwork and furniture, ceramics, glass, etc.; drawings and paintings by F. E. Church, W. Homer and other 19th-century American artists; closed for renovation till 2013; library of 70,000 vols, incl. 8,000 rare books; 1,000 items: books, journals, guides, ephemera; 13,000 drawings and 4,300 black and white photographs; Dir BILL MOGGRIDGE; Pres. BETH COMSTOCK (acting); Sec. JUDY FRANCIS ZANKEL; Treas. ERIC A. GREEN; Curatorial Dir CARA McCARTY.

Dia Beacon Riggio Galleries: Three Beekman St, Beacon, NY 12508; tel. (845) 440-0100; fax (845) 440-0092; e-mail info@diaart.org; internet www.diaart.org/sites/main/beacon; f. 2003; attached to Dia Art Foundation; art from the 1960s to the present; Dir PHILIPPE VERGNE; Curator YASMIL RAYMOND.

El Museo del Barrio: 1230 Fifth Ave, 104th St, New York, NY 10029; tel. (212) 831-7272; e-mail info@elmuseo.org; internet www.elmuseo.org; f. 1969; 6,500 objects spanning more than 800 years of Latin American, Caribbean and Latino art, incl. pre-Columbian Taíno artefacts, traditional arts, 20th-century drawings, paintings, sculptures and installations, as well as prints, photography, documentary films, and video; Exec. Dir MARGARITA AGUILAR; Dir of Curatorial Programmes DEBORAH CULLEN; Chair. TONY BECHARA; Sec. MICHAEL J. GARCÍA; Treas. MARY McCAFFREY.

Everson Museum of Art: 401 Harrison St, Syracuse, NY 13202; tel. (315) 474-6064; fax (315) 474-6943; e-mail everson@everson.org; internet www.everson.org; f. 1897 as Syracuse Museum of Fine Arts, present location 1968; 11,000 objects, incl. American paintings, with 700 art works spanning over 2 centuries; 2,000 pieces of American Art pottery colln; 600 works on paper of 19th- and 20th-century art movements; 100 decorative objects; Exec. Dir STEVEN KERN; Pres. PATRICK PEDRO; Sec. EUGENIA BRIEVA; Treas. RICHARD DRISCOLL.

Frick Collection: 1 E 70th St, New York, NY 10021; tel. (212) 288-0700; fax (212) 628-4417; e-mail info@frick.org; internet www.frick.org; f. 1920; European paintings from 13th to 19th centuries; Italian Renaissance bronzes and furniture; Limoges enamels of the Renaissance; French 18th-century sculpture, furniture and porcelains; Oriental porcelains; works of art mostly assembled by industrialist Henry Clay Frick; library: see Libraries and Archives; Dir IAN WARDROPPER.

Grey Art Gallery: New York Univ., 100 Washington Sq. E, New York, NY 10003; tel. (212) 998-6780; fax (212) 995-4024; e-mail greyartgallery@nyu.edu; internet www.nyu.edu/greyart; f. 1927 as A. E. Gallatin's Museum of Living Art, present name 1975; attached to New York Univ.; collects, preserves, studies, documents, interprets and exhibits evidence of human culture; 6,000 objects of late-19th- and 20th-century works, ranging from Pablo Picasso's Bust of Sylvette to Joseph Cornell box and Chocolat Menier, from 1952; American paintings from the 1940s to the present.

Solomon R. Guggenheim Museum: 1071 Fifth Ave, 89th St, New York, NY 10128-0173; tel. (212) 423-3500; fax (212) 423-3650; e-mail visitorinfo@guggenheim.org; internet www.guggenheim.org/new-york/collections; f. 1937; Solomon R. Guggenheim's colln of non-objective painting; Peggy Guggenheim's colln of abstract and surrealist painting and sculpture; Justin K. Thannhauser's array of Impressionist, post-Impressionist and early modern masterpieces; Count Giuseppe Panza di Biumo's colln of European and American Minimalist, post-Minimalist, environmental, and conceptual art; library of 20,000 vols; Dir RICHARD ARMSTRONG; Chief Curator and Deputy Dir NANCY SPECTOR.

Harbor Defense Museum: 230 Sheridan Loop, Fort Hamilton Military Community, Brooklyn, NY 11252-5701; tel. (718) 630-4349; fax (718) 630-4888; internet www.harbordefensemuseum.com; f. 1825; US Army weapons, uniforms, small arms, cannons and accoutrements from 18th century to present; military art and historical items from Fort Hamilton; Dir PAUL MORANDO.

Hispanic Society of America Museum and Library: 613 W 155th St, New York, NY 10032; Audubon Terrace, Broadway, between 155th and 156th Sts, New York, NY 10032; tel. (212) 926-2234; fax (212) 690-0743; e-mail info@hispanicsociety.org; internet www.hispanicsociety.org; f. 1904; concentrates on culture of the Iberian Peninsula and Latin America: paintings, prints and drawings (14th century to present), sculpture (13th century to present), archaeology, decorative arts (ceramics, textiles, metalwork, furniture); library of 250,000 vols, 200,000 MSS, 15,000 vols printed before 1701; Dir Dr MITCHELL A. CODDING; Curator of Paintings and Drawings MARCUS BURKE; Curator of Iconography PATRICK LENAGHAN.

Jacques Marchais Museum of Tibetan Art: 338 Lighthouse Ave, Staten Island, NY 10306; tel. (718) 987-3500; fax (718) 351-0402; internet www.tibetanmuseum.org; f. 1948; colln of Jacques Marchais during the early 1920s through the late 1940s, incl. sculptures, thangka or scroll paintings, ritual artefacts, musical instruments, furniture and historic photographs of Tibet; Exec. Dir MEG VENTRUDO; Pres. BEVERLY GARCIA-ANDERSO; Sec. RUTH SPRUTE; Treas. GEORGE SIEGHARDT.

Jewish Museum: 1109 Fifth Ave, 92nd St, New York, NY 10128; tel. (212) 423-3200; fax (212) 423-3232; e-mail info@thejm.org; internet www.thejewishmuseum.org; f. 1904; explores scope and diversity of 4,000 years of Jewish art and culture through 27,000 objects; Dir CLAUDIA GOULD.

Metropolitan Museum of Art: 1000 Fifth Ave, New York, NY 10028-0198; tel. (212) 535-7710; e-mail communications@metmuseum.org; internet www.metmuseum.org; f. 1866; art of Africa, Oceania and the Americas; American paintings and sculpture; American decorative arts; ancient Near Eastern art; Asian art; drawings and prints; European paintings; European sculpture and decorative arts; Greek and Roman art; Islamic art; Robert Lehman Colln; medieval art; musical instruments; photographs; 20th-century art; 2m. works of art and 6,500 objects; library of 240,000 vols, 1,400 periodicals; photograph and slide library; Chair. DANIEL BRODSKY; Pres. EMILY K. RAFFERTY; Dir and CEO THOMAS P. CAMPBELL; publs *Metropolitan Museum of Art Bulletin*, *Metropolitan Museum Journal*, *Now at the Met*.

Museum of Chinese in America: 215 Centre St, New York, NY 10013; tel. (212) 619-4785; fax (212) 619-4720; e-mail info@mocanyc.org; internet www.mocanyc.org; f. 1980, present location 2009; collns incl. 60,000 letters and documents, business and organizational records, oral histories, clothing and textiles, photographs and precious artefacts of Chinese American history; colln and research centre in Mulberry St; Dir JESSICA CHAO; Curator and Dir of Exhibitions HERB HOI CHUN TAM; Co-Chair. MAYA LIN; Co-Chair. MEI-MEI TUAN; Sec. PATRICIA P. TANG; Treas. JONATHAN LEE.

Museum of Jewish Heritage: Edmond J. Safra Plaza, 36 Battery Pl., New York, NY 10280; tel. (646) 437-4202; e-mail info@mjhnyc.org; internet www.mjhnyc.org; f. 1997; 25,000 items on modern Jewish history and Holocaust; incl. 4,000 audio and video testimonies by Holocaust survivors, liberators, rescuers, Jews who served in the Allied Armies during Second World War; Dir Dr DAVID G. MARWELL; Sr Curator ESTHER BRUMBERG; Chair. ROBERT M. MORGENTHAU.

Museum of Modern Art: 11 W 53rd St, New York, NY 10019-5497; tel. (212) 708-

9400; fax (212) 708-9889; e-mail info@moma .org; internet www.moma.org; f. 1929; paintings, drawings, prints, sculptures, industrial and graphic design, photographs, architecture and design since 1880s; large colln of American, British, French, German and Russian films, 1,200 of which are available to educational organizations; colln of modern and contemporary photography in the world; daily film showings; organizes exhibitions worldwide in all the visual arts; library of 300,000 vols, incl. 300 periodicals and 40,000 vertical files; Dir GLENN D. LOWRY; Chair. JERRY I. SPEYER; Sec. PATTY LIPSHUTZ; Treas. RICHARD E. SALOMON.

Museum of the City of New York: 1220 Fifth Ave, 103rd St, New York, NY 10029; tel. (212) 534-1672; fax (212) 423-0758; e-mail info@mcny.org; internet www.mcny .org; f. 1923; colln of 1.4m. paintings, sculptures, prints, photographs, costumes, toys reflecting historical and modern New York city; Pres. and Dir SUSAN HENSHAW JONES; Chair. JAMES G. DINAN; Sec. JAMES P. DRUCKMAN; Treas. JANE B. O'CONNELL.

National Museum of the American Indian: George Gustav Heye Center, Alexander Hamilton U.S. Custom House, One Bowling Green, New York, NY 10004; tel. (212) 514-3700; fax (212) 514-3800; e-mail nmai-ny@si.edu; internet www.nmai.si.edu; f. 1989; attached to Smithsonian Instn; colln of the material culture of the native people of the W Hemisphere; 800,000 items from the colln of George Gustav Heye; film and audiovisual collns; paper archives; photography archive of more than 300,000 images; also located in Washington, DC; library of 40,000 vols, 90,000 photographs and negatives, 1,500 linear ft of records; Dir KEVIN GROVER.

Neue Galerie: Museum for German and Austrian Art, 1048 Fifth Ave, New York, NY 10028; tel. (212) 628-6200; fax (212) 628-8824; e-mail museum@neuegalerie.org; internet www.neuegalerie.org; f. 2001; early 20th-century German and Austrian art and design; Dir RENÉE PRICE; Pres. RONALD S. LAUDER.

Noble Maritime Collection: 1000 Richmond Terrace, Bldg D, Staten Island, NY 10301; tel. (718) 447-6490; fax (718) 447-6056; internet www.noblemaritime.org; f. 1987; preserves and interprets art and writings of marine artist, John A. Noble; House Boat Studio, Ship Model Gallery with colln from Sailors' Snug Harbor; sailing vessels, steamships and collns from the 18th, 19th and 20th centuries; Exec. Dir ERIN M. URBAN; Chair. JAMES J. DEVINE; Sec. KEVIN J. MAHONEY; Treas. JOHN J. PINTO.

Paley Center for Media: 25 W 52nd St, New York, NY 10019; tel. (212) 621-6800; fax (212) 621-6600; e-mail groupvisitsny@ paleycenter.org; internet www.paleycenter .org; f. 1975 as The Museum of Broadcasting, present name 2007; 150,000 television and radio programmes and advertisements reflecting the history of television and radio; incl. a screening room to browse and watch programmes; br. in Los Angeles, CA; Pres. and CEO PAT MITCHELL.

Rochester Museum & Science Center: 657 E Ave, Rochester, NY 14607-2177; tel. (585) 271-4320; fax (585) 271-5935; internet www.rmsc.org; f. 1912; collns of 1.2m. objects: incl. 164,000 history objects, 20,960 ethnology objects, 800,000 archaeology objects; RMSC's Natural Sciences colln incl. 26,000 specimens; Strasenburgh Planetarium; Cumming Nature Center: environmental education facility in Naples, NY; library of 25,000 vols, 1,400 serial titles,

60,000 archived documents, 40,000 photographs; Pres. KATE BENNETT.

Rubin Museum of Art: 150 W 17th St, New York, NY 10011; tel. (212) 620 5000; fax (212) 620-0628; e-mail info@rmanyc.org; internet www.rmanyc.org; f. 1999; museum of Himalayan art; 2,000 works of art incl. paintings, sculptures and textile of the Himalayan region incl. Nepal, Tibet and Bhutan as well as the inter-related traditions of India, Mongolia and China spanning a period from the 2nd to the 20th century; education centre; Chief Operating Officer PATRICK SEARS; Chief Curator JAN VAN ALPHEN.

Whitney Museum of American Art: 945 Madison Ave, 75th St, New York, NY 10021; tel. (212) 570-3600; fax (212) 570-1807; e-mail info@whitney.org; internet www .whitney.org; f. 1930; 19,000 paintings, sculptures, drawings, prints, photographs, films, videos and new media by more than 2,900 artists; library of 50,000 vols, 500 current periodicals; Dir ADAM D. WEINBERG; Chief Curator and Deputy Dir DONNA DE SALVO; Pres. NEIL G. BLUHM; Sec. JOANNE LEONHARDT CASSULLO; Treas. HENRY CORNELL.

Yager Museum of Art & Culture: POB 4020, Oneonta, NY 13820; tel. (607) 431-4480; e-mail museum@hartwick.edu; internet www.hartwick.edu/academics/ museum; f. 1929, present location 1967; attached to Hartwick College; 17,000 objects of fine arts, Upper Susquehanna Indian artefacts, SW pottery, baskets and rugs; Museum Coordinator DONNA ANDERSON.

Yeshiva University Museum: 15 W 16th St, New York, NY 10011; tel. (212) 294-8330; fax (212) 294-8335; e-mail info@yum.cjh.org; internet www.yumuseum.org; f. 1973; colln of more than 8,000 artefacts, incl. fine and folk art, ethnographic and archaeological artefacts, clothing and textiles, Jewish ceremonial objects, documents, books and MSS; colln represents 2,000 years of Jews living throughout the world; spec. colln incl. archaeological artefacts dating from the Bronze Age to the late antique period; Torah scroll and Tefillin of the Baal Shem Tov, founder of the Hassidic movement; Dir JACOB WISSE.

North Carolina

Ackland Art Museum: Univ. of North Carolina at Chapel Hill, POB 3400, Chapel Hill, NH 27599-3400; tel. (919) 966-5736; fax (919) 966-1400; e-mail ackland@email.unc .edu; internet www.ackland.org; f. 1958; attached to Univ. of North Carolina; 16,000 works of art; art glass colln dating from 1880s to 1950s; African art colln incl. ancient Nok terracotta sculpture; European paintings from Renaissance to 20th century; paintings and sculptures from modernist period; Dir EMILY KASS; Chief Curator PETER NISBET.

Asheville Art Museum: POB 1717, 2 S Pack Sq., Asheville, NC 28802-1717; tel. (828) 253-3227; fax (828) 257-4503; e-mail mailbox@ashevilleart.org; internet www .ashevilleart.org; f. 1948; 3,000 objects and 4,000 architectural drawings; 20th- and 21st-century American art; Exec. Dir PAMELA L. MYERS; Curator FRANK THOMSON.

Aurora Fossil Museum: POB 352, 400 Main St, Aurora, NC 27806-0352; tel. (252) 322-4238; fax (252) 322-2220; e-mail aurfosmus@yahoo.com; internet www .aurorafossilmuseum.com; f. 1976; colln incl. Pleistocene Age mastodon tusk and rare fossil cetacean skeleton; archaeology colln incl. stone tools, jewellery and cooking implements of native Americans from E North Carolina.

Bechtler Museum of Modern Art: 420 S Tryon St, Charlotte, NC 28202; tel. (704) 353-

9200; e-mail info@bechtler.org; internet www .bechtler.org; f. 2010; colln comprises mid-century modern art by artists incl. Alberto Giacometti, Joan Miro, Jean Tinguely and Barbara Hepworth; Pres. and CEO JOHN BOYER; Chair. CYNDEE PATTERSON; Sec. ROBERT S. LILIEN; Treas. LYNN GOOD.

Cape Fear Museum of History and Science: 814 Market St, Wilmington, NC 28401; tel. (910) 798-4350; fax (910) 798-4382; internet www.capefearmuseum.com; f. 1898; 50,000 objects (photographs, household items, industrial ltools etc.) on history, science and cultures of lower Cape Fear; Dir RUTH HAAS; Curator BARBARA ROWE.

Carolinas Aviation Museum: 4672 First Flight Dr., Charlotte, NC 28208; tel. (704) 359-8442; fax (704) 255-1651; e-mail info@ carolinasaviation.org; internet www .carolinasaviation.org; f. 1991; colln incl. aircraft, helicopters, equipment, gadgets and printed material spanning years of aviation history and accomplishments; Exec. Dir WALLY COPPINGER.

Chatham Historical Museum: POB 93, Pittsboro, NC 27312; e-mail history@ chathamhistory.org; internet www .chathamhistory.org; f. 1990; local history museum; colln incl. early settlement and formation of Chatham Co, colonial warrant signed by William Hooper who signed Declaration of Independence, 1880 census of agriculture and early maps; Pres. BARBARA PUGH; Sec. WINNCIE JANE HINNANT; Treas. DAN PERRY; Curator JANE PYLE.

Colburn Earth Science Museum: 2 S Pack Sq., Asheville, NC 28801-3521; tel. (828) 254-7162; e-mail colburngroupon@gmail.com; internet www.colburnmuseum.org; f. 1960 as Burnham S. Colburn Memorial Museum, present name 2002; 4,500 specimens incl. examples of 350 minerals in North Carolina; 500 fossil specimens; 1,000 cut gemstones from around the world; Dir VICKY BALLARD; Pres. JOSEPH NUNAN.

Cowan Museum: POB 950, 411 S Main St, Kenansville, NC 28349; tel. (910) 296-2149; internet www.cowanmuseum.com; f. 1848; artefacts incl. household utensils dating from 18th and 19th century that highlight early rural North Carolina and Duplin Co; Curator ILA O. COWAN.

Fine Art Museum: 199 Centennial Dr., Cullowhee, NC 28723; tel. (828) 227-3591; fax (828) 227-7632; e-mail museum@wcu .edu; internet www.wcu.edu/museum; f. 2005; attached to Western Carolina Univ.; 1,200 pieces of contemporary fine art since 1945 and craft media by regional, nat. and int. artists; Dir DENISE DRURY.

Gaston County Museum: POB 429, Dallas, NC 28034; 131 W Main St, Dallas, NC; tel. (704) 922-7681; e-mail museum@co.gaston.nc .us; internet www.gastoncountymuseum.org; f. 1975; 5,000 objects, 20,000 documents and 400,000 photos on Gaston Co dating from the 1500s to 21st century; Dir JEFF PRUETT; Chair. BRENT MESSER; Sec. JOHN BROOKS; Treas. VAN NOBLETT; Curator STEPHANIE ELLIOTT.

Greensboro Historical Museum: 130 Summit Ave, Greensboro, NC 27401; tel. (336) 373-2043; fax (336) 373-2204; internet www.greensborohistory.org; f. 1924; 25,000 items incl. militaria, costumes, textiles and decorative arts; MSS, photographs, printed materials and artwork dating from 1700 to present; 11,000 American artefacts from 1979 excavations; Dir LINDA EVANS (acting).

Gregg Museum of Art & Design: POB 7306, Raleigh, NC 27695-7306; tel. (919) 515-3503; e-mail gregg@ncsu.edu; internet www .ncsu.edu/gregg; f. 1992, present name and status 1998; attached to North Carolina State Univ.; 20,000 objects incl. textiles, ceramics, photography, glass and sculpture; Native American art and artefacts; Dir ROGER MANLEY; Pres. JIM CLARK; Treas. JON W. BARTLEY.

Mint Museum: 2730 Randolph Rd, Charlotte, NC 28207; tel. (704) 337-2000; internet www.mintmuseum.org; f. 1936; contemporary art colln incl. paintings, drawings, sculptures and photography; American art colln incl. fed. portraiture, 19th century landscape paintings and early 20th-century realism; 12,500 objects of decorative arts holdings from England and continental Europe, American art pottery and Asian porcelain; 1 br; library of 15,000 vols; Chair. RICHARD T. WILLIAMS.

Morehead Planetarium and Science Center: CB 3480, UNC-CH, Chapel Hill, NC 27599; tel. (919) 962-1236; fax (919) 962-1238; e-mail mhplanet@unc.edu; internet www.moreheadplanetarium.org; f. 1947; educational programmes for adults and children; daily planetarium shows; digital video theatre; Star Theatre; exhibitions; Dir TODD BOYETTE; Dir for Finance and Admin. SUSAN DURHAM; publ. *Sundial*.

Nasher Museum of Art at Duke University: 2001 Campus Dr., Durham, NC 27705; tel. (919) 684-5135; fax (919) 681-8624; e-mail nasherinfo@duke.edu; internet nasher.duke.edu; f. 1969 as Duke Univ. Museum of Art, present name 2005; colln incl. 10,000 works of medieval art, art of Americas, antiquities, Russian art, modern and int. contemporary art, traditional African art and Asian art; Dir KIMERLY RORSCHACH.

North Carolina Museum of Art: 4630 Mail Services Centre, Raleigh, NC 27607-6494; 2110 Blue Ridge Rd, Raleigh, NC 27607-6494; tel. (919) 839-6262; fax (919) 733-8034; internet ncartmuseum.org; f. 1924; colln incl. European paintings from Renaissance to 19th century, African, ancient American, pre-Columbian and Oceanic art, and Jewish ceremonial objects; library of 40,000 vols; Dir LAWRENCE J. WHEELER; Chief Curator LINDA JOHNSON DOUGHERTY; publ. *Preview* (4 a year).

North Carolina Museum of History: Five E Edenton St, Raleigh, NC 27601-1011; tel. (919) 807-7900; fax (919) 733-8655; internet ncmuseumofhistory.org; f. 1898, present name 1965; 150,000 artefacts representing 6 centuries of North Carolina history; Dir KENNETH B. HOWARD; Curator ROANN BISHOP; Curator JEANNE MARIE WARZESKI.

North Carolina Museum of Natural Sciences: 11 W Jones St, Raleigh, NC 27601-1029; tel. (919) 733-7450; fax (919) 733-1573; internet www.naturalsciences.org; f. 1879 as North Carolina State Museum; colln of 3m. specimens focusing on zoology, geology and paleontology of North Carolina and SE USA; Dir Dr BETSY M. BENNETT.

Reynolda House Museum of American Art: POB 7287, Winston-Salem, NC 27109-7287; 2250 Reynolda Rd, Winston-Salem, NC 27106; tel. (336) 758-5150; e-mail reynolda@reynoldahouse.org; internet www.reynoldahouse.org; f. 1967; American art colln of painting and sculpture from 3 centuries, dating from colonial period to present; architectural drawings, documents, oral histories and photographs; 700 articles of clothing, representing 2 generations of the Reynolds Family from 1890 to 1965; library of 3,650 vols; Exec. Dir ALLISON C. PERKINS.

Weatherspoon Art Museum: POB 26170, UNC Greensboro, Greensboro, NC 27402-6170; tel. (336) 334-5770; fax (336) 334-5907; e-mail weatherspoon@uncg.edu;

internet weatherspoon.uncg.edu; f. 1941; attached to Univ. of North Carolina; 6,000 works incl. modern and contemporary American art; American art dating from 1900 to present; Lenoir C. Wright colln of Japanese wood block prints; Dir NANCY DOLL.

North Dakota

Bonanzaville: 1351 W Main Ave, POB 719, West Fargo, ND 58078; tel. (701) 282-2822; fax (701) 282-7606; internet www.bonanzaville.com; f. 1955; attached to Cass Co Historical Soc.; 400,000 artefacts in 43 historical bldgs; Eugene Dahl Car Museum, Eagles Air Museum, Horse Drawn Vehicle Bldg, Law Enforcement Museum, Medical Display, Melroe Tractor Bldg, Moum Agricultural Bldg and Telephone Museum; Exec. Dir TROY WHITE; Pres. ROBERT CLARKE; Treas. PAUL MEYERS; Curator ANDREW NIELSEN.

Dakota Dinosaur Museum: 200 E. Museum Dr., Dickinson, ND 58601; tel. (701) 225-3466; e-mail info@dakotadino.com; internet www.dakotadino.com; f. 1987; geological and paleontological specimens of dinosaurs; skeletal casts replicas of real bones; dinosaur sculptures; Dir and Curator ALICE LEAGUE; Dir and Curator LARRY LEAGUE.

Dickinson Museum Center: 188 Museum Dr. E, Dickinson, ND 58601; tel. (701) 456-6225; fax (701) 456-7994; e-mail info@dickinsonmuseumcenter.org; internet www.dickinsonmuseumcenter.org; Joachim Regional Museum: art and history exhibits of regional significance; Museum Dir DANIELLE STUCKLE.

Fargo Air Museum: 1609 19th Ave N, Fargo, ND 58102; tel. (701) 293-8043; fax (701) 293-8103; internet www.fargoairmuseum.org; colln of aircrafts; Chair. REX A. HAMMARBACK; Sec. TIMOTHY McPHERSON; Treas. ROBERT THIBIDEAU.

North Dakota Museum of Art: 261 Centennial Dr., Grand Forks, ND 58202; tel. (701) 777-4195; fax (701) 777-4425; e-mail ndmoa@ndmoa.com; internet www.ndmoa.com; f. 1975 as Univ. of North Dakota Art Galleries, present name and status 1981; contemporary, int. art in all media starting with the early 1970s; colln contemporary Native American art; Dir LAUREL REUTER.

Pembina State Museum: Off Interstate 29, 805 Highway 59, Pembina, ND 58271; tel. (701) 328-2666; fax (701) 328-3710; e-mail histsoc@nd.gov; internet www.history.nd.gov/historicsites/pembina; attached to State Historical Soc. of North Dakota; 2 exhibition galleries; observation tower offering a grand view of the Red River Valley; pre-glacial fossils; bone and stone tools; frontier military forts; colln highlights current trends in industry, agriculture, and recreation in NE North Dakota; temporary exhibitions; natural history, history, archaeology and ethnology; collection items range from a 10,000 year old mastodon to a 1915 homesteader's claim shack to 1990s youth soccer equipment; Dir MERLAN PAAVERUD.

Pioneer Trails Regional Museum: 12 First Ave NE, POB 78, Bowman, ND 58623; tel. (701) 523-3600; e-mail ptrm@ptrm.org; internet www.ptrm.org; colln and research on anthropology, archaeology, astronomy, botany, genealogy, local history and paleontology.

Plains Art Museum: 704 First Ave N, Fargo, ND 58102; tel. (701) 232-3821; fax (701) 293-1082; e-mail museum@plainsart.org; internet plainsart.org; f. 1965 as Red River Art Center, present name 1975; 3,000 works incl. nat. and regional contemporary art, traditional American Indian art and traditional folk art; Hannaher's, Inc. Print

Studio, Dawson Studio and Goldberg Resource Library; Dir and CEO COLLEEN SHEEHY; Chair. ARLETTE PRESTON; Sec. KATE HAUGAN; Treas. JIM HAMBRICK.

Prairie Village Museum: 102 HWY 2 SE, POB 232, Rugby, ND 58368-2444; tel. (701) 776-7606; e-mail prairievillagemuseum@gmail.com; internet www.prairievillagemuseum.com; f. 1964; colln incl. bldgs, artefacts, household items, clothing, buggies, automobiles and farm machinery dating from late 1880s to the present, focussing on turn of the century; Exec. Dir CATHY JELSING.

Ohio

Akron Art Museum: 1 S High, Akron, OH 44308; tel. (330) 376-9185; fax (330) 376-1180; e-mail mail@akronartmuseum.org; internet www.akronartmuseum.org; f. 1922 as Akron Art Institute, present name 1980; 5,000 art works produced from 1850 to the present; public colln of glass by artist Paul Stankard; library of 11,000 vols, 38 journals, 5,200 artist biographical files; Dir and CEO Dr MITCHELL KAHAN.

Allen Memorial Art Museum: c/o Oberlin College, 87 N Main St, Oberlin, OH 44074; tel. (440) 775-8665; fax (440) 775-8799; internet www.oberlin.edu/amam; f. 1917; attached to Oberlin College; colln of 14,000 works of art incl. European and American paintings and sculpture from 15th century to present; Asian paintings, scrolls, sculpture and decorative art, incl. ukiyo-e prints, African, Pre-Columbian and ancient art and photographs; Dir Dr STEPHANIE WILES.

Butler Institute of American Art: The Beecher Center, 524 Wick Ave, Youngstown, OH 44502; tel. (330) 743-1107; fax (330) 743-9567; e-mail info@butlerart.com; internet www.butlerart.com; f. 1919; 20,000 individual works spanning 4 centuries; Marine colln; impressionist works; early 20th-century works; contemporary works; brs in Salem and Howland Township; Dir and Chief Curator Dr LOUIS A. ZONA.

Canton Museum of Art: 1001 Market Ave N, Canton, OH 44702; tel. (330) 453-7666; fax (330) 453-1034; internet www.cantonart.org; f. 1935 as Little Civic Art Gallery, present name 1995; colln of American watercolours of 19th and 20th centuries and contemporary ceramics; Exec. Dir M. J. ALBACETE; Pres. DONALD JENSEN; Sec. GLEN BECKER; Treas. RON VAN HORN.

Cincinnati Art Museum: 953 Eden Park Dr., Cincinnati, OH 45202; tel. (513) 639-2995; fax (513) 721-0129; e-mail information@cincyart.org; internet www.cincinnatiartmuseum.org; f. 1881; colln incl. ancient art of Egypt, Greece, Rome and Near and Far Eastern art, art of Africa and the Americas, costume and textiles, prints, drawings, photographs, paintings, sculpture, decorative art, and contemporary art; colln of ancient Nabataean art, Herbert Greer French colln of old master prints and colln of European and American portrait miniatures; temporary exhibitions; library of 52,000 vols, 250,000 pamphlets and clippings; Chair. LARRY A. SHEAKLEY; Chief Curator Dr JAMES CRUMP; Dir AARON BETSKY (acting); Pres. GEORGE H. VINCENT; publ. *CANVAS* (6 a year).

Cleveland Museum of Art: 11150 E Blvd, Cleveland, OH 44106; tel. (216) 421-7340; fax (216) 421-0411; e-mail info@clevelandart.org; internet www.clevelandart.org; f. 1913; archives; collns incl. African art, American painting and sculpture, ancient Egyptian, near East, Greek and Roman art, art of the Americas, decorative arts and design, drawings, Chinese art, contemporary art, European painting and sculpture from 1500 to 1800, modern European painting and sculpture, Indian and SE Asian art, Japanese and Korean art, medieval art, photographs, prints, textiles and Islamic art; temporary exhibitions; library of 450,000 vols; Chair. R. STEVEN KESTNER; Dir, Pres. and CEO Dr DAVID FRANKLIN; Sec. SARAH S. CUTLER; Treas. JANET G. ASHE; publ. *Cleveland Studies in the History of Art* (1 a year).

Cleveland Museum of Natural History: One Wade Oval Dr., University Circle, Cleveland, OH 44106-1767; tel. (216) 231-4600; fax (216) 231-5919; internet www.cmnh.org; f. 1920; research and colln in fields of archaeology, botany, cultural anthropology, invertebrate paleontology, invertebrate zoology, mineralogy, ornithology, physical anthropology, vertebrate paleontology, vertebrate zoology; 5m. artefacts and specimens incl. the Hamann-Todd Osteological Colln; protects 4,500 acres of rare natural habitats throughout Northeast Ohio; Shafran Planetarium; Mueller Observatory (incl. 10$\frac{1}{2}$-inch Warner and Swasey telescope built in 1899); Wade Gallery (colln of 1,500 gems and minerals); library: Harold T. Clark Library of 60,000 vols (incl. 40,000 periodicals and 20,000 books), 1,000 Rare Book Colln; Exec. Dir and CEO Dr EVALYN GATES; Pres. A. CHACE ANDERSON; Sec. GORDON D. KINDER; Treas. JONATHON L. GRIMM; publs *Explorer* (4 a year), *Kirtlandia* (scientific papers), *Tracks* (6 a year).

Columbus Museum of Art: 480 E Broad St, Columbus, OH 43215; tel. (614) 221-6801; e-mail info@cmaohio.org; internet www.columbusmuseum.org; colln of late 19th- and early 20th-century American and European modern art; regional collns of woodcarvings; paintings and lithographs; photographs; Philip and Suzanne Schiller Colln of American Social Commentary Art 1930–70; Exec. Dir NANNETTE V. MACIEJUNES; Pres. JAY VORYS; Sec. LOANN W. CRANE; Treas. MICHAEL A. PETRECCA.

Dayton Art Institute: 456 Belmonte Park N, Dayton, OH 45405; tel. (937) 223-5277; fax (937)223-3140; e-mail info@daytonart.org; internet www.daytonartinstitute.org; f. 1919; collns of 26,000 objects spanning 5,000 years of art history, incl. ancient, European, Oceanic, Asian, Pre-Columbian and American fine and decorative art; outdoor sculptures; Chair. ROB CONNELLY; Exec. Dir MICHAEL R. ROEDIGER.

Kennedy Museum of Art: Lin Hall, Ohio Univ., Athens, OH 45701; tel. (740) 593-1304; fax (740) 593-1305; e-mail kennedymuseum@ohio.edu; internet www.ohio.edu/museum; attached to Ohio Univ.; colln of 8,000 objects incl. SW Native American arts and crafts, 700 Navajo weavings, 1,200 jewellery items and silver work, post-1945 print colln, 20th-century American Art and works on paper; 300 objects of African art incl. textiles, sculpture, jewellery, clothing and ceremonial items; Dir EDWARD E. PAULEY; Curator PETRA KRALICKOVA; publ. *KMA Magazine* (2 a year).

Kent State University Museum: 515 Hilltop Dr., POB 5190, Rockwell Hall, Kent, OH 44242-0001; E Main St and S Lincoln St, Kent, OH 44242-0001; tel. (330) 672-3450; fax (330) 672-3218; e-mail museum@kent.edu; internet www.kent.edu/museum; f. 1985; colln of 20,000 objects incl. American glass, clothing and textiles, furniture, paintings and decorative arts; Dir JEAN DRUESEDOW; Curator Asst Prof. SARA HUME.

Massillon Museum: 121 Lincoln Way E, Massillon, OH 44646; tel. (330) 833-4061; fax (330) 833-2925; internet www.massillonmuseum.org; f. 1933 as Baldwin Museum, present name 1938; 100,000 objects

that incl. paintings and prints, ceramics, glass, photographs, textiles, costumes, military artefacts, city records, agricultural equipment, Native American objects, quilts, books, musical instruments, medical equipment, furniture, toys, household equipment and circus memorabilia; 60,000 photographs; 18,000 archival and reference documents; 700 geological specimens and fossils; Exec. Dir and Curator ALEXANDRA NICHOLIS; Chair. JUDY PAQUELET; Treas. and Sec. MAUDE SLAGLE.

Miami University Art Museum: 801 S Patterson Ave, Oxford, OH 45056; tel. (513) 529-2232; e-mail artmuseum@muohio.edu; internet arts.muohio.edu/art-museum; f. 1978; 16,000 artworks incl. prints, paintings and sculptures; incl. Outdoor Sculpture Park; William Holmes McGuffey Museum (open by appointment); Charles M. Messer Leica Camera Colln; Dir Dr ROBERT S. WICKS.

National Museum of the US Air Force: 1100 Spaatz St, Wright-Patterson Air Force Base, OH 45433-7102; tel. (937) 255-3286; e-mail nationalmuseum.usaf@wpafb.af.mil; internet www.nationalmuseum.af.mil; f. 1923; displays of historical events, individuals and materials incl. 360 aircraft and missiles; preservation of milestones in aerospace technology; study of aviation and aerospace history; Research Center available by appointment only; 12 field museums; 7 heritage centres; Dir JOHN L. HUDSON; Sr Curator TERRY AITKEN.

Ohio River Museum: 601 Front St, Marietta, OH 45750; tel. (740) 373-3750; e-mail cmmoriv@ohiohistory.org; internet ohsweb.ohiohistory.org/places/se09; attached to Ohio Historical Soc.; colln depicting origins and natural history of the Ohio River and history of steamboat on the Ohio River system; colln of boat building, mussels and tool and equipment from steamboat era; Site Man. F. BARMANN.

Southern Ohio Museum: 825 Gallia St, Portsmouth, OH 45662; tel. (740) 354-5629; e-mail info@somacc.com; internet www.somacc.com; f. 1979; Charles and William Wertz Colln: 10,000 prehistoric Native American objects; Anna Louise Stanton Doll Colln of 18th, 19th and early 20th century in bisque, china, papier mache and tin; Carl Ackerman Colln: 10,000 historic local photographs; Art of the Ancients Colln: 10,000 objects aging from 1,500 to 8,000 years old; library of 1,000 vols; Dir PEGI WILKES; Chief Curator SARA JOHNSON.

Springfield Museum of Art: 107 Cliff Park Rd, Springfield, OH 45501; tel. (937) 325-4673; internet www.springfieldart.museum; f. 1946 as Springfield Art Asscn, present name 1989; works of Berenice Abbott, George Bellows, Robert Brackman, Alfred T. Bricher, Thomas Doughty, Emil S. Carlsen, Ethel Cook, Stuart Davis and Charles Demuth; Dir ANN FORTESCUE; Curator CHARLOTTE GORDON.

Taft Museum of Art: 316 Pike St, Cincinnati, OH 45202; tel. (513) 241-0343; fax (513) 241-7762; e-mail taftmuseum@taftmuseum.org; internet www.taftmuseum.org; f. 1820, present name and status 1932; European and American master paintings; Chinese ceramics and works of art; European decorative arts; 17th- to 19th-century watches; pieces of early 19th-century American furniture and European and American sculptures; Dir and CEO DEBORAH EMONT SCOTT; Chief Curator LYNNE AMBROSINI.

Toledo Museum of Art: POB 1013, Toledo, OH 43697; 2445 Monroe St, Toledo, OH 43620; tel. (419) 255-8000; internet www.toledomuseum.org; f. 1901; 30,000 works of art: American and European painting, his-

tory of art in glass, ancient Greek, Roman and Egyptian works, Asian and African art, medieval art, sculpture, decorative arts, graphic arts, and modern and contemporary art; sculpture garden and glass pavilion; Dir and CEO BRIAN P. KENNEDY; Chair. ELIZABETH BRADY; Vice-Chair. and Sec. JOHN S. SZUCH; Vice-Chair. and Treas. GEORGE L. CHAPMAN; Chief Curator CAROLYN PUTNEY.

Zanesville Museum of Art: 620 Military Rd, Zanesville, OH 43701; tel. (740) 452-0741; internet www.zanesvilleart.org; colln of Ohio glass and pottery, decorative arts ancient to Tiffany and works by Cezanne, Grandma Moses, Lautrec, Matisse, Picasso, Rembrandt, Rubens; Asian, Indian, African, Pre-Columbian collns; Madame Alexander Doll Colln; Dir SUSAN TALBOT-STANAWAY.

Oklahoma

Cherokee Strip Museum: 2617 W Fir Ave, Perry, OK 73077-7903; tel. (580) 336-2405; e-mail csmuseum@okhistory.org; internet www.cherokee-strip-museum.org; f. 1968; attached to Oklahoma Historical Soc.; artefacts, photographs and documents tracing history of the Cherokee Outlet and its people; original furnishings and memorabilia of Henry S. Johnston and fmr gov., Henry Bellmon; beadwork artefacts of Otoe-Missouria Indians; music room; tamac pottery; guns and lawmen; early 1900s kitchen; Historical Facility Man. PEGGY HAXTON.

Cherokee Strip Regional Heritage Center: 507 S Fourth St, Enid, OK 73701; tel. (580) 237-1907; fax (580) 234-1055; e-mail csrhcinfo@okhistory.org; internet www.csrhc.org; f. 1960, present location 1975, present name and status 2005; attached to Oklahoma Historical Soc.; living history area, Humphrey Heritage Village, which is colln of 4 historically significant blgs incl. 1893 US Land Office; Dir ANDI HOLLAND; Curator DAVE KENNEDY; Chair. LEW O. WARD; Sec. DARON RUDY; Treas. Dr DAVID RUSSELL.

Fred Jones Jr Museum of Art: 555 Elm Ave, Norman, OK 73019-3003; tel. (405) 325-3272; fax (405) 325-7696; e-mail museuminfo@ou.edu; internet www.ou.edu/fjjma.html; f. 1936, present name 1992; attached to Univ. of Oklahoma; 16,000 objects incl. Eugene B. Adkins Colln andJames T. Bialac Native American Art Colln, French Impressionism, 20th-century American painting and sculpture, traditional and contemporary Native American art, art of the Southwest, ceramics, photography, contemporary art, Asian art and graphics from 16th century to the present; Dir GHISLAIN D'HUMIERES.

International Photography Hall of Fame & Museum: Science Museum Oklahoma, 2100 NE 52nd St, Oklahoma City, OK 73111; tel. (405) 424-4055; fax (405) 424-4058; e-mail info@iphf.org; internet www.iphf.org; f. 1965; Photographic Equipment Colln; Photographic Images Colln; Pres. JOHN W. NAGEL; Sec. DAVID HANLON; Exec. Dir MICHAEL R. SCALF, SR.

Mabee-Gerrer Museum of Art: 1900 W MacArthur Dr., Shawnee, OK 74804; tel. (405) 878-5300; fax (405) 878-5133; e-mail info@mgmoa.org; internet www.mgmoa.org; f. 1919; Egyptian, Greek and Roman objects; art from the Middle Ages and Renaissance through early 20th century and Native American, African, Oceanic and E cultural artefacts; Dir and Chief Curator DANE POLLEI; Chair. PAUL HAMMOND; Treas. CHRIS RICK.

Museum of the Western Prairie: 1100 Memorial Dr., Altus, OK 73521; tel. (580) 482-1044; e-mail muswestpr@okhistory.org; internet www.okhistory.org/outreach/

museums/westernprairie.html; attached to Oklahoma Historical Soc.; showcases natural history to industrial history of SW Oklahoma; Dir JENNIE BUCHANAN.

National Cowboy & Western Heritage Museum: 1700 NE 63rd St, Oklahoma City, OK 73111; tel. (405) 478-2250; fax (405) 478-4714; e-mail info@nationalcowboymuseum .org; internet www.nationalcowboymuseum .org; f. 1955; classic and contemporary Western art; colln of American cowboy, rodeos, Native American culture, Victorian firearms, frontier military and Western performers; sponsors educational programs and scholarly research; Donald C. & Elizabeth M. Dickinson Research Center; Pres. ROBERT A. FUNK.

Oklahoma City Museum of Art: 415 Couch Dr., Oklahoma City, OK 73102; tel. (405) 236-3100; e-mail info@okcmoa.com; internet www.okcmoa.com; f. 1989 by merger of Oklahoma Art Center with Oklahoma Museum of Art; paintings, prints, photographs and sculptures of American, European, post-war and contemporary art from 1945 to present; drawings and prints from 16th century to the present; art glass; library of 5,000 vols; Chair. ELBY J. BEAL; Pres. and CEO GLEN GENTELE; Sec. JOHN R. BOZALIS; Treas. PETER B. DELANEY; publ. *CONNECT* (3 a year).

Oklahoma History Center: 800 Nazih Zuhdi Dr., Oklahoma City, OK 73105; tel. (405) 522-5248; fax (405) 522-5402; e-mail okhc@okhistory.org; internet www .okhistorycenter.org; attached to Oklahoma Historical Soc.; 50 topics and 2,000 artefacts reflecting Oklahoma's past; Dir Dr DEE HENDERSON.

Oklahoma Territorial Museum: 402 E Oklahoma, Guthrie, OK 73044; tel. (405) 282-1889; e-mail guthriecomplex@okhistory .org; internet www.okhistory.org/outreach/ museums/territorialmuseum.html; attached to Oklahoma Historical Soc.; artefacts, photographs and paintings showcasing history of Oklahoma's Territorial period; Carnegie Library; Dir NATHAN V. TURNER.

Philbrook Museum of Art: POB 52510, Tulsa, OK 74152; 2727 S Rockford Rd, Tulsa, OK 74114; tel. (918) 749-7941; e-mail curator@philbrook.org; internet www .philbrook.org; African art; American and European paintings and sculptures; Asian art; Italian Renaissance; George R. Kravis, II Design Colln; modern and contemporary art; native American art; outdoor sculpture; works on paper; library of 15,000 vols, 125 periodicals; Chief Curator CATHERINE WHITNEY.

Pioneer Heritage Townsite Center: 201 N Ninth St, Frederick, OK 73542; tel. (580) 335-5844; e-mail pioneer@okhistory.org; internet www.okhistory.org/outreach/ museums/pioneertownsite.html; f. 1977; attached to Oklahoma Historical Soc.; house structures, barn and churches of 1920s; Tillman County Historical Museum exhibits life in SW Oklahoma community during territorial period, World Wars and Depression era; implement shed exhibits tractors, harrows, plows, grain separators and other pieces of early farm machinery from late 1800s to 1950s.

Pioneer Woman Museum: 701 Monument Rd, Ponca City, OK 74604-3910; tel. (580) 765-6108; e-mail piown@okhistory.org; internet www.okhistory.org/outreach/ museums/pioneerwoman.html; f. 1958; attached to Oklahoma Historical Soc.; preserves legacy of women from all races, creeds and nationalities who have contributed to devt of Oklahoma; Pioneer Woman Statue; Dir JEAN WINCHESTER.

Price Tower Arts Center: 510 Dewey Ave, Bartlesville, OK 74003; tel. (918) 336-4949; e-mail dwoodall@pricetower.org; internet pricetower.org; 3,000 works of art; Exec. Dir TIMOTHY L. BORUFF; publ. *The View*.

Route 66 Museum: 2229 W Gary Blvd, Clinton, OK 73601; tel. (580) 323-7866; e-mail rt66mus@okhistory.org; internet www.route66.org; f. 1968 as Museum of the Western Trails, present status 1991, present name 1995; attached to Oklahoma Historical Soc.; vehicles and artefacts exhibiting history and culture of each decade concerning road construction, transportation, lodging, restaurants, garages, curio shops; Dir PAT SMITH.

Sam Noble Museum: 2401 Chautauqua Ave, Norman, OK 73072-7029; tel. (405) 325-4712; fax (405) 325-7699; internet www .snomnh.ou.edu; f. 1899; attached to Univ. of Oklahoma; 7m. objects and specimens in 12 collns: archaeology, ethnology, herpetology, ichthyology, invertebrates, invertebrate paleontology, mammalogy, ornithology, Native American languages, paleobotany and micropaleontology, Okla colln of genomic resources and vertebrate paleontology; Dir Dr MICHAEL A. MARES.

Science Museum Oklahoma: 2100 NE 52nd St, Oklahoma City, OK 73111-7107; tel. (405) 602-6664; fax (405) 602-3768; e-mail communications@sciencemuseumok .org; internet www.sciencemuseumok.org; f. 1962 as Oklahoma Science and Arts Foundation, present name 2004; planetarium and Dome Theatre; Chair. JAMES W. FARRIS; Pres. DONALD R. OTTO; Sec. KYM KOCH THOMPSON.

Sherwin Miller Museum of Jewish Art: 2021 E 71st St, Tulsa, OK 74136; tel. (918) 492-1818; fax (918) 492-1888; e-mail director@jewishmuseum.net; internet jewishmuseum.net; f. 1965, present name 2000; colln of 10,000 artefacts showing 5,000 year history of the Jewish people from pre-Canaanite era through settling of the Jewish community in Tulsa and the American SW; Julius and Gertrude Livingston Oklahoma Jewish Archives, Tulsa Jewish Genealogical Soc. and Markovitz Jewish Genealogy Study and Research Center; Exec. Dir ARTHUR FELDMAN; Curator Dr KAREN YORK.

Spiro Mounds Archaeological Center: 18154 First St, Spiro, OK 74959; tel. (918) 962-2062; e-mail spiro@okhistory.org; internet www.okhistory.org/outreach/ museums/spiromounds.html; f. 1978; attached to Oklahoma Historical Soc.; 150-acre site encompassing 12 southern mounds containing evidence of an Indian culture that occupied the site from AD 850 to 1450; organizes solstice and equinox alignment tours; Dir DENNIS PETERSON.

Thomas Gilcrease Museum: 1400 N Gilcrease Museum Rd, Tulsa, OK 74127-2100; tel. (918) 596-2700; internet www.gilcrease .org; f. 1949; attached to Univ. of Tulsa; anthropological colln of 250,000 specimens, covering prehistoric and historic archaeology and ethnographic materials from Native American, Hispanic and Anglo-American cultural traditions; 10,000 paintings, drawings, prints and sculptures from colonial times to the present; library of 100,000 vols of rare books, MSS and archival material; Exec. Dir Dr DUANE H. KING; Chair. HANS C. HELMERICH; Sec. JOAN B. ATKINSON.

Oregon

3D Center of Art & Photography: 1928 NW Lovejoy, Portland, OR 97209; tel. (503) 227-6667; internet www.3dcenter.us; f. 1994; history of 3-D: antique stereocards to View-Master, contemporary 3-D photography, len-

ticulars, anaglyphs and computer generated 3-D art; Dir STACY WEBB.

A. R. Bowman Memorial Museum: 246 N Main St, Prineville, OR 97754; tel. (541) 447-3715; e-mail bowmuse@netscape.net; internet www.bowmanmuseum.org; f. 1971; historical and genealogical exhibits and research; Exec. Dir GORDON GILLESPIE.

Albany Regional Museum: 136 Lyon St S, Albany, OR 97321; tel. (541) 967-7122; e-mail armuseum@peak.org; internet www .armuseum.com; f. 1980; artefacts, documents and photographs depicting history and culture of Albany, Oregon, and its immediate surroundings; Chair. LARRY BARDELL; Sec. MARY JACQ BURCK; Treas. MICHAEL KOK.

Classic Aircraft Aviation Museum, Inc.: POB 91430, Portland, OR 97291-0430; 3005 NE Cornell Rd, Hillsboro, OR 97125; tel. (503) 693-1414; internet www.classicaircraft .org; acquisition, restoration and operation of classic military aircraft and aviation artefacts; educational programmes about the jet age and cold-war period; aerospace technology; Dir Dr DOUG DONKEL.

Coos Art Museum: 235 Anderson Ave, Coos Bay, OR 97420; tel. (541) 267-3901; e-mail info@coosart.org; internet www.coosart.org; f. 1950 as Coos Artist League; 550 pieces of atwork, incl. contemporary fine art prints and original works in all media by Pacific NW artists.

Grants Pass Museum of Art: POB 966, Grants Pass, OR 97528; 229 SW 'G' St, Grants Pass, OR 97526; tel. (541) 479-3290; fax (541) 479-1218; e-mail museum@ gpmuseum.com; internet www.gpmuseum .com; f. 1979 as Gallery One; Exec. Dir CHRIS PONDELICK; Pres. SUSAN EILEEN BURNES; Sec. ERVA ZABEL; Treas. DON STOCKING.

Jordan Schnitzer Museum of Art: 1223 Univ. of Oregon, Eugene, OR 97403-1233; 1430 Johnson Lane Eugene, Eugene, OR 97403; tel. (541) 346-3027; fax (541) 346-0976; e-mail jsmadesk@uoregon.edu; internet jsma.uoregon.edu; f. 1933, present name 2005; attached to Univ. of Oregon; galleries featuring 13,000 objects of American, Chinese, European, Japanese, Korean, and S Asian art; Gordon Gilkey Research Center; animation classes, UO Geography Seminars and photography courses; Pres. GREG FITZ-GERALD; Exec. Dir JILL HARTZ.

Museum of Natural and Cultural History: 1680 E 15th Ave, Eugene, OR 97403-1224; tel. (541) 346-3024; fax (541) 346-5334; e-mail mnh@uoregon.edu; internet natural-history.uoregon.edu; f. 1935 as Oregon State Museum of Anthropology and UO Museum of Natural History; attached to Univ. of Oregon; 1m. ethnographic and archaeological objects; 100,000 fossils and biological specimens from Oregon, the Pacific Northwest and around the world; Native American cultural and archaeological artefacts, spanning 15,000 years; incl. cache of 10,000-year-old sagebrush bark sandals, extensive fossil collns, several hundred w Indian baskets made before 1900; Dir JON ERLANDSON; publ. *University of Oregon Anthropological Papers* (irregular).

Oregon Historical Society Museum: 1200 SW Park Ave, Portland, OR 97205; tel. (503) 222-1741; fax (503) 221-2035; e-mail orhist@ ohs.org; internet www.ohs.org; f. 1898; 85,000 artefacts of local history; library of 30,000 vols, 25,000 maps, 12,000 linear ft of MSS, 4,000 serials titles, 6,000 vertical files, 16,000 rolls of microfilm, 8.5m. ft of film and video cassettes, 10,000 oral history cassettes, 2.5m. photographs; Exec. Dir KERRY TYMCHUK; Pres. Dr JERRY E. HUDSON; Sec. Dr

LESLEY HALLICK; Treas. PAT RITZ; publ. *Oregon Historical Quarterly* (4 a year).

Oregon Sports Hall of Fame and Museum: 8500 SE McLoughlin Blvd, Suite 101, Portland, OR 97222; tel. (503) 227-7466; e-mail info@oregonsportshall.org; internet www.oregonsportshall.org; f. 1978; Oregon's athletic history; seminars and programmes concerning history and participation in sports; presently closed for relocation; Exec. Dir MIKE ROSE; Pres. CHUCK RICHARDS; Sec. and Treas. GREG HITCHCOCK.

Pennsylvania

Academy of Natural Sciences: 1900 Benjamin Franklin Parkway, Philadelphia, PA 19103-1195; tel. (215) 299-1000; e-mail presidentsoffice@ansp.org; internet www.ansp.org; f. 1812; attached to Drextel Univ.; 17m. specimens; collns incl. butterflies and dinosaurs; dioramas; a fusion of art and science; library of 200,000 vols; Pres. and CEO GEORGE W. GEPHART, JR; publs *Notulae Naturae* (irregular), *Proceedings of the Academy of Natural Sciences of Philadelphia*, *Special Publications*.

American Philosophical Society Museum: Richardson Hall, Second Fl., 431 Chestnut St, Philadelphia, PA 19106; Philosophical Hall, 104 S Fifth St, Philadelphia, PA 19106; tel. (215) 440-3442; fax (215) 238-0340; e-mail museum@amphilsoc.org; internet www.apsmuseum.org; 3,000 artefacts and fine art objects of 18th century; portraits of founding fathers; models of inventions; scientific instruments made by or relating to David Rittenhouse and other early APS members; plant specimens collected by Lewis and Clark; Benjamin Franklin's personal belongings; Dir and Curator Dr SUE ANN PRINCE.

American Swedish Historical Museum: 1900 Pattison Ave, Philadelphia, PA 19145; tel. (215) 389-1776; fax (215) 389-7701; e-mail info@americanswedish.org; internet www.americanswedish.org; f. 1926; contributions by Swedes and Swedish-Americans since the mid-17th century; 12 galleries dedicated to all major historical and cultural aspects of Swedish accomplishments; exhibition on New Sweden Colony (1638–1655); colln of letters, documents and designs by John Ericsson; library of 11,000 vols, primary source genealogical documents and sources; Chair. JOHN MCCANN; Exec. Dir TRACEY BECK; Curator CARRIE HOGAN.

Barnes Foundation Gallery, Collections and Arboretum: 300 N Latch's Lane, Merion, PA 19066-1729; tel. (610) 667-0290; fax (610) 664-4026; e-mail info@barnesfoundation.org; internet www.barnesfoundation.org; f. 1922; offers courses in visual literacy and the philosophy and appreciation of art; colln of 1,000 paintings, incl. works by El Greco, Titian, Goya, Rubens, Cézanne, Renoir, Modigliani, Soutine, Picasso, Matisse and Van Gogh; sculpture, antique furniture and wrought iron; Arboretum, school with courses in botany, horticulture and landscape design; Teacher Institute with courses in visual arts and environmental and horticultural studies; library of 4,000 vols; Chair. Dr BERNARD C. WATSON; Sec. JACQUELINE F. ALLEN; Treas. STEPHEN J. HARMELIN.

Berman Museum of Art: 601 E Main St, Collegeville, PA 19426-1000; tel. (610) 409-3500; fax (610) 409-3664; internet www.ursinus.edu/netcommunity; f. 1989; attached to Ursinus College; 4,000 paintings, prints, drawings, sculpture, decorative and cultural objects; paper colln of 1,500 pieces of art by Durer, Rembrandt, and Cézanne; early 20th-century New York and Philadel-

phia School artists; Op and Pop Art compositions; paintings and prints of Francoise Gilot; colln of Pennsylvania German art and artefacts; Dir LISA TREMPER HANOVER.

Brandywine River Museum: POB 141, Chadds Ford, PA 19317; tel. (610) 388-2700; e-mail inquiries@brandywine.org; internet www.brandywinemuseum.org; f. 1971; colln of works by 3 generations of Wyeths; colln of American illustration, still life and landscape painting; library of 3,500 vols, 22,000 items, incl. portfolios and scrapbooks, films and video cassettes, sound cassettes and phonograph records, historic calendars and posters, exhibition posters and brochures, photographs, ephemera such as clippings, tear sheets, book jackets and archival materials related to various artists; Dir JAMES H. DUFF; Curator VIRGINIA H. O'HARA.

Carnegie Museum of Art: 4400 Forbes Ave, Pittsburgh, PA 15213-4080; tel. (412) 622-3131; e-mail cma-development@carnegiemuseums.org; internet web.cmoa.org; f. 1895; 101,477 objects; contemporary art incl. film and video works; works of American art from the late 19th century, French impressionist and post-impressionist paintings and European and American decorative arts from the late 17th century to the present; Ailsa Mellon Bruce Galleries, Heinz Architectural Center, Hall of Architecture and Hall of Sculpture; Chair. WILLIAM E. HUNT; Dir LYNN ZELEVANSKY.

Carnegie Museum of Natural History: 4400 Forbes Ave, Pittsburgh, PA 15213; tel. (412) 622-3131; e-mail cmnhweb@carnegiemnh.org; internet www.carnegiemnh.org; f. 1896; Alcoa Foundation Hall of American Indians; Benedum Hall of Geology; Bonehunters Quarry; Botany Hall; Cenozoic Hall: Hall of African Wildlife; Hall of Fossil Mammals; Hall of North American Wildlife; Hillman Hall of Minerals and Gems; Polar World: Wyckoff Hall of Arctic Life; Walton Hall of Ancient Egypt; spec. colln of Dinosaurs spanning the Mesozoic era; library of 132,000 vols, 5,400 periodical titles; Dir Dr SAMUEL M. TAYLOR; publ. *Annals of Carnegie Museum* (4 a year).

Carnegie Science Center: 1 Allegheny Ave, Pittsburgh, PA 15212-5850; tel. (412) 237-3400; fax (412) 237-3375; internet www.carnegiesciencecenter.org; f. 1991; 400 interactive exhibits; 3 live demonstration theatres; 4-storey Imax dome theatre; 36,000-sq. ft sport science exhibition; a planetarium, Cold War submarine moored in Pittsburgh's Ohio River; model-railway display; working foundry; Tesla coil and Van de Graaff generator; interactive exhibits featuring robotics, cryogenics and lasers; Buhl Planetarium and Institute of Popular Science; Co-Dir RON BAILLIE; Co-Dir ANN METZGER.

Earth and Mineral Sciences Museum and Art Gallery: 16 Deike Bldg, University Park, PA 16802-5000; tel. (814) 865-6336; fax (814) 863-7708; e-mail museum@ems.psu.edu; internet www.ems.psu.edu/outreach/museum; attached to College of Earth and Mineral Sciences, Pennsylvania State Univ. in State College; displays minerals like azurite and velvet malachite from Bisbee, Arizona; amazonite crystals from the Pikes' Peak, Colorado; 22,000 specimens of fossils, rocks and minerals; collns of glasses, ceramics, metals, plastics, synthetic materials, old mining and scientific equipment and archaeological artefacts; spec. colln: 100 mine safety lamps and scientific instruments and specimens of Frederick Augustus Genth; Chair. MARK PATZKOWSKY; Dir RUSS GRAHAM.

Everhart Museum of Natural History, Science and Art: 1901 Mulberry St, Scran-

ton, PA 18510-2390; tel. (570) 346-7186; fax (570) 346-0652; e-mail general.information@everhart-museum.org; internet everhart-museum.org; f. 1908; colln of historic and contemporary American paintings; colln of Dorflinger glass; American folk art; works from Native American sources, pre-Columbian and S American objects, Africa, China, Japan, India, Indonesia, Korea and Tibet; colln of rocks, fossils, minerals, plant specimens, shell coral and a wet specimen; Chair. JOSEPH T. WRIGHT; Sec. MICHELE HUGHES; Treas. KEN M. MARQUIS.

Fort Pitt Museum: Point State Park, 101 Commonwealth Pl, Pittsburgh, PA 15222; tel. (412) 281-9285; e-mail membership@heinzhistorycenter.org; internet www.heinzhistorycenter.org; f. 1969; attached to Senator John Heinz History Center; W Pennsylvania's early history through interactive exhibits and artefacts; life-like museum figures; W Pennsylvania's role during the French and Indian War and the American Revolution; Dir ALAN GUTCHESS.

Franklin Institute Science Museum: 222 N 20th St, Philadelphia, PA 19103; tel. (215) 448-1200; fax (215) 448-1235; e-mail curatorial@fi.edu; internet www.fi.edu; f. 1934; Imax Theater, 3D theatre; exhibits and demonstrations in physical sciences and technology; workshops and teacher training; Fels Planetarium Theater; Chair. MARSHA R. PERELMAN; Pres. and CEO Dr DENNIS M. WINT; publ. *Journal*.

Frick Art & Historical Center: 7227 Reynolds St, Pittsburgh, PA 15208; tel. (412) 371-0600; e-mail info@thefrickpittsburgh.org; internet www.thefrickpittsburgh.org; f. 1881; fine and decorative arts, cars, carriages, bldgs and other items related to the Frick family's life in Pittsburgh; works on paper by Jean-François Millet, a group of Renaissance and Baroque bronzes; colln of early Renaissance painting and 18th-century French painting and decorative art; Frick Art museum, Clayton and Car and Carriage Museum; Dir BILL BODINE; Dir of Curatorial Affairs SARAH J. HALL; Chair. DAVID A. BROWNLEE; Sec. CAROL A. WORD; Treas. MATTHEW J. TEPLITZ.

Hoyt Institute of Fine Arts: 124 E Leasure Ave, New Castle, PA 16101; tel. (724) 652-2882; fax (724) 657-8786; e-mail hoyt@hoytartcenter.org; internet www.hoytartcenter.org; Shenango China Colln, WPA Poster Colln and Louis J. G. Buehler colln; arts classes, workshops and annual exhibits; library of 1,000 vols; Exec. Dir KIMBERLY KOLLER-JONES.

Penn Museum–University of Pennsylvania Museum of Archaeology and Anthropology: 3260 South St, Philadelphia, PA 19104; tel. (215) 898-4000; fax (215) 898-0657; e-mail info@museum.upenn.edu; internet www.penn.museum; f. 1887; 1m. objects from Egypt, Mesopotamia, Canaan and Israel, Mesoamerica, Asia and the ancient Mediterranean world; artefacts from native peoples of the Americas and Africa; library of 100,000 vols, archives with 300,000 photographic items and more than 600m. of textual records; Dir Dr RICHARD HODGES; Chair. MICHAEL J. KOWALSKI; publ. *Expedition* (3 a year).

Pennsylvania Academy of the Fine Arts: 118–128 N Broad St, Philadelphia, PA 19102; tel. (215) 972-7600; fax (215) 569-0153; internet www.pafa.org; f. 1805; 19th- and 20th-century American paintings, sculptures, and works on paper; Albert M. Greenfield American Art Resource; library of 16,000 vols, 55 current periodical subscriptions, 20,000 slides; Pres. and CEO DAVID R. BRIGHAM; Sr Curator ROBERT COZZOLINO;

Chair. KEVIN F. DONOHOE; Sec. HERBERT S. RIBAND, JR; Treas. THOMAS L. BENNETT.

Philadelphia History Museum: 15 S Seventh St, Philadelphia, PA 19106; tel. (215) 685-4830; fax (215) 685-4837; e-mail info@ philadelphiahistory.org; internet www .philadelphiahistory.org; f. 1938; 10,500 objects and 800 paintings by Philadelphia artists like Charles Wilson Peale and his sons; portraits of local and nat. leaders: William Penn, Benjamin Franklin, and John Quincy Adams; spec. colln incl. objects from Balch Institute of Ethnic Studies and CIGNA; Exec. Dir and CEO CHARLES CROCE; Sr Curator JEFFREY R. RAY; Pres. JAMES J. MAZZARELLI, JR; Sec. LISA YANG; Treas. GREGORY KLEIBER.

Philadelphia Museum of Art: POB 7646, Philadelphia, PA 19101-7646; tel. (215) 763-8100; fax (215) 236-4465; e-mail mpr@ philamuseum.org; internet www .philamuseum.org; f. 1876; 230,000 works of art, incl. paintings, prints, sculpture and silver from medieval to contemporary times representing European, American, and Far Eastern art; library of 200,000 vols; Chair. CONTANCE H. WILLIAMS; Dir and CEO TIMOTHY RUB; publ. *Bulletin* (irregular).

Attached Museum:

   Rodin Museum: POB 7646, Benjamin Franklin Parkway, 22nd St, Philadelphia, PA 19101-7646; tel. (215) 568-6026; e-mail visitorservices@philamuseum.org; internet www.rodinmuseum.org; f. 1923, present status 1939; houses 130 sculptures; Chair. BARBARA ARONSON.

Reading Public Museum: 500 Museum Rd, Reading, PA 19611-1425; tel. (610) 371-5850; fax (610) 371-5632; e-mail museum@ readingpublicmuseum.org; internet www .readingpublicmuseum.org; f. 1904, present status 1992; colln of Pennsylvania German folk art; an Egyptian mummy; 25-acre arboretum; Neag Planetarium; Dir and CEO JOHN GRAYDON SMITH; Chair. KATHLEEN KLEPPINGER; Sec. LEIGH A. RYE; Treas. SOCRATES J. GEORGEADIS.

State Museum of Pennsylvania: 300 N St, Harrisburg, PA 17120-0024; tel. (717) 787-4980; fax (717) 783-4558; e-mail bhager@ state.pa.us; internet www.statemuseumpa .org; f. 1905; 4,000,000 objects of archaeology, community and domestic life, fine arts, paleontology and geology, industry and technology, popular culture and political history and zoology and botany; incl. planetarium; Dir DAVID W. DUNN (acting).

Suzanne H. Arnold Art Gallery: Lebanon Valley College, 101 N College Ave, Annville, PA 17003-1400; tel. (717) 867-6445; e-mail gallery@lvc.edu; internet www.lvc.edu/ gallery; attached to Lebanon Valley College; works from the 16th century to the present: edieval manuscripts, Renaissance prints, Japanese woodcuts, and Pop Art, as well as installations, drawings; paper colln; African and Inuit art; Dir Dr BARBARA McNULTY.

Westmoreland Museum of American Art: 221 N Main St, Greensburg, PA 15601; tel. (724) 837-1500; fax (724) 837-2921; e-mail info@wmuseumaa.org; internet www .wmuseumaa.org; f. 1949; 3,400 objects, incl. American and SW Pennsylvania art; Dir and CEO JUDITH HANSEN O'TOOLE; Chief Curator BARBARA L. JONES.

Widener University Art Gallery: 1 University Pl., Chester, PA 19013; tel. (610) 499-1189; internet www.widener.edu/about/ artgallery; Alfred O. Deshong Colln of 19th- and 20th-century American paintings; 19th-century European paintings; 18th- and 19th-century Asian art; colln of African and

Oceanic pottery and pre-Columbian pottery from Peru; Collns Man. REBECCA M. WARDA.

Woodmere Art Museum: 9201 Germantown Ave, Philadelphia, PA 19118; tel. (215) 247-0476; fax (215) 247-2387; e-mail education@woodmereartmuseum.org; internet www.woodmereartmuseum.org; f. 1940; 3,000 works of art incl. paintings, antique rugs, statuary, vases and objects of art dating from the 18th and 19th centuries; 9 galleries and salons; Dir and CEO Dr WILLIAM R. VALERIO; Curator Dr MATTHEW PALCZYNSKI.

Rhode Island

Annmary Brown Memorial: 21 Brown St, Providence, RI 02912; tel. (401) 863-2942; e-mail barbara_schulz@brown.edu; internet library.brown.edu/about/amb; f. present status 1948; attached to Brown Univ.; European and American paintings dating from 17th to 20th century; 105 British swords from Cyril and Harriet Mazansky British Sword Colln; Univ. Curator ROBERT EMLEN.

David Winton Bell Gallery: List Art Center, Brown Univ., 64 College St, Providence, RI 02912; tel. (401) 863-2932; fax (401) 863-9323; internet www.brown.edu/bellgallery; f. 1971; attached to Brown Univ.; 4,000 works of art dating from 16th century to present; Dir JO-ANN CONKLIN; Curator Dr IAN ALDEN RUSSELL.

Haffenreffer Museum of Anthropology: 300 Tower St, Bristol, RI 02809; tel. (401) 253-8388; fax (401) 253-1198; e-mail haffenreffermuseum@brown.edu; internet brown.edu/facilities/haffenreffer; attached to Brown Univ.; 110,000 items of ethnographic and archaeological interest mainly from North America but also from Latin America, Africa, Middle East and Asia, incl. 60,000 objects collected by Rudolf F. Haffenreffer; Herbert Spinden Photographic Archive of 20,000 images and documents relating to Central American archaeology and ethnography from the early 20th century, incl. many images of important archaeological sites that have since been altered or destroyed; Kensinger Colln with 5,000 photographs and related field notes and texts from anthropologist Ken Kensinger's research with the Cashinahua of Peru in 1960s; Conti Colln has 3,000 photographs dating from the late 1950s to early 1970s taken by Rhode Island photographer Gino Conti, primarily on the Hopi, Apache and Navaho reservations, and also in Mexico; library of 10,000 vols; Dir STEVEN LUBAR; Deputy Dir and Chief Curator KEVIN P. SMITH.

Museum of Art, Rhode Island School of Design: 224 Benefit St, Providence, RI 02903; tel. (401) 454-6500; fax (401) 454-6556; e-mail museum@risd.edu; internet www.risd.edu; f. 1877; 84,000 objects, incl. 19th century American paintings, contemporary art paintings dating from 1960 to present; decorative arts colln: European and American decorative arts from Medieval period to present, Asian Art spanning 5,000 years; Dir JOHN W. SMITH.

Museum of Primitive Art and Culture: 1058 Kingstown Rd, Suite 5, Peace Dale, RI 02879; tel. (401) 783-5711; internet www .primitiveartmuseum.org; f. 1892; 15,000 archaeological and ethnological objects; colln incl. chopping tool from E Africa that dates to 2m. years ago, prehistoric stone artefacts from New England, Stone Age artefacts from Europe; Curator SARAH PEABODY TURNBAUGH.

National Museum of American Illustration: Vernon Court, 492 Bellevue Ave, Newport, RI 02840; tel. (401) 851-8949; fax (401) 851-8974; e-mail art@americanillustration .org; internet www.americanillustration.org; f. 1998; housed in Vernon Court, an adapta-

tion of an 18th-century French château built in 1898; American Imagist Colln of 2,000 original works by Maxfield Parrish, Norman Rockwell, J. C. Leyendecker, Howard Pyle, N. C. Wyeth, Charles Dana Gibson, Henry Hutt, James Montgomery Flagg, Howard Chandler Christy, John Falter; comprises original art works, prints (open and ltd edns), as well as significant memorabilia, vintage materials, artefacts (such as Rockwell's first paint box and Parrish's stippling paint brushes) and photographic materials; Chair. LAURENCE S. CUTLER; Dir JUDY GOFFMAN CUTLER.

Newport Art Museum & Art Association: 76 Bellevue Ave, Newport, RI 02840; tel. (401) 848-8200; fax (401) 848-8205; e-mail info@newportartmuseum.org; internet www .newportartmuseum.org; f. 1912 as Art Asscn of Newport, present bldg 1916; colln on visual arts of Newport and SE New England; dating from late 18th century to present; Exec. Dir ELIZABETH A. GODDARD; Curator NANCY WHIPPLE GRINNELL; Curator TARA ECENARRO.

Pettaquamscutt Historical Society Museum: Old Washington County Jail, 2636 Kingstown Rd, Kingston, RI 02881; tel. (401) 783-1328; e-mail pettaquamscutt@ yahoo.com; internet www.pettaquamscutt .org; f. 1958; colln incl. artefacts and decorative arts, MSS and furniture dating from mid-19th to mid-20th century; Pres. H. GRAHAM NYE; Sec. SANDY McCAW; Treas. MARY KEANE; Dir LORI URSO.

South Carolina

American Military Museum: 360 Concord St, Suite 9, Charleston, SC 29401; tel. (843) 577-7000; e-mail info@ americanmilitarymuseum.org; internet www .americanmilitarymuseum.org; f. 1987; artefacts from 14 American conflicts dating from Revolutionary War to ongoing conflicts in Iraq and Afghanistan; colln incl. headgear, edged weapons, guns, rifles, patches, insignia, personal equipment, medals, decorations, belts, flags and other military artefacts from the US Army, Navy, Air Force, Marines and Coast Guard.

Anderson County Museum: 202 E Greenville St, Anderson, SC 29624; tel. (864) 260-4737; fax (864) 332-5320; internet andersoncountymuseum.org; 20,000 diverse artefacts incl. history of Anderson co; library of 1,600 vols, 2,000 historic photos; Curator ALISON HINMAN.

Avery Research Center for African American History and Culture: College of Charleston, 66 George St, Charleston, SC 29424; tel. (843) 953-7609; fax (843) 953-7607; e-mail averyresearchcenter@cofc.edu; internet avery.cofc.edu; f. 1985; attached to College of Charleston; colln incl. African and African American history; Exec. Dir PATRICIA WILLIAMS-LESSANE.

Bob Campbell Geology Museum: 140 Discovery Lane, Clemson, SC 29634-0130; tel. (864) 656-4600; e-mail bcgm@clemson .edu; internet www.clemson.edu/public/ geomuseum; f. 1998; attached to Clemson Univ.; colln incl. 10,000 rocks, minerals, fossils, carvings, gemstones and artefacts such as Native American tools; Dir Dr PATRICK McMILAN.

Bob Jones University Museum and Gallery: 1700 Wade Hampton Blvd, Greenville, SC 29614; tel. (864) 770-1331; fax (864) 770-1306; e-mail contact@bjumg.org; internet bjumg.org; f. 1948; European old master paintings in America dating from 14th to 19th century; Russian Icon colln dating from 14th to 20th century; 200 pieces of Gothic to 19th century furniture; 1,000 ancient artefacts; educational satellite facility at Heritage Green.

Charleston Museum: 360 Meeting St, Charleston, SC 29403; tel. (843) 722-2996; fax (843) 722-1784; e-mail info@charlestonmuseum.org; internet www .charlestonmuseum.org; f. 1773; colln incl. weaponry dating from 18th to 20th century, civil war artefacts and silver artefacts dating from colonial era to Victorian age; Heyward-Washington House, Joseph Manigault House, Dill Sanctuary; Pres. Dr JOHN RASHFORD; Dir Dr JOHN R. BRUMGARDT.

Cherokee County History & Arts Museum: Cherokee Historical and Preservation Society Inc., POB 8113, 301 College Dr., Gaffney, SC 29340; tel. (864) 489-3988; fax (864) 489-8541; e-mail chaps@cherokeecountyhistory.org; internet www .cherokeecountyhistory.org; f. 2008; 2,000 exhibits on Native Americans, American revolution and geology.

Columbia Museum of Art: POB 2068, 1515 Main St, Columbia, SC 29202; tel. (803) 799-2810; internet www.columbiamuseum.org; f. 1950; 6,000 objects incl. European and American fine and decorative art spanning centuries, Asian art and antiquities; Exec. Dir KAREN BROSIUS; Chief Curator WILL SOUTH.

Florence Museum of Art, Science and History: 558 Spruce St, Florence, SC 29501; tel. (843) 662-3351; fax (803) 753-9922; e-mail florencemuseum@me.com; internet www.florencemuseum.org; African colln: weaponry, tools and vessels from tribal cultures; Civil War colln: 1,000 items incl. uniforms, battle swords and guns; antiques from Mesopotamia, ancient Egypt, Babylonia, ancient Greece and Rome; Exec. Dir ANDREW R. STOUT.

Gibbes Museum of Art: 135 Meeting St, Charleston, SC 29401; tel. (843) 722-2706; fax (843) 720-1682; e-mail research@gibbesmuseum.org; internet www .gibbesmuseum.org; f. 1905 as Gibbes Memorial Art Gallery; 10,000 works of fine art, mainly American works with a Charleston or Southern connection; 18th-, 19th- and early 20th-century paintings, works on paper (prints, drawings, watercolours, photographs), miniature portraits and sculpture; Exec. Dir and Chief Curator ANGELA D. MACK.

Greenville County Museum of Art: 420 College St, Greenville, SC 29601; tel. (864) 271-7570; fax (864) 271-7579; e-mail info@greenvillemuseum.org; internet www .greenvillemuseum.org; Southern colln of American art dating from colonial times to present; portraits from the 1700s and art from 19th and 20th centuries; contemporary art colln incl. features artists such as Josef Albers, Jasper Johns and Andy Warhol; Dir THOMAS W. STYRON.

McKissick Museum: 816 Bull St, Columbia, SC 29208; tel. (803) 777-7251; fax (803) 777-2829; e-mail mckscal@mailbox.sc.edu; internet www.cas.sc.edu/mcks; f. 1976; attached to College of Arts and Sciences, Univ. of South Carolina; collns dating to 1801 incl. natural science specimens, traditional and contemporary crafts, textiles, political memorabilia, fine and decorative arts, art glass and material culture objects; Exec. Dir Dr JANE PRZYBYSZ.

Slave Relics Museum: 208 Carn St, Walterboro, SC 29488; tel. (843) 549-9130; e-mail info@slaverelics.org; internet www .slaverelics.org; colln incl. historical artefacts, documents, photographs and memorabilia on African American culture; artefacts used by enslaved Africans dating from 1750

to mid-1800s; Curator and Pres. DANNY DRAIN.

South Carolina Confederate Relic Room & Military Museum: 301 Gervais St, Columbia, SC 29201; tel. (803) 737-8095; fax (803) 737-8099; internet www.crr.sc.gov; f. 1896, present status 1998; attached to South Carolina Budget and Control Board; military history museum of state; colln of military material of Revolutionary War, Mexican War, Civil War, Spanish-American War, First World War and Second World War; colln incl. images of troops stationed on Mexican Border in 1916, crew of Second World War light cruiser and USS Columbia CL-56; Dir ALLEN ROBERSON.

South Carolina State Museum: 301 Gervais St, Columbia, SC 29201; tel. (803) 898-4921; e-mail publicrelations@scmuseum.org; internet www.southcarolinastatemuseum .org; f. 1988; 70,000 artefacts; art, cultural history, natural history, science and technology; Stringer Discovery Center; travelling exhibits; Exec. Dir WILLIAM CALLOWAY.

South Dakota

Dacotah Prairie Museum: POB 395, Aberdeen, SD 57402-0395; 21 S Main St, Aberdeen, SD 57401; tel. (605) 626-7117; e-mail dpm@brown.sd.us; internet www .dacotahprairiemuseum.com; f. 1938 as N South Dakota History Museum, present name and status 1970; colln of 40,000 artefacts; works of local and regional artists; 55 mounted specimens from North America, Africa and India; Dir SUE GATES; Pres. NINA VILHAUER; Sec. JACIE SCHLEY.

Dakota Discovery Museum: 1300 McGovern Ave, Mitchell, SD 57301; tel. (605) 996-2122; e-mail info@dakotadiscovery.com; internet dakotadiscovery.com; f. 1939; sculptures of Merriwether Lewis and William Clark by James Earle Fraser; historic village complex; American Indian beadwork and porcupine quillwork incl. clothing, bags, ceremonial regalia, utilitarian objects, horse gear, dolls and missionary items; exhibit incl. Plains Indians, Fur Trade, Dakota Territory, Railroading, Farming and Ranching, 1930s Great Depression; Exec. Dir and Curator LORI HOLMBERG.

Deadwood's Adams Museum: 54 Sherman St, Deadwood, SD 57732; tel. (605) 578-1714; fax (605) 578-1194; internet adamsmuseumandhouse.org/adamsmuseum .php; f. 1930; artefacts, folk art colln, Lakota bead and quill work, Potato Creek Johnny's gold nugget, historic photographs and maps rep. of art and natural history of the Black Hills and Wild Bill, Calamity Jane and Deadwood Dick; Chair. Dr DAVID WOLFF; Sec. and Treas. CARLA CANEVA; Curator ARLETTE HANSEN.

Heritage Center: c/o Red Cloud Indian School, 100 Mission Dr., Pine Ridge, SD 57770; tel. (605) 867-8257; e-mail heritagecenter@redcloudschool.org; internet www.redcloudschool.org/museum; f. 1982 as museum; attached to Red Cloud Indian School; Native American fine arts and Lakota tribal arts and history; 2,000 paintings, drawings and sculptures; Dir PETER STRONG; Curator MARY BORDEAUX.

Journey Museum: 222 New York St, Rapid City, SD 57701; tel. (605) 394-6923; fax (605) 394-6940; internet www.journeymuseum .org; incl. Museum of Geology on campus of the South Dakota School of Mines and Technology, South Dakota Historical Soc.'s Archeology Research Center, US Dept of Interior, Indian Arts and Craft Board's Sioux Indian Museum, Minnilusa Historical Assocn and City of Rapid City Duhamel Plains Indian Artifact Colln; colln of archaeology, geology,

paleontology, space science, Sioux Indian Museum, W Native gardens and Duhamel Colln of Native American artefacts; Exec. Dir RAY SUMMERS.

Museum of the South Dakota State Historical Society: South Dakota Cultural Heritage Center, 900 Governors Dr., Pierre, SD 57501-2217; tel. (605) 773-3458; fax (605) 773-6041; internet history.sd.gov/museum; f. 1901; attached to US Dept of Tourism; 3 galleries of local history; travelling exhibitions; 29,000 artefacts; colln of Lakota materials and internationally significant objects that document European arrival on northern plains; military colln; Dir JAY S. SMITH; Pres. BRAD TENNANT; Curator of Collns DANIEL BROSZ; Curator of Exhibits KATHRYN HIGDON; Curator of Interpretation RONETTE RUMPCA; publs *Hoofprints* (6 a year), *South Dakota History* (4 a year).

National Music Museum: c/o Univ. of South Dakota, 414 E Clark St, Vermillion, SD 57069; tel. (605) 677-5306; fax (605) 677-6995; e-mail nmm@usd.edu; internet orgs .usd.edu/nmm; f. 1973; attached to Univ. of South Dakota; 15,000 American, European and non-Western instruments; 2 18th-century grand pianos; 500 instruments made in late 19th and early 20th centuries; brass, woodwind and stringed instruments by 17th-and 18th-century Nürnberg craftsmen, incl. mems of the Haas and Oberlender families, Ernst Busch, Paul Hainlein and Jacob Denner; 17th- and 18th-century Dutch woodwind instruments by Richard Haka, Hendrik Richters, Philip Borkens and Abraham van Aardenberg; Witten-Rawlins Colln of early Italian stringed instruments; library of 5,000 vols, 20,000 periodicals; Exec. Dir Dr MARGARET DOWNIE BANKS; Chair. TOM LILLIBRIDGE; Sec. MARILYN NYBERG; Treas. JACK POWELL.

Pioneer Museum: POB 361, Hot Springs, SD 57747; 301 N Chicago St, Hot Springs, SD 57747; tel. (605) 745-5147; e-mail pioneer@pioneer-museum.com; internet www .pioneer-museum.com; f. 1961 as elementary school; attached to Fall River County Historical Soc.; 600 historical pieces of art by local artists, incl. paintings and sculpted sandstone, alabaster, marble pieces, historic photographs, tapestries and quilts; handcrafted tools, old washing machines, wood cook stoves and kerosene lamps; replica of 19th-century classroom and country store; Man. WANDA AABURG; Pres. JIM BINGHAM; Sec. CAROL SIDES; Treas. JOHN PENCE.

South Dakota Agricultural Heritage Museum: c/o South Dakota State Univ., 925 11th St, POB 601, Brookings, SD 57007; tel. (605) 688-6226; fax (605) 688-6303; e-mail sdsu.agmuseum@sdstate.edu; internet www.sdstate.edu/agmuseum; attached to South Dakota State Univ.; exhibits incl. tractors and farm equipment, 1882 homestead claim shack, recreated 1915 farmhouse and historic photographs on South Dakota history, agricultural technology and rural life; Eugene Beckman Archive: original sales brochures, operators manuals, parts lists and sales premiums dating from the 1880s through the early 1960s; Dir MAC HARRIS.

South Dakota Art Museum: Medary Ave and Harvey Dunn St, POB 2250, Brookings, SD 57007; tel. (605) 688-5423; fax (605) 688-4445; e-mail sdsu_sdam@sdstate.edu; internet www.sdstate.edu/ southdakotaartmuseum; f. 1970; attached to South Dakota State Univ.; collns incl. paintings by Harvey Dunn, Native American Art (incl. clothing, quillwork, moccasins, headdresses, bags, beadwork, pipes, pottery, baskets and tools from N American Plains;

MUSEUMS AND ART GALLERIES

pottery, jewellery and rugs from SW and baskets and carvings from NW Coast of N America), Marghab Linens of 1930s–70s, Paul Goble, Native American works by Oscar Howe; photographs, paintings, sculptures, ceramics, prints and textiles of South Dakota artists; temporary exhibitions; Dir LYNN VERSHOOR; Pres. MARILYN DeLONG; Sec. MAREE LARSON; Treas. JACK STENGEL.

University Art Galleries: c/o Univ. of South Dakota, 414 E Clark St, Vermillion, SD 57069; tel. (605) 677-3177; fax (605) 677-5988; e-mail uag@usd.edu; internet www.usd .edu/uag; f. 1977; attached to Univ. of South Dakota; 1,600 pieces esp. of South Dakota artists, contemporary art, Northern Plains American Indian Art, Asian and African study collns; colln of Oscar Howe paintings; Dir ALISON ERAZMUS.

W. H. Over Museum of Natural and Cultural History: 1110 Ratingen St, Vermillion, SD 57069; tel. (605) 677-5228; internet www.whovermuseum.org; f. 1912, present name 1949; attached to Univ. of South Dakota; colln of natural history materials of the state and region; Sioux artefacts, historic photographic portraits of legendary leaders and daily life of the tribes of the upper Missouri river; 500 stereographic cards of Stanley J. Morrow's photographs about the Indians, the US Army, the river trade and booming mining towns during the post-Civil War period; Pres. MAXINE JOHNSON; Sec. Dr ROBERT FREESE; Treas. Dr CHARLES ESTEE.

Tennessee

American Museum of Science and Energy: 300 S Tulane Ave, Oak Ridge, TN 37830; tel. (865) 576-3200; e-mail information@amse.org; internet www.amse .org; f. 1949 as American Museum of Atomic Energy, present location 1975, present name 1978; attached to US Dept of Energy; operated by Enterprise Advisory Services, Inc.; one of the world's largest energy exhibitions, with live demonstrations, computers and films on all energy forms and uses; Dir DAVID SINCERBOX; Deputy Dir KEN MAYES.

Art Museum of University of Memphis (AMUM): 142 CFA Bldg, Memphis, TN 38152-3200; tel. (901) 678-2224; fax (901) 678-5118; e-mail artmuseum@memphis.edu; internet www.memphis.edu/amum; f. 1981 as Univ. Gallery, present name and status 1994; attached to College of Communication and Fine Arts; Egyptian antiquities, 180 objects of Sub-Saharan African art, 1,000 works on paper; cultural artefacts incl. Japanese armour, flintlock duelling pistols, Ethiopian spear points, Navaho textiles and ancient Greco-Roman glass; Dir LESLIE LUEBBERS.

Beechcraft Heritage Museum: POB 550, 570 Old Shelbyville Highway, Tullahoma, TN 37388; tel. (931) 455-1974; fax (931) 455-1994; e-mail info@ beechcraftheritagemuseum.org; internet www.beechcraftheritagemuseum.org; f. 1973 Staggerwing Museum Foundation, present name 2007; aviation museum tracing lineage of Beechcraft airplanes; 30 airplane models, aviation artefacts and memorabilia.

Belz Museum of Asian & Judaic Art: 119 S Main St, Concourse Level, Memphis, TN 38103; tel. (901) 523-2787; fax (901) 523-8603; e-mail info@belzmuseum.org; internet www.belzmuseum.org; f. 1998 as Peabody Place Museum; Asian art colln: 900 objects dating from 202BC to early 20th century incl. jades, ivories, sculptures, paintings, ceramics and textiles; colln of Judaica, Russian lacquer boxes, contemporary glass, Italian

mosaics and mineral specimens; Dir BELINDA D. FISH; Chair and CEO JACK BELZ.

Cowan Railroad Museum: POB 53, 108 Front St, Cowan, TN 37318-0053; tel. (931) 967-3078; e-mail secretary@ cowanrailroadmuseum.org; internet www .cowanrailroadmuseum.org; f. 1976; colln of 1000 historic railroad and Cowan city artefacts, period costumes, photographs, tools, documents, old maps and out-of-print railroad books; Pres. MARK LEDBETTER; Sec. MARYANN KNOWLES; Treas. DAVID ELLENBURG.

Dixon Gallery & Gardens: 4339 Park Ave, Memphis, TN 38117; tel. (901) 761-5250; fax (901) 682-0943; internet www.dixon.org; f. 1976; 2,000 objects incl. French and American Impressionist paintings and significant holdings of German and English porcelain; Chair. STEPHEN C. REYNOLDS; Pres. D. STEPHEN MORROW; Sec. CHRISTINE P. RICHARDS; Treas. WILLIAM C. LOSCH; Dir KEVIN SHARP.

Frank H. McClung Museum: Univ. of Tennessee, 1327 Circle Park Dr., Knoxville, TN 37996-3200; tel. (865) 974-2144; fax (865) 974-3827; e-mail museum@utk.edu; internet mcclungmuseum.utk.edu; f. 1961; attached to Univ. of Tennessee; colln in anthropology, archaeology, decorative arts, local history and natural history; Dir JEFFERSON CHAPMAN.

Hunter Museum of American Art: 10 Bluff View, Chattanooga, TN 37403; tel. (423) 267-0968; fax (423) 267-9844; internet www.huntermuseum.org; f. 1952 as George Thomas Hunter Gallery of Art, present name 1975; American art from Colonial period to present; colln incl. paintings, works on paper, sculpture, furniture and contemporary studio glass; Chair. NORMA P. MILLS; Sec. MARK A. RAMSEY; Treas. CRAIG HOLLEY; Exec. Dir DANIEL E. STETSON; Chief Curator ELLEN SIMAK.

Knoxville Museum of Art: 1050 World's Fair Park, Knoxville, TN 37916-1653; tel. (865) 525-6101; fax (865) 546-3635; e-mail info@knoxart.org; internet www.knoxart.org; f. 1961, fmrly Dulin Gallery of Art, present location 1990; coll incl. 700 objects representing 20th- and 21st-century works on paper, paintings, mixed media works, sculpture and fine craft; Chair. JAY McBRIDE; Exec. Dir DAVID L. BUTLER.

McMinn County Living Heritage Museum: POB 889, Athens, TN 37371; 522 W Madison Ave, Athens, TN 37303; tel. and fax (423) 745-0329; internet www .livingheritagemuseum.com; colln of 7,000 artefacts on culture and history of SE Tennessee region from first settlers in the mid-1700s to the 1940s; Pres. LAURIE POWELL; Sec. BARRY WILLIS; Treas. TOM BIDDLE; Exec. Dir ASHLEY RUSH.

Memphis Brooks Museum of Art: 1934 Poplar Ave, Memphis, TN 38104; tel. (901) 544-6200; fax (901) 725-4071; internet www .brooksmuseum.org; f. 1916 as Brooks Memorial Art Gallery, present name 1983, present status 1989; 8,500 works of art incl. Italian Renaissance and Baroque, British, French Impressionists and 20th-century artists; 19th- and 20th-century sculpture and decorative arts, incl. period furniture and textiles; ancient Greek and Mediterranean art; library of 5,000 vols; Pres. W. MARK PARKER; Sec. NATHAN A. BICKS; Dir CAMERON KITCHIN.

Reece Museum: POB 70660, East Tennessee State Univ., Johnson City, TN 37614-1701; tel. (423) 439-4392; fax (423) 439-4283; e-mail reecemus@etsu.edu; internet www .etsu.edu/cass/reece; f. 1961; attached to East Tennessee State Univ.; colln on regional art and history; Civil War artefacts; Native American colln incl. stone axes; Dir THERESA BURCHETT.

Tennessee Museum of Aviation: POB 5587, Sevierville, TN 37864-5587; 135 Air Museum Way, Sevierville, TN 37862; tel. (865) 908-0171; fax (865) 908-8421; e-mail info@tnairmuseum.com; internet www .tnairmuseum.com; f. 2001; exhibits tracing timeline of military aviation history and Tennessee aviation history; CEO and Chair. R. NEAL MELTON.

Tennessee State Museum: 505 Deaderick St, Nashville, TN 37243-1120; tel. (615) 741-2692; e-mail museuminfo@tnmuseum.org; internet www.tnmuseum.org; f. 1817; artefacts from Paleolithic, Archaic, Woodland and Mississippian periods; 15,000 years old mastodon bones; 3,000 years old early ceremonial pottery; Civil War artefacts incl. uniforms, battle flags and weapons; Exec. Dir LOIS RIGGINS-EZZELL; Chief Curator DAN POMEROY.

West Tennessee Regional Art Center: 1200 Main St, Humboldt, TN 38343; tel. (731) 784-1787; internet www.wtrac.tn.org; f. 1994; Caldwell Colln: sculpture, watercolor paintings, drawings, prints and lithographs, pastels and silk-screens; Chair. CHARLES GUY; Sec. LOIS CURRIE; Treas. CAROLYN BARNETT; Curator BILL HICKERSON.

Texas

Amarillo Museum of Art: POB 447, Amarillo, TX 79178; 2200 S Van Buren St, Amarillo, TX 79109-2407; tel. (806) 371-5050; e-mail amoa@actx.edu; internet www .amarilloart.org; f. 1967; early American modernist paintings; European paintings from 17th to 19th century; Asian art colln incl. rep. textiles from Middle East with examples from 8th to 20th century; S and SE Asian sculpture incl. Buddhist and Hindu objects dating from 2nd century BC Gandharan works to 9th-century Java and 14th-century Khmer sculpture; Pres. T. JAY REEVES; Sec. MIKE LADD; Treas. BARRY WILSON; Dir KIM MAHAN.

Amon Carter Museum of American Art: 3501 Camp Bowie Blvd, Fort Worth, TX 76107-2695; tel. (817) 738-1933; fax (817) 665-4315; e-mail visitors@cartermuseum.org; internet www.cartermuseum.org; f. 1961; American paintings from 19th and 20th centuries; 100 sculptures by artists like Frederic Remington and Charles M. Russell; 5,700 prints from lithographs of Mexican War; library of 150,000 vols; Dir ANDREW J. WALKER.

Art Museum of Southeast Texas: 500 Main St, Beaumont, TX 77701; tel. (409) 832-3432; e-mail info@amset.org; internet www.amset.org; f. 1950 as Beaumont Art Museum, inc. 1950, present name and location 1987; 1,000 art works of modern and contemporary American art focusing on Texas and contemporary folk art (dating from 19th to 21st century); Exec. Dir LYNN CASTLE; Pres. J. MITCHELL SMITH; Sec. CARLA ALLEN; Treas. RUSS WADDILL.

Blanton Museum of Art: Univ. of Texas at Austin, 1 University Station D1303, Austin, TX 78712; Univ. of Texas at Austin, 200 E MLK, Austin, TX 78701; tel. (512) 471-7324; fax (512) 471-7023; e-mail info@ blantonmuseum.org; internet www .blantonmuseum.org; f. 1963 as Univ. Art Museum, present name 1997; attached to Univ. of Texas at Austin; 17,000 objects incl. 300 European paintings, predominantly Italian Renaissance and Baroque; American art colln incl. 4,000 paintings, prints, drawings and sculptures dating from 1875 to present; 2,000 works of Latin American art; Dir SIMONE J. WICHA; Chair. JUDY TATE.

Dallas Museum of Art: 1717 N Harwood, Dallas, TX 75201; tel. (214) 922-1200; fax

(214) 954-0174; e-mail mediarelations@ dallasmuseumofart.org; internet www .dallasmuseumofart.org; f. 1903, present location 1984; more than 23,000 works of art from around the world; arts of Africa, Asia and Pacific; Indonesian textiles; architectural and shrine objects from S Asia; Egyptian antiquities; contemporary art since 1945; American art from pre-Columbian times to the mid-20th century; 19th- century and early modern European paintings and sculpture; N American and European decorative arts; Wendy and Emery Reves Colln, Faith and Charles Bybee Colln of American Furniture; prints, drawings, photographs; art works from c. 3000BC to the fall of the Roman Empire; library: reference library of 65,000 vols, spec. collns: ethnography, artists' files; Chair. DEEDIE ROSE; Dir MAXWELL L. ANDERSON; Pres. JOHN R. EAGLE; Sec. ANN V. HOBSON; Treas. VICTOR D. ALMEIDA.

Dishman Art Museum: POB 10027, Lamar Univ., Beaumont, TX 77710; tel. (409) 880-8959; fax (409) 880-1799; internet dept.lamar .edu/cofac/deptart/dishman.asp; f. 1983; attached to Lamar Univ.; colln incl. 50 prints from European and American artists of late 19th and early 20th centuries; 19th-century African masks and ceramic vessels and figures from Mexico; Dir Dr JESSICA DANDONA.

Ellen Noël Art Museum of the Permian Basin: 4909 University Blvd, Odessa, TX 79762; tel. (432) 550-9696; fax (432) 550-9226; internet www.noelartmuseum.org; f. 1985 as Art Institute for the Permian Basin, present name 1995; American art dating from 1860 to present; 800 art works incl. paintings, sculptures, ceramics, glass, works on paper and photography; Exec. Dir LES REKER.

El Paso Museum of Art: One Arts Festival Plaza, El Paso, TX 79901; tel. (915) 532-1707; fax (915) 532-1010; e-mail arts@elpasotexas .gov; internet www.elpasoartmuseum.org; f. 1959; 5,000 works of art incl. 12th–18th-century European art; 2,500 works on paper dating from 16th to 20th century; contemporary art focusing on SW region; American art dating from early 19th century to 20th century; Dir Dr MICHAEL A. TOMOR; Sr Curator Dr PATRICK SHAW CABLE.

Hall of State: c/o Dallas Historical Soc., POB 150038, Dallas, TX 75315-0038; 3939 Grand Ave, Dallas, TX 75210; tel. (214) 421-4500; fax (214) 421-7500; internet www .dallashistory.org; f. 1936; attached to Dallas Historical Soc. (see Learned Societies); museum and archives of Texas and Dallas history; colln incl. 3,000,000 historic documents, 30,000 historic photographs, 10,000 garments; library of 14,000 vols, 15,000 museum artefacts and 3m. archival items; Exec. Dir JACK BUNNING; Dir JACK BUNNING; Collns Man. ALAN OLSON.

Kimbell Art Museum: 3333 Camp Bowie Blvd, Fort Worth, TX 76107-2792; tel. (817) 332-8451; fax (817) 877-1264; e-mail curators@kimbellmuseum.org; internet www .kimbellart.org; f. 1972; colln of 350 works of art incl. Asian, European, African, pre-Columbian and Oceanic art dating from 3BC to mid-20th century; Dir ERIC M. LEE.

Longview Museum of Fine Arts: POB 3484, Longview, TX 75606; 215 E Tyler St., Downtown, Longview, TX 75606; tel. (903) 753-8103; fax (903) 753-8217; e-mail fineart@ lmfa.org; internet www.lmfa.org; f. 1958; 300 pieces of art work incl. drawings, paintings, photographs, pottery, prints, sculpture, woodblock and paper works; Dir RENEE HAWKINS.

McNay Art Museum: 6000 N New Braunfels, POB 6069, San Antonio, TX 78209-0069;

6000 N New Braunfels, San Antonio, TX 78209; tel. (210) 824-5368; e-mail info@ mcnayart.org; internet www.mcnayart.org; f. 1950; Medieval and Renaissance art colln incl. paintings, fragments of altarpieces and portraits; 19th- and 20th-century European and American paintings and sculptures; 19th- and 20th-century French, American and Mexican prints and drawings; 2,000 rare books; Chair. TOM FROST; Pres. JOAN BUZZINI HURD; Sec. SARAH E. HARTE; Treas. BILL MCCARTNEY; Dir WILLIAM J. CHIEGO; Chief Curator RENE P. BARILLEAUX.

Meadows Museum: 5900 Bishop, Southern Methodist Univ., Dallas, TX 75205-0357; tel. (214) 768-2516; fax (214) 768-1688; e-mail meadows@smu.edu; internet smu.edu/ meadowsmuseum; f. 1962; attached to Southern Methodist Univ.; modern works by Picasso and Juan Gris; Renaissance altarpieces, monumental Baroque canvases, exquisite Rococo oil sketches, poly-chrome wood sculptures, Impressionist landscapes, modernist abstractions; Dir Dr MARK ROGLÁN.

Menil Collection: 1515 Sul Ross St, Houston, TX 77006; tel. (713) 525-9400; fax (713) 525-9444; e-mail info@menil.org; internet www.menil.org; f. 1987; 16,000 paintings, sculptures, decorative objects, prints, drawings, photographs and rare books; library of 30,000 vols; Chair. LOUISA STUDE SAROFIM; Pres. HARRY C. PINSON; Sec. ADELAIDE DE MENIL CARPENTER; Dir JOSEF HELFENSTEIN.

Modern Art Museum of Fort Worth: 3200 Darnell St, Fort Worth, TX 76107; tel. (817) 738-9215; fax (817) 735-1161; e-mail info@ themodern.org; internet www.themodern .org; f. 1892; colln incl. 2,600 works of modern and contemporary int. art; Curator ANDREA KARNES.

Museum of Fine Arts Houston: 1001 Bissonnet St, Houston, TX 77005; tel. (713) 639-7300; fax (713) 639-7399; e-mail guestservices@mfah.org; internet www.mfah .org; f. 1900; 63,000 artworks; art of the ancient world; European painting and sculpture; Far Eastern art; art of Africa, Oceania and the Americas; decorative arts; prints and drawings; film and video; modern art; photography; textiles and costume; 2 major museum bldgs, the Caroline Wiess Law Bldg and the Audrey Jones Beck Bldg; 2 facilities for the Glassell School of Art, the Studio School for Adults and the Glassell Jr School; 2 house museums that exhibit decorative arts, Bayou Bend Colln and Gardens and Rienzi; the Lillie and Hugh Roy Cullen Sculpture Garden; 18 acres of public gardens; library of 146,000 vols, 83,000 slides; Chair. MEREDITH J. LONG; Dir GWENDOLYN H. GOFFE; publ. *MFA Today* (6 a year).

San Angelo Museum of Fine Arts: 1 Love St, San Angelo, TX 76903; tel. (325) 653-3333; fax (325) 658-6800; e-mail museum@ samfa.org; internet www.samfa.org; f. 1981; 276 objects of American crafts since 1945, ceramic arts, Mexican and Mexican-American art of all eras and contemporary American ceramics; Dir HOWARD TAYLOR.

San Antonio Museum of Art: 200 W Jones Ave, San Antonio, TX 78215; tel. (210) 978-8100; e-mail ancientart@samuseum.org; internet www.samuseum.org; f. 1925 as San Antonio Museum Asscn, present name and status 1994; colln incl. 17th–20th-century European art, Greek and Roman sculptures; contemporary colln incl. works of 20th century and 500 Asian objects; Dir Dr KATIE LUBER.

San Jacinto Museum of History: 1 Monument Circle, La Porte (Houston), TX 77571-9585; tel. (281) 479-2421; fax (281) 479-2428; e-mail sjm@sanjacinto-museum.org; internet

www.sanjacinto-museum.org; f. 1939; attached to San Jacinto Museum of History Asscn and Texas State Parks and Wildlife Comm.; 17,000 items and 700 linear ft of MSS from TX, New Spain, US and Mexico; documents since the 15th century; colln of Mayan, Aztec and Mexican artefacts; exhibits history of Texas region from 1519 to 1900; library of 30,000 vols, 250,000 documents and MSS; Chair. ROBERT B. HIXON; Pres. LARRY SPASIC; Dir J. C. MARTIN; Curator ELIZABETH APPLEBY.

Stark Museum of Art: 712 Green Ave, Orange, TX 77630-5721; tel. (409) 886-2787; fax (409) 883-6361; e-mail info@ starkmuseum.org; internet www .starkmuseum.org; f. 1978; colln incl. 19th- and 20th-century W American art and artefacts; decorative arts incl. glass and porcelain; rare books and MSS; Man. Dir Dr SARAH E. BOEHME.

Strake Jesuit Art Museum: 8900 Bellaire Blvd, Houston, TX 77036-4699; tel. (713) 490-8117; fax (713) 774-6427; internet www .strakejesuit.org; f. 1996; attached to Strake Jesuit College Preparatory; 300 art works incl. Egyptian antiquity and Mayan culture; Registrar PAM HOWARD.

Texas Memorial Museum: 2400 Trinity St, Austin, TX 78705; tel. (512) 471-1604; fax (512) 471-4794; internet www.utexas.edu/ tmm; f. 1936; attached to Univ. of Texas; natural history of Texas, the Southwest and Latin America, minerals, dinosaurs, fossils, palaeontology, vertebrate and invertebrate zoology, geology, entomology; Dir EDWARD C. THERIOT; publ. *Pearce-Sellards Series*.

Trammell & Margaret Crow Collection of Asian Art: 2010 Flora St, Dallas, TX 75201; tel. (214) 979-6430; fax (214) 979-6439; internet www.crowcollection.org; f. 1998; colln incl. pieces from China, Japan, India and SE Asia spanning 3500BC to early 20th century; Dir AMY LEWIS HOFLAND; Curator Dr CARON SMITH.

Tyler Museum of Art: 1300 S Mahon Ave, Tyler, TX 75701; tel. (903) 595-1001; fax (903) 595-1055; e-mail info@tylermuseum .org; internet www.tylermuseum.org; f. 1971; colln incl. 1,500 paintings, prints, photographs and sculpture; works by early and contemporary Texas artists; Dir KIMBERLEY BUSH TOMIO.

Utah

BYU Museum of Art: BYU Museum of Art, N Campus Dr., Provo, UT 84602; tel. (801) 422-8287; e-mail moa@byu.edu; internet cfacweb.byu.edu/departments/moa; attached to BYU College of Fine Arts and Communication, Brigham Young Univ.; 17,000 objects: on American art from the late 18th century to the present, incl. painting, photography, prints and sculpture; Hudson River School landscape paintings and American impressionism.

BYU Museum of Paleontology: 1683 N Canyon Rd, Provo, UT 84602-3300; tel. (801) 422-3680; fax (801) 422-7919; internet cpms .byu.edu/esm; f. 1976; attached to Brigham Young Univ.; fossil vertebrate colln of over 17,000 specimens ranging from Devonian fish (380m. years ago) to Pleistocene mammoths and cave fossils (15,000 years ago), with primary focus on dinosaurs from the Intermountain W; Curator and Man. Dr RODNEY D. SCHEETZ.

Chase Home Museum of Utah Folk Arts: 900 S 600E, Liberty Park, Salt Lake City, UT 84105-1519; tel. (801) 236-7548; state-owned colln of contemporary folk art; Ethnic Folk Arts Gallery, Native American Gallery, Occupational Folk Arts Gallery, Rural Folk Arts Gallery.

Orem Heritage Museum: SCERA Center for the Arts, 745 S State St, Second Fl., Orem, UT 84058; internet www.scera.org; f. 1933; attached to SCERA Center for the Arts; 30,000 artefacts depicting history of Orem; Pres. and CEO ADAM J. ROBERTSON.

USU Eastern Prehistoric Museum: 451 E 400N, Price, UT 84501; 155 E Main St, Price, UT; tel. (435) 613-5060; fax (435) 637-2514; e-mail castlecountryvisitorinfo@gmail.com; internet www.ceu.edu/museum; f. 1961 as Carbon College Prehistoric Museum; attached to College of Eastern Utah, Utah State Univ.; colln of prehistoric artefacts; Museum Dir. KEN CARPENTER; Chair. KEN FLECK.

Utah Museum of Fine Arts: Marcia and John Price Museum Bldg, 410 Campus Center Dr., Salt Lake City, UT 84112-0350; tel. (801) 581-7332; fax (801) 585-5198; internet umfa.utah.edu; f. 1951; attached to Univ. of Utah; 18,000 original objects of African art, American art, American Indian art, ancient Greek and Roman art, art of the Pacific Islands, Austrian art, Cambodian art, Chinese art, decorative arts, Dutch art, Egyptian art, English art, Flemish art, French art, German art, Italian art, Japanese art, Nazi-era provenance research project, Pre-Columbian art, Scottish art, Spanish art, Thai art; Exec. Dir GRETCHEN DIETRICH.

Vermont

Bennington Museum: 75 Main St, Bennington, VT 05201-2885; tel. (802) 447-1571; e-mail info@benningtonmuseum.org; internet www.benningtonmuseum.org; f. 1852, present name and status 1954; colln incl. paintings and sculptures by Vermont artists, maps, books and military artefacts; artefacts dating from early 18th century to present; library of 8,000 vols; Chair. RAYMOND BOLTON; Sec. PATRICIA GUERERRO; Treas. LARAINE SMITH.

Dorset Historical Society: POB 52, Route 30, Kent Hill Rd, Dorset, VT 05251; tel. (802) 867-0331; fax (802) 867-0412; e-mail info@dorsetvthistory.org; internet dorsetvthistory.org/museum; colln incl. Republic of Vermont coins dating 1785-1788 and iron tools dating 19th century; Pres. DICK HITTLE; Sec. RUTH STEWART; Treas. AL ECKHARDT; Curator JON MATHEWSON.

Fairbanks Museum and Planetarium: 1302 Main St, Saint Johnsbury, VT 05819; tel. (802) 748-2372; internet www.fairbanksmuseum.org; f. 1889; colln of 1,75,000 objects incl. 75,000 natural history specimens, 95,000 historical artefacts and 5,000 ethnological items representing Oceania, Africa, Egypt, Japan and native North America; archives colln incl. Civil War records, photographic materials, personal papers and institutional records; historical colln incl. 19th century agricultural, industrial and household objects; museum incl. planetarium; Chair. ARTHUR S. BROOKS; Exec. Dir CHARLES C. BROWNE.

Henry Sheldon Museum of Vermont History: 1 Park St, Middlebury, VT 05753-1334; tel. (802) 388-2117; e-mail info@henrysheldonmuseum.org; internet www.henrysheldonmuseum.org; f. 1882; colln on Vermont's furniture, paintings, documents and artefacts; colln incl. portraits, paintings, household objects; personal artefacts; textiles and clothing; Assoc. Dir MARY MANLEY.

Lake Champlain Maritime Museum: 4472 Basin Harbor Rd, Vergennes, VT 05491; tel. (802) 475-2022; fax (802) 475-2953; e-mail info@lcmm.org; internet www.lcmm.org; f. 1985; colln incl. original small watercraft built over last 150 years; shipwrecks and recovered artefacts; Chair. DAR-

CEY HALE; Sec. FRANCES FOSTER; Treas. GARY FARRELL; Exec. Dir ARTHUR B. COHN.

Middlebury College Museum of Art: Mahaney Center for Arts, Route 30, Middlebury, VT 05753; tel. (802) 443-5007; fax (802) 443-2069; internet museum.middlebury.edu; f. 1968 as Johnson Gallery, present name 1992; 2,500 works spanning from 4BC to the present; Asian art, American and European paintings and sculptures dating from Renaissance to 19th century; Asian art, antiques, photography, 19th-century European and American sculptures and contemporary prints; Dir RICHARD SAUNDERS; Chief Curator EMMIE DONADIO.

Robert Hull Fleming Museum: 61 Colchester Ave, Univ. of Vermont, Burlington, VT 05405; tel. (802) 656-0750; fax (802) 656-8059; e-mail fleming@uvm.edu; internet www.uvm.edu/~fleming; f. 1931; attached to Univ. of Vermont; 20,000 objects spanning history of civilization; art and artefacts from Ancient Egypt, Africa, Asia, Europe and America; Dir JANIE COHEN.

Shelburne Museum: POB 10, Shelburne, VT 05482; 6000 Shelburne Rd, Shelburne, VT 05482; tel. (802) 985-3346; fax (802) 985-2331; e-mail info@shelburnemuseum.org; internet shelburnemuseum.org; f. 1947; colln incl. decorative arts, design, 19th-century American folk art, 19th- and 20th-century decoys, quilts, carriages, artefacts dating from 17th-20th century; painting colln incl. French Impressionists and 400 American works dating from 18th to 20th century; Chair. JAMES PIZZAGALLI; Sec. ALICE COONEY FRELINGHUYSEN; Treas. PAUL PERRAULT.

Southern Vermont Arts Center: POB 617 West Rd, Manchester, VT 05254; 930 SVAC Dr., West Road, Manchester, VT 05254; tel. (802) 362-1405; fax (802) 362-3274; e-mail info@svac.org; internet www.svac.org; colln of 800 art works from 9th and 20th century; colln incl. works by Luigi Lucioni; Pres. STANLEY S. STROUP; Exec. Dir JOSEPH M. MADEIRA.

Southern Vermont Natural History Museum: Route 9, Hogback Mountain, Marlboro, VT 05363; tel. (802) 464-0048; e-mail museum@sover.net; internet www.vermontmuseum.org; f. 1996; colln incl. 600 native New England birds and mammals in 150 small dioramas; Exec. Dir EDWARD METCALFE.

St Johnsbury Athenaeum: 1171 Main St, St Johnsbury, VT 05819; tel. (802) 748-8291; e-mail inform@stjathenaeum.org; internet www.stjathenaeum.org; f. 1873; colln incl. works from American and European artists dating from late 18th century to mid-19th century; Chair. WILLIAM MARSHALL; Sec. EILEEN BOLAND; Treas. BRENDA MARIE WILKINS; Exec. Dir MATTHEW POWERS.

Woodstock Historical Society: 26 Elm St, Woodstock, VT 05091; tel. (802) 457-1822; e-mail info@woodstockhistorical.org; internet woodstockhistorical.org; f. 1943; colln incl. exhibits of furniture, fine art, clothing, textiles, silver, ceramics, photographs and early American toys; Dir JACK ANDERSON.

Virginia

Chrysler Museum of Art: 245 W Olney Rd, Norfolk, VA 23510; tel. (757) 664-6200; fax (757) 664-6201; e-mail museum@chrysler.org; internet www.chrysler.org; f. 1933, present name and status 1971; colln incl. 10,000 glass objects spanning 3,000 years, European painting and sculptures dating from Renaissance to present, American paintings and sculptures, contemporary art since 1945 and decorative art; library of 106,000 vols; Chair. MACON F. BROCK; Sec. MAURICE A. JONES; Dir WILLIAM HENNESSEY; Curator JEFF HARRISON.

Colonial Williamsburg: POB 1776, Williamsburg, VA 23187-1776; tel. (757) 229-1000; e-mail mcottrill@cwf.org; internet www.history.org; Colonial Williamsburg incl. DeWitt Wallace Decorative Arts museum and Abby Aldrich Rockefeller Folk Art museum; colln incl. colonial and contemporary folk art; furniture, metals, ceramics, paintings and prints dating from 17th to 19th centuries; Pres. and CEO COLIN G. CAMPBELL.

Colonial Williamsburg Foundation: POB 1776, Williamsburg, VA 23187-1776; tel. (757) 229-1000; fax (757) 220-7702; e-mail cwres@cwf.org; internet www.history.org; f. 1926; 301-acre outdoor living history museum with nearly 500 preserved, restored and reconstructed bldgs; 90 acres of period gardens and greens; demonstration of 18 historic trades; incl. DeWitt Wallace Decorative Arts Museum, Bassett Hall, Kimball Theatre and Abby Aldrich Rockefeller Folk Art Museum; library: John D. Rockefeller, Jr Library of 75,000 vols, 45,000 MSS, 55,000 architectural plans; Pres. COLIN G. CAMPBELL; publ. *Colonial Williamsburg* (3 a year).

Danville Museum of Fine Arts and History: 975 Main St, Danville, VA 24541; tel. (434) 793-5644; fax (434) 799-6145; internet www.danvillemuseum.org; f. 1974; colln incl. 19th century art by artists like Jean Joseph Weertz, Edward Gay and Harvey Young, American Modern art, decorative arts and artefacts related to Civil War; Pres. GLENN N. SCARBORO; Treas. THOMAS W. FREEZE; Exec. Dir LYNNE BJARNESEN.

Eleanor D. Wilson Museum: POB 9679, 8009 Fishburn Dr., Roanoke, VA 24020-1679; tel. (540) 362-6532; e-mail wilsonmuseum@hollins.edu; internet www.hollins.edu/museum; attached to Hollins Univ.; colln incl. 1000 art objects incl. paintings, photographs and works on paper; Dir AMY MOORE-FIELD.

Fredericksburg Area Museum and Cultural Center: 1001 Princess Anne St, Fredericksburg, VA 22401; tel. (540) 371-3037; e-mail info@famcc.org; internet www.famcc.org; f. 1986; colln incl. objects significant to Fredericksburg and surrounding areas of Stafford, Spotsylvania, King George and Caroline; colln incl. 8,000 individual objects and artefacts on Fredericksburg area history; Chair. ANDREW WITHERS; Pres. and CEO ELLEN KILLOUGH; Sec. TERESA D'ORAZIO; Treas. RICK PEARCE.

Gari Melchers Home and Studio: Belmont, 224 Washington St, Fredericksburg, VA 22405; tel. (540) 654-1015; fax (540) 654-1785; e-mail garimelchers@umw.edu; internet garimelchers.umw.edu; f. 1955; colln incl. 1,677 paintings and drawings by Gari Melchers, 414 works by other artists, 3000 items of furniture, decorative objects and books; Dir DAVID BERRETH; Curator JOANNA CATRON.

Hampton University Museum: Hampton Univ., Hampton, VA 23668; tel. (757) 727-5308; fax (757) 727-5170; e-mail museum@hamptonu.edu; internet museum.hamptonu.edu; f. 1868; colln incl. 9,000 objects on African American fine arts, traditional African, native American, native Hawaiian, Pacific Island and Asian art; Dir NASHID MADYUN.

Hermitage Museum and Gardens: 7637 North Shore Rd, Norfolk, VA 23505; tel. (757) 423-2052; fax (757) 423-2410; e-mail info@thehermitagemuseum.org; internet www.thehermitagemuseum.org; f. 1942; colln incl. 40,000 objects spanning 5,000 years of art history from over 30 countries; colln incl. fine and decorative art objects; Pres. K. MAXWELL

DALE; Treas. F. NASH BILISOLY; Sec. ELEANOR A. LEWIS; Exec. Dir MELANIE MATHEWES.

Longwood Center for the Visual Arts (LCVA): 29 N Main St, Farmville, VA 23901; tel. (434) 395-2206; fax (434) 392-6441; internet www.longwood.edu/lcva; f. 1978; attached to Longwood Univ.; colln incl. Ziegler and Brumfield colln of African art, Rowe colln of Chinese art, Cole colln of 19th-century Bohemian and European glass, English pottery and Meissen porcelain, American works by Thomas Sully and James McNeil Whistler and 19th-century decorative arts; Dir KATHY JOHNSON BOWLES.

Mariners' Museum: 100 Museum Dr., Newport News, VA 23606; tel. (757) 596-2222; fax (757) 591-7320; e-mail frontdeskstaff@marinersmuseum.org; internet www.mariner.org; f. 1930; int. maritime colln of c. 35,000 artefacts; incl. Peter W. Ifland Colln of Navigation Instruments (169 navigation pieces covering 5 centuries), Edwin Levick Colln of 30,000 photographs (yachting events and America's Cup races), artefacts and archives of the Civil War ironclad USS Monitor; library: see Libraries and Archives; Chair. JOHN R. LAWSON, JR; Pres. and Chief Exec. WILLIAM B. COGAR; Chief Curator LYLES FORBES.

Muscarelle Museum of Art: College of William and Mary, POB 8795, Williamsburg, VA 23187-8795; tel. (757) 221-2700; fax (757) 221-2711; e-mail museum@wm.edu; internet web.wm.edu/muscarelle; f. 1983; attached to College of William & Mary; colln incl. Colonial American, 17th- and 18th-century English portraits, prints and drawings from 16th to 20th centuries representing American and European artists, Japanese prints and German Expressionist works; Dir Dr AARON H. DE GROFT.

Taubman Museum of Art: 110 Salem Ave SE, Roanoke, VA 24011; tel. (540) 342-5760; internet www.taubmanmuseum.org; colln incl. 2,050 pieces incl. decorative arts, American art, 3,500-year-old Egyptian Ushabiti ceramic figures and contemporary art works by Roanoke artists; Chair. PATRICIA P. KERMES; Sec. THOMAS L. MCKEON; Treas. DAVID J. WINE; Exec. Dir DAVID MICKENBERG.

University of Virginia Art Museum: Thomas H. Bayly Bldg, 155 Rugby Rd, POB 400119, Charlottesville, VA 22904-4119; tel. (434) 924-3592; fax (434) 924-6321; internet www.virginia.edu/artmuseum; f. 1935; colln incl. 12,000 objects on American and European paintings, works on paper, sculptures dating from 15th to 20th centuries, ancient Mediterranean art and Asian art; Dir BRUCE BOUCHER.

Virginia Historical Society: POB 7311, Richmond, VA 23221-0311; tel. (804) 358-4901; fax (804) 355-2399; internet www.warmuseum.org; f. 1831; colln incl. genealogical materials, maps, paintings, prints, postcards, weapons, militaria, glass plate negatives and 19th–21st century photographs; Chair. W. TAYLOR REVELEY, III.

Virginia Museum of Fine Arts: 200 North Blvd, Richmond, VA 23220-4007; tel. (804) 340-1400; fax (804) 340-1548; internet www.vmfa.museum; f. 1936; state-wide network of local and regional arts orgs and loan programme offering exhibition material to affiliated groups; film programmes; permanent collns incl. Russian Imperial jewelled objects by Fabergé, ancient Greek, Roman and Byzantine objects and sculptures; Indian, Chinese, Japanese, medieval, renaissance, and baroque paintings and sculptures; Himalayan colln; Art Nouveau and Art Deco colln; European and American decorative arts, prints, sculpture and paintings; contemporary art; library of 134,500 vols; Assoc.

Dir SANDRA C. RUSAK; publ. *Calendar* (6 a year).

Virginia War Museum: 9285 Warwick Blvd, Newport News, VA 23607; tel. (757) 247-8523; fax (757) 247-8627; e-mail virginiawarmuseum@nngov.com; internet www.warmuseum.org; f. 1923; colln incl. uniforms, weapons and art work from Revolutionary War to Vietnam War; overview of US military history from 1775 to present; Pres. WARREN SHINDLE; Sec. LAWRENCE MUNNIKHUYSEN, III; Treas. (vacant).

Washington

Aberdeen Museum of History: 111 E Third St, Aberdeen, WA 98520; tel. (360) 533-1976; e-mail museum@aberdeen-museum.org; internet www.aberdeen-museum.org; f. 1981; housed in the Aberdeen Armory Bldg; colln of armoury.

Anacortes Museum: 1305 Eighth St, Anacortes, WA 98221; tel. (360) 293-1915; fax (360) 293-1929; e-mail coa.museum@cityofanacortes.org; internet museum.cityofanacortes.org; f. 1958; Dir STEVE OAKLEY; Curator of Collns JUDY HAKINS.

Bainbridge Island Historical Museum: 215 Ericksen Ave, NE, Bainbridge Island, WA 98110; tel. (206) 842-2773; fax (206) 842-0914; internet www.bainbridgehistory.org/museum.php; f. 1949; 3,500 artefacts and documents and more than 4,000 photographs that depict life on Bainbridge Island from 1854 to the present; Curator RICK CHANDLER; Exec. Dir HENRY R. (HANK) HELM.

Bellevue Arts Museum: 510 Bellevue Way, NE, Bellevue, WA 98004; tel. (425) 519-0770; fax (425) 637-1799; e-mail info@bellevuearts.org; internet www.bellevuearts.org; f. 1947, present bldg 2001, present name 2005; Managing Dir LARRY WRIGHT; Dir of Curatorial Affairs STEFANO CATALANI.

National Museum of American Jewish History: 101 S Independence Mall E, Philadelphia, PA 19106-2517; tel. (215) 923-3811; internet www.nmajh.org; f. 1740 as Synagogue of the American Revolution; repository with more than 25,000 artefacts that relate to the daily occupational, domestic, religious and communal aspects of American Jewish life; Pres. and CEO MICHAEL ROSENZWEIG.

Seattle Art Museum: 1300 First Ave, Seattle, WA 98101-2003; tel. (206) 625-8900; fax (206) 654-3135; e-mail pr@seattleartmuseum.org; internet www.seattleartmuseum.org; f. 1906; 23,000 objects: Aboriginal and Oceanic art, African art, American art, ancient Mediterranean and Islamic art, decorative arts, European arts, Japanese and Korean art, modern and contemporary art, Native and Mesoamerican art, textiles; 2 research libraries and a lending library for educators; Pres. WINNIE STRATTON; Sec. STEWART LANDEFEL; Treas. ROBERT STRONG.

Attached Museums:

Olympic Sculpture Park: 2901 W Ave, Seattle, WA 98121; tel. (206) 654-3100; fax (206) 332-1371; f. 1999; waterfront site for exhibition of sculptures.

Seattle Asian Art Museum: 1400 E Prospect St, Volunteer Park, Seattle, WA 98112-3303; tel. (206) 654-3100; fax (206) 654-3191; Chinese, South Asian and SE Asian Art.

Washington State History Museum: 1911 Pacific Ave, Tacoma, WA 98402; tel. (253) 272-3500; fax (253) 272-9518; e-mail researchcenter@wshs.wa.gov; internet www.washingtonhistory.org/wshm; f. 1996; attached to Washington State Historical Soc.; Great Hall of Washington History,

History Lab Learning Center; Dir JENNIFER KILMER; publ. *Columbia* (1 a year).

West Virginia

Clay Center for the Arts and Sciences of West Virginia: 1 Clay Sq., Charleston, WV 25301; tel. (304) 561-3570; internet www.theclaycenter.org; f. 2003; Avampato Discovery Museum, Maier Foundation Performance Hall, Juliet Museum of Art and Walker Theater; 806 objects incl. works on paper by American artists from 19th and 20th centuries; outdoor sculptures; Chair. ELLEN CAPPELLANTI; Pres. and CEO Dr JUDITH L. WELLINGTON; Sec. FONDA ELLIOT; Treas. CHARLES M. AVAMPATO.

Harpers Ferry National Historical Park: POB 65, Harpers Ferry, WV 25425; tel. (304) 535-6029; fax (304) 535-6244; internet www.nps.gov/hafe; historic photographs, technical drawings, rare postcards and contemporary images; E deciduous forest with different plant species, 170 bird and 30 mammal species; Superintendent REBECCA HARRIET.

Huntington Museum of Art: 2033 McCoy Rd, Huntington, WV 25701; tel. (304) 529-2701; fax (304) 529-7447; internet www.hmoa.org; collns incl. folk art, prints, sculptures, silver, touma, glass; Herman P. Dean Firearms colln; Daywood Colln; art glass colln incl. Wilbur Myers Glass Colln; Dr Marion C. Korstanje Colln of Natural History Prints; Winslow Anderson Colln of Haitian Art (incl. 156 paintings, metal artefacts and wooden sculptures); Touma Near Eastern Colln (art objects from Middle E, Ottoman Turkey, Central Asian Republics, Indian subcontinent, North Africa and Moorish Spain); American colln (incl. Native American works from N, Central and S America); European paintings, sculptures, drawings and prints from mid-16th century up to mid-20th century; incl. C. Fred Edwards Conservatory of subtropical plants; library of 20,000 vols in James D. Francis Art Library; Pres. LEE OXLEY; Sec. JOAN WEISBERG; Treas. BRANDON ROISMAN; Exec. Dir MARGARET MARY LAYNE; Sr Curator JENINE CULLIGAN.

Museum of American Glass in West Virginia: POB 574, Weston, WV 26452; 230 Main Ave, Weston, WV; tel. (304) 269-5006; e-mail wvmuseumofglass@aol.com; internet www.magwv.com; f. 1993; artefacts of handmade glass incl. bottles to lightening rod balls, telegraph insulators to glass used in automobiles, pressed to blown tableware of 18th century rep. of history of glass artists, places and competing companies.

Museums of Oglebay Institute: Oglebay Resort, Wheeling, WV; tel. (304) 242-7272; internet www.oionline.com/museums; f. 1930; Mansion Museum, Oglebay Institute Glass Museum of 3,000 artefacts of Wheeling Glass made from 1829–1939, incl. cut lead crystal, Victorian art glass, Peachblow, pattern and depression and Northwood's carnival glass; Northwood Gallery incl. crystal, carnival, coloured and opalescent glassware; organizes history lectures, appraisal events and educational activities; Dir CHRISTIN BYRUM; Curator MEGAN CLARK.

Museum of the Berkeley Springs: POB 99, Berkeley Springs, WV 25411; e-mail history@museumoftheberkeleysprings.com; internet www.museumoftheberkeleysprings.com; colln on geology of Berkeley Springs: relief map and quartz crystals, tools, arrowheads and locator map of Native Americans telling 8,500 years of local history, ketches by Porte Crayon, historic swimsuits, photos and sit-up steam cabinet; bottle cappers and signs, silica products and photographs; artefacts from Washington Elm; Pres. DAVID MILBURN; Exec. Dir TAMME MARGGRAF.

West Virginia State Museum at the Cultural Center: Capitol Complex, 1900 Kanawha Blvd E, Charleston, WV 25305-0300; tel. (304) 558-0220; fax (304) 558-2779; internet www.wvculture.org/agency/cultcenter.html; f. 1890 as West Virginia Historical and Antiquarian Soc., present bldg 1976; attached to West Virginia Div. of Culture and History; local art and history; also houses state archives and state museum; operates 6 historic sites and museums; Museum Dir CHARLES MORRIS, III; publ. *Artworks* (4 a year).

Wisconsin

Charles Allis Art Museum: 1801 N Prospect Ave, Milwaukee, WI 53202; tel. (414) 278-8295; fax (414) 278-0335; internet www.charlesallis.org; f. 1911; 19th-century French and American Paintings, Chinese and Japanese porcelains, Renaissance bronzes, Japanese netsuke and antique furnishings; Exec. Dir MARIA COSTELLO; Curator MARTHA MONROE.

Chazen Museum of Art: 800 University Ave, Madison, WI 53706; tel. (608) 263-2246; internet www.chazen.wisc.edu; f. 1970 as Elvehjem Art Center, present name 2005; attached to Univ. of Wisconsin–Madison; colln of 20,000 works of art incl. paintings, sculptures, drawings and watercolours; prints of American, European, Asian and ancient art; photography and applied and decorative arts incl. architectural decoration, beadwork, baskets and textiles, ceramics, glass and metalwork, medallic art and coins; Dir RUSSELL PANCZENKO.

Door County Maritime Museum: 120 N Madison Ave, Sturgeon Bay, WI 54235; tel. (920) 743-5958; fax (920) 743-9483; e-mail info@dcmm.org; internet www.dcmm.org; exhibits shipyards producing fishing trawlers, Navy vessels, ore carriers and yachts; Cana Island Lighthouse and Gills Rock Museum; Sturgeon Bay Museum; Exec. Dir BOB DESH; Curator JOHN MOGA.

Haggerty Museum of Art: Marquette Univ., POB 1881, Milwaukee, WI 53201-1881; tel. (414) 288-1669; e-mail haggertym@marquette.edu; internet www.marquette.edu/haggerty; f. 1889; attached to Marquette Univ.; Dir WALLY MASON.

Kenosha Public Museum: 5500 First Ave, Kenosha, WI 53140; tel. (262) 653-4140; internet www.kenosha.org/museum; f. 1933; 70,000 works, incl. 1,000 works in fine arts colln; decorative and fine arts, natural science specimens and cultural artefacts, related to world cultures, Native Americans, zoology, geology, fossils and fine and decorative arts; Dir PEGGY GREGORSKI.

Leigh Yawkey Woodson Art Museum: 700 N 12th St, Franklin and 12th Sts, Wausau, WI 54403-5007; tel. (715) 845-7010; fax (715) 845-7103; e-mail museum@lywam.org; internet www.lywam.org; f. 1976; colln of 2,000 works of art, incl. paintings, drawings and field sketches, prints (etchings, engravings, woodcuts, and screenprints), photographs, 125 Victorian glass baskets, 20th-century utilitarian and decorative glassware and porcelains, 100 Royal Worcester porcelain bird figurines and historic and contemporary glass vessel forms and sculptural objects; Dir KATHY FOLEY.

Madison Museum of Contemporary Art: 227 State St, Madison, WI 53703; tel. (608) 257-0158; fax (608) 257-5722; e-mail flash@mmoca.org; internet www.mmoca.org; f. present location 2006; colln of 5,000 artworks incl. works of 20th and 21st centuries paintings, sculpture, photography, prints and drawings; Dir STEPHEN FLEISCHMAN; Pres.

JIM YEHLE; Sec. WILLIAM DEATLEY; Treas. DAVID STEIN.

Milwaukee Art Museum: 700 N Art Museum Dr., Milwaukee, WI 53202; tel. (414) 224-3200; fax (414) 271-7588; e-mail mam@mam.org; internet www.mam.org; f. 1957 as Milwaukee Art Center; 20,000 works of art, incl. collns of American decorative arts, German Expressionist prints and paintings, folk and Haitian art, and American art after 1960; George Mann Niedecken Archives; Landfall Press Archives; Rogovin Colln of photographs of working-class families; Herzfeld Foundation Print, Drawing, and Photography Study Center; library of 20,000 vols; Dir and CEO DANIEL T. KEEGAN; Chief Curator BRADY ROBERTS.

Milwaukee Public Museum: 800 W Wells St, Milwaukee, WI 53233-1478; tel. (414) 278-2702; fax (414) 278-6100; e-mail museumnews@mpm.edu; internet www.mpm.edu; photographic colln of 300,000 images; anthropology colln of 120,000 artefacts of world cultural areas of the Americas, Africa and Oceania; geology colln of fossils, minerals and rocks; 250,000 specimens of preserved plants and plant material in botanical colln; 250,000 historical objects from Egyptian mummies to 20th-century Milwaukee clothing and manufactures; vertebrate and invertebrate zoology colln; planetarium; library of 100,000 vols; Chair. RICHARD A. MEEUSEN; Pres. and CEO JAY WILLIAMS; Sec. and Treas. CHARLES I. HENDERSON.

Museum of Wisconsin Art: 300 S 6th Ave, West Bend, WI 262-334-9638; tel. (262) 334-9638; fax (262) 334-8080; internet wisconsinart.org; f. 1961 as West Bend Gallery of Fine Arts, present name 2007; Carl von Marr colln and Early Wisconsin Regional Art colln; 2,000 works of art; Wisconsin Art Archive with 8,000 files on Wisconsin art, artists and library of research material on state art and history; Exec. Dir THOMAS D. LIDTKE; Pres. DALE KENT; Sec. VIRGI DRISCOLL; Treas. RAYMOND LIPMAN.

Neville Public Museum: 210 Museum Place, Green Bay, WI 54303-2760; tel. (920) 448-4460; fax (920) 448-4458; e-mail generalinfo@nevillepublicmuseum.org; internet www.nevillepublicmuseum.org; f. 1915, present name and status 1927; 100,000 3-D historic and prehistoric artefacts; photograph colln of approx. 1m. images and 4m. ft of news film; archival repository of MSS, public records, maps, newspapers and spec. collns library; Dir ROLF JOHNSON; Chair. KRAMER ROCK; Sec. DAVID PAMPERIN; Treas. DIANE FORD.

Oshkosh Public Museum: 1331 Algoma Blvd, Oshkosh, WI 54901; tel. (920) 236-5799; e-mail museum_info@ci.oshkosh.wi.us; internet www.oshkoshmuseum.org; f. 1924; colln of 250,000 objects incl. fine, folk and decorative arts, textiles, toys, natural history specimens, Native American objects and historic artefacts; 47,000 historic photographs and 1,078 linear ft of archival records; Dir BRAD LARSON; Curator DEBRA DAUBERT.

Racine Art Museum: POB 187, Racine, WI 53401-0187; 441 Main St, Racine, WI 53403; tel. (262) 638-8300; fax (262) 898-1045; internet www.ramart.org; f. 1941 as Charles A. Wustum Museum of Fine Arts; 5,000 objects in ceramics, fibers, glass, metals and wood; Wustum Museum; Exec. Dir BRUCE W. PEPICH; Pres. STEPHANIE LAZZERONI; Sec. KRAIG BRYANT; Treas. JAMES WALKER.

Rahr—West Art Museum: 610 N Eight St, Manitowoc, WI 54220; tel. (920) 686-3090; fax (920) 683-5047; e-mail rahrwest@manitowoc.org; internet www.manitowoc.org/index.aspx?nid=1006; 19th-, 20th- and

21st-century contemporary art and decorative arts with emphasis on American art and int. and regional US and Wisconsin art; Pres. AMY FRICKE WEIGEL; Dir GREG VADNEY.

Trout Museum of Art: Reigel Bldg, 111 W College Ave, Appleton, WI 54911; tel. (920) 733-4089; fax (920) 733-4149; e-mail info@troutmuseum.org; internet www.troutmuseum.org; f. 1972 as Appleton Gallery of Art, present name 2010; colln of 150 works of art incl. American, European, Asian and African paintings, sculptures and decorative objects rep. of 400 years of art history; Exec. Dir TIMOTHY RILEY; Pres. MICHAEL CISLER; Sec. WENDY SCHMIDT; Treas. PRATEEK MEHROTRA.

Villa Terrace Decorative Arts Museum: 2220 N Terrace Ave, Milwaukee, WI 53202; tel. (414) 271-3656; fax (414) 271-3986; internet projects.tsrnet.com/cavt/development/villa; f. 1923; furnishings and works of art from 15th through 18th centuries; Colnik colln of 200 pieces of ironwork; Renaissance Garden; Exec. Dir MARIA COSTELLO; Curator MARTHA MONROE.

Wisconsin Historical Museum: 30 N Carroll St, Madison, WI 53703; tel. (608) 264-6555; fax (608) 264-6575; e-mail museum@wisconsinhistory.org; internet www.wisconsinhistoricalmuseum.org; attached to Wisconsin Historical Soc.; 110,000 historical objects and 400,000 archaeological artefacts documenting the history of Wisconsin from prehistoric times to the present; spec. collns incl. anthropology, business and technology, costumes and textiles, domestic life, political and military life; Dir JENNIFER KOLB; Chief Curator PAUL G. BOURCIER.

Wisconsin Maritime Museum: 75 Maritime Dr., Manitowoc, WI 54220; tel. (920) 684-0218; fax (920) 684-0219; e-mail museum@wisconsinmaritime.org; internet www.wisconsinmaritime.org; f. 1970 as Manitowoc Submarine Memorial Asscn; colln of model ships and boats, operating steam engine, displays of historic vessels and marine engines, and the Wisconsin Waterways and Little Lakefarer's Rooms; Second World War submarine USS Cobia; library of 8,000 vols, 40,000 photographs, 300 linear ft of MSS materials; Exec. Dir NORMA BISHOP; Curator JOHN LARNER.

Wisconsin Veterans Museum: 30 W Mifflin St, Madison, WI 53703; tel. (608) 267-1799; internet www.wisvetsmuseum.com; f. 1901; attached to Wisconsin Dept of Veterans Affairs; 23,000 artefacts incl. uniforms, equipment, armament, flags, insignia, decorations, personal items and souvenirs; battle flag colln and archives; Wisconsin Nat. Guard Museum; Dir MICHAEL TELZROW.

Wright Museum of Art: Beloit College, 700 College St, Beloit, WI 53511; tel. (608) 363-2702; fax (608) 363-2248; e-mail wright@beloit.edu; internet www.beloit.edu/wright; f. 1930; attached to Beloit College; 6,000 works of art incl. American Impressionism, Modernist paintings, 19th-century plaster casts, German Expressionism, ancient art, Asian art, landscapes, portraiture and Japanese Modern print; Dir JOY ELIZABETH BECKMAN.

Wyoming

Buffalo Bill Historical Center: 720 Sheridan Ave, Cody, WY 82414; tel. (307) 587-4771; fax (307) 578-4090; e-mail info@bbhc.org; internet www.bbhc.org; f. 1917 as Buffalo Bill Museum, present name 1950; incl. Whitney Gallery of Western Art (paintings, sculpture and prints of the American W from early 19th century through present), Plains Indian Museum (collns of Plains Indian art and artefacts), Cody Firearms Museum (colln of 5,000 American and European firearms on devt of firearms from 16th century to the present), McCracken Research Library and Draper Museum of Natural History (research on natural environment and human cultures of the American W, focusing on the Greater Yellowstone region); library of 30,000 vols, 300 MSS and 500,000 photographs; Chair. BARRON G. COLLIER, II; Exec. Dir and CEO BRUCE B. ELDREDGE.

Carbon County Museum: 904 W Walnut, Rawlins, WY 82301; tel. (307) 328-2740; fax (307) 328-2666; e-mail carbonc@wyoming.com; internet www.carboncountymuseum.org; colln on the Union Pacific Railroad, pioneers, residents and outlaws, Native Americans and agriculture; Thomas Edison exhibit; Dir TIFFANY WILSON; Chair. GENE CARRICO (acting); Sec. DAVID THROGMORTON; Treas. LEON CORPUZ.

Cheyenne Frontier Days Old West Museum: 4610 Carey Ave, POB 2720, Cheyenne, WY 82003; tel. (307) 778-7290; fax (307) 778-7288; e-mail info@oldwestmuseum.org; internet www.oldwestmuseum.org; f. 1978; 60,000 artefacts incl. paintings, sculptures, historic clothing dating to 1850 and artefacts related to art and material culture of the American W; Exec. Dir AMIEE REESE; Pres. Dr JIM MCSHANE; Sec. Dr RICK DAVIS; Treas. GENE ENGRAV.

Hulett Museum and Art Gallery: POB 103, Hulett, WY 82720; 115 Highway 24, Hulett, WY 82720; tel. (307) 467-5292; e-mail hulettmuseum@rtconnect.net; internet hulettmuseum.org; f. 2010; colln of prehistoric and historic artefacts related to history and culture of NE Wyoming; Dir MITCH MAHONEY.

Jim Gatchell Memorial Museum: POB 596, Buffalo, WY 82834; 100 Fort St, Buffalo, WY 82834; tel. (307) 684-9331; e-mail jmuseum@vcn.com; internet www.jimgatchell.com/jim_gatchell_memorial_museum; f. 1900 as Buffalo Pharmacy; 14,000 artefacts incl. documents, photographs, firearms, clothing and wagons related to history of Johnson Co with emphasis on its Frontier Era; Dir JOHN GAVIN; Pres. DAVE OSMUNDSEN; Sec. BARBARA MADSEN; Treas. SALLY RAMSBOTTOM.

National Museum of Wildlife Art: 2820 Rungius Rd, Jackson Hole, WY 83002; tel. (307) 733-5771; e-mail info@wildlifeart.org; internet www.wildlifeart.org; f. 1987 as Wildlife of the American West Art Museum; 5,000 pieces of art portraying wildlife, dating from 2500BC to the present; European and American painting and sculpture; colln of American art from the 19th and 20th centuries recording European exploration of the American West; spec. collns incl. Carl Rugius Colln, John Clymer Colln, American Bison Colln, Dellenback Colln, JKM Colln; art library and archives; incl. Nat. Elk Refuge; Chair. STEPHANIE BRENNAN; Pres. and CEO Dr JAMES C. McNUTT; Sec. JUDSON BALL; Treas. DAVID WALSH.

Nicolaysen Art Museum: 400 E Collins St, Casper, WY 82601; tel. (307) 235-5247; internet www.thenic.org; f. 1967; 6,265 objects, incl. paintings, sculptures, textiles, drawings, photographs, prints and works on paper; spec. collns: Conrad Schwiering Studio and Illustrations by Carl Link; Discovery Center; Exec. Dir CONNIE GIBBONS; Chair. JENNIFER TRUE; Sec. CRAIG VALDEZ; Curator LISA HATCHADOORIAN.

University of Wyoming Art Museum: 2111 Willet Dr., Laramie, WY 82072; tel. (307) 766-6622; fax (307) 766-3520; e-mail uwartmus@uwyo.edu; internet www.uwyo.edu/artmuseum; f. 1972; 8,000 art objects incl. European and American paintings, prints, sculpture and drawings; spec. collns of 18th- and 19th-century Japanese Ukiyo-e prints, 15th- through 19th-century Persian and Indian miniature paintings, 20th-century Haitian art, 20th-century Japanese netsuke, 20th-century and contemporary photography, and Rapa Nui, African and Native American artefacts; 15th-century Old Master prints, French Rococo, German Expressionism, Fauvism, Modernism, Surrealism, Abstract Expressionism and Contemporary Art; outdoor sculptures; Dir and Chief Curator SUSAN MOLDENHAUER; Pres. RUTH ARNOLD; Sec. and Treas. JACQUE BUCHANAN.

Wyoming Dinosaur Center & Dig Sites: 110 Carter Ranch Rd, POB 868, Thermopolis, WY 82443; tel. (307) 864-2997; fax (307) 864-5762; e-mail wdinoc@wyodino.org; internet www.wyodino.org; museum with interpretive displays, dioramas, life-size dinosaur mounts, exhibits covering all facets of early life; colln incl. fossil fish from Scotland, flying reptiles from Brazil, marine reptiles from Russia and Switzerland and fossil dinosaur eggs from China and Argentina; fossil preparation laboratory; 80 dig sites in Warm Springs Ranch; Research Center; Casting Laboratory; Dir of Science SCOTT HARTMAN; Gen. Man. ANGIE GUYON.

Wyoming State Museum: Barrett Bldg, 2301 Central Ave, Fourth Fl., Cheyenne, WY 82002; tel. (307) 777-2416; fax (307) 777-5375; e-mail wsm@state.wy.us; internet wyomuseum.state.wy.us; f. 1895; themed galleries: Barber Gallery, Drawn to this Land, Hands-on History Room, Living in Wyoming, RIP–Rex in Pieces, Swamped with Coal, The Wild Bunch, Wyoming's Story; travelling exhibits; colln of structures, bldg furnishings, personal artefacts, tools and equipment, recreational artefacts, societal artefacts, ethnographic artefact, archaeology and natural history; Museum Supervisor MANNY VIGIL.

Universities and Colleges

(Arranged alphabetically by State)

ALABAMA

AIR UNIVERSITY

55 LeMay Plaza S, Maxwell AFB, Montgomery, AL 36112-6335
Telephone: (334) 953-2014
Fax: (334) 953-3379
Internet: www.au.af.mil/au
Founded 1946
State control
Pres. and Commander: Lt Gen. DAVID S. FADOK
Vice-Pres. for Academic Affairs: Dr BRUCE MURPHY
Registrar: LLOYD L. WILSON
Library Dir: Dr JEFF LUZIUS
Library: 2.9m. vols, 5,30,000 military documents, 4,29,000 bound periodical vols, 4,33,000 maps and charts, 9,09,000 microforms
Number of students: 500
Publication: *Air and Space Power Journal* (4 a year).

ALABAMA AGRICULTURAL AND MECHANICAL UNIVERSITY

POB 908, Hunstville, AL 35762
4900 Meridian St, Huntsville, AL 35810-1015
Telephone: (256) 372-5000
E-mail: info@aamu.edu
Internet: www.aamu.edu
Founded 1875 as Huntsville Normal School, present name 1969
State control
Academic year: August to May
Pres.: Dr ANDREW HUGINE, JR
Exec. Vice-Pres. and Chief Operating Officer: Dr KEVIN ROLLE
Vice-Pres. for Academic Affairs and Provost: Dr DANIEL WIMS
Vice-Pres. for Business and Finance: RALPH JOHNSON
Vice-Pres. for Research and Devt: Dr ROSE M. YATES
Vice-Pres. for Student Affairs: JEFFERY T. BURGIN, JR
Registrar: CEDRIC ARRINGTON
Dir and Head of Public and Information Services: GARY BUSH (acting)
Library of 339,272 vols, 2,200 journals
Number of teachers: 348
Number of students: 5,814

DEANS

College of Agricultural and Environmental Studies: Dr ROBERT TAYLOR
Arts and Sciences: Dr MATTHEW EDWARDS
College of Business and Public Affairs: Dr AMIN SARKAR
College of Education, Humanities and Behavioral Sciences: Dr CURTIS E. MARTIN
College of Engineering, Technology and Physical Sciences: Dr TRENT MONTGOMERY
School of Graduate Studies: Dr VANN NEWKIRK
Univ. College: Dr JUARINE STEWART

ALABAMA STATE UNIVERSITY

915 S Jackson St, POB 271, Montgomery, AL 36101-0271
Telephone: (334) 229-4100
Fax: (334) 229-6637
E-mail: wharris@alasu.edu
Internet: www.alasu.edu
Founded 1867 as Lincoln Normal School, present name and status 1969
State control
Academic year: September to May
Pres.: Dr WILLIAM H. HARRIS
Exec. Vice-Pres. and Chief Operating Officer: Dr JOHN F. KNIGHT, JR
Vice-Pres. for Academic Affairs and Provost: Dr ALFRED SMITH
Vice-Pres. for Admin. Services: Dr LEON FRAZIER
Vice-Pres. for Business and Finance: Dr FREDDIE GALLOT
Vice-Pres. for Institutional Advancement: ZILLAH FLUKER
Vice-Pres. for Student Affairs: Dr WILLIAM P. HYTCHE
Vice-Pres. for Univ. Relations: DANIELLE KENNEDY
Univ. Librarian and Learning Resources: Dr JANICE FRANKLIN
Library of 507,374 vols (incl. 304,944 books, 74,659 e-books, 127,771 bound journals), 6,026 periodical titles (1,597 physical titles and 4,429 e-journals)
Number of teachers: 270
Number of students: 5,096
Publications: *ASU Today, Sciences@ASU*

DEANS

College of Business Administration: Dr LEQUITA BOOTH
College of Education: Dr JOHN GOODEN (acting)
College of Health Sciences: Dr STEVEN B. CHESBRO
College of Liberal Arts and Social Sciences: Dr LEON C. WILSON

College of Science, Mathematics and Technology: Dr CAJETAN M. AKUJUOBI
College of Visual and Performing Arts: Dr TOMMIE H. STEWART
Div. of Aerospace Studies–Air Force ROTC: Lt Col DAWN DAVIS
School of Graduate Studies: Dr WILLIAM A. PERSON
School of Music: Dr HORACE B. LAMAR, Jr
Univ. College: Dr EVELYN HODGE

AMRIDGE UNIVERSITY

POB 240240, Montgomery, AL 36117-3553
1200 Taylor Rd, Montgomery, AL 36117-3553
Telephone: (334) 387-7524
Fax: (334) 387-3878
E-mail: admissions@amridgeuniversity.edu
Internet: www.amridgeuniversity.edu
Founded 1942 as Montgomery Bible School, present name 2008
Private control
Academic year: August to August
Pres.: Dr MICHAEL C. TURNER
Vice-Pres. for Academic Affairs: Dr STANLEY DOUGLAS PATTERSON
Registrar: ELAINE TARENCE
Librarian: TERENCE SHERIDAN
Library: 150,000 journals, 20m. monographs

DEANS

College of Business and Leadership: Dr KENYETTA MCCURTY
College of General Studies: ROGER SHEPHERD (acting)
School of Human Services: Dr KENYETTA MCCURTY
Turner School of Theology: Dr RODNEY CLOUD (acting)

ATHENS STATE UNIVERSITY

300 N Beaty St, Athens, AL 35611-1999
Telephone: (256) 233-8100
Fax: (256) 233-8163
Internet: www.athens.edu
Founded 1822 as Athens Female Acad., present status 1975, present name 1988
State control
Academic year: August to July
Pres.: ROBERT K. GLENN
Provost and Vice-Pres. for Academic Affairs: RONALD CROMWELL
Vice-Pres. for Advancement: RICK MOULD
Vice-Pres. for Enrolment and Student Support Services: JIM HUTTO
Vice-Pres. for Financial Affairs: MIKE MCCOY
Dir of Admissions and Records: NECEDAH HENDERSON
Registrar: TERESA SUIT
Library Dir: Prof. Dr ROBERT BURKHARDT
Library of 100,000 vols
Number of teachers: 69
Number of students: 3,500

DEANS

College of Arts and Sciences: RONALD FRITZE
College of Business: Dr LINDA SHONESY
College of Education: Prof. DEBRA BAIRD

AUBURN UNIVERSITY

Auburn, AL 36849
Telephone: (334) 844-4000
Fax: (334) 844-6179
E-mail: registrar@auburn.edu
Internet: www.auburn.edu
Founded 1856 as East Alabama Male College, present name and status 1960
State control
Academic year: August to July
Pres.: Dr JAY GOGUE

Exec. Vice-Pres. and Chief Financial Officer: Dr DONALD L. LARGE, JR
Vice-Pres. for Academic Affairs and Interim Provost: Dr TIMOTHY BOOSINGER
Vice-Pres. for Devt: JANE PARKER
Vice-Pres. for Research and Assoc. Provost: Dr JOHN M. MASON, JR
Vice-Pres. for Student Affairs: Dr AINSLEY CARRY
Registrar: LAURA ANN FOREST
Dean of Libraries: Dr BONNIE MACEWAN
Library of 3,459,542 bound vols, 2,718,948 microfilms, 39,318 current periodicals, 256,354 maps, govt documents
Number of teachers: 1,358
Number of students: 25,469
Publications: *Alabama Cooperative Extension System* (1 a year), *Auburn Magazine* (4 a year), *Auburn University Research* (1 a year), *AU Daily, Beyond Auburn* (4 a year), *Engineering Research Activities* (1 a year), *Facts and Figures* (every 2 years), *Glomerata* (1 a year), *Graduate & Undergraduate* (1 a year), *Southern Humanities Review* (4 a year), *The Auburn Pharmacist* (4 a year), *The Auburn Plainsman* (48 a year), *The Auburn Veterinarian* (4 a year), *The Circle* (4 a year), *Tiger Cub* (1 a year)

DEANS

College of Agriculture: Dr WILLIAM BATCHELOR
College of Architecture, Design and Construction: Dr VINI NATHAN
College of Business: Prof. Dr BILL C. HARDGRAVE
College of Education: Dr BETTY LOU WHITFORD
College of Engineering: Dr LARRY BENEFIELD
College of Forestry and Wildlife Sciences: Dr JAMES P. SHEPARD
College of Human Sciences: Dr JUNE HENTON
College of Liberal Arts: Dr ANNE-KATRIN GRAMBERG
College of Nursing: Prof. Dr GREGG E. NEWSCHWANDER
College of Pharmacy: Dr R. LEE EVANS
College of Sciences and Mathematics: Prof. Dr CHARLES SAVRDA
College of Veterinary Medicine: Dr CALVIN JOHNSON
Graduate School: Dr GEORGE FLOWERS

AUBURN UNIVERSITY AT MONTGOMERY

POB 244023, Montgomery, AL 36124-4023
Telephone: (334) 244-3000
Fax: (334) 244-3920
E-mail: askaum@aum.edu
Internet: www.aum.edu
Founded 1967
State control
Academic year: August to August
Chancellor: Dr JOHN G. VERES, III
Vice-Chancellor for Advancement: CAROLYN C. GOLDEN
Vice-Chancellor for Financial Affairs: WANDA C. MEADOWS
Vice-Chancellor for Outreach and Strategic Initiatives: Dr KATHERINE A. JACKSON
Provost: Dr JENNIFER A. BROWN
Dean of Students: Dr JAN LYN
Registrar: ELIZABETH WARD
Dean of Libraries: LUCY FARROW
Library of 325,000 vols, 1,600 periodicals, 10,00,000 fed. govt documents, 15,000 journal titles
Number of students: 5,200

DEANS

School of Business: Dr W. RHEA INGRAM
School of Education: Dr SAMUEL FLYNT
School of Liberal Arts: Dr MICHAEL BURGER

School of Nursing: Dr GREGG NEWSCHWANDER
School of Sciences: Dr KAREN STINE

BIRMINGHAM—SOUTHERN COLLEGE

900 Arkadelphia Rd, Birmingham, AL 35254
Telephone: (205) 226-4600
Fax: (205) 226-4627
Internet: www.bsc.edu
Founded 1918 by merger of Southern Univ. (f. 1856) and Birmingham College (f. 1898)
Private control
Academic year: August to August
Offers bachelors degree in Arts, Fine Arts, Music, Musical Arts, Music Education, Science
Pres.: Gen. CHARLES C. KRULAK
Provost: Dr MARK S. SCHANTZ
Vice-Pres. for Admin.: LANE ESTES
Vice-Pres. for Communications: BILL WAGNON
Vice-Pres. for Enrolment Management: Dr KATHLEEN GREER ROSSMANN
Vice-Pres. for Finance: ELI PHILLIPS
Vice Pres. for Information Technology: ANTHONY HAMBEY
Vice Pres. for Institutional Advancement: PAT ANDERSON-FLOWERS
Vice-Pres. for Student Devt: Dr DAVID EBERHARDT
Library Dir: CHARLOTTE FORD
Library of 257,000 vols, 57,000 govt documents, 35,000 periodicals, 47,000 microfiches, 20,000 microfilms, audiovisual items, recordings, slides
Number of teachers: 106
Number of students: 1,521

CONCORDIA COLLEGE—SELMA

POB 2470, Selma, AL 36703
1712 Broad St, Selma, AL 36701
Telephone: (334) 874-5700
Fax: (334) 874-5755
E-mail: admissions@concordiaselma.edu
Internet: www.concordiaselma.edu
Founded 1922 as Alabama Luther College, present name 1981, present status 1994
Private control
Academic year: August to May
Bachelor degree programmes in business and education
Pres.: Rev. Dr TILAHUN MEKONNEN MENDEDO
Dean of Instruction: Dr DOREEN MOYO
Library Dir: J. SCOTT WHITING
Library of 55,000 vols, 100 periodicals and 3,000 e-books
Number of students: 650

FAULKNER UNIVERSITY

5345 Atlanta Highway, Montgomery, AL 36109
Telephone: (334) 386-7140
Fax: (334) 386-7143
E-mail: admissions@faulkner.edu
Internet: www.faulkner.edu
Founded 1942 as Montgomery Bible College; present name 1985
Private control
Academic year: August to July
Campuses at Huntsville, Birmingham, Montgomery, Mobile
Pres.: Dr BILLY D. HILYER
Vice-Pres. for Academic Affairs: JACK TUCCI
Vice-Pres. for Advancement: BEN BRUCE
Vice-Pres. for Enrolment Management: KEITH MOCK
Vice-Pres. for Finance: WILMA PHILLIPS
Registrar: DON REYNOLDS
Dean of Students: FAIRES AUSTIN

Dir of Admissions: NEIL SCOTT
Dir of Libraries: BARBARA KELLY
Library of 100,000 vols

DEANS

College of Arts and Sciences: Prof. DAVE RAMPERSAD
College of Biblical Studies: Prof. CECIL MAY
College of Business: Prof. DAVE A. KHADANGA
College of Education: JENDIA GRISSETT
Jones School of Law Admin.: CHARLES NELSON

HERITAGE CHRISTIAN UNIVERSITY

POB HCU, Florence, AL 35630
3625 Helton Dr., Florence, AL 35630
Telephone: (256) 766-6610
Fax: (256) 760-0981
E-mail: hcu@hcu.edu
Internet: www.hcu.edu
Founded 1971 as Int. Bible College; present name 2000
Private control
Academic year: August to July
Offers courses in Bible and theology
Pres.: DENNIS JONES
Vice-Pres. and Dean of Academic Affairs: Prof. Dr BILL BAGENTS
Vice-Pres. for Operations: PAT MOON
Vice-Pres. for Univ. Advancement: PHILIP GOAD
Dean of Students: BRAD MCKINNON
Registrar: CHARLOTTE ORR
Librarian: JAMIE COX
Library of 61,000 vols.

HUNTINGDON COLLEGE

1500 E Fairview Ave, Montgomery, AL 36106-2148
Telephone: (334) 833-4222
Fax: (334) 833-4347
E-mail: admiss@huntingdon.edu
Internet: www.huntingdon.edu
Founded 1854 as Tuskegee Female College, present name 1935
Private control
Academic year: August to July
Depts of art, biology, business, chemistry, communication studies, history and political science, language and literature, mathematics, music, psychology, religion, sport science and physical education, teacher education, pre-professional studies
Pres.: J. CAMERON WEST
Provost and Dean of College: SIDNEY J. STUBBS
Treasurer and Sr Vice-Pres. for Planning and Admin.: JAY A. DORMAN
Vice Pres. for College and Alumni Relation: ANTHONY J. LEIGH
Vice-Pres. for Enrolment Management: LAURA HINDS DUNCAN
Vice-Pres. for Student Life and Dean of Students: FRANK R. PARSONS, JR
Dir for Library: Prof. ERIC A. KIDWELL
Library of 180,693 vols
Number of teachers: 115
Number of students: 1,123

JACKSONVILLE STATE UNIVERSITY

700 Pelham Rd N, Jacksonville, AL 36265-1602
Telephone: (256) 782-5781
E-mail: info@jsu.edu
Internet: www.jsu.edu
Founded 1883 as Jacksonville State Normal School, present name and status 1966
State control
Academic year: August to July

Pres.: BILL MEEHAN
Provost and Vice-Pres. for Academic and Student Affairs: Dr REBECCA O. TURNER
Vice-Pres. for Admin. and Business Affairs: CLINT CARLSON (acting)
Vice-Pres. for Information Technology: VINSON HOUSTON
Vice-Pres. for Institutional Advancement: Dr CHARLES LEWIS
Dean of Library Services: JOHN-BAUER GRAHAM
Library of 600,000 vols
Number of teachers: 384 (265 full-time, 119 part-time)
Number of students: 9,077

DEANS

College of Arts and Sciences: Dr J. E. WADE
College of Commerce and Business Admin.: Dr BILL FIELDING
College of Education and Professional Studies: Dr JOHN HAMMETT
College of Graduate Studies and Continuing Education: Dr BILL CARR
College of Nursing and Health Sciences: Dr SARAH LATHAM

JUDSON COLLEGE

302 Bibb St, Marion, AL 36756
Telephone: (334) 683-5100
Fax: (334) 683-5147
E-mail: admissions@judson.edu
Internet: www.judson.edu
Founded 1838 as Judson Female Institute, present name 1903
Private control
Academic year: August to July
Offers arts majors and programmes incl. medicine, dentistry, law and engineering
Pres.: DAVID EARL POTTS
Vice-Pres. and Academic Dean: SARA BLISS KISER
Vice-Pres. and Dean of Students: SANDRA S. FOWLER
Vice-Pres. for Admissions and Financial Aid: CHARLOTTE S. CLEMENTS
Vice-Pres. for Advancement and Gen. Counsel: JOSEPH W. MATHEWS, JR
Vice-Pres. for Business Affairs: DENNIS FRODSHAM
Registrar: ELEANOR C. DRAKE
Dir of Library Services: GEORGE WASHBURN
Library of 70,000 vols
Number of students: 300
Publications: *The Ivy Vine, The Scrimshaw* (1 a year).

MILES COLLEGE

POB 39800, Birmingham, AL 35208
5500 Myron Massey Blvd, Fairfield, AL 35064
Telephone: (205) 929-1000
Fax: (205) 929-1453
E-mail: admissions@miles.edu
Internet: www.miles.edu
Founded 1898 as Miles Memorial College, present name 1941
Private control
Academic year: August to July
Academic divs: business and accounting, communications, education, humanities, natural sciences and mathematics, social and behavioural sciences
Pres.: Dr GEORGE T. FRENCH, JR
Sr Vice-Pres. of Finance and Admin.: DIANA KNIGHTON
Dean and Vice-Pres. of Academic Affairs: Dr EMMANUEL CHEKWA
Dean of Students Affairs: GRIENA KNIGHT
Dir of College Relations: Dr RICKY LEE

Dir. of Institutional Planning and Devt: W. FRANK TOPPING
Library of 90,000 vols, 6,000 periodicals
Number of teachers: 135
Number of students: 1,800

OAKWOOD UNIVERSITY

7000 Adventist Blvd NW, Huntsville, AL 35896
Telephone: (256) 726-7000
Fax: (256) 726-7154
E-mail: admission@oakwood.edu
Internet: www.oakwood.edu
Founded 1896 as Oakwood Industrial School, present name and status 2008
Private control
Academic year: July to June
Areas of study incl. biological sciences, business and information systems, chemistry, communication and fine arts education, education, English and foreign languages, family and consumer science, health and physical education, history and political science, mathematics and computer sciences, music, nursing, psychology, religion and theology, social work
Pres.: Dr LESLIE N. POLLARD
Provost and Sr Vice-Pres.: Dr R. TIMOTHY MCDONALD
Vice-Pres. for Academic Affairs: Dr C. GARLAND DULAN
Dir of Admissions: JOYCE SMITH
Dir of Library Services: PAULETTE MACLEAN JOHNSON
Library of 71,608 vols
Number of teachers: 176 (106 full-time, 70 part-time)
Number of students: 2,006 (1,953 undergraduate, 53 graduate)

SAMFORD UNIVERSITY

800 Lakeshore Dr., Birmingham, AL 35229
Telephone: (205) 726-2011
Fax: (205) 726-2654
Internet: www.samford.edu
Founded 1841 as Howard College, present name and status 1965
Private control
Academic year: June to May
Pres.: ANDREW WESTMORELAND
Provost and Exec. Vice-Pres.: Dr J. BRADLEY CREED
Vice-Pres. for Business and Financial Affairs: HARRY B. BROCK, III
Vice-Pres. for Operations and Planning: SARAH C. LATHAM
Vice-Pres. for Student Affairs and Enrolment Management: R. PHIL KIMREY
Vice-Pres. for Univ. Advancement: W. RANDALL PITTMAN
Dean of Admission: JASON BLACK
Dean of Academic Services and Registrar: PAUL G. AUCOIN
Library Dir: KIMMETHA HERNDON
Number of teachers: 252
Number of students: 4,715
Publications: *American Journal of Trial Advocacy* (3 a year), *Cumberland Lawyer* (2 a year), *Cumberland Law Review* (3 a year), *Seasons Magazine* (4 a year, online), *Samford University Catalog* (1 a year, online), *The Beeson Journal* (1 a year), *The Educational Collaborative*

DEANS

Beeson Divinity School: Prof. Dr TIMOTHY F. GEORGE
Brock School of Business: HOWARD FINCH (acting)
Cumberland School of Law: Dr JOHN L. CARROLL

Howard College of Arts and Sciences: DAVID W. CHAPMAN
Ida V. Moffett School of Nursing: Prof. NENA F. SANDERS
McWhorter School of Pharmacy: Prof. Dr CHARLES D. SANDS, III
Orlean Bullard Beeson School of Education and Professional Studies: Prof. Dr JEANIE ANN BOX
School of Arts: JOSEPH HOPKINS

SOUTHEASTERN BIBLE COLLEGE

2545 Valleydale Rd, Birmingham, AL 35244-2083
Telephone: (205) 970-9200
Fax: (205) 970-9207
E-mail: info@sebc.edu
Internet: www.sebc.edu
Founded 1935 as Birmingham School of the Bible, present name 1952, present status 1962
Private control
Academic year: August to May
Depts of arts and sciences, Biblical studies, education
Pres.: Dr DONALD W. HAWKINS
Provost and Vice-Pres. for Education: Dr VICKI L. WOLFE
Vice-Pres. for Advancement: CLIFF MCARDLE
Vice-Pres. for Devt: CLIFF MCARDLE
Vice-Pres. for Operations: PAUL WILLARD
Dean of Student Life and Dir. of Admissions: KRISTIE HARRICK
Dir of Institutional Effectiveness and Research: Dr PETER REOCH
Registrar: JOEL WOLFE
Dir of Library Services: PAUL A. ROBERTS
Library of 35,000 vols.

SPRING HILL COLLEGE

4000 Dauphin St, Mobile, AL 36608
Telephone: (251) 380-4000
Fax: (251) 460-2186
E-mail: admit@shc.edu
Internet: www.shc.edu
Founded 1830
Private control
Academic year: August to May
Faculties of communication, fine and performing arts, language and literature, library and information resource services, nursing, philosophy and theology, sciences, social sciences,
Pres.: Rev. RICHARD P. SALMI
Provost: Dr GEORGE E. SIMS
Vice-Pres. for Advancement: SAMANTHA CHURCH
Vice-Pres. for Accounting and Finance: RHONDA M. SHIRAZI
Vice-Pres. for Devt: JEFFREY HILPERTS
Vice-Pres. for Student Affairs and Dean of Students: JOSEPH W. DEIGHTON
Chief Information Officer: MARGARET MASSEY
Registrar: STUART MOORE
Dir of Library: GENTRY LANKEWICZ HOLBERT
Library of 192,313 vols
Number of teachers: 135 (84 full-time, 51 part-time)
Number of students: 1,460 (1,194 full-time, 266 part-time)

DEANS

Biology: Dr DONALD CULBERSON
Business: Dr SERGIO CASTELLO
Chemistry, Physics and Engineering: Dr LESLI BORDAS
Communication Arts: Dr SHAREE BROUSSARD
English: Dr CATHERINE SWENDER
Fine and Performing Arts: Rev. STEPHEN CAMPBELL
Foreign Languages: Dr COLETTE WINDISH

History: Dr TOM WARD
Mathematics: DANIEL CYPHERT
Nursing: Dr TERRAN MATHERS
Philosophy: Dr JOANNA FORSTROM
Political Science and Law: Dr ROBERT HARDING
Psychology: Dr ROYCE SIMPSON
Sociology: Dr HAROLD DORTON
Teacher Education: Dr LORI AULTMAN
Theology: Rev. CHRISTOPHER VISCARDI

STILLMAN COLLEGE

POB 1430, Tuscaloosa, AL 35403-9990
3601 Stillman Blvd, Tuscaloosa, AL 35401
Telephone: (205) 349-4240
E-mail: admissions@stillman.edu
Internet: www.stillman.edu
Founded 1876 as Tuscaloosa Institute, present name 1948
Private control
Academic year: August to July
Pres.: Dr ERNEST MCNEALEY
Vice-Pres. for Academic Affairs: Dr CHRISTOPHER JEFFRIES
Vice-Pres. for External Affairs: EDDIE B. THOMAS
Vice-Pres. for Fiscal Affairs: SAMA MONDEH
Vice-Pres. for Retention: CHARLOTTE CARTER
Vice-Pres. for Student Affairs: Dr SHARON WHITTAKER-DAVIS
Dean of Enrolment Management: GEORGE LEE
Dean of the Library: ROBERT J. HEATH
Library of 117,550 vols, 410 periodicals
Number of teachers: 60
Number of students: 1,000

DEANS

Arts and Sciences: Dr MARY JANE KROTZER
Professional Education: LINDA BRADFORD

TALLADEGA COLLEGE

627 W Battle St, Talladega, AL 35160
Telephone: (256) 761-0206
Fax: (256) 761-9206
E-mail: admissions@talladega.edu
Internet: www.talladega.edu
Founded 1867 as Swayne School, present name and status 1869
Private control
Academic year: August to May (2 semesters)
Pres.: Dr BILLY C. HAWKINS
Provost and Vice-Pres. for Academic Affairs: Dr EVELYN M. WHITE
Vice-Pres. for Admin. and Finance: Dr GERALD WILLIAMS
Vice-Pres. for Institutional Advancement: CASANDRA D. BLASSINGAME
Dean of Enrolment Management: FLORETTA J. DORTCH
Dean of Student Affairs: JACQUELINE PADDIO
Registrar: LINDSEY L BARNETTE
Library Dir: Dr JOSEPH MCDONALD
Library of 130,000 vols
Number of teachers: 35
Number of students: 702

DEANS

Div. of Business and Admin.: ERIC HELVY (acting)
Div. of Humanities and Fine Arts: TRELLIE JEFFERS (acting)
Div. of Natural Sciences and Mathematics: Prof. Dr CHARLIE M. STINSON
Eunice Walker Div. of Social Sciences and Education: Dr EDWARD HALL

TROY UNIVERSITY

Troy, AL 36082
Telephone: (334) 670-3000
Fax: (334) 670-3735

E-mail: ask@troy.edu
Internet: www.troy.edu
Founded 1887 as Troy State Normal School, present name 2004
Academic year: August to May
Colleges of arts and sciences, business, communication and fine arts, education, health and human services
Chancellor: Dr JACK HAWKINS, JR
Sr Vice-Chancellor for Student Services and Admin.: Dr JOHN R. DEW
Sr Vice-Chancellor for Academic Affairs: Dr EARL INGRAM
Sr Vice-Chancellor for Advancement and External Relations: JOHN W. SCHMIDT
Sr Vice-Chancellor for Finance and Business Affairs: JAMES M. BOOKOUT
Sr Vice-Chancellor for Student Services and Admin.: JOHN R. DEW
Exec. Vice-Chancellor and Provost: Dr ED D. ROACH
Registrar: VICKIE MILES
Dean for Libraries: Dr HENRY R. STEWART
Dean for Student Services: HERBERT E. REEVES
Library of 334,000 vols
Number of teachers: 265
Number of students: 5,100 .

CONSTITUENT UNIVERSITIES

Troy University, Dothan

500 Univ. Dr., Dothan, AL 36303
Telephone: (334) 9836556
Fax: (334) 9836322
Internet: ask@troy.edu
Internet: dothan.troy.edu
Founded 1887 as Troy State Normal School, present name 2004
Academic year: August to August
Vice-Chancellor: Dr DON JEFFREY
Dean for Student Services: ROBERT G. WILLIS
Campus Registrar: LISA J. BOUTWELL
Dir for Library Services: CHRIS SHAFFER
Number of students: 1,855

DEANS

College of Arts and Sciences: Dr ROBERT SAUNDERS
College of Business Admin.: Dr ADAIR GILBERT
College of Education: Dr SANDRA LEE JONES

Troy University, Montgomery

231 Montgomery St, PO Drawer 4419, Montgomery, AL 361034419
Telephone: (334) 241-9576
Fax: (334) 241-9590
E-mail: libweb@troy.edu
Internet: montgomery.troy.edu
Academic year: August to May
Vice-Chancellor: RAY WHITE
Dean for Student Services: Dr CHARLES WESTERN
Campus Registrar: LYNN LEWIS
Library Dir: KENT SNOWDEN
Library of 32,000 vols, 50,000 e-books

DEANS

College of Arts and Sciences: Dr WILLIAM S. RICHARDSON
College of Business: Dr JAMES SIMPSON
College of Education: Dr LEN KITCHENS

Troy University, Phenix City

1 Univ. Pl., Phenix City, AL 36869
Telephone: (334) 448-5106
Fax: (334) 448-5229
Internet: phenix.troy.edu
Academic year: August to August
Vice-Chancellor: Dr DAVE WHITE
Campus Registrar: CHRISTOPHER WAID

Dean for Student Services: JACK MILLER

DEANS

College of Business Admin.: Dr CHERIE FRETWELL
College of Counselling and Psychology: Dr KATHRYN NESS
College of Education: Dr LARRY THACKER

TUSKEGEE UNIVERSITY

Tuskegee, AL 36088
1200 W Montgomery Rd, Tuskegee Inst, AL 36088
Telephone: (334) 727-8011
Fax: (334) 727-5750
E-mail: admissions@mytu.tuskegee.edu
Internet: www.tuskegee.edu
Founded 1881
Private control
Academic year: August to July
Pres.: Dr GIBERT L. ROCHON
Provost and Vice-Pres. for Academic Affairs: Dr LUTHER S. WILLIAMS
Vice-Pres. for Finance and Chief Financial Officer: STEPHEN A. MARTIN
Vice-Pres. for Devt.: CHERYL M. THOMAS
Vice-Pres. for Student Affairs and Enrolment Management: Dr CYNTHIA D. SELLERS
Dean of Students: PETER J. SPEARS
Registrar: EDRICE D. LEFTWICH
Dir of Library Services: JUANITA M. ROBERTS
Library of 250,000 vols, 1,000 periodicals
Number of teachers: 266
Number of students: 3,000

DEANS

Andrew F. Brimmer College of Business and Information Science: Dr TEJINDER SARA
College of Agriculture and Environmental and Natural Sciences: Dr WALTER H. HILL
College of Engineering, Architecture and Physical Science: Dr LEGAND L. BURGE, JR
College of Liberal Arts and Education: Dr CARLTON E. MORRIS
College of Veterinary Medicine, Nursing and Allied Health: Dr TSEGAYE HABTEMARIAM
Robert R. Taylor School of Architecture and Construction Science: Dr RICHARD K. DOZIER

UNITED STATES SPORTS ACADEMY

One Academy Dr., Daphne, AL 36526
Telephone: (251) 626-3303
Fax: (251) 625-1035
E-mail: academy@ussa.edu
Internet: www.ussa.edu
Founded 1972
Private control
Academic year: September to August
Offers degrees in sports science, sports management
Pres. and CEO: Dr THOMAS P. ROSANDICH
Vice-Pres.: Dr T. J. ROSANDICH
Exec. Sec.: CANELA STEINER
Dean of Admin. and Finance: HOLLY MCLELLAN
Dir of Doctoral Studies: Dr FRED CROMARTIE
Dir of Student Services: Dr TIMOTHY FOLEY
Registrar: SARA COLE
Dir for Library and Archivist: GREG TYLER
Library: 1m. vols
Number of teachers: 32
Number of students: 873
Publications: The Academy (2 a year), The Sport Digest (4 a year, online (thesportdigest.com)), The Sport Journal (4 a year, online (www.thesportjournal.org)).

UNIVERSITY OF ALABAMA

POB 870100, Tuscaloosa, AL 35487-0134
Telephone: (205) 348-6010
Fax: (205) 348-3312
E-mail: registrar@ua.edu
Internet: www.ua.edu
Founded 1831
State control
Academic year: August to May
Pres.: Dr JUDY BONNER
Provost and Vice-Pres. for Academic Affairs: Dr JUDY L. BONNER
Vice-Pres. for Financial Affairs and Treas.: Dr LYNDA GILBERT
Vice-Pres. for Research: JOE BENSON
Vice-Pres. for Student Affairs and Vice Provost for Academic Affairs: Dr MARK D. NELSON
Vice-Pres. for Univ. Advancement: Dr PAMELA H. PARKER
Exec. Sec.: MARGARET SMITH
Dean of Students: Dr TIM HEBSON
Dean of Libraries: Prof. LOUIS A. PITSCHMANN
Library: see Libraries and Archives
Number of teachers: 1,501
Number of students: 31,747
Publications: Alabama Alumni Magazine (4 a year), Alabama Business (4 a year), Alabama Heritage (4 a year), Alabama Law Review (5 a year), Alabama Research Magazine (1 a year), Alabama Review (4 a year), Law and Psychology Review (1 a year)

DEANS

Capstone College of Nursing: Prof. SARA E. BARGER
College of Arts and Sciences: Dr ROBERT F. OLIN
College of Communication and Information Sciences: LOY SINGLETON
College of Community Health Sciences: Dr THADDEUS P. M. ULZEN
College of Continuing Studies: Dr CAROLYN DAHL
College of Education: Dr JAMES E. MCLEAN
College of Engineering: CHARLES KARR
College of Human Environmental Sciences: Dr MILLA D. BOSCHUNG
Culverhouse College of Commerce and Business Admin.: Dr J. MICHAEL HARDIN
Graduate School: Dr DAVID A. FRANCKO
Honors College: Dr SHANE SHARPE
School of Law: Dr KENNETH RANDALL
School of Social Work: LUCINDA L. ROFF

UNIVERSITY OF ALABAMA AT BIRMINGHAM

1530 Third Ave S, Birmingham, AL 35294-1150
Telephone: (205) 934-4011
Fax: (205) 975-8505
E-mail: president@uab.edu
Internet: www.uab.edu
Founded 1936, present name and status 1969
State control
Pres.: Dr CAROL Z. GARRISON
Provost: Dr LINDA LUCAS
Sr Vice-Pres.: Dr RAY L. WATTS
Vice-Pres. for Devt., Alumni and External Relations: Dr SHIRLEY SALLOWAY KAHN
Vice-Pres. for Financial Affairs and Admin.: RICHARD L. MARGISON
Vice-Pres. for Information Technology: Dr DOUG RIGNEY
Vice-Pres. Research and Economic Devt: Dr RICHARD B. MARCHASE
Library: 1m. vols (Mervyn H. Sterne Library), 358,858 vols (Lister Hill Library of the Health Sciences); 2,125 current periodicals (Sterne), 1,809 current periodicals (Lister Hill)

Number of teachers: 2,244 (2,090 full-time)
Number of students: 17,575
Publications: UAB Magazine (4 a year), UAB Reporter (52 a year)

DEANS

College of Arts and Sciences: THOMAS M. DILORENZO
Graduate School: Dr BRYAN D. NOE
School of Business: Prof. Dr DAVID R. KLOCK
School of Dentistry: Dr MICHAEL S. REDDY
School of Education: Prof. DEBORAH L. VOLTZ
School of Engineering: Dr MELINDA LALOR
School of Health Professions: Dr HAROLD P. JONES
School of Medicine: Dr RAY L. WATTS
School of Nursing: Dr DOREEN C. HARPER
School of Optometry: Dr ROD W. NOWAKOWSKI
School of Public Health: Prof. Dr MAX MICHAEL, III

UNIVERSITY OF ALABAMA IN HUNTSVILLE

301 Sparkman Dr., Huntsville, AL 35899
Telephone: (256) 824-1000
Fax: (256) 890-6538
E-mail: admitme@uah.edu
Internet: www.uah.edu
Founded 1950, present status 1969
State control
Academic year: August to July
Pres.: Dr ROBERT A. ALTENKIRCH
Provost and Exec. Vice-Pres. for Academic Affairs: Dr VISTASP KARBHARI
Vice-Pres. for Diversity: DELOIS SMITH
Vice-Pres. for Finance and Admin. and Interim Vice-Pres. for Univ. Advancement: RAY M. PINNER
Vice-Pres. for Research: Dr JOHN HORACK
Dean for Students: Dr REGINA HYATT
Dir for Institutional Research: DEBBIE STOWERS
Dean for Library: Dr DAVID MOORE
Library of 302,503 vols, 27,633 current serial titles, 544,303 microforms, 2,677 audiovisual materials, 61,249 e-books
Number of teachers: 486
Number of students: 7,629

DEANS

College of Business Administration: Dr CARON ST JOHN
College of Engineering: Prof. Dr SHANKAR MAHALINGAM
College of Liberal Arts: Dr GLENN T. DASHER
College of Nursing: Dr C. FAY RAINES
College of Science: Dr JOHN D. FIX
Graduate Studies: Dr RHONDA KAY GAEDE

UNIVERSITY OF MOBILE

5735 College Parkway, Mobile, AL 36613-2842
Telephone: (251) 675-5990
Fax: (251) 675-6293
Internet: www.umobile.edu
Founded 1961 as Mobile College, present name 1993
Private control
Academic year: May to August
Pres.: Dr MARK R. FOLEY
Chancellor: Dr WILLIAM K. WEAVER, JR
Vice-Pres. for Academic Affairs: Dr AUDREY C. EUBANKS
Vice-Pres. for Business Affairs: J. STEPHEN LEE
Vice-Pres. for Devt and Institutional Advancement: BRIAN BOYLE
Vice-Pres. for Enrolment Management: KIM LEOUSIS
Vice-Pres. for Student Devt: KIMBERLY B. LEOUSIS

Dean of Academic Services and Registrar: Dr DONALD BERRY

Dir of Library Services: JEFFREY D. CALAMETTI

Library of 64,504 vols, 143,605 microfiches, 950 periodical titles

Number of teachers: 111 full-time

Number of students: 1,987

DEANS

College of Arts and Sciences: Dr DWIGHT STEEDLEY

Centre for Adult Programs: Dr PAMELA S. BUCHANAN

Graduate Programs: Dr ANNE LOWERY

School of Business: Dr JANE FINLEY

School of Christian Studies: Dr CECIL TAYLOR

School of Education: Dr PETER KINGSFORD

School of Nursing: RICHARD MCELHANEY

UNIVERSITY OF MONTEVALLO

Montevallo, AL 35115

Telephone: (205) 665-6000

Fax: (205) 665-6003

E-mail: registrar@montevallo.edu

Internet: www.montevallo.edu

Founded 1896 as Alabama Girls Industrial School, present name and status 1969

State control

Academic year: August to August

Pres.: JOHN W. STEWART, III

Vice-Pres. for Academic Affairs: Dr MARY BETH ARMSTRONG

Sr Vice-Pres. for Admin. Affairs: Dr MICHELLE R. JOHNSTON

Vice-Pres. for Business Affairs: DeANNA SMITH

Vice-Pres. for Student Affairs: Dr KIMBERLY BARRETT

Registrar: SHAYNE GERVAIS

Dir of Admissions: GREG EMBRY

Dir of Libraries: KATHLEEN LOWE

Library of 248,132 vols, 7,51,618 microfilms items, 2,523 audiovisual items, 868 current periodicals

Number of teachers: 210 (135 full-time and 75 part-time)

Number of students: 3,100

DEANS

College of Arts and Sciences: Dr MARY BETH ARMSTRONG

College of Education: ANNA MCEWAN

College of Fine Arts: WILLIAM T. CLOW

Stephens College of Business: Prof. Dr STEPHEN H. CRAFT

UNIVERSITY OF NORTH ALABAMA

1 Harrison Plaza, Florence, AL 35632-0001

Telephone: (256) 765-4608

Fax: (205) 765-4329

E-mail: registrar@una.edu

Internet: www.una.edu

Founded 1830 as LaGrange College, present name and status 1872

State control

Academic year: August to July (2 semesters)

Pres.: WILLIAM G. CALE, JR

Provost and Vice-Pres. for Academic Affairs: Dr JOHN G. THORNELL

Vice-Pres. for Business and Financial Affairs: Dr STEVEN SMITH

Vice-Pres. for Student Affairs: Dr DAVID P. SHIELDS, JR

Vice-Pres. for Univ. Advancement: Dr ALAN MEDDERS

Registrar: TINA SHARP

Dir of Library Services: MELVIN D. DAVIS

Library of 328,456 vols, 900,000 microform items, 7,800 audiovisual items, 2,145 current periodicals, 200,000 e-books

Number of teachers: 285 (201 full-time, 84 part-time)

Number of students: 7,100

DEANS

College of Arts and Sciences: Dr VAGN HANSEN

College of Business: Dr KERRY P. GATLIN

College of Education: Dr DONNA JACOBS

College of Nursing and Allied Health: Dr BIRDIE I. BAILEY

UNIVERSITY OF SOUTH ALABAMA

307 University Blvd, Mobile, AL 36688-0002

Telephone: (251) 460-6101

E-mail: admiss@usouthal.edu

Internet: www.southalabama.edu

Founded 1963

State control

Academic year: August to May (3 semesters)

Pres.: GORDON MOULTON

Sr Vice-Pres. for Academic Affairs: Dr DAVID JOHNSON

Sr Vice-Pres.: Dr ANDRZEJ WIERZBICKI

Vice-Pres. for Devt and Alumni Relations: Dr JOSEPH F. BUSTA, JR

Vice-Pres. for Financial Affairs: M. WAYNE DAVIS

Vice-Pres. for Research: Dr JAMES J. CONNORS

Vice-Pres. for Student Affairs: Dr JOHN W. SMITH

Registrar: MELISSA M. WOLD

Dean of Graduate School: Dr B. KEITH HARRISON

Dean of Students: Dr MICHAEL A. MITCHELL

Dean of Libraries: Dr RICHARD J. WOOD

Library of 515,914 vols

Number of teachers: 1,085 (759 full-time, 326 part-time)

Number of students: 14,769

DEANS

College of Arts and Sciences: Dr ANDRZEJ WIERZBICKI

College of Education: Dr RICHARD L. HAYES

College of Engineering: Dr JOHN W. STEADMAN

College of Medicine: Dr SAMUEL J. STRADA

College of Nursing: Dr DEBRA C. DAVIS

Covey College of Allied Health Professions: Dr RICHARD E. TALBOTT

Graduate School: Dr KEITH HARRISON

Mitchell College of Business: Dr CARL C. MOORE

School of Computing: Dr ALEC F. YASINSAC

School of Continuing Education and Special Programs: Dr VAUGHN S. MILLNER

UNIVERSITY OF WEST ALABAMA

Livingston, AL 35470

Telephone: (205) 652-3400

Fax: (205) 652-3522

E-mail: admissions@uwa.edu

Internet: www.uwa.edu

Founded 1835, present name and status 1995

State control

Academic year: August to July

Pres.: Dr RICHARD D. HOLLAND

Provost: Dr DAVID M. TAYLOR

Vice-Pres. for Financial Affairs: T. RAIFORD NOLAND

Vice-Pres. for Institutional Advancement: CLEMIT W. SPRUIELL

Vice-Pres. for Student Affairs: DANNY BUCKALEW

School of Graduate Studies: Dr KATHY CHANDLER

Dir of Library: Prof. Dr NEIL SNIDER

Library of 250,000 vols

Number of teachers: 92

Number of students: 2,261

DEANS

College of Business: Dr KEN TUCKER

College of Education: Dr KATHY CHANDLER

College of Liberal Arts: Dr TIM EDWARDS

College of Natural Sciences and Mathematics: Dr VENKAT SHARMA

ALASKA

ALASKA BIBLE COLLEGE

POB 289, Glennallen, AK 99588

Telephone: (907) 822-3201

Fax: (907) 822-5027

E-mail: info@akbible.edu

Internet: www.akbible.edu

Founded 1966

Private control

Academic year: August to May (2 semesters)

Pres.: NICK RINGGER

Vice-Pres. for Academic Affairs: KEVIN NEWMAN

Vice-Pres. for Student Devt: BOB WENDT

Librarian: PAM HORST

Registrar: CAROL REIMER

Library of 30,500 vols, over 200 magazines and periodicals

Number of teachers: 10

Number of students: 45

ALASKA PACIFIC UNIVERSITY

4101 University Dr., Anchorage, AK 99508

Telephone: (907) 561-1266

Fax: (907) 562-0615

E-mail: infodesk@alaskapacific.edu

Internet: www.alaskapacific.edu

Founded 1957 as Alaska Methodist Univ., present name 1978

Academic year: September to August

Pres.: Dr DON BANTZ

Academic Dean: TRACY M. STEWART

Registrar: DONNA DOUGHERTY

Library of 400,000 vols, shared with Univ. of Alaska, Anchorage

Number of teachers: 80

Number of students: 689

ILISAGVIK COLLEGE

POB 749, 100 Stevenson St, Barrow, AK 99723

Telephone: (907) 852-3333

Fax: (907) 852-2729

Internet: www.ilisagvik.cc

Founded 1986 as North Slope Higher Education Center

Private control

Pres.: Dr BROOKE GONDARA

Dean of Students and Institutional Devt: PEARL BROWER

Library Dir: DAVID ONGLEY.

PRINCE WILLIAM SOUND COMMUNITY COLLEGE (PWSCC)

POB 97, 303 Lowe St, Valdez, AK 99686

Telephone: (907) 834-1600

Fax: (907) 834-1691

Internet: www.pwscc.edu

Founded 1978

Private control

Academic year: May to August

Some of the Bachelors courses are provided in partnership with Univ. of Alaska Anchorage and Univ. of Alaska Southeast

Pres.: DOUG A. DESORCIE

Academic Advisor: ROBYN PAUL

Dir for Student Services: CHRISTOPHER WASHKO

Dir for Training: B. J. WILLIAMS

Head Librarian: MOLLIE GOOD
Number of students: 1,500 (incl. on-campus, distance, part-time and full-time)

UNIVERSITY OF ALASKA STATEWIDE SYSTEM

POB 757500, Fairbanks, AK 99775
Suite 206, Butrovich Bldg, Fairbanks, AK 99775
Telephone: (907) 450-8100
Fax: (907) 450-8101
E-mail: syserve@alaska.edu
Internet: www.alaska.edu

Founded 1917 as Alaska Agricultural College and School of Mines; univ. status 1935; consists of 3 multi-campus 4-year univs, community college
Pres.: PATRICK K. GAMBLE
Vice-Pres. for Academic Affairs: DANIEL J. JULIUS
Vice-Pres. for Finance and Admin.: JOE TRUBACZ
Vice-Pres. for Research: Dr DANIEL J. JULIUS
Vice-Pres. for Univ. Relations: CARLA BEAM
Number of teachers: 2,332 (statewide)
Number of students: 32,711 (statewide)
Publs program catalogues from various units of the univ.

CONSTITUENT UNIVERSITIES
University of Alaska Anchorage: POB 141629, Anchorage, AK 99514-1629; tel. (907) 786-1480; fax (907) 786-4888; e-mail enroll@uaa.alaska.edu; internet www.uaa.alaska.edu; Chancellor and CEO TOM CASE; 20,554 students.
University of Alaska Fairbanks: POB 757520, Fairbanks, AK 99775; tel. (907) 474-7211; internet www.uaf.edu; Chancellor and CEO BRIAN ROGERS; 1,049 teachers; 11,034 students.
University of Alaska Southeast: 11120 Glacier Highway, Juneau, AK 99801; tel. (907) 796-6000; fax (907) 796-6162; e-mail uas.info@uas.alaska.edu; internet www.uas.alaska.edu; Chancellor JOHN PUGH; Vice-Chancellor CAROL GRIFFIN.

ARIZONA

AMERICAN INDIAN COLLEGE OF THE ASSEMBLIES OF GOD

10020 N 15th Ave, Phoenix, AZ 85021-2199
Telephone: (602) 944-3335
Fax: (602) 943-8299
E-mail: aicadm@aicag.edu
Internet: www.aicag.edu
Founded 1957
Private control
Academic year: August to May
Depts of business administration, Christian ministries and education
Pres.: Dr DAVID L. DEGARMO
Vice-Pres. for Academic Affairs: Dr JOSEPH J. SAGGIO
Vice-Pres. for Student Devt: Rev. VINCE ROUBIDEAUX
Dir for Enrolment Services: SANDRA GONZALEZ
Dir for Financial Services: Rev. PAUL G. HENNING
Registrar: JENNIFER ROUBIDEAUX
Library Dir: Rev. JOHN S. ROSE
Library of 20,000 vols
Number of teachers: 21 (7 full-time, 14 part-time)
Number of students: 80

ARIZONA CHRISTIAN UNIVERSITY

2625 E Cactus Rd, Phoenix, AZ 85032
Telephone: (602) 489-5300
Fax: (602) 404-2159
E-mail: info@arizonachristian.edu
Internet: arizonachristian.edu
Founded 1960 as Southwestern Conservative Baptist Bible College, present name and status 2011
Private control
Academic year: August to August
Depts of behavioural studies, biblical studies, business administration, Christian ministries, elementary education, secondary education, music ministry, pre-law and pre-med
Pres.: LEN MUNSIL
Provost and Sr Vice-Pres.: Dr GARY DAMORE
Sr Vice-Pres. and Chief Financial Officer: DIANE CATLIN
Academic Dean: Dr W. PERRY BAKER
Vice-Pres. for Enrolment and Marketing: HEATHER KIM
Dean for Students: CHUCK HUNTER
Registrar: LAMBERT CRUZ
Dir for Library Services: SEAN J. MCNULTY
Library of 25,000 vols, 20,000 e-books, 13,900 e-journals and magazines
Number of teachers: 85 (18 full-time, 67 part-time)

ARIZONA STATE UNIVERSITY

University Dr. and Mill Ave Tempe, AZ 85287
Telephone: (480) 965-9011
E-mail: askasu@asu.edu
Internet: www.asu.edu
Founded 1885
State control
Pres.: Dr MICHAEL M. CROW
Exec. Vice-Pres. and Provost: ELIZABETH D. CAPALDI
Exec. Vice-Pres. and Chief Financial Officer: MORGAN OLSEN
Sr Vice-Pres. for Academic Affairs: Prof. Dr DAVID YOUNG
Sr Vice-Pres. for Educational Outreach and Student Services: JAMES RUND
Vice-Pres. and Chief of Staff: JAMES O'BRIEN
Vice-Pres. and Exec. Vice-Provost for Online and Extended Education: Dr MERNOY HARRISON
Registrar: LOU ANN DENNY
Univ. Librarian: SHERRIE SCHMIDT
Library: see Libraries and Archives
Number of teachers: 1,800 (full-time)
Number of students: 72,254
Publications: *ASU Magazine* (4 a year), *Canyon Voices* (online (canyonvoices.asu.edu)), *TRIVIA: Voices of Feminism* (online (www.triviavoices.com))

DEANS
Barrett, The Honors College: MARK JACOBS
College of Liberal Arts and Sciences: ROBERT E. PAGE, JR
College of Nursing and Health Innovation: Dr TERI BRITT PIPE
College of Public Programs: JONATHAN KOPPELL
College of Technology and Innovation: MITZI MONTOYA
Graduate College: Dr MARIA T. ALLISON
Herberger Institute for Design and the Arts: KWANG-WU KIM
Ira A. Fulton Schools of Engineering: PAUL JOHNSON
Mary Lou Fulton Teachers College: Dr MARI KOERNER
New College of Interdisciplinary Arts and Sciences: Dr ELIZABETH LANGLAND
Sandra Day O'Connor College of Law: DOUGLAS SYLVESTER

School of Sustainability: SANDER VAN DER LEEUW
University College: Dr FREDERICK C. COREY
W. P. Carey School of Business: ROBERT MITTELSTAEDT
Walter Cronkite School of Journalism and Mass Communication: CHRISTOPHER CALLAHAN

DINÉ COLLEGE

1 Circle Dr., Route 12, Tsaile, AZ 86556-0067
Telephone: (928) 724-6600
E-mail: info@dinecollege.edu
Internet: www.dinecollege.edu
Founded 1968
Tribal control
Campuses at Chinle, Ganado, Kayenta, Tuba City, Window Rock in Arizona, Shiprock and Crownpoint in New Mexico
Pres.: Dr MAGGIE GEORGE
Vice-Pres. for Academic and Student Affairs: KY TRAVIS
Vice-Pres. for Admin. and Finance: RONALD R. BELLOLI
Library of 90,000 vols, 3,000 video cassettes and DVDs, 600 magazines, newspapers, journals and microforms
Number of teachers: 60
Number of students: 1,657

EVEREST COLLEGE PHOENIX

10400 N 25th Ave, Suite 190, Phoenix, AZ 85021
Telephone: (602) 942-4141
Fax: (602) 943-0960
Internet: www.everestcollegephoenix.edu
Founded 1982 as Academy of Business College, present name 2009
Private control
Offers Bachelors degrees in criminal justice and business administration; campus in Mesa
Pres.: Dr EDWARD JOHNSON
Provost: Dr MICHAEL BERRY
Pres. for Phoenix Campus: TODD MCDONALD
Pres. for Mesa Campus: MARY RITTER
Academic Dean: JOELLYN SCHNURR
Dir for Admissions: NICK THORESON
Sr Registrar: ROSALIND PEREIRA
Librarian: DIANA FURMAN.

FRANK LLOYD WRIGHT SCHOOL OF ARCHITECTURE

POB 4430, Scottsdale, AZ 85261
Telephone: (480) 860-2700
Fax: (480) 860-8472
E-mail: info@taliesin.edu
Internet: taliesin.edu
Founded 1932 as Taliesin Fellowship, present name 1960
Private control
Pres. and CEO: ANNE MALEY
Dean: VICTOR SIDY
Dir of Academic Affairs: MADALENA MAESTRI
Dir for Admissions, Financial Aid and Registrar: PAMELA STEFANSSON
Dir for Libraries: ELIZABETH DAWSARI
Library of 27,000 vols.

GRAND CANYON UNIVERSITY

POB 11097, Phoenix, AZ 85061-1097
3300 W Camelback Rd, Phoenix, AZ 85017-3030
Telephone: (602) 639-7500
Internet: www.gcu.edu
Founded 1949 as Grand Canyon College, present name 1989
Private control

Academic year: August to August

Pres.: Dr KATHY PLAYER

Provost and Chief Academic Officer: Dr CHERI ST ARNAULD

CEO: BRIAN MUELLER

Exec. Vice-Pres.: Dr STAN MEYER

Sr Vice-Pres. for Campus Devt: ROBERT MACHEN

Vice-Pres. for Academic Compliance and Univ. Registrar: JENNIFER LECH

Vice-Pres. for Student Services and Dean for Students: TIM GRIFFIN

Library of 155,000 vols

Number of students: 40,000

DEANS

College of Arts and Sciences: Dr MARK WOODEN

College of Doctoral Studies: Dr HANK RADDA

College of Education: Dr KIMBERLY A. LA PRADE

College of Fine Arts and Production: CLAUDE N. PENSIS

College of Nursing: Dr ANNE M. MCNAMARA

Ken Blanchard College of Business: Dr W. KEVIN BARKSDALE

NORTHCENTRAL UNIVERSITY

10000 E University Dr., Prescott Valley, AZ 86314

Telephone: (928) 541-7777

Fax: (928) 541-7817

E-mail: information@ncu.edu

Internet: www.ncu.edu

Founded 1996

Private control

CEO: GEORGE A. BURNETT

Pres. and Provost: Dr CLINTON D. GARDNER

Vice-Provost: Dr SCOTT W. M. BURRUS

Dir for Library Services: ED SALAZAR

DEANS

Graduate School: Dr GREGORY T. BRADLEY

School of Behavioural and Health Sciences: Dr HEATHER FREDERICK

School of Business and Technology Management: Dr A. LEE SMITH

School of Education: Dr CINDY K. KNOTT

NORTHERN ARIZONA UNIVERSITY

700 S Osborne Dr., Flagstaff, AZ 86011

Telephone: (928) 523-9011

Internet: www.nau.edu

Founded 1899

State control

Academic year: August to May

36 Campuses throughout Arizona

Pres.: Dr JOHN D. HAEGER

Provost and Vice-Pres. for Academic Affairs: Dr LIZ GROBSMITH

Vice-Provost for Undergraduate Studies: Dr KAREN PUGLIESI

Exec. Vice-Pres.: Dr M. J. MCMAHON

Sr Vice-Pres. for Enrolment Management and Student Affairs: DAVID BOUSQUET

Vice-Pres. for Admin. and Finance: JENNUS BURTON

Vice-Pres. for Institutional Research: Dr PATRICIA HAEUSER

Vice-Pres. for Research: Dr LAURA HUENNEKE

Vice-Pres. for Univ. Advancement: MASON GERETY

Dean and Univ. Librarian: CYNTHIA CHILDREY

Library: 1.4m. vols

Number of teachers: 864

Number of students: 25,364

Publication: *Horizons*

DEANS

College of Arts and Letters: Dr MICHAEL VINCENT

College of Education: Dr GYPSY M. DENZINE

College of Engineering, Forestry and Natural Sciences: Dr PAUL W. JAGODZINSKI

College of Health and Human Services: Dr LESLIE SCHULZ

College of Social and Behavioural Sciences: Dr MICHAEL R. STEVENSON

Graduate College: Dr RAMONA MELLOTT

W. A. Franke College of Business: Dr MASON GERETY

PRESCOTT COLLEGE

220 Grove Ave, Prescott, AZ 86301

Telephone: (928) 350-2100

Fax: (928) 776-5242

E-mail: admissions@prescott.edu

Internet: www.prescott.edu

Founded 1966

Private control

Academic year: September to August

Campus at Tuscon, Arizona; offers courses in abstract art, agroecology, counselling psychology, creative writing, ecopsychology, education, environmental education and interpretation, fine arts, human development, humanities, human ecology, management, outdoor adventure and teacher education

Pres.: Dr KRISTIN R. WOOLEVER

Provost and Exec. Vice-Pres. for Academic Affairs: Dr PAUL BURKHARDT

Chief Operating Officer: CATHERINE BOLAND

Registrar: MARY TREVOR

Library Dir: RICH LEWIS

Library of 23,900 vols

Number of teachers: 60 (full-time)

Number of students: 1,100

Publications: *Alligator Juniper* (1 a year, print and online (www.prescott.edu/experience/publications/alligatorjuniper)), *Transitions*.

SOUTHWEST COLLEGE OF NATUROPATHIC MEDICINE & HEALTH SCIENCES

2140 E Broadway Rd, Tempe, AZ 85282

Telephone: (480) 858-9100

Fax: (480) 858-9116

E-mail: admissions@scnm.edu

Internet: www.scnm.edu

Founded 1993

Private control

Pres. and CEO: Dr PAUL A. MITTMAN

Exec. Vice-Pres. for Academic and Clinical Affairs: CHRISTINE L. GIRARD

Vice-Pres. for Devt: VONISE PETERSEN

Vice-Pres. for Finance and Admin.: MARION DAVIS

Vice-Pres. for Student Affairs: MELISSA WINQUIST

Dean for Medical Education: JONI OLEHAUSEN

Dean for Faculty and Curriculum Devt: Dr BECKY B. CLARK

Library of 15,000 vols, 200 journal titles

Number of students: 337

Publication: *SCNM Now* (2 a year).

SOUTHWEST UNIVERSITY OF VISUAL ARTS

2525 N Country Club Rd, Tucson, AZ 85716

Telephone: (520) 325-0123

E-mail: admissions@suva.edu

Internet: www.suva.edu

Founded 1983 as Art Center Design College, present name and status 2011

Private control

Campus at Albuquerque, New Mexico

Pres.: SHARMAN R. WOODS

Chief Academic Officer: MARVIN R. WOODS

Library of 5,000 vols, 250 video cassettes, 200 CD-ROMs, 80 magazine subscriptions, 3 newspaper subscriptions.

THUNDERBIRD SCHOOL OF GLOBAL MANAGEMENT

1 Global Pl., Glendale, AZ 85306-6000

Telephone: (602) 9787000

Fax: (602) 978-7008

E-mail: admissions@thunderbird.edu

Internet: www.thunderbird.edu

Founded 1946 as The American Institute for Foreign Trade, present name 1997

Private control

Academic year: September to August

Campuses in China, Switzerland, Mexico and Russia

Pres.: Prof. Dr ÁNGEL CABRERA

Sr Vice-Pres. for Exec. Education: Dr DENNIS BALTZLEY

Vice-Pres. for Institutional Advancement and and Chief Devt Officer: Dr JOAN NEICE

Chief Academic Officer and Dean for the School: Prof. Dr DAVID BOWEN

Chief Financial Officer: TIM PROPP

Dean for Faculty: Dr DALE DAVISON

Dean for Research: Dr MANSOUR JAVIDAN

Registrar: DONNA METZGER

Dir for Library: CAROL HAMMOND

Number of students: 1,275

Publications: *Thunderbird Global Impact Report* (1 a year), *Thunderbird International Business Review* (6 a year), *Thunderbird Magazine* (2 a year)

DEANS

Accounting: DALE L. DAVISON

Economics: JOHN F. MATHIS

Executive Education: DAVID BOWEN

PROFESSORS

Applied Accounting: DALE DAVISON

Applied Entrepreneurship: STEVEN STRALSER

Applied Family Business: ERNESTO POZA

Global Entrepreneurship: ROBERT HISRICH

Global Management: MARY TEAGARDEN

Int. Finance: JOHN F. MATHIS

Int. Studies: MARTIN SOURS

Management: ANDREW INKPEN

Management: CHRISTINE PEARSON

Management: DAVID BOWEN

Management: MANSOUR JAVIDAN

Management: KANNAN RAMASWAMY

Marketing: ROBERT WIDING

Risk Management: JOHN O'CONNELL

Supply Chain Management: JOSEPH CAVINATO

UNIVERSITY OF ADVANCING TECHNOLOGY

2625 W Baseline Rd, Tempe, AZ 85283-1056

Telephone: (602) 383-8228

Fax: (602) 383-8222

E-mail: admissions@uat.edu

Internet: www.uat.edu

Founded 1983 as CAD Institute, present name 2002

Private control

Academic year: September to August

Technology disciplines incl. advancing computer science, artificial life programming, computer forensics, game design, game programming, human-computer interaction, network security, robotics and embedded systems, strategic technology development, technology forensics, technology product design, and web and social media technologies

Pres.: JASON D. PISTILLO
Provost and Dean: DAVID B. BOLMAN
Vice-Pres. for Finance: ROBERT L. WRIGHT
Dean for Academic Affairs: REBECCA R. WHITEHEAD
Dean for Admissions and Student Support: CHRYS PISTILLO
Dean for Online Education: MICHAEL ERWIN
Dean for Student and Employer Affairs: MEREDITH BARHAM
Registrar: JUDITH DRAYER
Academic Librarian: SUSAN WHITE
Library of 10,000 books, CD-ROMs and video cassettes
Number of teachers: 73 (full-time and part-time)
Number of students: 1,052 (incl. 420 online, 66 graduates)
Publication: *Journal of Advancing Technology* (2 a year).

UNIVERSITY OF ARIZONA

Tucson, AZ 85721
Telephone: (520) 621-2211
Fax: (602) 621-9118
E-mail: admissions@arizona.edu
Internet: www.arizona.edu
Founded 1885
State control
Academic year: August to May (2 terms)
Pres.: Dr EUGENE G. SANDER
Provost and Sr Vice-Pres. for Academic Affairs: JACQUELINE MOK
Sr Vice-Pres. for Research: LESLIE TOLBERT
Vice-Pres. for External Relations: JAIME GUTIERREZ
Vice-Pres. for Legal Affairs and Gen. Counsel: LYNNE WOOD
Vice-Pres. for Research, Graduate Studies and Economic Devt: LESLIE TOLBERT
Vice-Pres. for Student Affairs: MELISSO VITO
Dean for Admissions: Dr KASEY URQUIDEZ
Dean for Univ. Libraries: CARLA STOFFLE
Library: see Libraries and Archives
Number of teachers: 2,400 (f.t.e.)
Number of students: 38,057 (29,719 undergraduate, 6,962 graduate, 1,376 professional and medical)
Publications: *Arizona and the West* (history, 4 a year), *Arizona Law Review*, *Arizona Quarterly* (literature), *Books of the Southwest*, *Bulletin*, *Business and Economic Review* (12 a year), *Hispanic American Historical Review* (4 a year), *Record*

DEANS

College of Agriculture and Life Sciences: Dr SHANE C. BURGESS
College of Architecture and Landscape Architecture: JANICE CERVELLI
College of Education: Dr RONALD W. MARX
College of Engineering: Dr JEFFREY GOLDBERG
College of Fine Arts: JORY HANCOCK
College of Humanities: Dr MARY WILDNER-BASSETT
Colleges of Letters, Arts and Science: Dr JOAQUIN RUIZ (Exec. Dean)
College of Medicine: Dr STEVEN GOLDSCHMID
College of Nursing: Dr JOAN SHAVER
College of Optical Sciences: Dr THOMAS L. KOCH
College of Pharmacy: Dr J. LYLE BOOTMAN
College of Science: Dr JOAQUIN RUIZ
College of Social and Behavioural Sciences: Dr JOHN P. JONES, III
Eller College of Management: Dr LEONARD M. JESSUP
Graduate College: Dr ANDREW C. COMRIE
Honors College: Dr PATRICIA MACCORQUODALE
James E. Rogers College of Law: Dr LAWRENCE PONOROFF

Mel and Enid Zuckerman College of Public Health: Dr IMAN HAKIM
Outreach College: Dr MICHAEL A. PROCTOR
UA South: Dr JAMES SHOCKEY

PROFESSORS

College of Agriculture and Life Sciences:

ALLEN, R. E., Animal Science; Nutritional Sciences
AX, R. L., Animal Science; Obstetrics and Gynaecology
BEATTIE, B. R., Agricultural and Resource Economics
BOURQUE, D. P., Biochemistry; Molecular and Cellular Biology
BOWERS, W. S., Entomology
BRUSSEAU, M. L., Soil, Water and Environmental Sciences; Hydrology and Water Resources
BURAS, N., Hydrology and Water Resources
BYRNE, D. N., Entomology
CALDWELL, R. L., Soil, Water and Environmental Sciences; Communication
CATE, R. M., Family and Consumer Sciences
CHANDLER, V. L., Plant Science; Molecular and Cellular Biology
CHRISTENSON, J. A., Agricultural and Resource Economics
COATES, W. E., Arid Lands
COLBY, B. G., Agricultural and Resource Economics; Hydrology and Water Resources
COLLIER, R. J., Animal Science
COLLINS, J. K., Veterinary Science and Microbiology
CORY, D. C., Agricultural and Resource Economics
COX, D. E., Agriculture Education
DANIEL, T. C., Renewable Natural Resources; Psychology
DENISE, R. K., Animal Science
DENNEHY, T. J., Entomology
DESTEIGUER, J. E., Renewable Natural Resources
FFOLLIOTT, P. F., Watershed Management; Arid Lands
FOSTER, K. E., Arid Lands
GALBRAITH, D. W., Plant Science
GAY, L. W., Watershed Management
GERBA, C. P., Soil, Water and Environmental Sciences; Microbiology and Immunology
GIACOMELLI, G. A., Agricultural and Biosystems Engineering
GIMBLETT, H. R., Renewable Natural Resources; Landscape Architecture
GLENN, E. P., III, Soil, Water and Environmental Sciences; Wildlife and Fisheries Science
GOLL, D. E., Nutritional Sciences; Biochemistry
GUNATILAKA, L., Arid Lands
HAGEDORN, H. H., Entomology
HARTSHORNE, D. J., Nutritional Sciences; Biochemistry
HATCH, K. L., Agricultural and Biosystems Engineering
HAWES, M. C., Plant Pathology
HAWKINS, R. H., Watershed Management; Hydrology and Water Resources
HUETE, A. R., Soil, Water and Environmental Sciences
INNES, R. D., Agricultural and Resource Economics; Economics
JENSEN, M. H., Plant Science
JOENS, L. A., Veterinary Science and Microbiology
KALTENBACH, C., Animal Science
KENNEDY, C. K., Plant Pathology; Molecular and Cellular Biology
KNIGHT, J. A., Jr, Agriculture Education
LARKINS, B. A., Plant Science; Molecular and Cellular Biology
LEONARD, R. T., Plant Science

LIGHTNER, D. V., Veterinary Science and Microbiology
MCCLARAN, M. P., Range Management
MCCLURE, M. A., Plant Pathology
MCDANIEL, R. G., Plant Science
MCLAUGHLIN, S. P., Arid Lands
MCPHERSON, G. R., Renewable Natural Resources
MAIER, R. M., Soil, Water and Environmental Sciences
MANNAN, R. W., Wildlife and Fisheries Science
MARCHELLO, J. A., Animal Science; Nutritional Sciences
MARSH, S. E., Arid Lands; Geography and Regional Development; Renewable Natural Resources
MILLER, G. M., Agriculture Education
MONKE, E. A., Agricultural and Resource Economics
MORAN, N. A., Ecology and Evolutionary Biology; Entomology
PEPPER, I. L., Soil, Water and Environmental Sciences
POE, S. E., Agricultural and Biosystems Engineering
RAY, D. T., Plant Science
REID, C. P., Renewable Natural Resources
RIDLEY, C. A., Family and Consumer Sciences; Psychology
ROHRBAUGH, M. J., Family and Consumer Sciences; Psychology
ROTH, R. L., Agricultural and Biosystems Engineering
ROWE, D. C., Family and Consumer Sciences; Psychology
RUYLE, G. B., Range Management
SANDER, E. G., Biochemistry; Nutritional Sciences
SCHOWENGERDT, R., Arid Lands; Electrical and Computer Engineering; Optical Sciences
SCHURG, W. A., Veterinary Science and Microbiology; Animal Science
SHAW, W. W., Wildlife and Fisheries Science
SHIM, S., Family and Consumer Sciences
SILVERTOOTH, J. C., Soil, Water and Environment Sciences; Plant Science
SLACK, D. C., Agricultural and Biosystems Engineering
SONGER, J. G., Veterinary Science and Microbiology
STERLING, C. R., Veterinary Science and Microbiology
TABASHNIK, B., Entomology
THOMPSON, G. D., Agricultural and Resource Economics
VANETTEN, H. D., Plant Pathology
VIERLING, E., Biochemistry; Molecular and Cellular Biology
WARRICK, A. W., Soil, Water and Environmental Sciences; Hydrology and Water Resources
WHEELER, D. E., Entomology
WIERENGA, P. J., Soil, Water and Environmental Sciences
WILSON, P. N., Agricultural and Resource Economics
WOLFE, F. H., Nutritional Sciences
ZWOLINSKI, M. J., Watershed Management

College of Architecture and Landscape Architecture:

ALBANESE, C. A., Architecture
CHALFOUN, N. V., Architecture
ERIBES, R. A., Planning; Architecture
MALO, A., Architecture
MATTER, F. S., Planning; Architecture
ROSENBLOOM, S., Planning; Architecture
SAN MARTIN, I. J., Architecture
STAMM, W. P., Architecture

College of Education:

ALEAMONI, L. M., Special Education, Rehabilitation and School Psychology

AMES, W. S., Teaching and Teacher Education
ANDERS, P. L., Language, Reading and Culture
ANTIA, S. D., Special Education, Rehabilitation and School Psychology
CARTER, K. J., Teaching and Teacher Education
DOYLE, W., Teaching and Teacher Education
GOOD, T. L., Educational Psychology
GOODMAN, Y. M., Language, Reading and Culture
GRIFFEY, D. C., Physical Education
LESLIE, L., Higher Education
LEVIN, J. R., Educational Psychology
LEVIN, J. S., Higher Education
McCARTY, T. L., Language, Reading and Culture
MAKER, C. J., Special Education, Rehabilitation and School Psychology
MISHRA, S. P., Special Education, Rehabilitation and School Psychology
MOLL, L. C., Language, Reading and Culture
MORRIS, R. J., Special Education, Rehabilitation and School Psychology
OBRZUT, J. E., Special Education, Rehabilitation and School Psychology
RHOADES, G. D., Higher Education (H)
RUIZ, R., Language, Reading and Culture
SABERS, D. L., Educational Psychology
SALES, A. P., Special Education, Rehabilitation and School Psychology
SHORT, K. G., Language, Reading and Culture
SLAUGHTER, S. A., Higher Education
STREITMATTER, J. L., Educational Psychology
TAYLOR, J. L., Educational Administration
UMBREIT, J., Special Education, Rehabilitation and School Psychology
VALMONT, W. J., Language, Reading and Culture
WOODARD, D. B., Higher Education

College of Engineering:
ARNOLD, R. G., Chemical Engineering
ASKIN, R. G., Systems and Industrial Engineering
BAHILL, A. T., Systems and Industrial Engineering
BALES, R. C., Hydrology and Water Resources
BALSA, T. F., Aerospace and Mechanical Engineering
BASSETT, R. L., Hydrology and Water Resources
BIRNIE, D. P. III, Materials Science and Engineering; Electrical and Computer Engineering
BREWS, J. R., Electrical and Computing Engineering
BUDHU, M., Civil Engineering and Engineering Mechanics
BURAS, N., Hydrology and Water Resources
CALVERT, P. D., Materials Science and Engineering
CELLIER, F. E., Electrical and Computer Engineering
CETAS, T. C., Aerospace and Mechanical Engineering; Electrical and Computer Engineering
CHAMPAGNE, F. H., Aerospace and Mechanical Engineering
CHEN, C. F., Aerospace and Mechanical Engineering
COLBY, B. G., Hydrology and Water Resources
CONTRACTOR, D., Civil Engineering and Engineering Mechanics
DAVENPORT, W. G., Materials Science and Engineering
DAVIS, D. R., Hydrology and Water Resources

DESAI, C., Civil Engineering and Engineering Mechanics
DEYMIER, P. A., Materials Science and Engineering
EHSANI, M. R., Civil Engineering and Engineering Mechanics
FASEL, H. F., Aerospace and Mechanical Engineering
FRANTZISKONIS, G. N., Civil Engineering and Engineering Mechanics
GANAPOL, B. D., Hydrology and Water Resources
HALDAR, A., Civil Engineering and Engineering Mechanics
HAWKINS, R. H., Hydrology and Water Resources
HEINRICH, J. C., Aerospace and Mechanical Engineering
HIGLE, J. L., Systems and Industrial Engineering
HISKEY, J. B., Materials Science and Engineering
JACKSON, K. A., Materials Science and Engineering; Optical Sciences
KECECIOGLU, D. B., Aerospace and Mechanical Engineering
KERSCHEN, E. J., Aerospace and Mechanical Engineering
KOSTUK, R. K., Electrical and Computer Engineering; Optical Sciences
KULATILAKE, P., Mining and Geological Engineering
KUNDU, T., Civil Engineering and Engineering Mechanics
LOURI, A., Electrical and Computer Engineering
LYNCH, D. C., Materials Science and Engineering
MADDOCK, T., III, Hydrology and Water Resources
MADENCI, E., Aerospace and Mechanical Engineering
MARCELLIN, M. W., Electrical and Computer Engineering
MIRCHANDANI, P. B., Systems and Industrial Engineering; Electrical and Computer Engineering
NEUMAN, S. P., Hydrology and Water Resources
NIKRAVESH, P. E., Aerospace and Mechanical Engineering
OHANLON, J. F., Electrical and Computer Engineering
PALUSINSKI, O. A., Electrical and Computer Engineering
PETERSON, T. W., Chemical and Environmental Engineering (H)
POIRIER, D. R., Materials Science and Engineering
PRINCE, J. L., III, Electrical and Computer Engineering
RAGHAVAN, S., Materials Science and Engineering
RAMBERG, J. S., Systems and Industrial Engineering
RAMOHALLI, K. N., Aerospace and Mechanical Engineering
REAGAN, J. A., Electrical and Computer Engineering; Optical Sciences
ROZENBLIT, J. W., Electrical and Computer Engineering
SAADATMANESH, H., Civil Engineering and Engineering Mechanics
SCHOOLEY, L. C., Electrical and Computer Engineering
SCHOWENGERDT, R., Electrical and Computer Engineering; Optical Sciences
SEN, S., Systems and Industrial Engineering
SHADMAN, F., Chemical Engineering
SHUTTLEWORTH, W. J., Hydrology and Water Resources
SIMMONS, J. H., Materials Science and Engineering; Optical Sciences
SIMON, B. R., Aerospace and Mechanical Engineering

SOROOSHIAN, S., Hydrology and Water Resources; Systems and Industrial Engineering
STERNBERG, B. K., Mining and Geological Engineering
STRICKLAND, R. N., Electrical and Computer Engineering; Optical Sciences
SUNDARESHAN, M. K., Electrical and Computer Engineering
SZIDAROVSZKY, F., Systems and Industrial Engineering; Hydrology and Water Resources
SZILAGYI, M. N., Electrical and Computer Engineering
UHLMANN, D. R., Materials Science and Engineering; Optical Sciences
VALDES, J. B., Civil Engineering and Engineering Mechanics; Hydrology and Water Resources
VARADY, R. G., Hydrology and Water Resources
VRUDHULA, S. B. K., Electrical and Computer Engineering
WANG, F., Systems and Industrial Engineering
WEINBERG, M. C., Materials Science and Engineering
WENDT, J. O. L., Chemical and Environmental Engineering
WILLIAMS, J. G., Nuclear and Energy Engineering
WILLIAMS, S. K., Materials Science and Engineering
WYGNANSKI, I. J., Aerospace and Mechanical Engineering
YEH, T.-C. J., Hydrology and Water Resources
ZEIGLER, B. P., Electrical and Computer Engineering
ZIOLKOWSKI, R. W., Electrical and Computer Engineering

College of Fine Arts:
ASIA, D. I., Music
BOELTS, J. G., Art
CALDWELL, C. B., Media Arts
CHABOT, A. M., Art
CHAMBERLAIN, B. B., Music
COOK, G. D., Music
CROFT, M. F., Art
CUTIETTA, R. A., Music
DEMING, C. J., Media Arts
DIETZ, W. D., Music
DIXON, H. W., Theatre Arts
ERVIN, T. R., Music
FAN, P., Music
FERNANDEZ, N., Music
GEOFFRION, M. M., Art
GREER, W. D., Art
HAMMAN, D. L., Music
HAMMOND, H., Art
HANCOCK, J. L., Dance
HANSON, G. I., Music
HASKELL, J. R., Music
HEDDEN, S. K., Music
HITNER, C. V., Art
JONES, H. H., Art
KASHY, J. L., Music
KIRKBRIDE, J. E., Music
KOLOSICK, J. T., Music
LOWE, M., Dance
McLAUGHLIN, C. M., Music
MURPHY, E. W., Music
O'BRIEN, J. P., Music
PARRY, E. C., III, Art
PATTERSON, R. T., Music
POLK, A. W., Art
POWELL, G. C., Music
QUIROZ, A. J., Music
ROE, C. R., Music
ROGERS, B. J., Art
SEVIGNY, M. J., Art
TUCCI, A. D., Theatre Arts
TUNKARA, M. S., Art
WIMMER, G. E., Art
WINSLOW, D. J., Theatre Arts

ZUMBRO, N. L., Music

College of Humanities:
AIKEN, S. H., English
ARIEW, R. A., French and Italian
BABCOCK, B. A., English
BECK, J., French and Italian
BOWEN, R., English
CANFIELD, J. D., English
CHANDOLA, A. C., East Asian Studies
CHISHOLM, D. H., German Studies
CLASSEN, A., German Studies
COMPITELLO, M. A., Spanish and Portuguese
DAHOOD, R., English
DAYAN, J., English
DRYDEN, E. A., English
ENOS, T., English
EPSTEIN, W. H., English
EVANS, E. J., English
EVERS, L. J., English
FIELDER, G. E., Russian and Slavic Languages
FIORE, R. L., Spanish and Portuguese
GARRARD, J. G., Russian and Slavic Languages
GILABERT, J. J., Spanish and Portuguese
GONZALEZ, R. D., English
GUTSCHE, G. J., Russian and Slavic Languages
GYURKO, L. A., Spanish and Portuguese
HOGLE, J. E., English
HOUSTON, R. W., English
KIEFER, F. P., Jr, English
KINKADE, R. P., Spanish and Portuguese
KOLODNY, A., English
KUNNIE, J. E., African-American Studies
LEONARD, A., Jr, Classics; Near Eastern Studies
MCKNIGHT, B. E., East Asian Studies
MARTINSON, S. D., German Studies
MEDINE, P. E., English
MILLER, J. R., English
MILLER, T. P., English
MOMADAY, N. S., English
MONSMAN, G. C., English
NANTELL, J. A., Spanish and Portuguese
ORLEN, S. L., English
PENNER, J. D., English
PIALORSI, F. P., English
POVERMAN, C. E., English
PROMIS, J. M. O., Spanish and Portuguese
RAVAL, S. S., English
RIVERO, E. S., Spanish and Portuguese
SALDATE, M., IV, Education Foundations and Administration
SAVILLE-TROIKE, M., English
SCHULZ, R. A., German Studies
SCRUGGS, C. W., English
SHELTON, R. W., English
SKINNER, M. B., Classics
SOLOMON, J., Classics
SOREN, H. D., Classics
TAO, C-L. P., East Asian Studies
TAO, J-S., East Asian Studies
TAPAHONSO, L., American Indian Studies
TATUM, C. M., Spanish and Portuguese
TERPENING, R. H., French and Italian
TROIKE, R. C., English
ULREICH, J. C., Jr, English
VANCE, T. J., East Asian Studies
VOYATZIS, M. E., Classics
WAUGH, L. R., French and Italian
WILD, P. T., English
WITTIG, M. M., French and Italian; Women's Studies

Eller College of Business and Public Administration:
BLOCK, M. K., Economics
BRUCKS, M. L., Marketing
BURGOON, J. K., Communication
CHEN, H., Management Information Systems
CONNOLLY, T., Management and Policy
COX, J. C., Economics

DROR, M., Management Information Systems
DYL, E. A., Finance
FELIX, W. L., Accounting
FISHBACK, P. V., Economics
GILLILAND, S. W., Management and Policy
HECKLER, S. E., Marketing
IACOBUCCI, D. M., Marketing
ISAAC, M. R., Economics
KANTOR, S. E., Economics
LIBECAP, G. D., Economics
MCCABE, K. A., Economics
MILWARD, H. B., Public Administration and Policy; Management and Policy
NUNAMAKER, J. F., Jr, Management Information Systems
OAXACA, R. L., Economics
RAM, S., Management Information Systems
RAPOPORT, A., Management and Policy
SHENG, O. R. L., Management Information Systems
SILVERS, A. L., Public Administration and Policy
SMITH, K. R., Economics
TAYLOR, L. D., Economics
WALKER, M. A., Economics
WALLENDORF, M., Marketing
WALLER, W. S., Accounting
ZUPAN, M. A., Economics

James E. Rogers College of Law:
ANAYA, S. J.
ANDREWS, A. W.
ATWOOD, B. A.
AUSTIN, G. W.
BRAUCHER, J.
CHIORAZZI, M. G.
DOBBS, D. B.
GANTZ, D. A.
GLENNON, R. J., Jr, Law and Public Policy
HEGLAND, K. F.
HENDERSON, R. C.
KORN, J. B.
KOZOLCHYK, B.
MASSARO, T. M.
MAUET, T. A.
OBIORA, L. A.
RATNER, J. R.
SCHNEYER, T. J.
SCHUESSLER, T. L.
SILVERMAN, A.
SPECE, R. G., Jr
WEISS, E. J.
WILLIAMS, R. A., Jr
WOODS, W. D., Jr

College of Medicine:
AHMANN, F. R., Medicine; Surgery
AKPORIAYE, E., Microbiology and Immunology
ALBERTS, D. S., Medicine; Pharmacology; Public Health
ALECK, K. A., Clinical Paediatrics
ALPERT, J. S., Medicine
AMPEL, N. M., Medicine
ATWATER, A. E., Physiology
BALDWIN, A. L., Physiology
BARANKO, P. V., Clinical Professor
BARKER, S. J., Anaesthesiology
BARNES, G. R., Jr, Clinical Professor
BARRETT, H. H., Optical Sciences; Radiology
BARTON, L. L., Paediatrics
BERG, R. A., Paediatrics
BERNSTEIN, H., Microbiology and Immunology
BOWDEN, G. T., Radiation Oncology; Pharmacology and Toxicology
BOYWER, T. D., Medicine
BRANDENBURG, R. O., Medicine
BRAUN, E. J., Physiology
BUCHSBAUM, H. W., Clinical Neurology
BURT, J. M., Physiology; Surgery
BUXER, J. B., Clinical Professor
CANFIELD, L. M., Public Health
CARMONA, R. H., Clinical Surgery

CARTER, D. E., Pharmacology and Toxicology
CETAS, T. C., Radiation Oncology
CHAMBLISS, L., Clinical Obstetrics and Gynaecology
CLEWELL, W. H., Clinical Professor
COULL, B. M., Neurology; Medicine
COULTHARD, S. W., Clinical Surgery
CRAIG, A. D., Jr, Cell Biology and Anatomy
CROSS, H. E., Clinical Ophthalmology
CUNNIFF, C. M., Paediatrics; Clinical Obstetrics and Gynaecology
CUNNINGHAM, J. T., Clinical Medicine
DALLAS, W. J., Optical Sciences; Radiology
DALTON, W. S., Medicine
DANTZLER, W. H., Physiology
DASPIT, C. P., Clinical Surgery
DAVIS, T. P., Pharmacology
DELLON, A. L., Clinical Professor
DEMEURE, M. J., Surgery
DORR, R. T., Pharmacology
DRESNER, M. L., Clinical Surgery
DRYDEN, R. M., Clinical Opthalmology
DUCKWORTH, W. C., Clinical Medicine
DUNCAN, B. R., Paediatrics; Public Health
ELLIOT, J., Clinical Obstetrics and Gynaecology
ERENBERG, A., Clinical Paediatrics
ESCOBAR, P. L., Clinical Medicine
EWY, G. A., Medicine
FAGAN, T. C., Medicine
FELICETTA, J. V., Clinical Medicine
FISHBURNE, J. I., Jr, Clinical Obstetrics and Gynaecology
FLINK, I. L., Medicine
FREGOSI, R. F., Physiology
FRENCH, E. D., Pharmacology
FREUNDLICH, I. M., Clinical Professor
FRIEDMAN, R. L., Microbiology and Immunology
GALGIANI, J. N., Medicine
GANDOLFI, A. J., Anaesthesiology; Pharmacology and Toxicology
GAREWAL, H. S., Medicine
GATENBY, R. A., Radiology
GELENBERG, A. J., Psychiatry
GERNER, E. W., Radiation Oncology
GHISHAN, F. K., Paediatrics; Physiology
GILLIES, R. J., Radiology
GLATTKE, T. J., Surgery
GLEASON, D. M., Clinical Surgery
GLICKMAN, S. I., Clinical Surgery
GMITRO, A. F., Radiology; Optical Sciences
GOLDMAN, S., Surgery; Medicine
GORE, R. W., Physiology; Cell Biology and Anatomy
GRAHAM, A. R., Pathology
GRANA, W. A., Orthopaedic Surgery
GREEN, S. A., Public Health
GROGAN, T. M., Pathology
GROSS, R. A., Clinical Medicine
GROSSMAN, M., Clinical Medicine
GRUENER, R. P., Physiology
HABIB, M. P., Clinical Medicine
HADJIPAVLOU, A. G., Clinical Surgery
HALE, F. A., Clinical Family and Community Medicine
HALONEN, M. J., Pharmacology; Microbiology; Medicine
HAMEROFF, S. R., Anaesthesiology
HAMILTON, A. J., Surgery; Clinical Radiation Oncology; Psychology
HANSEN, R. C., Medicine; Paediatrics
HARRIS, D. T., Microbiology and Immunology
HATCH, K. D., Obstetrics and Gynaecology
HAUSSLER, M. R., Biochemistry
HAYNES, R. J., Clinical Surgery
HEINE, M. W., Obstetrics and Gynaecology
HENDIN, B. A., Clinical Neurology
HERMAN, R. M., Pharmacology
HERSH, E. M., Medicine; Microbiology and Immunology
HOYER, P. B., Physiology
HUNT, K. R., Clinical Radiology
HUNTER, T. B., Radiology

HUTTER, J. J., Paediatrics
ISERSON, K. V., Emergency Medicine
JOHNSON, D. G., Medicine; Pharmacology
KALIVAS, J., Clinical Medicine
KAPLAN, A. M., Clinical Paediatrics
KATZ, M. A., Medicine; Physiology
KAY, M., Microbiology and Immunology; Medicine
KERN, K. B., Medicine
KLOTZ, S. A., Medicine
LANCE, M. P., Medicine
LANE, R. D., Psychiatry
LEIBOWITZ, A. I., Clinical Medicine
LESLIE, J. B., Clinical Anaesthesiology
LEVINE, B. E., Clinical Medicine
LEVINE, N., Medicine
LEVINE, R. B., Neurobiology; Physiology
LEVY, P., Clinical Medicine
LIEN, Y-H. H., Medicine; Physiology
LISSE, J. R., Medicine
LOHMAN, T. G., Physiology
LUKAS, R. J., Pharmacology
McCARTY, R. J., Clinical Medicine
McCLURE, C. L., Clinical Family and Community Medicine
McCUSKEY, R. S., Cell Biology and Anatomy; Physiology
McDONAGH, P. F., Surgery; Physiology
McLOONE, J. B., Clinical Psychiatry
McMULLEN, N. T., Cell Biology and Anatomy; Neurology
MALAN, T. P., Anaesthesiology
MALONE, J. M., Clinical Surgery
MARCHALONIS, J. J., Microbiology and Immunology; Pathology; Medicine
MARSHALL, J. R., Public Health; Medicine
MARSHALL, W. N., Jr, Clinical Paediatrics
MARTINEZ, F., Paediatrics
MATTOX, J. H., Public Health; Clinical Obstetrics and Gynaecology
MEISLIN, H. W., Emergency Medicine
MICHAEL, U. F., Clinical Medicine
MILLER, J. M., Ophthalmology; Optical Sciences
MILLER, T. P., Medicine
MILLS, J. L., Surgery
MOHER, L. M., Clinical Family and Community Medicine
MORGAN, W. J., Paediatrics; Physiology
MORKIN, E., Medicine; Physiology; Pharmacology
MORRISON, D. A., Medicine; Radiology
NAGLE, R. B., Pathology; Cell Biology and Anatomy; Surgery
NOLTE, J., Cell Biology and Anatomy
OBER, R. R., Clinical Ophthalmology
OLESON, J. R., Radiation Oncology
ORTIZ, A., Public Health
OTTO, C. W., Anaesthesiology
OUTWATER, E. K., Radiology
OVITT, T. W., Radiology
PALMER, C. M., Clinical Anaesthesiology
PAYNE, C. M., Microbiology and Immunology
PEIRCE, J. C., Clinical Medicine
PELLETIER, K. R., Clinical Professor
PENG, Y-M., Medicine
PETERSEN, E. A., Medicine; Family and Community Health; Public Health
PETERSEN, S. R., Clinical Professor
PHIBBS, B. P., Clinical Medicine
PINNAS, J. L., Clinical Professor
PORRECA, F., Pharmacology; Anaesthesiology
PORTER, J. M., Clinical Surgery
POTTER, R. L., Psychiatry
POWIS, G., Pathology; Pharmacology
PURDON, T. F., Clinical Obstetrics and Gynaecology
PUST, R. E., Family and Community Medicine; Public Health
PUTNAM, C. W., Surgery; Pharmacology
QUAN, S. F., Medicine; Anaesthesiology
RACY, J. C., Psychiatry
RAMSAY, E. G., Surgery

RANCE, N. E., Pathology; Neurology; Cell Biology and Anatomy
RAY, C. G., Clinical Pathology
REED, K. L., Obstetrics and Gynaecology
REICHLIN, S., Medicine
REIMAN, E. M., Psychiatry
REKATE, H. L., Clinical Surgery
REYNA, V. F., Surgery; Medicine
RIMSZA, M. E., Clinical Paediatrics
RIZKALLAH, T. H., Clinical Obstetrics and Gynaecology
ROBBINS, R. A., Medicine
ROEHRIG, H., Radiology
ROESKE, W. R., Medicine; Pharmacology
ROSENFELD, P. A., Clinical Obstetrics and Gynaecology
RUNYAN, R. B., Cell Biology and Anatomy
RYAN, K. J., Pathology; Microbiology and Immunology
SABBAGH, A. H., Clinical Professor
SAMPLINER, R. E., Medicine
SANDERS, A. B., Emergency Medicine
SANOWSKI, R. A., Clinical Medicine
SATTENSPIEL, E., Clinical Obstetrics and Gynaecology
SCHIFF, M., Clinical Surgery
SCHILLER, W. R., Clinical Surgery
SCHMITZ, G. L., Clinical Surgery
SCHORR, W. F., Clinical Medicine
SCHUMACHER, M. J., Paediatrics; Medicine
SECOMB, T. W., Physiology
SEEGER, J. F., Radiology
SETHI, G. K., Surgery
SHAH, J. H., Medicine; Radiology
SHAPIRO, W. R., Clinical Neurology
SHEHAB, Z. M., Clinical Paediatrics; Clinical Pathology
SHISSLAK, C. M., Public Health; Family and Community Medicine, Psychology
SIBLEY, W. A., Neurology
SILVERMAN, H. D., Clinical Family and Community Medicine
SIPES, I. G., Pharmacology and Toxicology; Anaesthesiology
SKINNER, P. H., Family and Community Medicine
SLOVITER, R. S., Pharmacology; Neurology
SNYDER, R. W., Ophthalmology
SOBONYA, R. E., Pathology
SONNTAG, V. K. H., Clinical Surgery
SPAITE, D. W., Emergency Medicine
SPETZLER, R. F., Surgery
STERN, L. Z., Medicine
STERN, R. G., Clinical Radiology
STONE, H. H., Clinical Surgery
STUART, D. G., Physiology
SURWIT, E. A., Clinical Obstetrics and Gynaecology
SZIVEK, J. A., Orthopaedic Surgery
TAETLE, R., Medicine
TISCHLER, M. E., Biochemistry; Medicine; Physiology
TOLBERT, L. P., Neurobiology; Cell Biology and Anatomy
ULMER, D. D., Clinical Medicine
UNGER, E. C., Radiology
VALENZUELA, T. D., Emergency Medicine
VAN WYCK, D., Medicine
VILLAR, H. V., Surgery; Radiation Oncology
WEIL, A. T., Clinical Public Health
WEINSTEIN, R. S., Pathology
WEISS, B. D., Clinical Family and Community Medicine
WEISS, J. C., Clinical Paediatrics
WHITNEY, P. J., Clinical Surgery
WILLIAMS, C. L., Surgery
WILLIAMS, R. L., Clinical Paediatrics
WILLIAMS, S. K., Surgery; Physiology
WITTE, C. L., Surgery
WITTE, M. H., Surgery
WITTEN, M. L., Paediatrics
WOOLFENDEN, J. M., Radiology
WOOSLEY, R. L., Pharmacology; Medicine
WRIGHT, S. H., Physiology
YAMAMURA, H. I., Pharmacology; Biochemistry; Psychiatry

YATES, A., Clinical Family and Community Medicine
YUDELL, A., Clinical Neurology

College of Nursing:
BADGER, T. A.
GLITTENBERG, J. E.
ISENBERG, M. A.
MOORE, I. M.
PARSONS, L. C.
PHILLIPS, L. R.
REED, P. G.
VERRAN, J. A.
WOODTLI, M. A.

College of Pharmacy:
BOOTMAN, J. L., Pharmacy Practice and Science; Pharmaceutical Sciences; Public Health
CARTER, D. E., Pharmacology and Toxicology
COLE, J. R., Medicinal Chemistry; Pharmaceutical Sciences
CONSROE, P. F., Pharmacology and Toxicology
COONS, S. J., Pharmacy Practice and Science; Public Health
DRAUGALIS, J., Pharmacy Practice and Science; Pharmaceutical Sciences
GANDOLFI, A. J., Pharmacology; Pharmacology and Toxicology
HURLEY, L., Medicinal Chemistry–Pharmacology and Toxicology; Medicinal Chemistry–Pharmaceutical Sciences
JACOBSON, E. L., Pharmacology and Toxicology
JACOBSON, M. K., Medicinal Chemistry–Pharmacology and Toxicology
LIEBLER, D. C., Pharmacology and Toxicology
McQUEEN, C. A., Pharmacology and Toxicology
MAYERSOHN, M., Pharmaceutical Sciences
MURPHY, J. E., Pharmacy Practice and Science; Pharmaceutical Sciences
NOLAN, P. E., Pharmacy Practice and Science; Pharmaceutical Sciences
REGAN, J. W., Pharmacology and Toxicology
SCHRAM, K. H., Pharmaceutical Sciences
SIPES, I. G., Pharmacology and Toxicology
SLOVITER, R. S., Pharmacology
TIMMERMANN, B., Pharmacology and Toxicology; Pharmaceutical Sciences
TONG, T. G., Pharmacy Practice and Science; Pharmacology and Toxicology
YALKOWSKY, S. H., Pharmaceutical Sciences

College of Science:
ADAMOWICZ, L., Chemistry
ANDREWS, G. R., Computer Science
ANGEL, J. R. P., Astronomy; Optical Sciences
APOSHIAN, H. V., Molecular and Cellular Biology; Pharmacology
ARMSTRONG, N. R., Chemistry; Optical Sciences
ARNETT, W. D., Astronomy
ATKINSON, G. H., Chemistry; Optical Sciences
BALDWIN, T. O., Biochemistry
BARRETT, B. R., Physics
BARTON, M. D., Geosciences
BAYLES, K. A., Speech and Hearing Science
BECK, S. L., Geosciences
BETTERTON, E. A., Atmospheric Sciences
BICKEL, W. S., Physics
BIRKY, C. W., Jr, Ecology and Environmental Biology
BOURQUE, D. P., Biochemistry; Molecular and Cellular Biology
BOWDEN, G. T., Radiation Oncology; Pharmacology and Toxicology; Molecular and Cellular Biology
BOYNTON, W. V., Lunar and Planetary Laboratory; Planetary Sciences

BREDAS, J.-L. E., Chemistry
BRILLIANT, M. H., Paediatrics; Molecular and Cellular Biology
BROWER, D. L., Molecular and Cellular Biology; Biochemistry
BROWN, M. F., Chemistry; Biochemistry
BROWN, R. H., Planetary Sciences; Lunar and Planetary Laboratory; Astronomy
BURD, G. D., Molecular and Cellular Biology; Cell Biology and Anatomy; International Studies
BURROWS, A. S., Physics; Astronomy
BUTLER, R. F., Geosciences; Arizona Research Laboratories
CALDER, W. A., III, Ecology and Evolutionary Biology
CHANDLER, V. L., Plant Science; Molecular and Cellular Biology
CHASE, C. G., Geosciences
COHEN, A. S., Geosciences; Ecology and Environmental Biology
CRANFIELD, L. M., Biochemistry; Public Health
CRESS, A. E., Radiation Oncology; Molecular and Cellular Biology
CUSANOVICH, M. A., Biochemistry; Chemistry
CUSHING, J. M., Mathematics
DAVIES, R., Atmospheric Sciences
DAVIS, O. K., Geosciences
DEAN, J. S., Dendrochronology; Anthropology
DEBRAY, S. K., Computer Science
DECELLES, P. G., Geosciences
DENTON, M. B., Chemistry; Geosciences
DIECKMANN, C. L., Biochemistry; Molecular and Cellular Biology
DOWNEY, P. J., Computer Science
DRAKE, M. J., Planetary Sciences; Lunar and Planetary Laboratory; Arizona Research Laboratories; Geosciences
ENEMARK, J. H., Chemistry
ERCOLANI, N. M., Mathematics
ERICKSON, R. P., Paediatrics; Molecular and Cellular Biology
FANG, L.-Z., Physics
FARIS, W. G., Mathematics
FINK, U., Lunar and Planetary Laboratory; Planetary Sciences
FLASCHKA, H., Mathematics
FLESSA, K. W., Geosciences
FORSTER, K. I., Psychology
FRIEDLANDER, L., Mathematics
GANGULY, T., Geosciences
GARCIA, J. D., Physics
GAY, D. A., Mathematics
GEHRELS, A. M. J. T., Lunar and Planetary Laboratory; Planetary Sciences
GEHRELS, G. E., Geosciences
GLASS, R. S., Chemistry
GLATTKE, T. J., Speech and Hearing Science; Surgery
GREENBERG, R. J., Planetary Sciences; Teaching and Teacher Education
GREENLEE, W. M., Mathematics
GRIMES, W. J., Biochemistry; Molecular and Cellular Biology
GROVE, L. C., Mathematics
GUPTA, R., Computer Science
HALLICK, R. B., Biochemistry
HAUSSLER, M. R., Biochemistry
HAYNES, C. V., Geosciences
HERMAN, B. M., Atmospheric Sciences
HILDEBRAND, J. G., Neurobiology; Biochemistry
HOLLAND, A. L., Speech and Hearing Science
HRUBY, V. J., Chemistry; Arizona Research Laboratories; Biochemistry
HSIEH, K. C., Physics
HUBBARD, W. B., Lunar and Planetary Laboratory; Planetary Sciences
HUGHES HALLETT, D. J., Mathematics
HUGHES, M. K., Dendrochronology; Watershed Management
IMPEY, C. D., Astronomy

JOHNS, K. A., Physics
JOHNSON, R. A., Geosciences
JOKIPII, J. R., Planetary Sciences; Lunar and Planetary Laboratory; Astronomy
KELLER, P. C., Chemistry
KENNEDY, C. K., Plant Pathology; Molecular and Cellular Biology
KENNEDY, T. G., Mathematics; Physics
KENNICUTT, R. C., Astronomy
KRIEG, P. A., Cell Biology and Anatomy; Molecular and Cellular Biology
KUKOLICH, S. G., Chemistry
LARSON, H. P., Lunar and Planetary Laboratory; Planetary Sciences
LEAVITT, S. W., Dendrochronology
LEVERMORE, C. D., Mathematics
LEWIS, J. S., Lunar and Planetary Laboratory; Planetary Sciences
LICHTENBERGER, D. L., Chemistry
LIEBERT, J. W., Astronomy
LITTLE, J. W., Biochemistry; Molecular and Cellular Biology
LOMEN, D. O., Mathematics
LOVELOCK, D., Mathematics
LUNINE, J. I., Planetary Sciences; Lunar and Planetary Laboratory; Arizona Research Laboratories; Physics
McCALLUM, W. G., Mathematics
McCULLEN, J. D., Physics
McINTYRE, L., Jr, Physics
MAIER, R., Mathematics; Physics
MARDER, S. R., Chemistry; Optical Sciences
MARKOW, T. A., Ecology and Environmental Biology
MASH, E. A., Jr., Chemistry
MAZUMDAR, S., Physics; Optical Sciences
MELIA, F., Physics; Astronomy
MELOSH, H. J., Lunar and Planetary Laboratory; Planetary Sciences; Geosciences
MENDELSON, N. H., Molecular and Cellular Biology
MICHOD, R. E., Ecology and Evolutionary Biology
MIESFELD, R. L., Biochemistry; Molecular and Cellular Biology
MITTAL, Y. D., Mathematics
MOLONEY, J. V., Mathematics; Optical Sciences
MORAN, N. A., Ecology and Environmental Biology; Entomology
MOUNT, D. W., Molecular and Cellular Biology; Ecology and Environmental Biology; Biochemistry
MULLEN, S. L., Atmospheric Sciences; Hydrology and Water Resources
MYERS, E. W., Jr, Computer Science; Molecular and Cellular Biology
NEWELL, A. C., Mathematics; Arizona Research Laboratories
O'BRIEN, D. F., Chemistry; Biochemistry
OCHMAN, H., Biochemistry; Ecology and Environmental Biology; Molecular and Cellular Biology
OVERPECK, J. T., Geosciences
PALMER, J. N., Mathematics
PARKER, R. R., Molecular and Cellular Biology; Biochemistry
PARRISH-JONES, J. T., Geosciences
PATCHETT, P. J., Geosciences; Arizona Research Laboratories
PATRASCIOIU, A. N., Physics
PEMBERTON, J. E., Chemistry
POLT, R. L., Chemistry
POMEAU, Y., Mathematics
RAFELSKI, J., Physics; Arizona Research Laboratories
RIEKE, G. H., Astronomy; Planetary Sciences; Lunar and Planetary Laboratory
RIEKE, M. J., Astronomy
ROSENZWEIG, M. L., Ecology and Evolutionary Biology
RUIZ, J., Geosciences
RUTHERFOORD, J. P., Physics
RYCHLIK, M. R., Mathematics
SALZMAN, W. R., Chemistry

SARCEVIC, I., Physics
SCADRON, M. D., Physics
SCHAFFER, W. M., Ecology and Evolutionary Biology
SCHLICHTING, R. D., Computer Science
SCHMIDT, G. D., Astronomy
SHAKED, M., Mathematics
SHUPE, M. A., Physics
SMITH, M. A., Chemistry
SNODGRASS, R. T., Computer Science
STEIN, D. L., Physics
STEVENSON, F. W., Mathematics
STRITTMATTER, P. A., Astronomy
SWETNAM, T. W., Dendrochronology
SWINDLE, T. D., Lunar and Planetary Laboratory; Planetary Sciences; Geosciences
TABOR, M., Mathematics; Applied Mathematics; Physics
THAKUR, D. S., Mathematics
THOMPSON, R. I., Astronomy
TIFFT, W. G., Astronomy
TISCHLER, M. E., Biochemistry; Medicine; Physiology
TITLEY, S. R., Geosciences
TOMASKO, M. G., Lunar and Planetary Laboratory
TOUBASSI, E., Mathematics
TOUSSAINT, W. D., Physics
VANETTEN, H. D., Plant Pathology; Molecular and Cellular Biology
VELEZ, W. Y., Mathematics
VENABLE, D. L., Ecology and Evolutionary Biology
VIERLING, E., Biochemistry; Molecular and Cellular Biology
VON HOFF, D. D., Medicine; Pathology; Molecular and Cellular Biology
WALKER, F. A., Chemistry; Biochemistry
WALLACE, T. C., Jr, Geosciences
WARD, S., Molecular and Cellular Biology; Ecology and Environmental Biology
WELLS, M. A., Biochemistry
WILLOUGHBY, S. S., Mathematics
WINFREE, A. T., Ecology and Environmental Biology
WING, W. H., Physics; Optical Sciences; Arizona Research Laboratories; International Studies
WOJTKOWSKI, M. P., Mathematics
WOOLF, N. J., Astronomy
WYSOCKI, V. H., Chemistry; Biochemistry
YELLE, R. V., Planetary Sciences; Lunar and Planetary Laboratory
ZAKHAROV, V. E., Mathematics
ZANDT, G., Geosciences
ZIURYS, L. M., Chemistry; Astronomy

College of Social and Behavioural Sciences:

ADAMS, E. C., Anthropology
ANDERSON, K. S., History
ANNAS, J. E., Philosophy
BARNES, C. A., Psychology
BASSO, E. B., Anthropology
BECHTEL, R. B., Psychology; Renewable Natural Resources
BECKER, J. V., Psychology; Psychiatry
BEEZLEY, W. H., History
BERGENSEN, A. J., Sociology
BERNSTEIN, A. E., History
BERNSTEIN, G. L., History
BEVER, T. G., Psychology; Linguistics; Cognitive Science
BONINE, M. E., Near Eastern Studies; Geography and Regional Development
BOOTZIN, R. R., Psychology; Psychiatry
BUCHANAN, A. E., Philosophy
CHALMERS, D. J., Philosophy
CHAVES, M. A., Sociology
CLARKE, J. W., Political Science
COSGROVE, R. A., History
DANIEL, T. C., Psychology; Renewable Natural Resources
DE LA TORRE, A. I., Mexican American Studies–Public Health

DEAN, J. S., Dendrochronology; Anthropology
DEMERS, R. A., Linguistics
DEUTSCH, S. J., History
DEVER, W. G., Near Eastern Studies
DINNERSTEIN, L., History
DINNERSTEIN, M., Women's Studies
DOBSON, M. V., Ophthalmology
EATON, R. M., History
ESTRADA, A. L., Mexican American Studies
FERNANDEZ, C., Sociology
FINAN, T. J., Anthropology
FISH, P. R., Anthropology
FORSTER, K. I., Psychology
FUCHS, E., Near Eastern Studies; Judaic Studies
GALASKIEWICZ, J. J., Sociology
GAMAL, A. S., Near Eastern Studies
GARCIA, J. A., Political Science
GARCIA, J. R., History
GARRETT, M. F., Psychology; Linguistics; Speech and Hearing Studies
GIBSON, L. J., Geography
GLISKY, E. L., Psychology
GLITTENBERG, J. E., Nursing; Psychiatry; Anthropology
GOLDMAN, A. I., Philosophy
GREENBERG, J. B., Anthropology
GUMERMAN, G. J., Anthropology
HAMMOND, M., Linguistics
HARNISH, R. M., Philosophy; Linguistics
HEALEY, R. A., Philosophy
HILL, J. H., Anthropology
HURT, C. D., Information Resources and Library Science; Communication
JACOB, C. S., Communication
JOHNSON, J. W., Journalism
KARANT-NUNN, S. C., History
KASZNIAK, A. W., Psychology; Psychiatry; Neurology
KENNEDY, E. J., Women's Studies; Anthropology
KING, J. E., Psychology; Anthropology
KRAMER, C., Anthropology
LANGENDOEN, D. T., Linguistics
LANSING, J. S., Anthropology
LONGACRE, W. A., Anthropology
MCNAUGHTON, B. L., Psychology; Physiology
MCPHERSON, J. M., Sociology
MALONEY, J. C., Philosophy
MARSH, S. E., Arid Lands; Geography and Regional Development
MARSTON, S., Geography and Regional Development
MARTINEZ, O., History
MISHLER, W. T., II, Political Science
MOLM, L. D., Sociology
MORBECK, M. E., Anthropology
MORILL, C. K., Sociology; Psychology; Communication
MULLIGAN, G. F., Geography and Regional Development
NADEL, L., Psychology
NADER, H., History
NICHOLS, R. L., History
NICHTER, M., Anthropology; Public Health
NORRANDER, B., Political Science
OLSEN, J. W., Anthropology
PAREZO, N. J., American Indian Studies; Anthropology
PETERSON, M. A., Psychology
PHILIPS, S. U., Anthropology
PIATTELLI-PALMARINI, M., Cognitive Science
PLANE, D., Geography and Regional Development
POLLOCK, J. L., Philosophy
RAGIN, C. C., Sociology
REID, J. J., Jr, Anthropology
ROHRBAUGH, M. J., Psychology; Family and Consumer Sciences
ROWE, D. C., Family and Consumer Sciences; Psychology
SALES, B. D., Psychology; Psychiatry; Law
SCHIFFER, M. B., Anthropology
SCHLEGEL, A. E., Anthropology

SCHMIDTZ, D. J., Philosophy; Economics
SCHWARTZ, G. E., Psychology; Psychiatry; Neurology; Medicine
SCHWARTZ, J. E., Political Science
SECHREST, L., Psychology
SHARKEY, J. E., Journalism
SHELDON, B. E., Information Resources and Library Science
SHERIDAN, T. E., Anthropology
SHOHAM, V., Psychology
SILVERS, A. L., Public Administration and Policy
SMITH, C. D., Jr, Near Eastern Studies
SMITH-LOVIN, D. L., Sociology
SNOW, D. A., Sociology
STEVENS, S. J., Research Professor
STINI, W. A., Anthropology; Family and Community Medicine; Public Health
SULLIVAN, M. P., Political Science
VOLGY, T. J., Political Science
WALKER, H. A., Sociology
WEINER, D. R., History
WELSH, W. A., Political Science; Family and Consumer Medicine
WENK, G. L., Psychology; Neurology
WILLIAMS, E. J., Political Science
WILLIAMS, J. M., Psychology
ZEGURA, S. L., Anthropology
ZEPEDA, O., Linguistics

Arizona International College:
AMEGAGO, M. M. K.
BIXBY, B. R.
BUKHARDT, P. E.
BURGESS, K. H.
CONTERIS, H. J.
DURAN-CERDA, D. M.
FERNANDO, J. L.
GRIJALVA, M. A.
HELGERT, J. P.
PELTIER, J.
POPE, E. R.
SCOTT, A. G.
SHERMAN, P. M.
SPATARO, L. P.
TAL, K.

Optical Sciences Center:
DERENIAK, E. L., Optical Sciences; Electrical and Computer Engineering
FALCO, C. M., Optical Sciences; Arizona Research Laboratories
FRIEDEN, B. R., Optical Sciences
GIBBS, H. M., Optical Sciences
MANSURIPUR, M., Optical Sciences
MARATHAY, A. S., Optical Sciences
MEYSTRE, P., Optical Sciences; Physics
PEYGHAMBARIAN, N. N., Optical Sciences; Materials Science and Engineering
POWELL, R. C., Optical Sciences; Materials Science and Engineering
SARGENT, M., III, Optical Sciences
SARID, D., Optical Sciences; Arizona Research Laboratories
SASIAN, J. M., Optical Sciences; Astronomy
SHACK, R. V., Optical Sciences
SHOEMAKER, R. L., Optical Sciences; Chemistry; Radiology
WRIGHT, E. M., Optical Sciences; Physics
WYANT, J. C., Optical Sciences; Electrical and Computer Engineering

Other academic units:
ACOSTA, J. J., Military Science Tactics
CHRISTMAN, W. E., Naval Science
DYCHE, D. D., Military Aerospace Studies
WILKINSON, R. H., Humanities Programme

ATTACHED RESEARCH INSTITUTE
Mount Graham International Observatory: operated by Steward Observatory, the research arm of the Dept of Astronomy; see separate entry under Research Institutes.

UNIVERSITY OF PHOENIX

1625 W Fountainhead Parkway, Tempe, AZ 85282-2371

Telephone: (480) 966-9577
Internet: www.phoenix.edu

Founded 1976
Private control

163 Campuses and learning centres in the USA, Canada and Puerto Rico; internet-based degree courses

Pres.: Dr BILL PEPICELLO
Provost and Sr Vice-Pres.: ALAN DRIMMER
Sr Vice-Pres. for Academic Research: ADAM HONEA
Vice-Pres. for Academic Admin.: LEE FINKEL
Vice-Pres. for Academic Operations: RUSS PADEN

Number of teachers: 32,000
Number of students: 470,800

DEANS
College of Criminal Justice and Security: Dr JAMES J. NESS
College of Education: Dr MEREDITH CURLEY
College of Humanities: Dr BARB BADERMAN
College of Information Systems and Technology: Dr BLAIR SMITH
College of Natural Sciences: Dr HINRICH EYLERS
College of Nursing: Dr PAMELA FULLER
College of Social Sciences: Dr LYNN HALL
School of Advanced Studies: Dr JEREMY MORELAND
School of Business: Dr BILL BERRY

WESTERN INTERNATIONAL UNIVERSITY

9215 N Black Canyon Highway, Phoenix, AZ 85021

Telephone: (602) 943-2311
Fax: (602) 371-8637
E-mail: wiuinfo@apollogrp.edu
Internet: www.west.edu

Founded 1978
Private control

Campuses at Scottsdale, Chandler, Tempe, and Peoria in Arizona, and in China, India and Netherlands; offers bachelors degrees and MBA in business admin., management, information technology, finance, marketing and int. business

Pres.: TRACY LORENZ
Provost: Dr BARBARA BADERMAN
Vice-Pres. for Information Technology
Vice-Pres. for Strategy and Devt: ALLYSON POOLEY
Vice-Pres. for Univ. Services: KRIS MCCALL
Sr Dir for Finance: HEIDI PHIPPS
Dir for Enrolment: MELISSA MACHUCA
Dir for Enrolment: AMY KWIATKOWSKI
Registrar: HUE HASLIM.

ARKANSAS

ARKANSAS BAPTIST COLLEGE

1621 Dr Martin Luther King Dr., Little Rock, AR 72202

Telephone: (501) 370-4000
Fax: (501) 372-7992
Internet: www.arkansasbaptist.edu

Founded 1884 as Minister's Institute, present name 1885
Private control

Schools of arts and sciences, business and religious studies

Pres.: Dr O. FITZGERALD HILL
Exec. Vice-Pres. and Chief Financial Officer: BILLY OWENS

Vice-Pres. for Academic Affairs: Dr HOWARD O. GIBSON
Registrar: FREDDIE FOX
Library Dir: JOYCE CAMPBELL

DEANS

School of Business: Dr HOWARD O. GIBSON

ARKANSAS STATE UNIVERSITY

POB 179, 2105 Aggie Rd, Admin. Bldg, Room 202, State Univ., AR 72467
Telephone: (870) 972-2100
Fax: (870) 972-2036
E-mail: admissions@astate.edu
Internet: www.astate.edu
Founded 1909 as a regional agricultural training school, present name and status 1967
State control
Academic year: August to July
Main campus in Jonesboro, also campuses in Beebe, Mountain Home, Newport, Heber Springs and Paragould; Technical Center at Marked Tree
Pres.: Dr CHARLES L. WELCH
Chancellor: Dr G. DANIEL HOWARD
Exec. Vice Chancellor and Provost: Dr GLEN JONES
Vice-Chancellor for Finance and Admin.: ED KREMERS
Vice-Chancellor for Student Affairs: Dr WILLIAM R. STRIPLING
Vice-Chancellor for Univ. Advancement: CRISTIAN A. MURDOCK
Registrar: TRACY FINCH
Dean for Library and Information Services: JEFF BAILEY
Library of 536,900 vols, 531,307 fed. and state documents, 482,122 microforms
Number of teachers: 632
Number of students: 21,801 (ASU System)

DEANS

College of Agriculture and Technology: Dr DAVID BEASLEY
College of Business: Dr LEN FREY
College of Communications: Dr OSA AMIENYI
College of Education: Dr GREGORY MEEKS
College of Engineering: Dr DAVID B. BEASLEY
College of Fine Arts: Dr DALE MILLER
College of Humanities and Social Sciences: Dr CAROL O'CONNOR
College of Nursing and Health Professions: Dr SUSAN N. HANRAHAN
College of Sciences and Mathematics: Dr ANDREW NOVOBILSKI
Continuing Education and Community Outreach: Dr BEVERLY GILBERT
Graduate School: Dr ANDREW SUSTICH
Honors College: Dr ANDREW SUSTICH
Univ. College: Dr LYNITA COOKSEY

ARKANSAS TECH UNIVERSITY

1605 Coliseum Dr., Russellville, AR 72801
Telephone: (479) 968-0389
Fax: (479) 964-0839
E-mail: tech.enroll@atu.edu
Internet: www.atu.edu
Founded 1909, present name and status 1976
Pres.: Dr ROBERT CHARLES BROWN
Vice-Pres. for Academic Affairs: Dr JOHN W. WATSON
Sr Vice-Pres. for Admin. and Finance: DAVID C. MOSELEY
Vice-Pres. for Devt: JAYNE W. JONES
Vice-Pres. for Student Services and Univ. Relations: SUSIE NICHOLSON
Chancellor for Ozark Campus: Dr JO ALICE BLONDIN
Registrar: TAMMY RHODES
Dir for Library: WILLIAM A. PARTON

Library of 160,000 vols, 810,000 microforms, 110,000 govt documents, 10,000 multimedia titles and 1,245 current periodicals
Number of teachers: 400
Number of students: 9,814

DEANS

College of Applied Sciences: Prof. Dr WILLIAM HOEFLER
College of Arts and Humanities: Prof. Dr H. MICHEAL TARVER
College of Business: Dr ED BASHAW
College of Education: Prof. ELDON CLARY
College of Natural and Health Sciences: JEFF ROBERTSON
College of Professional Studies and Community Outreach: MARY ANN ROLLANS
Graduate College: Dr MARY B. GUNTER

CENTRAL BAPTIST COLLEGE

1501 College Ave, Conway, AR 72034
Telephone: (501) 329-6872
Fax: (501) 329-2941
E-mail: info@cbc.edu
Internet: www.cbc.edu
Founded 1952 as Conway Baptist College, present name 1962
Private control
Depts of behavioural sciences, Bible, business, fine arts, health and physical education, literature and language arts, maths and science, and social studies
Pres.: TERRY KIMBROW
Vice-Pres. for Academic Affairs: Dr GARY McALLISTER
Vice-Pres. for Advancement: SANCY FAULK
Vice-Pres. for Financial Affairs: DONNA GRAY
Dir for Student Services: BOBBY SULLIVAN
Registrar: PHYLIS HOFFMANN
Library Dir: RACHEL WHITTINGHAM
Library of 40,000 vols
Number of teachers: 50 (full-time and part-time)
Number of students: 742

CROWLEY'S RIDGE COLLEGE

100 College Dr., Paragould, AR 72450
Telephone: (870) 236-6901
Fax: (870) 236-7748
Internet: www.crc.edu
Founded 1964
Private control
Offers courses in Biblical studies and business administration
Pres.: KEN HOPPE
Vice-Pres. for Academic Affairs: PHIL WILKERSON
Vice-Pres. for Advancement: RICHARD JOHNSON
Vice-Pres. for Student Affairs: ART SMITH
Dir for Admissions: NANCY JONESHILL
Registrar: PAUL McFADDEN
Library of 12,000 vols
Publication: CRC Insider (2 a year).

HARDING UNIVERSITY

915 E Market Ave, Searcy, AR 72143
Telephone: (501) 279-4000
Fax: (501) 279-4865
E-mail: admissions@harding.edu
Internet: www.harding.edu
Founded 1924 as Harding College, by merger of Arkansas Christian College with Harper College, present name 1979
Private control
Pres.: DAVID B. BURKS
Provost and Vice-Pres. for Academic Affairs: Prof. Dr LARRY L. LONG

Vice-Pres. for Univ. Advancement: MIKE WILLIAMS
Vice-Pres. and Dean of Students: Dr DAVID COLLINS
Registrar: JANICE HURD
Dir for Library: ANN DIXON
Library of 373,133 vols, 4,951 cassettes, 817 CDROMs, 688 maps, 837 periodical subscriptions
Number of teachers: 301
Number of students: 7,155
Publication: Harding Magazine

DEANS

College of Arts and Humanities: Dr J. WARREN CASEY
College of Bible and Religion: Dr MONTE COX
College of Business Administration: Dr BRYAN D. BURKS
College of Education: Prof. Dr LEWIS FINLEY
College of Nursing: Prof. Dr CATHLEEN M. SCULTZ
College of Pharmacy: Dr JULIE HIXSON-WALLACE
College of Sciences: Prof. Dr TRAVIS THOMPSON
Honors College: Dr J. WARREN CASEY
International Programmes: Dr JEFFREY T. HOPPER

HENDERSON STATE UNIVERSITY

1100 Henderson St, Arkadelphia, AR 71999-0001
Telephone: (870) 230-5000
Fax: (870) 230-5147
Internet: www.hsu.edu
Founded 1890 as Arkadelphia Methodist College, present status 1929
State control
Academic year: August to May
Pres.: BOBBY G. JONES
Provost and Vice-Pres. for Academic Affairs: Dr VERNON G. MILES
Vice-Pres. for Finance and Admin.: LECIA FRANKLIN
Vice-Pres. for Student Services: CHAD FIELDING
Dir for Univ. Relations and Admissions: VIKITA HARDWRICK
Registrar: TOM GATTIN
Dir for Library: ROBERT YEHL
Library of 300,000 vols
Number of teachers: 166 (full-time)
Number of students: 3,779
Publication: FORGE (1 a year)

DEANS

Ellis College of Arts and Sciences: Dr MARALYN SOMMER
Graduate School: Dr KENNETH D. TAYLOR
School of Business: Dr JEFFREY L. HAMM
Teachers College: Dr JUDY HARRISON

HENDRIX COLLEGE

1600 Washington Ave, Conway, AR 72032
Telephone: (501) 329-6811
Fax: (501) 450-1200
Internet: www.hendrix.edu
Founded 1876 as Central Institute, present name 1931
Private control
Depts of humanities, interdisciplinary and pre-professional programmes, natural sciences, social sciences
Pres.: Dr J. TIMOTHY CLOYD
Provost and Dean for the College: Dr ROBERT ENTZMINGER
Exec. Vice-Pres. and Dean for Advancement: ELLIS ARNOLD
Vice-Pres. for Enrolment and Dean for Admissions: KAREN FOUST

Vice-Pres. for Student Affairs: JIM WILTGEN
Registrar: XINYING WANG
Library Dir: AMANDA MOORE

Library of 190,000 vols
Number of teachers: 108 (full-time)
Number of students: 1,426

JOHN BROWN UNIVERSITY

2000 W University St, Siloam Springs, AR 72761

Telephone: (479) 5249500
E-mail: jbuinfo@jbu.edu
Internet: www.jbu.edu

Founded 1919 as Southwestern Collegiate Institute, present name 1934
Private control
Academic year: July to June

Undergraduate academic divs: biblical studies, business, communication and fine arts, education, engineering and construction management, general studies, humanities and social sciences, natural sciences; depts in the graduate studies div.: Christian ministry, counselling, leadership and ethics

Pres.: Dr CHARLES POLLARD
Vice-Pres. for Academic Affairs: Dr ED ERICSON, III
Vice-Pres. for Enrolment Management: DON CRANDALL
Vice-Pres. for Finance and Admin.: KIM HADLEY
Vice-Pres. for Student Devt: Dr STEPHEN BEERS
Vice-Pres. for Univ. Advancement: Dr JAMES KRALL
Dean for Graduate Studies: Dr RICHARD ELLIS
Dean for Undergraduate Studies: Dr ROBERT NORWOOD
Registrar: BECKY LAMBERT
Dir for Library Services: MARY HABERMAS

Library of 120,000 vols (incl. 14,000 periodicals and 11,000 e-books)
Number of teachers: 123 (68 full-time, 55 adjunct)
Number of students: 2,183

LYON COLLEGE

POB 2317, 2300 Highland Rd, Batesville, AR 72503-2317

Telephone: (870) 307-7000
Fax: (870) 307-7001
E-mail: admissions@lyon.edu
Internet: www.lyon.edu

Founded 1872 as Arkansas College, present name 1994
Private control
Academic year: August to May

Divs of business and economics, fine arts, humanities, language and literature, math and science, social science, international programmes

Pres.: Prof. Dr DONALD V. WEATHERMAN
Vice-Pres. for Academic Services and Dean for Faculty: Dr VIRGINIA F. WRAY
Vice-Pres. for Admin.: DAVID L. HERINGER
Vice-Pres. for Business and Finance: KENNETH J. RUETER
Vice-Pres. for Enrollment Services: DENNY G. BARDOS
Vice-Pres. for Institutional Advancement: TIMOTHY L. BRUNER
Vice-Pres. for Student Life and Dean of Students: Dr F. BRUCE JOHNSTON
Registrar: DONALD R. TAYLOR
Library Dir: DEAN COVINGTON

Library of 215,000 vols, 20,000 periodical subscriptions
Number of teachers: 45
Number of students: 650

Publication: *Piper Magazine.*

OUACHITA BAPTIST UNIVERSITY

410 Ouachita St, Arkadelphia, AR 71998

Telephone: (870) 245-5000
Fax: (870) 245-5412
Internet: www.obu.edu

Founded 1886 as Ouachita Baptist College, present name and status 1965
Private control
Academic year: June to May

Pres.: Dr REX M. HORNE, JR
Vice-Pres. for Academic Affairs: Prof. STAN POOLE
Vice-Pres. for Admin. Services: BRETT POWELL
Vice-Pres. for Devt: TERRY PEEPLES
Vice-Pres. for Institutional Advancement: WESLEY KLUCK
Vice-Pres. for Student Services and Dean of Students: KELDON HENLEY
Chancellor: BEN ELROD
Registrar and Dir for Admissions: JUDY JONES
Dir for Library Services: Prof. Dr RAY GRANADE

Library of 150,000 vols, 1,000 current serial titles
Number of teachers: 108 (full-time)
Number of students: 1,594

DEANS

Chesley and Elizabeth Pruet School of Christian Studies: Dr J. DANIEL HAYS
Frank D. Hickingbotham School of Business: BRYAN MCKINNEY
J. D. Patterson School of Natural Sciences: Dr JOE JEFFERS
Michael D. Huckabee School of Education: MERRIBETH D. BRUNING
School of Fine Arts: D. SCOTT HOLSCLAW
School of Humanities: Dr JEFF ROOT
School of Interdisciplinary Studies: STAN POOLE
W. H. Sutton School of Social Sciences: RANDALL D. WIGHT

PHILANDER SMITH COLLEGE

900 W Daisy L. Gatson Bates Dr., Little Rock, AR 72202

Telephone: (501) 375-9845
Fax: (501) 370-5277
E-mail: registrar@philander.edu
Internet: www.philander.edu

Founded 1877 as Walden Seminary, present name 1882
Private control
Academic year: August to July

Divs of business and economics, education, humanities, natural and physical sciences, and social sciences

Pres.: Dr WALTER M. KIMBROUGH
Vice-Pres. for Academic Affairs: Dr FRANK JAMES
Vice-Pres. for Enrolment Management: DAVID D. PAGE
Vice-Pres. for Fiscal Affairs: TERRY WALLACE
Vice-Pres. for Institutional Advancement: Dr SHANNON FLEMING
Vice-Pres. for Student Affairs: Dr STACY DOWNING
Registrar: BERTHA OWENS
Head Librarian: TERESA OJEZUA

Library of 46,000 vols.

SOUTHERN ARKANSAS UNIVERSITY

100 E University, Magnolia, AR 71753-5000

Telephone: (870) 235-4000
Internet: www.saumag.edu

Founded 1911 as Third District Agricultural School, present name 1976
State control
Academic year: August to July

Pres.: Prof. Dr DAVID F. RANKIN
Vice-Pres. for Academic Affairs: Dr DAVID L. CROUSE
Vice-Pres. for Admin. and Gen. Counsel: ROGER W. GILES
Vice-Pres. for Facilities: CHARLES J. LEWIS
Vice-Pres. for Finance: DARRELL MORRISON
Vice-Pres. for Student Affairs: Dr DONNA Y. ALLEN
Dean for Students: SANDRA SMITH
Dean for Enrolment Services: SARAH JENNINGS
Registrar: Dr ED NIPPER
Library Dir: DANIEL PAGE

Library of 150,000 vols
Number of students: 3,400 (2,944 undergraduate, 435 graduate)

DEANS

College of Business: Dr LISA TOMS
College of Education: Prof. Dr ZAIDY MOHD-ZAIN
College of Liberal and Performing Arts: Prof. Dr TREY BERRY
College of Science and Technology: Prof. Dr SCOTT MCKAY
School of Graduate Studies: Prof. Dr KIM BLOSS-BERNARD

UNIVERSITY OF ARKANSAS SYSTEM

2404 N University Ave, Little Rock, AR 72207

Telephone: (501) 686-2500
Fax: (501) 686-2506
Internet: www.uasys.edu

Founded 1871 as Arkansas Industrial Univ., present name 1899
State control

Pres.: DONALD R. BOBBITT
Vice-Pres. for Academic Affairs: DANIEL E. FERRITOR
Vice-Pres. for Admin.: ANN KEMP
Vice-Pres. for Finance: BARBARA A. GOSWICK
Vice-Pres. for Univ. Relations: MELISSA K. RUST
Gen. Counsel: FRED HARRISON
Number of students: 70,000.

CONSTITUENT UNIVERSITIES

University of Arkansas at Little Rock

2801 S University Ave, Little Rock, AR 72204

Telephone: (501) 569-3000
Internet: ualr.edu

Founded 1927, present name and status 1969

Chancellor: Dr JOEL E. ANDERSON
Provost and Vice-Chancellor for Academic Affairs: Dr SANDRA ROBERTSON
Vice-Chancellor for Educational, Student Services and Student Life: Dr CHARLES W. DONALDSON
Vice-Chancellor for Finance and Admin.: Dr ROBERT ADAMS
Vice-Chancellor for Univ. Advancement: BILL WALKER
Dean for Library: WANDA DOLE

Library of 500,000 vols, 11,000 e-books, 28,000 journals, 3,600 periodicals
Number of teachers: 1,202 (675 full-time, 527 part-time)
Number of students: 13,000

Publications: *Arkansas Journal of Social Change and Public Service, The Journal of Appellate Practice and Process, UALR Law Review* (4 a year, online (ualr.edu/lawreview))

DEANS

College of Arts, Humanities and Social Sciences: Dr DEBORAH BALDWIN
College of Business: Dr JANE WAYLAND

College of Education: Dr ANGELA MAYNARD SEWALL
College of Professional Studies: Dr ANGELA BRENTON
College of Science and Mathematics: Dr MICHAEL A. GEALT
Donaghey College of Engineering and Information Technology: Dr ERIC SANDGREN
Graduate School: Dr PATRICK J. PELLICANE
William H. Bowen School of Law: Prof. JOHN DIPIPPA

University of Arkansas at Monticello

Monticello, AR 71655
Telephone: (870) 460-1026
Fax: (870) 460-1933
Internet: www.uamont.edu
Founded 1909, present status 2003
Chancellor: H. JACK LASSITER
Provost and Vice-Chancellor for Academic Affairs: Dr R. DAVID RAY
Vice-Chancellor for Advancement and Univ. Relations: CLAY BROWN
Vice-Chancellor for Finance and Admin.: JAY JONES
Vice-Chancellor for Student Affairs: JAY HUGHES
Vice-Chancellor for UAM College of Technology Crossett: LINDA RUSHING
Vice-Chancellor for UAM College of Technology McGehee: BOB WARE
Dean for Students: SCOTT KUTTENKULER
Dean for Enrolment Management and Dir for Admissions: MARY WHITING
Registrar: Dr DEBBIE K. BRYANT
Library Dir: SANDRA CAMPBELL
Library of 500,000 vols (incl. 1,200 current periodicals)
Number of teachers: 100
Number of students: 3,638 (3,506 undergraduate, 132 graduate)

DEANS

School of Agriculture: Dr KELLY BRYANT
School of Arts and Humanities: MARK SPENCER
School of Business: Dr LOUIS JAMES
School of Computer Information Systems: BRIAN HAIRSTON
School of Education: Dr PEGGY DOSS
School of Forest Resources: Dr PHIL TAPPE
School of Mathematics and Natural Sciences: MORRIS BRAMLETT
School of Nursing: PAM GOUNER
School of Social and Behavioural Sciences: Dr THOMAS SPRINGER

University of Arkansas at Pine Bluff

1200 N University Dr., Pine Bluff, AR 71601
Telephone: (870) 575-8000
Internet: www.uapb.edu
Founded 1873, present status 1972
Chancellor: LAWRENCE A. DAVIS, JR
Vice-Chancellor for Academic Affairs: Dr MARY E. BENJAMIN
Vice-Chancellor for Finance and Admin.: PAULINE THOMAS
Registrar: ERICA W. FULTON
Library Dir: EDWARD J. FONTENETTE
Library of 362,653 vols, 466 journals
Number of students: 3,710

DEANS

Honors College: Dr CAROLYN F. BLAKELY
School of Agriculture, Fisheries and Human Sciences: Dr JAMES O. GARNER, JR
School of Business and Management: CARLA M. MARTIN
School of Education: Dr CALVIN JOHNSON
University College: Dr JEWELL M. WALKER

University of Arkansas, Fayetteville

1 Univ. of Arkansas, Fayetteville, AR 72701
Telephone: (479) 575-2000
Fax: (479) 575-7515
E-mail: uofa@uark.edu
Internet: www.uark.edu
Founded 1871
Academic year: August to May
Chancellor: Dr G. DAVID GEARHART
Provost and Vice-Chancellor for Academic Affairs: SHARON GABER
Vice-Provost for Enrolment Management and Dean for Admissions: SUZANNE MCCRAY
Vice-Chancellor for Advancement: BRADFORD E. CHOATE
Vice-Chancellor for Finance and Admin.: Dr DONALD O. PEDERSON
Vice-Chancellor for Govt and Community Relations: RICHARD B. HUDSON
Vice-Chancellor for Student Affairs and Dean for Students: Dr DANIEL PUGH
Registrar: DAVE DAWSON
Dean for Libraries: CAROLYN HENDERSON ALLEN
Library: see Libraries and Archives
Number of teachers: 989
Number of students: 23,199 (19,027 undergraduate, 3,773 graduate, 399 law)
Publications: *Arkansas Land & Life Magazine* (2 a year), *Arkansas Law Notes* (1 a year, online (lawnotes.law.uark.edu)), *Arkansas Law Record* (2 a year), *Arkansas Law Review* (4 a year, print and online (lawreview.law.uark.edu)), *Bumpers College Alumni Magazine, Discovery, Inquiry: The Undergraduate Research Journal* (online (inquiry.uark.edu)), *Journal of Food Law & Policy, Journal of Islamic Law & Culture* (2 a year), *Research Frontiers* (2 a year, online (researchfrontiers.uark.edu))

DEANS

Clinton School of Public Service: JAMES L. RUTHERFORD
College of Education and Health Professions: Prof. Dr TOM E. C. SMITH
College of Engineering: Prof. ASHOK SAXENA
Dale Bumpers College of Agricultural, Food and Life Sciences: MICHAEL E. VAYDA
Fay Jones School of Architecture: JEFF SHANNON
Graduate School and Int. Education: TODD G. SHIELDS
Honors College: BOB MCMATH
J. W. Fulbright College of Arts and Sciences: Prof. Dr ROBIN A. ROBERTS
Sam M. Walton College of Business: Dr DAN L. WORRELL
School of Continuing Education and Academic Outreach: Dr PAULINE RANKIN
School of Law: Dr STACY L. LEEDS

University of Arkansas for Medical Sciences

4301 W Markham St, Little Rock, AR 72205
Telephone: (501) 686-7000
Internet: www.uams.edu
Founded 1879, present status 1911
Chancellor: Dr DAN RAHN
Vice-Chancellor for Academic Affairs and Chief Academic Officer: Dr JEANNE K. HEARD
Vice-Chancellor for Admin. and Governmental Affairs: TOM S. BUTLER
Vice-Chancellor for Campus Operations: MARK KENNEDAY
Vice-Chancellor for Devt and Alumni Affairs: LANCE BURCHETT
Vice-Chancellor for Information Technology and Chief Information Officer: DAVID L. MILLER

Vice-Chancellor for Regional Programs: Dr MARK MENGEL
Vice-Chancellor for Research: Dr LARRY CORNETT
Dir for Admissions: MARY MCCLAIN
Registrar: KRISTINE STUMP
Library Dir: MARY L. RYAN
Library of 42,038 vols (incl. 35,342 titles)
Number of teachers: 1,354
Number of students: 2,820
Publications: *Seek* (4 a year), *UAMS Journal, UAMS Medical Center Magazine*

DEANS

College of Health Related-Professions: Dr DOUGLAS L. MURPHY
College of Medicine: Dr DEBRA FISER
College of Nursing: Dr LORRAINE FRAZIER
College of Pharmacy: Dr STEPHANIE GARDNER
College of Public Health: Dr JAMES M. RACZYNSKI
Graduate School: Dr ROBERT E. MCGEHEE

University of Arkansas—Fort Smith

5210 Grand Ave, POB 3649, Fort Smith, AR 72913-3649
Telephone: (479) 788-7000
Internet: www.uafs.edu
Founded 1928, present status 2002
Chancellor: Dr PAUL B. BERAN
Provost and Sr Vice-Chancellor: Dr RAY WALLACE
Vice-Chancellor for Operations: Dr KYLE PARKER
Vice-Chancellor for Student Affairs: Dr LEE KREHBIEL
Vice-Chancellor for Univ. Advancement: Dr MARTA LOYD
Vice-Chancellor for Univ. Relations: MARK HORN
Dir for Admissions: MARK LLOYD
Dir for Library Services: ROBERT FRIZZELL
Number of students: 7,587
Publications: *Azahares, Bell Tower* (2 a year)

DEANS

College of Applied Science and Technology: Dr GEORGIA M. HALE
College of Business: Prof. Dr STEVE WILLIAMS
College of Education: JOHN R. JONES
College of Health Sciences: Prof. Dr CAROLYN MOSLEY
College of Humanities and Social Sciences: Dr HENRY Q. RINNE
College of Languages and Communication: Dr JOE HARDIN
College of Science, Technology, Engineering and Mathematics: MARK ARANT
College of Student Success: DIANA ROWDEN

UNIVERSITY OF CENTRAL ARKANSAS

201 Donaghey Ave, Conway, AR 72035
Telephone: (501) 450-5000
Fax: (501) 450-5734
E-mail: admissions@uca.edu
Internet: www.uca.edu
Founded 1907 as Arkansas State Normal School, present name 1975
State control
Academic year: August to August
Pres. and Gen. Counsel: TOM COURTWAY
Provost and Vice-Pres. for Academic Affairs: Dr LANCE R. GRAHN
Vice-Pres. for Enrolment Management: Dr ROBERT W. PARRENT
Vice-Pres. for Finance and Admin.: DIANE NEWTON
Vice-Pres. for Institutional Advancement and Devt: SHELLEY MEHL
Vice-Pres. for Student Services: RONNIE WILLIAMS

Vice-Pres. for Univ. and Govt Relations: JEFF PITCHFORD
Dean for Students: Dr GARY ROBERTS
Registrar: ANTHONY D. SITZ
Library Dir: ART LICHTENSTEIN
Library of 400,000 vols
Number of teachers: 382 (full-time)
Number of students: 11,163

DEANS

College of Business: Dr PATRICIA CANTRELL
College of Education: Dr DIANA POUNDER
College of Fine Arts and Communication: Dr ROLLIN POTTER
College of Health and Behavioural Sciences: Dr NEIL W. HATTLESTAD
College of Liberal Arts: Dr MAURICE A. LEE
College of Natural Science and Mathematics: Dr STEPHEN ADDISON
Graduate School: Dr ELAINE McNIECE
Honors College: Prof. Dr RICK SCOTT
Undergraduate Studies: Dr T. CLAY ARNOLD

UNIVERSITY OF THE OZARKS

415 N College Ave, Clarksville, AR 72830-2880

Telephone: (501) 979-1000
Fax: (501) 979-1355
E-mail: admiss@ozarks.edu
Internet: www.ozarks.edu

Founded 1834 as Cane Hill School, present location 1891, present name 1987
Private control

Divs of business, communications and government, education, humanities and fine arts, sciences and mathematics

Pres.: Dr RICK NIECE
Provost and Vice-Pres. for Academic Affairs: Dr DANIEL TADDIE
Exec. Vice-Pres.: STEVE EDMISTEN
Dean for Admissions and Financial Aid: JANA HART
Dean for Enrolment Management: KIM MYRICK (acting)
Dean for Students: JOE HOING
Registrar: WILMA HARRIS
Library Dir: STUART STELZER
Library of 80,000 vols, 40,000 govt documents, 10,000 microfilms, 12,000 bound periodicals, 480 current periodicals
Number of teachers: 49
Number of students: 630

WILLIAMS BAPTIST COLLEGE

60 W Fulbright Ave, Walnut Ridge, AR 72476
Telephone: (870) 886-6741
Fax: (870) 886-3924
E-mail: admissions@wbcoll.edu
Internet: www.wbcoll.edu

Founded 1941 as Southern Baptist College, present name 1991
Private control

Depts of art, business, Christian ministries, education, English, history, music, natural science and psychology

Pres.: Dr JEROL B. SWAIM
Vice-Pres. for Academic Affairs: Prof. Dr KENNETH M. STARTUP
Vice-Pres. for Enrolment Management and Student Affairs: ANGELA FLIPPO
Vice-Pres. for Institutional Advancement and Alumni Affairs: ERIC TURNER
Dir for Admissions: AARON ABBOTT
Dean for Students: SUSAN WATSON
Registrar: TONYA BOLTON
Dir for Library Services: PAMELA MERIDITH
Library of 75,000 vols
Number of students: 691

CALIFORNIA

ACADEMY OF ART UNIVERSITY

79 New Montgomery St, Fourth Fl., San Francisco, CA 94105-3410
Telephone: (415) 274-2208
Fax: (415) 618-6278
E-mail: info@academyart.edu
Internet: www.academyart.edu

Founded 1929 as Acad. of Art College, present name 2004
Private control
Academic year: September to August

Schools of advertising, animation and visual effects, architecture, computer arts, digital arts and communication, fashion, fine art, graphic design, illustration, industrial design, interior architecture and design, motion pictures and television, new media, photography

Pres.: Dr ELISA STEPHENS
Library Dir: DEBRA SAMPSON (acting)
Library of 47,800 vols, 275 periodicals
Number of teachers: 1,368
Number of students: 18,093

ALLIANT INTERNATIONAL UNIVERSITY

10455 Pomerado Rd, San Diego, CA 92131-1799
Telephone: (866) 825-5426
E-mail: admissions@alliant.edu
Internet: www.alliant.edu

Founded 2001 by merger of California School of Professional Psychology (f. 1969) and United States Int. Univ. (f. 1927)
Private control
Academic year: August to May

6 Campuses in Fresno, Irvine, Los Angeles, Sacramento, San Diego, San Francisco; also in Mexico (Mexico City)

Pres.: Dr GEOFFREY COX
Provost and Vice-Pres. for Academic Affairs: Dr RUSS NEWMAN
Vice-Pres. for Devt and Univ. Relations: JOHN DE MICHELE
Vice-Pres. for Finance and CFO: JEANINE HAWK
Vice-Pres. for Int. Relations: TERENCE BARBER
Vice-Pres. for Admin. and Gen. Counsel: JENNIFER TREESE WILSON
Vice-Pres. for Undergraduates: Dr ERIC GRAVENBERG
Chief Human Resources Officer: KRISTINA COMBS
Dir of Communications: NICOLETTE TOUSSAINT
Dean for Students: Dr CRAIG BREWER
Univ. Librarian: SCOTT ZIMMER
Library of 136,471 vols, 10,065 online vols, 375 print journals, 4,945 electronic journals, 55 research databases, 3,007 video cassettes and DVDs, 892 audio cassettes, 4,463 psychological tests
Number of teachers: 200
Number of students: 4,236

DEANS

Alliant School of Management: Dr CHESTER HASKELL
California School of Forensic Studies: Dr ERIC HICKEY
California School of Professional Psychology: Dr MORGAN SAMMONS
Hufstedler School of Education: Dr KAREN SCHUSTER WEBB
San Francisco Law School: JANE GAMP

AMERICAN BAPTIST SEMINARY OF THE WEST

2606 Dwight Way, Berkeley, CA 94704-3029
Telephone: (510) 841-1905
Fax: (510) 841-2446
E-mail: admissions@absw.edu
Internet: www.absw.edu

Founded 1871 as California College, present name 1968, present location 1974
Private control (part of the Graduate Theological Union)

Graduate areas of study: biblical studies, theology, ethics, church history, arts of ministry, history, social sciences, foreign languages, social theory, psychology, art, liturgical studies, Christian spirituality

Pres.: Dr PAUL M. MARTIN
Vice-Pres.: MICHELLE M. HOLMES
Dean of Faculty: JUDY YATES SIKER
Registrar and Dir for Student Services: NANCY SVENSSON.

AMERICAN CONSERVATORY THEATER

30 Grant Ave, 6th Fl., San Francisco, CA 94108-5800
Telephone: (415) 834-3200
E-mail: hr@act-sf.org
Internet: www.act-sf.org

Founded 1965
Private control
Language of instruction: English
Academic year: September to May

Graduate area of study: fine arts

Chair.: NANCY LIVINGSTON
Pres.: RUSTY REUFF
Artistic Dir: CAREY PERLOFF
Conservatory Dir: MELISSA SMITH
Exec. Dir: ELLEN RICHARD
Library of 10,000 vols (incl. playscripts, books, video cassettes, language and music compact discs and tapes, music scores, and theatre journals)
Number of students: 3,000

AMERICAN FILM INSTITUTE

2021 N Western Ave, Los Angeles, CA 90027-1657
Telephone: (323) 856-7600
Fax: (323) 467-4578
E-mail: information@afi.com
Internet: www.afi.com

Founded 1967
Private control

Depts of cinematography, directing, editing, producing, production design, screenwriting, sound, stage and post-production facilities

Pres. and CEO: BOB GAZZALE
Chair.: HOWARD STRINGER
Dean: ROBERT MANDEL
Artistic Dir: ROGER BIRNBAUM
Artistic Dir: FRANK PIERSON
Exec. Vice-Dean: JOE PETRICCA
Vice-Dean for Fellow Affairs: CAROLYN BROOKS
Vice-Dean for Production and Post-Production: PHILLIP LINSON
Library of 10,000 vols, 100 journals, 5,000 film scripts, 4,000 television scripts, 2,500 DVDs; spec. collns Martin Scorsese, Fritz Lang, Robert Aldrich, Charles Feldman.

AMERICAN JEWISH UNIVERSITY

15600 Mulholland Dr., Bel Air, CA 90077
Telephone: (310) 476-9777
E-mail: admissions@ajula.edu
Internet: www.ajula.edu

Founded 2007 by merger of Brandeis-Bardin Institute (f. 1941) with Univ. of Judaism (f. 1947)
Private control
Academic year: August to May
Campus at Brandeis
Pres.: Dr ROBERT D. WEXLER
Provost: Dr STUART J. SIGMAN
Sr Vice-Pres. and Chief Advancement Officer: JAY A. STREAAR
Vice-Pres. for Academic Affairs: Dr LOIS HECHT OPPENHEIM
Vice-Pres. for Business, Admin. and Technology: ZOFIA YALOVSKY
Vice-Pres. for Devt: JAY STREAR
Vice-Pres. for Finance, Admin. and Technology: ZOFIA YALOVSKY
Rector: Dr ELLIOT DORFF
Dir of Sigi Ziering Institute: Dr MICHAEL BERENBAUM
Registrar: ARNIE WEISBERG
Library Dir: PAUL MILLER
Library of 120,000 vols
Publication: *Vision Magazine* (1 a year)

DEANS

College of Arts and Sciences: Dr STUART J. SIGMAN
Graduate Center for Education: Dr MIRIAM HELLER STERN
Graduate School of Nonprofit Management: NINA LIEBERMAN
Whizin Center for Continuing Education: Dr GADY LEVY
Ziegler School of Rabbinic Studies: BRADLEY SHAVIT ARTSON

ARGOSY UNIVERSITY

601 S Lewis St, Orange, CA 92868
Telephone: (714) 620-3700
Fax: (714) 620-3801
Internet: www.argosy.edu
Founded 2001 by merger of American Schools of Professional Psychology, Medical Institute of Minnesota and Univ. of Sarasota
Campuses: Atlanta, GA; Chicago, IL; Dallas, TX; Denver, CO; Honolulu, HI; Nashville, TN; Orange County, CA; Phoenix, AZ; San Diego, CA; Santa Monica, FL; Schaumburg, IL; Seattle, WA; Tampa, FL; Twin Cities (Minneapolis and St Paul), MN; Washington, DC
State control
Chancellor: Dr CRAIG D. SWENSON
Exec. Vice-Pres.: Dr ERIC EVENSON
Vice-Pres. for Academic Affairs: Dr KATHRYN J. TOOREDMAN
Vice-Pres. for Admissions: JEFF CROSS
Vice-Pres. for Finance: KEN STEVENS
Dir for Library Services: CLARA WILLIAMS

DEANS

College of Business: Dr CYNTHIA LARSON
College of Education: Dr CYNTHIA KUCK
College of Health Sciences: Dr KRISTIN BENSON
College of Psychology and Behavioural Sciences: Dr SUSAN SANCES
College of Undergraduate Studies: Dr RUKMANI JAYARAMAN

ART CENTER COLLEGE OF DESIGN

1700 Lida St, Pasadena, CA 91103
Telephone: (626) 396-2200
Fax: (626) 405-9104
E-mail: proffice@artcenter.edu
Internet: www.artcenter.edu
Founded 1930, present name 1965
Private control
Language of instruction: English

Academic year: September to August
Undergraduate courses in advertising, environmental design, film, fine art media, graphic design, illustration, photography and imaging, product design, transportation design; graduate courses in Film, art, industrial design, media design, criticism and theory
Pres. and CEO: LORNE BUCHMAN
Provost: FRED FEHLAU
Vice-Pres. and Chief Financial Officer: RICHARD HALUSCHAK
Vice-Pres. for Int. Initiatives: MARIANA AMATULLO
Sr Vice-Pres. for Real Estate and Operations: GEORGE FALARDEAU
Chief Human Resources Officer: NANCY DUGGAN
Vice-Pres. for Marketing and Communications: ARWIN DUFFY
Vice-Pres. for Admissions: KIT BARON
Vice-Pres. for Student Gallery: STEPHEN L. NOWLIN
Chief Officer for Student Affairs: JEFFREY HOFFMAN
Vice-Pres. and Library Dir: ELIZABETH GALLOWAY
Registrar: WILLIAM GARTRELL
Number of teachers: 375
Number of students: 1,781

AZUSA PACIFIC UNIVERSITY

901 East Alosta Ave, POB 7000, Azusa, CA 91702-7000
Telephone: (626) 969-3434
Internet: www.apu.edu
Founded 1899 as Training School for Christian Workers, present name and status 1981
Private control
Pres. and CEO: Dr JON R. WALLACE
Pres. for Legal Affairs and Community Relations: Dr MARK S. DICKERSON
Exec. Vice-Pres.: DAVID E. BIXBY
Exec. Vice-Pres.: JOHN C. REYNOLDS
Sr Vice-Pres. for Student Life and Dean of Students: Dr TERRY A. FRANSON
Vice-Pres. for Enrollment Management: DAVID HUNTER
Provost: Dr MARK STATON (acting)
Vice-Provost for Graduate Programs and Research: PAUL W. GRAY
Vice-Provost for Undergraduate Programs: DIANE J. GUIDO
Library of 240,000 vols, media items, 703,000 microforms, 1,900 serial titles, 140 online databases, 46,000 electronic titles
Number of teachers: 1,074 (incl. 354 full-time, 41 part-time, 679 adjunct)
Number of students: 9,258

DEANS

Center for Adult and Professional Studies: FRED GARLETT
College of Liberal Arts and Sciences: DAVID L. WEEKS
School of Behavioural and Applied Sciences: ROSEMARY LIEGLER
School of Business and Management: ILENE L. SMITH-BEZJIAN
School of Education: HELEN EASTERLING WILLIAMS
School of Music: DONALD NEUFELD (acting)
School of Nursing: AJA TULLENERS LESH
School of Theology: T. SCOTT DANIELS

BIOLA UNIVERSITY

13800 Biola Ave, La Mirada, CA 90639-0001
Telephone: (562) 903-6000
Fax: (562) 903-4761
E-mail: president@biola.edu
Internet: www.biola.edu

Founded 1908, present status 1981
Private control
Pres.: Dr BARRY COREY
Provost and Sr Vice-Pres.: DAVID P. NYSTROM
Vice-Provost for Faculty Devt and Univ. Assessment: CHRIS GRACE
Vice-Provost for Undergraduate Education: CAROL TAYLOR
Vice-Pres. for Business and Financial Affairs: MICHAEL PIERCE
Vice-Pres. for Univ. Advancement: ADAM MORRIS
Vice-Pres. for Univ. Services: GREG BALSANO
Dean of Student Affairs: JOHN W. BACK
Sr Director for Enrollment Management: GREGORY VAUGHAN
Library of 270,000 vols, 1,100 current periodicals
Number of teachers: 252
Number of students: 3,447

DEANS

Cook School of Intercultural Studies: Dr F. DOUGLAS PENNOYER
Crowell School of Business: LARRY D. STRAND
Fine Arts and Communication: DOUG TARPLEY
Humanities and Social Sciences: CASSANDRA VAN ZANDT
Rosemead School of Psychology: Dr CLARK D. CAMPBELL
School of Education: Dr JUNE HETZEL
Sciences: WALT STANGL
Talbot School of Theology: Dr DENNIS H. DIRKS

BROOKS INSTITUTE

27 E Cota St, Santa Barbara, CA 93101
Telephone: (805) 585-8000
E-mail: admissions@brooks.edu
Internet: www.brooks.edu
Founded 1945
Private control
Areas of study: photography, visual communications, visual journalism, film and video production
Pres.: JOHN CALMAN.

CALIFORNIA BAPTIST UNIVERSITY

8432 Magnolia Ave, Riverside, CA 92504
Telephone: (951) 689-5771
Fax: (951) 351-1808
E-mail: admissions@calbaptist.edu
Internet: www.calbaptist.edu
Founded 1950
Pres.: Dr RONALD L. ELLIS
Provost: Dr JONATHAN K. PARKER
Vice-Pres. for Finance and Admin.: MARK HOWE
Vice-Pres. for Institutional Advancement: Dr ARTHUR CLEVELAND
Vice-Pres. for Marketing and Communication: Dr MARK A. WYATT
Vice-Pres. for Enrollment and Student Services: KENT DACUS
Dean of Students: ANTHONY LAMMONS
Registrar: SHAWNN KONING
Dir of Library Services and Information Technology: ERICA MCLAUGHLIN
Library of 100,000 vols, 36,000 microfiches, 500 journals, 1,600 video cassettes, 800 classical music CDs, 800 DVDs
Number of teachers: 51 full-time
Number of students: 3,400

DEANS

College of Allied Health: Dr CHARLES D. SANDS
College of Arts and Sciences: Dr JAMES LU
School of Behavioural Sciences: Dr H. BRUCE STOKES

Dr. Robert K. Jabs School of Business: Dr ANDREW HERRITY
School of Christian Ministries: Dr CHRIS MORGAN
Dr. Bonnie G. Metcalfe School of Education: Dr JOHN SHOUP
School of Engineering: Dr ANTHONY DONALDSON
Shelby and Ferne Collinsworth School of Music: Dr GARY BONNER
School of Nursing: Dr CONSTANCE L. MILTON

CALIFORNIA COLLEGE OF THE ARTS

1111 Eighth St, San Francisco, CA 94107-2247
Telephone: (415) 703-9500
Fax: (415) 703-9539
E-mail: info@cca.edu
Internet: www.cca.edu
Founded 1907
Academic year: September to May
Campuses in Oakland and San Francisco
Pres.: STEPHEN BEAL
Provost: MARK BREITENBERG
Sr Vice-Pres. of Advancement: SUSAN AVILA
Vice-Pres. of Communications: CHRIS BLISS
Vice-Pres. of Enrollment Management: SHERI MCKENZIE
Dean of Students: LIZ POINTER
Dir of Libraries: JANICE WOO
Library of 73,000 vols, 2,500 online periodicals, 500,000 images and 150,000 slides
Number of teachers: 326
Number of students: 1,860
Publications: *Design Book Review* (4 a year), *Glance* (2 a year).

ATTACHED INSTITUTES

Center for Art and Public Life: tel. (510) 594-3757; fax (510) 594-3769; e-mail center@cca.edu; internet center.cca.edu; f. 1998; Dir SANJIT SETHI.

Wattis Institute for Contemporary Arts: tel. (415) 551-9210; fax (415) 551-9209; e-mail wattis@cca.edu; internet www.wattis.org; f. 1998; forum for presentation and discussion of local, nat. and int. contemporary culture; Dir JENS HOFFMAN.

CALIFORNIA INSTITUTE OF INTEGRAL STUDIES

1453 Mission St, San Francisco, CA 94103
Telephone: (415) 575-6100
Fax: (415) 575-1628
Internet: www.ciis.edu
Founded 1968
Pres.: JOSEPH L. SUBBIONDO
Academic Vice-Pres.: JUDIE WEXLER
Dean of Students and Alumni: RICHARD BUGGS
Dir of Communications and Marketing: VALERIE BUSH
Dir of Devt: DOROTEA REYNA
Dir of Diversity and Human Resources: L'ESA GUILIAN
Dir of Facilities and Operations: JONATHAN MILLS
Dir of Finance: KEN ABIKO
Dir of Financial Aid: MICHAEL SZKOTAK
Dir of Information Technology Services: SCOTT CILIBERTI
Dir of Public Programs: KARIM BAER
Dir of Undergraduate Studies: MICHELLE ENG
Registrar: NANCY HAGER
Library Dir: LISE DYCKMAN
Library of 35,000 vols, 300 periodicals, 1,300 audio and video titles
Number of teachers: 55 full-time, 11 part-time
Number of students: 1,005

BA in Interdisciplinary Studies; School of Professional Psychology (1 PhD and 4 MA programmes); School of Consciousness and Transformation (7 MA and 6 PhD programmes).

CALIFORNIA INSTITUTE OF TECHNOLOGY

Mail Code 206-31, Pasadena, CA 91125
1200 East California Blvd, Pasadena, CA 91125
Telephone: (626) 395-6811
Fax: (626) 795-1547
Internet: www.caltech.edu
Founded 1891 as Throop University, present name 1921
Private control
Academic year: September to June
Pres.: Dr JEAN-LOU CHAMEAU
Provost: Dr EDWARD STOLPER
Vice-Provost: Dr MORY GHARIB
Vice-Provost: Dr MELANY HUNT
Gen. Counsel: VICTORIA STRATMAN
Vice-Pres. for Business and Finance: DEAN W. CURRIE
Vice-Pres. for Devt and Institute Relations: PETER B. DERVAN
Vice-Pres. for Marketing and Communications: (vacant)
Vice-Pres. for Student Affairs: Prof. ANNEILA SARGENT (acting)
Dir of Admissions: JARRID WHITNEY
Dean of Graduate Studies: Prof. JOSEPH E. SHEPHERD
Controller and Chief Financial Accountant: MATTHEW BREWER
Sec.: MARY L. WEBSTER
Registrar: MARY NEARY MORLEY
Univ. Librarian: KIMBERLY DOUGLAS
Library of 825,498 vols
Number of teachers: 489 (incl. professorial, visiting, research)
Number of students: 2,175
Publication: *Engineering and Science*

CHAIRMEN OF DIVISIONS

Biology: STEPHEN L. MAYO
Chemistry and Chemical Engineering: JACQUELINE K. BARTON
Engineering and Applied Science: ARES J. ROSAKIS
Geological and Planetary Sciences: KENNETH A. FARLEY
Humanities and Social Sciences: JONATHAN N. KATZ
Physics, Mathematics and Astronomy: B. THOMAS SOIFER

PROFESSORS

ABELSON, J. N.
ABU-MOSTAFA, Y. S., Electrical Engineering and Computer Science
ADOLPHS, R., Psychology and Neuroscience and Biology
ALLMAN, J. M., Neurobiology
ALVAREZ, R. M., Political Science
ANDERSEN, R. A., Neuroscience
ANDERSON, D. J., Biology
ANTONSSON, E. K., Mechanical Engineering
ARNOLD, F. H., Chemical Engineering and Biochemistry
ASCHBACHER, M., Mathematics
ATTARDI, G., Molecular Biology
ATWATER, H. A., Jr, Applied Physics and Materials Science
AVOUAC, J., Geology
BALTIMORE, D., Biology
BARR, A. H., Computer Science
BARTON, J. K., Chemistry
BEAUCHAMP, J. L., Chemistry
BECK, J. L., Engineering and Applied Science
BELLAN, P. M., Applied Physics
BERCAW, J. E., Chemistry

BHATTACHARYA, K., Mechanics and Materials Science
BJORKMAN, P. J., Biology
BLAKE, G. A., Cosmochemistry, Planetary Sciences, Chemistry
BORDER, K. C., Economics
BORODIN, A., Mathematics
BOSSAERTS, P. L., Finance
BRADY, J. F., Chemical Engineering and Mechanical Engineering
BRENNEN, C. E., Mechanical Engineering
BREWER, J., History and Literature
BRONNER-FRASER, M., Biology
BROWN, M. E., Astronomy
BRUCK, J., Computation and Neural Systems and Electrical Engineering
BRUNO, O. P., Applied and Computational Mathematics
BUCHWALD, J. Z., History
BURDICK, J. W., Mechanical Engineering and Bioengineering
CALEGARI, D., Mathematics
CAMERER, C. F., Economics
CAMPBELL, J. L., Chemistry and Biology
CANDES, E. J. D., Applied and Computational Mathematics
CHAMEAU, J., Civil Engineering, Environmental Science and Engineering, Mechanical Engineering
CHANDY, K. M., Computer Science
CLAYTON, R. W., Geophysics
COHEN, J. G., Astronomy
COLONIUS, T. E., Mechanical Engineering
CROSS, M. C., Theoretical Physics
CVITANIC, J., Mathematical Finance
DAVIDSON, E. H., Cell Biology
DAVIS, M. E., Chemical Engineering
DERVAN, P. B., Chemistry
DESHAIES, R., Biology
DICKINSON, M. H., Bioengineering
DIMOTAKIS, P. E., Aeronautics, Applied Physics
DJORGOVSKI, S. G., Astronomy
DOUGHERTY, D. A., Chemistry
DOYLE, J. C., Control and Dynamical Systems, Electrical Engineering and Bioengineering
DUBIN, J. A., Economics
DUNPHY, W. G., Biology
EFFROS, M., Electrical Engineering
EILER, J. M., Geochemistry
EISENSTEIN, J. P., Physics, Applied Physics
ELACHI, C., Electrical Engineering and Planetary Science
ELLIS, R. S., Astronomy
ENSMINGER, J. E., Anthropology
FARLEY, K. A., Geochemistry
FEINGOLD, M., History
FILIPPONE, B. W., Physics
FLACH, M., Mathematics
FLAGAN, R. C., Chemical Engineering, Environmental Science and Engineering
FRASER, S. E., Biology, Bioengineering
FULTZ, B. T., Materials Science and Applied Physics
GHARIB, M., Aeronautics and Bioengineering
GODDARD, W. A., III, Chemistry, Materials Science and Applied Physics
GOEREE, J. K., Economics
GOODSTEIN, D. L., Physics and Applied Physics
GOODWIN, D. G., Mechanical Engineering and Applied Physics
GRAY, H. B., Chemistry
GRETHER, D. M., Economics
GROTZINGER, J. P., Geology
GRUBBS, R. H., Chemistry
GURNIS, M. C., Geophysics
HAILE, S. M., Materials Science and Chemical Engineering
HAJIMIRI, S., Electrical Engineering
HALL, J. F., Civil Engineering
HARRISON, F. A., Physics and Astronomy
HEATH, J. R., Chemistry
HEATON, T. H., Engineering Seismology
HELMBERGER, D. V., Geophysics

HERING, J. G., Environmental Science and Engineering
HITCHCOCK, C. R., Philosophy
HITLIN, D. G., Physics
HOFFMAN, P. T., History and Social Science
HOFFMANN, M. R., Environmental Science
HOU, Y. T., Applied and Computational Mathematics
HUGHES, E. W., Physics
HUNT, M. L., Mechanical Engineering
INGERSOLL, A. P., Planetary Science
JOHNSON, W. L., Engineering and Applied Science
KAMIONKOWSKI, M., Theoretical Physics and Astrophysics
KATZ, J. N., Political Science
KECHRIS, A. S., Mathematics
KENNEDY, M. B., Biology
KIEWIET, D. R., Political Science
KIMBLE, H. J., Physics
KIRSCHVINK, J. L., Geobiology
KITAEV, A., Theoretical Astrophysics and Computer Science
KOCH, C., Computation and Neural Systems
KONISHI, M., Behavioural Biology
KORMOS-BUCHWALD, D. L., History
KORNFIELD, J. A., Chemical Engineering
KOUSSER, J. M., History and Social Science
KULKARNI, S. R., Astronomy and Planetary Science
KUPPERMANN, A., Chemical Physics
LA BELLE, J., English
LANGE, A. E., Physics
LAURENT, G. J., Biology and Computation and Neural Systems
LEDYARD, J. O., Economics and Social Sciences
LESTER, H. A., Biology
LEWIS, N. S., Chemistry
LIBBRECHT, K. G., Physics
LORDEN, G. A., Mathematics
LOW, S., Computer Science and Electrical Engineering
MCAFEE, R. P., Business Economics and Management
MCELIECE, R. J., Electrical Engineering
MCGILL, T. C., Applied Physics
MCKEOWN, R. D., Physics
MCKOY, B. V., Theoretical Chemistry
MACMILLAN, D. W. C., Chemistry
MAKAROV, N. G., Mathematics
MARCUS, R. A., Chemistry
MARSDEN, J. E., Engineering and Control and Dynamical Systems
MARTIN, A. J., Computer Science
MARTIN, D. C., Physics
MAYO, S. L., Biology and Chemistry
MEIRON, D. I., Applied and Computational Mathematics and Computer Science
MEYEROWITZ, E. M., Biology
MURRAY, R. M., Control and Dynamical Systems
NEWMAN, D. K., Geobiology and Biology
NEWMAN, H. B., Physics
OGURI, H., Theoretical Physics
OH, H., Mathematics
OKUMURA, M., Chemical Physics
ORDESHOOK, P. C., Political Science
ORTIZ, M., Aeronautics and Mechanical Engineering
PALFREY, T. R., III, Economics and Political Science
PARKER, C. S., Biochemistry
PATTERSON, P. H., Biology
PERONA, P., Electrical Engineering
PETERS, J. C., Chemistry
PHILLIPS, R., Applied Physics and Mechanical Engineering
PHILLIPS, T. G., Physics
PHINNEY, E. S., III, Theoretical Astrophysics
PIGMAN, G. W., III, English
PINE, J., Physics
PLOTT, C. R., Economics and Political Science
POLITZER, H. D., Theoretical Physics
PORTER, F. C., Physics
PRESKILL, J. P., Theoretical Physics

PRINCE, T. A., Physics
PSALTIS, D., Electrical Engineering
PULLIN, D. I., Aeronautics
RAMAKRISHNAN, D., Mathematics
RAVICHANDRAN, G., Aeronautics and Mechanical Engineering
READHEAD, A. C. S., Astronomy
REES, D. C., Chemistry
RICHARDS, J. H., Organic Chemistry and Biochemistry
ROSAKIS, A. J., Aeronautics and Mechanical Engineering
ROSENSTONE, R. A., History
ROSENTHAL, J., Economics
ROSSMAN, G. R., Mineralogy
ROTHENBERG, E., Biology
ROUKES, M. L., Physics, Applied Physics and Bioengineering
RUTLEDGE, D. B., Electrical Engineering
SALEEBY, J. B., Geology
SARGENT, A. I., Astronomy
SARGENT, W. L. W., Astronomy
SCHERER, A., Electrical Engineering, Applied Physics, and Physics
SCHRODER, P., Computer Science and Applied and Computational Mathematics
SCHULMAN, L. J., Computer Science
SCHUMAN, E. M., Biology
SCHWARZ, J. H., Theoretical Physics
SCOVILLE, N. Z., Astronomy
SEINFELD, J. H., Chemical Engineering
SHEPHERD, J. E., Aeronautics and Mechanical Engineering
SHERMAN, R. P., Economics and Statistics
SHIMOJO, S., Biology
SIEH, K. E., Geology
SIMON, B. M., Mathematics and Theoretical Physics
SOIFER, B. T., Physics
SPITZER, M. L., Law and Social Science
STEIDEL, C. C., Astronomy
STERNBERG, P. W., Biology
STEVENSON, D. J., Planetary Science
STOCK, J. M., Geology and Geophysics
STOLPER, E. M., Geology
STOLTZ, B. M., Chemistry
STONE, E. C., Physics
STRAUSS, J. H., Biology
TAI, Y., Electrical Engineering and Mechanical Engineering
THORNE, K. S., Theoretical Physics
TIRRELL, D. A., Chemistry and Chemical Engineering
TOMBRELLO, T. A., Physics
TROIAN, S., Applied Physics, Aeronautics, and Mechanical Engineering
TROMP, J., Geophysics
VAHALA, K. J., Applied Physics
VAIDYANATHAN, P. P., Electrical Engineering
VARSHAVSKY, A. J., Cell Biology
WALES, D. B., Mathematics
WANG, Z., Chemical Engineering
WEINSTEIN, A. J., Physics
WEINSTEIN, C., English
WEITEKAMP, D. P., Chemical Physics
WENNBERG, P. O., Atmospheric Chemistry and Environmental Science and Engineering
WERNICKE, B. P., Geology
WILSON, R. M., Mathematics
WISE, M. B., High Energy Physics
WOLD, B. J., Molecular Biology
WOODWARD, J. F., Philosophy
YARIV, A., Applied Physics and Electrical Engineering
YEH, N., Physics
YUNG, Y. L., Planetary Science
ZEWAIL, A. H., Chemical Physics, Physics
ZINN, K., Biology
ZMUIDZINAS, J., Physics

CALIFORNIA INSTITUTE OF THE ARTS

24700 McBean Parkway, Valencia, CA 91355-2397

Telephone: (661) 255-1050
Fax: (661) 253-7710
E-mail: info@calarts.edu
Internet: www.calarts.edu

Founded 1961 by merger of Los Angeles Conservatory of Music (f. 1883) and Chouinard Art Institute (f. 1921)
Academic year: September to May

Pres.: STEVEN D. LAVINE
Vice-Pres. for Admin.: D. DEAN HOUCHIN
Vice-Pres. and Chief Advancement Officer: BIANCA ROBERTS
Vice-Pres. for Spec. Projects: LYNN R. ROSENFELD
Provost: JAQUELINE ELAM (acting)
Registrar: NANCY WHITTEMORE
Vice Pres. for Int. Relations: CAROL KIM
Dean of Library and Information Resources: JEFFREY GATTEN
Dean of Students: YVONNE GUY

Library of 90,000 vols
Number of teachers: 314
Number of students: 1,467
Publications: *Black Clock* (2 a year), *CalArts Magazine* (2 a year)

DEANS

Herb Alpert School of Music at CalArts Richard Seaver Distinguished Chair in Music: DAVID ROSENBOOM
School of Art: THOMAS LAWSON
School of Critical Studies: MICHAEL BRYANT, JANET SARBANES (acting)
School of Film and Video: STEVE ANKER
School of Theatre: TRAVIS PRESTON
Sharon Disney Lund School of Dance: STEPHAN KOPLOWITZ

CALIFORNIA LUTHERAN UNIVERSITY

60 West Olsen Rd, Thousand Oaks, CA 91360-2787

Telephone: (805) 493-3820
Fax: (805) 493-3114
E-mail: media@callutheran.edu
Internet: www.callutheran.edu

Founded 1959; attached to Evangelical Lutheran Church in America
Private control

Pres.: Dr CHRIS KIMBALL
Provost and Vice-Pres. for Academic Affairs: LEANNE NEILSON
Vice-Pres. for Admin. and Finance: KAREN DAVIS
Vice-Pres. for Student Affairs and Dean of Students: WILLIAM ROSSER
Vice-Pres. for Univ. Advancement: R. STEPHEN WHEATLY
Registrar: MARIA KOHNKE
Librarian: KENNETH PFLUEGER

Library of 110,416 vols
Number of teachers: 256 (118 full-time, 138 part-time)
Number of students: 3,021

DEANS

College of Arts and Sciences: Dr JOAN L. GRIFFIN
Graduate School of Education: Prof. GEORGE J. PETERSEN
School of Management: Dr CHARLES MAXEY

CALIFORNIA MARITIME ACADEMY

200 Maritime Academy Dr., Vallejo, CA 94590

Telephone: (707) 654-1000
Fax: (707) 654-1001

E-mail: humanresources@csum.edu
Internet: www.csum.edu

Founded 1929 as California Nautical School, present name 1938; attached to specialized campus of California State Univ.

State control

Academic year: September to May

Degrees in marine transportation, global studies and maritime affairs, marine engineering technology, mechanical engineering, facilities engineering technology, business admin., int. business and logistics

Pres.: Dr WILLIAM B. EISENHARDT

Provost and Vice-Pres. for Academic Affairs: Dr GERALD S. JACUBOWSKI

Vice-Pres. for Admin. and Finance: KURT LOHIDE

Vice Pres. for Advancement and Executive Dir: THOMAS C. DUNWORTH

Academic Dean: STEPHEN PRONCHICK

Library of 35,000 vols, 270 periodicals

Number of students: 850

Publication: *Cal Maritime Magazine* (2 a year).

CALIFORNIA POLYTECHNIC STATE UNIVERSITY

1 Grand Ave, San Luis Obispo, CA 93407

Telephone: (805) 756-1111
Fax: (805) 756-5400
E-mail: admissions@calpoly.edu
Internet: www.calpoly.edu

Founded 1901 as California Polytechnic School, present name 1972

Academic year: September to June

Pres.: JEFFREY D. ARMSTRONG

Provost and Vice-Pres. for Academic Affairs: Dr ROBERT D. KOOB

Vice-Pres. for Student Affairs: CORNEL MORTON

Vice-Pres. for Univ. Advancement: SANDRA OGREN

Dean of Library Services: MICHAEL D. MILLER

Library of 600,000 books, 45,000 online journals, 750 print journals, 195 article databases

Number of teachers: 1,047

Number of students: 19,325

Publications: *Cal Poly Today* (4 a year), *Mustang Daily*

DEANS

College of Agriculture, Food and Environmental Sciences: Dr DAVID J. WEHNER
College of Architecture and Environmental Design: R. THOMAS JONES
College of Engineering: Dr ERLING SMITH
College of Liberal Arts: LINDA HALISKY
College of Science and Mathematics: PHILIP S. BAILEY
Orfalea College of Business: DAVE CHRISTY
School of Education: Dr ROBERT DETWEILER

CALIFORNIA STATE POLYTECHNIC UNIVERSITY, POMONA

3801 W Temple Ave, Pomona, CA 91768

Telephone: (909) 869-7659
Internet: www.csupomona.edu

Founded 1938

Pres.: J. MICHAEL ORTIZ

Provost and Vice-Pres. for Academic Affairs: Dr MARTEN L. denBOER

Vice-Pres. for Admin. Affairs and Chief Financial Officer: Dr EDWIN A. BARNES

Chief Information Officer Instructional and Information Technology: STEPHANIE DODA

Vice-Pres. for Student Affairs: Dr DOUGLAS R. FREER

Vice-Pres. for Univ. Advancement: SCOTT WARRINGTON

Registrar: MARIA L. MARTINEZ

Library Dean: Dr RAY WANG
Library: 2.4m. books, microfilms, maps, 3,000 periodicals, 2,800 online journals
Number of teachers: 3,000
Number of students: 21,000
Publication: *Panorama* (1 a year)

DEANS

College of Agriculture: LESTER C. YOUNG
College of Business Admin.: RICHARD S. LAPIDUS
College of Education and Integrative Studies: Dr PEGGY KELLY
College of Engineering: Dr MAHYAR AMOUZEGAR
College of Environmental Design: MICHAEL WOO
College of Letters, Arts and Social Sciences: Dr SHARON HILLES
College of Science: MANDAYAM SRINIVAS
College of the Extended Univ.: Dr UEI-JIUN FAN
Collins School of Hospitality Management: ANDREW FEINSTEIN

CALIFORNIA STATE UNIVERSITY SYSTEM

401 Golden Shore, Long Beach, CA 90802-4210

Telephone: (562) 951-4000
Internet: www.calstate.edu

Coordinating HQ for 23 state univs

Chancellor: CHARLES B. REED

Number of teachers: 43,000

Number of students: 412,000

Publications: *Annual Fact Book* (1 a year), *CSU Leader* (12 a year).

CALIFORNIA STATE UNIVERSITY, BAKERSFIELD

9001 Stockdale Highway, Bakersfield, CA 93311-1022

Telephone: (661) 654-2456
Fax: (661) 664-3194
E-mail: excellence@csub.edu
Internet: www.csub.edu

Founded 1970

Academic year: September to June

Pres.: Dr HORACE MITCHELL

Provost and Vice-Pres. for Academic Affairs: SORAYA M. COLEY

Vice-Pres. for Business and Admin. Services: MICHAEL A. NEAL

Vice-Pres. for Student Affairs: Dr JOHN HULTSMAN

Vice-Pres. for Univ. Advancement: SORAYA M. COLEY

Dean of Libraries: RODNEY M. HERBSBERGER

Library of 521,199 vols, 30,000 e-journals and e-books

Number of teachers: 469

Number of students: 7,800

DEANS

School of Arts and Humanities: RICHARD COLLINS
School of Business and Public Administration: Dr JOHN EMERY
School of Natural Sciences, Mathematics and Engineering: Dr JULIO R. BLANCO
School of Social Sciences and Education: Dr KATHLEEN M KNUTZEN

CALIFORNIA STATE UNIVERSITY, CHICO

400 West First St, Chico, CA 95929

Telephone: (530) 898-4636
Internet: www.csuchico.edu

Founded 1889 as Chico Normal School, present name 1972

Pres.: Dr PAUL J. ZINGG

Provost and Vice-Pres. for Academic Affairs: SANDRA M. FLAKE

Vice-Pres. for Business and Finance: LORRAINE B. HOFFMAN

Vice-Provost for Information Resources: WILLIAM POST

Vice-Pres. for Student Affairs: DREW CALANDRELLA

Vice-Pres. for Univ. Advancement: RICHARD ELLISON

Library Services Dir: CAROLYN DUSENBURY

Library of 634,000 vols, 2m. documents

Number of teachers: 960

Number of students: 15,500

DEANS

College of Agriculture: Dr JENNIFER RYDER FOX
College of Behavioural and Social Sciences: Dr GAYLE E. HUTCHINSON
College of Business: Dr MIKE WARD
College of Communication and Education: MAGGIE PAYNE
College of Engineering, Computer Science and Construction Management: Dr MIKE WARD
College of Humanities and Fine Arts: Dr JOEL ZIMBELMAN
College of Natural Sciences: Dr FREDERIKA (FRAKA) HARMSEN
Graduate Studies: E. K. PARK

CALIFORNIA STATE UNIVERSITY, DOMINGUEZ HILLS

1000 E Victoria St, Carson, CA 90747

Telephone: (310) 243-3696
Fax: (310) 243-3858
Internet: www.csudh.edu

Founded 1960 as South Bay State College

Pres.: Dr MILDRED GARCIA

Provost and Vice-Pres. for Academic Affairs: Dr MITCH MAKI (acting)

Vice-Pres. for Admin. and Finance: MARY ANN RODRIGUEZ

Vice-Pres. for Enrollment Management and Student Affairs: SUSAN E. BORREGO

Vice-Pres. for Univ. Advancement: GREG SAKS

Registrar: BRANDY McLELLAND

Dean of Univ. Library: SANDRA PARHAM

Library of 440,000 vols, 687,800 microfilms and 2,200 current periodicals

Number of teachers: 623 (incl. 279 full-time, 344 part-time)

Number of students: 13,854

DEANS

College of Arts and Humanities: Dr CAROL A. TUBBS (acting)
College of Business Administration and Public Policy: Dr KAYE BRAGG (acting)
College of Extended and International Education: Dr MARGARET GORDON
College of Natural Behavioural Sciences: Dr LAURA ROBLES
College of Professional Studies: Dr ANUPAMA JOSHI (acting)

CALIFORNIA STATE UNIVERSITY, EAST BAY

25800 Carlos Bee Blvd, Hayward, CA 94542-3000

Telephone: (510) 885-3000
Fax: (510) 885-3808
Internet: www.csuhayward.edu

Founded 1957

Also has a Concord Campus and a Oakland Center

Pres.: LEROY M. MORISHITA

Provost and Vice-Pres. for Academic Affairs: Dr JAMES L. J. HOUPIS

Vice-Pres. for Admin. and Finance: BRAD WELLS

Vice-Pres. for Planning and Enrollment Management and Student Affairs: Dr LINDA DALTON

Vice-Pres. for Univ. Advancement: ROBERT BURT

Chief Information Officer: (vacant)

Univ. Librarian: MYOUNG-JA LEE KWON

Library of 700,000 vols

Number of teachers: 506

Number of students: 12,889

DEANS

College of Business and Economics: TERRI SWARTZ

College of Education and Allied Studies: Dr CAROLYN NELSON

College of Letters, Arts and Social Sciences: KATHELEEN ROUNTREE

College of Science: MICHAEL LEUNG

CALIFORNIA STATE UNIVERSITY, FRESNO

5241 N Maple Ave, Fresno, CA 93740-8027

Telephone: (559) 278-4240

E-mail: outreach@listserv.csufresno.edu

Internet: www.csufresno.edu

Founded 1911 as Fresno State Normal School

Academic year: August to December,January to May (2 semesters)

Pres.: Dr JOHN D. WELTY

Provost and Vice-Pres. for Academic Affairs: Dr WILLIAM A. COVINO

Vice-Pres. for Admin. and Chief Financial Officer: CYNTHIA TENIENTE-MATSON

Vice-Pres. for Student Affairs: Dr PAUL M. OLIARO

Vice-Pres. for Univ. Advancement: Dr PETER N. SMITS

Assoc. Vice-Pres. and Dean of Undergraduate Studies: Dr DENNIS NEF

Dean of Library Services: PETER MCDONALD

Library: 1m. vols, 60,000 e-journals, magazines and newspapers, colln of e-books

Number of teachers: 1,100 (incl. full-time and part-time)

Number of students: 21,500

DEANS

College of Arts and Humanities: Dr VIDA SAMIIAN

College of Health and Human Services: Dr ANDREW HOFF

College of Science and Mathematics: Dr ANDREW HOFF

College of Social Sciences: LUZ GONZALEZ

Craig School of Business: ROBERT HARPER

Jordan College of Agricultural Sciences and Technology: CHARLES BOYER

Kremen School of Education and Human Development: PAUL BEARE

Lyles College of Engineering: Dr RAM NUNNA

CALIFORNIA STATE UNIVERSITY, FULLERTON

POB 34080 Fullerton, CA 92834-9480

800 N College Blvd, Fullerton, CA 92831-3599

Telephone: (657) 278-2011

E-mail: outreach@fullerton.edu

Internet: www.fullerton.edu

Founded 1957

Pres.: MILTON A. GORDON

Exec. Vice-Pres.: JUDITH A. ANDERSON

Vice-Pres. for Academic Affairs: STEVEN N. MURRAY (acting)

Vice-Pres. for Admin. and Finance: WILLIE J. HAGAN

Vice-Pres. for Student Affairs: SILAS H. ABREGO (acting)

Vice-Pres. for Univ. Advancement: PAMELA HILLMAN

Vice-Pres. for Information and Technology: AMIR DABIRIAN

Registrar: MELISSA WHATLEY

Univ. Librarian: RICHARD C. POLLARD

Library of 1,279,172 vols, 1,149,348 microforms, 10,049 maps, 8,087 films and video cassettes

Number of teachers: 2,000 (incl. full-time and part-time)

Number of students: 34,912

DEANS

College of the Arts: JOE ARNOLD

College of Communications: WILLIAM BRIGGS

College of Education: Dr CLAIRE C. CAVALLARO (acting)

College of Engineering and Computer Science: RAMAN UNNIKRISHNAN

College of Health and Human Development: Dr SHARI G. MCMAHAN

College of Humanities and Social Sciences: Dr ANGELA DELLA VOLPE

College of Natural Sciences and Mathematics: Dr ROBERT A. KOCH (acting)

Mihaylo College of Business and Economics: ANIL K. PURI

CALIFORNIA STATE UNIVERSITY, LONG BEACH

1250 Bellflower Blvd, Long Beach, CA 90840-0115

Telephone: (562) 985-4111

Internet: www.csulb.edu

Founded 1949 as Los Angeles-Orange County State College, present name 1972

Public control

Pres.: F. KING ALEXANDER

Provost and Sr Vice-Pres. for Academic Affairs: Dr DONALD J. PARA

Vice-Pres. for Admin. and Finance: MARY STEPHENS

Vice-Pres. for Student Services: Dr DOUGLAS W. ROBINSON

Vice-Pres. for Univ. Relations and Devt: ANDREA TAYLOR

Dean of Library Services: ROMAN KOCHAN

Library of 1,096,089 vols, 1,503,457 microfilms, 35,080 non-book materials, 2,110 current periodicals

Number of teachers: 2,128 (948 full-time, 1,180 part-time)

Number of students: 33,419

DEANS

College of the Arts: RAYMOND TORRES-SANTOS

College of Business Administration: MICHAEL E. SOLT

College of Continuing and Professional Education: JEET JOSHEE

College of Education: MARQUITA GRENOT-SCHEYER

College of Engineering: FOROUZAN GOLSHANI

College of Health and Human Services: KENNETH I. MILLAR

College of Liberal Arts: GERRY RIPOSA

College of Natural Sciences and Mathematics: LAURA KINGSFORD

CALIFORNIA STATE UNIVERSITY, LOS ANGELES

5151 State University Dr., Los Angeles, CA 90032-8530

Telephone: (323) 343-3901

Fax: (323) 343-6306

E-mail: admission@calstatela.edu

Internet: www.calstatela.edu

Founded 1947

Pres.: JAMES M. ROSSER

Provost and Vice-Pres. for Academic Affairs: Dr ASHISH VAIDYA

Vice-Pres. for Admin. and Chief Financial Officer: LISA CHAVEZ

Vice-Pres. for Information Technology Services: PETER QUAN

Vice-Pres. for Institutional Advancement: KYLE C. BUTTON

Vice-Pres. for Student Affairs: ANTHONY R. ROSS

Dean of Graduate Studies and Research: ALAN E. MUCHLINSKI

Dean of Undergraduate Studies: ALFREDO G. GONZALEZ (acting)

Univ. Librarian: ALICE KAWAKAMI (acting)

Library: 1m. vols, 200 historical and geographical atlases, 4,500 periodicals and newspapers

Number of teachers: 888

Number of students: 18,000

DEANS

College of Arts and Letters: Dr PETER MCALLISTAR

College of Business and Economics: JAMES A. GOODRICH

Charter College of Education: Dr MARY FALVEY

College of Engineering, Computer Science and Technology: Dr H. KEITH MOO-YOUNG

College of Health and Human Services: Dr BEATRICE YORKER (acting)

College of Natural and Social Sciences: Dr JIM HENDERSON

CALIFORNIA STATE UNIVERSITY, MONTEREY BAY

100 Campus Center, Seaside, CA 93955-8001

Telephone: (831) 582-3000

E-mail: moreinfo_prospective@csumb.edu

Internet: csumb.edu

Founded 1994

Academic year: August to May

Pres.: Dr DIANE F. HARRISON

Provost and Vice-Pres. for Academic Affairs: Dr KATHRYN CRUZ-URIBE

Vice-Pres. for Admin. and Finance: KEVIN SAUNDERS

Vice-Pres. for Devt: Dr CHRIS HASEGAWA

Vice-Pres. for Student Affairs: Dr RONNIE HIGGS

Vice-Pres. for Univ. Advancement: Dr PATTI HIRAMOTO

Dir of the Library: BILL ROBNETT

Library of 65,000 vols

Number of teachers: 280

Number of students: 4,790

DEANS

College of Arts, Humanities, and Social Sciences: Dr RENEE R. CURRY

College of Professional Studies: Dr BRIAN SIMMONS

College of Science, Media Arts, and Technology: Dr MARSHA MOROH

College of Univ. Studies and Programmes: Dr CHRIS HASEGAWA (acting)

CALIFORNIA STATE UNIVERSITY, NORTHRIDGE

18111 Nordhoff St, Northridge, CA 91330

Telephone: (818) 677-1200

Fax: (818) 677-3766

E-mail: admissions@csun.edu

Internet: www.csun.edu

Founded 1958 as Los Angeles State College, present name 1972

Academic year: August to to May

Pres.: Dr JOLENE KOESTER

Provost and Vice-Pres. for Academic Affairs: Dr HARRY HELLENBRAND

Vice-Pres. for Admin. and Finance: THOMAS MCCARRON

Vice-Pres. for Information Technology: HILARY BAKER
Vice-Pres. for Operations: JULIE WANKE
Vice-Pres. for Student Affairs: Dr WILLIAM WATKINS
Vice-Pres. for Univ. Advancement: Dr VANCE T. PETERSON
Dir of Admissions and Records: ERIC FORBES
Dean of Univ. Library: Dr MARK STOVER
Library: 1.4m vols (incl. 1.1m books, 250,000 periodicals), 3.2m. microforms, 53,000 e-journals, 274,713 e-books, 2,300 print journals, 14,200 sound recordings, 12,700 film and video recordings, 60,000 photographs
Number of teachers: 4,000
Number of students: 36,000

DEANS

College of Business and Economics: Dr WILLIAM JENNINGS
College of Engineering and Computer Science: Dr S. K. RAMESH
College of Extended Learning: JOYCE FEUCHT-HAVIAR
College of Health and Human Development: Dr SYLVIA A. ALVA
College of Humanities: Dr ELIZABETH SAY
College of Science and Mathematics: JERRY STINNER
College of Social and Behavioural Sciences: STELLA THEODOULOU
Michael D. Eisner College of Education: MICHAEL D. SPAGNA
Mike Curb College of Arts, Media and Communication: W. ROBERT BUCKER
Tseng College: JOYCE FEUCHT-HAVIAR

CALIFORNIA STATE UNIVERSITY, SACRAMENTO

6000 J St, Sacramento, CA 95819-6056
Telephone: (916) 278-6011
Fax: (916) 278-6664
E-mail: infodesk@csus.edu
Internet: www.csus.edu
Founded 1947 as Sacramento State College
Academic year: September to May
Pres.: ALEXANDER GONZALEZ
Provost and Vice-Pres. for Academic Affairs: JOSEPH F. SHELEY
Vice-Pres. for Admin.: STEPHEN G. GARCIA
Vice-Pres. for Student Affairs: Dr LORI VARLOTTA
Vice-Pres. for Univ. Affairs: CAROLE HAYASHINO
Dir of Library Systems: CARLOS RODRIGUEZ
Library: 2m. vols
Number of teachers: 1,295
Number of students: 27,033
Publications: *Calaveras Station* (1 a year), *Capitol University Journal* (2 a year)

DEANS

College of Arts and Letters: EDWARD S. INCH
College of Business Administration: Dr SANJAY VARSHNEY
College of Continuing Education: Dr ALICE TOM
College of Education: VANESSA SHEARED
College of Engineering and Computer Science: EMIR JOSÉ MACARI
College of Health and Human Services: Dr FRED D. BALDINI
College of Natural Sciences and Mathematics: Dr JILL M. TRAINER
College of Social Sciences and Interdisciplinary Studies: Dr CHARLES GOSSETT

CALIFORNIA STATE UNIVERSITY, SAN BERNARDINO

5500 University Parkway, San Bernardino, CA 92407-2318
Telephone: (909) 880-5000

Fax: (909) 880-5903
E-mail: moreinfo@csusb.edu
Internet: www.csusb.edu
Founded 1960 as San Bernardino-Riverside State College, present name 1972
Academic year: September to September
Liberal arts college with several applied programmes offering a broad range of first degrees, several teaching credentials and Masters degrees in selected fields
Pres.: ALBERT K. KARNIG
Provost and Vice-Pres. for Academic Affairs: Dr ANDREW BODMAN
Vice-Pres. for Admin. and Finance: BOB GRADNER
Vice-Pres. for Information Resources and Technology: LORAINE M. FROST
Vice-Pres. for Student Affairs: Dr FRANK L. RINCÓN
Vice-Pres. for Univ. Advancement: LARRY SHARP
Univ. Librarian: CEASAR CABALLERO
Library of 720,000 vols, 2,400 current periodicals and serial publications, also maps, microfilms, musical scores, CD-ROMs; depository for CA state and fed. govt documents
Number of teachers: 2,100
Number of students: 17,500

DEANS

College of Arts and Letters: Dr ERI F. YASUHARA
College of Business and Public Administration: Dr LAWRENCE C. ROSE
College of Education: Dr JAY FIENE
College of Extended Learning: Dr TATIANA KARMANOVA
College of Natural Sciences: DAVID MAYNARD
College of Social and Behavioural Sciences: Dr JAMAL R. NASSAR

CALIFORNIA STATE UNIVERSITY, SAN MARCOS

333 S Twin Oaks Valley Rd, San Marcos, CA 92096-0001
Telephone: (760) 750-4000
E-mail: registrar@csusm.edu
Internet: www.csusm.edu
Founded 1979
Academic year: September to May
Pres.: Dr KAREN S. HAYNES
Chancellor: CHARLES B. REED
Provost and Vice-Pres. for Academic Affairs: EMILY F. CUTRER
Vice-Pres. for Community Engagement: Dr JAN JACKSON
Vice-Pres. for Finance and Admin.: LINDA HAWK
Vice-Pres. for Student Affairs: Dr ELOISE STIGLITZ
Vice-Pres. for Univ. Advancement: NEAL HOSS
Dean of Library: BARBARA PREECE
Library of 290,444 vols (incl. books, periodicals and documents), 38,955 e-journals, 47,068 e-books, 3,798 sound recordings, 8,192 film and video recordings
Number of teachers: 232
Number of students: 9,722

DEANS

College of Business Administration: Dr REGINA EISENBACH
College of Education, Health and Human Services: Dr DON CHU
College of Science and Mathematics: Dr KATHERINE KANTARDJIEFF
Extended Learning: MIKE SCHRODER
Graduate Studies: Dr GERARDO M. GONZÁLEZ
School of Nursing: JUDY PAPENHAUSEN

CALIFORNIA STATE UNIVERSITY, STANISLAUS

1 University Circle, Turlock, CA 95382
Telephone: (209) 667-3122
Fax: (209) 667-3333
Internet: www.csustan.edu
Founded 1960
Pres.: Dr HAMID SHIRVANI
Provost and Vice-Pres. for Academic Affairs: Dr JAMES T STRONG
Vice-Pres. for Business and Finance: RUSS GIAMBELLUCA
Vice-Pres. for Univ. Advancement: SUSANA GAJIC-BRUEYA
Assoc. Vice-Pres. for Enrollment and Student Affairs: Dr SUZANNE ESPINOZA
Vice-Pres. for Faculty Affairs and Human Resources: DENNIS W. SHIMEK
Dean of Admissions and Registrar: LISA BERNARDO
Dean of Library Services: ANNIE HOR
Library of 361,000 vols, 2,000 current periodicals, 1.3m. microfilms, 4,700 sound and video recordings, govt documents, special colln of children's literature
Number of teachers: 443 (incl. 265 full-time and 178 part-time)
Number of students: 8,305

DEANS

College of the Arts: Dr DARYL JOSEPH MOORE
College of Business Administration: Dr LINDA NOWAK
College of Education: Dr KATHY NORMAN
College of Human and Health Sciences: Dr JUNE BOFFMAN
College of Humanities and Social Sciences: Dr JAMES A. TUEDIO
College of Natural Sciences: Dr ROBERT MARINO

CHAPMAN UNIVERSITY

1 University Dr., Orange, CA 92866
Telephone: (714) 997-6815
Internet: www.chapman.edu
Founded 1861 as Hesperian College in Woodland
Private (Disciples of Christ) Liberal Arts
Pres.: Dr JAMES L. DOTI
Provost and Exec. Vice-Pres.: Dr DANIELE STRUPPA
Exec. Vice-Pres. for Finance and Admin.: GARY BRAHM
Vice-Chancellor and Dean for Enrollment Management: MIKE PELLY
Vice-Chancellor for Student Affairs and Dean of Students: Dr JERRY PRICE
Exec. Vice-Pres. for Univ. Advancement: SHERYL BOURGEOIS
Registrar: Dr JACK F. FARRELL
Dean of the Libraries: CHARLENE BALDWIN
Library: 593,000 vols
Number of teachers: 646 (349 full-time, 297 part-time)
Number of students: 6,398

DEANS

College of Educational Studies: Dr DON N. CARDINAL
College of Performing Arts: WILLIAM HALL (acting)
George L. Argyros School of Business and Economics: Dr ARTHUR KRAFT
Lawrence and Kristina Dodge College of Film and Media Arts: BOB BASSETT
Schmid College of Science and Technology: Dr MENAS KAFATOS
School of Law: SCOTT HOWE
Wilkinson College of Humanities and Social Sciences: PATRICK QUINN

CHURCH DIVINITY SCHOOL OF THE PACIFIC

2451 Ridge Rd, Berkeley, CA 94709-1217

Telephone: (510) 204-0700
Fax: (510) 644-0712
E-mail: info@cdsp.edu
Internet: www.cdsp.edu

Founded 1893
Private control (part of the Graduate Theological Union)
Academic year: August to May
Areas of study: divinity, theological studies, arts, ministry

Pres. and Dean: Rev. Dr W. MARK RICHARDSON
Vice-Pres. for Admin.: STEVE ARGYRIS
Vice-Pres. for Advancement: JERRY CAMPBELL
Dean of Academic Affairs: Dr LINDA L. CLADER
Dean of School for Deacons: RODERICK B. DUGLISS
Dean of Students: L. ANN HALLISEY
Registrar: MARGO WEBSTER.

CLAREMONT GRADUATE UNIVERSITY

150 E 10th St, Claremont, CA 91711

Telephone: (909) 621-8000
Fax: (909) 621-8390
E-mail: information@cgu.edu
Internet: www.cgu.edu

Founded 1925
Masters and doctoral degrees in 22 professional and academic disciplines

Pres.: DEBORAH A. FREUND
Provost and Exec. Vice-Pres. for Academic Affairs: JACOB ADAMS
Asst Vice-Pres. for Advancement: MIKE AVILA
Sr Vice-Pres. for Finance and Admin.: Dr STEVEN N. GARCIA

Library: 2m. vols (incl. e-books and journals)
Number of teachers: 169 (81 full-time, 88 part-time)
Number of students: 2,188

DEANS

Peter F. Drucker and Masatoshi Ito Graduate School of Management: HIDEKI YAMAWAKI
School of the Arts and Humanities: JANET FARRELL BRODIE
School of Behavioural and Organizational Sciences: Dr STEWART I. DONALDSON
School of Community and Global Health: C. ANDERSON JOHNSON
School of Educational Studies: MARGARET GROGAN
School of Information Systems and Technology: Dr THOMAS A. HORAN
School of Mathematical Sciences: ELLIS CUMBERBATCH
School of Politics and Economics: JEAN SCHROEDEL
School of Religion: TAMMI J. SCHNEIDER

CLAREMONT MCKENNA COLLEGE

500 E Ninth St, Claremont, CA 91711-6400

Telephone: (909) 621-8000
Fax: (909) 621-8495
E-mail: deanofstudents@cmc.edu
Internet: www.cmc.edu

Founded 1946
Academic year: August to May (2 semesters)
Liberal arts college with emphasis on business and public affairs; mem. of the Claremont Colleges

Pres.: Prof. PAMELA BROOKS GANN
Dean of the Faculty and Vice-Pres. for Academic Affairs: GREGORY D. HESS

Vice-Pres. for Business and Admin. and Treas.: ROBIN J. ASPINALL
Vice-Pres. for Devt and External Relations: ERNIE ISEMINGER
Vice-Pres. for Student Affairs: JEFFERSON HUANG
Assoc. Vice-Pres. for Devt: STEVE SIEGEL
Dean for Students: MARY SPELLMAN
Registrar and Dir for Institutional Research: ELIZABETH MORGAN
Chief Technology Officer: CYNTHIA HUMES

Library: 2m. vols
Number of teachers: 134
Number of students: 1,211

CLAREMONT SCHOOL OF THEOLOGY

1325 N College Ave, Claremont, CA 91711-3199

Telephone: (909) 447-2500
Fax: (909) 626-7062
E-mail: president@cst.edu
Internet: www.cst.edu

Founded 1885 as Maclay College of Theology, present location 1957
Private control
Academic year: September to May

Pres.: Dr JERRY D. CAMPBELL
Vice-Pres. for Academic Affairs and Dean of Faculty: Dr PHILIP CLAYTON
Vice Pres. for Admin. and Finance: LYNN O'LEARY-ARCHER
Vice Pres. for Devt: DUANE DYER
Chief Financial Officer: JOAN FROST
Registrar: JENNIE J. ALLEN
Dir for the Library: JOHN DICKASON

Library of 210,000 vols, 650 print subscriptions, 6,000 e- journals

Publication: *Claremont Journal of Religion* (online).

CLEVELAND CHIROPRACTIC COLLEGE

10850 Lowell Ave, Overland Park, KS 66210

Telephone: (913) 234-0600
Fax: (323) 906-2094
E-mail: la.admissions@cleveland.edu
Internet: www.cleveland.edu

Founded 1911, present status 2011
Academic year: September to August
Private control

Depts of basic sciences, diagnostic sciences, chiropractic sciences, clinical sciences, humanities and social sciences, physical and life sciences

Pres.: Dr CARL S. CLEVELAND, III
Provost: ASHLEY E. CLEVELAND
Chief Operating Officer: JEFF KARP
Vice-Pres. for Campus Relations: D. CLARK BECKLEY
Dir for Student Services: JALONNA BOWIE
Dir for Admissions: MELISSA DENTON
Dir for Library: MARCIA THOMAS

Library of 15,000 vols, 350 journal subscriptions, 7,000 e-journals, 75,000 microfiche files
Number of students: 568

Publication: *Clevelander*.

COGSWELL POLYTECHNICAL COLLEGE

1175 Bordeaux Dr., Sunnyvale, CA 94089-9772

Telephone: (408) 541-0100
Fax: (408) 747-0764
E-mail: info@cogswell.edu
Internet: www.cogswell.edu

Founded 1887
Private control
Academic year: January to August

Areas of study: 3-D animation, 3-D modelling, computer engineering, digital arts engineering, digital audio, entertainment design, game design, software engineering
Chancellor: CHARLES H. HOUSE
Pres.: LISA KEMP
Vice-Pres. for Finance and Admin.: REJINO CASTANEDA
Vice-Pres. for Information Technology: Dr ANDREY FEDIN
Dean for College: MICHAEL MARTIN
Dean of Information Technology: Dr ANDREY FEDIN
Dean for Institutional Advancement: BONNIE PHELPS
Dean for Student Life: BARB BLOOM
Registrar: JILL MUSICK
Librarian: BRUCE DAHMS

Number of teachers: 55 (12 full-time, 43 part-time)
Number of students: 288 (182 full-time, 106 part-time)

Library of 12,000 vols, 100 periodicals.

COLEMAN UNIVERSITY

8888 Balboa Ave, San Diego, CA 92123-1506

Telephone: (858) 499-0202
Fax: (858) 499-0233
E-mail: admissions@coleman.edu
Internet: www.coleman.edu

Founded 1963 as Coleman College, present name 2008
Private control

Depts of bioinformatics, graphic design, information systems, networks and security; campus: San Marcos

Pres.: PAUL PANESAR
Vice-Pres. for Academics: SHERYL RIDENS
Vice-Pres.: DARLENE ANKTON
Registrar: KAREN HYNES
Librarian (San Diego): MANNY BERNAD
Number of students: 1,000

COLUMBIA COLLEGE HOLLYWOOD

18618 Oxnard St, Tarzana, CA 91356-1411

Telephone: (818) 345-8414
Fax: (818) 345-9053
E-mail: info@columbiacollege.edu
Internet: www.columbiacollege.edu

Founded 1951
Private control

Areas of study: cinema, television and video production

Pres.: RICHARD KOBRITZ
Dean for College: ALAN L. GANSBERG
Dean for Student Services: Dr YOLANDA DAWSON
Sr. Dir for Finance: RICHARD CROWE
Dir for Admissions: CARMEN MUNOZ
Dir for Information Technology and Production Services: RONALD REEVES
Registrar: DEBORAH LOWE
Librarian: MARA BURNS

Library of 10,000 vols.

CONCORDIA UNIVERSITY IRVINE

1530 Concordia W, Irvine, CA 92612-3203

Telephone: (949) 854-8002
Fax: (949) 854-6894
E-mail: info@cui.edu
Internet: www.cui.edu

Founded 1973 as Christ College Irvine, present name 1993
Private control
Academic year: August to May

Pres.: Dr KURT KRUEGER
Provost and Exec. Vice-Pres.: Dr MARY. SCOTT

Assoc. Provost and Vice-Pres. for Academic Affairs: Dr PETER SENKBEIL
Exec. Vice-Pres. for Univ. Advancement: TIM JAEGER
Exec. Vice Pres. for External Relations: STEPHEN CHRISTENSEN
Vice-Pres. for Business Operations and Information Technology: ALAN K. RUDI
Vice-Pres. for Student Services: Dr GARY R. MCDANIEL
Dean for Students: Dr DEREK VERGARA
Dean for Academic Records and Registrar: Prof. KENNETH CLAVIR
Dir for Library Services: CAROLINA BARTON
Library of 92,000 vols
Number of teachers: 100 (full-time)
Number of students: 3,362
Publication: *Concordia Today* (online)

DEANS

Christ College: Dr STEVEN P. MUELLER
School of Arts and Sciences: Dr TIMOTHY L. PREUSS
School of Business and Professional Studies: Dr TIMOTHY C. PETERS (acting)
School of Education: Dr JANICE E. NELSON

DOMINICAN SCHOOL OF PHILOSOPHY & THEOLOGY

2301 Vine St, Berkeley, CA 94708
Telephone: (510) 849-2030
Fax: (510) 849-1372
E-mail: info@dspt.edu
Internet: www.dspt.edu
Founded 1851, present name 1976
Private control
Language of instruction: English
Academic year: August to June
Pres.: Rev. MICHAEL SWEENEY
Vice-Pres. for Admin.: PETER MACLEOD
Academic Dean: CHRISTOPHER RENZ
Registrar: TERESA OLSON
Library of 440,000 vols, 1,500 periodical subscriptions and 292,000 non-book holdings
Number of teachers: 20 (14 full-time, 6 part-time)
Number of students: 103
Publication: *Ad Gentes.*

DOMINICAN UNIVERSITY OF CALIFORNIA

50 Acacia Ave, San Rafael, CA 94901-2298
Telephone: (415) 457-4440
Fax: (415) 485-3205
E-mail: chilly@dominican.edu
Internet: www.dominican.edu
Founded 1890 as a women's college, present name 2000
Private control
Academic year: August to May
Br. campus: Ukiah Center
Pres.: Dr MARY B. MARCY
Provost: Dr KENNETH J. PORADA
Exec. Vice-Pres. and Chief Academic Officer: Dr LUÍS MARÍA R. CALINGO
Exec. Dir for Library: GARY GORKA
Library of 100,000 vols, 375 periodicals
Number of teachers: 223
Number of students: 2,278

DEANS

School of Arts, Humanities and Social Sciences: Dr NICOLA PITCHFORD
School of Business and Leadership: Dr DAN MOSHAVI
School of Education and Counseling Psychology: Dr EDWARD KUJAWA
School of Health and Natural Sciences: Dr MARTHA A. NELSON

FIELDING GRADUATE UNIVERSITY

2112 Santa Barbara St, Santa Barbara, CA 93105-3538
Telephone: (805) 687-1099
E-mail: admissions@fielding.edu
Internet: www.fielding.edu
Founded 1974
Private control
Pres.: Dr RICHARD S. MEYERS
Provost and Sr Vice-Pres.: Dr GLORIA J. WILLINGHAM
Assoc. Provost for Enrolment Management: MONIQUE SNOWDEN
Assoc. Provost for Research and Learning: Dr DANIEL R. SEWELL
Vice Pres.: LISA LEWIS
Vice Pres. for Univ. Advancement and Devt: Dr DAVID EDELMAN
Vice-Pres. for Human Resources and Admin.: Dr ANNA J. MCDONALD
Dir for Library Services: LESLIE MATHEWS
Number of teachers: 131 (75 full-time, 56 part-time)
Number of students: 1,300
Publication: *Fielding Focus*

DEANS

School of Educational Leadership and Change: Dr MURIO BORUNDA
School of Human and Organization Development: Dr CHARLES MCCLINTOCK
School of Psychology: Dr GERARDO RODRIQUEZ-MENENDEZ

FIVE BRANCHES UNIVERSITY

200 Seventh Ave, Santa Cruz, CA 95062
Telephone: (831) 476-9424
Fax: (831) 476-8928
E-mail: receptionist@fivebranches.edu
Internet: www.fivebranches.edu
Founded 1984 as Five Brs Institute
Private control
Languages of instruction: English, Chinese, Korean
Academic year: programme begins in August and February
Areas of study: acupuncture, Chinese herbology, traditional Chinese medicine, Western medicine and natural sciences; campus at San Jose
Pres.: RON ZAIDMAN
Vice-Pres. for Academic Affairs and Academic Dean: JOANNA ZHAO
Dir for Admissions: ELEONOR MENDELSON
Registrar and Dir for Student Services: ANA LOBATO
Library of 7,000 vols
Number of teachers: 200
Number of students: 500

DEANS

Traditional Chinese Medicine: JOANNA ZHAO

FRANCISCAN SCHOOL OF THEOLOGY

1712 Euclid Ave, Berkeley, CA 94709-1294
Telephone: (510) 848-5232
Fax: (510) 549-9466
E-mail: info@fst.edu
Internet: www.fst.edu
Founded 1854 as Mission Santa Barbara, present name 1968
Private control
Offers Masters in arts, divinity, ministry, theology; continuing education programme
Pres. and Rector: Fr JOSEPH P. CHINNICI
Academic Dean: Prof. WILLIAM J. SHORT
Chief Financial Officer: CAROLYN RODKIN
Number of students: 100

FRESNO PACIFIC BIBLICAL SEMINARY

1717 S Chestnut Ave, Fresno, CA 93702
Telephone: (559) 453-2317
Fax: (559) 453-2355
E-mail: fresno@mbseminary.edu
Internet: seminary.fresno.edu
Founded 1955; attached to Fresno Pacific Univ.
Private control
Academic year: August to August
MAs in Christian ministry, divinity, intercultural mission, marriage, family and child counselling, New Testament, Old Testament, theology; diplomas in Anglican studies, Christian studies, congregational care, evangelism and church planting, integration, Presbyterian studies, women in ministry; campuses at Langley and Winnipeg in Canada
Pres.: JIM HOLM
Academic Dean: LYNN JOST
Dean for Students: RICK BARTLETT
Chief Financial Officer: LINDA BOWMAN
Registrar: LORI JAMES
Librarian: RICHARD RAWLS
Library of 150,000 vols
Number of teachers: 11
Number of students: 143

FRESNO PACIFIC UNIVERSITY

1717 S Chestnut Ave, Fresno, CA 93702-4709
Telephone: (209) 453-2000
Fax: (209) 453-2007
Internet: www.fresno.edu
Founded 1944 as Pacific Bible Institute, present name 1997
Private control
Academic year: August to May
Campuses at Bakersfield, N Fresno, Visilia, Merced and Fresno
Pres.: Dr D. MERRILL EWERT
Provost and Vice-Pres. for Enrolment Management: Dr STEVE VARVIS
Vice-Pres. and Chief Information Officer: ALAN OURS
Vice-Pres. for Advancement and Univ. Relations: MARK DEFFENBACHER
Vice-Pres. for Finance and Business Affairs: DIANE CATLIN
Library Dir: KEVIN ENNS-REMPEL
Library of 145,000 vols
Number of teachers: 70
Number of students: 1,453

DEANS

School of Business: DENNIS LANGHOFER
School of Education: GARY GRAMENZ
School of Humanities, Religion and Social Sciences: Dr KEVIN REIMER
School of Natural Sciences: Dr KAREN CIANCI

FULLER THEOLOGICAL SEMINARY

135 N Oakland Ave, Pasadena, CA 91182
Telephone: (626) 584-5200
E-mail: admissions@fuller.edu
Internet: www.fuller.edu
Founded 1947
Private control
Regional campuses: California Coast, Northern California, Northwest, Southwest, Colorado and Texas
Pres.: Dr RICHARD J. MOUW
Provost and Sr. Vice-Pres.: C. DOUGLAS MCCONNELL
Vice-Pres. for Enrolment and Student Affairs: WENDY WAKEMAN
Vice-Pres. for Finance: JOHN W. WARD
Vice-Pres. for Seminary Advancement: JOE B. WEBB

Registrar: DAVID E. KIEFER
Library Dir: MICHAEL D. MURRAY

Library of 500,000 vols, 10,000 e-journals, 10,000 e-books, 3,400 print periodicals, 900 nat. and int. journals and 800 monographic serials
Number of teachers: 80
Number of students: 4,500

DEANS

School of Intercultural Studies: Dr C. DOUGLAS MCCONNELL
School of Psychology: Dr WINSTON E. GOODEN
School of Theology: Dr HOWARD LOEWEN

GOLDEN GATE BAPTIST THEOLOGICAL SEMINARY

201 Seminary Dr., Mill Valley, CA 94941-3163

Telephone: (415) 380-1300
Fax: (415) 380-1302
E-mail: admissions@ggbts.edu
Internet: www.ggbts.edu

Founded 1944
Private control
Academic year: August to August

Br. campuses: Northern California Campus, CA; Southern California Campus, CA; Pacific Northwest Campus, WA; Arizona Campus, AZ; Rocky Mountain Campus, CO
Pres.: Dr JEFF IORG
Vice-Pres. for Academic Affairs: Dr D. MICHAEL MARTIN
Vice-Pres. for Business and Finance: GARY GROAT
Vice-Pres. for Institutional Advancement: Dr THOMAS O. JONES
Vice-Pres. for Enrollment and Student Services: Dr ADAM GROZA
Registrar: JENNIFER PEACH
Dir of Library Services: KELLY CAMPBELL
Number of teachers: 23 full-time
Number of students: 2,057

GOLDEN GATE UNIVERSITY

536 Mission St, San Francisco, CA 94105-2968

Telephone: (415) 442-7000
Fax: (415) 442-7807
Internet: www.ggu.edu

Founded 1901
Private control
Campuses: Silicon Valley, Los Angeles and San Francisco (California), and Seattle (Washington)
Pres.: Dr DAN ANGEL
Vice-Pres. for Academic Affairs: Dr BARBARA H. KARLIN
Vice-Pres. for Finance: SWAGAT KAJALE
Vice-Pres. for Operations: BOB HITE
Dir for Enrolment Services: LOUIS D. RICCARDI
Dir for Univ. Library: JANICE CARTER
Library of 75,000 vols, 75,000 e-book vols
Number of teachers: 264 (incl. full-time and part-time)
Number of students: 3,605
Publication: *GGU magazine* (3 a year)

DEANS

Edward S. Ageno School of Business: PAUL FOUTS
School of Accounting: Dr MARY P. CANNING
School of Law: Dr DRUCILLA STENDER RAMEY
School of Taxation: Dr MARY P. CANNING
Undergraduate Programmes: CHERRON HOPPES

HARVEY MUDD COLLEGE

301 Platt Blvd, Claremont, CA 91711-5901

Telephone: (909) 621-8000
Fax: (909) 621-8360
E-mail: president@hmc.edu
Internet: www.hmc.edu

Founded 1955
Private control
Academic year: August to May

Liberal arts college; mem. of Claremont Univ. Consortium; depts of biology, chemistry, computer science, engineering, humanities, social sciences and arts, mathematics, physics
Pres.: MARIA KLAWE
Vice-Pres. for Student Affairs and Dean for Students: MAGGIE BROWNING
Vice-Pres. and Chief Information Officer: JOSEPH VAUGHAN
Vice-Pres. for Academic Affairs and Dean for Faculty: ROBERT CAVE
Vice-Pres. for Admin. and Finance: ANDREW DORANTES
Vice-Pres. for Admission and Financial Aid: THYRA BRIGGS
Vice-Pres. for College Advancement: DAN MACALUSO
Vice-Pres. for Computing and Information Services and Chief Information Officer: JOSEPH VAUGHAN
Registrar: NOEL KELLER
Librarian: JOHN MCDONALD
Library: 1m. vols (shared with the Claremont Colleges)
Number of teachers: 82 (full-time and part-time)
Number of students: 756

HOLY NAMES UNIVERSITY

3500 Mountain Blvd, Oakland, CA 94619-1699

Telephone: (510) 436-1000
Fax: (510) 436-1199
E-mail: admissions@hnu.edu
Internet: www.hnu.edu

Founded 1868
Private control
Academic year: August to July
Coeducational liberal arts college
Pres.: Dr WILLIAM J. HYNES
Vice-Pres. for Academic Affairs and Dean of Faculty: BETH MARTIN
Vice-Pres. for Finance and Admin.: STUART KOOP
Vice-Pres. for Institutional Advancement: DAV CVITKOVIC
Vice-Pres. for Mission Effectiveness: Sr CAROL SELLMAN
Vice-Pres. for Student Affairs and Enrolment Services: MICHAEL MILLER
Vice-Pres. for Univ. Advancement: RICHARD ORTEGA
Dir for Library Services: KAREN SCHEINDER
Library of 30,000 vols, 50,000 e-books
Number of teachers: 121
Number of students: 1,331

HOPE INTERNATIONAL UNIVERSITY

2500 E Nutwood Ave, Fullerton, CA 92831

Telephone: (714) 879-3901
Fax: (714) 681-7451
E-mail: gradinfo@hiu.edu
Internet: www.hiu.edu

Founded 1928 as Pacific Bible Seminary, present name 1997
Private control
Academic year: August to March

Educational centres at Corona and Orange (California), and Everett (Washington)
Pres.: Dr JOHN DERRY

Vice-Pres. for Academic Affairs: Dr PAUL ALEXANDER
Vice-Pres. for Business and Finance: FRANK SCOTTI
Vice-Pres. for Enrolment Management: TERESA SMITH
Vice-Pres. for Institutional Advancement: MICHAEL MULRYAN
Vice-Pres. for Student Affairs: MARK COMEAUX
Registrar: RON ARCHER
Dir for Library Services: ROBIN HARTMAN
Library of 65,000 vols
Number of teachers: 165
Number of students: 1,300

DEANS

College of Arts and Science: Dr STEVEN D. EDGINGTON
College of Business and Management: Dr JAMES D. WOEST
College of Education: Dr GEORGE E. WEST
College of Ministry and Biblical Studies: Dr JOE GRANA
College of Psychology and Counseling: Dr LAURA L. STEELE
Pacific Christian College: STEVEN D. EDGINGTON

HUMBOLDT STATE UNIVERSITY

One Harpst St, Arcata, CA 95521-8299

Telephone: (707) 826-3011
E-mail: welcome@humboldt.edu
Internet: www.humboldt.edu

Founded 1913
Academic year: August to May
Pres.: ROLLIN C. RICHMOND
Provost and Vice-Pres. for Academic Affairs: ROBERT SNYDER
Vice-Pres. for Admin. Affairs: BURT NORDSTROM
Vice-Pres. for Student Affairs: Dr PEG L. BLAKE
Vice-Pres. for Univ. Advancement: FRANK WHITLATCH
Dean of Enrollment Management: JEAN BUTLER
Dir for Institutional Research and Planning: JACQUELINE NAGATSUKA
Registrar: HILARY DASHIELL
Dean for the Library: TERESA L. GRENOT
Library of 560,000 vols, 650 atlases, 8,000 CDs, 6,000 VHS, 1,000 DVDs
Number of teachers: 517
Number of students: 7,902

DEANS

College of Arts, Humanities and Social Sciences: KEN AYOOB
College of Natural Resources and Sciences: STEVE SMITH
College of Professional Studies: JOHN LEE

HUMPHREYS COLLEGE

6650 Inglewood Ave, Stockton, CA 95207

Telephone: (209) 478-0800
Fax: (209) 478-8721
E-mail: college_president@humphreys.edu
Internet: www.humphreys.edu

Founded 1896 as Stockton Business College, present name 1947
Private control
Academic year: September to September
Campuses in Modesto and Stockton
Pres.: Dr ROBERT G. HUMPHREYS
Dean for Admin.: WILMA OKAMOTO-VAUGHN
Dean for Instruction: JESS BONDS
Registrar: MARIA J. GARCIA-MILLER
Librarian: STANISLAV PERKNER
Number of students: 1,172

DEANS

Laurence Drivon School of Law: L. PATRICK PIGGOTT

ITT TECHNICAL INSTITUTE

9680 Granite Ridge Dr., San Diego, CA 92123
Telephone: (858) 571-8500
Internet: itt-tech.edu
Founded 1969
Private control
Academic year: September to September

140 Campuses in 38 states; Breckinridge School of Nursing, School of Business, School of Criminal Justice, School of Drafting and Design, School of Electronics Technology, School of Health Sciences, School of Information Technology
Dir: JOHN A. BYERS
Dean: CORNELL R. HOKE
Registrar: COLLEEN HEBDING
Number of students: 70,000

JOHN F. KENNEDY UNIVERSITY

100 Ellinwood Way, Pleasant Hill, CA 94523-4817
Telephone: (925) 969-3450
Fax: (510) 254-6964
E-mail: proginfo@jfku.edu
Internet: www.jfku.edu
Founded 1964
Private control
Affiliate of Nat. Univ. System; campuses at: Pleasant Hill, San Jose, Berkeley and Costa Mesa
Chancellor: Dr JERRY C. LEE
Pres.: Dr STEVEN STARGARDTER
Provost: DIANA PAQUE
Academic Vice-Pres.: IRVING BERKOWITZ
Vice-Pres. for Academic Affairs: DONALD CAMPBELL
Vice-Pres. for Institutional Research, Planning and Assessment: SANDI TATMAN
Vice-Pres. for Advancement: ANNE MARIE TAYLOR
Vice-Pres. for Enrolment Services: K. SUE DUNCAN
Dir for Human Resources: THERESA RODGERS
Registrar: MICHAEL RAINE
Univ. Librarian: CLAUDIA CHESTER
Library of 100,000 vols, 1,000 print journals, 18,000 e-journals and 50,000 e-books
Number of teachers: 687
Number of students: 2,000

DEANS

College of Continuing Education: Dr JOSHUA LACHS
College of Graduate and Professional Studies: RUTH FASSINGER
College of Law: BARBIERI
College of Undergraduate Studies: MICHAEL GRANEY-MULHOLLAND
Extended Univ.: JOSHUA LACHS

LA SIERRA UNIVERSITY

4500 Riverwalk Parkway, Riverside, CA 92515
Telephone: (951) 785-2000
Fax: (951) 785-2901
E-mail: info@lasierra.edu
Internet: www.lasierra.edu
Founded 1922 as La Sierra Acad., present name 1990
Private Control
Academic year: September to June
Pres.: Dr RANDAL R. WISBEY
Provost: Dr STEVE PAWLUK
Vice-Pres. for Advancement and Univ. Relations: Dr NORMAN YERGEN

Vice-Pres. for Enrolment Services: DAVID LOFTHOUSE
Vice-Pres. for Financial Admin.: DAVID GERIGUIS
Vice-Pres. for Student Life: YAMI BAZAN
Registrar: FAYE SWAYZE
Library Dir: KITTY SIMMONS
Library of 260,395 vols, 646289 audiovisual material, 50,121 electronic books
Number of teachers: 110 (full-time)
Number of students: 2,199
Publications: *Adventist Heritage* (4 a year), *La Sierra University*

DEANS

College of Arts and Sciences: Dr ADENY SCHMIDT
School of Business: Dr JOHN THOMAS
School of Education: Dr ED BOYATT
School of Religion: Dr JOHN W. WEBSTER

LIFE CHIROPRACTIC COLLEGE WEST

25001 Industrial Blvd, Hayward, CA 94545
Telephone: (510) 780-4500
Fax: (510) 780-4525
Internet: www.lifewest.edu
Founded 1976 as Pacific States Chiropractic College, present name 1981
Private control
Academic year: September to June
Pres.: Dr BRIAN D. KELLY
Chief Financial Officer: REZA BADIEE
Dean for College: Dr JOSEPH FERGUSON
Dean for Health Center: Dr SCOTT DONALDSON
Exec. Dir for Enrolment: CARLOS R. ALICEA
Dir for Student Services, Job Location and Devt: JACKIE BIRON
Dir for Research: Dr DALE JOHNSON
Dir for Financial Aid: BRENDA R. JOHNSON
Registrar: ROBBIE SHERWOOD
Library Dir: ANNETTE OSENGA.

LIFE PACIFIC COLLEGE

1100 W Covina Blvd, San Dimas, CA 91773
Telephone: (909) 599-5433
Fax: (909) 599-6690
E-mail: info@lifepacific.edu
Internet: www.lifepacific.edu
Founded 1923, L.I.F.E. Bible College
Private control
Academic year: August to May
Pres.: Dr ROBERT FLORES
Vice-Pres. for Academic Affairs: Dr TERRY SAMPLES
Dir for Advancement: LYNNETTE LOZOYA
Dir for Institutional Research: BRUCE PRIMROSE
Chief Financial Officer: Rev. JARROD KULA
Dean for Students: J. J. PETERSON
Registrar: BRITTANY ADAMS
Librarian: KEITH DAWSON.

LOMA LINDA UNIVERSITY

Loma Linda, CA 92350
Telephone: (909) 558-1000
Fax: (909) 558-0242
E-mail: admissions.app@llu.edu
Internet: www.llu.edu
Founded 1905
Private control
Pres. and CEO: Dr RICHARD H. HART
Sr Vice-Pres. for Clinical Faculty: RICARDO PEVERINI
Sr Vice-Pres. for Educational Affairs: RONALD L. CARTER
Sr Vice-Pres. for Faculty Practice: DAVID WREN
Sr Vice-Pres. for Finance: STEVEN MOHR

Sr Vice-Pres. for Health Admin.: DANIEL FONTOURA
Sr Vice-Pres. for Human Resource Management and Risk Management: MARK L. HUBBARD
Sr Vice-Pres. for Managed Care: ZAREH SARRAFIAN
Sr Vice-Pres. for Strategic Planning: MICHAEL H. JACKSON
Exec. Vice-Pres. for Finance and Admin. and Chief Financial Officer: KEVIN J. LANG
Exec. Vice-Pres. for Hospital Affairs: RUTHITA J. FIKE
Exec. Vice-Pres. for Medical Affairs: H. ROGER HADLEY
Exec. Vice-Pres. for Univ. Affairs: RICHARD H. HART
Vice Pres. and CIO for Academia: DAVID P. HARRIS
Vice Pres. and CIO for Health Ministries: RICHARD HERGERT
Vice-Pres. for Allied Health Professions Education: CRAIG R. JACKSON
Vice-Pres. for Dentistry: CHARLES J. GOODACRE
Vice-Pres. for Diversity: LESLIE N. POLLARD
Vice-Pres. for Finance: ROD NEAL
Vice-Pres. for Graduate Medical Education: DANIEL W. GIANG
Vice-Pres. for Graduate Studies Education: ANTHONY J. ZUCCARELLI
Vice-Pres. for Healthcare Business Devt and Govt Relations: MEL SAUDER
Vice-Pres. for Nursing Education: MARILYN M. HERMANN
Vice-Pres. for Patient Care Services: ELIZABETH J. DICKINSON
Vice-Pres. for Public Affairs: W. AUGUSTUS CHEATHAM
Vice-Pres. for Quality: Dr JAMES PAPPAS
Vice-Pres. for Religious Education: Dr JON PAULIEN
Vice-Pres. for Spiritual Life and Wholeness: Dr GERALD R. WINSLOW
Dir of Libraries: CARLENE DRAKE
Library of 317,368 vols
Number of teachers: 1,393 (full-time)
Number of students: 4,212

DEANS

School of Allied Health Professions: Dr CRAIG R. JACKSON
School of Dentistry: Dr CHARLES J. GOODACRE
School of Medicine: Dr ROGER HADLEY
School of Nursing: Dr MARILYN H. HERMANN
School of Pharmacy: Dr W. WILLIAM HUGHES
School of Public Health: Dr JAMES KYLE
School of Religion: Dr JON PAULIEN
School of Science and Technology: BEVERLY J. BUCKLES

LOYOLA MARYMOUNT UNIVERSITY

1 LMU Dr., Los Angeles, CA 90045-2659
Telephone: (310) 338-2700
Internet: www.lmu.edu
Founded 1911, present name 1973
Private control
Academic year: August to May
Pres.: Dr DAVID W. BURCHAM
Chancellor: PATRICK J. CAHALAN
Sr Vice-Pres.: DAVID W. BURCHAM
Sr Vice-Pres. for Academic Affairs and Chief Academic Officer: Dr JOSEPH HELLIGE
Sr Vice-Pres. for Admin.: EVELYNNE B. SCARBOROUGH
Sr Vice-Pres. for Business and Finance: THOMAS FLEMING
Sr Vice-Pres. for Student Affairs: Dr ELENA M. BOVE
Sr Vice-Pres. for Univ. Relations: DENNIS SLON
Vice-Pres. for Communications and Govt Relations: KATHLEEN FLANAGAN

Vice-Pres. for Devt and Alumni Relations: BEDFORD MCINTOSH
Dir of Graduate Admissions: CHAKÉ KOUYOUMJIAN
Dean of Univ. Libraries: KRISTINE BRANCOLINI
Library of 561,498 vols (289,201 main campus; 272,297 Law School)
Number of teachers: 507 (full-time)
Number of students: 9,070 (5,797 undergraduate, 1,961 graduate and 1,312 Law School)

DEANS

Bellarmine College of Liberal Arts: PAUL TIYAMBE ZELEZA
College of Business Administration: Dr DENNIS W. DRAPER
College of Communication and Fine Arts: Prof. BARBARA J. BUSSE
Frank R. Seaver College of Science and Engineering: Dr RICHARD G. PLUMB
Loyola Law School: Dr VICTOR J. GOLD
School of Education: Dr SHANE P. MARTIN
School of Film and Television: STEPHEN UJLAKI

MASTER'S COLLEGE

21726 Placerita Canyon Rd, Santa Clarita, CA 91321
Telephone: (661) 259-3540
Fax: (661) 288-1037
E-mail: admissions@masters.edu
Internet: www.masters.edu
Founded 1927 as Los Angeles Baptist Theological Seminary, present name 1985
Private control
Areas of study: biblical counselling, biblical studies, biological and physical science, business, communication, computer and information sciences, English, history and political studies, home economics, liberal studies, mathematics, music, physical education, teacher education, divinity, theology
Pres.: Dr JOHN MACARTHUR
Exec. Vice-Pres. and Provost: Dr MARK TATLOCK
Vice-Pres. for Academic Affairs: Dr JOHN HUGHES
Vice-Pres. of Advancement: MARK AYDELOTTE
Vice-Pres. for Enrolment Management: Dr PAUL BERRY
Vice-Pres. for Finance: JASON HARTUNG
Vice-Pres. for Operations: ROBERT L. HOTTON
Dean for Student Life: JOE KELLER
Chief Operating Officer and Chief Information Officer: NATE PRINCE
Dir for Library Services: JOHN STONE
Library of 143,000 vols
Number of teachers: 70
Number of students: 1,100

MENLO COLLEGE

1000 El Camino Real, Atherton, CA 94027-4301
Telephone: (650) 543-3887
Fax: (650) 543-4102
E-mail: advancement@menlo.edu
Internet: www.menlo.edu
Founded 1927 as Menlo Junior College, present name 1949
Private control
Depts of communication, liberal arts and management
Pres.: Dr JAMES KELLY
Provost: Dr JIM WOOLEVER
Vice-Pres. for Student Services: DAVID PLACEY
Academic Dean: LOWELL PRATT
Dean for Business and Academic Affairs: DALE HOCKSTRA

Dean for Arts and Sciences: MARILYN THOMAS
Sr Assoc. Dir for Admissions: BOB WILMS
Dir for Financial Aid: ANNE HEATON-DUNLAP
Dir for Enrolment Management: CINDY MCGREW
Dean for Library and Information Services: C. BRIGID WELCH
Number of students: 750
Publication: *Advantage*.

MILLS COLLEGE

5000 MacArthur Blvd, Oakland, CA 94613
Telephone: (510) 430-2255
Fax: (510) 430-3298
E-mail: admission@mills.edu
Internet: www.mills.edu
Founded 1852 as Young Ladies' Seminary, as a college 1885
Private control
Academic year: August to May
Liberal arts college for women; co-educational graduate programmes
Pres.: Dr ALECIA A. DeCOUDREAUX
Provost and Dean of the Faculty: SANDRA GREER
Vice-Pres. and Gen. Counsel: THERESE LEONE
Vice-Pres. for Admin. and Human Resources: LESA HAMMOND
Vice-Pres. for Finance and Treas.: JAMIE NICKEL
Vice-Pres. for Operations and Chief of Staff: RENÉE JADUSHLEVER
Vice-Pres. for Institutional Advancement: CYNTHIA BRANDT STOVER
Dean for Undergraduate Admission: GIULIETTA AQUINO
Dean for Student Life: JOI D. LEWIS
Library of 240,000 vols; spec. collns 12,000 vols and 10,000 MSS, incl. Shakespeare's First Folio, a Mozart MSS, leaf from a Gutenberg Bible and 3,100 journals
Number of teachers: 203 (100 full-time, 103 part-time)
Number of students: 1,555
Publications: *580 Split* (1 a year), *Mills Academic Research Journal* (1 a year, online), *The Walrus* (1 a year), *Womanist, A Women of Color Journal* (1 a year)

DEANS

Fine Arts: MARY-ANN MILFORD
Graduate Literary Studies: CYNTHIA SCHEINBERG
Letters: RUTH SAXTON
Lorry I. Lokey Graduate School of Business: Dr DEBORAH MERRILL-SANDS
Natural Sciences and Education: LINDA KROLL
School of Education: KATHERINE SCHULTZ
Social Sciences: LAURA NATHAN

MONTEREY INSTITUTE OF INTERNATIONAL STUDIES: A GRADUATE SCHOOL OF MIDDLEBURY COLLEGE

460 Pierce St, Monterey, CA 93940
Telephone: (831) 647-4123
Fax: (831) 647-6405
E-mail: info@miis.edu
Internet: www.miis.edu
Founded 1955 as Monterey Institute of Foreign Studies, present name 2010
Academic year: September to June
Pres.: SUNDER RAMASWAMY
Provost: AMY SANDS
Dean for Student Services: TATE MILLER
Exec. Dir Institutional Advancement: KEVIN WASBAUER
Exec. Dir. for Finance: JAI SHANKAR
Exec. Dir for Strategic Planning and Technology: AMY MCGILL

Exec. Dir for Communications: JASON WARBURG
Library Dir: PETER LIU
Library of 100,000 vols, 500 print periodicals
Number of teachers: 117 (68 full-time, 49 part-time)
Number of students: 780

DEANS

Graduate School of International Policy and Management: YUWEI SHI
Graduate School of Translation, Interpretation and Language Education: RENEE JOURDENAIS

MOUNT ST MARY'S COLLEGE

Chalon Campus: 12001 Chalon Rd, Los Angeles, CA 90049-1599
Telephone: (310) 954-4000
Fax: (310) 954-4379
E-mail: mountnews@msmc.la.edu
Internet: www.msmc.la.edu
Founded 1925
Private control
Academic year: June to May
Liberal arts and sciences college primarily for women; depts of American studies, art, biological sciences, business admin., education, English, film and social justice, gerontology, history, humanities, language and culture, music, nursing, philosophy, physical sciences and mathematics, physical therapy, political science, psychology, religious studies, social work, sociology; campus in Doheny
Pres.: Dr ANN McELANEY-JOHNSON
Provost and Academic Vice-Pres.: Dr ELEANOR SIEBERT
Vice-Pres. for Admin. and Finance: CHRIS K. McALARY
Vice-Pres. for Information Support Service and Enrolment Management: LARRY SMITH
Vice-Pres. for Institutional Advancement: Dr STEPHANIE CUBBA
Vice-Pres. for Student Affairs: Dr JANE LINGUA
Dir of Libraries: CLAUDIA REED
Library of 140,000 vols
Number of teachers: 185
Number of students: 2,480 (1,980 undergraduates, 500 graduates)
Publication: *Mount Magazine* (2 a year).

NATIONAL UNIVERSITY

11255 N Torrey Pines Rd, La Jolla, CA 92037-1011
Telephone: (858) 642-8000
Fax: (858) 642-8708
E-mail: advisor@nu.edu
Internet: www.nu.edu
Founded 1971
Private control
Academic year: August to January
26 Learning centres throughout California; campuses at Carlsbad, La Mesa, Mission Valley, Rancho Bernardo, South Bay, Spectrum Business Park
Pres.: PATRICIA E. POTTER
Provost: Dr EILEEN D. HEVERON
Chancellor: Dr JERRY C. LEE
Exec. Vice-Pres.: Dr JOHN F. CADY
Exec. Vice-Pres. for Business and Regional Operation: RICHARD E. CARTER
Vice-Chancellor for Organizational Devt: Dr GARY FROST
Vice-Pres. for Admin and Business: KEVIN CASEY
Vice-Pres. for Advancement and Alumni Relations: MAGGIE T. WATKINS
Vice-Pres. for Regional Operations and Marketing: VIRGINIA BENEKE

Vice-Pres. for Strategic Planning: RICHARD C. JOY

Vice-Pres. for Student Services: Dr JOSEPH ZAVALA

Vice-Pres. for Univ. Relations: ROBERT FREELEN

Dean for Graduate Studies: (vacant)

Library Dir: ANNE MARIE SECORD

Library of 200,000 vols

Number of teachers: 1,096 (140 full-time, 85 assoc., 871 adjunct)

Number of students: 17,090 (full-time)

DEANS

College of Letters and Sciences: Dr MICHAEL MCANEAR

School of Business and Management: Dr RONALD UHLIG

School of Education: Dr KEN FAWSON

School of Engineering, Technology and Media: Dr JOHN A. CICERO

School of Health and Human Services: MICHAEL LACOURSE

NAVAL POSTGRADUATE SCHOOL

Public Affairs Office, Code 004, 1 University Circle, Monterey, CA 93943-5001

Telephone: (831) 656-2023

Fax: (831) 656-3238

E-mail: pao@nps.edu

Internet: www.nps.edu

Founded 1909 as School of Marine Engineering, present name 1919, present location 1951

State control

Academic year: October to September

Pres.: Vice-Admiral DANIEL T. OLIVER

Exec. Vice-Pres. and Provost: Dr LEONARD A. FERRARI

Vice-Provost for Academic Affairs: Dr DOUG MOSES

Vice-Pres. for Finance and Admin.: COLLEEN NICKLES

Vice-Pres. for Information Resources and Chief Information Officer: Dr CHRISTINE M. HAKSA

Vice-Pres. and Dean for Research: Dr KARL VAN BIBBER

Dean for Students: ALAN G. POINDEXTER

Univ. Librarian: ELEANOR UHLINGER

Library of 1,063,696 vols (incl. microform)

Number of teachers: 359

Number of students: 2,376

DEANS

Graduate School of Business and Public Policy: Dr WILLIAM R. GATES

Graduate School of Engineering and Applied Sciences: Dr PHILIP DURKEE

Graduate School of Operational Information Sciences: Dr PETER PURDUE

School of International Graduate Studies: Dr JAMES J. WIRTZ

NOTRE DAME DE NAMUR UNIVERSITY

1500 Ralston Ave, Belmont, CA 94002

Telephone: (650) 508-3500

Fax: (650) 508-3736

E-mail: pr@ndnu.edu

Internet: www.ndnu.edu

Founded 1851, chartered 1868, present location 1923

Private control

Pres.: Dr JUDITH MAXWELL GREIG

Provost: Dr DIANA DEMETRULIAS

Vice-Pres. for Advancement: MICHAEL J. ROMO

Vice-Pres. for Campus Life: RAYMOND JONES

Vice-Pres. for Enrolment Management: HERNAN BUCHELI

Vice-Pres. for Finance and Admin.: HENRY ROTH

Dean for Enrolment: JARRID WHITNEY

Librarian: Dr KLAUS MUSMANN

Registrar: SANDRA LEE

Library of 120,000 vols, 300 periodicals

Number of teachers: 103 (full-time)

Number of students: 1,790 (full-time and part-time)

DEANS

College of Arts and Sciences: Dr JOHN LEMMON

School of Business and Management: Dr BARBARA CAULLEY

School of Education and Leadership: Dr JOANNE ROSSI

OCCIDENTAL COLLEGE

1600 Campus Rd, Los Angeles, CA 90041

Telephone: (323) 259-2500

Fax: (323) 259-2958

E-mail: admission@oxy.edu

Internet: www.oxy.edu

Founded 1887

Private control

Academic year: August to May

Courses in American studies, art history and visual arts, Asian studies, biochemistry, biology, chemistry, cognitive science, critical theory and social justice, diplomacy and world affairs, economics, education, English and comparative literary studies, English writing, environmental programmes, geology, German, Russian, and classical studies, global affairs, history, kinesiology, mathematics, music, philosophy, physics, politics, psychobiology, psychology, religious studies, sociology, Spanish and French literary studies, Theatre, women's studies/gender studies

Pres.: Dr JONATHAN VEITCH

Vice-Pres. for Academic Affairs and Dean for the College: Dr JORGE GONZALEZ

Vice-Pres. for Admin.: MICHAEL P. GROENER

Vice-Pres. for Finance and Planning: AMOS HIMMELSTEIN

Vice-Pres. for Information Resources and Chief Information Officer: PAMELA MCQUESTEN

Vice-Pres. for Legal Affairs and Gen. Counsel: Dr SANDRA COOPER

Vice-Pres. for Student Affairs and Dean for Students: BARBARA J. AVERY

Vice-Pres. and Dean for Admission and Financial Aid: VINCE CUSEO

Sr. Vice-Pres. for Institutional Advancement and External Relations: DENNIS COLLINS

Registrar: VICTOR T. EGITTO

Librarian: EMILY BERGMAN

Library of 500,000 items (books, video and audio recordings and microfilms) and 1,255 current periodicals

Number of teachers: 169

Number of students: 2,102

OTIS COLLEGE OF ART AND DESIGN

9045 Lincoln Blvd, Los Angeles, CA 90045

Telephone: (310) 665-6800

Fax: (310) 665-6821

E-mail: admissions@otis.edu

Internet: www.otis.edu

Founded 1918

BAs in architecture/landscape/interiors, communication arts, digital media, fashion design, fine arts, interactive product design, toy design; MAs in fine arts, public practice, writing

Pres.: SAMUEL HOI

Provost: KERRY WALK

Vice-Pres. for Administrative and Financial Services: WILLIAM SCHAEFFER

Vice-Pres. for Enrolment Management: MARC MEREDITH

Vice-Pres. of Institutional Advancement: CARRIE STEWART

Dean for Admissions: YVETTE SOBKY

Dean for Student Affairs: LAURA KIRALLA

Registrar: ANNA MANZANO

Dir for Library: SUE MABERRY

Library of 25,000 vols, 5,000 videos and DVDs, 150 periodicals

Number of teachers: 200

Number of students: 1,200

PACIFIC LUTHERAN THEOLOGICAL SEMINARY

2770 Marin Ave, Berkeley, CA 94708

Telephone: (510) 524-5264

Fax: (510) 524-2408

E-mail: seminaryrelations@plts.edu

Internet: plts.edu

Founded 1950

Private control

MAs in Christian ministry, divinity and theological studies; partnership with Luther Seminary in St Paul, Minnesota

Academic year: September to May

Pres.: Dr PHYLIS ANDERSON

Vice-Pres. for Advancement: CINDY CARROLL

Academic Dean: MICHAEL AUNE

Dir for Admissions: Dr Rev. STEVEN CHURCHILL

Dean for Faculty: MICHAEL B. AULNE

Dean for Students and Registrar: CHERYL HEUER

Library Dir: ROBERT BENEDETTO

Library of 450,000 vols, 1,500 journal subscriptions, 290,000 other media holdings

Number of teachers: 150

Number of students: 1,350

PACIFIC OAKS COLLEGE

55 Eureka St, Pasadena, CA 91103

Telephone: (626) 529-8500

Fax: (626) 577-3502

E-mail: president@pacificoaks.edu

Internet: www.pacificoaks.edu

Founded 1945

Private control

Courses in human devt, marital and family therapy, teacher education programmes

Pres.: EZAT PARNIA

Provost: Dr MICHAEL HOROWITZ

Vice-Pres. for Institutional Advancement: KERRY NEAL

Registrar: MARSHA FRANKER

Librarian: NERMINE HANNA

Library of 17,000 vols

Number of teachers: 71

Number of students: 1,281

Publication: *Voices* (2 a year)

DEANS

College of Education: Dr KALANI BEYER

College of Human Development and Family Studies: Dr KALANI BEYER

Online Learning: Dr MARCIA MOODY

PACIFIC SCHOOL OF RELIGION

1798 Scenic Ave, Berkeley, CA 94709-1323

Telephone: (510) 849-8200

Fax: (510) 845-8948

E-mail: psrinfo@psr.edu

Internet: www.psr.edu

Founded 1866 as Pacific Theological Seminary, present name 1916; attached to Graduate Theological Union

Private control

Academic year: September to May

Pres.: RIESS POTTERVELD

Vice-Pres. for Academic Affairs and Dean: Dr TAT-SIONG BENNY LIEW
Vice-Pres. for Institutional Advancement: KATHI MCSHANE
Chief Financial Officer: STEVE ARGYRIS
Registrar: DELPHINE HWANG
Dir for Badè Museum: AARON BRODY
Library Dir: ROBERT BENETTO
Library of 700,000 vols
Number of teachers: 35 (15 core, 20 adjunct)
Number of students: 248

PACIFIC UNION COLLEGE

One Angwin Ave, Angwin, CA 94508
Telephone: (707) 965-6336
Fax: (707) 965-6671
E-mail: pr@puc.edu
Internet: www.puc.edu
Founded 1882
Private control
Academic year: September to June

Liberal arts college; depts of aviation, biology, business admin. and economics, chemistry, communication, computer science, education, English, exercise science, health and nutrition, history, honours, mathematics, modern languages, music, nursing, physics, psychology and social work, religion, visual arts
Pres.: Dr HEATHER KNIGHT
Vice-Pres. for Academic Admin. and Academic Dean: Dr NANCY LECOURT
Vice-Pres. for Advancement: Dr CAROLYN HAMILTON
Vice-Pres. for Financial Admin. and Chief Financial Officer: Dr DAVE LAURENCE
Vice-Pres. for Student Services: Dr LISA BISSELL PAULSON
Registrar: MARLO WATERS
Chair of Library Services: ADUGNAW WORKU
Library of 153,898 vols
Number of teachers: 135 (94 full time, 41 part time)
Number of students: 1,530
Publication: *PUC Viewpoint* (4 a year).

PACIFICA GRADUATE INSTITUTE

249 Lambert Rd, Carpinteria, CA 93013
Telephone: (805) 969-3626
Fax: (805) 565-1932
E-mail: contact@pacifica.edu
Internet: www.pacifica.edu
Founded 1976

Depts of clinical psychology, counselling psychology, depth psychology, depth psychotherapy, humanities, mythological studies
Chancellor: Dr STEPHEN AIZENSTAT
Pres.: Dr CAROL S. PEARSON
Provost: Dr PATRICIA KATSKY
Chief Financial Officer: DAVID HENKEL
Dean for Academic Affairs: Dr CINDY CARTER
Dir for Admissions: WENDY OVEREND
Dir for Institutional Advancement and Public Relations: ERIK H. DAVIS
Dir for Library Services: ALAIN DUSSERT
Registrar: FRANCINE MATAS.

PALO ALTO UNIVERSITY

1791 Arastradero Rd, Palo Alto, CA 94304
Telephone: (800) 818-6136
Fax: (650) 433-3888
E-mail: admissions@paloaltou.edu
Internet: www.paloaltou.edu
Founded 1975 as Pacific Graduate School of Psychology, present name 2009
Private control

Undergraduate and graduate and doctoral programmes; offers business psychology, clinical psychology, neuropsychology; psych-

ology and social action; mental health counselling
Pres.: Dr ALLEN D. CALVIN
Vice-Pres. for Academic Affairs: Dr WILLIAM FROMING
Registrar: NORA MARQUEZ.

PARDEE RAND GRADUATE SCHOOL

1776 Main St, Santa Monica, CA 90407-2138
Telephone: (310) 393-0411
Fax: (310) 451-6978
E-mail: prgs@prgs.edu
Internet: www.prgs.edu
Founded 1970
Private control

Areas of study: economics, empirical analysis, modelling and computational methods, policy analysis, science and technology, social and behavioural sciences
Dean: Dr SUSAN L. MARQUIS
Number of teachers: 154
Number of students: 110

PATTEN UNIVERSITY

2433 Coolidge Ave, Oakland, CA 94601
Telephone: (510) 261-8500
Fax: (510) 534-4344
E-mail: admissions@patten.edu
Internet: www.patten.edu
Founded 1944
Private control

Depts of art, biblical studies, Christian leadership, church ministries, communications, education, liberal studies for teaching, music, organizational management, pastoral studies, psychology, urban missions, youth ministry
Pres.: Dr GARY R. MONCHER
Academic Vice-Pres. and Provost: Dr KENNETH ROMINES
Vice-Pres. for Univ. Services: DARLA E. CUADRA
Vice-Pres. for Finance and Admin.: ANDREW M. GANES
Dean for Enrolment Services: ROBERT OLIVERA
Dean for Student Services: SHARON BARTA
Library Dir: ANN ZEMENS
Library of 35,000 vols, 180 periodicals.

PEPPERDINE UNIVERSITY

24255 Pacific Coast Highway, Malibu, CA 90263
Telephone: (310) 506-4000
Internet: www.pepperdine.edu
Founded 1937 as college, present status 1970
Private control

Pres. and Chief Exec. Officer: ANDREW K. BENTON
Chancellor: Dr CHARLES B. RUNNELS
Provost and Chief Academic Officer: Dr DARRYL TIPPENS
Exec. Vice-Pres. and Chief Operating Officer: GARY HANSON
Sr Vice-Pres. for Investments and Chief Investment Officer: JEFF PIPPIN
Sr Vice-Pres. for Planning, Information and Technology: Dr NANCY MAGNUSSON
Vice-Pres. for Advancement and Public Affairs: KEITH HINKLE
Dean for Admission and Enrolment Management: PAUL A. LONG
Dean for Int. Programs: CHARLES HALL
Dean for Libraries: MARK S. ROOSA
Dean for Student Affairs: MARK DAVIS
Registrar: HUNG V. LE
Library: 7 libraries with a combined colln of 1m. vols
Number of teachers: 300 (full-time)

Number of students: 7,700
Publication: *Pepperdine People Magazine*

DEANS
Frank R. Seaver College of Letters, Arts, and Sciences: RICK MARRS
George L. Graziadio School of Business and Management: LINDA A. LIVINGSTONE
Graduate School of Education and Psychology: MARGARET WEBER
School of Law: DEANELL REECE TACHA
School of Public Policy: JAMES R. WILBURN

PROFESSORS
Frank R. Seaver College of Letters, Arts, and Sciences:
ADJEMIAN, C., Mathematics
ADLER, R., Marketing
ARDOIN, B., Communication
BAIM, D., Economics and Finance
BAIRD, D., History
BANKS, J., Management and Organizational Behaviour
BATCHELDER, R., Economics
BUCHANAN, R. W., Communication
CALDWELL, D. E., Social Sciences
CARROLL, L. A., English
CASEY, M. W., Communication
CHANDLER, R., Communication
CHESNUTT, R. D., Religion
CLEGG, C., English
CLOUD, D. C., Accounting
COBB, G., Music
COLLINGS, M. R., English
DAVIS, S., Biology
DOWDEY, D., German
DUNPHY, M., Physical Education
FALKNER, A., Art
FELTNER, M., Sports Medicine
GAMBILL, K., English
GANSKE, J., Chemistry
GIBONEY, S., Education
GIBSON, D., Philosophy
GOSE, M. D., Education
GREEN, D. B., Chemistry
HANCOCK, D. L., Mathematics
HART, G. W., English
HENDERSON, J., Theatre
HUGHES, R. T., Religion
KATS, L., Biology
LANGFORD, M., French
LOVE, S., Religion
LOWRY, D. N., Communication
MACRAE, H., Sports Medicine
MACRAE, P., Sports Medicine
MADDOX, R. B., Mathematics
MARRS, R. R., Religion
MARTIN, K. L., Biology
MONSMA, S., Political Science
MURRIE, M., Telecommunications
MYERS, V., English
NEILSON, G., Theatre
PARKENING, C., Music
PAYNE-PALACIO, J., Nutritional Science
PHILLIPS, W., Physics
PIASENTIN, J., Art
PULLEN, M., Music
REINECK, L., English
SESHAN, V., Management
SEXTON, R. L., Social Sciences
SHATZER, M., Communication
SHORES, D., Broadcasting
STRACHE, C. V., Physical Education
SUMMERS, M. R., Business Administration
SWARTZENDRUBER, D., Biology
THOMAS, J., English
THOMASON, P. B., Spanish
THOMPSON, D., Mathematics
TYLER, R. L., Religion
WARFORD, S., Computer Science
WEBB, G. T., Japanese Cultural History
WHITE, J. B., Chemistry
WILSON, J. F., New Testament
YATES, J. E., Organizational Behaviour and Management

George L. Graziadio School of Business and Management:

BLEUEL, W. H., Quantitative Methods
BUSKIRK, B. D., Marketing
DARDEN, C. E., Organization and Management
DUDLEY, T. J., Quantitative Methods
FLIEGE, S., Quantitative Methods
FOJTIK, C. W., Marketing
GERTMENIAN, W., Economics
GOODRICH, J., Int. Business
HAGAN, A. J., Economics
HALL, O. P., Jr, Quantitative Methods
HESSE, R., Quantitative Methods
HITCHIN, D. E., Management
HOISMAN, A. J., Behavioural Science
HUNT, C. J., Jr, Business Law
LARSON, W. G., Business Law
MALLINGER, M., Organization Behaviour
MARTINOFF, J. T., Finance
MOTAMEDI, K. K., Organization and Management
NICKLES, M. D., Economics
PENDERGHAST, T. F., Quantitative Methods
PETRO, F. A., Accounting
REISMAN, G., Economics
RICHARDSON, J. E., Marketing
RIERDAN, R. C., Behavioural Science
ROCKEY, E., Behavioural Science
SAMUELSON, B. A., Accounting
SANFORD, E., Economics
SHAFER, W., Accounting
SIEGEL, S., Technology Management
STANLEY, D. J., Finance and Accounting
STROM, W. L., Behavioural Science
VARDIABASIS, D., Economics
YOUNG, T. W., Economics

School of Education and Psychology:

ASAMEN, J. K., Psychology
COZOLINO, L. J., Psychology
FOY, D., Psychology
GARCIA, C. L., Education
HARRELL, S. P., Psychology
HEDGESPETH, J., Psychology
HIATT-MICHAEL, D., Education
HIBBS, C., Psychology
INGRAM, B., Psychology
LEVY, D. A., Psychology
LOWE, D. W., Psychology
McCALL, C., Research Methods
McMANUS, J. F., Education
MARTINEZ, T., Psychology
NEELY, F. W., Psychology
PAULL, R., Education
POLIN, L. G., Education
ROWE, D., Psychology
SÁNCHEZ, M., Education
SCHMIEDER-RAMIREZ, J., Education
SHAFRANSKE, E. P., Psychology
STEPHENS, R., Education

School of Law:

ALFORD, R. P.
BOST, T. G.
BOYD, K. L.
BUCHAN, L.
CALDWELL, H. M.
CHASE, C. A.
COCHRAN, R. F., Jr
COE, J. J., Jr
GAFFNEY, E. M., Jr
GASH, J. A.
GOODMAN, C. C.
GRADISHER, M. R.
GRAFFY, C. P.
JAMES, B.
KERR, C. L.
KERR, J. E.
KNAPLUND, K. S.
LEVINE, S. J.
LOWRY, L. R.
McCRORY, J. P.
McDERMOTT, A. X.
McDONALD, B. P.
McGOLDRICK, J. M., Jr

MARTIN, D. W.
MENDOZA, A.
MILLER, A.
NELSON, C. I.
OGDEN, G. L.
PERRIN, L. T.
POPOVICH, R.
PUSHAW, R. J.
ROBINSON, P.
SAXER, S. R.
SCARBERRY, M. S.
SEYMOUR, A. D.
SMITH, M. L.
WENDEL, P. T.
WESTON, M. A.

School of Public Policy:

LLOYD, G., Public Policy
McALLISTER, E., Public Policy
MONSMA, S. V., Political Science
SEXTON, R., Economics
VAN EATON, C., Public Policy
VARDIABASIS, D., Economics
WILSON, J. Q., Public Policy

PITZER COLLEGE

1050 N Mills Ave, Claremont, CA 91711-6110

Telephone: (909) 621-8000
E-mail: admission@pitzer.edu
Internet: www.pitzer.edu

Founded 1963; attached to Claremont Colleges

Private control

Language of instruction: English

Academic year: August to May

Pres.: Dr LAURA SKANDERA TROMBLEY
Vice-Pres. for Academic Affairs and Dean for Faculty: ALAN JONES
Vice-Pres. for Admin. and Treas.: YUET LEE
Vice-Pres. and Dean for Admission and Financial Aid: ANGEL B. PÉREZ
Vice-Pres. for College Advancement: ADRIAN STEVENS
Vice-Pres. for Marketing and Public Relations and Marketing: ANNA CHANG
Vice-Pres. for Student Affairs: JIM MARCHANT
Registrar: EVA PETERS
Librarian: ALBERTA WALKER

Library: 2m. vols, 70,000 periodicals

Number of teachers: 75

Number of students: 1,000

POINT LOMA NAZARENE UNIVERSITY

3900 Lomaland Dr., San Diego, CA 92106-2810

Telephone: (619) 849-2200
Fax: (619) 849-2579
E-mail: admissions@ptloma.edu
Internet: www.pointloma.edu

Founded 1902 as Pacific Bible College, present name 1998

Private control

Academic year: August to May

Depts of art and design, biology, chemistry, communication and theatre, family and consumer sciences, history and political science, kinesiology, literature, journalism and modern languages, mathematics, information and computer sciences, music, physics and eng., psychology, sociology and social work; campuses in Arcadia, Bakersfield and Mission Valley

Pres.: Dr BOB BROWER
Provost and Chief Academic Officer: Dr KERRY D. FULCHER
Vice-Pres. for External Relations: JOSEPH E. WATKINS, III
Vice-Pres. for Financial Affairs: GEORGE R. LATTER
Vice-Pres. for Spiritual Devt: MICHAEL A. PITTS

Vice-Pres. for Student Devt: CAYE BARTON SMITH
Vice-Pres. for Univ. Advancement: DANIEL J. MARTIN
Dir for Admissions: SCOTT SHOEMAKER
Dir for Learning Services: Dr FRANK QUINN
Number of students: 3,500

DEANS

Fermanian School of Business: Dr KEN ARMSTRONG
School of Education: Dr GARY L. RAILSBACK
School of Nursing: Dr BARB TAYLOR
School of Theology and Christian Ministry: Dr RON BENEFIEL

POMONA COLLEGE

333 N College Way, Claremont, CA 91711-6312

Telephone: (909) 621-8000
Internet: www.pomona.edu

Founded 1887

Private control

Coe-ducational, nonsectarian, undergraduate college of liberal arts and sciences

Pres.: DAVID W. OXTOBY
Vice-Pres. for Academic Affairs and Dean of the College: CECILIA CONRAD
Vice-pres. for Advancement: CHRISTOPHER PONCE
Vice-Pres. for Devt: CHRIS PONCE
Vice-Pres. and Dean for Students: MIRIAM FELDBLUM
Vice-Pres. for Planning: RICHARD FASS
Vice-Pres. and Treas.: KAREN SISSON
Dean of Admissions and Financial Aid: SETH ALLEN
Registrar: MARGARET ADORNO

Library: 1.9m. vols

Number of teachers: 191

Number of students: 1,560

Publication: *Pomona College Magazine* (3 a year).

SAINT MARY'S COLLEGE OF CALIFORNIA

1928 St Mary's Rd, Moraga, CA 94556

Telephone: (925) 631-4000
Internet: www.stmarys-ca.edu

Founded 1863

Private control

Pres.: Dr RONALD GALLAGHER
Provost and Vice-Pres. for Academic Affairs: Dr BETHAMI DOBKIN
Vice-Pres. for Advancement and Planning: Bro. STANISLAUS SOBCZYK
Vice-Pres. for College Communications and Vice-Provost for Enrollment: MICHAEL BESEDA
Vice-Pres. for Devt: Dr KEITH E. BRANT
Vice-Pres. for Finance: PETER A. MICHELL
Dean of Academic Resources: PAT KREITZ
Vice-Provost for Academic Affairs: FRANCES SWEENEY
Vice-Provost for Student Life: Dr JANE CAMARILLO

Library of 200,000 vols, 1,100 current periodicals

Number of teachers: 192 (full-time)

Number of students: 3,917

DEANS

Kalmanovitz School of Education: Dr PHYLLIS METCALF-TURNER
School of Economics and Business Administration: Dr ZHAN LI
School of Liberal Arts: Dr STEPHEN WOOLPERT
School of Science: Dr Prof. ROY WENSLEY

SAMRA UNIVERSITY OF ORIENTAL MEDICINE

3545 Wilshire Blvd., Suite 355, Los Angeles, CA 90010

Telephone: (213) 381-1700
Internet: www.samra.edu
Founded 1965
Private control
Languages of instruction: English, Chinese, Korean
Academic year: October to September
Areas of study: acupuncture theory; anatomy; basic sciences; Chinese herbology; Chinese medical theory; Oriental medicine; physiology
Pres.: Dr TAE CHEONG CHOO
Vice-Pres.: Dr BYUNG S. HONG
Provost: Dr KAATSUYUKI SAKAMOTO
Academic Dean: DEANNIE JANOWITZ
Registrar: ELIZABETH GOMEZ
Librarian: GAN YE
Library of 7,000 items.

SAMUEL MERRITT UNIVERSITY

3100 Telegraph Ave, Oakland, CA, 94609

Telephone: (510) 869-6511
Fax: (510) 869-6525
E-mail: information@samuelmerritt.edu
Internet: www.samuelmerritt.edu
Founded 1909, present name 2009
Campuses in Oakland, Sacramento, San Francisco and San Mateo
Pres. and CEO: SHARON DIAZ
Academic Vice-Pres. and Provost: Dr SCOT FOSTER
Vice-Pres. for Enrollment and Student Services: JOHN GARTEN-SHUMAN
Vice-Pres. for Finance and Admin.: GREGORY GINGRAS
Library Dir: MARCUS BANKS
Library of 13,896 vols, 26,697 bound journals, 474 current periodicals
Number of teachers: 251 (110 full-time, 141 part-time)
Number of students: 1,400

DEANS

School of Nursing: Dr AUDREY BERMAN
School of Podiatric Medicine: Dr JOHN N. VENSON

SAN DIEGO CHRISTIAN COLLEGE

2100 Greenfield Dr., El Cajon, CA 92019

Telephone: (619) 201-8700
Fax: (619) 201-8749
E-mail: admissions@sdcc.edu
Internet: www.sdcc.edu
Founded 1970 as Christian Heritage College, present name 2005
Private control
Academic year: September to May
Depts of aviation, adult professional studies (degree completion), biblical studies, business, communication, education, English, history and social science, kinesiology, mathematics, music, psychology, biological science
Pres.: Dr PAUL AGUE
Vice-Pres. of Academic Affairs: JON DePRIEST
Vice-Pres. for Student Life: JON DePRIEST
Vice-Pres. for Enrolment and Marketing: MITCH FISK
Vice-Pres. for Admin. and Finance: KEN YODER
Dean for Admin. and Finance: ROBERT JENSEN
Dean for Students: STEVE JENKINS
Registrar: SUSIE PARKS
Dir for Library Services: RUTH MARTIN
Library of 119,850 vols
Number of students: 403

Publication: *IMPACT* (1 a year).

SAN DIEGO STATE UNIVERSITY

5500 Campanile Dr., San Diego, CA 92182-8000

Telephone: (619) 594-5200
Internet: www.sdsu.edu
Founded 1897 as San Diego Normal School, present name 1970
Academic year: May to May
Pres.: ELLIOT HIRSHMAN
Provost for Academic Affairs: NANCY A. MARLIN
Vice-Pres. for Business and Financial Affairs: SALLY F. ROUSH
Vice-Pres. for Univ. Relations and Devt: MARY RUTH CARLETON
Vice-Pres. for Research and Dean of Graduate Affairs: STEPHEN WELTER
Vice-Pres. for Student Affairs: JAMES R. KITCHEN
Exec. Dir for Enrolment Services: SANDRA COOK
Dean of Library: GALE ETSCHMAIER
Library of 1,342,735 vols, 644,028 govt documents
Number of teachers: 1,795 (985 full-time, 810 part-time)
Number of students: 30,016 (24,590 undergraduate, 5,426 graduate)
Publications: *360: The Magazine of San Diego State University*, *Fiction International* (1 a year), *Journal of Borderlands Studies* (2 a year), *Mobilization* (3 a year), *Pacific Coast Council on Latin-American Studies* (2 a year), *Pacific Review: A West Coast Arts Review Annual*, *Poetry International* (1 a year)

DEANS

College of Arts and Letters: PAUL WONG
College of Business Admin.: MICHAEL R. CUNNINGHAM
College of Education: Dr RIC A. HOVDA
College of Engineering: Dr DAVID T. HAYHURST
College of Extended Studies: JOE SHAPIRO
College of Health and Human Services: MARILYN NEWHOFF
College of Professional Studies and Fine Arts: JOYCE M. GATTAS
College of Sciences: STANLEY MALOY
Graduate Division: STEVEN WELTER
Imperial Valley Campus: DAVID PEARSON
Undergraduate Division: GEOFFREY W. CHASE

SAN FRANCISCO ART INSTITUTE

800 Chestnut St, San Francisco, CA 94133

Telephone: (415) 771-7020
E-mail: admissions@sfai.edu
Internet: www.sfai.edu
Founded 1871 as San Francisco Art Asscn, present name 1961
Private control
Academic year: August to May
Areas of study: design and technology, filmmaking, liberal arts, new genres, painting, photography, printmaking, sculpture
Pres.: CHARLES DESMARAIS
Sr Vice-Pres. for Finance and Admin.: JUDY LOGAN
Vice-Pres. and Dean for Academic Affairs: Dr JEANNENE PRZYBLYSKI
Vice-Pres. for Enrolment: ELIZABETH O'BRIEN
Vice-Pres. for Academic Planning and Facilities: JENNIFER STEIN
Vice-Pres. for Devt and Alumni Relations: CYNTHIA PERRY COLEBROOK
Vice-Pres. for Advancement: KATHY LOWRY
Dean for Students: YUNNY YIP

Library of 26,000 vols.

SAN FRANCISCO CONSERVATORY OF MUSIC

50 Oak St, San Francisco, CA 94102-6011

Telephone: (415) 864-7326
Fax: (415) 503-6299
Internet: www.sfcm.edu
Founded 1917 as Ada Clement Piano School, present name 1923
Private control
Depts of brass, chamber music, conducting, composition, guitar, keyboards, percussion, strings, voice, woodwinds; undergraduate and graduate degrees, postgraduate diplomas
Pres.: COLIN MURDOCH
Vice-Pres. for Advancement: BESS TOUMA
Vice-Pres. for Finance and Admin.: KATHRYN WITTENMYER
Dean: MARY ELLEN POOLE
Dir. of Admission: MELISSA COCCO-MITTEN
Registrar: JONAS WRIGHT
Head Librarian: KEVIN McLAUGHLIN
Library of 60,000 vols, incl. 38,000 scores and parts, 15,000 audio visual items, 12,500 books and 77 periodicals
Number of teachers: 112 (32 full-time, 80 part-time)
Number of students: 400

SAN FRANCISCO STATE UNIVERSITY

1600 Holloway Ave, San Francisco, CA 94132

Telephone: (415) 338-1111
Fax: (415) 338-2514
E-mail: sfsuinfo@sfsu.edu
Internet: www.sfsu.edu
Founded 1899 as San Francisco State Normal School
Academic year: August to DecemberJanuary to MayJune to August (3 semesters)
Pres.: Dr ROBERT A. CORRIGAN
Provost and Vice-Pres. for Academic Affairs: Dr SUE V. ROSSER
Exec. Vice-Pres. for Admin. and Finance and Chief Financial Officer: LEROY M. MORISHITA
Vice-Pres. for Student Affairs and Dean of Students: J. E. (PENNY) SAFFOLD
Vice-Pres. for Univ. Advancement: ROBERT J. NAVA (acting)
Registrar: SUZANNE DMYTRENKO
Univ. Librarian: DEBORAH C. MASTERS
Library of 1,160,869 items, incl; 2,557,985 microforms, 193,202 audiovisual items, 17,119 subscription periodicals
Number of teachers: 1,591
Number of students: 29,718

Publication: *SF State Magazine*

DEANS

College of Arts and Humanities: PAUL SHERWIN
College of Behavioural and Social Sciences: JOEL KASSIOLA
College of Business: CARAN COLVIN
College of Ethnic Studies: KENNETH P. MONTEIRO
College of Extended Learning: GAIL WHITAKER
College of Health and Human Services: DON TAYLOR (acting)
College of Science and Engineering: SHELDON AXLER
Graduate College of Education: Dr JACOB E. PEREA

SAN FRANCISCO THEOLOGICAL SEMINARY

105 Seminary Rd, San Anselmo, CA 94960
Telephone: (415) 451-2800
Fax: (415) 451-2851
E-mail: info@sfts.edu
Internet: www.sfts.edu
Founded 1871; attached to Graduate Theological Union
Private control
Pres.: Dr Rev. JAMES L. MCDONALD
Vice-Pres. for Academic Affairs and Dean for the Seminary: Dr ELIZABETH LIEBERT
Vice-Pres. for Admin. and Finance and Chief Financial Officer: BARBARA BRENNER BUDER
Vice-Pres. for Institutional Advancement: Rev. SCOTT SHELDON
Dean: Dr ELIZABETH LIEBERT
Registrar: Dr POLLY COOTE
Library Dir (GTU): ROBERT BENETTO
Librarian (SFTS): MICHAEL PETERSON
Library of 100,000 vols.

SAN JOSÉ STATE UNIVERSITY

1 Washington Sq., San José, CA 95192
Telephone: (408) 924-1000
Internet: www.sjsu.edu
Founded 1857
Pres.: MOHAMMAD QAYOUMI
Provost and Vice-Pres. for Academic Affairs: Dr ELLEN JUNN
Vice-Pres. for Admin. and Finance: SHAWN BIBB
Vice-Pres. for Student Affairs: WILLIAM NANCE
Vice-Pres. for Univ. Advancement: NANCY BUSSANI
Librarian: ROBERT BRUCE
Library of 900,000 vols, 3,500 periodical titles
Number of teachers: 627 (full-time)
Number of students: 30,236

DEANS

Charles W. Davidson College of Engineering: Dr BELLE WEI
College of Applied Sciences and Arts: Dr CHARLES BULLOCK
College of Business: Dr DAVID M. STEELE
College of Humanities and the Arts: KARL TOEPFER
College of Science: J. MICHAEL PARRISH
College of Social Sciences: SHEILA BIENENFELD
Connie L. Lurie College of Education: ELAINE CHIN
Continuing Education: MARK NOVAK

SANTA CLARA UNIVERSITY

500 El Camino Real, Santa Clara, CA 95053
Telephone: (408) 554-4000
Internet: www.scu.edu
Founded 1851 as Santa Clara College, present name 1985
Private control
Academic year: September to June
Chancellor: WILLIAM REWAK
Pres.: MICHAEL ENGH
Provost: DENNIS C. JACOBS
Vice-Pres. for Admin. and Finance: ROBERT WARREN
Vice-Pres. for Enrolment Management: MICHAEL SEXTON
Vice-Pres. for Univ. Relations: ROBERT GUNSALUS
Gen. Counsel: JOHN OTTOBONI
Registrar: MONICA AUGUSTIN
Univ. Librarian: ELIZABETH SALZER
Library of 800,000 vols, law library of 370,000 vols

Number of teachers: 852 (461 full-time, 391 part-time)
Number of students: 8,846
Publications: *Explore* (2 a year), *Santa Clara Law* (2 a year), *Santa Clara Magazine* (4 a year), *STS Nexus* (2 a year)

DEANS

College of Arts and Sciences: W. ATOM YEE (acting)
Jesuit School of Theology: KEVIN F. BURKE
Leavey School of Business: Dr DREW STARBIRD
School of Education and Counselling Psychology: ATOM YEE
School of Engineering: GODFREY MUNGAL
School of Law: DONALD J. POLDEN

SAYBROOK UNIVERSITY

747 Front St, Third Fl., San Francisco, CA 94111-1920
Telephone: (415) 433-9200
Fax: (415) 433-9271
E-mail: info@saybrook.edu
Internet: www.saybrook.edu
Founded 1971 as Saybrook Graduate School and Research Center
Academic year: September to July
Pres.: Dr MARK SCHULMAN
Exec. Vice-Pres.: Dr ARTHUR C. BOHART, Jr
Vice-Pres. for Academic Affairs: Dr DANIEL SEWELL
Vice-Pres. for Marketing and Enrolment Management: SIGRID BADINELLI
Vice-Pres. for Operations and CFO: MICHAEL CAIRNS
Dir for Admissions: CATHLEEN FUSCO
Dir for Research and Library Services: NOAH LOWENSTEIN
Registrar: AARON HIATT
Number of teachers: 114 (20 executive, 22 consulting, 72 part-time)
Number of students: 525
Publication: *International Journal of Transpersonal Studies* (1 a year)

DEANS

Graduate College of Mind-Body Medicine: JAMES S. GORDON
Graduate College of Psychology and Humanistic Studies: Dr ROBERT SCHMITT
LIOS Graduate College of Leadership Studies: CYNTHIA FITZGERALD

SCRIPPS COLLEGE

1030 Columbia Ave, Claremont, CA 91711
Telephone: (909) 621-8000
Internet: www.scrippscollege.edu
Founded 1926; attached to Claremont Colleges
Private control
Pres.: LORI BETTISON-VARGA
Vice-Pres. and Dean of Admission and Financial Aid: PATRICIA F. GOLDSMITH
Vice-Pres. and Dean of Faculty: Dr AMY MARCUS-NEWHALL
Vice-Pres. for Devt and College Relations: MARTHA H. KEATES
Vice-Pres. for Enrolment: VICTORIA ROMERO
Vice-Pres. for Financial and Business Affairs: JOANNE M. COVILLE
Vice-Pres. for Institutional Advancement: MIKE ARCHIBALD
Vice-Pres. for Student Affairs and Dean of Students: REBECCA R. LEE
Librarian: JUDY HARVEY SAHAK
Library of 110,000 vols in Denison Library and 10,000 in Rare Book Room
Number of teachers: 95 (69 full-time and 26 part-time)
Number of students: 859

SIMPSON UNIVERSITY

2211 College View Dr., Redding, CA 96003
Telephone: (530) 224-5600
Fax: (530) 226-4861
E-mail: registrar@simpsonu.edu
Internet: www.simpsonu.edu
Founded 1921 as Simpson Bible Institute, Simpson College 1971
Private control
Academic year: September to July
Pres.: Dr LARRY J. MCKINNEY
Provost: Dr STANLEY CLARK
Exec. Vice-Pres. and and Treas. and Chief Financial Officer: BRADLEY E. WILLIAMS
Vice-Pres. for Advancement: GORDON B. FLINN
Vice-Pres. for Enrolment Management: Dr HERB TOLBERT
Vice-Pres. for Student Devt: Dr RICHARD BROWN
Dean for Education: GLEE R. BROOKS
Dir ASPIRE Programme: PATTY TAYLOR
Registrar: WENDY RIDDLE
Dir for Library Services: LARRY L. HAIGHT
Library of 70,000 vols
Number of students: 1,216

DEANS

A. W. Tozer Theological Seminary: Dr SARAH SUMNER
School of Continuing Studies: PATTY TAYLOR
School of Education: Dr GLEE BROOKS
School of Traditional Undergraduate Studies: ROBIN DUMMER

SONOMA STATE UNIVERSITY

1801 E Cotati Ave, Rohnert Park, CA 94928-3609
Telephone: (707) 664-2880
Fax: (707) 664-2505
Internet: www.sonoma.edu
Founded 1960 as Sonoma State College, present name and status 1978
Academic year: August to June
Pres.: Dr RUBEN ARMIÑANA
Provost and Vice-Pres. for Academic Affairs: Dr ANDREW ROGERSON
Chief Financial Officer and Vice-Pres. for Admin. and Finance: Dr LAURENCE FURUKAWA-SCHLERETH
Vice-Pres. for Univ. Devt: ERIK GREENY
Vice-Pres. for Student Affairs and Enrolment Management: MATTHEW LOPEZ-PHILLIPS
Vice-Pres. for Univ. Affairs: DAN CONDRON
Library Dean: Dr BARBARA BUTLER
Library of 670,000 vols, 35,000 periodicals and 275,000 items
Number of teachers: 1,511
Number of students: 8,921

DEANS

School of Arts and Humanities: Dr THAINE STEARNS
School of Business and Economics: Dr WILLIAM SILVER
School of Education: Dr CARLOS AYALA
School of Extended Education: Dr MARK MERICKEL
School of Science and Technology: Dr LYNN STAUFFER
School of Social Sciences: Dr ELAINE LEEDER

SOUTHERN CALIFORNIA COLLEGE OF OPTOMETRY

2575 Yorba Linda Blvd, Fullerton, CA 92831-1699
Telephone: (714) 870-7226
Fax: (714) 879-0481
Internet: www.scco.edu
Founded 1904
Private control

Pres.: Dr KEVIN L. ALEXANDER
Vice-Pres. and Dean for Academic Affairs: Dr Prof. MORRIS S. BERMAN
Vice-Pres. and Dean for Clinical Affairs: Dr JULIE A. SCHORNACK
Vice-Pres. for Advancement and Marketing: PAUL A. STOVER
Vice-Pres. for Financial Affairs and Chief Financial Officer: LISA K. ALBERS
Vice-Pres. for Student Affairs: Dr LORRAINE I. VOORHEES
Librarian: DONNA JEAN MATTHEWS
Library of 10,000 vols, 6,500 bound journals and 300 current periodicals
Number of teachers: 80 (full-time and part-time)
Number of students: 381
Publications: *Alumniscope* (2 a year), *SCCO Admissions Catalog* (every 2 years).

SOUTHERN CALIFORNIA UNIVERSITY OF HEALTH SCIENCES

16200 E Amber Valley Dr., Whittier, CA 90604-4051
Telephone: (562) 947-8755
E-mail: admissions@scuhs.edu
Internet: www.scuhs.edu
Founded 1911 as Los Angeles College of Chiropractic
Pres.: Dr JOHN SCARINGE
Vice-Pres. for Academic Affairs: TODD KNUDSEN
Vice-Pres. of Admin. and Finance: THOMAS ARENDT
Vice-Pres. for Institutional Advancement: REGINA WEBSTER
Assoc. Vice-Pres. for Student Affairs: GEOFFREY JOWETT
Chief Financial Officer: ROGER JENKINS

DEANS

College of Acupuncture and Oriental Medicine: Dr WEN-SHUO WU
Los Angeles College of Chiropractic: MICHAEL SACKETT

SOUTHWESTERN LAW SCHOOL

3050 Wilshire Blvd, Los Angeles, CA 90010
Telephone: (213) 738-6700
Fax: (213) 383-1688
E-mail: admissions@swlaw.edu
Internet: www.swlaw.edu
Founded 1911
Private control
Academic year: August to July
Dean and CEO: BRYANT G. GARTH
Vice-Dean for Academic Affairs: AUSTEN L. PARRISH
Assoc. Dean for Academic Admin.: DOREEN E. HEYER
Assoc. Dean for Career Services: GARY J. GREENER
Assoc. Dean for Institutional Advancement: DEBRA L. LEATHERS
Assoc. Dean for Library Services: LINDA WHISMAN
Assoc. Dean for Research: ARTHUR F. MCEVOY
Assoc. Dean for Students and Diversity Affairs: H. NYREE GRAY
Assoc. Dean and Gen. Counsel: PATRICK PYLE
Assoc. Dean for Public Affairs: LESLIE R. STEINBERG
Asst Dir for Admissions: LISA M. GEAR
Dir for Financial Aid: WAYNE MAHONEY
Dir for Registration and Academic Records: CAROLYN HAITH
Chief Financial Officer: PAUL KALUSH
Chief Information Systems Officer: BO SUZOW
Chief Operating Officer: JANICE A. MANIS
Library of 500,000 vols
Number of teachers: 56 (full-time)

Number of students: 1,050
Publications: *Journal of International Media and Entertainment Law, Southwestern Journal of International Law, Southwestern Law Review.*

SAINT MARY'S COLLEGE OF CALIFORNIA

1928 St Mary's Rd, Moraga, CA 94556
Telephone: (925) 631-4000
Internet: www.stmarys-ca.edu
Founded 1863
Private control
Pres.: Dr RONALD GALLAGHER
Provost and Vice-Pres. for Academic Affairs: Dr BETHAMI DOBKIN
Vice-Pres. for Advancement and Planning: Bro. STANISLAUS SOBCZYK
Vice-Pres. for College Communications and Vice-Provost for Enrollment: MICHAEL BESEDA
Vice-Pres. for Devt: Dr KEITH E. BRANT
Vice-Pres. for Finance: PETER A. MICHELL
Dean of Academic Resources: PAT KREITZ
Vice-Provost for Academic Affairs: FRANCES SWEENEY
Vice-Provost for Student Life: Dr JANE CAMARILLO
Library of 200,000 vols, 1,100 current periodicals
Number of teachers: 192 (full-time)
Number of students: 3,917

DEANS

Kalmanovitz School of Education: Dr PHYLLIS METCALF-TURNER
School of Economics and Business Administration: Dr ZHAN LI
School of Liberal Arts: Dr STEPHEN WOOLPERT
School of Science: Dr Prof. ROY WENSLEY

ST PATRICK'S SEMINARY & UNIVERSITY

320 Middlefield Rd, Menlo Park, CA 94025
Telephone: (650) 325-5621
Fax: (650) 323-5447
E-mail: info@stpatricksseminary.org
Internet: www.stpatricksseminary.org
Founded 1898
Private control
Academic year: September to May
Chancellor: Dr Rev. GEORGE H. NIEDERAUER
Pres., Rector and Vice-Chancellor: Dr Rev. JAMES L. MCKEARNEY
Vice-Pres. and Sec.: Rev. JOHN C. WESTER
Vice-Pres. for Advancement: CHRISTOPHER GRASSO
Vice-Pres. for Business and Finance: JENNIFER MORRIS
Academic Dean: Rev. GLADSTONE STEVENS
Dean for Students: Rev. VINCENT D. BUI
Registrar: NURIA ORTIZ
Library Manager: LAUREN JOHN
Library of 100,000 vols, 250 periodicals.

STANFORD UNIVERSITY

450 Serra Mall, Stanford, CA 94305-2004
Telephone: (650) 723-2300
Internet: www.stanford.edu
Founded 1885
Private control
Academic year: September to June
Pres.: Dr JOHN HENNESSY
Provost: Dr JOHN ETCHEMENDY
Vice-Pres. and Gen. Counsel: DEBRA L. ZUMWALT
Vice-Pres. for Alumni Affairs: HOWARD WOLF
Vice-Pres. for Business Affairs and CFO: RANDALL S. LIVINGSTON
Vice-Pres. for Devt: MARTIN SHELL

Vice-Pres. for Land, Bldgs and Real Estate: ROBERT REIDY
Vice-Pres. for Public Affairs: DAVID DEMAREST
Vice-Pres., Stanford Linear Accelerator Center: WILLIAM J. MADIA
Registrar: THOMAS C. BLACK
Vice-Provost for Graduate Education: PATRICIA GUMPORT
Vice-Provost for Undergraduate Education: HARRY ELAM
Vice-Provost and Dean of Research: ANN ARVIN
Univ. Librarian: MICHAEL KELLER
Library: see Libraries and Archives
Number of teachers: 1,903
Number of students: 15,666
Publications: *Journal of Law, Business and Finance* (2 a year), *Stanford Environmental Law Journal* (2 a year), *Stanford Humanities Review* (2 a year), *Stanford Journal of International Law* (2 a year), *Stanford Law Review* (6 a year), *Stanford Social Innovation Review* (4 a year)

DEANS

Continuing Studies: CHARLES JUNKERMAN
Graduate School of Business: GARTH SALONER
School of Earth Sciences: PAMELA A. MATSON
School of Education: CLAUDE STEELE
School of Engineering: JAMES D. PLUMMER
School of Humanities and Sciences: RICHARD SALLER
School of Law: LARRY KRAMER
School of Medicine: Dr PHILIP PIZZO

PROFESSORS

AAKER, J. L., Graduate School of Business
ADLER, J. R., Jr, Neurosurgery
ADMATI, A. R., Graduate School of Business
ALBANESE, C., Surgery
ALBERS, G. W., Neurology
ALDRICH, R. W., Molecular and Cell Physiology
ALEXANDER, J. C., Law
ALEXANDER, S. R., Paediatrics
AMEMIYA, T., Economics
ANDERSEN, H., Chemistry
ANDERSON, R. U., Jr, Urology
ANDRIACCHI, T. P., Mechanical Engineering
APOSTOLIDES, J.-M., French and Italian
ARBER, D., Pathology
ARIAGNO, R. L., Paediatrics
ARVIN, A. M., Paediatrics
ATHEY, S. C., Economics
ATLAS, S. W., Radiology
ATTANASAIO, O., Economics
AYDIN, A., Geology and Environmental Sciences
AZIZ, K., Petroleum Engineering
BABCOCK, B., Law
BACHRACH, L. K., Paediatrics
BAER, U., German Studies
BAKER, B. S., Biological Sciences
BAKER, K., History
BAMBOS, N., Management Science and Engineering
BANDURA, A., Psychology
BANKMAN, A. J., Law
BARCHIESI, A., Classics
BARLEY, S., Management Science and Engineering
BARNETT, D., Materials Science and Engineering
BARNETT, W., Graduate School of Business
BARON, D. P., Graduate School of Business
BARON, E. J., Pathology
BARON, J. N., Graduate School of Business
BARRES, B. A., Neurobiology
BARSH, G. S., Paediatrics
BARTH, M. E., Graduate School of Business
BARTH, R. A., Radiology
BAUGH, J., Education
BEACH, D., Mechanical Engineering
BEASLEY, M., Applied Physics

BEAVER, W. H., Graduate School of Business
BEININ, J. S., History
BENDER, J., English
BENDOR, J., Graduate School of Business
BENITZ, W. E., Paediatrics
BERGER, K., Music
BERMAN, R. A., German Studies
BERNHARDT, E., German Studies
BERNHEIM, B. D., Economics
BERNSTEIN, B., History
BERNSTEIN, D., Paediatrics
BEROZA, G. C., Geophysics
BETTINGER, J. R., Communication
BIELEFELDT, C. W., Religious Studies
BIENENSTOCK, A. I., Stanford Synchrotron Radiation Laboratory
BIRD, D. K., Geological and Environmental Sciences
BLACK, B. S., Law
BLAND, R. D., Paediatrics
BLANDFORD, R., Stanford Linear Acceleration Center
BLASCHKE, T., Medicine
BLAU, H. M., Molecular Pharmacology
BLOCH, D. A., Health Research and Policy
BLOCK, S. M., Applied Physics
BLOOM, E., Stanford Linear Accelerator Center
BLUMENKRANZ, M. S., Ophthalmology
BOBO, L., Sociology
BOOTHROYD, J. C., Microbiology and Immunology
BORJA, R. I., Civil and Environmental Engineering
BOSKIN, M., Economics
BOWER, G. H., Psychology
BOWMAN, C., Mechanical Engineering
BOXER, S., Chemistry
BOYD, S. P., Electrical Engineering
BOYER, A. L., Radiation Oncology
BRADY, D., Graduate School of Business
BRANDEAU, M. L., Management Science and Engineering
BRATMAN, M., Philosophy
BRAUMAN, J. J., Chemistry
BRAUND, S., Classics
BRAVMAN, J. C., Materials Science and Engineering
BREIDENBACH, M., Stanford Linear Accelerator Center
BRESNAHAN, T., Economics
BRESNAN, J., Linguistics
BROCK-UTNE, J. G., Anaesthesia
BRODSKY, J. B., Anaesthesia
BRODSKY, S., Stanford Linear Accelerator Center
BROTHERSTON, J. G., Spanish and Portuguese
BROWN, G. H., English
BROWN, J. M., Radiation Oncology
BROWN, P. O., Biochemistry
BRUMFIEL, G., Mathematics
BRUNGER, A. T., Molecular and Cellular Physiology
BRUTLAG, D. L., Biochemistry
BRYK, A., Education
BUC, P. C., History
BULOW, J. I., Graduate School of Business
BUMP, D. W., Mathematics
BURCHAT, P. R., Physics
BURGELMAN, R. A., Graduate School of Business
BURKE, D. L., Stanford Linear Accelerator Center
BUTCHER, E. C., Pathology
BYER, R., Applied Physics
BYERS, T. H., Management Science and Engineering
CABRERA, B., Physics
CALLAN, E., Education
CAMARILLO, A. M., History
CAMPBELL, A. M., Biological Sciences
CANTWELL, B., Aeronautics, Astronautics
CARLSON, R., Management Science and Engineering
CARLSON, R. W., Medicine
CARLSSON, G., Mathematics

CARNOY, M., Education
CARRAGEE, E. J., Orthopaedic Surgery
CARROLL, G. R., Graduate School of Business
CARSON, C., History
CARSTENSEN, L. L., Psychology
CARTER, D., Mechanical Engineering
CARTER, S., Asian Languages
CASEY, E. B., English
CASPER, G., Law
CASPER, R., Psychiatry
CASTLE, T., English
CHAFE, C. D., Music
CHAMBERLAIN, C. P., Geological and Environmental Sciences
CHAN, P. H., Neurosurgery
CHANG, F. K., Aeronautics and Astronautics
CHAO, A. W., Stanford Linear Accelerator Center
CHERITON, D. R., Computer Science
CHIEN, Y. K., Microbiology and Immunology
CHRISTENSEN, R. M., Aeronautics and Astronautics
CHU, G., Medicine
CHU, S., Physics
CIOFFI, J. M., Electrical Engineering
CLAERBOUT, J. F., Geophysics
CLARK, E., Linguistics
CLARK, H. H., Psychology
CLAYBERGER, C. A., Paediatrics
CLEARY, M. L., Pathology
CLEMENS, B. M., Materials Science and Engineering
COHEN, H. J., Paediatrics
COHEN, M., French and Italian
COHEN, P. J., Mathematics
COHEN, R. L., Mathematics
COHEN, S. E., Anaesthesia
COHEN, S. N., Genetics
COLE, G. M., Law
COLLMAN, J. P., Chemistry
CONTI, M., Gynaecology and Obstetrics
COOK, K. S., Sociology
COOKE, J. P., Medicine
COOPER, A., Medicine
CORK, L., Comparative Medicine
CORN, W., Art, Art History
CORNELL, C. A., Civil and Environmental Engineering
COTTLE, R. W., Management Science and Engineering
COVER, T. M., Electrical Engineering
COX, D., Electrical Engineering
COX, K. L., Paediatrics
CRABTREE, G., Pathology
CRASWELL, R., Law
CROSS, P. C., Structural Biology
CUTKOSKY, M. R., Mechanical Engineering
DAHL, G. V. H., Paediatrics
DAINES, R., Law
DALLY, W. J., Electrical Engineering
DAMON, W., Education
DARLING-HAMMOND, L., Education
DAUSKARDT, R. H., Materials Science and Engineering
DAVID, P. A., Economics
DAVIS, M. M., Microbiology and Immunology
DAVIS, R., Biochemistry
DEIERLEIN, G. G., Civil and Environmental Engineering
DE KRUYFF, R. H., Paediatrics
DE MARZO, P. M., Graduate School of Business
DEMBO, A., Mathematics
DEMENT, W. C., Psychiatry
DE MICHELI, G., Electrical Engineering
DENNY, M. W., Biological Sciences
DEVINE, A., Classics
DIACONIS, P., Statistics
DILL, D. L., Computer Science
DIMOPOULOS, S., Physics
DIRZO, R., Biological Sciences
DIXON, L. J., Stanford Linear Accelerator Center
DOLAN, J., Drama
DONALDSON, S., Radiation Oncology
DONIACH, S., Applied Physics

DONOHO, D., Statistics
DORFAN, J., Stanford Linear Accelerator Center
DORFMAN, L., Neurology
DRELL, P. S., Stanford Linear Accelerator Center
DRUZIN, M. L., Obstetrics and Gynaecology
DUFFIE, J. D., Graduate School of Business
DUNBAR, R. B., Geological and Environmental Sciences
DUPUY, J.-P., French and Italian
DURBIN, P. A., Mechanical Engineering
DURHAM, W., Anthropological Sciences
DURLOFSKY, L. J., Petroleum Engineering
DUTTON, R., Electrical Engineering
EATON, J. K., Mechanical Engineering
ECKERT, P., Linguistics
EFRON, B., Statistics
EGBERT, P., Ophthalmology
EHRLICH, P. R., Biological Sciences
EISEN, A. M., Religious Studies
EISENHARDT, K. M., Management Science and Engineering
EISNER, E. W., Education
EL GAMAL, A., Electrical Engineering
ELAM, H. J., Jr, Drama
ELIASHBERG, J., Mathematics
ENGE, P. K., Aeronautics and Astronautics
ENGLAND, P., Sociology
ENGLEMAN, E., Pathology
EPEL, D., Biological Sciences
ERNST, W. G., Geology, Environmental Sciences
ESQUIVEL, C., Surgery
ETCHEMENDY, J. W., Philosophy
EVANS, J. M., English
EVERITT, C. W. F., Hansen Laboratory
FAINSTAT, T., Obstetrics and Gynaecology
FAJARDO, L., Pathology
FALKOW, S., Microbiology and Immunology
FARHAT, C., Mechanical Engineering
FATHMAN, C., Medicine
FAURE, B. R., Religious Studies
FAYER, M., Chemistry
FEARON, J. D., Political Science
FEE, W., Surgery
FEINSTEIN, C. B., Psychiatry
FEJER, M. M., Applied Physics
FELDMAN, D., Medicine
FELDMAN, M. W., Biological Sciences
FELSTINER, J., English
FEREJOHN, J. A., Political Science
FERGUSON, J., Cultural and Social Anthropology
FERNALD, R. D., Psychology
FERNEYHOUGH, B., Music
FERRELL, J. E., Jr, Molecular Pharmacology
FETTER, A. L., Physics
FIELD, C., Biological Sciences
FIELDS, K., English
FIKES, R. E., Computer Science
FINDLEN, P., History
FIORINA, M. P., Political Science
FIRE, A., Pathology
FISH, K. J., Anaesthesia
FISHER, G., Law
FISHER, R. S., Neurology
FISHKIN, J., Communication
FISHKIN, S. F., English
FLANAGAN, R., Graduate School of Business
FLEISHMAN, L., Slavic Languages and Literature
FLIEGELMAN, J. W., English
FOLLESDAL, D., Philosophy
FORD, J. M., Psychiatry
FORD, R. T., Law
FORTMANN, S. P., Medicine
FOSTER, G., Graduate School of Business
FOWLER, M. B., Medicine
FRANCKE, U., Genetics
FRANK, C., Chemical Engineering
FREEDMAN, E., History
FREIDIN, G., Slavic Languages and Literature
FRIED, B., Law
FRIEDLANDER, L., English
FRIEDMAN, J. H., Statistics

FRIEDMAN, L. M., Law
FRIEDMAN, M., Philosophy
FRIES, J. F., Medicine
FROELICHER, V. F., Medicine
FULLER, G. G., Chemical Engineering
FULLER, M. T., Developmental Biology
FURTHMAYR, H., Pathology
GABA, D. M., Anaesthesia
GABRIELLI, J., Psychology
GALLI, S. J., Pathology
GAMBHIR, S., Radiology
GAMBLE, J. G., Orthopaedic Surgery
GARBER, A. M., Medicine
GARCIA-MOLINA, H., Computer Science
GARNER, C. C., Psychiatry
GARWIN, E. L., Stanford Linear Accelerator Center
GELLER, E., Anaesthesia
GIACCIA, A. J., Radiation Oncology
GIACOMINI, J. C., Medicine
GIBBONS, J. F., Electrical Engineering
GILLY, W. F., Biological Sciences
GILSON, R. J., Law
GIROD, B., Electrical Engineering
GIUDICE, L. C., Obstetrics and Gynaecology
GLADER, B. E., Paediatrics
GLASSER, T. L., Communication
GLAZER, G. M., Radiology
GLICK, I., Psychiatry
GLOVER, G. H., Radiology
GLYNN, P. W., Management Science and Engineering
GOLDSTEIN, J. L., Political Science
GOLDSTEIN, P. L., Law
GOLUB, G. H., Computer Science
GOODE, R., Surgery
GOODMAN, S. B., Functional Restoration
GORDON, D. M., Biological Sciences
GORELICK, S. M., Geological and Environmental Sciences
GORIS, M., Radiology
GOSLING, J. A., Surgery
GOTLIB, I. H., Psychology
GOULD, J., Paediatrics
GOULDER, L. H., Economics
GRAHAM, S. A., Geological and Environmental Sciences
GRANOVETTER, M., Sociology
GRAY, R., Electrical Engineering
GRECO, R. S., Surgery
GREELY, H. T., Law
GREENBERG, H., Medicine
GREENBERG, P., Medicine
GREENE, R., English
GREGG, R. C., Religious Studies
GREIF, A., Economics
GRENADIER, S. R., Graduate School of Business
GREY, T. C., Law
GROSSMAN, P. L., Education
GRUENFELD, D. H., Graduate School of Business
GRUMET, F. C., Pathology
GRUNDFEST, J. A., Law
GRUSKY, D. B., Sociology
GUIBAS, L. J., Computer Science
GUILLEMINAULT, C., Psychiatry
GUMBRECHT, J. U., French and Italian
GUMPORT, P. J., Education
HABER, S. H., History
HAERTEL, E. H., Education
HAKUTA, K., Education
HALL, R., Economics
HAMMER, L. D., Paediatrics
HAMMOND, P., Economics
HANAWALT, P. C., Biological Sciences
HANCOCK, S. L., Radiation Oncology
HANLEY, F. L., Cardiothoracic Surgery
HANNAH, D., Art, Art History
HANNAN, M., Graduate School of Business
HANRAHAN, P. M., Computer Science
HANSON, R., Mechanical Engineering
HARO, M.-P., Spanish and Portuguese
HARRIS, J. M., Geophysics
HARRIS, J. S., Electrical Engineering
HARRIS, S. E., Electrical Engineering

HARRISON, J. M., Graduate School of Business
HARRISON, R. P., French and Italian
HARSH, G. R., IV, Neurosurgery
HASTIE, T. J., Statistics
HAUSMAN, W., Management Science and Engineering
HEDMAN, G.-B., Stanford Synchrotron Radiation Laboratory
HELLER, H. C., Biological Sciences
HELLER, T. C., Law
HENDRICKSON, M. R., Pathology
HENNESSY, J., Electrical Engineering
HENSLER, D. R., Law
HENTZ, V. R., Surgery
HERFKENS, R. J., Radiology
HERSCHLAG, D., Biochemistry
HERTZENBERG, L. A., Genetics
HERZOG, T., History
HESSELINK, L., Electrical Engineering
HIMEL, T. M., Stamford Linear Accelerator Center
HINTON, S., Music
HINTZ, R., Paediatrics
HLATKY, M. A., Health Research and Policy
HODDER, I., Cultural and Social Anthropology
HODGSON, K., Chemistry
HOFFMAN, A. R., Medicine
HOLLOWAY, D., Political Science
HOPPE, R., Radiation Oncology
HORNE, R. N., Petroleum Engineering
HORNING, S. J., Medicine
HOROWITZ, L., Psychology
HOROWITZ, M. A., Electrical Engineering
HOTSON, J. R., Neurology
HOWARD, R. A., Management Science and Engineering
HOYME, H. E., Paediatrics
HSUEH, A., Obstetrics and Gynaecology
HUESTIS, W., Chemistry
HUNT, S., Medicine
INAN, U. S., Electrical Engineering
INGLE, J., Geological and Environmental Sciences
ISHII, K., Mechanical Engineering
IYENGAR, S., Communication
JACKLER, R., Otolaryngology and HNS
JACOBS, C. D., Medicine
JAFFE, R. A., Anaesthesia
JAMESON, A., Aeronautics and Astronautics
JARDETZKY, O., Molecular Pharmacology
JARDETZKY, T., Structural Biology
JAROS, J. A., Stanford Linear Accelerator Center
JEFFREY, R. B., Radiology
JOHNSTONE, I. M., Statistics
JONES, P., Biological Sciences
JOURNEL, A., Petroleum Engineering
JUEL, C., Education
KAHN, J., Electrical Engineering
KAHN, M. S., Art, Art History
KAHN, S., Stanford Linear Accelerator Center
KAISER, A. D., Biochemistry
KALLOSH, R., Physics
KAMAE, T., Stanford Linear Accelerator Center
KAPITULNIK, A., Applied Physics
KAPP, D. S., Radiation Oncology
KARL, T. L., Political Science
KARLAN, P., Law
KASEVICH, M., Physics
KATZNELSON, Y., Mathematics
KAY, M., Linguistics
KAY, M. A., Paediatrics
KAZOVSKY, L. G., Electrical Engineering
KEEFFE, M., Medicine
KELLEY, D. M., Mechanical Engineering
KELMAN, M. G., Law
KENDIG, J., Anaesthesia
KENNEDY, D. M., History
KERCKHOFF, S. P., Mathematics
KERNER, J. A., Paediatrics
KESSLER, D. P., Graduate School of Business
KESSLER, R., Urology
KHATIB, O., Computer Science
KHAVARI, P. A., Dermatology

KHOSLA, C. S., Chemical Engineering
KILLEN, J. D., Medicine
KIM, S. K., Developmental Biology
KING, A. C., Health Research and Policy
KINGSLEY, D. M., Developmental Biology
KIPARSKY, P., Linguistics
KIREMIDJIAN, A. S., Civil and Environmental Engineering
KIRKEGAARD, K, Microbiology and Immunology
KIRST, M., Education
KITANIDIS, P. K., Civil and Environmental Engineering
KLAUSNER, M., Law
KLEIN, R. G., Anthropological Studies
KLENOW, P., Economics
KNIGHT, R., Geophysics
KNUDSEN, E. I., Neurobiology
KOBILKA, B. K., Medicine
KOCHERLAKOTA, N., Economics
KOLLMAN, N. S., History
KOOL, E. T., Chemistry
KOPITO, R. R., Biological Sciences
KORAN, L. M., Psychiatry
KORNBERG, R. D., Structural Biology
KOSEFF, J. R., Civil and Environmental Engineering
KOSEK, J., Pathology
KOVACH, R. L., Geophysics
KRAEMER, F. B., Medicine
KRAEMER, H., Psychiatry
KRAMER, R. M., Graduate School of Business
KRANE, E. J., Anaesthesia
KRASNER, S., Political Science
KRASNOW, M. A., Biochemistry
KRAWINKLER, H., Civil and Environmental Engineering
KRAWITZ, J., Communication
KREHBIEL, K., Graduate School of Business
KRENSKY, A. M., Paediatrics
KREPS, D., Graduate School of Business
KROO, I. M., Aeronautics and Astronautics
KROSNICK, J. A., Communication
KRUGER, C. H., Mechanical Engineering
KRUMBOLTZ, J. D., Education
KRUMMEL, T. M., Surgery
KURZ, M., Economics
LABAREE, D., Education
LAI, T. L., Statistics
LAITIN, D., Political Science
LAM, M. S., Computer Science
LANE, A. T., Dermatology
LANE, B., Radiology
LATOMBE, J.-C., Computer Science
LATTIN, J. M., Graduate School of Business
LAU, L. J., Economics
LAUGHLIN, R., Physics
LAVORI, P. W., Health Research and Policy
LAW, K. H., Civil and Environmental Engineering
LAZEAR, E. P., Graduate School of Business
LECKIE, J., Civil and Environmental Engineering
LEE, H. L., Graduate School of Business
LEHMAN, I. R., Biochemistry
LEIFER, L., Mechanical Engineering
LEITH, D., Stanford Linear Accelerator Center
LEIVICK, J. R., Art and Art History
LELE, S. K., Aeronautics and Astronautics
LEMLEY, M., Law
LENOIR, T., History
LEPPER, M., Psychology
LERER, S., English
LESSIG, L., Law
LEUNG, L. L., Medicine
LEVIN, B., Linguistics
LEVITT, L. J., Medicine
LEVITT, M., Structural Biology
LEVITT, R. E., Civil and Environmental Engineering
LEVY, R., Medicine
LEVY, S., Medicine
LEWIS, M. E., Asian Languages
LI, J., Mathematics
LINDE, A., Physics

LINK, M., Paediatrics
LIOU, J., Geological and Environmental Sciences
LIPSICK, J., Pathology
LITT, I., Paediatrics
LIU, T.-P., Mathematics
LOAGUE, K., Geological and Environmental Sciences
LOEW, G. A., Stanford Linear Accelerator Center
LONG, S., Biological Sciences
LONGAKER, M. T., Surgery
LORIG, K., Medicine
LOUGEE CHAPPELL, C., History
LOWE, D. R., Geological and Environmental Sciences
LUENBERGER, D. G., Management Science and Engineering
LUNSFORD, A., English
LUTH, V., Stanford Linear Acceleration Center
LUTHY, R. G., Civil and Environmental Engineering
MCADAM, D., Sociology
MCCALL, M., Classics
MCCLUSKEY, E. J., Electrical Engineering
MCCONNELL, S. K., Biological Sciences
MACCORMACK, R., Aeronautics and Astronautics
MCDERMOTT, R., Education
MCDEVITT, H. O., Microbiology and Immunology
MCDONALD, J. G., Graduate School of Business
MCDOUGALL, I. R., Radiology
MCGINN, R. E., Management Science and Engineering
MCGUIRE, J., Dermatology
MCKAY, D., Structural Biology
MCKINNON, R. I., Economics
MCLAUGHLIN, M. W., Education
MCMAHAN, U. J., Neurobiology
MCMILLAN, R. J., Graduate School of Business
MCNICHOLS, M., Graduate School of Business
MCNUTT, M. K., Geophysics
MACURDY, T., Economics
MADIX, R. J., Chemical Engineering
MAHOOD, G. A., Geological and Environmental Sciences
MALENKA, R. C., Psychiatry
MANCALL, M., History
MANNA, Z., Computer Science
MARINA, N., Paediatrics
MARKMAN, E., Psychology
MARKUS, H., Psychology
MARMOR, M., Ophthalmology
MARTIN, J., Graduate School of Business
MARTIN, R. P., Classics
MATHESON, G. O., Orthopaedic Surgery
MATHEWS, M. V., Music
MATIN, A., Microbiology and Immunology
MATSON, P. A., Geological and Environmental Sciences
MAVKO, G. M., Geophysics
MAZZEO, R. R., Mathematics
MENDELSON, H., Graduate School of Business
MENDEZ, M. A., Law
MENDOZA, F. S., Paediatrics
MENG, T. H.-Y., Electrical Engineering
MERIGAN, T., Medicine
MEYER, T. W., Medicine
MICHELSON, P. F., Physics
MIGNOT, E., Psychiatry
MIHM, F. G., Anaesthesia
MILGRAM, R. J., Mathematics
MILGROM, P., Economics
MILLER, D. A. B., Electrical Engineering
MILLER, D. C., Cardiothoracic Surgery
MILLER, D. T., Graduate School of Business
MILLER, E., Geological and Environmental Sciences
MINTS, G., Philosophy
MITCHELL, J. C., Computer Science
MITCHELL, R. S., Cardiothoracic Surgery
MOBLEY, W. C., Neurology

MOCARSKI, E. S., Microbiology and Immunology
MOCHLY-ROSEN, D., Molecular Pharmacology
MOE, T. M., Political Science
MOERNER, W. E., Chemistry
MOIN, P., Mechanical Engineering
MOLDOWAN, J. M., Geological and Environmental Sciences
MONISMITH, S. G., Civil and Environmental Engineering
MOONEY, H. A., Biological Sciences
MOOS, R. H., Psychiatry
MORA-MANGANO, C., Anaesthesia
MORAVCSIK, J. M., Philosophy
MORETTI, F., English
MORRIS, I., Classics
MORRIS, R. E., Cardiothoracic Surgery
MOSS, R. B., Paediatrics
MOTWANI, R., Computer Science
MUNGAL, M. G., Mechanical Engineering
MURRAY, W., Management Science and Engineering
MUSEN, M. A., Medicine
MYERS, B., Medicine
MYERS, R. M., Genetics
NAIMARK, N., History
NAPEL, S. A., Radiology
NASS, C. I., Communications
NEALE, M. A., Graduate School of Business
NELSON, D. V., Mechanical Engineering
NELSON, W. J., Molecular and Cell Physiology
NETZ, R., Classics
NEWSOME, W. T., III, Neurobiology
NISHI, Y., Electrical Engineering
NISHIMURA, D. G., Electrical Engineering
NOLL, R., Economics
NUR, A., Geophysics
NUSSE, R., Developmental Biology
OAKES, D. D., Surgery
OI, J., Political Science
OKIMOTO, D. I., Political Science
OLCOTT, C., IV, Surgery
OLKIN, I., Statistics
OLSHEN, R., Health Research and Policy
OLZAK, S., Sociology
OMARY, M. B., Medicine
O'REILLY, C. A., III, Graduate School of Business
ORGEL, S., English
ORNSTEIN, D., Mathematics
ORR, F., Petroleum Engineering
ORTOLANO, L., Civil and Environmental Engineering
OSGOOD, B. G., Electrical Engineering
OSHEROFF, D., Physics
OWEN, A. B., Statistics
OYER, P. E., Cardiothoracic Surgery
PADILLA, A., Education
PALUMBI, S., Biological Sciences
PALUMBO-LIU, D. J., Comparative Literature
PAPANICOLAOU, G. C., Mathematics
PARHAM, P., Structural Biology
PARKER, G. G. C., Graduate School of Business
PARKER, P., English
PARNES, J. R., Medicine
PATE-CORNELL, E., Management Science and Engineering
PATELL, J., Graduate School of Business
PATERSON, J., Stanford Linear Accelerator Center
PAULRAJ, A., Electrical Engineering
PAULSON, B., Civil and Environmental Engineering
PEA, R., Education
PEARL, R., Anaesthesia
PEASE, R., Electrical Engineering
PECORA, R., Chemistry
PELC, N. J., Radiology
PENCAVEL, J., Economics
PERKASH, I., Urology
PERLROTH, M. G., Medicine
PERRY, J., Philosophy
PERRY, W., Management Science and Engineering

PESKIN, M., Stanford Linear Accelerator Center
PETERS, P. S., Linguistics
PETERSEN, J., Medicine
PETROSIAN, V., Physics
PFEFFER, J., Graduate School of Business
PFEFFER, S. R., Biochemistry
PFEFFERBAUM, A., Psychiatry
PFLEIDERER, P., Graduate School of Business
PHELAN, P., Drama
PHILIP, A. G. S., Paediatrics
PHILLIPS, D., Education
PHIZACKERLEY, R. P., Stanford Synchrotron Radiation Laboratory
PIANETTA, P., Stanford Synchrotron Radiation Laboratory
PINSKY, P. M., Mechanical Engineering
PIZZO, P. A., Paediatrics
PLUMMER, J., Electrical Engineering
POLAN, M., Obstetrics and Gynaecology
POLHEMUS, R., English
POLINSKY, A., Law
POLLARD, D. D., Geological and Environmental Sciences
POPP, R., Medicine
PORTEUS, E., Graduate School of Business
POWELL, W. W., Education
PRATT, M., Spanish and Portuguese
PREDMORE, M., Spanish and Portuguese
PRESCOTT, C., Stanford Linear Accelerator Center
PRINCE, D. A., Neurology
PRINZ, F. B., Mechanical Engineering
PROBER, C. G., Paediatrics
PROCTOR, R., History
QUERTERMOUS, T., Medicine
QUINN, H., Stanford Linear Accelerator Center
RABIN, R. L., Law
RABINOVITCH, M., Paediatrics
RADIN, M., Law
RAJAN, M. V., Graduate School of Business
RAKOVE, J., History
RAMIREZ, F., Education
RAMPERSAD, A., English
RAMSAUR, M. F., Drama
RECHT, L., Neurology
REEVES, B., Communication
REHM, M. R., Drama
REICHELSTEIN, S. J., Graduate School of Business
REINHARD, M., Civil and Environmental Engineering
REISS, A. L., Psychiatry
REISS, P. C., Graduate School of Business
REITZ, B., Cardiothoracic Surgery
REMINGTON, J. S., Medicine
RHINE, W. D., Paediatrics
RHODE, D. L., Law
RICE, C., Political Science
RICHTER, B., Stanford Linear Accelerator Center
RICKFORD, J., Linguistics
RIDGEWAY, C., Sociology
RIGGS, D., English
RINSKY, L. A., Orthopaedic Surgery
RISCH, N. J., Genetics
RIVERS, D., Political Science
RIZK, N. W., Medicine
ROBERTS, D. F., Communication
ROBERTS, D. J., Graduate School of Business
ROBERTS, E. S., Computer Science
ROBERTS, R. L., History
ROBERTSON, C. R., Chemical Engineering
ROBINSON, J. A., Political Science
ROBINSON, O. W., III, German Studies
ROBINSON, P., History
ROCK, S. M., Aeronautics and Astronautics
RODRIGUE, A., History
ROMANO, J., Statistics
ROMER, P., Graduate School of Business
RORTY, R., Comparative Literature
ROSALDO, R. I., Jr, Cultural and Social Anthropology
ROSENTHAL, M. H., Anaesthesia
ROSS, L., Psychology

ROTH, B., Mechanical Engineering
ROTH, R. A., Molecular Pharmacology
ROTH, W., Psychiatry
ROUGHGARDEN, J., Biological Sciences
ROUSE, R. V., Pathology
RUBIN, K., Mathematics
RUDD, P., Medicine
RUFFINELLI-ALTESOR, J., Spanish and Portuguese
RUMELHART, D. E., Psychology
RUTH, R. D., Stanford Linear Accelerator Center
SAG, I. A., Linguistics
SAGAN, S. D., Political Science
SAIDMAN, L. J., Anaesthesia
SALDIVAR, R., English
SALISBURY, J. K., Computer Science
SALONER, G., Graduate School of Business
SALVATIERRA, O., Jr, Surgery
SAMUELSON, K., Communication
SAPOLSKY, R. M., Biological Sciences
SARASWAT, K., Electrical Engineering
SARGENT, T. J., Economics
SARNOW, P., Microbiology and Immunology
SAUNDERS, M. A., Management Science and Engineering
SAUSSY, C. P. H., Comparative Literature
SCANDLING, J., Medicine
SCHATZBERG, A., Psychiatry
SCHEIDEL, W., Classics
SCHENDEL, S. A., Surgery
SCHERRER, P. H., Physics
SCHIEBERGER, L., History
SCHINDLER, R., Stanford Linear Accelerator Center
SCHNAPP, J. T., French and Italian
SCHNEIDER, S., Biological Sciences
SCHNITTGER, I., Medicine
SCHOEN, R., Mathematics
SCHOOLNIK, G. K., Medicine
SCHROEDER, J. S., Medicine
SCHUPBACH, Slavic Languages and Literatures
SCHURMAN, D., Functional Restoration
SCOTT, M. P., Developmental Biology
SEGAL, I. R., Economics
SEGALL, P., Geophysics
SELLS, P., Linguistics
SERRES, M., French and Italian
SHAFER, S. L., Anaesthesia
SHANKS, M., Classics
SHAPIRO, L., Developmental Biology
SHAQFEH, E. S. G., Chemical Engineering
SHAVELSON, R., Education
SHAW, K., Graduate School of Business
SHEEHAN, J. J., History
SHEEHAN, T., Religious Studies
SHEIKH, J. T., Psychiatry
SHEN, Z.-X., Applied Physics
SHENKER, S. H., Physics
SHORTLIFFE, L., Urology
SHOVEN, J., Economics
SHUER, L. M., Neurosurgery
SIBLEY, R. K., Pathology
SIEGMUND, D. O., Statistics
SIEMANN, R., Stanford Linear Accelerator Center
SIKIC, B. I., Medicine
SILVERBERG, G. D., Neurosurgery
SILVERMAN, N., Paediatrics
SIMON, L., Mathematics
SIMONI, R., Biological Sciences
SIMONSON, I., Graduate School of Business
SINCLAIR, R., Materials Science and Engineering
SINGH, K., Ophthalmology
SINGLETON, K., Graduate School of Business
SKEFF, K. M., Medicine
SLEEP, N., Geophysics
SMITH, S. J., Molecular and Cell Physiology
SMITH, T. I., Physics
SNIDERMAN, P., Political Science
SNIPP, C. M., Sociology
SO, S. K. S., Surgery
SOLOMON, E., Chemistry
SOMERO, G., Biological Sciences

SOMERVILLE, C., Biological Sciences
SOMMER, F. G., Radiology
SPAIN, D., Surgery
SPIEGEL, D., Psychiatry
SPRINGER, G., Aeronautics and Astronautics
SPUDICH, J. A., Biochemistry
SRINIVASAN, V., Graduate School of Business
STAMEY, T. A., Urology
STANSKI, D. R., Anaesthesia
STANSKY, P. D. L., History
STEBBINS, J., Geological and Environmental Sciences
STEELE, C. M., Psychology
STEFANICK, M., Medicine
STEINBERG, G. K., Neurosurgery
STEINER, H., Psychiatry
STEINMAN, L., Neurology
STEPHENS, S., Classics
STEVENS, D., Medicine
STEVENSON, D., Paediatrics
STIPEK, D. J., Education
STOHR, J., Stanford Synchrotron Radiation Laboratory
STREET, R. L., Civil and Environmental Engineering
STRNAD, J. F., Law
STROBER, M., Education
STROBER, S., Medicine
SULLIVAN, K., Law
SUSSKIND, L., Physics
SUSSMAN, H., Pathology
SUTTON, R. I., Management Science and Engineering
SWAIN, J., Medicine
SWARTZ, J. R., Chemical Engineering
SWEENEY, J., Management Science and Engineering
SWITZER, P., Statistics
TAKEUCHI, M. R., Art and Art History
TALLENT, E., English
TATUM, C. B., Civil and Environmental Engineering
TAYLOR, C., Psychiatry
TAYLOR, J. B., Economics
TAYLOR, K. A., Philosophy
TESSIER-LAVIGNE, M., Biological Sciences
THOMAS, E. A. C., Psychology
THOMPSON, B. H., Jr, Law
THOMPSON, D. G., Psychiatry
THOMPSON, S., Biological Sciences
TIBSHIRANI, R. J., Health Research and Policy
TINKLENBERG, J., Psychiatry
TOBAGI, F., Electrical Engineering
TOMPKINS, L., Medicine
TRIADAFILOPOULOS, G., Medicine
TROST, B., Chemistry
TRUDELL, J. R., Anaesthesia
TSIEN, R., Molecular and Cellular Physiology
TULJAPURKAR, S., Biological Sciences
TUMA, N., Sociology
TURNER, P., Art and Art History
TVERSKY, B., Psychology
TYLER, G., Electrical Engineering
UMETSU, D. T., Paediatrics
VALANTINE, H. A., Medicine
VALDES, G., Education
VAN BENTHEM, J. F., Philosophy
VAN DAM, J., Medicine
VAN HORNE, J. C., Graduate School of Business
VAN MEURS, K. P., Paediatrics
VEINOTT, A. F., Jr, Management Science and Engineering
VINOGRAD, R. E., Art and Art History
VITOUSEK, P., Biological Sciences
WAGONER, R. V., Physics
WALBOT, V., Biological Sciences
WALD, M. S., Law
WALDER, A. G., Sociology
WALDRON, K. J., Mechanical Engineering
WALKER, D., Education
WANDELL, B. A., Psychology
WANG, J., Asian Languages
WANG, P., Medicine
WANG, T. S.-F., Pathology
WARNKE, R., Pathology

WASOW, T., Linguistics
WATT, W., Biological Sciences
WAYMOUTH, R. M., Chemistry
WEBER, C., Drama
WEIN, L. M., Graduate School of Business
WEINGAST, B. R., Political Science
WEISBERG, R., Law
WEISSMAN, I., Pathology
WENDER, P., Chemistry
WEYANT, J. P., Management Science and Engineering
WHANG, S., Graduate School of Business
WHITE, B., Mathematics
WHITE, R., History
WHITMORE, I., Surgery
WHITTEMORE, A., Health Research and Policy
WHYTE, R. I., Cardiothoracic Surgery
WIDROW, B., Electrical Engineering
WILSON, D. M., Paediatrics
WINE, J., Psychology
WINEBERG, S., Education
WINOGRAD, T., Computer Sciences
WOJCICKI, S. G., Physics
WOLAK, F. A., Economics
WOLF, A., Anthropological Sciences
WOLF, B. J., Art and Art History
WOLFF, T., English
WONG, H.-S., Electrical Engineering
WONG, S.-W. S., Electrical Engineering
WOOD, A. W., Philosophy
WOOD, R., Philosophy
WOOLEY, B. A., Electrical Engineering
WRIGHT, G., Economics
XIE, Y., Sociology
YAMAMOTO, Y., Electrical Engineering
YANAGISAKO, S. J., Cultural and Social Anthropology
YARBRO-BEJARANO, Y., Spanish and Portuguese
YAU, H.-T., Mathematics
YE, Y., Management Science and Engineering
YEARLEY, L., Religious Studies
YESAVAGE, J., Psychiatry
YOCK, P. G., Medicine
ZARE, R. N., Chemistry
ZARINS, C. K., Surgery
ZHANG, S., Physics
ZIPPERSTEIN, S. J., History
ZOBACK, M., Geophysics

STARR KING SCHOOL FOR THE MINISTRY

2441 LeConte Ave, Berkeley, CA 94709-1209
Telephone: (510) 845-6232
Fax: (510) 845-6273
E-mail: starrking@sksm.edu
Internet: www.sksm.edu

Founded 1904 as Pacific Unitarian School for the Ministry, present name 1941; attached to Graduate Theological Union
Private control
Academic year: September to May
Pres.: Dr. Rev REBECCA A. PARKER
Provost: IBRAHIM ABDURRAHMAN FARAJAJÉ
Vice-Pres. for Academic Affairs and Dean of Faculty: Rev. Dr DORSEY BLAKE
Vice-Pres. for Advancement: KELLY FLOOD
Vice-Pres. for Finance and Admin.: THOMAS SMITH
Dean for Students: BECKY LEYSER
Dir for Continuing and Online Education: CATHLEEN YOUNG
Library Dir: BONNIE HARDWICK
Registrar: KATRINA CROSWELL
Library of 365,000 vols.

THOMAS AQUINAS COLLEGE

10,000 N Ojai Rd, Santa Paula, CA 93060
Telephone: (805) 525-4417
Fax: (805) 525-9342
E-mail: admissions@thomasaquinas.edu
Internet: www.thomasaquinas.edu

Founded 1971
Private control
Offers Bachelors degrees in liberal arts
Private control
Academic year: September to June
Pres.: Dr MICHAEL F. MCLEAN
Vice-Pres.: JOHN W. NEUMAYR
Vice-President for Devt and General Counsel: JOHN QUINCY MASTELLER
Vice-Pres. for Finance and Admin.: PETER L. DELUCA
Dean: Dr BRIAN T. KELLY
Registrar: MARK KRETSCHMER
Librarian: VILTIS JATULIS
Library of 72,000 vols
Number of teachers: 37
Number of students: 358
Publication: *The Aquinas Review* (2 a year).

THOMAS JEFFERSON SCHOOL OF LAW

1155 Island Ave, San Diego, CA 92101
Telephone: (619) 297-9700
Fax: (619) 294-4713
E-mail: admissions@tjsl.edu
Internet: www.tjsl.edu
Founded 1969
Private control
Academic year: June to August
Pres. and Dean: RUDY HASL
Library Dir: PATRICK MEYER
Library of 200,000 vols.

UNIVERSITY OF CALIFORNIA

Office of the Pres., 12th Fl., 1111 Franklin St, Oakland, CA 94607-5200
E-mail: ucinfo@ucapplication.net
Internet: www.universityofcalifornia.edu
Founded 1869
10 Campuses
Pres.: MARK G. YUDOF
Provost and Exec. Vice-Pres. for Academic Affairs: Dr WYATT R. HUME
Exec. Vice-Pres. for Univ. Affairs: BRUCE B. DARLING
Vice-Pres. for Agriculture and Natural Resources: W. R. GOMES
Vice-Pres. for Budget: LARRY HERSHMAN
Vice-Pres. for Clinical Services Devt: WILLIAM H. GURTNER
Vice-Pres. for Financial Management: ANNE BROOME
Vice-Pres. for Health Affairs: RORY HUME
Vice-Pres. for Investments: MARIE N. BERGREN
Vice-Pres. for Laboratory Admin.: S. ROBERT FOLEY
Vice-Pres. for Legal Affairs: CHARLES F. ROBINSON
Vice-Pres. for Student Affairs: JUDY K. SAKAKI
Library: see Libraries and Archives
Number of teachers: 8,776
Number of students: 220,000.

CONSTITUENT CAMPUSES

University of California, Berkeley

Berkeley, CA 94720
Telephone: (510) 642-6000
Internet: www.berkeley.edu
Founded 1868
State control
Chancellor: ROBERT J. BIRGENEAU
Exec. Vice-Chancellor and Provost: GEORGE W. BRESLAUER
Vice-Chancellor for Admin. and Finance: JOHN WILTON
Vice-Chancellor for Equity and Inclusion: GIBOR BASRI

Vice-Chancellor for Facilities Services: EDWARD J. DENTON
Vice-Chancellor for Research: GRAHAM FLEMING
Vice-Chancellor for Student Affairs: HARRY LE GRANDE
Vice-Chancellor for Univ. Relations: SCOTT BIDDY
Univ. Librarian: THOMAS C. LEONARD
Number of teachers: 2,082 (1,582 full-time, 500 part-time)
Number of students: 36,142 (25,885 undergraduate, 10,257 graduate)

DEANS

College of Chemistry: RICHARD A. MATHIES
College of Engineering: SHANKAR SASTRY
College of Environmental Design: JENNIFER WOLCH
College of Letters and Science: MARK RICHARDS
College of Natural Resources: J. KEITH GILLESS
Graduate School of Education: JUDITH WARREN LITTLE
Graduate School of Journalism: NEIL HENRY
Richard and Rhoda Goldman School of Public Policy: HENRY BRADY
School of Information: ANNALEE SAXENIAN
School of Law: CHRISTOPHER F. EDLEY, Jr
School of Optometry: DENNIS LEVI
School of Public Health: STEPHEN SHORTELL (acting)
School of Social Welfare: LORRAINE MIDANIK
Walter A. Haas School of Business: RICHARD K. LYONS

University of California, Davis

1 Shields Ave, Davis, CA 95616
Telephone: (530) 752-1011
Fax: (530) 752-6363
Internet: www.ucdavis.edu
Founded 1905
State control
Academic year: September to June
Chancellor: LINDA KATEHI
Provost and Exec. Vice-Chancellor: RALPH HEXTER
Vice-Chancellor for Admin. and Resource Management: JOHN A. MEYER
Vice-Chancellor for Human Health Sciences: CLAIRE POMEROY
Vice-Chancellor for Research: HARRIS LEWIN
Vice-Chancellor for Student Affairs: FRED WOOD
Vice-Chancellor for Univ. Relations: BEVERLY SANDEEN
Vice-Provost for Academic Personnel: MAUREEN STANTON
Vice-Provost for Information and Educational Technology: PETER SIEGEL
Vice-Provost for Undergraduate Studies: PATRICA TURNER
Vice-Provost for Univ. Outreach and Int. Programs: WILLIAM B. LACY
Univ. Librarian: RANDOLPH SIVERSON (acting)
Library: see Libraries and Archives
Number of teachers: 2,558
Number of students: 32,153
Publications: *BizLawJournal.com* (online), *CA&ES Outlook* (2 a year), *Environs* (2 a year), *Journal of International Law Policy* (2 a year), *Journal of Juvenile Law and Policy* (2 a year), *Migration News* (12 a year), *The Horse Report* (4 a year), *UC Davis Law Review* (4 a year)

DEANS

Betty Irene Moore School of Nursing: HEATHER YOUNG
College of Agricultural and Environmental Sciences: NEAL K. VAN ALFEN
College of Biological Sciences: JAMES E. K. HILDRETH

College of Education: HAROLD G. LEVINE
College of Engineering: ENRIQUE LAVERNIA (acting)
Div. of Humanities, Arts and Cultural Studies: JESSIE ANN OWENS
Div. of Mathematics and Physical Sciences: WINSTON KO
Div. of Social Sciences: GEORGE R. MANGUN
Graduate School of Management: STEVEN CURRALL
Graduate Studies: JEFFERY C. GIBELING
School of Law: KEVIN JOHNSON
School of Medicine: CLAIRE POMEROY
School of Veterinary Medicine: MICHAEL D. LAIRMORE
Univ. Extension: DENNIS F. PENDLETON

PROFESSORS

College of Agricultural and Environmental Sciences (150 Mrak Hall, 1 Shields Ave, Davis, CA 95616; tel. (530) 752-0107; fax (530) 752-9049; internet www.aes.ucdavis.edu):

Faculty of Agricultural and Resource Economics:

ALSTON, J. M.
CAPUTO, M. R.
CARMAN, H.
CARTER, C. A.
CHALFANT, J. A.
FARZIN, Y. H.
GREEN, R. D.
HAVENNER, A.
HEIEN, D. M.
HOWITT, R. E.
JARVIS, L. S.
MARTIN, P. L.
MORRISON PAUL, C. J.
PARIS, Q.
ROZELLE, S.
SEXTON, R. J.
SUMNER, D. A.
TAYLOR, J. E.
VOSTI, S. A.
WILEN, J. E.
WILLIAMS, J.

Faculty of Agronomy and Range Science:

DEMMENT, M. W.
DENISON, R. F.
DVORAK, J.
FOIN, T. C.
GENG, S.
GEPTS, P. L.
JERNSTEDT, J.
PHILLIPS, D. A.
PLANT, R. E.
RAINS, D. W.
RICE, K. J.
TEUBER, L. R.
TRAVIS, R. L.
VAN KESSEL, C.
WILKENS, T.

Faculty of Animal Science:

ADAMS, T. E.
ANDERSON, G. B.
BERGER, T. J.
CALVERT, C. C.
DE PETERS, E. J.
DOROSHOV, S. I.
FADEL, J. G.
FAMULA, T. R.
GALL, G. A.
HUNG, S. S.
KING, A. J.
KLASING, K. C.
LEE, Y. B.
MEDRANO, J. F.
MENCH, J. A.
MILLAM, J. R.
OBERBAUER, A. M.
PRICE, E. O.
ROSER, J. F.
WEATHERS, W. W.
WILSON, B. W.

ZINN, R. A.

Faculty of Biological and Agricultural Engineering under the College of Agricultural and Environmental Sciences:

PIEDRAHITA, R. H.
UPADHYAYA, S. K.

Faculty of Entomology:

CAREY, J. R.
CRANSTON, P. S.
DINGLE, H.
EDMAN, J. D.
EHLER, L. E.
GRANETT, J.
GULLAN, P. J.
HAMMOCK, B. D.
KARBAN, R.
KAYA, H. K.
KIMSEY, L. S.
LEAL, W. S.
PAGE, R. E.
PARRELA, M. P.
PENG, Y. S. C.
ROSENHEIM, J. A.
SCOTT, T. W.
ULLMAN, D. E.
WARD, P. S.

Faculty of Environmental Design:

GOTELLI, D. E.
HARRISON, P.
LAKY, G.
RIVERS, V. Z.
SHAWCROFT-GUARINO, B.

Faculty of Environmental Horticulture:

BARBOUR, M. G.
BERRY, A. M.
BURGER, D. W.
DURZAN, D. J.
HARDING, J. A.
LIETH, J. H.
REID, M. S.
WU, L. L.

Faculty of Environmental Science and Policy:

GOLDMAN, C. R.
HARRISON, S. P.
HASTINGS, A. M.
JOHNSTON, R. A.
ORLOVE, B. S.
QUINN, J. F.
REJMANKOVA, E.
RICHERSON, P. J.
SABATIER, P. A.
SIH, A.
WILLIAMS, S. L.

Faculty of Environmental Toxicology:

CHERR, G. N.
DENISON, M. S.
KADO, N. Y.
KNEZOVICH, J. P.
MATSUMURA, F.
MILLER-SEARS, M. G.
RICE, R. H.
SHIBAMOTO, T.
TJEERDEMA, R. S.

Faculty of Food Science and Technology:

BAMFORTH, C. W.
BANDMAN, E.
DUNGAN, S. R.
GERMAN, J. B.
GUINARD, J.
HAARD, N. F.
KROCHTA, J. M.
MCCARTHY, M. J.
OGRYDZIAK, D. M.
O'MAHONY, M. A.
PRICE, C. W.
REID, D. S.
SHOEMAKER, C. F.
SINGH, R. P.
SMITH, G. M.

Faculty of Human and Community Development:

ALDWIN, C.

BARTON, K.
BRUSH, S. B.
BRYANT, B. K.
CONGER, R. D.
GE, X.
HARPER, L. V.
KENNEY, M. F.
LACY, W. B.
MOMSEN, J.
OBER, B. A.
SMITH, M. P.
WELLS, M. J.

Faculty of Land, Air and Water Resources:

BAHRE, C. J.
BLEDSOE, C. S.
CARROLL, J. J.
CASEY, W. H.
DAHLGREN, R. A.
FLOCCHINI, R. G.
FOGG, G. E.
GRISMER, M. E.
GROTJAHN, R.
HOPMANS, J. W.
HSIAO, T. C.
LAUCHLI, A. E.
NATHAN, T. R.
PAW U, K. T.
RECK, R. A.
RICHARDS, J. M.
ROLSTON, D. E.
SCOW, K. M.
SHELTON, M. L.
SILK, M. W.
SINGER, M. J.
SOUTHARD, R. J.
USTIN, S. L.
WEARE, B. C.
ZASOSKI, R. J.

Faculty of Landscape Architecture:

ALLAN, N.
FRANCIS, M.
MACCANNELL, E. D.

Faculty of Nematology:

CASWELL-CHAN, E. P.
FERRIS, H.
JAFFEE, B. A.
NADLER, S. A.
WILLIAMSON, V. M.

Faculty of Nutrition:

ALLEN, L. H.
BROWN, K. G.
CLIFFORD, A. J.
DEWEY, K. G.
GRIVETTI, L. E.
KEEN, C. L.
LONNERDAL, B. L.
MCDONALD, R. B.
RUCKER, R. B.
SCHNEEMAN, B. O.
STERN, J. S.

Faculty of Plant Pathology:

BOSTOCK, R. M.
BRUENING, G.
COOK, D. R.
DAVIS, R. M.
DUNIWAY, J. M.
FALK, B. W.
GILBERTSON, R. L.
GILCHRIST, D. G.
GORDON, T. R.
KADO, C. I.
KIRKPATRICK, B. C.
MACDONALD, J. D.
RONALD, P. C.
TYLER, B. M.
VAN ALFEN, N.
WEBSTER, R. K.

Faculty of Pomology:

BLUMWALD, E.
BROWN, P. H.
DANDEKAR, A. M.
DEJONG, T. M.
GRADZIEL, T. M.

KADER, A. A.
LABAVITCH, J. M.
POLITO, V. S.
SHACKEL, K. A.
SHAW, D. V.
SUTTER, E. G.
WEINBAUM, S.

Faculty of Textiles and Clothing:

HSIEH, Y.
KAISER, S. B.
PAN, N.
RUCKER, M. H.

Faculty of Vegetable Crops:

BAYER, D. E.
BLOOM, A. J.
BRADFORD, K. J.
JACKSON, L. E.
MICHELMORE, R. W.
NEVINS, D. J.
QUIROS, C. F.
SALTVEIT, M. E.
YODER, J. I.

Faculty of Viticulture and Oenology:

BISSON, L. F.
BOULTON, R. B.
HEYMANN, H.
MATTHEWS, M. A.
MEREDITH, C. P.
NOBLE, A. C.
WALKER, M. A.
WATERHOUSE, A. L.
WILLIAMS, L. E.

Faculty of Wildlife, Fish and Conservation Biology:

ANDERSON, D. W.
BOTSFORD, L. W.
CARO, T. M.
CECH, J. J.
EADIE, J. M.
ELLIOTT-FISK, D. L.
MOYLE, P. B.
VAN VUREN, D.

School of Education (2077 Academic Surge Bldg, 1 Shields Ave, Davis, CA 95616; tel. (530) 752-8019; fax (530) 752-5411):

DUGDALE, S. S.
FIGUEROA, R. A.
GANDARA, P.
LEVINE, H. G.
MERINO, B. J.
MURPHY, S.
SANDOVAL, J. H.
WAGNER, J. C.
WATSON-GEGEO, K. A.
YOUNG, I. P.

College of Engineering (1050 Engineering Unit II, 1 Shields Ave, Davis, CA 95616; tel. (530) 752-0553; fax (530) 752-8058; internet engineering.ucdavis.edu):

Faculty of Biological and Agricultural Engineering under the College of Engineering:

DELWICHE, M. J.
GILES, D. K.
HARTSOUGH, B. R.
HILLS, D. J.
JENKINS, B. M.
MCCARTHY, K. L.
MILES, J. A.
RUMSEY, T. R.
SLAUGHTER, D. C.
UPADHYAYA, S. K.
WALLENDER, W. W.

Faculty of Biomedical Engineering:

BENHAM, C. J.
CHERRY, S. R.
FERRARA, K. W.
INSANA, M. F.
SAVAGEAU, M. A.
SIMON, I.

Faculty of Chemical Engineering and Materials Science:

BROWNING, N. D.
GATES, B. C.
GIBELING, J. C.
GROZA, J. R.
HIGGINS, B. G.
HOWITT, D. G.
JACKMAN, A. P.
McCOY, B. J.
McDONALD, K. A.
MUKHERJEE, A. K.
NAVROTSKY, A.
PALAZOGLU, A. N.
PHILLIPS, R. J.
POWELL, R. L.
RISBUD, S. H.
RYU, D. D. Y.
SHACKELFORD, J. F.
STROEVE, P.
WHITAKER, S.

Faculty of Civil and Environmental Engineering:

ARULANANDAN, K.
BOULANGER, R.
CHANG, D. P.
DAFALIAS, Y. F.
DARBY, J. L.
GINN, T.
IDRISS, I. M.
KAVVAS, M. L.
KUTTER, B. L.
LAROCK, B. E.
LUND, J. R.
MARINO, M. A.
MOKHTARIAN, P. L.
NIEMEIER, D. A.
RAMEY, M. R.
RUNDLE, J. B.
SPERLING, D.
YOUNIS, B.

Faculty of Computer Science:

BAI, Z.
BRUNO, J.
FARRENS, M. K.
GUSFIELD, D.
HAMANN, B.
JOY, K. I.
LEVITT, K. N.
MARTEL, C. U.
MATLOFF, N. S.
MUKHERJEE, B.
OLSSON, R. A.
ROGAWAY, P. W.
RUSCHITZKA, M. G.

Faculty of Electrical and Computer Engineering:

ABDEL-GHAFFAR, K. A.
BRANNER, G. R.
CHANG, T. S.
COLINGE, J. P.
CURRENT, K. W.
DING, Z.
FEHER, K.
FORD, G. E.
HALEY, S. B.
HERITAGE, J. P.
HUNT, C. E.
HURST, P. J.
KNOESEN, A.
LEVY, B. C.
LEWIS, S. H.
OKLOBDZIJA, V. G.
REDINBO, G. R.
REED, T. R.
SMITH, R. L.
SPENCER, R. R.
TIEN, N. C.
WANG, S.
YOO, S. B.

Faculty of Engineering:

MUNIR, Z. A.

Faculty of Engineering—Applied Science:

BALDIS, H. A.
CRAMER, S. P.
FREEMAN, R. R.
HWANG, D. Q.
JENSEN, N. G.
KOLNER, B. H.
KROL, D.
LAUB, A. J.
LUHMANN, N. C.
MAX, N. L.
McCURDY, W. C.
MILLER, G. H.
OREL, A. E.
ROCKE, D. M.
RODRIGUE, G.
VEMURI, V.
YEH, Y.

Faculty of Mechanical and Aeronautical Engineering:

BAUGHN, J. W.
CHATTOT, J. J.
DAVIS, R. J.
DWYER, H. A.
FAROUKI, R. T.
FRANK, A. A.
HAFEZ, M. M.
HESS, R. A.
HUBBARD, M.
HULL, M. L.
KARNOPP, D. C.
KENNEDY, I. M.
KOLLMANN, W.
MARGOLIS, D. L.
RAVANI, B.
REHFIELD, L. W.
SARIGUL-KLIJN, N.
SHAW, B. D.
VAN DAM, C. P.
VELINSKY, S. A.
WEXLER, A. S.
WHITE, B. R.
YAMAZAKI, K.

School of Law (1013 King Hall, 1 Shields Ave, Davis, CA 95616; tel. (530) 752-0243; fax (530) 752-4704; internet www.kinghall .ucdavis.edu):

AMANN, D. M.
AYER, J. D.
BROWNSTEIN, A. E.
DOBRIS, J. C.
DOREMUS, H.
FEENEY, F. F.
GANDARA, A.
GLENNON, M. J.
GROSSMAN, G. S.
HILLMAN, R. W.
IMWINKELRIED, E. J.
JOHNSON, K. R.
JOO, T. W.
KURTZ, L. A.
LEWIS, E. A.
OAKLEY, J. B.
PERSCHBACHER, R. R.
POULOS, J. W.
REYNOSO, C.
SIMMONS, D. L.
WEST, M. S.
WOLK, B. A.
WYDICK, R. C.

College of Letters and Science (200 Social Sciences and Humanities Bldg, 1 Shields Ave, Davis, CA 95616; tel. (530) 752-0392; fax (530) 752-3440; internet www.ls.ucdavis .edu):

Faculty of African American and African Studies:

OLUPONA, J. K.
STEWART, J. O.
TURNER, P. A.

Faculty of American Studies:

BLAIR, C.
FRANKENBERG, R.

MECHLING, J. E.
SMITH, M.

Faculty of Anthropology:

BETTINGER, R. L.
BORGERHOFF-MULDER, M.
DONHAM, D. L.
HARCOURT, A. H.
JOSEPH, S.
McHENRY, H. M.
RODMAN, P. S.
SMITH, C. A.
SMITH, D. G.
SMITH, J. S.
SRINIVAS, S.
WINTERHALDER, B. P.
YENGOYAN, A. A.

Faculty of Art History and Art Studio:

ATKINSON, C.
BILLS, T. B.
COLLINS, H. M.
HENDERSON, W.
HERSHMAN, L.
HOLLOWELL, D.
MACLEOD, D. S.
PULS, L. A.
RUDA, J.
WERFEL, G. S.

Faculty of Asian American Studies:

HAMAMOTO, D. Y.
HING, B. O.
SUE, S.

Faculty of Chemistry:

BALCH, A. L.
BRITT, R. D.
FAWCETT, W. R.
FINK, W. H.
GERVAY HAGUE, J.
JACKSON, W. M.
KAUZLARICH, S.
KELLY, P. B.
KURTH, M. J.
LAMAR, G. N.
LEBRILLA, C. B.
MEARES, C. F.
MOLINSKI, T.
NANTZ, M
NG, C. Y.
POWER, P. P.
ROCK, P. A.
SCHORE, N. E.
STUCHEBRUKHOV, A.
TINTI, D. S.
TRUE, N. S.
TUCKER, S. C.

Faculty of Chicana/o Studies:

CHABRAM-DERNE, A.
DE LA TORRE, A.
MONTOYA, M.

Faculty of Communication:

BELL, R. A.
BERGER, C. R.
MOTLEY, M. T.

Faculty of Comparative Literature:

BLANCHARD, M. E.
FINNEY, G.
LARSEN, N. A.
LU, S. H.
MURAV, H. L.
SCHEIN, S. L.
SCHIESARI, J.
SCHILDGEN, B. P.
TORRANCE, R. M.

Faculty of Comparative Research:

SKINNER, G. W.

Faculty of East Asian Languages and Cultures:

BORGEN, R.
YEH, M.

Faculty of Economics:

BONANNO, G.
CAMERON, A.

CLARK, G.
FEENSTRA, R. C.
HOOVER, K. D.
LINDERT, P. H.
MAKOWSKI, L.
OLMSTEAD, A. L.
QUINZII, M.
SHEFFRIN, S. M.
SILVESTRE, J.
WALTON, G. M.
WOO, W. T.

Faculty of English:

ABBOTT, D. P.
BYRD, W. M.
DALE, P. A.
DIEHL, J. F.
FERGUSON, M. W.
FREED, L. R.
GILBERT, S. M.
HAYS, P. L.
LANGLAND, E.
LEVIN, R. A.
LOKKE, K.
MCPHERSON, S. J.
MAJOR, C.
MORRIS, L. A.
OSBORN, M.
OWENS, L. D.
ROBERTSON, D. A.
SCHLEINER, W.
SIMMONS, S.
SIMPSON, D. E.
SNYDER, G. S.
VAN LEER, D. M.
WADDINGTON, R. B.
WATKINS, E. P.
WILLIAMSON, A. B.
ZENDER, K. F.

Faculty of French and Italian:

BLANCHARD, M. E.
CANNON, J.
DUTSCHKE, D. J.
MANOLIU, M. I.
VAN DEN ABBEELE, G.

Faculty of Geology:

CARLSON, S. J.
DAY, H. W.
DEWEY, J. F.
KELLOGG, L. H.
LESHER, C. E.
MONTAÑEZ, I. P.
MOORES, E. M.
MOUNT, J. F.
SCHIFFMAN, P.
SPERO, H. J.
TURCOTTE, D. L.
TWISS, R. J.
VERMEIJ, G.
VEROSUB, K. L.
ZIERENBERG, R. A.

Faculty of German and Russian:

BERND, C. A.
DRUZHNIKOV, Y.
MCCONNELL, W.
MENGES, K. R.
RANCOUR-LAFERRIERE, D.
SCHAEFFER, P. M.

Faculty of History:

BAUER, A. J.
BIALE, D.
BRANTLEY, C. L.
BROWER, D. R.
CADDEN, J.
HAGEN, W. W.
HALTTUNEN, K.
HOLLOWAY, T. H.
KUDLICK, C. J.
LANDAU, N. B.
MANN, S. L.
MARGADANT, T. W.
METCALF, B. O.
PRICE, D. C.
ROSEN, R. E.

SMITH, M.
SPYRIDAKIS, S.
TAYLOR, A. S.
WALKER, C. E.

Faculty of Linguistics:

BENWARE, W. A.
OJEDA, A. E.
TIMM, L. A.

Faculty of Mathematics:

BORGES, C. R.
BRAMSON, M. D.
CHEER, A. Y.
DIEDERICH, J. R.
EDELSON, A. L.
FUCHS, D. B.
GRAVNER, J.
HAAS, J.
HUNTER, J. K.
KRENER, A. J.
KUPERBERG, G. J.
MILTON, E. O.
MOGILNER, A.
MULASE, M.
NACHTERGAELE, B.
PUCKETT, E. G.
SAITO, N.
SALLEE, G. T.
SCHWARZ, A.
SHKOLLER, S.
SILVIA, E. M.
TEMPLE, J. B.
THOMPSON, A. A.
THURSTON, W. P.
TRACY, C. A.
WETS, R. J.

Faculty of Music:

BAUER, R.
BUSSE BERGER, A. M.
FRANK, A. D.
HOLOMAN, D. K.
NUTTER, D. A.
ORTIZ, P. V.
REYNOLDS, C. A.

Faculty of Native American Studies:

HERNANDEZ-AVILA, I.
LONGFISH, G. C.
MACRI, M. J.
MONTEJO, V. D.
VARESE, S.

Faculty of Philosophy:

CUMMINS, R. C.
DWORKIN, G.
GRIESEMER, J. R.
JUBIEN, M.
KING, J. C.
NEANDER, K. L.
TELLER, P.
WEDIN, M. V.
WILSON, G. M.

Faculty of Physics:

ALBRECHT, A. J.
BECKER, R. H.
CARLIP, S.
CHAU, L.
CHIANG, S.
CORRUCCINI, L. R.
COX, D. L.
FADLEY, C. S.
FONG, C.
GUNION, J. F.
KISKIS, J. E.
KLEIN, B. M.
KO, W. T.
LANDER, R.
PELLETT, D. E.
PICKETT, W. E.
SCALETTAR, R. T.
SINGH, R. R.
TRIPATHI, S. M.
YAGER, P. M.
ZHU, X.
ZIMANYI, G.

Faculty of Political Science:

HUCKFELDT, R. R.
JACKMAN, R. W.
NINCIC, M.
PETERMAN, L. I.
ROTHCHILD, D. S.
SIVERSON, R. M.
STONE, W. J.
WADE, L. L.

Faculty of Psychology:

ACREDOLO, L. P.
CAPITANIO, J. P.
COSS, R. G.
ELMS, A. C.
EMMONS, R. A.
ERICKSEN, K. P.
GOODMAN, G. S.
HARRISON, A. A.
HENRY, K. R.
HEREK, G. M.
JOHNSON, J. T.
KROLL, N. E.
KRUBITZER, L. A.
LONG, D. L.
MANGUN, G. R.
MENDOZA, S. P.
OWINGS, D. H.
PARKS, T. E.
POST, R. B.
SHAVER, P. R.
SIMONTON, D. K.
SOMMER, R.
WIDAMAN, K. F.

Faculty of Religious Studies:

JANOWITZ, N.
LAI, W. W.

Faculty of Sociology:

BLOCK, F.
COHEN, L. E.
CRAMER, J. C.
FELMLEE, D. H.
GOLDSTONE, J. A.
HALL, J. R.
JACKMAN, M. R.
JOFFE, C.
LOFLAND, L. H.
MCCARTHY, W. D.
SMITH, V. A.
WALTON, J. T.
WOLF, D. L.

Faculty of Spanish and Classics:

ARMISTEAD, S. G.
BLAKE, R. J.
GONZÁLEZ, C.
LARSEN, N. A.
ROLLER, L. E.
SCARI, R. M.
TRAILL, D. A.
VERANI, H. J.

Faculty of Statistics:

BERAN, R. J.
BURMAN, P.
JOHNSON, W. O.
MACK, Y. P.
MUELLER, H. G.
ROUSSAS, G. G.
SAMANIEGO, F. J.
SHUMWAY, R. H.
UTTS, J. M.
WANG, J.-L.

Faculty of Theatre and Dance:

ANDERSON, S. P.
IACOVELLI, J. C.
SELLERS-YOUNG, B. A.
SHANNON, P.

Faculty of Women and Gender Studies:

KUHN, A. K.
NEWTON, J.
RABINE, L. W.

Division of Biological Sciences (202 Life Sciences Addition, 1 Shields Ave, Davis, CA

95616; tel. (530) 752-0410; fax (530) 752-2604; internet www.dbs.ucdavis.edu):

Biological Science:
CHANG, E. S.

Evolution and Ecology:
CHESSON, P. L.
DOYLE, J. A.
GILLESPIE, J. H.
GOTTLIEB, L. D.
GREY, R. D.
GROSBERG, R. K.
LANGLEY, C. H.
PEARCY, R. W.
REJMANEK, M.
SANDERSON, M. J.
SCHOENER, T. W.
SHAFFER, H. B.
SHAPIRO, A. M.
STAMPS, J. A.
STANTON, M. L.
STRONG, D. R.
TOFT, C. A.
TURELLI, M.
WAINWRIGHT, P. C.

Microbiology:
ARTZ, S. W.
BAUMANN, P.
HEYER, W. D.
KOWALCZYKOWSKI, S. C.
MANNING, J. S.
MEEKS, J. C.
NELSON, D. C.
PRIVALSKY, M. L.
STEWART, V. J.
ROTH, J. R.

Molecular and Cellular Biology:
ARMSTRONG, P. B.
BASKIN, R. J.
BURTIS, K. C.
CALLIS, J.
CLEGG, J. S.
CROWE, J. H.
DAHMUS, M. E.
DOI, R. H.
ERICKSON, C. A.
ETZLER, M. E.
GASSER, C. S.
HEDRICK, J. L.
HJELMELAND, L. M.
KIGER, J. A.
LAGARIAS, J. C.
MYLES, D.
RODRIGUEZ, R. L.
SCHMID, C. W.
SHOLEY, J. M.
SEGEL, I. H.

Neurobiology, Physiology and Behaviour:
CARSTENS, E. E.
FULLER, C. A.
HORWITZ, B. A.
ISHIDA, A. T.
MULLONEY, B.
PAPPONE, P. A.
SILLMAN, A. J.
WEIDNER, W. J.
WILSON, M. C.
WOOLLEY, D. E.

Plant Biology:
DELMER, D. P.
HARADA, J. J.
LUCAS, W. J.
MURPHY, T. M.
O'NEILL, S. D.
ROST, T. L.
SINHA, N.
STEMLER, A. J.
SUNDARESEN, V.
THEG, S. M.
VANDERHOEF, L. N.

Graduate School of Management (106 AOB4, 1 Shields Ave, Davis, CA 95616; tel. (530) 752-7399; fax (530) 752-2924; e-mail gsm@

ucdavis.edu; internet www.gsm.ucdacvis.edu):
BARBER, B.
BIGGART, N. W.
BUNCH, D. S.
CLARK, P. K.
GERSTNER, E.
GRIFFIN, P. A.
MAHER, M.
PALMER, D.
SMILEY, R. H.
SWAMINATHAN, A.
TOPKIS, D. M.
TSAI, C.-L.
WOODRUFF, D.

School of Medicine (Med Sci 1c, Room 102 Campus, 1 Shields Ave, Davis, CA 95616; tel. (530) 752-4028; fax (530) 752-1532; internet www-med.ucdavis.edu):

Department of Anaesthesiology and Pain Medicine:
ANTOGNINI, J. F.

Department of Biological Chemistry:
BRADBURY, E. M.
HAGERMAN, P. J.
HERSHEY, J. W.
HJELMELAND, L. M.
HOLLAND, M. J.
JUE, T.
KUNG, H.-J.
TROY LI, F. A.

Department of Cell Biology and Human Anatomy:
ERICKSON, K. L.
FITZGERALD, P.
KUMARI, V.
MEIZEL, S.
PRIMAKOFF, P.
TUCKER, R. P.

Department of Dermatology:
GRANDO, S. A.
HUNTLEY, A. C.
ISSEROFF, R. R.
LIU, F.-T.
ZIBOH, V. A.

Department of Epidemiology and Preventive Medicine:
BECKETT, L. A.
CHEN, M. S.
GOLD, E. B.
LEIGH, J. P.
SCHENKER, M. B.
WINTEMUTE, G. J.

Department of Family and Community Medicine:
BERTAKIS, K. D.
CALLAHAN, E. J.
FRANKS, P.
MELNIKOW, J.
NESBITT, T. S.
NUOVO, J.

Department of Human Physiology:
CALA, P. M.
CARLSEN, R. C.
CURRY, F. E.
O'DONNELL, M. E.
TURGEON, J. L.
WIDDICOMBE, J.
WISE, P.

Department of Internal Medicine:
ALBERTSON, T. E.
AMSTERDAM, E. A.
AOKI, T.
BERGLUND, L.
BONHAM, A. C.
COHEN, S. H.
CROSS, C. E.
DEGREGORIO, M.
DENARDO, S. J.
DEPNER, T. A.
FITZGERALD, F. T.

GANDARA, D. R.
GERSHWIN, M. E.
HALSTED, C. H.
HINSHAW, V. S.
KAPPAGODA, C. T.
KARAKAS, S. E.
KAUFMAN, M. P.
KAYSEN, G.
KRAVITZ, R.
LAM, K.
LAST, J. A.
LEUNG, J.
LOEWY, E.
MARTIN, R. B.
MATTHEWS, H. R.
MEYERS, F. J.
PARSONS, G. H.
PIMSTONE, N. R.
POLLARD, R. B.
POWELL, J. S.
PRINDIVILLE, T. P.
REDDI, A. H.
RICHMAN, C. M.
ROBBINS, J. A.
ROBBINS, R. L.
RUTLEDGE, J. C.
SCHAEFER, S.
SIEGEL, D.
SILVA, J.
STEBBINS, C. L.
ZERN, M.

Department of Medical Microbiology and Immunology:
BEAMAN, B. L.
DANDEKAR, S.
PAPPAGIANIS, D.
SYVANEN, M.
THEIS, J. H.

Medicine:
ANDERS, T. F.
SELDIN, M. F.

Department of Neurological Surgery:
BERMAN, R. F.
BOGGAN, J. E.
LYETH, B. G.
MATTHEWS, D. L.
MUIZELAAR, J. P.
SCHWARTZKROIN, P. A.

Department of Neurology:
DE CARLI, C.
GORIN, F. A.
JAGUST, W. J.
KWEE, I.
MANGUN, G. R.
MASELLI, R. A.
REMLER, M. P.
RICHMAN, D. P.
SEYAL, M.

Department of Obstetrics and Gynaecology:
BOYERS, S.
GILBERT, W. M.
OVERSTREET, J. W.
SMITH, L. H.

Department of Ophthalmology:
CHALUPA, L. M.
KELTNER, J. L.
MANNIS, M. J.
WERNER, J. S.

Department of Orthopaedic Surgery:
BENSON, D. R.
RAB, G. T.
RODRIGO, J. J.
SZABO, R. M.

Department of Otolaryngology:
DONALD, P. J.

Department of Paediatrics:
HAGERMAN, R. J.
JOAD, J. P.
MAKKER, S. P.
PHILIPPS, A. F.
SHERMAN, M. P.

STYNE, D. M.
TARANTAL, A. F.
WENMAN, W. M.

Department of Pathology:

CARDIFF, R. D.
ELLIS, W. G.
GREEN, R.
JIALAL, I.
KOST, G. J.
LARKIN, E. C.
LUCIW, P. A.

Department of Pharmacology:

BONHAM, A. C.
CHUANG, R. Y.
HENDERSON, G. L.

Department of Plastic Surgery:

STEVENSON, T. R.

Department of Psychiatry:

AMARAL, D. G.
HENDREN, R. L.
JONES, E. G.
KNAPP, P. K.
MADDOCK, R. J.
MORRISON, T. L.
ROGERS, S. J.

Department of Radiation Oncology:

BOGREN, H. G.
BOONE, J. M.
BRUNBERG, J. A.
BUONOCORE, M. H.
KATZBERG, R. W.
KUBO, H.
LATCHAW, R. E.
LINK, D. P.
McGAHAN, J. P.
MOORE, E. H.
ROSENQUIST, C. J.
SEIBERT, J. A.
STADAINIK, R. C.
VIJAYAKUMAR, S.

Department of Surgery:

FOLLETTE, D. M.
GREENHALGH, D. G.
HOLCROFT, J. W.
SEGEL, L. D.
WISNER, D. H.
WOLFE, B. M.

Department of Urology:

DE VERE WHITE, R. W.
STONE, A. R.

School of Veterinary Medicine (tel. (530) 752-1360; fax (530) 752-2801; internet www .vetmed.ucdavis.edu):

Faculty of Anatomy, Physiology and Cell Biology:

BRUSS, M. L.
GIETZEN, D. W.
HART, B. L.
HYDE, D. M.
PINKERTON, K. E.
PLOPPER, C. G.
RAYBOULD, M. J.
STOVER, S. M.
TABLIN, F.
WU, R.

Faculty of Medicine and Epidemiology:

ARDANS, A. A.
CARLSON, G. P.
CARPENTER, T. E.
COWGILL, L. D.
FELDMAN, E. C.
GARDNER, I.
GEORGE, L. W.
HEDRICK, R. P.
HIRD, D. W.
IHRKE, P. J.
KITTLESON, M. D.
LING, G. V.
MADIGAN, J. E.
NELSON, R. W.
PEDERSEN, N. C.

SMITH, B. P.
THOMAS, W. P.
THURMOND, M. C.
WALSH, D. A.
WHITE, S. D.
WILSON, W. D.

Faculty of Molecular Biosciences:

BUCKPITT, A. R.
CORTOPASSI, G. I.
GIRI, S. N.
HANSEN, R. J.
PESSAH, I. N.
ROGERS, Q. R.
SEGALL, H. J.
VULLIET, P. R.

Faculty of Pathology, Microbiology and Immunology:

BARTHOLD, S. W.
BOYCE, W. M.
CHRISTOPHER, M. W.
CONRAD, P. A.
GERSHWIN, L. J.
HIGGINS, R. J.
LEFEBVRE, R. B.
LOWENSTINE, L. J.
MACLACHLAN, N. J.
MILLER, C. J.
MOORE, P. F.
MUNSON, L.
MURPHY, F. A.
OSBURN, B. I.
STOTT, J. L.
WILSON, D. W.
YILMA, T.
ZINKL, J. G.

Faculty of Population Health and Reproduction:

BALL, B. A.
BONDURANT, R. H.
CHOMEL, B. B.
CLIVER, D. O.
CULLOR, J. S.
FARVER, T. B.
HART, L. A.
LAM, K. M.
LASLEY, W. L.
LIU, I. K.
MURRAY, J. D.
TANNENBAUM, J.

Faculty of Surgical and Radiological Sciences:

BUYUKMIHCI, N. C.
GREGORY, C. R.
HASKINS, S. C.
HILDEBRAND, S. V.
HORNOF, W. J.
ILKIW, J.
JONES, J. H.
LECOUTEUR, R. A.
MADEWELL, B. R.
NYLAND, T. G.
O'BRIEN, T. R.
PASCOE, J. R.
PASCOE, P. J.
SNYDER, J. R.
STEFFEY, E. P.
THEON, A. P.
VASSEUR, P.
VERSTRAETE, F. J. M.
WISNER, E. R.

University of California, Irvine

Irvine, CA 92697

Telephone: (949) 824-5011

Internet: www.uci.edu

Founded 1965

State control

Chancellor: MICHAEL V. DRAKE

Exec. Vice-Chancellor and Provost: MICHAEL R. GOTTFREDSON

Vice-Chancellor for Admin. and Business Services: WENDELL C. BRASE

Vice-Chancellor for Planning and Budget: MEREDITH MICHAELS

Vice-Chancellor for Research: JOHN C. HEMMINGER

Vice-Chancellor for Student Affairs: THOMAS A. PARHAM

Vice-Chancellor for Univ. Advancement: GREGORY R. LEET

Univ. Librarian (vacant)

Library of 2,250,000 vols and 22,000 current periodicals

Number of teachers: 1,520

Number of students: 26,984

Publication: *UCI* Gen. Catalogue (1 a year)

DEANS

Claire Trevor School of the Arts: JOSEPH S. LEWIS, III

Donald Bren School of Information and Computer Sciences: HAL STERN (acting)

Henry Samueli School of Engineering: GREGORY WASHINGTON

Paul Merage School of Business: ANDREW J. POLICANO (acting)

School of Biological Sciences: ALBERT BENNETT

School of Humanities: VICKI L. RUIZ

School of Law: ERWIN CHEMERINSKY

School of Medicine: RALPH V. CLAYMAN

School of Physical Sciences: KENNETH C. JANDA

School of Social Ecology: VALERIE JENNESS

School of Social Sciences: BARBARA DOSHER

University of California, Los Angeles (UCLA)

405 Hilgard Ave, Los Angeles, CA 90095-9000

Telephone: (310) 825-4321

Internet: www.ucla.edu

Founded 1919

Chancellor: GENE D. BLOCK

Exec. Vice-Chancellor and Provost: SCOTT WAUGH

Vice-Chancellor for Academic Personnel: CAROLE GOLDBERG

Vice-Chancellor for Admin. Affairs: JACK POWAZEK

Vice-Chancellor for External Affairs: RHEA TURTELTAUB

Vice-Chancellor for Finance, Budget and Capital Programmes: STEVEN A. OLSEN

Vice-Chancellor for Health Sciences: A. EUGENE WASHINGTON

Vice-Chancellor for Legal Affairs: KEVIN REED

Vice-Chancellor for Research: JAMES STEVEN ECONOMOU

Vice-Chancellor for Student Affairs: JANINA MONTERO

Vice-Chancellor (Graduate Studies) and Dean of Graduate Division: ROBIN L. GARRELL

Univ. Librarian: GARY STRONG

Library: 8m. vols, 90,000 periodicals

Number of teachers: 4,016

Number of students: 39,252

DEANS

Anderson School of Management: JUDY OLIAN

Continuing Education and UCLA Extension: CATHY SANDEEN

David Geffen School of Medicine: A. EUGENE WASHINGTON

Graduate Div.: ROBIN L. GARRELL

Graduate School of Education and Information Studies: AIMEE DORR

Henry Samueli School of Engineering and Applied Science: VIJAY DHIR

School of the Arts and Architecture: CHRISTOPHER WATERMAN

School of Dentistry: NO-HEE PARK

School of Law: RACHEL F. MORAN

School of Nursing: COURTNEY LYDER

School of Public Affairs: FRANKLIN GILLIAM, JR
School of Public Health: LINDA ROSENSTOCK
School of Theater, Film and Television: TERI SCHWARTZ

University of California, Merced

POB 2039, Merced, CA 95344
5200 N Lake Rd., Merced, CA 95343
Telephone: (209) 228-4400
Internet: www.ucmerced.edu
Founded 2005
Chancellor: DOROTHY LELAND
Exec. Vice-Chancellor and Provost: KEITH E. ALLEY
Vice-Chancellor for Admin.: MARY E. MILLER
Vice-Chancellor for Research: SAMUEL TRAINA
Vice-Chancellor for Student Affairs: JANE FIORI LAWRENCE
Vice-Chancellor for Univ. Relations: DAVID HOSLEY
Chief Information Officer: RICHARD M. KOGUT
Univ. Librarian: DONALD BARLCA
Number of teachers: 80
Number of students: 5,200

DEANS

Graduate Studies: SAMUEL TRAINA
School of Engineering: E. DANIEL HIRLEMAN
School of Natural Sciences: JUAN MEZA
School of Social Sciences, Humanities and Arts: MARK ALDENDERFER

University of California, Riverside

900 University Ave, Riverside, CA 92521
Telephone: (909) 787-1012
Fax: (909) 787-3866
Internet: www.ucr.edu
Founded 1954
State control
Academic year: September to June
Chancellor: Dr TIMOTHY P. WHITE
Exec. Vice-Chancellor and Provost: DALLAS RABENSTEIN
Vice-Chancellor Finance and Business Operations: GRETCHEN BOLAR
Vice-Chancellor for Admin.: AL DIAZ
Vice-Chancellor for Public Service and Int. Programmes: JOHN F. AZZARETTO
Vice-Chancellor for Research: Dr CHARLES F. LOUIS
Vice-Chancellor for Student Affairs: JAMES W. SANDOVAL
Vice-Chancellor for Univ. Advancement: PETER A. HAYASHIDA
Registrar: ELIZABETH C. BENNETT
Univ. Librarian: Dr RUTH JACKSON
Library of 2,368,843 vols, 2,151 serial subscriptions and 1,772,053 microforms
Number of teachers: 615 (f.t.e.)
Number of students: 19,000

DEANS

Bourns College of Engineering: REZA ABBASCHIAN
College of Humanities, Arts and Social Sciences: STEPHEN CULLENBERG
College of Natural and Agricultural Sciences: MARYLYNN V. YATES
Div. of Biomedical Sciences: Dr CRAIG V. BYUS
Graduate Div.: JOSEPH W. CHILDERS
Graduate School of Education: DOUG MITCHELL
School of Business Administration: YUNZENG WANG

University of California, San Diego

9500 Gilman Dr., La Jolla, CA 92093
Telephone: (858) 534-2230
Fax: (858) 534-5355
Internet: ucsd.edu
State control
Academic year: September to June

Chancellor: MARYE ANNE FOX
Exec. Vice-Chancellor for Academic Affairs: SURESH SUBRAMANI
Vice-Chancellor for External and Business Affairs: STEVEN W. RELYEA
Vice-Chancellor for Health Sciences: DAVID A. BRENNER
Vice-Chancellor for Marine Sciences and Dir of Scripps Institution of Oceanography: TONY D. HAYMET
Vice-Chancellor for Research: SANDRA A. BROWN
Vice-Chancellor for Resource Management and Planning: GARY MATTHEWS
Vice-Chancellor for Student Affairs: PENNY RUE
Provost of Revelle College: DON WAYNE
Provost of John Muir College: SUSAN SMITH (acting)
Provost of Thurgood Marshall College: ALLAN HAVIS
Provost of Earl Warren College: STEVEN ADLER
Provost of Eleanor Roosevelt College: ALAN HOUSTON
Provost of Sixth College: JIM LIN
Registrar: GABRIEL OLSEZEWSKI
Librarian: BRIAN SCHOTTLAENDER
Number of teachers: 1,205
Number of students: 29,324

Publication: *USCD Perspectives*

DEANS

Div. of Arts and Humanities: SETH LERER
Divi. of Biological Sciences: STEVE KAY
Div. of Physical Sciences: MARK THIEMENS
Div. of Social Sciences: JEFFREY L. ELMAN
Jacobs School of Engineering: FRIEDER SEIBLE
Rady School of Management: ROBERT S. SULLIVAN
School of Int. Relations and Pacific Studies: PETER COWHEY
School of Medicine: DAVID A. BRENNER
Scripps Instn of Oceanography: TONY HAYMET
Skaggs School of Pharmacy and Pharmaceutical Sciences: PALMER TAYLOR

University of California, San Francisco

Third and Parnassus Ave, San Francisco, CA 94143
Telephone: (415) 476-9000
Fax: (415) 476-9634
Internet: www.ucsf.edu
Founded 1864
Chancellor: Dr SUSAN DESMOND-HELLMANN
Exec. Vice-Chancellor and Provost: Dr JEFFREY BLUESTONE
Sr Vice-Chancellor: STEVE BARCLAY
Sr Vice-Chancellor for Finance and Admin.: JOHN E. PLOTTS
Sr Vice-Chancellor for Strategic Communications and Univ. Relations: BARBARA J. FRENCH
Vice-Chancellor for Medical Affairs: DAVID KESSLER
Exec. Dir Institute for Biomedical Research: REGIS KELLY
Registrar: DOUGLAS CARLSON
Librarian: KAREN BUTTER
Library of 821,492 vols
Number of teachers: 2,400
Number of students: 4,051

DEANS

Graduate Div.: Dr JOSEPH CASTRO
School of Dentistry: Dr JOHN FEATHERSTONE
School of Medicine: Dr SAM HAGWOOD
School of Nursing: Dr DAVID VLAHOV
School of Pharmacy: MARY-ANNE KODA-KIMBLE

University of California, Santa Barbara

Santa Barbara, CA 93106
Telephone: (805) 893-8000
Internet: www.ucsb.edu
Founded 1909, present status 1944
Academic year: September to June
Chancellor: HENRY T. YANG
Exec. Vice-Chancellor: GENE LUCAS
Vice-Chancellor for Admin. Services: DONNA J. CARPENTER
Vice-Chancellor for Institutional Advancement: JOHN M. WIEMANN
Vice-Chancellor for Research: MICHAEL S. WITHERELL
Vice-Chancellor for Student Affairs: MICHAEL D. YOUNG
Asst Chancellor for Budget and Planning: TODD G. LEE
Registrar: MARSHA BANKSTON (acting)
Univ. Librarian: DENISE STEPHENS
Library: 3m. vols, 540,000 maps, 4,100 MSS collns, 5m. cartographic images and aerial photos
Number of teachers: 1,050
Number of students: 21,685

DEANS

Bren School of Environmental Science and Management: STEVEN D. GAINES
College of Creative Studies: BRUCE TIFFNEY
College of Engineering: ROD C. ALFERNESS
College of Letters and Science: DAVID MARSHALL
Gevirtz Graduate School of Education: JANE CLOSE CONOLEY
Graduate Div.: GALE M. MORRISON
Humanities and Fine Arts: Dr DAVID MARSHALL
Science: PIERRE WILTZIUS
Social Sciences: Dr MELVIN L. OLIVER
Undergraduate Education: MARY NISBET (acting)

University of California, Santa Cruz

1156 High St, Santa Cruz, CA 95064
Telephone: (831) 459-2131
Fax: (831) 459-0146
E-mail: admissions@ucsc.edu
Internet: www.ucsc.edu
Founded 1962
Academic year: September to June
Chancellor: GEORGE R. BLUMENTHAL (acting)
Campus Provost and Exec. Vice-Chancellor: Dr ALISON GALLOWAY
Vice-Provost for Academic Affairs: HERBERT LEE
Vice-Provost and Dean of Undergraduate Education: WILLIAM A. LADUSAW
Vice-Provost and Dean of Univ. Extension: MARK CIOC
Vice-Chancellor for Business and Admin. Services: CHRISTINA L. VALENTINO
Vice-Chancellor for Planning and Budget: MEREDITH MICHAELS
Vice-Chancellor for Research: BRUCE H. MARGON
Vice-Chancellor for Student Affairs: SUSAN HANSEN (acting)
Vice-Chancellor for Univ. Relations: DONNA M. MURPHY
Exec. Director of Admissions and Univ. Registrar: KEVIN BROWNE
Univ. Librarian: VIRGINIA STEEL
Library of 1,350,000 vols, 15,000 periodicals, 800,000 microforms, 500 other items (maps, slides, audio and visual recordings)
Number of teachers: 542 (ladder-rank faculty)
Number of students: 16,332

DEANS

Div. of Arts: DAVID YAGER
Div. of Humanities: WILLIAM A. LADUSAW

Div. of Physical and Biological Sciences: PAUL KOCH
Div. of Social Sciences: SHELDON KAMIENIECKI
Jack Baskin School of Engineering: ARTHUR RAMIREZ

UNIVERSITY OF LA VERNE

1950 Third St, La Verne, CA 91750

Telephone: (909) 593-3511
Fax: (909) 953-0965
Internet: laverne.edu

Founded 1891 as Lordsburg College, present name 1977
Private control
Academic year: September to June
9 Regional campuses

Pres.: DEVORAH LIEBERMAN
Provost and Vice-Pres. for Academic Affairs: ROBERT NEHER
Exec. Vice-Pres.: PHILIP A. HAWKEY
Vice-Pres. for Enrolment Management: HOMA SHABAHANG
Vice-Pres. for Univ. Relations: JEAN BJERKE
Registrar: MARILYN DAVIES
Dean of Student Affairs: LORETTA RAHMANI
Librarian: TAYLOR RUHL
Library of 337,000 vols
Number of teachers: 220 (85 full-time, 135 part-time)
Number of students: 7,500

DEANS

College of Arts and Sciences: Dr JONATHAN L. REED
College of Business and Public Management: Dr ABE HELOU
College of Education and Organization Leadership: Dr MARK GOOR
College of Law: Prof. ALLEN K. EASLEY

UNIVERSITY OF REDLANDS

POB 3080, 1200 E Colton Ave, Redlands, CA 92373-0999

Telephone: (909) 793-2121
Fax: (909) 793-2029
Internet: www.redlands.edu

Founded 1907
Private control

Pres.: Dr JAMES R. APPLETON
Vice-Pres. and Dean for Student Life: CHARLOTTE G. BURGESS
Vice-Pres. for Academic Affairs: DAVID FITE
Sr Vice-Pres. for Finance and Admin.: PHILLIP DOOLITTLE
Vice-Pres. for Univ. Relations: NEIL MACREADY
Registrar: CHARLOTTE LUCEY
Library Dir: JEAN SWANSON
Library of 280,000 vols
Number of teachers: 551
Number of students: 4,080
Publication: Redlands

DEANS

College of Arts and Sciences: Dr KATHY OGREN
School of Business: Dr STUART NOBLE-GOODMAN
School of Education: Dr JAMES VALADEZ
School of Music: Dr ANDREW R. GLENDENING

UNIVERSITY OF SAN DIEGO

5998 Alcala Park, San Diego, CA 92110

Telephone: (619) 260-4600
E-mail: admissions@sandiego.edu
Internet: www.sandiego.edu

Founded 1949
Private control

Pres.: Dr MARY E. LYONS

Exec. Vice-Pres. and Provost: Dr JULIE H. SULLIVAN
Vice-Pres. for Business Services and Admin.: LEENDERT R. HERING
Vice-Pres. for Mission and Ministry: DANIEL J. DILLABOUGH
Vice-Pres. for Student Affairs: CARMEN M. VAZQUEZ
Vice-Pres. for Univ. Relations: Dr TIMOTHY L. O'MALLEY
Librarian: EDWARD STARKEY
Library of 500,000 vols and 2,200 current periodicals
Number of teachers: 845 (402 full-time, 443 part-time)
Number of students: 8,317
Publications: Journal of Contemporary Legal Issues (2 a year), Law Review (4 a year), San Diego International Law Journal (2 a year)

DEANS

College of Arts and Sciences: Dr MARY K. BOYD
Hahn School of Nursing and Health Sciences: Dr Prof. SALLY BROSZ HARDIN
Joan B. Kroc School of Peace Studies: Dr WILLIAM R. HEADLEY
School of Business Administration: Dr DAVID PYKE
School of Law: Dr STEPHEN FERRUOLO
School of Leadership and Education Sciences: Dr PAULA A. CORDEIRO

UNIVERSITY OF SAN FRANCISCO

2130 Fulton St, San Francisco, CA 94117-1080

Telephone: (415) 422-5555
Fax: (415) 422-2303
Internet: www.usfca.edu

Founded 1855
Private control
Academic year: September to May

Pres.: Dr Rev. STEPHEN A. PRIVETT
Provost and Vice-Pres. for Academic Affairs: Dr JENNIFER E. TURPIN
Chancellor: Rev. JOHN LO SCHIAVO
Vice-Pres. for Business and Finance: CHARLIE CROSS
Vice-Pres. for Int. Relations: STANLEY D. NEL
Vice-Pres. for Univ. Advancement: DAVID F. MACMILLAN
Vice-Pres. for Univ. Life: Dr MARGARET M. HIGGINS
Gen. Counsel: DONNA DAVIS
Dean for Academic and Enrolment Services: ELIZABETH J. JOHNSON
Dean for the Univ. Library: TYRONE H. CANNON
Library of 593,543 vols
Number of teachers: 290
Number of students: 8,568
Publications: Maritime Law Journal (2 a year), USF Law Review (4 a year)

DEANS

Colleges of Arts and Sciences: Dr MARCELO CAMPERI
School of Education: Dr WALTER GMELCH
School of Law: Dr JEFFREY S. BRAND
School of Management: Dr MICHAEL J. WEBBER
School of Nursing and Health Professions: Dr JUDITH F. KARSHNER

UNIVERSITY OF SOUTHERN CALIFORNIA

University Park Campus, Los Angeles, CA 90089

Telephone: (213) 740-2311
Internet: www.usc.edu

Founded 1880

Academic year: August to May
Private control

Pres.: C. L. MAX NIKIAS
Provost and Sr Vice-Pres. for Academic Affairs: ELIZABETH GARRETT
Sr Vice-Pres. for Admin.: TODD R. DICKEY
Sr Vice-Pres. for Finance and Chief Financial Officer: ROBERT ABELES
Sr Vice-Pres. for Univ. Advancement: ALBERT R. CHECCIO
Vice-Pres. for Admissions and Planning: KATHERINE HARRINGTON
Gen. Counsel and Sec.: CAROL MAUCH AMIR
Dean of Libraries: CATHERINE QUINLAN
Library: see Libraries and Archives
Number of teachers: 3,400 (full-time)
Number of students: 38,000
Publications: USC Chronicle, USC Trojan Family (4 a year)

DEANS

Annenberg School for Communication and Journalism: ERNEST J. WILSON, III
Davis School of Gerontology: GERALD C. DAVISON
Dornsife College of Letters, Arts and Sciences: HOWARD GILLMAN
Gould School of Law: ROBERT K. RASMUSSEN
Herman Ostrow School of Dentistry: AVISHAI SADAN
Keck School of Medicine: CARMEN A. PULIAFITO
Leventhal School of Accounting: JAMES G. ELLIS
Marshall School of Business: JAMES G. ELLIS
Roski School of Fine Arts: ROCHELLE STEINER
Rossier School of Education: KAREN SYMMS GALLAGHER
School of Architecture: QINGYUN MA
School of Cinematic Arts: ELIZABETH M. DALEY
School of Pharmacy: R. PETE VANDERVEEN
School of Social Work: MARILYN L. FLYNN
School of Theatre: MADELINE PUZO
Sol Price School of Public Policy: JACK H. KNOTT
Thornton School of Music: ROBERT A. CUTIETTA
Viterbi School of Engineering: YANNIS C. YORTSOS

PROFESSORS

Distinguished and University Professors:
ARBIB, MICHAEL A., Biological Sciences and Biomedical Engineering
ARMSTRONG, LLOYD, Jr, Physics and Education
BENNIS, WARREN, Business Admin.
BRAUDY, LEO B., English and American Literature
CAPRON, ALEXANDER M., Law and Medicine
COHEN, MARSHALL, Emeritus of Philosophy and Law
COWAN, GEOFFREY, Communication Leadership
EASTERLIN, RICHARD A., Economics
FINCH, CALEB, Gerontology and Biological Sciences
GOLOMB, SOLOMON W., Electrical Engineering and Mathematics
HELLWARTH, ROBERT W., Physics
JORDAN, THOMAS, Geophysics and Earth Sciences
KINDER, MARSHA, Comparative Literature
PIKE, MALCOLM CECIL, Preventive Medicine
SHIH, JEAN C., Cell and Neurobiology
STARR, KEVIN O., History and Policy, Planning and Devt
TIERNEY, WILLIAM G., Higher Education
TOULMIN, STEPHEN E., Anthropology, Int. Relations and Religion
WATERMAN, MICHAEL S., Biological Sciences and Mathematics
ARNHEIM, NORMAN, Biological Sciences
BENNIS, WARREN, English

CORAGHESSAN BOYLE, T., English
EVERETT, PERCIVAL, Cinematic Arts
HARRIS, MARK JONATHAN, Theory and Composition
HARTKE, STEPHEN, Preventive Medicine
HENDERSON, BRIAN E., Biochemistry and Molecular Biology
JONES, PETER A., Paediatrics
KAUFMAN, FRANCINE R., Molecular Microbiology and Immunology
LAI, MICHAEL M. C., Business
LAWLER, EDWARD E., III, Medicine
LEVINE, ALEXANDRA M., Chemistry
OLAH, GEORGE A., Medicine
RAHIMTOOLA, SHAHBUDIN H., Cardiothoracic Surgery
STARNES, VAUGHN A., Pharmaceutical Sciences
WOLF, MICHAEL A., Biological Sciences and Biomedical Engineering

School of Gerontology:
BENGTSON, V. L.
BONDAREFF, W.
CRIMMINS, E.
DAVIES, K.
FINCH, C.
GATZ, M.
KNIGHT, R.
PYNOOS, J.
SCHNEIDER, E. L.
SCHNEIDER, L.
SILVERSTEIN, M.
WILBER, K.
ZELINSKI, E.

School of Law:
ALTMAN, S. A.
ARMOUR, J. D.
BICE, S. H.
BRECHT, A. O.
CAPRON, A. M.
COWAN, G.
CRUZ, D. B.
DUDZIAK, M. L.
ESTRICH, S.
FINEGAN, E. J.
GARET, R. R.
GARRETT, E.
GILLMAN, H.
GRIFFITH, T. D.
GROSS, A. J.
HADFIELD, G.
KEATING, G. C.
KLERMAN, D. M.
KURAN, T.
LEFCOE, G.
LEVINE, M. L.
LYON, T. D.
MCCAFFERY, E. J.
MARMOR, A.
MURPHY, K. J.
SAKS, E. R.
SCHOR, H. M.
SHAPIRO, M. H.
SIMON, L. G.
SLAWSON, W. D.
SMITH, E. M.
SPITZER, M. L.
STOLZENBERG, N. M.
STONE, C. D.
TALLEY, E. L.
WHITEBREAD, C. H.

School of Medicine:
ADLER, R.
AHMADI, J.
AKMAL, M.
ALKANA, R.
ANDERSON, W.
ANN, D.
APUZZO, M.
ASKANAS, V.
AZEN, S.
BAEHNER, R.
BALLARD, C.
BEART, R., Jr

BERGMAN, R.
BERNE, T.
BERNSTEIN, L.
BEYDOUN, S.
BONDAREFF, W.
BOYD, S.
BREMNER, C.
BRENNER, P.
BRINTON, R.
BROEK, D.
BUCHANAN, T.
CADENAS, E.
CAMPESE, V.
CHANDRASOMA, P.
CHUI, H.
CHUONG, C.-M.
CLARK, F.
COLLETTI, P.
CONTI, P.
COSTIN, G.
COTE, R.
CRAFT, C.
CRANDALL, E.
DANENBERG, P.
DE JUAN, E., Jr
DE MEESTER, T.
DECLERCK, Y.
DEMETRIADES, D.
DENNERT, G.
DIZEREGA, G.
DUBEAU, L.
DWYER, J.
ELKAYAM, U.
EL-SHAHAWY, M.
ENGEL, W.
EPSTEIN, A.
FARLEY, R.
FEINSTEIN, D.
FRANK, G.
GAYNON, P.
GEFFNER, M.
GIANNOTTA, S.
GILL, P.
GILLES, F.
GILLILAND, F.
GILSANZ, V.
GOMER, C.
GONG, H., Jr
GOODWIN, T.
GORAN, M.
GOVINDARAJAN, S.
GRANT, E.
GROFFEN, J.
GRUSHKIN, C.
HAHN, R.
HAILE, R.
HALLS, J.
HAMMOND, G.
HAYS, D.
HAYWOOD, L.
HEISTERKAMP, N.
HENDERSON, B.
HILL, A.
HINTON, D.
HODGMAN, J.
HODIS, H.
HOFMAN, F.
HOHN, A.
HORWITZ, D.
HSIEH, C.-L.
HUANG, H.
HUMAYUN, M.
HURVITZ, D.
ISRAEL, R.
IWAKI, Y.
JACOBS, R.
JELLIFFE, R.
JOHNSON, C.
JOHNSON, C.
JOHNSON, D.
JONES, P.
KALRA, V.
KAPLOWITZ, N.
KAPTEIN, E.
KAST, W. M.
KATKHOUDA, N.

KAUFMAN, F.
KEANE, J.
KEDES, L.
KEENS, T.
KILBURN, K.
KLONER, R.
KOHN, D.
KORSCH, B.
KOSS, M.
LAINE, L.
LAMB, H.
LAUG, W.
LAWLOR, M.
LEE, A.
LEVINE, A.
LEVY, D.
LEWIS, A.
LIEBER, M.
LIESKOVSKY, G.
LU, S.
LUMB, P.
MCCOMB, J.
MCDONOUGH, A.
MCMILLAN, M.
MCNEILL, T.
MACK, T.
MAHOUR, G.
MARKLAND, F.
MARTIN, W.
MATTINGLY, C.
MAXSON, R.
MEISELMAN, H.
MENDEZ, R.
MILLER, C.
MINCKLER, D.
MIRCHEFF, A.
MISHELL, D., Jr
MISHRA, S.
MORROW, C.
MULL, J.
MURPHREE, A.
NATHWANI, B.
NELSON, M.
NEWTH, C.
NICOLOFF, J.
NIMNI, M.
O'LEARY, D.
OU, J.-H.
PARKMAN, R.
PATTENGALE, P.
PATZAKIS, M.
PAULSON, R.
PENTZ, M.
PETERS, J. M.
PIKE, M.
PLATZKER, A.
PORTNOY, B.
POWARS, D.
PRESS, M.
PRESTON-MARTIN, S.
QUISMORIO, F.
RADIN, D.
RAHIMTOOLA, S.
RALLS, K.
RAO, N.
RASHEED, S.
REYNOLDS, C.
RICE, D.
RICHARDSON, J.
ROSS, R.
ROY, S.
ROY-BURMAN, P.
RUDE, R.
RYAN, S., Jr
SADUN, A.
SATTLER, F.
SCHECHTER, J.
SCHNEIDER, L.
SEEGER, R.
SEGALL, H.
SELBY, R.
SENER, S.
SHARMA, O.
SHERWIN, R.
SHIBATA, D.
SHIH, J.

SHOUPE, D.
SHRIVASTAVA, P.
SHULMAN, I.
SIEGEL, M.
SIEGEL, S.
SILBERMAN, H.
SILKA, M.
SILVERSTEIN, M.
SINATRA, F.
SINGH, M.
SKINNER, D.
SMITH, R.
SOHAL, R.
SOKOL, R.
STALLCUP, M.
STANLEY, P.
STARNES, V.
STELLWAGEN, R.
STOHL, W.
STOHLMAN, S.
STRAM, D.
SUSSMAN, S.
TAKAHASHI, M.
TAYLOR, C.
TENG, E.
THOMAS, D.
THORDARSON, D.
TOKES, Z.
TOLO, V.
TRICHE, T.
TSUKAMOTO, H.
VANGSNESS, T., Jr
VARMA, R.
VESELY, L.
WARBURTON, D.
WEAVER, F.
WEBER, J.
WEINBERG, K.
WEINER, L.
WEISS, M.
WETZEL, R.
WILLIAMS, R.
WOOD, B.
WOODLEY, D.
WU, P.
WU-WILLIAMS, A.
YELLIN, A.
YING, S.-Y.
YU, M.
ZEE, C.-S.
ZEIDLER, A.
ZELMAN, V.

School of Music:
BEER, H., Conducting
BERG, S., Jazz Studies
BROWN, B. A., Music History
CRAVENS, T., Winds and Percussion
CROCKETT, D., Composition
DEHNING, W., Choral and Sacred Music
GLAZE, G., Vocal Arts
GORDON, S., Keyboard Studies
HARTKE, S. N., Composition
HOPKINS, J. F., Composition
LAURIDSEN, M., II, Composition
LEONARD, R., Strings
LESEMANN, F., Composition
LIVINGSTON, L., Conducting
MASON, T. D., Jazz Studies
MCCURDY, R. C., Jazz Studies
MCINNES, D., Strings
PERRY, J., Keyboard Studies
POLLACK, D., Keyboard Studies
SCHOENFELD, E., Strings
SIMMS, B., Music History
THOMAS, W. E. L., Electro-Acoustic Media
TICHELI, F., IV, Composition
TYLER, J., Early Music Performance, Music
History

School of Pharmacy:
ALKANA, R. L.
ANN, D.
BRINTON, R.
BURCKHART, G.
CADENAS, E.
CHAN, T. M.

JOHNSON, D.
SHEN, W.-C.
SHIH, J. C.
SOHAL, R.
STIMMEL, G. L.
WOLF, W.

School of Policy, Planning and Development:
BANERJEE, T.
CAIDEN, G.
COOPER, T.
FERRIS, J. M.
GABRIEL, S. A.
GIULIANO, G.
GORDON, P.
GRADDY, E.
GREENWALD, H.
HEIKKILA, E.
KREIGER, M. H.
LOPEZ-LEE, D.
MAZMANIAN, D.
MELNICK, G.
MYERS, D.
MYRTLE, R.
NEWLAND, C.
PACHON, H.
PETAK, W.
RICHARDSON, H.
SLOANE, D.
SUNDEEN, R., Jr
TANG, S.-Y.
VON WINTERFELDT, D.
WHOLEY, J. S.

School of Social Work:
BREKKE, J.
CHI, I.
ELL, K.
FLYNN, M.
JANSSON, B.
MCCROSKEY, J.
MONDROS, J.
MOR-BARAK, M.
STONER, M.
TRICKETT, P.

School of Theatre:
CARNICKE, S. M.
HOUSTON, V.
PUZO, M.

UNIVERSITY OF THE PACIFIC

3601 Pacific Ave, Stockton, CA 95211
Telephone: (209) 946-2211
E-mail: admission@pacific.edu
Internet: www.pacific.edu
Founded 1851 as California Wesleyan College, present name 1961
Private control
Academic year: August to May
Main campus in Stockton; Pacific McGeorge School of Law in Sacramento; Arthur A. Dugoni School of Dentistry in San Francisco
Pres.: PAMELA A. EIBECK
Provost: Dr MARIA G. PALLAVICINI
Vice-Pres. for Devt: CHRISTOPHER JOHNSTON
Vice-Pres. for Business and Finance: PATRICK CAVANAUGH
Vice-Pres. for Student Life: Dr ELIZABETH GRIEGO
Vice-Pres. for External Relations: TED LELAND
Dean for the Library: C. BRIGID WELCH
Library of 281,769 vols, 1,361 periodicals, 689,462 microforms
Number of teachers: 444 (all campuses)
Number of students: 7,000 (all campuses)
Publications: Contact Point (3 a year), De Minimis, Pacifican, Pacific Historian, Pacific Law, Pacific Review

DEANS

Arthur A. Dugoni School of Dentistry: Dr PATRICK J. FERRILLO, JR
College of the Pacific: Dr THOMAS W. KRISE

Conservatory of Music: GIULIO M. ONGARO
Eberhardt School of Business: LEWIS R. GALES
Gladys L. Benerd School of Education: LYNN BECK
McGeorge School of Law: ELIZABETH RINDS-KOPF PARKER
School of Engineering and Computer Science: Dr RAVI JAIN
School of International Studies: Dr CYNTHIA WAGNER WEICK
Research and Graduate Studies: Dr JIN K. GONG
Thomas J. Long School of Pharmacy and Health Sciences: PHILIP OPPENHEIMER

UNIVERSITY OF WEST LOS ANGELES

9800 S La Cienega Blvd, 12th Fl., Inglewood, CA 90301-4423
Telephone: (310) 342-5200
Fax: (310) 342-5295
Internet: www.uwla.edu
Founded 1966
Private control
Campuses in W Los Angeles and the San Fernando Valley
Pres.: ROBERT W. BROWN
Vice-Pres. for Student Affairs: Dr ROBERT W. ADAMS
Dean: BASIL G. DEZES
Dir of Enrolment: JOHN MCTEAGUE
Dir of Facilities: RON BEATTY
Dir of Operations (San Fernando Valley Campus): PAT GALASSO
Dir of Student Services: PAT MYERS
Assoc. Dean and Registrar: TONI O'NEAL
Librarian: JESSE ALDAVA
Library of 34,000 vols
Number of teachers: 40 (3 full-time, 37 adjunct)
Number of students: 350
Publication: UWLA Law Review (2 a year)

DEANS

School of Law: BASIL GEORGE DEZES
School of Paralegal Studies: MARLENE AMERA ALHANDY

VANGUARD UNIVERSITY OF SOUTHERN CALIFORNIA

55 Fair Dr., Costa Mesa, CA 92626-9601
Telephone: (714) 556-3610
Fax: (714) 957-9317
E-mail: kanolf@vanguard.edu
Internet: www.vanguard.edu
Founded 1920 as Southern California Bible School, present name and status 1999
Private control
Courses incl. business and management, communication and arts, education, humanities, natural sciences and mathematics, psychology and religion
Pres.: Dr CAROL A. TAYLOR
Provost and Vice-Pres. for Academic Affairs: Dr JEFF HITTENBERGER
Vice-Pres. for Business and Finance: LETTIE COWIE
Vice-Pres. for Enrolment Management: KIM JOHNSON
Vice-Pres. for Student Affairs: ANN HAMILTON
Vice-Pres. for Univ. Advancement: KELLY KANNWISCHER
Dean of Students: LINDA HARTZELL
Registrar: JUDY K. HAMILTON
Head Librarian: ALISON ENGLISH
Library of 135,500 vols, 1,053 periodicals
Number of teachers: 175 (62 full-time, 113 part-time)
Number of students: 1,961
Publication: Vanguard Magazine (4 a year)

DEANS

School for Professional Studies: Dr PAUL COX

WESTERN STATE UNIVERSITY COLLEGE OF LAW

1111 N State College Blvd, Fullerton, CA 92831-3014

Telephone: (714) 738-1000
Fax: (714) 441-1748
E-mail: adm@wsulaw.edu
Internet: www.wsulaw.edu

Founded 1966
Private control
Academic year: August to May

Criminal Law Practice Center, Business Law Center, Legal Clinic and Trial Practice Programme

Dean and Pres.: WILLIAM E. ADAMS
Assoc. Dean of Academic Affairs: SUSAN KELLER
Dir of Criminal Law Practice Center: DAVID FRAKT
Dir of Legal Clinic: TERENCE W. ROBERTS
Library Dir: PATRICIA HARRIS O'CONNOR (acting)

Number of teachers: 62 (28 full-time, 34 adjunct)
Number of students: 500

WESTERN UNIVERSITY OF HEALTH SCIENCES

309 East Second St, Pomona, CA 91766-1854

Telephone: (909) 6236116
E-mail: admissions@westernu.edu
Internet: www.westernu.edu

Founded 1977 as College of Osteopathic Medicine of the Pacific, present name 1996
Private control

Pres.: Dr PHILIP PUMERANTZ
Provost and Chief Operating Officer: GARY M. GUGELCHUK
Treas. and Chief Financial Officer: KEVIN D. SHAW
Vice-Pres. for Human Resources: HOWARD M. PARDUE
Vice-Pres. for Research and Biotechnology: STEVEN J. HENRIKSEN
Vice-Pres. for Enrolment Management and Student Affairs: BEVERLY A. GUIDRY
Library Dir: PATRICIA VADER
Number of students: 1,425

DEANS

College of Allied Health Professions: Dr STEPHANIE D. BOWLIN
College of Biomedical Sciences: Dr MICHEL BAUDRY
College of Dental Medicine: Dr STEVEN W. FRIEDRICHSEN
College of Graduate Nursing: KAREN HANFORD
College of Optometry: Dr ELIZABETH HOPPE
College of Osteopathic Medicine of the Pacific: CLINTON E. ADAMS
College of Podiatric Medicine: Dr LAWRENCE B. HARKLESS
College of Pharmacy: Dr DANIEL ROBINSON
College of Veterinary Medicine: Dr PHILLIP D. NELSON

WESTMINSTER SEMINARY CALIFORNIA

1725 Bear Valley Parkway, Escondido, CA 92027

Telephone: (760) 480-8474
Fax: (760) 480-0252
E-mail: info@wscal.edu
Internet: www.wscal.edu

Founded 1979
Private control

Academic year: September to May

Offers MDiv and MA in biblical studies, theological studies, historical theology, Christian studies

Pres.: Dr W. ROBERT GODFREY
Exec. Vice-Pres.: STEVEN OEVERMAN
Vice-Pres. for Advancement: DAWN G. DOORN
Academic Dean: Dr J. V. FESKO
Dean of Students: Dr JULIUS J. KIM
Registrar: BRIAN J. MILLS
Library Dir: JOHN BALES

Library of 120,000 vols, 260 periodicals
Number of teachers: 25 (12 full-time)
Number of students: 150

WHITTIER COLLEGE

POB 634, 13406 E Philadelphia, Whittier, CA 90608-4413

Telephone: (562) 907-4200
Fax: (562) 907-4870
E-mail: president@whittier.edu
Internet: www.whittier.edu

Founded 1887
Private control

Liberal arts, business and law

Pres.: Dr SHARON D. HERZBERGER
Vice-Pres. and Dean of Students: JEANNE ORTIZ
Vice-Pres. for Academic Affairs and Dean of the Faculty: CHARLOTTE BORST
Vice-Pres. for Advancement: ELIZABETH POWER ROBISON
Vice-Pres. for Enrolment: LISA MEYER
Vice-Pres. for Finance and Admin.: JAMES DUNKELMAN
Registrar: WILLIAM GARTRELL
Assoc. Library Dir: LAUREL CRUMP

Library of 250,000 vols, 44,000 microfilms, 300 current periodicals; spec. collns: John Greenleaf Whittier, Quakers
Number of teachers: 100 (full-time)
Number of students: 1,500

Publications: *The Rock* (3 a year), *Whittier Law Review*

DEANS

Whittier Law School: PENELOPE BRYAN

WILLIAM JESSUP UNIVERSITY

333 Sunset Blvd, Rocklin, CA 95765

Telephone: (916) 577-2200
Fax: (916) 577-2203
E-mail: information@jessup.edu
Internet: www.jessup.edu

Founded 1939 as San Jose Bible College, present name and status 2004
Private control
Academic year: September to May

Areas of study: Bible and theology, business administration, Christian education, English, history, intercultural studies, liberal studies, music, pastoral ministry, psychology, public policy and youth ministry; br. campus at San Jose

Pres.: JOHN JACKSON
Vice-Pres. for Academic Affairs: Dr DENNIS JAMESON
Vice-Pres. for Advancement: JOSEPH D. WOMACK
Vice-Pres. for Finance and Admin.: GENE DE YOUNG
Vice-Pres. for Student Devt: PAUL BLEZIEN
Registrar: TINA PETERSEN
Library Dir: KEVIN PISCHKE

Library of 34,000 vols
Number of students: 896

WOODBURY UNIVERSITY

7500 Glenoaks Blvd, Burbank, CA 91510-7846

Telephone: (818) 767-0888
E-mail: info@woodbury.edu
Internet: www.woodbury.edu

Founded 1884 as Woodbury Business College; present name 1974
Private control
Academic year: August to August
Br. campus at San Diego

Pres.: Dr LUIS CALINGO
Vice-Pres. for Academic Affairs: DAVID M. ROSEN
Vice-Pres. for Student Devt: PHYLLIS CREMER
Vice-Pres. for Enrolment Management and Univ. Marketing: DON E. ST. CLAIR
Vice-Pres. for Finance and Admin.: KEN JONES
Vice-Pres. for Information Technology and Planning: STEVE DYER
Vice-Pres. for Univ. Advancement: RICHARD M. NORDIN
Dir for Library Services: NEDRA PETERSON
Number of students: 1,500

DEANS

Institute of Transdisciplinary Studies: Dr DOUGLAS J. CREMER
School of Architecture: NORMAN MILLAR
School of Business: Dr ANDRÈ B. VAN NIEKERK
School of Media, Culture and Design: Dr EDWARD M. CLIFT

WRIGHT INSTITUTE

2728 Durant Ave, Berkeley, CA 94704

Telephone: (510) 841-9230
Fax: (510) 841-0167
E-mail: info@wi.edu
Internet: www.wi.edu

Founded 1968
Private control
Academic year: September to June
Area of study: clinical psychology

Pres.: PETER DYBWAD
Vice-Pres. for Finance and Admin. Affairs: TRICIA O'REILLY
Dean: Dr CHUCK ALEXANDER
Dir for Clinical Training: GILBERT NEWMAN
Dir of Clinical Services: CRYSTAL A. JOHNSON
Registrar: GINNY MORGAN
Library Dir: JASON STRAUSS

Library of 10,000 items, 1,100 journals.

COLORADO

ADAMS STATE COLLEGE

208 Edgemont Blvd, Alamosa, CO 81101

Telephone: (719) 587-7011
Fax: (719) 587-7522
E-mail: ascadmit@adams.edu
Internet: www.adams.edu

Founded 1921
State control

Depts of art, biology, business administration, chemistry, communications, computer science, earth sciences, English, history/government/philosophy, human performance and physical education, interdisciplinary studies, mathematics, music, nursing, physics, psychology, sociology, Spanish, teacher education, theatre

Pres.: Dr DAVID P. SVALDI
Vice-Pres. for Academic Affairs: Dr FRANK NOVOTNY
Sr Vice-Pres. for Enrolment Management and Programme Devt: Dr MICHAEL MUMPER

Vice-Pres. for Finance and Govt Relations: BILL MANSHEIM
Asst Vice-Pres. for Student Affairs: KENNETH MARQUEZ
Dir for Student Support Services: DEBORAH WHITE
Registrar: M. BELEN MAESTAS
Dir for Library: DAVID GOETZMAN

Library of 127,024 vols, 1,350 maps, 2,748 videos and DVDs, 13,577 microfilm reels, 338 periodical subscriptions, 119,289 unique titles and editions
Number of teachers: 123 (full-time and part-time)
Number of students: 3,701

COLLEGE FOR FINANCIAL PLANNING

8000 E Maplewood Ave, Suite 200, Greenwood Village, CO 80111
Telephone: (303) 220-1200
Fax: (303) 220-1810
E-mail: cffpenrollmentgroup@apollogrp.edu
Internet: www.cffp.edu
Founded 1972
Private control
Pres.: JOHN SEARS
Vice-Pres. for Academic Affairs: Dr JESSE B. ARMAN.

COLORADO CHRISTIAN UNIVERSITY

8787 W Alameda Ave, Lakewood, CO 80226
Telephone: (303) 963-3000
Fax: (303) 963-3001
E-mail: admission@ccu.edu
Internet: www.ccu.edu
Founded 1989 by merger of Colorado Christian College and Colorado Baptist Univ.
Private control
Academic year: August to August
Pres.: WILLIAM L. ARMSTRONG
Vice-Pres. for Academic Affairs: Dr CHERRI PARKS
Vice-Pres. for Business Affairs and Chief Financial Officer: DANIEL L. COHRS
Vice-Pres. for Student Devt: JAMES S. MCCORMICK
Vice-Pres. for Devt: PAUL J. ELDRIDGE
Asst Vice-Pres. for Admin. Services: RON W. BENTON
Registrar: LINDA PERCIANTE
Library Dir: GAYLE C. GUNDERSON

Library of 100,000 vols, 9,300 reference titles, 1,500 video cassettes, 200 audio cassettes, 2,500 music CDs
Number of teachers: 334
Number of students: 4,000

DEANS
College of Adult and Graduate Studies, Business and Technology Division: Dr MELLANI J. DAY
College of Adult and Graduate Studies, Curriculum and Instruction Education Division: Dr WENDY ELLIOT WENDOVER
College of Adult and Graduate Studies, Nursing and Sciences Division: Dr BARBARA J. WHITE
College of Adult and Graduate Studies, Social Sciences and Humanities Division: Prof. Dr LAVERNE K. JORDAN
School of Business and Leadership: Dr GARY W. EWEN
School of Education: Dr SARA DALLMAN
School of Humanities and Sciences: Dr WILLIAM R. SAXBY
School of Music: STEVEN T. TAYLOR
School of Theology: Dr SID BUZZELL

COLORADO COLLEGE

14 E Cache La Poudre St, Colorado Springs, CO 80903
Telephone: (719) 389-6000
Fax: (719) 389-6933
E-mail: communications@coloradocollege.edu
Internet: www.coloradocollege.edu
Founded 1874
Private control

American cultural studies, anthropology, art, Asian studies, biology, chemistry, classics, comparative literature, drama and dance, East Asian languages, economics and business, education, English, environmental science, feminist and gender studies, geology, German, history, mathematics and computer science, music, philosophy, physics, political science, psychology, religion, Romance languages, Russian, sociology, sport science, Southwest studies

Pres.: JILL TIEFENTHALER
Vice-Pres. for Advancement: STEPHEN ELDER
Vice-Pres. for Finance and Admin. and Treas.: ROBERT MOORE
Vice-Pres. for Enrolment Management: MARK HATCH
Vice-Pres. for Information Management: DAVE ARMSTRONG
Vice-Pres. for Student Life: MIKE EDMONDS
Dean for College and Faculty: SUSAN ASHLEY
Registrar: PHIL APODOCA
Library Dir: CAROL DICKERSON

Number of teachers: 140
Number of students: 2,040

COLORADO MESA UNIVERSITY

1100 N Ave, Grand Junction, CO 81501-3122
Telephone: (970) 248-1020
Fax: (970) 248-1973
Internet: www.coloradomesa.edu
Founded 1925 as Grand Junction Junior College, present name 2011
State control
Academic year: August to May

Depts of art, biological sciences, business, computer science, mathematics and statistics, health sciences, kinesiology, languages, literature and mass communication, mechanical engineering partnership program, physical and environmental sciences, social and behavioural sciences, teacher education and theatre; campuses in Montrose and Grand Junction in Colorado

Pres.: TIMOTHY E. FOSTER
Vice-Pres. for Academic Affairs: Dr CAROL FUTHEY
Vice-Pres. for Admin. Services and Finance: PATRICK DOYLE
Vice-Pres. for Student Services: JOHN MARSHALL
Dir of Admissions: JARED MEIER
Registrar: HOLLY TEAL
Dir of Library: ELIZABETH BRODAK (acting)

Library of 395,200 vols, 59,300 current journals, 30,500 e-books and documents, 82,375 govt docs, 12,248 audiovisual items, 17,390 maps
Number of teachers: 230 (full-time)
Number of students: 8,844 (8,766 undergraduate, 60 graduate, 18 exclusively extended studies)

COLORADO MOUNTAIN COLLEGE

802 Grand Ave, Glenwood Springs, CO 81601
Telephone: (970) 945-8691
Fax: (970) 947-8324
E-mail: joinus@coloradomtn.edu
Internet: www.coloradomtn.edu
Founded 1967

State control
Academic year: May to April
Offers Bachelors degrees in business administration and sustainability studies; 11 campuses
Pres.: Dr STANLEY JENSEN
Sr Vice-Pres.: Dr JILL BOYLE
Sr Vice-Pres. for Academic Affairs: Dr BRAD TYNDALL
Vice-Pres. for Student Affairs: BRAD BANKHEAD
Vice-Pres. for Institutional Effectiveness: Dr MEETA GOEL
Vice-Pres. and Chief Information Officer: SCOTT COWDREY
Number of students: 25,000

COLORADO SCHOOL OF MINES

1500 Illinois St, Golden, CO 80401-1887
Telephone: (303) 273-3000
Fax: (303) 273-3278
E-mail: presoffice@mines.edu
Internet: www.mines.edu
Founded 1874
State control

Engineering education and applied science related to earth, energy, materials and environment

Pres.: BILL SCOGGINS
Provost and Exec. Vice-Pres.: Dr TERENCE PARKER
Exec. Vice-Pres. for Univ. Advancement: BRIAN WINKELBAUER
Sr Vice-Pres. for Finance and Admin.: JOSEPH TRUBACZ
Vice-Pres. for Research and Technology Transfer: Dr JOHN POATE
Vice-Pres. for Student Life: Dr DANIEL FOX
Dean for Graduate Studies: Dr THOMAS M. BOYD
Dir for Enrolment Management: HEATHER BOYD
Chief Information Officer: DEREK WILSON
Dir for Library: JOANNE LERUD HECK

Library of 200,000 vols, 900 print journals, 30,000 e-journals, 30,000 e-books, 500,000 govt publs, 453,000 microforms and 172,000 maps
Number of teachers: 200
Number of students: 5,000

Publications: *Energy and the Earth*, *High Grade* (online (highgrade.mines.edu)), *Mines Magazine* (3 a year, online (minesmagazine.com)).

COLORADO STATE UNIVERSITY

Fort Collins, CO 80523
Telephone: (970) 491-6444
Fax: (970) 491-0501
E-mail: presofc@lamar.colostate.edu
Internet: www.colostate.edu
Founded 1870 as Colorado Agricultural College, present name 1957
State control
Pres.: Dr TONY FRANK
Provost and Exec. Vice-Pres.: Prof. Dr RICK MIRANDA
Vice-Pres. for Advancement: BRETT ANDERSON
Vice-Pres. for Enrolment and Access: Dr ROBIN BROWN
Vice-Pres. for Information Technology and Dean for Libraries: Dr PATRICK J. BURNS
Vice-Pres. for Research: WILLIAM H. FARLAND
Vice-Pres. for Student Affairs: Dr BLANCHE M. HUGHES
Vice-Pres. for Univ. Operations: AMY PARSONS

Library: see Libraries and Archives
Number of teachers: 1,540
Number of students: 30,450

DEANS

College of Agricultural Sciences: Dr CRAIG BEYROUTY

College of Applied Human Sciences: Dr JEFF MCCUBBIN

College of Business: Dr AJAY MENON

College of Engineering: Dr SANDRA WOODS

College of Liberal Arts: Dr ANN M. GILL

College of Natural Sciences: Prof. JANICE L. NERGER

College of Veterinary Medicine and Biomedical Sciences: Dr LANCE PERRYMAN

Warner College of Natural Resources: JOYCE BERRY

COLORADO STATE UNIVERSITY— PUEBLO

2200 Bonforte Blvd, Pueblo, CO 81001-4901

Telephone: (719) 549-2100

Fax: (719) 549-2419

E-mail: info@colostate-pueblo.edu

Internet: www.colostate-pueblo.edu

Founded 1933 as S Colorado Junior College, present status 1965, present name 2003

State control

Pres.: LESLEY A. DI MARE

Provost and Vice-Pres. for Academic Affairs: Dr RICK KREMINSKI

Dean for Student Affairs: Dr ZAV DADABHOY

Dean for Univ. Library: RHONDA GONZALES

Library of 350,000 vols, 12,000 CDs, DVDs and video cassettes, 40,000 print and online journals

Number of teachers: 398 (188 full-time, 210 part-time)

Number of students: 5,246

DEANS

College of Education, Engineering and Professional Studies: Prof. HECTOR R. CARRASCO

College of Humanities and Social Sciences: ROY B. SONNEMA

College of Science and Mathematics: Dr DAVID W. LEHMPUHL

Division of Continuing Education: Dr JAMES MALM

Graduate Studies: Dr MEL DRUELINGER

Hasan School of Business: SUE HANKS

COLORADO TECHNICAL UNIVERSITY

4435 N Chestnut St, Colorado Springs, CO 80907

Telephone: (719) 598-0200

Fax: (719) 598-3740

E-mail: help@coloradotech.edu

Internet: www.coloradotech.edu

Founded 1965

Private control

Academic year: October to September

Campuses in Colorado Springs, Denver, Kansas City, Pueblo and Sioux Falls

CEO: JEREMY WHEATON

Chancellor and Chief Academic Officer: Dr DAVID LEASURE

Provost: Dr CONNIE JOHNSON

Vice-Provost: Dr CHRIS DAVIS

Vice-Pres. for Admissions: KEITH ARMSTRONG

Vice-Pres. for Finance: JENNIFER BRIAR

Vice-Pres. for Student Affairs: MARK GASCHE

Vice-Pres. for Operations: ERIC STORTZ

Registrar: ROLAND RUDAS

Librarian: KAY BURMAN

DEANS

College of Business and Management: JOSEPH HEINZMAN, JR

College of Engineering and Computer Science: Dr BRUCE HARMON

DENVER SEMINARY

POB 100000, Denver, CO 80250-0100

6399 S Santa Fe Dr., Littleton, CO 80120

Telephone: (303) 761-2482

Fax: (303) 761-8060

E-mail: info@denverseminary.edu

Internet: www.denverseminary.edu

Founded 1950

Private control

Academic year: September to May

Pres.: Dr MARK YOUNG

Chancellor: GORDON MACDONALD

Provost and Dean: Dr RANDY MACFARLAND

Vice-Pres. for Advancement: Dr JIM HOWARD

Vice-Pres. for Enrolment Management: BOB FOMER

Vice-Pres. of Finance: DEBBIE KELLAR

Vice-Pres. for Student Services: ROBERT JONES

Dir for Admissions: CHRISTINE MULLER

Registrar: PAM BETKER

Dir for Library: Dr KEITH P. WELLS

Library of 175,000 vols, 250 periodical subscriptions

Number of teachers: 27

Number of students: 1,030

Publications: *Denver Seminary Magazine, The Denver Journal*.

FORT LEWIS COLLEGE

1000 Rim Dr., Durango, CO 81301-3999

Telephone: (970) 247-7010

E-mail: admission@fortlewis.edu

Internet: www.fortlewis.edu

Founded 1911

State control

Pres.: Dr DENE KAY THOMAS

Provost and Vice-Pres. for Academic Affairs: Dr BARBARA MORRIS

Vice-Pres. for Finance and Admin.: STEVEN SCHWARTZ

Vice-Pres. for Student Affairs: Dr GLENNA WITT SEXTON

Dir for Admission and Advising: ANDREW BURNS

Registrar: KATHY KENDALL

Dir for Library: ASTRID OLIVER

Library of 175,000 vols

Number of teachers: 261

Number of students: 3,685

DEANS

School of Arts, Humanities and Social Sciences: Dr LINDA SCHOTT

School of Business Administration: Dr GARY LINN

School of Natural and Behavioural Sciences: Dr MAUREEN BRANDON

ILIFF SCHOOL OF THEOLOGY

2201 S University Blvd, Denver, CO 80210-4798

Telephone: (303) 744-1287

Fax: (303) 777-0164

E-mail: info@iliff.edu

Internet: www.iliff.edu

Founded 1892

Private control

Academic year: September to August

Pres.: DAVID TRICKETT

Academic Vice-Pres. and Dean for Faculty: ALBERT HERNANDEZ

Vice-Pres. for Institutional Advancement: PEGGY SANDGREN

Dean for Enrolment and Student Services: DAVID WORLEY

Registrar: CARMEN BACA DOSTER

Dir for Library and Information Services: Dr DEBORAH CREAMER

Library of 248,000 vols, 900 periodical subsriptions, 56,000 microforms

Number of teachers: 14

Number of students: 300

JONES INTERNATIONAL UNIVERSITY

9697 E Mineral Ave, Centennial, CO 80112

Telephone: (303) 784-8904

Fax: (303) 799-0966

E-mail: info@jonesinternational.edu

Internet: www.jiu.edu

Founded 1993

Private control

Pres.: RICHARD COX, JR

Chancellor: GLENN R. JONES

Exec. Vice-Chancellor: BRUCE CUNNINGHAM

Sr Vice-Pres., Admin. and Human Resources: AMY THRALL

Chief Academic Officer: MARIJANE AXTELL PAULSEN

Chief Information Officer: JOHN E. JENNINGS

Library of 45,000 vols of e-books

DEANS

School of Business: Dr DANETTE LANCE

School of Education: Dr JOANNE MAYPOLE

METROPOLITAN STATE COLLEGE OF DENVER

POB 173362, Denver, CO 80217-3362

1059 Ninth St Park, Denver, CO

Telephone: (303) 556-2400

Internet: www.mscd.edu

Founded 1965

State control

Academic year: August to May

Campuses at Northglenn and Greenwood Village

Pres.: Dr STEPHEN M. JORDAN

Provost and Vice-Pres. for Academic Affairs: Dr VICKI GOLICH

Vice-Pres. for Admin. and Finance: NATALIE LUTES

Vice-Pres. for Advancement and External Relations: ERIN TRAPP

Vice-Pres. for Student Services: (vacant)

Dean for Student Life: EMILIA PAUL

Registrar: PAULA MARTINEZ

Univ. Librarian: MARY M. SOMERVILLE

Library: 1m. traditional print and media items

Number of teachers: 1,451 (540 full-time, 911 part-time)

Number of students: 24,000

Publication: *Metrosphere* (1 a year)

DEANS

School of Business: Dr ANN MURPHY

School of Letters, Arts and Sciences: Dr JOAN LAURA FOSTER

School of Professional Studies: Dr SANDRA D. HAYNES

NAROPA UNIVERSITY

2130 Arapahoe Ave, Boulder, CO 80302

Telephone: (303) 444-0202

Fax: (303) 444-0410

E-mail: infodesk@naropa.edu

Internet: www.naropa.edu

Founded 1974 as Naropa Institute

Private control

Academic year: August to July (3 semesters)

BAs in contemplative psychology, early childhood education, environmental studies, interdisciplinary studies, music, religious studies, traditional eastern arts, visual arts and writing and literature, fine arts in performance; MAs in contemplative education, creative writing, divinity, environmental leadership, fine arts, Indo-Tibetan Buddhism, religious studies, counselling psychology (contemplative, somatic transpersonal), writing and poetics

Pres.: JOHN WHITEHOUSE COBB (acting)
Provost and Vice-Pres. for Academic Affairs: Dr CAROL A. BLACKSHIRE-BELAY
Vice-Pres. for Student Affairs and Enrolment Management: CHERYL BARBOUR
Dir for Library and Archives: NICHOLAS WEISS

Library of 26,000 vols, 100 periodicals; spec. collns incl. 15,000 original Tibetan texts in 2,200 vols, 6,000 audiocassette recordings of events held at Naropa Univ.
Number of students: 1,063 (445 undergraduate, 618 graduate)

NATIONAL THEATRE CONSERVATORY

1101 13th St, Denver, CO 80204-2154
Telephone: (303) 893-4000
E-mail: ntc@dcpa.org
Internet: www.denvercenter.org
Founded 1984; attached to Denver Center for the Performing Arts
Private control

Area of study: fine arts

Pres. of Denver Center for the Performing Arts: RANDY WEEKS
Dir for Education and Dean: DANIEL RENNER
Registrar: KATE AMBERG
Librarian: LINDA ELLER

Library of 30,000 single scripts and anthologies.

NAZARENE BIBLE COLLEGE

1111 Academy Park Loop, Colorado Springs, CO 80910-3704
Telephone: (719) 884-5000
Fax: (719) 884-5199
E-mail: info@nbc.edu
Internet: www.nbc.edu
Founded 1964
Private control
Languages of instruction: English, Spanish
Academic year: September to May

Pres.: Dr HAROLD B. GRAVES, JR
Vice-Pres. for Academic Affairs: Dr GARY W. STREIT
Vice-Pres. for Finance: J. MIKE ARRAMBIDE
Dean for Online Education: Dr ALAN D. LYKE
Registrar: Dr JAY W. OTT
Library Dir: Prof. ANN M. ATTIG

Number of teachers: 155 (9 full-time, 146 part-time)
Number of students: 3,024 (1,410 online, 1,614 on campus)

Publication: Voice and Vision.

REGIS UNIVERSITY

3333 Regis Blvd, Denver, CO 80221-1099
Telephone: (303) 458-4126
Fax: (303) 964-5473
E-mail: enrolsvc@regis.edu
Internet: www.regis.edu
Founded 1877 as Las Vegas College, present name 1921
Private control
Academic year: August to August

Campuses in Aurora, Broomfield, Colorado Springs, Englewood, Fort Collins and Longmont in Colorado, and Las Vegas in Nevada

Pres.: MICHAEL J. SHEERAN
Vice-Pres. for Academic Affairs: PATRICIA LADEWIG
Vice-Pres. for Univ. Relations: JULIE CROCKETT
Dir for Admissions: VIC DAVOLT

Dean for Libraries: IVAN GAETZ
Library of 260,000 vols, 2,500 periodicals
Number of teachers: 270
Number of students: 14,609 (7,119 undergraduate, 7,490 graduate)
Publications: Human Development Magazine (2 a year), Regis University Magazine (2 a year)

DEANS

College for Professional Studies: Dr HEINZ BUSCHANG (acting)
Regis College: PAUL D. EWALD
Rueckert-Hartman College for Health Professions: Prof. Dr JANET L. HOUSER

ROCKY MOUNTAIN COLLEGE OF ART AND DESIGN

1600 Pierce St, Denver, CO 80214
Telephone: (303) 753-6046
Fax: (303) 759-4970
Internet: www.rmcad.edu
Founded 1963
Private control

Courses in animation, art education, communications design (graphic design), fine arts, game art, illustration, interior design; online degree programmes

Pres. and Provost: Dr MARIA PUZIFERRO
Dean for Academics: Dr KIKI GILDERHUS

Library of 14,000 vols, 8,700 digital images, 100,000 digital art and design images, 1,700 DVDs
Number of teachers: 45 (full-time)
Number of students: 600

UNITED STATES AIR FORCE ACADEMY

2304 Cadet Dr., Suite 320, Colorado Springs, CO 80840-5016
Telephone: (719) 333-2990
Internet: www.usafa.af.mil
Founded 1954
State control

Divs of basic sciences, engineering, humanities, social sciences

Superintendent: Lt Gen. MICHAEL C. GOULD
Vice-Superintendent: Col TAMRA RANK
Dean for Faculty: Brig. Gen. DANA H. BORN

Library of 1,898,549 vols
Number of teachers: 600
Number of students: 4,000

UNIVERSITY OF COLORADO

1800 Grant St, Suite 800, Denver, CO 80203
Telephone: (303) 860-5600
Fax: (303) 860-5610
E-mail: officeofthepresident@cu.edu
Internet: www.cu.edu
Founded 1876
State control

Pres.: BRUCE D. BENSON
Sr Vice-Pres. and Chief of Staff: LEONARD DINEGAR
Vice-Pres. and Academic Affairs Officer: KATHLEEN BOLLARD
Vice-Pres. and Chief Financial Officer: KELLY FOX
Vice-Pres. and Univ. Counsel: DANIEL J. WILKERSON
Vice-Pres. for Communication: KEN MCCONNELLOGUE
Vice-Pres. for Govt Relations: TANYA MARES KELLY-BOWRY

Number of teachers: 4,300
Number of students: 57,739 (all campuses).

CONSTITUENT CAMPUSES

University of Colorado at Boulder

Boulder, CO 80309
Telephone: (303) 492-1411
E-mail: homepage@colorado.edu
Internet: www.colorado.edu
Founded 1877

Chancellor: PHILIP P. DiSTEFANO
Provost and Exec. Vice-Chancellor for Academic Affairs: RUSSELL MOORE
Sr Vice-Chancellor and Chief Financial Officer: RIC PORRECA
Vice-Chancellor for Admin.: JEFFREY LIPTON
Vice-Chancellor for Diversity, Equity and Community Engagement: ROBERT BOSWELL
Vice-Chancellor for Research: STEIN STURE
Vice-Chancellor for Student Affairs: DEB COFFIN
Registrar: BARBARA TODD
Dean for Students: KAREN RAFORTH
Dean for Libraries: JAMES WILLIAMS, II
Library: see Libraries and Archives
Number of teachers: 3,799 (2,723 full-time, 1,076 part-time)
Number of students: 29,884 (24,757 undergraduate, 5,127 graduate)
Publications: Arctic and Alpine Research (4 a year), Colorado Alumnus (10 a year), Colorado Arts & Sciences Magazine (4 a year, online (artsandsciences.colorado.edu/ magazine)), Colorado Business Review (12 a year), Colorado Engineer, Colorado Journal of International Environmental Law and Policy (2 a year), English Language Notes, Journal on Telecommunications and High Technology Law, University of Colorado Law Review (4 a year)

DEANS

College of Architecture and Planning: MARK GELERNTER
College of Arts and Sciences: TODD GLEESON
College of Engineering and Applied Science: ROBERT DAVIS
College of Music: DANIEL SHER
Continuing Education and Professional Studies: ANNE HEINZ
Graduate School: JOHN A. STEVENSON
Leeds School of Business: DAVID IKENBERRY
School of Education: LORRIE SHEPARD
School of Law: PHILIP J. WEISER

University of Colorado at Colorado Springs

1420 Austin Bluffs Pkwy, Colorado Springs, CO 80918
Telephone: (719) 255-8227
Fax: (719) 255-3716
Internet: www.uccs.edu

Chancellor: Prof. Dr PAMELA S. SHOCKLEY-ZALABAK
Provost and Exec. Vice-Chancellor for Academic Affairs: MARGARET A. BACON
Vice-Chancellor for Admin. and Finance: BRIAN D. BURNETT
Vice-Chancellor for Student Success and Enrolment Management: HOMER WESLEY
Vice-Chancellor for Univ. Advancement: MARTIN WOOD
Registrar: JOHN SALNAITIS
Dean forLibrary: Prof. TERI R. SWITZER

Library of 408,018 vols, 451,923 microforms, 396,572 govt documents/maps, 9,720 audiovisual items
Number of teachers: 514
Number of students: 13,500

DEANS

Beth-El College of Nursing and Health Sciences: Dr NANCY SMITH
College of Business and Administration: Dr VENKATESHWAR REDDY

College of Education: Dr MARY L. SNYDER

College of Engineering and Applied Science: Dr R. DANDAPANI

College of Letters, Arts and Sciences: Dr THOMAS M. CHRISTIENSEN

Graduate School: Dr JENENNE P. NELSON

University of Colorado at Denver and Health Sciences Center

POB 173364, Denver, CO 80217-3364

1250 14th St, Denver, CO 80217

Telephone: (303) 556-2400

Internet: www.ucdenver.edu

Founded 1912, present name and status 2009

Chancellor: JERRY WARTGOW

Exec. Vice-Chancellor for Anschutz Medical Campus: LILLY MARKS

Provost and Vice-Chancellor for Academic and Student Affairs: RODERICK NAIRN

Vice-Chancellor for Admin. and Finance: JEFFREY PARKER

Vice-Chancellor for Research: RICHARD J. TRAYSTMAN

Dean for Faculty: J. C. BOSCH

Univ. Librarian: MARY M. SOMERVILLE

Number of teachers: 4,497

Number of students: 29,000 (incl. Denver, Aurora and online)

Publication: *The EDition*

DEANS

Business School: SUEANN AMBRON

College of Architecture and Planning: Prof. MARK GELERNTER

College of Arts and Media: Dr DAVID DYNAK

College of Engineering and Applied Science: Dr MARC INGBER

College of Liberal Arts and Sciences: Prof. Dr DANIEL J. HOWARD

College of Nursing: Dr PATRICIA MORITZ

Colorado School of Public Health: Dr JUDITH ALBINO

Graduate School: BARRY SHUR

School of Education and Human Development: Dr REBECCA KANTOR

School of Dental Medicine: Dr DENISE KASSEBAUM

School of Medicine: Dr RICHARD D. KRUGMAN

Skaggs School of Pharmacy and Pharmaceutical Sciences: RALPH ALTIERE

School of Public Affairs: Prof. PAUL TESKE

UNIVERSITY OF DENVER

2199 S University Blvd, Denver, CO 80208

Telephone: (303) 871-2000

Fax: (303) 871-4000

Internet: www.du.edu

Founded 1864 as Colorado Seminary, present name 1880

Private control

Academic year: September to May

Chancellor: ROBERT COOMBE

Provost: GREGG KVISTAD

Vice-Chancellor for Business and Financial Affairs: CRAIG W. WOODY

Vice-Chancellor for Enrolment Services: THOMAS F. WILLOUGHBY

Vice-Chancellor for Univ. Advancement: SCOTT LUMPKIN

Vice-Chancellor for Univ. Communications: KEVIN CARROLL

Registrar: DENNIS BECKER

Dean and Dir for Library: NANCY ALLEN

Library of 1,897,000 vols

Number of teachers: 639 (full-time)

Number of students: 11,842 (5,455 undergraduate, 6,387 graduate)

Publications: *Denver Law Journal* (4 a year), *Denver Law Journal of International Law and Policy* (4 a year, online (djilp.org)), *Family Law Quarterly*, *GSSW Magazine* (2 a year), *The Centre Report* (4 a year), *The University of Denver Law Review, The University of Denver Water Law Review* (2 a year, online (law.du.edu/index.php/university-of-denver-water-law-review)), *Transportation Law Journal* (3 a year, online (law.du.edu/index.php/transportation-law-journal)), *University of Denver Magazine* (4 a year, print and online (blogs.du.edu/today/content/magazine))

DEANS

Daniels College of Business: Prof. Dr CHRISTINE RIORDAN

Division of Arts, Humanities and Social Sciences: ANNE MCCALL

Division of Natural Sciences and Mathematics: ANDREI KUTATELADZE

Graduate School of Professional Psychology: Prof. PETER BUIRSKI

Graduate School of Social Work: Dr JAMES HERBERT WILLIAMS

Josef Korbel School of International Studies: CHRISTOPHER ROBERT HILL

Morgridge College of Education: Dr GREGORY ANDERSON

School of Engineering and Computer Science: MICHAEL KEABLES

Sturm College of Law: MARTIN J. KATZ

University College of Professional and Continuing Education: JAMES R. DAVIS

Women's College: Dr LYNN M. GANGONE

UNIVERSITY OF NORTHERN COLORADO

501 20 St, Greeley, CO 80639

1862 10th Ave, Greeley, CO 80639

Telephone: (970) 351-1890

Fax: (970) 351-1837

E-mail: admissions@unco.edu

Internet: www.unco.edu

Founded 1889 as State Normal School, present name 1970

State control

Academic year: August to May (2 semesters)

Pres.: KAY NORTON

Provost and Sr Vice-Pres.: ROBBYN WACKER (acting)

Sr Vice-Pres. for Finance and Admin.: MICHELLE QUINN

Vice-Pres. for Devt and Alumni Relations: VICTORIA L. GORRELL

Vice-Pres. and Gen. Counsel: DAN SATRIANA

Vice-Pres. for Univ. Relations: CHARLES LEONHARDT

Dean for Students: Dr KATRINA RODRIGUEZ

Registrar: CHARLIE COUCH

Dean for Libraries: HELEN REED

Library: 1.5m. vols

Number of teachers: 705 (491 full-time, 214 part-time)

Number of students: 12,499 (10,231 undergraduate, 2,268 graduate)

DEANS

College of Education and Behavioural Sciences: Dr EUGENE P. SHEEHAN

College of Humanities and Social Sciences: DAVID CALDWELL

College of Natural and Health Sciences: DENISE A. BATTLES

College of Performing and Visual Arts: Dr ANDREW JAY SVEDLOW

Monfort College of Business: DONALD GUDMUNDSON

University College: Dr THOMAS SMITH

UNIVERSITY OF THE ROCKIES

555 E Pikes Peak Ave, Colorado Springs, CO 80903-3612

Telephone: (719) 442-0505

Fax: (719) 389-0359

E-mail: admissions@rockies.edu

Internet: www.rockies.edu

Founded 1998 as Colorado School of Professional Psychology, present name 2007

Private control

Pres.: Dr CHARLITA SHELTON

Provost: Dr TINA J. PARSCAL

Vice-Pres.: Dr ROBERT EDELBROCK

Vice-Pres. for Academic Affairs, Online: Dr LINDA HIEMER

Dean for Research: DEBORA SCHEFFEL

Dir for Student Services: Dr SERENE PRITCHETT

Dir for Online Admissions: ADAM FORREST

Registrar: ERIK GASKILL

Library Dir: TRINA PURCELL

Library of 3,000 vols

DEANS

School of Organizational Leadership: Dr J. STEPHEN KIRKPATRICK

School of Professional Psychology: Dr DAVID STEPHENS

WESTERN STATE COLLEGE OF COLORADO

600 N Adams St, Gunnison, CO 81231

Telephone: (970) 943-0120

Fax: (970) 943-7069

E-mail: admissions@western.edu

Internet: www.western.edu

Founded 1901, fmrly Colorado State Normal School, present name 1923

State control

Depts of accounting, anthropology, art, biology, business administration, chemistry, communication and theatre, computer information science, economics, education, English, environmental studies, exercise and sport science, French, geography, geology, history, mathematics, music, philosophy, physics, politics and government, psychology, recreation and outdoor education, sociology, Spanish

Pres.: Dr JAY W. HELMAN

Vice-Pres. for Academic Affairs: Prof. JESSICA YOUNG

Vice-Pres. for Finance and Admin.: BRAD BACA

Vice-Pres. for Student Affairs and Dean for Students: GARY PIERSON

Dir for Admissions and Assoc. Vice-Pres. for Enrolment Services: TIM ALBERS

Registrar: DEBRA CLARK

Library Dir: NANCY GAUSS

Library of 435,000 vols, 700 periodicals, 1,461 video cassettes; spec. colln of books and govt documents about Colorado

Number of teachers: 143

Number of students: 2,300

CONNECTICUT

ALBERTUS MAGNUS COLLEGE

700 Prospect St, New Haven, CT 06511-1189

Telephone: (203) 773-8550

Fax: (203) 773-5248

E-mail: admissions@albertus.edu

Internet: www.albertus.edu

Founded 1925

Private control

Academic year: August to May

Offers bachelor degree in arts, science, fine arts; graduate programmes incl. art therapy, education, liberal studies, leadership, business and management

Pres.: Dr JULIA M. MCNAMARA

Provost and Vice-Pres. for Academic Affairs: Dr JOHN J. DONOHUE

Vice-Pres. for Devt and Alumni Relations: CAROLYN BEHAN KRAUS

Vice-Pres. for Finance and Treas.: JEANNE MANN
Vice-Pres. for Institutional Advancement and Planning: ROBERT J. BUCCINO
Dean of Admissions and Financial Aid: RICHARD J. LOLATTE
Dean of Student Services: MAUREEN V. MORRISON
Registrar: CLAUDIA A. SCHIAVONE
Dir of Library and Information Services: ANNE LEENEY-PANAGROSSI

Library of 100,000 vols, 650 periodical titles, 2,000 audiovisual titles, 24,316 e-journals, 54,108 e-books
Number of teachers: 75
Number of students: 2,250

CENTRAL CONNECTICUT STATE UNIVERSITY

1615 Stanley St, New Britain, CT 06050
Telephone: (860) 832-2278
Fax: (860) 832-1781
E-mail: admissions@ccsu.edu
Internet: www.ccsu.edu
Founded 1849 as New Britain Normal School, present name and status 1983
State control
Academic year: September to May
Pres.: Prof. Dr JACK W. MILLER
Provost and Vice-Pres. for Academic Affairs: Dr CARL R. LOVITT
Vice-Pres. for Institutional Advancement: CHRISTOPHER J. GALLIGAN
Vice-Pres. for Student Affairs: Dr LAURA TORDENTI
Chief Admin. Officer: Dr RICHARD R. BACHOO
Chief Financial Officer: CHARLENE CASA-MENTO
Chief Information Officer: JAMES ESTRADA
Dean of Students: JANE M. HIGGINS
Registrar: SUSAN PETROSINO
Dir of Library Services: CARL ANTONUCCI

Library of 665,605 vols, 3,000 periodicals, govt docs, Polish Heritage Colln of 17,000 vols
Number of teachers: 968 (440 full-time, 528 part-time)
Number of students: 12,521 (10,092 undergraduate, 2,429 graduate)

DEANS

Carol A. Ammon School of Arts and Sciences: Dr SUSAN E. PEASE
School of Business: Dr SIAMACK SHOJAI (acting)
School of Education and Professional Studies: Dr MITCHELL SAKOFS
School of Engineering and Technology: Prof. Dr ZDZISLAW B. KREMENS
School of Graduate Studies: Prof. Dr PAULETTE A. LEMMA

CHARTER OAK STATE COLLEGE

55 Paul J. Manafort Dr., New Britain, CT 06053-2150
Telephone: (860) 515-3800
Fax: (860) 760-6047
E-mail: admissions@charteroak.edu
Internet: www.cosc.edu
Founded 1973
State control
Offers bachelors degree in arts and science, business, health care, public safety, information systems
Pres.: ED KLONOSKI
Provost: Dr SHIRLEY M. ADAMS
Chief Financial and Admin. Officer: CLIFFORD S. WILLIAMS
Academic Dean of Undergraduate Programmes: Dr DANA A. WILKIE
Dean of Marketing and Enrolment Services: HARRY E. WHITE

Dean and Chief Information Officer: GEORGE F. CLAFFEY, JR
Registrar: JENNIFER WASHINGTON
Number of students: 2,278

CONNECTICUT COLLEGE

270 Mohegan Ave, New London, CT 06320-4196
Telephone: (860) 447-1911
Fax: (860) 439-4301
E-mail: admission@conncoll.edu
Internet: www.conncoll.edu
Founded 1911
Academic year: August to May
Centres of arts and technology, environment, int. studies and liberal arts, public policy and community action, race and ethnicity
Pres.: Dr LEO I. HIGDON, JR
Vice-Pres. for Admin.: ULYSSES B. HAMMOND
Vice-Pres. for Advancement: GREGORY T. WALDRON
Vice-Pres. for College Relations: PATRICIA M. CAREY
Vice-Pres. for Information Services and College Librarian: Dr W. LEE HISLE
Vice-Pres. for Finance: PAUL MARONI
Provost and Dean of the Faculty: Prof. ROGER BROOKS
Dean of Admissions and Financial Aid: MARTHA C. MERRILL
Dean of College: ARMANDO BENGOCHEA
Dean of Student Life: JOCELYN BRIDDELL
Dean of Studies: THERESA AMMIRATI
Registrar: BETH LABRIOLA

Library of 555,578 vols, 438,170 govt. documents, 94,710 audiovisual, 1,325 journals and 6,675 e-journals
Number of teachers: 178 (full-time)
Number of students: 1,912
Publication: CC (4 a year).

EASTERN CONNECTICUT STATE UNIVERSITY

83 Windham St, Willimantic, CT 06226-2295
Telephone: (860) 465-5000
Fax: (860) 465-4485
E-mail: admissions@easternct.edu
Internet: www.easternct.edu
Founded 1889, refounded as Willimantic State College 1959, present name 1983
State control
Academic year: August to May
Pres.: Dr ELSA M. NÚÑEZ
Exec. Vice-Pres.: Dr MICHAEL PERNAL
Vice-Pres. for Academic Affairs: Dr RHONA FREE
Vice-Pres. for Finance and Admin.: JAMES R. HOWARTH
Vice-Pres. for Institutional Advancement: KENNETH J. DeLISA
Vice-Pres. for Student Affairs: Dr KENNETH M. BEDINI
Dean of Students: WALTER DIAZ
Registrar: JENNIFER HUOPPI
Dir of Admissions: CHRISTOPHER DORSEY
Dir of Library Services: PATRICIA S. BANACH

Library of 311,320 vols
Number of teachers: 361 (184 full-time, 177 part-time)
Number of students: 5,606

DEANS

School of Arts and Sciences: Prof. Dr CARMEN R. CID
School of Continuing Education: Dr SHELLY GIMÉNEZ
School of Educational and Professional Studies: Dr JAIME GOMEZ

FAIRFIELD UNIVERSITY

1073 North Benson Rd, Fairfield, CT 06824-5195
Telephone: (203) 254-4000
Fax: (203) 254-4199
E-mail: admis@fairfield.edu
Internet: www.fairfield.edu
Founded 1942
Private control
Academic year: September to May
Pres.: Rev. JEFFREY P. von ARX
Sr Vice-Pres.for Academic Affairs: Dr PAUL J. FITZGERALD
Vice-Pres. for Admin. and Chief of Staff: Dr MARK C. REED
Vice-Pres. for Advancement: STEPHANIE B. FROST
Vice-Pres. for Finance and Treas.: JULIE L. DOLAN
Vice-Pres. for Student Affairs: Dr THOMAS C. PELLEGRINO
Dean of Students: KAREN DONOGHUE
Registrar: ROBERT C. RUSSO
Dir. of Library Services: JOAN OVERFIELD

Library of 325,166 vols, 888,554 microforms, 9,615 audiovisual items, 4,478 e-books, 1,796 periodicals
Number of teachers: 517 (251 full-time, 266 part-time)
Number of students: 5,061 (3,843 undergraduates, 1,218 graduates)

DEANS

Charles F. Dolan School of Business: Dr DONALD E. GIBSON
College of Arts and Sciences: Dr ROBBIN CRABTREE
Graduate School of Education and Allied Professions: Dr SUSAN DOUGLAS FRANZOSA
School of Engineering: Dr JACK BEAL
School of Nursing: Dr JSUZANNE CAMPBELL
Univ. College Continuing Studies: Dr EDNA F. WILSON

GOODWIN COLLEGE

1 Riverside Dr., East Hartford, CT 06118
Telephone: (860) 528-4111
Fax: (860) 291-9550
Internet: www.goodwin.edu
Founded 1999, present status 2004
Private control
Academic year: August to August
Offers bachelor programmes in health science, child study, nursing, organizational studies
Pres.: MARK SCHEINBERG
Exec. Vice-Pres. and Provost: ANN CLARK
Vice-Pres. for Academic Affairs: JUDITH D. ZIMMERMAN
Vice-Pres. for College Relations and Advancement: TODD ANDREWS
Vice-Pres. for Enrolment Services: DANIEL NOONAN
Vice-Pres. for Finance and Chief Financial Officer: JERRY EMLET
Vice-Pres. for Institutional Effectiveness: JANET JEFFORD
Registrar: DENISE SCHWABE
Dean of Students: SANDY WIRTH
Library Dir: MARILYN NOWLAN
Number of teachers: 261
Number of students: 3,116
Publication: Goodwin Magazine.

HARTFORD SEMINARY

77 Sherman St, Hartford, CT 06105-2260
Telephone: (860) 509-9500
Fax: (860) 509-9509
E-mail: info@hartsem.edu
Internet: www.hartsem.edu

Founded 1913 by merger of Hartford Theological Seminary, Hartford School of Religious Education and Kennedy School of Missions; present name 1981
Private control
Academic year: September to June

Center for Faith in Practice, Hartford Institute for Religion Research, Duncan Black Macdonald Center for the Study of Islam and Christian-Muslim Relations
Pres.: Dr HEIDI HADSELL
Academic Dean: Prof. Dr JAMES NIEMAN
Chief Devt Officer: JONATHAN LEE
Registrar and Dir of Academic Services: KAREN ROLLINS
Library Dir: Dr STEVEN BLACKBURN
Library of 92,000 vols, 300 periodicals
Publications: *Conversations in Religion and Theology* (4 a year), *The Muslim World* (4 a year), *Reviews in Religion and Theology* (4 a year).

HOLY APOSTLES COLLEGE & SEMINARY

33 Prospect Hill Rd, Cromwell, CT 06416-2027
Telephone: (860) 632-3010
Fax: (860) 632-3030
E-mail: admissions@holyapostles.edu
Internet: www.holyapostles.edu
Founded 1956 as Holy Apostles Seminary; present name 1972
Private control
Academic year: August to May
Offers BA degree programmes in liberal arts, MA degree in pastoral studies, philosophy, theology
Chancellor: Most Rev. MICHAEL R. COTE
Pres. and Rector: Very Rev. DOUGLAS L. MOSEY
Vice-Rector: Rev. Dr JOHN HILLIER
Vice-Pres. for Academic Affairs: Rev. Dr GREGOIRE J. FLUET
Vice-Pres. for Admin. Affairs: Dr JAMES F. PAPILLO
Registrar: Dr CYNTHIA TOOLIN
Dir of Library Services: CLARE ADAMO
Library of 60,000 vols, 200 newspapers, journals and periodicals.

LINCOLN COLLEGE OF NEW ENGLAND

2279 Mt Vernon Rd, Southington, CT 06489
Telephone: (860) 628-4751
Fax: (860) 628-6444
Internet: www.lincolncollegene.edu
Founded 2009 by merger Clemens College and Briarwood College
Private control
Academic year: August to August
Campuses in Hartford, Suffield; offers bachelor degree programmes in criminal justice, funeral service management, health information admin.
Pres.: KATHRYN S. REGJO
Vice-Pres. for Academic Affairs: Dr GIL LINNE
Vice-Pres. for Admin.: KEVIN MILLER
Vice-Pres. for Admissions: ANTHONY REICH
Vice-Pres. for Operations and Student Affairs: SPENCER W. MCNIVEN
Exec. Vice-Pres. and Chief Financial Officer: KEVIN MILLER
Dean of Academic Affairs: Dr STEVEN GOLDSMITH
Registrar: STEPHANIE CROMBIE
Dir of Library Services: VALERI WALLACE
Number of students: 1,064

LYME ACADEMY COLLEGE OF FINE ARTS

84 Lyme St, Old Lyme, CT 06371
Telephone: (860) 434-5232
Fax: (860) 434-8725
E-mail: admissions@lymeacademy.edu
Internet: www.lymeacademy.edu
Founded 1976
Private control
Academic year: August to May
Offers bachelor of fine arts degrees in drawing, illustration, painting, sculpture
Pres. and CEO: DEBRA PETKE
Vice-Pres. for Academic Affairs and Interim Dean: SALLY SEAMAN
Vice-Pres. for Devt: FRITZ JELLINGHAUS
Registrar: JIM FALCONER
Co-Dir of Admissions: JESSIE MCCOY
Co-Dir of Admissions: OLWEN LOGAN
Number of students: 85

MITCHELL COLLEGE

437 Pequot Ave, New London, CT 06320
Telephone: (860) 701-5000
Fax: (860) 701-5090
E-mail: admissions@mitchell.edu
Internet: www.mitchell.edu
Founded 1938
Private control
Academic year: August to May
Offers bachelors degree in arts, science
Pres.: Dr MARY ELLEN JUKOSKI
Vice-Pres. for Academic Affairs and Dean of College: Dr LAURENCE M. CONNER
Vice-Pres. for Student Affairs and Dean of Students: DIANE MILLER
Registrar: KEVIN P. KELLY
Dir of Library and Information Services: SUZANNE BARTELS
Number of students: 952 (808 full-time, 144 part-time)

PAIER COLLEGE OF ART, INC.

20 Gorham Ave Hamden, CT 06514-3902
Telephone: (203) 287-3031
Fax: (203) 287-3021
E-mail: admissions@paiercollegeofart.edu
Internet: www.paiercollegeofart.edu
Founded 1946 as Paier School of Applied Art, present name and status 1982
Private control
Academic year: August to May (2 semesters)
Courses incl. fine arts, graphic design, illustration, interior design, photography
Pres.: JONATHAN E. PAIER
Vice-Pres. and Dean of Admissions: DANIEL LEWIS PAIER
Dean of College: FRANCIS REXFORD COOLEY
Dir. of Admin. Services: ANGELA DEROSE
Librarian: BETH R. HARRIS.

POST UNIVERSITY

POB 2540, 800 Country Club Rd, Waterbury, CT 06723-2540
Telephone: (203) 596-4500
Fax: (203) 596-4602
E-mail: admissions@post.edu
Internet: www.post.edu
Founded 1890 as Matoon Shorthand School, present name and status 2004
Private control
Academic year: September to May
Pres. and CEO: Dr TOM SAMPH
Provost: Dr DONALD MROZ
Vice-Pres. for Academic Affairs: Dr WILLIAM H. MCDONALD
Vice-Pres. for Finance and Admin.: SCOTT T. ALLEN
Dean of Students: ERICA KLUGE

Dir. of Admissions: JAY E. MURRAY
Registrar: KEITH GAUVIN
Library Dir: TRACY A. RALSTON
Library of 61,116 vols, 10,943 govt documents, 400 periodicals
Number of teachers: 217 (37 full-time, 180 part-time)
Number of students: 863

DEANS

John P. School of Public Service: RICHARD STROMPF
Post College: JAMES F. NARDOZZI (acting)
School of Business: Dr DONALD MROZ
School of Education: JANE BAILEY

QUINNIPIAC UNIVERSITY

275 Mount Carmel Ave, Hamden, CT 06518-1908
Telephone: (203) 582-8600
Fax: (203) 582-8654
E-mail: admissions@quinnipiac.edu
Internet: www.quinnipiac.edu
Founded 1929
Private control
Academic year: June to May
Pres.: JOHN L. LAHEY
Sr Vice-Pres. for Academic and Student Affairs: MARK THOMPSON
Sr Vice-Pres. for Admin.: RICHARD FERGUSON
Sr Vice-Pres. for Finance: PATRICK HEALY
Vice-Pres. and Dean of Admissions: JOHN ISAAC MOHR
Vice-Pres. and Dean of Students: MANUEL CARREIRO
Vice-Pres. for Devt and Alumni Affairs: DONALD WEINBACH
Vice-Pres. for Public Affairs: LYNN BUSHNELL
Registrar: DOROTHY LAURIA
Dean of Graduate Student Affairs: GINA FRANK
Library Dir: CHARLES M. GETCHELL, JR
Library of 466,000 vols
Number of teachers: 671 (350 full-time, 321 part-time)
Number of students: 8,400
Publications: *Quinnipiac Magazine* (2 a year), *Quinnipiac Law Magazine* (2 a year), *Quinnipiac University Business Magazine* (2 a year)

DEANS

College of Arts and Sciences: Dr JOHANNES BERGMANN
Frank H. Netter, M. D., School of Medicine: Dr BRUCE KOEPPEN
School of Business: MATTHEW L. O'CONNOR
School of Communications: LEE KAMLET
School of Education: CYNTHIA DUBEA
School of Health Sciences: Dr EDWARD R. O'CONNOR
School of Law: Dr BRAD SAXTON
School of Nursing: Dr JEAN LANGE

RENSSELAER AT HARTFORD

275 Windsor St, Hartford, CT 06120-2910
Telephone: (860) 548-2400
Fax: (860) 548-7887
E-mail: info@ewp.rpi.edu
Internet: www.ewp.rpi.edu
Founded 1955; attached to Rensselaer Polytechnic Institute, New York
Private control
Academic year: September to July (3 terms)
Offers MA in computer science, engineering and information technology, management; computer science and engineering graduate certificate programmes
Vice-Pres. and Dean: JOHN A. MINASIAN
Vice-Provost and Dean: LESTER GERHARDT
Dean of Admin.: Dr DAVID L. RAINEY (acting)

Registrar: DORIS M. MATSIKAS
Library Dir: MARY S. DIXEY
Library of 44,000 vols, 490 periodicals, 400 journals and 36,000 e-journals
Number of teachers: 135 (35 full-time, 100 part-time)
Number of students: 2,100

SACRED HEART UNIVERSITY

5151 Park Ave, Fairfield, CT 06825-1000
Telephone: (203) 371-7999
Fax: (203) 365-7509
E-mail: enroll@sacredheart.edu
Internet: www.sacredheart.edu

Founded 1963
Private control

Campuses in Fairfield, Griswold, Ireland, Luxembourg, Stamford, Trumbull

Pres.: Dr JOHN J. PETILLO
Sr Vice-Pres. for Finance and Admin.: MICHAEL J. KINNEY
Sr Vice-Pres. for Student Affairs and Athletics: JAMES M. BARQUINERO
Provost and Vice-Pres. for Academic Affairs: Dr LAURA NIESEN DE ABRUNA
Vice-Pres. for Strategic Planning and Admin.: Dr DAVID L. COPPOLA
Vice-Pres. for Univ. Advancement: MEGAN ROCK
Dean of Students: LARRY WIELK
Registrar: DONNA J. PERRONE
Univ. Librarian: Dr PETER GAVIN FERRIBY
Library of 180,000 vols
Number of teachers: 622 (222 full-time, 400 part-time)
Number of students: 6,400 (incl. 3,488 full-time undergraduates, 685 part-time undergraduates, 2,234 graduates)

DEANS

College of Arts and Sciences: Dr SEAMUS CAREY
College of Health Professions: Dr PATRICIA W. WALKER
Isabelle Farrington College of Education: PATRICIA W. WALKER
John F. Welch College of Business: Dr RUPENDRA PALIWAL
Univ. College: MARY LOU DEROSA

ST VINCENT'S COLLEGE

2800 Main St, Bridgeport, CT 06606
Telephone: (203) 576-5278
Fax: (203) 576-5318
E-mail: registrar@stvincentscollege.edu
Internet: www.stvincentscollege.edu

Founded 1905
Private control
Academic year: August to May (2 semesters)

Degree programmes incl. general studies, medical assisting, nursing, radiography

Pres. and CEO: Dr MARTHA K. SHOULDIS
Sr Vice-Pres. for Finance and Interim Chief Financial Officer: JOHN GLECKER
Vice-Pres. and Dean: JOANNE R. WOLFERTZ
Dean of Academic Services: SUSAN CAPASSO
Dir of Admin. Services: JANICE N. FAYE
Dir of Admissions: JOSEPH P. MARRONE
Registrar: JOSEPH MACIONUS
Librarian: VICKY JACOBSON
Number of students: 585

SOUTHERN CONNECTICUT STATE UNIVERSITY

501 Crescent St, New Haven, CT 06515-1355
Telephone: (203) 392-5200
Fax: (203) 392-5705
E-mail: gradinfo@southernct.edu
Internet: www.southernct.edu

Founded 1893, present name 1959

State control
Academic year: August to May

Pres.: Prof. MARY A. PAPAZIAN
Exec. Vice-Pres.: JAMES E. BLAKE
Vice-Pres. for Academic Affairs and Interim Provost: MARIANNE KENNEDY
Vice-Pres. for Institutional Advancement: GREGG CRERAR
Vice-Pres. for Student and Univ. Affairs: PETER TROIANO
Registrar: KIMBERLY LAING
Dir of Library Services: CHRISTINA D. BAUM
Library of 300,000 vols
Number of teachers: 1,053 (438 full-time, 615 part-time)
Number of students: 11,769 (incl. 8,496 undergraduates, 3,273 graduates)

DEANS

School of Arts and Sciences: DONNA JEAN FREDEEN
School of Business: ELLEN DURNIN
School of Education: MICHAEL SAMPSON
School of Graduate Studies: HOLLY CRAWFORD
School of Health and Human Services: GREGORY J. PAVEZA

TRINITY COLLEGE

300 Summit St, Hartford, CT 06106-3100
Telephone: (860) 297-2000
Fax: (860) 297-2257
E-mail: registrar.office@trincoll.edu
Internet: www.trincoll.edu

Founded 1823
Private control
Academic year: August to May

American studies, anthropology, art history, biology, chemistry or biochemistry, classics, computer science, economics, educational studies, engineering, English, environmental science, history, int. studies, Jewish studies, mathematics, modern languages and literature, music, neuroscience, philosophy, physics, political science, psychology, public policy and law, religion, sociology, studio arts, theatre and dance, women, gender and sexuality

Pres.: JAMES F. JONES, JR
Vice-Pres. for Academic Affairs and Dean of the Faculty: Prof. Dr RENA FRADEN
Vice-Pres. for College Advancement: RONALD A. JOYCE
Vice-Pres. for Finance and Operations and Treas.: PAUL MUTONE
Vice-Pres. for Strategic Planning, Admin. and Affirmative Action: PAULA A. RUSSO
Dean of Admissions and Financial Aid: LARRY DOW
Dean of Multicultural Affairs: KARLA SPURLOCK-EVANS
Dean of Students: FREDERICK ALFORD
Registrar: PATRICIA MCGREGOR
Librarian: Prof. RICHARD S. ROSS
Library: 1m. vols, 7,00,000 items incl. microforms, 13,000 current periodicals, 21,852 audiovisual materials, govt documents
Number of teachers: 185 (full-time)
Number of students: 2,248 (2,144 undergraduate, 104 graduate)

Publications: *Reporter*, *Review*, *Trinity Papers*, *Trinity Reporter* (3 a year), *Tripod*.

UNITED STATES COAST GUARD ACADEMY

31 Mohegan Ave, New London, CT 06320-8103
Telephone: (860) 444-8444
Internet: www.uscga.edu

Founded 1876 as School of Instruction for the Revenue Marine; present name 1915

State control
Faculties of engineering, humanities, management, mathematics, science

Superintendent: Rear Admiral SANDRA L. STOSZ
Dean of Academics: Dr KURT J. COLELLA
Dir of Admissions: STEVE FINTON
Registrar: DONALD E. DYKES
Library Dir: (vacant)
Library of 178,000 vols, 55,000 periodicals
Number of teachers: 125
Number of students: 1,046

UNIVERSITY OF BRIDGEPORT

126 Park Ave, Bridgeport, CT 06604-5620
Telephone: (203) 576-4552
Fax: (203) 576-4941
E-mail: admit@bridgeport.edu
Internet: www.bridgeport.edu

Founded 1927 as Junior College of Connecticut, present name and status 1947
Private control
Academic year: September to May

Pres.: NEIL ALBERT SALONEN
Vice-Pres. for Academic Affairs and Interim Provost: HANS VAN DER GIESSEN
Vice-Pres. for Admin. and Finance: Dr SUSAN D. WILLIAMS
Vice-Pres. for Facilities: GEORGE ESTRADA
Vice-Pres. for Graduate Studies and Research: Dr TAREK M. SOBH
Vice-Pres. for Int. Programmes: Dr THOMAS J. WARD
Vice-Pres. for Univ. Relations: MARY-JANE FOSTER
Dean of Admissions: BRYAN J. GROSS
Dean of Student Affairs: KENNETH M. HOLMES
Registrar: CHRISTIAN HANSEN
Univ. Librarian: DIANE MIRVIS
Library of 243,586 vols, 1,051,159 microforms, 3,342 video and audio items, 45,712 serial subscriptions
Number of teachers: 124 (full-time)
Number of students: 4,805

DEANS

College of Chiropractice: FRANK A. ZOLLI
College of Naturopathic Medicine: ELIZABETH PIMENTEL
Fones School of Dental Hygiene: Dr MARGARET H. ZAYAN
Int. College: Dr THOMAS J. WARD
School of Arts and Sciences: Dr STEPHEN HEALEY
School of Business: Dr ROBERT GILMORE
School of Continuing and Professional Studies: MICHAEL J. GIAMPAOLI
School of Education: Dr ALLEN P. COOK
School of Engineering: Dr TAREK M. SOBH

UNIVERSITY OF CONNECTICUT

352 Mansfield Rd, Storrs, CT 06269
Telephone: (860) 486-2000
Internet: www.uconn.edu

Founded 1881 as The Storrs Agricultural School, present name 1939
State control
Academic year: September to May

Campuses in Avery Point, Greater Hartford, Stamford, Torrington, Waterbury

Pres.: Prof. Dr SUSAN HERBST
Provost and Exec. Vice-Pres. for Academic Affairs: MUN CHOI
Sr Vice-Provost and Vice-Pres. for Research: SUMAN SINGHA
Vice-Pres. for Enrolment Planning and Management: WAYNE LOCUST
Vice-Pres. for Health Affairs: PHILIP E. AUSTIN

Vice-Pres. and Chief Financial Officer: RICHARD GRAY

Vice-Pres.for Economic Devt: MARY HOLZ-CLAUSE

Vice-Pres. for Student Affairs: Dr JOHN R. SADDLEMIRE

Library: see under Libraries and Archives

Number of teachers: 1,330

Number of students: 30,525

Publications: *Connecticut Insurance Law Journal* (2 a year), *Connecticut Journal of International Law* (2 a year), *Connecticut Law Review* (4 a year), *Connecticut Public Interest Law Journal* (online), *MELUS* (4 a year), *The Connecticut Economy* (4 a year), *UConn Magazine* (3 a year), *University Today* (52 during academic year, online)

DEANS

College of Agriculture and Natural Resources: GREGORY J. WEIDEMANN

College of Liberal Arts and Sciences: Dr JEREMY TEITELBAUM

Graduate School: KENT HOLSINGER

Neag School of Education: THOMAS C. DEFRANCO

School of Business: JOHN A ELLIOTT

School of Dental Medicine: Dr R. LAMONT MACNEIL

School of Education: THOMAS DE FRANCO

School of Engineering: MUN Y. CHOI

School of Fine Arts: Dr BRID GRANT

School of Law: Prof. JEREMY R. PAUL

School of Medicine: Dr FRANK M TORTI

School of Nursing: Dr REGINA CUSSON

School of Pharmacy: Dr ROBERT L. MCCARTHY

School of Social Work: Prof. Dr SALOME RAHEIM

PROFESSORS

College of Agriculture and Natural Resources (1376 Storrs Rd, Unit 4066, Storrs, CT 06269-4066; tel. (860) 486-2917; fax (860) 486-5113; e-mail canrdean@uconn.edu; internet www.canr.uconn.edu):

ADAMS, R. G., Jr, Entomology

BERKOWITZ, G., Plant Science

BLASIAK, M. M., Plant Science

BRAND, M. H., Plant Science

BRAVO-URETA, B. E., Agricultural Economics

BULL, N. H., Extension

BUSHMICH, S., Pathobiology

CIVCO, D. L., Natural Resources Management

CLARK, R. M., Nutritional Sciences

CLAUSEN, J. C., Natural Resources Management and Engineering

COTTERILL, R. W., Agricultural Economics

DARRE, M. J., Animal Science

FAUSTMAN, L. C., Animal Science

FERNANDEZ, M. L., Nutritional Sciences

FLETCHER, D., Animal Science

FREAKE, H. C., Nutritional Sciences

GARMENDIA, A., Pathobiology

GEARY, S. J., Pathobiology

GREGER, J., Nutritional Sciences

GUILLARD, K., Plant Science

HART, I. C., Animal Science

HOAGLUND, T. A., Animal Science

KERR, K. M., Pathobiology

KHAN, M. I., Pathology

KOO, S. I., Nutritional Sciences

LEE, L. K., Agriculture and Resource Economics

LI, Y., Plant Science

LOPEZ, R. A., Agricultural Economics

LOVE, C., Extension

MCAVOY, R. J., Plant Science

PAGOULATOS, E., Agricultural Economics

PEREZ-ESCAMILLA, R., Nutritional Sciences

POMEROY, R., Agricultural and Resource Economics

ROBBINS, G. A., Natural Resources

RODRIGUEZ, N., Nutritional Sciences

SILBART, L. K., Allied Health Sciences

SINGHA, S., Horticulture

VAN KRUININGEN, H. J., Pathobiology

WARNER, G., Natural Resources Management and Engineering

YANG, X., Animal Science

YANG, X. (H.), Natural Resources Management and Engineering

ZINN, S. A., Animal Science

College of Liberal Arts and Sciences (215 Glenbrook Rd, Unit 4098, Storrs, CT 06269-4098; tel. (860) 486-2713; fax (860) 486-0304; internet www.clas.uconn.edu):

ABE, K., Mathematics

ABIKOFF, W., Mathematics

ADAMS, E., Ecology and Evolutionary Biology

ALBERT, A. D., Molecular and Cell Biology

ANDERSON, G. J., Ecology and Evolutionary Biology

ANDERSON, S., Human Development and Family Studies

ANDERSON, S. L., Philosophy

ANSELMENT, R. A., English

AUSTIN, P. E., Economics

AZIMI, F., History

BAILEY, W. F., Chemistry

BARNES-FARRELL, J., Psychology

BARRECA, R. R., English

BASS, R., Mathematics

BASU, A. K., Chemistry

BAXTER, D. L., Philosophy

BEALL, J. C., Philosophy

BENSON, C. D., English

BENSON, D. R., Molecular and Cell Biology

BERENTSON, W., Geography

BERTHELOT, A., Modern and Classical Languages (French)

BEST, P. E., Physics

BIGGS, F., English

BIRGE, R. R., Physics

BLANK, T. O., Human Development and Family Studies

BLEI, R. C., Mathematics

BLOOM, L. Z., English

BOBALJIK, J., Linguistics

BOHLEN, W. F., Marine Sciences

BOHN, R. K., Chemistry

BOSKOVIC, Z., Linguistics

BOSTER, J. S., Anthropology

BOYER, M. A., Political Science

BRADFIELD, S., English

BROADHEAD, R. S., Sociology

BROWN, R. D., History

BUCK, R. W., Communication Sciences

BUCKLEY, R. N., History

BUCKLIN, A., Marine Sciences

CAIRA, J. N., Ecology and Evolutionary Biology

CALABRESE, A., Linguistics

CARELLO, C. A., Psychology

CARSTENSEN, F. V., Economics

CELESTIN, R., Modern and Classical Languages (French)

CHAFFIN, R., Psychology

CHAPPLE, W. D., Physiology and Neurobiology

CHAZDON, R. L., Ecology and Environmental Biology

CHEN, M. H., Statistics

CHEN, T. T., Molecular and Cell Biology

CHOI, Y. S., Mathematics

CLARK, A., Philosophy

CLIFFORD, J. G., Political Science

COELHO, C. A., Communication Sciences

COLWELL, R. K., Ecology and Evolutionary Biology

COMPRONE, J. J., English

CORMIER, V. F., Physics

COSGEL, M. M., Economics

COSTIGLIOLA, F., History

COTE, R., Physics

CRAWFORD, M., Psychology

CRIVELLO, J. F., Physiology and Neurobiology

CROMLEY, E. K., Geography

CROMLEY, R. G., Geography

CROTEAU, M. E., Journalism

DALMOLIN, E. F., Modern and Classical Languages (French)

DAM, H. G., Marine Sciences

D'ANDRELE, R., Anthropology

DASHEFSKY, A. M., Sociology

DAVID, C. W., Chemistry

DAVIS, J. A., History

DEBLAS, A. L., Physiology and Neurobiology

DESCH, C. E., Jr, Ecology and Evolutionary Biology

DEY, D. K., Statistics

DULACK, T., English

DUNNE, G. V., Physics

DUSSART, J. T., Psychology

DUTTA, N. K., Physics

EBY, C. V., English

ELDER, C. L., Philosophy

ERICKSON, P. I., Anthropology

EYLER, E. E., Physics

FARNEN, R. F., Political Science

FEIN, D. A., Psychology

FISHER, J. D., Psychology

FITZGERALD, W. F., Marine Sciences

FOWLER, C. A., Psychology

FRANK, H. A., Chemistry

FRANKLIN, W., English

FULLERTON, R. J., Jr, Aerospace Studies

GAI, M., Physics

GALLO, R. V., Physiology and Neurobiology

GIBSON, G. N., Physics

GILBERT, H. R., Communication Sciences

GINE, E., Mathematics

GLASBERG, D. S., Sociology

GLAZ, J., Statistics

GLAZ, S., Mathematics

GOGARTEN, J. P., Molecular and Cell Biology

GOMES, M. A., Modern and Classical Languages (Spanish)

GOODHEART, L. B., History

GOODSTEIN, L., Sociology

GORDON, R. B., Modern and Classical Languages (French)

GOULD, P. L., Physics

GREEN, J. A., Psychology

GROSS, R. A., History

GUENOUN, S., Modern and Classical Languages (French)

GUI, C., Mathematics

HAAS, A. H., Mathematics

HALLWOOD, C. P., Economics

HAMILTON, D. S., Physics

HANDWERKER, W. P., Anthropology

HANINK, D. M., Geography

HANSON, B. C., Political Science

HARKNESS, S., Human Development and Family Studies

HARRIS, S., English

HARVEY, C., Military Science

HASENFRATZ, R., English

HENRY, C. S., Ecology and Evolutionary Biology

HIGONETT, M. R., English

HISKES, R. P., Political Science

HOGAN, P. C., English

HOLLENBERG, D. C., English

HOLSINGER, K. E., Ecology and Evolutionary Biology

HOLZWORTH, J., Psychology

HOWELL, A. R., Chemistry

JAVANAINEN, J. M., Physics

JOESTEN, R. L., Chemistry

JOHNSON, B. T., Psychology

JONES, S. P., English

KALICHMAN, S., Psychology

KAPPERS, L. A., Physics

KENDALL, D. A., Molecular and Cell Biology

KENNY, D. A., Psychology

KHARCHENCO, V., Physics

KNECHT, D. A., Molecular and Cell Biology

KNOBLAUCH, V. L., Economics

KOLTRACHT, I., Mathematics
KOVNER, A., Physics
KREMER, J. N., Marine Sciences
KUMAR, C. V., Chemistry
KUO, L., Statistics
KUPPERMAN, J. J., Philosophy
LANGLOIS, R. N., Economics
LES, D. H., Ecology and Environmental Biology
LEWIS, C. W., Political Science
LILLO-MARTIN, D. C., Linguistics
LIN, C. A., Communication Sciences
LINNEKIN, J. S., Anthropology
LoTURCO, J. J., Physiology and Neurobiology
LOWE, C. A., Psychology
LUYSTER, R. W., Philosophy
LYNCH, M. P., Philosophy
LYNES, M. A., Molecular and Cell Biology
McBREATY, S. A., Anthropology
McBREEN, E., Human Development and Family Studies
McKENNA, P. J., Mathematics
MACKINNON, R. D., Geography
MACLEOD, G. G., English
McMANUS, G. B., Marine Sciences
MADYCH, W. R., Mathematics
MAKOWSKY, V. A., English
MALLETT, R. L., Physics
MANNHEIM, P. O., Physics
MARCUS, P. I., Molecular and Cell Biology
MARKUS, E., Psychology
MARSDEN, J., English
MASCIANDARO, F., Modern and Classical Languages (Italian)
MASON, R., Marine Sciences
MAXSON, S. C., Psychology
MEYER, M., English
MEYERS, D. T., Philosophy
MICELI, T. J., Economics
MICHEL, R. G., Chemistry
MILLER, D. B., Psychology
MILLER, R. L., English
MILLER, S. S., Modern and Classical Languages (Classics and Hebrew)
MOISEFF, A., Physiology and Neurobiology
MUKHOPADHYAY, N., Statistics
MURPHY, B., English
MUSIEK, F., Communication Sciences
NAIGLES, L. R., Psychology
NAPLES, N., Sociology
NEUMANN, M., Mathematics
NOLL, K. M., Molecular and Cell Biology
O'DONNELL, J., Marine Sciences
OLSHEVASKY, V., Mathematics
OSLEEB, J. P., Geography
PAPADIMITRAKOPOULOUS, F., Chemistry
PEASE, D. M., Physics
PETERSON, C. W., Physics
PETERSON, R. S., English
PHILLIPS, R. L., Philosophy
PICKERING, S. F., English
PRATTO, F., Psychology
RAVISHANKER, N., Statistics
RAWITSCHER, G. H., Physics
RAY, S. C., Economics
REITER, H. L., Political Science
RENFRO, J. L., Physiology and Neurobiology
RICKARDS, J. P., Psychology
RIGAZIO-DIGILIO, S., Human Development and Family Studies
ROBINSON, J., Human Development and Family Studies
ROCKWELL, R. C., Sociology
ROE, S. A., History
ROSS, S. L., Economics
RUSLING, J. F., Chemistry
SABATELLI, R., Human Development and Family Studies
SALAMONE, J. D., Psychology
SANDERS, C. R., Sociology
SCHAEFER, C. W., Ecology and Evolutionary Biology
SCHLICHTING, C. D., Ecology and Environmental Biology

SCHWENK, K., Ecology and Environmental Biology
SEGERSON, K., Economics
SEHULSTER, J. R., Psychology
SHOEMAKER, N., History
SIDNEY, S. J., Mathematics
SILANDER, J. A., Ecology and Evolutionary Biology
SILVESTRINI, B. G., History
SIMON, C. M., Ecology and Environmental Biology
SIMONSEN, W., Public Policy
SMITH, M. B., Chemistry
SMITH, W. W., Physics
SNYDER, L. B., Communication Sciences
SONSTROEM, D. A., English
SPALDING, K., History
SPIEGEL, E. S., Mathematics
STRAUSBAUGH, L. D., Molecular and Cell Biology
STWALLEY, W. C., Physics
SUIB, S. L., Chemistry
SUNG, C. S. P., Chemistry
SUPER, C. M., Human Development and Family Studies
SWADLOW, H. A., Psychology
SWANSON, M. S., Physics
TAYLOR, R. L., Sociology
TEITELBAUM, J., Mathematics
TESCHKE, C., Molecular and Cell Biology
THORSON, R. M., Ecology and Evolutionary Biology
TOLLEFSON, J. L., Mathematics
TORGERSEN, T. L., Marine Sciences
TROYER, L., Sociology
TRUMBO, S., Ecology and Evolutionary Biology
TUCHMAN, G., Sociology
TURCHIN, P., Ecology and Environmental Biology
TURVEY, M. T., Psychology
VAN DER HULST, H. G., Linguistics
VILLEMEZ, W. J., Sociology
VITALE, R. A., Statistics
WAGNER, D., Ecology and Evolutionary Biology
WALLACE, M., Sociology
WALLER, A. L., History
WANG, Y., Statistics
WEAKLIEM, D. L., Sociology
WELLS, K. D., Ecology and Evolutionary Biology
WHEELER, S. C., Philosophy
WHITLATCH, R. B., Marine Sciences
WILKENFELD, R. B., English
WILSON, R. A., Anthropology
WISENSALE, S., Human Development and Family Studies
WORCESTER, W. A., Journalism
YARISH, C., Ecology and Evolutionary Biology
YEAGLE, P. L., Molecular and Cell Biology
ZIRAKZADEH, C. E., Political Science

Neag School of Education (249 Glenbrook Rd, Unit 2064C, Storrs, CT 06269-2064; tel. (860) 486-3813; fax (860) 486-0210; internet www.education.uconn.edu):

ARMSTRONG, L. E., Kinesiology
BONANNON, R., Physical Therapy
BRAY, M., Educational Psychology
BROWN, S. W., Educational Psychology
DeFRANCO, T., Curriculum and Instruction
DENEGAR, C. R., Physical Therapy
DOYLE, M. A., Curriculum and Instruction
GOODKIND, T. B., Curriculum and Instruction
HASSON, S. M., Physical Therapy
JUNDA, M. E., Educational Leadership
KARAN, O. C., Educational Psychology
KEHLE, T. J., Educational Psychology
KRAEMER, W. J., Kinesiology
LEU, D. J., Curriculum and Instruction
McGUIRE, J. M., Educational Psychology
MARESH, C. M., Kinesiology
REAGAN, T. G., Curriculum and Instruction

REIS, S. M., Educational Psychology
SCHWAB, R. L., Educational Leadership
SHECKLEY, B. G., Educational Leadership
SMEY, J. W., Physical Therapy
STEPHENS, R., Educational Leadership
SUGAI, G., Educational Psychology
SWAMINATHAN, H., Educational Psychology

Ratcliffe Hicks School of Agriculture (1376 Storrs Rd, Unit 4090, Storrs, CT 06269-4090; tel. (860) 486-2920; e-mail acadprog@uconn.edu; internet www.cag.uconn.edu/rh/rh).

School of Business (2100 Hillside Rd, Unit 1041, Storrs, CT 06269-1041; tel. (860) 486-2314; fax (860) 486-0889; e-mail contact@business.uconn.edu; internet www.sba.uconn.edu):

BIGGS, S. F., Accounting
CARRAFIELLO, V. A., Business Law
CLAPP, J. M., Finance
COULTER, R. H., Marketing
EARLEY, P. C., Management
FOX, K. H., Business Law
GARFINKEL, R. S., Operations Research and Information Management
GHOSH, C., Finance
GIACOTTO, C., Finance
GOES, P. B., Operations and Information Management
GOPAL, R., Operations Research and Information Management
HARDING, J., Finance
HEGDE, S. P., Finance
HUSSEIN, M. E., Accounting
JAIN, S. C., Marketing
KLEIN, L. S., Finance
KUMAR, V., Marketing
LUBATKIN, M. J., Management
MARSDEN, J. R., Operations Research and Information Management
MATHIEU, J. E., Management
NAIR, S. K., Operations Research and Information Management
O'BRIEN, T. J., Finance
POWELL, G. N., Management
SANTERRE, R., Finance
SEWALL, M. A., Marketing
SIRMANS, C. F., Finance and Real Estate
VEIGA, J. F., Management
WILLENBORG, M., Accounting

School of Dental Medicine (263 Farmington Ave, Farmington, CT 06030; tel. (860) 679-2000; internet sdm.uchc.edu):

AGAR, J., Reconstructive Sciences
BEAZOGLOU, T., Craniofacial Sciences
D'AMBROSIO, J., Oral Health and Diagnostic Services
DEALY, C., Reconstructive Sciences
DONGARI-BAGTZOGLOU, A., Oral Health and Diagnostic Services
EISENBERG, E., Oral Health and Diagnostic Sciences
FRANK, M. E., Oral Health and Diagnostic Sciences
FREILICH, M., Reconstructive Sciences
GOLDBERG, A. J., Reconstructive Sciences
GOUPIL, M., Craniofacial Sciences
HAND, A., Craniofacial Sciences
KAZEMI, R., Reconstructive Sciences
KELLY, J. R., Reconstructive Sciences
KOSHER, R., Reconstructive Sciences
LITT, M. D., Oral Health and Diagnostic Sciences
LURIE, A. G., Oral Health and Diagnostic Sciences
MacNEIL, R., Oral Health and Diagnostic Sciences
MEIERS, J., Reconstructive Sciences
MINA, M., Craniofacial Sciences
NANDA, R., Craniofacial Sciences
NEWITTER, D., Reconstructive Sciences
NICHOLS, F., Oral Health and Diagnostic Sciences
PENDRYS, D., Oral Health and Diagnostic Services

PETERSON, D. E., Oral Health and Diagnostic Sciences
REISINE, S., Oral Health and Diagnostic Sciences
ROBINSON, P., Oral Health and Diagnostic Sciences
ROSSOMANDO, E. P., Craniofacial Sciences
SAFAVI, K., Craniofacial Sciences
SHAFER, D., Craniofacial Sciences
SPANGBERG, L. S. W., Oral Health and Diagnostic Sciences
TANZER, J. M., Oral Health and Diagnostic Sciences
TAYLOR, T., Reconstructive Sciences
TRUMMEL, C. L., Oral Health and Diagnostic Sciences
UPHOLT, W., Reconstructive Sciences
ZHU, Q., Craniofacial Sciences

School of Engineering (261 Glenbrook Rd, Unit 2237, Storrs, CT 06269-2237; tel. (860) 486-2221; fax (860) 486-0318; internet www .engr.uconn.edu):
ACCORSI, M. L., Civil and Environmental Engineering
ACHENIE, L. E., Chemical, Materials and Biomolecular Engineering
AINDOW, M., Chemical, Materials and Biomolecular Engineering
AMMAR, R. A., Computer Science and Engineering
ANWAR, A. F. M., Electrical and Computer Engineering
BAGTZOGLOU, A., Civil and Environmental Engineering
BANSAL, R., Electrical and Systems Engineering
BAR-SHALOM, Y., Electrical and Computer Engineering
BARKER, K., Computer Science and Engineering
BERGMAN, T. L., Mechanical Engineering
BRODY, H. D., Chemical, Materials and Biomolecular Engineering
CETEGEN, B., Mechanical Engineering
COOPER, D. J., Chemical, Materials and Biomolecular Engineering
DEMURJIAN, S. A., Computer Science and Engineering
DEWOLF, J. T., Civil and Environmental Engineering
ENDERLE, J. D., Electrical and Computer Engineering
ENGEL, G. L., Computer Science and Engineering and Electrical and Systems Engineering
EPSTEIN, H. I., Civil and Environmental Engineering
ERKEY, C., Chemical, Materials and Biomolecular Engineering
FAGHIRI, A., Mechanical Engineering
FOX, M. D., Electrical and Computer Engineering
FRANTZ, G. C., Civil and Environmental Engineering
IVAN, J. N., Civil Engineering
JAIN, F. C., Electrical and Computer Engineering
JAVIDI, B., Electrical and Computer Engineering
JORDAN, E. H., Mechanical Engineering
KATTAMIS, T. Z., Materials Science and Engineering
KAZEROUNIAN, K., Mechanical Engineering
LUH, P. B., Electrical and Computer Engineering
MAGNUSSON, R., Electrical and Computer Engineering
MARCUS, H. L., Chemical, Materials and Biomolecular Engineering
OLGAC, N., Mechanical Engineering
OR, D., Civil and Electrical Engineering
PATTIPATI, K. R., Electrical and Computer Engineering
PETERS, T. J., Computer Science and Engineering

PITCHUMANI, R., Mechanical Engineering
RAJASEKARAN, S., Computer Science and Engineering
REIFSNIDER, K. L., Mechanical Engineering
SAMMES, N. M., Mechanical Engineering
SHAW, L. L., Chemical, Materials and Biomolecular Engineering
SHAW, M. T., Chemical, Materials and Biomolecular Engineering
SHIN, D. G., Computer Science and Engineering
SMITH, E., Civil and Environmental Engineering
TAYLOR, G. W., Electrical and Computer Engineering
WEISS, R. A., Chemical, Materials and Biomolecular Engineering
WILLETT, P. K., Electrical and Computer Engineering
ZHANG, B., Mechanical Engineering
ZHU, Q., Electrical and Computer Engineering

School of Fine Arts (830 Bolton Rd, Unit 1128, Storrs, CT 06269-1128; tel. (860) 486-3016; fax (860) 486-5845; internet www.sfa .uconn.edu):
ARM, T. E., Music
BASS, W. R., Music
CROW, L. J., Dramatic Arts
ENGLISH, G. M., Dramatic Arts
FRANKLIN, J. F., Dramatic Arts
FROGLEY, A., Music
FUCHS, K., Music
GIVENS, J., Art and Art History
MCDONALD, R. A., Dramatic Arts
MARTINEZ, A., Art
MAZZOCCA, A. N., Art
MILLER, R. F., Music
MILLS, D. L., Music
MOLETTE, C. W., Dramatic Arts
MUIRHEAD, D. D., Art
MYERS, K. M., Art and Art History
OGUIBE, O., Art and Art History
RENSHAW, J. H., Music
ROCCOBERTON, B. P. Jr, Dramatic Arts
RYKER, K., Dramatic Arts
SABATINE, J., Dramatic Arts
STANLEY, G., Music
STERN, A. S., Dramatic Arts
TALVACCHIA, B. L., Art
THORPE, J. K., Art
WOODS, D. G., Music

School of Law (65 Elizabeth St, Hartford, CT 06105-2290; tel. (860) 570-5000; fax (860) 570-5128; internet www.law.uconn.edu):
BAKER, T. E.
BARNES, R. D.
BECKER, L. E., Jr
BERGER, B.
BERMAN, P. S.
BIRMINGHAM, R. L.
CALLOWAY, D. A.
DAILEY, A. C.
DICKERSON, L.
FERNOW, T. O.
FISCHL, R. M.
GUSTAFSON, K.
JANIS, M. W.
KAY, R. S.
KIRK, D.
KURLANTZICK, L. S.
LEVIN, L. C.
LINDSETH, P.
MCCOY, P.
MCLEAN, W. E.
MORAWETZ, T. H.
OQUENDO, A. R.
ORLAND, L.
PARKER, R. W.
PAUL, J.
POMP, R. D.
SIEGELMAN, P.
STARK, J. H.
STRASSER, K. A.
TONDRO, T. J.

UTZ, S. G.
WEISBROD, C. A.
WHITMAN, R.
WILF, S.

School of Medicine (263 Farmington Ave, Farmington, CT 06030-1912; tel. (860) 679-2000; fax (860) 679-1371; internet medicine .uchc.edu):
ALBERTSON, P. C., Surgery
ALTMAN, A. J., Paediatrics
ARNOLD, A., Medicine
BABOR, T. F., Community Medicine and Health Care
BARBARESE, E., Neuroscience
BAUER, L. O., Psychiatry
BENN, P. A., Genetics and Developmental Biology
BERNSTEIN, L., Neuroscience
BIGAZZI, P. E., Pathology and Laboratory Medicine
BROWNER, B. O., Orthopaedic Surgery
BRUDER, M. E., Paediatrics
CAMPBELL, W. A., Obstetrics and Gynaecology
CARMICHAEL, G. G., Genetics and Developmental Biology
CARSON, J. H., Molecular, Microbial and Structural Biology
CHERNIAK, M. G., Medicine
CLOUTIER, M., Paediatrics
CONE, R. E., Immunology
CUSHMAN, R. A., Family Medicine
DAS, A. K., Molecular, Microbial and Structural Biology
DAS, D. K., Surgery
DECKERS, P. J., Surgery
EIPPER, E. A., Molecular, Microbial and Structural Biology
EISENBERG, S., Molecular, Microbial and Structural Biology
FEDER, H. M., Jr, Family Medicine
FEIN, A., Cell Biology
FEINSTEIN, M. B., Cell Biology
FIFIELD, J., Family Medicine
FOROUHAR, F., Pathology and Laboratory Medicine
FORTINSKY, R. H., Medicine
GOLDSCHNEIDER, I., Immunology
GRANT-KELS, J. M., Dermatology
GRASSO, J. A., Cell Biology
GREENSTEIN, R. M., Genetics and Developmental Biology
GRONOWICZ, G. F., Surgery
GROSS, J. B., Anaesthesiology
HANSEN, M., Medicine
HESSELBROCK, V. M., Psychiatry
HLA, T. R., Cell Biology
HUEY, L., Psychiatry
HURLEY, M. M., Medicine
JAFFE, L., Cell Biology
KADDEN, R. M., Psychiatry
KIM, D. O., Neuroscience
KING, S. M., Molecular, Microbial and Structural Biology
KLOBUTCHER, L. A., Molecular, Microbial and Structural Biology
KOEPPEN, B. M., Medicine
KOPPEL, D. E., Molecular, Microbial and Structural Biology
KRANZLER, H. R., Psychiatry
KREAM, B., Medicine
KREUTZER, D. L., Pathology
KUCHEL, G., Medicine
KUWADA, S., Neuroscience
LALANDE, M., Genetics and Developmental Biology
LE FRANCOIS, L., Medicine
LEVINE, J. B., Medicine
LIANG, B. T., Medicine
LIEBERMAN, J., Orthopaedic Surgery
LOEW, L. M., Cell Biology
LORENZO, J. A., Medicine
MAINS, R. E., Neuroscience
MAULIK, N., Surgery
MAXWELL, G. D., Neuroscience

MAYER, B., Genetics and Developmental Biology
MOREST, D. K., Neuroscience
MUKHOPADHYAY, B., Medicine
OLIVER, D. L., Neuroscience
O'ROURKE, J. T., Immunology
OZOLS, J., Molecular, Microbial and Structural Biology
PACHTER, J., Cell Biology
PAPPANO, A. J., Cell Biology
PELUSO, J. J., Cell Biology
PETRY, N., Psychiatry
POTASHNER, S. J., Neuroscience
RADOLF, J. D., Medicine
RAJAN, T. V., Pathology and Laboratory Medicine
RATZAN, S. K., Paediatrics
ROSENBERG, D., Medicine
RUNOWICZ, C. D., Obstetrics and Gynaecology
SANDERS, M. M., Pathology and Laboratory Medicine
SARFARAZI, M., Surgery
SCHENSUL, S., Community Medicine and Health Care
SETLOW, P., Molecular, Microbial and Structural Biology
SIMON, R. H., Surgery
SRIVASTAVA, P. K., Immunology
STEVENS, R., Community Medicine and Health Care
TENNEN, H., Community Medicine and Health Care
TRAHIOTIS, C., Neuroscience
TRESTMAN, R., Medicine
TSIPOURAS, P., Genetics and Developmental Biology
WELLER, S. K., Molecular, Microbial and Structural Biology
WHITE, B. A., Cell Biology
WHITE, W. B., Medicine
WIKEL, S. K., Immunology
WINOKUR, A., Psychiatry
WOLFSON, L. I., Neurology
WU, C. H., Medicine
WU, G. Y., Medicine

School of Nursing (231 Glenbrook Rd, Storrs, CT 06269-2026; tel. (860) 486-3716; fax (860) 486-0001; internet www.nursing.uconn.edu):

BAVIER, A., Nursing
BECK, C. L., Nursing
CUSSON, R., Nursing
KOERNER, B. L., Nursing
NEAFSEY, P. J., Nursing

School of Pharmacy (69 N Eagleville Rd, Storrs, CT 06268; tel. (860) 486-2121; fax (860) 486-1553; internet pharmacy.uconn .edu):

BURGESS, D. J., Pharmaceutics
GERALD, M. C., Pharmacology
LANGNER, R. O., Pharmacology
MCCARTHY, R. L., Pharmacy Practice
MORRIS, J. B., Toxicology
PIKAL, M. J., Pharmaceutics
WHITE, C. M., Pharmacy Practice

School of Social Work (1798 Asylum Ave, West Hartford, CT 06117-2698; tel. (860) 570-9118; fax (860) 570-9419; e-mail swadmission@uconn.edu; internet www.ssw .uconn.edu):

DAVIDSON, K. W.
FISHER, R.
GITTERMAN, A.
HEALY, L. M.
HESSELBROCK, M. N.
HUMPHREYS, N. A.
JOHNSON, H. C.

Whetten Graduate Center (438 Whitney Rd Ext., Storrs, CT 06269-1152; tel. (860) 486-3617; fax (860) 486-6739; e-mail gradschool@ uconn.edu; internet www.grad.uconn.edu).

UNIVERSITY OF HARTFORD

200 Bloomfield Ave, West Hartford, CT 06117-1599
Telephone: (860) 768-4100
Fax: (860) 768-4378
E-mail: uofhart@hartford.edu
Internet: www.hartford.edu

Founded 1957 by merger of Hartford Art School, Hartt College of Music, Hillyer College
Private control
Academic year: September to August (2 semesters)

Pres.: Dr WALTER HARRISON
Provost: SHARON L. VASQUEZ
Vice-Pres. for Finance and Admin.: AROSHA JAYAWICKREMA
Vice-Pres. for Institutional Advancement: CHRISTINE PINA
Vice-Pres. for Student Affairs: J. LEE PETERS
Vice-Pres. for Univ. Relations: JOHN J. CARSON
Dean of Admissions: RICHARD A. ZEISER
Dean of Graduate Studies: PETER DIFFLEY
Asst Provost and Dean of Faculty Devt: H. FREDERICK SWEITZER
Assoc. Provost and Dean of Undergraduate Studies: GUY CHARLES COLARULLI
Registrar: DOREEN LAY
Dir of Univ. Libraries: RANDI ASHTON-PRITTING

Library of 606,154 vols
Number of teachers: 848 (347 full-time, 501 part-time)
Number of students: 7,400

DEANS

Barney School of Business: Dr JAMES W. FAIRFIELD-SONN
College of Arts and Sciences: Dr JOSEPH C. VOELKER
College of Education, Nursing and Health Professions: Prof. Dr RALPH O. MUELLER
College of Engineering, Technology and Architecture: Dr LOUIS T. MANZIONE
Hartford Art School: NANCY M. STAURT (acting)
Hartt School: Dr AARON A. FLAGG
Hillyer College: Dr DAVID H. GOLDENBERG

UNIVERSITY OF NEW HAVEN

300 Boston Post Rd, West Haven, CT 06516
Telephone: (203) 932-7000
Fax: (203) 932-3060
E-mail: adminfo@newhaven.edu
Internet: www.newhaven.edu

Founded 1920
Private control
Academic year: August to May

Pres.: Prof. Dr STEVEN H. KAPLAN
Provost and Sr Vice-Pres. for Academic and Student Affairs: Dr DAVID P. DAUWALDER
Vice-Pres. for Enrolment Management: Dr JAMES MCCOY
Vice-Pres. for Finance and Treas.: GEORGE S. SYNODI
Vice-Pres. for Univ. Advancement: RICHARD J. TUCHMAN
Assoc. Vice-Pres. for Facilities: LOUIS ANNINO
Dean of Students and Assoc. Vice-Pres. of Student Affairs: REBECCA JOHNSON
Registrar: LYNN M. KOHRN
Librarian: HANKO DOBI

Library of 231,414 vols, 144,120 print documents
Number of teachers: 599 (170 full-time, 429 part-time)
Number of students: 5,543 (4,607 undergraduates, 1,778 graduates)
Publication: *Essays in Arts and Sciences*

DEANS

College of Arts and Sciences: Dr LOURDES ALVAREZ
College of Business and Arts: LAWRENCE FLANAGAN
Henry C. Lee College of Criminal Justice and Forensic Sciences: Dr MARIO THOMAS GABOURY
Tagliatela College of Engineering: Dr RONALD S. HARICHANDRAN
Univ. College: MARSHA HAM

UNIVERSITY OF SAINT JOSEPH

1678 Asylum Ave, West Hartford, CT 06117
Telephone: (860) 232-4571
Fax: (860) 231-8396
E-mail: admissions@sjc.edu
Internet: www.usj.edu

Founded 1932
Private control
Academic year: September to August

Pres.: Dr PAMELA TROTMAN REID
Provost: Dr MICHELLE KALIS
Vice-Pres. for Enrolment Management: GARY L. SHERMAN
Vice-Pres. for Finance and Admin.: SHAWN HARRINGTON
Vice-Pres. for Institutional Advancement: DOUGLAS NELSON
Vice-Pres. for Student Affairs and Dean of Students: Dr CHERYL A. BARNARD
Registrar: ALLISON MISKY
Dir of Library: LINDA GEFFNER

Library of 141,600 vols (incl. books, e-books and e-journals)
Number of teachers: 110 (full-time)
Number of students: 2,592

DEANS

School of Education: Dr KATHLEEN A. BUTLER
School of Graduate and Professional Studies: Dr DANIEL NUSSBAUM
School of Health and Natural Sciences: Dr SANDRA AFFENITO
School of Humanities and Social Sciences: Dr WAYNE STEELY
School of Pharmacy: Dr JOSEPH R. OFOSU

WESLEYAN UNIVERSITY

45 Wyllys Ave, Middletown, CT 06459
Telephone: (860) 685-2000
Fax: (860) 685-3001
E-mail: admission@wesleyan.edu
Internet: www.wesleyan.edu

Founded 1831
Private control
Academic year: September to May

Pres.: Dr MICHAEL S. ROTH
Provost and Vice-Pres. for Academic Affairs: Prof. Dr ROB ROSENTHAL
Vice-Pres. for Finance and Admin.: JOHN C. MEERTS
Vice-Pres. for Student Affairs: MICHAEL J. WHALEY
Vice-Pres. for Univ. Relations: BARBARA-JAN WILSON
Registrar: ANNA C. G. VAN DER BURG
Dean of Admissions and Financial Aid: NANCY HARGRAVE MEISLAHN
Univ. Librarian: PATRICIA TULLY

Library: 1.2m. vols
Number of teachers: 375
Number of students: 3,370 (undergraduates and postgraduates)
Publication: *History and Theory*

DEANS

Arts and Humanities: Prof. ANDREW CURRAN
Natural Sciences and Mathematics: Prof. ISHITA MUKERJI

Social Sciences and Interdisciplinary Programmes: Prof. GARY SHAW

WESTERN CONNECTICUT STATE UNIVERSITY

181 White St, Danbury, CT 06810
Telephone: (203) 837-8210
Fax: (203) 837-8338
E-mail: admissions@wcsu.edu
Internet: www.wcsu.edu
Founded 1903
State control
Academic year: August to May
Pres.: JAMES W. SCHMOTTER
Provost and Vice-Pres. for Academic Affairs: Dr JANE MCBRIDE GATES
Vice-Pres. for Finance and Admin.: PAUL REIS
Vice-Pres. for Student Affairs: WALTER B. BERNSTEIN
Chief Information Officer: LORRAINE CAPOBIANCO
Dean of Graduate Studies and External Programs: Dr BURTON PERETTI
Dean of Student Affairs: WALTER CRAMER
Registrar: LOURDES CRUZ
Dir of Library Services: Dr ED O'HARA
Number of teachers: 528 (226 full-time and 302 part-time)
Number of students: 6,407 (4,845 full-time and 1,562 part-time)

DEANS

Ancell School of Business: ALLEN D. MORTON
School of Arts and Sciences: Dr ABBEY ZINK
School of Professional Studies: MARYANN ROSSI
School of Visual and Performing Arts: Prof. Dr DANIEL GOBLE

YALE UNIVERSITY

POB 208234, New Haven, CT 06520-8234
Telephone: (203) 432-2550
Fax: (203) 432-7105
E-mail: student.questions@yale.edu
Internet: www.yale.edu
Founded 1701, named Yale College 1718, present name and status 1861
Private control
Pres.: Dr RICHARD CHARLES LEVIN
Provost: Dr PETER SALOVEY
Vice-Pres. and Gen. Counsel: Dr DOROTHY KATHRYN ROBINSON
Vice-Pres. and Sec.: Dr LINDA KOCH LORIMER
Vice-Pres. for Devt: INGE THERESIA REICHENBACH
Vice-Pres. for Finance and Business Operations: SHAUNA RYAN KING
Vice-Pres. for Human Resources and Admin.: MICHAEL ALLAN PEEL
Vice-Pres. for New Haven and State Affairs and Campus Devt: Dr BRUCE D. ALEXANDER
Vice-Pres. for West Campus Planning and Program Devt: Dr SCOTT ALLAN STROBEL
Univ. Registrar: GABRIEL G. OLSZEWSKI
Librarian: Dr SUSAN GIBBONS
Library: see Libraries and Archives
Number of teachers: 3,810
Number of students: 13,647 (incl. 5,279 undergraduate, 6,381 graduate
Publications: *American Journal of Science, American Scientist, Journal of American Oriental Society, Journal of Biological Chemistry, Journal of Industrial Ecology* (4 a year), *Journal of Music Theory, Journal of the History of Medicine and Allied Sciences, Theatre Magazine* (3 a year), *Yale Alumni Magazine* (1 a year), *Yale French Studies, Yale Human Rights and Development Law Journal* (1 a year), *Yale Journal of Biology and Medicine* (4 a year), *Yale Journal of Health Policy, Law and Ethics* (2 a year), *Yale Journal of International Law* (2 a year), *Yale Journal of Law and Feminism* (2 a year), *Yale Journal of Law and the Humanities* (2 a year), *Yale Journal on Regulation, Yale Law and Policy Review, Yale Law Journal* (8 a year), *Yale Literary Magazine* (2 a year), *Yale Review, Yale Scientific Magazine* (4 a year)

DEANS

School of Architecture: ROBERT A. M. STERN
School of Art: ROBERT STORR
Divinity School: HAROLD W. ATTRIDGE
School of Drama: JAMES BUNDY
School of Engineering and Applied Science: T. KYLE VANDERLICK
School of Forestry and Environmental Studies: PETER CRANE
Law School: ROBERT C. POST
School of Management: EDWARD A. SNYDER
School of Medicine: ROBERT J. ALPERN
School of Music: ROBERT BLOCKER
School of Nursing: MARGARET GREY
School of Public Health: PAUL D. CLEARY
Graduate School of Arts and Sciences: THOMAS D. POLLARD
Yale College: MARY MILLER

PROFESSORS
(Some staff serve in more than one faculty)

School of Architecture:

ALEXLEY, J. W.
BEEBY, T. H., Architectural Design
BLOOMER, K. C., Architectural Design
GARVIN, A., Urban Planning and Devt
HAYDEN, D., Architecture and Urbanism
KOETTER, F. H.
PLATTUS, A. J.
PURVES, A., Architectural Design
STERN, R. A. M.

School of Art:

BARTH, F., Painting and Printmaking
BENSON, R. M., Photography
DE BRETTEVILLE, S. L., Graphic Design
LYTLE, W. R., Painting
PAPAGEORGE, T., Photography
REED, R. J., Jr, Painting and Printmaking
STOCKHOLDER, J., Sculpture

Faculty of Arts and Sciences (Yale College and Graduate School):

ACKERMAN, B., Law and Political Science
ADAIR, R. K., Physics
ADAMS, M. McC., Philosophy, Religious Studies
ADAMS, R. M., Philosophy
ADORNO, R., Spanish
AGNEW, J.-C., American Studies and History
ALEXANDER, J. C., Sociology
ALEXANDROV, V. E., Slavic Languages and Literatures
ALHASSID, Y., Physics
ALTMAN, S., Biology
ALTONJI, J., Economics
AMANAT, A., History
ANDERSON, S. R., Linguistics
ANDREW, D., Comparative Literature, Film Studies
ANDREWS, D. W. K., Economics and Statistics
ANGULIN, D., Computer Science
APPADURAI, A., Int. Studies
APPELQUIST, T. W., Physics
AUSTIN, D. J., Chemistry
AVNI, O., French
BAILYN, C., Astronomy, Physics
BALTAY, C., Physics and Astronomy
BANAC, I., History
BARRON, A., Statistics
BATISTA, V. S., Chemistry
BEALS, R. W., Mathematics
BENHABIB, S., Philosophy, Political Science
BERCOVICI, D., Geology and Geophysics
BERNER, R. A., Geology and Geophysics

BERNSTEIN, I. B., Mechanical Engineering and Physics
BERRY, S. T., Economics
BERS, V., Classics
BEWLEY, T. F., Economics
BLOCH, R. H., French
BLOOM, H. I., English Language and Literature
BLOOM, P., Psychology and Linguistics
BOBZIEN, S., Philosophy
BOORMAN, S. A., Sociology
BÖWERING, G. H., Religious Studies
BRACKEN, P., Management and Political Science
BRAINARD, W. C., Economics
BRAUND, S. M., Classics
BRISMAN, L., English Language and Literature
BRODHEAD, R. H., American Studies, English Language and Literature
BROMLEY, D. A., Physics
BROMWICH, D., English Language and Literature
BROOKS, P., Comparative Literature and French
BROWN, D. J., Economics
BROWN, T. H., Psychology and Physiology
BROWNELL, K. D., Psychology
BRUDVIG, G., Chemistry
BURGER, R. L., Anthropology
BUSHKOVITCH, P. A., History
BUSS, L. W., Ecology and Evolutionary Biology, Geology and Geophysics
BUTLER, J., History and American Studies, Religious Studies
CAMERON, D. R., Political Science
CAMPBELL, J., English Language and Literature
CARBY, H. V., African American Studies and American Studies
CASSON, A. W., Mathematics
CASTEN, R., Physics
CHANG, J. T., Statistics
CHANG, K.-I. S., East Asian Languages and Literatures
CHANG, R. K., Applied Physics, Physics and Electrical Engineering
CHU, B.-T., Mechanical Engineering
CLARK, K., Comparative Literature and Slavic Languages and Literatures
COIFMAN, R. R., Mathematics and Computer Science
COLEMAN, J., Philosophy
CRABTREE, R. H., Chemistry
CROSS, R. J., Jr, Chemistry
CROTHERS, D. M., Chemical Engineering, Chemistry and Molecular Physics and Biochemistry
DAVIS, D., Sociology
DE LA MORA, J. F., Mechanical Engineering
DELLAPORTA, S., Biology
DEMOS, J. P., Religious Studies, Near Eastern Languages and Civilizations, and History
DENNING, M., American Studies
DE ROSE, K., Philosophy
DEVORET, M., Applied Physics and Physics
DIMOCK, W. C., American Studies, English Language and Literature
DONOGHUE, M. J., Ecology and Environmental Biology
DORSEY, J., Computer Science
DOUDNA, J., Molecular Biophysics and Biochemistry
DUDLEY, K., American Studies
DUNCAN, J., Diagnostic Radiology, Electrical Engineering
DUVAL, E. M., French
EIRE, C. M. N., History and Religious Studies
EISENSTAT, S. C., Computer Science
ELIMELECH, M., Chemical Engineering
ENGEL, E., Economics
ENGELMAN, D. M., Molecular Biophysics and Biochemistry
ENGELSTEIN, L., History

ERRINGTON, J. J., Anthropology, East Asian Languages and Literatures
EVENSON, R. E., Economics
FAIR, R. C., Economics
FALLER, J. W., Jr, Chemistry
FARAGHER, J. M., American Studies, History
FEIGELBAUM, J., Computer Science
FEIT, W., Mathematics
FELMAN, S., French and Comparative Literature
FISCHER, M. J., Computer Science
FLAVELL, R. A., Immunobiology and Biology
FLEURY, P., Engineering and Applied Physics, Physics
FOLTZ, W. J., African Studies and Political Science
FOSTER, B. R., Near Eastern Languages and Civilizations
FRAADE, S. D., Religious Studies
FRANK, R., English Language and Literature
FREEDMAN, P. H., History
FRENKEL, I. B., Mathematics
FRY, P. H., English Language and Literature
GADDIS, J. L., History
GAREN, A., Molecular Biophysics and Biochemistry
GARLAND, H., Mathematics
GAUTHIER, J. A., Geology and Geophysics
GEANAKOPLOS, J., Economics
GELERNTNER, D., Computer Science
GERBER, A., Political Science
GHOSH, S., Molecular Biophysics and Biochemistry
GILMORE, G., African American Studies, History
GILROY, P., Sociology and African American Studies
GIRVIN, S. M., Physics and Applied Physics
GLIER, I., Germanic Languages and Literatures
GOLDBERG, P., Economics
GOLDBLATT, H., Medieval Slavic Languages and Literatures
GOLDSMITH, M. H., Biology
GOLDSMITH, T. H., Biology
GOLDSTEIN, L. M., Linguistics
GOMEZ, A., Mechanical Engineering
GONZÁLEZ ECHEVERRÍA, R. O., Hispanic and Comparative Literatures
GOODYEAR, S. S., English Language and Literature
GORDON, R. B., Geology and Geophysics
GORDON, R. W., History, Law
GRAEDEL, T., Geology and Geophysics
GREEN, D., Political Science
GRIFFITH, E. H., African and African American Studies
GRINDLEY, N. D. F., Molecular Biophysics and Biochemistry
GROBER, R., Applied Physics and Physics
GRUENDLER, B., Near Eastern Languages and Civilizations
GUICHARNAUD, J. E., French
GUINNANE, T., Economics and History
GUTAS, D., Near Eastern Languages and Civilizations
HALLER, G. L., Chemical Engineering and Chemistry
HAMADA, K., Economics
HAMILTON, A. D., Chemistry
HAMLIN, C., Germanic Languages and Literatures and Comparative Literature
HAMMER, L., English Language and Literature
HANSEN, V., History
HARMS, R. W., African Studies, History
HARRIES, K., Philosophy
HARRIS, J., Physics
HARSHAV, B., Comparative Literature
HARTIGAN, J. A., Statistics
HARTWIG, J. F., Chemistry
HAYDEN, D., American Studies

HAYES, C., Religious Studies
HENRICH, V. E., Applied Sciences, Physics
HERSEY, G. L., History of Art
HICKEY, L. J., Geology and Geophysics
HILL, A., Anthropology
HOLE, F., Anthropology
HOLFORD, T., Public Health and Statistics
HOLLOWAY, J. S., History
HOLMES, F. L., History
HOMANS, M. B., English, Women's and Gender Studies
HORN, L. R., Linguistics
HORVÁTH, C. G., Chemical Engineering
HUDAK, P., Computer Science
HYMAN, P. E., Modern Jewish History
IACHELLO, F., Physics and Chemistry
INSLER, S., Linguistics
JACKSON, K. D., Spanish and Portuguese
JACOBS, C., Comparative Literature
JACOBSON, M. F., African American Studies, American Studies, History
JAYNES, G. D., Economics, African Studies and African American Studies
JESHION, R., Philosophy
JOHNSON, M. A., Chemistry
JOHNSON, M. K., Psychology
JONES, P. W., Mathematics
JORGENSEN, W. L., Chemistry
JOSEPH, G. M., History
KAGAN, D., Classics and History
KAGAN, S., Classics, Philosophy
KAMENS, E., East Asian Languages and Literatures
KANKEL, D. R., Biology
KARATO, S., Geology and Geophysics
KAVANAGH, T., French
KAZDIN, A. E., Psychology
KEANE, E., Economics
KEIL, F. C., Psychology and Linguistics
KELLY, W. W., Anthropology
KENNEDY, P. M., History
KENNEY, J., Astronomy
KEVLES, D. J., History
KIERNAN, B. F., History
KLEIN, M. J., History of Science and Physics
KLEINER, D. E. E., Classics and History of Art
KLEVORICK, A. K., Economics
KONIGSBERG, W., Molecular Biophysics and Biochemistry
KUTZINSKY, V. M., English Language and Literature, African American Studies and American Studies
LaFRANCE, M., Psychology, Women's and Gender Studies
LANG, S., Mathematics
LARSON, R. B., Astronomy
LAWLER, T., English Language and Literature
LAYTON, B. R., Religious Studies and Near Eastern Languages and Civilizations
LEE, R., Mathematics
LEVIN, R. C., Economics
LIFTON, R., Medicine, Genetics, Molecular Biophysics and Biochemistry
LONG, M. B., Mechanical Engineering and Applied Physics
MA, T.-P., Electrical Engineering and Applied Physics
McDERMOTT, D. V., Computer Science
MacDOWELL, S. W., Physics
MacNAB, R. M., Molecular Biophysics and Biochemistry
MANDELBROT, B. B., Mathematics
MANLEY, L. G., English Language and Literature
MARCUS, I. G., Jewish History
MARGULIS, G. A., Mathematics
MARMOR, T., Public Management and Political Science
MARTIN, D., Religious Studies
MATTHEWS, J. F., History and Classics
MAYER, E., Anthropology
MAYHEW, D. R., Political Science
MAZZOTTA, G., Italian

MENDELSOHN, R., Economics, Forestry and Enviromental Studies, Management
MENOCAL, M. R., Spanish
MERRIMAN, J. M., History
MILLER, C. L., French, and African and African American Studies
MILLER, G., Molecular Bophysics and Biochemistry
MOCHRIE, S., Physics and Applied Physics
MONTGOMERY, D., History
MOORE, P. B., Chemistry and Molecular Biophysics and Biochemistry
MOOSEKER, M. S., Biology and Cell Biology
MORGAN, R. P., Theory of Music
MORRIS, S., Economics
MORSE, A. S., Computer Science, Electrical Engineering
MUSSER, C., American Studies, Film Studies
NALEBUFF, B., Economics
NARENDRA, K. S., Electrical Engineering
NOVICK, A., Ecology and Environmental Biology
ORNSTON, L. N., Biology
ORSZAG, S. A., Mathematics
OUTKA, G., Philosophy and Christian Ethics
PARK, J., Geology and Geophysics
PARKER, P. D. M., Physics
PATTERSON, A., English Language and Literature
PATTERSON, L., English Language and Literature
PEARCE, D. G., Economics
PETERSON, L. H., English Language and Literature
PEUCKER, B., Germanic Languages and Literatures
PFEFFERLE, L. D., Chemical Engineering
PHILLIPS, P. C. B., Economics and Statistics
PIATETSKI-SHAPIRO, I., Mathematics
PLANTINGA, L. B., History of Music
POLAK, B., Economics
POLLARD, D. B., Statistics and Mathematics
POWELL, J. R., Ecology and Environmental Biology
PROBER, D. E., Applied Physics, Physics
QUINT, D. L., English and Comparative Literature
RAE, D. W., Political Science and Management
RANIS, G., Int. Economics
RAWSON, C., English Language and Literature
READ, N., Physics and Applied Physics
REED, M. A., Electrical Engineering and Applied Physics
REGAN, L. J., Molecular Biophysics and Biochemistry
RILEY, M. A., Ecology and Environmental Biology
ROACH, J. R., Theatre and English
ROBINSON, F. C., English
ROEDER, S., Biology
ROEMER, J. E., Economics, Political Science
ROGERS, J., English Language and Literature
ROKHLIN, V., Computer Science and Mathematics
ROSE-ACKERMAN, S., Jurisprudence, Law and Political Science
ROSENBAUM, J. L., Biology
ROSENBLUTH, F. M., Political Science
ROSNER, D. E., Chemical Engineering
RUDDLE, F. H., Biology and Genetics
RUSSETT, B. M., Political Science and Int. Relations
RUSSETT, C. E., History
RYE, D. M., Geology and Geophysics
SACHDEV, S., Physics and Applied Physics
SALOVEY, P., Epidemiology and Public Health, Psychology
SALTZMAN, W. M., Chemical Engineering
SAMMONS, J. L., Germanic Languages and Literatures
SANDWEISS, J., Physics

SANNEH, L., History, Divinity
SAUNDERS, M., Chemistry
SCARF, H. E., Economics
SCHEFFLER, H. W., Anthropology
SCHEPARTZ, A., Chemistry
SCHMIDT, M. P., Physics
SCHULTZ, M. H., Computer Science
SCHULZ, T. P., Economics and Demography
SCHWARTZ, S. B., History
SCOTT, J. C., Political Science and Anthropology
SEILACHER, A., Geology and Geophysics
SHANKAR, R., Physics and Applied Physics
SHAPIRO, I., Political Science
SHIN, S.-J., Philosophy
SHUBIK, M., Economics
SHULMAN, R. G., Chemistry, Molecular Biophysics and Biochemistry
SILBERSCHATZ, A., Computer Science
SIMPSON, W. K., Near Eastern Languages and Civilizations
SINGER, J. L., Psychology
SIU, H. F., Anthropology
SKINNER, B. J., Geology and Geophysics
SKOWRONEK, S., Political Science and Social Science
SMITH, R. B., Geology and Geophysics
SMITH, S. B., Political Science
SMOOKE, M. D., Mechanical Engineering
SNYDER, M., Molecular Biophysics and Biochemistry
SOFIA, S., Astronomy
SÖLL, D. G., Molecular Biophysics and Biochemistry, Biology and Chemistry
SOMMERFIELD, C. M., Physics
SPENCE, J. D., History
SREENIVASAN, K. R., Mechanical Engineering, Physics and Applied Physics
SRINIVASAN, T. N., Economics
STEITZ, T. A., Chemistry, Molecular Biophysics and Biochemistry
STEPTO, R. B., English, African American Studies, American Studies
STERNBERG, R. J., Psychology and Education
STIMSON, H. M., Linguistics, East Asian Languages and Literatures
STONE, A. D., Physics and Applied Physics
STOUT, H. S., History, Religious Studies and American Studies, American Christianity
STROBEL, S., Molecular Biophysics and Biochemistry
SUMMERS, W. C., History of Medicine and Science, Molecular Biophysics and Biochemistry, Therapeutic Radiology
SUNDER, S., Accounting, Economics and Finance
SZELENYI, I., Sociology
SZWED, J. F., Anthropology, African and African American Studies and American Studies
THOMPSON, R. F., African American Studies and History of Art
TREAT, J., East Asian Languages and Literatures
TRUMPENER, K., English and Comparative Literature
TULLY, J. C., Chemistry, Physics and Applied Physics
TUREKIAN, K. K., Geology and Geophysics
TURNER, F. M., History
TURNER, H. A., Jr, History
UDRY, C., Economics
URRY, C. M., Physics and Astrophysics
VACCARO, P. H., Chemistry
VAISNYS, J. R., Ecology and Environmental Biology, Electrical Engineering
VALENTINE, A. M., Chemistry
VALESIO, P., Italian
VALIS, N., Spanish and Portuguese
VAN ALTENA, W. F., Astronomy
VENCLOVA, T., Slavic Languages and Literatures
VERONIS, G., Geology and Geophysics
VRBA, E. S., Geology and Geophysics

WAGNER, A. R., Psychology
WAGNER, G. P., Ecology and Environmental Biology
WALZ, J. Y., Chemical Engineering
WARD, D. C., Genetics, Molecular Biophysics and Biochemistry
WARNER, J. H., American Studies, History, History of Medicine
WATTS, D. P., Anthropology
WEINSTEIN, S., Religious Studies, Buddhist Studies and East Asian Languages and Literatures
WEISS, H., Near Eastern Archaeology, Near Eastern Languages and Civilizations, and Anthropology
WELSH, A., English Language and Literature
WETTLAUFER, J., Geology and Geophysics, Physics
WEXLER, L., American Studies
WHEELER, S., Law and the Social Sciences
WIKSTROM, L. L., Chemical Engineering
WILSON, R., Religious Studies
WINTER, J., History
WOOD, J. L., Chemistry
WOODALL, J. M., Electrical Engineering
WRIGHT, C. M., History of Music
WRIGHTSON, K., History
WYMAN, R. J., Biology
WYNN, K., Psychology
YEAZELL, R. B., English Language and Literature
ZELLER, M. E., Physics
ZIEGLER, F. E., Chemistry
ZIGLER, E. F., Psychology
ZILM, K. W., Chemistry
ZINN, R. J., Astronomy
ZUCKER, S. W., Computer Science and Electrical Engineering
ZUCKERMAN, G. J., Mathematics

Divinity School:
ADAMS, M. Mc., Historical Theology
ATTRIDGE, H. W., New Testament
BARTLETT, D. L., Preaching and Christian Communication
COLLINS, A. Y., Old Testament Interpretation and Criticism
DITTES, J. E., Pastoral Theology and Psychology
FARLEY, M. A., Christian Ethics
FASSLER, M. E., Music History and Liturgy
KELSEY, D. H., Theology
MURRAY, T., Organ
OGLETREE, T. W., Theological Ethics
OUTKA, G., Philosophy and Christian Ethics
SANNEH, L. O., Missions and World Christianity and History
SPINKS, B. D., Liturgical Studies
STOUT, H. S., American Religious History
VOLF, M., Systematic Theology
WILSON, R. R., Old Testament and Religious Studies

School of Drama:
BUNDY, J.

School of Forestry and Environmental Studies:
ASHTON, M. S., Silviculture and Forest Ecology
BERLYN, G. P., Anatomy and Physiology of Trees
BREWER, G. D., Resource Policy and Management
BURCH, W. R., Jr, Natural Resource Management
DOVE, M. R., Social Ecology
ESTY, D. C., Environmental Law and Policy
GRAEDEL, T. E., Industrial Ecology
GREGOIRE, T. G., Forest Management
KELLERT, S. R., Social Ecology
LYONS, J. R., Natural Resource Management
MENDELSOHN, R., Forest Policy
MONTAGNINI, F., Tropical Forestry

OLIVER, C. D., Forest Policy
REPETTO, R., Economics and Sustainable Devt
SCHMITZ, O. J., Population and Community Ecology
SICCIAMA, T. G., Forest Ecology
SPETH, J. G., Environmental Policy and Sustainable Devt
WARGO, J. P., Environmental Risk Analysis, Political Science

School of Law:
ACKERMAN, B. A., Law and Political Science
AMAR, A. R., Law
AYRES, I., Law
BALKIN, J. M., Constitutional Law and the First Amendment
BRILMAYER, L., Int. Law
BURT, R. A., Law
CARTER, S. L., Law
CHUA, A. L., Law
COLEMAN, J. L., Jurisprudence and Philosophy
CURTIS, D. E., Law
DALTON, H. L., Law
DAMASKA, M. R., Law
DAYS, D. S., III, Law
DEUTSCH, J. G., Law
DIGNAM, B., Law
DUKE, S. B., Law
ELLICKSON, R. C., Property and Urban Law
ESTY, D. C., Environmental Law and Policy
FISS, O. M., Law
GEWIRTZ, P. D., Constitutional Law
GOLDSTEIN, A. S., Law
GORDON, R. W., Law and Legal History
GRAETZ, M. J., Law
HANSMANN, H. B., Law
KAHAN, D. M., Law
KAHN, P. W., Law and the Humanities
KLEVORICK, A. K., Law and Economics
KOH, H. H., Int. Law
LANGBEIN, J. H., Law and Legal History
LUCHT, C. L., Law
MASHAW, J. L., Law
PETERS, J. K., Law
POTTENGER, J. L., Law
PRIEST, G. L., Law and Economics
REISMAN, W. M., Int. Law
RESNIK, J., Law
ROMANO, R., Law
ROSE, C. M., Law and Organization
ROSE-ACKERMAN, S., Jurisprudence (Law School and Dept of Political Science)
RUBENFELD, J., Law
SCHUCK, P. H., Law
SCHULTZ, V., Law and Social Sciences
SIEGEL, R., Law
SIMON, J. G., Law
SOLOMON, R. A., Law
STITH, K., Law
WEDGWOOD, R., Law
WHITMAN, J. Q., Comparative and Foreign Law
WIZNER, S., Law
YOSHINO, K., Law

Yale School of Management:
BRACKEN, P., Management and Political Science
BREWER, G. D., Resource Policy and Management
CHEN, ZH., Finance
CHEVALIER, J. A., Finance and Economics
DHAR, R., Marketing
FEINSTEIN, J., Economics
GARSTKA, S., Practice of Management
GARTEN, J. E., Practice of Int. Trade and Finance
GOETZMANN, W., Management and Finance Studies
IBBOTSON, R., Practice of Finance
INGERSOLL, J. E., Jr, Int. Trade and Finance
KAPLAN, E., Management Sciences, Public Health
LI, L., Production Management

LÓPEZ-DE-SILANES, F., Finance and Economics
MACAVOY, P., Management Studies
MARMOR, T. R., Public Policy and Management
NALEBUFF, B., Economics and Management
OSTER, S. M., Management and Entrepreneurship
POLAK, B., Economics and Management
RAE, D. W., Management
ROUWENHORST, K. G., Finance
SCOTT MORTON, F. M., Economics
SEN, S. K., Organization, Management and Marketing
SHUBIK, M. S., Mathematical Institutional Economics
SPIEGEL, M., Finance
SUNDER, S., Accounting, Economics and Finance
SWERSEY, A. J., Operations Research
VROOM, V. H., Organization and Management, Psychology
WELCH, I., Finance
WITTINK, D. R., Management and Marketing

School of Medicine:
AGHAJANIAN, G. K., Psychiatry and Pharmacology
ANDERSON, K. S., Pharmacology
ANDIMAN, W. A., Paediatrics and Epidemiology and Public Health
ANDREWS, N. W., Cell Biology, Microbial Pathogenesis
ANDRIOLE, V. T., Internal Medicine
ANYAN, W. R., Paediatrics
ARONSON, P. S., Internal Medicine and Cellular and Molecular Physiology
ASKENASE, P. W., Internal Medicine
BAKER, M. D., Emergency Medicine, Paediatrics
BALTIMORE, R. S., Paediatrics, Infectious Diseases and Epidemiology and Public Health
BARASH, P. G., Anaesthesiology
BARNSTABLE, C. J., Neurobiology, Ophthalmology and Visual Science
BARON, R., Orthopaedics and Rehabilitation, Internal Medicine and Cell Biology
BARTOSHUK, L. M., Surgery
BATSFORD, W. P., Internal Medicine
BEARDSLEY, G. P., Paediatric Haematology and Pharmacology
BEHRMAN, H. R., Obstetrics and Gynaecology
BELSKY, J. L., Internal Medicine
BERLINER, N., Genetics and Internal Medicine
BIA, F. J., Medicine and Laboratory Medicine
BIA, M. J., Medicine
BINDER, H. J., Cellular and Molecular Physiology, Digestive Diseases and Internal Medicine
BLATT, S. J., Psychiatry and Psychology
BOLOGNIA, J. L., Dermatology
BOOSS, J., Neurology and Laboratory Medicine
BORON, W. F., Cellular and Molecular Physiology
BOTHWELL, A., Immunobiology
BOTTOMLY, H. K., Immunobiology and Molecular, Cellular and Developmental Biology
BOULPAEP, E. L., Cellular and Molecular Physiology
BOWERS, M. B., Jr, Psychiatry
BOYER, J. L., Digestive Diseases, Internal Medicine
BRACKEN, M. B., Epidemiology and Public Health, Chronic Disease Epidemiology, Neurology
BRASH, D. E., Genetics, Therapeutic Radiology
BRAVERMAN, I. M., Dermatology

BROADUS, A. E., Internal Medicine and Cellular and Molecular Physiology
BROWN, T. H., Cellular and Molecular Physiology, Psychology
BUCALA, R., Medicine
BUNNEY, B. S., Psychiatry and Pharmacology
BURRELL, M. I., Diagnostic Radiology
BURROW, G. N., Obstetrics and Gynaecology
BYRNE, T. N., Neurology and Medicine
CABIN, H., Internal Medicine
CADMAN, E. C., Internal Medicine
CAPLAN, M., Cellular and Molecular Physiology
CARPENTER, T. O., Endocrinology, Paediatrics
CARTER, D., Pathology
CENTRELLA, M., Surgery
CHAMBERS, S. K., Obstetrics and Gynaecology
CHANDLER, W. K., Cellular and Molecular Physiology
CHASE, H. S., Jr, Medicine
CHENG, Y.-C., Pharmacology
CHOI, Y., Laboratory Medicine, Pathology
CLEARY, J. P., Internal Medicine
CLEMAN, M., Internal Medicine
COCA-PRADOS, M., Ophthalmology and Visual Science
COHEN, L. B., Cellular and Molecular Physiology
COHEN, L. S., Internal Medicine
COLEMAN, D., Medicine
COLLINS, J. G., Anaesthesiology
COOLEY, L., Cell Biology, Genetics
COONEY, L. M., Jr, Internal Medicine
COSTA, J. C., Pathology
CRAFT, J., Immunobiology, Medicine
CRESSWELL, P., Immunobiology
CULLEN, M. R., Medicine, Occupational and Environmental Medicine, Public Health
CURTIS, A. M., Diagnostic Radiology
DANNIES, P. S., Pharmacology
DAW, N. W., Ophthalmology and Visual Science
DE CAMILLI, P. V., Cell Biology
DEISSEROTH, A. B., Internal Medicine
DE LUCA, V. A., Internal Medicine
D'ESCOPO, N. D., Internal Medicine
DE VITA, V. T., Internal Medicine
DI MAIO, D., Genetics
DOBBINS, J. W., Internal Medicine
DONABEDIAN, R. K., Laboratory Medicine
DU BOIS, A. B., Epidemiology and Public Health, and Cellular and Molecular Physiology
DUFFY, T. P., Internal Medicine
DUNCAN, C. C., Neurosurgery and Paediatrics
DUNCAN, J., Diagnostic Radiology
EDBERG, S. C., Internal Medicine, Laboratory Medicine
EHRENKRANZ, R. A., Neonatology, Obstetrics and Gynaecology, Paediatrics
EHRENWERTH, J., Anaesthesiology
EHRLICH, B., Pharmacology and Cellular and Molecular Biology
ELEFTERIADES, J. A., Surgery
ELIAS, J. A., Medicine
FARBER, L. R., Internal Medicine
FERRO-NOVICK, S., Cell Biology
FINKELSTEIN, F. O., Internal Medicine
FISCH, D., Epidemiology of Microbial Diseases
FISCHER, D. S., Internal Medicine
FISCHER, J. J., Therapeutic Radiology
FLAVELL, R., Immunobiology, Molecular, Cellular and Developmental Biology
FLOCH, M. H., Internal Medicine
FLYNN, S. D., Pathology, Surgery
FORBUSH, B., III, Cellular and Molecular Physiology
FORGET, B. G., Medicine and Genetics
FORMAN, B. H., Internal Medicine
FORREST, J. N., Jr, Medicine

FRIEDLAENDER, G. E., Orthopaedics and Rehabilitation
FRIEDLAND, G. H., Epidemiology, Medicine
GALÁN, J., Cell Biology, Microbial Pathogenesis
GEIBEL, J. P., Surgery
GENEL, M., Paediatrics
GHOSH, S., Immunobiology, Molecular Biophysics and Biochemistry, Molecular, Cellular and Developmental Biology
GIEBISCH, G. H., Cellular and Molecular Physiology
GIFFORD, R. H., Internal Medicine
GLAZER, P. M., Therapeutic Radiology and Genetics
GLICKMAN, M. G., Diagnostic Radiology and Surgery
GOLDMAN-RAKIC, P., Neurobiology, Neurology
GOLDSTEIN, S. A. N., Cellular and Molecular Physiology, Paediatrics
GONZALEZ, C., Ophthalmology and Visual Science, Paediatrics
GORE, J. C., Diagnostic Radiology
GORELICK, F., Internal Medicine, Digestive Diseases and Cell Biology
GREEN, B., Surgery
GREENFELD, D. G., Psychiatry
GREER, C., Neurobiology, Neurosurgery
GRIFFITH, B., Laboratory Medicine
GRIFFITH, E. E. H., Psychiatry
GROSS, I., Neonatology, Obstetrics and Gynaecology, Paediatrics
GROSZMANN, R. J., Digestive Diseases, Internal Medicine
GUSBERG, R. J., Surgery
HAFFTY, B. G., Therapeutic Radiology
HAYSLETT, J. P., Medicine
HEALD, P. W., Dermatology
HEBERT, S. C., Cellular and Molecular Physiology, Medicine
HENDLER, E. D., Internal Medicine
HENINGER, G. R., Psychiatry
HERBERT, P. N., Internal Medicine
HIERHOLZER, W. J., Internal Medicine and Epidemiology
HINES, R. L., Anaesthesiology
HOCKFIELD, S., Neurology
HOFFER, P. B., Diagnostic Radiology
HOFFMAN, J. F., Cellular and Molecular Physiology
HOLBROOK, N. J., Geriatrics
HOLFORD, T. R., Epidemiology and Public Health
HORWICH, A. L., Genetics and Paediatrics
HOSTETTER, M. K., Paediatrics
IANNINI, P. B., Internal Medicine
INNIS, R. B., Psychiatry and Pharmacology
INOUYE, S. K., Geriatrics
INSOGNA, K. L., Internal Medicine
JACOBS, S. C., Psychiatry
JACOBY, R. O., Comparative Medicine
JAFFE, C. C., Diagnostic Radiology and Internal Medicine
JAMIESON, J. D., Cell Biology
JANEWAY, C., Immunobiology and Molecular, Cellular and Developmental Biology
JATLOW, P. I., Laboratory Medicine and Psychiatry
JOINER, K. A., Internal Medicine, Cell Biology and Infectious Diseases
JOKL, P., Orthopaedics and Rehabilitation
KACZMAREK, L. K., Cellular and Molecular Physiology and Pharmacology
KAETZ, H. W., Internal Medicine
KAIN, Z., Anaesthesiology, Paediatrics
KANTOR, F. S., Internal Medicine
KAPADIA, C. R., Internal Medicine
KASHGARIAN, M., Pathology and Molecular, Cellular and Developmental Biology
KASL, S. V., Chronic Disease Epidemiology
KAVATHAS, P., Genetics, Immunobiology, Laboratory Medicine
KELLER, M. S., Diagnostic Radiology and Paediatrics
KENNEY, J. D., Internal Medicine

KICKBUSCH, I. S., Epidemiology and Public Health
KIDD, K. K., Genetics, Molecular, Cellular and Developmental Biology, and Psychiatry
KIER, E. L., Diagnostic Radiology
KIM, J. H., Pathology
KINDER, B. K., Surgery
KLIGER, A. S., Internal Medicine
KOCSIS, J. D., Neurology
KOPF, G. S., Surgery
KOSTEN, T. R., Psychiatry
KRUMHOLZ, H. M., Epidemiology and Public Health, Internal Medicine
KRYSTAL, J. H., Psychiatry
LAMOTTE, R. H., Anaesthesiology
LANDRY, M., Laboratory Medicine
LANNIN, D. R., Surgery
LAWSON, J. P., Diagnostic Radiology, Orthopaedics and Rehabilitation
LEADERER, B. P., Public Health, Environmental Studies
LEDER, S. B., Surgery
LEFFELL, D. J., Dermatology
LENTZ, T. L., Cell Biology
LESSER, R. L., Neurology, Ophthalmology and Visual Science
LEVANTHAL, J. M., Nursing, Paediatrics and Child Study Center
LEVINE, R. A., Laboratory Medicine
LEVINE, R. J., Internal Medicine
LEVITIN, H., Internal Medicine
LEVY, L. L., Neurology
LEVY, S. R., Neurology
LIFTON, R. P., Medicine and Genetics
LISTER, G., Jr, Paediatrics and Anaesthesiology
LORBER, M. I., Surgery
LYTTON, B., Surgery, Urology
MCCARTHY, P., Paediatrics, Nursing
MCCARTHY, S., Diagnostic Radiology
MCCLENNAN, B. L., Diagnostic Radiology
MCCORMICK, D., Neurology
MCGLASHAN, T. H., Psychiatry
MCMAHON-PRATT, D., Epidemiology of Microbial Diseases
MCPHEDRAN, P., Laboratory Medicine and Internal Medicine
MADRI, J. A., Pathology
MAHNENSMITH, R., Medicine
MAHONEY, M. J., Genetics, and Obstetrics and Gynaecology, and Paediatrics
MAKUCH, R. W., Epidemiology and Public Health
MALAWISTA, S. E., Medicine
MARCHESI, S. L., Pathology and Laboratory Medicine
MARCHESI, V. T., Pathology, Cell Biology
MARIEB, N. J., Internal Medicine
MARKS, L. E., Environmental Health Sciences
MARSH, J. C., Internal Medicine
MATTHAY, R. A., Medicine
MAZURE, C. M., Psychiatry
MELLMAN, I. S., Cell Biology and Immunobiology
MENT, L. R., Paediatrics and Neurology
MERIKANGAS, K. R., Chronic Disease Epidemiology, Psychiatry
MERSON, M. H., Epidemiology and Public Health
MILLER, I. G., Jr, Epidemiology and Public Health, Molecular Biophysics and Biochemistry, Paediatrics
MILLER, P. L., Anaesthesiology
MILSTONE, L. M., Dermatology
MOCZYDLOWSKI, E. G., Cellular and Molecular Physiology, Pharmacology
MODLIN, I. M., Surgery
MOGHADDAM, B., Neurobiology, Psychiatry
MOOSEKER, M., Cell Biology
MORROW, J. S., Molecular, Cellular and Developmental Biology, Pathology
MOSER, M., Internal Medicine
MOYER, M. S., Paediatrics
NAIM, A., Psychiatry

NAIR, S., Internal Medicine
NATH, R., Therapeutic Radiology
NOVICK, P., Cell Biology
O'MALLEY, S. S., Psychiatry
PATTON, C. L., Epidemiology of Microbial Diseases
PELKER, R. R., Orthopaedics and Rehabilitation
PERILLIE, P. E., Internal Medicine
PERSING, J. A., Surgery and Neurosurgery
PESCHEL, R. E., Therapeutic Radiology
PEZZIMENTI, J. F., Internal Medicine
PIEPMEIER, J. M., Neurosurgery
POBER, J. S., Pathology, Dermatology and Immunobiology
QUAGLIARELLO, V. J., Medicine
RABINOVICI, R., Surgery
RADDING, C. M., Genetics and Molecular Biophysics and Biochemistry
RAFFERTY, T. D., Anaesthesiology
RAKIC, P., Neurology and Neurobiology
RAPPEPORT, J., Internal Medicine
RASTEGAR, A., Medicine
REDMOND, D. E., Jr, Psychiatry and Neurosurgery
RENSHAW, T., Orthopaedics and Rehabilitation
RICHARDS, F. F., Internal Medicine
RISCH, H. A., Chronic Disease Epidemiology
ROCKWELL, S. C., Pharmacology, Therapeutic Radiology
ROEDER, S., Genetics, Molecular, Cellular and Developmental Biology
ROSE, J. K., Pathology and Cell Biology
ROSENBAUM, S., Anaesthesiology
ROSENFIELD, A. T., Diagnostic Radiology
ROSENHECK, R. A., Epidemiology and Public Health, Psychiatry
ROTH, R. H., Jr, Psychiatry and Pharmacology
ROUNSAVILLE, B. J., Psychiatry
RUDDLE, F., Genetics, Molecular, Cellular and Developmental Biology
RUDDLE, N. H., Epidemiology of Microbial Diseases, Immunobiology
RUDNICK, G., Pharmacology
SACKS, F. L., Internal Medicine
SANTOS-SACCHI, J., Surgery
SARTORELLI, A. C., Pharmacology
SASAKI, C. T., Surgery
SCHATZ, D., Immunobiology
SCHLESSINGER, J., Pharmacology
SCHOEN, R., Internal Medicine
SCHOTTENFELD, R. S., Psychiatry
SCHWARTZ, I. R., Surgery
SCHWARTZ, P. E., Obstetrics and Gynaecology
SEASHORE, J. H., Surgery
SEASHORE, M. R., Genetics, Paediatrics
SEGAL, S. S., Cellular and Molecular Physiology
SESSA, W. C., Pharmacology
SHAPIRO, E. D., Epidemiology and Public Health, Paediatrics, Nursing
SHAW, C., Diagnostic Radiology
SHAYWITZ, A. E., Neurology, Paediatrics
SHAYWITZ, S. E., Paediatrics
SHERTER, C. B., Internal Medicine
SHERWIN, R. S., Internal Medicine
SHULMAN, G. I., Internal Medicine, and Cellular and Molecular Physiology
SIEGEL, N. J., Medicine, Paediatrics
SIGWORTH, F. J., Cellular and Molecular Physiology
SILVERMAN, D., Anaesthesiology
SINATRA, R., Anaesthesiology
SIVARAJAN, M., Anaesthesiology
SLAYMAN, C. L., Cellular and Molecular Physiology
SLAYMAN, C. W., Genetics and Cellular and Molecular Physiology
SLEDGE, W. H., Psychiatry
SMITH, B. R., Internal Medicine, Laboratory Medicine, Paediatrics
SNOW, D. L., Psychiatry

SNYDER, E. L., Laboratory Medicine
SPENCER, D. D., Neurosurgery
SPENCER, S. S., Neurology
SPIRO, H. M., Internal Medicine
STERN, D. F., Pathology
STITT, J. T., Cellular and Molecular Physiology, Epidemiology and Environmental Health Sciences
STRITTMATTER, S. M., Neurobiology, Neurology
SULAVIK, S. B., Internal Medicine
SUMMERS, W. C., Therapeutic Radiology, Molecular Biophysics and Biochemistry, and Genetics
SUMPIO, B. E., Surgery
TAMBORLANE, W. V., Paediatrics
TATTERSALL, P., Laboratory Medicine and Genetics
TAYLOR, K. J., Diagnostic Radiology
TIGELAAR, R. E., Dermatology and Immunobiology
TINETTI, M., Medicine, Epidemiology and Public Health
TOULOUKIAN, R. J., Paediatrics, Surgery
TRAUBE, M., Digestive Diseases, Internal Medicine
UDELSMAN, R., Surgery
ULLU, E., Cell Biology, Medicine
VAN DEN POL, A., Neurosurgery
WACKERS, F. J., Diagnostic Radiology and Medicine
WALSH, T. J., Neurology, Ophthalmology and Visual Science
WARD, D. C., Genetics, Molecular Biophysics and Biochemistry
WARDLAW, S. C., Laboratory Medicine
WARREN, G., Cell Biology
WAXMAN, S. G., Neurology, Neurobiology
WEISS, R. M., Surgery, Urology
WEISSMAN, S. M., Genetics and Internal Medicine
WESTCOTT, J. A., Diagnostic Radiology
WHITE, R. I., Jr, Diagnostic Radiology
WRIGHT, F. S., Internal Medicine and Cellular and Molecular Physiology
ZARET, B. L., Diagnostic Radiology, Medicine
ZELTERMAN, D., Epidemiology and Public Health
ZONANA, H. V., Psychiatry

School of Music:

AGAWU, K., Theory of Music
AKI, S., Violin
BERMAN, B., Piano
BRESNICK, M. I., Composition
CHOOKASIAN, L., Voice and Opera
DUFFY, T. C.
FASSLER, M. E.
FORTE, A., Theory of Music
FRANK, C., Piano
GOTTLIEB, G., Percussion
HARTH, S., Violin
HAWKSHAW, P., History of Music
LADERMAN, E., Composition
LEVINE, J., Viola
MURRAY, T., Organ
OUNDJIAN, P., Violin
PARISOT, A. S.
REPHANN, R.
ROSAND, E., History of Music
ROSEMAN, R., Oboe
RUFF, W. H., Jr.
SHIFRIN, D., Clarinet
SMITH, L. L.
SWALLOW, J. W., Brass and Ensemble Performance
TIRRO, F. P.
YARICK-CROSS, D., Voice

School of Nursing:

BURST, H. V., Nursing
DIERS, D. K., Nursing
DIXON, J. K., Nursing
FUNK, M., Nursing
GILLISS, C. L., Nursing
GREY, M., Nursing

KNAFL, K. A., Nursing
KNOPF, M. T., Oncology Nursing
KRAUSS, J. B., Nursing
MILONE-NUZZO, P., Nursing
MINARKI, P., Nursing
WILLIAMS, A., Nursing

DELAWARE

DELAWARE STATE UNIVERSITY

1200 N Dupont Highway, Dover, DE 19901-2277

Telephone: (302) 857-6290
Fax: (302) 857-6352
E-mail: admissions@desu.edu
Internet: www.desu.edu

Founded 1891 as State College for Colored Students, present name and status 1993
State control
Academic year: August to DecemberJanuary to May (2 semesters)
2 Satellite campuses: Sussex County campus and Wilmington campus
Pres.: Dr HARRY LEE WILLIAMS (acting)
Provost and Vice-Pres. for Academic Affairs: Dr ALTON THOMAS
Vice-Pres. for Finance and Admin.: AMIR MOHAMMADI
Vice-Pres. for Institutional Advancement: CAROLYN CURRY
Vice-Pres. for Research: NOUREDDINE MELIKECHI
Vice-Pres. for Student Affairs: KEMAL M. ATKINS
Dean for Univ. Libraries: Dr REBECCA BATSON
Registrar: TERELL D. HOLMES
Dir for Admissions: LAWITA G. CHEATHAM
Library: see Libraries and Archives
Number of teachers: 198
Number of students: 3,819

DEANS

College of Agriculture and Related Sciences: Dr DYREMPLE B. MARSH
College of Arts Humanities and Social Sciences: Prof. MARSHALL STEVENSON
College of Business: Dr SHELTON RHODES
College of Education, Health and Public Policy: Dr JOHN N. AUSTIN
College of Mathematics, Natural Science and Technology: Dr NOUREDDINE MELIKECHI
School of Graduate Studies and Research: Dr MICHAEL CASSON

GOLDEY-BEACOM COLLEGE

4701 Limestone Rd, Wilmington, DE 19808
Telephone: (302) 998-8814
Fax: (302) 996-5408
E-mail: gbc@gbc.edu
Internet: www.gbc.edu

Founded 1886 as Wilmington Commercial College, present name 1951
Private control
Academic year: August to May
Areas of study: business, computer information systems, criminal justice, economics, English and psychology
Pres.: MOHAMMAD ILYAS
Vice-Pres.: GARY L. WIRT
Vice-Pres. for Admin. and Finance: KRISTINE M. SANTOMAURO
Academic Dean: ALISON BOORD WHITE
Dean for Enrolment Management: JANE H. LYSLE
Dean for Student Affairs: BERNADETTE H. WIMBERLEY
Dir for Admissions: LARRY EBY
Dean for Information Technology: EMILY JACKSON
Number of students: 1,600

UNIVERSITY OF DELAWARE

Newark, DE 19716
Telephone: (302) 831-2792
Fax: (302) 831-6905
E-mail: registrar@udel.edu
Internet: www.udel.edu

Founded 1743 as Free School, present status and name 1921
State control
Academic year: June to May
Pres.: Dr PATRICK T. HARKER
Provost: TOM APPLE (acting)
Sr Vice-Provost for Research and Strategic Initiatives: MARK A. BARTEAU
Deputy Provost: NANCY BRICKHOUSE
Exec. Vice-Pres. and Univ. Treas.: SCOTT R. DOUGLASS
Vice-Pres. and Chief of Staff: PATRICIA PLUMMER WILSON
Vice-Pres. and Gen. Counsel: LAWRENCE WHITE
Vice-Pres. and Univ. Sec.: PIERRE D. HAYWARD
Vice-Pres. for Devt and Alumni Relations: MONICA M. TAYLOR
Vice-Pres. for Facilities and Auxiliary Services: DAVID SINGLETON
Vice-Pres. for Finance and Admin.: JENNIFER J. J. DAVIS
Vice-Pres. for Information Technologies: CARL JACOBSON
Vice-Pres. for Student Life: MICHAEL A. GILBERT
Dean for Library Services: MATHEW SIMON
Library: see Libraries and Archives
Number of teachers: 1,131
Number of students: 21,489 (17,092 undergraduate, 3,617 graduate and 780 professional)
Publications: *DEconstruction*, *UD Research* (online (www.udel.edu/researchmagazine))

DEANS

Alfred Learner College of Business and Economics: Prof. BRUCE WEBBER
College of Agriculture and Natural Resources: Prof. ROBIN MORGAN
College of Arts and Science: Prof. GEORGE WATSON
College of Earth, Ocean and Environment: NANCY TARGETT
College of Engineering: BABATUNDE A. OGUNNAIKE
College of Health Sciences: Dr KATHLEEN S. MATT
College of Education and Human Development: Prof. LYNN OKAGAKI (acting)

PROFESSORS

ABRAMS, B. A., Economics
ACKERMAN, B. P., Psychology, Linguistics
ADAMS, F., Philosophy
ADVANI, S. G., Mechanical Engineering
AGARWAL, S. K., Mechanical Engineering
AGUIRRE, B. E., Sociology and Criminal Justice
ALCHON, S. A., History
ALLEN, H. E., Civil Engineering
ALLMENDINGER, D. F., Jr, History
AMER, P. D., Computer and Information Sciences, Electrical and Computer Engineering
AMES, D. L., Urban Affairs and Public Policy, Geography
ANDERSEN, M. L., Sociology and Criminal Justice, Women's Studies
ANDERSON, L. G., Marine Studies, Economics
ANDREWS, D. C., English
ANGELL, T. S., Mathematical Sciences
ARCE, G. R., Electrical and Computer Engineering, Marine Studies
ARDIS, A. L., English
ARENSON, M. A., Music
ATHANASSOGLOU-KALLMYER, N., Art History

BACH, R. D., Chemistry and Biochemistry
BACHMAN, R, Sociology and Criminal Justice
BADIEY, M., Marine Studies
BARNEKOV, T. K., Urban Affairs and Public Policy
BAROUDI, J., Accounting and Management Information Systems
BARR, S. M., Bartol Research Institute
BARTEAU, M. A., Chemical Engineering, Chemistry and Biochemistry
BEAR, G. G., Education
BEASLEY, J. C., English
BEEBE, T. P., Jr, Chemistry and Biochemistry
BELLAMY, D. P., Mathematical Sciences
BENNETT, J., English
BENNETT, R. B., English
BERIS, A. N., Chemical Engineering
BERNHARDT, S. A., Writing
BERNSTEIN, J. A., History
BEST, J., Sociology and Criminal Justice
BIEBER, J. W., Bartol Research Institute
BIEDERMAN, K., Finance
BILINSKY, Y., Political Science and International Relations
BINDER-MACLEOD, S. A., Physical Therapy
BLITS, J. H., Education, Political Science and Int. Relations
BOLTON, R. C., Art
BONCELET, C. G., Electrical and Computer Engineering
BOULD, S., Sociology and Criminal Justice, Individual and Family Studies, Women's Studies
BOYER, J. S., Marine Biochemistry and Biophysics, Plant and Soil Sciences
BOYLAN, A. M., History, Women's Studies
BRAUN, T. E. D., Comparative Literature, Foreign Languages and Literatures
BRICKHOUSE, N., Education
BRILL, T. B., Chemistry and Biochemistry
BROADBRIDGE, P., Mathematical Sciences
BROCK, D. H., English
BROCKMANN, R. J., English
BROWN, F., English
BROWN, H. E., Art, Art Conservation, Art History, Museum Studies
BROWN, J. L., Foreign Languages and Literatures
BROWN, R. F., Philosophy
BROWN, R. P., Theatre
BROWN, S. D., Chemistry and Biochemistry
BROWNING, J. E., Theatre
BROWNING, W. L., Theatre
BUCHANAN, T. S., Mechanical Engineering
BUCKMASTER, D. A., Accounting and Management Information Systems
BURMEISTER, J. L., Chemistry and Biochemistry
BURNSIDE, J., Animal and Food Sciences, Biological Sciences
BUTKIEWICZ, J. L., Economics
BYRNE, J. M., Urban Affairs and Public Policy, Marine Studies
CALLAHAN, D. F., History
CALLAHAN, R. A., History
CAMPBELL, L. L., Biological Sciences
CARBERRY, M. S., Computer and Information Sciences, Linguistics
CARON, D. M., Entomology and Applied Ecology
CAROTHERS, M. L., Art
CARR, C. L., Music
CARROLL, R. B., Plant and Soil Sciences
CARSON, D., Biological Sciences
CASE, J., Computer and Information Sciences
CAVINESS, B. F., Computer and Information Sciences, Mathematical Sciences
CHAJES, M. J., Civil and Environmental Engineering
CHAPMAN, H. P., Art History
CHEN, J. G., Chemical Engineering, Materials Science and Engineering
CHOU, T. W., Mechanical Engineering
CHUI, S.-T., Bartol Research Institute
CHURCH, T. M., Marine Studies, Chemistry and Biochemistry

CICALA, G. A., Psychology
CINCIN-SAIN, B., Marine Studies, Political Science and International Relations, Urban Affairs and Public Policy
COGBURN, L. A., Animal and Food Sciences
COHEN, L. H., Psychology
COLE, P., Linguistics
COLLINS, G. E., Computer and Information Sciences
COLLINS, N. E., Bioresources Engineering
COLMAN, R. F., Chemistry and Biochemistry
COLTON, D. L., Mathematical Sciences
COOK-IOANNIDIS, P., Mathematical Sciences
CORNELL, H. V., Biological Sciences
COTUNGA, N., Nutrition and Diatetics
COURTRIGHT, J. A., Communications
CURTIS, J. C., History
CURTIS, L. A., Biological Sciences, Marine Studies
CUSTER, J. F., Anthropology
DAVIS, S., Political Science and International Relations
DAVISON, R. A., English
DAWSON, C., English
DEAN, J. M., English
DEBESSAY, A., Accounting and Management Information Systems
DEINER, P. L., Individual and Family Studies
DE LEON, P. A., Biological Sciences
DEL FATTORE, J., English, Legal Studies
DEMICCIO, F. J., Hotel, Restaurant and Institutional Management
DENSON, C. D., Chemical Engineering
DENTEL, S. K., Civil and Environmental Engineering
DEXTER, S. C., Marine Studies, Materials Science and Engineering
DHURJATI, P., Chemical Engineering
DI LORENZO, T. M., Psychology
DIRENZO, G., Sociology and Criminal Justice
DOHMS, J. E., Immunology and Microbiology
DONALDSON-EVANS, M. P., Foreign Languages and Literatures
DOREN, D. J., Chemistry and Biochemistry
DUGGAN, L. G. J., History
DURBIN, P. T., Philosophy, Urban Affairs and Public Policy
DYBOWSKI, C. R., Chemistry and Biochemistry
EBERT, G. L., Mathematical Sciences
EISENBERGER, R. W., Psychology
ELIAS, J. G., Electrical and Computer Engineering
ELSON, C. M., Legal Studies, Corporate Governance
EPIFANIO, C., Marine Studies
ERMANN, M. D., Sociology and Criminal Justice
EVANS, D. H., Chemistry and Biochemistry
EVENSON, P. A., Bartol Research Institute
FAGHRI, A., Civil and Environmental Engineering
FANELLI-KUCZMARSKI, M. T., Nutrition and Diatetics
FARACH-CARSON, M. C., Biological Sciences
FERRETTI, R., Education, Psychology
FITZMAURICE, C., Theatre
FLYNN, P. D., English
FOU, C.-M., Physics and Astronomy
FRETT, J. J., Plant and Soil Sciences
FUHRMANN, J. J., Plant and Soil Sciences
GAERTNER, S. L., Psychology
GAFFNEY, P. M., Marine Studies
GAISSER, T. K., Bartol Research Institute
GALLAGHER, J. L., Marine Studies
GALVIN, M. E., Materials Science and Engineering
GAO, G.-R., Electrical and Computer Engineering
GARLAND, H., Business Administration
GARVINE, R. W., Marine Studies, Civil and Environmental Engineering
GATES, B. T., English, Women's Studies
GEHRLEIN, W. V., Business Administration
GELB, J., Jr, Animal and Food Sciences

GEMPESHAW, C. M., II, Economics, Food and Resource Economics
GIBSON, A. E., Art History
GILBERT, R. P., Mathematical Sciences, Marine Studies, Computer and Information Sciences
GILLESPIE, J. W., Jr, Materials Science and Engineering
GINZBERG, M. J., Accounting and Management Information Systems, Business Administration
GLASS, B. P., Geology, Marine Studies
GLUTTING, J. J., Education
GLYDE, H. R., Physics and Astronomy
GOLDSTEIN, L. F., Political Science and Int. Relations
GOLINKOFF, R. M., Education, Linguistics, Psychology
GOODMAN, S., English
GREEN, P., Plant and Soil Sciences
GREENBERG, M. D., Mechanical Engineering
GRIFFITHS, L., Animal and Food Sciences
GRUBB, F. J., Economics, History
HAAS, K. C., Sociology and Criminal Justice
HABER, C., History
HADJIPANAYIS, G., Physics and Astronomy
HALIO, J. L., Communications, Comparative Literature, English, Theatre
HALL, H. B., Philosophy
HALL, S. J., Health and Exercise Sciences
HALLENBECK, D. J., Mathematical Sciences
HALPRIN, A., Physics and Astronomy
HAMILTON, C., Nutrition and Diatetics
HAMPEL, R., Education
HANEY, M. H., Electrical and Computer Engineering
HANS, V. P., Sociology and Criminal Justice
HAREVEN, T. K., Individual and Family Studies, History
HASLETT, B. J., Communications, Psychology, Women's Studies
HASLETT, D. W., Philosophy
HASTINGS, S. E., Food and Resource Economics
HAUS, H.-U., Theatre
HAWK, J. A., Plant and Soil Sciences
HAYES, E. R., Nursing
HELMLING, S., English
HERMAN, B. L., Art History, History
HERMAN, D., Music
HEWITT, K. H., Military Science
HEYRMAN, C. L., History
HIEBERT, J., Education
HIGGINBOTHAM, E., Sociology and Criminal Justice
HILDEBRANDT, D. J., Music
HOFFECKER, C. E., History
HOFFMAN, J. E., Psychology
HOFFMAN, S. D., Economics, Women's Studies
HOFSTETTER, F., Education
HOLMES, L. W., Art
HOOVER, D. G., Animal and Food Sciences
HOUGH-GOLDSTEIN, J. A., Entomology and Applied Ecology
HSIAO, G. C., Mathematical Sciences
HUANG, C. P., Civil and Environmental Engineering, Marine Studies
HUDDLESTON, M. W., Political Science and Interntional Relations, Urban Affairs and Public Policy
HUNSPERGER, R. G., Electrical and Computer Engineering
HURT, J. J., History
IH, C. S., Electrical and Computer Engineering, Marine Studies
ILVENTO, T. W., Food and Resource Economics
INCIARDI, J. A., Sociology and Criminal Justice
INGERSOLL, D. E., Political Science and International Relations
INTRAUB, H., Psychology
IZARD, C., Psychology
JACKSON, M. D., English
JAIN, M. K., Chemistry and Biochemistry

JOHNSON, H. B., Black American Studies, History
JOHNSON, M. V., Chemistry and Biochemistry
JONES, J. M., Psychology
JONES, S. K., Accounting and Management Information Systems
JORDAN, R. R., Geology
KALER, E. W., Chemical Engineering
KALKSTEIN, L. S., Geography
KALLAL, M. J., Consumer Studies
KAPLAN, D. W., Education
KARLSON, R. H., Biological Sciences
KEELER, C., Animal and Food Sciences
KENNEDY, J. A., Mathematical Sciences
KERR, A. D., Civil and Environmental Engineering
KERRANE, K., English
KIKUCHI, S., Civil and Environmental Engineering
KIRBY, J. T., Civil and Environmental Engineering, Marine Studies
KIRCHMAN, D. L., Marine Studies
KIRWAN, A. D., Jr, Marine Studies
KITTO, S. L., Plant and Soil Sciences
KLEMAS, V. V., Marine Studies, Electrical and Computer Engineering
KLINZING, D. G., Individual and Family Studies
KLOCKARS, C. B., Sociology and Criminal Justice
KMIEC, E. B., Biological Sciences
KOBAYASHI, N., Civil and Environmental Engineering, Marine Studies
KOFORD, K. J., History, Economics, Political Science and International Relations
KOLCHIN, P. R., History
KOLODZEY, J., Electrical and Computer Engineering
KRAFT, J. C., Geology, Marine Studies
KUNG, L., Animal and Food Sciences
KUSHMAN, J. E., Consumer Studies
LAMBRECHT, M., Nursing
LANE, R., Art
LATHROP, T. A., Foreign Languages and Literatures
LAZENBIK, F., Mathematical Sciences
LEATHERS, D. J., Geography
LEAVENS, P. B., Geology
LEITCH, T. M., English
LEJA, M., English
LEMIEUX, B., Plant and Soil Sciences
LENHOFF, A. M., Chemical Engineering
LESHCHINSKY, P. E., Civil and Environmental Engineering
LEUNG, C. N., Physics and Astronomy
LEWIS, K. A., Business
LI, W., Mathematical Sciences
LINK, C. R., Economics
LLOYD, E. L., Computer and Information Sciences
LUTHER, G. W., Marine Studies, Chemistry and Biochemistry, Civil and Environmental Engineering
MACDONALD, J., Physics and Astronomy
MAGEE, J., Political Science and International Relations
MANGONE, G. J., Legal Studies, Marine Studies
MANRAI, A. K., Business Administration
MANRAI, L., Business Administration
MARKS, C. C., Black American Studies, Sociology and Criminal Justice
MARTIN, R. E., Geology
MASON, C. E., Entomology and Applied Ecology
MASON, D. M., Food and Resource Economics
MASTERSON, F. A., Psychology
MATTHAEUS, W. H., Bartol Research Institute
MAY, G., History
MELL, D. C., English
MEYER, D. H., History
MEYER, W. H., Political Science and International Relations
MILLER, G. E., English
MILLER, J. B., Economics

MILLER, M. J., Political Science and International Relations
MILLER, S., Sociology and Criminal Justice, Women's Studies
MILLS, D. L., Electrical and Computer Engineering
MONK, P. B., Mathematics
MOODY, W. B., Education, Mathematical Sciences
MORGAN, R. W., Agriculture and Food Sciences, Biology, Chemistry and Biochemistry
MORRISON, J. L., Consumer Studies
MULLAN, D. J., Bartol Research Institute
MULLIGAN, J., Economics
MUNSON, M. S. B., Chemistry and Biochemistry
MURRAY, F. B., Education, Psychology
NANDAKUMAR, R., Education
NASHED, M. Z., Mathematical Sciences, Electrical Engineering
NEES, L. P., Art History
NEEVES, R. E., Health and Exercise Science
NELSON, F. E., Geography
NELSON, M., English
NELSON, P., Food and Resource Economics
NESS, N. F., Bartol Research Institute
NEWTON, J. E., Black American Studies
NICHOLS, R. D., Art
NIGG, J. M., Sociology and Criminal Justice
NORTHMORE, D. P. M., Psychology
OLIVER, J. K., Political Science and International Relations, Marine Studies
O'NEILL, J. B., Economics
OPILA, R. L., Materials Science and Engineering
OWOCKI, S. P., Bartol Research Institute
PALKOVITZ, R. J., Individual and Family Studies
PALLEY, M. L., Political Science and International Relations, Women's Studies
PALMER, L. M., Philosophy, Women's Studies
PARSONS, G. R., Marine Studies, Economics
PAULANKA, B. J., Nursing
PAULY, T. H., English
PERSE, E. M., Communications
PETERS, D. L., Individual and Family Studies, Urban Affairs and Public Policy
PETERSON, L. W., Music
PFAELZER, J., English
PIFER, E. I., Communications, Comparative Literature, English
PIKA, J. A., Political Science and International Relations
PILL, W. G., Plant and Soil Sciences
PITTEL, S., Bartol Research Institute
PIZZOLATO, T. D., Plant and Soil Sciences
PIZZUTO, J. E., Geology
PONG, D., History
POPE, C. R., Animal and Food Sciences
POTTER, L. D., English
PRODAN, J. C., Music
PURNELL, L., Nursing
RABOLT, J. F., Materials Science and Engineering
RAFFEL, J. A., Urban Affairs and Public Policy, Political Science and International Relations
RATHS, J., Education
REEDY, C. L., Museum Studies, Art History, Urban Affairs and Public Policy
REIDEL, L., Theatre
REYNOLDS, H. T., Political Science and International Relations, Urban Affairs and Public Policy
RHEINGOLD, A. L., Chemistry and Biochemistry
RICH, D., Urban Affairs and Public Policy, Political Science and International Relations
RICHARDS, J. G., Health and Exercise Sciences
RICHARDS, M. P., English
RIDGE, D., Chemistry and Biochemistry
RITTER, W. F., Bioresources Engineering
ROBBINS, C., Sociology and Criminal Justice

ROBBINS, S. L., Theatre
ROBINSON, C. E., English
ROE, P. G., Anthropology
ROSELLE, D. P., Mathematics
ROSENBERGER, J. K., Microbiology
ROTH, R. R., Entomology and Applied Ecology
RUARK, G., English
RUSSELL, T. W. F., Chemical Engineering
SAFER, E. B., English
SANDLER, S. I., Chemical Engineering, Chemistry and Biochemistry
SANIGA, E. M., Business Administration
SATINOFF, E., Psychology
SAUNDERS, B. D., Computer and Information Sciences, Mathematical Sciences
SAYDAM, T., Computer and Information Sciences
SCARPITTI, F. R., Sociology and Criminal Justice
SCHWARTZ, L. W., Mechanical Engineering, Mathematical Sciences
SCHWARTZ, N. B., Anthropology
SCHWEDA-NICHOLSON, N. L., Legal Studies, Linguistics
SCHWEITZER, R. L., Economics
SEIDMAN, L. S., Economics
SELEKMAN, J. A., Nursing
SETHI, A. S., Computer and Information Sciences
SETTLE, R. F., Economics
SETTLES, B. H., Individual and Family Studies
SHAFI, M., Foreign Languages and Literatures
SHAFI, Q., Bartol Research Institute
SHARNOFF, M., Physics and Astronomy
SHARP, J. H., Marine Studies
SHIPMAN, H. L., Physics and Astronomy
SIDEBOTHAM, S. E., History
SIGNORIELLI, N., Communications
SIMMONS, D. T., Biological Sciences
SIMONS, R. F., Psychology
SIMS, J. T., Plant and Soil Sciences
SKOPIK, S. D., Biological Sciences
SLOYER, C. W., Jr, Mathematical Sciences
SMITH, J. L., Nutrition and Dietetics
SNIDER, O. S., Animal and Food Sciences
SNYDER-MACKLER, L., Physical Therapy, Philosophy
SOLES, J. R., Political Science and International Relations
SPARKS, D. L., Civil and Environmental Engineering, Chemistry and Biochemistry, Plant and Soil Sciences
SPINSKI, V., Art
STANEV, T., Bartol Research Institute
STARK, C., English
STARK, R. M., Mathematical Sciences, Civil and Environmental Engineering
STETSON, M. H., Biological Sciences
STONER, J. H., Art Conservation
ST PIERRE, E. K., Accounting and Management Information Systems
STRAIGHT, R., Arts
STRASSER, S., History
STRECKFUSS, R. J., Music
SVENDSEN, I. A., Civil and Environmental Engineering, Marine Studies
SWASEY, J. E., Plant and Soil Sciences
SWEENEY, J. E., Theatre
SYLVES, R. T., Political Science and Int. Relations, Marine Studies, Urban Affairs and Public Policy
SZALEWICZ, K., Physics and Astronomy
SZERI, A. Z., Mechanical Engineering
TABER, D. F., Chemistry and Biochemistry
TALLAMY, D. W., Entomology and Applied Ecology
TARGETT, N. M., Marine Studies
TARGETT, T. E., Marine Studies
THEOPOLD, K. H., Chemistry and Biochemistry
THIBAULT, B., Foreign Languages and Literatures
THORPE, C., Chemistry and Biochemistry

TIERNEY, K. J., Sociology and Criminal Justice
TILMON, H. D., Food and Resource Economics
TOENSMEYER, U. C., Food and Resource Economics
TOLLES, B. F., Jr, Art History, History, Museum Studies
TURKEL, G. M., Sociology and Criminal Justice
ULLMAN, W. J., Marine Studies, Geology
UNGER, D. G., Individual and Family Studies
UNRUH, K., Physics and Astronomy
VARMA, R. D., Economics
VASILAS, B. L., Plant and Soil Sciences
VENEZKY, R., Education, Computer and Information Sciences, Linguistics
VICKERY, C. E., Nutrition and Dietetics
VINSON, J. R., Mechanical Engineering; Marine Studies
VUKELICH, C., Individual and Family Studies
WAGNER, N. J., Chemical Engineering
WAGNER, R. C., Biological Sciences
WALKER, J. H., Theatre
WALKER, J. M., English
WARREN, R., Urban Affairs and Public Policy; Political Science and International Relations
WATSON, G. H., Physics and Astronomy
WEBSTER, F., Marine Studies
WEDEL, A. R., Communications, Linguistics, Foreign Languages and Literatures
WEHMILLER, J. F., Geology, Marine Studies
WEISS, J. J., Art
WHITE, C. E., Jr, Accounting and Management Information Systems
WHITE, H. B., III, Chemistry and Biochemistry
WILDER, M. S., Urban Affairs and Public Policy
WILKINS, D. J., Mechanical Engineering
WILLMOTT, C. J., Geography, Marine Studies
WIRTH, M. J., Chemistry and Biochemistry
WOLTERS, R. B., History
WONG, K.-C., Marine Studies
WOOD, T. K., Entomology and Applied Ecology
WOOL, R. P., Chemical Engineering
YAGODA, B., English
YAN, X.-H., Marine Studies
ZINN, M. A., Music
ZIPSER, R. A., Foreign Languages and Literatures
ZUCKERMAN, M., Psychology

WESLEY COLLEGE

120 N State St, Dover, DE 19901
Telephone: (302) 736-2300
E-mail: info@wesley.edu
Internet: www.wesley.edu
Founded 1873 as Wilmington Conf. Acad., present name 1918
Private control
Academic year: August to May
2 Campuses: New Castle and Dover Air Force Base
Pres.: Dr WILLIAM N. JOHNSTON
Exec. Vice-Pres. and Provost: Dr BETTE S. COPLAN
Vice-Pres. for Academic Affairs: Dr PATRICIA DWYER
Vice-Pres. for Finance and Dir of Human Resources: ERIC R. NELSON
Vice-Pres. for Institutional Advancement: CHRIS A. WOOD
Dean for Students: MARY-ALICE OZECHOSKI
Dean for Enrolment Management: Dr HOWARD BALLENTINE
Registrar: RAYANN FRYATT
Library Dir: ROGER GETZ
Library of 100,000 vols 20,000 e-journals
Number of students: 2,500
Publication: Wesley Magazine (2 a year).

WIDENER UNIVERSITY SCHOOL OF LAW

Delaware Campus: POB 7474, 4601 Concord Pike, Wilmington, DE 19803-0474
Harrisburg Campus: POB 69381, 3800 Vartan Way, Harrisburg, PA 17106-9381

Telephone: (302) 477-21703 (Delaware)
E-mail: lawadmissions@widener.edu
Internet: law.widener.edu

Founded 1971
Private control
Academic year: August to May
Pres.: JAMES HARRIS
Assoc. Provost and Dean for Law School: LINDA L. AMMONS
Dean for Student Affairs: KEITH E. SEALING
Asst Dean forBusiness and Admin.: VERNE R. SMITH
Dir for Information Technology: SHARON BUCZALA
Dir for Admissions: ERIC M. KNISKERN
Registrar: DOROTHY HEMPHILL
Number of teachers: 198 (78 full-time, 120 part-time)
Number of students: 1,600
Publications: *Delaware Journal of Corporate Law* (2 a year), *Widener Journal of Law, Economics and Race* (online (www.wjler.org)), *Widener Law Journal* (1 a year), *Widener Law Review* (1 a year).

WILMINGTON UNIVERSITY

320 N DuPont Highway, New Castle, DE 19720-6491

Telephone: (302) 356-4636
Fax: (302) 328-5902
E-mail: infocenter@wilmu.edu
Internet: www.wilmu.edu

Founded 1968 as Wilmington College, present name 2007
Private control
Academic year: 3 semesters
Campuses: Wilson Graduate Center, Middletown, Dover, Dover Air Force Base, Georgetown, Rehoboth Beach and N Wilmington, New Jersey
Pres.: Dr JACK P. VARSALONA
Provost and Vice-Pres. for Academic Affairs: BETTY J. CAFFO
Chief Financial Officer and Vice-Pres. for Financial Affairs: HEATHER A. O'CONNELL
Vice-Pres. for Admin. Affairs: CAROLE D. PITCHER
Vice-Pres. for Student Affairs: LAVERNE T. HARMON
Librarian: JAMES A. BRADLEY
Registrar: ELIZABETH P. JORDAN
Library of 117,000 vols
Number of students: 15,000
Publication: *WilmU* (2 a year)

DEANS

College of Arts and Sciences: Dr DOREEN TURNBO
College of Business: Dr DONALD W. DURANDETTA
College of Education: Dr JOHN C. GRAY
College of Health Professions: Dr DENISE Z. WESTBROOK
College of Social and Behavioral Sciences: CHRISTIAN A. TROWBRIDGE
College of Technology: Dr EDWARD L. GUTHRIE

DISTRICT OF COLUMBIA

AMERICAN UNIVERSITY

4400 Massachusetts Ave, NW, Washington, DC 20016

Telephone: (202) 885-1000

Fax: (202) 885-3265
E-mail: admissions@american.edu
Internet: www.american.edu
Private control
Academic year: August to December,January to July (2 semesters)
Liberal arts curriculum; doctoral instn
Pres.: NEIL KERWIN
Provost: SCOTT A. BASS
Vice Pres., Chief Legal Counsel and Sec.: MARY E. KENNARD
Vice-Pres. for Campus Life and Dean of Students: GAIL SHORT HANSON
Vice-Pres. for Communications: TERESA FLANNERY
Vice-Pres. for Devt and Alumni Relations: THOMAS J. MINAR
Vice-Pres. for Finance and Treas.: DONALD L. MYERS
Dean for Academic Affairs: Dr PHYLLIS PERES (acting)
Registrar: ALICE POEHLS
Univ. Librarian: BILL MAYER
Library of 701,518 vols, 20,000 e-books, 258,000 digitized primary source materials, 41,000 media and sound recordings and 14,245 musical scores
Number of teachers: 750 (full-time)
Number of students: 12,033 (6,657 undergraduates, 3,620 graduates, 1,756 law)
Publications: *Folio*, *Intercultural Management Quarterly*, *Journal of International Service* (2 a year), *Pharmakon*

DEANS

College of Arts and Sciences: PETER STARR
Kogod College of Business Administration: MICHAEL J. GINZBERG
School of Communication: LARRY KIRKMAN
School of International Service: JAMES GOLDGEIER
School of Public Affairs: WILLIAM M. LEOGRANDE (acting)
Washington College of Law: CLAUDIO M. GROSSMAN

CATHOLIC UNIVERSITY OF AMERICA

620 Michigan Ave, NE, Washington, DC 20064

Telephone: (202) 319-5000
Internet: www.cua.edu

Founded 1887
Private control
Academic year: September to August
Pres.: JOHN H. GARVEY
Provost: Dr JAMES BRENNAN
Vice-Pres. for Enrolment Management: Dr W. MICHAEL HENDRICKS
Vice-Pres. for Finance and Treas.: CATHY R. WOOD
Vice-Pres. for Institutional Advancement: H. KEN DEDOMINICIS
Vice-Pres. for Student Life: SUSAN D. PERVI
Vice-Pres. for Univ. Relations and Chief of Staff: FRANK G. PERSICO
Assoc. Vice-Pres. and Univ. Registrar: ADRIANA FARELLA
Gen. Counsel: Dr LAWRENCE MORRIS
Univ. Librarian: STEPHEN CONNAGHAN
Library: 3.9m. vols (incl. books, e-books, microforms and audiovisual materials).
Number of teachers: 797
Number of students: 6,894 (3,633 undergraduate, 3,261 graduate)
Publications: *Catholic University Law Review*, *CommLaw Conspectus: Journal of Communications Law and Policy*, *Journal of Contemporary Health Law and Policy*, *Journal of Law, Philosophy and Culture*, *Pierre d'angle*, *Review of Metaphysics*, *The Catholic Historical Review* (4

a year), *The Jurist: Studies in Church Law and Ministry*, *U.S. Catholic Historian*

DEANS

Benjamin T. Rome School of Music: Dr GRAYSON WAGSTAFF
Columbus School of Law: VERYL MILES
Metropolitan School of Professional Studies: Dr SARA THOMPSON
Nat. Catholic School of Social Service: Dr JAMES R. ZABORA
School of Architecture and Planning: RANDALL OTT
School of Arts and Sciences: Dr LAWRENCE R. POOS
School of Canon Law: Rev. ROBERT KASLYN
School of Engineering: Dr CHARLES C. NGUYEN
School of Library and Information Science: Dr INGRID HSIEH-YEE
School of Nursing: Dr PATRICIA MCMULLEN
School of Philosophy: Dr JOHN C. MCCARTHY
School of Theology and Religious Studies: Rev. MARK MOROZOWICH

CORCORAN COLLEGE OF ART AND DESIGN

500 17th St, NW, Washington, DC 20006-4804

Telephone: (202) 639-1800
Fax: (202) 639-1830
E-mail: admissions@corcoran.org
Internet: www.corcoran.edu

Founded 1890
Private control
Academic year: August to December,January to May (2 semesters)
Campuses in Downtown and Georgetown
Provost and Chief Academic Officer: CATHERINE ARMOUR
Dean for Enrolment: Dr CHRISTINE LEICHLITER
Dean for Students: JOHN DICKSON
Dean for Undergraduate Studies: ANDY GRUNDBERG
Registrar: CURREN MCLANE
Library Dir: MARIO ASCENCIO
Library of 35,000 vols, 32,000 slides, 1,200 DVDs, 190 periodicals subscription
Number of students: 615 (347 undergraduate, 268 graduate)

GALLAUDET UNIVERSITY

800 Florida Ave, NE, Washington, DC 20002-3695

Telephone: (202) 651-5000
Fax: (202) 651-5508
E-mail: public.relations@gallaudet.edu
Internet: www.gallaudet.edu

Founded 1864 as Columbia Instn for the Instruction of the Deaf and Dumb and Blind, present name 1954
Academic year: August to May
Liberal education and career devt for deaf and hard of hearing students; incl. a museum
Pres.: Dr ALAN HURWITZ
Provost: Dr STEPHEN WEINER
Vice-Pres. for Admin. and Finance: PAUL KELLY
Vice-Pres. for Devt and Alumni Relations: Dr LYNNE MURRAY
Chief Enrolment and Management Officer: CHARITY REEDY-HINES
Dean for Student Affairs: DWIGHT BENEDICT
Dir for Library Services: SARAH HAMRICK
Library of 200,000 vols
Number of teachers: 234
Number of students: 1,793 (1,100 undergraduate, 433 graduate, 201 professional studies and 59 English Language Institute)

Publications: *Gallaudet Today* (2 a year), *Perspectives in Education and Deafness* (4 a year)

DEANS

College of Liberal Arts, Sciences and Technologies: Dr ISAAC AGBOOLA
Graduate School and Professional Programmes: Dr CAROL ERTING

GEORGE WASHINGTON UNIVERSITY

2121 I St, NW, Washington, DC 20052
Telephone: (202) 994-1000
Fax: (202) 994-9025
Internet: www.gwu.edu
Founded 1821 as Columbian College, present name 1994
Private control
Academic year: September to May

3 Campuses: Foggy Bottom and Mount Vernon in Washington, DC, and the GW Virginia Science and Technology Campus in Ashburn, Virginia

Pres.: STEVEN KNAPP
Provost and Exec. Vice-Pres. for Academic Affairs: Dr STEVEN R. LERMAN
Sr Vice-Provost for Academic Affairs and Planning: FORREST MALTZMAN
Sr Vice-Pres. and Sr Vice-Provost for Student and Academic Support Services: ROBERT A. CHERNAK
Sr Vice-Pres. and Gen. Counsel: BETH NOLAN
Exec. Vice-Pres. and Treas.: LOUIS H. KATZ
Vice-Pres. for Advancement: MICHAEL MORSBERGER
Vice-Pres. for Devt and Alumni Relations: MICHAEL J. MORSBERGER
Vice-Pres. for External Relations: LORRAINE VOLES
Vice-Pres. for Research: LEO M. CHALUPA
Vice-Pres. and Sec.: ARISTIDE J. COLLINS, JR
Registrar: ELIZABETH AMUNDSON
Univ. Librarian: JACK A. SIGGINS
Library: see under Libraries and Archives
Number of teachers: 2,220
Number of students: 25,260

Publications: *GW Review* (2 a year), *The American Intellectual Property Law Association Quarterly Journal*, *The Federal Circuit Bar Journal (FCBJ)* (4 a year), *The George Washington International Law Review* (4 a year), *The George Washington Law Review* (6 a year), *The Journal of Energy and Environmental Law* (2 a year), *The Public Contract Law Journal* (4 a year), *Wooden Teeth* (2 a year)

DEANS

College of Professional Studies: Dr ALI ESKANDARIAN
Columbian College of Arts and Sciences: PEG BARRATT
Elliott School of Int. Affairs: MICHAEL E. BROWN
Graduate School of Education and Human Development: MICHAEL J. FEUER
Law School: PAUL SCHIFF BERMAN
School of Business: Dr DOUG GUTHRIE
School of Engineering and Applied Science: Dr DAVID S. DOLLING
School of Medicine and Health Sciences: JEFFREY S. AKMAN
School of Public Health and Health Services: Dr LYNN R. GOLDMAN
School of Nursing: Dr JEAN JOHNSON

PROFESSORS

(Some professors serve in more than one school)

Columbian School of Arts and Sciences and Elliott School of International Affairs:

ABRAMSON, F. P., Pharmacology, Chemistry
ABRAVANEL, E., Psychology

ADAMS, G. M., Int. Affairs
ALBRIGHT, J. W., Microbiology and Immunology
ALLEN, C. J., Anthropology, Int. Affairs
ANDERSON, J. C., Art
ARNDT, R. A., Physics
ARTERTON, F. C., Political Management
ASKARI, H. G., Business, Int. Affairs
ATKIN, M. A., History
AUSTIN, J. F., Sociology
AZAR, I., Spanish and Human Sciences
BAGINSKI, F. E., Mathematics
BAILEY, J. M., Biochemistry and Molecular Biology
BECKER, W. H., History and Int. Affairs
BELL, D., Anthropology
BERKOWITZ, E. D., History
BERMAN, B. L., Physics
BHALA, R., Law, Int. Affairs
BLACK, A. M., History and Int. Affairs
BLOSSOM, N. H., Interior Design
BORRIELLO, J., Psychology
BOULIER, B. L., Economics
BRADLEY, M. D., Economics, Int. Affairs
BRISCOE, W. J., Physics
BROCK, G. W., Telecommunications
BROWN, N. J., Political Science, Int. Affairs
BURNS, J. R., Zoology
CARESS, E. A., Chemistry
CAWS, P. J., Philosophy
CHAVES, J., Chinese
CHIAPPINELLI, V. A., Basic Science, Pharmacology, Neurological Surgery
CHURCHILL, R. P., Philosophy
CORDES, J. J., Economics and Int. Affairs
COSTIGAN, C. C., Design
COTTROL, R. J., Law, History, Sociology
DAVIS, H., Strategic Management and Int. Affairs
DEERING, C. J., Political Science
DONALDSON, R. P., Biology
DUNNING, R. M., Jr, Economics
EAST, M. A., Int. Affairs and Political Science
ETZIONI, A., Sociology
FALK, J. E., Operations Research
FEIGELBAUM, H. B., Political Science, Int. Affairs
FERRER, J., Jr, Business, Int. Affairs
FISHER, E. A., Classics
FRIEDLER, G., Engineering and Applied Science, Statistics
FUERTH, L., Int. Affairs
GALLO, L. L., Biochemistry and Molecular Biology
GANZ, R. N., Jr, English
GARNER, N. C., Theatre
GASTWIRTH, J. L., Statistics and Economics
GLICK, I. I., Mathematics
GOLDFARB, R. S., Economics
GOLDSTEIN, A. L., Biochemistry and Molecular Biology
GOW, D. D., Anthropology, Int. Affairs
GRIFFITH, W. B., Philosophy
GRINKER, R. R., Anthropology, Int. Affairs, Human Sciences
GUENTHER, R. J., Music
GUPTA, M. M., Mathematics
HARDING, H., Int. Affairs, Political Science
HARTMANN, H., Women's Studies
HENIG, J. R., Political Science
HILTEBEITEL, A. J., Religion, Human Sciences
HOLMES, D. E., Clinical Psychology
HORTON, J. O., American Civilization and History
HOTEZ, P. J., Microbiology, Tropical Medicine, Global Health, Int. Affairs
HOWE, G. W., Psychology
INDERFURTH, K. F., Int. Affairs
JACOBSON, L. B., Theatre
JOHNSON, K. E., Anatomy
JUDSON, H. F., History
JUNGHENN, H. D., Mathematics
KAMINSKI, G. L., Economics, Int. Affairs
KATZ, I. J., Mathematics

KENNEDY, D. K., History, Int. Affairs
KENNEDY, K. A., Pharmacology and Genetics
KENNEDY, R. E., Jr, European History
KIM-RENAUD, Y. K., Korean Language and Culture, Int. Affairs
KING, M. M., Chemistry
KLAMER, A., Economics, Int. Affairs
KLARÉAN, P. F., History, Int. Affairs
KNOWLTON, R. E., Biology
KUIPERS, J. C., Anthropology, Int. Affairs, Human Sciences
KUMAR, A., Biochemistry, Molecular Biology and Genetics
KWOKA, J. E., Jr, Economics
LABADIE, P. A., Economics
LACHIN, J. M., III, Statistics, Biostatistics
LADER, M. P., Art
LADISCH, S., Paediatrics, Biochemistry and Molecular Biochemistry
LAKE, J. L., Photography
LEHMAN, D. R., Physics
LENGERMANN, P. M., Sociology
LEWIS, J. F., Geology
LILLIEFORS, H. W., Statistics
LINEBAUGH, C. W., Speech and Hearing, Medicine
LIPSCOMB, D. L., Biology
LOGSDON, J. M., Political Science, Int. Affairs
LONGSTRETH, R. W., American Civilization
LUDLOW, G., French, Int. Affairs
McALEAVEY, D. W., English
McCLINTOCK, C., Political Science, Int. Affairs
McGRATH, D. C., Jr, Geography, Urban and Regional Planning
MADDOX, J. H., English
MAHMOUD, H. M., Statistics
MANDEL, H. G., Pharmacology
MANHEIM, J. B., Political Communications and Political Science
MAXIMON, L. C., Physics
MAZZUCHI, T. A., Operations Research, Engineering Management
MERGEN, B. M., American Civilization
MILLAR, J. R., Economics and Int. Affairs
MILLER, B. D., Anthropology, Int. Affairs
MILLER, J. A., English, American Studies
MILLER, J. C., Psychology
MILLER, J. H., Chemistry
MOLINA, S. B., Art
MUFTIC, S., Computer Science
NASR, S. H., Islamic Studies
NAU, H. R., Political Science and Int. Affairs
NAYAK, T. K., Statistics
OFFERMAN, L. R., Psychology
OZDOGAN, T., Ceramics
PACKER, R. K., Biology
PALMER, P. M., American Civilization, Women's Studies
PARKE, W. C., Physics
PARSONS, D. O., Economics
PASTER, G. K., English
PATIERNO, S. R., Pharmacology, Genetics
PECK, L. L., History
PELZMAN, J., Economics and Int. Affairs
PERRY, D. C., Pharmacology
PETERSON, R. A., Psychology, Psychiatry and Behavioural Sciences
PEUSNER, K. D., Anatomy
PLOTZ, J. A., English, Human Sciences
POPPEN, P. J., Psychology
POST, J. M., Psychiatry, Political Psychology, Int. Affairs
PRZYTYCKI, J. H., Mathematics
RAMAKER, D. E., Chemistry
RASKIN, M., Policy Studies
REDDAWAY, P., Political Science and Int. Affairs
REICH, B., Political Science and Int. Affairs
REICH, W., Int. Affairs, Ethics and Human Behaviour
REISS, D., Psychiatry and Behavioural Science, Medicine, Psychology

RIBUFFO, L. P., History
ROBINSON, E. A., Jr, Mathematics
ROBINSON, L. F., Art
ROBLES, F., Int. Marketing, Int. Affairs
ROSENAU, J. N., Int. Affairs
ROTHBLAT, L. A., Psychology, Anatomy
ROWE, W. F., Forensic Sciences
ROWLEY, D. A., Chemistry
RYCROFT, R. W., Int. Science and Technology Policy, Int. Affairs
SACHAR, H. M., History, Int. Affairs
SALAMON, L. B., English, Human Sciences
SAPERSTEIN, M. E., Jewish History
SASHKIN, M., Human Resource Devt
SCHAFFNER, R. F., Medical Humanities, Philosophy
SCHWANDT, D. R., Human Resource Devt
SCOTT, D. W., Microbiology and Immunology, Anatomy and Cell Biology
SEAVEY, O. A., English
SHAMBAUGH, D. L., Political Science and Int. Affairs
SHAO, X.-Q., Anthropology
SIGELMAN, C. K., Psychology
SIGELMAN, L., Political Science
SINGPURWALLA, N. D., Operations Research, Statistics
SMITH, S. C., Economics, Int. Affairs
SODARO, M. J., Political Science and Int. Affairs
SOLAND, R. M., Operations Research
SPECTOR, R. H., History and Int. Affairs
SQUIRES, G. D., Sociology
STEINHARDT, R., Law, Int. Affairs
STEN, C. W., English
STEPHENS, G. C., Geology
STERLING, C. H., Media and Public Affairs, Telecommunication
THIBAULT, J. F., French, Human Sciences
THORNTON, R. C., History and Int. Affairs
TROPEA, J. L., Sociology
TROST, R. P., Economics
TUCH, S. A., Sociology
ULLMAN, D. H., Mathematics
VANDERHOEK, J. Y., Biochemistry and Molecular Biology
VERTER, J. L., Statistics
VLACH, J. M., American Civilization, Anthropology
VON BARGHAHN-CALVETTI, B. A., Art
WADE, A. G., Theatre
WALLACE, D. D., Jr, Religion
WALLACE, R. A., Sociology
WALSH, R. J., Anatomy and Cell Biology
WARREN, C., Communication
WATSON, H. S., Economics
WEGLICKI, W. B., Medicine, Physiology
WEINER, R. J., Int. Business, Int. Affairs
WEITZER, R., Sociology
WERLING, L. L., Pharmacology
WILLIAMS, R. L., Naval Science
WINSLOW, E. K., Behavioural Sciences
WIRTZ, P. W., Management Science, Psychology
WITHERS, M. R., Dance
WOLCHIK, S. L., Political Science and Int. Affairs
WOOD, B., Human Origins, Human Evolutionary Anatomy
WOODWARD, W. T., Painting
WRIGHT, J. F., Jr, Drawing and Graphics
YEIDE, H. E., Jr, Religion
YEZER, A., Economics
ZIOLKOWSI, J. E., Classics

School of Business and Public Management:
ACHROL, R. S., Marketing
ADAMS, W. C., Public Admin.
ARTERTON, F. C., Political Management
BABER, W. R., Accountancy
BAGCHI, P. K., Business Admin.
BARNHILL, T. M., Finance
CARSON, J. H., Management Science
CHERIAN, E. J., Information Systems
CHITWOOD, S. R., Public Admin.
COYNE, J. P., Management Science

DAVIS, H. J., Strategic Management
DIVITA, S. F., Marketing
DYER, R. F., Business Admin.
FOLKERTS, J., Media and Public Affairs
FORMAN, E. H., Management Science
GLASCOCK, J. L., Finance
GRANGER, M. J., Management Science
HALAL, W. E., Management Science
HANDORF, W. C., Finance
HARMON, M. M., Public Admin.
HARVEY, J. B., Management Science
HAWKINS, D. E., Tourism Studies, Tourism Policy, Medicine
HILMY, J., Accountancy
INFELD, D. L., Public Admin., Health Services Management and Policy
JAQUES, E., Management Science
KEE, J. E., Public Admin.
KLOCK, M. S., Finance
KUMAR, K. R., Accountancy
LAUTER, G. P., Int. Business
LENN, D. J., Strategic Management and Public Policy
LOBUTS, J. F., Jr, Management Science
McSWAIN, C. J., Public Admin.
MADDOX, L. M., Business Admin.
MANHEIM, J. B., Media and Public Affairs, Political Science
NEWCOMER, K. E., Public Admin.
PAIK, C.-M., Accountancy and Quantitative Methods
PARK, Y. S., International Business
PERRY, J. H., Jr, Business Admin.
PHILLIPS, S. M., Finance
RAU, P. A., Business Admin.
ROBERTS, S. V., Media and Public Affairs
ROBLES, F., Int. Marketing and Int. Affairs
SHELDON, D. R., Accountancy
SOYER, R., Management Science
STERLING, C. H., Media and Public Affairs, Telecommunication
STERN, C., Media and Public Affairs
TRACHTENBERG, S. J., Public Admin.
UMPLEBY, S. A., Management Science
WEINER, R. J., Int. Business and Int. Affairs
WIRTZ, P. W., Management Science, Psychology
WORTH, M. J., Nonprofit Management

School of Engineering and Applied Science:
BERKOVICH, S. Y., Engineering and Applied Science
BOCK, P. S., Engineering
BRIER, G. R., Engineering Management
CARROLL, R. L., Jr, Engineering and Applied Science
CHOI, H.-A., Engineering and Applied Science
COOPER, P. A., Engineering
DEASON, J. P., Engineering Management, Systems Engineering
DELLA TORRE, E., Engineering and Applied Science
DIGGES, K. H., Engineering and Applied Science
EDELSON, B. L., Engineering
EISNER, H., Engineering Management
FELDMAN, M. B., Engineering and Applied Science
FRIEDER, G., Engineering and Applied Science, Statistics
GARRIS, C. A., Engineering
GILMORE, C. M., Engineering and Applied Science
HAQUE, M. I., Engineering and Applied Science
HARRALD, J. R., Engineering Management
HARRINGTON, R. J., Engineering and Applied Science
HELGERT, H. J., Engineering and Applied Science
HELLER, R. S., Engineering and Applied Science
HOFFMAN, L. J., Engineering and Applied Science

JONES, D. L., Engineering
KAHN, W. K., Engineering and Applied Science
KAUFMAN, R. E., Engineering
KYRIAKOPOULOS, N., Engineering
LANG, R. H., Engineering and Applied Science
LEE, J. D.-Y., Engineering and Applied Science
LIEBOWITZ, H., Engineering and Applied Science
LOEW, M. H., Engineering
MAHMOOD, K., Engineering
MARTIN, C. D., Engineering and Applied Science
MAURER, W. D., Engineering and Applied Science
MAZZUCHI, T. A., Operations Research, Engineering Management
MELTZER, A. C., Engineering and Applied Science
MURPHREE, E. L., Jr, Engineering Management, Systems Engineering
MYERS, M. K., Engineering and Applied Science
NAGEL, D. J., Engineering
NARAHARI, B., Engineering and Applied Science
PARDAVI-HORVATH, M., Engineering and Applied Science
PELTON, J. N., Engineering
PICKHOLTZ, R. L., Engineering and Applied Science
POST, J. M., Engineering Management, Political Psychology, Int. Affairs, Psychiatry and Behavioural Sciences
ROPER, W. E., Engineering and Applied Science
SANDUSKY, R. R., Jr, Engineering and Applied Science
SARKANI, S., Engineering Management, Systems Engineering
SIBERT, J. L., Engineering and Applied Science
SZU, H., Engineering
TOLSON, R. H., Engineering and Applied Science
TONG, T. W., Mechanical Engineering
VOJCIC, B. R., Engineering and Applied Science
WASYLKIWSKYJ, W., Engineering and Applied Science
WATERS, R. C., Engineering Management
YOUSSEF, A., Engineering and Applied Science
ZAGHLOUL, M. E., Engineering and Applied Science

Law School:
ADELMAN, M. J.
BANZHAF, J. F., III
BARRON, J. A.
BENITEZ, A. M.
BHALA, R.
BLOCK, C. D.
BRATTON, W. W.
BROWN, K. B.
BUTLER, P.
CAHN, N. R.
CARTER, W. B.
CHEH, M. M.
CLARK, B. R.
CRAVER, C. B.
CUNNINGHAM, L. E.
DIENES, C. T.
FRIEDENTHAL, J. H.
GABALDON, T. A.
GUTMAN, J. S.
IZUMU, C. L.
JOHNSTON, G. P.
JONES, S. R.
KOVACIC, W. E.
LEE, C.
LEES, F. J.
LERNER, R. L.
LUPU, I. C.

LYMAN, J. P.
MAGGS, G. E.
MEIER, J. S.
MEYER, P. H.
MITCHELL, L. E.
MORGAN, T. D.
PAGEL, S. B.
PARK, R. E.
PERONI, R. J.
PETERSON, T. D.
PIERCE, R. J., Jr
RAVEN-HANSEN, P.
REITZE, A. W., Jr
ROBINSON, D., Jr
SALTZBURG, S. A.
SCHECHTER, R. E.
SCHWARTZ, J. I.
SELMI, M.
SIEGEL, J. R.
SIRULNIK, E. S.
SOHN, L. B.
SOLOMON, L. D.
SPANOGLE, J. A.
STEINHARDT, R. G.
STRAND, J. H.
TRANGSRUD, R. H.
TURLEY, J. R.
TUTTLE, R.
WILMARTH, A. E., Jr
YOUNG, M. K.
ZUBROW, L. E.

School of Medicine and Health Sciences:
ABRAMSON, F. P., Pharmacology, Chemistry
ADELSON, E., Medicine
ADVANI, M., Psychiatry and Behavioural Sciences
AHLGREN, J. D., Medicine, Pharmacology
ALBERT, M., Medicine
ALBRIGHT, J., Microbiology and Tropical Medicine
AMIRI, S., Paediatrics
AMMERMAN, B., Neurological Surgery
APUD, J., Psychiatry and Behavioural Sciences
ARLING, B., Medicine
ARONS, B., Psychiatry and Behavioural Sciences
ASCENSAO, J., Medicine
AUGUST, G. P., Paediatrics
BACHMAN, L., Anaesthesiology, Critical Care Medicine, Paediatrics
BAILEY, J. M., Biochemistry and Molecular Biology
BANK, W. O., Radiology and Neurological Surgery
BARAF, H., Medicine
BARNHILL, R., Dermatology, Pathology
BARR, N., Surgery, Health Care Sciences
BARRY, P., Medicine, Health Care Sciences
BARTH, W. F., Medicine
BATSHAW, M., Paediatrics
BATTEY, J., Surgery
BATTLE, C., Paediatrics
BECKER, A., Obstetrics and Gynaecology
BECKER, K. L., Medicine and Physiology, Experimental Medicine
BELMAN, A. B., Urology and Paediatrics
BENNETT, H., Paediatrics
BERBERIAN, B. J., Dermatology
BERENSON, R., Health Care Sciences
BERNAD, P., Neurology
BERNSTEIN, L., Medicine
BERRY, G., Paediatrics
BIGELOW, L., Psychiatry and Behavioural Sciences
BLANK, A., Psychiatry and Behavioural Sciences
BORENSTEIN, D., Medicine
BORUM, M., Medicine
BOWLES, L. T., Surgery
BRAUN, M., Dermatology
BRILL, D., Medicine
BRILL, W., Medicine
BRONSTHER, O., Surgery

BROWN, B., Psychiatry and Behavioural Sciences
BROWN, H., Ophthalmology
BUKRINSKY, M., Microbiology and Tropical Medicine
BULAS, D., Radiology, Paediatrics
BURMAN, K., Medicine
BURNS, W., Pathology
BURRIS, B., Psychiatry
BYRNE, J., Paediatrics, Epidemiology and Biostatistics
BYRON, H., Ophthalmology
CAHAN, J., Surgery, Health Care Sciences
CALLENDER, C., Surgery
CAMPOS, J. M., Paediatrics, Pathology, Microbiology and Tropical Medicine
CANTER, J., Surgery
CAPUTY, A., Neurological Surgery
CARLSON, D., Obstetrics and Gynaecology
CAWLEY, J., Prevention and Community Health, Health Care Sciences
CHAMBERLAIN, J., Paediatrics
CHANDRA, R., Pathology, Paediatrics
CHANG, P., Medicine
CHATOOR-KOCH, I. M., Psychiatry and Behavioural Sciences and Paediatrics
CHENG, T. O., Medicine
CHERTOFF, J., Psychiatry and Behavioural Sciences
CHIAPPINELLI, V., Pharmacology and Neurological Surgery
CHIN, M., Anaesthesiology and Critical Care Medicine
CHODOFF, P., Psychiatry and Behavioural Sciences
CHUSED, J., Psychiatry and Behavioural Sciences, Paediatrics
COGEN, P., Neurological Surgery, Paediatrics
COHEN, G. D., Health Care Sciences, Psychiatry and Behavioural Sciences
COHEN, L., Paediatrics
COHEN, M., Surgery
COHEN-MANSFIELD, J., Health Care Sciences, Prevention and Community Health
COLBERG-POLEY, A., Paediatrics, Biochemistry and Molecular Biology
COLEMAN, R., Paediatrics
COLEMAN, R., Psychiatry and Behavioural Sciences
COLICE, G., Medicine
COMAS-DIAZ, L., Psychiatry and Behavioural Sciences
COOK, C., Pathology
COONEY, F., Neurological Surgery
COOPER, B., Medicine
CORSO, P., Surgery
COTLOVE, E., Psychiatry and Behavioural Sciences
COWAN, C., Ophthalmology
COX, G., Emergency Medicine
CYTRYN, L., Psychiatry and Behavioural Sciences
D'ANGELO, L. J., Paediatrics, Prevention and Community Health, Medicine
DANIEL, D., Psychiatry and Behavioural Sciences
DANOVITCH, S., Medicine
DAVIS, D., Psychiatry and Behavioural Sciences
DAVIS, D. O., Radiology, Neurology and Neurological Surgery
DAVIS, G., Microbiology and Tropical Medicine
DENNIS, M., Neurological Surgery
DePALMA, L., Pathology, Anatomy and Cell Biology
DIAMOND, D., Psychiatry and Behavioural Sciences
DIAMOND, R., Medicine
DLUHY, J., Psychiatry and Behavioural Sciences
DOMAN, D., Medicine
DOPPELHEUER, J., Obstetrics and Gynaecology

DOSA, S., Medicine
DRUY, E. M., Radiology
DUBEY, A., Obstetrics and Gynaecology
DUFOUR, D. R., Pathology
DYER, C., Psychiatry and Behavioural Sciences
EATON, J., Psychiatry and Behavioural Sciences
ECONOMOPOULOS, B., Anaesthesiology and Critical Care Medicine
EDELSON, R., Neurology
EDELSTEIN, S., Emergency Medicine, Anaesthesiology and Critical Care Medicine
EICHELBERGER, M. R., Surgery and Paediatrics
EIG, B., Paediatrics
EIN, D., Medicine
EIN, T., Obstetrics and Gynaecology
EIST, H., Psychiatry and Behavioural Sciences
ELLWOOD, L., Health Care Sciences
EL-MOHANDES, A., Prevention and Community Health, Paediatrics, Obstetrics and Gynaecology
ERSHLER, W., Medicine
EVANS, F. B., Psychiatry and Behavioural Sciences
FAIRBANKS, D., Surgery
FALK, N., Medicine, Health Care Sciences
FALK, R., Obstetrics and Gynaecology
FEIGIN, D., Radiology
FELDMAN, B., Surgery, Health Care Sciences, Paediatrics
FELDMAN, I., Surgery
FIELDS, A., Anaesthesiology and Critical Care Medicine
FINKELSTEIN, J. D., Medicine
FISCHER, R., Medicine
FRAM, D., Psychiatry and Behavioural Sciences
FRANK, J., Psychiatry and Behavioural Sciences
FRASER, C., Pharmacology, Microbiology and Tropical Medicine
FUCHS, M., Medicine
GAARDER, K., Psychiatry and Behavioural Sciences
GAASTERLAND, D., Ophthalmology
GAHRES, E., Obstetrics and Gynaecology
GALLO, L., Biochemistry and Molecular Biology
GALLO, V., Paediatrics, Pharmacology
GEELHOED, G. W., International Medicine and Surgery
GEORGE, D., Psychiatry and Behavioural Sciences
GERSHEN, B., Medicine
GIAUME, C., Anatomy and Cell Biology
GILBERT, C., Obstetrics and Gynaecology
GILLANDERS, R., Obstetrics and Gynaecology
GILLMAN, R., Psychiatry and Behavioural Sciences
GINDOFF, P. R., Obstetrics and Gynaecology
GINSBERG, A. L., Medicine
GIORDANO, J. M., Surgery
GLASER, B., Ophthalmology
GLASSMAN, L., Radiology
GLATT, M., Paediatrics, Psychiatry and Behavioural Sciences
GOLD, M., Medicine
GOLDSTEIN, A., Biochemistry and Molecular Biology
GOLDSTEIN, H., Medicine
GOLDSTEIN, K., Medicine
GOLDSTEIN, S., Medicine
GOODENHOUGH, D. J., Radiology
GOODMAN, S., Psychiatry and Behavioural Sciences
GOODWIN, F., Psychiatry and Behavioural Sciences
GORDIN, F., Medicine
GORDON, G., Psychiatry and Behavioural Sciences

GORELICK, K., Psychiatry and Behavioural Sciences
GRAETER, J., Orthopaedic Surgery
GRANATIR, W., Psychiatry and Behavioural Sciences
GRAVITZ, M., Psychiatry and Behavioural Sciences
GREENBERG, L. W., Paediatrics
GREENE, C., Paediatrics
GREENSPAN, S., Psychiatry and Behavioural Sciences, Paediatrics
GRIFFITH, J. L., Psychiatry and Behavioural Sciences, Neurology
GROSS, P., Urology
GROSS, R., Psychiatry and Behavioural Sciences
GROSSMAN, J. H., Obstetrics and Gynaecology, Microbiology and Tropical Medicine, Prevention and Community Health
GUIDOTTI, T., Environmental Occupational Health, Medicine
GULYA, A., Surgery
GUNTHER, S. F., Orthopaedic Surgery
GUTIERREZ, G., Medicine, Anaesthesiology and Critical Care Medicine
HAAS, M., Psychiatry and Behavioural Sciences
HAAS, S., Orthopaedic Surgery
HAIDER, R., Medicine
HANNALLAH, R. S., Anaesthesiology and Critical Care Medicine, Paediatrics
HARISIADIS, L. A., Radiology
HARSHBARGER, J., Pathology
HARTMAN, G., Surgery, Paediatrics
HASSAN, M., Obstetrics and Gynaecology
HAUDENSCHILD, C. C., Pathology and Medicine
HAWLEY, R., Anatomy and Cell Biology
HECKMAN, B., Medicine
HEINTZE, A., Obstetrics and Gynaecology
HELLER, N., Psychiatry and Behavioural Sciences
HELMKAMP, B., Obstetrics and Gynaecology
HENSON, D., Pathology
HERER, G. R., Paediatrics
HERSH, S., Psychiatry and Behavioural Sciences, Paediatrics
HILL, M. C., Radiology
HOFFMAN, D., Epidemiology and Biostatistics, Global Health
HOFFMAN, E., Paediatrics, Biochemistry and Molecular Biology
HOLBROOK, P. R., Anaesthesiology and Critical Care Medicine, Paediatrics
HOLLAND, C. A., Paediatrics
HOPPING, S., Surgery
HOTEZ, P., Microbiology and Tropical Medicine, Global Health, Epidemiology and Biostatistics
HOWARD, W. J., Medicine
HOWE, G., Psychiatry and Behavioural Sciences
HSIA, J., Medicine
HURLEY, J., Paediatrics
HUTTON, J., Surgery
ISSA, F., Psychiatry and Behavioural Sciences
JAAFAR, M., Ophthalmology, Paediatrics
JACOBSEN, F., Psychiatry and Behavioural Sciences
JACOBSON, J., Neurological Surgery
JAFFE, L., Radiology
JANATI, A., Neurology
JEROME, M., Obstetrics and Gynaecology
JOHNSON, F., Pathology
JOHNSON, K., Anatomy and Cell Biology, Obstetrics and Gynaecology
JOSEPH, D., Psychiatry and Behavioural Sciences
JOSEPH, J., Paediatrics, Epidemiology and Biostatistics
JOSHI, P., Psychiatry and Behavioural Sciences, Paediatrics
KAFKA, J., Psychiatry and Behavioural Sciences
KALINER, M., Medicine

KAMANI, N., Paediatrics
KAO, G., Dermatology
KAPIKIAN, A., Paediatrics
KAPLAN, K., Psychiatry and Behavioural Sciences, Paediatrics
KAPLAN, R., Anaesthesiology and Critical Care Medicine, Paediatrics
KARCHER, D., Pathology
KATZ, A., Pathology
KATZ, B., Ophthalmology
KATZ, N., Surgery
KATZ, R., Dermatology, Paediatrics
KATZ, R. J., Medicine and Emergency Medicine
KATZ, S., Urology
KAUFMAN, R., Engineering, Anatomy and Cell Biology
KAUFMAN, R., Medicine
KELLEHER, J., Physiology and Experimental Medicine
KELLY, J. J., Neurology and Neurological Surgery
KENNEDY, K., Pharmacology, Genetics
KESHISHIAN, J., Surgery
KHOURY, A., Obstetrics and Gynaecology
KIMMEL, P. L., Medicine
KIRBY, E., Psychiatry and Behavioural Sciences
KIRKPATRICK, J., Surgery
KLINE, P., Medicine
KNELLER, M., Radiology
KNOLL, S., Surgery
KOBRINE, A., Neurological Surgery
KOCH, E., Obstetrics and Gynaecology
KOENIG, K., Emergency Medicine
KOVAL, N., Medicine
KOZLOFF, L., Surgery
KREBS, H., Obstetrics and Gynaecology
KRESSEL, B., Medicine
KUEHL, K., Paediatrics
KUMAR, A., Biochemistry and Molecular Biology, Genetics
KUSHNER, D. C., Radiology and Paediatrics
KUSHNER, E., Psychiatry and Behavioural Sciences
LACHER, D., Pathology
LADISCH, S., Paediatrics, Biochemistry and Molecular Biology
LAKSHMAN, R., Medicine, Biochemistry and Molecular Biology
LANDAU, B., Psychiatry and Behavioural Sciences, Paediatrics
LANDO, H., Medicine
LANE, H., Medicine
LARSEN, J. W., Jr, Obstetrics and Gynaecology
LAURENO, R., Neurology
LAWS, E., Neurological Surgery
LAZAR, S., Psychiatry and Behavioural Sciences
LAZARUS, A., Obstetrics and Gynaecology
LE GOLVAN, P., Pathology
LEATHERBURY, L., Paediatrics
LEFKOWITZ, L., Paediatrics, Health Care Sciences
LEMP, M., Ophthalmology
LEVI, L., Psychiatry and Behavioural Sciences
LEVINE, P., Epidemiology and Biostatistics, Medicine
LEVITT, R., Obstetrics and Gynaecology
LEVY, L., Radiology
LEW, S., Medicine
LEWIS, J., Medicine
LEWIS, R., Orthopaedic Surgery
LIEBERMAN, E., Psychiatry and Behavioural Sciences
LIEBERMAN, M., Medicine
LINDSAY, J., Medicine
LIOTTA, L., Pathology
LIPSIUS, S., Psychiatry and Behavioural Sciences, Obstetrics and Gynaecology
LIPSON, A., Medicine
LITOVITZ, T., Emergency Medicine
LITTMAN, B., Obstetrics and Gynaecology
LOO, T., Pharmacology

LOWE, J., Paediatrics
LUBAN, N. C., Paediatrics and Pathology
LUKE, J., Pathology
LURIE, N., Medicine
LYNN, D. J., Health Care Sciences and Medicine
MCAFEE, J., Radiology
MACDONALD-GINZBURG, M. G., Paediatrics
MCDOWELL, R., Paediatrics
MCGILL, W. A., Anaesthesiology and Critical Care Medicine, Paediatrics
MACHT, S., Surgery
MCKNEW, D., Paediatrics
MADDOX, J., Obstetrics and Gynaecology
MAHDAVI, I., Paediatrics
MAJD, M., Radiology and Paediatrics
MALAWER, M. M., Orthopaedic Surgery
MANDEL, H. G., Pharmocology
MANDLER, R., Neurology and Neurological Surgery
MANYAK, M. J., Urology, Microbiology and Tropical Medicine
MARINOFF, S., Obstetrics and Gynaecology
MARLOW, J., Obstetrics and Gynaecology
MARTIN, D., Obstetrics and Gynaecology
MARTIN, G. R., Paediatrics
MASTERS, E. C., Obstetrics and Gynaecology
MASTROYANNIS, C., Obstetrics and Gynaecology
MASUR, H., Medicine
MAYER, T., Emergency Medicine
MECKLENBURG, F., Obstetrics and Gynaecology
MERIKANGAS, J., Psychiatry and Behavioural Science
MEYER, J., Medicine
MIDGLEY, F. M., Surgery and Paediatrics
MILLER, G., Psychiatry and Behavioural Sciences
MILOWE, I., Paediatrics
MOAK, J. P., Paediatrics
MONDZAC, A., Medicine
MOODY, S., Anatomy and Cell Biology
MOSKOVITZ, P., Orthopaedic Surgery, Neurological Surgery
MUFARRIJ, I., Obstetrics and Gynaecology
MULLAN, F., Health Care Sciences, Paediatrics, Prevention and Community Health
MURPHY, R., Ophthalmology
NACHNANI, G., Medicine
NASHEL, D., Medicine
NASR, M., Psychiatry and Behavioural Sciences
NAWAB, E., Obstetrics and Gynaecology
NEVIASER, R. J., Orthopaedic Surgery
NEWMAN, K., Surgery, Paediatrics
NEWMAN, M., Medicine
NG, L., Neurology
NICKLAS, R., Medicine
NICOLAS, J., Paediatrics, Pharmacology
NIERMAN, W., Biochemistry and Molecular Biology
NIGRA, T., Dermatology, Paediatrics
NOWAK, J., Psychiatry and Behavioural Sciences
OBOLER, A., Medicine
OCHSENSCHLAGER, D. W., Paediatrics and Emergency Medicine
O'KIEEFE, D., Medicine
OLDFIELD, E., Neurological Surgery
OMMAYA, A., Neurological Surgery
O'NEILL, J., Ophthalmology
ORENSTEIN, J., Pathology
ORKIN, B., Surgery
PACKER, R. J., Neurology and Paediatrics
PALOMBI, J., Psychiatry and Behavioural Sciences, Paediatrics
PAN, J., Obstetrics and Gynaecology
PARENTI, D., Medicine, Microbiology and Tropical Medicine
PARKER, P., Paediatrics
PARKS, M., Ophthalmology, Paediatrics
PATEL, R. I., Anaesthesiology and Critical Care Medicine, Paediatrics

PATIERNO, S., Pharmacology, Genetics, Environmental Occupational Health
PAWLSON, L. G., Healthcare Sciences, Medicine, Health Services Management and Policy
PEDREIRA, F., Paediatrics
PEEBLES, P., Paediatrics
PEELE, R., Psychiatry and Behavioural Sciences
PERMAN, G., Psychiatry and Behavioural Sciences
PERRY, D., Pharmacology
PETROVITCH, C., Anaesthesiology and Critical Care Medicine
PEUSNER, K., Anatomy and Cell Biology
PHILLIPS, M., Medicine
PILLAI, M., Medicine
PLATIA, E. V., Medicine
POLIS, M., Emergency Medicine
POLLACK, M. M., Anaesthesiology and Critical Care Medicine, Paediatrics
POST, J., Psychiatry and Behavioural Sciences
POTOLICCHIO, S. J., Neurology and Neurological Surgery
POTTER, B. M., Radiology and Paediatrics
POVAR, G., Health Care Sciences, Medicine
POWERS, D., Obstetrics and Gynaecology
PRINCIPATO, J., Surgery
PROTOS, P., Obstetrics and Gynaecology
PULASKI, R., Neurology
PUMPHREY, R., Surgery
PUTNAM, J., Medicine
PYATT, R., Radiology
RABSON, A., Pathology
RAIS-BAHRMANI, K., Paediatrics
RANKIN, J., Psychiatry and Behavioural Sciences
RANKIN, R., Psychiatry and Behavioural Sciences
RAPOPORT, J., Psychiatry and Behavioural Sciences, Paediatrics
RATNER, R., Psychiatry and Behavioural Sciences
REAMAN, G. H., Paediatrics
REICH, W., Psychiatry and Behavioural Sciences
REISS, D., Psychiatry and Behavioural Sciences, Medicine and Psychology
RESTAK, R., Neurology
RICKLES, F., Medicine, Paediatrics
RIEGELMAN, R., Epidemiology and Biostatistics, Medicine, Health Care Sciences
RIEGER, R., Paediatrics, Psychiatry and Behavioural Sciences
ROBBINS, D. C., Medicine
ROBERTSON, W. W., Orthopaedic Surgery
ROBINOWITZ, C., Psychiatry and Behavioural Sciences
ROBINSON, L., Psychiatry and Behavioural Sciences
RODRIGUEZ-GARCIA, R., Global Health, Prevention and Community Health, International Affairs
ROSENBAUM, S., Health Policy, Health Services Management and Leadership, Health Care Sciences
ROSENBERG, J., Medicine
ROSENBLUM, S., Psychiatry and Behavioural Sciences
ROSENQUIST, G. C., Paediatrics
ROSENSTEIN, J., Anatomy and Cell Biology, Neurological Surgery
ROSS, M., Obstetrics and Gynaecology
ROTHMAN, B., Obstetrics and Gynaecology
ROTSZTAIN, A., Medicine
RUBOVITS-SEITZ, P., Psychiatry and Behavioural Sciences
RUCKMAN, R. N., Paediatrics
RUDZKI, C., Medicine
RUSHTON, H. G., Urology and Paediatrics
SADIN, H., Medicine
SARIN, P., Environmental Occupational Heath, Biochemistry and Molecular Biology
SCALETTAR, R., Medicine

SCHECHTER, G. P., Medicine
SCHEER, J., Health Care Sciences
SCHLEIN, P., Medicine
SCHNEIDER, M., Medicine
SCHWARTZ, A., Pathology
SCHWARTZ, R., Paediatrics, Health Care Sciences
SCOTT, D., Immunology, Anatomy and Cell Biology
SCOTT, J., Emergency Medicine
SCOTT, S., Medicine
SEIBEL, N., Paediatrics
SEIDES, S., Medicine
SEKHAR, L. N., Neurological Surgery
SEMERJIAN, H., Urology
SEVER, J. L., Paediatrics, Microbiology and Tropical Medicine, Obstetrics and Gynaecology
SHARGEL, M., Medicine
SHESSER, R. F., Emergency Medicine, Medicine, Environmental Occupational Health
SHORE, M., Paediatrics
SHORT, B. L., Paediatrics
SHRIER, D., Psychiatry and Behavioural Sciences, Paediatrics
SIDAWY, A. N., Surgery
SIDAWY, M., Pathology
SILBER, T. J., Paediatrics, Global Health, Prevention and Community Health
SILVA, C., Surgery
SILVER, S., Pathology, Prevention and Community Health, Medicine
SIMON, D., Medicine
SIMON, G. L., Medicine, Biochemistry and Molecular Biology, Microbiology and Tropical Medicine
SIMON, J., Obstetrics and Gynaecology
SINGH, N., Paediatrics, Health Care Sciences, Global Health
SLUZKI, C., Psychiatry and Behavioural Sciences
SLY, R. M., Paediatrics
SMITH, L., Surgery
SMITH, M., Emergency Medicine
SMOLLER, B., Psychiatry and Behavioural Sciences
SOLDIN, S. J., Paediatrics, Pathology
SOLOMON, F., Psychiatry and Behavioural Sciences
SOREL, E., Psychiatry and Behavioural Sciences
SOUTHBY, R., Global Health, Health Care Sciences, Health Policy
SPAGNOLO, S. V., Medicine
STAR, R., Medicine
STARK, W., Psychiatry and Behavioural Sciences, Paediatrics
STEIN, M., Psychiatry and Behavioural Sciences, Paediatrics
STEINBERG, W. M., Medicine
STEINFELD, H., Medicine
STERN, M., Psychiatry and Behavioural Sciences
STEVENS, C., Psychiatry and Behavioural Sciences
STOCK, M., Medicine and Health Care Sciences
STOCKTON, W., Psychiatry and Behavioural Sciences
STONE, A., Health Care Sciences, Medicine
STOPAK, B., Neurological Surgery
STOPAK, S., Ophthalmology
STRASSBURGER, F., Paediatrics
STRICKLAND, D., Biochemistry and Molecular Biology
TAUBER, L., Neurological Surgery
TAUBIN, J., Medicine, Health Care Sciences
TAVASSOLI, F., Pathology
TAYLOR, D., Psychiatry and Behavioural Sciences
TETTE, A., Surgery
THOMAS, J., Psychiatry and Behavioural Sciences
THOMPSON, A., Medicine
TIEVSKY, G., Radiology

TRAMONT, E., Medicine
TROUT, H., Surgery
TRUJILLO, N., Medicine
TSOKOS, G., Paediatrics
TUAZON, C. U., Medicine
TUCHMAN, M., Paediatrics, Biochemistry and Molecular Biology
TURNER, M., Dermatology
USHER, M., Psychiatry and Behavioural Sciences
VAN BREDA, A., Radiology
VANDERHOEK, J., Biochemistry and Molecular Biology
VARGHESE, P. J., Medicine and Paediatrics
VELASQUEZ, M. T., Medicine
VENBRUX, A., Radiology, Surgery
VIRMANI, R., Pathology
WALETZKY, J., Psychiatry and Behavioural Sciences
WALKER, G., Biochemistry and Molecular Biology
WALSH, R., Anatomy and Cell Biology, Neurological Surgery
WARGOTZ, E., Pathology
WARREN, N., Dermatology
WARTOFSKY, L., Medicine
WATKIN, D., Medicine
WEGLICKI, W. B., Medicine, Physiology and Experimental Medicine
WEINBERGER, D., Psychiatry and Behavioural Sciences
WEINSTEIN, S., Neurology, Paediatrics
WEISS, H., Medicine
WEISS, L., Medicine
WELBORN, L. G., Anaesthesiology and Critical Care Medicine, Paediatrics
WERLING, L., Pharmacology, Neurological Surgery
WHERRY, D., Surgery
WHITE, P. H., Medicine and Paediatrics
WILKINSON, R., Medicine
WILLIAMS, C. M., Dermatology and Pathology
WILLIAMS, J. F., Anaesthesiology and Critical Care Medicine, Health Services Management and Policy
WILLIAMS, M., Pathology
WILLIAMS, S., Obstetrics and Gynaecology
WINKLES, J., Biochemistry and Molecular Biology
WISNESKI, L., Medicine
WITTENBERG, R., Psychiatry and Behavioural Sciences
WOLFE, M., Medicine
WOLIN, S., Psychiatry and Behavioural Sciences
WOLMAN, S., Pathology
WOOD, B., Anthropology, Anatomy and Cell Biology
WRIGHT, D. C., Neurological Surgery
YODAIKEN, R., Pathology, Health Care Sciences
YOO, D., Medicine
YU, G., Urology
ZAJTCHUK, R., Surgery
ZALAL, G. H., Surgery and Paediatrics
ZALESKE, D., Orthopaedic Surgery, Paediatrics
ZEMAN, R., Radiology
ZIMMERMAN, M., Ophthalmology
ZINNER, J., Psychiatry and Behavioural Sciences

School of Public Health and Health Services:
BILES, B., Health Policy
BORZI, P., Health Policy
BOYD, N. R., Prevention and Community Health
CAWLEY, J. F., Prevention and Community Health
D'ANGELO, L. J., Prevention and Community Medicine
DARR, K. J., Health Services Management and Leadership
EASTAUGH, S. R., Health Services Management and Leadership

EL-MOHANDES, A., Prevention and Community Medicine
GREENBERG, W., Health Economics
GUIDOTTI, T. L., Environmental and Occupational Health
HIDALGO, J., Health Policy
HIRSCH, R. P., Epidemiology and Biostatistics
LACHIN, J., Epidemiology and Biostatistics
LEVINE, P. H., Epidemiology and Biostatistics, Environmental and Occupational Health
MICHAELS, D., Environmental and Occupational Health
MILLER, W. C., Exercise Science
PAUP, D. C., Exercise Science
RIEGELMAN, R. K., Epidemiology and Biostatistics
RODRIGUEZ-GARCIA, R., Center for International Health
ROSSELLO, P., Global Health
SARIN, P., Environmental and Occupational Health
SOUTHBY, R. M. F., Global Health, Health Policy
SULLIVAN, P. A., Exercise Science
WINDSOR, R. A., Prevention and Community Medicine

Graduate School of Education and Human Development:

CASTLEBERRY, M. S., Special Education
CONFESSORE, G. J., Higher Education Administration
CUMMINGS, W. K., International Education
DEW, D. W., Counselling, Psychiatry and Behavioural Sciences
EL-KHAWAS, E. H., Education Policy
FERRANTE, R., Education
FREUND, M. B., Special Education
FUTRELL, M. H., Education
HEDDESHEIMER, J. C., Counselling, Psychiatry and Behavioural Sciences
HOARE, C. H., Human Devt and Human Resource Devt
HOLMES, D. H., Education
HOWERTON, E. B., Jr, Education
IANACONE, R. N., Special Education
KOCHHAR-BRYANT, C. A., Special Education
LINKOWSKI, D. C., Counselling, Psychology and Behavioural Sciences
LYNCH, S. H., Teacher Preparation, Special Education
MAZUR, A. J., Special Education
MULLER, R. O., Educational Research
PALEY, N. B., Elementary Education
PARATORE, S. R., Education
ROTBERG, I. C., Education Policy
SASHKIN, M., Human Resource Devt
SCHWANDT, D. R., Human Resource Devt
SHOTEL, J. R., Special Education
TAYMANS, J. H., Special Education
WATSON, A., Higher Education Admin.
WEST, L. L., Special Education
WHITAKER, R., Higher Education

GEORGETOWN UNIVERSITY

3700 O St, NW, Washington, DC 20057
Telephone: (202) 687-0100
E-mail: guadmiss@georgetown.edu
Internet: www.georgetown.edu
Founded 1789
Private control
Campus in Doha, Qatar
Pres.: JOHN J. DEGIOIA
Provost: Dr JAMES J. O'DONNELL
Sr Vice-Pres., Chief Operating Officer and Treas.: CHRISTOPHER L. AUGOSTINI
Sr Vice-Pres. for Research and Chief Technology Officer: Dr SPIROS DIMOLITSAS
Sr Vice-Pres. for Strategic Devt: DANIEL R. PORTERFIELD
Exec. Vice-Pres. and Exec. Dean of the School of Medicine: Dr HOWARD FEDEROFF

Exec. Vice-Pres. and Dean of Law Center: Dr WILLIAM TREANOR
Vice-Pres. and Chief Human Resources Officer: MARY ANN MAHIN
Vice-Pres. for Advancement: R. BARTLEY MOORE
Vice-Pres. for Facilities and Student Housing: KAREN S. FRANK
Vice-Pres. for Financial Planning and Analysis: DAVID RUBENSTEIN
Vice-Pres. and Gen. Univ. Counsel: STEPHANIE TSACOUMIS
Vice Pres. for Information Services and Chief Information Officer: KEVIN C. MURPHY
Vice-Pres. for Institutional Diversity and Equity: ROSEMARY KILKENNY
Vice-Pres. for Mission and Ministry: Rev. KEVIN O'BRIEN
Vice-Pres. for Public Affairs: ERIK SMULSON
Vice-Pres. for Student Affairs and Dean of Students: TODD A. OLSON
Dean for Medical Education: Dr STEPHEN RAY
Dean for Research: Dr ROBERT CLARKE
Vice-Pres. of Technology Commercialization: Dr CLAUDIA CHERNEY STEWART
Vice-Pres. for Univ. Safety: ROCCO DELMONACO, JR
Registrar: JOHN Q. PIERCE, IV
Librarian: ARTEMIS G. KIRK
Library: see Libraries and Archives
Number of teachers: 2,188 (1,282 full-time, 906 part-time)
Number of students: 16,871 (7,553 undergraduate, 5,832 graduate, 3,486 professional)
Publications: *American Criminal Law Review, Georgetown Immigration Law Journal, Georgetown International Environmental Law Review* (4 a year), *Georgetown Journal of Gender and the Law* (3 a year), *Georgetown Journal of International Law* (4 a year), *Georgetown Journal of Law & Modern Critical Race Perspectives* (2 a year), *Georgetown Journal of Law & Public Policy* (2 a year), *Georgetown Journal of Legal Ethics* (4 a year), *Georgetown Journal on Poverty Law & Policy* (3 a year), *Georgetown Law Journal* (6 a year), *Georgetown Magazine* (4 a year), *Georgetown Medical Bulletin* (3 a year), *Georgetown Public Policy Review, Gnovis* (online (www.gnovisjournal.org)), *Lombardi Magazine* (4 a year), *Law and Policy in International Business* (3 a year), *The Anthem, The Hoya* (104 a year), *The Tax Lawyer* (irregular), *The Voice* (52 a year)

DEANS

Edmund A. Walsh School of Foreign Service: CAROL LANCASTER
Georgetown College: CHESTER L. GILLIS
Georgetown Law: WILLIAM M. TREANOR
Graduate School of Arts and Sciences: GERALD M. MARA
Robert Emmett McDonough School of Business: DAVID A. THOMAS
School of Medicine: Dr STEPHEN RAY MITCHELL
School of Nursing and Health Studies: Dr MARTIN Y. IGUCHI
School of Continuing Studies: Dr ROBERT L. MANUEL

PROFESSORS

Edmund A. Walsh School of Foreign Service:
ALBRIGHT, M.
ANDERSON, J.
BAILEY, J.
CANZONERI, M.
CHICKERING, R.
CROCKER, C.
CUDDINGTON, J.
CUMBY, R. E.
ESPOSITO, J. L.
GALLUCCI, R. L.

HADDAD, Y. Y.
HOWE, H. M.
HUDSON, M. C.
IKENBERRY, G. J.
KEELY, C. B.
KLINE, J. M.
KROGH, P. F.
LAKE, A.
LANGAN, J.
LIEBER, R.
MCHENRY, D.
MCNEILL, J. R.
MIKELL, G.
MORAN, T. H.
PIRTLE, C. E.
RAMO, F.
REARDON-ANDERSON, J.
STENT, A.
STITES, R.
STOWASSER, B.
SUBIRATS, J.
TABAK, F.
TILLMAN, S. P.
TUCKER, N. B.
VALENZUELA, A.
VIKSNINS, G. J.
VOLL, J.
WEISS, C.
WINTERS, F. X.
YOST, C.

Law School:
ABERNATHY, C. F.
ALEINIKOFF, T. A.
AREEN, J. C.
BABCOCK, H.
BAUMAN, J. D.
BLOCH, S. L.
BLOCHE, M. G.
BYRNE, J. P.
CAMPBELL, A. J.
CARTER, B. E.
CASHIN, S. D.
CHUSED, R. H.
COHEN, J. E.
COHEN, S. B.
COHN, S. L.
COLE, D. D.
COOK, A. E.
COPACINO, J. M.
DASH, S.
DIAMOND, R. D.
DINH, V. D.
DONAHOE, D. R.
DRINAN, R. F.
EDELMAN, P. B.
ERNST, D. R.
FEINERMAN, J. V.
FELDBLUM, C. R.
FELDMAN, H. L.
GINSBURG, M. D.
GOLDBERG, S. P.
GOLDBLATT, S. H.
GOSTIN, L. O.
GOTTESMAN, M. H.
GULATI, G. M.
GUSTAFSON, C. H.
HAFT, R. J.
HAY, A. M.
HEINZERLING, L.
JACKSON, J. H.
JACKSON, V. C.
JORDAN, E. C.
KATYAL, N. K.
KING, P. A.
KOPLOW, D. A.
LANGEVOORT, D. C.
LAWRENCE, C. R., III
LAZARUS, R. J.
LUBAN, D. J.
MACKLIN, L. W. S.
MATSUDA, M. J.
MENKEL-MEADOW, C. J.
MLYNIEC, W. J.
MURPHY, J. G., Jr
NORTON, E. H.

OAKLEY, R. L.
OLDHAM, J. C.
O'SULLIVAN, J. R.
PAGE, J. A.
PEARLMAN, R. A.
PELLER, G.
PERDUE, W. C.
PITOFSKY, R.
QUINN, K. P.
RAMSFIELD, J. J.
REGAN, M. C., Jr
ROE, R. L.
ROSS, S. D.
ROTHSTEIN, P. F.
SALOP, S. C.
SCHOTLAND, R. A.
SCHRAG, P. G.
SCHWARTZ, W. F.
SEIDMAN, L. M.
SPANN, G. A.
STROMSETH, J. E.
STUMBERG, R. K.
TAGUE, P. W.
TARULLO, D. K.
THOMAS, J. R.
TUSHNET, M. V.
VÁZQUEZ, C. M.
VUKOWICH, W. T.
WASSERSTROM, S. J.
WEIDENBRUCH, P. P., Jr
WEISS, E. B.
WERRO, F.
WEST, R. L.
WILLIAMS, W. W.

McDonough School of Business:
AGGARWAL, R.
ANDREASEN, A. R.
BIES, R. J.
BRENKERT, G. G.
COOKE, T. B.
DROMS, W. G.
ERNST, R.
FEKRAT, M. A.
FERDOWS, K.
GRANT, R.
JOHANSSON, J. K.
LEVY, M. B.
MCCABE, D. M.
MAYO, J. W.
MAZZOLA, J. B.
MICELI, M. P.
NOLLEN, S. D.
ORD, J. K.
PARKER, R. S.
POWERS, J. J., Jr
QUINN, D. P.
REINSCH, L.
STATEN, M. E.
THOMAS, R. J.
WALKER, D. A.

School of Nursing and Health Studies:
BAIGIS, J.
EVANS, C.
FILERMAN, G.
RAMEY, C.
RAMEY, S.

Undergraduate School:
AGGARWAL, R., School of Business
ALATIS, J. E., Linguistics and Modern Greek
ALBRECHT, J. W., Economics
ALBRIGHT, M. K., Practice of Diplomacy
ANDERLINI, L., Economics
ANDREASEN, A. R., School of Business
ASTARITA, T., History
BABB, V., English
BAIGIS, J., Nursing
BAILEY, J. J., Government and School of Foreign Service
BARNES, S. H., Govt and School of Foreign Service
BARROWS, E. M., Biology
BATES, R. D., Jr, Chemistry
BEAUCHAMP, T. L., Philosophy

BENKE, G., Mathematics
BENSKY, R. D., French
BETZ, P. F., English
BIES, R. J., School of Business
BRADLEY, Rev, D. J. M., Philosophy
BRENKERT, G. G., School of Business
BROUGH, J. B., Philosophy
BROWN, D. M., History
BYRNES, A. S., German
CALVERT, S., Psychology
CALVEZ, J.-Y., Government
CANZONERI, M. B., Economics and School of Foreign Service
CAREY, G. W., Government
CHANG, D.-C., Mathematics
CHAPMAN, G. B., Biology
CHAPMAN, T., School of Nursing and Health Studies
CHICKERING, R., History and School of Foreign Service
CIMA, G. G., English
COLLINS, J. B., History
COLLINS, S. M., Economics
COOKE, T. B., School of Business
CROCKER, C. A., Strategic Studies in School of Foreign Service
CUDDINGTON, J. T., Economics and School of Foreign Service
CUMBY, R. E., International Business Diplomacy
CURRAN, R. E., History
CURRIE, J. F., Physics
DAVIS, W., Philosophy
DENNING, D. E., Computer Science
DROMS, W.M G., School of Business
ENGLER, H., Mathematics
ERNST, R., School of Business
ESPOSITO, J. L., Center for Muslim–Christian Understanding
EVANS, M. D., Economics
FASOLD, R. H W., Linguistics
FEKRAT, M. A., School of Business
FERDOWS, K.A, School of Business
FILERMAN, G., Health Studies
FINKEL, N. J., Psychology
GALE, I., Economics
GALLUCCI, R. L., School of Foreign Service
GIBERT, S. P., Government
GLAVIN, J. J., English
GODSON, R., Government
GOLDFRANK, D. M., History
GOMEZ-LOBO, A., Philosophy
GOODMAN, A. E., School of Foreign Service
GORMLEY, W. T., Government and Public Policy
GRANT, R. M., School of Business
GUSTAFSON, T., Government
HADDAD, Y. Y., School of Foreign Service
HALL, C. M., Sociology
HAUGHT, J. F., Theology
HEELAN, P. A., Philosophy
HENDERSON, E. J., Biology
HILTON, A. H., Art
HIRSH, J. C., English
HOLMER, J. M., English
HOWARD, D. V., Psychology
HUDSON, M. C., Arab Studies
IKENBERRY, G. J., School of Foreign Service
IRIZARRY, E. D., Spanish
JANKOWSKY, K. R., German
JOHANSSON, J. K., School of Business
JOHNSON, R. M., History
JOYNER, C. C., Government
KALYANASUNDARAM, B., Computer Science
KAZIN, M., History
KELTNER, B., School of Nursing and Health Studies
KERTESZ, M., Chemistry
KING, T. M., Theology
KIRKPATRICK, J. J.
KLINE, J. M., School of Foreign Service
KONÉ, A., French
KORD, S. T., German
KROGH, P. F., School of Foreign Service
KUHN, S. T., Philosophy
LAGNESE, J. E., Mathematics

LAKE, A., School of Foreign Service
LARUBIA-PRADO, F., Spanish
LEVY, M. B., School of Business
LIEBER, R. J., Govt
MCAULIFFE, J. D., Georgetown College
MCCABE, D. M., School of Business
MCDONALD, W. F., Sociology
MCHENRY, D. F., School of Foreign Service
MCKEOWN, E., Theology
MCNAMARA, D., Sociology
MCNEILL, J. R., School of Foreign Service and History
MCNELIS, P. D., Economics and School of Foreign Service
MADDOX, L. B., English
MARTIRE, D. E., Chemistry
MARULLO, S., Sociology
MASSOUD-MOGHADDAM, F., Psychology
MAZZOLA, J. B., School of Business
MICELI, M. P., School of Business
MIKELL, G., Sociology and School of Foreign Service
MORAN, T. H., Int. Business Diplomacy
MORRIS, M. A., Slavic Languages
MUJICA, B. L., Spanish
MURPHY, G. R., German
NEALE, J. H., Biology
NISHIOKA, D. J., Biology
NOLLEN, S. D., School of Business
O'BRIEN, G., English
ORD, J. K., School of Business
PARKER, R. S., School of Business
PARROTT, W. G., Psychology
PFORDRESHER, J. C., English
PHILLIPS, D. A., Psychology
POPE, M. T., Chemistry
PRELINGER, E. A., Art
PUTO, C. P., School of Business
QUINN, D., School of Business
RAGUSSIS, M., English
RAMEY, C. T., School of Nursing and Health Studies
RAMEY, S. L., School of Nursing and Health Studies
RAPPAPORT, J., Spanish and School of Foreign Service
REARDON-ANDERSON, J., School of Foreign Service
REINSCH, N. LAMAR, Jr, School of Business
ROBINSON, D. N., Psychology
ROSENBLATT, J. P., English
ROSHWALD, A., History
RUEDY, J. D., History
RYDING, K. C., Arabic
SANDEFUR, J. T., Jr, Mathematics
SCHALL, J. V., Govt
SCHIFFRIN, D., Linguistics
SCHURER, W., School of Business
SCHWARTZ, M., Economics
SCOLLON, R. T., Linguistics
SERENE, J. W., Physics
SEVERINO, R., Italian
SHAHID, I., Arabic
SHERMAN, N.
SITTERSON, J. C., Jr, English
SLEVIN, J. F., English
SMITH, B. R., English
STEINBERG, D. I., School of Foreign Service
STENT, A., Govt
STITES, R., History and School of Foreign Service
STOWASSER, B., Arabic and School of Foreign Service
SWEENEY, R. J., School of Business
SZITTYA, P. R., English
TAMBASCO, A. J., Theology
TANNEN, D.
TAYLOR, D. W., Biology
THOMAS, R. J., School of Business
TUCKER, J. E., History
TUCKER, N. B., School of Foreign Service and History
VALENZUELA, A., Government
VEATCH, R. M., Philosophy
VELAUTHAPILLAI, M., Computer Science
VERECKE, W., Philosophy

VIKSNINS, G. J., Economics and School of Foreign Service
VOLL, J. O., School of Foreign Service and History
VROMAN, S., Economics
WALKER, D. A., School of Business
WALTERS, L. B., Jr, Philosophy
WAYNE, S. J., Govt
WEISS, C., School of Foreign Service
WEISS, R. G., Chemistry
WILCOX, W. C., Govt
WINTERS, F. X., School of Foreign Service
YANG, D. C., Chemistry
YOST, C. A., School of Foreign Service

HOWARD UNIVERSITY

2400 Sixth St, NW, Washington, DC 20059
Telephone: (202) 806-6100
Fax: (202) 806-5934
Internet: www.howard.edu
Founded 1867
Private control
Academic year: August to May (2 terms)
Pres.: Dr SIDNEY A. RIBEAU
Provost and Sr Vice-Pres. for Academic Affairs and Health Sciences: Dr LASALLE LEFFALL
Sr Vice-Pres. and Sec.: Dr ARTIS HAMPSHIRE-COWAN
Sr Vice-Pres., Chief Financial Officer and Treas.: ROBERT TAROLA
Sr Vice-Pres. and Exec. Dean for Health Sciences: Dr EVE J. HIGGINBOTHAM
Sr Vice-Pres. for Strategic Planning and External Affairs: Dr HASSAN MINOR
Sr Vice-Pres. and Sec.: ARTIS G. HAMPSHIRE-COWAN
Exec. Vice-Pres. and Chief Operating Officer: TROY A. STOVALL
Vice-Pres. for Research and Compliance: Dr FLORENCE BONNER
Vice-Pres. for Devt and Alumni Relations: NESTA BERNARD
Vice-Pres. for Student Affairs: Dr BARBARA GRIFFIN
Gen. Counsel: NORMA LEFTWICH
Dir for Libraries: ARTHUREE R. WRIGHT
Library: see Libraries and Archives
Number of teachers: 1,288 (1,082 full-time, 206 part-time)
Number of students: 10,594
Publications: *Howard Journal of Communications* (4 a year), *Howard Law Journal* (1 year), *Howard Magazine*, *Human Rights and Globalization Law Review*, *Journal of Negro Education* (4 a year), *Journal of Religious Thought* (2 a year), *The Jurist* (2 a year)

DEANS

College of Arts and Sciences: Dr JAMES DONALDSON
College of Dentistry: Dr LEO E. ROUSE
College of Medicine: Dr MARK S. JOHNSON
College of Nursing and Allied Health Sciences: Dr MARY HILL
College of Pharmacy: Dr ANTHONY K. WUTOH
Graduate School: Dr CHARLES L. BETSEY
School of Business: Dr BARRON HARVEY
School of Communications: Dr CHUKA ONWU-MECHILI
School of Divinity: Dr ALTON POLLARD, III
School of Education: Dr LESLIE FENWICK
School of Engineering, Architecture and Computer Sciences: Dr JAMES MITCHELL
School of Law: Dr KURT L. SCHMOKE
School of Social Work: Dr CUDORE L. SNELL

INSTITUTE OF WORLD POLITICS

1521 16th St, NW, Washington, DC 20036-1464
Telephone: (202) 462-2101

E-mail: info@iwp.edu
Internet: www.iwp.edu
Founded 1990, present status 2005
Private control
Academic year: September to July
Offers Master's degrees in statecraft and nat. security affairs, statecraft and int. affairs and strategic intelligence studies
Pres.: Dr JOHN LENCZOWSKI
Exec. Vice-Pres.: DOUGLAS MILLS
Vice-Pres. for Academic Affairs and Academic Dean: Dr CHARLES ROGER SMITH
Vice-Pres. for Finance and Admin.: JIM HOLMES
Vice-Pres. for Institutional Advancement: TRICIA LLOYD
Dir for Libraries and Information Services: JAMES STAMBAUGH
Registrar: HASANNA BENSON-TYUS
Library of 30,000 vols.

NATIONAL INTELLIGENCE UNIVERSITY

200 MacDill Blvd, Washington, DC 20340-5100
Telephone: (202) 231-3319
E-mail: jmic@dia.mil
Internet: www.ni-u.edu
Founded 1962 as Defense Intelligence School, present name 2011
State control
Academic year: August to July
Pres.: DAVID R. ELLISON
Provost: Dr SUSAN M. STUDDS
Registrar: ERIC H. STUPAR
Dir for Library: DENISE M. CAMPBELL
Library of 70,000 vols, 550 journals
Number of teachers: 82 (41 full-time, 41 part-time)
Number of students: 624

DEANS

College of Strategic Intelligence: Dr VANCE R. SKARSTEDT
School of Science and Technology Intelligence: Dr BRIAN R. SHAW

NATIONAL DEFENSE UNIVERSITY

300 Fifth Ave SW, Marshall Hall, Fort Lesley J. McNair, Washington, DC 20319-5066
Telephone: (202) 685-4700
Internet: www.ndu.edu
Founded 1924 as Army Industrial College
State control
Academic year: August to July
5 Colleges: College of Int Security Affairs, Industrial College of the Armed Forces, Information Resources Management College, Jt Forces Staff College and Nat. War College
Pres.: Vice-Admiral ANN E. RONDEAU
Sr Vice-Pres. for Int. Programmes and Outreach: NANCY McELDOWNEY
Vice-Pres. for Academic Affairs: Dr JOHN W. YAEGER
Vice-Pres. for Research: Dr HANS BINNENDIJK
Number of teachers: 348
Number of students: 4,066
Publications: *Joint Force Quarterly*, *Prism* (4 a year).

PONTIFICAL FACULTY OF THE IMMACULATE CONCEPTION AT THE DOMINICAN HOUSE OF STUDIES

487 Michigan Ave, NE, Washington, DC 20017-1585
Telephone: (202) 495-3820
Fax: (202) 495-3873
E-mail: registrar@dhs.edu
Internet: www.dhs.edu

Founded 1902 as The College of the Immaculate Conception, present name 1988
Private control
Languages of instruction: Greek, Latin
Academic year: August to May
Chancellor: Very Rev. CARLOS AZPIROZ
Vice-Chancellor: Very Rev. BRIAN MULCAHY
Pres.: Very Rev. Prof. STEVEN BOGUSLAWSKI
Vice-Pres. and Academic Dean: Rev. Prof. GABRIEL B. O'DONNELL
Registrar: TOBIAS NATHE
Treas.: SHAUNA ROYE
Librarian: JOHN MARTIN RUIZ
Library of 56,500 vols, 2,500 titles in specialized reference, Dominican and rare books collns
Number of teachers: 25
Number of students: 86
Publication: *The Thomist* (online (www.thomist.org)).

POTOMAC COLLEGE

4000 Chesapeake St, NW, Washington, DC 20016
Telephone: (202) 686-0876
Fax: (202) 686-0818
E-mail: admissions@potomac.edu
Internet: www.potomac.edu
Founded 1991
Private control
Academic year: January to December
Courses in accounting, business management, international business, information systems management, network security management; campus in N Virginia
Pres.: C. CATHLEEN RAFFAELI
Vice-Pres. for Academic Affairs: Dr CATHY EBERHART
Vice-Pres. for Human Resources and Student Affairs: DEEDY GIBBS
Library of 6,500 vols, 60 print periodicals, 50,000 e-books.

TRINITY WASHINGTON UNIVERSITY

125 Michigan Ave, NE, Washington, DC 20017
Telephone: (202) 884-9000
Fax: (202) 884-9229
E-mail: president@trinitydc.edu
Internet: www.trinitydc.edu
Founded 1897
Private control
Pres.: Dr PATRICIA McGUIRE
Provost and Vice-Pres. for Academic Affairs: Dr VIRGINIA BROADDUS
Chief Financial Officer: BARBARA LETTIERE
Vice-Pres. for Institutional Advancement: ANN PAULEY
Dean for Education: SUELLEN MEARA
Dean for Student Services: MEECHIE BOWIE
Registrar: MARVA BOSWELL
Dir for Library: JACOB BERG
Library: over 200,000 vols
Number of teachers: 59 full-time
Number of students: 2,555
Publications: *Trinilogue*, *Trinity Magazine* (3 a year), *Trinity Times*

DEANS

College of Arts and Sciences: Dr ELIZABETH CHILD
School of Education: Dr SUELLEN MEARA
School of Nursing and Health Professions: Dr MARY ROMANELLO
School of Professional Studies: Dr TELAEKAH BROOKS

UNIVERSITY OF THE DISTRICT OF COLUMBIA

4200 Connecticut Ave, NW, Washington, DC 20008

Telephone: (202) 274-5000
Fax: (202) 274-6341
E-mail: udcadmission@udc.edu
Internet: www.udc.edu

Founded 1851 as Miner Normal School
Academic year: August to May

Pres.: Dr ALLEN L. SESSOMS
Provost and Vice-Pres. for Academic Affairs: Dr KEN BAIN
Vice-Pres. for Facilities Management: BARBARA JUMPER
Vice-Pres. for Govt Relations: AIMEE OCCHETTI
Vice-Pres. for Student Affairs: Dr VALERIE L. EPPS (acting)
Vice-Pres. for Univ. Relations and Public Affairs: ALAN ETTER
Gen. Counsel: Dr CRAIG W. PARKER
Chief of Staff and Vice-Pres. of Operations: STAN JACKSON
Dean for Library: ALBERT J. CASCIERO
Number of students: 9,660

DEANS

College of Agriculture, Urban Sustainability and Environmental Sciences: Dr GLORIA WYCHE MOORE
College of Arts and Sciences: (vacant)
David A. Clarke School of Law: Dr KATHERINE S. BRODERICK
School of Business and Public Admin.: Dr RICHARD F. BEBEE
School of Engineering and Applied Sciences: BEVERLY HARTLINE (acting)

WASHINGTON THEOLOGICAL UNION

6896 Laurel St, NW, Washington, DC 20012

Telephone: (202) 726-8800
Fax: (202) 726-1716
E-mail: info@wtu.edu
Internet: www.wtu.edu

Founded 1968 as Coalition of Religious Seminaries, present name 1969
Private control
Academic year: August to May

Pres.: Very Rev. FREDERICK J. TILLOTSON
Academic Dean: ANNE E. McLAUGHLIN (acting)
Dir for Enrolment Services: CYNTHIA CAMERON
Dir for Institutional Advancement: JOAN KNETEMANN
Registrar: Rev. BARTHOLOMEW J. MERELLA
Dir for Library: (vacant)
Library of 130,000 vols
Number of students: 250

WESLEY THEOLOGICAL SEMINARY

4500 Massachusetts Ave NW, Washington, DC 20016

Telephone: (202) 885-8600
Fax: (202) 885-8605
E-mail: admiss@wesleysem.edu
Internet: www.wesleyseminary.edu

Founded 1882 as Westminster Theological Seminary, present name and location 1958
Private control
Academic year: August to May
2 Campuses

Pres.: Rev. Dr DAVID F. McALLISTER-WILSON
Vice-Pres. for Devt: Dr MICHAEL T. BRADFIELD
Vice-Pres. for Finance and Admin.: JUNE R. STOWE
Vice-Pres. for Int. Relations: KYUNGLIM SHIN LEE
Dean: AMY ODEN
Dean: BRUCE C. BIRCH

Registrar: ELEANOR GEASE
Dir of Library: DAVID WILLIAM FAUPEL
Library of 175,000 vols, 400 journals subscriptions
Number of students: 1,000

FLORIDA

AVE MARIA SCHOOL OF LAW

1025 Commons Circle, Naples, FL 34119

Telephone: (239) 687-5300
E-mail: info@avemarialaw.edu
Internet: www.avemarialaw.edu

Founded 1999 at Ann Arbor, Michigan, present location 2009
Private control
Academic year: August to May

Pres. and Dean: Prof. Dr EUGENE R. MILHIZER
Assoc. Dean of Academic Affairs: PATRICK QUIRK
Assoc. Dean for Student Affairs: KAYE A. CASTRO
Dir of Admissions: MICHELE CONNOR
Dir of Devt and External Affairs: JOHN KNOWLES
Dir of Finance and Admin.: VIRGINIA TRAVER
Registrar: ANGELA KOJIRO
Dir of Law Library: ROBERTA STUDWELL
Library of 400,000 vols
Publications: *International Law Journal, Law Review.*

AVE MARIA UNIVERSITY

5050 Ave Maria Blvd, Ave Maria, FL 34142-9505

Telephone: (239) 280-2500
Fax: (239) 280-2559
E-mail: admissions@avemaria.edu
Internet: www.avemaria.edu

Founded 1998 as Ave Maria Institute
Private control
Academic year: August to July

Depts of biology and chemistry, economics, history, literature, mathematics and physics, philosophy, politics, sacred music, theology

Pres. and CEO: H. JAMES TOWEY
Chancellor: THOMAS S. MONAGHAN
Chief Financial Officer: PAUL R. RONEY
Sr Vice-Pres. for Academic Affairs: JOHN E. SITES
Vice-Pres. for Enrolment and Marketing: DENNIS GRACE
Vice Pres. for Institutional Advancement: Dr LOUIS TRAINA
Vice-Pres. for Student Affairs and Dean of Students: Dr DANIEL DENTINO
Vice-Pres. for Univ. Relations: (vacant)
Dean of Faculty: Dr MICHAEL A. DAUPHINAIS
Dir of Admission: JASON FABAZ
Registrar: STEPHANIE E. NEGIP
Dir of Library Services: TERENCE GALLAGHER (acting)

Library of 200,000 vols, 25,000 bound periodicals, 10,000 rare books colln
Number of teachers: 28 (12 full-time, 16 adjunct)
Number of students: 109

BAPTIST COLLEGE OF FLORIDA

5400 College Dr., Graceville, FL 32440-1898

Telephone: (850) 328-2660
Fax: (850) 263-9026
E-mail: admissions@baptistcollege.edu
Internet: www.baptistcollege.edu

Founded 1943 as Florida Baptist Institute, present name and status 2000
Private control
Academic year: August to July

Offers bachelor degrees in biblical studies, Christian counselling, business leadership, education, English, history, min. studies, music; offers masters degree in Christian studies

Pres.: Dr THOMAS A. KINCHEN
Sr Vice-Pres.: Prof. Dr R. C. HAMMACK
Vice-Pres. for Development: CHARLES R. PARKER
Dean of Students: Dr ROGER RICHARDS
Registrar: STEPHANIE W. ORR
Dir of Library Services: JOHN E. SHAFFETT, JR
Number of students: 625

Publication: *Echoes* (4 a year).

BARRY UNIVERSITY

11300 NE Second Ave, Miami Shores, FL 33161-6695

Telephone: (305) 899-3000
Fax: (305) 899-3100
E-mail: admissions@mail.barry.edu
Internet: www.barry.edu

Founded 1940
Private control
Academic year: August to May

Pres.: Sis. Dr LINDA BEVILACQUA
Gen. Counsel: DAVID DUDGEON
Provost: Dr LINDA M. PETERSON
Vice-Pres. for Business and Finance: D. BRUCE EDWARDS
Vice-Pres. for Institutional Advancement: (vacant)
Vice-Pres. for Legal Affairs: JOHN WALKER
Vice-Pres. for Student Affairs: Dr SCOTT SMITH
Registrar: CYNTHIA CHRUSZCZYK
Library Dir: TOM MESSNER

Library of 950,000 vols, 2,880 periodicals, 1,200 journals and 541,560 microforms
Number of teachers: 311 full-time
Number of students: 6,924

DEANS

Adrian Dominican School of Education: Dr TERRY PIPER
College of Arts and Sciences: Dr KAREN A. CALLAGHAN
College of Health Sciences: Dr PEGGE BELL
D. Inez Andreas School of Business: Dr TOMISLAV MANDAKOVIC
Dwayne O. Andreas School of Law: Dr LETICIA M. DIAZ
Ellen Whiteside McDonnell School of Social Work: Dr PHYLLIS SCOTT
Frank J. Rooney School of Adult and Continuing Education: Dr CAROL-RAE SODANO
School of Human Performance and Leisure Sciences: Dr DARLENE KLUKA
School of Podiatric Medicine: Dr JEFFREY JENSEN

BEACON COLLEGE

105 E Main St, Leesburg, FL 34748

Telephone: (352) 787-7660
Fax: (352) 787-0721
E-mail: admissions@beaconcollege.edu
Internet: www.beaconcollege.edu

Founded 1989
Private control
Academic year: August to June

Offers academic degree programmes to students with learning disabilities; offers bachelor degrees in computer information systems, human services, liberal studies

Pres.: Dr JOHN M. HUTCHINSON
Vice-Pres. for Academic Affairs: Dr SHELLY CHANDLER
Vice-Pres. for Finance and Admin.: CALVIN SANSON

Vice-Pres. for Institutional Advancement and Alumni Relations: Dr WALTER ZIE-LINSKI

Vice-Pres. for Student Services: Dr ROBERT BRIDGEMAN

Dir of Admissions: BRENDA MELI

Registrar: DAVID BROWN

Dir of Library Resources: DIANNA WADE

Library of 23,000 vols, 38,000 e-books, 100 periodicals, 1000 audiovisuals and 600 items in learning disabilities colln

Number of students: 130

BETHUNE—COOKMAN COLLEGE

640 Dr Mary McLeod Bethune Blvd, Daytona Beach, FL 32114-3099

Telephone: (386) 481-2000

Fax: (386) 481-2010

E-mail: bronson@cookman.edu

Internet: www.cookman.edu

Founded 1904 as Daytona Educational and Industrial Training School, present name 1924, present status 2007

Private control

Academic year: August to April

Pres.: Dr TRUDIE KIBBE REED

Vice-Pres. for Academic Affairs: Dr DORCAS McCoy

Vice-Pres. for Institutional Advancement: Dr HIRAM POWELL

Vice-Pres. for Institutional Effectiveness: Dr RAY SHACKELFORD

Vice-Pres. for Student Affairs: DWAUN J. WARMACK (acting)

Chief Financial Officer: Dr RONALD DOWDY

Chief Information Officer: FRANKLIN E. PATTERSON

Registrar: ANNIE REDD

Dir of Library Learning: Dr TASHA LUCAS-YOUMANS

Library of 130,000 vols

Number of teachers: 361 (full-time)

Number of students: 3,600

Publication: *Undergraduate Research Journal* (1 a year)

DEANS

School of Arts and Humanities: Dr JAMES BROOKS

School of Business: Dr AUBREY E. LONG

School of Education: Dr CAROL JOHNSON

School of Graduate and Professional Studies: Dr DARRYL FRAZIER

School of Nursing: Dr WILLIE MAE SESSION

School of Science, Engineering and Mathematics: Dr HERBERT THOMPSON

School of Social Sciences: Dr IAN PAYTON

BROWARD COLLEGE

111 E Las Olas Blvd, Fort Lauderdale, FL 33301

Telephone: (954) 201-7350

Fax: (954) 201-7379

Internet: www.broward.edu

Founded 1960, present name and status 2008

State control

Academic year: August to August

Campuses: Judson A. Samuels S campus, N campus; offers bachelor of applied science degree in information technology, nursing, supervision and management, teacher education, technology management

Pres.: Dr J. DAVID ARMSTRONG, JR

Provost and Sr Vice-Pres. for Academic Affairs and Student Success: Dr LINDA HOWDYSHELL

Sr Vice-Pres. for Admin.: THOMAS W. OLLIFF

Vice-Pres. for Advancement: NANCY R. BOTERO

Vice-Pres. for Finance: JAYSON IROFF

Vice-Pres. for Information Technology and Institutional Effectiveness: PATTI BARNEY

Vice-Pres. for Student Affairs and Enrolment Management: ANGELIA N. MILLENDER

Dean of Student Affairs: DAVID ASENCIO

Registrar and Assoc. Vice-Pres. for Student Affairs: WILLIE J. ALEXANDER

Dean of Univ. and College Library: MIGUEL MENENDEZ

Publication: *P'an Ku.*

CARLOS ALBIZU UNIVERSITY

2173 NW 99th Ave, Miami, FL 33172-2209

Telephone: (305) 593-1223

Fax: (305) 592-7930

Internet: mia.albizu.edu

Founded 1966, present name and status 2000

Private control

Campus in San Juan; offers degree courses in business admin., education, English, psychology

Pres.: Dr ILEANA RODRIGUEZ-GARCIA

Chancellor of Miami campus: Dr CARMEN S. ROCA

Chancellor of San Juan campus: Dr JOSÉ J. CABIYA

Dir of Finance: EUNICE PIERRE-LOUIS

Dir of Student Services: PETER RUBIO

Registrar: FINA CAMPA

Library Dir: MARY BISHOP.

CHIPOLA COLLEGE

3094 Indian Circle, Marianna, FL 32446

Telephone: (850) 526-2761

Internet: www.chipola.edu

Founded 1947 as Chipola Jr College, present name and status 2003

Courses incl. bachelor of science in nursing and bachelor of business admin.

State control

Academic year: August to August

Pres.: Dr GENE PROUGH

Sr Vice-Pres. for Instruction: Dr SARAH CLEMMONS

Vice-Pres. for Finance: STEVE YOUNG

Vice-Pres. for Student Affairs: Dr JAYNE ROBERTS

Dean of Institutional Devt and Planning: GAIL HARTZOG

Registrar: KATHY REHBERG

Dir of Library Services and Distance Learning: Dr LOU KIND

Number of students: 2,000

DEANS

School of Business and Technology: Dr JAMES P. FROH

School of Education: Dr LOU CLEVELAND

School of Health Sciences: VICKIE W. STEPHENS

CLEARWATER CHRISTIAN COLLEGE

3400 Gulf-to-Bay Blvd, Clearwater, FL 33759-4595

Telephone: (727) 726-1153

Fax: (727) 726-8597

E-mail: admissions@clearwater.edu

Internet: www.clearwater.edu

Founded 1966, present status 2008

Private control

Academic year: August to May

Areas of study incl. biblical studies, business, education, fine arts, humanities, sciences

Pres.: Prof. Dr JACK KLEM

Vice-Pres. for Academic Affairs: Prof. Dr MARY C. DRAPER

Vice-Pres. for Financial Affairs: RANDY T. LIVINGSTON

Vice-Pres. for Institutional Advancement: TERRY D. WILD

Vice-Pres. for Student Life: RYAN DUPEE

Registrar: THOMAS CANNON, JR

Dean of Students: TODD BARTON

Dir of Library: ELIZABETH WERNER

Library of 100,000 vols

Number of teachers: 51 (incl. 32 full-time)

Number of students: 561

COLLEGE OF CENTRAL FLORIDA

3001 SW College Rd, Ocala, FL 34474-4415

Telephone: (352) 873-5800

Fax: (352) 291-4450

E-mail: library@cf.edu

Internet: www.cf.edu

Founded 1966 by merger of Hampton Jr College and Central Florida Jr College, present name and status 2010

State control

Academic year: August to August

Campuses: Citrus, Levy centre, Hampton centre; offers bachelor degrees courses in applied science, science

Interim Pres. and Sr Vice-Pres. for Admin. and Finance: Dr JAMES D. HARVEY

Vice-Pres. for Citrus Campus: Dr VERNON LAWTER

Vice-Pres. for Institutional Advancement: JOAN M. STEARNS

Vice-Pres. for Instructional Affairs: Dr MARK PAUGH

Vice-Pres. for Student Affairs: Dr TIMOTHY G. WISE

Dean of Enrolment Management: LYN POWELL

Dean of Student Services: HENRI BENLOLO

Dean of Learning Resource Centre: RICHARD BAZILE

Library of 65,000 vols

Number of teachers: 116

Number of students: 18,836

Publications: *CF Connection* (2 a year), *Imprints* (1 a year), *In The Write Mind* (1 a year).

DAYTONA STATE COLLEGE

1200 W Int. Speedway Blvd, Daytona Beach, FL 32114-2817

Telephone: (386) 506-3000

Internet: www.daytonastate.edu

Founded 1957 as Daytona Beach Jr College, present status 2006, present name 2008

State control

Academic year: August to June

Campuses in DeLand, Flagler/Palm Coast, New Smyrna Beach-Edgewater

Pres.: Dr CAROL W. EATON

Exec. Vice-Pres. and Gen. Counsel: BRIAN BABB

Sr Vice-Pres. for Academic Affairs: Dr MICHAEL VITALE

Sr Vice-Pres. for Admin. and Accounting and Chief Financial Officer: DENNIS MICARE

Sr Vice-Pres. for Enrolment, Student Devt and Marketing: Dr THOMAS LoBASSO

Dean of Institutional Research: SUSAN ANTILLON

Number of students: 35,000

Publication: *Ole' Literary Magazine*

DEANS

College of Online Studies: ROBERT SAUM

Mori Hosseini College of Hospitality Management: COSTA MAGOULAS

School of Adult Education: KATRINA BELL

School of Health and Wellness: WILLIAM DUNNE

ECKERD COLLEGE

4200 54th Ave S, St Petersburg, FL 33711

Telephone: (727) 867-1166

Fax: (727) 866-2304
E-mail: admissions@eckerd.edu
Internet: www.eckerd.edu

Founded 1958 as Florida Presbyterian College, present name and status 1972
Private control
Academic year: August to May

Liberal arts college; courses incl. bachelor degrees in arts, chemistry, science

Pres.: Dr Donald R. Eastman, III
Vice-Pres. and Dean of Special Programmes: James E. Deegan
Vice-Pres. and Sec. of College: Lisa Mets
Vice-Pres. for Academic Affairs and Dean of Faculty: Dr Betty H. Stewart
Vice-Pres. for Advancement: Matthew S. Bisset
Vice Pres. for Business and Finance: Christopher P. Brennan
Vice-Pres. for Student Life and Dean of Students: Dr James J. Annarelli
Dir of Admissions: Maria Furtado
Dean of Admissions and Financial Aid: John F. Sullivan
Registrar: Linda Swindall
Dir of Library Services: Jamie Gill

Library of 150,000 vols, 20,000 journals
Number of teachers: 163 (109 full-time, 54 part-time)
Number of students: 1,832

EDISON STATE COLLEGE

8099 College Parkway, Fort Myers, FL 33919
Telephone: (239) 489-9300
E-mail: president@edison.edu
Internet: www.edison.edu

Founded 1962, present name 2008
State control
Academic year: August to June

Campuses in Charlotte co, Collier co, Hendry/Glades centre

District Pres.: Kenneth P. Walker
Gen. Counsel: Mark Lupe
Vice-Pres. for Academic Affairs: Dr Erin Harrel
Vice-Pres. for Financial Services: Gina Doeble
Vice-Pres. for Strategic Initiatives: Edith Pendleton
Charlotte Campus Pres.: Dr Patricia Land
Vice-Pres. and Provost of Henry/Glades Centre and Interim Collier Campus Pres.: Dr Robert R. Jones
Registrar: Billee Silva
Dean of Student Services: Patricia Newell
District Dean of Learning Resources and Vice-Pres. for Strategic Initiatives: Dr Edith Pendleton

Number of teachers: 132 (full-time)
Number of students: 25,027

DEANS

School of Education and Charter Schools: Erin Harrel
School of Health Sciences: (vacant)
School of Nursing: (vacant)

EDWARD WATERS COLLEGE

1658 Kings Rd, Jacksonville, FL 32209-6199
Telephone: (904) 470-8000
Fax: (904) 470-8048
Internet: www.ewc.edu

Founded 1866, present name 1892
Private control
Academic year: August to May

Liberal arts college; degree programmes incl. biology, business admin., communications, criminal justice, elementary education, mathematics, music

Pres.: Dr Nathaniel Glover, Jr
Exec. Vice-Pres.: Dr Eurmon Hervey, Jr

Vice-Pres. for Academic Affairs: Dr Bertha D. Minus
Vice-Pres. for Business and Finance: Randolph Mitchell
Vice-Pres. for Student Affairs and Enrolment Management: Dr James B. Ewers, Jr
Dean of Faculty: Dr Reuben Perechi
Registrar: Lindsey Barnette
Library Dir: Carmella Martin

Library of 30,000 vols, 147 periodicals
Number of students: 839

EMBRY—RIDDLE AERONAUTICAL UNIVERSITY

600 S Clyde Morris Blvd, Daytona Beach, FL 32114-3900
Telephone: (386) 226-6000
Fax: (386) 226-6307
E-mail: dbadmit@erau.edu
Internet: www.erau.edu

Founded 1926 as Embry-Riddle School of Aviation; present name 1970
Private control
Academic year: September to August

Pres.: Dr John P. Johnson
Sr Exec. Vice-Pres. for Academics and Research: Christina Frederick-Recascino
Sr Exec. Vice-Pres. and Chief Financial Officer: Eric Weekes
Vice-Pres. for Institutional Advancement: Daniel Montplaisir
Vice-Pres. for Devt: Pat Ramsey
Chief Information Officer: Cindy Bixler
Exec. Vice-Pres. and Chief Academic Officer for Daytona Beach Campus: Dr Richard Heist
Library Dir: Dr Anne Marie Casey

Library of 116,227 vols, 2,078 periodicals
Number of teachers: 341 (249 full-time, 92 part-time)
Number of students: 9,585 (4,496 undergraduates, 5,089 graduates)

DEANS

College of Arts and Sciences: Dr Bill Grams
College of Aviation: Dr Tim Brady
College of Business: Dr Michael Williams
College of Engineering: Dr Maj Mirmirani

CAMPUSES

Embry-Riddle Aeronautical University—Prescott, Arizona Campus

3700 Willow Creek Rd, Prescott, AZ 86301-3720
Telephone: (928) 777-6600
Fax: (928) 777-3806
E-mail: pradmfrm@erau.edu
Internet: prescott.erau.edu

Founded 1978
Private control
Academic year: September to August

Exec. Vice-Pres. and Chief Academic Officer for Prescott Campus: Dr Frank Ayers
Library Dir: Sarah Thomas

Library of 34,000 vols
Number of teachers: 111 (81 full-time, 30 part-time)
Number of students: 3,359 (1,654 undergraduate, 1,705 graduate)

DEANS

College of Arts and Sciences: Dr Archie Dickey
College of Aviation: Dr Gary Northam
College of Engineering: Dr Ron Madler

Embry-Riddle Aeronautical University—Worldwide

600 S Clyde Morris Blvd, Daytona Beach, FL 32114-3900
Telephone: (386) 226-6910

Fax: (386) 226-6984
E-mail: worldwide@erau.edu
Internet: worldwide.erau.edu

Comprises Centre for Distance Learning, College of Career Education; operates in the USA, Europe

Exec. Vice-Pres. and Chief Academic Officer for Worldwide Campus: Dr John R. Watret
Dean of Academic Affairs for Central Region: Dr Mark Friend
Dean of Academic Affairs for Eastern Region: Dr Bernard Cordial
Dean of Academic Affairs for Int. Region: Bill Muldoon
Dean of Academic Affairs for Western Region: Dr Katherine Moran
Registrar: Edward Trombley, III
Library Dir: Anne Marie Casey

Library of 116,227 vols, 2,078 periodicals
Number of teachers: 2,531 (121 full-time, 2,410 part-time)
Number of students: 27,261 (20,046 undergraduate, 7,215 graduate)

EVEREST UNIVERSITY

Suite 400, 6 Hutton Centre Dr., Santa Ana, FL 92707
Telephone: (714) 427-3000
Fax: (714) 427-5111
Internet: www.everest.edu

Founded 1890, fmrly Florida Metropolitan Univ., present name and status 2007
Private control

Campuses in Brandon, Lakeland, Jacksonville, Largo, Melbourne, Orange Park, S Orlando, N Orlando, Pompano Beach, Tampa

Chair. and CEO: David G. Moore
Pres. and Chief Operating Officer: Anthony Digiovanni
Sr Vice-Pres. for Academic Affairs: Dr Mary H. Barry

Number of students: 11,000 (all campuses)

FLAGLER COLLEGE

74 King St, St Augustine, FL 32084
Telephone: (904) 829-6481
Fax: (904) 826-0094
E-mail: admissions@flagler.edu
Internet: www.flagler.edu

Founded 1968
Private control
Academic year: August to June (2 semesters)
Language of instruction: English

Offers bachelors degree in arts, fine arts, public admin.

Chancellor: Dr William T. Proctor
Pres.: Dr William T. Abare, Jr
Vice-Pres. for Business Services: Kenneth S. Russom
Vice-Pres. for Enrolment Management: Marc G. Williar
Vice-Pres. for Institutional Advancement: F. Mark Whittaker
Dean of Academic Affairs: Dr Alan Woolfolk
Dean of Student Services: Daniel P. Stewart
Registrar: Miriam Roberson
Dir of Library Services: Jennifer M. Eason

Library of 92,010 vols, 132,994 e-books, 1,877 microform, 4,922 audiovisual material, 533 periodicals
Number of students: 2,678

FLORIDA AGRICULTURAL AND MECHANICAL UNIVERSITY

1601 Martin Luther King Jr Blvd, Tallahassee, FL 32307
Telephone: (850) 599-3000
Fax: (850) 599-3069

Internet: www.famu.edu

Founded 1887, present name 1909
State control
Academic year: August to June

Pres.: Dr JAMES H. AMMONS
Provost and Vice-Pres. for Academic Affairs:
CYNTHIA HUGHES HARRIS
Gen. Counsel: AVERY D. McKNIGHT
Vice-Pres. for Admin. and Financial Services:
TERESA HARDEE
Vice-Pres. for Devt: CARLA S. WILLIS
Vice-Pres. for Student Affairs: WILLIAM HUDSON, JR
Vice-Pres. for Univ. Relations: SHARON P.
SAUNDERS
Chief Communications Officer: SHARON SAUNDERS
Dir of Libraries: LAUREN B. SAPP
Library: 1m. vols, 98,538 current periodicals,
192,000 microforms, 76,000 non-print
items
Number of teachers: 532
Number of students: 12,161

DEANS

School of Architecture: RODNER WRIGHT
College of Arts and Sciences: Dr RALPH W.
TURNER
College of Education: GENNIVER C. BELL
College of Engineering Sciences, Technology
and Agriculture: Dr MAKOLA ABDULLAH
College of Law: LeROY PERNELL
College of Pharmacy and Pharmaceutical
Sciences: HENRY LEWIS, III
FAMU/FSU College of Engineering: Dr
CHING-JEN CHEN
School of Allied Health Sciences: Dr BARBARA
MOSLEY
School of Business and Industry: Dr
SHAWNTA FRIDAY-STROUD
School of Gen. Studies: Dr DOROTHY HENDERSON
School of Graduate Studies, Research and
Continuing Education: Dr CHANTA M. HAYWOOD
School of Journalism and Graphic Communication: Dr JAMES E. HAWKINS
School of Nursing: Dr RUENA NORMAN

FLORIDA ATLANTIC UNIVERSITY

777 Glades Rd, POB 3091, Boca Raton, FL
33431

Telephone: (561) 297-3000
Fax: (561) 297-2758
E-mail: admissions@fau.edu
Internet: www.fau.edu

Founded 1964
State control

Campuses in Boca Raton, Dania Beach,
Davie, Fort Lauderdale, Jupiter, Treasure
Coast; also Open Univ. and Continuing Education Div. (Fort Lauderdale), Harbor Br.
Marine Sciences Bldg (Fort Pierce) and
SeaTech (ocean engineering research and
graduate education centre, Dania Beach)

Pres.: Dr MARY JANE SAUNDERS
Univ. Provost and Chief Academic Officer: Dr
BRENDA CLAIBORNE
Sr Vice-Pres. for Student Affairs: Dr CHARLES
BROWN
Vice-Pres. for Research: Dr BARRY T. ROSSON
Vice-Pres. for Univ. Advancement: RANDY
TALBOT
Univ. Registrar: HARRY E. DeMIK
Dean of Univ. Libraries: Dr WILLIAM MILLER
Library: 2.5m. vols incl. books, periodicals,
govt documents, microforms, maps, media
and other materials, 200,000 e-books,
20,000 e-journals
Number of teachers: 1,067 (1,040 full-time,
27 part-time)
Number of students: 28,325 (15,838 full-
time, 12,487 part-time)

Publications: *Coastlines Literary Magazine,
Florida Atlantic Comparative Studies
Journal, Journal of the Fantastic in the
Arts*

DEANS

Charles E. Schmidt College of Medicine: Dr
DAVID J. BJORKMAN
Charles E. Schmidt College of Science: Dr
GARY W. PERRY
Christine E. Lynn College of Nursing: Dr
MARLAINE SMITH
College for Design and Social Inquiry: Dr
ROSALYN CARTER
College of Business: Dr J. DENNIS COATES
College of Education: Dr VALERIE J. BRISTOR
College of Engineering and Computer Science: Dr MOHAMMAD ILYAS
Dorothy F. Schmidt College of Arts and
Letters: Prof. Dr HEATHER COLTMAN
Graduate College: Dr BARRY T. ROSSON
Harriet L. Wilkes Honors College: Dr JEFFREY BULLER

FLORIDA CHRISTIAN COLLEGE

1011 Bill Beck Blvd, Kissimmee, FL 34744

Telephone: (407) 847-8966
Fax: (321) 206-2007
E-mail: fcc@fcc.edu
Internet: www.fcc.edu

Founded 1975, present name 1981
Private control
Academic year: August to May

Bachelor programmes incl. Bible, Bible and
humanities, children's min. Christian min.,
counselling, cross-cultural min., educational
leadership, elementary education, musical
arts, music and worship min., organizational
leadership, non-profit management, preaching, youth and family min.

Pres.: WILLIAM K. BEHRMAN
Exec. Vice-Pres.: Dr TERRY ALLCORN
Vice-Pres. for Academics: Dr BRIAN D. SMITH
Vice-Pres. for Finance: RENEE COOK
Dir of Institutional Research: BRUCE DUSTERHOFT
Registrar: DIANE ADAMS
Librarian: LINDA STARK
Number of teachers: 16
Number of students: 380

Publication: *Sonlife* (2 a year).

FLORIDA COLLEGE

119 N Glen Arven Ave, Temple Terrace, FL
33617-5578

Telephone: (813) 988-5131
Fax: (813) 899-6772
E-mail: admissions@floridacollege.edu
Internet: www.floridacollege.edu

Founded 1946 as Florida Christian College,
present name 1963
Private control
Academic year: August to May

Offers degree programmes in business
admin., communication, education, music

Pres.: Dr H. E. PAYNE, JR
Vice-Pres. for Academic and Student Affairs:
DOUGLAS H. C. NORTHCUTT
Dir of Enrolment Management: PAUL J.
CASEBOLT
Dir of Institutional Devt: DOUGLAS R. NERLAND
Academic Dean: DANIEL W. PETTY
Dean of Student Services: BRIAN CRISPELL
Registrar: BETH ANN GRANT
Library Dir: WANDA D. DICKEY
Library of 150,000 vols, 22,000 periodicals

Publication: *Florida College Magazine*.

FLORIDA GULF COAST UNIVERSITY

10501 FGCU Blvd S, Fort Myers, FL 33965-
6565

Telephone: (239) 590-1000
Fax: (239) 590-1010
E-mail: admissions@fgcu.edu
Internet: www.fgcu.edu

Founded 1991
State control
Academic year: August to May

Pres.: Dr WILSON G. BRADSHAW
Provost and Vice-Pres. for Academic Affairs:
Dr RONALD B. TOLL
Vice-Pres. for Admin. Services and Finance:
STEVE L. MAGIERA
Vice-Pres. for Student Affairs: Dr J. MICHAEL
ROLLO
Vice-Pres. for Univ. Advancement: Dr ROSEMARY M. THOMAS
Dir of Graduate Studies: Dr GREG TOLLEY
Dean of Students: Dr MICHELE YOVANOVICH
Gen. Counsel: VEE LEONARD
Univ. Registrar: SUSAN BYARS
Library Dean: Dr KATHLEEN F. MILLER
Library of 314,785 vols, 123,917 govt publs,
40,863 periodicals, 23,968 e-books, 94,211
e-journals
Number of teachers: 3,067
Number of students: 12,047

DEANS

College of Arts and Sciences: Prof. Dr DONNA
HENRY
College of Education: Prof. Dr MARCI GREENE
College of Health Professions: Prof. Dr
MITCHELL L. CORDOVA
College of Professional Studies: TONY A.
BARRINGER
Lutgert College of Business: Dr HUDSON
ROGERS
U. A. Whitaker College of Engineering: Prof.
Dr SUSAN M. BLANCHARD

FLORIDA HOSPITAL COLLEGE OF HEALTH SCIENCES

671 Winyah Dr., Orlando, FL 32803-1226

Telephone: (407) 303-5619
Fax: (407) 303-5671
Internet: www.fhchs.edu

Founded 1992, present status 2008
Private control
Academic year: August to August (3 semesters)

Courses in nuclear medicine technology,
nursing, occupational therapy, radiologic sciences

Pres.: Dr DAVID E. GREENLAW
Sr Vice-Pres. for Academic Admin.: Dr
DONALD E. WILLIAMS
Sr Vice-Pres. for Financial Admin.: ROBERT
CURREN
Vice Pres. for Academic Admin. for Educational Technology and Distance Education:
Dr DAN LIM
Vice-Pres. for Operations: RUBEN MARTINEZ
Vice-Pres. for Student Services: STEPHEN
ROCHE
Library Dir: DEANNA FLORES.

FLORIDA INSTITUTE OF TECHNOLOGY

150 W University Blvd, Melbourne, FL
32901-6975

Telephone: (321) 674-8030
Fax: (321) 674-8004
E-mail: admission@fit.edu
Internet: www.fit.edu

Founded 1958, present name and status 1966
Private control
Academic year: August to May (3 semesters)

Pres.: Dr ANTHONY JAMES CATANESE
Sr Vice-Pres. and Chief Devt Officer: DOR-OTHY A. ALLEN
Sr Vice-Pres. and Chief Financial Officer: Dr ROBERT E. NIEBUHR
Exec. Vice-Pres. and Chief Operating Officer: Dr T. DWAYNE McCAY
Vice-Pres. and Chief Financial Officer: JACK ARMUL
Vice-Pres. for Academic Affairs: (vacant)
Vice-Pres. for Research: FRANK KINNEY
Vice-Pres. for Student Affairs: Dr RANDALL L. ALFORD
Registrar: CHARLOTTE YOUNG
Dir of Undergraduate Admission: MICHAEL J. PERRY
Dean of Students: RODNEY B. BOWERS
Dir of Libraries: Dr CELINE LANG
Library of 117,000 vols, 228,000 govt documents, 32,000 journals
Number of teachers: 616 (234 full-time, 382 part-time)
Number of students: 8,980

DEANS

College of Aeronautics: Dr KENNETH P. STACKPOOLE
College of Engineering: Dr FREDRIC M. HAM
College of Psychology and Liberal Arts: Prof. Dr MARY BETH KENKEL
College of Science: Prof. Dr HAMID K. RASSOUL
Nathan M. Bisk College of Business: Prof. Dr S. ANN BECKER
School of Extended Studies: (vacant)

FLORIDA INTERNATIONAL UNIVERSITY

11200 SW Eighth St, Miami, FL 33199
Telephone: (305) 348-2000
Internet: www.fiu.edu
Founded 1965
State control
Academic year: August to August
Campuses: Biscayne Bay, FIU Broward-Pines Centre, Engineering Centre, FIU Downtown, FIU College of Architecture and Arts, Wolfsonian-FIU
Pres.: Dr MARK B. ROSENBERG
Provost, Exec. Vice-Pres. and Chief Operating Officer: Dr DOUGLAS WARTZOK
Sr Vice-Pres. for Admin. and Chief Financial Officer: Dr KENNETH A. JESSELL
Sr Vice-Pres. for Information Technology and Chief Information Officer: ROBERT GRILLO
Sr Vice-Pres. for Univ. Advancement: HOWARD R. LIPMAN
Sr Vice-Pres. for External Relations: SANDRA B. GONZALEZ-LEVY
Vice-Pres. for Research: Dr ANDRÉS G. GIL
Vice-Pres. for Student Affairs: Dr ROSA L. JONES
Gen. Counsel: M. KRISTINA RAATTAMA
Dean of Univ. Libraries: LAURA K. PROBST
Library: 1.7m. vols, 9,700 current periodicals, maps, microforms, govt documents, archives, rare books
Number of teachers: 1,100 (full-time)
Number of students: 46,000

DEANS

Chaplin School of Hospitality and Tourism Management: Dr MIKE HAMPTON
College of Architecture and Arts: BRIAN SCHRINER
College of Arts and Sciences: Dr KENNETH G. FURTON
College of Business Admin.: Dr JOYCE J. ELAM
College of Education: DELIA C. GARCIA
College of Engineering and Computing: Prof. Dr AMIR MIRMIRAN
College of Law: R. ALEXANDER ACOSTA

College of Nursing and Health Sciences: Prof. Dr ORA STRICKLAND
Herbert Wertheim College of Medicine: Dr JOHN A. ROCK
Honors College: Dr LESLEY A. NORTHUP
Robert Stempel College of Public Health and Social Work: MICHELE CICCAZZO
School of Journalism and Mass Communication: Prof. Dr RAUL REIS
Univ. College: JOYCE J. ELAM
Univ. Graduate School: Dr LAKSHMI N. REDDI

FLORIDA MEMORIAL UNIVERSITY

15800 N W 42nd Ave, Miami Gardens, FL 33054-6155
Telephone: (305) 626-3600
Fax: (954) 714-3769
E-mail: admit@fmuniv.edu
Internet: www.fmuniv.edu
Founded 1941 by merger of Florida Baptist Institute and Florida Baptist Acad., present name and status 2006
Private control
Academic year: August to July
Pres.: Dr HENRY LEWIS, III
Provost and Vice-Pres. for Academic Affairs: Dr MAKOLA M. ABDULLAH
Vice-Pres. for Admin.: Dr HAROLD R. CLARKE, JR
Vice-Pres. for Business and Fiscal Affairs: TONY VALENTINE
Vice-Pres. for Institutional Advancement: Dr ADRIENE B. WRIGHT
Vice-Pres. for Student Affairs: Dr DANNEAL JONES, JR
Registrar: LELIA ALLEN-EFFORD
Dir of Library: GLORIA OSWALD
Library of 127,000 vols, 700 current periodicals
Number of teachers: 94 (full-time)
Number of students: 2,242

DEANS

School of Arts and Sciences: WILLIAM E. HOPPER, JR
School of Business: Prof. Dr ABBASS ENTESSARI
School of Education: Prof. Dr MILDRED E. BERRY

FLORIDA NATIONAL COLLEGE

4425 W Jose Regueiro 20th Ave, Hialeah, FL 33012
Telephone: (305) 821-3333
Fax: (305) 362-0595
E-mail: admissions@mm.fnc.edu
Internet: www.fnc.edu
Founded 1988 as Florida Int. Institute, present name 1989
Private control
Academic year: August to August (3 semesters)
Academic divs incl. allied health, business and economics, English, humanities and fine arts, nursing
Pres.: Dr MARÍA CRISTINA REGUEIRO
Vice-Pres. for Academic Affairs: CARIDAD SÁNCHEZ
Vice-Pres. for Assessment and Research and Dir of Financial Aid: OMAR SÁNCHEZ
Vice-Pres. for Operations: FRANK ANDREU
Dir of Admission: GUILLERMO ARAYA
Dir of Student Services: MAKEDA MEEKS
Registrar: JOSE LUIS VALDES
Library Dir: PATRICK BYRNES
Library of 32,045 vols.

FLORIDA SOUTHERN COLLEGE

111 Lake Hollingsworth Dr., Lakeland, FL 33801-5698
Telephone: (863) 680-4111
Fax: (863) 680-4120
E-mail: fscadm@flsouthern.edu
Internet: www.flsouthern.edu
Founded 1883 as South Florida Institute, present name 1935
Private control
Academic year: August to July
Pres.: Dr ANNE B. KERR
Provost and Vice-Pres. for Academic Affairs: Dr KYLE FEDLER
Vice-Pres. for Advancement: Dr MATTHEW R. THOMPSON
Vice-Pres. for Enrolment Management: Dr JOHN P. GRUNDIG
Vice-Pres. for External Relations: Dr ROBERT H. TATE
Vice-Pres. for Finance and Admin.: V. TERRY DENNIS
Vice-Pres. for Student Life: Dr CAROLE R. OBERMEYER
Dir of Library: RANDALL M. MacDONALD
Library of 175,213 vols, 15,412 audiovisuals
Number of teachers: 107
Number of students: 2,319 (2,185 undergraduates, 134 graduates)

DEANS

Barney Barnett School of Business and Economics: Dr WILLIAM L. RHEY
School of Arts and Sciences: Dr JAMES T. BYRD
School of Education: TRACY D. TEDDER
School of Nursing and Health Sciences: Prof. Dr JOHN M. WELTON

FLORIDA STATE COLLEGE AT JACKSONVILLE

501 W State St, Jacksonville, FL 32202-4076
Telephone: (904) 633-5950
Fax: (904) 633-5955
E-mail: justask@fscj.edu
Internet: www.fscj.edu
Founded 1966, present name 2009
State control
Academic year: August to August
Schools of arts and sciences, aviation, business, construction, manufacturing and architecture, culinary arts and hospitality, digital media and entertainment technology, education, health sciences, information technology, public safety and security, transportation
Pres.: Dr STEVEN R. WALLACE
Vice-Pres. and Provost: JUDITH BILSKY
Exec. Vice-Pres. for Instruction and Student Services: Dr DONALD W. GREEN, JR
Vice-Pres. for Admin. Services: STEVEN P. BOWERS
Vice-Pres. for Institutional Advancement: ROBERT STAMP
Vice-Pres. for Student Devt and Community Education: Dr TRACY A. PIERCE
Gen. Counsel and Vice-Pres. for Strategic Initiatives: JEANNE MILLER
Academic Dean: WENDY NORFLEET
Library of 257,473 vols, 23,320 audiovisual colln
Number of teachers: 2,147 (394 full-time, 1,753 part-time)
Number of students: 80,000

FLORIDA STATE UNIVERSITY

600 W College Ave, Tallahassee, FL 32306
Telephone: (850) 644-6200
Fax: (850) 644-0197
E-mail: admissions@admin.fsu.edu
Internet: www.fsu.edu

Founded 1851 as Seminary W of Suwannee River, present name and status 1947

State control

Academic year: August to April (2 semesters)

Satellite campus in Panama city, Florida

Chancellor of the State Univ. System: CHARLES REED

Pres.: Dr ERIC J. BARRON

Provost and Exec. Vice-Pres. for Academic Affairs: Dr GARNETT S. STOKES

Sr Vice-Pres. for Finance and Admin.: JOHN R. CARNAGHI

Vice-Pres. for Planning and Programmes: Dr ROBERT B. BRADLEY

Vice-Pres. for Research: Prof. Dr KIRBY W. KEMPER

Vice-Pres. for Student Affairs: MARY B. COBURN

Vice-Pres. for Univ. Relations: ELIZABETH MARYANSKI

Dean of the Faculties and Deputy Provost: Dr JENNIFER N. BUCHANAN

Dean of Graduate School: NANCY MARCUS (acting)

Dean of Students: Dr JEANINE WARD-ROOF

Dean of Undergraduate Studies: KAREN L. LAUGHLIN

Registrar: MAXWELL CARRAWAY

Dean of Univ. Libraries: JULIA ZIMMERMAN

Library: see Libraries and Archives

Number of teachers: 1,956

Number of students: 40,000

DEANS

College of Applied Studies: DONALD FOSS

College of Arts and Sciences: SAM HUCKABA

College of Business: Prof. CARYN L. BECK-DUDLEY

College of Communication and Information: Dr LAWRENCE C. DENNIS

College of Criminology and Criminal Justice: Prof. Dr THOMAS BLOMBERG

College of Education: Prof. Dr MARCY P. DRISCOLL

College of Engineering: Prof. JOHN COLLIER

College of Human Sciences: Dr BILLIE J. COLLIER

College of Law: Prof. DONALD J. WEIDNER

College of Medicine: Prof. Dr JOHN P. FOGARTY

College of Motion Picture Arts: Prof. Dr FRANK PATTERSON

College of Music: Prof. Dr DON GIBSON

College of Nursing: Prof. Dr DIANNE SPEAKE

College of Social Sciences and Public Policy: Prof. Dr DAVID W. RASMUSSEN

College of Social Work: Prof. Dr NICHOLAS F. MAZZA

College of Visual Arts, Theatre and Dance: Dr SALLY E. MCRORIE

GULF COAST STATE COLLEGE

5230 W Highway 98, Panama City, FL 32401

Telephone: (850) 769-1551

Internet: www.gulfcoast.edu

Founded 1957, present name 2011

State control

Academic year: August to May

Campus in Gulf; academic divs incl. business and technology, business, continuing and community education, health sciences, language and literature, mathematics, natural sciences, public safety, social sciences, visual and performing arts, wellness and athletics

Pres.: Dr JIM KERLEY

Vice-Pres. for Academic Affairs: GEORGE BISHOP

Vice-Pres. for Admin. and Finance: JOHN MERCER

Dir of Enrolment Services: SHARON TODD

Dir of Library Services: LORI DRISCOLL

Library of 100,000 vols, 275 journals, magazines and newspapers.

HOBE SOUND BIBLE COLLEGE

11298 SE Gomez Ave, POB 1065, Hobe Sound, FL 33455-1065

Telephone: (772) 546-5534

Fax: (772) 545-1422

E-mail: info@hsbc.edu

Internet: www.hsbc.edu

Founded 1960

Private control

Academic year: August to May

Offers bachelors of art in ministerial studies

Pres.: P. DANIEL STETLER

Academic Dean: Dr CLIFFORD W. CHURCHILL

Dir of Admin. Services: WESLEY HOLDEN

Dir of Admissions: JOANNA WETHERALD

Dir of Advancement: JONATHAN HEATH

Dir of Finances: KENDALL STRAIGHT

Dir of Institutional Advancement: JONATHAN HEATH

Dean of Students: JOHN S. JONES

Registrar: ANN FRENCH

Librarian: KELLY CASTORO

Library of 30,000 vols.

HODGES UNIVERSITY

2655 Northbrooke Dr., Naples, FL 34119

Telephone: (239) 513-1122

E-mail: admissions@hodges.edu

Internet: www.hodges.edu

Founded 1990 as Int. College, present name and status 2007

Private control

Academic year: September to August

Campus in Fort Myers

Pres.: Dr TERRY P. MCMAHAN

Exec. Vice-Pres. for Academic Affairs: Dr JEANETTE BROCK

Exec. Vice-Pres. for Admin.: JOHN WHITE

Vice-Pres. for Information Technology and Facilities Management: DAVE RICE

Vice-Pres. for Student Devt: RON BOWMAN

Vice-Pres. for Student Enrolment Management: RITA LAMPUS

Vice-Pres. for Student Records Management: CAROL MORRISON

Vice-Pres. for Univ. Advancement: PHIL MEMOLI

Dean of Students: Prof. Dr MARCIA BROOKS

Registrar: JENNA KAISER

Dir of Library: CAROLYNN VOLZ

Library of 30,000 vols, 59,000 e-books

Number of teachers: 158 (81 full-time, 77 part-time)

Number of students: 2,940

DEANS

Fisher School of Technology: Dr MIKE NELSON

Johnson School of Business: Dr NANCEY WYANT

Liberal Arts: ELSA ROGERS

Nichols School of Professional Studies: Dr KAREN LOCKLEAR

School of Allied Health: Dr CARLENE HARRISON

INDIAN RIVER STATE COLLEGE

3209 Virginia Ave, Fort Pierce, FL 34981-5596

Telephone: (772) 462-4772

E-mail: admissions-info@irsc.edu

Internet: www.irsc.edu

Founded 1959, present name and status 1970

State control

Academic year: August to August

Campuses in Chastain, Dixon Hendry, Mueller, St Lucie W; offers bachelor degree courses in applied science, biology, digital media, education, nursing

Pres.: Dr EDWIN R. MASSEY

Vice-Pres. for Academic Affairs: ANTHONY IACONO

Vice-Pres. for Admin. and Finance: BARRY A. KEIM

Vice-Pres. for Institutional Effectiveness: Dr CHRISTINA T. HART

Vice-Pres. for Instructional Services: Dr MARY G. LOCKE

Vice-Pres. for Student Affairs: FRANK L. WATKINS, JR

Number of students: 34,000

JACKSONVILLE UNIVERSITY

2800 University Blvd N, Jacksonville, FL 32211-3394

Telephone: (904) 256-8000

Fax: (904) 256-7012

E-mail: admissions@ju.edu

Internet: www.ju.edu

Founded 1934, present name and status 1958

Private control

Academic year: 3 semesters

Pres.: Dr KERRY D. ROMESBURG

Sr Vice-Pres. for Academic Affairs: Dr LOIS S. BECKER

Sr Vice-Pres. for Enrolment Management: TERRY WHITTUM

Vice-Pres. for Finance and Admin.: Dr GEORGE SCADUTO

Vice-Pres. for Student Life: Dr JOHN BALOG

Vice-Pres. for Univ. Advancement: MICHAEL HOWLAND

Dean of Students: Dr BRYAN COKER

Registrar: CAROLYN A. BARRETT

Dir of Library: DAVID JONES

Library of 572,000 vols

Number of teachers: 271 (166 full-time, 105 part-time)

Number of students: 3,554

Publication: *Wave* (2 a year)

DEANS

College of Arts and Sciences: Dr DOUGLAS M. HAZZARD

College of Fine Arts: BILL HILL

Davis College of Business: Dr WILLIAM M. CROSBY

School of Education: Dr CHRISTINA RAMIREZ-SMITH

School of Nursing: Dr JUDITH ERICKSON

JONES COLLEGE

5353 Arlington Expressway, Jacksonville, FL 32211-5588

Telephone: (904) 743-1122

Fax: (904) 743-4446

E-mail: info@jones.edu

Internet: www.jones.edu

Founded 1918

Private control

Academic year: September to August (3 semesters)

Areas of study incl. allied health management, business admin., computer information systems; offers bachelors degree in allied health management, business admin., computer information systems, elementary education, interdisciplinary studies, legal assistant

Pres.: Dr FRANK MCCAFFERTY

Dean of College: DEE THORNTON

Dir of Admissions: LINDA VAUGHN.

KEISER UNIVERSITY

1500 NW 49th St, Fort Lauderdale, FL 33309

Telephone: (954) 776-4456

Fax: (954) 771-4894

E-mail: admissions@keiseruniversity.edu

Internet: www.keiseruniversity.edu

Founded 1977 as Keiser School, present name and status 2006
Private control
Campuses in Daytona Beach, Fort Myers, Jacksonville, Lakeland, Melbourne, Miami, Orlando, Pembroke Pines, Port St. Lucie, Sarasota, Tallahassee, Tampa, West Palm Beach.
Chancellor and CEO: Dr ARTHUR KEISER
Vice-Chancellor for Academic Affairs: Dr WILLIAM RITCHIE
Vice-Chancellor for Student Advancement and Community Relations: BELINDA KEISER
Library of 111,740 vols
Number of students: 13,000

LYNN UNIVERSITY

3601 N Military Trail, Boca Raton, FL 33431-5598
Telephone: (561) 237-7000
Fax: (561) 237-7100
E-mail: admission@lynn.edu
Internet: www.lynn.edu
Founded 1962 as Marymount College, present name 1991
Private control
Academic year: September to May
Pres. and CEO: Dr KEVIN McANDREW ROSS
Chief Information Officer: Dr CHRISTIAN G. BONIFORTI
Sr Vice-Pres. for Admin.: GREGORY MALFITANO
Vice-Pres. for Academic Affairs: Prof. Dr GREGG COX
Vice-Pres. for Devt and Alumni Affairs: JUDI NELSON
Vice-Pres. for Student Life: Dr PHIL RIORDAN
Gen. Counsel: MARGARET E. RUDDY
Library Dir: CHARLES L. KUHN
Library of 270,000 vols (incl. books, periodicals, video cassettes, microforms)
Number of students: 2,109 (1,660 undergraduate, 449 graduate)

DEANS

College of Business and Management: Dr THOMAS KRUCZEK
College of Education: Dr CRAIG A. MERTLER
College of Hospitality Management: Dr JOSEPH A. ROONEY
College of Int. Communication: Prof. Dr DAVID L. JAFFE
College of Liberal Education: Dr KATRINA CARTER-TELLISON
Conservatory of Music: Prof. Dr JON ROBERTSON
School of Aeronautics: Major Dr JEFFREY C. JOHNSON

MIAMI DADE COLLEGE

300 N E Second Ave, Miami, FL 33132-2204
Telephone: (305) 237-8888
Fax: (305) 237-3109
E-mail: mdcinfo@mdc.edu
Internet: www.mdc.edu
Founded 1960 as Dade County Jr College, present name and status 2003
State control
Academic year: August to April
Campuses in Doral, Hialeah, Homestead, Miami; offers bachelor degree courses in applied science, science
Pres.: Dr EDUARDO J. PADRÓN
Provost: Dr ROLANDO MONTOYA
Vice-Provost For Education: Dr PAMELA G. MENKE
Exec. Dir and CEO: GLENN KAUFHOLD
Number of teachers: 668
Number of students: 174,000
Publication: *MCD Magazine.*

MIAMI INTERNATIONAL UNIVERSITY OF ART & DESIGN

1501 Biscayne Blvd, Suite 100, Miami, FL 33132-1418
Telephone: (305) 428-5700
Fax: (305) 374-5933
Internet: www.artinstitutes.edu/miami
Founded 1965
Private control
Academic year: July to June
Courses incl. bachelor of arts, science and master of arts, fine arts
Pres.: ERIKA FLEMING
Vice-Pres. for Admin and Financial Services: JOE GIANNATTASIO
Dean of Academic Affairs: PAUL COX
Dean of Student Affairs: JOHN OSBORNE
Sr Dir of Admissions: KEVIN RYAN
Library of 23,000 vols and 200 periodicals.

NEW COLLEGE OF FLORIDA

5800 Bay Shore Rd, Sarasota, FL 34243-2109
Telephone: (941) 487-5000
Fax: (941) 487-5010
E-mail: admissions@ncf.edu
Internet: www.ncf.edu
Founded 1960
State control
Academic year: August to May (2 semesters)
Pres.: Prof. Dr GORDON E. MICHALSON, JR
Provost and Vice-Pres. of Academic Affairs: Prof. Dr STEPHEN MILES
Vice-Pres. for Admin. and Finance: JOHN U. MARTIN
Dean of Students: WENDY BASHANT
Dean of Enrolment Services and Information Technology: KATHLEEN KILLION
Registrar: KATHLEEN ALLEN
Dean of the Library: Dr BRIAN DOHERTY
Library of 285,897 vols, 1,174 current serials received, 540,234 microforms, 165 e-books, 8,400 audiovisual, 4,210 video cassettes
Number of teachers: 71 (full-time)
Number of students: 801

PROFESSORS

Division of Humanities:

CARRASCO, M. E., Art History
CUOMO, G. R., German Language and Literature
EDIDIN, A. Z., Philosophy
HASSOLD, C., Art History
LANGSTON, D. C., Philosophy and Religion
MICHALSON, G. E., Humanities

Division of Natural Sciences:

BEULIG, A., Biology
DEMSKI, L. S., Biology
GILCHRIST, S., Biology
LOWMAN, M., Biology and Environmental Studies
RUPPEINER, G., Physics
SCUDDER, P., Chemistry

Division of Social Sciences:

ANTHONY, A. P., Art History
DOENECKE, J., History
ELLIOTT, C., Economics
LEWIS, E., Political Science
STROBEL, F., Economics
VESPERI, M. D., Anthropology

NORTHWEST FLORIDA STATE COLLEGE

100 College Blvd, Niceville, FL 32578-1295
Telephone: (850) 678-5111
Fax: (850) 729-5208
E-mail: registrar@nwfsc.edu
Internet: www.nwfsc.edu
Founded 1964 as Okaloosa-Walton Jr College, present name and status 2008

State control
Academic year: August to May (3 semesters)
Campuses in Chautauqua Centre, Fort Walton Beach, Eglin AF Base Centre, Hurlburt Field Centre, Robert L. F. Sikes Education Centre, S Walton Centre; depts of adult gen. education, advanced technology and design, athletics, health and fitness, business and computer technology, English and communications, humanities, fine and performing arts, mathematics, nursing and allied health, public safety
Pres.: Dr TY HANDY
Vice-Pres. for Academic Affairs: Dr SASHA L. JARRELL
Vice-Pres. for Admin. Services: Dr GARY YANCEY
Registrar and Dean of Enrolment Services: CHRISTINE C. BISHOP
Library Dir: JANICE HENDERSON
Library of 106,260 vols, 5,701 audiovisuals, 30,000 e-books
Number of teachers: 310 (95 full-time and 215 part-time)
Number of students: 17,021

NOVA SOUTHEASTERN UNIVERSITY

3301 College Ave, Fort Lauderdale-Davie, FL 33314-7796
Telephone: (954) 262-8000
Fax: (954) 262-3811
E-mail: admissions@nova.edu
Internet: www.nova.edu
Founded 1994, by merger of Nova Univ., Southeastern Univ. of Health Sciences
Private control
Academic year: July to June
Pres. and CEO: Dr GEORGE L. HANBURY, II
Chancellor of Health Professions Div.: Dr FREDERICK LIPPMAN
Provost and Exec. Vice-Pres. for Academic Affairs: Dr FRANK DE PIANO
Exec. Vice-Pres. and Chief Operating Officer: JACQUELINE A. TRAVISANO
Vice-Pres. for Community and Govt Affairs: Dr LARRY A. CALDERON
Vice-Pres. for Enrolment and Student Services: STEPHANIE G. BROWN
Vice-Pres. for Financial Operations: W. DAVID HERON
Vice-Pres. for Information Services and Univ. Librarian: DONALD E. RIGGS
Vice-Pres. for Institutional Advancement: Dr JOE PINEDA
Vice Pres. for Institutional Effectiveness: Dr RONALD CHENAIL
Exec. Dir for Univ. Relations: DAVID C. DAWSON
Dean for Student Affairs: Dr BRAD A. WILLIAMS
Registrar: ELAINE POFF
Library: 1.4m. vols
Number of teachers: 723
Number of students: 29,000
Publications: *Digressions* (1 a year), *Farquhar Student Journal* (2 a year (online)), *ILSA Journal of International and Comparative Law* (3 a year), *International Travel Law Journal* (3 a year), *Internet Journal of Allied Health Sciences and Practice* (6 a year), *Nova Law Review* (3 a year), *Nova Lawyer* (1 a year), *Peace and Conflict Studies* (2 a year), *The Qualitative Report* (4 a year), *Viewpoint* (3 a year)

DEANS

Abraham S. Fischler School of Education: Dr H. WELLS SINGLETON
Center for Psychological Studies: Dr KAREN S. GROSBY
College of Dental Medicine: Dr ROBERT UCHIN
College of Health Care Sciences: Dr RICHARD E. DAVIS

College of Medical Sciences: Dr HAROLD E. LAUBACH
College of Nursing: Dr MARCELLA RUTHERFORD
College of Optometry: Dr DAVID S. LOSHIN
College of Osteopathic Medicine: Dr ANTHONY J. SILVAGNI
College of Pharmacy: Dr ANDRÉS MALAVÉ
Farquhar College of Arts and Sciences: Dr DONALD ROSENBLUM
Fischler School of Education and Human Services: Dr H. WELLS SINGLETON (Dean and Provost)
Graduate School of Computer and Information Sciences: Dr ERIC S. ACKERMAN
Graduate School of Humanities and Social Sciences: Dr HONGGANG YANG
H. Wayne Huizenga School of Business and Entrepreneurship: Dr J. PRESTON JAMES
Mailman Segal Centre for Human Development: Dr RONI COHEN LIEDERMAN
Oceanographic Center: Prof. Dr RICHARD E. DODGE
School of Humanities and Social Sciences: Dr HONGGANG YANG
Shepard Broad Law Center: Prof. ATHORNIA STEELE
Univ. School: Dr JEROME S. CHERMAK

PALM BEACH ATLANTIC UNIVERSITY

POB 24708, West Palm Beach, FL 33416-4708
901 S Flagler Dr., West Palm Beach, FL 33401
Telephone: (561) 803-2000
E-mail: admit@pba.edu
Internet: www.pba.edu
Founded 1968
Campuses in Orlando, Wellington
Private control
Academic year: August to May
Pres.: Dr WILLIAM M. B. FLEMING, JR
Provost: Prof. Dr JOSEPH A. KLOBA
Vice-Pres. and Chief Financial Officer: GEORGE GALL
Vice-Pres. for Enrolment Services: BUCKLEY A. JAMES
Vice-Pres. for Student Devt: Dr MARY ANN SEARLE
Dean of Students: KEVIN ABEL
Registrar: AUDREY SCHOFIELD
Library Dean: STEVEN BAKER
Library of 350,000 vols
Number of teachers: 156 (full-time)
Number of students: 3,663

DEANS

Catherine T. MacArthur School of Leadership: Prof. Dr JIM LAUB
Gregory School of Pharmacy: Prof. Dr MARY FERRILL
Rinker School of Business: Prof. Dr LESLIE TURNER
School of Arts and Sciences: Prof. Dr BARTON STARR
School of Communication and Media: Dr DUANE MEEKS
School of Education and Behavioural Studies: Dr GENE SALE
School of Ministry: Prof. Dr RANDY RICHARDS
School of Music and Fine Arts: Prof. Dr LLOYD MIMS
School of Nursing: Prof. Dr JOANNE MASELLA

PALM BEACH STATE COLLEGE

4200 Congress Ave, Lake Worth, FL 33461-4796
Telephone: (561) 868-3350
Fax: (561) 868-3584
E-mail: enrollmt@palmbeachstate.edu
Internet: www.palmbeachstate.edu

Founded 1933 as Palm Beach Jr College, present status 2009, present name 2010
State control
Academic year: August to August
Campuses in Belle Glade, Boca Raton, Palm Beach Gardens, W Palm Beach; offers bachelors degree courses in applied sciences, sciences
Pres.: Dr DENNIS P. GALLON
Vice-Pres. for Academic Affairs: Dr SHARON A. SASS
Vice-Pres. for Admin. and Business Services: RICHARD A. BECKER
Vice-Pres. for Student Services and Enrolment Management: PATRICIA J. ANDERSON
Provost: Dr MARÍA M. VALLEJO
Gen. Counsel: DENISE WALLACE
Registrar: EDWARD MUELLER
Library of 10,000 vols, 2,000 journals and periodicals
Number of students: 51,248

PENSACOLA STATE COLLEGE

1000 College Blvd, Pensacola, FL 32504
Telephone: (850) 484-1000
Fax: (850) 484-1711
E-mail: askus@pensacolastate.edu
Internet: www.pensacolastate.edu
Founded 1948 as Pensacola Jr College, present name and status 2010
State control
Academic year: August to August
Campuses in Pensacola, Milton, Warrington; depts of allied health, biological sciences, education, engineering, English and communications, health science, history, languages and social sciences, mathematics, nursing, performing arts, physical sciences, visual arts
Pres.: Dr C. EDWARD MEADOWS
Vice-Pres. for Academic Affairs: Dr ERIN SPICER
Vice-Pres. for Business Affairs: GEAN ANN EMOND
Vice-Pres. for Instructional Affairs: Dr MARTIN GONZALEZ
Vice-Pres. for Student Affairs and Gen. Counsel: THOMAS J. GILLIAM, JR
Dean of Milton Campus: Dr ANTHEA AMOS
Number of teachers: 584 (184 full-time, 400 part-time)
Number of students: 28,000

POLK STATE COLLEGE

999 Ave H NE, Winter Haven, FL 33881-4299
Telephone: (863) 297-1000
Fax: (863) 297-1023
E-mail: registrar@polk.edu
Internet: www.polk.edu
Founded 1964, present name and status 2009
State control
Academic year: August to August
Campuses in Lakeland, Winter Haven; offers bachelors degree in applied science
Pres.: Dr EILEEN HOLDEN
Vice-Pres. for Academic and Student Services: Dr KENNETH ROSS
Vice-Pres. for Admin. and Chief Financial Officer: PETER S. ELLIOTT
Provost for Lakeland Campus: STEVE HULL
Provost for Winter Haven Campus: Dr SHARON E. MILLER
Dir of Financial Services: (vacant)
Dir of Institutional Research, Effectiveness and Planning: PETER USINGER
Library of 93,000 vols
Number of teachers: 100 (full-time)
Number of students: 12,900

RINGLING COLLEGE OF ART AND DESIGN

2700 N Tamiami Trail, Sarasota, FL 34234-5895
Telephone: (941) 3515100
Fax: (941) 3597517
E-mail: admissions@ringling.edu
Internet: www.ringling.edu
Founded 1931
Private control
Academic year: August to May
Courses incl. advertising design, business of art and design, computer animation, digital filmmaking, gen. fine arts, game art and design, graphic and interactive communication, illustration, interior design, motion design, photography and digital imaging
Pres.: Dr LARRY R. THOMPSON
Vice-Pres. for Academic Affairs: MELODY WEILER
Vice-Pres. for Finance and Admin.: TRACY A. WAGNER
Vice-Pres. for Institutional Advancement: (vacant)
Vice-Pres. for Student Life and Dean of Students: Dr TAMMY S. WALSH
Dean of Admissions: JAMES H. DEAN
Dir of Library Services: KATHLEEN LIST
Library of 55,000 vols, 6,100 DVDs and audiovisual items, 350 periodicals, 127,000 35-mm slides
Number of teachers: 130
Number of students: 1,300

ROLLINS COLLEGE

1000 Holt Ave, Winter Park, FL 32789-4499
Telephone: (407) 646-2000
Fax: (407) 646-1502
E-mail: admission@rollins.edu
Internet: www.rollins.edu
Founded 1885
Private control
Academic year: September to May
Pres.: Dr LEWIS M. DUNCAN
Provost and Vice-Pres. for Academic Affairs: Dr CAROL M. BRESNAHAN
Vice-Pres. for Business and Finance and Treas.: JEFFREY G. EISENBARTH
Vice-Pres. for Institutional Advancement: RONALD J. KORVAS
Vice-Pres. for Planning and Dean of College: Dr LAURIE M. JOYNER
Dean of Admissions and Enrolment: DAVID G. ERDMANN
Dean of Faculty: Dr ROBERT SMITHER
Dean of Student Affairs: Dr KAREN L. HATER
Library Dir: JONATHAN MILLER
Library of 303,000 vols, 1,600 current periodicals
Number of teachers: 210
Number of students: 3,272 (2,615 undergraduate, 657 graduate).
Publications: *Alumni Record* (4 a year), *Brushing* (1 a year)

DEANS

College of Arts and Sciences: Dr ROBERT SMITHER
College of Professional Studies: Dr DEBRA K. WELLMAN
Crummer Graduate School of Business: CRAIG M. McALLASTER
Hamilton Holt School: Dr DEBRA K. WELLMAN

SAINT LEO UNIVERSITY

33701 State Rd 52, POB 6665, Saint Leo, FL 33574-6665
Telephone: (352) 588-8200
Fax: (352) 588-8654
E-mail: news@saintleo.edu
Internet: www.saintleo.edu

Founded 1889, present name and status 1999
Private control
Academic year: August to April (2 semesters)
Pres.: Dr ARTHUR F. KIRK, JR
Vice-Pres. for Academic Affairs: Dr MARIBETH DURST
Vice-Pres. for Business Affairs and Chief Financial Officer: FRANK MEZZANINI
Vice-Pres. for Enrolment and Online Programs: KATHRYN MCFARLAND
Vice-Pres. for Student Services: Dr EDWARD DADEZ
Dir of Univ. Advancement: DAVID OSTRANDER
Registrar: KAREN HATFIELD
Dir of Library Services: BRENT SHORT
Library of 152,584 vols
Number of teachers: 1,287
Number of students: 15,565

DEANS

Donald R. Tapia School of Business: Dr MICHAEL NASTANSKI
School of Arts and Sciences: Dr MARY T. SPOTO
School of Education and Social Services: Dr CAROL G. WALKER

ST JOHNS RIVER STATE COLLEGE

5001 St Johns Ave, Palatka, FL 32177-3807
Telephone: (386) 312-4200
Fax: (386) 312-4292
E-mail: bachelorsprograms@sjrstate.edu
Internet: www.sjrstate.edu

Founded 1958 as St Johns River Jr College, present name and status 2010
State control
Academic year: August to August
Campuses in Orange Park, Palatka, St Augustine
Pres. and Chair.: JOE H. PICKENS
Exec. Vice-Pres.: MELISSA C. MILLER
Vice-Pres. for Academic Affairs: Dr MELANIE A. BROWN
Vice-Pres. for Admin. Affairs: ANNETTE W. BARRINEAU
Vice-Pres. for Business Affairs: ALBERT P. LITTLE
Vice-Pres. for Devt and External Affairs: CAROLINE D. TINGLE
Vice-Pres. for Finance and Admin.: ALBERT P. LITTLE
Vice-Pres. for Research and Institutional Effectiveness: Dr ROSALIND M. HUMERICK
Vice-Pres. for Student Affairs: Dr GILBERT L. EVANS, JR
Chief Information Officer: PAUL M. HAWKINS
Provost for St Augustine Campus: Dr GREGORY K. MCLEOD
Provost for Orange Park Campus: JAMES C. ROY
Dir of Admissions and Records: SUSANNE LINEBERGER
Dean of Library Services: CARMEN M. CUMMINGS
Library of 65,000 vols, 3,000 journals, 30,000 e-books
Number of teachers: 113 (full-time)
Number of students: 7,468 (2,501 full-time, 4,967 part-time)

DEANS

Allied Health: Dr THOMAS D. BAXTER
Arts and Sciences: Dr LAURA L. BOILINI
Florida School of Arts: ALAN R. HENTSCHEL
Nursing: Dr MARY ANNE LANEY

ST JOHN VIANNEY COLLEGE SEMINARY

2900 SW 87th Ave, Miami, FL 33165-3244
Telephone: (305) 223-4561
Fax: (305) 223-0650
E-mail: sjvcsadmin@gmail.com

Internet: www.sjvcs.edu

Founded 1959 as St John Vianney Seminary; present name 1977
Private control
Offers Catholic education, priestly formation
Rector and Pres.: Rev. ROBERTO GARZA
Dean of Students: Rev. LUCIEN E. PIERRE
Academic Dean: Dr RAMÓN J. SANTOS
Registrar: BONNIE DE ANGULO
Library Dir: MARIA RODRIGUEZ
Library of 50,000 vols
Number of teachers: 22

ST PETERSBURG COLLEGE

POB 13489, St Petersburg, FL 33733-3489
Telephone: (727) 341-4772
Fax: (727) 341-3231
E-mail: information@spcollege.edu
Internet: www.spcollege.edu

Founded 1927 as St Petersburg Jr College, present name and status 2002
State control
Academic year: August to July
Pres.: Dr WILLIAM D. LAW, JR
Sr Vice-Pres. for Academic and Student Affairs: Dr ANNE M. COOPER
Sr Vice-Pres. for Admin., Business Services and Information Technology: Dr DOUGLAS S. DUNCAN
Vice-Pres. for Economic Devt and Innovative Projects: DENNIS L. JONES
Vice-Pres. for Institutional Advancement: FRANCES Z. NEU
Gen. Counsel: SUZANNE GARDNER (acting)
Dir of Learning Resources: JOSEPH LEOPOLD
Library of 250,000 vols, 25,000 e-journals and periodicals and 57,000 e-books
Number of teachers: 1,738 (309 full-time, 1,429 part time)
Number of students: 33,938

DEANS

College of Education: KIMBERLY HARTMAN
College of Health Sciences: TAMI J. GRZESIKOWSKI
College of Nursing: SUSAN BAKER (acting)
College of Public Safety Admin.: BRIAN FRANK
College of Technology and Management: GREGORY NENSTIEL
Paralegal Studies: SUSAN DEMERS
School of Veterinary Technology: Dr RICHARD M. FLORA

ST THOMAS UNIVERSITY

16401 NW 37th Ave, Miami Gardens, Miami, FL 33054-6459
Telephone: (305) 628-6546
Fax: (305) 628-6591
E-mail: signup@stu.edu
Internet: www.stu.edu

Founded 1961 as Biscayne College, present name and status 1984
Private control
Academic year: August to May
Pres.: Rev. FRANKLYN M. CASALE
Provost and Chief Academic Officer: Dr GREGORY S. CHAN
Vice-Pres. for Admin. and Chief Financial Officer: TERRENCE L. O'CONNOR
Vice-Pres. for Planning and Enrolment: Dr BEATRIZ GONZALEZ ROBINSON
Vice-Pres. for Student Affairs: Dr SARAH SHUMATE
Vice-Pres. for Univ. Advancement: BEVERLY S. BACHRACH
Dean of Academic Support: BARBARA SINGER
Dean of Enrolment: ANDRE LIGHTBOURN
Dean of Graduate Studies: Dr JOSEPH A. IANNONE
Dean of Undergraduate Studies: Dr GUIYOU HUANG

Dean of Students: ISSAC M. CARTER
Registrar: IRAIDA ACEBO
Library Admin.: JONATHAN C. ROACH
Library of 275,106 vols, 99,000 e-books, 600 print journal, newspaper titles
Number of teachers: 113 (54 full-time, 59 part-time)
Number of students: 2,501
Publications: Journal of Multidisciplinary Research, St Thomas Law Review (1 a year)

DEANS

Biscayne College of Liberal Arts and Social Sciences: Prof. Dr SCOTT C. ZEMAN
School of Business: Prof. Dr J. ANTONIO VILLAMIL
School of Law: Prof. Dr DOUGLAS E. RAY
School of Leadership Studies: Dr SUSAN B. ANGULO
School of Science, Technology and Engineering Management: Dr WIM F. A. STEELANT
School of Theology and Ministry: MARY CARTER WAREN

ST VINCENT DE PAUL REGIONAL SEMINARY

10701 S Military Trail, Boynton Beach, FL 33436-4899
Telephone: (561) 732-4424
Fax: (561) 737-2205
Internet: www.svdp.edu

Founded 1963
Private control
Academic year: August to May (2 semesters)
Offers master of art, divinity
Rector, Pres. and Dean of Formation: Rev. KEITH BRENNAN
Vice-Rector and Dean of Human Formation: Rev. JOSÉ N. ALFARO
Academic Dean: Rev. Dr DEACON DENNIS T. DEMES
Dean of Pastoral Formation: Rev. LOUIS GUERIN
Dean of Spiritual Formation: Rev. STEPHEN OLDS
Treas. and Campus Admin.: KEITH PARKER
Library Dir: ARTHUR G. QUINN
Library of 81,000 vols, 3,000 bound periodicals, 1,500 audiovisuals
Number of teachers: 30
Publication: St Vincent's (2 a year).

SCHILLER INTERNATIONAL UNIVERSITY—FLORIDA

(For general information, see entry for Schiller International University in Germany chapter)

8560 Ulmerton Rd, Largo, FL 33771
Telephone: (727) 474-4080
Fax: (727) 734-0359
E-mail: admissions@schiller.edu
Internet: www.schiller.edu

Founded 1964
Private control
Academic year: September to June (3 semesters)

Int. campuses in France, Germany, Spain; offers degrees in business admin., financial planning, interdisciplinary studies, int. business, int. economics, int. hospitality and tourism, int. management, int. relations and diplomacy, management of information technology
Pres.: MICHELE GEIGLE
Provost: ANGELA CARNEY
Registrar: STEPHANIE HAGEN
Librarian: JEANNE GROSSMAN
Number of teachers: 40
Number of students: 250

SEMINOLE STATE COLLEGE OF FLORIDA

100 Weldon Blvd, Sanford, FL 32773-6199
Telephone: (407) 708-2106
Fax: (407) 708-2029
E-mail: admissions@seminolestate.edu
Internet: www.seminolestate.edu
Founded 1966 as Seminole Jr College, present name and status 2009
State control
Academic year: August to July
Campuses in Altamonte Springs, Heathrow, Oviedo, Sanford/Lake Mary; offers bachelor degrees in applied science, science
Pres.: Dr E. ANN McGEE
Exec. Vice-Pres. for Admin. Services and Chief Financial Officer: Dr JOE SARNOVSKY
Vice-Pres. for Academic Affairs and Chief Academic Officer: JIM HENNINGSEN
Vice-Pres. for Information Technology and Resources and Chief Information Officer: DICK HAMANN
Vice-Pres. for Student Affairs and Chief Student Affairs Officer: Dr MARCIA ROMAN
Dean of Libraries and Learning Technology: PATRICIA S. DeSALVO
Number of teachers: 784 (552 full-time, 232 part-time)
Number of students: 32,771

SOUTHEASTERN UNIVERSITY

1000 Longfellow Blvd, Lakeland, FL 33801
Telephone: (863) 667-5000
Fax: (863) 667-5200
E-mail: info@seu.edu
Internet: www.seu.edu
Founded 1935 as South-Eastern Bible Institute, present name and status 2005
Private control
Academic year: August to May (3 semesters)
Pres.: Dr KENT INGLE
Exec. Vice-Pres.: DEL CHITTIM
Vice-Pres. for Academic Affairs: Prof. Dr WILLIAM HACKETT
Vice-Pres. for Enrolment Management: ROY ROWLAND, IV
Vice-Pres. for Finance and Admin.: DAN MORTENSEN
Vice-Pres. for Student Devt: CHRIS OWENS
Vice-Pres. for Univ. Advancement: BRIAN C. CARROLL
Registrar: LINDA KELSO
Dir of Admission: BETANIA TORRES
Dean of Student Services: DARRELL HARDT
Dean of Library Services: GRACE VEACH
Library of 100,000 vols, 800 periodicals, 32,000 e-books
Number of teachers: 98
Number of students: 2,900

DEANS

College of Arts and Sciences: Dr GORDON MILLER
College of Business and Legal Studies: Dr R. JOSEPH CHILDS
College of Christian Ministries and Religion: Dr ROBERT HOULIHAN
College of Education: Dr DOUG ROTH

STATE COLLEGE OF FLORIDA, MANATEE—SARASOTA

POB 1849, Bradenton, FL 34206
5840 26 St W, Bradenton, FL 34207
Telephone: (941) 752-5000
Fax: (941) 752-8185
E-mail: records@scf.edu
Internet: www.scf.edu
Founded 1957 as Manatee Jr College, present name and status 2009
State control

Academic year: August to August (3 semesters)
Campuses in Lakewood Ranch, Venice
Pres.: Dr LARS A. HAFNER
Vice-Pres. for Academic Quality and Success: Dr W. JACK CROCKER
Vice-Pres. for Baccalaureate Programmes: Dr MICHAEL J. MEARS
Vice-Pres. for Business and Admin. Services: CAROL PROBSTFELD
Vice-Pres. for Educational and Student Services: DONALD BOWMAN
Library Dir: TRACY ELLIOTT
Library of 96,670 vols, 292 periodicals and 34,319 e-books,
Number of teachers: 136 (full-time)
Number of students: 11,500

DEANS

Nursing and Health Professions: Dr BONNIE HESSELBERG

STETSON UNIVERSITY

421 N Woodland Blvd, DeLand, FL 32723
Telephone: (386) 822-7100
Fax: (904) 822-8925
E-mail: admissions@stetson.edu
Internet: www.stetson.edu
Founded 1883 as DeLand Acad., DeLand Univ. 1887, present name 1889
Private control
Academic year: August to July
Campus in St Petersburg; satellite centres in Celebration, Tampa
Pres.: Dr WENDY B. LIBBY
Provost and Vice-Pres. for Academic Affairs: Dr ELIZABETH PAUL
Vice-Pres. for Business and Chief Operating Officer: Dr F. ROBERT HUTH, JR
Vice-Pres. for Campus Life: RINA TOVAR
Vice-Pres. for Enrolment Management: JOEL BAUMAN
Vice-Pres. for Students Affairs and Dean of Students: CHRISTOPHER M. KANDUS-FISHER
Vice-Pres. for Univ. Relations: CAROL L. JULIAN
Dean for Admissions: REBECCA R. ECKSTEIN
Registrar: TERRI M. RICHARDS
Library of 330,000 vols and 245,000 govt documents
Number of teachers: 195 (full-time, DeLand campus)
Number of students: 3,255 (2,505 in DeLand, 750 at College of Law in St Petersburg)
Publications: *Alumni Magazine, Stetson Lawyer-Alumni Magazine* (2 a year), *Stetson University Magazine* (2 a year), *The Cupola* (2 a year), *Touchstone* (1 a year), *Visual* (2 a year)

DEANS

College of Arts and Sciences: Dr GRADY W. BALLENGER
College of Law: Prof. Dr ROYAL C. GARDNER
School of Business Administration: Dr STUART MICHELSON
School of Music: Prof. Dr JEAN OHLSSON WEST

UNIVERSITY OF CENTRAL FLORIDA

POB 160000, Orlando FL 32816
4000 Central Florida Blvd, Orlando, FL 32816
Telephone: (407) 823-2000
Fax: (407) 823-5625
E-mail: admission@mail.ucf.edu
Internet: www.ucf.edu
Founded 1963 as Florida Technological Univ., present name 1978
State control
Academic year: August to August (3 semesters)

Pres.: Dr JOHN C. HITT
Provost and Exec. Vice-Pres.: Dr TONY WALDROP
Vice-Pres. and Chief of Staff: Dr JOHN F. SCHELL
Vice-Pres. for Admin. and Finance: WILLIAM F. MERCK, II
Vice-Pres. for Devt and Alumni Relations: ROBERT J. HOLMES, JR
Vice-Pres. for Research and Commercialization: Dr M. J. SOILEAU
Vice-Pres. for Student Devt and Enrolment Services: Dr MARIBETH EHASZ
Vice-Pres. for Univ. Relations: Dr DANIEL C. HOLSENBECK
Dean of Undergraduate Studies and Vice-Provost: Dr ELLIOT VITTES
Registrar: Dr DENNIS J. DULNIAK
Dir of Univ. Libraries: BARRY B. BAKER
Library: 2m. vols, 593,000 e-books, 326,310 govt. documents, 29,659 current periodicals, 3,092,514 microforms, 50,517 audiovisual items
Number of teachers: 1,827
Number of students: 58,587

DEANS

Burnett Honors College: Prof. Dr ALVIN WANG
College of Arts and Humanities: Dr JOSÉ FERNÁNDEZ
College of Business Admin.: Dr FOARD F. JONES
College of Education: Dr SANDRA L. ROBINSON
College of Engineering and Computer Science: Dr MARWAN A. SIMAAN
College of Graduate Studies: PATRICIA BISHOP
College of Health and Public Affairs: Dr MICHAEL L. FRUMKIN
College of Medicine: Dr DEBORAH C. GERMAN
College of Nursing: JEAN D'MEZA LEUNER
College of Optics and Photonics: Prof. Dr BAHAA E. A. SALEH
College of Sciences: Prof. Dr MICHAEL D. JOHNSON
Rosen College of Hospitality Management: Dr ABRAHAM PIZAM

UNIVERSITY OF FLORIDA

Gainesville, FL 32611-3150
Telephone: (352) 392-3261
Fax: (352) 392-2115
E-mail: gradschool@ufl.edu
Internet: www.ufl.edu
Founded 1853, present name 1905
State control
Academic year: August to September
Pres.: Dr JAMES BERNARD MACHEN
Provost and Sr Vice-Pres. for Academic Affairs: Dr JOE GLOVER
Sr Vice-Pres. for Health Affairs: Dr DAVID S. GUZICK
Vice-Pres. and Chief Information Officer: Dr ELIAS ELDAYRIE
Vice-Pres. and Gen. Counsel: JAMIE LEWIS KEITH
Vice-Pres. for Business Affairs and Economic Devt: CURTIS REYNOLDS
Vice-Pres. for Devt and Alumni Affairs: THOMAS J. MITCHELL
Vice-Pres. and Chief Financial Officer: MATTHEW FAJACK
Vice-Pres. for Enrolment Management and Assoc. Provost: Dr ZINA EVANS
Vice-Pres. for Research: WINFRED M. PHILLIPS
Vice-Pres. for Student Affairs: DAVE KRATZER
Vice-Pres. for Univ. Relations: JANE ADAMS
Univ. Registrar: STEPHEN J. PRITZ, JR
Dean of Students: Dr JEN DAY SHAW
Dean of Univ. Libraries: JUDITH RUSSELL
Library: see Libraries and Archives
Number of teachers: 5,434

Number of students: 52,271 (36,386 undergraduate, 15,885 graduate)

Publications: *Florida Historical Quarterly*, *Journal of Politics*, *Southern Folklore Quarterly*, *University of Florida Law Review*, *UF Law*

DEANS

College of Agricultural and Life Sciences: Dr TERESA BALSER

College of Dentistry: Prof. Dr TERESA A. DOLAN

College of Design, Construction and Planning: Prof. Dr CHRISTOPHER SILVER

College of Education: Prof. Dr GLENN E. GOOD

College of Engineering: CAMMY R. ABERNATHY

College of Fine Arts: LUCINDA LAVELLI

College of Health and Human Performance: Prof. Dr STEVE M. DORMAN

College of Journalism and Communications: Prof. Dr JOHN W. WRIGHT, II

College of Liberal Arts and Sciences: PAUL J. D'ANIERI

College of Medicine: Dr MICHAEL L. GOOD

College of Nursing: Dr KATHLEEN ANN LONG

College of Pharmacy: Prof. Dr WILLIAM H. RIFFEE

College of Public Health and Health Professions: Dr MICHAEL G. PERRI

College of Veterinary Medicine: Dr GLEN F. HOFFSIS

Graduate School: Dr HENRY FRIERSON

Institute of Food and Agricultural Sciences: Dr MILLIE FERRER-CHANCY

Levin College of Law: ROBERT JERRY

Warrington College of Business Admin.: JOHN KRAFT

UNIVERSITY OF MIAMI

Coral Gables, FL 33124

Telephone: (305) 284-2211

Fax: (305) 284-4985

E-mail: admission@miami.edu

Internet: www.miami.edu

Founded 1925

Private control

Academic year: September to May (2 terms)

Pres.: DONNA E. SHALALA

Provost and Exec. Vice-Pres.: Dr THOMAS J. LEBLANC

Sr Vice-Pres. for Business and Finance and Chief Financial Officer: JOSEPH T. NATOLI

Sr Vice-Pres. for Medical Affairs: Dr PASCAL J. GOLDSCHMIDT

Sr Vice-Pres. for Univ. Advancement and External Affairs: SERGIO M. GONZALEZ

Vice-Pres., Gen. Counsel and Sec. of the Univ.: AILEEN M. UGALDE

Vice-Pres. for Finance and Treas.: JOHN R. SHIPLEY

Vice-Pres. for Enrolment Management and Continuing Studies: PAUL M. OREHOVEC

Vice-Pres. for Govt Affairs: RODOLFO J. FERNANDEZ

Vice-Pres. for Information Technology and Chief Information Officer: STEVE CAWLEY

Vice-Pres. for Student Affairs: PATRICIA A. WHITELY

Dean of Undergraduate Education and Sr Vice-Provost: WILLIAM SCOTT GREEN

Dean of Libraries: WILLIAM D. WALKER

Library: 4.1m. vols, 86,740 current serials titles, 83,789 e-journals, 630,755 e-books, 4m. microforms, 176,052 audiovisual materials

Number of teachers: 3,084 (2,617 full-time, 467 part-time)

Number of students: 16,068 (14,736 full-time, 1,332 part-time)

Publications: *Journal of Inter-American Studies* (4 a year), *Medicine* (3 a year), *Miami* (3 a year), *World Affairs* (4 a year)

DEANS

College of Arts and Sciences: Dr LEONIDAS G. BACHAS

College of Engineering: Dr JAMES M. TIEN

Graduate School: Dr TERRI A. SCANDURA

Miller School of Medicine: Dr PASCAL J. GOLDSCHMIDT

Phillip and Patricia Frost School of Music: Dr SHELTON G. BERG

Rosenstiel School of Marine and Atmospheric Sciences: Dr RONI AVISSAR

School of Architecture: ELIZABETH PLATER-ZYBERK

School of Business Admin.: Dr EUGENE W. ANDERSON

School of Communication: GREGORY J. SHEPHERD

School of Education: Dr ISAAC PRILLELTENSKY

School of Law: Dr PATRICIA D. WHITE

School of Nursing and Health Studies: NILDA P. PERAGALLO

UNIVERSITY OF NORTH FLORIDA

1 UNF Dr, Jacksonville, FL 32224-2645

Telephone: (904) 620-1000

Fax: (904) 620-2299

E-mail: admissions@unf.edu

Internet: www.unf.edu

Founded 1972

State control

Academic year: August to August

Pres.: Prof. JOHN A. DELANEY

Provost and Vice-Pres. for Academic Affairs: Dr MARK E. WORKMAN

Vice-Pres. and Chief of Staff: Dr THOMAS S. SERWATKA

Vice-Pres. and Gen. Counsel: KAREN J. STONE

Vice-Pres. for Admin. and Finance: SHARI SHUMAN

Vice-Pres. for Institutional Advancement: Dr PIERRE N. ALLAIRE

Vice-Pres. for Student and Int. Affairs: Dr MAURICIO GONZALEZ

Dean of Continuing Education: ROBERT L. WOOD

Dean of Graduate School: Dr LEN ROBERSON

Dean for Undergraduate Studies: Dr JEFFREY COKER

Dean of Library: Dr SHIRLEY HALLBLADE

Library of 840,423 vols, 2,800 serial journals, 32,875 e-journals, 53,252 e-books, 21,521 audio items, 8,753 video materials, 8,528 maps, 1.5m. microforms

Number of teachers: 510 (full-time)

Number of students: 16,317 (13,711 undergraduate, 1,804 graduate)

DEANS

Brooks College of Health: Prof. Dr PAMELA S. CHALLY

Coggin College of Business Admin.: Prof. Dr AJAY SAMANT

College of Arts and Sciences: Dr BARBARA A. HETRICK

College of Computing, Engineering and Construction: Dr MARK A. TUMEO

College of Education and Human Services: Dr LARRY DANIEL

UNIVERSITY OF SOUTH FLORIDA

4202 E Fowler Ave, Tampa, FL 33620

Telephone: (813) 974-2011

E-mail: info@admin.usf.edu

Internet: www.usf.edu

Founded 1956

State control

Academic year: August to July (3 semesters

Campuses in Lakeland, Sarasota-Manatee, St Petersburg

Pres.: Dr JUDY LYNN GENSHAFT

Provost and Exec. Vice-Pres.: Dr RALPH WILCOX

Sr Vice-Pres. for Research, Innovation and Global Affairs: Dr KAREN A. HOLBROOK

Sr Vice-Pres. for Univ. Advancement: JOEL MOMBERG

Vice-Pres. for Admin. Affairs: SANDY LOVINS

Vice-Pres. of Student Affairs: Dr JENNIFER MENINGALL

Chief Operating Officer: JOHN LONG

Regional Chancellor and Campus Chief Exec. Officer for Lakeland: Dr MARSHALL GOODMAN

Regional Chancellor and Campus Chief Exec. Officer for Sarasota-Manatee: Dr ARTHUR M. GUILFORD

Regional Chancellor and Campus Chief Exec. Officer for St Petersburg: Dr MARGARET SULLIVAN

Dean of Graduate School: Dr KAREN LILLER

Dean of Undergraduate Studies: Dr W. ROBERT SULLINS

Exec. Dir of Univ. College: Dr SANDRA COOPER

Registrar: LINDA ERICKSON

Dean of Libraries: WILLIAM A. GARRISON

Library of 2,556,031 vols, 82,706 serials

Number of teachers: 1,820 (1,679 full-time, 141 part-time)

Number of students: 47,214 (35,799 undergraduate, 8,833 graduate)

DEANS

College of Arts and Sciences: Prof. Dr ERIC EISENBERG

College of Behavioural and Community Sciences: Dr CATHERINE BATSCHE

College of Business: Dr ROBERT L. FORSYTHE

College of Education: Dr COLLEEN S. KENNEDY

College of Engineering: Prof. Dr JOHN M. WIENCEK

College of Graduate Studies: Dr KAREN LILLER

College of Marine Science: Dr JACQUELINE E. DIXON

College of Medicine: Dr STEPHEN K. KLASKO (acting)

College of Nursing: Dr PATRICIA A. BURNS

College of Public Health: Dr DONNA PETERSEN

College of the Arts: Dr BARTON LEE

Honors College: Dr STUART SILVERMAN

UNIVERSITY OF SOUTH FLORIDA ST. PETERSBURG

140 Seventh Ave S, St Petersburg, FL 33701

Telephone: (727) 873-4873

Fax: (727) 873-4329

E-mail: admissions@usfsp.edu

Internet: www.usfsp.edu

Founded 1965, present name and status 1968

State control

Academic year: September to August

Regional Chancellor and CEO: Dr MARGARET SULLIVAN

Regional Vice-Chancellor for Academic Affairs: NORINE NOONAN

Regional Vice-Chancellor for Admin. and Financial Services: ASHOK K. DHINGRA

Regional Vice-Chancellor for External Affairs: HELEN LEVINE

Dean of Library: CAROL HIXSON

Library of 204,839 vols

Number of teachers: 160 (full-time)

Number of students: 4,000

DEANS

College of Arts and Sciences: Dr FRANK A. BIAFORA

College of Business: Dr MALING EBRAHIMPOUR

College of Education: Dr BILL HELLER

College of Marine Science: Dr JACQUELINE E. DIXON

UNIVERSITY OF TAMPA

401 W Kennedy Blvd, Tampa, FL 33606-1490
Telephone: (813) 253-3333
Fax: (813) 258-7398
E-mail: admissions@ut.edu
Internet: www.ut.edu
Founded 1931, present name and status 1933
Private control
Academic year: August to July
Pres.: Dr RONALD L. VAUGHN
Provost and Vice Pres. for Academic Affairs:
  Dr JANET M. MCNEW
Vice-Pres. for Admin. and Finance: RICHARD
  W. OGOREK
Vice-Pres. for Devt and Univ. Relations:
  DANIEL T. GURA
Vice-Pres. for Enrolment: DENNIS NOSTRAND
Vice-Pres. for Operations and Planning: Dr
  LINDA W. DEVINE
Dean of Students: STEPHANIE RUSSELL HOLZ
Dir of Macdonald-Kelce Library: MARLYN R.
  PETHE
Registrar: MICHELLE PELAEZ
Library of 275,297 vols, 1,600 periodicals,
  49,301 microforms, 7,335 audiovisual
  items, 32,536 e-books, spec. collns, partial
  depository for US govt documents
Number of teachers: 534 full-time
Number of students: 6,738 full-time
Publications: *Pinter Review* (2 a year),
  Tampa Review (2 a year), *UT Journal* (3
  a year)

DEANS

College of Arts and Letters: Dr HAIG MARDIR-
  OSIAN
College of Natural and Health Sciences: Dr
  JAMES GORE
College of Social Sciences, Mathematics and
  Education: Dr ANNE V. GORMLY
John H. Sykes College of Business: Dr F.
  FRANK GHANNADIAN

UNIVERSITY OF WEST FLORIDA

Bldg 10, 11000 Univ. Parkway, Pensacola,
  FL 32514-5750
Telephone: (850) 474-2000
Fax: (850) 474-3360
E-mail: admissions@uwf.edu
Internet: www.uwf.edu
Founded 1965
State control
Academic year: August to August
Pres.: Dr JUDY BENSE
Vice-Pres. for Academic Affairs and Interim
  Provost: DAVID MARKER
Gen. Counsel: LEE GORE
Exec. Vice-Pres.: HAROLD M. WHITE, JR
Vice-Pres. for Admin. Affairs: Dr MATTHEW
  ALTIER
Vice-Pres. for Student Affairs: Dr KEVIN W.
  BAILEY
Vice-Pres. for Univ. Advancement: Dr KYLE
  MARRERO
Registrar: ANN H. DZIADON
Dean of Libraries: ROBERT DUGAN
Library of 840,125 vols, 4,588 serial sub-
  scriptions, 1,693,620 microforms, 714,729
  govt. documents, 3,811 maps, 108,195 e-
  books
Number of teachers: 342
Number of students: 12,021

DEANS

College of Arts and Sciences: Prof. Dr JANE
  HALONEN
College of Business: Prof. Dr EDWARD
  RANELLI
College of Professional Studies: Dr PAM
  NORTHRUP

WARNER UNIVERSITY

13895 Highway 27, Lake Wales, FL 33859
Telephone: (863) 638-1426
Fax: (863) 638-2503
E-mail: admissions@warner.edu
Internet: www.warner.edu
Founded 1968 as Warner Southern College,
  present name and status 2008
Private control
Academic year: August to May
Pres.: Dr GREGORY V. HALL
Vice-Pres. and Chief Academic Officer: Prof.
  Dr JAMES MOYER
Vice-Pres. for Advancement: DORIS B.
  GUKICH
Vice-Pres. for Advancement: DORIS GUKICH
Vice-Pres. for Enrolment Management and
  Marketing: DAWN RAFOOL
Dean of Students: Dr WENDI SANTEE
Registrar: SARA FASEL KANE
Dir of Learning Resource Centre: SHERILL
  HARRIGER
Library of 95,000 vols and 8,000 periodicals
Number of teachers: 118
Number of students: 1,017

DEANS

School of Business: Prof. Dr CATHY LEWIS-
  BRIM
School of Education: Prof. Dr BILL RIGEL
School of Ministry, Arts and Sciences: Prof.
  Dr STEVEN DARR

WEBBER INTERNATIONAL UNIVERSITY

POB 96, Babson Park, FL 33827
1201 N Scenic Highway, Babson Park, FL
  33827
Telephone: (836) 638-1431
Fax: (836) 638-2823
E-mail: admissions@webber.edu
Internet: www.webber.edu
Founded 1927
Private control
Academic year: June to May (4 semesters)
Offers bachelors in business admin, gen.
  business studies; masters in business admin.
Pres.: Dr KEITH WADE
Vice-Pres. for Enrolment and Student Record
  Services: KATHY WILSON
Vice-Pres. for Finance: CHRISTINA JORDON
Vice-Pres. for Institutional Advancement:
  STEVE WARNER
Academic Dean: Dr CHARLES SHIEH
Dean of Student Life: Dr JOHANNA DE VER-
  TEUIL
Registrar and Dir for Financial Aid: KATHY
  WILSON
Head Librarian: SUE DUNNING
Number of teachers: 44 (19 full-time, 25
  adjunct)
Number of students: 718 (670 undergradu-
  ate, 48 graduate)

GEORGIA

ABRAHAM BALDWIN AGRICULTURAL COLLEGE

2802 Moore Highway, Tifton, GA 31793-2601
Telephone: (229) 391-5001
Fax: (229) 391-5051
E-mail: abacinfo@abac.edu
Internet: www.abac.edu
Founded 1908, present name and status 1933
State control
Academic year: August to July (2 semesters)
Pres.: Dr DAVID C. BRIDGES
Vice-Pres. for Academic Affairs: Dr NILES M.
  REDDICK

Vice-Pres. for External Affairs and Advance-
  ment: KEITH D. BARBER
Dir for Enrolment Management: DONNA
  WEBB
Library Dir: MARIE DAVIS
Number of students: 3,284
Publication: *Pegasus* (1 a year)

DEANS

School of Agriculture and Natural Resources:
  Prof. Dr TIMOTHY MARSHALL
School of Business: Prof. Dr JEFF GIBBS
School of Human Sciences: Dr DARBY T.
  SEWELL
School of Liberal Arts: Prof. Dr BOBBIE
  ROBINSON
School of Nursing and Health Sciences: Dr
  WANDA GOLDEN
School of Science and Mathematics: Prof. Dr
  RAY N. BARBER

AGNES SCOTT COLLEGE

141 E College Ave, Decatur, GA 30030
Telephone: (404) 471-6000
Fax: (404) 471-6067
E-mail: admission@agnesscott.edu
Internet: www.agnesscott.edu
Founded 1889
Private control
Academic year: August to May
Depts of Africana studies, anthropology, art
  and art history, Asian studies, biochemistry
  and molecular biology, biology, chemistry,
  classics, economics, education, English,
  environmental and sustainability studies,
  film and media studies, French and German,
  history, human rights, int. relations, math-
  ematics, music, neuroscience, philosophy,
  physical education and athletics, physics
  and astronomy, political science, psychology,
  public health, religious studies, sociology and
  anthropology, Spanish, theatre and dance,
  women studies
Pres.: Dr ELIZABETH KISS
Vice-Pres. for Academic Affairs and Dean of
  College: Prof. Dr CAROLYN J. STEFANCO
Vice-Pres. for Business and Finance: JOHN P.
  HEGMAN
Vice-Pres. for Enrolment and Dean of Admis-
  sion: LAURA E. MARTIN
Vice-Pres. for College Advancement: Dr
  ROBERT J. PARKER
Vice-Pres. for Student Life and Dean of
  Students: DONNA A. LEE
Dir of Admissions: ALEXA WOOD GAERA
Registrar: ANGELA B. DEWBERRY
Dir of Library Services: ELIZABETH BAGLEY
Library of 236,551 vols, 54,126 e-books,
  26,731 audiovisual items, 40,072 current
  periodicals
Number of teachers: 95
Number of students: 871

ALBANY STATE UNIVERSITY

504 College Dr., Albany, GA 31705
Telephone: (229) 430-4600
E-mail: enrollmentservices@asurams.edu
Internet: www.asurams.edu
Founded 1903 as Albany Bible and Manual
  Training Instn, present name and status
  1996
Pres.: Dr EVERETTE J. FREEMAN
Vice-Pres. for Academic Affairs: Dr ABIODUN
  OJEMAKINDE
Vice-Pres. for Fiscal Affairs: LARRY WAKE-
  FIELD
Vice-Pres. for Institutional Advancement:
  CLIFFORD PORTER
Vice-Pres. for Student Affairs: Dr EDGAR L.
  BERRY
Dir of Enrolment Services: JAMES BURRELL
Dean of Graduate School: RANI GEORGE

Registrar: ARNA ALBRITTEN
Dir of Library Services: Dr LAVERNE L. MCLAUGHLIN
Library of 900,000 vols
Number of teachers: 148 (full-time)
Number of students: 6,711

DEANS

College of Arts and Humanities: Dr LEROY E. BYNUM, JR
College of Business: KATHALEENA MONDS
College of Education: Dr KIMBERLY KING-JUPITER
College of Sciences and Health Professions: JOYCE JOHNSON

ARMSTRONG ATLANTIC STATE UNIVERSITY

11935 Abercorn St, Savannah, GA 31419
Telephone: (912) 344-2576
E-mail: adm-info@armstrong.edu
Internet: www.armstrong.edu
Founded 1935 as Armstrong Jr College, present name and status 1996
State control
Academic year: August to May
Pres.: Dr LINDA M. BLEICKEN
Vice-Pres. for Academic Affairs and Dean of Faculty: Dr ANNE THOMPSON
Vice-Pres. for Advancement: SCOTT JOYNER
Vice-Pres. for Business and Finance: DAVID CARSON
Vice-Pres. for Student Affairs: Dr KEITH BETTS
Registrar: JUDY GINTER
Librarian: DOUG FRAZIER
Library of 200,000 vols, 1,000 journals, 18,000 audiovisuals
Number of teachers: 258 (full-time)
Number of students: 7,493 (6,813 undergraduate, 680 graduate)
Publications: *AMT Marquee* (1 a year), *Calliope*

DEANS

College of Education: Dr PATRICIA WACHHOLZ
College of Health Professions: DONNA BROOKS
College of Liberal Arts: LAURA BARRETT
College of Science and Technology: Dr ROBERT GREGERSON

ART INSTITUTE OF ATLANTA

6600 Peachtree Dunwoody Rd, NE, 100 Embassy Row, Atlanta, GA 30328-1649
Telephone: (770) 394-8300
Fax: (770) 394-0008
E-mail: aiaadm@aii.edu
Internet: www.artinstitutes.edu/atlanta
Founded 1949 as Massey Business College; present name 1975
Private control
Academic year: October to September
Br. campuses in Charleston, N Virginia, Tennessee, Virginia Beach, Washington; degree programmes in culinary arts, design, fashion, general education, media arts
Pres.: JO ANN KOCH
Vice-Pres. for Human Resources: JOSELYN C. CASSIDY
Sr Dir of Admissions: JOY MCCLURE
Dir of Admin. and Financial Services: CHRIS SCHWARZER
Dean of Academic Affairs: Dr DAN GARLAND
Dean of Student Affairs: Dr APRIL SHAVKIN
Registrar: DIANA HILL
Library Dir: GAYLE MEIER
Library of 40,000 vols, 4,000 video materials, 150 periodicals
Number of teachers: 250
Number of students: 3,319

AUGUSTA STATE UNIVERSITY

2500 Walton Way, Augusta, GA 30904-2200
Telephone: (706) 737-1444
E-mail: admissions@aug.edu
Internet: www.aug.edu
Founded 1783 as Acad. of Richmond County; present name and status 1996
State control
Academic year: August to July
Pres.: Dr WILLIAM A. BLOODWORTH, JR
Vice-Pres. for Academic Affairs: CAROL J. RYCHLY (acting)
Vice-Pres. for Business Operations: THERESE ROSIER
Vice-Pres. for Student Services and Dean of Students: Dr JOYCE A. JONES
Registrar and Dir of Admissions: KATHERINE H. SWEENEY
Library Dir: Dr CAMILLA REID
Library of 435,000 vols incl. 50,000 e-books
Number of teachers: 200 (full-time)
Number of students: 6,500

DEANS

College of Arts and Sciences: Prof. Dr ROBERT R. PARHAM
College of Education: Prof. Dr GORDON EISENMAN
Hull College of Business Admin.: Prof. Dr MARC D. MILLER,
Pamplin College of Arts and Sciences: Dr ROBERT PARHAM (acting)

BAUDER COLLEGE

384 Northyards Blvd, NW, Suites 190 and 400, Atlanta, GA 30313
Telephone: (404) 237-7573
Fax: (404) 237-1619
E-mail: admissions@bauder.edu
Internet: atlanta.bauder.edu
Founded 1964
Private control
Programmes in bachelor of science incl. business admin., criminal justice, information technology, paralegal studies
Pres.: Dr CHARLES A. TAYLOR
Head Librarian: MARY KAYE HOOKER
Library of 12,000 vols, 150 journals, 52,000 e-books.

BERRY COLLEGE

2277 Martha Berry Highway, NW, Mount Berry, GA 30149
Telephone: (706) 232-5374
E-mail: admissions@berry.edu
Internet: www.berry.edu
Founded 1902 as Boys' Industrial School
Private control
Academic year: August to August (3 semesters)
Pres.: Dr STEPHEN R. BRIGGS
Provost: Dr KATHERINE M. WHATLEY
Vice-Pres. for Advancement: BETTYANN M. O'NEILL
Vice-Pres. for Enrolment Mangement: Dr GARY WATERS
Vice-Pres. for Finance: BRIAN ERB
Vice-Pres. for Student Affairs and Dean of Students: DEBBIE E. HEIDA
Dir of Admissions: BRETT E. KENNEDY
Registrar: LINDA A. TENNANT
Library Dir: SHERRE L. HARRINGTON
Library of 700,000 vols incl. print and microform, 1,700 journals, 104,871 govt documents
Number of teachers: 126
Number of students: 2,093 (1,944 undergraduate, 149 graduate)

DEANS

Campbell School of Business: Dr JOHN R. GROUT
Charter School of Education and Human Sciences: Prof. Dr JACQUELINE M. MCDOWELL
Evans School of Humanities, Arts and Social Sciences: Prof. Dr THOMAS D. KENNEDY
School of Mathematical and Natural Sciences: Prof. Dr D. BRUCE CONN

BEULAH HEIGHTS UNIVERSITY

POB 18145, 892 Berne St, SE, Atlanta, GA 30316
Telephone: (404) 627-2681
Fax: (404) 627-0702
E-mail: admissionsinfo@beulah.org
Internet: www.beulah.org
Founded 1918 as Beulah Heights Bible Institute, present name and status 2006
Private control
Academic year: August to May (3 semesters)
Bachelors of arts in leadership studies, religious studies, masters of business admin., divinity
Pres.: Dr BENSON M. KARANJA
Vice-Pres. for Academic Programme Devt: Dr ANGELITA HOWARD
Vice-Pres. and Dean of Academic Affairs: Dr JAMES B. KEILLER
Vice-Pres. for Finance: TAMMY GUELFO
Vice-Pres. for Student Life and Enrolment Management: SHAWN ADAMS
Registrar: JACQUELYN B. ARMSTRONG
Dir of Admissions: JOHN DREHER
Dir of Library Service: PRADEEP K. DAS
Library of 45,000 vols
Number of teachers: 35
Number of students: 2,100

BRENAU UNIVERSITY

500 Washington St, SE, Gainesville, GA 30501
Telephone: (770) 534-6100
Fax: (770) 538-4701
E-mail: admissions@brenau.edu
Internet: www.brenau.edu
Founded 1878 as Georgia Baptist Female Seminary, present name and status 1992
Private control
Academic year: July to August
Campuses in Augusta, Kings Bay, North Atlanta, South Atlanta
Pres.: Dr ED L. SCHRADER
Provost and Vice-Pres. for Academic Affairs: Dr NANCY KRIPPEL
Exec. Vice-Pres. and Chief Financial Officer: Dr WAYNE DEMPSEY
Sr Vice-Pres.for Enrolment Management and Student Services: SCOTT BRIELL
Sr Vice-Pres. for Institutional Devt: JIM BARCO
Vice-Pres. for External Relations: MATT THOMAS
Registrar and Dir of Student Records: BARBARA WILSON
Dean of Library Services: MARLENE GIGUERE
Library of 85,000 vols, 60,000 e-books, 16,000 e-journals and magazines
Number of students: 2,768
Publication: *The Window* (4 a year)

DEANS

College of Business and Mass Communication: Dr BILL LIGHTFOOT
College of Education: Prof. Dr DAVID L. BARNETT
College of Fine Arts and Humanities: Dr ANDREA BIRCH
College of Health and Science: Prof. Dr GALE HANSEN STARICH

Graduate School: Dr GALE HANSEN STARICH

BREWTON-PARKER COLLEGE

Highway 280, 201 David-Eliza Fountain Circle, POB 197, Mount Vernon, GA 30445

Telephone: (912) 583-2241
Fax: (912) 583-4498
E-mail: admissions@bpc.edu
Internet: www.bpc.edu

Founded 1904 as Union Baptist Institute; present name 1978
Private control
Academic year: August to June

Divs of arts and letters, business, education, religion and philosophy

Pres.: Dr MIKE SIMONEAUX
Provost: Dr CHRISTOPHER JONES
Vice-Pres. for College Advancement: JESSICA JAMES
Vice-Pres. for Enrolment Services: JIM BEALL
Chief Financial Officer: NATASHA MASON
Chief Information Officer: DAVID KIGHT
Dean of Students: SHERRIE HELMS
Registrar: SARA CROWE
Dir of Library: ANN C. HUGHES

Library of 80,000 vols
Number of teachers: 89 (43 full-time, 46 part-time)
Number of students: 778

Publication: *Oracle* (1 a year).

CLARK ATLANTA UNIVERSITY

223 James P. Brawley, Atlanta, GA 30314-4389

Telephone: (404) 880-8000
E-mail: cauadmissions@cau.edu
Internet: www.cau.edu

Founded 1988 by merger of Atlanta Univ. (f. 1865) and Clark College (f. 1869)
Private control
Academic year: August to July (3 semesters)

Pres.: Dr CARLTON E. BROWN
Provost and Vice-Pres. for Academic Affairs: Dr JOSEPH H. SILVER, SR
Vice-Pres. for Enrolment Services and Student Affairs: Dr CARL E. JONES
Vice-Pres. for Finance and Business Services and Chief Financial Officer: LUCILLE MAUGÉ
Vice-Pres. for Institutional Advancement and Univ. Relations: (vacant)
Vice-Pres. for Research and Sponsored Programmes: Dr MARCUS W. SHUTE
Gen. Counsel: LANCE DUNNINGS
Dean of Graduate Studies: Dr BETTYE CLARK
Dean of Undergraduate Studies: Dr ALEXA B. HENDERSON
Dir of Library Services: LORETTA PARHAM

Library: 1.6m. vols incl. 43,000 e-books, 867,000 microforms, 314,000 govt documents, 17,000 theses and dissertations, 35,000 bound periodicals, 1,500 current periodicals, 7,000 audiovisual material
Number of teachers: 300 (175 full-time)
Number of students: 3,941 (3,267 undergraduate, 674 graduate)

DEANS

School of Arts and Sciences: Dr SHIRLEY WILLIAMS-KIRKSEY
School of Business Admin.: Prof. Dr LYDIA FLOYD
School of Education: Dr SEAN S. WARNER
Whitney M. Young, Jr School of Social Work: Prof. Dr VIMALA PILLARI

CLAYTON STATE UNIVERSITY

2000 Clayton State Blvd, Morrow, GA 30260
Telephone: (678) 466-4000
Fax: (678) 466-4169

E-mail: registrar@clayton.edu
Internet: www.clayton.edu

Founded 1969 as Clayton Jr College; present name and status 2005
State control
Academic year: August to May

Pres.: Prof. Dr THOMAS J. HYNES, JR
Provost and Vice-Pres. for Academic Affairs: Dr MICHEAL CRAFTON
Vice-Pres. for Business and Operations: CORLIS CUMMINGS
Vice-Pres. for External Relations: STEVE STEPHENS
Vice-Pres. for Information Technology and Services: Dr JOHN BRYAN (acting)
Vice-Pres. for Student Affairs: Dr BRIAN HAYNES
Registrar: REBECCA GMEINER
Dean of Library: Dr GORDON N. BAKER

Library of 116,201 vols, 372 journals, 27,693 e-books
Number of teachers: 213 (197 full-time)
Number of students: 6,900

DEANS

College of Arts and Sciences: Prof. Dr NASSER MOMAYEZI
College of Business: Prof. Dr ALPHONSO OGBUEHI
College of Health: Dr LISA EICHELBERGER
College of Information and Mathematical Sciences: Prof. Dr LILA F. ROBERTS
School of Graduate Studies: GWENDOLYN JONES HAROLD

COLLEGE OF COASTAL GEORGIA

One College Dr., Brunswick, GA 31520

Telephone: (912) 279-5700
Fax: (912) 262-3072
E-mail: admiss@ccga.edu
Internet: www.ccga.edu

Founded 1961 as Brunswick College, present name and status 2008
State control
Academic year: August to May (2 semesters)

Pres.: Dr VALERIE A. HEPBURN
Vice-Pres. for Academic Affairs: Dr PHILIP J. MASON
Vice-Pres. for Student Affairs: Dr GERALD KIEL
Vice-Pres. for Business Affairs: JEFF PRESTON
Chief Advancement Officer: ELIZABETH K. WEATHERLY
Chief Information Officer: GERI CHAPMAN CULBREATH
Dir of Admissions and Orientation: (vacant)
Registrar: LISA LESSEIG
Dean of Library Science: DEBORAH HOLMES

Number of teachers: 84
Number of students: 3,465

Publications: *College of Coastal Georgia*, *Pulse of Camden* (1 a year), *Seaswells* (1 a year)

DEANS

School of Arts, Humanities and Social Sciences: Prof. Dr M. KAREN HAMBRIGHT
School of Business and Public Affairs: Prof. Dr WILLIAM STEWART MOUNTS, JR
School of Education and Teacher Preparation: Dr KENT LAYTON
School of Mathematics and Natural Sciences: Dr KEITH E. BELCHER
School of Nursing and Health Sciences: Dr PATRICIA KRAFT

COLUMBIA THEOLOGICAL SEMINARY

POB 520, Decatur, GA 30031-0520
701 S Columbia Dr., Decatur, GA 30030-4118

Telephone: (404) 378-8821
Fax: (404) 377-9696

E-mail: admissions@ctsnet.edu
Internet: www.ctsnet.edu

Founded 1828, present name 1925
Private control
Academic year: September to May

Offers master of arts in divinity, educational ministry, ministry, practical theology, theological studies, theology

Pres.: Dr STEPHEN A. HAYNER
Exec. Vice-Pres. and Dean of Faculty: Dr DEBORAH F. MULLEN
Vice-Pres. for Business and Finance: J. MARTIN SADLER
Vice-Pres. for Institutional Advancement: DOUG TAYLOR
Dean of Students and Vice-Pres. for Student Services: Dr JOHN E. WHITE
Registrar: MIKE MEDFORD
Dir of Advancement Services: C. J. DRYMON
Library Dir: Dr SARA MYERS

Library of 165,000 vols, 878 current periodicals, 41,000 microforms
Number of teachers: 36
Number of students: 500

Publication: *Journal for Preachers* (4 a year).

COLUMBUS STATE UNIVERSITY

4225 University Ave, Columbus, GA 31907

Telephone: (706) 507-8800
E-mail: pr@colstate.edu
Internet: www.columbusstate.edu

Founded 1958
State control
Academic year: August to June

Pres.: Dr TIMOTHY S. MESCON
Provost and Vice-Pres. for Academic Affairs: Dr TOM HACKETT
Vice-Pres. for Business and Finance: TOM HELTON
Vice-Pres. for Student Affairs and Enrolment Management: Dr GINA L. SHEEKS
Vice-Pres. for Univ. Advancement: REX WHIDDON
Chief Information Officer: ABRAHAM GEORGE
Dean of Students: AARON REESE
Registrar: JOHN BROWN
Dean of Libraries: MARK FLYNN

Library of 375,000 vols, 11,400 multimedia materials, 1.3m. microfilm and microfiche
Number of teachers: 481 (296 full-time, 185 part-time)
Number of students: 8,307

DEANS

College of Arts: Dr RICHARD BAXTER, JR
College of Business and Computer Science: Dr LINDA U. HADLEY
College of Education and Health Professions: Dr BARBARA BUCKNER
College of Letters and Sciences: Dr DAVID J. LANOUE
D. Abbott Turner College of Business and Computer Science: Dr LINDA HADLEY

COVENANT COLLEGE

14049 Scenic Highway, Lookout Mountain, GA 30750-4164

Telephone: (706) 820-1560
Fax: (706) 820-0893
E-mail: info@covenant.edu
Internet: www.covenant.edu

Founded 1955
Private control
Academic year: August to May (2 semesters)

Pres.: Dr NIEL NIELSON
Vice-Pres. for Academic Affairs: Dr JEFFREY B. HALL
Vice-Pres. for Advancement: TROY DUBLE
Vice-Pres. for Student Devt and Dean of Students: BRAD VOYLES

Registrar and Dean of Records: RODNEY MILLER

Dir of Admissions and Church Relations: MATTHEW BRYANT

Dir of Library Services: TAD MINDEMAN

Library of 100,000 vols, 90,000 e-books, 10,000 e-journals, magazines and newspapers

Number of teachers: 62 (full-time)

Number of students: 1,030

Publication: *The View*

DEANS

Education and Social Science: Prof. Dr JAMES L. DREXLER

Humanities: Prof. Dr PAUL J. MORTON

Organizational Management and Instructional Technology: Dr GINNER W. HUDSON

Sciences: Prof. Dr JEROME D. WENGER

DALTON STATE COLLEGE

650 College Dr., Dalton, GA 30720

Telephone: (706) 272-4436

Fax: (706) 272-2530

E-mail: admissions@daltonstate.edu

Internet: www.daltonstate.edu

Founded 1963 as Dalton Jr College, present name and status 1998

State control

Academic year: August to May (2 semesters)

Pres.: Dr JOHN O. SCHWENN

Vice-Pres. for Academic Affairs: Dr SANDRA STONE

Vice-Pres. for Enrolment and Student Services: Dr JODI S. JOHNSON

Vice-Pres. for Fiscal Affairs: SCOTT A. BAILEY

Registrar: PATRICIA A. KRESL

Library Dir: LYDIA F. KNIGHT

Library of 135,597 vols, 200 current periodicals, 59,609 e-books

Number of teachers: 250 (170 full-time, 80 part-time)

Number of students: 5,485

DEANS

School of Business: Prof. Dr DONNA MAYO

School of Education: Prof. Dr CALVIN MEYER

School of Liberal Arts: Prof. Dr MARY NIELSEN

School of Sciences and Mathematics: Dr RANDALL GRIFFUS

School of Nursing: Prof. Dr CORDIA STARLING

School of Social Work: Prof. Dr SPENCER ZEIGER

School of Technology: Prof. Dr CHARLES DAVID JOHNSON

EMMANUEL COLLEGE

POB 129, Franklin Springs, GA 30639-0129

181 Springs St, Franklin Springs, GA 30639

Telephone: (706) 245-2874

Fax: (706) 245-4424

E-mail: admissions@ec.edu

Internet: www.ec.edu

Founded 1919 as Franklin Springs Institute; present name and status 1939

Private control

Academic year: August to May (3 semesters)

Pres.: Dr MICHAEL S. STEWART

Vice-Pres. for Academic Affairs: Dr JOHN R. HENZEL

Vice-Pres. for Devt: BRIAN JAMES

Vice-Pres. for Enrolment and Marketing: WENDY D. VINSON

Vice-Pres. for Finance: KEVIN L. CRAWFORD

Vice-Pres. for Student Life: JASON L. CROY

Dean of Students: TIM HARRISON

Registrar: DEBRA F. GRIZZLE

Library Dir: JOY SLIFE

Library of 95,000 vols

Number of students: 800

DEANS

School of Arts and Sciences: Dr LESLIE BOUCHER

School of Business: JENNIFER LESTER-BENSON

School of Christian Ministries: Rev. TRACY REYNOLDS

School of Education: Dr VICKI HOLLINSHEAD

EMORY UNIVERSITY

Atlanta, GA 30322

Telephone: (404) 727-6123

E-mail: admiss@learnlink.emory.edu

Internet: www.emory.edu

Founded 1836 as Emory College, present name and status 1915

Private control

Academic year: August to May

Pres.: JAMES W. WAGNER

Provost and Exec. Vice-Pres. for Academic Affairs: Dr EARL LEWIS

Vice-Provost for Academic Affairs: LISA A. TEDESCO

Exec. Vice-Pres. for Finance and Admin.: MICHAEL J. MANDL

Exec. Vice-Pres. for Health Affairs: Dr S. WRIGHT CAUGHMAN

Sr Vice-Pres. and Gen. Counsel: STEPHEN D. SENCER

Sr Vice-Pres. and Dean of Campus Life: JOHN L. FORD

Sr Vice-Pres. for Devt and Alumni Relations: SUSAN CRUSE

Vice-Pres. and Deputy to the Pres.: Dr GARY S. HAUK

Vice-Pres. and Sec. of the Univ.: Dr ROSEMARY M. MAGEE

Vice-Pres. for Communications and Marketing: RON SAUDER

Vice-Provost and Dean of the Graduate Study: LISA A. TEDESCO

Registrar: TOM MILLEN

Vice-Provost and Dir of Libraries: RICHARD E. LUCE

Library of 3,662,882 vols

Number of teachers: 3,046 (full-time)

Number of students: 13,893 (12,773 full-time, 1,120 part-time)

Publications: *Academic Exchange* (6 a year), *Emory Bankruptcy Developments Journal* (2 a year), *Emory International Law Review* (2 a year), *Emory Law Journal* (6 a year), *Emory Health* (4 a year), *Emory Lawyer* (2 a year), *Emory Magazine* (4 a year), *Emory Medicine* (3 a year), *Emory Nursing* (2 a year), *Goizueta Business Magazine* (3 a year), *Methodist Review* (1 a year), *New Vico Studies* (1 a year), *Practical Matters*, *Public Health Magazine* (2 a year), *Quadrangle* (2 a year)

DEANS

Candler School of Theology: Prof. Dr JANICE LOVE

Emory College of Arts and Sciences: Prof. Dr ROBIN FORMAN

Goizueta Business School: Prof. Dr LAWRENCE M. BENVENISTE

Graduate School: LISA A. TEDESCO

Nell Hodgson Woodruff School of Nursing: Prof. Dr LINDA A. McCAULEY

Oxford College: Prof. STEPHEN H. BOWEN

Rollins School of Public Health: Dr JAMES W. CURRAN

School of Law: Prof. Dr ROBERT A. SCHAPIRO

School of Medicine: Dr THOMAS J. LAWLEY

PROFESSORS

AABERG, T. M., Ophthalmology

ABRAMOWITZ, A., Political Science

ABRAMOWSKY, C. R., Pathology

ABRAMS, H. E., Law

ADAMSON, W. L., History

AGNEW, R. S., Sociology

ALARCON, R., Psychiatry/Behavioural Sciences

ALAVI, M., Information Strategy

ALBRECHT, T. E., Music

ALDRIDGE, D. P., Sociology

ALEXANDER, F. S., Law

ALEXANDER, G. E., Neurology

ALEXANDER, R. W., Medicine

ALLITT, P., History

AN-NA'IM, A., Law

ANSARI, A. A., Pathology

ANSEL, J. C., Dermatology

ARMELAGOS, G., Anthropology

ARTHUR, T. C., Law

AUSTIN, H., Epidemiology

BAJAJ, K., Physics

BARLETT, P., Anthropology

BARON, M., Radiology

BARROW, D., Neurosurgery

BARSALOU, L., Psychology

BAUERLEIN, M., English

BAUMGARTNER, B. R., Radiology

BEARD, L., Accounting

BECKER, E. R., Health Policy and Management

BEDERMAN, D. J., Law

BEIK, W., History

BENSTON, G. J., Finance

BERMAN, H. J., Law

BERNSTEIN, A., Law

BERNSTEIN, K. E., Pathology

BERRY, A. J., Anaesthesiology

BESSEMBINDER, H., Finance

BLACK, M., Political Science

BLAKE, D. A., Pharmacology

BLUMENTHAL, D. R., Judaic Studies

BONDI, R. C., Church History

BONNEFIS, P., French and Italian

BOOTHE, R., Psychology

BORING, J. R., III, Epidemiology

BOSS, J., Microbiology/Immunology

BOSTWICK, J., III, Plastic Surgery

BOSWELL, T. E., Sociology

BRACHMAN, P., International Health

BRAITHWAITE, R., Behavioural Science and Health Education

BRANCH, W. T., General Medicine

BRANN, A. W., Neurology, Paediatrics

BRIGHT, D. F., Classics and Comparative Literature

BROGAN, D. J., Biostatistics

BROWN, P. J., Anthropology

BROWN, W. V., Medicine (Lipids)

BROWNLEY, M. W., English

BRYAN, J. A., Pathology

BUGGE, J. M., English

BUSS, M. J., Religion

BUZBEE, W., Law

CALABRESE, R., Biology

CARNEY, W. J., Law

CARPENTER, L., English

CARR, D., Philosophy

CARTER, E. B., Biology

CARUTH, C., English

CASARELLA, W. J., Radiology

CATLIN, P. A., Rehabilitation Medicine

CAUGHMAN, S. W., Dermatology

CHAKRABORTY, H., Biostatistics

CHEN, R. L., Physics

CHENG, X., Biochemistry

CHIMOWITZ, M. I., Neurology

CHIRINKO, R., Economics

CHOPP, R., Systematic Theology

CHURCH, R., Ophthalmology

CLEMENTS, S. D., Cardiology

CLOUD, A. M., Law

COHEN, C., Pathology

COLE, J. A., Anthropology

COMPANS, R. W., Microbiology/Immunology

CONN, D. L., Rheumatology

CONN, P. J., Pharmacology

COOK, D. A., Film Studies

COOPER, R., Practice of Cost Management, Accounting

COPE, T., Physiology
CORNISH, J. D., Paediatrics
COURTRIGHT, P., Asian Studies
CRAVER, J. M., Cardiothoracic Surgery
CURRAN, J. M., Public Health
DANNER, D. J., Genetics
DAVIS, D. C., Medicine
DAVIS, L. W., Oncology
DAVIS, M., Psychiatry/Behavioural Sciences
DAVIS, P., Radiology
DE WAAL, F. B. M., Psychology, Primate Behaviour
DEANGRADE, J. R., Orthopaedics
DECONCINI, B., Religion
DELONG, M. R., Neurology
DICLEMENTE, R. J., Behavioural Science and Health Education
DIGIROLAMO, M., Medicine (Geriatrics)
DILORIO, C., Behavioural Science and Health Education
DINGLEDINE, R. J., Pharmacology
DOERNBERG, R. L., International Legal Studies
DOETSCH, P., Biochemistry
DONHAM, D. L., Anthropology
DOUGLAS, J. S., Medicine (Cardiology)
DUFFUS, D. A., Mathematic and Computer Science
DUKE, M., Psychology
DUNBAR, S., Adult and Elder Health
DUNCAN, M., Law
EATON, D. C., Physiology
ECKMAN, J. R., Haematology/Oncology
EDELHAUSER, H., Ophthalmology
EDMONDSON, D. E., Biochemistry
ELMER, W. A., Biology
ELSAS, L. J., II, Medical Genetics, Paediatrics
EMORY, E., Psychology
ENGELHARD, G., Educational Studies
ENGLAND, P., Physical Education
ENGLISH, A. W., Cell Biology
EPSTEIN, M., Russian and East Asian Languages and Culture
FALEK, A., Psychiatry/Behavioural Sciences
FAMILY, F., Physics
FARLEY, M. M., Infectious Diseases
FELICIANO, D. V., Surgery, Trauma/Critical Care
FELNER, J. M., Medicine (Cardiology)
FINK, A. S., General Surgery
FINNERTY, V. M., Biology
FIVUSH, R., Psychology
FLANDERS, W. D., Epidemiology
FLANNERY, J., Performing Arts
FLEMING, L. L., Orthopaedics
FLYNN, T. R., Philosophy
FONG, P., Physics
FOSTER, F. S., English
FOTION, N., Philosophy
FOWLER, J., Theology
FOX-GENOVESE, E., History
FRANCH, R., Medicine (Cardiology)
FRANKEL, B., Psychiatry/Behavioural Sciences
FREER, R. D., Law
FYFE, D., Paediatrics
GARCIA, E. V., Radiology
GARROW, D. J., Law
GELLER, R. J., Paediatrics
GIDDENS, D., Medical School Administration
GILES, M. W., Political Science
GOLDSMITH, D., Chemistry
GOODING, L. R., Microbiology/Immunology
GOODMAN, M., Radiology
GOULD, K., Primate Research
GOULD, R., Mathematic and Computer Science
GOUZOULES, H., Psychology
GOZANSKY, N. E., Law
GRAVANIS, M. B., Pathology
GREENAMYRE, T. J., Neurology
GREENE, D. K., History
GRIFFIN, J. B., Psychiatry/Behavioural Sciences
GRINDON, A. J., Pathology
GROSSNIKLAUS, H., Ophthalmology

GRUBER, W., English
GUNN, R. B., Physiology
GUNNEMANN, J., Social Ethics, Theology
GUTTERMAN, M., Law
GUTTIERREZ-MOUAT, R., Spanish
GUYTON, R., Cardiothoracic Surgery
HABER, M. J., Biostatistics
HAHN, C., Educational Studies
HALLORAN, M. E., Biostatistics
HANSON, S. R., Biomedical Engineering
HARARI, J., French and Italian
HARTGRAVES, A., Accounting
HARTLE, A., Philosophy
HARTZELL, H. C., Cell Biology
HATCHER, R. A., Gynaecology/Obstetrics
HAY, P., Law
HAYES, J. H., Theology (Old Testament)
HEAVEN, M., Chemistry
HERMAN, C., Pathology
HERRON, C., French and Italian
HICKS, A., Sociology
HILL, C. L., Chemistry
HOGUE, C., Epidemiology
HOLIFIELD, E. B., Theology
HOLLADAY, C. R., Theology (New Testament)
HOLLAND, B., Psychiatry/Behavioural Sciences
HOLTZMAN, S. G., Pharmacology
HOPKINS, L. C., Neurology
HOROWITZ, I. R., Gynaecology/Obstetrics
HUDSON, T., Radiology
HUG, C. C., Academic Affairs
HUMPHREY, D. R., Physiology
HUNTER, H. O., Law
HUNTER, R. J., Theology
HUTTON, W. C., Orthopaedics
HUYNH, B. H., Physics
INSEL, T. R., Psychiatry/Behavioural Sciences
IRVINE, J., Educational Studies
IUVONE, P. M., Pharmacology
JAFFE, S. L., Psychiatry/Behavioural Sciences
JENSEN, P., Pathology
JINKS-ROBERTSON, S., Biology
JOHNSON, L. T., Theology
JOHNSON, R., Chemistry
JOHNSON, T. C., Health, Physical Education and Dance
JOHNSTON, J. H., English
JONES, D. P., Biochemistry
JONES, E., Cardiothoracic Surgery
JONES, G., Biology
JORDAN, M., Religion
JOSEPH, R., Political Science
JOYNER, R. W., Paediatrics
JUDOVITZ, D., French and Italian
JUSTICE, J. B., Chemistry
KAHN, R. A., Biochemistry
KALAIDJIAN, W., English
KANTER, K. R., Cardiothoracic Surgery
KAPP, J., Ophthalmology
KARP, I., Liberal Arts, African Studies
KASLOW, N., Psychiatry/Behavioural Sciences
KAUFMAN, M. J., Chemistry
KAUFMAN, S., Radiology
KELLER, J. W., Radiation Oncology
KELLERMANN, A., Emergency Medicine
KERTZ, C. L., Accounting
KINKADE, J. M., Biochemistry
KLEHR, H., Politics and History
KLEIN, L., Gynaecology/Obstetrics
KLEINBAUM, D., Epidemiology
KLUGMAN, K. P., International Health
KNAUFT, B. M., Anthropology
KOHLI, A., Marketing
KONNER, M., Anthropology
KONSYNSKI, B., Business
KOVAC, S. R., Gynaecology/Obstetrics
KUHAR, M. J., Pharmacology
KULL, A., Law
KUSHNER, H., Science and Society
KUTNER, M., Biostatistics
KUTNER, N., Rehabilitation Medicine
LAMBETH, J. D., Biochemistry
LANGBERG, J. J., Cardiology, Electrophysiology
LAUER, S., Oncology, Paediatrics

LAWLEY, T. J., Medical School Administration
LAWRENCE, E. C., Medicine
LESSER, J., History, Latin American and Caribbean Studies
LETZ, R., Behavioural Science and Health Education
LEVEY, A. I., Neurology
LEVIN, B., Biology
LEVINSON, R. M., Medicine
LEVY, R., Psychiatry/Behavioural Sciences
LEWIS, W., Pathology
LIEBESKIND, L. S., Chemistry
LIN, M. C., Physical Chemistry
LINVILLE, K. B., Academic Affairs
LIOTTA, D. C., Chemistry
LIPSTADT, D., Judaic Studies
LIVINGSTON, D., Philosophy
LOLLAR, J. S., Haematology/Oncology
LONG, R. A., African Studies
LONG, T., Theology
LONGINI, I. M., Biostatistics
LOWE, W. J., Theology
LUCCHESI, J., Biology
LUSKIN, M. B., Cell Biology
LUTZ, L. J., Family and Preventive Medicine
LYNN, D., Chemistry
MABERLY, G., International Health
MCCAREY, B. E., Ophthalmology
MCCAULEY, R., Philosophy
MCDOWELL, J. J., Psychology
MCGINLEY, P. H., Radiation/Oncology
MCGOWAN, J. E., Epidemiology
MACON, E. J., Medicine
MCQUAIDE, M. M., Sociology
MADARA, J. L., Pathology
MAHAVIER, W. S., Mathematics and Computer Science
MAJMUDAR, B., Pathology
MAKKREEL, R. A., Philosophy
MANDELL, A. J., Psychiatry/Behavioural Sciences
MANSOUR, K., Cardiothoracic Surgery
MARSHALL, F. F., Urology
MARTIN, L. G., Radiology
MARTIN, R. C., Religion
MARTORELL, R., International Health
MARZILLI, L. G., Chemistry
MATTOX, D. E., Otolaryngology
MAYTON, W. T., Law
MEINERT, W. J., Family and Preventive Medicine
MERRILL, A. H., Biochemistry
MILLER, J. I., Cardiothoracic Surgery
MILLER, M., Law
MILLER, S. B., General Medicine
MINNEMAN, K. P., Pharmacology
MITCH, W. E., Medicine (Renal)
MOHANTY, J. N., Philosophy
MORAN, C., Microbiology/Immunology
MORGAN, E. T., Pharmacology
MOROKUMA, K., Chemistry
MORRIS, D. C., Cardiology
MURRAY, J., Adult and Elder Health
MUTH, R. D., Economics
NAHMIAS, A. J., Infectious Diseases, Paediatrics
NASSAR, V. H., Pathology
NAURIGHT, L. P., Adult and Elder Health
NEILL, D. B., Psychology
NEMEROFF, C., Psychiatry/Behavioural Sciences
NEWBY, G., Middle Eastern Studies
NEWSOM, C. A., Old Testament
NEYLAN, J. F., Medicine
NICHOLS, T. R., Physiology
NOE, B., Cell Biology
NOWICKI, S., Psychology
O'DAY, G. R., Theology
OLIKER, V., Mathematics and Computer Science
OLIVER, H. P., Religion
O'SHEA, H. S., Adult and Elder Health
OUSLANDER, J. G., Geriatric Medicine
PACKARD, R., International Health, History
PADWA, A., Chemistry

PARTIN, C., Health, Physical Education and Dance
PASCAL, R. R., Pathology
PASTOR, R., International Relations/Political Science
PATTERSON, R., Philosophy
PATTERSON, R. E., Cardiology
PEDERSON, L., English
PENNELL, J. N., Law
PERKOWITZ, S., Physics
PESKOWITZ, M., Religion
PETERSEN, K. W., Cell Biology
PETTIGREW, R., Radiology
PHILLIPS, L. S., Endocrinology
PINTER, M., Physiology
PLOTSKY, P. M., Psychiatry/Behavioural Sciences
PLUMMER, A., Medicine
POHL, J., Medicine
POLING, C. V., Art History
POLLET, R. J., Medicine
POMERANTZ, G., Journalism
POWELL, M. L., Nursing
POWNALL, G., Accounting
RAMBUSS, R., English
RAMOS, H. S., General Medicine
RANDALL, H. W., Gynaecology/Obstetrics
REAL, L., Biology
RECTOR, A. M., Law
REED, W. L., English
REMINGTON, T. F., Political Science
RICHEY, R., Theology
RICKETTS, R., Surgery, Paediatrics
RIMLAND, D., Infectious Diseases
ROARK, J., History
ROBBINS, V., Religion
ROCHAT, P., Psychology
ROCK, J. A., Gynaecology/Obstetrics
RODL, V., Mathematics and Computer Science
ROSENBERG, A., Psychiatry/Behavioural Sciences
ROTHENBERG, R. B., Family and Preventive Medicine
RUBIN, P. H., Economics
RUBINSON, R., Sociology
RUSCHE, H., English
RYAN, P. B., Environmental and Occupational Health
SALAM, A., Surgery (Vascular)
SALE, W. S., Cell Biology
SALIERS, D. E., Theology
SALMON, M. E., Nursing
SALTMAN, R. B., Health Policy and Management
SANDS, J. M., Medicine
SARAL, R., Medicine
SCHAFFER, B. K., Economics
SCHINAZI, R. F., Paediatrics
SCHISLER, C., Music History
SCHMID, R., Mathematics and Computer Science
SCHUCHARD, R., English
SCOTT, J., Cell Biology
SCOTT, J. R., Microbiology/Immunology
SEBEL, P., Anaesthesiology
SEWELL, C. W., Pathology
SHAFER, W. M., Microbiology/Immunology
SHANOR, C. A., Law
SHAPIRO, M. M., Psychology
SHAPIRO, W., Political Science
SHAPPELL, R., Physical Education
SHARP, E., Nursing
SHERMAN, S., Genetics
SHETH, J., Marketing
SHORE, B., Anthropology
SHULMAN, J. A., Medicine
SHURE, D., Biology
SIDELL, N., Gynaecology/Obstetrics
SILVERMAN, M. E., Medicine
SIMONS, J. W., Medicine
SITTER, J. E., English
SKANDALAKIS, J. E., Surgical Anatomy and Technique
SLATER, N. W., Classics
SMITH, G. R., Law

SMITH, K., Haematology/Oncology
SMITH, L. E., Theology
SMITH, R. B., III, Surgery
SNAREY, J., Human Development and Ethics, Psychology
SOCOLOW, S. M., History, Latin American and Caribbean Studies
SOLOMON, A. R., Dermatology
SPITZNAGEL, J. K., Microbiology/Immunology
SPRAWLS, P., Radiological Services
SRIVASTAVA, R., Marketing
STEIN, D., Emergency Medicine
STEIN, D. G., Psychology
STEIN, K. W., Middle East Research
STERK, C. E., Behavioural Science and Health Education
STERN, B. J., Neurology
STERNBERG, P., Ophthalmology
STOKES, D., Biology
STONE, J., Medicine
STRICKLAND, O., Nursing
STULTING, R. D., Ophthalmology
SUNDERAM, V. S., Mathematics and Computer Science
SUNG, Y. F., Anaesthesiology
SYBERS, R. G., Radiology
SYMBAS, P., Cardiothoracic Surgery
TARCAN, Y., Radiology
TAYLOR, A., Nuclear Medicine, Radiology
TERRELL, T. P., Law
THOMAS, L.-G., III, Business Organization and Management
THORPE, K. E., Health Policy and Management
TIPTON, S. M., Theology
TORRES, W. E., Radiology
TUNE, L., Psychiatry/Behavioural Sciences
TUSA, R., Neurology
VAN DER VYVER, J., International Law
VANDALL, F. J., Law
VARADY, T., Law
VERENE, D. P., III, Philosophy
VINTEN-JOHANSEN, J., Cardiothoracic Surgery
VON WURTTEMBERG, A., Sanskrit
WAINER, B. E., Pathology, Geriatric Medicine
WALKER, E., Psychology
WALKER, H. K., Medicine
WALKER, T. G., Political Science
WALLEN, K., Psychology, Primate Research
WALLER, J. L., Anaesthesiology
WALTER, P. F., Medicine
WALTMAN, P., Mathematics and Computer Science
WARING, G. O., Ophthalmology
WARREN, S., Genetics
WATTS, N. B., Endocrinology
WATTS, R. L., Neurology
WAYMIRE, G., Marketing
WEATHERS, D. R., Pathology
WEBER, C. J., General Surgery
WEINTRAUB, W. S., Medicine
WEISS, B., Pathology
WEISS, J., Psychiatry/Behavioural Sciences
WEISS, S. A., Pathology
WENGER, N. K., Medicine
WHITE, D. F., Liberal Arts
WHITE, S., History
WHITESIDES, T. E., Orthopaedics
WILCOX, W. D., Paediatrics
WILKINSON, K. D., Biochemistry
WILLIAMS, W. H., Cardiothoracic Surgery
WILSON, M., Primate Research
WINOGRAD, E., Psychology
WITTE, J., Law
WOLF, S. L., Rehabilitation Medicine
WOOD, J. G., Cell Biology
WOOD, W. C., Surgical Oncology
WORKOWSKI, K. A., Infectious Diseases
WORTHMAN, C., Anthropology
YOUNG, J., Epidemiology
YOUNG, L., Physiology
ZAIDAN, J. R., Anaesthesiology
ZIEGLER, H. K., Microbiology/Immunology
ZUMPE, D., Psychiatry/Behavioural Sciences

FORT VALLEY STATE UNIVERSITY

1005 State University Dr., Fort Valley, GA 31030-4313

Telephone: (478) 825-6211
Fax: (478) 825-6394
E-mail: registrar1@fvsu.edu
Internet: www.fvsu.edu

Founded 1895 as Fort Valley High and Industrial School, present name and status 1996
State control
Academic year: July to June

Pres.: Prof. Dr LARRY EUGENE RIVERS
Exec. Vice-Pres. and Chief Legal Officer: Dr CANTER BROWN
Vice-Pres. for Academic Affairs: Dr JULIUS SCIPIO
Vice-Pres. for Business and Finance: HENRY SPINKS
Vice-Pres. for Business and Finance: HENRY SPINKS
Vice-Pres. for External Affairs: Dr MELODY L. CARTER
Vice-Pres. for Student Affairs and Enrolment Management: WILLIE L. WILLIAMS
Dir of Admissions: DONAVON COLEY
Registrar: SHAREE J. LAWRENCE
Librarian: Dr ANNIE M. PAYTON

Library of 191,806 vols
Number of teachers: 202 (153 full-time, 49 part-time)
Number of students: 3,500

DEANS

College of Agriculture, Family Sciences and Technology: Dr GOVINDARAJAN KANNAN
College of Arts and Sciences: Dr B. KEITH MURPHY
College of Education: Dr EDWARD HILL
College of Graduate Studies and Extended Education: Dr ANNA R. HOLLOWAY

GAINESVILLE STATE COLLEGE

POB 1358, Gainesville, GA 30503
3820 Mundy Mill Rd, Oakwood, GA 30566

Telephone: (678) 717-3639
Fax: (678) 717-3751
E-mail: info@gsc.edu
Internet: www.gsc.edu

Founded 1966 as Gainesville Jr College, present name and status 2005
State control
Campus in Oconee

Pres.: Dr MARTHA T. NESBITT
Vice-Pres. and CEO for Oconee Campus: Dr MARGARET VENABLE
Vice-Pres. for Academic Affairs: Dr AL PANU
Vice-Pres. for Business and Finance: PAUL GLASER
Vice-Pres.for Institutional Advancement: MARY TRANSUE
Vice-Pres. for Student Affairs: Dr TOM G. WALTER
Chief Information Officer: BRANDON E. HAAG
Dean of Students and Assoc. Vice-Pres.: ALICIA CAUDILL
Registrar: JANICE C. HARTSOE
Dean of Libraries: Dr DEBORAH PROSSER
Number of students: 8,568 (5,229 full-time, 3,339 part-time)

DEANS

School of Business, Education, Health and Wellness: Dr MARYELLEN S. COSGROVE
School of Humanities and Fine Arts: Prof. Dr ERIC SKIPPER
School of Science, Technology, Engineering and Mathematics: Dr DANNY LAU (acting)
School of Social Sciences: Dr H. LEE CHEEK, JR

GEORGIA COLLEGE AND STATE UNIVERSITY

231 W Hancock St, Milledgeville, GA 31061

Telephone: (478) 445-5004
Fax: (478) 445-5151
E-mail: admissions@gcsu.edu
Internet: www.gcsu.edu

Founded 1889 as Georgia Normal and Industrial College, present name and status 1996
State control
Pres.: Dr STANLEY PRECZEWSKI
Provost and Vice-Pres. for Academic Affairs: Dr SANDRA JORDAN
Gen. Counsel: MARC CARDINALLI
Vice-Pres. for Admin. and Operations: Dr PAUL JONES
Vice-Pres. for External Relations and Univ. Advancement: AMY AMASON
Vice-Pres. for Institutional Research and Enrolment Management: Dr PAUL JONES
Vice-Pres. for Student Affairs and Dean of Students: Dr BRUCE HARSHBARGER
Dir of Libraries: NANCY DAVIS BRAY

Library of 200,000 vols, 37,118 journals, 37,920 federal documents, 23,500 print and electronic periodicals, partial depository for US govt documents
Number of teachers: 316 (full-time)
Number of students: 6,737 (5,715 undergraduate, 1,022 graduate)

DEANS

College of Arts and Sciences: KENNETH J. PROCTER
College of Health Sciences: Dr SANDRA GANGSTEAD
J. Whitney Bunting College of Business: Dr MATTHEW LIAO-TROTH
John H. Lounsbury College of Education: Dr JANE HINSON

GEORGIA HEALTH SCIENCES UNIVERSITY

1120 15th St, Augusta, GA 30912

Telephone: (706) 721-0211
E-mail: admissions@georgiahealth.edu
Internet: www.georgiahealth.edu

Founded 1828 as Medical Academy of Georgia, present name 2011
State control
Pres.: Dr RICARDO AZZIZ
Provost and Exec. Vice-Pres. for Academic Affairs: Dr GRETCHEN CAUGHMAN
Sr Vice-Pres. for Admin. and Chief Admin. Officer: Dr WILLIAM BOWES
Sr Vice-Pres. for Advancement and Community Relations and Chief Devt Officer: SUSAN L. BARCUS
Sr Vice-Pres. for Finance and Chief Financial Officer: DENNIS ROEMER
Sr Vice-Pres. for Research: Dr MARK HAMRICK
Vice-Pres. for Instruction and Enrolment Management and Assoc. Provost: Dr ROMAN CIBIRKA
Vice-Pres. for Institutional Effectiveness: BETH BRIGDON
Vice-Pres. for Student Services and Devt: KEVIN FRAZIER
Chief Information Officer: HELEN THOMPSON
Registrar: HEATHER METRESS, RITA GARNER
Dir of Libraries: Prof. Dr DAVID KING

Library of 164,984 vols, 4,000 periodicals
Number of teachers: 1,027 (651 full-time,)
Number of students: 2,442

Publications: GHSU Today Magazine (3 a year), MCG Tomorrow (1 a year), Scope, Word of Mouth Magazine (3 a year)

DEANS

College of Allied Health Sciences: Prof. Dr ANDREW BALAS
College of Dental Medicine: Dr CONNIE L. DRISKO
College of Graduate Studies: Dr EDWARD INSCHO
College of Nursing: Prof. Dr LUCY MARION
Medical College of Georgia: Dr PETER F. BUCKLEY

GEORGIA INSTITUTE OF TECHNOLOGY

225 North Avenue NW, Atlanta, GA 30332

Telephone: (404) 894-2000
Internet: www.gatech.edu

Founded 1885, present name 1948
State control
Academic year: August to May
Pres.: Dr G. P. PETERSON
Provost and Exec. Vice-Pres. for Academic Affairs: Dr RAFAEL L. BRAS
Sr Vice Provost for Academic Affairs: ANDERSON D. SMITH
Exec. Vice-Pres. for Admin. and Finance: STEVEN G. SWANT
Vice-Pres. for Devt: BARRETT H. CARSON
Vice-Pres. for Institute Diversity: Dr ARCHIE W. ERVIN
Exec. Vice-Pres. for Research: Dr STEPHEN E. CROSS
Vice-Pres. for Student Affairs: Dr WILLIAM D. SCHAFER
Exec. Dir of Govt and Community Relations: DENE H. SHEHEANE
Registrar: RETA PIKOWSKY
Dean of Libraries: CATHERINE MURRARY-RUST

Library of 2,549,845 vols (incl. books, serial backfiles and govt documents), 4,668,536 microforms, 325,350 audiovisual materials, 46,017 current serial subscriptions
Number of teachers: 1,106
Number of students: 20,941

Publications: Blue Print, Research Horizons, The Technique

DEANS

College of Architecture: Prof. ALAN BALFOUR
College of Computing: Prof. ZVI GALIL
College of Engineering: Prof. GARY S. MAY
College of Management: Prof. STEVE SALBU
College of Sciences: Prof. Dr PAUL HOUSTON
Ivan Allen College of Liberal Arts: Prof. JACQUELINE JONES-ROYSTER

GEORGIA SOUTHERN UNIVERSITY

POB 8024, Statesboro, GA 30460
1332 S Dr., Statesboro, GA 30458

Telephone: (912) 478-4636
Fax: (912) 478-1156
E-mail: admissions@georigasouthern.edu
Internet: www.georgiasouthern.edu

Founded 1906
State control
Academic year: August to July
Pres.: Prof. Dr BROOKS A. KEEL
Provost: Dr WILLIAM T. MOORE
Vice-Pres. for Business and Finance: Dr RONALD J. CORE
Vice-Pres. for Research: Dr CHARLES E. PATTERSON
Vice-Pres. for Student Affairs and Enrolment Management: Dr TERESA ELAINE THOMPSON
Vice-Pres. for Univ. Advancement: SALINDA ARTHUR
Registrar: T. MICHAEL DEAL
Dean of the Library: W. BEDE MITCHELL

Library of 1,579,038 vols incl. 761,163 govt documents, 896,011 microforms
Number of teachers: 784 (759 full-time)

Number of students: 19,691 (17,044 undergraduates, 2,647 graduate)

DEANS

Allen E. Paulson College of Science and Technology: Dr BRET DANILOWICZ
College of Business Admin.: Dr RONALD SHIFFLER
College of Education: Dr THOMAS R. KOBALLA, JR
College of Engineering and Information Technology: MOHAMMAD DAVOUD
College of Health and Human Sciences: Prof. Dr JEAN BARTELS
College of Liberal Arts and Social Sciences: Dr MICHAEL R. SMITH
Jack N. Averitt College of Graduate Studies: Dr CHARLES PATTERSON
Jiann-Ping Hsu College of Public Health: Prof. Dr LYNN D. WOODHOUSE

GEORGIA SOUTHWESTERN STATE UNIVERSITY

800 GSW State Univ. Dr., Americus, GA 31709

Telephone: (229) 928-1273
E-mail: gswapps@canes.gsw.edu
Internet: www.gsw.edu

Founded 1906 as Third Agricultural and Mechanical School; present name 1996
State control
Academic year: August to May
Pres.: Dr KENDALL BLANCHARD
Vice-Pres. for Academic Affairs and Dean of Faculty: Dr BRIAN U. ADLER
Vice-Pres. for Business and Finance: W. CODY KING
Vice-Pres. for Student Affairs: Dr SAMUEL T. MILLER
Vice-Pres. for Univ. Relations: (vacant)
Vice-Pres. for Enrolment Management: Dr GAYE S. HAYES
Registrar: KRISTA SMITH
Dean of the Library: VERA J. WEISSKOPF

Library of 190,000 vols
Number of teachers: 108
Number of students: 3,046 (2,811 undergraduate, 235 graduate)

DEANS

College of Arts and Sciences: Dr KELLY McCOY
School of Business Admin.: Dr LIZ WILSON
School of Computing and Mathematics: Dr BORIS V. PELTSVERGER
School of Education: Prof. Dr LETTIE J. WATFORD
School of Nursing: Prof. Dr SANDRA DANIEL

GEORGIA STATE UNIVERSITY

POB 3965, Atlanta, GA 30302-3965

Telephone: (404) 651-2500
Fax: (404) 413-2002
Internet: www.gsu.edu

Founded 1913
State control
Academic year: August to May
Pres.: Dr MARK P. BECKER
Provost and Sr Vice-Pres. for Academic Affairs: Dr RISA PALM
Sr Vice-Pres. for Finance and Admin.: JERRY RACKLIFFE
Vice-Pres. for Devt: WALTER MASSEY
Vice-Pres. for Research and Economic Devt: JAMES WEYHENMEYER
Vice-Pres. for Student Affairs: Dr DOUGLASS F. COVEY
Registrar: SHARI PIOTROWSKI SCHWARTZ
Dean of Libraries: NANCY H. SEAMANS

Library of 3,444,343 vols
Number of teachers: 1,142 (full-time)
Number of students: 32,000

Publications: *GSU Magazine* (4 a year), *Health and Human Review* (2 a year), *Law Review* (4 a year), *State of Business Magazine* (2 a year), *The Forecast for the Nation* (4 a year)

DEANS

Andrew Young School of Policy Studies: MARY BETH WALKER (acting)

Byrdine F. Lewis School of Nursing and Health Professions: Dr MARGARET C. WILMOTH

College of Arts and Sciences: Dr WILLIAM J. LONG

College of Education: Prof. Dr RANDY W. KAMPHAUS

College of Law: Dr STEVEN J. KAMINSHINE (acting)

Honors College: Dr LARRY BERMAN

J. Mack Robinson College of Business: Dr H. FENWICK HUSS

GORDON COLLEGE

419 College Dr., Barnesville, GA 30204

Telephone: (678) 359-5555

Fax: (678) 359-5080

E-mail: gordon@gdn.edu

Internet: www.gdn.edu

Founded 1852 as Barnesville Male and Female High School, present name and status 2006

State control

Academic divs incl. business and social science, humanities, mathematics and natural sciences, nursing and health sciences, teacher education

Pres.: Dr MAX BURNS

Vice-Pres. for Academic Affairs: ED WHEELER

Vice-Pres. for Business Affairs: Dr LEE FRUITTICHER

Vice-Pres. for Institutional Advancement: RHONDA TOON

Vice-Pres. for Student Affairs: Dr DENNIS R. CHAMBERLAIN

Dir of Admissions: BENNETT FERGUSON

Registrar: JANET BARRAS

Library Dir: NANCY ANDERSON

Library of 102,757 vols, 27,417 e-books, 9,637 microfilms, 4,785 audiovisual materials

Number of teachers: 229 (115 full-time, 114 part-time)

Number of students: 5,000

INTERDENOMINATIONAL THEOLOGICAL CENTER

700 Martin Luther King, Jr Dr., SW, Atlanta, GA 303144143

Telephone: (404) 527-7700

Fax: (404) 527-0901

E-mail: info@itc.edu

Internet: www.itc.edu

Founded 1958

Private control

Academic year: September to May

Pres.: Rev. Dr RONALD EDWARD PETERS

Provost and Exec. Vice-Pres. for Academic Services: Dr TEMBA MAFICO

Vice-Pres. for Financial and Admin. Services: ELIZABETH LITTLEJOHN

Dir of Institutional Advacement: Dr GEORGE THOMPSON

Registrar: BOBBIE HALL

Library Dir: LORETTA PARHAM

Library of 383,000 vols, 43,000 e-books, 867,000 microforms, 3,14,000 govt documents, 17,000 theses and dissertations, 35,000 bound periodicals, 1,500 current periodical subscriptions

Publications: *Journal of the Interdenominational Theological Center* (2 a year), *The Lantern* (1 a year)

DEANS

Charles H. Mason Theological Seminary: HAROLD D BENNETT

Gammon Theological Seminary: ALBERT MOSLEY

Johnson C. Smith Theological Seminary: PAUL T. ROBERTS

Morehouse School of Religion: G. MARTIN YOUNG

Phillips School Of Theology: MARVIN FRANK THOMAS

Turner Theological Seminary: JOHN FRANK GREEN

KENNESAW STATE UNIVERSITY

1000 Chastain Rd, Kennesaw, GA 30144

Telephone: (770) 423-6000

E-mail: ksuadmit@kennesaw.edu

Internet: www.kennesaw.edu

Founded 1966 as Kennesaw Jr College; present name 1996

State control

Academic year: August to May

Pres.: Dr DANIEL S. PAPP

Provost and Vice-Pres. for Academic Affairs: Prof. Dr WILLIAM KEN HARMON

Vice-Pres. for External Affairs: ARLETHIA PERRY-JOHNSON

Vice-Pres. for Research and Dean of Graduate Studies: Dr CHARLES AMLANER

Vice-Pres. for Student Success: Dr JEROME RATCHFORD

Vice-Pres. for Univ. Advancement: JOE MEEKS

Registrar and Assoc. Vice-Pres. for Enrolment Services: KIM WEST

Library Dir: BETTY CHILDRES

Library of 600,000 vols and govt publs

Number of teachers: 1,277 (737 full-time, 540 part-time)

Number of students: 23,452 (21,467 undergraduates, 1,985 graduate)

DEANS

Bagwell College of Education: Dr ARLINDA J. EATON

Coles College of Business: Dr KATHY SCHWAIG

College of Continuing and Professional Education: BARBARA S. CALHOUN

College of Health and Human Services: Dr RICHARD L. SOWELL

College of Humanities and Social Sciences: Dr RICHARD VENGROFF

College of Science and Mathematics: Prof. Dr RONALD H. MATSON

College of the Arts: Prof. JOSEPH D. MEEKS

Univ. College: Prof. Dr RALPH J. RASCATI

LAGRANGE COLLEGE

601 Broad St, LaGrange, GA 30240-2999

Telephone: (706) 880-8000

Fax: (706) 880-8358

Internet: www.lagrange.edu

Founded 1831, present name 1934

Private control

Academic year: September to May

Major areas of study incl. accountancy, art and design, biochemistry, biology, business management, chemistry, computer science, early childhood education, English, exercise science, history, mathematics, music, nursing, political science, psychology, religion, sociology, Spanish, theatre arts

Pres.: Dr DAN MCALEXANDER

Provost and Chief Academic Officer: Prof. Dr DAVID L. GARRISON

Exec. Vice-Pres. for Admin.: PHYLLIS D. WHITNEY

Vice-Pres. for Academic Affairs and Dean: Dr JAY K. SIMMONS

Vice-Pres. for Advancement: WILLIAM JONES

Dir for Enrolment Management and Admissions: RICHARD DANA PAUL

Vice-Pres. for Finance and Operations: MARTIN E. PIRRMAN

Dean of Students: Prof. Dr JACK C. SLAY, JR

Registrar: JIMMY HERRING

Library Dir: LOREN PINKERMAN

Library of 190,000 vols

Number of teachers: 75

Number of students: 994

LIFE UNIVERSITY

1269 Barclay Circle, Marietta, GA 30060

Telephone: (770) 426-2600

Fax: (770) 426-2895

E-mail: admissions@life.edu

Internet: www.life.edu

Founded 1974 as Life Chiropractic College; present name and status 1996

Private control

Pres.: Dr GUY F. RIEKEMAN

Provost and Exec. Vice-Pres.: Dr BRIAN J. MCAULAY

Vice-Pres. for Operations and Finance: WILLIAM D. JARR

Vice-Pres. for Univ. Advancement: GREG HARRIS

Exec. Dir of Enrolment Management: Dr GARY SULLENGER

Exec. Dir of Student Services: MARC SCHNEIDER

Registrar: BRIAN SHERES

Library Dir: SUSAN A. STEWART

Number of teachers: 126

Number of students: 2,609

Publications: *Today's Chiropractic LifeStyle* (6 a year), *Your Extraordinary LIFE* (3 a year)

DEANS

College of Chiropractic Science: Dr LESLIE KING

College of Graduate Studies and Research: Dr CATHERINE FAUST

College of Undergraduate Studies: Dr MICHAEL SMITH

MACON STATE COLLEGE

100 College Station Dr., Macon, GA 31206-5145

Telephone: (478) 471-2700

Fax: (478) 757-2621

E-mail: mscinfo@maconstate.edu

Internet: www.maconstate.edu

Founded 1968 as Macon Jr College, present name and status 1997

State control

Campus in Warner Robins

Pres.: Dr JEFFERY S. ALLBRITTEN

Provost and Vice-Pres. for Academic Affairs: Dr MARTHA VENN

Vice-Pres. for External Affairs and Continuing Studies: ALBERT J. ABRAMS

Vice-Pres. for Fiscal Affairs: NANCY STROUD

Vice-Pres. for Student Affairs and Enrolment Management: Dr MELANIE MCCLELLAN

Chief Information Officer: ROGER DIXON

Dean of Students: LYNN W. MCCRANEY

Registrar: TOM WAUGH

Library Dir: PAT BORCK

Library of 7,373 vols

Number of teachers: 187

Number of students: 5,702

DEANS

School of Arts and Sciences: Dr RONALD WILLIAMS

School of Business: Dr VARKEY K. TITUS

School of Education: Dr M. ANN LEVETT (acting)

School of Information Technology: Dr ALEX KOOHANG

School of Nursing and Health Sciences: Dr REBECCA CORVEY

MERCER UNIVERSITY

1400 Coleman Ave, Macon, GA 31207-0001

Telephone: (478) 301-2500

Fax: (478) 301-2108

E-mail: info@mercer.edu

Internet: mercer.edu

Founded 1833, present name and status 1838

Private control

Academic year: August to May

Campuses in Atlanta, Savannah

Pres.: Dr WILLIAM D. UNDERWOOD

Provost: Dr D. SCOTT DAVIS

Exec. Vice-Pres. for Admin. and Finance: Dr JAMES S. NETHERTON

Sr Vice-Pres. and Gen. Counsel: Dr WILLIAM G. SOLOMON, IV

Sr Vice-Pres. for Atlanta Campus: Dr RICHARD V. SWINDLE

Sr Vice-Pres. for Enrolment Management: Dr PENNY L. ELKINS

Sr Vice-Pres. for Univ. Advancement: JOHN A. PATTERSON

Vice-Pres. and Dean of Students: Dr DOUGLAS R. PEARSON

Dean of Students for Atlanta Campus: CLAIRE CORDELL DYES

Registrar and Vice-Provost: Dr MARILYN MINDINGALL

Dean of Univ. Libraries: ELIZABETH D. HAMMOND

Library of 796,693 vols, 1,000 current periodicals, 4,400 audio items, US govt documents

Number of teachers: 742

Number of students: 7,300

Publications: *Inside Mercer, Mercer Lawyer* (2 a year), *The Business Advisor, The Law Letter* (2 a year), *The Mercer Engineer, The Mercerian* (2 a year)

DEANS

College of Continuing and Professional Studies: Dr PRISCILLA R. DANHEISER

College of Liberal Arts: Dr LAKE LAMBERT

College of Pharmacy and Health Sciences: Prof. Dr HEWITT W. MATTHEWS

Eugene W. Stetson School of Business and Economics: Dr D. SCOTT DAVIS

Georgia Baptist College of Nursing: Prof. Dr LINDA A. STREIT

James and Carolyn McAfee School of Theology: Prof. R. ALAN CULPEPPER

School of Engineering: Prof. Dr WADE H. SHAW

School of Medicine: Dr WILLIAM F. BINA, III

Tift College of Education: Dr CARL R. MARTRAY

Townsend School of Music: Dr DAVID KEITH

Walter F. George School of Law: Prof. GARY SIMSON

MIDDLE GEORGIA COLLEGE

1100 Second St, SE, Cochran, GA 31014

Telephone: (478) 934-6221

Fax: (478) 934-3403

E-mail: admissions@mgc.edu

Internet: www.mgc.edu

Founded 1884 as Middle Georgia Agricultural and Mechanical Jr College, present name and status 1929

State control

Academic year: May to May

Campuses in Dublin, Eastman; academic divs incl. aviation management, business, fiscal affairs, humanities, science, mathematics and engineering, social science education

Pres.: Dr W. MICHAEL STOY

Vice-Pres. for Academic Affairs: Dr MARY LOU FRANK

Vice-Pres. for Fiscal Affairs: LYNN HOBBS

Vice-Pres. for Student and Public Affairs: JENNIFER BRANNON

Registrar and Dir of Admissions: JOHN EDGE

Dir of Library Resources: PAUL E. ROBARDS

Library of 55,000 vols, 933 periodicals.

MOREHOUSE COLLEGE

830 Westview Dr., SW, Atlanta, GA 30314

Telephone: (404) 681-2800

Fax: (404) 572-3668

E-mail: admissions@morehouse.edu

Internet: www.morehouse.edu

Founded 1867 as Augusta Institute, present name and status 1913

Private control

Pres.: Prof. Dr ROBERT M. FRANKLIN, JR

Provost and Sr Vice-Pres. for Academic Affairs: WELDON JACKSON

Vice-Pres. for Business and Finance: SHEILA JACOBS

Vice-Pres. for Campus Operations: ANDRÉ BERTRAND

Vice-Pres. for Institutional Advancement: PHILLIP HOWARD

Vice-Pres. for Student Services: WILLIAM BYNUM, JR

Dean of Admissions: KEVIN L. WILLIAMS

Library Dir: LORETTA PARHAM

Library of 404,000 vols, 31,000 bound journals, 1,500 current serials, 7,600 audiovisual materials

Number of teachers: 217 (164 full-time, 53 part-time)

Number of students: 2,800

Publications: *Inside Morehouse, Journal of Negro History, Morehouse Magazine* (1 a year)

DEANS

Div. of Business and Economics: JOHN E. WILLIAMS

Div. of Humanities and Social Science: Dr TOBE JOHNSON

Div. of Science and Mathematics: Dr JOHN K. HAYNES

MOREHOUSE SCHOOL OF MEDICINE

720 Westview Dr., SW, Atlanta, GA 30310-1495

Telephone: (404) 752-1500

Fax: (404) 752-1512

Internet: www.msm.edu

Founded 1975 as School of Medicine at Morehouse College; present name 1981

Private control

Academic year: July to May

Depts of community health and preventive medicine, family medicine, internal medicine, medical education, microbiology, biochemistry and immunology, neurobiology, obstetrics and gynaecology, pathology and anatomy, paediatrics, pharmacology and toxicology, physiology, psychiatry and behavioural sciences, surgery,

Pres.: Dr JOHN E. MAUPIN, JR

Dean and Exec. Vice-Pres.: Dr VALERIE MONTGOMERY RICE

Sr Vice-Pres. for Admin. and Chief Financial Officer: DONNETTA S. BUTLER

Vice-Pres. for Institutional Advancement: SALLY DAVIS

Vice-Pres. and Sr Assoc. Dean: Dr SANDRA HARRIS-HOOKER

Chief Information Officer: CIGDEM DELANO

Gen. Counsel: HAROLD JORDAN

Registrar: DERRECK PRESSLEY

Library Dir: JOE SWANSON, JR

Library of 80,000 vols

Number of teachers: 204

Number of students: 329

Publication: *MSM Magazine* (1 a year).

NORTH GEORGIA COLLEGE AND STATE UNIVERSITY

82 College Circle, Dahlonega, GA 30597

Telephone: (706) 864-1400

Fax: (706) 864-1478

E-mail: admissions@northgeorgia.edu

Internet: www.northgeorgia.edu

Founded 1873 as North Georgia Agricultural College, present name and status 1996

State control

Academic year: August to May

Pres.: Prof. Dr BONITA JACOBS

Vice-Pres. for Academic Affairs: Dr PATRICIA DONAT (acting)

Vice-Pres. for Business and Finance: FRANK J. McCONNELL

Vice-Pres. for Exec. Affairs: BILLY WELLS

Vice-Pres. for Institutional Advancement: Dr ANDREW J. LEAVITT

Vice-Pres. for Student Affairs: Col. TOM PALMER

Chief Information Officer: Dr BRYSON PAYNE

Registrar: JILL BRADY

Dir of Library Services: SHAWN TONNER

Library of 180,000 vols (incl. print and e-books), 40,000 electronic and print periodicals

Number of teachers: 362

Number of students: 6,100

Publications: *Honores: The NGCSU Journal of Undergraduate Research* (2 a year), *North Georgia Leader* (2 a year)

DEANS

Mike Cottrell School of Business: Dr RICHARD OATES

School of Arts and Letters: Dr CHRISTOPHER JESPERSEN

School of Education: Dr ROBERT O. MICHAEL

School of Science and Health Professions: Prof. Dr MICHAEL S. BODRI

OGLETHORPE UNIVERSITY

4484 Peachtree Rd, NE, Atlanta, GA 30319

Telephone: (404) 261-1441

Fax: (404) 364-8500

E-mail: admission@oglethorpe.edu

Internet: www.oglethorpe.edu

Founded 1835

Private control

Academic year: September to May

Offers bachelor of arts, science

Pres.: Dr LAWRENCE M. SCHALL

Provost and Vice-Pres. for Academic Affairs: Dr DENISE VON HERRMANN

Vice-Pres. for Business and Finance: MIKE HORAN

Vice-Pres. for Devt and Alumni Relations: PETER A. ROONEY

Vice-Pres. for Enrolment and Financial Aid: LUCY LEUSCH

Registrar: GAIL MEIS

Dir of Library: ANNE A. SALTER

Library of 150,000 bound vols, 1,600 DVDs

Number of teachers: 116

Number of students: 1,230

Publications: *Telefunkin', The Flying Petrel* (4 a year), *The Tower* (2 a year), *Yamacraw* (1 a year).

PAINE COLLEGE

1235 15th St, Augusta, GA 30901-3182

Telephone: (706) 821-8200

Fax: (706) 821-8373

Internet: www.paine.edu

Founded 1882, present name and status 1903
Private control
Academic year: August to May
Pres.: Dr GEORGE C. BRADLEY
Provost and Vice-Pres. for Academic Affairs:
MARCUS TILLERY
Vice-Pres. and Dean of Student Affairs: TINA
CARDENAS
Vice-Pres. for Admin. and Fiscal Affairs:
LEROY SUMMERS, JR
Vice-Pres. for Institutional Devt: BRANDON
BROWN
Registrar: CASTINE RHOADES WILLIAMS
Dir of Library: LYN DENNISON
Library of 122,752 vols, periodicals, elec-
tronic resources
Number of teachers: 129 (60 full-time)
Number of students: 925
Publications: *The Lion* (1 a year), *The Paine
Magazine* (4 a year)

DEANS

School of Arts and Sciences: Dr EMILY ALLEN
WILLIAMS
School of Professional Studies: Dr STEVEN L.
THOMAS

PIEDMONT COLLEGE

POB 10, 165 Central Ave, Demorest, GA
30535
Telephone: (706) 778-3000
Fax: (706) 778-0701
E-mail: ugrad@piedmont.edu
Internet: www.piedmont.edu
Founded 1897 as J. S. Green Collegiate
Institute, present name 1903
Private control
Academic year: August to May
Campus in Athens
Pres.: Dr JAMES F. MELLICHAMP
Admissions: CINDY PETERSON
Registrar: LINDA WOFFORD
Dir of Library Services: ROBERT GLASS
Library of 95,000 vols
Number of teachers: 120
Number of students: 2,700

DEANS

School of Arts and Sciences: Dr STEVEN
NIMMO
School of Business: Prof. Dr JOHN M. MISNER
School of Education: Dr BOB CUMMINGS
School of Nursing: Prof. Dr LINDA SCOTT

POINT UNIVERSITY

2605 Ben Hill Rd, East Point, GA 30344
Telephone: (404) 761-8861
Internet: point.edu
Founded 1937 as Atlanta Christian College,
present name 2011
Private control
Academic year: August to May
Depts of Biblical studies, business, counsel-
ling and human services, education, fine arts,
humanities and general studies, math and
science
Pres.: DEAN C. COLLINS
Chief Academic Officer and Vice-Pres. for
Adult and Professional Studies: Dr W.
DARRYL HARRISON
Vice-Pres. for Academic Affairs: Dr KIMBERLY
C. MACENCZAK
Vice-Pres. for Admin. and Chief Financial
Officer: JEFF HAVERLY
Vice-Pres. for Advancement: EMMA W. MOR-
RIS
Vice-Pres. for Business and Finance: JEFFREY
A. HAVERLY
Vice-Pres. for Enrolment Management:
STACY BARTLETT

Vice-Pres. for Institutional Effectiveness: Dr
DENNIS E. GLENN
Vice-Pres. for Student Devt and Dean of
Chapel: SAMUEL W. HUXFORD
Dir of Admission: TIFFANY SCHOENOFF
Registrar: LISA SELLERS
Library Dir: Prof. MICHEAL L. BAIN
Library of 80,000 vols
Number of teachers: 26 (full-time)
Number of students: 1,288

REINHARDT UNIVERSITY

7300 Reinhardt College Circle, Waleska, GA
30183-2981
Telephone: (770) 720-5600
Fax: (770) 720-5602
E-mail: admissions@reinhardt.edu
Internet: www.reinhardt.edu
Founded 1883 as Reinhardt Acad., present
name and status 2010
Private control
Academic year: August to May
Pres.: Dr J. THOMAS ISHERWOOD
Vice-Pres. and Dean for Academic Affairs: Dr
ROBERT L. DRISCOLL
Vice-Pres. for Finance and Admin.: ROBERT
G. MCKINNON
Vice-Pres. for Institutional Advancement
and External Affairs: JOELLEN B. WILSON
Vice-Pres. for Student Affairs and Dean of
Students: Dr ROGER R. LEE
Registrar: JANET M. RODNING
Library Dir: MICHAEL MARTINEZ
Library of 70,730 vols, periodicals, microfilm,
microfiche
Number of teachers: 60 (full-time)
Number of students: 1,154

DEANS

McCamish School of Business: Dr DONALD D.
WILSON, JR
Price School of Education: Dr JAMES L.
CURRY, JR
School of Arts and Humanities: Dr A. WAYNE
GLOWKA
School of Mathematics and Sciences: Prof. Dr
WILLIAM J. DE ANGELIS
School of Music: Dr DENNIS K. MCINTIRE

SAVANNAH COLLEGE OF ART AND DESIGN

POB 77300, Atlanta, GA 30357-1300
1600 Peachtree St, NE, Atlanta, GA 30309
Telephone: (404) 253-2700
Fax: (404) 253-3466
E-mail: scadatl@scad.edu
Internet: www.scad.edu
Founded 1978
Private control
Academic year: August to May
Campuses in Hong Kong, Lacoste, Savannah
Pres. and Co-Founder: PAULA S. WALLACE
Chief Academic Officer: TOM FISCHER
Vice-Pres. for Academic Support: Dr GOKHAN
OZAYSIN
Vice-Pres. for Business and Finance: DAVID
LEOPARD
Vice-Pres. for Enrolment Management:
SCOTT LINZEY
Vice-Pres. for Student Success: PHIL ALLETTO
Exec. Dir of Institutional Advancement:
MCLEAN HOOFF
Dean of Library Services: DEBORAH IRENE
PROSSER
Library of 40,000 vols, 370 periodicals
Number of teachers: 720
Number of students: 11,000

DEANS

School of Building Arts: CHRISTIAN SOTTILE
School of Communication Arts: JOHN LOWE

School of Design: VICTOR ERMOLI
School of Fashion: MICHAEL FINK
School of Film, Digital Media and Performing
Arts: PETER WEISHAR
School of Fine Arts: STEVE BLISS
School of Foundation Studies: MAUREEN
GARVIN
School of Liberal Arts: ROBERT EISINGER

SAVANNAH STATE UNIVERSITY

3219 College St, Savannah, GA 31404
Telephone: (912) 3568-4778
Fax: (912) 356-2998
E-mail: registrar@savannahstate.edu
Internet: www.savannahstate.edu
Founded 1890 as Georgia State Industrial
College, present name and status 1996
State control
Academic year: August to May
Pres.: Dr CHERYL DAVENPORT DOZIER
Vice-Pres. for Academic Affairs: Dr MOSTAFA
SARHAN
Vice-Pres. for Business and Financial
Affairs: EDWARD B. JOLLEY, JR
Vice-Pres. forUniv. Advancement: (vacant)
Vice-Pres. for Student Affairs: Dr IRVIN
CLARK
Library Dir: MARY JO FAYOYIN
Library of 190,209 vols, 30,000 bound peri-
odicals, 548,273 microforms and print peri-
odical subscriptions, 4,000 audiovisuals
Number of teachers: 357 (157 full-time, 43
part-time)
Number of students: 4,080

DEANS

College of Business Admin.: Prof. Dr MOS-
TAFA SARHAN
College of Liberal Arts And Social Sciences:
Dr MICHAEL SCHROEDER
College of Sciences And Technology: Dr
DERREK B. DUNN

SHORTER UNIVERSITY

315 Shorter Ave, Rome, GA 30165-4298
Telephone: (706) 291-2121
Fax: (706) 236-1515
E-mail: admissions@shorter.edu
Internet: www.shorter.edu
Founded 1873 as Cherokee Baptist Female
College, present name 2010
Private control
Academic year: August to May (2 semesters)
Pres.: Dr DONALD V. DOWLESS
Provost: Dr L. CRAIG SHULL
Vice-Pres. for Advancement: BERT EPTING
Vice-Pres. for Devt and Alumni: SUZANNE
SCOTT (acting)
Vice-Pres. for Enrolment Management: Dr
JOHN HEAD
Vice-Pres. for Finance and Chief Financial
Officer: STEPHANIE OWENS
Vice-Pres. for Student Affairs and Dean of
Students: Dr. DEBRA FAUST
Vice-Pres. for University Management: BERT
EPTING
Dir of Admissions: PATRICK MCELHANEY
Registrar: BRANDI BERGER
Dir of Libraries: DEWAYNE WILLIAMS
Library of 144,673 vols, 8,230 microforms,
65,397 audiovisual materials, 51,199 e-
books
Number of teachers: 417 (99 full-time, 318
part-time)
Number of students: 3,775
Publications: *Shorter Magazine* (1 a year),
The Chimes (1 a year)

DEANS

College of Adult and Professional Programs:
Dr BARBARA FINN

College of Arts and Sciences: Dr SABRENA R. PARTON

Robert H. Ledbetter College of Business: Dr ROBERT DARVILLE, III

School of Education: Dr SANDRA LESLIE

School of Fine and Performing Arts: Dr ALAN WINGARD

School of Nursing: Dr VANICE W. ROBERTS

School of Science and Mathematics: Dr CRAIG ALLEE

SOUTH UNIVERSITY

709 Mall Blvd, Savannah, GA 31406-4805

Telephone: (912) 201-8000

E-mail: susavadm@southuniversity.edu

Internet: www.southuniversity.edu

Founded 1899 as Draughon's Practical Business College, present name and status 2001

Private control

Academic year: September to September

Campuses in Alabama, Austin, Florida, Michigan, Ohio, South Carolina, Texas, Virginia

Chancellor: JOHN T. SOUTH, III

Vice-Chancellor for Academic Affairs: Dr STEVEN K. YOHO

Vice-Chancellor for Finance: CHAD THOMPSON

Vice-Chancellor for South Univ. Campuses: Dr DAN PETERSON

Vice-Pres. for Academic Affairs: Dr LESLIE BAUGHMAN

Registrar: ANITA MACIAS

Dir of Univ. Libraries: KATE SAWYER

Number of students: 23,764

DEANS

College of Arts and Sciences: Dr JOHN MICHAEL BROOKS

College of Business: Dr STEVEN K. YOHO (acting)

College of Creative Art and Design: Dr LESLIE BAUGHMAN

College of Health Professions: Dr A. WILLIAM PAULSEN

College of Nursing: Dr MARY WALKER

School of Pharmacy: Prof. Dr JAMES E. WYNN

SOUTHERN POLYTECHNIC STATE UNIVERSITY

1100 S Marietta Parkway, Marietta, GA 30060-2896

Telephone: (678) 915-7778

Fax: (678) 915-3202

E-mail: admiss@spsu.edu

Internet: www.spsu.edu

Founded 1948 as Technical Institute, present name and status 1996

State control

Academic year: August to August

Pres.: Dr LISA A. ROSSBACHER

Vice-Pres. for Academic Affairs: Dr ZVI SZAFRAN

Vice-Pres. for Advancement: RON DEMPSEY

Vice-Pres. for Business and Finance: BILL PRIGGE

Vice-Pres. for Student and Enrolment Services: Dr RON R. KOGER

Dir for Admissions: GARY BUSH

Library Dir: Dr JOYCE WHITE MILLS

Library of 129,954 vols, 994 periodicals and newspapers, 3,490 microforms, 330 audiovisual materials

Number of teachers: 200 (full-time)

Number of students: 5,514

DEANS

School of Architecture and Construction Management: Dr WILSON C. BARNES

School of Arts and Sciences: Dr THOMAS NELSON

School of Computing and Software Engineering: Dr HAN REICHGELT

School of Engineering Technology and Management: Prof. Dr THOMAS R. CURRIN

School of Engineering Technology and Management: Dr RAY JEFFREY

SPELMAN COLLEGE

350 Spelman Lane, SW, Atlanta, GA 30314-4399

Telephone: (404) 681-3642

Fax: (404) 223-1428

Internet: www.spelman.edu

Founded 1881 as Atlanta Baptist Female Seminary, present name 1924

Private control

Academic year: August to May

Offers bachelor of arts, science

Pres.: Dr BEVERLEY DANIEL TATUM

Provost and Vice-Pres. for Academic Affairs: Dr JOHNNELLA E. BUTLER

Vice-Pres. for Business and Financial Affairs and Treasurer: ROBERT D. FLANIGAN, JR

Vice-Pres. for Devt: KASSANDRA JOLLEY

Vice-Pres. for Enrolment Management: ARLENE CASH

Vice-Pres. for Institutional Advancement: KASSANDRA JOLLEY

Vice-Pres. for Student Affairs: Dr DARNITA KILLIAN

Academic Dean: Dr CYNTHIA NEAL SPENCE

Dean of Undergraduate Studies: Dr DESIREE S. PEDESCLEAUX

Registrar: Dr FREDERICK A. FRESH

Library Dir: LORETTA PARHAM

Library of 383,000 vols, 3,000 e-books, 867,000 microforms, 314,000 govt documents, 17,000 theses and dissertations, 35,000 bound periodicals, 1,500 current periodicals

Number of teachers: 156

Number of students: 2,177

THOMAS UNIVERSITY

1501 Millpond Rd, Thomasville, GA 31792-7636

Telephone: (229) 226-1621

Fax: (229) 227-6888

E-mail: admissions@thomasu.edu

Internet: www.thomasu.edu

Founded 1950 as Birdwood Jr College; present name 2000

Private control

Academic year: August to May

Depts of arts and sciences, business, education, human services, nursing, social work

Pres.: Dr GARY BONVILLIAN

Provost and Vice-Pres. for Academic Affairs: ANN LANDIS

Vice-Pres. for Finance and Admin.: TIM KLOCKO

Vice-Pres. for Institutional Advancement: RICHARD A. MUNROE

Exec. Dir of Enrolment Management and Student Affairs: MICKY WEST

Dir of Admissions: KERRI KNIGHT

Registrar: LACEY HARRISON

Dir of Library Services: AMBER BROCK

Library of 31,000 vols, 160 periodicals and newspapers

Number of teachers: 120 (50 full-time, 70 part-time)

Number of students: 1,109 (863 undergraduate, 246 graduate)

TOCCOA FALLS COLLEGE

107 N Chapel Dr., POB 800777, Toccoa Falls, GA 30598

Telephone: (706) 886-6831

Fax: (706) 282-6020

E-mail: admissions@tfc.edu

Internet: www.tfc.edu

Founded 1907

Private control

Academic year: August to May

Pres.: Dr W. WAYNE GARDNER

Provost: Dr BARBARA K. BELLEFEUILLE

Vice-Pres. for Academic Affairs: Dr W. BRIAN SHELTON

Vice-Pres. for Advancement: JAMES HANSEN

Vice-Pres. for Business and Finance: GREGG SCHULTE

Vice-Pres. for Institutional Advancement: JAMES HANSEN

Vice-Pres. for Student Devt: LEE YOWELL

Registrar: KELLY G. VICKERS

Dir of Information Services: PATRICIA FISHER

Library of 150,000 vols and 175 current subscriptions

Number of teachers: 71

Number of students: 750

DEANS

School of Arts and Sciences: Prof. Dr KIERAN CLEMENTS

School of Christian Ministries: Dr W. BRIAN SHELTON

School of Professional Studies: Prof. Dr THOMAS COUNCIL

TRUETT MCCONNELL COLLEGE

100 Alumni Dr., Cleveland, GA 30528

Telephone: (706) 865-2134

Fax: (706) 865-3110

E-mail: admissions@truett.edu

Internet: www.truett.edu

Founded 1947

Private control

Academic year: August to July (2 semesters)

Degree programmes incl. bachelor of arts in business admin., world missions; bachelor of science in education, psychology

Pres.: Dr EMIR FETHI CANER

Vice-Pres. for Academic Services: Dr BRAD REYNOLDS

Vice-Pres. for Advancement: Dr DANIEL MOOSBRUGGER

Vice-Pres. for Business Admin.: Dr DAVID ARMSTRONG

Vice-Pres. for Student Services and Athletic Dir: CHRIS EPPLING

Dir of Admissions: NATHAN RAYNOR

Registrar: MELISSA FORTNER

Library Dir: JANICE WILSON.

UNIVERSITY OF GEORGIA

Athens, GA 30602

Telephone: (706) 542-3000

E-mail: reghelp@uga.edu

Internet: www.uga.edu

Founded 1785

State control

Pres.: Dr MICHAEL F. ADAMS

Provost and Sr Vice-Pres. for Academic Affairs: Prof. JERE W. MOREHEAD

Sr Vice-Pres. for External Affairs: THOMAS S. LANDRUM

Sr Vice-Pres. for Finance and Admin.: TIMOTHY P. BURGESS

Vice-Pres. for Instruction: Dr LAURA D. JOLLY

Vice-Pres. for Public Service and Outreach: Dr JENNIFER FRUM

Vice-Pres. for Research: Dr DAVID C. LEE

Vice-Pres. for Student Affairs: Dr RODNEY D. BENNETT

Registrar: JAN HATHCOTE

Univ. Librarian: Dr WILLIAM GRAY POTTER

Library: 4.7m. vols

Number of teachers: 2,807

Number of students: 34,765 (26,571 undergraduate, 8,194 graduate)

Publications: *Environmental Ethics* (4 a year), *Georgia Economic Outlook* (1 a year), *Georgia Historical Quarterly* (4 a year), *Georgia Journal of College Student Affairs* (2 a year), *Georgia Journal of Ecological Anthropology* (1 a year), *Georgia Journal of International and Comparative Law* (3 a year), *Georgia Magazine* (4 a year), *Georgia Pharmacist Magazine* (1 a year), *Georgia Pharmacist Quarterly* (4 a year), *Georgia Preceptor* (4 a year), *Georgia Science Teacher* (3 a year), *Impact Interactive* (a service-learning magazine project, 1 a year), *Journal of Agribusiness* (2 a year), *Journal of Business Research* (12 a year), *Journal of Public Service and Outreach* (3 a year), *Journal of Research and Development in Education* (4 a year), *State and Local Government Review* (3 a year), *Teaching Georgia Government* (3 a year), *The Aesculapian* (4 a year), *The Georgia Advocate* (3 a year), *The Georgia Review* (4 a year), *Toxicology Digest* (4 a year)

DEANS

College of Agricultural and Environmental Sciences: Dr JAY SCOTT ANGLE
College of Education: Dr ARTHUR M. HORNE
College of Environment and Design: Dr DANIEL NADENICEK
College of Family and Consumer Sciences: Dr LINDA KIRK FOX
College of Pharmacy: Dr SVEIN ØIE
College of Public Health: Dr PHILLIP L. WILLIAMS
Franklin College of Arts and Sciences: Dr HUGH RUPPERSBURG
Graduate School: Dr MAUREEN GRASSO
Grady College of Journalism and Mass Communication: Dr E. CULPEPPER CLARK
Odum School of Ecology: Dr JOHN GITTLEMAN
School of Law: Prof. Dr REBECCA H. WHITE
School of Public and Int. Affairs: Dr THOMAS P. LAUTH
School of Social Work: Prof. Dr MAURICE C. DANIELS
School of Veterinary Medicine: Dr SHEILA W. ALLEN
Terry College of Business: Dr ROBERT SUMICHRAST
Warnell School of Forestry and Natural Resources: Prof. Dr MICHAEL CLUTTER

UNIVERSITY OF WEST GEORGIA

1601 Maple St, Carrollton, GA 30118
Telephone: (678) 839-5000
Fax: (678) 839-4747
E-mail: admiss@westga.edu
Internet: www.westga.edu
Founded 1906, present status 1995, present name 2005
State control
Academic year: August to July
Pres.: Dr BEHERUZ N. SETHNA
Provost and Vice-Pres. for Academic Affairs: Dr MICHAEL HORVATH
Vice-Pres. for Business and Finance: JAMES SUTHERLAND
Vice-Pres. for Student Affairs and Enrolment Management: Dr SCOT LINGRELL
Vice-Pres. for Univ. Advancement: Dr BILL ESTES
Chief Information Officer: KATHY KRAL
Registrar: DONNA HALEY
Dir of Admissions: JUSTIN BARLOW
Dir of Institutional Research and Planning: Dr EBENEZER KOLAJO
Dean of Libraries: LORENE FLANDERS
Library of 850,195 vols, 65,301 current serials subscriptions (paper, microform and electronic), 197,300 microforms, 11,634 audiovisual items, 20,000 maps and charts
Number of teachers: 600 (434 full-time, 166 part-time)

Number of students: 11,646 (10,029 undergraduate, 1,617 graduate)
Publications: *Just the Facts, Studies in the Social Sciences* (1 a year), *West Georgia College Faculty Research Review* (1 a year)

DEANS

College of Arts and Humanities: Dr RANDY J. HENDRICKS
College of Education: Dr KIM METCALF
College of Science and Mathematics: Dr BRUCE LANDMAN
College of Social Sciences: Prof. Dr N. JANE MCCANDLESS
Graduate School: Dr CHARLES W. CLARK
Honors College: Dr MICHAEL HESTER
Richards College of Business: Dr FAYE McINTYRE
School of Nursing: Prof. Dr KATHRYN M. GRAMS

VALDOSTA STATE UNIVERSITY

1500 N Patterson St, Valdosta, GA 31698
Telephone: (229) 245-6517
Fax: (229) 333-5482
E-mail: admissions@valdosta.edu
Internet: www.valdosta.edu
Founded 1906, present name and status 1993
State control
Academic year: January to December
Pres.: Dr LOUIS H. LEVY
Provost and Vice-Pres. for Academic Affairs: Dr PHILIP GUNTER
Vice-Pres. for Finance and Admin.: SUE E. MITCHELL
Vice-Pres. for Student Affairs and Dean of Students: RUSSELL MAST
Vice-Pres. for Univ. Advancement: JOHN D. CRAWFORD (acting)
Registrar: STANLEY JONES
Library Dir: Dr ALAN BERNSTEIN
Library of 549,683 vols
Number of teachers: 616
Number of students: 13,089
Publication: *The Journal of Southwest Georgia History* (4 a year)

DEANS

College of Arts and Sciences: Dr CONNIE L. RICHARDS
College of Nursing: Dr ANITA HUFFT
College of the Arts: Dr JOHN GASTON (acting)
Division of Social Work: Dr MARTHA M. GIDDINGS
Graduate School: Dr ALFRED F. FUCIARELLI
Harley Langdale, Jr College of Business Admin.: Prof. Dr L. WAYNE PLUMLY, JR
James L. and Dorothy H. Dewar College of Education: Dr KARLA HULL

WESLEYAN COLLEGE

4760 Forsyth Rd, Macon, GA 31210
Telephone: (478) 477-1110
Fax: (478) 757-4030
Internet: www.wesleyancollege.edu
Founded 1836 as Georgia Female College, present name 1917
Private control
Academic year: August to May
Divs of fine arts, humanities, natural sciences and mathematics, professional studies, social and behavioural sciences
Pres.: Dr RUTH AUSTIN KNOX
Vice-Pres. for Academic Affairs and Dean of College: VIVIA L. FOWLER
Vice-Pres. for Business and Fiscal Affairs and Treas.: RICHARD P. MAIER
Vice-Pres. for Enrolment Services: CHARLES STEPHEN FARR
Vice-Pres. for Institutional Advancement: SUSAN T. WELSH

Vice-Pres. for Student Affairs: PATRICIA M. GIBBS
Registrar: PATRICIA R. HARDEMAN
Library Dir: SYBIL McNEIL
Library of 142,579 vols, 33,000 microforms, 500 periodicals
Number of teachers: 79
Number of students: 683

YOUNG HARRIS COLLEGE

One College St, POB 68, Young Harris, GA 30582
Telephone: (706) 379-5125
E-mail: admissions@yhc.edu
Internet: www.yhc.edu
Founded 1886
Private control
Academic year: June to May
Pres.: Dr CATHY COX
Sr Vice-Pres. for Finance and Admin.: DAVID LEOPARD
Vice-Pres. for Academic Affairs: Dr RONALD ROACH
Vice-Pres. for Advancement: JAY T. STROMAN
Vice-Pres. for Business and Controller: WADE BENSON
Vice-Pres. for Enrolment Management and External Relations: CLINTON G. HOBBS
Vice-Pres. for Planning and Assessment: ROSEMARY ROYSTON
Vice-Pres. for Student Devt: SUSAN ROGERS
Registrar: TAMMY GIBSON
Dean of Library Services: DAWN LAMADE
Library of 50,000 vols, 50,000 e-books
Number of students: 900
Publications: *Communique* (1 a year), *Echoes Magazine* (1 a year), *Legacy* (1 a year)

DEANS

Div. of Fine Arts: Prof. Dr KEITH DeFOOR
Div. of Humanities: Prof. Dr RUTH B. LOOPER
Div. of Mathematics and Science: Prof. Dr PAUL T. ARNOLD
Div. of Social and Behavioural Science: Prof. Dr B. LEE MARCH

HAWAII

BRIGHAM YOUNG UNIVERSITY, HAWAII CAMPUS

55–220 Kulanui St, Laie, Oahu, HI 96762
Telephone: (808) 675-3211
Internet: www.byuh.edu
Founded 1875 as Brigham Young Acad.
Private control
Pres.: Dr STEVEN C. WHEELWRIGHT
Vice-Pres. for Academics: Dr MAX L. CHECKETTS
Vice-Pres. for Admin. Services: MICHAEL B. BLISS
Vice-Pres. for Student Devt and Services: Dr DEBBIE HIPPOLITE WRIGHT
Vice-Pres. for Univ. Advancement: V. NAPUA BAKER
Chief Information Officer: JIM NILSON
Registrar: VERNELLE LAKATANI
Univ. Librarian: MICHAEL ALDRICH
Library of 163,000 vols
Number of teachers: 109
Number of students: 2,802

DEANS

College of Business, Computing and Govt: Dr GLADE TEW
College of Human Devt: JOHN BAILEY
College of Language, Culture and Art: PHILLIP McARTHUR
College of Math and Science: JEFF BURROUGHS

CHAMINADE UNIVERSITY

3140 Waialae Ave, Honolulu, HI 96816-1578
Telephone: (808) 735-4711
Fax: (808) 735-4870
E-mail: admissions@chaminade.edu
Internet: www.chaminade.edu
Founded 1955
Private control
Academic year: August to May
Pres.: Bro. BERNARD PLOEGER
Provost: Dr LARRY OSBORNE
Vice-Pres. for Finance and Facilities: Dr
DANIEL GILMORE
Dean for Enrolment Management: JOY
BOUEY
Dean for Students: GRISSEL BENITEZ-HODGE
Dir for Information Services and Library:
SHARON LEPAGE
Registrar: JOHN MORRIS
Library of 75,000 vols
Number of teachers: 75 full-time
Number of students: 2,822
Publications: *Aulama*, *Chaminade Literary
Review* (2 a year)

DEANS

Division of Behavioral Sciences: Dr ROBERT
SANTEE
Division of Business and Communication: Dr
BARBARA POOLE-STREET (acting)
Division of Education: Dr DAVID GROSSMAN
Division of Humanities and Fine Arts: Dr
DAVID L. COLEMAN
Division of Natural Sciences and Mathemat-
ics: Dr HELEN TURNER

HAWAII PACIFIC UNIVERSITY

1164 Bishop St, Honolulu, HI 96813
Telephone: (808) 544-0200
Fax: (808) 544-9323
E-mail: hr@hpu.edu
Internet: www.hpu.edu
Founded 1965 as Hawai'i Pacific College,
present name 1990
Private control
Academic year: September to June
Windward campus and Downtown campus
Pres.: Dr GEOFFREY. BANNISTER
Sr Vice-Pres. for Academic Affairs: Dr JOHN
KEARNS
Vice-Pres. for Community Relations: NANCY
ELLIS
Vice-Pres. for Enrolment Management:
SCOTT STENSRUD
Vice-Pres. for Human Resources: CLAIRE
COOPER
Vice-Pres. for Institutional Research and
Academic Support: LESLIE CORREA
Vice-Pres. for Student Support Services:
JEFFREY PHILPOTT
Registrar: KELLY NASHIRO-YOSHIDA
Librarian: KATHLEEN CHEE
Library of 180,000 vols, 11,000 periodicals
Number of teachers: 587
Number of students: 7,800
Publications: *Hawaii Pacific Review* (1 a
year), *Kalamalama* (12 a year), *The Voice*
(2 a year), *Wanderlust* (1 a year)

DEANS

College of Business Administration: Dr
DEBORAH CROWN
College of Humanities and Social Sciences:
Dr STEVEN C. COMBS
College of Natural and Computational Sci-
ences: Dr ANDREW M. BRITTAIN
College of Nursing and Health Sciences: Dr
RANDY M. CAINE

UNIVERSITY OF HAWAI'I SYSTEM

2444 Dole St, Honolulu, HI 96822
Telephone: (808) 956-8111
Fax: (808) 956-5286
Internet: www.hawaii.edu
Founded 1907 as College of Agriculture and
Mechanic Arts
State control
Academic year: January to December
10 Campuses: 3 univs and 7 community
colleges in Hawai'i, Honolulu, Kapiolani,
Kauai, Leeward, Maui, Windward
Academic year: August to May
Pres.: M. R. C. GREENWOOD
Provost and Exec. Vice-Pres. for Academic
Affairs: LINDA JOHNSRUD
Vice-Pres. for Admin.: SAM CALLEJO
Vice-Pres. for Budget and Finance: HOWARD
TODO
Vice-Pres. for Information Technology: DAVID
LASSNER
Vice-Pres. for Legal Affairs and Univ. Gen.
Counsel: DAROLYN LENDIO
Vice-Pres. for Research: JAMES GAINES
Vice-Pres. for Student Affairs and Univ.
Relations: ROCKNE FREITAS
Librarian: DIANE PERUSHEK
Library: 3.5m. vols
Number of teachers: 3,310
Number of students: 60,090

Publications: *Asian Perspectives* (2 a year,
archaeology for Asia and the Pacific),
Asian Theatre Journal (2 a year, journal
of the Asscn for Asian Performance), *Buddhist–Christian Studies* (1 a year, journal
of the Soc. for Buddhist–Christian Studies), *Biography* (4 a year, interdisciplinary
biographical scholarship), *The Contemporary Pacific* (2 a year, island affairs), *China
Review International* (2 a year, reviews of
scholarly literature in Chinese studies),
Journal of World History (4 a year, journal
of the World History Asscn), *Ka Ho'oilina*
(2 a year, journal of Hawaiian language
sources), *Korean Studies* (2 a year, multi-
disciplinary journal on Korea and Koreans
abroad), *Manoa* (2 a year, new writing
from America, the Pacific and Asia),
Oceanic Linguistics (2 a year, current
research on languages of the Oceanic
area), *Pacific Science* (4 a year, biological
and physical sciences of the Pacific region),
Philosophy East & West (4 a year, comparative philosophy), *Journal of Modern
Literature in Chinese* (2 a year, bilingual),
*Yearbook of the Association of Pacific Coast
Geographers* (1 a year), *Yishu* (4 a year,
contemporary Chinese art).

CONSTITUENT CAMPUSES

University of Hawai'i at Hilo

200 W Kawili St, Hilo, HI 96720-4091
Telephone: (808) 974-7414
Fax: (808) 933-0861
E-mail: uhhadm@hawaii.edu
Internet: www.hilo.hawaii.edu
Founded 1947 as Hawaii Vocational School,
present name 1970
Academic year: August to May
Chancellor: Dr DONALD STRANEY
Number of teachers: 230
Number of students: 4,079

DEANS

College of Agriculture, Forestry and Natural
Resource Management: BRUCE MATHEWS
College of Arts and Sciences: RANDY Y.
HIROKAWA
College of Business and Economics: HARRY
HENNESSEY
College of Pharmacy: Dr JOHN M. PEZZUTO

University of Hawai'i at Manoa

2500 Campus Rd, Honolulu, HI 96822
Telephone: (808) 956-8111
Internet: manoa.hawaii.edu
Founded 1907
Academic year: August to May
Chancellor: Dr VIRGINIA S. HINSHAW
Number of teachers: 1,209
Number of students: 20,337

DEANS

College of Arts and Humanities: THOMAS
BINGHAM
College of Education: Dr CHRISTINE K. SOR-
ENSEN
College of Engineering: Dr PETER E. CROUCH
College of Languages, Linguistics and Lit-
erature: ROBERT . BLEY-VROMAN
College of Natural Sciences: WILLIAM L.
DITTO
College of Social Sciences: DENISE E. KONAN
College of Tropical Agriculture and Human
Resources: SYLVIA YUEN
Graduate Division: PATRICIA COOPER
Hawai'inuiākea School of Hawaiian Know-
ledge: MAENETTE AH NEE-BENHAM
John A. Burns School of Medicine: Dr JERRIS
HEDGES
Myron B. Thompson School of Social Work:
Dr NOREEN MOKUAU
Outreach College: WILLIAM G. CHISMAR
School of Architecture: CLARK E. LLEWELLYN
School of Nursing and Dental Hygiene: Dr
MARY G. BOLAND
School of Ocean and Earth Science and
Technology: BRIAN TAYLOR
School of Pacific and Asian Studies: EDWARD
J. SHULTZ
School of Travel Industry Management: Dr
JUANITA LIU
Shidler College of Business: V. VANCE ROLEY
William S. Richardson School of Law: Prof.
AVI SOIFER

University of Hawai'i—West O'ahu

96–129 Ala Ike, Pearl City, HI 96782
Telephone: (808) 454-4700
Fax: (808) 453-6075
E-mail: info@uhwo.hawaii.edu
Internet: westoahu.hawaii.edu
Founded 1976
Academic year: August to May
Divs of humanities, professional studies,
social sciences
Chancellor: GENE I. AWAKUNI
Number of teachers: 41
Number of students: 1,471

IDAHO

BOISE BIBLE COLLEGE

8695 W Marigold St, Boise, ID 83714
Telephone: (208) 376-7731
Fax: (208) 376-7743
Internet: www.boisebible.edu
Founded 1945
Private control
Academic year: July to June
Chancellor: Dr CHARLES A. CRANE
Pres.: Dr TERRY E. STINE
Academic Dean: CHARLES H. FABER
Dean for Students: TRAVIS JACOB
Dir for Admissions: RUSSELL GROVE
Dir for Devt: DAVID DAVOLT
Dir for Enrolment Services: ROSS A. KNUDSEN
Librarian: GLENNIS THOMAS
Library of 35,500 vols
Number of teachers: 15
Number of students: 175

BOISE STATE UNIVERSITY

1910 Univ. Dr., Boise, ID 83725
Telephone: (208) 426-1000
Fax: (208) 426-4001
E-mail: communications@boisestate.edu
Internet: www.boisestate.edu

Founded 1932
State control
Pres.: Dr BOB KUSTRA
Provost and Vice-Pres. for Academic Affairs:
Dr MARTIN SCHIMPF
Vice-Pres. for Finance and Admin.: STACY A.
PEARSON
Vice-Pres. for Student Affairs: Dr LISA HAR-
RIS
Vice-Pres. for Univ. Advancements: ROSE-
MARY REINHARDT
Registrar: KRIS MARIE COLLINS
Dean for Univ. Libraries: Dr MARILYN MOODY
Library of 573,452 vols; 10,097 reference
books; 94,459 bound periodicals; 51,399 e-
books; 88,362 periodicals, newspapers, and
serials; 1,443,488 microforms; 19,490 non-
print materials; 92,459 maps and 7,047
MSS
Number of teachers: 2,092
Number of students: 19,664

DEANS

College of Applied Technology: VERA
MCCRINK
College of Arts and Sciences: Dr TONY ROARK
College of Business and Economics: Dr
PATRICK SHANNON
College of Education: Dr DIANE BOOTHE
College of Engineering: Dr AMY J. MOLL
College of Health Science: Dr TIM DUNNAGAN
College of Social Sciences and Public Affairs:
Dr MELISSA LAVITT
Extended Studies: MARK WHEELER
Graduate College: Dr JOHN R. PELTON

BRIGHAM YOUNG UNIVERSITY—
IDAHO

525 S Center St, Rexburg, ID 83460
Telephone: (208) 496-1411
E-mail: ask@byui.edu
Internet: www.byui.edu

Founded 1888 as Bannock Stake Acad.
Private control
Academic year: 3 semesters
Pres.: KIM B. CLARK
Academic Vice-Pres.: FENTON L. BROADHEAD
Vice-Pres. for Advancement: HENRY J. EYR-
ING
Vice-Pres. for Univ. Resource: CHARLES N.
ANDERSEN
Vice-Pres. for Student Services and Activ-
ities: KEVIN MIYASAKI
Dean for Students: KIP HARRIS
Institutional Research and Assessment Dir:
SCOTT BERGSTROM
Chief Information Officer: SPALDING JUGGA-
NAIKLO
Library Dir: MARTIN H. RAISH
Registrar: KYLE MARTIN
Library of 200,000 vols, 330,000 e-books,
100,000 e-journals, 10,000 videos and
DVDs
Number of students: 15,000

DEANS

College of Agriculture and Life Sciences: VAN
CHRISTMAN
College of Business and Communication:
ROBYN BERGSTROM
College of Education and Human Develop-
ment: STEVE DENNIS
College of Language and Letters: JOHN IVERS
College of Performing and Visual Arts: KEVIN
BROWER

College of Physical Sciences and Engineer-
ing: KENDALL PECK
Continuing Education: CHAD PRICE
Foundations and Interdisciplinary Studies:
JON LINFORD

COLLEGE OF IDAHO

2112 Cleveland Blvd, Caldwell, ID 83605
Telephone: (208) 459-5011
Fax: (208) 459-5175
E-mail: admissions@albertson.edu
Internet: www.collegeofidaho.edu

Founded 1891 as College of Idaho, present
name 2007
Private control
Academic year: September to June
Pres.: Dr MARVIN HENBERG
Vice-Pres. for Academic Affairs and Dean for
Faculty: Dr MARK SMITH
Vice-Pres. for Advancement: MICHAEL VAN-
DERVELDEN
Vice-Pres. for Finance and Admin.: PETRA
CARVER
Vice-Pres. for Student Affairs and Dean for
Students: PAUL BENNION
Dir for Admissions: BRUCE SMITH
Exec. Dir for Devt: MICHAEL VANDERVELDEN
Library Dir: CHRISTINE SCHUTZ
Library of 185,000 vols; 10,000 journals,
magazines and newspapers; 75,000 govt
documents
Number of teachers: 60 (full-time)
Number of students: 1,055
Publications: *Catalog* (1 a year), *Quest* (3 a
year).

IDAHO STATE UNIVERSITY

921 S Eighth Ave, Pocatello, ID 83209
Telephone: (208) 236-0211
Fax: (208) 236-4000
Internet: www.isu.edu

Founded 1901
State control
Pres.: ARTHUR C. VAILAS
Provost and Vice-Pres. for Academic Affairs:
Dr BARBARA ADAMCIK
Vice-Pres. for Finance and Admin.: JAMES
FLETCHER
Vice-Pres. for Univ. Advancement: Dr KENT
TINGLEY
Vice-Pres. for Student Affairs: Dr PATRICIA
TERRELL
Registrar: ROSS RUCHTI
Librarian: KAY FLOWERS
Library of 995,525 vols (incl. books, bound
periodicals and govt documents), 34,428
microfilms, 1,847,083 microfiches and
microcards, 44,257 maps and 2,938 current
periodicals
Number of teachers: 770
Number of students: 14,489

DEANS

College of Arts and Letters: KANDI TURLEY-
AMES
College of Business: Dr KREGG AYTES
College of Education: DEBORAH L. HEDEEN
College of Pharmacy: Dr PAUL CADY
College of Science and Engineering: Dr
GEORGE IMEL
College of Technology: Dr MARILYN E. DAVIS
Graduate School: Dr NICOLE R. HILL

LEWIS-CLARK STATE COLLEGE

500 Eighth Ave, Lewiston, ID 83501
Telephone: (208) 792-5272
Fax: (208) 792-2822
E-mail: registrar@lcsc.edu
Internet: www.lcsc.edu

Founded 1893 as Lewiston State Normal
School, present name 1971
State control
Academic year: August to May
Pres.: J. ANTHONY FERNÁNDEZ
Provost and Vice-Pres. for Academic Affairs:
Dr CARMEN SIMONE
Vice-Pres. for Finance and Admin.: CHET
HERBST
Dean for Academic Programmes: (vacant)
Dean for Community Programmes: KATHY
MARTIN
Dean for Student Services: ANDREW HANSON
Dean for Professional-Technical Pro-
grammes: Dr ROB LOHRMEYER
Registrar: NIKOL LUTHER
Dir for Library Services: SUSAN NIEWENHOUS
Library of 251,000 vols
Number of teachers: 180
Number of students: 4,200

NORTHWEST NAZARENE
UNIVERSITY

623 S Univ. Blvd, Nampa, ID 83686-5897
Telephone: (208) 467-8011
Fax: (208) 467-8645
Internet: www.nnu.edu

Founded 1913
Private control
Pres.: Dr DAVID ALEXANDER
Vice-Pres. for Academic Affairs: Dr BURTON
J. WEBB
Vice-Pres. for Enrolment and Marketing:
STACEY BERGGREN
Vice-Pres. for Financial Affairs: DAVE PETER-
SON
Vice-Pres. for Spiritual and Leadership Devt:
FRED FULLERTON
Vice-Pres. for Student Devt: CAREY COOK
Registrar: NANCY AYERS
Dir of Library Services: SHARON I. BULL
Library of 120,000 vols, 850 current period-
icals, 600,000 vols of microforms, non-print
materials and govt documents
Number of teachers: 105 (full-time)
Number of students: 2,020 (1,322 under-
graduate, 698 graduate)

DEANS

School of Arts, Humanities and Social Sciences: RON E. PONSFORD
School of Business, Economics and Leadership: Dr STEVE MOUNTJOY
School of Education, Social Work and Counseling: JIM BADER

UNIVERSITY OF IDAHO

875 Perimeter Dr., Moscow, ID 83844
Telephone: (208) 885-6326
Fax: (208) 885-9119
E-mail: registrar@uidaho.edu
Internet: www.uidaho.edu

Founded 1889
Pres.: Dr M. DUANE NELLIS
Provost and Exec. Vice-Pres.: DOUGLAS D.
BAKER
Vice-Pres. for Finance and Admin.: RON
SMITH
Vice-Pres. for Research and Economic Devt:
JOHN K. MCIVER
Vice-Pres. for Univ. Advancement: CHRIS
MURRAY
Registrar: RETA PIKOWSKY
Dean for the Library: LYNN BAIRD
Dean for Students: Dr BRUCE PITMAN
Library of 936,738 vols, 105,493 microforms,
642,199 govt documents, 786,882 govt
documents on microfiche, 207,087 maps
and 5,305 current periodicals
Number of teachers: 3,159
Number of students: 12,312

DEANS

College of Agriculture and Life Sciences: Dr JOHN HAMMEL
College of Art and Architecture: MARK HOVERSTEN
College of Business and Economics: Dr JOHN MORRIS
College of Education: Dr CORI MANTLE-BROMLEY
College of Engineering: LARRY STAUFFER
College of Graduate Studies: Dr JIE CHEN
College of Law: Dr DONALD L. BURNETT, Jr
College of Letters, Arts and Social Sciences: KATHERINE G. AIKEN
College of Natural Resources: KURT PREGITZER
College of Science: SCOTT A. WOOD

ILLINOIS

ADLER SCHOOL OF PROFESSIONAL PSYCHOLOGY

17 N Dearborn St, Chicago, IL 60602
Telephone: (312) 662-4000
Fax: (312) 662-4099
E-mail: information@adler.edu
Internet: www.adler.edu
Founded 1952 as Alfred Adler Institute of Chicago, present name 1991
Private control
Academic year: June to June
Campus in Vancouver, Canada
Pres.: Dr RAYMOND E. CROSSMAN
Vice-Pres. for Academic Affairs: Dr MARTHA CASAZZA
Vice-Pres. for Admin.: JO BETH CUP
Vice-Pres. for Finance and Technology: JEFFREY GREEN
Vice-Pres. for Institutional Advancement: ANTHONY CHIMERA
Dean for Vancouver Campus: Dr LARRY AXELROD
Dir for Library Services: KERRY COCHRANE
Library of 10,000 vols, 350 audiovisual materials
Number of teachers: 30
Publication: *Gemeinschaftsgefühl* (1 a year, Social Interest).

AMERICAN INTERCONTINENTAL UNIVERSITY

231 N Martingale Rd, Sixth Fl., Schaumburg, IL 60173
Telephone: (877) 701-3800
E-mail: aiuaadministration@aiuniv.edu
Internet: www.aiuniv.edu
Founded 1970
Private control
Schools of business, criminal justice, design, education and information technology; campuses in Atlanta (Georgia), Houston (Texas), Weston (Florida); int. campus in London (UK)
Pres. and Chancellor: Dr GEORGE MILLER
Provost and Chief Academic Officer: GREGORY G. WASHINGTON
Vice-Provost: Dr. JOHN CAMPBELL
Sr Vice-Pres. for Finance and Admin.: NATE SWANSON
Vice-Pres. for Student Affairs: LEON KELLEY
Registrar: Dr. RAGINI BILOLIKAR.

AUGUSTANA COLLEGE

639 38th St, Rock Island, IL 61201-2296
Telephone: (309) 794-7000
Fax: (309) 794-7422
E-mail: admissions@augustana.edu
Internet: www.augustana.edu
Founded 1860

Private control
Academic year: September to May
Courses in accounting, art, art education, art history, biochemistry, biology, business admin., chemistry, classics, communication sciences and disorders, computer science/mathematics, earth science teaching, economics, elementary and secondary education, English, French, geography, geology, German, history, mathematics, pre-medicine, music, music education, music performance, philosophy, physics, political science, psychology, religion, Scandinavian, sociology, Spanish, speech communication, studio art, theatre
Pres.: STEVEN C. BAHLS
Vice-Pres. for Devt: LYNN E. JACKSON
Vice-Pres. for College: W. KENT BARNDS
Dean and Chief Academic Officer: Dr PAREENA G. LAWRENCE
Dean for Admissions: DANE ROWLEY
Dean for Students: Dr EVELYN S. CAMPBELL
Registrar: LIESL A. FOWLER
Dir of the Library: CARLA TRACY
Library of 244,368 vols
Number of teachers: 184 (135 full-time, 49 part-time)
Number of students: 2,500

AURORA UNIVERSITY

347 S Gladstone Ave, Aurora, IL 60506-4892
Telephone: (630) 892-6431
Fax: (630) 844-5463
E-mail: admission@aurora.edu
Internet: www.aurora.edu
Founded 1893 as Mendota Seminary, present name 1985
Private control
Academic year: September to May
Campus at Williams Bay, Wisconsin
Pres.: Dr REBECCA L. SHERRICK
Provost: Dr ANDREW P. MANION
Exec. Vice-Pres. for Advancement: THEODORE PARGE
Sr Vice-Pres. for George Williams Campus: Dr JOHN PYLE
Vice-Pres. for Admin.: THOMAS HAMMOND
Vice-Pres. for Community Relations: SARAH RUSSE
Vice-Pres. for Devt and Alumni Relations: TERI TOMASZKIEWICZ
Vice-Pres. for Enrolment: Dr DONNA DeSPAIN
Vice-Pres. for Finance: BETH REISSENWEBER
Vice-Pres. for Student Life: LORA DE LACEY
Vice-Pres. for Univ. Communications: STEVEN McFARLAND
Registrar: KATE MALE
Dir for Univ. Library: JOHN LAW
Library of 99,000 vols, 7,000 multimedia materials, 210 periodical subscriptions
Number of teachers: 155
Number of students: 4,400

DEANS

College of Arts and Sciences: Dr SAIB OTHMAN
College of Education: Dr DONALD C. WOLD
College of Professional Studies: Dr JODI KOSLOW-MARTIN
School of Continuing Education: Dr LINDA OLBINSKI

BENEDICTINE UNIVERSITY

5700 College Rd, Lisle, IL 60532-0900
Telephone: (630) 829-6000
Fax: (630) 829-6091
E-mail: admissions@ben.edu
Internet: www.ben.edu
Founded 1887 as St Procopius College
Private control
Academic year: September to May
Campus at Springfield

Pres.: Dr WILLIAM J. CARROLL
Provost and Vice-Pres. for Academic Affairs: Dr DONALD B. TAYLOR
Exec. Vice-Pres.: CHARLES GREGORY
Vice-Pres. for Enrolment Services: KARI GIBBONS
Dir for Admissions: KATHLEEN SCHOTTENHAMEL
Registrar: BOB BOSANAC
Univ. Librarian: JACK FRITTS
Library of 100,000 vols, 15,000 periodicals, 120 databases
Number of teachers: 598 (117 full-time, 7 part-time, 474 adjunct)
Number of students: 6,857 (3,825 undergraduate, 3,032 graduate)
Publication: *Voices Magazine* (3 a year)

DEANS

College of Business: Dr SANDRA L. GILL
College of Education and Health Services: Dr ALAN GORR
College of Liberal Arts: Dr MARÍA DE LA CÁMARA
College of Science: Dr BART NG
Moser College of Adult and Professional Studies: Dr MICHAEL CARROLL

BLACKBURN COLLEGE

700 College Ave, Carlinville, IL 62626
Telephone: (217) 854-3231
Fax: (217) 854-3713
E-mail: info@blackburn.edu
Internet: www.blackburn.edu
Founded 1837
Private control
Academic year: August to May
Depts of accounting, art, biology, business and economics, chemistry, communications, computer science, criminal justice, education, engineering, English, history, mathematics, medical technology, performing arts, philosophy and religion, physical education, physics, political science, pre-law, pre-professional, psychology, Spanish
Pres.: MIRIAM R. PRIDE
Provost: Dr JEFFERY P. APER
Vice-Pres. for Admin. and Finance: HEATHER BIGARD
Dir for Admissions: ALISHA KAPP
Dean for Students: HEIDI HEINZ
Registrar: DIANNA M. RUYLE
Head Librarian: CAROL SCHAEFER
Library of 70,000 vols
Number of teachers: 53 (38 full-time, 15 part-time)
Number of students: 600

BRADLEY UNIVERSITY

1501 W Bradley Ave, Peoria, IL 61625
Telephone: (309) 676-7611
E-mail: admissions@bradley.edu
Internet: www.bradley.edu
Founded 1897, present name and status 1946
Private control
Pres.: JOANNE K. GLASSER
Provost and Vice-Pres. for Academic Affairs: Dr DAVID GLASSMAN
Vice-Pres. for Advancement: PATRICK VICKERMAN
Vice-Pres. for Business Affairs: GARY ANNA
Vice-Pres. for Student Affairs: Dr ALAN GALSKY
Registrar: KATHERINE M. BEATY
Exec. Dir for Library: BARBARA A. GALIK
Library: 1.2m. vols (incl. 510,297 books, bound periodicals and govt documents, 787,169 microforms)
Number of teachers: 350 (full-time)
Number of students: 6,000 (5,200 undergraduate, 800 graduate)

Publications: *Bradley Hilltopics* (4 a year), *Bradley Works*

DEANS

College of Education and Health Sciences: Dr JOAN SATTLER
College of Engineering and Technology: Dr RICHARD T. JOHNSON
College of Liberal Arts and Sciences: Dr CLAIRE ETAUGH
Foster College of Business Administration: Dr ROBERT SCOTT
Graduate School: Dr ALBERTO DELGADO
Slane College of Communications and Fine Arts: Dr JEFFREY H. HUBERMAN

CATHOLIC THEOLOGICAL UNION

5401 S Cornell Ave, Chicago, IL 60615-5698
Telephone: (773) 371-5400
E-mail: admissions@ctu.edu
Internet: www.ctu.edu
Founded 1968
Private control
Academic year: September to June

Depts of biblical literature and languages, historical and doctrinal studies, intercultural studies and ministries, spirituality and pastoral ministry, and word and worship

Pres.: Rev. DONALD SENIOR
Vice-Pres. and Academic Dean: Sis. BARBARA REID
Vice-Pres. for Admin. and Finance: MICHAEL W. CONNORS
Registrar: MARÍA DE JESÚS LEMUS
Library Dir: MELODY LAYTON MCMAHON
Library of 150,000 vols, 500 periodicals
Publication: *New Theology Review*.

CHAMBERLAIN COLLEGE OF NURSING

3005 Highland Parkway, Downers Grove, IL 60515
Fax: (630) 512-8888
E-mail: info@chamberlain.edu
Internet: www.chamberlain.edu
Founded 1889
Private control

Campuses in Florida, Arizona, Texas, Illinois, Virginia, Missouri, Ohio and Indiana

Pres.: Dr SUSAN L. GROENWALD
Vice-Pres. for Academic Affairs: Dr WILLIAM RICHARD COWLING, III
Vice-Pres. for Campus Operations: MARIE HALLINAN
Dir for Admissions: LARRY VEENEMAN
Dir for Finance: TAE KANG
Dir for Online Programmes: BRENDA HAMMERSLEY
Dir for Student Services: JUNE MARLOWE.

CHICAGO SCHOOL OF PROFESSIONAL PSYCHOLOGY

350 N Orleans, Suite 1050, Chicago, IL 60654-1822
Telephone: (312) 329-6600
Fax: (312) 644-3333
E-mail: admissions@thechicagoschool.edu
Internet: www.thechicagoschool.edu
Founded 1979
Private control
Academic year: October to August

Campuses in Chicago, Los Angeles, Irvine, Westwood, Washington, DC; courses in applied behaviour analysis, clinical psychology graduate programme, continuing professional education, counselling psychology graduate programmes, forensic psychology graduate programmes, industrial organizational and business psychology programmes, school psychology; online courses

Pres.: Dr MICHELE NEALON-WOODS
Vice-Pres. for Academic Affairs: Dr ORLANDO TAYLOR
Vice-Pres. for Admissions: MAGDALEN KELLOGG
Vice-Pres. for Finance and Admin.: CAROLE ROBERTSON
Vice-Pres. for Student Affairs: Dr JENNIFER STRIPE PORTILLO
Registrar: ANA DEL CASTILLO
Dir for Library Services: INDU AGGARWAL
Number of students: 3,500
Publication: *INSIGHT* (2 a year).

CHICAGO STATE UNIVERSITY

9501 S King Dr., Chicago, IL 60628-1598
Telephone: (773) 995-2000
Internet: www.csu.edu
Founded 1867 as a teacher training school, present name 1971
State control
Academic year: August to May (2 terms)

Pres.: Dr WAYNE WATSON
Provost and Sr Vice-Pres. for Academic Affairs: Dr SANDRA WESTBROOKS
Sr Vice-Pres. for Admin. and Finance: GLEN MEEKS
Vice-Pres. for Enrolment Management: ANDRE BELL
Dir for Admissions: MATTHEW HARRISON
Registrar: CARNICE HILL
Dean for Library and Learning Resources: Dr RICHARD DARGA (acting)
Number of teachers: 470 (350 full-time, 120 part-time)
Number of students: 7,000
Publications: *CSU Excellence Magazine* (2 a year), *Illinois Schools Journal* (1 a year), *Reflections* (12 a year)

DEANS

College of Arts and Sciences: Dr DAVID KANIS
College of Business: Dr DERRICK K. COLLINS
College of Education: Dr SYLVIA GIST
College of Health Sciences: Dr JOSEPH BALOGUN
College of Pharmacy: Dr MIRIAM A. MOBLEY SMITH
Continuing Education and Non-Traditional Degree Programmes: NELLIE MAYNARD
Honors College: Dr RICHARD G. MILO
School of Graduate and Professional Studies: Dr JUSTIN K. AKUJIEZE

CHICAGO THEOLOGICAL SEMINARY

1407 E 60th St, Chicago, IL 60637
Telephone: (773) 896-2400
Fax: (773) 643-1334
E-mail: admissions@ctschicago.edu
Internet: www.ctschicago.edu
Founded 1855
Private control
Academic year: September to May

Offers postgraduate courses in arts, divinity, religious leadership, sacred theology; doctoral courses in ministry, philosophy

Pres.: Dr ALICE HUNT
Vice-Pres. for Devt: MEGAN DAVIS-OCHI
Vice-Pres. for Finance and Admin.: STEPHEN MANNING
Academic Dean: Prof. Dr KEN STONE
Dir for Enrolment Management: KIM KING
Registrar: ELENA JIMENEZ
Librarian: Rev. Dr NEIL W. GERDES
Library of 50,500 vols, 100 periodicals.

COLUMBIA COLLEGE CHICAGO

600 S Michigan Ave, Chicago, IL 60605
Telephone: (312) 663-1600
E-mail: admissions@colum.edu

Internet: www.colum.edu
Founded 1890 as Columbia School of Oratory, present name 1997
Private control

Pres.: Dr WARWICK L. CARTER
Vice-Pres. and Gen. Counsel: ANNICE M. KELLY
Vice-Pres. for Academic Affairs and Interim Provost: Dr LOUISE LOVE
Vice-Pres. for Campus Environment: ALICIA BERG
Vice-Pres. for Institutional Advancement: Dr ERIC WINSTON
Vice-Pres. for Student Affairs: MARK KELLY
Dean for Students: SHARON WILSON-TAYLOR
Dean for the Library: JO CATES (acting)
Library of 306,807 vols, 1,255 print serials, 46,978 e-books, 58,375 e-journals, 37,888 multimedia materials
Number of teachers: 1,167
Number of students: 11,922 (11,400 undergraduate, 522 graduate)
Publications: *@LAS* (1 a year), *Court Green* (1 a year), *DEMO*, *Echo magazine* (2 a year), *Fictionary*, *Hair Trigger* (1 a year), *South Loop Review: Creative Nonfiction+Art* (1 a year)

DEANS

School of Fine and Performing Arts: Dr ELIZA NICHOLS
School of Liberal Arts and Sciences: Dr DEBORAH H. HOLDSTEIN
School of Media Arts: Dr ROBIN BARGAR

CONCORDIA UNIVERSITY CHICAGO

7400 Augusta St, River Forest, IL 60305-1402
Telephone: (708) 771-8300
Internet: www.cuchicago.edu
Founded 1864
Private control
Academic year: August to May (2 semesters)

Pres.: Rev. Dr JOHN F. JOHNSON
Sr Vice-Pres. for Academics: Dr MANFRED B. BOOS
Sr Vice-Pres. for Univ. Advancement: Dr ALAN C. KLAAS
Sr Vice-Pres. for Univ. Planning and Research: ALAN E. MEYER
Vice-Pres. for Admin.: Dr DENNIS WITTE
Vice-Pres. for Enrolment and Marketing: EVELYN BURDICK
Vice-Pres. for Student Life and Leadership and Dean for students: JEFFREY C. HYNES
Registrar: CONSTANCE K. PETTINGER
Dir for Library Services: YANA V. SERDYUK
Library of 160,000 vols, 140 periodical subscriptions, 480,000 ERIC microfiche documents
Number of students: 5,134 (1,451 undergraduate, 3,683 graduate)
Publication: *Forester Magazine*

DEANS

College of Arts and Sciences: Dr GARY E. WENZEL
College of Business: Dr GEORGE VUKOTICH
College of Education: Dr KEVIN BRANDON
College of Graduate and Innovative Programmes: Prof. Dr THOMAS P. JANDRIS

DEPAUL UNIVERSITY

1 E Jackson Blvd, Chicago, IL 60604
Telephone: (312) 362-8000
E-mail: dpcl@depaul.edu
Internet: www.depaul.edu

Founded 1898, present name and status 1907
Campuses at Lincoln Park, Loop, Naperville, O'Hare, Oak Forest and Rolling Meadows
Private control

Pres.: Rev. Dr DENNIS H. HOLTSCHNEIDER
Chancellor: Rev. JOHN T. RICHARDSON
Provost: Dr HELMUT P. EPP
Exec. Vice-Pres.: Dr ROBERT L. KOZOMAN
Sr Vice-Pres. for Advancement: MARY C. FINGER
Sr Vice-Pres. for Enrolment Management and Marketing: Dr DAVID H. KALSBEEK
Vice-Pres. and Gen. Counsel: JOSÉ D. PADILLA
Vice-Pres. for Community, Govt and Int. Affairs: J. D. BINDENAGEL
Vice-Pres. for Devt: DAVID LIVELY
Vice-Pres. for Finance: BONNIE FRANKEL
Vice-Pres. for Institutional Diversity and Equity: ELIZABETH F. ORTIZ
Vice-Pres. for Student Affairs: JAMES R. DOYLE
Registrar: NANCY GALL
Dir for Libraries: JAMES GALBRAITH

Library of 799,756 vols, 28,319 e-books, 100,774 microforms, 2,168 ft archives, 47,056 e-journals, 31,237 spec. collns
Number of teachers: 938 (full-time)
Number of students: 25,398 (16,384 undergraduates, 7,983 graduate, 1,031 law)
Publications: *Business & Commercial Law Journal* (2 a year, online (laworgs.depaul.edu/journals/bclj)), *DePaul Journal of Art, Technology and Intellectual* (2 a year), *De Paul Magazine* (4 a year), *Journal for Social Justice* (online (laworgs.depaul.edu/journals/social_justice)), *Journal of Health and Hospital Law* (12 a year), *Law Review* (4 a year, online (laworgs.depaul.edu/journals/lawreview)), *Philosophy Today* (4 a year)

DEANS

College of Computing and Digital Media: Dr DAVID MILLER
College of Communication: Dr JACQUELINE TAYLOR
College of Education: Dr PAUL ZIONTS
College of Law: Dr GREGORY MARK
College of Liberal Arts and Social Sciences: Dr CHARLES S. SUCHAR
College of Science and Health: Dr JERRY CLELAND
Driehaus College of Business: Dr RAY WHITTINGTON
School for New Learning: Dr MARISA ALICEA
School of Music: Dr DONALD E. CASEY
Theatre School: JOHN CULBERT

DEVRY UNIVERSITY

Highland Landmark V, 3005 Highland Parkway, Downers Grove, IL 60515-5683
Telephone: (602) 216-7700
Fax: (602) 943-4108
E-mail: info@devry.edu
Internet: www.devry.edu

Founded 1931 as DeForest Training School, present name and status 2002
Private control
Academic year: November to October
90 Campus locations in the USA and Canada

Pres.: DAVID J. PAULDINE
Provost and Vice-Pres. for Academic Affairs: Dr DONNA M. LORAINE
Vice-Pres. for Enrolment Management: ERIKA R. ORRIS
Vice-Pres. for Student and Career Services: CLAUDE TOLAND
Univ. Librarian: GLENN FERDMAN

Library of 375,000 vols, 80,000 e-book titles (25 campus libraries)
Number of teachers: 700 (full-time)
Number of students: 85,000 (incl. online)

DEANS

College of Business and Management: Dr OSCAR GUTIERREZ

College of Engineering and Information Science: JOHN GIANCOLA
College of Health Sciences: Dr JOSEPH YORK
College of Liberal Arts and Sciences: Dr DONNA REKAU
College of Media Arts and Technology: Dr BRIAN BETHUNE
Keller Graduate School of Management: Dr DONNA M. LORAINE

DOMINICAN UNIVERSITY

7900 W Div. St, River Forest, IL 60305
Telephone: (708) 366-2490
Fax: (708) 524-5990
Internet: www.dom.edu

Founded 1901 as St Clara College in Wisconsin, present name 1997
Private control
Academic year: May to April

Pres.: DONNA M. CARROLL
Sr Vice-Pres. for Admin.: AMY McCORMACK
Provost and Vice-Pres. for Academic Affairs: CHERYL JOHNSON-ODIM
Vice-Pres. for Enrolment Management: MARY ANN ROWAN
Vice-Pres. for Univ. Advancement: GRACE CICHOMSKA
Vice-Pres. for Mission and Min.: DIANE KENNEDY
Dean for Students: TRUDI GOGGIN
Registrar: MICHAEL P. MILLER
Univ. Librarian: Dr INEZ RINGLAND

Library of 250,000 vols, 30,000 periodicals
Number of teachers: 394 (156 full-time, 238 part-time)
Number of students: 3,612 (1,953 undergraduate, 1,659 graduate)
Publications: *Dominican* (online (www.dom.edu/magazine)), *World Libraries* (2 a year)

DEANS

Brennan School of Business: Dr ARVID C. JOHNSON
Graduate School of Library and Information Science: Prof. Dr SUSAN ROMAN
Graduate School of Social Work: Dr CHARLIE STOOPS (acting)
Rosary College of Arts and Sciences: Prof. Dr JEFFREY CARLSON
School of Education: Dr COLLEEN REARDON

EASTERN ILLINOIS UNIVERSITY

600 Lincoln Ave, Charleston, IL 61920-3099
Telephone: (217) 581-5000
Internet: www.eiu.edu

Founded 1895
State control
Academic year: August to June

Pres.: Dr WILLIAM L. PERRY
Provost and Vice-Pres. for Academic Affairs: Dr BLAIR M. LORD
Vice-Pres. for Student Affairs: Dr DANIEL P. ADLER
Vice-Pres. for Univ. Advancement: BOB MARTIN
Dean for Enrolment Management: FRANK HOHENGARTEN
Registrar: G. SUE HARVEY
Dean for Library Services: Dr ALLEN LANHAM

Library of 978,209 vols, 1.2m. microtexts, maps, music scores and pamphlets
Number of teachers: 753 (613 full-time, 140 part-time)
Number of students: 11,630 (9,970 undergraduate, 1,660 graduate)

DEANS

College of Arts and Humanities: BONNIE IRWIN
College of Education and Professional Studies: DIANE H. JACKMAN

College of Sciences: GODSON OBIA
Graduate School: Dr ROBERT M. AUGUSTINE
Honors College: JOHN STIMAC
Lumpkin College of Business and Applied Sciences: Dr MAHYAR IZADI
School of Continuing Education: Dr WILLIAM C. HINE

EAST-WEST UNIVERSITY

816 S Michigan Ave, Chicago, IL 60605
Telephone: (312) 939-0111
Fax: (312) 939-0083
E-mail: info@eastwest.edu
Internet: www.eastwest.edu

Founded 1980
Private control
Academic year: September to August

Depts of behavioural and social sciences, biology, business administration, computer and information science, English and communications, electronics engineering technology, mathematics, office administration

Chancellor: Dr M. WASIULLAH KHAN
Provost: Dr MADHU JAIN
Dean for Enrolment Management: MAZIN SAFAR
Dir for Devt: JUDY BACON
Registrar: AMAL MATARI
Librarian: Dr EKKEHARD-TEJA WILKE

Library of 26,000 vols, 2,500 films, 150 periodical subscriptions, 30 e-book reference sets
Number of teachers: 43 (full-time)
Number of students: 1,170

ELMHURST COLLEGE

190 Prospect Ave, Elmhurst, IL 60126-3296
Telephone: (630) 617-3500
Fax: (630) 617-3282
E-mail: admit@elmhurst.edu
Internet: public.elmhurst.edu

Founded 1871, present name 1924
Private control
Academic year: August to May

Depts of art, biology, business and economics, chemistry, communication arts and sciences, computer science and information systems, education, English, foreign languages and literatures, geography and geosciences, history, kinesiology, mathematics, music, nursing, philosophy, physics, political science, psychology, sociology, theology and religion, urban studies

Pres.: Dr S. ALAN RAY
Sr Vice-Pres. for Finance and Admin.: DENISE JONES
Vice-Pres. for Academic Affairs and Dean for Faculty: ALZADA J. TIPTON
Vice-Pres. and Chief Information Officer: JAMES KULICH
Vice-Pres. for Communications and Public Affairs: JAMES W. WINTERS
Vice-Pres. for Devt and Alumni Relations: JOSEPH R. EMMICK
Dean for Admission: GARY ROLD
Dean for Students: EILEEN SULLIVAN
Dir for Library: SUSAN SWORDS STEFFEN

Library of 320,000 vols
Number of teachers: 136 (full-time)
Number of students: 3,410

EUREKA COLLEGE

300 E College Ave, Eureka, IL 61530-1500
Telephone: (309) 467-3721
Fax: (309) 467-6386
E-mail: admissions@eureka.edu
Internet: www.eureka.edu

Founded 1855
Private control
Academic year: August to May

Divs of education, fine and performing arts, humanities, science and mathematics, social sciences and business

Pres.: Dr J. DAVID ARNOLD
Provost and Dean for College: Dr PHILIP ACREE CAVALIER
Vice-Pres. for Admissions, Communications and Integrated Marketing: Dr BRIAN SAJKO
Vice-Pres. for Devt and Alumni Relations: MARC PASTERIS
Dean for Admissions and Financial Aid: KURT KRILE
Dean for Students: BROOKE CAMPBELL
Library Dir: ANTHONY GLASS
Library of 80,000 vols, 300 periodical subsriptions
Number of teachers: 44
Number of students: 800

GARRETT-EVANGELICAL THEOLOGICAL SEMINARY

2121 Sheridan Rd, Evanston, IL 60201
Telephone: (847) 866-3900
Fax: (847) 467-0689
E-mail: seminary@garrett.edu
Internet: www.garrett.edu
Founded 1853 as Garrett Biblical Institute, present name and status 1974
Private control
Academic year: September to July

Masters degrees in art and music ministry, Christian education and pastoral care, divinity, theological studies; doctoral degrees in Christian education and congregational studies, ethics and history, liturgical studies and Biblical studies, pastoral theology, personality and culture, theology

Pres.: PHILIP AMERSON
Academic Dean and Vice-Pres. for Academic Affairs: Dr LALLENE RECTOR
Vice-Pres. for Devt: DAVID HEETLAND
Dean for Students: Rev. CYNTHIA A. WILSON
Dir for Academic Studies and Registrar: VINCE MCGLOTHIN-ELLER
Library Dir: Dr BETH SHEPPARD
Library of 300,000 vols
Number of teachers: 36
Number of students: 400
Publication: *Aware Magazine* (4 a year).

GOVERNORS STATE UNIVERSITY

1 University Parkway, University Park, IL 60466-0975
Telephone: (708) 534-5000
Fax: (708) 534-8399
E-mail: gsunow@govst.edu
Internet: www.govst.edu
Founded 1969
State control

Pres.: ELAINE P. MAIMON
Provost and Vice-Pres. for Academic Affairs: TERRY ALLISON
Exec. Vice-Pres., Chief of Staff and Treas.: Dr GEBEYEHU EJIGU
Vice-Pres. for Institutional Advancement: JOAN VAUGHAN
Vice-Pres. and Gen. Counsel: ALEXIS KENNEDY
Registrar: MICHELLE SMITH-WILLIAMS
Dean for Library Services: DIANE DATES CASEY
Library of 459,994 vols, 28,930 audiovisual materials, 449 linear ft MSS.
Number of teachers: 300
Number of students: 7,788

DEANS

College of Arts and Sciences: Prof. REINHOLD HILL
College of Business and Public Administration.: Dr ELLEN FOSTER-CURTIS

College of Education: DEBORAH BORDELON
College of Health and Human Services: Dr ELIZABETH CADA

GREENVILLE COLLEGE

315 E College Ave, Greenville, IL 62246-1145
Telephone: (618) 664-2800
Fax: (618) 664-1748
Internet: www.greenville.edu
Founded 1892
Private control
Academic year: July to June
Pres.: Dr LARRY LINAMEN
Provost: Dr RANDALL BERGEN
Vice-Pres. for Advancement: WALTER FENTON
Vice-Pres. for Enrolment: MICHAEL RITTER
Vice-Pres. for Finance: DANA FUNDERBURK
Vice-Pres. and Dean for Student Devt: Dr NORMAN HALL
Registrar: MICHELLE SUSSENBACH
Dir for Library: JANE HOPKINS
Library of 114,059 vols
Number of teachers: 163 (68 full-time, 95 part-time)
Number of students: 1,605
Publication: *Record* (2 a year)

DEANS

School of Arts and Sciences: Dr BRADLEY S. SHAW
School of Education: Dr VICKIE COOK
School of Professional Studies: Dr DAVE HOLDEN

HARRINGTON COLLEGE OF DESIGN

2nd Fl., 200 W Madison St, Chicago, IL 60606-3433
Telephone: (877) 939-4975
Fax: (312) 939-8005
Internet: www.harrington.edu
Founded 1931, fmrly Harrington Institute of Interior Design, present name 2003
Private control

Courses in communication design, digital photography and interior design

Pres.: BOB NACHTSHEIM
Sr Dir for Admissions: BRYAN LAMBERT
Registrar: SAM DELAROSA
Dir for Library Services: LEIGH GATES
Library of 27,000 vols, 16,000 e-books, 125 journal and newspaper titles, 35,000 digital images, 500 videos, DVDs and CDs
Number of teachers: 70
Number of students: 508

HEBREW THEOLOGICAL COLLEGE

7135 N Carpenter Rd, Skokie, IL 60077
Telephone: (847) 982-2500
Fax: (847) 674-6381
E-mail: htc@htc.edu
Internet: www.htc.edu
Founded 1919, present name 1921
Private control
Chancellor: Dr JEROLD ISENBERG
Vice-Pres. for Admin.: SENDER KUTNER
Dir for Admissions: JOSHUA ZISOOK
Dir for Devt: GERSHON SEIF
Registrar and Financial Aid Officer: SHMUEL LEIB SCHUMAN
Library of 70,000 vols

DEANS

Blitstein Institute for Women: Dr ESTHER SHKOP
Men's College Division: MICHAEL A. MYERS

ILLINOIS COLLEGE

1101 W College Ave, Jacksonville, IL 62650
Telephone: (217) 245-3000
Fax: (217) 245-3034
E-mail: info@ic.edu
Internet: www.ic.edu
Founded 1829
Private control

Divs of humanities, natural science, social sciences

Pres.: Dr AXEL D. STEUER
Vice-Pres. for Academic Affairs and Dean for College: Dr ELIZABETH H. TOBIN
Vice-Pres. for Business Affairs: FRANK G. WILLIAMS
Vice-Pres. for Devt and Alumni Relations: PHILIP HOOD
Vice-Pres. for Enrolment Management and College Marketing: STEPHANIE ELPERS CHIPMAN
Vice-Pres. for Student Affairs and Dean for Students: Dr MALINDA L. CARLSON
Registrar: Dr GLEN W. CLATTERBUCK
Librarian: MARTIN H. GALLAS
Library of 143,000 vols, 600 journal subscriptions, 10,000 microfilm and microfiche items
Number of teachers: 52
Number of students: 1,000

ILLINOIS COLLEGE OF OPTOMETRY

3241 S Michigan Ave, Chicago, IL 60616-3878
Telephone: (312) 949-7400
Fax: (312) 949-7680
E-mail: admissions@ico.edu
Internet: www.ico.edu
Founded 1872
Private control
Academic year: August to May

Degrees offered: Doctor of Optometry, Bachelor of Science in Visual Science; in conjunction with the Univ. of Chicago, Master of Science, Doctor of Philosophy

Pres.: Dr AROL AUGSBURGER
Vice-Pres. for Academic Affairs and Interim Dean: STEPHANIE MESSNER
Vice-Pres. for Devt: DAVID KORAJCZYK
Registrar: LAVERN YOUNG
Library Dir: (vacant)
Library of 22,000 vols
Number of teachers: 84 (49 full-time, 35 part-time)
Number of students: 639
Publication: *ICO Matters* (3 a year).

ILLINOIS INSTITUTE OF ART— CHICAGO

350 N Orleans St, Chicago, IL 60654
Telephone: (312) 280-3500
Internet: www.artinstitutes.edu/chicago
Founded 1916 as Commercial Arts School, present name and status 1995
Private control

Depts of culinary, design, fashion, general education, media arts

Pres.: JOHN BALESTER JENKINS
Vice-Pres. for Academic Affairs: VESNA GRBOVIC
Vice-Pres. and Sr Dir for Admissions: JANIS K. ANTON
Dean for Student Affairs: BETTY KOURASIS
Registrar: LaVONDRA L. LACEY
Library Dir: JULIET S. TEIPEL
Library of 33,000 vols, 600,000 images.

ILLINOIS INSTITUTE OF TECHNOLOGY

3300 S Federal St, Chicago, IL 60616-3793
Telephone: (312) 567-3000
Internet: www.iit.edu

Founded 1940 by merger of Armour Institute of Technology (f. 1892) with Lewis Institute (f. 1896)
Private control

Pres.: Dr JOHN L. ANDERSON
Provost and Sr Vice-Pres. for Academic Affairs: ALAN W. CRAMB
Vice-Pres. and Gen. Counsel: MARY ANN SMITH
Vice-Pres. for External Affairs: DAVID BAKER
Vice-Pres. for Finance and Admin.: PATRICIA LAUGHLIN
Vice-Pres. for Institutional Advancement: ELIZABETH J. HUGHES
Vice-Pres. for Int. Affairs: Prof. DARSH WASAN
Dean for Student Affairs: KATHERINE MURPHY STETZ
Registrar: REBECCA NICHOLES
Dean for Libraries: CHRISTOPHER STEWART
Library: see Libraries and Archives
Number of teachers: 551 (295 full-time, 256 part-time)
Number of students: 7,787
Publications: *ece@iit* (1 a year), *Employee Rights and Employment Policy*, *iitmagazine* (3 a year), *Seventh Circuit Review* (2 a year), *Vectors* (1 a year)

DEANS

Armour College of Engineering: NATACHA DEPAOLA
Chicago-Kent College of Law: Prof. HAROLD J. KRENT
College of Architecture: DONNA V. ROBERTSON
College of Psychology: Dr M. ELLEN MITCHELL
College of Science and Letters: R. RUSSELL BETTS
Institute of Design: PATRICK WHITNEY
School of Applied Technology: C. ROBERT CARLSON
Stuart School of Business: Dr HARVEY KAHALAS

ILLINOIS STATE UNIVERSITY

Normal, IL 61790
Telephone: (309) 438-2111
E-mail: admissions@illinoisstate.edu
Internet: illinoisstate.edu

Founded 1857
State control

Pres.: Dr AL BOWMAN
Provost and Vice-Pres. for Academic Affairs: Dr SHERI NOREN EVERTS
Vice-Pres. for Finance and Planning: Dr DANIEL LAYZELL
Vice-Pres. for Student Affairs: Dr LARRY DIETZ
Vice-Pres. for Univ. Advancement: ERIN MINNÉ
Registrar: JESS RAY
Dean for Univ. Libraries: Dr SOHAIR F. WASTAWY
Library of 1,610,271 vols, 38,395 e-journals, 48,527 multimedia titles, 2,541 print journals
Number of teachers: 1,205
Number of students: 21,080 (18,535 undergradute, 2,545 graduate; on-campus)

DEANS

College of Applied Science and Technology: Dr JEFFERY A. WOOD
College of Arts and Sciences: GREGORY B. SIMPSON
College of Business: Dr SCOTT D. JOHNSON
College of Education: Dr DEBORAH J. CURTIS

College of Fine Arts: Dr JAMES MAJOR (acting)
Mennonite College of Nursing: Prof. Dr JANET WESSEL KREJCI

ILLINOIS WESLEYAN UNIVERSITY

1312 Park St, Bloomington, IL 61702
Telephone: (309) 556-1000
Fax: (309) 556-3411
E-mail: iwuadmit@iwu.edu
Internet: www.iwu.edu

Founded 1850
Private control
Academic year: August to May

Schools of music, theatre, art and nursing

Pres.: RICHARD F. WILSON
Provost and Dean for Faculty: JONATHAN GREEN
Vice-Pres. for Advancement: MARTIN W. SMITH
Vice-Pres. for Student Affairs and Dean for Students: KARLA CARNEY-HALL
Dean for Admissions: TONY BANKSTON
Dean for Enrolment Management: IRV EPSTEIN
Registrar: LESLIE BETZ
Univ. Librarian: KAREN SCHMIDT
Library of 368,317 vols
Number of teachers: 182 (full-time)
Number of students: 2,090
Publications: *Illinois Wesleyan University Quarterly*, *IWU Magazine*.

INSTITUTE FOR CLINICAL SOCIAL WORK

Robert Morris Center, 401 S State St, Suite 822, Chicago, IL 60605
Telephone: (312) 935-4232
Fax: (312) 935-4255
E-mail: info@icsw.edu
Internet: www.icsw.edu

Founded 1981
Private control

Pres.: Dr MARTIN LAUB
Dean: Dr AMY ELDRIDGE
Dir for Student Affairs: KAREN BLOOMBERG
Librarian: SCOT AUSBORN

Number of teachers: 45
Number of students: 90

JOHN MARSHALL LAW SCHOOL

315 S Plymouth Court, Chicago, IL 60604
Telephone: (312) 427-2737
E-mail: admission@jmls.edu
Internet: www.jmls.edu

Founded 1899
Private control
Academic year: August to May

Advocacy and dispute resolution, global legal studies, tax, employee benefits, fair housing, information technology and privacy, intellectual property, international business and trade, real estate

Dean: JOHN E. CORKERY (acting)
Assoc. Dean for Academic Affairs: RALPH RUEBNER
Assoc. Dean for Admission and Student Affairs: Dr WILLIAM B. POWERS
Assoc. Dean for Advanced Studies and Research: KATHRYN J. KENNEDY
Asst Dean for Institutional Affairs: JOHN M. MCNAMARA
Assoc. Dean for Outreach and Planning: RORY DEAN SMITH
Chief Financial Officer: CYNTHIA SAH
Registrar: ANNA JOHNSON
Library Dir: JUNE HSIAO LIEBERT (acting)
Library of 254,585 vols
Number of teachers: 77

Number of students: 1,546 (1,139 undergraduate, 407 graduate)
Publications: *Journal of Computer and Information Law*, *The John Marshall Law Review*, *The John Marshall Law School Review of Intellectual Property Law*.

JUDSON UNIVERSITY

1151 N State St, Elgin, IL 60123-1498
Telephone: (847) 628-2500
Fax: (847) 695-0712
E-mail: askthecabinet@judsonu.edu
Internet: www.judsonu.edu

Founded 1913 as undergraduate div. of Northern Seminary, present name and status 2007
Private control
Campus at Rockford, Illinois

Pres.: Dr JERRY B. CAIN
Provost and Vice-Pres. for Academic Affairs: Dr DALE H. SIMMONS
Vice-Pres. for Business Affairs: JOHN POTTER
Vice-Pres. for External Relations: TORY GUM
Vice-Pres. and Dean for Student Affairs: LEANN PAULEY HEARD
Exec. Dir for Enrolment Services: NANCY BINGER
Registrar: VIRGINIA L. GUTH
Library Dir: LARRY C. WILD
Library of 91,000 vols
Number of teachers: 103 (40 full-time, 63 part-time)
Number of students: 1,200
Publication: *Judson today* (online (www.judsonu.edu/judsontoday))

DEANS

College of Liberal Arts and Sciences: Dr LANETTE POTEETE-YOUNG
School of Art, Design and Architecture: Dr CURTIS J. SARTOR
School of Education: Dr KATHLEEN E. MILLER
School of Leadership and Business: Dr THOMAS H. BERLINER

KENDALL COLLEGE

900 N North Branch St, Chicago, IL 60642
Telephone: (312) 752-2000
Fax: (312) 752-2057
E-mail: admissions@kendall.edu
Internet: www.kendall.edu

Founded 1934 as Evanston Collegiate Institute, present name 1950
Private control
Academic year: November to October

Pres.: EMILY WILLIAMS KNIGHT
Provost: Dr GWEN HILLESHEIM
Dean for Student Affairs: KIMBERLY SKARR
Registrar: ALEX UNDERWOOD
Dir for Library Services: IVA FREEMAN
Library of 35,000 vols
Number of teachers: 32
Number of students: 4,155

DEANS

School of Business: MICHELLE COUSSENS
School of Culinary Arts: RENEE ZONKA
School of Education: Dr PAUL T. BUSCENI
School of Hospitality Management: JEFFREY CATRETT

KNOWLEDGE SYSTEMS INSTITUTE

3420 Main St, Skokie, IL 60076
Telephone: (847) 679-3135
Fax: (847) 679-3166
E-mail: info@ksi.edu
Internet: www.ksi.edu

Founded 1978
Private control

Offers Masters degree in information technology and computer science
Chancellor: Dr SHI-KUO CHANG
Dean for Academic Affairs: Dr FREDERICK THULIN
Exec. Dir: JUDY PAN
Dir for Research: Dr HUBERT KORDYLEWSKI
Library Dir: JILL FRANKLIN.

KNOX COLLEGE

2 E South St, Galesburg, IL 61401-4999
Telephone: (309) 341-7000
Fax: (309) 341-7090
E-mail: admission@knox.edu
Internet: www.knox.edu
Founded 1837
Private control
Programmes in arts, humanities, sciences and social sciences
Pres.: Dr TERESA L. AMOTT
Vice-Pres. for Academic Affairs and Dean for College: Prof. LAWRENCE B. BREITBORDE
Vice-Pres. for Advancement: BEVERLY HOLMES
Vice-Pres. for Enrolment and Dean for Admission: PAUL STEENIS
Vice-Pres. for Finance and Admin. Services: THOMAS B. AXTELL
Dean for Students: DEBRA SOUTHERN
Library Dir: JEFFREY DOUGLAS
Library of 350,000 vols, 14,000 periodicals
Number of teachers: 120 (104 full-time, 16 part-time)
Number of students: 1,420 (undergraduate)
Publications: *Catch* (2 a year), *Knox Magazine* (4 a year).

LAKE FOREST COLLEGE

555 N Sheridan Rd, Lake Forest, IL 60045
Telephone: (847) 234-3100
Fax: (847) 735-6291
E-mail: president@lakeforest.edu
Internet: www.lakeforest.edu
Founded 1857 as Lake Forest Univ.
Private control
Academic year: August to May
Liberal arts college
Pres.: STEPHEN D. SCHUTT
Provost and Dean for Faculty: MICHAEL T. ORR
Vice-Pres. for Admissions and Career Services: WILLIAM J. MOTZER, JR
Vice-Pres. for Business Affairs: LESLIE T. CHAPMAN
Vice-Pres. for Devt and Alumni Relations: RICH BARTOLOZZI
Dean for Students: ROB FLOT
Registrar: RUTHANE BOPP
Dir for Library and Information Technology: JAMES R. CUBIT
Library of 281,079 vols, 2,540 journals, magazines and newspapers, 4,778 videos and DVDs, 1,904 music recordings
Number of teachers: 116
Number of students: 1,493
Publications: *Collage, Tusitala*.

LAKE FOREST GRADUATE SCHOOL OF MANAGEMENT

Conway Park, 1905 W Field Court, Lake Forest, IL 60045-4824
Telephone: (847) 234-5005
Fax: (847) 295-3656
E-mail: question@lfgsm.edu
Internet: www.lakeforestmba.edu
Founded 1946
Private control
Academic year: August to June

Campuses at Chicago and Schaumburg in Illinois
Pres. and CEO: JOHN N. POPOLI
Vice-Pres. for Finance and Admin.: MALCOLM C. DOUGLAS
Vice-Pres. for Devt: STASIA ZWISLER
Vice-Pres. for Information Technology: GREG KOZAK
Vice-Pres. for Research, Devt and Innovation: KATHY M. LECK
Dir for Admissions: CAROLYN BRUNE
Registrar: CHRISTINE L. PERLSTROM
Number of teachers: 120 (all adjunct faculty)
Number of students: 825

LEWIS UNIVERSITY

1 University Parkway, Romeoville, IL 60446-2200
Telephone: (815) 838-0500
Fax: (815) 838-9456
E-mail: admissions@lewisu.edu
Internet: www.lewisu.edu
Founded 1932
Private control
Pres.: Bro. JAMES GAFFNEY
Provost: Dr STEPHANY SCHLACHTER
Exec. Vice-Pres.: WAYNE DRAUDT
Sr Vice-Pres. for Enrolment Management: RAYMOND KENNELLY
Sr Vice-Pres. for Finance and Facilities: ROBERT C. DEROSE
Vice-Pres. for Student Services: JOSEPH FALESE
Vice-Pres. for Univ. Advancement: LEONARD BERTOLINI
Dir for Admissions: RYAN COCKERILL
Registrar: ROBERT KEMPIAK
Library Dir: Dr JULIE KRAHL
Library of 145,000 vols, 600 current periodicals, 2,500 video cassettes
Number of teachers: 200 (full-time)
Number of students: 6,500

DEANS

College of Arts and Sciences: Dr BONNIE BONDAVALLI
College of Business: Dr RAMI KHASAWNEH
College of Education: Dr JEANETTE M. MINES
College of Nursing and Health Professions: Dr PEGGY RICE
School for Professional and Continuing Education: Dr WALTER PEARSON

LEXINGTON COLLEGE

310 S Peoria St, Chicago, IL 60607
Telephone: (312) 226-6294
Fax: (312) 226-6405
E-mail: admissions@lexingtoncollege.edu
Internet: www.lexingtoncollege.edu
Private control
Women's college; offers Bachelors of applied science degree in hospitality management
Pres.: MARY HUNT
Academic Dean: Dr JOLENE BIRMINGHAM
Dir for Devt: KATHERINE CASKEY
Dir for Marketing and Enrolment: VERONICA NORTH
Registrar: LISA LEONARD
Librarian: JOSEPHINE KUJAWA
Library of 3,000 vols.

LINCOLN CHRISTIAN UNIVERSITY

100 Campus View Dr., Lincoln, IL 62656
Telephone: (217) 732-3168
E-mail: admissions@lincolnchristian.edu
Internet: www.lincolnchristian.edu
Founded 1944
Private control
Academic year: August to May

Campuses at Bloomington and Danville in Illinois, and Las Vegas in Nevada; offers doctoral degrees in ministry
Pres.: Dr KEITH H. RAY
Provost: Dr CLAY ALAN HAM
Vice-Pres. for Enrolment Management: KRISTA J. BROOKS
Vice-Pres. for Finance: ANDREA SHORT
Vice-Pres. for Student Devt: BRIAN MILLS
Vice-Pres. for Univ. Advancement: GORDON VENTURELLA
Registrar: SHAWN SMITH
Library Dir: NANCY J. OLSON
Library of 184,944 vols
Number of teachers: 44
Number of students: 1,085

DEANS

Hargrove School of Adult and Graduate Studies: Dr TOM TANNER
Seminary: Dr DINELLE FRANKLAND
Undergraduate Studies: Dr NEAL WINDHAM

LOYOLA UNIVERSITY CHICAGO

1032 W Sheridan Rd, Chicago, IL 60660
Telephone: (773) 274-3000
E-mail: admission@luc.edu
Internet: www.luc.edu
Founded 1870 as St Ignatius College, present name and status 1909
Private control
Academic year: August to May
3 Campuses in Chicago and Maywood, Illinois, and 1 in Italy
Pres.: Rev. MICHAEL J. GARANZINI
Provost: Dr JOHN PELISSERO
Sr Vice-Pres. and Gen. Counsel: ELLEN KANE MUNRO
Sr Vice-Pres. for Admin. Services: THOMAS M. KELLY
Sr Vice-Pres. for Advancement: JONATHAN HEINTZELMAN
Vice-Pres. for Information Services and Chief Information Officer: SUSAN M. MALISCH
Vice-Pres. for Facilities: PHILIP KOSIBA
Vice-Pres. for Student Devt: Dr ROBERT D. KELLY
Registrar: CLARE KORINEK
Dean of Libraries: ROBERT SEAL
Library of 900,000 vols, 3,600 periodical subscriptions
Number of teachers: 650 (full-time)
Number of students: 16,040
Publications: *Children's Legal Rights Journal* (4 a year), *International Law Review* (2 a year), *Loyola Law* (2 a year), *Loyola Magazine, Loyola World, Stritch M.D.*

DEANS

College of Arts and Sciences: Dr FRANK FENNELL (acting)
Graduate School: Dr SAMUEL ATTOH
Graduate School of Business: Dr KATHLEEN A. GETZ
Marcella Niehoff School of Nursing: Dr VICKI A. KEOUGH
School of Business Administration: Dr KATHLEEN A. GETZ
School of Communication: Dr DON HEIDER
School of Continuing and Professional Studies: Dr JANET V. DEATHERAGE (acting)
School of Education: Dr DAVID PRASSE
School of Law: DAVID N. YELLEN
School of Social Work: Prof. Dr DARRELL P. WHEELER
Stritch School of Medicine: Dr LINDA BRUBAKER

LUTHERAN SCHOOL OF THEOLOGY AT CHICAGO

1100 E 55th St, Chicago, IL 60615
Telephone: (773) 256-0700

Fax: (773) 256-0782
E-mail: admissions@lstc.edu
Internet: www.lstc.edu
Founded 1962 by merger of Augustana Theological Seminary, Grand View Seminary, Chicago Lutheran Theological Seminary and Suomi Theological Seminary
Private control
Academic year: September to May
Areas of study incl. biblical studies, environmental ministry and interfaith, religion and science and urban ministry
Pres.: PHILIP HOUGEN
Vice-Pres. for Advancement: MARK VAN SCHARREL
Vice-Pres. for Operations: BOB BERRIDGE
Dean for Students: TERRY BAEDER
Dir for Admissions: SCOTT CHALMERS
Registrar: PATRICIA A. BARTLEY
Dir for Library: CHRISTINE WENDEROTH
Library of 400,000 vols
Number of teachers: 19
Number of students: 290
Publications: *Currents in Theology and Mission* (6 a year), *Epistle* (3 a year).

McCORMICK THEOLOGICAL SEMINARY

5460 S University Ave, Chicago, IL 60615
Telephone: (773) 947-6300
Fax: (773) 947-6273
E-mail: admit@mccormick.edu
Internet: mccormick.edu
Founded 1829 as Indiana Seminary, present name 1884
Private control
Academic year: September to June
Doctoral degree in ministry programmes and Masters degree in discipleship development, theology, urban ministry and divinity
Pres.: FRANK M. YAMADA
Vice-Pres. for Academic Affairs and Dean for Faculty: LUIS RIVERA
Vice-Pres. for Admin. and Finance: DAVID CRAWFORD
Vice-Pres. for Student Affairs and Dean for Students: CHRISTINE VOGEL
Sr Dir for Seminary Relations and Devt: SAM EVANS
Registrar: JIM COURTNEY
Dir for Library: CHRISTINE WENDEROTH
Library of 400,000 vols
Number of teachers: 16 (full-time)
Number of students: 150

McKENDREE UNIVERSITY

701 College Rd, Lebanon, IL 62254
Telephone: (618) 537-4481
E-mail: info@mckendree.edu
Internet: www.mckendree.edu
Founded 1828 as Lebanon Seminary, present name and status 2007
Private control
Academic year: August to May
College of arts and sciences; schools of business, education, and nursing and health professions; campuses at Scott AFB, Illinois, and Louisville and Radcliff in Kentucky
Pres.: Dr JAMES M. DENNIS
Provost and Dean for Univ.: Dr CHRISTINE BAHR
Sr Vice-Pres.: VICTORIA DOWLING
Vice-Pres. for Admin. and Finance: SALLY MAYHEW
Vice-Pres. for Admission and Financial Aid: CHRISTOPHER HALL
Vice-Pres. for Research, Planning and Technology: Dr MARY BORNHEIMER
Vice-Pres. for Student Affairs and Dean for Students: Dr JONI BASTIAN

Exec. Dir for Kentucky Campuses: Dr DARREL HARDT
Registrar: DEBORAH L. LARSON
Dir for Library: REBECCA L. SCHREINER
Library of 70,000 vols
Number of teachers: 99 (full-time)
Number of students: 3,220 (2,355 undergraduate, 865 graduate)

DEANS

Graduate School: Dr JOSEPH CIPFL

MacMURRAY COLLEGE

447 E College Ave, Jacksonville, IL 62650
Telephone: (217) 479-7000
Fax: (217) 245-0405
E-mail: publicinformation@mac.edu
Internet: www.mac.edu
Founded 1846 as Illinois Conf. Female Acad., present name and status 1955
Private control
Divs of business and social sciences, education, fine arts and humanities, interdisciplinary and pre-professional programmes, and natural and health sciences
Pres.: Dr COLLEEN HESTER
Vice-Pres. for Academic and Student Affairs: JOHN L. BAILEY
Dean for Students: MARTIN SABOLO
Dir for Admissions: ALICIA ZEONE
Registrar: Prof. Dr ALLAN A. METCALF
Library Dir: SUSAN EILERING
Library of 130,000 vols, 125 periodicals
Number of teachers: 53
Number of students: 550
Publications: *Mac News* (2 a year), *Montage* (1 a year).

MEADVILLE LOMBARD THEOLOGICAL SCHOOL

610 S Michigan Ave, Chicago, IL 60605
Telephone: (773) 256-3000
Fax: (312) 327-7002
Internet: www.meadville.edu
Founded 1844
Private control
Academic year: September to June
Pres.: Prof. LEE BARKER
Provost: Prof. SHARON WELCH
Vice-Pres. for Finance and Admin.: DEBORAH BIEBER
Registrar: (vacant)
Dean for Library: Rev. Dr NEIL W. GERDES
Library of 140,000 vols, 120 periodicals
Number of teachers: 9
Number of students: 101

MEDICINE SHIELD COLLEGE PROGRAM—AMERICAN INDIAN ASSOCIATION OF ILLINOIS/NATIVE AMERICAN EDUCATIONAL SERVICES

6554 N Rockwell, Chicago, IL 60659
Telephone and fax (773) 338-8320
E-mail: dpwiese@aol.com
Internet: www.chicago-american-indian-edu.org
Founded 1974, present name and status 2007; attached to Eastern Illinois Univ.
Private control
Languages of instruction: English, Ojibwe, Lakota
Academic year: August to May
Areas of study: general studies, public policy, with emphasis on tribal knowledge, community service, community developmentt and leadership
Pres.: DORENE WIESE
Dean of AIAI Campus: LOLA HILL
Registrar: Dr MELANIE CLOUD

Head Librarian: MELANIE CLOUD
Library of 10,000 vols
Number of teachers: 8
Number of students: 30

METHODIST COLLEGE OF NURSING

415 NE St Mark Ct, Peoria, IL 61603
Telephone: (309) 672-5513
Fax: (309) 671-8303
Internet: www.mcon.edu
Founded 1900, present name and status 2001
Private control
Pres.: Dr KIMBERLY A. JOHNSTON
Dean for Academic Affairs: Dr LINDA PENDERGAST
Dean for Enrolment Management: DAVID PETERSON
Registrar: ANN GAREY
Library Coordinator: MELISSA HUDAK
Number of teachers: 47 (30 full-time, 17 part-time)
Number of students: 547 (446 undergraduate, 101 graduate)

MIDSTATE COLLEGE

411 W Northmoor Rd, Peoria, IL 61614-3558
Telephone: (309) 692-4092
Fax: (309) 692-4873
E-mail: midstate@midstate.edu
Internet: www.midstate.edu
Founded 1888, present name 1970
Private control
Depts of business administration, health information technology, allied health, general studies, realtime reporting, accounting, paralegal services and administration professional
Pres. and CEO: MEREDITH N. BUNCH
Chief Academic Dean: MARGARET STARR
Dir for Student Affairs: RHONDA URBAN
Dir for Library Services: ZACHARY BROWN
Number of teachers: 81

MIDWESTERN UNIVERSITY

555 31st St, Downers Grove, IL 60515
Telephone: (630) 515-6171
E-mail: admissil@midwestern.edu
Internet: www.midwestern.edu
Founded 1900 as American College of Osteopathic Medicine and Surgery, present name and status 1993
Private control
Academic year: September to May
Campus at Glendale, Arizona
Pres. and CEO: Dr KATHLEEN H. GOEPPINGER
Exec. Vice-Pres. and Chief Operating Officer: Dr ARTHUR G. DOBBELEARE
Sr Vice-Pres. and Chief Financial Officer: GREGORY J. GAUS
Vice-Pres. for Clinical Education: GEORGE T. CALEEL
Vice-Pres. for Human Resources and Admin.: ANGELA L. MARTY
Vice-Pres. for Univ. Relations: Dr KAREN D. JOHNSON
Dean for Student Services: Dr TERESA DOMBROWSKI
Registrar: SUE HARDWIDGE
Dir for Library Services: NATALIE REED
Number of students: 4,400

DEANS

Basic Sciences: Dr JOHN R. BURDICK
College of Dental Medicine—Downers Grove Campus: M. A. J. MACNEIL
College of Dental Medicine—Glendale Campus): Dr RUSSELL GILPATRICK
College of Health Sciences—Downers Grove Campus: Dr FRED D. ROMANO

College of Health Sciences—Glendale Campus: Dr JACQUELYN M. SMITH
Arizona College of Optometry: DONALD E. JARNAGIN
Chicago College of Osteopathic Medicine: KAREN J. NICHOLS
Arizona College of Osteopathic Medicine: LORI A. KEMPER
Chicago College of Pharmacy: Dr NANCY FJORTOFT
College of Pharmacy—Glendale: Dr DENNIS J. McCALLIAN

MILLIKIN UNIVERSITY

1184 W Main St, Decatur, IL 62522-2084
Telephone: (217) 424-6211
Fax: (217) 424-3993
Internet: www.millikin.edu
Founded 1901
Private control
Academic year: August to May
Pres.: Dr HAROLD G. JEFFCOAT
Vice-Pres. for Academic Affairs: BARRY PEARSON
Vice-Pres. for Enrolment: Dr RICHARD DUNSWORTH
Vice-Pres. for Finance and Business Affairs: RICK RIEDER
Vice-Pres. for Univ. Devt: PEGGY S. LUY
Dean for Admission and Financial Aid: STACEY HUBBARD
Dean for Student Devt: RAPHAELLA PRANGE (acting)
Registrar: WALT WESSELL
Dir for Library: CYNTHIA FULLER
Library of 189,000 vols, 1,000 periodicals, 53,000 e-journals, 82,000 e-books
Number of teachers: 249
Number of students: 2,340 (2,300 undergraduate, 40 graduate)
Publications: Collage (1 a year), *Millikin University Quarterly, Quarterly Economic and Financial Forecast*

DEANS

College of Arts and Sciences: Dr RANDY BROOKS
College of Fine Arts: LAURA LEDFORD
College of Professional Studies: Dr DEBORAH SLAYTON (acting)
Tabor School of Business: Dr JAMES G. DAHL

MONMOUTH COLLEGE

700 E Broadway, Monmouth, IL 61462-1998
Telephone: (309) 457-2131
Fax: (309) 457-2310
E-mail: info@monmouthcollege.edu
Internet: www.monmouthcollege.edu
Founded 1853
Private control
Language of instruction: English, French, German, Greek, Japanese, Latin, Spanish
Academic year: August to May
Pres.: Dr MAURI A. DITZLER
Vice-Pres. for Devt and College Relations: MOLLY A. BALL
Vice-Pres. for Enrolment Management: OMAR G. CORREA
Vice-Pres. for Finance and Business: DONALD GLADFELTER
Vice-Pres. for Student Life and Dean for Students: JACQUELYN CONDON
Dean for Faculty: DAVID M. TIMMERMAN
Registrar: CHRISTINE JOHNSTON
Library Dir: J. RICHARD SAYRE
Library of 333,000 vols
Number of teachers: 121 (84 full-time, 37 part-time)
Number of students: 1,308
Publication: *Monmouth College Magazine* (2 a year).

MOODY BIBLE INSTITUTE

820 N LaSalle Blvd, Chicago, IL 60610
Telephone: (312) 329-4000
E-mail: pr@moody.edu
Internet: www.moody.edu
Founded 1886 as Chicago Evangelization Soc., present name 1900
Private control
Academic year: August to May
Br. campuses in Spokane, Washington, and Plymouth, Michigan
Pres.: Dr PAUL NYQUIST
Provost and Dean of Education: JUNIAS VENUGOPAL
Exec. Vice-Pres. and Chief Operating Officer: STEVEN MOGCK
Vice-Pres. and Gen. Counsel: STEPHEN OAKLEY
Vice-Pres. for Educational Resources: WILLIAM W. BLOCKER
Vice-Pres. for Information Systems: FRANK W. LEBER, JR
Vice-Pres. for Student Services: THOMAS SHAW
Registrar: TIMOTHY C. WIEGERT
Library Dir: JAMES PRESTON
Library of 216,318 vols
Number of teachers: 83 (full-time)

DEANS

Education: JUNIAS VENUGOPAL
Moody Theological Seminary: JOHN JELINEK
Undergraduate School: LARRY DAVIDHIZAR

NATIONAL LOUIS UNIVERSITY

Chicago Campus, 122 S Michigan Ave, Chicago, IL 60603-3032
Telephone: (312) 621-9650
Fax: (312) 621-3057
E-mail: nluinfo@nl.edu
Internet: www.nl.edu
Founded 1886 as Miss Harrison's Training School, present name 1990
Private control
Campuses in Skokie, Lisle, Wheeling and Elgin (Illinois), Milwaukee and Beloit (Wisconsin), Tampa (Florida) and Nowy Sacz (Poland)
Pres.: Dr NIVINE MEGAHED
Provost: Dr CHRISTINE QUINN
Vice-Pres. for Devt: REBECCA STIMSON
Vice-Pres. for Enrolment Management: BOBBI BIRINGER
Vice-Pres. for Finance and Admin.: KENT KAY
Vice-Pres. for Institutional Advancement: (vacant)
Dir for Admissions: KEN KASPRZAK
Vice-Pres. for Operational Services: WILLIAM ROBERTS
Registrar: KENNETH GILSON
Dean for Library: KATHLEEN WALSH
Library of 125,000 vols
Number of teachers: 246
Number of students: 10,063 (2,213 undergraduate, 7,850 graduate)
Publication: *nlu today*

DEANS

College of Arts and Sciences: STEPHEN THOMPSON
College of Management and Business: WALTER ROETTGER
National College of Education: Dr ALISON HILSABECK

NATIONAL UNIVERSITY OF HEALTH SCIENCES

200 E Roosevelt Rd, Lombard, IL 60148
Telephone: (630) 629-2000
Internet: www.nuhs.edu

Founded 1906 as Nat. School of Chiropractic, present name 2000
Private control
Br. campuses in Florida
Pres.: Dr JAMES F. WINTERSTEIN
Vice-Pres. for Academic Services: VINCENT DeBONO
Vice-Pres. for Admin. Services: TRACY McHUGH
Vice-Pres. for Business Services: RONALD MENSCHING
Dean for Students: DANIEL DRISCOLL
Registrar: YESENIA MALDONADO
Chair. for Learning Resource Centre: JOYCE WHITEHEAD
Library of 15,000 vols
Publications: *Journal of Chiropractic Humanities* (online), *Journal of Chiropractic Medicine* (4 a year), *Journal of Manipulative and Physiological Therapeutics*

DEANS

College of Allied Health Sciences: Dr RANDY SWENSON
College of Professional Studies—Florida Campus: Dr JOSEPH STIEFEL
College of Professional Studies—Lombard Campus: Dr NICHOLAS TRONGALE
Lincoln College of Post-Professional, Graduate and Continuing Education: Dr JONATHAN SOLTYS

NORTH CENTRAL COLLEGE

30 N Brainard St, Naperville, IL 60540
Telephone: (630) 637-5100
Fax: (630) 637-5121
E-mail: admissions@noctrl.edu
Internet: www.northcentralcollege.edu
Founded 1861, fmrly Plainfield College
Private control
Academic year: September to June
Liberal arts college; offers graduate programmes in business administration, education, leadership studies, liberal studies, management information systems, web and internet applications
Pres.: Dr HAROLD WILDE
Vice-Pres. for Academic Affairs and Dean for Faculty: Dr R. DEVADOSS PANDIAN
Vice-Pres. for Business Affairs: PAUL H. LOSCHEIDER
Vice-Pres. for Enrolment Management, Athletics and Student Affairs: LAURIE HAMEN
Vice-Pres. for Institutional Advancement: RICK SPENCER
Registrar: JONATHAN PICKERING
Dir for Library Services: JOHN J. SMALL
Library of 150,000 vols, 3,400 journals
Number of teachers: 252 (133 full-time, 119 part-time)
Number of students: 2,973 (2,713 undergraduate, 260 graduate)

NORTH PARK UNIVERSITY

3225 W Foster Ave, Chicago, IL 60625-4895
Telephone: (773) 244-6200
Internet: www.northpark.edu
Founded 1891, present name and status 1997
Private control
Pres.: Dr DAVID L. PARKYN
Provost: Dr JOSEPH JONES
Exec. Vice-Pres. and Chief Financial Officer: CARL BALSAM
Vice-Pres. for Devt and Alumni Affairs: MARY SURRIDGE
Vice-Pres. for Enrolment and Marketing: NATHAN MOUTTET
Vice-Pres. for Student Devt and Dean for Students: Dr ANDREA NEVELS
Registrar: AARON SCHOOF
Library Dir: SARAH ANDERSON

Library of 443,665 vols, 995 journals, 28 newspapers
Number of teachers: 125 (full-time)
Number of students: 3,128 (1,852 undergraduate, 1,002 graduate/seminary, 274 continuing studies)

DEANS

College of Arts and Sciences: CHARLES PETERSON
School of Adult Learning: Dr BRYAN J. WATKINS
School of Business and Non-profit Management: Prof. Dr WESLEY E. LINDAHL
School of Education: Dr REBECCA NELSON
School of Music: CRAIG JOHNSON
School of Nursing: Prof. LINDA DUNCAN
Theological Seminary: LINDA CANNELL

NORTHEASTERN ILLINOIS UNIVERSITY

5500 N St Louis Ave, Chicago, IL 60625-4699
Telephone: (773) 583-4050
Fax: (773) 442-4900
E-mail: admrec@neiu.edu
Internet: www.neiu.edu
Founded 1867 as a teacher training instn
State control
Pres.: SHARON K. HAHS
Provost and Vice-Pres. for Academic Affairs: VICKI ROMAN-LAGUNAS (acting)
Vice-Pres. for Finance and Admin.: MARK D. WILCOCKSON
Vice-Pres. for Institutional Advancement: MELBA RODRIGUEZ
Vice-Pres. for Student Affairs: Dr FRANK E. ROSS
Dir for Admissions: CLAUDIA MERCADO
Dean for Students: Dr MICHAEL T. KELLY
Registrar: DANIEL R. WEBER
Univ. Librarian: BRADLEY F. BAKER
Library of 651,005 vols (and Regional Archives Depository)
Number of teachers: 488 (325 full-time, 163 part-time)
Number of students: 11,000

DEANS

College of Arts and Sciences: Dr WAMUCII NJOGU
College of Business and Management: Dr AMY B. HIETAPELTO
College of Education: Dr MAUREEN D. GILLETTE
Graduate College: Dr MARCELO SZTAINBERG

NORTHERN SEMINARY

660 E Butterfield Rd, Lombard, IL 60148
Telephone: (630) 620-2180
Fax: (630) 620-2190
E-mail: info@seminary.edu
Internet: www.seminary.edu
Founded 1913
Private control
Campuses at Chicago, Lombard, Rockford; online programmes
Pres.: Dr ALISTAIR BROWN
Dean for Academic Programmes: Dr KAREN WALKER-FREEBURG
Dean for Students: Dr RICKY FREEMAN
Registrar: MARILYN MAST HEWITT
Library Dir and Dean for Academic Admin.: BLAKE WALTER
Library of 55,000 vols, 175 journals, 8,000 e-books
Number of teachers: 32
Number of students: 200

NORTHERN ILLINOIS UNIVERSITY

1425 W Lincoln Highway, DeKalb, IL 60115-2828
Telephone: (815) 753-1000
Fax: (815) 753-8686
E-mail: admissions@niu.edu
Internet: www.niu.edu
Founded 1895, fmrly Northern Illinois State Normal School, present name and status 1957
State control
Academic year: August to May
Pres.: JOHN G. PETERS
Exec. Vice-Pres. and Provost: RAYMOND W. ALDEN, III
Exec. Vice-Pres. for Finance and Facilities: EDDIE R. WILLIAMS
Vice-Pres. for Outreach, Engagement and Information Technologies: ANNE C. KAPLAN
Vice-Pres. for Research and Graduate Studies: LISA C. FREEMAN
Vice-Pres. for Student Affairs and Enrolment Management: Dr BRIAN O. HEMPHILL
Vice-Pres. for Univ. Advancement: MICHAEL P. MALONE
Vice-Pres. for Univ. Relations: KATHY BUETTNER
Dean for Univ. Libraries: PATRICK J. DAWSON
Library: 2m. vols, 1,343,933 govt documents, 21,267 current periodicals, 3,000,087 microfilm units, 6,000 e-journals
Number of teachers: 1,185
Number of students: 22,990 (17,306 undergraduate, 5,365 graduate, 319 law)
Publications: *Applied and Computational Control, Signals and Circuits* (1 a year), *Crossroads: An Interdisciplinary Journal of Southeast Asian Studies* (2 a year), *George Eliot–George Henry Lewes Studies* (1 or 2 a year), *International Economic Journal* (4 a year), *International Journal of Sociology of the Family* (2 a year), *International Review of Modern Sociology* (2 a year), *Journal of Political and Military Sociology* (2 a year), *Names: A Journal of Onomastics* (4 a year), *Popular Music and Society* (4 a year), *Style Journal* (4 a year), *The Journal of Burma Studies* (1 a year), *Thresholds in Education* (4 a year)

DEANS

College of Business: DENISE D. SCHOENBACHLER
College of Education: Dr LA VONNE I. NEAL
College of Engineering and Engineering Technology: PROMOD VOHRA
College of Health and Human Sciences: MARY PRITCHARD
College of Law: JENNIFER ROSATO
College of Liberal Arts and Sciences: CHRISTOPHER K. MCCORD
College of Visual and Performing Arts: RICHARD HOLLY
Graduate School: Dr BRADLEY G. BOND (acting)

NORTHWESTERN UNIVERSITY

633 Clark St, Evanston, IL 60208
Telephone: (847) 491-3741
E-mail: ug-admission@northwestern.edu
Internet: www.northwestern.edu
Founded 1851
Private control
Academic year: September to June
Campuses at Evanston and Chicago in Illinois, and Doha in Qatar
Pres.: MORTON O. SCHAPIRO
Provost: DANIEL I. LINZER
Sr Vice-Pres. for Business and Finance: EUGENE S. SUNSHINE
Vice-Pres. and Chief Investment Officer: WILLIAM H. MCLEAN

Vice-Pres. and Gen. Counsel: THOMAS G. CLINE
Vice-Pres. for Admin. and Planning: MARILYN MCCOY
Vice-Pres. for Alumni Relations and Devt: ROBERT MCQUINN
Vice-Pres. for Information Technology and Chief Information Officer: SEAN REYNOLDS
Vice-Pres. for Research: JOSEPH T. WALSH, JR
Vice-Pres. for Student Affairs: PATRICIA TELLES-IRVIN
Vice-Pres. for Univ. Relations: ALAN K. CUBBAGE
Registrar: JACQUALYN CASAZZA
Dean for Libraries: SARAH M. PRITCHARD
Library: see Libraries and Archives
Number of teachers: 2,500 (full-time)
Number of students: 16,475 (8,367 undergraduate, 8,108 graduate)
Publications: *Journal of Criminal Law and Criminology* (4 a year, online (www.law.northwestern.edu/jclc)), *Journal of International Human Rights* (online (www.law.northwestern.edu/journals/jihr)), *Journal of International Law and Business* (3 a year, online (www.law.northwestern.edu/journals/jilb)), *Journal of Law and Social Policy* (online (www.law.northwestern.edu/journals/njlsp)), *Northwestern Journal of Technology and Intellectual Property* (online (scholarlycommons.law.northwestern.edu/njtip)), *Northwestern Perspective* (4 a year), *Northwestern University Journal of International Law and Business* (3 a year, online (www.law.northwestern.edu/journals/jilb)), *Northwestern University Law Review* (4 a year, online (www.law.northwestern.edu/journals/lawreview)), *Tri-Quarterly* (3 a year, online (triquarterly.org)), *The Reporter* (4 a year)

DEANS

Feinberg School of Medicine: ERIC G. NEILSON
Graduate School: DWIGHT A. MCBRIDE
Henry and Leigh Bienen School of Music: TONI-MARIE MONTGOMERY
J. L. Kellogg School of Management: SALLY BLOUNT
Judd A. and Marjorie Weinberg College of Arts and Sciences: SARAH MANGELSDORF
Medill School of Journalism, Media, Integrated Marketing Communications: JOHN LAVINE
Northwestern Univ. in Qatar: EVERETTE DENNIS
Robert R. McCormick School of Engineering and Applied Science: JULIO OTTINO
School of Communication: BARBARA J. O'KEEFE
School of Continuing Studies: THOMAS F. GIBBONS
School of Education and Social Policy: PENELOPE L. PETERSON
School of Law: DANIEL B. RODRIGUEZ

OLIVET NAZARENE UNIVERSITY

1 University Ave, Bourbonnais, IL 60914-2345
Telephone: (815) 939-5011
E-mail: admissions@olivet.edu
Internet: www.olivet.edu
Founded 1907, fmrly Illinois Holiness Univ., present name 1986
Private control
Pres.: Dr JOHN C. BOWLING
Vice-Pres. for Academic Affairs and Academic Dean: Dr GREGG CHENOWETH
Vice-Pres. for Finance: Dr DOUGLAS PERRY
Vice-Pres. for Graduate and Continuing Education: Dr RYAN D. SPITTAL

Vice-Pres. for Institutional Advancement: Dr BRIAN ALLEN

Vice-Pres. for Student Devt and Dean for Students: Rev. Dr WALTER (WOODY) WEBB

Dir for Admissions: SUSAN WOLFF

Registrar: JIM KNIGHT

Library Dir: KATHY BOYENS

Library of 160,000 vols, 900 current periodicals, 100,000 other items (maps, pamphlets, sheet-music, microforms, govt documents)

Number of teachers: 100

Number of students: 4,600

DEANS

College of Arts and Sciences: Dr JANNA McLEAN

School of Education: Dr JAMES UPCHURCH

School of Graduate and Continuing Studies: Dr JEFFREY WILLIAMSON

School of Professional Studies: Dr DENNIS CROCKER

School of Theology and Christian Ministry: Dr CARL LETH

PRINCIPIA COLLEGE

1 Maybeck Pl., Elsah, IL 62028-9720

Telephone: (618) 374-2131

Fax: (618) 374-5122

E-mail: registrar@principia.edu

Internet: www.principiacollege.edu

Founded 1910, present status 1932

Private control

Liberal arts courses

Pres.: Prof. Dr JONATHAN PALMER

Dean for Academics: Prof. Dr SCOTT SCHNEBERGER

Dean for Students: DORSIE GLEN

Dean for Enrolment Management: BRIAN McCAULEY

Registrar: PATRICIA W. LANGTON

Library Dir: LISA ROBERTS

Library of 125,000 vols

Number of teachers: 95

Number of students: 526

QUINCY UNIVERSITY

1800 College Ave, Quincy, IL 62301-2699

Telephone: (217) 222-8020

Fax: (217) 228-5479

E-mail: admissions@quincy.edu

Internet: www.quincy.edu

Founded 1860, present name and status 1993

Private control

Divs of behavioural and social sciences, fine arts and communication, humanities and science and technology

Pres.: Dr ROBERT A. GERVASI (acting)

Vice-Pres. for Academic Affairs: Dr TERESA I. REED

Vice-Pres. for Business and Finance: TIM WEIS

Vice-Pres. for Enrolment Management: SYNDI L. PECK

Vice-Pres. for Mission and Min.: Fr JOHN DOCTOR

Vice-Pres. for Student Affairs: Dr TIFFANY QUINZE

Registrar: BARBARA WELLMAN

Dean for Library and Information Resources: PATRICIA TOMCZAK

Library of 210,000 vols

Number of teachers: 153

Number of students: 1,424

Publications: *Communication Magazine*, *QUniverse Magazine*

DEANS

School of Business: Dr CYNTHIA HALIEMUN

School of Education: Dr ANN BEHRENS

RESURRECTION UNIVERSITY

3 Erie Court, Third Fl., Oak Park, IL 60302

Telephone: (708) 763-6530

E-mail: admissions@resu.edu

Internet: www.resu.edu

Founded 1914 as West Suburban School of Nursing, present name 2010

Private control

Offers BSc in health informatics and information management, nursing; MSc in nursing

Pres.: Dr BETH A. BROOKS

Chief Financial Officer: Dr THERESA SCANLAN

Exec. Dir for Marketing and Admissions: DESLA MANCILLA

Dir for Student Services: CARMELITA GEE

Dean for Nursing: Prof. Dr SANDIE SOLDWISCH

Registrar: EDY COOPER

Librarian: ERIC HERNANDEZ

Number of students: 230

ROBERT MORRIS UNIVERSITY

401 S State St, Chicago, IL 60605

Telephone: (312) 935-6800

Fax: (312) 935-4182

E-mail: enroll@robertmorris.edu

Internet: www.robertmorris.edu

Founded 1965, present name and status 2005

Private control

Campuses at Aurora, Bensenville, Chicago, Elgin, Orland Park, Peoria, Schaumburg, Springfield and Waukegan

Pres.: MICHAEL P. VIOLLT

Provost: MABLENE KRUEGER

Sr Vice-Pres. for Enrolment Management: NICOLE FARINELLA

Sr Vice-Pres. for Resource Admin.: DEBORAH BRODZINSKI

Vice-Pres. for Academic Admin.: KATHLEEN SUHAJDA

Vice-Pres. for Business Affairs: RONALD M. ARNOLD

Vice-Pres. for External Affairs: MARIE GIACOMELLI

Vice-Pres. for Information Systems: LISA CONTRERAS

Vice-Pres. for Student Affairs: ANGELA JORDAN

Registrar: STELLA MACH

Library Dir: SUE DUTLER

Library of 190,000 vols (incl. all campuses)

Number of students: 3,519

Publications: *egg* (1 a year), *Full Bleed*, *Radius*, *SCOPE*

DEANS

College of Liberal Arts: PAULA DIAZ

College of Nursing and Health Studies: Dr JANET HAGGERTY DAVIS

Institute of Art and Design: JANICE KAUSHAL

Institute of Technology and Media: BASIM KHARTABIL

Morris Graduate School of Management: Dr KAYED AKKAWI

School of Business Administration: LARRY NIEMAN

ROCKFORD COLLEGE

5050 E State St, Rockford, IL 61108

Telephone: (815) 226-4000

Fax: (815) 226-4119

Internet: www.rockford.edu

Founded 1847, present name 1892

Private control

Divs of arts and humanities; science, mathematics and nursing; social and behavioural sciences and education

Pres.: Dr ROBERT HEAD

Exec. Vice-Pres. and Dean of College: Dr STEPHANIE QUINN

Vice-Pres. for College Devt: JOHN McNAMARA

Vice-Pres. for Enrolment Management: BARRETT BELL

Vice-Pres. for Institutional Advancement: BERNARD SUNDSTEDT

Dean for Students: BRADLEY KNOTTS

Registrar: ANNA JATTKOWSKI-HUDSON

Library Dir: Dr JAN FIGA

Library of 1,437,953 vols and 500 current periodicals, 795 linear ft archives

Number of teachers: 71 (full-time)

Number of students: 1,350

Publications: *Decus* (3 a year), *Rockford College Literary Magazine (RCLM)*.

ROOSEVELT UNIVERSITY

Wabash Bldg, Room 116, 425 S Wabash Ave, Chicago, IL 60605

Telephone: (312) 341-3500

E-mail: gradadmission@roosevelt.edu

Internet: www.roosevelt.edu

Founded 1945 as Thomas Jefferson College, present name and status 1959

Private control

Campuses at Chicago and Schaumburg in Illinois

Pres.: Dr CHARLES R. MIDDLETON

Provost and Exec. Vice-Pres.: Dr JAMES GANDRE

Sr Vice-Pres. for Finance and Admin.: MIROSLAVA MEJIA KRUG

Vice-Pres. for Enrolment Management and Student Services: Dr SALLYE McKEE

Vice-Pres. for Government Relations and Univ. Outreach: LESLEY D. SLAVITT

Vice-Pres. for Institutional Advancement and Chief Advancement Officer: PATRICK M. WOODS

Sr Dir for Admission: JOANNE CANYON-HELLER

Registrar: SHELIA COFFIN

Univ. Librarian: RICHARD M. UTTICH

Library of 374,000 vols

Number of teachers: 500

Number of students: 6,620

Publications: *Business and Society*, *Roosevelt University Magazine*

DEANS

Chicago College of Performing Arts: HENRY FOGEL

College of Arts and Science: Dr LYNN Y. WEINER

College of Education: HOLLY STADLER

College of Pharmacy: Dr GEORGE E. MacKINNON, III

Evelyn T. Stone College of Professional Studies: GREG BUCKLEY

Walter E. Heller College of Business: TERRI FRIEL

ROSALIND FRANKLIN UNIVERSITY OF MEDICINE AND SCIENCE

3333 Green Bay Rd, North Chicago, IL 60064

Telephone: (847) 578-3000

E-mail: helpdesk@rosalindfranklin.edu

Internet: www.rosalindfranklin.edu

Founded 1912 as Chicago Hospital-College of Medicine

Private control

Academic year: July to June

Pres. and CEO: K. MICHAEL WELCH

Exec. Vice-Pres. and Chief Operating Officer: MARGOT A. SURRIDGE

Vice-Pres. for Academic Affairs: Dr WENDY RHEAULT

Vice-Pres. for Faculty Affairs: Dr TIMOTHY HANSEN

Vice-Pres. for Institutional Advancement: TINA M. ERICKSON
Vice-Pres. for Research: Dr RONALD KAPLAN
Chief Financial Officer: ROBERTA LANE
Registrar: CINDY FRIESEN
Dir of Library: BONNIE J. WATTERSON
Library of 119,000 vols, 2,000 biomedical journals
Number of teachers: 989 (157 full-time, 104 part-time, 728 volunteer)
Number of students: 2,026

DEANS

Chicago Medical School: Dr RUSSELL ROBERTSON
College of Health Professions: Dr WENDY RHEAULT
College of Pharmacy: Dr GLORIA MEREDITH
Dr William M. Scholl College of Podiatric Medicine: Dr NANCY PARSLEY
School of Graduate and Postdoctoral Studies: Dr JOSEPH X. DiMARIO

RUSH UNIVERSITY

Suite 440, 600 S Paulina St, Chicago, IL 60612
Telephone: (312) 942-5000
E-mail: rush_admissions@rush.edu
Internet: www.rushu.rush.edu
Founded 1972
Private control
Academic year: September to June (3 terms)
Pres. and Chief Operating Officer: PETER W. BUTLER
CEO: Dr LARRY J. GOODMAN
Provost: THOMAS A. DEUTSCH
Vice-Provost: Dr LOIS K. HALSTEAD
Registrar: WILLIAM F. KARNOSCAK
Library Dir: CHRISTINE D. FRANK
Library of 108,380 vols, 41,228 book titles, 253 e-books, 4,300 e-journals
Number of teachers: 2,900
Number of students: 2,000

DEANS

College of Health Sciences: DAVID SHELLEDY (acting)
College of Nursing: Dr MELANIE C. DREHER
Graduate College: Dr PAUL M. CARVEY
Rush Medical College: Dr THOMAS A. DEUTSCH

SAINT ANTHONY COLLEGE OF NURSING

5658 E State St, Rockford, IL 61108-2468
Telephone: (815) 395-5091
Fax: (815) 227-2275
E-mail: info@sacn.edu
Internet: www.sacn.edu
Founded 1915 as Saint Anthony School of Nursing, present name 1990
Private control
Academic year: August to May
Pres.: Dr TERESE ANN BURCH
Dean for Graduate Affairs and Research: Dr SHANNON LIZER
Dean for Undergraduate Affairs: Dr BETH M. CARSON
Assoc. Dean for Support Services: NANCY SANDERS
Dir for Learning Resource Centre: HEATHER KLEPITSCH
Librarian: MARY DUMAR
Library of 2,700 vols, 200 print and 1,000 online periodicals
Number of teachers: 17 (f.t.e.)
Number of students: 232 (185 undergraduate, 47 graduate)

ST AUGUSTINE COLLEGE

1345 W Argyle St, Chicago, IL 60640
Telephone: (773) 878-7989
Fax: (773) 878-3897
Internet: www.staugustine.edu
Founded 1980
Private control
4 Campuses in Chicago; offers Bachelors degree in social work
Pres.: ANDREW SUND
Vice-Pres. for Institutional Advancement: ALFREDO CALIXTO
Vice-Pres. for Technology, Research and Systems: PAUL HECK
Dean for Academic and Student Affairs: Dr BRUNO BONDAVALLI
Dean for Instruction: LEE MALTBY
Dir for Financial Aid: MARIA ZAMBONINO
Number of teachers: 100

SAINT FRANCIS MEDICAL CENTER COLLEGE OF NURSING

511 NE Greenleaf St, Peoria, IL 61603-3783
Telephone: (309) 655-2201
Fax: (309) 624-8973
E-mail: conadmissions@osfhealthcare.org
Internet: www.sfmccon.edu
Founded 1905 as St Francis Hospital School of Nursing, present name 1985
Private control
Academic year: August to May
Pres.: Dr PATRICIA A. STOCKERT
Dean for Undergraduate Programme: Dr SUZANNE BROWN
Dean for Graduate Programme: Dr JANICE F. BOUNDY
Assoc. Dean for Institutional Research: Dr MARY C. SHOEMAKER
Asst Dean for Support Services: KEVIN STEPHENS
Dir for Admissions and Registrar: JANICE FARQUHARSON
Librarian: LESLIE E. MENZ
Library of 7,556 vols, 1,840 periodicals, 123 professional journals
Number of teachers: 44 (32 full-time, 12 part-time)
Number of students: 452 (333 undergraduate, 119 graduate)

ST JOHN'S COLLEGE

729 E Carpenter St, Springfield, IL 62702
Telephone: (217) 525-5628
Fax: (217) 757-6870
E-mail: information@stjohnscollegespringfield.edu
Internet: www.stjohnscollegespringfield.edu
Founded 1886
Private control
Depts of continuing education and nursing
Chancellor and Dean: Prof. Dr BRENDA RECCHIA JEFFERS
Student Devt Officer: BETH BEASLEY
Admissions Officer and Registrar: LINDA QUIGLEY
Library Dir: KITTY WRIGLEY
Number of teachers: 18
Number of students: 93

SAINT XAVIER UNIVERSITY

3700 W 103rd St, Chicago, IL 60655
Telephone: (773) 298-3000
Fax: (773) 779-9061
E-mail: admission@sxu.edu
Internet: www.sxu.edu
Founded 1846, present name and status 1992
Private control
Academic year: August to May

Campus at Orlando Park, Illinois
Pres.: Dr CHRISTINE M. WISEMAN
Provost: Dr ANGELA DURANTE
Vice-Pres. for Business and Finance: RAYMOND P. CATANIA
Vice-Pres. for Student Affairs: JOHN P. PELRINE, JR
Vice-Pres. for Student Recruitment and Enrolment Planning: Dr KATHLEEN CARLSON
Vice-Pres. for Univ. Advancement: Dr STEVEN J. MURPHY
Vice-Pres. for Univ. Mission and Heritage: Dr SUSAN M. SANDERS
Vice-Pres. for Univ. Relations: ROBERT C. TENCZAR, JR
Librarian and Library Dir: MARK A. VARGAS
Library of 120,000 vols, 5,000 DVDs, 45,000 journals, 8,000 music scores, 7,000 music albums and 6,000 video cassettes
Number of teachers: 444 (192 full-time, 14 part-time, 252 adjunct)
Number of students: 4,709 (2,993 undergraduate, 1,716 undergraduate)
Publication: Saint Xavier Magazine (2 a year)

DEANS

College of Arts and Sciences: Prof. Dr KATHLEEN ALAIMO
Graham School of Management: Dr JAMES D. BRODZINSKI
School for Continuing and Professional Studies: Dr LESLIE M. PETTY
School of Education: Dr BEVERLY GULLEY
School of Nursing: Dr GLORIA JACOBSON

SCHOOL OF THE ART INSTITUTE OF CHICAGO

37 S Wabash Ave, Chicago, IL 60603
Telephone: (312) 629-6100
Fax: (312) 263-0141
E-mail: admiss@saic.edu
Internet: www.saic.edu
Founded 1866 as Chicago Acad. of Design
Private control
Academic year: September to May
Depts of architecture, art education, art history, art and technology studies, ceramics, design for emerging technologies, fashion design, fiber and material studies, film, video and new media, liberal arts, painting and drawing, performance, photography, print media, sculpture, sound, visual communication, visual and critical studies and writing
Pres.: Dr WALTER E. MASSEY
Provost: ELISSA TENNY
Vice-Provost: PAUL COFFEY
Vice-Pres. for Enrolment Management: ROSE MILKOWSKI
Dean for Faculty: LISA WAINWRIGHT
Dean for Graduate Studies: CANDIDA ALVAREZ
Dean for Undergraduate Studies: TIFFANY HOLMES
Library of 400,000 vols, 1,200 current serial subscriptions
Number of teachers: 568 (141 full-time and 427 part-time
Number of students: 3,221 (2,487 undergraduate, 734 graduate)

SEABURY-WESTERN THEOLOGICAL SEMINARY

8765 W Higgins Rd, Evanston, IL 60631
Telephone: 773-380-6780
Fax: (847) 328-9624
E-mail: seabury@seabury.edu
Internet: www.seabury.edu
Founded 1933 by merger of Seabury Divinity School (f. 1858) with Western Theological Seminary (f. 1883)

Private control
Academic year: September to June
Dean and Pres.: ROBERT G. BOTTOMS
Vice-Pres. and Chief Operating Officer: ELIZABETH BUTLER JAMESON
Academic Dean: Prof. ELLEN K. WONDRA
Dir for Finance and Admin.: MARK MILIOTTO
Registrar: PEGGY PEARSON
Dir for Library: BETH SHEPPARD
Library of 300,000 vols
Number of students: 92

SHIMER COLLEGE

3424 S State St, Chicago, IL 60616
Telephone: (312) 235-3500
Fax: (312) 235-3501
Internet: www.shimer.edu
Founded 1853
Private control
Courses in liberal arts: humanities, natural sciences and social sciences
Pres.: EDWARD NOONAN
Vice-Pres. for Academic Affairs and Dean for College: BARBARA STONE
Vice-Pres. for Enrolment Management and Student Services and Dean for Students: B. DAVID GALT
Chief Financial Officer: SANDRA COLLINS
Dir for Devt: MARY PAT BARBARIE
Registrar: JIM ULRICH
Library Dir: COLLEEN MCCARROLL
Library of 20,000 vols
Number of teachers: 13 (11 full-time, 2 part time)
Number of students: 100 (undergraduate)

SOUTHERN ILLINOIS UNIVERSITY CARBONDALE

Carbondale, IL 62901-6899
Telephone: (618) 453-2121
Fax: (618) 453-5362
E-mail: joinsiuc@siu.edu
Internet: www.siuc.edu
Founded 1869
State control
Chancellor: Dr RITA CHENG
Pres.: Dr GLENN POSHARD
Provost and Vice-Chancellor: Dr JOHN NICKLOW
Vice-Chancellor for Admin. and Finance: KEVIN D. BAME
Vice-Chancellor for Institutional Advancement: (vacant)
Vice-Chancellor for Research and Graduate Dean: JOHN A. KOROPCHAK
Dean for Students: PETER GITAU
Dean for Library: DAVID H. CARLSON
Library of 3,203,455 vols, 58,246 current serials, 4,633,365 microform units, 312,153 govt documents, 89,050 rare books, 18,610 linear ft MSS and archives
Number of teachers: 1,598 (full-time and part-time)
Number of students: 19,817

DEANS

College of Agricultural Sciences: TODD A. WINTERS
College of Applied Sciences and Arts: TERRY A. OWENS
College of Business: J. DENNIS CRADIT
College of Education and Human Services: JOHN BENSHOFF
College of Engineering: JOHN J. WARWICK
College of Liberal Arts: KIMBERLY KEMPF-LEONARD
College of Mass Communication and Media Arts: GARY P. KOLB
College of Science: Dr JAY C. MEANS
Graduate School: JOHN A. KOROPCHAK
School of Law: CYNTHIA FOUNTAINE

School of Medicine: Dr J. KEVIN DORSEY

SOUTHERN ILLINOIS UNIVERSITY EDWARDSVILLE

Edwardsville, IL 62026-1151
Telephone: (618) 650-2000
Fax: (618) 650-3837
Internet: www.siue.edu
Founded 1957
State control
Academic year: August to May
Chancellor: VAUGHN VANDEGRIFT
Pres.: Dr GLENN POSHARD
Provost and Vice-Chancellor for Academic Affairs: ANN M. BOYLE
Vice-Chancellor for Admin.: KENNETH R. NEHER
Vice-Chancellor for Student Affairs: NARBETH R. EMMANUEL
Vice-Chancellor for Univ. Relations: PATRICK D. HUNDLEY
Dean for Students: JAMES KLENKE
Dean for Library and Information Services: Dr REGINA MCBRIDE
Library of 808,094 vols, 1,675,875 microforms, 26,708 current periodicals, 33,063 audiovisual items
Number of teachers: 899 (619 full-time, 280 part-time)
Number of students: 14,235
Publications: *Papers on Language and Literature* (4 a year, online (www.siue.edu/pll)), *Sou'wester* (2 a year, online (www.siue.edu/english/sw))

DEANS

College of Arts and Sciences: Dr ALDEMARO ROMERO
Graduate Studies and Research: Dr JERRY WEINBERG
School of Business: Dr GARY GIAMARTINO
School of Dental Medicine: BRUCE E. ROTTER
School of Education: Dr BETTE S. BERGERON
School of Engineering: Dr HASAN SEVIM
School of Nursing: Dr MARCIA MAURER
School of Pharmacy: Dr GIREESH V. GUPCHUP

SPERTUS—A CENTER FOR JEWISH LEARNING & CULTURE

610 S Michigan Ave, Chicago, IL 60605
Telephone: (312) 322-1700
E-mail: info@spertus.edu
Internet: www.spertus.edu
Founded 1924
Private control
Academic year: September to August
Pres. and CEO: Prof. Dr HAL M. LEWIS
Dean and Chief Academic Officer: Prof. Dr DEAN P. BELL
Library of 110,000 vols; spec. colln: 1,500 rare books dating from 15th–20th centuries; Chicago Jewish Archives
Number of teachers: 49
Number of students: 300

TELSHE YESHIVA–CHICAGO

3535 W Foster Ave, Chicago, IL 60625
Telephone: (773) 463-7738
Private control
Areas of study: rabbinical and Talmudic education
Pres.: Rabbi AVRAHAM LEVIN
Number of students: 74

TRINITY CHRISTIAN COLLEGE

6601 W College Dr., Palos Heights, IL 60463-0929
Telephone: (708) 597-3000
E-mail: admissions@trnty.edu

Internet: www.trnty.edu
Founded 1959
Private control
Academic year: August to May
Programmes of study in accounting, art and design, biology, business, business communication, chemistry, church and ministry leadership, communication arts, computer science, economics, education, English, exercise science, geology, Greek, history, information systems, mathematics, music, nursing, philosophy, physical education, physics, political science, psychology, science, social work, sociology, Spanish, special education, theology
Pres.: Dr STEVEN TIMMERMANS
Provost: Dr ELIZABETH A. RUDENGA
Vice-Pres. for Admissions and Marketing: PETER HAMSTRA
Vice-Pres. for Business and Finance: JAMES BELSTRA
Vice-Pres. for Campus Devt: Dr GEORGE VANDER VELDE
Vice-Pres. for Devt: LARRYL HUMME
Vice-Pres. for Student Devt: GINNY CARPENTER
Registrar: CHRISTOPHER HUANG
Library Dir: MARCILLE FREDERICK
Library of 68,000 vols, 30,000 journals, magazines and newspapers
Number of students: 1,470

TRINITY COLLEGE OF NURSING & HEALTH SCIENCES

2122 25th Ave, Rock Island, IL 61201
Telephone: (309) 779-7700
E-mail: admissions@trinitycollegeqc.edu
Internet: www.trinitycollegeqc.edu
Founded 1898
Private control
Chancellor: Dr SUSAN C. WAJERT
Dir for Student Services and External Relations: JOANN M. LAY
Dean for Nursing and Health Sciences: TRACY L. POELVOORDE
Registrar: CARA BANKS
Librarian: MARY VICKREY
Number of students: 238

TRINITY INTERNATIONAL UNIVERSITY

2065 Half Day Rd, Deerfield, IL 60015
Telephone: (847) 945-8800
Fax: (847) 317-8097
Internet: www.tiu.edu
Founded 1897, present name and status 1995
Private control
Campuses in California, Florida, Illinois; online programmes
Chancellor: KENNETH L. MEYER
Pres.: Dr G. CRAIG WILLIFORD
Provost and Exec. Vice-Pres.: JEANETTE L. HSIEH
Sr Vice-Pres. for Academic Affairs: Dr ROBERT HERRON
Sr Vice-Pres. for Business and Finance and Chief Financial Officer: J. MICHAEL PICHA
Sr Vice-Pres. for Education: Dr TITE TIÉNOU
Sr Vice-Pres. for Enrolment: ROGER L. KIEFFER
Sr Vice-Pres. for Information Technology and Planning: STEVE GEGGIE
Sr Vice-Pres. for Student Affairs and Dean of Students: Dr WILLIAM O. WASHINGTON
Sr Vice-Pres. for Univ. Advancement: Dr DAVID HOAG
Registrar: ROBERT M. BOSANAC
Univ. Librarian: ROBERT H. KRAPOHL
Library of 233,000 bound vols, 170,000 microform vols, 2,000 current periodicals, 2 microform collns of English literature

from 15th–17th centuries, items from collns of Dr Carl F. H. Hentry and Dr Wilbur Smith

Number of teachers: 100

Number of students: 2,864 (1,280 undergraduate, 1,584 graduate)

Publications: *The Trillium* (2 a year), *Trinity Journal* (2 a year), *Trinity Magazine* (2 a year)

DEANS

Trinity College: Dr ROBERT W. HERRON

Trinity Evangelical Divinity School: Prof. Dr TITE TIÉNOU

Trinity Graduate School: Dr ROBERT W. HERRON

Trinity Law School: MYRON STEEVES

CONSTITUENT COLLEGES

Trinity College

E-mail: tcadmissions@tiu.edu
Internet: undergrad.tiu.edu

PROFESSORS

GRADDY, W. E., English
MOULDER, W. J., Biblical Studies
POINTER, S. R., History
SATRE, P. J., Music

Trinity Evangelical Divinity School

E-mail: tedsadm@tiu.edu
Internet: www.teds.edu

PROFESSORS

AVERBECK, R. E., Old Testament and Semitic Languages
BEITZEL, B. J., Old Testament and Semitic Languages
CANNELL, L. M., Educational Mins
CARSON, D. A., New Testament
COLE, G. A., Biblical and Systematic Theology
ELMER, D. H., Educational Ministries
FEINBERG, P. D., Biblical and Systematic Theology
HIEBERT, P. G., Mission and Anthropology
HOFFMEIER, J. K., Old Testament and Ancient Near Eastern History and Archaeology
KILNER, J. F., Bioethics and Contemporary Culture
NETLAND, H. A., Mission and Evangelism
NYQUIST, J. W., Mission and Evangelism
OSBORNE, G. R., New Testament
SENTER, M. H., Educational Mins
VAN GEMEREN, W. A., Old Testament and Semitic Languages
WOODBRIDGE, J. D., Church History and the History of Christian Thought
YOUNGER, K. L., Jr, Old Testament, Semitic Languages and Near Eastern History

Trinity Graduate School

E-mail: tgsadm@tiu.edu
Internet: graduate.tiu.edu

PROFESSORS

KILNER, J. F., Bioethics and Contemporary Culture
TIÉNOU, T., Theology of Mission

UNIVERSITY OF CHICAGO

5801 S Ellis Ave, Chicago, IL 60637

Telephone: (773) 702-1234
Internet: www.uchicago.edu

Founded 1890
Private control
Academic year: September to June

Pres.: ROBERT J. ZIMMER
Provost: THOMAS F. ROSENBAUM
Exec. Vice-Pres.: DAVID A. GREENE
Vice-Pres. and Chief Investment Officer: MARK A. SCHMID
Vice-Pres. and Dean for College Admissions and Financial Aid: JAMES G. NONDORF
Vice-Pres. and Gen. Counsel: BETH A. HARRIS
Vice-Pres. and Sec. for Univ.: DAVID B. FITHIAN
Vice-Pres. for Admin. and Chief Financial Office: NIM CHINNIAH
Vice-Pres. for Alumni Relations and Devt: THOMAS J. FARRELL
Vice-Pres. for Campus Life and Dean for Students: KIMBERLY M. GOFF-CREWS
Vice-Pres. for Research and Nat. Laboratories: DONALD H. LEVY
Registrar: ANDREW HANNAH
Dir for Libraries and Univ. Librarian: JUDITH NADLER

Library: see Libraries and Archives
Number of teachers: 2,188 (full-time)
Number of students: 15,626 (5,134 undergraduate, 10,492 graduate, professional and other)

Publications: *American Art: Smithsonian American Art Museum* (3 a year), *American Journal of Education* (4 a year), *American Journal of Human Genetics* (12 a year), *American Journal of Sociology* (6 a year), *American Naturalist* (12 a year), *Astronomical Journal* (12 a year), *Astrophysical Journal* (36 a year and 12 supplements a year), *Chicago Journal of International Law* (2 a year, online (cjil.uchicago.edu)), *Classical Philology* (4 a year), *Clinical Infectious Diseases* (24 a year), *Comparative Education Review* (4 a year), *Crime and Justice* (1 a year), *Critical Inquiry* (4 a year), *Current Anthropology* (5 a year), *Economic Development and Cultural Change* (4 a year), *Elementary School Journal* (5 a year), *Ethics: An International Journal of Social, Political and Legal Philosophy* (4 a year), *History of Religions* (4 a year), *International Journal of American Linguistics* (4 a year), *International Journal of Plant Sciences* (6 a year), *Isis* (4 a year, plus *Current Bibliography* as 5th issue), *Journal of Accounting Research* (online (www.chicagobooth.edu/jar)), *Journal of British Studies* (4 a year), *Journal of Business* (4 a year), *Journal of Consumer Research: An Interdisciplinary Quarterly*, *Journal of Econometrics* (online (www.journals.elsevier.com/journal-of-econometrics)), *Journal of Geology* (6 a year), *Journal of Infectious Diseases* (24 a year), *Journal of Labor Economics* (4 a year), *Journal of Law & Economics* (2 a year), *Journal of Legal Studies* (2 a year), *Journal of Modern History* (4 a year), *Journal of Near Eastern Studies* (4 a year), *Journal of Political Economy* (6 a year), *Journal of Religion* (4 a year), *Journal of the American Musicological Society* (3 a year), *Law & Social Inquiry* (4 a year), *Library Quarterly*, *Modern Philology* (4 a year), *Ocean Yearbook* (1 a year), *Osiris* (1 a year), *Philosophy of Science* (5 a year), *Physiological and Biochemical Zoology* (6 a year), *Publications of the Astronomical Society of the Pacific* (12 a year), *Quantitative Marketing and Economics*, *Quarterly Review of Biology*, *Signs: Journal of Women in Culture and Society* (4 a year), *Social Service Review* (4 a year), *Supreme Court Economic Review* (1 a year), *Supreme Court Review* (1 a year), *University of Chicago Law Review* (4 a year, online (lawreview.uchicago.edu)),

University of Chicago Legal Forum (1 a year, online (legal-forum.uchicago.edu)), *Winterthur Portfolio: A Journal of American Material Culture* (3 a year)

DEANS

Biological Sciences Division and the Pritzker School of Medicine: KENNETH S. POLONSKY
Chicago Booth School of Business: SUNIL KUMAR
Divinity School: MARGARET M. MITCHELL
Division of Humanities: MARTHA T. ROTH
Division of the Physical Sciences: ROBERT A. FEFFERMAN
Division of the Social Sciences: JOHN MARK HANSEN
Graham School of Continuing Liberal and Professional Studies: DANIEL W. SHANNON
Harris School of Public Policy Studies: COLM O'MUIRCHEARTAIGH
Law School: MICHAEL H. SCHILL
School of Social Service Administration: NEIL B. GUTERMAN
The College: JOHN W. BOYER

UNIVERSITY OF ILLINOIS

Urbana, IL 61801

Telephone: (217) 333-1000
Fax: (217) 333-5733
E-mail: infosource@uillinois.edu
Internet: www.uillinois.edu

Founded 1867
State control
Pres.: Prof. Dr ROBERT A. EASTER
Vice-Pres. and Chief Financial Officer: WALTER K. KNORR
Vice-Pres. for Academic Affairs: CHRISTOPHE PIERRE
Vice-Pres. for Health Affairs.: JOE G. N. GARCIA
Vice-Pres. for Research: Dr LAWRENCE B. SCHOOK

Number of teachers: 5,649 (f. t. e.)
Number of students: 77,635 (3 campuses).

CONSTITUENT CAMPUSES

University of Illinois at Chicago

601 S Morgan St, Chicago, IL 60607-7113

Telephone: (312) 413-3350
Fax: (312) 413-3393
Internet: www.uic.edu

Founded 1982 by merger of Medical Center campus with Chicago Circle campus

Chancellor: PAULA ALLEN-MEARES
Provost and Vice-Chancellor for Academic Affairs: LON S. KAUFMAN
Vice-Chancellor for Administrative Services: MARK DONOVAN
Vice-Chancellor for Devt: PENELOPE HUNT
Vice-Chancellor for External Affairs: WARREN CHAPMAN
Vice-Chancellor for Human Resources: JOHN LOYA
Vice-Chancellor for Research: MITRA DUTTA
Vice-Chancellor for Student Affairs: BARBARA HENLEY
Univ. Librarian: MARY CASE (acting)

Library: 1.9m. vols
Number of teachers: 2,574 (f. t. e.)
Number of students: 27,580 (16,911 undergraduate, 8,012 graduate, 2,657 professional)

DEANS

College of Applied Health Sciences: BO FERNHALL
College of Architecture and the Arts: JUDITH R. KIRSHNER
College of Business Admin.: MICHAEL PAGANO
College of Dentistry: BRUCE GRAHAM
College of Education: VICTORIA CHOU

College of Engineering: PETER C. NELSON
College of Liberal Arts and Sciences: ASTRIDA TANTILLO
College of Medicine: DIMITRI T. AZAR
College of Medicine at Peoria: SARA L. RUSCH (Regional Dean)
College of Medicine at Rockford: MARTIN LIPSKY (Regional Dean)
College of Nursing: TERRI E. WEAVER
College of Pharmacy: JERRY L. BAUMAN
College of Urban Planning and Public Affairs: MICHAEL PAGANO
Graduate College: KAREN J. COLLEY
Honors College: BETTE L. BOTTOMS
Jane Addams College of Social Work: CREASIE FINNEY HAIRSTON
School of Public Health: PAUL BRANDT-RAUF

University of Illinois at Springfield

1 University Plaza, Springfield, IL 62703-5407
Telephone: (217) 206-6600
Fax: (217) 206-6511
E-mail: admissions@uis.edu
Internet: www.uis.edu

Founded 1969 as Sangamon State Univ., present name and status 1995

Chancellor: SUSAN J. KOCH
Vice-Chancellor for Academic Affairs: LYNN PARDIE
Vice-Chancellor for Student Affairs: TIMOTHY L. BARNETT
Registrar: BRIAN CLEVENGER
Dean for Library and Univ. Librarian: JANE TREADWELL

Library of 566,000 vols, 30,000 e-books, 4,848 films, DVDs and video cassettes, 1,863,000 microforms, 200,000 govt documents
Number of students: 5,174 (3,197 undergraduate, 1,977 graduate)
Publication: *Illinois Issues* (12 a year, online (illinoisissues.uis.edu))

DEANS

College of Business and Management: RONALD D. MCNEIL
College of Education and Human Services: JAMES W. ERMATINGER
College of Liberal Arts and Sciences: JAMES W. ERMATINGER
College of Public Affairs and Admin.: PINKY S. WASSENBERG

University of Illinois at Urbana-Champaign

901 W Illinois St, Urbana, IL 61801
Telephone: (217) 333-1000
E-mail: admissions@illinois.edu
Internet: www.uiuc.edu

Founded 1867, present name 1885

More than 80 centres, laboratories, and institutes on the Urbana-Champaign campus that perform research for govt agencies and industry

Chancellor: PHYLLIS M. WISE
Provost and Vice-Chancellor for Academic Affairs: RICHARD WHEELER
Vice-Chancellor for Institutional Advancement: JAMES SCHROEDER
Vice-Chancellor for Public Engagement: STEVEN SONKA
Vice-Chancellor for Research: ROBERT EASTER
Vice-Chancellor for Student Affairs: C. RENEE ROMANO

Library: see Libraries and Archives
Number of teachers: 3,078
Number of students: 42,605
Publications: *Creating Engineers for the 21st Century*, *Health Care, Transportation and Security*, *Illinois Journal of Mathematics*, *LASNews* (online (www.las.illinois.edu/alumni/magazine)), *Water Energy Food*

DEANS

College of Agricultural, Consumer and Environmental Sciences: ROBERT J. HAUSER
College of Applied Health Sciences: TANYA M. GALLAGHER
College of Business: LARRY DEBROCK
College of Education: MARY KALANTZIS
College of Engineering: Prof. ILESANMI ADESIDA
College of Fine and Applied Arts: ROBERT B. GRAVES
College of Law: Prof. BRUCE P. SMITH
College of Liberal Arts and Sciences: Dr RUTH V. WATKINS
College of Media: Prof. JAN SLATER
College of Medicine at Urbana-Champaign: Dr URETZ J. OLIPHANT
College of Veterinary Medicine: HERB WHITELEY
Graduate College: DEBASISH DUTTA
Graduate School of Library and Information Science: JOHN UNSWORTH
School of Labour and Employment Relations: Prof. JOEL CUTCHER-GERSHENFELD
School of Social Work: Prof. WYNNE KORR

PROFESSORS

College of Agricultural, Consumer and Environmental Sciences:

AHERIN, R. A., Farm Safety
ANSELIN, L. E., Econometrics, Regional Economics
BAHR, J. M., Reproductive Physiology
BAIANU, I. C., Food Chemistry
BANWART, W. L., Soil Chemistry
BARRICK, R. K., Human and Community Devt
BARRY, P. J., Agricultural Finance
BELLER, A. H., Family Economics
BELOW, F. E., Plant Physiology
BERENBAUM, M. R., Insect Ecology
BERGER, L. L., Ruminant Nutrition
BLASCHEK, H. P., Food Microbiology
BOAST, C. W., Soil Physics
BODE, L. E., Power and Machinery
BOHNERT, H. J., Molecular Biology and Genomics of Plant Stress
BRADEN, J. B., Natural Resource and Environmental Economics
BREWER, M. S., Food Science
BRISKIN, D. P., Plant Physiology, Plant Biochemistry
BULLOCK, D. G., Crop Production and Biometry
BURIAK, P., Technical Systems Management
CAMPION, D. R., Animal Growth and Devt
CARR, T. R., Meat Science
CHASSY, B. M., Food Microbiology and Biotechnology
CHERYAN, M., Processing, Food and Biochemical Engineering
CHICOINE, D. L., State and Local Govt Finance
CHOW, P., Wood Science
CHRISTIANSON, L. L., Structures and Environment
CLARK, J. H., Ruminant Nutrition
COOKE, P. S., Veterinary Biosciences, Morphology
D'ARCY, C. J., Virology
DARMODY, R. G., Pedology
DAVID, M. B., Biogeochemistry
DAWSON, J. O., Tree Physiology
DIAMOND, A. M., Human Nutrition
DOCAMPO, R., Microbiology and Immunology
DONG, F. M., Food Science and Human Nutrition
DONOVAN, S. M., Nutrition
DRACKLEY, J. K., Nutrition
DUDLEY, J. W., Plant Genetics
EASTER, R. A., Animal Nutrition

ECKHOFF, S. R., Food and Bioprocess Engineering
ELLIS, M., Swine Nutrition
ENDRESS, A. G., Environmental Stress Physiology
ERDMAN, J. W., Nutrition
FAHEY, G. C., Animal Sciences, Nutritional Biochemistry
FARRAND, S. K., Molecular Biology
FAULKNER, D. B., Beef Extension
GARCIA, P., Agricultural Marketing and Price Analysis
GASKINS, H. R., Animal Sciences
GERTNER, G. Z., Forest Biometrics
GOOD, D. L., Agricultural Marketing
GRAY, M. E., Integrated Pest Management and Extension
GROSSMAN, M., Genetics
GROSSMAN, M. R., Agricultural Law
HANSEN, L. G., Pharmacology and Toxicology
HARPER, J. G., Agricultural Education
HAUSER, R. J., Agricultural Marketing and Price Analysis
HEICHEL, G. H., Plant Physiology
HELFERICH, W. G., Nutrition, Food Toxicology
HESS, R. A., Morphology/Toxicology
HIRSCHI, M. C., Soil and Water Extension
HOEFT, R. G., Soil Fertility and Extension
HOLLIS, G. R., Swine Extension
HURLEY, W. L., Lactation
HUTJENS, M. F., Dairy Extension
HYMOWITZ, T., Plant Genetics and Genetic Engineering
IRWIN, M. E., Int. Entomology
IRWIN, S. H., Agricultural Marketing and Price Analysis
ISSERMAN, A. M., Rural Economic Devt
JEFFERY, E. H., Toxicology, Food Science and Human Nutrition, Veterinary Biosciences
JONES, R. L., Soil Mineralogy and Ecology
JUVIK, J. A., Plant Genetics
KALITA, P. K., Soil and Water Association
KELLEY, K. W., Animal Sciences
KESLER, D. J., Reproductive Physiology
KOLB, F. L., Small Grain Breeding and Genetics
KORBAN, S. S., Plant Genetics
KRAMER, L. F., Applied Family Studies
KUHLENSCHMIDT, M. S., Microbiology
LARSON, R. A., Environmental Chemistry
LARSON, R. W., Family Ecology
LAYMAN, D. K., Nutrition
LEWIN, H. A., Biotechnology
LILA, M. A., Plant Physiology
LINS, D. A., Finance
LITCHFIELD, J. B., Food and Bioprocess Engineering
LONG, S. P., Photosynthesis and Environmental Sciences
MCKEITH, F. K., Meat Science
MACKIE, R. I., Animal Sciences, Microbiology
MARTIN, S. E., Food Microbiology
MERCHEN, N. R., Animal Sciences, Ruminant Nutrition
MILLER, G. Y., Veterinary Pathobiology
MORGANOSKY, M. A., Consumer and Retail Marketing
MORRIS, S. A., Processing Association
MULVANEY, R. L., Soil Fertility, Soil Chemistry, Soil Microbiology
MURPHY, M. R., Animal Sciences, Ruminant Nutrition
NAFZIGER, E. D., Crop Production and Extension
NELSON, R. L., Plant Genetics
NIBLACK, T. L., Cyst Nematode Management and Extension
NOEL, G. R., Nematology
NOVAKOFSKI, J. E., Animal Sciences, Meat Science
O'BRIEN, W. D., Electrical and Computer Engineering

OLSON, K. R., Soil Conservation, Soil Management, Pedology
ORT, D. R., Plant Physiology
PARRETT, D. F., Meat Animal Evaluation
PARSONS, C. M., Poultry Nutrition and Management
PATAKY, J. K., Epidemiology
PAUL, A. J., Small Animal Extension and Medicine
PAULSEN, M. R., Food and Bioprocess Engineering
PECK, T. R., Soil Chemistry and Extension
PERLMAN, A. L., Speech and Hearing
PERSHING, R. L., Power and Machinery
PETTIGREW, J. E., Animal Sciences, Swine Nutrition
PLECK, E. H., Human and Community Devt, History
PLECK, J. H., Human Devt and Family Studies
PLEWA, M. J., Plant Genetics/Environmental Mutagens
PORTIS, A. R., Plant Biochemistry
PUEPPKE, S. G., Plant Pathology
RAHEEL, M., Textiles and Clothing
REBEIZ, C. A., Plant Biochemistry and Plant Physiology
ROLFE, G. L., Forest Ecology and Environmental Studies
SALAMON, S. B., Community Studies, Family Studies
SCHMIDT, S. J., Food Chemistry
SCHOOK, L. B., Comparative Genomics
SHANKS, R. D., Genetics
SHAPIRO, C. H., Human and Community Devt
SINGLETARY, K. W., Nutrition
SKIRVIN, R. M., Horticulture
SMITH, R. D., Epidemiology and Preventive Medicine
SOFRANKO, A. J., Rural Sociology
SONKA, S. T., Agricultural Management
SPOMER, L. A., Plant Physiology
STEFFEY, K. L., Forage and Field Crop Insects and Extension
STUCKI, J. W., Soil Chemistry
SWANSON, B. E., Int. Agricultural Education, Int. Extension Technology Transfer
TIAN, L., Power and Machinery Association
TRUPIN, S. R., Obstetrics and Gynaecology
UCHTMANN, D. L., Agricultural Law
UNNEVEHR, L. J., Agricultural Marketing and Policy
VAN ES, J. C., Rural Sociology
VODKIN, L. O., Soybean Genetics and Genetic Engineering
WALLIG, M. A., Veterinary Pathobiology
WANSINK, B. C., Marketing and Agricultural Economics
WAX, L. M., Plant Physiology and Weed Science
WEATHERHEAD, P. J., Behavioural Ecology
WEIGEL, R. M., Epidemiology and Preventive Medicine
WEINZIERL, R. A., Fruit, Vegetable, and Livestock Insects
WHEELER, M. B., Reproductive Physiology
WHITE, B. A., Microbiology
WHITE, D. G., Fungal Diseases of Corn
WIDHOLM, J. M., Plant Physiology and Genetic Engineering
WILKINSON, H. T., Turfgrass Diseases
WILLIAMS, D. J., Horticulture
ZHANG, Q., Power and Machinery Association

College of Applied Health Studies:
BOILEAU, R. A., Kinesiology
CHAMBERS, R. D., Speech and Hearing Science
CHODZKO-ZAJKO, W., Kinesiology
FESENMAIER, D. R., Leisure Studies
GALLAGHER, T. M., Speech and Hearing Science
GOOLER, D. M., Speech and Hearing Science

HENGST, J., Speech and Hearing Science
IWAMOTO, G., Kinesiology
JOHNSON, C. J., Speech and Hearing Science
KUEHN, D. P., Speech and Hearing Science
LANSING, C. R., Speech and Hearing Science
MCAULEY, E., Kinesiology
O'ROURKE, T., Community Health
PERLMAN, A. L., Speech and Hearing Science
PROCTOR, F. A., Speech and Hearing Science
REIS, J., Community Health
SCHIRO-GEIST, C., Community Health
WATKIN, K. L., Speech and Hearing Science
WATKINS, R. V., Speech and Hearing Science
YAIRI, E., Speech and Hearing Science

College of Business:
ABDEL-KHALIK, A. R., Accountancy
ALSTON, L. J., Economics
ARNOULD, R. J., Economics
BAER, A., Economics
BECK, P. J., Accountancy
BERA, A. K., Economics
BERNHARDT, D., Economics
BLAIR, C., Management Science/Process Management
BLAIR, C. E., Business Admin.
BROWN, C. E., Accountancy
BRUECKNER, J. K., Economics
CHAN, L. K. C., Finance
CHENG, J. L., Business Admin., Int. Business
CHHAJED, D., Business Admin., Program Management Science/Process Management
CHO, I. K., Economics
COLWELL, P. F., Finance and Real Estate Research
CONLEY, J. P., Economics
D'ARCY, S. P., Finance
DEBROCK, L., Economics
ENGELBRECHT-WIGGANS, R., Business Admin., Management Science/Process Management
FINNERTY, J. E., Finance
GAHVARI, F., Economics
GENTRY, J. A., Finance
GIERTZ, J. F., Economics
GOTTHEIL, F. M., Economics
GRIFFIN, A., Business Admin., Marketing
GRINOLS, E. L., Economics
HALPERIN, R. M., Accountancy
HESS, J. D., Business Admin.
IKENBERRY, D., Finance
JEGADEESH, N., Finance
KAHN, C. M., Finance and Economics
KANNAN, S., Finance
KINDT, J., Business Law
KLEINMUNTZ, D. N., Business Admin., Strategic Management
KOENKER, R., Economics
KRASA, S., Economics
KWON, Y. K., Accountancy
LAKONISHOK, J., Finance
LANSING, P., Business Admin., Business Law
LEBLEBICI, H., Business Admin., Organizational Behaviour
LINS, D. A., Finance, Agricultural and Consumer Economics
LYNGE, M. J., Jr, Finance
MONAHAN, G. E., Business Admin., Management Science/Process Management
MONROE, K. B., Marketing
NEAL, L. D., Economics
NEUMANN, F. L., Accountancy Executive Leadership
NORTHCRAFT, G., Organizational Behaviour
OLDHAM, G., Organizational Behaviour
PEARSON, N. D., Finance
PENNACCHI, G. G., Finance

QUALLS, W. J., Business Admin., Marketing
RASHID, S., Economics
RESEK, R. W., Economics
ROSZKOWSKI, M. E., Business Admin., Business Law
SETH, A., Business Admin., Strategic Management
SHAFER, W. J., Economics
SHAVITT, S., Business Admin., Marketing
SHAW, M. J., Commerce and Business Admin., Marketing
SOLOMON, I., Accountancy
SUDHARSHAN, D., Business Admin., Marketing
TAUB, B., Economics
VILLAMIL, A. P., Economics
WANSINK, B., Marketing
WEISBACH, M. S., Finance
WILLIAMS, S. R., Economics
WON, Y., Accountancy
YANNELIS, N. C., Economics
ZIEBART, D. A., Accountancy

College of Communications:
BREWER, W. F., Psychology
CHRISTIANS, C., Communications
DASH, L., Journalism
DAVIS, S., Folklore and Folklife
DELIA, J. G., Communication and Human Relations
DENZIN, N., Sociology
DESSER, D., Cinema Studies, Speech Communication
GAINES, W., Journalism
HARRINGTON, W., Journalism
HELLE, S., Advertising and Journalism
LIEBOVICH, L. W., Mass Communications
MCCARTHY, C., Education, Curriculum Theory
MCCHESNEY, R. W., Library and Information Science
MERRITT, R. L., Int. Relations, Political Science
NERONE, J., Media Studies
O'GUINN, T., Advertising and Business Admin.
PRESS, A., Media Studies, Speech Communication
RICH, R., Law, Political Science
ROTZOLL, K., Advertising
SCHILLER, D., Communication, Library and Information Science
SRULL, T., Advertising
TREICHLER, P. A., Linguistics, Criticism and Interpretive Theory
WILLIAMS, B., Political Science
YATES, R., Journalism

College of Education:
ALEXANDER, K.
ANDERSON, R.
ANDERSON, T.
ARMBRUSTER, B.
BAROODY, A.
BARRERA, R.
BRAGG, D.
BRESLER, L.
BURBULES, N.
CHADSEY, J.
CLIFT, R.
CORDOVA-WENTLING, R. M.
CZIKO, G.
FEINBERG, W.
GARCIA, G.
GREENE, J.
HALLE, J.
HARRIS, V.
HUNTER, R.
IKENBERRY, S. R.
JOHNSON, S.
LEVIN, J.
LOEB, J.
MCCLURE, E.
MCCOLLUM, J.
MCCONKIE, G.
MIRON, L.

PERRY, M.
RENZAGLIA, A.
RIZVI, F.
ROUNDS, J.
RUSCH, F.
SCHWANDT, T.
STAHL, S.
TRAVERS, K.
TRENT, W.
WARD, J.
WESTBURY, I.
WILLIS, A.

College of Engineering:
ABELSON, J. R., Materials Science and Engineering
ADRIAN, R. J., Mechanical and Industrial Engineering, Theoretical and Applied Mechanics
AGHA, G., Computer Science
AHERIN, R., Agricultural Engineering
AHUJA, N., Engineering
ALKIRE, R. C., Chemical and Biomolecular Engineering
AREF, H., Physics, Theoretical and Applied Mechanics
AVERBACK, R. S., Materials Science and Engineering
AXFORD, R., Nuclear, Plasma and Radiological Engineering
BALACHANDAR, S. B., Theoretical and Applied Mechanics
BASAR, T., Electrical and Computer Engineering
BAYM, G. A., Physics
BECK, D. H., Physics
BERGMAN, L. A., Aeronautical and Astronautical Engineering
BLAHUT, R., Electrical and Computer Engineering
BRAATZ, R. D., Chemical and Biomolecular Engineering
BRAGG, M. B., Aeronautical and Astronautical Engineering
BREWSTER, M. Q., Mechanical and Industrial Engineering
BUCKIUS, R. O., Mechanical and Industrial Engineering
BUCKMASTER, J. D., Aeronautical and Astronautical Engineering, Theoretical and Applied Mechanics
BULLARD, C. W., Mechanical and Industrial Engineering
BURIAK, P., Agricultural Engineering
BURTON, R. L., Aeronautical and Astronautical Engineering
CAHILL, D. G., Materials Science and Engineering
CAMPBELL, E., Computer Science
CARLSON, D. E., Theoretical and Applied Mechanics
CEPERLEY, D. M., Physics
CHANG, Y.-C., Physics
CHEW, W., Engineering
CHIANG, T.-C., Physics
CHRISTIANSON, L., Agricultural Engineering
CLEGG, R. M., Physics
COLEMAN, J., Electrical and Computer Engineering
CONRY, T. F., General Engineering
CONWAY, B. A., Aeronautical and Astronautical Engineering
COOK, H. E., Gen. Engineering
COOPER, S. L., Physics
CRAIG, J., Mechanical and Industrial Engineering
DANTZIG, J. A., Mechanical and Industrial Engineering
DAVIS, W. J., Gen. Engineering
DEBEVEC, P. T., Physics
DEJONG, G., Computer Science
DEVOR, R. E., Mechanical and Industrial Engineering
ECKHOFF, S., Agricultural Engineering
ECKSTEIN, J. N., Physics

ECONOMY, J., Materials Science and Engineering
EHRLICH, G., Materials Science and Engineering
ERREDE, S. M., Physics
FENG, M., Electrical and Computer Engineering
FERREIRA, P. M., Mechanical and Industrial Engineering
FLYNN, C. P., Physics
FRADKIN, E. H., Physics
GEIL, P. H., Materials Science and Engineering
GEORGIADIS, J. G., Mechanical and Industrial Engineering
GLADDING, G. E., Physics
GOLDBART, P. M., Physics, Gen. Engineering
GOLDENFELD, N. D., Physics
GOLLIN, G. D., Physics
GRANICK, S., Chemical and Biomolecular Engineering, Materials Science and Engineering, Physics
GRATTON, E., Physics
GREENE, J. E., Materials Science and Engineering, Physics
GREENE, L. H., Physics
GRUEBELE, M. H., Physics
HABER, R. B., Theoretical and Applied Mechanics
HAJEK, B., Engineering
HAN, J., Computer Science
HEATH, M. T., Computer Science
HERTZOG, D. W., Physics
HESS, K., Physics
HIGDON, J. J. L., Chemical and Biomolecular Engineering
HIRSCHI, M., Agricultural Engineering
HODDESON, L., Physics
HOLONYAK, N., Physics
HRNJAK, P. S., Mechanical and Industrial Engineering
HUANG, T., Electrical Engineering
HUANG, Y. Y., Mechanical and Industrial Engineering, Theoretical and Applied Mechanics
HWU, W.-M., Electrical and Computer Engineering
IYER, R., Engineering
JACOBI, A. M., Mechanical and Industrial Engineering
JACOBSON, S. H., Mechanical and Industrial Engineering
JAMISON, R. D., Materials Science and Engineering
JONES, B. G., Nuclear, Plasma and Radiological Engineering, Mechanical and Industrial Engineering
KALE, L., Computer Science
KAPOOR, S. G., Mechanical and Industrial Engineering
KATZ, S., Physics
KERKHOVEN, T., Computer Science
KIM, K., Nuclear, Plasma and Radiological Engineering
KLEIN, M. V., Physics
KOGUT, J. B., Physics
KRIER, H., Mechanical and Industrial Engineering
KRIVEN, W. M., Materials Science and Engineering
KUMAR, P., Electrical and Computer Engineering
KUSHNER, M., Engineering
KUSHNER, M. J., Physics
KUSHNER, M. K., Chemical and Biomolecular Engineering
KWIAT, P. G., Physics
LAMB, F. K., Physics
LAWRENCE, F. V., Jr, Materials Science and Engineering
LECKBAND, D. E., Chemical and Biomolecular Engineering
LEE, K. D., Aeronautical and Astronautical Engineering
LEGGETT, A. J., Physics

LISS, TONY M., Physics
LOTH, E., Aeronautical and Astronautical Engineering
MAKRI, N., Physics
MARTIN, R. M., Physics
MASEL, R. I., Chemical and Biomolecular Engineering
MEDANIC, J. V., Gen. Engineering
MESEGUER, J., Computer Science
MILEY, G. H., Nuclear, Plasma and Radiological Engineering
MOSER, R. D., Theoretical and Applied Mechanics
MOUSCHOVIAS, T. C., Physics
MUNSON, D., Jr, Electrical and Computer Engineering
NAHRSTEDT, K., Computer Science
NAMACHCHIVAYA, N. S., Aeronautical and Astronautical Engineering
NAYFEH, M. H., Physics
NEWELL, T. A., Mechanical and Industrial Engineering
OONO, Y., Physics
PADUA, D., Computer Science
PANDHARIPANDE, V. R., Physics
PATEL, J., Engineering
PAULSEN, M., Agricultural Engineering
PAYNE, D. A., Materials Science and Engineering
PEARLSTEIN, A. J., Mechanical and Industrial Engineering, Theoretical and Applied Mechanics
PENG, J.-C., Physics
PHILLIPS, J. W., Theoretical and Applied Mechanics
PHILLIPS, P. W., Physics
PHILLIPS, W. R. C., Theoretical and Applied Mechanics
PINES, D., Physics
PITT, L., Computer Science
PONCE, J., Computer Science
PRICE, R. L., Gen. Engineering
PRUSSING, J. E., Aeronautical and Astronautical Engineering
REED, D., Computer Science
REIS, H. L. M., Gen. Engineering
RIAHI, D. N., Theoretical and Applied Mechanics
ROBERTSON, I. M., Materials Science and Engineering
ROBINSON, I. K., Physics
ROCKETT, A., Materials Science and Engineering
ROGERS, J. A., Materials Science and Engineering
RUZIĆ, D. N., Nuclear, Plasma and Radiological Engineering
SALAMON, M. B., Physics
SCHULTEN, K. J., Physics
SCHWEIZER, K. S., Chemical and Biomolecular Engineering, Materials Science and Engineering
SEEBAUER, E. G., Chemical and Biomolecular Engineering
SEHITOGLU, H., Mechanical and Industrial Engineering
SELEN, M. A., Physics
SENTMAN, L. H., Aeronautical and Astronautical Engineering
SHA, L., Computer Science
SHAPIRO, S. L., Physics
SINGER, C., Nuclear, Plasma and Radiological Engineering
SKEEL, R. D., Computer Science
SLICHTER, C. P., Physics
SNIR, M., Computer Science
SOCIE, D. F., Mechanical and Industrial Engineering
SOTTOS, N. R., Theoretical and Applied Mechanics
SPONG, M. W., Gen. Engineering
STACK, J. D., Physics
STEWART, D. S., Theoretical and Applied Mechanics
STONE, M., Physics

STUBBINS, J. F., Nuclear, Plasma and Radiological Engineering
SULLIVAN, J. D., Physics
THALER, J. J., Physics
THOMAS, B. G., Mechanical and Industrial Engineering
THURSTON, D. L., Gen. Engineering
TORRELLAS, J., Computer Science
TORTORELLI, D. A., Mechanical and Industrial Engineering, Theoretical and Applied Mechanics
TUCKER, C. L., III, Mechanical and Industrial Engineering
VAN HARLINGEN, D. J., Physics
VANKA, S. P., Mechanical and Industrial Engineering
WAH, B., Electrical and Computer Engineering
WALKER, J. S., Mechanical and Industrial Engineering
WATSON, W. D., Physics
WEAVER, J. H., Materials Science and Engineering, Physics
WEAVER, R. L., Theoretical and Applied Mechanics
WEISSMAN, M. B., Physics
WHITE, S. R., Aeronautical and Astronautical Engineering
WILTZIUS, P., Materials Science and Engineering, Physics
WISS, J. E., Physics
WOLFE, J. P., Physics
ZUKOSKI, C. F., Chemical and Biomolecular Engineering

College of Fine and Applied Arts:
ALBRECHT, J. G., Architecture
ALEXANDER, R., Music
ALI, M. M., Architecture
ANDERSON, J. R., Architecture
ANTHONY, K. H., Architecture
ARENDS, M., Industrial Design
BASKINGER, M., Graphic Design
BELLAFIORE, V., Landscape Architecture
BOGNAR, B., Architecture
BULLOCK, W., Industrial Design
CAMERON, M., Music
CARLSON, W., Glass
CONLIN, K. F., Theatre
DALHEIM, E., Music
DI VIRGILIO, N., Music
DRY, C., Architecture
EWALD, M., Music
FINEBERG, J., Art History
FORREST, C. W., Urban and Regional Planning
GARNER, J. S., Architecture
GOGGIN, N., Narrative Media
GRAVES, R., Theatre
GRUCZA, L., Painting
HARKNESS, T., Landscape Architecture
HARRIS, J. B., Theatre
HEDEMAN, A. D., Art History
HEDLUND, R., Music
HEILES, W., Music
HILL, J. W., Music
HOBSON, I., Music
HOPKINS, L., Landscape Architecture
HOPKINS, L. D., Urban and Regional Planning
HOSTETTER, E., Art History
ISSERMAN, A., Urban and Regional Planning
JAKLE, J., Landscape Architecture
KEENE, J. F., Music
KENDRICK, B., Painting
KEYS, H., Theatre
KIM, M. K., Architecture
KIM, T. J., Urban and Regional Planning
KINDERMAN, W., Music
KNAAP, G. J., Urban and Regional Planning
KOVATCH, R., Ceramics
KRAMER, K., Music
McFARQUHAR, R., Theatre
MACHALA, K., Music

MARTENS, C., Foundation
METTEM, A., Foundation
NETTLES, B., Photography
OUSTERHOUT, R. G., Architecture
PERKINS, K. A., Theatre
PLUMMER, H. S., Architecture
RICHTMEYER, D., Music
ROMM, R., Music
ROWAN, D., Printmaking
SCHAFFER, P., Music
SCHWARTZ, R., Painting
SIENA, J., Music
SILVER, C., Urban and Regional Planning
SOCHA, D., Printmaking
SQUIERM, J., Narrative Media
STOLTZFUS, F., Music
STONE, S., Music
SULLIVAN, D., Theatre
THEIDE, B. J., Metals
TIPEI, S., Music
TURINO, T., Music
VAN LAARM, T., Painting
WADLEIGH, H., Dance
WARD, T. R., Music
WARFIELD, J. P., Architecture
WESCOAT, J. L., Landscape Architecture
WILLIAMS, B., Urban and Regional Planning
WYATT, S. A., Music

College of Law:
BALL, C. A.
BELL, G.
BOYLE, F. A.
COLOMBO, J. D.
DAVEY, W. J.
FINKIN, M. W.
FREYFOGLE, E. T.
GEERDES, C. E.
HARRIS, O. F., Jr
HURD, H. M.
KAPLAN, R. L.
KINPORTS, K.
LEIPOLD, A. D.
McADAMS, R. H.
MAGGS, P. B.
MEYER, D. D.
PAINTER, R. W.
PFANDER, J. E.
REYNOLDS, L. A.
RIBSTEIN, L. E.
RICH, R. F.
ROSS, S. F.
SHOBEN, E. W.
TABB, C. J.
TARR, N. W.
TERRY, C. T.
ULEN, T. S.

College of Liberal Arts and Sciences:
ACCAD, E., French
ADELMAN, G., English
ALEXANDER, S., Mathematics
ALKIRE, R. C., Chemical and Biomolecular Engineering
ANGIONE, R. J., Astronomy
AUGSPURGER, C., Animal Biology, Plant Biology
BAILLARGEON, R., Psychology
BARON, D., English
BASS, J. D., Geology
BASSETT, T. J., Geography
BATZLI, G. O., Animal Biology
BAYM, G. A., Physics
BAYM, N., English
BEAK, P., Chemistry
BEARD, K., Atmospheric Sciences
BELFORD, R. L., Chemistry
BELMONT, A. S., Cell and Structural Biology, Biophysics
BERENBAUM, M. R., Entomology
BERNDT, B. C., Mathematics
BEST, P. M., Molecular and Integrative Physiology, Biophysics, Neuroscience and Bioengineering
BETHKE, C. M., Geology
BLAKE, D. B., Geology

BLAKE, N., Comparative Literature, Slavic Languages and Literature
BOCK, J. K., Psychology
BOHN, P. W., Chemistry
BOHNERT, H., Plant Biology and Crop Sciences
BOURGAIN, J., Mathematics
BRAATZ, R. D., Chemical and Biomolecular Engineering
BRECHIN, S., Sociology
BREWER, D. J., Anthropology
BREWER, W. F., Psychology
BRISKIN, D., Natural Resources and Environmental Sciences, Plant Biology
BRISTOL, E., Slavic Languages and Literature
BROWNE, G. M., Classics
BUDESCU, D., Psychology
BUSH, D. R., Plant Biology
CALDER, W. M., III, Classics
CAPWELL, C., Music
CARMEN, I. H., Political Science
CARRINGER, R. L., Cinema Studies, English
CASSELL, A. K., Italian and Comparative Literature
CHAI, L., English
CHEESEMAN, J., Plant Biology
CHEN, W.-P., Geology
CHENG, C-C., East Asian Languages and Culture
CHU, Y.-H., Astronomy
CLARK, R. A., Speech Communication
CLEGG, R. M., Physics and Biophysics
COATES, R. M., Chemistry
COHEN, N. J., Psychology
CONLEY, T. M., Speech Communication
CONTRACTOR, N., Speech Communication
CROFTS, A. R., Biochemistry
CRONAN, J. E., Microbiology, Biochemistry
DADE, E. C., Mathematics
D'ANGELO, J. P., Mathematics
DELCOMYN, F., Entomology
DELEY, H., French
DELIA, J. G., Speech Communication
DELL, G. S., Psychology
DeLUCIA, E., Plant Biology
DENMARK, S. E., Chemistry
DENZIN, N., Cinema Studies
DESSER, D., Cinema Studies
DeVRIES, A. L., Animal Biology
DIENER, E. F., Psychology
DLOTT, D. D., Chemistry
DRASGOW, F., Psychology
DUTTA, S., Mathematics
FAGYAL, Z., French
FENG, A. S., Molecular and Integrative Physiology, Biophysics, Bioengineering, and Neuroscience
FITZGERALD, L., Psychology
FOSSUM, R. M., Mathematics
FRANCIS, G. K., Mathematics
FRAZZETTA, T. H., Animal Biology
FRIEDMAN, P., English
FRITZSCHE, P., History
FÜREDI, Z., Mathematics
GABRIEL, M., Psychology
GARBER, P. A., Anthropology
GARCIA, P., Agricultural Economics
GARRETT, P., English
GENNIS, R. B., Biochemistry, Chemistry, Biophysics
GERLACH, U. H., Germanic Languages and Literature
GERLT, J. A., Biochemistry, Chemistry and Biophysics, Basic Medical Science
GEWIRTH, A. A., Chemistry
GIROLAMI, G. S., Chemistry
GLASER, M., Biochemistry, Basic Medical Sciences
GOLATO, P., French
GOLD, P. E., Psychology
GOODMAN, D. G., East Asian Languages and Culture
GOTTLIEB, A., Anthropology
GRAHAM, P., English

GRANICK, S., Chemical and Biomolecular Engineering
GRAY, M. E., Entomology
GRAYSON, D. R., Mathematics
GREENOUGH, W. T., Psychology
GROVE, D., Anthropology
GRUEBELE, M., Chemistry
GUIBBOR, A., English
GUMPORT, R. I., Biochemistry, Basic Medical Sciences
HABOUSH, W., Mathematics
HADLEY, A. O., French
HANNON, B. M., Geography
HAWISHER, G. E., English
HE, X., Statistics
HELLER, W., Psychology
HELMAN, S. I., Molecular and Integrative Physiology, Biophysics, and Bioengineering
HENSON, C. W., Mathematics
HEWINGS, G. J. D., Geography
HIGDON, J. J. L., Chemical and Biomolecular Engineering
HILDEBRAND, A. J., Mathematics
HINKKANEN, A., Mathematics
HITCHINS, K., History
HOCK, H. H., Linguistics
HSUI, A. T., Geology
HUALDE, J. I., Linguistics and Spanish, Italian, and Portuguese
HUBERT, L., Psychology
IBEN, I., Jr, Physics
IMREY, P., Statistics
IRWIN, D., Psychology
IRWIN, M. E., Entomology
IVANOV, S. V., Mathematics
JACOBSON, H., Classics
JAEGER, C. S., Cinema Studies
JAEGER, S., Comparative Literature
JAHER, F. C., Cinema Studies
JAHIEL, E., Cinema Studies, French
JAKLE, J. A., Geography
JAKOBSSON, E., Molecular and Integrative Physiology, Biochemistry, Biophysics, Bioengineering, and Neuroscience
JOCKUSCH, C. G., Mathematics
JOHNSON, D. L., Geography
JURASKA, J., Psychology
KALINKE, M. E., Germanic Languages and Literature
KATZ, S., Mathematics
KATZENELLENBOGEN, B. S., Molecular and Integrative Physiology
KATZENELLENBOGEN, J. A., Chemistry
KELLER, J. D., Anthropology
KELLY, B., English
KEMPER, B. W., Molecular and Integrative Physiology, Cell and Structural Biology
KIBBEE, D., French
KIM, C. W., Linguistics, East Asian Languages and Culture
KIRKPATRICK, R. J., Geology
KLEMPERER, W. G., Chemistry
KLEPINGER, L. L., Anthropology
KLUEGEL, J., Sociology
KNOTT, J. H., Political Science
KOENKER, D. P., History
KOSTOCHKA, A. V., Mathematics
KRAMER, A., Psychology
KRANZ, D. M., Biochemistry
KUKLINSKI, J. H., Political Science
LAMB, F. K., Physics
LAUGHLIN, P. R., Psychology
LAUTERBUR, P. C., Chemistry
LECKBAND, D. E., Chemistry, Chemical and Biomolecular Engineering
LEHMAN, F. K., Anthropology
LEWIS, R. B., Anthropology
LIEBERMAN, L., English
LISY, J. M., Chemistry
LOEB, P. A., Mathematics
LOTZ, H. P., Mathematics
LOVE, J. L., History
McCARTHY, T., Philosophy
McDONALD, J. D., Chemistry
McDONALD, R., Psychology

McKIM, R., Religious Studies, Philosophy
McLAFFERTY, S., Geography
McLINDEN, L., Mathematics
McMAHAN, J., Philosophy
MAHER, P., Philosophy
MAK, M., Atmospheric Sciences
MAKRI, N., Chemistry
MALL, L., French
MALPELI, J. G., Psychology
MANGELSDORF, S., Psychology
MARDEN, J., Statistics
MARSHAK, S., Geology
MARTINSEK, A., Statistics
MASEL, R. I., Chemical and Biomolecular Engineering
MATHY, J.-P., French, Comparative Literature
MICHELSON, B., English
MILES, J. B., Mathematics
MILLER, G., Psychology
MILLER, P., Psychology
MILLER, P., Speech Communication
MOHR, R., Philosophy
MOORE, J. S., Chemistry
MORGAN, J. L., Linguistics
MORRISSEY, J. H., Biochemistry
MORTIMER, A., French
MOUSCHOVIAS, T., Physics and Astrophysics
MURAV, H., Slavic Languages and Literature, Comparative Literature
MUSUMECCI, A., Italian
NARDULLI, P. F., Political Science
NEDERVEEN-PIETERSE, J., Sociology
NEELY, C., English
NIKOLAEV, I., Mathematics
NUZZO, R., Chemistry
O'KEEFE, D. J., Speech Communication
OLDFIELD, E., Chemistry
ONO, K., Asian American Studies
ORDAL, G. W., Biochemistry, Basic Medical Science
ORT, D. R., Plant Biology
PACKARD, J., East Asian Languages and Culture
PAHRE, R., Political Science
PAIGE, K. N., Animal Biology
PALENCIA-ROTH, M., Comparative Literature
PALMORE, J. I., Mathematics
PANDHARIPANDE, R., Linguistics, Religious Studies, Sanskrit, Comparative Literature
PANDHARIPANDE, V., Physics
PARK, D., Psychology
PARKER, R. D., English
PHILLIPS, P. W., Physics
PHILLIPS, T. L., Plant Biology
PILLAY, A., Mathematics
PINDERHUGHES, D. M., Political Science, Afro-American Studies
PINES, D., Physics and Electrical and Computer Engineering
PITARD, W. T., Religious Studies
PORTON, G. G., Religious Studies, History, Comparative Literature
POWERS, R., English
PRESS, A., Speech Communication
QUIRK, P. J., Political Science
RAPPAPORT, J., Psychology
RAUBER, R., Atmospheric Sciences
RAUCHFUSS, T. B., Chemistry
REZNICK, B., Mathematics
RHOADS, B. L., Geography
RICH, R. F., Political Science
ROBERTSON, H. M., Entomology
ROBINSON, D. J. S., Mathematics
ROBINSON, G. E., Entomology, Political Science
ROBINSON, S. K., Animal Biology
ROBINSON, W., Atmospheric Sciences
ROEDIGER, D., Afro-American Studies
ROGERS, J. A., Chemistry
RONCADOR, S. M., Brazilian, Portuguese and Lusophone Literatures
ROSENBLATT, J., Mathematics
ROSS, B., Psychology

ROTMAN, J., Mathematics
ROY, E., Psychology
RUAN, Z.-J., Mathematics
SAHINIDIS, N. V., Chemical and Biomolecular Engineering
SANSONE, D., Classics
SCHACHT, R., Philosophy
SCHEELINE, A., Chemistry
SCHEHR, L., French
SCHLESINGER, M., Atmospheric Sciences
SCHULER, M. A., Cell and Structural Biology, Biochemistry
SCHULTEN, K., Chemistry
SCHUPP, P., Mathematics
SCHWEIZER, K. S., Chemistry, Chemical and Biomolecular Engineering
SEEBAUER, E. G., Chemical and Biomolecular Engineering
SEIGLER, D. S., Plant Biology
SHAFTER, A. W., Astronomy
SHAPIRO, M., English
SHAPIRO, S. L., Physics and Astronomy
SHAPLEY, J. R., Chemistry
SHAPLEY, P. A., Chemistry
SHEARER, C. A., Plant Biology
SHERWOOD, O. D., Molecular and Integrative Physiology
SHOBEN, E. J., Psychology
SIMPSON, D., Statistics
SLIGAR, S. G., Chemistry
SMITH, S. G., Chemistry
SNIEZEK, J. A., Psychology
SOFFER, O., Anthropology
SOUSA, R., Portuguese, Spanish and Comparative Literature
SRULL, T. K., Psychology
STEFFEY, K. L., Entomology
STILLINGER, N. B., English
STOLARSKY, K. B., Mathematics
SULLIVAN, Z., English
SUSLICK, K. S., Chemistry
SWANSON, D. L., Political Science, Speech Communication
SWEEDLER, J. V., Chemistry
TALBOT, E. J., French
TEARE, S., Electrical Engineering
THOMPSON, L. A., Astronomy
THOMPSON, J., English
TOBY, R. P., East Asian Languages and Culture
TODOROVA, M., History
TUMANOV, A. E., Mathematics
ULLOM, S. V., Mathematics
UNNEVEHR, L., Agricultural and Consumer Economics
VALENTE, J., English
VAN DEN DRIES, L., Mathematics
WALLACE, J., Philosophy
WALSH, J., Atmospheric Sciences
WASSERMAN, S., Psychology, Statistics
WATSON, W. D., Physics and Astronomy
WATTS, E., English
WEATHERHEAD, P. J., Animal Biology, Natural Resources, Environmental Sciences
WEBBINK, R. F., Astronomy
WEINZIERL, R. A., Entomology
WEISSBERG, R., Political Science
WEST, D. B., Mathematics
WHITT, G. S., Animal Biology
WHITTEN, N. E., Jr, Anthropology
WICKENS, C., Psychology
WIECKOWSKI, A., Chemistry
WILCOX, J., Spanish
WILHELMSON, R., Atmospheric Sciences
WILSON, B. J., Speech Communication
WOESE, C. I., Microbiology and Animal Biology
WRAIGHT, C. A., Biochemistry and Plant Biology
WRIGHT, D., English
WRIGHT, R., Germanic Languages and Literature, Cinema Studies
WU, J.-M., Mathematics
WUEBBLES, D. J., Atmospheric Sciences
YU, G. T., Political Science
ZIMMERMAN, S. C., Chemistry

ZINNES, D., Political Science
ZUKOSKI, C. F., Chemical and Biomolecular Engineering

College of Medicine:

BAKER, D. H., Internal Medicine
BELMONT, A. S., Cell and Structural Biology
BEST, P. M., Molecular and Integrative Physiology, Physiology, Biophysics, Bioengineering and Neuroscience
BOILEAU, R. A., Internal Medicine
BUETOW, M. K., Paediatrics and Adolescent Health
CLEGG, R. M., Physics and Biophysics
CRASS, J. R., Internal Medicine
CROFTS, A. R., Biochemistry and Biophysics
CRONAN, J. E., Microbiology, Biochemistry and Microbiology
DONCHIN, E., Internal Medicine
ENSRUD, E. R., Internal Medicine
ERDMAN, J. W., Jr, Internal Medicine
ESSEX-SORLIE, D. L., Internal Medicine
FARRAND, S., Microbiology and Plant Pathology
FENG, A. S., Physiology, Biophysics, Bioengineering and Neuroscience
FREEDMAN, P., Internal Medicine
GARDNER, J. F., Microbiology
GELFAND, V. I., Cell and Structural Biology
GENNIS, R. B., Biochemistry, Chemistry, Biophysics
GERLT, J. A., Biochemistry, Chemistry and Biophysics, Basic Medical Sciences
GILLETTE, M. U., Cell and Structural Biology
GILLETTE, R., Molecular and Integrative Physiology, Biophysics
GLASER, M., Biochemistry and Biophysics
GREENOUGH, W. T., Psychiatry, Cell and Structural Biology, Psychology and Psychiatry
GUMPORT, R. I., Biochemistry, Basic Medical Sciences
HELMAN, S. I., Physiology, Biophysics and Bioengineering
JAKOBSSON, E., Physiology, Biochemistry, Biophysics
JEFFERY, E., Pharmacology
KATZENELLENBOGEN, B. S., Cell and Structural Biology, Molecular and Integrative Physiology
KAUFMAN, S. J., Cell and Structural Biology
KEMPER, B. W., Cell and Structural Biology, Pharmacology, Molecular and Integrative Physiology
KIRBY, R. W., Internal Medicine
KRANZ, D. M., Biochemistry
LAYMAN, D. K., Internal Medicine
LEVY, A., Pathology
MARSHALL, W. P., Internal Medicine
MILLER, C. G., Microbiology
MILLER, G. A., Psychiatry
MORRISSEY, J. H., Biochemistry
NELSON, R. A., Internal Medicine
OLSEN, G., Microbiology and Biophysics
ORDAL, G. W., Biochemistry, Basic Medical Science
POLLARD, J. W., Internal Medicine
PRABHUDESAI, M., Pathology
RAMIREZ, V. D., Physiology and Neuroscience
ROBBINS, A. W., Internal Medicine
ROBERTSON, H. M., Cell and Structural Biology, Entomology
ROBINSON, G. E., Cell and Structural Biology, Entomology
RUEDA, J. L., Psychiatry
SALYERS, A., Microbiology
SCHULER, M. A., Cell and Structural Biology, Biochemistry, Plant Biology
SCHWARTZ, B. S., Biochemistry
SHAPIRO, D. J., Biochemistry
SHERWOOD, O. D., Physiology

SIEGEL, I. A.
SLIGAR, S. G., Biochemistry, Chemistry, Physiology and Biophysics, Medicine
SWITZER, R. L., Biochemistry, Basic Medical Sciences
WEYHENMEYER, J., Pathology
WILLIAMS, B., Pathology
WOESE, C. R., Microbiology
WRAIGHT, C. A., Biochemistry, Biophysics, Plant Biology

College of Veterinary Medicine:

ANDREWS, J. J., Veterinary Pathobiology
ARDEN, W. A., Veterinary Clinical Medicine
BEASLEY, V. R., Veterinary Biosciences
BENSON, G. J., Veterinary Clinical Medicine, Veterinary Anaesthesiology and Comparative Medicine
CAMPBELL, K. L., Veterinary Clinical Medicine
CLARKSON, R. B., Veterinary Clinical Medicine, Veterinary Biosciences
COOKE, P. S., Veterinary Biosciences
DOCAMPO, R., Veterinary Pathobiology
GOETZ, T. E., Veterinary Clinical Medicine
GROSS, D. R., Veterinary Biosciences
HANSEN, L. G., Veterinary Biosciences
HASCHEK-HOCK, W. M., Veterinary Pathobiology
HESS, R. A., Veterinary Biosciences
JOHNSON, A. L., Veterinary Clinical Medicine
KITRON, U. D., Veterinary Pathobiology
KUHLENSCHMIDT, M. S., Veterinary Pathobiology
LOCK, T. F., Veterinary Clinical Medicine
MANOHAR, M., Veterinary Biosciences
MARRETTA, S. M., Veterinary Clinical Medicine
MEERDINK, G. L., Toxicology
MILLER, G. Y., Veterinary Pathobiology, Veterinary Clinical Medicine
OTT, R. S., Veterinary Clinical Medicine, Veterinary Medicine Administration
PAUL, A. J., Veterinary Pathobiology
RAFFE, M. R., Veterinary Clinical Medicine
SCHANTZ, S. L., Veterinary Biosciences
SEGRE, M., Veterinary Pathobiology
SISSON, D. D., Veterinary Clinical Medicine
SMITH, R. D., Veterinary Pathobiology
TRANQUILLI, W. J., Veterinary Clinical Medicine
TROUTT, H. F., Veterinary Clinical Medicine
VALLI, V. E. O., Veterinary Pathobiology
VIMR, E. R., Veterinary Pathobiology
WALLIG, M. A., Veterinary Pathobiology
WEIGEL, R. M., Veterinary Pathobiology
WHITELEY, H. E., Veterinary Pathobiology
ZACHARY, J. F., Veterinary Pathobiology

School of Labour and Employment Relations:

DRASGOW, F.
FEUILLE, P.
LAWLER, J.
LEROY, M.
MARTOCCHIO, J.
NORTHCRAFT, G.
OLDHAM, G.
OLSON, C.

UNIVERSITY OF ST FRANCIS

500 Wilcox St, Joliet, IL 60435
Telephone: (815) 740-3400
Fax: (815) 740-5032
E-mail: information@stfrancis.edu
Internet: www.stfrancis.edu

Founded 1920
Private control
Academic year: August to May

Pres.: Dr MICHAEL J. VINCIGUERRA
Provost and Vice-Pres. for Academic Affairs: Dr FRANK PASCOE
Vice-Pres. for Admin. and Finance: ELIZABETH LAKEN

Vice-Pres. for Admissions and Enrollment Services: CHARLES M. BEUTEL
Vice-Pres. for Mission Integration and Min.: Sis. MARY ELIZABETH IMLER
Dir of Libraries: TERRY COTTRELL

Library of 134,800 vols
Number of teachers: 310
Number of students: 3,321 (1,822 undergraduate, 1,499 graduate)

DEANS

College of Arts and Sciences: Dr ROBERT W. KASE
College of Business and Health Administration: Dr CHRISTOPHER CLOTT
College of Education: Dr JOHN GAMBRO
College of Nursing: Dr CAROL J. WILSON

UNIVERSITY OF SAINT MARY OF THE LAKE—MUNDELEIN SEMINARY

1000 E Maple Ave, Mundelein, IL 60060
Telephone: (847) 566-6401
E-mail: info@usml.edu
Internet: www.vocations.org

Founded 1844 as Saint Mary's College, present name 2000
Private control

Offers Masters degrees in divinity, liturgy and liturgical studies; doctoral degree in ministry

Rector and Pres.: Very Rev. DENNIS J. LYLE
Provost: Rev. THOMAS FRANZMAN
Vice-Rector for Academic Affairs: Rev. THOMAS A. BAIMA
Vice-Rector for Seminary Admin.: Rev. JAMES PRESTA
Vice-Pres. for Facilities: STAN RYS
Vice-Pres. for Finance: JOHN LEHOCKY
Vice-Pres. for Institutional Advancement: MARK J. TERESI
Dean for Formation: Rev. KEVIN J. FEENEY
Library Dir: LORRAINE OLLEY

Library of 200,000 vols, 434 periodicals

Publications: *Chicago Studies* (3 a year, online (www.chicagostudies.org)), *Interconnections: Journal of Catholic Seminary Studies* (online (www.usml.edu/journal)), *The Bridge* (print and online (www.usml.edu/publications/bridge)).

VANDERCOOK COLLEGE OF MUSIC

3140 S Federal St, Chicago, IL 60616-3731
Telephone: (312) 225-6288
Fax: (312) 225-5211
E-mail: vandercook@vandercook.edu
Internet: www.vandercook.edu

Founded 1909
Private control

Pres.: Dr CHARLES T. MENGHINI
Dean for Graduate Studies: RUTH RHODES
Dean for Undergraduate Studies: KAYE CLEMENTS
Dir for Admissions and Retention: AMY LENTING
Registrar: CAROLYN BERGHOFF
Head Librarian: ROB DELAND

Library of 14,653 vols
Number of teachers: 6
Number of students: 230

WESTERN ILLINOIS UNIVERSITY

1 University Circle, Macomb, IL 61455-1380
Telephone: (309) 298-1414
Fax: (309) 298-4444
E-mail: info@wiu.edu
Internet: www.wiu.edu

Founded 1899
State control
Academic year: August to May

Pres.: Dr JACK THOMAS
Provost and Academic Vice-Pres.: Dr KEN-
NETH S. HAWKINSON
Vice-Pres. for Administrative Services: JULIE
DEWEES
Vice-Pres. for Advancement and Public Ser-
vices: BRAD BAINTER
Vice-Pres. for Student Services: Dr GARY
BILLER
Registrar: ANGELA NICOLE LYNN
Dean for Univ. Libraries: Dr PHYLIS C. SELF
Library of 1,150,000 vols
Number of teachers: 615 (full-time)
Number of students: 12,554
Publications: *Essays in Literature, Western
Illinois Magazine*

DEANS

College of Arts and Sciences: Dr SUSAN
MARTINELLI-FERNANDEZ
College of Business and Technology: Dr TOM
EREKSON
College of Education and Human Services:
Dr STERLING SADDLER
College of Fine Arts and Communication: Dr
SHARON EVANS

WHEATON COLLEGE

501 College Ave, Wheaton, IL 60187-5593
Telephone: (630) 752-5000
Fax: (630) 752-5555
Internet: www.wheaton.edu
Founded 1860
Private control
Academic year: August to May
Pres.: Dr PHILIP G. RYKEN
Provost: Dr STANTON JONES
Vice-Pres. for Advancement and Alumni
Relations: Dr R. MARK DILLON
Vice-Pres. for Finance and Treas.: Dr DALE A.
KEMP
Vice-Pres. for Student Devt: Dr PAUL CHEL-
SEN
Registrar: PEGGY KING
Librarian: LISA RICHMOND
Library of 1,113,924 vols (incl. 370,000
books), 7,833 current periodicals
Number of teachers: 291 (198 full-time, 93
part-time)
Number of students: 3,000 (2,400 under-
graduate, 600 graduate)
Publication: *Kodon Literary Magazine* (3 a
year)

DEANS

Conservatory, Arts and Communication: Dr
MICHAEL WILDER
Graduate School: Dr JEFFREY A. MOSHIER
Humanities and Theological Studies: Dr JILL
PELÁEZ BAUMGAERTNER
Information and Technology: Dr GARY N.
LARSON
Natural and Social Sciences: Prof. Dr DOR-
OTHY F. CHAPPELL

INDIANA

AMERICAN COLLEGE OF
EDUCATION

101 W Ohio St, Suite 1200, Indianapolis, IN
46204
Telephone: (800) 280-0307
E-mail: ace.admissions@ace.edu
Internet: www.ace.edu
Founded 2005, fmrly Barat College (f. 1858)
Private control
Offers online Masters degree in education
Pres.: Dr SANDRA DORAN

Assoc. Provost and Sr Vice-Pres. for Institu-
tional Effectiveness and Assessment: Dr
SHAWNTEL LANDRY
Vice-Pres. for Curriculum and Devt: LANA
SLOAN
Vice-Pres. for Enrolment and Student Ser-
vices: AMY LANGFORD
Vice-Pres. for Online Learning and Technol-
ogy: CHANCE SPIKER
Vice-Pres. for Professional Devt: Dr STACEY
HUGHES
Academic Dean: Dr MARY BOLD
Chief Financial Officer: MICHAEL BRISKEY
Registrar: LYNDIA WAGNER
Dir for Library: Dr SANDRA AL-ABDULMUNEM.

ANDERSON UNIVERSITY

1100 E Fifth St, Anderson, IN 46012
Telephone: (765) 649-9071
Fax: (765) 641-3015
E-mail: info@anderson.edu
Internet: www.anderson.edu
Founded 1917
Private control
Academic year: August to May
Pres.: Dr JAMES L. EDWARDS
Provost and Vice-Pres. for Academic Affairs
and Dean: Dr MARIE S. MORRIS
Vice-Pres. for Advancement: ROBERT L. COFF-
MAN
Vice-Pres. for Finance and Treas.: DANA S.
STUART
Vice-Pres. for Student Affairs: Dr BRENT
BAKER
Dir for Admissions: JOE DAVIS
Registrar: ARTHUR J. LEAK
Dir for Univ. Libraries: Dr JANET BREWER
Library of 285,144 vols, 56,925 microfiche,
25,926 periodicals, 17,968 govt documents,
6,633 e-books, 2,342 video cassettes, 1,162
DVDs, 7,789 reference books
Number of teachers: 206 (144 full-time, 62
part-time)
Number of students: 2,565 (2,022 under-
graduate, 543 graduate)

DEANS

College of Science and Humanities: Dr D.
BLAKE JANUTOLO
College of the Arts: Dr JEFFREY E. WRIGHT
Falls School of Business: TERRY TRUITT
School of Adult Learning: Dr ALEZA D.
BEVERLY
School of Education: Dr JAN FULKERSON
School of Nursing: KAREN WILLIAMS
School of Theology: Dr DAVID L. SEBASTIAN

ASSOCIATED MENNONITE BIBLICAL
SEMINARY

3003 Benham Ave, Elkhart, IN 46517-1999
Telephone: (574) 295-3726
Fax: (574) 295-0092
E-mail: admissions@ambs.edu
Internet: www.ambs.edu
Founded 1958
Private control
Courses in Christian formation, divinity,
peace studies and theological studies; br.
campus at North Newton (Kansas)
Pres.: Dr SARA WENGER SHENK
Vice-Pres. for Advancement Admin.: RON
RINGENBERG
Academic Dean: REBECCA SLOUGH
Dir for Enrolment and Student Services: S.
ROBERT ROSA
Dir for Devt: MISSY KAUFFMAN SCHROCK
Registrar: SCOTT JANZEN
Dir for Library Services: EILEEN K. SANER
Library of 109,000 vols
Number of teachers: 15
Number of students: 180

Publication: *Vision: A Journal for Church
and Theology* (2 a year).

BALL STATE UNIVERSITY

2000 W University Ave, Muncie, IN 47306
Telephone: (765) 289-1241
E-mail: askus@bsu.edu
Internet: www.bsu.edu
Founded 1918 as Indiana State Normal
School E Div., present name 1965
State control
Academic year: August to May
Pres.: JO ANN M. GORA
Provost and Vice-Pres. for Academic Affairs:
TERRY KING
Vice-Pres. for Business Affairs and Treas.:
RANDY HOWARD
Vice-Pres. for Enrolment, Marketing and
Communications: TOM TAYLOR
Vice-Pres. for Information Technology: PHI-
LIP REPP
Vice-Pres. for Student Affairs and Dean for
Students: KAY BALES
Vice-Pres. for Univ. Advancement: Dr HUD-
SON AKIN
Registrar: NANCY CRONK
Dean for Univ. Libraries: ARTHUR W. HAFNER
Library: 1.5m. vols (incl. microfilms and
audiovisual items), 4,000 current period-
icals
Number of teachers: 836 (full-time)
Number of students: 22,147
Publications: *Ball State Alumnus* (6 a year),
Indiana Mathematics Teacher (2 a year),
International Journal of Social Education,
Odyssey (1 a year), *Proceedings of the
Indiana Academy of Social Sciences* (1 a
year), *Teacher Educator* (4 a year)

DEANS

College of Applied Sciences and Technology:
Prof. MITCHELL WHALEY
College of Architecture and Planning: Prof.
GUILLERMO VASQUEZ DE VELASCO
College of Communication, Information and
Media: ROGER LAVERY
College of Fine Arts: Prof. ROBERT A. KVAM
College of Sciences and the Humanities: Dr
MICHAEL MAGGIOTTO
Honors College: Prof. JAMES RUEBEL
Miller College of Business: RAJIB SANYAL
Teachers' College: Prof. JOHN JACOBSON
Univesity College: Dr MARILYN BUCK

BETHANY THEOLOGICAL SEMINARY

615 National Rd W, Richmond, IN 47374-
4019
Telephone: (765) 983-1800
Fax: (765) 983-1840
E-mail: contactus@bethanyseminary.edu
Internet: www.bethanyseminary.edu
Founded 1905 as Bethany Bible School,
present name 1963
Private control
Academic year: August to May
Masters degree in arts and divinity
Pres.: RUTHANN KNECHEL JOHANSEN
Academic Dean: STEVEN SCHWEITZER
Exec. Dir for Institutional Advancement:
LOWELL FLORY
Exec. Dir for Student and Business Services
and Treas.: BRENDA REISH
Dir for Admissions: TRACY STODDART PRIMO-
ZICH
Dir for Student Devt: AMY GALL RITCHIE
Dir for Academic Services and Registrar:
APRIL VANLONDEN
Number of teachers: 16
Number of students: 63
Publication: *Wonder & Word* (2 a year).

BETHEL COLLEGE

1001 Bethel Circle, Mishawaka, IN 46545
Telephone: (574) 807-7000
Fax: (574) 257-3277
E-mail: info@bethelcollege.edu
Internet: www.bethelcollege.edu
Founded 1947
Private control
Academic year: August to May
Br. campuses at Elkhart, Fort Wayne, Winona Lake (Indiana); extension centres in Michigan
Pres.: Dr STEVEN R. CRAMER
Sr Vice-Pres.: Prof. Dr DENNIS D. ENGBRECHT
Vice-Pres. for Academic Services: Dr BRADLEY D. SMITH
Vice-Pres. for College Relations: Dr C. ROBERT LAURENT
Vice-Pres. for Devt: TERRY A. ZEITLOW
Vice-Pres. for Student Devt: Dr SHAWN M. HOLTGREN
Registrar: JEANNE FOX
Dir for Library Services: Dr CLYDE R. ROOT
Number of teachers: 219
Number of students: 2,100

DEANS

Division of Arts and Humanities: Dr TOM VISKER
Division of Professional and Graduate Studies: Dr BRADLEY SMITH
Division of Sciences: Dr ROB MYERS
School of Nursing: Dr CAROL DOROUGH

BUTLER UNIVERSITY

4600 Sunset Ave, Indianapolis, IN 46208
Telephone: (317) 940-6000
Fax: (317) 940-9930
E-mail: info@butler.edu
Internet: www.butler.edu
Founded 1855
Private control
Pres.: JAMES M. DANKO
Provost and Vice-Pres. for Academic Affairs: KATHRYN MORRIS
Vice-Pres. for Enrolment Management: TOM WEEDE
Vice-Pres. for Operations: GERALD CARLSON
Vice-Pres. for Student Affairs: LEVESTER JOHNSON
Vice-Pres. for Univ. Advancement: MARK HELMUS
Registrar: SONDREA OZOLINS
Dean for Libraries: LEWIS MILLER
Library of 330,000 vols, 20,000 e-books, 35,000 e-journal subscriptions, 16,000 audiovisual materials, 17,000 musical scores
Number of teachers: 339 (full-time)
Number of students: 4,667

Publication: Real

DEANS

College of Business: CHUCK WILLIAMS
College of Communication: Prof. WILLIAM NEHER
College of Education: Dr ENA SHELLEY
College of Liberal Arts and Sciences: Dr JAY R. HOWARD
College of Pharmacy and Health Sciences: MARY H. ANDRITZ
Jordan College of Fine Arts: Dr RONALD CALTABIANO

CALUMET COLLEGE OF ST JOSEPH

2400 New York Ave, Whiting, IN 46394
Telephone: (219) 473-4215
Fax: (219) 473-4259
E-mail: admissions@ccsj.edu
Internet: www.ccsj.edu

Founded 1951
Private control
Academic year: September to August
Divs of liberal arts and professional studies
Pres.: Dr DANIEL LOWERY
Vice-Pres. for Academic Affairs: Dr JOI PATTERSON
Vice-Pres. for Student Life and Dean for Students: MELISHA HENDERSON
Dir for Enrolment Management: MARY SEVERA
Dir for Devt: MICHAEL SPICCIA
Registrar: DIANA FRANCIS
Library Dir: MARCIA KEITH
Library of 110,000 vols, 74 periodicals, 1,417 multimedia items
Number of teachers: 60
Number of students: 1,259

CHRISTIAN THEOLOGICAL SEMINARY

1000 W 42nd St, Indianapolis, IN 46208
Telephone: (317) 924-1331
Fax: (317) 923-1961
E-mail: admissions@cts.edu
Internet: www.cts.edu
Founded 1910 as Butler School of Religion, present name and status 1958
Private control
Academic year: September to May
Pres.: MATTHEW MYER BOULTON
Vice-Pres. and Co-Academic Dean: Dr HOLLY HEARON
Vice-Pres. and Co-Academic Dean: Dr K. BERNIE LYON
Vice-Pres. for Seminary Advancement: MELISSA HICKMAN
Registrar: MATT SCHLIMGEN
Library Dir: LORNA A. SHOEMAKER
Library of 210,000 vols (incl. 1,000 periodicals)
Number of teachers: 44
Number of students: 300

Publications: Encounter, Link.

CONCORDIA THEOLOGICAL SEMINARY

6600 N Clinton St, Fort Wayne, IN 46825-4996
Telephone: (260) 452-2100
Fax: (260) 452-2121
E-mail: info@ctsfw.edu
Internet: www.ctsfw.edu
Founded 1846
Private control
Academic year: September to May
Masters and doctoral degrees in divinity, ministry, sacred theology
Pres.: Rev. Dr LAWRENCE R. RAST, JR
Vice-Pres. for Institutional Advancement: R. RADCLIFFE FINCH
Academic Dean: Rev. Dr CHARLES A. GIESCHEN
Dir for Enrolment Management and Dean for Students: THOMAS P. ZIMMERMAN
Dean for Graduate Studies: Prof. KLAUS DETLEV SCHULZ
Registrar: BARBARA A. WEGMAN
Dir of Library Services: Rev. Prof. ROBERT V. ROETHEMEYER
Library of 152,000 vols
Number of teachers: 25
Number of students: 321

Publications: Concordia Theological Quarterly (4 a year), For the Life of the World.

DEPAUW UNIVERSITY

POB 37, Greencastle, IN 46135-0037
Telephone: (765) 658-4800

Fax: (317) 658-4177
E-mail: admission@depauw.edu
Internet: www.depauw.edu
Founded 1837 as Indiana Asbury Univ., present name 1884
Private control
Academic year: August to May
Liberal arts programmes and interdisciplinary study programmes
Pres.: Dr BRIAN W. CASEY
Exec. Vice-Pres. and Dean of the Faculty: Dr NEAL ABRAHAM
Vice-Pres. for Academic Affairs: Prof. Dr DAVID THORP HARVEY
Vice-Pres. for Admission and Financial Aid: DANIEL LEE MEYER
Vice-Pres. for Advancement: MARCIA SLOAN LATTA
Vice-Pres. for Finance and Admin.: BRADLEY ALAN KELSHEIMER
Vice-Pres. for Student Life and Dean for Students: CINDY BABINGTON
Registrar: Dr KENNETH J. KIRKPATRICK
Dir for Libraries: RICK PROVINE
Library of 400,000 vols
Number of teachers: 234
Number of students: 2,390

Publication: DePauw Magazine.

EARLHAM COLLEGE

801 National Rd W, Richmond, IN 47374-4095
Telephone: (765) 983-1200
Fax: (765) 983-1560
E-mail: admissions@earlham.edu
Internet: www.earlham.edu
Founded 1847, present name and status 1859
Private control
Academic year: August to May
Liberal arts college
Pres.: DAVID DAWSON
Provost: NELSON BINGHAM
Vice-Pres. for Academic Affairs and Academic Dean: GREG MAHLER
Vice-Pres. for Finance and Operations: SENA LANDEY
Vice-Pres. for Institutional Advancement: JAMES McKEY
Vice-Pres. and Dean for Student Devt: CHERYL PRESLEY
Vice-Pres. and Dean for Admissions and Financial Aid: NANCY SINEX (acting)
Registrar: BONITA WASHINGTON-LACEY
Dir for the Library: NEAL BAKER (acting)
Library of 400,834 vols
Number of teachers: 101 (93 full-time, 8 part-time)
Number of students: 1,181 (undergraduate)

Publication: The Earlhamite (2 a year).

FRANKLIN COLLEGE

101 Branigin Blvd, Franklin, IN 46131-2623
Telephone: (317) 738-8000
Fax: (317) 736-8013
E-mail: admissions@franklincollege.edu
Internet: www.franklincollege.edu
Founded 1834
Private control
Academic year: August to May
Divs of business, computing and mathematics, education, fine arts, humanities, journalism, natural sciences and social sciences
Chancellor: (vacant)
Pres.: Dr JAMES G. MOSELEY
Vice-Pres. for Academic Affairs and Dean for College: Dr DAVID G. BRAILOW
Vice-Pres. for Enrolment and Student Affairs: ALAN P. HILL
Vice-Pres. for Institutional Advancement: JAMES B. MEYER

Dean for Students: ELLIS F. HALL
Registrar: MATTHEW R. JONES
Dir for Library: RONALD L. SCHUETZ
Library of 107,000 vols, 6,000 video cassettes, 300 journal subscriptions, 17,000 e-journals and newspapers
Number of teachers: 66 (full-time)
Number of students: 1,060

GOSHEN COLLEGE

1700 S Main St, Goshen, IN 46526
Telephone: (574) 535-7000
Fax: (219) 535-7660
E-mail: info@goshen.edu
Internet: www.goshen.edu
Founded 1894 as Elkhart Institute of Science
Private control
Liberal arts courses
Pres.: Dr JAMES E. BRENNEMAN
Vice-Pres. for Academic Affairs and Academic Dean: Dr ANITA STALTER
Vice-Pres. for Finance: JIM HISTAND
Vice-Pres. for Institutional Advancement: JIM CASKEY
Vice-Pres. for Student Life and Dean for Students: WILLIAM J. BORN
Registrar: STANLEY W. MILLER
Library Dir: LISA GUEDEA CARREÑO
Library of 135,000 vols, 400 periodical subscriptions
Number of teachers: 112 (82 full-time, 30 part-time)
Number of students: 1,000
Publications: *Bulletin* (online (blog.goshen.edu/bulletin)), *Mennonite Quarterly Review* (4 a year, online (www.goshen.edu/mqr)).

GRACE COLLEGE AND SEMINARY

200 Seminary Dr., Winona Lake, IN 46590
Telephone: (574) 372-5100
Fax: (574) 372-5263
E-mail: admissions@grace.edu
Internet: www.grace.edu
Founded 1937, present status 1994
Private control
Academic year: August to July
Pres.: Dr RONALD E. MANAHAN
Provost: Dr WILLIAM J. KATIP
Vice-Pres. for Advancement: Dr JOHN R. BOAL
Vice-Pres. for Academic and Student Services: Dr JAMES E. SWANSON
Chief Financial Officer: G. STEPHEN POPENFOOSE
Dean for Enrolment Management: CINDY N. SISSON
Dir for Admissions: MARK POHL
Registrar: STEVEN T. CARLSON
Dir for Library Services: TONYA FAWCETT
Library of 150,000 vols
Number of teachers: 118
Number of students: 1,700

DEANS

School of Adult and Community Education: Prof. Dr STEPHEN A. GRILL
School of Arts and Sciences: Prof. Dr MARK M. NORRIS
School of Behavioural Science: Prof. E. MICHAEL GRILL
School of Business: Prof. JEFFREY K. FAWCETT
School of Education: LAURINDA A. OWEN
School of Ministry Studies: Prof. Dr JEFFREY GILL

HANOVER COLLEGE

POB 108, Hanover, IN 47243
484 Ball Dr., Hanover, IN 47243
Telephone: (812) 866-7000

E-mail: info@hanover.edu
Internet: www.hanover.edu
Founded 1827
Private control
Divs of arts and letters, natural sciences, humanities and social sciences
Pres.: Dr SUE DEWINE
Vice-Pres. for Academic Affairs and Dean for Faculty: STEVE JOBE
Vice-Pres. for College Advancement: DENNIS HUNT
Vice-Pres. for Enrolment Management: JON RIESTER
Vice-Pres. and Dean for Student Life: DAVID YEAGER
Dean for Admission: CHRISTOPHER GAGE
Registrar: KEN PRINCE
Dir for Library: KENNETH E. GIBSON
Library of 3,000 vols, 314,000 govt documents, 6,700 audiovisual items, 52,000 microforms, 2,000 periodicals
Number of teachers: 71
Number of students: 1,100
Publication: *The Hanoverian*.

HOLY CROSS COLLEGE

54515 State Rd, 933N, POB 308, Notre Dame, IN 46556
Telephone: (574) 239-8377
Fax: (574) 239-8323
E-mail: admissions@hcc-nd.edu
Internet: www.hcc-nd.edu
Founded 1966
Private control
Pres.: Dr JOHN R. PAIGE
Exec. Vice-Pres.: Dr TINA HOLLAND
Vice-Pres. for Mission Advancement: ROBERT KLOSKA
Vice-Pres. for Operations: DANIEL HAVERTY
Dean for Admissions and Enrolment Management: MARIE E. BENSMAN
Dean for Students: DANIEL COCHRAN
Dir for Library Services: MARY ELLEN HEGEDUS
Library of 20,000 vols, 140 periodicals, 8,000 journals and newspapers
Number of students: 500

HUNTINGTON UNIVERSITY

2303 College Ave, Huntington, IN 46750
Telephone: (219) 356-6000
Fax: (219) 359-4086
E-mail: admissions@huntington.edu
Internet: www.huntington.edu
Founded 1897
Private control
Academic year: September to May
Liberal arts courses
Pres.: Dr G. BLAIR DOWDEN
Sr Vice-Pres. for Academic Affairs and Dean for Faculty: Dr A. NORRIS FRIESEN
Sr Vice-Pres. for Strategy and Graduate and Adult Programmes: Dr ANN C. McPHERREN
Vice-Pres. for Enrolment Management and Marketing: JEFFREY C. BERGGREN
Vice-Pres. for Student Life: Dr RONALD L. COFFEY
Vice-Pres. for Univ. Relations: JOHN W. PAFF
Registrar: SARAH J. HARVEY
Dir for Library Services: ANITA GRAY
Library of 200,000 vols, 60,000 e-books
Number of teachers: 68
Number of students: 1,262

INDIANA INSTITUTE OF TECHNOLOGY

1600 E Washington Blvd, Fort Wayne, IN 46803
Telephone: (260) 422-5561

Fax: (260) 422-7696
E-mail: admissions@indianatech.edu
Internet: www.indianatech.edu
Founded 1930, present name 1963
Private control
Campuses at Fishers, Greenwood, Huntington, Kendallville, Mishawaka, Munster, Plainfield, Shelbyville and Warsaw
Pres.: Dr ARTHUR E. SNYDER
Vice-Pres. for Academic Affairs: Dr DOUGLAS PERRY
Vice-Pres. for Enrolment Management: ALLISON CARNAHAN
Vice-Pres. for Institutional Advancement: MARK RICHTER
Library Dir: CONNIE SCOTT
Library of 33,000 vols
Number of teachers: 50
Number of students: 5,000

DEANS

College of Business: Dr JEFFREY A. ZIMMERMAN
College of Engineering: DAVE ASCHLIMAN
College of General Studies: Dr DOTY LATUSZEK
School of Computer Sciences: DAVE ASCHLIMAN

INDIANA STATE UNIVERSITY

200 N Seventh St, Terre Haute, IN 47809-1902
419 Rankin Hall, 210 N Seventh St, Terre Haute, IN 47809
Telephone: (812) 237-6311
Fax: (812) 237-2291
E-mail: admissions@indstate.edu
Internet: www.indstate.edu
Founded 1865 as Indiana State Normal School, present name and status 1965
State control
Academic year: August to May
Pres.: Dr DANIEL J. BRADLEY
Provost and Vice-Pres. for Academic Affairs: C. JACK MAYNARD
Gen. Counsel and Sec. of the Univ.: MELONY A. SACOPULOS
Vice-Pres. for Enrolment Management, Marketing and Communication: JOHN E. BEACON
Vice-Pres. for Student Affairs and Dean for Students: CARMEN TILLERY
Registrar: APRIL HAY
Dean for Library Services: ALBERTA D. COMER
Library of 1,344,592 vols
Number of teachers: 446 (full-time)
Number of students: 11,494
Publications: *Cognitive Technology* (2 a year), *Folklore Historian* (1 a year), *Grassland* (1 a year), *Hoosier Folklore*, *Indiana English* (3 a year), *Indiana State University Magazine* (3 a year, online (www.isu-magazine.com)), *Midwestern Folklore* (2 a year), *Snowy Egret*, *The Hoosier Science Teacher* (4 a year, online (www.indstate.edu/scied/thstforms.htm)), *The Indiana Council of Teachers of Mathematics Journal—Mathematics Teacher* (2 a year), *Tonic* (1 a year), *Via Solaris* (print)

DEANS

Bayh College of Education: Dr BRADLEY V. BALCH
College of Arts and Sciences: Dr JOHN D. MURRAY
College of Graduate and Professional Studies: Dr JAY D. GATRELL
College of Nursing, Health and Human Services: Dr RICHARD WILLIAMS
College of Technology: Dr BRADFORD SIMS
Scott College of Business: Dr NANCY J. MERRITT

INDIANA UNIVERSITY

107 S. Indiana Ave, Bloomington, IN 47405-7000

Telephone: (812) 855-4848
Internet: www.iu.edu

Founded 1820 as a state seminary, present status 1852
State control

Pres.: MICHAEL A. McROBBIE
Exec. Vice-Pres.: CHARLES R. BANTZ
Exec. Vice-Pres.: KAREN HANSON
Exec. Vice-Pres. for Univ. Regional Affairs, Planning and Policy: JOHN APPLEGATE
Vice-Pres. and Chief Financial Officer: NEIL D. THEOBALD
Vice-Pres. and Gen. Counsel: DOROTHY J. FRAPWELL
Vice-Pres. for Diversity, Equity and Multicultural Affairs: EDWIN C. MARSHALL
Vice-Pres. for Information Technology and Chief Information Officer: BRADLEY C. WHEELER
Vice-Pres. for Public Affairs and Govt Relations: MIKE SAMPLE
Vice-Pres. for Research: JORGE JOSÉ
Dean for Univ. Libraries: BRENDA JOHNSON

Number of teachers: 8,685 (all campuses)
Number of students: 109,445 (all campuses)

Publication: *Research & Creative Activity*.

CONSTITUENT CAMPUSES

Indiana University Bloomington

107 S Indiana Ave, Bloomington, IN 47405-7000

Telephone: (812) 855-4848
E-mail: iuadmit@indiana.edu
Internet: www.iub.edu

Founded 1820 as a state seminary, present name 1838

Provost and Chief Academic Officer: KAREN HANSON
Vice-Provost for Enrolment Management: Dr DAVID B. JOHNSON
Vice-Provost for Faculty and Academic Affairs: THOMAS GIERYN
Vice-Provost for Research: P. SARITA SONI
Vice-Provost for Undergraduate Education: SONYA STEPHENS
Dir for Admissions: MARY ELLEN ANDERSON
Dean for Students: Dr HAROLD GOLDSMITH
Registrar: MARK McCONAHAY
Dean for Univ. Libraries: BRENDA JOHNSON

Library: see Libraries and Archives
Number of teachers: 2,973
Number of students: 42,464

Publications: *American Historical Review* (5 a year), *American Journal of Semiotics* (4 a year), *Anthropological Linguistics* (4 a year, online (www.indiana.edu/~anthling)), *Business Horizons* (6 a year), *Indiana Business Review* (4 a year, online (www.ibrc.indiana.edu/ibr)), *Indiana Law Journal* (4 a year, online (ilj.law.indiana.edu)), *Indiana Magazine of History* (4 a year, online (www.indiana.edu/~imaghist)), *Indiana Slavic Studies* (1 a year), *Indiana University Mathematics Journal* (4 a year), *Journal of American History* (4 a year), *Journal of Asian History* (2 a year), *Journal of Chemical Physics* (52 a year), *Journal of Folklore Research* (3 a year, print and online (scholarworks.iu.edu/journals/index.php/jfr)), *Journal of Mathematical Physics* (12 a year), *Journal of Slavic Linguistics* (2 a year), *Journal of the Experimental Analysis of Behavior* (6 a year), *Kelley Magazine* (2 a year), *Phi Delta Kappan* (10 a year), *SPEA Magazine*, *Teaching & Learning* (2 a year), *Victorian Studies* (4 a year)

DEANS

College of Arts and Sciences: LARRY SINGELL
Hutton Honors College: MATTHEW AUER
Jacobs School of Music: GWYN RICHARDS
Kelley School of Business: DANIEL C. SMITH
Maurer School of Law: Prof. LAUREN ROBEL (acting)
School of Continuing Studies: Prof. DANIEL CALLISON
School of Education: Prof. GERARDO GONZÁLEZ
School of Health, Physical Education and Recreation: MOHAMMED R. TORABI
School of Informatics and Computing: ROBERT B. SCHNABEL
School of Journalism: Prof. BRADLEY HAMM
School of Library and Information Science: Prof. Dr DEBORA SHAW
School of Nursing: MARION BROOME
School of Optometry: Dr JOSEPH A. BONANNO
School of Public and Environmental Affairs: Dr JOHN D. GRAHAM
School of Social Work: Dr MICHAEL A. PATCHNER
Univ. Graduate School: JAMES WIMBUSH

Indiana University East

2325 Chester Blvd, Richmond, IN 47374-1289

Telephone: (765) 973-8200
Fax: (765) 973-8237
E-mail: eawelcc@indiana.edu
Internet: www.iue.edu

Chancellor: Dr NASSER H. PAYDAR
Exec. Vice-Chancellor for Academic Affairs: LARRY RICHARDS
Vice-Chancellor for Admin. and Finance: DAN DOOLEY
Dean for Students: MARY BLAKEFIELD
Library Dir: FRANCES YATES

Library of 85,000 vols
Number of teachers: 204 (87 full-time, 117 part-time)
Number of students: 3,823 (3,725 undergraduate, 98 graduate)

DEANS

School of Business and Economics: DAVID W. FRANTZ
School of Education: MARILYN WATKINS
School of Humanities and Social Sciences: KATHERINE FRANK
School of Natural Science and Mathematics: NEIL SABINE
School of Nursing: KAREN CLARK

Indiana University Kokomo

2300 S Washington St, Kokomo, IN 46904-9003

Telephone: (317) 453-2000
E-mail: iuadmis@iuk.edu
Internet: www.iuk.edu

Founded 1932 as Kokomo Junior College, present status 1970

Chancellor: Dr MICHAEL HARRIS
Exec. Vice-Chancellor for Academic Affairs: SUE SCIAME-GIESECKE
Vice-Chancellor for Admin. and Finance: ROY TAMIR
Vice-Chancellor for Public Affairs and Advancement: PENNY LEE
Vice-Chancellor for Student Affairs: JACK THARP
Dean for Library: RHONDA ARMSTRONG

Library of 112,000 vols, 5,000 multimedia items
Number of teachers: 167
Number of students: 3,109

DEANS

School of Arts and Sciences: Dr ERV BOSCHMANN
School of Business: Dr FRANK WADSWORTH
School of Education: Dr PAUL C. PAESE

School of Nursing: Dr LINDA WALLACE
School of Public and Environmental Affairs: Dr ROBERT DIDIE

Indiana University Northwest

3400 Broadway, Gary, IN 46408-1197

Telephone: (219) 980-6500
Fax: (219) 981-4219
E-mail: admit@iun.edu
Internet: www.iun.edu

Founded 1963

Chancellor: Dr WILLIAM J. LOWE
Exec. Vice-Chancellor for Academic Affairs: Dr DAVID J. MALIK
Vice-Chancellor for Admin.: JOSEPH PELLICCIOTTI
Vice-Chancellor for Student Services Admin.: ERNEST SMITH
Dir for Admissions: LINDA TEMPLETON
Registrar: JEFF JOHNSTON
Dir for Library Services: TIMOTHY SUTHERLAND

Library of 200,000 vols (incl. books and periodicals), 200,000 govt documents
Number of teachers: 360 (160 full-time, 200 part-time)
Number of students: 6,035

DEANS

College of Arts and Sciences: Dr MARK S. HOYERT
College of Health and Human Services: Dr PATRICK BANKSTON
School of Business and Economics: ANNA S. ROMINGER
School of Continuing Studies: Dr DANIEL J. CALLISON
School of Education: Dr STANLEY E. WIGLE

Indiana University—Purdue University at Fort Wayne

2101 E Coliseum Blvd, Fort Wayne, IN 46805-1499

Telephone: (260) 481-6812
Internet: www.ipfw.edu

Founded 1964
Academic year: August to May

Chancellor: MICHAEL A. WARTELL
Vice-Chancellor for Academic Affairs: WILLIAM J. McKINNEY
Vice-Chancellor for Financial Affairs: WALTER J. BRANSON
Vice-Chancellor for Student Affairs: GEORGE S. McCLELLAN
Dir for Admissions: CAROL B. ISAACS
Registrar: PATRICK A. McLAUGHLIN
Library Dean: CHERYL TRUESDELL

Library of 311,094 vols, 1,500 current periodicals, 106,114 govt publs, 537,778 microforms, audiovisual items
Number of teachers: 400 (full-time)
Number of students: 14,000

DEANS

College of Arts and Sciences: Dr CARL N. DRUMMOND
College of Education and Public Policy: Prof. BARRY KANPOL
College of Engineering, Technology and Computer Science: Prof. MAX YEN
College of Health and Human Services: Prof. ANN OBERGFELD
College of Visual and Performing Arts: CHUCK O'CONNOR
Richard T. Doermer School of Business: Dr OTTO H. CHANG

Indiana University—Purdue University at Indianapolis

420 University Blvd, Indianapolis, IN 46202

Telephone: (317) 274-5555
Fax: (317) 278-1862
E-mail: apply@iupui.edu

Internet: www.iupui.edu
Founded 1969
Chancellor: CHARLES R. BANTZ (acting)
Exec. Vice-Chancellor and Dean for Faculties: UDAY P. SUKHATME
Vice-Chancellor for External Affairs: AMY CONRAD WARNER
Vice-Chancellor for Finance and Admin.: DAWN RHODES
Vice-Chancellor for Research: KODY VARAH-RAMYAN
Vice-Chancellor for Student Life: ZEBULUN DAVENPORT
Dean for Univ. Library: DAVID LEWIS
Library of 650,000 vols, 4,000 periodicals and journals
Number of teachers: 2,500
Number of students: 30,566

DEANS

Herron School of Art: VALERIE EICKMEIER
Honors College: JANE LUZAR
Kelley School of Business: Prof. DANIEL C. SMITH
Purdue School of Engineering and Technology: Dr DAVID J. RUSSOMANNO
Robert H. McKinney School of Law: Prof. GARY R. ROBERTS
School of Allied Health and Rehabilitation Sciences: Dr AUGUSTINE AGHO
School of Dentistry: Prof. JOHN N. WILLIAMS, JR
School of Education: GERARDO M. GONZALEZ
School of Informatics: ROBERT B. SCHNABEL
School of Journalism: Prof. JAMES W. BROWN
School of Liberal Arts: Prof. WILLIAM BLOMQUIST
School of Library and Information Science: Prof. Dr DEBORA SHAW
School of Medicine: Prof. D. CRAIG BRATER
School of Nursing: Dr MARION E. BROOME
School of Physical Education and Tourism Management: Dr JAY GLADDEN
School of Public and Environmental Affairs: Dr JOHN D. GRAHAM
School of Science: Prof. Dr SIMON J. RHODES
School of Social Work: Dr MICHAEL A. PATCHNER
University College: Prof. Dr KATHY E. JOHNSON

Indiana University South Bend

POB 7111, 1700 Mishawaka Ave, South Bend, IN 46634-7111
Telephone: (574) 520-5005
Internet: www.iusb.edu
Founded 1916 as Central High School
Chancellor: Dr UNA RAE MECK
Exec. Vice-Chancellor for Academic Affairs: ALFRED J. GUILLAUME, JR
Vice-Chancellor for Admin. and Fiscal Affairs: WILLIAM O'DONNELL
Vice-Chancellor for Public Affairs and Univ. Advancement: ILENE SHEFFER
Vice-Chancellor for Student Affairs and Enrolment Management: JEFF JONES
Dean for Library Services: VICKI BLOOM
Library of 323,498 vols, 58,000 e-journals, 100,000 e-books
Number of teachers: 562 (301 full-time, 261 part-time)
Number of students: 8,385

DEANS

College of Health Sciences: Dr MARY JO REGAN-KUBINSKI
College of Liberal Arts and Sciences: Dr ELIZABETH DUNN
Raclin School of the Arts: MARVIN CURTIS
School of Business and Economics: Dr ROBERT DUCOFFE
School of Education: Dr DAVID HORVATH

Indiana University Southeast

4201 Grant Line Rd, New Albany, IN 47150
Telephone: (812) 941-2000
E-mail: admissions@ius.edu
Internet: www.ius.edu
Founded 1941, present name and status 1968
Academic year: August to May
Chancellor: Dr SANDRA R. PATTERSON-RANDLES
Vice-Chancellor for Academic Affairs: Dr GILBERT W. ATNIP
Vice-Chancellor for Admin. and Finance: DANA C. WAVLE
Vice-Chancellor for Student Affairs: Dr RUTH C. GARVEY-NIX
Registrar: BRITTANY HUBBARD
Dir for Library Services: C. MARTIN ROSEN
Library of 585,000 vols (incl. microforms), 1,200 current periodicals
Number of students: 7,200
Publication: *Journal of Business Disciplines*

DEANS

School of Arts and Letters: SAMANTHA EARLEY
School of Business: Dr ALAN JAY WHITE
School of Education: Dr GLORIA MURRAY
School of Natural Sciences: EMMANUEL OTU
School of Nursing: MIMI McKAY
School of Social Sciences: JOE WERT

INDIANA WESLEYAN UNIVERSITY

4201 S Washington St, Marion, IN 46953
Telephone: (765) 674-6901
Fax: (765) 677-2499
E-mail: admissions@indwes.edu
Internet: www.indwes.edu
Founded 1920 as Marion College, present name and status 1998
Private control
Academic year: September to April
Education centres in Indiana, Kentucky and Ohio
Pres.: Dr HENRY L. SMITH
Provost and Chief Academic Officer: Dr DAVID WRIGHT
Exec. Vice-Pres.: Dr KEITH NEWMAN
Vice-Pres. for Enrolment Management: KRIS DOUGLAS
Vice-Pres. for Student Devt: MICHAEL MOFFITT
Vice-Pres. for Wesley Seminary: WAYNE SCHMIDT
Registrar: KIMBERLY NICHOLSON
Library Dir: SHEILA CARLBLOM
Library of 133,396 vols
Number of teachers: 1,010 (f. t. e.)
Number of students: 15,872

DEANS

College of Adult and Professional Studies: Dr BRIDGET AITCHISON
College of Arts and Sciences: Dr DARLENE BRESSLER
Graduate School: Dr JIM FULLER
School of Nursing: Dr BARBARA IHRKE

ITT TECHNICAL INSTITUTE

9511 Angola Court, Indianapolis, IN 46268-1119
Telephone: (317) 875-8640
Internet: www.itt-tech.edu
Founded 1956
Private control
Areas of study: automated manufacturing technology, computer and electronics engineering technology, computer drafting and design, computer visualization technology, computer-aided drafting and design technology, electronics engineering technology, information systems security, information technology–computer network systems, information technology–multimedia, information technology–software applications and programming, information technology–web development, technical project management for electronic commerce; 130 campuses in 35 states
Pres.: Dr EUGENE W. FEICHTNER
Sr Vice-Pres. and Chief Academic Officer: Dr P. MICHAEL LINZMAIER
Vice-Pres. for Learning Technologies: JOHN P. TRIMBLE
Vice-Pres. for Student Services: JONATHAN H. PATTERSON
Registrar: HARRIET ALLEN
Librarian: ANN C. LEE
Number of students: 80,000 (all campuses)

MANCHESTER COLLEGE

604 E College Ave, North Manchester, IN 46962
Telephone: (260) 982-5000
E-mail: admitinfo@manchester.edu
Internet: www.manchester.edu
Founded 1860 as Roanoke Classical Seminary, present name 1889, present status 1932
Private control
Liberal arts and professional courses
Pres.: JO YOUNG SWITZER
Exec. Vice-Pres.: Dr DAVID F. McFADDEN
Vice-Pres. and Dean for Academic Affairs: GLENN SHARFMAN
Vice-Pres. for College Advancement: MICHAEL EASTMAN
Vice-Pres. for Student Devt: BETH SWEITZER-RILEY
Dir for Admissions: ADAM HOHMAN
Registrar: LILA D. HAMMER
Dir for Library: ROBIN J. GRATZ
Library of 160,000 vols
Number of teachers: 75 (full-time)
Number of students: 1,320
Publication: *Manchester Magazine* (4 a week).

MARIAN UNIVERSITY

3200 Cold Spring Rd, Indianapolis, IN 46222-1997
Telephone: (317) 955-6000
Fax: (317) 955-6448
E-mail: admissions@marian.edu
Internet: www.marian.edu
Founded 1851 as St Francis Normal, present name and status 2009
Private control
Academic year: August to May
Pres.: Dr DANIEL J. ELSENER
Exec. Vice-Pres. and Provost: Dr THOMAS J. ENNEKING
Vice-Pres. for Admin. and Gen. Counsel: DEBORAH A. LAWRENCE
Vice-Pres. for Institutional Advancement: JOHN FINKE
Vice-Pres. for Student Affairs and Dean for Students: RUTH RODGERS
Dean for Academic Affairs: WILLIAM B. HARTING
Registrar: JACK HILL
Librarian: KELLEY F. GRIFFITH
Library of 135,000 vols
Number of teachers: 156 (93 full-time, 63 part-time)
Number of students: 2,300

DEANS

Clark H. Byrum School of Business: Dr RUSS KERSHAW
College of Osteopathic Medicine: PAUL EVANS
School of Education: Dr LINDAN B. HILL
School of Liberal Arts: Dr JAMES NORTON, III

School of Mathematics and Sciences: Dr LOREN BERTOCCI
School of Nursing: Prof. ANITA SICCARDI

MARTIN UNIVERSITY

2171 Avondale Pl., Indianapolis, IN 46218
Telephone: (317) 543-3235
Fax: (317) 543-4790
Internet: www.martin.edu
Founded 1977 as Martin Centert College, present name and status 1990
Private control
Academic year: August to July
Pres.: Dr CHARLOTTE WESTERHAUS-RENFROW
Provost and Vice-Pres. for Academic Affairs: Dr MARTIN GREENAN
Vice-Pres. for Admin.: WILLIAM WOODSON
Vice-Pres. for Enrolment Management and Student Affairs: SALATHA WILLIS
Vice-Pres. for Institutional Research and Sponsored Programs: Dr BRIAN L. STEUER-WALD
Dir for Admissions: THERESA BUTLER
Registrar: RUDELL MOORE
Number of teachers: 48 (30 full-time, 18 adjunct)
Number of students: 1,407

DEANS

College of Business and Social Sciences: NICOLE C. BARNETT
School of Justice Studies: Dr J. S. SMITH
School of Liberal Arts: Dr KATHLEEN BARLOW
School of Mathematics and Sciences: Dr GLORIA M. AMENY-DIXON

OAKLAND CITY UNIVERSITY

138 N Lucretia St, Oakland City, IN 47660
Telephone: (800) 737-5125
Fax: (812) 749-1433
E-mail: ocuadmit@oak.edu
Internet: www.oak.edu
Founded 1885 as Oakland City College, present name and status 1995
Private control
Academic year: August to May
Pres.: Dr RAY G. BARBER
Provost: Dr MICHAEL J. ATKINSON
Vice-Pres. for Admin. and Finance: Dr ROBERT E. YEAGER
Dir for Devt and Advancement: BRIAN BAKER
Dir for Admissions: KIM HELDT
Registrar: BETTY BURNS
Library Dir: Dr DENISE J. PINNICK
Number of teachers: 66
Number of students: 1,477 (1,321 undergraduate, 156 graduate and professional)
Publication: The Connection (4 a year)

DEANS

Chapman School of Religious Studies: DANNY DUNIVAN
School of Arts and Sciences: Dr CLAUDINE D. CUTCHINE
School of Business: MICHAEL J. BURCH
School of Education: Dr MARY JO BEAUCHAMP

PURDUE UNIVERSITY

1031 Hovde Hall, West Lafayette, IN 47907-1031
Telephone: (765) 494-4600
Fax: (765) 494-7875
E-mail: admissions@purdue.edu
Internet: www.purdue.edu
Founded 1869
State control
Academic year: August to May
Chancellor: MICHAEL A. WARTELL
Pres.: FRANCE A. CÓRDOVA

Exec. Vice-Pres. for Academic Affairs and Provost: TIMOTHY D. SANDS
Vice-Pres. for Devt: LISA D. CALVERT
Vice-Pres. for Ethics and Compliance: ALYSA CHRISTMAS ROLLOCK
Vice-Pres. for Information Technology and Chief Information Officer: GERARD McCARTNEY
Vice-Pres. for Research: RICHARD O. BUCKIUS
Vice-Pres. for Student Affairs: MELISSA EXUM
Registrar: ROBERT A. KUBAT
Dean for Libraries: JAMES L. MULLINS
Library: see Libraries and Archives
Number of teachers: 5,133 (system wide)
Number of students: 74,759 (system wide)
Publications: Engineering Impact, Innovation, Inside Purdue, Perspective, THiNK (1 a year)

DEANS

College of Agriculture: JAY T. AKRIDGE
College of Education: MARYANN SANTOS DE BARONA
College of Engineering: LEAH H. JAMIESON
College of Health and Human Sciences: CHRISTINE M. LADISCH
College of Liberal Arts: IRWIN H. WEISER
College of Pharmacy: CRAIG K. SVENSSON
College of Science: JEFFREY T. ROBERTS
College of Technology: GARY BERTOLINE
Graduate School: MARK J. T. SMITH
Krannert Graduate School of Management: P. CHRISTOPHER EARLEY
School of Veterinary Medicine: WILLIE M. REED

UNIVERSITY BRANCHES

Purdue University Calumet

2200 169th St, Hammond, IN 463232094
Telephone: (219) 989-2400
Fax: (219) 989-2775
E-mail: adms@calumet.purdue.edu
Internet: www.purduecal.edu
State control
Chancellor: Dr THOMAS L. KEON
Vice-Chancellor for Academic Affairs: Dr RALPH V. ROGERS
Vice-Chancellor for Admin. Services: JAMES K. JOHNSTON
Vice-Chancellor for Advancement: DANIEL HENDRICKS
Vice-Chancellor for Student Affairs: SARAH HOWARD
Vice-Chancellor for Information Services: FRANK CERVONE
Registrar: ANNE AGOSTO-SEVERA
Dir for Learning and Research Services: TAMMY S. GUERRERO
Library of 264,000 vols
Number of teachers: 598
Number of students: 9,807 (8,664 undergraduate, 1,143 graduate)

DEANS

School of Education: Dr ALICE G. ANDERSON
School of Engineering, Mathematics and Science: Dr MICHAEL C. HENSON
School of Liberal Arts and Social Sciences: Dr RON CORTHELL
School of Management: Dr MARTINE DUCHA-TELET
School of Nursing: Dr PEGGY GERARD
School of Technology: Dr NIAZ LATIF

Purdue University North Central

1401 S U.S. 421, Westville, IN 46391
Telephone: (219) 872-0527
Fax: (219) 785-5355
E-mail: admissions@pnc.edu
Internet: www.pnc.edu
Founded 1967
State control

Chancellor: Dr JAMES B. DWORKIN
Vice-Chancellor for Academic Affairs: KAREN SCHMID
Vice-Chancellor for Admin.: STEPHEN R. TURNER
Vice-Chancellor for Enrolment Management and Student Services: PAUL McGUINNESS
Registrar: GEORGE ROYSTER
Librarian: K. R. JOHNSON
Number of teachers: 288 (125 full-time, 163 part-time)
Number of students: 5,279

DEANS

College of Business: Prof. Dr ALAN G. KRABBENHOFT
College of Engineering and Technology: Prof. Dr LARRYL MATTHEWS
College of Liberal Arts: Prof. Dr S. REX MORROW
College of Science: Prof. Dr KEITH SCHWIN-GENDORF

ROSE—HULMAN INSTITUTE OF TECHNOLOGY

5500 Wabash Ave, Terre Haute, IN 47803
Telephone: (812) 877-1511
Fax: (812) 877-8001
E-mail: admissions@rose-hulman.edu
Internet: www.rose-hulman.edu
Founded 1874 as Rose Polytechnic Institute, present name 1971
Private control
Depts of applied biology and biomedical engineering, chemical engineering, chemistry and biochemistry, civil engineering, computer science and software engineering, electrical and computer engineering, engineering management, humanities and social sciences, mathematics, mechanical engineering and physics and optical engineering
Pres.: MATT BRANAM
Vice-Pres. and Chief Admin. Officer: ROBERT A. COONS
Vice-Pres. for Academic Affairs: PHILLIP J. CORNWELL
Vice-Pres. for Enrolment Management: JAMES A. GOECKER
Vice-Pres. for Student Affairs and Dean for Students: PETER A. GUSTAFSON
Vice-Pres. for Institutional Advancement: RICKEY N. McCURRY
Dean for Faculty: WILLIAM KLINE
Dir for Admissions: LISA NORTON
Registrar: TIMOTHY J. PRICKEL
Library Dir: RICHARD BERNIER
Library of 70,000 vols, 22,000 vols of periodicals, 1,500 NASA and NATO documents
Number of teachers: 177 (163 full-time, 14 part-time)
Number of students: 1,980 (1,985 undergraduate, 85 graduate)
Publication: Echoes.

SAINT JOSEPH'S COLLEGE

POB 870, Rensselaer, IN 47978
1498 S College Ave, Rensselaer, IN 47978
Telephone: (219) 866-6000
Fax: (219) 866-6100
E-mail: admissions@saintjoe.edu
Internet: www.saintjoe.edu
Founded 1889
Private control
Liberal arts courses
Pres.: Dr F. DENNIS RIEGELNEGG
Vice-Pres. for Academic Affairs: Dr DANIEL J. BLANKENSHIP
Vice-Pres. for Institutional Advancement and Marketing: Dr MAUREEN V. EGAN
Dean for Students: Dr LESLIE FRERE
Registrar: CAROL A. BURNS

Library Dir: CATHERINE SAYLERS
Library of 134,628 vols, 22,096 audiovisual
items, 67,069 microforms, 2,500 e-books
Number of teachers: 101 (full-time and part-
time)
Number of students: 1,033
Publication: *Contact*.

SAINT MARY-OF-THE-WOODS COLLEGE

1 St Mary of Woods College, Saint Mary-of-
the-Woods, IN 47876
Telephone: (812) 535-5151
Fax: (812) 535-5010
E-mail: smwc@smwc.edu
Internet: www.smwc.edu
Founded 1840
Private control
Academic year: August to May
Liberal arts courses
Pres.: Dr DOTTIE L. KING
Co-Chancellor: Dr BARBARA DOHERTY
Co-Chancellor: Dr JEANNE KNOERLE
Vice-Pres. for Academic Affairs: Dr JANET
CLARK
Vice-Pres. for Finance and Admin.: GORDON
AFDAHL
Vice-Pres. for Student Life: VICKI KOSOWSKY
Registrar: SUSAN MEIER
Library Dir: JUDITH TRIBBLE
Library of 150,000 vols
Number of teachers: 67
Number of students: 1,700

Publication: *Aurora* (2 a year).

SAINT MARY'S COLLEGE

Notre Dame, IN 46556
Telephone: (219) 284-4000
E-mail: admission@saintmarys.edu
Internet: www.saintmarys.edu
Founded 1844
Private control
Liberal arts courses
Pres.: CAROL ANN MOONEY
Sr Vice-Pres. and Dean for Faculty: PATRICIA
FLEMING
Vice-Pres. for College Relations: SHARI RODRI-
GUEZ
Vice-Pres. for Enrolment Management:
MONA C. BOWE
Vice-Pres. for Mission: VERONIQUE WIEDOWER
Vice-Pres. for Finance and Admin.: RICHARD
SPELLER
Vice-Pres. for Student Affairs: KAREN JOHN-
SON
Dir for Admission: KRISTIN MCANDREW
Registrar: TODD NORRIS
Library Dir: JANET FORE
Library of 260,000 vols, 2,000 journals
Number of students: 1,500 (full-time)
Publications: *Chimes* (1 a year), *Courier*
(online (www3.saintmarys.edu/courier)),
The Avenue.

SAINT MEINRAD SEMINARY AND SCHOOL OF THEOLOGY

200 Hill Dr., St Meinrad, IN 47577
Telephone: (812) 357-6611
Fax: (812) 357-6964
E-mail: theology@saintmeinrad.edu
Internet: www.saintmeinrad.edu
Founded 1857
Private control
Academic year: August to July (2 semesters)
Offers Masters in divinity, theological stud-
ies and art (catholic thought and life) pro-
grammes
Pres. and Rector: Rev. DENIS ROBINSON

Vice-Rector: Rev. GODFREY MULLEN
Academic Dean: Dr ROBERT ALVIS
Dir for Enrolment: Rev. BRENDAN MOSS
Library Dir: DAN KOLB
Library of 170,000 vols, 300 periodicals,
2,000 rare books
Number of teachers: 31
Number of students: 136

TAYLOR UNIVERSITY

236 W Reade Ave, Upland, IN 46989-1001
Telephone: (317) 998-2751
Fax: (317) 998-4925
E-mail: admissions@taylor.edu
Internet: www.taylor.edu
Founded 1846
Private control
Academic year: September to May (3 terms)
Pres.: Dr GENE B. HABECKER
Chancellor: Dr JAY KESLER
Provost: Dr STEPHEN S. BEDI
Vice-Pres. for Enrolment Management and
Marketing: STEPHEN MORTLAND
Vice-Pres. for Student Devt and Dean for
Students: Dr SKIP TRUDEAU
Vice-Pres. for Univ. Advancement: Dr BEN
SELLS
Dir for Admissions: AMY BARNETT
Registrar: JANET SHAFFER
Univ. Librarian: DAN BOWELL
Library of 235,114 vols
Number of teachers: 138 (full-time)
Number of students: 2,424 (1,919 under-
graduate, 369 distance learning, 136
graduate)
Publications: *Parnassus*, *Profile*, *Taylor Uni-
versity Magazine*

DEANS

School of Business: Dr LAWRENCE BELCHER
School of Liberal Arts: Dr THOMAS JONES
School of Natural and Applied Sciences: Dr
MARK BIERMANN
School of Professional and Graduate Studies:
Dr CONNIE LIGHTFOOT

TCM INTERNATIONAL INSTITUTE

POB 24560, 6337 Hollister Dr., Indianapolis,
IN 46224
Telephone: (317) 299-0333
Fax: (317) 290-8607
E-mail: tcm@tcmi.org
Internet: www.tcmi.edu
Founded 1982 as Summer Seminary
Private control
Campus in Austria; provides courses in
Belarus, Bulgaria, Czech Republic, Estonia,
Hungary, Moldova, Poland, Romania, Russia
and Ukraine
Pres. and CEO: Dr DONALD ANTHONY TWIST
N American Vice-Pres.: DAVID WRIGHT
Dir for Academic Services: SUE ABEGGLEN
Dir for Operations: CAROL FIELDS
Dir for Global Outreach: DEBBIE POER
Dir for Assessment: RICHARD JUSTICE
Library of 16,000 vols.

TRINE UNIVERSITY

1 University Ave, Angola, IN 46703-1764
Telephone: (260) 665-4100
Fax: (260) 665-4292
E-mail: admit@trine.edu
Internet: www.trine.edu
Founded 1884 as Tri-State Normal College,
present name 2008
Private control
Campuses at Angola, Fort Wayne, Scherer-
ville, South Bend/Mishawaka, Columbus,
Logansport and Indianapolis

Pres.: Dr EARL D. BROOKS, II
Sr Vice-Pres.: MICHAEL R. BOCK
Vice-Pres. for Academic Affairs: Dr DAVID R.
FINLEY
Vice-Pres. for Alumni and Devt: KENT
STUCKY
Vice-Pres. for Enrolment Management:
SCOTT J. GOPLIN
Vice-Pres. for Finance: JODY GREER
Vice-Pres. for Student Services: RANDY
WHITE
Registrar: DEBBIE HELMSING
Dir for Library and Information Services:
KRISTINA BREWER
Number of teachers: 65
Number of students: 2,339

Publications: *Discover*, *Trine Magazine*

DEANS

Allen School of Engineering and Technology:
Dr V. K. SHARMA
Franks School of Education: Dr SUZANNE VAN
WAGNER
Jannen School of Arts and Sciences: Dr JOHN
SHANNON
Ketner School of Business: Dr V. K. SHARMA
School of Professional Studies: DAVID W.
WOOD

UNIVERSITY OF EVANSVILLE

1800 Lincoln Ave, Evansville, IN 47722
Telephone: (812) 488-2000
Fax: (812) 479-2320
E-mail: admission@evansville.edu
Internet: www.evansville.edu
Founded 1854 as Moores Hill Male and
Female Collegiate Institute, present name
and status 1967
Private control
Academic year: August to May
Pres.: Dr THOMAS A. KAZEE
Sr Vice-Pres. for Academic Affairs: Dr JOHN
MOSBO
Vice-Pres. for Enrolment Services: Dr TOM
BEAR
Vice-Pres. for Institutional Advancement:
JOHN BARNER
Vice-Pres. for Fiscal Affairs and Admin.:
JEFFREY WOLF
Vice-Pres. for Students Affairs and Dean for
Students: DANA CLAYTON
Dir for Univ. Relations: LUCY HIMSTEDT
Dean for Admission: DON VOS
Registrar: AMY BRANDEBURY
Univ. Librarian: WILLIAM LOUDEN
Library of 274,123 vols, 678 journals, 14,000
e-journals, 472,469 microform units,
12,687 audiovisual items
Number of teachers: 192
Number of students: 2,934

DEANS

College of Arts and Sciences: JEAN BECKMAN
College of Education and Health Sciences: Dr
LYNN R. PENLAND
College of Engineering and Computer Sci-
ence: Dr PHILIP GERHART
Schroeder Family School of Business Admin-
istration: Dr STEPHEN STANDIFIRD

UNIVERSITY OF INDIANAPOLIS

1400 E Hanna Ave, Indianapolis, IN 46227
Telephone: (317) 788-3368
Internet: www.uindy.edu
Founded 1902, present name 1986
Private control
Academic year: September to August (2
semesters)
Campus in Athens, Greece; partnership sites
in Asia and Central America
Pres.: Dr BEVERLEY J. PITTS

Exec. Vice-Pres. and Provost: Dr DEBORAH BALOGH
Vice-Pres. for Research, Planning and Int. Partnership: Dr MARY MOORE
Vice-Pres. for Student Affairs and Enrolment: MARK WEIGAND
Vice-Pres. for Univ. Advancement: JAMES SMITH
Dir for Admissions: RON WILKS
Registrar: Dr MARY BETH BAGG
Library Dir: FRANCESCA BUSCH

Library of 150,000 vols, 600 periodicals
Number of teachers: 500 (full-time and part-time)
Number of students: 5,345 (main campus)

DEANS

College of Arts and Sciences: Dr JENNIFER DRAKE (acting)
College of Health Sciences: Dr STEPHANIE KELLY
Ecumenical Programmes: Dr MICHAEL CARTWRIGHT
School for Adult Learning: Dr PATRICIA JEFFERSON
School of Business: Dr SHEELA YADAV
School of Education: Dr KATHRYN MORAN
School of Nursing: Dr ANNE THOMAS
School of Psychological Sciences: Dr RICK HOLIGROCKI

UNIVERSITY OF NOTRE DAME

300 Main Bldg, Notre Dame, IN 46556
Telephone: (574) 631-5000
E-mail: admissions@nd.edu
Internet: www.nd.edu

Founded 1842 as l'Université de Notre Dame du Lac
Private control
Academic year: August to May

Pres.: Rev. JOHN I. JENKINS
Provost: Dr THOMAS G. BURISH
Exec. Vice-Pres.: JOHN F. AFFLECK-GRAVES
Vice-Pres. and Gen. Counsel: MARIANNE CORR
Vice-Pres. and Chief Information Officer: RONALD D. KRAEMER
Vice-Pres. for Research: ROBERT J. BERNHARD
Vice-Pres. for Student Affairs: Rev. THOMAS P. DOYLE
Vice-Pres. for Univ. Relations: LOUIS M. NANNI
Dir for Admissions: ROBERT MUNDY
Registrar: CHUCK HURLEY
Univ. Librarian: DIANE P. WALKER

Library: see Libraries and Archives
Number of teachers: 1,085 (982 full time, 103 part-time)
Number of students: 11,985

Publications: *Academy of Management Review*, *Acroterion* (1 a year), *American Journal of Jurisprudence* (print and online (www.nd.edu/~ndlaw/ajj)), *American Midland Naturalist: An International Journal of Ecology, Evolution and Environment* (online (www.nd.edu/~ammidnat)), *Journal of College and University Law* (online (www.nd.edu/~jcul)), *Journal of Legislation* (online (www.nd.edu/~ndlaw/jleg)), *Journal of Multicultural Counseling and Development*, *Juggler* (2 a year, online (www.nd.edu/~juggler)), *Nineteenth-Century Contexts* (online (www.nd.edu/~ncc)), *Notre Dame Journal of Formal Logic* (online (www.nd.edu/~ndjfl)), *Notre Dame Journal of Law, Ethics and Public Policy* (2 a year, print and online (www.nd.edu/~ndlaw/jlepp)), *Notre Dame Law Review* (online (ndlawreview.org)), *Notre Dame Magazine* (4 a year, online (magazine.nd.edu)), *Notre Dame Philosophical Review* (online (ndpr.nd.edu/recent-reviews)), *Notre Dame Review* (print and online (ndreview.nd.edu)), *Religion and Literature* (3 a year, online (religionandlit.nd.edu)), *Review of Politics* (online (www.nd.edu/~rop)), *Technical Review*

DEANS

College of Arts and Letters: JOHN T. MCGREEVY
College of Engineering: PETER K. KILPATRICK
College of Science: GREGORY P. CRAWFORD
First Year of Studies: HUGH R. PAGE, Jr
Graduate School: GREGORY E. STERLING
Law School: NELL JESSUP NEWTON
Mendoza College of Business: Dr CAROLYN Y. WOO
School of Architecture: MICHAEL N. LYKOUDIS

PROFESSORS

College of Arts and Letters:

ALDOUS, J., Sociology
AMERIKS, K., Philosophy
ANADON, J., Romance Languages and Literature
APPLEBY, R. S., History
ARNOLD, P., Political Science
AUNE, D. E., Theology
AYO, N., Liberal Studies
BARBER, S. A., Political Science
BARTELL, E., Economics
BIDDICK, K., History
BLACHLY, A., Music
BLANTZ, T. E., History
BOBIK, J., Philosophy
BORKOWSKI, J. G., Psychology
BOULTON, M. B., Romance Languages and Literatures
BOWER, J., Music
BRADLEY, K. R., Classics
BRADSHAW, P. F., Theology
BROGAN, J. V., English
BRUNS, G. L., English
BURRELL, D. B., Philosophy
BUSTAMANTE, J. A., Psychology, Sociology
BUTTIGIEG, J. A., English
CACHEY, T., Romance Languages and Literatures
CARDENAS, G., Psychology
CRAFTON, D., Film, Television and Theatre
CRAMER, C., Music
CUMMINGS, E. M., Psychology
CUNNINGHAM, L. S., Theology
DALEY, S. J., Theology
DALLMAYR, F., Political Theory
DaMATTA, R., Anthropology
DAVID, M., Philosophy
DAY, J. D., Psychology
DELANEY, C. F., Philosophy
DePAUL, M., Philosophy
DETLEFSEN, M., Philosophy
DOODY, M. A., English Literature
DOUGHERTY, J. P., English
DOUTHWAITE, J., Romance Languages and Literatures
DOWTY, A., Political Science
DUNNE, J. S., Theology
DUTT, A., Economics
DYE, K., Music
EMERY, K., Jr, Program of Liberal Studies
FLINT, T., Philosophy
FOX, C. B., English
FRANCIS, M. J., Political Science
FREDDOSO, A. J., Philosophy
FREDMAN, S., English
FRESE, D., English
GERNES, S. G., English
GERSH, S., Medieval Studies
GIBBONS, L., English, Film, Television and Theatre
GODMILOW, J., Film, Television and Theatre
GUTTING, G., Philosophy
HAIMO, E. T., Music
HALLINAN, M. W., Sociology
HALTON, E., Sociology
HAMBURG, G., History
HAMLIN, C., History

HART, K., English
HERO, R. E., Political Science
HIGGINS, P., Music
HOLLAND, P. D., Film, Television and Theatre
HÖSLE, V., German and Russian Languages and Literatures
HOWARD, D. A., Philosophy
HOWARD, G. S., Psychology
JAKSIC, I., History
JEMIELITY, T. J., English
JENSEN, R., Economics
JOHANSEN, R. C., Political Science
JOHNSON, M., Theology
JOY, L. S., Philosophy
KAVENY, M., Theology
KIM, K., Economics
KLINE, E. A., English
KOMMERS, D. P., Political Science
KREMER, W. J., Art, Art History and Design
KRIEG, R. A., Theology
KSELMAN, T., History
LAPIDGE, M., English
LEAHY, W. H., Economics
LOPEZ, G., Political Science
LOUX, M. J., Philosophy
McADAMS, A. J., Political Science
McBRIEN, R. P., Theology
McINERNY, R., Philosophy
McKENNA, J. J., Anthropology
MAINWARING, S., Political Science
MANIER, E., Philosophy
MANN, G. L., English
MARSDEN, G. M., History
MARULLO, T., German and Russian Languages and Literature
MATTHIAS, J. E., English
MAXWELL, S. E., Psychology
MEIER, J. P., Theology
MOODY, P., Political Science
MURRAY, J., History
NEYREY, S. J., Theology
NICGORSKI, W. J., Political Science, Program of Liberal Studies
NOBLE, T., Medieval Institute
NORTON, R. E., German and Russian Languages and Literatures
O'BRIEN O'KEEFFE, K., English
O'DONNELL, G., Political Science
O'REGAN, C., Theology
O'ROURKE, W. A., English
PILKINTON, M. C., Film, Television and Theatre
PLANTINGA, A., Philosophy
POPE-DAVIS, D., Psychology
POWER, F. C., Liberal Studies, Psychology
PROFIT, V. B., German and Russian Languages and Literatures
ROCHE, M., German Language and Literature, Philosophy
ROOS, J., Political Science
ROS, J., Economics
ROSENBERG, C., Art, Art History and Design
SAYERS, V., English
SAYRE, K. M., Philosophy
SCHLERETH, T. J., American Studies
SCHMUHL, R., American Studies
SCULLY, T. R., Political Science
SEIDENSPINNER-NÚÑEZ, D., Romance Languages and Literatures
SHEERIN, D., Classics, Theology
SHRADER-FRECHETTE, K., Philosophy, Biological Sciences
SKURSKI, R., Economics
SLAUGHTER, T., History
SLOAN, P. R., Liberal Studies
SMYTH, J., History
STERBA, J., Philosophy
STERLING, G. E., Theology
SWARTZ, T., Economics
TURNER, J., History
ULRICH, E., Theology
VALENZUELA, J. S., Sociology
VANDEN BOSSCHE, C., English
VANDERKAM, J. C., Theology

VAYRYNEN, R., Political Science
WALSHE, A. P., Political Science
WALTON, J., English
WATSON, S., Philosophy
WEGS, R., History
WEIGERT, A., Sociology
WEITHMAN, P., Philosophy
WELLE, J., Romance Languages and Literatures
WERGE, T., English
WHITMAN, T., Psychology
YOUENS, S., Music
ZIAREK, E., English

College of Engineering
Department of Aerospace and Mechanical Engineering:
ATASSI, H. M., Aero-acoustics
BATILL, S. M., Design
CORKE, T. C., Fluid Mechanics
DUNN, P. F., Particle Dynamics
INCROPERA, F. P., Heat Transfer
JUMPER, E. J., Aerodynamics
MUELLER, T. J., Fluid Mechanics
NELSON, R. C., Aerodynamics
OVAERT, T., Manufacturing
PAOLUCCI, S., Fluid Mechanics
RENAUD, J. E., Design
SEN, M., Heat Transfer
SKAAR, S. B., Control
THOMAS, F. O., Fluid Mechanics

Department of Chemical Engineering:
BRENNECKE, J. F.
CHANG, H.-C.
KANTOR, J. C.
LEIGHTON, D. T.
MCCREADY, M. J.
MCGINN, P. J.
MILLER, A. E.
SCHMITZ, R. A.
STADTHERR, M. A.
STRIEDER, W. C.
VARMA, A.
WOLF, E. E.

Department of Civil Engineering and Geological Sciences:
BURNS, P. C.
KAREEM, A.
SILLIMAN, S. E.
TAYLOR, J. I.

Department of Computer Science and Engineering:
BOWYER, K.
CHEN, D. Z.
KOGGE, P. M.
UHRAN, J., Jr

Department of Electrical Engineering:
ANTSAKLIS, P. J.
BAUER, P. H.
BERNSTEIN, G. H.
COLLINS, O.
COSTELLO, D. J.
FUJA, T. E.
HUANG, Y.-F.
LENT, C. S.
MERZ, J. L.
POROD, W.
ROSENTHAL, J.
SAIN, M. K.
SEABAUGH, A. C.
STEVENSON, R. L.

College of Science:
ALBER, M. S., Mathematics
APRAHAMIAN, A., Physics
ARNOLD, G. B., Physics
ASMUS, K.-D., Chemistry and Biochemistry
BARABASI, A.-L., Physics
BASU, S. C., Chemistry and Biochemistry
BELOVSKY, G. E., Biological Sciences
BENDER, H. A., Biological Sciences
BERRY, H. G., Physics
BESANSKY, N. J., Biological Sciences
BIGI, I. I., Physics

BLACKSTEAD, H. A., Physics
BOTTEI, R. S., Chemistry and Biochemistry
BUECHLER, S. A., Mathematics
BUNKER, B. A., Physics
CAO, J., Mathematics
CASON, N. M., Physics
COLLINS, F. H., Biological Sciences
CONNOLLY, F. X., Mathematics
CREARY, X., Chemistry and Biochemistry
DOBROWOLSKA-FURDYNA, M., Physics
DUMAN, J., Biological Sciences
DWYER, W. G., Mathematics
FAYBUSOVICH, L. E., Mathematics
FEHLNER, T. P., Chemistry and Biochemistry
FRASER, M. J., Jr, Biological Sciences
FRAUENDORF, S. G., Physics
FURDYNA, J. K., Physics
GARG, U., Physics
GOERRES, J., Physics
HAHN, A. J., Mathematics
HELLENTHAL, R., Biological Sciences
HELQUIST, P., Chemistry and Biochemistry
HIMONAS, A. A., Mathematics
HOWARD, A., Mathematics
HU, B., Mathematics
HYDE, D. R., Biological Sciences
HYDER, A. K., Research Physics
JACOBS, D. C., Chemistry and Biochemistry
JOHNSON, A. L., Biological Sciences
JOHNSON, W. R., Physics
JONES, G. L., Physics
KNIGHT, J. F., Mathematics
KOLATA, J. J., Physics
KULPA, C. F., Biological Sciences
LAMBERTI, G. A., Biological Sciences
LAPPIN, A. G., Chemistry and Biochemistry
LEPRAPPIER, F., Mathematics
LIVINGSTON, A. E., Physics
LODGE, D. M., Biological Sciences
LOSECCO, J. M., Physics
MARINO, J. P., Chemistry and Biochemistry
MATHEWS, G. J., Physics
MEISEL, D., Chemistry and Biochemistry
MERZ, J. L., Physics
MIGLIORE, J. C., Mathematics
MILLER, M. J., Chemistry and Biochemistry
NEWMAN, K. E., Physics
NOWAK, T. L., Chemistry and Biochemistry
O'TOUSA, J. E., Biological Sciences
PAONI, N., Chemistry and Biochemistry
RETTIG, T. W., Physics
ROSENTHAL, J. J., Mathematics
RUCHTI, R. C., Physics
SAPIRSTEIN, J. R., Physics
SCHEIDT, W. R., Chemistry and Biochemistry
SERIANNI, A. S., Chemistry and Biochemistry
SEVERSON, D. W., Biological Sciences
SEVOV, S., Chemistry and Biochemistry
SHAW, M.-C., Mathematics
SHEPHARD, W. D., Physics
SHRADER-FRECHETTE, K., Biological Sciences
SMITH, B. D., Chemistry and Biochemistry
SMYTH, B., Mathematics
SNOW, D. M., Mathematics
SOMMESE, A. J., Mathematics
STANTON, N. K., Mathematics
STOLZ, S. A., Mathematics
TAYLOR, L. R., Mathematics
TENNISWOOD, M. P., Biological Sciences
WARCHOL, J., Physics
WAYNE, M. R., Physics
WELSH, J. E. J., Biological Sciences
WIESCHER, M. C. F., Physics
WILLIAMS, E. B., Mathematics
WONG, P.-M., Mathematics
XAVIER, F., Mathematics

Law School:
BARRETT, M.
BAUER, J. P.
BENNETT, G.

BLAKEY, G. R.
BRADLEY, G. V.
DUTILE, F. N.
GUNN, A.
GURULE, J.
JACOBS, R. F.
KAVENY, M. C.
KELLENBERG, C. L.
KOMMERS, D. P.
MENDEZ, J. E.
MOONEY, C. A.
O'HARA, P.
PHELPS, T. G.
PRATT, W. F., Jr
RODES, R. E., Jr
SECKINGER, J. H.
SHELTON, D. L.
SMITHBURN, E.
TIDMARSH, J.

Mendoza College of Business:
AFFLECK-GRAVES, J., Finance and Business Economics
BRETZ, R., Management and Administrative Sciences
CONLON, E. J., Management and Administrative Sciences
COSIMANO, T. F., Finance and Business Economics
ENDERLE, G., Marketing
ETZEL, M. J., Marketing
FRECKA, T. J., Accountancy
GRESIK, T., Finance and Business Economics
GUILTINAN, J. P., Marketing
GUNDLACH, G. T., Marketing
HARTVIGSEN, D. B., Management and Administrative Sciences
HUANG, R. D., Finance and Business Economics
KEANE, J. G., Management and Administrative Sciences
KEATING, B. P., Finance and Business Economics
KENNEDY, J. J., Marketing
KRAJEWSKI, L., Management and Administrative Sciences
MCDONALD, W. D., Finance and Business Economics
MATTA, K. F., Management and Administrative Sciences
MILANI, K. W., Accountancy
MITTELSTAEDT, H. F., Accountancy
MORRIS, M. H., Accountancy
MURPHY, P. E., Marketing
NICHOLS, W. D., Accountancy
RAMANAN, R., Accountancy
REILLY, F. K., Finance and Business Economics
RICCHIUTE, D. N., Accountancy
RUESCHHOFF, N. G., Accountancy
SCHAEFER, T., Accountancy
SCHULTZ, P., Finance and Business Economics
SHEEHAN, R. G., Finance and Business Economics
SIMON, D. T., Accountancy
TAVIS, L. A., Finance and Business Economics
URBANY, J., Marketing
VECCHIO, R. P., Management and Administrative Sciences
WILKIE, W. L., Marketing
WITTENBACH, J. L., Accountancy

School of Architecture:
AMICO, R.
CROWE, N.
LYKOUDIS, M.
SMITH, T. G.
WESTFALL, C. W.

UNIVERSITY OF SAINT FRANCIS

2701 Spring St, Fort Wayne, IN 46808-3994
Telephone: (260) 399-7999

Fax: (260) 399-8152
E-mail: admis@sf.edu
Internet: www.sf.edu
Founded 1890 as Saint Francis College, present name and status 1998
Private control
Academic year: August to May
Pres.: Sis. M. ELISE KRISS
Provost: Prof. Dr ROLF W. DANIEL
Exec. Vice-Pres.: Dr STACY J. ADKINSON
Vice-Pres. for Finance: RICHARD BIENZ
Vice-Pres. for Student Life and Dean for Students: SHARON K. MEJEUR
Vice-Pres. for Univ. Relations: Dr DONALD F. SCHENKEL
Registrar: FRANK CONNOR
Dir for Library Services: KARLA ALEXANDER
Library of 68,000 vols, 450 periodical subscriptions
Number of teachers: 142
Number of students: 2,300

DEANS

Business: HELEN MURRAY
Creative Arts: RICK CARTWRIGHT
Keith Busse School of Business and Entrepreneurial Leadership: HELEN J. MURRAY
School of Arts and Sciences: Dr MATT SMITH
School of Creative Arts: RICK CARTWRIGHT
School of Health Sciences: Dr NANCY GILLESPIE
School of Professional Studies: Dr JANE SWISS

UNIVERSITY OF SOUTHERN INDIANA

8600 University Blvd, Evansville, IN 47712-3596
Telephone: (812) 464-8600
Fax: (812) 465-7154
E-mail: enroll@usi.edu
Internet: www.usi.edu
Founded 1965 as the Evansville Campus of Indiana State Univ., present name and status 1985
State control
Academic year: August to May
Pres.: Prof. Dr LINDA L. M. BENNETT
Provost and Vice-Pres. for Academic Affairs: Dr RONALD S. ROCHON
Vice-Pres. for Finance and Admin.: MARK ROZEWSKI
Vice-Pres. for Govt and Univ. Relations: CYNTHIA S. BRINKER
Registrar: SANDY FRANK
Dir for Library: MARTHA NIEMEIER
Library of 244,622 vols, 88,720 vols of govt documents, 576,304 microform units, 33,946 e-journals, 975 linear ft MSS
Number of teachers: 660 (339 full-time, and 321 part-time)
Number of students: 10,820
Publication: USI Magazine (online (www.usi.edu/magazine))

DEANS

College of Business: Dr MOHAMMED KHAYUM
College of Liberal Arts: MICHAEL K. AAKHUS
College of Nursing and Health Professions: Dr NADINE A. COUDRET
Pott College of Science and Engineering: Dr SCOTT A. GORDON

VALPARAISO UNIVERSITY

Valparaiso, IN 46383-6493
Telephone: (219) 464-5000
Fax: (219) 464-5381
E-mail: university.relations@valpo.edu
Internet: www.valpo.edu
Founded 1859, present name and status 1906
Private control
Pres.: Dr MARK A. HECKLER

Provost and Exec. Vice-Pres. for Academic Affairs: Dr MARK R. SCHWEHN
Vice-Pres. for Admin. and Finance: CHARLEY E. GILLESPIE
Vice-Pres. for Enrolment Management: MICHAEL JOSEPH
Vice-Pres. for Institutional Advancement: LISA HOLLANDER
Vice-Pres. for Student Affairs: Dr BONNIE L. HUNTER
Dean for Library Services: BRAD EDEN
Library of 451,000 vols, 262,068 printed monographic vols, 78,563 journals, 3,536 films
Number of teachers: 220 (full-time)
Number of students: 4,000
Publication: Valpo Magazine

DEANS

Christ College (The Honors College): Dr MEL PIEHL
College of Arts and Sciences: Dr JON T. KILPINEN
College of Business: Dr ROY AUSTENSEN (acting)
College of Engineering: Dr KRAIG J. OLEJNICZAK
College of Nursing: Dr JANET BROWN
Graduate School and Continuing Education: Dr DAVID ROWLAND
School of Law: JAY CONISON

VINCENNES UNIVERSITY

1002 N First St, Vincennes, IN 47591
Telephone: (800) 742-9198
Fax: (812) 888-4380
E-mail: vuadmit@vinu.edu
Internet: www.vinu.edu
Founded 1801
State control
Pres.: Dr DICK HELTON
Provost and Vice-Pres. for Instructional Services and Dean for Faculty: Dr RONALD M. DAVIS
Dir for Admissions: CHRISTIAN BLOME
Dean for Students: JOHN LIVERS
Registrar: DONNA JO WEAVER
Dean for Learning Resources Centre: ROBERT A. SLAYTON

DEANS

Business and Public Service: NICOLAS SPINA
Extended Studies: DON KAUFMAN
Health Sciences and Human Performance: JANA VIECK
Humanities: CHARLES W. REINHART
Science and Mathematics: PETER IYERE
Social Sciences and Performing Arts: ERIC MARGERUM
Technology and Aviation Technology Centre: ARTHUR H. HAASE

WABASH COLLEGE

301 W Wabash Ave, Crawfordsville, IN 47933
Telephone: (765) 361-6100
Fax: (765) 361-6437
E-mail: admissions@wabash.edu
Internet: www.wabash.edu
Founded 1832
Private control
Liberal arts courses
Pres.: Dr PATRICK E. WHITE
Dean for Admissions and Financial Aid: STEVEN J. KLEIN
Dean for College: Dr GARY A. PHILLIPS
Dean for College Advancement: JOSEPH R. EMMICK
Dean for Students: MICHAEL P. RATERS
Registrar: Dr JULIE A. OLSEN
Librarian: JOHN LAMBORN

Library of 434,460 vols, 5,530 current periodicals, 162,000 govt documents, 11,151 audiovisual titles
Number of teachers: 89
Number of students: 910
Publication: Columns.

IOWA

AIB COLLEGE OF BUSINESS

2500 Fleur Dr., Des Moines, IA 50321
Telephone: (515) 244-4221
Fax: (515) 244-6773
E-mail: admissions@aib.edu
Internet: www.aib.edu
Founded 1921 as American Institute of Business
Private control
Academic year: September to August
Pres.: NANCY WILLIAMS
Vice-Pres. for Academic Affairs: Dr SUSAN CIGELMAN
Vice-Pres. for Student Life: TERRY WILSON
Chief Academic Officer: CHRISTY ROLAND
Chief Financial Officer: PAUL WINGET
Dir for Admissions: STEVE OLSEN
Registrar: RANDY TERRONEZ
Library Dir: LESLIE BINTNER
Number of teachers: 71 (22 full-time, 49 part-time)
Number of students: 937

ALLEN COLLEGE

1825 Logan Ave, Waterloo, IA 50703
Telephone: (319) 226-2000
Fax: (319) 226-2010
E-mail: allencollegeadmissions@ihs.org
Internet: www.allencollege.edu
Founded 1925 as Allen Memorial Hospital School of Nursing, present name 1996
Private control
Academic year: August to May (2 semesters)
Chancellor: Prof. Dr JERRY D. DURHAM
Vice-Chancellor for Academic Affairs: Dr NANCY KRAMER
Dir for Student Services: JOANNA RAMSDEN-MEIER
Coordinator for Library/Media Services: Dr RUTH LINGXIN YAN
Number of teachers: 23
Number of students: 500

DEANS

School of Health Sciences: Prof. Dr PEGGY FORTSCH
School of Nursing: Prof. Dr KENDRA WILLIAMS-PEREZ

ASHFORD UNIVERSITY

400 N Bluff Blvd, Clinton, IA 52732
Telephone: (563) 242-4023
E-mail: admissions@ashford.edu
Internet: www.ashford.edu
Founded 1918 as Mount St Clare College, present name and status 2005
Private control
Pres.: Dr ELIZABETH TICE
Provost: REBECCA WARDLOW
Vice-Pres. for Admissions: ALICE PARENTI
Univ. Registrar: KIRK MORRISON
Library Dir: FLORA S. LOWE
Library of 101,000 vols, 650 periodicals and journals, 70,000 microforms, 700 audio visual titles
Number of teachers: 52 (26 full-time, 26 part-time)
Number of students: 495 (461 undergraduate, 34 graduate)

DEANS

College of Business and Professional Studies: Dr CHARLES R. MINNICK
College of Education: Dr JOEN ROTTLER
College of Health, Human Services and Science: Dr BARBARA PHILIBERT
College of Liberal Arts: Dr WILLIAM C. LOWE

BRIAR CLIFF UNIVERSITY

POB 2100, Sioux City, IA 51104-0100
3303 Rebecca St, Sioux City, IA 51104-2324
Telephone: (712) 279-5200
Fax: (712) 279-1632
E-mail: admissions@briarcliff.edu
Internet: www.briarcliff.edu

Founded 1930 as Briar Cliff College, present name 2001
Private control
Academic year: September to May

Programmes in accounting, art, biology, business administration, chemistry, computer science, criminal justice, elementary education, English, environmental science, graphic design, health, physical education, and recreation, history, human resource management, mass communications, management information systems, mathematics, medical technology, music, new media, nursing, political science, psychology, radiological technology, secondary education, social research, social work, Spanish, sports science, theatre, theology, writing

Pres.: BEVERLY A. WHARTON
Provost, Vice-Pres. for Academic Affairs and Academic Dean: Dr WILLIAM T. MANGAN
Vice-Pres. for Enrolment Management: SHARISUE WILCOXON
Vice-Pres. for Institutional Advancement: CRAIG McGARRY
Vice-Pres. for Student Devt: STEVEN JANOWIAK
Registrar: DEIDRE ENGEL
Library Dir: DEB ROBERTSON
Library of 100,000 vols
Number of teachers: 51
Number of students: 1,100

Publications: Briar Cliff University Magazine, The Briar Cliff Review.

BUENA VISTA UNIVERSITY

610 W Fourth St, Storm Lake, IA 50588
Telephone: (712) 749-2351
Fax: (712) 749-2037
Internet: www.bvu.edu

Founded 1891, present name and status 1995
Private control
Academic year: September to May

Pres.: FREDERICK V. MOORE
Vice-Pres. for Academic Affairs and Dean for Faculty: Dr DAVID EVANS
Vice-Pres. for Enrolment Management: JOHN KLOCKENTAGER
Vice-Pres. for Institutional Advancement: KENNETH CONVERSE
Vice-Pres. for Student Services and Dean for Students: Dr MARY GILL
Registrar: NILA HOUSKA
Univ. Librarian: JAMES R. KENNEDY

Library of 147,000 vols, 29,000 periodicals
Number of teachers: 80 (full-time)
Number of students: 2,599

DEANS

Harold Walters Siebens School of Business: Dr ELIZABETH THROOP
School of Communication and Arts: Prof. Dr MICHAEL WHITLATCH
School of Education and Exercise Science: (vacant)
School of Science: BENJAMIN DONATH

School of Social Science, Philosophy and Religion: Prof. Dr DIXEE BARTHOLOMEW-FEIS

CENTRAL COLLEGE

812 University, Pella, IA 50219
Telephone: (877) 462-3687
Fax: (641) 628-5983
E-mail: admission@central.edu
Internet: www.central.edu

Founded 1853; attached to Reformed Church
Private control

Programmes in accounting, actuarial science, anthropology, art, athletic training, biology, business management, chemistry, communication studies, computer science, economics, elementary education, English, environmental studies, exercise science, french, general studies, German studies, history, information systems, international management, international studies, linguistics, mathematics, mathematics/computer science, music, music education, natural science, philosophy, physics, political science, psychology, religion, secondary education, social science, sociology, Spanish, theatre; pre-professional programmes: architecture, chiropractics, dentistry, engineering, law, medicine, nursing, occupational therapy, optometry, pharmacy, physical therapy, podiatric medicine, veterinary medicine; overseas study centres in France, Austria, Spain, Wales, England, Yucatan, China and the Netherlands
Academic year: August to May

Pres.: Dr MARK PUTNAM
Vice-Pres. for Academic Affairs and Dean for Faculty: Dr MARY MORTON-STREY
Vice-Pres. for Advancement: DAVE SUTPHEN
Vice-Pres. for Finance and Admin. and Treas.: MARGARET TUNGSETH
Vice-Pres. for Student Enrolment Management: CAROL WILLIAMSON
Dean for Student Life: ERIC JONES
Registrar: STEPHANIE HENNING
Library Dir: NATALIE H. HUTCHINSON

Library of 200,000 vols, 4,000 music scores and anthologies
Number of teachers: 89 (full-time)
Number of students: 1,600

Publication: The Central Ray.

CLARKE UNIVERSITY

1550 Clarke Dr., Dubuque, IA 52001-3198
Telephone: (563) 588-6300
Fax: (563) 588-6789
E-mail: clarke-info@clarke.edu
Internet: www.clarke.edu

Founded 1843, present name and status 2010
Private control
Academic year: August to May

Depts of accounting and business admin., art and art history, athletic training, biology, chemistry, communication, computer science, drama and speech, education, history/political science, language and literature, mathematics, music, nursing, philosophy, physical therapy, psychology, religious studies and social work

Pres.: Dr JOANNE M. BURROWS
Provost and Vice-Pres. for Academic Affairs: JOAN LINGEN
Vice-Pres. for Institutional Advancement: BILL BIEBUYCK
Vice-Pres. for Enrolment Management: BETH TRIPLETT
Vice-Pres. for Student Life: KATHLEEN ZANGER
Registrar: KRISTI DROESSLER
Library Dir: SUE LEIBOLD

Library of 121,000 vols
Number of teachers: 120

Number of students: 1,232

Publications: Catalyst (1 a year), CLARKE: The Magazine of Clarke University, Tenth Muse (1 a year).

COE COLLEGE

1220 First Ave, NE, Cedar Rapids, IA 52402
Telephone: (319) 399-8500
Fax: (319) 399-8816
E-mail: admission@coe.edu
Internet: www.coe.edu

Founded 1851 as School for the Prophets, present name 1881
Private control
Academic year: August to May

Majors in accounting, African-American studies, American studies, art, Asian studies, athletic training, biochemistry, biology, business admin., chemistry, computer science, economics, education, English, English as a second language, environmental science, French, French studies, gender studies, general science, German, German studies, historical studies, history, interdisciplinary, literature, mathematics, molecular biology, music, nursing, philosophy, physical education, physics, political science, pre-professional programmes, psychology, public relations, religion, sociology, Spanish, Spanish studies, speech, theatre arts, writing

Pres.: Dr JAMES R. PHIFER
Vice-Pres. for Academic Affairs and Dean for Faculty: Dr MARIE BAEHR
Vice-Pres. for Admin. and Enrolment Services: MICHAEL WHITE
Vice-Pres. for Advancement: RICHARD MEISTERLING
Vice-Pres. for Student Affairs: LOU STARK
Dean for Admission: JULIE STAKER
Registrar: Dr EVELYN MOORE
Dir for Library Services: JILL JACK

Library of 300,000 vols, 1,100 current periodicals, 10,000 microforms, 16,000 audiovisual items, 33,500 print and online periodicals
Number of teachers: 138 (80 full-time, 58 part-time)
Number of students: 1,350

Publication: Courier (4 a year).

CORNELL COLLEGE

600 First St, SW, Mount Vernon, IA 52314-1098
Telephone: (319) 895-4000
Fax: (319) 895-4492
E-mail: admission@cornellcollege.edu
Internet: www.cornellcollege.edu

Founded 1853 as Iowa Conf. Seminary, present name 1857
Private control

Depts of art, biology, chemistry, computer science, economics and business, education, English, geology, history, kinesiology, languages, mathematics, music, philosophy, physics, politics, psychology, religion, sociology and anthropology, theatre and communications studies

Pres.: JONATHAN BRAND
Vice-Pres. for Academic Affairs and Dean for College: R. JOSEPH DIEKER
Vice-Pres. for Alumni and College Advancement: PETER WILCH
Vice-Pres. for Enrolment and Dean for Admissions: JONATHAN STROUD
Vice-Pres. for Student Affairs: JOHN HARP
Registrar: JONNA HIGGINS-FREESE
Dir for Library: PAUL WAELCHLI

Library of 190,000 vols
Number of teachers: 82
Number of students: 1,200

DES MOINES UNIVERSITY

3200 Grand Ave, Des Moines, IA 50312-4198
Telephone: (515) 271-1400
Fax: (515) 271-1578
E-mail: info@dmu.edu
Internet: www.dmu.edu

Founded 1898 as Dr S. S. Still College of Osteopathy, present name 1999
Private control
Pres. and CEO: Dr ANGELA L. WALKER FRANKLIN
Provost: Dr KAREN MCLEAN
Vice-Pres. for Admin. Services: STEPHEN DENGLE
Vice-Pres. for Institutional Advancement: SUE HUPPERT
Vice-Pres. for Student Services: MARY ANN ZUG
Registrar: KATHY L. SCAGLIONE
Library Dir: LARRY D. MARQUARDT
Library of 26,000 medical vols, 30,000 bound journals, 3,000 e-journals
Number of students: 1,700
Publication: *DMU Magazine* (4 a year)

DEANS

College of Health Sciences: Dr JODI L. CAHALAN
College of Osteopathic Medicine: Dr KENDALL REED
College of Podiatric Medicine and Surgery: Dr ROBERT M. YOHO
University Research: Dr JEFFREY GRAY

DIVINE WORD COLLEGE

102 Jacoby Dr. SW, POB 380, Epworth, IA 52045-0380
Telephone: (319) 876-3353
E-mail: dwcinfo@dwci.edu
Internet: www.dwci.edu

Founded 1931 as St Paul's Mission House, present name 1964
Private control
Academic year: August to May
Courses in cross-cultural studies, philosophy and religious studies
Pres.: Rev. TIMOTHY LENCHAK
Vice-Pres. for Academic Affairs: Dr MATHEW KANJIRATHINKAL
Vice-Pres. for Devt: TERRY SYKORA
Vice-Pres. for Formation and Dean for Students: Rev. KHIEN MAI LUU
Vice-Pres. for Recruitment and Admissions: LEN UHAL
Registrar: DEBORAH HIRSCH
Library Dir: DANIEL BOICE
Library of 90,000 vols, 350 magazines.

DORDT COLLEGE

498 Fourth Ave, NE, Sioux Center, IA 51250
Telephone: (712) 722-6000
Fax: (712) 722-1185
E-mail: admissions@dordt.edu
Internet: www.dordt.edu

Founded 1955
Private control
Languages of instruction: English, Dutch, Spanish, Latin
Academic year: August to May
Liberal arts courses
Pres.: Dr CARL E. ZYLSTRA
Provost: Dr ERIK HOEKSTRA
Vice-Pres. for Academic Affairs: Dr ROCKNE MCCARTHY
Vice-Pres. for College Advancement: JOHN BAAS
Vice-Pres. for Student Services: KEN BOERSMA
Exec. Dir for Admissions: QUENTIN VAN ESSEN

Registrar: JIM BOS
Dir for Library Services: SHERYL TAYLOR
Library of 285,000 vols, 300 journals, magazines and newspapers, 58,500 e-titles
Number of teachers: 80 (full-time)
Number of students: 1,402
Publication: *Pro Rege* (4 a year).

DRAKE UNIVERSITY

2507 University Ave, Des Moines, IA 50311-4505
Telephone: (515) 271-2011
Fax: (515) 271-3977
E-mail: admission@drake.edu
Internet: www.drake.edu

Founded 1881
Private control
Academic year: September to May (2 semesters)
Pres.: Dr DAVID E. MAXWELL
Provost: SUE WRIGHT
Vice-Pres. for Admission and Financial Aid: TOM DELAHUNT
Vice-Pres. for Alumni and Devt: JOHN SMITH
Dean for Students: Dr SENTWALI BAKARI
Registrar: NANCY GEIGER
Dean for Cowles Library: RODNEY HENSHAW
Dir for Law Library: JOHN EDWARDS
Library of 514,886 vols, 1,900 journals, 107,995 govt documents, 2,500 audiovisual items, 35,703 e-books
Number of teachers: 417 (237 full-time, 180 part-time)
Number of students: 4,377 (3,202 undergraduate, 1,175 graduate)
Publications: *Drake Blue* (online (www.drake.edu/magazine)), *Drake Law Review*, *Drake Update*

DEANS

College of Arts and Sciences: Dr JOSEPH LENZ
College of Business and Public Admin.: CHARLES C. EDWARDS, JR
College of Pharmacy and Health Sciences: RAYLENE ROSPOND
Drake Law School: ALLAN W. VESTAL
School of Education: JANET MCMAHILL
School of Journalism and Mass Communication: CHARLES C. EDWARDS, JR

EMMAUS BIBLE COLLEGE

2570 Asbury Rd, Dubuque, IA 52001
Telephone: (563) 588-8000
Fax: (563) 588-1216
E-mail: info@emmaus.edu
Internet: www.emmaus.edu

Founded 1941
Private control
Academic year: August to May
Depts of business, Christian education, computer studies, counselling, general education, intercultural studies, music, teacher education
Pres.: KENNETH A. DAUGHTERS
Chancellor: Dr DANIEL H. SMITH
Vice-Pres. for Academic Affairs: LISA L. BEATTY
Vice-Pres. for Admin. and Finance: Dr MARK A. PRESSON
Vice-Pres. for Advancement: Dr STEVEN R. WITTER
Vice-Pres. for Student Devt: JONATHAN W. GLOCK
Registrar: KATHRYN L. VAN DINE
Librarian: JOHN H. RUSH
Library of 120,000 vols
Number of teachers: 25
Number of students: 283
Publication: *Journey Magazine*.

FAITH BAPTIST BIBLE COLLEGE AND THEOLOGICAL SEMINARY

1900 NW Fourth St, Ankeny, IA 50023
Telephone: (515) 964-0601
Fax: (515) 964-1638
E-mail: admissions@faith.edu
Internet: www.faith.edu

Founded 1921 as Omaha Bible Institute, present name 1967
Private control
Academic year: August to May
Divs of Bible and theology, Christian studies, general education
Pres.: Dr JAMES D. MAXWELL, III
Vice-Pres. for Academic Services and Dean for College: Dr JEFFERY G. NEWMAN
Dean for Seminary: Dr ERNIE SCHMIDT
Dir for Enrolment: MARK DAVIS
Dean for Students: SHON LUNDBERG
Registrar: DAVID STOUT
Head Librarian: Dr JOHN HARTOG, II
Library of 69,000 vols, 395 periodicals, 2,000 video cassettes and DVDs, 4,800 audio cassettes and CDs, 4,800 microfiche
Number of teachers: 34
Number of students: 302

GRACELAND UNIVERSITY

1 University Pl., Lamoni, IA 50140
Telephone: (641) 784-5423
Fax: (641) 784-5480
E-mail: admissions@graceland.edu
Internet: www.graceland.edu

Founded 1895
Private control
Academic year: August to May
Campus at Independence (Missouri)
Pres.: Dr JOHN D. SELLARS
Vice-Pres. for Academic Affairs and Dean for Faculty: PARRIS R. WATTS
Vice-Pres. for Business and Admin. Services: JANICE K. TIFFANY
Vice-Pres. for Enrolment Management: LOUISE CUMMINGS-SIMMONS
Vice-Pres. for Institutional Advancement: KELLY W. EVERETT
Vice-Pres. for Institutional Effectiveness: Dr KATHLEEN M. CLAUSON BASH
Dir for Admissions: KEVIN BROWN
Dean for Students: MARIAN KILLPACK
Registrar: JOYCE LIGHTHILL
Dir for Library Services: FRANCIS ACLAND
Library of 119,233 vols, 526 periodical and newspaper subscriptions, 2,139 records, cassettes and CDs, 618 DVDs and video cassettes
Number of teachers: 79 (full-time)
Number of students: 2,271 (1,710 full-time, 561 part-time)

DEANS

C. H. Sandage School of Business: Dr STEVEN L. ANDERS
College of Liberal Arts and Studies: Dr GARY HEISSERER
Edmund J. Gleazer School of Education: Dr TAMMY E. EVERETT
School of Nursing: Dr CLAUDIA D. HORTON
Seminary: Dr DON COMPIER

GRAND VIEW UNIVERSITY

1200 Grandview Ave, Des Moines, IA 50316
Telephone: (515) 263-2800
Fax: (515) 263-6095
E-mail: admissions@grandview.edu
Internet: www.grandview.edu

Founded 1896, present name and status 2008
Private control
Academic year: August to May (2 semesters)

Divs of humanities, natural science, nursing and social science
Pres.: KENT L. HENNING
Provost and Vice-Pres. for Academic Affairs: Dr MARY ELIZABETH STIVERS
Vice-Pres. for Admin. and Finance: ADAM J. VOIGTS
Vice-Pres. for Advancement: WILLIAM BURMA
Vice-Pres. for Enrolment Management: DEBBIE M. BARGER
Vice-Pres. for Student Affairs: Dr JAY PRESCOTT
Dir for Admissions: DIANE JOHNSON SCHAEFER
Registrar: DEBORAH GANNON
Library Dir: PAMELA REES
Number of teachers: 190 (90 part-time, 100 part-time)
Number of students: 2,230

GRINNELL COLLEGE

1121 Park St, Grinnell, IA 50112-1690
Telephone: (641) 269-4000
Fax: (641) 269-3408
E-mail: askgrin@grinnell.edu
Internet: www.grinnell.edu
Founded 1846
Private control
Divs of humanities, science and social studies
Pres.: RAYNARD S. KINGTON
Vice-Pres. for Academic Affairs and Dean for College: PAULA V. SMITH
Vice-Pres. for College Services: JOHN W. KALKBRENNER
Vice-Pres. for Devt and Alumni Relations: BETH HALLORAN
Vice-Pres. for Student Affairs: W. HOUSTON DOUGHARTY
Dean for Admission: DOUG BADGER (acting)
Registrar: CHERYL CHASE
Librarian: RICHARD FYFFE
Library of 817,849 vols, 39,745 audio visual materials, 2,000 periodicals and journals, 140,000 e-books
Number of teachers: 214 (161 full-time, 53 part-time)
Number of students: 1,597

IOWA STATE UNIVERSITY

Ames, IA 50011
Telephone: (515) 294-4111
E-mail: contact@iastate.edu
Internet: www.iastate.edu
Founded 1858 as Iowa Agricultural College and Model Farm, present status 1959
State control
Pres.: Prof. STEVEN LEATH
Exec. Vice-Pres. and Provost: ELIZABETH HOFFMAN
Vice-Pres. for Extension and Outreach: CATH-ANN KRESS
Vice-Pres. for Research and Economic Devt: SHARRON QUISENBERRY
Vice-Pres. for Student Affairs: THOMAS L. HILL
Registrar: KATHY M. JONES
Dean for Library Services: OLIVIA M. MADISON
Library: see Libraries and Archives
Number of teachers: 1,740
Number of students: 28,682
Publications: Ethos (2 a year, print and online (www.ethosmagazine.org)), Inquiry, Iowa Stater, Iowa State University Veterinarian, IVisions, Marston Muses, Outlook, The Agriculturist, The Gentle Doctor (2 a year), The Iowa Engineer

DEANS
College of Agriculture and Life Sciences: WENDY WINTERSTEEN

College of Business Administration: Prof. LABH S. HIRA
College of Design: LUIS RICO-GUTIERREZ
College of Engineering: Dr JONATHAN WICKERT
College of Human Sciences: PAMELA WHITE
College of Liberal Arts and Sciences: DAVID OLIVER
College of Veterinary Medicine: Dr LISA K. NOLAN
Graduate College: DAVID K. HOLGER

IOWA WESLEYAN COLLEGE

601 N Main St, Mount Pleasant, IA 52641
Telephone: (319) 385-8021
E-mail: admit@iwc.edu
Internet: www.iwc.edu
Founded 1842, present name 1912
Private control
Divs of business, education, fine arts, human studies, language and literature, nursing, science, mathematics and computer studies
Pres.: Dr JAY K. SIMMONS
Vice-Pres. for Academic Affairs: Dr NANCY ERICKSON
Vice-Pres. and Dean for Student Life: Dr LINDA BUCHANAN
Vice-Pres. for Institutional Relations: JERRY THOMAS
Dean for Admissions: MARK PETTY
Registrar: PATTY BROKKEN
Library Dir: PAULA KINNEY
Library of 108,427 vols
Number of teachers: 42
Number of students: 863
Publication: Purple & White.

KAPLAN UNIVERSITY

1801 E Kimberly Rd, Suite one, Davenport, IA 52807
Telephone: (563) 355-3500
E-mail: infoku@kaplan.edu
Internet: portal.kaplanuniversity.edu
Founded 1937 as American Institute of Commerce, present name and status 2004
Private control
Campuses in Maryland, Maine and Nebraska; learning centres in Indiana, Maryland, Missouri and Wisconsin
Pres. for Kaplan Univ. Group: GREGORY MARINO
Pres.: Dr WADE DYKE
Provost: Dr GERI MALANDRA
Vice-Provost for Academic Affairs: Dr KARA VANDAM
Vice-Provost for Governance and Admin.: Dr KEITH SMITH
Dir for Library Services: JENNIE VER STEEG
Library of 50,000 vols of e-books
Number of teachers: 4,500
Number of students: 61,000 (online and campus-based)

DEANS
College of Arts and Sciences: Dr SARA SANDER
Concord Law School: GREG BRANDES
School of Business and Management: Dr THOMAS C. BOYD
School of Criminal Justice: TIM PARDUE
School of General Education: Dr JODY DEKORTE
School of Graduate Education: Dr DREW ROSS
School of Health Sciences: Dr GINGER CAMERON
School of Information Systems and Technology: Dr DAVID DEHAVEN
School of Legal Studies: FRANK DIMARINO
School of Nursing: SHELIA BURKE

LORAS COLLEGE

1450 Alta Vista St, Dubuque, IA 52004-0178
Telephone: (563) 588-7100
Fax: (563) 588-7119
E-mail: admissions@loras.edu
Internet: www.loras.edu
Founded 1839, present name 1939
Private control
Courses in accounting, art-studio, athletic training, archaeology/cultural interpretation, biochemistry, biology, business, business finance, business management, business marketing, Catholic studies, chemistry, computer science, criminal justice, economics, electromechanical engineering, elementary education, English literature, English writing, gender studies, Greek and Roman studies, history, integrated visual arts, int. studies, iIish studies, management information systems, mathematics, media studies, music/music education, philosophy, physics-applied, politics, psychology, public relations, publishing, religious studies, social work, sociology, Spanish, sport management, sport science, theatre, world literature
Pres.: JAMES E. COLLINS
Provost: Dr CHERYL R. JACOBSEN
Vice-Pres. for Institutional Advancement: PAMELA S. GERAD
Vice-Pres. for Finance and Admin. Services: STEPHEN J. SCHMALL
Dean for Students: ARTHUR W. SUNLEAF
Registrar: J. T. BROWN
Library Dir: JOYCE MELDREM
Library of 440,000 vols, 8,000 current periodicals
Number of teachers: 141
Number of students: 1,576
Publication: Loras College Magazine (print and online (www.loras.edu/magazine)).

LUTHER COLLEGE

700 College Dr., Decorah, IA 52101-1045
Telephone: (563) 387-2000
Fax: (563) 387-2158
E-mail: admissions@luther.edu
Internet: www.luther.edu
Founded 1861
Private control
Academic year: September to July (2 semesters)
Majors/minors in accounting, African studies, anthropology, art, arts management, athletic training, biblical languages, biology, business (management), chemistry, classical studies, classics, communication studies, computer science, economics, education, English, environmental studies, French, German, Greek, health, history, int. management studies, Latin, Latin American studies, management, management information systems, mathematics, mathematics/statistics, museum studies, music, music management, nursing, philosophy, physical education, physics, political science, psychology, religion, resource management, Russian studies, Scandinavian studies, social work, sociology, Spanish, speech/theatre, sports management, theatre/dance management, women's and gender studies
Pres.: Dr RICHARD L. TORGERSON
Vice-Pres. and Dean for Student Life: Dr ANN HIGHUM
Vice-Pres. for Academic Affairs and Dean for Faculty: Dr KEVIN KRAUS
Vice-Pres. for Devt: KEITH J. CHRISTENSEN
Vice-Pres. for Enrolment Management: (vacant): SCOT SCHAEFFER
Vice-Pres. for Finance and Admin.: DIANE TACKE
Dir for Admissions: DEREK HARTL
Registrar: DOUGLAS KOSCHMEDER

Library Head: ANDREA BECKENDORF
Library of 340,000 vols, 800 periodicals, 63,000 e-books
Number of teachers: 178 (full-time)
Number of students: 2,500

MAHARISHI UNIVERSITY OF MANAGEMENT

Fairfield, IA 52557
Telephone: (641) 472-7000
Fax: (641) 472-1179
E-mail: admissions@mum.edu
Internet: www.mum.edu

Founded 1971 as Maharishi International Univ., present name 1995
Private control
Academic year: August to June
Pres.: Dr BEVAN MORRIS
Exec. Vice-Pres.: Dr CRAIG PEARSON
Chief Admin. Officer: Dr DAVID STREID
Dean for Admissions: NICHOLAS ROSANIA
Dean for Faculty: Dr CATHERINE GORINI
Dean for Student Life: ELLEN AKST JONES
Registrar: TOM ROWE
Library Dir: MARTIN SCHMIDT
Library of 144,000 vols
Number of teachers: 80
Number of students: 1,238

DEANS

College of Arts and Sciences: Dr SCOTT HERRIOTT
College of Computer Science and Mathematics: Dr GREGORY GUTHRIE
Graduate School: Dr FRED TRAVIS

MERCY COLLEGE OF HEALTH SCIENCES

928 Sixth Ave, Des Moines, IA 50309-1239
Telephone: (515) 643-3180
Fax: (515) 643-6698
E-mail: admissions@mchs.edu
Internet: www.mchs.edu

Founded 1899 as Mercy Hospital Training School, present name and status 1995
Private control
Pres.: BARBARA Q. DECKER
Provost and Vice-Pres. for Academic Affairs: ELIZABETH RITT
Vice-Pres. for Admissions and Advancement: BRIAN TINGLEFF
Registrar: CAROLYN BUCKLIN
Library Dir: EILEEN HANSEN
Library of 14,738 vols, 158 journals
Number of students: 729
Publications: Mercy Messenger (12 a year, online (www.mchs.edu/mercy-messenger.cfm)), VitalSigns (2 a year)

DEANS

School of Allied Health: THERESA SMITH
School of Liberal Arts and Sciences: Dr JEANNINE MATZ
School of Nursing: Dr SHIRLEY BEAVER

MORNINGSIDE COLLEGE

1501 Morningside Ave, Sioux City, IA 51106
Telephone: (712) 274-5000
Fax: (712) 274-5101
E-mail: msadm@morningside.edu
Internet: www.morningside.edu
Founded 1894
Private control
Depts of art, biology, business administration, chemistry, computer and application programming, computer science, corporate communication, education, engineering physics, English, history, mass communication, mathematics, music, nursing, philoso-

phy, political science, psychology, religious studies, Spanish and theatre
Pres.: JOHN C. REYNDERS
Vice-Pres. for Academic Affairs and Dean for College: Dr WILLIAM C. DEEDS
Vice-Pres. for Institutional Advancement: TOM RICE
Vice-Pres. for Student Services and Admissions: TERRI CURRY
Dean for Enrolment: ROBBIE ROHLENA
Registrar: MARY PESHEK
Dir for Library Services: DARIA BOSSMAN
Library of 117,330 vols, 3,575 sound recordings, 8,869 micofilms, 76,285 microfiche
Number of teachers: 75
Number of students: 1,200
Publications: Student Health 101, The Kiosk, The Morningsider.

MOUNT MERCY UNIVERSITY

1330 Elmhurst Dr., NE, Cedar Rapids, IA 52402-4798
Telephone: (319) 363-8213
Fax: (319) 363-5270
E-mail: admission@mtmercy.edu
Internet: www.mtmercy.edu

Founded 1924 as Mount Mercy Acad., present name and status 2010
Private control
Academic year: August to May

Depts of business, communications, education, history, literature and arts, natural and applied sciences, nursing and psychology, politics and justice, philosophy, religion and campus ministry, sociology and social work
Pres.: Dr CHRISTOPHER R. L. BLAKE
Provost and Vice-Pres. for Academic Affairs: Dr MELODY GRAHAM (acting)
Vice-Pres. for Enrolment and Student Life: Dr SUE OATEY
Vice-Pres. for Devt: DUFF RIDGEWAY
Registrar: JASON CLAPP
Dir for Library Services: MARILYN MURPHY
Library of 140,000 vols
Number of teachers: 148 (80 full-time, 68 part-time)
Number of students: 1,824

NORTHWESTERN COLLEGE

101 Seventh St, SW, Orange City, IA 51041-1996
Telephone: (712) 707-7100
Fax: (712) 707-7247
E-mail: admissions@nwciowa.edu
Internet: www.nwciowa.edu

Founded 1882, resent name and status 1960
Private control
Academic year: August to May

Depts of art, biology, business/economics, chemistry, communications, computer science, education, English/writing and rhetoric, foreign languages, history, humanities, kinesiology, mathematics, music, nursing, philosophy, physics, political science, psychology, religion/Christian education, social work, sociology, theatre and speech
Pres.: GREGORY E. CHRISTY
Provost: Dr JASPER LESAGE
Vice-Pres. for Advancement: JAY WIELENGA
Dean for Enrolment Management: KENTON PAULS
Dean for Faculty: Dr ADRIENNE FORGETTE
Dean for Student Life: Dr JOHN G. BROGAN
Registrar: SANDY VAN KLEY
Dir for Library: Dr TIM SCHLAK
Library of 129,000 vols
Number of teachers: 134 (85 full-time and 49 part-time)
Number of students: 1,211

PALMER COLLEGE OF CHIROPRACTIC

1000 Brady St, Davenport, IA 52803
Telephone: (563) 884-5000
Fax: (563) 884-5414
E-mail: admissions.ia@palmer.edu
Internet: www.palmer.edu

Founded 1897 as Palmer School and Cure, present name 1961

Campuses at Port Orange (Florida) and San Jose (California)

Chancellor: Dr DENNIS M. MARCHIORI
Vice-Chancellor for Academic Affairs: ROBERT E. PERCUOCO
Vice-Chancellor for Admin. and Chief Financial Officer: THOMAS L. TIEMEIER
Vice-Chancellor for Clinic Affairs: KURT WOOD
Vice-Chancellor for Enrolment: Dr J. MICHAEL NOVAK
Vice-Chancellor for Institutional Advancement: Dr ROBERT LEE
Vice-Chancellor for Research: Dr CHRISTINE GOERTZ
Vice-Chancellor for Student Success: Dr KEVIN A. CUNNINGHAM
Vice-Chancellor for Support Services: ROBERT E. LEE
Provost for Davenport Campus: DAN WEINTERT
Registrar: MINDY LEAHY
Dir for Libraries: DENNIS PETERSON
Library of 85,000 vols
Number of students: 2,341
Publication: Streams from the Fountainhead (2 a year).

ST AMBROSE UNIVERSITY

518 W Locust St, Davenport, IA 52803-2898
Telephone: (319) 333-6000
Fax: (319) 333-6243
E-mail: admit@sau.edu
Internet: www.sau.edu

Founded 1882, present name and status 1987
Private control
Pres.: Dr JOAN LESCINSKI
Vice-Pres. for Academic and Student Affairs: Dr PAUL KOCH
Vice-Pres. for Advancement: JEANNE KOBUSZEWSKI
Vice-Pres. for Enrolment Management: JOHN COOPER
Library Dir: MARY HEINZMAN
Library of 150,000 vols
Number of teachers: 356
Number of students: 3,567 (2,829 undergraduate, 815 graduate)
Publication: Scene Magazine

DEANS

College of Arts and Sciences: Dr ARON R. AJI
College of Business: DAVID O'CONNELL
College of Education and Health Sciences: Dr SANDRA CASSADY
Graduate and Adult Education: Dr REGINA MATHESON

SIMPSON COLLEGE

701 North C St, Indianola, IA 50125-1297
Telephone: (515) 961-6251
Fax: (515) 961-1498
E-mail: admiss@simpson.edu
Internet: www.simpson.edu
Founded 1860
Private control
Academic year: August to May
Campuses at West Des Moines and Ankeny; depts of art, biology and environmental science, business administration and economics, chemistry and physics, communication

studies, computer science, education, English, history, mathematics, music, philosophy, political science, psychology, social sciences, sport science and health education, theatre arts, world language and culture studies and women's and gender studies

Pres.: JOHN W. BYRD
Vice-Pres. for Academic Affairs and Academic Dean: STEVE GRIFFITH
Vice-Pres. for College Advancement: BOB LANE
Vice-Pres. for Enrolment: DEB TIERNEY
Vice-Pres. for Student Devt and Dean for Students: JAMES THORIUS
Registrar: JODY RAGAN
Librarian: CYNTHIA M. DYER

Library of 155,761 vols
Number of teachers: 87
Number of students: 2,035 (1485 full-time, 550 part-time)

Publication: *The Simpson Magazine* (4 a year).

UNIVERSITY OF DUBUQUE

2000 University Ave, Dubuque, IA 52001
Telephone: (319) 589-3000
Fax: (563) 589-3690
Internet: www.dbq.edu

Founded 1852
Private control

Schools of business, liberal arts, professional programmes and theology

Pres.: Rev. Dr JEFFREY F. BULLOCK
Vice-Pres. and Dean for Seminary: Prof. BRADLEY LONGFIELD
Vice-Pres. for Academic Affairs: MARK WARD
Vice-Pres for Enrolment Management, Marketing and Univ. Relations: SUSAN SMITH
Vice-Pres for Enrolment Management, Marketing and Univ. Relations: PETER SMITH
Vice-Pres. and Dean of Student Life: Dr MICK MIYAMOTO
Dean for Admission: JESSE JAMES
Registrar: LIZ OLSEN
Univ. Librarian: MARY ANN KNEFEL

Library of 182,502 vols, 3,051 multimedia items, 417 periodicals
Number of students: 1,000

UNIVERSITY OF IOWA

1 Jessup Hall, Iowa City, IA 52242-1316
2222 Old Highway 218S, Iowa City, IA 52242-1602
Telephone: (319) 335-3500
Fax: (319) 335-0807
E-mail: admissions@uiowa.edu
Internet: www.uiowa.edu

Founded 1847
State control
Academic year: August to May (2 terms and summer session)

Pres.: SALLY MASON
Exec. Vice-Pres. and Provost: P. BARRY BUTLER
Sr Vice-Pres. and Treas.: DOUGLAS K. TRUE
Vice-Pres. for Research and Economic Devt: JORDEN COHEN
Vice-Pres. of Student Life: THOMAS R. ROCKLIN
Dir for Admissions: MICHAEL BARRON
Registrar: LAWRENCE J. LOCKWOOD
Univ. Librarian: NANCY L. BAKER

Library: see Libraries and Archives
Number of teachers: 1,700
Number of students: 30,893 (21,565 undergraduate, 5,617 graduate, 3,711 professional)

Publications: *Journal of Communication Inquiry* (4 a year), *Iowa Law Review* (5 a year, online (www.uiowa.edu/~ilr)), *Syllecta Classica* (1 a year, online (www.uio-

wa.edu/~classics/syllecta)), *The Iowa Review* (3 a year, online (iowareview.uiowa.edu)), *Walt Whitman Quarterly Review* (4 a year, print and online (ir.uiowa.edu/wwqr))

DEANS

College of Dentistry: DAVID C. JOHNSEN
College of Education: MARGARET S. CROCCO
College of Engineering: ALEC B. SCRANTON
College of Law: GAIL B. AGRAWAL
College of Liberal Arts and Sciences: LINDA MAXSON
College of Nursing: RITA FRANTZ
College of Pharmacy: DONALD LETENDRE
College of Public Health: SUSAN CURRY
Graduate College: JOHN C. KELLER
Henry B. Tippie College of Business: WILLIAM C. HUNTER
Roy J. and Lucille A. Carver College of Medicine: PAUL ROTHMAN

UNIVERSITY OF NORTHERN IOWA

1227 W 27th St, Cedar Falls, IA 50614
Telephone: (319) 273-2311
Fax: (319) 273-3509
E-mail: admissions@uni.edu
Internet: www.uni.edu

Founded 1876
State control
Academic year: July to June

Pres.: Dr BENJAMIN J. ALLEN
Exec. Vice-Pres. and Provost: Dr GLORIA J. GIBSON
Vice-Pres. for Student Affairs: Dr TERRENCE HOGAN
Vice-Pres. for Admin. and Financial Services: MICHAEL HAGER
Exec. Dir for Univ. Relations: JAMES E. O'CONNOR
Dir for Admissions: CHRISTIE M. KANGAS
Dean of Students: LYN REDINGTON
Registrar: PHILIP L. PATTON
Dean for Library: KATHERINE F. MARTIN

Library of 973,231 vols, 252,048 govt documents, 1,124,239 microform units, 41,438 maps, 7,968 audio visual materials, 175,348 periodicals, 52,924 e-journals, 77,877 e-books
Number of teachers: 832 (649 full-time, 183 part-time)
Number of students: 13,168

Publications: *American Journal of Undergraduate Research* (4 a year), *Argumentation and Advocacy* (4 a year), *Iowa Council for the Social Studies (ICSS) Journal* (1 a year), *Iowa Journal of Communication* (4 a year, online (www.uni.edu/commstudies/ica/journal/journal.htm)), *Journal of Assessment and Accountability in Educator Preparation*, *Journal of Contemporary Ethnography* (2 a year), *Journal of Economics (MVEA)* (2 a year), *The North American Review* (4 a year), *Universitas* (2 a year, online (www.uni.edu/universitas))

DEANS

College of Business Administration: Dr FARZAD MOUSSAVI
College of Education: Dr DWIGHT C. WATSON
College of Humanities, Arts and Sciences: Dr JOEL K. HAACK
College of Social and Behavioural Science: Dr PHILIP MAUCERI
Continuing Education and Special Programmes: KENT M. JOHNSON
Graduate College: Dr MIKE LICARI

UPPER IOWA UNIVERSITY

POB 1857, 605 Washington St, Fayette, IA 52142
Telephone: (563) 425-5200
Fax: (563) 425-5271
E-mail: info@uiu.edu
Internet: www.uiu.edu

Founded 1857
Private control
Academic year: August to May

Divs of business, education, liberal arts and science and mathematics

Pres.: Dr ALAN G. WALKER
Sr Vice-Pres. and Chief Academic Officer: Dr DAVID CHOWN
Sr Vice-Pres. for Academic Extension: Dr WILLIAM DUFFY
Vice-Pres. for Admissions and Financial Aid: JOBYNA JOHNSTON
Vice-Pres. for Advancement, Devt and Alumni Relations: WENDELL SNODGRASS
Sr Vice-Pres. for External Affairs: ANDREW WENTHE
Registrar: HOLLY STREETER
Dir for Library Services: BECKY WADIAN

Library of 155,108 vols
Number of teachers: 574
Number of students: 6,600

WALDORF COLLEGE

106 S Sixth St, Forest City, IA 50436
Telephone: (641) 585-2450
Fax: (641) 585-8194
E-mail: admissions@waldorf.edu
Internet: www.waldorf.edu

Founded 1903, present status 2001
Private control
Academic year: August to July

Liberal arts courses; online degree programmes

Pres.: Dr BOB ALSOP
Vice-Pres. for Academic Affairs and Dean for College: SCOTT SEARCY
Vice-Pres. for Operations: RICK COOPER
Dir for Admissions: SCOTT PITCHER
Dean for Students: JASON RAMAKER
Registrar: TWYLAH KRAGEL
Library Dir: AMY HILL

Library of 90,000 vols
Number of students: 600

WARTBURG COLLEGE

100 Wartburg Blvd, Waverly, IA 50677
Telephone: (319) 352-8200
Fax: (319) 352-8514
E-mail: admissions@wartburg.edu
Internet: www.wartburg.edu

Founded 1852
Private control
Academic year: September to June

Depts of accounting, art, art education, biochemistry, biology, business admin., chemistry, church music, communication arts, communication design, communication studies, community sociology, computer information systems, computer science, economics, education, engineering science, English, exploring, fitness management, history, interdepartmental major, int. relations, mathematics, medical technology, modern languages, music education, music performance, music therapy, philosophy, physical education, physics, political science, psychology, religion, social work, sociology, writing

Pres.: Dr DARREL D. COLSON
Vice-Pres. for Academic Affairs and Dean for Faculty: Dr FRED RIBICH
Vice-Pres. for Enrolment Management: Dr EDITH J. WALDSTEIN

Vice-Pres. for Institutional Advancement: SCOTT LEISINGER
Vice-Pres. for Student Life and Dean for Students: Dr DEBORAH LOERS
Registrar: SHEREE COVERT
Librarian: CHRIS SCHAFER
Library of 130,000 vols
Number of teachers: 109 (full-time)
Number of students: 1,805
Publication: *Wartburg Magazine* (3 a year, print and online (www.wartburg.edu/magazine)).

WARTBURG THEOLOGICAL SEMINARY

POB 5004, Dubuque, IA 52004-5004
333 Wartburg Pl., Dubuque, IA 52003-7797
Telephone: (563) 589-0200
Fax: (563) 589-0333
E-mail: admissions@wartburgseminary.edu
Internet: www.wartburgseminary.edu
Founded 1854
Private control
Offers Masters in arts, diaconal ministry, divinity and theology
Pres.: Dr STANLEY N. OLSON
Vice-Pres. for Mission Support: Rev. Dr LEN HOFFMANN
Academic Dean: Prof. Dr CRAIG NESSAN
Dir for Admissions: Rev. KARLA WILDBERGER
Registrar: Dr KEVIN ANDERSON
Dir for Library: SUSAN EBERTZ
Library of 92,000 vols
Number of teachers: 21
Number of students: 190

WILLIAM PENN UNIVERSITY

201 Trueblood Ave, Oskaloosa, IA 52577
Telephone: (641) 673-1076
Fax: (641) 673-1396
E-mail: admissions@wmpenn.edu
Internet: www.wmpenn.edu
Founded 1873 as Penn College, present name and status 2000
Private control
Academic year: August to May
Pres.: Dr ANN M. FIELDS
Vice-Pres. for Academic Affairs: Dr MARJORIE WELCH
Vice-Pres. for Advancement: SHERRI L. TAYLOR
Vice-Pres. for Student Services and Enrolment Management: JOHN OTTOSSON
Registrar: PATRICK MCADAMS
Librarian: JULIE HANSEN
Number of teachers: 55
Number of students: 1,650
Publication: *Penn & Ink* (2 a year)

DEANS

College of Arts, Sciences and Professional Studies: Dr NOEL STAHLE
College for Working Adults: Dr MARJORIE WELCH

KANSAS

BAKER UNIVERSITY

POB 65, Baldwin City, KS 66006-0065
618 Eighth St, Baldwin City, KS 66006
Telephone: (785) 594-6451
Fax: (785) 594-8425
E-mail: admission@bakeru.edu
Internet: www.bakeru.edu
Founded 1858 (chartered)
Private control
Pres.: Dr PATRICIA N. LONG

Exec. Vice-Pres. for Admin. Services: SUSAN LINDAHL
Vice-Pres. for Enrolment Management and Student Devt: MARK BANDRE
Vice-Pres. for Univ. Advancement: LYN LAKIN
Dean for Students: CASSY BAILEY
Univ. Registrar: RUTH MILLER
Dir for Library Services: KATHLEEN R. BRADT
Library of 108,652 vols, 399 periodicals
Number of teachers: 162 (77 full-time, 85 part-time)
Number of students: 3,536

DEANS

College of Arts and Sciences: Dr RAND ZIEGLER
School of Education: Dr PEGGY HARRIS
School of Nursing: Dr KATHLEEN HARR
School of Professional and Graduate Studies: Dr PEGGY HARRIS

BARCLAY COLLEGE

607 N Kingman, Haviland, KS 67059
Telephone: (620) 862-5252
Fax: (620) 862-5403
E-mail: admissions@barclaycollege.edu
Internet: www.barclaycollege.edu
Founded 1917 as Kansas Central Bible Training School, present name 1990
Private control
Divs of biblical studies, general studies and liberal arts
Pres.: Dr ROYCE FRAZIER
Provost: Dr ADRIAN HALVERSTADT
Vice-Pres. for Student Services: KEVIN LEE
Dir for Library Services: PAT HALL
Library of 62,000 vols
Number of teachers: 30
Number of students: 250

BENEDICTINE COLLEGE

1020 N Second St, Atchison, KS 66002-1499
Telephone: (913) 367-5340
Fax: (913) 367-6566
Internet: www.benedictine.edu
Founded 1858, present name 1971
Private control
Academic year: August to May
Depts of arts and communication, business and public policy, education, health, humanities, science and mathematics, social and behavioural science
Pres.: STEPHEN D. MINNIS
Vice-Pres. for Academic Affairs and Dean of College: Dr KIMBERLY J. SHANKMAN
Vice-Pres. for Advancement: KELLY J. VOWELS
Vice-Pres. for Student Life: LINDA HENRY
Dean for Enrolment Management: PETE HELGESEN
Registrar: LINDA HERNDON
Library Dir: STEVEN GROMATZKY
Library of 320,000 vols, 340 current periodicals
Number of teachers: 52
Number of students: 1,909
Publications: *Loomings* (1 a year), *Raven Review*.

BETHANY COLLEGE

335 E Swensson St, Lindsborg, KS 67456-1895
Telephone: (785) 227-3380
Fax: (785) 227-2004
E-mail: admissions@bethanylb.edu
Internet: www.bethanylb.edu
Founded 1881 as Bethany Acad., present name and status 1889
Private control

Academic year: August to May
Depts of accounting, art, athletic training, biology, business, chemistry, Christian min., coaching, communication, computer applications, criminal justice, economics, education, engineering, English, finance, foreign, language, forensic, science, global studies, health sciences, history, int. management, management, marketing, mathematics, multicultural studies, music, philosophy, physical education, physics, political science, psychology, religion, spec. education, sports management, theatre
Pres.: Dr EDWARD F. LEONARD, III
Provost and Dean for College: Dr EUGENE BALES
Vice-Pres. for Advancement: JIM RUBLE
Dean for Student Life: FREDA STRACK
Registrar: JILL MEGREDY
Dir for Library Services: DENISE CARSON
Library of 115,000 vols
Number of teachers: 54
Number of students: 622

BETHEL COLLEGE

300 E 27th St, North Newton, KS 67117-1716
Telephone: (316) 283-2500
Fax: (316) 284-5286
E-mail: admissions@bethelks.edu
Internet: www.bethelks.edu
Founded 1887
Private control
Courses in arts, nursing, sciences, social work
Pres.: PERRY WHITE
Vice-Pres. for Academic Affairs: Dr BRAD BORN
Vice-Pres. for Admissions: TODD MOORE
Vice-Pres. for Advancement: SONDRA KOONTZ
Vice-Pres. for Student Life: WELDON MARTENS
Registrar: RODNEY FREY
Co-Dir for Libraries: GAIL NILES STUCKY
Co-Dir for Libraries: BARBARA THIESEN
Co-Dir for Libraries: JOHN THIESEN
Library of 125,000 vols
Number of teachers: 59 (36 full-time, 23 part-time)
Number of students: 523
Publications: *Context*, *Mennonite Life* (4 a year).

CENTRAL BAPTIST THEOLOGICAL SEMINARY

6601 Monticello Rd, Shawnee, KS 66226-3513
Telephone: (913) 667-5700
Fax: (913) 371-8110
Internet: www.cbts.edu
Founded 1901
Private control
Academic year: June to May
Doctoral and Masters degree in divinity, ministry, theological studies
Pres.: Prof. Dr MOLLY T. MARSHALL
Exec. Vice-Pres.: GEORGE N. TOWNSEND
Vice-Pres. for Institutional Advancement: JOHN W. GRAVLEY
Dean for Seminary: Prof. Dr ROBERT E. JOHNSON
Library Dir: VANCE THOMAS.

CENTRAL CHRISTIAN COLLEGE OF KANSAS

1200 S Main St, POB 1403, McPherson, KS 67460
Telephone: (620) 241-0723
Fax: (620) 241-6032
E-mail: admissions@centralchristian.edu

Internet: www.centralchristian.edu

Founded 1884 as Orleans Seminary, present name 1999

Private control

Offers Bachelors of science in ministry and business

Pres.: HAL HOXIE

Vice-Pres. for Academics: Dr LEONARD F. FAVARA

Vice-Pres. for Advancement: CALVIN HAWKINS

Vice-Pres. for Finance and Admissions: J. DAVID FERRELL

Registrar: BEV KELLEY

Library Dir: JUDY STOCKSTILL.

DONNELLY COLLEGE

608 N 18th St, Kansas City, KS 66102

Telephone: (913) 621-8700

Fax: (913) 621-8719

E-mail: admissions@donnelly.edu

Internet: www.donnelly.edu

Founded 1949

Private control

Academic year: August to June (3 semesters)

Offers Bachelors in arts and applied sciences in organizational leadership

Pres.: Dr STEVE LaNASA

Vice-Pres. for Institutional Effectiveness: FRANCES SANDERS

Vice-Pres. for Student Affairs: DONETTE ALONZO

Registrar: AMBER BLOOMFIELD-MARTINEZ

Number of students: 1,100

EMPORIA STATE UNIVERSITY

1200 Commercial St, Emporia, KS 66801-5087

Telephone: (620) 341-1200

Fax: (316) 341-5073

E-mail: go2esu@emporia.edu

Internet: www.emporia.edu

Founded 1863, present status 1976, present name 1977

State control

Pres.: Dr H. EDWARD FLENTJE

Provost and Vice-Pres. for Academic Affairs and Student Life: TERESA MEHRING

Assoc. Provost for Enrolment Management: JAMES E. WILLIAMS

Vice-Pres. for Admin. and Fiscal Affairs: RAYMOND A. HAUKE

Registrar: ELAINE HENRIE

Dean for Univ. Libraries and Archives: JOHN B. SHERIDAN

Library of 711,000 vols

Number of teachers: 254

Number of students: 5,976 (3,846 undergraduate, 2,130 postgraduate)

Publications: *ESU Business World* (4 a year), *Flint Hills Review* (1 a year), *Kansas School Naturalist* (4 a year), *Spotlight* (4 a year)

DEANS

College of Liberal Arts and Sciences: MARIE C. MILLER

Graduate School: KATHY ERMLER

School of Business: Dr JOSEPH WEN

School of Library and Information Management: Dr GWEN ALEXANDER

Teachers College: Dr PHIL BENNETT

FORT HAYS STATE UNIVERSITY

Sheridan Hall 204, 600 Park St, Hays, KS 67601-4099

Telephone: (785) 628-4000

Internet: www.fhsu.edu

Founded 1902

State control

Academic year: August to May

Pres.: Dr EDWARD H. HAMMOND

Provost: LAWRENCE V. GOULD (acting)

Vice-Pres. for Admin. and Finance: MIKE BARNETT

Vice-Pres. for Student Affairs: Dr TISA MASON

Dir for Admissions: TRICIA CLINE

Registrar: Dr JOEY LINN

Library Dir: JOHN ROSS

Library of 300,000 vols, 500,000 vols in govt document section

Number of teachers: 300

Number of students: 12,802

DEANS

College of Arts and Sciences: PAUL W. FABER

College of Business and Leadership: MARK BANNISTER

College of Education and Technology: ROBERT F. SCOTT

College of Health and Life Sciences: JEFF BRIGGS

Graduate Studies and Research: TIM CROWLEY

Virtual College: DENNIS KING

FRIENDS UNIVERSITY

2100 W University Ave, Wichita, KS 67213

Telephone: (316) 295-5000

Fax: (316) 295-5060

E-mail: learn@friends.edu

Internet: www.friends.edu

Founded 1898

Private control

Academic year: July to June

Pres.: Prof. Dr T. J. ARANT

Vice-Pres. for Academic Affairs: Dr JOHN YODER

Vice-Pres. for Admin. and Finance: RANDALL C. DOERKSEN

Vice-Pres. for Univ. Relations: HERVEY W. WRIGHT, III

Vice-Pres. for Student Affairs: CAROLE OBERMEYER

Registrar: HEIDI HOSKINSON

Library Dir: Prof. MAX BURSON

Library of 100,000 vols

Number of teachers: 79

Number of students: 2,800

Publication: *Focus* (4 a year)

DEANS

College of Adult and Professional Studies: Dr JO LOBERTINI

College of Business, Arts, Sciences and Education: Dr STEVEN PETERS

Graduate School: Dr EVELYN C. HUME

HASKELL INDIAN NATIONS UNIVERSITY

155 Indian Ave, Lawrence, KS 66046

Telephone: (785) 749-8404

Fax: (785) 749-8406

Internet: www.haskell.edu

Founded 1884 as United States Indian Industrial Training School, present name 1993

Tribal control

Academic year: August to May

Divs of arts and sciences, business, education

Pres.: CHRIS REDMAN

Vice-Pres. for Academic Affairs: Dr VENIDA CHENAULT

Vice-Pres. for Univ. Services: CLYDE PEACOCK

Dir for Admissions: DOROTHY D. STITES

Registrar: MANNY KING

Library Dir: Dr MARILYN RUSSELL

Number of students: 900

KANSAS STATE UNIVERSITY

Manhattan, KS 66506

Telephone: (785) 532-6011

Fax: (785) 532-6393

E-mail: k-state@k-state.edu

Internet: www.k-state.edu

Founded 1863

State control

Academic year: August to May

Pres.: Dr KIRK H. SCHULZ

Provost and Sr Vice-Pres.: APRIL MASON

Sr Vice-Provost for Academic Affairs: RUTH DYER

Vice-Pres. for Research: Prof. R. W. TREWYN

Vice-Pres. for Admin. and Finance: BRUCE A. SHUBERT

Vice-Pres. for Communications and Marketing: JEFFERY B. MORRIS

Vice-Pres. for Student Life and Dean for Students: PAT BOSCO

Chief of Staff and Dir for Community Relations: JACKIE L. HARTMAN

Dir for Governmental Relations: SUE PETERSON

Library: see Libraries and Archives

Number of teachers: 1,251

Number of students: 23,863

Publications: *K-Stater Alumni Magazine*, *Perspectives Research Magazine* (5 a year)

DEANS

College of Agriculture: JOHN FLOROS

College of Architecture, Planning and Design: TIMOTHY DE NOBLE

College of Arts and Sciences: PETER DORHOUT

College of Business Administration: Prof. ALI R. MALEKZADEH

College of Education: MICHAEL C. HOLEN

College of Engineering: Dr JOHN ENGLISH

College of Human Ecology: Dr VIRGINIA MOXLEY

College of Technology and Aviation: DENNIS KUHLMAN

College of Veterinary Medicine: RALPH C. RICHARDSON

Continuing Education: SUE MAES

Graduate School: Dr CAROL SHANKLIN

KANSAS WESLEYAN UNIVERSITY

100 E Claffin Ave, Salina, KS 67401-6196

Telephone: (785) 827-5541

Fax: (785) 827-0927

E-mail: admissions@kwu.edu

Internet: www.kwu.edu

Founded 1886

Private control

Divs of applied arts and sciences, fine arts, humanities, nursing, social sciences

Pres. and CEO: Dr FLETCHER M. LAMKIN

Provost and Exec. Vice-Pres.: Dr WAYNE LOWEN

Vice-Pres. for Admissions: WILLIAM P. TANNER

Vice-Pres. for Finance and Admin.: WAYNE SCHNEIDER

Dir for Admissions: STEVE BERRY

Dir for Enrolment and Financial Services: GLENNA ALEXANDER

Registrar: DENISE HOEFFNER

Dir for Library Services: JAMES CORBLY

Library of 75,938 vols

Number of teachers: 45 (40 full-time, 5 part-time)

Number of students: 825

MCPHERSON COLLEGE

POB 1402, 1600 E Euclid, McPherson, KS 67460

Telephone: (620) 242-0400

Fax: (620) 241-8443

E-mail: admiss@mcpherson.edu

Internet: www.mcpherson.edu
Founded 1887 as McPherson College and Institute, present name 1898
Private control
Academic year: September to May

Depts of art, behavioural science, business, English, health, physical education and recreation, history, mathematics and information technology, modern language, music, natural sciences, philosophy and religion, teacher education, technology, theatre

Pres.: MICHAEL P. SCHNEIDER
Provost: Dr KENT EATON
Vice-Pres. for Academic Affairs: Dr KENT EATON
Vice-Pres. for Admissions: DAVID BARRETT
Vice-Pres. for Advancement: AMANDA GUTIERREZ
Dean for Students: LaMONTE ROTHROCK
Dir for Library Services: MARY HESTER
Number of teachers: 42
Number of students: 620

MANHATTAN CHRISTIAN COLLEGE

1415 Anderson Ave, Manhattan, KS 66502
Telephone: (785) 539-3571
Fax: (785) 539-0832
E-mail: admit@mccks.edu
Internet: www.mccks.edu
Founded 1927 as Christian Workers Univ., present name 1971
Private control
Academic year: August to May

Depts of Bible and theology, general studies, practical ministries

Pres.: KEVIN INGRAM
Vice-Pres. for Academic Affairs: RANDY INGMIRE
Vice-Pres. for Institutional Advancement: VERN HENRICKS
Vice-Pres. for Student Life: Dr RICK L. WRIGHT
Dir for Library Services: MARY ANN BUHLER
Library of 40,000 vols, 2,600 journals, 3,000 e-books
Number of teachers: 24
Number of students: 406

MIDAMERICA NAZARENE UNIVERSITY

2030 E College Way, Olathe, KS 66062-1899
Telephone: (913) 782-3750
Fax: (913) 791-3290
E-mail: info@mnu.edu
Internet: www.mnu.edu
Founded 1966
Private control
Academic year: August to April

Divs of business, Christian ministry and formation, education and counselling, liberal arts and sciences, nursing and health science

Pres.: JAMES H. DIEHL
Vice-Pres. for Academic Affairs: Dr STEPHEN W. RAGAN
Vice-Pres. for Enrolment Devt: (vacant)
Vice-Pres. for Student Devt: RANDY BECKUM
Vice-Pres. for Univ. Advancement: JON D. NORTH
Dir for Admissions: WARREN ROGERS
Registrar: JAMES GARRISON
Librarian: Dr RODNEY BIRCH
Library of 400,000 vols
Number of teachers: 123
Number of students: 1,778

NEWMAN UNIVERSITY

3100 McCormick Ave, Wichita, KS 67213-2097
Telephone: (316) 942-4291

Fax: (316) 942-4483
E-mail: admissions@newmanu.edu
Internet: www.newmanu.edu
Founded 1933 as Sacred Heart Junior College, present name 1998
Private control
Offers courses in Colorado, Oklahoma, SE Kansas and W Kansas

Pres.: Dr NOREEN M. CARROCCI
Provost and Vice-Pres. for Academic Affairs: MICHAEL AUSTIN
Vice-Pres. for Finance and Admin.: MARK B. DRESSELHAUS
Vice-Pres. for Institutional Advancement: THOMAS E. BORREGO
Dean for Admissions: JOHN CLAYTON
Dean for Students: LAURA NICHOLAS
Registrar: SHIRLEY RUEB
Dir for Library Services: JOSEPH FORTE
Number of teachers: 191
Number of students: 2,071
Publications: *Challenge* (online (challenge.newmanu.edu)), *Sheridan Edwards Review* (1 a year)

DEANS

College of Graduate and Continuing Studies: Dr AUDREY CURTIS HANE
College of Undergraduate Studies: Dr DAVID SHUBERT

OTTAWA UNIVERSITY

1001 S Cedar St, Ottawa, KS 66067
Telephone: (785) 242-5200
Fax: (785) 229-1020
E-mail: admiss@ottawa.edu
Internet: www.ottawa.edu
Founded 1865
Private control
Academic year: June to May

Campuses at Mesa, Phoenix and Tempus (Arizona), Indiana, Kansas City, Wisconsin; divs of arts and sciences, business and education

Pres.: KEVIN C. EICHNER
Provost and Chief Academic Officer: Dr TERRY HAINES
Vice-Pres. for Admin.: J. CLARK RIBORY
Vice-Pres. for Univ. Advancement: PAUL BEAN
Vice-Pres. and Provost for College: Dr DENNIS TYNER
Asst Vice-Pres. for Enrolment Management: BILL HAMMOND
Registrar: KAREN ADAMS
Dir for Library Services: GLORIA CREED-DIKEOGU
Library of 84,000 vols, 186 periodicals
Number of teachers: 59
Number of students: 2,503 (full-time)

PITTSBURG STATE UNIVERSITY

1701 South Broadway, Pittsburg, KS 66762
Telephone: (620) 231-7000
Fax: (620) 235-6003
E-mail: psuinfo@pittstate.edu
Internet: www.pittstate.edu
Founded 1903
State control

Pres.: Dr STEVEN A. SCOTT
Provost and Vice-Pres. for Academic Affairs: Dr LYNETTE J. OLSON
Vice-Pres. for Admin. and Campus Life: JOHN D. PATTERSON
Vice-Pres. for Univ. Advancement: J. BRADFORD HODSON
Dean for Enrolment Management: WILLIAM A. IVY
Registrar: DEBBIE GREVE
Dean for Library Services: DAVID P. BUNNELL

Library of 350,000 vols, 71,000 e-books, 4,900 periodicals, 23,000 e-periodicals
Number of teachers: 325
Number of students: 7,000

DEANS

College of Arts and Sciences: Prof. Dr KARL KUNKEL
College of Education: Prof. Dr HOWARD W. SMITH
College of Technology: Dr BRUCE DALLMAN
Gladys A. Kelce College of Business: Dr PAUL W. GRIMES
Graduate School: Dr PEGGY SNYDER

SOUTHWESTERN COLLEGE

100 College St, Winfield, KS 67156-2499
Telephone: (620) 229-6000
Fax: (620) 229-6224
E-mail: scadmit@sckans.edu
Internet: www.sckans.edu
Founded 1885
Private control
Academic year: August to May
Courses in business, education, liberal arts, music

Pres.: Dr W. RICHARD MERRIMAN, JR
Vice-Pres. for Academic Affairs and Dean for Faculty: Dr J. ANDREW SHEPPARD
Vice-Pres. for Institutional Advancement: MIKE FARRELL
Vice-Pres. for Student Life: DAWN PLEAS-BAILEY
Dir for Admission: MARLA SEXSON
Registrar: STACY TOWNSLEY
Library Dir: VERONICA MCASEY
Library of 50,000 vols, 100,000 e-books, 5,000 DVDs and CDs, 35,000 journal subscriptions
Number of teachers: 48 (full-time)
Number of students: 1,401 (691 full-time, 710 part-time)

STERLING COLLEGE

125 W Cooper, Sterling, KS 67579
Telephone: (620) 278-2173
Fax: (620) 278-3188
E-mail: admissions@sterling.edu
Internet: www.sterling.edu
Founded 1887 as Cooper Memorial College, present name 1920
Private control

Majors incl. art and graphic design, athletic training, biology, business admin., chemistry, Christian ministries, communication and theatre arts, culinary arts, elementary education, English, exercise science, graphic design and effects, history, ind. interdisciplinary, mathematics, music, music education, psychology, religious and philosophical studies

Pres.: Dr PAUL J. MAURER
Vice-Pres. for Academic Affairs: Dr GREG KERR
Vice-Pres. for Enrolment: DENNIS DUTTON
Vice-Pres. for Institutional Advancement: MARVIN DEWEY
Vice-Pres. for Student Life: TINA WOHLER
Registrar: JANET CAYWOOD
Library Dir: VALORIE STARR
Library of 85,000 vols
Number of teachers: 32
Number of students: 736
Publication: *Sterling*.

TABOR COLLEGE

400 South Jefferson, Hillsboro, KS 67063
Telephone: (620) 947-3121
Fax: (620) 947-2607
E-mail: admissions@tabor.edu

Internet: www.tabor.edu
Founded 1908
Private control
Academic year: August to May

Divs of education, humanities, natural and mathematical sciences, pre-professional programmes, social science and applied arts

Pres.: Dr JULES GLANZER
Vice-Pres. for Academic Affairs and Academic Dean: Dr FRANK E. JOHNSON
Vice-Pres. for Advancement: JAMES ELLIOTT
Vice-Pres. for Enrolment Management: RUSTY ALLEN
Vice-Pres. for Student Life, Learning and Formation: JIM PAULUS
Registrar: DEANNE DUERKSEN
Dir for Library Services: ROBIN OTTOSON

Library of 53,000 vols, 150 periodicals
Number of teachers: 65
Number of students: 721

Publication: *Connection*.

UNITED STATES ARMY COMMAND AND GENERAL STAFF COLLEGE

100 Stimson Ave, Fort Leavenworth, KS 66027-1352

Telephone: (913) 684-7313
E-mail: usarmy.leavenworth.tradoc.mbx .cgsc-ussd@mail.mil
Internet: usacac.army.mil/cac2/cgsc

Founded 1882 as School of Application for Cavalry and Infantry, present name 1947; attached to Combined Arms Center-Leader Devt and Education
State control
Academic year: August to June

Depts of army tactics, command and leadership, distance education, joint, interagency and multinational operations, logistics and resource operations and military history; 3 satellite campuses: Fort Belvoir and Fort Lee in Virginia and Fort Gordon in Georgia

Commanding Gen.: Lt Gen. DAVID G. PERKINS
Deputy Commandant: Col MICHAEL J. JOHNSON (acting)
Dean for Academics: Dr WENDELL CHRISTOPHER KING.

UNIVERSITY OF KANSAS

Room 230, 1450 Jayhawk Blvd, Lawrence, KS 66045

Telephone: (785) 864-2700
Fax: (785) 864-4120
E-mail: chancellor@ku.edu
Internet: www.ku.edu

Founded 1864
State control
Academic year: August to May

Chancellor: BERNADETTE GRAY-LITTLE
Provost and Exec. Vice-Chancellor: JEFFREY S. VITTER
Sr Vice-Provost for Academic Affairs: SARA THOMAS ROSEN
Vice-Provost for Enrolment Management: MATT MELVIN
Vice-Provost for Faculty Devt: MARY LEE HUMMERT
Vice-Provost for Admin. and Finance: DIANE GODDARD
Vice-Provost for Student Success: TAMMARA DURHAM
Vice-Chancellor and Dean for Edwards Campus: Dr ROBERT M. CLARK
Vice-Chancellor for Research and Graduate Studies: STEVE WARREN
Chief Information Officer: BOB LIM
Registrar: (vacant)
Dean for Libraries: LORRAINE HARICOMBE

Library: see Libraries and Archives
Number of teachers: 2,525
Number of students: 29,462

Publications: *American Studies Journal* (4 a year, online (journals.ku.edu/index.php/ amerstud)), *Auslegung* (2 a year), *Biodiversity Informatics*, *Chimères* (online (www2.ku.edu/~chimeres)), *Folklorica*, *Indigenous Nations Studies Journal*, *Journal of Applied Behavior Analysis*, *Journal of Dramatic Theory and Criticism* (2 a year), *Journal of Kansas Entomological Society*, *Journal of Public Administration Research and Theory*, *Journal of Social and Clinical Psychology*, *Kansas Academy of Science Transactions*, *Kansas Journal of Law and Public Policy* (3 a year), *Kansas Law Review* (5 a year), *KU Law Magazine* (2 a year), *La Coronica: A Journal of Medieval Spanish Language and Literature*, *Latin American Theatre Review* (2 a year), *Middle School Journal*, *Paleontological Contributions* (online (paleo.ku.edu/ contributions.html)), *Research Opportunities in Renaissance Drama*, *Russkij Tekst*, *Slovene Linguistic Studies*, *Social Thought and Research*, *The Nabokovian*, *Treatise on Invertebrate Paleontology*, *Yearbook of German-American Studies*

DEANS

College of Liberal Arts and Sciences: DANNY J. ANDERSON
Graduate Studies: SARA ROSEN
School of Architecture, Design and Planning: JOHN C. GAUNT
School of Business: NEELI BENDAPUDI
School of Education: RICK GINSBERG
School of Engineering: Dr STUART R. BELL
School of Journalism and Mass Communications: ANN M. BRILL
School of Law: STEPHEN MAZZA
School of Music: ROBERT L. WALZEL, JR
School of Pharmacy: KENNETH L. AUDUS
School of Social Welfare: MARY ELLEN KONDRAT

ATTACHED MEDICAL CENTRE

University of Kansas Medical Center

3901 Rainbow Blvd, Kansas City, KS 66160

Telephone: (913) 588-5000
Fax: (913) 588-1412
Internet: www.kumc.edu

Founded 1905

Exec. Vice-Chancellor: Dr BARBARA F. ATKINSON
Sr Vice-Chancellor for Academic and Student Affairs: Dr KAREN MILLER
Vice-Chancellor for Admin.: EDWARD PHILLIPS
Vice-Chancellor for Research: Dr PAUL TERRANOVA
Dean for Student Services: Dr DOROTHY KNOLL
Registrar: Dr CHRIS MEIERS

Number of teachers: 890
Number of students: 3,178

DEANS

Graduate Studies: Dr ALLEN B RAWITCH
School of Allied Health: Prof. KAREN MILLER
School of Medicine: Dr H. DAVID WILSON
School of Nursing: Dr KAREN MILLER

UNIVERSITY OF SAINT MARY

4100 S Fourth St, Leavenworth, KS 66048-5082

Telephone: (913) 682-5151
Fax: (913) 758-6140
E-mail: admissions@stmary.edu
Internet: www.stmary.edu

Founded 1923, present name and status 2003
Private control
Academic year: August to July

Campuses at Overland Park, Shawnee and Wyandotte County in Kansas; depts of

behavioural sciences, criminology and psychology, business, account and sport management, education, fine arts, history, political science and global studies, information systems and technology and healthcare informatics, language and literature, natural sciences, nursing, physical therapy and theology, philosophy, pastoral ministry

Pres.: Dr DIANE STEELE
Vice-Pres. for Academic Affairs: Dr BRYAN F. LE BEAU
Vice-Pres. for Finance and Admin. Services: DALE L. CULVER
Dir for Enrolment Management: KEN WUERZBERGER
Dean for Students: Dr LISA BECKENBAUGH
Registrar: MARY PAT DUTTON
Dir for Library: PENELOPE LONERGAN

Library of 118,195 vols
Number of teachers: 31 (full-time)
Number of students: 1,000

Publication: *Aspire*.

WASHBURN UNIVERSITY

1700 SW College Ave, Topeka, KS 66621

Telephone: (785) 670-1010
Fax: (785) 670-1048
E-mail: admissions@washburn.edu
Internet: www.washburn.edu

Founded 1865 as Lincoln College, present name and status 1952
State control
Academic year: August to May

Pres.: Dr JERRY B. FARLEY
Provost and Vice-Pres. for Academic Affairs: Dr RANDALL PEMBROOK
Vice-Pres. for Admin. and Treas.: RICHARD L. ANDERSON
Vice-Pres. for Student Life: Dr DENISE C. OTTINGER
Registrar: Dr WANDA DOLE
Dean for Univ. Libraries: Dr ALAN BEARMAN

Library of 320,000 vols, 1,700 periodicals
Number of teachers: 300
Number of students: 7,230

Publications: *Alumni Magazine* (4 a year), *Circuit Rider*, *KAW*, *Washburn Update*

DEANS

College of Arts and Sciences: Dr GORDON D. McQUERE
School of Applied Studies: Dr WILLIAM S. DUNLAP
School of Business: Dr DAVID SOLLARS
School of Law: THOMAS J. ROMIG
School of Nursing: Prof. Dr MONICA SCHEIBMEIR

WICHITA STATE UNIVERSITY

1845 Fairmont St, Wichita, KS 67260

Telephone: (316) 978-3456
Fax: (316) 978-3174
Internet: www.wichita.edu

Founded 1894 as Fairmount College (Congregational), present status 1964
State control

Pres.: Dr DONALD L. BEGGS
Provost: Prof. KEITH H. PICKUS
Vice-Pres. and Gen. Counsel: TED D. AYRES
Vice-Pres. for Admin. and Finance: MARY L. HERRIN
Vice-Pres. for Campus Life and Univ. Relations: WADE A. ROBINSON
Registrar: WILLIAM E. WYNNE
Dean for Univ. Libraries: DONALD GILSTRAP

Library of 1,243,272 vols, 1,187,960 microfilms and microfiche, 528,592 govt documents, 4,759 linear ft of archives and MSS
Number of teachers: 546
Number of students: 15,100

Publications: *Mikrokosmos* (1 a year), *The Shocker* (print and online (webs.wichita.edu/dt/shockermag/show))

DEANS

College of Education: Dr SHARON IORIO
College of Engineering: Dr ZULMA TORO-RAMOS
College of Fine Arts: Dr RODNEY E. MILLER
College of Health Professions: Prof. Dr PETER A. COHEN
Fairmount College of Liberal Arts and Sciences: Dr WILLIAM D. BISCHOFF
Graduate School: Dr J. DAVID MCDONALD
W. Frank Barton School of Business: Dr DOUGLAS HENSLER

KENTUCKY

ALICE LLOYD COLLEGE

100 Purpose Rd, Pippa Passes, KY 41844
Telephone: (606) 368-6000
Fax: (606) 368-2125
E-mail: admissions@alc.edu
Internet: www.alc.edu
Founded 1923 as Caney Jr College, present status 1982
Private control
Academic year: August to May
Offers bachelor of arts, science
Pres.: JOE A. STEPP
Exec. Vice-Pres.: JAMES STEPP
Vice-Pres. for Academic Affairs and Academic Dean: Prof. CLAUDE L. CRUM
Vice-Pres. for Business Affairs: DAVID JOHNSON
Dean of Student and Community Life: SCOTT CORNETT
Dir of Admissions: ANGELA PHIPPS
Registrar: THELMARIE THORNSBERRY
Library Dir: ANDREW BUSROE
Library of 3,000 vols in Appalachian colln
Number of teachers: 32
Number of students: 508

ASBURY THEOLOGICAL SEMINARY

204 N Lexington Ave, Wilmore, KY 40390
Telephone: (859) 858-3581
E-mail: admissions.office@asburyseminary.edu
Internet: www.asburyseminary.edu
Founded 1923
Private control
Academic year: September to May
Campus in Florida Dunnam
Pres.: Prof. Dr TIMOTHY C. TENNENT
Provost and Vice-Pres. for Academic Affairs: Dr LESLIE A. ANDREWS
Vice-Pres. for Community Formation: Dr MARILYN ELLIOTT
Vice-Pres. for Enrolment Management and Student Services: KEVIN BISH
Vice-Pres. for Finance and Admin.: BRYAN BLANKENSHIP
Vice-Pres. for Florida Campus: Dr GENEVA SILVERNAIL
Vice-Pres. for Seminary Advancement and Communications: JAY MANSUR
Vice-Pres. for Florida Dunnam Campus: Dr GENEVA SILVERNAIL
Exec. Dir of Libraries: PAUL A. TIPPEY
Library of 247,000 vols
Number of teachers: 62
Number of students: 1,778
Publications: *The Asbury Herald* (3 a year), *The Asbury Journal*

DEANS

Beeson International Center for Biblical Preaching and Church Leadership: Dr THOMAS F. TUMBLIN
E. Stanley Jones School of World Mission and Evangelism: Dr TERRY C. MUCK
School of Biblical Interpretation: Dr DAVID R. BAUER
School of Practical Theology: Dr ANNE K. GATOBU
School of Theology and Formation: Dr JAMES R. THOBABEN
School of Urban Ministries: Dr ZAIDA MALDONADO PÉREZ

ASBURY UNIVERSITY

One Macklem Dr., Wilmore, KY 40390
Telephone: (859) 858-3511
Fax: (859) 858-3921
E-mail: admissions@asbury.edu
Internet: www.asbury.edu
Founded 1890 as Kentucky Holiness College, present name and status 2010
Private control
Academic year: August to May
Campus in Florida
Pres.: Prof. Dr SANDRA C. GRAY
Provost and Chief Academic Officer: Dr JONATHAN S. KULAGA
Vice-Pres. for Business Affairs and Treas.: Dr CHARLIE D. FISKEAUX
Vice-Pres. for Institutional Advancement and Gen. Counsel: GREG SWANSON
Vice-Pres. for Student Devt: Dr MARK TROYER
Academic Dean: Prof. Dr BONNIE BANKER
Registrar: WILLIAM A. HALL
Dir of Library Services: MORGAN A. TRACY
Library of 150,000 vols
Number of teachers: 155
Number of students: 1,638
Publication: *The Ambassador*

DEANS

College of Arts and Sciences: Dr STEVE K. CLEMENTS
School of Communication Arts: Dr JAMES R. OWENS
School of Education: Dr VERNA J. LOWE
School of Graduate and Professional Studies: Dr JONATHAN S. KULAGA (acting)

BELLARMINE UNIVERSITY

2001 Newburg Rd, Louisville, KY 40205-0671
Telephone: (502) 272-8000
Fax: (502) 272-8033
E-mail: admissions@bellarmine.edu
Internet: www.bellarmine.edu
Founded 1950 as Bellarmine College, present name and status 2000
Private control
Academic year: August to May
Pres.: Dr JOSEPH J. MCGOWAN, JR
Provost: Dr DORIS A. TEGART
Vice-Pres. for Academic Affairs: Dr CAROLE C. PFEFFER
Vice-Pres. for Admin. and Finance: ROBERT L. ZIMLICH
Vice-Pres. for Admin. and Student Services: Dr ROBERT L. ZIMLICH
Vice-Pres. for Devt and Alumni Relations: GLENN F. KOSSE
Vice-Pres. for Enrolment Management: SEAN J. RYAN
Vice-Pres. for Student Affairs: Dr FRED W. RHODES
Dean of Graduate Admissions: Dr SARA Y. PETTINGILL
Dean of Students: HELEN-GRACE RYAN
Dean of Undergraduate Admissions: TIMOTHY A. STURGEON
Registrar: ANN OLSEN

Library Dir: Dr JOHN K. STEMMER
Library of 118,000 vols, 350 periodical subscriptions, 47,000 ebooks
Number of teachers: 150 (full-time)
Number of students: 3,249
Publication: *Bellarmine Magazine* (4 a year)

DEANS

Annsley Frazier Thornton School of Education: Prof. Dr ROBERT B. COOTER, JR
Bellarmine College: Dr WILLIAM E. FENTON
Donna and Allan Lansing School of Nursing and Health Sciences: Dr SUSAN H. DAVIS
Regional Center for Environmental Studies: Dr ROBERT W. KINGSOLVER
School of Communication: Dr LARA NEEDHAM
School of Continuing and Professional Studies: Dr MICHAEL D. MATTEI
W. Fielding Rubel School of Business: Prof. Dr DANIEL L. BAUER

BEREA COLLEGE

101 Chestnut St, Berea, KY 40404
Telephone: (859) 985-3000
Fax: (859) 985-3915
E-mail: askadmissions@berea.edu
Internet: www.berea.edu
Founded 1855 as dist. school, present name and status 1869
Private control
Academic year: August to May
Bachelor of arts, sciences in 32 majors
Pres.: Dr LYLE D. ROELOFFS
Academic Vice-Pres. and Dean of Faculty: Prof. Dr CHAD BERRY
Vice-Pres. for College Relations and Devt: MICHELLE JANSSEN
Vice-Pres. for Finance: JEFFREY AMBURGEY
Vice-Pres. for Operations and Sustainability: STEVE KARCHER
Dir of Library Services: ANNE CHASE
Library of 450,000 vols
Number of teachers: 144
Number of students: 1,500
Publications: *Apollon—The Undergraduate eJournal* (apollonejournal.org), *Berea College Magazine* (1 a year).

BRESCIA UNIVERSITY

717 Frederica St, Owensboro, KY 42301-3023
Telephone: (270) 685-3131
E-mail: admissions@brescia.edu
Internet: www.brescia.edu
Founded 1950, present name 1998
Private control
Academic year: August to May
Divs of fine arts, humanities, mathematics and natural science; schools of business, education, social and behavioural sciences
Pres.: Rev. LARRY HOSTETTER
Vice-Pres. and Dean of Student Devt: JAMES FITZPATRICK
Vice-Pres. for Academic Affairs: SIS. CHERYL CLEMONS
Vice-Pres. for Business and Finance: DALE CECIL
Vice-Pres. for Enrolment: CHRISTOPHER HOUK
Vice-Pres. for Institutional Advancement: TODD BROCK
Registrar: SIS. HELENA FISCHER
Dir of Library Services: SIS. JUDITH NELL RINEY
Number of teachers: 60
Number of students: 697

CAMPBELLSVILLE UNIVERSITY

1 University Dr., Campbellsville, KY 42718-2799
Telephone: (270) 789-5000

Fax: (270) 789-5050
E-mail: admissions@campbellsville.edu
Internet: www.campbellsville.edu
Founded 1906
Private control
Academic year: August to July
Pres.: Dr MICHAEL V. CARTER
Vice-Pres. for Academic Affairs: Dr FRANKLIN D. CHEATHAM
Vice-Pres. for Admissions and Student Services: DAVID WALTERS
Vice-Pres. for Church and External Relations: JOHN E. CHOWNING
Vice-Pres. for Devt: J. BENJI KELLY
Vice-Pres. for Finance and Admin.: OTTO TENNANT
Vice-Pres. for Regional and Professional Education: Dr H. KEITH SPEARS
Dean of Student Services: JOSH ANDERSON
Dir of Library Services: Dr JOHN RUSSELL BIRCH

Library of 95,000 vols
Number of teachers: 350
Number of students: 1,800

DEANS

Carver School of Social Work and Counselling: Dr DARLENE EASTRIDGE
College of Arts and Sciences: Dr MARY WILGUS
Porter and Bouvette School of Business and Economics: Prof. Dr PATRICIA H. COWHERD
School of Education: Dr BRENDA A. PRIDDY
School of Music: Dr J. ROBERT GADDIS
School of Nursing: Prof. Dr ROBERT J. WADE
School of Theology: Prof. Dr JOHN HURTGEN

CENTRE COLLEGE

600 W Walnut St, Danville, KY 40422
Telephone: (859) 238-5200
Fax: (859) 236-6226
E-mail: admission@centre.edu
Internet: www.centre.edu
Founded 1819
Private control
Academic year: August to May
Major courses incl. anthropology, sociology art history, art (studio), behavioural neuroscience, biochemistry and molecular biology, biology, chemical physics, chemistry, classical studies, computer science, dramatic arts, economics, education, English, financial economics, French, German studies, govt, history, int. studies, mathematics, music, philosophy, physics, psychology, religion, Spanish
Pres.: JOHN ALLEN ROUSH
Vice-Pres. for Academic Affairs and Dean of College: Prof. Dr STEPHANIE L. FABRITIUS
Vice-Pres. and Dean of Student Life: RANDY HAYS
Vice-Pres. for College Relations: Dr RICHARD W. TROLLINGER
Vice-Pres. for Finance and Treas.: JOHN E. CUNY
Dean of Admission and Student Financial Planning: ROBERT M. NESMITH
Registrar: TIMOTHY P. CULHAN
Library Dir: STANLEY R. CAMPBELL

Library of 375,000 vols, 28,000 e-journals and 32,000 e-books
Number of teachers: 120
Number of students: 1,300

CLEAR CREEK BAPTIST BIBLE COLLEGE

300 Clear Creek Rd, Pineville, KY 40977
Telephone: (606) 337-3196
Fax: (606) 337-2372
E-mail: ccbbc@ccbbc.edu
Internet: www.ccbbc.edu

Founded 1926 as Clear Creek Mountain Springs, Inc., present name and status 1986
Private control
Academic year: August to May
Offers bachelor in arts in Church ministries and leadership, missions and Evangelism, pastoral ministry
Pres.: Dr DONNIE FOX
Academic Dean: Prof. Dr MALCOLM HESTER
Dean of Institutional Advancement: Dr JAY SULFRIDGE
Dean of Student Affairs: DAVID WADE
Dir of Admissions: BILLY HOWELL
Registrar: BRENDA HESTER
Dir of Library Services: MARGE CUMMINGS
Library of 37,000 vols, 42,000 monographs, 230 print periodicals
Number of teachers: 22
Number of students: 187

EASTERN KENTUCKY UNIVERSITY

521 Lancaster Ave, Richmond, KY 40475
Telephone: (859) 622-1000
Fax: (859) 622-1020
E-mail: admissions@eku.edu
Internet: www.eku.edu
Founded 1906 as Eastern Kentucky State Normal School, present name and status 1966
State control
Academic year: August to May
Pres.: Dr DOUG WHITLOCK
Provost and Vice-Pres. for Academic Affairs: Dr JANNA VICE
Vice-Pres. for Administration: JAMES STREET
Vice-Pres. for Enrolment Management, Marketing and Univ. Relations: LIBBY WACHTEL (acting)
Vice-Pres. for Financial Affairs: BARRY POYNTER
Vice-Pres. for Student Affairs: Dr JAMES CONNEELY
Vice-Pres. for Univ. Advancement: JOSEPH FOSTER
Exec. Dir of Govt Relations: JIM CLARK
Registrar: TINA DAVIS
Dean of Libraries: BETINA GARDNER
Library of 837,945 vols, 3,565 current periodicals, 1,410,522 current periodicals
Number of teachers: 667 (full-time)
Number of students: 16,567
Publication: *The Eastern Magazine*

DEANS

College of Arts and Sciences: Dr JOHN WADE
College of Business and Technology: Prof. Dr ROBERT B. ROGOW
College of Education: Dr BILL PHILIPS
College of Health Sciences: Dr DEBORAH WHITEHOUSE (acting)
College of Justice and Safety: Dr ALLEN AULT

FRONTIER NURSING UNIVERSITY

POB 528, 195 School St, Hyden, KY 41749
Telephone: (606) 672-2312
Fax: (606) 672-3776
E-mail: fnu@frontier.edu
Internet: www.frontierschool.edu
Founded 1939 as Frontier Graduate School of Midwifery, present name and status 2011
Private control
Offers master of science in nursing
Pres. and Dean: SUSAN STONE
Assoc. Dean of Academic Affairs: JOYCE KNESTRICK
Assoc. Dean of Family Nursing: JULIE MARFELL
Assoc. Dean of Midwifery and Women's Health: SUZAN ULRICH
Assoc. Dean of Research: JANET ENGSTROM

Dir of Library Services: BILLIE ANNE GEBB.

GEORGETOWN COLLEGE

400 East College St, Georgetown, KY 40324-1696
Telephone: (502) 863-8000
Fax: (502) 868-8891
E-mail: president@georgetowncollege.edu
Internet: www.georgetowncollege.edu
Founded 1787, present status 1829
Offers bachelors of arts, music, music education, science; master of arts in education
Private control
Academic year: July to June
Pres.: Dr WILLIAM H. CROUCH, JR
Provost and Academic Dean: Dr ROSEMARY A. ALLEN
Vice-Pres., Chief Financial Officer and Treas.: JAMES A. MOAK, JR
Vice-Pres. for Enrolment Management: GARVEL KINDRICK
Vice-Pres. for Institutional Advancement: ROY LOWDENBACK
Vice-Pres. for Student Life and Dean of Students: Dr TODD GAMBILL
Dean of Education: YOLANDA CARTER
Registrar: WINNIE BRATCHER
Library Dir: SUSAN MARTIN
Library of 185,267 vols, 733 current periodicals, 4,064 audiovisual items
Number of teachers: 161 (116 full-time, 45 part-time)
Number of students: 1,818

KENTUCKY CHRISTIAN UNIVERSITY

100 Academic Parkway, Grayson, KY 41143-2205
Telephone: (606) 474-3000
Fax: (606) 474-3155
E-mail: knights@kcu.edu
Internet: www.kcu.edu
Founded 1919 as Christian Normal Institute, present name and status 2004
Private control
Academic year: August to May
Chancellor: Dr KEITH P. KEERAN
Pres.: Dr JEFFREY K. METCALF
Exec. Vice-Pres.: JOHN L. DUNDON
Sr Vice-Pres. and Provost: Dr JEFF METCALF
Vice-Pres. for Academic Affairs: Dr PERRY STEPP
Vice-Pres. for Business and Finance: BILL BONDURANT
Vice-Pres. for Univ. Advancement: LARRY MONROE
Dean of Student Services: RON ARNETT
Dir of Admissions: SHEREE GREER
Registrar: ANDREA STAMPER
Library Dir: NAULAYNE ENDERS
Library of 100,000 vols, 200 print journals, 100,000 e-books, 17,000 e-journal titles
Number of teachers: 32
Number of students: 580

DEANS

Graduate School: DAVID FIENSY
Keeran School of Education: Dr KAREN FORD
Sack School of Bible and Ministry: Prof. Dr DAVID FIENSY
School of Arts and Sciences: Dr JOHN WINELAND
School of Business: Prof. Dr TIM NISCHAN
School of Music: Dr WES GOLIGHTLY
School of Social Work and Human Services: MARGARET MCLAUGHLIN
Yancey School of Nursing: ABIGAIL LEIGH BECK

KENTUCKY MOUNTAIN BIBLE COLLEGE

POB 10, Vancleve, KY 41385-0010
855 Kentucky Highway 541, Vancleve, KY 41339
Telephone: (606) 693-5000
Fax: (888) 742-1124
E-mail: kmbc@kmbc.edu
Internet: www.kmbc.edu

Founded 1931 as Kentucky Mountain Bible Institute; present name and status 1989
Private control
Academic year: August to May

Study programmes incl. Christian Education, Christian Ministry, Communication, Elementary Education, Ministerial, Missions, Music Ministry, Nursing
Pres.: Dr PHILIP SPEAS
Exec. Vice-Pres. and Vice-Pres. for Academic Affairs: THOMAS H. LORIMER
Vice-Pres. for Business Affairs: DOUG DUNN
Vice-Pres. for Devt: Dr JOHN ELDON NEIHOF
Dean of Students: JAMES NELSON
Registrar: RICHARD ENGLEHARDT
Librarian: PATRICIA ANN BOWEN

Library of 30,000 vols
Number of teachers: 16
Number of students: 85

KENTUCKY STATE UNIVERSITY

400 East Main St, Frankfort, KY 40601
Telephone: (502) 597-6000
E-mail: admissions@kysu.edu
Internet: www.kysu.edu

Founded 1886 as State Normal School for Colored Persons, present name and status 1972
State control
Academic year: August to May

Pres.: Dr MARY EVANS SIAS
Vice-Pres. for Academic Affairs and Interim Provost: Dr MAC A. STEWART
Vice-Pres. for Admin., External Relations and Devt: HINFRED MCDUFFIE
Vice-Pres. for Finance and Business Affairs: ALICE BURSEY JOHNSON
Vice-Pres. for Student Affairs and Enrolment Management: Dr RUBYE WILLIAM JONES
Gen. Counsel: LORI A. DAVIS
Registrar: JOHN B. MARTIN
Dir of Libraries: SHEILA A. STUCKEY

Library of 700,000 vols
Number of teachers: 149
Number of students: 2,315

DEANS

College of Agriculture, Food Science and Sustainable Systems: Dr TEFERI TSEGAYE
College of Arts, Social Sciences and Interdisciplinary Studies: Dr SAM O. OLEKA
College of Business and Computer Science: Dr TSEHAI ALEMAYEHU
College of Mathematics, Science, Technology and Health: Dr CHARLES BENNETT
College of Professional Studies: Dr GASHAW LAKE

KENTUCKY WESLEYAN COLLEGE

3000 Frederica St, Owensboro, KY 42301
Telephone: (270) 926-3111
Fax: (270) 926-3196
E-mail: admissions@kwc.edu
Internet: www.kwc.edu

Founded 1866, present status 1947
Private control
Academic year: August to May

Depts of behavioural sciences, biology and zoology, centre for business studies, chemistry, cross disciplinary, communication arts, education, English, history and political science, mathematics and physics, modern languages, pre-professional programmes, kinesiology and health promotion, religion and philosophy
Pres.: Prof. Dr CRAIG TURNER
Vice-Pres. for Academic Affairs and Dean of College: Dr PAULA DEHN
Vice-Pres. for External Affairs: RICHARD BOROWSKI
Vice-Pres. for Finance and Treas.: CINDRA K. STIFF
Vice-Pres. for Student Services: SCOTT KRAMER
Dir of Admissions: RASHAD SMITH
Registrar: JENNIFER VAUGHAN
Dir of Library: PATRICIA MCFARLING

Library of 150,000 vols incl. books, periodicals, govt documents, audiovisual materials
Number of teachers: 69
Number of students: 802

LEXINGTON THEOLOGICAL SEMINARY

631 South Limestone St, Lexington, KY 40508
Telephone: (859) 252-0361
Fax: (859) 281-6042
E-mail: admissions@lextheo.edu
Internet: www.lextheo.edu

Founded 1865 as College of the Bible, present name 1965
Private control

Offers masters programmes in divinity, arts, pastoral studies, ministry
Pres.: CHARISSE GILLETT
Vice-Pres. for Academic Affairs: Prof. Dr RICH WEIS
Vice-Pres. for Advancement: JAMES M. WRAY, JR
Chief Financial Officer: LAURA DAVIS
Dir of Admissions: ERIN CASH
Registrar: WINDY KIDD
Librarian: DOLORES YILIBUW

Library of 165,000 vols, 200 periodicals
Number of teachers: 24
Number of students: 56
Publication: *Lexington Theological Quarterly* (4 a year).

LINDSEY WILSON COLLEGE

210 Lindsey Wilson St, Columbia, KY 42728
Telephone: (270) 384-2126
Fax: (270) 384-8200
E-mail: info@lindsey.edu
Internet: www.lindsey.edu

Founded 1903 as Lindsey Wilson Training School; present name 1923, present status 1986
Private control
Academic year: August to May

Liberal arts college; Kentucky campuses: Ashland, Big Stone Gap, Cincinnati, Columbia, Cumberland, Danville, Elizabethtown, Florence, Gallatin, Hazard, Henderson, Hilsboro, Hopkinsville, Lexington, Mount Gay, London, Louisville, Madisonville, Maysville, Paducah, Prestonsburg, Radcliff, WythevilleScottsville, Shelbyville and Somerset; Virginia campuses: Wytheville, Richlands
Pres.: WILLIAM T. LUCKEY, JR
Chancellor: JOHN B. BEGLEY
Vice-Pres. for Academic Affairs: BETTIE STARR
Vice-Pres. for Admin. and Finance: ROGER DRAKE
Vice-Pres. for Development: KEVIN A. THOMPSON
Vice-Pres. for Educational Outreach and Student Financial Services: DENISE FUDGE

Vice-Pres. for Student Services and Enrolment Management: L. DEAN ADAMS
Dean of Admissions: TRACI POOLER
Dean of Students: CHRISTOPHER SCHMIDT
Registrar: SUE COOMER
Library Dir: PHILIP HANNA

Library of 500,000 vols
Number of teachers: 107
Number of students: 2,310

LOUISVILLE PRESBYTERIAN THEOLOGICAL SEMINARY

1044 Alta Vista Rd, Louisville, KY 40205
Telephone: (502) 895-3411
Fax: (502) 895-1096
E-mail: admissions@lpts.edu
Internet: www.lpts.edu

Founded 1901 by merger of Danville Theological Seminary and Louisville Presbyterian Seminary
Private control
Academic year: August to May

Programmes offered incl. doctor of ministry, master of arts in spirituality, master of divinity
Pres.: Prof. Dr MICHAEL JINKINS
Vice-Pres. for Academic Affairs and Dean of Seminary: Dr SUSAN R. GARRETT
Vice-Pres. for Finance and Chief Financial Officer: PATRICK A. CECIL
Dean of Students: SUSAN R. GARRETT
Dir of Admissions and Recruitment: CHERI HARPER
Registrar: DAVID GRAY
Dir of Library and Information Technology Services: Prof. ANGELA MORRIS (acting)

Library of 175,000 vols, 12,000 microforms and 7,000 audiovisual items
Number of teachers: 21
Number of students: 230

PROFESSORS

ADENEY, F., Evangelism and Global Mission
BOS, J., Bible and Old Testament
BROGDON, L., New Testament and Black Church Studies
COOK, C., Pastoral Care and Counselling
CRAIGO-SNELL, S., Theology
ELWOOD, C., Historical Theology
GARRETT, S., New Testament
HESTER, D., Pastoral Theology
JINKINS, M., Theology
JOHNSON, K., Historical Theology and Church History
KIRKPATRICK, C., Ecumenical Studies and Global Ministries
MUMFORD, D., Homiletics
PAUW, A., Doctrinal Theology
REISTROFFER, D., Ministry
SOARDS, M., New Testament
TOWNSEND, L., Pastoral Ministry and Pastoral Care and Counselling
WALKER, E. J., Pastoral Care and Counseling
WIGGER, J., Christian Education
WILLIAMSON, S., Theological Ethics

MID-CONTINENT UNIVERSITY

99 E Powell Rd, Mayfield, KY 42066
Telephone: (270) 247-8521
Fax: (270) 247-3115
E-mail: mcc@midcontinent.edu
Internet: www.midcontinent.edu

Founded 1949, present name and status 2004
Private control
Academic year: August to July

Pres.: Dr ROBERT J. IMHOFF
Exec. Vice-Pres.: CHARLES W. FORD
Vice-Pres. for Academic Affairs: Prof. Dr STEPHEN D. WILSON
Vice-Pres. for Devt: Dr LARRY STEWART
Vice-Pres. for Finance and Admin.: ANDREW STRATTON

Dean of Students and Int. Affairs: KOBY MILLER
Dir of Admissions: CHRISTOPHER AUSTIN
Registrar: YVONNE YATES
Library Dean: Dr RAY LYTLE
Library of 40,000 vols, 200 periodicals, 1,600 audiovisual items
Number of students: 2,000

DEANS

Baptist College of Arts and Sciences: Dr JAMIE SUMMERVILLE
James W. Cecil Baptist College of the Bible: Dr LARRY ORANGE

MIDWAY COLLEGE

512 East Stephens St, Midway, KY 40347
Telephone: (859) 846-4421
Fax: (859) 846-5817
Internet: www.midway.edu
Founded 1847 as Kentucky Female Orphan School; present name 1978
Private control
Academic year: August to May
Pres.: Dr WILLIAM B. DRAKE, JR
Vice-Pres. for Academic Affairs: (vacant)
Vice-Pres. for Business Affairs: LYEN CREWS
Vice-Pres. for College Relations and Devt: JUDY MARCUM
Vice-Pres. and Dean of Enrollment Management: Dr JAMES WOMBLES
Vice-Pres. and Assoc. Dean of School for Career Devt: Dr WILLIAM BROWN
Provost and Dean of Women's College: SARAH H. LAWS
Registrar: P. EDWARD PRESLER
Dir of Library Services: CATHY REILENDER
Number of teachers: 48 (full-time)
Number of students: 1,200

MOREHEAD STATE UNIVERSITY

150 University Blvd, Morehead, KY 40351
Telephone: (606) 783-2221
Fax: (606) 783-2678
E-mail: admissions@moreheadstate.edu
Internet: www.moreheadstate.edu
Founded 1887 as Morehead Normal School, present name and status 1966
State control
Academic year: August to May
Pres.: Dr WAYNE D. ANDREWS
Provost and Vice-Pres. for Academic Affairs: KARLA HUGHES
Vice-Pres. for Admin. and Fiscal Services: MICHAEL R. WALTERS
Vice-Pres. for Devt: BARBARA A. ENDER
Vice-Pres. for Planning and Budgets: BETH G. PATRICK
Vice-Pres. for Student Life: MADONNA WEATHERS
Vice-Pres. for Univ. Advancement: JAMES SHAW
Registrar: ROSLYN PERRY
Dean of Library Services: Dr DAVID GREGORY (acting)
Library: 5m. vols, 2,500 periodicals
Number of teachers: 440 (320 full-time, 120 part-time)
Number of students: 10,000
Publication: Inscape (2 a year)

DEANS

Caudill College of Arts, Humanities and Social Sciences: Dr M. SCOTT MCBRIDE
College of Business and Public Affairs: Dr ROBERT ALBERT
College of Education: Dr CATHY GUNN
College of Science and Technology: Dr ROGER MCNEIL
Institute for Regional Analysis and Public Policy: Dr DAVID RUDY

MURRAY STATE UNIVERSITY

102 Curris Centre, Murray, KY 42071
Telephone: (270) 809-3011
Fax: (270) 809-3413
E-mail: msu.admissions@murraystate.edu
Internet: www.murraystate.edu
Founded 1922
State control
Language of instruction: English
Academic year: August to May
Pres.: Dr RANDY J. DUNN
Provost and Vice-Pres. for Academic Affairs: Prof. Dr BONNIE S. HIGGINSON
Vice-Pres. for Finance and Admin. Services: THOMAS W. DENTON
Vice-Pres. for Institutional Advancement: JAMES F. CARTER
Vice-Pres. for Student Affairs: Dr DONALD E. ROBERTSON
Gen. Counsel: JOHN P. RALL
Dean of Libraries: ADAM L. MURRAY
Library of 401,663 vols of monographs, 124,147 vols of periodicals, 215,649 govt documents
Number of teachers: 578 (421 full-time, 157 part-time)
Number of students: 10,623 (8,664 undergraduate, 1,959 graduate)
Publications: Blue and Gold (alumni magazine), Chrysalis, JMC Journal, New Madrid, Notations

DEANS

Academic Outreach and Continuing Education: Dr BRIAN VAN HORN
Arthur J. Bauernfeind College of Business: Dr TIMOTHY S. TODD
College of Education: Dr RENEE CAMPOY
College of Health Sciences and Human Services: Dr SUSAN MULLER
College of Humanities and Fine Arts: Dr TED BROWN
College of Science, Engineering and Technology: Dr STEPHEN H. COBB
Hutson School of Agriculture: Dr TONY BRANNON
School of Nursing: Dr MARCIA B. HOBBS

NORTHERN KENTUCKY UNIVERSITY

Nunn Dr., Highland Heights, KY 41099
Telephone: (859) 572-5100
Fax: (859) 572-5566
E-mail: gradprog@nku.edu
Internet: www.nku.edu
Founded 1968 as Northern Kentucky State College; present name 1976, present status 1973
State control
Academic year: August to May
Pres.: Dr JAMES C. VOTRUBA
Vice-Pres. for Academic Affairs and Provost: Dr GAIL W. WELLS
Vice-Pres. for Admin. and Financeand Treas.: KENNETH H. RAMEY
Vice-Pres. for Legal Affairs and Gen. Counsel: SARA L. SIDEBOTTOM
Vice-Pres. for Student Affairs: Dr LISA B. RHINE
Vice-Pres. for Univ. Advancement: GERARD A. ST AMAND
Dean of Students: Dr JEFFREY N. WAPLE
Registrar: KIMBERLY K. TAYLOR
Assoc. Provost of Libraries: ARNE ALMQUIST
Library of 814,318 vols, 37,037 e-books
Number of teachers: 530 (full-time)
Number of students: 15,748 (10,712 full-time, 5,036 part-time)
Publication: Northern (2 a year)

DEANS

College of Arts and Sciences: Prof. Dr SAMUEL J. ZACHARY

College of Education and Human Services: MARK WASICSKO
College of Health Professions: Prof. Dr DENISE ROBINSON
College of Informatics: Dr KEVIN KIRBY
Haile/US Bank College of Business: Prof. Dr RICHARD H. KOLBE
Salmon P. Chase College of Law: Prof. Dr DENNIS HONABACH

SAINT CATHARINE COLLEGE

2735 Bardstown Rd, St Catharine, KY 40061
Telephone: (859) 336-5082
E-mail: admissions@sccky.edu
Internet: www.sccky.edu
Founded 1931
Private control
Pres.: WILLIAM D. HUSTON
Exec. Vice-Pres.: ROGER MARCUM
Vice-Pres. for Academic Affairs: Dr DON GILES
Vice-Pres. for Advancement: JENNA COPPLE
Vice-Pres. for Enrolment Management and Dean of Students: Dr VICTORIA GUTHRIE
Vice-Pres. for Finance and Admin.: GARY ROBINSON
Registrar: ANITA FOSTER
Dir of Admissions: PAUL PRESTA
Dir of Library Services: ILONA BURDETTE
Library of 22,000 vols, 100 journals and periodicals, 1,000 audiovisual items
Number of students: 850

DEANS

Graduate School: Dr SIS. MARY ANGELA SHAUGHNESSY
School of Arts and Sciences: Rev. Dr ROBERT SLOCUM
School of Health and Human Sciences: Dr HARRY NICKENS
School of Professional Studies: Dr DAVID ARNOLD

SOUTHERN BAPTIST THEOLOGICAL SEMINARY

2825 Lexington Rd, Louisville, KY 40280
Telephone: (502) 897-4011
Fax: (502) 899-1770
E-mail: admissions@sbts.edu
Internet: www.sbts.edu
Founded 1859
Private control
Academic year: August to May
Pres.: Prof. Dr R. ALBERT MOHLER, JR
Sr Vice-Pres. for Academic Admin.: Dr RUSSELL D. MOORE
Sr Vice-Pres. for Institutional Admin.: DAN S. DUMAS
Sr Vice-Pres. for Institutional Advancement: JASON K. ALLEN
Vice-Pres. for Academic Innovation: Dr RANDY L. STINSON
Vice-Pres. for Business Services: R. CRAIG PARKER
Vice-Pres. for Extension Education: Prof. Dr MARK T. COPPENGER
Vice-Pres. for Research and Assessment: Prof. Dr GREGORY A. WILLS
Vice-Pres. for Student Services: DANIEL E. HATFIELD
Dean of Students: LAWRENCE A. SMITH
Registrar: NORMAN CHUNG
Librarian and Assoc. Vice-Pres. for Academic Resources: BRUCE L. KEISLING
Library: 1m. vols incl. 384,500 vols of books, periodicals, audiovisual items
Number of teachers: 130
Number of students: 2,890
Publications: Southern Baptist Journal of Theology (4 a year), Southern Seminary Magazine (4 a year)

DEANS

Billy Graham School of Missions and Evangelism: Dr ZANE G. PRATT
Boyce College: Dr DAN DeWITT
School of Church Ministries: Dr RANDY L. STINSON
School of Theology: Prof. Dr RUSSELL D. MOORE

SPALDING UNIVERSITY

845 South Third St, Louisville, KY 40203
Telephone: (502) 585-9911
Fax: (502) 585-7158
E-mail: admissions@spalding.edu
Internet: www.spalding.edu
Founded 1814, present name and status 1984
Private control
Academic year: July to June
Pres.: Dr TORI MURDEN McCLURE
Provost: Prof. Dr LEWIS RANDY STRICKLAND
Vice-Pres. for Univ. Advancement: JEFFREY L. ASHLEY
Dean of Enrolment Management: CHRISTOPHER HART
Dean of Students, Student Devt and Campus Life: Dr RICHARD HUDSON
Dir of Admissions: PATRICIA GOODMAN
Chief Financial Officer: MARK HOHMANN
Registrar: JENNIFER GOHMANN
Library Dir: JACQUELINE YOUNG
Library of 200,000 vols, 22,000 bound journals, 450 current periodical subscriptions
Number of teachers: 250
Number of students: 2,400

DEANS

College of Business and Communication: Dr DIANE TOBIN
College of Education: Dr BEVERLY KEEPERS
College of Health and Natural Sciences: JOANNE BERRYMAN
College of Social Sciences and Humanities: Dr JOHN JAMES

SULLIVAN UNIVERSITY

3101 Bardstown Rd, Louisville, KY 40205
Telephone: (502) 456-6505
Fax: (502) 454-4880
E-mail: admissions@sullivan.edu
Internet: www.sullivan.edu
Founded 1962 as Sullivan Business College, present name and status 2000
Private control
Academic year: September to September (4 quarters)
Campuses in Fort Knox, Lexington
Chancellor: A. R. SULLIVAN
Pres.: Dr GLENN D. SULLIVAN
Exec. Vice-Pres.: Dr BILL NOEL
Sr Vice-Pres.: TOM DAVISSON
Vice-Pres. for Academic Affairs and Chief Academic Officer: JAY MARR
Vice-Pres. for Enrolment Management: JIM CRICK
Vice-Pres. for Finance: SHELTON BRIDGES
Vice-Pres. for Student Services and Dean of Students: CHRIS ERNST
Dean of Graduate School: Prof. Dr ERIC S. HARTER
Registrar: LESLEY CASH
Dir of Libraries: Prof. CHARLES BROWN
Library of 20,000 vols
Number of teachers: 38
Number of students: 2,001

DEANS

College of Business and Admin.: KEN MORAN
College of Information and Computer Technology: VIRGINIA GODWIN
College of Pharmacy: Dr HIEU TRAN
General Education: MARGIE GALLO

Institute for Legal Studies: NICK RIGGS
National Center for Hospitality Studies: KEITH LERNE
School of Accountancy: TIM SWENSON

THOMAS MORE COLLEGE

333 Thomas More Parkway, Crestview Hills, KY 41017-3495
Telephone: (859) 341-5800
Fax: (859) 344-3444
E-mail: admissions@thomasmore.edu
Internet: www.thomasmore.edu
Founded 1921 as Villa Madonna College, present name 1968
Private control
Academic year: June to May
Programmes of study incl. accountancy, art, biology, business administration, chemistry, communication, computer information systems, criminal justice, economics, education, English, environmental science, foreign languages, forensic science, gerontology, history, humanities, international studies, mathematics, medical laboratory science, music, nursing, philosophy, physics, political science, pre-engineering, pre-legal studies, pre-med, pre-veterinary, psychology, sociology, sports and entertainment marketing, theatre, theology, web design
Pres.: Sis. MARGARET A. STALLMEYER
Vice-Pres. for Academic Affairs: Dr BRADLEY BIELSKI
Vice-Pres. for Finance: PETER W. AAMODT
Vice-Pres. for Institutional Advancement: CATHY L. SILVERS
Vice-Pres. for Student Services: MATTHEW H. WEBSTER
Dean of Students: EBONY GRIGGS-GRIFFIN
Registrar: KELLY GOYETTE
Dir of Library: JAMES M. McKELLOGG
Library of 112,665 vols
Number of teachers: 149 (74 full-time, 75 part-time)
Number of students: 1,832

TRANSYLVANIA UNIVERSITY

300 North Broadway, Lexington, KY 40508-1797
Telephone: (859) 233-8300
Fax: (859) 233-8797
E-mail: admissions@transy.edu
Internet: www.transy.edu
Founded 1780 as Transylvania Seminary, present name and status 1908
Private control
Academic year: August to July
Academic divs incl. business and economics, education, physical education and exercise science, fine arts, humanities, natural sciences and mathematics, social sciences
Pres.: Dr R. OWEN WILLIAMS
Vice-Pres. and Dean of the College: WILLIAM F. POLLARD
Vice-Pres. for Advancement: KIRK PURDOM
Vice-Pres. for Finance and Business: MARC A. MATHEWS
Vice-Pres. for Enrolment and Dean of Admissions: BRADLEY L GOAN
Vice-Pres. for Student Affairs and Dean of Students: MICHAEL K. VETTER
Registrar: JIM MONAGHAN MILLS
Dir of Library: SUSAN M. BROWN
Library of 130,000 vols
Number of teachers: 96
Number of students: 1,100

UNION COLLEGE

310 College St, Barbourville, KY 40906-1499
Telephone: (606) 546-4151
Fax: (606) 546-1217

Internet: www.unionky.edu
Founded 1795
Private control
Academic year: July to June
Depts of business, educational studies, English and communications, history, religious studies, languages, fine and performing arts, natural sciences, nursing and health sciences, psychology, social and behavioural sciences, wellness, human performances and recreation management
Pres.: Dr THOMAS J. McFARLAND (acting)
Academic Dean: Dr LARRY INKSTER (acting)
Vice-Pres. for Advancement: DENISE WAINSCOTT
Vice-Pres. for Business and Financial Services: STEVE HOSKINS
Dean of Admissions and Financial Aid: ANDRE WASHINGTON
Dean of Education: Dr ROBERT SWANSON
Dean of Enrolment Management: JERRY JACKSON
Dean of Student Life: DEBBIE D'ANNA
Registrar: KATHY WEBB
Dir of Library Services: TARA L. COOPER
Library of 162,646 vols, 439,794 microforms
Number of teachers: 213
Number of students: 2,133

UNIVERSITY OF KENTUCKY

Lexington, KY 40506
Telephone: (859) 257-9000
Fax: (859) 257-3823
E-mail: admissions@uky.edu
Internet: www.uky.edu
Founded 1865 as Agricultural and Mechanical College of Kentucky Univ., present name 1916
State control
Academic year: August to May
Pres.: Dr ELI CAPILOUTO
Provost: KUMBLE R. SUBBASWAMY (acting)
Exec. Vice-Pres. for Devt: D. MICHAEL RICHEY
Exec. Vice-Pres. for Finance and Admin.: FRANK A. BUTLER
Vice-Pres. for Facilities Management: BOB WISEMAN
Vice-Pres. for Institutional Diversity: JUDY JACKSON
Vice-Pres. for Institutional Research, Planning and Effectiveness: HEIDI ANDERSON
Vice-Pres. for Student Affairs: ROBERT C. MOCK, JR
Vice-Pres. for Univ. Relations: THOMAS W. HARRIS
Gen. Counsel: BARBARA W. JONES (acting)
Chief Information Officer: VINCE J. KELLEN
Dir of Admissions and Registrar: DONALD E. WITT
Dean of Libraries: TERRY BIRDWHISTELL
Library: see Libraries and Archives
Number of teachers: 2,165 full-time
Number of students: 27,108
Publications: *Alzheimer's Disease Review* (4 a year), *Colloquia Germanica* (4 a year), *Disclosure (Lexington)* (1 a year), *Growth and Change* (urban and regional policy, 4 a year), *Kentucky Law Journal* (4 a year), *Kentucky Review* (2 a year), *L'Esprit Createur* (4 a year), *Retiarius: commentarii periodici Latini* (1 a year)

DEANS

College of Agriculture: Dr M. SCOTT SMITH
College of Arts and Sciences: Prof. Dr MARK LAWRENCE KORNBLUH
College of Communications and Information Studies: Dr DAN O'HAIR
College of Dentistry: Dr SHARON P. TURNER
College of Design: MICHAEL A. SPEAKS
College of Education: Prof. Dr MARY JOHN O'HAIR

College of Engineering: Dr THOMAS W. LESTER
College of Fine Arts: Dr MICHAEL S. TICK
College of Health Sciences: Dr SHARON R. STEWART
College of Law: Prof. DAVID A. BRENNEN
College of Medicine: Dr FREDERICK C. DE BEER
College of Nursing: Prof. Dr JANE M. KIRSCHLING
College of Pharmacy: Prof. Dr TIMOTHY S. TRACY
College of Public Health: Dr STEPHEN W. WYATT
College of Social Work: Prof. Dr JAMES P. ADAMS, JR
Gatton College of Business and Economics: Prof. Dr DAVID W. BLACKWELL
Graduate School: JEANNINE BLACKWELL

UNIVERSITY OF LOUISVILLE

2301 S Third St, Louisville, KY 40292
Telephone: (502) 852-5555
Fax: (502) 852-7160
E-mail: admitme@louisville.edu
Internet: www.louisville.edu
Founded 1798 as Jefferson Seminary, present name and status 1846
State control
Academic year: August to May
Pres.: Dr JAMES R. RAMSEY
Provost: Dr SHIRLEY C. WILLIHNGANZ (acting)
Vice-Pres. for External Affairs: Dr DAN HALL
Vice-Pres. for Finance: MICHAEL J. CURTIN
Exec. Vice-Pres. for Research and Innovation: Dr WILLIAM M. PIERCE, JR
Vice-Pres. for Student Affairs: Dr TOM JACKSON, JR (acting)
Vice-Pres. for Univ. Advancement: A. KEITH INMAN
Registrar: SCOTT BURKS (acting)
Dean of Univ. Libraries: Prof. ROBERT FOX (acting)
Library of 2,275,328 vols, 30,650 e-books, 10,814 audiovisual items, 2,230,500 microforms, 12,118 current serial titles
Number of teachers: 2,319 (1,659 full-time, 660 part-time)
Number of students: 22,249 (16,924 full-time, 5,325 part-time)
Publications: The Cardinal, Inside U of L

DEANS

College of Arts and Sciences: Prof. Dr J. BLAINE HUDSON
College of Business: R. CHARLES MOYER
College of Education and Human Devt: Dr W. BLAKE HASELTON
J. B. Speed School of Engineering: Dr NEVILLE G. PINTO
Louis D. Brandeis School of Law: Prof. JIM CHEN
Raymond A. Kent School of Social Work: TERRY L. SINGER
School of Dentistry: Dr JOHN J. SAUK
School of Interdisciplinary and Graduate Studies: Dr BETH A. BOEHM
School of Medicine: Dr TONI GANZEL
School of Music: Prof. Dr CHRISTOPHER P. DOANE
School of Nursing: Prof. Dr MARCIA J. HERN
School of Public Health and Information Sciences: Dr RICHARD D. CLOVER (acting)

UNIVERSITY OF PIKEVILLE

147 Sycamore St, Pikeville, KY 41501
Telephone: (606) 218-5250
Fax: (606) 218-5269
Internet: www.upike.edu
Founded 1889, present name and status 2011
Private control
Academic year: August to July

Pres.: Dr PAUL E. PATTON
Vice-Pres. for Academic Affairs: THOMAS R. HESS
Vice-Pres. for Devt: Dr ERIC A. BECHER
Vice-Pres. for Finance and Business Affairs: DOUGLAS LANGE
Vice-Pres. for Student Services and Dean of Students: RONALD D. DAMRON
Dir of Admissions: GARY JUSTICE
Registrar: GIA POTTER
Library Dir: KAREN S. EVANS
Library of 72,673 vols
Number of teachers: 62
Number of students: 1,510 (1,201 undergraduate, 309 postgraduate)

DEANS

College of Arts and Science: THOMAS R. HESS
Kentucky College of Osteopathic Medicine: Dr BOYD R. BUSER

UNIVERSITY OF THE CUMBERLANDS

6191 College Station Dr., Williamsburg, KY 40769
Telephone: (606) 549-2200
Fax: (606) 539-4534
E-mail: admiss@ucumberlands.edu
Internet: www.ucumberlands.edu
Founded 1889 as Williamsburg Institute, present name and status 2005
Private control
Academic year: August to August
Areas of study incl. business administration, education, public relations, religion, science, theatre arts and journalism
Pres.: JIM TAYLOR
Vice-Pres. for Academic Affairs: Dr LARRY COCKRUM
Vice-Pres. for Business Services: STEVE MORRIS
Vice-Pres. for Institutional Advancement: SUE WAKE
Vice-Pres. for Student Services: Dr MICHAEL COLGROVE
Registrar: CHUCK DUPIER
Dir of the Library: JANICE WREN
Library of 155,000 vols
Number of teachers: 112
Number of students: 3,300 (1,746 undergraduate, 1,554 graduate)

WESTERN KENTUCKY UNIVERSITY

1906 College Heights Blvd, Bowling Green, KY 42101
Telephone: (270) 745-0111
Fax: (270) 745-4830
E-mail: wku@wku.edu
Internet: www.wku.edu
Founded 1907, present name and status 1966
State control
Academic year: August to July
Pres.: Dr GARY A. RANSDELL
Provost and Vice-Pres. for Academic Affairs: Dr A. GORDON EMSLIE
Vice-Pres. for Devt and Alumni Relations: KATHRYN R. COSTELLO
Vice-Pres. for Finance and Admin.: K. ANN MEAD
Vice-Pres. for Information Technology: Dr ROBERT OWEN
Vice-Pres. for Institutional Advancement: THOMAS S. HILES
Vice-Pres. for Research: Dr GORDON C. BAYLIS
Vice-Pres. for Student Affairs: HOWARD BAILEY
Registrar: FREIDA EGGLETON
Dir of Admissions: SCOTT GORDON
Dean of Libraries: CONNIE FOSTER
Library of 729,070 vols, 161,463 bound periodicals, 936,779 govt documents, 2,236,014

microforms, 6,984 MSS, 29,906 audiovisual items
Number of teachers: 747 (full-time)
Number of students: 20,903

DEANS

College of Education and Behavioural Sciences: Prof. Dr SAM EVANS
College of Health and Human Services: Dr JOHN A. BONAGURO
Gordon Ford College of Business: Dr JEFF KATZ
Ogden College of Science and Engineering: Dr BLAINE FERRELL
Potter College of Arts and Letters: Dr DAVID LEE
Univ. College: Dr DENNIS K. GEORGE

LOUISIANA

CENTENARY COLLEGE OF LOUISIANA

POB 41188, Shreveport, LA 71134-1188
2911 Centenary Blvd, Shreveport, LA 71104
Telephone: (318) 869-5011
Fax: (318) 869-5010
E-mail: president@centenary.edu
Internet: www.centenary.edu
Founded 1845 by merger of College of Louisiana and Centenary College
Private control
Academic year: June to May
Pres.: Dr B. DAVID ROWE
Provost and Dean of College: Dr MICHAEL HEMPHILL
Vice-Pres. for Advancement: SCOTT RAWLES
Vice-Pres. for Finance and Admin.: BILL BALLARD
Vice-Pres. for Enrolment Services: MONTY CURTIS
Vice-Pres. for Student Devt: BETSY EAVES
Dean of Students: MARK MILLER
Dir of Admissions: GAIL ROBINSON
Registrar: Dr GARY YOUNG
Dir of Library Services: CHRISTY J. WRENN
Library of 251,477 vols, 179,934 online journal, 358 print journals
Number of teachers: 64 (full-time)
Number of students: 805 (undergraduate)
Publication: Pandora

DEANS

Frost School of Business: Dr CHRISTOPHER L. MARTIN
Hurley School of Music: Prof. GALE ODOM

DILLARD UNIVERSITY

2601 Gentilly Blvd, New Orleans, LA 70122
Telephone: (504) 283-8822
Fax: (504) 816-4895
E-mail: admissions@dillard.edu
Internet: www.dillard.edu
Founded 1930 by merger of New Orleans Univ. and Straight College
Private control
Academic year: June to May
Pres.: Dr JAMES E. LYONS, SR
Provost and Sr Vice-Pres. for Academic Affairs: Dr PHYLLIS DAWKINS
Exec. Vice-Pres.: Dr WALTER L. STRONG
Provost and Sr Vice-Pres. for Academic Affairs: Dr PHYLLIS WORTHY DAWKINS
Chief Financial Officer: WANDA BROOKS
Vice-Pres. for Student Affairs: Dr CHRISTOPHER CAMERON
Registrar: PAMELA ENGLAND
Dean of Library: CYNTHIA J. CHARLES
Library of 105,128 vols, 295 current periodicals, 1,150 microfilms, 320 audiovisual items, 88,000 e-books

Number of teachers: 127 (82 full-time, 45 part-time)
Number of students: 1,249
Publication: *Dillard Today* (1 a year)

DEANS

College of Arts and Sciences: Prof. Dr ROBERT A. COLLINS
College of Business: Prof. Dr CHRISTIAN V. FUGAR
College of General Studies: Dr DOROTHY SMITH
College of Professional Studies: Dr LAURA V. ROUZAN
School of Science, Technology, Engineering and Mathematics: Prof. Dr JOHN E. WILSON

LOUISIANA COLLEGE

1140 College Dr., Pineville, LA 71359
Telephone: (318) 487-7259
E-mail: admissions@lacollege.edu
Internet: www.lacollege.edu
Founded 1906
Private control
Academic year: August to August
Pres.: Dr JOE AQUILLARD
Exec. Vice-Pres.: Dr TIMOTHY L. JOHNSON
Vice-Pres. for Academic Affairs: Dr TIM SEARCY
Vice-Pres. for Business Affairs and Chief Financial Officer: RANDALL HARGIS
Vice-Pres. for Institutional Advancement: Rev. TIMOTHY JOHNSON
Vice-Pres. for Student Devt and Dean of Students: Dr PEGGY PACK
Registrar: CAROLYN DENNIS
Dir of Library: W. TERRY MARTIN
Library of 135,000 vols, 199,000 govt documents, 75,000 microfilm, 500 journals, 41,000 e-books, 13,200 e-journals
Number of teachers: 109
Number of students: 1,459

DEANS

Caskey School of Divinity: Prof. Dr CHARLES QUARLES
Div. of Fine Arts and Media: Dr FRED GUILBERT
Judge Paul Pressler School of Law: J. MICHAEL JOHNSON
School of Education: Dr RANDALL E. ESTERS
School of Nursing and Allied Health: Prof. Dr KIMBERLY J. SHARP

LOUISIANA STATE UNIVERSITY SYSTEM

3810 W Lakeshore Dr., Baton Rouge, LA 70808
Telephone: (225) 578-2111
Fax: (225) 578-5524
Internet: www.lsusystem.edu
Founded 1860
Academic year: August to July
Pres.: Dr WILLIAM L. JENKINS
Vice-Pres. for Academic Affairs and Technology Transfer: CAROLYN H. HARGRAVE
Vice-Pres. for Student and Academic Support Services and Chief of Staff: MIKE GARGANO
Chief Financial Officer and Asst Vice-Pres. for Budget and Finance: WENDY SIMONEAUX.

CONSTITUENT UNIVERSITIES

Louisiana State University

Baton Rouge, LA 70803
Telephone: (225) 578-6977
Fax: (225) 578-5982
E-mail: admissions@lsu.edu
Internet: www.lsu.edu
Founded 1860

State control
Academic year: August to August
Chancellor: Dr MICHAEL V. MARTIN
Exec. Vice-Chancellor and Provost: Dr JOHN MAXWELL HAMILTON
Vice-Chancellor and Chief Financial Officer: ERIC MONDAY
Vice-Chancellor for Research and Economic Devt: Dr THOMAS R. KLEI
Vice-Chancellor for Strategic Initiatives: Dr ISIAH M. WARNER
Vice-Chancellor for Student Life and Enrolment: Dr KURT KEPPLER
Exec. Dir of Univ. College: PAUL IVEY
Dean of Students and Assoc. Vice-Chancellor: Dr K. C. WHITE
Dean of Univ. Libraries: JENNIFER CARGILL
Registrar: ROBERT K. DOOLOS
Library of 3,664,826 vols, 6,778,517 microforms, 12m. MSS, 25,900 audiovisual, 549,153 maps, 1,01,615 current periodicals, 3,68,604 e-books, 97,105 e-periodicals
Number of teachers: 1,236 (1,176 full-time, 60 part-time)
Number of students: 28,771 (23,686 undergraduate, 5,085 graduate)

DEANS

College of Agriculture: Dr KENNETH KOONCE
College of Art and Design: KENNETH E. CARPENTER
College of Education: Prof. LAURA F. LINDSAY
College of Engineering: Dr RICHARD KOUBEK
College of Humanities and Social Sciences: Prof. Dr GAINES M. FOSTER
College of Music and Dramatic Arts: LAURENCE KAPTAIN
College of Science: Prof. Dr KEVIN R. CARMAN
E. J. Ourso College of Business Admin.: Prof. ELI JONES
Graduate School: Prof. GARY L. BYERLY
Honors College: Dr NANCY CLARK
Manship School of Mass Communication: Prof. JERRY CEPPOS
School of Coast and Environment: Prof. CHRIS D'ELIA
School of Library and Information Science: Dr BETH M. PASKOFF
School of Social Work: Dr DAPHNE S. CAIN
School of Veterinary Medicine: Dr PETER F. HAYNES

Louisiana State University, Alexandria

8100 Highway 71S, Alexandria, LA 71302-9121
Telephone: (318) 473-6417
Fax: (318) 473-6418
E-mail: contact@lsua.edu
Internet: www.lsua.edu
Founded 1960, present status 2002
State control
Academic year: August to May
Offers bachelor degrees in biology, business administration, communication studies, criminal justice, elementary education, English, history, mathematics, nursing, psychology
Chancellor: Dr DAVID P. MANUEL
Provost and Vice-Chancellor for Academic and Student Affairs: Dr BARBARA S. HATFIELD
Vice-Chancellor for Finance and Admin. Services: DAVID WESSE
Registrar: TERESA SEYMOUR
Dir of the Library: Dr BONNIE HINES
Library of 166,700 vols, 19,000 microfilms
Number of teachers: 111 (full-time)
Number of students: 2,613

Louisiana State University, Shreveport

One University Pl., Shreveport, LA 71115
Telephone: (318) 797-5000
Internet: www.lsus.edu

Founded 1967
State control
Academic year: August to May (2 semesters)
Chancellor: Dr VINCENT J. MARSALA
Provost and Vice-Chancellor for Academic Affairs: Dr PAUL D. SISSON
Vice-Chancellor for Business Affairs: MICHAEL T. FERRELL
Vice-Chancellor for Student Affairs: Dr GLORIA W. RAINES
Vice-Chancellor for Univ. Devt: Dr JOHNETTE H. MAGNER
Registrar and Dean of Enrolment Services: MICKY P. DIEZ
Dean of Student Affairs: Dr RANDY R. BUTTERBAUGH
Dean of Library: Dr ALAN D. GABEHART
Library of 250,000 vols, 2,000 periodicals, 68,000 e-books, 45,000 e-journals
Number of teachers: 140 (full-time)
Number of students: 4,562
Publications: *Bulletin of the Museum of Life Sciences* (2 a year), *LSUS Magazine*, *Spectra* (1 a year), *North Louisiana Historical Journal* (3 a year)

DEANS

College Arts and Sciences: Dr LAWRENCE E. ANDERSON
College of Business, Education and Human Devt: Dr DAVID GUSTAVSON
Continuing Education and Public Service: TISHA SAMHAM
Graduate Studies: (vacant).

OTHER CONSTITUENT INSTITUTIONS

Louisiana State University Health Sciences Center, New Orleans

433 Bolivar St, New Orleans, LA 70112
Telephone: (504) 568-4808
E-mail: registrar@lsuhsc.edu
Internet: www.lsuhsc.edu
Founded 1931
State control
Academic year: August to August
Chancellor: Dr LARRY H. HOLLIER
Vice-Chancellor For Academic Affairs: Dr JOSEPH M. MOERSCHBAECHER, III
Vice-Chancellor For Admin. And Finance: RONALD E. SMITH
Registrar: W. BRYANT FAUST, IV
Dir of Libraries: DEBORAH SIBLEY
Library of 238,000 vols, 3,000 audiovisual titles, 200 print journals
Number of students: 2,500

DEANS

School of Allied Health Professions: Dr J. M. CAIRO
School of Dentistry: Prof. Dr HENRY A. GREMILLION
School of Graduate Studies: Prof. JOSEPH M. MOERSCHBAECHER, III
School of Medicine: Prof. Dr STEVE NELSON
School of Nursing: Prof. Dr DEMETRIUS J. PORCHE
School of Public Health: Dr ELIZABETH T. H. FONTHAM

Louisiana State University Health Sciences Center, Shreveport

1501 Kings Highway, POB 33932, Shreveport, LA 71103-3932
Telephone: (318) 675-5000
E-mail: shvreg@lsuhsc.edu
Internet: www.lsuhscshreveport.edu
Founded 1976 as Univ. hospital, present status 1978, present name 1999
State control
Academic year: June to June
Chancellor: Dr ROBERT A. BARISH
Vice-Chancellor for Admin.: JOHN T. DAILEY

Registrar: KIMBERLY CARMEN
Library Dir: MARIANNE COMEGYS
Library of 190,000 vols, 1,017 e-books
Number of students: 829

DEANS

School of Allied Health Professions: Dr
JOSEPH MCCULLOCH
School of Graduate Studies: Dr SANDRA C.
ROERIG
School of Medicine: Dr ANDREW L. CHESSON,
JR

Paul M. Hebert Law Center

One E Campus Dr., Louisiana State Univ.,
Baton Rouge, LA 70803-1000
Telephone: (225) 578-8646
Fax: (225) 578-8202
E-mail: info@law.lsu.edu
Internet: www.law.lsu.edu
Founded 1906 as LSU Law School, present
name 1979; attached to Louisiana State
University
State control
Academic year: August to July (3 semesters)
Programmes incl. civil and int. law, intellec-
tual property law, environmental law
Chancellor: Prof. JACK M. WEISS
Vice-Chancellor: Prof. CHRISTOPHER PIETRUSZ-
KIEWICZ
Vice-Chancellor for Academic Affairs: Prof.
ERICK V. ANDERSON
Vice-Chancellor for Faculty Devt and Insti-
tutional Assessment: Prof. RAYMOND T.
DIAMOND
Vice-Chancellor for Finance and Business
Affairs: Prof. N. GREGORY SMITH
Dir of Admissions: JAKE T. HENRY, III
Dir of Student Affairs and Registrar:
MICHELE FORBES
Dir of Library and Information Services:
BETH WILLIAMS
Library of 850,000 vols, 160,000 vols of court
records
Number of teachers: 38 (full-time)
Publications: *LSU Law, Louisiana Law
Review.*

LOYOLA UNIVERSITY NEW ORLEANS

6363 St Charles Ave, New Orleans, LA 70118
Telephone: (504) 865-3240
Fax: (504) 865-2787
E-mail: admit@loyno.edu
Internet: www.loyno.edu
Founded 1904 as Loyola College, present
status 1912, present name 1996
Private control
Academic year: August to July
Pres.: Rev. Dr KEVIN W. WILDES
Provost and Vice-Pres. for Academic Affairs:
Dr EDWARD J. KVET
Vice-Pres. for Enrolment Management: SAL-
VADORE A. LIBERTO
Vice-Pres. for Finance and Admin.: JAY
CALAMIA
Vice-Pres. for Institutional Advancement:
WILLIAM BISHOP
Vice-Pres. for Student Affairs: Dr M. L.
PETTY
Vice-Pres. for Enrolment Management: SAL-
VADORE A. LIBERTO
Dir of Admissions: KEITH E. GRAMLING
Dean of Libraries: DEBORAH POOLE
Library of 371,000 vols, 36,000 journals,
27,000 e-books
Number of teachers: 275
Number of students: 4,982 (2,965 under-
graduates)
Publications: *JustSouth Quarterly* (4 a year),
Loyola Executive (2 a year), *Loyola Law
Review* (4 a year), *Loyola Lawyer* (2 a

year), *Loyola Magazine* (4 a year), *New
Orleans Review* (4 a year)

DEANS

College of Business: Dr WILLIAM B. LOCANDER
College of Humanities and Natural Sciences:
Dr JO ANN MORAN CRUZ Jr
College of Law: Prof. Dr MARÍA PABÓN LÓPEZ
College of Music and Fine Arts: Prof. Dr
DONALD BOOMGAARDEN
College of Social Sciences: Prof. Dr LUIS
MIRÓN

NEW ORLEANS BAPTIST THEOLOGICAL SEMINARY

3939 Gentilly Blvd, New Orleans, LA 70126
Telephone: (504) 282-4455
Fax: (504) 816-8023
E-mail: nobts@nobts.edu
Internet: www.nobts.edu
Founded 1917 as Baptist Bible Institute,
present name 1946
Private control
Pres.: Dr CHARLES S. KELLEY, JR
Provost: Dr STEVE W. LEMKE
Vice-Pres. for Business Affairs: L. CLAY
CORVIN
Dean of Admissions and Registrar: Dr PAUL
GREGOIRE
Dean of Libraries: Dr JEFF GRIFFIN
Library of 290,000 vols
Number of teachers: 70
Number of students: 3,000 (1926 full-time)

DEANS

Graduate Studies: Prof. JERRY BARLOW
Leavell College: Prof. Dr L. THOMAS STRONG,
III

NOTRE DAME SEMINARY

2901 S Carrolton Ave, New Orleans, LA
70118-4391
Telephone: (504) 866-7426
Fax: (504) 866-3119
E-mail: registrar@nds.edu
Internet: www.nds.edu
Founded 1923
Private control
Academic year: August to May
Divinity, theological studies; hispanic minis-
try programme, human formation, pastoral
dept, spiritual formation
Chancellor: ARCHBISHOP OF NEW ORLEANS
Pres. and Rector: Rev. JOSÉ I LAVASTIDA
Academic Dean: MINH PHAN
Registrar: CYNTHIA GARRITY
Dir of Library: THOMAS B. BENDER, IV
Library of 95,000 vols incl. 12,000 bound
periodicals, 165 periodicals
Number of teachers: 30
Number of students: 154 (full-time)

OUR LADY OF HOLY CROSS COLLEGE

4123 Woodland Dr., New Orleans, LA 70131-
7399
Telephone: (504) 394-7744
Fax: (504) 391-2421
E-mail: admissions@olhcc.edu
Internet: www.olhcc.edu
Founded 1916 as Holy Cross Normal, present
name 1960
Private control
Academic year: August to July
Undergraduate programmes incl. allied
health, biology, business admin., counselling
and behavioural sciences, education, Eng-
lish, general studies, history, nursing, social
sciences, theology; offers masters degree in
arts, education, theology

Pres.: Dr MYLES M. SEGHERS
Provost: Prof. Dr PATRICIA PRECHTER
Vice-Pres. for Finance and Operations: Sis.
MARJORIE A. HEBERT
Registrar: ROBERT MITCHELL
Dean of Admissions and Student Affairs:
KATHARINE GONZALES
Dir of Library Services: Sis. HELEN FONTENOT
Library of 201,807 vols
Number of teachers: 154 (52 full-time, 102
part-time)
Number of students: 1,260 (997 undergradu-
ate, 263 graduate)

OUR LADY OF LAKE COLLEGE

7434 Perkins Rd, Baton Rouge, LA 70808
Telephone: (225) 768-1700
Fax: (225) 768-0811
E-mail: registrar@ololcollege.edu
Internet: www.ololcollege-edu.org
Founded 1923, present name and status 1995
Private control
Academic year: August to July (3 semesters)
Pres.: Prof. Dr SANDRA S. HARPER
Exec. Vice-Pres. for Academic and Student
Affairs: Prof. Dr DAVID ENGLAND
Vice-Pres. for Finance and Admin.: HOA T.
NGUYEN
Vice-Pres. for Planning and Institutional
Effectiveness: TRACY W. MOLIDOR
Dean of Student Services: Dr PHYLLIS L.
SIMPSON
Dir of Enrolment Management: REBECCA
CANNON
Registrar: RYAN F. GARRITY
Dean of Library: TRAVIS DUDLEY
Library of 30,000 print and e-book vols, 300
periodicals, 1,700 audiovisual items
Number of teachers: 80 (full-time)
Number of students: 1,860

DEANS

School of Arts, Sciences and Health Professions: Dr KATHERINE H. KRIEG
School of Nursing: Dr JENNIFER BECK

SAINT JOSEPH SEMINARY COLLEGE

75376 River Rd, St Benedict, LA 70457
Telephone: (985) 867-2299
Fax: (985) 327-1085
E-mail: acsec@sjasc.edu
Internet: www.sjasc.edu
Private control
Programmes offered incl. bachelors in phil-
osophy and liberal arts, philosophy and
theological studies
Pres.-Rector: Rev. GREGORY M. BOQUET
Dean of Academic Affairs: Dr RUSS POTTLE
Dean of Students: Rev. KILLIAN TOLG
Registrar: CASEY EDLER
Library Dir: BONNIE BESS WOOD
Library of 50,000 vols, 10,000 bound serials,
137 current serial titles, 1,500 audiovisual
materials
Number of teachers: 26
Number of students: 194

SOUTHERN UNIVERSITY SYSTEM

J. S. Clark Admin. Bldg, Fourth Fl., Baton
Rouge, LA 70813
Telephone: (225) 771-4500
Fax: (225) 771-5522
Internet: www.sus.edu
Founded 1880
State control
Pres.: Dr RONALD MASON, JR
Vice-Pres. for Academic and Student Affairs:
KASSIE FREEMAN
Vice-Pres. for Finance and Business Affairs:
KEVIN APPLETON

Vice-Pres. for Information and Technology Management: TONY MOORE
Vice-Pres. for Institutional Advancement: ERNIE TROY HUGHES.

CONSTITUENT INSTITUTIONS

Southern University and A & M College

POB 9374, Baton Rouge, LA 70813
Telephone: (225) 771-4500
Internet: web.subr.edu
Founded 1880
State control
Academic year: August to May (2 semesters)
Chancellor: Dr JAMES L. LLORENS
Exec. Vice-Chancellor and Interim Provost: Dr JANET RAMI
Vice-Chancellor for Finance and Admin.: FLANDUS MCCLINTON, JR
Vice-Chancellor for Research and Strategic Initiatives: Dr MICHAEL STUBBLEFIELD
Vice-Chancellor for Student Affairs: Dr BRANDON DUMAS (acting)
Registrar: D'ANDREA LEE
Dean of Libraries: Prof. EMMA BRADFORD PERRY
Library of 112,858 vols, 744,000 microforms, 34,380 audiovisual materials
Number of teachers: 354
Number of students: 7,627
Publication: *The Southern Digest*

DEANS

College of Agricultural, Family and Consumer Sciences: Dr DEWITT JONES
College of Arts and Humanities: Dr JOYCE O'ROURKE
College of Business: Dr DONALD ANDREWS
College of Education: Dr VERJANIS ANDREWS PEOPLES
College of Engineering: Dr HABIB P. MOHAMADIAN
College of Sciences: Dr ROBERT H. MILLER, JR
Graduate School: Dr MWALIMU SHUJAA
Honors College: Dr ELLA KELLEY
Nelson Mandela School of Public Policy and Urban Affairs: Dr WILLIAM ARP, III
School of Architecture: LONNIE WILKINSON
School of Nursing: Dr CHERYL TAYLOR

Southern University at New Orleans

6400 Press Dr., New Orleans, LA 70126
Telephone: (504) 286-5000
Fax: (504) 284-5481
Internet: www.suno.edu
Founded 1956
State control
Academic year: August to May (2 semesters)
Chancellor: Dr VICTOR UKPOLO
Vice-Chancellor for Academic Affairs: Dr DAVID ADEGBOYE
Vice-Chancellor for Admin. and Finance: WOODIE WHITE
Vice-Chancellor for Enrolment Services and Student Affairs: Dr DONNA GRANT
Vice-Chancellor for Univ. Advancement: GLORIA BARTLEY MOULTRIE
Registrar: GILDA DAVIS
Library Dir: SHATIQUA MOSBY-WILSON
Library: 9,000 e-books
Number of students: 3,165
Publication: *The Journal of Urban Education*

DEANS

College of Arts and Sciences: Dr HENRY EFESOA-MOKOSSO
College of Business and Public Administration: Dr IGWE UDEH
College of Education and Human Development: Dr LOUISE S. KALTENBAUGH
School of Graduate Studies: Dr IRA NEIGHBORS
School of Social Work: Dr BEVERLY C. FAVRÉ

TULANE UNIVERSITY

6823 St Charles Ave, New Orleans, LA 70118
Telephone: (504) 865-5000
Fax: (504) 865-5202
E-mail: pr@tulane.edu
Internet: tulane.edu
Founded 1834 as Medical College of Louisiana; present name and status 1884
Private control
Academic year: August to May (2 semesters)
Pres.: Prof. SCOTT S. COWEN
Provost and Sr Vice-Pres. for Academic Affairs: Dr MICHAEL A. BERNSTEIN
Exec. Vice-Pres. for Univ. Relations and Development: YVETTE M. JONES
Sr Vice-Pres.: BENJAMIN P. SACHS
Sr Vice-Pres. for Operations and Chief Financial Officer: ANTHONY P. LORINO
Vice-Pres. for Administrative Services: ANNE P. BAÑOS
Vice-Pres. for Enrolment Management and Registrar: EARL RETIF
Vice-Pres. for Student Affairs and Dean of Students: MICHAEL H. HOGG
Gen. Counsel: VICTORIA D. JOHNSON
Registrsar: EARL D. RETIF
Dean of Libraries and Academic Information Resources: Dr LANCE D. QUERY
Library: see Libraries and Archives
Number of teachers: 1,100
Number of students: 13,359 (8,339 undergraduate)

DEANS

A. B. Freeman School of Business: Prof. Dr IRA SOLOMON
Graduate School: Prof. MICHAEL HERMAN
Law School: DAVID D. MEYER
Newcomb-Tulane College: Prof. Dr JAMES MACLAREN
School of Architecture: Prof. KENNETH SCHWARTZ
School of Continuing Studies: Dr RICHARD A. MARKSBURY
School of Liberal Arts: Prof. Dr CAROLE HABER
School of Medicine: Prof. BENJAMIN P. SACHS
School of Public Health and Tropical Medicine: Prof. Dr PIERRE BUEKENS
School of Science and Engineering: Prof. Dr NICHOLAS J. ALTIERO
School of Social Work: Dr RONALD E. MARKS

UNIVERSITY OF LOUISIANA SYSTEM

1201 N Third St, Suite 7-300, Baton Rouge, LA 70802
Telephone: (225) 342-6950
E-mail: rmoffett@uls.state.la.us
Internet: www.ulsystem.net
Founded 1974 as Board of Trustees for State Colleges and Universities, present name 1995
Number of students: 83,000 at 8 univs
Pres.: Dr RANDY MOFFETT
Provost and Vice-Pres. for Academic and Student Affairs: Dr BRAD O'HARA
Vice-Pres. for Admin. and Gen. Counsel: DIANNE IRVINE
Vice-Pres. for Business and Finance: ROBBIE ROBINSON
Vice-Pres. for Research and Performance Assessment: Dr BEATRICE BALDWIN.

CONSTITUENT INSTITUTIONS

Grambling State University

403 Main St, Grambling, LA 71245
Telephone: (318) 247-3811
Fax: (318) 274-6172
E-mail: admissions@gram.edu
Internet: www.gram.edu
Founded 1901

State control
Academic year: August to May
Pres.: Dr FRANK G. POGUE
Provost and Vice-Pres. for Academic Affairs: Dr CONNIE WALTON
Vice-Pres. of Finance: LEON SANDERS
Vice-Pres. for Institutional Advancement: Dr KENOYE EKE
Registrar: PATRICIA J. HUTCHERSON
Dir of Library Services: FELIX E. UNAEZE (acting)
Library of 294,000 vols
Number of teachers: 238
Number of students: 4,994

DEANS

College of Arts and Sciences: Dr EVELYN WYNN
College of Business: Dr CARL N. WRIGHT
College of Education: Dr WYNETTA Y. LEE
College of Professional Studies: Dr RAMA M. TUNUGUNTLA
School of Graduate Studies and Research: Dr JANET GUYDEN

Louisiana Tech University

Ruston, LA 71272
Telephone: (318) 257-0211
Fax: (318) 257-2928
E-mail: iso@latech.edu
Internet: www.latech.edu
Founded 1894 as Louisiana Industrial Institute and College, present name and status 1970
State control
Academic year: June to May (2 semesters)
Pres.: Dr DANIEL D. RENEAU
Exec. Vice-Pres.: Dr TERRY M. MCCONATHY
Vice-Pres. for Academic Affairs: Dr KENNETH W. REA
Vice-Pres. for Admin. Affairs: Dr KENNETH W. REA
Vice-Pres. for Finance and Admin.: JOSEPH R. THOMAS, JR
Vice-Pres. for Research and Devt: Dr LESLIE K. GUICE
Vice-Pres. for Student Affairs: Dr JAMES M. KING
Vice-Pres. for Univ. Advancement: CORRE STEGALL
Dean of Enrolment Management: PAMELA R. FORD
Registrar: ROBERT D. VENTO
Dean of Library Services: MICHAEL DiCARLO
Library of 3,715,805 vols incl. 462,696 bound vols, 62,931 e-books, 1,933 periodical titles, 578,081 microforms, 2,269,644 govt documents, 396 audiovisual materials, 40,124 maps
Number of teachers: 374
Number of students: 11,581

DEANS

College of Applied and Natural Sciences: Prof. Dr JAMES D. LIBERATOS
College of Business: Dr JAMES R. LUMPKIN
College of Education: Dr DAVID GULLATT
College of Engineering and Science: Prof. Dr STAN A. NAPPER, Jr
College of Liberal Arts: Dr DONALD P. KACZVINSKY
Graduate School and Univ. Research: Dr TERRY M. MCCONATHY

McNeese State University

4205 Ryan St, Lake Charles, LA 70609
Telephone: (337) 475-5000
Fax: (337) 475-5012
E-mail: amillet@mcneese.edu
Internet: www.mcneese.edu
Founded 1939 as Lake Charles Jr College, present name and status 1970
State control

Academic year: August to May

Pres.: Dr PHILLIP C. WILLIAMS

Provost and Vice-Pres. for Academic and Student Affairs: Dr JEANNE DABOVAL

Vice-Pres. for Admin. and Student Affairs: Dr KALIL LEYOUB

Vice-Pres. for Business Affairs: Dr EDDIE P. MECHE

Vice-Pres. for Univ. Advancement: RICHARD REID

Dean of Enrolment Management: STEPHANIE TARVER

Dean of Student Services: Dr TOBY W. OSBURN

Dir of Admissions: KARA SMITH

Registrar: APRIL MILLET

Library Dir: DEBBIE JOHNSON-HOUSTON

Library of 400,000 vols

Number of teachers: 317 (full-time)

Number of students: 8,941

Publications: *The Log* (1 a year), *The McNeese Arena* (1 a year), *The McNeese Review* (1 a year), *The McNeese Update* (3 a year)

DEANS

Burton College of Education: Dr WAYNE FETTER

College of Business: Dr MITCHELL ADRIAN

College of Engineering and Engineering Technology: Dr NIKOS KIRITSIS

College of Liberal Arts: Dr RAY MILES

College of Nursing: Dr PEGGY L. WOLFE

College of Science: Dr GEORGE MEAD, JR

William J. Doré, Sr. School of Graduate Studies: Dr GEORGE MEAD

Nicholls State University

Thibodaux, LA 70310

Telephone: (985) 446-8111

E-mail: grad-stu@nicholls.edu

Internet: www.nicholls.edu

Founded 1948 as Francis T. Nicholls Jr College of Louisiana State Univ., present name and status 1970

State control

Academic year: January to December (2 semesters)

Pres.: Prof. Dr STEPHEN T. HULBERT

Exec. Vice-Pres.: LAWRENCE HOWELL

Vice-Pres. for Academic Affairs: Dr ALLAYNE BARRILLEAUX

Vice-Pres. for Institutional Advancement: Dr DAVID E. BOUDREAUX

Vice-Pres. for Student Affairs and Enrolment Services: Dr EUGENE A. DIAL, JR

Dir of Graduate Studies: BETTY A. KLEEN

Registrar: KELLY J. RODRIGUE

Library Dir: Prof. Dr ROBERT J. BREMER

Library of 450,000 vols and periodicals, 350,000 catalogued fed. and state documents, 40,000 e-books, 380,000 microforms

Number of teachers: 278 (full-time)

Number of students: 6,050

DEANS

College of Arts and Sciences: Dr JOHN P. DOUCET

College of Business Admin.: Dr SHAWN MAULDIN

College of Education: Dr J. STEVEN WELSH

College of Nursing and Allied Health: Prof. Dr SUE WESTBROOK

Univ. College and John Folse Culinary Institute: Prof. Dr ALBERT DAVIS

Northwestern State University of Louisiana

Natchitoches, LA 71497-0002

Telephone: (318) 357-6011

Fax: (318) 357-4223

E-mail: academicservices@nsula.edu

Internet: www.nsula.edu

Founded 1884 as state normal school, present name and status 1970

State control

Academic year: August to August

Pres.: Dr RANDALL J. WEBB

Vice-Pres. for Academic and Student Affairs and Acting Provost: Dr LISA ABNEY

Vice-Pres. for Business Affairs and Controller: CARL JONES

Vice-Pres. for External Affairs: JERRY D. PIERCE

Vice-Pres. for Technology, Research and Economic Development: Dr DARLENE WILLIAMS

Vice-Pres. for Student Affairs: Dr PATRICE MOULTON (acting)

Vice-Pres. for University Affairs: Dr MARCUS JONES

Dean of Students: CHRISTOPHER MAGGIO

Registrar: LILLIE FRAZIER BELL

Dir of Libraries: ABBIE LANDRY

Library of 322,270 vols incl. books and serial vols, 295,166 print material and 27,104 e-books, 458,000 govt documents, 5,500 audiovisual items, 50,000 journals, newspapers and magazines

Number of teachers: 278 (full-time)

Number of students: 9,191

Publication: *Southern Studies* (4 a year)

DEANS

College of Arts, Letters, Graduate Studies and Research and Graduate School: Dr STEVE HORTON

College of Business: Dr MARGARET KILCOYNE (acting)

College of Education and Human Devt: Dr VICKIE S. GENTRY (acting)

College of Nursing and Allied Health: Dr NORANN Y. PLANCHOCK

College of Science, Technology and Business: Dr AUSTIN L. TEMPLE, JR

Southeastern Louisiana University

SLU 10784, Hammond, LA 70402

Telephone: (985) 549-2000

Fax: (985) 549-5882

E-mail: admissions@selu.edu

Internet: www.selu.edu

Founded 1925 as Hammond Jr College, present status 1970

State control

Academic year: June to May

Pres.: Dr JOHN L. CRAIN

Provost and Vice-Pres. for Academic Affairs: Dr TAMMY BOURG

Vice-Pres. for Admin. and Finance: STEPHEN SMITH

Vice-Pres. for Student Affairs: Dr MARVIN L. YATES

Vice-Pres. for Univ. Advancement: WENDY J. LAUDERDALE

Dean of Research and Graduate Studies: Dr JERALD AINSWORTH

Library Dir: ERIC JOHNSON

Library of 365,831 vols, 3,779 serial subscriptions, 816,501 microforms, 50,705 audiovisual materials, 71,370 e-books, 244,630 govt documents

Number of teachers: 630 (524 full-time, 106 part-time)

Number of students: 15,414

Publications: *Economic Reporter* (4 a year), *Louisiana Literature* (2 a year), *Nineteenth Century Studies* (1 a year), *The Pick* (2 a year)

DEANS

College of Arts, Humanities and Social Sciences: Dr KAREN FONTENOT

College of Business: Dr RANDY SETTOON

College of Education and Human Devt: Dr JOHN C. FISCHETTI

College of Nursing and Health Studies: Dr ANN K. CARRUTH

College of Science and Technology: Dr DANIEL MCCARTHY

PROFESSORS

ALESSI, H., Counseling and Human Development

BEAUBOUEF, T., Computer Science and Industrial Technology

BEDELL, J., English

BELL, J., History and Political Science

BLACKWOOD, C., Visual Arts

BOND, E., Nursing

BOND, W., Biological Sciences

BONNETTE, J., Computer Science and Industrial Technology

BOSTIC, M., Computer Science and Industrial Technology

BUDDEN, M., Marketing and Supply Chain Management

CANNON, G., Mathematics

CAPPEL, S., Management

CARR, S., Teaching and Learning

CARRUTH, A., Nursing

CARRUTH, P., Accounting

CHILDERS, G., Biological Sciences

COPE, R., Marketing and Supply Chain Management

CROTHER, B., Biological Sciences

DEALWIS, T., Mathematics

DOUGHTY, M., Chemistry and Physics

DRANGUET, C., History and Political Science

DUGGAL, R., Business Administration and Finance

ELLIOTT, C., Teaching and Learning

FAUST, J., English

FELLOM, M., Music and Dramatic Arts

FICK, T., English

FONT, W., Biological Sciences

FORREST, B., History and Political Science

FREDELL, J., English

FULWILER, J., Educational Leadership and Technology

GERMAN, H., English

GOLD, E., English

GONZALEZ-PEREZ, M., History and Political Science

GUTTHY, A., Foreign Languages and Literature

HIGGINBOTHAM, T., Computer Science and Industrial Technology

HOLMES, L., Chemistry and Physics

HSING, Y., Business Administration and Finance

HYDE, B., Nursing

JAMAL, A., Marketing and Supply Chain Management

JONES, M., Marketing and Supply Chain Management

KABZA, L., Mathematics

KEARNEY, M., English

KEDDY, P., Biological Sciences

KEOWN, G., Visual Arts

KING, P., Management

KOLB, K., Foreign Languages and Literature

KRAEMER, R., Kinesiology and Health Studies

LANE, E., Educational Leadership and Technology

LEWIS, B., Sociology and Criminal Justice

LI, S., Mathematics

LONGMAN, D., General Studies

LOUTH, R., English

MCALLISTER, C., English

MCALLISTER, H., Psychology

MCKAY, S., Marketing and Finance

MARSHALL, M., Foreign Languages and Literature

MEEKER, B., Nursing

MERINO, D., Mathematics

MIRANDO, J., Communication

MUNCHAUSEN, L., Chemistry and Physics

NAQUIN, M., Kinesiology and Health Studies

NELSON, E., Biological Sciences

NEUERBURG, K., Mathematics

NORTON, W., Biological Sciences

OESCHER, J., Education Leadership and Technology
PARENT, F., Sociology and Criminal Justice
PARTRIDGE, M., Teaching and Learning
PEDERSEN, K., Mathematics
PHILLIPS, C., Management
PRYOR, S., Nursing
RAMSEY, R., Management
REYES, E., Mathematics
RIEDEL, M., Sociology and Criminal Justice
ROLLING, P., Counselling and Human Development
SCHEPKER, S., Music and Dramatic Arts
SCHULDT, B., Marketing and Supply Chain Management
SHAFFER, G., Biological Sciences
STIEGLER, L., Communication Sciences and Disorders
SUBER, S., Music and Dramatic Arts
SYNOVITZ, L., Kinesiology and Health Studies
TITARD, P., Accounting
TRAVER, A., Accounting
VOLDMAN, Y., Music and Dramatic Arts
WADLINGTON, E., Teaching and Learning
WAIKAR, A., Marketing and Supply Chain Management
WALTER, J., English
WHITE, M., Biological Sciences
WYLD, D., Management
YEARGAIN, J., Management

University of Louisiana at Lafayette

104 University Circle, Lafayette, LA 70504-1732
Telephone: (337) 482-1000
Fax: (337) 482-6195
E-mail: enroll@louisiana.edu
Internet: www.louisiana.edu
Founded 1898 as Southwestern Louisiana Industrial Institute, present status 1960, present name 1999
State control
Academic year: June to May
Pres.: Dr E. JOSEPH SAVOIE
Provost and Vice-Pres. for Academic affairs: Dr STEVE LANDRY
Vice-Pres. for Admin. and Finance: JERRY L. LEBLANC
Vice-Pres. for Enrolment Management and Registrar: Dr DEWAYNE BOWIE
Vice-Pres. for Research and Graduate Studies: Dr ROBERT E. TWILLEY
Vice-Pres. for Student Affairs: RAYMOND BLANCO
Vice-Pres. for Univ. Advancement: KENNETH ARDOIN
Dean of Students: EDWARD PRATT
Dir of Library: Dr CHARLES TRICHE
Library: 1m. vols, 2m. microforms, 6,000 serial titles
Number of teachers: 700 (600 full-time, 100 part-time)
Number of students: 16,885 (15,321 undergraduates, 1,564 graduates)
Publications: *Attakapas Gazette* (4 a year), *Louisiana History* (4 a year), *Southwestern Review* (1 a year)

DEANS

B. I. Moody III College of Business Admin.: Dr JOBY JOHN (acting)
College of Education: Dr GERALD CARLSON
College of Engineering: Dr MARK E. ZAPPI
College of General Studies: Dr PHEBE A. HAYES
College of Liberal Arts: Dr DAVID BARRY
College of the Arts: H. GORDON BROOKS, II
College of Nursing and Allied Health Professions: Dr GAIL POIRRIER
Graduate School: Dr DAVID BREAUX
Ray P. Authement College of Sciences: Dr BRADD CLARK

University of Louisiana at Monroe

700 University Ave, Monroe, LA 71209
Telephone: (318) 342-1000
Fax: (318) 342-5161
Internet: www.ulm.edu
Founded 1931 as Ouachita Parish Jr College, present status 1970, present name 1999
State control
Academic year: May to June
Pres.: Dr NICK J. BRUNO
Exec. Vice-Pres.: Dr STEPHEN RICHTERS
Vice-Pres. for Academic Affairs: Dr ERIC PANI
Vice-Pres. for Business Affairs: DAVE NICKLAS
Vice-Pres. for Student Affairs: Dr WAYNE BRUMFIELD
Vice-Pres. for Univ. Advancement: Dr DON SKELTON
Dir of Admissions: JENNIFER MALONE
Registrar: ANTHONY MALTA
Dean of the Library: DONALD R. SMITH
Library of 633,818 vols, incl. 193,935 govt documents, 2,939 current periodicals, 555,603 microform vols
Number of teachers: 521
Number of students: 8,595

DEANS

College of Arts and Sciences: Dr MICHAEL CAMILLE
College of Business Admin.: Dr RONALD BERRY
College of Education and Human Devt: Dr SANDRA M. LEMOINE
College of Health Sciences: Dr DENNY RYMAN
College of Pharmacy: Dr BENNY L. BLAYLOCK

University of New Orleans

2000 Lakeshore Dr., New Orleans, LA 70148
Telephone: (504) 280-6000
Fax: (504) 280-5522
E-mail: admissions@uno.edu
Internet: www.uno.edu
Founded 1958 as Louisiana State Univ. in New Orleans, present name 1974
State control
Academic year: August to May (2 semesters)
Pres.: PETER J. FOS
Provost and Vice-Chancellor for Academic and Student Affairs: Dr LOUIS V. PARADISE
Vice-Chancellor for Campus Services (vacant)
Vice-Chancellor for External Affairs: RACHEL A. KINCAID
Vice-Chancellor for Financial Services, Comptroller and Chief Financial Officer: LINDA K. ROBISON
Vice-Chancellor for Governmental and Community Affairs: RACHEL A. KINCAID
Vice-Chancellor for Research and Sponsored Programs: Dr SCOTT WHITTENBURG
Univ. Registrar: ALEX ARCENEAUX
Dir of Admissions: ANDY J. BENOIT
Dean of Library Services: Dr SHARON MADER
Library of 800,000 vols, 3,000 current periodicals, 2m. microforms, 91,000 print and electronic journals, 139,000 e-books
Number of teachers: 605
Number of students: 11,276 (8,345 undergraduate, 2,931 graduate)
Publications: *Metropolitan Report* (4 a year), *New Orleans Real Estate Market Survey* (2 a year), *Review of Business and Economics Research* (2 a year), *Statistical Abstract of Louisiana* (3 a year), *UNO Magazine* (4 a year)

DEANS

College of Business Admin.: Dr JOHN A. WILLIAMS
College of Education and Human Devt: Dr APRIL WHATLEY BEDFORD, JR

College of Engineering: Dr NORMA JEAN MATTEI
College of Liberal Arts: Prof. Dr SUSAN KRANTZ
College of Sciences: Dr STEVEN G. JOHNSON
Graduate School: Dr SCOTT WHITTENBURG

XAVIER UNIVERSITY OF LOUISIANA

One Drexel Dr., New Orleans, LA 70125
Telephone: (504) 486-7411
Fax: (504) 520-7388
E-mail: apply@xula.edu
Internet: www.xula.edu
Founded 1925
Private control
Academic year: August to May (2 semesters)
Pres.: Dr NORMAN C. FRANCIS
Sr Vice-Pres. for Academic Affairs: Dr LOREN JAMES BLANCHARD
Sr Vice-Pres. for Admin.: CALVIN S. TREGRE
Vice-Pres. for Fiscal Affairs: EDWARD J. PHILLIPS
Vice-Pres. for Institutional Advancement: Dr KENNETH ANTHONY ST CHARLES
Vice-Pres. for Student Services: JOSEPH K. BYRD
Dean of Admissions: WINSTON D. BROWN
Registrar: AVIS M. STUARD
Librarian: ROBERT E. SKINNER
Library of 200,000 vols, 30,000 e-books, 1,900 periodicals and newspapers 721,000 microforms
Number of teachers: 240 (full-time)
Number of students: 3,399
Publication: *Xavier Gold* (1 a year)

DEANS

College of Arts and Sciences: Dr ANIL KUKREJA
College of Pharmacy: Dr KATHLEEN B. KENNEDY
Graduate School: Dr ALVIN J. RICHARD

MAINE

BANGOR THEOLOGICAL SEMINARY

Two College Circle, POB 411, Bangor, ME 04402-0411
Telephone: (207) 942-6781
Fax: (207) 990-1267
E-mail: ajaehnig@bts.edu
Internet: www.bts.edu
Founded 1814
Private control
Academic year: September to May
Campus in Portland; graduate programmes incl. master of arts, divinity, ministry
Pres.: Rev. Dr ROBERT S. GROVE-MARKWOOD
Vice-Pres. for Advancement: REBECCA WRIGHT
Academic Dean: STEVEN LEWIS
Dir of Admissions: ADREA JAEHNIG
Registrar: DANIELLE R. LAVINE
Library Dir: LORRAINE McQUARRIE
Library of 124,000 vols
Number of teachers: 50
Number of students: 162 (full-time)

BATES COLLEGE

Two Andrews Rd, Lewiston, ME 04240-6028
Telephone: (207) 786-6255
Fax: (207) 786-6025
E-mail: admission@bates.edu
Internet: www.bates.edu
Founded 1855
Private control
Academic year: September to May (2 semesters)

Major academic programmes incl. anthropology, art and visual culture, biology, chemistry, dance, economics, English, French, geology, German, history, mathematics, music, philosophy, physics, politics, psychology, religious studies, rhetoric, Russian, sociology, Spanish, theatre

Pres.: NANCY J. CABLE
Vice-Pres. for Academic Affairs and Dean of Faculty: Dr PAMELA J. BAKER
Vice-Pres. for College Advancement: KELLY K. KERNER
Vice-Pres. and Dean of Enrolment and External Affairs: Dr NANCY J. CABLE
Vice-Pres. for Finance and Admin. and Treas.: TERRY J. BECKMANN
Vice-Pres. for Information and Library Services and Librarian: Dr EUGENE LEE WIEMERS
Dean of Admissions: (vacant)
Dean of Students: TEDD R. GOUNDIE
Registrar: MARY K. MESERVE

Library of 610,000 vols, 184,000 e-books, 52,500 e-journals
Number of teachers: 206
Number of students: 1,725

BOWDOIN COLLEGE

3900 College Station, Brunswick, ME 04011
Telephone: (207) 725-3000
Fax: (207) 725-3123
E-mail: admissions@bowdoin.edu
Internet: www.bowdoin.edu
Founded 1794
Private control
Academic year: August to July

Liberal arts college; academic programmes incl. anthropology, arts, computer science, mathematics, economics, education, French, German, govt and legal studies, Italian, neuroscience, Russian, science, Spanish, theatre, visual arts

Pres.: BARRY MILLS
Sr Vice-Pres. for Finance and Admin. and Treas.: S. CATHERINE LONGLEY
Sr Vice-Pres. for Planning and Devt and Sec.: WILLIAM A. TORREY
Vice-Pres. for Institutional Planning and Assessment: REBECCA BRODIGAN
Chief Information Officer: MITCHEL W. DAVIS
Dean for Academic Affairs: CRISTLE COLLINS JUDD
Dean of Admissions and Financial Aid: SCOTT A. MEIKLEJOHN
Dean of Student Affairs: TIMOTHY W. FOSTER
Registrar: JAN BRACKETT
Librarian: SHERRIE BERGMAN

Library of 1,034,168 vols, 29,864 audiovisual items, 915 microform, periodical titles
Number of teachers: 216
Number of students: 1,775

Publications: Bowdoin Magazine (4 a year), Bowdoin Forum (int. affairs, 1 a year).

COLBY COLLEGE

4000 Mayflower Hill, Waterville, ME 04901-8840
Telephone: (207) 859-4000
Fax: (207) 859-4055
E-mail: admissions@colby.edu
Internet: www.colby.edu
Founded 1813 as Maine Literary and Theological Instn, present name 1896
Private control
Academic year: September to May
Languages of instruction: French, Spanish, Italian

Depts of administration, humanities, interdisciplinary studies, natural sciences, social sciences

Pres.: Dr WILLIAM D. ADAMS

Vice-Pres. for Academic Affairs and Dean of Faculty: LORI G. KLETZER
Vice-Pres. for Admin. and Treas.: DOUGLAS C. TERP
Vice-Pres. and Dean of Admissions and Financial Aid: TERESA E. COWDRY
Vice-Pres. for College Relations: MICHAEL D. KISER
Vice-Pres. for Devt and Alumni Relations: DEBORAH DUTTON COX
Vice-Pres. of Student Affairs and Dean of Students: JAMES S. TERHUNE
Registrar: ELIZABETH N. SCHILLER
Dir of Libraries: CLEMENT P. GUTHRO

Library of 489,436 vols, 37,839 serial titles, 24,768 audiovisual items, 61,000 microforms 750,663 e-books
Number of teachers: 200 (162 full-time, 38 part-time)
Number of students: 1,815

Publications: Colby (4 a year), Colby Library Quarterly, Colby Perspective.

COLLEGE OF THE ATLANTIC

105 Eden St, Bar Harbor, ME 04609
Telephone: (207) 288-5015
Fax: (207) 288-4126
E-mail: inquiry@coa.edu
Internet: www.coa.edu
Founded 1969
Private control
Academic year: September to June

Academic areas incl. arts and design, environmental sciences, human studies

Pres.: DAVID HALES
Academic Dean: KEN HILL
Dean of Admission: SARAH BAKER
Dean of Devt: LYNN BOULGER
Admin. Dean: ANDREW GRIFFITHS
Registrar: JUDITH ALLEN
Library Dir: JANE HULTBERG

Library of 36,000 vols, 475 periodicals
Number of teachers: 44 (29 full-time, 15 part-time)
Number of students: 359

Publication: COA (2 a year).

HUSSON UNIVERSITY

1 College Circle, Bangor, ME 04401
Telephone: (207) 941-7100
Fax: (207) 941-7935
E-mail: admit@husson.edu
Internet: www.husson.edu
Founded 1898, present name and status 2008
Private control
Academic year: September to May
Pres. and CEO: Dr ROBERT A. CLARK
Provost and Chief Academic Officer: LYNNE COY-OGAN
Exec. Vice-Pres.: BEN HASKELL
Vice-Pres. for Admin. and Finance and Chief Financial Officer: CRAIG HADLEY
Vice-Pres. for Admin.: JOHN RUBINO
Vice-Pres. for Advancement: THOMAS MARTZ
Dir of Admissions: CARLENA BEAN
Dean of Students: SHARON WILSON-BARKER
Registrar: NANCY FENDERS
Head Librarian: AMY AVERRE

Number of teachers: 90
Number of students: 2,800

Publications: Crosscut (1 a year), The Ledger

DEANS

College of Business: RONALD NYKIEL
College of Health and Education: BARBARA HIGGINS
New England School of Communications: BEN HASKELL
School of Graduate Studies: MICHAEL W. MULLANE
School of Pharmacy: RODNEY LARSON

School of Science and Humanities: FRANCIS A. HUBBARD

MAINE COLLEGE OF ART

522 Congress St, Portland, ME 04101
Telephone: (207) 775-3052
Fax: (207) 772-5069
E-mail: info@meca.edu
Internet: www.meca.edu
Founded 1882 as part of Portland Soc. of Art, present status 1982, present name 1992
Private control
Academic year: August to May

Academic programmes incl. art history, ceramics, new media, foundation, painting, photography, graphic design, printmaking, illustration, public engagement, liberal arts, sculpture, metalsmithing and jewelry, woodworking and furniture design

Pres.: DONALD TUSKI
Exec. Vice-Pres.: BETH ELICKER
Vice-Pres. for Academic Affairs and Dean of College: IAN ANDERSON
Vice-Pres. for Advancement and College Relations: TIMOTHY W. KANE
Vice-Pres. for Enrolment: RICK LONGO
Registrar: ANNE DENNISON
Dir of Admissions: GRACE HOPKINS-LISLE
Library Dir: MOIRA STEVEN

Library of 33,000 vols, 100 periodicals, 52,000 slides
Number of teachers: 53
Number of students: 380 (350 undergraduate, 30 graduate)

MAINE MARITIME ACADEMY

Castine, ME 04420-5000
Telephone: (207) 326-2206
Fax: (207) 326-2510
E-mail: admissions@mma.edu
Internet: www.mainemaritime.edu
Founded 1941
State control
Academic year: September to April

Depts of arts and sciences, engineering, physical education; Corning School of Ocean Studies; Loeb-Sullivan School of Int. Business and Logistics

Pres.: Dr WILLIAM J. BRENNAN
Vice-Pres. for Academic Affairs and Academic Dean: Dr JOHN BARLOW
Vice-Pres. for Enrolment Management: JEFF LOUSTAUNAU
Vice-Pres. for Finance, Admin. and Govt Affairs: RICHARD R. ERICSON
Chief Advancement Officer: ELEANOR WILLMANN
Dean of Student Services: DEIDRA DAVIS
Dir of Admissions: JEFFREY C. WRIGHT
Registrar: CHRISTINA STEPHENS
Dir of Library Services: BRENT HALL

Library of 99,614 vols, 326 periodicals, 5,093 maps
Number of teachers: 118
Number of students: 970

SAINT JOSEPH'S COLLEGE OF MAINE

278 Whites Bridge Rd, Standish, ME 04084-5263
Telephone: (207) 892-6766
Fax: (207) 893-7861
E-mail: info@sjcme.edu
Internet: www.sjcme.edu
Founded 1912
Private control
Academic year: June to May (2 semesters)

Academic programmes in biology, business admin., chemistry, classics, communications, criminal justice, elementary education, English, environmental science, environmental studies, exercise science fitness, exercise science specialist, history, literature and American culture, marine science, mathematics, nursing, philosophy, physical education teaching, political science, psychology, sociology, sports management, theology

Pres.: Dr KENNETH LEMANSKI
Exec. Vice-Pres.: JOHN ZERILLO
Vice-Pres. for Academic Affairs and Dean of College: Dr RANDALL KREIG
Vice-Pres. and Chief Financial Officer: PHILIP A. YAUCH
Vice-Pres. for Enrolment Management: KATHLEEN DAVIS
Vice-Pres. for Institutional Advancement: MICHAEL DEMPSEY
Chief Admin. Officer: JANET LaFLAMME
Dean of Admissions: VINCENT J. KLOSKOWSKI
Dean of Student Life: REIS HAGERMAN
Dir of Library Services: SHELLY DAVIS

Library: over 100,000 vols, 6,000 e-books, 41,000 e-journals
Number of teachers: 96 (53 full-time; 43 part-time)
Number of students: 5,128 (750 full-time; 446 part-time; 3,932 external)

THOMAS COLLEGE

180 West River Rd, Waterville, ME 04901-5097

Telephone: (207) 859-1111
Fax: (207) 859-1114
E-mail: info@thomas.edu
Internet: www.thomas.edu

Founded 1894 as Keist Business College, present name 1962, present status 1963
Private control
Academic year: September to May

Academic programmes incl. business and management, communications, criminal justice, finance, forensic psychology

Pres.: Dr GEORGE R. SPANN
Provost and Vice-Pres. for Academic Affairs: Prof. Dr THOMAS EDWARDS
Sr Vice-Pres. and Chief Financial Officer: BETH B. GIBBS
Vice-Pres. for Advancement: ROBERT MOORE
Vice-Pres. for Enrolment Management: ROBERT CALLAHAN
Vice-Pres. for Information Services: CHRISTOPHER H. RHODA
Vice-Pres. for Student Affairs: LISA DESAUTELS-POLIQUIN
Dean of Institutional Advancement: FRAN DAY
Registrar: MEGHAN REITCHEL
Library Dir: LISA AURIEMMA

Library of 30,000 vols
Number of students: 594

Publication: *Thomas Magazine*.

UNITY COLLEGE

90 Quaker Hill Rd, Unity, ME 04988
Telephone: (207) 948-3131
Fax: (207) 948-6277
E-mail: admissions@unity.edu
Internet: www.unity.edu

Founded 1965

Divs incl. environmental programmes, wildlife conservation, marine biology and liberal studies
Private control
Academic year: September to May

Pres.: STEPHEN MULKEY
Sr Vice-Pres. for Academic Affairs: Dr WILLIAM R. TRUMBLE
Vice-Pres. for College Devt: JOSEPH GALLI
Vice-Pres. for Finance and Admin.: DEBORAH CRONIN

Dean of Enrolment Management: ALISA JOHNSON
Dean for Student Affairs: GARY ZANE
Dir of Admissions: KAY FIEDLER
Registrar: HOLLY A. HEIN
Library Dir: MELORA R. NORMAN

Library of 50,000 vols, 400 periodicals
Number of teachers: 53 (30 full-time, 23 part-time)
Number of students: 578

UNIVERSITY OF MAINE SYSTEM

16 Central St, Bangor, ME 04401
Telephone: (207) 973-3201
Fax: (207) 973-3209
E-mail: moreinfo@maine.edu
Internet: www.maine.edu

Founded 1968

Chancellor: JAMES H. PAGE
Vice-Chancellor for Academic and Student Affairs: JAMES BREECE
Vice-Chancellor for Admin. and Finance: REBECCA WYKE
Exec. Dir: ROSA REDONNETT

Number of teachers: 1,327
Number of students: 30,080 (total across 7 univs).

CONSTITUENT INSTITUTIONS

University of Maine

Orono, ME 04469
Telephone: (207) 581-1865
Fax: (207) 581-1213
E-mail: um-admit@maine.edu
Internet: www.umaine.edu

Founded 1862 as Maine College of Agriculture and Mechanic Arts, present name and status 1897
State control
Academic year: September to May (2 semesters)

Pres.: PAUL W. FERGUSON
Provost and Sr Vice-Pres. for Academic Affairs: Dr SUSAN J. HUNTER
Vice-Pres. for Admin. and Finance: JANET E. WALDRON
Vice-Pres. for Devt: ERIC ROLFSON
Vice-Pres. for Research: Dr MICHAEL J. ECKARDT
Vice-Pres. for Student Affairs and Dean of Students: ROBERT Q. DANA
Dean of Graduate Studies: DANIEL H. SANDWEISS
Dean of Libraries: JOYCE RUMERY

Library of 1,171,107 vols, 17,480 periodicals, 1.67m. microforms, 2.37m. govt documents, spec. colln on marine studies incl. 13,300 books and journals
Number of teachers: 608
Number of students: 11,168

Publications: *Agricultural Experimental Station Publications, Maine Studies, UMaine Today Magazine* (4 a year), *Technology Experiment Station Publications*

DEANS

College of Education and Human Devt: ANNE E. POOLER
College of Engineering: Prof. DANA HUMPHREY
College of Liberal Arts and Sciences: Prof. Dr JEFF HECKER
College of Natural Sciences, Forestry and Agriculture: EDWARD ASHWORTH
Honors College: CHARLIE SLAVIN
Maine Business School: Prof. Dr IVAN MANEV

University of Maine at Augusta

46 University Dr., Augusta, ME 04330-9410
Telephone: (207) 621-3000

Fax: (207) 621-3116
E-mail: uma-info@maine.edu
Internet: www.uma.edu

Founded 1965, present status 1971
State control
Academic year: August to May (2 semesters)
Campus in Bangor

Pres.: Dr ALLYSON HUGHES HANDLEY
Provost and Interim Vice-Pres. for Academic Affairs: Dr JOSEPH SZAKAS
Vice-Pres. for Enrolment Services: JONATHAN H. HENRY
Vice-Pres. for Finance and Admin.: ELLEN J. SCHNEITER
Exec. Dir of Admin. Services: SHERI STEVENS
Dean of Extended Campus Learning: Dr THOMAS E. ABBOTT
Dean of Students: KATHLEEN DEXTER
Registrar: ANN CORBETT
Dean of Libraries and Distance Learning: Dr THOMAS E. ABBOTT

Library of 81,000 vols
Number of teachers: 100 (full-time)
Number of students: 5,000

DEANS

College of Arts and Sciences: GILLIAN JORDAN
College of Professional Studies: Dr BRENDA McALEER

University of Maine at Machias

116 O'Brien Ave, Machias, ME 04654-1397
Telephone: (207) 255-1200
Fax: (207) 255-4864
E-mail: ummadmissions@maine.edu
Internet: www.umm.maine.edu

Founded 1909
State control
Academic year: September to May

Major areas of study incl. biology, business and entrepreneurial studies, college studies, education, English and book arts, environmental recreation and tourism management, environmental studies, interdisciplinary fine arts, liberal studies, marine biology, psychology and community studies

Pres.: Dr CYNTHIA E. HUGGINS
Provost and Vice-Pres. for Academic Affairs: STUART G. SWAIN
Vice-Pres. for Admin. and Finance: THOMAS L. POTTER
Dean of Enrolment Management: MICHAEL MATTISON
Registrar: MARY STOVER
Dir of Library: ANGELYNN KING

Library of 94,000 vols, 15,000 journals
Number of teachers: 36
Number of students: 1,000

University of Maine at Presque Isle

181 Main St, Presque Isle, ME 04769-2888
Telephone: (207) 768-9400
Fax: (207) 768-9608
E-mail: admissions@umpi.edu
Internet: www.umpi.edu

Founded 1903 as Aroostook State Normal School, present name and status 1971
State control
Academic year: September to May

Colleges of arts and sciences, professional programs, education; programmes in art, athletic training and health, applied science, biology, business and int. studies, criminal justice, elementary education, English, exercise science/physical education, environmental studies, history, liberal studies, mathematics, medical laboratory technology, physical education, professional communication, psychology, recreation/leisure services, social work, teacher education, world languages; bachelors of applied science and honours programmes

Pres.: Prof. Dr LINDA SCHOTT
Provost and Vice-Pres. for Academic Affairs: Dr MICHAEL SONNTAG
Vice-Pres. for Admin. and Finance: CHARLES BONIN
Dean of Students: CHRISTINE L. CORSELLO
Dir of Admissions: ERIN BENSON
Registrar: KATHY DAVIS
Library Dir: JOANNE WALLINGFORD
Library of 458,500 vols
Number of students: 1,453
Publication: *Upcountry* (online).

University of Maine, Farmington

246 Main St, Farmington, ME 04938
Telephone: (207) 778-7000
Fax: (207) 778-8193
E-mail: umfadmit@maine.edu
Internet: www.umf.maine.edu
Founded 1864 as Western State Normal School, present name and status 1970
State control
Academic year: August to May (2 semesters)
Pres.: THEODORA J. KALIKOW
Vice-Pres. for Academic Affairs and Provost: Prof. DANIEL P. GUNN
Vice-Pres. for Admin.: RYAN LOW
Vice Pres. for Enrolment Management and Marketing: ROBERTO NOYA
Vice-Pres. for Student and Community Services: F. CELESTE BRANHAM
Dir of Admissions: JAMIE MARCUS
Dir of Library: FRANKLIN D. ROBERTS
Library of 105,000 vols
Number of teachers: 125
Number of students: 2,000

DEANS

College of Arts and Sciences: ROBERT L. LIVELY
College of Education, Health and Rehabilitation: KATHERINE W. YARDLEY

University of Maine, Fort Kent

23 University Dr., Fort Kent, ME 04743
Telephone: (207) 834-7500
Fax: (207) 973-3296
E-mail: umfkadm@maine.edu
Internet: www.umfk.edu
Founded 1878 as Madawaska Training School, present name and status 1970
State control
Academic year: September to May
Academic divs incl. arts and humanities, education, natural and behavioural sciences, nursing
Pres.: WILSON G. HESS
Vice-Pres. for Academic Affairs and Dean of Faculty: Dr RACHEL E. ALBERT
Vice-Pres. for Admin. and Interim Dean of Enrolment Management: JOHN D. MURPHY
Registrar: DONALD M. RAYMOND
Dir. of Admissions: JILL M. CAIRNS
Dir of Information Services: LESLIE E. KELLY
Library of 48,280 vols, 118,452 e-books, 183 periodicals, 6,024 microforms, 40,088 e-journals
Number of teachers: 68
Number of students: 1,109

University of Southern Maine

POB 9300, Portland, ME 04104-9300
Telephone: (207) 780-4141
Fax: (207) 780-4933
E-mail: usmadm@usm.maine.edu
Internet: www.usm.maine.edu
Founded 1878
Campuses in Gorham, Lewiston-Auburn
State control
Academic year: September to May
Pres.: Dr SELMA BOTMAN

Provost and Vice-Pres. for Academic Affairs: Dr JOHN R. WRIGHT
Vice-Pres. for Univ. Advancement: MEG WESTON
Dir of Admission: SCOTT STEINBERG
Dean of Graduate Studies: DAHLIA LYNN
Registrar: STEVEN G. RAND
Librarian: DAVID NUTTY
Library of 484,000 volumes
Number of teachers: 351
Number of students: 9,564

DEANS

College of Arts, Humanities and Sciences: Dr LYNN M. KUZMA
College of Management and Human Services: Prof. Dr JOSEPH MCDONNELL
College of Science, Technology and Health: Prof. ANDREW ANDERSON
Lewiston-Auburn College: Dr JOYCE GIBSON
School of Law: PETER PITEGOFF

UNIVERSITY OF NEW ENGLAND

11 Hills Beach Rd, Biddeford, ME 04005
Telephone: (207) 283-0171
Fax: (207) 282-6379
E-mail: admissions@une.edu
Internet: www.une.edu
Founded 1939 as College Séraphique; present name and status 1978; merged with Westbrook College (f. 1831) 1996
Campus in Portland
Private control
Academic year: September to May
Pres.: Dr DANIELLE N. RIPICH
Provost and Vice-Pres. for Academic Affairs: Dr JOHN L. WILLIAMS
Vice-Pres. for Campus Services: WILLIAM J. BOLA
Vice-Pres. for Fiscal Affairs: NICOLE TRUFANT
Vice-Pres. for Institutional Advancement: THOMAS E. WHITE
Vice-Pres. for Operations: BILL J. BOLA
Vice-Pres. for Research and Dean of Graduate Studies: Dr TIMOTHY FORD
Vice-Pres. for Student Affairs: CYNTHIA SMITH FORREST
Dean of Enrolment Management: S. GATO
Dean of Students: MARK NAHORNEY
Registrar: JOAN M. MONAHAN
Dean of Library Services: ANDREW J. GOLUB
Number of teachers: 148
Number of students: 7,330

DEANS

College of Arts and Sciences: Dr JEANNE A. K. HEY
College of Dental Medicine: Dr JAMES J. KOELBL
College of Osteopathic Medicine: Dr MARC B. HAHN
College of Pharmacy: Dr GAYLE A. BRAZEAU
Westbrook College of Health Professions: Dr DAVID M. WARD

MARYLAND

CAPITOL COLLEGE

11301 Springfield Rd, Laurel, MD 20708
Telephone: (301) 369-2800
Fax: (301) 953-1442
E-mail: admissions@capitol-college.edu
Internet: www.capitol-college.edu
Founded 1927 as Capitol Radio Engineering Institute, present location 1980
Private control
Pres. and CEO: Dr MICHAEL T. WOOD
Vice-Pres. for Academic Affairs and Chief Academic Officer: Dr WILLIAM MACONACHY
Vice-Pres. for College Advancement and Chief Advancement Officer: MICHAEL GIBBS

Vice-Pres. for Finance and Admin. and Chief Financial Officer: DERICK VEENSTRA
Vice-Pres. for Planning and Assessment and Chief Technical Officer: DIANNE VEENSTRA
Dean for Student Life: MELINDA BUNNELL-RHYNE
Dir for Library Services: RICK A. SAMPLE
Library of 10,000 vols
Number of teachers: 57
Number of students: 801 (630 undergraduate, 171 graduate)

DEANS

School of Business and Information Sciences: Dr HELEN G. BARKER
School of Business and Information Sciences: (vacant)

GOUCHER COLLEGE

1021 Dulaney Valley Rd, Baltimore, MD 21204-2794
Telephone: (410) 337-6000
Fax: (410) 337-6504
E-mail: admissions@goucher.edu
Internet: www.goucher.edu
Founded 1885
Private control
Academic year: August to May
Pres.: SANFORD J. UNGAR
Provost: MARC ROY
Vice-Pres. and Dean of Students: GAIL NEVERDON EDMONDS
Vice-Pres. for Devt and Alumni Affairs: JANET WILEY
Vice-Pres. for Enrolment Management: MICHAEL O'LEARY
Vice-Pres. for Finance: TOM PHIZACKLEA
Vice-Pres for Govt and Community Relations: WENDY BELZER LITZKE
Registrar: ANDREW WESTFALL
Librarian: NANCY MAGNUSON
Number of teachers: 173 (full-time and part-time)
Number of students: 2,350

Publications: *Donnybrook Fair* (1 a year), *Preface, Quindecim, The Goucher Quarterly*.

HOOD COLLEGE

401 Rosemont Ave, Frederick, MD 21701-8575
Telephone: (301) 663-3131
Fax: (301) 694-7653
Internet: www.hood.edu
Founded 1893 as Woman's College of Frederick, present name 1912
Academic year: August to May
Pres.: Dr RONALD J. VOLPE
Provost and Vice-Pres. for Academic Affairs: Dr KATHERINE CONWAY-TURNER
Sr Vice-Pres. for Finance and Treas.: CHARLES MANN
Vice-Pres. for Undergraduate and Graduate Enrolment Management: Dr KATHLEEN C. BANDS
Vice-Pres. for Institutional Advancement: NANCY GILLECE
Vice-Pres. for Student Life and Dean of Students: OLIVIA G. WHITE
Dean for Graduate School: ALLEN FLORA
Registrar: NANETTE MARKEY
Library Dir: JAN SAMET O'LEARY
Library of 185,000 vols
Number of teachers: 136 (107 full-time, 29 part-time)
Number of students: 2,435
Publication: *Hood Magazine* (4 a year).

JOHNS HOPKINS UNIVERSITY

3400 N Charles St, Baltimore, MD 21218
Telephone: (410) 516-8000
Internet: www.jhu.edu

Founded 1876
Private control
Academic year: September to June

Pres.: RONALD J. DANIELS
Provost and Sr Vice-Pres. for Academic Affairs: LLOYD B. MINOR
Sr Vice-Pres. for External Affairs and Devt: MICHAEL C. EICHER
Sr Vice-Pres. for Finance and Admin.: DANIEL G. ENNIS
Sr Vice-Pres. and Chief of Staff: CLARENCE D. ARMBRISTER
Vice-Pres. and Gen. Counsel: STEPHEN S. DUNHAM
Vice-Pres. for Communications and Public Affairs: GLENN M. BIELER
Vice-Pres. for Devt and Alumni Relations: FRITZ W. SCHROEDER
Vice-Pres. for Finance and Treas.: (vacant)
Vice-Pres. for Govt and Community Affairs: THOMAS S. LEWIS
Vice-Pres. for Human Resources: CHARLENE MOORE HAYES
Vice-Pres. for Medicine: EDWARD D. MILLER
Registrar: HEDY SCHAEDEL
Dean for Univ. Libraries: WINSTON TABB
Library: see Libraries and Archives
Number of teachers: 519
Number of students: 6,971 (5,038 undergraduate, 1,933 graduate)
Publications: *Cardiovascular Report* (4 a year), *Conquest, HeadLines, Hopkins BrainWise* (3 a year), *Hopkins Children's, Hopkins Medicine Magazine, Johns Hopkins Medicine Magazine, NeuroNow, On Target, Promise and Progress*

DEANS

Bloomberg School of Public Health: MICHAEL J. KLAG
Carey Business School: PHILLIP PHAN
School of Advanced International Studies: Dr JESSICA P. EINHORN (acting)
School of Education: DAVID ANDREWS
School of Medicine: EDWARD D. MILLER
School of Nursing: MARTHA N. HILL (acting)
Whiting School of Engineering: NICHOLAS P. JONES
Zanvyl Krieger School of Arts and Sciences: KATHERINE NEWMAN

PROFESSORS

Bloomberg School of Public Health:

ALEXANDER, C. S., Population and Family Health Sciences
ANDERSON, G. F., Health Policy and Management
ANTHONY, J. C., Mental Hygiene
ARMENIAN, H. K., Epidemiology
BAKER, S. P., Health Policy and Management
BAKER, T. D., Int. Health
BEATY, T. H., Epidemiology
BECKER, S., Population and Family Health Sciences
BERTRAND, J. T., Population and Family Health Sciences
BLACK, R., Int. Health
BREITNER, J. C. S., Mental Hygiene
BRENNER, M. H., Health Policy and Management
BREYSSE, P., Environmental Health Sciences
BROOKMEYER, R., Biostatistics
BROWN, T. R., Biochemistry and Molecular Biology
BRYANT, F. R., Biochemistry and Molecular Biology
BURKE, D. S., Int. Health
CABALLERO, B., Int. Health

CELENTANO, D., Epidemiology
CHANDRASEGARAN, S., Environmental Health Sciences
CHOW, L., Population and Family Health Sciences
COHEN, B. H., Epidemiology
COMSTOCK, G. W., Epidemiology
CULOTTA, V., Environmental Health Sciences
DANNENBERG, A. M., Environmental Health Sciences
DIENER-WEST, M., Biostatistics
EATON, W. W., Mental Hygiene
ENSMINGER, M. E., Health Policy and Management
FADEN, R., Health Policy and Management
FEINLEIB, M., Epidemiology
FITZGERALD, R. S., Environmental Health Sciences
GIELEN, A., Health Policy and Management
GILMAN, R., Int. Health
GOLDBERG, A. M., Environmental Health Sciences
GOLDMAN, L., Environmental Health Sciences
GORDIS, L., Epidemiology
GOSTIN, L., Health Policy and Management
GRAY, R. H., Population and Family Health Sciences
GRIFFIN, D. E., Molecular Microbiology and Immunology
GROOPMAN, J. D., Environmental Health Sciences
GROSSMAN, L., Biochemistry and Molecular Biology
GUILARTE, T. R., Environmental Health Sciences
GUYER, B., Population and Family Health Sciences
HALSEY, N., Int. Health
HARDWICK, J. M., Molecular Microbiology and Immunology
HELZLSOUER, K., Epidemiology
HENDERSON, D. A., Int. Health
HILL, K. H., Population and Family Health Sciences
HUANG, P. C., Biochemistry
JAKAB, G. J., Environmental Health Sciences
KASPER, J. A., Health Policy and Management
KATZ, J., Int. Health
KENSLER, T. W., Environmental Health Sciences
KETNER, G. W., Molecular Microbiology and Immunology
KIM, Y. J., Population and Family Health Sciences
KLEEBURGER, S., Environmental Health Sciences
KRAG, S. S., Biochemistry and Molecular Biology
KUMAR, N., Molecular Microbiology and Immunology
LAWRENCE, R. S., Health Policy and Management
LEAF, P. J., Mental Hygiene
LEVIN, D. E., Biochemistry
LIANG, K. Y., Biostatistics
LINKS, J. M., Environmental Health Sciences
MACKENZIE, E. J., Health Policy and Management
MCMACKEN, R., Biochemistry and Molecular Biology
MARGOLIK, J., Molecular Microbiology and Immunology
MARKHAM, R., Molecular Microbiology and Immunology
MATANOSKI, G. M., Epidemiology
MEINERT, C. L., Epidemiology
MILLER, P. S., Biochemistry and Molecular Biology
MITZNER, W. A., Environmental Health Sciences

MORLOCK, L., Health Policy and Management
MORROW, R., Int. Health
MOSLEY, W. H., Population and Family Health Sciences
MUÑOZ, A., Epidemiology
NATHANSON, C. A., Population and Family Health Sciences
NAVARRO, V., Health Policy and Management
NELSON, K., Epidemiology
PAIGE, D. M., Population and Family Health Sciences
PICKART, C. M., Biochemistry
PIERCE, N. F., Int. Health
PIOTROW, P. T., Population and Family Health Sciences
POWE, N. R., Epidemiology
REINKE, W. A., Int. Health
RISBY, T., Environmental Health Sciences
ROHDE, C. A., Biostatistics
ROSE, N. R., Molecular Microbiology and Immunology
ROTER, D., Health Policy and Management
ROYALL, R. M., Biostatistics
SACK, D., Int. Health
SACK, R. B., Int. Health
SALKEVER, D. S., Health Policy and Management
SAMET, J., Epidemiology
SANTOSHAM, M., Int. Health
SCHOENRICH, E. H., Health Policy and Management
SCHWARTZ, B., Environmental Health Sciences
SCOCCA, J. J., Biochemistry
SCOTT, A. L., Molecular Microbiology and Immunology
SHAH, K. V., Molecular Microbiology and Immunology
SOMMER, A., Epidemiology
SPANNHAKE, E., Environmental Health Sciences
STARFIELD, B., Health Policy and Management
STEINHOFF, M., Int. Health
STEINWACHS, D. M., Health Policy and Management
STRICKLAND, P. T., Environmental Health Sciences
STROBINO, D. M., Population and Family Health Sciences
SZKLO, M., Epidemiology
TERET, S. P., Health Policy and Management
TIELSCH, J. M., Int. Health
TONASCIA, J., Biostatistics
TRPIS, M., Molecular Microbiology and Immunology
TRUSH, M. A., Environmental Health Sciences
TS'O, P. O. P., Biochemistry and Molecular Biology
TSUI, A. O., Population and Family Health Sciences
WAGNER, H. N., Environmental Health Sciences
WANG, M., Biostatistics
WEINER, J. P., Health Policy and Management
WEST, K., Int. Health
WRIGHT, W. W., Biochemistry and Molecular Biology
YAGER, J., Environmental Health Sciences
ZABIN, L. S., Population and Family Health Sciences
ZEGER, S., Biostatistics
ZIRKIN, B., Biochemistry and Molecular Biology

Carey School of Business:

AGRESTI, W., Business Studies
ANIKEEF, M., Business Studies
DADA, M., Business Studies
LIEBOWITZ, J., Business Studies
PHAN, P., Business Studies

School of Medicine:

ABELOFF, M. D., Oncology, Medicine
ACHUFF, S. C., Medicine
ADKINSON, N. F., Jr, Medicine
ADLER, R., Ophthalmology and Neuroscience
AGNEW, W. S., Physiology and Neuroscience
AGRE, P. C., Biological Chemistry and Medicine
AMBINDER, R. F., Oncology, Pathology, Pharmacology and Molecular Science
AMZEL, L. M., Biophysics and Biophysical Chemistry
ANHALT, G. J., Dermatology and Pathology
ASKIN, F. B., Pathology
ATOR, N. A., Psychiatry
AUGUST, J. T., Pharmacology and Molecular Sciences, Oncology
BARBARAN, J. M., Neuroscience, Psychiatry
BARKER, L. R., Medicine
BARTLETT, J. G., Medicine
BAUGHMAN, K. L., Medicine
BAUMGARTNER, W. A., Surgery and Cardiac Surgery
BAYLESS, T. M., Medicine
BAYLIN, S. B., Oncology and Medicine
BEACHY, P. A., Molecular Biology and Genetics
BECKER, D. M., Medicine
BECKER, L. C., Medicine
BELL, W. R., Medicine
BERG, J. M., Biophysics and Biophysical Chemistry
BIGELOW, G. E., Psychiatry and Behavioural Sciences
BOCHNER, B. S., Medicine
BOEKE, J. D., Molecular Biology and Genetics
BOITNOTT, J. K., Pathology
BOROWITZ, M. J., Pathology, Oncology
BOTTOMLEY, P. A., Radiology and Radiological Science, Nuclear Magnetic Resonance Research, Biomedical Engineering and Medicine
BRANDT, J., Psychiatry
BREAKEY, W. R., Psychiatry
BREM, H., Neurological Surgery, Oncology
BRESSLER, N. M., Ophthalmology
BRESSLER, S. B., Ophthalmology
BRIEGER, G. H., History of Science, Medicine and Technology
BRINKER, J. A., Medicine
BROONER, R. K., Psychiatry
BRUSHART, T. M., Orthopaedic Surgery, Surgery, Plastic Surgery and Neurology
BULKLEY, G. B., Surgery
BURDICK, J. F., Surgery
BURGER, P. C., Pathology, Oncology Center, Neurological Surgery
BURKE, P. J., Oncology Center, Medicine
BURTON, J. R., Medicine
CALKINS, H. G., Medicine and Paediatrics
CAMERON, J. L., Surgery, Oncology
CAMPBELL, J. N., Neurological Surgery
CAMPOCHIARO, P. A., Ophthalmology and Neuroscience
CAPUTE, A. J., Paediatrics
CARSON, B. S., Neurological Surgery, Oncology, Paediatrics and Plastic Surgery
CARTER, H. B., Urology and Oncology
CASELLA, J. F., Paediatrics, Oncology Center
CASERO, R. J., Jr, Oncology
CATALDO, M. F., Psychiatry and Paediatrics
CHAISSON, R. E., Medicine
CHAKRAVARTI, A., Medicine and Paediatrics
CHAN, D. W., Pathology, Oncology, Radiology and Radiological Science, Urology
CHANDRA, N., Medicine
CHANG, A. Y., Oncology
CHAO, E. Y., Orthopaedic Surgery and Biomedical Engineering

CHARACHE, P., Pathology, Oncology, Medicine
CHATTERJEE, S. B., Paediatrics
CIVIN, C. I., Oncology, Paediatrics
CLEMENTS, J. E., Comparative Medicine, Neurology and Pathology
COFFEY, D. S., Urology, Oncology, Pharmacology and Molecular Sciences
COLE, P. A., Pharmacology and Molecular Sciences
COLOMBANI, P. M., Surgery, Paediatric Surgery, Oncology
CORDEN, J. L., Molecular Biology and Genetics
CORNBLATH, D. R., Neurology
COTTER, R. J., Pharmacology and Molecular Sciences, Biophysics and Biophysical Chemistry
CRAIG, N. L., Molecular Biology and Genetics
CRAIG, S. W., Biological Chemistry and Pathology
CUMMINGS, C. W., Otolaryngology—Head and Neck Surgery, Oncology
CUTTING, G. R., Paediatrics and Medicine
DANG, C. V., Medicine, Oncology, Pathology
DANNALS, R. F., Radiology, Radiological Science and Nuclear Medicine
DAVIDSON, N. E., Oncology
DAWSON, T., Neurology and Neuroscience
DE JUAN, E., Jr, Ophthalmology
DELATEUR, B. J., Physical Medicine and Rehabilitation
DENCKLA, M. B., Neurology and Paediatrics
DEPAULO, J. R., Psychiatry
DESIDERIO, S. V., Molecular Biology and Genetics
DEVREOTES, P. N., Biological Chemistry, Cell Biology and Anatomy
DICELLO, J. F., Oncology
DIEHL, A. M., Medicine
DIETZ, H. C., Paediatrics
DONEHOWER, R. C., Oncology and Medicine
DONOWITZ, M., Medicine
DOVER, G. J., Paediatrics and Oncology
DRACHMAN, D. B., Neurology and Neuroscience
EGGLESTON, P. A., Paediatrics
EISELE, D. W., Otolaryngology—Head and Neck Surgery, Anaesthesiology, Critical Care Medicine, Oncology and Urology
ENGLUND, P. T., Biological Chemistry
EPSTEIN, J. I., Pathology, Oncology, Urology
EROZAN, Y. S., Pathology
ETTINGER, D. S., Oncology, Medicine
FAJARDO, L. L., Radiology and Radiological Science, Diagnostic Radiology and Oncology
FEINBERG, A. P., Medicine and Oncology
FINKELSTEIN, D., Ophthalmology
FISHMAN, E. K., Radiology and Radiological Science, Diagnostic Radiology, Oncology
FORASTIERE, A. A., Oncology, Otolaryngology—Head and Neck Surgery
FORTUIN, N. J., Medicine
FOX, H. E., Gynaecology and Obstetrics
FRASSICA, F. J., Orthopaedic Surgery and Oncology
FREEMAN, J. M., Neurology and Paediatrics
FRIED, L. P., Medicine
FROST, J. J., Radiology and Radiological Science, and Nuclear Medicine and Neuroscience
FUCHS, P. A., Otolaryngology—Head and Neck Surgery, Biomedical Engineering and Neuroscience
GARCIA, J. G., Medicine
GEARHART, J. D., Gynaecology and Obstetrics, Comparative Medicine and Physiology
GEARHART, J. P., Urology and Paediatrics
GERSTENBLITH, G., Medicine
GIARDIELLO, F. M., Medicine, Oncology, Pathology

GIBSON, D. W., Pharmacology and Molecular Sciences
GOLDBERG, M. F., Ophthalmology
GOLDSTEIN, G. W., Neurology and Paediatrics
GORDIS, L., Paediatrics
GORDON, B., Neurology
GOTTSCH, J. D., Ophthalmology
GREEN, W. R., Ophthalmology and Pathology
GREENOUGH, W. B., III, Medicine
GREIDER, C. W., Molecular Biology and Genetics, Oncology
GRIFFIN, J. W., Neurology, Neuroscience and Pathology
GRIFFITH, L. S., Medicine
GRIFFITHS, R. R., Psychiatry and Neuroscience
GROSSMAN, S. A., Oncology, Medicine and Neurological Surgery
GUGGINO, W. B., Physiology and Paediatrics
GUYTON, D. L., Ophthalmology
HALPERIN, H. R., Medicine, Biomedical Engineering
HAMILTON, R. G., Medicine
HANDLER, J. S., Medicine
HANLEY, D. F., Neurology, Anaesthesiology and Critical Care Medicine
HAPONIK, E. F., Medicine
HARMON, J. W., Surgery
HARRIS, J. C., Jr, Psychiatry and Paediatrics
HART, G. W., Biological Chemistry
HAWKINS, B. S., Ophthalmology
HAYWARD, G. S., Pharmacology and Molecular Sciences, Oncology and Pathology
HAYWARD, S. D., Pharmacology and Molecular Sciences, Oncology and Pathology
HELLMAN, D. B., Medicine
HENDRY, S. H., Neuroscience
HEPTINSTALL, R. H., Pathology
HESS, A. D., Oncology and Pathology
HOLTZMAN, N. A., Paediatrics
HRUBAN, R. H., Pathology, Oncology
HUBBARD, A. L., Cell Biology, Anatomy and Physiology
HUGANIR, R. L., Neuroscience
HUGGINS, G. R., Gynaecology and Obstetrics
HUNGERFORD, D. S., Orthopaedic Surgery
HUTCHINS, G. M., Pathology
ISAACS, J. T., Oncology and Urology
ISAACS, W. B., Urology, Oncology
JABS, D. A., Ophthalmology and Medicine
JABS, E. W., Paediatrics, Medicine, Surgery and Plastic Surgery
JACKSON, J. B., Pathology
JASINSKI, D. R., Medicine
JOHNS, R. A., Anaesthesiology and Critical Care Medicine
JOHNS, R. J., Medicine
JOHNSON, K. O., Neuroscience and Biomedical Engineering
JOHNSON, R. T., Neurology, Molecular Biology, Genetics and Neuroscience
JOHNSTON, M. V., Neurology and Paediatrics
JONES, B., Radiology and Radiological Sciences, Diagnostic Radiology
JONES, R. J., Oncology
KAN, J. S., Paediatrics
KASHIMA, H. K., Otolaryngology—Head and Neck Surgery, Oncology
KASS, D. A., Medicine and Biomedical Engineering
KAVOUSSI, L. R., Urology
KELEN, G. D., Emergency Medicine
KELLY, T. J., Jr, Molecular Biology and Genetics
KICKLER, T. S., Pathology, Oncology and Medicine
KIM, K. S., Paediatrics
KINZLER, K. W., Oncology

KIRSCH, J. R., Anaesthesiology and Critical Care Medicine
KLAG, M. J., Medicine
KLEIN, A. S., Surgery
KOCH, W., Otolaryngology, Oncology
KOEHLER, R. C., Anaesthesiology and Critical Care Medicine
KOSTUIK, J., Orthopaedic Surgery and Neurological Surgery
KUNCL, R. W., Neurology
KURMAN, R. J., Gynaecology and Obstetrics, Pathology
KWITEROVICH, P. O., Jr, Paediatrics and Medicine
LADENSON, P. W., Medicine, Oncology and Pathology
LANE, M. D., Biological Chemistry
LAWSON, E. E., Paediatrics
LEDERMAN, H. M., Paediatrics
LEE, S., Molecular Biology and Genetics
LENZ, F. A., Neurological Surgery
LEONG, K. W., Biomedical Engineering
LESSER, R. P., Neurology, Neurological Surgery
LEVINE, D. M., Medicine
LEVINE, M. A., Paediatrics and Medicine
LI, G., Emergency Medicine
LICHTENSTEIN, L. M., Medicine
LIETMAN, P. S., Medicine, Paediatrics, Pharmacology and Molecular Sciences
LILLEMOE, K. D., Surgery
LIU, J., Pharmacology and Molecular Sciences, Neuroscience
LONG, D. M., Neurological Surgery
LOUGHLIN, G. M., Paediatrics
LYKETSOS, C. G., Psychiatry
MCARTHUR, J. C., Neurology
MCCARTHY, E. F., Jr, Pathology, Orthopaedic Surgery
MCCAUL, M. E., Psychiatry
MACGLASHAN, D. W., Medicine
MCHUGH, P. R., Psychiatry
MCKHANN, G. M., Neurology and Neuroscience
MCKUSICK, V. A., Medicine
MCMILLAN, J. A., Paediatrics
MALONEY, P. C., Physiology
MANN, R. B., Pathology, Oncology
MANSON, P. N., Surgery and Plastic Surgery
MARBAN, E., Medicine and Physiology
MASSOF, R. W., Ophthalmology
MAUGHAN, W. L., Medicine and Biomedical Engineering
MAUMENEE, I. E., Ophthalmology
MERZ, W. G., Pathology
MEYER, R. A., Neurological Surgery and Biomedical Engineering
MEZEY, E., Medicine
MIGEON, B. R., Paediatrics
MIGEON, C. J., Paediatrics
MILDVAN, A. S., Biological Chemistry
MILLER, E. D., Anaesthesiology and Critical Care Medicine
MILLER, N. R., Ophthalmology and Neurology, Neurological Surgery
MINOR, L. B., Otolaryngology—Head and Neck Surgery, Biomedical Engineering, Neuroscience
MOLLIVER, M. E., Neuroscience and Neurology
MONTELL, C., Biological Chemistry and Neuroscience
MONTZ, F. J., Gynaecology and Obstetrics, Oncology
MOORE, T. H., Medicine
MORAN, T. H., Psychiatry
MOSER, H. W., Neurology and Paediatrics
MOSTWIN, J. L., Urology
MUNSTER, A. M., Surgery and Plastic Surgery
MURPHY, D. B., Cell Biology and Anatomy
MURPHY, P. A., Medicine and Molecular Biology and Genetics
NAIDU, S., Neurology, Paediatrics
NATARAJAN, V., Medicine

NATHANS, J., Molecular Biology and Genetics, Neuroscience and Ophthalmology
NESS, P. M., Pathology and Medicine
NICHOLS, D. G., Anaesthesiology, Critical Care Medicine
NIPARKO, J. K., Otolaryngology—Head and Neck Surgery
NORTH, R., Neurological Surgery, Anaesthesiology and Critical Care Medicine
PARDOLL, D. M., Oncology, Medicine and Pathology
PARTIN, A., Urology
PEARLSON, G. D., Psychiatry
PEDERSEN, P. L., Biological Chemistry
PERLER, B. A., Surgery
PERMUTT, S., Medicine
PETRI, M., Medicine
PIANTADOSI, S., Oncology
PITHA-ROWE, P. M., Oncology
PLOTNICK, L., Paediatrics
POPEL, A. S., Biomedical Engineering
POWE, N. R, Medicine
PRICE, D. L., Pathology, Neurology and Neuroscience
QUIGLEY, H. A., Ophthalmology
QUINN, T. C., Medicine
RABINS, P. V., Psychiatry
RACUSEN, L., Pathology
RAJA, S. N., Anaesthesiology and Critical Care Medicine
REED, R. R., Molecular Biology and Genetics and Neuroscience
REEVES, R. H., Physiology
REPKA, M. X., Ophthalmology, Paediatrics
RICHARDSON, M. A., Otolaryngology—Head and Neck Surgery
RIGAMONTI, D., Neurological Surgery, Radiology and Radiological Science, Neuroradiology
RONNETT, G. V., Neuroscience, Neurology
ROSE, G. D., Biophysics and Biophysical Chemistry
ROSE, K. D., Cell Biology and Anatomy
ROSENSTEIN, B. J., Paediatrics
ROSENTHAL, D. L., Pathology, Gynaecology and Obstetrics, Oncology
ROSS, C. A., Psychiatry and Neuroscience
ROTHSTEIN, J. D., Neurology and Neuroscience
ROWE, P. C., Paediatrics
RUFF, C. B., Cell Biology, Anatomy and Orthopaedic Surgery
RYUGO, D. K., Otolaryngology—Head and Neck Surgery, Neuroscience
SACHS, M. B., Biomedical Engineering and Neuroscience, Otolaryngology—Head and Neck Surgery
SAUDEK, C. D., Medicine
SAUDER, D. N., Dermatology
SCHACHAT, A. P., Ophthalmology and Oncology
SCHEIN, O. D., Ophthalmology
SCHLEIMER, R. P., Medicine
SCHMIDT, C. W., Jr, Psychiatry
SCHNAAR, R. L., Pharmacology, Molecular Sciences and Neuroscience
SCHNECK, J., Pathology
SCHRAMM, L. P., Biomedical Engineering and Neuroscience
SCHWARZ, K., Paediatrics
SCIUBBA, J. J., Otolaryngology—Head and Neck Surgery, Dermatology, Pathology
SEMENZA, G. L., Paediatrics
SHAPER, J. H., Oncology
SHAPIRO, E. P., Medicine
SHAPIRO, T. A., Medicine
SHARKIS, S. J., Oncology
SHORTLE, D. R., Biological Chemistry, Biophysics and Biophysical Chemistry
SHOUKAS, A. A., Biomedical Engineering
SIDRANSKY, D., Otolaryngology – Head and Neck Surgery, Urology, Oncology, Pathology
SIEGELMAN, S. S., Radiology and Radiological Science
SILICIANO, R. F., Medicine

SINGER, H. S., Neurology and Paediatrics
SLAVNEY, P. R., Psychiatry and Medicine
SMITH, K. D., Paediatrics
SMITH, P. L., Medicine
SNYDER, S. H., Neuroscience, Pharmacology, Molecular Sciences and Psychiatry
SOLLNER-WEBB, B. T., Biological Chemistry
SOMMER, A., Ophthalmology
SPIVAK, J. L., Medicine and Oncology
SPONSELLER, P. D., Orthopaedic Surgery
STARK, W. J., Jr, Ophthalmology
STITZER, M. L., Psychiatry
STRAIN, E. C., Psychiatry
SYLVESTER, J. T., Medicine
TALALAY, P., Pharmacology and Molecular Sciences
TEAFORD, M. F., Cell Biology and Anatomy
TERRY, P. B., Medicine
THAKOR, N. V., Biomedical Engineering
THOMAS, G. H., Paediatrics and Pathology
TOMASELLI, G. F., Medicine
TRAILL, T. A., Medicine
TRAYSTMAN, R. J., Anaesthesiology and Critical Care Medicine
TSO, M. D., Ophthalmology and Pathology
UNDEM, B. J., Medicine
VALLE, D. L., Paediatrics and Ophthalmology
VAN ZIJL, P. C., Radiology and Radiological Sciences, Nuclear Magnetic Resonance, Biophysics and Biophysical Chemistry
VOGELSANG, G. B., Oncology
VOGELSTEIN, B., Oncology and Pathology
VON DER HEYDT, R., Neuroscience
WALLACH, E. E., Gynaecology and Obstetrics
WALSER, M., Pharmacology and Molecular Sciences and Medicine
WALSH, P.C., Urology
WAND, G. S., Medicine, Psychiatry
WATKINS, L., Jr, Surgery and Cardiac Surgery
WEISHAMPEL, D. B., Cell Biology and Anatomy
WEISS, J. L., Medicine
WEST, S., Ophthalmology
WHARAM, M. D., Jr, Oncology, Paediatrics, Radiology and Radiological Science and Neurological Surgery
WIGLEY, F. M., Medicine
WILLIAMS, G. M., Surgery
WINCHURCH, R. A., Surgery
WINKELSTEIN, J. A., Paediatrics, Medicine and Pathology
WINSLOW, R. L., Biomedical Engineering
WISE, R. A., Medicine
WOLBERGER, C., Biophysics and Biophysical Chemistry
WONG, D. F., Radiology and Radiological Science, and Nuclear Medicine
WORLEY, P. F., Neuroscence and Neurology
YARDLEY, J. H., Pathology
YASTER, M., Anaesthesiology and Critical Care Medicine
YAU, K., Neuroscience and Ophthalmology
YEO, C. J., Surgery and Oncology
YOLKEN, R. H., Paediatrics
YOUNG, E. D., Biomedical Engineering and Neuroscience, Otolaryngology—Head and Neck Surgery
YOUSEM, D. M., Radiology and Radiological Science, Neuroradiology
YUE, I. D., Biomedical Engineering and Neuroscience
ZACUR, H. A., Gynaecology and Obstetrics
ZEE, D. S., Neurology and Neuroscience, Ophthalmology and Otolaryngology—Head and Neck Surgery
ZEIMER, R., Ophthalmology
ZEITLIN, P. L., Paediatrics
ZERHOUNI, E. A., Radiology and Radiological Science, Diagnostic Radiology and Biomedical Engineering
ZIEVE, P. D., Medicine
ZINK, C., Comparative Medicine and Pathology

ZWEIER, J. L., Medicine

Whiting School of Engineering:

ANANDARAJAH, A., Civil Engineering
ANDREOU, A. G., Electrical and Computer Engineering
AWERBUCH, B., Computer Science
BALL, W. P., Geography and Environmental Engineering
BETENBAUGH, M. J., Chemical Engineering
BOLAND, J., Geography and Environmental Engineering
BOUWER, E. J., Geography and Environmental Engineering
BRUSH, G. S., Geography and Environmental Engineering
BUSCH-VISHNIAC, I. J., Mechanical Engineering
CAMMARATA, R., Materials Science and Engineering
CHEN, S., Mechanical Engineering
CHIRIKJAN, G., Mechanical Engineering
DAVIDSON, F. M., Electrical and Computer Engineering
DONOHUE, M., Chemical Engineering
DOUGLAS, A. S., Mechanical Engineering
ELLIS, J. H., Geography and Environmental Engineering
FILL, J. A., Mathematical Sciences
GERMAN, D., Mathematical Sciences
GOODRICH, M. T., Computer Science
GOUTSIAS, J. I., Electrical and Computer Engineering
GREEN, R. E., Jr, Materials Science and Engineering
HAGER, G. D., Computer Science
HAN, S.-P., Mathematical Sciences
HANKE, S., Geography and Environmental Engineering
HEMKER, K. J., Mechanical Engineering
HOBBS, B. F., Geography and Environmental Engineering
IGUSA, T., Civil Engineering
JELINEK, F., Electrical and Computer Engineering
JONES, N. P., Civil Engineering
JOSEPH, R. I., Electrical and Computer Engineering
KAPLAN, A. E., Electrical and Computer Engineering
KATZ, J., Mechanical Engineering
KATZ, J. L., Chemical Engineering
KHURGIN, J. B., Electrical and Computer Engineering
KNIO, O., Mechanical Engineering
KOSARAJU, S. R., Computer Science
MASSON, G. M., Computer Science
MENEVEAU, C. V., Mechanical Engineering
MEYER, G. G. L., Electrical and Computer Engineering
MILLER, M., Biomedical Engineering
MILLER, M. I., Electrical and Computer Engineering
NAIMAN, D. Q., Mathematical Sciences
O'MELIA, C. R., Geography and Environmental Engineering
PANG, J.-S., Mathematical Sciences
PARLANGE, M. B., Geography and Environmental Engineering
PAULAITIS, M. E., Chemical Engineering
PRIEBE, C. E., Mathematical Sciences
PRINCE, J. L., Electrical and Computer Engineering
PROSPERETTI, A., Mechanical Engineering
RAMESH, K. T., Mechanical Engineering
REVELLE, C., Geography and Environmental Engineering
RUGH, W. J., Electrical and Computer Engineering
SCHEINERMAN, E. R., Mathematical Sciences
SCHOENBERGER, E. J., Geography and Environmental Engineering
SEARSON, P. C., Materials Science and Engineering
SHARPE, W. N., Jr, Mechanical Engineering

SMITH, S. F., Computer Science
STEBE, K., Chemical Engineering
STONE, A. T., Geography and Environmental Engineering
TAYLOR, R. H., Computer Science
WEINERT, H. L., Electrical and Computer Engineering
WIERMAN, J. C., Mathematical Sciences
WILCOCK, P. R., Geography and Environmental Engineering
WOLFF, L. B., Computer Science
WOLMAN, M. G., Geography and Environmental Engineering

School of Advanced International Studies (1730 Massachusetts Ave, Washington, DC 20036):

AJAMI, F., Middle East Studies
BARRET, S., Int. Relations
BODNAR, G., Int. Finance
CALLEO, D. P., European Studies
COHEN, E. A., Strategic Studies
CORDEN, W. M., Int. Economics
DORAN, C. F., Canadian Studies and Int. Relations
FRANK, I., Int. Economics
FUKUYAMA, F., Political Economy
GLEIJESES, P., US Foreign Policy and Latin American Studies
GOODELL, G. E., Int. Devt
GRILLI, E., Int. Economics
JACKSON, K. D., Asian and South East Asia Studies
LAMPTON, D. M., Asian Studies
MANDELBAUM, M., US Foreign Policy
PARROTT, B., Russian and Eurasian Studies
PEARSON, C. S., Int. Economics
RIEDEL, J. C., Int. Economics
ROETT, R., Latin American Studies and Western Hemisphere Programs
THAYER, N. B., Asian Studies
WEDGEWOOD, J. D., Int. Law and Organization
ZARTMAN, I. W., African Studies

School of Nursing:

ALLEN, J., Preventive Cardiology
BERK, R. A., Psychometrics and Statistics
CAMPBELL, J., Community Health
DONALDSON, S., Physiology and Biophysics
FRALIC, M., Nursing Management
GASTON-JOHANSSON, F., Research Utilization and Pain
HILL, M., Adult Health

Zanvyl Krieger School of Arts and Sciences:

ACHINSTEIN, P., Philosophy
ALEXANDER, K., Sociology
ANDERSON, A., English
ANDERSON, W., Romance Languages and Literatures
ARRIGHI, G., Sociology
BAGGER, J., Physics and Astronomy
BALL, G., Psychology
BALL, L., Economics
BARNETT, B., Physics and Astronomy
BECKWITH, S., Physics and Astronomy
BEEMON, K., Biology
BELL, D., History
BENNETT, C. L., Physics and Astronomy
BERRY, S., History
BESSMAN, M., Biology
BETT, R., Philosophy
BLUMENFELD, B. J., Physics and Astronomy
BOARDMAN, J. M., Mathematics
BOWEN, K., Chemistry
BRAND, L., Biology
BRIEGER, G., History of Science, Medicine and Technology
BROHOLM, C., Physics and Astronomy
BROOKS, J., History
BRYAN, B. M., Near Eastern Studies
BURZIO, L., Cognitive Science
CAMERON, S., English
CAMPE, R., German
CARROLL, C., Economics

CASTRO-KLARÉN, S., Romance Languages and Literatures
CHERLIN, A., Sociology
CHIEN, C.-L., Physics and Astronomy
CHIEN, C.-Y., Physics and Astronomy
CONE, R. A., Biophysics
CONNOLLY, W., Political Science
COOPER, J., Political Science
COOPER, J. S., Near Eastern Studies
CORCES, V., Biology
CRENSON, M., Political Science
CUMMINGS, M., Political Science
DAGDIGIAN, P., Chemistry
DAS, V., Anthropology
DAVID, S., Political Science
DAVIDSEN, A., Physics and Astronomy
DEFAUX, G., Romance Languages and Literatures
DEMPSEY, C., History of Art
DETIENNE, M., Classics
DIETZE, G., Political Science
DITZ, T., History
DIXON, S., Writing Seminars
DOERING, J., Chemistry
DOMOKOS, G., Physics and Astronomy
DRAPER, D., Chemistry
DRAPER, D., Biophysics and Chemistry
EBERT, J. D., Biology
EDIDIN, M., Biology
EGETH, H., Psychology
FALK, A., Physics and Astronomy
FAMBROUGH, D., Biology
FELDMAN, G., Physics and Astronomy
FELDMAN, P., Physics and Astronomy
FERGUSON, F., English
FERRY, J., Earth and Planetary Sciences
FISHER, G. W., Earth and Planetary Sciences
FLATHMAN, R. C., Political Science
FORD, H., Physics and Astronomy
FORNI, P., Romance Languages and Literatures
FORSTER, E., Humanities Center
FREIRE, E., Biology, Biophysics
FRIED, M., Humanities Center, History of Art
GALAMBOS, L. P., History
GALLAGHER, M., Psychology
GARVEN, G., Earth and Planetary Sciences
GERSOVITZ, M., Economics
GINSBERG, B., Political Science
GOLDBERG, J., English
GONZÁLEZ, E., Romance Languages and Literatures
GORDON, R., Sociology
GREENE, J., History
GROSSMAN, A., English
GROSSMAN, J., Political Science
HARDIE, L. A., Earth and Planetary Sciences
HARRINGTON, J., Economics
HECKMAN, T., Physics and Astronomy
HEDGECOCK, E., Biology
HENRY, R., Physics and Astronomy
HERTZ, N., Humanities Center
HOLLAND, P., Psychology
HOYT, M. A., Biology
HUANG, R. C., Biology
IRWIN, J., Writing Seminars
JOHNSON, M., History
JUSCZYK, P., Psychology
KAGAN, R., History
KARGON, R. H., History of Science, Medicine and Technology
KARLIN, K., Chemistry
KARNI, E., Economics
KATZ, R., Political Science
KECK, M., Political Science
KESSLER, H., History of Art
KHAN, M. A., Economics
KINGSLAND, S., History of Science, Medicine and Technology
KNIGHT, F., History
KOHN, M., Sociology
KOLYVAGIN, V., Mathematics

KOVESI-DOMOKOS, S., Physics and Astronomy
KROLIK, J., Physics and Astronomy
LANDAU, B., Cognitive Science
LATTMAN, E., Biophysics
LEE, Y. C., Biology
LEE, Y. K., Physics and Astronomy
LEGENDRE, G., Cognitive Science
LESLIE, S., History of Science, Medicine and Technology
LEYS, R., Humanities Center
LYKKEN, J., Physics and Astronomy
MCCARTER, P. K., Jr, Near Eastern Studies
MCCARTY, R., Biology
MCCLOSKEY, M., Cognitive Science
MCGARRY, J., Writing Seminars
MACCINI, L., Economics
MACKSEY, R., Humanities Center
MAGUIRE, H., History of Art
MARSH, B., Earth and Planetary Sciences
MELION, W., History of Art
MEYER, G., Chemistry
MINICOZZI, W. P., Mathematics
MOFFITT, R., Economics
MOON, M., English
MOOS, H. W., Physics and Astronomy
MORAVA, J., Mathematics
MORGAN, P., History
MOUDRIANAKIS, E., Biology
NÄGELE, R., German
NEUFELD, D., Physics and Astronomy
NEWMAN, S., Introduction to Policy Analysis (Policy Studies)
NICHOLS, S., Humanities Center
NICHOLS, S., Romance Languages and Literature
NIRENBERG, D., History
NORMAN, C., Physics and Astronomy
OLSON, P. L., Earth and Planetary Sciences
ONO, T., Mathematics
OSBORN, T., Earth and Planetary Sciences
PAGDEN, A., History
PANDEY, G., Anthropology
PAULSON, R., English
PEVSNER, A., Physics and Astronomy
POLAND, D., Chemistry
POSNER, G. H., Chemistry
PRIVALOV, P., Biology
REICH, D., Physics and Astronomy
ROBBINS, M., Physics and Astronomy
ROSEMAN, S., Biology
ROSS, D., History
ROWE, W., History
RUSSELL-WOOD, A. J. R., History
RUSSO, E., Romance Languages and Literature
RYNASIEWICZ, R., Philosophy
SALAMON, L., Political Science
SCHLEIF, R., Biology
SCHROER, T., Biology
SCHWARTZ, G. M., Near Eastern Studies
SHALIKA, J., Mathematics
SHAPIRO, A., Classics
SHEARN, A., Biology
SHIFFMAN, B., Mathematics
SHOKUROV, V. A., Mathematics
SIEBER, H., Romance Languages and Literatures
SILVERSTONE, H. J., Chemistry
SISSA, G., Classics
SMOLENSKY, P., Cognitive Science
SOGGE, C., Mathematics
SPIEGEL, G., History
SPRUCK, J., Mathematics
STANLEY, S., Earth and Planetary Sciences
STEPHENS, W., Romance Languages and Literatures
STROBEL, D., Earth and Planetary Sciences
SVERJENSKY, D., Earth and Planetary Sciences
SWARTZ, M., Physics and Astronomy
SZALAY, A., Physics and Astronomy
TESANOVIC, Z., Physics and Astronomy
TOWNSEND, C., Chemistry
VEBLEN, D., Earth and Planetary Sciences
VISHNIAC, E., Physics and Astronomy

WALKER, J. C., Physics and Astronomy
WALKOWITZ, J., History
WALTERS, R., History
WEISS, D., History of Art
WENTWORTH, R., Mathematics
WESTBROOK, R., Near Eastern Studies
WILLIAMS, M., Philosophy
WILSON, G., Philosophy
WILSON, W. S., Mathematics
WOLF, S., Philosophy
WOODSON, S. A., Biophysics
WYSE, R., Physics and Astronomy
YANTIS, S., Psychology
YARKONY, D., Chemistry
YOUNG, H. P., Economics
ZELDICH, S., Mathematics
ZUCKER, S., Mathematics

LOYOLA UNIVERSITY MARYLAND

4501 N Charles St, Baltimore, MD 21210-2699

Telephone: (410) 617-2000
Fax: (410) 617-2176
Internet: www.loyola.edu

Founded 1852 as Loyola College, present name and status 2009
Private control
Academic year: August to May

Pres.: Rev. BRIAN F. LINNANE
Exec. Vice-Pres.: Dr SUSAN DONOVAN
Vice-Pres. for Academic Affairs: TIMOTHY SNYDER
Vice-Pres. for Admin.: TERRENCE SAWYER
Vice-Pres. for Advancement: MEGAN GILLICK
Vice-Pres. for Finance and Treas.: RANDALL D. GENTZLER
Vice-Pres. for Enrolment Management and Communications: MARC M. CAMILLE
Vice-Pres. for Student Devt and Dean for Students: Dr SUSAN M. DONOVAN
Library Dir: JOHN MCGINTY

Library of 400,000 vols
Number of teachers: 397 (full-time)
Number of students: 6,080 (3,863 undergraduate, 2,217 graduate)

DEANS

Loyola College of Arts and Sciences: Rev. JAMES MIRACKY
School of Education: Dr L. MICKEY FENZEL
Sellinger School of Business and Management: Dr KARYL B. LEGGIO

MARYLAND INSTITUTE COLLEGE OF ART

1300 W Mount Royal Ave, Baltimore, MD 21217

Telephone: (410) 669-9200
Fax: (410) 669-9206
E-mail: pr@mica.edu
Internet: www.mica.edu

Founded 1826
Private control
Academic year: August to May

Pres.: FRED LAZARUS, IV
Vice-Pres. for Admission and Financial Aid: THERESA LYNCH BEDOYA
Provost and Vice-Pres. for Academic Affairs: GUNALAN NADARAJAN
Vice-Pres. for Advancement: MICHAEL FRANCO
Vice-Pres. for Fiscal Affairs and Chief Financial Officer: DOUGLAS MANN
Vice-Pres. for Operations: MICHAEL MOLLA
Vice-Pres. for Student Affairs and Dean of Students: J. DAVIDSON PORTER
Vice-Pres for Technology Systems and Services: TOM HYATT
Registrar: CHRISTINE PETERSON
Dir for Library: FLORENCE THORP

Library: 64,000 monographs, 325 current periodical subscriptions, 5,500 full-text

journal titles, 35,000 digital images, 215,000 slides and 5,000 DVDs and videos
Number of teachers: 178
Number of students: 2,169 (1,863 undergraduate, 306 graduate)

DEANS

Centre of Art Education: KAREN CARROLL
School for Professional and Continuing Studies: DAVID GRACYALNY

MCDANIEL COLLEGE

Two College Hill, Westminster, MD 21157-4390

Telephone: (410) 848-7000
Fax: (410) 857-2729
E-mail: pio@mcdaniel.edu
Internet: www.mcdaniel.edu

Founded 1867 as W Maryland College, present name 2002
Private control
Academic year: August to June

Liberal arts and sciences; teacher certification courses; offers Masters courses in deaf education, gerontology and human services management

Pres.: ROGER N. CASEY
Provost and Dean of the Faculty: THOMAS M. FALKNER
Vice-Pres. for Admin. and Finance: ETHAN A. SEIDEL
Vice-Pres. for Enrolment Management and Dean of Admissions: FLORENCE W. HINES
Vice-Pres. for Institutional Advancement: RICHARD G. KIEF
Dean and Vice-Pres. for Student Affairs: BETH R. GERL
Registrar: JAN KIPHART
Library Dir: JESSAME FERGUSON

Library of 200,000 vols
Number of teachers: 135
Number of students: 3,160 (1,600 undergraduate, 1,560 graduate)

MORGAN STATE UNIVERSITY

1700 E Coldspring Lane, Baltimore, MD 21251

Telephone: (443) 885-3333
E-mail: info@morgan.edu
Internet: www.morgan.edu

Founded 1867 as Centenary Biblical Institute, present status 1939
State control
Academic year: August to May

Pres.: Dr DAVID WILSON
Provost and Vice-Pres. for Academic Affairs: Dr T. JOAN ROBINSON
Vice-Pres. for Finance and Management: RAYMOND VOLLMER
Vice-Pres. for Institutional Advancement: CHERYL Y. HITCHCOCK
Vice-Pres. for Planning and Information Technology: Dr JOSEPH POPOVICH
Vice-Pres. for Student Affairs: TANYA RUSH (acting)
Gen. Counsel: JULIE GOODWIN
Dir for Library: Dr RICHARD BRADBERRY

Library of 400,000 vols
Number of teachers: 1,500
Number of students: 8,200

DEANS

College of Liberal Arts: Dr M'BARE N'GOM
School of Architecture and Planning: Dr MARY ANNE AKERS
School of Business and Management: Dr OTIS A. THOMAS
School of Community Health and Policy: Dr ALLAN NOONAN
School of Computer, Mathematical and Natural Sciences: Dr JOSEPH A. WHITTAKER

School of Education and Urban Studies: Dr PATRICIA L. WELCH

School of Engineering: Dr EUGENE M. DELOATCH

School of Graduate Studies: Dr MARK GARRISON

School of Social Work: Dr ANNA McPHATTER

MOUNT ST MARY'S UNIVERSITY

16300 Old Emmitsburg Rd, Emmitsburg, MD 21727

Telephone: (301) 447-6122
Fax: (301) 447-5755
E-mail: admissions@msmary.edu
Internet: www.msmary.edu

Founded 1805
Private control
Academic year: January to December

Pres.: THOMAS H. POWELL
Provost and Vice-Pres. for Academic Affairs: Dr DAVID B. REHM
Exec. Vice-Pres.: DAN S. SOLLER
Vice-Pres. and Seminary Rector: STEVEN P. ROHLFS
Vice-Pres. for Univ. Advancement: ROBERT J. BRENNAN
Vice-Pres. for Business and Finance: MICHAEL S. MALEWICKI
Vice-Pres. for Enrolment Management: MICHAEL A. POST
Vice-Pres. for Univ. Affairs: PAULINE A. ENGELSTÄTTER
Registrar: MARGOT C. RHOADES
Dean for Library: CHARLES L. KUHN
Library of 200,000 vols, 2,000 DVDs and VHS cassettes-documentaries
Number of teachers: 120 (98 full-time, 22 part-time)
Number of students: 2,118
Publication: *Mount Magazine* (2 a year)

DEANS

College of Liberal Arts: JOSHUA P. HOCHSCHILD
Richard J. Bolte Sr School of Business: Dr WILLIAM G. FORGANG
School of Education and Human Services: Dr BARBARA MARTIN PALMER
School of Natural Science and Mathematics: Dr DAVID W. BUSHMAN

NOTRE DAME OF MARYLAND UNIVERSITY

4701 N Charles St, Baltimore, MD 21210
Telephone: (410) 435-0100
Fax: (410) 532-6287
E-mail: admiss@ndm.edu
Internet: www.ndm.edu

Founded 1873 as Notre Dame of Maryland Collegiate Institute, present name 2011
Private control
Academic year: August to May

Pres.: Dr JAMES CONNEELY
Vice-Pres. for Academic Affairs: Sis. CHRISTINE DE VINNE
Dir for Admissions: LARRY SHATTUCK
Dir for Library: JOHN McGINTY
Library of 400,000 vols, 16,000 media items (DVDs, CDs and videos)
Number of teachers: 104 (full-time)
Number of students: 2,929

DEANS

School of Arts and Sciences: Dr DEBRA FRANKLIN
School of Education: SHARON SLEAR
School of Nursing: Dr KATIE COOK
School of Pharmacy: Dr ANNE LIN

SOJOURNER-DOUGLASS COLLEGE

200 N Central Ave, Baltimore, MD 21202
Telephone: (410) 276-0306
Fax: (410) 276-1810
Internet: www.sdc.edu

Founded 1972 as Homestead Montebello Center, present status 1980
Private control
Academic year: August to May

6 Campuses: Edgewater, Bahamas, Cambridge, Owings Mills, Lanham and Salisbury
Pres.: Dr CHARLES W. SIMMONS
Provost and Vice-Pres. for Academic Affairs: Dr MARIAN STANTON
Vice-Pres. for Admin. and Fiscal Affairs: DONALD HUTCHINS
Chief Librarian: OMOWALI ALI
Number of teachers: 44
Number of students: 444

ST JOHN'S COLLEGE

60 College Ave, Annapolis, MD 21401
Telephone: (410) 626-2522
Fax: (410) 269-7916
E-mail: admissions@sjca.edu
Internet: www.stjohnscollege.edu

Founded 1696 as King William's School, present name and status 1784
Private control
Academic year: August to May

For Santa Fe campus, see under New Mexico
Pres.: CHRISTOPHER B. NELSON
Vice-Pres. for Advancement: BARBARA GOYETTE
Dean: PAMELA KRAUS
Treas.: BRONTE D. JONES
Registrar: DANIEL E. CROWE
Dir for Admissions: SARAH MORSE
Dir for Alumni Relations: JO ANN MATTSON
Library Dir: CATHERINE DIXON
Library of 100,000 vols
Number of teachers: 69
Number of students: 450
Publications: *The College* (3 a year), *The St. John's Review*.

ST MARY'S COLLEGE OF MARYLAND

18952 E Fisher Rd, St Mary's City, MD 20686-3001
Telephone: (240) 895-2000
Fax: (240) 895-5001
E-mail: admissions@smcm.edu
Internet: www.smcm.edu

Founded 1840, present name 1964
State control
Academic year: August to May

Pres.: Dr JOSEPH URGO
Vice-Pres. for Academic Affairs and Dean of Faculty: Dr BETH RUSHING
Vice-Pres. for Advancement: Dr MAUREEN SILVA
Vice-Pres. for Business and Finance: Dr THOMAS J. BOTZMAN
Vice-Pres. and Dean for Admissions and Financial Aid: Dr PATRICIA GOLDSMITH
Dean for Students: Dr LAURA BAYLESS
Dir for Library: Dr CELIA RABINOWITZ
Library of 200,000 vols
Number of teachers: 227 (139 full-time, 88 part-time)
Number of students: 2,017 (1,982 undergraduate, 35 graduate)
Publication: *The Mulberry Tree* (2 a year).

ST MARY'S SEMINARY & UNIVERSITY

5400 Roland Ave, Baltimore, MD 21210-1994
Telephone: (410) 864-4000
Fax: (410) 433-1384

E-mail: admissions@stmarys.edu
Internet: www.stmarys.edu

Founded 1791
Private control

Vice-Chancellor, Pres. and Rector: Rev. Dr THOMAS HURST
Vice-Rector: Rev. TIMOTHY KULBICKI
Vice-Pres. for Advancement and Human Resources: ELIZABETH L. VISCONAGE
Vice-Pres. for Finance: RICHARD G. CHILDS
Dean for Students: Rev. EDWARD J. GRISWOLD
Dir for Information Services: ARRYN MILNE
Registrar: PAULA THIGPEN

Library of 22,000 vols, 130,000 monographs, 390 periodical subscriptions
Number of teachers: 45 (21 full-time, 24 part-time)
Number of students: 120 (75 full-time, 45 part-time)

DEANS

Ecumenical Institute of Theology: Dr MICHAEL J. GORMAN
School of Theology: Rev. TIMOTHY KULBICKI

TAI SOPHIA INSTITUTE

7750 Montpelier Rd, Laurel, MD 20723
Telephone: (410) 888-9048
Fax: (410) 888-9004
Internet: www.tai.edu

Founded 1974 as College of Chinese Acupuncture, present name 2000
Private control

Courses in acupuncture, Chinese herbs, health coaching, herbal studies, medical herbalism, nutrition and integrative health, therapeutic herbalism, transformative leadership and social change, and wellness coaching

Pres. and CEO: FRANK VITALE
Provost and Exec. Vice-Pres. for Academic Affairs: Dr JUDITH K. BROIDA
Vice-Pres. for Admin. and Gen. Counsel: LOUISE GUSSIN
Vice-Pres. for Business and Financial Services: MARC LEVIN
Vice-Pres. for Marketing and Enrolment Management: LISA CONNELLY-DUGGAN
Number of students: 439

UNIFORMED SERVICES UNIVERSITY OF THE HEALTH SCIENCES

4301 Jones Bridge Rd, Bethesda, MD 20814
Telephone: (301) 295-3101
E-mail: admissions@mxa.usuhs.mil
Internet: www.usuhs.mil

Founded 1972

Pres.: Dr CHARLES S. RICE
Vice-Pres. and Chief Information Officer: TIMOTHY RAPP
Vice-Pres. for Exec. Affairs: WILLIAM BESTER
Vice-Pres. for Finance and Admin.: STEPHEN RICE
Vice-Pres. for Research: Dr STEVEN KAMINSKY
Vice-Pres. for Teaching and Research Support: Dr VERNON D. SCHINSKI
Registrar: GAIL HEWITT-CLARKE
Number of teachers: 433 (on campus)
Number of students: 2,410

DEANS

F. Edward Hébert School of Medicine: Dr LARRY W. LAUGHLIN
Graduate School of Nursing: Dr ADA SUE HINSHAW

UNITED STATES NAVAL ACADEMY

121 Blake Rd, Annapolis, MD 21402-5000
Telephone: (410) 293-1000
Fax: (410) 293-3735

E-mail: pao@usna.edu
Internet: www.usna.edu
Founded 1845 as Naval School, present name 1850
State control
Academic year: August to May
Superintendent: Vice Admiral MICHAEL H. MILLER
Commandant of Midshipmen: Capt. ROBERT E. CLARK, II
Academic Dean and Provost: WILLIAM C. MILLER
Dean of Admissions: STEPHEN B LATTA
Registrar: Dr CHRISTOPHER A. DAVIS
Librarian: JAMES RETTIG
Library: see Libraries and Archives
Number of teachers: 574
Number of students: 4,350 midshipmen
Publications: *Lucky Bag* (1 a year), *Shipmate* (online), *Trident*.

UNIVERSITY OF MARYLAND SYSTEM

3300 Metzerott Rd, Adelphi, MD 20783-1690
Telephone: (301) 445-2756
Fax: (301) 445-4761
E-mail: webnotes@usmd.edu
Internet: www.usmd.edu
Founded 1988 by merger of 5 Univ. of Maryland instns and 6 mems of the State Univ. and College System of Maryland
State control
12 Instns, 2 regional higher education centres and a system office
Chancellor: Dr WILLIAM ENGLISH KIRWAN
Sr Vice-Chancellor for Academic Affairs: IRWIN GOLDSTEIN
Vice-Chancellor for Admin. and Finance: JOSEPH VIVONA
Vice-Chancellor for Advancement: LEONARD R. RALEY
Vice-Chancellor for Communications: ANNE MOULTRIE
Vice-Chancellor for Govt Relations: PATRICK J. HOGAN
Number of teachers: 13,982 (8,206 full-time, 5,776 part-time)
Number of students: 155,607.

CONSTITUENT UNIVERSITIES

Bowie State University

14000 Jericho Park Rd, Bowie, MD 20715-9465
Telephone: (301) 860-4000
E-mail: gradadmissions@bowiestate.edu
Internet: www.bowiestate.edu
Founded 1865 as Baltimore Normal School, present name and status 1988
Academic year: September to May
Pres.: Dr MICKEY L. BURNIM
Provost and Vice-Pres. for Academic Affairs: Dr KAREN JOHNSON SHAHEED
Vice-Pres. and Gen. Counsel: ANTIONETTE MARBRAY
Vice-Pres. for External Relations: MAITLAND DADE
Vice-Pres. for Finance and Admin.: Dr KARL B. BROCKENBROUGH
Vice-Pres. for Institutional Advancement: Dr RICHARD LUCAS
Vice-Pres. for Student Affairs: Dr ARTIE L. TRAVIS
Dean for Library: MARIAN RUCKER-SHAMU
Library of 280,000 vols
Number of teachers: 346 (190 full-time, 156 part-time)
Number of students: 5,617 (4,111 undergraduate, 1,506 graduate)

DEANS

College of Arts and Sciences: Dr GEORGE ACQUAAH,
College of Business: Dr ANTHONY NELSON
College of Education: Dr TRAKI TAYLOR-WEBB
College of Professional Studies: Dr ELLIOTT PARRIS
Graduate School: Dr COSMAS U. NWOKEAFOR

Coppin State University

2500 W North Ave, Baltimore, MD 21216-3698
Telephone: (410) 951-3000
Fax: (410) 523-7351
E-mail: admissions@coppin.edu
Internet: www.coppin.edu
Founded 1900 as Colored High School, present name 2004
Academic year: August to May
Pres.: Dr REGINALD S. AVERY
Provost and Vice-Pres. for Academic Affairs: Dr RONNIE L. COLLINS
Vice-Pres. for Admin. and Finance: DICK SIEMER
Vice-Pres. for Enrolment Management: Dr REGINALD G. L. ROSS
Vice-Pres. for Information Technology: Dr AHMED M. EL-HAGGAN (acting)
Vice-Pres. for Institutional Advancement: DOUGLAS DALZELL
Vice-Pres. for Student Affairs: Dr FRANKLIN D. CHAMBERS
Dir of Institutional Research: Dr OYEBANJO LAJUBUTU
Dir of Univ. Relations: URSULA BATTLE
Dir of Library: Dr MARY E. WANZA
Registrar: Dr MARGARET W. TURNER
Library of 81,742 vols, 286,929 microform titles, 705 current periodicals
Number of teachers: 238
Number of students: 3,567 (3,003 undergraduate, 564 graduate)
Publication: *Journal of Minority Affairs* (1 a year)

DEANS

Helene Fuld School of Nursing: Dr MARCELLA A. COPES
Honors College: RON L. COLLINS, SR
School of Arts and Sciences: Dr ALCOTT ARTHUR
School of Education: Dr EDNA SIMMONS
School of Graduate Studies: Dr MARY E. OWENS-SOUTHALL
School of Management Science and Economics: Dr SADIE GREGORY
School of Professional Studies: Dr BEVERLY J. O'BRYANT

Frostburg State University

101 Braddock Rd, Frostburg, MD 21532-2303
Telephone: (301) 687-4000
Fax: (301) 687-4737
E-mail: fsuadmissions@frostburg.edu
Internet: www.frostburg.edu
Founded 1898 as State Normal School, present name and status 1987
Pres.: Dr JONATHAN C. GIBRALTER
Provost and Vice-Pres. for Academic Affairs: Dr STEPHEN J. SIMPSON
Vice-Pres. for Admin. and Finance: DAVID ROSE
Vice-Pres. for Economic Devt: STEPHEN SPAHR
Vice-Pres. for Student and Educational Services: Dr THOMAS L. BOWLING
Vice-Pres. for Univ. Advancement: B. J. DAVISSON, II
Registrar: JAY HEGEMAN
Dir for Admissions: TRISHA GREGORY
Dir for Library: Dr DAVID M. GILLESPIE
Library of 5,000,000 vols
Number of teachers: 305

Number of students: 5,385 (4,755 undergraduate, 630 graduate)
Publications: *Bittersweet, Joining the Conversation, Nightsun, Profile*

DEANS

College of Business: AHMAD TOOTOONCHI
College of Education: Dr CLARENCE GOLDEN
College of Liberal Arts and Sciences: Dr JOSEPH HOFFMAN

Salisbury University

1101 Camden Ave, Salisbury, MD 21801
Telephone: (410) 543-6000
Fax: (410) 677-5025
Internet: www.salisbury.edu
Founded 1922
Academic year: August to May
Pres.: Dr JANET DUDLEY-ESHBACH
Provost and Vice-Pres. for Academic Affairs: Dr DIANE ALLEN
Vice-Pres. for Admin. and Finance: BETTY CROCKETT
Vice-Pres. for Student Affairs: Dr DANE FOUST
Vice-Pres. for Univ. Advancement (vacant)
Registrar: JACQUELINE MORAN MAISEL
Dean for Enrolment Management: JANE DANÉ
Dean for Libraries and Instructional Resources: Dr MARTHA ZIMMERMAN
Library of 254,151 vols, 4,467 audiovisual items
Number of teachers: 579 (388 full-time, 191 part-time)
Number of students: 8,606 (7,892 undergraduate, 714 graduate)
Publications: *Literature/Film Quarterly* (4 a year), *Panorama* (2 a year), *Shoreline, SU Magazine, SU Today* (irregular)

DEANS

Franklin P. Perdue School of Business: Dr BOB G. WOOD
Fulton School: MAARTEN PEREBOOM
Henson School of Science and Technology: Dr KAREN L. OLMSTEAD,
Seidel School of Education and Professional Studies: Dr DENNIS PATANICZEK

Towson University

8000 York Rd, Towson, MD 21252-0001
Telephone: (410) 704-2000
E-mail: admissions@towson.edu
Internet: www.towson.edu
Founded 1866 as State Normal School, present location 1915, present name 1997
Academic year: September to May
Pres.: MARAVENE S. LOESCHKE
Provost and Vice-Pres. for Academic Affairs: MARCIA G. WELSH
Vice-Pres. for Admin. and Finance and Chief Fiscal Officer: MARK BEHM
Vice-Pres. for Economic and Community Outreach: DYAN BRASINGTON
Vice-Pres. for Student Affairs: DEBRA MORIARTY
Vice-Pres. for Univ. Advancement: Dr GARY N. RUBIN
Registrar: DAVID DECKER
Dir for Admissions: LOUISE SHULACK (acting)
Dean for Libraries: DEBORAH NOLAN
Library of 579,824 vols
Number of teachers: 1,644 (841 full-time, 803 part-time)
Number of students: 21,464 (17,517 undergraduate, 3,947 graduate)
Publications: *Grub Street* (1 a year), *iMagazine, Towson Alumni Magazine* (3 a year), *Tower Echoes* (1 a year), *Towson Journal of International Affairs, Transitions* (1 a year)

DEANS

College of Business and Economics: SHOREH KAYNAMA

College of Education: Dr RAYMOND P. LORION

College of Fine Arts and Communication: SUSAN E. PICINICH

College of Health Professions: CHARLOTTE E. EXNER

College of Liberal Arts: TERRY CONNEY

Honors College: JOSEPH McGINN

Jess and Mildred Fisher College of Science and Mathematics: DAVID A. VANKO

University of Baltimore

1420 N Charles St, Baltimore, MD 21201

Telephone: (410) 837-4200

E-mail: intladms@ubalt.edu

Internet: www.ubalt.edu

Founded 1925

Pres.: ROBERT L. BOGOMOLNY

Provost and Sr Vice-Pres. for Academic Affairs: JOSEPH S. WOOD

Sr Vice-Pres. for Admin. and Finance: HARRY SCHUCKEL

Sr Vice-Pres. for Enrolment Management and Student Affairs: MIRIAM KING

Vice-Pres. for Institutional Advancement: THERESA SILANSKIS

Dir for Library: LUCY HOLMAN

Library of 400,000 vols

Number of teachers: 167

Number of students: 6,442 (3,257 undergraduate, 2,041 graduate, 1,144 law)

Publications: *The Reporter, University of Baltimore Magazine* (2 a year)

DEANS

College of Public Affairs: STEPHEN L. PERCY

Robert G. Merrick School of Business: DARLENE BRANNIGAN SMITH

School of Law: F. MICHAEL HIGGINBOTHAM

Yale Gordon College of Arts and Sciences: JEFFREY SAWYER (acting)

University of Maryland, Baltimore

620 W Lexington St, Baltimore, MD 21201

Telephone: (410) 706-3100

Internet: www.umaryland.edu

Founded 1807

Pres.: Dr JAY A. PERMAN

Vice-Pres. for Academic Affairs: ROGER J. WARD

Vice-Pres., Chief Admin. and Finance Officer: KATHLEEN M. BYINGTON

Vice-Pres. and Chief Govt and Community Affairs Officer: T. SUE GLADHILL

Vice-Pres. and Chief Enterprise and Economic Devt Officer: JAMES L. HUGHES

Vice-Pres. for Medical Affairs: Dr E. ALBERT REECE

Vice-Pres. for Planning and Accountability: PETER N. GILBERT

Sr Univ. Counsel: SUSAN GILLETTE

Library of 613,407 vols

Number of teachers: 2,515

Number of students: 6,349 (772 undergraduate, 5,577 graduate)

Publication: *Maryland Magazine* (1 a year)

DEANS

Dental School: CHRISTIAN S. STOHLER

Graduate School: (vacant)

School of Law: PHOEBE A. HADDON

School of Medicine: Dr E. ALBERT REECE

School of Nursing: Dr JANET D. ALLAN

School of Pharmacy: Dr NATALIE D. EDDINGTON

School of Social Work: Dr RICHARD P. BARTH

University of Maryland, Baltimore County

1000 Hilltop Circle, Baltimore, MD 21250

Telephone: (410) 455-1000

E-mail: admissions@umbc.edu

Internet: umbc.edu

Founded 1963

Academic year: September to May

Pres.: FREEMAN A. HRAQBOWSKI, III

Provost and Sr Vice-Pres. for Academic Affairs: PHILIP ROUS

Vice-Pres. for Admin. and Finance: LYNNE SCHAEFER

Vice-Pres. for Information Technology: JOHN SUESS

Vice-Pres. for Institutional Advancement: GREGORY SIMMONS

Vice-Pres. for Research: GEOFFREY P. SUMMERS

Vice-Pres. for Student Affairs: NANCY YOUNG

Gen. Counsel: DAVID GLEASON

Dir of Library: LARRY WILT

Library: 1m.

Number of teachers: 766 (475 full-time, 291 part-time)

Number of students: 13,199 (10,573 undergraduate, 2,626 graduate)

DEANS

College of Arts, Humanities and Social Sciences: JOHN W. JEFFRIES

College of Engineering and Information Technology: WARREN DeVRIES

College of Natural and Mathematical Sciences: WILLIAM LaCOURSE

Erickson School: JUDAH RONCH

Graduate School: JANET RUTLEDGE

School of Social Work: Dr RICHARD BARTH

University of Maryland, College Park

College Park, MD 20742-5260

Telephone: (301) 405-1000

Fax: (301) 314-9443

Internet: www.umd.edu

Founded 1856 as Maryland Agricultural College

Academic year: September to May

Pres.: Dr WALLACE D. LOH

Provost and Sr Vice-Pres.: Dr ANN WYLIE

Vice-Pres. for Admin. Affairs: ROBERT M. SPECTER

Vice-Pres. for Information Technology and Chief Information Officer: BRIAN VOSS

Vice-Pres. for Research: Dr PATRICK G. O'SHEA

Vice-Pres. for Student Affairs: Dr LINDA M. CLEMENT

Vice-Pres. for Univ. Relations: BRODIE REMINGTON

Registrar: ADRIAN R. CORNELIUS

Dean for Library Services: Dr PATRICIA STEELE

Library of 3,816,713 vols

Number of teachers: 4,248 (367,567 f.t.e.)

Number of students: 37,641

DEANS

A. James Clark School of Engineering: Dr DARRYLL PINES

College of Agriculture and Natural Resources: Dr CHENG-I WEI

College of Arts and Humanities: BONNIE THORNTON-DILL

College of Behavioural and Social Sciences: Dr JOHN R. TOWNSHEND

College of Computer, Mathematical and Natural Sciences: JAYANTH BANAVAR

College of Education: DONNA L. WISEMAN

College of Information Studies: Dr JENNIFER J. PREECE

Graduate School: Dr CHARLES CARAMELLO

Philip Merrill College of Journalism: KEVIN KLOSE

Robert H. Smith School of Business: G. ANAND ANANDALINGAM

School of Architecture, Planning and Preservation: DAVID CRONRATH

School of Public Health: JANE CLARK

School of Public Policy: DONALD KETTL

University of Maryland, Eastern Shore

One Backbone Rd, Princess Anne, MD 21853

Telephone: (410) 651-2200

Fax: (410) 651-6105

E-mail: umesadmissions@umes.edu

Internet: www.umes.edu

Founded 1886 as Delaware Conf. Acad., present name 1970, present status 1988

Pres.: Dr MORTIMER H. NEUFVILLE

Vice-Pres. for Academic Affairs: Dr CHARLES WILLIAMS

Vice-Pres. for Admin. Affairs: Dr RONNIE HOLDEN

Vice-Pres. for Student Affairs and Enrolment Management: Dr ANTHONY L. JENKINS

Vice-Pres. for Institutional Advancement: GAINS HAWKINS

Vice-Pres. for Technology and Commercialization: Dr RONALD G. FORSYTHE

Dean for Library Services: Dr ELLIS B. BETECK

Library of 211,000 vols

Number of teachers: 212

Number of students: 3,166

DEANS

School of Agricultural and Natural Sciences: Dr JURGEN SCHWARZ (acting)

School of the Arts and Professions: Dr T. H. BAUGHMAN

School of Business and Technology: Dr AYODELE J. ALADE

School of Graduate Studies: Dr JENNIFER M. KEANE-DAWES

School of Pharmacy and Health Professions: Dr NICHOLAS RONALD BLANCHARD

University of Maryland, University College

3501 University Blvd, E, Adelphi, MD 20783

Telephone: (240) 582-2509

Fax: (301) 985-7678

E-mail: umucinfo@info.umuc.edu

Internet: www.umuc.edu

Founded 1947

Academic year: August to May

Pres.: JAVIER MIYARES

Provost: Dr GREG VON LEHMEN (acting)

Vice-Pres. and Chief Financial Officer: EUGENE D. LOCKETT, JR

Vice-Pres. and Chief of Staff: ANDREA Y. HART

Vice-Pres. and Dir: Dr ALLAN J. BERG

Vice-Pres. for Enrolment Management: SEAN CHUNG

Vice-Pres. for the Dept of Defence Relations: JOHN F. JONES, JR

Vice-Pres. for Information Technology: PETER C. YOUNG

Vice-Pres. for Institutional Advancement: CATHY SWEET-WINDHAM

Interim Vice-Pres. and Dir for UMUC Asia: Dr ALLAN J. BERG

Vice-Pres. and Dir for UMUC Europe: Dr ALLEN J. BERG

Vice-Pres. and Gen. Counsel: NANCY WILLIAMSON

Library of 1,337

Number of teachers: 3,108 worldwide

Number of students: 92,211 worldwide

DEANS

Graduate School of Management and Technology: Dr ROBERT GOODWIN

School of Undergraduate Studies: Dr MARIE A. CINI

STEVENSON UNIVERSITY

1525 Greenspring Valley Rd, Stevenson, MD 21153-0641

Telephone: (410) 486-7001
E-mail: admissions@mail.vjc.edu
Internet: www.stevenson.edu

Founded 1947, fmrly Villa Julie College, present name 2008
Private control
Academic year: August to May
Campuses in Baltimore, Greenspring and Owings Mills

Pres.: Dr KEVIN J. MANNING
Exec. Vice-Pres. for Academic Affairs and Dean of Staff: Dr PAUL D. LACK
Exec. Vice-Pres. and Chief Financial Officer: TIMOTHY M. CAMPBELL
Vice-Pres. for Univ. Advancement: STEVENSON W. CLOSE, Jr
Registrar: TRACY R. BOLT
Dir for Library Services: MAUREEN A. BECK

Library of 100,000 vols
Number of students: 3,929 (2,985 undergraduate, 357 graduate)

DEANS

Brown School of Business and Leadership: NORMAN ENDLICH
School of Design: KEITH D. KUTCH
School of Education: DEBORAH S. KRAFT
School of Humanities and Social Sciences: Dr JAMES GERARD SALVUCCI
School of the Sciences: Dr SUSAN T. GORMAN

WASHINGTON ADVENTIST UNIVERSITY

7600 Flower Ave, Takoma Park, MD 20912

Telephone: (301) 891-4000
Fax: (301) 891-4167
E-mail: info@wau.edu
Internet: www.wau.edu

Founded 1904 as Washington Training Institute, present name and status 2009
Private control

Pres.: Dr WEYMOUTH SPENCE
Provost: SUSAN HORNSHAW
Sr Vice-Pres. for Operations: GERALD ANDERSON
Exec. Vice-Pres. for Finance: PATRICK FARLEY
Vice-Pres. for Advancement and Alumni Relations: BRUCE PEIFER
Vice-Pres. for Min.: BARAKA MUGANDA
Vice-Pres. for Student Life: JEAN WARDEN
Registrar: Dr EMILE JOHN
Librarian: LEE WISEL

Library of 140,000 vols
Number of teachers: 47
Number of students: 1,212

Publications: The Columbia Journal (2 a year), Golden Memories, Montage (1 a year), Reunion (4 a year)

DEANS

School of Arts and Social Sciences: GASPAR COLON
School of Graduate and Professional Studies: Dr JUDE EDWARDS
School of Health Professions, Science and Wellness: GINA BROWN

WASHINGTON BIBLE COLLEGE/ CAPITAL BIBLE SEMINARY/EQUIP INSTITUTE

6511 Princess Garden Parkway, Lanham, MD 20706

Telephone: (301) 552-1400
Fax: (301) 552-2775
E-mail: iadmissions@bible.edu
Internet: www.bible.edu

Founded 1938 by merger of 3 Bible institutes
Private control

Academic year: July to June
Br in Springfield, Virginia

Pres.: Dr GEORGE M. HARTON
Library Dir: WILLIAM A. BANKS

Library of 93,057 vols
Number of teachers: 49
Number of students: 502

WASHINGTON COLLEGE

300 Washington Ave, Chestertown, MD 21620-1197

Telephone: (410) 778-2800
Fax: (410) 778-7850
E-mail: wc_admissions@washcoll.edu
Internet: www.washcoll.edu

Founded 1782
Private control
Academic year: September to July
Offers divs: humanities, natural sciences and mathematics, and social sciences

Pres.: MITCHELL B. REISS
Provost and Dean of the College: JOHN B. TAYLOR
Sr Vice-Pres. for Finance and Admin.: JAMES MANARO
Exec. Vice-Pres.: JOSEPH L. HOLT
Vice-Pres. for Admissions and Enrolment Management: KEVIN COVENEY
Vice-Pres. for Advancement: GRETCHEN DWYER
Vice-Pres. for College Relations: MEREDITH DAVIES HADAWAY
Vice-Pres. and Dean for Student Affairs: MELA DUTKA
Registrar: JENNIFER BERSHON
College Librarian: RUTH SHOGE

Library of 200,000 vols
Number of teachers: 149
Number of students: 1,400

Publications: Apeiron (1 a year), The Collegian (12 a year), The Pegasus (1 a year), Treason, Washington College Review (1 a year), Washington College International Studies Review.

MASSACHUSETTS

AMERICAN INTERNATIONAL COLLEGE

100 State St, Springfield, MA 01109

Telephone: (413) 737-7000
Fax: (413) 205-3051
E-mail: inquiry@aic.edu
Internet: www.aic.edu

Founded 1885
Private control
Academic year: September to May

Pres.: Dr VINCENT M. MANIACI
Exec. Vice-Pres. for Academic Affairs: Dr GREGORY T. SCHMUTTE
Exec. Vice-Pres. for Admin.: RICHARD BEDARD
Vice-Pres. for Admissions Services: PETER J. MILLER
Vice-Pres. for Enrolment Management: LINDA DAGRADI
Vice-Pres. for Finance: Dr THOMAS E. DYBICK
Vice-Pres. for Student Affairs: Dr BLAINE K. STEVENS
Exec. Dir for Institutional Advancement: HEATHER CAHILL
Registrar: DIANE FURTEK
Dir of Library Services: ESTELLE SPENCER

Library of 189,000 vols
Number of teachers: 167 (84 full-time, 83 part-time)
Number of students: 3,598 (3,059 undergraduate, 539 graduate)

DEANS

School of Arts and Sciences: Dr VICKIE L. HESS
School of Business Admin.: Dr LEA A. JOHNSON
School of Continuing Education: Dr ROLAND E. HOLSTEAD
School of Health Sciences: Dr CAROL A. JOBE

AMHERST COLLEGE

POB 5000, Amherst, MA 01002-5000

Telephone: (413) 542-2000
Fax: (413) 542-2327
E-mail: info@amherst.edu
Internet: www.amherst.edu

Founded 1821
Private control
Academic year: September to May

Depts of American studies, anthropology and sociology, Asian languages and civilizations, astronomy, biology, black studies, chemistry, classics, economics, English, European studies, fine arts, French, geology, German, history, law, jurisprudence, and social thought, mathematics and computer science, music, neuroscience, philosophy, physical education and athletics, physics, political science, psychology, religion, Russian, Spanish, theater and dance, women's and gender studies

Pres.: Dr CAROLYN A. MARTIN
Chief Advancement Officer: MEGAN MOREY
Dean of Admission and Financial Aid: THOMAS A. PARKER
Dean of Faculty: GREGORY S. CALL
Dean of Students: ALLEN HART
Registrar: KATHLEEN M. GOFF
Librarian: BRYN GEFFERT

Library of 1,023,085 vols, 595,296 media items
Number of teachers: 195 (full-time)
Number of students: 1,795

Publication: Amherst Magazine (4 a year).

ANDOVER NEWTON THEOLOGICAL SCHOOL

210 Herrick Rd, Newton Centre, MA 02459

Telephone: (617) 964-1100
Fax: (617) 965-9756
E-mail: admissions@ants.edu
Internet: www.ants.edu

Founded 1807 as Andover Theological Seminary, present name 1965; attached to Boston Theological Institute
Private control
Academic year: August to May
Offers masters degree in divinity, ministry, religious education, theological research, theological studies

Pres.: Rev. Dr NICK CARTER
Vice-Pres. for Academic Affairs and Dean of the Faculty: SARAH B. DRUMMOND
Vice-Pres. for Finance and Operations: YI JUNG
Vice-Pres. for Institutional Advancement: JENNIFER CRAIG
Vice-Pres. for Strategic Initiatives and Dean of Students and Community Life: NANCY NIENHUIS
Registrar: NAYDA AQUILA
Dir of Enrolment: MARGARET L. CARROLL
Dir of Library: JEFFREY L. BRIGHAM

Library of 260,000 vols
Number of teachers: 91
Number of students: 480

ANNA MARIA COLLEGE

50 Sunset Lane Paxton, MA 01612

Telephone: (508) 849-3300
Fax: (508) 849-3229

E-mail: admissions@annamaria.edu
Internet: www.annamaria.edu
Founded 1946
Private control
Academic year: August to May (2 semesters)
Divs of business, law and public policy, environmental, natural and technological sciences, fine arts, humanities and int. studies, human devt and human services
Pres.: Dr JACK P. CALARESO
Exec. Vice-Pres.: MARY LOU RETELLE
Vice-Pres. for Academic Affairs: BILLYE AUCLAIR
Vice-Pres. for Student Affairs and Dean of Retention: ANDREW KLEIN
Dean of Students: Dr JOSEPH FARRAGHER
Dir of Institutional Advancement: BRIDGET HAVARD
Registrar: BARBARA ZAWALICH
Dir of Library: RUTH PYNE
Library of 95,000 vols
Number of teachers: 223
Number of students: 1,498

ASSUMPTION COLLEGE

500 Salisbury St, Worcester, MA 01609-1296
Telephone: (508) 767-7000
Fax: (508) 756-1780
E-mail: admiss@assumption.edu
Internet: www.assumption.edu
Founded 1904
Private control
Academic year: September to May (2 semesters)
Divs of art and music, business studies, economics and global studies, education, English, modern and classical languages and cultures, history, human services and rehabilitation studies, mathematics and computer science, natural sciences, philosophy, political science, psychology, social and rehabilitation services, sociology and anthropology, theology
Pres.: Dr FRANCESCO C. CESAREO
Provost and Academic Vice-Pres.: FRANCIS LAZARUS
Exec. Vice-Pres. for Finance and Admin. and Treas.: CHRISTIAN W. MCCARTHY
Vice-Pres. for Enrolment Management: EVAN E. LIPP
Vice-Pres. for Institutional Advancement: (vacant)
Vice-Pres. for Student Affairs: Dr CATHERINE M. WOODBROOKS
Dean of Admissions: KATHLEEN M. MURPHY
Dean of Campus Life: NANCY CRIMMIN
Dean of College: MARY LOU ANDERSON
Dean of Continuing Education: (vacant)
Dean of Undergraduate Studies: ELOISE KNOWLTON
Registrar: DAVID W. AALTO
Dir of Library: DORIS ANN SWEET
Library of 216,668 vols
Number of teachers: 287
Number of students: 2,787
Publication: Assumption College Magazine (4 a year).

BABSON COLLEGE

231 Forest St, Babson Park, MA 02457-0310
Telephone: (781) 235-1200
Fax: (617) 239-5614
E-mail: ugradadmission@babson.edu
Internet: www.babson.edu
Founded 1919 as Babson Institute, present name 1969
Private control
Academic year: August to August
Pres.: LEONARD A. SCHLESINGER
Provost and Chief Academic Officer: Dr SHAHID ANSARI

Vice-Pres. and Gen. Counsel: JONATHAN MOLL
Vice-Pres. for Admin.: MARY ROSE
Vice-Pres. for Devt: DIANA PRESCOTT ZAIS
Vice-Pres. for Finance and Chief Financial Officer: PHILIP SHAPIRO
Dean of Admissions: GRANT GOSSELIN
Dean of Faculty: CAROLYN HOTCHKISS
Dean of Student Affairs: BETSY NEWMAN
Dir of Libraries: (vacant)
Library of 132,024 vols
Number of teachers: 250
Number of students: 3,342
Publication: Babson Magazine (4 a year)

DEANS
Babson Exec. Education: ELAINE EISENMAN
F. W. Olin Graduate School of Business: RAGHU TADEPALLI
Undergraduate School: Dr DENNIS HANNO

BARD COLLEGE AT SIMON'S ROCK

84 Alford Rd, Great Barrington, MA 01230
Telephone: (413) 644-4400
Fax: (413) 528-7365
E-mail: admit@simons-rock.edu
Internet: www.simons-rock.edu
Founded 1966
Private control
Academic year: August to May
Divs of arts, languages and literature, mathematics and computing, science, social studies
Pres.: LEON BOTSTEIN
Provost and Vice-Pres.: Dr PETER LAIPSON
Exec. Vice-Pres.: DIMITRI PAPADIMITRIOU
Vice-Pres. for Early College Policies and Programmes: LESLIE DAVIDSON
Dean of Academic Affairs: ANNE O'DWYER
Dean of the College: M. LESLIE DAVIDSON
Dean of Student Affairs: ROBERT GRAVES
Registrar: HEIDI-BETH ROTHBERG
Dir of Library: BRIAN MIKESELL
Library of 90,772 vols
Number of teachers: 40
Number of students: 350

BAY PATH COLLEGE

588 Longmeadow St, Longmeadow, MA 01106
Telephone: (413) 565-1000
Fax: (413) 565-1103
E-mail: contact@baypath.edu
Internet: www.baypath.edu
Founded 1897 as Bay Path Institute, present name 1988
Private control
Academic year: August to May
Campus in Burlington, Sturbridge
Pres.: Dr CAROL A. LEARY
Provost and Vice-Pres. for Academic Affairs: Dr MELISSA MORRISS-OLSON
Vice-Pres. for Academic and Admin. Technology: Dr DAVID M. DEMERS
Vice-Pres. for Finance and Admin. Services: MICHAEL J. GIAMPIETRO
Vice-Pres. for Institutional Advancement: KATHLEEN M. BOURQUE
Vice-Pres. for Planning and Student Devt: CARON T. HOBIN
Registrar: LAURA K. LANDER
Dir of Library and Information Services: MICHAEL MORAN
Library of 49,713 vols, 84,824 e-books, 412 periodicals, 4,410 microform units, 2,495 video items, 1,414 DVDs, 6,176 streaming films, 202 audio CDs
Number of teachers: 68
Number of students: 2,191

DEANS
Arts and Sciences: Dr MICHAEL KONIG
Education: Dr LIZ FLEMING
Management and Social Justice: Dr GEOFFREY MILLS

BECKER COLLEGE

Weller Academic Bldg, 61 Sever St, Worcester, MA 01609
Telephone: (508) 791-9241
Fax: (508) 831-7505
E-mail: info@becker.edu
Internet: www.becker.edu
Founded 1784 as Leicester Acad., present name 1990
Private control
Academic divs incl. animal studies, business, criminal justice and legal studies, design, education and psychology, nursing and exercise sciences
Pres.: Dr ROBERT E. JOHNSON
Sr Vice-Pres. and Chief Financial Officer: Dr DAVID A. ELLIS
Vice-Pres. for Academic Affairs and Dean of College: Dr ELIZABETH V. FULLER
Vice-Pres. for Devt and Alumni Affairs: DEAN J. HICKEY
Vice-Pres. for Institutional Advancement Dean: J. HICKEY
Vice-Pres. for Student Affairs and Dean of Students: KENNETH S. CAMERON
Dean of Enrolment Management: KAREN SCHEDIN
Registrar: NIKKI ANDREWS
Dir of Libraries: GARRETT EASTMAN
Library of 73,500 vols
Number of students: 1,800

BENJAMIN FRANKLIN INSTITUTE OF TECHNOLOGY

41 Berkeley St, Boston, MA 02116
Telephone: 617.423.4630
Fax: 617.482.3706
E-mail: admissions@bfit.edu
Internet: www.bfit.edu
Founded 1908
Private control
Academic year: September to May (2 semesters)
Depts of architectural technology, automotive technology, electrical technology, electronics engineering technology, mechanical engineering technology, medical electronics engineering technology, ophthalmic assisting
Pres.: GEORGE C. CHRYSSIS
Academic Dean: ANTHONY BENOIT
Dean of Enrolment Management: MIKE BOSCO
Dean of Students: BRIAN BICKNELL
Chief Financial Officer: KEITH DROPKIN
Dir of Admissions: MARVIN LOISEAU
Dir of Devt: JULIANA FIELD
Registrar: JAMES KLASEN
Dir. of Library Services: SHARON BONK
Library of 73,000 vols incl. newspapers, 300 journals
Number of teachers: 167
Number of students: 564

BENTLEY UNIVERSITY

175 Forest St, Waltham, MA 02452
Telephone: (781) 891-2000
Fax: (781) 891-2569
E-mail: ugadmission@bentley.edu
Internet: www.bentley.edu
Founded 1917 as school of accounting and finance, present name and status 2008
Private control
Pres.: Dr GLORIA CORDES LARSON

Provost and Vice-Pres. for Academic Affairs: Dr MICHAEL J. PAGE
Vice-Pres. for Business and Finance and Treas.: PAUL CLEMENTE
Vice-Pres. for Devt, Corporate and Alumni Affairs: JOHN W. MOSSER
Vice-Pres. for Enrolment Management: JOANN C. MCKENNA
Vice-Pres. for Information Technology: TRACI A. LOGAN
Vice-Pres. for Student Affairs: KATHLEEN L. YORKIS
Vice-Pres. for Univ. Advancement: WILLIAM TORREY
Gen. Counsel: Dr JUDITH A. MALONE
Exec. Dir of Academic Technology, Library and Online Learning: PHIL KNUTEL
Library of 192,566 vols
Number of teachers: 471 (290 full-time, 181 part-time)
Number of students: 5,691 (4292 undergraduate, 1,399 graduate)
Publication: *Business in the Contemporary World* (4 a year)

DEANS

Arts and Sciences: Dr DANIEL L. EVERETT
Business and the McCallum Graduate School: Dr ROY A. WIGGINS

BERKLEE COLLEGE OF MUSIC

1140 Boylston St, Boston, MA 02215-3695
Telephone: (617) 266-1400
Fax: (617) 536-2047
E-mail: admissions@berklee.edu
Internet: www.berklee.edu
Founded 1945 as Schillinger House of Music, present name 1970
Private control
Academic year: September to August (3 semesters)
Campus in Valencia
Pres.: ROGER H. BROWN
Sr Vice-Pres. for Academic Affairs and Provost: LAWRENCE J. SIMPSON
Sr Vice-Pres. for Institutional Advancement: CINDY ALBERT LINK
Vice-Pres. for Admin.: JOHN ELDERT
Vice-Pres. for Enrolment: MARK CAMPBELL
Vice-Pres. for External Affairs: THOMAS P. RILEY
Vice-Pres. for Finance: AMELIA KOCH
Vice-Pres. for Student Affairs and Dean of Students: LAWRENCE E. BETHUNE
Dean of Admissions: DAMIEN BRACKEN
Registrar: MICHAEL HAGERTY
Dean of Learning Resources: GARY HAGGERTY
Library of 27,779 vols, 33,430 recordings, 23,302 musical scores, 23,764 lead sheets, 450 periodicals
Number of teachers: 524
Number of students: 4,131

DEANS

Continuing Education: DEBORAH L. CAVALIER
Music Technology Div.: S. JAY KENNEDY
Professional Education Div.: DARLA S. HANLEY,
Professional Performance Div.: MATT MARAVUGLIO
Professional Writing and Music Technology Div.: KARI H. JUUSELA

BLESSED JOHN XXIII NATIONAL SEMINARY

558 South Ave, Weston, MA 02493-2699
Telephone: (781) 899-5500
Fax: (781) 899-9057
E-mail: seminary@blessedjohnxxiii.edu
Internet: www.blessedjohnxxiii.edu
Founded 1964
Private control

Academic year: September to May
Areas of study incl. divinity, pre-theology
Rector and Pres.: Rev. WILLIAM B. PALARDY
Academic Dean and Registrar: Dr ANTHONY KEATY
Dean of Seminarians: Rev. THOMAS F. SCHMITT
Dir of Pastoral Ministry Programmes: Rev. MICHAEL A. J. ALFANO
Dir of Pre-Theology Programme: Dr JOHN F. MILLARD
Dir of Spiritual Formation: Rev. PAUL E. MICELI
Library Dir: Sis. JACQUELINE MILLER
Library of 67,000 vols
Number of teachers: 20
Number of students: 73

BOSTON ARCHITECTURAL COLLEGE

320 Newbury St, Boston, MA 02115
Telephone: (617) 262-5000
Fax: (617) 585-0121
E-mail: admissions@the-bac.edu
Internet: www.the-bac.edu
Founded 1889 as Boston Architectural Club, present name 1944
Private control
Schools architecture, design studies, interior design, landscape design
Pres.: Dr THEODORE LANDSMARK
Provost and Academic Vice-Pres.: JULIA HALEVY
Exec. Vice-Pres.: JAMES T. DUNN
Vice-Pres. for Finance and Admin.: KATHY ROOD
Vice-Pres. for Institutional Advancement: CHRISTOPHER COX
Dean of Enrolment and Student Financial Services: JAMES RYAN
Dean of Research and Assessment: HERB CHILDRESS
Dean of Students and Assoc. Provost: RICHARD GRISWOLD
Dir of Admissions: RICHARD MOYER
Dir of Student Devt: KARA PEET
Registrar: ANN ROYALL
Dir of Library: SUSAN LEWIS
Library of 45,700 vols, 45,000 slides, 7,000 images
Number of teachers: 485
Number of students: 1,096 (621 undergraduate, 475 graduate)

BOSTON COLLEGE

140 Commonwealth Ave, Chestnut Hill, MA 02467
Telephone: (617) 552-8000
Fax: (617) 552-0798
E-mail: gsasinfo@bc.edu
Internet: www.bc.edu
Founded 1863
Private control
Academic year: September to May
Campuses in Brighton, Newton
Pres.: Rev. WILLIAM P. LEAHY
Provost and Dean of Faculties: CUTBERTO GARZA
Exec. Vice-Pres.: PATRICK J. KEATING
Vice-Pres. for Facilities Management: DANIEL BOURQUE
Vice-Pres. for Finance and Treas.: PETER C. MCKENZIE
Vice-Pres. for Student Affairs: Dr PATRICK ROMBALSKI
Dir of Libraries: JEROME YAVARKOVSKY
Library of 2,594,750 vols, 300,000 e-books
Number of teachers: 1,215 (737 full time, 478 part time)
Number of students: 14,625

Publications: *Boston College Environmental Affairs Law Review* (4 a year), *Boston College International and Comparative Law Review* (2 a year), *Boston College Law Review* (5 a year), *Boston College Third World Law Journal* (2 a year), *Catholic Education: A Journal of Inquiry and Practice, Journal of Educational Change, Journal of Technology, Learning, and Assessment, Learning Disability Quarterly, Lonergan Workshop Journal* (1 a year), *Philosophy and Social Criticism* (6 a year), *Religion and the Arts* (4 a year), *The Community, Work and Family Journal, The Journal of Corporate Citizenship, Uniform Commercial Code Reporter-Digest* (4 a year)

DEANS

Carroll School of Management: ANDREW C. BOYNTON
College and Graduate School of Arts and Sciences: DAVID QUIGLEY
Graduate School of Social Work: Prof. ALBERTO GODENZI
Law School: Prof. Dr VINCENT D. ROUGEAU
Lynch School of Education: Prof. Dr MAUREEN KENNY
School of Theology and Ministry: MARK S. MASSA
William F. Connell School of Nursing: Prof. Dr SUSAN GENNARO
Woods College of Advancing Studies: JAMES A. WOODS

PROFESSORS

Carroll School of Management (140 Commonwealth Ave, Chestnut Hill, MA 02467; tel. (617) 552-3932; fax (617) 552-2208; e-mail carrollschool.dean@bc.edu):

BARTUNEK, J., Organization Studies
CAMPANELLA, F. B., Finance
CLOTE, P., Computer Science
CRONIN, M., Operations and Strategic Management
FERSON, W. E., Finance
GIPS, J., Computer Science
GRAVES, S., Operations and Strategic Management
HOLDERNESS, C. G., Finance
KANE, E. J., Finance
MARCUS, A., Finance
NIELSEN, R., Organization Studies
O'BRIEN, C., Business Law
PARKER, F. J., Business Law
RAELIN, J., Operations and Strategic Management
RINGUEST, J., Operations and Strategic Management
RITZMAN, L., Operations and Strategic Management
SAFIZADEH, M. H., Operations and Strategic Management
STRAUBING, H., Computer Science
TAGGART, R., Finance
TEHRANIAN, H., Finance
TORBERT, W. R., Organization Studies
TWOMEY, D. P., Business Law
WADDOCK, S., Operations and Strategic Management
WILSON, G. P., Accounting
WOODSIDE, A., Marketing
WRIGHT, A., Accounting

College and Graduate School of Arts and Sciences (140 Commonwealth Ave, Chestnut Hill, MA 02467-3961; tel. (617) 552-2800; fax (617) 552-2154; e-mail casdean@bc.edu):

ANDERSON, J., Economics
ANNUNZIATO, A., Biology
ARNOTT, R., Economics
ASH, A., Mathematics
BAGLIVO, J., Mathematics
BANUAZIZI, A., Psychology
BARTH, J. R., English
BEDELL, K., Physics

BELSLEY, D., Economics
BERGER, P., Fine Arts
BERNAUER, J. W., Philosophy
BLAKE, R., Fine Arts
BLANCHETTE, O., Philosophy
BODENHEIMER, R., English
BOMBOLAKIS, E. G., Geology and Geophysics
BROIDO, D. A., Physics
BROWN, S., Theology
BROWNELL, H., Psychology
BRUCKNER, M. T., Romance Languages
BRUELL, C., Political Science
BUCKLEY, M., Theology
BUNIE, A., History
BURGESS, D., Biology
BYRNE, P. H., Philosophy
CAHILL, L., Theology
CARPENTER, D. E., Romance Languages
CLARKE, M. J., Chemistry
CLEARY, J. J., Philosophy
CLOONEY, F. X., Theology
CLOTE, P., Biology
COBB-STEVENS, R., Philosophy
COX, D., Economics
CRANE, M., English
CRONIN, J., History
DAVIDOVITS, P., Chemistry
DERBER, C., Sociology
DI BARTOLO, B., Physics
DIETRICH, D., Theology
EASTON, R., Psychology
EBEL, J. E., Geology and Geophysics
EGAN, H., Theology
EYKMAN, C., German Studies
FAULKNER, R. K., Political Science
FLANAGAN, J. F., Philosophy
FLEMING, R., History
FOURKAS, J. T., Chemistry
FRIEDBERG, S., Mathematics
GARCIA, J., Philosophy
GOIZUETA, R., Theology
GOLLOP, F. M., Economics
GOTTSCHALK, P., Economics
GRAY, P., Psychology
GROOME, T. H., Theology
GUILLEMIN, J., Sociology
HACHEY, T. E., History
HAFNER, D. L., Political Science
HASKIN, D., English
HEINEMAN, J., History
HEPBURN, J. C., Geology and Geophysics
HERBECK, D., Communications
HESSE-BIBER, S., Sociology
HIBBS, T., Philosophy
HIMES, M., Theology
HOFFMAN, C., Biology
HOLLENBACH, D., Theology
HOLMSTROM, L. L., Sociology
HOVEYDA, A. H., Chemistry
IRELAND, P., Economics
KANTROWITZ, E. R., Chemistry
KARP, D. A., Sociology
KEARNEY, R., Philosophy
KELLY, C. J., Political Science
KELLY, T. R., Chemistry
KEMPA, K., Physics
KENNEDY, T. F., Music
KENNEY, M., Mathematics
KIRSCHNER, D. A., Biology
KRAUS, M., Economics
KREEFT, P. J., Philosophy
LAMB, M., Theology
LANDY, M., Political Science
LEE, T. O., Music
LEWBEL, A., Economics
LEWIS, P., English
LIEM, R., Psychology
LOWRY, S., Sociology
LYDENBERG, R., English
McFADDEN, D. L., Chemistry
McLAUGHLIN, L. W., Chemistry
MADIGAN, A., Philosophy
MANNING, R., History
MARIANI, P., English
MATELSKI, M., Communications

MATSON, S., English
MEISSNER, W., Theology
MELNICK, R. S., Political Science
MEYERHOFF, G. R., Mathematics
MICHALCZYK, J., Fine Arts
MILLER, S. J., Chemistry
MUNNELL, A. H., Finance
MUSKAVITCH, M., Biology
NAUGHTON, M., Physics
NETZER, N., Fine Arts
NORTHRUP, D., History
NUMAN, M., Psychology
PARIS, J. J., Theology
PERKINS, P., Theology
PFOHL, S. J., Sociology
PHILIPPIDES, D. M. L., Classics
QUINN, J., Economics
RASMUSSEN, D. M., Philosophy
REEDER, M., Mathematics
REINERMAN, A. J., History
RESLER, M., German Studies
RESTUCCIA, F., English
RICHARDSON, A., English
RICHARDSON, W. J., Philosophy
RINTALA, M., Political Science
ROBERTS, M. F., Chemistry
ROSS, R. S., Political Science
ROY, D. C., Geology and Geophysics
RUSSELL, J. A., Psychology
SARDELLA, D. J., Chemistry
SCHERVISH, P. G., Sociology
SCHIANTARELLI, F., Economics
SCHLOZMAN, K. L., Political Science
SCHOR, J., Sociology
SCHRADER, R., English
SCOTT, L. T., Chemistry
SCOTT-JONES, D., Psychology
SEGAL, U., Economics
SEYFRIED, T., Biology
SHELL, S., Political Science
SHOLL, M. J., Psychology
SMITH, J. H., Mathematics
SMYER, M., Psychology
SNAPPER, M. L., Chemistry
TAMINIAUX, J., Philosophy
TAYLOR, D., English
THIE, P. R., Mathematics
VALETTE, R. M., Romance Languages
VAUGHAN, D., Sociology
WEILER, P., History
WILLIAMSON, J. B., Sociology
WILSON, C. P., English
WILT, J., English
WINNER, E., Psychology
WOLFE, A., Political Science
WOLFF, L., History

Graduate School of Social Work (140 Commonwealth Ave, Chestnut Hill, MA 02467; tel. (617) 552-4020; fax (617) 552-2374; e-mail gssw@bc.edu):

BLYTHE, B.
GODENZI, A.
IATRIDIS, D. S.
KAYSER, K.
MALUCCIO, A. N.

Law School (885 Centre St, Newton Center, MA 02459; tel. (617) 552-8550; fax (617) 552-2851):

AULT, H. J.
BARON, C. H.
BLOOM, R. M.
BRODIN, M. S.
BROWN, G. D.
COQUILLETTE, D. R.
CUNNINGHAM, L.
FITZGIBBON, S. T.
GOLDFARB, P.
HILLINGER, I. M.
HOWE, R.-A. W.
KATZ, S. N.
KOHLER, T. C.
McMORROW, J. A.
PLATER, Z. J. B.
REPETTI, J. R.
ROGERS, J. S.

SOIFER, A.
SPIEGEL, M.
WELLS, C.
WIRTH, D. A.
YEN, A. C.-C.

Lynch School of Education (140 Commonwealth Ave, Chestnut Hill, MA 02467; tel. (617) 552-4200; fax (617) 552-0812; e-mail gsoe@bc.edu):

AIRASIAN, P. W.
ALTBACH, P. G.
BLUSTEIN, D.
BRABECK, M. M.
BRISK, M. E.
CASEY, M. B.
COCHRAN-SMITH, M.
DACEY, J. S.
DUDLEY-MARLING, C.
HANEY, W. M.
HARGREAVES, A.
HAUSER-CRAM, P.
HELMS, J. E.
LADD, G. T.
LERNER, J. V.
LYKES, M. B.
MADAUS, G. F.
MULLIS, I. V. S.
PINE, G. J.
PULLIN, D. C.
SHIRLEY, D. L.
STARRATT, R. J.
TWOMEY, E.
WALSH, M. E.
YOUN, E. I. K.

William F. Connell School of Nursing (140 Commonwealth Ave, Chestnut Hill, MA 02467; tel. (617) 552-4250; fax (617) 552-0745):

BURGESS, A. W.
DUFFY, M. E.
FRY, S. T.
HAWKINS, J. W.
JONES, D. A.
MUNRO, B. H.
ROY, Sr, C.
VESSEY, J. A.
WARDLE, M. G.

BOSTON COLLEGE SCHOOL OF THEOLOGY AND MINISTRY

140 Commonwealth Ave, Chestnut Hill, MA 02467-3800
9 Lake St, Brighton, MA 02135-3841
Telephone: (617) 552-6501
Fax: (617) 552-0811
E-mail: stmadmissions@bc.edu
Internet: www.bc.edu/schools/stm

Founded 2008 by merger of Weston Jesuit School of Theology with Institute of Religious Education and Pastoral Ministry
Private control
Academic year: August to DecemberJanuary to August (2 semesters)
Offers bachelors degree in sacred theology; masters degree in pastoral ministry, religious education, theology
Dean: MARK MASSA
Asst Dean and Dir of Admissions: SEAN PORTER
Assoc. Dean of Finance and Admin.: JOHN STACHNIEWICZ
Assoc. Dean of Student Affairs: JACQUELINE REGAN
Librarian: ESTHER GRISWOLD
Library of 2,440,000 vols.

BOSTON CONSERVATORY

8 The Fenway, Boston, MA 02215
Telephone: (617) 536-6340
Fax: (617) 912-9101
E-mail: admissions@bostonconservatory.edu

Internet: www.bostonconservatory.edu
Founded 1867
Private control
Academic year: September to May
Divs of dance, music, theatre
Pres.: RICHARD ORTNER
Vice President of Academic Affairs, Dean and Chief Academic Officer: PATRICIA HOY
Vice-Pres. for Admin., Student Affairs and Dean of Students: CARMEN GRIGGS
Vice President of Finance and Planning: ERIC NORMAN
Dir of Admissions: MEGHAN CADWALLADER
Dir of Devt: EILEEN MENY
Registrar: GREGORY KARAS
Dir of Library: JENNIFER HUNT

Library of 40,000 vols
Number of teachers: 160
Number of students: 730 (522 undergraduate, 208 graduate)

BOSTON GRADUATE SCHOOL OF PSYCHOANALYSIS

1581 Beacon St, Brookline, MA 02446
Telephone: (617) 277-3915
Fax: (617) 277-0312
E-mail: bgsp@bgsp.edu
Internet: www.bgsp.edu
Founded 1973
Private control
Academic year: September to June (2 semesters)
Campus in New York; offers MA and doctorate degrees in Psychoanalysis, Psychoanalysis and Culture, Psychoanalytic Counselling
Pres.: Dr JANE SNYDER
Vice-Pres. for Finance and Institutional Relations: Dr CAROL M. PANETTA
Dean of Graduate Studies: Dr LYNN PERLMAN
Dir of Financial Aid, Admissions Coordinator, Int. Student Services: STEPHANIE WOOLBERT
Registrar: ALLISON WILLIAMS
Dir of Library Services: AMY COHEN-ROSE

Library of 5,000 vols incl. journals
Number of teachers: 68
Number of students: 206

BOSTON UNIVERSITY

One Silber Way, Boston, MA 02215
Telephone: (617) 353-2000
Fax: (617) 353-9695
E-mail: admissions@bu.edu
Internet: www.bu.edu
Founded 1839 as Newbury Biblical Institute, present name 1869
Private control
Academic year: September to May (2 semesters)
Pres.: Dr ROBERT A. BROWN
Provost: Prof. Dr JEAN MORRISON
Sr Vice-Pres. for External Affairs: Dr STEPHEN P. BURGAY
Sr Vice-Pres., Chief Financial Officer and Treas.: MARTIN J. HOWARD
Sr Vice-Pres., Gen. Counsel and Sec. of Board of Trustees: Dr TODD L. C. KLIPP
Exec. Vice-Pres.: JOSEPH P. MERCURIO
Vice-Pres. for Admin. Services: PETER FIEDLER
Vice-Pres. for Auxiliary Services: PETER P. SMOKOWSKI
Vice-Pres. for Devt and Alumni Relations: SCOTT G. NICHOLS
Vice-Pres. for Enrolment and Student Affairs: Dr LAURIE A. POHL
Vice-Pres. for Govt and Community Affairs: EDWARD KING
Vice-Pres. for Operations: GARY W. NICKSA
Vice-Pres. and Assoc. Provost for Global Operations: WILLIS G. WANG

Vice-Pres. and Assoc. Provost for Research: Dr ANDREI A. RUCKENSTEIN
Dean of Students: KENNETH ELMORE
Registrar: FLORENCE BERGERON
Dir of Library: ROBERT HUDSON
Library: see Libraries and Archives
Number of teachers: 2,628
Number of students: 31,766
Publications: *Arion, Boston University Law Review, Journal of Education, Journal of Field Archaeology*

DEANS
College and Graduate School of Arts and Sciences: Prof. Dr VIRGINIA SAPIRO
College of Communication: THOMAS E. FIEDLER
College of Engineering: Prof. Dr KENNETH R. LUTCHEN
College of Fine Arts: BENJAMÍN E. JUÁREZ
College of General Studies: Dr LINDA S. WELLS
Henry M. Goldman School of Dental Medicine: Prof. JEFFREY W. HUTTER
Metropolitan College: Dr JAY A. HALFOND
Sargent College of Health and Rehabilitation Sciences: Prof. Dr GLORIA S. WATERS
School of Education: Dr HARDIN L. K. COLEMAN
School of Hospitality Administration: Dr CHRISTOPHER MULLER
School of Law: Prof. MAUREEN O'ROURKE
School of Management: Prof. KENNETH W. FREEMAN
School of Medicine: KAREN H. ANTMAN
School of Public Health: ROBERT F. MEENAN
School of Social Work: Prof. GAIL S. STEKETEE
School of Theology: Prof. MARY ELIZABETH MULLINO MOORE

BRANDEIS UNIVERSITY

415 South St, Waltham, MA 02454-9110
Telephone: (781) 736-2000
Fax: (781) 736-8699
E-mail: admissions@brandeis.edu
Internet: www.brandeis.edu
Founded 1948
Private control
Academic year: August to May (2 semesters)
Pres.: Dr FREDERICK M. LAWRENCE
Sr Vice-Pres. and Chief of Staff: Dr DAVID BUNIS
Provost and Chief Academic Officer: Dr STEVE A. N. GOLDSTEIN
Sr Vice-Pres. and Gen. Counsel: Dr JUDITH R. SIZER
Sr Vice-Pres. for Admin.: MARK COLLINS
Sr Vice-Pres. for Finance and Chief Financial Officer: FRANCES A. DROLETTE
Sr Vice-Pres. for Communications and External Affairs: ANDREW GULLY
Sr Vice-Pres. of Institutional Advancement: NANCY K. WINSHIP
Sr Vice-Pres. for Students and Enrolment: ANDREW FLAGEL
Vice-Pres. for Student Affairs and Dean of Student Life: RICK SAWYER
Assoc. Vice-Pres. for Univ. Affairs: JOHN HOSE
Registrar: Dr MARK HEWITT
Provost for Library and Technology Services and Chief Information Officer: Dr JOHN UNSWORTH
Library of 1,202,654 vols, 103,883 current serial subscriptions, 950,712 microforms, 40,021 audiovisual materials, 352,502 e-books
Number of teachers: 507 (364 full-time, 143 part-time)
Number of students: 5,828 (3,504 undergraduate, 2,324 graduate)
Publications: *Brandeis Magazine* (3 a year), *Catalyst* (2 a year)

DEANS
College of Arts and Sciences: Prof. Dr SUSAN J. BIRREN
Graduate School of Arts and Sciences: Prof. Dr MALCOLM W. WATSON
Heller School for Social Policy and Management: Prof. Dr LISA M. LYNCH
International Business School: Dr BRUCE MAGID

BRIDGEWATER STATE UNIVERSITY

131 Summer St, Bridgewater, MA 02325
Telephone: (508) 531-1000
Fax: (508) 531-1707
E-mail: admission@bridgew.edu
Internet: www.bridgew.edu
Founded 1840 as Bridgewater Normal School, present name 2010
State control
Academic year: September to May (2 semesters)
Pres.: Dr DANA MOHLER-FARIA
Provost and Vice-Pres. for Academic Affairs: Dr HOWARD B. LONDON
Vice-Pres. for Admin. and Finance: MIGUEL GOMES, JR (acting)
Vice-Pres. for External Affairs: Dr EDWARD MINNOCK
Vice-Pres. for Student Affairs: Dr D. DAVID OSTROTH
Vice-Pres. for Univ. Advancement and Strategic Planning: BRYAN BALDWIN (acting)
Registrar: IRENE CHECKOVICH
Dir of Libraries: Dr MICHAEL A. SOMMERS
Library of 340,258 vols
Number of teachers: 309 (full-time)
Number of students: 11,201

DEANS
Bartlett College of Science and Mathematics: Dr ARTHUR GOLDSTEIN
College of Education and Allied Studies: Dr ANNA BRADFIELD
College of Graduate Studies: Dr WILLIAM S. SMITH
College of Humanities and Social Sciences: Dr HOWARD B. LONDON (acting)
College of Science and Mathematics: Dr ARTHUR GOLDSTEIN
Ricciardi College of Business: Dr MARIAN M. EXTEJT

CAMBRIDGE COLLEGE

1000 Massachusetts Ave, Cambridge, MA 02138-5304
Telephone: (617) 868-1000
Fax: (617) 349-3561
E-mail: admit@cambridgecollege.edu
Internet: www.cambridgecollege.edu
Founded 1971
Private control
Academic year: September to August
Founder and Chancellor: EILEEN M. BROWN
Pres.: DEBORAH C. JACKSON
Exec. Vice-Pres.: Dr EZAT PARNIA
Provost and Vice-Pres. for Academic Affairs: Dr ELWOOD ROBINSON
Vice-Pres. for College Affairs: Dr JOSEPH DAISY
Vice-Pres. for Finance and Admin.: KIM GAZZOLA
Vice-Pres. for Institutional Advancement: PATRICIA F. DENN
Dean of Enrolment Management: ELAINE LAPOMARDO
Dean of Student Affairs: REGINA ROBINSON
Dir of Admissions: DENISE HAILE
Registrar: L. MARK SLAWSON
Number of teachers: 718
Number of students: 8,300

DEANS

School of Education: Dr N. ALAN SHEPPARD (acting)

School of Management: Dr MARY ANN JOSEPH (acting)

School of Psychology and Counselling: Prof. Dr NITI SETH

School of Undergraduate Studies: Prof. JAMES STEPHEN LEE

BRANCH CAMPUSES

Cambridge College, California: 8686 Haven Ave, Rancho Cucamonga, CA 91730; tel. (909) 635-0250; fax (909) 635-0253; Dir GREGORY WHITE.

Cambridge College, Georgia: 753 Broad St, Suite 1000, Augusta, GA 30901; tel. (706) 821-3965; fax (706) 821-3793; Dir SHARLOTTE EVANS.

Chesapeake Campus: Suite 300, 1403 Greenbrier Parkway, Chesapeake, VA 23320; tel. (757) 424-0333; fax (757) 424-1140; e-mail chesapeake@cambridgecollege .edu; Dir JIM WALDMAN.

Lawrence Campus: Lawrence Center, 60 Island St, Lawrence, MA 01840-1835; tel. (978) 738-0502; fax (978) 738-9655; e-mail lawrence@cambridgecollege.edu; Dir DOLORES C. CALAF.

Memphis Campus: Oak Ridge Bldg, Suite 401, 8000 Centerview Parkway, Cordova, TN 38018; tel. (901) 755-9399.

Puerto Rico Center: , 268 Ponce de Leon Ave, Suite 1400, Hato Rey, San Juan, PR 00918; tel. (787) 296-1101; e-mail puertorico@cambridgecollege.edu.

Springfield Campus: 570 Cottage St, Springfield, MA 01104; tel. (413) 747-0204; fax (413) 747-0613; e-mail springfield@ cambridgecollege.edu; Dir TERESA FORTE.

CLARK UNIVERSITY

950 Main St, Worcester, MA 01610-1477

Telephone: (508) 793-4411

Fax: (508) 793-8821

E-mail: admissions@clarku.edu

Internet: www.clarku.edu

Founded 1887

Private control

Academic year: August to May

Areas of study incl. art history, Asian studies, biology, business admin., chemistry and biochemistry, education, engineering, geography, history, physics

Pres.: Prof. Dr DAVID P. ANGEL

Provost and Vice-Pres. for Academic Affairs: Prof. Dr DAVIS BAIRD

Exec. Vice-Pres.: JAMES E. COLLINS

Vice-Pres. for Govt and Community Affairs: JACK FOLEY

Vice-Pres. for Planning and Budget: ANDREA MICHAELS

Vice-Pres. for Univ. Advancement: C. ANDREW MCGADNEY

Dean of Admissions and Financial Aid: DON HONEMAN

Dean of College and Associate Provost: Prof. Dr WALTER WRIGHT

Dean of Graduate Studies and Associate Provost: PRISCILLA ELSASS

Dean of Research and Associate Provost: Dr NANCY BUDWIG

Dean of Students: DENISE DARRIGRAND

Registrar: REBECCA HUNTER

Librarian: GWENDOLYNE ARTHUR

Library of 584,350 vols

Number of teachers: 197 (full-time)

Number of students: 2,209 (undergraduate)

Publications: *Clark University News, Economic Geography, Idealistic Studies.*

COLLEGE OF THE HOLY CROSS

One College St, Worcester, MA 01610-2395

Telephone: (508) 793-2011

Fax: (508) 793-3030

Internet: www.holycross.edu

Founded 1843

Private control

Academic year: August to May (2 semesters)

Depts of African studies, American sign language/deaf studies, Asian studies, biochemistry, biological psychology, biology, chemistry, Chinese, classics, economics and accounting, education, engineering, English, environmental studies, French, German, gerontology studies, graduate studies, history, Italian, Latin American and Latino studies, mathematics and computer science, medieval and renaissance studies, modern languages and literatures, music, naval science (NROTC), peace and conflict studies, philosophy, physics, political science, pre-business, pre-law, premedical and pre-dental studies, psychology, religious studies, Russian, Russian and Eastern European studies, science coordinator, sociology and anthropology, Spanish, studies in world literature, theatre, visual arts, women's and gender studies

Pres.: Rev. PHILIP L. BOROUGHS

Sr Vice-Pres.: FRANK VELLACCIO

Vice-Pres. for Academic Affairs and Dean of College: Dr TIMOTHY R. AUSTIN

Vice-Pres. for Admin. and Finance: MICHAEL J. LOCHHEAD

Vice-Pres. for Devt and Alumni Relations: (vacant)

Vice-Pres. for Student Affairs and Dean of Students: JACQUELINE D. PETERSON

Gen. Counsel: Dr TIMOTHY F. MINES

Registrar: PATRICIA RING

Dir of Library Services: KATHLEEN M. CARNEY

Library of 650,000 vols, 4,500 print and e-journals

Number of teachers: 325 (258 full-time, 67 part-time)

Number of students: 2,872

Publications: *Interfaces* (2 a year), *Fosforo, Holy Cross Magazine* (4 a year), *The Holy Cross Journal of Law and Public Policy* (1 a year), *The Purple, The Purple Patcher* (1 a year).

CONWAY SCHOOL

332 South Deerfield Rd, POB 179, Conway, MA 01341-0179

Telephone: (413) 369-4044

Fax: (413) 369-4032

Internet: www.csld.edu

Founded 1972, present status 1989

Private control

Offers MA in landscape planning and design

Dir: PAUL CAWOOD HELLMUND

Assoc. Dir for Admissions and Communication: MOLLIE BABIZE

Assoc. Dir of Finance, Operations and Community Projects: DAVE NORDSTROM

Library of 3,000 vols.

CURRY COLLEGE

1071 Blue Hill Ave, Milton, MA 02186

Telephone: (617) 333-0500

Fax: (617) 333-2114

E-mail: curryadm@curry.edu

Internet: www.curry.edu

Founded 1879 as School of Elocution and Expression; present name 1943

Private control

Academic year: September to May

Campus in Plymouth; depts of applied technology communication, education, fine and

applied arts, humanities, interdisciplinary studies, management, natural sciences and mathematics, nursing, politics and history, psychology, sociology and criminal justice

Pres.: Dr KENNETH K. QUIGLEY, JR

Chief Academic Officer: Dr DAVID POTASH

Chief Devt Officer: CHRISTOPHER LAWSON

Chief Financial Officer: RICHARD F. SULLIVAN

Dean of Admission: JANE P. FIDLER

Dean of Continuing Education and Graduate Studies: Dr RUTH D. SHERMAN

Dean of Faculty: Dr CASSANDRA VOLPE HORII

Dean of Institutional Planning: Dr SUSAN W. PENNINI

Dean of Students: MARYELLEN M. COLLITON KILEY

Registrar: MARIKA HAMILTON

Dir of Library: Prof. EDWARD TALLENT

Number of teachers: 450

Number of students: 3,880

DEAN COLLEGE

99 Main St, Franklin, MA 02038-1994

Telephone: (508) 541-1900

Fax: (508) 541-8726

E-mail: admission@dean.edu

Internet: www.dean.edu

Founded 1865, present name 1994

Private control

Academic year: August to May

Schools of arts, business, dance, liberal arts and sciences, professional and continuing studies, theatre

Pres.: Dr PAULA M. ROONEY

Vice-Pres. for Academic Affairs and Planning: Dr LINDA M. RAGOSTA

Vice-Pres. for College Operations and Human Resources: Dr PETER MARTEL

Vice-Pres. for Enrolment Services and Marketing: JOHN F. MARCUS

Vice-Pres. for Financial Services and Treas.: DANIEL A. MODELANE

Vice-Pres. for Institutional Advancement: COLEEN P. RESNICK

Vice-Pres. for Student Devt and Retention: Dr CINDY T. KOZIL

Registrar: NANCY C. SULLIVAN

Library of 32,000 vols, 105 periodicals

Number of students: 1,600

EASTERN NAZARENE COLLEGE

23 East Elm Ave, Quincy, MA 02170

Telephone: (617) 745-3000

Fax: (617) 745-3929

E-mail: admissions@enc.edu

Internet: www1.enc.edu

Founded 1900

Private control

Academic year: September to May (2 semesters)

Depts incl. biology, business, chemistry, education, history, mathematics, movement arts, music, social work

Pres.: Dr CORLIS MCGEE

Provost and Dean of the College: Dr TIMOTHY WOOSTER

Vice-Pres. for Enrolment: JEFFREY A. WELLS

Vice-Pres. for Finance: JAN WEISEN

Vice-Pres. for Institutional Advancement: Dr SCOTT TURCOTT

Vice-Pres. for Student Devt: VERNON WESLEY

Dir of Admissions: ANDREW WRIGHT

Registrar: MARGARET BALLARD

Dir of Library Services: SUSAN WATKINS

Library of 126,465 vols

Number of teachers: 52

Number of students: 1,075

DEANS

Adult and Graduate Studies: Dr LINDA SCOTT

ELMS COLLEGE

291 Springfield St, Chicopee, MA 01013-2839
Telephone: (413) 594-2761
Fax: (413) 592-4871
Internet: www.elms.edu
Founded 1928
Private control
Academic year: September to May

Liberal arts college; divs of business and law, communication sciences and disorders, education, humanities and fine arts, natural sciences, mathematics and technology, nursing, social sciences

Pres.: Dr JAMES H. MULLEN, Jr
Vice-Pres. for Academic Affairs: Dr WALTER C. BREAU
Vice-Pres. for Finance and Admin.: BRIAN E. DOHERTY
Vice-Pres. for Institutional Advancement: KEVIN M. EDWARDS
Vice-Pres. for Student Affairs: JOHN KELLER
Dir of Admission: JOSEPH WAGNER
Registrar: LAURA LANDER
Dir of Library: PATRICIA BOMBARDIES
Library of 103,000 vols, 684 periodicals
Number of teachers: 167 (67 full-time, 10 part-time, 90 adjunct)
Number of students: 1,355

Publication: *Elms College Magazine*.

EMERSON COLLEGE

120 Boylston St, Boston, MA 02116-4624
Telephone: (617) 824-8500
Fax: 617-824-8609
E-mail: admission@emerson.edu
Internet: www.emerson.edu
Founded 1880
Private control
Academic year: August to May

Pres.: Dr LEE PELTON (acting)
Vice-Pres. and Gen. Counsel: CHRISTINE HUGHES
Vice-Pres. for Academic Affairs: LINDA MOORE
Vice-Pres. for Admin. and Finance: MAUREEN MURPHY
Vice-Pres. for Devt and Alumni Relations: BARBARA RUTBERG
Vice-Pres. for Enrolment: M. J. KNOLL-FINN
Vice-Pres. for Institutional Advancement: DONALD C. MAIN
Dean of Students: RONALD LUDMAN
Registrar: WILLIAM F. DEWOLF
Dir of Library: ROBERT FLEMING
Library of 125,000 vols
Number of teachers: 465
Number of students: 4,290 (3,453 undergraduate, 837 graduate)

Publications: *Berkeley Beacon* (2 a week), *Emerson Review* (2 a year), *Expression: The Magazine for Alumni and Friends of Emerson College* (3 a year), *Omnivore* (2 a year)

DEANS

Graduate Studies: RICHARD ZAUFT
Liberal Arts: AMY ANSELL
School of Arts: DANIEL TOBIN
School of Communication: JANIS ANDERSEN

EMMANUEL COLLEGE

400 The Fenway, Boston, MA 02115
Telephone: (617) 735-9715
Fax: (617) 735-9801
E-mail: enroll@emmanuel.edu
Internet: www.emmanuel.edu
Founded 1919
Private control
Academic year: May to May

Pres.: Sis. JANET EISNER

Exec. Vice-Pres. and Chief Operating Officer: NEIL BUCKLEY
Vice-Pres. for Academic Affairs: JOYCE DE LEO
Vice-Pres. for Devt and Alumni Relations: JOAN CALDWELL (acting)
Vice-Pres. for Finance and Admin.: NEIL BUCKLEY
Vice-Pres. of Student Affairs: Dr PATRICIA A. RISSMEYER
Library Dir: Dr SUSAN VON DAUM THOLL (acting)
Library of 140,000 vols, 2,000 journals
Number of teachers: 80
Number of students: 2,500

DEANS

Arts and Sciences: Dr WILLIAM C. LEONARD

ENDICOTT COLLEGE

376 Hale Street, Beverly, MA 01915
Telephone: (978) 927-0585
Fax: (978) 927-0084
E-mail: admission@endicott.edu
Internet: www.endicott.edu
Founded 1939
Private control
Academic year: June to August

Pres.: Dr RICHARD E. WYLIE
Exec. Vice-Pres. and Vice-Pres. for Finance: LYNNE B. O'TOOLE
Vice-Pres.: Dr MARY HUEGEL
Vice-Pres. for Admissions and Financial Aid: THOMAS J. REDMAN
Vice-Pres. for Institutional Advancement: DAVID VIGNERON
Vice-Pres. for Student Affairs: Dr BEVERLY DOLINSKY
Registrar: ANITA MCFARLANE
Dir of Library: BRIAN COURTEMANCHE
Library of 116,876 vols, 124,809 e-periodicals
Number of teachers: 367 (112 full-time, 255 part-time)
Number of students: 4,650

DEANS

School of Arts and Sciences: Dr GENE WONG
School of Business: Dr AMY BELL ROSS
School of Communication: Dr LAUREL HELLERSTEIN
School of Education: Dr SARA QUAY
School of Hospitality Management: Dr WILLIAM SAMENFINK
School of Nursing: Dr KELLY FISHER
School of Sport Science and Fitness Studies: Dr DEBORAH SWANTON
School of Visual and Performing Arts: MARK TOWNER
Undergraduate College: Dr LAURA ROSSI-LE
Van Loan School of Graduate and Professional Studies: Dr MARY HUEGEL

EPISCOPAL DIVINITY SCHOOL

99 Brattle St, Cambridge, MA 02138
Telephone: (617) 868-3450
Fax: (617) 864-5385
E-mail: admissions@eds.edu
Internet: www.eds.edu
Founded 1974 by merger of Philadelphia Divinity School (f. 1857) with Episcopal Theological School (f. 1867)
Private control
Academic year: September to May

Offers degrees in divinity, ministry, theological studies

Pres. and Dean: Very Rev. Dr KATHERINE HANCOCK RAGSDALE
Academic Dean: Dr ANGELA BAUER-LEVESQUE
Vice-Pres. for Institutional Advancement: HUGO DE LA ROSA
Dean of Student and Community Life: MIRIAM GELFER

Registrar: LISA HOWELL
Library Dir: ESTHER A. GRISWOLD
Library of 232,000 vols
Number of teachers: 22
Number of students: 68 (full-time)

FISHER COLLEGE

118 Beacon St, Boston, MA 02116
Telephone: (617) 236-8800
Fax: (617) 236-5473
E-mail: admissions@fisher.edu
Internet: www.fisher.edu
Founded 1903
Private control
Academic year: September to May

Schools of art, business and management, nursing

Pres.: Dr THOMAS M. MCGOVERN
Vice-Pres. for Academic Affairs: JANET KUSER
Vice-Pres. for Admin.: RHONDA PIERONI
Vice-Pres. for Finance: STEVEN RICH
Dean of Admissions: ROBERT MELARAGNI
Dean of Students: SHIELA LALLY
Registrar: ROSA CADENA
College Librarian: JOSHUA MCKAIN

Publication: *Fisher Today* (2 a year).

FITCHBURG STATE UNIVERSITY

160 Pearl St, Fitchburg, MA 01420-2697
Telephone: (978) 665-3000
Fax: (978) 665-3693
E-mail: admissions@fitchburgstate.edu
Internet: www.fitchburgstate.edu
Founded 1894 as State Normal School, present name 2010
State control
Academic year: September to June (2 semesters)

Pres.: Dr ROBERT V. ANTONUCCI
Vice-Pres. for Academic Affairs: Dr ROBIN E. BOWEN
Vice-Pres. for Finance and Admin.: JAY BRY
Vice President for Institutional Advancement: CHRISTOPHER HENDRY
Dean of Enrolment Management and Dir of Financial Aid: PAMELA MCCAFFERTY
Dir of Admissions: KAY REYNOLDS
Registrar: LINDA DUPELL
Dir of Library: ROBERT FOLEY

Library of 210,790 vols, 478,000 microforms, 500 periodicals, 1,000 e-books, 43,000 e-journals
Number of teachers: 196 (full-time)
Number of students: 6,891 (4,172 undergraduate, 2,791 graduate)

Publication: *Contact* (1 a year)

DEANS

Education: ELAINE E. FRANCIS
Graduate and Continuing Education: CATHERINE CANNEY

FRAMINGHAM STATE COLLEGE

100 State St, POB 9101, Framingham, MA 01701-9101
Telephone: (508) 620-1220
Fax: (508) 626-4592
E-mail: admissions@framingham.edu
Internet: www.framingham.edu
Founded 1839

Depts incl. art and music, biology, chemistry and food science, communication arts, computer science, economics and business admin.
State control
Academic year: September to May (2 semesters)

Pres.: Dr TIMOTHY J. FLANAGAN

Sr Vice-Pres. for Admin. and Finance: Dr DALE M. HAMEL
Vice-Pres. for Academic Affairs: Dr LINDA VADEN-GOAD
Vice-Pres. for Enrolment and Student Devt: SUSANNE H. CONLEY
Vice-Pres. for Univ. Advancement: CHRISTOPHER P. HENDRY
Dean of Graduate and Continuing Education: Dr SCOTT GREENBERG
Dean of Students: Dr MELINDA K. STOOPS
Registrar: MARK R. POWERS
Dir of Library Services: BONNIE MITCHELL (acting)
Library of 344,185 vols
Number of teachers: 196
Number of students: 6,415 (4,321 undergraduate, 2,094 graduate)
Publication: *Alumni Magazine* (1 a year).

FRANKLIN W. OLIN COLLEGE OF ENGINEERING

Olin Way, Needham, MA 02492-1200
Telephone: (781) 292-2300
Fax: (781) 292-2344
E-mail: info@olin.edu
Internet: www.olin.edu
Founded 1997
Private control
Academic year: August to May
Academic programmes in engineering incl. electrical and computer engineering, mechanical engineering
Pres.: Dr RICHARD K. MILLER
Provost and Dean of Faculty: VINCENT P. MANNO
Exec. Vice-Pres. and Treas.: STEPHEN P. HANNABURY
Vice-Pres. for Admin. and Finance: STEPHEN P. HANNABURY
Exec. Vice-Pres. for Devt, Family and Alumni Relations: J. THOMAS KRIMMEL
Vice-Pres. for External Relations and Dean of Admission: Dr CHARLES S. NOLAN
Vice-Pres. for Innovation and Research: SHERRA E. KERNS
Dean of Student Life: Dr ROGER C. CRAFTS
Registrar: LINDA T. CANAVAN
Dir of Library: DIANNA MAGNONI
Number of teachers: 37
Number of students: 346
Publication: *Journal of Asynchronous Learning Networks* (2–4 a year)

PROFESSORS

BOURNE, J., Electrical and Computer Engineering
DONIS-KELLER, H., Biology and Art
HOLT, S. S., Physics
KERNS, D., Electrical Engineering
KERNS, S., Electrical and Computer Engineering
MILLER, R., Mechanical Engineering
PRATT, G., Electrical and Computer Engineering

GORDON COLLEGE

255 Grapevine Rd, Wenham, MA 01984
Telephone: (978) 927-2300
Fax: (978) 524-3704
E-mail: info@gordon.edu
Internet: www.gordon.edu
Founded 1889 as Boston Missionary Training School; present name after merger with Barrington College 1985
Academic year: August to July (2 semesters)
Divs of economics, education, fine arts, humanities, mathematics and computer science, psychology, social work, sociology
Pres.: Dr D. MICHAEL LINDSAY
Provost: Dr MARK L. SARGENT

Sr Vice-Pres. for Finance and Admin.: MICHAEL J. AHEARN
Exec. Vice-Pres. and Chief of Staff: DANIEL B. TYMANN
Vice-Pres. for Marketing and Strategic Communications: RICHARD D. SWEENEY, JR
Vice-Pres. for Development: SANDRA L. BUTTERS
Vice-Pres. for Enrolment: SILVIO VAZQUEZ
Vice-Pres. for Student Devt and Dean of Students: BARRY J. LOY
Dean of College Planning: Dr STEPHEN C. MACLEOD
Registrar: CAROL A. HERRICK
Dir of Library Services: Dr MYRON SCHIRER-SUTER
Library of 190,000 vols, 74,000 e-books, 51,150 print and online journals
Number of teachers: 173 (98 full-time, 75 part-time)
Number of students: 1,573
Publication: *STILLPOINT* (2 a year).

GORDON-CONWELL THEOLOGICAL SEMINARY

130 Essex St, South Hamilton, MA 01982
Telephone: (978) 468-7111
Fax: (978) 468-6691
E-mail: admrep@gcts.edu
Internet: www.gordonconwell.edu
Founded 1969 by merger of Conwell School of Theology (f. 1884) with Gordon Divinity School (f. 1889)
Private control
Academic year: September to May
Br. campuses in Boston, Charlotte, Jacksonville; degree programmes incl. arts, divinity, ministry, theology
Pres.: Prof. Dr DENNIS HOLLINGER
Provost: Prof. Dr FRANK JAMES
Dean of Faculty: CAROL KAMINSKI
Exec. Vice-Pres. and Chief Financial Officer: ROBERT S. LANDREBE
Vice-Pres. for Advancement: KURT DRESCHER
Academic Dean: BARRY H. COREY
Dean of Enrolment Management and Registrar: SCOTT POBLENZ
Dean of Students: LISE SCHLUETER
Head Librarian: FREEMAN BARTON
Library of 250,000 vols
Number of teachers: 48
Number of students: 986

HAMPSHIRE COLLEGE

893 West St, Amherst, MA 01002
Telephone: (413) 549-4600
Fax: (413) 582-5584
E-mail: admissions@hampshire.edu
Internet: www.hampshire.edu
Founded 1965
Private control
Academic year: September to June
Pres.: JONATHAN LASH
Sec.: BETH WARD
Vice-Pres. for Academic Affairs and Dean of Faculty: Prof. ALAN GOODMAN
Vice-Pres. for Finance and Admin. and Treas.: MARK K. SPIRO
Chief Advancement Officer: CLAY BALLANTINE
Dean of Students: DAWN ELLINWOOD
Dir of Admissions and Financial Aid: JULIE RICHARDSON
Dir of Library and College Archivist: SUSAN DAYALL (acting)
Library of 121,837 vols, 64,469 e-books, 9,712 journals, 56,041 e-journals
Number of teachers: 100
Number of students: 1,530

DEANS

School of Cognitive Science: LAURA SIZER

School of Critical Social Inquiry: ANNIE ROGERS
School of Humanities, Arts and Cultural Studies: NORMAN HOLLAND
School of Interdisciplinary Arts: ELLEN DONKIN
School of Natural Science: JASON TOR
School of Social Science: BARBARA YNGVESSON

HARVARD UNIVERSITY

Massachusetts Hall, Cambridge, MA 02138
Telephone: (617) 495-1000
Fax: (617) 495-8821
Internet: www.harvard.edu
Founded 1636
Private control
Academic year: September to June
Pres.: Prof. Dr DREW GILPIN FAUST
Provost: Prof. Dr ALAN M. GARBER
Vice-Pres. and Sec.: MARC GOODHEART
Treas.: JAMES ROTHENBERG
Exec. Vice-Pres.: KATHERINE N. LAPP
Vice-Pres. for Admin.: TOM VAUTIN
Vice-Pres. for Alumni Affairs and Devt: TAMARA ROGERS
Vice-Pres. for Finance and Chief Financial Officer: DAN SHORE
Vice-Pres. and Gen. Counsel: ROBERT IULIANO (acting)
Dir of Univ. Library: ROBERT DARNTON
Library: 17m. vols
Number of teachers: 12,100 (2,100 non-medical, 10,000 medical)
Number of students: 21,000

DEANS

Continuing Education and Univ. Extension: MICHAEL SHINAGEL
Faculty of Arts and Sciences: Prof. Dr MICHAEL D. SMITH
Graduate School of Design: Prof. MOHSEN MOSTAFAVI
Graduate School of Arts and Sciences: Prof. RICHARD TARRANT
Harvard Business School: Dr NITIN NOHRIA
Harvard College: Prof. Dr EVELYNN M. HAMMONDS
Harvard Divinity School: Prof. Dr WILLIAM A. GRAHAM
Harvard Graduate School of Education: Prof. KATHLEEN MCCARTNEY
Harvard Law School: Prof. Dr MARTHA MINOW
Harvard Medical School: Prof. Dr JEFFREY S. FLIER
Harvard School of Dental Medicine: Prof. Dr R. BRUCE DONOFF
Harvard School of Public Health: Prof. Dr JULIO FRENK
John F. Kennedy School of Government: Prof. Dr DAVID T. ELLWOOD
Radcliffe Institute for Advanced Study: Prof. Dr LIZABETH COHEN
School of Engineering and Applied Sciences: Prof. Dr CHERRY A. MURRAY

PROFESSORS

Graduate School of Arts and Sciences (University Hall, Cambridge, MA 02138; tel. (617) 495-1566; internet www.fas.harvard.edu):

ABERNATHY, F. H., Mechanical Engineering
ALESINA, A., Economics and Government
ALEXIOU, M., Modern Greek Studies, Comparative Literature
ALT, J. E., Government
ANDERSON, D., Applied Mathematics
ANDERSON, J. G., Atmospheric Chemistry
ASHTON, P. S., Forestry
AZIZ, M., Materials Science
BARANCZAK, S., Polish Language and Literature
BAR-YOSEF, O., Prehistoric Archaeology
BATES, R. H., Government

BAZZAZ, F. A., Biology
BENHABIB, S., Government
BENSON, L. D., English Literature
BERCOVITCH, S., English and American Literature and Language, Comparative Literature
BERG, H. C., Molecular and Cellular Biology, Physics
BIAGIOLI, M., History of Science
BIEWENER, A., Biology
BISSON, T. N., Medieval History
BLACKBOURN, D., History
BLIER, S., History of Art and Architecture
BLOXHAM, J., Geophysics
BOBO, L., Sociology and Afro-American Studies
BOIS, Y.-A., Modern Art
BOL, P., Chinese History
BOLITHO, H., Japanese History
BOSS, K. J., Biology
BOSSERT, W. H., Science
BOTT, R., Mathematics
BOYM, S., Slavic Languages and Literature, Comparative Literature
BRANDT, A., History of Science
BRANTON, D., Biology
BRINKMANN, R., Music
BROCKETT, R. W., Electrical Engineering and Computer Science
BRYSON, W., History of Art and Architecture
BUELL, L., English
BURGARD, P., German
BUTLER, J. N., Applied Chemistry
CAMERON, A., Astrophysics
CAMPBELL, J. Y., Applied Economics
CARAMAZZA, A., Psychology
CATON, S., Contemporary Arab Studies
CAVANAGH, P., Psychology
CAVANAUGH, C., Biology
CAVES, R. E., Political Economy
CHAMBERLAIN, G., Economics
CHANDRA, P., Indian and South Asian Art
CHEATHAM, T. E., Computer Science
COATSWORTH, J., Latin American Affairs
COELHO, J.-F., Portuguese Language and Literature, Comparative Literature
COHEN, L., History
COLEMAN, K., Latin
COLEMAN, S. R., Science
COLTON, T., Government and Russian Studies
CONLEY, T., Romance Languages and Literature
COOPER, R., International Economics
COREY, E. J., Organic Chemistry
COTT, N. F., History
CRAIG, A. M., History
CRANSTON, E. A., Japanese Literature
CROMPTON, A. W., Natural History
CUTLER, D., Economics
DAMROSCH, L., Literature
DAVIDOVSKY, M., Music
DAWSON, M., Government
DEMPSTER, A. P., Theoretical Statistics
DEVORE, B. I., Biological Anthropology
DOMINGUEZ, J. I., International Affairs
DONOGHUE, D., English and American Literature and Language
DONOGHUE, M., Biology
DOWLING, J., Natural Sciences
DUFFY, J., Byzantine Philology and Literature
DZIEWONSKI, A. M., Science
ECK, D. L., Comparative Religion and Indian Studies
ECKERT, C., Korean History
EHRENREICH, H., Science
EKSTROM, G., Geology and Geophysics
ELKIES, N., Mathematics
ELLISON, P., Anthropology
ENGELL, J., English and Comparative Literature
EPPS, B., Romance Languages and Literature

ERIKSON, R. L., Cellular and Developmental Biology
EVANS, A., Materials Engineering
EVANS, D. A., Chemistry
FANGER, D. L., Literature
FARRELL, B., Meteorology
FASH, W., Central American and Mexican Archaeology and Ethnology
FELDMAN, G., Science
FELDSTEIN, M. S., Economics
FERGUSON, N., History
FERNANDEZ-CIFUENTE, L., Romance Languages and Literature
FIDO, F., Romance Languages and Literature
FIELD, G. B., Applied Astronomy
FISHER, D., Physics
FISHER, P. J., English and American Literatures
FLEMING, D. H., American History
FLIER, M., Ukrainian Philology
FORD, P., Celtic Languages and Literature
FRANKLIN, M., Physics
FREEMAN, R. B., Economics
FRIEDEN, J., Government
FRIEDMAN, B. M., Political Economy
FRIEND, C., Chemistry
FUDENBERG, D., Economics
GABRIELSE, G., Physics
GALISON, P., History of Science and of Physics
GARBER, M., English
GATES, H., Humanities
GAYLORD, M., Romance Languages and Literature
GELBART, W. M., Molecular and Cellular Biology
GEORGI, H. M., Physics
GIENAPP, W., History
GILBERT, D., Psychology
GILBERT, W.
GLASHOW, S. L., Physics
GLAUBER, R. J., Physics
GOLDFARB, W., Modern Mathematics and Mathematical Logic
GOLDIN, C., Economics
GOLOVCHENKO, J., Physics
GORDON, A., History
GORDON, R. G., Chemistry
GRABOWICZ, G. G., Ukrainian Literature
GRAHAM, W. A., History of Religion and Islamic Studies
GREEN, J. R., Political Economy
GREENBLATT, S., English and American Literature and Language
GRILICHES, Z., Economics
GRINDLAY, J. E., Astronomy
GROSS, B. H., Mathematics
GROSZ, B., Computer Science
GUIDOTTI, G., Biochemistry
GUILLORY, J., English
GUTHKE, K. S., German Art and Culture
GUZZETTI, A. F., Visual Arts
HACKMAN, J., Social and Organizational Psychology
HALL, P., Government
HALPERIN, B. I., Mathematics and Natural Philosophy
HANKINS, J., History
HARDACRE, H., Japanese Religions and Society
HARRINGTON, A., History of Science
HARRINGTON, J. J., Environmental Engineering
HARRIS, J. C., English and Folklore
HARRIS, J. D., Mathematics
HARRIS, J. M., Jewish Studies
HARRISON, S. C., Biochemistry and Molecular Biology
HART, O., Economics
HARTL, D., Biology
HASTINGS, J., Natural Sciences
HEIMERT, A. E., American Literature
HEINRICHS, W. P., Arabic
HELLER, E., Physics
HELPMAN, E., Economics

HENRICHS, A. M., Greek Literature
HERSCHBACH, D. R., Science
HERZFELD, M., Anthropology
HIGGINBOTHAM, E. B., Afro-American Studies, History
HIGONNET, P. L.-R., French History
HO, Y. C., Engineering and Applied Mathematics
HOFFMAN, P., Geology
HOFFMANN, S. H.
HOLLAND, H. D., Geology
HOLM, R. H., Chemistry
HOOLEY, J., Psychology
HOROWITZ, P., Physics
HOWE, R., Engineering
HUEHNERGARD, J. D., Semitic Philology
HUTCHINSON, J. W., Applied Mechanics
HUTH, J., Physics
IRIYE, A., American History
JACOB, D., Atmospheric Chemistry, Environmental Engineering
JACOBSEN, E., Chemistry
JACOBSEN, S. B., Geochemistry
JAFFE, A. M., Mathematics and Theoretical Science
JARDINE, A., Romance Languages and Literature
JASANOFF, J., Linguistics
JENKINS, F., Zoology and Biology
JOHNSON, B., Law and Psychiatry in Society
JONES, C. P., Classics and History
JONES, R. V., Applied Physics
JORGENSON, D. W., Economics
KAFADAR, C., Turkish Studies
KAGAN, J., Psychology
KAISER, W. J., English and Comparative Literature
KALAVREZOU, I., Byzantine Art
KATZ, L., Economics
KAZHDAN, D., Mathematics
KEENAN, E. L., History
KELLY, T., Music
KELMAN, H. C., Social Ethics
KIELY, R. J., English
KILLIP, C., Visual and Environmental Studies
KILSON, M. L., Government
KING, G., Government
KIRBY, W., History
KIRSHNER, R. P., Astronomy
KISHLANSKY, M., History
KLECKNER, N., Biochemistry and Molecular Biology
KLEINMAN, A. M., Medical Anthropology
KLEMPERER, W. A., Chemistry
KNOLL, A., Biology
KOERNER, J., History of Art and Architecture
KORNAI, J., Economics
KORSGAARD, C., Philosophy
KOSSLYN, S. M., Psychology
KRONAUER, R. E., Mechanical Engineering
KRONHEIMER, P., Mathematics
KUGEL, J. L., Classical and Modern Jewish and Hebrew Literature and Comparative Literature
KUHN, P. A., History and East Asian Languages and Civilizations
KUNG, H., Electrical Engineering and Computer Science
KUNO, S., Linguistics
LAMBERG-KARLOVSKY, C. C., Archaeology and Ethnology
LANGER, E. J., Psychology
LEE, L., Chinese Literature
LEVIN, R., Music
LEVINE, N., History of Art and Architecture
LEWALSKI, B., History and Literature, English Literature
LEWIN, D. B., Music
LEWIS, H. R., Computer Science
LEWONTIN, R. C., Biology
LIEBER, C., Chemistry
LIEBERSON, S., Sociology
LIEM, K., Ichthyology

LOCKWOOD, L. H., Music
LOEB, A., Astronomy
LOSICK, R. M., Biology
MCCANN, D., Korean Literature
MCCARTHY, J. J., Biological Oceanography
MCCORMICK, M., History
MCDONALD, C., Romance Languages and Literatures
MCELROY, M. B., Environmental Studies
MACFARQUHAR, R., History and Political Science
MACHINIST, P., Hebrew and Other Oriental Languages
MCMAHON, A., Molecular and Cellular Biology
MCMAHON, T. A., Applied Mechanics and Biology
MCMULLEN, C., Mathematics
MCNALLY, R., Personality Psychology
MAHER, B. A., Psychology of Personality
MAIER, C. S., European Studies
MALMSTAD, J., Slavic Languages and Literatures
MANIATIS, T. P., Molecular and Cellular Biology
MANKIW, N. G., Economics
MANSFIELD, H. C., Government
MARGLIN, S. A., Economics
MARSDEN, P. V., Sociology
MARTIN, L., Government
MARTIN, P. C., Pure and Applied Physics
MASKIN, E. S., Economics
MAY, E. R., American History
MAYBURY-LEWIS, D. H., Anthropology
MAZUR, B., Mathematics
MAZUR, E., Physics
MEDOFF, J. L., Labour and Industry
MEISTER, M., Molecular and Cellular Biology
MELTON, D. A., Molecular and Cellular Biology
MENDELSOHN, E. I., History of Science
MESELSON, M. S., Natural Sciences
MITCHELL, R., Applied Biology
MITCHELL, S. A., Scandinavian and Folklore
MITTEN, D. G., Classical Art and Archaeology
MORALEJO, S., Fine Arts
MORAN, R., Philosophy
MORRIS, C., Statistics
MOTTAHEDEH, R., History
MURDOCH, J. E., History of Science
MYERS, A., Chemistry and Chemical Biology
NAGY, G. J., Classical Greek Literature and Comparative Literature
NAKAYAMA, K., Psychology
NARAYAN, R., Astronomy
NECIPOGLU, G., Islamic Art
NELSON, D. R., Physics
NOZICK, R., Philosophy
O'CATHASAIGH, T., Irish Studies
O'CONNELL, R. J., Geophysics
OETTINGER, A., Applied Mathematics, Information Resources Policy
OWEN, E., Middle East History
OWEN, S.
OZMENT, S. E., Ancient and Modern History
PALUMBI, S., Biology
PARK, K., History of Science, Women's Studies
PARSONS, C., Philosophy
PATTERSON, O., Sociology
PAUL, W., Applied Physics
PEARSALL, D. A., English Literature
PEDERSON, S., History
PERALTA, E., Molecular Neurobiology
PERKINS, D. H., Political Economy
PERRY, E., Government
PERSHAN, P. S., Applied Physics
PERTILE, L., Romance Languages and Literature, Comparative Literature
PETERSON, P., Government
PFISTER, D. H., Systematic Botany

PHARR, S. J., Japanese Politics
PIERCE, N., Biology
PIERSON, P., Government
PILBEAM, D. R., Social Sciences
PINNEY, G., Classical Archaeology and Art
PRENTISS, M., Physics
PRESS, W. H., Astronomy, Physics
PUTNAM, H. W.
PUTNAM, R. D., Political Science
RABIN, M. O., Computer Science
RANDS, B., Music
RENTSCHLER, E., German
RESKIN, B., Sociology
RICE, J. R., Engineering Sciences and Geophysics
ROBERTSON, E., Molecular and Cellular Biology
ROBINSON, A. R., Geophysical Fluid Dynamics
ROGERS, P. P., Environmental Engineering
ROSEN, S., National Security and Military Affairs
ROSENTHAL, R., Social Psychology
RUBIN, D. B., Statistics
RUBIN, J., Japanese Humanities
RUDENSTINE, N., English and American Literature and Language
RUSSELL, J., Armenian Studies
RUVOLO, M., Anthropology
RYAN, J. L., German and Comparative Literature
SACKS, G. E., Mathematical Logic
SACKS, P., English and American Literature and Language
SANDEL, M. J., Government
SCANLON, T., Natural Religion, Moral Philosophy and Civil Policy
SCARRY, E., Aesthetics and the General Theory of Value
SCHACTER, D., Psychology
SCHMID, W., Mathematics
SCHOR, N., Romance Languages and Literature
SCHREIBER, S. L., Chemistry
SEGAL, C., Classics
SEN, A., Economics, Philosophy
SEPTIMUS, B., Jewish History and Sephardic Civilization
SHAKHNOVICH, E., Chemistry and Chemical Biology
SHAPIRO, I. I.
SHEARMAN, J.
SHELEMAY, K., Music
SHELL, M., English and Comparative Literature
SHEPSLE, K., Government
SHIEBER, S., Computer Science
SHLEIFER, A., Economics
SILVERA, I. F., Natural Sciences
SIMON, E., Germanic Languages and Literature
SIU, Y. T., Mathematics
SKJAERVO, P., Iranian
SKOCPOL, T. R., Government, Sociology
SOLBRIG, O. T., Biology
SOLLORS, W., English Literature, Afro-American Studies
SOMMER, D., Romance Languages and Literature
SØRENSEN, A. B., Sociology
SPAEPEN, F. A., Applied Sciences
STAGER, L., Archaeology of Israel
STEINKELLER, P., Assyriology
STERNBERG, S. Z., Mathematics
STEVENS, P. F., Biology
STILGOE, J. R., History of Landscape
STONE, H. A., Applied Mathematics, Chemical Engineering
STONE, P. J., Psychology
STROMINGER, J. L., Biochemistry
SULEIMAN, S. R., Civilization of France, Comparative Literature
SZPORLUK, R., Ukrainian History
TAI, H., Sino-Vietnamese History
TAMBIAH, S. J., Anthropology

TARRANT, R. J., Latin Language and Literature
TATAR, M. M., German
TAUBES, C. H., Mathematics
TAYLOR, R. L., Mathematics
THERNSTROM, S., History
THOMAS, R., Greek and Latin
THOMPSON, D., Political Philosophy
TINKHAM, M., Physics
TODD, W. M., Slavic Languages and Literature, Comparative Literature
TOMLINSON, P. B., Biology
TROMP, J., Geophysics
TU, W.-M., Chinese History and Philosophy
TUCK, R., Government
ULRICH, L., Early American History
VAFA, C., Physics
VAIL, H., History
VALIANT, L. G., Computer Science and Applied Mathematics
VAN DER KUIJP, L., Tibetan and Himalayan Studies
VAN DER MERWE, N. J., Scientific Archaeology
VENDLER, H.
VERBA, S.
VERDINE, G., Bio- and Organic Chemistry
VOGEL, E. F., Social Sciences
WANG, J. C., Biochemistry and Molecular Biology
WARREN, K., Anthropology
WATERS, M., Sociology
WATKINS, C. W., Linguistics and Classics
WATSON, J., Chinese Society
WEITZMAN, M., Economics
WESTERVELT, R., Physics
WHITE, S. H., Psychology
WHITESIDES, G. M., Chemistry
WILLIAMSON, J. G., Economics
WILSON, R., Physics
WINSHIP, C., Sociology
WINTER, I. J., Fine Arts
WISSE, R., Yiddish Literature and Comparative Literature
WITZEL, E., Sanskrit
WOFSEY, S., Atmospheric and Environmental Studies
WOLFF, C., Music
WOMACK, J., Latin American History and Economics
WOOLLACOTT, R. M., Biology
WRANGHAM, R., Anthropology
WU, T. T., Applied Physics
YALMAN, N. O., Social Anthropology and Middle Eastern Studies
YANG, W., Electrical Engineering and Computer Science
YAU, S., Mathematics
ZIOLKOWSKI, J., Medieval Latin and Comparative Literature

Graduate School of Design (Office of Admissions, 48 Quincy St, Suite 422, Cambridge, MA 02138; tel. (617) 495-5453; fax (617) 495-8849; e-mail admissions@gsd.harvard.edu; internet www.gsd.harvard.edu):
ALTSHULER, A., Urban Policy and Planning
BAIRD, G., Architecture
FORMAN, R. T. T., Landscape Ecology
GOMEZ-IBAÑEZ, J. A., Urban Planning and Public Policy
HARGREAVES, G., Landscape Architecture
HAYS, M., Architectural Theory
KOOLHAAS, R., Architecture and Urban Design
KRIEGER, A., Urban Design
MACHADO, R., Architecture and Urban Design
MONEO, J. R., Architecture
MORI, T., Architecture
PEISER, R., Real Estate Development
POLLALIS, S. N., Design Technology and Management
ROWE, P. G., Architecture and Urban Design

SCHODEK, D. L., Architectural Technology
SILVETTI, J. S., Architecture
SMITH, C., Architectural History
STEINITZ, C. F., Landscape Architecture and Planning
STILGOE, J. R., History of Landscape Development
VAN VALKENBURGH, M., Landscape Architecture
VIGIER, F. C., Regional Planning

Graduate School of Education (111 Longfellow Hall, 13 Appian Way, Cambridge, MA 021388; tel. (617) 495-3414; fax (617) 496-3577; e-mail gseadmissions@harvard.edu; internet www.gse.harvard.edu):

CHAIT, R.
DUCKWORTH, E. R.
ELGIN, C. Z.
ELMORE, R. F.
FISCHER, K. W.
GARDNER, H. E.
HARRIS, P.
JOHNSON, S. M.
JUEL, C.
KORETZ, D.
LAWRENCE-LIGHTFOOT, S.
LIGHT, R. J.
MCCARTNEY, K.
MURNANE, R.
MURPHY, J. T.
ORFIELD, G., Education and Social Policy
PERKINS, D.
REUBEN, J.
SELMAN, R. L.
SINGER, J. D.
SNOW, C. E.
SUÁREZ-OROZCO, M.
WILLETT, J. B.

Harvard Business School (Communications Office, Harvard Business School, Soldiers Field, Boston, MA 02163; tel. (617) 495-6000; e-mail news@hbs.edu; internet www.hbs.edu):

AMABILE, T. M., Entrepreneurial Management
APPLEGATE, L. M., General Management
AUSTIN, J. E., Business, Government and International Economy
BADARACCO, J. L., General Management
BAKER, G. P., III, Organizations and Markets
BALDWIN, C. Y., Organizations and Markets
BARTLETT, C. A., General Management
BARTON, D. A., Technology and Operations Management
BEER, M., Organizational Behaviour
BELL, D. E., Marketing
BOWEN, H. K., Technology and Operations Management
BOWER, J. L., General Management
BRADLEY, S. P., Competition and Strategy
BRANDENBERGER, A. M., Competition and Strategy
BRUNS, W. J., Jr, Accounting and Control
CASH, J. I., Jr, Service Management
CAVES, R. E., Competition and Strategy
CHRISTENSEN, C. J., Control
CLARK, K. B., Dean of the Faculty
CRANE, D. B., Finance
CRUM, M. C., Finance
DATAR, S., Accounting and Control
DEIGHTON, J. A., Marketing
DESHPANDÉ, R., Marketing
FERGUSON, N., Business, Government and the International Economy
FROOT, K. A., Finance
FRUHAN, W. E., Jr, Finance
GABARRO, J. J., Organizational Behaviour
GARVIN, D. A., General Management
GHEMAWAT, P., Competition and Strategy
GREYSER, S. A., Marketing
HAMMOND, J. H., Technology and Operations Management
HAWKINS, D. F., Accounting and Control

HAYES, R. H., Technology and Operations Management
HEALY, P. M., Accounting and Control
HERZLINGER, R. E., Accounting and Control
HILL, L. A., Organizational Behaviour
IANSITI, M., Technology and Operations Management
IBARRA, H., Organizational Behaviour
JENSEN, M. C., Organizations and Markets
KANTER, R. M., General Management
KAPLAN, R. S., Accounting and Control
KESTER, W. C., Finance
KOHLBERG, E., Competition and Strategy
KOTTER, J. P., Organizational Behaviour
LIGHT, J. O., Finance
LORSCH, J. W., Organizational Behaviour
MCCRAW, T. K., Business, Government and International Economy
MCFARLAN, F. W., General Management
MCKENNEY, J. L., Management Information Systems
MASON, S. P., Finance
MERTON, R. C., Finance
MEYER, R. F., Managerial Economics
MILLS, D. Q., Human Resource Management
MONTGOMERY, C. A., Competition and Strategy
NOHRIA, N., Organizational Behaviour
NOLAN, R. L., General Management
PAINE, L. S., General Management
PALEPU, K. G., Accounting and Control
PEROLD, A. F., Finance
PIPER, T. R., Finance
PISANO, G., Technology and Operations Management
PODOLNY, J.
PORTER, M. E., Competition and Strategy
QUELCH, J.
RANGAN, V. K., Marketing
REILING, H. B., Finance
ROTEMBERG, J. J., Business, Government and International Economy
ROTH, A. E., Negotiation and Decision Making.
RUBACK, R. S., Finance
SAHLMAN, W. A., Entrepreneurial Management
SALTER, M. S., Organizations and Markets
SASSER, W. E., Jr, Service Management
SCHLESINGER, L. A., Service Management
SCOTT, B. R., Business, Government and International Economy
SEBENIUS, J. K., Negotiation and Decision Making
SHAPIRO, R. D., Technology and Operations Management
SILK, A. J., Marketing
SIMONS, R. L., Accounting and Control
SLOANE, C. S., Organizational Behaviour
STEVENSON, H. H., Entrepreneurial Management
STOBAUGH, R. B., Production and Operations Management
TEDLOW, R. S., Business, Government and International Economy
TUFANO, P., Finance
TUSHMAN, M. L., Organizational Behaviour
UPTON, D. M., Technology and Operations Management
VIETOR, R. H. K., Business, Government and International Economy
WELLS, L. T., Jr, Business, Government and International Economy
WHEELWRIGHT, S. C., Technology and Operations Management
YOFFIE, D. B., Competition and Strategy
YOSHINO, M. Y., General Management
ZALTMAN, G., Marketing
ZUBOFF, S., Organizational Behaviour

Harvard Divinity School (Office of Admissions and Financial Aid, Room 214, 14 Divinity Ave, Cambridge, MA 02138; tel. (617) 495-5796; e-mail admissions@hds.harvard.edu; internet www.hds.harvard.edu):

AHMED, L., Women's Studies in Religion
BOVON, F., New Testament
COAKLEY, S., Theology
COX, H. G., Theology
CURRASCO, D., Religion, America and Anthropology
DYCK, A., Ethics
ECK, D., Comparative Religion
FIORENZA, F. S., Roman Catholic Theological Studies
GOMES, P. J., Christian Morals
GRAHAM, W., Middle Eastern Studies
GYATSO, J., Comparative Religion
HALL, D. D., American Religious History
HANSON, P. D., Hebrew Bible/Old Testament
KING, K. L., New Testament Studies and Gnosticism
LEVENSON, J. D., Jewish Studies
ORSI, R., History of Religion
SCHÜSSLER FIORENZA, E., New Testament and Ministerial Studies
SULLIVAN, L., History of Religion
THIEMANN, R. F., Theology

Harvard Law School (1563 Massachusetts Avenue, Cambridge, MA 02138; tel. (617) 495-3100; e-mail jdadmiss@law.harvard.edu; internet www.law.harvard.edu):

ALFORD, W.
ANDREWS, W. D.
BARTHOLET, E., Public Interest
BEBCHUK, L. A., Law, Economics, Finance
BELLOW, G.
BREWER, S.
CHARNY, D.
CLARK, R. C.
DERSHOWITZ, A. M.
DESAN, C.
DONAHUE, C.
EDLEY, C. F.
ELHAUGE, E.
FALLON, R. H.
FIELD, M.
FISHER, W.
FRUG, G. E.
GLENDON, M. A.
GUINIER, L.
HALPERIN, D. I.
HANSON, J.
HAY, B. L.
HERWITZ, D. R.
HEYMANN, P. B.
HORWITZ, M. J., Legal History
JACKSON, H.
KAPLOW, L.
KAUFMAN, A. L.
KENNEDY, D. M.
KENNEDY, D. W., General Jurisprudence
KENNEDY, R. L.
KRAAKMAN, R. H.
LESSIG, L.
MANSFIELD, J. H.
MARTIN, H. S.
MELTZER, D. J.
MICHELMAN, F. I.
MILLER, A. R.
MINOW, M.
MNOOKIN, R.
NESSON, C. R.
OGLETREE, C., Jr
PARKER, R. D.
RAKOFF, T. D., Administrative Law
RAMSEYER, M.
ROSENBERG, M. D.
SANDER, F. E. A.
SARGENTICH, L. D.
SCOTT, H. S., International Financial Systems
SHAPIRO, D. L.
SHAVELL, S. M., Law and Economics
SINGER, J. W.
SLAUGHTER, A.-M.
STEIHER, C.
STEINER, H. J.
STONE, A. A., Law and Psychiatry

TRIBE, L. H., Constitutional Law
UNGER, R. M.
VAGTS, D. F., International Law
VISCUSI, W. K.
VORENBERG, J.
WARREN, A. C.
WARREN, E.
WEILER, J. H. H.
WEILER, P. C.
WEINREB, L. L.
WESTFALL, D.
WHITE, L.
WILKINS, D. B.
WOLFMAN, B.

Harvard Medical School (25 Shattuck St, Boston, MA 02115; tel. (617) 432-1000; e-mail admissions_office@hms.harvard.edu; internet hms.harvard.edu):

ABBAS, A. K., Pathology
ABBOTT, W. M., Surgery
ADAMS, D. F., Radiology
ADELSTEIN, S. J., Medical Biophysics
AISENBERG, A. C., Medicine
AKINS, C. W., Surgery
ALBERT, M. S., Psychiatry
ALI, H. H., Anaesthesia
ALONSO, A. W., Psychiatry
ALPER, C., Paediatrics
ALT, F. W., Genetics
ANDERSON, E., Comparative Anatomy
APPLEBURY, M. L., Ophthalmology
ARKY, R., Medicine
ARNAOUT, M. A., Medicine
ARNDT, K. A., Dermatology
ATHANASOULIS, C. A., Radiology
AUSIELLO, D. A., Medicine
AUSTEN, K. F., Medicine
AUSTEN, W. G., Surgery
AUSUBEL, F., Genetics
AVRUCH, J., Medicine
BACH, F., Surgery
BADEN, H., Dermatology
BAIM, D., Medicine
BALDESSARINI, R. J., Psychiatry
BARBIERI, R., Obstetrics, Gynaecology and Reproductive Biology
BARLOW, C. F., Neurology
BARNETT, G. O., Medicine
BARSAMIAN, E. M., Surgery
BARSKY, A. J., III, Psychiatry
BEAL, M. F., Neurology
BEAN, B. P., Neurobiology
BEARDSLEE, W., Psychiatry
BECKWITH, J. R., Microbiology and Molecular Genetics
BELFER, M. L., Psychiatry
BENACERRAF, B. R., Obstetrics, Gynaecology and Reproductive Biology
BENDER, W. W., Biological Chemistry, Molecular Pharmacology
BENES, F. M., Psychiatry
BENJAMIN, T. L., Pathology
BERKOWITZ, R. S., Obstetrics, Gynaecology and Reproductive Biology
BERNFIELD, M., Paediatrics
BERSON, E. L., Ophthalmology
BIEDERMAN, J., Psychiatry
BIGGERS, J., Cell Biology
BIRD, E. D., Neuropathology
BISTRIAN, B. R., Medicine
BLACK, P. M., Neurosurgery
BLENIS, J., Cell Biology
BLOCH, K. J., Medicine
BONVENTRE, J. V., Medicine
BORUS, J. F., Psychiatry
BRADY, T., Radiology
BRANDT, A. M., History of Medicine
BRAUNWALD, E., Medicine
BREAKEFIELD, X. O., Neurology
BRENNAN, T., Medicine
BRENNER, B., Medicine
BRENNER, M. B., Medicine
BREWSTER, D., Surgery
BROTMAN, A. W., Psychiatry
BROWN, E. M., Medicine

BRUGGE, J. S., Cell Biology
BUCHANAN, J. R., Medicine
BUCKLEY, M. J., Surgery
BUNN, H. F., Medicine
BURAKOFF, S. J., Paediatrics
BURGESON, R. E., Dermatology
BURROWS, P. E., Radiology
CANELLOS, G. P., Medicine
CANTLEY, L. C., Medicine
CANTOR, H. I., Pathology
CAPLAN, D. N., Neurology
CAREY, M. C., Medicine
CARPENTER, C. B., Medicine
CASSEM, E. H., Psychiatry
CAVINESS, V. S., Jr, Child Neurology and Mental Retardation
CEPKO, C. L., Genetics
CHABNER, B., Medicine
CHEN, L. B., Pathology
CHIN, W. W., Medicine
CHRISTIANI, D. C., Medicine
CHURCH, G. H., Genetics
CHYLACK, L. T., Jr, Ophthalmology
CLAPHAM, D. E., Neurobiology
CLEARY, P. D., Medical Sociology
CLEVELAND, R. H., Radiology
CLOUSE, M. E., Radiology
COEN, D. M., Biological Chemistry, Molecular Pharmacology
COHEN, B. M., Psychiatry
COHEN, J. B., Neurobiology
COHN, L. H., Surgery
COLDITZ, G. A., Medicine
COLE, J. O., Psychiatry
COLEMAN, C. N., Radiation Oncology
COLES, R., Psychiatry and Medical Humanities
COLLIER, R. J., Microbiology and Molecular Genetics
COLLINS, J. J., Surgery
COLLINS, P., Pathology
COLODNY, A. H., Surgery
COLVIN, R. B., Pathology
COMPTON, C. C., Pathology
COOPER, G. M., Pathology
COREY, D. P., Neurobiology
CORSON, J. M., Pathology
COSIMI, A. B., Surgery
COTRAN, R., Pathology
COYLE, J. T., Psychiatry
CRONE, R., Anaesthesia
CROWLEY, W. F., Jr, Medicine
CRUM, C. P., Pathology
CRUMPACKER, C., Medicine
DAGGETT, W. M., Surgery
D'AMORE, P. A., Ophthalmology
DATTA, S., Anaesthesiology
DAVID, J. R., Medicine
DAVIDOVITCH, Z., Orthodontics
DAVIS, K. R., Radiology
DAWSON, D. M., Neurology
DELBANCO, T., Medicine
DEMLING, R. H., Surgery
DESANCTIS, R. W., Medicine
DESROSIERS, R. C., Microbiology, Molecular Genetics
DEUEL, T. F., Medicine
DEWOLF, W. C., Surgery
DIAMANDOPOULOS, G. T., Pathology
DOGON, I. L., Operative Dentistry
DONAHOE, P. K., Surgery
DONOFF, R. B., Oral and Maxillofacial Surgery
DORF, M. E., Pathology
DORSEY, J. L., Medicine
DORWART, R., Psychiatry
DOUGLASS, C. W., Dental Care Administration
DOWLING, J. E., Ophthalmology
DRAZEN, J. M., Medicine
DRETLER, S. P., Surgery
DRYJA, T. P., Jr, Ophthalmology
DVORAK, A. M., Pathology
DVORAK, H. F., Pathology
DZAU, V. J., Medicine
EARLS, F. J., III, Child Psychiatry

EBERLEIN, T. J., Surgery
EDELMAN, R., Radiology
EISENSTEIN, B., Medicine
EPSTEIN, A., Medicine
EPSTEIN, F., Medicine
ERIKSSON, E., Surgery
EZEKOWITZ, R. A. B., Paediatrics
FEDERMAN, D. D., Medicine and Medical Education
FEIN, R., Medical Economics
FINBERG, R. W., Medicine
FINK, M., Surgery
FISCHBACH, G. D., Neurobiology
FISHMAN, M. C., Medicine
FLEISHER, G. R., Paediatrics
FLETCHER, C., Pathology
FLETCHER, R., Ambulatory Care and Prevention
FLETCHER, S., Ambulatory Care and Prevention
FLIER, J. S., Medicine
FOLKMAN, M. J., Paediatric Surgery
FOSTER, C. S., Ophthalmology
FOX, I. H., Medicine
FRAENKEL, D. G., Microbiology
FRANK, R., Health Economics in Health Care Policy
FREI, E., III, Medicine
FRIED, M. P., Otology and Laryngology
FRIEDMAN, E., Ophthalmology
FRIGOLETTO, F. D., Jr, Obstetrics and Gynaecology
FURIE, B., Medicine
FURSHPAN, E. J., Neurobiology
GALABURDA, A., Neurology and Neuroscience
GALLI, J. J., Pathology
GARNICK, M. B., Medicine
GEHA, R. S., Paediatrics
GELBER, R. D., Paediatrics
GELMAN, S., Anaesthesia
GIMBRONE, M. A., Pathology
GIPSON, I. K., Ophthalmology
GLICKMAN, R. M., Medicine
GLIMCHER, L. H., Medicine
GLIMCHER, M. J., Orthopaedic Surgery
GOETINCK, P. F., Dermatology
GOITEIN, M., Radiation Therapy
GOLDBERG, A. L., Cell Biology
GOLDBERG, I. H., Pharmacology
GOLDHABER, P., Periodontology
GOLDMAN, H., Pathology
GOLDMAN, P., Biological Chemistry and Molecular Pharmacology
GOLDMANN, D. A., Paediatrics
GOLDSTEIN, D. P., Obstetrics, Gynaecology and Reproduction
GOLDWYN, R. M., Surgery
GOOD, B. J., Medical Anthropology
GOOD, M. J. D., Social Medicine
GOODENOUGH, D. A., Anatomy and Cell Biology
GOODMAN, H. M., Genetics
GOYAL, R. K., Medicine
GRAGOUDAS, E., Ophthalmology
GREEN, H., Cell Biology
GREENBERG, M. E., Neurology, Neuroscience
GREENBERG, R. M., Psychiatry
GREENE, R. E., Radiology
GREENES, R. A., Radiology
GRIFFIN, J., Medicine
GRILLO, H. C., Surgery
GRISCOM, N. T., Radiology
GROOPMAN, J. E., Medicine
GROWDON, J. H., Neurology
GRUNEBAM, H. U., Psychiatry
GUNDERSON, J. G., Psychiatry
GUREWICH, V., Medicine
GUSELLA, J. F., Genetics
GUTHEIL, T. G., Psychiatry
HABENER, J. F., Medicine
HABER, E., Medicine
HALES, C. A., Medicine
HALL, F. M., Radiology
HALL, J. E., Orthopaedic Surgery

HANDIN, R. I., Medicine
HARLOW, E. E., Genetics
HARRIS, J. R., Radiation Oncology
HARRIS, N. L., Pathology
HARRIS, W. H., Orthopaedic Surgery
HARRISON, S. C., Biological Chemistry and Molecular Biology
HAUSER, S. T., Psychiatry
HAVENS, L. L., Psychiatry
HAY, D. I., Oral Biology
HAY, E. D., Embryology
HAYES, W. C., Biomechanics
HAYNES, H. A., Dermatology
HEALY, G. B., Otolaryngology
HECHTMAN, H. B., Surgery
HEDLEY-WHYTE, E. T., Pathology
HEDLEY-WHYTE, J., Anaesthesia and Respiratory Therapy
HEMLER, M., Pathology
HENDREN, W. H., III, Paediatric Surgery
HENNEKENS, C. H., Ambulatory Care and Prevention
HERNDON, J. H., Orthopaedic Surgery
HERZOG, D. B., Psychiatry
HIATT, H. H., Medicine
HICKEY, P. R., Anaesthesia
HIROSE, T., Ophthalmology
HIRSCH, M. S., Medicine
HOBSON, J. A., Psychiatry
HOGLE, J. M., Biological Chemistry and Molecular Pharmacology
HOLLENBERG, N. K., Radiology
HOLMES, G. L., Neurology
HOLMES, L. B., Paediatrics
HORTON, E. S., Medicine
HOWLEY, P. M., Comparative Pathology
HUBEL, D. H., Neurophysiology
HUNT, R. D., Comparative Pathology
IEZZONI, L. I., Medicine
INGWALL, J. S., Medicine
INUI, T. S., Ambulatory Care and Prevention
ISSELBACHER, K. J., Medicine
IZUMO, S., Medicine
JACOBSON, A. M., Psychiatry
JAIN, R. K., Radiation Oncology
JAKOBIEC, F. A., Ophthalmology
JANDL, J. H., Medicine
JELLINCK, M. S., Paediatrics
JENIKE, M. A., Psychiatry
JOHNSON-POWELL, G., Child Psychiatry
JOLESZ, F. A., Radiology
JONAS, R., Surgery
JONES, H. R., Neurobiology
JOSEPHSON, M., Medicine
KABAN, L. B., Oral and Maxillofacial Surgery
KAHN, C. R., Medicine
KARCHMER, A. W., Medicine
KARNOVSKY, M. J., Pathological Anatomy
KASPER, D. L., Medicine
KASSER, J. R., Orthopaedic Surgery
KAUFMAN, D. S., Medicine
KAZEMI, H., Medicine
KESSLER, R., Health Care Policy
KHANTZIAN, E., Psychiatry
KHURI, S. F., Surgery
KIEFF, E. D., Medicine
KINET, J. P., Pathology
KING, G. L.
KINGSTON, R., Genetics
KIRSCHNER, M. W., Medicine and Cell Biology
KISSIN, I., Anaesthesia
KITZ, R. J., Research and Teaching in Anaesthetics and Anaesthesia
KLAGSBRUN, M., Surgery
KLEINMAN, A. M., Medical Anthropology
KLIBANSKI, A., Medicine
KNIPE, D. M., Microbiology and Molecular Genetics
KOLODNER, R. D., Biological Chemistry and Molecular Pharmacology
KOLTER, R. G., Microbiology and Molecular Genetics
KOMAROFF, A. L., Medicine

KOSIK, K. S., Neurology
KRANE, S. M., Clinical Medicine
KRAVITZ, E. A., Neurobiology
KRESSEL, H. Y., Radiology
KRIS, A., Psychiatry
KRONENBERG, H. M., Medicine
KUFE, D. W., Medicine
KUNKEL, L. M., Genetics
KUPPER, T., Dermatology
LAING, F. C.
LAMONT, J. T., Medicine
LARSEN, P. R., Medicine
LEBOWITZ, R. L., Radiology
LEDER, P., Genetics
LEFFERT, R. D., Orthopaedic Surgery
LESSELL, S., Ophthalmology
LETVIN, N., Medicine
LEVITON, A., Neurology
LEVITSKY, S., Surgery
LI, F. P., Medicine
LIANG, M., Medicine
LIBBY, P., Medicine
LIBERMAN, M. C., Physiology
LIN, E. C. C., Microbiology and Molecular Genetics
LIPSITT, D. R., Psychiatry
LIVINGSTON, D. M., Medicine
LIVINGSTONE, M. S., Neurobiology
LOCK, J. E., Paediatrics
LOEFFLER, J. S., Radiation Oncology
LOGERFO, F. W., Surgery
LOVEJOY, F. H., Jr, Paediatrics
LOWENSTEIN, E., Anaesthesia
LUX, S. E., IV, Paediatrics
MCCARLEY, R. W., Psychiatry
MCCORMICK, M. C., Paediatrics
MCDOUGAL, W. S., Surgery
MCINTOSH, K., Paediatrics
MACK, J. E., Psychiatry
MCKEON, F. D., Cell Biology
MCLOUD, T. C., Radiology
MCNEIL, B. J., Health Care Policy
MANKIN, H. J., Orthopaedic Surgery
MANNICK, J. A., Surgery
MANSCHRECK, T. C., Psychiatry
MARGOLIES, M. N., Surgery
MARTIN, J. B., Neurology
MARTYN, J. A. J., Anaesthesia
MASLAND, R. H., Neuroscience
MATTHYSSE, S., Psychiatry
MAY, J., Surgery
MAYER, J. E., Jr, Surgery
MAYER, R. J., Medicine
MEKALANOS, J. J., Microbiology and Molecular Genetics
MELLO, N. K., Psychology
MENDELSON, J. H., Psychiatry
MEYER, J. E., Radiology
MIHM, M. C., Jr, Dermatopathology
MILLER, K. W., Anaesthesiology
MIRIN, S. M., Psychiatry
MISHLER, E. G., Social Psychology
MITCHISON, T. J., Cell Biology
MODELL, A. H., Psychiatry
MOELLERING, R. C. Jr, Medical Research
MONACO, A. P., Surgery
MONGAN, J., Health Care Policy
MONTGOMERY, W. W., Otolaryngology
MONTMINY, M., Cell Biology
MOORE, G. T., Ambulatory Care and Prevention
MORGAN, J. P., Medicine
MORRIS, C. N., Health Care Policy
MORSE, W. H., Psychobiology
MORTON, C. C., Obstetrics and Gynaecology
MOSKOWITZ, M. A., Neurology
MULLIGAN, R., Genetics
MURPHY, J. M., Psychiatry
NADELSON, C., Psychiatry
NADLER, L. M., Medicine
NADOL, J. B., Jr, Otolaryngology
NATHAN, D. G., Paediatrics
NEEDLEMAN, H. L., Paediatric Dentistry
NEER, E. J., Medicine
NESSON, H. R., Medicine
NEUTRA, M. R., Paediatrics

NEWBURGER, J. W., Paediatrics
NEWHOUSE, J. P., Health Care Policy
NOTMAN, M. T., Psychiatry
NOVELLINE, R. A., Radiology
OJEMANN, R. G., Surgery
OLSEN, B. R., Anatomy
ORKIN, S. H., Paediatrics
PALFREY, J. S., Paediatrics
PARRISH, J. A., Dermatology
PAUL, D. L., Neurobiology
PENNEY, J. B., Jr, Neurology
PEPPERCORN, M. A., Medicine
PERRIMON, N., Genetics
PFEFFER, M. A., Medicine
PIER, G. B., Pathology
PINKUS, G. S., Pathology
PIZZO, P., Paediatrics
PLATT, O., Paediatrics
PLOEGH, H. L., Pathology
PODOLSKY, D. K., Medicine
POSS, R., Orthopaedic Surgery
POTTER, D. D., Neurobiology
POTTS, J. T., Jr, Clinical Medicine
POUSSAINT, A. F., Psychiatry
RABKIN, M. T., Medicine
RANDO, R. R., Biological Chemistry and Molecular Pharmacology
RAO, A., Pathology
RAPOPORT, T. A., Cell Biology
RAVIOLA, E., Neurobiology
REICH, P., Psychiatry
REID, L., Pathology
REINHERZ, E. L., Medicine
REMOLD, H. G., Medicine
REPPERT, S. M., Paediatrics
RETIK, A. B., Surgery
RICHARDSON, C. C., Biological Chemistry and Molecular Pharmacology
RICHIE, J. P., Surgery
RIORDAN, J. F., Biochemistry
RITZ, J., Medicine
ROBERTS, T. M., Pathology
ROBINSON, D. R., Medicine
ROSEN, F. S., Paediatrics
ROSEN, S. S., Pathology
ROSENBERG, R. D., Medicine
ROSENBLATT, M., Molecular Medicine
ROSENTHAL, D. I., Radiology
ROSENTHAL, D. S., Medicine
ROSNER, B. A., Medicine
ROTHENBERG, A., Psychiatry
RUDERMAN, J. V., Anatomy and Cell Biology
RUSSELL, P. S., Surgery
RUVKUN, G. B., Genetics
SACHS, B. P., Obstetrics, Gynaecology and Reproductive Medicine
SACHS, D. H., Surgery
SAITO, H., Biological Chemistry and Molecular Pharmacology
SALLAN, S. E., Paediatrics
SALZMAN, C., Psychiatry
SAMUELS, M. A., Neurology
SAPER, C. B., Neurology
SCHIFF, I., Gynaecology
SCHILDKRAUT, J. J., Psychiatry
SCHLOLLSMAN, S. F., Medicine
SCHNEEBERGER, E. E., Pathology
SCHNIPPER, L. E., Medicine
SCHOEN, F. J., Pathology
SCHUR, P. H., Medicine
SCOTT, R. M., Surgery
SEED, B., Genetics
SEIDMAN, C. E., Medicine
SEIDMAN, J. G., Genetics
SELKOE, D. J., Neurology
SELMAN, R. L., Psychology
SELTZER, S. E., Radiology
SELWYN, A., Medicine
SERHAN, C. N., Anaesthesia
SHANNON, D. C., Paediatrics
SHEFFER, A. L., Medicine
SHIPLEY, W. U., Radiation Therapy
SHKLAR, G., Oral Pathology
SHORE, M. F., Psychiatry
SIDMAN, R. L., Neuropathology

SILBERT, J. E., Medicine
SILEN, W., Surgery
SILVER, P. A., Biological Chemistry and Molecular Pharmacology
SIMEONE, J. F., Radiology
SIMON, B., Psychiatry
SKILLMAN, J. J., Surgery
SKLAR, J. L., Pathology
SLEDGE, C. B., Orthopaedic Surgery
SMITH, A. R., Radiation Oncology
SOBER, A. J., Dermatology
SODROSKI, J. G., Pathology
SONIS, S. T., Oral Medicine and Oral Pathology
SOUBA, W. W., Surgery
SPEALMAN, R. D., Psychobiology
SPECTOR, M., Orthopaedic Surgery
SPEIZER, F. E., Medicine
SPIEGELMAN, B. M., Biological Chemistry and Molecular Pharmacology
SPIRO, R. G., Biological Chemistry
SPRINGER, T. A., Pathology
STEER, M. L., Surgery
STEINMAN, T. I., Medicine
STERN, R. S., Dermatology
STILES, C. D., Microbiology and Molecular Genetics
STONE, A. A., Law and Psychiatry
STOSSEL, T. P., Medicine
STREILEIN, J. W., Ophthalmology
STREWLER, G. J., Medicine
STRICHARTZ, G. R., Anaesthesia
STROM, T. B., Medicine
STRUHL, K., Biological Chemistry and Molecular Pharmacology
SUIT, H. D., Radiation Oncology
SUKHATME, V. P., Medicine
SWARTZ, M. N., Medicine
SZOSTAK, J. W., Genetics
TABIN, C. J., Genetics
TASHJIAN, A. H., Jr, Biological Chemistry and Molecular Pharmacology
TAUBMAN, M. A., Oral Biology
TAYLOR, G. A., Radiology
TERHORST, C. P., Medicine
THIBAULT, G. E., Medicine
THIER, S. O., Medicine and Health Care Policy
THRALL, J. H., Radiology
TILNEY, N. L., Surgery
TOMKINS, R. G., Surgery
TOSTESON, D. C., Cell Biology
TREVES, S. T., Radiology
TSUANG, M. T., Psychiatry
TYLER, H. R., Neurology
UTIGER, R. D., Medicine
VACANTI, J. P., Surgery
VAILLANT, G. E., Psychiatry
VAN PRAAGH, R., Pathology
VOLPE, J. J., Neurology
WAGNER, G., Biological Chemistry and Molecular Pharmacology
WALKER, W. A., Nutrition and Paediatrics
WALSH, C. T., Biological Chemistry and Molecular Pharmacology
WARSHAW, A. L., Surgery
WEINBERG, A. N., Medicine
WEINBERGER, S. E., Medicine
WEINBLATT, M. E., Medicine
WEINER, H. L., Neurology
WEINSTEIN, H. J., Paediatrics
WEINSTEIN, M. C., Medicine
WEIR, G. C., Medicine
WEISS, S. T., Medicine
WEISSMAN, B. N., Radiology
WELLER, P. F., Medicine
WEYMAN, A. E., Medicine
WHITE, A. A., III, Orthopaedic Surgery
WHITTEMORE, A., Surgery
WILLETT, W. C., Medicine
WILLIAMS, G. H., Medicine
WILMORE, D. W., Surgery
WILSON, T. H., Cell Biology
WINKELMAN, J. W., Pathology
WINSTON, F. M., Genetics
WITTENBERG, J., Radiology

WOHL, M. E., Paediatrics
WOLF, G. L., Radiology
WOLF, M. A., Medicine
WOLFF, C., Anaesthesia
WOLFF, P. H., Psychiatry
WRAY, S. H., Neurology
YARMUSH, M., Surgery
YOUNG, A. B., Neurology
YOUNG, R. H., Pathology
YUNIS, E. J., Pathology
ZAPOL, W. M., Anaesthesia
ZERVAS, N. T., Neurosurgery
ZETTER, B. R., Surgery
ZINNER, M., Surgery

Harvard School of Dental Medicine (Office of Admissions, DMD, 188 Longwood Ave, Boston, MA 02115; tel. (617) 432-1443; e-mail hsdm_dmd_admissions@hsdm.harvard.edu; internet www.hsdm.harvard.edu):

DOGON, I. L., Restorative Dentistry
DONOFF, R. B., Oral and Maxillofacial Surgery
DOUGLASS, C. W., Oral Health Policy and Epidemiology
GOLDHABER, P., Periodontology
HAY, D. I., Oral Biology
KABAN, L. B., Oral and Maxillofacial Surgery
OLSEN, B. R., Oral Biology
SHKLAR, G., Oral Pathology
SONIS, S. S., Oral Medicine and Diagnostic Sciences
TAUBMAN, M. A., Oral Biology

Harvard School of Public Health (158 Longwood Avenue, Boston, MA 02115-5810; tel. (617) 432-1031; fax (617) 432-7080; e-mail admissions@hsph.harvard.edu; internet www.hsph.harvard.edu):

ALONSO, W., Population and International Health
BERKMAN, L. F., Health and Social Behaviour
BLENDON, R. J., Health Policy and Management
BLOOM, D. E., Population and International Health
BRAIN, J. D., Environmental Health
BRENNAN, T. A., Health Policy and Management
CHEN, L. C., Population and International Health
CHRISTIANI, D. C., Environmental Health
COOK, E. F., Epidemiology
DAVID, J. R., Tropical Public Health
DEGRUTTOLA, V. G., Biostatistics
DEMPLE, B. F., Toxicology
DYCK, A. J., Population and International Health
EARLS, F. J., Maternal and Child Health
EPSTEIN, A. M., Health Policy and Management
ESSEX, M. E., Cancer Biology
FINEBERG, H. V., Administration
FREDBERG, J. J., Environmental Health
GLIMCHER, L. H., Cancer Biology
GOLDMAN, P., Nutrition
GRAHAM, J. D., Health Policy and Management
HARN, D. A., Tropical Public Health
HARRINGTON, D. P., Biostatistics
HARRINGTON, J. J., Environmental Health
HEMENWAY, D., Health Policy and Management
HILL, A. G., Population and International Health
HSIAO, W. C., Health Policy and Management
KELSEY, K. T., Environmental Health
KOUTRAKIS, P., Environmental Health
LAGAKOS, S. W., Biostatistics
LAIRD, N. M., Biostatistics
LEE, T., Immunology and Infectious Diseases
LEVINS, R., Population and International Health

LI, F. P., Epidemiology
LITTLE, J. B., Cancer Biology
McCORMICK, M. C., Maternal and Child Health
MONSON, R. R., Epidemiology and Environmental Health
MUELLER, N. E., Epidemiology
MURRAY, C., Population and International Health
NEWHOUSE, J. P., Health Policy and Management
PAGANO, M., Biostatistics
PIESSENS, W. F., Tropical Public Health
PROTHROW-STITH, D. B., Health Policy and Management
REICH, M. R., Population and International Health, and Health Policy and Management
ROBERTS, M. J., Health Policy and Management
ROBINS, J. M., Epidemiology and Biostatistics
RYAN, L. M., Biostatistics
SAMSON, L. D., Molecular and Cellular Toxicology
SMITH, T. J., Environmental Health
SORENSON, G., Health and Social Behaviour
SPEIZER, F. E., Environmental Health
SPENGLER, J. D., Environmental Health
SPIELMAN, A., Tropical Public Health
STAMPFER, M. J., Nutrition and Epidemiology
TARLOV, A., Health Policy and Management
TASHJIAN, A. H., Jr, Toxicology
TRICHOPOULOS, D. V., Epidemiology
WALKER, A. M., Epidemiology
WARE, J. H., Biostatistics
WEI, L. J., Biostatistics
WEINSTEIN, M. C., Health Policy, Management and Biostatistics
WILLETT, W. C., Epidemiology and Nutrition
WIRTH, D. F., Tropical Public Health
ZELEN, M., Biostatistics

John F. Kennedy School of Government (79 John F. Kennedy St, Cambridge, MA 02138; tel. (617) 495-1100; e-mail admissions@hks .harvard.edu; internet www.ksg.harvard .edu):

ALLISON, G. T., Government
ALTSHULER, A., Urban Policy and Planning
APPLBAUM, A., Ethics and Public Policy
AVERY, C., Public Policy
BANE, M. J., Domestic Social Policy
BORJAS, G., Immigration
CARTER, A. B., International and National Security
CLARK, W. C., International Science, Public Policy and Human Development
DOTY, P. M., Public Policy
ELLWOOD, D., Income Support and Social Welfare Policy
FRANKEL, J., Capital Formation and Growth
GERGEN, D., Public Management and Leadership
GOLDSMITH, S., Practice of Public Management
GOMEZ-IBANEZ, J. A., Public Policy and Urban Policy
GRINDLE, M. S., International Development
HAUSMANN, R., Practice of Economic Development
HOGAN, W., Public Policy and Management
HOLDREN, J., Science and Energy Policy
IGNATIEFF, M., Human Rights Practice
JASANOFF, S., Science and Public Policy
JENCKS, C., US Domestic Social Policy
JUMA, C., Practice of International Development
KALT, J., International Political Economy
KELMAN, S. J., Public Management
KEYSSAR, A., History and Social Policy

LAWRENCE, R. Z., International Trade
LEONARD, H., Public Management
LIGHT, R., Education
MANSBRIDGE, J., Democratic Governance
MOORE, M. H., Criminal Justice Policy and Management
NEWHOUSE, J. P., Health Policy and Management
NEWMAN, K., Sociology of Labour Markets
NYE, J., International Affairs and Democratic Governance
ORREN, G. R., Public Policy
PATTERSON, T., Press and Politics
PORTER, R., Business and Government
PUTNAM, R., Democratic Governance
RODRIK, D., International Trade and Development
ROSENSWEIG, M., Public Policy
RUGGIE, J., International Affairs
SAICH, A., International Affairs
SCHAUER, F., First Amendment
SPARROW, M., Practice of Public Management
STAVINS, R. N., Environmental Economics
THOMPSON, D., Political Philosophy
VELASCO, A., International Finance and Development
WILSON, W. J., Urban Sociology
WISE, D., Political Economy
ZECKHAUSER, R. J., Political Economy

HEBREW COLLEGE

160 Herrick Rd, Newton Centre, MA 02459
Telephone: (617) 559-8600
Fax: (617) 559-8601
E-mail: admissions@hebrewcollege.edu
Internet: www.hebrewcollege.edu
Founded 1921
Private control
Academic year: September to May
Pres.: Rabbi DANIEL L. LEHMANN
Vice-Pres. for Devt: MICHAEL GILBERT
Provost: Dr BARRY MESCH
Dean of Faculty: KAREN REISS MEDWED
Dir of Recruitment and Admissions: DAVID MICLEY
Dir of Student Life: DAVID LIST
Registrar: MARILYN JAYE
Library Dir: HARVEY SUKENIC
Library of 125,000 vols
Number of teachers: 43
Number of students: 200

DEANS

Hebrew College Online: NATHAN EHRLICH
Rabbinical School: Rabbi SHARON COHEN ANISFELD
School of Jewish Music: Dr BRIAN J. MAYER (acting)
Shoolman Graduate School of Jewish Education: MICHAEL SHIRE

HELLENIC COLLEGE–HOLY CROSS GREEK ORTHODOX SCHOOL OF THEOLOGY

50 Goddard Ave, Brookline, MA 02445-7496
Telephone: (617) 731-3500
Fax: (617) 850-1460
E-mail: admissions@hchc.edu
Internet: www.hchc.edu
Founded 1937 as Holy Cross Theological School
Private control
Academic year: September to May
Academic programmes incl. classics and Greek studies, elementary education, human devt, literature and history, management and leadership, religious studies
Pres.: Rev. NICHOLAS C. TRIANTAFILOU
Chief Operating Officer: JAMES D. KARLOUTSOS
Dean of Hellenic College: DEMETRIOS KATOS

Dean of Holy Cross: Fr THOMAS FITZGERALD
Registrar: ALBA PAGAN
Library Dir: Very Rev. Dr JOACHIM COTSONIS
Library of 75,000 vols
Number of teachers: 15
Number of students: 209 (77 undergraduate, 132 graduate)

HULT INTERNATIONAL BUSINESS SCHOOL

1 Education St, Cambridge, MA 02141
Telephone: (617) 746-1990
Fax: (617) 746-1991
E-mail: admissions@hult.edu
Internet: www.hult.edu
Founded 1964 as Arthur D. Little School of Management, present name 2003
Private control
Campuses in Boston, Dubai, London, San Francisco, Shanghai; offers masters degree in digital marketing, finance, int. business, int. business management, int. marketing, social entrepreneurship
Pres. and Chair.: Dr STEPHEN HODGES
Vice-Pres. for Academic Affairs: Dr RICHARD J. JOSEPH
Chief Academic Officer and Chief Operating Officer: Dr MUKUL KUMAR
Dean of Academic Affairs: Dr RICHARD J. JOSEPH
Registrar: NICOLE GREGOIRE
Librarian: JOHN WALSH
Number of teachers: 38
Number of students: 59

LABOURÉ COLLEGE

2120 Dorchester Ave, Dorchester, MA 02124
Telephone: (617) 296-8300
E-mail: admissions@laboure.edu
Internet: www.laboure.edu
Founded 1892 as Carney Hospital Training School for Nurses, present name 1993
Private control
Academic year: July to August
Academic divs incl. health information technology, neurodiagnostic technology, nursing, radiation therapy, nutrition and food management
Pres.: Dr MAUREEN SMITH (acting)
Vice-Pres. and Dean of Student Affairs: KAREN M. MASTERS
Vice-Pres. and Dir of Institutional Advancement: CATHERIN PHILBIN
Chief Financial Officer: MARK VIRELLO
Dean of Academic Affairs: Dr PAULA VOSBURGH
Registrar: JOHN SACCO
Dir of Library: ANDREW CALO
Number of teachers: 67
Number of students: 620

LASELL COLLEGE

1844 Commonwealth Ave, Newton, MA 02466
Telephone: (617) 243-2000
Fax: (617) 243-2380
E-mail: info@lasell.edu
Internet: www.lasell.edu
Founded 1851
Private control
Academic year: September to May
Pres.: MICHAEL B. ALEXANDER
Vice-Pres. for Academic Affairs: Dr JAMES OSTROW
Vice-Pres. for Business and Finance: Dr MICHAEL J. HOYLE
Vice-Pres. for Institutional Advancement: RUTH S. SHUMAN

Vice-Pres. for Enrolment Management: KATHLEEN M. O'CONNOR
Vice-Pres. for Student Affairs: DIANE AUSTIN
Registrar: DIANNE POLIZZI
Dir of Library: MARILYN NEGIP
Library of 61,822 vols, 31,140 e-journals
Number of teachers: 331
Number of students: 1,600

DEANS

Graduate and Professional Studies: Dr JOAN E. DOLAMORE
School of Allied Health and Sports Studies: Dr LISA BORTMAN
School of Arts and Sciences: Dr STEVEN BLOOM
School of Business and Information Technology: Dr K. BREWER DORAN
Undergraduate Education: STEVEN BLOOM

LESLEY UNIVERSITY

29 Everett St, Cambridge, MA 02138-2790
Telephone: (617) 349-8300
Fax: (617) 349-8717
E-mail: info@lesley.edu
Internet: www.lesley.edu
Founded 1909 as Lesley School, present name and status 2000
Private control
Academic year: September to May
Pres.: Dr JOSEPH B. MOORE
Provost and Vice-Pres. for Academic Affairs: Dr SELASE WILLIAMS
Vice-Pres. for Admin.: MARYLOU BATT
Vice-Pres. for Advancement: RANDY STABILE
Vice-Pres. for Budgeting and Financial Planning: ML DYMSKI
Vice-Pres. and Chief Financial Officer: BERNICE BRADIN
Vice-Pres. for Enrolment Management: JEFFREY HANDLER
Vice-Pres. for Urban Initiatives: WILLIAM DANDRIDGE
Dean of Faculty: LISA FIORE
Dean of Lesley College: Dr MARY COLEMAN
Dean for Student Life and Academic Devt: Dr NATHANIEL MAYS
Registrar: MELISSA JANOT
Dir of Libraries: PATRICIA PAYNE
Library of 100,000 vols
Number of teachers: 190
Number of students: 8,566 (2,329 undergraduate, 6,237 graduate)
Publication: *Journal of Pedagogy, Pluralism and Practice* (irregular)

DEANS

Art Institute of Boston: STAN TRECKER
Graduate School of Arts and Social Sciences: Dr CATHERINE KOVEROLA
Graduate School of Education: Dr JONATHON H. GILLETTE
Lesley College: Prof. Dr MARY D. COLEMAN

LONGY SCHOOL OF MUSIC

27 Garden St, Cambridge, MA 02138
Telephone: (617) 876-0956
E-mail: music@longy.edu
Internet: www.longy.edu
Founded 1915
Private control
Academic year: August to June (2 semesters)
Offers Masters of music degrees in chamber music, collaborative piano, composition and theory, Dalcroze eurhythmics, early music, experiential education, large ensembles, mind and body studies, modern American music, music history and interdisciplinary studies, opera, organ, percussion, piano, strings, voice and woodwind, brass
Pres.: KAREN L. ZORN

Dean for Conservatory: WAYMAN CHIN
Chief Financial Officer: HOWARD LEVY
Dir for Devt: KIMBERLEE LABONTE
Dir for Library: ROY RUDOLPH
Number of teachers: 158
Number of students: 235

MASSACHUSETTS COLLEGE OF ART AND DESIGN

621 Huntington Ave, Boston, MA 02115
Telephone: (617) 879-7000
Fax: (617) 232-0050
E-mail: admissions@massart.edu
Internet: www.massart.edu
Founded 1873
Private control
Academic year: September to May

Academic programmes incl. animation, architectural design, art history, art teacher education, ceramics, community education, community studio education, fashion design, fibres, film/video, glass, graphic design, history of art, illustration, industrial design, jewellery and metalsmithing, museum education, painting, photography, printmaking, sculpture, studio education

Pres.: Dr DAWN BARRETT
Sr Vice-Pres. for Academic Affairs: Dr MAUREEN KELLY
Exec. Vice-Pres.: KURT STEINBERG
Vice-Pres. for Admin. and Finance and Chief Operating Officer: KURT STEINBERG
Vice-Pres. for Institutional Advancement: HUNTER O'HANIAN
Vice-Pres. for Student Devt: MAUREEN KEEFE
Library Dir: PAUL DOBBS
Library of 95,000 vols
Number of teachers: 263
Number of students: 2,426

Publication: *Folio* (2 a year).

MASSACHUSETTS COLLEGE OF LIBERAL ARTS

375 Church St, North Adams, MA 01247
Telephone: (413) 662-5000
Fax: (413) 662-5580
E-mail: admissions@mcla.edu
Internet: www.mcla.mass.edu
Founded 1894 as North Adams Normal School , present name 1997
Public control
Academic year: September to May

Depts of art, arts management, athletic training, biology, business admin., chemistry, computer science, education, English and communications, fine and performing arts, history, political science and geography, mathematics, modern language, philosophy, physical education, physics, political science and public policy, psychology, sociology, anthropology and social work, women studies

Pres.: Dr MARY K. GRANT
Vice-Pres. for Academic Affairs: Dr CYNTHIA F. BROWN
Vice-Pres. for Admin. and Finance: Dr JAMES STAKENAS
Vice-Pres. for Enrolment and External Relations: DENISE RICHARDELLO
Chief Advancement Officer: MARIANNE DRAKE
Dean of Academic Affairs: Dr MONICA NESET JOSLIN
Dean of Students: CHARLOTTE F. DEGEN
Registrar: STEVEN P. KING (acting)
Assoc. Dean for Library Services: MAUREEN HORAK (acting)
Library of 172,000 vols, 500 print periodicals, 300,000 microforms, 4,000 online journals
Number of students: 1,890 (1,680 undergraduate, 210 graduate)

MASSACHUSETTS COLLEGE OF PHARMACY AND HEALTH SCIENCES

179 Longwood Ave, Boston, MA 02115-5896
Telephone: (617) 732-2800
Fax: (617) 732-2801
E-mail: admissions@mcphs.edu
Internet: www.mcphs.edu
Founded 1823 as Massachusetts College of Pharmacy, present name 1979
Private control
Campuses in Manchester, Worcester
Pres.: CHARLES F. MONAHAN, JR
Provost and Vice-Pres. for Academic Affairs: Dr GEORGE E. HUMPHREY
Exec. Vice-Pres., Chief Operating Officer and Chief Financial Officer: RICHARD J. LESSARD
Vice-Pres. for Devt and Chief of Staff: MARGUERITE C. JOHNSON
Dean of Students and Asst Provost for Student Affairs: JEAN JOYCE-BRAD
Vice-Pres. for Finance and Admin.: RICHARD J. LESSARD
Exec. Dir of Admission: KATHLEEN RYAN
Registrar: MARJORIE MCMAHON
Dean of Library and Learning Resources: RICHARD KAPLAN
Library of 88,065 vols incl. e-books and journals, 43,616 e-journals, 800 periodicals
Number of teachers: 229
Number of students: 5,334

DEANS

Forsyth School of Dental Hygiene: Dr LINDA D. BOYD
School of Arts and Sciences: Dr DELIA CASTRO ANDERSON
School of Health Sciences: Dr JAMES BLAGG
School of Medical Imaging and Therapeutics: Dr FRANCES KEECH (acting)
School of Nursing: Dr CAROL ELIADI
School of Optometry: LESLEY WALLS
School of Physical Therapy, Worcester: Dr LINDA TSOUMAS
School of Pharmacy, Boston: Dr DOUGLAS J. PISANO
School of Pharmacy, Worcester/Manchester: Dr MICHAEL J. MALLOY
School of Physician Assistant Studies: (vacant)
School of Radiologic Sciences: Dr K. CYRUS WHALEY (acting)

MASSACHUSETTS INSTITUTE OF TECHNOLOGY

77 Massachusetts Ave, Cambridge, MA 02139-4307
Telephone: (617) 253-1000
Fax: (617) 253-8000
E-mail: registrar-www@mit.edu
Internet: www.mit.edu
Founded 1861
Private control
Academic year: September to May
Pres.: Prof. Dr L. RAFAEL REIF
Chancellor: Prof. W. ERIC L. GRIMSON
Provost: (vacant)
Exec. Vice-Pres. and Treas.: ISRAEL RUIZ
Vice-Pres. and Gen. Counsel: R. GREGORY MORGAN
Vice-Pres. for Finance: MICHAEL W. HOWARD
Vice-Pres. for Institute Affairs and Corporation Sec.: Dr KIRK KOLENBRANDER
Vice-Pres. for Research and Associate Provost: Prof. Dr CLAUDE R. CANIZARES
Vice-Pres. for Resource Devt: JEFFREY L. NEWTON
Dean for Graduate Education: Prof. Dr CHRISTINE ORTIZ
Dean for Undergraduate Education: Prof. Dr DANIEL E. HASTINGS
Dean for Student Life: CHRIS COLOMBO

Registrar: MARY R. CALLAHAN
Dir for Libraries: ANN J. WOLPERT
Library of 3,583,060 vols
Number of teachers: 1,018
Number of students: 10,894 (4,384 undergraduate, 6,510 graduate)
Publications: *Sloan Management Review* (4 a year), *Technology Review* (24 a year)

DEANS

School of Architecture and Planning: Prof. ADÈLE NAUDÉ SANTOS
School of Engineering: Prof. Dr IAN A. WAITZ
School of Humanities, Arts and Social Sciences: Prof. DEBORAH K. FITZGERALD
School of Science: Prof. MARC A. KASTNER
Sloan School of Management: Prof. Dr DAVID C. SCHMITTLEIN

PROFESSORS

(Some professors serve in more than one department)

School of Architecture and Planning (77 Massachusetts Ave, Room 7-231, Cambridge, MA 02139-4307; tel. (617) 253-4401; fax (617) 253-9417; e-mail sap-info@mit.edu; internet sap.mit.edu):

Department of Architecture:
ANDERSON, S., History and Architecture
BEINART, J., Architecture
CHANG, Y. H., Architecture (Head)
DE MONCHAUX, J., Architecture and Urban Planning
DENNIS, M., Architecture
GLICKSMAN, L. R., Building Technology
JARZOMBEK, M., History and Architecture
JONAS, J., Visual Arts
JONES, C., History of Art
KNIGHT, T., Design and Computation
MITCHELL, W. J., Architecture, Media Arts and Sciences
NORFORD, L., Building Technology
RABBAT, N., History of Architecture
SANTOS, A. N., Architecture and Urban Planning
SPIRN, A. W., Landscape Architecture and Planning
STINY, G., Design and Computation
WAMPLER, J., Architecture
WESCOAT, J., Architecture
WODICZKO, K., Visual Arts

Department of Urban Studies and Planning:
AMSDEN, A., Political Economy
CIOCHETTI, B. A., Practice of Real Estate
CLAY, P., Urban Studies and Planning
DAVIS, D., Political Sociology
FERREIRA, J., Urban Studies and Operations Research
FOGELSON, R. M., Urban Studies and History
FRENCHMAN, D., Urban Design
GAKENHEIMER, R., Urban Planning
GELTNER, D., Real Estate Finance
KEYES, L. C., City and Regional Planning
LEVY, F. S., Urban Economics
McDOWELL, C., Practice of Community Development
OSTERMAN, P., Human Resources and Management
POLENSKE, K. R., Regional Political Economy and Planning
REIN, M., Social Policy
SANYAL, B., Urban and Regional Planning
SPIRN, A., Landscape Architecture and Planning
SUSSKIND, L. E., Urban and Environmental Planning
TENDLER, J., Political Economy
VALE, L. J., Urban Design and Planning (Head)
WHEATON, W. C., Urban Economics
Program in Media Arts and Sciences:
GERSHENFELD, N., Media Arts and Sciences

ISHII, H., Media Arts and Sciences
MACHOVER, T., Music and Media
MAEDA, J., Design and Computation
MITCHELL, W. J., Architecture and Media Arts and Sciences
NEGROPONTE, N. P., Media Technology
PENTLAND, A. P., Media Arts and Sciences
PICARD, R., Media Arts and Sciences
RESNICK, M., Media Arts and Sciences and Learning Research (Head)
VERCOE, B., Media Arts and Sciences

School of Engineering (77 Massachusetts Ave, Room 1-206, Cambridge, MA 02139-4307; tel. (617) 253-3291; fax (617) 253-8549; e-mail engineering@mit.edu; internet engineering.mit.edu):

Department of Aeronautics and Astronautics:

CRAWLEY, E. F., Aeronautics and Astronautics and Engineering Systems
DEYST, J. J., Aeronautics and Astronautics
DRELA, M., Aeronautics and Astronautics
EPSTEIN, A. H., Aeronautics and Astronautics
GREITZER, E. M., Aeronautics and Astronautics
HALL, S. R., Aeronautics and Astronautics
HANSMAN, R. J., Aeronautics and Astronautics and Engineering Systems
HARRIS, W. L., Aeronautics and Astronautics
HASTINGS, D. E., Aeronautics and Astronautics, Engineering Systems
HOFFMAN, J. A., Practice of Astronautics
HOW, J. P., Aeronautics and Astronautics
LAGACÉ, P. A., Aeronautics and Astronautics, Engineering Systems
LEVESON, N. G., Aeronautics and Astronautics, Engineering Systems
LIEBECK, R., Practice of Aerospace Engineering
MARTÍNEZ-SÁNCHEZ, M., Aeronautics and Astronautics
NEWMAN, D. J., Aeronautics and Astronautics, Engineering Systems
NIGHTINGALE, D. J., Practice of Aeronautics and Astronautics and Engineering Systems
ODONI, A. R., Aeronautics and Astronautics and Civil and Environmental Engineering
PERAIRE, J., Aeronautics and Astronautics
WAITZ, I. A., Aeronautics and Astronautics (Head)
WIDNALL, S. E., Aeronautics and Astronautics and Engineering Systems
WILLIAMS, B. C., Aeronautics and Astronautics
YOUNG, L. R., Astronautics, Health Sciences and Technology

Department of Biological Engineering:

BELCHER, A. M., Materials Science and Biological Engineering
CHAKRABORTY, A., Chemical Engineering, Chemistry and Biological Engineering
DEDON, P. C., Toxicology and Biological Engineering
DELONG, E. F., Environmental and Biological Engineering
DEWEY, C. F., Jr, Mechanical Engineering and Biological Engineering
ESSIGMAN, J. M., Chemistry, Toxicology and Biological Engineering
FOX, J. G., Toxicology
GRIFFITH, L. G., Biological and Mechanical Engineering
GRODZINSKY, A. J., Electrical, Mechanical and Biological Engineering
KAMM, R. D., Biological and Mechanical Engineering
KLIBANOV, A. M., Chemistry and Biological Engineering
LANGER, R. S., Chemical and Biolomedical Engineering

LAUFFENBURGER, D. A., Biological Engineering, Biology and Chemical Engineering (Head)
LODISH, H. F., Biology and Biological Engineering
MATSUDAIRA, P. T., Biology and Biological Engineering
SAMSON, L. D., Toxicology and Biological Engineering
SASISEKHARAN, R., Biological Engineering and Health Sciences and Technology
SCHAUER, D. B., Biological Engineering and Comparative Medicine
SO, P. T., Mechanical and Biological Engineering
SURESH, S., Materials Science and Bioengineering
TANNENBAUM, S. R., Toxicology and Chemistry
THILLY, W. G., Toxicology
TIDOR, B., Bioengineering and Computer Science
WITTRUP, K. D., Chemical Engineering and Bioengineering
YANNAS, I. V., Polymer Science and Bioengineering

Department of Chemical Engineering:

ARMSTRONG, R. C., Chemical Engineering
BARTON, P., Chemical Engineering
BLANKSCHTEIN, D., Chemical Engineering
CHAKRABORTY, A., Chemical Engineering, Chemistry and Biological Engineering
COHEN, R. E., Chemical Engineering
COLTON, C. K., Chemical Engineering
COONEY, C. L., Chemical and Biochemical Engineering
DEEN, W. M., Chemical Engineering
GLEASON, K. K., Chemical Engineering
HAMMOND, P., Chemical Engineering
HATTON, T. A., Chemical Engineering Practice
JENSEN, K. F., Chemical Engineering (Head)
LANGER, R. S., Chemical and Biomedical Engineering
LAUFFENBURGER, D. A., Biological Engineering, Chemical Engineering and Biology
McRAE, G. J., Chemical Engineering
RUTLEDGE, G. C., Chemical Engineering
SAWIN, H. H., Chemical and Electrical Engineering
SMITH, K. A., Chemical Engineering
STEPHANOPOULOS, G., Chemical Engineering
STEPHANOPOULOS, GRE., Chemical Engineering
TESTER, J. W., Chemical Engineering
TROUT, B., Chemical Engineering
WANG, D. I. C., Chemical Engineering
WITTRUP, K. D., Chemical Engineering and Biological Engineering

Department of Civil and Environmental Engineering:

BARNHART, C., Civil and Environmental Engineering
BEN-AKIVA, M., Civil and Environmental Engineering
BRAS, R. L., Civil and Environmental Engineering and Earth, Atmospheric and Planetary Sciences
BUYUKOZTURK, O., Civil and Environmental Engineering
CHISHOLM, S., Civil and Environmental Engineering and Biology
CONNOR, J. J., Jr, Civil and Environmental Engineering
DELONG, E., Civil and Environmental Engineering and Biological Engineering
DE NEUFVILLE, R. L., Civil and Environmental Engineering, Engineering Systems
EINSTEIN, H. H., Civil and Environmental Engineering

ELTAHIR, E., Civil and Environmental Engineering
ENTEKHABI, D., Civil and Environmental Engineering
GIBSON, L., Materials Science and Engineering, Civil and Environmental Engineering and Mechanical Engineering
GSCHWEND, P., Civil and Environmental Engineering
HEMOND, H. F., Civil and Environmental Engineering
JAILLET, P., Civil and Environmental Engineering (Head)
KAUSEL, E., Civil and Environmental Engineering
LARSON, R. C., Civil and Environmental Engineering and Engineering Systems
LERMAN, S. R., Civil and Environmental Engineering
McLAUGHLIN, D. B., Civil and Environmental Engineering
MADSEN, O. S., Civil and Environmental Engineering
MARKS, D. H., Civil and Environmental Engineering, Engineering Systems
MEI, C. C., Civil and Environmental Engineering
MOAVENZADEH, F., Civil and Environmental Engineering, Engineering Systems
NEPF, H., Civil and Environmental Engineering
ODONI, A. R., Aeronautics and Astronautics and Civil and Environmental Engineering
ROOS, D., Engineering Systems and Civil and Environmental Engineering
SHEFFI, Y., Civil and Environmental Engineering, Engineering Systems
SIMCHI-LEVI, D., Civil and Environmental Engineering, Engineering Systems
SUSSMAN, J. M., Civil and Environmental Engineering, Engineering Systems
ULM, F.-J., Civil and Environmental Engineering
VENEZIANO, D., Civil and Environmental Engineering
WHITTLE, A. J., Civil and Environmental Engineering
WILSON, N. H. M., Civil and Environmental Engineering

Department of Electrical Engineering and Computer Science:

ABELSON, H., Computer Science and Engineering
AGARWAL, A., Computer Science and Engineering
AKINWANDE, A., Electrical Engineering
ANTONIADIS, D., Electrical Engineering
ARVIND, Computer Science and Engineering
BAGGEROER, A. B., Engineering and Mechanical Engineering
BERS, A., Electrical Engineering
BERTSEKAS, D. P., Electrical Engineering
BERWICK, R. C., Computer Science and Engineering and Computational Linguistics
BHATIA, S., Electrical Engineering and Health Sciences and Technology
BONING, D., Electrical Engineering and Computer Science
BRAIDA, L. B. D., Electrical Engineering and Health Sciences and Technology
BROOKS, R. A., Computer Science and Engineering
CHAN, V. W. S., Electrical Engineering
CHANDRAKASAN, A., Electrical Engineering
DAHLEH, M. A., Electrical Engineering
DAVIS, R., Computer Science and Engineering
DEL ALAMO, J. A., Electrical Engineering
DEVADAS, S., Electrical Engineering and Computer Science
DRESSELHAUS, M. S., Electrical Engineering and Physics

FONSTAD, C. G., Jr, Electrical Engineering
FREEMAN, D. M., Computer Science and Engineering
FUJIMOTO, J. G., Electrical Engineering
GALLAGER, R. G., Electrical Engineering
GIFFORD, D. K., Computer Science and Engineering
GOLDWASSER, S., Computer Science and Engineering
GRAY, M. L., Medical and Electrical Engineering
GRAY, P. E., Electrical Engineering
GRIMSON, W. E. L., Medical Engineering (Head)
GRODZINSKY, A. J., Electrical, Mechanical and Biological Engineering
GUTTAG, J. V., Computer Science and Engineering
HENNIE, F. C., III, Computer Science and Engineering
HORN, B. K., Computer Science and Engineering
HOYT, J. L., Electrical Engineering
HU, Q., Electrical Engineering
IPPEN, E. P., Electrical Engineering and Physics
JAAKKOLA, T. S., Computer Science and Engineering
JACKSON, D. N., Computer Science and Engineering
KAASHOEK, M. F., Computer Science and Engineering
KAEBLING, L. P., Computer Science and Engineering
KAERTNER, F. X., Electrical Engineering
KARGER, D. R., Computer Science and Engineering
KASSAKIAN, J. G., Electrical Engineering
KIRTLEY, J. L., Jr, Electrical Engineering
KOLODZIEJSKI, L. A., Electrical Engineering
LANG, J. H., Electrical Engineering
LEE, H.-S., Electrical Engineering
LEEB, S. B., Electrical and Mechanical Engineering
LEISERSON, C. E., Computer Science and Engineering
LIM, J. S., Electrical Engineering
LISKOV, B. H., Engineering
LOZANO-PÉREZ, T., Computer Science and Engineering
LYNCH, N. A., Software Science and Engineering
MAGNANTI, T. L., Management Science and Electrical Engineering
MARK, R. G., Health Sciences and Technology and Electrical Engineering and Computer Science
MEDARD, M., Electrical Engineering
MEGRETSKI, A., Electrical Engineering
MEYER, A. R., Computer Science and Engineering
MICALI, S., Computer Science and Engineering
MINSKY, M. L., Media Arts and Sciences and Computer Science and Engineering
MITTER, S. K., Electrical Engineering and Engineering Systems
MOSES, J., Computer Science and Engineering and Engineering Systems
OPPENHEIM, A. V., Engineering
ORLANDO, T. P., Electrical Engineering
PARKER, R. R., Electrical Engineering and Nuclear Science and Engineering
PARRILO, P., Electrical Engineering and Computer Science
PEAKE, W. T., Electrical and Bioengineering
PENFIELD, P. L., Jr, Electrical Engineering
RAM, R. J., Electrical Engineering
REIF, L. R., Emerging Technology
RIVEST, R. L., Computer Science and Engineering
ROBERGE, J. K., Electrical Engineering
RUBINFELD, R., Computer Science and Engineering

RUS, D. L., Computer Science and Engineering
SAWIN, H. H., Chemical Engineering and Electrical Engineering
SCHINDALL, J. E., Practice
SCHMIDT, M. A., Electrical Engineering
SHAPIRO, J. H., Electrical Engineering
SMITH, A. C., Electrical Engineering
SMITH, H. I., Electrical Engineering
SODINI, C. G., Electrical Engineering
STAELIN, D. H., Electrical Engineering
STEVENS, K. N., Electrical Engineering and Health Sciences and Technology
SUDAN, M., Computer Science and Engineering
SUSSMAN, G. J., Electrical Engineering
SZOLOVITS, P., Computer Science and Engineering and Health Sciences and Technology
TELLER, S., Computer Science and Engineering
TIDOR, B., Electrical Engineering and Computer Science and Biological Engineering
TROXEL, D. E., Electrical Engineering
TSITSIKLIS, J. N., Electrical Engineering and Computer Science
VERGHESE, G. C., Electrical Engineering
WARD, S. A., Computer Science and Engineering
WARDE, C., Electrical Engineering
WHITE, J. K., Electrical Engineering
WILLSKY, A. S., Electrical Engineering
WILSON, G. L., Electrical and Mechanical Engineering
WINSTON, P. H., Engineering
WORNELL, G. W., Electrical Engineering
WYATT, J. L., Electrical Engineering
ZAHN, M., Electrical Engineering
ZUE, V. M., Electrical Engineering and Computer Science

Department of Materials Science and Engineering:

ALLEN, S. M., Physical Metallurgy
BALLINGER, R., Materials Science and Engineering and Nuclear Science and Engineering
BELCHER, A. M., Materials Science and Engineering and Biological Engineering
CARTER, W. C., Materials Science and Engineering
CEDER, G., Materials Science and Engineering
CHIANG, Y.-M., Ceramics
CIMA, M., Engineering
CLARK, J. P., Materials Systems
EAGAR, T. W., Materials Engineering and Materials Systems
FITZGERALD, E. A., Materials Science and Engineering
GIBSON, L., Materials Science and Engineering, Civil and Environmental Engineering and Mechanical Engineering
HOBBS, L. W., Materials Science and Nuclear Science and Engineering
HOSLER, D., Archaeology and Ancient Technology
JENSEN, K. F., Chemical Engineering, Materials Science and Engineering
KIMERLING, L. C., Materials Science and Engineering
LECHTMAN, H., Archaeology and Ancient Technology
MAYES, A. M., Polymer Physics
ROSS, C., Materials Science
RUBNER, M. F., Materials Science and Engineering
SADOWAY, D. R., Metallurgy
SURESH, S., Materials Science and Engineering and Mechanical Engineering
THOMAS, E. L., Materials Science and Engineering (Head)
THOMPSON, C. V., Materials Science and Engineering

TULLER, H. L., Ceramics and Electronic Materials
WUENSCH, B. J., Ceramics
YIP, S., Nuclear Science and Materials Science Engineering

Department of Mechanical Engineering:

ABEYARATNE, R., Mechanics
AKYLAS, T. R., Mechanical Engineering
ANAND, L., Mechanical Engineering
ASADA, H., Engineering
BAGGEROER, A., Mechanical, Ocean and Electrical Engineering
BATHE, K.-J., Mechanical Engineering
BOYCE, M. C., Mechanical Engineering (Head)
BRISSON, J. G., II, Mechanical Engineering
CHEN, G., Mechanical Engineering
CHENG, W. K., Mechanical Engineering
CHRYSSOSTOMIDIS, C., Ocean Science and Engineering and Mechanical and Ocean Engineering
CHUN, J. H., Mechanical Engineering
CRAVALHO, E. G., Mechanical Engineering
D'ARBELOFF, A., Practice of Mechanical Engineering and Management
DEWEY, C. F., Jr, Mechanical Engineering and Bioengineering
DUBOWSKY, S., Mechanical Engineering and Aeronautics and Astronautics
GHONIEM, A. F., Mechanical Engineering
GIBSON, L., Materials Science and Engineering and Mechanical Engineering and Environmental Engineering
GLICKSMAN, L., Mechanical Engineering and Architecture
GOSSARD, D. C., Mechanical Engineering
GRAVES, S., Mechanical Engineering and Management
GRIFFITH, L., Teaching Innovation, Mechanical and Biological Engineering
GRODZINSKY, A. J., Mechanical, Electrical and Biological Engineering
GUTOWSKI, T. G., Mechanical Engineering
HARDT, D. E., Mechanical Engineering
HART, D., Mechanical Engineering
HEYWOOD, J. B., Mechanical Engineering
HOGAN, N. J., Mechanical Engineering and Brain and Cognitive Science
HUNTER, I. W., Mechanical Engineering
KAMM, R. D., Mechanical and Biological Engineering
KAZIMI, M. S., Mechanical and Nuclear Engineering
LANGER, R. S., Mechanical, Chemical and Biological Engineering
LEEB, S. B., Mechanical and Electrical Engineering and Computer Science
LEONARD, J. J., Mechanical and Ocean Engineering
LIEHARD, J., Mechanical Engineering
LLOYD, S., Mechanical Engineering
MCKINLEY, G. H., Teaching Innovation and Mechanical Engineering
MAKRIS, N. C., Mechanical and Ocean Engineering
MARCUS, H., Marine Systems
MEI, C. C., Engineering, Mechanical and Civil Engineering
MIKIC, B. B., Mechanical Engineering
MILGRAM, J., Mechanical and Ocean Engineering
PARKS, D. M., Mechanical Engineering
PATERA, A. T., Engineering
PATRIKALAKIS, N. M., Engineering, Mechanical and Ocean Engineering
ROWELL, D., Mechanical Engineering
SACHS, E. M., Mechanical Engineering
SCHMIDT, H., Mechanical and Ocean Engineering
SCLAVOUNOS, P., Mechanical Engineering and Naval Architecture
SEERING, W. P., Mechanical Engineering
SLOCUM, A., Mechanical Engineering
SLOTINE, J.-J. E., Mechanical Engineering and Brain and Cognitive Sciences

SMITH, J. L., Jr, Mechanical Engineering
So, P. T., Mechanical and Biological Engineering
SURESH, S., Biological Engineering and Materials Science and Engineering
TRIANTAFYLLOU, M., Mechanical and Ocean Engineering
TRUMPER, D. L., Mechanical Engineering
VANDIVER, J. K., Mechanical and Ocean Engineering
VEST, C. M., Mechanical Engineering
WALLACE, D., Mechanical Engineering
WELSH, M. S., Practice of Naval Construction and Engineering
WIERZBICKI, T., Applied Mechanics
WILLIAMS, J. H., Jr, Teaching Excellence, Mechanical Engineering and Writing and Humanistic Studies
WILSON, G. L., Electrical and Mechanical Engineering
YANNAS, I. V., Mechanical Engineering, Polymer Science and Biological Engineering
YOUCEF-TOUMI, K., Mechanical Engineering
YUE, D. K.-P., Engineering, Mechanical and Ocean Engineering

Department of Nuclear Science and Engineering:

APOSTOLAKIS, G., Nuclear Science and Engineering and Engineering Systems
BALLINGER, R. G., Nuclear Science and Engineering and Materials Science and Engineering
CORY, D. G., Nuclear Science and Engineering
FREIDBERG, J. P., Nuclear Science and Engineering
GOLAY, M. W., Nuclear Science and Engineering
HOBBS, L. W., Materials Science and Nuclear Science and Engineering
HUTCHINSON, I. H., Nuclear Science and Engineering (Head)
KADAK, A. C., Practice, Nuclear Science and Engineering
KAZIMI, M. S., Nuclear Engineering and Mechanical Engineering
LESTER, R. K., Nuclear Science and Engineering
PARKER, R. R., Electrical Engineering and Nuclear Science and Engineering
YANCH, J. C., Nuclear Science and Engineering
YIP, S., Nuclear Science and Engineering and Materials Science and Engineering

Engineering Systems Division:

ALLEN, T. J., Management and Engineering Systems
APOSTOLAKIS, G., Engineering Systems
BARNHART, C., Civil and Environmental Engineering and Engineering Systems
CARROLL, J., Behavioural and Policy Sciences and Engineering Systems
CLARK, J. P., Materials Systems and Engineering Systems
CRAWLEY, E. F., Aeronautics and Astronautics and Engineering Systems
CUSUMANO, M., Management and Engineering Systems
DE NEUFVILLE, R., Civil and Environmental Engineering and Engineering Systems
EAGAR, T. W., Materials Engineering and Engineering Systems
EPPINGER, S. D., Management Science and Engineering Systems
FINE, C., Management and Engineering Systems
GRAVES, S. C., Management and Engineering Systems
HANSMAN, J., Aeronautics and Astronautics and Engineering Systems
HARDT, D. E., Mechanical Engineering and Engineering Systems

HASTINGS, D., Aeronautics and Astronautics and Engineering Systems
KOCHAN, T. A., Management and Engineering Systems
LAGACÉ, P. A., Aeronautics and Astronautics and Engineering Systems
LARSON, R., Civil and Environmental Engineering and Engineering Systems
LEVESON, N., Aeronautics and Astronautics and Engineering Systems
LLOYD, S., Mechanical Engineering and Engineering Systems
MADNICK, S., Information Technology and Engineering Systems
MARKS, D. H., Civil and Environmental Engineering and Engineering Systems
MINDELL, D., History of Engineering and Manufacturing and Engineering Systems
MITTER, S., Electrical Engineering and Engineering Systems
MOAVENZADEH, F., Civil and Environmental Engineering and Engineering Systems
MONIZ, E., Physics and Engineering Systems
MOSES, J., Computer Science and Engineering Systems
NEWMAN, D. J., Aeronautics and Astronautics and Engineering Systems
ROOS, D., Civil and Environmental Engineering and Engineering Systems (Co-Dir)
SEERING, W. P., Mechanical Engineering and Engineering Systems
SHEFFI, Y., Engineering Systems and Civil and Environmental Engineering (Head)
SIMCHI-LEVI, D., Civil and Environmental Engineering and Engineering Systems
STERMAN, J., Management and Engineering Systems
SUSSMAN, J. M., Civil and Environmental Engineering and Engineering Systems
UTTERBACK, J., Management and Innovation and Engineering Systems
WELSCH, R., Statistics and Management Science and Engineering Systems
WIDNALL, S., Aeronautics and Astronautics and Engineering Systems

School of Humanities, Arts and Social Sciences (77 Massachusetts Ave, Room E51-255, Cambridge, MA 02139-4307; tel. (617) 253-3450; e-mail shass-www@mit.edu; internet shass.mit.edu):

Department of Economics:

ACEMOGLU, K. D., Economics
ANGELETOS, G.-M., Economics
ANGRIST, J., Economics
AUTOR, D., Economics
BANERJEE, A., Economics
BLANCHARD, O. J., Economics
CABALLERO, R., Economics (Head)
CHERNOZHUKOV, V., Economics
DIAMOND, P. A., Economics
DUFLO, E., Poverty Alleviation and Development Economics
ELLISON, G., Economics
FINKELSTEIN, A., Economics
GIBBONS, R. S., Management and Economics
GREENSTONE, M., Environmental Economics
GRUBER, J., Economics
HARRIS, J. E., Economics
HAUSMAN, J. A., Economics
HOLMSTRÖM, B. R., Economics (Head)
JOSKOW, P. L., Economics and Management
NEWEY, W. K., Economics
PIORE, M. J., Political Economy
POTERBA, J. M., Economics
ROSE, N., Economics
ROSS, S., Finance and Economics
SCHMALENSEE, R. L., Management and Economics

SNYDER, J., Political Science and Economics
TEMIN, P., Economics
THUROW, L. C., Management and Economics
TOWNSEND, R., Economics
WERNING, I., Economics
WHEATON, W. C., Economics and Urban Studies

Department of Linguistics and Philosophy:

BYRNE, A., Philosophy
CHOMSKY, N. A., Linguistics
FLYNN, S., Second Language Acquisition
FOX, D., Linguistics
GIBSON, E. A., Cognitive Science
HASLANGER, S., Philosophy
HEIM, I., Linguistics
HOLTON, R., Philosophy
IATRIDOU, S., Linguistics
KENSTOWICZ, M., Linguistics
LANGTON, R., Philosophy
McGEE, V., Philosophy
MIYAGAWA, S., Japanese Language and Culture, Linguistics
O'NEIL, W., Linguistics
PESETSKY, D., Linguistics
SINGER, I., Philosophy
STALNAKER, R., Philosophy
STERIADE, D., Linguistics
VON FINTEL, K., Linguistics
WEXLER, K. N., Psychology and Linguistics
YABLO, S., Philosophy

Department of Political Science:

ANSOLABEHERE, S. D., Political Science
BERGER, S., Political Science
CHOUCRI, N., Political Science
LOCKE, R. M., Entrepreneurship and Political Science
PIORE, M. J., Political Economy and Political Science
POSEN, B. R., Political Science
SAMUELS, R. J., Political Science
SNYDER, J. M., Political Science and Economics
STEWART, C., III, Political Science (Head)
VAN EVERA, S. W., Political Science

Foreign Languages and Literatures Section:

DE COURTIVRON, I., French Studies (Head)
GARRELS, E., Spanish and Latin American Studies
MIYAGAWA, S., Japanese Language and Culture, Linguistics
TURK, E. B., French Studies and Film
WANG, J., Chinese Languages and Culture

History Section:

DOWER, J. W., History
FOGELSON, R. M., History and Urban Studies
KHOURY, P. S., History
McCANTS, A. E. C., History (Head)
MAIER, P., History
RITVO, H., History
SMITH, M. R., History of Technology
WOOD, E. A., History

Literature Section:

BUZARD, J., Literature (Head)
DONALDSON, P. S., Literature
HENDERSON, D., Literature
HILDEBIDLE, J., Literature
JENKINS, H., III, Comparative Media Studies and Literature
KIBEL, A. C., Literature
PERRY, R., Literature and Women's Studies
TAPSCOTT, S. J., Literature
THORBURN, D., Literature
URICCHIO, W., Comparative Media Studies

Music and Theater Arts Section:

BRODY, A., Theater Arts
CHILD, P., Music
DEFRANTZ, T., Theater Arts
HARBISON, J., Music
HARRIS, E. T., Music
LINDGREN, L., Music

SONENBERG, J., Theater Arts
THOMPSON, M. A., Music
VERCOE, B., Media Arts and Sciences
ZIPORYN, E., Music

Program in Anthropology:

FISCHER, M. M. J., Anthropology and Science and Technology Studies
HOWE, J., Anthropology
JACKSON, J. E., Anthropology
SILBEY, S., Sociology and Anthropology (Head)

Program in Comparative Media Studies:

JENKINS, H., III, Humanities, Comparative Media Studies and Literature
URICCHIO, W., Comparative Media Studies

Program in Science, Technology and Society:

FISCHER, M. M. J., Humanities
FITZGERALD, D. K., History of Technology
MANNING, K. R., Rhetoric and the History of Science
MINDELL, D. A., History of Engineering and Manufacturing, Engineering Systems (Dir)
POSTOL, T. A., Science, Technology and Nat. Security Policy
SMITH, M. R., History of Technology
TURKLE, S. R., Social Studies of Science and Technology
WILLIAMS, R. H., History of Science and Technology

Program in Writing and Humanistic Studies:

KANIGEL, R., Science Writing
LEVENSON, T., Science Writing
MANNING, K. R., Rhetoric and the History of Science
PARADIS, J., Writing (Program Head)
WILLIAMS, J. H., Engineering
WILLIAMS, R. H., History of Science and Technology

School of Science (77 Massachusetts Ave, Room 6-123, Cambridge, MA 02139; tel. (617) 253-8900; fax (617) 253-8901; e-mail scnc@mit.edu; internet web.mit.edu/science):

Department of Biology:

AMON, A., Biology
BAKER, T., Biology
BARTEL, D. P., Biology
BELL, S., Biology
CHEN, J., Biology
CHISHOLM, S. W., Civil and Environmental Engineering and Biology
CONSTANTINE-PATON, M., Biology
FINK, G. R., Genetics
GERTLER, F., Biology
GROSSMAN, A. D., Biology
GUARENTE, L. P., Biology
HOPKINS, N. H., Biology
HORVITZ, H. R., Biology
HOUSMAN, D. E., Cancer Research and Biology
HYNES, R. O., Cancer Research
IMPERIALI, B., Chemistry and Biology
JACKS, T. E., Biology
JAENISCH, R., Biology
KAISER, C., Biology (Head)
KING, J. A., Biology
KRIEGER, M., Biology, Molecular Genetics
LANDER, E., Biology
LAUFFENBURGER, D., Bioengineering, Chemical Engineering and Biology
LEES, J. A., Biology
LINDQUIST, S., Biology
LODISH, H. F., Biology and Bioengineering
MATSUDAIRA, P., Biology and Bioengineering
NEWMAN, D. K., Biology
ORR-WEAVER, T., Biology
PAGE, D., Biology
PARDUE, M. L., Biology
PLOEGH, H., Biology
QUINN, W., Neurobiology
RAJBHANDARY, U. L., Molecular Biology
RICH, A., Biophysics

SAMSON, L., Toxicology and Biological Engineering
SAUER, R. T., Biology
SHARP, P. A., Biology
SHENG, M., Neuroscience
SINSKEY, A. J., Microbiology
SIVE, H. L., Biology
SOLOMON, F., Biology
STEINER, L. A., Immunology
STUBBE, J., Chemistry and Biology
TONEGAWA, S., Biology and Neuroscience
WALKER, G. C., Biology
WEINBERG, R. A., Cancer Research
WILSON, M., Neurobiology
YOUNG, R. A., Biology

Department of Brain and Cognitive Sciences:

ADELSON, E. H., Visual Sciences
BEAR, M., Neuroscience
BERWICK, R. C., Computational Linguistics
BIZZI, E., Brain Sciences and Human Behaviour
BROWN, E. N., Computational Neuroscience and Health Sciences and Technology
CHOROVER, S. L., Psychology
CONSTANTINE-PATON, M., Biology
CORKIN, S. H., Behavioural Neuroscience
DESIMONE, R., Neuroscience
GABRIELI, J., Health Sciences and Technology and Cognitive Neuroscience
GIBSON, E., Cognitive Sciences
GRAYBIEL, A. M., Neuroanatomy
HEIN, A., Experimental Psychology
HOCKFIELD, S., Neuroscience
HOGAN, N., Mechanical Engineering
KANWISHER, N. G., Cognitive Neuroscience
MILLER, E. K., Visual Neuroscience
POGGIO, T. A., Brain Sciences and Human Behaviour
POTTER, M. C., Psychology
PRELAC, D., Management
QUINN, W. G., Neurobiology
RICHARDS, W. A., Cognitive Sciences
SCHILLER, P. H., Medical Engineering and Medical Physics
SCHNEIDER, G. E., Neuroscience
SEUNG, H. S., Computational Neuroscience
SHENG, M. H.-T., Neurobiology
SLOTINE, J.-J. E., Mechanical Engineering and Information Sciences
SUR, M., Neuroscience (Head)
TONEGAWA, S., Biology and Neuroscience
TSAI, L.-H., Neuroscience
WEXLER, K. N., Psychology and Linguistics
WILSON, M., Neuroscience
WURTMAN, R. J., Neuropharmacology

Department of Chemistry:

BAWENDI, M. G., Chemistry
BUCHWALD, S. L., Chemistry
CEYER, S. T., Chemistry
CUMMINS, C. C., Chemistry
DANHEISER, R. L., Chemistry
DEUTCH, J. M., Chemistry
DRENNAN, C. L., Chemistry
ESSIGMANN, J. M., Chemistry and Toxicology
FIELD, R. W., Chemistry
FU, G. C., Chemistry
GRIFFIN, R. G., Chemistry
IMPERIALI, B., Chemistry and Biology
KLIBANOV, A. M., Chemistry and Bioengineering
LIPPARD, S. J., Chemistry
NELSON, K. A., Chemistry
NOCERA, D. G., Energy Chemistry
PETERS, J. C., Chemistry
SCHROCK, R. R., Chemistry
SILBEY, R. J., Chemistry
STUBBE, J., Chemistry and Biology
SWAGER, T. M., Chemistry (Head)
TANNENBAUM, S. R., Chemistry and Toxicology
TOKMAKOFF, A., Chemistry

Department of Earth, Atmospheric and Planetary Sciences:

BINZEL, R. P., Planetary Sciences
BOWRING, S. A., Geology
BOYLE, E. A., Ocean Geochemistry
BURCHFIEL, B. C., Geology
ELLIOT, J. L., Planetary Astronomy and Physics
EMANUEL, K. A., Atmospheric Science
ENTEKHABI, D., Civil and Environmental Engineering and Earth, Atmospheric and Planetary Sciences
EVANS, J. B., Geophysics
FLIERL, G. R., Oceanography
FREY, F. A., Geochemistry
GROVE, T. L., Geology
HAGER, B. H., Earth Sciences
HERRING, T. A., Geophysics
LINDZEN, R. S., Meteorology
MARSHALL, J., Atmospheric and Oceanic Sciences
MORGAN, F. D., Geophysics
PLUMB, R. A., Meteorology
PRINN, R. G., Atmospheric Chemistry
RIZZOLI, P. M., Physical Oceanography
ROTHMAN, D. H., Geophysics
ROYDEN, L., Geology and Geophysics
SUMMONS, R. E., Geobiology
TOKSÖZ, M. N., Geophysics
VAN DER HILST, R., Geophysics
WISDOM, J., Planetary Sciences
WUNSCH, C. I., Physical Oceanography
ZUBER, M. T., Planetary Sciences and Geophysics (Head)

Department of Mathematics:

ARTIN, M., Mathematics
BENNEY, D. J., Applied Mathematics
BERGER, B., Applied Mathematics
BEZRUKAVNIKOV, R., Mathematics
CHENG, H., Applied Mathematics
COLDING, T. H., Mathematics
DUDLEY, R. M., Mathematics
EDELMAN, A., Applied Mathematics
ETINGOF, P. I., Mathematics
FREEDMAN, D. Z., Applied Mathematics
GOEMANS, M., Applied Mathematics
GUILLEMIN, V. W., Mathematics
HELGASON, S., Mathematics
JERISON, D. S., Mathematics
KAC, V., Mathematics
KLEIMAN, S., Mathematics
KLEITMAN, D. J., Applied Mathematics
LEIGHTON, F. T., Applied Mathematics
LUSZTIG, G., Mathematics
MCKERNAN, J., Mathematics
MATTUCK, A. P., Mathematics
MELROSE, R. B., Mathematics
MILLER, H. R., Mathematics
MROWKA, T., Mathematics
POONEN, B., Mathematics
ROGERS, H., Jr, Mathematics
ROSALES, R. R., Applied Mathematics
SEIDEL, P., Mathematics
SHEFFIELD, S., Mathematics
SHOR, P., Applied Mathematics
SINGER, I. M., Mathematics
SIPSER, M., Applied Mathematics (Head)
STAFFILANI, G., Mathematics
STANLEY, R. P., Applied Mathematics
STRANG, W. G., Mathematics
STROOCK, D. W., Mathematics
TOOMRE, A., Applied Mathematics
VOGAN, D. A., Jr, Mathematics

Department of Physics:

ASHOORI, R., Physics
BECKER, U. J., Physics
BELCHER, J. W., Physics
BENEDEK, G. B., Physics and Biological Physics
BERTOZZI, W., Physics
BERTSCHINGER, E., Physics (Head)
BUSZA, W., Physics
CANIZARES, C. R., Physics
CHAKRABARTY, D., Physics

CHEN, M., Physics
COPPI, B., Physics
DRESSELHAUS, M. S., Physics and Electrical Engineering
ELLIOT, J. L., Earth, Atmospheric and Planetary Sciences and Physics
FARHI, E., Physics
FELD, M. S., Physics
FISHER, P. H., Physics
FREEDMAN, D., Mathematics and Physics
GREYTAK, T. J., Physics
GUTH, A. H., Physics
HEWITT, J. N., Physics
IPPEN, E. P., Electrical Engineering and Physics
JACKIW, R. W., Physics
JAFFE, R. L., Physics and Science
JOANNOPOULOS, J. D., Physics
JOSS, P. C., Physics
KARDAR, M., Physics
KASTNER, M., Physics
KETTERLE, W., Physics
KOWALSKI, S. B., Physics
LEE, P. A., Physics
LEVITOV, L., Physics
LEWIN, W. H. G., Physics
LITSTER, J. D., Physics
MATTHEWS, J. L., Physics
MILNER, R. G., Physics
MONIZ, E. J., Physics
NEGELE, J. W., Physics
PORKOLAB, M., Physics
PRITCHARD, D. E., Physics
RAJAGOPAL, K., Physics
RAPPAPORT, S. A., Physics
REDWINE, R. P., Physics
SCHECHTER, P., Astrophysics
SEUNG, H. S., Computational Neuroscience and Physics
TAYLOR, W., Physics
TING, S. C. C., Physics
WEN, X.-G., Physics
WILCZEK, F., Physics
WYSLOUCH, B., Physics
ZWIEBACH, B., Physics

Whitaker College of Health Sciences and Technology (77 Massachusetts Ave, Room E25-519, Cambridge, MA 02139; tel. (617) 258-4418; fax (617) 253-7498; internet hst .mit.edu):

BENEDEK, G. B., Physics and Biological Physics and Health Sciences and Technology
BRAIDA, L. D., Electrical Engineering and Health Sciences and Technology
COHEN, R. J., Biomedical Engineering
CRAVALHO, E. G., Mechanical Engineering and Health Sciences and Technology
EDELMAN, E. R., Health Sciences and Technology
GABRIELI, J., Health Sciences and Technology, Brain and Cognitive Sciences
GEHRKE, L., Health Sciences and Technology
GRAY, M. L., Medical and Electrical Engineering
HOUSMAN, D. E., Biology
LANGER, R. S., Chemical and Biomedical Engineering and Health Sciences and Technology
MARK, R. G., Health Sciences and Technology and Electrical Engineering and Computer Science
SINSKEY, A. J., Biology and Health Sciences and Technology
SZOLOVITS, P., Computer Science and Engineering and Health Sciences and Technology
WURTMAN, R. J., Neuropharmacology and Health Sciences and Technology
YOUNG, L. R., Astronautics and Health Sciences and Technology

Harvard-MIT Division of Health Sciences and Technology

BHATIA, S. N., Health Sciences and Technology, and Electrical Engineering and Computer Science
BROWN, E. N., Health Sciences and Technology, and Computational Neuroscience
FREEMAN, D. M., Electrical Engineering
LANGER, R. S., Chemical and Biomedical Engineering, and Health Sciences and Technology
SASISEKHARAN, R., Biological Engineering, and Health Sciences and Technology

Sloan School of Management (50 Memorial Dr., Cambridge, MA 02142; tel. (617) 253-2659; fax (617) 258-9739; e-mail communication@sloan.mit.edu; internet mitsloan.mit.edu):

ANCONA, D. G., Management
ASQUITH, P., Finance
BARNETT, A. I., Operations Research and Management and Management Science
BERNDT, E. R., Applied Economics
BERTSIMAS, D., Management
BITRAN, G. R., Management
BRYNJOLFSSON, E., Management Science
CARROLL, J. S., Management
COX, J. C., Finance
CUSUMANO, M. A., Management
EPPINGER, S. D., Management
FERNÁNDEZ, R. M., Management
FINE, C. H., Management
FREUND, R. M., Management Science
GIBBONS, R. S., Management
GRAVES, S. C., Management
HAUSER, J. R., Marketing
HENDERSON, R. M., Management
HOLMSTROM, B. R., Economics and Management
JOHNSON, S., Entrepreneurship
JOSKOW, P. L., Economics and Management
KOCHAN, T. A., Management
KOTHARI, S. P., Accounting
LESSARD, D. R., Int. Management
LITTLE, J. D. C., Marketing
LO, A. W., Finance
LOCKE, R., Entrepreneurship
MADNICK, S. E., Information Technology and Engineering Systems
MAGNANTI, T. L., Management Science and Electrical Engineering
MALONE, T. W., Management
MYERS, S. C., Financial Economics
ORLIKOWSKI, W. J., Communication Sciences
ORLIN, J. B., Management
OSTERMAN, P., Human Resources and Management
PINDYCK, R. S., Finance and Economics
PRELEC, D., Management
ROBERTS, E. B., Management
ROSS, S. A., Financial Economics
SCHMALENSEE, R. L., Management and Economics
SCHMITTLEIN, D. C., Management
SIMESTER, D., Management Science
STERMAN, J., Computer Studies
STOKER, T. M., Management and Economics
THUROW, L. C., Management and Economics
URBAN, G. L., Management
UTTERBACK, J., Management and Innovation
VAN MAANEN, J. E., Management
VON HIPPEL, E. A., Management
WANG, J., Finance
WATTS, R. L., Accounting
WELSCH, R. E., Statistics and Management Science
WERNERFELT, B., Management
YATES, J., Management

MASSACHUSETTS MARITIME ACADEMY

101 Academy Dr., Buzzards Bay, MA 02532
Telephone: (508) 830-5000
Fax: (508) 830-5077
E-mail: info@maritime.edu
Internet: www.maritime.edu

Founded 1891 as Massachusetts Nautical Training School; present name 1942
State control
Academic year: August to June

Depts of engineering, humanities, international maritime business, environmental protection, safety and emergency management, marine transportation, science and mathematics, social science

Pres.: RICHARD G. GURNON
Vice-Pres. for Academic Affairs and Dean: BRADLEY K. LIMA
Vice-Pres. for Admin. and Finance: MICHAEL A. JOYCE
Vice-Pres. for Advancement: HOLLY A. KNIGHT
Vice-Pres. for Enrolment Management: ELIZABETH STEVENSON
Vice-Pres. for External Relations and Finance: MICHAEL A. JOYCE
Vice-Pres. for Operations: FRANCIS X. McDONALD
Vice-Pres. for Student Services: EDWARD J. ROZAK
Dir of Admissions: ROY FULGUERAS
Dean of Graduate Studies and Continuing Education: Dr JAMES J. McDONALD
Registrar and Asst Dean: MICHAEL R. CUFF
Dir of Library: SUSAN S. BERTEAUX

Number of teachers: 52
Number of students: 770

MASSACHUSETTS SCHOOL OF LAW AT ANDOVER

500 Federal St, Andover, MA 01810
Telephone: (978) 681-0800
Fax: (978) 681-6330
E-mail: mslaw@mslaw.edu
Internet: www.mslaw.edu
Founded 1988
Private control
Academic year: July to July

Academic programmes in business and corporate law, civil litigation, communications sports and entertainment law, criminal law, environmental law, family law, finance and asset management law, intellectual property, media, information law, juvenile law, labour law, land use and planning, litigation, real estate

Dean: Prof. Dr LAWRENCE R. VELVEL
Dir of Admissions: PAULA COLBY-CLEMENTS
Registrar: LOUISE ROSE
Dir of Information Resources: JUDITH WOLFE

Library of 60,000 vols.

MASSACHUSETTS SCHOOL OF PROFESSIONAL PSYCHOLOGY

221 Rivermoor St, Boston, MA 02132
Telephone: (617) 327-6777
Fax: (617) 327-4447
E-mail: admissions@mspp.edu
Internet: www.mspp.edu
Private control
Academic year: January to December

Pres.: NICHOLAS COVINO
Provost: Dr DAN KING
Vice-Pres. for Finance and Operations: PATRICK CAPOBIANCO
Dean of Students: Dr FRANCES V. MERVYN
Dir of Admissions: MARIO MURGA
Registrar: EILEEN O'DONNELL
Librarian: MATTHEW KRAMER

DEANS

Advanced Graduate Studies: Dr STANLEY BERMAN

Clinical Psychology Dept: Dr ALAN DODGE BECK

MERRIMACK COLLEGE

315 Turnpike St, North Andover, MA 01845

Telephone: (978) 837-5000

Fax: (978) 837-5222

E-mail: regoff@merrimack.edu

Internet: www.merrimack.edu

Founded 1947

Private control

Academic year: September to May

Pres.: Dr CHRISTOPHER E. HOPEY

Provost and Vice-Pres. for Academic Affairs: JOSEPHINE MODICA-NAPOLITANO

Vice-Pres. for Admin. and Gen. Counsel: CHRISTINE ABOWITZ

Vice-Pres. for Enrolment Management, Planning and Strategy: KURT THIEDE

Vice-Pres. for Finance and Chief Financial Officer: MARK VADALA

Vice-Pres. for Mission and Student Affairs: Rev. RAYMOND DLUGOS

Dean of Admissions: MARK BARRETT

Registrar: ELAINE GRELLE

Dir of Library: KATHRYN GEOFFRIONSCANNELL

Library of 125,000 vols, 1,069 current periodicals

Number of teachers: 139

Number of students: 2,000

Publication: *Merrimack Magazine* (4 a year)

DEANS

Francis E. Girard School of Business and International Commerce: MARK CORDANO

School of Education: DAN BUTIN

School of Liberal Arts: MICHAEL ROSSI

School of Science and Engineering: MARY NOONAN

MGH INSTITUTE OF HEALTH PROFESSIONS

36 First Ave, Charleston Navy Yard, Boston, MA 02129-4557

Telephone: (617) 726-2947

Fax: (617) 726-3716

E-mail: admissions@mghihp.edu

Internet: www.mghihp.edu

Founded 1980

Private control

Academic year: September to August

Pres.: Prof. Dr JANIS P. BELLACK

Provost and Vice-Pres. for Academic Affairs: Prof. Dr ALEX F. JOHNSON

Vice-Pres. for Finance and Admin.: ATLAS D. EVANS

Chief Devt Officer: HARRIET S. KORNFELD

Academic Dean: KEVIN KEARNS

Dean of Student Affairs: CAROLYN F. LOCKE

Registrar and Asst Dean of Students: JAMES V. VITAGLIANO

Librarian: JESSICA BELL

Library of 50,000 vols

Number of teachers: 81 (66 full-time, 15 part-time)

Number of students: 1,111 (694 full-time, 417 part-time)

DEANS

School of Health and Rehabilitation Sciences: Prof. Dr LESLIE G. PORTNEY

School of Nursing: Dr LAURIE LAUZON CLABO

MONTSERRAT COLLEGE OF ART

23 Essex St, POB 26, Beverly, MA 01915

Telephone: (978) 921-4242

Fax: (978) 921-4268

E-mail: admiss@montserrat.edu

Internet: www.montserrat.edu

Founded 1970 as Montserrat School of Visual Arts

Private control

Academic year: September to May (3 semesters)

Areas of study incl. animation and interactive media, art education, graphic design, illustration, interdisciplinary arts, liberal arts, painting and drawing, photography and video, printmaking, sculpture

Pres.: Dr STEPHEN D. IMMERMAN

Dean of Admissions and Enrolment Management: RICK LONGO

Dean of College Relations: JO BRODERICK

Dean of Devt: HOWARD AMIDON

Dean of Faculty and Academic Affairs: LAURA TONELLI

Dean of Students: MAUREEN WARK

Registrar: THERESA SKELLY

Librarian: CHERI COE

Library of 15,000 vols, 90 periodicals

Number of teachers: 63

Number of students: 390 (undergraduate)

MOUNT HOLYOKE COLLEGE

50 College St, South Hadley, MA 01075

Telephone: (413) 538-2000

Fax: (413) 538-2391

E-mail: admission@mtholyoke.edu

Internet: www.mtholyoke.edu

Founded 1837 as Mount Holyoke Female Seminary, present name 1893

Private control

Academic year: September to May

Areas of study incl. ancient studies, art studio, chemistry, economics, engineering, geology, music, psychology, sociology, theatre arts, statistics

Pres.: LYNN C. PASQUERELLA

Vice-Pres. for Academic Affairs and Dean of Faculty: CHRISTOPHER BENFEY (acting)

Vice-Pres. for Devt: CHARLES J. HAIGHT

Vice-Pres. for Enrollment and College Relations: DIANE ANCI

Vice-Pres. for Finance and Admin. and Treas.: BEN HAMMOND

Vice-Pres. for Student Affairs and Dean of College: CERRI BANKS

Dean of Students and Assoc. Dean of the College: RENE DAVIS

Dean of Studies: GEOFFREY SUMI

Registrar: ELIZABETH PYLE

Chief Information Officer and Exec. Dir of Library, Information and Technology Services: CHARLOTTE SLOCUM PATRIQUIN

Library of 750,000 vols, 1,300 periodicals

Number of teachers: 283

Number of students: 2,362

Publications: *Vista* (2 a year), *Alumnae Quarterly* (4 a year).

MOUNT IDA COLLEGE

777 Dedham St, Newton, MA 02459

Telephone: (617) 928-4500

Fax: (617) 928-4507

E-mail: registrar@mountida.edu

Internet: www.mountida.edu

Founded 1899 as Women's Private High School

Private control

Academic year: August to May

Schools of animal science, arts and sciences, business, design

Pres.: Dr LANCE CARLUCCIO

Vice-Pres. for Academic Affairs: Dr ELLEN BEAULIEU

Vice-Pres. for Devt and Dir of External Relations: Dr DEBORAH HIRSCH

Vice-Pres. for Enrollment Management and Marketing: MAUREEN MORIARTY

Vice-Pres. for Finance and Admin.: CHERYL ST PIERRE-SLEBODA

Vice-Pres. for Student Affairs: Dr ELIZABETH TRUE

Dean of Academic Services: ALYCE CURTIS

Dean of Graduate Studies and Continuing Education: Dr LOIS NUNEZ

Registrar: MAUREEN MORIARTY

Dean of Information Technology and Learning Resources: MARJORIE LIPPINCOTT

Library of 120,000 titles

Number of teachers: 100

Number of students: 1,429

NATIONAL GRADUATE SCHOOL OF QUALITY MANAGEMENT

186 Jones Rd, Falmouth, MA 02540

Telephone: (508) 457-1313

Fax: (508) 457-5347

E-mail: info@ngs.edu

Internet: www.ngs.edu

Founded 1993

Private control

Academic year: January to December

Offers degree programmes in business administration, science

Pres. and Founder: Dr ROBERT GEE

Vice-Pres. for Enrollment Management: VIRGINIA PETISCE

Registrar: VANESSA HOFFMAN

Number of teachers: 252

Number of students: 393 (full-time)

NEW ENGLAND COLLEGE OF BUSINESS AND FINANCE

10 High St, Boston, MA 02110-1605

Telephone: (617) 951-2350

Fax: (617) 951-2533

E-mail: info@necb.edu

Internet: www.necb.edu

Founded 1909 as American Banking Institute, present name 2008

Private control

Academic year: January to December

Offers BSc in business administration; MSc in business ethics and compliance, finance

Pres.: Dr HOWARD E. HORTON

Provost: Prof. Dr CHRISTOPHER WEIR

Sr Vice-Pres. for Student Services: PAULA BRAMANTE

Dean of Academic Affairs: Dr CHRISTIAN BROCATO

Dean of Undergraduate Studies: ROGER PAO

Registrar: ROBERT WAGSTAFF

Librarian: Prof. JEFFREY C. CRONIN.

NEW ENGLAND COLLEGE OF OPTOMETRY

424 Beacon St, Boston, MA 02115

Telephone: (617) 266-2030

Fax: (617) 424-9202

E-mail: admissions@neco.edu

Internet: www.neco.edu

Founded 1894 as Klein School of Optics; present name 1976

Private control

Academic year: September to May

Depts of advanced care, biomedical sciences, primary care and speciality, vision sciences

Pres.: Prof. Dr CLIFFORD SCOTT

Vice-Pres. for Admin.: JOHN CURRAN

Vice-Pres. and Dean of Academic Affairs: Prof. Dr BARRY FISCH

Vice-Pres. and Dean of Students, Admin. and Alumni: Dr TERRANCE B. NEYLON

Vice-Pres. for Devt: LARRY RAFF

Vice-Pres. for Institutional Advancement: NANCY BROUDE
Vice-Pres. for Professional Services: ROGER WILSON
Chief Financial Officer and Treas.: BRUCE BERNIER
Dir of Admissions: Dr TALINE FARRA
Registrar: GLENDA UNDERWOOD
Dir of Library Services: KRISTIN MOTTE
Library of 11,000 vols, 200 journals
Number of teachers: 77
Number of students: 425

NEW ENGLAND CONSERVATORY OF MUSIC

290 Huntington Ave, Boston, MA 02115-5018
Telephone: (617) 585-1100
Fax: (617) 585-1115
E-mail: admission@newenglandconservatory.edu
Internet: necmusic.edu
Founded 1867
Private control
Academic year: September to May
Academic programmes in chamber music, composition, historical performance and world music, jazz and contemporary improvisation, music history and theory, music in education, piano, orchestral and wind ensemble conducting, orchestral instruments, orchestras, wind ensembles, voice and opera
Pres.: TONY WOODCOCK
Provost and Dean of College: THOMAS NOVAK
Sr Vice-Pres. for Finance and Operations: EDWARD R. LESSER
Vice-Pres. for Institutional Advancement: DON JONES
Dean of Preparatory and Continuing Education: LESLIE WU FOLEY
Dean of Students: THOMAS HANDEL
Dir of Admissions: CHRIS DALY
Registrar: ROBERT WINKLEY
Dir of Libraries: JEAN MORROW
Library of 150,000 vols
Number of teachers: 400
Number of students: 750
Publications: *Journal for Learning through Music* (1 a year), *Notes* (2 a year).

NEW ENGLAND INSTITUTE OF ART

10 Brookline Place W, Brookline, MA 02445-7295
Telephone: (617) 739-1700
E-mail: neiaregistrar@aii.edu
Internet: www.artinstitutes.edu/boston
Founded 1952 as Norm Prescott School of Broadcasting, present name 2003
Private control
Academic year: January to August
Bachelor of science degree programmes in advertising, audio and media technology, digital film-making and video production, fashion and retail management, graphic design, interior design, media arts and animation, photography, sound and motion picture technical arts, web design and interactive media
Pres.: DAVID WARREN
Dean of Academic Affairs: RICHARD KETTNER-POLLEY
Dir of Admin. and Financial Services: ROSS SORACI
Sr Dir of Admissions: LINDA ROBERTS
Registrar: DAWN NORRIS
Dir of Library: MARY ANN TRICARICO
Number of teachers: 156 (49 full-time, 107 part-time)
Number of students: 1,483

NEW ENGLAND LAW—BOSTON

154 Stuart St, Boston, MA 02116
Telephone: (617) 451-0010
Fax: (617) 422-7201
E-mail: admit@nesl.edu
Internet: www.nesl.edu
Founded 1908 as Portia Law School, present name 2008
Private control
Academic year: August to May
Offers degree in advanced legal studies
Dean: JOHN F. O'BRIEN
Dir of Admissions: MICHELLE L'ETOILE
Dir of Student Services: JACQUI PILGRIM
Registrar: DAVID BERTI
Library Dir: Prof. ANNE M. ACTON
Library of 321,000 vols
Number of teachers: 87 (37 full-time, 50 part-time)
Number of students: 1,135 (800 full-time, 335 part-time)
Publications: *New England Journal of Comparative and International Law* (1 a year), *New England Journal on Criminal and Civil Confinement* (2 a year), *New England Law Review* (4 a year).

NEWBURY COLLEGE

129 Fisher Ave, Brookline, MA 02445
Telephone: (617) 730-7000
Fax: (617) 731-9618
E-mail: admissions@newbury.edu
Internet: www.newbury.edu
Founded 1962
Private control
Academic year: August to May (2 semesters)
Schools of arts, science and design, business and management, hotel and restaurant management
Pres.: HANNAH M. McCARTHY
Exec. Vice-Pres.: JOSEPH CHILLO
Exec. Vice-Pres. for Enrolment: JOSEPH CHILLO
Vice-Pres. for Academic Affairs and Dean of the College: Dr HANNAH LEVERTOV
Vice-Pres. for Devt: CLARE McCULLY
Vice-Pres. for Finance and Chief Financial Officer: JOYCE HANLON
Vice-Pres. for Student Affairs: PAUL MARTIN
Registrar: RACHELLE MAZZA-BORRELLI
Dir of Library Services: PETER G. OBUCHAN
Number of teachers: 1,025

NICHOLS COLLEGE

POB 5000, Dudley, MA 01571
124 Center Rd, Dudley, MA 01571
Telephone: (508) 213-1560
Fax: (508) 213-2225
E-mail: admissions@nichols.edu
Internet: www.nichols.edu
Founded 1815 as Nichols Acad., present name and status 1971
Academic year: August to May (2 semesters)
Campuses in Auburn, Devens, Worcester; areas of study incl. accounting, business administration, business communications, business economics, criminal justice management, English, history, mathematics, psychology
Pres.: Dr SUSAN WEST ENGELKEMEYER
Provost and Sr Vice-Pres.: Dr ALAN J. REINHARDT
Vice-Pres. and Dean of Student Services: BRIAN McCOY
Vice-Pres. for Admin.: MICHAEL J. STANTON
Vice-Pres. for College Advancement: WILLIAM C. PIECZYNSKI
Vice-Pres. for Enrolment and Marketing: THOMAS R. CAFARO

Vice-Pres. for Information Services: KEVIN F. BRASSARD
Vice-Pres. for Student Affairs and Dean of Students: Dr BRIAN T. McCOY
Registrar: BETIN ROBICHAUD
Dir of Library: JIM DOUGLAS
Library of 67,000 vols
Number of teachers: 50
Number of students: 1,592 (1,343 undergraduate, 249 graduate)
Publication: *Nichols College Magazine*.

NORTHEASTERN UNIVERSITY

360 Huntington Ave, Boston, MA 02115
Telephone: (617) 373-2000
Fax: (617) 373-8780
E-mail: admissions@neu.edu
Internet: www.northeastern.edu
Founded 1898
Private control
Academic year: August to August
Pres.: Dr JOSEPH E. AOUN
Provost and Sr Vice-Pres. for Academic Affairs: STEPHEN DIRECTOR
Sr Vice-Pres. and Gen. Counsel: RALPH MARTIN
Sr Vice-Pres. for Admin. and Finance: JOHN H. McCARTHY
Sr Vice-Pres. for Enrolment Management and Student Affairs: PHILOMENA MANTELLA
Sr Vice-Pres. for Exec. Affairs: MARK PUTNAM
Sr Vice-Pres. for External Affairs: MICHAEL ARMINI
Sr Vice-Pres. for Univ. Advancement: DIANE MACGILLIVRAY
Vice-Pres. for Devt: LUANNE M. KIRWIN
Dean of Library: WILLIAM WAKELING
Library of 932,999 vols, 206,507 e-books, 1,489,153 microforms, 70,225 serial titles, 59,926 e-journals, 23,437 audiovisual items, 143,905 govt documents
Number of teachers: 1,033
Number of students: 20,530

DEANS

Bouvé College of Health Sciences: Dr TERRY FULMER
College of Arts, Media and Design: Dr XAVIER COSTA
College of Business Admin.: Prof. Dr HARRY LANE (acting)
College of Computer and Information Science: LARRY FINKELSTEIN
College of Engineering: ALLEN SOYSTER
College of Professional Studies: Dr JOHN G. LABRIE
College of Science: Dr J. MURRAY GIBSON
College of Social Sciences and Humanities: GEORGES VAN DEN ABBEELE
School of Law: Prof. EMILY E. SPIELER

PINE MANOR COLLEGE

400 Heath St, Chestnut Hill, MA 02467
Telephone: (617) 731-7000
Fax: (617) 731-7199
E-mail: admission@pmc.edu
Internet: www.pmc.edu
Founded 1911 as a post-secondary div. of Dana Hall School; present name and status 1977
Private control
Academic year: September to May
Depts of biology, communication, community health, creative writing, English, history, management and organizational change, psychology, social and political systems, visual arts
Pres.: Dr ALANE K. SHANKS
Vice-Pres. for Finance and Business: BETSY ESPE

Vice-Pres. for Institutional Advancement:
SUSAN WEBBER
Dean of College: Dr WILLIAM B. VOGELE
Dir of Admissions: ELAINE VINCENT
Dean of Student Services and Community
Engagement: WHITNEY RETALLIC
Registrar: JEFF MEI
Library Dir: SARAH WOOLF (acting)
Library of 70,000 vols
Number of teachers: 66
Number of students: 486

REGIS COLLEGE

235 Wellesley St, Weston, MA 02493-1571
Telephone: (781) 768-7000
Fax: (781) 768-8339
E-mail: admission@regiscollege.edu
Internet: www.regiscollege.edu
Founded 1927
Private control
Academic year: September to June
Pres.: Dr ANTOINETTE M. HAYS
Vice-Pres. for Academic Affairs: PAULA HAR-
BECKE
Vice-Pres. for Enrolment and Marketing:
PAUL VACCARO
Vice-Pres. for Finance and Business: THOMAS
G. PISTORINO
Vice-Pres. for Student Affairs: LYNN TRIPP
COLEMAN
Chief Devt Officer: MIRIAM FINN SHERMAN
Dean of Students: Dr KARA KOLOMITZ
Dir of Admission: WANDA ESTHER SURIEL
Registrar: ESTHER A. GHAZARIAN
Dir of Library: LYNN TRIPLETT
Library of 133,000 vols
Number of teachers: 106 (71 full-time, 85
part-time)
Number of students: 1,800
Publications: *Hemetera*, *Regis Today* (2 a
year)

DEANS

School of Liberal Arts, Education and Social
Sciences: Dr ELIZABETH CAWLEY
School of Nursing Sciences and Health Pro-
fessions: ANTOINETTE HAYS

SALEM STATE UNIVERSITY

352 Lafayette St, Salem, MA 01970
Telephone: (978) 542-6000
Fax: (978) 542-6336
E-mail: admissions@salemstate.edu
Internet: www.salemstate.edu
Founded 1854 as Salem Normal School,
present name 2010
State control
Academic year: September to May (2 semes-
ters)
Pres.: Dr PATRICIA MAGUIRE MESERVEY
Exec. Vice-Pres.: Dr STANLEY CAHIL
Provost and Vice-Pres. for Academic Affairs:
Dr KRISTIN ESTERBERG
Exec. Vice-Pres. for Student Life: Dr STANLEY
P. CAHILL
Vice-Pres. for Finance and Facilities:
ANDREW SOLL
Vice-Pres. for Institutional Advancement:
CYNTHIA MCGURREN
Dean of Students: JAMES G. STOLL
Dean of Library: SUSAN E. CIRILLO
Library of 225,000 vols
Number of teachers: 779 (333 full-time, 446
part-time)
Number of students: 9,646 (6,241 full-time,
3,405 part-time

DEANS

Bertolon School of Business: Dr K. BREWER
DORAN

College of Health and Human Services: Dr
NEAL DeCHILLO
School of Arts and Sciences: Dr JUDE V.
NIXON
School of Graduate Studies: Dr CAROL A.
GLOD
School of Professional and Continuing Edu-
cation: Dr ARLENE T. GREENSTEIN

ST JOHN'S SEMINARY

127 Lake St, Brighton, MA 02135
Telephone: (617) 254-2610
Fax: (617) 787-2336
E-mail: contact@sjs.edu
Internet: www.sjs.edu
Founded 1884
Private control
Academic year: September to May
Offers degrees in divinity, ministry, philoso-
phy, theology
Rector: Rev. ARTHUR L. KENNEDY
Vice-Rector: Rev. CHRISTOPHER O'CONNOR
Dean of Faculty: Rev. STEPHEN E. SALOCKS
Dean of Students: Rev. CHRISTOPHER K.
O'CONNOR
Dir of Communication and Devt: Dr KATH-
LEEN HECK
Dir of Finance and Operations: RICHARD A.
FLAHERTY
Librarian: Rev. Mgr LAURENCE W. McGRATH
Library of 171,000 vols
Number of teachers: 22
Number of students: 80 (full-time)
Publication: *The Saint John's Seminary
Magazine* (2 a year).

SCHOOL OF THE MUSEUM OF FINE ARTS

230 The Fenway, Boston, MA 02115
Telephone: (617) 267-6100
Fax: (617) 424-6271
E-mail: admissions@smfa.edu
Internet: www.smfa.edu
Founded 1876
Academic year: September to May
Areas of study incl. film, painting and per-
formance, studio art
Pres.: CHRISTOPHER BRATTON
Provost and Dir of Devt: DAN POTEET
Vice-Pres. and Dean of Enrolment: ERIC
THOMPSON
Vice-Pres. for Institutional Advancement
and External Relations: ANNE COWIE
Dean of Admissions: ERIC THOMPSON
Dean of Faculty: FRITZ BUEHNER
Dean of School: DEBORAH H. DLUHY
Registrar: DAN JOHNSON
Librarian: DARIN MURPHY
Library of 130,000 vols
Number of teachers: 145 (full-time)
Number of students: 785 (612 undergradu-
ate and diploma, 173 graduate)

SIMMONS COLLEGE

300 The Fenway, Boston, MA 02115
Telephone: (617) 521-2000
Fax: (617) 521-3199
E-mail: ugadm@simmons.edu
Internet: www.simmons.edu
Founded 1899
Private control
Academic year: September to May
Pres.: HELEN G. DRINAN
Provost: CHARLENA SEYMOUR
Sr Vice-Pres. for Admin. and Finance and
Treas.: STEFANO FALCONI
Vice-Pres. and Gen. Counsel: KATHY ROGERS
Vice-Pres. for Advancement: MARIANNE LORD

Vice-Pres. for Marketing and Admission:
CHERYL HOWARD
Dean of Student Life: SARAH NEIL
Registrar: DONNA DOLAN
Dir of Libraries: DAPHNE HARRINGTON
Library of 225,000 vols, 53,000 journals,
8,000 audiovisual items
Number of teachers: 548 (231 full-time, 317
part-time)
Number of students: 5,003
Publications: *Abafazi*, *Essays and Studies*,
Now, *Sidelines* (2 a year), *Simmons News*,
Simmons Review (3 a year)

DEANS

College of Arts and Sciences: Prof. Dr RENÉE
WHITE
Graduate School of Library and Information
Sciences: Dr MICHÈLE V. CLOONAN
School of Management: CATHY MINEHAN
School of Nursing and Health Studies: Dr
JUDY BEAL
School of Social Work: Dr STEFAN KRUG

SMITH COLLEGE

Northampton, MA 01063
Telephone: (413) 584-2700
Fax: (413) 585-2123
E-mail: admission@smith.edu
Internet: www.smith.edu
Founded 1871
Private control
Academic year: September to May
Areas of study incl. computer science, dance,
E Asian languages and cultures, E Asian
studies, economics, education and child
study, engineering, English language and
literature, environmental science and policy,
film studies
Pres.: CAROL T. CHRIST
Provost and Dean of Faculty: MARILYN R.
SCHUSTER
Vice-Pres. for Advancement: PATRICIA JACK-
SON
Vice-Pres. for Campus Life and Dean of
College: MAUREEN MAHONEY
Vice-Pres. for Finance and Admin.: RUTH
CONSTANTINE
Vice-Pres. for Devt: PATRICIA JACKSON
Dean of Admission: DEBRA D. SHAVER
Dean of Students: JULIANNE OHOTNICKY
Registrar: TRICIA O'NEILL
Dir of Libraries: CHRISTOPHER LORING
Library of 1,200,000 vols
Number of teachers: 303 (287 full-time, 16
part-time)
Number of students: 2,781 (2,682 under-
graduate, 99 postgraduate)
Publications: *Alumnae Quarterly* (4 a year),
Amazonian Literary Review (1 a year),
Meridians.

SPRINGFIELD COLLEGE

263 Alden St, Springfield, MA 01109-3797
Telephone: (413) 748-3000
Fax: (413) 748-3746
E-mail: admissions@spfldcol.edu
Internet: www.spfldcol.edu
Founded 1885
Private control
Academic year: August to May
Pres.: Dr RICHARD B. FLYNN
Exec. Vice-Pres.: JILL F. RUSSELL
Vice-Pres. for Academic Affairs: Dr JEAN A.
WYLD
Vice-Pres. for Devt and Alumni Relations:
JOHN WHITE
Vice-Pres. for Finance and Admin.: JOHN
MAILHOT
Vice-Pres. for Institutional Advancement:
DAVID FRABONI

Vice-Pres. for Student Affairs: Dr DAVID G. BRAVERMAN
Registrar: KEITH INGALLS
Dir of Library: ANDREA TAUPIER
Library of 187,358 vols, 25,586 bound periodicals
Number of teachers: 205 full-time
Number of students: 3,407

DEANS

School of Arts, Science and Professional Studies: Dr ANNE HERZOG
School of Health, Physical Education, and Recreation: Dr CHARLES REDMOND
School of Health Sciences and Rehabilitation Studies: Dr DAVID J. MILLER
School of Human Services: Dr ROBERT J. WILLEY, JR
School of Social Work: Dr FRANCINE J. VECCHIOLLA

STONEHILL COLLEGE

320 Washington St, Easton, MA 02357
Telephone: (508) 565-1000
Fax: (508) 565-1500
E-mail: admissions@stonehill.edu
Internet: www.stonehill.edu
Founded 1948
Private control
Academic year: September to May

Areas of study incl. computer science, criminology, history, interdisciplinary studies, mathematics, philosophy

Pres.: Rev. MARK T. CREGAN
Vice-Pres. for Academic Affairs and Provost: KATIE CONBOY
Vice-Pres. for Advancement: FRANCIS X. DILLON
Vice-Pres. for Enrolment Management and Marketing: CHRISTOPHER LYDON
Vice-Pres. for Finance and Treas.: JEANNE FINLAYSON
Vice-Pres. for Mission: Rev. JOHN DENNING
Vice-Pres. for Student Affairs: Rev. JOHN DENNING
Dean of Faculty: KAREN TALENTINO
Registrar: JOHN PESTANA
Dir of Library: SUSAN CONANT

Library of 194,587 vols
Number of teachers: 151 (full-time)
Number of students: 2,617

Publication: *Stonehill Alumni Magazine* (2 a year).

SUFFOLK UNIVERSITY

8 Ashburton Place, Boston, MA 02108-2770
Telephone: (617) 573-8000
Fax: (617) 573-8353
E-mail: admission@suffolk.edu
Internet: www.suffolk.edu
Founded 1906 as Suffolk School of Law, present name 1937
Private control
Academic year: September to August
Int. campus in Spain; satellite campus in Lawrence

Pres.: JAMES MCCARTHY
Provost and Academic Vice-Pres.: BARRY BROWN (acting)
Vice-Pres. and Treas.: DANIELLE MANNING (acting)
Vice-Pres. for Enrolment Planning and Management: WALTER CAFFEY
Vice-Pres. for Govt Relations and Community Affairs: JOHN A. NUCCI
Dean of College: KENNETH S. GREENBERG
Dean of Student Affairs: NANCY C. STOLL
Dir of Law Library: BETSY MCKENZIE

Library of 241,000 vols, 2,070 periodicals, 396,250 microforms
Number of teachers: 400

Number of students: 9,563

Publications: *Journal of Health & Biomedical Law* (2 a year), *Journal of High Technology Law*, *Salamander* (2 a year), *Suffolk Alumni Magazine* (4 a year), *Suffolk Business Magazine* (1 a year), *Suffolk Law School Alumni Magazine* (2 a year), *Suffolk Transnational Law Review* (2 a year), *Suffolk University Law Review* (4 a year), *The Advocate*, *The Suffolk Journal*, *Venture* (1 a year)

DEANS

College of Arts and Sciences: KENNETH S. GREENBERG
Law School: CAMILLE A. NELSON
Sawyer Business School: WILLIAM J. O'NEILL, JR

TUFTS UNIVERSITY

Medford, MA 02155
Telephone: (617) 628-5000
E-mail: admissions.inquiry@ase.tufts.edu
Internet: www.tufts.edu
Founded 1852
Private control
Academic year: September to May
Campuses in Boston, France, Grafton, Somerville, Talloires

Pres.: ANTHONY P. MONACO
Provost and Sr Vice-Pres.: PEGGY NEWELL
Exec. Vice-Pres.: PATRICIA L. CAMPBELL
Vice-Pres. for Finance and Treas.: THOMAS S. MCGURTY
Vice-Pres. for Information Technology and Chief Information Officer: DAVID KAHLE
Vice-Pres. for Operations: RICHARD W. REYNOLDS
Vice-Pres. for Univ. Advancement: BRIAN K. LEE
Vice-Pres. for Univ. Relations: MARY R. JEKA
Dean of Student Affairs: BRUCE REITMAN
Dean of Student Services: PAUL STANTON
Dean of Admissions and Financial Aid: LAURIE A. HURLEY
Dir of Library: JEFF KOSOKOFF

Library of 1,214,414 vols, contained in 4 libraries on 3 campuses
Number of teachers: 1,263
Number of students: 9,658

Publications: *International Journal of Middle East Studies*, *Tufts Health and Nutrition Letter*, *Tufts Journal*, *Tufts Medicine*, *Tufts Veterinary Medicine* (2 a year)

DEANS

Cummings School of Medicine: DEBORAH T. KOCHEVAR
Fletcher School of Law and Diplomacy: STEPHEN W. BOSWORTH
Gerald J. and Dorothy Friedman School of Nutrition Science and Policy: ROBIN KANAREK
Graduate School of Arts and Sciences: LYNNE PEPALL
Jonathan M. Tisch College of Citizenship and Public Service: NANCY WILSON
Sackler School of Graduate Biomedical Sciences: NAOMI ROSENBERG
School of Arts and Sciences: JOANNE BERGER-SWEENEY
School of Dental Medicine: HUW F. THOMAS
School of Engineering: LINDA M. ABRIOLA
School of Medicine: HARRIS BERMAN

PROFESSORS

ADELMAN, L., Pathology
ADLER, D., Psychiatry
AFSAR, M., Electrical and Computer Engineering
ALEXANDER, S., Paediatric Dentistry
ALONSO, J., Romance Languages
AMATO, R., Paediatrics

AMBADDY, N., Psychology
AMMONS, E., English
AMPOLA, M., Paediatrics
ARIAS, I., Physiology
AUNER, J., Music
AZZOUNI, J., Philosophy
BACHOVCHIN, W., Biochemistry
BACOW, L., Public Health and Family Medicine
BAGHDIANTZ-MCCABE, I., History
BANKOFF, M., Radiology
BANKS, H., Orthopaedic Surgery
BARRETT, D., Urology
BAUM, J., Ophthalmology
BEINFELD, M., Pharmacology and Experimental Therapeutics
BELSKY, M., Orthopaedic Surgery
BERESFORD, J., Obstetrics and Gynaecology
BERG, J., Clinical Sciences
BERKMAN, E., Medicine
BERMAN, H., Public Health and Family Medicine
BERNSTEIN, J., Music
BERRY, J., Political Science
BHARUCHA, J., Neuroscience
BIANCHI, D., Paediatrics
BIERBAUM, B., Orthopaedic Surgery
BIRKETT, D., Surgery
BLACHER, R., Psychiatry
BLOOMQUIST, E., Physiology
BLUMENTHAL, S., Psychiatry
BOGHOSIAN, B., Mathematics
BORGERS, C., Mathematics
BOUDREAU, F., Obstetrics and Gynaecology
BOYER, M., Public Health and Family Medicine
BRATT, R., Urban and Environmental Policy and Planning
BRAWERMAN, G., Biochemistry
BRIDGES, R., Biomedical Sciences
BRISS, B., Orthodontics
BRODER, M., Medicine
BRODY, C., Computer Science
BRONSON, R., Biomedical Sciences
BROWN, B., Paediatrics
BROWN, W., Neurology
BROWN, W., Psychiatry
BULLOCK, P., Biochemistry
BURKMAN, R., Obstetrics and Gynaecology
BUSHNELL, E., Psychology
CALLOW, A., Surgery
CAMER, S., Surgery
CAMILLI, A., Molecular Biology and Microbiology
CARPINITO, G., Urology
CARTER, B., Radiology
CASSADY, J., Radiation Oncology
CASTELLOT, J., Anatomy and Cellular Biology
CAVAZOS, L., Public Health and Family Medicine
CEBE, P., Physics and Astronomy
CELLI, B., Medicine
CEPEDA, M., Anaesthesiology
CETRULO, C., Obstetrics and Gynaecology
CHAPMAN, R., Prosthodontics and Operative Dentistry
CHAPRA, S., Civil and Environmental Engineering
CHARM, S., Biochemistry
CHECHILE, R., Psychology
CHELMOW, D., Obstetrics and Gynaecology
CHEN, J., General Dentistry
CHEW, F., Biology
CHOI, I., Radiology
CHONG, F., Pathology
COCHRAN, B., Physiology
COCHRANE, D., Biology
COE, N., Surgery
COFFIN, J., Microbiology—Basic Science
COHEN, I., Psychiatry
CONKLIN, J., Sociology
CONNOLLY, N., Anaesthesiology
COOK, R., Psychology
COOPER, A., Pathology
COSGROVE, G., Neurosurgery
COTTER, S., Clinical Sciences

CRANE, G., Classics
CRAVEN, D., Medicine
CRISCITIELLO, M., Medicine
DAMASSA, D., Anatomy and Cellular Biology
DARLING, D., Radiology
DAVIS, J., Paediatrics
DAWSON-HUGHES, B., Medicine
DENNETT, D., Philosophy
DESFORGES, J., Medicine
DEVIGNE, R., Political Science
DEWALD, R., Chemistry
DICE, J., Physiology
DIGGES, D., English
DODMAN, N., Clinical Sciences
DOGEL, Y., Pathology
DOHERTY, R., Prosthodontics and Operative Dentistry
DRACHMAN, V., History
DRAPKIN, M., Medicine
DUCIBELLA, T., Obstetrics and Gynaecology
DUKER, J., Ophthalmology
DUNLAP, K., Neuroscience
DWYER, J., Medicine
EASTERBROOKS, A., Child Development
EDGERS, L., Civil and Environmental Engineering
ENGELKING, L., Biomedical Sciences
ENGELKING, L., Physiology
ENGELMAN, R., Surgery
EPSTEIN, L., Psychiatry
EPSTEIN, S., Medicine
ERNST, S., Biology
ESTES, N., Medicine
FANBURG, B., Medicine
FEIG, L., Biochemistry
FEINGOLD, D., Dermatology
FELDMAN, D., Child Development
FERNANDEZ-ARMESTO, F., History
FERRONE, J., Orthopaedic Surgery
FIELDING, R., Medicine
FLAX, M., Pathology
FLORES, A., Paediatrics
FLYNN, C., English
FLYTZANI-STEPHANOPOULOS, M., Chemical Engineering
FOLSTEIN, M., Psychiatry
FORD, L., Physics and Astronomy
FORGAC, M., Physiology
FOSTER, E., Pathology
FRANK, E., Physiology
FRANTZ, I., Paediatrics
FREEMAN, R., Surgery
FREIDBERG, S., Neurosurgery
FRIEDBERG, R., Pathology
FRIEDMAN, L., Medicine
FRIEDMANN, P., Surgery
FRISKEN, S., Computer Science
FYLER, J., English
GAASCH, W., Medicine
GALBURT, R., Oral and Maxillofacial Surgery
GALPER, J., Medicine
GANDA, K., General Dentistry
GANG, D., Pathology
GARLICK, J., Cell, Molecular, Developmental Biology
GARVEN, G., Geology
GASARIAN, A., Romance Languages
GELFAND, J., Medicine
GEORGAKIS, C., Chemical Engineering
GERMAIN, M., Medicine
GILL, M., Psychiatry
GITTLEMAN, S., German, Russian, Asian Languages and Literatures
GOLDBERG, E., Microbiology—Basic Science
GOLDBERG, M., Orthopaedic Surgery
GOLDENBERG, D., Medicine
GOLDIN, B., Public Health and Family Medicine
GOLDSTEIN, G., Physics and Astronomy
GONZALEZ, F., Mathematics
GOODMAN, E., Paediatrics
GORBACH, S., Public Health and Family Medicine
GORSON, K., Neurology
GOTTLIEB, A., Dermatology
GRACE, N., Medicine

GRADY, G., Medicine
GREEN, D., Endodontics
GREENBLATT, D., Pharmacology and Experimental Therapeutics
GREIF, R., Mechanical Engineering
GUERTIN, R., Physics and Astronomy
GUNTHER, L., Physics and Astronomy
GUSS, D., Anthropology
GUTIERREZ, M., Mathematics
HAAS, T., Chemistry
HAHN, M., Mathematics
HALL, S., Anaesthesiology
HAMMER, N., Prosthodontics and Operative Dentistry
HAMMER, R., Psychiatry
HAMPF, F., Radiology
HAND, R., Medicine
HANNENBERG, A., Anaesthesiology
HARDER, D., Psychology
HARRINGTON, J., Medicine
HARTMANN, E., Psychiatry
HARTNELL, G., Radiology
HASSELBLATT, B., Mathematics
HAWLEY, C., Periodontology
HAYDON, P., Neuroscience
HAYES, C., Public Health and Community Service
HEIJIN, C., Psychiatry
HENNEMAN, P., Emergency Medicine
HERMAN, I., Physiology
HERN, D., Prosthodontics and Operative Dentistry
HESKETH, P., Medicine
HIBBERD, P., Medicine
HIGBY, D., Medicine
HIGGENS, T., Medicine
HILL, N., Medicine
HINDS, P., Radiation Oncology
HINES, E., Civil and Environmental Engineering
HIRATA, H., German, Russian, Asian Languages and Literatures
HIRAYAMA, H., Prosthodontics and Operative Dentistry
HOLCOMB, P., Psychology
HOMER, M., Radiology
HOPWOOD, J., Electrical and Computer Engineering
HOWE, E., Romance Languages
HSU, L., Psychiatry
HUBER, B., Pathology
HUGHES, W., Physiology
HUVOS, A., Medicine
INOUYE, C., German, Russian, Asian Languages and Literatures
IOANNIDES, Y., Economics
ISBERG, R., Microbiology—Basic Science
ISLAM, S., Civil and Environmental Engineering
JACKENDOFF, R., Philosophy
JACKSON, F., Neuroscience
JACOB, M., Neuroscience
JACOB, R., Computer Science
JACOBSON, S., Anatomy and Cellular Biology
JALAL, A., History
JANKOWSKI, J., Psychiatry
JAY, D., Physiology
JENNINGS, J., Urban and Environmental Policy and Planning
JENSEN, H., Paediatrics
JIANG, L., Medicine
JOHNSON, V., German, Russian, Asian Languages and Literatures
JONES, E., Paediatrics
JOSEPH, P., Sociology
KACHANOV, M., Mechanical Engineering
KAHN, M., Oral Pathology
KANAREK, R., Psychology
KAPLAN, D., Biomedial Engineering
KARAS, R., Medicine
KARMODY, C., Otolaryngology/Head and Neck Surgery
KASSIRER, J., Medicine
KAUER, J., Neuroscience
KEANE, T., Psychiatry
KENLER, K., Obstetrics and Gynaecology

KENNEY, P., Surgery
KENNISON, R., Obstetrics and Gynaecology
KENNY, J., Chemistry
KILARU, P., Anaesthesiology
KILMER, M., Mathematics
KISLIUK, R., Biochemistry
KLAPHOLZ, H., Obstetrics and Gynaecology
KLAUBER, G., Urology
KLINGEMANN, H., Medicine
KONSTAM, M., Medicine
KOPELMAN, R., Medicine
KOPIN, A., Medicine
KOSCH, P., Paediatrics
KOSOWSKY, B., Medicine
KREAM, R., Pharmacology
KRETSCHMAR, C., Paediatrics
KRIMSKY, S., Urban and Environmental Policy and Planning
KRINSKY, N., Biochemistry
KROLL, A., Ophthalmology
KULIG, J., Paediatrics
KUMAMOTO, C., Molecular Biology and Microbiology
KUMAR, K., Chemistry
KUMAR, M., Biomedical Sciences
LANG, K., Physics and Astronomy
LASSER, R., Electrical and Computer Engineering
LAU, J., Medicine
LAURENT, P., History
LAURENZI, G., Medicine
LECHAN, R., Medicine
LEE, M., Medicine
LEIVILLE-WEBSTER, C., Clinical Sciences
LERNER, R., Child Development
LEUPP, G., History
LEVESQUE, P., Anaesthesiology
LEVEY, A., Medicine
LEVINE, H., Medicine
LEVY, S., Molecular Biology and Microbiology
LEWIS, S., Biology
LIBERTINO, J., Urology
LICHTENSTEIN, A., Public Health and Family Medicine
LINSENMAYER, T., Anatomy and Cellular Biology
LIPTZIN, B., Psychiatry
LISCUM, L., Physiology
LITVAK, J., English
LO, T., Radiation Oncology
LOPEZ, M., Surgery
LUNDY, L., Obstetrics and Gynaecology
MCCARTHY, H., Surgery
MCCARTHY, J., Orthopaedic Surgery
MCCAULEY, R., Radiology
MACDONNELL, K., Medicine
MACKEY, W., Surgery
MADIAS, N., Medicine
MADOFF, M., Public Health and Family Medicine
MAHLER, D., Anaesthesiology
MALAMY, M., Microbiology—Basic Science
MALCHOW, H., History
MANN, W., Physics and Astronomy
MANNO, V., Mechanical Engineering
MARCHANT, D., Obstetrics and Gynaecology
MARRONE, S., History
MAZZOTTI, J., Romance Languages
MEHTA, N., General Dentistry
MEIRI, K., Anatomy and Cellular Biology
MEISSNER, H., Paediatrics
MENDELSOHN, M., Medicine
METCALF, G., Economics
MEYDANI, S., Immunology
MICZEK, K., Psychiatry
MICZEK, K., Psychology
MILLER, E., Electrical and Computer Engineering
MILLER, K., Medicine
MILNER, L., Paediatrics
MIRKIN, S., Biology
MIRKIN, S., Genetics
MITCHELL, G., Obstetrics and Gynaecology
MOORE, C., Microbiology—Basic Science
MOREHEAD, J., Anatomy and Cellular Biology
MORGAN, J., Medicine

MULHOLLAND, D., History
MUNSAT, T., Neurology
MURPHY, R., Medicine
MUST, A., Public Health and Family Medicine
NAGINSKI, I., Romance Languages
NAIMI, S., Medicine
NALEBUFF, E., Orthopaedic Surgery
NAPIER, A., Physics and Astronomy
NAPIER, S., German, Russian, Asian Languages and Literatures
NASRAWAY, S., Surgery
NAVAB, F., Medicine
NEUMANN, P., Medicine
NEWBERG, A., Radiology
NIELSEN, H., Paediatrics
NITECKI, Z., Mathematics
NOLLER, K., Obstetrics and Gynaecology
NOONAN, J., Electrical and Computer Engineering
NORMAN, G., Economics
NORTON, R., Medicine
O'DONNELL, K., Surgery
O'DONNELL, T., Surgery
O'GRADY, J., Obstetrics and Gynaecology
OHMAN, J., Medicine
O'LEARY, D., Radiology
OLIVER, W., Physics and Astronomy
ORDOVAS, J., Genetics
OSTRANDER, S., Sociology
OTIS, C., Pathology
OXENKRUG, G., Psychiatry
PAGE, D., Surgery
PAIS, V., Urology
PALMER, C., Public Health and Community Service
PANDIAN, N., Medicine
PANJWANI, N., Ophthalmology
PAPAGEORGE, M., Oral and Maxillofacial Surgery
PAPAS, A., General Dentistry
PATTERSON, J., Medicine
PAUKER, S., Medicine
PAUL, R., Radiology
PAYNE, D., Surgery
PECHENIK, J., Biology
PENNINCK, D., Clinical Sciences
PEPPER, M., Public Health and Family Medicine
PEREIRA, B., Medicine
PERRIN, E., Paediatrics
PERRIN, M., Pathology
PERRONE, R., Medicine
PLAUT, A., Medicine
POLAK, J., Radiology
PORTNEY, K., Political Science
PREIS, D., Electrical and Computer Engineering
QUINTO, E., Mathematics
RABINOVICI, R., Surgery
RABSON, A., Pathology
RANKIN, C., Endodontics
REECE, R., Paediatrics
REED, J., Biology
REICHLIN, S., Medicine
REID, P., Classics
REITER, E., Paediatrics
REUBEN, S., Anaesthesiology
REUTER, K., Radiology
REYNOLDS, R., Anaesthesiology
RICHARD, M., Philosophy
RICHARDS, D., Economics
RICHMOND, J., Orthopaedic Surgery
RIDGE, J., Geology
ROAF, E., Anaesthesiology
ROBBINS, A., Public Health and Family Medicine
ROBERTS, P., Surgery
ROGERS, C., Mechanical Engineering
ROHRER, R., Surgery
ROMERO, C., German, Russian, Asian Languages and Literatures
ROMERO, L., Biology
ROSE, D., Medicine
ROSENBERG, I., Physiology

ROSENBERG, M., Oral and Maxillofacial Surgery
ROSENBERG, N., Pathology
ROSENBLATT, M., Physiology
ROWLAND, T., Paediatrics
RUBENSTEIN, J., Medicine
RUBY, L., Orthopaedic Surgery
RUSH, J., Clinical Sciences
RUSSELL, R., Medicine
SABIN, T., Neurology
SADEGHI-NEJAD, A., Paediatrics
SADOWSKY, N., Radiology
SAFAII, H., Pathology
SAHAGIAN, G., Physiology
SAIGAL, A., Mechanical Engineering
SAMO, R., Radiology
SANAYEI, M., Civil and Environmental Engineering
SAPERSTEIN, G., Environmental and Population Health
SAWKAT, A., Pharmacology and Experimental Therapeutics
SCHAEFER, E., Medicine
SCHALLER, J., Paediatrics
SCHLIEMANN, A., Education
SCHMIDT, K., Anaesthesiology
SCHNEPS, J., Physics and Astronomy
SCHOETZ, D., Surgery
SCHOLZ, F., Radiology
SCHREIBER, J., Paediatrics
SCHULTZ, M., Chemistry
SCHWARTZ, A., Clinical Sciences
SEDDON, J., Ophthalmology
SELKER, H., Medicine
SENELICK, L., Drama and Dance
SHADER, R., Pharmacology
SHAUGHNESSY, A., Public Health and Family Medicine
SHEN, E., Pathology
SHIKORA, S., Surgery
SHOEMAKER, C., Biomedical Sciences
SHUCART, W., Neurosurgery
SIEGEL, E., Biology
SILBERMAN, E., Psychiatry
SILVA, J., Medicine
SINGH, I., Prosthodontics and Operative Dentistry
SKIEST, D., Medicine
SLIWA, K., Physics and Astronomy
SMITH, G., Philosophy
SMITH, L., Obstetrics and Gynaecology
SMITH, T., Political Science
SNYDMAN, D., Medicine
SONENSCHEIN, A., Microbiology—Basic Science
SONNENSCHEIN, C., Anatomy and Cellular Biology
SORBERA, R., Oral and Maxillofacial Surgery
SORGER, K., Pathology
SOTO, A., Anatomy and Cellular Biology
SOUVAINE, D., Computer Science
SPOLAORE, E., Economics
STEARNS, N., Medicine
STECHENBERG, B., Paediatrics
STEER, M., Surgery
STELLER, M., Obstetrics and Gynaecology
STOLOW, R., Chemistry
STRAUSS, G., Medicine
STROM, J., Medicine
SUNG, N., Chemical Engineering
SYLVIA, W., Jr, Prosthodontics and Operative Dentistry
TALAMO, B., Neuroscience
TARLOV, S., Neuroscience
TAYLOR, H., Psychology
TEIXIDOR I BIGAS, M., Mathematics
TERES, D., Medicine
TERRES, G., Physiology
TERRONO, A., Orthopaedic Surgery
THEOHARIDES, T., Pharmacology and Experimental Therapeutics
THORLEY-LAWSON, D., Pathology
TICKLE-DEGNEN, L., Occupational Therapy
TILLMAN, H., General Dentistry
TISCHLER, A., Pathology
TOBIN, R., Physics and Astronomy

TRIMMER, B., Biology
TSICHLIS, P., Medicine
TUERK, I., Urology
TURKSOY-MARCUS, R., Obstetrics and Gynaecology
TURNER, R., Orthopaedic Surgery
TWITCHELL, T., Neurology
TZIPORI, S., Biomedical Sciences
UEDA, R., History
UMLAS, J., Pathology
VALAES, T., Paediatrics
VAN ETTEN, R., Medicine
VILENKIN, A., Physics and Astronomy
VOGEL, R., Civil and Environmental Engineering
WAIT, R., Surgery
WALT, D., Chemistry
WANKE, C., Medicine
WAX, F., Dermatology
WAZER, D., Radiation Oncology
WECHSLER, J., Art and Art History
WEILER, K., Education
WEINER, A., Oral Diagnostic
WEINSTOCK, J., Medicine
WEISS, R., Mathematics
WERTLEIB, D., Child Development
WIDMER, G., Biomedical Sciences
WILL KUO, L., Orthodontics
WILSON, I., Medicine
WILSON, J., English
WINN, P., History
WITTENBERG, S., Medicine
WLEZIEN, R., Mechanical Engineering
WOLF, M., Child Development
WOLFE, L., Paediatrics
WONG, J., Medicine
WORTIS, H., Pathology
WRIGHT, A., Microbiology—Basic Science
WU, J., Neurosurgery
YEE, A., Biochemistry
YUCEL, R., Radiology
ZAMENHOF, R., Radiation Oncology
ZINMAN, L., Urology

UNIVERSITY OF MASSACHUSETTS

225 Franklin St, 33rd Fl., Boston, MA 02110
333 S St, Suite 400, Shrewsbury, MA 01545-4169

Telephone: (617) 287-7100
Internet: www.massachusetts.edu

Founded 1863 as Massachusetts Agricultural College, present name 1947

Pres.: ROBERT L. CARET
Exec. Vice-Pres.: JAMES R. JULIAN
Sr Vice-Pres. for Academic Affairs, Student Affairs and Int. Relations: Dr MARCELLETTE G. WILLIAMS
Vice-Pres. for Admin. and Finance, Treas. and Controller: CHRISTINE M. WILDA
Vice-Pres. for Economic Devt: THOMAS CHMURA
Vice-Pres. for Information Services, Chief Information Officer and CEO for UMasOnline: DAVID GRAY
Vice-Pres. for Management and Fiscal Affairs and Treas.: STEPHEN LENHARDT
Vice-Pres. for Univ. Advancement: KATHERINE V. SMITH
Number of students: 60,000.

CONSTITUENT UNIVERSITIES

University of Massachusetts, Amherst
Amherst, MA 01003
Telephone: (413) 545-0111
Fax: (413) 545-2328
Internet: www.umass.edu

Founded 1863 as Massachusetts Agricultural College, present name and status 1947
State control
Academic year: September to June
Chancellor: Dr ROBERT C. HOLUB

Provost and Sr Vice-Chancellor for Academic Affairs: JAMES V. STAROS
Vice-Chancellor for Admin. and Finance: JAMES SHEEHAN
Vice-Chancellor for Devt and Alumni Relations: MICHAEL A. LETO
Vice Chancellor for Research and Engagement: MICHAEL MALONE
Vice-Chancellor for Student Affairs and Campus Life: JEAN KIM
Vice-Chancellor for Univ. Relations: JOHN KENNEDY
Dean of Students: ENKU GELAYE
Registrar: JOHN LENZI
Dir of Libraries: JAY SCHAFER
Library: 8m. vols
Number of teachers: 1,174 (full-time)
Number of students: 27,569
Publication: *The Massachusetts Review* (4 a year)

DEANS

College of Engineering: Dr THEODORE DJAFERIS
College of Humanities and Fine Arts: JULIA C. HAYES
College of Natural Resources and the Environment: STEVE GOODWIN
College of Natural Sciences and Mathematics: GEORGE M. LANGFORD
College of Social and Behavioral Sciences: ROBERT S. FELDMAN
Commonwealth College: Dr PRISCILLA M. CLARKSON
Graduate School: JOHN MULLIN
Isenberg School of Management: MARK A. FULLER
School of Education: CHRISTINE B. McCORMICK
School of Nursing: Dr STEPHEN J. CAVANAGH
School of Public Health and Health Sciences: C. MARJORIE AELION

ASSOCIATED INSTITUTE

Stockbridge School of Agriculture: Amherst, MA 01003; tel. (413) 545-2222; fax (413) 577-0242; e-mail stockbridgeschool@nre.umass.edu; internet www.umass.edu/stockbridge; f. 1918; Dir MARTHA G. BAKER.

University of Massachusetts, Boston

100 Morrissey Blvd, Boston, MA 02125-3393
Telephone: (617) 287-5000
Fax: (617) 265-6040
E-mail: enrollment.info@umb.edu
Internet: www.umb.edu
Founded 1852 as Girls' High School, present name and status 1982
State control
Academic year: September to June
Chancellor: J. KEITH MOTLEY
Provost and Sr Vice-Chancellor for Academic Affairs: WINSTON LANGLEY
Vice-Chancellor for Admin. and Finance: ELLEN M. O'CONNOR
Vice-Chancellor for Athletics and Recreation, Special Projects and Programs: CHARLIE TITUS
Vice-Chancellor for Enrollment Management: KATHLEEN S. TEEHAN
Vice-Chancellor for Student Affairs: PATRICK K. DAY
Vice-Chancellor for Univ. Advancement: GINA CAPPELLO
Library of 600,000 vols
Number of teachers: 1,038
Number of students: 15,454

DEANS

College of Education and Human Devt: FELICIA L. WILCZENSKI
College of Liberal Arts: EMILY McDERMOTT
College of Management: PHILIP L. QUAGLIERI

College of Nursing and Health Sciences: MARION WINFREY
College of Public and Community Service: ANNA MADISON
College of Science and Mathematics: ANDREW GROSOVSKY
Graduate Studies and Intercollegiate Programs: JOAN LIEM
John W. McCormack Graduate School of Policy Studies: STEPHEN CROSBY
University College: PHILIP DI SALVIO

University of Massachusetts, Dartmouth

285 Old Westport Rd, N Dartmouth, MA 02747-2300
Telephone: (508) 999-8000
Fax: (508) 999-8901
E-mail: admissions@umassd.edu
Internet: www.umassd.edu
Founded 1895
State control
Academic year: September to May
Chancellor: Dr JEAN F. MacCORMACK
Provost and Vice-Chancellor for Academic and Student Affairs: Dr JOHN W. FARRINGTON
Vice-Chancellor, Chief Operating Officer for Admin. and Fiscal Services: DEBORAH McLAUGHLIN
Dir of Undergraduate Admissions: MICHAEL LYNCH
Registrar: Dr CARNELL JONES, JR
Dean of Library Services: TERRANCE BURTON
Library of 457,879 vols
Number of teachers: 636 (380 full-time, 256 part-time)
Number of students: 9,225
Publications: *Portuguese Literary and Cultural Studies* (1 a year), *TEMPER* (1 a year)

DEANS

Charlton College of Business: Dr RICHARD PEGNETTER
College of Arts and Sciences: Dr WILLIAM HOGAN
College of Engineering: Dr ROBERT E. PECK
College of Nursing: Dr JAMES A. FAIN
College of Visual and Performing Arts: Dr ADRIAN TIÓ
Professional and Continuing Education: Dr JOY McGUIRL-HODLEY
School of Education, Public Policy and Civic Engagement: Dr ISMAEL RAMERIZ-SOTO
School of Law: Prof. MICHAEL G. HILLINGER
School of Marine Science and Technology: Dr STEVEN E. LOHRENZ

University of Massachusetts, Lowell

1 University Ave, Lowell, MA 01854
Telephone: (978) 934-4000
Fax: (978) 934-3000
Internet: www.uml.edu
Founded 1894 as Lowell Normal School, , present name and status 1991
State control
Academic year: September to June
Chancellor: MARTY MEEHAN
Exec. Vice-Chancellor: Dr JACQUELINE MOLONEY
Provost and Vice-Chancellor for Academic Affairs: Dr AHMED ABDELAL
Vice-Chancellor for Admin., Finance and Facilities: JOANNE YESTRAMSKI
Vice-Chancellor for Advancement: EDWARD CHIU
Vice-Chancellor for Univ. Relations: PATRICIA McCAFFERTY
Vice-Chancellor for Admin., Finance, Facilities and Technology: JOANNE YESTRAMSKI
Dean of Enrolment and Student Success: THOMAS TAYLOR

Dean of Student Affairs: LARRY SIEGEL
Registrar: PATRICIA A. DUFF
Library of 453,486 vols (incl. books, serials, microforms, audiovisual materials, e-books)
Number of teachers: 683 (473 full-time, 543 part-time)
Number of students: 15,431 (9,026 undergraduate, 3,702 graduate, 2,703 continuing education)
Publication: *New Solutions* (environmental and occupational health policy, 4 a year)

DEANS

Education: ANITA GREENWOOD
Engineering: JOHN TING
Fine Arts, Humanities and Social Sciences: NINA COPPENS
Health and Environment: SHORTIE McKINNEY
Marine Sciences: ROBERT GAMACHE
School of Management: KATHRYN CARTER
Sciences: ROBERT TAMARIN

University of Massachusetts Medical School

55 Lake Avenue N, Worcester, MA 01655
Telephone: (508) 856-2000
Fax: (508) 856-3629
E-mail: ummscommunications@umassmed.edu
Internet: www.umassmed.edu
Founded 1962
State control
Chancellor: Dr MICHAEL F. COLLINS
Vice-Chancellor: EDWARD J. KEOHANE
Vice-Chancellor for Admin. and Finance: ROBERT E. JENAL
Vice-Chancellor and Chief Operating Officer: JOYCE A. MURPHY
Vice-Chancellor for Devt: CHARLIE J. PAGNAM
Vice-Chancellor for Faculty Affairs: Dr LUANNE THORNDYKE
Vice-Chancellor for Operations: ROBERT E. JENAL
Vice-Chancellor for Univ. Relations: ALBERT SHERMAN
Dean and Exec. Deputy Chancellor: TERRY R. FLOTTE
Registrar: MICHAEL F. BAKER
Dir of Library Services: ELAINE R. MARTIN
Number of teachers: 810
Number of students: 2,683 (full-time)

DEANS

Graduate School of Biomedical Sciences: Dr ANTHONY CARRUTHERS (acting)
Graduate School of Nursing: Dr PAULETTE SEYMOUR ROUTE
School of Medicine: Dr TERRY R. FLOTTE

WELLESLEY COLLEGE

106 Central St, Wellesley, MA 02481
Telephone: (781) 283-1000
Fax: (781) 283-3650
E-mail: admission@wellesley.edu
Internet: www.wellesley.edu
Founded 1870
Private control
Liberal arts college for women; depts of Africana studies, anthropology, art, astronomy, biological sciences, chemistry, classical studies, computer science, E Asian languages and literatures, economics
Pres.: H. KIM BOTTOMLY
Provost and Dean of College: ANDREW SHENNAN
Vice-Pres. for Admin. and Planning: PATRICIA M. BYRNE
Vice-Pres. for Finance and Treas.: ANDREW B. EVANS
Dean of Admissions: JENNIFER DESJARLAIS

Dean of Students: DEBRA DeMEIS (acting)
Registrar and Asst Dean of College: CAROL SHANMUGARATNAM
Chief Information Officer, Library and Technology Services: GANESAN RAVISHANKER
Library: 1.68m. vols, 32,000 sound and video recordings, 16,000 maps
Number of teachers: 326 (251 full-time, 75 part-time)
Number of students: 2,344 (2,190 full-time, 154 part-time)

WENTWORTH INSTITUTE OF TECHNOLOGY

550 Huntington Ave, Boston, MA 02115-5998
Telephone: (617) 989-4590
Fax: (617) 989-4591
E-mail: admissions@wit.edu
Internet: www.wit.edu
Founded 1904
Private control
Academic year: August to May
Pres.: Dr ZORICA PANTIC
Vice-Pres. of Academic Affairs and Provost: RUSSELL PINIZZOTTO
Vice-Pres. for Finance: BOB TOTINO
Vice-Pres. for Enrolment Management and Student Affairs: KEIKO BROOMHEAD
Vice-Pres. for Institutional Advancement: BRENDA CROSS-SANCHEZ
Registrar: MATTHEW BURKE
Library Dir: WALTER PUNCH
Library of 75,000 vols
Number of teachers: 139 (full-time)
Number of students: 3,892
Publication: *Wentworth Magazine* (2 a year)

DEANS

College of Architecture, Design and Construction Management: GLENN WIGGINS
College of Arts and Sciences: PATRICK HAFFORD
College of Engineering and Technology: FREDERICK DRISCOLL
College of Professional and Continuing Education: LARRY CARR

WESTERN NEW ENGLAND UNIVERSITY

1215 Wilbraham Rd, Springfield, MA 01119
Telephone: (413) 782-3111
Fax: (413) 782-1746
E-mail: ugradmis@wne.edu
Internet: www.wne.edu
Founded 1919
Private control
Pres.: ANTHONY S. CAPRIO
Provost and Vice-Pres. for Academic Affairs: JERRY A. HIRSCH
Vice-Pres. for Advancement: BEVERLY DWIGHT
Vice-Pres. for Enrolment Management: CHARLES R. POLLOCK
Vice-Pres. for Finance and Admin.: WILLIAM KELLEHER
Vice-Pres. for Marketing and External Affairs: BARBARA A. CAMPANELLA
Vice-Pres. for Student Affairs and Dean of Students: JEANNE HART-STEFFES
Assoc. Dean for Library and Information Resources: PAT NEWCOMBE
Library of 783,000 vols
Number of teachers: 205 (full-time)
Number of students: 3,700

DEANS

College of Arts and Sciences: SAEED GHAHRAMANI
College of Business: JULIE SICILIANO
College of Engineering: CARL RATHMANN
College of Pharmacy: EVAN ROBINSON

School of Law: ARTHUR R. GAUDIO

WESTFIELD STATE UNIVERSITY

POB 1630, Westfield, MA 01086-1630
577 Western Ave, Westfield, MA 01086
Telephone: (413) 572-5300
E-mail: admissions@wsc.ma.edu
Internet: www.wsc.ma.edu
Founded 1838
State control

Majors in art, biology, business management, computer information systems, computer science, criminal justice, economics, education, English, environmental sciences, French, general science, history, mass communication, mathematics, movement science, multicultural and ethnic studies, music, philosophy, political science, psychology, regional planning, social work, sociology, Spanish, theatre arts, women's studies
Pres.: EVAN DOBELLE
Vice-Pres. for Academic Affairs: Dr LIZ PRESTON
Vice-Pres. for Admin. and Finance: JERRY HAYES
Vice-Pres. for Advancement and College Relations: ROBERT ZIOMEK
Vice-Pres. for Enrolment Management: CAROL PERSSON
Vice-Pres. for Student Affairs: Dr CARLTON PICKRON
Registrar: JOHN OHOTNICKY
Library Dir: THOMAS RAFFENSPERGER
Library of 136,000 vols
Number of teachers: 170
Number of students: 3,200

WHEATON COLLEGE

26 East Main St, Norton, MA 02766-2322
Telephone: (508) 286-8200
Fax: (508) 285-8276
E-mail: info@wheatoncollege.edu
Internet: www.wheatoncollege.edu
Founded 1834 as female seminary
Private control

Depts of African studies, African American studies, American studies, ancient studies, anthropology, art history, studio art, Asian studies, astronomy, biochemistry, biology, chemistry, classics, computer science, devt studies, diaspora studies, economics, education, English, environmental science, environmental studies, family studies, French, German, Greek, Hispanic studies, history, int. relations, Italian studies, Latin, Latin American studies, legal studies, management, mathematics, mathematics and computer science, mathematics and economics, music, philosophy, physics and astronomy, political science, psychobiology, psychology, public policy studies, religion, Russian and Russian studies, sociology, statistics, theatre studies and dance, urban studies, women's studies
Pres.: RONALD A. CRUTCHER
Provost: LINDA EISENMANN
Vice-Pres. for College Advancement: MARY M. CASEY
Vice-Pres. for Enrollment and Marketing: GAIL BERSON
Vice-Pres. for Finance and Admin.: (vacant)
Vice-Pres. for Student Affairs and Dean of Students: LEE BURDETTE WILLIAMS
Registrar and Dean of Academic Systems: PATRICIA BROWN SANTILLI
Dir of Library Collns and Access: GLORIA L. BARKER
Library of 352,700 vols
Number of teachers: 150 (full-time)
Number of students: 1,600

Publications: *Quarterly Magazine*, *Wheaton Matters*.

WHEELOCK COLLEGE

200 The Riverway, Boston, MA 02215
Telephone: (617) 879-2000
Fax: (617) 879-2276
E-mail: registrar@wheelock.edu
Internet: www.wheelock.edu
Founded 1888 as Chauncy-Hall School
Private control
Academic year: September to May
Pres.: JACKIE JENKINS-SCOTT
Vice-Pres. for Academic Affairs: Dr JULIE E. WOLLMAN
Vice-Pres. and Chief Financial Officer: ANNE MARIE MARTORANA
Vice-Pres. for Campus Life and Information Services: ROY SCHIFILLITI
Vice-Pres. for Enrolment Management and Student Success and Chief Diversity Officer: Dr ADRIAN K. HAUGABROOK
Vice-Pres. for Institutional Advancement and Devt: LINDA WELTER
Dean of Students: BARBARA MORGAN
Dir of Academic Resources and Library: BRENDA ECSEDY
Library of 85,000 vols
Number of teachers: 65 (full-time)
Number of students: 1,237
Publication: *Magazine*

DEANS

School of Arts and Sciences: Dr SHIRLEY MALONE-FENNER
School of Education, Social Work, Child Life and Family: DONNA McKIBBENS

WILLIAMS COLLEGE

Hopkins Hall, 880 Main St, Williamstown, MA 01267
Telephone: (413) 597-3131
E-mail: admission@williams.edu
Internet: www.williams.edu
Founded 1793
Private control

Depts of American studies, anthropology, art, Asian studies, astronomy, astrophysics, biology, chemistry, Chinese, classics, comparative literature, computer science, economics, English, French, geosciences, German, history, Japanese, literary studies, mathematics and statistics, music, philosophy, physics, political economy, political science, psychology, religion, Russian, sociology, Spanish, theatre, women's and gender studies
Pres.: ADAM FAULK
Provost: WILLIAM J. LENHART
Vice-Pres. for Finance and Admin. and Treas.: FREDERICK W. PUDDESTER
Vice-Pres. for Operations: STEPHEN P. KLASS
Vice-Pres. for Strategic Planning and Institutional Diversity: MIKE REED
Dean of College: KAREN MILL
Dean of Faculty: WILLIAM G. WAGNER
Dir of Admission: DICK NESBITT
Registrar: CHARLES R. TOOMAJIAN, JR
Librarian: DAVID M. PILACHOWSKI
Library of 885,000 vols, 61,000 rare books, 30,500 paper and e-periodicals, 480,000 microtexts, 30,000 sound recordings, 11,000 video cassettes, 368,000 govt documents
Number of teachers: 320
Number of students: 2,053

WORCESTER POLYTECHNIC INSTITUTE

100 Institute Rd, Worcester, MA 01609-2280
Telephone: (508) 831-5000

Fax: (508) 831-5753
E-mail: president@wpi.edu
Internet: www.wpi.edu

Founded 1865 as Worcester Co Free Institute of Industrial Science
Private control
Academic year: August to May

Pres.: DENNIS D. BERKEY
Exec. Vice-Pres. and Chief Financial Officer: JEFFREY S. SOLOMON
Provost and Vice-Pres. for Academic Affairs: ERIC OVERSTROM
Sr Vice-Pres. for Enrolment and Institutional Strategy: KRISTIN TICHENOR
Vice-Pres. for Student Affairs and Campus Life: JANET RICHARDSON
Chief Information Officer: DEBORAH SCOTT
Registrar: HEATHER L. JACKSON
Dean of Library Services: TRACEY LEGER-HORNBY

Library of 225,000 vols
Number of teachers: 324
Number of students: 5,303 (3,746 undergraduate, 1,557 graduate)

DEANS

Arts and Sciences: Dr KAREN KASHMANIAN OATES
Corporate and Professional Education: STEPHEN P. FLAVIN
Engineering: SELÇUK GÜÇERI
School of Business: Dr MARK RICE

WORCESTER STATE UNIVERSITY

486 Chandler St, Worcester, MA 01602-2597
Telephone: (508) 929-8000
Fax: (508) 929-8191
E-mail: admissions@worcester.edu
Internet: www.worcester.edu

Founded 1874 as Worcester Normal School, present name and status 2010

Depts of biology, business admin. and economics, communication, computer science, criminal justice, education, health sciences, history and political science, languages and literature, mathematics, nursing, philosophy, physical and earth sciences, psychology, sociology, visual and performing arts
Private control
Academic year: September to May

Pres.: BARRY M. MALONEY
Vice-Pres. for Academic Affairs: Dr CHARLES CULLUM
Vice-Pres. for Admin. and Finance: KATHY EICHELROTH
Vice-Pres. for Institutional Advancement: THOMAS M. McNAMARA
Vice-Pres. for Student Affairs: Dr SIBYL BROWNLEE
Registrar: JULIE A. CHAFFEE
Library Dir: JAMES E. HOGAN

Library of 149,662 vols
Number of teachers: 411
Number of students: 5,369

Publications: *Journal of Graduate Research* (1 a year), *Worcester Statement* (2 a year).

MICHIGAN

ADRIAN COLLEGE

110 S Madison St, Adrian, MI 49221-2575
Telephone: (517) 265-5161
Fax: (517) 264-3856
E-mail: admissions@adrian.edu
Internet: www.adrian.edu

Founded 1859
Private control
Academic year: September to May

Depts of accounting and business, art and design, biology, chemistry, communication arts and sciences, earth science, economics, English, environmental science/studies, exercise science/physical education, history, interior design, mathematics, modern languages and cultures, music, philosophy/religion, physics, political science, psychology, sociology, social work and criminal justice, teacher education, theatre

Pres.: Dr JEFFREY R. DOCKING
Exec. Vice-Pres.: CYNTHIA BEAUBIEN
Vice-Pres. and Dean for Academic Affairs: Dr AGNES CALDWELL
Vice-Pres. for Devt: RONALD L. REEVES
Vice-Pres. for Enrolment: FRANK J. HRIBAR
Dean for Students: KRISTI HOTTENSTEIN
Registrar: BRIDGETTE WINSLOW
Head Librarian: DAVID CRUSE

Library of 150,000 vols
Number of teachers: 71
Number of students: 1,650

ALBION COLLEGE

611 E Porter St, Albion, MI 49224
Telephone: (517) 629-1000
Fax: (517) 629-0476
E-mail: admission@albion.edu
Internet: www.albion.edu

Founded 1835
Private control
Academic year: August to May

Depts of anthropology and sociology, art, art history, athletic training, biology, chemistry, computer science, earth science, economics and management, English, ethnic studies, French, geological sciences, German, history, international studies, mathematics, music, philosophy, physical education, physics, political science, psychology, public policy, religious studies, Spanish, speech communication, theatre, women's and gender studies

Pres.: Dr DONNA RANDALL
Provost: Dr SUSAN P. CONNER
Vice-Pres. for Finance and Admin.: Dr MICHAEL L. FRANDSEN
Vice-Pres. for Institutional Advancement and Interim Vice-Pres. for Enrolment Management: Dr JOSHUA D. MERCHANT
Vice-Pres. for Student Affairs and Dean of Students: Dr SALLY WALKER
Dir for Admission: MANDY DUBIEL
Registrar: Dr ANDREW M. DUNHAM
Dir for Library: MICHAEL VAN HOUTEN
Dir for Library: CLAUDIA DIAZ

Library of 357,416 vols, 19,605 microforms, 51,316 video cassettes and audiovisual items, 124,171 e-books
Number of teachers: 130
Number of students: 1,514

Publication: *Io Triumphe!* (print and online (www.albion.edu/ia/alumniengagement/io-triumphe)).

ALMA COLLEGE

614 W Superior St, Alma, MI 48801
Telephone: (989) 463-7111
Fax: (989) 463-7057
E-mail: admissions@alma.edu
Internet: www.alma.edu

Founded 1886
Private control

Depts of health sciences, humanities, natural sciences and social sciences
Pres.: Dr JEFF ABERNATHY
Provost and Vice-Pres. for Academic Affairs: Dr MICHAEL L. SELMON
Vice-Pres. for Advancement: CAROL HYBLE
Vice-Pres. for Enrolment: Dr KAREN S. KLUMPP
Vice-Pres. for Student Life: NICHOLAS A. PICCOLO
Dir for Admissions: BOB GARCIA
Registrar: SUSAN M. DEEL
Library Dir: CAROL ZEILE

Library of 246,000 vols, 1,200 periodicals
Number of teachers: 139 (87 full-time, 52 part-time)
Number of students: 1,417

ANDREWS UNIVERSITY

Berrien Springs, MI 49104
Telephone: (269) 471-7771
Fax: (269) 471-3228
E-mail: enroll@andrews.edu
Internet: www.andrews.edu

Founded 1874, present name 1960
Private control
Academic year: August to May

Pres.: Dr NIELS-ERIK ANDREASEN
Provost: Dr ANDREA LUXTON
Vice-Pres. for Enrolment Management: STEPHEN PAYNE
Vice-Pres. for Financial Admin.: LAWRENCE SCHALK
Vice-Pres. for Student Life: FRANCES FAEHNER
Vice-Pres. for Univ. Advancement: DAVID A. FAEHNER
Gen. Counsel: BRENT G. T. GERATY
Registrar: Dr EMILIO GARCIA-MARENKO
Dean for Libraries: LAWRENCE W. ONSAGER

Library of 743,694 vols, 2,800 periodicals
Number of teachers: 301
Number of students: 3,547

Publications: *Andrews University Seminary Studies* (2 a year), *Christian Leadership Journal*, *Focus* (4 a year), *Journal for Research in Christian Education*, *Missions Journal*

DEANS

College of Arts and Sciences: KEITH E. MATTINGLY
College of Technology: VERLYN BENSON
School of Architecture: CAREY CARSCALLEN
School of Business Administration: ALLEN STEMBRIDGE
School of Education: JAMES R. JEFFERY
School of Graduate Studies and Research: CHRISTON ARTHUR
SDA Theological Seminary: DENIS FORTIN

AQUINAS COLLEGE

1607 Robinson Rd, SE, Grand Rapids, MI 49506-1799
Telephone: (616) 632-8900
Fax: (616) 732-4589
E-mail: admissions@aquinas.edu
Internet: www.aquinas.edu

Founded 1886
Private control
Academic year: August to May (2 semesters)

College of liberal arts
Pres.: Dr C. JUAN OLIVAREZ
Provost and Dean for Faculty: Dr CHARLES D. GUNNOE, JR
Vice-Pres for Enrolment Management: PAULA T. MEEHAN
Vice-Pres for Institutional Advancement: GREGORY W. MCALEENAN
Registrar: CECELIA MESLER
Dir for Library: FRANCINE PAOLINI
Dir for Library: SHELLIE JEFFRIES
Library of 110,000 vols, 991 periodicals and over 16,000 non-print items
Number of teachers: 192 (90 full-time, 102 part-time)
Number of students: 2,200

Publications: *Aquinas Magazine* (4 a year), *Presidential Perspectives* (2 a year).

BAKER COLLEGE

1050 W Bristol Rd, Flint, MI 48507
Telephone: (810) 766-4250
Fax: (810) 766-4279
Internet: www.baker.edu

Founded 1911, present status 1985
Private control
Academic year: September to August

Areas of study: business, education, engineering and technology, health, human service, office administration and computers; 9 campuses, 6 br. locations and online programmes
Pres. and CEO: F. JAMES CUMMINS
Vice-Pres. for Academics: Dr CANDACE A. JOHNSON
Vice-Pres. for Career Services: YVONNE LANGLEY
Vice-Pres. for Student Services: GERALD MCCARTY, II
Registrar: ROBERT MARTIN
Number of students: 43,000

CALVIN COLLEGE

3201 Burton, SE, Grand Rapids, MI 49546
Telephone: (616) 526-6000
Fax: (616) 526-8551
E-mail: info@calvin.edu
Internet: www.calvin.edu

Founded 1876
Private control
Academic year: September to May

Pres.: Dr GAYLEN J. BYKER
Provost: CLAUDIA DeVRIES BEVERSLUIS
Vice-Pres. for Admin., Finance and Information Services: HENRY E. DeVRIES, II
Vice-Pres. for Advancement: KEN ERFFMEYER
Vice-Pres. for Enrolment Management: RUSSELL BLOEM
Vice-Pres. for Student Life: SHIRLEY VOGELZANG HOOGSTRA
Registrar: THOMAS STEENWYK
Dir for Library: GLENN A. REMELTS

Library of 648,581 vols, 143,072 bound journal vols, 28,017 e-journals, 808,547 microforms, 12,956 DVDs, audio cassettes and CD-ROMs, 1,537 journal subscriptions
Number of teachers: 388
Number of students: 3,967

Publication: *Fides et Historia* (2 a year).

CALVIN THEOLOGICAL SEMINARY

3233 Burton St, SE, Grand Rapids, MI 49546
Telephone: (616) 957-6036
Fax: (616) 957-6101
E-mail: admission@calvinseminary.edu
Internet: www.calvinseminary.edu

Founded 1876
Private control

Areas of study: divinity, ministry, theological studies
Pres.: Rev. JULIUS PLANTINGA MEDENBLIK
Vice-Pres. for Academic Affairs: (vacant)
Dean for Academic Programs: RONALD FEENSTRA
Dir for Admissions: MATTHEW COOKE
Dean for Faculty: LYLE BIERMA
Registrar: JOAN BEELEN
Librarian: PAUL FIELDS
Number of teachers: 30
Number of students: 300 (full-time)

Publications: *Calvin Theological Journal* (2 a year), *Calvin Theological Seminary Forum* (3 a year), *Stromata* (1 a year).

CENTRAL MICHIGAN UNIVERSITY

Mount Pleasant, MI 48859
Telephone: (989) 774-4000
Fax: (989) 774-3665
E-mail: cmuadmit@cmich.edu
Internet: www.cmich.edu

Founded 1892
State control
Academic year: August to May

Pres.: Dr GEORGE E. ROSS
Provost and Exec. Vice-Pres.: E. GARY SHAPIRO
Vice-Pres. for Devt and External Relations: KATHLEEN WILBUR
Vice-Pres. for Finance and Admin. Services: DAVID A. BURDETTE
Registrar: KAREN HUTSLAR
Dean for Students: TONY VOLSIN
Dean for Libraries: THOMAS J. MOORE

Library of 1,025,000 vols, 3,570 periodical and newspaper subscriptions, 1,320,000 microforms
Number of teachers: 751 (full-time)
Number of students: 28,389

Publication: *Michigan Historical Review* (2 a year)

DEANS
College of Business Administration: CHARLES CRESPY
College of Communication and Fine Arts: SALMA GHANEM
College of Education and Human Services: KATHRYN KOCH
College of Graduate Studies: ROGER COLES
College of Humanities and Social and Behavioural Sciences: PAMELA GATES
College of Medicine: ERNIE YODER
College of Science and Technology: Dr IAN R. DAVISON
Herbert H. and Grace A. Dow College of Health Professions: CHRISTOPHER D. INGERSOLL

CLEARY UNIVERSITY

3601 Plymouth Rd, Ann Arbor, MI 48105
Telephone: (734) 332-4477
Fax: (734) 332-4646
E-mail: admissions@cleary.edu
Internet: www.cleary.edu

Founded 1883 as Cleary School of Penmanship, present name and status 2002
Private control
Academic year: September to June

Campus at Howell; extension sites at Dearborn Heights and Flint

Pres. and CEO: THOMAS P. SULLIVAN
Provost and Vice-Pres. for Academic Affairs: Dr VINCENT P. LINDER
Dir for Univ. Libraries: JANE ELLEN INNES
Number of teachers: 105
Number of students: 1,000

DEANS
College of Applied Business Science: CLYDE RIVARD
College of Business Innovation and Applied Technology: DAWN MARKELL
College of Graduate Studies: Dr SADHANA ALANGAR
College of Management: DAVID CASTLEGRANT

COLLEGE FOR CREATIVE STUDIES

201 E Kirby, Detroit, MI 48202-4034
Telephone: (313) 664-7400
Fax: (313) 827-2739
E-mail: admissions@collegeforcreativestudies.edu
Internet: www.collegeforcreativestudies.edu

Founded 1906 as Detroit Soc. of Arts and Crafts, present name 2001
Private control
Academic year: September to May

Areas of study: advertising design, crafts, fine arts, graphic design, illustration, photography, product design, transportation design, liberal arts
Pres.: RICHARD L. ROGERS
Vice-Pres. for Admin. and Finance: ANNE BECK
Vice-Pres. for Institutional Advancement: NINA HOLDEN
Dean for Enrolment Services: JULIE HINGELBERG
Dean for College: IMRE MOLNAR
Registrar: NADINE HAGOORT
Librarian: BETH WALKER

Library of 40,000 vols, 250 periodicals, 120,000 images, 90,000 slides
Number of teachers: 250
Number of students: 1,339

CONCORDIA UNIVERSITY—ANN ARBOR

4090 Geddes Rd, Ann Arbor, MI 48105
Telephone: (734) 995-7300
Fax: (734) 995-4610
E-mail: admission@cuaa.edu
Internet: www.cuaa.edu

Founded 1963 as Concordia Lutheran Junior College, present status 1976, present name 2001
Private control
Academic year: September to May

CEO: Dr RUSSELL NICHOLS
Pres.: RANDALL W. LUECKE (acting)
Vice-Pres. for Academic Affairs: Dr ROSS STUEBER
Dir for Admissions: BENJAMIN D. LIMBACK
Registrar: COLLEEN CLELAND
Dir for Library Services: BRENDA BURROUGHS
Number of teachers: 47
Number of students: 770

DEANS
School of Arts and Sciences: Dr ROBERT MCCORMICK
School of Education: Dr DENNIS GENIG

CORNERSTONE UNIVERSITY

1001 E Beltline Ave NE, Grand Rapids, MI
49525-5897

Telephone: (616) 949-5300
Fax: (616) 222-1418
E-mail: admissions@cornerstone.edu
Internet: www.cornerstone.edu

Founded 1941, present name and status 1999
Private control
Academic year: August to May

Campuses in Kalamazoo and Zeeland; Asia
Baptist Theological Seminary in Singapore;
Grand Rapids Theological Seminary in Min-
nesota; divs of Bible, business, communica-
tion and media studies, fine arts, history and
social science, humanities, kinesiology, reli-
gion and minstry, science and mathematics,
teacher education
Chancellor: Dr W. WILBERT WELCH
Pres.: Dr JOSEPH M. STOWELL, III
Provost: Dr RICK OSTRANDER
Exec. Vice-Pres.: MARC FOWLER
Sr Vice-Pres. for Univ. Advancement: WIL-
LIAM KNOTT
Vice-Pres. and Academic Dean for Grand
Rapids Theological Seminary: Dr JOHN
VERBERKMOES
Registrar: GAIL DUHON
Library Dir: FRED SWEET
Number of teachers: 64
Number of students: 2,600 (1,800 under-
graduate, 800 graduate)
Publication: *Cornerstone Magazine* (1 a
year).

CRANBROOK ACADEMY OF ART

POB 801, 39221 Woodward Ave, Bloomfield
Hills, MI 48303-0801

Telephone: (248) 645-3300
Fax: (248) 646-0046
E-mail: caaadmissions@cranbrook.edu
Internet: www.cranbrookart.edu

Founded 1904
Private control
Academic year: September to May

Divs of 2D design, 3D design, architecture,
ceramics, fiber, metalsmithing, painting,
photography, print media, sculpture
Dir: REED KROLOFF
Dean for Admissions and Registrar: KATHAR-
INE WILLMAN
Library Dir: JUDY DYKI
Library of 25,000 vols
Number of teachers: 10 (full-time)
Number of students: 150

DAVENPORT UNIVERSITY

415 East Fulton, Grand Rapids, MI 49503

Telephone: (616) 451-3511
Fax: (616) 732-1142
E-mail: info@davenport.edu
Internet: www.davenport.edu

Founded 1866 as Grand Rapids Business
College, present name 2000
Private control
Academic year: September to August

30 Campuses throughout Michigan and N
Indiana
Pres.: RICHARD J. PAPPAS
Exec. Vice-Pres. for Academics and Provost:
LINDA RINKER
Exec. Vice-Pres. for Advancement: DENNIS
WASHINGTON
Exec. Vice-Pres. for Enrolment and Student
Services: LARRY POLSELLI
Exec. Vice-Pres. for Univ. Relations and
Communications: KIM BRUYN
Exec. Dir for Library: SALLY PAGE
Number of teachers: 1,200

Number of students: 13,000

DEANS

College of Arts and Sciences: Dr TOM LONE-
RGAN
College of Health Professions: KAREN DALEY
College of Technology: MICHAEL CLANCY
Donald W. Maine College of Business: IRENE
BEMBENISTA

EASTERN MICHIGAN UNIVERSITY

18 Welch, Ypsilanti, MI 48197

Telephone: (734) 487-1849
Fax: (734) 487-7170
E-mail: undergraduate.admissions@emich
.edu
Internet: www.emich.edu

Founded 1849 as Michigan State Normal
School, present name and status 1959
State control
Academic year: September to April

Pres.: Dr SUSAN W. MARTIN
Provost and Vice-Pres. for Academic Affairs:
(vacant)
Vice Pres. For Advancement: TOM STEVICK
Vice-Pres. for Student Affairs and Enroll-
ment Management: BERNICE LINDKE
Registrar: (vacant)
Dean for Library: TARA LYNN FULTON
Library of 2,000,000 vols, 129,847 periodicals
Number of teachers: 700 (full-time)
Number of students: 23,000

DEANS

College of Arts and Science: THOMAS VENNER
College of Business: DAVID MIELKE
College of Education: JANN JOSEPH
College of Health and Human Services:
MURALI NAIR
College of Technology: MORELL BOONE
Graduate School: DEB deLASKI-SMITH

FERRIS STATE UNIVERSITY

1201 S State St, CSS 301, Big Rapids, MI
49307

Telephone: (231) 591-2000
Fax: (231) 591-3944
E-mail: admissions@ferris.edu
Internet: www.ferris.edu

Founded 1884
State control
Academic year: August to May

Pres.: DAVID L. EISLER
Provost and Vice-Pres. for Academic Affairs:
FRITZ ERICKSON
Vice-Pres. for Admin. and Finance: JERRY L.
SCOBY
Vice-Pres. for Diversity and Inclusion: Dr
DAVID PILGRIM
Vice-Pres. for Student Affairs: Dr DANIEL
BURCHAM
Vice-Pres. for Univ. Advancement and Mar-
keting: JOHN WILLEY
Dean for Library Systems and Operations:
LEAH MONGER
Library of 370,000 vols and periodicals,
45,000 e-journals, newspapers and maga-
zines
Number of teachers: 561 (full-time)
Number of students: 14,381

DEANS

College of Allied Health Sciences: Dr JULIE
COON
College of Arts and Sciences: KAREN STRASSER
College of Business: Dr DAVID M. NICOL
College of Education and Human Services:
Dr MICHELLE A. JOHNSTON
College of Engineering Technology: Dr RON
MCKEAN
College of Pharmacy: Dr STEPHEN DURST

Michigan College of Optometry: Dr MICHAEL
CRON
University College: Dr WILLIAM POTTER

FINLANDIA UNIVERSITY

601 Quincy St, Hancock, MI 49930

Telephone: (906) 482-5300
Fax: (906) 487-7509
E-mail: admissions@finlandia.edu
Internet: www.finlandia.edu

Founded 1896
Private control
Academic year: August to July (3 semesters)

Pres.: Dr PHILIP R. JOHNSON
Exec. Vice-Pres. for Academic and Student
Affairs: TYANN LINDELL
Exec. Vice-Pres. for External Affairs and
Chief Advancement Officer: DUANE AHO
Univ. Registrar: EVELYN GOKE
Head Librarian: BETH MARTIN
Library of 50,000 vols, 300 periodicals, 500
video cassettes, 13,000 e-books
Number of students: 500
Publication: *the Bridge* (3 a year)

DEANS

College of Health Sciences: Dr FREDI DE
YAMPERT
International School of Art and Design:
DENISE VANDEVILLE
International School of Business: Prof. TERRY
MONSON
Suomi College of Arts and Sciences: Dr
CHRISTINE O'NEIL

GRACE BIBLE COLLEGE

POB 910, 1011 Aldon St, SW, Grand Rapids,
MI 49509

Telephone: (616) 538-2330
Fax: (616) 538-0599
E-mail: info@gbcol.edu
Internet: www.gbcol.edu

Founded 1939 as Milwaukee Bible Institute,
present name 1961
Private control
Academic year: August to May

Pres.: Dr KEN B. KEMPER
Vice-Pres. for Academics: PAUL R. SWEET
Vice-Pres. for Community Life: BRIAN P.
SHERSTAD
Dir for Enrolment: KEVIN GILLIAM
Dir for Library: KATHY MOLENKAMP
Number of teachers: 29
Number of students: 149

Publication: *The Journey*.

GRAND VALLEY STATE UNIVERSITY

1 Campus Dr., Allendale, MI 49401-9403

Telephone: (616) 331-5000
E-mail: admissions@gvsu.edu
Internet: www.gvsu.edu

Founded 1960
State control
Academic year: August to April

Campuses at Muskegon, Holland, Grand
Rapids and Traverse City (Michigan)
Pres.: Dr THOMAS J. HAAS
Provost and Vice-Pres. for Academic Affairs:
Dr GAYLE R. DAVIS
Vice-Provost for Student Affairs and Dean
for Students: Dr H. BART MERKLE
Vice-Pres. for Devt: MARIBETH G. WARDROP
Vice-Pres. for Finance and Admin.: JIM
BACHMEIER
Vice-Pres. for Inclusion and Equity: Dr
JEANNE J. ARNOLD
Vice-Pres. for Univ. Relations: MATTHEW E.
MCLOGAN
Univ. Counsel: THOMAS A. BUTCHER

Registrar: LYNN BLUE
Dean for Univ. Libraries: LEE VAN ORSDEL
Library of 750,000 vols, 557,000 e-journals and books
Number of teachers: 837
Number of students: 24,662

DEANS

Brooks College of Interdisciplinary Studies: Dr WENDY J. WENNER
College of Community and Public Service: Dr GEORGE GRANT, JR
College of Education: Dr ELAINE COLLINS
College of Health Professions: Dr ROY H. OLSSON, JR
College of Liberal Arts and Sciences: Dr FREDERICK J. ANTCZAK
Graduate Studies: JEFFREY POTTEIGER
Kirkhof College of Nursing: Dr CYNTHIA A. MCCURREN
Padnos College of Engineering and Computing: Dr PAUL D. PLOTKOWSKI
Seidman College of Business: Dr H. JAMES WILLIAMS

GREAT LAKES CHRISTIAN COLLEGE

6211 W Willow Highway, Lansing, MI 48917
Telephone: (517) 321-0242
Fax: (517) 321-5902
E-mail: glcc@glcc.edu
Internet: www.glcc.edu
Founded 1949 as Great Lakes Bible College, present name 1992
Private control
Academic year: August to May

Areas of study: Bible/theology, Christian education, Christian ministries, cross-cultural ministry, family life education, history, interpersonal and organizational communication, music, psychology/counselling, youth ministry
Pres.: LAWRENCE L. CARTER
Vice-Pres. for Academic Affairs: DAVID RICHARDS
Vice-Pres. for Enrolment Management: LLOYD SCHARER
Vice-Pres. for Institutional Advancement: PHILIP E. BEAVERS
Dean for Student Affairs: BETSY CARTER
Registrar: BRIAN SLENSKI
Dir for Library Services: JAMES ORME
Library of 52,000 vols, 20,000 e-books
Number of teachers: 14
Number of students: 192

HILLSDALE COLLEGE

33 E College St, Hillsdale, MI 49242
Telephone: (517) 437-7341
Fax: (517) 437-3923
E-mail: admissions@hillsdale.edu
Internet: www.hillsdale.edu
Founded 1844
Private control
Areas of study: accounting, art, biology, chemistry, classical studies, computational mathematics, economics, education (elementary and secondary), English, financial management, French, German, history, marketing management, mathematics, music, philosophy, physical education, physics, political science, psychology, religion, Spanish, speech, theatre
Pres.: LARRY P. ARNN
Provost: DAVID M. WHALEN
Vice-Pres. for Admin.: RICHARD PÉWÉ
Vice-Pres. for External Affairs: DOUGLAS JEFFREY
Vice-Pres. for Institutional Advancement: JOHN CERVINI
Vice-Pres. for Student Affairs: DIANE PHILIPP
Dir for Admissions: JEFFREY S. LANTIS

Registrar: DOUGLAS MCARTHUR
Library Dir: DAN KNOCH
Library of 300,000 vols, 1,000 e-books, 61,000 microforms, 8,000 audio and visual items, 1,600 journals
Number of teachers: 115
Number of students: 1,400
Publication: *Imprimis* (12 a year).

HOPE COLLEGE

POB 9000, 69 E 10th St, Holland, MI 49422-9000
Telephone: (616) 395-7000
Fax: (616) 395-7922
E-mail: admissions@hope.edu
Internet: www.hope.edu
Founded 1866
Private control
Academic year: August to May
Pres.: Dr JAMES E. BULTMAN
Provost: Dr R. RICHARD RAY, JR
Vice-Pres. and Chief Financial Officer: TOM BYLSMA
Vice-Pres. for Admissions: WILLIAM C. VAN-DERBILT
Vice-Pres. for Student Devt and Dean for Students: Dr RICHARD FROST
Registrar: CAROL DE JONG
Dir for Libraries: KELLY JACOBSMA
Library of 370,000
Number of teachers: 203
Number of students: 3,230
Publication: *Opus* (2 a year)

DEANS

Arts and Humanities: Dr WILLIAM D. REYNOLDS
Natural and Applied Sciences: Dr MOSES N. F. LEE
Social Sciences: Dr SCOTT VANDER STOEP

KALAMAZOO COLLEGE

1200 Academy St, Kalamazoo, MI 49006-3295
Telephone: (269) 337-7000
Fax: (269) 337-7390
E-mail: admission@kzoo.edu
Internet: www.kzoo.edu
Founded 1833 as Michigan and Huron Institute, present name 1855
Private control
Academic year: September to June
Divs of fine arts, humanities, interdisciplinary studies, natural sciences and mathematics, modern and classical languages and literatures, physical education, social sciences
Pres.: Dr EILEEN WILSON-OYELARAN
Provost: Dr MICHAEL A. MCDONALD
Vice-Pres. for College Advancement: VICTORIA GORRELL
Vice-Pres. for Student Devt and Dean for Students: SARAH WESTFALL
Dean for Enrollment: JOELLEN L. SILBERMAN
Dean for Admission: ERIC STAAB
Registrar: ALYCE BRADY
Dir for Library: STACY A. NOWICKI
Library of 330,000 vols
Number of teachers: 103 (full-time)
Number of students: 1,348

KETTERING UNIVERSITY

1700 W Third Ave, Flint, MI 48504-6214
Telephone: (810) 762-9500
Fax: (810) 762-9837
E-mail: admissions@kettering.edu
Internet: www.gmi.edu
Founded 1919, present name and status 1998
Private control

Depts of business, chemistry and biochemistry, computer science, electrical and computer engineering, industrial and manufacturing engineering, liberal arts, mathematics, mechanical engineering, physics
Pres.: Dr ROBERT K. MCMAHAN, JR
Provost and Vice-Pres. for Academic Affairs: Dr ROBERT L. SIMPSON
Vice-Pres. for Admin. and Finance: (vacant)
Vice-Pres. for Admissions and Enrolment Services: (vacant)
Vice-Pres. for Univ. Advancement: JACK STOCK (acting)
Vice-Pres. for Student Life and Dean for Students: BETSY HOMSHER
Registrar: SHEILA RUPP
Dir for Library Services: Dr CHARLES D. HANSON
Library of 180,000 vols, 1,900 periodicals
Number of teachers: 135
Number of students: 3,200

KUYPER COLLEGE

3333 E Beltline NE, Grand Rapids, MI 49525
Telephone: (616) 222-3000
E-mail: admissions@kuyper.edu
Internet: www.kuyper.edu
Founded 1939 as Reformed Bible Institute, present name and status 1970
Private control
Academic year: August to April
Areas of study: Bible and theology, cross-cultural studies, educational ministries, general education, liberal arts, physical education, pre-seminary studies, professional education, social work and youth ministry
Pres.: Dr NICHOLAS V. KROEZE
Provost and Vice-Pres. for Academic Admin.: Dr MELVIN J. FLIKKEMA
Vice-Pres. for Enrolment Management: RYAN STRUCK-VANDER HAAK
Vice-Pres. for College Advancement: KEN CAPISCIOLTO
Academic Dean: Dr TAMARA ROSIER
Dir for Library Services: DIANNE ZANDBERGEN
Library of 600,000 vols, 150 periodicals
Number of teachers: 56 (19 full-time, 37 part-time)
Number of students: 344

LAKE SUPERIOR STATE UNIVERSITY

650 W Easterday Ave, Sault Ste Marie, MI 49783
Telephone: (906) 632-6841
Fax: (906) 635-2111
E-mail: admissions@lssu.edu
Internet: www.lssu.edu
Founded 1946 as Sault Ste Marie Br. of Michigan College of Mining and Technology, present name 1987
State control
Academic year: September to May
Pres.: Dr TONY MCLAIN
Provost and Vice-Pres. for Academic Affairs: MORRIE WALWORTH
Vice-Pres. for Enrolment Services: WILLIAM EILOLA
Vice-Pres. for Finance: SHERRY BROOKS
Vice-Pres. for Student Affairs: KEN PERESS
Registrar: NANCY NEVE
Dean for Library: (vacant)
Library of 130,000 vols, 850 periodicals, 75,000 microforms
Number of teachers: 121
Number of students: 2,398

DEANS

College of Arts, Letters, Social Sciences and Emergency Services: Dr PAIGE GORDIER

College of Business, Engineering, and Economic Development: Dr DAVID R. FINLEY (acting)
College of Natural and Mathematical Sciences: Dr BARBARA KELLER
College of Nursing, Recreation Studies and Exercise Science: (vacant)
Great Lakes Academy: Dr MELVIN L. WAISANEN
School of Education: DONNA FIEBELKORN

LAWRENCE TECHNOLOGICAL UNIVERSITY

21000 W Ten Mile Rd, Southfield, MI 48075-1058
Telephone: (248) 204-4000
Fax: (248) 204-3727
E-mail: admissions@ltu.edu
Internet: www.ltu.edu
Founded 1932
Private control
Academic year: August to May
Pres. and CEO: Dr LEWIS N. WALKER
Provost and Chief Academic Officer: Dr MARIA J. VAZ
Vice-Pres. for Finance and Admin.: LINDA L. HEIGHT
Vice-Pres. for Univ. Advancement: STEPHEN E. BROWN
Dean for Students: KEVIN FINN
Registrar: NOREEN G. FERGUSON
Library Dir: GARY R. COCOZZOLI
Number of teachers: 452
Number of students: 4,500
Publication: *Prism* (1 a year)

DEANS

College of Architecture and Design: GLEN S. LEROY
College of Arts and Sciences: Dr HSIAO-PING MOORE
College of Engineering: Dr NABIL F. GRACE
College of Management: Dr LOUIS A. DEGENNARO

MADONNA UNIVERSITY

36600 Schoolcraft Rd, Livonia, MI 48150-1173
Telephone: (734) 432-5300
Fax: (734) 432-5393
E-mail: muinfo@madonna.edu
Internet: www.madonna.edu
Founded 1947
Private control
Academic year: September to July
Pres.: Dr ROSE MARIE KUJAWA
Vice-Pres. for Academic Admin.: Dr ERNEST NOLAN
Vice-Pres. for Student Services: Dr CONNIE TINGSON-GATUZ
Vice-Pres. for Univ. Advancement: ANDREA NODGE
Univ. Registrar: DINA DuBUIS
Dir for Library Services: JOANNE LUMMETTA
Library of 163,678 vols
Number of teachers: 274
Number of students: 4,000
Publications: *Madonna Now*, *Revelations* (2 a year)

DEANS

College of Arts and Humanities: Dr KATHLEEN MARTIN O'DOWD
College of Education: Dr KAREN OBSNIUK
College of Nursing and Health: Dr TERESA L. C. THOMPSON
College of Science and Mathematics: Dr TED F. BIERMANN
College of Social Sciences: Dr KAREN L. ROSS
Graduate School: Dr EDITH RALEIGH

Outreach and Distance Learning: Dr JAMES NOVACK
School of Business: Dr STUART R. ARENDS

MARYGROVE COLLEGE

8425 W McNichols Rd, Detroit, MI 48221
Telephone: (313) 927-1200
Fax: (313) 927-1345
E-mail: info@marygrove.edu
Internet: www.marygrove.edu
Founded 1905
Private control
Academic year: September to April
Pres.: Dr DAVID J. FIKE
Vice-Pres. for Academic Affairs: JANE HAMMANG-BUHL
Vice-Pres. for Finance and Admin.: BILL JOHNSON
Vice-Pres. for Institutional Advancement: KENNETH MALECKE
Vice-Pres. for Student Affairs and Enrolment Management: Dr JULIANA MOSLEY
Dir for Learning Resource Centre: DOLORES NOEL
Library of 84,015 vols, 371 periodicals
Number of teachers: 64
Number of students: 1,188 (780 undergraduate, 408 graduate)
Publications: *Contact* (1 a year), *Maxis Review* (1 a year)

DEANS

Arts and Sciences: Dr JUDITH A. HEINEN
Education: CHRISTINE KOENIG SEGUIN
Extended Learning: Dr BRENDA D. BRYANT
Fine Arts: ROSE DE SLOOVER
Professional Studies: JANE HAMMANG-BUHL

MICHIGAN JEWISH INSTITUTE

6890 W Maple, West Bloomfield, MI 48322
Telephone: (248) 414-6900
Fax: (248) 414-6907
E-mail: info@mji.edu
Internet: www.mji.edu
Founded 1994
Private control
Academic year: September to August
Areas of study: business and information systems, computer information systems, Judaic studies
Pres. and Chief Financial Officer: KASRIEL SHEMTOV
Sr Vice-Pres. and Dean for Academic Admin.: Dr T. HERSHEL GARDIN
Librarian and Registrar: KAREN ROBERTSON-HENRY.

MICHIGAN SCHOOL OF PROFESSIONAL PSYCHOLOGY

26811 Orchard Lake Rd, Farmington Hills, MI 48334-4512
Telephone: (248) 476-1122
Fax: (248) 476-1125
Internet: www.mispp.edu
Founded 1980 as Center for Humanistic Studies, present name 2006
Private control
Academic year: August to July (3 semesters)
Pres.: Dr KERRY MOUSTAKAS
Vice-Pres.: DIANE K. ZALAPI
Program Dir: Dr LEE BACH
Registrar: HEATHER N. RIGBY
Academic Librarian: CANDI WILSON
Library of 7,000 vols, 20 journal subscriptions, 270 instructional audio visual materials
Number of students: 149

MICHIGAN STATE UNIVERSITY

East Lansing, MI 48824
Telephone: (517) 355-6560
Fax: (517) 355-4670
E-mail: presmail@msu.edu
Internet: www.msu.edu
Founded 1855 as Agricultural College of the State of Michigan, present status 1955, present name 1964
State control
Academic year: August to May (2 terms)
Pres.: LOU ANN K. SIMON
Provost and Vice-Pres. for Academic Affairs: KIM A. WILCOX
Vice-Pres. for Governmental Affairs: MARK BURNHAM
Vice-Pres. for Legal Affairs and Gen. Counsel: ROBERT A. NOTO
Vice-Pres. for Research and Graduate Studies: J. IAN GRAY
Vice-Pres. for Student Affairs and Services: Dr DENISE B. MAYBANK
Vice-Pres. for Univ. Advancement: ROBERT W. GROVES
Vice-Pres. for Univ. Relations: HEATHER SWAIN
Registrar: NICOLE G. ROVIG (acting)
Dir for Libraries: CLIFFORD H. HAKA
Library: see Libraries and Archives
Number of teachers: 4,900
Number of students: 47,131
Publications: *Centennial Review* (3 a year), *MSU Alumni Magazine* (4 a year), *The Engaged Scholar Magazine* (1 a year, print and online (engagedscholar.msu.edu))

DEANS

College of Agriculture and Natural Resources: DOUGLAS BUHLER
College of Arts and Letters: KAREN A. WURST
College of Communication Arts and Sciences: PAMELA WHITTEN
College of Education: ROBERT FLODEN
College of Engineering: SATISH UDPA
College of Human Medicine: MARSHA D. RAPPLEY (acting)
College of Law: JOAN HOWARTH
College of Music: JAMES FORGER
College of Natural Science: R. JAMES KIRKPATRICK
College of Nursing: MARY MUNDT
College of Osteopathic Medicine: WILLIAM D. STRAMPEL
College of Social Science: MARIETTA L. BABA
College of Veterinary Medicine: CHRISTOPHER M. BROWN
Eli Broad College of Business and Eli Broad Graduate School of Management: STEFANIE LENWAY
Honors College: Dr CYNTHIA JACKSON-ELMOORE
James Madison College: SHERMAN GARNETT
Lyman Briggs College: ELIZABETH SIMMONS
Residential College in Arts and Humanities: STEPHEN L. ESQUITH (acting)

PROFESSORS

(Departments may be attached to more than one college)

College of Nursing:
ALLEN, G. D.
COLLINS, C.
GIFT, A. G.
GIVEN, B. A.
ROTHERT, M. L.

Department of Accounting:
ARENS, A. A.
BUZBY, S. L.
DILLEY, S. C.
GRAY, J.
HAKA, S.
MCCARTHY, W. E.
MEAD, G. C.

O'CONNOR, M. C.
OUTSLAY, E.
SHIELDS, M. D.
SOLLENBERGER, H. M.
WARD, D. D.

Department of Advertising:

PRATT, C.
REECE, B. B.
SALMON, C.
VANDENBERGH, B. G.

Department of Agricultural Economics:

BATIE, S. S.
BERNSTEN, R. H.
BLACK, J. R.
CRAWFORD, E.
HAMM, L. G.
HARSH, S. B.
HARVEY, L. R.
HILKER, J. H.
HOEHN, J.
KELSEY, M. P.
LEHOLM, A. G.
MOSER, C. H.
MYERS, R. J.
NOTT, S. B.
PIERSON, T. R.
RICKS, D. J.
ROBISON, L. J.
SCHMID, A. A.
SCHWAB, G.
STAATZ, J. M.
VAN RAVENSWAAY, E.
WEBER, M.

Department of Agricultural Engineering:

BAKKER-ARKEMA, F. W.
BICKERT, W. G.
BROOK, R.
GERRISH, J.
LOUDON, T. L.
MROZOWSKI, T.
SEGERLIND, L. J.
SRIVASTAVA, A.
STEFFE, J. F.
SURBROOK, T. C.
VAN EE, G. R.
VON BERNUTH, R.

Department of American Thought and Language:

ABRAHAMS, E. C.
BECKWITH, G. M.
BRATZEL, J. N.
BRESNAHAN, R. J.
BUNGE, N. L.
CHAMBERLAIN, W.
COOPER, D. D.
D'ITRI, P. A.
ELLISTON, S. F.
HOPPENSTAND, G. C.
LADENSON, J. R.
LUNDE, E.
MCKINLEY, B. E.
NOVERR, D. A.
ROUT, K.
SOMERS, P. P., Jr
STEINBERG, M.
THOMAS, F. R.
ZIEWACZ, L. E.

Department of Animal Science:

ALLEN, M. S.
AULERICH, R. J.
BEEDE, D. K.
BENSON, M. E.
BUCHOLTZ, H. F.
BURSIAN, S.
DENNIS BANKS, B.
ERICKSON, R. W.
FERRIS, T. A.
FOGWELL, R.
HAWKINS, D. R.
HOGBERG, M. G.
IRELAND, J.
MELLENBERGER, R. W.
RAHN, A. P.

RITCHIE, H. D.
RUST, S. R.
SHELLE, J. E.
VARGHESE, S. K.
YOKOYAMA, M. T.

Department of Anthropology:

CHARTKOFF, J.
CLELAND, C. E.
CLIMO, J.
DERMAN, W.
DWYER, D.
GALLIN, B.
GOLDSTEIN, L. G.
LOVIS, W. A.
POLLARD, H. P.
ROBBINS, L. H.
SAUER, N.
SPIELBERG, J.
WHITEFORD, S.

Department of Art:

BANDES, S. J.
DEUSSEN, P. W.
FAGAN, J. E.
FUNK, R.
GLENDINNING, P.
KILBOURNE, W. G.
KUSZAI, J. J.
LAWTON, J. L.
MACDOWELL
STANFORD, L. O.
TARAN, I. Z.
VANLIERE, E. N.
WOLTER, K. H.

Department of Audiology and Speech Sciences:

CASBY, M.
EULENBERG, J. B.
MOORE, E. J.
PUNCH, J. L.
RAKERD, B. S.
SMITH, L. L.
STOCKMAN, I. G.

Department of Biochemistry and Molecular Biology:

BIEBER, L. L.
FERGUSON-MILLER, S.
FRAKER, P. J.
GREEN, P. G.
HOLLINGSWORTH, R. I.
KAGUNI, J. M.
KAGUNI, L. S.
KINDEL, P. K.
KROOS, L. R.
MCCORMICK, J. J.
MCGROARTY, E. J.
MCINTOSH, L.
MAHER, V. M.
PREISS, J.
RAIKHEL, N. V.
REVZIN, A.
SCHINDLER, M. S.
SMITH, W. L.
TRIEZENBERG, S. J.
WANG, J. L.
WATSON, J. T.
WILSON, J. E.

Department of Botany and Plant Pathology:

DEZOETEN, G. A.
EKERN, F. F.
EWERS, F. W.
FULBRIGHT, D. W.
HAMMERSCHMIDT, R.
HART, L. P.
HOLLENSEN, R.
JONES, A. L.
KEEGSTRA, K. G.
KENDE, H.
KLOMPARENS, K. L.
MURPHY, P. G.
NADLER, K. D.
OHLROGGE, J. B.
POFF, K. L.
SAFIR, G. R.

SEARS, B.
TAGGART, R.
VARGAS, J. M., JR
WALTON, J. D.
WEBBER, P. J.
WOLK, C. P.
ZEEVAART, J. A. D.

Department of Chemical Engineering:

BERGLUND, K.
DALE, B.
DRZAL, L. T.
HAWLEY, M. C.
JAYARAMAN, K.
MILLER, D. J.
NARAYAN, R.
PETTY, C. A.
WORDEN, R. M.

Department of Chemistry:

ALLISON, J.
BABCOCK, G. T.
CHANG, C. K.
CROUCH, S. R.
CUKIER, R. I.
DUNBAR, K.
FROST, J.
HARRISON, J. F.
HUNT, K. C.
HUNT, P. M.
KANATZIDES, M. G.
LEROI, G. E.
MCGUFFIN, V. L.
MCHARRIS, W. C.
MORRISSEY, D. J.
PINNAVAIA, T. J.
RATHKE, M. W.
REUSCH, W. H.
MALECZKA, R.
WAGNER, P. J.
WULFF, W. D.

Department of Civil and Environmental Engineering:

BALADI, G.
DAVIS, M. L.
HARICHANDRAN, R. S.
HATFIELD, F.
LYLES, R. W.
MCKELVEY, F.
SOROUSHIAN, P.
TAYLOR, W. C.
VOICE, T. C.

Department of Communication:

ATKIN, C. K.
BOSTER, F. J.
DONOHUE, W.
SMITH, S. W.

Department of Computer Science and Engineering:

CHUNG, M.-J.
DILLON, L. K.
GREENBERG, L.
HUGHES, H. D.
JAIN, A. K.
MUTKA, M.
NI, L. M.
PRAMANIK, S.
STOCKMAN, G. C.
WEINSHANK, D. J.
WOJCIK, A. S.

Department of Counseling, Educational Psychology and Special Education:

AMES, C.
BECKER, B. J.
CLARK, C. M.
CREWE, N. M.
DICKSON, W. P.
ENGLERT, C. S.
FLODEN, R. E.
HAPKIEWICZ, W. C.
JUNE, L. N.
LEAHY, M. J.
LOPEZ, F. G.
MEHRENS, W. A.
PALAS, A. M.

PERNELL, E.
PHILLIPS, S. E.
PRAWAT, R.
RECKASE, M. D.
SCHMIDT, W. H.
SMITH, G.
SPIRO, R. J.
STEWART, D. A.
YELON, S. L.

Department of Crop and Soil Sciences:
BOYD, S. A.
CHRISTENSON, D. R.
CRUM, J. R.
FOSTER, E. F.
FREED, R. D.
GOODMAN, E.
HARWOOD, R. R.
JACOBS, L. W.
JOHNSTON, T. J.
KELLS, J. D.
KELLY, J. D.
LEEP, R. H.
LEMME, G. D.
LENSKI, R. E.
MOKMA, D. L.
PAUL, E. A.
PENNER, D.
PIERCE, F. J.
RENNER, K. A.
RITCHIE, J. T.
ROBERTSON, G. P.
SMUCKER, A. J. M.
THOMASHOW, M.
TIEDJE, J. M.
WARNCKE, D. D.

Department of Economics:
ALLEN, B. T.
BAILLIE, R. T.
BALLARD, C. L.
BIDDLE, J. E.
BOYER, K. D.
BROWN, B. W.
CHOI, J. P.
DAVIDSON, C.
FISHER, R. C.
GODDEERIS, J. H.
HOLZER, H. J.
KREININ, M. E.
LIEDHOLM, C. E.
LINZ, S. J.
MACKEY, M. C.
MARTIN, L. W.
MATUSZ, S. J.
MENCHIK, P. L.
MEYER, J.
NEUMARK, D. B.
OBST, N. P.
PECCHENINO, R. A.
SCHMIDT, P. J.
SEGERSTROM, P. S.
STRAUSS, J. A.
WILSON, J. D.
WOODBURY, S. A.
WOOLDRIDGE, J.

Department of Educational Administration:
CHURCH, R. L.
CUSICK, P. A.
DAVIS, M.
FAIRWEATHER, J.
GRANDSTAFF, M. E.
IGNATOVICH, F. R.
KAAGAN, S. S.
MOORE, K. M.
PLANK, D. N.
ROMANO, L. G.
SIMON, L. A. K.
SYKES, G.
TURNER, M.
WEILAND, S.

Department of Electrical and Computer Engineering:
ASMUSSEN, J., Jr
DELLER, J.
FISHER, P. D.

FOUKE, J. M.
KHALIL, H.
NYQUIST, D. P.
PIERRE, P. A.
REINHARD, D. K.
ROTHWELL, E. J.
SALAM, F. M.
SCHLUETER, R. A.
SHANBLATT, M.
SIEGEL, M.
TUMMALA, R. L.
WEY, C.-L.

Department of English:
ATHANASON, A. N.
BANKS, J. S.
BRUNNER, D. D.
CRANE, M.
DEWHURST, C. K.
DULAI, S. S.
FISHBURN, K. R.
GASS, S. M.
GOCHBERG, D. S.
GOODSON, A. C.
GROSS, B. E.
HARROW, K.
HILL, J. L.
JOHNSEN, W.
LANDRUM, L. N.
LUDWIG, J. B.
McCLINTOCK, J. I.
McGUIRE, P. C.
MARTIN, R. A.
MATHESON, L. M.
MEINERS, R. K.
O'DONNELL, P. J.
PAANANEN, V. N.
PENN, W. S.
POGEL, N.
ROBINSON, R. F.
ROSENBERG, D. M.
SEATON, J.
SKEEN, A. C.
SMITHERMAN, G.
STALKER, J. C.
STOCK, P. L.
TAVORMINA, M. T.
UPHAUS, R. W.
VINCENT, W. A.
WAKOSKI, D.
WHALLON, W.
WILSON, M.

Department of Entomology:
AYERS, G. S.
BESAW, L. C.
BIRD, G. W.
DELFOSSE, E. S.
GAGE, S.
GRAFIUS, E. J.
HOLLINGWORTH, R. M.
MERRITT, R. W.
MILLER, J. R.
POSTON, F. L.
RAIKHEL, A.
SCRIBER, J. M.
SMITLEY, D. R.
STEHR, F. W.
VANTASSELL, E.
WHALON, M. E.
ZABIK, M. J.

Department of Epidemiology:
PARETH, N.
PATHAK, P. K.

Department of Family and Child Ecology:
AMES, B. D.
BARRATT, M. S.
BOBBITT, N.
BOGER, R.
GRIFFORE, R.
IMIG, D. R.
IMIG, G. L.
JOHNSON, D. J.
KEITH, J. G.
KOSTELNIK, M.
LUSTER, T. J.

McADOO, H. P.
MILLER, J. R.
PHENICE, L.
SCHIAMBERG, L. B.
SODERMAN, A. K.
TAYLOR, C. S.
WALKER, R.
WHIREN, A. P.
YOUATT, J. P.

Department of Family and Community Medicine:
AGUWA, M. I.
BORDINAT, S. M.
CUMMINGS, M.
KURTZ, M.
PAPSIDERO, J.

Department of Family Practice:
ALEXANDER, E.
BRODY, H.
GERARD, R.
GIVEN, C. W.
HICKNER, J.
OGLE, K. S.
PATHAK, D. R.
WHITTIER, H. L.

Department of Finance:
BOOTH, G. G.
GRUNEWALD, A. E.
HENRY, J. B.
KHANNA, N.
LASHBROOKE, E. C., JR
O'DONNELL, J. L.
RAINEY, J. F.
SIMONDS, R. R.
STENZEL, P.

Department of Fisheries and Wildlife:
BATIE, R. E.
D'ITRI, F.
DOBSON, T. A.
GARLING, D. L.
JOHNSON, D. I.
PEYTON, R. B.
PRINCE, H. H.
TAYLOR, W. W.

Department of Food Science and Human Nutrition:
BENNINK, M. R.
BOND, J. T.
BOOREN, A. M.
CASH, J. N.
CHENOWETH, W. L.
GRAY, I. J.
HEGARTY, P. V.
HOERR, S. M.
LINZ, J. E.
PESTKA, J. J.
ROMSOS, D. R.
SMITH, D. M.
SONG, W. O.
UEBERSAX, M. A.
ZABIK, M.
ZILE, M. H.

Department of Forestry:
DICKMANN, D. I.
KEATHLEY, D. E.
KIELBASO, J. J.
KOELLING, M. R.
McDONOUGH, M.
POTTER-WITTER, K. L.

Department of Geography:
CAMPBELL, D. J.
CHUBB, M.
COREY, K. E.
GROOP, R. E.
HAMLIN, R.
HARMAN, J. R.
HINOJOSA, R.
LIM, G.-C.
MANSON, G. A.
MEHRETU, A.
OLSON, J. M.
SCHAETZL, R. J.

SKOLE, D. L.
THOMAS, J.
WILLIAMS, J.
WITTICK, R. I.

Department of Geological Sciences:

ANSTEY, R. L.
CAMBRAY, F. W.
FUJITA, K.
LARSON, G. J.
LONG, D. T.
SIBLEY, D. F.
TROW, J. W.
VELBEL, M. A.
VOGEL, T. A.

Department of History:

ANDERSON, J. R.
EADIE, J. W.
FISHER, A.
GLIOZZO, C. A.
HINE, D. C.
LAURENCE, R. R.
LEVINE, P. D.
MARCUS, H. G.
MOCH, L. P.
RADDING, C. M.
REED, H. A.
ROBINSON, D. W.
SCHOENL, W. J.
SIEGELBAUM, L. H.
SILVERMAN, H.
STEWART, G. T.
SWEENEY, J. M.
THOMAS, R. W.
THOMAS, S. J.
VIETH, J. K.
WILBUR, E.

Department of Horticulture:

BIERNBAUM, J. A.
CAMERON, A. C.
CARLSON, W. H.
DILLEY, D. R.
FLORE, J. A.
HANCOCK, J. F.
HANSON, E. J.
HEINS, R. D.
HERNER, R. C.
HOWELL, G. S.
IEZZONI, A. F.
LOESCHER, W. H.
NAIR, M.
PERRY, R. L.
SINK, K. C.
WIDDERS, I. E.
ZANDSTRA, B. H.

Department of Human Environment and Design:

SONTAG, M. S.
STERNQUIST, B.
STEWART, D. G.

Department of Internal Medicine:

HUGHES, M. J.
OTTEN, R. F.
PYSH, J. J.
RISTOW, G. E.

Department of Kinesiology:

DUMMER, G.
FELTZ, D. L.
HAUBENSTRICKER, J. L.
MALINA, R. M.
PIVARNIK, J. M.

Department of Large Animal Clinical Sciences:

AMES, N. K.
BAKER, J. C.
BARTLETT, P. C.
CARON, J. P.
DERKSEN, F. J.
HERDT, T.
HOLLAND, R. E.
KANEENE, J. B.
KING, L. J.
LLOYD, J. W.

MATHER, E. C.
NACHREINER, R. F.
NICKELS, F. A.
ROBINSON, N. E.
ROOK, J. S.
SEARS, P. M.
SPRECHER, D. J.
STICK, J. A.
STRAW, B. E.

Department of Linguistics and Germanic, Slavic, Asian and African Languages:

ABBOTT, B. K.
BELGARDT, R.
FALK, J. S.
HUDSON, G.
JUNTUNE, T. W.
LIN, Y.-H.
LOCKWOOD, D. G.
MCCONEGHY, P.
PAULSELL, P.
PETERS, G. F.
PRESTON, D.
SENDICH, M.
WILKINS, W. K.
WURST, K. A.

Department of Management:

BARRICK, M.
HOLLENBECK, J. R.
MOCH, M. K.
RUBIN, P. A.
WAGNER, J. A., III

Department of Marketing and Supply Chain Management:

ALLEN, J. W.
BOWERSOX, D. J.
CALANTONE, R. J.
CAVUSGIL, S. T.
CLOSS, D.
DROGE, C. L.
HARRELL, G. D.
MELNYK, S. A.
NARASIMHAN, R.
NASON, R. W.
SONG, X.-X. M.
VICKERY, S. K.
WILSON, R. D.

Department of Materials Science and Mechanics:

ALTIERO, N. J.
CASE, E. D.
CLOUD, G. L.
GRUMMON, D. S.
HUBBARAD, R. P.
LIU, D.
MUKHERJEE, K.
PENCE, T. J.
SOUTAS-LITTLE, R. W.
SUBRAMANIAN, K. N.

Department of Mathematics:

AKBULUT, S.
BAO, P.
BLAIR, D. E.
BROWN, W. C.
CHEN, B.-Y.
DRACHMAN, B.
DUNNINGER, D. R.
FINTUSHEL, R. A.
FRAZIER, M. W.
HALL, J. I.
HESTENES, M.
HILL, R. O.
IVANOV, N.
KUAN, W. E.
KURTZ, J. C.
LAMM, P. K.
LAPPAN, G.
LAPPAN, P. A.
LI, T. Y.
LO, C. Y.
LUDDEN, G. D.
MCCARTHY, J. D.
MACCLUER, C. R.
MASTERSON, J. J.

MEIERFRANKENFELD, U.
MORAN, D. A.
NEWHOUSE, S. E.
OW, W. H.
PALMER, E. M.
PARKER, T. H.
PLOTKIN, J. M.
ROTTHAUS, C.
SAGAN, B. E.
SCHUUR, J. D.
SEEBECK, C. L.
SENK, S. L.
SHAPIRO, J. H.
SLEDD, W. T.
SONNEBORN, L. M.
SREEDHARAN, V. P.
TREIL, S.
ULRICH, B.
VOLBERG, A.
WALD, J. W.
WANG, C.-Y.
WEIL, C. E.
WINTER, D. L.
WINTER, M. J. K.
WOLFSON, J. G.
WONG, P. K.
ZEIDAN, V. M.
ZHOU, Z.

Department of Mechanical Engineering:

FOSS, J. F.
LLOYD, J. R.
MCGRATH, J.
MEDICK, M. A.
RADCLIFFE, C. J.
ROSENBERG, R. C.
SCHOCK, H. J.
SHAW, S. W.
SHIK, T.
THOMPSON, B. S.
WICHMAN, I. S.

Department of Medicine:

ABELA, G. S.
DIMITROV, N. V.
DIPETTE, D. J.
GOSSAIN, V. V.
HASSOUNA, H. I.
HOLMES-ROVNER, M.
HOPPE, R.
JONES, J. W.
MAYLE, J. E.
NEIBERG, A. D.
PENNER, J. A.
ROSENMAN, K. D.
SCHWARTZ, K. A.
SMITH, R. C.
STEIN, G. E.
SWANSON, G. M.
WANG, D. H.

Department of Microbiology and Molecular Genetics:

BAGDASARIAN, M.
BERTRAND, H.
BREZNAK, J. A.
BRUBAKER, R. R.
CONRAD, S. E.
CORNER, T.
DAZZO, F.
DEBRUIJN, F. J.
DODGSON, J. B.
ESSELMAN, W.
FLUCK, M. M.
GARRITY, G. M.
HAUG, A.
HAUSINGER, R. P.
JACKSON, J. H.
KIERSZENBAUM, F.
MAES, R. K.
MULKS, M. H.
ORIEL, P. J.
PATTERSON, M. J.
PATTERSON, R.
REDDY, C. A.
REUSCH, R. N.
SNYDER, L. R.

VELICER, L. F.
WALKER, R. D.

Department of Obstetrics, Gynecology and Reproductive Biology:

MARSHALL, J. F.
VASILENKO, P.

Department of Osteopathic Manipulative Medicine:

RECHTIEN, J. J.
REYNOLDS, H.
WARD, R. C.

Department of Osteopathic Surgical Specialities:

BECKMEYER, H. E.
HARDING, S. A.
HAUT, R. C.
HOGAN, M. J.
JACOBS, A. W.

Department of Park, Recreation and Tourism Resources:

BRISTOR, J. L.
FRIDGEN, J.
HOLECEK, D. F.
RASMUSSEN, G. A.
STYNES, D. J.
VAN DER SMISSEN, B.

Department of Pathology:

BELL, T. G.
HARKEMA, J. R.
KREHBIEL, J.
LOVELL, K. L.
MACKENZIE, C.
MULLANEY, T. P.
PADGETT, G. A.
REED, W. M.
RHEUBEN, M. B.
TVEDTEN, H.
WILLIAMS, C. S. F.
YAMINI, B.

Department of Pediatrics:

BREITZER, G. M.
MAGEN, M.
SCHNEIDERMAN, D. O.

Department of Pediatrics and Human Development:

CHANG, C. C.
FISHER, R.
GORDON, R.
KALLEN, D. J.
KAUFMAN, D. B.
KULKARNI, R.
KUMAR, A.
MURRAY, D. L.
NETZLOFF, M. L.
SCOTT-EMUAKPOR, A.
SEAGULL, E. A.
SPARROW, A. W.
TROSKO, J. E.

Department of Pharmacology and Toxicology:

ATCHISON, W. D.
BARMAN, S.
BENNETT, J. L.
BRASELTON, W. E., JR
FINK, G. D.
FISCHER, L. J.
GALLIGAN, J. J.
GEBBER, G. L.
GOODMAN, J. I.
KAMINSKI, N. E.
MOORE, K. E.
ROTH, R. A.
THORNBURG, J.

Department of Philosophy:

ANDRE, J. A.
ASQUITH, P. D.
BENJAMIN, M.
ESQUITH, S. L.
FLECK, L. M.
FRYE, M.
GARELICK, H. M.

HALL, R. J.
HANNA, J. F.
KOCH, D. F.
KOTZIN, R. H.
LAWSON, B. E.
MCCRACKEN, C. J.
MILLER, B.
PETERSON, R. T.
TOMLINSON, T.

Department of Physical Medicine and Rehabilitation:

HALLGREN, R.
HINDS, W. C.
KAUFMAN, D.
STANTON, D. F.

Department of Physics and Astronomy:

ABOLINS, M. A.
AUSTIN, S. M.
BALDWIN, J. A.
BASS, J.
BAUER, W. W.
BENENSON, W.
BERZ, M. M.
BORYSOWICZ, J.
BROCK, R. L.
BROMBERG, C. M.
BROWN, B. A.
DANIELEWICZ, P.
DUXBURY, P. M.
DYKMAN, M. I.
GALONSKY, A. I.
GOLDING, B.
HARRISON, M. J.
HARTMANN, W. M.
HUSTON, J. W.
KASHY, E.
LINNEMAN, J. T.
LYNCH, W. G.
MAHANTI, S. D.
POLLACK, G. L.
POPE, B. G.
PRATT, W. P., JR
PUMPLIN, J. C.
REPKO, W. W.
SHERRILL, B. M.
SIGNELL, P. S.
SIMKIN, S. M.
SMITH, H. A.
STEIN, R. F.
THOENNESSEN, M.
THORPE, M. F.
TOMANEK, D.
TUNG, W. K.
WEERTS, H. J.
WESTFALL, G. D.
ZELENVINSKY, V.

Department of Physiology:

ADAMS, T.
HASLAM, S. Z.
HEIDEMANN, S.
HOOTMAN, S. R.
JUMP, D. B.
KREULEN, D. L.
MEYER, R. A.
PETROPOULOS, E. A.
RIEGLE, G. D.
ROOT-BERNSTEIN, R. S.
SPARKS, H.
SPIELMAN, W. S.
TIEN, H. T.
ZIPSER, B.

Department of Political Science:

ABRAMSON, P. R.
ALLEN, W. B.
BRATTON, M.
FINIFTER, A. W.
HALL, M. G.
HAMMOND, T. H.
HULA, R. C.
KNOTT, J. H.
MELZER, A.
OSTROM, C. W., JR
ROHDE, D. W.
SILVER, B. D.

STEIN, B. N.
WAGMAN, J.
WEINBERGER, J. W.

Department of Psychiatry:

BIELSKI, R. J.
COLENDA, C.
OSBORN, G. G.
ROSEN, L. W.
STOFFELMAYR, B.
VAN EGEREN, L. F.
WERNER, A.
WILLIAMS, D. H.

Department of Psychology:

ABELES, N.
BARCLAY, A. M.
BOGAT, G. A.
CALDWELL, R. A.
CARR, T. H.
DAVIDSON, W., II
FERREIRA, M. F.
FITZGERALD, H. E.
FORD, J. K.
HARRIS, L. J.
HENDERSON, J. M.
HUNTER, J. E.
ILGEN, D. R.
JACKSON, L. A.
KARON, B. P.
KERR, N. L.
KOSLOWSKI, S. W.
LEVINE, R. L.
LOMBARDI, V. L.
MESSE, L. A.
NUNEZ, A. A.
PAULUS, G. S.
SCHMITT, N. W.
SISK, C. L.
STOLLAK, G. E.
VON EYE, A. A.
WOOD, G.
ZACKS, J. L.
ZACKS, R. T.

Department of Radiology:

FALLS, W. M.
GOTTSCHALK, A.
HALPERT, R. D.
JOHNSON, J. I.
POTCHEN, E. J.
ROSS, L. M.
WALKER, B. E.

Department of Religious Studies:

GREENE, J. T.
VERSLUIS, A.
WELCH, A. T.

Department of Resource Development:

BARNES-MCCONNELL, P.
BRONSTEIN, D. A.
DERSCH, E.
FEAR, F. A.
KAKELA, P. J.
KAMRIN, M. A.
NICKEL, P. E.
ROWAN, G.
SCHULTINK, G.
WRIGHT, D.

Department of Romance and Classical Languages:

COLMEIRO, J. F.
DONOHOE, J. I.
FIORE, R. L.
FRANCESE, J.
GRAY, E. F.
JOSEPHS, H.
KOPPISCH, M.
MANSOUR, G. P.
MARINO, N. F.
PORTER, L. M.
SNOW, J. T.
TYRRELL, W. B.

Department of Small Animal Clinical Sciences:

ARNOCZKY, S. P.

BRADEN, T. D.
DECAMP, C. E.
EVANS, A. T.
EYSTER, G. E.
FLO, G. L.
HAUPTMAN, J.
JOHNSON, C.
MOSTOSKY, U. V.
PROBST, C. W.
ROSSER, E. J.
SCHALL, W. D.
WALSHAW, R.

Department of Sociology:
BOKEMEIER, J.
BROMAN, C. L.
BUSCH, L. M.
CONNER, T. L.
GALLIN, R. S.
GOLD, S. J.
HAMILTON, R. S.
HILL, R. C.
JOHNSON, N. E.
KAPLOWITZ, S.
MANNING, P. K.
PERLSTADT, H.
RUMBAUT, R. G.
SHLAPENTOKH, V.
VANDERPOOL, C. K.
WILEY, D.
ZINN, M. B.

Department of Statistics and Probability:
ERICKSON, R. V.
FABIAN, V.
FELDMAN, D.
GARDINER, J. C.
GILLILAND, D. C.
HANNAN, J. F.
KOUL, H. L.
LePAGE, R. D.
MANDREKAR, V.
PAGE, C. F.
RAMAMOORTHI, R. V.
SALEHI, H.
STAPLETON, J.

Department of Surgery:
DEAN, R. E.
HARKEMA, J.
OSUCH, J. R.
TOLEDO, L. H.

Department of Teacher Education:
ALLEMAN, J. E.
ANDERSON, C. W.
ANDERSON, K.
ANDERSON, L. M.
BADER, L. A.
BARNES, H. L.
BOOK, C.
BROPHY, J. E.
CHERRYHOLMES, C.
EDWARDS, P. A.
FEATHERSTONE, J.
FERRINI-MUNDY, J.
FLORIO-RUANE, S.
GALLAGHER, J. J.
JOYCE, W. W.
KENNEDY, M. M.
KOZIOL, S. M.
LABAREE, D. F.
LANIER, J. E.
LANIER, P. E.
LITTLE, T.
NEMSER, S. F.
PEARSON, P. D.
PURCELL-GATES, V.
PUTNAM, J. G.
RIETHMILLER, P. L.
ROEHLER, L. R.
SCHWILLE, J.
SEDLAK, M. W.
WEST, B. B.
WHEELER, C.

Department of Telecommunication:
BIOCCA, F. A.

GREENBERG, B. S.
HEETER, C. J.
LA ROSE, R. J.
LEVY, M. R.
LITMAN, B. R.
MODY, B.
MUTH, T. A.
STEINFIELD, C.
WILDMAN, S. S.
WILLIAMS, G. A.

Department of Theatre:
DURR, D. L.
RUTLEDGE, F. C.
RUTLEDGE, G.
SCHUTTLER, G.

Department of Zoology:
AGGARWAL, S. K.
ATKINSON, J. W.
BAND, R. N.
BEAVER, D. L.
BROMLEY, S. C.
BURTON, T. M.
BUSH, G. L.
CATHEY, B.
CLEMENS, L. G.
COOPER, W. E.
DYER, F. C.
EILAND, L. C.
GIESY, J. P.
HALL, D. J.
HILL, R. W.
HOLEKAMP, K. E.
HUGGETT, R. J.
MUZZALL, P. M.
PEEBLES, C.
ROBBINS, L. G.
SNIDER, R. J.
STEVENSON, R. J.
STRANEY, D.
WEBBER, M. M.

Division of Human Pathology:
JONES, M.
KUMAR, K.
SANDER, C. M.
SIEW, S.

James Madison College:
AYOOB, M.
BANKS, R. F.
DORR, R. F.
GARNETT, S. W.
GRAHAM, N. A.
HOEKSTRA, D. J.
RUBNER, M.
SCHECHTER, M.
SEE, K. O.
WALTZER, K.
ZINMAN, M. R.

Lyman Briggs School:
EBERT-MAY, D.
INGRAHAM, E. C.
MERCURO, N.
SAYED, M. M. A.
SIMPSON, W. A.
SPEES, S. T.

National Superconducting Cyclotron Laboratory:
BLOSSER, H. G.
GELBKE, C. K.
HANSEN, P. G.
YORK, R. C.

Office of Medical Education Research and Development:
ABBETT, W. S.
ANDERSON, W. A.
FARQUAR, L. J.
HENRY, R. C.
MOLIDOR, J. B.

School of Criminal Justice:
BONNER, R. W.
BYNUM, T. S.
CARTER, D. L.
HORVATH, F. S.

HUDZIK, J. K.
MASTROFSKI
MORASH, M. A.
NALLA, M. K.
SIEGEL, J.
SMITH, C. E.
STEWART, C. S.

School of Hospitality Business:
CICHY, R.
KASAVANA, M. L.
KNUTSON, B. J.
NINEMEIER, J. D.
SCHMIDGALL, B. H.

School of Journalism:
BOSSEN, H. S.
COTE, W. E.
DAVENPORT, L. D.
DETJEN, J. T.
FICO, F.
LACY, S. R.
MOLLOY, J. D.
SOFFIN, S. I.
SPANIOLO, J. D.

School of Labor and Industrial Relations:
BLOCK, R. N.
CURRY, T. H.
KOSSEK, E. E.
KRUGER, D. H.
MOORE, M. L.
REVITTE, J.
SMITH, P. R.
TOBEY, S. H.
VANDE VORD, N.
WOLKINSON, B. W.

School of Music:
CARMAN, O. W.
CATRON, D. L.
DAN, R. M.
DONAKOWSKI, C.
ELL, F. W.
FORGER, D. M.
FORGER, J. B.
GREGORIAN, L.
HUTCHESON, J. T.
JOHNSON, M. E.
JOHNSON, T. O.
KRATUS, J. K.
LeBLANC, A.
LULLOFF, J. P.
MOON, Y. H.
NEWMAN, J.
OLSON, C.
RUGGIERO, C. H.
SINDER, P. N.
SMITH, C. K.
STOLPER, D.
TIMS, F. C.
VERDEBR, E. L.
VERDEBR, W.
VOTAPEK, R. J.
WARD, B. W.
WHITWELL, J. L.
ZARA, M.

School of Packaging:
BURGESS, C. J.
DOWNES, T. W.
GIACIN, J. R.
HARTE, B.
HUGHES, H. A.
LOCKHART, H. E.
SELKE, S. E. M.

School of Social Work:
ANDERSON, G. R.
DUANE, E. A.
FREDDOLINO, P. P.
HAROLD, R. D.
HERRICK, J. M.
LEVANDE, D. I.
WHITEMAN, V. L.

Centers and Other Administrative Units:
BLINN, L. V.
BOWMAN, H. E.

CARROLL, T. W.
KAUFMAN, G.
LOPUSHINSKY, T.
NERENZ, D. R.
NOVICKI, D. J.
ROSENTHAL, W. H.
SIERRA, L.
VORRO, J.
WILLIAMS, J. G.

Medical Technology Program:
DAVIS, G. L.

Undergraduate University Division:
CURRY, B. P.

Urban Affairs Programs:
DARDEN, J. T.
LANG, M.
SCHWEITZER, J. H.
THORNTON, D.

W. K. Kellogg Biological Station:
GROSS, K. L.
KLUG, M. J.
KNEZEK, B. D.
MITTELBACH, G. G.
TESSIER, A. J.

MICHIGAN TECHNOLOGICAL UNIVERSITY

1400 Townsend Dr., Houghton, MI 49931-1295
Telephone: (906) 487-1885
E-mail: mtu4u@mtu.edu
Internet: www.mtu.edu
Founded 1885 as Michigan Mining School, present name 1964
State control
Academic year: August to April
Pres.: Dr GLENN D. MROZ
Provost and Vice-Pres. for Academic Affairs: Dr MAX SEEL
Vice-Pres. for Admin.: ELLEN HORSCH
Vice-Pres. for Advancement: SHEA MCGREW
Vice-Pres for Governmental Relations: Dr DALE TAHTINEN
Vice-Pres. for Research: Dr DAVID D. REED
Vice-Pres. for Student Affairs: Dr LES COOK
Univ. Librarian and Dir for Library: ELLEN MARKS
Number of teachers: 464
Number of students: 7,148
Publications: Michigan Tech Magazine (3 a year), Michigan Tech Research Magazine (1 a year)

DEANS

College of Engineering: TIMOTHY J. SCHULZ
College of Sciences and Arts: Dr BRUCE E. SEELY
School of Business and Economics: DARRELL RADSON
School of Forest Resources and Environmental Science: MARGARET GALE
School of Technology: JAMES FRENDEWEY

NORTHERN MICHIGAN UNIVERSITY

1401 Presque Isle Ave, Marquette, MI 49855-5301
Telephone: (906) 227-1000
Fax: (906) 227-2204
Internet: www.nmu.edu
Founded 1899 as Northern State Normal School, present name and status 1963
State control
Academic year: August to May
Pres.: LESLIE E. WONG
Provost and Vice-Pres. for Academic Affairs: Dr PAUL LANG
Vice-Pres. for Finance and Admin.: R. GAVIN LEACH
Assoc. Provost for Student Services and Enrolment: WILLIAM BERNARD

Dir for Admissions: GERRI DANIELS
Registrar: KIM ROTUNDO
Dean for Academic Information Services: DARLENE WALCH
Library of 478,745 vols, 522,903 govt docs
Number of teachers: 496
Number of students: 9,252

DEANS

College of Academic Information Services: DARLENE WALCH
College of Arts and Sciences: Dr MICHAEL BROADWAY
College of Graduate Studies: TERRY SEETHOFF
College of Professional Studies: HARVEY WALLACE
Walker L. Cisler College of Business: Dr JAMAL RASHED

NORTHWOOD UNIVERSITY

4000 Whiting Dr., Midland, MI 48640-2398
Telephone: (989) 837-4200
Fax: (989) 837-4490
E-mail: miadmit@northwood.edu
Internet: www.northwood.edu
Founded 1959, present name and status 2006
Private control
Academic year: September to May
Areas of study: arts, business administration, computer information systems, health care; campuses at West Palm Beach (Florida) and Cedar Hill (Texas)
Pres. and CEO: KEITH A. PRETTY
Exec. Vice-Pres. and Chief Academic Officer: Dr KRISTIN STEHOUWER
Vice-Pres. for Marketing and Enrolment Management: JOHN YOUNG
Vice-Pres. for Univ. Advancement: ARNOLD D'AMBROSIO
Provost for Michigan Campus: WILLIAM BATEMAN
Library Dir: SANDRA POTTS
Library of 60,000 vols, 300 periodicals, 50 DVDs
Number of teachers: 61
Number of students: 3,284
Publication: Idea (4 a year, online (www.northwood.edu/idea)).

OAKLAND UNIVERSITY

Telephone: (248) 370-2100
Internet: www.oakland.edu
Founded 1957, present name 1963
State control
Academic year: September to August (2 semesters, 2 sessions)
Pres.: Dr GARY D. RUSSI
Provost and Interim Sr Vice-Pres. for Academic Affairs: VIRINDER K. MOUDGIL
Vice-Pres. for Devt, Alumni and Community Engagement: ERIC BARRITT
Vice-Pres. for Finance and Admin.: JOHN W. BEAGHAN
Vice-Pres. for Govt Relations: ROCHELLE A. BLACK
Vice-Pres. for Student Affairs and Enrolment Management: MARY BETH SNYDER
Dean for Library: ADRIENE LIM
Library of 747,000 vols, 1.1m. microfiche
Number of teachers: 534 (full-time)
Number of students: 19,379 (15,838 undergraduate, 3,541 graduate)

DEANS

College of Arts and Sciences: RONALD A. SUDOL
Oakland Univ. William Beaumont School of Medicine: Prof. Dr ROBERT FOLBERG
School of Business Administration: MOHAN TANNIRU
School of Educational and Human Services: MARY L. OTTO

School of Engineering and Computer Science: PIETER FRICK
School of Health Sciences: KENNETH HIGHTOWER
School of Nursing: LINDA THOMPSON-ADAMS

OLIVET COLLEGE

320 S Main St, Olivet, MI 49076
Telephone: (616) 749-7000
Fax: (616) 749-7121
Internet: www.olivetcollege.edu
Founded 1844
Private control
Academic year: August to July
Depts of business administration, education, health, physical education, recreation and sport (HPERS), humanities, mathematics and computer science, natural and physical science, social science, visual and performing arts
Pres.: Dr STEVEN M. COREY
Provost and Dean for College: Prof. Dr MARIA G. DAVIS
Vice-Pres. for Admin.: LARRY COLVIN
Vice-Pres. and Dean for Student Life: Dr LINDA LOGAN
Dir for Admissions: MELISSA CASAREZ
Registrar: LESLIE SULLIVAN
Dir for Library: ELAINE HOELTZEL
Library of 90,000 vols, 500 periodicals
Number of teachers: 92
Number of students: 1,136

ROBERT B. MILLER COLLEGE

450 North Ave, Battle Creek, MI 49017-3397
Telephone: (269) 660-8021
Fax: (269) 565-2180
E-mail: info@millercollege.edu
Internet: www.millercollege.edu
Founded 2005
Private control
Pres.: DAVE HARRIS
Vice-Pres. for Student Services: CHAD DANIELSON
Registrar: JACKIE WASHBURN

DEANS

Elizabeth H. Binda School of Education: SEAN KOTTKE
School of Arts and Science: HARRY ADAMSON
School of Business: DAVE FISHER
School of Nursing: THERESA DAWSON

ROCHESTER COLLEGE

800 W Avon Rd, Rochester Hills, MI 48307
Telephone: (248) 218-2000
Fax: (248) 650-6060
E-mail: admissions@rc.edu
Internet: www.rc.edu
Founded 1959 as North Central Christian College, present name 1997
Private control
Academic year: August to May
Divs of arts and sciences, extended learning and business, nursing, professional studies
Pres.: Prof. RUBEL SHELLY
Provost and Chief Academic Officer: Dr JOHN D. BARTON
Vice-Pres. for Enrolment Services: KLINT PLEASANT
Academic Dean: KATRINA VANDERWOUDE
Dir for Assessment and Institutional Research: MARK MANRY
Dean for Students: BRIAN E. COLE
Registrar: REBEKAH PINCHBACK
Dir for Library Services: ALISON KELLER
Number of teachers: 37
Number of students: 864
Publication: The Shield.

SACRED HEART MAJOR SEMINARY

2701 Chicago Blvd, Detroit, MI 48206

Telephone: (313) 883-8500
Fax: (313) 868-6440
E-mail: information@shms.edu
Internet: www.aodonline.org/shms

Founded 1919 as Sacred Heart Seminary, present name 1988
Private control

Areas of study: arts, pastoral studies and divinity, philosophy, theology

Rector and Pres.: Rev. JEFFREY M. MONFORTON
Vice-Rector and Dean for Seminarians: Rev. GERARD BATTERSBY
Dean for Institute for Min.: JANET DIAZ
Dean for Studies: Rev. TODD LAJINESS
Library Dir: KAREN RAE MEHAFFEY

Library of 115,000 vols, 17,600 bound periodicals, 500 journals
Number of teachers: 69 (39 full-time, 30 part-time)
Number of students: 410 (235 undergraduate, 175 graduate)

SAGINAW VALLEY STATE UNIVERSITY

7400 Bay Rd, University Center, MI 48710

Telephone: (989) 964-4000
Fax: (989) 790-0180
E-mail: admissions@svsu.edu
Internet: www.svsu.edu

Founded 1963
State control
Academic year: August to August

Pres.: Dr ERIC R. GILBERTSON
Provost and Vice-Pres. for Academic Affairs: Dr DONALD J. BACHAND
Exec. Vice-Pres. for Admin. and Business Affairs: JIM MULADORE
Vice-Pres. for Enrolment Management: JAMES DWYER
Vice-Pres. for Student Affairs and Dean for Students: MERRY JO BRANDIMORE
Library Dir: LINDA FARYNK

Library of 233,000 vols, 9,000 e-books, 25,000 media items, 370,000 microforms, 24,000 journals
Number of teachers: 294
Number of students: 10,790

Publication: *Reflections*

DEANS

College of Arts and Behavioural Sciences: Dr MARY HEDBERG
College of Business and Management: JILL WETMORE
College of Education: Dr SUSIE EMOND
College of Science, Engineering and Technology: DEBORAH HUNTLEY
Crystal M. Lange College of Health and Human Services: JUDITH P. RULAND

SIENA HEIGHTS UNIVERSITY

Telephone: (517) 263-0731
Fax: (517) 264-7702
E-mail: admissions@sienaheights.edu
Internet: www.sienaheights.edu

Founded 1919, present name 1998
Private control
Academic year: August to May

Campuses at Battle Creek, Benton Harbor, Jackson, Lansing, Southfield and Monroe in Michigan

Pres.: Dr PEG ALBERT
Vice-Pres. for Academic Affairs: SHARON WEBER

Vice-Pres. for Enrolment Management: C. PATRICK PALMER
Vice-Pres. for Institutional Advancement: MITCHELL P. BLONDE
Dean for Students: MICHAEL ORLANDO
Dir for Admissions: SARA A. JOHNSON
Registrar: BRENDA K. DOREMUS
Dir for Library: ROBERT W. GORDON

Library of 136,082 vols
Number of teachers: 220 (70 full-time, 150 adjunct)
Number of students: 2,408 (2,097 undergraduate, 311 graduate)

Publications: *Reflections* (3 a year), *Spectra* (6 a year)

DEANS

College of Arts and Sciences: Dr MARK SCHERSTEN
College for Professional Studies: DEBORAH CARTER
Graduate College: Dr ANNE HOOGHART

SPRING ARBOR UNIVERSITY

106 E Main St, Spring Arbor, MI 49283

Telephone: (517) 750-1200
Fax: (517) 750-2108
E-mail: admissions@arbor.edu
Internet: www.arbor.edu

Founded 1873, present name 2001
Private control

Pres.: Dr CHARLES H. WEBB
Provost and Chief Academic Officer: Dr BETTY J. OVERTON-ADKINS
Vice-Pres. for Enrolment Services: MATT S. OSBORNE
Vice-Pres. for Finance and Admin.: JERRY L. WHITE
Vice-Pres. for Student Devt and Learning: KIM K. HAYWORTH
Vice-Pres. for Technology Services: JEFF EDWARDS
Vice-Pres. for Univ. Advancement: BRENT ELLIS
Registrar: TIM WIEGERT
Library Dir: ROY MEADOR

Library of 120,300 vols
Number of teachers: 87 (full-time)
Number of students: 4,195

DEANS

Gainey School of Business: Dr JAMES COE
School of Arts and Sciences: ROGER VARLAND
School of Education: LINDA SHERRILL
School of Graduate and Professional Studies: NATALIE GIANETTI

THOMAS M. COOLEY LAW SCHOOL

POB 13038, Lansing, MI 48901
300 South Capitol Ave, Lansing, MI 48933

Telephone: (517) 371-5140
Fax: (517) 334-5718
E-mail: admissions@cooley.edu
Internet: www.cooley.edu

Founded 1972
Private control
Academic year: September to August

Campuses at Lansing, Grand Rapids, Auburn Hills and Ann Arbor in Michigan

Pres. and Dean: DON LEDUC
Assoc. Dean for Enrolment and Student Services: Dr PAUL ZELENSKI
Assoc. Dean for Faculty: Prof. CHARLES P. CERCONE
Assoc. Dean for Devt and Alumni Relations: JAMES ROBB
Registrar: SHERIDA WYSOCKI
Assoc. Dean for Library and Instructional Support: DUANE STROJNY

Library of 650,000 vols
Number of teachers: 402 (123 full-time, 279 adjunct)
Number of students: 4,001

Publications: *Art and Museum Law Journal*, *Benchmark: The Thomas M. Cooley Law School Magazine*, *Journal of Practical and Clinical Law* (3 a year), *Thomas M. Cooley Law Review*.

UNIVERSITY OF DETROIT MERCY

POB 19900, 4001 W McNichols Rd, Detroit, MI 48221-3038

Telephone: (313) 993-1000
E-mail: admissions@udmercy.edu
Internet: www.udmercy.edu

Founded 1877 as Detroit College, chartered as univ. 1911, merged with Mercy College of Detroit in 1990
Private control

Pres.: Dr ANTOINE M. GARIBALDI
Vice-Pres. for Academic Affairs and Provost: PAMELA ZARKOWSKI
Vice-Pres. for Enrolment and Student Affairs: DENISE WILLIAMS MALLETT
Vice-Pres. for Univ. Advancement: GREGORY CASCIONE
Dean for Student Life: MONICA WILLIAMS
Registrar: DIANE M. PRAET
Dean for Univ. Libraries: MARGARET AUER

Library of 830,000 vols, 86,900 journals, 12,000 audiovisual items, 1m. microforms, 91,500 e-books, 90,000 govt documents
Number of teachers: 336 (full-time)
Number of students: 5,335

DEANS

College of Business Administration: Dr JOSEPH G. EISENHAUER
College of Engineering and Science: LEO HANIFIN
College of Health Professions: Dr CHRISTINE M. PACINI
College of Liberal Arts and Education: Dr ROY FINKENBINE
School of Architecture: WILL WITTIG
School of Dentistry: MERT AKSU
School of Law: LLOYD A. SEMPLE

UNIVERSITY OF MICHIGAN

Ann Arbor, MI 48109

Telephone: (734) 764-1817
E-mail: info@umich.edu
Internet: www.umich.edu

Founded 1817
State control
Language of instruction: English
Academic year: September to August

Pres.: MARY SUE COLEMAN
Provost and Exec. Vice-Pres. for Academic Affairs: Prof. PHILIP J. HANLON
Vice-Pres. for Devt: JERRY A. MAY
Vice-Pres. for Govt Relations: CYNTHIA H. WILBANKS
Vice-Pres. for Research: Dr STEPHEN R. FORREST
Vice-Pres. for Student Affairs: E. ROYSTER HARPER
Vice-Pres. and Gen. Counsel: SUELLYN SCARNECCHIA
Vice-Pres. and Sec.: SALLY J. CHURCHILL
Univ. Registrar: PAUL A. ROBINSON
Exec. Dir for Admissions: THEODORE L. SPENCER
Univ. Librarian and Dean for Libraries: PAUL N. COURANT

Library: see Libraries and Archives
Number of teachers: 6,086 (f. t. e.)
Number of students: 42,716

Publications: *Dividend* (2 a year), *Emergence*, *Espanol*, *Findings* (2 a year), *Innov-*

ator (1 a year), *LSA Magazine, Medicine at Michigan, Michigan Alumnus* (4 a year), *Michigan Engineer* (2 a year), *Michigan Quarterly Review* (online (www.michigan-quarterlyreview.com)), *Montage* (online (www.montage.umich.edu)), *Movement, Muse* (online (www.music.umich.edu/muse)), *Ongoing* (2 a year, print and online (ssw.umich.edu/Ongoing)), *Portico* (2 a year, print and online (www.tcaup.umich.edu/publications/portico)), *SI Information, State & Hill* (print and online (www.fordschool.umich.edu/state-and-hill)), *Stewards* (online (snre.umich.edu/stewards)), *The University of Michigan Today* (4 a year, online (michigantoday.umich.edu))

DEANS

A. Alfred Taubman College of Architecture and Urban Planning: MONICA PONCE DE LEON
College of Engineering: DAVID C. MUNSON, JR
College of Literature, Science and the Arts: TERRENCE J. MCDONALD
College of Pharmacy: FRANK J. ASCIONE
Gerald R. Ford School of Public Policy: SUSAN M. COLLINS
Horace H. Rackham School of Graduate Studies: JANET WEISS
Law School: EVAN CAMINKER
Medical School: JAMES O. WOOLLISCROFT
School of Art and Design: BRYAN ROGERS
School of Dentistry: PETER POLVERINI
School of Education: DEBORAH BALL
School of Information: JEFFREY MACKIE-MASON
School of Kinesiology: RONALD ZERNICKE
School of Music, Theatre and Dance: CHRISTOPHER KENDALL
School of Natural Resources and Environment: MARIE MIRANDA (acting)
School of Nursing: KATHLEEN M. POTEMPA
School of Public Health: MARTIN PHILBERT
School of Social Work: LAURA LEIN
Stephen M. Ross School of Business: ALISON DAVIS-BLAKE

PROFESSORS

A. Alfred Taubman College of Architecture and Urban Planning (2000 Bonisteel Blvd, Ann Arbor, MI 48109-2069; tel. (734) 764-1300; fax (734) 763-2322; internet taubmancollege.umich.edu):

BURESH, T.
CONSTANT, C.
DEWAR, M.
FISHMAN, R.
GILES, H.
GROAT, L.
HILL, E.
KELBAUGH, D.
LEINBERGER, C.
LEVINE, J.
MURRAY, M.
PONCE DE LEON, M.
RAY, M.
THOMAS, J.
WINEMAN, J.

Gerald Ford School of Public Policy (Joan and Sanford Weill Hall, 735 S State St, Ann Arbor, MI 48109-3091; tel. (734) 764-3490; fax (734) 763-9181; internet www.fordschool.umich.edu):

AXELROD, R.
CHAMBERLIN, J.
COHEN, D.
COLLINS, S.
CORCORAN, M.
COURANT, P.
DANZIGER, S.
DANZIGER, S.
DEARDORFF, A.
DINARDO, J.
DOMINGUEZ, K.

GERBER, E.
HALL, R.
HOUSE, J.
JACOB, B.
LEVITSKY, M.
RABE, B.
SIMON, C.
SVEJNAR, J.

College of Engineering (tel. (734) 647-7000; fax (734) 647-7001; internet www.engin.umich.edu):

ADRIAENS, P., Civil and Environmental Engineering
ARMSTRONG, T., Industrial Operations
ARRUDA, E., Mechanical Engineering
ASHTON-MILLER, J., Biomedical Engineering
ASHTON-MILLER, J., Mechanical Engineering
ASSANIS, D., Mechanical Engineering
ATKINS III, D., COE EECS—CSE Division
ATREYA, A., Mechanical Engineering
ATREYA, S., Atmospheric, Oceanic and Space Science.
ATZMON, M., Nuclear Engineering and Radiological Science
AUSTIN, T., COE EECS—CSE Division
BARBER, J., Mechanical Engineering
BARKER, J., Atmospheric, Oceanic and Space Science.
BAVEJA, S., COE EECS—CSE Division
BECK, R., Naval Architecture and Marine Dept
BERNITSAS, M., Naval Architecture and Marine Dept
BERNSTEIN, D., Aerospace Engineering
BHATTACHARYA, P., COE EECS—ECE Division
BIELAJEW, A., Nuclear Engineering and Radiological Science
BLAAUW, D., COE EECS—CSE Division
BLAAUW, D., COE EECS—ECE Division
BORENSTEIN, J., Mechanical Engineering
BOUGHER, S., Atmospheric, Oceanic and Space Science.
BOYD, I., Aerospace Engineering
BOYD, J., Atmospheric, Oceanic and Space Science
BOZER, Y., Industrial Operations
BULKLEY, J., Civil and Environmental Engineering
BURNS, M., Chemical Engineering
CAIN, C., Biomedical Engineering
CARROLL, M., Atmospheric, Oceanic and Space Science.
CECCIO, S., Mechanical Engineering
CESNIK, C., Aerospace Engineering
CHAO, X., Industrial Operations
CHEN, P., COE EECS—CSE Division
COMBI, M., Space Physics Research Lab
DAHM, W., Aerospace Engineering
DASKIN, M., Industrial Operations
DOWLING, D., Mechanical Engineering
DOWNAR, T., Nuclear Engineering and Radiological Science
DRAKE, R., Atmospheric, Oceanic and Space Science.
DRISCOLL, J., Aerospace Engineering
DUENYAS, I., Industrial Operations
DURFEE, E., COE EECS—CSE Division
EL-TAWIL, S., Civil and Environmental Engineering
ENGLAND, A., COE EECS—ECE Division
FESSLER, J., COE EECS—ECE Division
FISK, L., Atmospheric, Oceanic and Space Science.
FLEMING, R., Nuclear Engineering and Radiological Science
FOGLER, H., Chemical Engineering Dept
FORREST, S., COE EECS—ECE Division
FREUDENBERG, J., COE EECS—ECE Division
FRIEDMANN, P., Aerospace Engineering
GALLIMORE, A., Aerospace Engineering

GALVANAUSKAS, A., COE EECS—ECE Division
GHOSH, A., Materials Science and Engineering
GIANCHANDANI, Y., COE EECS—ECE Division
GILCHRIST, B., COE EECS—ECE Division
GILGENBACH, R., Nuclear Engineering and Radiological Science
GLOECKLER, G., Atmospheric, Oceanic and Space Science
GLOTZER, S., Chemical Engineering
GOLDMAN, R., Materials Science and Engineering.
GOMBOSI, T., Atmospheric, Oceanic and Space Science
GREEN, P., Materials Science and Engineering.
GRIZZLE, J., COE EECS—ECE Division
GROSH, K., Mechanical Engineering
GROTBERG, J., Biomedical Engineering
GULARI, E., Chemical Engineering
HALLORAN, J., Materials Science and Engineering.
HANSEN, W., Civil and Environmental Engineering
HAYES, J., COE EECS—CSE Division
HAYES, K., Civil and Environmental Engineering
HERO III, A., COE EECS—ECE Division
HERRIN, G., Industrial Operations
HE, Z., Nuclear Engineering and Radiological Science
HISKENS, I., COE EECS—ECE Division
HOLLAND, J., COE EECS—CSE Division
HOLLISTER, S., Biomedical Engineering
HOLLOWAY, J., Nuclear Engineering and Radiological Science
HONEYMAN, P., COE EECS—CSE Division
HRYCIW, R., Civil and Environmental Engineering
HULBERT, G., Mechanical Engineering
HU, S., Mechanical Engineering
IOANNOU, P., Civil and Environmental Engineering
ISLAM, M., COE EECS—ECE Division
JAGADISH, H., COE EECS—CSE Division
JAHANIAN, F., COE EECS—CSE Division
JONES, J., Materials Science and Engineering.
KABAMBA, P., Aerospace Engineering
KANICKI, J., COE EECS—ECE Division
KANNATEY-ASIBU JR, E., Mechanical Engineering
KANTOWITZ, B., Industrial Operations
KATOPODES, N., Civil and Environmental Engineering
KAVIANY, M., Mechanical Engineering
KEARFOTT, K., Nuclear Engineering and Radiological Science
KEYSERLING, W., Industrial Operations
KIEFFER, J., Materials Science and Engineering.
KIERAS, D., COE EECS—CSE Division
KIKUCHI, N., Mechanical Engineering
KIPKE, D., Biomedical Engineering
KIVELSON, M., Atmospheric, Oceanic and Space Science.
KOLMANOVSKY, I., Aerospace Engineering
KOREN, Y., Mechanical Engineering
KOTA, S., Mechanical Engineering
KOTOV, N., Chemical Engineering
KOZYRA, J., Space Physics Research Lab
KRUSHELNICK, K., Nuclear Engineering and Radiological Science
KUIPERS, B., COE EECS—CSE Division
KUO, A., Mechanical Engineering
KUSHNER, M., COE EECS—ECE Division
LAFORTUNE, S., COE EECS—ECE Division
LAINE, R., Materials Science and Engineering
LAIRD, J., COE EECS—CSE Division
LARSEN, E., Nuclear Engineering and Radiological Science
LARSON, R., Chemical Engineering Dept

College of Literature, Science and the Arts (500 S State St, Ann Arbor, MI 48109; tel. (734) 764-0322; fax (734) 764-2697; internet www.lsa.umich.edu):

DENVER, R., Molecular Cellular and Developmental Biology
DERKSEN, H., Mathematics
DESHPANDE, M., Asian Languages and Cultures
DESHPANDE, M., Linguistics
DILLARD, A., CAAS
DISCH, L., Political Science
DISCH, L., Women's Studies
DOERING, C., Mathematics
DOLGACHEV, I., Mathematics
DOMINGUEZ, K., Economics
DOUGLAS, S., Communication Studies
DOWD, G., American Culture
DOWD, G., History
DUAN, C., Molecular Cellular and Developmental Biology
DUANMU, S., Linguistics
DUNLAP, P., Ecology and Evolutionary Biology
DUREN, P., Mathematics
DWORKIN, S., Linguistics
DWORKIN, S., Romance Languages and Literature
ECCLES, J., Psychology
ELEY, G., History
ELLIS, N., Psychology
ELLISON, J., American Culture
ELLSWORTH, P., Psychology
ENDELMAN, T., History
EPSTEIN, S., Linguistics
ESTABROOK, G., Ecology and Evolutionary Biology
EVRARD, A., Physics
EWING, R., Geological Sciences
FALLER, L., English Language and Literature
FEATHERMAN, D., Sociology
FEELEY-HARNIK, G., Anthropology
FIERKE, C., Chemistry
FINE JR, J., History
FINK, W., Ecology and Evolutionary Biology
FISHER, D., Geological Sciences
FLANNERY, K., Anthropology
FLORIDA, N., Asian Languages and Cultures
FOMIN, S., Mathematics
FORNAESS, J., Mathematics
FRANCIS, A., Chemistry
FRANZESE JR, R., Political Science
FREEDMAN, J., American Culture
FREEDMAN, J., English Language and Literature
FREESE, K., Physics
FRICKE, T., Anthropology
FRIER, B., Classical Studies
FULTON, W., Mathematics
GAGOS, T., Classical Studies
GAINES, K., CAAS
GAINES, K., History
GARBRAH, K., Classical Studies
GARCIA SANTO-TOMAS, E., Romance Languages and Literature
GAZDA, E., History of Art
GELMAN, S., Psychology
GERDES, D., Physics
GERE, A., English Language and Literature
GIBBARD, A., Philosophy
GIDLEY, D., Physics
GINGERICH, P., Geological Sciences
GITELMAN, Z., Political Science
GLICK, G., Chemistry
GOLDBERG, D., Ecology and Evolutionary Biology
GOLDENBERG, E., Political Science
GOLDSTEIN, L., English Language and Literature
GONZALEZ, R., Psychology
GOODISON, L., CAAS
GOODISON, L., English Language and Literature
GOODMAN, D., History
GOODMAN, D., Women's Studies
GOODSON III, T., Chemistry

GRAHAM-BERMANN, S., Psychology
GREGERSON, L., English Language and Literature
GRIESS JR, R., Mathematics
GROVES, R., Sociology
GUNNING, S., American Culture
GUNNING, S., CAAS
GUNNING, S., English Language and Literature
GUTMANN, M., History
HALL, R., Political Science
HALPERIN, D., English Language and Literature
HANCOCK, D., History
HANLON, P., Mathematics
HANNOOSH, M., Romance Languages and Literature
HARTMANN, L., Astronomy
HEATH, J., Linguistics
HERBERT, S., Classical Studies
HERRERO-OLAIZOLA, A., Romance Languages and Literature.
HERRMANN, A., English Language and Literature
HERRMANN, A., Women's Studies
HERWITZ, D., Comparative Literature
HERWITZ, D., History of Art
HERWITZ, D., Philosophy
HINES JR, J., Economics
HOCHSTER, M., Mathematics
HOLLAND, P., Psychology
HOUSE, J., Sociology
HOWARD, J., American Culture
HOWARD, J., English Language and Literature
HSING, T., Statistics
HUESMANN, L., Communication Studies
HUME, R., Molecular Cellular and Developmental Biology
HUNTER, M., Ecology & Evolutionary Biology
HUTCHINGS, V., Political Science
INGLEHART, R., Political Science
IRVINE, J., Anthropology
ITO, K., Asian Languages and Cultures
JACKSON, J., Psychology
JACKSON, J., Political Science
JACKSON, S., Near Eastern Studies
JACKSON, T., Mathematics
JACOBSON, D., Philosophy
JANKO, R., Classical Studies
JI, L., Mathematics
JONIDES, J., Psychology
JONSSON, M., Mathematics
JORDAN, A., English Language and Literature.
JOYCE, J., Philosophy
JUSTER, S., History
KANE, G., Physics
KAPLAN, S., Psychology
KARLSEN, C., History
KARNI, S., Mathematics
KEANE JR, E., Anthropology
KEATING, D., Psychology
KEENER, R., Statistics
KELLER-COHEN, D., Linguistics
KELLEY, M., American Culture
KELLEY, M., History
KENNEDY, R., Chemistry
KESLER, S., Geological Sciences
KILIAN, L., Economics
KIMBALL, M., Economics
KIMELDORF, H., Sociology
KINDER, D., Political Science
KITAYAMA, S., Psychology
KIVELSON, V., History
KLING II, G., Ecology and Evolutionary Biology
KLIONSKY, D., Molecular Cellular and Developmental Biology
KNYSH, A., Near Eastern Studies
KOLLMAN, K., Political Science
KONDRASHOV, A., Ecology and Evolutionary Biology
KOPELMAN, R., Chemistry
KOREEDA, M., Chemistry

KOTTAK, C., Anthropology
KRASNY, R., Mathematics
KRISCH, J., Physics
KRIZ, I., Mathematics
KUWADA, J., Molecular Cellular and Developmental Biology
LAGARIAS, J., Mathematics
LAITNER, J., Economics
LAMBROPOULOS, V., Classical Studies
LAMBROPOULOS, V., Comparative Literature
LAM, D., Economics
LANGE, R., Geological Sciences
LARSON, K., English Language and Literature
LAZARSFELD, R., Mathematics
LEE, F., Psychology
LEGASSICK, T., Near Eastern Studies
LEHMAN, J., Ecology and Evolutionary Biology
LEVINE, D., Political Science
LEVINSON, M., English Language and Literature.
LEWIS, R., Psychology
LIEBERMAN, V., History
LINDNER, R., History
LIN, S., Asian Languages and Cultures
LOEB, L., Philosophy
LOHMANN, K., Geological Sciences
LOPEZ JR, D., Asian Languages and Cultures
LORD, C., Psychology
LORENZON, W., Physics
LOVE, T., Psychology
LUBMAN, D., Chemistry
LUMA, J., Psychology
LUPIA, A., Political Science
MACDONALD, M., History
MADDOCK, J., Molecular Cellular and Developmental Biology
MANNHEIM, B., Anthropology
MARCUS, J., Anthropology
MAREN, S., Psychology
MARKOVITS, A., Germanic Languages and Literature.
MARKOVITS, A., Political Science
MARKUS, G., Political Science
MARSH, E., Chemistry
MASUZAWA, T., Comparative Literature
MASUZAWA, T., History
MATEO, M., Astronomy
MATZGER, A., Chemistry
MCCRACKEN, P., Romance Languages and Literature.
MCCRACKEN, P., Women's Studies
MCDONALD, T., History
MCKAY, T., Physics
MEBANE JR, W., Political Science
MEBANE JR, W., Statistics
MEGGINSON, R., Mathematics
MERLIN, R., Physics
MEYER, D., Psychology
MEYERHOFF, M., Chemistry
MICHAILIDIS, G., Statistics
MICHALOWSKI, P., Near Eastern Studies
MILLER, P., Mathematics
MITANI, J., Anthropology
MIZRUCHI, M., Sociology
MONTGOMERY, H., Mathematics
MONTGOMERY, J., Chemistry
MOORE, D., History
MORANTZ-SANCHEZ, R., History
MORRIS, M., Chemistry
MORRISON, F., Psychology
MORROW, J., Political Science
MOSS, T., English Language and Literature
MRAZEK, R., History
MUKASA, S., Geological Sciences
MURPHY, S., Statistics
MUSTATA, M., Mathematics
MYERS, P., Ecology and Evolutionary Biology
NADELHOFFER, K., Ecology and Evolutionary Biology
NAGATA, D., Psychology

NAIR, V., Statistics
NEAL, H., Physics
NESSE, R., Psychology
NEUMAN, W., Communication Studies
NEWMAN, M., Physics
NISBETT, R., Psychology
NORICH, A., English Language and Literature
NORNES, M., Asian Languages and Cultures
NORNES, M., Screen Arts and Cultures
NOVAK, W., History
NUSSBAUM, R., Ecology and Evolutionary Bio
OCONNOR, B., Ecology and Evolutionary Biology
O'FOIGHIL, D., Ecology and Evolutionary Biology
OLSON, S., Psychology
ORR, B., Physics
O'SHEA, J., Anthropology
OWEN, R., Geological Sciences
OWUSU, M., Anthropology
OYSERMAN, D., Psychology
PACHELLA, R., Psychology
PAGE, S., Political Science
PAIGE, J., Sociology
PASCUAL, M., Ecology and Evolutionary Biology
PAULSON, W., Romance Languages and Literature
PECORARO, V., Chemistry
PEDRAZA, S., Sociology
PENNER-HAHN, J., Biophysics
PENNER-HAHN, J., Chemistry
PERLMUTTER, M., Psychology
PERNICK, M., History
PETERSON, C., Psychology
PICHERSKY, E., Molecular Cellular and Developmental Biology
PITCHER, M., CAAS
POTTER, D., Classical Studies
POTTS, A., History of Art
POWERS, M., History of Art
PRASAD, G., Mathematics
PRICE, R., Psychology
QIAN, J., Physics
RABKIN, E., English Language and Literature
RAILTON, P., Philosophy
RAITHEL, G., Physics
RAMAMOORTHY, A., Biophysics
RAMAMOORTHY, A., Chemistry
RAMIREZ-CHRISTENSEN, E., Asian Languages and Cultures
RAMMUNY, R., Near Eastern Studies
RAUCH, J., Mathematics
RAYMOND, P., Molecular Cellular and Developmental Biology
REUTER-LORENZ, P., Psychology
RHODE, P., Economics
RICHSTONE, D., Astronomy
RILES, J., Physics
ROBERTSON, J., Anthropology
ROBINSON, T., Psychology
ROHANI, P., Ecology and Evolutionary Biology
ROHANI, P., Study of Complex Systems
RONEN, O., Slavic Languages and Literature
ROOT, M., History of Art
ROSENBERG, W., History
ROTHMAN, E., Statistics
RUAN, Y., Mathematics
RUETSCHE, L., Philosophy
RUFF, L., Geological Sciences
SALANT, S., Economics
SAMEROFF, A., Psychology
SANDELANDS, L., Psychology
SANDER, L., Physics
SARTER, M., Psychology
SAVIT, R., Physics
SAXONHOUSE, A., Political Science
SCANNELL, G., Communication Studies
SCHIEFELBEIN JR, J., Molecular Cellular and Developmental Biology

SCHOENFELDT, M., English Language and Literature
SCHULENBERG, J., Psychology
SCHWARZ, N., Psychology
SCODEL, R., Classical Studies
SCOTT, G., Mathematics
SCOTT, R., History
SEARS, E., History of Art
SEIFERT, C., Psychology
SELLERS, R., Psychology
SENSION, R., Chemistry
SHAMMAS, A., Comparative Literature
SHAMMAS, A., Near Eastern Studies
SHAPIRO, M., Economics
SHIPAN, C., Political Science
SIEBERS, T., English Language and Literature
SIEGFRIED, S., History of Art
SIEGFRIED, S., Women's Studies
SILVERMAN, R., CAAS
SILVERMAN, R., History of Art
SIMON, C., Mathematics
SINOPOLI, C., Anthropology
SKLAR, L., Philosophy
SLEMROD, J., Economics
SMEREKA, P., Mathematics
SMITH, J., Psychology
SMITH, J., Economics
SMITH, K., Mathematics
SMITH, L., Economics
SMITH, S., English Language and Literature
SMITH, S., Women's Studies
SMOCK, P., Sociology
SMOLLER, J., Mathematics
SMUTS, B., Psychology
SOMERS, M., Sociology
SPATZIER, R., Mathematics
SPETH, J., Anthropology
STAFFORD, F., Economics
STAM, A., Political Science
STEIN, H., CAAS
STEINMETZ, G., Germanic Languages and Literature
STEINMETZ, G., Sociology
STEMBRIDGE, J., Mathematics
STENSONES, B., Mathematics
STEWART, A., Psychology
STEWART, A., Women's Studies
SULLIVAN, T., Sociology
SUNY, R., History
SVEJNAR, J., Economics
TANG, X., Asian Languages and Cultures
TANG, X., Comparative Literature
TARDIF, T., Psychology
TARLE, G., Physics
TERRENATO, N., Classical Studies
TESAR, L., Economics
TESSLER, M., Political Science
THOMASON, R., Linguistics
THOMASON, R., Philosophy
THOMASON, S., Linguistics
THORNTON, A., Sociology
THORNTON III, J., History
THUN, R., Physics
TOMAN, J., Slavic Languages and Literature
TONOMURA, H., History
TRAUB, V., English Language and Literature
TRAUB, V., Women's Studies
TRAUGOTT, M., Communication Studies
TRAUTMANN, T., History
TSEBELIS, G., Political Science
TUCKER, P., Ecology and Evolutionary Biology
UHER, C., Physics
URIBE-AHUMADA, A., Mathematics
VAN DAM, R., History
VANDERMEER, J., Ecology and Evolutionary Biology
VAN DER PLUIJM, B., Geological Sciences
VAN DER VOO, R., Geological Sciences
VAN KEKEN, P., Geological Sciences
VEDEJS, E., Chemistry
VERSHYNIN, R., Mathematics

VICINUS, M., English Language and Literature
VINOVSKIS, M., History
VOLLING, B., Psychology
VON ESCHEN, P., American Culture
VON ESCHEN, P., History
WALD, A., English Language and Literature
WALTER, L., Geological Sciences
WALTER, N., Chemistry
WALTON JR, H., Political Science
WALTON, K., Philosophy
WANG, N., Statistics
WASSERMAN, A., Mathematics
WEBB, P., Ecology and Evolutionary Biology
WEISSKOPF, T., Economics
WELLMAN, H., Psychology
WELLS, J., Physics
WERNER, E., Ecology and Evolutionary Biology
WHALLON JR, R., Anthropology
WHATLEY, W., Economics
WILLIAMS, M., Anthropology
WILLIAMS, R., English Language and Literature
WILLIS, R., Economics
WILSON, M., Ecology and Evolutionary Biology
WINTER, D., Psychology
WINTER, D., Mathematics
WOLPOFF, M., Anthropology
WRIGHT, H., Anthropology
WU, S., Mathematics
XIE, Y., Sociology
YAEGER, P., English Language and Literature
YAEGER, P., Women's Studies
YATES, J., Psychology
YBARRA, O., Psychology
YOCUM, C., Molecular Cellular and Developmental Biology
YOFFEE, N., Anthropology
YOFFEE, N., Near Eastern Studies
YOUNG, V., Mathematics
ZHANG, J., Ecology and Evolutionary Biology
ZHANG, J., Psychology
ZHANG, Y., Geological Sciences
ZHOU, B., Physics
ZUCKER, R., Psychology

College of Pharmacy (428 Church St, Ann Arbor, MI 48109-1065; tel. (734) 764-7312; fax (734) 763-2022; internet pharmacy.umich.edu):

AMIDON, G. E.
AMIDON, G. L.
ASCIONE, F.
BAGOZZI, R.
BERARDI, R.
CRIPPEN, G.
JOHNSON, C.
LARSEN, S.
LEE, K.
MOSBERG, H.
MUELLER, B.
SCHWENDEMAN, S.
SHERMAN, D.
SHIMP, L.
SHOWALTER, H.
SMITH, D.
WELAGE, L.
WOODARD, R.
YANG, V.

Law School (625 S State St, Ann Arbor, MI 48109-1215; tel. (734) 764-1358; fax (734) 763-9375; internet www.law.umich.edu):

ALVAREZ, A.
AVI-YONAH, R.
BAGENSTOS, S.
BARR, M.
BENY, L.
CAMINKER, E.
CLARK, S.
COOPER, E.

CRANE, D.
CRAWFORD, S.
CROLEY, S.
DUQUETTE, D.
EISENBERG, R.
ELLSWORTH, P.
EVANS, A.
FRIEDMAN, R.
FRIER, B.
FROST, P.
GROSS, S.
HALBERSTAM, D.
HATHAWAY, J.
HERZOG, D.
HINES JR, J.
HORWITZ, J.
KAHN, D.
KATZ, E.
KHANNA, V.
KRIER, J.
LAYCOCK, D.
LITMAN, J.
LOGUE, K.
MACKINNON, C.
MCCORMACK, B.
MENDELSON, N.
MILLER, W.
MORAN, D.
NOVAK, W.
PARSON, E.
PAYTON, S.
POTTOW, J.
PRIMUS, R.
PRITCHARD, A.
RADIN, M.
RATNER, S.
REGAN, D.
REIMANN, M.
REINGOLD, P.
RINE, N.
SANTACROCE, D.
SCARNECCHIA, S.
SCHLANGER, M.
SCHNEIDER, C.
SCHROTH, A.
SCOTT, R.
WAGGONER, L.
WEST, M.
WHITE, J.
WHITMAN, C.

Ross School of Business (701 Tappan St, Ann Arbor, MI 48109-1234; tel. (734) 763-5796; fax (734) 763-7804; internet www.bus.umich .edu):

ADRIAENS, P.
AHUJA, G.
ANDERSON, E.
ASHFORD, S.
BAGOZZI, R.
BAKER, W.
BATRA, R.
BROCKBANK, J.
BUCHMUELLER, T.
CAMERON, K.
CAPOZZA, D.
DAVIS, G.
DEGRAFF, J.
DOLAN, R.
DUENYAS, I.
DUTTON, J.
FEINBERG, F.
FORNELL, C.
GLADWIN, T.
GORDON, M.
HINES JR, J.
HOPP, W.
IMHOFF JR, E.
INDJEJIKIAN, R.
JACKSON, W.
KAUL, G.
KENNEDY, R.
KIM, E.
KINNEAR, T.
KRISHNA, A.
KRISHNAN, M.

LAFONTAINE, F.
LANEN, W.
LENK, P.
LI, H.
LIM, L.
LOVEJOY, W.
LUNDHOLM, R.
LYON, T.
MANCHANDA, P.
MASTEN, S.
MUIR, D.
NARAYANAN, M.
OSWALD, L.
PRAHALAD, C.
QUINN, R.
RAMASWAMY, V.
SANDELANDS, L.
SCHIPANI, C.
SCHRIBER, T.
SEVERANCE, D.
SEYHUN, H.
SIEDEL III, G.
SLEMROD, J.
SPREITZER, G.
SUSLOW, V.
SUTCLIFFE, K.
SVEJNAR, J.
TALBOT, F.
TICHY, N.
WALSH, J.
WEICK, K.
WEISS, J.
WESTPHAL, J.
ZHANG, L.
ZIMMERMAN, M.

School of Art and Design (2000 Bonisteel Blvd, Ann Arbor, MI 48109-2069; tel. (734) 764-0671; fax (734) 936-0469; internet art-design.umich.edu):

COGSWELL JR, J.
HERWITZ, D.
INUZUKA, S.
JACKSON, W.
JACOBSEN, C.
LEONARD, J.
MARINARO, L.
MOSS, T.
NUNOO-QUARCOO, F.
OVERMYER JR, R.
PORTER, M.
RODEMER, C.
ROGERS, B.
SMITH, S.
WEST, E.

School of Dentistry (1011 N University, Ann Arbor, MI 48109-1078; tel. (734) 763-6933; fax (734) 647-6805; e-mail ddsadmissions@ umich.edu; internet www.dent.umich.edu):

BAGRAMIAN, R.
BAYNE, S.
BRADLEY, R.
BROOKS, S.
CLARKSON, B.
EBER, R.
FASBINDER, D.
FEINBERG, S.
FRANCESCHI, R.
GIANNOBILE, W.
HELMAN, J.
HEYS, D.
HOLLAND, G.
HU, J.
JOHNSON, L.
KAPILA, S.
KOHN, D.
KREBSBACH, P.
LANTZ, M.
LOPATIN, D.
MA, P.
MCCAULEY, L.
MCDONALD, N.
MCNAMARA JR, J.
MISTRETTA, C.
NOR, J.
O'BRIEN, W.

PETERS, M.
POLVERINI, P.
RAZZOOG, M.
RICHARDS, P.
SIMMER, J.
STEFANAC, S.
TAICHMAN, R.
TAYLOR, G.
WANG, H.
WOOLFOLK, M.
YAMAN, P.

School of Education (610 E University Ave, Ann Arbor, MI 48109-1259; tel. (734) 764-9470; internet www.soe.umich.edu):

BALL, D.
BASS, H.
BATES, P.
BLUMENFELD, P.
BOWMAN, P.
BURKHARDT, J.
CARLISLE, J.
COHEN, D.
COOK, C.
CRAIG, H.
DESJARDINS, S.
GERE, A.
JACOB, B.
KING, P.
KRAJCIK, J.
LAMPERT, M.
LARSEN-FREEMAN, D.
LEE, V.
MCCALL, B.
MILLER, K.
MIREL, J.
MOJE, E.
MOSS, P.
NEUMAN, S.
PALINCSAR, A.
PETERS, C.
REX, L.
ROWAN, B.
SCHLEPPEGRELL, M.
SELLERS, R.
SILVER, E.
SONGER, N.
ST JOHN, E.
STONE III, C.
WIXSON, K.

School of Kinesiology (tel. (734) 647-9856; fax (734) 647-2808; internet www.kines.umich .edu):

BORER, K.
CARTEE, G.
CORNWELL, T.
EDINGTON, D.
FORT, R.
KATCH, V.
ROSENTRAUB, M.
ULRICH, B.
ULRICH, D.
ZERNICKE, R.

School of Information (4322 N Quad, 105 S State St, Ann Arbor, MI 48109-1285; tel. (734) 964-9376; fax (734) 764-2475; e-mail info@umich.edu; internet www.si.umich .edu):

ACKERMAN, M.
ATKINS III, D.
BLOUIN JR, F.
CHEN, Y.
COHEN, M.
CRAWFORD, S.
DURRANCE, J.
FINHOLT, T.
KING, J.
MARKEY, K.
MASON, J.
POLLACK, M.
RADEV, D.
RESNICK, P.
VAN HOUWELING, D.

School of Music, Theatre and Dance (E. V. Moore Bldg, 1100 Baits Dr., Ann Arbor, MI

48109-2085; tel. (734) 764-0583; fax (734) 763-5097; internet www.music.umich.edu):

AARON, R.
BLACKSTONE, J.
BORDERS, J.
CULVER, R.
DAUGHERTY, M.
DEYOUNG JR, G.
DICKERSON, G.
ELLIOTT, A.
EVERETT, W.
FOGEL, J.
FREDRICKSEN, E.
FULCHER, J.
GANNETT, D.
GENNE, B.
GORDON, C.
GREENE, A.
GUCK, M.
HAITHCOCK, M.
JENNINGS, A.
KAENZIG, F.
KANE, A.
KATZ, M.
KENDALL, C.
KERR, P.
KIBBIE, J.
KIESLER, K.
KING, N.
KORSYN, K.
LAM, J.
MASON, M.
MCCARTHY, M.
MEAD, A.
MONTS, L.
NAGEL, L.
NEVILLE-ANDREWS, J.
PARMENTIER, E.
POGGI, G.
RUSH, S.
RUSH, S.
SARATH, E.
SCHOENFIELD, P.
SCHOTTEN, Y.
SHENG, B.
SHIPPS, S.
SIMONI, M.
SINTA, D.
SKELTON, J.
SPARLING, P.
STEIN, L.
UDOW, M.
VERRETT, S.
WEST, S.
WILEY, R.
WOODS, L.

School of Natural Resources and Environment (Dana Bldg, 440 Church St, Ann Arbor, MI 48109-1041; tel. (734) 764-6453; fax (734) 936-2195; internet www.snre.umich.edu):

AGRAWAL, A.
ALLAN, J.
BIERBAUM, R.
BROWN, D.
BRYANT JR, B.
BULKLEY, J.
BURTON, G.
DIANA, J.
GLADWIN, T.
GRESE, R.
HOFFMAN, A.
HUNTER, M.
KAPLAN, R.
KEOLEIAN, G.
LOW, B.
LYON, T.
MOHAI, P.
MOORE, M.
NASSAUER, J.
PARSON, E.
PERFECTO, I.
SCAVIA, D.
WEBB, P.
WILEY, M.
YAFFEE, S.

ZAK, D.

School of Nursing (Room 1160, 400 N Ingalls, Ann Arbor, MI 48109-5482; tel. (734) 763-5985; fax (734) 936-3644; e-mail sn-osams@ umich.edu; internet www.nursing.umich .edu):

ALGASE, D.
BOYD, C.
KALISCH, B.
KALISCH, P.
KETEFIAN, S.
LARSON, J.
LOVELAND-CHERRY, C.
NORTHOUSE, L.
POHL, J.
POTEMPA, K.
PRESSLER, S.
REDMAN, R.
SAMPSELLE, C.
SCISNEY-MATLOCK, M.
STEIN, K.
TITLER, M.
VILLARRUEL, A.
WILLIAMS, R.

School of Public Health (1415 Washington Heights, 1700 SPH I, Ann Arbor, MI 48109-2029; tel. (734) 763-5425; fax (734) 763-5455; e-mail sph.web@umich.edu; internet www .sph.umich.edu):

ABECASIS, G.
ALEXANDER, J.
BATTERMAN, S.
BOEHNKE, M.
BUCHMUELLER, T.
CHATTERS, L.
CLARK, N.
CONNELL, C.
DIEZ ROUX, A.
FOXMAN, B.
FRANZBLAU, A.
FRIES, B.
GALEA, S.
GERONIMUS, A.
GOOLD, S.
GRAZIER, K.
GRIFFITH, J.
HARLOW, S.
HARRIS, C.
HIRTH, R.
HU, H.
ISRAEL, B.
JACOBSON, P.
JANZ, N.
KALBFLEISCH, J.
KARDIA, S.
KAZANJIAN, P.
KEELER, G.
KOOPMAN, J.
KRAUSE, N.
LANTZ, P.
LEPKOWSKI, J.
LIANG, J.
LITTLE, R.
LOCH-CARUSO, R.
LONGWORTH, Z.
MCLAUGHLIN, C.
MEADOWS, P.
MONTO, A.
MORGENSTERN, H.
NEIGHBORS, H.
NORTON, E.
NRIAGU, J.
PETERSON, K.
PEYSER, P.
PHILBERT, M.
RAGHUNATHAN, T.
RESNICOW, K.
RICHARDSON, R.
ROBINS, T.
SHOPE, J.
SMITH, D.
SONG, P.
SOWERS, M.
STRECHER, V.
TAYLOR, J.

TSODIKOV, A.
VILLARRUEL, A.
WARNER, K.
WHEELER, J.
WILSON, M.
ZELLERS, E.
ZIMMERMAN, M.

School of Social Work (1080 S University Ave, Ann Arbor, MI 48109-1106; tel. (734) 764-3309; fax (734) 936-1961; internet www .ssw.umich.edu):

BURGIO, L.
CHECKOWAY, B.
DANZIGER, S.
DELVA, J.
DUNKLE, R.
FALLER, K.
GANT, L.
GOLDMAN, K.
GUTIERREZ, L.
INGERSOLL-DAYTON, B.
LEIN, L.
OYSERMAN, D.
POWELL, T.
ROOT, L.
SAUNDERS, D.
SIEFERT, K.
TAYLOR, R.
TOLMAN, R.
TROPMAN, J.
TUCKER, D.

REGIONAL CAMPUSES

University of Michigan—Dearborn

4901 Evergreen Rd, Dearborn, MI 48128-1491

Telephone: (313) 593-5000
Fax: (313) 593-5452
Internet: www.umd.umich.edu

Founded 1959
State control
Academic year: September to August

Chancellor: Dr DANIEL LITTLE
Provost and Vice-Chancellor for Academic Affairs: Dr CATHERINE A. DAVY
Vice-Chancellor for Enrollment Management and Student Life: STANLEY E. HENDERSON
Vice-Chancellor for Govt Relations: EDWARD J. BAGALE
Vice-Chancellor for Institutional Advancement (vacant)
Registrar: ADRIENNE KELLUM MCDAY
Dir for Library: ELAINE LOGAN

Number of teachers: 381 (full-time)
Number of students: 8,600

DEANS

College of Arts, Sciences and Letters: Dr JEROLD L. HALE
College of Business: Dr KIM SCHATZEL
College of Education: Dr EDWARD SILVER
College of Engineering and Computer Science: Dr SUBRATA SENGUPTA

University of Michigan—Flint

302 E Kearsley, Flint, MI 48502-1950
Telephone: (313) 762-3000
Fax: (313) 762-3687
E-mail: admissions@umflint.edu
Internet: www.umflint.edu

Founded 1956
State control
Academic year: July to June

Chancellor: Dr RUTH J. PERSON
Provost and Vice-Chancellor for Academic Affairs: Dr GERARD VOLAND
Vice-Chancellor for Admin.: DAVID BARTHELMES
Vice-Chancellor for Student Affairs: MARY-JO SEKELSKY
Registrar: KAREN ARNOULD
Librarian: BOB HOUBECK

Library of 865,795 vols
Number of teachers: 372 (full-time)
Number of students: 8,262 (6,959 under-
graduate, 1,303 graduate)

DEANS

College of Arts and Sciences: Dr D. J. TRELA
School of Education and Human Services: Dr
BOB BARNETT
School of Health Professions and Studies:
DAVID GORDON
School of Management: Dr VAHID LOTFI (act-
ing)

WALSH COLLEGE OF ACCOUNTANCY AND BUSINESS ADMINISTRATION

POB 7006, Troy, MI 48007-7006
3838 Livernois, Troy, MI 48083
Telephone: (248) 689-8282
Fax: (248) 689-0938
E-mail: admissions@walshcollege.edu
Internet: www.walshcollege.edu

Founded 1922 as Walsh Institute of Account-
ancy, present name 1968
Private control
Academic year: September to September

Areas of study: accounting, finance, health
care, management; campus at Novi (Michi-
gan); univ. centres at Clinton Township,
Harper Woods and Port Huron in Michigan
Pres. and CEO: STEPHANIE W. BERGERON
Exec. Vice-Pres. and Chief Academic Officer:
Dr MICHAEL LEVENS
Vice-Pres. for Enrolment Management: JOHN
W. LICHTENBERG
Vice-Pres. for Human Resources and Admin.:
ELIZABETH A. BARNES
Registrar: KAREN HILLEBRAND
Library Dir: Dr JONATHAN CAMPBELL
Library of 27,000 vols, 250 periodicals
Number of students: 3,147 (1,122 under-
graduate, 2,025 graduate)

Publication: *The Walsh Journal*.

WAYNE STATE UNIVERSITY

1309 Faculty/Admin. Bldg, Detroit, MI 48202
Telephone: (313) 577-2424
Fax: (313) 577-2198
E-mail: emoen@oia.wayne.edu
Internet: www.wayne.edu

Founded 1868, present status 1933
State control
Academic year: August to May

Pres.: ALLAN GILMOUR
Provost and Sr Vice-Pres. for Academic
Affairs: RONALD T. BROWN
Vice-Pres. and Gen. Counsel: LOUIS LESSEM
Vice-Pres. for Devt and Alumni Affairs:
DAVID RIPPLE
Vice-Pres. for Govt Affairs: HARVEY HOLLINS,
III
Vice-Pres. for Research: HILARY RATNER
Dean for Univ. Libraries: SANDRA G. YEE

Library: see Libraries and Archives
Number of teachers: 1,816 (full-time)
Number of students: 31,505

DEANS

College of Education: CAROLYN M. SHIELDS
College of Engineering: FARSHAD FOTOUHI
College of Fine, Performing and Communi-
cation Arts: MATTHEW SEEGER
College of Liberal Arts and Sciences: ROBERT
L. THOMAS
College of Nursing: BARBARA K. REDMAN
Eugene Applebaum College of Pharmacy and
Health Sciences: LLOYD YOUNG
Graduate School: HILARY RATNER
Irvin D. Reid Honors College: JERRY HERRON
Law School: ROBERT ACKERMAN

School of Business Administration: MAR-
GARET L. WILLIAMS
School of Medicine: VALERIE PARISI
School of Social Work: CHERYL WAITES

PROFESSORS

College of Education
Admin. and Organizational Studies:
BRANDENBURG, D.
DEMONT, R.
GIPSON, J. H.
MORRISON, G.
RICHEY, R.
Teacher Education:
BALE, J.
KAPLAN, L.
PETERSON, J. M.
RONEY, R.
SMITH, G.
WHITIN, D.
Theoretical and Behavioural Foundations:
HILLMAN, S.
MARCOTTE, D.
MARKMAN, B. S.
PIETROFESA, J.
SAWILOWSKY, S.

College of Engineering
Chemical Engineering:
GULARI, E.
HUANG, Y.
NG, K.
PUTATUDNA, S.
ROTHE, E. W.
Civil Engineering:
AKTAN, H. M.
DATTA, T. K.
FU, G.
MILLER, C.
Electrical and Computer Engineering:
AUNER, G.
ERLANDSON, R.
HASSOUN, M.
HUANG, C.
LIN, F.
SILVERSMITH, D.
SINGH, H.
SIY, P.
WANG, L.
YING, H.
Industrial and Manufacturing Engineering:
PLONKA, F.
SINGH, N.
Mechanical Engineering:
BERDICHEVSKY, V.
GIBSON, R.
IBRAHIM, R.
MAI, M.-C.
RIVIN, E.
SINGH, T.
TAN, C.-A.
TARAZA, D.
WHITMAN, A. B.
WU, S.
YANG, K.-H.

College of Fine, Performing and Communi-
cation Arts
Art and Art History:
HEGARTY, J.
JACKSON, M.
MARTIN, R.
NAWARA, J.
ROBARE, D.
ROSAS, M.
WILLIAMS, P.
ZAJAC, J.
Communication:
SEEGER, M.
Music:
MARKOU, K.

Theatre:
CALARCO, J.
KAUSHANSKY, L.
MAGIDSON, D.
PULLIN, N.
SCHRAEDER, T.
THOMAS, J.

College of Liberal Arts
Africana Studies:
BOYD, M. (H)
HUTCHFUL, E.
Anthropology:
MONTILUS, G.
SANKAR, A.
Classics, Greek and Latin:
MCNAMEE, K.
Criminal Justice:
STACK, S.
ZALMAN, M.
Economics:
BRAID, R.
LEE, L.
ROSSANA, A.
SPURR, S.
English:
BARTON, E.
BRILL, L.
BURGOYNE, R.
COLEMBA, H.
HARRIS, W.
LANDRY, D.
LELAND, C.
LINDBERG, K.
MAROTTI, A.
RAY, R.
SCRIVENER, M.
SKLAR, E.
VLASOPOLOS, A.
WASSERMAN, R.
History:
BUKOWCZYK, J.
FAUE, E.
HYDE, C.
RAUCHER, A.
SMALL, M.
Humanities:
COGAN, M.
Philosophy:
GRANGER, H.
LOMBARD, L.
MCKINSEY, T.
YANAL, R.
Political Science:
ABBOTT, P. R.
BLEDSOE, T.
DOWNING, R. G.
ELDER, C.
FINO, S.
PARRISH, C.
Romance Languages and Literatures:
DITOMMASO, A.
HIGUERO, F.
STIVALE, C.
Sociology:
ESHLEMAN, J. R.
GELFAND, D.
HANKIN, J.
SENGSTOCK, M.
WARSHAY, L.

College of Lifelong Learning
Interdisciplinary Studies Program:
ARONSON, A. R.
BAILS, J. G.
GLABERMAN, M.
KLEIN, J.
MAIER, C. L.
RASPA, R. N.
SCHINDLER, R.

WRIGHT, R. H.

College of Nursing:
AROIAN, K.
HOUGH, E.
NIES, M.
OERMANN, M.
PIPER, B. A.
RICE, V.

College of Science

Biology:

ARKING, R.
FREEMAN, D.
GREENBERG, M.
HEBERLEIN, G.
HOUGH, R.
MIZUKAMI, H.
MOORE, W. S.
SMITH, P. D.
TAYLOR, J.

Chemistry:

BHAGWAT, A.
CHA, J.-K.
LINVELDT, R.
McCLAIN, W.
MONTGOMERY, J.
POOLE, C.
RABAN, J. P.
ROMANO, L.
RORABCHER, D.
SCHLEGEL, H.

Computer Science:

GOEL, N.
REYNOLDS, R.

Mathematics:

BACHELIS, G. F.
BRENTON, L.
CHOW, P.-L.
COHN, W.
GLUCK, D. H.
HANDEL, D.
KHAN, S.
KHASMINSKII, R.
KLEIN, J.
KOROSTELEV, A.
LIANG, T.
MAGAARD, K.
MAKAR-LIMANOV, L.
MALCOLMSON, P.
MENALDI, J. L.
MORDUKHOVICH, B.
OKOH, F.
RHEE, C.
SCHOCHET, C. L.
SCHREIBER, B. H.
SUN, T.-C.
YIN, G.
ZHANG, Z.

Nutrition and Food Science:

JEN, C.
KLURFELD, D. M.
SHELEF, L.

Physics:

BELLWIED, R.
CHANG, J. J.
CORMIER, T.
DUNIFER, G.
KARCHIN, P.
KAUPPILA, W. E.
KEYES, P. H.
KUO, P. K.
MORGAN, C.
NAIK, R.
SAPERSTEIN, A. M.
STEIN, T. S.

Psychology:

ALEXANDER, S.
COSCINA, D.
FIRESTONE, I. J.
FITZGERALD, J.
KAPLAN, K.
KILBEY, M. M.

LABOUVIE-VIEF, G.
LEVY, S.
URBERG, K.
WEISFELD, G.

College of Urban, Labour and Metropolitan Affairs

Clarence Hillberry Prof. of Urban Affairs:

GALSTER, G.

Coleman A. Young Prof. of Urban Affairs:

YOUNG, A. H.

Geography and Urban Planning:

BOYLE, R. M.
RESSE, L.
SINCLAIR, R.

Urban and Labor Studies:

BATES, T.
BROWN, D. R.
COOKE, W.
MASON, P.
SMOCK, S. M.
WOLMAN, H.
YOUNG, H.

Law School:

BROWN, K.
BURNHAM, W.
CALKINS, S.
DANNIN, E.
FRIEDMAN, J. M.
HENNING, P.
LITMAN, J.
McINTYRE, M. J.
MOGK, J.
SCHENK, A.

Eugene Applebaum College of Pharmacy and Health Sciences

Anaesthesia:

COOK, K. A.
CRAWFORTH, K. L.
HAGLUND, V. L.
MANGAHAS, P.
WALCZYK, M. L.
WORTH, P. A.

Clinical Laboratory Science:

ALDRIGE, G.
CASTILLO, J. B.
HARAKE, B.
WALLACE, A. M.

Mortuary Science:

BURDA-MASTROGIANIS, L.
FRADE, P.
FRITTS-WILLIAMS, M. L.
HUNTOON, R.

Occupational and Environmental Health Sciences:

BASSETT, D.
BHALLA, D.
KERFOOT, E. J.
TAFFE, B.
WARNER, P. O.

Occupational Therapy:

BROWN, K.
ESDAILE, S.
LUBORSKY, M.
LYSACK, C.
POWELL, N.

Pharmaceutical Sciences:

ABRAMSON, H.
BOLARIN, D.
COMMISSARIS, R.
CORCORAN, G. B.
FULLER, G. C.
GIBBS, R.
HIRATA, F.
LINDBLAD, W.
LOUIS-FERDINAND, R. T.
PITTS, D. K.
SVENSSON, C. K.
WORMSER, H.
WOSTER, P. M.

Pharmacy Practice:

CAPPELLETTY, D.
EDWARDS, D. J.
FAGAN, S.
JABER, L. A.
KALE-PRADHAN, P. B.
KEYS, P.
MILLER, M.
MOSER, L. R.
MUNZENBERGER, P. J.
RHONEY, D.
RYBAK, M. J.
SCHUMANN, W.
SINGH, R.
SLAUGHTER, R. L.
SMITH, G. B.
SMYTHE, M. A.
STEVENSON, J. G.
TISDALE, J. E.
VIVIAN, J. C.
WILSON, J.

Physical Therapy:

AMUNDSEN, L.
CARLSON, C.
DROVIN, J.
DUNLEAVY, K.
McNEVIN, N.
TALLEY, S.

Physician Assistant Studies:

FRICK, J.
NORMILE, H.
SIDDIQUE, M.
TODD, K.
WORMSER, H.

Radiation Therapy Technology:

CHADWELL, D.
KEMPA, A.

School of Business Administration

Accounting:

BILLINGS, B.
REINSTEIN, A.
SPAULDING, A.
VOLZ, W.

Finance and Business Economics:

HAMILTON, J.
SOMERS, T.
SPENCER, M.

Management:

MARTIN, J. E.
OSBORN, R. N.

Marketing:

BELTRAMINI, R.
CANNON, H.
JACKSON, G.
KELLY, J.
RIORDAN, E.
RYMER, J.
YAPRAK, A.

School of Medicine

Anaesthesiology:

BROWN, E. (H)

Anatomy:

BERNSTEIN, M.
GOODMAN, M.
GOSHGARIAN, H.
HAZLETT, L.
LASKER, G.
MAISEL, H.
MEYER, D.
MITCHELL, J. A.
MIZERES, N. J.
POURCHO, R.
RAFOLS, J.
ROHER, A.
SKOFF, R.

Audiology:

RINTELMANN, W. F. (H)

Biochemistry:

BROOKS, S.

BROWN, R. K.
EDWARDS, B.
EVANS, D.
JOHNSON, R.
LEE, C. P.
ROSEN, B.
ROWND, R.
VINOGRADOV, S.

Cardiology:

KLONER, R.
WYNNE, J.

Community Medicine:

WALLER, J.

Dermatology and Syphilology:

BIRMINGHAM, D.
HASHIMOTO, K.

Family Medicine:

DALLMAN, J.
GALLAGHER, R. E.
WERNER, P.

Immunology and Microbiology:

BERK, R.
BOROS, D. L.
BROWN, W. J.
DEGUISTI, D.
HAZLEH, L.
JEFFRIES, C.
KAPLAN, J.
KONG, Y.-C.
LEFFORD, M.
LEON, M.
LEVIN, S.
LISAK, R.
MONTGOMERY, P. C.
PALCHAUDHURI, S.
SOBEL, J.
SUNDICK, R.
SWANBORG, R. H.
WEINER, L. M.

Internal Medicine:

AL-SARRAF, M.
BAGCHI, N.
BERGSMAN, K. L.
BISHOP, C. R.
BRENNAN, M.
CLAPPER, I.
CORBETT, T.
FERNÁNDEZ-MADRID, F. B.
GRUNBERGER, G.
HEILBRUN, L.
HEPPNER, G.
KESSEL, D.
LERNER, S.
LEWIS, B. M.
LUM, L.
LYNNE-DAVIS, P.
MCDONALD, F.
MACK, R.
MAJUMDAR, A.
MARSH, J.
MIGDAL, S.
MILLER, R.
MUTCHNICK, M.
NAKEFF, A.
PRASAD, A. S.
PURI, P.
RESNICK, L.
SAMSON, M.
SANTEN, R.
SENSENBRENNER, L.
SOBEL, J.
SOWERS, J.
SPEARS, J.
TALMERS, F.
TRANCHIDA, L.
VAITKEVICIUS, V.
VALDIVIESO, M.
VALERIOTE, F.
WYNNE, J.

Neurology:

BENJAMINS, J. A.
CHUGANI, H.

DORE-DUFFY, P.
LEWITT, P.
LISAK, R.
NIGRO, M.

Neurosurgery:

DIAZ, F. G.
THOMAS, L. M.

Obstetrics and Gynaecology:

ABEL, E.
AGER, J.
BEHRMAN, S. J.
BERMAN, R.
COTTON, D.
DEPPE, G.
EVANS, M.
FREEDMAN, R.
LANCASTER, W.
MAMMEN, E.
MARIONA, F.
MILLER, O.
MOGHISSI, K.
POLAND, M.
ROMERO, R.
SACCO, A. G.
SHERMAN, A.
SOBEL, J.
SOKOL, R.
STRYKER, J.
SUBRAMANIAN, M.

Ophthalmology:

ESSNER, E.
FRANK, R. N.
JAMPEL, R. S.
PUKLIN, J.
SHICHI, H.
SHIN, D.
SPOOR, T.

Orthopaedic Surgery:

FITZGERALD, R.
MANOLI II, A.
RYAN, J.

Otolaryngology:

COHN, A. M.
DRESCHER, D.
DWORKIN, J.
JACOBS, J.
MATHOG, R. H.

Paediatrics:

BEN-YOSEPH, Y.
BRANS, Y. W.
CASH, R.
CHUGANI, H.
COHEN, S.
COLLINS, J.
DAJANI, A. S.
EPSTEIN, M.
FAROOKI, Z.
FLEISCHMANN, L.
GRUSKIN, A.
GUTAI, J.
KAPLAN, J.
KAUFFMAN, R.
LUM, L.
LUSHER, J.
NIGRO, M.
OSTREA, E.
PINSKY, W. W.
RAUMDRANATH, Y.
ROBIN, A.
SAMAIK, A.
SARNAIK, A.
SENSENBRENNER, L.
SHANKARIAN, G.
SLOVIS, T.

Pathology:

BEDROSSIAN, C.
BROWN, W.
CRISSMAN, J.
DALE, E.
EVANS, M.
GIACOMELLI, F. E.
HONN, K.

KURKINEN, M.
MAMMEN, E.
MILLER, D.
PALUTKE, M.
PERRIN, E. V.
RAZ, A.
SHEAHAN, D.
SPITZ, W. U.
THIBERT, R.
WEINER, L.
WIENER, J.
ZAK, B.

Pharmacology:

ANDERSON, G.
BANNON, M.
CHOPRA, D.
DUTTA, S.
GOLDMAN, H.
HIRATA, F.
HOLLENBERG, P. F.
KESSEL, D.
MARKS, B.
NOVAK, R.
SLOANE, B.
WAKADE, A.

Physiology:

BARRACO, R.
CHURCHILL, P. C.
DUNBAR, J. C.
FOA, P.
GALA, R.
HONG, F. T.
LAWSON, D.
MCCOY, L. E.
MAMMEN, E.
NYBOER, J.
PENNEY, D.
PHILLIS, J. W.
RAM, J.
RILLEMA, J. A.
SEEGERS, W.
WALZ, D. A. (H)

Psychiatry:

BANNON, M.
FISCHHOFF, J.
FREEDMAN, R.
GALLOWAY, M.
KAPATOS, G.
KUHN, D.
LEWITT, P.
LUBY, E.
LYCAKI, H.
POHL, R.
ROSENBAUM, A.
ROSENZWEIG, N.
SARWER-FONER, G.
SCHORER, C.
SITARAM, N.
UHDE, T.

Radiation Oncology:

HERSKOVIC, A. M.
HONN, K. V.
MARUYAMA, Y.
ORTON, C. G.
PORTER, A.

Radiology:

KLING, G.
SOULEN, R.
WOLLSCHLAEGER, G.

Surgery:

BERGUER, R.
FROMM, D.
KLEIN, M.
LEDGERWOOD, A. M.
LUCAS, C.
PHILIPPART, A.
ROSENBERG, J. C.
SILVA, Y. J.
STEPHENSON, L.
SUGAWA, C.
WALT, A. J.
WEAVER, A. W.
WILSON, R. F.

Urology:
JAFFER, D.
MONTIE, J.
PERLMUTTER, A. D.
PONTES, J.
School of Social Work:
BEVERLY, C.
BRANDALL, J.
MOXLEY, D.
University Libraries
Library and Information Science:
ALBRITTON, R. L.
BAKER, L. M.
BROWN-SYED, C. L.
EZELL, C. L.
FIELD, J. J.
HOLLEY, R.
JOHNSON, N. B.
MIKA, J.
NEAVILL, G. B.
POWELL, R.
SPITERI, L. F.

WESTERN MICHIGAN UNIVERSITY

1903 W Michigan Ave, Kalamazoo, MI 49008-5200
Telephone: (269) 387-1000
E-mail: ask-wmu@wmich.edu
Internet: www.wmich.edu
Founded 1903, present name and status 1957
State control
Academic year: July to June
Pres.: Dr JOHN M. DUNN
Provost and Vice-Pres. for Academic Affairs: Dr TIMOTHY J. GREENE
Vice-Provost for Enrolment Management: KEITH HEARIT
Vice-Pres. for Government Affairs and Univ. Relations: GREGORY J. ROSINE
Vice-Pres. for Devt and Alumni Relations: JAMES S. THOMAS
Vice Pres. of Diversity and Inclusion: Dr MARTHA B. WARFIELD
Vice-Pres. for Research: Dr DANIEL M. LITYNSKI
Vice-Pres. for Student Affairs: DIANE K. ANDERSON
Registrar: CARRIE CUMMING
Dean for Univ. Libraries: Dr JOSEPH G. REISH
Library of 4,949,153 vols, 52,673 periodical titles
Number of teachers: 1,437
Number of students: 25,086
Publications: *Analysis of Verbal Behaviour* (1 a year), *Behavior Analyst* (2 a year), *Caribe* (2 a year, jtly with Western Michigan Univ. in Kalamazoo, Univ. of Northern Florida in Jacksonville and Marquette Univ. of Milwaukee), *Cistercian Institute Publications* (1 a year), *Comparative Drama* (4 a year), *Journal of Comparative Religion* (online), *Journal of Sociology and Social Welfare* (4 a year), *Medieval Prosopography* (2 a year), *Medieval Review* (online), *Medievally Speaking* (2 a year), *Mid-American Journal of Business* (4 a year), *Old English Newsletter* (4 a year), *Proceedings of the Heraclitean Society* (1 a year), *Reading Horizons Journal* (4 a year), *Studies in Iconography* (1 a year), *Teaching Ethics Journal: The Journal for the Society for Ethics Across the Curriculum* (1 a year), *The Hilltop Review: A Journal of Western Michigan University Graduate Research* (2 a year), *The Parkview Edition* (2 a year), *Third Coast* (2 a year), *WMU Magazine* (2 a year), *WMU Research Magazine* (2 a year), *Yearbook of Langland Studies* (1 a year)

DEANS
College of Arts and Sciences: Dr ALEXANDER J. ENYEDI
College of Aviation: DAVID M. POWELL
College of Education and Human Devt: Dr VAN COOLEY
College of Engineering and Applied Sciences: Dr ANTHONY J. VIZZINI
College of Fine Arts: Dr MARGARET M. MERRION
College of Health and Human Services: Dr EARLIE M. WASHINGTON
Graduate College: Dr SUSAN STAPLETON
Haworth College of Business: Dr KAY M. PALAN
Lee Honors College: Dr NICOLAS A. ANDREADIS

WESTERN THEOLOGICAL SEMINARY

101 E 13th St, Holland, MI 49423
Telephone: (616) 392-8555
Fax: (616) 392-2072
E-mail: admissions@westernsem.edu
Internet: www.westernsem.edu
Founded 1866
Private control
Academic year: September to May
Areas of study: divinity, ministry, theology, social work
Pres.: Dr TIMOTHY L. BROWN
Dean and Vice-Pres. for Academic Affairs: Dr LEANNE VAN DYK
Vice-Pres. for Advancement and Communications: JOHN NORDSTROM
Dir for Admissions: Dr MARK POPPEN
Dean for Students: Dr MATT FLODING
Registrar: PAT DYKHUIS
Library Dir: PAUL M. SMITH
Library of 100,000 vols
Number of teachers: 18
Number of students: 230

MINNESOTA

ADLER GRADUATE SCHOOL

550 E 78th St, Richfield, MN 55423
Telephone: (612) 861-7554
Fax: (612) 861-7559
E-mail: info@alfredadler.edu
Internet: www.alfredadler.edu
Founded 1967 as Minnesota Adlerian Soc., present status 1991, present name 2004
Private control
Offers Masters degree in Adlerian counselling and psychotherapy
Pres.: Dr DANIEL A. HAUGEN
Academic Vice-Pres. and Dean: Dr DAVID J. MATHIEU
Vice-Pres. for Finance: LESLIE ROHDE
Dir for Admissions and Student Services: EVELYN HAAS
Registrar: JEANETTE MAYNARD NELSON.

AUGSBURG COLLEGE

2211 Riverside Ave S, Minneapolis, MN 55454
Telephone: (612) 330-1000
Fax: (612) 330-1649
E-mail: augpres@augsburg.edu
Internet: www.augsburg.edu
Founded 1869
Private control
Areas of study: accounting, American Indian studies, biology, business administration, chemistry, communication studies, computer science, economics, education, engineering, finance, health education, history, international relations, management information systems, marketing, mathematics, medieval studies, metro-urban studies, modern languages, music, philosophy, physical education, physics, political science, psychology, religion, sociology, theatre arts, women's studies
Pres.: PAUL C. PRIBBENOW
Vice-Pres.: CHRISTINE SZAJ
Vice-Pres. for Academic Affairs and Dean for College: BARBARA FARLEY
Vice-Pres. for Enrolment Management: JULIE EDSTROM
Vice-Pres. for Finance and Admin.: TAMMY McGEE
Vice-Pres. for Institutional Advancement: JEREMY WELLS
Vice-Pres. for Student Affairs: ANN GARVEY
Vice-Pres. and Chief Information Officer: LEIF ANDERSON
Registrar: WAYNE KALLESTAD
Dir for Library Services: JANE ANN NELSON
Library of 190,000 vols
Number of teachers: 305 (125 full-time, 180 part-time)
Number of students: 4,054
Publication: *Augsburg Now* (4 a year).

BETHANY LUTHERAN COLLEGE

700 Luther Dr., Mankato, MN 56001
Telephone: (507) 344-7000
Fax: (507) 344-7376
E-mail: admissions@blc.edu
Internet: www.blc.edu
Founded 1911 as Bethany Ladies College
Private control
Liberal arts college
Pres.: Dr DAN R. BRUSS
Vice-Pres. for Student Affairs: STEVE JAEGER
Dean for Academic Affairs: ERIC WOLLER
Dean for Admissions: DON WESTPHAL
Registrar: MARY JO STARKSON
Dir for Library Services: ORRIN AUSEN
Library of 68,000 vols
Number of teachers: 71
Number of students: 612
Publication: *Bethany Report*.

BETHEL UNIVERSITY

3900 Bethel Dr., St Paul, MN 55112-6999
Telephone: (651) 638-6400
Fax: (651) 638-6008
E-mail: buadmissions-cas@bethel.edu
Internet: www.bethel.edu
Founded 1871, present name 2004
Private control
Academic year: August to June
School of the churches of the Baptist Gen. Conf.; 3 seminaries in Minnesota, California and Pennsylvania
Pres.: JAMES H. BARNES, III
Provost and Exec. Vice-Pres.: DAVID CLARK
Sr Vice-Pres. for Finance and Admin.: KATHLEEN J. NELSON
Sr Vice-Pres. for Strategic Planning and Research: JOSEPH D. LALUZERNE
Sr Vice-Pres. for Univ. Relations: PAT MAZOROL
Vice-Pres. for Devt: BRUCE W. ANDERSON
Vice-Pres. for Student Life: EDEE SCHULZE
Registrar: KATRINA CHAPMAN
Dir for Univ. Libraries: DAVID STEWART
Library of 146,026 vols, 21,027 e-books, 35,405 journals, 5,000 audio resources, 6,596 video resources
Number of teachers: 237 (207 at colleges and graduate school, 30 at seminary)
Number of students: 6,400

DEANS
Bethel Seminary: DAVID CLARK (acting)

College of Adult and Professional Studies: DICK CROMBIE
College of Arts and Sciences: DEB HARLESS
Graduate School: DICK CROMBIE

CAPELLA UNIVERSITY

Capella Tower, 225 S Sixth St, Ninth Fl., Minneapolis, MN 55402
Telephone: (612) 339-8650
Fax: (612) 977-5060
E-mail: info@capella.edu
Internet: www.capella.edu
Founded 1993 as Graduate School of America, present name and status 1999
Private control
Pres.: Dr DEBORAH BUSHWAY
Provost: Dr CHARLES TIFFIN
Number of teachers: 1,604
Number of students: 35,755

DEANS

Harold Abel School of Social and Behavioural Sciences: DAVID CHAPMAN
School of Business and Technology: Dr WILLIAM REED (acting)
School of Education: Dr BARBARA BUTTS WILLIAMS
School of Public Service Leadership: SUZANNE HOLMES
School of Undergraduate Studies: FERANDA WILLIAMSON

CARLETON COLLEGE

1 N College St, Northfield, MN 55057
Telephone: (507) 222-4000
Fax: (507) 222-4526
E-mail: admissions@carleton.edu
Internet: www.carleton.edu
Founded 1866
Private control
Academic year: September to June (3 semesters)

Depts of African-American studies; American studies; Arabic; archaeology; art and art history; Asian languages and literatures; Asian studies; biochemistry; biology; chemistry; cinema and media studies; classical languages; cognitive science; computer science; cross cultural studies; economics; educational studies; English; environmental studies; European studies; French and Francophone studies; geology; German; Hebrew; history; international relations; Latin American studies; linguistics; literary and cultural studies; mathematics; medieval and renaissance studies; music; neuroscience; philosophy; physics and astronomy; political science; physical education, athletics and recreation; psychology; religion; Russian; sociology and anthropology; Spanish; theatre and dance; women's and gender studies; off-campus studies, pre-med and summer academic programmes
Pres.: STEVEN G. POSKANZER
Vice-Pres. and Dean for Admissions and Financial Aid: PAUL THIBOUTOT
Vice-Pres. and Treas.: FREDERICK ROGERS
Vice-Pres. for External Relations: DON HASSELTINE
Vice-Pres. for Student Devt and Dean for Students: HUDLIN WAGNER
Dean for College: BEVERLY NAGEL
Registrar: ROGER LASLEY
Librarian: SAM DEMAS
Library of 563,581 vols of books, 446,089 e-books, 39,060 e-journals, 11,886 spec. collns, 278,138 vols of govt documents, 12,490 media colln
Number of teachers: 235
Number of students: 1,991
Publication: Carleton College Voice.

COLLEGE OF SAINT BENEDICT

37 S College Ave, St Joseph, MN 56374-2099
Telephone: (320) 363-5011
Fax: (320) 363-5050
E-mail: admission@csbsju.edu
Internet: www.csbsju.edu
Founded 1913
Catholic liberal arts college for women partnered with Saint John's Univ. for men; depts of fine arts, humanities, natural sciences, social sciences, interdisciplinary and pre-professional programmes
Private control
Pres.: Dr MARYANN BAENNINGER
Chief of Staff: KATHRYN ENKE
Provost: RITA KNUESEL
Vice-Provost: JOE DES JARDINS
Vice-Pres. for Admission: CAL MOSLEY
Vice-Pres. for Finance and Admin.: SUSAN PALMER
Vice-Pres. for Institutional Advancement: KIMBERLY MOTES
Vice-Pres. for Student Devt: MARY GELLER
Academic Dean: Dr RICHARD ICE
Dean for Students: JODY TERHAAR
Dir for Libraries and Media: KATHY PARKER
Library of 640,000 vols
Number of teachers: 198 (170 full-time, 28 part-time)
Number of students: 2,086
Publications: CSB/SJU Magazine, Saint Benedict's, Studio One (1 a year), The Record.

COLLEGE OF ST SCHOLASTICA

1200 Kenwood Ave, Duluth, MN 55811-4199
Telephone: (218) 723-6000
Fax: (218) 723-5991
E-mail: admissions@css.edu
Internet: www.css.edu
Founded 1912
Private control
Academic year: September to August
Extended campuses at Brainerd, St Cloud, St Paul and Rochester in Minnesota
Pres.: Dr LARRY GOODWIN
Vice-Pres. for Academic Affairs: Dr ELIZABETH DOMHOLDT
Vice-Pres. for Enrolment Management: ERIC BERG
Vice-Pres. for College Advancement: MARGOT ZELENZ
Vice-Pres. for Student Life and Dean for Students: STEVE LYONS
Registrar: GEORGE BEATTIE
Library Dir: KEVIN MCGREW
Library of 127,400 vols
Number of teachers: 399 (183 full-time, 12 part-time, 204 adjunct)
Number of students: 4,014

DEANS

School of Arts and Letters: Dr TAMMY OSTRANDER
School of Business and Technology: Prof. Dr KURT R. LINBERG
School of Education: JO OLSEN
School of Health Sciences: RONDELL BERKELAND
School of Nursing: Dr MARTHA WITRAK
School of Sciences: GERALD HENKEL-JOHNSON

COLLEGE OF VISUAL ARTS

344 Summit Ave, St Paul, MN 55102
Telephone: (651) 757-4000
Fax: (651) 757-4010
E-mail: info@cva.edu
Internet: www.cva.edu
Founded 1924
Private control

Areas of study: fine arts, graphic design, illustration, photography
Pres. and Chief Academic Officer: ANN LEDY
Vice-Pres. for Admin. and Institutional Research and Gen. Counsel: Dr SUSAN SHORT
Dir for Admissions: ELYAN PAZ
Dir for Student Life: ANNE WHITE
Registrar: LOIS CANEDAY
Library Dir: KATHRYN HEUER
Library of 10,200 vols, 31,000 slides, 300 video recordings, 40 journals
Number of teachers: 65
Number of students: 250

CONCORDIA COLLEGE

901 Eighth St S, Moorhead, MN 56562
Telephone: (218) 299-4000
Fax: (218) 299-3947
E-mail: admissions@cord.edu
Internet: www.cord.edu
Founded 1891
Private control
Areas of study: education, liberal arts, nursing
Pres.: Dr WILLIAM J. CRAFT
Provost and Dean for College: Dr MARK KREJCI
Vice-Pres. for Advancement: TERESA L. HARLAND
Vice-Pres. for Enrolment: STEVEN M. SCHUETZ
Registrar: NANCY PENNA
Library Dir: SHARON HOVERSON
Library of 300,000 vols, 50 newspapers, 1,200 periodicals
Number of teachers: 194 (full-time)
Number of students: 2,800
Publication: Concordia Magazine (2 a year).

CONCORDIA UNIVERSITY, ST PAUL

275 Syndicate St N, St Paul, MN 55104-5494
Telephone: (651) 641-8278
Fax: (651) 603-6320
E-mail: admission@csp.edu
Internet: www.csp.edu
Founded 1893
Private control
Academic year: August to May
Pres.: Rev. THOMAS RIES
Sr Vice-Pres.: Dr ERIC LAMOTT
Exec. Vice-Pres.: Dr CHERYL CHATMAN
Vice-Pres. for Academic Affairs: LONN MALY
Vice-Pres. for Finance: Rev. MICHAEL DORNER
Vice-Pres. for Univ. Advancement: RUSTY SELTZ
Registrar: TONI SQUIRES
Dir for Library Services: Dr CHARLOTTE KNOCHE
Library of 152,000 vols
Number of teachers: 344 (83 full-time, 261 part-time)
Number of students: 2,800

DEANS

College of Arts and Sciences: Dr DAVID LUMPP
College of Business and Organizational Leadership: Dr BRUCE CORRIE
College of Education: DON HELMSTETTER
College of Vocation and Ministry: Rev. Dr DAVID LUMPP

CROSSROADS COLLEGE

920 Mayowood Rd SW, Rochester, MN 55902
Telephone: (507) 288-4563
Fax: (507) 288-9046
E-mail: academic@crossroadscollege.edu
Internet: www.crossroadscollege.edu

Founded 1913 as Int. Christian Bible College Asscn, present name 2002
Private control
Academic year: August to May
Offers degrees in Biblical thought and literature, business administration, counselling psychology, family, youth and community, general ministry, general studies, intercultural studies, music, pastoral leadership
Pres. and Vice-Pres. for Advancement: MICHAEL KILGALLIN
Vice-Pres. for Academics: Prof. CLAUDIO DIVINO
Vice-Pres. for Admin. and Finance: ROGER LANGSETH
Vice-Pres. for Student Devt: TIM MCKINNEY
Dir for Admissions: CHRISTOPHER WILLIAMS
Registrar: ROBERT DAMON
Dir for Library: JIM GODSEY
Library of 35,000 vols, 300 periodicals
Number of teachers: 21
Number of students: 184

CROWN COLLEGE

8700 College View Dr., St Bonifacius, MN 55375
Telephone: (952) 446-4100
Fax: (952) 446-4149
E-mail: info@crown.edu
Internet: www.crown.edu
Founded 1916, present name 1992
Private control
Academic year: August to May
Depts of Biblical and theological studies, business and sport management, Christian ministry, communication arts, humanities and social sciences, mathematics and science, music, nursing, teacher education
Pres.: Dr RICK MANN
Vice-Pres. for Academic Affairs: Dr SCOTT H. MOATS
Vice-Pres. for Advancement: WENDY G. EDGAR
Vice-Pres. for Enrolment Services and Marketing: MIKE PRICE
Vice-Pres. for Finance and Operations: DAVID TARRANT
Vice-Pres. for Student Devt: MIKE SOHM
Registrar: CHERYL FISK
Dir for Library: Dr DENNIS INGOLGSLAND
Library of 160,000 vols), 70,000 microforms, 209,000 e-books, 46,000 journals
Number of teachers: 65
Number of students: 1,200
Publication: *Bridge*

DEANS

Graduate School and Online Studies: Dr JAMES HUNTER

DUNWOODY COLLEGE OF TECHNOLOGY

818 Dunwoody Blvd, Minneapolis, MN 55403-1192
Telephone: (612) 374-5800
Fax: (612) 374-4128
E-mail: info@dunwoody.edu
Internet: www.dunwoody.edu
Founded 1914
Private control
Offers Bachelors of science in applied management, health informatics, industrial engineering technology, interior design
Pres.: Dr RICH WAGNER
Sr Vice-Pres.: ROBERT DOTY
Vice-Pres. for Devt and Alumni Relations: MARK SKIPPER
Registrar: YUN BOK CHRISTENSON
Librarian: KRISTINA OBERSTAR
Number of students: 1,409

GUSTAVUS ADOLPHUS COLLEGE

800 W College Ave, St Peter, MN 56082
Telephone: (507) 933-8000
Fax: (507) 933-7041
E-mail: admission@gustavus.edu
Internet: www.gustavus.edu
Founded 1862
Private control
Academic year: September to June
Divs of education, fine arts, humanities, natural sciences and mathematics, social sciences
Pres.: JACK R. OHLE
Provost and Dean for College: Dr MARK J. BRAUN
Vice-Pres. for Enrolment Management: Dr THOMAS M. CRADY
Vice-Pres. for Institutional Advancement: THOMAS W. YOUNG
Vice-Pres. for Student Life and Dean for Students: Dr JONES VANHECKE
Registrar: KRISTIANNE WESTPHAL
Library Chair.: BARBARA FISTER
Library of 250,000 vols
Number of teachers: 277 (205 full-time, 72 part-time)
Number of students: 2,448 (f. t. e.)

HAMLINE UNIVERSITY

1536 Hewitt Ave, St Paul, MN 55104-1284
Telephone: (612) 523-2800
E-mail: admission@hamline.edu
Internet: www.hamline.edu
Founded 1854
Private control
Campus at Minneapolis (Minnesota)
Pres.: LINDA HANSON
Vice-Pres. for Academic and Student Affairs: DAVID STERN
Dean for Students: ALAN SICKBERT
Dir for Admission: MILYON TRULOVE
Univ. Registrar: TIMOTHY TRAFFIE
Dir for Bush Memorial Library: DIANE CLAYTON
Dir of Bush Memorial Library: JULIE ROCHAT
Dir of Law Library: GRACE M. MILLS
Library of 230,000 vols
Number of teachers: 152
Number of students: 4,900
Publications: *Hamline*, *Hamline Law Review*, *Journal of Law and Religion*, *Journal of Public Law and Policy*

DEANS

College of Liberal Arts: JOHN MATACHEK
School of Business: Dr ANNE M. MCCARTHY
School of Education: Dr LARRY HARRIS
School of Law: DONALD LEWIS

LUTHER SEMINARY

2481 Como Ave, St Paul, MN 55108
Telephone: (651) 641-3456
Fax: (651) 523-1609
E-mail: infodesk@luthersem.edu
Internet: www.luthersem.edu
Founded 1917
Private control
Academic year: September to May
Offers degrees in arts, divinity, ministry, philosophy, sacred music, social work, theology
Pres.: Rev. Dr RICHARD H. BLIESE
Vice-Pres. for Academic Affairs: DAVID EVERETT
Vice-Pres. for Seminary Relations: TOM JOLIVETTE
Vice-Pres. for Admin. and Finance: DONALD LEWIS
Vice-Pres. for Student Affairs and Enrolment: CARRIE CARROLL

Academic Dean: LESLIE ORTIZ
Dir for Admissions: SARA WILHELM GARBERS
Registrar: DIANE DONCITS
Dir for Library Services: PAUL DANIELS
Library of 250,000 vols
Number of teachers: 45
Number of students: 806

MACALESTER COLLEGE

1600 Grand Ave, St Paul, MN 55105-1899
Telephone: (612) 696-6000
Fax: (612) 696-6500
E-mail: admissions@macalester.edu
Internet: www.macalester.edu
Founded 1874
Private control
Areas of study: humanities and fine arts, natural sciences, social sciences
Pres.: BRIAN C. ROSENBERG
Provost and Dean for Faculty: KATHLEEN M. MURRAY
Vice-Pres. for Admin. and Finance: DAVID WHEATON
Vice-Pres. for Advancement: THOMAS P. BONNER
Vice-Pres. for Student Affairs: LAURIE B. HAMRE
Dean for Admissions and Financial Aid: LORNE T. ROBINSON
Dean for Students: JIM HOPPE
Registrar: JAYNE NIEMI
Library Dir: TERESA FISHEL
Library of 400,000 vols
Number of teachers: 165 (full-time)
Number of students: 1,987
Publication: *Macalester Today* (4 a year, print and online (www.macalester.edu/news/macalestertoday)).

MARTIN LUTHER COLLEGE

1995 Luther Court, New Ulm, MN 56073-3300
Telephone: (507) 354-8221
Fax: (507) 354-8225
E-mail: mlcadmit@mlc-wels.edu
Internet: www.mlc-wels.edu
Founded 1995 by merger of Dr Martin Luther College (f. 1884) with Northwestern College (f. 1865)
Private control
Academic year: August to May
Pres.: Rev. MARK G. ZARLING
Vice-Pres. for Academics: Dr DAVID O. WENDLER
Vice-Pres. for Admin.: Prof. STEVEN R. THIESFELDT
Vice-Pres. for Enrolment Management: Prof. PHILIP M. LEYRER
Vice-Pres. for Student Life: JEFFREY L. SCHONE
Dir for Admissions: MARK STEIN
Registrar: GWEN KRAL
Library Dir: DAVID GOSDECK
Number of teachers: 82
Number of students: 717

DEANS

Educational Ministry: Prof. KURT WITTMERSHAUS
Pastoral Ministry: Prof. DANIEL BALGE

MAYO MEDICAL SCHOOL, COLLEGE OF MEDICINE

200 First St, SW, Rochester, MN 55905
Telephone: (507) 284-3627
Fax: (507) 266-5298
E-mail: medschooladmissions@mayo.edu
Internet: www.mayo.edu/mms
Private control
Dean: KEITH D. LINDOR

Assoc. Dean for Student Affairs: PATRICIA L. BARRIER
Registrar: DELORES BARTZ
Library of 400,003 vols, 4,712 journals, 4,082 e-journals, 92,626 book titles
Number of students: 50
Publications: *Mayo Alumni* (4 a year), *Mayo Clinic Proceedings* (12 a year).

MINNEAPOLIS COLLEGE OF ART AND DESIGN

2501 Stevens Ave, Minneapolis, MN 55404
Telephone: (612) 874-3700
Fax: (612) 874-3701
E-mail: info@mcad.edu
Internet: www.mcad.edu
Founded 1886 as Minneapolis School of Fine Arts
Private control
Academic year: September to May
Divs of design, fine arts, liberal arts, media arts, science
Pres.: JAY COOGAN
Vice-Pres. for Academic Affairs: Prof. VINCE LEO
Vice-Pres. for Admin.: PAM NEWSOME-PROCH-NIAK
Vice-Pres. for Enrolment Management: WILLIAM MULLEN
Vice-Pres. for Institutional Advancement: JOAN GRATHWOL OLSON
Vice-Pres. for Student Affairs: SUSAN CALMENSON
Dir for Continuing Studies: HOWARD ORANSKY
Registrar: JACQUELINE CHESTNUT
Library Dir: SUZANNE DEGLER
Library of 60,000 vols
Number of teachers: 65
Number of students: 700
Publication: *MCAD Magazine*.

MINNESOTA STATE COLLEGES AND UNIVERSITIES

30 E Seventh St, Suite 350, St Paul, MN 55101-7804
Telephone: (612) 296-8012
Fax: (612) 297-5550
E-mail: chancellor@so.mnscu.edu
Internet: www.mnscu.edu
Founded 1995
Sate control
Academic year: August to May
Incorporates 31 colleges and univs, incl. 24 two-year colleges and 7 state univs
Chancellor: STEVEN J. ROSENSTONE
Vice-Chancellor for Academic and Student Affairs: Dr DOUGLAS KNOWLTON
Vice-Chancellor for Advancement: MICHAEL DOUGHERTY
Number of students: 250,000 (system-wide)
Publication: *The Minnesota State Colleges & Universities Magazine* (2 a year).

CONSTITUENT UNIVERSITIES

Bemidji State University

1500 Birchmont Ave, NE, Bemidji, MN 56601-2699
Telephone: (218) 755-2001
Fax: (218) 755-4048
E-mail: admissions@bemidjistate.edu
Internet: www.bemidjistate.edu
Founded 1919
Pres.: Dr RICHARD HANSON
Provost and Vice-Pres. for Academic Affairs: ROBERT J. GRIGGS
Vice-Pres. for Finance and Admin.: WILLIAM MAKI

Vice-Pres. for Student Devt and Enrolment: Dr MARY WARD
Dir for Admissions: MARYJO CHIRPICH
Registrar: MICHELLE FRENZEL
Dean for Library Services: ROBERT GRIGGS
Library of 400,000 vols, 900 periodicals
Number of teachers: 220 (full-time)
Number of students: 5,000
Publication: *Horizons*

DEANS

College of Arts and Sciences: Dr P JOAN POOR
College of Business, Technology and Communication: Dr CAROL L. NIELSEN
College of Health Sciences and Human Ecology: Dr PATRICIA L. ROGERS
School of Graduate Studies: Dr PATRICIA L. ROGERS

Metropolitan State University

700 E Seventh St, St Paul, MN 55106-5000
Telephone: (616) 793-1300
Fax: (616) 772-7738
Internet: www.metrostate.edu
Founded 1971
Pres.: Dr SUE K. HAMMERSMITH
Provost and Vice-Pres. for Academic Affairs: GARY SEILER
Vice-Pres. for Admin. and Finance: MURTUZA SIDDIQUI
Vice-Pres. for Student Affairs and Enrolment Management: TRENDA BOYUM-BREEN
Vice-Pres. for Univ. Advancement: ROBERT HEUERMANN
Dir for Admissions: JULIO VARGAS-ESSEX
Registrar: DARYL JOHNSON
Dean for Library and Information Services: BRUCE WILLMS (acting)
Number of teachers: 820 (168 full-time, 652 part-time)
Number of students: 9,606

DEANS

College of Arts and Sciences: BECKY L. OMDAHL
College of Management: PAUL HUO
College of Nursing and Health Sciences: ANN LEJA
College of Professional Studies: DANIEL ABEBE
First College: DANIEL ABEBE
School of Law Enforcement and Criminal Justice: VIRGINIA LANE

Minnesota State University, Mankato

309 Wigley Admin. Center, Mankato, MN 56001
Telephone: (507) 389-1111
Fax: (507) 389-6200
E-mail: presidentsoffice@mnsu.edu
Internet: www.mnsu.edu
Founded 1868 as Mankato Normal School, present name 1999, present status 2009
Academic year: August to May
Pres.: Dr RICHARD DAVENPORT
Vice-Pres. for Academic and Student Affairs: Dr SCOTT R. OLSON
Vice-Pres. for Finance and Admin.: RICHARD J. STRAKA
Vice-Pres. for Technology: ED CLARK
Vice-Pres. for Univ. Advancement: DOUG MAYO
Assoc. Vice-Pres. for Student Affairs and Enrolment Management: Dr DAVID P. JONES
Dean for Students: MARY DOWD
Registrar: MARCIUS BROCK
Dean for Library Services: JOAN ROCA
Library of 693,973 vols
Number of teachers: 640
Number of students: 15,000

Publications: *Blue Earth Review* (online (english.mnsu.edu/blueearth)), *Today* (3 a year)

DEANS

College of Allied Health and Nursing: HARRY KRAMPF
College of Arts and Humanities: WALTER ZAKAHI
College of Business: Dr BRENDA FLANNERY
College of Education: Dr JEAN HAAR
College of Extended Learning: BECKY COPPER-GLENZ
College of Graduate Studies and Research: Dr BARRY RIES
College of Science, Engineering and Technology: Dr VIJENDRA AGARWAL
College of Social and Behavioural Sciences: Dr KIM GREER

Minnesota State University Moorhead

1104 Seventh Ave, S, Moorhead, MN 56563
Telephone: (218) 236-2011
Fax: (218) 236-2168
E-mail: admissions@mnstate.edu
Internet: www.mnstate.edu
Founded 1887, present status 1975, present name 2000
Academic year: August to May
Pres.: Dr EDNA MORA SZYMANSKI
Provost and Sr Vice-Pres. for Academic Affairs: Dr ANNE E. BLACKHURST
Vice-Pres. for Enrolment Management: DIANE SOLINGER
Vice-Pres. for Finance and Admin. Affairs: JAN MAHONEY
Vice-Pres. for Student Affairs: WARREN K. WIESE
Registrar: RUSSELL CURLEY
Dean for Instructional Resources: BRITTNEY GOODMAN
Library of 595,000 vols
Number of teachers: 547
Number of students: 8,500

DEANS

College of Arts and Humanities: TIM BORCHERS
College of Business and Industry: MARSHA WEBER
College of Education and Human Services: TERI WALSETH
College of Social and Natural Sciences: MICHELLE MALOTT
University College: DENISE GORSLINE

St Cloud State University

720 Fourth Ave, S, St Cloud, MN 56301-4498
Telephone: (320) 308-0121
E-mail: scsu4u@stcloudstate.edu
Internet: www.stcloudstate.edu
Founded 1869, present status 1975
Academic year: August to July
Pres.: EARL H. POTTER, III
Provost and Vice-Pres. for Academic Affairs: DEVINDER MALHOTRA
Vice-Pres. for Admin. Affairs: STEVE LUDWIG
Vice-Pres. for Student Life and Devt: WANDA OVERLAND
Vice-Pres. for Univ. Advancement: CRAIG WRUCK
Dean for Learning Resources Services: RUTH ZIETLOW
Library: 2.767m. vols (incl. 570,000 books, 1.9m. microforms incl. fed. and state documents, 1,000 print periodicals, 15,000 e-periodicals, 1,500 maps, 26,000 media items)
Number of teachers: 650
Number of students: 17,231
Publications: *Dimensions* (2 a year), *Upper Mississippi Harvest* (1 a year)

DEANS

College of Liberal Arts: MARK SPRINGER
College of Science and Engineering: DAVID DEGROOTE
Herberger Business School: DIANA LAWSON
School of Education: OSMAN ALAWIYE
School of Health and Human Services: MONICA DEVERS
School of Public Affairs: ORN BODVARSSON

Southwest Minnesota State University

1501 State St, Marshall, MN 56258-1598

Telephone: (507) 537-7021
Fax: (507) 537-7154
Internet: www.smsu.edu

Founded 1963
Academic year: August to May

Pres.: Dr RONALD A. WOOD
Provost and Vice-Pres. for Academic and Student Affairs: Dr BETH WETHERBY
Vice-Pres. for Finance and Admin.: DEBRA KERKAERT
Assoc. Vice-Pres. for Advancement: WILLIAM MULSO
Dean for Students: SCOTT CROWELL
Registrar: PATRICIA CARMODY
Univ. Librarian: KATHLEEN ASHE

Library of 160,000 vols
Number of teachers: 142
Number of students: 6,585

DEANS

College of Arts, Letters and Sciences: Dr JAN LOFT
College of Business, Education, Graduate and Professional Studies: Dr RAPHAEL ONYEAGHALA

Winona State University

POB 5838, 175 W Mark St, Winona, MN 55987

Telephone: (507) 457-5000
Fax: (507) 457-2415
E-mail: admissions@winona.edu
Internet: www.winona.edu

Founded 1858
Academic year: August to May

Pres.: Dr JUDITH A. RAMALEY
Provost and Vice-Pres. for Academic Affairs: NANCY O. JANNIK
Vice-Pres. for Finance and Admin. Services: KURT LOHIDE (acting)
Vice-Pres. for Student Life and Devt: CONNIE GORES
Vice-Pres. for Univ. Advancement: JAMES C. SCHMIDT
Dean for Students: KAREN JOHNSON
Dean for Library: THOMAS BREMER

Library of 350,000 vols (incl. 220,000 books, 125,000 bound periodicals, 8,000 video cassettes and DVDs, 1,000 current print periodical subscriptions)
Number of teachers: 350
Number of students: 8,896

Publication: *Currents*

DEANS

College of Business: JAMES MURPHY
College of Education: HANK RUBIN
College of Liberal Arts: RALPH TOWNSEND
College of Nursing and Health Science: WILLIAM MCBREEN
College of Science and Engineering: HAROLD ORNES (acting)

NORTH CENTRAL UNIVERSITY

910 Elliot Ave, Minneapolis, MN 55404

Telephone: (612) 343-4400
Fax: (612) 343-4778
E-mail: info@northcentral.edu
Internet: www.northcentral.edu

Founded 1930 as North Central Bible Institute, present name 1998
Private control
Academic year: August to May

Depts of arts and sciences, Bible and theology, business administration, Carlstrom deaf studies, church leadership, education, English, fine arts, intercultural studies and languages, social and behavioural sciences

Pres.: Dr GORDON ANDERSON
Vice-Pres. for Academic Affairs and Academic Dean: Dr THOMAS BURKMAN
Vice-Pres. for Advancement: PAUL FREITAG
Vice-Pres. for Student Devt: MIKE NOSSER
Vice-Pres. for Univ. Relations and Enrolment: NATE RUCH
Dir for Admissions: JOSHUA MARTIN
Registrar: CODY SCHMITZ
Dir for Library: MELODY REEDY

Library of 70,000 vols
Number of teachers: 88
Number of students: 1,204

NORTHWESTERN COLLEGE

3003 Snelling Ave, N, St Paul, MN 55113-1598

Telephone: (651) 631-5100
Fax: (651) 628-3301
E-mail: admissions@nwc.edu
Internet: www.nwc.edu

Founded 1902
Private control
Academic year: August to May

Depts of art and design, Biblical and theological studies, biology and biochemistry, business, Christian ministries, communication, education, English and literature, history and related fields, mathematics and engineering, music, physical education, health and kinesiology, psychology, world languages

Pres.: Dr ALAN S. CURETON
Sr Vice-Pres. for Academic Affairs: Dr JANET SOMMERS
Vice-Pres. for Institutional Advancement: AMY BRAGG CAREY
Vice-Pres. for Student Life: MATT HILL
Dean for Faculty: Dr MARK D. BADEN
Registrar: ANDREW L. SIMPSON
Library Dir: RUTH MCGUIRE

Library of 100,000 vols, 17,000 periodicals
Number of teachers: 117
Number of students: 3,000

NORTHWESTERN HEALTH SCIENCES UNIVERSITY

2501 W 84th St, Bloomington, MN 55431

Telephone: (952) 888-4777
E-mail: info@nwhealth.edu
Internet: www.nwhealth.edu

Founded 1941 as Northwestern College of Chiropractic, present name and status 1999
Private control

Pres.: MARC T. ZIEGLER
Provost and Vice-Pres. for Academic Affairs: MICHAEL R. WELLES
Sr Vice-Pres.: CHARLES E. SAWYER
Exec. Vice-Pres.: JAMES E. MCDONALD
Vice-Pres. for Admin.: ROSS B. DUGAS
Vice-Pres. for Research: Dr GERT BRONFORT
Dean for Student Affairs and Enrolment Management: Dr EMILY J. TWEED
Registrar: RUTH ANN MARKS
Dir for Library Services: DELLA SHUPE

Number of teachers: 138
Number of students: 859

DEANS

College of Acupuncture and Oriental Medicine: MARK MCKENZIE

College of Chiropractic: RENÉE M. DEVRIES
College of Undergraduate Health Sciences: DALE K. HEALEY
School of Massage Therapy: DALE K. HEALEY

OAK HILLS CHRISTIAN COLLEGE

1600 Oak Hills Rd, SW, Bemidji, MN 56601

Telephone: (218) 751-8670
Fax: (218) 751-8825
E-mail: oakhills@oakhills.edu
Internet: www.oakhills.edu

Founded 1946 as Oak Hills Christian Training School, present name 1998
Private control

Areas of study: biblical studies, Christian ministries, general education

Pres.: Dr STEVEN HOSTETTER
Vice-Pres. for Advancement: JOAN BERNTSON
Dean for the College: Dr STEVEN WARE
Dir for Admissions: JOHN ENGQUIST
Registrar: MARY HANNAH
Library and Technology Dir: KEITH BUSH

Library of 23,000 vols
Number of teachers: 20
Number of students: 125

RASMUSSEN COLLEGE

8565 Eagle Point Circle, Lake Elmo, MN 55042

Telephone: (651) 259-6600
Fax: (651) 259-6601
Internet: www.rasmussen.edu

Founded 1900 as Rasmussen Practical School of Business
Private control

Divs of business, education, health sciences, nursing, technology and design, justice studies; campuses in Minnesota, Illinois, Florida, Wisconsin and North Dakota;

Pres.: KRISTI A. WAITE
Vice-Pres. for Academic Affairs: CARIE ANN POTENZA
Vice-Pres. for Academic Services: GRETA FERKEL
Vice-Pres. for Admissions: SUSAN M. HAMMERSTROM
Vice-Pres. for Student Affairs: TAWNIE L. CORTEZ
Dir for Library and Learning Resources: EMILY O'CONNOR

Number of teachers: 1,000
Number of students: 15,000

ST CATHERINE UNIVERSITY

2004 Randolph Ave, St Paul, MN 55105

Telephone: (651) 690-6000
Fax: (651) 690-6024
E-mail: admission@stkate.edu
Internet: www.stkate.edu

Founded 1905, present name and status 2009
Private control

Campus at Minneapolis (Minnesota); liberal arts univ. for women

Pres.: ANDREA J. LEE
Sr Vice-Pres.: COLLEEN HEGRANES
Vice-Pres. for Enrolment Management and Student Affairs: Dr BRIAN BRUESS
Vice-Pres. for External Relations: MARJORIE MATHISON HANCE
Vice-Pres. for Finance and Admin.: THOMAS ROONEY
Registrar: CINDY EGENESS
Dir for Libraries, Media Services and Archives: CAROL JOHNSON

Library of 252,107 vols
Number of teachers: 261
Number of students: 5,328

DEANS

Henrietta Schmoll School of Health: PENE-LOPE MOYERS

School of Business and Leadership: Dr PAULA KING

School of Humanities, Arts and Sciences: Dr ALAN SILVA

School of Professional Studies: Dr MARYANN JANOSIK

SAINT JOHN'S UNIVERSITY

POB 2000, Collegeville, MN 56321
Telephone: (320) 363-2011
Fax: (320) 363-2778
E-mail: admission@csbsju.edu
Internet: www.csbsju.edu
Founded 1857
Academic year: August to May
Private control

Liberal arts college for men partnered with College of Saint Benedict for women; depts of fine arts, humanities, natural science, social science

Pres.: Dr MICHAEL HEMASETH
Provost for Academic Affairs: RITA KNUESEL
Academic Dean: Dr RICHARD ICE
Vice-Pres. for Finance and Admin.: DICK ADAMSON
Vice-Pres. for Institutional Advancement: ROB CULLIGAN
Vice-Pres. for Student Devt: DOUG MULLIN
Dir for Libraries and Media: KATHY PARKER

Library of 640,538 vols, 121,394 microforms, 19,145 govt documents, 33,108 current serial titles, 116,741 e-books
Number of teachers: 180 (154 full-time, 26 part-time)
Number of students: 2,016

SAINT MARY'S UNIVERSITY OF MINNESOTA

700 Terrace Heights, Winona, MN 55987-1399
Telephone: (507) 457-6987
Fax: (507) 457-1633
E-mail: admissions@smumn.edu
Internet: www.smumn.edu
Founded 1912
Private control

Campus at Minneapolis (Minnesota); centres at Apple Valley, Rochester, Minnetonka, Oakdale, Nairobi, Kenya and Jamaica
Chancellor: Dr LOUIS DeThOMASIS
Pres.: WILLIAM MANN
Sr Vice-Pres. for Univ. Advancement: Dr STEVEN E. TITUS
Exec. Vice-Pres. and Gen. Counsel: ANN E. MERCHLEWITZ
Vice-Pres. for Academic Affairs: Dr DONNA ARONSON
Vice-Pres. for the College: JAMES M. BEDTKE
Registrar: YUNGE DUTTON
Library Dir: LAURA OANES
Library of 180,000 vols, 750 periodicals
Number of teachers: 589
Number of students: 6,058
Publication: Saint Mary's Magazine

DEANS

School of Business: THOMAS MARPE
School of Education: SCOTT SORVAAG
School of Humanities and Sciences: Dr ELIZABETH A. THROOP
School of the Arts: MICHAEL CHARRON

ST OLAF COLLEGE

1520 St Olaf Ave, Northfield, MN 55057-1098
Telephone: (507) 786-2222
Fax: (507) 786-3986
Internet: www.stolaf.edu

Founded 1874
Private control
Academic year: September to May
Areas of study: fine arts, natural and mathematical sciences, social sciences and humanities
Pres.: DAVID R. ANDERSON
Provost and Dean for College: MARCI SORTOR
Vice-Pres. and Dean for Enrolment: MICHAEL KYLE
Vice-Pres. and Treas.: ALAN NORTON
Vice-Pres. for Advancement and College Relations: MICHAEL STITSWORTH
Vice-Pres. for Student Life and Dean for Students: GREG KNESER
Registrar: MARY CISAR
Dir for the Library Services: ROBERTA LEMBKE
Library of 420,000 vols, 22,000 media items, 5000 periodicals, 18,000 scores
Number of teachers: 256 (f. t. e.)
Number of students: 3,179
Publication: St Olaf Magazine (3 a year).

UNITED THEOLOGICAL SEMINARY OF THE TWIN CITIES

3000 Fifth St, NW, New Brighton, MN 55112-2598
Telephone: (651) 633-4311
Fax: (651) 633-4315
E-mail: info@unitedseminary.edu
Internet: www.unitedseminary.edu
Private control
Areas of study: in divinity, ministry, religious leadership
Pres.: MARY E. McNAMARA
Vice-Pres. for Devt: JIM OLSEN
Vice-Pres. for Finance and Admin.: TOM LOCKHART
Dean for the Seminary: SUSAN K. EBBERS
Dir for Admissions: GLEN N. HERRINGTON-HALL
Registrar: SUSAN HASTINGS
Library Dir: SUSAN K. EBBERS
Library of 83,000 vols
Number of teachers: 27
Number of students: 112 (full-time)
Publication: ARTS: The Arts in Religious and Theological Studies (2 a year).

UNIVERSITY OF MINNESOTA

100 Church St, SE, Minneapolis, MN 55455
6 Morrill Hall, 100 Church St, SE, Minneapolis, MN 55455-0110
Telephone: (612) 625-5000
Fax: (612) 624-6369
E-mail: feedback@tc.umn.edu
Internet: www1.umn.edu
Founded 1851
State control
Academic year: September to May
Pres.: Dr ERIC W. KALER
Vice-Provost for Student Affairs: GERALD RINEHART
Sr Vice-Pres. for Academic Affairs and Provost: E. THOMAS SULLIVAN
Sr Vice-Pres. for System Academic Admin.: ROBERT J. JONES
Vice-Pres. and Chief Financial Officer: RICHARD PFUTZENREUTER
Vice-Pres. and Chief Information Officer: ANN HILL DUIN
Vice-Pres. for Research: R. TIMOTHY MULCAHY
Vice-Pres. for Univ. Services: KATHLEEN O'BRIEN
Gen. Counsel: MARK ROTENBERG
Librarian: WENDY P. LOUGEE
Library: see Libraries and Archives
Number of teachers: 4,168 (system-wide)

Number of students: 69,221 system-wide (52,557 Twin Cities campus)

DEANS

Carlson School of Management: SRI ZAHEER
College of Biological Sciences: ROBERT ELDE
College of Continuing Education: MARY NICHOLS
College of Design: THOMAS FISHER
College of Education and Human Devt: JEAN K. QUAM
College of Food, Agricultural and Natural Resource Sciences: ALLEN S. LEVINE
College of Liberal Arts: JAMES A. PARENTE, JR
College of Pharmacy: MARILYN K. SPEEDIE
College of Science and Engineering: STEVEN L. CROUCH
College of Veterinary Medicine: TREVOR R. AMES (acting)
Graduate School: HENNING SCHROEDER
Humphrey School of Public Affairs: ERIC SCHWARTZ
Law School: Prof. DAVID WIPPMAN
Medical School: AARON FRIEDMAN
School of Dentistry: JUDITH BUCHANAN
School of Nursing: Prof. CONNIE W. DELANEY
School of Public Health: JOHN R. FINNEGAN, JR

PROFESSORS

Accounting (Carlson School of Management, 321 19th Ave, S, Suite 3-110, Minneapolis, MN 55455-0438; tel. (612) 624-7511; fax (612) 626-1335; e-mail macct@umn.edu; internet www.carlsonschool.umn.edu/master-accountancy/index.aspx):

AMERSHI, A.
DICKHAUT, J.
JOYCE, E.
KANODIA, C.
RAYBURN, J.

Aerospace Engineering and Mechanics (107 Akerman Hall, 110 Union St, SE, Minneapolis, MN 55455-0153; tel. (612) 625-8000; fax (612) 626-1558; e-mail dept@aem.umn.edu; internet www.aem.umn.edu):

BALAS, G.
BEAVERS, G. S.
CANDLER, G. V.
FOSDICK, R. L.
GARRARD, W. L.
LEO, P.
WILSON, T. A.

African-American and African Studies (810 Social Sciences Bldg, 267 19th Ave, S, Minneapolis, MN 55455; tel. (612) 624-9847; e-mail aaas@umn.edu; internet aaas.umn.edu):

FARAH, C.
ISAACMAN, A. F.
McCURDY, R.
NIMTZ, A.
PORTER, P. W.
SCOTT, E.

Agricultural, Food and Environmental Education (320 Vocational and Technical Education Bldg, 1954 Buford Ave, St Paul, MN 55108; tel. (612) 624-2221; fax (612) 625-2798; internet www.cehd.umn.edu/olpd/grad-programs/afee):

KRUEGER, R.
PETERSON, R.

Agronomy and Plant Genetics (411 Borlang Hall, 1991 Upper Burford Circle, St Paul, MN 55108-6026; tel. (612) 625-7773; fax (612) 625-1268; e-mail agro@umn.edu; internet agronomy.cfans.umn.edu):

BECKER, R. L.
CARDWELL, V. B.
DURGAN, B. R.
EHLKE, N. J.
GENGENBACH, B. G.
GRONWALD, J. W.
GUNSOLUS, J. L.

HARDMAN, L. L.
HICKS, D. R.
JONES, R. J.
JUNG, H. J.
LUESCHEN, W. E.
ORF, J. H.
PHILLIPS, R. L.
RINES, H. W.
SHEAFFER, C. C.
SIMMONS, S. R.
SOMERS, D. A.
STUTHMAN, D. D.
VANCE, C. P.
WYSE, D. L.

American Studies (104 Scott Hall, 72 Pleasant St, SE, Minneapolis, MN 55455; tel. (612) 624-4190; fax (612) 624-3858; e-mail amstdy@umn.edu; internet americanstudies .umn.edu):

MAY, E. T.
MAY, L.
NOBLE, D.
PRELL, R. E.
YATES, G. G.

Anaesthesiology (B-515 Mayo Memorial Bldg (MMC 294), 420 Delaware St, SE, Minneapolis, MN 55455; tel. (612) 624-9990; fax (612) 624-2363; internet www.anesthesiology .umn.edu):

BEEBE, D. S.
BELANI, K. G.
IAIZZO, P. A.
PALAHNIUK, R. J.

Animal Science (305 Haecker Hall, 1364 Eckles Ave, St Paul, MN 55108-6118; tel. (612) 624-2722; fax (612) 625-5789; internet www.ansci.umn.edu):

CROOKER, B. A.
DAYTON, W. R.
EL HALAWANI, M. E.
FOSTER, D. N.
HANSEN, L. B.
HATHAWAY, M. R.
HAWTON, J. D.
HUNTER, A. G.
JOHNSON, D. G.
JOHNSTON, L. J.
LINN, J. G.
MARX, G. D.
NOLL, S. N.
O'GRADY, S. M.
OSBORN, J. W.
PONCE DE LEÓN, F. A.
RENEAU, J. K.
SEYKORA, A.
SHURSON, G. C.
STERN, M. D.
WHEATON, J. E.
WHITE, M. E.

Anthropology (395 Humphrey Center, 301 19th Ave, S, Minneapolis, MN 55453; tel. (612) 625-3400; fax (612) 625-3095; e-mail anth@umn.edu; internet www.cla.umn.edu/ anthropology):

GIBBON, G.
GUDEMAN, S.
INGHAM, J. M.
MILLER, F. C.
RAHEJA, G. G.
WELLS, P.

Applied Economics (231 Ruttan Hall, 1994 Buford Ave, St Paul, MN 55108; tel. (612) 625-1222; fax (612) 625-6245; e-mail apecdept@umn.edu; internet www.apec.umn .edu):

APLAND, J. D.
EASTER, K. W.
EIDMAN, V. R.
GARTNER, W. C.
KING, R. P.
KINSEY, J. L.
LEVINS, R. L.
MORSE, G. W.

OLSEN, K. D.
PARLIAMENT, C. D.
PEDERSON, E. D.
POLASKY, S.
ROE, T. L.
RUNGE, C. F.
RUTTEN, V. W.
SCHUH, G. E.
SENAUER, B. H.

Architecture (Rapson Hall, Room 145, 89 Church St, Minneapolis, MN 55455; tel. (612) 624-7866; fax (612) 624-5743; e-mail archinfo@umn.edu; internet arch.design .umn.edu):

FISHER, T.
LaVINE, L.
ROBINSON, J. W.
ROCKCASTLE, G.
SATKOWSKI, L.

Art (405 21st Ave, Minneapolis, MN 55455; tel. (612) 625-8096; fax (612) 625-7881; e-mail artdept@umn.edu; internet artdept .umn.edu):

BETHKE, K. E.
HOARD, C. C.
KATSIAFICAS, D.
MORGAN, C.
PHARIS, M.
PORTRATZ, W. E.
ROSE, T. A.

Art History (338 Heller Hall, 271 19th Ave, S, Minneapolis, MN 55455; tel. (612) 624-4500; fax (612) 626-8679; e-mail arthist@umn.edu; internet www.arthist.umn.edu):

ASHER, F. M.
COOPER, F.
McNALLY, S.
MARLING, K. A. R.
POOR, R. J.
WEISBERG, G.

Astronomy (356 Tate Lab of Physics, 116 Church St, SE, Minneapolis, MN 53455; tel. (612) 624-0211; fax (612) 626-2029; internet www.astro.umn.edu):

DAVIDSON, K. D.
DICKEY, J. M.
GEHRZ, R. D.
HUMPHREYS, R. M.
JONES, T.
JONES, T. W.
KUHI, L.
RUDNICK, L.
SKILLMAN, E.
WOODWARD, P. R.

Biochemistry, Molecular Biology and Biophysics (6-155 Jackson Hall, 321 Church St, SE, Minneapolis, MN 55455; tel. (612) 625-6100; fax (612) 625-2163; e-mail bmbb@umn.edu; internet www.cbs.umn.edu/bmbb):

ALLEWELL, N. M.
ANDERSON, J. S.
ARMITAGE, I. M.
BANASZAK, L. J.
BARRY, B. A.
BERNLOHR, D. A.
BLOOMFIELD, V. A.
CONTI-FINE, B. M.
DAS, A.
DEMPSEY, M. E.
FLICKINGER, M. C.
FUCHS, J. A.
HOGENKAMP, H. P. C.
HOOPER, A. B.
HOWARD, J. B.
KOERNER, J. F.
LA PORTE, D. C.
LIPSCOMB, J. D.
LIVINGSTON, D. M.
LOUIS, C. F.
LOVRIEN, R. E.
MAYO, K. H.
NELSESTUEN, G. L.
OEGEMA, T. R.

OHLENDORF, D. H.
SANDERS, M. M.
SCHOTTEL, J. S.
THOMAS, D. D.
TOWLE, H. C.
TSONG, T.
VAN NESS, B. G.
WACKETT, L. P.

Bioethics (N-504 Boynton, 410 Church St, SE, Minneapolis, MN 55455; tel. (612) 624-9440; fax (612) 624-9108; e-mail bioethx@ umn.edu; internet www.ahc.umn.edu/ bioethics):

BEBEAU, M.
BURK, D.
CRANFORD, R.
KANE, R.
MAYO, D.

Biomedical Engineering (7–105 Hasselmo Hall, 312 Church St, SE, Minneapolis, MN 55455; tel. (612) 624-4507; fax (612) 626-6583; e-mail bmedus@umn.edu; internet bme .umn.edu):

POLLA, D.
SIEGEL, R.
TRANQUILLO, R.

Biostatistics (A-460 Mayo Bldg (MMC 303), 420 Delaware St, SE, Minneapolis, MN 55455; tel. (612) 624-4655; fax (612) 626-0660; internet www.sph.umn.edu/ biostatistics):

CARLIN, B.
CONNETT, J.
DUNSMUIR, W.
GOLDMAN, A.
LE, C.
LOUIS, T.
NEATON, J.
TWEEDIE, R.

Biosystems and Agricultural Engineering (213 Biosystems and Agricultural Engineering, 1390 Eckles Ave, St Paul, MN 55108; tel. (612) 625-7733; fax (612) 624-3005; e-mail bae@gaia.bae.umn.edu; internet www.bae .umn.edu):

BHATTACHARYA, M.
CLAYTON, C. J.
JACOBSEN, L. D.
JANNI, K. A.
MOREY, R. V.
NIEBER, J. L.
RUAN, R.
WILCKE, W. F.

Biotechnology Institute (240 Gortner Lab, 1479 Gortner Ave, St Paul, MN 55108-6106; tel. (612) 624-6774; fax (612) 625-5780; e-mail bti@umn.edu; internet www.bti.umn .edu):

BROOKER, R.
FLICKINGER, M.
SADOWSKY, M.
SHERMAN, D.
SRIENC, F.
URRY, D.
WACKETT, L.

Business and Industry Education (425 Vocational and Technical Education Bldg, 1954 Buford Ave, St Paul, MN 55108; tel. (612) 624-3004; fax (612) 624-4720; internet education.umn.edu/wcfe/bie):

BROWN, J.
LAMBRECH, J.
LEWIS, T.
McLEAN, G.
PUCEL, D.

Chemical Engineering and Materials Science (151 Amundson Hall, 421 Washington Ave, SE, Minneapolis, MN 55455-0132; tel. (612) 625-1313; fax (612) 626-7246; e-mail bates@ cems.umn.edu; internet www.cems.umn .edu):

BATES, F.

CARETTA, R.
CARR, R. W.
CARTER, B.
CHELIKOWSKY, J. R.
CUSSLER, E. L.
DAVIS, H. T.
DERBY, J.
EVANS, D. F.
GEANKOPLIS, C. J.
GERBERICH, W. W.
HU, W. S.
KELLER, K. H.
MCCORMICK, A.
MACOSKO, C. W.
PALMSTROM, C.
SCHMIDT, L. D.
SCRIVEN, L. E.
SEIDEL, R.
SHORES, D. A.
SMYRL, W. H.
SRIENC, F.
TRANQUILLO, R.
WARD, M. D.

Chemistry (139 Smith Hall, 207 Pleasant St, SE, Minneapolis, MN 55455; tel. (612) 624-6000; fax (612) 6626-7541; internet www.chem.umn.edu):

BARANY, G.
BLOOMFIELD, V. A.
CARR, P. W.
CRAMER, C. J.
DAVIS, H. T.
ELLIS, J. E.
GENTRY, W. R.
GLADFELTER, W. L.
GRAY, G. R.
HOYE, T.
KASS, S.
LEOPOLD, K.
LIPSKY, S.
LODGE, T.
MANN, K. R.
MILLER, L. L.
NOLAND, W. E.
PIGNOLET, L. H.
QUE, L.
RAFTERY, M.
STANKOVICH, M. T.
TOLMAN, W.
TRUHLAR, D. G.

Child Development (51 E River Parkway, Minneapolis, MN 55455; tel. (612) 624-0526; fax 612 624-6373; e-mail icd@umn.edu; internet www.cehd.umn.edu/icd):

BAUER, P.
COLLINS, W. A.
CRICK, N.
EGELAND, B. R.
GUNNAR, M. R.
MARATSOS, M. P.
MASTEN, A. S.
NELSON, C.
PICK, A. D.
PICK, H. L., Jr
SROUFE, L. A.
WEINBERG, R. A.
YONAS, A.

Civil Engineering (122 Civil Engineering Bldg, 500 Pillsbury Dr., SE, Minneapolis, MN 55455-0116; tel. (612) 625-5522; fax (612) 626-7750; e-mail cive@umn.edu; internet www.ce.umn.edu):

ARNDT, R. E. A.
BREZONIK, P. L.
CROUCH, S. L.
DETOURNAY, E.
DRESCHER, A.
FOUFOULA-GEORGIOU, E.
FRENCH, C. W.
GULLIVER, J. S.
MICHALOPOULOS, P.
PARKER, G. N.
SEMMENS, M. J.
STEFAN, G.

STOLARSKI, H. K.
STRACK, O. D. L.
VOLLER, V. R.

Classical and Near Eastern Studies (245 Nicholson Hall, 216 Pillsbury Dr., SE, Minneapolis, MN 55455; tel. (612) 625-5353; fax (612) 624-4894; e-mail cnes@umn.edu; internet cnes.cla.umn.edu):

BELFIORE, E.
CLAYTON, T.
COOPER, F.
DOUGLAS, S.
MCNALLY, S.
OLSON, T.
SONKOWSKY, R. P.
STAVROU, T.

Classical Civilization Program (330 Folwell Hall, 9 Pleasant St, SE, Minneapolis, MN 55455; tel. (612) 625-7565):

AKEHURST, F. R.
BELFIORE, E.
CLAYTON, T.
COOPER, F.
LIBERMAN, A.
SONKOWSKY, R.
TRACY, J.
WILSON, L.

Clinical and Population Sciences (225 Veterinary Teaching Hospitals, 1352 Boyd Ave/1365 Gortner Ave, St Paul, MN 55108; tel. (612) 625-7755; fax (612) 625-6241; e-mail amesx001@tc.umn.edu; internet www.cvm.umn.edu):

AMES, T. R.
BLAHA, T. C.
FAHNING, M. L.
FARNSWORTH, R. J.
FETROW, J. P.
JOO, H. S.
MOLITOR, T. M.
MORRISON, R. B.
PIJOQAN, C. J.
PULLEN, M. M.
SEGUIN, B. E.
TURNER, T. A.

Clinical Pharmacology (6-120 Jackson Hall, 321 Church St, SE, Minneapolis, MN 55455-0217; tel. (612) 626-4460; fax (612) 625-8408; internet www.pharmacology.med.umn.edu):

HOLZMAN, J. L.
HUNNINGHAKE, D.
PENTEL, P.
YEE, D.

Cognitive Sciences (205 Elliot Hall, 75 East River Rd, Minneapolis, MN 55455; tel. (612) 626-3570; fax (612) 626-7253; e-mail cogsci@umn.edu; internet www.cogsci.umn.edu/index.shtml):

CHILDERS, T.
GEORGOPOULOS, A.
GINI, M.
GUNDEL, J.
JOHNSON, P.
KERSTEN, D.
LEGGE, G.
MARATSOS, M.
NELSON, C.
OVERMIER, B.
PICK, A.
PICK, H.
SAMUELS, J.
SPEAKS, C.
UGURBIL, K.
VAN DEN BROEK, P.
VIEMEISTER, N.
WADE, M.
YONAS, A.

Communication Disorders (115 Shevlin Hall, 164 Pillsbury Dr., SE, Minneapolis, MN 55455; tel. (612) 624-3322; fax (612) 624-7586; e-mail cdis@tc.umn.edu; internet www.cdis.umn.edu):

CARNEY, A. E.

REICHLE, J. E.
SPEAKS, C. E.
WINDSOR, J.

Communication Studies (225 Ford Hall, 221 Church St, SE, Minneapolis, MN 55455; tel. (612) 624-5800; internet www.comm.umn.edu):

BROWNE, D. R.
CAMPBELL, K.
HEWES, D.
SCHIAPPA, E.

Community Health Education (300 W Bank Office Bldg, 1300 52nd St, Minneapolis, MN 55455; tel. (612) 624-1878; fax (612) 624-0315; internet www.sph.umn.edu/programs/che):

FORSTER, J.
GARRAD, J.
JEFFREY, R. W.
LANDO, H. A.
LUEPKER, R. V.
LYTLE, P.
MCGOVERN, P.
PERRY, C. L.
PIRIE, P. L.
VENMGA, R.
WAGENAAR, A. C.

Computer Science and Engineering (4-192 Keller Hall, 200 Union St, SE, Minneapolis, MN 55455; tel. (612) 625-4002; fax (612) 625-0572; e-mail admissions@cs.umn.edu; internet www.cs.umn.edu):

BOLEY, D. L.
DU, D.
DU, D. Z.
FOX, D.
GINI, M. L.
JANARDAN, R.
KUMAR, V.
NORBERG, A. L.
PAPANIKOLOPOULOUS, W.
PARK, H.
SAAD, Y.
SHEKHAR, S.
SHRAGOWITZ, E.
SRIVASTAVA, A.
TRIPATHI, A. R.
YEW, P.

Counseling and Student Personnel Psychology (250 Education Sciences Bldg, 56 E River Rd, Minneapolis, MN 55455-0364; tel. (612) 624-6827; fax (612) 624-8241; e-mail cspp@umn.edu; internet www.cehd.umn.edu/edpsych/programs/cspp):

HUMMEL, T.
ROMANO, J.
SKOVHOLT, T.
VEACH, P.

Cultural Studies and Comparative Literature (235 Nicholson Hall, 216 Pillsbury Dr., SE, Minneapolis, MN 55455; tel. (612) 624-8099; fax (612) 625-4170; internet cscl.umn.edu):

BRENNAN, T.
LEPPERT, R.
MOWITT, J.
SARLES, H. B.
SCHULTE-SASSE, J.

Curriculum and Instruction (125 Peik Hall, 159 Pillsbury Dr., SE, Minneapolis, MN 55455; tel. (612) 625-4006; fax (612) 624-8277; e-mail ciinfo@umn.edu; internet www.cehd.umn.edu/ci):

AVERY, P.
BEACH, R. W.
COGAN, J.
DILLON, D.
GRAVES, M.
JOHNSON, R.
LAMBRECHT, J.
LAWRENZ, F.
MANNING, J. C.
O'BRIEN, D.

POST, T.
TAYLOR, B.

Dental Research Center for Biomaterials and Biomechanics (16-212 Malcolm Moos Health Sciences Tower, 515 Delaware St, SE, Minneapolis, MN 55455; tel. (612) 625-0950; fax (612) 626-1484):

COMBE, E.
DOUGLAS, W.

Dermatology (4-240 Phillips-Wangensteen Bldg, 516 Delaware St, SE, Minneapolis, MN 55455; tel. (612) 625-8625; fax (612) 624-6678; internet www.dermatology.umn.edu):

HORDINSKY, M.
KING, R.

Design, Housing, and Apparel (240 McNeal Hall of Home Econ., 1985 Buford Ave, St Paul, MN 55108; tel. (612) 624-9700; fax (612) 624-2750; internet dha.che.umn.edu):

ANGELL, W.
DeLONG, M.
EICHER, J.
GUERIN, D.
JOHNSON, K.

Ecology, Evolution, and Behaviour (100 Ecology Bldg, 1987 Upper Buford Circle, St Paul, MN 55108; tel. (612) 625-5200; fax (612) 624-6777; internet www.cbs.umn.edu/eeb):

ALSTAD, D.
BARNWELL, F.
BEATTY, J.
CORBIN, K.
CURTSINGER, J.
CUSHING, E.
LANYON, S.
MEGARD, R.
MORROW, P.
NEUHAUSER, C.
PACKER, C.
PUSEY, A.
REGAL, P.
SHAW, R.
SINIFF, D.
STARFIELD, A.
STERNER, R. W.
TILMAN, G. D.
ZINK, R.

Economics (1035 Walter W Heller Hall, 271 19th Ave, S, Minneapolis, MN 55455; tel. (612) 625-6353; fax (612) 624-0209; e-mail econdept@econ.umn.edu; internet www.econ.umn.edu):

ALLEN, B.
BOLDRIN, M.
CHARI, V. V.
CHIPMAN, J. S.
ECKSTEIN, Z.
FELDMAN, R. D.
FOSTER, E.
HOLMES, T.
HURWICZ, L.
JONES, L.
KEHOE, T.
KOCHERLAKOTA, N.
McLENNAN, A.
PRESCOTT, E. C.
RICHTER, M. K.
RUSTICHOTRI, A.
RUTTAN, V.
SCHUH, G. E.
SWAN, C.
WERNER, J.

Education for Work and Community (425 Vocational and Technical Education Bldg, 1954 Buford Ave, St Paul, MN 55108; tel. (612) 624-3004; fax (612) 624-4720; internet education.umn.edu/wcfe/wcfe):

BROWN, J.
KRUEGER, R.
LEWIS, T.
PETERSON, R.
THOMAS, R.

Educational Policy and Administration (330 Wulling Hall, 86 Pleasant St, SE, Minneapolis, MN 55455; tel. (612) 624-1006; fax (612) 624-3377; e-mail edpagrad@umn.edu; internet www.education.umn.edu/edpa):

AMMENTORP, W. M.
CHAPMAN, D. W.
COGAN, J. J.
FRY, G. W.
HEARN, J. C.
LEWIS, D. R.
LEWIS, T.
SEASHORE, R.

Educational Psychology (204 Burton Hall, 178 Pillsbury Dr., SE, Minneapolis, MN 55455; tel. (612) 624-1698; fax (612) 624-8241; e-mail epsy-adm@umn.edu; internet www.education.umn.edu/edpsych):

BART, W. M.
BRUININKS, R.
CHRISTENSON, S.
DAVISON, M. L.
DENO, S.
HARWELL, M.
HUMMEL, T.
HUPP, S.
JOHNSON, D. W.
LAWRENZ, F.
McCONNELL, S.
McEVOY, M.
MARUYAMA, G.
PELLEGRINI, A.
ROMANO, J.
SAMUELS, S. J.
SKOVHOLT, T. M.
TENNYSON, R.
van den BROEK, P.
VEACH, P. M.
YSSELDYKE, J.

Electrical and Computer Engineering (4-178 Electrical Engineering/Computer Science, 200 Union St, SE, Minneapolis, MN 55455; tel. (612) 625-3300; fax (612) 625-4583; internet www.ece.umn.edu):

COHEN, P. I.
GEORGIOU, T.
GIANNAKIS, G.
GOPINATH, A.
KAVEH, M.
KIEFFER, J. C.
KIEHL, R.
KINNEY, L. L.
KUMAR, K. S. P.
LEE, E. B.
LEGER, J.
LILJA, D.
MAZIAR, C.
MOHAN, N.
MOON, J.
NATHAN, M.
PARHI, K.
PERIA, W. T.
POLLA, D.
ROBBINS, W. P.
RUDEN, P.
TANNENBAUM, A.
TEWFIK, A.
WOLLENBERG, B. F.

Emergency Medicine (A-624 Mayo Memorial Bldg (MMC 911), 420 Delaware St, SE, Minneapolis, MN 55455; tel. (612) 626-6911; fax (612) 626-2352):

AMSTERDAM, J.
CLINTON, J.
KNOPP, R.
LING, L.
RUIZ, E.

English (207 Lind Hall, 207 Church St, SE, Minneapolis, MN 55455; tel. (612) 625-3363; fax (612) 624-8228; internet english.cla.umn.edu):

BALES, K.
BRENNAN, T.

BRIDWELL-BOWLES, L.
BROWNE, M. D.
CLAYTON, T.
ELFENBEIN, A.
ESCURE, G.
FIRCHOW, P. E.
GARNER, S.
GRIFFIN, E. M.
HALEY, D.
HAMPL, P. M.
HANCHER, M.
HIRSCH, G.
KENDALL, C.
MINER, V.
MOWITT, J.
RABINOWITZ, P.
REED, P. J.
ROSS, D.
ROTH, M.
SOLOTAROFF, R.
SPRENGNETHER, M.
WEINSHEIMER, J.

English as a Second Language (214 Nolte Center for Continuing Education, 315 Pillsbury Dr., SE, Minneapolis, MN 55455; tel. (612) 624-3331; fax (612) 624-4579; e-mail eatarone@tc.umn.edu; internet www.iles.umn.edu/esl.htm):

COHEN, A.
TARONE, E.

Entomology (219 Hodson Hall, 1980 Folwell Ave, St Paul, MN 55108; tel. (612) 624-3636; fax (612) 625-5299; e-mail entodept@tc.umn.edu):

ANDOW, D. A.
ASCERNO, M. E.
HIEMPEL, G. E.
HOLZENTHAL, R. W.
HUTCHINSON, W. G.
KURTTI, T. J.
MESCE, R. D.
MOON, R. D.
OSTLIE, K. R.
RADCLIFFE, E. B.
RAGSDALE, D. W.
WALGENBACH, D. D.

Environmental and Occupational Health (1260 Mayo Memorial Bldg (MMC 807), 420 Delaware St, SE, Minneapolis, MN 55455; tel. (612) 626-0900; fax (612) 626-4837; internet www.umn.edu/eoh):

GERBERICH, S.
SEXTON, K.
SWACKHAMER, D.
TOSCANO, W.
VESLEY, D.

Epidemiology (300 West Bank Office Bldg, 1300 52nd St, Minneapolis, MN 55455; tel. (612) 624-1878; fax (612) 624-0315; internet www.epi.umn.edu):

BROWN, J. E.
CROW, R. S.
FINNEGAN, J. R.
FOLSOM, A. R.
FORSTER, J. L.
GARRAD, J.
GLASSER, S. P.
HIMES, J. M.
JACOBS, D. R.
JEFFEREY, R. W.
LANDO, H. A.
LUEPKER, R. V.
McGOVERN, P.
MENOTTI, A.
PERRY, C. L.
PIRIE, P. L.
SHAHAR, E.
STORY, M. T.
VENINGA, R.
WAGENAAR, A. C.

Experimental and Clinical Pharmacology (7-159 Weaver-Densford Hall, 308 Harvard St, SE, Minneapolis, MN 55455; tel. (612) 626-

9937; fax (612) 625-9931; internet www
.pharmacy.umn.edu):

CLOYD, J. C.
FLETCHER, C. V.
GROSS, C.
GUAY, D. R.
HANLON, J. T.
LACKNER, J. E.
MANN, K. J.
ROTSCHAFER, J. C.
ZASKE, D. E.

Family Education (325 Vocational and Technical Education Bldg, 1954 Buford Ave, St
Paul, MN 53708; tel. (612) 624-3010; fax
(612) 625-6798; internet education.umn.edu/
wcfe/fe):

THOMAS, R.

Family Practice and Community Health (6-
240 Phillips-Wangensteen Bldg, 516 Delaware St, SE, Minneapolis, MN 55455; tel.
(612) 624-2622; fax (612) 624-5930; internet
www.med.umn.edu/fp):

BLAND, C. J.
COLEMAN, E.
GJEROINGEN, D.
KEENAN, J.
SIMON ROSSER, B. R.

Family Social Science (290 McNeal Hall of
Home Econ., 1985 Buford Ave, St Paul, MN
55108; tel. (612) 625-1900; fax (612) 625-
4227; internet fsos.che.umn.edu):

BAUER, J.
BOSS, P.
DANES, S.
DETZNER, D.
DOHERTY, W.
GROTEVANT, H. D.
HOGAN, M. J.
MADDOCK, J.
RETTIG, K.
ROSENBLATT, P.
TURNER, W.

Finance (3-122 Carlson School of Management, 321 19th Ave, S, Minneapolis, MN
55455; tel. (612) 624-2888; fax (612) 626-
1335; internet www.csom.umn.edu):

ALEXANDER, G.
BENVENISTE, L.
BOYD, J.
LEVINE, R.
NANTELL, T.

Fisheries and Wildlife (200 Hodson Hall,
1980 Folwell Ave, St Paul, MN 55455; tel.
(612) 624-3600; fax (612) 625-5299; internet
www.fw.umn.edu):

ADELMAN, I.
ANDERSON, D.
COHEN, Y.
COOPER, J.
CUTHBERT, F.
KAPUSCINSKI, A.
PERRY, J.
SMITH, D.
SORENSEN, P.
SPANGLER, G.

Food Science and Nutrition (225 Food Science and Nutrition, 1334 Eckles Ave, St
Paul, MN 55108; tel. (612) 624-1290; fax
(612) 625-5272; e-mail fscn@mail.coafes.umn
.edu; internet fscn.che.umn.edu):

ADDIS, P. B.
BRADY, L. J.
CSALLANY, A. S.
FULCHER, R. G.
LABUZA, T. P.
MCKAY, L. L.
REINECCIUS, G. A.
SLAVIN, J. L.
SMITH, D. E.
TATINI, S. R.
VICKERS, Z. M.
WARTHESEN, J. J.

Forest Resources (115 Green Hall, 1530
North Cleveland Ave, St Paul, MN 53108;
tel. (612) 624-3400; fax (612) 625-5212;
e-mail fr@forestry.umn.edu; internet www
.cnr.umn.edu/fr):

ANDERSON, D. H.
BAUER, M. E.
BAUGHMAN, M. J.
BLINN, C. R.
BROOKS, K. N.
BURK, T. E.
EK, A. R.
ELLEFSON, P. B.
PERRY, J. A., II
REICH, P. B.
ROSE, D. W.

French and Italian (260 Folwell Hall, 9
Pleasant St, SE, Minneapolis, MN 55455;
tel. (612) 624-4308; fax (612) 624-6021;
e-mail frit@umn.edu; internet cla.umn.edu/
frit):

AKEHURST, F. R. P.
NOAKES, S.
PAGANINI, M.

General College (25 Appleby Hall, 128 Pleasant St, SE, Minneapolis, MN 55455; tel. (612)
625-3339; fax (612) 625-0704; internet www
.gen.umn.edu):

BROTHEN, T. F.
COLLINS, T. G.
GIDMARK, J. B.
HIGHBEE, J. H.
MOORE, R. C.
ROBERTSON, D. F.
YAHNKE, R. E.

Genetics, Cell Biology and Development (6-
160 Jackson Hall, 321 Church St, SE,
Minneapolis, MN 55455; tel. (612) 624-3110;
fax (612) 626-6140; e-mail gcd@mail.med
.umn.edu; internet www.gcd.med.umn.edu):

BAUER, G. E.
BERMAN, J. G.
BERRY, S.
BROOKER, R. J.
ERLANDSEN, S. L.
FAN, D. P.
FARAS, A. H.
GOLDSTEIN, S. F.
HACKETT, P. B.
HAMILTON, D. W.
HERMAN, R. K.
HERMAN, W. S.
JOHNSON, R. G.
KING, R. A.
KURIYAMA, P. A.
LEFEBVRE, P. A.
LINCK, R. W.
MCIVOR, R. S.
MAGEE, P. T.
O'CONNOR, M. B.
ORR, H. T.
SILFLOW, C. D.
SIMMONS, M. J.
SNUSTAD, D. P.
SORENSON, R. L.
VANNESS, B. G.

Geography (414 Social Sciences Bldg, 267
19th Ave, S, Minneapolis, MN 55455; tel.
(612) 625-6080; fax (612) 624-1044; e-mail
geog@geog.umn.edu; internet www.geog
.umn.edu):

ADAMS, J. S.
BROWN, D. A.
GERSMEHL, P. J.
HART, J. F.
HSU, M. L.
LEITNER, H.
MCMASTER, R. B.
MARTIN, J. A.
SAMATOR, A. I.
SCOTT, E. P.
SHEPPARD, E. S.
SKAGGS, R. H.

Geology and Geophysics (108 Pilsbury Hall,
310 Pilsbury Dr., SE, Minneapolis, MN
55455; tel. (612) 624-1333; fax (612) 625-
3819; e-mail geology@umn.edu; internet
www.geo.umn.edu):

ALEXANDER, E. C., Jr
BANERJEE, S. K.
EDWARDS, R. L.
HUDLESTON, P.
ITO, E.
KOHLSTEDT, D.
KOHLSTEDT, S. G.
MOREY, G. B.
MOSHOWITZ, B.
MURTHY, V. R.
PAOLA, C.
PFANNKUCH, H. O.
SEYFRIED, W. E., Jr
SOUTHWICK, D.
STOUT, J.
TEYSSIER, C.
YUEN, D.

German, Scandinavian, and Dutch (205
Folwell Hall, 9 Pleasant St, SE, Minneapolis,
MN 55455; tel. (612) 625-2080; fax (612) 624-
8297; internet www.folwell.umn.edu/gsd):

FIRCHOW, E. S.
HASSELMO, N.
HOUE, P.
JOERES, R. B.
LIBERMAN, A.
PARENTE, J., Jr
SCHULTE-SASSE, J.
STOCKENSTRÖM, G.
TERAOKA, A.
ZIPES, J.

Gerontology (D-312 Mayo Memorial Bldg
(MMC 197), 420 Delaware St, SE, Minneapolis, MN 55455; tel. (612) 624-3904; fax
(612) 624-8448; e-mail coa@tc.umn.edu;
internet www.umn.edu/coa):

AHLBURG, D.
BORN, D.
BOSS, P.
BOULT, C.
CLOYD, J.
CURTSONGER, J.
DETZNER, D.
DIFABIO, R.
DURFEE, W.
DYSKEN, M.
EUSTIS, N.
FELDMAN, B.
GARRARD, J.
GERSHEENSON, C.
GUAY, D.
HANCOCK, P.
HANLON, J.
HELLER, L.
KANE, R.
KANE, R.
KELLER, L.
KIVNICK, H.
LACKNER, T.
LARSON, A.
LE, C.
MCGUE, M.
MEYERS, S.
MILES, S.
PARK, R.
QUAM, J.
SCHONDEMEYER, S.
SEYBOLD, V.
SNYDER, M.
SWIONTKOWSKI, M.
THOMAS, D.
WADE, M.
WYMAN, J.
ZIMMERMAN, S.

Healthcare Management (3-140 Carlson
School of Management, 321 19th Ave, S,
Minneapolis, MN 55455; tel. (612) 624-8814;
internet   www.csom.umn.edu/

facultydepartments/departments/healthcaremgmt/healthcaremgmt.cfm):

BEGUN, J.
CHRISTIANSON, J.
WECKWERTH, V.

Health Ecology (15-136 Malcolm Moos Health Sciences Tower, 515 Delaware St, SE, Minneapolis, MN 55455; tel. (612) 625-1191; fax (612) 626-6096; e-mail tlpash@maroon.tc.umn.edu; internet www.umn.edu/dental/department/prevsei/div_hecology.html):

BEBEAU, M.
BORN, D.
DIANGELIS, A.
MARTENS, L.

Health Informatics (777 Mayo Memorial Bldg (MMC 511), 420 Delaware St, SE, Minneapolis, MN 55455; tel. (612) 625-8440; fax (612) 625-7166; e-mail grad@email.labmed.umn.edu; internet www.hinf.umn.edu):

CONNELLY, D.
FINKELSTEIN, S.
GATEWOOD, L.
SPEEDIE, S.

Health Informatics Graduate Programme (777 Mayo Memorial Bldg (MMC 511), 420 Delaware St, SE, Minneapolis, MN 55455; tel. (612) 625-8440; fax (612) 625-7166; e-mail grad@email.labmed.umn.edu; internet www.hinf.umn.edu):

CONNELLY, D.
ELLIS, L.
FAN, D.
FINKELSTEIN, S.
FRICTON, J.
GATEWOOD, L.
HARRIS, I.
JOHNSON, P.
McQUARRIE, D.
PATTERSON, R.
SPEEDIE, S.
WHOLEY, D.
WILCOX, G.

Health Services Research and Policy, Division of (15-200 Phillips-Wangensteen Bldg, 516 Delaware St, SE, Minneapolis, MN 55455; tel. (612) 624-6151; fax (612) 624-2196; e-mail ihsr@umn.edu; internet www.hsr.umn.edu):

CHRISTIANSON, J.
DOWD, B.
FELDMAN, R.
GARRARD, J.
HANLON, J.
KANE, R.
KANE, R.
KRALEWSKI, J.
LURIE, N.
McBEAN, M.
MOSCOVICE, I.
NYMAN, J.
SWIONTKOWSKI, M.
VENNIGA, R.

History (614 Social Sciences Bldg, 267 19th Ave, S, Minneapolis, MN 55455; tel. (612) 624-2800; fax (612) 624-7096; internet www.hist.umn.edu):

ALTHOLZ, J. L.
BACHRACH, B. S.
BERMAN, H.
EVANS, J.
EVANS, S.
FARMER, E. L.
GOOD, D.
ISAACMAN, A. F.
McCAA, R.
MAYNES, M. J.
MENARD, R. R.
MUNHOLLAND, J. K.
NOONAN, T. S.
PHILLIPS, C.

PHILLIPS, W.
REYERSON, K.
RUGGLES, S.
SAMAHA, J.
STAVROU, T. G.
THAYER, J. A.
TRACY, J.
VECOLI, R. J.
WALTNER, A.

History of Medicine (511A Diehl Hall, 505 Essex St, SE, Minneapolis, MN 55455; tel. (612) 624-4416; fax (612) 625-7938; internet www.med.umn.edu/history/home.htm):

EYLER, J. M.

History of Science and Technology (381 Tate Lab of Physics, 116 Church St, SE, Minneapolis, MN 55455; tel. (612) 624-7069; fax (612) 624-4578; internet www.physics.umn.edu):

BEATTY, J.
KOHLSTEDT, S. G.
NORBERG, A. L.
SEIDEL, R. W.
SHAPIRO, A. E.

Hormel Institute (801 16th Avenue, NE, Austin, MN 55912; tel. (507) 433-8804; fax (507) 437-9606; internet www.smig.net/hi):

BROCKMAN, H. L.
BROWN, R. E.
DONG, Z.
KISS, Z.
SCHMID, H. H. O.

Horticultural Science (305 Alderman Hall, 1970 Rolwell Ave, St Paul, MN 55108; tel. (612) 624-5300; fax (612) 624-4941; internet www.hort.agri.umn.edu):

BECKER, R. L.
BROWN, D. L.
COHEN, J. D.
GARDNER, G. M.
HOOVER, E. E.
LI, P. H.
LUBY, J. J.
MARKHART, A. H., III
OLIN, P. J.
PELLETT, H. M.
PRESTON, D.
ROSEN, C. J.
SOWOKINOS, J. R.
WHITE, D. B.
WILDUNG, D. K.

Human Genetics (4-122 Malcolm Moos Health Sciences Tower, 515 Delaware St, SE, Minneapolis, MN 55455; tel. (612) 624-8111; fax (612) 626-7031; internet www.ihg.med.umn.edu):

BERRY, S.
CONKLIN, K.
HACKETT, P.
KERSEY, J.
KING, R.
McIVOR, R. S.
MOSER, K.
ORR, H.
SOMIA, M.
VANNESS, B.
WHITLEY, C.

Human Resource Development and Adult Education (425 Vocational and Technical Education Bldg, 1954 Buford Ave, St Paul, MN 55108; tel. (612) 624-3004; fax (612) 624-4720; internet education.umn.edu/wcfe/hrd/default.html):

BROWN, J.
LEWIS, T.
McLEAN, G.
PUCEL, D.
SWANSON, R.

Human Sexuality (180 West Bank Office Bldg, 1300 52nd St, Minneapolis, MN 55455; tel. (612) 625-1500; fax (612) 626-8311):

COLEMAN, E.
ROSSER, S.

Humphrey School of Public Affairs (300 Hubert H. Humphrey Center, 301 19th Ave, S, Minneapolis, MN 55455; tel. (612) 625-9505; fax (612) 625-3513; internet www.hhh.umn.edu):

ADAMS, J.
ARCHIBALD, S.
BRANDL, J.
BRYSON, J.
EUSTIS, N.
FENNELLY, K.
HOENACK, S.
KAPSTEIN, E.
KELLER, K.
KENNEY, S.
KLEINER, M.
KUDRLE, R.
MARKUSEN, A.
MYERS, S. L., Jr
SCHUH, G. E.

Industrial Relations (3-300 Carlson School of Management, 321 19th Ave, S, Minneapolis, MN 55455; tel. (612) 624-2500; fax (612) 624-8360; internet www.irc.csom.umn.edu):

AHLBURG, D.
ARVEY, R.
BEN-NER, A.
BOGNANNO, M.
FOSSUM, J.
REMINGTON, J.
SCOVILLE, J.
WHITMAN, A.
ZAIDI, M.

Information and Decision Sciences (3-365 Carlson School of Management, 321 19th Ave, S, Minneapolis, MN 55455; tel. (612) 624-8030; fax (612) 626-1316; internet www.csom.umn.edu):

ADAMS, C. R.
CHERVANY, N. L.
CURLEY, S.
DAVIS, G. B.
JOHNSON, P. E.
KAUFFMAN, R. J.

Jewish Studies Center (339 Folwell Hall, 9 Pleasant St, SE, Minneapolis, MN 55455; tel. (612) 624-4914):

BACHRACH, B.
BERMAN, H.
BRUSTEIN, W.
PRELL, R. V.-E.
ZIPES, J.

Journalism and Mass Communication (111 Murphy Hall, 206 Church St, SE, Minneapolis, MN 55455; tel. (612) 625-9824; fax (612) 626-8251; internet sjmc.umn.edu):

DICKEN-GARCIA, H.
FABER, R. J.
FANG, I. E.
HANSEN, K. A.
KIRTLEY, J. E.
LEE, C. C.
ROBERTS, N. L.
SULLIVAN, D.
WACKMAN, D. B.

Kinesiology (220 Cooke Hall, 1900 University Ave, SE, Minneapolis, MN 55455; tel. (612) 625-5300; fax (612) 625-7700; internet education.umn.edu/kls/kinesiology/default.html):

KANE, J.
LEON, A.
WADE, M.

Laboratory Medicine and Pathology (D-242 Mayo Memorial Bldg (MMC 609), 420 Delaware St, SE, Minneapolis, MN 55455; tel. (612) 625-9171; fax (612) 625-0617; internet www.borg.labmed.umn.edu/ateam.html):

AHMED, K.

APPLE, F.
BALFOUR, H. J.
BROWN, D. M.
CLARK, B.
ECKFELDT, J.
ELLIS, L.
FERRIERI, P.
FINKELSTEIN, S.
FURCHT, L. T.
GARRY, V.
GATEWOOD, L. C.
HALBERG, F.
HAUS, E.
HECHT, S.
HORWITZ, C.
JESSURUN, J.
KERSEY, J. H.
LEBIEN, T.
MCCARTHY, J.
MCCULLOUGH, J. J.
MCIVOR, S.
MALEJKA-GIGANTI, D.
MANIVEL, C.
MESCHER, M.
ORR, H.
RAO, G.
ROSE, A.
SHIMIZU, Y.
STANLEY, M.
TSAI, M.
WATTENBERG, L.
WELLS, C.
WHITE, J.
WILSON, M.

Landscape Architecture (1425 University Ave, SE, Minneapolis, MN 55455; tel. (612) 625-6860; fax (612) 625-0710; internet www .cala.umn.edu/landscape_architecture/land-scape.html):

NECKAR, L.
PITT, D.

Law (285 Mondale Hall, 229 19th Ave, S, Minneapolis, MN 55455; tel. (612) 625-1000; fax (612) 625-2011; internet www.law.umn .edu):

ADAMS, E.
BEFORT, S.
BURK, P.
BURKHART, A.
CHEN, J.
COOPER, L. J.
DRIPPS, D.
ERICKSON, M.
FARBER, D. A.
FELD, B. C.
FELLOWS, M. L.
FRASE, R. S.
GIFFORD, D. J.
KELLY, B.
KOEPPEN, B.
MARSHALL, D. P.
MATHESON, J.
MORRISON, F. L.
MUNDSTOCK, G.
OKEDIJI, R.
PAULSEN, M.
POWELL, J.
SAMAHA, A.
SCHOETTLE, F.
SHARPE, C.
STEIN, R. A.
TONRY, M. H.
WEISS, F.
WEISSBRODT, D. S.
WOLF, S.
YOUNGER, J.
YUDOF, M.

Life Course Center (1014 Social Sciences Bldg, 267 19th Ave, S, Minneapolis, MN 55455; tel. (612) 624-6333; fax (612) 624-7020; internet www.soc.umn.edu/research/aboutlcc.htm):

KRUTTSCHNITT, C.
LASLETT, B.

MALMQUIST, C.
MORTIMER, J.
STRYKER, R.

Limnological Research Center (220 Pillsbury Hall, 310 Pillsbury Dr., SE, Minneapolis, MN 55455; tel. (612) 624-7005; fax (612) 625-3819; internet lrc.geo.umn.edu):

BANERJEE, S. K.
CUSHING, E. J.
EDWARDS, L.
ITO, E.
JOHNSON, T. C.
MEGARD, R. O.

Linguistics (214 Nolte Center for Continuing Education, 315 Pillsbury Dr., SE, Minneapolis, MN 55455; tel. (612) 624-3331; fax (612) 624-4579; e-mail umling@tc.umn.edu):

GUNDEL, J.

Marketing and Logistics Management (3-150 Carlson School of Managment, 321 19th Ave, S, Minneapolis, MN 55455; tel. (612) 624-5055; fax (612) 624-8804; internet www.csom .umn.edu/wwwpages/depts/mktg/mktgdept .htm):

HOUSTON, M.
JOHN, D.
JOHN, G.
LOKEN, B.
MEYERS-LEVY, J.
ROERING, K.
RUEKERT, R.
WALKER, O.

Mathematics (127 Vincent Hall, 206 Church St, SE, Minneapolis, MN 55455; tel. (612) 625-2004; fax (612) 626-2017; e-mail dpt@ math.umn.edu; internet www.math.umn .edu):

ADAMS, S.
AGARD, S.
ANDERSON, G.
ARNOLD, D.
ARONSON, D.
BAXTER, J.
BOBKOV, S.
BRAMSON, M.
CALDERER, M. C.
COCKBURN, B.
FESHBACH, M.
FRISTEDT, B.
GARRETT, P.
GOLDMAN, J.
GRAY, L.
GULLIVER, R.
HARRIS, M.
HEJHAL, D.
JAIN, N.
JODEIT, M.
KAHN, D.
KEYNES, H.
KRYLOV, N.
LITTMAN, W.
LOWENGRUB, J.
LUSKIN, M.
LYUBEZNIK, G.
MCCARTHY, C.
MCGEHEE, R.
MARDEN, A.
MESSING, W.
MEYERS, N.
MILLER, W., Jr
MOECKEL, R.
NI, W.-M.
ODLYZKO, A.
OLVER, P.
OTHMER, H.
POLACIK, P.
PRIKRY, K.
REINER, V.
REITICH, F.
REJTO, P.
ROBERTS, J.
SAFONOV, M.
SANTOSA, F.
SELL, G.

SPERBER, S.
STANTON, D.
STORVICK, D.
WEBB, P.
WHITE, D.

Mechanical Engineering (1100 Mechanical Engineering, 111 Church St, SE, Minneapolis, MN 55455; tel. (612) 625-0705; fax (612) 626-1854; e-mail mech-eng-info@me.umn .edu; internet www.me.umn.edu):

ARORA, S. R.
BAR-COHEN, A.
DAVIDSON, J.
DONATH, M.
DURFEE, W.
ERDMAN, A. G.
GIRSHICK, S.
HEBERLEIN, J.
KITTLESON, D. B.
KLAMECHI, B.
KUEHN, T. H.
KULACKI, F.
KVÅLSETH, T. O.
LEWIS, J.
MCMURRY, P. H.
MARPLE, V. A.
PUI, D.
RAMALINGAM, S.
RAMSEY, J. W.
SIMON, T. W.
SPARROW, E. M.
STARR, P.
STELSON, K.
STRYKOWSKI, P.
TAMMA, K.

Medical Biotechnology (7-105 Basic Sciences and Biomedical Engineering, 312 Church St, SE, Minneapolis, MN 55455; tel. (612) 626-2366; fax (612) 625-1121; internet www.med .umn.edu/imb):

FURCHT, L.
MCCARTHY, J.
MCCULLOUGH, J.
RAO, G.

Medical Technology (15-170 Phillips-Wangensteen Bldg, 516 Delaware St, SE, Minneapolis, MN 55455; tel. (612) 625-9490; fax (612) 625-5901; e-mail medtech@tc.umn .edu):

TSAI, M.
WELLS, C.

Medicinal Chemistry (8-101 Weaver-Densford Hall, 308 Harvard St, SE, Minneapolis, MN 55455; tel. (612) 624-9919; fax (612) 624-0139; internet www.pharmacy.umn.edu):

ABUL-HAJJ, Y. J.
HANNA, P. E.
HECHT, S. S.
JOHNSON, R. L.
NAGASAWA, H. T.
PORTOGHESE, P. S.
REMMEL, R. P.
SHIER, W. T.
SPEEDIE, M. K.
VINCE, R.

Medicine (100 Philips-Wangensteen Bldg, 516 Delaware St, SE, Minneapolis, MN 55455; tel. (612) 625-7140):

ANAND, I.
ASINGER, R.
BACHE, R.
BANTLE, J.
BEHRENS, T.
BENDITT, D.
BILLINGTON, C.
BITTERMAN, P.
BLUMENTHAL, M.
BOND, J.
CHESLER, E.
CHRISTIANSON, J.
COHN, J. N.
COLLINS, A.
CROSSLEY, K.

DANIELS, B.
DAVIES, S.
DUANE, W.
FROHNERT, P.
FROM, A.
GEORGOPOULOS, A.
GLASSER, S.
GOLDSMITH, S.
GOODMAN, J.
GRAY, R.
GRIMM, R.
HAASE, A.
HEBBEL, R.
HERTZ, M.
HOLTZMAN, J.
HOSTETTER, T.
HOWE, R.
HUNNINGHAKE, D.
INGBAR, D.
JANOFF, E.
JOHNSON, G.
JOHNSON, J.
KAHN, J.
KASISKE, B.
KEANE, W.
KENNEDY, H.
KING, R.
KUBO, S.
LAKE, J.
LEDERLE, F.
LEVINE, A.
LEVITT, M. D.
LUEPKER, R.
LUIKART, S.
LURIE, N.
McCLAVE, P.
MAHOWALD, M.
MARIASH, C.
MARINI, J.
MESSNER, R.
MILES, S.
MILLER, J.
MILLER, L.
MILLER, W.
MOLDOW, C.
MUELLER, D.
NICHOL, K.
NIEWOEHNER, D.
NUTTALL, F. O.
PALLER, M.
PENTEL, P.
PETERSON, B.
PETERSON, P. K.
PIERACH, C.
POPKIN, M.
RAIJ, L.
RAO, K.
RAVDIN, J.
ROSENBERG, A.
ROSENBERG, M.
RUBINS, H.
SABATH, L. D.
SIMON, G.
SKUBITZ, K.
STEER, C.
TAYLOR, A.
UGURBIL, K.
VERCELLOTTI, G.
VERFAILLIE, C.
WEIR, E. K.
WEISDORF, D.
WHITE, C.
WILLIAMS, D.
WILSON, R.
WOLF, S.
YEE, D.

Microbial Biochemistry and Biotechnology (156 Gortner Laboratory, 1479 Gortner Ave, St Paul, MN 55108; tel. (612) 625-3785; fax (612) 625-5780; internet www.cbs.umn.edu/bmbb):

ANDERSON, J. S.
FLICKINGER, M. C.
HOOPER, A. B.
SCHOTTEL, J. L.

Microbiology (1460 Mayo Memorial Bldg (MMC 196), 420 Delaware St, SE, Minneapolis, MN 55455; tel. (612) 624-6190; fax (612) 626-0623; e-mail micro@lenti.med.umn .edu; internet www.microbiology.med.umn .edu):

BERMAN, J.
CLEARY, P. P.
DUNNY, G.
DWORKIN, M.
FARAS, A. J.
HAASE, A.
HANSON, R.
JENKINS, M.
JOHNSON, R. C.
MAGEE, P. T.
PLAGEMANN, P. G. W.
SCHLIEVERT, P. M.
SHERMAN, D.

Molecular and Cellular Therapy (D-242 Mayo Memorial Bldg (MMC 609), 420 Delaware St, SE, Minneapolis, MN 55455; tel. (612) 626-3272; fax (612) 625-0617; internet www.mbbnet.umn.edu/institutes/cmct):

McCULLOUGH, J.
MILLER, J.

Molecular Biology (6-155 Jackson Hall, 321 Church St, SE, Minneapolis, MN 55455; tel. (612) 625-6100; fax (612) 625-2163; internet www.cbs.umn.edu/bmbb):

DAS, A.
FUCHS, J. A.
LaPORTE, D. C.
LIVINGSTON, D. M.
SANDERS, M. M.
TOWLE, H. C.
VanNESS, B. G.

Music (100 Donald N. Ferguson Hall, 2106 4th St, S, Minneapolis, MN 55455; tel. (612) 624-5740; fax (612) 626-2200; internet www .music.umn.edu):

ANDERSON, J.
ASHWORTH, T.
BALDWIN, D.
BRAGINSKY, A.
CHERLIN, M.
GARRETT, M.
GRAYSON, D.
HAACK, P.
JACKSON, D.
KIRCHHOFF, C.
KONKOLL, K.
LANCASTER, T.
LUBET, A.
McCURDY, R.
MAURICE, G.
O'REILLY, S.
REMENIKOVA, T.
SHOCKLEY, R.
SUTTON, V.
WARE, D. C.
WELLER, L.
ZAIMONT, J. L.

Naval Science (203 Armory Bldg, 15 Church St, SE, Minneapolis, MN 55455; tel. (612) 625-6677; fax (612) 624-5030; e-mail nrotc@ umn.edu; internet www.umn.edu/nrotc):

FREY, W.

Neurology (12-100 Phillips-Wangensteen Bldg (MMC 295), 516 Delaware St, SE, Minneapolis, MN 55455; tel. (612) 625-9900; fax (612) 625-7950; internet www.neurology .umn.edu):

ANSARI, K.
ASHE, K.
CRANFORD, R.
ETTINGER, M.
GEORGOPOULOS, A.
IADECOLA, C.
KENNEDY, W. R.
KLASSEN, A. C.
KNOPMAN, D.

KRIEL, R.
LOCKMAN, L.
MAHOWALD, M.
MORIARTY, G.
NELSON, C.
PARRY, G.
RAMIREZ-LASSEPAS, M.
ROSS, E. M.
ROTTENBERG, D.
SHAPIRO, E.
TRUWITT, C.
WIRTSCHAFTER, J.

Neuroscience (6-145 Jackson Hall, 321 Church St, SE, Minneapolis, MN 55455; tel. (612) 626-6800; fax (612) 626-5009; internet www.neurosci.umn.edu):

CARROLL, M.
ELDE, R.
EL-FAKAHANY, E.
ENGELAND, W.
FLANDERS, M.
GEORGOPOULOS, A.
GIESLER, G., Jr
IADECOLA, C.
JUHN, S.
LARSON, A.
LETOURNEAU, P.
LEVINE, A.
McLOON, S.
MANTYH, P.
MILLER, R.
NEWMAN, E.
POPPELE, R.
SANTI, P.
SEYBOLD, V.
SOECHTING, J.
SORENSON, P.
SPARBER, S.
UGURBIL, K.
WILCOX, G.

Neurosurgery (D-429 Mayo Memorial Bldg (MMC 96), 420 Delaware St, SE, Minneapolis, MN 55455; tel. (612) 624-6666; fax (612) 624-0644; internet www.neuro.umn.edu):

EFANGE, S. M. N.
HALL, W. A.
KUCHARCZYK, J.
LOW, W. C.
MAXWELL, R. E.
ROCKSWOLD, G. L.
WIRTSCHAFTER, J. D.

Nuclear Medicine (2-449 Fairview Univ. Medical Center (MMC 292), 420 Delaware St, SE, Minneapolis, MN 55455; tel. (612) 273-4092; fax (612) 273-1950; internet www .med.umn.edu/radiology):

ANDERSON, Q.
EFRANGE, S.
GOMES, M.

Nursing (6-101 Weaver-Densford Hall, 308 Harvard St, SE, Minneapolis, MN 55455; tel. (612) 624-9600; fax (612) 626-2359; internet www.nursing.umn.edu):

BEARINGER, L.
DISCH, J.
EDWARDSON, S.
GROSS, C.
HODGE, F.
LEONARD, B.
WYMAN, J.

Obstetrics, Gynaecology and Women's Health (12-211 Malcolm Moos Health Sciences Tower, 515 Delaware St, SE, Minneapolis, MN 55455; tel. (612) 626-3111; fax (612) 626-0665; internet www.med.umn.edu/obgyn):

CARSON, L.
DE JONGE, C.
GAZIANO, E. P.
KNOX, G. E.
LEUNG, B. S.
MARTENS, M. G.
OKAGAKI, T.

POTISH, R.
RAMAKRISHAN, S.
THOMPSON, T. R.
TROFATTER, K. F.
TWIGGS, L. B.

Operations and Management Science (3-150 Carlson School of Management, 321 19th Ave, S, Minneapolis, MN 55455; tel. (612) 624-7010; fax (612) 624-8804; internet carlsonschool.umn.edu/csom/deptinfo.html):

ANDERSON, J. C.
CHERVANY, N.
HILL, A. V.
NACHTSHEIM, C.
SCHROEDER, R. G.

Ophthalmology (9th Fl., Phillips-Wangensteen Bldg, 516 Delaware St, SE, Minneapolis, MN 55455; tel. (612) 625-4400; fax (612) 626-3119; internet www.med.umn.edu/ophthalmology):

DOUGHMAN, D. J.
GREGERSON, D. S.
KRACHMER, J. H.
NELSON, J. D.
SUMMERS, C. G.
WIRTSCHAFTER, J. D.

Oral Sciences (17-252 Malcolm Moos Health Sciences Tower, 515 Delaware St, SE, Minneapolis, MN 55455; tel. (612) 624-9123; fax (612) 626-2651; internet www1.umn.edu/dental/department/oralsci/dep_oral.html):

ANDERSON, D. L.
COMBE, E.
DELONG, R.
DOUGLAS, W. H.
GERMAINE, G. R.
LILJEMARK, W. F.
ROHRER, M.
SCHACHTELE, C. F.
SHAPIRO, B. L.

Orthodontics (6-320 Malcolm Moos Health Sciences Tower, 515 Delaware St, SE, Minneapolis, MN 55455; tel. (612) 625-5110; fax (612) 626-2571):

SPEIDEL, T. M.

Orthopaedic Surgery (350 Variety Club Research Center, 401 E River Rd, Minneapolis, MN 55455; tel. (612) 625-1177; fax (612) 625-6032):

LEWIS, J. L.
OEGEMA, T., Jr
OGILVIE, J.
SWIONTKOWSKI, M.
THOMPSON, R. C., Jr

Otolaryngology (8-240 Phillips-Wangensteen Bldg (MMC 396), 516 Delaware St, SE, Minneapolis, MN 55455; tel. (612) 625-3200; fax (612) 625-2101):

ADAMS, G.
GIEBINK, G. S.
JUHN, S. K.
MAISEL, R.
MARGOLIS, R.
NELSON, D.
SANTI, P.

Paediatric Dentistry (6-150 Malcolm Moos Health Sciences Tower, 515 Delaware St, SE, Minneapolis, MN 55455; tel. (612) 624-1985; fax (612) 629-2900; internet www1.umn.edu/dental/department/prevsci/div_pediatric.html):

BEIRAGHI, S.
MOLLER, K.
TILL, M.

Paediatrics (13-118 Phillips-Wangensteen Bldg, 516 Delaware St, SE, Minneapolis, MN 55455; tel. (612) 624-3113; fax (612) 626-6601):

BALFOUR, H.
BELANI, K.
BERRY, S.
BLAZAR, B.

BLUM, R.
BLUMENTHAL, M.
BROWN, D. M.
CHAVERS, B.
CLAWSON, C. C.
FERRIERI, P.
FISH, A.
GEORGIEFF, M.
GIEBINK, G. S.
HULL, H.
INGBAR, D.
JOHNSON, D.
KAPLAN, E.
KASHTAN, C.
KERSEY, J.
KIM, Y.
KING, R.
KOHEN, D.
KRIEL, R.
LOCKMAN, L.
MAMMEL, M.
MAUER, S. M.
MOLLER, J.
NELSON, C.
NEVINS, T.
OGILVIE, J.
RAMSAY, N.
REMAFEDI, G.
RESNICK, M.
ROBISON, L.
SHAPIRO, E.
SHARP, H.
SINAIKO, A.
STORY, M.
SUMMERS, G.
THOMPSON, T.
TRUWIT, C.
WAGNER, J.
WANGENSTEEN, O. D.
WARWICK, W.
WHITE, J.
WHITLEY, C.

Periodontology (7-368 Malcolm Moos Health Sciences Tower, 515 Delaware St, SE, Minneapolis, MN 55455; tel. (612) 625-5400; fax (612) 626-2652; internet www.umn.edu/dental/department/prevsci/div_perio.html):

BAKDASH, B.
HERZBERG, M. C.
PHILSTROM, B. L.
WOLFF, L. F.

Pharmaceutical Care and Health Systems (7-159 Weaver-Densford Hall, 308 Harvard St, SE, Minneapolis, MN 55455; tel. (612) 626-9938; e-mail tesda001@tc.umn.edu; internet www.pharmacy.umn.edu):

CIPOLLE, R. J.
MORLEY, P. C.
SCHONDELMEYER, S. W.
STRAND, I. M.
WEAVER, L. C.

Pharmaceutics (9-177 Weaver-Densford Hall, 308 Harvard St, SE, Minneapolis, MN 55455; tel. (612) 624-5151; fax (612) 626-2125; internet www.pharmacy.umn.edu/resgrad/pceutics/pharmaceuticshome.html):

BRAECKMAN, R.
FREY II, W. H.
GRANT, D. J. W.
RESCIGNO, A.
SAWCHUK, R. J.
SIEGEL, R. A.
SURYANARAYANAN, R. G.

Pharmacology (6-120 Jackson Hall, 321 Church St, SE, Minneapolis, MN 55455; tel. (612) 625-9997; fax (612) 625-8408; internet www.pharmacology.med.umn.edu):

BEATTIE, C. W.
CONTI-FINE, B.
EL-ZAKAHANY, E.
HANNA, P. E.
HOLTZMAN, J. L.
HUNNINGHAKE, D. B.
LAW, P.

LEE, H. C.
LOH, H. H.
PENTEL, P. R.
SINAIKO, A. R.
SLADEK, N. E.
SPARBER, S. B.
THAYER, A.
WILCOX, G. L.
WOOD, W. G.
YEE, D.
ZIMMERMAN, B. G.

Philosophy (831 Walter W. Heller Hall, 271 19th Ave, S, Minneapolis, MN 55455; tel. (612) 625-6563; fax (612) 624-8380; internet philosophy.umn.edu):

BOWIE, N.
DAHL, N. O.
EATON, M. M.
GIERE, R.
GUNDERSON, K.
HANSON, W. H.
HELLMAN, G.
HOPKINS, J. S.
KAC, M.
LEWIS, D.
LONGINO, H.
OWENS, J.
PETERSON, S.
SAVAGE, C. W.
SCHEMAN, N.
WALLACE, J. R.

Philosophy of Science (746 Walter W. Heller Hall, 271 19th Ave, S, Minneapolis, MN 55455; tel. (612) 625-6635; fax (612) 626-8380; internet www.mcps.umn.edu):

GIERE, R.
GUNDERSON, K.
HANSON, W.
HELLMAN, G.
LONGINO, H.
SAVAGE, C. W.
SHAPIRO, A.
STUEWER, R.

Physical Medicine and Rehabilitation (500 Boynton (MMC), Minneapolis, MN 55455; tel. (612) 626-4050; fax (612) 624-6686; internet www.mcps.umn.edu):

DI FABIO., R.
PATTERSON, R.

Physics and Astronomy (148 Tate Lab of Physics, 116 Church St, SE, Minneapolis, MN 55455; tel. (612) 624-7375; fax (612) 624-4578; internet www.physics.umn.edu):

BROADHURST, J. H.
CAMPBELL, C. E.
CATTELL, C.
CUSHMAN, P.
DAHLBERG, E. D.
ELLIS, P. J.
GOLDMAN, A. M.
GROSBERG, A.
HALLEY, J. W.
HELLER, K. J.
HUANG, C. C.
KAKALIOS, J.
KAPUSTA, J. I.
LARKIN, A.
LYSAK, R. L.
MARSHAK, M. L.
PEPIN, R. O.
PETERSON, E. A.
POLING, K.
RUDAZ, S.
RUDDICK, K.
RUSACK, R.
SHIFMAN, M.
SHKLOVSKII, B.
VAINSHTEIN, A.
VALLS, O. T.
VOLOSHIN, M.
WALSH, T. F.

Physiology (6-125 Jackson Hall, 321 Church St, SE, Minneapolis, MN 55455; tel. (612)

625-5902; fax (612) 625-5149; internet physiology.med.umn.edu):

DI SALVO, J.
IAIZZO, P.
LEVITT, D.
LOW, W.
O'GRADY, S.
OSBORN, J.
WANGENSTEEN, O. D.
WEIR, K. E.

Plant Biology (220 Biological Sciences Center, 1445 Gortner Ave, St Paul, MN 55108; tel. (612) 625-1234; fax (612) 625-1738; e-mail pbio@ux.acs.umn.edu; internet www.cbs.umn.edu/plantbio/pbio):

BIESBOER, D. D.
BRAMBL, R.
CHARVAT, L.
GLEASON, F. K.
KOUKKARI, W. L.
MCLAUGHLIN, D. J.
OLSZEWSKI, N. E.
SNUSTAD, P. D.
VANDENBOSCH, K.
WETMORE, C. M.
WICK, S.

Plant Pathology (495 Borlaug Hall, 1991 Upper Buford Circle, St Paul, MN 55108; tel. (612) 625-8200; fax (612) 625-9728; internet www.plpa.agri.umn.edu):

BLANCHETTE, R. A.
GROTH, J. V.
JONES, R. K.
KINKEL, L. L.
KRUPA, S. V.
LARSEN, P. O.
LOCKHART, B. E.
MACDONALD, D. H.
NYVALL, R. F.
PERCICH, J. A.
PFLEGER, F. L.
WINDELS, C. E.
YOUNG, N. D.
ZEYEN, R. J.

Political Science (1414 Social Sciences Bldg, 267 19th Ave, S, Minneapolis, MN 55455; tel. (612) 624-4144; fax (612) 626-7599; internet www.polisci.umn.edu):

DIETZ, M.
DUVALL, R.
FARR, J.
FLANIGAN, W. H.
FOGELMAN, E.
JACOBS, L.
KVAVIK, R.
NIMITZ, A.
ROSENSTONE, S.
SCOTT, T. M.
SHIVELY, W. P.

Psychiatry (F-282/2A W, 2450 Riverside Ave S, Minneapolis, MN 55455; tel. (612) 273-9800; fax (612) 273-9779; e-mail madso0009@umn.edu; internet www.med.umn.edu/psychiatry):

CARROLL, M.
ECKERT, E.
EL-FAKAHANY, E.
HARTMAN, B.
HATSUKAMI, D.
KROLL, J.
MACKENZIE, T.
SCHULTZ, C.

Psychiatry Research (628 Diehl Hall (MMC 392), 505 Essex St, SE, Minneapolis, MN 55455; tel. (612) 626-4034; fax (612) 624-8939):

CARROLL, M. E.
EL-FAKAHANY, E.
HATSUKAMI, D.

Psychological Foundations of Education (206 Burton Hall, 178 Pillsbury Drive, SE, Minneapolis, MN 55455; tel. (612) 624-6083; fax

(612) 624-8241; internet www.coled.umn.edu/edpsych/default.html):

BART, W.
DAVISON, M.
HARWELL, H.
JOHNSON, D.
LAWRENZ, F.
MARUYAMA, G.
PELLEGRINI, A.
SAMUELS, S. J.
TENNYSON, R.
VAN DEN BROEK, P.

Psychology (N-218 Elliot Hall, 75 East River Rd, Minneapolis, MN 55455; tel. (612) 625-4042; fax (612) 626-2079; internet www.psych.umn.edu):

BORGIDA, E.
BOUCHARD, T. J.
BURKHARDT, D. A.
BUTCHER, J. N.
CAMPBELL, J. P.
CUDECK, R.
DAVIS, E. R.
DUNETTE, M.
FOX, P.
GARMEZY, N.
HANSEN, J. I.
KERSTEN, D.
LEON, G. R.
LYKKEN, D.
MCGUE, M.
MATOWIDLOS, S.
MOTOWIDLO, S.
OVERMIER, J. B.
PATRICK, C.
SACKETT, D.
SNYDER, M.
TELLEGEN, A.
VIEMEISTER, N. F.
WEISS, D. J.

Public Health Administration (D-359 Mayo Memorial Bldg (MMC 97), 420 Delaware St, SE, Minneapolis, MN 55455; tel. (612) 625-9480; fax (612) 624-5920; internet www.hsr.umn.edu):

MCBEAN, M.
VENINGA, R.

Public Health Nutrition (300 W Bank Office Bldg, 1300 52nd St, Minneapolis, MN 55455; tel. (612) 624-1818; fax (612) 624-0315; internet www.epi.umn.edu):

BROWN, J. E.
HIMES, J. H.
JEFFERY, R. W.
LUEPKER, R. V.
PERRY, C.
STORY, M. T.

Radiology (2-300 Fairview Univ. Medical Center (MMC 292), 420 Delaware St, SE, Minneapolis, MN 55455; tel. (612) 273-6004; fax (612) 273-1470; internet www.med.umn.edu/radiology):

EFANGE, S.
GARWOOD, M.
HU, X.
HUNTER, D.
JEROSCH-HERALD, M.
KIEFFER, S.
KIM, S.
KUCHARCZYK, J.
REINKE, D.
RITENOUR, E. R.
STEENSON, C.
STILLMAN, A.
TRUWIT, C.
UGURBIL, K.

Recreation and Sports Studies (220 Cooke Hall, 1900 University Ave, SE, Minneapolis, MN 55455; tel. (612) 625-5300; fax (612) 626-7700; internet www.kls.umn.edu):

KANE, M. J.
MCAVOY, L.

Regulatory Biochemistry (374 Gortner Lab, 1479 Gortner Ave, St Paul, MN 55108; tel. (612) 624-3622; internet www.cbs.umn.edu/bmbb):

BERNLOHR, D. A.
CONTI-FINE, B. M.
DEMPSEY, M. E.
KOERNER, J. F.
LOUIS, C. F.
NELSESTUEN, G. L.
OEGEMA, T. G.
RAFTERY, M. A.

Rhetoric (4 Classroom Office Bldg, 1994 Buford Ave, St Paul, MN 55108; tel. (612) 624-3445; fax (612) 624-3617; internet www.rhetoric.umn.edu):

BECKER, S.
BERKEKOTTER
GROSS, A. G.
LAY, M. M.
MCDOWELL, E. E.
MARCHAND, W. M.
MIKELONIS, V. M.
WAHLSTROM, B. J.
WHARTON, W. K.

Rural Sociology and Community Analysis (230 Peters Hall, 1404 Gortner Ave, St Paul, MN 55108; tel. (612) 625-4779; fax (612) 625-3746; internet ssw.che.umn.edu/centers.htm#crsca):

MCTAVISH, D.
MENANTEAU, D.
MEYERS, S. S.

St Anthony Falls Laboratory (2 Third Ave, SE, Minneapolis, MN 55414; tel. (612) 627-4010; fax (612) 627-4609; internet www.umn.edu/safl):

ARNDT, R.
FARELL, C.
FOUFOULA-GEORGIOU, E.
GULLIVER, J.
PAOLA, C.
PARKER, G.
SONG, C.
STEFAN, H.
VOLLER, V.

School Psychology (344 Elliot Hall, 75 E River Rd, Minneapolis, MN 55455; tel. (612) 624-4156; fax (612) 624-0879; internet education.umn.edu/edpsych):

CHRISTENSON, S.
MCCONNELL, S.
YSSELDYKE, J.

Scientific Computation (Graduate Programme) (7-125 Weaver Densford Hall, 308 Harvard St, SE, Minneapolis, MN 55455; tel. (612) 626-2601; fax (612) 626-4429):

ANDERSON, R.
BOLEY, D.
CANDLER, G.
CHELIKOWSKY, J.
COCKBURN, B.
CRAMER, C.
DERBY, J.
EBNER, T.
FONTOULA-GEORGIO, E. F.
FRIEDMAN, A.
KERSTEN, D.
KUMAR, V.
LOWENGRUB, J.
LUSKIN, M.
NIEBER, J.
OTHMER, H.
PARK, H.
PATANKAR, S.
SAAD, Y.
SCRIVEN, L. E.
SELL, G.
SONG, C.
SRIVASTAVA, J.
STECH, H.
THOMAS, D.
TIERNEY, L.

TRUHLAR, D.
TWETIK, A. H.
VOLLER, V.
WILCOX, G.
WOODWARD, P.
YUEN, D.

Slavic and Central Asian Languages and Literatures (214 Nolte Center for Continuing Education, 315 Pillsbury Dr., SE, Minneapolis, MN 55455; tel. (612) 624-3331; fax (612) 624-4579; e-mail iles@umn.edu):

BASHIRI, I.
JAHN, G.

Small Animal Clinical Sciences (C-339 Veterinary Teaching Hospitals, 1352 Boyd Ave and 1365 Gortner Ave, St Paul, MN 55108; tel. (612) 625-7744; fax (612) 624-0751):

ARMSTRONG, P. J.
BISTNER, S.
FEENEY, D.
HARDY, R.
JESSEN, C.
KLAUSNER, J.
LIPOWITZ, A.
OSBORNE, C.
POLZIN, D.
REDIG, P.
WALLACE, L.

Social Administrative and Clinical Pharmacy (7-155 Weaver-Densford Hall, 308 Harvard St, SE, Minneapolis, MN 55455; tel. (612) 624-2973; fax (612) 625-9931; internet www.pharmacy.umn.edu):

CIPOLLE, R. J.
GARRARD, J. M.
GATEWOOD, L. C.
LANGLEY, P. C.
MORLEY, P. C.
SCHONDELMEYER, S. W.
SPEEDIE, S. M.
STRAND, L. M.
WEAVER, L. C.
WECKWERTH, V. E.
ZASKE, D. E.

Social Work (105 Peters Hall, 1404 Gortner Ave, St Paul, MN 55108; tel. (612) 625-1220; fax (612) 624-3744; internet ssw.che.umn.edu):

BAIZERMAN, M.
BEKER, J.
EDLESON, J.
GILGUN, J.
HOLLISTER, D.
KIVNICK, H.
MENANTEAU, D.
MEYERS, S.
QUAM, J.
ROONEY, R.
UMBREIT, M.
WELLS, S.

Sociology (909 Social Sciences Bldg, 267 19th Ave, S, Minneapolis, MN 55455; tel. (612) 624-4300; fax (612) 624-7020; internet www.soc.umn.edu):

AMINZADE, R.
ANDERSON, J.
ANDERSON, R. E.
GALASKIEWICZ, J.
KNOKE, D.
KRUTTSCHNITT, C.
LASLETT, B.
LEIK, R. K.
MALMQUIST, C.
MARINI, M.
MORTIMER, J.
NELSON, J. I.
STRYKER, R.

Soil, Water, and Climate (439 Borlaug Hall, 1991 Upper Buford Circle, St Paul, MN 55108; tel. (612) 625-1244; fax (612) 625-2208; internet www.soils.agri.umn.edu):

ALLAN, D. L.
ANDERSON, J. L.

BAKER, J. M.
BLOOM, P. R.
CLAPP, C.
COOPER, T. H.
DOWDY, R. H.
GRAHAM, P. H.
GUPTA, S. C.
HALBACH, T. R.
KOSKINEN, W. C.
LAMB, J. A.
MALZER, G.
MOLINA, J. A.
MONCRIEF, J. F.
MULLA, D. J.
NATER, E. A.
RANDALL, G. W.
REHM, G. W.
REICOSKY, D. C.
ROBERT, P. C.
ROSEN, C. J.
RUSSELLE, M. P.
SADOWSKI, M. J.
SCHMITT, M. A.
SEELEY, M. W.

Spanish and Portuguese (34 Folwell Hall, 9 Pleasant St, SE, Minneapolis, MN 55455; tel. (612) 625-5858; fax (612) 625-3549; internet spansport.cla.umn.edu):

JARA, R.
SPADACCINI, N.
VIDAL, H.

Special Education Programs (227 Burton Hall, 178 Pillsbury Drive, SE, Minneapolis, MN 55455; tel. (612) 624-2342; fax (612) 626-9627; internet education.umn.edu/edpsych):

DENO, S.
HUPP, S.
McEVOY, M.

Statistics (313 Ford Hall, 224 Church St, SE, Minneapolis, MN 55455; tel. (612) 625-8046; fax (612) 624-8858; internet www.stat.umn.edu):

BINGHAM, C.
CHALONER, K.
COOK, R. D.
DICKEY, J.
EATON, M. L.
GEISSER, S.
GEYER, C.
HAWKINS, D.
MEEDEN, G.
OEHLERT, G.
SUDDERTH, W. D.
TIERNEY, L.
WEISBERG, S.

Strategic Management and Organization (3-353 Carlson School of Management, 321 19th Ave, S, Minneapolis, MN 55455; tel. (612) 624-5232; fax (612) 626-1316; internet www.csom.umn.edu/wwwpages/depts/smo):

BROMILEY, P.
ERICKSON, W. B.
LENWAY, S.
MAITLAND, I.
MARCUS, A.
NICHOLS, M.
SAPIENZA, H.
VAN DE VEN, A.

Structural Biology and Biophysics (140 Gortner Laboratory, 1479 Gortner Ave, St Paul, MN 55108; tel. (612) 625-6100; e-mail bmbb@biosci.cbs.umn.edu; internet www.cbs.umn.edu/bmbb):

ARMITAGE, I. M.
BANASZAK, L. J.
BARRY, B. A.
BLOOMFIELD, V. A.
HOGENKAMP, H. P.
HOWARD, J. B.
LIPSCOMB, J. D.
LOVRIEN, R. E.
MAYO, K. H.
OHLENDORF, D. H.

THOMAS, D. D.
TSONG, T. Y.

Surgery (11-100 Phillips-Wangensteen Bldg (MMC 195), 516 Delaware St, SE, Minneapolis, MN 55455; tel. (612) 625-1400; fax (612) 625-8496; internet www.surg.umn.edu):

BOLMAN, R. M., III
BUCHWALD, H.
CERRA, F.
CUNNINGHAM, B.
DALMASSO, A.
DRIES, D.
DUNN, D.
ENGELAND, W.
EYLER, J.
FOKER, J.
GOODALE, R. L.
GRUESSNER, R.
LAKE, J.
LEE, J. T.
LEVINE, A.
LYTE, M.
McQUARRIE, D. G.
MATAS, A.
MILLER, L.
MOLINA, E.
PARK, S.
PAYNE, W.
RODRIGUEZ, J.
ROTHENBERGER, D. A.
SAKO, Y.
SHUMWAY, S.
SUTHERLAND, D.
WARD, H.
WELLS, C.

Surgical Sciences (11-100 Phillips-Wangensteen (MMC 195), 516 Delaware St, SE, Minneapolis, MN 55455; tel. (612) 625-1400):

DALMASSO, A.
ENGELAND, W.
EYLER, J.
WELLS, C.

Theatre Arts and Dance (580 Rarig Center, 330 21st Ave, S, Minneapolis, MN 55455; tel. (612) 625-6699; fax (612) 625-6334; e-mail theatre@umn.edu; internet cla.umn.edu/theater):

BROCKMAN, C. L.
KOBIALKA, M.
REID, B.

Therapeutic Radiology/Radiation Oncology (M-26 Masonic Cancer Center (MMC 494), 424 Harvard St, SE, Minneapolis, MN 55455; tel. (612) 626-6146; fax (612) 624-5445; internet www.ahc.umn.edu):

LEE, C. K.
LEVITT, S. H.
POTISH, R. A.
SONG, C. W.
VALLERA, D.

TMJ/Orofacial Pain (6-320 Malcolm Moos Health Sciences Tower, 515 Delaware St, SE, Minneapolis, MN 55455; tel. (612) 624-3130; fax (612) 626-0138):

FRICTON, J.

Toxicology Graduate Program (244 Veterinary Diagnostic Lab, 1333 Gortner Ave, St Paul, MN 55108; tel. (612) 625-8787; fax (612) 624-8707; internet www.mvdl.umn.edu):

ABUL-HAJJ, Y.
BROWN, D.
CARLSON, R.
DiSALVO, J.
DREWES, L.
HANNA, P.
MURPHY, M.
NAGASAWA, H.
NIEMI, G.
PROHASKA, J.
SCHOOK, L.
SPARBER, S.

WALLACE, K.

Urban Studies (348 Social Sciences Bldg, 267 19th Ave, S, Minneapolis, MN 55455; tel. (612) 626-1626; fax (612) 624-1044; internet urbanstudies.cla.umn.edu):

ADAMS, J. S.
FISHER, T.
GALASKIEWICZ, J.
LEITNER, H.
RUNGE, C. F.
SCOTT, T.
SHEPPARD, E.

Urologic Surgery (A-597 Mayo Memorial Bldg (MMC 394), 420 Delaware St, SE, Minneapolis, MN 55455; tel. (612) 625-9933):

HULBERT, J.

Veterinary Diagnostic Medicine (277 Veterinary Diagnostic Lab, 1333 Gortner Ave, St Paul, MN 55108; tel. (612) 625-8787; internet www.mvdl.umn.edu):

COLLINS, J.
GOYAL, S.
HAYDEN, D.
KURTZ, H.
O'BRIEN, T.
WALSER, M.

Veterinary Pathobiology (205 Veterinary Science, 1971 Commonwealth Ave, St Paul, MN 55108; tel. (612) 625-5255; fax (612) 625-5203; internet www.cvm.umn.edu):

BEITZ, A. J.
BEY, R. F.
BROWN, D. R.
FLETCHER, T. F.
GALLANT, E. M.
HALVORSON, D. A.
LARSON, A. A.
MAHESWARAN, S. K.
MURTAUGH, M. M.
NAGARAJA, K. V.
SHARMA, J. M.
STROMBERG, B. E.
WEISS, D. J.

Women's Studies (425 Ford Hall, 277 Church St, SE, Minneapolis, MN 55455; tel. (612) 624-6006; fax (612) 624-3573; internet womenstudy.cla.umn.edu):

KAMINSKY, A.
LONGINO, H.
SCHEMAN, N.

Wood and Paper Science (203 Kaufert Lab of Forest Products and Wood Science, 2004 Folwell Ave, St Paul, MN 55108; tel. (612) 625-5200; fax (612) 625-6286; internet www.cnr.umn.edu/wps):

BOWYER, J.
MASSEY, J.
SARKANEN, S.
SCHMIDT, E.

Work, Community and Family Education (Adm 210 Vocational and Technical Education Bldg, 1954 Buford Ave, St Paul, MN 55108; tel. (612) 625-3757; fax (612) 624-2231; e-mail wcfe@umn.edu; internet education.umn.edu/wcfe):

BROWN, J.
LAMBRECHT, J.
LEWIS, T.
MCLEAN, G.
PETERSON, R.
PUCEL, D.
SWANSON, R.
THOMAS, R.

OTHER CAMPUSES

University of Minnesota, Crookston

2900 University Ave, Crookston, MN 56716
Telephone: (218) 281-8020
Fax: (218) 281-8050
E-mail: umcinfo@umn.edu
Internet: www1.crk.umn.edu

Founded 1966, present name 1988
State control
Academic year: August to May

Depts of agriculture and natural resources, business and mathematics, liberal arts and education, science and technology

Chancellor: CHARLES H. CASEY
Sr Vice-Chancellor for Academic and Student Affairs: THOMAS BALDWIN
Dir for Admissions and Enrolment Management: AMBER EVANS-DAILY
Registrar: ROBERT NELSON
Dir for Library Services: OWEN WILLIAMS
Number of teachers: 49 (full time)
Number of students: 2,653

PROFESSORS

ALI, ADEL, Computer Software Technology and Information Technology Management
BRORSON, S., Marketing and Management
DEL VECCHIO, R., Agriculture and Natural Resources
GELLER, J., Sociology
KNOWLTON, D., Art and Sciences
MARX, G., Agricultural, Food and Environmental Sciences
NEET, S., Art and Sciences
PETERSON, W. C., Art and Sciences
PETERSON, W., Mathematics
SELZLER, B., Art and Sciences
SVEDARSKY, W. D., Natural Resources
WINDELS, C., Agricultural, Food and Environmental Sciences

University of Minnesota, Duluth

1049 University Dr., Duluth, MN 55812
Telephone: (218) 726-8000
Fax: (218) 726-6186
E-mail: sknill@d.umn.edu
Internet: www.d.umn.edu

Founded 1895 as Normal School at Duluth
Academic year: September to May

Chancellor: LENDLEY C. BLACK
Exec. Vice-Chancellor for Academic Affairs: BILIN TSAI
Vice-Chancellor for Student Life: LISA ERWIN
Vice-Chancellor for Finance and Operations: JOHN KING
Vice-Chancellor for Advancement: WILLIAM WADE
Dir for Admissions: BETH ESSELSTROM
Library Dir: BILL SOZANSKY

Library of 261,609 vols, 268,225 e-books, 27,941 media items, 81,587 e-journals, 109,956 print govt documents, 26,194 electronic govt documents
Number of teachers: 589 (454 full-time, 135 part-time)
Number of students: 11,806

DEANS

College of Education and Human Service Professions: PAUL N. DEPUTY
College of Liberal Arts: SUSAN MAHER
College of Science Engineering: JAMES P. RIEHL
Labovitz School of Business and Economics: KJELL R. KNUDSEN (acting)
Medical School Duluth: GARY DAVIS
School of Fine Arts: WILLIAM E. PAYNE
Swenson College of Science and Engineering: PENNY MORTON

PROFESSORS

ADAMS, S. J., English
ANDERSON, A. C., Music
ANDERSON, C., Economics
ANDREWS, I. T., Biology
BACIG, T., Sociology—Anthropology
BARTLETT, E., Women's Studies
BELOTE, L., Sociology—Anthropology
BRUSH, G., Art
BRUSH, L., Art

BURNS, S. G., Electrical and Computer Engineering
CAPLE, R., Chemistry
CARLSON, H., Education
CARLSON, R. M., Chemistry
CASTLEBERRY, S., Management Studies
CROUCH, D., Computer Science
DAS, A., Psychology
DEPUTY, P. N., Communication Sciences and Disorders
DREWES, L., Biochemistry and Molecular Biology
DUFF, T., Finance and Management Information Sciences
DURGUNOGLA, A. Y., Psychology
EISENBERG, R. M., Pharmacology
ELLIOT, B. A., Behavioural Sciences
ELLIOT, B. A., Family Medicine
EVANS, J., Chemistry
FALK, D., Social Work
FEROZ, E., Accounting
FETZER, J., Philosophy
FIRLING, C., Biology
FLEISCHMAN, W., Sociology—Anthropology
FUGELSO, M., Industrial Engineering
FULKROD, J., Chemistry
GALLIAN, J. A., Mathematics and Statistics
GORDON, R., Psychology
GRANT, J. A., Geological Sciences
GREEN, R., Mathematics and Statistics
HAFFERTY, F., Behavioural Sciences
HARRISS, D. K., Chemistry
HEDIN, T., Art
HEDMAN, S., Biology
HELLER, L. J., Medical and Molecular Physiology
HILLER, J., Physics
HOLST, T., Geological Sciences
JAMES, B., Mathematics and Statistics
JAMES, K. L., Mathematics and Statistics
JANKOFSKY, K. P., English
JESSWEIN, W. A., Economics
JOHNSON, T., Industrial Engineering
JOHNSON, T. C., Geological Sciences
JORDAN, T. F., Physics
KARIM, M. R., Biology
KENDALL, L. A., Industrial Engineering, MSc in Engineering Management
KLEMER, A., Biology
KLUEG, J., Art
KNOPP, L. M., Jr, Geography
KRAMER, J., Social Work
KRITZMIRE, J., Music
LAUNDERGAN, J. C., Sociology—Anthropology
LETTENSTROM, D., Art
LEY, E., Health, Physical Education and Recreation
LICHTY, R. W., Economics
LIEVANO, R., Finance and Management Information Sciences
LINDEKE, R., Industrial Engineering
LINN, M. D., Composition
LIU, Z., Mathematics and Statistics
MCCARTHY, D. A., Education
MCCLURE, B., Psychology
MAGNUSON, V. R., Chemistry
MAIOLO, J. C., English
MARCHESE, R., Sociology—Anthropology
MARTIN, K. A., Theatre
MAYO, D., Philosophy
MERRIER, P., Finance and Management Information Sciences
MILLER, K., Psychology
MILLER-CLEARY, L., English
MIZUKO, M. I., Communications Sciences and Disorders
MORTON, R., Geological Sciences
NEWSTROM, J. W., Management Studies
OJAKANGAS, R. W., Geological Sciences
PASTOR, J., Biology
PETERSON, J. M., Economics
PIERCE, J. L., Management Studies
POE, D., Chemistry
PROHASKA, J., Biochemistry and Molecular Biology
RAAB, R. L., Economics

RED HORSE, J. G., American Indian Studies
REGAL, J., Pharmacology
REGAL, R., Mathematics and Statistics
RICHARDS, C., Biology
RIEHL, J. P., Chemistry
RILEY, K., Composition
ROUFS, T. G., Sociology—Anthropology
RUBENFELD, S., Management Studies
SEVERSON, A. R., Anatomy and Cell Biology
SEYBOLT, R., Foreign Languages and Literatures
SHARP, P., Political Science
SHEHADEH, N., Electrical and Computer Engineering
SHEPHARD, M., Social Work
SMITH, D., Sociology—Anthropology
STACHOWITZ, M., Electrical and Computer Engineering
STECH, H., Mathematics and Statistics
STEINNES, D. N., Economics
STORCH, N. T., History
STUECHER, U., Psychology
SUNNAFRANK, M., Communication
SYDOR, M., Physics
THOMPSON, L. C., Chemistry
TRACHTE, G., Pharmacology
TROLANDER, J., Women's Studies
TROLANDER, J. A., History
TSAI, B., Chemistry
WALLACE, K., Biochemistry and Molecular Biology
WARD, P., Pathology and Laboratory Medicine
WEGREN, T., Music
WOLD, S., Music
WONG, S., Finance and Management Information Sciences
ZEITZ, E., Foreign Languages and Literatures
ZHDANKIN, V., Chemistry
ZIEGLER, R., Medical Microbiology and Immunology

University of Minnesota, Morris

600 E Fourth St, Morris, MN 56267
Telephone: (320) 589-6035
Fax: (320) 589-6051
E-mail: petersdk@mrs.umn.edu
Internet: www.morris.umn.edu
Founded 1960
Academic year: August to May
Divs of education, humanities, science and mathematics, social sciences
Chancellor: JACQUELINE JOHNSON
Vice-Chancellor for Academic Affairs and Dean: Dr BART D. FINZEL
Vice-Chancellor for Student Affairs: SANDRA OLSON-LOY
Library Dir: LeANN DEAN
Number of teachers: 121
Number of students: 1,700

PROFESSORS

AHERN, W. H., History
CABRERA, V., Modern Languages
CARLSON, J. A., Music
COTTER, J., Geology
DEMOS, V. P., Sociology
FRENIER, M. D., History
GARARASO, P., Philosophy
GOOCH, V., Biology
GUYOTTE, R., History
HINDS, H. E., Jr, History
HOPPE, D. M., Biology
INGLE, J. S., Art Studio
KISSOCK, C. M., Education
KLINGER, E., Psychology
LEE, J., Political Science
LEE, M.-L., Modern Languages
LOPEZ, A. A., Computer Science
NELLIS, J. G., Art Studio
O'REILLY, M. F., Mathematics
PAYNE, T. R., Theatre Arts
PETERSON, F. W., Art History
PURDY, D. H., English

SCHUMAN, S., English
SUNGUR, E., Mathematics
TOGEAS, J. B., Chemistry
VAN ALSTINE, J. B., Geology

University of Minnesota, Rochester

111 S Broadway, Suite 300, Rochester, MN 55904
Telephone: (507) 258-8001
Fax: (507) 258-8004
E-mail: umrinfo@umn.edu
Internet: www.r.umn.edu
Founded 1959, present status 2000
Academic year: August to May
Areas of study: adult education/human resource development, business and management, education, fine arts, health sciences, interpreting, nursing, occupational therapy, public health, social work, technology
Chancellor: Dr STEPHEN LEHMKUHLE
Vice-Chancellor for Academic Affairs: Dr CLAUDIA NEUHAUSER
Asst Vice-Chancellor for Admin.: GAIL SAUTER
Asst Vice-Chancellor for Institutional Advancement: JAY HESLEY
Asst Vice-Chancellor for Student Affairs: KENDRA WEBER
Dir for Admissions: JADE GRABAU
Librarian: MARY BETH SANCOMB-MORAN
Number of teachers: 11
Number of students: 273

UNIVERSITY OF ST THOMAS

2115 Summit Ave, St Paul, MN 55105
Telephone: (651) 962-5000
Fax: (651) 962-6504
E-mail: admissions@stthomas.edu
Internet: www.stthomas.edu
Founded 1885
Private control
Academic year: September to May
Pres.: Rev. DENNIS DEASE
Exec. Vice-Pres and Chief Academic Officer: Dr SUSAN HUBER
Exec. Vice-Pres and Chief Admin. Officer: Dr MARK DIENHART
Vice-Pres. for Information Resources and Technologies: Dr SAMUEL J. LEVY
Vice-Pres. for Mission: JOHN MALONE
Vice-Pres. for Student Affairs: JANE CANNEY
Vice-Pres. for Univ. and Govt Relations: DOUG HENNES
Registrar: PAUL J. SIMMONS
Librarian: DANIEL GJELTEN
Library of 730,000 vols, 95,000 e-books, 40,000 journals
Number of teachers: 847 (439 full-time, 408 part-time)
Number of students: 10,534 (6,176 undergraduate, 4,358 graduate)
Publications: B. Magazine (2 a year), Logos: A Journal of Catholic Thought and Culture (4 a year), New Hibernia Review (4 a year), Perspectives Magazine (2 a year), St. Thomas Lawyer (2 a year), St. Thomas Magazine (3 a year), Summit Avenue Review

DEANS

College of Applied Professional Studies: Dr BRUCE KRAMER
College of Arts and Sciences: Dr MARISA KELLY
Opus College of Business: Dr CHRISTOPHER PUTO
School of Divinity: Dr CHRISTOPHER THOMPSON
School of Engineering: Dr DONALD WEINKAUF
School of Law: THOMAS MENGLER
School of Social Work: Dr BARBARA SHANK

WALDEN UNIVERSITY

155 Fifth Ave S, Suite 100, Minneapolis, MN 55401
Telephone: (866) 492-5336
Fax: (410) 843-8104
Internet: www.waldenu.edu
Founded 1970
Private control
Divs of counselling and social service, education and leadership, health sciences, management, nursing, psychology, public policy and administration
Pres.: JONATHAN A. KAPLAN
Provost: Dr DENISE DeZOLT
Exec. Vice-Pres.: Dr CYNTHIA G. BAUM
Vice-Pres. for Education Policy and Regulation: Dr BONNIE COPELAND
Vice-Pres. for Operations: BRETT LUNDEEN
Chief Academic Officer: Dr ERIC RIEDEL
Dir for Admissions: DEVON LOETZ
Registrar: EVE DAUER
Dir for Library Services: (vacant)
Library of 50,000 vols of journals, 100,000 e-books and 1.5m. dissertations
Number of teachers: 2,500
Number of students: 46,500
Publications: International Journal of Applied Management and Technology, Journal of Social, Behavioral and Health Sciences, Journal of Social Change, Walden Alumni Magazine.

WILLIAM MITCHELL COLLEGE OF LAW

875 Summit Ave, St Paul, MN 55105-3076
Telephone: (651) 227-9171
Fax: (651) 290-6414
E-mail: admissions@wmitchell.edu
Internet: www.wmitchell.edu
Founded 1900
Private control
Academic year: August to May
Pres. and Dean: ERIC S. JANUS
Vice-Pres. for Information Technology Services: JAMES VILLARS
Vice-Pres. for Institutional Advancement: LINDA KEILLOR BERG
Vice-Pres. for Student Affairs and Dean for Students: DANIEL THOMPSON
Dir for Admissions: KENDRA DANE
Registrar: JIM STEVENS
Assoc. Dean for Information Resources: SIMON CANICK
Number of teachers: 90 (40 full-time, 50 adjunct)
Number of students: 1,025
Publications: Mitchell on Law, William Mitchell Law Raza Journal (online (web.wmitchell.edu/lawraza)), William Mitchell Law Review (4 a year)

PROFESSORS

BYRNE, A.
COLBERT, B.
DUBE, D.
EASLEY, A.
ERLINDER, P.
HAUGEN, P.
HAYDOCK, R.
HAYNSWORTH, H.
HEIDENREICH, D.
HOGG, J.
IIJIMA, A.
JANUS, E.
JORDAN, M.
JUERGENS, A.
KIRWIN, K.
KLASS, A.
KLEINBERGER, D.
KNAPP, P.
KRISHNAN, J.
KUNZ, C.

LEVINE, R.
LOGAN, W.
MOY, C.
MURPHY, R.
OH, P.
OLIPHANT, R.
PANNIER, R.
PORT, K.
PRINCE, D.
RADSAN, J.
ROBERTS, E.
ROY, D.
SCALLEN, E.
SCHAUMANN, N.
SCHMEDMAN, D.
SONSTENG, J.
STEENSON, M.
VER PLOEG, C.
VER STEEGH, N.
WINER, A.

MISSISSIPPI

ALCORN STATE UNIVERSITY

1000 ASU Dr., Alcorn State, MS 39096-7500
Telephone: (601) 877-6100
Fax: (601) 877-2975
E-mail: president@alcorn.edu
Internet: www.alcorn.edu
Founded 1871 as Alcorn Univ., present name and status 1974
State control
Academic year: August to May
Pres.: Dr M. CHRISTOPHER BROWN, II
Provost and Exec. Vice-Pres. for Academic Affairs: Dr SAMUEL L. WHITE
Sr Vice-Pres. for Finance and Administrative Services and Chief Financial Officer: Dr BETTY ROBERTS
Vice-Pres. for Business Affairs: CAROLYN HINTON
Vice-Pres. for Institutional Affairs: MARCUS D. WARD
Vice-Pres. for Student Affairs: E. CHERYL PONDER
Registrar: JIMMY SMITH
Dean for Libraries: Dr BLANCHE SANDERS
Library of 366,116 vols
Number of teachers: 213
Number of students: 4,018
Publications: *Alcorn* (1 a year), *Alcornite* (1 a year), *ASU Today* (2 a year, online)

DEANS

Newtie J. Boyd Academic Support Center: Dr EDWARD VAUGHN
School of Agriculture, Research, Extension and Applied Sciences: Dr BARRY L. BEQUETTE
School of Arts and Sciences: Dr NORRIS EDNEY (acting)
School of Business: Dr VIVEK BHARGAVA
School of Education and Psychology: Dr ROBERT CARR
School of Graduate Studies: Dr DONZEL LEE
School of Nursing: Dr LINDA GODLEY

BELHAVEN UNIVERSITY

1500 Peachtree St, Jackson, MS 39202
Telephone: (601) 968-5940
Fax: (601) 968-9998
E-mail: admission@belhaven.edu
Internet: www.belhaven.edu
Founded 1883 as Belhaven College, present name 2010
Private control
Academic year: August to May
Campuses in Atlanta (Georgia), Chattanooga and Memphis (Tennessee), Houston (Texas), Orlando (Florida)
Pres.: Dr ROGER PARROTT

Sr Vice-Pres. and Provost: Dr DANIEL CARL FREDERICKS
Vice-Pres. for Campus Operations: TOM PHILLIPS
Vice-Pres. for Student Affairs and Athletics: SCOTT LITTLE
Vice-Pres. for Univ. Advancement: KEVIN RUSSELL
Chief Financial Officer: VIRGINIA HENDERSON
Dean for Faculty: Dr CURT BECK
Dean for Student Life: GREG HAWKINS
Dir for Admissions: SUZANNE SULLIVAN
Registrar: DONNA WEEKS
Dir for Library: SUSAN SPRINGER
Library of 125,000 vols, 34,000 e-books
Number of teachers: 195 (51 full-time, 144 adjunct)
Number of students: 3,245 (1,091 undergraduate, 550 graduate)

DEANS

Honors College: Dr MELISSA HAUSE
School of Arts and Sciences: Dr GLENN SUMRALL
School of Business: Dr RALPH A. MASON, III
School of Education: Dr SANDRA L. RASBERRY

BLUE MOUNTAIN COLLEGE

POB 160, Blue Mountain, MS 38610
201 W Main, Blue Mountain, MS 38610
Telephone: (662) 685-4771
Fax: (662) 685-4776
Internet: www.bmc.edu
Founded 1873
Private control
Academic year: August to May (2 semesters)
Depts of biblical and associated studies, business, education, fine arts and speech, kinesiology and health studies, language and literature, mathematics and natural science, social and behavioural sciences
Pres.: Dr BETTYE ROGERS COWARD
Vice-Pres. for Academic Affairs: SHARON ENZOR
Vice-Pres. for Planning, Assessment, Graduate Studies and Spec. Programmes: JANICE NICHOLSON
Academic Dean: GARTH E. RUNION
Dean for Enrolment Services and Student Life: JACK MOSER
Dir for Admissions: MARIA TEEL
Registrar: SHEILA FREEMAN
Dir for Library Services: DEREK CASH
Library of 60,500 vols, 36,094 e-books
Number of teachers: 30
Number of students: 550

DELTA STATE UNIVERSITY

1003 W Sunflower Rd, Cleveland, MS 38733
Telephone: (662) 846-3000
Fax: (662) 846-4014
E-mail: admissions@deltastate.edu
Internet: www.deltastate.edu
Founded 1924 as Delta State Teachers College, present name and status 1974
State control
Academic year: August to July (2 semesters)
Pres.: Dr JOHN M. HILPERT
Provost and Vice-Pres. for Academic Affairs: Dr ANN C. LOTVEN
Vice-Pres. for Finance and Admin.: GREG REDLIN
Vice-Pres. for Student Affairs: Dr WAYNE BLANSETT
Vice-Pres. for Univ. Relations: Dr MICHELLE ROBERTS
Dean for Enrolment Management and Dir for Admissions: Dr DEBBIE HESLEP
Dean for Graduate Studies: Dr ALBERT NYLANDER
Registrar: JOHN ELLIOTT
Dir for Library Services: JEFF SLAGELL

Library of 360,000 vols
Number of teachers: 270
Number of students: 4,000

DEANS

College of Arts and Sciences: Dr PAUL HANKINS
College of Business: Dr BILLY MOORE
College of Education: Dr LESLIE GRIFFIN
Graduate and Continuing Studies: Dr ALBERT B. NYLANDER
Robert E. Smith School of Nursing: Dr LIZABETH CARLSON

JACKSON STATE UNIVERSITY

1400 John R. Lynch St, Administration Tower, Jackson, MS 39217-0280
Telephone: (601) 979-2121
Fax: (601) 979-2399
E-mail: admappl@jsums.edu
Internet: www.jsums.edu
Founded 1877 as Natchez Seminary, present name and status 1974
State control
Academic year: August to August (2 semesters)
Pres.: Dr CAROLYN MEYERS
Provost and Vice-Pres. for Academic Affairs: Prof. Dr MARK G. HARDY
Vice-Pres. for Business and Finance: MICHAEL THOMAS
Vice-Pres. for Information and Process Management: Dr WILLIE G. BROWN
Vice-Pres. for Research and Fed. Relations: Dr FELIX A. OKOJIE
Vice-Pres. for Student Life: Dr MARCUS A. CHANAY
Registrar: ALFRED JACKSON
Dean for Library and Information Resources: Dr MELISSA DRUCKERY
Library of 376,566 vols
Number of teachers: 502 (382 full-time, 120 part-time)
Number of students: 8,903
Publication: *Blue and White Flash* (4 a year)

DEANS

College of Business: Dr GLENDA GLOVER
College of Education and Human Development: Dr DANIEL WATKINS
College of Liberal Arts: Dr DOLLYE M. E. ROBINSON
College of Public Service: Dr MARIO AZEVEDO
College of Science, Engineering and Technology: Dr PAUL B. TCHOUNWOU
Division of Graduate Studies: Dr DORRIS R. ROBINSON GARDNER
Division of International Studies: ALLY MACK

MILLSAPS COLLEGE

1701 N State St, Jackson, MS 39210-0001
Telephone: (601) 974-1000
Fax: (601) 974-1059
E-mail: admissions@millsaps.edu
Internet: www.millsaps.edu
Founded 1890
Private control
Academic year: August to May (2 semesters)
Pres.: Dr ROBERT PEARIGEN
Sr Vice-Pres. for Academic Affairs and Dean of College: Dr S. KEITH DUNN
Vice-Pres. for Finance: LOUISE BURNEY
Vice-Pres. for Institutional Advancement: CHARLES R. LEWIS
Vice-Pres. for Institutional Planning and Assessment: TERRI HUDSON
Vice-Pres. and Dean for Students: Dr BRIT KATZ
Dean for Admissions: MICHAEL THORP
Dean for Faculty: DAVID DAVIS
Librarian: THOMAS HENDERSON

Library of 209,900 vols, 631 print journals, 7,000 e-journals

Number of teachers: 97 (full-time)

Number of students: 1,118 (1,013 undergraduate, 105 graduate)

Publications: *Promenade* (1 a year), *Stylus* (2 a year)

DEANS

Else School of Management: Dr KIMBERLY BURKE

MISSISSIPPI COLLEGE

200 S Capitol St, Clinton, MS 39056

Telephone: (601) 925-3000

Fax: (601) 925-3481

E-mail: admissions@mc.edu

Internet: www.mc.edu

Founded 1826 as Hampstead Acad., present name 1830

Private control

Academic year: August to May (2 semesters)

Pres.: Dr LEE G. ROYCE

Vice-Pres. for Academic Affairs: Dr RON HOWARD

Vice-Pres. for Admin. and Govt Relations: Dr STEVE STANFORD

Vice-Pres. for Advancement: Dr BILL TOWNSEND

Vice-Pres. for Enrolment Management and Student Affairs: Dr JIM TURCOTTE

Vice-Pres. for Planning and Assessment and Dean for Graduate Studies: Dr DEBBIE NORRIS

Chief Financial Officer: DONNA LEWIS

Chief Information Officer: BILL CRANFORD

Library Dir: KATHLEEN HUTCHISON

Library of 253,818 vols

Number of teachers: 194 (full-time)

Number of students: 5,270 (3,238 undergraduate, 1,457 graduate, 575 law)

DEANS

School of Business: Prof. Dr MARCELO EDUARDO

School of Christian Studies and the Arts: Prof. WAYNE VANHORN

School of Education: Prof. Dr DON W. LOCKE

School of Humanities and Social Sciences: Prof. Dr GARY K. MAYFIELD

School of Law: Prof. Dr JAMES H. ROSENBLATT

School of Nursing: Prof. Dr MARY JEAN PADGETT

School of Science and Mathematics: Prof. Dr STAN BALDWIN

MISSISSIPPI STATE UNIVERSITY

POB 5325, Mississippi State, MS 39762

Telephone: (662) 325-2323

Fax: (662) 325-7455

E-mail: msuinfo@ur.msstate.edu

Internet: www.msstate.edu

Founded 1878 as Agricultural and Mechanical College of State of Mississippi, present name 1958

State control

Academic year: August to May

Pres.: Dr MARK E. KEENUM

Provost and Exec. Vice-Pres. for Academic Affairs: JEROME A. GILBERT

Vice-Pres. for Agriculture, Forestry and Veterinary Medicine: GREGORY BOHACH

Vice-Pres. for Budget and Planning: DON ZANT

Vice-Pres. for Devt and Alumni: JOHN RUSH

Vice-Pres. for Research and Economic Devt: DAVID R. SHAW (acting)

Vice-Pres. for Student Affairs: WILLIAM KIBLER

Chief of Staff and Chief Financial Officer: MICHAEL J. McGREVEY

Gen. Counsel: JOAN LUCAS

Registrar: BUTCH STOKES

Dean for Graduate School: Dr LOUIS R. D'ABRAMO

Dean for Libraries: FRANCES COLEMAN

Library of 2,124,341 vols, 70,331 journals

Number of teachers: 1,352

Number of students: 20,424

DEANS

College of Agriculture and Life Sciences: Dr GEORGE HOPPER

College of Architecture, Art and Design: JAMES L. WEST

College of Arts and Sciences: Dr GARY L. MYERS

College of Business: SHARON OSWALD

College of Education: Dr RICHARD BLACKBOURN

College of Forest Resources: GEORGE M. HOPPER

College of Veterinary Medicine: KENT H. HOBLET

James Worth Bagley College of Engineering: SARAH A. RAJALA

Judy and Bobby Shackouls Honors College: CHRISTOPHER A. SNYDER

MISSISSIPPI UNIVERSITY FOR WOMEN

1100 College St, Columbus, MS 39701

Telephone: (662) 329-4750

Fax: (662) 241-7481

E-mail: admissions@muw.edu

Internet: www.muw.edu

Founded 1884

State control

Academic year: August to May

Pres.: Dr JIM BORSIG

Provost and Vice-Pres. for Academic Affairs: Dr EVERETT E. CASTON

Vice-Pres. for Finance and Admin.: NORA R. MILLER

Vice-Pres. for Institutional Advancement: KEN KENNEDY

Vice-Pres. for Student Services: JENNIFER MILES

Dean of Library Services: GAIL GUNTER

Library of 426,900 vols

Number of teachers: 128

Number of students: 3,314

DEANS

College of Arts and Sciences: Dr THOMAS C. RICHARDSON

College of Business and Legal Studies: ANNE BALAZS

College of Education and Human Sciences: Dr SUE JOLLY-SMITH

College of Nursing and Speech Language Pathology: Dr SHEILA V. ADAMS

School of Professional Studies: Dr WILLIAM S. STEWART

MISSISSIPPI VALLEY STATE UNIVERSITY

14000 Highway 82, W, Itta Bena, MS 38941-1400

Telephone: (662) 254-9041

Fax: (662) 254-3759

E-mail: admsn@mvsu.edu

Internet: www.mvsu.edu

Founded 1946 as Mississippi Vocational College, present name and status 1974

State control

Academic year: August to July (2 semesters)

Pres.: Dr DONNA H. OLIVER

Provost and Exec. Vice-Pres. for Academic Affairs: Dr ANNA M. HAMMOND

Vice-Pres. for Business and Finance: JAMES WASHBURN

Vice-Pres. for Student Affairs, Enrolment Management and Diversity: Dr JERALD ADLEY

Vice-Pres. for Univ. Advancement: ANGELA Y. GETTER

Registrar: MAXCINE B. RUSH

Library Dir: Dr MANTRA HENDERSON

Library of 213,860 vols, 402 periodicals, 2,200 e-periodicals, 42,000 e-books, 4,026 video titles

Number of teachers: 112

Number of students: 2,452

DEANS

College of Arts and Sciences: Dr TAZINSKI LEE

College of Education: PATRICIA BROOKS

College of Professional Studies: Dr CURRESSIA M. BROWN

Graduate School: RICKEY HILL

REFORMED THEOLOGICAL SEMINARY

5422 Clinton Blvd, Jackson, MS 39209-3099

Telephone: (601) 923-1600

Fax: (601) 923-1654

E-mail: rts.jackson@rts.edu

Internet: www.rts.edu

Founded 1966

Private control

Academic year: June to May (2 semesters)

Campuses in Atlanta (Georgia), Charlotte (North Carolina), Jackson (Mississippi), Houston (Texas), Memphis (Tennessee), Oviedo (Florida), McLean (Virginia),

Chancellor and CEO: Dr ROBERT C. CANNADA, JR

Pres. (Atlanta Campus): JOHN SOWELL

Pres. (Jackson Campus): Dr GUY RICHARDSON

Pres. (Orlando Campus): DONALD W. SWEETING

Exec. Vice-Pres.: ROBERT T. BRIDGES

Chief Academic Officer: ROBERT J. CARA

Chief Devt and Communications Officer: LYNWOOD C. PEREZ

Chief Financial Officer: BRADLEY TISDALE

Dir for Admissions and Dean for Students: BRIAN GAULT

Chief Registrar: KIAMA J. LEE

Dir for Libraries: BYRON L. CONLEY

Library of 150,000 vols

Number of teachers: 105

Number of students: 600

Publication: *Ministry & Leadership* (4 a year).

RUST COLLEGE

150 Rust Ave, Holly Springs, MS 38635

Telephone: (662) 252-8000

Fax: (662) 252-6107

E-mail: admissions@rustcollege.edu

Internet: www.rustcollege.edu

Founded 1866 as Asbury Methodist Episcopal Church, present name and status 1915

Private control

Academic year: August to April

Divs of business, education, humanities, science and mathematics, social science

Pres.: Dr DAVID L. BECKLEY

Vice-Pres. for Academic Affairs: Dr PAUL C. LAMPLEY

Vice-Pres. for Devt: Dr ISHMELL H. EDWARDS

Vice-Pres. for Finance and Business: DON MANNING-MILLER

Dean for Student Affairs: CAROLYN HYMON

Registrar: CLARENCE E. SMITH

Head Librarian: ANITA W. MOORE

Library of 120,000 vols, 300 periodicals

Number of teachers: 59

Number of students: 1,029

SOUTHEASTERN BAPTIST COLLEGE

4229 Highway 15, N, Laurel, MS 39440

Telephone: (601) 426-6346
Fax: (601) 426-6347
E-mail: info@southeasternbaptist.edu
Internet: www.southeasternbaptist.edu

Founded 1948
Private control
Academic year: August to July

Areas of study: business administration and management, Bible studies, general studies

Pres.: Dr MEDRISK SAVELL
Exec. Vice-Pres.: JOSEPH HARRIS
Academic Dean: Dr AARON PARKER
Dean for Students: GREG HILLMAN
Dir for Admissions: RONNIE KITCHENS
Dir for Information Technology: HUBERT DYESS
Librarian: AMY HINTON

Library of 30,000 vols
Number of students: 63

TOUGALOO COLLEGE

500 West County Line Rd, Tougaloo, MS 39174

Telephone: (601) 977-7700
Fax: (601) 977-7739
Internet: www.tougaloo.edu

Founded 1869 as teacher training school, present name 1916
Private control
Academic year: August to May (2 semesters)

Pres.: Dr BEVERLEY WADE HOGAN
Provost and Exec. Vice-Pres. for Academic Affairs: Dr BETTYE PARKER-SMITH
Vice-Pres. for Facilities Management: KELLE MENOGAN, SR
Vice-Pres. for Finance and Admin. and Chief Financial Officer: Dr CYNTHIA MELVIN
Vice-Pres. for Information Technology: TERRY JORDAN
Vice-Pres. for Institutional Advancement: SANDRA A.M. BOWIE (acting)
Vice-Pres. for Student Affairs: FRED ALEXANDER
Dir for Admissions: JUNO JACOBS
Registrar: CAROLYN EVANS

Library of 139,600 vols
Number of teachers: 73
Number of students: 916

Publications: *The Harambee* (12 a year), *Tougaloo News* (3 a year)

DEANS

Division of Education, Supervision and Instruction: Dr PAMELA RUSS
Division of Humanities: Dr ANDREA MONTGOMERY
Division of Natural Science: Dr RICHARD McGINNIS
Division of Social Sciences: Dr KAMAL ABDEL-RAHMAN

UNIVERSITY OF MISSISSIPPI

POB 1848, University, MS 38677-1848
University Ave, University, MS 38677

Telephone: (662) 915-7211
Fax: (662) 915-7486
E-mail: admissions@olemiss.edu
Internet: www.olemiss.edu

Founded 1844
State control

Schools of medicine, dentistry, nursing, health related professions are constituents of the Univ. of Mississippi Medical Center, located in Jackson, Mississippi

Chancellor: Dr DANIEL W. JONES
Pres. and Chief Exec. Officer of the Univ. Foundation: WENDELL WEAKLEY

Provost and Vice-Chancellor for Academic Affairs: MORRIS H. STOCKS
Vice-Chancellor for Finance and Admin.: LARRY D. SPARKS
Vice-Chancellor for Research and Sponsored Programmes: ALICE M. CLARK
Vice-Chancellor for Student Affairs: LARRY RIDGEWAY (acting)
Registrar and Dir for Admissions: CHARLOTTE FANT (acting)
Dean for Libraries: JULIA ROLES

Library: 1.9m. vols, 218,625 current periodicals, 184,757 e-journals, 366,145 e-books
Number of teachers: 779 (full-time)
Number of students: 20,844

Publications: *Law School, Medical Center*

DEANS

College of Liberal Arts: Dr GLENN W. HOPKINS
DeSoto Center: Dr FANNYE LOVE
Graduate School: Dr CHRISTY M. WYANDT
Meek School of Journalism and New Media: Prof. Dr WILL NORTON, JR
Patterson School of Accountancy: Prof. Dr MARK WILDER
Sally McDonnell Barksdale Honors College: Dr DOUGLASS SULLIVAN-GONZÁLEZ
School of Applied Sciences: Prof. Dr CAROL MINOR BOYD
School of Business Administration: Dr KEN B. CYREE
School of Education: Dr DAVID ROCK
School of Engineering: Dr ALEXANDER CHENG
School of Law: Dr RICHARD GERSHON
School of Nursing: Prof. Dr KIM HOOVER
School of Pharmacy: Prof. Dr DAVID D. ALLEN
Tupelo Center: Dr JAMES PATE

UNIVERSITY OF MISSISSIPPI MEDICAL CENTER

2500 N State St, Jackson, MS 39216

Telephone: (601) 984-1080
Fax: (601) 984-1079
Internet: www.umc.edu

Founded 1955; attached to Univ. of Mississippi
State control
Academic year: August to May (2 semesters)

Chancellor: Dr DANIEL W. JONES
Vice-Chancellor for Health Affairs: Dr JAMES KEETON
Assoc. Vice-Chancellor for Academic Affairs: Dr HELEN R. TURNER
Assoc. Vice-Chancellor for Research: Dr JOHN E. HALL
Chief Admin. Officer: DAVID POWE
Chief Financial Officer: JAMES L. WENTZ
Chief Information Officer: CHARLES R. ENICKS
Registrar: BARBARA WESTERFIELD
Library Dir: SUSAN CLARK

Library of 252,759 vols, 38,345 microforms, 2,615 audiovisual materials, 348 e-books, 1,894 journals
Number of teachers: 587
Number of students: 2,500

DEANS

School of Dentistry: Dr GARY REEVES
School of Graduate Studies: Dr JOEY GRANGER
School of Health-Related Professions: Dr BEN L. MITCHELL
School of Medicine: Dr JAMES KEETON,
School of Nursing: Dr KIM HOOVER
School of Pharmacy: Dr DAVID D. ALLEN

UNIVERSITY OF SOUTHERN MISSISSIPPI

POB 5001, 118 College Dr., Hattiesburg, MS 39406-0001

Telephone: (601) 266-1000

Fax: (601) 266-5148
E-mail: admissions@usm.edu
Internet: www.usm.edu

Founded 1910 as Mississippi Normal College
State control
Academic year: August to May (2 semesters)
Campus at Long Beach (Mississippi)

Pres.: Dr MARTHA D. SAUNDERS
Provost: Dr DENIS WIESENBURG
Vice-Pres. for Admin. Affairs: CHAD DRISKELL
Vice-Pres. for Advancement: BOB PIERCE
Vice-Pres. for Research: Dr DENIS WIESENBURG
Vice-Pres. for Student Affairs: Dr JOSEPH S. PAUL
Dean for Univ. Admissions: Dr KRISTI MOTTER
Dean for Univ. Libraries: CAROLE KIEHL

Library: 1.3m. vols
Number of teachers: 650
Number of students: 17,254 (14,096 undergraduate, 3,158 graduate)

Publications: *Journal of Mississippi History, Mississippi Review, Southern Quarterly*

DEANS

College of Arts and Letters: Dr STEVEN MOSER
College of Business: Prof. Dr LANCE NAIL
College of Education and Psychology: Prof. Dr ANN P. BLACKWELL
College of Health: Dr MICHAEL FORSTER
College of Science and Technology: Dr JOE B. WHITEHEAD, JR
Graduate School: Dr SUSAN A. SILTANEN
Honors College: Dr DAVID R. DAVIES

WILLIAM CAREY UNIVERSITY

498 Tuscan Ave, Hattiesburg, MS 39401-5499

Telephone: (601) 318-6051
Fax: (601) 318-6454
E-mail: admissions@wmcarey.edu
Internet: www.wmcarey.edu

Founded 1892 as Pearl River Boarding School
Private control
Academic year: August to August
Campuses at Biloxi (Mississippi) and New Orleans (Louisiana)

Pres. and CEO: Dr TOMMY KING
Vice-Pres. for Academic Affairs: Dr GARRY M. BRELAND
Vice-Pres. for Advancement and Church Relations: SCOTT HUMMEL
Vice-Pres. for Business Affairs and Chief Financial Officer: GRANT GUTHRIE
Vice-Pres. for Institutional Effectiveness and Planning: Dr BENNIE R. CROCKETT, JR
Vice-Pres. for Medical Education: MICHAEL K. MURPHY
Vice-Pres. for Student Services: BRENDA F. WALDRIP
Graduate Dean: Dr FRANK G. BAUGH
Dean for Enrolment Management and Records: Dr WILLIAM N. CURRY
Registrar: GAYLE KNIGHT
Dir for Libraries and Learning Resources: CHERYL LAUGHLIN

Library of 127,000 resources, 40,000 e-books, 43,000 e-journals
Number of teachers: 80 (full-time)
Number of students: 2,172

DEANS

College of Osteopathic Medicine: DARRELL E. LOVINS
Cooper School of Missions and Biblical Studies: Dr DANIEL P. CALDWELL
Joseph and Nancy Fail School of Nursing: Dr JANET K. WILLIAMS

Ralph and Naomi Noonkester School of Arts and Letters: Dr MYRON C. NOONKESTER
School of Business: Dr CHERYL D. DALE
School of Education: Dr BARRY MORRIS
School of Natural and Behavioral Sciences: Dr FRANK G. BAUGH
Winters School of Music: Dr DON ODOM

MISSOURI

AQUINAS INSTITUTE OF THEOLOGY

23 S Spring Ave, St Louis, MO 63108-3323
Telephone: (314) 256-8800
Fax: (314) 256-8888
E-mail: info@ai.edu
Internet: www.ai.edu
Founded 1925
Private control
Academic year: August to May

Divs of Aquinas ministry formation programme, health care mission, lay spiritual formation, pastoral studies-catechesis of the good shepherd, theology, preaching
Chancellor: BRUNO CADORÉ
Pres.: RICHARD PEDDICORD
Vice-Pres. and Academic Dean: Dr GREGORY HEILLE
Dir for Admissions and Financial Aid: DAVID WERTHMANN
Dir for Finance and Admin.: THOMAS BARBARAK
Dean for Students: GEORGE BOUDREAU
Registrar: JULIE QUINT
Librarian: KATHLEEN TEHAN
Number of teachers: 35
Number of students: 200 (full-time)

ASSEMBLIES OF GOD THEOLOGICAL SEMINARY

1435 N Glenstone Ave, Springfield, MO 65802-2131
Telephone: (417) 268-1000
Fax: (417) 268-1001
E-mail: agts@agts.edu
Internet: www.agts.edu
Founded 1972 as Assemblies of God Graduate School, present name 1984
Private control
Academic year: September to July
Depts of Bible and theology, global missions, practical theology
Pres.: Dr BYRON D. KLAUS
Academic Dean: STEPHEN LIM
Dir for Enrolment Management: MARIO GUERREIRO
Registrar: GENEVA M. HEISKELL
Dir for Library Services: JOSEPH F. MARICS, JR
Library of 86,000 vols, 70,000 microforms, 4,000 audiovisual material, 500 current periodical subscriptions
Number of teachers: 15
Number of students: 550

A. T. STILL UNIVERSITY

800 W Jefferson St, Kirksville, MO 63501
Telephone: (660) 626-2121
Fax: (660) 626-2672
E-mail: admissions@atsu.edu
Internet: www.atsu.edu
Founded 1892 as Kirksville College of Osteopathic Medicine, present name 1993
Private control
Academic year: August to June
Br. campus at Mesa, Arizona
Pres.: Dr JACK MAGRUDER
Vice-Pres. for Academic Affairs: (vacant)
Vice-Pres. for Institutional Advancement: ROBERT L. BASHAM (acting)

Vice-Pres. for Research, Grants and Information Systems: Dr JOHN HEARD, JR
Vice-Pres. for Student Affairs and Dean for Students: RON GABER
Registrar: DEANNA HUNSAKER
Library Dir: DOUG BLANSIT
Library of 80,000 vols, 4,500 audiovisual items
Number of teachers: 100
Number of students: 3,293
Publication: First Impressions (2 a year)

DEANS
Arizona School of Dentistry and Oral Health: Dr JACK DILLENBERG
Arizona School of Health Sciences: Dr BARBARA MAXWELL
Kirksville College of Osteopathic Medicine: Dr JEFF A. SUZEWITS
School of Health Management: Dr KIMBERLY O'REILLY
School of Osteopathic Medicine in Arizona: Dr THOMAS E. McWILLIAMS

AVILA UNIVERSITY

11901 Wornall Rd, Kansas City, MO 64145
Telephone: (816) 942-8400
Fax: (816) 942-3362
E-mail: admission@avila.edu
Internet: www.avila.edu
Founded 1916, present name and status 2001
Private control
Pres.: Dr RONALD A. SLEPITZA
Provost and Vice-Pres. for Academic Affairs: Dr MARIE JOAN HARRIS, SR
Vice-Provost and Vice-Pres. for Information Services: Dr SUE KING
Vice-Pres. for Advancement and External Relations: ANGIE HEER
Vice-Pres. for Finance and Admin. Services: PAUL BOOKMEYER
Dean for Students: DARBY GOUGH
Registrar: DAVE DEITCH
Librarian: KATHLEEN FINEGAN
Library of 74,658 vols, 500 periodicals
Number of teachers: 65
Number of students: 1,818

DEANS
College of Liberal Arts and Social Sciences: Prof. Dr CHARLENE GOULD
School of Business: Dr RICHARD WOODALL
School of Education: Prof. Dr SUE ELLEN McCALLEY
School of Nursing: Prof. Dr SUSAN H. FETSCH
School of Science and Health: Dr LARRY GARRISON SULLIVAN
School of Visual and Communication Arts: Dr DOTTY HAMILTON

BAPTIST BIBLE COLLEGE AND GRADUATE SCHOOL

628 E Kearney St, Springfield, MO 65803
Telephone: (417) 268-6000
Fax: (417) 268-6694
E-mail: info@gobbc.edu
Internet: www.gobbc.edu
Founded 1950
Private control
Academic year: August to May
Chancellor: Dr LELAND KENNEDY
Pres.: JIM EDGE
Vice-Pres. for Academic Affairs: Dr GREGORY T. CHRISTOPHER
Dean for Students: RAY ADAMS
Dir for Institutional Research: LESA CHASTAIN
Dean for Baptist Bible Graduate School: WAYNE SLUSSER
Registrar: TERRY ALLCORN
Dir for Library Services: JON JONES

Library of 82,000 vols, 270 current periodical subscriptions
Number of teachers: 28
Number of students: 805 (746 undergraduate, 59 graduate)

CALVARY BIBLE COLLEGE AND THEOLOGICAL SEMINARY

15800 Calvary Rd, Kansas City, MO 64147-1341
Telephone: (816) 322-0110
Fax: (816) 331-4474
E-mail: admissions@calvary.edu
Internet: www.calvary.edu
Founded 1961 by merger of Kansas City Bible College (f. 1932) and Midwest Bible College (f. 1938), Calvary Theological Seminary (f. 1966) as Graduate Div. of Calvary Bible College, present name 1992
Private control
Academic year: August to May

Depts of Bible and theology, biblical counselling, education, general studies, intercultural studies, ministry studies, music, non-traditional studies, theatre arts
Pres.: Dr JAMES L. CLARK
Vice-Pres. and Academic Dean: Dr TEDDY BITNER
Vice-Pres. and Academic Dean for Seminary: Dr THOMAS BAURAIN
Vice-Pres. for Operations: RANDY L. GRIMM
Dean for Students: CORY TROWBRIDGE
Dir for Admissions: BOB CRANK
Registrar: LARRY SPRY
Librarian: HANNAH BITNER
Library of 62,000 vols
Number of teachers: 39
Number of students: 337 (283 undergraduate, 54 graduate)

CENTRAL BIBLE COLLEGE

3000 N Grant Ave, Springfield, MO 65803
Telephone: (417) 833-2551
Fax: (417) 833-5478
E-mail: info@cbcag.edu
Internet: www.cbcag.edu
Founded 1922
Private control
Academic year: August to April

Divs of arts and sciences, Biblical education, church ministries, fine arts and communications, missions and evangelism
Pres.: Dr GARY A. DENBOW
Vice-Pres. for Academic Affairs: Dr DAVID ARNETT
Vice-Pres. for Operations: DAVID WILLEMSEN
Vice-Pres. for Student Devt: Rev. Dr JIM P. VIGIL
Librarian: LYNN ANDERSON
Library of 177,512 vols, 11,000 periodical vols, 4,130 journals, 8,000 books and reference sources
Number of teachers: 47 (29 full-time, 18 part-time)
Number of students: 626

CENTRAL CHRISTIAN COLLEGE OF THE BIBLE

911 E Urbandale Dr., Moberly, MO 65270
Telephone: (660) 263-3900
Fax: (660) 263-3936
E-mail: admissions@cccb.edu
Internet: www.cccb.edu
Founded 1957
Private control
Language of instruction: English
Academic year: August to May

Areas of study: biblical research, Christian counselling, Christian education, Christian ministries, cross-cultural ministry, preaching, youth and family ministry

Chancellor: LLOYD M. PELFREY

Pres.: Dr RONALD L. OAKES

Vice-Pres. for Academics: Dr DAVID B. FINCHER

Vice-Pres. for Student Devt and Enrolment: RICHARD REXRODE

Vice-Pres. for Advancement: PHILIP MARLEY

Registrar: FAITH M. AXTON

Library Dir: PATTY AGEE

Number of teachers: 25

Number of students: 315

Publication: *The Sentinel* (2 a year).

CENTRAL METHODIST UNIVERSITY

411 Central Methodist Sq., Fayette, MO 65248

Telephone: (660) 248-3391

E-mail: admissions@centralmethodist.edu

Internet: www.centralmethodist.edu

Founded 1854

Private control

Academic year: August to May

Divs of accounting, business and economics, English, fine and performing arts, foreign languages, health professions, mathematics and computer science, philosophy and religion, professional education, science, social sciences

Pres.: Dr MARIANNE E. INMAN

Vice-Pres. and Dean for the Univ.: Dr RITA GULSTAD

Vice-Pres. for Advancement: DONNA MERRELL

Vice-Pres. for Campus Life: JAMES WEBSTER

Vice-Pres. for Finance and Admin.: JULEE SHERMAN

Vice-Pres. for Information Services: CHAD GAINES

Dir for Information Resources: CYNTHIA DUDENHOFFER

Library of 100,000 vols

Number of teachers: 159

Number of students: 3,420

Publications: *Inscape* (1 a year), *The Talon* (2 a year).

CLEVELAND CHIROPRACTIC COLLEGE

10850 Lowell Ave, Second Fl., Overland Park, Kansas, MO 66210

Telephone: (913) 234-0600

Fax: (913) 234-0906

E-mail: kc.admissions@cleveland.edu

Internet: www.cleveland.edu

Founded 1922 as Central Chiropractic College; present name 1924

Private control

Academic year: September to August

Areas of study: biological sciences, health promotion, human biology

Pres.: Dr CARL S. CLEVELAND, III

Provost: ASHLEY E. CLEVELAND

Vice-Pres. for Campus Relations: D. CLARK BECKELY

Dir for Admissions: MELISSA DENTON

Dir for Research: MARK T. PFEFER

Dir for Student Services: JALONNA BOWIE

Library Dir: MARCIA M. THOMAS

Library of 14,800 vols

Number of students: 502

COLLEGE OF THE OZARKS

Point Lookout, MO 65726

Telephone: (417) 334-6411

Fax: (417) 335-2618

E-mail: admiss4@cofo.edu

Internet: www.cofo.edu

Founded 1906 as School of the Ozarks, present name 1990

Private control

Academic year: August to May

Depts of accounting, agriculture, art, biology, business administration, chemistry, computer sciences, criminal justice, education, English, family and consumer sciences, foreign languages, graphic arts, history, hotel and restaurant management, mass communications, mathematics-physics, military science, music, nursing, philosophy and religion, physical education, political science, psychology, sociology, speech communication, technology, theatre

Pres.: Dr JERRY C. DAVIS

Exec. Vice-Pres.: M. FRED MULLINAX

Vice-Pres.: Dr HOWELL W. KEETER

Dean for Admin.: Dr MARVIN R. SCHOENECKE

Dean for the College: Dr ERIC W. BOLGER

Dean for Students: NICK SHARP

Registrar: FRANCES L. FOMAN

Library Supervisor: PATTI TURNER

Library of 119,000 vols

Number of teachers: 83 (full-time)

Number of students: 1,345

Publication: *Ozark Visitor* (4 a year).

COLUMBIA COLLEGE

1001 Rogers St, Columbia, MO 65216

Telephone: (573) 875-8700

Fax: (573) 875-7209

E-mail: admissions@ccis.edu

Internet: www.ccis.edu

Founded 1851 as Christian Female College, present name 1970

Private control

Academic year: August to July

Areas of study: art, business administration, computer and mathematical sciences, criminal justice administration and human services, education, history and social sciences, humanities, science; 23 extension campuses throughout the USA

Pres.: Dr GERALD T. BROUDER

Exec. Vice-Pres. and Dean for Academic Affairs: Dr TERRY B. SMITH

Vice-Pres. for Adult Higher Education: MIKE RANDERSON

Dean for Student Affairs: FAYE BURCHARD

Library Dir: JANET CARUTHERS

Library of 80,000 vols

Number of teachers: 59

Number of students: 25,000

CONCEPTION SEMINARY COLLEGE

POB 501, Conception, MO 64433

Telephone: (660) 944-2821

Fax: (660) 944-2800

E-mail: communications@conception.edu

Internet: www.conception.edu

Founded 1886 as College of New Engelberg, present name 1972

Private control

Pres. and Rector: SAMUEL RUSSELL

Library Dir: Bro. THOMAS SULLIVAN

Number of teachers: 32

Number of students: 80

CONCORDIA SEMINARY

801 Seminary Pl., St Louis, MO 63105

Telephone: (314) 505-7000

Fax: (314) 505-7001

E-mail: admissions@csl.edu

Internet: www.csl.edu

Founded 1839

Private control

Academic year: September to May

Pres.: Rev. Dr DALE A. MEYER

Provost: Prof. ARTHUR D. BACON

Exec. Vice-Pres. for Academic Affairs: Prof. Dr ANDREW H. BARTELT

Sr Vice-Pres. for Enrolment Management: MICHAEL J. REDEKER

Sr Vice-Pres. for Financial Planning and Admin.: MICHAEL A. LOUIS

Registrar: BETH MENNEKE

Dir for Library Services: DAVID O. BERGER

Library of 270,000 vols

Number of teachers: 55

Number of students: 534 (full-time)

Publications: *Around the Tower, Concordia Journal, Concordia Seminary Magazine.*

COTTEY COLLEGE

1000 W Austin, Nevada, MO 64772

Telephone: (417) 667-8181

Fax: (417) 667-8103

E-mail: enrollmgt@cottey.edu

Internet: www.cottey.edu

Founded 1884

Private control

Offers Bachelor of arts in English, environmental studies, international relations and business

Pres.: Dr JUDY ROBINSON ROGERS

Vice-Pres. for Academic Affairs: Dr CATHRYN G. PRIDAL

Vice-Pres. for Admin. and Finance: MARY HAGGANS

Vice-Pres. for Enrolment Management: RICK EBER

Vice-Pres. for Student Life: MARI ANNE PHILLIPS

Vice-Pres. for Institutional Advancement: STUART LANG

Dir for Admission: JUDI STEEGE

Registrar: MARCIA MORTON

Dir for Library: BECKY KIEL

Library of 50,000 vols

Number of students: 350

COVENANT THEOLOGICAL SEMINARY

12330 Conway Rd, St Louis, MO 63141

Telephone: (314) 434-4044

Fax: (314) 434-4819

E-mail: info@covenantseminary.edu

Internet: www.covenantseminary.edu

Founded 1956

Private control

Academic year: September to May

Pres.: Dr BRYAN CHAPELL

Vice-Pres. for Academics and Dean for Faculty: Dr MARK DALBEY

Sr Dir for Admissions and Alumni: JEREMY KICKLIGHTER

Dean for Students: MIKE HIGGINS

Registrar: BETSY GASOSKE

Library Dir: JAMES C. PAKALA

Library of 68,000 vols

Number of teachers: 42

Number of students: 435 (full-time)

Publication: *Covenant Magazine* (3 a year).

COX COLLEGE

1423 N Jefferson Ave, Springfield, MO 65802

Telephone: (417) 269-3401

Fax: (417) 269-3581

E-mail: admissions@coxcollege.edu

Internet: www.coxcollege.edu

Founded 1907 as Burge Deaconess Training School for Nurses, present name 2008

Private control

Academic year: August to May

Offers Bachelors and Masters degrees in nursing

Pres.: Dr ANNE BRETT

Vice-Pres. for Academic Affairs: Dr MARTIN SELLERS
Vice-Pres. for Student Services: DAVID SCHOOLFIELD
Dir for Admissions: LINDY BIGLIENI
Dean for Information Services: WILMA BUNCH
Number of students: 650

DEANS

Health Science: SONYA HAYTER
Nursing: PATRICIA WAGNER

CULVER-STOCKTON COLLEGE

1 College Hill, Canton, MO 63435
Telephone: (573) 288-6000
Fax: (573) 288-6611
E-mail: admission@culver.edu
Internet: www.culver.edu
Founded 1853
Academic year: August to May

Divs of business, education and applied arts, fine arts, humanities and social sciences, natural and mathematical sciences

Pres.: RICHARD D. VALENTINE
Vice-Pres. for Academic Affairs: Dr D'ANN CAMPBELL
Vice-Pres. for Advancement: ERIC BARKLEY
Dean for the College: Dr DAVID WILSON
Dir for Admission: MISTY MCBEE
Registrar: CHRIS HUEBOTTER
Librarian: SHARON K. UPCHURCH
Library of 164,266 vols
Number of teachers: 50
Number of students: 752

Publication: *Chronicle* (2 a year).

DRURY UNIVERSITY

900 N Benton Ave, Springfield, MO 65802
Telephone: (417) 873-7879
Fax: (417) 873-7435
E-mail: drury@drury.edu
Internet: www.drury.edu
Founded 1873
Private control

Liberal arts college; divs of fine arts, humanities, mathematics and sciences, social sciences

Pres.: TODD PARNELL
Vice-Pres. for Academic Affairs and Dean for College: CHARLES TAYLOR
Vice-Pres. for Admin. Services: BILL SCORSE
Vice-Pres. for Alumni and Devt: Dr KRYSTAL MC CULLOCH
Vice-Pres. for Campus Operations and Sustainability: PETER RADECKI
Vice-Pres. for Enrolment Management: DAWN HILES
Vice-Pres. for Student Affairs and Dean for Students: TIJUANA JULIAN
Registrar: GALE BOUTWELL
Library Dir: POLLY BORUFF-JONES
Library of 180,000 vols, 550 periodicals
Number of teachers: 118 (f. t. e.)
Number of students: 1,618

EDEN THEOLOGICAL SEMINARY

475 E Lockwood Ave, St Louis, MO 63119-3192
Telephone: (314) 961-3627
Fax: (314) 918-2535
E-mail: dwindler@eden.edu
Internet: www.eden.edu
Founded 1850
Private control

Areas of study: biblical studies, ethics, historical and theological studies, ministry studies

Pres.: Rev. Dr DAVID M. GREENHAW
Exec. Vice-Pres.: RICK WALTERS

Vice-Pres. for Institutional Advancement: BRYCE KRUG
Dir for Admin.: AL SCHON
Dir for Devt: JACQUELINE HAMILTON
Academic Dean: Rev. Dr DEBORAH KRAUSE
Dean for Students: Rev. CARL SCHENCK
Registrar: MICHELLE WOBBE
Library Dir: MICHAEL P. BODDY
Library of 86,000 vols
Number of teachers: 24
Number of students: 131 (full-time)

EVANGEL UNIVERSITY

1111 N Glenstone Ave, Springfield, MO 65802
Telephone: (417) 865-2815
Fax: (417) 865-9599
Internet: www.evangel.edu
Founded 1955
Private control
Academic year: September to May

Depts of behavioural sciences, business, communication, education, humanities, music, kinesiology, science and technology, social sciences, theology

Pres.: Dr ROBERT H. SPENCE
Vice-Pres. for Academic Affairs: Dr GLENN H. BERNET, JR
Vice-Pres. for Business and Finance: GEORGE CRAWFORD
Vice-Pres. for Enrolment Management: Dr ANDY DENTON
Vice-Pres. for Institutional Advancement: JIM WILLIAMS
Vice-Pres. for Student Devt: Dr DAVID BUNDRICK
Registrar: CATHY WILLIAMS
Library Dir: DALE JENSEN
Library of 120,000 vols
Number of teachers: 100
Number of students: 2,168

FONTBONNE UNIVERSITY

6800 Wydown Blvd, St Louis, MO 63105
Telephone: (314) 862-3456
Fax: (314) 889-1451
Internet: www.fontbonne.edu
Founded 1923
Private control
Pres.: DENNIS C. GOLDEN
Vice-Pres. for Academic Affairs: JOHN BRUNO
Vice-Pres. for Finance and Admin.: GARY ZACK
Vice-Pres. for Institutional Advancement: SANDRA LEHRER
Vice-Pres. for Student Affairs: RANDI WILSON
Registrar: MAZIE MOORE
Univ. Librarian: SHARON MCCASLIN
Library of 90,020 vols, 510 periodicals
Number of teachers: 315
Number of students: 2,532

GLOBAL UNIVERSITY

211 S Glenstone Ave, Springfield, MO 65804
Telephone: (417) 862-9533
Fax: (417) 862-0863
E-mail: info@globaluniversity.edu
Internet: www.globaluniversity.edu
Private control
Languages of instruction: English, French, Spanish
Pres.: Dr GARY L. SEEVERS
Provost: Dr ROBERT A. LOVE
Vice-Provost and Dean for Education: JOHN G. NILL
Vice-Pres. for Center for Evangelism and Discipleship: BART BAGWELL
Vice-Pres. for Global Operations: JOSEPH A. SZABO
Dir for Library Services: RUSS LANGFORD

Library of 25,000 vols

DEANS

Berean School of the Bible: Dr RANDY J. HEDLUN
Graduate School of Theology: Dr CARL W. CHRISNER
Undergraduate School of Bible and Theology: WILLARD D. TEAGUE

HANNIBAL-LAGRANGE UNIVERSITY

2800 Palmyra Rd, Hannibal, MO 63401
Telephone: (573) 221-3675
Fax: (573) 221-6594
E-mail: admissions@hlg.edu
Internet: www.hlg.edu
Founded 1858, present name and status 2010
Private control

Divs of business and computer information systems, Christian studies, fine arts, humanities, natural science and mathematics, social science, nursing and allied health

Pres.: Dr WOODROW W. BURT
Vice-Pres. for Academic Affairs: DAVID J. PELLETIER
Vice-Pres. for Enrolment Management: RAYMOND W. CARTY
Vice-Pres. for Institutional Advancement: STEVE MILLER
Registrar: BETH CRUM (acting)
Library Dir: JULIE A. ANDRESEN
Library of 135,000 vols, 300 periodicals
Number of teachers: 46
Number of students: 1,150

Publication: *Reflections*.

HARRIS-STOWE STATE UNIVERSITY

3026 Laclede Ave, St Louis, MO 63103
Telephone: (314) 340-3300
Fax: (314) 340-3399
E-mail: admissions@hssu.edu
Internet: www.hssu.edu
Founded 1857, present name and status 2005
State control

Pres.: Dr ALBERT WALKER
Vice-Pres. for Academic Affairs: Dr DWYANE SMITH
Exec. Dir for Enrolment Management: LASHANDA BOONE
Dean for Student Affairs: CHARLES GOODEN
Registrar: CHAUVETTE MCELMURRY
Library Dir: BARBARA N. NOBLE
Library of 87,000 vols
Number of teachers: 82
Number of students: 1,980

DEANS

Anheuser-Busch School of Business: Dr FATEMEH ZAKERY
College of Arts and Sciences: Dr LATEEF ADELANI
College of Education: Dr LATISHA SMITH

KANSAS CITY ART INSTITUTE

4415 Warwick Blvd, Kansas City, MO 64111-1820
Telephone: (816) 472-4852
E-mail: info@kcai.edu
Internet: www.kcai.edu
Founded 1885
Private control
Academic year: August to May

Schools of liberal arts, fine arts and design, electronic arts

Pres.: Dr JACQUELINE CHANDA
Exec. Vice-Pres. for Admin.: RONALD CATTELINO
Vice-Pres. and Chief Information Officer: LARRY DICKERSON

Vice-Pres. for Academic Affairs: Dr MARK SALMON
Vice-Pres. for Advancement: PAM SIBERT
Vice-Pres. for Communications: ANNE CANFIELD
Vice-Pres. for Enrolment Management and Student Achievement: Dr BAMBI BURGARD
Registrar: ANDREA KHAN
Library Dir: M. J. POEHLER
Library of 30,000 vols, 111,160 slides
Number of students: 746

Publication: *Sprung Formal* (1 a year).

KANSAS CITY UNIVERSITY OF MEDICINE AND BIOSCIENCES

1750 Independence Ave, Kansas City, MO 64106-1453
Telephone: (816) 654-7000
Fax: (816) 283-2484
E-mail: admissions@kcumb.edu
Internet: www.kcumb.edu
Founded 1916 as Kansas City College of Osteopathy and Surgery, present name and structure 2004
Private control
Academic year: August to July
Pres. and CEO: H. DANNY WEAVER
Exec. Vice-Pres. for Academic and Medical Affairs: DARIN HAUG
Vice-Pres. for Advancement: BETH DOLLASE
Vice-Pres. for Enrolment Management and Registrar: HEIDI TERRY
Vice-Pres. for Finance and Admin.: JAMES PARK
Vice-Pres. for Univ. Relations: NATALIE LUTZ
Dir for Admissions: PATTI HARPER
Dir for Library: MARILYN J. DEGEUS
Number of teachers: 48
Number of students: 1,108
Publications: *KCUMB Communicator* (2 a year), *VOICES Magazine*

DEANS

College of Biosciences: DOUG RUSHING
College of Osteopathic Medicine: DARIN HAUG

KENRICK-GLENNON SEMINARY

5200 Glennon Dr., St Louis, MO 63119
Telephone: (314) 792-6100
Fax: (314) 792-6500
Internet: www.kenrick.edu
Founded 1898
Private control
Academic year: August to May
Pres. and Rector: JOHN HORN
Vice-Rector: GREGORY MIKESCH
Vice-Rector for Admin. and Finance: Rev. DONALD EDWARD HENKE
Academic Dean: Dr JOHN L. GRESHAM
Dean for Students and Dir for Admissions: Rev. PAUL ROTHSCHILD
Dir for Devt: KATE GUYOL
Registrar: JOE MEIERGERD
Dir for Library: MARY ANN AUBIN
Library of 80,000 vols
Number of students: 110 (30 undergraduate, 80 graduate)

LINCOLN UNIVERSITY

820 Chestnut St, Jefferson City, MO 65101
Telephone: (573) 681-5000
Fax: (573) 681-5566
E-mail: enroll@lincolnu.edu
Internet: www.lincolnu.edu
Founded 1866 as Lincoln Institute, present name and status 1921
State control
Academic year: August to July
Pres.: Dr CAROLYN R. MAHONEY

Provost and Vice-Pres. for Academic Affairs: Dr ANN HARRIS
Vice-Pres. for Admin.: CURTIS E. CREAGH
Vice-Pres. for Student Affairs: THERESSA FERGUSON
Vice-Pres. for Univ. Advancement: BENECIA WILLIAMS
Dir for Admissions: ROXANNE SEIDNER
Dean for Library Services and Univ. Archives: JEROME OFFORD, JR
Library of 204,948 vols, 58 periodicals, 190 serial microform titles
Number of teachers: 179
Number of students: 3,388

DEANS

College of Agricultural and Natural Sciences: Dr STEVE MEREDITH
College of Arts and Letters: Dr RUTHI STURDEVANT
College of Behavioral and Technological Sciences: Dr RUTHI STURDEVANT
College of Professional Studies: Dr LINDA S. BICKEL

LINDENWOOD UNIVERSITY

209 S Kingshighway, St Charles, MO 63301
Telephone: (636) 949-2000
E-mail: admissions@lindenwood.edu
Internet: www.lindenwood.edu
Founded 1827
Private control
Academic year: August to May
Pres.: Dr JAMES D. EVANS
Provost and Vice-Pres. for Academic Affairs: Dr JANN R. WEITZEL
Vice-Pres. for Operations: JULIE MUELLER
Vice-Pres. for Institutional Advancement: Dr LUCY MORROS
Vice-Pres. for Student Devt: JOHN OLDANI
Vice-Pres. for Belleville Campus: JERRY BLADDICK
Dean for Students: TERRY RUSSELL
Dean for Library Services: ELIZABETH MACDONALD
Library of 93,822 vols, 218 journals, 400 audio books
Number of teachers: 100
Number of students: 7,570
Publications: *Arrow Rock*, *Connection* (4 a year), *Journal of International and Global Studies*, *Lindenwood University Academics* (1 a year), *LindenWord* (2 a year), *The Confluence*, *The Lindenwood Review*

DEANS

School of American Studies: DAVID KNOTTS
School of Business and Entrepreneurship: ROGER ELLIS
School of Communications: MIKE WALL
School of Education: CYNTHIA BICE
School of Fine and Performing Arts: Prof. DONNELL WALSH
School of Humanities: MICHAEL WHALEY
School of Human Services: Assoc. Prof. CARLA MUELLER
School of Sciences: MARILYN ABBOTT

LOGAN COLLEGE OF CHIROPRACTIC/UNIVERSITY PROGRAMS

1851 Schoettler Rd, POB 1065, Chesterfield, MO 63006-1065
Telephone: (636) 227-2100
Fax: (636) 207-2424
E-mail: loganadm@logan.edu
Internet: www.logan.edu
Founded 1935
Private control
Academic year: September to April
Pres.: Dr GEORGE A. GOODMAN

Vice-Pres. for Academic Affairs: Dr CARL W. SAUBERT, IV (acting)
Vice-Pres. for Admin. Affairs: SHARON K. KEHRER
Vice-Pres. for Enrolment Management: Dr BOYD A. BRADSHAW
Vice-Pres. for Institutional Advancement: PATRICIA C. JONES
Dir for Admissions: STEVE HELD
Dean for Research and Devt: Dr RODGER TEPE
Dean for Student Services: JAMES PAINE
Registrar: JOHN-HERBERT JAFFRY
Dir for Library: CHABHA HOCINE TEPE
Library of 12,000 vols, 240 journals, 23,050 media items
Number of teachers: 87 (45 full-time, 42 part-time)
Number of students: 1,001

MARYVILLE UNIVERSITY OF SAINT LOUIS

650 Maryville University Dr., St Louis, MO 63141
Telephone: (314) 529-9300
Fax: (314) 542-9085
E-mail: admissions@maryville.edu
Internet: www.maryville.edu
Founded 1872
Private control
Academic year: August to May
Pres.: Dr MARK LOMBARDI
Vice-Pres. for Academic Affairs: Dr MARY ELLEN FINCH
Vice-Pres. for Admin. and Finance: Dr LARRY HAYS
Vice-Pres. for Enrolment: JEFF MILLER
Vice-Pres. for Institutional Advancement: TOM ESCHEN
Vice-Pres. for Student Life and Dean for Students: NINA CALDWELL
Registrar: STEPHANIE ELFRINK
Dean of Library: Dr GENIE MCKEE
Library of 252,550 vols, 213,465 books, 62,337 current serials
Number of teachers: 283
Number of students: 3,900

Publication: *Maryville Magazine*

DEANS

College of Arts and Sciences: Dr DANIEL SPARLING
John E. Simon School of Business: Dr PAMELA HORWITZ
School of Education: Dr SAM HAUSFATHER
School of Health Professions: Dr CHARLES J. GULAS

MIDWESTERN BAPTIST THEOLOGICAL SEMINARY

5001 N Oak Trafficway, Kansas City, MO 64118
Telephone: (816) 414-3700
Fax: (816) 414-3799
E-mail: admissions@mbts.edu
Internet: www.mbts.edu
Founded 1957
Private control
Academic year: August to July
Pres.: Dr R. PHILIP ROBERTS
Sr Vice-Pres. for Institutional Advancement: ANTHONY W. ALLEN
Vice-Pres. for Academic Devt: JERRY SUTTON
Vice-Pres. for Institutional Effectiveness: RODNEY A. HARRISON
Vice-Pres. for Student Devt: DAVID M. MCALPIN
Registrar: MIKE HAWKINS
Dir for Library Services: CRAIG KUBIC
Library of 110,000 vols
Number of teachers: 30

Number of students: 253 (full-time)

Publications: *Midwestern Journal of Theology* (2 a year), *The Midwestern* (4 a year).

MISSOURI BAPTIST UNIVERSITY

1 College Park Dr., Saint Louis, MO 63141-8698

Telephone: (314) 434-1115
Fax: (314) 434-7596
E-mail: admissions@mobap.edu
Internet: www.mobap.edu

Founded 1957 as campus extension of Hannibal-LaGrange College, present name 1999

Private control

Academic year: August to April

Divs of business, education, fine arts, health and sport sciences, humanities, natural sciences, social and behavioural sciences; graduate programmes; campuses at Franklin Co, Hillsboro and Moscow Mills (Missouri)

Pres.: Dr R. ALTON LACEY
Provost and Sr Vice-Pres. for Academic Affairs: Dr ARLEN R. DYKSTRA
Sr Vice-Pres. for Institutional Advancement: KEITH ROSS
Vice-Pres. for Enrolment Services: TERRY DALE CRUSE
Vice-Pres. for Student Devt: Dr ANDY CHAMBERS (acting)
Vice-Pres. for Graduate Studies: Dr CLARK TRIPLETT
Dir for Admissions: AARON BLACK
Dir for Library Services: NITSA HINDELEH

Number of teachers: 151
Number of students: 5,201 (1,359 graduate, 3,842 undergraduate)

Publication: *MBU Magazine*.

MISSOURI SOUTHERN STATE UNIVERSITY

3950 E Newman Rd, Joplin, MO 64801-1595

Telephone: (417) 625-9300
Fax: (417) 659-4497
E-mail: info@mssu.edu
Internet: www.mssu.edu

Founded 1937 as Joplin Junior College, present name and status 2003

State control

Academic year: June to May

Pres.: Dr BRUCE W. SPECK (acting)
Vice-Pres. for Academic Affairs: Dr A. J. ANGLIN
Vice-Pres. for Business Affairs: ROB YUST
Vice-Pres. for Devt: Dr MARK PARSONS
Vice-Pres. for Student Affairs: DARREN FULLERTON
Registrar: CHERYL DOBSON
Library Dir: WENDY L. MCGRANE

Library of 274,000 vols, 754,000 microform items
Number of teachers: 289
Number of students: 5,802 (5,751 undergraduate, 51 graduate)

DEANS

Graduate Studies and Lifelong Learning: Dr JO KROLL
Robert W. Plaster School of Business Admin.: Dr BEVERLY BLOCK
School of Arts and Sciences: Dr RICHARD MILLER
School of Education: Dr GLENN COLTHARP
School of Technology: Dr TIA M. STRAIT

MISSOURI STATE UNIVERSITY

901 S National Ave, Springfield, MO 65897

Telephone: (417) 836-5000
Fax: (417) 836-6777
E-mail: info@missouristate.edu

Internet: www.missouristate.edu

Founded 1905, present name 2005

State control

Campuses at Mountain Grove and West Plains (Missouri) and in Dalian (People's Republic of China)

Pres.: CLIF SMART
Provost: Dr FRANK EINHELLIG
Vice-Pres. for Admin. and Information Services: KEN MCCLURE
Vice-Pres. for Diversity and Inclusion: Dr KENNETH COOPWOOD
Vice-Pres. for Research and Economic Devt: Dr JIM BAKER
Vice-Pres. for Student Affairs and Dean for Students: Dr EARLE DOMAN
Vice-Pres. for Univ. Advancement: BRENT DUNN
Dean for Library Services: NEOSHA MACKEY

Library of 609,852 vols, 827,099 govt docs, 871,618 units of microform, 29,373 audio visual titles, 184,580 maps, 4,750 current periodicals
Number of teachers: 816 (649 full-time, 167 part-time)
Number of students: 22,866

DEANS

College of Arts and Letters: Dr CAREY ADAMS
College of Business Administration: Dr STEPHANIE BRYANT
College of Education: Dr DENNIS KEAR
College of Health and Human Services: Dr HELEN REID
College of Humanities and Public Affairs: Dr VICTOR MATTHEWS
College of Natural and Applied Sciences: Dr TAMERA JAHNKE
Graduate College: Dr PAWAN KAHOL

MISSOURI VALLEY COLLEGE

500 E College, Marshall, MO 65340

Telephone: (660) 831-4000
Fax: (660) 831-4003
Internet: www.moval.edu

Founded 1889

Private control

Academic year: August to July

Pres.: Dr BONNIE L. HUMPHREY
Vice-Pres. for Institutional Advancement: ERIC SAPPINGTON
Vice-Pres. for Enrolment Management and Operations: TOM D. FIFER
Chief Academic Officer: Dr SHARON WEISER
Dir for Admissions: TENNILLE LANGDON
Dean for Student Affairs: HEATH MORGAN
Registrar: MARSHA LASHLEY
Library Dir: PAMELA K. REEDER

Library of 70,000 vols
Number of teachers: 55 (full-time)
Number of students: 1,476

DEANS

Education: Dr EARL WELLBORN
Graduate Studies: Dr JOHN GAULT
Mathematics and Sciences: Dr KATHERINE ADAMS
School of Nursing and Health Sciences: Dr KARLA BRUNTZEL

MISSOURI WESTERN STATE UNIVERSITY

4525 Downs Dr., St Joseph, MO 64507

Telephone: (816) 271-4200
E-mail: admission@missouriwestern.edu
Internet: www.missouriwestern.edu

Founded 1915 as St Joseph Junior College, present name 1969, present name and status 2005

State control

Academic year: August to May

Pres.: Dr ROBERT A. VARTABEDIAN
Provost and Vice-Pres. for Academic Affairs: Dr JEANNE DAFFRON
Vice-Pres. for Financial Planning and Admin.: MELVIN F. KLINKNER
Vice-Pres. for Student Affairs: ESTHER PERÁLEZ
Vice-Pres. for Univ. Advancement: DAN NICOSON
Registrar: SUSAN BRACCIANO
Library Dir: JULIA SCHNEIDER

Library of 226,000 vols, 1,200 journals and state govt documents
Number of teachers: 200
Number of students: 6,296 (6,135 undergraduate, 161 graduate)

Publications: *The Saint Joseph Palette*, *Western Magazine* (3 a year)

DEANS

Graduate Studies: Dr BRIAN CRONK
Liberal Arts and Sciences: Dr MURRAY NABORS
Professional Studies: Dr PHILIP S. NITSE
Steven L. Craig School of Business: Dr PHILIP S. NITSE
Western Institute: GORDON MAPLEY

NAZARENE THEOLOGICAL SEMINARY

1700 E Meyer Blvd, Kansas City, MO 64131

Telephone: (816) 268-5400
Fax: (816) 268-5500
E-mail: enroll@nts.edu
Internet: www.nts.edu

Founded 1944

Private control

Academic year: August to May

Pres.: Dr DAVID A. BUSIC
Dean for Admin. and Student Services: Dr D. MARTIN BUTLER
Dean for the Faculty: Dr ROGER HAHN
Registrar and Dir for Admissions: PAMELA ASHER
Dir for Library Services: DEBRA L. BRADSHAW

Library of 150,000 vols, 320 periodicals
Number of teachers: 35 (11 full-time, 24 part-time)
Number of students: 250 (full-time)

Publication: *Didache*.

NORTHWEST MISSOURI STATE UNIVERSITY

800 University Dr., Maryville, MO 64468

Telephone: (660) 562-1562
Fax: (660) 562-1993
E-mail: admissions@nwmissouri.edu
Internet: www.nwmissouri.edu

Founded 1905

State control

Academic year: August to August

Pres.: Dr JOHN JASINSKI
Provost: Dr DOUGLAS DUNHAM
Vice-Pres. for Student Affairs: Dr MATT BAKER
Vice-Pres. for Univ. Advancement: MICHAEL JOHNSON
Vice-Pres. for Univ. Relations: MITZI LUTZ
Registrar: TERRI VOGEL
Dir for Academic and Library Services: Dr LESLIE GALBREATH

Library of 368,000 vols, 30,000 e-periodicals
Number of teachers: 227
Number of students: 7,225

Publication: *Northwest Alumni Magazine* (2 a year)

DEANS

College of Arts and Sciences: Dr CHARLES A. MCADAMS

College of Education and Human Services: Dr JOYCE PIVERAL
Graduate School: Dr GREGORY HADDOCK
Melvin D. and Valorie G. Booth College of Business and Professional Studies: Dr GREGORY HADDOCK
Missouri Academy: Dr CLEO SAMUDZI

PARK UNIVERSITY

8700 NW River Park Dr., Parkville, MO 64152
Telephone: (816) 741-2000
Fax: (816) 741-4911
E-mail: admissions@park.edu
Internet: www.park.edu
Founded 1875
Private control
Academic year: August to July
40 Campuses in 21 states; online degree programme
Pres.: Dr MICHAEL DROGE
Provost and Vice-Pres. for Academic Affairs: Dr JERRY D. JORGENSEN
Vice-Pres. for Distance Learning: Dr THOMAS W. PETERMAN
Vice-Pres. for Finance and Admin.: DORLA WATKINS
Vice-Pres. for Univ. Advancement: LAURIE D. MCCORMACK
Vice-Pres. and Gen. Counsel: ROGER HERSHEY
Assoc. Vice-Pres. for Student Affairs: CLARINDA H. CREIGHTON
Registrar: (vacant)
Dir for Library Systems: ANN SCHULTIS
Library of 155,000 vols, 1,000 periodicals, 4,000 reels of microfilm
Number of teachers: 100
Number of students: 1,194
Publications: *Narva* (1 a year), *Scholasticus* (1 a year), *Scribe*

DEANS

College of Liberal Arts and Sciences: Dr JANE WOOD
Hauptmann School for Public Affairs: LAURIE DIPADOVA-STOCKS
School for Education: Dr MICHELLE MYERS
School of Business: Prof. Dr BRAD KLEINDL

RANKEN TECHNICAL COLLEGE

4431 Finney Ave, St Louis, MO 63113
Telephone: (314) 286-4809
Fax: (314) 286-3309
E-mail: admissions@ranken.edu
Internet: www.ranken.edu
Founded 1907
Private control
Offers Bachelor of science in architectural technology and applied management
Pres.: STAN SHOUN
Vice-Pres. for Education: DONALD J. POHL
Vice-Pres. for Finance and Admin.: PETER T. MURTAUGH
Vice-Pres. for Student Success: JOHN E. WOOD
Dean for Academic Affairs: CRYSTAL A. HERRON
Library of 20,000 vols.

RESEARCH COLLEGE OF NURSING

2525 E Meyer Blvd, Kansas City, MO 64132
Telephone: (816) 995-2800
Internet: www.researchcollege.edu
Founded 1905 as German Hospital Training School for Nurses
Private control
Academic year: August to May (2 semesters)
Pres. and Dean: Dr NANCY O. DEBASIO

Assoc. Dean of Academic Programmes: (vacant)
Dir for Graduate Programmes: Dr LYNN WARMBRODT
Dir for Student Affairs: LORI VITALE
Dir for Learning Resource Centre: TOBEY STOSBERG
Number of students: 400

ROCKHURST UNIVERSITY

1100 Rockhurst Rd, Kansas City, MO 64110
Telephone: (816) 501-4000
Fax: (816) 501-4588
E-mail: admission@rockhurst.edu
Internet: www.rockhurst.edu
Founded 1910
Private control
Academic year: August to May
Pres.: Rev. THOMAS B. CURRAN
Vice-Pres. for Academic Affairs: Dr SHARON HOMAN
Vice-Pres. for Advancement: BOB GRANT
Vice-Pres. for Mission and Min.: WILLIAM OULVEY
Vice-Pres. for Student Devt and Athletics: Dr MATT QUICK
Vice-Pres. for Univ. Advancement: Dr JANE LAMPO
Assoc. Vice-Pres. for Admin.: MATT HEINRICH
Assoc. Vice-Pres. for Enrolment Services: LANE RAMEY
Registrar: MINDA THROWER
Dir of Library: LAURIE HATHMAN
Library of 100,000 vols
Number of teachers: 208
Number of students: 3,000
Publication: *Rockhurst Magazine*

DEANS

College of Arts and Sciences: Dr TIMOTHY MCDONALD
Helzberg School of Management: Dr JAMES M. DALEY
Research College of Nursing: Dr NANCY O. DEBASIO
School of Graduate and Professional Studies: Dr JEFFREY R. BREESE

SAINT LOUIS CHRISTIAN COLLEGE

1360 Grandview Dr., Florissant, MO 63033
Telephone: (314) 837-6777
Fax: (314) 837-8291
E-mail: admissions@slcconline.edu
Internet: www.slcconline.edu
Founded 1956
Private control
Academic year: July to June
Areas of study: Christian ministry, educational ministries, intercultural and urban missions, preaching ministry, worship and music ministry
Pres.: Dr GUTHRIE VEECH
Vice-Pres. for Operations: JUDY LINCOLN
Academic Dean: MICHAEL CHAMBERS
Dir for Admissions: CARRIE CHAPMAN
Dean for Students: CHRISTINE CABLE
Registrar: CINDY BINGAMON
Library Man.: MATTHEW DEWITT
Library of 41,000 vols, 150 periodicals, 16,000 microforms, 3,000 audio cassettes, 400 video cassettes
Number of teachers: 9
Number of students: 301

ST LOUIS COLLEGE OF PHARMACY

4588 Parkview Pl., St Louis, MO 63110-1088
Telephone: (314) 367-8700
Fax: (314) 446-8304
E-mail: admissions@stlcop.edu
Internet: www.stlcop.edu

Founded 1864
Private control
Academic year: August to July
Pres.: Dr JOHN A. PIEPER
Vice-Pres. for Academic Affairs: Dr WENDY DUNCAN-HEWITT
Vice-Pres. for Advancement: BRETT T. SCHOTT
Vice-Pres. for Enrolment Services: GLORIA J. VERTREES
Vice-Pres. for Finance and Admin.: GARY G. TORRENCE
Vice-Pres. for Student Affairs: Dr KIMBERLY J. KILGORE
Registrar and Dir for Admissions: PENELOPE MYERS BRYANT
Dir for Library: JILL NISSEN
Library of 54,000 vols
Number of teachers: 88 (full-time)
Number of students: 1,260

DEANS

Arts and Sciences: Dr KIMBERLY J. KILGORE
Pharmacy: Dr WENDY DUNCAN-HEWITT

SAINT LOUIS UNIVERSITY

1 N Grand Blvd, St Louis, MO 63103
Telephone: (314) 977-2500
Fax: (314) 977-3412
E-mail: admitme@slu.edu
Internet: www.slu.edu
Founded 1818
Private control
Academic year: September to May (2 terms)
Pres.: Rev. LAWRENCE H. BIONDI
Provost: JOE WEIXLMANN
Vice-Pres. for Academic Affairs: Dr MANOJ PATANKAR
Vice-Pres. for Advancement: JEFF FOWLER
Vice-Pres. for Enrolment and Retention Management: JAY GOFF
Vice-Pres. for Facilities Management and Civic Affairs: KATHLEEN T. BRADY
Vice-Pres. for Mission and Min.: PAUL STARK
Vice-Pres. for Research: Dr RAYMOND TAIT
Vice-Pres. for Student Devt: KENT PORTER-FIELD
Vice-Pres. and Gen. Counsel: WILLIAM R. KAUFFMAN
Registrar: JANEL ESKER
Asst Provost for Libraries: GAIL M. STAINES
Library: see Libraries and Archives
Number of teachers: 3,121 (1,301 full-time, 1,820 part-time)
Number of students: 13,200 (8,100 undergraduate, 5,100 graduate)
Publications: *African American Review, Boulevard, Forum for Social Economics, Journal of Gerontology: Social Sciences, Institute of Jesuit Sources, Journal of Health Law and Policy* (2 a year), *Journal of Herpetology, Journal of Policy History, Journal of Urban Affairs, Manuscripta* (2 a year), *Pageoph, Public Law Review* (2 a year), *Review for Religious, Saint Louis University Law Journal, Studies in the Spirituality of Jesuits, The Modern Schoolman* (4 a year), *Theology Digest* (4 a year), *Universitas, Warsaw Trans Atlantic Law Journal*

DEANS

College of Arts and Sciences: MICHAEL D. BARBER
College of Education and Public Service: Dr GERARD FOWLER
College of Philosophy and Letters: MICHAEL BARBER
Doisy College of Health Sciences: Dr CHARLOTTE ROYEEN
John Cook School of Business: Dr ELLEN F. HARSHMAN
Madrid Campus: Dr PAUL VITA

Parks College of Engineering, Aviation and Technology: Dr KRISHNASWAMY RAVINDRA
School for Professional Studies: Dr JENNIFER GIANCOLA
School of Law: ANNETTE CLARK
School of Medicine: PHILIP O. ALDERSON
School of Nursing: Dr TERI A. MURRAY
School of Public Health: EDWIN TREVATHAN
School of Social Work: Dr GERARD FOWLER

PROFESSORS

ABELL, B. F., Meteorology
AL-JUREIDINI, S. B., Paediatrics
ALBERT, S. G., Internal Medicine
ALDRIDGE, R. D., Biology
AMINE, L. S., Marketing
AMON, E., Obstetrics and Gynaecology
ANDERSON, E. L., Internal Medicine
ANDERSON, R. O., Communication
ARMBRECHT, H. J., Internal Medicine
ARTAL, R., Obstetrics and Gynaecology
ASPINWALL, N., Biology
AZZAM, F. J., Anaesthesiology
BACON, B. R., Internal Medicine
BAJAJ, S. P., Internal Medicine
BALDASSARE, J. J., Pharmacological and Physiological Sciences
BALFOUR, I. C., Paediatrics
BANKS, W. A., Internal Medicine
BARBER, M. D., Philosophy
BARENKAMP, S. J., Paediatrics
BARMANN, L. F., American Studies
BARRY, R. C., Paediatrics
BASTANI, B., Internal Medicine
BAUDENDISTEL, L. J., Anaesthesiology
BELLONE, C. J., Molecular Microbiology and Immunology
BELSHE, R. B., Internal Medicine
BENOFY, L. P., Physics
BENOIT, R. P., English
BENTLEY, D. W., Internal Medicine
BERNHARDT, P., Biology
BIONDI, L. H., Modern Languages
BJERREGAARD, P., Internal Medicine
BLASKIEWICZ, R. J., Obstetrics and Gynaecology
BOHMAN, J. P., Philosophy
BOLLA, R. I., Biology
BRENNAN, D. G., Communication Sciences and Disorders
BRENNAN, W. C., Social Work
BRESLIN, R. D., Educational Leadership and Higher Education
BROCKHAUS, R. H., Management
BROWN, W. W., Internal Medicine
BROWNSON, R. C., Community Health
BUCHOLZ, R. D., Surgery
BULLER, R. M., Molecular Microbiology and Immunology
BURDGE, R. E., Orthopaedic Surgery
BURGIN, R. W., Communication
BURKE, W. J., Neurology
BURTON, F. R., Internal Medicine
CANTWELL, J. C., Mathematics and Mathematical Computer Science
CASE, M. E., Pathology
CERVENKA, P. A., Law
CHAITMAN, B. R., Internal Medicine
CHAPNICK, B. M., Pharmacological and Physiological Sciences
CHARRON, W. C., Philosophy
CHEN, S.-C., Paediatrics
CHINNADURAI, G., Molecular Virology
CHOATE, J. W., Obstetrics, Gynaecology and Women's Health
CHU, J.-Y., Paediatrics
CHUNG, H. D., Pathology
COHEN, J. D., Internal Medicine
COOPER, M. H., Anatomy and Neurobiology
COSCIA, C., Biochemistry and Molecular Biology
COUNTE, M. A., Health Administration
CREER, M. H., Pathology
CRITCHLOW, D. T., History
CROSSLEY, D. J., Geophysics
CUMMINGS, S. B., Public Policy Studies

CZYSZ, P. A., Aerospace Engineering
DAHMS, T. E., Anaesthesiology
DAVENPORT, G., Psychology
DELESPESSE, J. B., Aerospace Studies (ROTC)
DEMELLO, D. E., Pathology
DEUEL, R. K., Neurology
DIBISCEGLIE, A., Internal Medicine
DIECK, H. A., Chemistry
DIXIT, V. V., Physics
DORE, I. I., Law
DORSETT, D., Biochemistry and Molecular Biology
DOWDY, J., Mathematics and Mathematical Computer Science
DOYLE, J. P., Philosophy
DOYLE, R. E., Comparative Medicine
DUCKRO, P. N., Community and Family Medicine
DUNSFORD, J. E., Law
ELICEIRI, G. L., Pathology
ELLSWORTH, M. L., Pharmacological and Physiological Sciences
FARRIS, B. E., Jr, Sociology
FEMAN, S. S., Ophthalmology
FERGUSON, D. J., Orthodontics
FERMAN, M. A., Aerospace and Mechanical Engineering
FETE, T. J., Paediatrics
FIORE, A. C., Surgery
FISHER, J. T., Theological Studies
FITCH, C. D., Internal Medicine
FITZGIBBON, S. A., Law
FLETCHER, J. W., Internal Medicine
FLICK, L. H., Community Health
FLIESLER, S. J., Ophthalmology
FORD, C. E., Mathematics and Mathematical Computer Science
FORRESTER, T., Pharmacological and Physiological Science
FRANKOWSKI, S., Law
FREESE, R. W., Mathematics and Mathematical Computer Science
GALE, J. B., Paediatrics
GANNON, P., Psychiatry and Human Behaviour
GARCIA, P., Modern Languages
GARVIN, P. J., Surgery
GIBBONS, J. L., Psychology
GILNER, F. H., Psychology
GILSINAN, J. F., Public Policy Studies
GOLDMAN, R. L., Law
GOLDNER, J. A., Law
GOLDSTEIN, J. K., Law
GORSE, G. J., Internal Medicine
GRADY, M. P., Educational Studies
GRAFF, R. J., Surgery
GRAHAM, M. A., Pathology
GRANDGENETT, D. P., Molecular Virology
GREANEY, T. L., Law
GREEN, MAURICE, Molecular Virology
GREEN, MICHAEL, Molecular Microbiology and Immunology
GRIFFING, G. T., Internal Medicine
GROSSBERG, G. T., Psychiatry and Human Behaviour
GUITHUES, H. J., Finance
HAIRE-JOSHU, D. L., Community Health
HALLETT, G. L., Philosophy
HAMRICK, L. C., Modern Languages
HANDAL, P. J., Psychology
HARRIS, S. G., Mathematics and Mathematical Computer Science
HEANEY, R. M., Internal Medicine
HEBDA, J. J., Mathematics and Mathematical Computer Science
HEIBERG, E., Radiology
HERRMANN, R. B., Geophysics, Earth and Atmospheric Sciences
HITCHCOCK, J. F., History
HOMAN, S. M., Community Health
HOOVER, R. G., Pathology
HORVATH, F. L., Physician Assistant Education
HOWARD, A. J., Law
HRUBETZ, J., Nursing

HUANG, J. S., Biochemistry and Molecular Biology
HUGHES, H. M., Psychology
JANNEY, C. G., Pathology
JENNINGS, J. P., Accounting
JOHNSON, F. E., Surgery
JOHNSON, R. G., Surgery
JOHNSON, S. H., Law
JOHNSON, T. H., Modern Languages
JOIST, J. H., Pathology
JOS, C. J., Psychiatry and Human Behaviour
KALLIONGIS, J. E., Mathematics and Mathematical Computer Science
KAMINSKI, D. L., Surgery
KAO, M. S., Obstetrics and Gynaecology
KARUNAMOORTHY, S. N., Aerospace and Mechanical Engineering
KATZ, B. M., Research Methodology
KATZ, J. A., Management
KAUFMAN, N. H., Law
KAVANAUGH, J. F., Philosophy
KEENAN, W. J., Paediatrics
KEITHLEY, J. P., Accounting
KELLOGG, R. T., Psychology
KENNEDY, D. J., Internal Medicine
KERN, M. J., Internal Medicine
KIM, S. H., Finance
KIM, Y. S., Pharmacological and Physiological Sciences
KIMMEY, J. R., Community Health
KLEIN, C., Biochemistry and Molecular Biology
KNUEPFER, M. M., Pharmacological and Physiological Sciences
KNUTSEN, A. P., Paediatrics
KOLMER, E., American Studies
KORN, J. H., Psychology
KORNBLUTH, J., Pathology
KOWERT, B. A., Chemistry
KRAMER, T. J., Psychology
KURZ, R. S., Health Administration
KWAK, N. K., Decision Sciences and MIS
KWON, I. W., Decision Sciences and MIS
LABOVITZ, A. J., Internal Medicine
LAGUNOFF, D., Pathology
LANE, B. C., Theological Studies
LANG, J. M., Psychiatry and Human Behaviour
LECHNER, A. J., Pharmacological and Physiological Sciences
LEGUEY-FEILLEUX, J. R., Political Science
LEIPPE, M. R., Psychology
LEVARY, R. R., Decision Sciences and MIS
LEWIS, J. E., Law
LIN, Y. J., Meteorology, Earth and Atmospheric Sciences
LIU, M.-S., Pharmacological and Physiological Sciences
LOMPERIS, T. J., Political Science
LONGO, W. E., Surgery
LONIGRO, A. J., Internal Medicine
LUISIRI, A., Radiology
LYNCH, R. E., Paediatrics
MCCLURE, H. L., Aviation Science
MCGOWAN, J. R., Accounting
MCGUIRE, R. A., Communication Sciences and Disorders
MCLEOD, F. G., Theological Studies
MCSWEENEY, M., Nursing Research
MAGILL, G., Health Care Ethics
MALONE, L. J., Jr, Chemistry
MANCINI, M. J., American Studies
MANOR, D., Aerospace and Mechanical Engineering
MARGOLIS, R. B., Psychiatry and Human Behaviour
MARSKE, C. E., Sociology
MARTIN, D. S., Radiology
MARTIN, K. J., Internal Medicine
MATTFELDT-BEMAN, M., Nutrition and Dietetics
MATUSCHAK, G. M., Internal Medicine
MAYDEN, R. L., Biology
MEDOFF, J., Biology
MENGEL, M. B., Community and Family Medicine

METHENY, N. A., Adult and Gerontological Nursing
MEYER, A. E., Communication
MILLER, D. D., Internal Medicine
MILLER, D. K., Internal Medicine
MILLER, S. W., Marketing
MITCHELL, B. J., Geophysics, Earth and Atmospheric Sciences
MOBERG, T. F., Research Methodology
MODRAS, R. E., Theological Studies
MOISAN, T. E., English
MONTELEONE, J. A., Paediatrics
MONTELEONE, P. L., Paediatrics
MOORADIAN, A. D., Internal Medicine
MOORE, J. T., Meteorology, Earth and Atmospheric Sciences
MOORE, T. L., Internal Medicine
MORLEY, J. E., Internal Medicine
MUNZ, D. C., Psychology
MURDICK, N. L., Educational Studies
MURPHY, D. T., Modern Languages
MURRAY, R. L. E., Mental Health, Family, Community, and Systems Nursing
NAGABHUSHAN, B. L., Aerospace and Mechanical Engineering
NAUNHEIM, K. S., Surgery
NEEDHAM, C. A., Law
NEVINS, F. M., Law
NIKOLAI, R. J., Orthodontics
NOFFSINGER, J. E., Paediatrics
NOGUCHI, A., Paediatrics
O'BRIEN, J. C., Law
O'CONNOR, D. M., Paediatrics
OHAR, J. A., Internal Medicine
OLIVER, J. M., Psychology
ORDOWER, H. M., Law
O'TOOLE, M. L., Obstetrics and Gynaecology
PADBERG, W. H., Social Work
PALETTA, C. E., Surgery
PANNETON, W. M., Anatomy and Neurobiology
PARKER, G. E., Management
PAULY, J. J., Communication
PERMAN, W. H., Radiology
PERRY, E. I., History
PERRY, H. M., Internal Medicine
PERRY, L. C., History
PERRY, S. A., Adult and Gerontological Nursing
PETERSON, G. J., Surgery
PETRUSKA, P. J., Internal Medicine
PIERRON, R. L., Orthopaedic Surgery
POLLARD, C. A., Community and Family Medicine
PUNZO, V. C., Philosophy
PURO, S., Political Science
RAHMAN, H., Electrical Engineering
RANA, W.-U.-Z., Anatomy and Neurobiology
RAO, G. V., Earth and Atmospheric Sciences
RAO, P. S., Paediatrics
RAVINDRA, K., Aerospace and Mechanical Engineering
RAY, R., Internal Medicine
REBORE, R. W., Educational Leadership and Higher Education
REESE, C., Mental Health, Family, Community and Systems Nursing
REIMERS, H. J., Internal Medicine
RENARD, G. J., Jr, Theological Studies
ROHLIK, J., Law
ROMEIS, J. C., Health Services Research
ROSS, M. J., Psychology
ROY, T. S., Radiation Oncology
RUCKDESCHEL, R. A., Social Work
RUDDY, T. M., History
RUH, M. F., Pharmacological and Physiological Sciences
RUH, T. S., Pharmacological and Physiological Sciences
RYERSE, J. S., Pathology
SALIMI, Z., Radiology
SALINAS-MADRIGAL, L., Pathology
SALSICH, P. W., Jr, Law
SAMSON, W. K., Pharmacological and Physiological Sciences
SANCHEZ, J. M., History

SANTHANAM, T. S., Physics
SCALZO, A. J., Paediatrics
SCHLAFLY, D. L., Jr, History
SCHMITZ, H. H., Health Administration
SCHMITZ, P. G., Internal Medicine
SCHULZE, I. T., Molecular Microbiology and Immunology
SCOTT, J. F., English
SEITZ, N. E., Finance
SELHORST, J. B., Neurology
SEVERSON, J. G., Jr, Biology
SHANER, M. C., Management
SHAPIRO, M. J., Surgery
SHEA, W. M., Theological Studies
SHIELDS, J. B., Radiology
SHIPPEY, T. A., English
SILBERSTEIN, M. J., Radiology
SILVERBERG, A. B., Internal Medicine
SLAVIN, R. G., Internal Medicine
SLY, W. S., Biochemistry and Molecular Biology
SMITH, G. S., Surgery
SMITH, K., Jr, Surgery
SOTELO-AVILA, C., Pathology
SPAZIANO, V. T., Chemistry
SPRAGUE, R. S., Internal Medicine
STACEY, L. M., Physics
STANTON, C. M., Educational Leadership and Higher Education
STARK, W., Biology
STEINHARDT, G. F., Urology, Surgery
STEVENS, T. C., Mathematics and Mathematical Computer Science
STOEBERL, P. A., Management
STOLZER, A. J., Aviation Science
STRATMAN, H. G., Internal Medicine
STRETCH, J. J., Social Work
STUMP, D. V., English
STUMP, E. A., Philosophy
SWANSTROM, T., Public Policy Studies
SWIERKOSZ, E. M., Pathology
TAIT, R. C., Psychiatry and Human Behaviour
TAN, Y., Anatomy and Neurobiology
TERRY, N., Law
THACKER, W. D., Physics
THOMAS, C. W., Biomedical Engineering
THOMAS, D. R., Internal Medicine
TOCE, S. S., Paediatrics
TOLBERT, D. L., Anatomy and Neurobiology
TOMAZIC, T. J., Research Methodology
TREADGOLD, W., History
TRUE, W. R., Community Health
TSAU, C. M., Mathematics and Mathematical Computer Science
TUCHLER, D. J., Law
ULTMANN, M. H., Paediatrics
VAGO, S., Sociology
VAN DER BERG, S., English
VIRGO, K. S., Surgery
VOGLER, C. A., Pathology
VOGLER, G. A., Comparative Medicine
WACKER, W. D., Mathematics and Mathematical Computer Science
WALENTIK, C. A., Paediatrics
WARREN, K. F., Political Science
WATSON, S., Law
WEBB, K., Community and Family Medicine
WEBER, T. R., Surgery
WEBSTER, R. O., Internal Medicine
WEINBERGER, A. M., Law
WEIXLMANN, J., English
WELCH, P. J., Economics
WERNET, S. P., Social Work
WESTFALL, T. C., Pharmacological and Physiological Sciences
WHITING, R. B., Internal Medicine
WHITMAN, B., Paediatrics
WILLIAMS, D. R., Law
WILLMORE, L. J., Jr, Neurology
WINN, H. N., Obstetrics and Gynaecology
WOLD, W. S. M., Molecular Microbiology and Immunology
WOLINSKY, F. D., Health Administration
WOLVERSON, M. K., Radiology
WONGSURAWAT, N., Internal Medicine

WOOD, E. G., Paediatrics
WOOD, T. T., Art and Art History
YEAGER, F., Finance
YOUNG, P. A., Anatomy and Neurobiology
ZAHM, D. S., Anatomy and Neurobiology
ZASSENHAUS, H. P., Molecular Microbiology and Immunology
ZENSER, T. V., Internal Medicine

SAINT PAUL SCHOOL OF THEOLOGY

5123 E Truman Rd, Kansas City, MO 64127
Telephone: (816) 483-9600
Fax: (816) 483-9605
E-mail: admiss@spst.edu
Internet: www.spst.edu
Private control

Campus at Oklahoma City (Oklahoma)

Pres.: Dr MYRON F. McCOY
Vice-Pres. for Academic Affairs and Dean: Prof. DON COMPIER
Vice-Pres. for Advancement: JIM OMAN
Dir for Admissions: LEE JOHNSON
Registrar: BRENDA BARROWS
Dir for Library and Information Services: LOGAN S. WRIGHT

Library of 100,000 vols, 500 journals
Number of teachers: 41
Number of students: 280

SCHOOL OF PROFESSIONAL PSYCHOLOGY AT FOREST INSTITUTE

2885 W Battlefield, Springfield, MO 65807-3952
Telephone: (417) 823-3477
Fax: (417) 823-3442
Internet: www.forest.edu
Founded 1979
Private control

Pres.: Dr MARK SKRADE
Vice-Pres. for Academic Affairs: BRIAN NEDWEK
Vice-Pres. for Enrolment Services: DAWN MEDLEY
Registrar: CAROLYN SMITH
Library Services Man.: RENEE McHENRY

Library of 5,500 vols, 208 journals and newspapers, 440 video cassettes
Number of students: 300

SOUTHEAST MISSOURI STATE UNIVERSITY

One University Plaza, Cape Girardeau, MO 63701
Telephone: (314) 651-2000
Fax: (314) 651-5061
Internet: www.semo.edu
Founded 1873
State control

Pres.: Dr KENNETH W. DOBBINS
Provost: Dr RONALD ROSATI
Vice-Pres. for Admin. and Enrolment Management: DENNIS HOLT
Vice-Pres. for Univ. Advancement: WAYNE SMITH
Registrar: SANDRA L. HINKLE
Dir of Library: Dr DAVID STARRETT

Library of 430,000 vols, 287,000 govt docs, 2,000 magazines and journals, 1.2m. microforms
Number of teachers: 401
Number of students: 10,101

DEANS

College of Education: Dr TAMELA RANDOLPH
College of Health and Human Services: LORETTA PRATER
College of Liberal Arts: Dr FRANK BARRIOS
College of Science and Mathematics: Dr CHRIS McGOWAN

Donald L. Harrison College of Business: Dr GERALD MCDOUGALL

School of Extended Learning: GERALD S. MCDOUGALL

School of Graduate Studies: Dr BILL EDDLEMAN

School of Polytechnic Studies: Dr CHRIS MCGOWAN

School of University Studies and Academic Information Services: DAVID STARRETT

SOUTHWEST BAPTIST UNIVERSITY

1600 University Ave, Bolivar, MO 65613
Telephone: (417) 328-5281
Fax: (417) 326-1514
E-mail: admitme@sbuniv.edu
Internet: www.sbuniv.edu
Founded 1878 as Southwest Baptist College, present name 1981
Private control
Campuses at Mountain View, Salem, Springfield (Missouri)
Pres.: Dr C. PAT TAYLOR
Provost: Dr WILLIAM BROWN
Vice-Pres. for Admin.: RON MAUPIN
Vice-Pres. for Enrolment Management: Dr STEPHANIE MILLER
Vice-Pres. for Information and Technology Services: Dr BOB MCGLASSON
Vice-Pres. for Univ. Relations: Dr R. STANTON NORMAN
Dean for Students: ROB HARRIS
Registrar: JOHN CREDILLE
Dean for Library Services: EDWARD W. WALTON (acting)
Library of 129,000 vols
Number of teachers: 106
Number of students: 3,600
Publication: *SBU Life*

DEANS

College of Business and Computer Science: Dr KENNETH E. BANDY
College of Education and Social Science: Dr LINDA WOODERSON
College of Science and Mathematics: Dr PERRY A. TOMPKINS
Courts Redford College of Theology and Min.: Dr RODNEY REEVES
Geneva Casebolt College of Music, Arts and Letters: JEFFERY WATERS
St John's College of Nursing and Health Sciences: Dr MARTHA BAKER

STEPHENS COLLEGE

1200 E Broadway, Columbia, MO 65215
Telephone: (573) 442-2211
Fax: (573) 876-7165
E-mail: info@stephens.edu
Internet: www.stephens.edu
Founded 1833
Private control
Academic year: August to May
Pres.: Dr DIANNE LYNCH
Vice-Pres. for Academic Affairs: NANCY CORNWELL
Vice-Pres. for Enrolment Management: CHRIS COLLIER
Vice-Pres. for Finance and Admin.: LINDI OVERTON
Vice-Pres. for Student Services: DEB DUREN
Registrar: LINDA SHARP
Library Dir: CORRIE HUTCHISON
Library of 134,672 vols
Number of teachers: 55 (full-time)
Number of students: 864

DEANS

Liberal Arts: MIMI HEDGES
School of Design and Fashion: MONICA MCMURRY

School of Performing Arts: Prof. BETH LEONARD

TRUMAN STATE UNIVERSITY

100 E Normal, Kirksville, MO 63501
Telephone: (660) 785-4000
Fax: (660) 785-7456
E-mail: admissions@truman.edu
Internet: www.truman.edu
Founded 1867 as North Missouri Normal School and Commercial College, present name 1996
State control
Academic year: August to May
Pres.: Dr TROY D. PAINO
Provost and Vice-Pres. for Academic Affairs: RICHARD COUGHLIN
Registrar: MARGARET HERRON
Dean for Libraries: RICHARD COUGHLIN
Library of 335,144 vols, 7,283 spec. collns vol, 2,237 vols of archives, 3,860 rare books
Number of teachers: 358
Number of students: 6,090 (5,600 undergraduate, 250 graduate, 240 int.)
Publications: *Detours* (2 a year), *Truman Review* (3 a year, print and online (alumni.truman.edu/trumanreview)), *Windfall* (1 a year)

DEANS

School of Arts and Letters: Dr PRISCILLA RIGGLE
School of Business: Dr DEBRA KERBY
School of Health Sciences and Education: Dr JANET L. GOOCH
School of Science and Mathematics: Dr JONATHAN GERING
School of Social and Cultural Studies: Dr DOUG DAVENPORT

UNIVERSITY OF CENTRAL MISSOURI

POB 800, Warrensburg, MO 64093
Telephone: (660) 543-4111
Fax: (660) 543-8517
E-mail: admit@ucmo.edu
Internet: www.ucmo.edu
Founded 1871, present name and status 2006
State control
Academic year: August to May
Pres.: Dr CHARLES M. AMBROSE
Provost: Dr GEORGE WILSON
Vice-Provost for Enrolment Management: Dr RICHARD D. SLUDER
Vice-Pres. for Admin. and Finance: JOHN F. MERRIGAN
Vice-Pres. for Univ. Advancement: Dr JASON S. DRUMMOND
Gen. Counsel: HANK SETSER
Dir for Admissions: ANN E. NORDYKE
Registrar: TERI BOWMAN
Dean for Library Services: MOLLIE DINWIDDIE
Library: 2m. vols, 2,500 newspaper and periodical subscriptions, 829,100 microforms
Number of teachers: 451
Number of students: 11,351 (2,183 graduate, 9,168 undergraduate)

DEANS

College of Arts, Humanities and Social Sciences: Dr GERSHAM NELSON
College of Education: Dr MICHAEL WRIGHT
College of Health and Human Services: Dr RICHARD SLUDER
College of Health, Science and Technology: Dr ALICE GREIFE
Harmon College of Business Administration: Dr ROGER J. BEST
Honors College: JOSEPH D. LEWANDOWSKI
School of Graduate and Extended Studies: Dr JOSEPH VAUGHN

UNIVERSITY OF MISSOURI SYSTEM

Columbia, MO 65211
Telephone: (573) 882-2011
Fax: (573) 882-2721
E-mail: mu4u@missouri.edu
Internet: www.umsystem.edu
Founded 1839
State control
Pres.: STEPHEN J. OWENS
Sr Assoc. Vice-Pres. for Academic Affairs: Dr STEVEN W. GRAHAM
Vice-Pres. for Finance and Admin.: NATALIE KRAWITZ
Vice-Pres. for Govt Relations: STEPHEN C. KNORR
Vice-Pres. for Human Resources: ELIZABETH RODRIGUEZ
Vice-Pres. for Information Technology: Dr GARY K. ALLEN
Vice-Pres. for Research and Economic Devt: Dr MICHAEL F. NICHOLS
Library: see Libraries and Archives
Number of teachers: 7,814
Number of students: 71,596.

CONSTITUENT CAMPUSES

University of Missouri—Columbia

104 Jesse Hall, Columbia, MO 65211
Telephone: (573) 882-7881
E-mail: mu4u@missouri.edu
Internet: www.missouri.edu
Founded 1839
Academic year: August to May
Chancellor: Dr BRADY J. DEATON
Provost: BRIAN FOSTER (acting)
Vice-Provost for Enrolment Management: ANN KORSCHGEN
Vice-Chancellor for Admin. Services: JACQUELYN JONES
Vice-Chancellor for Devt and Alumni Relations: THOMAS HILES
Vice-Chancellor for Research: ROBERT DUNCAN
Vice-Chancellor for Student Affairs: CATHY SCROGGS
Registrar: BRENDA SELMAN
Dir for Admissions: BARBARA RUPP
Library of 3,612,144 vols, 7.5m. microforms, 1.7m. govt documents and 53,394 journals
Number of teachers: 2,072
Number of students: 33,805

DEANS

College of Agriculture, Food and Natural Resources: THOMAS PAYNE
College of Arts and Sciences: MICHAEL O'BRIEN
College of Business: JOAN GABEL
College of Education: DANIEL CLAY
College of Engineering: JAMES E. THOMPSON
College of Human Environmental Sciences: STEPHEN JORGENSEN
College of Veterinary Medicine: NEIL OLSON
Graduate School: GEORGE JUSTICE
School of Health Professions: RICHARD OLIVER
School of Journalism: DEAN MILLS (acting)
School of Law: R. LAWRENCE DESSEM
School of Medicine: ROBERT CHURCHILL
School of Nursing: JUDITH FITZGERALD MILLER

University of Missouri—Kansas City

301 Admin. Center, 5100 Rockhill Rd, Kansas City, MO 64110-2499
301 Admin. Center, 5115 Oak St, Kansas City, MO 64112
Telephone: (816) 235-1101
Fax: (816) 235-5588
E-mail: umkcchancellor@umkc.edu
Internet: www.umkc.edu
Founded 1929
Academic year: August to July

Chancellor: LEO E. MORTON
Exec. Vice-Chancellor and Provost: Dr GAIL HACKETT
Vice-Chancellor for Finance and Admin. Affairs: SHARON LINDENBAUM
Vice-Chancellor for Student Affairs: MELVIN C. TYLER
Vice-Chancellor for Univ. Advancement: CURT CRESPINO
Dir for Admissions: DORETTA KIDD (acting)
Registrar: DOUG SWINK
Dean for Libraries: Dr SHARON L. BOSTICK
Library of 1,313,266 vols, 1,459,439 microforms, 202,156 e-books, 129,943 vol govt publs, 7,523 video cassettes and DVDs
Number of teachers: 1,883
Number of students: 15,143

DEANS

College of Arts and Sciences: WAYNE VAUGHT
Conservatory of Music and Dance: PETER WITTE
Henry W. Bloch School of Management: Dr TENG-KEE TAN
School of Biological Sciences: LAWRENCE DREYFUS
School of Computing and Engineering: KEVIN Z. TRUMAN
School of Dentistry: MARSHA A. PYLE
School of Education: Dr WANDA J. BLANCHETT
School of Graduate Studies: Dr DENIS M. MEDEIROS
School of Law: ELLEN SUNI
School of Medicine: BETTY M. DREES
School of Nursing: Dr LORA LACEY-HAUN
School of Pharmacy: Dr RUSSELL B. MELCHERT

Missouri University of Science and Technology

106 Parker Hall, 300 W 13th St, Rolla, MO 65409-1060
Telephone: (573) 341-4114
Fax: (573) 341-6306
E-mail: admissions@mst.edu
Internet: www.mst.edu
Founded 1870, fmrly Univ. of Missouri-Rolla, present name and status 2008
Academic year: August to July

Divs of arts and humanities, business and social sciences, engineering, sciences and computing
Chancellor: WARREN K. WRAY
Provost and Exec. Vice-Chancellor for Academic Affairs: ROBERT W. SCHWARTZ
Vice-Provost and Dean for Enrolment Management: LAURA K. STOLL
Vice-Chancellor for Admin. Services: F. STEPHEN MALOTT
Vice-Chancellor for Student Affairs: Dr DEBRA ROBINSON
Vice-Chancellor for Univ. Advancement: JOAN NESBITT
Registrar: DEANNE JACKSON
Library Dir: ANDREW STEWART
Library of 388,000 vols
Number of teachers: 497 (398 full-time, 99 part-time)
Number of students: 7,500 (5,650 undergraduate, 1,850 graduate)
Publication: *Missouri S&T*.

University of Missouri—St Louis

1 University Blvd, St Louis, MO 63121-4400
Telephone: (314) 516-5000
Fax: (314) 516-5378
E-mail: admissions@umsl.edu
Internet: www.umsl.edu
Founded 1963
Academic year: August to July
Chancellor: Prof. Dr THOMAS F. GEORGE
Provost and Vice-Chancellor for Academic Affairs: Prof. GLEN H. COPE

Vice-Chancellor for Managerial and Technological Services: Prof. Dr JAMES M. KRUEGER
Vice-Chancellor for Univ. Advancement: MARTIN F. LEIFELD
Vice-Provost for Research: Prof. NASSAR ARSHADI
Vice-Provost for Student Affairs: CURTIS C. COONROD
Dir for Admissions: ALAN BYRD
Registrar: LINDA SILMAN
Dean for Libraries: CHRISTOPHER R. DAMES
Library: 1.2m. vols, 1.2m. govt documents, 1.3m. microfilm units, 3,966 audiovisual units, 10,567 e-books
Number of teachers: 1,447
Number of students: 16,800

Publications: *Theory and Society Journal*, *UMSL Magazine* (2 a year)

DEANS

College of Arts and Sciences: RONALD YASBIN
College of Business Administration: N. KEITH WOMER
College of Education: Dr KATHLEEN HAYWOOD
College of Fine Arts and Communication: JAMES E. RICHARDS
College of Nursing: Dr SUSAN DEAN-BAAR
College of Optometry: LARRY J. DAVIS
Continuing Education: WILLIAM T. WALKER
Graduate School: JUDITH WALKER DE FELIX
Pierre Laclede Honours College: Dr ROBERT M. BLISS
UMSL/WU Joint Undergraduate Engineering Program: Dr BERNARD FELDMAN

PROFESSORS

ALTHOF, W., Educational Psychology
ANDERSON, K. C., Art and Art History
BERKOWITZ, M. W., Educational Psychology
BIRD, A., Business Admin.
BOHAN, R. L., Art and Art History
BREAUGH, J., Business Administration
BURSIK, R. J., Criminology and Criminal Justice
CALSYN, R. J., Psychology
CAMPBELL, J. F., Business Administration
CARROLL, J. C., English
CHICKOS, J., Chemistry
CHUI, C., Mathematics and Computer Science
COCHRAN, J. A., Educational Leadership Policy
COKER, A. A., Theatre and Dance
COOK, S., English
COREY, J. Y., Chemistry
COSMOPOULOS, M., Anthropology
COTTONE, R. R., Counseling (College of Education)
CURRY, G. D., Criminology and Criminal Justice
DIBOOGLU, S., Economics
EBEST, S. B., English
ESBENSEN, F. A., Criminology and Criminal Justice
EVEN, Y., Art and Art History
EYSSELL, T. H., College of Business Admin.
FEIGENBAUM, S. K., Economics
FLORES, R. A., Physics and Astronomy
FRIEDLANDER, R. J., Mathematics and Computer Science
FUNG, H. G., Business Administration
GERTEIS, L. S., History
GILLINGHAM, J. R., History
GOKEL, G. W., Center for Nanoscience
GRADY, F. W., English
GRANGER, C. R., Biology
HANDEL, P. H., Physics and Astronomy
HARBACH, B. C., Music
HARRIS, M. M., Business Administration
HARRIS, W. R., Chemistry
HENSON, B. L., Physics and Astronomy
HUNT, J. H., Biology
HURLEY, A., History
JANSON, M. A., Business Administration

JIANG, Q., Mathematics and Computer Science
JONES, E., Political Science
JOSHI, K., Business Administration
KELLOGG, E. A., Biology
KYLE, W. C., Education—Teaching and Learning
LACITY, M. C., Business Administration
LANKFORD, E. L., Art and Art History
LAURITSEN, J. L., Criminology and Criminal Justice
LAWRENCE, E. C., Business Administration
LEE, R. K., Nursing
LEVENTHAL, J. J., Physics and Astronomy
LOISELLE, B. A., Biology
LUI, J., Center for Nanoscience
McPHAIL, T. L., Theatre and Dance
MARQUIS, R. J., Biology
MARTINICH, J. S., Business Administration
MITCHELL, R. H., History
MOSS, F. E., Physics and Astronomy
MUNDY, R. A., Center for Transportation Studies
MUNSON, R., Philosophy
MURRAY, J. Y., College of Business Administration
MURRAY, M. D., Theatre and Dance
MUSHABEN, J. M., Political Science
NAUSS, R. M., Business Administration
O'BRIEN, J. J., Chemistry
OHALLMHURAIN, G., Music
PARKER, P. G., Biology
PATTERSON, M. L., Psychology
PECK, C. K., Optometry
POPE, M. L., Counseling (College of Education)
RAO, A. P., Mathematics and Computer Science
RAY, R. J., Music
RICHARDS, J., Music
RICHARDSON, L. I., Educational Leadership and Policy
RICKLEFS, R. E., Biology
ROBERTSON, D. B., Political Science
ROCHESTER, J. M., Political Science
RONEN, D., Business Administration
ROSE, D. C., Economics
ROSENFELD, R. B., Criminology and Criminal Justice
ROSS, S. A., Philosophy
ROWAN, S. W., History
SABHERWAL, R., Business Administration
SAUL, E. W., Teaching and Learning
SAUTER, V. L., Business Administration
SCHWANTES, C. A., History
SCHWARTZ, H. E., English
SEGAL, U. A., Social Work
SHERRADEN, M. S., Social Work
SHYMANSKY, J. A., Teaching and Learning
SILVA, G. E., Political Science
SIMMONS, P. E., Teaching and Learning
SMITH, L. D., College of Business Administration
SORENSEN, R. L., Economics
SPILLING, C., Chemistry
STEIN, L., Political Science
STEVENS, P. F., Biology
TANG, M. Z., Biology
TAYLOR, G. T., Psychology
TOULIATOS, D. H., Music
VANDENBERG, B. R., Psychology
WALL, E. W., English
WANG, X., Biology
WHITE, L. H., Economics
WILKENS, L. A., Biology
WILKING, B. A., Physics and Astronomy
WILLIAMS, L. V., Foreign Languages and Literature
WILLMAN, F., Music
WINKLER, A. E., Economics
WOLFE, P., English
WRIGHT, R. T., Criminology and Criminal Justice
YOUNGER, D., Art and Art History
ZARUCCHI, J. M., Art and Art History
ZENI, J. E., English

WASHINGTON UNIVERSITY IN SAINT LOUIS

POB 1089, 1 Brookings Dr., Saint Louis, MO 63130-4899

Telephone: (314) 935-6000
Fax: (314) 935-4290
E-mail: admissions@wustl.edu
Internet: www.wustl.edu

Founded 1853 as Eliot Seminary, present name 1857
Private control
Academic year: August to May

Chancellor: Prof. Dr MARK S. WRIGHTON
Provost and Exec. Vice-Chancellor for Academic Affairs: EDWARD S. MACIAS
Exec. Vice-Chancellor for Alumni and Devt Programmes: DAVID T. BLASINGAME
Exec. Vice-Chancellor for Admin.: HENRY S. WEBBER
Exec. Vice-Chancellor and Gen. Counsel: MICHAEL R. CANNON
Vice-Chancellor for Finance: BARBARA A. FEINER
Vice-Chancellor of Govt and Community Relations: PAMELA S. LOKKEN
Vice-Chancellor for Research: EVAN D. KHARASCH
Vice-Chancellor for Students: SHARON STAHL
Vice-Chancellor for Scholarly Resources and Dean for Libraries: SHIRLEY K. BAKER
Number of teachers: 1,089 (932 full-time, 157 part-time)
Number of students: 13,908 (11,823 full-time, 2,085 part-time)
Publication: *Washington Magazine* (6 a year)

DEANS

Faculty of Arts and Sciences: GARY S. WIHL
George Warren Brown School of Social Work: EDWARD F. LAWLOR
Graduate School of Arts and Sciences: RICHARD J. SMITH
Olin Business School: MAHENDRA R. GUPTA
Sam Fox School of Design and Visual Arts: CARMON COLANGELO
School of Engineering and Applied Science: RALPH S. QUATRANO
School of Law: KENT D. SYVERUD
School of Medicine: LARRY J. SHAPIRO

WEBSTER UNIVERSITY

470 E Lockwood Ave, St Louis, MO 63119-3194

Telephone: (314) 968-6900
Fax: (314) 968-7112
E-mail: admissions@webster.edu
Internet: www.webster.edu

Founded 1915, present name and status 1983
Private control
Academic year: August to May

Chancellor: NEIL J. GEORGE
Pres.: Dr ELIZABETH J. STROBLE
Provost and Sr Vice-Pres.: JULIAN Z. SCHUSTER
Vice-Pres. for Enrolment Management and Student Affairs: PAUL CARNEY
Vice-Pres. for Devt and Alumni Programmes: FAITH D. MADDY
Vice-Pres. and Interim Chief Information Officer: KENNETH FREEMAN
Registrar: DON MORRIS
Dean for Univ. Library: EILEEN CONDON
Library of 299,000 vols
Number of teachers: 2,689 (912 full-time, 1,777 part-time)
Number of students: 22,000

DEANS

College of Arts and Sciences: DAVID CARL WILSON
George Herbert Walker School of Business and Technology: Dr BENJAMIN OLA AKANDE

Leigh Gerdine College of Fine Arts: PETER SARGENT
School of Communications: DEBRA CARPENTER
School of Education: BRENDA FYFE

WESTMINSTER COLLEGE

Fulton, MO 65251

Telephone: (573) 592-6241
Fax: (573) 642-5217
E-mail: westminster@westminster-mo.edu
Internet: www.westminster-mo.edu

Founded 1851 as Fulton College, present name 1853
Private control
Academic year: August to May
Divs of humanities, natural and mathematical sciences, social sciences

Pres.: Dr GEORGE B. FORSYTHE
Vice-Pres. and Chief Information Officer: SCOTT LOWE
Vice-Pres. and Dean for Enrolment Services: GEORGE WOLF
Vice-Pres. and Dean for Student Life: Dr STEPHANIE KRAUTH
Vice-Pres. and Dir for Churchill Institute: ROB HAVERS
Vice-Pres. for Academic Affairs and Dean for Faculty: Dr CAROLYN PERRY
Vice-Pres. for Institutional Advancement: JOHN COMERFORD
Registrar: PHYLLIS MASEK
Dir for Library Services: ANGELA GERLING
Library of 121,073 vols
Number of teachers: 72
Number of students: 1,102

WILLIAM JEWELL COLLEGE

500 College Hill, Liberty, MO 64068

Telephone: (816) 781-7700
Fax: (816) 415-5005
E-mail: admission@william.jewell.edu
Internet: www.jewell.edu

Founded 1849
Private control
Academic year: September to May
Liberal arts college

Pres.: DAVID L. SALLEE
Provost: ANNE C. DEMA
Vice-Pres. for Academic Affairs and Dean: TIMOTHY E. FULOP
Vice-Pres. for Enrolment and Student Affairs: Dr RICHARD P. WINSLOW
Vice-Pres. for Finance and Operations: BRIAN CLEMONS
Vice-Pres. for Institutional Advancement: Dr CHAD J. JOLLY
Registrar: ED LANE
Systems Librarian: STEVEN BAILEY
Library of 260,119 vols
Number of teachers: 128
Number of students: 1,500
Publication: *Achieve Magazine*.

WILLIAM WOODS UNIVERSITY

1 University Ave, Fulton, MO 65251

Telephone: (573) 642-2251
Fax: (573) 592-1146
E-mail: admissions@williamwoods.edu
Internet: www.williamwoods.edu

Founded 1870 as William Woods College, present name and status 1993
Private control
Academic year: August to May
Divs of art, behavioural and social sciences, business and economics, education, equestrian studies, human performance and science, humanities; campuses at Blue Springs, Branson, Columbia, Jefferson City (Missouri)

Pres.: Prof. Dr JAHNAE H. BARNETT

Vice-Pres.: SCOTT T. GALLAGHER
Vice-Pres. and Dean for Academic Affairs: Prof. Dr SHERRY MCCARTHY
Vice-Pres. and Dean for Graduate College: Prof. MICHAEL WESTERFIELD
Vice-Pres. for Finance: CALE FESSLER
Vice-Pres. for Graduate College Recruitment: Dr ROBERT FESSLER
Dean for Admissions: SARAH MUNNS
Dean for Student Life: VENITA MITCHELL
Registrar: TARA DEIERLING
Library Dir: ERLENE DUDLEY

Library of 160,000 vols
Number of teachers: 352 (52 full-time, 300 part-time)
Number of students: 3,500

MONTANA

CARROLL COLLEGE

1601 N Benton Ave, Helena, MT 59625

Telephone: (406) 447-4300
Fax: (406) 447-4533
Internet: www.carroll.edu

Founded 1909
Private control
Academic year: August to May

Pres.: Dr THOMAS EVANS
Vice-Pres. for Finance and Admin.: LORI PETERSON
Vice-Pres. for Institutional Advancement: TOM MCCARVEL
Vice-Pres. for Student Life: Dr JIM D. HARDWICK
Academic Dean: JOHN SCHARF
Registrar: CATHERINE DAY
Library Dir: CHRISTIAN FRAZZA

Library of 85,000 vols, 2,000 titles, 150 periodicals, 90,000 monographs
Number of teachers: 85
Number of students: 1,502

CHIEF DULL KNIFE COLLEGE

POB 98, Lame Deer, MT 59043

Telephone: (406) 477-6215
Internet: www.cdkc.edu

Founded 1975, fmrly known as Dull Knife Memorial College, present name 2001
Tribal control
Academic year: August to May

Pres.: Dr RICHARD LITTLEBEAR
Vice-Pres.: WILLIAM WERTMAN
Dean for Academic Affairs: MICHELE CURLEE
Dean for Student Affairs: ZANE SPANG

Library of 24,688 vols.

MONTANA STATE UNIVERSITY

POB 172000, 100 Culbertson Hall, Bozeman, MT 59717-2000

Telephone: (406) 994-0211
Fax: (406) 994-2893
E-mail: president@montana.edu
Internet: www.montana.edu

Founded 1893

Pres.: Dr WADED CRUZADO
Provost and Vice-Pres. for Academic Affairs: Dr MARTHA A. POTVIN
Vice-Pres. for Admin. and Finance: TERRY LEIST
Vice-Pres. for Research, Creativity and Technology Transfer: THOMAS MCCOY
Vice-Pres. for Student Success: Dr ALLEN YARNELL
Dean for Students: MATTHEW CAIRES
Dean for Libraries: TAMARA MILLER
Dir for Admissions: RONDA RUSSELL

Library of 34,000 vols, 1,200 linear ft MSS materials

Number of teachers: 847 (592 full-time, 255 part-time)
Number of students: 14,153

DEANS

College of Agriculture: JEFF JACOBSEN
College of Arts and Architecture: JOSEPH FEDOCK
College of Business: SUSAN DANA
College of Education, Health and Human Development: LARRY BAKER
College of Engineering: ROBERT MARLEY
College of Letters and Science: PAULA LUTZ
College of Nursing: HELEN MELLAND
Gallatin College Programs: ROBERT HIETALA
Graduate School: CARL FOX

MONTANA STATE UNIVERSITY—BILLINGS

1500 Univ. Dr., Billings, MT 59101
Telephone: (406) 657-2011
Fax: (406) 657-2299
E-mail: admissions@msubillings.edu
Internet: www.msubillings.edu
Founded 1927 as Eastern Montana College, present name 1995
State control
Academic year: September to May
Chancellor: Dr ROLF GROSETH
Provost and Academic Vice-Chancellor: Dr MARK PAGANO
Vice-Chancellor for Admin. Services: TERRIE IVERSON
Vice-Chancellor for Student Affairs: Dr STACY KLIPPENSTEIN
Library Dir: BRENT ROBERTS
Library of 281,258 vols
Number of teachers: 342 (150 full-time, 192 part-time)
Number of students: 4,300

DEANS

College of Allied Health Professions: Dr DIANE DUIN
College of Arts & Sciences: Dr TASNEEM KHALEEL
College of Business: Dr TIMOTHY J. WILKINSON
College of Education: Dr MARY SUSAN FISHBAUGH
College of Technology: Dr MARSHA RILEY

MONTANA STATE UNIVERSITY—GREAT FALLS COLLEGE OF TECHNOLOGY

2100 16th Ave S, Great Falls, MT 59405
Telephone: (406) 771-4300
Fax: (406) 771-4317
E-mail: information@msugf.edu
Internet: www.msugf.edu
Founded 1969, present name and status 1994; attached to Montana State Univ.
State control
Pres.: WADED CRUZADO
Dean and CEO: Dr GWENDOLYN G. JOSEPH
Exec. Dir for Human Resources: MARY KAY BONILLA
Exec. Dir for College Relations: PAM PARSONS
Exec. Dir for Institutional Research and Planning: WENDY DOVE
Number of teachers: 113 (41 full-time, 72 part-time)
Number of students: 2,569

MONTANA STATE UNIVERSITY—NORTHERN

POB 7751, 300 W 11th St, Havre, MT 59501
Telephone: (406) 265-3700
Fax: (406) 265-3777
E-mail: admissions@msun.edu
Internet: www.msun.edu

Founded 1929
State control
Baccalaureate courses in arts and sciences, business, nursing, teacher education, technology; Masters courses in education; br. educational centres in Great Falls and Lewistown
Chancellor: Dr JAMES LIMBAUGH
Provost and Vice-Chancellor for Academic Affairs: Dr ROSALYN TEMPLETON
Dean for Students and Registrar: LINDSEY BROWN
Library Dir: VICKI GIST
Library of 100,000 vols
Number of teachers: 80
Number of students: 1,215

MONTANA TECH

1300 W Park St, Butte, MT 59701
Telephone: (406) 496-4256
Fax: (406) 496-4710
E-mail: enrollment@mtech.edu
Internet: www.mtech.edu
Founded 1893; attached to Univ. of Montana
State control
Academic year: June to May
Chancellor: Dr DONALD M. BLACKKETTER
Vice-Chancellor for Academic Affairs and Research: Dr DOUG M. ABBOTT
Vice-Chancellor for Admin. and Finance: MAGGIE PETERSON
Vice-Chancellor for Devt and Advancement: TRACI O'NEILL
Vice-Chancellor for Student Affairs and Dean for Students: PAUL BEATTY
Dir for Enrolment Management: TONY CAMPEAU
Registrar: KATHY WILLIAMS
Dir for Library: ANN ST CLAIR
Number of teachers: 212
Number of students: 2,803
Publications: Catalog, MNews, The Technocrat

DEANS

College of Letters, Sciences, and Professional Studies: Dr DOUG COE
College of Technology: Dr JOHN M. GARIC
Graduate School: JOE FIGUEIRA
School of Mines and Engineering: Dr PETER KNUDSEN

ROCKY MOUNTAIN COLLEGE

1511 Poly Dr., Billings, MT 59102-1796
Telephone: (406) 657-1000
Fax: (406) 259-9751
E-mail: president@rocky.edu
Internet: www.rocky.edu
Founded 1947 by merger of Deer Lodge (f. 1878), Wesleyan College and Billings Polytechnic Institute
Private control
Academic year: August to May
Pres.: Dr MICHAEL R. MACE (acting)
Vice-Pres. for Academic Affairs: ANTHONY PILTZ
Vice-Pres. for Admissions: KELLY EDWARDS
Vice-Pres. for Advancement: GREG KOHN
Dir of Library: WILLIAM KEHLER
Library of 86,600 vols
Number of teachers: 83 (45 full-time, 38 part-time)
Number of students: 800
Publication: Rocky Today.

SALISH KOOTENAI COLLEGE

POB 70, Pablo, MT 59855
58138 US Highway 93, Pablo, MT 59855
Telephone: (406) 275-4800

Fax: (406) 275-4801
Internet: www.skc.edu
Founded 1976 as br. campus of Flathead Valley Community College, present name and status 1981
Tribal control
Academic year: September to June
Pres.: Dr LUANA ROSS
Academic Vice-Pres.: CARMEN TAYLOR
Vice-Pres. of Business Affairs: (vacant)
Dir for Library: FRED NOEL.

UNIVERSITY OF GREAT FALLS

1301 20th St, S, Great Falls, MT 59405
Telephone: (406) 791-5202
Fax: (406) 791-5393
E-mail: enroll@ugf.edu
Internet: www.ugf.edu
Founded 1932 as Great Falls Junior College for Women, present name 1995
Private control
Liberal arts college; 4-year and 2-year degree courses in education, human services and professional counselling
Pres.: Dr EUGENE J. MCALLISTER
Provost and Academic Vice-Pres.: Dr RICHARD MCDOWELL
Vice-Pres. for Enrolment Management: CHARLENE BROWN
Vice-Pres. for Finance and Human Resources: STACEY EVE
Vice-Pres. for Philanthropy: TENIS TENNYSON
Dir for Admissions and Records: R. HENSLEY
Information Services Librarian: SUSAN LEE
Registrar: KERRI KOTESKEY
Library of 97,353 vols
Number of teachers: 80
Number of students: 950

UNIVERSITY OF MONTANA

32 Campus Dr., Missoula, MT 59812
Telephone: (406) 243-0211
Fax: (406) 243-2797
Internet: www.umt.edu
Founded 1893
Pres.: Dr ROYCE C. ENGSTROM
Provost and Vice-Pres. for Academic Affairs: Dr PERRY J. BROWN
Exec. Vice-Pres.: JAMES P. FOLEY
Vice-Pres. for Admin. and Finance: ROBERT A. DURINGER
Vice-Pres. for Research and Devt: DAVID FORBES
Vice-Pres. for Student Affairs: Dr TERESA BRANCH
Registrar: EDWIN D. JOHNSON
Dean for Students: Dr CHARLES COUTURE
Dean of Libraries: BONNIE ALLEN
Library of 700,000 vols, 77,600 US govt documents
Number of teachers: 450
Number of students: 13,019

DEANS

College of Arts and Sciences: CHRISTOPHER COMER
College of Forestry and Conservation: Dr JAMES BURCHFIELD
College of Health Professions and Biomedical Sciences: Dr VERNON R. GRUND
College of Technology: BARRY GOOD
College of Visual and Performing Arts: STEPHEN KALM
Div. of Continuing Education: SHARON ALEXANDER
Graduate School: STEPHEN SPRANG
Phyllis J. Washington College of Education and Human Sciences: ROBERTA EVANS
School of Business Administration: Dr LARRY D. GIANCHETTA

School of Extended and Lifelong Learning:
Dr ROGER MACLEAN
School of Journalism: PEGGY KUHR (acting)
School of Law: Prof. IRMA S. RUSSELL

UNIVERSITY OF MONTANA WESTERN

710 S Atlantic St, Dillon, MT 59725
Telephone: (406) 683-7331
Fax: (406) 683-7493
E-mail: admissions@umwestern.edu
Internet: www.umwestern.edu
Founded 1893
State control
Academic year: September to June
Chancellor: Dr RICHARD STOREY
Provost and Vice-Chancellor for Academic
Affairs: Dr KARL ULRICH
Asst Provost: DONNA ROUSE
Vice-Chancellor for Admin. and Finance:
SUSAN BRIGGS
Dean for Outreach and Research: ANNELIESE
RIPLEY
Dean for Students: C. NICOLE HAZELBAKER
Dir for Admissions: CATHERINE REDHEAD
Dir for Devt and Alumni Relations: AMBERLY
PAHUT
Registrar: JASON KARCH
Library Dir: MICHAEL SCHULZ
Number of teachers: 50
Number of students: 1,379 (1,185 full-time,
194 part-time)

NEBRASKA

BELLEVUE UNIVERSITY

1000 Galvin Rd S, Bellevue, NE 68005
Telephone: (402) 293-2000
Fax: (402) 293-2020
E-mail: servicedesk@bellevue.edu
Internet: www.bellevue.edu
Founded 1966, present name and status 1994
Private control
Campuses in Midwest-Nebraska, Iowa and
South Dakota
Pres.: Dr MARY B. HAWKINS
Vice-Pres. for Academic Affairs: DONNA N.
MCDANIEL
Dean for Students: MICHELLE EPPLER
Registrar: PHILLIP E. CHAPMAN
Library Dir: ROBIN BERNSTEIN
Library of 105,000 vols
Number of teachers: 62
Number of students: 9,000
Publication: *The View*

DEANS

College of Arts and Sciences: Dr THERESE
MICHELS
College of Business: Dr RODERIC HEWLETT
College of Information Technology: MARY
DOBRANSKY
College of Professional Studies: Dr MARTHA
MUÑOZ

CHADRON STATE COLLEGE

1000 Main St, Chadron, NE 69337
Telephone: (308) 432-6000
Fax: (308) 432-6464
E-mail: inquire@csc.edu
Internet: www.csc.edu
Founded 1911
State control
Academic year: August to May (2 semesters)
Pres.: Dr JANIE C. PARK
Vice-Pres. for Academic and Student Affairs:
Dr LOIS VEATH
Vice-Pres. for Admin. and Finance: DALE
GRANT

Vice-Pres. for Enrolment Management and
Student Services: Dr R. RANDY RHINE
Registrar: DALE WILLIAMSON
Library Dir: MILTON WOLF
Library of 200,000 vols
Number of teachers: 101 (full-time)
Number of students: 2,759

DEANS

School of Business, Entrepreneurship,
Applied and Mathematical Sciences and
Sciences: Dr JOEL R. HYER
School of Education, Human Performance,
Counseling, Psychology and Social Work:
Dr MARGARET R. CROUSE
School of Liberal Arts: Dr CHARLES E. SNARE

CLARKSON COLLEGE

101 S 42nd St, Omaha, NE 68131-2739
Telephone: (402) 552-3100
Fax: (402) 552-6057
E-mail: admiss@clarksoncollege.edu
Internet: www.clarksoncollege.edu
Founded 1884
Private control
Areas of study: nursing and health care
administration
Pres.: Dr LOUIS W. BURGHER
Vice-Pres. for Academic Affairs: Dr JODY
WOODWORTH
Vice-Pres. for Operations: TONY DAMEWOOD
Dir for Admissions: DENISE WORK
Registrar: MICHELE STIRTZ
Dir for Library Services: NANCY RALSTON
Number of teachers: 26
Number of students: 980

COLLEGE OF SAINT MARY

7000 Mercy Rd, Omaha, NE 68106-2377
Telephone: (402) 399-2400
Fax: (402) 399-2341
E-mail: academicaffairs@csm.edu
Internet: www.csm.edu
Founded 1923
Private control
Academic year: August to August
Divs of arts and sciences, health care profes-
sions, professional studies, graduate studies;
campus in Lincoln (Nebraska)
Pres.: Dr MARYANNE STEVENS
Vice-Pres. for Academic Affairs: Dr CHRIS-
TINE PHARR
Vice-Pres. for Enrolment Services: JOE SZEJK
Vice-Pres. for Finance and Admin.: SARAH
KOTTICH
Vice-Pres. for Institutional Advancement:
VERLYN SCHUELER
Vice-Pres. for Student Devt: Dr TARA KNUD-
SON CARL
Registrar: DEBBIE NUGEN
Library Dir: SARAH WILLIAMS
Number of teachers: 54
Number of students: 1,000
Publication: *College of Saint Mary Magazine*
(3 a year).

CONCORDIA UNIVERSITY—
NEBRASKA

800 N Columbia Ave, Seward, NE 68434
Telephone: (402) 643-3651
Fax: (402) 643-4073
E-mail: info@cune.edu
Internet: www.cune.edu
Founded 1894
Private control
Academic year: August to May
Pres. and CEO: Rev. Dr BRIAN L. FRIEDRICH
Provost: Rev. Dr JENNY MUELLER-ROEBKE
Assoc. Provost: Dr LISA ASHBY

Chief Financial Officer: DAVID KUMM
Vice-Pres. for Enrolment Management, Stu-
dent Services and Athletics: SCOTT SEEVERS
Vice-Pres. for Institutional Advancement:
Rev. RICHARD MADDOX
Registrar: EDWIN SIFFRING
Dir for Library Services: PHILIP HENDRICKSON
Library: see Libraries and Archives
Number of teachers: 65
Number of students: 2,200
Publications: *Broadcaster, Issues in Chris-
tian Education* (3 a year)

DEANS

College of Arts and Sciences: Dr BRENT
ROYUK
College of Education: Dr RON BORK

CREIGHTON UNIVERSITY

2500 California Plaza, Omaha, NE 68178
Telephone: (402) 280-2700
Fax: (402) 280-2727
Internet: www.creighton.edu
Founded 1878, chartered 1879; attached to
Soc. of Jesus
Private control
Academic year: August to May
Pres.: TIMOTHY R. LANNON
Vice-Pres. for Academic Affairs: Prof.
PATRICK J. BORCHERS
Vice-Pres. for Admin.: JOHN L. WILHELM
Vice-Pres. for Finance: JAN D MADSEN
Vice-Pres. for Health Sciences: DONALD R.
FREY
Vice-Pres. for Information Technology: BRIAN
A. YOUNG
Vice-Pres. for Student Services and Dean for
Students: Dr JOHN C. CERNECH
Vice-Pres. for Univ. Relations: (vacant)
Gen. Counsel: JAMES S. JANSEN
Registrar: PATRICIA GRAFELMAN HALL
Dir for Alumni Memorial Library: MICHAEL J.
LACROIX
Library of 916,571 vols, 1.9m. microforms
Number of teachers: 985 (759 full-time, 226
part-time)
Number of students: 7,730
Publications: *Creighton Law Review* (4 a
year), *Creighton University Magazine* (4 a
year)

DEANS

Arts and Sciences: Dr ROBERT J. LUEGER
Business Administration: Dr ANTHONY R.
HENDRICKSON
Dentistry: MARK A. LATTA
Graduate School: GAIL M. JENSEN
Law: Prof. MARIANNE CULHANE
Medicine: ROWEN K. ZETTERMAN
Nursing: Dr ELEANOR V. HOWELL
Pharmacy and Health Professions: J. CHRIS-
TOPHER BRADBERRY
University College: GAIL M. JENSEN

PROFESSORS

ABEL, P., Pharmacology
AGRAWAL, D., Biomedical Sciences
ALLEN, R., Pathology
ANDERSON, R., Internal Medicine
ANDERSON, T., Law School Instruction
BAECHLE, T., Exercise Sciences
BEISEL, K., Biomedical Sciences
BERTONI, J., Neurology
BEWTRA, C., Pathology
BHATIA, S., Adult and Child Psychiatry
BIRMINGHAM, E., Law School Instruction
BROCK, B., Education
BRUMBACK, R., Pathology
BUCKO, R., Sociology
CARLSON, J., Philosophy
CASALE, T., Internal Medicine
CASEY, M., Obstetrics and Gynaecology

CHENG, S., Mathematics and Computer Sciences
CHERNEY, M., Physics
CHIOU, R., Urological Surgery
CHU, C., Adult Psychiatry
CIPOLLA, S., Physics
CLARK, T., Political Science and International Relations
CULLEN, D., Internal Medicine
DALLON, C., Law School Instruction
DEWAN, N., Internal Medicine
DICKEL, C., Education
DOWD, JR, F., Pharmacology
ECKERSON, J., Exercise Sciences
FEEZELL, R., Philosophy
FENNER, G., Law School Instruction
FILIPI, C., General Surgery
FITZGIBBONS, JR, R., General Surgery
FLECKY, M., Fine and Performing Arts
FLEMING, A., Obstetrics and Gynaecology
FLETCHER, S., Paediatric Cardiology
FORSE, R., General Surgery
FRITZSCH, B., Biomedical Sciences
GAINES, R., General Surgery
GALLAGHER, J., Internal Medicine
GATALICA, Z., Pathology
GOSS, E., MacAllister Chair
GREEN, J., Law School Instruction
GREENSPOON, L., Klutznick Chair
HADDAD, A., Center for Health Policy and Ethics
HALLWORTH, R., Biomedical Sciences
HAMM, M., Graff Chair in Catholic Theology
HARMLESS, J., Theology
HARPER, C., Sociology
HAUSER, R., Theology
HE, Z., Biomedical Sciences
HEANEY, R., University Chair
HOPP, R., Paediatric Allergy
HULCE, M., Chemistry
KELLY, M., Law School Instruction
KROGSTAD, J., Accounting
LANSPA, S., Internal Medicine
LAPPE, J., Internal Medicine
LEAK, G., Psychology
LOGGIE, B., Surgery Oncology
LOVAS, S., Biomedical Sciences
LYNCH, H., Preventive Medicine
McGUIRE, M., Orthopaedic Surgery
McLAUGHLIN WITTEBORT, B., Biomedical Sciences
MACK, R., Law School Instruction
MALIK, D., Mathematics and Computer Sciences
MALINA, B., Theology
MANGRUM, R., Yossem Chair
MATTSON, B., Chemistry
MELILLI, K., Law School Instruction
MOHIUDDIN, S., Internal Medicine
MOOSS, A., Cardiology Education
MORDESON, J., Mathematics and Computer Sciences
MORSE, E., Law School Instruction
MUELLER, J., Theology
MURPHY, R., Biomedical Sciences
MURRAY, J., Philosophy
MURRAY, T., Pharmacology
MURTHY, V., Economics and Finance
NAIR, C., Cardiology Education
NAIR, P., Computer Science
NATH, R., McGraw Chair
NEUMEISTER, K., Law School Instruction
O'BRIEN, J., Internal Medicine
O'KEEFE IV, J., Theology
PEARSON, E., Law School Instruction
PETTY, F., Psychiatry Research
PETZEL, D., Biomedical Sciences
QUINN, T., Biomedical Sciences
RAVAL, V., Accounting
RECKER, R., Internal Medicine
RENDELL, M., Internal Medicine
RENO, R., Theology
RICH, E., Internal Medicine
ROY-HEWITSON, L., Modern Languages and Literatures
SARMA, D., Pathology

SEGER, J., Physics
SIMKINS, R., Theology
SPENCER, B., English
STEPHENS, W., Philosophy
STONE, N., Psychology
SUGIMOTO, J., Cardiac Surgery
SULLIVAN, P., Psychiatry Research
TEPLY, L., Law School Instruction
VOLKMER, R., Law School Instruction
WELIE, J., Center for Health Policy and Ethics
WHITE, M., Law School Instruction
WHITE, R., Philosophy
WHITTEN, R., Law School Instruction
WILLIAMS, M., Cardiology
WILSON, D., Forensic Psychiatry
WINGENDER, J., Economics and Finance
WORKMAN, J., Management and Marketing
WRIGHT, W., Kenefick Chair in Humanities
YEE, J., Biomedical Sciences
ZACH, T., Paediatric Newborn Medicine
ZACHARIAS, G., English
ZEHNDER, J., Environmental and Atmospheric Sciences

DOANE COLLEGE

1014 Boswell, Crete, NE 68333
Telephone: (402) 826-2161
Fax: (402) 826-8600
E-mail: admissions@doane.edu
Internet: www.doane.edu

Founded 1872
Private control

Divs of fine arts and humanities, economics and business, science, mathematics, and information science and technology, social sciences and education; campuses at Lincoln and Grand Island (Nebraska)

Pres.: Dr JACQUE CARTER
Vice-Pres. for Academic Affairs and Dean for the Faculty: Dr JOHN M. BURNEY
Vice-Pres. for Admission: JOEL WEYAND
Vice-Pres. for Advancement: JERRY WOOD
Vice-Pres. for Student Leadership: KIM JACOBS
Vice-Pres. for Finance and Admin.: JULIE SCHMIDT
Vice-Pres. for Information Services: MIKE CARPENTER
Registrar: DENISE ELLIS
Library Dir: JAYNE GERMER

Library of 221,435 vols
Number of teachers: 104
Number of students: 2,950

GRACE UNIVERSITY

1311 S Ninth St, Omaha, NE 68108-3629
Telephone: (402) 449-2800
Fax: (402) 341-9587
E-mail: admissions@graceuniversity.edu
Internet: www.graceuniversity.edu

Founded 1943 as Grace Bible Institute, present name 1995
Private control
Academic year: August to June

Pres.: Dr JAMES P. ECKMAN
Exec. Vice-Pres.: MICHAEL JAMES
Dir for Admissions: TARA KOTH
Academic Dean: Dr JOHN D. HOLMES
Dean for Enrolment Management: CHRIS PRUITT
Dean for Student Services: DEB OSMANSON
Registrar: KRIS J. UDD
Library Dir: BEN BRICK

Number of teachers: 15
Number of students: 578 (509 undergraduate, 69 graduate)

HASTINGS COLLEGE

710 N Turner, Hastings, NE 68901
Telephone: (402) 463-2402
Internet: www.hastings.edu

Founded 1882
Private control

Depts of art, biology, chemistry, communication arts, computer science, English, foreign languages and literatures, history, humanities, mathematics, music, nursing, philosophy, physical education, physics, political science, psychology, sociology, teacher education, theatre

Pres.: DENNIS TROTTER
Vice-Pres. for Academic Affairs: CLARK HENDLEY
Vice-Pres. for Enrollment Management: MJ HUEBNER
Vice-Pres. for Finance and Admin.: KAY LANGSETH
Vice-Pres. for Student Affairs: JOAN McCARTHY
Registrar: DAN PETERS
Librarian: ROBERT NEDDERMAN

Library of 140,000 vols, 525 print journals
Number of teachers: 69
Number of students: 1,150

MIDLAND UNIVERSITY

900 N Clarkson St, Fremont, NE 68025
Telephone: (402) 941-6250
Fax: (402) 721-0250
E-mail: info@midlandu.edu
Internet: www.midlandu.edu

Founded 1883, present name and status 2010
Private control
Academic year: August to May
Liberal arts college

Pres.: Dr BENJAMIN E. SASSE
Vice-Pres.: GREG FRITZ
Vice-Pres. for Academic Affairs: Dr STEVE BULLOCK
Vice-Pres. for Finance and Admin.: JODI BENJAMIN
Dir for Admissions: ELIZA FERZELY
Dir for Library: Dr THOMAS E. BOYLE

Library of 114,000 vols
Number of teachers: 55
Number of students: 950

NEBRASKA CHRISTIAN COLLEGE

12550 S 114th St, Papillion, NE 68046
Telephone: (402) 935-9400
Fax: (402) 935-9500
E-mail: info@nechristian.edu
Internet: www.nechristian.edu

Founded 1944
Private control
Academic year: August to May (2 semesters)

Areas of study: biblical studies, Christian education, church music, deaf ministries, family life ministry, general studies, missions, pastoral ministries, youth ministries

Pres. and CEO: RICHARD D. MILLIKEN
Vice-Pres. for Academics and Chief Academic Officer: MARK S. KRAUSE
Dir for Admissions: BRIAN TAYLOR
Dean for Students: DAVID HUSKEY
Registrar: MARK HUDDLESTON
Librarian: LINDA LU LLOYD

Number of teachers: 24
Number of students: 162

NEBRASKA METHODIST COLLEGE OF NURSING AND ALLIED HEALTH

720 N 87th St, Omaha, NE 68114
Telephone: (402) 354-7000
E-mail: admissions@methodistcollege.edu
Internet: www.methodistcollege.edu

Founded 1891 as Diploma School of Nursing, present status 1985

Private control

Divs of arts and sciences, health professions, professional development, nursing

Pres.: Dr DENNIS JOSLIN

Vice-Pres. for Academic Affairs: Dr KENNETH RYALLS

Vice-Pres. for Student Affairs: Dr KRISTINE HESS

Dir for Enrolment Services and Admissions: SARA HANSON

Dean for Students: Dr MELISSA HOFFMAN

Registrar: MELINDA STONER

Library Dir: BEVERLY SEDLACEK

Library of 12,000 vols

Number of teachers: 60

Number of students: 700

NEBRASKA WESLEYAN UNIVERSITY

5000 St Paul Ave, Lincoln, NE 68504-2794

Telephone: (402) 466-2371

Fax: (402) 465-2179

E-mail: info@nebrwesleyan.edu

Internet: www.nebrwesleyan.edu

Founded 1887

Private control

Pres.: FREDERIK OHLES

Provost: JUDITH MUYSKENS

Vice-Pres. for Advancement: JOHN GREVING

Vice-Pres. for External Relations: PATTY KARTHAUSER

Vice-Pres. for Finance and Admin.: CLARK CHANDLER

Dir for Admissions: DAVID DUZIK

Dean for Students: PETER ARMSTRONG

Registrar: BETTE OLSON

Univ. Librarian: JOHN MONTAG

Library of 200,000 vols

Number of teachers: 109

Number of students: 2,100

DEANS

College of Liberal Arts and Sciences: Dr KATHY WOLFE

University College: Dr JACK SIEMSEN

PERU STATE COLLEGE

POB 10, 600 Hoyt St, Peru, NE 68421

Telephone: (402) 872-3815

E-mail: admissions@peru.edu

Internet: www.peru.edu

Founded 1867

Pres.: Dr DAN HANSON

Vice-Pres. for Academic Affairs: Dr TODD L. DREW

Vice-Pres. for Admin. and Finance: BRUCE BATTERSON

Vice-Pres. for Enrolment Management and Student Affairs: MICHAELA WILLIS

Library Dir: ROGER BECKER

Library of 600,000 vols

Number of teachers: 47

Number of students: 1,745

DEANS

Graduate Studies: GREG SEAY

School of Arts and Sciences: Dr PATRICK FORTNEY

School of Education: Dr JODI KUPPER

School of Professional Studies: GREG GALARDI

SAINT GREGORY THE GREAT SEMINARY

800 Fletcher Rd, Seward, NE 68434-8145

Telephone: (402) 643-4052

Fax: (402) 643-6964

E-mail: sggs@stgregoryseminary.edu

Internet: www.stgregoryseminary.edu

Founded 1997

Private control

Academic year: August to May (2 semesters)

Rector: Rev. JOHN T. FOLDA

Academic Dean: Rev. JEFFREY R. EICKHOFF

Librarian: Dr TERRENCE D. NOLLEN

Library of 33,000 vols.

UNION COLLEGE

3800 S 48th St, Lincoln, NE 68506

Telephone: (402) 486-2600

Fax: (402) 486-2895

E-mail: ucinfo@ucollege.edu

Internet: www.ucollege.edu

Founded 1891

Private control

Academic year: August to May

Divs of business and computer science, fine arts, health sciences, human development, humanities, religion, science, mathematics

Pres.: Dr JOHN WAGNER

Vice-Pres. for Academic Admin.: MALCOLM RUSSELL

Vice-Pres. for Advancement: LuANN DAVIS

Vice-Pres. for Enrolment and Student Financial Affairs: NADINE NELSON

Vice-Pres. for Student Services: LINDA WYSONG BECKER

Registrar: MICHELLE YOUNKIN

Library Dir: SABRINA RILEY

Library of 176,653 vols

Number of teachers: 73

Number of students: 886

Publication: *CORDmagazine* (2 a year).

UNIVERSITY OF NEBRASKA

Telephone: (402) 472-2111

Fax: (402) 472-1237

Internet: www.nebraska.edu

Founded 1869

State control

Pres.: JAMES B. MILLIKEN

Provost and Exec. Vice-Pres.: LINDA R. PRATT

Vice-Pres. and Gen. Counsel: JOEL D. PEDERSEN

Vice-Pres. for Business and Finance: DAVID E. LECHNER

Vice-Pres. for Univ. Affairs: SHARON STEPHAN

Number of teachers: 4,582 (3,460 full-time, 1,122 part-time)

Number of students: 42,798.

CONSTITUENT CAMPUSES

University of Nebraska at Kearney

905 W 25th St, Kearney, NE 68849-0601

Telephone: (308) 865-8441

Fax: (308) 865-8157

Internet: www.unk.edu

Founded 1903

Chancellor: DOUGLAS A. KRISTENSEN

Vice-Chancellor for Academic Affairs: CHARLES BICAK

Vice-Chancellor for Business and Finance: BARBARA L. JOHNSON

Vice-Chancellor for Univ. Relations: CURTIS CARLSON

Dean for Student Affairs: Dr JOSEPH A. ORAVECZ

Registrar: KIMRA F. SCHIPPOREIT

Dean for Libraries: JANET WILKE

Library of 250,000 vols, 210,000 print titles, 11,000 e-books, 114,000 periodical vols, 275,000 USA govt documents, 17,000 state govt documents

Number of teachers: 425 (307 full-time, 118 part-time)

Number of students: 5,702

DEANS

College of Business and Technology: TIM BURKINK

College of Education: ED SCANTLING

College of Fine Arts and Humanities: Dr WILLIAM JURMA

College of Graduate Studies and Research: KENYA TAYLOR

College of Natural and Social Sciences: JOHN C. LA DUKE

University of Nebraska at Lincoln

1400 R St, Lincoln, NE 68588-0419

Telephone: (402) 472-7211

Fax: (402) 472-5110

Internet: www.unl.edu

Founded 1869

Chancellor: HARVEY S. PERLMAN

Sr Vice-Chancellor for Academic Affairs: Dr ELLEN WEISSINGER

Vice-Chancellor for Business and Finance: CHRISTINE A. JACKSON

Vice-Chancellor for Research and Economic Devt: Dr PREM PAUL

Vice-Chancellor for Student Affairs: Dr JUAN FRANCO

Vice-Pres. and Vice-Chancellor for Institute of Agriculture and Natural Resources: Dr RONNIE GREEN

Dean for Univ. Libraries: JOAN R. GIESECKE

Library: see Libraries and Archives

Number of teachers: 2,094 (1,697 full-time, 397 part-time)

Number of students: 22,185

Publications: *Nebraska Journal of Economics and Business, Nebraska Law Review, Prairie Schooner* (4 a year), *Quarterly Journal of Finance and Accounting, University of Nebraska Studies*

DEANS

College of Agricultural Sciences and Natural Resources: Dr STEVEN S. WALLER

College of Architecture: Dr JAMES O'HANLON

College of Arts and Sciences: DAVID MANDERSCHEID

College of Business Administration: Dr DONDE PLOWMAN

College of Education and Human Sciences: Dr MARJORIE KOSTELNIK

College of Engineering: TIMOTHY WEI

College of Fine and Performing Arts: CHRISTIN MAMIYA

College of Journalism and Mass Communications: Dr GARY KEBBEL

College of Law: Dr SUSAN POSER

Graduate Studies: PATRICK DUSSAULT

University of Nebraska at Omaha

6001 Dodge St, Omaha, NE 68182

Telephone: (402) 554-2100

Fax: (402) 554-3555

Internet: www.unomaha.edu

Founded 1908

Chancellor: Dr JOHN CHRISTIANSEN

Sr Vice-Chancellor for Academic and Student Affairs: Dr B. J. REED

Dir for Univ. Relations: TIMOTHY KALDAHL

Dean for Univ. Library: STEPHEN SHORB

Library of 700,000 vols, 1.7m. micro-material items, 2,300 print subscriptions, 45,000 e-subscriptions

Number of teachers: 884 (490 full-time, 394 part-time)

Number of students: 11,657

DEANS

College of Arts and Sciences: Dr DAVID BOOCKER

College of Business Administration: Dr LOUIS POL

College of Communication, Fine Arts and Media: GAIL F. BAKER

College of Education: NANCY EDICK
College of Information Science and Technology: HESHAM H. ALI
College of Public Affairs and Community Service: JOHN BARTLE (acting)
Graduate Studies: Dr DEBORAH SMITH-HOWELL
International Studies and Programs: THOMAS E. GOUTTIERRE

University of Nebraska Medical Center

42nd and Emile, Omaha, NE 68198
Telephone: (402) 559-4000
Fax: (402) 559-4396
E-mail: unmcgraduatestudies@unmc.edu
Internet: www.unmc.edu
Founded 1880, present status 1902
Chancellor: Dr HAROLD M. MAURER
Vice-Chancellor for Academic Affairs: Dr DAVID CROUSE
Vice-Chancellor for External Affairs: ROBERT D. BARTEE
Vice-Chancellor for Research: Dr JENNIFER LARSEN
Library Dir: Dr NANCY N. WOELFL
Library of 249,000 vols, 67,700 monographs and textbooks, 479 e-books, 6,700 e-journals
Number of teachers: 1,156 (951 full-time, 205 part-time)
Number of students: 3,253

DEANS

College of Dentistry: Dr JOHN REINHARDT
College of Medicine: BRADLEY BRITIGAN
College of Nursing: Dr JULIANN SEBASTIAN
College of Pharmacy: Dr COURTNEY FLETCHER
College of Public Health: Dr AYMAN EL-MOHANDES
Graduate Studies: Dr DAVID A. CROUSE
School of Allied Health Professions: Dr KYLE P. MEYER

WAYNE STATE COLLEGE

1111 Main St, Wayne, NE 68787
Telephone: (402) 375-7000
E-mail: admissions@wsc.edu
Internet: www.wsc.edu
Founded 1910
State control
Academic year: August to July (2 semesters)
Pres.: CURT FRYE
Vice-Pres. and Dean for Students: Dr JEFF CARSTENS
Vice-Pres. for Academic Affairs: Dr ROBERT McCUE
Vice-Pres. for Admin. and Finance: JEAN DALE
Vice-Pres. for Devt: PHYLLIS CONNER
Library Dir: DAVE GRABER
Library of 350,000 vols
Number of teachers: 125 (full-time)
Number of students: 3,571

DEANS

School of Arts and Humanities: Dr JAMES F. O'DONNELL
School of Business and Technology: Dr VAUGHN BENSON
School Education and Counseling: Dr NEAL SCHNOOR
School of Natural and Social Sciences: Dr JON DALAGER

YORK COLLEGE

1125 E Eighth St, York, NE 68467
Telephone: (402) 363-5600
Fax: (402) 363-5623
E-mail: president@york.edu
Internet: www.york.edu
Founded 1890

Private control
Academic year: August to May
Offers Bachelors in liberal arts and Masters of Arts in education
Chancellor: WAYNE BAKER
Pres.: Dr STEVE W. ECKMAN
Vice-Pres. for Admissions: WILLIE SANCHEZ
Vice-Pres. for Advancement: BRENT MAGNER
Vice-Pres. for Student Devt and Dean for Students: Dr SHANE MOUNTJOY
Academic Dean: Dr TRACEY WYATT
Registrar: TOD J. MARTIN
Dir for Library: KEN GUNSELMAN
Number of teachers: 49
Number of students: 507

NEVADA

MORRISON UNIVERSITY

10315 Professional Circle, Suite 201, Reno, NV 89521
Telephone: (866) 381-6050
Fax: (775) 850-0711
E-mail: info@morrisonuniversity.com
Internet: anthem.edu/morrison
Founded 1902 as Nevada Business Institute, present name 1999; attached to Anthem Education
Private control
Academic year: September to September
Offers business-related education and training; Bachelors and Masters degree programmes
Chancellor and CEO: Dr JAMES D. HUTTON
Pres.: MARY MORRISON-LEMBERES
Exec. Vice-Pres.: NORMAN W. SEROSKI
Vice-Pres. for Academics: Dr JOHN BURRUEL
Registrar: GERRE YOUNG
Library Dir: USHA MEHTA
Number of teachers: 20
Number of students: 239

NEVADA SYSTEM OF HIGHER EDUCATION

2601 Enterprise Rd, Reno, NV 89512
Telephone: (775) 784-4901
Fax: (775) 784-1127
Internet: system.nevada.edu
Chancellor: DAN KLAICH
Vice-Chancellor for Academic and Student Affairs: CRYSTAL ABBA
Vice-Chancellor for Finance: MARK STEVENS
Vice-Chancellor for Health Sciences: Dr MARCIA TURNER
Vice-Chancellor for Information Technology: STEVEN ZINK.

CONSTITUENT INSTITUTIONS

College of Southern Nevada

W Charleston Campus, 6375 W. Charleston Blvd, Las Vegas, NV 89146
Telephone: (702) 651-5000
Internet: www.csn.edu
Founded 1971
3 Main campuses and multiple academic sites throughout the S Nevada area
Pres.: Dr MICHAEL D. RICHARDS
Sr Vice-Pres. for Finance and Admin.: PATRICIA CHARLTON
Vice-Pres. for Student Affairs: Dr CHEMENE CRAWFORD
Vice-Pres. for Academic Affairs: Dr DARREN DIVINE
Number of teachers: 1,468 (492 full-time, 976 part-time)
Number of students: 43,561 (11,742 full-time, 31,819 part-time)

DEANS

School of Advanced and Applied Technologies: Dr MICHAEL SPANGLER
School of Arts and Letters: WENDY WEINER
School of Business, Hospitality and Public Services: HYLA WINTERS
School of Education, Behavioral and Social Sciences: CHARLES OKEKE
School of Science & Mathematics: SALLY JOHNSTON
Ralph & Betty Engelstad School of Health Sciences: PATRICIA CASTRO

Great Basin College

1500 College Parkway, Elko, NV 89801
Telephone: (775) 738-8493
Fax: (775) 738-8771
Internet: www.gbcnv.edu
Founded 1967
Career and technical education; community education; fine arts; health science; humanities and social sciences; mathematics, science, business, and computing
Pres. and Vice-Pres. for Student Services: LYNN MAHLBERG
Vice-Pres. for Academic Affairs: Dr MIKE McFARLANE
Library of 46,828 vols, 656 microfilms and 113 subscriptions
Number of students: 3,835

Nevada State College

1125 Nevada State Dr., Henderson, NV 89002
Telephone: (702) 992-2130
Fax: (702) 992-2111
E-mail: admissions@nsc.nevada.edu
Internet: www.nsc.nevada.edu
Founded 2002
Pres.: Dr BART PATTERSON
Provost and Exec. Vice-Pres.: Dr ERIKA BECK
Sr Vice-Pres. for Finance and Admin.: HARRY E. NEEL, JR
Library of 14,000 vols
Number of students: 3,000

DEANS

School of Education: Dr JIM LaBUDA
School of Liberal Arts and Sciences: Dr ANDY KUNIYUKI
School of Nursing: Dr SHIRLEE J. SNYDER

University of Nevada, Las Vegas

4505 S Maryland Parkway, Las Vegas, NV 89154
Telephone: (702) 895-3011
E-mail: admissions@unlv.edu
Internet: go.unlv.edu
Founded 1957
Academic year: August to May
Pres.: Dr NEAL SMATRESK
Exec. Vice-Pres. and Provost: Dr MICHAEL BOWERS
Vice-Pres. for Advancement: Dr WILLIAM G. BOLDT
Vice-Pres. for Diversity Initiatives and Govt Affairs: LUIS VALERA
Sr Vice-Pres. for Finance and Business: GERRY BOMOTTI
Vice-Pres. for Student Affairs: Dr JUANITA FAIN
Vice-Pres. for Research and Dean of the Graduate College: Dr RONALD SMITH
Assoc. Vice-Pres. for Community Relations: SCHYLER RICHARDS
Sr Assoc. Vice-Pres. for Devt: NANCY STROUSE
Registrar: JEFF HALVERSON
Dean of Libraries: PATRICIA A. IANNUZZI
Library: 3m. vols
Number of teachers: 3,100
Number of students: 27,364

DEANS

College of Education: Dr WILLIAM SPEER
College of Fine Arts: Dr JEFFREY P. KOEP
College of Graduate Studies: Dr RON SMITH
College of Health Sciences: Dr CAROLYN SABO
College of Liberal Arts: Dr CHRISTOPHER C. HUDGINS
College of Sciences: Dr TIMOTHY L. PORTER
Greenspun College of Urban Affairs: Dr LEE BERNICK
Honors College: Dr PETER L. STARKWEATHER
Howard R. Hughes College of Engineering: Dr RAMA VENKAT
Lee Business School: PAUL JARLEY
William F. Harrah College of Hotel Administration: DONALD D. SNYDER
William S. Boyd School of Law: JOHN VALERY WHITE

University of Nevada, Reno

1664 N Virginia St, Reno, NV 89557-0208
Telephone: (775) 784-1110
Fax: (775) 784-6429
E-mail: asknevada@unr.edu
Internet: www.unr.edu

Founded 1874 as State Univ. of Nevada in Elko, present location 1885
Academic year: August to May

Pres.: Dr MARC JOHNSON
Exec. Vice-Pres. and Provost: Dr HEATHER HARDY
Vice-Provost for Extended Studies: Dr FRED HOLMAN
Vice-Provost for Instruction and Undergraduate Programmes: Dr WILLIAM CATHEY
Vice-Pres. for Admin. and Finance: RONALD ZUREK
Vice-Pres. for Devt and Alumni Relations: JOHN K. CARUTHERS
Vice-Pres. for Information Technology and Dean of Libraries: STEVEN D. ZINK
Vice-Pres. for Marketing and Communications: CINDY POLLARD
Vice-Pres. for Research: MARSHA READ
Vice-Pres. for Student Services: SHANNON ELLIS
Registrar: MELISSA N. CHOROSZY

Library: 1.1m. vols
Number of teachers: 941
Number of students: 17,679

Publication: *Electronic Journal of Science Education* (4 a year)

DEANS

College of Agriculture, Biotechnology, and Natural Resources: RON PARDINI
College of Business.: GREG MOSIER
College of Education: CHRISTINE CHENEY
College of Engineering: EMMANUEL MARAGAKIS
College of Liberal Arts: SCOTT CASPER
College of Science: JEFF THOMPSON
Cooperative Extension: KAREN HINTON
Division of Health Sciences: DENISE MONTCALM
Donald W. Reynolds School of Journalism and Advanced Media Studies: WILLIAM WINTER
Extended Studies: FRED B. HOLMAN
Graduate School: MARSHA READ
School of Medicine: Dr THOMAS L. SCHWENK

Western Nevada College

2201 W College Parkway, Carson City, NV 89703
Telephone: (775) 445-3000
E-mail: info_desk@wnc.edu
Internet: www.wnc.edu

Founded 1971
3 Campuses: Carson City Campus, Douglas Campus and Fallon Campus
Public control
Academic year: August to May

Pres.: Dr CAROL LUCEY
Vice-Pres. for Finance and Admin. Services: DANIEL NEVERETT
Dir for Information and Marketing Services: ANNE HANSEN

Library of 46,000 vols, 185 magazines, 12 newspaper subscriptions, 1,000 maps and 18,000 full-text journals
Number of students: 5,300

SIERRA NEVADA COLLEGE

999 Tahoe Blvd, Incline Village, NV 89451-9500
Telephone: (775) 831-1314
Fax: (775) 831-1696
E-mail: admissions@sierranevada.edu
Internet: www.sierranevada.edu

Founded 1969
Private control
Academic year: August to May

Liberal arts college; interdisciplinary curriculum combining entrepreneurial thinking and environmental, social, economic and educational sustainability

Pres.: Dr LYNN GILLETTE
Provost and Exec. Vice-Pres.: SHANNON BEETS
Dean of Faculty: DAN O'BRYAN
Registrar: ROSEANNA BEENK
Library Dir: Dr BETTS MARKLE

Number of teachers: 130
Number of students: 1,300 (500 undergraduate, 800 graduate)

NEW HAMPSHIRE

CHESTER COLLEGE OF NEW ENGLAND

40 Chester St, Chester, NH 03036
Telephone: (603) 887-4401
Fax: (603) 887-1777
E-mail: admissions@chestercollege.edu
Internet: chestercollege.edu

Founded 1965 as White Pines College, present status 1999, present name 2002
Private control
Academic year: August to May (2 semesters)

Areas of study: creative writing, fine arts, graphic design and communication arts, interdisciplinary arts, photography and media arts, professional writing

Pres. and CEO: Dr ROBERT A. BAINES
Vice-Pres. for Academic Affairs and Student Services: LAURA IVES
Vice-Pres. for Admission and Marketing: ANTHONY PADILLA
Vice-Pres. for Operations and Finance: RICHARD BENOIT
Registrar: BARBARA GILL
Dir for Library Services: ERIC CRAPO

Library of 24,000 vols, 80 periodicals
Number of teachers: 49 (12 full-time, 37 part-time)
Number of students: 200

COLBY-SAWYER COLLEGE

541 Main St, New London, NH 03257-7835
Telephone: (603) 526-3000
Fax: (603) 526-3452
E-mail: colbyweb@colby-sawyer.edu
Internet: www.colby-sawyer.edu

Founded 1837 as New London Acad., present name 1975
Private control
Academic year: September to May (2 semesters)

Depts of business administration, education, environmental studies, exercise and sport sciences, fine and performing arts, health

studies, humanities, natural sciences, nursing, social sciences

Pres.: THOMAS C. GALLIGAN, JR
Academic Vice-Pres. and Dean for Faculty: DEBORAH A. TAYLOR
Vice-Pres. for Admin.: DOUGLAS C. ATKINS
Vice-Pres. for Advancement: ELIZABETH A. CAHILL
Vice-Pres. for Enrolment Management: GREGORY W. MATTHEWS
Vice-Pres. for Finance and Treas.: TODD EMMONS
Vice-Pres. for Student Devt and Dean for Students: DAVID A. SAUERWEIN
Academic Dean: BURTON KIRKWOOD
Registrar: CAROLE H. PARSONS
Library Dir: CARRIE THOMAS

Number of teachers: 118
Number of students: 1,250

DANIEL WEBSTER COLLEGE

20 University Dr., Nashua, NH 03063-1300
Telephone: (603) 577-6000
Fax: (603) 577-6001
E-mail: registrar@dwc.edu
Internet: www.dwc.edu

Founded 1965 as New England Aeronautical Institute
Private control
Academic year: August to May (2 semesters)

Pres.: ROBERT E. MYERS
Provost and Vice-Pres. of Academic Affairs: Dr MICHAEL FISHBEIN
Vice-Pres. for Advancement and Alumni Affairs: GAIL M. GARCEAU
Vice-Pres. for Business, Finance and Operations: THOMAS N. DICONZA
Vice-Pres. for Student Affairs: SUSAN C. ELSASS
Dean of Students: MICHELLE O'MALLEY
Registrar: MARILYN NIEUWEBOER
Library Dir: SUSAN WAGNER

Library of 34,000 vols
Number of teachers: 60
Number of students: 650

DEANS

School of Arts and Sciences: Dr KATHLEEN M. HIPP
School of Aviation and Sciences: JONATHAN PROHASKA
School of Business, Management and Professional Studies: Dr RONALD E. LIVINGSTON
School of Engineering and Computer Sciences: Dr NICHOLAS BERTOZZI

DARTMOUTH COLLEGE

6016 McNutt Hall, Hanover, NH 03755
Telephone: (603) 646-1110
Fax: (603) 646-2266
E-mail: contact@dartmouth.edu
Internet: www.dartmouth.edu

Founded 1769
Private control
Academic year: June to June

Pres.: JIM YONG KIM
Provost: CAROL L. FOLT (acting)
Sr Vice-Pres. for Advancement: CAROLYN A. PELZEL
Exec. Vice-Pres. and Chief Financial Officer: STEVEN N. KADISH
Vice-Pres. and Chief Human Resources Officer: MYRON S. McCOO
Vice-Pres. and Chief Information Officer: ELLEN WAITE-FRANZEN
Vice-Pres. for Campus Planning and Facilities: LINDA L. SNYDER
Vice-Pres. for Devt: THOMAS W. HERBERT
Vice-Pres. for Finance: MICHAEL WAGNER
Dean for Admissions and Financial Aid: MARIA LASKARIS
Registrar: MEREDITH H. BRAZ

Dean for Libraries: JEFFREY L. HORRELL (acting)

Library of 2,677,605 vols, 368,000 e-books, 24,000 video items, 192,000 maps, 450,000 photographs, 2,587,446 microforms, 55,382 current, 72,000 digital resources

Number of teachers: 1,004

Number of students: 6,141 (4,248 undergraduate, 1,893 graduate)

Publications: *Dartmouth Engineer* (2 a year), *Dartmouth Medicine* (4 a year), *Encrucijada* (online), *Linguistic Discovery* (online), *Tuck Today*

DEANS

College: CHARLOTTE H. JOHNSON (acting)

Faculty of Arts and Sceinces: MICHAEL MASTANDUNO (acting)

Geisel School of Medicine: WILEY W. SOUBA, JR (acting)

Graduate Studies: BRIAN POGUE

Thayer School of Engineering: JOSEPH J. HELBLE (acting)

Tuck School of Business: PAUL DANOS

PROFESSORS

Note: some professors serve in more than one department

Humanities

Department of African and African-American Studies:

ALVERSON, H. S., Anthropology
AMADIUMI, I., Religion
COOK, W., English
HALL, R. L., Sociology
KASFIR, N. M., Govt
LANGFORD, G. M., Biology
PEASE, D. L., English
SPITZER, L., History
WALKER, K., French and Italian
WILDER, C., History

Department of Art History:

JORDAN, J., Modern Art
KENSETH, J., Renaissance and Baroque Art

Department of Asian and Middle Eastern Languages and Literatures:

ALLAN, S., Chinese
GLINERT, L., Hebrew

Department of Classics:

BRADLEY, E. M., Greek and Latin Literature, Roman and Early Christian Art and Architecture
RUTTER, J. B., Classical Art and Archaeology, Archaeology of the Aegean
SCOTT, W. C., Greek and Latin Literature, Classical Drama, Homer
TATUM, J., Greek and Latin Literature, Ancient Fiction, the Classical Tradition, Roman Comedy

Department of Comparative Literature:

COOK, W., English
CREWE, J., English
GAYLORD, A. T., English
GEMUNDEN, G., German
GLINERT, J. A., Asian, Middle Eastern Languages and Literature
GREEN, M. J., French and Italian
HEFFERNAN, J. W., English
HIGGINS, L. A., French and Italian
HIRSCH, M., French and Italian
JEWELL, K. J., French and Italian
KOPPER, J. M., Russian
KRITZMAN, L. D., French and Italian
LAWRENCE, A., Film

Department of English:

BOOSE, L., English
COOK, W., English
CREWE, J., English and Comparative Literature
GAYLORD, A., English
HEBERT, E., English
HEFFERNAN, J. A. W., English

HUNTINGDON, C., English
McKEE, P., English
MATHIS, C., English and Creative Writing
RENZA, L., English
SACCIO, P., English and Shakespearean Studies
SILVER, B. R., English
SLEIGH, T., English
TRAVIS, P. W., English
WYKES, P., English

Department of Film and Television Studies:

LAWRENCE, A.

Department of French and Italian:

GREEN, M.
HIGGINS, L.
HIRSCH, M.
JEWELL, K.
KRITZMAN, L. D.
RASSIAS, J.
WALKER, K. L.

Department of German:

DUNCAN, B., German Language
GEMÜNDEN, G., German, Comparative Literature
SCHER, S. P., German, Comparative Literature

Department of Linguistics and Cognitive Science:

ALVERSON, H. S., Anthropology
DUNBAR, K., Education and Psychology
DUNCAN, B., German
GLINERT, L. H., AMELL
GRENOBLE, L., Russian
HUGHES, H. C., Psychology
JAHNER, E. A., English and Native American Studies
MOOR, J. H., Philosophy
PETTITO, L. A., Education and Psychology
SCHERR, B. P., Russian
SINNOTT-ARMSTRONG, W. P., Philosophy
SORENSEN, R. A., Philosophy
TAUBE, J., Psychology
TRAVIS, P. W., English
WALKER, K. L., French and Italian
WOLFORD, G. L., Psychology

Department of Music:

APPLETON, J. H.
O'NEAL, M.
PINKAS, S.

Department of Philosophy:

DRIVER, J.
GERT, B.
MOOR, J. H.
SINNOTT-ARMSTRONG, W.
SORENSEN, R.

Department of Religion:

ACKERMAN, S.
AMADIUME, I., African Religions
FRANKENBERRY, N., Philosophy of Religion, Women and Religion, Science and Religion
GREEN, R. M., Religious Ethics, Business Ethics
HENRICKS, R. G., Religions of China

Department of Russian:

GRENOBLE, L.
KOPPER, J.
LOSEFF, L.
SCHERR, B.

Department of Spanish and Portuguese:

BUENO-CHAVEZ, R.
PASTOR, B.

Department of Studio Art:

FRANK MOSS, B., IV
RANDALL, C.
THOMPSON, E.

Department of Theatre:

CRICKARD, L.
GAFFNEY, P.
GRENOBLE, L.

SPICER, M.

Women and Gender Studies:

ACKERMAN, S., Religion
AMADIUMI, I., Religion
BOOSE, L. E., English
DARROW, M. H., History
DOMOSH, M., Geography
FOWLER, L. L., Govt
FRANKENBERRY, N. K., Religion
GARROD, A. G., Education
GREEN, M. J., French and Italian
HIGGINS, L. A., French and Italian
HIRSCH, M., French and Italian
JEWELL, K. J., French and Italian
LAWRENCE, A., Film
SILVER, B. R., English
SPITZER, L., History

Science

Department of Biological Sciences:

BERGER, E. M., Molecular Genetics, Cell Biology
FOLT, C. L., Aquatic Ecology
GILBERT, J. J., Ecology, Aquatic Biology
GUERINOT, M. L., Molecular Genetics, Microbiology
HOLMES, R. T., Animal Behaviour, Ecology
LANGFORD, G. M., Cell Biology
McCLUNG, C. R., Molecular Genetics
McPEEK, M. A., Community Ecology, Evolution
PEART, D. R., Population and Community Ecology, Forest Ecology
SLOBODA, R. D., Cell Biology, Neurobiology
WITTERS, L. A., Human Biology, Endocrinology/Metabolism

Department of Chemistry:

BELBRUNO, J. J.
BRAUN, C. L.
CANTOR, R. S.
DITCHFIELD, R.
GRIBBLE, G. W.
HUGHES, R. P.
JACOBI, P. A.
LEMAL, D. M.
LIPSON, J. E. G.
SODERBERG, R. H.
SPENCER, T. A.
WILCOX, D. E.
WINN, J. S.

Department of Computer Science:

DONALD, B. R.
DRYSDALE, R. L., III
KOTZ, D. F.
MAKEDON, F. S.
ROCKMORE, D.

Department of Environmental Studies:

FRIEDLAND, A.
HOWARTH, R.
SHEPHERD, J.
VIRGINIA, R.

Department of Mathematics:

ARKOWITZ, M. A.
BAUMGARTNER, J. E.
BICKEL, T. F.
BOGART, K. P.
DOYLE, P.
GORDON, C. S.
GROSZEK, M.
LAHR, C. D.
POMERANCE, C. B.
ROCKMORE, D. N.
SHEMANSKE, T. R.
WALLACE, D. I.
WEBB, D. L.
WILLIAMS, D. P.

Department of Physics and Astronomy:

FESEN, C. G.
FESEN, R. A.
GLEISER, M.
HUDSON, M. K.
LaBELLE, J. W.
LAWRENCE, W. E.

MONTGOMERY, D. C.
MOOK, D. E.
THORSTENSEN, J. R.
WEGNER, G. A.
WYBOURNE, M. N.

Social Sciences

Department of Anthropology:

ALVERSON, H.
EICKELMAN, D. F.
ENDICOTT, K.
KAN, S.
NICHOLS, D. L.

Department of Economics:

BLANCHFLOWER, D. G.
FISCHEL, W. A.
GUSTMAN, A. L.
IRWIN, D. A.
KOHN, M.
MARION, N. P.
SAMWICK, A. A.
SCOTT, J. T.
SKINNER, J.
STAIGER, D. O.
VENTI, S. F.

Department of Education:

DUNBAR, K.
GARROD, A.
PETITTO, L. A.

Department of Geography:

DOMOSH, M.
MAGILLIGAN, F. J.
WRIGHT, R. A.

Department of Government:

FOWLER, L. L.
FREEDMAN, J. O.
KASFIR, N. M.
LEBOW, R. N.
MASTANDUNO, M.
SA'ADAH, M. A.
WINTERS, R. F.

Department of History:

CALLOWAY, C.
CROSSLEY, P. K.
DARROW, M.
ERMARTH, H. M.
GARTHWAITE, G. R.
NAVARRO, M.
NELSON, J. B.
SHEWMAKER, K. E.
SPITZER, L.
WHELAN, H. W.
WILDER, C. S.
WRIGHT, J.

Department of Latin American, Latino and Caribbean Studies:

BUENO-CHAVEZ, R., Spanish and Portuguese
NAVARRO, M., History
NICHOLS, D. L., Anthropology
PASTOR, B., Spanish and Portuguese
WALKER, K. L., French and Italian
WRIGHT, R., Geography

Department of Native American Studies:

CALLOWAY, C. G.
KAN, S.
NICHOLS, D. L.

Department of Psychological and Brain Sciences:

DUNBAR, K., Cognitive Psychology
GAZZANIGA, M. S., Cognitive Neuroscience
GRAFTON, S., Functional Brain Imaging
HEATHERTON, T. F., Experimental Social Neuroscience, Personality and Motivation
HUGHES, H. C., Electrophysiological and Psychophysical Studies of Sensory Processing in Humans
HULL, J. G., Structure of Self-knowledge and Function of Self-regulatory Systems
JERNSTEDT, G. C., Learning, Instructional Design Theory, Evaluation Research

KLECK, R. E., Experimental Social Communication Processes
MACRAE, C. N., Social Cognition
MORRIS, W. N., Mood and Emotion
PETITTO, L. A., Cognitive Psychology and Psycholinguistics
TAUBE, J. S.
WOLFORD, G. L.

Department of Sociology:

CAMPBELL, J. L.
HALL, R. L.
PARSA, M.

Dartmouth Medical School (1 Rope Ferry Rd, Hanover, NH 03755-1404; tel. (603) 650-1200; fax (603) 650-1202; e-mail dms.administration@dartmouth.edu; internet www.dartmouth.edu/dms):

ADDANTE, R. R., Oral-Maxillofacial Surgery and Anaesthesiology
AHLES, T. A., Psychiatry
ALTO, W. A., Community and Family Medicine
AMBROS, V. R., Genetics
AuBUCHON, J. P., Pathology and Haematology-Oncology
BALDWIN, J. C., Surgery
BANKER, B. Q., Pathology
BARLOWE, C. K., Biochemistry
BARON, J. A., General Internal Medicine and Community and Family Medicine
BARTELS, S. J., Psychiatry
BARTLETT, D., Physiology
BATALDEN, P. B., Paediatrics and Community and Family Medicine
BAUGHMAN, R. D., Dermatology
BEISSWENGER, P. J., Medicine
BERGER, B. J., Psychiatry
BERMAN, S. A., Medicine
BERNAT, J. L., Neurology
BERNINI, P. M., Surgery (Orthopaedics)
BIRD, H. H., Anaesthiology
BLACK, W. C., Radiology
BOYLE, W. E., Paediatrics and Community and Family Medicine
BRINCKERHOFF, C. E., Medicine and Biochemistry
BRINCK-JOHNSER, T., Pathology
BROOKS, J. G., Paediatrics
BROWN, F. E., Plastic Surgery
BURCHARD, K. W., Surgery and Anaesthesiology
BYOCK, I. R., Anaesthiology
BZIK, D. J., Microbiology and Immunology
CAMPBELL, D. G., Surgery (Ophthalmology)
CARPENTER, S. J., Anatomy
CENDRON, M., Surgery
CHAMBERS, W. F., Anatomy
CHANG, T. Y., Biochemistry
CHEUNG, A., Microbiology and Immunology
CLENDENNING, W. E., Medicine
COHEN, J. A., Medicine
COLACCHIO, T. A., Surgery
COLE, C. N., Biochemistry and Genetics
COLE, M. D., Pharmacology and Toxicology
COMPTON, D. A., Biochemistry
CORNELL, C. J., Haematology-Oncology and Paediatrics
CORNELL, G. G., Medicine
CORSON, J. A., Psychiatry
CORWIN, H. L., Medicine and Anaesthesiology
CRAIG, R. W., Pharmacology, Toxicology
CRICHLOW, R. W., Surgery
CROMWELL, L. D., Radiology and Neurosurgery
CRONENWETT, J. L., Surgery
CROW, H. C., Radiology
DARNALL, R. A., Paediatrics and Physiology
DAUBENSPECK, A., Physiology
DeLEO, J. A., Anaesthesiology
DIETRICH, A. J., Community and Family Medicine
DMITROVSKY, E., Pharmacology and Toxicology
DONEGAN, J. O., Otolaryngology

DOW, R. W., Surgery
DRAKE, R. E., Psychiatry; Community and Family Medicine
DUHAIME, A.-C., Surgery
DUNLAP, J. C., Genetics and Biochemistry
EASTMAN, A., Pharmacology and Toxicology
EDWARDS, W. H., Paediatrics
EISENBERG, B. L., Surgery
ERNSTOFF, L. T., Haematology-Oncology
ERNSTOFF, M. S., Haematology-Oncology
FANGER, M. W., Microbiology and Immunology
FEJES-TOTH, A. N., Physiology
FEJES-TOTH, G., Physiology
FERM, V. H., Anatomy
FISHER, E. S., Community and Family Medicine
FLOOD, A. B., Community and Family Medicine
FRANK, J. E., Paediatrics
FREY, W. G., Medicine
FRIEDMAN, M. J., Psychiatry, Pharmacology and Toxicology
FROMM, H., Gastroenterology
GALLAGHER, J. D., Anaesthesiology
GALTON, V. A., Physiology
GLASS, D. D., Anaesthesiology
GOODMAN, D. C., Paediatrics
GORMLEY, E. A., Surgery
GOSSELIN, R. E., Pharmacology and Toxicology
GRAFTON, S. T., Medicine
GREEN, A. I., Psychiatry
GREEN, R. L., Psychiatry
GREEN, W. R., Microbiology and Immunology
GREENBERG, R., Community and Family Medicine
GUYRE, P. M., Physiology
HAMILTON, J. W., Pharmacology, Toxicology
HARBAUGH, R. E., Surgery (Neurosurgery) and Radiology
HARBURY, H. A., Biochemistry
HARTMAN, G. S., Anaesthiology
HAZARD, R. G., Orthopaedics
HEAD, J. M., Surgery
HEANEY, J. A., Surgery
HENDERSON, J. V., Community and Family Medicine
HENDERSON, L. P., Physiology
HICKEY, W. F., Pathology
HOFNAGEL, D., Paediatrics
HOLMES, G. L., Medicine
HUG, E. B., Medicine
INSELBURG, J. W., Microbiology
ISRAEL, M. A., Paediatrics and Genetics
JACOBS, N. J., Microbiology
KARAGAS, M., Community and Family Medicine
KARL, R. C., Surgery
KASPER, L. H., Medicine
KELLEY, M. L., Medicine
KERRIGAN, C. L., Surgery
KING, B. H., Psychiatry
KLAUS, S. N., Medicine
KLEIN, R. Z., Paediatrics
KOOP, C. E., Surgery
KORC, M., Medicine
KOVAL, K. J., Orthopaedics
LANE, F. W., Medicine
LAYTON, W. M., Anatomy
LEITER, J. C., Physiology and Medicine
LEVIN, D. L., Paediatrics and Anaesthesiology
LEVINE, G. M., Community and Family Medicine
LEWIS, L. D., Medicine
LIENHARD, G. E., Biochemistry
LITTLE, G. A., Paediatrics; Obstetrics and Gynaecology
LLEWELLYN-THOMAS, H. A., Community and Family Medicine
LONGNECKER, D. S., Pathology
LOROS, J. J., Biochemistry and Genetics
LUBIN, M., Microbiology

McALLISTER, T. W., Psychiatry
McCANN, F. V., Physiology
McCOLLUM, R. W., Community and Family Medicine
McDANIEL, M. D., Anatomy
McINTYRE, D. R., Medicine
MAHLER, D. A., Medicine
MANGANIELLI, P. D., Obstetrics and Gynaecology
MARON-PADILLA, M., Pathology
MARRIN, C. A. S., Surgery
MAUE, R. A., Medicine
MAURER, L. H., Medicine
MAYOR, M. B., Surgery (Orthopaedics)
MEMOLI, V. A., Pathology
MODLIN, J. F., Paediatrics
MOESHLER, J. B., Paediatrics
MOGIELNICKI, R. P., General Internal Medicine
MOHANDAS, T. K., Pathology
MUESER, K. T., Psychiatry; Community and Family Medicine
MUNCK, A. U., Physiology
NAITOVE, A., Surgery
NATTIE, E. E., Physiology
NELSON, E. C., Community and Family Medicine
NELSON, W. H., Psychiatry
NEMIAH, J. C., Psychiatry
NIERENBERG, D. W., Pharmacology and Toxicology
NODA, L. H., Biochemistry
NOELLE, R. J., Microbiology and Immunology
NOLL, W. W., Paediatrics
NORDGREN, R. E., Paediatrics
NORTH, W. G., Physiology
NUGENT, W. C., Surgery
NYE, R. E., Physiology
O'CONNOR, G. T., Community and Family Medicine
O'DONNELL, J. F., Medicine
ONION, D. K., Community and Family Medicine
OXMAN, T. E., Psychiatry; Community and Family Medicine
PAYSON, H. E., Psychiatry
PEARLMAN, J. D., Medicine
PFEFFERKORN, E. R., Microbiology
PLUME, S. K., Surgery
QUILL, T. J., Anaesthesiology
RAVARIS, C. L., Psychiatry
REGAN-SMITH, M. G., Rheumatology; Community and Family Medicine
REEVES, A. G., Medicine
RIGBY, W. F. C., Microbiology and Immunology
ROBERTS, D. W., Surgery (Neurosurgery)
ROEBUCK, W. D., Pharmacology and Toxicology
ROGERS, C. C., Medicine
ROLETT, E. L., Medicine
ROSENBERG, S. D., Psychiatry
ROTHSTEIN, R. I., Medicine
ROUS, S. N., Surgery
ROZYCKI, A. A., Paediatrics
RUECKERT, F., Surgery
ST GERMAIN, D. L., Medicine
ST JOHN, W. M., Physiology
SANDERS, J. H., Surgery
SARGENT, J. D., Paediatrics
SATEIA, M. J., Psychiatry
SAUNDERS, R. L., Surgery
SAYKIN, A. J., Psychiatry
SCHNED, A. R., Pathology
SCHWARTZMAN, J. D., Pathology
SCORNIK, O. A., Biochemistry
SILBERFARB, P. M., Psychiatry and Medicine
SIMONS, M., Cardiology; Pharmacology and Toxicology
SKINNER, J. S., Community and Family Medicine
SMITH, B. D., Obstetrics and Gynaecology
SMITH, R. P., Pharmacology and Toxicology
SOBEL, R., Psychiatry

SOKOL, H. W., Physiology
SOLOW, C., Psychiatry
SORENSON, G. D., Pathology
SPECK, N. A., Biochemistry
SPENCER, S. K., Dermatology and Surgery (Dermatology)
SPIEGEL, P. K., Radiology
SPIELBERG, S. P., Paediatrics
STANTON, B. A., Physiology
STAUFFER, M. W., Pathology
STOKES, D. C., Paediatrics
STRICKLER, J. C., Medicine
STYS, S. J., Obstetrics and Gynaecology (Maternal-Foetal Medicine)
SUTTON, J. E., Surgery
SWARTZ, H. M., Radiology; Community and Family Medicine; Physiology
TOSTESON, A. N., Community and Family Medicine
TOSTESON, T. D., Community and Family Medicine
TRUMPOWER, B. L., Biochemistry
VALTIN, H., Physiology
VAN LEEUWIN, D. J., Medicine
VARNUM, J. W., Hospital Administration
VIDAVER, R. M., Psychiatry
VON REYN, C. F., Medicine
WADE, W. F., Microbiology
WALLACE, A. G., Medicine
WALSH, D. B., Surgery
WASSON, J. H., Community and Family Medicine
WEINSTEIN, J. N., Surgery (Orthopaedics); Community and Family Medicine
WELCH, H. G., Community and Family Medicine
WENNBERG, J. E., Community and Family Medicine
WICKNER, W. T., Biochemistry
WILKINSON, R. H., Radiology
WILLIAMSON, P. D., Medicine
WIRA, C. R., Physiology
YEAGER, M. P., Anaesthesiology
YEO, K.-T. J., Pathology
YOUNG, R. D., Obstetrics and Gynaecology
ZACHARSKI, L. R., Medicine
ZUBKOFF, M., Community and Family Medicine
ZWOLAK, R. M., Surgery

Thayer School of Engineering (14 Engineering Dr., Hanover, NH 03755; tel. (603) 646-2230; fax (603) 646-3856; e-mail thayer.receptionist@dartmouth.edu; internet engineering.dartmouth.edu):

BAKER, I.
CUSHMAN-ROISIN, B.
CYBENKO, G.
GARMIRE, E.
GRAEVE, R. J.
HUTCHINSON, C. E.
KANTROWITZ, A. R.
KENNEDY, F. E.
LOTKO, W.
LYNCH, D. R.
PAULSEN, K. D.
PETRENKO, V. F.
RICHTER, H. J.
SCHULSON, E. M.
STRATTON, W. D.
TAYLOR, S.
WYMAN, C. E.

Tuck School of Business Administration (100 Tuck Hall, Hanover, NH 03755; tel. (603) 646 8825; fax (603) 646-1308; e-mail tuck.admissions@tuck.dartmouth.edu; internet www.tuck.dartmouth.edu):

ARGENTI, P. A., Management and Corporate Communication
BAKER, K. R., Management
BERNARD, A., Int. Economics
BLAYDON, C. C., Management
DANOS, P., Business Admin.
DAVENI, R. A., Strategic Management
ECKBO, B. E., Finance
FINKELSTEIN, S., Management

FRENCH, K. R., Finance
GOVINDARAJAN, V., Int. Business
GREENHALGH, L., Management
HANSEN, R. G., Business Admin.
HELFAT, C. E., Strategy and Technology
JOHNSON, M. E., Operations Management
JOYCE, W. F., Strategy and Organizational Theory
KELLER, K. L., Marketing
KELLER, P. A., Management
LAPORTA, R., Finance
MASSEY, J. A., Int. Business
MUNTER, M. M., Management Communication
NESLIN, S. A., Marketing
POWELL, S. G., Business Admin.
PYKE, D. F., Business Admin.
ROGALSKI, R. J., Investments
SHANK, J. K., Managerial Accounting and Management Control
STICKNEY, C. P., Management
ZUBKOFF, M., Health Economics and Management

FRANKLIN PIERCE UNIVERSITY

40 University Dr., Rindge, NH 03461-0060
Telephone: (603) 899-4000
Fax: (603) 899-4394
E-mail: admissions@franklinpierce.edu
Internet: www.franklinpierce.edu

Founded 1962 as Franklin Pierce College, present name and status 2007
Private control
Academic year: September to May (2 semesters)
Campuses at Concord, Lebanon, Portsmouth, Manchester in New Hampshire and Goodyear in Arizona
Pres.: Dr JAMES F. BIRGE
Provost and Vice-Pres. for Academic Affairs: Dr KIM MOONEY
Vice-Pres. for College Relations: EVELYN BUCHANAN
Vice-Pres. for Enrolment Management: WILLIAM P. HAWKINS
Vice-Pres. for Finance and Admin. and Chief Financial Officer: RICHARD A. MARSHALL
Vice-Pres. for Institutional Advancement: AHMAD BOURA
Vice-Pres. for Student Affairs: Dr JAMES P. EARLE
Dir for Admissions: LINDA QUIMBY
Registrar: Dr SUSAN R. CHAMBERLIN
Dir for Library Services: CARISSA M. CARISSA M. DELIZIO

Library of 132,015 vols, 13,365 serial subscriptions
Number of teachers: 65
Number of students: 2,305
Publication: *Pierce Radius* (2 a year)

DEANS

College of Graduate and Professional Studies: Dr PATRICIA BROWN

HESSER COLLEGE

3 Sundial Ave, Manchester, NH 03103
Telephone: (603) 668-6660
Fax: (603) 621-8994
E-mail: admissions@hesser.edu
Internet: www.hesser.edu

Founded 1900 as Hesser Business College, present status 2006
Private control

Areas of study incl. allied health, arts and sciences, business, criminal justice, early childhood education; 5 regional locations: Concord, Manchester, Nashua, Portsmouth, Salem

Pres.: Dr JACQUELYN ARMITAGE

Vice-Pres. for Academic Affairs: Dr GREGORY FOWLER
Vice-Pres. for Finance and Admin.: JOSEPH A. SERGI
Vice-Pres. for Operations: MAUREEN ZNOJ
Academic Dean: Dr JAN WYATT
Dir for Admissions: KRISTOPHER GOODMAN
Registrar: SUSAN PROVENCHER
Dir for Library Services: ADA KEMP

Library of 25,552 vols, 50,000 e-books, 1,639 audiovisual items, 170 periodicals.

NEW ENGLAND COLLEGE

98 Bridge St, Henniker, NH 03242
Telephone: (603) 428-2000
Fax: (603) 428-3155
E-mail: admission@nec.edu
Internet: www.nec.edu

Founded 1946
Private control
Academic year: September to May (2 semesters)

Divs of education, liberal arts and sciences, management

Pres.: Dr MICHELE D. PERKINS
Vice-Pres. for Academic Affairs: Dr HILTON HALLOCK
Vice-Pres. for Enrolment and Marketing: Dr BARBARA LAYNE
Vice-Pres. for Finance and Admin.: PAULA A. AMATO
Vice-Pres. for Strategic Priorities and Institutional Advancement: Dr JAMES GARVEY
Vice-Pres. for Student Devt and Dean for Student Affairs: E. JOSEPH PETRICK
Dean for Admission: DIANE RAYMOND
Dean for Graduate and Professional Studies: NELLY LEJTER
Dean for Students: LORI RUNKSMEIER
Registrar: FRANK L. HALL
Library Dir: KATHERINE VAN WEELDEN

Library of 100,000 vols, 200 periodicals
Number of teachers: 76 (51 full-time, 25 part-time)
Number of students: 1,000

Publication: *Entelechy International: A Journal of Contemporary Ideas* (1 a year).

RIVIER COLLEGE

420 South Main St, Nashua, NH 03060
Telephone: (603) 888-1311
Fax: (603) 897-8883
E-mail: admissions@rivier.edu
Internet: www.rivier.edu

Founded 1933, present status 1935, present location 1941
Private control
Academic year: September to May

Liberal arts college; areas of study: biology, chemistry, communications, criminal justice, human development, mathematics, modern languages, sociology

Pres.: Sis. PAULA MARIE BULEY
Vice-Pres. for Academic Affairs: Sis. THERESE LAROCHELLE
Vice-Pres. for Enrolment Management: DAVID BOISVERT
Vice-Pres. for Finance and Admin.: JOSEPH A. FAGAN
Vice-Pres. for Student Devt: LYNN JANSKY
Academic Dean: Dr ALBERT DeCICCIO
Registrar: KEVIN GATELY
Library Dir: DANIEL SPEIDEL

Library of 90,000 vols, 45,000 e-books
Number of teachers: 74 (full-time)
Number of students: 2,289

Publication: *InSight: Rivier Academic Journal*.

SAINT ANSELM COLLEGE

100 St Anselm Dr., Manchester, NH 03102-1310
Telephone: (603) 641-7000
Fax: (603) 641-7116
E-mail: admission@anselm.edu
Internet: www.anselm.edu

Founded 1889
Private control
Academic year: August to May (2 semesters)

Liberal arts college; depts of. criminal justice, economics and business, humanities, nursing, philosophy, politics, theology

Pres.: Fr JONATHAN DeFELICE
Exec. Vice-Pres.: Dr SUZANNE K. MELLON
Vice-Pres. for Academic Affairs and Dean for College: AUGUSTINE KELLY
Vice-Pres. for Student Affairs: Dr JOSEPH M. HORTON
Dean for Admission: NANCY DAVIS GRIFFIN
Registrar: MARY ANN ERICSON
Librarian: JOSEPH W. CONSTANCE, JR

Library of 240,000 vols, 1,100 periodical titles, 75,000 microforms
Number of teachers: 171 (137 full-time, 34 part-time)
Number of students: 1,899

SOUTHERN NEW HAMPSHIRE UNIVERSITY

2500 N River Rd, Manchester, NH 03106
Telephone: (603) 626-9100
E-mail: info@snhu.edu
Internet: www.snhu.edu

Founded 1932 as New Hampshire School of Accounting and Secretarial Science, present name and status 2001
Private control
Academic year: August to May (2 semesters)
Campuses in Maine, Nashua, Portsmouth, Salem

Pres.: Dr PAUL J. LeBLANC
Provost and Sr Vice-Pres. for Academic Affairs: Dr PATRICIA A. LYNOTT
Sr Vice-Pres. for Academics, Student Success and Operations: YVONNE SIMON
Sr Vice-Pres. for Finance and Admin.: WILLIAM McGARRY
Vice-Pres. for Devt and Human Resources: PAMELA HOGAN
Vice-Pres. for Enrolment Management: BRAD POZNANSKI
Vice-Pres. for Institutional Advancement: DONALD BREZINSKI
Dean for Students: HEATHER LORENZ
Registrar: Dr JENNIFER DiSTEFANO
Dean for Library: KATHRYN GROWNEY

Library of 109,000 vols, 53,146 e-journals
Number of teachers: 100
Number of students: 6,400

DEANS

Continuing Education: CAROL BATKER
School of Arts and Sciences: Dr KAREN ERICKSON
School of Business: Dr WILLIAM J. GILLETT
School of Education: Dr MARY S. HEATH

THOMAS MORE COLLEGE OF LIBERAL ARTS

6 Manchester St, Merrimack, NH 03054
Telephone: (603) 880-8308
Fax: (603) 880-9280
E-mail: admissions@thomasmorecollege.edu
Internet: www.thomasmorecollege.edu

Founded 1978
Private control
Academic year: September to May (2 semesters)

Areas of study: history, law, literature, philosophy, politics, theology

Pres.: Dr WILLIAM EDMUND FAHEY
Vice-Pres. for Admin.: CLINT HANSON
Vice-Pres. for Institutional Advancement: CHARLIE McKINNEY
Academic Dean: Prof. Dr CHRISTOPHER OLAF BLUM
Dean for Students: WALTER J. THOMPSON
Dir for Admissions: MARK SCHWERDT
Registrar: CHRISTOPHER BLUM
Librarian: SAMUEL SCHMITT

Library of 40,000 vols, 7,500 periodicals
Number of teachers: 9
Number of students: 82

Publication: *Second Spring: An International Journal of Faith and Culture* (2 a year).

UNIVERSITY SYSTEM OF NEW HAMPSHIRE

Dunlap Center, 25 Concord Rd, Durham, NH 03824-3545
Telephone: (603) 862-1800
Fax: (603) 862-0908
E-mail: usnh.chancellor@unh.edu
Internet: www.usnh.edu

Founded 1963
State control

Chancellor: Dr EDWARD R. MacKAY
Vice-Chancellor and Treas.: Dr KEN CODY
Assoc. Vice-Chancellor for Academic and Student Affairs: TOM FRANKE
Assoc. Vice-Chancellor for Govt Affairs: KATHLEEN K. SALISBURY
Gen. Counsel and Sec.: RONALD F. RODGERS
Number of students: 30,998.

CONSTITUENT INSTITUTIONS

Granite State College

8 Old Suncook Rd, Concord, NH 03301
Telephone: (603) 228-3000
Fax: (603) 513-1389
E-mail: ask.granite@granite.edu
Internet: www.granite.edu

Founded 1972 as School of Continuing Studies, present name and status 2005
Academic year: July to June (2 semesters)
Regional campuses at Claremount, Conway, Rochester

Pres.: Dr TODD J. LEACH
Dean for Academic Affairs: Dr SHEILA TAYLOR-KING
Dean for Enrolment Management: M. B. LUFKIN
Dean for Finance and Admin.: LISA L SHAWNEY
Dean for Students and External Engagement: TESSA H. McDONNELL
Registrar: KAREN KING

Number of teachers: 323 (adjunct)
Number of students: 33,127

Keene State College

229 Main St, Keene, NH 03435
Telephone: (603) 352-2276
E-mail: admissions@keene.edu
Internet: www.keene.edu

Founded 1909 as Keene Normal School, present name and status 1963
State control
Academic year: September to May (2 semesters)

Pres.: Dr HELEN F. GILES-LEE
Provost and Vice-Pres. for Academic Affairs: Dr EMILE NETZHAMMER
Vice-Pres. for Advancement: MARYANN LaCROIX LINDBERG
Vice-Pres. for Finance and Planning: Dr JAY V. KAHN

Vice-Pres. for Student Affairs: Dr ANDREW ROBINSON
Dean of Library: IRENE HEROLD
Registrar: TOM RICHARD
Library of 326,000 vols, 900 periodicals, newspapers and audiovisual materials
Number of teachers: 455 (197 full-time, 258 part-time)
Number of students: 5,738
Publication: *Keene State Today*

DEANS

School of Arts and Humanities: Dr NONA FIENBERG
School of Professional and Graduate Studies: Dr MELINDA TREADWELL
School of Science and Social Sciences: GORDON LEVERSEE

Plymouth State University

17 High St, Plymouth, NH 03264-1595
Telephone: (603) 535-5000
Fax: (603) 535-2654
E-mail: plymouthadmit@plymouth.edu
Internet: www.plymouth.edu
Founded 1871 as teacher training school, present name 2003
State control
Academic year: September to May (2 semesters)
Pres.: Dr SARA JAYNE STEEN
Provost and Vice-Pres. for Academic Affairs: Dr JULIE N. BERNIER
Vice-Pres. for Enrolment Management and Student Affairs: RICHARD A. BARTH
Vice-Pres. for Finance and Admin.: STEPHEN J. TASKAR
Vice-Pres. for Univ. Advancement: SALLY C. HOLLAND
Registrar: GEORGE GILMORE
Dean of Library and Academic Support Services: DAVID BERONA
Library of 349,394 vols
Number of teachers: 187
Number of students: 7,500 (4,300 undergraduate, 2,262 graduate)
Publications: *Anthology of Teachers' Writing* (1 a year), *Centripetal* (2 a year), *Plymouth Magazine* (2 a year), *The New Hampshire Journal of Education* (1 a year), *Writing across the Curriculum* (1 a year)

DEANS

College of Arts and Sciences: Dr CYNTHIA W. VASCAK
College of Business Administration: Prof. Dr TRENT E. BOGGESS
College of Education, Health and Human Services: Dr GAIL F. MEARS
Frost School of Continuing and Professional Education: Dr NANCY S. BETCHART

University of New Hampshire

105 Main St, Durham, NH 03824
Telephone: (603) 862-1234
Fax: (603) 862-0077
E-mail: admissions@unh.edu
Internet: www.unh.edu
Founded 1866 as New Hampshire College of Agriculture and the Mechanic Arts, present name 1923
Public control
Academic year: September to May (2 semesters)
Pres.: Dr MARK W. HUDDLESTON
Provost and Exec. Vice-Pres. for Academic Affairs: Dr JOHN D. ABER
Vice-Pres. for Advancement: PETER WEILER
Vice-Pres. for Finance and Admin.: Dr DICK CANNON
Vice-Pres. for Student and Academic Services: Dr MARK RUBINSTEIN
Dir for Admissions: ROBERT McGANN

Registrar: KATHRYN P. FORBES
Dean for University Libraries: Dr SHERRY VELLUCCI
Library of 1,555,475 vols
Number of teachers: 1,027 (621 full-time, 406 part-time)
Number of students: 15,172 (12,609 undergraduate, 2,563 graduate)
Publications: *IDEA: The Intellectual Property Law Review* (4 a year), *Inquiry* (undergraduate research journal), *Main Street Magazine*, *Portuguese Studies Review*, *Seafare* (jtly with Univ. of Maine), *UNH-LAW* (2 a year), *UNH Magazine* (3 a year), *University of New Hampshire Law Review* (1 a year)

DEANS

College of Engineering and Physical Sciences: Dr SAMUEL MUKASA
College of Health and Human Services: Dr NEIL VROMAN
College of Liberal Arts: Dr KENNETH FULD
College of Life Sciences and Agriculture: JON M. WRAITH
Graduate School: Dr HARRY J. RICHARDS
University of New Hampshire School of Law: JOHN T. BRODERICK, JR
University of New Hampshire at Manchester: Dr SALLY WARD
Whittemore School of Business and Economics: Dr DANIEL E. INNIS

NEW JERSEY

BERKELEY COLLEGE

44 Rifle Camp Rd, Woodland Park, NJ 07424
Telephone: (973) 278-5400
Fax: (973) 278-9141
E-mail: info@berkeleycollege.edu
Internet: berkeleycollege.edu
Founded 1931
Private control
Academic year: September to July
Pres.: Dr DARIO A. CORTES
Provost: Dr GLEN ZEITZER
Sr Vice-Pres. and Chief Financial Officer: DONALD DEVINE, II
Sr Vice-Pres. for Enrolment Management: DIANE RECINOS
Sr Vice-Pres. for Govt Relations: TERI DUDA
Vice-Pres. for Operations: MARK WAGENER
Vice-Pres. for Student Accounts: EILEEN LOFTUS-BERLIN
Vice-Pres. for Student Devt and Campus Life: ED HUGHES
Vice-Pres. for Library Services: MARLENE DOTY
Number of students: 8,900
Publication: *Berkley College Viewbook*

DEANS

School of Business: Dr JOHN RAPANOS
School of Liberal Arts: Dr DONALD KIEFFER
School of Professional Studies: Dr JUDITH KORNBERG

BLOOMFIELD COLLEGE

467 Franklin St, Bloomfield, NJ 07003
Telephone: (973) 748-9000
Fax: (973) 748-0916
E-mail: admission@bloomfield.edu
Internet: www.bloomfield.edu
Founded 1868 as German Theological Seminary
Private control
Academic year: August to August
Pres.: RICHARD A. LEVAO
Sr Vice-Pres. for Admin. and Finance: JOHN CROSS

Vice-Pres. for Academic Affairs and Dean for Faculty: MARION TERENZIO
Vice-Pres. for Enrolment Management: ADAM CASTRO
Vice-Pres. for Institutional Advancement: KWI BRENNAN
Vice-Pres. for Student Affairs and Dean for Students: PATRICK LAMY
Dir for Admission: NICOLE CIBELLI
Registrar: EILEEN POLAZZI
Library Dir: DAN FIGUEREDO
Library of 70,000 vols
Number of teachers: 181
Number of students: 2,000

CALDWELL COLLEGE

120 Bloomfield Ave, Caldwell, NJ 07006
Telephone: (973) 618-3000
Fax: (973) 618-3600
E-mail: admissions@caldwell.edu
Internet: www.caldwell.edu
Founded 1939
Private control
Academic year: August to May
Humanities; physical and biological sciences, and mathematics; and social sciences
Pres.: Dr NANCY H. BLATTNER
Vice-Pres. for Academic Affairs: Dr PATRICK PROGAR
Vice-Pres. for Enrolment Management: JOSEPH L. POSILLICO
Vice-Pres for Finance and Admin.: JACK RAINEY
Vice-Pres. for Institutional Effectiveness: SHEILA N. O'ROURKE
Vice-Pres. for Devt and Alumni Affairs: KEVIN BOYLE
Vice-Pres. and Dean for Student Life: Sis. KATHLEEN TUITE
Librarian: Dr PETER PANOS
Library of 142,356 vols
Number of teachers: 184
Number of students: 2,300 (1,599 full-time)

CENTENARY COLLEGE

400 Jefferson St, Hackettstown, NJ 07840-9930
Telephone: (908) 852-1400
Fax: (908) 979-4359
E-mail: admissions@centenarycollege.edu
Internet: www.centenarycollege.edu
Founded 1867
Private control
Academic year: August to June
Campuses in Hackettstown, Parsippany, Edison and Long Valley
Pres.: Dr BARBARA-JAYNE LEWTHWAITE
Provost and Vice-Pres. for Academic Affairs: JAMES PATTERSON
Vice-Pres. for Finance and Chief Financial Officer: ROGER ANDERSON
Sr Vice-Pres. for College Relations and Marketing: DIANE P. FINNAN
Vice-Pres. for Information Systems: NORMAN W. RANKIS
Dean for Students: Rev. DAVID JONES
Registrar: Dr THOMAS BRUNNER
Library Dir: NANCY MADACSI
Library of 100,000 vols
Number of teachers: 150 (full-time, adjunct)
Number of students: 970
Publications: *The Centenarian*, *Viewbooks*

DEANS

School of International Programs: Dr JOSEPH P. LINSKEY
School of Professional Studies: DEIRDRE LETSON

COLLEGE OF NEW JERSEY

POB 7718, 2000 Pennington Rd, Ewing, NJ 08628-0718

Telephone: (609) 771-1855
Internet: www.tcnj.edu

Founded 1855 as New Jersey State Normal School, present name 1996
Academic year: August to May

Pres.: R. BARBARA GITENSTEIN
Provost and Vice-Pres. for Academic Affairs: SUSAN BAKEWELL-SACHS
Vice-Provost: MARK KINSELICA
Vice-Pres. for Admin. and Finance: PETER L. MILLS
Vice-Pres. for College Relations and Advancement: MATHEW GOLDEN
Vice-Pres. for Devt and Alumni Affairs: JOHN MARCY
Vice-Pres. for Student Affairs: JAMES M. NORFLEET
Registrar: FRANK COOPER
Dean of the Library and Information Services: TARAS PAVLOVSKY
Library of 562,000 vols, 13,000 video recordings, 21,000 sound recordings, 30,000 periodical titles, 11,000 reference colln
Number of teachers: 994
Number of students: 7,115 (6460 undergraduate, 655 graduate)
Publication: *TCNJ Magazine*

DEANS

School of Arts and Communication: Dr JOHN C. LAUGHTON
School of Business: Dr WILLIAM KEEP (acting)
School of Education: Dr MARK S. KISELICA
School of Engineering: Dr STEVEN SCHREINER
School of Humanities and Social Sciences: Dr BENJAMIN RIFKIN
School of Nursing, Health, and Exercise Science: Dr MARCIA BLICHARZ
School of Science: Dr JEFFREY M. OSBORN

COLLEGE OF SAINT ELIZABETH

Two Convent Rd, Morristown, NJ 07960-6989

Telephone: (973) 290-4000
E-mail: apply@cse.edu
Internet: www.cse.edu

Founded 1899
Private control
Academic year: August to May

Pres.: Sis. FRANCIS RAFTERY
Vice-Pres. and Dean for Academic Affairs: Dr JAMES S. DLUGOS
Vice-Pres. for Finance and Admin. and Treas.: MARIA CAMMARATA
Vice-Pres. for Institutional Advancement: DEBORAH M. MCCREERY
Vice-Pres. for Student Life and Dean for Students: KATHERINE M. BUCK
Dean for Graduate Programmes: Dr JACQUELINE MCGLADE
Dean of Women's College and Undergraduate Studies: Dr CAROL A. STROBECK
Library Dir: AMIRA UNVER
Library of 188,000 vols, 450 periodical subscriptions
Number of teachers: 250
Number of students: 2,112

DREW UNIVERSITY

36 Madison Ave, Madison, NJ 07940

Telephone: (973) 408-3000
Fax: (973) 408-3080
Internet: www.drew.edu

Founded 1867
Private control
Academic year: September to May

Pres.: VIVIAN BULL

Provost and Academic Vice-Pres.: PAMELA GUNTER-SMITH
Vice-Pres. for Admin. and Univ. Relations: MARGARET E. L. HOWARD
Vice-Pres. for Enrolment Management: RENEE VOLAK
Vice-Pres. for Finance and Business Affairs: HOWARD BUXBAUM
Vice-Pres. for Univ. Advancement: JAY ANGELETTI
Dean for Campus Life and Student Affairs: SARA WALDRON
Dean for Libraries: ANDREW D. SCRIMGEOUR
Registrar: HORACE TATE
Library of 300,000 vols
Number of teachers: 155 (full-time)
Number of students: 2,716
Publication: *Drew Magazine* (3 a year)

DEANS

Caspersen School of Graduate Studies: ROBERT READY
College of Liberal Arts: JONATHAN LEVIN
Theological School: JEFFREY KUAN

FAIRLEIGH DICKINSON UNIVERSITY

1000 River Rd, Teaneck, NJ 07666

Telephone: (201) 692-2000
E-mail: grad@fdu.edu
Internet: www.fdu.edu

Founded 1942, present status 1956
Private control
Academic year: August to May

Campuses at Morris County and Teaneck in New Jersey, Oxfordshire in UK and Vancouver in Canada

Pres.: Dr J. MICHAEL ADAMS
Provost and Sr Vice-Pres. for Academic Affairs: Dr CHRISTOPHER A. CAPUANO
Sr Vice-Pres. for Univ. Advancement: RICHARD REISS
Vice-Pres. and Chief Information Officer: NEAL STURM
Vice-Pres. for Finance and Treas.: Dr HANIA FERRARA
Vice-Pres. for Enrolment Management: JONATHAN WEXLER
Gen. Counsel: JOHN M. CODD
Univ. Librarian: JAMES MARCUM
Library of 650,000 vols
Number of teachers: 836 (262 full-time, 574 part-time)
Number of students: 12,112 (8,585 undergraduate, 3,527 graduate)
Publications: *FDU Magazine*, *Journal of Psychology and the Behavioral Sciences* (1 a year), *The Literary Review* (4 a year)

DEANS

Anthony J. Petrocelli College of Continuing Studies: KENNETH T. VEHRKENS
Maxwell Becton College of Arts and Sciences (Florham-Madison Campus): Dr GEOFFREY WEINMAN
Silberman College of Business: Dr WILLIAM M. MOORE
Univ. College (Teaneck-Hackensack Campus): Dr PATTI A. MILLS
Wroxton College: Dr NICHOLAS D. J. BALDWIN

FELICIAN COLLEGE

262 S Main St, Lodi, NJ 07644-2117

Telephone: (201) 559-6000
Fax: (201) 559-6188
E-mail: admissions@inet.felician.edu
Internet: www.felician.edu

Founded 1923 as Immaculate Conception Normal School, present name 1967
Private control
Academic year: August to May

Campuses at Lodi and Rutherford

Pres.: Sis. THERESA MARY MARTIN
Provost and Vice-Pres. for Academic Affairs: Sis. MARY ROSITA BRENNAN
Sr Exec. Vice-Pres.: Dr CHARLES J. ROONEY
Exec. Vice-Pres. for Admin. and Finance: MARC J. CHALFIN
Vice-Pres. for College Services: ROBERT DECKER
Vice-Pres. for Enrolment Management: ARTHUR D. GOON
Vice-Pres. for Student Affairs: MARY TARCILIA JUCHNIEWICZ
Vice-Pres. for Institutional Advancement: CELESTE A. ORANCHAK
Registrar: JUNE FINN
Dir for Library Services: PAUL GLASSMAN
Library of 115,000 vols, 360 print periodicals, 20,000 online journals, 43,000 e-books, 80,000 microforms
Number of teachers: 30
Number of students: 2,400

DEANS

Div. of Arts and Sciences: Dr EDWARD KUBERSKY
Div. of Business and Management Sciences: Dr BETH CASTIGLIA
Div. of Nursing and Health Management: Dr MURIEL M. SHORE
Div. of Teacher Education: Dr DONNA M. BARRON-BAKER

GEORGIAN COURT UNIVERSITY

900 Lakewood Ave, Lakewood, NJ 08701-2697

Telephone: (732) 364-2700
Fax: (732) 987-2000
E-mail: admissions@georgian.edu
Internet: www.georgian.edu

Founded 1908 as Mount Saint Mary College and Acad., present name 1924
Private control
Academic year: September to May

Pres.: Dr ROSEMARY E. JEFFRIES
Provost: EVELYN SAUL QUINN
Chief Financial Officer: RONALD RECK
Dir for Library Services: LAURA GEWISSLER
Library of 157,000 vols, 782 journals
Number of teachers: 272 (105 full-time, 167 adjunct)
Number of students: 2,555 (1,772 undergraduate, 783 graduate)
Publication: *The Fountain Spray*

DEANS

School of Arts and Sciences: Dr RITA SMITH KIPP
School of Business: Dr JANICE WARNER
School of Education: Dr JACQUELINE E. KRESS

KEAN UNIVERSITY

1000 Morris Ave, Union, NJ 07083

Telephone: (908) 737-5326
E-mail: admitme@kean.edu
Internet: www.kean.edu

Founded 1855, present name 1997
Academic year: September to June

Pres.: Dr DAWOOD FARAHI
Exec. Vice-Pres. for Operations: PHILIP CONNELLY
Vice-Pres. for Academic Affairs: Dr JEFFREY TONEY (acting)
Vice-Pres. for Institutional Advancement and Research: Dr KRISTIE REILLY
Vice-Pres. for Student Affairs: JANICE MURRAY-LAURY (acting)
Registrar: KENNETH WOLPIN
Univ. Librarian: LUIS RODRIGUEZ
Library of 275,000 vols
Number of teachers: 342 (full-time)
Number of students: 15,939

Publication: *Kean Magazine*

DEANS

College of Business and Public Management: Dr KATHRYN MARTELL
College of Education: Dr SUSAN POLLIRSTOK
College of Humanities and Social Sciences: Dr KENNETH DOLLARHIDE
College of Natural, Applied and Health Sciences: Dr GEORGE CHANG (acting)
Nathan Weiss Graduate College: Dr STEVEN LORENZET
School of Visual and Performing Arts: HOLLY LOGUE

MONMOUTH UNIVERSITY

400 Cedar Ave, West Long Branch, NJ 07764-1898

Telephone: (732) 571-3400
E-mail: gradadm@monmouth.edu
Internet: www.monmouth.edu

Founded 1933 as Monmouth Jr College, present name and status 1995
Private control

Pres.: PAUL G. GAFFNEY, II
Provost and Vice-Pres. for Academic Affairs: THOMAS PEARSON
Vice-Pres. for Administrative Services: PATRICIA SWANNACK
Vice-Pres. for Enrolment Management: ROBERT D. MCCAIG
Vice-Pres. for Finance: WILLIAM G. CRAIG
Vice-Pres. for Student and Community Services: MARY ANNE NAGY
Vice-Pres. for Univ. Advancement: Dr JEFFERY N. MILLS
Vice-Pres. and Gen. Counsel: GREY J. DIMENNA
Dean for Library: Dr DR. RAVINDRA SHARMA
Library of 252,500 vols, 1,250 periodicals
Number of teachers: 397 (full-time and part-time)
Number of students: 5,311 (4,037 undergraduate, 1,274 graduate)
Publication: *Monmouth University Magazine*

DEANS

Graduate School: Dr DATTA V. NAIK
Honors School: Dr KEVIN L. DOOLEY
Leon Hess Business School: DONALD MOLIVER
Marjorie K. Unterberg School of Nursing and Health Studies: Dr JANET MAHONEY
School of Education: LYNN ROMEO
School of Science: MICHAEL A. PALLADINO
School of Social Work: Dr ROBIN S. MAMA
Wayne D. McMurray School of Humanities and Social Sciences: Dr STANTON GREEN

MONTCLAIR STATE UNIVERSITY

Montclair, NJ 07043

Telephone: (973) 655-4000
Fax: (973) 655-5455
E-mail: undergraduate.admissions@montclair.edu
Internet: www.montclair.edu

Founded 1908 as The New Jersey State Normal School, present name 1994
Academic year: September to May

Pres.: Dr SUSAN A. COLE
Provost and Vice-Pres. for Academic Affairs: WILLARD P. GINGERICH
Vice-Pres. for Finance and Treas.: DONALD C. CIPULLO
Vice-Pres. for Human Resources: JUDITH T. HAIN
Vice-Pres. for Student Devt and Campus Life: Dr KAREN PENNINGTON
Vice-Pres. for Univ. Advancement: JACK T. SHANNON
Vice-Pres. for Univ. Facilities: GREGORY W. BRESSLER
Dean for Library Services: JUDITH LIN HUNT

Library of 500,000 vols, 2,000 serials
Number of teachers: 1,275 (509 full-time, 766 part-time)
Number of students: 18,498

DEANS

College of Education and Human Services: ADA BETH CUTLER
College of Humanities and Social Sciences: MARIETTA MORRISSEY
College of Science and Mathematics: Dr ROBERT PREZANT
College of the Arts: Dr GEOFFREY W. NEWMAN
Graduate School: Dr JOAN C. FICKE
School of Business: Dr E. LaBRENT CHRITE

NEW BRUNSWICK THEOLOGICAL SEMINARY

17 Seminary Pl., New Brunswick, NJ 08901-1196

Telephone: (732) 247-5241
Fax: (732) 249-5412
E-mail: info@nbts.edu
Internet: www.nbts.edu

Founded 1784
Private control
Academic year: September to May

2 Campuses: New Brunswick, New Jersey, and St John's campus at Queens, New York

Pres.: GREGG ALAN MAST
Academic Dean: RENEE HOUSE
Dean for Students: JESSICA J. DAVIS
Dir for Library: CHRISTOPHER BRENNAN
Library of 150,000 vols, 10,000 periodicals
Number of teachers: 30
Number of students: 200

NEW JERSEY CITY UNIVERSITY

2039 Kennedy Blvd, Jersey City, NJ 07305-1597

Telephone: (201) 200-2000
Fax: (201) 200-2044
E-mail: admissions@njcu.edu
Internet: www.njcu.edu

Founded 1927 as New Jersey State Normal School, present name and status 1998
State control
Academic year: September to May

Pres.: Dr CARLOS HERNÁNDEZ
Vice-Pres. for Academic Affairs: Dr JOANNE Z. BRUNO
Vice-Pres. for Admin. and Finance: AARON ASKA
Vice-Pres. for Student Affairs: Dr JOHN MELENDEZ
Vice-Pres. for Univ. Advancement: Dr WILLIAM FELLENBERG
Library Dir: GRACE F. BULAONG
Number of teachers: 784 (243 full-time, 4 part-time, 537 adjunct)
Number of students: 8,703 (6,639 undergraduate, 1,689 graduate, 375 continuing)
Publications: *Academic Forum, Gothic Magazine* (1 a year), *Journal of the Imagination in Language Learning* (1 a year), *PATHS, Transformations* (2 a year)

DEANS

College of Professional Studies: Dr SANDRA BLOOMBERG
Deborah Cannon Partridge Wolfe College of Education: Dr ALLAN A. DE FINA
William J. Maxwell College of Arts and Sciences: Dr BARBARA FELDMAN

NEW JERSEY INSTITUTE OF TECHNOLOGY

University Heights, Newark, NJ 07102-1982
Telephone: (973) 596-3000
Fax: (973) 642-4380

E-mail: information@njit.edu
Internet: www.njit.edu

Founded 1881 as Newark Technical School
Pres.: JOEL S. BLOOM
Provost and Sr Vice-Pres. for Academic Affairs: Dr IAN GATLEY
Sr Vice-Pres. for Admin. and Treas.: HENRY A. MAUERMEYER
Sr Vice-Pres. for Research and Devt: Dr DONALD H. SEBASTIAN
Vice-Pres. for Academic and Student Services: JACK GENTUL
Vice-Pres. for Human Resources: Dr THEODORE JOHNSON
Vice-Pres. for Univ. Advancement: Dr CHARLES R. DEES, JR
Gen. Counsel: Dr HOLLY STERN
Dean of Admissions: KATHRYN KELLY
Registrar: JOSEPH THOMPSON
Librarian: RICHARD T. SWEENEY
Library of 170,186 vols, 356 journal subscriptions
Number of teachers: 490 (408 full-time, 82 adjunct)
Number of students: 9,558 (6,604 undergraduate, 2,954 graduate)
Publication: *NJIT Magazine*

DEANS

Albert Dorman Honors College: ATAM DHAWAN
College of of Architecture and Design: URS P. GAUCHAT
College of Computing Sciences: NARAIN GEHANI
College of Science and Liberal Arts: Dr FADI P. DEEK
Newark College of Engineering: SUNIL SAIGAL (acting)
School of Management: PIUS J. EGBELU

PRINCETON THEOLOGICAL SEMINARY

POB 821, 64 Mercer St, Princeton, NJ 08542-0803

Telephone: (609) 921-8300
Fax: (609) 924-2973
E-mail: admissions@ptsem.edu
Internet: www.ptsem.edu

Founded 1812
Private control
Academic year: September to May

Pres.: IAIN R. TORRANCE
Sr Vice-Pres., Chief Operating Officer and Treas.: JOHN W. GILMORE
Vice-Pres. for Information Technology: ADRIAN BACKUS
Vice-Pres. for Investment and Chief Investment Officer: JUDITH W. HEAGSTEDT
Vice-Pres. for Seminary Relations: ROSEMARY C. MITCHELL
Vice-Pres. for Strategy and Dir for Continuing Education: CHARLES KALMBACH
Dean for Academic Affairs: Prof. JAMES F. KAY
Dean for Student Life: CATHY COOK DAVIS
Registrar: DAVID H. WALL
Librarian: DONALD A. VORP
Library of 1,229,734 vols
Number of teachers: 44
Number of students: 539

Publication: *Theology Today* (4 a year).

PRINCETON UNIVERSITY

Princeton, NJ 08544
Telephone: (609) 258-3000
Fax: (609) 258-6743
E-mail: uaoffice@princeton.edu
Internet: www.princeton.edu

Founded 1746 as College of New Jersey, present name and status 1896

Private control
Academic year: September to May

Pres.: SHIRLEY M. TILGHMAN
Provost: CHRISTOPHER L. EISGRUBER
Exec. Vice-Pres.: MARK BURSTEIN
Vice-Pres. and Sec.: ROBERT K. DURKEE
Vice-Pres. for Campus Life: CYNTHIA CHER-
REY
Vice-Pres. for Devt: ELIZABETH BOLUCH WOOD
Vice-Pres. for Facilities: MICHAEL E. MCKAY
Vice-Pres. for Finance and Treas.: CAROLYN
N. AINSLIE
Vice-Pres. for Human Resources: LIANNE
SULLIVAN-CROWLEY
Vice-Pres. for Information Technology and
Chief Information Officer: BETTY LEYDON
Gen. Counsel: PETER G. MCDONOUGH
Dean for Admission: JANET LAVIN RAPELYE
Dean for College: VALERIE SMITH
Dean for Faculty: DAVID P. DOBKIN
Dean for Religious Life and Chapel: ALISON
L. BODEN
Dean for Research: A. J. STEWART SMITH
Dean for Undergraduate Students: KATH-
LEEN DEIGNAN
Registrar: POLLY WINFREY GRIFFIN
Librarian: KARIN A. TRAINER
Library: see Libraries and Archives
Number of teachers: 1,152 (full-time, part-
time, visiting)
Number of students: 7,731 (5,149 under-
graduate, 2,582 graduate)
Publications: *American Foreign Policy*,
Annals of Mathematics (6 a year), *Business
Today* (2 a year), *Nassau Literary Review*,
Prism Magazine, *Princeton Journal of
Bioethics*, *Princeton Tory*, *The Princeton
Tiger*, *World Politics* (4 a year)

DEANS

Graduate School: WILLIAM B. RUSSEL
School of Architecture: STANLEY T. ALLEN
School of Engineering and Applied Science:
H. VINCENT POOR
Woodrow Wilson School of Public and Inter-
national Affairs: CHRISTINA H. PAXSON

PROFESSORS

ABBATE, C., Music
ABREU, D. J., Economics
ACTON, F. S., Electrical Engineering and
Computer Science
ADELMAN, J. I., Latin American Studies
AGAWU, V. K., African Studies
AIT-SAHALIA, Y., Economics
AIZENMAN, M., Physics
AKSAY, I., Chemical Engineering
ALLEN, L. C., Chemistry
ALTMANN, J., Ecology and Evolutionary Biol-
ogy
APPIAH, K., Afro-American Studies
ARMSTRONG, C. M., Art and Archaeology
ARNOLD, R. D., Politics and Public Affairs
ASHENFELTER, O. C., Economics
ATKINS, S. D., Classics
AUSTIN, R. H., Physics
AXTMANN, R. C., Chemical Engineering
BABBITT, M. B., Music
BABBY, L. H., Slavic Language and Litera-
ture
BAGLEY, R. W., Art and Archaeology
BAHCALL, N., Astrophysical Science
BARTELS, L. M., Public and International
Affairs
BAUMOL, W. J., Economics
BELLOS, D. M., Romance Languages and
Literatures
BENABOU, R. J.-M., Economics and Public
Affairs
BENACERRAF, P., Philosophy
BENDER, M. L., Geosciences
BENTLEY, G. E., English Literature
BENZIGER, J. B., Chemical Engineering
BERMAN, S. L., Comparative Literature
BERNANKE, B., Economics and Public Affairs

BERNASEK, S. L., Chemistry
BERNHEIM, B. D., Economics
BERRY, C. H., Economics and Public Affairs
BHATT, R. N., Electrical Engineering
BILLINGTON, D. P., Civil Engineering
BLINDER, A. S., Economics
BOCARSLY, A. B., Chemistry
BOGDONOFF, S. M., Aeronautical, Mechanical
and Aerospace Engineering
BOLTON, P., Finance, Economics
BONINI, W. E., Geophysics and Geological
Engineering, Civil Engineering
BOON, J. A., Anthropology
BOYER, M. C., Architecture
BRACCO, F., Mechanical and Aerospace
Engineering
BRADFORD, D. F., Economics and Public
Affairs
BRANSON, W. H., Economics and Inter-
national Affairs
BROACH, J. R., Molecular Biology
BROADIE, S. W., Philosophy
BRODSKY LACOUR, C. J., Comparative Litera-
ture
BROMBERT, V. H., Romance Languages and
Literatures and Comparative Literature
BROWDER, W., Mathematics
BROWN, C. F., Jr, Comparative Literature
BROWN, G. L., Mechanical and Aerospace
Engineering
BROWN, P. F., Art and Archaeology
BROWN, P. R., History
BUNNELL, P. C., History of Photography and
Modern Art; Art and Archaeology
BURGESS, J. P., Philosophy
CALAPRICE, F. P., Physics
CALLAN, C. G., Jr, Physics
CAMPBELL, B. A., Psychology
CAR, R., Chemistry
CARMONA, R. A., Operations Research and
Financial Engineering
CARRASACO, D., Religion
CASE, A. C., Economics and Public Affairs
CATES, G. D., Jr, Physics
CAVA, R. J., Chemistry
CELIA, M. A., Civil and Environmental
Engineering
CHAIKIN, P. M., Physics
CHAMPLIN, E. J., Humanities; Classics
CHANCES, E. B., Slavic Languages and Lit-
eratures
CHANG, S.-Y. A., Mathematics
CHASE, A. M., Biology
CHAZELLE, B. M., Computer Science
CHENG, S. I., Aeronautical Engineering
CHILDS, W. A. P., Art and Archaeology
CHOU, C.-P., East Asian Studies
CHOU, S. Y., Engineering
CHOW, G. C., Economics, Political Economy
CHRISTODOULOU, D., Mathematics
CINLAR, E., Civil Engineering
CLARK, D., Computer Sciences
CLINTON, J. W., Near Eastern Studies
COALE, A. J., Economics and Public Affairs
COFFIN, D. R., Art and Archaeology
COHEN, M. R., Near Eastern Studies
COLE, M. D., Molecular Biology
COLLCUTT, M. C., East Asian Studies
CONWAY, J. H., Applied and Computational
Mathematics
COOPER, J., Psychology
COOPER, J. M., Philosophy
CORNGOLD, S. A., Germanic Languages
COX, E. C., Biology
ČURČIĆ, S., Art and Archaeology
CURSCHMANN, M. J. H., Germanic Languages
DAHLEN, F. A., Geological and Geophysical
Sciences
DANIELSON, M. N., Politics and Public Affairs
DANSON, L. N., English
DARLEY, J. M., Psychology
DARNTON, R. C., History
DAUBECHIES, I. C., Mathematics
DAVIDSON, R. C., Astrophysical Sciences
DAVIES, H. M., Religion

DEATON, A. S., Economics and International
Affairs
DEBENEDETTI, P. G., Engineering
DIAMOND, M. L., Religion
DÍAZ-QUIÑONES, A., Romance Languages and
Literatures
DI BATTISTA, M. A., English and Comparative
Literature
DICKINSON, B. W., Electrical Engineering
DIIULIO, J. J., Politics and Public Affairs
DILLIARD, I., Journalism and Public Relations
DIMAGGIO, P. J., Sociology
DISMUKES, G. C., Chemistry
DIXIT, A. K., Economics and International
Affairs
DOBBIN, F. R., Sociology
DOBKIN, D. P., Electrical Engineering and
Computer Science
DOIG, J. W., Politics and Public Affairs
DOYLE, M. W., Public and International
Affairs
DRAINE, B. T., Astrophysical Sciences
DRYER, F. L., Mechanical and Aerospace
Engineering
EBERT, R. P., Germanic Languages and
Literatures
EMERSON, C. G., Slavic Languages and
Literatures
ENGELSTEIN, L., History
ENQUIST, L. W., Molecular Biology
ERMOLAEV, H., Slavic Languages and Litera-
tures
ESPENSHADE, T. J., Sociology
EVANS, A. G., Engineering
FAGLES, R., Comparative Literature
FALK, R. A., International Law, Politics, and
International Affairs
FALTINGS, G., Mathematics
FARBER, H. S., Economics
FEENEY, D. C., Classics
FEFFERMAN, C., Mathematics
FISCH, N. J., Astrophysical Sciences
FISKE, S. T., Psychology
FITCH, V. L., Physics
FLEMING, J. V., English and Comparative
Literature
FLINT, S. J., Molecular Biology
FLOUDAS, C. A., Chemical Engineering
FORCIONI, A., Comparative Literature
FORD, A. L., Classics
FORREST, S. R., Electrical Engineering
FOSTER, H. F., Art and Archaeology
FRANKFURT, H. G., Philosophy
FRASSICA, P., Romance Languages and Lit-
eratures
FREEDMAN, R. W. B., Comparative Literature
FREIDIN, R. A., Ccl of the Humanities
FRESCO, J. R., Life Sciences
FRIEDBERG, A. L., Politics and International
Affairs
GAGER, J. G., Jr, Religion
GANDELSONAS, M. I., Architecture
GARON, S. M., History and East Asian Stud-
ies
GARVEY, G., Politics
GEDDES, R. L., Architecture
GEISON, G. L., History and History of Science
GEORGE, R. P., Jurisprudence
GIBBS, N., Journalism and Council of
Humanities
GIRGUS, J. S., Psychology
GLASSMAN, I., Mechanical and Aerospace
Engineering
GLUCKSBERG, S., Psychology
GOLDMAN, M. P., English
GOLDMAN, N. J., Demography and Public
Affairs
GOLDSTON, R. J., Astrophysical Sciences
GOODMAN, J., Astrophysical Sciences
GOSSMAN, J. L., Romance Languages and
Literatures
GOTT, J. R., III, Astrophysical Sciences
GOULD, E., Psychology
GOULD, J. L., Biology
GOWA, J., Politics

GOWIN, E. W., Council of the Humanities and Visual Arts
GRAF, F., Classics
GRAFTON, A. T., History
GRANT, P., Biology
GRAVES, M., Architecture
GREENSTEIN, F. I., Politics
GROSS, C. G., Psychology
GROSSMAN, G. M., Economics and Business Policy
GROTH, E. J., III, Physics
GROVES, J. T., Chemistry
GRUNER, S. M., Physics
GUL, F. R., Economics
GUNN, J. E., Astronomy
GUNNING, R. C.
GUTMANN, A., Politics
HAHN, B., Germanic Languages and Literatures
HALDANE, F. D. M., Physics
HAMMOUDI, A., Anthropology and Near East Studies
HAMORI, A. P., Near Eastern Studies
HANIOGLU, M. S., Near Eastern Studies
HAPPER, W., Physics
HARMAN, G. H., Philosophy
HARTOG, H. A., History
HELD, I. M., Geological and Geophysical Sciences, Atmospheric and Oceanic Sciences
HERBST, J. I., Politics and International Affairs
HIMMELFARB, M., Religion
HINDERER, W., Germanic Languages and Literatures
HOCHSCHILD, J. L., Politics and Public Affairs
HOEBEL, B. G., Psychology
HOFFMANN, L.-F., Romance Languages
HOLLANDER, R. B., Jr, European and Comparative Literature
HOLLISTER, L. S., Geological and Geophysical Sciences
HOLMES, P. J., Mechanical and Aerospace Engineering
HONORE, B. E., Economics
HOPFIELD, J. J., Molecular Biology
HORN, H. S., Biology
HOWARTH, W. L., English
HSIANG, W.-C., Mathematics
HUET, M.-H., Romance Languages and Literatures
ISSAWI, C., Near Eastern Studies
ITZKOWITZ, N., Near Eastern Studies
JACOBS, B. L., Psychology
JAFFE, P. R., Civil and Environmental Engineering
JAHN, R. G., Aerospace Sciences
JAMES, H., History
JAMESON, A., Mechanical and Aerospace Engineering
JEFFREY, P., Music
JENNINGS, M. W., Germanic Languages and Literatures
JHA, N. K., Electrical Engineering
JOHNSON, C. L., English
JOHNSON, M., Psychology
JOHNSON-LAIRD, P. N., Psychology
JOHNSTON, M., Philosophy
JONES, M., Chemistry
JORDON, W. C., History
KAHN, A., Electrical Engineering
KAHN, V. A., English and Comparative Literature
KAHNEMAN, D., Psychology
KASTER, R. A., Latin Language and Literature
KATEB, G., Politics
KATZ, N. M., Mathematics
KAUFMANN, T. D., Art and Archaeology
KELLER, G., Geological and Geophysical Sciences
KELLER, S., Sociology
KELLEY, S., Politics
KENEN, P. B., Economics and International Finance
KEVREKIDIS, Y. G., Chemical Engineering

KINCHLA, R. A., Psychology
KING, E. L., Language, Literature, and Civilization of Spain
KLAINERMAN, S., Mathematics
KLEBANOV, I. R., Mathematical Physics
KNAPP, G. R., Astrophysical Sciences
KNOEPFLMACHER, U. C., English
KOBAYASHI, H., Electrical Engineering and Computer Science
KOCHEN, S. B., Mathematics
KOHLI, A., Politics and International Affairs
KOHN, J. J., Mathematics
KOLLAR, J., Mathematics
KOMUNYAKAA, Y., Council of the Humanities and Creative Writing
KORNHAUSER, A. L., Civil Engineering
KOSTIN, M. D., Chemical Engineering
KRIPKE, S., Philosophy
KROMMES, J. A., Astrophysical Sciences
KUNG, S.-Y., Electrical Engineering
LAKE, P. G., History
LAM, S.-H., Mechanical and Aerospace Engineering
LAMB, J., English
LAMONT, M., Sociology
LANGE, V., Modern Languages
LANGLOIS, J. D., Jr, East Asian Studies
LANSKY, P., Music
LA PAUGH, A. S., Computer Science
LAU, N.-C., Geosciences and Atmospheric and Oceanic Sciences
LAW, C. K., Mechanical and Aerospace Engineering
LEE, P. C. Y., Civil Engineering
LEE, R. B.-L., Engineering
LEHMANN, K. K., Chemistry
LEIBLER, S., Physics and Molecular Biology
LERNER, R., Architecture
LEVIN, S. A., Ecology and Evolutionary Biology
LEWIS, D. K., Philosophy
LEWIS, J. P., Economics and International Affairs
LI, K., Computer Science
LIEB, E. H., Mathematical Physics
LINK, E. P., East Asian Studies
LIPTON, R. J., Computer Science
LITTMAN, M. G., Mechanical and Aerospace Engineering
LIU, B., Electrical Engineering
LONGUENESSE, B. M., Philosophy
LOWRY, H. N., Ottoman and Modern Turkish Studies
LYON, S. A., Electrical Engineering
McDONALD, K. T., Physics
MACEDO, S. J., Politics
MACKEY, S., Music
McLANAHAN, S. S., Sociology and Public Affairs
McLENDON, G. L., Chemistry
McPHERSON, J. M., History
MAHLMAN, J. D., Geological and Geophysical Sciences, and Atmospheric and Oceanic Sciences
MAHONEY, M. S., History and History of Science
MAKINO, S., East Asian Studies
MALIK, S., Electrical Engineering
MALKIEL, B. G., Economics
MALKIEL, N. W., History
MAMAN, A., French, Romance Languages and Literatures
MARLOW, D. R., Physics
MARTIN, E., Anthropology
MARTIN, R. B., English
MATHER, J. N., Mathematics
MEYER, H., Art and Archaeology
MEYERS, P. D., Physics
MILES, R. B., Mechanical and Aerospace Engineering
MILLER, D. T., Psychology
MILLER, G. A., Psychology
MILLER, H. K., English
MITCHELL, L. C., English
MODARRESSI, H., Near Eastern Studies
MOREL, F. M., Geosciences

MORGAN, W. J., Geophysics
MULDOON, P. B., Humanities
MULVEY, J. M., Civil Engineering
MURRIN, J. M., History
NAQUIN, S., History
NASH, S. C., Romance Languages and Literature
NEHAMAS, A., Humanities, Philosophy and Comparative Literature
NELSON, J., Mathematics
NEWTON, A., Molecular Biology
NOLET, A. M., Geological and Geophysical Sciences
NORD, D. E., English
NORD, P. G., History
OBER, J., Classics
ONG, N.-P., Physics
ORLANSKI, I., Geological and Geophysical Sciences, and Atmospheric and Oceanic Sciences
OSTRIKER, J. P., Astrophysical Sciences
PACALA, S., Ecology
PACZYNSKI, B., Astrophysical Sciences
PAGE, L. A., Jr, Physics
PAGELS, E. H., Religion
PAINTER, N. I., History
PANAGIOTOPOULOS, A. Z., Chemical Engineering
PAVEL, T., Comparative Literature, and Romance Languages and Literatures
PAXSON, C. H., Economics and Public Affairs
PEEBLES, P. J. E., Physics
PETERSON, L. I., Computer Science
PETERSON, W. J., East Asian Studies
PHILANDER, S. G. H., Geological and Geophysical Sciences
PHINNEY, R. A., Geological and Geophysical Sciences
PINTO, J. A., Art and Archaeology
PIROUÉ, P. A., Physics
PLAKS, A. H., East Asian Studies
POLYAKOV, A., Physics
POOR, H. V., Electrical Engineering
PORTES, A., Sociology
POWELL, W. B., Civil Engineering
POWERS, H. S., Music
PRAKASH, G., History
PRENTICE, D. A., Psychology
PREVOST, J.-H., Civil Engineering
PRUCNAL, P. R., Electrical Engineering
PRUDHOMME, P. R., Chemical and Electrical Engineering
RABB, T. K., History
RABINBACH, A. G., History
RABITZ, H. A., Chemistry
RABOTEAU, A. J., Religion
REINHARDT, U. E., Economics and Public Affairs, and Political Economy
RICHARDSON, J., English
RIGOLOT, F., Romance Languages and Literatures
ROCHE, T. P., Jr, English
RODGERS, D. T., History
RODRIGUEZ-ITURBE, I., Civil and Environmental Engineering
ROMER, T., Politics and Public Affairs
ROSE, M. D., Molecular Biology
ROSEN, H. S., Economics
ROSEN, L., Anthropology
ROSENTHAL, H., Social Sciences
ROTHSCHILD, M., Economics and Public Affairs
ROYCE, B. S. H., Mechanical and Aerospace Engineering
ROZMAN, G. F., Sociology
RUBENSTEIN, A., Economics
RUBENSTEIN, D. I., Ecology and Evolutionary Biology
RUSSEL, W. B., Chemical Engineering
RYSKAMP, C. A., English
SARMIENTO, J. L., Geological and Geophysical Sciences
SARNAK, P. C., Mathematics
SAVILLE, D. A., Chemical Engineering
SCANLON, R. H., Civil Engineering
SCHAFER, P., Jewish Studies

SCHEDL, P. D., Molecular Biology
SCHEINKMAN, J. A., Economics
SCHERER, G. W., Civil and Environmental Engineering
SCHMIDT, L. E., Religion
SCHOWALTER, W. R., Engineering and Applied Science
SCHUPBACH, G. M., Molecular Biology
SCHUTT, C. E., Chemistry
SCHWARTZ, J., Chemistry
SCHWARTZ, S. C., Electrical Engineering
SCOLES, G., Chemistry
SEAWRIGHT, J. L., Council of Humanities
SEDGEWICK, R., Computer Science
SEMMELHACK, M. F., Chemistry
SEYMOUR, P. D., Mathematics, and Applied and Computational Mathematics
SHAFIR, E. B., Psychology
SHAPIRO, H. T., Economics and Public Affairs
SHAYEGAN, M., Electrical Engineering
SHEAR, T. L., Jr, Classical Archaeology
SHENK, T. E., Molecular Biology
SHIMIZU, Y., Art and Archaeology
SHOWALTER, E., English
SIGMUND, P. E., Politics
SILHAVY, T. J., Molecular Biology
SILVER, L. M., Molecular Biology
SIMS, C. A., Economics
SINAI, Y. G., Mathematics
SINGER, B. H., Public and International Affairs
SINGER, P. A. D., Bioethics
SITNEY, P. A., Council of Humanities
SLABY, S. M., Civil Engineering
SMITH, A. J., Physics
SMITH, J. A., Civil and Environmental Engineering
SMITH, J. C. O., Humanities
SMITH, J. W., Philosophy
SMITH, N., English
SMITS, A., Mechanical and Aerospace Engineering
SMOLUCHOWSKI, R., Solid State Sciences
SOANES, S., Philosophy
SOBOYEJO, W. O., Mechanical and Aerospace Engineering
SOCOLOW, R. H., Mechanical and Aerospace Engineering
SONER, H. M., Engineering and Finance
SOOS, Z. G., Chemistry
SPIRO, T. G., Chemistry
SPITZER, L., Jr, Astronomy
SROLOVITZ, D. J., Mechanical and Aerospace Engineering
STANSELL, M. C., History
STARR, P., Sociology
STEIGLITZ, K., Computer Science
STEIN, E. M., Mathematics
STEIN, S. J., History
STEINBERG, M., Biology
STEINHARDT, P. J., Physics
STENGEL, R. F., Mechanical and Aerospace Engineering
STOCK, J. B., Molecular Biology
STOUT, J. L., Religion
STURM, J. C., Electrical Engineering
SUCKEWER, S., Mechanical and Aerospace Engineering
SULEIMAN, E. N., Politics
SUNDARESAN, S., Chemical Engineering
SUO, Z., Mechanical and Aerospace Engineering
SUPPE, J. E., Geological and Geophysical Sciences
SURTZ, R. E., Romance Languages and Literatures
TARJAN, R. E., Computer Science
TATE, C. C., English
TAYLOR, H. F., Sociology
TAYLOR, J. H., Physics
TEISER, S. F., Buddhist Studies
TEYSSOT, G. M., Architecture
TIENDA, M., Demographic Studies
TIGNOR, R. L., History
TORQUATO, S., Civil Engineering

TOWNSEND, C. E., Slavic Languages and Literatures
TREISMAN, A., Psychology
TREMAINE, S. D., Astrophysical Sciences
TROTTER, H. F., Mathematics
TRUSSELL, T. J., Economics and Public Affairs
TSUI, D. C., Electrical Engineering
TUKEY, J. W., Science, Statistics
TURNER, E. L., Astrophysical Sciences
UDOVITCH, A. L., Near Eastern Studies
UITTI, K. D., Modern Languages, Romance Languages and Literatures
ULLMAN, R., International Affairs
VAN FRAASSEN, B. C., Philosophy
VAN HOUTEN, F. B., Geological and Geophysical Sciences
VANMARCKE, E., Civil Engineering
VERDU, S., Electrical Engineering
VERLINDE, H. L., Physics
VOLKER, P. A., International and Economic Policy
VON GOELER, S. E., Astrophysical Sciences
VON HIPPEL, F. N., Public and International Affairs
WACHTEL, M. A., Slavic Languages and Literatures
WAGNER, S., Electrical Engineering
WALLACE, W. L., Sociology
WARD, B. B., Geosciences
WARREN, S., Chemistry
WATSON, G. S., Statistics
WATSON, M. W., Economics and Public Affairs
WEI, J., Chemical Engineering
WEIGERT, M., Molecular Biology
WEINAN, E., Mathematics
WEISS, T. R., English and Creative Writing
WEITZMANN, K., Art and Archaeology
WEST, C., Afro-American Studies
WEST, C. R., Religion
WESTERGAARD, P. T., Music
WESTERN, B., Sociology
WHITE, L. T., Politics
WHITWELL, J. C., Chemical Engineering
WIESCHAUS, E. F., Biology
WIGHTMAN, A. S., Mathematical Physics
WILENTZ, R. S., History
WILES, A. J., Mathematics
WILKINSON, D. T., Physics
WILLIAMS, E. S., Humanities
WILLIG, R. D., Economics and Public Affairs
WILLIS, J. R., Near Eastern Studies
WILMERDING, J., American Art; Art and Archaeology
WILSON, J. F., Religion
WOLFSON, S. J., English
WOLPERT, J., Geography, Public Affairs and Urban Planning
WOOD, E. F., Civil Engineering
WOOD, M. G., English
WOODFORD, M. D., Economics and Banking
WUTHNOW, R. J., Sociology
YAO, A. L.-L., Computer Science
YU, Y. S., East Asian Studies
ZAKIAN, V. A., Molecular Biology
ZEITLIN, F. I., Classics
ZELIZER, V. A., Sociology
ZIOLKOWSKI, T. J., Germanic Languages and Literatures, and Comparative Literature

RAMAPO COLLEGE OF NEW JERSEY

505 Ramapo Valley Rd, Mahwah, NJ 07430-1680

Telephone: (201) 684-7500
Fax: (201) 684-7964
E-mail: admissions@ramapo.edu
Internet: www.ramapo.edu

Founded 1969
State control
Academic year: September to May

Pres.: Dr PETER PHILIP MERCER
Provost and Vice-Pres. for Academic Affairs: Dr BETH E. BARNETT

Vice-Pres. for Institutional Advancement: CATHLEEN DAVEY
Vice-Pres. for Student Affairs: Dr PAMELA M. BISCHOFF
Dean for Students: NANCY MACKIN
Registrar: CYNTHIA BRENNAN
Librarian: ELIZABETH SIECKE
Library of 170,000 vols, 5,000 DVDs
Number of teachers: 187
Number of students: 6,008

Publications: *Eastern Economic Journal* (4 a year), *Ramapo Magazine, Viewbook*

DEANS

Anisfield School of Business: Dr LEWIS M. CHAKRIN
School of American and International Studies: Dr HASSAN M. NEJAD
School of Contemporary Arts: STEVEN PERRY
School of Social Science and Human Services: Dr SAMUEL ROSENBERG
School of Theoretical and Applied Science: Dr EDWARD SAIFF

RICHARD STOCKTON COLLEGE OF NEW JERSEY

101 Vera King Farris Dr., Galloway, NJ 08205-9441

Telephone: (609) 652-1776
Internet: www.stockton.edu

Founded 1969 as Richard Stockton State College
Academic year: September to May

Pres.: Dr HERMAN J. SAATKAMP, JR
Provost and Exec. Vice-Pres.: HARVEY KESSELMAN
Vice-Pres. for Admin. and Finance: ROBERT D'AUGUSTINE
Vice-Pres. for Student Affairs: THOMASA GONZALEZ
Gen. Counsel: MELISSA E. HAGER
Registrar: JOSEPH J. LoSASSO
Library Dir: DAVID PINTO
Number of teachers: 282 (full-time)
Number of students: 8,108

DEANS

School of Arts and Humanities: ROBERT GREGG
School of Business: Dr JANET M. WAGNER
School of Education: Dr JOSEPH MARCHETTI
School of General Studies: G. JAN COLIJN
School of Graduate and Continuing Studies: Dr LEWIS LEITNER
School of Health Sciences: Dr Prof. BRENDA STEVENSON MARSHALL
School of Natural Sciences and Mathematics: Dr DENNIS WEISS
School of Social and Behavioral Sciences: Dr CHERYL R. KAUS

RIDER UNIVERSITY

2083 Lawrenceville Rd, Lawrenceville, NJ 08648-3099

Telephone: (609) 896-5000
Fax: (609) 896-8029
E-mail: admissions@rider.edu
Internet: www.rider.edu

Founded 1865 as Trenton Business College, present name and status 1994
Private control

Campuses in Lawrenceville and Princeton

Pres.: Dr MORDECHAI ROZANSKI
Provost and Vice-Pres. for Academic Affairs: Dr DONALD A. STEVEN
Vice-Pres. for Enrolment Management: JAMIE O'HARA
Vice-Pres. for Finance and Treas.: JULIE A. KARNS
Assoc. Vice-Pres. for Student Affairs: Dr ANTHONY CAMPBELL

Vice-Pres. for Univ. Advancement: JONATHAN MEER
Dean for Univ. Libraries: F. WILLIAM CHICKERING
Library of 481,000 vols, 650,000 microforms
Number of teachers: 250
Number of students: 5,800 (4,700 undergraduate, 1,100 graduate)
Publication: *Rider University Magazine*

DEANS

College of Business Admin.: Dr LARRY M. NEWMAN
College of Continuing Studies: BORIS VILIC
College of Liberal Arts, Education, and Sciences: Dr PATRICIA MOSTO
Westminster College of the Arts: ROBERT L. ANNIS

ROWAN UNIVERSITY

201 Mullica Hill Rd, Glassboro, NJ 08028
Telephone: (856) 256-4000
Fax: (856) 256-4444
E-mail: admissions@rowan.edu
Internet: www.rowan.edu
Founded 1923 as Glassboro Normal School, present name and status 1997
State control
Academic year: July to June
Campuses in Glassboro and Camden
Pres.: Dr ALI HOUSHMAND
Provost: Dr JAMES NEWELL
Vice-Pres. for Facilities and Operations: MICHAEL HARRIS
Vice-Pres. for Finance and Chief Financial Officer: JOSEPH SCULLY
Vice-Pres. for Student Life: RICHARD JONES
Vice-Pres. for Univ. Relations: THOMAS GALLIA
Registrar: MURIEL A. J. FRIERSON
Dean for Camden Campus: Dr TYRONE W. McCOMBS
Dean for Library Services: BRUCE WHITHAM
Library of 350,000 vols
Number of teachers: 1,049
Number of students: 11,816 (10,438 undergraduate, 1,378 graduate)
Publications: *Avant, Image, Rowan Magazine* (3 a year), *The Gallery, Venue*

DEANS

College of Communication: LORIN BASDEN ARNOLD
College of Education: Dr CAROL A. SHARP
College of Engineering: Dr STEVEN CHIN
College of Fine and Performing Arts: JOHN R. PASTIN
College of Graduate and Continuing Education: Dr HORACIO SOSA
College of Liberal Arts and Sciences: Dr PARVIZ ANSARI
Cooper Medical School: Dr PAUL KATZ
Rohrer College of Business: NIRANJAN PATI

RUTGERS, THE STATE UNIVERSITY OF NEW JERSEY

57 US Highway One, New Brunswick, NJ 08901-8554
Telephone: (732) 445-4636
Internet: www.rutgers.edu
Founded 1766 as Queen's College
State control
Academic year: September to May
Pres.: Dr RICHARD L. McCORMICK
Provost for Biomedical and Health Sciences: Dr CHRISTOPHER MOLLOY
Exec. Vice-Pres. for Academic Affairs: Dr RICHARD EDWARDS
Exec. Vice-Pres. for Devt and Alumni Relations: CAROL P. HERRING

Sr Vice-Pres. for Finance and Admin.: BRUCE C. FEHN
Sr Vice-Pres. and Gen. Counsel: JONATHAN R. ALGER
Sr Vice-Pres. for Lifelong Learning: Dr DAVID FEINGOLD
Vice-Pres. for Admin. and Public Safety: JAY KOHL
Vice-Pres. for Alumni Relations: DONNA THORNTON
Vice-Pres. for Continuous Education and Outreach: RAPHAEL J. CAPRIO
Vice-Pres. for Enrolment Management: COURTNEY O. McANUFF
Vice-Pres. for Faculty and Staff Resources: VIVIAN FERNANDEZ
Vice-Pres. for Int. and Global Affairs: Dr JOANNA REGULSKA
Vice-Pres. for Public Affairs: Dr PETER McDONOUGH, JR
Vice-Pres. for Research and and Economic Devt: Dr MICHAEL J. PAZZANI
Vice-Pres. for Student Affairs: Dr GREGORY S. BLIMLING
Vice-Pres. for Undergraduate Education: Dr BARRY QUALLS
Vice-Pres. for Univ. Budgeting: Dr NANCY S. WINTERBAUER
Vice-Pres. for Univ. Relations: KIM MANNING
Sec.: LESLIE A. FEHRENBACH
Camden Campus Chancellor: Dr WENDELL E. PRITCHETT
Newark Campus Chancellor: Dr PHILIP YEAGLE
Univ. Librarian: MARIANNE GAUNT
Library: see Libraries and Archives
Number of teachers: 7,000 (full-time and part-time)
Number of students: 58,000 (incl. 14,800 postgraduate)
Publications: *Journal of Law and Public Policy, Journal of Regulatory Economics* (4 a year), *Labor Studies Journal, Plant Molecular Biology Reporter, Public Budgeting and Finance, Public Productivity and Management Review, Raritan Review* (4 a year), *Rutgers Business Law Journal, Rutgers Computer and Technology Law Journal* (2 a year), *Rutgers Journal of Law & Religion, Rutgers Law Journal, Rutgers Law Record* (online (www.lawrecord.com)), *Rutgers Law Review, Rutgers Race and the Law Review, Signs Journal of Women in Culture and Society* (4 a year), *Society, The American Sociologist, Women's Rights Law Reporter* (4 a year)

DEANS

Camden Campus:
College of Arts and Sciences and the Graduate School: Dr KRISTIE LINDEN-MEYER
School of Business: Dr JAISHANKAR GANESH
School of Law: RAYMAN SOLOMON
School of Nursing: Dr JOANNE P. ROBINSON

New Brunswick Campus:
College of Nursing (New Brunswick and Newark Campus: Dr WILLIAM L. HOLZE-MER
Edward J. Bloustein School of Planning and Public Policy: JAMES W. HUGHES
Ernest Mario School of Pharmacy: Dr JOSEPH A. BARONE (acting)
Graduate School: Dr JEROME J. KUKOR (acting)
Graduate School of Applied and Professional Psychology: STANLEY B. MESSER
Graduate School of Education: RICHARD DE LISI
Mason Gross School of the Arts: GEORGE B. STAUFFER
Rutgers Business School (Newark and New Brunswick): GLENN SHAFER

School of Arts and Sciences: DOUGLAS GREENBERG
School of Communication and Information: JORGE REINA SCHEMENT
School of Engineering: THOMAS N. FARRIS
School of Environmental and Biological Sciences: ROBERT M. GOODMAN
School of Management and Labor Relations: SUSAN J. SCHURMAN (acting)
School of Social Work: KATHLEEN J. POTTICK (acting)

Newark Campus:
College of Arts and Sciences and University College: JAN ELLEN LEWIS (acting)
Graduate School: Dr GARY ROTH
School of Criminal Justice: TODD R. CLEAR
School of Law: Prof. JOHN J. FARMER, JR
School of Public Affairs and Admin.: Dr MARC HOLZER

SAINT PETER'S COLLEGE

2641 John F. Kennedy Blvd, Jersey City, NJ 07306-5997
Telephone: (201) 761-6000
E-mail: gradadmit@spc.edu
Internet: www.spc.edu
Founded 1872
Private control
Academic year: August to May
Pres.: Dr EUGENE J. CORNACCHIA
Provost and Vice-Pres. for Academic Affairs: Dr MARYLOU YAM
Vice-Pres. for Advancement: MICHAEL A. FAZIO
Vice-Pres. for Finance and Business: DENTON STARGEL
Vice-Pres. for Mission and Ministry: Fr MICHAEL L. BRADEN
Vice-Pres. for Enrolment Management and Marketing: Dr TERENCE PEAVY
Academic Dean: Dr VELDA GOLDBERG
Dir for Admissions: DAVID GRIFFEY
Registrar: STEVEN E. SMITH
Library Dir: Dr DAVID ORENSTEIN
Library of 260,000 vols
Number of teachers: 284 (117 full-time, 167 part-time)
Number of students: 2,987 (2,344 undergraduate, 643 graduate)
Publication: *Saint Peter's College Magazine*

DEANS

College of Arts and Sciences and School of Business Administration: Dr VELDA GOLDBERG
School of Professional and Continuing Studies: ELIZABETH KANE

SETON HALL UNIVERSITY

400 S Orange Ave, South Orange, NJ 07079
Telephone: (973) 761-9000
Fax: (973) 275-2040
E-mail: thehall@shu.edu
Internet: www.shu.edu
Founded 1856 as Seton Hall College, present status 1950
Private control
Academic year: August to May
Pres.: Dr A. GABRIEL ESTEBAN
Exec. Vice-Pres. and Provost: Dr LARRY A. ROBINSON
Exec. Vice-Pres. for Admin.: Sr PAULA M. BULEY
Vice-Pres. for Enrolment Management: Dr ALYSSA McCLOUD
Vice-Pres. for Finance and Technology: DENNIS J. GARBINI
Vice-Pres. for Mission and Min.: Mgr ANTHONY ZICCARDI
Vice-Pres. for Student Services: Dr TRACY H. GOTTLIEB

Vice-Pres. for Univ. Advancement: Dr G. GREGORY TOBIN

Vice-Pres. and Gen. Counsel: CATHERINE A. KIERNAN

Dean for Libraries: Dr CHRYSANTHY M. GRIECO

Library of 750,000 vols, 25,000 journals

Number of teachers: 909 (446 full-time, 463 part-time)

Number of students: 9,700 (5,300 undergraduate, 4,400 graduate)

Publications: *Journal of Diplomacy and International Relations* (2 a year), *Mid-Atlantic Journal of Business* (3 a year), *The Chesterton Review* (4 a year), *The Journal of Global Health Governance* (2 a year)

DEANS

College of Arts and Sciences: Dr JOAN F. GUETTI

College of Education and Human Services: Dr JOSEPH DE PIERRO

College of Nursing: Dr PHYLLIS SHANLEY HANSELL

Div. of Continuing Education and Professional Studies: Dr NANCY LOW-HOGAN

Immaculate Conception Seminary School of Theology: Mgr ROBERT COLEMAN

School of Health and Medical Sciences: Dr BRIAN B. SHULMAN

School of Law: PATRICK E. HOBBS

W. Paul Stillman School of Business: Dr JOYCE A. STRAWSER (acting)

Whitehead School of Diplomacy and International Relations: Dr JOHN K. MENZIES

STEVENS INSTITUTE OF TECHNOLOGY

Castle Point on Hudson, Hoboken, NJ 07030-5991

Telephone: (201) 216-5000

Fax: (201) 216-5520

Internet: www.stevens-tech.edu

Founded 1870

Private control

Pres.: Dr NARIMAN FARVARDIN

Provost and Univ. Vice-Pres.: GEORGE KORFIATIS

Vice-Pres. and Chief Admin. Officer: MAUREEN P. WEATHERALL

Vice-Pres. for Devt: ED EICHHORN

Vice-Pres. for Facilities and Community Relations: HENRY P. DOBBELAAR

Vice-Pres. for Finance, Chief Financial Officer and Treas.: RANDY L. GREENE

Vice-Pres., Gen. Counsel and Sec.: KATHY L. SCHULZ

Vice-Pres. for Univ. Research and Enterprise Devt: HELENA S. WISNIEWSKI

Dean for Admissions: DANIEL S. GALLAGHER

Dean for Graduate Studies: CHARLES L. SUFFEL

Library Dir: OURIDA OUBRAHAM

Library of 105,000 vols, 48,815 e-books, 43,887 e-journals

Number of teachers: 438

Number of students: 5,934 (2,234 undergraduate, 3,700 graduate)

DEANS

Charles V. Schaefer, Jr, School of Engineering and Science: Dr MICHAEL BRUNO

College of Arts and Letters: Dr LISA DOLLING

School of Systems and Enterprises: Dr DINESH VERMA

Wesley J. Howe School of Technology Management: Dr GREGORY PRASTACOS

THOMAS EDISON STATE COLLEGE

101 W State St, Trenton, NJ 08608-1176

Telephone: (888) 442-8372

Fax: (609) 984-8447

E-mail: info@tesc.edu

Internet: www.tesc.edu

Founded 1972

State control

Pres.: Dr GEORGE A. PRUITT

Vice-Pres. and Provost: WILLIAM J. SEATON

Vice-Pres. and Treas.: MICHAEL J. SCHEIRING

Vice-Pres. for Planning and Research: Dr PENELOPE S. BROUWER

Vice-Pres. for Public Affairs: JOHN P. THURBER

Registrar: SHARON SMITH

Number of students: 20,200

DEANS

Heavin School of Arts and Sciences: Dr SUSAN DAVENPORT

John S. Watson School of Public Service and Continuing Studies: Dr JOSEPH YOUNGBLOOD, II

School of Applied Science and Technology: Dr THOMAS G. DEVINE (acting)

School of Business and Management: Dr SUSAN P. GILBERT

W. Cary Edwards School of Nursing: Dr SUSAN McMULLEN O'BRIEN

UNIVERSITY OF MEDICINE & DENTISTRY OF NEW JERSEY

POB 1709, 65 Bergen St, Suite 701, Newark, NJ 07107-1709

Telephone: (973) 972-4300

E-mail: uhcontact@umdnj.edu

Internet: www.umdnj.edu

Founded 1970 as College of Medicine and Dentistry of New Jersey, present name and status 1981

Campuses at: Newark, Stratford, Camden, Piscataway/New Brunswick, Scotch Plains

Pres.: Dr DENISE V. RODGERS

Exec. Vice-Pres. for Academic and Clinical Affairs: Dr DENISE V. RODGERS

Sr Vice-Pres. and Gen. Counsel: LESTER ARON

Sr Vice-Pres. for Admin.: Dr CHRISTOPHER KOSSEFF

Sr Vice-Pres. for Finance: DENISE MULKERN

Sr Vice-Pres. for Govt and Community Affairs: JULANE MILLER-ARMBRISTER

Sr Vice-Pres. for Univ. Advancement and Communications: DIANE WEATHERS

Vice-Pres. for Information Services and Technology: DENISE ROMANO

Vice-Pres. for Research: Dr KATHLEEN W. SCOTTO

Univ. Librarian: JUDY COHN

Library of 4,521 vols, 65,600 monographs

Number of teachers: 2,391

Number of students: 5,915

Publications: *UMDNJ, UMDNJ Research*

DEANS

Graduate School of Biomedical Sciences: Dr KATHLEEN W. SCOTTO

New Jersey Dental School: Dr CECILE A. FELDMAN

New Jersey Medical School: Dr ROBERT L. JOHNSON

Robert Wood Johnson Medical School: Dr PETER S. AMENTA

School of Health Related Professions: Dr JULIE O'SULLIVAN MAILLET

School of Nursing: Dr SUSAN W. SALMOND

School of Osteopathic Medicine: Dr THOMAS A. CAVALIERI

School of Public Health: Dr GEORGE G. RHOADS

WILLIAM PATERSON UNIVERSITY OF NEW JERSEY

300 Pompton Rd, Wayne, NJ 07470

Telephone: (973) 720-2000

Internet: www.wpunj.edu

Founded 1855 as Paterson City Normal School, present name 1997

State control

Academic year: September to June

Pres.: Dr KATHLEEN WALDRON

Provost and Sr Vice-Pres. for Academic Affairs: Dr EDWARD B. WEIL

Vice-Pres. for Admin. and Finance: STEPHEN BOLYAI

Vice-Pres. for Enrolment Management: KRISTIN E. COHEN

Vice-Pres. for Institutional Advancement: PAMELA L. FERGUSON

Vice-Pres. for Student Devt: JOHN MARTONE

Registrar: MARK EVANGELISTA

Dean for Library Services: Dr ANNE CILIBERTI

Library of 303,545 vols

Number of teachers: 389 (full-time)

Number of students: 11,518 (10,085 undergraduate, 1,433 graduate)

DEANS

College of Arts and Communication: STEPHEN HAHN

College of Education: CANDACE BURNS

College of Humanities and Social Science: KARA RABBITT

College of Science and Health: Dr SANDRA DeYOUNG

Cotsakos College of Business: Dr SAM BASU

NEW MEXICO

EASTERN NEW MEXICO UNIVERSITY

1500 S Ave K, Portales, NM 88130

Telephone: (505) 562-1011

E-mail: enrollment.services@enmu.edu

Internet: www.enmu.edu

Founded 1934

State control

Pres.: Dr STEVEN GAMBLE

Vice-Pres. for Academic Affairs: Dr JAMIE LAURENZ

Vice-Pres. for Student Affairs: Dr JUDITH HAISLETT

Vice-Pres. for Univ. Relations and Enrolment Services: RONNIE BIRDSONG

Registrar: CRYSTAL CREEKMORE

Dir for Library: MELVETA WALKER

Library of 699,847 vols, 300 works of art

Number of teachers: 262

Number of students: 5,080

DEANS

College of Business: Dr D. CHRISTOPHER TAYLOR

College of Education and Technology: Dr JERRY HARMON

College of Fine Arts: Dr JOSEPH KLINE

College of Liberal Arts and Sciences: Dr MARY FANELLI AYALA

Graduate School: Dr LINDA WEEMS

INSTITUTE OF AMERICAN INDIAN AND ALASKA NATIVE CULTURE AND ARTS DEVELOPMENT

83 Avan Nu Po Rd, Santa Fe, NM 87508

Telephone: (505) 424-2300

Fax: (505) 424-4500

Internet: www.iaia.edu

Founded 1962

Tribal control

Areas of study: fine arts in creative writing, indigenous liberal studies, museum studies, new media arts, studio arts

Pres.: Dr ROBERT G. MARTIN

Dir for Institutional Advancement: KIRSTEN JASNA

Academic Dean: Dr ANN FILEMYR

Dir for Library Programmes: SARAH KOSTELECKY.

NAVAJO TECHNICAL COLLEGE

POB 849, Crownpoint, NM 87313

Telephone: (505) 786-4100
Fax: (505) 786-5644
Internet: www.navajotech.edu

Founded 1979
Tribal control
Academic year: August to May (2 semesters)

Pres.: Dr ELMER J. GUY
Dir for Institutional Devt: JASON ARVISO
Dean for Instruction: TOM DAVIS
Dean for Student Services: Dr LAWRENCE ISAAC, JR
Registrar: DELORIS BECENTI
Librarian: CLYDE HENDERSON

Library of 250,000 vols.

NEW MEXICO HIGHLANDS UNIVERSITY

POB 9000, Las Vegas, NM 87701

Telephone: (505) 425-7511
Fax: (505) 454-3069
E-mail: admissions@nmhu.edu
Internet: www.nmhu.edu

Founded 1893 as New Mexico Normal School, present name and status 1941
State control
Academic year: August to May (2 semesters)

Pres.: Dr JAMES A. FRIES
Vice-Pres. for Academic Affairs: GILBERT D. RIVERA
Assoc. Vice-Pres. for Finance and Admin. Services: LAWRENCE TRUJILLO
Dean for Student Affairs: Dr FIDEL TRUJILLO
Registrar and Dir for Admissions: JOHN COCA
Dir for Library Services: RUBEN F. ARAGON

Number of teachers: 120
Number of students: 3,809

DEANS

College of Arts and Sciences: Dr ROY LUJAN
School of Business Media and Technology: Dr MARGARET YOUNG
School of Education: Dr MICHAEL ANDERSON
School of Social Work: Dr ALFREDO GARCIA

NEW MEXICO STATE UNIVERSITY

POB 30001, Las Cruces, NM 88003-8001

Telephone: (505) 646-0111
Fax: (505) 646-1517
E-mail: president@nmsu.edu
Internet: www.nmsu.edu

Founded 1888 as Las Cruces College, present name and status 1960
State control
Academic year: August to May

Pres.: BARBARA COUTURE
Exec. Vice-Pres. and Provost: Dr WENDY K. WILKINS
Sr Vice-Pres. for Admin. and Finance: ANGELA M. THRONEBERRY
Sr Vice-Pres. for External Relations: BENJAMIN WOODS
Vice-Pres. for Economic Devt: GARREY CARRUTHERS
Vice-Pres. for Research: VIMAL CHAITANYA
Vice-Pres. for Student Success: BERNADETTE MONTOYA
Vice-Pres. for Univ. Advancement: DENNIS PRESCOTT
Dean for Library: Dr ELIZABETH TITUS

Library: 1m. vols, 431,225 bound and unbound govt docs, 1.3m. microforms
Number of teachers: 1,826
Number of students: 30,866

DEANS

College of Agriculture, Consumer and Environmental Sciences: LOWELL CATLETT
College of Arts and Sciences: CHRISTA SLATON
College of Business: GARREY CARRUTHERS
College of Education: MICHAEL MOREHEAD
College of Engineering: RICARDO JACQUEZ
College of Health and Social Services: TILA-HUAN ADERA
Graduate School: LINDA LACEY
Honors College: BILL EAMON

NEW MEXICO TECH

801 Leroy Pl., Socorro, NM 87801

Telephone: (575) 835-5434
Fax: (575) 835-5989
E-mail: admission@admin.nmt.edu
Internet: www.nmt.edu

Founded 1889 as New Mexico School of Mines, present name 1951
State control

Depts of biology, chemistry, civil and environmental engineering, computer science, electrical engineering, materials engineering, mathematics, mechanical engineering, mineral engineering, physics, psychology

Pres.: Dr DANIEL H. LÓPEZ
Vice-Pres. for Academic Affairs: Dr PETER GERITY
Vice-Pres. for Admin. and Finance: LONNIE G. MARQUEZ
Vice-Pres. for Research and Economic Devt: Dr VAN D. ROMERO
Vice-Pres. for Student and Univ. Relations: MELISSA JARAMILLO-FLEMING
Library Dir: LISA BEINHOFF

Library of 600,000 vols
Number of students: 2,009

NORTHERN NEW MEXICO COLLEGE

POB 160, El Rito, NM 87530

Telephone: (575) 581-4100
Fax: (505) 581-4130
Internet: www.nnmc.edu

Founded 1909 as Spanish American Normal School, present name and status 2005
State control
Academic year: August to July

Areas of study: biology, business administration, environmental science, information engineering technology, information technology, integrative healing, integrated studies, mathematics, mechanical engineering (solar energy), music (jazz studies), nursing, software engineering, teacher education; campus at Española (New Mexico)

Pres.: Dr NANCY BARCELÓ
Provost and Vice-Pres. for Academic Affairs: Dr ANTHONY SENA
Vice-Pres. for Admin.: DAVID SCHUTZ
Vice-Pres. for Student Services and Dir for Admissions: FRANK ORONA
Registrar: JAN C. DAWSON
Dir for Library: ISABEL RODARTE

Number of teachers: 198 (57 full-time, 141 part-time)
Number of students: 2,126

DEANS

College of Arts and Sciences: Dr MELLIS SCHMIDT
College of Community, Workforce and Career Technical Education: Dr CAMILLA BUSTAMANTE
College of Education: Dr CATHERINE BERRY-HILL

ST JOHN'S COLLEGE

1160 Camino Cruz Blanca, Santa Fe, NM 87501-4599

Telephone: (505) 984-6000
Fax: (505) 984-6003
E-mail: admissions@sjcsf.edu
Internet: www.sjcsf.edu

Founded 1696 as King William's School, present name 1784, Santa Fe campus 1964
Private control

For Annapolis br. see under Maryland

Pres.: MICHAEL P. PETERS
Dean: J. WALTER STERLING
Dir for Admissions: LARRY CLENDENIN
Registrar: MARLINE MARQUEZ SCALLY
Library Dir: JENNIFER SPRAGUE

Library of 65,000 vols
Number of teachers: 61
Number of students: 450

Publications: *Grout* (1 a year), *The Gadfly*.

SANTA FE UNIVERSITY OF ART AND DESIGN

1600 St Michael's Dr., Santa Fe, NM 87505-7634

Telephone: (505) 473-6011
Fax: (505) 473-6363
E-mail: admissions@santafeuniversity.edu
Internet: www.santafeuniversity.edu

Founded 1859 as St Michael's College, present name and status 2010
Private control
Academic year: August to August

Depts of art, contemporary music, creative writing and literature, graphic and digital design, liberal arts, moving image arts, performing arts, photography

Pres.: LARRY HINZ
Vice-Pres. for Academic Affairs: GERRY SNYDER
Dir for Admission: CHRISTINE GUEVARA
Dir for Enrolment: RICHARD FERGUSON
Registrar: MARY E. ANGELL
Dir for Library: VALERIE NYE

Library of 170,000 vols in Fogelson Library, also 2 spec. libraries: Chase Art History Library and Beaumont and Nancy Newhall Library
Number of teachers: 80 (full-time)
Number of students: 1,950 (750 full-time, 1,200 part-time)

SOUTHWESTERN COLLEGE

POB 4788, 3960 San Felipe Rd, Santa Fe, NM 87507

Telephone: (877) 471-5756
Fax: (505) 471-4071
E-mail: info@swc.edu
Internet: www.swc.edu

Founded 1976 as Quimby College
Private control

Masters programmes in art therapy, counselling; certificate programmes in action methods, art therapy, grief counselling, school counselling

Pres.: Dr JAMES MICHAEL NOLAN
Vice-Pres.: KATHERINE M. NINOS
Academic Dean: Dr WEBB GARRISON
Dir for Admissions: DRU PHOENIX
Registrar: ANDREA PACHECO
Librarian: LESLIE MONSALVE-JONES.

UNIVERSITY OF NEW MEXICO

Albuquerque, NM 87131

Telephone: (505) 277-0111
Fax: (505) 277-6809
E-mail: unmpres@unm.edu
Internet: www.unm.edu

Founded 1889
State control
Academic year: August to May

Pres.: Dr DAVID J. SCHMIDLY
Exec. Vice-Pres. for Academic Affairs and Provost: Dr SUZANNE TRAGER ORTEGA
Exec. Vice-Pres. for Admin.: DAVID W. HARRIS

Vice-Pres. for Equity and Inclusion: Dr JOSEPHINE DE LEON
Vice-Pres. for Research: Dr JULIA E. FULGHUM
Vice-Pres. for Student Affairs: ELISIO TORRES
Dean for Students: KIMMERLY KLOEPPEL
Registrar: ALEXANDER GONZALEZ
Dean for Univ. Libraries: MARTHA BEDARD
Library: see Libraries and Archives
Number of teachers: 3,736
Number of students: 28,079 (f. t. e.)

DEANS

Anderson School of Management: DOUGLAS M. BROWN (acting)
College of Arts and Sciences: Dr BRENDA J. CLAIBORNE
College of Education: Dr RICHARD HOWELL
College of Fine Arts: Dr JAMES LINNELL
College of Nursing: Dr NANCY RIDENOUR
Continuing Education: Dr RITA MARTINEZ-PURSON
Graduate Studies: Dr AMY WOHLERT
Pharm. D. College of Pharmacy: Dr DONALD GODWIN
School of Architecture and Planning: GERALDINE FORBES ISAIS (acting)
School of Engineering: Dr CATALIN ROMAN
School of Law: KEVIN WASHBURN
School of Medicine: PAUL B. ROTH
University College: PETER WHITE

PROFESSORS

ABDALLA, R. N., Art and Art History
ABRAMS, J., Medicine
ADAMSON, G. W., Special Education
AHLUWALIA, H. S., Physics and Astronomy
AHMED, N., Electrical and Computer Engineering
ALLEN, F. S., Chemistry
ALTENBACH, J. S., Biology
ALVERSON, D. C., Paediatrics
ANGEL, E. S., Electrical and Computer Engineering
ANGEL, R. M., Music
ANSPACH, J. F., Law
ATENCIO, A. C., Physiology
ATTERBOM, H. A., Health Promotion, Physical Education and Leisure Programmes
AVASTHI, P., Medicine
BACA, O. G., Biology
BAKER, W. E., Mechanical Engineering
BANKHURST, A. D., Medicine
BARBO, D. M., Obstetrics and Gynaecology
BARROW, T. F., Art and Art History
BARTLETT, L. A., English
BARTON, L. M., Biology
BASSALLECK, B., Physics and Astronomy
BASSO, K. H., Anthropology
BAWDEN, G. L., Anthropology
BEAR, D. G., Cell Biology
BEENE, L., English
BENNAHUM, D. A., Medicine
BENNAHUM, J., Theatre and Dance
BENNETT, M. D., Family and Community Medicine
BENZEL, E. C., Surgery
BERGEN, J. J., Spanish and Portuguese
BERGMAN, B. E., Law
BICKNELL, J. M., Neurology
BILLS, G. D., Linguistics
BIRKHOLZ, G. A., Nursing
BLACK, W. C., III, Pathology
BLACKWELL, P. J., Educational Foundations
BORDEN, T. A., Surgery
BORN, J. L., Pharmacy
BOWES, S., Educational Administration
BOYER, C. P., Mathematics and Statistics
BROGAN, J., Civil Engineering
BROOKSHIRE, D. S., Economics
BROWDE, M. B., Law
BROWN, F. L., Jr, Public Administration
BROWN, J., Biology
BRUECK, S. R. J., Electrical and Computer Engineering

BRYANT, H. C., Physics and Astronomy
BUCHNER, M. A., Mathematics and Statistics
BULLERS, W. I., Jr, Management
BURCHIEL, S. W., Pharmacy
BURNESS, H. S., Economics
BURR, S. L., Law
BURRIS, B. H., Sociology
BUSS, W., Pharmacology
BYBEE, J. L., Linguistics
CAHILL, K. E., Physics and Astronomy
CAPUTI, J. E., American Studies
CARDENAS, A. J., Spanish and Portuguese
CARLOW, T. J., Neurology
CAVES, C. M., Physics and Astronomy
CECCHI, J. L., Chemical and Nuclear Engineering
CHAMPOUX, J. E., Management
CHANDLER, C., Physics and Astronomy
CHANG, B. K., Medicine
CHAPDELAINE, M., Music
CHENG, J., Electrical and Computer Engineering
CHRISTENSEN, R. R., Mathematics and Statistics
CIVIKLY-POWELL, J. M., Communications and Journalism
CLARK, J. M., Music
CLOUGH, D. H., Nursing
COES, D. V., Management
COFER, L. F., Psychology
COHEN, E. B., Law Library
COLTON, D. L., Educational Administration
CONDON, J. C., Communication and Journalism
CONNELL-SZASZ, M., History
CORCORAN, G. B., Pharmacy
CORDOVA, I. R., Educational Administration
COUGHLIN, R., Sociology
COUTSIAS, E. A., Mathematics and Statistics
CRAVEN, D. L., Art and Art History
CRAWFORD, M. H., Medicine
CURET, L. B., Obstetrics and Gynaecology
DAIL, W. G., Jr, Anatomy
DAMICO, H., English
DATYE, A. K., Chemical and Nuclear Engineering
DAVIDSON, R., Librarianship
DAVIS, G. L., American Studies
DAVIS, L., Neurology
DAVIS, M., Radiology
DEKEYSER, J., Music
DELANEY, H. D., Psychology
DESIDERIO, R. J., Law
DEVRIES, R. C., Electrical and Computer Engineering
DICKINSON, W. E., Surgery
DIELS, J.-C. M., Physics and Astronomy
DIETERLE, B., Physics and Astronomy
DILLARD, J. F., Management
DINIUS, A., Dental Programme
DODSON, T. A., Music
DORATO, P., Electrical and Computer Engineering
DOUGHER, M. J., Psychology
DRENNAN, J., Orthopaedics
DUBAN, S. L., Paediatrics
DUMARS, C., Law
DUNCAN, M. H., Paediatrics
DURYEA, P. J., Education
DUSZYNSKI, D. W., Biology
EATON, R. P., Medicine
EFROMOVICH, S., Mathematics and Statistics
EL-GENK, M. S., Chemical and Nuclear Engineering
ELIAS, L., Medicine
ELLIOTT, P. C., Management
ELLIS, J. W., Law
ELLISON, J. A., Mathematics and Statistics
ENGELBRECHT, G. A., Counselling and Family Studies
ENKE, C. G., Chemistry
ERIBES, R. A., Architecture and Planning
ESTRIN, J. A., Anaesthesiology
ETULAIN, R., History
EVANS, W., Theatre and Dance
EWING, R. C., Earth Sciences

FEENEY, D., Psychology
FEINBERG, E. A., Art and Art History
FELBERG, L., Music
FIELD, F. R., Training and Learning Technologies
FINLEY, D., Physics and Astronomy
FISCHER, M. R., English
FISHBURN, W. R., Counselling and Family Studies
FLEMING, R. E., English
FLETCHER, M. P., General Library
FLEURY, P. A., Electrical and Computer Engineering
FORMAN, W. B., Medicine
FOUCAR, M. K., Pathology
FRANDSEN, K. D., Communication and Journalism
FRITZ, C. G., Law
FROELICH, J. W., Anthropology
FRONECH, D. K., Electrical and Computer Engineering
FRY, D., Surgery
GAINES, B., English
GALEY, W. R., Jr, Physiology
GALLAGHER, P. J., English
GARCIA, F. C., Political Science
GARRY, P. J., Pathology
GEISSMAN, J. W., Earth Sciences
GELL-MAN, M., Physics and Astronomy
GERDES, D. C., Modern and Classical Languages
GIBSON, A. G., Mathematics and Statistics
GILFEATHER, F., Mathematics and Statistics
GISSER, M., Economics
GLEW, R. H., Biochemistry
GLUCK, J. P., Psychology
GOMEZ-PALACIO, I., Law
GONZALES, R. A., Law
GONZALES-BERRY, E., Modern and Classical Languages
GOODMAN, R., Philosophy
GORDON, W. C., Psychology
GOSZ, J. R., Biology
GRANT, D., Management
GREENBERG, R. E., Paediatrics
GRIFFIN, L. E., Health Promotion, Physical Education and Leisure Programmes
GWIN, M. C., English
HAALAND, K. Y., Psychiatry
HADLEY, W. M., Pharmacy
HAHN, B., Art and Art History
HAIMAN, F. S., General Honours
HALL, G. E., Law
HALL, J., Civil Engineering
HALL, L. B., History
HARJO, J., Engineering
HARRIS, F., Political Science
HARRIS, M., Educational Foundations
HARRIS, R. J., Psychology
HART, F. M., Law
HARTSHORNE, M. F., Radiology
HASHIMOTO, F., Medicine
HAWKINS, C., Electrical and Computer Engineering
HEFFRON, W. A., Family and Community Medicine
HEGGEN, R. J., Civil Engineering
HENNEY, J. E., Medicine
HERMANN, M. S. G., Law
HERZON, F. S., Surgery
HEYWARD, V., Health Promotion, Physical Education and Leisure Programmes
HIGGINS, P. A., Nursing
HINTERBICHLER, K., Music
HOLDER, R. W., Chemistry
HOLLAN, J. D., Computer Science
HUACO, G. A., Sociology
HUMPHRIES, S., Jr, Electrical and Computer Engineering
JAFFE, I. S., Theatre and Dance
JAIN, R., Electrical and Computer Engineering
JAMSHIDI, M., Electrical and Computer Engineering
JEWELL, P. F., Surgery
JOHNSON, D. M., English

JOHNSON, G. V., Biology
JOHNSON, J. D., Paediatrics
JOHNSON, P. J., Psychology
JOHN-STEINER, V. P., Education
JONES, D., English
JOOST-GAUGIER, C., Art and Art History
JORDAN, S. W., Pathology
JUNGLING, K. C., Electrical and Computer Engineering
KARLSTROM, K. E., Earth Sciences
KARNI, S., Electrical and Computer Engineering
KASSICIEH, S. K., Management
KAUFFMAN, D., Chemical and Nuclear Engineering
KAUFMAN, A., Family, Community and Emergency Medicine
KEITH, S. J., Psychiatry
KELLEY, R. O., Anatomy
KELLY, H. W., Pharmacy
KELLY, S. G., Law
KELSEY, C. A., Radiology
KELSEY, C. W., Education
KENDALL, D. L., Electrical and Computer Engineering
KENKRE, V. M., Physics and Astronomy
KERN, R. W., History
KEY, C. R., Pathology
KISIEL, W., Pathology
KLEIN, C., Geology
KLEPPER, D. J., Medicine
KLINE, W., Education
KODRIC-BROWN, A., Biology
KOGOMA, T., Cell Biology
KORNFELD, M., Pathology
KOSTER, F. T., Medicine
KOVNAT, R., Law
KUCHARZ, W., Mathematics and Statistics
KUDO, A. M., Geology
KUES, B. S., Earth Sciences
LAFREE, G., Sociology
LAMPHERE, L., Anthropology
LANCASTER, J. B., Anthropology
LEWIS, S. L., Nursing
LIGON, J. D., Biology
LINDEMAN, R. D., Medicine
LINNELL, J., Theatre and Dance
LIPSCOMB, M. F., Pathology
LIPSKI, J., Modern Languages
LONG, V., Counselling and Family Studies
LOPEZ, A. S., Law
LORENZ, J., Mathematics and Statistics
LOTFIELD, R. B., Biochemistry
LOVE, E. B., Librarianship
LUCKASSON, R. A., Special Education
LUGER, G. F., Computer Science
LUMIA, R., Mechanical Engineering
LUTZ, W., Chemical and Nuclear Engineering
MCCARTHY, D. M., Medicine
MCCLELLAND, C. E., III, History
MCCONNELL, T. S., Pathology
MCCULLOUGH-BRABSON, E., Music
MCDANIEL, M., Psychology
MCFARLANE, D. R., Public Administration
MCGRAW, J., Physics and Astronomy
MCGUFFEE, L. J., Pharmacology
MACIEL, D. R., History
MCIVER, J. K., Physics and Astronomy
MCLAUGHLIN, J. C., Pathology
MCNAMARA, P. A., Sociology
MCNEIL, J., Electrical and Computer Engineering
MCPHERSON, D., English
MACPHERSON, W. T., Law
MAKI, G., Electrical and Computer Engineering
MALOLEPSY, J., Theatre and Dance
MANN, B. M., Mathematics and Statistics
MARTINEZ, J. G. R., Special Education
MATHEWSON, A. D., Law
MATTHEWS, J. A. J., Physics and Astronomy
MATTHEWS, O. P., Geography
MATWIYOFF, N. A., Cell Biology
MAY, G. W., Civil Engineering
MAY, P. A., Sociology
MEIZE-GROCHOWSKI, R., Nursing

MELADA, I. P., English
MENNIN, S. P., Anatomy
MERKX, G. W., Sociology
METTLER, F. A., Jr, Radiology
MIGNEAULT, R., Librarianship
MILLER, W. R., Psychology
MILSTEIN, M. M., Educational Administration
MOLD, C., Microbiology
MONEIM, M. S., Orthopaedics
MORAIN, S. A., Geography
MORET, B. M., Computer Science
MORRIS, D. M., Surgery
MORRIS, M. M., Education
MORROW, C., Chemistry
MOSELEY, P. L., Medicine
MURATA, G. H., Medicine
MURPHY, S. J., Paediatrics
NIEMCZYK, T. M., Chemistry
NORDHAUS, R. S., Architecture and Planning
NORWOOD, J. M., Law
NORWOOD, V. L., American Studies
NURNBERG, H. G., Psychiatry
NUTTALL, H. E., Jr, Chemical and Nuclear Engineering
OBENSHAIN, S. S., Paediatrics
OCCHIALINO, M., Law
OGILBY, P. R., Chemistry
OLIVER, J. M., Pathology
OLLER, J. W., Jr, Linguistics
OMDAHL, J. L., Biochemistry
OMER, G., Jr, Orthopaedics
ONDRIAS, M. R., Chemistry
ONNEWEER, C., Mathematics and Statistics
ORRISON, W. W., Radiology
ORTIZ, A. A., Anthropology
ORTIZ, J. V., Chemistry
OVERTURF, G. D., Paediatrics
OWENS, L. D., English
PABISCH, P. K., Foreign Languages and Literature
PADILLA, R. S., Dermatology
PAINE, R. T., Jr, Chemistry
PANITZ, J. A., Physics and Astronomy
PAPADOPOULOS, E. P., Chemistry
PAPIKE, J. J., Geology
PAPILE, L. A., Paediatrics
PARK, S. M., Chemistry
PARKMAN, A. M., Management
PARNALL, T., Law
PARTRIDGE, L. D., Physiology
PATHAK, P. T., Mathematics and Statistics
PEABODY, D. S., Cell Biology
PECK, R. E., English
PEREZ-GOMEZ, J. R., Music
PETERSON, S. L., Pharmacy
PHAM, C., Economics
PIPER, J., Music
PORTER, J., History
PREDOCK-LINNELL, J., Theatre and Dance
PRICE, R. M., Physics and Astronomy
PRINJA, A. K., Chemical and Nuclear Engineering
PRIOLA, D. V., Physiology
PYLE, R. R., Medicine
QUENZER, R. W., Medicine
RABINOWITZ, H., History
RADOSEVICH, R. R., Management
RAIZADA, V., Medicine
RAZANI, A., Mechanical Engineering
REBOLLEDO, T. D., Modern Languages
REED, W. D., Medicine
REES, B. L., Nursing
REEVES, T. Z., Public Administration
REHDER, R. R., Management
REID, R. A., Management
REMMER, K. L., Political Science
REYES, P., Biochemistry
RICHARDS, C. G., Mechanical Engineering
RIENSCHE, L. L., Comm. Disorders
ROBBINS, R. G., History
ROBIN, D. M., Foreign Languages and Literature
RODERICK, N. F., Chemical and Nuclear Engineering
RODRIGUEZ, A., Modern and Classical Languages

ROEBUCK, J., History
ROGERS, E. M., Communication and Journalism
ROLL, S., Psychology
ROMERO, L. M., Law
ROSENBERG, G. A., Neurology
ROSS, H. L., Sociology
ROSS, T. J., Civil Engineering
ROTH, P. B., Emergency Medicine
RUEBUSH, B. K., Psychiatry and Psychology
RUYBAL, S. E., Nursing
SAIERS, J. H., Medicine
SAIKI, J. H., Medicine
SALAND, L. C., Anatomy
SALVAGGIO, R., American Studies
SANTLEY, R. S., Anthropology
SARTO, G. E., Obstetrics and Gynaecology
SAVAGE, D. D., II, Pharmacology
SCALES, A. C., Law
SCALETTI, J. V., Microbiology
SCALLEN, T. J., Biochemistry
SCHADE, D. S., Medicine
SCHARNHORST, G. F., English and American Studies
SCHAU, C. G., Educational Foundations
SCHREYER, H. L., Mechanical Engineering
SCHUELER, G. F., Philosophy
SCHUETZ, J. E., Communication
SCHULTZ, C., Management
SCHUYLER, M. R., Medicine
SCHWARTZ, R. L., Law
SCHWERIN, K. H., Anthropology
SCOTT, P. B., Curriculum and Instruction in Multicultural Teacher Education
SEARLES, R. P., Medicine
SEMO, E., History
SEVERINO, S. K., Psychiatry
SHAHINPOOR, M., Mechanical Engineering
SHAMA, A., Management
SHANE, D. L., Nursing
SHELTON, S. P., Civil Engineering
SHIPMAN, V. C., Counselling and Family Studies
SHOMAKER, D. J., Nursing
SHULTIS, C. L., Music
SIBBITT, W. L., Jr, Medicine
SIEMBIEDA, W. J., Architecture and Planning
SIMONSON, D. G., Management
SKIPPER, B. J., Family, Community and Emergency Medicine
SKLAR, D. P., Emergency Medicine
SKLAR, L. A., Pathology
SMITH, B. T., Computer Science
SMITH, D. D., Special Education
SMITH, D. M., Chemical and Nuclear Engineering
SMITH, H. L., Management
SMITH, M. M., Counselling and Family Studies
SMITH, P. J., Special Education
SMITH, W. S., Jr, Foreign Languages and Literature
SNYDER, R. D., Neurology
SONNENBERG, A., Medicine
SOUTHALL, T. W., Art and Art History
SRUBEK, J., Art Education
STARR, G. P., Mechanical Engineering
STEINBERG, S. L., Mathematics and Statistics
STONE, A. P., Mathematics and Statistics
STRAUS, L. G., Anthropology
STRICKLAND, R. G., Medicine
STURM, F. G., Philosophy
SUMMERS, J. W., Cell Biology
SUTHERLAND, R. J., Psychology
SWINSON, D., Physics and Astronomy
SZASZ, F. M., History
TANDBERG, W. D., Emergency Medicine
TAYLOR, A. P., Architecture and Planning
TAYLOR, S. A., Law
THOMPSON, D. E., Mechanical Engineering
THOMSON, B. M., Civil Engineering
THORNHILL, A. R., Biology
THORSON, J. L., English
TIANO, S. B., Sociology
TOLMAN, J. M., Modern and Classical Languages

TOOLSON, E. C., Biology
TRINKAUS, E., Anthropology
TROTTER, J. A., Anatomy
TROUP, G. M., Pathology
TROUTMAN, W. G., Pharmacy
TUASON, V. B., Psychiatry
TURAN, M., Architecture and Planning
TURNER, P. H., Counseling and Family Studies
TYLER, M., Music
TZAMALOUKAS, A., Medicine
UHLENHUTH, E. H., Psychiatry
USCHER, N. J., Music
USEEM, B., Sociology
UTTON, A. E., Law
VALDES, N., Sociology
VANDERJAGT, D., Biochemistry
VAN DONGEN, R. D., Curriculum and Instruction in Multicultural Teacher Education
VOGEL, K. G., Biology
WALDMAN, J. D., Paediatrics
WALKER, B. R., Physiology
WALTERS, E. A., Chemistry
WANG, M.-L., Civil Engineering
WATERMAN, R. E., Anatomy
WEIGLE, M. M., Anthropology
WEISS, G. K., Physiology
WEISS, J. R., Nursing
WERNLEY, J. A., Surgery
WHEELAND, R. G., Dermatology
WHIDDEN, M. B., English
WHITE, P., English
WIESE, W., Family, Community and Emergency Medicine
WILDIN, M. W., Mechanical Engineering
WILKINS, E. S., Chemical and Nuclear Engineering
WILLIAMS, R. H., Electrical and Computer Engineering
WILLIAMSON, M. R., Radiology
WILLIAMSON, S. L., Radiology
WILLMAN, C. L., Pathology
WINOGRAD, P., Law
WITEMEYER, H., English
WOFSY, C., Mathematics and Statistics
WOLF, S. S., Law
WOLFE, D. M., Physics and Astronomy
WOLFE, J. D., Theatre and Dance
WOOD, C. J., Education Administration
WOOD, J. E., Mechanical Engineering
WOOD, W. F., Music
WOODWARD, L. A., Geology
WORRELL, R. V., Orthopaedics
WRIGHT, J. B., Library
YAGER, J., Psychiatry
YATES, T. L., Biology
ZAGER, P. G., Medicine
ZANNES, E., Communication and Journalism
ZEILIK, M., II, Physics and Astronomy
ZIMMER, W. J., Mathematics and Statistics
ZONGOLOWICZ, H. M.
ZUMWALT, R. E., Pathology

UNIVERSITY OF THE SOUTHWEST

6610 Lovington Highway, Hobbs, NM 88240

Telephone: (575) 392-6561
Fax: (575) 392-6006
E-mail: admission@usw.edu
Internet: www.usw.edu

Founded 1956 as Hobbs Baptist College, present name 2008
Private control

Pres.: Dr GARY A. DILL
Vice-Pres. for Academic and Technology Services and Dean for Faculty: Dr JAMES SMITH
Vice-Pres. for Admin. Services: Dr DEE MOONEY
Dean for Enrolment Services and Student Success: JORDAN BODINE
Dean for Students: TOM MULKEY
Dean for Library Services: JOHN McCANCE

Number of teachers: 50
Number of students: 590

DEANS

School of Business: Dr TOM WILSON
School of Education: Dr MARY HARRIS

WESTERN NEW MEXICO UNIVERSITY

POB 680, 1000 W College St, Silver City, NM 88062

Telephone: (505) 538-6011
Fax: (505) 538-6278
E-mail: admissions@wnmu.edu
Internet: www.wnmu.edu

Founded 1893
State control

Pres.: Dr JOHN E. COUNTS
Provost and Vice-Pres. for Academic Affairs: Dr FAYE VOWELL
Vice-Pres. for Institutional Advancement, Economic Devt and Community Affairs: LINDA KAY JONES (acting)
Vice-Pres. for Student Affairs and Enrolment Management: ISAAC BRUNDAGE
Dir for Admissions: DAN TRESSLER
Registrar: BETSY MILLER
Univ. Librarian: Dr GILDA BAEZA-ORTEGO (acting)

Library of 388,193 vols
Number of teachers: 65
Number of students: 3,337

DEANS

School of Applied Technology: ANTONIO MACIAS
School of Business Administration and Economics: Dr LAURIE BARFITT
School of Education: Dr PARTICIA MANZANARES-GONZALES
School of Health Sciences and Human Performance: E. WALKER
School of Nursing: PAT McINTIRE
School of Social Work: BETH WALKER

NEW YORK

ADELPHI UNIVERSITY

POB 701, One S Ave, Garden City, NY 11530-0701

Telephone: (516) 877-3000
Fax: (516) 877-3039
E-mail: admissions@adelphi.edu
Internet: www.adelphi.edu

Founded 1863 as Adelphi Aacd., present status 1929
Private control

Academic year: August to May

Off-campus centres: Hauppauge Education and Conference Center, Hudson Valley Center and Manhattan Center

Pres.: Dr ROBERT A. SCOTT
Provost and Sr Vice-Pres. for Academic Affairs: GAYLE D. INSLER
Sr Vice-Pres. and Treas.: TIMOTHY P. BURTON
Vice-Pres. for Admin. and Student Services: ANGELO B. PROTO
Vice-Pres. for Univ. Advancement: CHRISTIAN P. VAUPEL
Dean for Univ. Libraries: CHARLES W. SIMPSON

Library of 600,000 vols, 806,000 microforms, 33,000 audiovisual materials, 61,000 e-journals
Number of teachers: 988 (329 full-time, 659 part-time)
Number of students: 7,922 (6,101 full-time and 1,821 part-time)

Publications: Adelphi University Magazine (2 a year), Erudition (1 a year)

DEANS

College of Arts and Sciences: SAM L. GROGG

Gordon F. Derner Institute of Advanced Psychological Studies: JACQUES BARBER
Honors College: RICHARD GARNER
Robert B. Willumstad School of Business: RAKESH GUPTA
Ruth S. Ammon School of Education: JANE ASHDOWN
School of Nursing: PATRICK COONAN
School of Social Work: ANDREW SAFYER

ALBANY COLLEGE OF PHARMACY AND HEALTH SCIENCES

106 New Scotland Ave, Albany, NY 12208-3492

Telephone: (518) 694-7200
Fax: (518) 694-7202
E-mail: info@acphs.edu
Internet: www.acphs.edu

Founded 1881
Private control

Campuses in Albany and Vermont

Pres. and Dean: Dr JAMES J. GOZZO
Provost and Vice-Pres. for Academic Affairs: Dr MEHDI BOROUJERDI
Vice-Pres. for Devt: VICKI A. DILORENZO
Vice-Pres. for Enrolment Management: TIFFANY M. GUTIERREZ
Vice-Pres. for Institutional Advancement: VICKI A. DiLORENZO
Dean for Student Affairs: Assoc. Prof. JOHN DENIO
Dir of Finance and Business Affairs: WILLIAM M. CRONIN
Dir for Admissions: MATT STEVER
Dir for Library Services: SUE IWANOWICZ
Gen. Counsel: GERALD H. KATZMAN
Registrar: JUDY SCHMONSKY

Number of teachers: 130
Number of students: 1,851

Publications: Alembic Pharmakon (1 a year), Another Creative Perspective (1 a year), PostScript, President's Report (1 a year)

DEANS

School of Arts and Sciences: Dr DAVID W. CLARKE
School of Health Sciences: Prof. Dr HASSAN A. N. EL-FAWAL
School of Pharmacy and Pharmaceutical Sciences: Prof. Dr MEHDI BOROUJERDI

ALBANY LAW SCHOOL

80 New Scotland Ave, Albany, NY 12208-3494

Telephone: (518) 445-2311
Fax: (518) 445-2315
E-mail: info@albanylaw.edu
Internet: www.albanylaw.edu

Founded 1851
Private control

Academic year: July to June

Pres. and Dean: CONNIE MAYER
Vice-Pres. for Finance and Business: VICTOR E. RAUSCHER
Vice-Pres. for Institutional Advancement: HELEN ADAMS-KEANE
Registrar: JOANN FITZSIMMONS
Assoc. Dean and Dir for Library: HELANE DAVIS

Library of 700,000 vols
Number of teachers: 107 (55 full-time, 52 part-time)
Number of students: 687

Publications: Albany Government Law Review, Albany Law Journal of Science and Technology, Albany Law Review.

ALBANY MEDICAL COLLEGE

43 New Scotland Ave, Albany, NY 12208
Telephone: (518) 262-5634

E-mail: graduate-studies@mail.amc.edu

Internet: www.amc.edu/academic

Founded 1839; attached to Albany Medical Center

Private control

Dean and Exec. Vice-Pres. for Health Affairs: Dr VINCENT P. VERDILE

Dir for Admissions: Dr JOANNE H. NANOS

Librarian: SHERRY HARTMAN

Library of 150,000 vols, 2,700 journals

Number of teachers: 117

Number of students: 748 (566 postgraduate, 182 graduate)

ALFRED UNIVERSITY

1 Saxon Dr., Alfred, NY 14802-1205

Telephone: (607) 871-2115

Fax: (607) 871-2198

E-mail: admissions@alfred.edu

Internet: www.alfred.edu

Founded 1836

Private control

Academic year: August to May

Courses in engineering and art and design

Pres.: Dr CHARLES M. EDMONDSON

Provost and Vice-Pres. for Academic Affairs: Dr WILLIAM HALL

Vice-Pres. for Business and Finance: GIOVINA M. LLOYD

Vice-Pres. for Enrolment Management: EARL E. PIERCE

Vice-Pres. for Student Affairs: KATHY WOUGHTER

Vice-Pres. for Univ. Relations: STANLEY A. COLLA

Dir for Admissions: CORRY UNIS

Dean for Libraries: STEPHEN S. CRANDALL

Library of 288,000 vols

Number of teachers: 196 (156 full-time, 40 part-time)

Number of students: 2,393

Publications: *Alfred Reporter*, *Kanakadea* (1 a year)

DEANS

College of Liberal Arts and Sciences: Dr MARY McGEE

College of Professional Studies: Dr NANCY J. EVANGELISTA

Inamori School of Engineering: Dr DOREEN D. EDWARDS

School of Art and Design: LESLIE M. BELLAVANCE

BANK STREET COLLEGE OF EDUCATION

610 W 112th St, New York, NY 10025-1898

Telephone: (212) 875-4400

Fax: (212) 875-4678

E-mail: gradcourses@bankstreet.edu

Internet: www.bankstreet.edu

Founded 1916

Private control

Academic year: September to July

Pres.: Dr ELIZABETH D. DICKEY

Vice-Pres. for Finance and Admin. and Chief Operating Officer: FRANK NUARA

Vice-Pres. for Institutional Advancement: JOHN BORDEN

Dean for Continuing Education: FERN KHAN

Dean for College: JON SNYDER

Dean for Graduate School: VIRGINIA ROACH

Dir for Library: KRISTIN FREDA

Library of 123,215 vols

Number of teachers: 125

Number of students: 1,052

BARD COLLEGE

POB 5000, Annandale-on-Hudson, NY 12504-5000

Telephone: (845) 758-6822

E-mail: admission@bard.edu

Internet: www.bard.edu

Founded 1860 as St Stephen's College, present name 1934

Private control

Academic year: August to May

Divs: arts; languages and literature; science, mathematics, and computing; and social studies; Bard College Conservatory of Music

Pres.: LEON BOTSTEIN

Exec. Vice-Pres.: DIMITRI B. PAPADIMITRIOU

Vice-Pres. and Dean: MICHÈLE DOMINY

Vice-Pres. and Dean for Graduate Studies: NORTON BATKIN

Vice-Pres. for Academic Affairs: ROBERT L. MARTIN

Vice-Pres. for Admin.: JAMES BRUDVIG

Vice-Pres. for Devt and Alumni Affairs: DEBRA PEMSTEIN

Vice Pres. for Int. Affairs and Academic Programs and Dean for Int. Studies: JONATHAN BECKER

Vice-Pres. for Student Affairs: MARY BACKLUND

Dean for Studies: DAVID SHEIN

Registrar: PETER GADSBY

Dir for Libraries: JEFFREY KATZ

Library of 280,000 vols (incl. 14,000 journals in print and online)

Number of teachers: 224

Number of students: 2,000

Publications: *Bard College Catalogue*, *Bardian* (3 a year), *Bard Music Festival Book Series*, *BardPolitik*, *Conjunctions* (2 a year), *La Voz* (12 a year, The Voice, Spanish), *Words without Borders* (12 a year, online (www.wordswithoutborders.org)).

BORICUA COLLEGE

Audubon Terrace Campus: 3755 Broadway, 156th St, New York, NY 10032

Telephone: (212) 694-1000

Internet: www.boricuacollege.edu

Founded 1974

Private control

Academic year: 2 semesters

Campuses in Bronx, Brooklyn and Manhattan

Pres.: Dr VICTOR G. ALICEA

Treas.: SERAFIN MARIEL

Vice-Pres. and Chief Academic Officer: Dr SHIVAJI SENGUPTA

Vice-Pres. and Dean for Academic Affairs, Brooklyn Campus: MARIA MONTES MORALES

Vice-Pres. for Information Technology: IRVING RAMIREZ

Dir for Finance: ELIAS OYOLA

Library Dir: LIZA RIVERA

Library of 15,778 vols, 9,000 maps

Number of teachers: 40

Number of students: 1,100

BRIARCLIFFE COLLEGE

1055 Stewart Ave, Bethpage, NY 11714

Telephone: (516) 918-3600

Internet: www.briarcliffe.edu

Founded 1966

Private control

Campuses in Bethpage, Patchogue and Queens; courses in accounting, business administration, criminal justice, fine arts, healthcare, networking and computer technology and paralegal studies

Pres.: Dr GEORGE SANTIAGO, JR

Provost and Chief Academic Officer: Dr HUBERT BENITEZ

Vice-Pres. for Admissions: GABRIEL CASTANO

Vice-Pres. for Finance and Operations: LOU COMMISSO

Vice-Pres. for Student Affairs: KATHY GENUA

Dean for College: RACHEL ANDOSCIA

Dean for Students: KATHY GENUA

Registrar: VICTORIA LEVINE

Dir for Library Services: JENNIFER DeVITO

Library of 30,000 vols.

BROOKLYN LAW SCHOOL

250 Joralemon St, Brooklyn, NY 11201

Telephone: (718) 625-2200

Fax: (718) 780-0395

E-mail: admitq@brooklaw.edu

Internet: www.brooklaw.edu

Founded 1901, present bldg 1969

Private control

Academic year: August to May

Pres.: Prof. JOAN G. WEXLER

Dean: Prof. MICHAEL GERBER

Chief Financial Officer: LAURIE NEWITZ

Chief Information Officer: PHIL ALLRED

Dean for Admissions and Financial Aid: HENRY W. HAVERSTICK, III

Assoc. Dean for Academic Affairs: MICHAEL CAHILL

Assoc. Dean for Student Affairs: BERYL R. JONES-WOODIN

Dir for Alumni Relations: CAITLIN MONCK-MARCELLINO

Registrar: SUZANNE M. DENNIS

Assoc. Law Librarian: LINDA HOLMES

Number of students: 1,376 (1,204 full-time, 172 part-time)

Publications: *Brooklyn Journal of Corporate, Financial & Commercial Law*, *Brooklyn Journal of International Law*, *Brooklyn Law Review*, *Journal of Law and Policy*.

BRYANT & STRATTON COLLEGE

1259 Central Ave, Albany, NY 12205

Telephone: (518) 437-1802

Internet: www.bryantstratton.edu

Founded 1854

Private control

Campuses: Albany, Amherst, Buffalo, Rochester, Orchard Park, Syracuse and Liverpool in New York; Akron, Cleveland, Eastlake and Parma in Ohio; Hampton, N Chesterfield and Virginia Beach in Virginia; Glendale, Milwaukee and Wauwatosa in Wisconsin

Pres. and CEO: JOHN J. STASCHAK

Exec. Vice-Pres. and Sec.: FRANCIS J. FELSER

Vice-Pres.: DOREEN A. JUSTINGER

Vice-Pres. and Chief Academic Officer: BETH A. TARQUINO

Vice-Pres., Chief Financial Officer and Treas.: DAVID VADEN

Number of students: 14,000

CANISIUS COLLEGE

2001 Main St, Buffalo, NY 14208-1098

Telephone: (716) 883-7000

Fax: (716) 888-2525

E-mail: admissions@canisius.edu

Internet: www.canisius.edu

Founded 1870

Private control

Academic year: May to August,August to December,January to May (3 semesters)

Pres.: Rev. JOHN J. HURLEY

Vice-Pres. for Academic Affairs: Dr RICHARD A. WALL

Vice-Pres. for Business and Finance: PATRICK E. RICHEY

Vice-Pres. for Institutional Advancement: CRAIG T. CHINDEMI

Vice-Pres. for Student Affairs: ELLEN CONLEY
Registrar: BLAIR W. FOSTER
Assoc. Vice-Pres for Library and Information Services: Dr JOEL COHEN
Library of 425,000 vols, 24,000 full text e-periodicals
Number of teachers: 505 (230 full-time, 275 part-time)
Number of students: 5,111 (3,369 under-graduate, 1,742 graduate)
Publication: *NetGazette*

DEANS

College of Arts and Sciences: Dr DAVID EWING
Richard J. Wehle School of Business: Dr ANTONE ALBER
School of Education and Human Services: Dr MICHAEL PARDALES

CAZENOVIA COLLEGE

22 Sullivan St, Cazenovia, NY 13035
Telephone: (315) 655-7208
E-mail: admission@cazenovia.edu
Internet: www.cazenovia.edu
Founded 1824 as Seminary of the Genesee Conf., present name 1982
Private control
Academic year: September to May
Areas of study incl.: art and design, business and management, education, humanities, natural sciences, social and behavioural sciences
Pres.: Dr MARK JOHN TIERNO
Exec. Vice-Pres. and Chief Operation Officer: Dr SUSAN A. BERGER
Vice-Pres. for Academic Affairs and Dean for Faculty: Dr DONALD A. MCCRIMMON
Vice-Pres. for Enrolment Management and Dean for Admissions and Financial Aid: ROBERT A. CROOT
Vice-Pres. for Financial Affairs and Chief Financial Officer: MARK EDWARDS
Vice-Pres. for Institutional Advancement: CAROL M. SATCHWELL
Vice-Pres. for Student Devt and Dean for Student Life: C. JOSEPH BEHAN
Registrar: J. ZACHARY KELLEY
Library Dir: STANLEY J. KOZACZKA
Library of 90,000 vols, 2,200 cassettes and DVDs
Number of teachers: 150 (55 full-time, 95 part-time)
Number of students: 1,000 full-time

CHRIST THE KING SEMINARY

711 Knox Rd, E Aurora, NY 14052-0607
Telephone: (716) 652-8900
Fax: (716) 652-8903
E-mail: cksacad@cks.edu
Internet: www.cks.edu
Founded 1857 as St Bonaventure School and Seminary, present name 1974
Private control
Academic year: August to December, January to May (2 semesters)
Pres. and Rector: Rev. PETER J. DRILLING
Vice-Rector: Rev. GREGORY M. FAULHABER
Academic Dean: Dr DENNIS A. CASTILLO
Library Dir: TERESA LUBIENECKI
Library of 160,000 vols
Number of teachers: 25 (18 full-time, 7 adjunct)
Number of students: 96 (full-time)

CITY UNIVERSITY OF NEW YORK

535 E 80th St, New York, NY 10021
Telephone: (212) 794-5555
E-mail: academicaffairs@mail.cuny.edu
Internet: www.cuny.edu

Founded 1847 as Free Acad., present name 1961
State control
24 Colleges and instns in New York city, incl. 11 sr colleges, 7 community colleges
Chancellor: MATTHEW GOLDSTEIN
Exec. Vice-Chancellor and Chief Operating Officer: ALLAN H. DOBRIN
Exec. Vice-Chancellor and Univ. Provost: ALEXANDRA W. LOGUE
Sr Vice-Chancellor for Univ. Relations: JAY HERSHENSON
Sr Vice-Chancellor for Budget, Finance and Fiscal Policy: MARC V. SHAW
Vice-Chancellor for Community Colleges: EDUARDO MARTI
Vice-Chancellor for Research: GILLIAN SMALL
Vice-Chancellor for Student Affairs: FRANK D. SANCHEZ
Dir for Admission: RICHARD P. ALVAREZ
Dean for Advancement: CARLOS FLYNN
Univ. Dean for Education: JOAN M. LUCAR-IELLO
Univ. Dean for Libraries and Information Resources: CURTIS KENDRICK
Dean for Undergraduate Studies: KARRIN E. WILKS
Library: Combined libraries of 7.6m. vols, 30,000 periodicals
Number of teachers: 6,700 (full-time)
Number of students: 540,000
Publication: *Salute to Scholars* (2 a year).

CONSTITUENT COLLEGES AND SCHOOLS

Baruch College

One Bernard Baruch Way, 55 Lexington Ave, 24th St, New York, NY 10010
Telephone: (646) 312-1000
Internet: www.baruch.cuny.edu
Founded 1919
Pres.: MITCHEL B. WALLERSTEIN
Provost and Sr Vice-Pres. for Academic Affairs: JOHN BRENKMAN
Vice-Pres. for Admin. and Finance: MARY FINNEN
Vice-Pres. for College Advancement: MARK GIBBEL
Vice-Pres. for Student Affairs, Enrolment Management and Dean for Students: BEN CORPUS
Chief Librarian: ARTHUR DOWNING
Library of 450,000 vols, 160,000 e-books, 2m. units of microform
Number of teachers: 500 (full-time)
Number of students: 17,063 (13,120 under-graduate, 3,943 graduate)
Publications: *Baruch College Alumni Magazine* (2 a year), *Dollars & Sense* (1 a year), *Encounters*

DEANS

School of Public Affairs: DAVID BIRDSELL
Weissman School of Arts and Sciences: JEFFREY M. PECK
Zicklin School of Business: JOHN ELLIOTT

Brooklyn College

2900 Bedford Ave, Brooklyn, NY 11210
Telephone: (718) 951-5000
E-mail: adminqry@brooklyn.cuny.edu
Internet: www.brooklyn.cuny.edu
Founded 1930
Pres.: KAREN L. GOULD
Provost and Vice-Pres. for Academic Affairs: WILLIAM A. TRAMONTANO
Vice-Pres. for Enrolment Management: Dr STEPHEN E. JOYNER
Vice-Pres. for Finance and Admin.: ALAN GILBERT (acting)

Vice-Pres. for Institutional Advancement: Dr ANDREW SILLEN
Vice-Pres. for Student Affairs: Dr MILGA MORALES
Library: 1.5m. vols, 45,000 serials, 43,000 e-serials, 40,000 e-books
Number of teachers: 1,355 (558 full-time, 797 part-time)
Number of students: 16,822 (13,095 under-graduate, 3,727 graduate)
Publication: *Brooklyn College Magazine*

DEANS

School of Business: WILLIE HOPKINS
School of Education: DEBORAH SHANLEY
School of Humanities and Social Sciences: KIMBERLEY L. PHILLIPS
School of Natural and Behavioral Sciences: KLEANTHIS PSARRIS
School of Visual, Media and Performing Arts: MARIA ANN CONELLI

City College of New York

160 Convent Ave, New York, NY 10031
Telephone: (212) 650-7000
Fax: (212) 650-7584
E-mail: admissions@ccny.cuny.edu
Internet: www.ccny.cuny.edu
Founded 1847
Pres.: Dr LISA S. COICO
Provost and Vice-Pres. for Academic Affairs: MARTIN MOSKOVITS
Number of teachers: 457 (full-time)
Number of students: 15,000
Publication: *Working Education Magazine*

DEANS

Bernard and Anne Spitzer School of Architecture: GEORGE RANALLI
Division of Humanities and the Arts: GERALDINE MURPHY (acting)
Division of Interdisciplinary Studies at Center for Worker Education: JUAN CARLOS MERCADO
Division of Science: Dr RUTH STARK
Division of Social Sciences: MARILYN HOSKIN
Grove School of Engineering: JOSEPH BARBA
School of Education: DORIS CINTRÓN (acting)
Sophie Davis School of Biomedical Education: Dr MAURIZIO TREVISAN

College of Staten Island

2800 Victory Blvd, Staten Island, NY 10314
Telephone: (718) 982-2000
Fax: (718) 982-2500
E-mail: admissions@csi.cuny.edu
Internet: www.csi.cuny.edu
Founded 1976 by merger of Staten Island Community College (f. 1955) with Richmond College (f. 1965)
Academic year: August to May (2 semesters)
Pres.: Dr TOMAS D. MORALES
Provost and Sr Vice-Pres. for Academic Affairs: Dr WILLIAM J. FRITZ
Vice-Pres. for Finance and Admin.: IRA PERSKY (acting)
Vice-Pres. for Institutional Advancement and External Affairs: BARBARA R. ESHOO
Vice-Pres. for Student Affairs: Dr A. RAMONA BROWN
Chief Librarian: Dr WILMA L. JONES
Library of 243,000 vols, 110,400 e-books, 250 print journals, 42,800 e-journals, 140 e-resources, 3,000 films and videos, 5,000 sound recordings, 400 linear ft of archival materials
Number of teachers: 954 (358 full-time, 596 part-time)
Number of students: 13,858 (10,652 full-time)

Publications: *Caesura* (irregular), *Eye on CSI, Operation: Three-Legged Dolphin* (2 a year), *Serpentine, Third Rail*

DEANS

Division of Humanities and Social Sciences: Dr CHRISTINE FLYNN SAULNIER
Division of Science and Technology: Dr ALEX CHIGOGIDZE

CUNY Graduate School of Journalism

219 W 40th St, New York, NY 10018
Telephone: (646) 758-7700
E-mail: admissions@journalism.cuny.edu
Internet: www.journalism.cuny.edu
Founded 2006
Academic year: 3 semesters
Dean: Prof. STEPHEN B. SHEPARD
Library of 1,500 vols.

CUNY School of Law

65–21 Main St, Flushing, NY 11367
Telephone: (718) 340-4200
E-mail: admissions@mail.law.cuny.edu
Internet: www.law.cuny.edu
Founded 1973, present status 1994
Dean: MICHELLE J. ANDERSON
Library of 95,000 vols, 175,000 microforms
Number of teachers: 28 (full-time)
Number of students: 572
Publication: *CUNY Law Magazine*.

Graduate Center

365 Fifth Ave, New York, NY 10016-4309
Telephone: (212) 817-7000
E-mail: admissions@gc.cuny.edu
Internet: www.gc.cuny.edu
Founded 1961
Pres.: WILLIAM P. KELLY
Provost and Sr Vice-Pres.: CHASE F. ROBINSON
Library of 305,000 vols, 555,000 microforms, 8,258 electronic and print serials
Number of teachers: 334 (full-time)
Number of students: 4,524
Publication: *Folio Magazine*

DEANS

Humanities and Social Sciences: LOUISE LENNIHAN
Sciences: ANN S. HENDERSON
School of Professional Studies: JOHN MOGULESCU

Hunter College

695 Park Ave, New York, NY 10065
Telephone: (212) 772-4000
E-mail: admissions@hunter.cuny.edu
Internet: www.hunter.cuny.edu
Founded 1870
Pres.: JENNIFER J. RAAB
Provost and Vice-Pres.: VITA RABINOWITZ
Vice-Pres. for Student Affairs: EIJA AYRAVAINEN
Chief Operating Officer: LEONARD ZINNANTI (acting)
Number of teachers: 1,800 (full-time)
Number of students: 22,000
Publications: *Around Hunter, At Hunter, E Magazine*

DEANS

Hunter-Bellevue School of Nursing: GAIL McCAIN
School of Arts and Sciences: EREC R. KOCH
School of Education: DAVID STEINER
Schools of the Health Professions: Dr KEN OLDEN (acting)
Silberman School of Social Work: Dr JACQUELINE B. MONDROS

John Jay College of Criminal Justice

899 10th Ave, New York, NY 10019
Telephone: (212) 237-8000
E-mail: admissions@jjay.cuny.edu
Internet: www.jjay.cuny.edu
Founded 1964
Pres.: JEREMY TRAVIS
Provost and Sr Vice-Pres. of Academic Affairs: JANE BOWERS
Sr Vice-Pres. for Finance and Admin.: ROBERT PIGNATELLO
Vice-Pres. for Enrolment Management: RICHARD SAULNIER
Library of 300,000 vols
Number of teachers: 256 (full-time)
Number of students: 10,834
Publication: *John Jay Magazine*.

Lehman College

250 Bedford Park Blvd, W, Bronx, NY 10468
Telephone: (718) 960-8000
Internet: www.lehman.cuny.edu
Founded 1968
Pres.: Dr RICARDO R. FERNANDEZ
Provost and Sr Vice-Pres. for Academic Affairs: Dr JOSEPH W. RACHLIN
Vice-Pres. for Admin. and Finance: VINCENT W. CLARK
Vice-Pres. for Enrolment Management: Dr ROBERT C. TROY
Vice-Pres. for Institutional Advancement: MARIO DELLAPINA
Vice-Pres. for Student Affairs: JOSE MAGDALENO
Library of 575,160 vols
Number of teachers: 350 (full-time)
Number of students: 12,287 (9,863 undergraduate, 2,424 graduate)
Publication: *Lehman Today* (2 a year)

DEANS

School of Arts and Humanities: Dr TIMOTHY ALBORN
School of Continuing and Professional Studies: Dr MARZIE A. JAFARI
School of Education: Dr HARRIET R. FAYNE
School of Natural and Social Sciences: Dr EDWARD L. JARROLL

Medgar Evers College

1650 Bedford Ave, Brooklyn, NY 11225
Telephone: (718) 951-5000
Internet: www.mec.cuny.edu
Founded 1969
Pres.: Dr WILLIAM L. POLLARD
Provost and Sr Vice-Pres.: Dr HOWARD C. JOHNSON
Sr Vice-Pres. and Chief Operating Officer: Dr LLOYD A. BLANCHARD
Vice-Pres. for Student Support Services and Enrolment Management: Dr VINCENT BANREY
Library of 110,000 vols, 25,000 audiovisual items, 350 journals, magazines and newspapers
Number of teachers: 127 (full-time)
Number of students: 5,063

DEANS

College of Freshman Studies: (vacant)
School of Liberal Arts and Education: Dr CARLYLE VAN THOMPSON (acting)
School of Professional and Community Development: Dr SIMONE RODRIGUEZ-DORESTANT
School of Science, Health and Technology: Dr MOHSIN PATWARY

New York City College of Technology (CUNY)

300 Jay St, Brooklyn, NY 11201
Telephone: (718) 260-5400
E-mail: connect@citytech.cuny.edu
Internet: www.citytech.cuny.edu
Founded 1946 as New York State Institute for Applied Arts and Sciences, present status 1964, present name 2002
Academic year: August to June
Pres.: Dr RUSSELL K. HOTZLER
Provost and Vice-Pres. for Academic Affairs: Dr BONNE AUGUST
Vice-Pres. for Admin. and Finance: Dr MIGUEL CAIROL
Vice-Pres. for Enrolment and Student Affairs: Dr MARCELA KATZ ARMOZA
Chief Librarian: DARROW WOOD
Library of 392,317 vols, 86,339 periodical titles
Number of teachers: 1,262 (414 full-time, 848 part-time)
Number of students: 15,963
Publications: *2 Bridges Review* (online), *City Tech Writer* (1 a year), *Journal of Urban Technology, Nucleus* (4 a year), *Perspectives*

DEANS

School of Arts and Sciences: Dr PAMELA BROWN
School of Professional Studies: BARBARA GRUMET
School of Technology and Design: KEVIN HOM

Queens College

65–30 Kissena Blvd, Flushing, NY 11367
Telephone: (718) 997-5000
Internet: www.qc.edu
Founded 1937
Pres.: JAMES L. MUYSKENS
Provost and Vice-Pres. for Academic Affairs: JAMES STELLAR
Number of teachers: 637 (full-time)
Number of students: 4,600
Publication: *Queens Magazine*

DEANS

Div. of Arts and Humanities: WILLIAM McCLURE (acting)
Div. of Education: FRANCINE PETERMAN
Div. of Mathematics and Natural Sciences: Dr LARRY LIEBOVITCH

York College

94–20 Guy R. Brewer Blvd, Jamaica, NY 11451
Telephone: (718) 262-2000
Internet: www.york.cuny.edu
Founded 1966, fmrly Alpha College
Pres.: Dr MARCIA C. KEIZS
Provost and Sr Vice-Pres. for Academic Affairs: Dr IVELAW LLOYD GRIFFITH
Chief Operating Officer: RONALD C. THOMAS
Library of 160,000 vols, 55,000 reels of microfilm, 90,000 microfiche cards
Number of teachers: 144 (full-time)
Number of students: 6,030

DEANS

School of Arts and Sciences: Dr PANAYIOTIS MELETIES
School of Business and Information Systems: ALFRED NTOKO
School of Health and Behavioral Sciences: Dr LYNNE W. CLARK

CLARKSON UNIVERSITY

Eight Clarkson Ave, Potsdam, NY 13699-5500

Telephone: (315) 268-6400
Fax: (315) 268-7993
E-mail: admission@clarkson.edu
Internet: www.clarkson.edu

Founded 1896 as Thomas S. Clarkson Memorial School of Technology, present name and status 1984

Pres.: Dr ANTHONY G. COLLINS
Provost: Dr THOMAS E. YOUNG
Treas.: JAMES D. FISH
Vice-Pres. for Univ. Outreach and Student Affairs: KATHRYN B. JOHNSON
Dean for Admissions: BRIAN T. GRANT
Registrar: LYNN BROWN
Library Dir: MICHELLE L. YOUNG

Library of 500,000 vols, over 3,700 print and e-journals, 15,000 e-books
Number of teachers: 244 (221 full-time)
Number of students: 3,539 (3,018 undergraduate, 521 graduate)

Publication: *Clarkson*

DEANS

School of Arts and Sciences: PETER TURNER
School of Business: TIMOTHY F. SUGRUE
Wallace H. Coulter School of Engineering: GOODARZ AHMADI

COLGATE ROCHESTER CROZER DIVINITY SCHOOL

1100 S Goodman St, Rochester, NY 14620-2589

Telephone: (585) 271-1320
Fax: (585) 271-8013
E-mail: admissions@crcds.edu
Internet: www.crds.edu

Founded 1970 by merger of 3 theological seminaries, 1 missionary training school and 1 theological school
Private control
Academic year: September to May

Pres.: Dr MARVIN A. MCMICKLE
Vice-Pres. for Academic Life and Dean of Faculty: Rev. Dr STEPHANIE L. SAUVÉ
Vice-Pres. for Enrolment Services: MELISSA MORRAL
Vice-Pres. for Finance and Chief Financial Officer: GERALD VAN STRYDONCK
Vice-Pres. for Institutional Advancement: PATRICK HANLEY
Registrar: ANDREA MASON
Library Dir: MARGE NEAD

Library: 3m. vols
Number of teachers: 8

COLGATE UNIVERSITY

13 Oak Dr., Hamilton, NY 13346

Telephone: (315) 228-1000
Fax: (315) 228-7798
E-mail: admission@colgate.edu
Internet: www.colgate.edu

Founded 1819 as Baptist Education Soc., present name 1890
Private control
Academic year: August to May

4 Academic divs: humanities, natural sciences and mathematics, social sciences and university studies

Pres.: JEFFREY HERBST
Provost and Dean for Faculty: BRUCE SELLECK
Vice-Pres. and Dean for Admission: GARY L. ROSS
Vice-Pres. and Dean for College: SCOTT C. BROWN
Vice-Pres. for Finance and Admin.: DAVID HALE

Vice-Pres. for Communications: DEBRA K. TOWNSEND
Vice-Pres. for Institutional Advancement and Alumni Affairs: MURRAY L. DECOCK
Chief Information Officer: DAVID D. GREGORY
Controller: THOMAS O'NEILL
Registrar: GRETCHEN B. HERRINGER
Librarian: JOANNE A. SCHNEIDER

Library of 766,961 vols, 236,569 e-books, 551,803 microforms, 461,469 govt documents, 11,317 sound recordings, 869 print journals, 46,711 e-journals
Number of teachers: 286 (full-time)
Number of students: 2,900

Publication: *The Colgate Scene* (4 a year).

COLLEGE OF MOUNT SAINT VINCENT

6301 Riverdale Ave, Riverdale, NY 10471

Telephone: (718) 405-3267
E-mail: admissions.office@mountsaintvincent.edu
Internet: www.mountsaintvincent.edu

Founded 1847 as Acad. of Mount St Vincent, present name 1911
Private control

Pres.: CHARLES L. FLYNN, JR
Provost and Dean for Faculty: GUY LOMETTI
Exec. Vice-Pres. and Treas.: ABED ELKESHK
Vice-Pres. for Admission and Financial Aid: TIMOTHY NASH
Vice-Pres. for Business: MATTHEW MCDEVITT
Vice-Pres. for Information Technology: W. ADAM WICHERN, III
Vice-Pres. for Institutional Advancement and College Relations: MADELEINE MELKONIAN
Vice-Pres. for Student Affairs and Dean for Students: DIANNA C. DALE
Dir for Library: SEBASTIAN DERRY

Library of 150,000 vols
Number of teachers: 80
Number of students: 1,800

Publication: *The Underground*

DEANS

School for Professional and Continuing Studies: EDWARD MEYER
Undergraduate College: PAUL DOUILLARD

COLLEGE OF NEW ROCHELLE

29 Castle Pl., New Rochelle, NY 10805

Telephone: (914) 654-5000
Fax: (914) 654-5980
E-mail: info@cnr.edu
Internet: www.cnr.edu

Founded 1904 as the College of St Angela
Private control
Academic year: September to May

Campuses at New Rochelle, Brooklyn, Bronx, New York

Pres.: Dr JUDITH HUNTINGTON
Exec. Vice-Pres.: ELLEN CURRY DAMATO
Sr Vice-Pres. for Academic Affairs: Dr DOROTHY ESCRIBANO
Vice-Pres. for College Advancement: BRENNA SHEENAN MAYER
Vice-Pres. for Financial Affairs: KEITH BORGE
Vice-Pres. for Student Affairs: COLETTE GEARY
Dean for Library: ANA M. FONTOURA

Library of 220,000 vols
Number of teachers: 758 (118 full-time, 640 adjunct)
Number of students: 4,500

Publications: *Annales* (1 a year), *Phoenix* (4 a year)

DEANS

Graduate School: Dr MARIE RIBARICH

School of Arts and Sciences: Dr RICHARD THOMPSON
School of New Resources: Dr ELZA DINWIDDIE-BOYD
School of Nursing: Dr MARY ALICE DONIUS

COLLEGE OF SAINT ROSE

432 W Ave, Albany, NY 12203-1490

Telephone: (518) 454-5111
Fax: (518) 454-2013
E-mail: admit@mail.strose.edu
Internet: www.strose.edu

Founded 1920
Private control
Academic year: September to May

Pres.: Dr R. MARK SULLIVAN
Provost and Vice-Pres. for Academic Affairs: Dr DAVID SZCZERBACKI
Vice-Pres. for Enrolment Management: MARY M. GRONDAHL
Vice-Pres. of Finance and Admin.: MARCUS BUCKLEY
Vice-Pres. of Institutional Advancement: KARIN CARR
Vice-Pres. for Student Affairs: DENNIS MCDONALD
Registrar: JUDITH KELLY
Dir for Library Services: PETER KOONZ

Library of 223,627 vols
Number of teachers: 474
Number of students: 5,000

Publications: *Journal of Behavioral and Neuroscience Research, Journal of Undergraduate Research* (1 a year)

DEANS

Huether School of Business: SEVERIN CARLSON
School of Arts and Humanities: Dr LORNA SHAW
School of Mathematics and Sciences: RICHARD J. THOMPSON, JR
Thelma P. Lally School of Education: Dr MARGARET KIRWIN

COLLEGE OF WESTCHESTER

325 Central Ave, White Plains, NY 10606

Telephone: (914) 831-0200
E-mail: admissions@cw.edu
Internet: www.cw.edu

Founded 1915
Private control
Academic year: September to August

Schools of allied health, business, digital media, information technology

Pres.: KAREN SMITH
Vice-Pres.: MARY BETH DELBALZO
Vice-Pres. for Academic and Student Affairs: Dr JOANN MULQUEEN
Dir for Admissions: MATTHEW CURTIS
Dean for Faculty: GREG MARCARELLI
Dean for Student Academic Services: JEAN CARLSON
Library Dir: MONECIA SAMUEL.

COLUMBIA UNIVERSITY

116th St, Broadway, New York, NY 10027-6902

Telephone: (212) 854-1754
Fax: (212) 932-0418
E-mail: askcuit@columbia.edu
Internet: www.columbia.edu

Founded 1754 as King's College, present name and status 1896
Private control
Academic year: September to May

Pres.: LEE C. BOLLINGER
Provost: JOHN H. COATSWORTH
Sr Exec. Vice-Pres.: ROBERT KASDIN

Exec. Vice-Pres. for Arts and Sciences: NICHOLAS B. DIRKS

Exec. Vice-Pres. for Communications: DAVID M. STONE

Exec. Vice-Pres. for Devt and Alumni Relations: FRED VAN SICKLE

Exec. Vice-Pres. for Facilities: JOSEPH A. IENUSO

Exec. Vice-Pres. for Finance: ANNE SULLIVAN

Exec. Vice-Pres. for Govt and Community Affairs: MAXINE GRIFFITH

Exec. Vice-Pres. for Research: G. MICHAEL PURDY,

Exec. Vice-Pres. for Student and Admin. Services: JEFFREY F. SCOTT

Vice-Pres. for Information Services and Univ. Librarian: JAMES G. NEAL

Gen. Counsel: JANE E. BOOTH

Library: see Libraries and Archives

Number of teachers: 3,634

Number of students: 28,221

Publications: *Chemical Highlights, Columbia Business Law Review* (3 a year), *Columbia Human Rights Law Review, Columbia Journal of American Studies* (1 a year), *Columbia Journal of Environmental Law, Columbia Journal of Law & the Arts* (4 a year), *Columbia Journal of Transnational Law, Columbia Journalism Review* (6 a year), *Columbia Law Review, Current Musicology* (2 a year), *Germanic Review, Global Political Assessment, Journal of International Affairs* (2 a year), *Journal of the Ancient Near Eastern Society, Journal of Philosophy, Prospects: The Annual for American Cultural Studies, Renaissance Quarterly, Revista Hispánica Moderna* (2 a year), *Romanic Review* (4 a year), *Studies in American Indian Literature, The Astronomical Journal*

DEANS

College of Dental Medicine: Dr IRA LAMSTER

College of Physicians and Surgeons: LEE GOLDMAN

Columbia Business School: Prof. GLENN HUBBARD

Columbia College: Prof. JAMES J. VALENTINI

Columbia Journalism School: NICHOLAS LEMANN

Columbia Law School: DAVID M. SCHIZER

Faculty of Arts and Sciences: NICHOLAS B DIRKS

Fu Foundation School of Engineering and Applied Science: FENIOSKY PEÑA-MORA

Graduate School of Architecture, Planning and Preservation: MARK WIGLEY

Graduate School of Arts and Sciences: CARLOS J. ALONSO

Mailman School of Public Health: LINDA P. FRIED

School of the Arts: CAROL BECKER

School of Continuing Education: KRISTINE A. BILLMYER

School of General Studies: PETER J. AWN

School of International and Public Affairs: JOHN H. COATSWORTH

School of Nursing: BOBBIE BERKOWITZ

School of Social Work: JEANETTE C. TAKAMURA

PROFESSORS

Anaesthesiology:
FINCK, A. D.
FINSTER, M.
HILLEL, Z.
HYMAN, A. I.
MORISHIMA, H. O.
ORNSTEIN, E.
PANG, L.
PANTUCK, E. J.
SMILEY, R. M.
STONE, J. G.
THYS, D. M.
TRINER, L.

WEISSMAN, C.
YOUNG, W. L.

Anatomy and Cell Biology:
AMBRON, R.
APRIL, E. W.
BELLVE, A. R.
BRANDT, P.
BULINSKI, J. C.
GERSHON, M. D.
KESSIN, R. H.
ROLE, L. W.
SILVERMAN, A.-J.
TENNYSON, V. M. S.
TORAN-ALLERAND, C. D.

Anthropology:
ALLAND, A., Jr
COHEN, M. L.
COMBS-SCHILLING, M. E.
D'ALTROY, T.
HOLLOWAY, R. L.
MELNICK, D.
NEWMAN, K.
SKINNER, E. P.
TAUSSIG, M.

Applied Physics:
BOOZER, A. H.
CHU, C. K.
HERMAN, I. P.
MARSHALL, T. C.
MAUEL, M.
NAVRATIL, G.

Architecture, Planning and Preservation:
FRAMPTON, K.
GRAVA, S.
HERDEG, K.
HOLL, S.
MCINTYRE, L.
MCLEOD, M.
MARCUSE, P.
PLUNZ, R.
POLSHEK, J. S.
SASSEN, S. J.
SCLAR, E.
STERN, R. A. M.
TSCHUMI, B.
WRIGHT, G.

Art History and Archaeology:
BALLON, H. M.
BECK, J. H.
BERGDOLL, B. G.
BRILLIANT, R.
CONNORS, J.
FREEDBERG, D.
KRAUSS, R.
MIDDLETON, R.
MURASE, M. C.
MURRAY, S.
MYCK, A.
PASZTORY, E.
REFF, T.
ROSAND, D.
STALEY, A.

Arts:
FORMAN, M., Film
INSDORF, A., Film
SARRIS, A., Film

Astronomy:
APPLEGATE, J.
BAKER, N.
HALPERN, J. P.
HELFAND, D.
PATTERSON, J.
PRENDERGAST, K. H.
SPIEGEL, E. A.
VAN GORKOM, J.

Biochemistry and Molecular Biophysics:
FEIGELSON, P.
GOFF, S.
GOLD, A. M.
GOLDBERGER, R. F.
GOTTESMAN, M. E.
GREENWALD, I. S.

HENDRICKSON, W. A.
HIRSH, D. I.
HONIG, B.
JESSELL, T.
KRASNA, A. I.
SRINIVASAN, P. R.

Biological Sciences:
BOCK, W. J.
CHALFIE, M.
CHASIN, L. A.
COHEN, D. H.
KELLEY, D. B.
MACAGNO, E. R.
MANCINELLI, A.
MANLEY, J.
POLLACK, R.
POO, M.
PRIVES, C. L.
TZAGOLOFF, A.
ZUBAY, G. L.

Business:
ADLER, M.
ARZAC, E. R.
BARTEL, A.
BROCKNER, J.
BURTON, J. C.
CAPON, N.
DONALDSON, J.
EDWARDS, F.
FEDERGRUEN, A.
GIOVANNINI, A.
GLASSERMAN, P.
GLOSTEN, L. R.
GREEN, L.
GREENWALD, B. C. N.
GUPTA, S.
HARRIGAN, K.
HARRIS, T.
HEAL, G.
HOLBROOK, M.
HORTON, R.
HUBBARD, R. G.
HUBERMAN, G.
HULBERT, J. M.
ICHNIOWSKI, B. E.
KOHLI, R.
KOLESAR, P.
LEFF, N.
LEHMANN, D.
LICHTENBERG, F. R.
MELUMAD, N. D.
MISHKIN, F.
NOAM, E.
OHLSON, J.
PATRICK, H.
SELDEN, L.
SEXTON, D.
STARR, M.
SUNDARESAN, S.
THOMAS, J. K.
TUSHMAN, M.
WARREN, E. K.
WILKINSON, M.
ZIPKIN, P.

Chemical Engineering and Applied Chemistry:
CHEH, H. Y.
DURNING, C.
GRYTE, C.
LEONARD, E. F.
O'SHAUGHNESSY, B.
SPENCER, J.

Chemistry:
BENT, B. E.
BERNE, B. J.
BERSOHN, R.
BRESLOW, R.
DANISHEFSKY, S. J.
EISENTHAL, K. B.
FLYNN, G. W.
FRIESNER, R.
KATZ, T. J.
NAKANISHI, K.
PARKIN, G. F. R.

PECHUKAS, P.
STILL, W. C.
TURRO, N. J.
VALENTINI, J.

Civil Engineering and Engineering Mechanics:

DASGUPTA, G.
DIMAGGIO, F. L.
FRIEDMAN, M. B.
GJELSVIK, A.
GRIFFIS, F. H.
MEYER, C.
STOLL, R. D.
TESTA, R. B.
VAICAITIS, R.

Classics:

BAGNALL, R. S.
CAMERON, A.
COULTER, J. A.
SAID, S.
TARÁN, L.
ZETZEL, J.

Computer Science:

AHO, A. V.
ALLEN, P. K.
FEINER, S. K.
GALIL, Z.
GROSS, J. L.
KAISER, G.
KENDER, J.
MCKEOWN, K.
STOLFO, S.
TRAUB, J. F.
UNGER, S.
WOZNIAKOWSKI, M.
YEMINI, Y.

Dental and Oral Surgery:

CANGIALOSI, T. J.
DAVIS, M. J.
EFSTRATIADIS, S. S.
FORMICOLA, A. J.
HASSELGREN, B. G.
HILLS, H. L.
ISRAEL, H. A.
KAHN, N.
KLYVERT, M.
LAMSTER, I. B.
MOSS-SALENTIJN, L.
MYERS, R.
ODRICH, J.
ROSER, S. M.
TROUTMAN, K. C.
ZEGARELLI, D. J.

Dermatology:

BICKERS, D. R.

East Asian Languages and Cultures:

ANDERER, P.
HYMES, R.
LEDYARD, G. K.
SHIRANE, H.
SMITH, H. D., II
WANG, D. D.-W.
ZELIN, M.

Economics:

BHAGWATI, J.
BLOOM, D.
CHICHILNISKY, G.
CLARIDA, R.
DESAI, P.
DHRYMES, P.
DUTTA, P. K.
ERICSON, R.
FINDLAY, R.
HAYASHI, F.
LANCASTER, K.
MUNDELL, R.
PHELPS, E.
SACHS, J. D.
WATTS, H.
WELLISZ, S. H.

Electrical Engineering:

ACAMPORA, A.

ANASTASSIOU, D.
DIAMENT, P.
HEINZ, T.
LAZAR, A.
MEADOWS, H. E.
OSGOOD, R.
SCHWARTZ, M.
SEN, A. K.
STERN, T. E.
TEICH, M. C.
TSIVIDIS, Y.
WANG, W.
YANG, E. S.
ZUKOWSKI, C. A.

English and Comparative Literature:

BLOUNT, M.
DAMROSCH, D.
DELBANCO, A.
DOUGLAS, A.
EDEN, K.
FERGUSON, R.
FERRANTE, J.
HANNING, R.
HOWARD, J.
KASTAN, D.
KOCH, J. K.
KROEBER, K.
MARCUS, S.
MEISEL, M.
MENDELSON, E.
MILLER, D. A.
MIROLLO, J. V.
MORETTI, F.
O'MEALLY, R. G.
PETERS, J. S.
QUIGLEY, A.
ROSENBERG, J. D.
ROSENTHAL, M.
SEIDEL, M.
SHAPIRO, J.
SPIVAK, G. C.
STADE, G.
TAYLER, E. W.
YERKES, D.

French and Romance Philology:

BLOCH, R. H.
COMPAGNON, A.
CONDE, M.
FORCE, P.
LOTRINGER, S.
MAY, G.
MITTERAND, H.
RIFFATERRE, M.

Genetics and Development:

BESTOR, T.
CARLSON, M.
COSTANTINI, F.
EFSTRATIADIS, A.
GILLIAM, T. C.
OTT, J.
PAPAIOANNOU, V.
ROTHSTEIN, R. J.
SCHON, E. A.
STERN, C. D.
STRUHL, G.
WARBURTON, D.
WOLGEMUTH, D.

Geological Sciences:

BROECKER, W. S.
CHRISTIE-BLICK, N.
FAIRBANKS, R. G.
GORDON, A. L.
HAYES, D. E.
HAYS, J. O.
LANGMUIR, C.
MENKE, W.
MUTTER, J.
OLSEN, P.
RICHARDS, P. G.
SCHLOSSER, P.
SCHOLZ, C.
SIMPSON, H. J.
SYKES, L. R.
WALKER, D.

Germanic Languages:

ANDERSON, M. M.
HUYSSEN, A.
MULLER, H.
VON MUCKE, D. E.

History:

BILLOWS, R.
BLACKMAR, E.
BRINKLEY, A.
BULLIET, R.
BUSHMAN, R.
BYNUM, C.
CANNADINE, D.
DE GRAZIA, V.
DEAK, I.
FIELDS, B.
FONER, E.
GLUCK, C.
GOREN, A. A.
HAIMSON, L.
HARRIS, W. V.
HOWELL, M.
JACKSON, K. T.
KLEIN, H. S.
LYNCH, H. R.
MALEFAKIS, E. E.
MARABLE, M.
PAXTON, R.
ROTHMAN, D.
SCHAMA, S.
SHENTON, J. P.
SMIT, J. W.
STANISLAWSKI, M.
STEPAN, N.
STERN, F.
VON HAGEN, M. L.
WOLOCH, I.
WORTMAN, R.
WRIGHT, M.
YERUSHALMI, Y. H.

Industrial Engineering and Operations Research:

BIENSTOCK, D.
GALLEGO, G.
GOLDFARB, D.
KLEIN, M.
PINEDO, M.
SIGMAN, K.
YAO, D. D.-W.

International and Public Affairs:

MOLZ, R. K.
NELSON, R. R.
RODRIK, D.

Italian:

BAROLINI, T.
REBAY, L.

Journalism:

BELFORD, B.
BENEDICT, H.
CAREY, J. W.
GARLAND, P.
GOLDSTEIN, K. K.
ISAACS, S. D.
KONNER, J.

Krumb School of Mines:

BESHERS, D. N.
DUBY, P. F.
HARRIS, C. C.
SOMASUNDARAN, P.
THEMELIS, N. J.
YEGULALP, T. M.

Law:

BARENBERG, M.
BERGER, C. J.
BERGER, V.
BERMANN, G.
BLACK, B. A.
BLACK, B. S.
BLASI, V.
BRIFFAULT, R.
CHIRELSTEIN, M.
COFFEE, J. C.

CRENSHAW, K. W.
DAMROSCH, L.
EDGAR, H. S. H.
EDWARDS, R.
FARNSWORTH, E. A.
FINEMAN, M.
FLETCHER, G.
GARDNER, R.
GILSON, R. J.
GINSBURG, J. C.
GOLDBERG, V. P.
GOLDSCHMID, H. J.
GORDON, J. N.
GREENAWALT, R. K.
GREENBERG, J.
HOOVER, J.
JONES, W. K.
KORN, H. L.
LEEBRON, D. W.
LIEBMAN, J.
LIEBMAN, L.
LYNCH, G.
MOGLEN, E.
MONAGHAN, H.
NARASIMHAN, S.
NEUMAN, G. L.
PARKER, K. E.
RABB, H. S.
RAPACZYNSKI, A.
ROE, M. J.
SABEL, C. F.
SMIT, H.
SOVERN, M.
STONE, R.
STRAUSS, P. L.
THOMAS, K.
UVILLER, H. R.
WILLIAMS, P. J.
YOUNG, M.
YOUNG, W. F., Jr

Mathematics:

BASS, H.
FRIEDMAN, R.
GALLAGHER, P. X.
GOLDFELD, D.
JACQUET, H. M.
JORGENSEN, T.
KARATZAS, I.
KURANISHI, M.
MORGAN, J.
PHONG, D.
PINKHAM, H. C.

Mechanical Engineering:

CHEVRAY, R.
FREUDENSTEIN, F.
LONGMAN, R. W.
MODI, V.

Medicine:

AL-AWQATI, Q.
APPEL, G. B.
BAER, L. R.
BANK, A.
BIGGER, J. T.
BILEZIKIAN, J. P.
BUTLER, V. P., Jr
CALDWELL, L. P.
CANFIELD, R. E.
CANNON, P. J.
CHESS, L.
CIMINO, J. J.
CLAYTON, P. D.
CORTELL, S.
FIELD, M.
FRANCIS, C. K.
FRANTZ, A. G.
GIARDINA, E.-G.
GINSBURG, H. N.
GOLDBERG, I. J.
GRIECO, M. H.
HOLT, P. R.
JACOBS, T. P.
KEMP, H., Jr
LEGATO, M. J.
LEIFER, E.

LINDENBAUM, J.
LOEB, J.
MELCHER, G.
MORRIS, T. Q.
MORSE, J. E.
NEU, H. C.
PHILLIPS, G. B.
PI-SUNYER, F. X.
ROSNER, W.
SCHWARTZ, M. J.
TABAS, I. A.
TALL, A.
TAPLEY, D. F.
TAUB, R. N.
THOMSON, G. E.
TURINO, G. M.
WARDLAW, S.
WEINSTEIN, I. B.
WEISFELDT, M. L.
WEISS, H. J.

Microbiology:

CALAME, K. L.
FIGURSKI, D.
MITCHELL, A. P.
RACANIELLO, V. R.
SHORE, D. M.
SHUMAN, H. A.
SILVERSTEIN, S. J.
YOUNG, C.

Middle East and Asian Languages and Cultures:

BURRILL, K. R. F.
MADINA, M.
MIRON, D.
PRITCHETT, F.
RICCARDI, T.
SALIBA, G.
VAN DE MIEROOP, M.

Music:

BENT, I.
CHRISTENSEN, D.
EDWARDS, G.
FRISCH, W.
KRAMER, J.
LERDAHL, A. W.
PERKINS, L.
SISMAN, E.
TUCKER, M. T.

Neurological Surgery:

BRISMAN, R.
HOUSEPIAN, E. M.
MCMURTRY, J.
QUEST, D. O.
STEIN, B. M.

Neurology:

BRUST, J. C. M., Jr
COTE, L. J.
DE VIVO, D. C.
DI MAURO, S.
EMERSON, R. G.
FAHN, S.
GHEZ, C.
GOLD, A. P.
HALSEY, J., Jr
HAUSER, W. A.
KARLIN, A.
LATOV, N.
LOVELACE, R. E.
MAYEUX, R.
MOHR, J. P.
PEDLEY, T.
PENN, A. S.
ROWLAND, L. P.
SCHWARTZ, J.
SCIARRA, D.
STERN, Y.
WEXLER, N.

Nursing:

FULMER, T. T.
MUNDINGER, M. O.

Obstetrics and Gynaecology:

BOWE, E. T.

FERIN, M.
HEMBREE, W. C.
JAGIELLO, G.
LOBO, R. A.
NEUWIRTH, R. S.
TIMOR, I. E.
WILLIAMS, S. B.

Ophthalmology:

BEHRENS, M.
BITO, L.
DONN, A.
FARRIS, R. L.
FORBES, M.
GOURAS, P.
L'ESPERANCE, F., Jr
MOORE, S.
SPALTER, H.
SPECTOR, A.
SRINIVASAN, B.
TROKEL, S.
WORGUL, B. V.
YANNUZZI, L. A.

Orthopaedic Surgery:

DICK, H.
EFTEKHAR, N.
FIELDING, J. W.
GRANTHAM, S. A.
LAI, W. M.
MOW, V. C.
RATCLIFFE, A.
SHELTON, M. L.

Otolaryngology:

BLITZER, A.
CLOSE, L. G.
KHANNA, S. M.

Paediatrics:

COOPER, L. Z.
CUNNINGHAM, N.
DECKELBAUM, R. J.
DELL, R. B.
DRISCOLL, J. M.
GERSHON, A. A.
GERSONY, W. M.
HEAGARTY, M.
JACOBS, J.
KRONGRAD, E.
LEBLANC, W.
LEVINE, L.
MELLIN, G. W.
MELLINS, R. B.
NICHOLSON, J. F.
PIOMELLI, S.
SITARZ, A.
STARK, R.
WETHERS, D. L.
WINCHESTER, R. J.

Pathology:

AXEL, R.
DALLA-FAVERA, R.
GELLER, L. M.
GOLDMAN, J. E.
GREENE, L. A.
KAUFMAN, M.
KOHN, D. F.
LEFKOWITCH, J. H.
LIEM, R. K. H.
MASON, C. A.
PERZIN, K. H.
RICHART, R. M.
SHELANSKI, M. L.
SUCIU-FOCA, N.

Pharmacology:

BOYDEN, P.
GOLDBERG, D. J.
GRAZIANO, J. H.
HOFFMAN, B. F.
ROBINSON, R. B.
ROSEN, M. R.
SIEGELBAUM, S. A.
WIT, A. L.

Philosophy:

ALBERT, D.

BEROFSKY, B.
BILGRAMI, A.
GAIFMAN, H.
GOEHR, L. D.
LARMORE, C.
LEVI, I.
POGGE, T.
SIDORSKY, D.

Physical Education and Intercollegiate Athletics:

ROHAN, J. P.

Physics:

APRILE, E.
CHRIST, N. H.
GYULASSY, M.
HAILEY, C. J.
HARTMANN, S.
KAHN, S. M.
LEE, T. D.
LEE, W.
MUELLER, A.
NAGAMIYA, S.
RUDERMAN, M. A.
SCHWARTZ, M.
SCIULLI, F.
SHAEVITZ, M. H.
TUTS, P. M.
UEMURA, Y.
WEINBERG, E.
WILLIS, W. J.
ZAJC, W. A.

Physiology and Cellular Biophysics:

BLANK, M.
DODD, J.
FISCHBARG, J.
KANDEL, E. R.
LOW, M. G.
SCHACHTER, D.
SILVERSTEIN, S. C.
STERN, D.

Political Science:

ANDERSON, L.
BALDWIN, D.
BERNSTEIN, T. P.
BETTS, R. K.
BIALER, S.
CHALMERS, D. A.
COHEN, J. L.
CURTIS, G. L.
ELSTER, J.
FRANKLIN, J. H.
HAMILTON, C. V.
JERVIS, R. L.
JOHNSTON, D. C.
KATZNELSON, I. I.
KESSELMAN, M. J.
LEGVOLD, R.
MILNER, H.
NATHAN, A. N.
ROTHSCHILD, J.
RUGGIE, J.
SCHILLING, W. R.
SHAPIRO, R. Y.
SNYDER, J.
WESTIN, A. F.

Psychiatry:

BENNETT, R.
DEVANAND, D.
DOHRENWEND, B.
DUNTON, H. D.
EHRHARDT, A. A.
ENDICOTT, J.
ERLENMEYER-KIMLING, L.
FIEVE, R. R.
FISCHMAN, M. W.
FOLEY, A. R.
GLASSMAN, A. H.
GORMAN, J. M.
GURLAND, B. J.
HOFER, M.
JAFFE, J.
KLEBER, H. D.
KLEIN, D. F.

KLEIN, R. G.
KUPFERMANN, I.
PARDES, H.
PROHOVNIK, I.
RAINER, J.
RYAN, J.
SACKEIM, H. A.
SHAFFER, D.
SPITZER, R.
TAMIR, H.
WEISSMAN, M. M.

Psychology:

COOPER, L. A.
DWECK, C. S.
GALANTER, E. H.
GIBBON, J.
GRAHAM, N.
HIGGINS, E. T.
HOOD, D. C.
KRANTZ, D.
KRAUSS, R.
MATIN, L.
METCALFE, J.
MISCHEL, W.
TERRACE, H. S.

Public Health:

BAYER, R.
BRANDT-RAUF, P. W.
BROWN, L.
CHALLENOR, B. D.
COLOMBOTOS, J. L.
DAVIDSON, A.
DESPOMMIER, D. D.
FLEISS, J. L.
HASHIM, S. A.
HOWE, G. R.
KANDEL, D.
LEVIN, B.
LINK, B. G.
LO, S.-H.
MCCARTHY, J.
OTTMAN, R.
PEARSON, T. A.
PERERA, F. P.
ROSENFIELD, A. G.
SANTELLA, R. P.
SISK, J. E.
STRUENING, E. L.
TSAI, W.-Y.

Radiation Oncology:

AMOLS, H. I.
BRENNER, D. J.
GEARD, C.
HALL, E.
HEI, T. K.
SCHIFF, P. B.

Radiology:

ABLOW, R. C.
ALDERSON, P. O.
BERDON, W.
ESSER, P.
FELDMAN, F.
HILAL, S.
KING, D. L.
NEWHOUSE, J. H.
NICKOLOFF, E. L.
SILVER, A. J.

Rehabilitation Medicine:

DOWNEY, J. A.
EDELSTEIN, J. E.
LIEBERMAN, J. S.
MYERS, S. J.
NEUHAUS, B. E.
THORNHILL, H.

Religion:

AWN, J.
LINDT, G.
PROUDFOOT, W.
RUPP, G.
SOMERVILLE, R.
THURMAN, R.
WEISS-HALIVNI, D.

Slavic Languages:

BELKNAP, R. L.
GASPAROV, B.
MAGUIRE, R. A.
MILLER, F. J.
POPKIN, C.
REYFMAN, I.

Social Work:

AKABAS, S.
BLACK, R. B.
CLOWARD, R. A.
FELDMAN, R.
GARFINKEL, I.
GITTERMAN, A.
HESS, M. M.
IVANOFF, A.
KAMERMAN, S. B.
KIRK, S.
MCGOWAN, B.
MEYER, C. H.
MONK, A.
MULLEN, E. J.
POLSKY, H.
SCHILLING, R. F.
SCHINKE, S.
SIMON, B. L.
SOLOMON, R.

Sociology:

COLE, J. R.
GANS, H.
LITWAK, E.
RUGGIE, M.
SILVER, A. A.
SPILERMAN, S.
WHITE, H.

Spanish and Portuguese:

ALAZRAKI, J.
GRIEVE, P. E.
MARTINEZ-BONATI, F.
SILVER, P. W.
SOBEJANO, G.

Statistics:

DE LA PENA, V.
HEYDE, C. C.

Surgery:

ALTMAN, R. P.
CHIU, D. T. W.
FORDE, K.
HARDY, M. A.
HUGO, N.
LO GERFO, P.
MARKOWITZ, A.
NOWYGROD, R.
QUAEGEBEUR, J. M.
REEMTSMA, K.
ROSE, E. A.
SMITH, C. R.
SPOTNITZ, H. M.
STOLAR, C. J. H.
TILSON, M. D.

Urology:

BUTTYAN, R.
HENSLE, T. W.
OLSSON, C. A.
PUCHNER, P. J.
ROMAS, N. S.

AFFILIATED COLLEGES

Barnard College: 3009 Broadway, New York, NY 10027; tel. (212) 854-5262; fax (212) 854-9470; internet www.barnard.edu; f. 1889; Pres. DEBORA L. SPAR; Dean AVIS E. HINKSON; Provost and Dean for Faculty PAUL HERTZ (acting); Vice-Pres. for College Relations DOROTHY DENBURG; Vice-Pres. for Devt BRET SILVER; Vice-Pres. for Information Technology CAROL KATZMAN; Gen. Counsel JOMYSHA STEPHEN; Dean for Library and Academic Information Services LISA R. NORBERG; library of 300,000 vols; 375 ; 2,390 .

Teachers' College: 525 W 120th St, New York, NY 10027; tel. (212) 678-3000; internet www.tc.columbia.edu; Pres. Dr SUSAN H. FUHRMAN; Provost and Dean Dr THOMAS JAMES; Vice-Pres. for Devt and External Affairs SUZANNE M. MURPHY; Vice-Pres. for Finance and Admin. HARVEY SPECTOR; Gen. Counsel LORI E. FOX; library of 430,432 vols, 237,935 non-print items; 5,371 ; publ. *TC Today*.

CONCORDIA COLLEGE

171 White Plains Rd, Bronxville, NY 10708
Telephone: (914) 337-9300
Fax: (914) 395-4500
E-mail: admission@concordia-ny.edu
Internet: www.concordia-ny.edu
Founded 1881; attached to Concordia Univ. System
Private control
Academic year: August to May
Pres.: Dr VIJI GEORGE
Chief Financial Officer: DENNIS LONNERGAN
Vice-Pres. for Institutional Advancement: Dr PAUL GRAND PRÉ
Chief Academic Officer: SHERRY J. FRASER
Dean of College: SHERRY FRASER
Dean of Faculty: Dr MANDANA NAKHAI
Dean of Students: JOHN M. BAHR
Registrar: MARK E. BLANCO
Library Dir: WILLIAM PERRENOD

Number of teachers: 30
Number of students: 800 (undergraduate)
Publication: *The Concordia New Yorker* (1 a year)

DEANS

Experiential Learning: JOHN M. BAHR
Nursing: Dr SUSAN APOLD

COOPER UNION FOR THE ADVANCEMENT OF SCIENCE AND ART

30 Cooper Sq., New York, NY 10003-7120
Telephone: (212) 353-4100
Fax: (212) 353-4327
E-mail: admissions@cooper.edu
Internet: www.cooper.edu
Founded 1859
Private control
Academic year: September to May
Pres.: Dr JAMSHED BHARUCHA
Chair.: MARK EPSKIN
Vice-Pres. for Finance, Admin. and Treas.: T. C. WESTCOTT
Vice-Pres. for Devt: DEREK A. WITTNER
Vice-Pres. for External Affairs: RONNI DENES
Dean for Student Services: LINDA LEMIESZ
Registrar and Dean for Admissions: MITCHELL LIPTON
Library Dir: CAROL SALOMON (acting)

Library of 100,000 vols, 300 periodicals
Number of teachers: 228
Number of students: 1,000
Publication: *At Cooper Union* (2 a year)

DEANS

Albert Nerken School of Engineering: SIMON BEN-AVI (acting)
Faculty of Humanities and Social Sciences: WILLIAM GERMANO
Irwin S. Chanin School of Architecture: ANTHONY VIDLER
School of Art: SASKIA BOS

CORNELL UNIVERSITY

Day Hall Lobby, Ithaca, NY 14853
Telephone: (607) 254-4636
Fax: (607) 254-6225
E-mail: info@cornell.edu
Internet: www.cornell.edu
Founded 1865 opened 1868

State and private control
Academic year: September to May
Pres.: DAVID J. SKORTON
Provost: W. KENT FUCHS
Provost for Medical Affairs: LAURIE H. GLIMCHER
Vice-Pres. for Alumni Affairs and Devt: CHARLES T. PHLEGAR
Vice-Pres. for Facilities Services: KYU-JUNG WHANG
Vice-Pres. for Finance and Chief Financial Officer: JOANNE M. DESTEFANO
Vice-Pres. for Govt and Community Relations: STEPHEN PHILIP JOHNSON
Vice-Pres. for Human Resources: MARY G. OPPERMAN
Vice-Pres. for Planning and Budget: ELMIRA MANGUM
Vice-Pres. for Student and Academic Services: SUSAN H. MURPHY
Vice-Pres. for Univ. Communications: THOMAS W. BRUCE
Vice-Pres. for Univ. Relations: GLENN C. ALTSCHULER
Dean of Univ. Faculty: WILLIAM FRY
Dean of Students: KENT L. HUBBELL
Univ. Counsel and Sec. of the Corpn: JAMES J. MINGLE
Univ. Librarian: ANNE R. KENNEY

Library: see under Libraries and Archives
Number of teachers: 1,564
Number of students: 22,254

Publications: *Administrative Science Quarterly, Agricultural Finance Review, Andean Past* (academic), *Association, Biological Control of Turfgrass Diseases, Colloqui: Cornell Journal of Planning and Urban Issues, Communique (Ithaca), Cornell Alumni Magazine, Cornell East Asia Series* (academic), *Cornell Engineering Magazine* (2 a year), *Cornell Enterprise, Cornell Field Crops and Soils Handbook, Cornell Hospitality Quarterly, Cornell Hotel School* (magazine), *Cornell International Law Journal* (3 a year), *Cornell Journal of Architecture* (academic), *Cornell Journal of Law and Public Policy, Cornell Law Review* (6 a year), *Cornell Lunatic, Cornell Modern Indonesia Project Publications, Cornell Phonetics Laboratory, Cornell Plantations Magazine, Cornell Recommendations for Commercial Florist Crops, Cornell Recommendations for Field Crops, Cornell Recommendations for Pest Control for Commercial Production and Maintenance of Trees and Shrubs, Cornell Science and Technology Magazine, Cornell Working Papers in Linguistics, Epoch* (3 a year), *Ezra* (4 a year), *Hotelie* (3 a year), *Human Ecology, Indonesia* (2 a year), *Industrial and Labor Relations Review, Industry Perspectives: A White Paper Series from Cornell, Journal of Empirical Legal Studies, LINK* (2 a year), *Living Bird, N K A, Philosophical Review, Traces* (Korean, Chinese, English and Japanese), *Weil Cornell Medicine*

DEANS

College of Agriculture and Life Sciences: KATHRYN J. BOOR
College of Architecture, Art and Planning: KENT KLEINMAN
College of Arts and Sciences: G. PETER LEPAGE
College of Engineering: LANCE R. COLLINS
College of Human Ecology: ALAN D. MATHIOS
College of Veterinary Medicine: MICHAEL I. KOTLIKOFF
Faculty of Computing and Information Science: DANIEL P. HUTTENLOCHER
Graduate School: BARBARA A. KNUTH
Law School: STEWART J. SCHWAB
Samuel Curtis Johnson Graduate School of Management: L. JOSEPH THOMAS

School of Continuing Education and Summer Sessions: GLENN C. ALTSCHULER
School of Hotel Administration: MICHAEL D. JOHNSON
School of Industrial and Labor Relations: HARRY C. KATZ
Weill Graduate School of Medical Sciences: DAVID P. HAJJAR

PROFESSORS

College of Agriculture and Life Sciences (260 Roberts Hall, Ithaca, NY 14853-5905; tel. (607) 255-2241; e-mail cals-studentservices@cornell.edu; internet www.cals.cornell.edu):

Animal Science:

AUSTIC, R.
BAUMAN, D.
BELL, A.
BLAKE, R.
BUTLER, W.
CHASE, L.
CURRIE, W.
EVERETT, R.
FOX, D.
GALTON, D.
GOREWIT, R.
HINTZ, H.
JOHNSON, P.
OLTENACU, P.
PARKS, J.
PELL, A.
POLLAK, E.
QUAAS, R.
THONNEY, M.

Applied Economics and Management:

BARRETT, C.
BILLS, N.
BOISVERT, R.
CHAPMAN, L.
CHRISTY, R.
CONRAD, J.
KAISER, H.
KANBUR, R.
KNOBLAUCH, W.
LADUE, E.
LEE, D.
LESSER, W.
MCLAUGHLIN, E.
MOUNT, T.
NOVAKOVIC, A.
RAJ, S.
SCHULZE, W.
STREEFER, D.
TAUER, L.
WANSINK, B.
WHITE, G.

Biological and Environmental Engineering:

ALBRIGHT, L.
ANESHANSLEY, D.
COOKE, J.
DATTA, A.
GEBREMEDHIN, K.
HAITH, D.
JEWELL, W.
PARLANGE, J.-Y.
SCOTT, N.
SPANSWICK, R.
STEENHUIS, T.
TIMMONS, M.
WALKER, L.
WALTER, M.

Communication:

BOOTH, J.
GAY, G.
OSTMAN, R.
WALTHER, J.

Crop and Soil Sciences:

CHERNEY, J.
COX, W.
DEGLORIA, S.
DUXBURY, J.
FICK, G.
MCBRIDE, M.

OBENDORF, R.
SETTER, T.
VAN ES, H.

Developmental Sociology:

BROWN, D.
EBERTS, P.
FELDMAN, S.
GEISLER, C.
GURAK, D.
HIRSCHL, T.
LYSON, T.
MCMICHAEL, P.
PFEFFER, M.

Earth and Atmospheric Sciences:

COLUCCI, S.
COOK, K.
RIHA, S.
WILKS, D.

Ecology and Evolutionary Biology:

CHABOT, B.
DHONDT, A.
FEENY, P.
FITZPATRICK, J.
HARRISON, R.
HARVELL, C.
HOWARTH, R.
MCCLURE, P.
MARKS, P.
MORIN, J.
ROOT, R.
WINKLER, D.

Education:

CAFFARELLA, R.
CAMP, W.

Entomology:

AGNELLO, A.
HOFFMANN, M.
LIEBHERR, J.
NYROP, J.
PECKARSKY, B.
REISSIG, W.
ROELOFS, W.
RUTZ, D.
SCOTT, J.
SHELTON, A.
SHIELDS, E.
SODERLUND, D.
STRAUB, R.
TINGEY, W.

Food Science:

ACREE, T.
BARBANO, D.
BATT, C.
BRADY, J., Jr
DURST, R.
GRAVANI, R.
HANG, Y.
HOTCHKISS, J.
HRADZINA, G.
LAWLESS, H.
LEE, C.
MILLER, D.
REGENSTEIN, J.
RIZVI, S.
SIEBERT, K.

Horticultural Sciences:

BROWN, S.
HARMAN, G.
LAKSO, A.
POOL, R.
REISCH, B.
TAYLOR, A.

Horticulture:

BASSUK, N.
BELLINDER, R.
BRIDGEN, M.
GOOD, G.
MILLER, W.
PETROVIC, A.
PRITTS, M.
WAKKINS, C.
WEILER, T.

WIEN, H.
WOLFE, D.

International Programs:

UPHOFF, N.

Landscape Architecture:

ADLEMAN, M.
GLEASON, K.
GOTTFRIED, H.
TRANCIK, R.
TROWBRIDGE, P.

Microbiology:

GHIORSE, W.
HELMANN, J.
WINANS, S.
ZINDER, S.

Molecular Biology and Genetics:

CALVO, J.
FOX, T.
GOLDBERG, M.
HANSON, M.
HENRY, S.
KEMPHUES, K.
LIS, J.
MACINTYRE, R.
ROBERTS, J.
SHALLOWAY, D.
TYE, B.
VOGT, V.
WU, R.

Natural Resources:

DECKER, D.
FAHEY, T.
GILLETT, J.
HULLAR, T.
KNUTH, B.
KRASNY, M.
LASSOIE, J.
MILLS, E.

Neurobiology and Behavior:

ADLER, K.
BRADBURY, J.
EISNER, T.
EMLEN, S.
HARRIS-WARRICK, R.
HOPKINS, C.
VEHRENCAMP, S.
WALCOTT, C.

Nutrition:

BENSADOUN, A.
LEVITSKY, D.
NOY, N.
PINSTRUP-ANDERSON, P.

Plant Biology:

BATES, D.
CREPET, W.
DAVIES, P.
DOYLE, J.
NASRALLAH, J.
NASRALLAH, M.
NIKLAS, K.
RODRIGUEZ, E.

Plant Breeding:

COFFMAN, W. R.
EARLE, E.
JOHN, M.
KRESOVICH, S.
MCCOUCH, S.
MUTSCHLER, M.
SORRELLS, M.
TANKSLEY, S.
VIANDS, D.

Plant Pathology:

ABAWI, G.
ALDWINCKLE, H.
BEER, S.
BERGSTROM, G.
BURR, T.
COLLMER, A.
DILLARD, H.
FRY, W.
HOCH, H.

HUDLER, G.
KOELLER, W.
LAZAROWITZ, S.
LORBEER, J.
LORIA, R.
MARTIN, G.
MILGROOM, M.
ROSENBERGER, D.
SEEM, R.
WILCOX, W.
ZITTER, T.

College of Architecture, Art and Planning (129 Sibley Dome, Ithaca, NY 14853; tel. (607) 255-9110; fax (607) 255-1900; e-mail aapdean@cornell.edu; internet www.aap .cornell.edu):

Architecture:

GOEHNER, W.
GREENBERG, D. P.
HASCUP, G.
HUBBELL, K.
MOSTAFAVI, M.
OTTO, C. F.
RICHARDSON, H.
WELLS, J.

Art:

KORD, V.
LOCEY, J.
SPECTOR, F.
SQUIER, J. L.
WALKINGSTICK, K.

City and Regional Planning:

AZIS, I.
BENERIA, L.
BOOTH, R.
CHRISOPHERSON, S.
CLAVEL, P.
DRENNAN, M.
FORESTER, J.
GOLDSMITH, W.
LEWIS, D.
OLPADWALA, P.
REARDON, K.

College of Arts and Sciences (172 Golden Smith Hall, Ithaca, NY 14853-3201; tel. (607) 255-4833; e-mail as_admissions@cornell.edu; internet www.arts.cornell.edu):

Anthropology:

GREENWOOD, D.
HENDERSON, J.
HOLMBERG, D.
MARCH, K.
SANGREN, P.
SIEGEL, J.
SMALL, M.

Asian Studies:

DE BARY, B.
GOLD, D.
GUNN, E.
MINKOWSKI, C.
SAKAI, N.
TAYLOR, K.

Astronomy:

CAMPBELL, D.
CHERNOFF, D.
CORDES, J.
GIERASCH, P.
GIOVANELLI, R.
GOLDSMITH, P.
HAYNES, M.
HERTER, T.
HOUCK, J.
NICHOLSON, P.
SQUYRES, S.
STACEY, G.
TERZIAN, Y.
VEVERKA, J.
WASSERMAN, I.

Chemistry and Chemical Biology:

ABRUNA, H.
BAIRD, B.
BEGLEY, T.

BURLITCH, J.
CARPENTER, B.
COATES, G.
COLLUM, D.
DAVIS, H.
DISALVO, F.
EALICK, S.
EZRA, G.
FAY, R.
FREED, J.
GANEM, B.
HINES, M.
HOFFMANN, R.
HOUSTON, P.
LEE, S.
LORING, R.
MEINWALD, J.
SOGAH, D.
WIDOM, B.
WOLCZANSKI, P.

Classics:

AHL, F.
CLINTON, K.
COLEMAN, J.
NUSSBAUM, A.
PELLICCIA, H.
PUCCI, P.
RAWLINGS, H., III
RUSTEN, J.

Comparative Literature:

CARMICHAEL, C.
COHEN, W.
KENNEDY, W.
MONROE, J.

Ecology and Systematics:

ELLNER, S.
GREENE, H.
HAIRSTON, N., Jr
KENNEDY, K.
POWER, A.
PROVINE, W.

Economics:

BASU, K.
BLUME, L.
COATE, S.
DAVIS, T.
EASLEY, D.
HONG, Y.
KIEFER, N.
LYONS, T.
MAJUMDAR, M.
MASSON, R.
MITRA, T.
POSSEN, U.
SHELL, K.
VOGELSANG, T.
WAN, H., Jr

English:

BOGEL, F.
BROWN, L.
CHASE, C.
CHEYFITZ, E.
CULLER, J.
FULTON, A.
GILBERT, R.
HERRIN, W.
HILL, T.
HITE, M.
JANOWITZ, P.
JEYIFO, B.
MCCALL, D.
MCCLANE, K., Jr
MCMILLIN, H.
MOHANTY, S.
MORGAN, R.
MURRAY, T.
PARKER, A.
SAMUELS, S.
SAWYER, P.
SCHWARZ, D.
SHAW, H.
SIEGEL, S.
SPILLERS, H.

VAUGHN, S.
WETHERBEE, W., III

German Studies:

ADELSON, L.
GROOS, A., Jr
HOHENDAHL, P.
KITTLER, W.
MARTIN, C.

Government:

BENSEL, R.
BUCK-MORSS, S.
BUNCE, V.
EVANGELISTA, M.
HERRING, R.
KATZENSTEIN, M.
KATZENSTEIN, P.
KRAMNICK, I.
LOWI, T.
MEBANE, W.
PONTUSSON, J.
RABKIN, J.
RUBENSTEIN, D.
SANDERS, M.
SHEFTER, M.
TARROW, S.
VANDEWALLE, N.

History:

ALTSCHULER, G.
BLUMIN, S.
CARON, V.
COCHRAN, S.
DEAR, P.
GREENE, S.
HULL, I.
HYAMS, P.
KAMMEN, M.
KAPLAN, S.
KOSCHMANN, J.
LACAPRA, D.
LOGEVALL, F.
MOORE, R.
NAJEMY, J.
NORTON, M.
PETERSON, C.
POLENBERG, R.
STEINBERG, M.
STRAUSS, B.
WASHINGTON, M.

History of Art:

KUNIHOLM, P.
LAZZARO, C.
RAMAGE, A.

Linguistics:

BOWERS, J.
COLLINS, C.
DIESING, M.
HARBERT, W.
MCCONNELL-GINET, S.
ROOTH, M.
ROSEN, C.
WHITMAN, J.
ZEC, D.

Mathematics:

BARBASCH, D.
BILLERA, L.
BROWN, K.
CHASE, S.
CONNELLY, R.
DENNIS, R. K.
DURRETT, R.
DYNKIN, E.
GROSS, L.
GUCKENHEIMER, J.
HATCHER, A.
HENDERSON, D.
HUBBARD, J.
HWANG, J. T.
ILIACHENKO, I.
KAHN, P.
LAWLER, G.
NERODE, A.
NUSSBAUM, M.
SALOFF-COSTE, L.

SCHATZ, A.
SEN, S.
SHORE, R.
SMILLIE, J.
SPEH, B.
STILLMAN, M.
STRICHARTZ, R.
THURSTON, W.
VOGTMANN, K.
WAHLBIN, L.
WEST, J.

Molecular Biology and Genetics:

AGUADRO, C.
BRETSCHER, A.
BROWN, W.
CLARK, A.
FEIGENSON, G.
HESS, G.
HINKLE, P.
HUFFAKER, T.
WILSON, D.
WOLFNER, M.

Music:

BILSON, M.
HARRIS-WARRICLE, R.
HSU, J.
ROSEN, D.
SIERRA, R.
STUCKY, S.
WEBSTER, J., Jr
ZASLAW, N.

Near Eastern Studies:

BRANN, R.
OWEN, D.
POWERS, D.

Neurobiology and Behavior:

BASS, A.
FETCHO, J.
HOWLAND, H.
HOY, R.
SEELEY, T.
SHERMAN, P.

Philosophy:

BOYD, R.
FINE, G.
IRWIN, T.
MACDONALD, S.
MILLER, R.
MOODY-ADAMS, M.
STURGEON, N.

Physics:

ALEXANDER, J.
AMBEGAOKAR, V.
ASHCROFT, N.
BERKELMAN, K.
BODENSCHATZ, E.
CASSEL, D.
DAVIS, J.
DUGAN, G.
ELSER, V.
FITCHEN, D.
GALIK, R.
GINSPARG, P.
GRUNER, S.
HAND, L.
HARTILL, D.
HENLEY, C.
HOFFSTAETTER, G.
LECLAIR, A.
LEE, D.
LEPAGE, G.
MCEUEN, P.
MERMIN, N.
NEUBERT, M.
PARPIA, J.
PATTERSON, J.
RALPH, D.
RICHARDSON, R.
RUBIN, D.
SETHNA, J.
SIEVERS, A., III
STEIN, P.
TALMAN, R.

TEUKOLSKY, S.
THORNE, R.
TYE, S.-H.
YAN, T.-M.
YORK, J.

Plant Biology:

TURGEON, E. G.

Programme on Ethics and Public Life:

SHUE, H.

Psychology:

BEM, D.
BEM, S.
CUTTING, J.
DARLINGTON, R.
DEVOOGD, T.
DUNNING, D.
EDELMAN, S.
FINLAY, B.
GILOVICH, T.
HALPERN, B.
JOHNSTON, R.
KRUMHANSL, C.
MAAS, J.
NEISSER, U.
REGAN, E.

Romance Studies:

BERGER, A.
CASTILLO, D.
GREENBERG, M.
KLEIN, R.
LEWIS, P.
LONG, K.
MIGIEL, M.
RESINA, J.

Russian Literature:

CARDEN, P.
POLLACK, N.
SENDEROVICH, S.
SHAPIRO, G.

Science and Technology Studies:

LYNCH, M.
PINCH, T.
REPPY, J.
ROSSITER, M.

Sociology:

HARRIS, D.
HECKATHORN, D.
MACY, M.
NEE, V.
STRANG, D.
SWEDBERG, R.

Theater, Film and Dance:

BATHRICK, D.
FELDSHUH, D.
GAINOR, J.
GOETZ, K.
LEVITT, B.

College of Engineering (Carpenter Hall, Ithaca, NY 14853-2201; tel. (607) 255-4326; fax (607) 255-9606; e-mail engr_admissions@ cornell.edu; internet www.engineering .cornell.edu):

Applied and Engineering Physics:

BROCK, J.
BUHRMAN, R.
COOL, T.
CRAIGHEAD, H.
GAETA, A.
KUSSE, B.
LINDAU, M.
LOVELACE, R.
SILCOX, J.
WEBB, W.
WISE, F.

Chemical Engineering:

ARCHER, L.
CLANCY, P.
COHEN, C.
KOCH, D.
OLBRICHT, W.

SHULER, M.
STEEN, P.

Civil and Environmental Engineering:

BRUTSAERT, W.
GOSSETT, J.
GRIGORIU, M.
HOVER, K.
INGRAFFEA, A.
KULHAWY, F.
LION, L.
LIU, P.
LOUCKS, D.
MEYBURG, A.
NOZICK, L.
O'ROURKE, T.
PEKOZ, T.
SANSALONE, M.
SCHULER, R.
SHOEMAKER, C.
STEDINGER, J.
TURNQUIST, M.

Computer Sciences:

ARMS, W.
BAILEY, G.
BIRMAN, K.
COLEMAN, T.
CONSTABLE, R.
ELBER, R.
GRIES, D.
HALPERN, J.
HOPCROFT, J.
HUTTENLOCHER, D.
KEDEM, K.
KOZEN, D.
PINGALI, K.
SCHNEIDER, F.
TARDOS, E.
VAN LOAN, C.
VAVASIS, S.

Earth and Atmospheric Sciences:

ALLMENDINGER, R.
BARAZANGI, M.
BROWN, L.
CATHLES, L.
CISNE, J.
GREENE, C.
ISACKS, B.
JORDAN, T.
KAY, R.
KAY, S.
PHIPPS MORGAN, J.
RHODES, F.
WHITE, W.

Electrical Engineering:

BERGER, T.
CHIANG, H.-D.
EASTMAN, L.
FARLEY, D., Jr
FINE, T.
FUCHS, W.
HAAS, Z.
HAMMER, D.
JOHNSON, C., Jr
KELLEY, M.
KINTNER, P., Jr
KLINE, R.
PARKS, T.
POLLOCK, C.
SEYLER, C.
SHEALY, J.
SPENCER, M.
TANG, C.-L.
THOMAS, R.
TIWARI, S.
TONG, L.
WICKER, S.

Materials Science and Engineering:

AST, D.
BLAKELY, J.
DIECKMANN, R.
GIANNELIS, E.
OBER, C.
RUOFF, A.

SASS, S.
VAN DOVER, R.

Mechanical and Aerospace Engineering:

AVEDISIAN, C.
BARTEL, D.
CAUGHEY, D.
COLLINS, L.
DAWSON, P.
GEORGE, A.
GOULDIN, F.
LEIBOVICH, S.
LOUGE, M.
MOON, F.
POPE, S.
TORRANCE, K.
WARHAFT, Z.
WILLIAMSON, C.
ZABARAS, N.

Operations Research and Industrial Engineering:

BLAND, R.
JACKSON, P.
LEWIS, A.
MUCKSTADT, J.
PROTTER, P.
RENEGAR, J.
RESNICK, S.
ROUNDY, R.
RUPPERT, D.
SAMORODNITSKY, G.
SHMOYS, D.
TODD, M.
TROTTER, L., Jr
TURNBULL, B.
WILLIAMSON, D.

Theoretical and Applied Mechanics:

BURNS, J.
CADY, K.
HEALEY, T.
HUI, CH.-Y.
JENKINS, J.
MUKHERJEE, S.
PHOENIX, S.
RAND, R.
RUINA, A.
SACHSE, W.
STROGATZ, S.
ZEHNDER, A.

College of Human Ecology (Martha Van Rensselaer Hall, Ithaca, NY 14853; tel. (607) 255-8774; fax (607) 255-3794; e-mail humec_admissions@cornell.edu; internet www.human.cornell.edu):

Design and Environmental Analysis:

BECKER, F.
ESHELMAN, P.
EVANS, G.
HEDGE, A.
JENNINGS, J.
LAQUATRA, J., Jr
SIMS, W.

Human Development and Family Studies:

BRUMBERG, J.
CECI, S.
COCHRAN, M.
DEPUE, R.
ECKENRODE, J.
GABARINO, J.
HAMILTON, S.
LUST, B.
PILLEMER, K.
ROBERTSON, S.
SAVIN-WILLIAMS, R.
WILLIAMS, W.

Nutrition:

BISOGNI, C.
BRANNON, P.
BRENNA, J.
GARZA, C.
HAAS, J.
HABICHT, J.-P.
OLSON, C.

PELTO, G.
RASMUSSEN, K.
SAHN, D.
STIPANUK, M.

Policy Analysis and Management:

AVERY, R.
BATTISTELLA, R.
BURKHAUSER, R.
GERNER, J.
KENTEL, D.
MATHIOS, A.
PARROT, A.
PETERS, H.
TROCHIM, W.
WHITE, W.

Textiles and Apparel:

CHU, CH.-CH.
LEMLEY, A.
LOKER, S.
NETRAVALI, A.
OBENDORF, S.

College of Veterinary Medicine (Ithaca, NY 14853-6401; tel. (607) 253-3000; fax (607) 253-3709; e-mail vet_admissions@cornell .edu; internet www.vet.cornell.edu):

Biomedical Sciences:

BEYENBACH, K.
DELAHUNTA, A.
FARNUM, C.
FORTUNE, J.
GILMOUR, R., Jr
HOUPT, K.
KOTLIKOFF, M.
LOEW, E.
MINOR, R.
NODEN, D.
QUARONI, A.
SCHIMENTI, J.
SCHLAFER, D.
SUAREZ, S.
SUMMERS, B.
YEN, A.

Clinical Sciences:

AINSWORTH, D.
BARR, S.
CENTER, S.
DIVERS, T.
DUCHARME, N.
FUBINI, S.
GILBERT, R.
GLEED, R.
HACKETT, R.
HORNBUCKLE, W.
KALLFELZ, F.
KOLLIAS, G., Jr
LUDDERS, J.
MILLER, W.
MOISE, N.
NIXON, A.
PAGE, R.
RANDOLPH, J.
SCOTT, D.
SMITH, D.
TENNANT, B.

Microbiology, Immunology and Parasitology:

ANTCZAK, D.
APPLETON, J.
BAINES, J.
BLOOM, S.
BOWMAN, D.
BOWSER, P.
DIETERT, R.
LUST, G.
MCGREGOR, D.
MARSH, J.
PARRISH, C.
RUSSELL, D.
SCHAT, K.

Molecular Medicine:

CERIONE, R.
GUAN, J.
OSWALD, R.

PAULI, B.
SCHWARK, W.
SHARP, G.
WEILAND, G.

Population Medicine and Diagnostic Services:

CHANG, Y.-F.
ERB, H.
GROHN, Y.
MOHAMMED, H.
SCHUKKEN, Y.
TORRES, A.
WHITE, M.

Law School (Myron Taylor Hall, Ithaca, NY 14853-4901; tel. (607) 255-0565; e-mail lawadmit@law.mail.cornell.edu; internet www.lawschool.cornell.edu):

ALEXANDER, G.
BARCELO, J., III
CLERMONT, K. M.
CLYMER, S.
EISENBERG, T.
FARINA, C.
GARVEY, S.
GERMAIN, C.
GREEN, R.
HAY, G. A.
HEISE, M.
HENDERSON, J., Jr
HILLMAN, R.
HOLDEN-SMITH, B.
JOHNSON, S. L.
LASSER, M.
LEHMAN, J.
MARTIN, P. W.
NDULO, M.
RACHLINSKI, J.
RILES, A.
ROSSI, F. F.
SCHWAB, S.
SHERWIN, E.
SHIFFRIN, S.
SILICIANO, J.
SIMSON, G. J.
SUMMERS, R. S.
TAYLOR, W.
WIPPMAN, D.

New York State College of Industrial and Labor Relations

Collective Bargaining:

DANIEL, C.
GROSS, J.
HURD, R.
KAHN, L.
KATZ, H.
KURUVILLA, S.
LIPSKY, D.
SALVATORE, N.
TURNER, L.

Employment and Disability Institute:

BRUYERE, S.

Human Resource Studies:

BRIGGS, V., Jr
DYER, L.
SNELL, S.
WRIGHT, P.

Labor Economics:

ABOWD, J.
BLAU, F.
BOYER, G.
EHRENBERG, R.
FIELDS, G.
HUTCHENS, R.
SMITH, R.

Organizational Behavior:

BACHARACH, S.
HAMMER, T.
LAWLER, E.
TOLBERT, P.

Social Statistics:

DICICCIO, T.

WELLS, M.

Samuel Curtis Johnson Graduate School of Management (Sage Hall, Ithaca, NY 14853-6201; tel. (607) 255-4526; fax (607) 255-0065; e-mail mba@cornell.edu; internet www .johnson.cornell.edu):

BENDANIEL, D.
BIERMAN, H., Jr
BLOOMFIELD, R.
DYCKMAN, T.
FRANK, R.
HART, S.
HASS, J.
HILTON, R.
ISEN, A.
JARROW, R.
LEE, C.
LIBBY, R.
MCADAMS, A.
MCCLAIN, J.
MICHAELY, R.
NELSON, M.
O'HARA, M.
ORMAN, L.
RAO, V.
RUSSO, J.
SMIDT, S.
SWAMINATHAN, B.
SWIERINGA, R.
THOMAS, L.
WALDMAN, M.

School of Hotel Administration (Statler Hall, Ithaca, NY 14853-6902; tel. (607) 255-9393; fax (607) 255.0021; e-mail hotelschool_admissions@cornell.edu; internet www.hotelschool.cornell.edu):

BROWNELL, J.
CORGEL, J.
DITTMAN, D.
ENZ, C.
GELLER, A.
HINKIN, T.
KIMES, S.
MUTKOSKI, S.
PENNER, R.
REDLIN, M.
SIGUAW, J.
THOMPSON, G.

Weill Cornell Medical College (1300 York Ave, New York, NY 10065; tel. (212) 746-5454; fax (212) 821-0576; e-mail cumc_admissions@med.cornell.edu; internet www.med.cornell.edu):

Anaesthesiology:

AMAR, D.
DESIDERIO, D.
DINNER, M., Clinical
HALPERN, N. A., Clinical
HARRISON, N., Pharmacology
HEMMINGS, H. C., Jr
KELLY, R. E., Clinical
LIEN, C. A., Clinical
MALHOTRA, V., Clinical
SAVARESE, J.
THOMAS, S. J.
THORNE, A. C., Clinical
WILSON, R. S.
YAO, F.-S. F., Clinical

Biochemistry:

BOSKEY, A. L.
BRESLOW, E. M. G.
COOPER, A. J. L.
MCGRAW, T. E.
MAXFIELD, F. R.
MENON, A. K.
NOVOGRODSKY, A.
ROBERTSON, H. D.
RUBIN, A. L.
RYAN, T. A.
STENZEL, K. H.
TATE, S. S.
WU, H.

Cardiothoracic Surgery:

ADKINS, M. S.
ALTORKI, N. K.
ISOM, O. W.
KRIEGER, K. H.
LARAGH, J. H., Medicine
TORTOLANI, A. J.

Cell and Developmental Biology:

BACHVAROVA, R. F.
FISCHMAN, D. A.
HAJJAR, K. A.
MIKAWA, T.
SATO, T. N.

Dermatology:

GRANSTEIN, R. D.
HALPERN, A. C.
VARGHESE, M. C.

Genetic Medicine:

RAFII, S.

Medicine:

ALLISON, J. P., Immunology
AUGUST, P.
BAJORIN, D. F.
BARDES, C. L., Clinical
BASSON, C. T.
BERMAN, E., Clinical
BOCKMAN, R. S.
BORER, J. S.
BOSL, G. J.
BROWN, A. E.
CARMEL, R.
CASPER, E. S.
CHANDRA, P., Clinical
CHARLSON, M. E.
CHEIGH, H., Clinical
CLARKSON, B. D.
CROW, M. K.
CRYSTAL, R. G.
DANNENBERG, A. J.
DEVEREUX, R. B.
DOSIK, H.
ETINGIN, O. R.
FAHEY, T. J., Jr, MClinical
FEIN, O. T., Clinical
FELDMAN, E. J.
FINNS, J. J.
FLOMENBAUM, N. E., Clinical
FUKS, Z. Y., Radiation Oncology
GIBOFSKY, A., Clinical
GOLDE, D. W.
GORDON, B., Clinical
GOTTO, A. M., Jr
GROEGER, J. S., Clinical
HAYES, J. G.
HEMPSTEAD, B. L.
HOUGHTON, A. N.
IMPERATO-MCGINLEY, J. L.
IVANSHKIV, L. B.
JACOBS, J. L., Clinical
JACOBSON, I. M., Clinical
JOHNSON, W. D.
KAGEN, L. J. A.
KELSEN, D. P.
KEMENY, N. E.
KIEHN, T. E., Clinical and Clinical Microbiology
KLEIN, H.
KLIGFIELD, P. D.
KOLESNICK, R. N.
KRIS, M. G.
KROWN, S. E.
KURTZ, R. C., Clinical
LACHS, M. S.
LAURENCE, J. C.
LERMAN, B. B.
LIPKIN, M.
LIVINGSTON, P. O.
LOCKSHIN, M. D.
MCCORMICK, B., Radiation Oncology
MARCUS, A. J.
MARKENSON, J. A., Clinical)
MARKS, P. A.
MAYER, K., Clinical

MESSINEO, F., Clinical
MEYER, B. R., Clinical
MINSKY, B., Radiation Oncology)
MOORE, A., Clinical
MOTZER, R. J.
MURRAY, H. W.
NACHMAN, R. L.
NANUS, D. M., Haematology, Oncology
NIMER, S. D.
NORTON, L.
OETTGEN, H. F.
OFFIT, K.
OKIN, P. M.
PAGET, S. A.
PAMER, E. G.
PAPE, J. W.
PECKER, M. S., Clinical
PFISTER, D. G.
PORTLOCK, C. S., Clinical
POSNETT, D. N.
PRITCHETT, R. A. R., Clinical
RAHAL, J. J.
RIGGIO, R. R., Clinical
RIVLIN, R. S.
ROBBINS, R. J.
ROBERTS, R. B.
ROMAN, M. J.
ROSEN, N.
ROSENFELD, I., Clinical
SAAL, S. D., Clinical
SALMON, J. E.
SALTZ, L. B.
SCHEIDT, S., Clinical
SCHEINBERG, D. A.
SCHER, H. I.
SCHUSTER, M. W., Clinical
SEPKOWITZ, K. A.
SHIKE, M.
SILVER, R. T.
SMITH, K. A.
SPRIGGS, D. R.
STEINBERG, C. R., Clinical
STEINGART, R. M.
STOVER, D. E., Clinical
STRAUS, D. J., Clinical
SUTHANTHIRAN, M.
THOMAS, H. M., III, Clinical
WADLER, S.
WEINSTEIN, A. M.
WEKSLER, B. B.
WEKSLER, M. E.
WHITE, D. A.
WINAWER, S. J.
WITTES, R.
WUEST, D. L., Pathology in Clinical
YAHALOM, J., Radiation Oncology

Microbiology and Immunology:

BARANY, F.
BROT, N.
COICO, R.
DING, A.
FALCK-PEDERSEN, E.
HOLLOMAN, W. K.
MOORE, J. P.
NAQI, S. A.
NATHAN, C.

Neurological Surgery:

GUTIN, P. H.
STEIG, P. E.

Neurology and Neuroscience:

APPEL, S. H., Neurology
BAKER, H., Neuroscience
BEAL, M. F.
BLASBERG, R. G., Neurology
BLASS, J.
BROOKS, D. C., Anatomy
CARONNA, J. J., Neurology (Clinical)
DANNON, M. J., Neurology (Clinical)
DEANGELIS, L. M., Neurology (Clinical)
FOLEY, K. M.
GIBSON, G. E., Neuroscience
IADECOLA, C.
LABAR, D. R.
LATOV, N.

MCDOWELL, F. H.
MILNER, T. A., Neuroscience
PASTERNAK, G. W.
PETITO, F. A., Neurology (Clinical)
PICKEL, V. M., Neuroscience
POLLACK, C. P., Neurology (Clinical)
POSNER, J. B.
RATAN, R. R.
ROSS, M. E.
RUBIN, M., Neurology (Clinical)
VICTOR, J. D.
VOLPE, B. T.
WAGNER, J. A.

Obstetrics and Gynaecology:

CAPUTO, T. A., Clinical
CHERVENAK, F. A.
GOSDEN, R. G.
LIU, H.-C., Reproductive Medicine
POST, R. C., Clinical
ROSENWAKS, Z.
SAXENA, B. B., Endocrinology)
SPITZER, M., Clinical
WITKIN, S. S., Immunology

Ophthalmology:

ABRAMSON, D. H.
COLEMAN, D. J.
RODRIGUEZ-BOULAN, E. J., Cell and Developmental Biology
SILVERMAN, R. H., Computer Science

Orthopaedic Surgery:

BURKE, G. W., Clinical
CORNELL, C. N., Clinical
CRAIG, E. V., Orthopaedic SurgeryClinical
HEALEY, J. H.
HELFET, D. L.
LANE, J. M.
LASKIN, R. S., Clinical
PELLICI, P. M., Clinical
ROOT, L., Clinical
SALVATI, E. A., Clinical
SCULCO, T. P., Clinical
TORZILLI, P. A., Applied Biomechanics
WARREN, R. F.
WEILAND, A. J., Plastic
WICKIEWICZ, T. L., Clinical
WILSON, P. D., Jr
WINDSOR, R. E., Clinical
WOLFE, S. W.
WRIGHT, T. M., Applied Biomechanics

Otorhinolaryngology:

SELESNICK, S. H.

Paediatrics:

BROMBERG, K.
BUSSEL, J. B.
CHUTORIAN, A. B.
COOPER, R. S., Ophthalmology
CUNNINGHAM-RUNDLES, S.
GERMAN, J. L.
GERSONY, W. M.
GIARDINA, P. V., Clinical
GLASS, L.
GREENWALD, B. M., Clinical
HILGARTNER, M. W.
KLEIN, A. A., Clinical
KOSOFSKY, B.
KRAUSS, A. N., Clinical
LEHMAN, T. J. A., Clinical
LOUGHLIN, G. M.
MENDEZ, H. A., Clinical
MOSCONA, A.
O'REILLY, R. J.
PERLMAN, J. M.
RAJEGOWDA, B., Clinical
RUBIN, D. H., Clinical
SOLOMON, G. E., Clinical/Neurology
STEINHERZ, P. G.

Pathology and Laboratory Medicine:

AKHTAR, M.
ALONSO, D. R.
BAERGEN, R., Clinical
BARRIOS, R.
BULLOUGH, P. G.
BURKE, M. D.

CAGLE, P. T.
CHADBURN, A.
CHAGANTI, R. S. K., Genetics
CHEN, Y. T.
CHEN-KIANG, S.
ELLENSON, L. H.
HAJJAR, D. P.
HODA, S. A. F., Clinical
HUVOS, A. G.
JONES, J. G.
KLIMSTRA, D. S.
KNOWLES, D. M.
LAND, G. A., Clinical
LAVI, E.
LEONARD, D. G. B.
LIEBERMAN, M. W.
LIPMAN, N. S., Veterinary Medicine
MCNUTT, N. S.
MODY, D. R.
MULLER, W. A.
PEERSCHKE, E. I. B.
PETROVIC, L. M.
REUTER, V. E.
ROSEN, P. P.
ROSENBLUM, M.
SALEEM, A., Pathology and LaboratoryClinical
SESHAN, S. V., Clinical
TRUONG, L. D., Clinical
WOLF, C. F. W., Clinical

Pharmacology:
BUCK, J.
GROSS, S. S.
GUDAS, L. J.
INTURRISI, C.
LEVI, R.
OKAMOTO, M.
REIDENBERG, M. M.
RIFKIND, A. B.
SZETO, H. H.
TOTH, M.

Physiology and Biophysics:
ANDERSEN, O. S.
GARDNER, D.
GRAFSTEIN, B.
HUANG, X.
MAACK, T.
MEHLER, E. L.
PALMER, L. G.
RAMIREZ, F.
ROUX, B.
WEINSTEIN, H.
WINDHAGER, E. E.

Psychiatry:
ADDONIZIO, G. C., Clinical
ALEXOPOULOS, G. S.
AUCHINCLOSS, E. L., Clinical
BARCHAS, J. D.
BREITBART, W.
BRUCE, M. L., Sociology
CAMPBELL, S. S., Psychology
CASEY, B. J., Developmental Psychobiology
CLARKIN, J. F., Clinical Psychology
FERRANDO, S. J., Clinical
FRIEDNAN, R. A., Clinical
GEARY, N. D., Psychology
GIBBS, J. A., Jr
HALMI, K. A.
HERTZIG, M. E.
HOLLAND, J. C. B.
KERNBERG, O. F.
KERNBERG, P. F.
KOCSIS, J. H.
LEDERBERG, M. S., Clinical
LEON, A. C., Biostatistics
MATTSON, M. R. A., Clinical
MEYERS, B. S.
PARDES, H.
PFEFFER, C. R.
POSNER, M. I., Psychology
SACKS, M. H.
SCHULBERG, H. C., Psychology
SHAMOIAN, C. A., Clinical
TARDIFF, K.

WILSON, P. G., Clinical
YOUNG, R. C.

Public Health:
BEGG, C. B., Biostatistics
BOTVIN, G. J., Psychology
DRUSIN, L. M., Clinical
FINKEL, M. L., Clinical
MILLMAN, R. B.
MUSHLIN, A. I.
RUCHLIN, H. S., Economics

Radiology:
ABRAMSON, S. J., Clinical
ADLER, R.
AMOLS, H. I., Physics
ANDERSON, L. L., Physics
AUH, Y. H.
BECKER, D. V.
BRILL, P.
CARAVELLI, J. F., Clinical
COHEN, M. A., Clinical
DECK, M. D. F.
DERSHAW, D. D.
DIVGI, C. R.
FINN, R. D., Physics
GAMSU, G.
GOBIN, Y. P.
GOLDSMITH, S. J.
HANN, L. E.
HEELAN, R. T.
HEIER, L. A., Clinical
HENSCHKE, C. I.
HERZOG, R. J.
HRICAK, H.
KOUTHCER, J. A.
KROL, G., Clinical
LARSON, S.
LI, G. C., Biophysics
LIBERMAN, L.
LING, C. C., Physics
MCCAULEY, D., Clinical
NORI, D., Clinical
PANICEK, D. M.
PAVLOV, H.
POTTER, M. R.
PRINCE, M. R.
ROSEN, N. S., Clinical
ROSENBLATT, R., Clinical
SOS, T. A.
SOSTMAN, H. D.
STRAUSS, H. W.
VALLABHAJOSULA, S., Radiopharmacy
WINCHESTER, P.
YANKELEVITZ, D. F.
ZAIDER, M., Physics
ZIMMERMAN, R. D.

Rehabilitation Medicine:
LIEBERMAN, J. S.
O'DELL, M. W., Clinical

Surgery:
BAINS, M. S., Clinical
BARIE, P. S.
BARONE, J. E., Clinical
BESSEY, P. Q.
BLUMGART, L. H.
BRENNAN, M. F.
CHASSIN, J. L., Clinical
CODY, H. S., III, Clinical
CORDEIRO, P. G.
EISENMAN, M. M.
FONG, Y.
GAGNER, M.
HURYN, J. M., Clinical Oral and Maxillofacial Surgery
ISRAEL, H. A., Clinical
KENT, K. C.
LAQUAGLIA, M. P.
MICHELASSI, F.
MILSOM, J. W.
OSBORNE, M. P.
PETREK, J. A.
PIZZI, W. F., Clinical
RUSCH, V. W.
SHAH, J. P., Clinical
SHAHA, A. R.

SMITH, B. H., Clinical
STAIANO-COICO, L., Microbiology
STOLAR, C. J.
STUBENBORD, W. T.
WISE, L.
WONG, G. Y., Statistics
WONG, W. D.
YURT, R. W.

Urology:
BANDER, N. H.
GOLDSTEIN, M.
GUILLONNEAU, B.
HERR, H. W.
SCARDINO, P. T.
SCHLEGEL, P. N.
SHEINFELD, J.
SOGANI, P. C., Clinical
VAUGHAN, E. D.

CULINARY INSTITUTE OF AMERICA

1946 Campus Dr., Hyde Park, NY 12538-1499

Telephone: (845) 452-9600
E-mail: admissions@culinary.edu
Internet: www.ciachef.edu
Founded 1946 as New Haven Restaurant Institute, present name 1951
Private control
Academic year: June to May
Campuses at Hyde Park, New York, San Antonio, Texas, St Helena, California, and Singapore

Pres.: Dr L. TIMOTH RYAN
Provost: MARK ERICKSON
Sr Vice-Pres. for Finance and Admin.: CHARLES A. O'MARA
Vice-Pres. for Admissions and Marketing: BRUCE D. HILLENBRAND
Vice-Pres. for Academic Affairs: Dr PETER RAINSFORD
Vice-Pres. for Admin. and Shared Services: RICHARD MIGNAULT
Vice-Pres. for Advancement and Business Devt: Dr VICTOR A. L. GIELISSE
Vice-Pres. for Strategic Initiatives and Industry Leadership: GREG DRESCHER
Dir for Library Services: EILEEN DE VRIES
Library of 84,000 vols, 4,000 DVDs and videos, 280 current periodical titles
Number of teachers: 150
Number of students: 2,900
Publication: *Food is Life* (online (www.foodislife.org))

DEANS

Liberal Arts and Business Management: Dr KATHLEEN MERGET

DAEMEN COLLEGE

4380 Main St, Amherst, NY 14226

Telephone: (716) 839-8225
Fax: (716) 839-8229
E-mail: admissions@daemen.edu
Internet: www.daemen.edu
Founded 1947 as Rosary Hill College, present name 1976
Private control
Academic year: September to May
Pres.: Dr EDWIN G CLAUSEN
Vice-Pres. for Academic Affairs and Dean for College: Dr MICHAEL S. BROGAN
Vice-Pres. for Business Affairs and Treas.: ROBERT C. BEISWANGER, JR
Vice-Pres. for Enrolment Management: PATRICIA RUPPERT BROWN
Vice-Pres. for External Affairs: DAVID A. CRISTANELLO
Vice-Pres. for Student Affairs and Dean of Students: RICHANNE C. MANKEY
Registrar: PAULETTE A. ANZELONE

Library of 100,000 vols, 24,000 full-text e-journals, over 37,000 e-books, and 600 print serials titles
Number of teachers: 120
Number of students: 2,958 (2095 undergraduate, 863 graduate)
Publication: *The Loom*

DEANS

Division of Arts and Sciences: KEVIN TELFORD
Division of Health and Human Services: RONALD J. SCHENK

DAVIS COLLEGE

400 Riverside Dr., Johnson City, NY 13790
Telephone: (607) 729-1581
Fax: (607) 729-2962
E-mail: info@davisny.edu
Internet: www.davisny.edu
Founded 1900 as Practical Bible Training School, present name 2004
Private control
Academic year: August to May
Offers courses in counselling, Christian ministries, int. ministries, pastoral studies and teaching English as a second language and youth ministries
Pres.: Dr DINO J. PEDRONE
Chief Academic Officer: Dr GILBERT A. PARKER
Chief Enrolment Officer: RICK CRAMER
Student Devt Officer: NICHOLE POST
Registrar: SPENCER KEY
Librarian: SHELLEY R. BYRON
Library of 70,000 vols
Number of teachers: 16
Number of students: 300

DOMINICAN COLLEGE

470 W Highway, Orangeburg, NY 10962
Telephone: (845) 359-7800
Fax: (845) 359-2313
E-mail: admissions@dc.edu
Internet: www.dc.edu
Founded 1952
Private control
Academic year: August to May
Offers courses in business, educational media, nursing, occupational therapy, physical therapy, teacher education and teachers of students who are blind or visually impaired
Pres.: Sis. MARY EILEEN O'BRIEN
Vice-Pres. for Academic Affairs and Academic Dean: Dr THOMAS S. NOWAK
Vice-Pres. for Enrolment Management: BRIAN G. FERNANDES
Vice-Pres. for Financial Affairs: CATHLEEN KENNY
Vice-Pres. for Institutional Advancement: DOROTHY CHRISTINE FILORAMO
Vice-Pres. for Student Devt and Dean for Students: DOHN E. HARSHBARGER
Registrar: MARY McFADDEN
Head Librarian: JOHN BARRIE
Library of 102,000 vols
Number of teachers: 40
Number of students: 1,855

DOWLING COLLEGE

150 Idle Hour Blvd, Oakdale, NY 11769
Telephone: (631) 244-3000
Fax: (631) 563-9681
E-mail: admissions@dowling.edu
Internet: www.dowling.edu
Founded 1955, present name 1968
Private control
Campuses in Melville, Oakdale and Shirley
Pres.: JEREMY D. BROWN

Interim Provost and Vice-Pres. for Corporate Programmes: Dr ELANA ZOLFO
Vice-Pres. for College Admin. and Student Affairs: DAVID RING
Vice-Pres. for Enrolment and Student Services: RONNIE MacDONALD
Library of 222,920 vols
Number of teachers: 121 (full-time)
Number of students: 6,300 (undergraduate and postgraduate)

DEANS

School of Arts and Sciences: Dr PAUL ABRAMSON
School of Education: Dr CLYDE PAYNE

D'YOUVILLE COLLEGE

320 Porter Ave, Buffalo, NY 14201-9985
Telephone: (716) 829-8000
Fax: (716) 829-7900
E-mail: admissions@dyc.edu
Internet: www.dyc.edu
Founded 1908
Private control
Offers Master's and doctoral programmes in health-related professions; 5-year programmes in education, dietetics, information technology, int. business, nursing, physical therapy and occupational therapy
Pres.: Sis. DENISE A. ROCHE
Sr Vice-Pres.: RICHARD WIESEN
Vice-Pres. for Academic Affairs: Dr ARUP SEN
Vice-Pres. of Admin. Services and External Relations
Vice-Pres. for Financial Affairs and Treas.: EDWARD A. JOHNSON
Vice-Pres. for Institutional Advancement: TIMOTHY G. BRENNAN
Vice-Pres. for Student Affairs and Enrolment Management: ROBERT P. MURPHY
Registrar: DION DALY
Dir for Admissions: RONALD H. DANNECKER
Library Dir: RAND BELLAVIA
Library of 127,000 vols
Number of teachers: 298 (178 full-time, 120 part-time)
Number of students: 3,142
Publication: *D'Mensions*.

ELMIRA COLLEGE

One Park Pl., Elmira, NY 14901
Telephone: (607) 735-1800
E-mail: admissions@elmira.edu
Internet: www.elmira.edu
Founded 1855
Private control
Academic year: July to August
Academic divs incl. business and economics, creative arts, humanities, mathematics and natural sciences, professional programmes and social and behavioural sciences
Pres.: Dr THOMAS KEITH MEIER
Vice-Pres. for Academic Affairs: Dr STEPHEN COLEMAN
Vice-Pres. and Dean for Student Life: JULIANNE BAUMANN
Vice-Pres. for Devt and Dean: SHERRY TROCINO
Vice-Pres. for Financial Affairs and Dean for Admin.: Dr ROBERT RUBLE
Dean for Library and Information Technology: ELIZABETH WAVLE-BROWN
Library of 250,000 vols, incl. 25,000 print and e-journals
Number of teachers: 78
Number of students: 1,200 (full-time)
Publications: *Callisophia, Sibyl*.

EXCELSIOR COLLEGE

Seven Columbia Circle, Albany, NY 12203-5159
Telephone: (518) 464-8500
Fax: (518) 464-8777
E-mail: admissions@excelsior.edu
Internet: www.excelsior.edu
Founded 1971 as Regents College, present name 2001
Private control
Centre in Washington DC
Pres.: JOHN F. EBERSOLE
Provost, Chief Academic Officer and Vice-Pres. for Institutional Research: MARY BETH HANNER
Vice-Pres. for Enrolment Management: CRAIG MASLOWSKY
Vice-Pres. for Extended Education and CEO: WAYNE BROWN
Vice-Pres. for Finance and Admin.: JOHN PONTIUS
Vice-Pres. for Human Resources and Admin. Services: EDMUND J. McTERNAN
Vice-Pres. for Information Technology: SUSAN O'HERN
Vice-Pres. for Institutional Advancement: CATHY KUSHNER
Vice-Pres. for Legal and Govt Affairs and Gen. Counsel: JOSEPH B. PORTER
Number of students: 30,000
Publication: *Live & Learn*

DEANS

School of Business and Technology: Dr JANE LeCLAIR
School of Health Sciences: Dr DEBORAH SOPCZYK
School of Liberal Arts: Dr SCOTT DALRYMPLE
School of Nursing: Dr MARY LEE POLLARD

FASHION INSTITUTE OF TECHNOLOGY

227 W 27th St, New York, NY 10001-5992
Telephone: (212) 217-7999
Fax: (212) 217-3761
E-mail: fitinfo@fitnyc.edu
Internet: www.fitnyc.edu
Founded 1944; attached to State Univ. of New York
State control
Academic year: August to May
Pres.: Dr JOYCE F. BROWN
Vice-Pres. for Academic Affairs: GIACOMO OLIVA
Vice-Pres. for Communications and External Relations: LORETTA LAWRENCE KEANE
Vice-Pres for Devt and Alumni Relations: DAWN B. DUNCAN
Vice-Pres. for Enrolment Management and Student Success: MARYBETH MURPHY
Vice-Pres for Finance and Admin. and Treas.: SHERRY F. BRABHAM
Vice-Pres. for Human Resources: ARTHUR E. BROWN, JR
Vice-Pres. for Information Technology: GREGG CHOTTINER
Gen. Counsel and Sec.: STEPHEN TUTTLE
Library Dir: Prof. NJ WOLFE
Library of 138,000 vols
Number of teachers: 1,007 (253 full-time, 754 part-time)
Number of students: 10,386 (10,166 undergraduate, 220 graduate)

DEANS

Jay and Patty Baker School of Business and Technology: DEBORAH KLESENSKI (acting)
School of Art and Design: JOANNE ARBUCKLE
School of Continuing and Professional Studies: (vacant)
School of Graduate Studies: JOANNE ARBUCKLE (acting)

School of Liberal Arts: Dr SCOTT STODDART

FIVE TOWNS COLLEGE

305 N Service Rd, Dix Hills, Long Island, NY 11746-5871
Telephone: (631) 656-2110
E-mail: info@ftc.edu
Internet: www.ftc.edu
Founded 1972
Private control
Academic year: August to May

Offers Bachelors, Masters and doctoral degrees in education, fine arts, mass communication, music

Pres.: Dr STANLEY G. COHEN
Provost and Dean for Academic Affairs: Dr ROGER H. SHERMAN
Dean for Admin.: MARTIN L. COHEN
Dean for Enrolment: JERRY L. COHEN
Dean for Students: SUSAN BARR
Registrar: MARA MALTZ
Library Dir: JOHN VANSTEEN
Library of 35,000 vols, 600 scores, 9,000 sound recordings, 2,300 video recordings, 500 periodicals titles
Number of teachers: 113 (36 full-time, 77 adjunct)
Number of students: 1,173 (1,106 undergraduate, 67 graduate)

FORDHAM UNIVERSITY

441 E Fordham Rd, Bronx, NY 10458
Telephone: (718) 817-1000
Fax: (718) 817-4925
E-mail: publicaff@fordham.edu
Internet: www.fordham.edu
Founded 1841 as St John's College, present status 1846, present name 1907
Private control
Academic year: July to June
Campuses in Bronx, New York and W Harrison
Pres.: Rev. JOSEPH M. MCSHANE
Provost: Dr STEPHEN FREEDMAN
Sr Vice-Pres. and Chief Financial Officer: JOHN J. LORDAN
Vice-Pres. for Academic Affairs: JUDITH MILLS
Vice-Pres. for Admin.: THOMAS A. DUNNE
Vice-Pres. for Devt and Univ. Relations: ROGER MILICI
Vice-Pres. for Enrolment: PETER A. STACE
Vice-Pres. for Finance: FRANK SIMIO
Vice-Pres. for Student Affairs: JEFFREY L. GRAY
Vice-Pres. for Technology: Dr FRANK SIRIANNI
Vice-Pres. for Univ. Mission and Min.: Rev. JOSEPH QUINN
Registrar: KENNETH POKROWSKI
Univ. Librarian: Dr JAMES MCCABE
Library: 2m. vols, 15,500 periodicals and 19,000 e-journals
Number of teachers: 1,121 (718 full-time, 403 part-time)
Number of students: 15,189 (8,427 undergraduate, 6,762 graduate)
Publications: *Fordham Magazine, International Philosophical Quarterly, Traditio* (1 a year)

DEANS

Fordham College at Lincoln Center: Dr ROBERT R. GRIMES
Fordham College at Rose Hill: Dr MICHAEL LATHAM
Gabelli School of Business: Dr DONNA RAPACCIOLI
Graduate School of Arts and Sciences: Dr NANCY BUSCH
Graduate School of Business Administration: Dr DAVID A. GAUTSCHI

Graduate School of Education: Prof. Dr JAMES J. HENNESSY
Graduate School of Religion and Religious Education: Dr JOHN P. HARRINGTON
Graduate School of Social Service: PETER B. VAUGHAN
School of Law: MICHAEL M. MARTIN
School of Professional and Continuing Studies: Dr ISABELLE FRANK

HAMILTON COLLEGE

198 College Hill Rd, Clinton, NY 13323
Telephone: (315) 859-4011
Fax: (315) 859-4457
E-mail: admission@hamilton.edu
Internet: www.hamilton.edu
Founded 1793 as Hamilton-Oneida Acad., chartered as Hamilton College 1812
Private control
Academic year: September to May

Areas of study incl. Africana studies; American studies; anthropology; art; art history; Asian studies; astronomy; biochemistry/molecular biology; biology; chemical physics; chemistry; Chinese; cinema and new media studies; classics; communication; comparative literature; computer science; creative writing; dance and movement studies; East Asian languages and literatures; economics; education studies; English and creative writing; environmental studies; foreign languages; French; geoarchaeology; geosciences; German studies; government; Hispanic studies; history; interdisciplinary concentration; Japanese; jurisprudence, law and justice studies; Latin American studies; mathematics; medieval and renaissance studies; music; neuroscience; philosophy; physics; psychology; public policy; religious studies; Russian studies; sociology; Spanish; theatre; women's studies; world politics

Pres.: JOAN HINDE STEWART
Vice-Pres. for Academic Affairs and Dean for Faculty: PATRICK REYNOLDS
Vice-Pres. for Admin. and Finance: KAREN LEACH
Vice-Pres. for Admission and Financial Aid: MONICA INZER
Vice-Pres. for Communications and Devt: DICK TANTILLO
Vice-Pres. for Information Technology and Interim Library Dir: DAVE SMALLEN
Vice-Pres. and Dean for Students: NANCY THOMPSON (acting)
Library of 500,000 vols
Number of teachers: 184 (full-time)
Number of students: 1,812
Publication: *Alumni Review.*

HARTWICK COLLEGE

POB 4020, Oneonta, NY 13820-4020
Telephone: (607) 431-4000
Fax: (607) 431-4154
E-mail: admissions@hartwick.edu
Internet: www.hartwick.edu
Founded 1797 as Hartwick Seminary
Private control
Academic year: September to May
Pres.: Dr MARGARET L. DRUGOVICH
Provost and Vice-Pres. for Academic Affairs: Dr MICHAEL G. TANNENBAUM
Vice-Pres. for College Advancement: JAMES BROSCHART
Vice-Pres. for Enrolment Management: DAVID B. CONWAY
Vice-Pres. for Finance and Chief Financial Officer: GEORGE ELLSBECK
Vice-Pres. for Institutional Advancement: JIM BROSCHART
Vice-Pres. for Student Affairs: Dr MEG NOWAK

Dean for Academic Affairs: GERALD HUNSBERGER
Dir for Admissions: JONATHAN KENT
Dir of Information Technology: DAVIS CONLEY
Dir for Institutional Research: MINGHUI WANG
Dir for Library and Information Resources: PAUL COLEMAN
Library of 355,776 vols
Number of teachers: 203 (105 full-time)
Number of students: 1,578

HEBREW UNION COLLEGE—JEWISH INSTITUTE OF RELIGION

The Brookdale Center, One W Fourth St, New York, NY 10012
Telephone: (212) 674-5300
Fax: (212) 388-1720
Internet: huc.edu
Founded 1875, present status 2011
Private control
Languages of instruction: English, Hebrew
Academic year: August to June
Schools of Rabbinical studies, graduate studies, education, Jewish nonprofit management, sacred music, biblical archaeology; campuses: Cincinnati in Ohio, Los Angeles in California, New York in New York, and Jerusalem in Israel
Pres.: Dr DAVID ELLENSON
Vice-Pres. for Academic Affairs: Dr MICHAEL MARMUR
Vice-Pres. for Finance and Admin.: SANDRA M. MILLS
Vice-Pres. for Institutional Advancement: Dr JANE F. KARLIN
Dean for Cincinnati Campus: Dr JONATHAN COHEN
Dean for Los Angeles Campus: JOSHUA HOLO
Dean for New York Campus: SHIRLEY IDELSON
Dean for Jerusalem Campus: NAAMAH KELMAN
Dir for Admissions: DEBORAH ABELSON
Registrar: CLYDE PARRISH
Dir for Libraries: Dr DAVID J. GILNER
Library of 130,000 vols
Number of teachers: 130
Number of students: 780
Publications: *American Jewish Archives Journal* (online (americanjewisharchives.org/journal)), *Hebrew Union College Annual.*

HILBERT COLLEGE

5200 S Park Ave, Hamburg, NY 14075
Telephone: (716) 649-7900
Fax: (716) 649-0702
E-mail: info@hilbert.edu
Internet: www.hilbert.edu
Founded 1957
Private control
Academic year: September to August
Divs of arts and science, criminal justice/forensic science, professional studies, social science
Pres.: Dr CYNTHIA ZANE
Provost and Vice-Pres. for Academic Affairs: Dr CHRISTOPHER HOLOMAN
Vice-Pres. for Business and Finance: RICHARD J. PINKOWSKI, JR
Vice-Pres. for Enrolment Management and Dean for Students: PETER S. BURNS
Vice-Pres. for Information Services: MICHAEL A. MURRIN
Vice-Pres. for Institutional Advancement: FRANCES VAUGHAN
Dir for Admissions: TIMOTHY LEE
Registrar: GEORGINA ADAMCHICK
Library Dir: WIL PROUT

Library of 36,500 vols, 50,000 e-journals and 1,300 videos and DVDs

Number of teachers: 125 (49 full-time, 76 part-time)

Number of students: 1,117 (1,089 undergraduate, 28 graduate)

Publications: *Hilbert Connections* (3 a year), *Hilbert Horizons*.

HOBART AND WILLIAM SMITH COLLEGES

300 Pulteney St, Geneva, NY 14456-3397

Telephone: (315) 781-3000

Fax: (315) 781-3400

E-mail: admissions@hws.edu

Internet: www.hws.edu

Founded 1822 (Hobart), 1908 (William Smith)

Academic year: August to May (2 semesters)

Operates under a coordinate college system; men graduate from Hobart College and women from William Smith College

Pres.: MARK D. GEARAN

Provost and Dean for Faculty: PAT MCGUIRE

Vice-Pres. for Communications: CATHY WILLIAMS

Vice-Pres. for Enrolment and Admissions: BOB MURPHY

Vice-Pres. for Finance: PETER POLINAK

Vice-Pres. for Human Resources: SANDRA BISSELL

Vice-Pres. for Institutional Advancement: ROBERT O'CONNOR

Vice-Pres. for Student Affairs: ROBB FLOWERS

Chief Information Officer: FRED DAMIANO

Dean for Hobart College: EUGEN BAER

Dean for William Smith College: SUSANNE MCNALLY

Treas.: PETER POLINAK

Library Dir: VINCE BOISSELLE

Library of 387,650 vols

Number of teachers: 207 (full-time)

Number of students: 2,224 (2,216 undergraduate, 8 graduate)

Publications: *The Pulteney St Survey* (3 a year), *The Seneca Review* (2 a year).

HOFSTRA UNIVERSITY

144 Hofstra Univ., Hempstead, NY 11549-1000

Telephone: (516) 463-6600

Fax: (516) 463-6096

E-mail: admission@hofstra.edu

Internet: www.hofstra.edu

Founded 1935

Private control

Academic year: August to May

Pres.: STUART RABINOWITZ

Provost and Sr Vice-Pres. for Academic Affairs: Dr HERMAN A. BERLINER

Sr Vice-Pres. for Planning and Admin.: Dr M. PATRICIA ADAMSKI

Vice-Pres. for Business Devt: RICHARD V. GUARDINO, JR

Vice-Pres. for Devt and Alumni Affairs: ALAN J. KELLY

Vice-Pres. for Enrolment Management: JESSICA EADS

Vice-Pres. for Facilities and Operations: JOSEPH M. BARKWILL

Vice-Pres. for Financial Affairs and Treas.: CATHERINE HENNESSY

Vice-Pres. for Information Technology: ROBERT W. JUCKIEWICZ

Vice-Pres. for Institutional Research and Assessment: STEPHANIE BUSHEY

Vice-Pres. for Legal Affairs and Gen. Counsel: DOLORES FREDRICH

Vice-Pres. for Student Affairs: SANDRA S. JOHNSON

Vice-Pres. for Univ. Relations: MELISSA KANE CONNOLLY

Dean for Library and Information Services: Dr DANIEL R. RUBEY (acting)

Library: 1.2m. vols

Number of teachers: 1,114

Number of students: 12,000

Publications: *Hofstra Magazine* (3 a year), *Pulse*

DEANS

Continuing Education: RICHARD V. GUARDINO, JR

Frank G. Zarb School of Business: Dr PATRICK J. SOCCI

Graduate Studies: LIORA P. SCHMELKIN

Hofstra College of Liberal Arts and Sciences: Dr BERNARD J. FIRESTONE (acting)

Hofstra North Shore-LIJ School of Medicine: Dr LAWRENCE G. SMITH

Hofstra Univ. Honors College: WARREN G. FRISINA

Maurice A. Deane School of Law: ERIC LANE

School of Communication: Dr EVAN W. CORNOG

School of Education and Human Services: Dr NANCY E. HALLIDAY

School of Engineering and Applied Science: Dr SIMON BEN-AVI

HOUGHTON COLLEGE

One Willard Ave, Houghton, NY 14744

Telephone: (585) 567-9200

E-mail: admission@houghton.edu

Internet: www.houghton.edu

Founded 1883

Private control

Academic year: August to June

Campus in W Seneca

Pres.: Dr SHIRLEY A. MULLEN

Academic Dean: LINDA MILLS WOOLSEY

Vice-Pres. for Advancement: BOB VAN WICKLIN

Vice-Pres. for Enrolment Management: WAYNE MACBETH

Vice-Pres. for Student Life: Dr SHARRA HYNES

Exec. Dir for Alumni Relations: DANIEL R. NOYES

Exec. Dir for Devt: SCOTT WADE

Dir for Library: DAVID STEVICK

Library of 255,000 vols, 10,000 scores, 30,000 journals subscription, 5,000 DVDs and VHS cassettes

Number of teachers: 136 (82 full-time)

Number of students: 1,200

Publication: *Houghton Magazine*.

IONA COLLEGE

715 N Ave, New Rochelle, NY 10801-1890

Telephone: (914) 633-2000

Fax: (914) 633-2642

E-mail: admissions@iona.edu

Internet: www.iona.edu

Founded 1940

Private control

Academic year: July to June

Campuses in New Rochelle and Rockland, New York

Pres.: Dr JOSEPH E. NYRE

Provost and Sr Vice-Pres. for Academic Affairs: Dr BRIAN J. NICKERSON

Sr Vice-Pres. for Finance and Admin.: JONATHAN IVEC

Sr Vice-Pres. for Advancement and External Affairs: PAUL J. SUTERA

Vice-Provost for Information Technology: JOANNE LAUGHLIN STEELE

Vice-Provost for Student Devt: CHARLES CARLSON

Dir for Libraries: RICHARD PALLADINO

Library of 266,883 vols (incl. books serial backfiles), 510,186 microforms, 742 serial titles, 4,077 audiovisual materials, 9,581 e-books

Number of teachers: 362

Number of students: 4,065

Publications: *Journal of Pastoral Counseling* (1 a year), *The Ionian*

DEANS

Hagan School of Business: Dr VINCENT J. CALLUZZO

School of Arts and Science: Dr JEANNE ZAINO

ITHACA COLLEGE

953 Danby Rd, Ithaca, NY 14850

Telephone: (607) 274-3011

Fax: (607) 274-1900

E-mail: admission@ithaca.edu

Internet: www.ithaca.edu

Founded 1892 as Ithaca Conservatory of Music

Private control

Academic year: August to May

Pres.: THOMAS R. ROCHON

Provost and Vice-Pres. for Academic Affairs: MARISA KELLY

Vice-Pres. for Enrolment Management: ERIC MAGUIRE

Vice-Pres. for Finance and Admin.: CARL E. SGRECCI

Vice-Pres. for Institutional Advancement: SHELLEY SEMMLER

Vice-Pres. for Student Affairs and Campus Life: BRIAN MCAREE

Vice-Pres. and Gen. Counsel: NANCY PRINGLE

Registrar: BRIAN SCHOLTEN

Librarian: LISABETH CHABOT

Library of 353,000 vols, 70,000 e-books, 36,000 microforms, 37,250 multimedia, 46,360 full-text serials

Number of teachers: 701 (478 full-time, 223 part-time)

Number of students: 6,760 (6,276 undergraduate, 484 graduate)

Publication: *ICView* (3 a year)

DEANS

Roy H. Park School of Communications: DIANE GAYESKI

School of Business: MARY ELLEN ZUCKERMAN

School of Health Sciences and Human Performance: JOHN SIGG

School of Humanities and Sciences: LESLIE W. LEWIS

School of Music: GREGORY WOODWARD

JEWISH THEOLOGICAL SEMINARY

3080 Broadway, New York, NY 10027

Telephone: (212) 678-8000

Fax: (212) 678-8947

E-mail: gsadmissions@jtsa.edu

Internet: www.jtsa.edu

Founded 1886

Private control

Academic year: August to May

Chancellor and Pres. of the Faculties: ARNOLD M. EISEN

Vice-Chancellor and Chief Operating Officer: Rabbi MICHAEL B. GREENBAUM

Vice-Chancellor and Chief Devt Officer: Rabbi MARC WOLF

Vice-Chancellor for Institutional Advancement: Rabbi CAROL DAVIDSON

Provost: Dr ALAN COOPER

Vice-Pres. for Student Affairs: Rabbi JOSEPH A. BRODIE

Chief Financial Officer: FRED SCHNUR

Dean for Academic Affairs: Dr STEPHEN GARFINKEL

Library Dir: NAOMI M. STEINBERGER (acting)

Library of 400,000 vols
Number of teachers: 110 (51 full-time, 59 part-time)
Number of students: 566
Publication: *Quntres: An Online Journal for the History, Culture, and Art of the Jewish Book* (1 a year)

DEANS

Albert A. List College of Jewish Studies: Dr SHULY RUBIN SCHWARTZ
Graduate School: Dr SHULY RUBIN SCHWARTZ
Rabbinical School: Rabbi DANIEL NEVINS
William Davidson Graduate School of Jewish Education: BARRY HOLTZ

JUILLIARD SCHOOL

60 Lincoln Center Plaza, New York, NY 10023-6588
Telephone: (212) 799-5000
E-mail: admissions@juilliard.edu
Internet: www.juilliard.edu
Founded 1905 as Institute of Musical Art, present name and status 1926
Private control
Incl. pre-college div., evening div. and music advancement programme
Pres.: JOSEPH W. POLISI
Provost and Dean: ARA GUZELIMIAN
Vice-Pres. and Dean for Academic Affairs: KAREN WAGNER
Vice-Pres. and Gen. Counsel: LAURIE A. CARTER
Vice-Pres. for Devt and Public Affairs: RICCARDO SALMONA
Vice-Pres. for Enrolment Management: JOAN D. WARREN
Vice-Pres. for Finance and Controller: CHRISTINE TODD
Vice-Pres. for Library and Information Resources: JANE GOTTLIEB
Registrar: KATHERINE GERTSON
Library of 23,000 vols, 7,300 music scores, 25,000 sound recordings, 140 MSS colln
Number of teachers: 309
Number of students: 846 (510 undergraduate)
Publication: *Juilliard Journal.*

KEUKA COLLEGE

141 Central Ave, Keuka Park, NY 14478
Telephone: (315) 279-5000
Fax: (315) 279-5216
E-mail: admissions@mail.keuka.edu
Internet: www.keuka.edu
Founded 1890
Private control
Academic year: August to May
Courses in dentistry, law, medicine, pharmacy, physical therapy, optometry, veterinary medicine; provides degree programmes in the People's Republic of China at 4 campus locations and at Viet Nam Nat. Univ. in Hanoi
Pres.: Dr JORGE L. DÍAZ-HERRERA
Exec. Vice-Pres.: CAROLANNE MARQUIS
Vice-Pres. for Academic Affairs: Dr ANNE K. WEED
Vice-Pres. for Finance and Admin.: JERRY HILLER
Vice-Pres. for the Centre for Professional Studies: Dr GARY SMITH
Vice-Pres. for Student Devt and Dean for Students: Dr JAMES BLACKBURN
Dean for Admissions and Marketing: FRED HOYLE
Dir for Library: LINDA PARK
Library of 88,061 vols, 79,093 titles, 21,194 periodicals, 4,021 microfilm reels, 8,939 e-books, 2,040 videos, CDs and DVDs

Number of teachers: 90 (79 full-time, 11 part-time)
Number of students: 1,979 (1,644 full-time, 335 part-time)
Publication: *Keuka Magazine*

DEANS

Center for Experiential Learning: Dr ANNE MARIE GUTHRIE

LE MOYNE COLLEGE

1419 Salt Springs Rd, Syracuse, NY 13214-1399
Telephone: (315) 445-4100
Fax: (315) 445-4540
Internet: www.lemoyne.edu
Founded 1946
Private control
Academic year: August to May
Pres.: Dr FRED P. PESTELLO
Provost and Vice-Pres. for Academic Affairs: Dr LINDA LeMURA
Vice-Pres. for Enrolment Management: DENNIS DePERRO
Vice-Pres. for Finance and Admin.: ROGER STACKPOOLE
Vice-Pres. for Institutional Advancement: Dr GREGORY STAHL
Vice-Pres. for Student Devt: Dr DEBORAH CADY MELZER
Dean for Admissions: DENNY NICHOLSON
Dir for Library: ROBERT C. JOHNSTON
Library of 242,233 vols
Number of teachers: 360
Number of students: 3,500 (2,800 undergraduate, 700 graduate)
Publication: *Le Moyne College Magazine*

DEANS

Division of Arts and Sciences: Dr J. BARRON BOYD, JR
School of Business: Dr WALLY ELMER

LIM COLLEGE

12 E 53rd St, New York, NY 10022
Telephone: (212) 752-1530
Fax: (212) 750-3432
E-mail: admissions@limcollege.edu
Internet: www.limcollege.edu
Founded 1939 as Laboratory Institute of Merchandising (LIM), present name 2009
Private control
Academic year: August to July
Areas of study incl.: fashion merchandising, management, marketing, visual merchandising
Pres.: ELIZABETH S. MARCUSE
Exec. Vice-Pres.: LINDA HARRIS PAOLILLO
Dean for Graduate Studies and Continuing Education: MILAN MILASINOVIĆ
Sr Vice-Pres. for Finance and Operation and Treas.: MICHAEL T. DONOHUE
Sr. Vice-Pres. for Academic and Student Affairs: Dr JO-ANN ROLLE
Vice-Pres. for Student Devt: Dr MICHAEL H. FERRY
Registrar: CAROLYN DISNEW
Dir for Library Services: GEORGE SANCHEZ
Library of 18,000 vols, 700DVDs, 125 periodical subscriptions, 70,000 e-books
Number of teachers: 187
Number of students: 1,595 (1,538 undergraduate, 57 graduate)

LONG ISLAND UNIVERSITY

720 N Blvd, Brookville, NY 11548-1327
Telephone: (516) 299-2000
Fax: (516) 299-2072
E-mail: attend@liu.edu
Internet: www.liu.edu

Founded 1926
Private control
Campuses in Brooklyn, Brookville (C.W. Post), Brentwood, Riverhead, Rockland and Westchester; Global College: People's Republic of China, Costa Rica and India
Pres.: Dr DAVID J. STEINBERG
Vice-Pres. for Academic Affairs: Dr JEFFREY KANE
Vice-Pres. for Finance and Treas.: ROBERT N. ALTHOLZ
Vice-Pres. for Information Technology: GEORGE BAROUDI
Vice-Pres. for Legal Services and Univ. Counsel: LYNETTE PHILLIPS
Vice-Pres. for Planning and Human Resources: Dr DANIEL J. RODAS
Vice-Pres. for Univ. Relations: RICHARD W. GORMAN
Provost for Brooklyn Campus: Dr GALE STEVENS HAYNES
Provost for C. W. Post Campus: Dr PAUL H. FORESTELL
Library: 2.6m. vols, incl. 50,000 e-books
Number of teachers: 1,596 (630 full-time, 966 part-time)
Number of students: 24,276 (9,734 undergraduate, 7,359 graduate)
Publication: *LIU Magazine* (2 a year)

DEANS

Arnold and Marie Schwartz College of Pharmacy and Health Sciences, Brooklyn Campus: Dr DAVID R. TAFT
College of Education and Information Sciences, C. W. Post Campus: Dr ROBERT HANNAFIN
College of Liberal Arts and Sciences, C. W. Post Campus: Dr KATHERINE HILL-MILLER
College of Management, C. W. Post Campus: FRANCIS N. BONSIGNORE
Global College, Brooklyn Campus: Dr ROBERT GLASS
Richard L. Conolly College of Liberal Arts and Sciences, Brooklyn Campus: Dr DAVID COHEN
School of Business, Public Administration and Information Sciences, Brooklyn Campus: MOHAMMED GHRIGA
School of Education, Brooklyn Campus: CECELIA TRAUGH
School of Health Professions, Brooklyn Campus: Dr BARRY S. ECKERT
School of Health Professions and Nursing, C. W. Post Campus: Dr MARYANN CLARK
School of Nursing, Brooklyn Campus: Dr HAZEL M. SANDERSON-MARCOUX (acting)
School of Visual and Performing Arts, C. W. Post Campus: NOEL ZEHLER

MANHATTAN COLLEGE

4513 Manhattan College Parkway, Riverdale, NY 10471
Telephone: (718) 862-8000
Fax: (718) 862-8014
E-mail: admit@manhattan.edu
Internet: www.manhattan.edu
Founded 1853, chartered as Manhattan College 1863
Private control
Academic year: August to May
Pres.: Dr BRENNAN O'DONNELL
Provost and Exec. Vice-Pres.: Dr WILLIAM CLYDE
Vice-Pres. for College Advancement: THOMAS MAURIELLO
Vice-Pres. for Enrolment Management: WILLIAM J. BISSET, JR
Vice-Pres. for Facilities: ANDREW RYAN
Vice-Pres. for Finance and Capital Projects: THOMAS J. RYAN
Vice-Pres. for Student Life: Dr RICHARD SATTERLEE

Registrar: LUZ M. TORRES
Dir for Admissions: DANA ROSE
Dir for Library: MAIRE I. DUCHON
Library of 230,000 vols, 3,000 media items, 20,000 periodical titles
Number of teachers: 201 (full-time)
Number of students: 3,500 (2,900 undergraduate, 600 graduate and continuing education)
Publications: *Manhattan Magazine* (2 a year), *Manhattan Monthly* (12 a year)

DEANS

School of Arts: Dr RICHARD K. EMMERSON
School of Business: Dr SALWA AMMAR
School of Education: Dr WILLIAM J. MERRIMAN
School of Engineering: Dr TIM J. WARD
School of Science: Dr CONSTANTINE E. THEODOSIOU

MANHATTAN SCHOOL OF MUSIC

120 Claremont Ave, New York, NY 10027-4689
Telephone: (212) 749-2802
E-mail: administration@msmnyc.edu
Internet: www.msmnyc.edu
Founded 1917
Academic year: July to May
Pres.: Dr ROBERT SIROTA
Vice-Pres. for External Affairs: SUSAN EBERSOLE
Vice-Pres. for Finance and Admin.: PAUL KELLEHER
Vice-Pres. for Instrumental Performance: DAVID GEBER
Dean for Students: ELSA JEAN DAVIDSON
Registrar: DAVID MCDONAGH
Dir for Library Services: PETER CALEB
Library of 95,000 vols, 33,000 sound recordings, 3,600 DVDs
Number of teachers: 250
Number of students: 926 (402 undergraduate, 453 non-doctoral graduate, 71 doctoral)

MANHATTANVILLE COLLEGE

Purchase, NY 10577
Telephone: (914) 694-2200
Fax: (914) 694-1732
E-mail: admissions@mville.edu
Internet: www.manhattanville.edu
Founded 1841 as Acad. of the Sacred Heart
Private control
Academic year: September to May
Pres.: JON CALVERT STRAUSS
Provost and Vice-Pres. for Academic Affairs: GAIL SIMMONS
Vice-Pres. for Admissions and Enrolment Management: KATHY FITZGERALD
Vice-Pres. for Finance: MARINA C. VASARHELYI
Vice-Pres. for Institutional Advancement: JOSE R. GONZALEZ
Vice-Pres. for Operations: J. GREGORY PALMER
Vice-Pres. for Student Affairs: DOUGLAS GEIGER
Library Dir: JEFF ROSEDALE (acting)
Library of 200,000 vols
Number of teachers: 103 (full-time)
Number of students: 2,700 (1,700 undergraduate, 1,000 graduate)
Publications: *Inkwell* (1 a year), *The Tower Yearbook*.

MARIST COLLEGE

3399 N Rd, Poughkeepsie, NY 12601
Telephone: (845) 575-3000
E-mail: admissions@marist.edu

Internet: www.marist.edu
Founded 1905 as St. Ann's Hermitage
Private control
Br. campus in Florence, Italy
Pres.: DENNIS J. MURRAY
Exec. Vice-Pres.: Dr GEOFFREY L. BRACKETT
Vice-Pres. for Academic Affairs and Dean for Faculty: Dr THOMAS WERMUTH
Vice-Pres. for Admission and Enrolment Planning: SEAN P KAYLOR
Vice-Pres. for Business Affairs and Chief Financial Officer: JOHN PECCHIA
Vice-Pres. for College Advancement: CHRISTOPHER M. DELGIORNO
Vice-Pres. for Information Technology: WILLIAM THIRSK
Vice-Pres. and Dean for Student Affairs: DEBORAH DICAPRIO
Registrar: JUDY IVANKOVIĆ
Librarian: JOHN MCGINTY
Library of 207,000 vols, 30,000 journals and newspapers, 5,000 audiovisual items
Number of teachers: 578 (228 full-time, 350 adjunct)
Number of students: 6,303 (4,536 undergraduate, 872 graduate, 569 adult continuing education)
Publication: *Foxtalk Magazine*

DEANS

School of Communication and the Arts: STEVEN RALSTON
School of Computer Science and Mathematics: ROGER NORTON
School of Global and Professional Programs: Dr LAUREN H. MOUNTY
School of Liberal Arts: Dr MARTIN B. SHAFFER
School of Management: ELMORE R. ALEXANDER
School of Science: Dr NEIL FITZGERALD
School of Social and Behavioral Science: Prof. MARGARET R. CALISTA

MARYMOUNT MANHATTAN COLLEGE

221 E 71st St, New York, NY 10021
Telephone: (212) 517-0400
Internet: marymount.mmm.edu
Founded 1936 as city campus of Marymount College, present name and status 1961
Private control
Academic year: August to July
Divs of accounting and business management, fine and performing arts, humanities, sciences, social sciences, interdisciplinary studies
Pres.: Dr JUDSON R. SHAVER
Exec Vice-Pres. for Finance and Admin.: PAUL CIRAULO
Vice-Pres. for Academic Affairs and Dean for the Faculty: DAVID PODELL
Vice-Pres. for Institutional Research and Planning: DEAN PETER H. BAKER
Vice-Pres. for Student Affairs and Dean for Students: CAROL JACKSON
Dean for Admissions: JIM ROGERS
Library Dir: DONNA HURWITZ
Library of 85,000 vols
Number of teachers: 142
Number of students: 2,000 (undergraduate)

MEDAILLE COLLEGE

18 Agassiz Circle, Buffalo, NY 14214
Telephone: (716) 880-2000
Fax: (716) 884-0291
E-mail: admissionsug@medaille.edu
Internet: www.medaille.edu
Founded 1875, present name and status 1968
Private control
Academic year: September to May
Campuses in Buffalo, Williamsville and Rochester in New York

Pres.: Dr RICHARD T. JURASEK
Provost and Vice-Pres. for Academic Affairs: Dr DOUGLAS W. HOWARD
Vice-Pres. for Business and Finance: MATTHEW CARVER
Vice-Pres. for College Relations: JOHN P. CRAWFORD
Vice-Pres. for Enrolment Management: GREGORY P. FLORCZAK
Chief Information Officer: BOB CHYKA
Dean for Students: AMY DEKAY
Registrar: KATHLEEN LAZAR
Library Dir: PAMELA JONES
Library of 54,000 vols
Number of teachers: 164
Number of students: 2,680 (1798 undergraduate, 882 graduate)
Publication: *Medaille College Magazine*

DEANS

School of Adult and Graduate Education: Dr JUDITH HOROWITZ
School of Education: Dr ILLANA LANE
Undergraduate College: Dr NORMAN R. MUIR

MERCY COLLEGE

555 Broadway, Dobbs Ferry, NY 10522
Telephone: (914) 674-7307
E-mail: admissions@mercy.edu
Internet: www.mercy.edu
Founded 1950
Private control
Academic year: September to May
Campuses in Dobbs Ferry, Bronx, Manhattan, White Plains, Yorktown Heights
Pres.: Dr KIMBERLY R. CLINE
Provost and Vice-Pres. for Academic Affairs: Dr MICHAEL B. SPERLING
Vice-Pres. for Enrolment Management: DEIRDRE WHITMAN
Vice-Pres. for Finance: JEANNE T. PLECENIK
Vice-Pres. for Institutional Advancement: DEBORAH SONTUPE
Dir for Admissions: MARCELLE HICKS
Dean for Library: Dr BRADLEE
Library of 215,000 vols
Number of teachers: 193 (full-time)
Number of students: 9,673 (4,103 full-time undergraduate)
Publication: *Engage*

DEANS

School of Business: LUCRETIA S. MANN (acting)
School of Education: Dr ALFRED S. POSAMENTIER
School of Health and Natural Sciences: Dr TOM OLSON
School of Liberal Arts: Dr MIRIAM SAHATDJIAN GOGOL
School of Social and Behavioral Sciences: Dr LOIS A. WIMS

METROPOLITAN COLLEGE OF NEW YORK

431 Canal St, New York, NY 10013
Telephone: (212) 343-1234
Fax: (212) 343-7399
E-mail: admissions@metropolitan.edu
Internet: www.metropolitan.edu
Founded 1964 as Women's Talent Corps, present name 2002
Private control
Academic year: January to AprilMay to AugustSeptember to December (3 semesters)
Pres.: VINTON THOMPSON
Sr Vice-Pres. and Chief Financial Officer: VINCENT MASSARO
Vice-Pres. for Enrolment Management: COLLETTE GARRITY

Dean for Students: DONA SOSA
Registrar: NOREEN SMITH
Dir for Library Services: JAY DATEMA
Library of 145,196 vols
Number of teachers: 179 (26 full-time, 153 part-time)
Number of students: 1,100

DEANS

Audrey Cohen School for Human Services and Education: Dr RUTH LUGO
School of Management: Dr HUMPHREY CROOKENDALE

MOLLOY COLLEGE

1000 Hempstead Ave, Kellenberg Hall, Rockville Centre, NY 11571-5002
Telephone: (516) 678-5000
E-mail: info@molloy.edu
Internet: www.molloy.edu
Founded 1955 as Molloy Catholic College for Women
Private control
Academic year: September to May
Pres.: Dr DREW BOGNER
Vice-Pres. for Academic Affairs and Dean for Faculty: Dr VALERIE COLLINS
Vice-Pres. for Advancement: EDWARD J. THOMPSON
Vice-Pres. for Enrolment Management: LINDA ALBANESE
Vice-Pres. for Finance and Treas.: MICHAEL A. McGOVERN
Vice-Pres. for Mission: Sr DOROTHY FITZGIBBONS
Vice-Pres. for Information Technology, Planning and Research: Dr ROBERT PATERSON
Vice-Pres. for Student Affairs: ROBERT HOULIHAN
Registrar: SUE FORTMAN
Library Dir: JUDITH BRINK-DRESCHER
Library of 80,000 vols, 400 periodicals
Number of teachers: 209
Number of students: 4,434 (3,414 undergraduate, 1,020 graduate)
Publications: Lions Land, Molloy Magazine, Molloy Matters

DEANS

Division of Business: Dr EDWARD WEIS
Division of Education: Dr MAUREEN WALSH
Division of Humanities: Dr A. NICHOLAS FARGNOLI
Division of Natural Sciences, Mathematics and Computer Science, Allied Heath Sciences and Speech Language-Pathology: Dr ANTHONY TOLVO
Division of Nursing: Dr JEANNINE D. MULDOON
Division of Social Sciences: Dr KATHLEEN MAURER SMITH

MONROE COLLEGE

2501 Jerome Ave, Bronx, NY 10468
Telephone: (718) 933-6700
Fax: (718) 364-3552
Internet: www.monroecollege.edu
Founded 1933 as Monroe School of Business
Private control
Academic year: September to August
Campuses in Bronx, New Rochelle and St Lucia
Pres.: STEPHEN J. JEROME
Sr Vice-Pres. and Chief Financial Officer: ANTHONY ALLEN
Exec. Vice-Pres.: ALEX EPHREM
Vice-Pres.: MARC JEROME
Vice-Pres. for Academics: KARENANN CARTY
Vice-Pres. for Admissions: W. JEFF WALLIS
Vice-Pres. for Student Financial Services: ROBERTA GREENBERG

Vice Pres. for Student Affairs: EVAN JEROME
Library of 50,000 vols

DEANS

King Graduate School: ROBERTA HARRIS
School of Allied Health Professions: JERRY KOSTROFF
School of Business and Accounting: MICHAEL MARINACCIO
School of Criminal Justice: MICHELE S. RODNEY
School of Education: Dr JOSEPHINE MOFFETT
School of Hospitality Management and the Culinary Arts: Dr FRANK C. COSTANTINO
School of Information Technology: Dr JANICE GIRARDI

MOUNT SAINT MARY COLLEGE

330 Powell Ave, Newburgh, NY 12550
Telephone: (845) 569-3100
Fax: (845) 562-6762
E-mail: admissions@msmc.edu
Internet: www.msmc.edu
Founded 1959
Private control
Academic year: May to May
Pres.: Fr KEVIN MACKIN
Vice-Pres. for Academic Affairs: IRIS J. TURKENKOPF
Vice-Pres. for College Advancement: JOSEPH VALENTI
Vice-Pres. for Enrolment Management: ART CRISS
Vice-Pres. for Finance and Admin. and Treas.: CATHLEEN KENNY
Vice-Pres. for Facilities and Operations: JAMES M. RAIMO
Vice-Pres. for Planning and Assessment: MARY HINTON
Chief Information Officer: DENNIS RUSH
Vice-Pres. for Student Affairs: HARRY STEINWAY
Registrar: DEBRA MILLER (acting)
Dir for Library: BARBARA WHITNEY PETRUZZELLI
Library of 90,247 vols, 28,743 online subscriptions
Number of teachers: 76 full-time, 141 part-time, 129 f.t.e.
Number of students: 2,700 (1,800 undergraduate)
Publication: Mount Saint Mary College Magazine.

NAZARETH COLLEGE

4245 E Ave, Rochester, NY 14618-3790
Telephone: (585) 389-2525
Fax: (585) 586-2452
E-mail: admissions@naz.edu
Internet: www.naz.edu
Founded 1924
Private control
Academic year: August to August
Pres.: DAAN BRAVEMAN
Vice-Pres. for Academic Affairs: SARA VARHUS
Vice-Pres. for Enrolment Management: THOMAS K. DARIN
Vice-Pres. for Finance and Treas.: MARGARET CASS FERBER
Vice-Pres. for Student Devt: KEVIN D. WORTHEN
Vice-Pres. for Institutional Advancement: KELLY E. GAGAN
Registrar: ANDREW H. MORRIS
Library Dir: CATHERINE DOYLE (acting)
Library of 266,000 vols, 2,004 serials
Number of teachers: 493 (157 full-time, 336 part-time)
Number of students: 3,102 (2,172 undergraduate, 930 graduate)

Publications: Connections (3 a year), Elbowroom (1 a year)

DEANS

College of Arts and Sciences: Dr DEBORAH DOOLEY
School of Education: Dr CRAIG HILL
School of Health and Human Services: Dr SHIRLEY SZEKERES
School of Management: GERARD F. ZAPPIA

NEW SCHOOL

66 W 12th St, New York, NY 10011
Telephone: (212) 229-5600
Fax: (212) 229-5330
E-mail: communications@newschool.edu
Internet: www.newschool.edu
Founded 1919
Private control
Academic year: August to May
Pres.: DAVID E. VAN ZANDT
Provost and Chief Academic Officer: TIM MARSHALL
Sr Vice-Pres. for Academic Affairs: BRYNA SANGER
Sr Vice-Pres. for Finance and Business: FRANK BARLETTA
Sr Vice-Pres. for Information Technology: SHELLEY E. REED
Sr Vice-Pres. for Student Services: LINDA ABRAMS REIMER
Vice-Pres. and Treas.: CRAIG BECKER
Vice-Pres. for Communications and External Affairs: PETER TABACK (acting)
Vice-Pres. for Devt and Alumni Relations: PAMELA BESNARD
Vice-Pres. for Enrolment Management: BOB GAY
Vice-Pres. for Legal Affairs and Gen. Counsel: ROY P. MOSKOWITZ
Library: 4.1m. vols
Number of teachers: 2,101 (415 full-time, 1,686 part-time)
Number of students: 11,677 (6,802 undergraduate, 1,167 full-time freshman, 3,708 graduate)
Publications: Constellations (4 a year), Graduate Faculty Philosophy Journal (2 a year), International Journal of Politics, Culture and Society (4 a year), Social Research (4 a year)

DEANS

Eugene Lang College the New School for Liberal Arts: STEPHANIE BROWNER
Mannes College the New School for Music: Dr RICHARD KESSLER
New School for Social Research: MICHAEL SCHOBER
Parsons the New School for Design: JOEL TOWERS
The New School for Public Engagement: DAVID SCOBEY

NEW YORK CHIROPRACTIC COLLEGE

2360 State Route 89, Seneca Falls, NY 13148
Telephone: (315) 568-3052
Fax: (315) 568-3087
E-mail: camsonline@nycc.edu
Internet: www.nycc.edu
Founded 1919 as Columbia Institute of Chiropractic
Private control
Academic year: May to June
Pres.: Dr FRANK J. NICCHI
Exec. Vice-Pres. and Provost: Dr MICHAEL A. MESTAN
Vice-Pres. for Enrolment Management: DIANE C. DIXON
Vice-Pres. for Finance and Admin. Services: SEAN J. ANGLIM

Vice-Pres. for Institutional Advancement: PETER VAN TYLE
Vice-Pres. for Institutional Quality and Assessment: DAVID R. ODIORNE
Dir for Admissions: MICHAEL LYNCH
Dean for Chiropractic Education: KAREN A. BOBAK
Dean for Research: Dr JEANMARIE R. BURKE
Dir for Library: BETHYN A. BONI
Library of 32,000 vols, more than 3,500 media titles, 200 journal titles
Number of students: 720
Publication: *Transitions Magazine*

DEANS

Chiropractic Clinical Education: WENDY L. MANERI
Finger Lakes School of Acupuncture and Oriental Medicine: JASON A. WRIGHT
Postgraduate aand Continuing Education: THOMAS A. VENTIMIGLIA

NEW YORK COLLEGE OF PODIATRIC MEDICINE

53 E 124th St, New York, NY 10035
Telephone: (212) 410-8147
Fax: (212) 876-7670
E-mail: enrollment@nycpm.edu
Internet: www.nycpm.edu
Founded 1911 as New York School of Chiropody, present name 1972
Private control
Academic year: July/August to May
Pres. and CEO: LOUIS L. LEVINE
Dean and Vice-Pres. for Academic Affairs: Dr MICHAEL J. TREPAL
Vice-Pres. for Admin.: JOEL A. STURM
Vice-Pres. for Information Technology and Operations: WILLIAM H. GRAHAM
Chief Financial Officer: GREG ONAIFO
Dean for Student Services: LAURENCE J. LOWY
Registrar: VERNESE PANNELL
Dir for Library Services: THOMAS P. WALKER
Library of 13,000 vols
Number of teachers: 119
Number of students: 283

DEANS

Division of Clinical Studies: Dr ROBERT ECKLES
Division of Pre-Clinical Sciences: Dr EILEEN DALY CHUSID
Graduate Medical Education: Dr ROBERT A. ECKLES
Medical Education: Dr MARK H. SWARTZ

NEW YORK INSTITUTE OF TECHNOLOGY

POB 8000, N Blvd, Old Westbury, NY 11568-0800
Telephone: (516) 686-1000
Fax: (516) 686-7613
E-mail: asknyit@nyit.edu
Internet: www.nyit.edu
Founded 1955
Private control
Academic year: September to May
Campuses in Old Westbury and Manhattan in NY; int. campuses in UAE, Jordan, Bahrain and People's Republic of China
Pres.: Dr EDWARD GUILIANO
Provost and Vice-Pres. for Academic Affairs: Dr RAHMAT SHOURESHI
Chief Financial Officer and Treas.: LEONARD AUBREY
Vice-Pres. for Academic Affairs and Dean for Faculty: ALEXANDRA W. LOGUE
Vice-Pres. for Devt: JOHN ELIZANDRO
Vice-Pres. for Enrolment, Communications and Marketing: Dr JACQUELYN NEALON

Vice-Pres. for Financial Affairs, Chief Financial Officer and Treas.: LEONARD AUBREY
Vice-Pres. for Health Sciences and Medical Affairs: Dr BARBARA ROSS-LEE
Vice-Pres. for Information Technology and Infrastructure: Dr NIYAZI BODUR
Vice-Pres. for Planning and Assessment: HARRIET ARNONE
Vice-Pres. for Student Affairs: JOE FORD
Gen. Counsel: CATHERINE R. FLICKINGER
Library of 100,000 vols, 13,000 e-books and videos
Number of teachers: 847 (283 full-time, 564 part-time)
Number of students: 14,000
Publication: *NYIT Magazine* (3 a year)

DEANS

College of Arts and Sciences: Dr ROGER YU
New York College of Osteopathic Medicine (NYCOM): Dr THOMAS SCANDALIS
School of Architecture and Design: JUDITH DIMAIO
School of Education: MICHAEL UTTENDORFER
School of Engineering and Computing Sciences: Dr NADA ANID
School of Health Professions: Dr PATRICIA M. CHUTE
School of Management: Dr JESS BORONICO

NEW YORK LAW SCHOOL

185 W Broadway, New York, NY 10013-2921
Telephone: (212) 431-2100
E-mail: admissions@nyls.edu
Internet: www.nyls.edu
Founded 1891
Private control
Academic year: August to May
Dean: Prof. ANTHONY CROWELL
Vice-Pres. for Finance and Admin.: FRED DEJOHN
Vice-Pres. and Assoc. Dean for Devt and Alumni Relations: SUZANNE J. S. DAVIDSON
Assoc. Dean for Academic Affairs: JETHRO K. LIEBERMAN
Assoc. Dean for Faculty Devt: Dr STEPHEN J. ELLMANN
Assoc. Dean for Professional Devt: Dr MARIANA HOGAN
Registrar: ORAL C. HOPE
Library Dir: CAMILLE BROUSSARD
Library of 500,000 vols
Number of teachers: 276 (94 full-time, 182 adjunct)
Number of students: 1,750
Publications: *Media Law & Policy* (3 a year), *New York Law School Law Review*, *New York Law School Magazine*.

NEW YORK MEDICAL COLLEGE

40 Sunshine Cottage Rd, Valhalla, NY 10595
Telephone: (914) 594-4000
Internet: www.nymc.edu
Founded 1860 as New York Homeopathic Medical College, present name 1938
Private control
Pres.: Dr ALAN KADISH
Provost: Dr RALPH A. O'CONNELL
Vice-Provost for Admin. and Finance and Sr Vice-Pres. for Finance: STEPHEN PICCOLO, JR
Vice-Pres. and Gen. Counsel: WALDEMAR A. COMAS
Vice-Pres. for Devt and Alumni Relations: JULIE A. KUBASKA
Vice-Pres. for Strategic Planning: WILLIAM A. STEADMAN, II
Registrar: Dr JUDITH A. EHREN
Assoc. Dean and Dir for Library: DIANA CUNNINGHAM

Library of 140,000 vols, 46,332 unique titles, 16,543 journal titles, 14,814 e-books
Number of teachers: 3,000
Number of students: 1,400

DEANS

Graduate School of Basic Medical Sciences: Dr FRANCIS L. BELLONI
School of Health Sciences and Practice: Dr ROBERT W. AMLER
School of Medicine: Dr WILLIAM A. STEADMAN, II

NEW YORK SCHOOL OF INTERIOR DESIGN

170 E 70th St, New York, NY 10021
Telephone: (212) 472-1500
Fax: (212) 472-3800
E-mail: info@nysid.edu
Internet: www.nysid.edu
Founded 1916, chartered in 1924
Private control
Academic year: September to July
Acting Pres. and Exec. Vice-Pres.: DAVID SPROULS
Vice-Pres. for Academic Affairs and Dean: ELLEN FISHER
Vice-Pres. for Enrolment Management: DAVID SPROULS
Vice-Pres. for Finance and Admin.: JANE CHEN
Dir for Library: SARAH FALLS
Library of 15,000 vols
Number of teachers: 90
Number of students: 730 (290 full-time, 440 part-time)

NEW YORK THEOLOGICAL SEMINARY

475 Riverside Dr., Suite 500, New York, NY 10115-0083
Telephone: (212) 870-1211
Fax: (212) 870-1236
E-mail: online@nyts.edu
Internet: www.nyts.edu
Founded 1900 as Bible Teachers' College, present name 1966
Private control
Academic year: August to May
Pres.: Prof. DALE T. IRVIN
Vice-Pres. for Academic Affairs and Academic Dean: Rev. Dr ELEANOR MOODY-SHEPHERD
Vice-Pres.: Dr LAURA PIRES-HESTER
Registrar: LYDIA RODRIGUEZ-BUMGARDNER
Dir for Library Services: Dr JERRY REISIG
Number of teachers: 35
Number of students: 650

NEW YORK UNIVERSITY

70 Washington Sq. S, New York, NY 10012
Telephone: (212) 998-1212
Internet: www.nyu.edu
Founded 1831
Private control
Academic year: September to May
Pres.: Dr JOHN SEXTON
Provost: Dr DAVID W. MCLAUGHLIN
Exec. Vice-Pres.: Dr MICHAEL ALFANO
Exec. Vice-Pres. for Finance and Information Technology: Dr MARTIN S. DORPH
Exec. Vice-Pres. for Operations: ALISON LEARY
Sr Vice-Pres., Gen. Counsel and Sec. for the Univ.: Dr BONNIE BRIER
Sr Vice-Pres. for Univ. Relations and Public Affairs: Dr LYNNE P. BROWN
Sr Vice-Pres. for Devt and Alumni Relations: Dr DEBRA A. LAMORTE

Vice-Pres. for Budget and Planning: ANTHONY P. JIGA
Vice-Pres. for Enrolment Management: RANDALL DEIKE
Vice-Pres. for Information Technology: MARILYN MCMILLAN
Vice-Pres. for Public Affairs: JOHN BECKMAN
Vice-Pres. for Public Resource Admin.: RICHARD N. BING
Vice-Pres. for Student Affairs: MARC L. WAIS
Sr Vice-Provost and Vice-Chancellor: Dr KATHERINE E. FLEMING
Sr Vice-Provost for Academic Policies: PIERRE HOHENBERG
Sr Vice-Provost for Planning: Dr RON ROBIN
Sr Vice-Provost for Research: Dr PAUL HORN
Sr Vice-Provost for Undergraduate Education and Univ. Life: LINDA G. MILLS
Sr Vice-Provost for Undergraduate Academic Affairs: Dr MATTHEW SANTIROCCO
Vice-Provost for Globalization and Multicultural Affairs: ULRICH BAER
Vice-Provost for Int. Education and Outreach: CAROL BRANDT
Vice-Provost for Science and Engineering Devt: GERARD BEN-AROUS
Registrar: ROGER PRINTUP
Dean for Libraries: CAROL A. MANDEL
Library: see Libraries and Archives
Number of teachers: 8,315
Number of students: 43,797 (22,097 undergraduate, 18,243 graduate, 3,457 first professionals)

Publications: *Clinical Law Review* (2 a year), *Environmental Law Journal* (3 a year), *I●CON, The International Journal of Constitutional Law* (4 a year), *Inquiry* (1 a year), *Journal of Accounting, Auditing and Finance* (4 a year), *Journal of International Financial Management and Accounting* (3 a year), *Journal of International Law and Politics* (4 a year), *Journal of Legislation and Public Policy* (2 a year), *Moot Court Casebook* (1 a year), *New York University Annual Survey of American Law* (4 a year), *New York University Law Review* (6 a year), *NYU Journal of Law & Business, Review of Law & Social Change* (6 a year), *Tax Law Review* (4 a year), *TDR: A Journal of Performance Studies* (4 a year), *The Journal of Law & Liberty, Victorian Literature and Culture* (2 a year), *Washington Square* (2 a year), *Women and Performance: a Journal of Feminist Theory* (2 a year), *Wordsworth Circle* (4 a year)

DEANS

College of Arts and Science: G. GABRIELLE STARR (acting)
College of Dentistry: Dr CHARLES N. BERTOLAMI
Gallatin School of Individualized Study: SUSANNE L. WOFFORD
Graduate School of Arts and Science: THOMAS J. CAREW
Leonard N. Stern School of Business: PETER BLAIR HENRY
NYU College of Nursing: Dr JUDITH HABER
NYU School of Medicine: ROBERT I. GROSSMAN
Robert F. Wagner Graduate School of Public Service: ELLEN SCHALL
School of Continuing and Professional Studies: ROBERT S. LAPINER
School of Law: RICHARD L. REVESZ
Silver School of Social Work: Dr LYNN VIDEKA
Steinhardt School of Culture, Education and Human Development: MARY M. BRABECK
Tisch School of the Arts: MARY SCHMIDT CAMPBELL

PROFESSORS

College of Arts and Science (100 Washington Square E, Room 910 New York, NY 10003-6688; internet www.nyu.edu/cas):
AARONSON, D., Psychology
AFFRON, C., French
ALEXANDER, J. J. G., Fine Arts
ALLEN, L. R., Psychology
AMENTA, E., Sociology
ANDERSEN, S. M., Psychology
ANDERSON, H. M., Spanish and Portuguese Languages and Literatures
AVELLANEDA, M., Mathematics
AVERILL, G., Music
AZMITIA, E. C., Biology, Neural Science
BACIC, Z., Chemistry
BAER, N. S., Conservation, Fine Arts
BAILEY, R., Music
BAKER, P. R., History
BALTIN, M. R., Linguistics
BARGH, J. A., Psychology
BAUMOL, W. J., Economics
BEAUJOUR, M., French
BEIDELMAN, T. O., Anthropology
BENDER, T., History
BENHABIB, J., Political Economy, Economics
BERENSON, E., History, French Studies
BERGER, M., Computer Science
BERMAN, S. M., Mathematics
BISHOP, T., French Literature, Comparative Literature
BLOCK, N., Philosophy, Psychology
BLOOM, H., English and American Literature, English
BOGHOSSIAN, P., Philosophy
BOGOMOLOV, F. A., Mathematics
BONFANTE, L., Classics
BOORMAN, S. H., Music
BRAMS, S. J., Politics
BRANDT, K. W.-G., Fine Arts
BRANDT, R. A., Physics
BRATHWAITE, K., Comparative Literature
BROWN, H. H., Jr, Physics
BROWN, J., Fine Arts
BROYDE, S., Biology
BRUNER, J., Psychology
BUDICK, B., Physics
BUENO DE MESQUITA, B., Politics
BURNS, F. J., Environmental Science
BURROWS, D. L., Music
BURROWS, W. E., Journalism and Mass Communication
CALHOUN, C. J., Sociology
CANARY, J. W., Chemistry
CANTOR, N. F., History, Comparative Literature, Sociology
CAPLIN, A., Economics
CAPPELL, S., Mathematics
CARNEVALE, P., Psychology
CARRASCO, M., Psychology and Neuroscience
CARRUTHERS, M. J., Literature
CHAIKEN, S., Psychology
CHAUDHURI, U., English
CHAZAN, R., Modern Jewish History
CHEEGER, J., Mathematics
CHELKOWSKI, P. J., Middle Eastern Studies
CHILDRESS, W. S., Mathematics
CHIOLES, J., Comparative Literature
CHUSID, M., Music
CLASTER, J. N., History
COHEN, B. S., Environmental Medicine
COHEN, J.-L., History of Architecture
COHEN, S. F., Russian Studies and History
COLE, R., Computer Science
COLLINS, C., English
COONS, E. E., Psychology, Neural Science
CORRADI, J. E., Sociology
CORUZZI, G. M., Biology
COSTA, M., Environmental Science
COSTELLO, J. R., Linguistics
DASH, J. M., French
DEIFT, P., Mathematics
DESPLAN, C., Biology

DEWAR, R. B. K., Computer Science
DIAWARA, M., Comparative Literature
DINER, H. R., American Jewish History, Hebrew and Judaic Studies, History
DINSHAW, C., English
DJEBAR, A., French
DOCTOROW, E. L., American Letters, English
DONOGHUE, D., English and American Letters
DOUBROVSKY, S., French
DOWNS, G. W., Jr, Politics
DUSTER, T., Sociology
DWORKIN, R., Law, Philosophy
EISLER, C., Fine Arts
ELBOURNE, P. D., Linguistics
ELLIS, M. H., Fine Arts
ENGEL, D., Holocaust Studies, Hebrew and Judaic Studies, and History
EVANS, H. L., Environmental Science
FAIRCHILD, S., Conservation
FARRAR, G., Physics
FELDMAN, S. M., Neural Science, Psychology
FELDMAN, Y. S., Hebrew Culture and Education
FERNANDEZ, R., Economics
FIELD, H. H., Philosophy
FINE, K., Philosophy
FLINN, C. J., Economics
FRECCERO, J., Italian, Comparative Literature
FRYDMAN, R., Economics
FURMANSKI, P., Biology
GALE, D., Economics
GANS, P. J., Chemistry
GARABEDIAN, P. R., Mathematics
GARLAND, D., Sociology
GATELY, D., Economics
GEACINTOV, N. E., Chemistry
GERSON, K., Sociology
GERSON, S., French
GERTLER, M., Economics
GILMAN, E. B., English
GILSENAN, M., Humanities, Middle Eastern Studies, Anthropology
GINSBURG, F., Anthropology
GITLIN, T., Journalism and Mass Communication, Education, Sociology
GOLDSTEIN, G. R., Dental Materials Science
GOLLWITZER, P. M., Psychology
GOODMAN, J., Mathematics
GOTTLIEB, A., Computer Science
GREENBERG, D. F., Sociology
GREENGARD, L., Mathematics
GREENLEAF, F. P., Mathematics
GRIFFIN, D., English
GRISHMAN, R., Computer Science
GROMOV, M., Mathematics
GROSS, J. T., Politics
GUILLORY, J., English
GURLAND, R. H., Philosophy
GUY, G. R., Linguistics
HAMEIRI, E., Mathematics
HANSEN, D., Ancient Middle Eastern Art and Archaeology
HARDIN, R., Politics
HARLEY, N. H., Environmental Science
HAROOTUNIAN, H., History
HARPER, P. B., English, American Studies
HARRINGTON, C., Politics
HARRISON, T., Anthropology
HAUSNER, M., Mathematics
HAVERKAMP, A., English
HAWKEN, M. J., Neural Science, Psychology
HEEGER, D. J., Psychology and Neural Science
HEILMAN, M., Psychology
HENDIN, J. G., English
HEYDEBRAND, W., Sociology
HEYNS, B., Sociology
HOFER, H., Mathematics
HOFFERT, M. I., Physics
HOFFMAN, M., Psychology
HOLLIER, D., French
HOROWITZ, R., Sociology

HOY, P. C., English
HSIUNG, J. C., Politics
HUGGINS, P., Physics
HULL, R. W., History
HÜPPAUF, B. R., German
HYMAN, I., Fine Arts
IVRY, A. L., Modern Jewish Thought, Hebrew and Judaic Studies, Middle Eastern Studies
JACOBY, L., Psychology
JAEGER, R. J., Environmental Science
JASSO, G., Sociology
JAVITCH, D., Comparative Literature, Italian
JOHNSON, P., History
JOLLY, C. J., Anthropology
JOVANOVIĆ, B., Economics
JUDT, A., European Studies, History
KALLENBACH, N. R., Chemistry
KAMM, F. M., Philosophy, Law
KAPLAN, F. E. S., Museum Studies
KAPLAN, M. A., Hebrew and Judaic Studies
KARCHIN, L., Music
KAYNE, R. S., Linguistics
KAZEMI, F., Politics, Middle Eastern Studies
KEDEM, Z. M., Computer Science
KELLEY, R. D. G., History
KINNELL, G., Creative Writing, English
KIRSHENBLATT-GIMBLETT, B., Performance Studies, Hebrew and Judaic Studies
KOHN, R. V., Mathematics
KOPCKE, G., Humanities
KRABBENHOFT, K., Spanish and Portuguese Languages and Literatures
KRAUSKOPF, J., Neural Science, Psychology
KRINSKY, C., Fine Arts
KRISER, D. B., Anthropology
KULICK, D., Anthropology
KUPPERMAN, K., History
LANDAU, S., Fine Arts
LANDY, M. S., Psychology, Neural Science
LAX, P. D., Mathematics
LeDOUX, J. E., Neural Science and Psychology
LeGEROS, R. Z., Dental Materials Science
LEHMAN, E. W., Sociology
LENNIE, P., Neural Science
LEVINE, B. A., Bible and Ancient Near Eastern Studies, Hebrew and Judaic Studies
LEVY, P. M., Physics
LIN, F.-H., Mathematics
LIPPMANN, M., Environmental Science
LOCKMAN, Z., Middle Eastern Studies, History
LOCKRIDGE, L. S., English
LOW, A., English
LOWENSTEIN, J. H., Physics
LUKES, S. M., Sociology
LYNCH, O. M., Urban Anthropology
McCHESNEY, R. D., Middle Eastern Studies
McKEAN, H. P., Mathematics
McLAUGHLIN, D. W., Mathematics
McNELIS, E. J., Chemistry
MAGNUSON, P. A., English
MAJDA, A. J., Mathematics
MANIN, B., Politics
MANOFF, R. K., Journalism and Mass Communication
MARINCOLA, M. D., Conservation
MARMOR, M., Environmental Medicine
MARSHALL, P., English
MARTIN, E., Anthropology
MARTÍNEZ, H. S., Spanish and Portuguese Languages and Literatures
MATHEWS, T. F., History of Art
MATTHEWS, T. J., Psychology, Neural Science
MATTINGLY, P., History
MAYNARD, J., English
MEAD, L. M., Politics
MEISEL, P., English
MICHELSON, A., Cinema Studies
MINCER, A., Physics
MISHRA, B., Computer Science

MITCHELL, C., Politics
MITCHELL, T., Politics, Middle Eastern Studies
MITSIS, P., Hellenic Culture and Civilization, Classics
MOLLOY, S., Spanish and Portuguese Languages and Literatures, Comparative Literature
MORTON, R. B., Politics
MOVSHON, J. A., Neural Science, Psychology
MURPHY, G. L., Psychology
MURPHY, L. B., Law, Philosophy
MYERS, F. R., Anthropology
NADIRI, M. I., Economics
NAGEL, T., Philosophy
NELKIN, D., Sociology
NEMETHY, P., Physics
NEWMAN, C. M., Mathematics
NICOLE, E., French
NIRENBERG, L., Mathematics
NOCHLIN, L., Modern Art
NOLAN, M., History
NYARKO, Y., Economics
O'CONNOR, D., Ancient Egyptian Art
OLDS, S., English
OLIVA, L. J., European Studies, History
OLLMAN, B., Politics
ORDOVER, J. A., Economics
OVERTON, M., Computer Science
PEACHIN, M., Classics
PEACOCKE, C., Philosophy
PELLI, D. G., Psychology, Neural Science
PERCUS, J. K., Mathematics, Physics
PERSELL, C. H., Sociology
PESKIN, C. S., Mathematics
PETERS, F. E., Middle Eastern Studies, Religious Studies, History
PINES, M. S., Dental Materials Science
PNUELI, A., Computer Science
POLLACK, R., Mathematics
POOVEY, M., English
PORRATI, M., Physics
POSNER, D., Fine Arts
POSNOCK, R., English
POSTAL, P. M., Linguistics
PRATT, M. L., Spanish and Portuguese
PRZEWORSKI, A., Politics
RAMSEY, J. B., Economics
RANDALL, R. S., Politics
RAPP, R., Anthropology
RAY, D., Economics
REGALADO, N. F., French
REIMERS, D. E., History
REISS, C. S., Biology
REISS, T. J., Comparative Literature
RICHARDSON, J., Philosophy
RICHARDSON, R. W., Physics
RINZEL, J., Neural Science, Mathematics
ROBINSON, E. J., Physics
ROELOFS, H. M., Politics
ROESNER, E. H., Music
RONELL, A., Germanic Languages and Literatures, Comparative Literature
ROSENBERG, L., Physics
ROSENBLUM, R., Modern European Art
ROSS, A., Comparative Literature
ROSS, K., Comparative Literature
ROSSMAN, T. G., Environmental Science
RUBLE, D. N., Psychology
RUDDICK, S., Philosophy
SAMMONS, J. T., History
SANDLER, L., Art History
SANTIROCCO, M. S., Classics
SARNAK, P., Mathematics
SCALLY, R. J., History, Classics
SCHAIN, M., Politics, French Studies
SCHECHNER, R., Performance Studies
SCHIEFFELIN, B. B., Anthropology
SCHIFFER, S., Philosophy
SCHIFFMAN, L. H., Hebrew and Judaic Studies
SCHLESINGER, R. B., Environmental Science
SCHLICK, T., Chemistry, Mathematics
SCHONBERG, E., Computer Science
SCHOTTER, A., Economics

SCHUCKING, E. L., Physics
SCHULMAN, A., Dental Materials Science
SCHUSTER, D. I., Chemistry
SCHWARTZ, J. T., Computer Science
SCHWEITZER, A., Humanities, Spanish and Portuguese Languages and Literatures, Comparative Literature
SCOTT, W., Biology
SCULLI, J., Physics
SEEMAN, N. C., Chemistry
SEIDMAN, E., Psychology
SEIGEL, J., History
SENNETT, R., Sociology, History
SHAPLEY, R. M., Sciences, Neural Science, Biology, Psychology
SHASHA, D., Computer Science
SHATAH, J., Mathematics
SHELLEY, M., Mathematics
SHINN, M., Psychology
SHOHAT, E., Art and Public Policy, Middle Eastern Studies
SHORE, R. E., Environmental Science
SHROUT, P., Psychology
SIDER, D., Classics
SIEBURTH, R., Comparative Literature, French
SIFAKIS, G. M., Hellenic Culture and Civilization, Classics
SILVER, K., Fine Arts, French Studies
SINGLER, J. V., Linguistics
SIRLIN, A., Physics
SKLAR, R., Cinema Studies
SMITH, M. S., Hebrew and Judaic Studies
SNODGRASS, J. G., Psychology
SOKAL, A. D., Physics
SOLOMON, S. D., Journalism and Mass Communication
SORENSEN, R. A., Philosophy
SOUCEK, P., Islamic Art
SPENCER, J. H., Computer Science, Mathematics
STAM, R., Cinema Studies
STEHLIN, S. A., History
STEPHENS, M., Journalism and Mass Communication
STIMPSON, C. R., Arts and Science
STOTZKY, G., Biology
STROKE, H. H., Physics
SUBIRATS, E., Spanish and Portuguese Languages and Literatures
SULLIVAN, E., Fine Arts
SZABOLCSI, A., Linguistics
TAYLOR, D., Performance Studies, Spanish
TING, L., Mathematics
TRACHTENBERG, M., History of Fine Arts
TROPE, Y., Psychology
TURNER, R., Art and Humanities
TYLER, T. R., Psychology
ULEMAN, J. S., Psychology
UNGER, I., History
UNGER, P., Philosophy
VARADHAN, S. R. S., Science, Mathematics
VITZ, E. B., French
VITZ, P. C., Psychology
VOLOGODSKII, A. V., Chemistry
WALEY-COHEN, J., History
WALKOWITZ, D., History
WEINEN, E., Mathematics
WEITZNER, H., Mathematics
WELKOWITZ, J., Psychology
WHITE, R., Anthropology
WIDLUND, O. B., Computer Science
WILSON, C. A., Economics
WILSON, S. R., Chemistry
WOLFF, E. N., Economics
WOLFSON, E., Hebrew Studies, Religious Studies
WRIGHT, M. H., Computer Science
XIN, Z., Mathematics
YAP, C. K., Computer Science
YAU, H.-T., Mathematics
YELLIN, V. F., Music
YOUNG, M. B., History
YÚDICE, G., Spanish and Portuguese and American Studies
ZASLAVSKY, G. M., Physics, Mathematics

ZHANG, J. Z. H., Chemistry
ZWANZIGER, D., Physics, Mathematics

College of Dentistry (345 E 24th St, New York, NY 10010; tel. (212) 998-9800; internet www.nyu.edu/dental):

BAHN, S., Biological Sciences, Medicine and Surgery
BRAL, M., Periodontics
CALAMIA, J., Restorative and Prosthodontics
CAUFIELD, P. W., Cariology and Operative Dentistry
GLICKMAN, R., Oral Maxillofacial Surgery
GOLDSTEIN, G., Prosthodontics
GUTTENPLAN, J., Basic Sciences (Biochemistry)
KATZ, R., Epidemiology and Health Promotion
KINNALLY, K., Basic Sciences
KIREMIDJIAN-SCHUMACHER, L., Basic Sciences
KUFTINEC, M., Orthodontics
LEGEROS, R., Implant Dentistry and Restorative and Prosthodontic Sciences
PINES, M., Biomaterials
REKOW, D., Basic Sciences and Craniofacial Biology and Orthodontics
ROSENBERG, P., Endodontics
ROY, M., Basic Sciences
SCHERER, W., Reconstructive and Comprehensive Care
SHIP, J. A., Oral Medicine
SINGH, I., Basic Sciences
SPIELMAN, A., Basic Science and Craniofacial Biology
TARNOW, D., Implant Dentistry
TERRACIO, L., Basic Sciences and Craniofacial Biology
VERNILLO, A., Oral Pathology

Institute of Fine Arts (One E 78th St, New York, NY 10075; tel. (212) 992-5800; fax (212) 992-5807; e-mail ifa.program@nyu.edu; internet www.nyu.edu/gsas/dept/fineart):

ALEXANDER, J. J. G., Fine Arts
BAER, N. S., Conservation
BROWN, J., Fine Arts
COHEN, J.-L., History of Architecture
EISLER, C., Fine Arts
ELLIS, M. H., Conservation
FAIRCHILD, S., Fine Arts
HANSEN, D. P., Fine Arts
KOPCKE, G. H., Humanities
MARINCOLA, M., Conservation
MATHEWS, T. F., History of Art
NOCHLIN, L., Modern Art
O'CONNOR, D., Ancient Egyptian Art
POSNER, D., Fine Arts
ROSENBLUM, R., Modern European Art, Fine Arts
SANDLER, L. F., Fine Arts
SOUCEK, P. P., Islamic Art
STORR, R., Modern Art
SULLIVAN, E. J., Fine Arts
TRACHTENBERG, M., History of Fine Arts
VARNEDOE, J. K. T., History of Art
WALLACE, L. A., Ancient Egyptian Art
WEIL-GARRIS BRANDT, K., Fine Arts
WESTERMANN, M., Fine Arts

Leonard N. Stern School of Business (Henry Kaufman Management Center, 44 W Fourth St, New York, NY 10012; tel. (212) 998-0100; internet www.stern.nyu.edu):

BALACHANDRAN, K. R., Accounting and Operations Management
BARDES, P., Accounting and Finance
BARTOV, E., Accounting, Business Ethics
BILDERSEE, J. S., Accounting
BRIEF, R., Statistics and Accounting
HIPSCHER, A., Accounting, Taxation and Business Law
JONES, S., Accounting, Taxation and Business Law
LIVNAT, J., Accounting
MORAN, M. J., Accounting

NICHOLS, C. W., Business Ethics
RONEN, J., Accounting
SORTER, G. H., Accounting and Law
WIESEN, J., Accounting, Taxation and Business Law
ZICKLIN, L., Accounting

Robert F. Wagner Graduate School of Public Service (The Puck Bldg, 295 Lafayette St, Second Fl., New York, NY 10012-9604; tel. (212) 998-7400; internet www.nyu.edu/wagner):

BERNE, R., Public Policy and Financial Management
BOISE, W. B., Public Administration
BOUFFORD, J. I., Health Policy and Public Service
BRECHER, C. M., Public and Health Administration
CHERKASKY, M., Health Policy and Management
FINKLER, S. A., Public and Health Administration, Accounting, and Financial Management
KOVNER, A., Public and Health Management
KROPF, R., Health Management
LEW, J. J., Public Administration
LIGHT, P., Public Service
MOSS, M., Urban Policy and Planning
RODWIN, V. G., Health Policy and Management
SCHALL, E., Health Policy and Management
SCHILL, M. H., Law and Urban Planning
SPARROW, R. L., Public Management
STAFFORD, W. W., Public Policy and Planning
STIEFEL, L., Economics
ZIMMERMAN, R., Planning and Public Administration

School of Law (40 Washington Sq. S, New York, NY 10012; tel. (212) 998-6100; internet www.law.nyu.edu):

ADLER, A. M., Law
ADLER, B. E., Law
ALLEN, W. T., Law and Business
ALSTON, P., Law
AMSTERDAM, A. G., Law
ANGELOS, C., Law
ARLEN, J., Law
BEEN, V. L., Law
BENKLER, Y., Law
BILLMAN, B. D., Law
BURNS, S. E., Clinical Law
CALDWELL, P. M., Law
CHASE, O. G., Law
CHEVIGNY, P. G., Law
COHEN, J. A., Law
CUNNINGHAM, N. B., Law
DAINES, R. M., Law
DALE, H. P., Philanthropy and the Law
DAVIS, P. C., Lawyering and Ethics
DORSEN, N., Law
DREYFUSS, R. C., Law
DWORKIN, R. M., Law
ESTREICHER, S., Law
EUSTICE, J. S., Taxation
FIRST, H., Law
FOX, E. M., Trade Regulation
FRIEDMAN, B., Law
GALOWITZ, P., Law
GARLAND, D. W., Law
GEISTFELD, M., Law
GILLERS, S., Law
GILLETTE, C. P., Contract Law
GOLOVE, D. M., Law
GUGGENHEIM, M. F., Clinical Law
HERSHKOFF, H., Law
HERTZ, R. A., Clinical Law
HOLMES, S. T., Law
JACOBS, J. B., Constitutional Law and the Courts
KAHAN, M., Law
KINGSBURY, B., Law
KORNHAUSER, L. A., Law

LAW, S. A., Law
LEVINSON, D., Law
LÓPEZ, G., Clinical Law
LOWENFELD, A. F., International Law
MAGUIGAN, H., Clinical Law
MALMAN, L. L., Law
MARTELL, L. A., Law
MERON, T., Law
MILLER, G. P., Law
MORAWETZ, N., Clinical Law
MURPHY, L., Law
NAGEL, T., Law
NELSON, W. E., Law
NEUBORNE, B., Law
NOBLE, R. K., Law
PILDES, R. H., Law
PRICE, M. K., Law
REID, J. P., Law
REVESZ, R. L., Law
RICHARDS, D. A. J., Law
SAGER, L., Law
SCHENK, D. H., Taxation
SCHILL, M. H., Law and Urban Planning
SCHMOLKA, L. L., Law
SCHULHOFER, S. J., Law
SCOTT, H. S., Law
SEXTON, J., Law
SHAVIRO, D. N., Law
SIEGEL, S., Law
SILBERMAN, L. J., Law
SORTER, G. H., Law
STEINES, J. P., Jr, Law
STEWART, R. B., Law
TAYLOR-THOMPSON, K. A., Clinical Law
THOMPSON, A. C., Law
UPHAM, F. K., Law
WEILER, J. H. H., Law
ZIMMERMAN, D. L., Law

School of Medicine (550 First Ave, New York, NY 10016; tel. (212) 263-7300; internet www.med.nyu.edu):

ABADIR, A. R., Anaesthesiology
ABELE, M. G., Radiology
ABRAMS, S., Psychiatry
ABRAMSON, S. B., Medicine, Rheumatology, Pathology
ADESNIK, M. B., Cell Biology
AIGES, H. W., Paediatrics
AL-ASKARI, S., Urology
ALBANO, A. M., Psychiatry
ALBOM, M. J., Dermatology
AMELAR, R. D., Urology
ANGRIST, B. M., Psychiatry
ARGYROS, T. G., Medicine
ARKEL, Y. S., Obstetrics and Gynaecology
ARLOW, J. A., Psychiatry
ARONOFF, M. S., Psychiatry
ARTMAN, M., Paediatric Surgery, Pharmacology
ASTON, S. J., Surgery
AUERBACH, R., Dermatology
AXEL, L., Radiology
AXELROD, F. B., Dysautonomia Treatment, Neurology
AYVAZIAN, L. F., Medicine
BAKER, R. G., Physiology, Neuroscience
BALDWIN, D. S., Medicine, Nephrology
BALLARD, H. S., Medicine
BARKIN, L., Psychiatry
BARRON, B. A., Obstetrics and Gynaecology
BASCH, R. S., Pathology
BASILICO, C., Microbiology
BAUMANN, F. G., Surgery
BEASLEY, R. W., Surgery, Plastic and Reconstructive Surgery
BEATTIE, C. N., Anaesthesiology
BECKER, J. A., Radiology
BELASCO, J. G., Microbiology
BELMAN, S., Environmental Medicine
BEN-YISHAY, Y., Rehabilitation Medicine
BENJAMIN, V., Neurosurgery
BERANBAUM, S. L., Radiology
BERCZELLER, P. H., Medicine
BERG, P., Medicine
BERGER, M. M., Psychiatry

BERKELEY, A. S., Obstetrics and Gynaecology
BERNSTEIN, R. L., Anaesthesiology
BHANOT, O. S., Environmental Medicine
BHARDWAJ, N., Medicine Physiology, Neuroscience Pharmacology
BIRNBAUM, B. A., Radiology
BLANCK, T. J. J., Anaesthesiology, Physiology, Neuroscience
BLASER, M., Internal Medicine, Microbiology
BLAUGRUND, S. M., Otolaryngology
BLOCK, J. M., Neurology
BLUM, H. P., Psychiatry
BLUM, M., Medicine, Endocrinology, Radiology
BODIAN, E. L., Dermatology
BOGART, B. I., Cell Biology
BORKOWSKY, W., Paediatrics
BOSLAND, M. C., Environmental Medicine, Urology
BOUFFORD, J. I., Paediatrics
BOXER, R. A., Paediatrics
BOYD, A. D., Surgery, Cardiothoracic Surgery
BRANCACCIO, R. R., Dermatology
BRODIE, J. D., Psychiatry
BROOME, J. D., Pathology
BROTMAN, A. W., Psychiatry
BROWN, E. R., Neurosurgery
BROWN, J. W., Neurology
BRUNO, M. S., Clinical Medicine
BUDMAN, D. R., Medicine, Oncology
BURAKOFF, S. J., Medicine, Oncology
BURDEN, S. J., Pharmacology
BURDOCK, E. I., Psychiatry
BURNS, F. J., Environmental Medicine
BUYON, J. P., Medicine, Rheumatology
BYSTRYN, J.-C., Dermatology
CAHILL, K. M., Medicine
CALANOG, A. M., Obstetrics and Gynaecology
CANCRO, R., Psychiatry
CAPAN, L., Anaesthesiology
CARR, R. E., Ophthalmology
CASTELLANOS, F. X., Child and Adolescent Psychiatry, Clinical Radiology
CHALFIN, L. S., Psychiatry
CHANDRA, M. M., Paediatrics
CHANDRA, R., Radiology
CHAO, M. V., Cell Biology
CHARAP, M. H., Medicine, General Medicine
CHARLES, N. C., Ophthalmology
CHARNEY, A. N., Medicine, Nephrology
CHASSIN, J. L., Surgery
CHESLER, M., Neurosurgery, Physiology and Neuroscience
CHESS, S., Psychiatry
CHIORAZZI, N., Medicine, Infectious Diseases and Immunology, Pathology
CHIU, D. T., Surgery, Plastic and Reconstructive Surgery
CITROME, L. L., Psychiatry
CLAPS, A. A., Paediatrics
COBRINIK, R., Paediatrics
COHEN, B. S., Environmental Medicine
COHEN, I. J., Ophthalmology
COHEN, N. L., Otolaryngology
COHEN, T., Medicine
COLLINS, A. H., Psychiatry
COLOMBO, A., Medicine
COLTRERA, J. T., Psychiatry
COOPER, J. S., Radiation Oncology
COOPER, N. S., Pathology
COOPER, P. R., Neurosurgery, Orthopaedic Surgery
COPLAN, N. L., Medicine
COSTA, M., Environmental Medicine, Pharmacology
COSTA E SILVA, J. A., Psychiatry
COWAN, N. J., Biochemistry
CRONSTEIN, B. N., Medicine, Rheumatology, Pathology, Pharmacology
CULLIFORD, A. T., Surgery, Cardiothoracic Surgery

CURTIN, J. P., Obstetrics and Gynaecology
D'AMICO, R. A., Ophthalmology
DANCIS, J., Paediatrics
DANILOWICZ, D. A., Paediatrics
DANTUONO, L. M., Obstetrics and Gynaecology
DAUM, F., Paediatrics
DAVID, R., Paediatrics
DAVIES, E. A., Paediatrics
DAVIS, J. E., Urology
DE LEON, M. J., Psychiatry
DEBROVNER, C. H., Obstetrics and Gynaecology
DEFENDI, V., Oncology, Pathology
DEGNAN, T. J., Medicine, Oncology
DELISI, L. E., Psychiatry
DELPHIN, E. S., Anaesthesiology
DEMOPOULOS, R. I., Pathology
DEPASQUALE, N. P., Medicine
DEUTSCH, B. G., Psychiatry
DEVINSKY, O., Neurology
DEWEY, S. L., Psychiatry
DHAWAN, V., Neurology
DILLER, L., Rehabilitation Medicine
DODICK, J. M., Ophthalmology
DOLGIN, M., Medicine, Cardiology
DRLICA, K. A., Microbiology
DUBIN, L., Urology
DUBNAU, D., Microbiology
DUBOIS, M. Y., Anaesthesiology
DUSTIN, M. L., Pathology
EBERSTEIN, A., Rehabilitation Medicine
EIDELBERG, D., Neurology, Neurosurgery
ELSBACH, P., Medicine
ENG, K., Surgery
EVANS, H. L., Environmental Medicine
FANTL, J. A., Obstetrics and Gynaecology
FARBER, S. J., Medicine, Nephrology
FARCON, E. M., Urology
FARCY, J.-P. C., Orthopaedic Surgery
FEINBERG, A. W., Medicine, Geriatrics
FEINER, H. D., Pathology
FERRIS, S. H., Psychiatry
FINGER, P. T., Ophthalmology
FINLAY, J. L., Paediatrics, Neurosurgery
FINLAY, J. R., Ophthalmology
FIRESTEIN, S. K., Psychiatry
FISCHEL, R. E., Psychiatry
FISHER, A. A., Dermatology
FISHER, M. M., Paediatrics
FISHER, Y. L., Ophthalmology
FISHMAN, G. I., Medicine, Cardiology, Physiology and Neuroscience, Pharmacology
FLOWER, R. W., Ophthalmology
FORMENTI, S. C., Medical Oncology
FOSTER, J. R., Psychiatry
FOX, A. C., Medicine, Cardiology
FRANCES, R. J., Psychiatry
FRANGIONE, B., Pathology, Psychiatry
FRANK, J., Cell Biology
FRANKEL, V. H., Orthopaedic Surgery
FRANKS, A. G., Jr, Dermatology
FREEDBERG, I. M., Dermatology, Cell Biology
FREEDMAN, M. L., Medicine, Geriatrics
FRENKEL, K., Environmental Medicine, Pathology
FRIEDMAN, H. S., Medicine
FRIEDMAN-KIEN, A. E., Dermatology
FROST, J. O., Otolaryngology
FURMANSKI, P., Pathology
GABRIEL, H. P., Psychiatry
GALANTER, M., Psychiatry
GALLOWAY, A. C., Surgery, Cardiothoracic Surgery
GARAY, S. M., Medicine, Pulmonary and Critical Care
GARDNER, E. P., Physiology and Neuroscience
GENIESER, N. B., Radiology
GEORGE, A. E., Radiology
GERONEMUS, R. G., Dermatology
GITTELMAN, M. I., Psychiatry
GLENN, J., Psychiatry
GLICKMAN, R. M., Medicine

GODSON, G. N., Biochemistry
GOLDBERG, E., Neurology
GOLDBERG, J. D., Environmental Medicine
GOLDBERGER, M., Psychiatry
GOLDFRANK, L. R., Medicine, Emergency Medicine, Surgery
GOLDRING, R. M., Medicine, Pulmonary and Critical Care
GOLDSTEIN, N., Psychiatry
GOLDSTEIN, S. R., Obstetrics and Gynaecology
GOLIMBU, C. N., Radiology
GOLIMBU, M. N., Urology
GOLOMB, F. M., Surgery, Surgical Oncology
GONEN, O., Radiology
GOODGOLD, A. L., Neurology, Radiology
GOPINATHAN, G., Neurology
GOUGE, T. H., Surgery
GRANT, A. D., Orthopaedic Surgery
GREBB, J. A., Psychiatry
GRECO, G. J., Ophthalmology
GREEN, M. R., Psychiatry
GREENE, J. B., Medicine
GREENSTEIN, V. C., Ophthalmology
GREGERSEN, P. K., Medicine, Rheumatology, Pathology
GRIECO, A. J., Medicine, General Medicine
GRIFO, J. A., Obstetrics and Gynaecology
GROSSI, E. A., Surgery, Cardiothoracic Surgery
GROSSMAN, R. I., Radiology, Neurosurgery, Neurology, and Physiology and Neuroscience
GROSSMAN, S., Psychiatry
GRUEN, P. H., Psychiatry
GUYER, D. R., Ophthalmology
HAGIN, R. A., Psychiatry
HAJDU, S. I., Pathology
HALPERIN, J. J., Neurology
HALPERT, E., Psychiatry
HARIN, A., Paediatrics
HARLAP, S., Obstetrics and Gynaecology
HARLEY, N. H., Environmental Medicine
HARPER, R. G., Paediatrics, Obstetrics and Gynaecology
HARRIS, H. W., Medicine, Pulmonary and Critical Care
HARRIS, M. N., Surgery, Surgical Oncology
HARRISON, R. M., Ophthalmology
HAZZI, C. G., Medicine
HEITLER, M. S., Paediatrics
HELPERN, J. A., Radiology, Psychiatry, Physiology and Neuroscience
HILLER, J. M., Psychiatry
HILLMAN, D. E., Physiology and Biophysics
HILZ, M. J., Neurology, Medicine
HIRSCH, C. S., Forensic Medicine, Pathology
HIRSCHHORN, R., Medicine, Genetics, Cell Biology, Paediatrics
HOFFMAN, I. R., Medicine
HOLZMAN, R. S., Medicine, Infectious Diseases and Immunology, Environmental Medicine
HOOD, R. M., Surgery
HORNBLASS, A., Ophthalmology
HOROWITZ, L., Medicine
HOROWITZ, M. H., Psychiatry
HORWITZ, S. T., Obstetrics and Gynaecology
HSU, L. Y.-F., Paediatrics, Obstetrics and Gynaecology
IOACHIM, H. L., Pathology
ISRAEL, J. S., Anaesthesiology
ITIL, T., Psychiatry
ITOH, M., Rehabilitation Medicine
JACOBS, A. J., Obstetrics and Gynaecology
JACOBS, D. R., Medicine
JACOBS, J. B., Otolaryngology
JACOBS, T. J., Psychiatry
JAFAR, J. J., Neurosurgery
JAFFE, W. L., Orthopaedic Surgery
JAHSS, M. H., Orthopaedic Surgery
JAVITT, D. C., Psychiatry
JAVITT, N. B., Medicine, Gastroenterology, Paediatrics

JELINEK, J. E., Dermatology
JELINEK, W. R., Biochemistry
JIMENEZ, A. C., Rehabilitation Medicine
JOHANSON, K.-E., Urology
JOHN, E. R., Psychiatry
JONAS, S., Neurology
JONG, A. Y., Psychiatry
JOYNER, A. L., Cell Biology, Physiology and Neuroscience
KAHN, E. I., Surgical Pathology, Clinical Paediatrics
KAHN, M. L., Cardiology
KALOGERAKIS, M. G., Psychiatry
KAMHOLZ, S. L., Medicine
KAMM, F. M., Medicine
KANOF, N. B., Dermatology
KANTOR, T. G., Medicine
KAPLAN, L. A., Pathology
KAPLAN, M. H., Medicine, Infectious Diseases and Immunology
KAPLAN, S. J., Clinical Psychiatry
KARPATKIN, M. H., Paediatrics
KARPATKIN, S., Medicine, Haematology
KATZ, J. L., Clinical Psychiatry
KATZ, L. A., Medicine, Nephrology
KATZ, S., Medicine
KATZ, S. E., Psychiatry
KEEGAN, A. F., Radiology
KEILL, S. L., Psychiatry
KELLY, P. J., Neurosurgery
KENAN, S., Orthopaedic Surgery
KENNEDY, J. T., Medicine
KERMANI, E. J., Psychiatry
KESSLER, R. E., Surgery
KHATAMEE, M. A., Obstetrics and Gynaecology
KING, S. A., Psychiatry
KITTREDGE, R. D., Radiology
KLEIN, H. L., Biochemistry, Medicine
KLEIN, I. L., Medicine, Endocrinology, Cell Biology
KLEIN, R. G., Psychiatry
KLEINBERG, D. L., Medicine, Endocrinology
KOCHEN, J. A., Paediatrics
KOHAN, S. L., Obstetrics and Gynaecology
KOLODNY, E. H., Neurology
KOMISAR, A., Otolaryngology
KOPF, A. W., Dermatology
KOPLEWICZ, H. S., Child and Adolescent Psychiatry, Clinical Paediatrics
KORELITZ, B. I., Medicine
KOVAL, K. J., Orthopaedic Surgery
KOZ, G., Psychiatry
KRAMER, E. L., Radiology
KRAMER, F. R., Microbiology
KRAMER, M., Psychiatry
KRASINSKI, K. M., Paediatrics, Environmental Medicine
KRASNER, R. C. J., Medicine
KREIBICH, G., Cell Biology
KREIS, W., Medicine, Oncology
KREY, L. C., Obstetrics and Gynaecology, Cell Biology
KRONZON, I., Medicine, Cardiology
KUHNS, T. R., Ophthalmology
KUMMER, F., Orthopaedic Surgery
KUPERSMITH, M. J., Neurology, Ophthalmology
KUSCHNER, M., Pathology, Environmental Medicine
LAJTHA, A. L., Psychiatry
LANE, M. E., Rehabilitation Medicine
LANYI, V. F., Rehabilitation Medicine
LASKA, E. M., Psychiatry
LASKIN, M., Psychiatry
LAVKER, R. M., Dermatology
LEE, M. H. M., Rehabilitation Medicine
LEE-HUANG, S., Biochemistry
LEGGIADRO, R. J., Paediatrics
LEHMAN, W. B., Orthopaedic Surgery
LEHMANN, R., Cell Biology
LEHNEIS, H. R., Rehabilitation Medicine
LEITMAN, B. S., Radiology
LEPOR, H., Urology, Pharmacology
LESSER, G. T., Medicine
LEVIN, R. I., Medicine, Cardiology

LEVINE, B. B., Medicine, Infectious Diseases and Immunology
LEVINE, D. N., Neurology
LEVINE, I. S., Psychiatry
LEVITZ, M., Obstetrics and Gynaecology
LEVY, D. E., Molecular Pathology
LEW, A., Psychiatry
LEWIS, D. O., Psychiatry
LIFSHITZ, K., Psychiatry
LIFSHITZ, M. S., Pathology
LILLESKOV, R. K., Psychiatry
LINDENMAYER, J.-P., Psychiatry
LIPKIN, G., Dermatology
LIPKIN, M., Jr, Medicine, Primary Care
LIPPMANN, M., Environmental Medicine
LISMAN, R., Ophthalmology
LITTMAN, D. R., Molecular Immunology, Pathology and Microbiology
LLINAS, R., Physiology and Neuroscience
LOCKWOOD, C. J., Obstetrics and Gynaecology
LOFTUS, T. A., Psychiatry
LOVECCHIO, J. L., Obstetrics and Gynaecology
LOWENSTEIN, J., Medicine, Nephrology
LUNTZ, M. H., Ophthalmology
LUSSKIN, R., Orthopaedic Surgery
LYNFIELD, J., Paediatrics
MA, D. M., Rehabilitation Medicine
MCCARTHY, J. G., Plastic Surgery
MAGRAMM, I., Ophthalmology
MAHONEY, C. J., Forensic Medicine
MALACH, M., Medicine
MANGER, W. M., Medicine
MANGIARDI, J. R., Neurosurgery
MANHEIMER, E. D., Medicine
MANNUZZA, S., Psychiatry
MARCOS, L. R., Psychiatry
MARGOLIS, R. U., Pharmacology
MARGOULEFF, D., Medicine, Nuclear Medicine
MARKOWITZ, J. F., Paediatrics
MARMOR, M., Environmental Medicine, Medicine, Pulmonary and Critical Care
MARSHALL, C. H., Radiology
MAS, F. G., Psychiatry
MASDEU, J. C., Neurology
MATTSSON, A., Psychiatry
MEGIBOW, A. J., Radiology
MEHL, S. J., Medicine
MEISELAS, L. E., Medicine, General Medicine
MEISLIN, A. G., Paediatrics
MERLINO, J. P., Psychiatry
MERUELO, D., Pathology
MESSITE, J., Environmental Medicine
MEYERSON, A. T., Psychiatry
MICHELIS, M. F., Medicine
MILANO, A. M., Medicine
MINDICH, L., Microbiology
MINUCHIN, P. P., Psychiatry
MINUCHIN, S., Psychiatry
MITNICK, H. J., Medicine
MONTEAGUDO, A., Obstetrics and Gynaecology
MORALES, P. A., Urology
MOSCATELLI, D. A., Cell Biology
MOSES, J. W., Medicine
MOSKOWITZ, P. K., Internal Medicine
MUGGIA, F. M., Oncology
NACHTIGALL, L. E., Obstetrics and Gynaecology
NACHTIGALL, R. H., Medicine
NAFTCHI, N. E., Rehabilitation Medicine
NAIDICH, D. P., Radiology
NAIDICH, J. B., Radiology
NARINS, R. S., Dermatology
NASS, R. D., Neurology
NEOPHYTIDES, A. N., Neurology
NEUBAUER, P. B., Psychiatry
NEWMAN, D., Psychiatry
NEZIROGLU, F. A., Psychiatry
NICHOLSON, C., Physiology and Neuroscience
NIXON, R. A., Psychiatry, Cell Biology

NORDIN, M., Orthopaedic Surgery, Environmental Medicine
NOVICK, R. P., Microbiology, Medicine, Pulmonary and Critical Care
NOZ, M. E., Radiology
NUSSENZWEIG, R. S., Medical and Molecular Parasitology
NUSSENZWEIG, V., Pathology
OBSTBAUM, S. A., Ophthalmology
O'HARE, D. B., Paediatrics
OLIVA-LOPEZ, E., Environmental Medicine
OPLER, L. A., Psychiatry
ORENTREICH, N., Dermatology
ORGEL, S., Psychiatry
ORLOW, S. J., Paediatric Dermatology
ORRIS, L., Environmental Medicine
ORT, P. J., Orthopaedic Surgery
OSTRER, H., Paediatrics, Pathology, Medicine
OVARY, Z., Pathology
PACHTER, H. L., Surgery
PACKER, S., Ophthalmology
PAHWA, S., Paediatrics
PANKOVICH, A. M., Orthopaedic Surgery
PAPERNIK, D. S., Psychiatry
PARISIEN, J. S., Orthopaedic Surgery
PARKS, W. P., Paediatrics, Microbiology
PASTERNACK, B. S., Environmental Medicine
PEARSON, J., Pathology
PELCOVITZ, D., Psychiatry
PELLICER, A. G., Pathology
PEPPER, B., Psychiatry
PERRY, R. I., Psychiatry
PESELOW, E. D., Psychiatry
PHILLIPS, R. A., Medicine
PHILLIPS-QUAGLIATA, J. M., Pathology
PINE, D. S., Psychiatry
PINTER, A., Microbiology
PLAINE, L., Urology
POMARA, N., Psychiatry
PORGES, R. F., Obstetrics and Gynaecology
PORTNOW, S. L., Psychiatry
POSNER, M. A., Orthopaedic Surgery
POST, R. C., Obstetrics and Gynaecology
POTMESIL, M., Radiology
POTTASH, A. C., Psychiatry
PRINCE, A. M., Pathology
QUARTERMAIN, D., Neurology, Physiology and Neuroscience
RACKOW, E., Medicine, Cardiology
RAFII, M., Radiology
RAICHT, R. F., Medicine, Gastroenterology
RAMSAY, D. L., Clinical Dermatology
RAUSEN, A. R., Paediatrics
RAYNOR, R. B., Neurosurgery
REEM, G. H., Pharmacology
REES, T. D., Surgery, Plastic and Reconstructive Surgery
REICH, T., Experimental Surgery
REISBERG, B., Psychiatry
RICHARDSON, M. A., Psychiatry
RIFKIN, D. B., Medicine and Cell Biology
RIGEL, D. S., Dermatology
RILES, T. S., Surgery
ROBBINS, E. S., Psychiatry
ROBBINS, H., Orthopaedic Surgery
ROBINS, P., Dermatology
ROGERS, B. O., Surgery
ROM, W. N., Jr, Medicine and Environmental Medicine
RON, D., Medicine, Endocrinology
ROSENBERG, Z. S., Radiology
ROSENBLUTH, J., Physiology and Neuroscience
ROSENFELD, D. L., Obstetrics and Gynaecology
ROSES, D. F., Surgery
ROSNER, R., Psychiatry
ROSSMAN, T. G., Environmental Medicine
ROTHSTEIN, A. A., Psychiatry
ROTROSEN, J. P., Psychiatry
ROUBIN, G. S., Medicine
ROVIT, R. L., Neurosurgery
ROWAN, R. L., Urology
ROY, A., Psychiatry

RUBERMAN, W., Environmental Medicine
RUBIN, S. E., Ophthalmology
RUDY, B., Physiology and Neuroscience, Biochemistry
RUOFF, M., Medicine
SABATINI, D. D., Cell Biology
SADOCK, B. J., Psychiatry
SADOCK, V. A., Psychiatry
SALZER, J. L., Neurology, Cell Biology
SAMUELS, H. H., Pharmacology and Medicine
SARNO, J. E., Jr, Rehabilitation Medicine
SARNO, M. T., Rehabilitation Medicine
SAXE, D. H., Surgery
SCHACHNE, L., Ophthalmology
SCHACHT, R. G., Paediatrics
SCHARFMAN, M. A., Psychiatry
SCHERR, L., Medicine, General Medicine
SCHLOSSMAN, A., Ophthalmology
SCHMIDT-SAROSI, C. L., Obstetrics and Gynaecology
SCHNEIDER, R. J., Microbiology
SCHOENFELD, M., Psychiatry
SCHREIBER, S. S., Clinical Medicine
SCHWARTZ, S., Medicine
SEDLIS, E., Paediatrics
SEIPLE, W. H., Ophthalmology
SHAPIRO, E., Urology
SHAW, L. N., Psychiatry
SHENGOLD, L. L., Psychiatry
SHORE, R. E., Environmental Medicine
SHUPACK, J. L., Dermatology
SIDTIS, J. J., Psychiatry
SIEGEL, C., Psychiatry
SIEGEL, I. M., Experimental Ophthalmology
SILBER, A., Psychiatry
SILVER, J., Medicine, Molecular Medicine, Pathology
SILVER, J. M., Psychiatry
SILVERBERG, M., Paediatrics
SILVERMAN, M. A., Psychiatry
SIMMS, H. H., Surgery
SIMON, E. J., Psychiatry, Pharmacology
SIMPSON, J. I., Physiology and Neuroscience
SINGER, M. H., Psychiatry
SKOLNICK, P., Psychiatry
SLABY, A. E., Psychiatry
SLAKTER, J. S., Ophthalmology
SLIPP, S., Psychiatry
SMALL, A. M., Psychiatry
SMITH, B. F., Ophthalmology
SMITH, I., Microbiology
SMITH, R. C., Psychiatry
SNYDER, C. A., Environmental Medicine
SOBERMAN, R. J., Medicine, Nephrology
SOLOMON, J. J., Environmental Medicine
SOLOWEY, A. C., Surgery
SOTER, N. A., Dermatology
SPATZ, M., Urology
SPEISER, P. W., Clinical Paediatrics
SPENCER, F. C., Surgery
SPEYER, J. L., Medicine, Oncology
SPITZER, M., Clinical Obstetrics and Gynaecology
SPRITZ, N., Medicine, Endocrinology
STEIGBIGEL, N. H., Medicine
STEINETZ, B. G., Environmental Medicine
STENSON, S. M., Ophthalmology
STERN, A., Pharmacology
STONE, E. A., Psychiatry
STONE, S. M., Paediatrics
SUGIMORI, M., Physiology and Neuroscience
SUN, T.-T., Dermatology
SUNSHINE, A., Medicine
SUSSMAN, N., Psychiatry
SVERDLIK, S. S., Rehabilitation Medicine
TAINTOR, Z. C., Psychiatry
TANCREDI, L. R., Psychiatry
TANG, M.-S., Environmental Medicine, Pathology Medicine
TAPPER, M. L., Medicine
TEEBOR, G. W., Pathology, Environmental Medicine

TESSLER, A. N., Urology
TESTA, N. N., Orthopaedic Surgery
THOMAS, A., Psychiatry
TICE, D. A., Surgery
TIMOR, I. E., Obstetrics and Gynaecology
TOBIAS, H., Medicine
TOLK, C. S., Psychiatry
TOMATIS, L., Environmental Medicine
TONIOLO, P. G., Environmental Medicine, Obstetrics and Gynaecology
TRUJILLO, M., Psychiatry
TUCHMAN, M., Medicine
TUNICK, P. A., Medicine, Cardiology
TZIMAS, N. A., Orthopaedic Surgery
VADASZ, C., Psychiatry
VALENTINE, F. T., Medicine, Infectious Diseases and Immunology
VANDERBERG, J. P., Medical and Molecular Parasitology
VAZQUEZ, C. I., Psychiatry
VILCEK, J. T., Microbiology
VINCIGUERRA, V. P., Medicine, Oncology
VOGEL, S. A., Psychiatry
VOLAVKA, J., Psychiatry
VORONTSOV, M. A., Physiology and Neuroscience
WAISMAN, J., Pathology
WALKER, P. S., Orthopaedic Surgery
WALLACH, R. C., Obstetrics and Gynaecology
WALLACH, S., Medicine
WALTZMAN, S. B., Otolaryngology
WAN, L. S., Obstetrics and Gynaecology
WANG, B. C., Anaesthesiology
WAPNIR, R. A., Paediatrics, Biochemistry
WARNER, R. S., Urology
WARSHAW, L. J., Environmental Medicine
WEINBERG, H. J., Neurology
WEINBERG, S., Dermatology
WEINSTEIN, H. C., Psychiatry
WEISSMANN, G., Medicine, Rheumatology
WELSH, H. K., Psychiatry
WEST, A. B., Pathology
WIKLER, N. S., Clinical Medicine
WILKES, B. M., Medicine, Nephrology
WISHNICK, M. M., Paediatrics
WITKOVSKY, P., Experimental Ophthalmology, Physiology and Neuroscience
WOLFF, B. B., Psychiatry
YANNUZZI, L. A., Ophthalmology
YARYURA-TOBIAS, J. A., Psychiatry
YOUNG, B. K., Obstetrics and Gynaecology
YOUNG, L. Y., Environmental Medicine
YUVIENCO, F. P., Urology
ZAVALA, F., Medical and Molecular Parasitology
ZELIKOVSKY, G., Urology
ZIDE, B. M., Surgery, Plastic and Reconstructive Surgery
ZIFF, E. B., Biochemistry
ZIMMON, D. S., Medicine, Gastroenterology
ZOLLA-PAZNER, S. B., Pathology
ZUCKER-FRANKLIN, D., Medicine, Haematology
ZUCKERMAN, J. D., Orthopaedic Surgery

Silver School of Social Work (One Washington Sq. N, New York, NY 10003-6654; tel. (212) 998-5910; fax (212) 995-4171; e-mail ssw.admissions@nyu.edu; internet www.nyu.edu/socialwork):

ANASTAS, J. W.
DANE, B.
ENGLAND, S.
FESTINGER, T. B.
GOLDSTEIN, E. G.
HOLDEN, G.
LANDSBERG, G.
MEENAGHAN, T. M.
MILLS, L. G.
MISHNE, J.
PADGETT, D.
SEINFELD, J.
STRAUSSNER, S. L.

Steinhardt School of Culture, Education and Human Development (82 Washington Sq. E, New York, NY 10003; tel. (212) 998-5030; internet www.nyu.edu/education):

CAROTHERS, S. C., Teaching and Learning
KOVNER, C., Nursing
McCLOWRY, S., Nursing
MAYHER, J. S., English Education
MILLER, M. C., Culture and Communication
NORMAN, E., Nursing
RICHARDSON, R., Higher Education
STAGE, F., Higher Education

Tisch School of the Arts (721 Broadway, 12th Fl., New York, NY 10003; tel. (212) 998-1800; internet www.nyu.edu/tisch):

CAMPBELL, M. S., Art and Public Policy
CANEMAKER, J., Film and Television
COOPER, P., Film and Television
DANCYGER, K., Film and Television
FROST, E. C., Film, Television and Radio
JENKIN, L., Dramatic Writing
KIMBRELL, M. A., Acting and Directing Studies
KIRSHENBLATT-GIMBLETT, B., Performance Studies
MARTIN, R., Art and Public Policy
MICHELSON, A., Cinema Studies
MILLER, T., Cinema Studies
NEIPRIS, J., Dramatic Writing
SCHECHNER, R., Performance Studies
SHOHAT, E., Art and Public Policy
SKLAR, R., Cinema Studies
SMITH, A. D., Performance Studies
STAM, R., Cinema Studies
STONEY, G. C., Film
TAYLOR, D., Performance Studies
WILLIS, D., Photography and Imaging

NIAGARA UNIVERSITY

NY 14109

Telephone: (716) 285-1212
Fax: (716) 286-8349
Internet: www.niagara.edu

Founded 1856 as College and Seminary of Our Lady of Angels
Private control

Pres.: Rev. JOSEPH L. LEVESQUE
Exec. Vice-Pres.: Dr BONNIE ROSE
Vice-Pres. for Academic Affairs: Dr TIMOTHY M. DOWNS
Vice-Pres. for Admin. Affairs: MICHAEL S. JASZKA
Vice-Pres. for Institutional Advancement: DONALD P. BIELECKI
Vice-Pres. for Student Life: Dr KEVIN HEARN
Dean for Admissions and Records: GEORGE C. PACHTER
Dir for Libraries: DAVID SCHOEN

Library of 279,793 vols
Number of teachers: 650 (130 full-time)
Number of students: 4,250 (3,300 undergraduate, 950 graduate)

Publications: *Aquila Literary Journal*, *Eagle* (4 a year, online (www.eagleonline.niagara.edu)), *Niagaran* (1 a year)

DEANS

College of Arts and Sciences: Dr NANCY E. McGLEN
College of Business Administration: Dr TEN-PAO LEE
College of Education: Dr DEBRA COLLEY
College of Hospitality and Tourism Management: Dr GARY D. PRATZEL

NYACK COLLEGE

One S Blvd, Nyack, NY 10960-3698
Telephone: (845) 358-1710
Fax: (845) 358-1751
E-mail: admissions@nyack.edu
Internet: www.nyack.edu

Founded 1882, fmrly Missionary Training Institute, present name 1972
Private control
Academic year: September to May
Campuses in New York city, New York, Washington, DC, and in Puerto Rico
Pres.: Dr MICHAEL G. SCALES
Provost and Vice-Pres. for Academic Affairs: Dr DAVID F. TURK
Exec. Vice-Pres. and Treas.: Dr DAVID C. JENNINGS
Vice-Pres. for Advancement: JEFFREY G. CORY
Vice-Pres. for Enrolment and Marketing: Dr ANDREA M. HENNESSY
Registrar: SUE HO
Dean for Library Services: LINDA POSTON
Library of 133,000 vols
Number of teachers: 305 (109 full-time, 196 adjunct)
Number of students: 3,263 (2040 undergraduate, 492 graduate, 731 Alliance Theological Seminary)

DEANS

Alliance Theological Seminary: Dr RONALD WALBORN
College of Arts and Sciences: Dr FERNANDO ARZOLA, JR
School of Business and Leadership: Dr ANITA UNDERWOOD
School of Education: Dr JoANN LOONEY
School of Music: Dr GLENN KOPONEN

PACE UNIVERSITY

One Pace Plaza, New York, NY 10038
Telephone: (866) 722-3338
E-mail: infoctr@pace.edu
Internet: www.pace.edu
Founded 1906
Private control
3 Campuses in New York City, Westchester and White Plains
Pres.: STEPHEN J. FRIEDMAN
Provost and Exec. Vice-Pres. for Academic Affairs: Dr HARRIET FELDMAN
Exec.Vice-Pres., Chief Financial Officer and Treas.: TOBY WINER
Vice-Pres. for Devt and Alumni Relations: JENNIFER BERNSTEIN
Vice-Pres. for Enrolment and Placement: ROBINA C. SCHEPP
Vice-Pres. for Information Technology: THOMAS A. HULL
Vice-Pres. for Univ Relations: MARIE J. TOULANTIS
Univ. Counsel: STEPHEN BRODSKY
Univ. Registrar: STEVEN L. JOHNSON
Univ. Librarian: WILLIAM J. MURDOCK (acting)
Library of 938,158 vols, 5,100 periodicals
Number of teachers: 1,200
Number of students: 12,704 (7,807 undergraduate, 4,042 graduate, 855 law graduate)

DEANS

College of Health Professions: Dr GERALDINE COLOMBRARO
Dyson College of Arts and Sciences: Dr NIRA HERRMANN
Lubin School of Business: NEIL S. BRAUN
School of Education: Dr ANDREA SPENCER
School of Law: Dr MICHELLE S. SIMON
Seidenberg School of Computer Science and Information Systems: Dr CONSTANCE A. KNAPP

PAUL SMITH'S COLLEGE

POB 265, Route 86 and 30, Paul Smiths, NY 12970-0265
Telephone: (518) 327-6227

Fax: (518) 327-6016
E-mail: admissions@paulsmiths.edu
Internet: www.paulsmiths.edu
Private control
Academic year: May to June
Pres.: Dr JOHN W. MILLS
Provost: Dr RICHARD NELSON
Vice-Pres. for Business and Finance: ANN MARIE SOMMA
Vice-Pres. for Enrolment Management: ERIC FELVER
Vice-Pres. for Information Systems: JAMES BUYEA
Vice-Pres. for Institutional Advancement: F. RAYMOND AGNEW
Registrar: Dr LORALYN TAYLOR
Dir for Educational Resources: NEIL SURPRENANT

DEANS

Division of Hospitality Resort and Culinary Management: ERNIE WILSON
Division of Forestry, Natural Resources and Recreation: Dr JEFFREY T. WALTON
Division of Science, Liberal Arts and Business: Dr PHILIP TAYLOR

PLAZA COLLEGE

74–09 37th Ave, Jackson Heights, NY 11372
Telephone: (718) 779-1430
E-mail: info@plazacollege.edu
Internet: www.plazacollege.edu
Founded 1916
Private control
Bachelor's in management and patient information management
Pres. and Provost: CHARLES E. CALLAHAN
Vice-Pres. for Financial Services: ELIZABETH K. CALLAHAN
Dean for Academic Affairs: MARIE DOLLA
Dean for Admin.: ROSE ANN BLACK
Dir for Library and Learning Resource Centre: KATHLEEN D'APRIX.

POLYTECHNIC INSTITUTE OF NEW YORK UNIVERSITY

Six MetroTech Center, Brooklyn, NY 11201
Telephone: (718) 260-3600
Fax: (718) 260-3136
E-mail: uadmit@poly.edu
Internet: www.poly.edu
Founded 1854 as Brooklyn Collegiate and Polytechnic Institute, fmrly Polytechnic Univ., present name and status 2008
Academic year: September to May
Campuses at Long Island, Manhattan and Westchester
Pres.: JERRY MACARTHUR HULTIN
Provost: Dr KATEPALLI SREENIVASAN
Vice-Pres.: BARBARA NOSEWORTHY
Vice-Pres. for Academic Affairs: Dr RICHARD S. THORSEN
Vice-Pres. for Finance and Business Affairs: DENNIS D. DINTINO
Vice-Pres. for Strategic Initiatives and Chief of Staff: ELIZABETH LUSSKIN
Dean for Admissions: JOY COLELLI
Dean for Student Affairs: ANITA FARRINGTON
Dir for Library Services: JANA STEVENS-RICHMAN
Number of teachers: 142 (full-time)
Number of students: 3,983
Publication: Cable.

PRATT INSTITUTE

200 Willoughby Ave, Brooklyn, NY 11205
Telephone: (718) 636-3600
Fax: (718) 636-3785
E-mail: info@pratt.edu
Internet: www.pratt.edu

Founded 1887
Academic year: August to May
Campuses in Brooklyn and Manhattan
Pres.: Dr THOMAS F. SCHUTTE
Provost: PETER BARNA
Vice-Pres. for Finance and Admin.: EDMUND RUTKOWSKI
Vice-Pres. for Institutional Advancement: TODD GALITZ
Vice-Pres. for Student Life: Dr HELEN MATUSOUR-AYRES
Registrar: LISLE HENDERSON
Dir for Libraries: RUSS ABELL
Library of 200,000 vols, incl. 600 periodicals, rare books and the college archives
Number of teachers: 1,000
Number of students: 4,733 (3,008 undergraduate, 1,725 graduate)
Publication: Prattfolio (2 a year)

DEANS

School of Architecture: TOM HANRAHAN
School of Art and Design: Dr CONCETTA M. STEWART
School of Information and Library Science: Dr TULA GIANNINI
School of Liberal Arts and Sciences: Dr ANDREW W. BARNES

RENSSELAER POLYTECHNIC INSTITUTE

110 Eighth St, Troy, NY 12180-3590
Telephone: (518) 276-6000
Fax: (518) 276-6003
E-mail: admissions@rpi.edu
Internet: www.rpi.edu
Founded 1824
Pres.: Dr SHIRLEY ANN JACKSON
Provost: PRABHAT HAJELA
Vice-Pres.: JOHN MINASIAN
Vice-Pres. for Admin.: CLAUDE ROUNDS
Vice-Pres. for Enrolment and Dean for Undergraduate and Graduate Admissions: PAUL MARTHERS
Vice-Pres. for Finance and Chief Financial Officer: VIRGINIA GREGG
Vice-Pres. for Human Resources: CURTIS POWELL
Vice-Pres. for Information Services and Technology and Chief Information Officer: JOHN KOLB
Vice-Pres. for Institute Advancement: BRENDA WILSON-HALE
Vice-Pres. for Student Life: TIMOTHY E. SAMS
Vice-Pres. for Strategic Communications and External Relations: WILLIAM WALKER
Registrar: SHARON KUNKEL
Dir for Libraries: BOB MAYO
Library of 475,000 vols, 3,117 periodicals, 100,000 slides
Number of teachers: 482 (377 full-time, 105 part-time)
Number of students: 6,914 (5,240 undergraduate, 1,184 graduate)

DEANS

Lally School of Management and Technology: THOMAS BEGLEY
School of Architecture: EVAN DOUGLIS
School of Engineering: DAVID ROSOWSKY (acting)
School of Humanities, Arts and Social Sciences: MARY SIMONI
School of Science: LAURIE LESHIN

ROBERTS WESLEYAN COLLEGE

2301 Westside Dr., Rochester, NY 14624-1997
Telephone: (585) 594-6000
Fax: (585) 594-6371
E-mail: admissions2@roberts.edu
Internet: www.roberts.edu

Founded 1866
Private control
Academic year: September to May
Liberal arts college; incl. Northeastern Seminary
Pres.: JOHN A. MARTIN
Provost and Sr Vice-Pres.: ROBERT ZWIER
Sr Vice-Pres. for Advancement and External Relations: JACK CONNELL
Sr Vice-Pres. and Treas.: JAMES E. CUTHBERT
Vice-Pres. for Academic and Student Support: NELSON W. HILL
Vice-Pres. for Admin.: RUTH LOGAN
Vice-Pres. for Admissions and Marketing: LINDA KURTZ
Registrar: LESA KOHR
Dir for Student Financial Services: STEPHEN FIELD
Dir for Library Services: AL KROBER
Library of 137,679 vols, 111,232 titles, 3,500 journals, 124,240 books
Number of teachers: 76
Number of students: 1,928
Publication: *Roberts Today* (4 a year)

DEANS

School of Liberal Arts and Sciences: JULIA GRIMM
School of Professional Studies: DAVID BASINGER

ROCHESTER INSTITUTE OF TECHNOLOGY

One Lomb Memorial Dr., Rochester, NY 14623-5603
Telephone: (585) 475-2411
E-mail: admissions@rit.edu
Internet: www.rit.edu
Founded 1829 as the Rochester Athenaeum
Private control
Pres.: Dr WILLIAM W. DESTLER
Provost and Sr Vice-Pres. for Academic Affairs: Dr JEREMY HAEFNER
Sr Vice-Pres. for Enrolment Management and Career Services: JAMES MILLER
Sr Vice-Pres. for Finance and Admin.: Dr JAMES H. WATTERS
Sr Vice-Pres. for Student Affairs: Dr MARY-BETH COOPER
Vice-Pres. for Devt and Alumni Relations: LISA CAUDA
Vice-Pres. for Govt and Community Relations: DEBORAH STENDARDI
Vice-Pres. for Research and Assoc. Provost: Dr RYNE RAFFAELLE
Vice-Pres. for Strategic Planning and Spec. Initiatives: KIT MAYBERRY
Dir of RIT Libraries: SHIRLEY BOWER
Library of 498,000 vols, 45,000 e-books, 30,000 e-journals, and 11,000 audio, film and video titles
Number of teachers: 1,533 (1,021 full-time, 16 part-time, 496 adjunct)
Number of students: 17,652 (14,753 undergraduate, 2,899 graduate)
Publication: *The University Magazine* (3 a year)

DEANS

B. Thomas Golisano College of Computing and Information Sciences: Dr ANDREW L. SEARS
College of Applied Science and Technology: Dr H. FRED WALKER
College of Health Sciences and Technology: Dr DANIEL B. ORNT
College of Imaging Arts and Sciences: LORRAINE JUSTICE
College of Liberal Arts: JAMES J. WINEBRAKE
College of Science: Dr SOPHIA MAGGELAKIS
E. Philip Saunders College of Business: Dr ASHOK RAO

Kate Gleason College of Engineering: Dr HARVEY PALMER
National Technical Institute for the Deaf: Dr GERAD BUCKLEY

ROCKEFELLER UNIVERSITY

1230 York Ave, New York, NY 10065
Telephone: (212) 327-8000
Fax: (212) 327-7974
E-mail: pubinfo@rockefeller.edu
Internet: www.rockefeller.edu
Founded 1901 as Rockefeller Institute for Medical Research, present status 1954, present name 1965
Centre for research and graduate education in biomedical sciences, chemistry, bioinformatics and physics; 73 laboratories
Pres.: MARC TESSIER-LAVIGNE
Vice-Pres. for Academic Affairs: MICHAEL W. YOUNG
Vice-Pres. for Devt: MAREN E. IMHOFF
Vice-Pres. for Educational Affairs and Dean: SIDNEY STRICKLAND
Vice-Pres. for Finance and Treas.: JAMES H. LAPPLE
Vice-Pres. for Human Resources: VIRGINIA HUFFMAN
Vice-Pres. for Medical Affairs: BARRY S. COLLER
Vice-Pres. for Scientific and Facility Operations: JOHN TOOZE
Vice-Pres. and Chief Investment Officer: AMY C. FALLS
Vice-Pres. and Gen. Counsel: HARRIET RABB
Corporate Sec.: JANE RENDALL (acting)
Librarian: CAROL A. FELTES
Library of 230,000 vols
Number of teachers: 250
Number of students: 545 (350 post-doctoral research, 170 doctoral, 25 MD–PhD)
Publications: *Journal of Cell Biology* (12 a year), *Journal of Clinical Investigation* (12 a year), *Journal of Experimental Medicine* (12 a year), *Journal of General Physiology* (12 a year).

SAGE COLLEGES

65 First St, Troy, NY 12180
Telephone: (518) 244-2000
Fax: (518) 244-6880
Internet: www.sage.edu
Founded 1916
Private control
Academic year: May to May
Pres.: Dr SUSAN C. SCRIMSHAW
Vice-Pres. for Academic Affairs: Dr SALLY A. LAWRENCE
Vice-Pres. for Finance and Admin.: WILLIAM BECKMAN
Vice-Pres. for Marketing and Enrolment Management: DAN LUNDQUIST
Dir for Libraries: LISA BRAINARD
Library of 200,000 vols, 60,000 vols of bound periodicals, 30,000 media items
Number of teachers: 160 (full-time)
Number of students: 3,000 (full-time)
Publications: *Connections*, *Crossroads*

DEANS

Russell Sage College: Dr SHARON P. ROBINSON
Sage College of Albany: Dr SAROLTA TAKACS
Esteves School of Education: Dr LORI QUIGLEY
Sage Graduate School of Health Sciences: ESTHER HASKVITZ
Sage Graduate School of Management: Dr DAN ROBESON

ST BONAVENTURE UNIVERSITY

3261 W State Rd, St Bonaventure, NY 14778
Telephone: (716) 375-2000
Fax: (716) 375-2005
Internet: www.sbu.edu
Founded 1855 as St Bonaventure's College, present name 1950
Academic year: August to June
Pres.: Sr MARGARET CARNEY
Provost and Vice-Pres. for Academic Affairs: Dr MICHAEL J. FISCHER
Vice-Provost for Student Life: RICHARD TRIETLEY, JR
Sr Vice-Pres. for Finance and Admin.: BRENDA L. McGEE
Vice-Pres. for Univ. Advancement: MARY DRISCOLL
Vice-Pres. for Univ. Relations: Dr EMILY F. SINSABAUGH
Registrar: HEATHER L. JACKSON
Dir for Library: PAUL J. SPAETH
Library of 325,000 vols, 11,500 reference titles, over 35,000 e-serials
Number of teachers: 160
Number of students: 2,017 (1,967 undergraduate)
Publications: *Bonadieu* (1 a year), *Bonaventure*, *Cithara* (2 a year), *Cord* (4 a year), *Laurel* (2 a year), *The Works of William of Ockham*

DEANS

School of Arts and Sciences: Dr WOLFGANG NATTER
School of Business: Dr CAROL M. FISCHER
School of Education: Dr JOSEPH E. ZIMMER
School of Franciscan Studies: Bro. F. EDWARD COUGHLIN
School of Graduate Studies: Dr PEGGY YEHL BURKE
School of Journalism and Mass Communication: Dr PAULINE HOFFMANN

ST FRANCIS COLLEGE

180 Remsen St, Brooklyn Heights, NY 11201
Telephone: (718) 522-2300
Internet: www.stfranciscollege.edu
Founded 1859 as St Francis Acad., present name and status 1884
Private control
Academic year: September to August
Graduate programmes in accounting and project management
Pres.: BRENDAN J. DUGAN
Exec. Vice-Pres.: JUNE McGRISKEN
Provost and Vice-Pres. for Academic Affairs: Dr TIMOTHY HOULIHAN
Vice-Pres. for Devt: THOMAS FLOOD
Dean for Students: Dr CHERYL HOWELL
Dir for Library Services: JAMES P. SMITH
Registrar: ROXANNE PERSAUD
Library of 177,000 vols
Number of teachers: 155
Number of students: 2,500
Publications: *Arthur Miller Journal* (2 a year), *ASEBL Journal*, *Assisi* (online).

ST JOHN FISHER COLLEGE

3690 E Ave, Rochester, NY 14618
Telephone: (585) 385-8000
Fax: (585) 385-8386
E-mail: admissions@sjfc.edu
Internet: www.sjfc.edu
Founded 1948
Private control
Academic year: September to June
Pres.: Dr DONALD E. BAIN
Provost and Dean: Dr RONALD J. AMBROSETTI
Sr Vice-Pres. for Enrolment Management and Planning: Dr GERARD J. ROONEY

Vice-Pres. for Finance and Business: Dr THOMAS E. O'NEIL
Vice-Pres. for Institutional Advancement: Dr WILLIAM J. O'CONNOR
Vice-Pres. for Student Affairs and Diversity Initiatives: Dr RICHARD DEJESÚS-RUEFF
Registrar: JULIE THOMAS
Dir for Library: MELISSA JADLOS
Library of 160,000 vols
Number of students: 3,100

DEANS

Bittner School of Business: Dr DAVID MARTIN
Ralph C. Wilson, Jr. School of Education: Dr WENDY PATERSON
School of Arts and Sciences: Dr DAVID PATE
Wegmans School of Nursing: Dr DIANNE COONEY MINER
Wegmans School of Pharmacy: Dr SCOTT A. SWIGART

ST JOHN'S UNIVERSITY

8000 Utopia Parkway, Queens, NY 11439
Telephone: (718) 990-2000
Fax: (718) 990-5723
E-mail: admhelp@stjohns.edu
Internet: www.stjohns.edu
Founded 1870, chartered 1871, re-chartered by Regents of the Univ. of the State of New York 1906
Private control
Academic year: September to May
Campuses at Queens, Staten Island, Manhattan and Oakdale in New York; global campuses at Rome in Italy and Paris in France
Pres.: Rev. DONALD J. HARRINGTON
Provost: Dr JULIA A. UPTON
Exec. Vice-Pres. for Mission and Student Services: Rev. JAMES J. MAHER
Sr Vice-Pres. and Chief of Staff: ROBERT D. WILE
Sr Vice-Pres. for Finance and Operations and Treas.: MARTHA HIRST
Sr Vice-Pres. for Human Resources and Strategic Planning: MARY T. HARPER HAGAN
Vice-Pres. and Sec. to the Univ.: Dr DOROTHY E. HABBEN
Vice-Pres. for Academic Support Services: Dr ANDRÉ MCKENZIE
Vice-Pres. for Community Relations: JOSEPH SCIAME
Vice-Pres. for Enrolment Management: BETH M. EVANS
Vice-Pres. for Institutional Research and Academic Planning: CLOVER HALL
Vice-Pres. for Int. Relations: Dr CECILIA CHANG
Vice-Pres. for Planning and Information Technology: Dr FRANK SIRIANNI
Vice-Pres. for Student Affairs: KATHRYN T. HUTCHINSON
Vice-Pres. for Univ. Min.: PAMELA SHEA-BYRNES
Gen. Counsel: JOSEPH E. OLIVA
Dean forf Libraries: Dr JAMES BENSON
Academic year: August to May
Library: 1.75m. vols
Number of teachers: 1,442
Number of students: 21,354 (15,720 undergraduate, 5,634 graduate)
Publications: *American Bankruptcy Institute Law Review* (2 a year), *Journal of Civil Rights and Economic Development* (4 a year), *St. John's Law Review* (4 a year), *New York International Law Review* (2 a year), *N.Y. Real Property Law Journal* (4 a year), *NY Litigator Law Journal* (irregular), *Professional Studies Review, Recipe, Res Gestae, St John's Today, St. John's Journal of International and Comparative Law* (online), *Sequoya Art and Literary Magazine, The Journal of Catholic Legal Studies, The Spectator, The Stormfront, The Torch, Vincentian Yearbook*

DEANS

College of Pharmacy and Allied Health Professions: ROBERT A. MANGIONE
College of Professional Studies: KATHLEEN VOUTÉ MACDONALD
Peter J. Tobin College of Business: Dr VICTORIA L. SHOAF
St John's College of Liberal Arts and Sciences: Dr JEFFERY FAGEN (acting)
School of Education: Dr JERROLD ROSS
School of Law: Prof. MICHAEL A. SIMONS

ST JOSEPH'S COLLEGE

245 Clinton Ave, Brooklyn, NY 11205
Telephone: (718) 940-5300
Internet: www.sjcny.edu
Founded 1916 as St Joseph's College for Women, present name 1970
Private control
Campuses in Brooklyn and Long Island
Pres.: Sis. ELIZABETH A. HILL
Provost: Sis. LORETTA MCGRANN
Vice-Pres. for Enrolment Management: THERESA LaROCCA-MEYER
Vice-Pres. for Institutional Advancement: NANCY CONNORS
Vice-Pres. for Planning: Dr THOMAS G TRAVIS
Chief Financial Officer: JOHN ROTH
Dean for Students: Dr SUSAN HUDEC
Dir for Library, Brooklyn: Dr WILLIAM MENG
Dir for Library, Long Island: TERRI CORBIN-HUTCHINSON
Library of 156,600 vols, 50,000 e-books and e-journals
Number of teachers: 640
Number of students: 5,837 (5,037 undergraduate, 800 graduate)

DEANS

School of Arts and Sciences (Brooklyn Campus): Dr RICHARD GREENWALD
School of Arts and Sciences (Long Island Campus): Dr CHRISTOPHER FROST
School of Professional and Graduate Studies: Dr THOMAS G. TRAVIS

SAINT JOSEPH'S SEMINARY, DUNWOODIE

201 Seminary Ave, Yonkers, NY 10704-1896
Telephone: (914) 968-6200
Fax: (914) 376-2019
E-mail: sjs@dunwoodie.edu
Internet: www.dunwoodie.edu
Founded 1896
Private control
Rector: Most Rev. GERALD T. WALSH
Academic Dean: Rev. KEVIN P. O'REILLY
Dean for Students and Admissions: Rev. ANDREW R. KING
Registrar: Sis. MARY FRANCES MILLS
Dir for Library Services: Sis. MONICA WOOD
Library of 103,000 vols, incl. 2,500 bound periodicals
Number of teachers: 22 (12 full-time, 10 part-time)

ST LAWRENCE UNIVERSITY

23 Romoda Dr., Canton, NY 13617
Telephone: (315) 229-5011
E-mail: admissions@stlawu.edu
Internet: www.stlawu.edu
Founded 1856
Private control
Academic year: August to May
Pres.: WILLIAM L. FOX

Vice-Pres. and Dean for Academic Affairs: VALERIE D. LEHR
Vice-Pres. and Dean for Admissions and Financial Aid: JEFFREY RICKEY
Vice-Pres. for Admin. Operations: THOMAS COAKLEY
Vice-Pres. for Communications: TOM EVELYN
Vice-Pres. for Finance and Treas.: KATHRYN L. MULLANEY
Vice-Pres. for Student Life: JOSEPH A. TOLLIVER
Vice-Pres. for Univ. Advancement: LAURA ELLIS
Sec.: ANGELA M. JOHNSTON
Registrar: CAROLYN FILIPPI
Librarian: MICHAEL ALZO BART HARLOE (acting)
Library: 1.5m. vols, incl. 417,000 govt documents, 1,900 print subscriptions, 597,000 microform units, over 6,100 videos
Number of teachers: 192 (171 full-time, 21 part-time)
Number of students: 2,457 (2,361 undergraduate, 96 graduate)
Publications: *Gridiron* (1 a year), *Laurentian* (1 a year), *St Lawrence Magazine* (4 a year).

ST THOMAS AQUINAS COLLEGE

125 Route 340, Sparkill, NY 10976
Telephone: (845) 398-4000
E-mail: admissions@stac.edu
Internet: www.stac.edu
Founded 1952
Private control
Academic year: August to May
Schools of arts and sciences, business, education
Pres.: Dr MARGARET MARY FITZPATRICK
Provost and Vice-Pres. for Academic Affairs: Dr L. JOHN DURNEY
Vice-Pres. for Admin. and Finance and Treas.: JOSEPH DONINI
Vice-Pres. for Enrolment Management and Campus Communications: VIN CRAPANZANO
Vice-Pres. for Institutional Advancement: KEVIN P. DUIGNAN
Vice-Pres. and Dean for Student Devt: Dr KIRK MANNING
Registrar: MILLIE ALEXIOU
Library Dir: (vacant)
Library of 95,000 vols, 420 magazines, newspapers, journals; 2,000 videos and DVDs
Number of students: 2,700

ST VLADIMIR'S ORTHODOX THEOLOGICAL SEMINARY

575 Scarsdale Rd, Yonkers, NY 10707-1699
Telephone: (914) 961-8313
Fax: (914) 961-4507
E-mail: info@svots.edu
Internet: www.svots.edu
Founded 1938
Private control
Academic year: August to May
Chancellor: Rev. Dr CHAD HATFIELD
Dean: Rev. Dr JOHN BEHR
Assoc. Dean for Academic Affairs: Dr JOHN BARNET
Assoc. Dean for Student Affairs: Rev. DAVID MEZYNSKI
Assoc. Chancellor for Finance: MELANIE RINGA
Dir for Admissions and Financial Aid: Dr DAVID WAGSCHAL
Librarian: ELEANA S. SILK
Library of 142,000 vols, 350 periodical subscriptions
Number of teachers: 14
Number of students: 55

Publication: *The St. Vladimir's Theological Quarterly*.

SARAH LAWRENCE COLLEGE

One Mead Way, Bronxville, NY 10708-5999
Telephone: (914) 395-2510
E-mail: slcadmit@sarahlawrence.edu
Internet: www.slc.edu
Founded 1926
Private control
Academic year: August to May
Pres.: KAREN R. LAWRENCE
Vice-Pres. for Admin.: THOMAS BLUM
Vice-Pres. for Advancement: CHARLES J. RASBERRY
Vice-Pres. for Communications and Marketing: Dr GERALD A. SCHORIN
Vice-Pres. for Finance and Operations: JOSEPH GIOVANNELLI
Dean for Admission and Financial Aid: AMY ABRAMS
Dean for College: Dr JERRILYNN D. DODDS
Dean for Graduate Studies: SUSAN GUMA
Dean for Student Affairs: Dr PAIGE CRANDALL
Dean for Studies and Student Life: Dr ALLEN GREEN (acting)
Dir for Library: SHA FAGAN
Registrar: DANIEL LICHT
Library of 200,000 vols
Number of teachers: 238
Number of students: 1,670 (1,328 undergraduate, 342 graduate)
Publications: *Revisionist* (online (www.revisionistslc.com)), *Sarah Lawrence Magazine*.

SCHOOL OF VISUAL ARTS

209 E 23 St, New York, NY 10010-3994
Telephone: (212) 592-2000
Fax: (212) 725-3587
E-mail: admissions@sva.edu
Internet: www.schoolofvisualarts.edu
Founded 1947 as Cartoonists and Illustrators School, present name 1956
Private control
Academic year: September to May
Pres.: DAVID RHODES
Exec. Vice-Pres.: ANTHONY P. RHODES
Provost: JEFFREY NESIN
Chief Financial Officer: GARY SHILLET
Exec. Dir for Student Affairs: JAVIER VEGA
Dir for Institutional Research: JEROLD L. DAVIS
Registrar: JON TODD
Library Dir: ROBERT LOBE
Library of 72,000 vols, 450 magazines and journals subscription
Number of teachers: 1,000
Number of students: 3,980 (3,416 undergraduate, 564 graduate)
Publication: *Visual Arts Journal*.

SEMINARY OF THE IMMACULATE CONCEPTION

440 W Neck Rd, Huntington, NY 11743
Telephone: (631) 423-0483
Fax: (631) 423-2346
E-mail: info@icseminary.edu
Internet: www.icseminary.edu
Founded 1930
Private control
Rector: Rev. Mgr PETER I. VACCARI
Vice-Rector: Rev. Mgr RICHARD HENNING
Academic Dean: Dr Sis. MARY LOUISE BRINK
Dean for Seminarians: Rev. NICHOLAS ZIEN-TARSKI
Dir for Library and Information Services: ELYSE HAYES

Library of 50,000 vols, 250 journals subscription, 600 audiovisual items, 4,000 old and rare books
Number of teachers: 14
Publication: *Seat of Wisdom* (online (www.seatofwisdomjournal.org)).

SIENA COLLEGE

515 Loudon Rd, Loudonville, NY 12211-1462
Telephone: (518) 783-2300
Fax: (518) 783-4293
E-mail: website@siena.edu
Internet: www.siena.edu
Founded 1937
Private control
Academic year: September to May
Pres.: Fr Dr KEVIN MULLEN
Vice-Pres. for Academic Affairs: Dr LINDA RICHARDSON
Vice-Pres. for Devt and External Affairs: DAVID SMITH
Vice-Pres. for Enrolment Management: NED JONES
Vice-Pres. for Finance and Admin.: PAUL STEC
Vice-Pres. for Student Affairs: Dr MARYELLEN GILROY
Chief of Staff: KEN PAULLI
Library Dir: GARY B. THOMPSON
Library of 360,430 vols, 5,000 journals
Number of teachers: 336 (206 full-time, 130 part-time)
Number of students: 3,792
Publications: *Pendragon* (1 a year), *The Saga* (1 a year)

DEANS

School of Business: Dr JEFFREY A. MELLO
School of Liberal Arts: Dr RALPH BLASTING
School of Science: Dr ALLAN WEATHERWAX

SKIDMORE COLLEGE

815 N Broadway, Saratoga Springs, NY 12866
Telephone: (518) 580-5000
Fax: (518) 580-5584
E-mail: info@skidmore.edu
Internet: www.skidmore.edu
Founded 1903 as Young Women's Industrial Club of Saratoga, present name and status 1922
Private control
Academic year: September to May
Liberal arts college
Pres.: PHILIP A. GLOTZBACH
Vice-Pres. for Academic Affairs: Dr SUSAN A. KRESS
Vice-Pres. for Advancement: MICHAEL CASEY
Vice-Pres. for Finance and Admin., Treas.: MICHAEL D. WEST
Dean for Faculty: BEAU BRESLIN
Dean for Spec. Programmes: Prof. PAUL CALHOUN
Dean for Student Affairs: W. ROCHELLE CALHOUN
Dean for Admissions and Student Aid: MARY LOU BATES
Dir for Alumni Affairs: MIKE SPOSILI
Librarian: RUTH S. COPANS
Registrar: DAVE DeCONNO
Library of 400,000 vols
Number of teachers: 248 (full-time)
Number of students: 2,400
Publications: *Salmagundi* (4 a year), *Scope* (3 a year).

STATE UNIVERSITY OF NEW YORK

State Univ. Plaza, 353 Broadway, Albany, NY 12246
Telephone: (518) 320-1100

E-mail: asksuny@suny.edu
Internet: www.suny.edu
Founded 1816
Chancellor: NANCY L. ZIMPHER
Provost and Exec. Vice-Chancellor: DAVID K. LAVALLEE
Sr Vice-Chancellor, Sec. and Gen. Counsel: WILLIAM F. HOWARD
Sr Vice-Chancellor for Community Colleges: JOHANNA DUNCAN-POITIER
Vice-Chancellor for Academic Programmes and Planning and Vice-Provost: ELIZABETH L. BRINGSJORD
Vice-Chancellor for Financial Services and Chief Financial Officer: BRIAN HUTZLEY
Vice-Chancellor for Global Affairs: MITCH LEVENTHAL
Vice-Chancellor for Human Resources: CURTIS L. LLOYD
Library: 18m. vols
Number of teachers: 33,455 (full-time)
Number of students: 467,845 (426,314 undergraduate, 41,531 graduate)
Publication: *SUNYergy* (4 a year, online).

CAMPUSES

University at Albany

1400 Washington Ave, Albany, NY 12222
Telephone: (518) 442-3305
Fax: (518) 442-5383
E-mail: geninfo@uamail.albany.edu
Internet: www.albany.edu
Founded 1844, present status 1962
Academic year: August to May
Pres.: GEORGE M. PHILIP
Provost and Vice-Pres. for Academic Affairs: SUSAN D. PHILLIPS
Vice-Pres. for Communications and Marketing: CATHERINE HERMAN
Vice-Pres. for Finance and Business: STEPHEN J. BEDITZ
Vice-Pres. for Research: JAMES A. DIAS
Vice-Pres. for Student Success: CHRISTINE A. BOUCHARD
Vice-Pres. for Univ. Devt: FARDIN SANAI
Vice-Provost for Enrolment Management: WAYNE A. LOCUST
Sr Counsel: JOHN H. REILLY
Chief Information Officer: CHRISTINE HAILE
Library of 1,613,524 vols
Number of teachers: 1,000
Number of students: 17,615 (12,959 undergraduate, 4,656 graduate)
Publication: *UAlbany*

DEANS

College of Arts and Sciences: Dr EDELGARD WULFERT
College of Computing and Information: PETER A. BLONIARZ
Rockefeller College of Public Affairs and Policy: DAVID L. ROUSSEAU
School of Business: Prof. DONALD SIEGEL
School of Criminal Justice: Prof. Dr ALAN LIZOTTE
School of Education: ROBERT L. BANGERT-DROWNS
School of Public Health: Dr PHILIP C. NASCA
School of Social Welfare: Prof. Dr KATHARINE BRIAR-LAWSON

Binghamton University

POB 6000, Binghamton, NY 13902-6000
4400 Vestal Parkway E, Binghamton, NY 13902
Telephone: (607) 777-2000
Fax: (607) 777-4000
E-mail: info@binghamton.edu
Internet: www.binghamton.edu
Founded 1946
Academic year: August to May

Pres.: Dr HARVEY G. STENGER
Provost and Vice-Pres. for Academic Affairs:
DONALD G. NIEMAN
Vice-Pres. for Admin.: JAMES VAN VOORST
Vice-Pres. for External Affairs: MARCIA CRA-
NER
Vice-Pres. for Research: BAHGAT SAMMAKIA
Vice-Pres. for Student Affairs: BRIAN ROSE
Library of 2,380,358 vols, 1,869, 980 micro-
forms, 81, 959 journal holdings, 2,671 CD
ROMs, 118,937 sound recordings, 120,955
maps, 3,518 video cassettes and DVDs and
212 e-databases
Number of teachers: 845
Number of students: 14,746 (11,861 under-
graduate and 2,885 graduate)
Publication: *Binghamton Magazine*

DEANS

College of Community and Public Affairs:
PATRICIA WALLACE INGRAHAM
Decker School of Nursing: Prof. Dr JOYCE
FERRARIO
Graduate School: NANCY E. STAMP
Harpur College of Arts and Sciences: (vacant)
School of Management: Dr UPINDER DHILLON
S. G. Grant Graduate School of Education:
Dr S. G. GRANT
Thomas J. Watson School of Engineering and
Applied Science: Dr KRISHNASWAMI SRIHARI

University at Buffalo

12 Capen Hall, Buffalo, NY 14260-1660
Telephone: (716) 645-2400
Fax: (716) 645-2895
E-mail: ubinfo@buffalo.edu
Internet: www.buffalo.edu
Founded 1846
Academic year: August to May
Pres.: SATISH K. TRIPATHI
Provost and Exec. Vice-Pres. for Academic
Affairs: BRUCE D. MCCOMBE
Senior Vice-Pres.: ROBERT J. WAGNER
Vice-Pres. for Devt and Alumni Relations:
NANCY L. WELLS
Vice-Pres. for Finance and Admin.: LAURA E.
HUBBARD
Vice-Pres. for Health Sciences: MICHAEL E.
CAIN
Vice-Pres. for Research and Economic Devt:
ALEXANDER N. CARTWRIGHT
Vice-Pres. for Univ. Life and Services: DEN-
NIS R. BLACK
Library: 3.6m. vols, 30,000 journals
Number of teachers: 2,259 (1,576 full-time,
683 part-time)
Number of students: 28,601 (19,058 under-
graduate, 9,543 graduate and professional)
Publications: *buffaloBOOKS, Intersight*

DEANS

College of Arts and Sciences: E. BRUCE
PITMAN
Graduate School of Education: Dr MARY H.
GRESHAM
Law School: MAKAU W. MUTUA
School of Architecture and Planning: ROBERT
G. SHIBLEY
School of Dental Medicine: Dr MICHAEL L.
GLICK
School of Engineering and Applied Sciences:
RAJAN BATTA (acting)
School of Management: ARJANG A. ASSAD
School of Medicine and Biomedical Sciences:
Dr MICHAEL E. CAIN
School of Nursing: Dr MARSHA L. LEWIS
School of Pharmacy and Pharmaceutical
Sciences: Dr WAYNE K. ANDERSON
School of Public Health and Health Profes-
sions: Dr LYNN T. KOZLOWSKI
School of Social Work: Prof. NANCY J. SMYTH

Stony Brook University

Stony Brook, NY 11794
Telephone: (631) 632-6000
E-mail: enroll@stonybrook.edu
Internet: www.stonybrook.edu
Founded 1957
Academic year: August to May
Pres.: SAMUEL L. STANLEY, JR
Provost and Sr Vice-Pres. for Academic
Affairs: DENNIS N. ASSANIS
Vice-Pres. for Economic Devt: YACOV SHA-
MASH
Vice-Pres. for Facilities and Services: BAR-
BARA CHERNOW
Vice-Pres. for Finance and Admin.: KAROL
KAIN GRAY
Vice-Pres. for Research: Dr JOHN HARMEN
MARBURGER, III
Library: 2.1 m., incl. 130,000 maps, 11,000
books and 8,000 DVDs
Number of teachers: 2,200
Number of students: 24,103

DEANS

College of Arts and Sciences: Dr NANCY
SQUIRES
College of Business: Dr MANUEL LONDON
College of Engineering and Applied Sciences:
YACOV SHAMASH
Graduate School: LAWRENCE MARTIN
School of Dental Medicine: Dr RAY C.
WILLIAMS
School of Health Technology and Manage-
ment: Dr CRAIG LEHMANN
School of Journalism: HOWARD SCHNEIDER
School of Marine and Atmospheric Sciences:
MINGHUA ZHANG
School of Medicine: Dr KENNETH KAUSHANSKY
School of Nursing: Dr LEE ANNE XIPPOLITOS
School of Professional Devt: Dr PAUL JAY
EDELSON
School of Social Welfare: Dr FRANCES L.
BRISBANE
Undergraduate Colleges: CHARLES ROBBINS.

UNIVERSITY COLLEGES

State University College at Brockport:
350 New Campus Dr., Brockport, NY 14420;
tel. (585) 395-2211; fax (585) 395-5452;
e-mail admit@brockport.edu; internet www
.brockport.edu; f. 1835; Pres. Dr JOHN R.
HALSTEAD; Provost and Vice-Pres. for Academic Affairs ANNE HUOT; Vice-Pres. for
Admin. and Finance LOUIS SPIRO; Vice-Pres.
for Advancement ROXANNE JOHNSTON; Vice-
Pres. for Enrolment Management and Student Affairs KATHRYN WILSON; Chief Communications Officer DAVID MIHALYOV; library
of 511,605 vols, 11,880 videos and DVDs,
107,000 periodicals; 594 teachers; 8,413 students (7,166 undergraduate, 1,247 graduate);
publ. *Kaleidoscope*

DEANS

School of the Arts, Humanities and Social
Sciences: DARWIN PRIOLEAU
School of Business Admin. and Economics:
Dr DANIEL PETREE
School of Education and Human Services:
DOUGLAS SCHEIDT

State University College at Buffalo: 1300
Elmwood Ave, Buffalo, NY 14222; tel. (716)
878-4000; fax (716) 878-6100; e-mail
admissions@buffalostate.edu; internet www
.buffalostate.edu; f. 1871; Pres. Dr AARON
PODOLEFSKY; Provost Dr DENNIS K PONTON;
Vice-Pres. for Finance and Management Dr
STANLEY KARDONSKY; Vice-Pres. for Student
Affairs HAL D. PAYNE; Assoc. Vice-Pres. for
Library MARYRUTH F. GLOGOWSKI; library of
675,000 vols; 1,792 (1,221 full-time, 571
part-time) teachers; 11,695 (9,788 undergraduate, 1,907 graduate) students

DEANS

Graduate School: Dr KEVIN J. RAILEY
School of Arts and Humanities: BENJAMIN C.
CHRISTY
School of Education: Dr PAUL G. THEOBALD
School of Natural and Social Sciences: Dr
MARK W. SEVERSON
School of the Professions: Dr KEVIN F.
MULCAHY
Univ. College: Dr SCOTT L. JOHNSON

State University College at Cortland:
POB 2000, Cortland, NY 13045-0900; tel.
(607) 753-2011; fax (607) 753-5998; internet
www2.cortland.edu/home; f. 1868; Pres. Dr
ERIK J. BITTERBAUM; Provost Vice-Pres. for
Student Affairs C. GREGORY SHARER; Vice-
Pres. for Finance and Management WILLIAM
E. SHAUT; Vice-Pres. for Institutional
Advancement RAYMOND D. FRANCO; Dir of
Libraries GAIL WOOD; 578 (301 full-time, 277
part-time) teachers; 7,358 students (6,310
undergraduate, 1,048 graduate)

DEANS

School of Arts and Sciences: R. BRUCE MAT-
TINGLY
School of Education: ANDREA LACHANCE
School of Professional Studies: JOHN COTTONE

State University College at Fredonia:
280 Central Ave., Fredonia, NY 14063; tel.
(716) 673-3111; fax (716) 673-3249; e-mail
admissions@fredonia.edu; internet www
.fredonia.edu; f. 1826; Pres. DENNIS L. HEF-
NER; Vice-Pres. Dr VIRGINIA SCHAEFER HOR-
VATH; Vice-Pres. for Univ. Advancement
DAVID TIFFANY; Assoc. Vice-Pres. for Admin.
JUDY LANGWORTHY; Dir of Admissions CHRIS-
TOPHER DEARTH; Librarian RANDY GADIKIAN;
474 (251 full-time; 223 part-time) teachers;
5,730 students (5,398 undergraduate, 332
graduate)

DEANS

College of Arts and Sciences: Dr JOHN
KIJINSKI
College of Education: Dr CHRISTINE GIVNER
School of Business: Dr RUSSELL BOISJOLY

State University College at Geneseo:
One College Circle, Geneseo, NY 14454; tel.
(585) 245-5000; fax (585) 245-5550; e-mail
admissions@geneseo.edu; internet www
.geneseo.edu; f. 1871; Pres. CHRISTOPHER C.
DAHL; Provost Dr CAROL LONG; Vice-Pres. for
Admin. and Finance Dr JAMES B. MILROY;
Registrar DELBERT BROWN; Dir of Libraries
CYRIL OBERLANDER; library of 516,700 vols;
265 (full-time) teachers; 5,038 students
(4,950 undergraduate, 88 graduate)

DEANS

Ella Cline Shear School of Education:
(vacant)
School of the Arts: Dr JONATHAN GONDER
School of Business: Dr MICHAEL SCHINSKI

State University College at New Paltz:
One Hawk Dr., New Paltz, NY 12561; tel.
(845) 257-2121; fax (845) 257-3209; e-mail
admissions@newpaltz.edu; internet www
.newpaltz.edu; f. 1828 as New Paltz Classic
Acad.; Pres. Dr DONALD P. CHRISTIAN; Provost
and Vice-Pres. for Academic Affairs CHERYL
B. TORSNEY; Vice-Pres. for Enrolment Management L. DAVID EATON; Dean of Library
CHUI-CHUN LEE; library of 500,000 vols; 325
(full-time) teachers; 7,885 students (6,582
undergraduate, 1,303 graduate)

DEANS

College of Liberal Arts and Science: JAMES
SCHIFFER
School of Business: HADI SALAVITABAR
School of Education: Dr KAREN N. BELL
School of Fine and Performing Arts: MARY
HAFELI

School of Science and Engineering: DANIEL FREEDMAN

State University College at Old Westbury: POB 210, Old Westbury, NY 11568-0210; tel. (516) 876-3000; fax (516) 876-3307; e-mail enroll@oldwestbury.edu; internet www.oldwestbury.edu; f. 1965; Pres. Dr CALVIN O. BUTTS, III; Provost and Vice-Pres. for Academic Affairs PATRICK O'SULLIVAN; Vice-Pres. for Enrolment Services MARYBOOK MARQUEZ BELL; Vice-Pres. for Student Affairs Dr ML LANGLIE; Registrar PATRICIA A. SMITH; Library Dir STEPHEN KIRKPATRICK; 122 (full-time) teachers; 3,300 students

DEANS

School of Business: Dr N. J. DELENER
School of Education: RUBEN GONZALEZ

State University College at Oneonta: 108 Ravine Parkway, Oneonta, NY 13820; tel. (607) 436-3500; e-mail admissions@oneonta.edu; internet www.oneonta.edu; f. 1889; academic year August to DecemberJanuary to May (2 semesters); Pres. Dr NANCY KLENIEWSKI; Vice-Pres. for Finance and Admin. TODD FOREMAN; Vice-Pres. for Student Devt STEVEN R. PERRY; Registrar MAUREEN P. ARTALE; Dir of Admissions KAREN BROWN; Dir of Library MARY LYNN BENSEN; library of 500,000 vols; 503 teachers (258 full-time, 245 part-time); 6,000 students.

State University College at Oswego: 7060 Route 104, Oswego, NY 13126-3599; tel. (315) 312-2500; fax (315) 312-3260; e-mail admiss@oswego.edu; internet www.oswego.edu; f. 1861 as Oswego Primary Teachers' Training School; Pres. DEBORAH F. STANLEY; Vice-Pres. for Academic Affairs and Provost LORRIE CLEMO; Vice-Pres. for Student Affairs and Enrolment JOSEPH F. GRANT, JR; Vice-Pres. for Admin. and Finance NICHOLAS LYONS; library of 450,000 vols; 8,212 students (7,212 undergraduate, 928 graduate)

DEANS

College of Liberal Arts and Sciences: RHONDA MANDEL
Graduate Studies: DAVID KING
School of Business: RICHARD SKOLNIK
School of Communication, Media and the Arts: FRITZ MESSERE
School of Education: PAM MICHEL

State University College at Plattsburgh: 101 Broad St, Plattsburgh, NY 12901; tel. (518) 564-2000; fax (518) 564-2045; e-mail admissions@plattsburgh.edu; internet www.plattsburgh.edu; Pres. Dr JOHN ETTLING; Provost and Vice-Pres. for Academic Affairs Dr JAMES LISZKA; Vice-Pres. for Institutional Advancement ANNE HANSEN; Vice-Pres. for Admin. JOHN R. HOMBURGER; Vice-Pres. for Student Affairs WILLIAM D. LAUNDRY; Dean of Library and Information Services CERISE G. OBERMAN; 6,496 students (5,906 undergraduate, 547 graduate)

DEANS

Arts and Sciences: Dr KATHLEEN LAVOIE
Education, Health, and Human Services Programs: Dr MICHAEL MORGAN
School of Business and Economics: Dr RAY GUYDOSH

State University College at Purchase: 735 Anderson Hill Rd, Purchase, NY 10577; tel. (914) 251-6000; fax (914) 251-6314; e-mail admissions@purchase.edu; internet www.purchase.edu; f. 1967; Pres. THOMAS J. SCHWARZ; Provost and Exec. Vice-Pres. for Academic Affairs BARBARA B. DIXON; Vice-Pres. for Enrolment Management DENNIS CRAIG; Vice-Pres. for Student Affairs ROBIN KAUFMAN; Dir of Library PATRICK CALLAHAN; 4,200 students

DEANS

School of the Arts: KEN TABACHNICK
School of Liberal Arts and Sciences: Dr SUZANNE KESSLER

State University Empire State College: Two Union Ave, Saratoga Springs, NY 12866; tel. (518) 587-2100; e-mail admissions@esc.edu; internet www.esc.edu; f. 1971; Pres. ALAN R. DAVIS; Provost and Vice-Pres. for Academic Affairs MEG BENKE; Vice-Pres. for Admin. PAUL TUCCI; Vice-Pres. for Enrolment Management and Student Services HUGH B. HAMMETT; 1,400 teachers (250 full-time, 1,150 part-time)

DEANS

Center for Distance Learning: TOM P. MACKEY
Harry Van Arsdale Jr Center for Labor Studies
School for Graduate Studies: ROBERT CLOUGHERTY

State University of New York at Potsdam: 44 Pierrepont Ave, Potsdam, NY 13676; tel. (315) 267-2000; e-mail admissions@potsdam.edu; internet www.potsdam.edu; f. 1816 as St Lawrence Acad., present status 1948; academic year August to May; Pres. JOHN F. SCHWALLER; Provost MARGARET MADDEN; Vice-Pres. for Institutional Effectiveness and Enrolment Management RICK A. MILLER; Dir of Libraries JENICA ROGERS; 4,423 students (3,988 undergraduate, 435 graduate)

DEANS

Crane School of Music: MICHAEL SITTON
School of Arts and Sciences: STEVEN MARQUSEE
School of Education and Professional Studies: PETER BROUWER

COLLEGES OF TECHNOLOGY

State University of New York College of Technology at Alfred: 10 Upper College Dr., Alfred, NY 14802; tel. (607) 587-4215; internet www.alfredstate.edu; f. 1908; Pres. Dr JOHN M. ANDERSON; Vice-Pres. for Academic Affairs Dr STEPHEN J. HAVLOVIČ; Vice-Pres. for Admin. and Enrolment VALERIE NIXON; Vice-Pres. for Student Affairs Dr STEVE TYRELL; Dir of Libraries DAVID HAGGSTROM; library of 59,000 vols, 141 journal titles and 96,854 full-text periodicals; 203 (full-time) teachers; 3,700 students

DEANS

School of Arts and Sciences: Dr TERRY TUCKER
School of Applied Technology: CRAIG R. CLARK
School of Management and Engineering Technology: Dr JOHN C. WILLIAMS

State University of New York College of Technology at Canton: 34 Cornell Dr., Canton, NY 13617; tel. (315) 386-7011; e-mail admissions@canton.edu; internet www.canton.edu; Pres. JOSEPH L. KENNEDY; Provost and Vice-Pres. for Academic Affairs Dr CARLI SCHIFFNER; Vice-Pres. for Student Affairs Dr MOLLY MOTT; Dir of Library Services MICHELLE CURRIER; 3,800 students

DEANS

Canino School of Engineering Technology: Dr DAVID J. WELLS
School of Business and Liberal Arts: Dr LINDA HEILMAN

State University of New York College of Agriculture and Technology at Cobleskill: State Route 7, Cobleskill, NY 12043; tel. (518) 255-5700; internet www.cobleskill.edu; e-mail admissions@cobleskill.edu; f. 1916; Officer-in-Charge CANDACE S. VANCKO; Provost and Vice-Pres. for Academic Affairs

DEBRA H. THATCHER; Vice-Pres. for Student Devt STEVEN M. ACKERKNECHT; Vice-Pres. for Institutional Advancement REGINA M. LAGATTA; Dean of Library ELIZABETH D. ORGERON; library of 77,000 vols, 5,400 audiovisual materials; 200 teachers

DEANS

School of Agriculture and Natural Resources: TIM W. MOORE
School of Business: MICHAEL J. MCCASKEY
School of Liberal Arts and Sciences: SUSAN J. ZIMMERMANN

State University of New York College of Technology at Delhi: Two Main St, Delhi, NY 13753-1190; internet www.delhi.edu; f. 1913; Pres. Dr CANDACE VANCKO; Provost Dr JOHN NADER; Vice-Pres. for Finance and Admin. CAROL BISHOP; Vice-Pres. for Student Life BARBARA JONES; Dir of Library PAM PETERS; library of 50,000 vols, 30,000 online magazines and journals; 3,100 students

DEANS

Applied Sciences and Technology Div.: Prof. DOMINIC MORALES
Business and Hospitality Div.: Dr MICHAEL PETRILLOSE
Liberal Arts and Sciences Div.: Dr VERN LINDQUIST

State University of New York College of Technology at Farmingdale: 2350 Broadhollow Rd, Farmingdale, NY 11735-1021; tel. (631) 420-2000; e-mail admissions@farmingdale.edu; internet www.farmingdale.edu; f. 1912; Pres. Dr W. HUBERT KEEN; Provost and Vice-Pres. for Academic Affairs Dr LUCIA CEPRIANO (acting); Sr Vice-Pres. and CFO GEORGE P. LAROSA; Vice-Pres. for Institutional Advancement PATRICK CALABRIA; Vice-Pres. for Student Affairs Dr TOM CORTI; Dir of Information Resources MICHAEL KNAUTH; 512 teachers; 6,988 students

DEANS

School of Arts and Sciences: Dr ELEANOR R. FAPOHUNDA
School of Business: Dr LORRAINE GREENWALD
School of Engineering Technology: Dr KAMAL SHAHRABI
School of Health Sciences: Dr MARIE HAYDEN-MILES

State University of New York College of Agriculture and Technology at Morrisville: POB 901, 80 Eaton St, Morrisville, NY 13408-0636; tel. (315) 684-6000; fax (315) 684-6427; e-mail admissions@morrisville.edu; internet www.morrisville.edu; Pres. RICHARD J. CARRENO; Vice-Pres. for Academic Affairs DAVID E. ROGERS; Dir of Libraries CHRISTINE RUDECOFF; library of 95,000 vols, 250 print magazine and newspaper subscriptions, 1,600 audio and video recordings

DEANS

School of Agriculture and Natural Resources: CHRISTOPHER L. NYBERG
School of General Studies: JEANNETTE H. EVANS
School of Liberal Arts: PAUL F. GRIFFIN
School of Science and Technology: CHRISTINE A. CRING

SPECIALIZED COLLEGES

State University Institute of Technology at Utica/Rome: 100 Seymour Rd, Utica, NY 13502; tel. (315) 792-7500; internet www.sunyit.edu; f. 1966; academic year August to May; Pres. Prof. BJONG WOLF YEIGH; Provost WILLIAM W. DURGIN; Vice-Pres. for Admin. BRUCE REICHEL; Registrar JOHN LASHER.

State University of New York College of Environmental Science and Forestry: One Forestry Dr., Syracuse, NY 13210; tel. (315) 470-6500; e-mail esfinfo@esf.edu;

internet www.esf.edu; f. 1911 as New York State College of Forestry at Syracuse Univ.; Pres. Dr CORNELIUS B. MURPHY, JR; Provost and Vice-Pres. for Academic Affairs BRUCE C. BONGARTEN; Vice-Pres. for Admin. JOSEPH L. RUFO; Vice-Pres. for Enrolment Management and Marketing ROBERT C. FRENCH; 174 teachers (127 full-time, 47 part-time); 2,718 students (543 graduate, 1,586 full-time and 587 part-time undergraduate).

State University of New York College of Optometry at New York City: 33 W 42nd St, New York, NY 10036; tel. (212) 938-4000; e-mail admissions@sunyopt.edu; internet www.sunyopt.edu; f. 1971; Chancellor Dr NANCY L. ZIMPHER; Pres. DAVID A. HEATH; Vice-Pres. and Dean for Academic Affairs Dr DAVID TROILO; Vice-Pres. for Admin. and Finance DAVID BOWERS; Vice-Pres. for Clinical Affairs Dr RICHARD SODEN; Vice-Pres. for Institutional Advancement ANN WARWICK; Vice-Pres. for Student Affairs Dr JEFFREY PHILPOTT; Dir of Library Services ELAINE WELLS; library of 40,000 vols; 126 teachers (60 full-time, 60 part-time); 315 students.

SUNY Downstate Medical Center: 450 Clarkson Ave, Brooklyn, NY 11203; tel. (718) 270-1000; fax (718) 270-4775; e-mail admissions@downstate.edu; internet www.downstate.edu; f. 1962; Pres. Dr JOHN C. LAROSA; Vice-Pres. and Chief Financial Officer ALAN DZIJA; Dir of Admissions Dr SHUSH-AWNA DEOLIVEIRA; library of 67,078 vols, 388,320 journals, 4,000 e-journals and 356 e-books

DEANS

College of Health-Related Professions: Dr DAWN MORTON-RIAS
College of Medicine: Dr IAN L. TAYLOR
College of Nursing: Dr DAISY CRUZ-RICHMAN
School of Graduate Studies: MARK STEWART
School of Public Health: Dr PASCAL JAMES IMPERATO

State University of New York Maritime College: Six Pennyfield Ave, Throggs Neck, NY 10465; tel. (718) 409-7200; e-mail admissions@sunymaritime.edu; internet www.sunymaritime.edu; Pres. Rear Admiral WENDI B. CARPENTER; Provost and Vice-Pres. for Academic Affairs Dr JOSEPH C. HOFFMAN, JR; 1,850 students.

Upstate Medical University: 750 E Adams St, Syracuse, NY 13210-2375; tel. (315) 464-5540; e-mail admiss@upstate.edu; internet www.upstate.edu; f. 1834; Pres. Dr DAVID R. SMITH; Sr Vice-Pres. for Admin. and Finance STEVEN C. BRADY; Sr Vice-Pres. for Hospital Affairs Dr JOHN MCCABE; Sr Vice-Pres. for Operations Dr WANDA M. THOMPSON; library of 220,160 vols, 730 e-books, 146,482 journals, 4,331 audiovisual items; 669 teachers (488 full-time, 181 part-time); 1,542 students

DEANS

College of Graduate Studies: Dr STEVEN GOODMAN
College of Health Professions: Dr HUGH W. BONNER
College of Medicine: Dr DAVID B. DUGGAN
College of Nursing: Dr ELVIRA SZIGETI

SYRACUSE UNIVERSITY

Syracuse, NY 13244-5040
Telephone: (315) 443-1870
E-mail: gradinfo@syr.edu
Internet: www.syr.edu
Founded 1870
Private control
Academic year: August to July
Campuses in Los Angeles, Washington DC, New York city; 8 overseas centres: Beijing,

People's Republic of China; Florence, Italy; Hong Kong; Istanbul, Turkey; London, United Kingdom; Madrid, Spain; Santiago, Chile; Strasbourg, France
Chancellor and Pres.: NANCY CANTOR
Vice-Chancellor and Provost: ERIC F. SPINA
Sr Vice-Pres. and Dean for Student Affairs: THOMAS V. WOLFE
Sr Vice-Pres. and Gen. Counsel: THOMAS EVANS
Sr Vice-Pres. for Public Affairs: KEVIN C. QUINN
Exec. Vice-Pres. for Advancement and External Affairs: THOMAS J. WALSH
Exec. Vice-Pres. and Chief Financial Officer: LOUIS G. MARCOCCIA
Vice-Pres. for Business Operations: JENA PRIDEAUX MCWHA
Vice-Pres. for Community Engagement and Economic Devt: MARILYN HIGGINS
Vice-Pres. for Enrolment Management: DONALD A. SALEH
Vice-Pres. for Information Technology and Chief Information Officer: CHRISTOPHER M. SEDORE
Vice-Pres. for Research: GINA LEE-GLAUSER
Registrar: MAUREEN BREED
Dean for Library: SUZANNE THORIN
Library: see Libraries and Archives
Number of teachers: 1,513 (981 full-time, 86 part-time, 446 adjunct)
Number of students: 20,407 (13,504 full-time undergraduate, 697 part-time undergraduate, 4,381 full-time graduate and law school, 1,825 part-time graduate and law school)
Publications: *Syracuse Law Review* (4 a year), *Syracuse University Magazine* (3 a year)

DEANS

College of Arts and Sciences: GEORGE M. LANGFORD
College of Law: HANNAH R. ARTERIAN
College of Visual and Performing Arts: ANN CLARKE
David B. Falk College of Sport and Human Dynamics: DIANE LYDEN MURPHY
Graduate School: BEN WARE
L. C. Smith College of Engineering and Computer Science: LAURA J. STEINBERG
Martin J. Whitman School of Management: MELVIN T. STITH
Maxwell School of Citizenship and Public Affairs: JAMES B. STEINBERG
School of Architecture: MARK ROBBINS
School of Education: DOUGLAS BIKLEN
School of Information Studies: ELIZABETH D. LIDDY
S. I. Newhouse School of Public Communications: LORRAINE BRANHAM
University College: BETHAIDA GONZÁLEZ

TOURO COLLEGE

27–33 W 23 St, New York, NY 10010
Telephone: (212) 463-0400
Fax: (212) 627-9144
Internet: www.touro.edu
Founded 1970
Private control
Campuses in: Manhattan, Brooklyn, Queens, Long Island, California, Florida, Nevada, Israel, Italy and Germany; incl. New York Medical College
Chancellor: DONIEL LANDER
Pres.: Dr ALAN KADISH
Sr Vice-Pres. and Chief Admin. Officer: ALAN P. SCHOOR
Sr Vice-Pres. and Chief Financial Officer: MELVIN NESS
Sr Vice-Pres. for College Affairs: MOSHE KRUPKA

Sr Vice-Pres. for Graduate and Professional Education: SHALOM Z. HIRSCHMAN
Vice-Pres. for Academic Affairs: Dr JAY SEXTER
Vice-Pres. for Institutional Advancement: ERIC LEVINE
Vice-Pres. for Int. Affairs: Dr ISRAEL SINGER
Vice-Pres. for Planning and Assessment and Dean of Students: ROBERT GOLDSCHMIDT
Vice-Pres. for Undergraduate Education and Dean of Faculties: Dr STANLEY L. BOYLAN
Dir for Libraries: BASHE SIMON
Library of 183,700 vols, incl. 550 print journals
Number of teachers: 4,930 (2,091 full-time, 1,317 part-time, 1,522 clinical)
Number of students: 19,000
Publication: *Touro Lawyer*

DEANS

Graduate School of Business: MICHAEL WILLIAMS
Graduate School of Education: Dr LaMAR P. MILLER
Graduate School of Jewish Studies: Dr MICHAEL SHMIDMAN
Graduate School of Psychology: Dr RICHARD WAXMAN
Graduate School of Social Work: Dr STEVEN HUBERMAN
Graduate School of Technology: Dr ISSAC HERSKOWITZ
School of Health Sciences: Dr LOUIS H. PRIMAVERA
Touro College of Osteopathic Medicine: Dr ROBERT B. GOLDBERG
Touro College Jacob D. Fuchsberg Law Center: LAWRENCE RAFUL
Touro College of Pharmacy: Dr STUART FELDMAN

UNIFICATION THEOLOGICAL SEMINARY

30 Seminary Dr., Barrytown, NY 12507
Telephone: (845) 752-3000
Fax: (845) 752-3014
E-mail: registrar@uts.edu
Internet: www.uts.edu
Founded 1975
Private control
Academic year: August to May
Extension centre in New York city
Pres.: Dr RICHARD A. PANZER
Vice-Pres. for Academic Affairs and Academic Dean: Dr KATHY WININGS
Dean for Students: PAUL RAJAN
Dean for New York City Extension Center: Dr KATHY WININGS
Dir for Admissions: DAVETTA ANN OGUNLOLA
Registrar: UTE DELANEY
Library Dir: Dr KEISUKE NODA
Library of 50,000 vols
Number of teachers: 20
Number of students: 100
Publication: *Journal of Unification Studies* (1 a year).

UNION COLLEGE

807 Union St, Schenectady, NY 12308
Telephone: (518) 388-6000
Fax: (518) 388-6986
E-mail: admissions@union.edu
Internet: www.union.edu
Founded 1795
Private control
Academic year: September to June
Courses in humanities, social sciences, sciences and engineering
Pres.: STEPHEN C. AINLAY
Vice-Pres. for Academic Affairs and Dean for Faculty: THERESE MCCARTY

Vice-Pres. for Admissions, Financial Aid and Enrolment: MATTHEW MALATESTA
Vice-Pres. for College Relations: STEPHEN DARE
Vice-Pres. for Finance and Admin.: DIANE BLAKE
Vice-Pres. for Student Affairs and Dean for Students: STEPHEN C. LEAVITT
Dir for Admissions: ANN FLEMING BROWN
Registrar: PENELOPE ADEY
College Librarian: THOMAS MCFADDEN

Library of 612,633 vols
Number of teachers: 202 (full-time)
Number of students: 2,170 (full-time)

Publications: *President's Report* (1 a year), *Union College Magazine* (4 a year).

UNION GRADUATE COLLEGE

80 Nott Terrace, Schenectady, NY 12308
Telephone: (518) 631-9900
Fax: (518) 631-9901
E-mail: info@uniongraduatecollege.edu
Internet: www.uniongraduatecollege.edu; attached to Union College
Private control
Academic year: May to June
Pres.: Dr LAURA SCHWEITZER
Vice-Pres. for Enrolment: JOANNE FITZGERALD
Vice-Pres. for Finance and Operations: JOSEPH M. MCDONALD
Vice-Pres. for Institutional Advancement: DAN CHRISTOPHER
Registrar and Dir for Admissions: RHONDA SHEEHAN
Dir for Library Services: MARY ANNE WALTZ

DEANS

School of Education: Dr PATRICK F. ALLEN
School of Engineering and Computer Science: ROBERT KOZIK
School of Management: BELA MUSITS

UNION THEOLOGICAL SEMINARY

3041 Broadway, 121st St, New York, NY 10027
Telephone: (212) 662-7100
E-mail: contactus@uts.columbia.edu
Internet: www.uts.columbia.edu
Founded 1836
Private control
Academic year: September to May
Pres.: Rev. Dr SERENE JONES
Exec. Vice-Pres.: FREDERICK DAVIE
Vice-Pres. for Finance and Operations: RICHARD A. MADONNA, JR
Vice-Pres. for Institutional Advancement: BOB BOMERSBACH
Academic Dean: ROSEMARY SKINNER KELLER
Dean for Academic Affairs: DAISY MACHADO
Dir for Admissions and Financial Aid: NICHELLE JENKINS
Registrar: EDITH T. HUNTER
Library Dir: SARA J. MYERS

Library of 700,000 vols
Number of teachers: 46
Number of students: 284

Publications: *The Union Seminary Quarterly Review, Union Now* (2 a year).

UNITED STATES MILITARY ACADEMY

606 Thayer Rd, West Point, NY 10996-1797
Telephone: (845) 938-4041
E-mail: admissions@usma.edu
Internet: www.usma.edu
Founded 1802
Superintendent: Lt-Gen. DAVID HUNTOON
Commandant of Cadets: Brig. Gen. THEODORE D. MARTIN

Dean for Academic Board: Brig. Gen. TIMOTHY TRAINOR
Vice-Dean of Education: Dr JEAN BLAIR
Dir for Academic Affairs: Dr BRUCE KEITH
Dir for Admissions: Col DEBORAH MCDONALD
Librarian and Assoc. Dean: Dr CHRISTOPHER BARTH

Library of 460,000 vols, 60,000 journals
Number of teachers: 562
Number of students: 4,400

UNIVERSITY OF ROCHESTER

500 Joseph C. Wilson Blvd, Rochester, NY 14627
Telephone: (585) 275-2121
Fax: (585) 461-4595
E-mail: admit@rochester.edu
Internet: www.rochester.edu
Founded 1850
Private control
Academic year: September to May (two terms)
Pres.: JOEL SELIGMAN
Provost and Exec. Vice-Pres.: RALPH KUNCL
Sr Vice-Pres. and Robert L. and Mary L. Sproull Dean of the Faculty of Arts, Sciences and Engineering: PETER LENNIE
Sr Vice-Pres. and Chief Advancement Officer: JAMES D. THOMPSON
Sr Vice-Pres. and Gen. Counsel: SUE S. STEWART
Sr Vice-Pres. for Admin. and Finance, Chief Financial Officer and Treas.: RONALD J. PAPROCKI
Sr Vice-Pres. for Health Sciences: BRADFORD C. BERK
Sr Vice-Pres. and Gen. Sec.: SUE S. STEWART
Vice-Pres. for Communications: BILL MURPHY
Sr Vice-Pres. for Institutional Resources: DOUGLAS W. PHILLIPS
Univ. Dean: PAUL J. BURGETT
Dean for Research: PAUL SLATTERY
Registrar: NANCY SPECK
Dean for River Campus Libraries: SUSAN GIBBONS

Library: see Libraries and Archives
Number of teachers: 2,000
Number of students: 8,568 (5,358 undergraduate, 3,210 graduate)

DEANS

Eastman School of Music: DOUGLAS LOWRY
Graduate Studies: WENDI HEINZELMAN
Hajim School of Engineering and Applied Sciences: ROBERT CLARK
Margaret Warner Graduate School of Education and Human Devt: RAFFAELLA BORASI
School of Arts and Sciences: JOANNA B. OLMSTED
School of Medicine and Dentistry: Dr MARK B. TAUBMAN
School of Nursing: KATHY H. RIDEOUT
Simon School of Business: MARK ZUPAN

US MERCHANT MARINE ACADEMY

300 Steamboat Rd, Kings Point, NY 11024-1699
Telephone: (516) 726-5800
Fax: (516) 773-5509
E-mail: admissions@usmma.edu
Internet: www.usmma.edu
Founded 1943
State control
Academic year: July to June
Superintendent and Academic Dean: Dr SHASHI KUMAR
Chief of Staff: Captain ERIC YORK WALLISCHECK
Dir for Admissions: Captain ROBERT JOHNSON
Librarian: GEORGE BILLY

Library of 180,000 vols
Number of teachers: 80

Number of students: 950 midshipmen

UTICA COLLEGE

1600 Burrstone Rd, Utica, NY 13502
Telephone: (315) 792-3006
Fax: (315) 792-3003
E-mail: admiss@utica.edu
Internet: www.utica.edu
Founded 1946
Private control
Academic year: August to August
Pres.: Dr TODD S. HUTTON
Provost and Vice-Pres. for Academic Affairs: Dr JUDITH A. KIRKPATRICK
Sr Vice-Pres. and Chief Advancement Officer: LAURA CASAMENTO
Vice-Pres. for Enrolment Management: PATRICK QUINN
Vice-Pres. for Financial Affairs and Treas.: R. BARRY WHITE
Vice-Pres. for Legal Affairs and Gen. Counsel: WALTER DESOCIO
Vice-Pres. for Planning and Analysis: CAROL MACKINTOSH
Vice-Pres. for Strategic Initiatives: JAMES BROWN
Vice-Pres. for Student Affairs: STEVE PATTARINI
Asst Vice-Pres. for Library and Information Technology Services: BEVERLY MARCOLINE

Library of 192,500 vols, 40,000 microform units, 1,250 serial subscriptions, 1,000 online journals
Number of teachers: 128 (full-time)
Number of students: 3,093 (2,537 undergraduate, and 736 graduate)

VASSAR COLLEGE

124 Raymond Ave, Poughkeepsie, NY 12604
Telephone: (845) 437-7000
Fax: (845) 437-7060
E-mail: admissions@vassar.edu
Internet: www.vassar.edu
Founded 1861
Academic year: September to May
Pres.: CATHERINE BOND HILL
Vice-Pres. for Alumni Affairs and Devt: CATHERINE BAER
Vice-Pres. for Finance and Treas.: ELIZABETH EISMEIER
Dir for College Relations: SUSAN DEKREY
Dean for College: CHRISTOPHER F. ROELLKE
Dean for Faculty: JONATHAN L. CHENETTE
Dean for Students: DAVID BROWN
Dean for Studies: JOANNE LONG
Registrar: COLLEEN R. MALLET
Dir for Libraries: SABRINA PAPE

Library: see Libraries and Archives
Number of teachers: 290
Number of students: 2,400

VAUGHN COLLEGE OF AERONAUTICS AND TECHNOLOGY

86-01 23rd Ave, Flushing, NY 11369
Telephone: (718) 429-6600
Fax: (718) 429-0256
E-mail: admissions@vaughn.edu
Internet: www.vaughn.edu
Founded 1932 as Casey Jones School of Aeronautics, present name 1986
Private control
Academic year: 2 semesters
Pres.: Dr JOHN C. FITZPATRICK
Vice-Pres. for Enrolment Services and Public Affairs: ERNIE SHEPELSKY
Vice-Pres. for Finance and Business Services: ROBERT WALDMANN
Vice-Pres. for Student Affairs: JOHN F. AGNELLI
Librarian: JO ANN JAYNE

Number of teachers: 119

Number of students: 1,704 (1,314 full-time, 390 part-time)

Publication: *Vaughn College Magazine* (2 a year).

VILLA MARIA COLLEGE

240 Pine Ridge Rd, Buffalo, NY 14225

Telephone: (716) 896-0700

Fax: (716) 896-0705

E-mail: admissions@villa.edu

Internet: www.villa.edu

Founded 1961

Private control

Specializes in arts and music

Pres.: Sis. MARCELLA MARIE GARUS

Vice-Pres. for Academic Affairs: Dr JANET R. REOHR

Vice-Pres. for Business Affairs: VINCENT GRIZANTI

Vice-Pres. for Devt: Sis. MARY MARCINE BOROWIAK

Vice-Pres. of Enrolment Management: RANDYLL BOWEN

Vice-Pres. for Student Affairs: Sis. MARY LOUIS RUSTOWICZ

Registrar: MELANY SHIELDS

Dir for Library Services: Sis. MARY ANNA FALBO

Number of students: 500

WAGNER COLLEGE

One Campus Rd, Staten Island, NY 10301

Telephone: (718) 390-3100

Fax: (718) 390-3105

E-mail: admissions@wagner.edu

Internet: www.wagner.edu

Founded 1883

Private control

Pres.: Dr RICHARD GUARASCI

Provost and Vice-Pres. for Academic Affairs: Dr LILY McNAIR

Dean for Admissions and Financial Aid: BOB HERR

Dean for Integrated Learning: PATRICIA TOOKER

Dean for Libraries: DOROTHY DAVISON

Library of 150,000 vols

Number of teachers: 100 (full-time)

Number of students: 2,150 (1,850 undergraduate, 300 graduate)

WEBB INSTITUTE

298 Crescent Beach Rd, Glen Cove, NY 11542-1398

Telephone: (516) 671-2213

Fax: (516) 674-9838

E-mail: inquiry@webb-institute.edu

Internet: www.webb-institute.edu

Founded 1889

Academic year: August to June

Courses in naval architecture and marine engineering

Pres.: Admiral ROBERT C. OLSEN, JR

Dir for Enrolment Management: WILLIAM MURRAY

Dir for Financial Affairs: ANDREW BERKO

Registrar: JOCELYN WILSON

Library Dir: PATRICIA PRESCOTT

Library of 50,000 vols

Number of teachers: 11 (full-time)

Number of students: 80

WELLS COLLEGE

170 Main St, Aurora, NY 13026

Telephone: (315) 364-3266

Fax: (315) 364-3227

E-mail: admissions@wells.edu

Internet: www.wells.edu

Founded 1868

Private control

Academic year: August to May

Women's liberal arts college

Pres.: LISA MARSH RYERSON

Provost and Dean for College: Dr CINDY J. SPEAKER

Vice-Pres. for Communications and Marketing: ANN S. ROLLO

Vice-Pres. for Advancement: MICHAEL McGREEVEY

Dean for Students: JOEL ANDREW McCARTHY

Dir for Admissions and Financial Aid: SUSAN RAITH SLOAN

Registrar: Dr ANDRE SIAMUNDELE

Treas.: JOHN DENTES

Dir for Library: MURIEL GODBOUT

Library of 218,000 vols

Number of teachers: 55

Number of students: 559

Publication: *Wells College Express* (4 a year).

YESHIVA UNIVERSITY

500 W 185th St, New York, NY 10033

Telephone: (212) 960-5400

Fax: (212) 960-0055

E-mail: yuadmit@yu.edu

Internet: www.yu.edu

Founded 1886

Private control

Languages of instruction: English, Hebrew

3 Campuses in Manhattan and 1 in Bronx

Pres.: Dr RICHARD M. JOEL

Chancellor: Dr NORMAN LAMM

Provost and Sr Vice-Pres. for Academic Affairs: Dr MORTON LOWENGRUB

Vice-Pres. and Chief of Staff: JOSH JOSEPH

Vice-Pres. for Admin.: JEFFREY ROSENGARTEN

Vice-Pres. for Business Affairs: J. MICHAEL GOWER

Vice-Pres. for Information Technology: MARC MILSTEIN

Vice-Pres. for Institutional Advancement: DANIEL T. FORMAN

Vice-Pres. for Legal Affairs, Sec. and Gen. Counsel: ANDREW J. LAUER

Vice-Pres. for Medical Affairs: Dr ALLEN M. SPIEGEL

Vice-Pres. for Univ. Affairs: HERBERT DOBRINSKY

Dean for Univ. Libraries: PEARL BERGER

Library: Hedi Steinberg Library: 170,000 vols; Mendel Gottesman Library of Hebraica: 300,000 vols; Pollack Library: 317,000 vols; all libraries access 50,000 e-journals, and 428,000 e-book titles

Number of teachers: 1,100

Number of students: 7,232 (2,856 undergraduate, 3,543 graduate, 289 seminary)

Publications: *Yeshiva University Review*, *Yeshiva University Today*

DEANS

Albert Einstein College of Medicine: Dr ALLEN M. SPIEGEL

Azrieli Graduate School of Jewish Education and Administration: Dr DAVID J. SCHNALL

Benjamin N. Cardozo School of Law: Dr MATTHEW DILLER

Bernard Revel Graduate School of Jewish Studies: Dr DAVID BERGER

Ferkauf Graduate School of Psychology: Dr LAWRENCE J. SIEGEL

Stern College for Women: Dr KAREN BACON

Syms School of Business: MOSES PAVA

Wurzweiler School of Social Work: Dr CARMEN ORTIZ HENDRICKS

Yeshiva College: Dr BARRY L. EICHLER

Yeshiva Programme and Mazer School of Talmudic Studies: YONA REISS

BARTON COLLEGE

POB 5000, Wilson, NC 27893-7000

Telephone: (252) 399-6300

Fax: (252) 399-6572

Internet: www.barton.edu

Founded 1902 as Atlantic Christian College, present name 1990

Private control

Academic year: September to May (2 semesters)

Pres.: Dr NORVAL C. KNETEN

Provost and Vice-Pres. for Academic Affairs: Dr JOHN P. MARSDEN

Vice-Pres. for Admin. and Finance: Dr KRIS LYNCH

Vice-Pres. for External Relations: Dr KELLY THOMPSON

Vice-Pres. for Student Affairs: GEORGE SOLAN

Dir of Admissions: AMANDA METTS

Registrar: SHEILA MILNE

Dir of Library: JASON FLEMING

Library of 169,000 vols, 22,000 e-books, 390 periodicals and newspapers, 13,000 e-periodicals

Number of teachers: 69 (full-time)

Number of students: 1,200

Publication: *Scope*

DEANS

School of Arts and Sciences: Dr TERRENCE L. GRIMES

School of Business: Dr JOHN J. BETHUNE

School of Education: Dr JACKIE ENNIS

School of Nursing: Dr SHARON I. SARVEY

School of Social Work: Dr BARBARA CONKLIN

BELMONT ABBEY COLLEGE

100 Belmont-Mt Holly Rd, Belmont, NC 28012-1802

Telephone: (704) 461-6700

Fax: (704) 461-6220

E-mail: admissions@bac.edu

Internet: www.belmontabbeycollege.edu

Founded 1876 as St. Mary's College, present name 1913, present status 1952

Private control

Academic year: August to May (2 semesters)

Academic programmes incl. applied psychology, biology, history, liberal studies, sports management, theology

Chancellor: Rev. PLACID SOLARI

Pres.: Dr WILLIAM K. THIERFELDER

Vice-Pres. for Academic Affairs and Dean of Faculty: Dr ANNE CARSON DALY

Vice-Pres. for Admin. and Finance: WAYNE SCROGGINS

Vice-Pres. for College Relations: KENNETH DAVISON, JR

Vice-Pres. for Enrolment Management and Student Affairs: Dr LUCAS LAMADRID

Dir of Admissions: ROGER JONES

Registrar: Fr DAVID BROWN

Dir of Library Services: DONALD BEAGLE

Library of 130,000 vols, 57,000 e-books, 13,000 old and rare books, 650 periodical titles

Number of teachers: 50

Number of students: 1,000

Publications: *Agora, Crossroads*.

BENNETT COLLEGE

Greensboro, NC 27401-3239

Telephone: (336) 517-2100

Fax: (336) 517-2166

E-mail: admiss@bennett.edu

Internet: www.bennett.edu

Founded 1873

Private control

Academic year: August to May (2 semesters)
Offers Bachelors degree in arts, fine arts, science, social work
Pres.: Dr JULIANNE MALVEAUX
Provost and Vice-Pres. for Academic Affairs: ESTHER TERRY
Vice-Pres. for Admin. Services: ANDRENA COLEMAN
Vice-Pres. for Business and Finance: LATONYA FLAMER
Vice-Pres. for Enrolment Management: LES FERRIER, JR
Vice-Pres. for Institutional Advancement: IRIS RAMEY
Registrar: KAREN GREEN
Library Dir: JOAN WILLIAMS
Library of 100,000 vols, 90,000 monographs, 36,000 e-books, 2,400 audiovisual items, 23,000 periodicals
Number of teachers: 61 (full-time)
Number of students: 736 (672 full-time, 64 part-time)

BREVARD COLLEGE

One Brevard College Dr., Brevard, NC 28712
Telephone: (828) 883-8292
E-mail: admissions@brevard.edu
Internet: www.brevard.edu
Founded 1934 by merger of Rutherford College with Weaver Methodist College
Private control
Academic year: August to May (2 semesters)
Major programmes incl. art, biology, business and organizational leadership, criminal justice, English, environmental science, environmental studies, exercise science, general science, health science studies, history, integrated studies, mathematics, music, music education, psychology, religious studies, theatre studies, wilderness leadership and experiential education
Pres.: Dr DAVID JOYCE
Vice-Pres. for Academic Affairs and Dean of Faculty: JOHN S. HARDT
Vice-Pres. for Admissions and Financial Aid: MATHEW COX
Vice-Pres. for Business and Finance: DEBORAH P. HALL
Vice-Pres. for Institutional Advancement: SUSAN L. COTHERN
Dean of Students: CHRISTOPHER J. HOLLAND
Registrar: AMY HERTZ
Dir of Library: MICHAEL M. MCCABE
Library of 58,000 vols, 120,000 e-books, 4,490 audiovisual materials, 200 periodicals, 22,000 e-journals
Number of teachers: 55 (full-time)
Number of students: 658

CABARRUS COLLEGE OF HEALTH SCIENCES

401 Medical Park Dr., Concord, NC 28025-2405
Telephone: (704) 403-1555
Fax: (704) 403-2077
E-mail: admissions@cabarruscollege.edu
Internet: www.cabarruscollege.edu
Founded 1942 as Cabarrus Co Hospital School of Nursing, present name 1996, present status 2000
Private control
Academic year: August to May (2 semesters)
Degree offered in health services leadership and management, medical imaging, nursing
Chancellor: Dr DIANNE O. SNYDER
Provost: Prof. Dr MEG PATCHETT
Dean of Admin. and Financial Services: MARK E. COLEMAN
Dean of Student Services and Enrolment Management: CHRISTINE L. CORSELLO
Registrar: MICHAEL SMITH

Librarian: EMILY PATRIDGE
Library of 6,000 vols, 1,000 video cassettes and journals
Number of students: 477

CAMPBELL UNIVERSITY

POB 567, Buie's Creek, NC 27506
Telephone: (910) 893-1200
Fax: (910) 893-1424
E-mail: buildyourfuture@campbell.edu
Internet: www.campbell.edu
Founded 1887 as Buies Creek Acad., present name 1979
Private control
Academic year: August to May (2 semesters)
Chancellor: Dr NORMAN ADRIAN WIGGINS
Pres.: Prof. Dr JEREMY M. WALLACE
Provost and Vice-Pres. for Academic Affairs: Dr M. DWAINE GREENE
Sr Vice-Pres. for Institutional Advancement: Dr JACK BRITT
Vice-Pres. for Business and Treas.: JIM ROBERTS
Vice-Pres. for Enrolment Management: Dr JOHN ROBERSON
Vice-Pres. for Institutional Advancement: BRITT DAVIS
Vice-Pres. for Student Life: Dr DENNIS BAZEMORE
Registrar: J. DAVID McGIRT
Dean of Library: Dr BORRÉE P. KWOK
Library of 225,000 vols, 129,000 e-books, 284 periodicals, 50,000 e-periodicals, 500,000 microforms
Number of teachers: 428 (175 full-time, 253 part-time)
Number of students: 9,400
Publications: Accolades (1 a year), Campbell Magazine (2 a year), Pine Burr (year book)

DEANS

College of Arts and Sciences: Prof. Dr MARK L. HAMMOND
College of Pharmacy and Health Sciences: Prof. Dr RONALD W. MADDOX
Divinity School: Prof. Dr ANDREW H. WAKEFIELD
Lundy-Fetterman School of Business: Dr BENJAMIN M. HAWKINS
Norman Adrian Wiggins School of Law: Prof. MELISSA ESSARY
School of Education: Dr KAREN P. NERY
School of Osteopathic Medicine: Dr JOHN M. KAUFFMAN

CATAWBA COLLEGE

2300 W Innes St, Salisbury, NC 28144
Telephone: (704) 637-4111
Fax: (704) 637-4222
E-mail: admission@catawba.edu
Internet: www.catawba.edu
Founded 1851
Private control
Academic year: (2 semesters)
Pres.: BRIEN LEWIS
Provost: Dr W. RICHARD STEPHENS, JR
Sr Vice-Pres. for Devt: THOMAS C. CHILDRESS
Vice-Pres. for Enrolment Management: LOIS H. WILLIAMS
Dean of Students: G. BEN SMITH
Registrar: P. CAROL GAMBLE
Library Dir: STEVEN MCKINZIE
Library of 200,000 vols
Number of teachers: 115 (72 full-time, 43 part-time)
Number of students: 1,300

DEANS

Adrian L., Jr and Dorothy L. Shuford School of Performing Arts: Dr BARRY SANG

Enoch A. and Dorothy H. Goodman School of Education: Dr JAMES STRINGFIELD
James F. and Gerry T. Hurley School of Arts and Sciences: Dr STEVEN COGGIN
Ralph W. Ketner School of Business: Dr PAMELA THOMPSON
School of Evening and Graduate Studies: Dr EDITH BOLICK

CHOWAN UNIVERSITY

1 University Pl., Murfreesboro, NC 27855
Telephone: (252) 398-6500
Fax: (252) 398-1190
E-mail: admissions@chowan.edu
Internet: www.chowan.edu
Founded 1848 as Chowan Baptist Female Institute, present name and status 2006
Private control
Academic year: August to July (2 semesters)
Pres.: Dr M. CHRISTOPHER WHITE
Provost and Vice-Pres. for Academic Affairs: Dr DANNY B. MOORE
Vice-Pres. of Business Affairs: DONNIE O. CLARY
Vice-Pres. of Devt: JOHN TAYLOE
Vice-Pres. for Enrolment Management and Dean of Admissions: R. CHAD HOLT
Vice-Pres. for Student Affairs: RANDY HARRELL
Dir of Univ. Relations: JOSH BARKER
Registrar: DONNA WOODARD
Exec. Dir of Library Services: GEORGIA E. WILLIAMS
Library of 230,000 vols, 29,000 periodicals
Number of teachers: 56 (full-time)
Number of students: 1,200
Publication: CU Today Magazine

DEANS

School of Arts and Sciences: Dr ROMEY PEAVLER
School of Business: Dr LINDA L. MILES
School of Education: Dr BRENDA S. TINKHAM
School of Liberal Arts: Dr JOHN DILUSTRO

DAVIDSON COLLEGE

POB 7171, Davidson, NC 28035-7171
209 Ridge Rd, Davidson, NC 28035
Telephone: (704) 894-2000
Fax: (704) 894-2016
E-mail: admission@davidson.edu
Internet: www.davidson.edu
Founded 1837
Private control
Academic year: August to May (2 semesters)
Br. campus in Lake; depts of anthropology, art biology, interdisciplinary studies, chemistry, classics, economics, English, environmental studies, French and Francophone studies, German studies, Hispanic studies, history, Latin American studies, mathematics, music, philosophy, physics, political science, psychology, religion, sociology, theatre
Pres.: Dr CAROL QUILLEN
Vice-Pres. for Academic Affairs and Dean of Faculty: CLARK G. ROSS
Vice-Pres. for College Relations: EILEEN KEELEY
Vice-Pres. for Finance and Admin.: EDWARD A. KANIA
Vice-Pres. for Student Life and Dean of Students: THOMAS C. SHANDLEY
Vice-Pres. and Dean of Admissions and Financial Aid: CHRISTOPHER J. GRUBER
Registrar: Dr HANSFORD M. EPES
Dir of Library: JILL GREMMELS
Library of 600,000 vols, 500,000 e-books, 200,000 fed. govt documents
Number of teachers: 162 (full-time)
Number of students: 1,756

Publications: *Davidson Journal* (4 a year), *Hobart Park* (literary, 1 a year), *Oak Row Report* (12 a year).

DUKE UNIVERSITY

Durham, NC 27708
Telephone: (919) 684-8111
Fax: (919) 684-4500
E-mail: registrar@duke.edu
Internet: www.duke.edu
Founded 1838 as Union Institute Soc. in Randolph Co, present name and status 1924
Private control
Academic year: September to August
Pres.: Prof. Dr RICHARD H. BRODHEAD
Chancellor for Health Affairs and CEO: Dr VICTOR J. DZAU
Provost: Prof. PETER LANGE
Exec. Vice-Pres. and Treas.: Dr TALLMAN TRASK, III
Vice-Pres. and Gen. Counsel: Dr PAMELA J. BERNARD
Vice-Pres. and Univ. Sec.: RICHARD RIDDELL
Vice-Pres. for Admin.: KYLE CAVANAUGH
Vice-Pres. for Alumni Affairs and Devt: ROBERT SHEPARD
Vice-Pres. for Durham and Regional Affairs: PHAIL WYNN, JR
Vice-Pres. for Information Technology and Chief Information Officer: TRACY FUTHEY
Vice-Pres. for Student Affairs: Dr LARRY MONETA
Registrar: BRUCE CUNNINGHAM
Univ. Librarian and Vice-Provost for Library Affairs: Dr DEBORAH JAKUBS

Library of 6,340,456 vols
Number of teachers: 1,779
Number of students: 14,746 (6,526 undergraduate, 8,220 graduate and professional)
Publications: *American Literary Scholarship* (1 a year), *American Literature* (4 a year), *American Speech* (4 a year), *boundary 2* (3 a year), *Camera Obscura* (4 a year), *Common Knowledge* (2 a year), *Comparative Studies of South Asia, Africa and the Middle East* (2 a year), *Duke Gifted Letter* (4 a year), *Duke Mathematical Journal* (15 a year), *Eighteenth-Century Life* (3 a year), *Environmental History* (4 a year), *Ethnohistory* (4 a year), *French Historical Studies* (4 a year), *GLQ: A Journal of Lesbian and Gay Studies* (4 a year), *Hispanic American Historical Review* (4 a year), *History of Political Economy* (4 a year), *Journal of Health Politics, Policy and Law* (6 a year), *Journal of Medieval and Early Modern Studies* (3 a year), *Lesbian and Gay Studies Newsletter* (3 a year), *Mediterranean Quarterly* (4 a year), *Modern Language Quarterly* (4 a year), *Nepantla: Views from the South* (3 a year), *Pedagogy* (3 a year), *Poetics Today* (4 a year), *Positions* (3 a year), *Public Culture* (3 a year), *Radical History Review* (3 a year), *Social Science History* (4 a year), *Social Text* (4 a year), *South Atlantic Quarterly* (4 a year), *Theater* (3 a year), *Transition* (4 a year)

DEANS

Divinity School: Prof. Dr RICHARD HAYS
Fuqua School of Business: Dr WILLIAM BOULDING
Graduate School: Prof. Dr DAVID BELL
Nicholas School of the Environment: WILLIAM L. CHAMEIDES
Pratt School of Engineering: Prof. Dr THOMAS C. KATSOULEAS
Sanford School of Public Policy: Prof. Dr BRUCE R. KUNIHOLM
School of Law: Dr DAVID F. LEVI

School of Medicine: Prof. Dr NANCY C. ANDREWS
School of Nursing: Prof. Dr CATHERINE L. GILLISS
Trinity College of Arts and Sciences: LAURIE L. PATTON

PROFESSORS

ABOU-DONIA, M. B., Pharmacology and Cancer Biology
ADDISON, W. A., Obstetrics and Gynaecology
AERS, D., English
AGARWAL, P. K., Computer Science
AKWARI, O. E., Surgery
ALBALA, D. M., Surgery
ALDRICH, J., Political Science
ALLARD, W. K., Mathematics
ALLEN, N. B., Medicine
ANDERSON, E. E., Surgery
ANDERSON, P. A. W., Paediatrics
ANDERSON, R. W., Surgery
ANDERSON, W. B., Ophthalmology
ANDREWS, E., Slavic Languages and Literature
ANLYAN, W. G., Surgery
ANSCHER, M. S., Radiation Oncology
APPLEWHITE, J. W., English
ASHER, S. R., Psychology, Social and Health Sciences
ASHTON, R. H., Business Administration
AUGUSTINE, G. J., Jr, Neurobiology
AVISSAR, R., Civil and Environmental Engineering
BAILLIE, J., Medicine
BAKER, H. A., English
BAKER, P. A., Earth and Ocean Sciences
BALDWIN, S. W., Chemistry
BARANGER, H. U., Physics
BARBER, R. T., Marine Sciences
BARR, R. C., Biomedical Engineering
BARTLETT, J. A., Medicine
BARTLETT, K., Law
BASHORE, T. M., Medicine
BASSETT, F. H., III, Surgery
BEALE, J. T., Mathematics
BEALE, S. S., Law
BECKWITH, S., English
BEEN, M. D., Biochemistry
BEHAR, V. S., Medicine
BEHRINGER, R. P., Physics
BEJAN, A., Mechanical Engineering
BELL, D. F., Romance Studies
BENFEY, P. N., Biology
BENNETT, G. V., Cell Biology
BENNETT, P. B., Anaesthesiology
BERATAN, D. N., Chemistry
BERCHUCK, A., Obstetrics and Gynaecology
BERGER, J. O., Statistics
BERTOZZI, A. L., Mathematics
BETTMAN, J. R., Business Administration
BIERMANN, A. W., Computer Science
BIGNER, D. D., Pathology
BISSET, G. S., III, Radiology
BLAND, K. P., Religion
BLAZER, D. G., Psychiatry and Behavioural Sciences
BLUMENTHAL, J. A., Psychiatry and Behavioural Sciences
BOATWRIGHT, M. T., Classical Studies
BOLLERSLEV, T., Economics
BOLLINGER, R. R., Surgery
BOLOGNESI, D. P., Surgery
BONAVENTURA, C. J., Marine Sciences
BONAVENTURA, J., Marine Sciences
BONK, J. F., Chemistry
BORCHARDT, F. L., Germanic Languages
BOSSEN, E. H., Pathology
BOULDING, W. F., Business Administration
BOWIE, J. D., Radiology
BOYLE, J. D. A., Law
BRADFORD, W. D., Pathology
BRADLEY, M., Business Administration
BRADY, D. J., Electrical and Computer Engineering
BRANDON, R. N., Philosophy
BREEDEN, D. T., Business Administration

BRIZEL, D. M., Radiation Oncology
BRODIE, H. K. H., Psychiatry and Behavioural Sciences
BROWN, A. S., Electrical and Computer Engineering
BROWN, H. L., Obstetrics and Gynaecology
BRUZELIUS, C., Art and Art History
BRYANT, R., Mathematics
BUCKLEY, E. G., Ophthalmology
BUCKLEY, P. J., Pathology
BUCKLEY, R. H., Paediatrics
BUEHLER, A., Health, Physical Education and Recreation
BURCH, JR, W. M., Medicine
BURIAN, P. H., Classical Studies
BURNS, B. J., Psychiatry and Behavioural Sciences
BURTON, R. M., Business Administration
BUTTERS, R. R., English
CALIFF, R. M., Medicine
CARIN, L., Electrical and Computer Engineering
CARON, M. G., Cell Biology
CARRINGTON, P. D., Law
CARROLL, B. A., Radiology
CARTER, J. H., Psychiatry and Behavioural Sciences
CARTMILL, M., Biological Anthropology and Anatomy
CASEY, P. J., Pharmacology and Cancer Biology
CHAFE, W. H., History
CHAO, N. J., Medicine
CHEN, Y., Paediatrics
CHIKARAISHI, D. M., Neurobiology
CHRISTENSEN, N. L., Earth and Environmental Sciences
CHRISTIE, G. C., Law
CLARK, E. A., Religion
CLARK, J. S., Biology
CLARK, R. L., Mechanical Engineering
CLARKE-PEARSON, D. L., Obstetrics and Gynaecology
CLAY, D., Classical Studies
CLEMENTS, D. A., III, Paediatrics
CLIPP, E. C., Nursing
CLOTFELTER, C., Public Policy Studies
CLUM, J. M., Theatre Studies
COBB, F. R., Medicine
COCKS, F. H., Mechanical Engineering
COFFMAN, T. M., Medicine
COHEN, H. J., Medicine
COHEN, W. M., Business Administration
COHN, J. A., Medicine
COIE, J. D., Psychology, Social and Health Sciences
COLEMAN, R. E., Radiology
COLEMAN, W. J., Business Administration
COLVIN, O. M., Medicine
COOK, D. R., Anaesthesiology
COOK, P. J., Public Policy Studies
COOKE, M., Asian and African Language and Literature
COREY, G. R., Medicine
CORLISS, B., Earth and Ocean Sciences
COSTANZO, P. R., Psychology, Social and Health Sciences
COSTELLO, E. J., Psychiatry and Behavioural Sciences
COX, J. D., Law
CRAWFORD, J., Medicine
CRENSHAW, J. L., Divinity
CROVITZ, H. F., Psychiatry and Behavioural Sciences
CROWDER, L. B., Marine Sciences
CROWLEY, T. J., Earth and Ocean Sciences
CRUMBLISS, A. L., Chemistry
CULLEN, B. R., Molecular Genetics and Microbiology
CULP, J. M., Law
DAVIDSON, C. N., English
DAVIDSON, J. R., Psychiatry and Behavioural Sciences
DAVIS, N. G., Classical Studies
DAWSON, J. R., Immunology

DE BELLIS, M. D., Psychiatry and Behavioural Sciences
DELLINGER, W. E., Law
DELONG, G. R., Paediatrics
DE MARCHI, N., Economics
DEMOTT, D., Law
DENEEF, A. L., English
DESANCTIS, G., Business Administration
DEWHIRST, M. W., Radiation Oncology
DI GIULIO, R. T., Earth and Environmental Sciences
DIPRETE, T. A., Sociology
DODGE, K. A., Public Policy Studies
DOWELL, E. H., Mechanical Engineering
ECKERMAN, C. O., Psychological and Brain Sciences
EDELSBRUNNER, H., Computer Science
EDWARDS, G. S., Physics
EFIRD, J. M., Divinity
ELLINWOOD, E. H., JR, Psychiatry and Behavioural Sciences
ELLIS, C. S., Computer Science
ENDOW, S. A., Cell Biology
ENGLISH, P. C., History
EPSTEIN, D. L., Ophthalmology
ERICKSON, C. J., Psychological and Brain Sciences
ERICKSON, H. P., Cell Biology
EVERETT, R. O., Law
FAIR, R. B., Electrical and Computer Engineering
FALLETTA, J. M., Paediatrics
FARMER, J. C., Surgery
FEINGLOS, M. N., Medicine
FISCHER, G. W., Business Administration
FISH, P. G., Political Science
FISHER, S. R., Surgery
FITZPATRICK, D., Neurobiology
FLANAGAN, O., Philosophy
FLEISHMAN, J., Law
FLOYD, C. E., JR, Radiology
FOREMAN, J. W., Paediatrics
FORWARD, R. B., Marine Sciences
FRANCES, A. J., Psychiatry and Behavioural Sciences
FRANCIS, J., Business Administration
FRANK, M. M., Paediatrics
FREEMARK, M. S., Paediatrics
FRIEDMAN, A. H., Surgery
FRIEDMAN, H. S., Paediatrics
FRIEDMAN, M., Biomedical Engineering
FULKERSON, W. J., JR, Medicine
GAINES, J. M., Literature
GARCIA-BLANCO, M. A., Molecular Genetics and Microbiology
GARCI-GOMEZ, M., Romance Studies
GARG, D. P., Mechanical Engineering
GASPAR, B., History
GAVINS, R., History
GELFAND, A., Statistics
GEORGE, L. K., Sociology
GEORGE, S. L., Biostatistics and Bioinformatics
GEORGIADE, G. S., Surgery
GEREFFI, G., Sociology
GILBOA, E., Surgery
GILLESPIE, M. A., Political Science
GILLIAM, B., Music
GLANDER, K. E., Biological Anthropology and Anatomy
GLOWER, D. D., JR, Surgery
GOCKERMAN, J. P., Medicine
GOLDBERG, R. N., Paediatrics
GOLDING, M. P., Philosophy
GOLDSCHMIDT, P. J., Medicine
GOLDSTEIN, L. B., Medicine
GOODMAN, P. C., Radiology
GOODWIN, C. D., Economics
GOODWYN, L. C., History
GOSHAW, A. T., Physics
GRABOWSKI, H. G., Economics
GRAHAM, D. A., Economics
GRANT, A. O., Medicine
GRANT, J. P., Surgery
GRANT, R. W., Political Science
GREENBERG, C. S., Medicine

GREENFIELD, J. C., JR, Medicine
GREENLEAF, A. L., Biochemistry
GREENSIDE, H., Physics
GREER, M. R., Romance Studies
GRIECO, J., Political Science
GRIFFITHS, P. A., Mathematics
HAAGEN, P. H., Law
HAFF, P. K., Earth and Ocean Sciences
HAIN, R., Mathematics
HALL, K. C., Mechanical Engineering
HALL, R. P., III, Medicine
HALL, W. C., Neurobiology
HALL, W. G., Psychological and Brain Sciences
HALPERIN, E. C., Radiation Oncology
HAMILTON, J. A., Psychology, Social and Health Sciences
HAMILTON, J. D., Medicine
HAMMES, G. G., Biochemistry
HAMMOND, C. B., Obstetrics and Gynaecology
HAN, M. Y., Physics
HANEY, A. F., Obstetrics and Gynaecology
HARER, J., Mathematics
HARMAN, C. M., Mechanical Engineering
HARRELSON, J. M., Surgery
HARVEY, C. R., Business Administration
HAUERWAS, S. M., Divinity
HAVIGHURST, C. C., Law
HAYNES, B. F., Medicine
HAYS, P. D., Divinity
HEALY, R. G., Earth and Environmental Sciences
HEINZ, E. R., Radiology
HEITMAN, J. B., Molecular Genetics and Microbiology
HEITZENRATER, R. P., Divinity
HELMS, C. A., Radiology
HERRUP, C. B., History
HERSHFIELD, M. S., Medicine
HERTZBERG, B. S., Radiology
HILL, G. B., Obstetrics and Gynaecology
HILL, R. L., Biochemistry
HILLERBRAND, H. J., Religion
HINTON, D. E., Earth and Environmental Sciences
HOCHMUTH, R. M., Mechanical Engineering
HOFFMAN, M. R., Pathology
HOLLOWAY, R. L., English
HOROWITZ, D. L., Law
HOUGH, J. F., Political Science
HOWELL, C. R., Physics
HSIEH, D. A., Business Administration
HSIEH, T., Biochemistry
HUANG, A. T., Medicine
HUBER, J. C., Business Administration
HYLANDER, W. L., Biological Anthropology and Anatomy
JAFFE, G. J., Ophthalmology
JAFFE, S., Music
JAMESON, F., Literature
JASZCZAK, R. J., Radiology
JENNINGS, R. B., Pathology
JENTLESON, B. W., Public Policy Studies
JIRTLE, R. L., Radiation Oncology
JOHNSON, G. A., Radiology
JOHNSON, K. M., Engineering
JOHNSON, V. E., Statistics
JOINES, W. T., Electrical and Computer Engineering
JONES, L. G., Divinity
JONES, R. H., Surgery
JONES, T., Law
KAMAKURA, W. A., Business Administration
KANE, W. H., Medicine
KAPLAN, A., Romance Studies
KARSON, J. A., Earth and Ocean Sciences
KATUL, G. G., Earth and Environmental Sciences
KATZ, D. F., Biomedical Engineering
KATZ, L. C., Neurobiology
KAY, R. F., Biological Anthropology and Anatomy
KEEFE, F. J., Psychiatry and Behavioural Sciences
KEENE, J. D., Molecular Genetics and Microbiology

KELLER, T. F., Business Administration
KELLEY, A. C., Economics
KELSOE, G. H., Immunology
KEOHANE, N. O., Political Science
KEOHANE, R., Political Science
KERN, F. H., Anaesthesiology
KIEHART, D. P., Biology
KILLENBERG, P. G., Medicine
KIMBROUGH, K. P., Economics
KINNEY, T. R., Paediatrics
KIRBY, M. L., Paediatrics
KISSLO, J. A., Medicine
KITSCHELT, H. P., Political Science
KLINTWORTH, G. K., Pathology
KOCH, W. J., Surgery
KOONZ, C., History
KORNBERG, A., Political Science
KORT, W. A., Religion
KRAMER, R. A., Earth and Environmental Sciences
KREDICH, N. M., Medicine
KREUZER, K. N., Biochemistry
KRISHNAN, K. R. R., Psychiatry and Behavioural Sciences
KROLIK, J. L., Electrical and Computer Engineering
KUHN, C. M., Pharmacology and Cancer Biology
KUNIHOLM, B. R., Public Policy Studies
KUO, P. C., Surgery
KURTZBERG, J., Paediatrics
KYLE, A. S., Business Administration
LADD, H., Public Policy Studies
LAHUSEN, T., Literature
LAND, K. C., Sociology
LANGE, D. L., Law
LANGE, P., Political Science
LAUGHHUNN, D. J., Business Administration
LAVINE, M. L., Statistics
LAWLER, G. F., Mathematics
LAWRENCE, B. B., Religion
LAYTON, H., Mathematics
LEE, P. P., Ophthalmology
LEFKOWITZ, R. J., Medicine
LEIGHT, G. S., Surgery
LEIGHTEN, P., Art and Art History
LENTRICCHIA, F., Literature
LEVIN, L. S., Surgery
LEWIN, A. Y., Business Administration
LEWIS, D. V., Paediatrics
LIDDLE, R. A., Medicine
LIN, N., Sociology
LIND, E. A., Business Administration
LINNEY, E. A., Molecular Genetics and Microbiology
LISCHER, R., Divinity
LIVINGSTONE, D. A., Biology
LOCHMULLER, C. H., Chemistry
LOCKHEAD, G. R., Psychological and Brain Sciences
LOGUE, P. E., Psychiatry and Behavioural Sciences
LONGINO, M., Romance Studies
LOONEY, J. G., Psychiatry and Behavioural Sciences
LOWE, J. E., Surgery
LYERLY, H. K., Surgery
LYLES, K. W., Medicine
LYNCH, J. G., Business Administration
MCCANN, R. L., Surgery
MCCARTHY, G., Radiology
MCCLAIN, P. D., Political Science
MCCLAY, D. R., Biology
MCCUEN, B. W., Ophthalmology
MCDONNELL, D. P., Pharmacology and Cancer Biology
MCELROY, M. B., Economics
MCGOVERN, F. E., Law
MCGOWN, L., Chemistry
MCINTOSH, T. J., Cell Biology
MACINTYRE, N. R., Medicine
MCLENDON, R. E., Pathology
MCNAMARA, J. O., Sr, Neurobiology
MCPHAIL, A. T., Chemistry
MADDEN, D. J., Psychiatry and Behavioural Sciences

MAHONEY, E. P., Philosophy
MALIN, P. E., Earth and Environmental Sciences
MARCH, J. S., Psychiatry and Behavioural Sciences
MARCUS, J., Divinity
MARINOS, P. N., Electrical and Computer Engineering
MARK, D. B., Medicine
MARK, J. B., Anaesthesiology
MARKS, L. B., Radiation Oncology
MARTINEZ, S., Radiology
MASON, R. M., Surgery
MASSEY, J. M., Medicine
MASSOUD, H. Z., Electrical and Computer Engineering
MATCHAR, D. B., Medicine
MAUSKOPF, S., History
MEANS, A. R., Pharmacology and Cancer Biology
MECK, W. H., Psychological and Brain Sciences
MEDINA, M. A., Civil and Environmental Engineering
METZLOFF, T. B., Law
MEYERS, C. L., Religion
MEYERS, E. M., Religion
MICKIEWICZ, E., Public Policy Studies
MIGNOLO, W., Literature
MILLER, M. A., History
MILLS, E., Pharmacology and Cancer Biology
MITCHELL, W. G., Business Administration
MODRICH, P. L., Biochemistry
MOI, T., Literature
MOON, R. E., Anaesthesiology
MOORE, J. O., Medicine
MOORMAN, C., Business Administration
MOREIRAS, A., Romance Studies
MORGAN, S. P., Sociology
MORRIS, J. J., Medicine
MORRIS, M., Law
MORRISON, D. R., Mathematics
MOSTELLER, R. P., Law
MUDIMBE, V., Literature
MUELLER, B., Physics
MUNGER, M. C., Political Science
NADLER, J. V., Pharmacology and Cancer Biology
NEEDHAM, D., Mechanical Engineering
NELSON, R. C., Radiology
NEVINS, J. R., Molecular Genetics and Microbiology
NEWGARD, C. B., Pharmacology and Cancer Biology
NEWMAN, M. F., Anaesthesiology
NICKLAS, R. B., Biology
NICOLELIS, M. A., Neurobiology
NIJHOUT, H. F., Biology
NIOU, E. S., Political Science
NOLTE, L. W., Electrical and Computer Engineering
NOWICKI, S., Biology
NUNLEY, J. A., II, Surgery
O'BARR, W. M., Cultural Anthropology
OH, S., Physics
OLSEN, E. A., Medicine
O'RAND, A. M., Sociology
OREN, R., Earth and Environmental Sciences
ORR, L., Romance Studies
OSTBYE, T., Community and Family Medicine
PALETZ, D. L., Political Science
PALMER, R. A., Chemistry
PALMER, R. G., Physics
PAPPAS, T. N., Surgery
PARDON, W. L., Mathematics
PARKERSON, G. R., Community and Family Medicine
PATZ, E. F., Radiology
PAULSON, D. F., Surgery
PAULSON, E. K., Radiology
PAYNE, C. M., History
PAYNE, J. W., Business Administration
PERFECT, J. R., Medicine
PERICAK-VANCE, M. A., Medicine
PETER, R. H., Medicine

PETROSKI, H., Civil and Environmental Engineering
PHILLIPS, H. R., III, Medicine
PIANTADOSI, C. A., Medicine
PIMM, S. L., Earth and Environmental Sciences
PIRRUNG, M. C., Chemistry
PISETSKY, D. S., Medicine
PIZZO, S. V., Pathology
POPE, D., English
PORTER, J. A., English
POWELL, H. J., Law
POWELL, R. J., Art and Art History
PREMINGER, G. M., Surgery
PRICE, D. E., Political Science
PRICE, E. R., English
PROSNITZ, L. R., Radiation Oncology
PROVENZALE, J. M., Radiology
PUROHIT, D., Business Administration
PURVES, D., Neurobiology
PUTALLAZ, M., Psychology, Social and Health Sciences
QUARLES, L. D., Medicine
QUILLIGAN, M., English
QUINN, N., Cultural Anthropology
RADTKE, R. A., Medicine
RADWAY, J. A., Literature
RAETZ, C. R. H., Biochemistry
RAJAGOPALAN, K. V., Biochemistry
RAMUS, J. S., Marine Sciences
RAUSHER, M. D., Biology
RAVIN, C. E., Radiology
RECKHOW, K. H., Earth and Environmental Sciences
REDDY, W. M., History
REED, M. C., Mathematics
REEDY, M. K., Cell Biology
REICHERT, W. M., Biomedical Engineering
REICHMAN, J. H., Law
REIF, J. H., Computer Science
REINSMOEN, N. L., Pathology
RELLER, L. B., Pathology
REMMER, K. L., Political Science
REPPY, W. A., Law
REYNOLDS, J. F., Biology
RICHARDS, J. F., History
RICHARDSON, C. J., Earth and Environmental Sciences
RICHARDSON, D. C., Biochemistry
RICHARDSON, J. S., Biochemistry
RICHTER, D. D., Earth and Environmental Sciences
RIGSBY, K. J., Classical Studies
ROBBOY, S. J., Pathology
ROCKEY, D. C., Medicine
ROCKMAN, H. A., Medicine
ROGGLI, V. L., Pathology
ROLAND, A., History
ROLLESTON, J. L., Germanic Languages
ROSE, D., Computer Science
ROSENBERG, A., Philosophy
ROTH, S., Psychology, Social and Health Sciences
ROWE, T. D., Law
RUBIN, D. C., Psychological and Brain Sciences
RYAN, T. J., Medicine
SABISTON, D. C., Surgery
SACKS, J., Statistics
ST CLAIR, E. W., Medicine
SAMULSKI, T. V., Radiation Oncology
SANDERS, D. B., Medicine
SANDERS, E. P., Religion
SANDERS, S. P., Paediatrics
SANFORD, D. H., Philosophy
SCHAEFFER, D. G., Mathematics
SCHANBERG, S. M., Pharmacology and Cancer Biology
SCHIFFMAN, S. S., Psychiatry and Behavioural Sciences
SCHLESINGER, W. H., Biology
SCHMALBECK, R. L., Law
SCHMECHEL, D. E., Medicine
SCHOEN, C. L., Mathematics
SCHOMBERG, D. W., Obstetrics and Gynaecology

SCHROEDER, C., Law
SCHULMAN, K. A., Medicine
SCHWAB, S. J., Medicine
SCHWARCZ, S. L., Law
SCHWARTZ, D. A., Medicine
SCHWARTZ-BLOOM, R. D., Pharmacology and Cancer Biology
SCHWINN, D. A., Anaesthesiology
SEIGLER, H. F., Surgery
SEXTON, D. J., Medicine
SHATZMILLER, J., History
SHAUGHNESSY, E. J., Mechanical Engineering
SHAW, A. J., Biology
SHAW, B. R., Chemistry
SHELBURNE, J. D., Pathology
SHENOLIKAR, S., Pharmacology and Cancer Biology
SHEPPARD, B. H., Business Administration
SHERWOOD, A., Psychiatry and Behavioural Sciences
SIEDOW, J. N., Biology
SIEGEL, L. M., Biochemistry
SIEGLER, I. C., Psychiatry and Behavioural Sciences
SIMEL, D. L., Medicine
SIMON, J. D., Chemistry
SIMON, S. A., Neurobiology
SIMONS, E. L., Biological Anthropology and Anatomy
SIMPSON, I. H., Sociology
SLOAN, F. A., Economics
SLOTKIN, T. A., Pharmacology and Cancer Biology
SMITH, B. C., Philosophy
SMITH, B. H., Literature
SMITH, K. K., Biology
SMITH, P. K., Surgery
SMITH, S. W., Biomedical Engineering
SMITH, T. P., Radiology
SNYDERMAN, R., Medicine
SOPER, J. T., Obstetrics and Gynaecology
SPENNER, K. I., Sociology
SPICER, L. D., Radiology
SPRAGENS, T. A., Political Science
SPRITZER, C. E., Radiology
STADDON, J. E. R., Psychological and Brain Sciences
STAELIN, R., Business Administration
STAMLER, J. S., Medicine
STANLEY, D. K., Classical Studies
STEEGE, D. A., Biochemistry
STEINMETZ, D. C., Divinity
STERN, M. A., Mathematics
STEWART, P., Romance Studies
STILES, G. L., Medicine
STRANDBERG, V. H., English
STRAUMAN, T. J., Psychology, Social and Health Sciences
STRITTMATTER, W. J., Medicine
STROHBEHN, J. W., Biomedical Engineering
SUGARMAN, J., Medicine
SULLENGER, B. A., Surgery
SULLIVAN, K. M., Medicine
SURIN, K. J., Literature
SURWIT, R. S., Psychiatry and Behavioural Sciences
SVETKEY, L. P., Medicine
SWARTZ, M. S., Psychiatry and Behavioural Sciences
TAN, T. Y., Mechanical Engineering
TAUCHEN, G. E., Economics
TAYLOR, C. R., Economics
TEDDER, T. F., Immunology
TELEN, M. J., Medicine
TERBORGH, J. W., Earth and Environmental Sciences
THOMAS, J., Romance Studies
THOMAS, J. E., Physics
THOMPSON, J. H., History
THOMPSON, R. J., Psychology, Social and Health Sciences
THOMPSON, W. M., Radiology
TIRYAKIAN, E. A., Sociology
TODD, R. L., Music
TOONE, E. J., Chemistry
TORGOVNICK, M., English

TORNOW, W., Physics
TOWER, E., Economics
TRAHEY, G. E., Biomedical Engineering
TRANGENSTEIN, J. A., Mathematics
TREEM, W. R., Paediatrics
TRIVEDI, K. S., Electrical and Computer Engineering
TRUSKEY, G. A., Biomedical Engineering
TURNER, B. S., Nursing
TURNER, D. A., Surgery
TYREY, E. L., Obstetrics and Gynaecology
ULSHEN, M. H., Paediatrics
UNDERKUFFLER, L. S., Law
URBANIAK, J. R., Surgery
UYENOYAMA, M. K., Biology
VAN ALSTYNE, W. W., Law
VANCE, J. M., Medicine
VAN ROMPAY, L., Religion
VAN SCHAIK, C., Biological Anthropology and Anatomy
VENAKIDES, S., Mathematics
VERNON, J. M., Economics
VIDMAR, N. J., Law
VILGALYS, R. J., Biology
VISWANATHAN, S., Business Administration
VOGEL, S., Biology
VON RAMM, O. T., Biomedical Engineering
WACKER, G. A., Divinity
WAINWRIGHT, G., Divinity
WALLACH, M. A., Psychological and Brain Sciences
WALTER, R. L., Physics
WALTHER, P. J., Surgery
WANG, P. P., Electrical and Computer Engineering
WARE, R. E., Paediatrics
WARNER, D. S., Anaesthesiology
WEBSTER, G. D., Surgery
WEBSTER, R. E., Biochemistry
WEINBERG, J. B., Medicine
WEINER, R. D., Psychiatry and Behavioural Sciences
WEINERTH, J. L., Surgery
WEINHOLD, K. J., Surgery
WEINTRAUB, E. R., Economics
WEISTART, J. C., Law
WELLER, H. R., Physics
WELLS, S. A., Surgery
WEST, M., Statistics
WHALEY, R. E., Business Administration
WHARTON, A. W., Art and Art History
WHITE, R. A., Biology
WIENER, J. B., Law
WILBUR, R. L., Biology
WILKINS, R. H., Surgery
WILKINSON, W. E., Biostatistics and Bioinformatics
WILLIAMS, C. L., Psychological and Brain Sciences
WILLIAMS, K. J., English
WILLIAMS, R. B., Psychiatry and Behavioural Sciences
WILLIAMS, R. S., Medicine
WILLIMON, W. H., Divinity
WILSON, J., Sociology
WILSON, J. A. P., Medicine
WILSON, K. H., Medicine
WILSON, R. L., Nursing
WINKLER, R. L., Business Administration
WITT, R. G., History
WOLBARSHT, M. L., Psychological and Brain Sciences
WOLFE, W. G., Surgery
WOLPERT, R. L., Statistics
WONG, D. B., Philosophy
WOOD, P. H., History
WRIGHT, J. R., Cell Biology
YANG, W., Chemistry
YARGER, W. E., Medicine
YOUNG, S. L., Medicine
ZALUTSKY, M. R., Radiology
ZHOU, X., Mathematics
ZHOU, X., Sociology
ZIPKIN, P. H., Business Administration

ELON UNIVERSITY

100 Campus Dr., Elon, NC 27244
Telephone: (336) 278-2000
Fax: (336) 278-7699
E-mail: admissions@elon.edu
Internet: www.elon.edu

Founded 1889 as Elon College, present name and status 2001
Private control
Academic year: September to May (2 semesters)

Pres.: Dr LEO M. LAMBERT
Exec. Vice-Pres.: GERALD L. FRANCIS
Provost and Vice-Pres. for Academic Affairs: STEVEN D. HOUSE
Sr Vice-Pres. for Business, Finance and Technology: GERALD O. WHITTINGTON
Vice-Pres. for Admissions and Financial Planning: SUSAN C. KLOPMAN
Vice-Pres. for Student Life and Dean of Students: G. SMITH JACKSON
Vice-Pres. for Univ. Advancement: JIM PIATT
Vice-Pres. for Univ. Communications: DANIEL J. ANDERSON
Dean and Univ. Librarian: KATE D. HICKEY

Library of 300,000 vols, 40,000 e-journals, 20,000 audiovisual items
Number of teachers: 364 (full-time)
Number of students: 5,916 (5,225 undergraduate, 691 graduate)

DEANS

Elon College, College of Arts and Sciences: Dr ALISON MORRISON-SHETLAR
Martha and Spencer Love School of Business: Dr SCOTT BUECHLER
School of Communications: Prof. Dr PAUL PARSONS
School of Education: Prof. Dr DAVID COOPER
School of Health Sciences: Dr ELIZABETH A. ROGERS
School of Law: Prof. Dr GEORGE R. JOHNSON, JR

GARDNER-WEBB UNIVERSITY

POB 997, Boiling Springs, NC 28017
110 S Main St, Boiling Springs, NC 28017
Telephone: (704) 406-4000
Fax: (704) 406-4261
E-mail: admissions@gardner-webb.edu
Internet: www.gardner-webb.edu

Founded 1905 as Boiling Springs High School; present name and status 1993
Private control
Academic year: August to May

Pres.: Prof. Dr ARNOLD FRANK BONNER
Provost and Sr Vice-Pres.: Dr BEN C. LESLIE
Vice-Pres. for Advancement: RALPH DIXON, JR
Vice-Pres. for Business and Finance: MIKE W. HARDIN
Vice-Pres. and Dean of Student Devt: BRUCE MOORE
Vice-Pres. for Enrolment Management: JACK BUCHANAN
Registrar: STEPHEN SAIN
Dean of Libraries: MARY ROBY

Library of 200,000 vols, 27,000 e-books
Number of teachers: 147 (full-time)
Number of students: 4,300

GREENSBORO COLLEGE

815 W Market St, Greensboro, NC 27401-1875
Telephone: (336) 272-7102
Fax: (336) 271-6634
E-mail: admissions@gborocollege.edu
Internet: www.greensboro.edu

Founded 1838
Private control
Academic year: August to May (2 semesters)

Depts of accounting, art, business admin. and economics, education, English and communication studies, French, history, kinesiology, mathematics and computer science, music, natural sciences, political science and legal admin., psychology, religion, sociology, Spanish, theatre

Pres.: Prof. Dr LAWRENCE D. CZARDA
Vice-Pres. for Academic Affairs and Dean of Faculty: Prof. PAUL L. LESLIE
Vice-Pres. for Enrolment Management and Marketing: COLLEEN F. MURPHY
Vice-Pres. for Institutional Advancement: CAROLYN KOZUCH DEFRANCESCO
Vice-Pres. for Student Affairs: ROBIN L. DANIEL
Dean of Students: ILONA T. OWENS
Dir of Admissions: JULIANNE SCHATZ
Registrar: CAROL G. WILLIAMS
Library Dir: CHRISTINE A. WHITTINGTON

Library of 500,000 vols
Number of teachers: 114 (64 full-time, 50 part-time)
Number of students: 1,250

Publication: *Points Of Pride* (1 a year).

GUILFORD COLLEGE

5800 W Friendly Ave, Greensboro, NC 27410
Telephone: (336) 316-2000
Fax: (336) 316-2949
E-mail: admission@guilford.edu
Internet: www.guilford.edu

Founded 1837 as New Garden Boarding School, present name and status 1888
Private control
Academic year: August to May (2 semesters)

Liberal arts college; areas of study incl. accounting, art, English, geology, integrative studies, int. political economy, peace and conflict studies, philosophy, physics, political science, psychology, sociology and anthropology, sport admin., theatre studies, visual arts

Pres.: Prof. Dr KENT JOHN CHABOTAR
Vice-Pres. for Academic Affairs and Academic Dean: ADRIENNE ISRAEL
Vice-Pres. for Admin.: JON VARNELL
Vice-Pres. for Advancement: MIKE POSTON
Vice-Pres. for Enrolment Services: RANDY DOSS
Vice-Pres. for Finance: GREG BURSAVICH
Vice-Pres. for Student Affairs and Dean of Students: AARON FETROW
Library Dir: LEAH MCGINNIS DUNN

Library of 240,000 vols incl. periodicals
Number of teachers: 132 (full-time)
Number of students: 2,739

Publications: *Journal of Undergraduate Mathematics* (2 a year), *Journal of Undergraduate Research in Physics* (2 a year), *The Greenleaf Review* (1 a year), *The Southern Friend* (2 a year).

HIGH POINT UNIVERSITY

833 Montlieu Ave, High Point, NC 27262-3598
Telephone: (336) 841-9000
Fax: (336) 841-4599
Internet: www.highpoint.edu

Founded 1924 as High Point College, present name 1991
Private control
Academic year: August to May (2 semesters)

Pres.: Dr NIDO R. QUBEIN
Provost and Vice-Pres. for Academic Affairs: Dr DENNIS G. CARROLL
Vice-Pres. and Chief of Staff: CHRISTOPHER DUDLEY
Vice-Pres. for Business Affairs: Dr DENNY G. BOLTON
Vice-Pres. for Enrolment: ANDY BILLS

Vice-Pres. for Institutional Advancement: BETH BRAXTON
Vice-Pres. for Student Life: GAIL C. TUTTLE
Dean of Students: Dr KEVIN SNYDER
Registrar: DIANA LEE ESTEY
Dir of Library Services: DAVID L. BRYDEN
Library of 310,000 vols
Number of teachers: 166 (full-time)
Number of students: 3,689 (undergraduate)
Publication: *HPU Magazine*

DEANS

College of Arts and Science: Dr CAROLE B. STONEKING
Earl N. Phillips School of Business: Dr JAMES B. WEHRLEY
Nido R. Qubein School of Communication: WILFRED TREMBLAY
Norcross Graduate School: Dr ALBERTA HERRON
School of Art and Design: TURPIN JOINS
School of Education: Dr MARIANN TILLERY

JOHNSON C. SMITH UNIVERSITY

100 Beatties Ford Rd, Charlotte, NC 28216
Telephone: (704) 378-1000
Fax: (704) 372-5746
E-mail: admissions@jcsu.edu
Internet: www.jcsu.edu
Founded 1867 as Biddle Memorial Institute, present name 1923
Private control
Academic year: August to May (2 semesters)
Pres.: Dr RONALD CARTER
Exec. Vice-Pres. and Chief Operating Officer: Dr ELFRED PINKARD
Vice-Pres. for Business and Finance: GERALD HECTOR
Vice-Pres. for Institutional Advancement: JOY PAIGE
Vice-Pres. for Student Affairs: JEFFREY SMITH
Dean of Enrolment Services: CATHERINE HURD
Dean of Students: CATHY JONES
Dir of Admissions: DWIGHT SANCHEZ
Registrar: KEISHA WILSON
Dir of Library Services: MONIKA RHUE
Library of 113,000 vols
Number of teachers: 97 (full-time)
Number of students: 1,543 (1,496 full-time, 47 part-time)
Publications: *The Treewell, Undergraduate Research Journal* (1 a year)

DEANS

College of Arts and Letters: JOSEPH TURNER
College of Professional Studies: Dr HELEN CALDWELL
College of Science, Technology, Engineering and Mathematics: Dr MAGDY ATTIA
Metropolitan College: Dr ZENOBIA EDWARDS

LAUREL UNIVERSITY

1215 Eastchester Dr., High Point, NC 27265
Telephone: (336) 887-3000
Fax: (336) 889-2261
E-mail: admissions@laureluniversity.edu
Internet: www.laureluniversity.edu
Founded 1903 as Greensboro Bible and Training School; present name 2011
Private control
Academic year: August to July (3 semesters)
Pres.: Dr LARRY McCULLOUGH
Exec. Vice-Pres.: Dr OWEN ALLEN
Academic Dean of Undergraduate Studies: Dr JOHN LINDSEY
Dean of Graduate Studies: Prof. Dr ROBERT BRUMLEY
Registrar: GREG WORKMAN
Dir of Library Services: APRIL LINDSEY
Library of 40,000 vols

Number of teachers: 18 (6 full-time, 12 part-time)
Number of students: 145

DEANS

Adult, Professional and Graduate Studies: GARY LOUNSBERRY
School of Management: Dr OWEN ALLEN

LEES-MCRAE COLLEGE

191 Main St, POB 128, Banner Elk, NC 28604
Telephone: (828) 898-5241
Fax: (828) 898-8814
E-mail: admissions@lmc.edu
Internet: www.lmc.edu
Founded 1900 as a girls' school; present name 1931
Private control
Academic year: August to May (2 semesters)
Academic programmes incl. Appalachian studies, art and design, athletic training, biology, business admin., communication arts, criminal justice, English, history, humanities, interdisciplinary studies, international studies, mathematics, musical theatre, outdoor adventure studies, performing arts studies, philosophy, psychology, religious studies, sport management, sport science
Pres.: Dr BARRY M. BUXTON
Vice-Pres. for Academic Affairs: Dr KACY E. CRABTREE
Vice-Pres. for Advancement: CAROLINE O. HART
Vice-Pres. for Enrolment Management: GINGER HANSEN
Vice-Pres. for Finance and Business Affairs: KEN BUCHANAN
Dean of Students: ALLISON NORRIS
Registrar: LYNN HINSHAW
Dir of Libraries: RUSSELL TAYLOR
Library of 100,000 vols, periodicals, microforms, audiovisual materials
Number of teachers: 50 (full-time)
Number of students: 900

LENOIR-RHYNE UNIVERSITY

625 Seventh Ave NE, Hickory, NC 28601-3984
Telephone: (828) 328-7300
Fax: (828) 328-7368
E-mail: admissions@lr.edu
Internet: www.lr.edu
Founded 1891 as Highland College, present name 2008
Private control
Academic year: August to May (2 semesters)
Pres.: Dr WAYNE POWELL
Provost: Dr LARRY HALL
Vice-Pres. for Admin. and Finance: PETER J. KENDALL
Vice-Pres. of Enrolment Management: RACHEL A. NICHOLS
Vice-Pres. for Institutional Advancement: Dr W. SCOTT SHRODE
Dean of Students: Dr KATIE PATTILLO FISHER
Dir of Admissions: KAREN B. FEEZOR
Registrar: KATHY HAHN
Dir of Library Services: RITA JOHNSON
Library of 160,000 vols
Number of teachers: 98 full-time
Number of students: 1,837

DEANS

College of Arts and Sciences: Prof. Dr DANIEL W. KISER
College of Education and Human Services: Dr HANK WEDDINGTON
College of Health Sciences: Prof. Dr KATHERINE PASOUR

College of Professional and Mathematical Studies: Prof. Dr WILLIAM M. MAUNEY
Graduate and Lifelong Learning Programmes: Dr AMY WOOD

LIVINGSTONE COLLEGE

701 W Monroe St, Salisbury, NC 28144-5213
Telephone: (704) 216-6000
E-mail: admissions@livingstone.edu
Internet: www.livingstone.edu
Founded 1879 as Zion Wesley Institute, present name 1887
Private control
Academic year: August to May (2 semesters)
Divs of business, education, social work and psychology, liberal arts, mathematics and sciences
Pres.: Dr JIMMY R. JENKINS, SR (acting)
Vice-Pres. for Academic Affairs: Dr LEROY SIMMONS
Vice-Pres. for Business and Finance: WILLIAM JAMES
Vice-Pres. for Institutional Advancement: HERMAN J. FELTON, JR
Vice-Pres. for Student Affairs: Dr STANLEY J. ELLIOTT
Registrar: WENDY R. JACKSON
Dir of Library Services: GWENDOLYN PEART
Library of 80,000 vols
Number of teachers: 81 (59 full-time, 22 part-time)
Number of students: 1,156 (1,146 full-time, 10 part-time)
Publications: *Bears' Tale* (1 a year), *The Livingstonian* (1 a year).

MARS HILL COLLEGE

POB 6663, Mars Hill, NC 28754
100 Athletic St, Mars Hill, NC 28754
Telephone: (828) 689-1201
Fax: (828) 689-1437
E-mail: admissions@mhc.edu
Internet: www.mhc.edu
Founded 1856 as French Broad Baptist Institute, present name 1859
Private control
Academic year: August to May (2 semesters)
Academic divs incl. humanities and social science, mathematics and natural sciences, professional programmes and interdisciplinary majors and minors
Pres.: Dr DAN G. LUNSFORD
Exec. Vice-Pres. and Vice-Pres. for Academic and Student Affairs: Dr JOHN W. WELLS
Vice-Pres. for Enrolment Management: CRAIG GOFORTH
Vice-Pres. for Finance: NEIL TILLEY
Vice-Pres. for Institutional Advancement: BUD CHRISTMAN
Registrar: EDITH L. WHITT
Library Dir: BEV ROBERTSON
Library of 90,000 vols
Number of teachers: 85
Number of students: 1,200

MEREDITH COLLEGE

3800 Hillsborough St, Raleigh, NC 27607-5298
Telephone: (919) 760-8600
Fax: (919) 760-2874
E-mail: admissions@meredith.edu
Internet: www.meredith.edu
Founded 1891 as Baptist Female Univ., present name 1909
Private control
Academic year: August to May (2 semesters)
Pres.: Dr JO ALLEN
Sr Vice-Pres. for Academic Admin.: DENISE ROTONDO

Vice-Pres. for Academic Planning and Programmes: ELIZABETH WOLFINGER
Vice-Pres. for Business and Finance: CRAIG BARFIELD
Vice-Pres. for College Programmes: Dr JEAN JACKSON
Vice-Pres. for Institutional Advancement: LENNIE BARTON
Dir of Admissions: JEN MILLER-HOGG
Registrar: AMANDA STEELE-MIDDLETON
Dean of Library Information Services: LAURA DAVIDSON

Library of 190,000 vols, 16,000 microforms, 3000 newspaper and journals
Number of teachers: 138 (full-time)
Number of students: 2,131 (1,826 undergraduate, 305 graduate)

DEANS

School of Business: Prof. Dr DENISE M. ROTONDO
School of Education: Prof. MARIE CHAMBLEE
School of Humanities and Social Science: Prof. Dr GARRY WALTON
School of the Arts: Prof. Dr REBECCA BAILEY

METHODIST UNIVERSITY

5400 Ramsey St, Fayetteville, NC 28311-1420

Telephone: (910) 630-7000
Fax: (910) 630-7317
E-mail: pmcevoy@methodist.edu
Internet: www.methodist.edu

Founded 1956 as Methodist College, present name and status 2006
Private control
Academic year: August to May

Pres.: Dr BEN E. HANCOCK, JR
Exec. Vice-Pres. and Academic Dean: Dr DELMAS S. CRISP, JR
Vice-Pres. for Business Affairs: GENE T. CLAYTON
Vice-Pres. for Enrolment Services: RICK LOWE
Vice-Pres. for Institutional Advancement: ROBIN DAVENPORT
Vice-Pres. for Planning and Evaluation: Dr DONALD LASSITER
Vice-Pres. for Student Devt and Services: WILLIAM WALKER
Dean of Admissions: JAMIE LEGG
Registrar: JASMIN BROWN
Dir of Library Services: TRACEY PEARSON

Library of 111,224 vols, 45,000 non-book holdings
Number of teachers: 214
Number of students: 2,400

DEANS

Reeves School of Business: JOSEPH F. DOLL
School of Arts and Humanities: Dr LORI BROOKMAN
School of Graduate Studies: Dr LORI BROOKMAN
School of Public Affairs: Dr BONITA BELCASTRO
School of Science and Human Development: Dr TAT W. CHAN

MID-ATLANTIC CHRISTIAN UNIVERSITY

715 N Poindexter St, Elizabeth City, NC 27909

Telephone: (252) 334-2000
Fax: (252) 334-2071
E-mail: admissions@macuniversity.edu
Internet: www.macuniversity.edu

Founded 1948 as Roanoke Bible College, present name 2009
Private control

Depts of arts and sciences, biblical studies, Christian ministry, marketplace ministry;

schools of professional studies, undergraduate studies

Pres.: Dr D. CLAY PERKINS
Vice-Pres. for Academic Affairs: Dr KEVIN W. LARSEN
Vice-Pres. for Devt: W. KEITH WOOD
Vice-Pres. for Enrolment Services: Dr KENDALL S. GREENE
Vice-Pres. for Finance: KURTIS L. KIGHT
Vice-Pres. for Student Life: Dr KENDALL S. GREENE
Registrar: JOAN U. SAWYER
Library Dir: TRISH GRIFFIN

Number of teachers: 17
Number of students: 194

MONTREAT COLLEGE

310 Gaither Circle, POB 1267, Montreat, NC 28757

Telephone: (828) 669-8011
Fax: (828) 669-0120
E-mail: admissions@montreat.edu
Internet: www.montreat.edu

Founded 1916 as Montreat Normal School, present name 1934
Private control
Academic year: August to May (2 Semesters)
Br. campuses in Asheville, Black Mountain, Charlotte, Morganton, Raleigh, Rocky Mount; schools of arts and sciences, professional and adult studies; graduate programmes in arts, sciences

Pres.: Dr DAN STRUBLE
Provost and Sr Vice-Pres.: Dr MARSHALL E. FLOWERS, JR
Vice-Pres. and Dean of Academics: Dr ABBY FAPETU
Vice-Pres. for Advancement: JOE B. KIRKLAND
Vice-Pres. for Enrolment and Marketing: JONATHAN E. SHORES
Vice-Pres. for Finance and Admin.: GEOFF BREMER
Vice-Pres. for Institutional Advancement: JOE KIRKLAND
Vice-Pres. for Student Services and Dean of Students: CHARLES A. LANCE
Dean of Admissions and Financial Aid: LISA LANKFORD
Registrar: MERRILL NIX MCCARTHY
Library Dir: ELIZABETH PEARSON

Number of teachers: 89
Number of students: 1,036
Publication: *Reflection.*

MOUNT OLIVE COLLEGE

634 Henderson St, Mount Olive, NC 28365

Telephone: (919) 658-2502
Fax: (919) 658-7180
E-mail: admissions@moc.edu
Internet: www.moc.edu

Founded 1951 as Mount Allen Jr College, present name 1970, present status 1980
Private control
Academic year: August to July (2 semesters)
Br. campuses in Goldsboro, Jacksonville, New Bern, Research Triangle Park, Washington, Wilmington

Pres.: Dr PHILIP PAUL KERSTETTER
Exec. Vice-Pres.: Dr CAROL G. CARRERE
Vice-Pres. for Academic Affairs: Prof. Dr ELLEN S. JORDAN
Vice-Pres. for Enrolment: Dr BARBARA R. KORNEGAY
Vice-Pres. for Finance: DEBRA SMITH
Vice-Pres. for Institutional Advancement: Dr KEVIN JEAN
Vice-Pres. for Student Affairs: DAN SULLIVAN
Registrar: DAVID BOURGEOIS
Dir of Library Services: PAMELA R. WOOD

Library of 100,000 vols, 7,500 journals and periodicals, 30,000 e-books
Number of teachers: 316 (88 full-time, 228 part-time)
Number of students: 5,000

DEANS

School of Arts and Sciences: Prof. Dr DAVID HINES
Tillman School of Business: Dr RONALD PRESSLEY

NORTH CAROLINA WESLEYAN COLLEGE

3400 N Wesleyan Blvd, Rocky Mount, NC 27804–8630

Telephone: (252) 985-5100
Fax: (252) 985-5199
E-mail: registrar@ncwc.edu
Internet: www.ncwc.edu

Founded 1956
Private control
Academic year: January to May

Liberal arts college; academic divs incl. business, education, mathematics and sciences, social sciences and humanities

Pres.: JAMES A. GRAY, III
Provost and Sr Vice-Pres. for Academic Affairs: Dr ROBERT JAY STUBBLEFIELD
Vice-Pres. for Enrolment Management: BILL ALLEN
Vice-Pres. for Finance: LOREN LOOMIS HUBBELL
Vice-Pres. for Student Affairs and Dean of Students: RANDY WILLIAMS
Dir of Library: KATHY WINSLOW

Library of 100,000 vols, 30,000 e-books
Number of teachers: 70
Number of students: 1,700

PEACE COLLEGE

15 E Peace St., Raleigh, NC 27604-1194

Telephone: (919) 508-2000
Fax: (919) 508-2326
Internet: www.peace.edu

Founded 1857 as Peace Institute
Private control
Academic year: August to May

Academic programmes in biology, business communication and media studies, education, English, liberal studies, musical theatre, political science, psychology, theatre

Pres.: Dr DEBRA M. TOWNSLEY
Provost: Dr DEBBIE COTTRELL
Vice-Pres. for Admin. and Chief Financial Officer: ROCKY YEARWOOD
Vice-Pres. for School of Professional Studies: Dr LAURIE ALBERT
Vice-Pres. for Enrolment Management: AMBER STENBECK

Library of 47,000 vols, 38,000 e-books
Number of students: 700

PFEIFFER UNIVERSITY

48380 US Highway 52, Misenheimer, NC 28109

Telephone: (704) 463-1360
Fax: (704) 463-1363
E-mail: admis@pfeiffer.edu
Internet: www.pfeiffer.edu

Founded 1885 as Oberlin Home and School, present name and status 1996
Private control
Academic year: August to May (2 semesters)
Br. campuses in Charlotte, Triangle

Pres.: Dr MICHAEL C. MILLER
Chief Operating Officer and Exec. Vice-Pres.: DAVID OLIVE

Provost and Vice-Pres. for Academic Affairs: Dr TRACY ESPY
Vice-Pres. for Advancement and Chief Operating Officer: BOBBY STEWART
Vice-Pres. for Enrolment Management and Marketing: MICHAEL POLL
Vice-Pres. for Finance and Chief Financial Officer: ROBIN LESLIE
Vice-Pres. for Student Devt and Dean of Students: Dr RUSS SHARPLES
Registrar: LOURDES SILVA
Library Dir: LARA LITTLE
Library of 132,471 vols, 29,735 microform units, 3,766 audiovisual materials, 22,115 e-journals
Number of teachers: 95 (full-time)
Number of students: 2,020 (1,018 undergraduate, 1,002 graduate)
Publication: *Pfeiffer Phoenix* (1 a year)

DEANS
Continuing Education and Adult Professional Studies: PAULITA BROOKER
School of Humanities: Prof. Dr DAVID HECKEL
School of Natural and Health Sciences: Dr MARK MCCALLUM
School of Religion: Dr DOUG HUME
School of Social and Behavioural Sciences: Prof. Dr DONALD POE, JR

QUEENS UNIVERSITY OF CHARLOTTE

1900 Selwyn Ave, Charlotte, NC 28274
Telephone: (704) 337-2200
Fax: (704) 337-2517
E-mail: admissions@queens.edu
Internet: www.queens.edu
Founded 1857 as Charlotte Female Institute, present name and status 2002
Private control
Academic year: August to May
Pres.: Dr PAMELA L. DAVIES
Provost and Vice-Pres. for Academic Affairs: Dr ABIODUN GOKE-PARIOLA
Vice-Pres. for Admin. and Chief Financial Officer: MATT PACKEY
Vice-Pres. for Enrolment Management: Dr BRIAN RALPH (acting)
Vice-Pres. for Univ. Advancement: JAMES BULLOCK
Registrar: EDWARD ADAMS
Univ. Librarian: Dr CAROL WALKER JORDAN
Library of 150,000 vols
Number of teachers: 109 (full-time)
Number of students: 2,600
Publication: *Odyssey* (4 a year)

DEANS
Blair College of Health and Presbyterian School of Nursing: Dr TAMA L. MORRIS
College of Arts and Sciences: Dr LYNN MORTON
Hayworth College for Adult Studies: KRISTA TILLMAN
James L. Knight School of Communication: VAN KING
McColl School of Business: Dr TERRY BRODERICK
Wayland H. Cato, Jr School of Education: Dr DARREL MILLER

SAINT AUGUSTINE'S COLLEGE

1315 Oakwood Ave, Raleigh, NC 27610-2298
Telephone: (919) 516-4000
E-mail: admissions@st-aug.com
Internet: www.st-aug.edu
Founded 1867
Private control
Academic year: August to May
Pres.: Dr DIANNE BOARDLEY SUBER
Exec. Vice-Pres.: LEON SCOTT

Vice-Pres. of Institutional Advancement and Devt: MARC A. NEWMAN
Dean of Students: DORIS BULLOCK
Registrar: CRYSTAL WILLIAMS
Dean of the Library Services: CLEVELL S. ROSEBORO, II
Library of 100,000 vols, 300 periodicals
Number of teachers: 100
Number of students: 1,600

DEANS
Div. of Allied Health: Dr HENGAMEH G. ALLEN
Div. of Business: KENT LUSK
Div. of Extended Studies: ROLAND BULLARD
Div. of Liberal Arts and Education: Dr M. IYAILU MOSES
Div. of Natural Sciences and Mathematics: MARK MELTON

SALEM COLLEGE

601 S Church St, Winston-Salem, NC 27101
Telephone: (336) 721-2600
Fax: (336) 917-5339
Internet: www.salem.edu
Founded 1772
Private control
Academic year: August to August
Areas of study incl. business administration, interior design, mathematics, philosophy and religion, sociology
Pres.: Dr SUSAN E. PAULY
Vice-Pres. for Academic Affairs and Student Affairs and Dean of College: Dr SUSAN CALOVINI
Vice-Pres. for Institutional Advancement: VICKI WILLIAMS SHEPPARD
Dean of Admissions and Financial Aid: KATHERINE KNAPP WATTS
Dean of Students: KRISPIN W. BARR
Dir of Admin.: ANNA BECK GALLIMORE
Registrar: MARK ASHLEY
Dir of Libraries: Dr ROSE A. SIMON
Library of 159,000 vols, 57,000 e-books, 24,000 e-periodicals
Number of teachers: 104 (full-time)
Number of students: 1,100

DEANS
Martha H. Fleer Center for Adult Education: SUZANNE WILLIAMS

SHAW UNIVERSITY

118 E South St, Raleigh, NC 27601
Telephone: (919) 546-8200
Fax: (919) 546-8301
E-mail: admissions@shawu.edu
Internet: www.shawu.edu
Founded 1865, present name and status 1875
Private control
Academic year: August to May (2 semesters)
Pres.: Dr DOROTHY COWSER YANCY
Exec. Vice-Pres.: MARTEL PERRY
Vice-Pres. for Academic Affairs: Dr MARILYN SUTTON-HAYWOOD
Vice-Pres. for Fiscal Affairs: DEBRA LATIMORE
Vice-Pres. for Institutional Advancement: ANITA BROWER
Vice-Pres. for Student Affairs and Admin.: Dr JEFFREY A. SMITH
Dean of Enrolment Management: ROCHELLE KING
Dean of Students: DORIS BULLOCK
Registrar: JODY HAMILTON-DAVIS
Dir of Library Services: CAROLYN PETERSON
Library of 130,000 vols, 127,000 microfiche units
Number of teachers: 240
Number of students: 2,722

DEANS
College of Arts and Sciences: Dr RENATA DUSENBURY
College of Graduate and Professional Studies: Dr GADDIS FAULCON
Divinity School: Dr BRUCE GRADY

SOUTHEASTERN BAPTIST THEOLOGICAL SEMINARY

POB 1889, Wake Forest, NC 27588
120 S Wingate St, Wake Forest, NC 27587
Telephone: (919) 761-2100
E-mail: admissions@sebts.edu
Internet: www.sebts.edu
Founded 1950
Private control
Academic year: August to May
Degrees offered incl. bachelor of arts in Christian studies, master of church music, divinity
Pres.: Dr DANIEL L. AKIN
Sr Vice-Pres. for Academic Admin. and Dean of Faculty: Dr KENNETH KEATHLEY
Sr Vice-Pres. for Business Admin.: RYAN R. HUTCHINSON
Vice-Pres. for Institutional Advancement: DENNIS DARVILLE
Vice-Pres. for Student Services and Dean of Students: Dr MARK LIEDERBACH
Dean of College: BRUCE R. ASHFORD
Registrar: SHELDON H. ALEXANDER
Dir for Library: SHAWN C. MADDEN
Library of 300,000 vols
Number of teachers: 80
Number of students: 1,500

ST ANDREWS UNIVERSITY

1700 Dogwood Mile, Laurinburg, NC 28352
Telephone: (910) 277-5555
Fax: (910) 277-5020
E-mail: admissions@sapc.edu
Internet: www.sapc.edu
Founded 1958 as St. Andrews Presbyterian College by merger of Flora Macdonald College (f. 1896) with Presbyterian Jr College (f. 1928), present name 2011; attached to Webber International Univ., Florida
Private control
Academic year: August to May
Academic programmes incl. biology, business admin., elementary education, English and creative writing, forensic science, sport and recreation studies
Pres.: PAUL BALDASARE
Vice-Pres. for Academic Affairs and Dean of College: Dr ROBERT J. HOPKINS
Vice-Pres. for Admin. and Dean of Students: GLENN BATTEN
Vice-Pres. for Business and Finance: TERRY LAUGHTER
Vice-Pres. for Enrolment Management: JEFF BENNETT
Registrar: DEBORAH A. SMITH
Library Dir: MARY MCDONALD
Library of 170,000 vols incl. e-books, 200 current periodicals
Number of teachers: 64 (30 full-time, 34 part-time)
Number of students: 741
Publication: *Cairn* (1 a year).

UNIVERSITY OF NORTH CAROLINA

910 Raleigh Rd, POB 2688, Chapel Hill, NC 27514
Telephone: (919) 962-1000
Fax: (919) 962-2751
Internet: www.northcarolina.edu
Founded 1789

Pres.: THOMAS W. ROSS
Sr Vice-Pres. for Academic Affairs: SUZANNE ORTEGA
Vice-Pres. and Gen. Counsel: LAURA LUGER
Vice-Pres. for Academic Planning: (vacant)
Vice-Pres. for Finance: CHARLIE PERUSSE
Vice-Pres. for Govt Relations: ANITA WATKINS
Vice-Pres. for Information Resources and Chief Information Officer: JOHN LEYDON
Vice-Pres. for Research: Dr STEVEN LEATH
Sec. of Univ.: BART CORGNATI
Number of students: 221,727.

CONSTITUENT UNIVERSITIES

Appalachian State University

Boone, NC 28608

Telephone: (828) 262-2000
Fax: (828) 262-3136
E-mail: admissions@appstate.edu
Internet: www.appstate.edu

Founded 1899 as Watauga Acad., present name 1967
Academic year: August to May (2 semesters)
Chancellor: Dr KENNETH E. PEACOCK
Provost and Exec. Vice-Chancellor: Dr LORI GONZALEZ
Vice-Chancellor for Business Affairs: GREGORY M. LOVINS
Vice-Chancellor for Student Devt: CINDY WALLACE
Vice-Chancellor for Univ. Advancement: SUSAN PETTYJOHN
Registrar: ANDREA WAWRZUSIN
Univ. Librarian: MARY REICHEL
Library of 925,290 vols, 1,542,256 microforms
Number of teachers: 871 (full-time)
Number of students: 17,344 (15,460 undergraduate, 1,884 graduate)
Publication: Appalachian Today (2 a year)

DEANS

College of Arts and Sciences: Dr ANTHONY G. CALAMAI
College of Business: Dr RANDAL K. EDWARDS
College of Education: Dr CHARLES DUKE
College of Fine and Applied Arts: Dr GLENDA TREADAWAY
College of Health Sciences: Dr FRED WHITT
Hayes School of Music: Dr WILLIAM PELTO
Research and Graduate Studies: Dr EDELMA D. HUNTLEY

East Carolina University

East Fifth St, Greenville, NC 27858-4353

Telephone: (252) 328-6131
E-mail: admis@ecu.edu
Internet: www.ecu.edu

Founded 1907
Academic year: August to May (2 semesters)
Chancellor: Dr STEVE BALLARD
Provost and Sr Vice-Chancellor for Academic Affairs: Dr MARILYN SHEERER
Vice-Chancellor for Admin. and Finance: Dr RICK NISWANDER
Vice-Chancellor for Research and Graduate Studies: Dr DEIRDRE MAGEEAN
Vice-Chancellor for Student Affairs: Dr VIRGINIA HARDY
Vice-Chancellor for Univ. Advancement: MICHAEL B. DOWDY
Registrar: ANGELA R. ANDERSON
Dir of Admissions: DONALD C. JOYNER
Dean of Academic Library and Learning Resources: LARRY BOYER
Library: 1.3m. vols
Number of teachers: 2,054
Number of students: 27,783
Publications: The Children's Folklore Review (2 a year), Tar River Poetry (2 a year), Technical Communication (4 a year), The North Carolina Folklore Journal (2 a year),

The North Carolina Literary Review (1 a year)

DEANS

Brody School of Medicine: Dr PAUL R. G. CUNNINGHAM
College of Allied Health Sciences: Prof. Dr STEPHEN THOMAS
College of Business: Dr STANLEY G. EAKINS
College of Education: Prof. Dr LINDA ANN PATRIARCA
College of Fine Arts and Communication: Dr MICHAEL DORSEY
College of Health and Human Performance: Dr GLEN GILBERT
College of Human Ecology: Dr JUDY SIGUAW
College of Nursing: Dr SYLVIA T. BROWN
College of Technology and Computer Science: Dr DAVID WHITE
Graduate School: Dr PAUL GEMPERLINE
Honors College: Dr RICHARD R. EAKIN
School of Dental Medicine: Dr D. GREGORY CHADWICK
Thomas Harriot College of Arts and Sciences: Dr ALAN WHITE

Elizabeth City State University

1704 Weeksville Rd, Elizabeth City, NC 27909

Telephone: (252) 335-3400
Fax: (252) 335-3731
E-mail: infoline@mail.ecsu.edu
Internet: www.ecsu.edu

Founded 1891 as a normal school; present name 1969
Academic year: August to May (2 semesters)
Chancellor: Dr WILLIE J. GILCHRIST
Provost and Vice-Chancellor for Academic Affairs: Dr ALI A. KHAN
Vice-Chancellor for Business and Finance and Chief Financial Officer: BENJAMIN DURANT
Vice-Chancellor for Institutional Advancement: WILLIAM G. SMITH
Vice-Chancellor for Student Affairs: Dr ANTHONY BROWN
Registrar: VINCENT L. BEAMON
Dir of Library Services: JUANITA MIDGETTE SPENCE
Number of teachers: 177 (full-time)
Number of students: 3,307 (2,914 full-time, 393 part-time)
Publication: ECSU Magazine (2 a year)

DEANS

School of Arts and Humanities: Dr MUREL JONES
School of Education and Psychology: Prof. Dr CHARLES CHERRY
School of Mathematics, Science and Technology: Dr HARRY BASS
Walter R. Davis School of Business and Economics: DAVID BEJOU

Fayetteville State University

1200 Murchison Rd, Fayetteville, NC 28301-4298

Telephone: (910) 672-1111
Fax: (910) 672-1414
E-mail: admissions@uncfsu.edu
Internet: www.uncfsu.edu

Founded 1867 as Howard School, present name and status 1969
Chancellor: Dr JAMES A. ANDERSON
Provost and Vice-Chancellor for Academic Affairs: Dr JON YOUNG
Vice-Chancellor and Chief of Staff: Dr THOMAS E. H. CONWAY, JR
Vice-Chancellor for Business and Finance: ROBERT L. BOTLEY
Vice-Chancellor for Institutional Advancement: ARTHUR G. AFFLECK

Vice-Chancellor for Student Affairs: Dr JANICE HAYNIE
Registrar: SARAH BAKER
Dir of Library Services: BOBBY C. WYNN

Library of 317,412 vols, 64,000 e-books, 1,005,010 microforms, 2,769 periodicals, 56 newspapers, 19,751 audiovisual items
Number of teachers: 248 (full-time)
Number of students: 5,781

DEANS

College of Arts and Sciences: Dr DAVID BARLOW
Graduate Studies: Dr LADELLE OLION
School of Business and Economics: Dr ASSAD TAVAKOLI
School of Education: Dr LEONTYE LEWIS
Univ. College: Dr JOHN BROOKS

North Carolina Agricultural and Technical State University

1601 E Market St, Greensboro, NC 27411

Telephone: (336) 334-7500
Fax: (336) 256-2715
E-mail: uadmit@ncat.edu
Internet: www.ncat.edu

Founded 1891 as Agricultural and Mechanical College, present name and status 1967
Chancellor: Dr HAROLD L. MARTIN, SR
Provost and Vice-Chancellor for Academic Affairs: Dr WINSER ALEXANDER
Vice-Chancellor for Business and Finance: ROBERT POMPEY, JR
Vice-Chancellor for Research and Economic Devt: Dr CELESTINE NTUEN
Vice-Chancellor for Student Affairs: Dr MELODY C. PIERCE
Vice-Chancellor for Univ. Advancement: ROBERT POMPEY, JR
Dean of Students: Dr JUDY RASHID
Registrar: LESTER LUGO
Dean of Library Services: VICKI COLEMAN
Library of 416,000 vols
Number of teachers: 549 (full-time)
Number of students: 10,881 (9,206 undergraduate, 1,675 graduate)
Publication: A&T Today (3 a year)

DEANS

College of Arts and Sciences: Prof. Dr NATHAN F. SIMMS
College of Engineering: Dr ROBIN N. COGER
Joint School of Nanoscience and Nanoengineering: Prof. Dr JAMES G. RYAN
School of Agriculture and Environmental Sciences: Dr WILLIAM RANDLE
School of Business and Economics: Dr QUIESTER CRAIG
School of Education: Dr WILLIAM B. HARVEY
School of Graduate Studies: Dr SANJIV SARIN
School of Nursing: Dr INEZ TUCK
School of Technology: Dr BENJAMIN UWAKWEH

North Carolina Central University

1801 Fayetteville St, Durham, NC 27707

Telephone: (919) 530-6100
Fax: (919) 530-7976
Internet: www.nccu.edu

Founded 1910 as Nat. Religious Training School and Chautauqua for the Colored Race, present name 1969
Academic year: August to May
Chancellor: Dr CHARLIE NELMS
Provost and Vice-Chancellor for Academic Affairs: Dr DEBBIE THOMAS
Vice-Chancellor and Chief of Staff: SUSAN HESTER
Vice-Chancellor for Admin. and Finance: WENDELL M. DAVIS
Vice-Chancellor for Institutional Advancement: LOIS D DELOATCH
Vice-Chancellor for Research and Economic Devt: Dr HAZELL REED

Vice-Chancellor for Student Affairs and Enrolment Management: Dr KEVIN D. ROME
Registrar: Dr JEROME GOODWIN
Dir of Library Services: Dr THEODOSIA SHIELDS
Library of 850,000 vols, 6,165 periodicals
Number of teachers: 388
Number of students: 8,645
Publication: *Campus Echo*

DEANS

College of Behavioural and Social Sciences: Dr ELWOOD L. ROBINSON
College of Liberal Arts: Dr CARLTON WILSON
College of Science and Technology: Dr ABDUL K. MOHAMMED
School of Business: Dr D. KEITH PIGUES
School of Education: Dr CECELIA STEPPE-JONES
School of Graduate Studies: Dr CHANTA HAYWOOD
School of Law: RAYMOND C. PIERCE
School of Library and Information Science: Dr IRENE OWENS
Univ. College: Dr ONTARIO WOODEN

North Carolina State University

Raleigh, NC 27695
Telephone: (919) 515-2011
Fax: (919) 515-5039
E-mail: undergrad_admissions@ncsu.edu
Internet: www.ncsu.edu
Founded 1887 as North Carolina College of Agriculture and Mechanic Arts, present name 1965
Academic year: August to May
Chancellor: Dr WILLIAM RANDOLPH. WOODSON
Provost and Exec. Vice-Chancellor: Dr WARWICK ARDEN
Vice-Chancellor and Gen. Counsel: EILEEN S. GOLDGEIER
Vice-Chancellor for Finance and Business: CHARLES D. LEFFLER
Vice-Chancellor for Research and Graduate Studies: Dr TERRI L. LOMAX
Vice-Chancellor for Student Affairs: THOMAS H. STAFFORD, JR
Vice-Chancellor for Univ. Advancement: NEVIN E. KESSELER
Registrar: Dr LOUIS D. HUNT
Vice-Provost and Dir of Libraries: SUSAN K. NUTTER
Library: 4.4m. vols, 400,000 e-books, 63,271 periodicals, 69,223 serials
Number of teachers: 2,078
Number of students: 34,376

DEANS

College of Agriculture and Life Sciences: Dr JOHNNY C. WYNNE
College of Design: MARVIN J. MALECHA
College of Education: Dr M. JAYNE FLEENER
College of Engineering: LOUIS MARTIN-VEGA
College of Humanities and Social Sciences: JEFFERY P. BRADEN
College of Management: Dr IRA R. WEISS
College of Natural Resources: Dr ROBERT BROWN
College of Physical and Mathematical Sciences: Dr DANIEL L. SOLOMON
College of Textiles: Dr A. BLANTON GODFREY
College of Veterinary Medicine: DAVID G. BRISTOL
Graduate School: DUANE K. LARICK
Undergraduate Academic Programmes: JOHN T. AMBROSE

University of North Carolina at Asheville

One University Heights, Asheville, NC 28804-3299
Telephone: (828) 251-6600

Fax: (828) 251-6482
E-mail: admissions@unca.edu
Internet: www.unca.edu
Founded 1927 as Buncombe County Jr College, present status 1969
Academic year: August to August (2 semesters)
Chancellor: Prof. Dr ANNE PONDER
Provost and Vice-Chancellor for Academic Affairs: Dr JANE K. FERNANDES
Vice-Chancellor for Finance and Campus Operations: JOHN G. PIERCE
Vice-Chancellor for Student Affairs: Dr BILL HAGGARD
Dean of Admissions: PATRICE MITCHELL
Registrar: DEBBIE RACE
Univ. Librarian (vacant)
Library of 275,323 vols, 9,185 audiovisual materials
Number of teachers: 211 (full-time)
Number of students: 3,700
Publication: *UNC Asheville Magazine*

DEANS

Humanities: Dr GWEN M. ASHBURN
Natural Sciences: Dr KEITH E. KRUMPE
Social Sciences: Dr JEFF KONZ

University of North Carolina at Chapel Hill

103 South Bldg, POB 9100, Chapel Hill, NC 27599-9100
Telephone: (919) 962-2211
Fax: (919) 962-1647
E-mail: unchelp@admissions.unc.edu
Internet: www.unc.edu
Founded 1795, present status 1931
Academic year: August to May
Chancellor: HOLDEN THORP
Exec. Vice-Chancellor and Provost: BRUCE W. CARNEY
Vice-Chancellor and Gen. Counsel: LESLIE STROHM
Vice-Chancellor for Finance and Admin.: KAROL KAIN GRAY
Vice-Chancellor for Research and Economic Devt: BARBARA ENTWISLE
Vice-Chancellor for Student Affairs: Dr WINSTON B. CRISP
Vice-Chancellor for Univ. Advancement: MATTHEW KUPEC
Univ. Registrar and Asst Provost: CHRISTOPHER DERICKSON
Assoc. Provost for Univ. Libraries and Dir of Academic Affairs: SARAH C. MICHALAK
Library: see under Libraries and Archives
Number of teachers: 3,518
Number of students: 29,137
Publications: *Baseline* (3 a year), *Centerpieces* (12 a year), *Current Contents* (4 a year), *Endeavors* (3 a year), *Southern Economic Journal* (4 a year), *The High School Journal* (4 a year)

DEANS

College of Arts and Sciences: Dr KAREN GIL
Eshelman School of Pharmacy: Dr ROBERT BLOUIN
General College: Dr CAROLYN CANNON
Gillings School of Global Public Health: Dr BARBARA K. RIMER
Graduate School: Dr STEVE MATSON
Kenan-Flagler Business School: Dr JAMES W. DEAN, JR
School of Dentistry: Dr JANE WEINTRAUB
School of Education: Prof. Dr BILL McDIARMID
School of Government: Dr MICHAEL R. SMITH
School of Information and Library Science: Dr GARY MARCHIONINI
School of Journalism and Mass Communication: Dr DULCIE STAUGHAN
School of Law: JOHN BOGER

School of Medicine: Dr WILLIAM L. ROPER
School of Nursing: Dr KRISTEN SWANSON
School of Social Work: Dr JACK M. RICHMAN
Summer School: Dr JAN YOPP

PROFESSORS

Allied Medical Programmes:
MITCHELL, M. M.
MITCHELL, R. U.
PETERS, R. W.
SAKATA, R.
YODER, D. E.

American Studies Curriculum:
ALLEN, R. C.
KASSON, J. S.

Anaesthesiology:
BOYSEN, P. G.
GHIA, J. N.
KAFER, E. R.
MUELLER, R. A.
NORFLEET, E. A.
SPIELMAN, F. J.
SPRAGUE, D. H.
VAUGHAN, R. W.

Anthropology:
CRUMLEY, C. L.
EVENS, T. M.
FINKLER, K.
HOLLAND, D. C.
JOHNSON, N. B.
LARSEN, C. S.
LUTZ, C. A.
PEACOCK, J. L., III
STEPONAITIS, V. P.
WINTERHALDER, B.

Art:
FOLDA, J. T., III
GRABOWSKI, S. E.
KINNAIRD, R. W.
MARKS, A. S.
NOE, J. L.
SHERIFF, M. D.
STURGEON, C.
ZABOROWSKI, D. J.

Biochemistry:
CAPLOW, M.
CARTER, C. W., JR
CHANEY, S. G.
ERREDE, B. J.
HERMANS, J.
LEE, D. C.
LENTZ, B. R.
MARZLUFF, W. F.
MEISSNER, G. W.
MORELL, P.
NAYFEH, S. N.
SANCAR, A.
SWANSTROM, R. I.
TIDWELL, P. F.
TRAUT, T. W.
VAN DYKE, T. A.
WOLFENDEN, R. V.

Biology:
BLOOM, K. S.
BOLLENBACHER, W. E.
DICKISON, W. C.
FEDUCCIA, J. A.
GENSEL, P. G.
GILBERT, L. I.
HARRIS, A. K., JR
MATSON, S. W.
MATTHYSSE, A. G.
PARKS, C. R.
PEET, R. K.
PETES, T. D.
PRINGLE, J. R.
QUATRANO, R. S.
SALMON, E. D.
SCOTT, T. K.
STAFFORD, D. W.
STIVEN, A. E.
WHITE, P. S.

WILEY, R. H., JR

Biomedical Engineering Programme:
LUCAS, C. N.
TSUI, B. M.

Biostatistics:
DAVIS, C. E.
HELMS, R. W.
KALSBEEK, W. D.
KOCH, G. G.
KUPPER, L. L.
MARGOLIN, B. H.
QUADE, D. E.
SEN, P. K.
SUCHINDRAN, C. M.
SYMONS, M. J.

Business Administration:
ALDER, R. S.
ANDERSON, C. R.
ARMSTRONG, G. M.
BATEMAN, T. S.
BAYUS, B. L.
BETTIS, R. A.
BLOCHER, E. J.
BLOOM, P. N.
COLLINS, J. H.
CONRAD, J. S.
EDWARDS, J. R.
ELVERS, D. A.
EVANS, J. P.
FISCHER, W. A.
HARTZELL, D. J.
KASARDA, J. D.
KLOMPMAKER, J. E.
LANDSMAN, W. R.
MCENALLY, R. W.
MANN, R. A.
MARUCHECK, A. E.
NEEBE, A. W.
PEIRCE, E. R.
PERREAULT, W. D., JR
PRINGLE, J. J.
RAVENSCRAFT, D. J.
RENDLEMAN, R. J.
ROBERTS, B. S.
RONDINELLI, D. A.
ROSEN, B.
RUBIN, D. S.
SHAPIRO, D. L.
SULLIVAN, R. S.
TILLMAN, R.
WAGNER, H. M.
WHYBARK, D. C.

Cell Biology and Anatomy:
BURRIDGE, K. W. T.
GRANGER, N. A.
HACKENBROCK, C. R.
HENSON, O. W., JR
HERMAN, B.
JACOBSON, K. A.
KOCH, W. E.
LAUDER, J. M.
LEMASTERS, J. J.
MONTGOMERY, R. L.
O'RAND, M. G.
PENG, H. B.
PETRUSZ, P.
RUSTIONI, A.
SADLER, T. W.
SULIK, K. K.

Chemistry:
BAER, T.
BROOKHART, M. S.
BUCK, R. P.
COKE, J. L.
CRIMMINS, M. T.
DESIMONE, J. M.
ERICKSON, B. W.
EVANS, S. A., JR
IRENE, E. A.
JICHA, D. C.
JOHNSON, C. S., JR
JORGENSON, J. W.
KROPP, P. J.

MEYER, T. J.
MILLER, R. E.
MURRAY, R. W.
PEDERSEN, L. G.
SAMULSKI, E. T.
SORRELL, T. N.
SPREMULLI, L. L.
TEMPLETON, J. L.
THOMPSON, N. L.
WIGHTMAN, R. M.

City and Regional Planning:
GODSCHALK, D. R.
GOLDSTEIN, H. A.
KAISER, E. J.
LACEY, L.
LUGER, M. I.
MALIZIA, E. E.
MOREAU, D. H.
ROHE, W. M.

Classics:
BROWN, E. L.
HOUSTON, G. W.
LINDERSKI, J.
MACK, S.
RACE, W. H.
RECKFORD, K. J.
SAMS, G. K.
STADTER, P. A.
WEST, W. C., III
WOOTEN, C. W.

Communication Studies:
BALTHROP, V. W.
COX, J. R., JR
DYSON, M. E.
GROSSBERG, L.
HORNE, G. C.
KINDEM, G. A.
LONG, B. W.
ROSENFELD, L. B.
WOOD, J. T.

Comparative Literature:
FURST, L. R.

Computer Science:
BROOKS, F. P., JR
FUCHS, H.
HALTON, J. H.
MAGO, G. A.
PIZER, S. M.
PLAISTED, D. A.
SMITH, J. B.
WEISS, S. F.

Curriculum, African and Afro-American Studies:
NYANG'ORO, J. E.
SELASSIE, B. H.

Curriculum, Asian Studies:
SEATON, J. P.

Curriculum, Linguistics and Non-West Languages:
HENDRICK, R. J.
MELCHERT, H. C.
TSIAPERA, M.

Curriculum, Public Policy Analysis:
DILL, D. D.
STEGMAN, M. A.

Dentistry:
ARNOLD, R. R.
AUKHIL, I.
BAWDEN, J. W.
BAYNE, S. C.
BECK, J. D.
BURKES, E. J.
CRENSHAW, M. A.
HANKER, J. S.
HERSHEY, H. G.
HEYMANN, H. O.
HUNT, R. J.
HUTCHENS, L. H., JR
JENZANO, J. W.
KUSY, R. P.
MCIVER, F. T.

MURRAH, V. A.
OFFENBACHER, S.
OLDENBURG, T. R.
PROFFIT, W. R.
ROBERSON, T. M.
SHUGARS, D. A.
SIMPSON, D. M.
STAMM, J. W.
STRAUSS, R. P.
TROPE, M.
TULLOCH, J. F. C.
TURVEY, T. A.
VANN, W. F., JR
WARREN, D. W.
WHITE, R. P.
WHITE, R. P., JR
WILLIAMS, R. C.
WRIGHT, J. T.
YAMAUCHI, M.
WOOD, M. T.

Dermatology:
BRIGGAMAN, R. A.
FINE, J. D.
O'KEEFE, E. J.

Developmental Disabilities Training Institute:
BAROFF, G. S.

Dramatic Art:
BARRANGER, M. S.
HAMMOND, D. A.
OWEN, R. A.
RAPHAEL, B. N.
TURNER, C. W.

Economics:
AKIN, J. S.
BENAVIE, A.
BLACK, S. W., III
BLAU, D. M.
CONWAY, P. J.
DARITY, W. A., JR
FIELD, A. J., JR
FRIEDMAN, J. W.
FROYEN, R. T.
GALLANT, A. R.
GALLMAN, R. E.
GUILKEY, D. K.
MROZ, T. A.
MURPHY, J. L.
ROSEFIELDE, S. S.
SALEMI, M. K.
STEWART, J. F.
TARASCIO, V. J.
TAUCHEN, H. V.

Education:
BALLEW, J. H.
BRANTLEY, J. C.
BROWN, D.
BROWN, F.
BURKE, W. I.
COOP, R. H.
CUNNINGHAM, J.
DAY, B. D.
FITZGERALD, W. J.
FRIERSON, H. T.
GALASSI, J. P.
GALLAGHER, J. J.
HENNIS, R. S.
HUNTER, R. C.
LILLIE, D. L.
MARSHALL, C.
MORRISON, J. L.
NOBLIT, G. W.
ODOM, S. L., JR
PALMER, W.
PRYZWANSKY, W. B.
SIMEONSON, R. J.
SPIEGEL, D. L.
STEDMAN, D. J.
STUCK, G. B.
TOM, A. R.
UNKS, G.
WARE, W. B.
WASIK, B. H.

WHITE, K. P.

Emergency Medicine:

TINTINALLI, J. E.

English:

ANDREWS, W. L.
AVERY, L. G.
BETTS, D. W.
DESSEN, A. C.
EBLE, C. C.
FLORA, J. M.
GLESS, D. J.
GREENE, J. L.
GURA, P. F.
HARMON, W. R.
HARRIS, T.
HENDERSON, M. G.
HOBSON, F. C., JR
KENNEDY, E. D.
KING, J. K.
LENSING, G. S., JR
LINDEMANN, E.
LUDINGTON, C. T., JR
MCGOWAN, J. P.
MOSKAL, J.
O'NEILL, P. P.
PATTERSON, D. W.
RAPER, J. R.
RUST, R. D.
SHAPIRO, A. R.
TAYLOR, B. W.
THOMPSON, J. P.
THORNTON, W.
WAGNER-MARTIN, L. C.
WHISNANT, D. E.
WITTING, J. S.
ZUG, C. G., III

Environmental Science and Engineering:

ANDREWS, R. N.
CHRISTAKOS, G.
CHRISTMAN, R. F.
CRAWFORD-BROWN, D. J.
DIGIANO, F. A.
FOX, D. L.
GLAZE, W. H.
GOLD, A.
JEFFRIES, H.
KAMENS, R. M.
LAURIA, D. T.
LEITH, D.
MILLER, C. T.
PFAENDER, F.
RAPAPORT, S. M.
REIST, P. C.
SINGER, P. C.
SOBSEY, M. D.
SWENBERG, J. A.
WATSON, J. E., JR
WHITTINGTON, D.

Epidemiology:

HEISS, G.
HULKA, B.
IBRAHIM, M. A.
SAVITZ, D. A.
SEED, J. R.

Family Medicine:

CURTIS, P.
FIELDS, K. B.
GWYTHER, R. E.
LEA, J. W.
OLSON, P. R.
REEB, K. G.
SLOANE, P. D.

Geography:

BAND, L. E.
BIRDSALL, S. S.
FLORIN, J. W.
GESLER, W. M.
GREENLAND, D. E.
JOHNSON, J. H., JR
MEADE, M.
MORIARTY, B. M.
PALM, R. I.
ROBINSON, P. J.

WALSH, S. J.
ZONN, L. E.

Geology:

BENNINGER, L. K.
CARTER, J. G.
DENNISON, J. M.
FULLAGAR, P. D.
POWELL, C. A.
TEXTORIS, D. A.

German:

KOELB, C. T.
MEWS, S. E.
PIKE, D. C.
ROBERGE, P. T.

History:

BARNEY, W. L.
BULLARD, M. M.
CHOJNACKI, S. J.
FILENE, P. G.
FINK, L. R.
FLETCHER, W. M.
GRIFFITHS, D. M.
HALL, J. D.
HARRIS, B. J.
HEADLEY, J. M.
HIGGINBOTHAM, R. D.
HUNT, M. H.
JARAUSCH, K. H.
KASSON, J. F.
KESSLER, L. D.
KOHN, R. H.
KRAMER, L. S.
LOTCHIN, R. W.
MCNEIL, G. R.
MCVAUGH, M. R.
MATHEWS, D. G.
NELSON, J. K.
PEREZ, L. A.
PFAFF, R. W.
SEMONCHE, J. E.
SOLOWAY, R. A.
TALBERT, R. J.
WATSON, H. L.
WILLIAMSON, J. R.

Information and Library Science:

CHATMAN, E. A.
DANIEL, E. H.
MORAN, B. B.
SHAW, W. M., JR

Institute of Government:

ALLRED, S.
BELL, A. F., II
BRANNON, J. G.
CAMPBELL, W. A.
CLARKE, S. H.
DELLINGER, A. M.
DRENNAN, J. C.
FARB, R. L.
FERRELL, J. S.
JOYCE, R. P.
LAWRENCE, D. M.
LINER, C. D.
LOEB, B. F., JR
MASON, J.
MESIBOV, L. L.
OWENS, D. W.
SMITH, M. R.
VOGT, A. J.
WHITAKER, G. P.

Journalism:

BLANCHARD, M. A.
BOWERS, T. A.
BROWN, J. D.
COLE, R. R.
ELAM, A. R.
LAUTERBORN, R. F.
LINDEN, T. R.
MEYER, P. E.
SHAVER, M. A.
SHAW, D. L.
SIMPSON, R. H.
STEVENSON, R. L.
STONE, C. S., JR

WALDEN, R. C.

Law:

BILIONIS, L. D.
BLAKEY, W.
BOGER, J. C.
BROOME, L. L.
BROUN, K. S.
BROWN, C. N.
BRYAN, P. L.
BYRD, R. G.
CALMORE, J. O.
CLIFFORD, D. F., JR
CONLEY, J. M.
CORRADO, M. L.
CRAIN, M. G.
DAYE, C. E.
GIBSON, S. E.
HASKELL, P. G.
HAZEN, T. L.
HORNSTEIN, D. T.
KALO, J. J.
LINK, R. C.
LOEWY, A. H.
MARKHAM, J. W.
MCUSIC, M. S.
ORTH, J. V.
ROSEN, R. A.
SHARP, S. B.
TURNIER, W. J.
WEGNER, J. W.
WEISBURD, A. M.
YARBROUGH, M. V.
ZELENAK, L. A.

Law Library:

GASAWAY, L. N.

Leisure Studies and Recreation Administration:

HENDERSON, K. A.

Marine Sciences:

BANE, J. M., JR
FRANKENBERG, D.
HAY, M. E.
KOHLMEYER, J. J.
MARTENS, C. S.
NEUMANN, A. C.
PAERL, H. W.
PETERSON, C. H.
SCHWARTZ, F. J.
WELLS, J. T.
WERNER, P. E.

Maternal and Child Health Care:

BUEXENS, P.
KOTCH, J. B.
KOTELCHUCK, M.
TSUI, A. O.
UDRY, J. R.

Mathematics:

ASSANI, I.
BRYLAWSKI, T. H.
CIMA, J. A.
DAMON, J. N.
EBERLEIN, P. B.
FOREST, M. G.
GEISSINGER, L. D.
GOODMAN, S. E.
GRAVES, W. H.
HAWKINS, J. M.
KERZMAN, N.
KUMAR, S.
PETERSEN, K. E.
PFALTZGRAFF, J. A.
PLANTE, J. F.
PROCTOR, R. A.
SCHLESSINGER, M.
SMITH, W. W.
STASHEFF, J.
TAYLOR, M. E.
VARCHENKO, A.
WAHL, J. M.
WILLIAMS, M.
WOGEN, W. R.

Medical Allied Health Prof.:
BAILEY, D.
LEGRYS, V. A.
SAKATA, R.
YODER, D. E.

Medicine:
BERKOWITZ, L. R.
BERNARD, S. A.
BONDURANT, S.
BOUCHER, R. C., JR
BOZYMSKI, E. M.
BRENNER, D. A.
BROMBERG, P. A.
CAREY, T. S.
CLEMMONS, D. R.
COHEN, M. S.
COHEN, P. L.
COLINDRES, R. E.
DEHMER, G. J.
DONOHUE, J. F.
DROSSMAN, D. A.
EARP, H. S., III
FALK, R. J.
FINN, W. F.
GABRIEL, D. A.
GETTES, L. S.
GONZALEZ, J. J.
GREGANTI, M. A.
GRIGGS, T. R.
HEIZER, W. D.
HOOLE, A. J.
HUANG, E. S.
KIZER, J. S.
KNOWLES, M. R.
LANE, T. W.
LIU, E. T.
MATTERN, W. D.
MITCHELL, B. S.
NUZUM, C. T.
ONTJES, D. A.
ORRINGER, E. P.
PAGANO, J. S.
RANSOHOFF, D. F.
ROBERTS, H.
ROGERS, C. S.
RUTALA, W. A.
SANDLER, R. S.
SARTOR, R. B.
SHEA, T. C.
SIMPSON, R. J., JR
SMITH, S. C.
SPARLING, P. F.
UNGARO, P. C.
WHITE, G. C., II
WILLIAMS, M. E.
WILLIS, P. W.
WINFIELD, J. B.
YOUNT, W. J.

Microbiology and Immunology:
BACHENHEIMER, S. L.
BOTT, K. F.
CANNON, J. G.
CLARKE, S. H.
EDGELL, M. H.
FRELINGER, J. A.
GILLIGAN, P. H.
GRIFFITH, J.
HAUGHTON, G.
HUTCHISON, C. A.
JOHNSTON, R. E.
KLAPPER, D. G.
NEWBOLD, J. E.
RAAB-TRAUB, N.
TING, J. P.
WYRICK, P. B.

Microelectronics—Chemistry:
IRENE, E. A.

Music:
BONDS, M. E.
FINSON, J. W.
KETCH, J. E.
McKINNON, J. W.
NADAS, J. L.

NEFF, S.
OEHLER, D. L.
SMITH, B.
WARBURTON, T. A.
ZENGE, M. W.

Neurology:
GREENWOOD, R. S.
HALL, C. D.
HOWARD, J. N.
MANN, J. D.
SUZUKI, K.

Nursing:
DALTON, J. B.
DAVIS, D. H.
DOUGHERTY, M. C.
FOGEL, C. I.
FREUND, C. M.
FUNK, S. G.
GOEPPINGER, J.
HARRELL, J. S.
KJERVIK, D. K.
MILES, M. S.
MILIO, N.
MISHEL, M. H.
SANDELOWSKI, M. J.

Obstetrics and Gynaecology:
DROEGEMUELLER, W.
FOWLER, W. C., JR
FRITZ, M. A.
GRANADOS
HASKILL, J. S.
PARISI, Y. M.
STEEGE, J. F.
WALTON, L. A.

Operations Research:
FISHMAN, G.
PROVAN, J. S.
STIDHAM,, S., JR
TOLLE, J. W.

Ophthalmology:
COHEN, K. L.
EIFRIG, D. E.
GRIMSON, B. S.
PEIFFER, R. L., JR

Paediatrics:
AYLSWORTH, A. S.
BOSE, C. L.
CARSON, J. L.
COLLIER, A. M.
COOPER, H. A.
D'ERCOLE, A. J.
FERNALD, G. W.
FRENCH, F. S.
HAMRICK, H.
HENDERSON, F. W.
HENRY, G. W.
INGRAM, D. L.
KRAYBILL, E. N.
LAWSON, E. E.
LEIGH, M. W.
LEVINE, M. D.
LODA, F. A.
LOHR, J. A.
ROBERTS, K. B.
SCHALL, S. A.
SIMMONS, M. A.
STILES, A. D.
UNDERWOOD, L. E.
WILLIAMS, R. G.
WILSON, E. M.
WOOD, R. E.

Pathology and Laboratory Medicine:
ANDERSON, N. N.
BELLINGER, D. A.
BENTLEY, S. A.
BOULDIN, T. W.
CHAPMAN, J. F.
CROSS, R. E.
FARBER, R. A.
FOLDS, J. D.
FORMAN, D. T.
GRISHAM, J. W.

HAMMOND, J. E.
JENNETTE, J. C.
KAUFMAN, D. G.
LORD, S. T.
MAEDA, N.
REISNER, H. M.
SILVERMAN, L. M.
SMITH, G. J.
SMITHIES, O.
SUZUKI, K. I.
TIDWELL, R. R.
TOPAL, M. D.
WEISSMAN, B. E.

Pharmacology:
CREWS, F. T.
DER, C. J.
DUDLEY, K. H.
GATZY, J. T., JR
GOZ, B.
HARDEN, T. K.
JULIANO, R. L.
KOLE, R.
McCARTHY, K. D.
SCARBOROUGH, G. A.
THURMAN, R. G.

Pharmacy:
BROUWER, K. R.
CAMPBELL, W. H.
COCOLAS, G. H.
ECKEL, F. M.
HADZIJA, B. W.
HALL, I. H.
HARTZEMA, A. G.
LEE, K. H.
PIEPER, J. A.
THAKKER, D. R.

Philosophy:
ANTONY, L. M.
BLACKBURN, S. W.
BOXILL, B. R.
HILL, T. E., JR
HOOKER, M.
LONG, D. C.
LYCAN, W. G.
MUNSAT, S. M.
POSTEMA, G. J.
RESNIK, M. D.
ROSENBERG, J. F.
SAYRE-McCORD, G. D.
SCHLESINGER, G.
SMYTH, R. A.

Physical Education, Exercise and Sport Science:
BILLING, J. E.
HYATT, R. W.
McMURRAY, R. G.
MUELLER, F. O.
PRENTICE, W. E., JR
SILVA, J. M.

Physics/Astronomy:
CARNEY, B. W.
CHRISTIANSEN, W. A.
CLEGG, T. B.
DOLAN, L. A.
DY, K. S.
FRAMPTON, P. H.
HERNANDEZ, J.
KARWOWSKI, H. J.
LUDWIG, E. J.
McNEIL, L. E.
NG, Y. J.
ROSE, J. A.
ROWAN, L. G.
SCHROEER, D.
THOMPSON, W. J.
VAN DAM, H.
YORK, J. W., JR

Physiology:
ARENDSHORST, W. J.
FABER, J. E.
FAREL, P. B.
FAUST, R. G.
FROEHNER, S. C.

LIGHT, A. R.
LUND, P. K.
McILWAIN, D. L.
OXFORD, G. S.
PERL, E. R.
REID, L. M.
SEALOCK, R. W.
STUART, A. E.
WHITSEL, B. L.

Political Science:
BEYLE, T. L.
CONOVER, P. J.
HARTLYN, J.
HUBER, E. H.
LOWERY, D. L.
MARKS, G. W.
PHAY, R. E.
RABINOWITZ, G.
RICHARDSON, R. J.
SCHOULTZ, L. G.
SCHWARTZ, J.
SEARING, D. D.
STEINER, J.
STEPHENS, J. D.
STIMSON, J. A.
WHITE, J. W.
WRIGHT, D. S.

Psychiatry:
BREESE, G. R., JR
GOLDEN, R. N.
HOUPT, J. L.
JANOWSKY, D. S.
LIEBERMAN, J. A.
LIGHT, K. C.
McCARTNEY, C. F.
MAILMAN, R. B.
MARCUS, L. M.
MESIBOV, G. B.
STABLER, B.
VAN BOURGONDIE, M. E.
WHITT, J. K.

Psychology:
BAUCOM, D. H.
CAIRNS, R. B.
CHAMBLESS, D. L.
DYKSTRA-HYLAND, L. A.
ECKERMAN, D. A.
FILLENBAUM, S.
GRAY-LITTLE, B.
HOLLINS, M.
INSKO, C. A.
JOHNSON, E. S.
ORNSTEIN, P.
SCHOPLER, J. H.
SHINKMAN, P. G.
THISSEN, D. M.
THOMPSON, V. D.
WALLSTEN, T. S.
YOUNG, F. W.

Public Health:
ROPER, W. L.

Health Behaviour and Health Education:
BAUMAN, K. E.
DEVELLIS, B. M.
EARP, J. L.
MUTRAN, E.
SORENSON, J.
STECKLER, A. B.

Health Policy and Administration:
JAIN, S.
KALUZNY, A. D.
KILPATRICK, K. E.
ROZIER, R. G.
VENEY, J. E.
ZELMAN, W. N.

Nutrition:
ANDERSON, J. J.
COLEMAN, R. A.
KOHLMEIER, L.
POPKIN, B. M.
ZEISEL, S. H.

Public Health Nursing:
ATWOOD, J. R.
SALMON, M. E.

Radiation Oncology:
CHANEY, E. L.
LEADON, S. A.
RALEIGH, J. A.
ROSENMAN, J. G.
TEPPER, J. E.
VARIA, M. A.

Radiology:
JAQUES, P. F.
JOHNSTON, R. E.
KWOCK, L.
LEE, J. K.
McCARTNEY, W. H.
MITTELSTAEDT, C. A.
MAURO, M. A.

Religious Studies:
ERNST, C. W.
HALPERIN, D. J.
KAUFMAN, P. I.
SASSON, J. M.
TYSON, R. W., JR
VAN SETERS, J.

Romance Languages:
BANDERA, C.
CASADO, P. G.
CERVIGNI, D. S.
CILVETI, A. L.
CLARK, F. M.
DOMINGUEZ, F. A.
HAIG, I. R. S., II
ILLIANO, A.
KING, L. D.
MALEY, C. A.
MASTERS, G. M.
RECTOR, M. P.
SALGADO, M. A.
SHERMAN, C. L.
VOGLER, F. W.

Slavic Languages:
DEBRECZENY, P.
JANDA, L. A.
LEVINE, M. G.

Social Medicine:
CHURCHILL, L. R.
CROSS, A. W.
DE FRIESE, G. H.
ESTROFF, S. E.
MADISON, D. L.
MORRISSEY, J. P.
RUNYAN, D. K.

Social Work:
BOWEN, G. L.
COOKE, P. W.
DOBELSTEIN, A. W.
EDWARDS, R. L.
FRASER, M. W.
GALINSKY, M. J.
HENLEY, H. C.
NELSON, G. M.
ORTHNER, D. K.
USHER, C. L.
WEIL, M. O.

Sociology:
ALDRICH, H. E.
BEARMAN, P. S.
BLAU, J. R.
ELDER, G. H.
ENTWISLE, B.
KALLEBERG, A. L.
KLEINMAN, S.
NEILSEN, F. D.
OBERSCHALL, A. R.
REED, J. S., JR
RINDFUSS, R. R.
SIMPSON, R. L.
UHLENBERG, P.

Statistics:
ADLER, R.

CARLSTEIN, E.
CHAKRAVARTI, I. M.
KALLIANPUR, G.
KARR, A. F.
KELLY, D. G.
LEADBETTER, M. R.
MARRON, J. S.
SIMONS, G.
SMITH, R. L.

Surgery:
BAKER, C. C.
BLIGHT, A. R.
BUNZENDAHL, H.
BURNHAM, S. J.
CARSON, C. C., III
HALL, J. W., III
KEAGY, B. A.
MANDEL, S. R.
MAXWELL, J. G.
MEYER, A. A.
NAKAYAMA, D. K.
OLLER, D. W.
PECK, M. D.
PILLSBURY, H. C, III
PRAZMA, J.
SHELDON, G. F.
SHOCKLEY, W. M.
SLOAN, G. M.
STAREK, P. J.
WEISSLER, M. C.
WILCOX, B. R.

Women's Studies Programme:
BURNS, E. J.
HOFFERT, S. D.

University of North Carolina at Charlotte

1028 Colvard Bldg, 9021 University City Blvd, Charlotte, NC 28223-0001

Telephone: (704) 687-8622
Fax: (704) 687-6483
E-mail: unccadm@uncc.edu
Internet: www.uncc.edu

Founded 1946 as an extension centre of Univ. of North Carolina, present status 1965
Academic year: August to May (2 semesters)
Chancellor: Dr PHILIP L. DUBOIS
Vice-Chancellor for Academic Affairs and Provost: Dr JOAN F. LORDEN
Vice-Chancellor for Business Affairs: ELIZABETH A. HARDIN
Vice-Chancellor for Research and Economic Devt: ROBERT G. WILHELM
Vice-Chancellor for Student Affairs: Dr ARTHUR JACKSON
Vice-Chancellor for Univ. Advancement: NILES SORENSEN
Univ. Registrar: CHRISTOPHER B. KNAUER
Univ. Librarian: STANLEY J. WILDER

Library of 1,097,642 vols, 381,964 e-books, 57,471 serial subscriptions, 2,191,663 microforms, 32,948 video and audio material
Number of teachers: 1,125
Number of students: 25,277 (20,283 undergraduate, 4,994 graduate)

DEANS

Belk College of Business: Dr STEVE H. OTT
College of Arts and Architecture: KENNETH A. LAMBLA
College of Computing and Informatics: Dr YI DENG
College of Education: Dr MARY LYNN CALHOUN
College of Health and Human Services: Dr NANCY FEY-YENSAN
College of Liberal Arts and Sciences: Dr NANCY A. GUTIERREZ
Graduate School: THOMAS L. REYNOLDS
William States Lee College of Engineering: Dr ROBERT E. JOHNSON

University of North Carolina at Greensboro

1400 Spring Garden St, Greensboro, NC 27402

Telephone: (336) 334-5000
Fax: (336) 334-3649
E-mail: registrar@uncg.edu
Internet: www.uncg.edu

Founded 1891 as a normal college, present status 1931, present name 1963
Academic year: August to May (2 semesters)
Chancellor: Dr LINDA P. BRADY
Provost and Vice-Chancellor for Academic Affairs: Dr DAVID H. PERRIN
Vice-Chancellor for Business Affairs: READE TAYLOR
Vice-Chancellor for Research and Economic Devt: Dr TERRI SHELTON
Vice-Chancellor for Student Affairs: Dr CHERYL M. CALLAHAN
Vice-Chancellor for Univ. Advancement: Dr PATRICIA W. STEWART
Dean of Students: Dr BRETT A. CARTER
Registrar: Dr KELLY ROWETT-JAMES
Dean of Univ. Libraries: ROSANN V. BAZIRJIAN
Library: 2.5m. vols, 60,000 journals, 300,000 e-books
Number of teachers: 1,068 (838 full-time, 230 part-time)
Number of students: 18,771
Publication: *UNCG Magazine*

DEANS

Bryan School of Business and Economics: Prof. Dr McRae C. BANKS
College of Arts and Sciences: Dr TIMOTHY D. JOHNSTON
Div. of Continual Learning: Dr ROBERT M. BROWN
Graduate School: Dr WILLIAM WIENER
Joint School of Nanoscience and Nanoengineering: Prof. Dr JAMES G. RYAN
Joseph M. Bryan School of Business and Economics: Dr MACRAE BANKS
Lloyd International Honors College: Dr JERRY PUBANTZ
School of Education: Dr KAREN WIXSON
School of Health and Human Sciences: Dr CELIA R. HOOPER
School of Music, Theatre and Dance: Dr JOHN J. DEAL
School of Nursing: Prof. Dr LYNNE G. PEARCEY

University of North Carolina at Pembroke

POB 1510, Pembroke, NC 28372-1510

Telephone: (910) 521-6000
Fax: (910) 521-6328
E-mail: registrar@uncp.edu
Internet: www.uncp.edu

Founded 1887 as Croatan Normal School, present status 1969
Academic year: August to May (2 semesters)
Chancellor: Prof. Dr KYLE R. CARTER
Provost and Vice-Chancellor for Academic Affairs: Dr KENNETH D. KITTS
Vice-Chancellor for Advancement: WENDY LOWERY
Vice-Chancellor for Business Affairs and Chief Financial Officer: R. NEIL HAWK
Vice-Chancellor for Enrolment Management: JACQUELINE H. CLARK
Vice-Chancellor for Student Affairs: Dr DIANE JONES
Registrar: SHARON KISSICK
Dean of Library Services: Dr ELINOR FOSTER
Library of 385,294 vols, 67,298 e-books, 700,185 microforms, 11,030 audiovisual material, 40,475 current serial titles
Number of teachers: 553
Number of students: 6,944
Publication: *UNCP Today* (alumni magazine)

DEANS

Graduate Studies: Dr SARA SIMMONS (acting)
College of Arts and Sciences: Dr MARK CANADA
School of Business: Dr RAMIN MAYSAMI (acting)
School of Education: Dr LEAH FIORETINO

University of North Carolina at Wilmington

601 S College Road, Wilmington, NC 28403-5931

Telephone: (910) 962-3000
Fax: (910) 962-3038
E-mail: admissions@uncw.edu
Internet: www.uncw.edu

Founded 1947 as Wilmington College, present name and status 1969
Academic year: August to May
Chancellor: GARY L. MILLER
Provost and Vice-Chancellor for Academic Affairs: Dr CATHY L. BARLOW
Vice-Chancellor for Business Affairs: CHARLES A. MAIMONE
Vice-Chancellor for Student Affairs: PATRICIA LEONARD
Vice-Chancellor for Univ. Advancement: MARY GORNTO
Dean of Students: MICHAEL A. WALKER
Registrar: GILBERT C. BOWEN
Librarian: SARAH WATSTEIN
Library of 1,071,435 vols, 30,715 e-books, 34,825 video items, 105,047 bound periodicals
Number of teachers: 964
Number of students: 13,145
Publications: *Arts and Sciences* (1 a year), *Connections* (1 a year), *Re:search* (1 a year), *UNCW Magazine* (3 a year)

DEANS

Cameron School of Business: Dr LAWRENCE S. CLARK
College of Arts and Sciences: Dr DAVID CORDLE
College of Health and Applied Human Sciences: Dr CHARLES J. HARDY
Graduate School: Dr ROBERT D. ROER
School of Nursing: Dr JAMES McCANN
Watson School of Education: Dr KENNETH TEITELBAUM

University of North Carolina School of the Arts

POB 12189 Winston-Salem, NC 27117-2189
1533 South Main St, Winston-Salem, NC 27127-2738

Telephone: (336) 770-3399
Fax: (336) 734-2900
E-mail: admissions@uncsa.edu
Internet: www.uncsa.edu

Founded 1963
Academic year: August to May
Chancellor: JOHN F. MAUCERI
Provost: DAVID NELSON
Dean of Students: WARD CALDWELL
Chief Academic Officer: DAVID NELSON
Chief Advancement Officer (vacant)
Univ. Sec.: AMANDA BALWAH
Registrar: ERIN MORIN
Dir of Library: VICKI L. WEAVIL
Library of 122,441 vols, 24,957 microforms, 75,945 audiovisual materials, 422 current serial
Number of teachers: 171 (127 full-time, 44 part-time)
Number of students: 1,182

DEANS

High School Academic Programmes: JILL LANE
School of Dance: BRENDA DANIELS

School of Design and Production: JOSEPH TILFORD
School of Drama: GERALD FREEDMAN
School of Film-Making: JORDAN KERNER
School of Music: WADE WEAST
Univ. Programmes: DEAN WILCOX

Western Carolina University

Cullowhee, NC 28723

Telephone: (828) 227-7211
Fax: (828) 227-7319
E-mail: admiss@wcu.edu
Internet: www.wcu.edu

Founded 1889, present name 1953, present status 1972
Academic year: August to May (2 semesters)
Chancellor: DAVID O. BELCHER
Provost: ANGELA BRENTON
Sr Vice-Chancellor for Academic Affairs: FRED HINSON
Vice-Chancellor for Admin. and Finance: ROBERT T. EDWARDS
Vice-Chancellor for Advancement and External Affairs: CLIFTON B. METCALF
Vice-Chancellor for Student Affairs: SAM MILLER
Dir of Admissions: PHIL CAULEY
Registrar: LARRY HAMMER (acting)
Dean of Library Service: DANA SALLY
Library of 702,000 vols incl. bound periodicals, 1,513,000 microfilm, 23,000 e-books, 3,330 current serials
Number of teachers: 457 (full-time)
Number of students: 9,429

DEANS

College of Arts and Sciences: Dr H. GIBBS KNOTTS
College of Business: Prof. DARRELL FRANKLIN PARKER
College of Education and Allied Professions: Dr PERRY SCHOON
College of Fine and Performing Arts: Dr ROBERT KEHRBERG
College of Health and Human Sciences: Dr LINDA SEESTEDT-STANFORD
Educational Outreach: REGIS GILMAN
Honors College: Dr BRIAN RAILSBACK
Kimmel School of Construction Management and Technology: Dr JAMES ZHANG
Research and Graduate Studies: Dr SCOTT HIGGINS

Winston-Salem State University

601 S Martin Luther King, Jr Dr., Winston-Salem, NC 27110

Telephone: (336) 750-2000
Fax: (336) 750-2079
E-mail: admissions@wssu.edu
Internet: www.wssu.edu

Founded 1892 as Slater Industrial Acad., present name 1963, present status 1972
Academic year: August to May
Chancellor: Dr DONALD J. REAVES
Provost and Vice-Chancellor for Academic Affairs: BRENDA A. ALLEN
Vice-Chancellor for Finance and Admin.: GERALD E. HUNTER
Vice-Chancellor for Student Affairs: Dr TRAE T. COTTON
Vice-Chancellor for Univ. Advancement: MICHELLE M. COOK
Registrar: SHARON HUSH
Dir of Library Services: Dr MAE L. RODNEY
Library of 158,858 vols
Number of teachers: 400 (full-time)
Number of students: 6,442
Publication: *Archway* (3 a year)

DEANS

College of Arts and Sciences: Dr CHARLES W. FORD, JR

School of Business and Economics: Dr Jessica Bailey

School of Graduate Studies and Research: Dr Fidelis M. Ikem

School of Health Science: Dr Peggy Valentine

Univ. College: Dr Michelle B. Releford

WAKE FOREST UNIVERSITY

1834 Wake Forest Rd, Winston-Salem, NC 27106

Telephone: (336) 758-5000

Fax: (336) 758-5669

E-mail: wfuadmis@wfu.edu

Internet: www.wfu.edu

Founded 1834, present name 1839

Private control

Academic year: August to May

Pres.: Prof. Dr Nathan O. Hatch

Provost: Dr Mark Welker

Sr Vice-Pres. of Finance and Admin. and Chief Financial Officer: Hof Milam

Vice-Pres. and Gen. Counsel: Dr J. Reid Morgan

Vice-Pres. for Student Life: Kenneth A. Zick

Vice-Pres. for Univ. Advancement: Mark A. Petersen

Dean of Admissions: Martha Blevins Allman

Univ. Registrar: Dr Harold Pace

Dean of Library: Dr Lynn Sutton

Library: 1.7m. vols, 4,500 journals, 50,000 e-journals

Number of teachers: 1,740 (1,158 full-time, 582 part-time)

Number of students: 7,344 (4,775 undergraduate, 2,569 graduate and professional)

DEANS

Divinity School: Prof. Dr Gail R. O'Day

Graduate School of Arts and Sciences: Dr Lorna Grindlay Moore

School of Business: Prof. Steven S Reinemund, Jr

School of Law: Dr Blake D. Morant

School of Medicine: Dr Edward Abraham

Wake Forest College: Prof. Dr Jacquelyn S. Fetrow

PROFESSORS

Graduate School of Arts and Sciences:

Abramson, J. S., Paediatrics

Adams, M. R., Comparative Medicine

Akman, S. A., Cancer Biology, Internal Medicine

Altman, D. G., Public Health Sciences

Anderson, J. P., Education

Aschner, M., Physiology and Pharmacology

Barefield, J. P., History

Bass, D. A., Medicine

Baxley, J. V., Mathematics

Beck, R. C., Psychology

Berry, M. J., Health and Exercise Science

Best, D. L., Psychology

Bo, W. J., Neurobiology and Anatomy

Bond, M. G., Neurobiology and Anatomy

Borwick, S. H., Music

Bowden, D. W., Biochemistry

Boyd, S. B., Religion

Brosnihan, K. B., Physiology and Pharmacology

Brown, D. G., Economics

Browne, C. L., Biology

Browne, R. A., Biology

Brunso-Bechtold, J. K., Neurobiology and Anatomy

Buckalew, V. M., Jr, Medicine (Nephrology)

Burke, G. L., Public Health Sciences

Busija, D. W., Physiology and Pharmacology

Byington, R. P., Public Health Sciences

Carmichael, R. D., Mathematics

Childers, S. R., Physiology and Pharmacology

Chilton, F. H., Internal Medicine

Claiborne, H. A., Jr, Biochemistry

Clarkson, T. B., Jr, Comparative Medicine

Collins, J. E., Religion

Conner, W. E., Biology

Cotton, N., English

Cramer, S. D., Cancer Biology, Internal Medicine

Crouse, J. R., III, Medicine (Endocrinology and Metabolism)

Cunningham, C. C., Biochemistry

Cunningham, P. M., Education

Curran, J. F., Biology

Daniel, L. W., Biochemistry

Deadwyler, S. A., Physiology

DeShazer, M. K., English

Dimock, R. V., Jr, Biology

Durant, R. H., Paediatrics and Public Health Sciences

Eisenach, J. C., Anaesthesia

Esch, G. W., Biology

Escott, P. D., History

Espeland, M. A., Public Health Sciences (Biostatistics)

Ettin, A. V., English

Eure, H. E., Biology

Feldman, S. R., Dermatology, Pathology

Ferrario, C. M., Surgical Sciences

Frankel, A. E., Medicine and Cancer Biology

Frey, D. E., Economics

Furberg, C. D., Medicine and Public Health Sciences

Gladding, S. T., Education

Grant, K. A., Physiology and Pharmacology, Comparative Medicine

Hall, M. A., Law and Public Health Sciences

Hamilton, W. S., Russian

Hans, J. S., English

Hayashi, E. K., Mathematics and Computer Science

Hazen, M. D., Communication

Hearn, T. K., Jr, Philosophy

Hendricks, J. E., Jr, History

Hinze, W. L., Chemistry

Holzwarth, G. M., Physics

Holzwarth, N. A. W., Physics

Howard, F. T., Mathematics

Hughes, M. L., History

Hutson, S. M., Biochemistry

Hyde, M. J., Communication Ethics

Jarrett, D. B., Physiology and Pharmacology

Johnston, W. D., English

Kammer, G. M., Internal Medicine

Kaplan, J. R., Comparative Medicine, Anthropology

Kerr, W. C., Physics

Kimball, C. A., Religion

Kirkman, E. E., Mathematics

Koman, L. A., Orthopaedics

Kondepudi, D. K., Chemistry

Kuberski, P., English

Kucera, L. S., Microbiology

Kuhn, R. E., Biology

Kuzmanovich, J., Mathematics

Lane, H. C., Biology

Leary, M. R., Psychology

Leonard, W. J., Divinity School

Litcher, J. H., Education

Lively, M. O., Biochemistry

Longino, C. F., Sociology, Public Health Sciences

Lorentz, W. B., Jr, Paediatrics

Lyles, D. S., Microbiology and Immunology

McCall, C. E., Medicine (Infectious Disease), Microbiology and Immunology

McMillan, J. J., Communication

McPhail, L. C., Biochemistry

Maine, B. G., English

Margitic, M. R., Romance Languages

Martin, D. R., Accountancy

Martin, J. A., Jr, Religion

Matthews, G. E., Physics

May, J. G., Mathematics

Meis, P. J., Obstetrics and Gynaecology

Melson, G. A., Chemistry

Messier, S. P., Health and Exercise Science

Miller, H. S., Medicine

Milner, J. O., Education

Mizel, S. B., Microbiology and Immunology

Moran, P. R., Radiology

Morgan, T. M., Public Health Sciences

Moss, W. M., English

Nader, M. A., Physiology and Pharmacology

Nielsen, L. N., Education

Noftle, R. E., Chemistry

O'Flaherty, J. T., Medicine

Oppenheim, R. W., Anatomy

Overing, G. R., English

Owen, J., Medicine

Parks, J. S., Pathology

Plemmons, R. J., Mathematics and Computer Science

Porrino, L. J., Physiology and Pharmacology

Prineas, R., Public Health Sciences

Reifler, B. V., Psychiatry

Rejeski, W. J., Health and Exercise Science

Ribisl, P. M., Health and Exercise Science

Rich, S. S., Public Health Sciences

Richman, C. L., Psychology

Roberts, D. C. S., Physiology and Pharmacology

Rose, J. C., Physiology, Obstetrics and Gynaecology

Rubin, B. K., Paediatrics, Physiology, and Pharmacology

Rudel, L. L., Comparative Medicine, Biochemistry

St Clair, R. W., Pathology (Physiology)

Samson, H. H., III, Physiology and Pharmacology, Comparative Medicine

Shapere, D., Philosophy and History of Science

Sherertz, R. J., Medicine

Shihabi, Z. K., Pathology (Clinical Chemistry)

Shively, C. A., Comparative Medicine, Psychology

Shumaker, S. A., Public Health Sciences

Sigal, G., English

Silver, W. L., Biology

Simonelli, J. M., Anthropology

Sinclair, M. L., History

Smith, E., Sociology, American Ethnic Studies

Smith, J. E., Physiology and Pharmacology

Smith, J. H., History

Smith, M. S., Art

Smith, P. B., Biochemistry

Sonntag, W. E., Physiology

Sorci-Thomas, M., Comparative Medicine

Stein, B. E., Neurobiology and Anatomy

Strandhoy, J. W., Pharmacology

Swofford, R. L., Chemistry

Taylor, T. C., Accountancy

Thomas, M. J., Biochemistry

Toole, J. F., Neurology

Torti, F. M., Cancer Biology, Internal Medicine

Tower, R. B., Jr, Taxation

Trible, P., Religion

Valbuena, O., English

van de Rijn, I., Microbiology and Immunology

Velez, R., Internal Medicine

Wagner, W. D., Comparative Medicine

Wasilauskas, B. L., Pathology (Clinical Microbiology)

Weaver, D. S., Anthropology

Webber, R. L., Dentistry, Medical Engineering

WEIGL, P. D., Biology
WEINBERG, R. B., Internal Medicine
WELKER, M. E., Chemistry
WELLS, B. R., Romance Languages
WHEELER, K. T., JR, Radiology
WILKERSON, J. E., JR, Accounting
WILLIAMS, A. J., History
WILLIAMS, J. K., Comparative Medicine
WILLIAMS, R. T., Physics
WILLINGHAM, M. C., Pathology
WILSON, E. G., English
WOODALL, J. N., Anthropology
WOODWARD, D. J., Physiology and Pharmacology
WYKLE, R. L., Biochemistry

Graduate School of Management:
BALIGA, B. R., Management
FLYNN, B. B., Operations Management
HARRIS, F. H. DE B., Managerial Economics and Finance
MEREDITH, J. R., Management
NARUS, J. A., Business Marketing
PATEL, A., Finance
RESNICK, B. G., Banking and Finance
SHOESMITH, G. L., Economics
SMUNT, T. L., Management

School of Business and Accountancy:
AKINC, U., Production and Operations Management
EWING, S., Management and Statistics
HARRISON, K., Management
JURAS, P., Academic Excellence
KNIGHT, L., Accounting
MARTIN, D., Financial Accounting
ROBIN, D., Business Ethics
TAYLOR, T., Accounting
TOWER, R., Taxation
WILKERSON, J., Accounting

School of Law:
ANDERSON, C. B.
BILLINGS, R. B.
CASTLEMAN, D. R.
CORBETT, L. H., JR
COVINGTON, I. B., III
CURTIS, M. K.
DAVIS, T.
FOY, H. M., III
GREBELDINGER, S. K.
HALL, M. A.
HERRING, B. O. H.
LOGAN, D. A.
MEWHINNEY, K.
MONTAQUILA, S. R.
NEWMAN, J. S.
PALMITER, A. R.
PARKER, D. L.
PARKER, J. W.
PARKER, M. F.
PEEPLES, R. A.
REYNOLDS, S.
ROBERTS, P. J.
ROBERTS, T. E.
ROSE, C. P., JR
ROSE, S.
SCHNEIDER, R. C., JR
SHORES, D. F.
STEELE, T. M.
TAYLOR, M. H.
WALKER, G. K.
WALSH, R. K.
WRIGHT, R. F., JR
ZICK, K. A., II

School of Medicine:
ABRAMSON, J. S., Paediatrics
ADAMS, M. R., Comparative Medicine
ADAMS, P. L., Internal Medicine (Nephrology)
ADCOCK, E. W., III, Paediatrics
AKMAN, S. A., Cancer Biology, Internal Medicine (Haematology/Oncology)
ALTMANN, D. G., Public Health Sciences (Social Sciences and Health Policy)
APPLEGATE, R. J., Internal Medicine (Cardiology)

APPLEGATE, W. B., Internal Medicine
ARGENTA, L. C., Surgical Sciences (Plastic/Reconstructive)
ASCHNER, M., Physiology and Pharmacology
ASSIMOS, D. G., Surgical Sciences (Urology)
BASS, D. A., Internal Medicine (Pulmonary Critical Care Medicine)
BECHTOLD, R. E., Radiological Sciences (Radiology)
BLEECKER, E. R., Internal Medicine (Pulmonary Critical Care Medicine)
BO, W. J., Neurobiology and Anatomy
BOND, M. G., Neurobiology and Anatomy
BOWDEN, D. W., Biochemistry
BOWTON, D. L., Anaesthesiology, Internal Medicine (Pulmonary Critical Care Medicine)
BROSNIHAN, K. B., Surgical Sciences (General)
BRUNSO-BECHTOLD, J. K., Neurobiology and Anatomy
BUCKALEW, V. M., JR, Internal Medicine (Nephrology)
BURKART, J. M., Internal Medicine (Nephrology)
BURKE, G. L., Public Health Sciences
BUSIJA, D. W., Physiology and Pharmacology
BUSS, D. H., Pathology
BUTTERWORTH, J. F., IV, Anaesthesiology
BYINGTON, R., Public Health Sciences (Epidemiology)
CHALLA, V. R., Pathology
CHENG, C.-P., Internal Medicine (Cardiology)
CHEW, F. S., Radiological Sciences (Radiology)
CHILDERS, S. R., Physiology and Pharmacology
CHILES, C., Radiological Sciences (Radiology)
CHILTON, F. L., Internal Medicine (Pulmonary Critical Care Medicine)
CLAIBORNE, A., Biochemistry
CLARKSON, T. B., Comparative Medicine
COATES, M. L., Family and Community Medicine
COOPER, M. R., Internal Medicine (Haematology/Oncology)
COVITZ, W., Paediatrics
CROUSE, J. R., III, Internal Medicine (Endocrinology/Metabolism)
CUNNINGHAM, C. C., Biochemistry
CURL, W. W., Surgical Sciences (Orthopaedics)
DANIEL, L. W., Biochemistry
DEAN, R. H., Surgical Sciences (General)
DENTON, W. H., Psychiatry and Behavioural Medicine
DEWAN, D. M., Obstetric Anaesthesiology
DILLARD, R. G., Paediatrics
DIXON, R. L., Radiological Sciences (Radiology)
DIZ, D. I., Surgical Sciences (General), Physiology and Pharmacology
DONOFRIO, P. D., Neurology (Neuromuscular Diseases)
DURANT, R. H., Paediatrics, Public Health Sciences
DYER, R. B., Radiological Sciences (Radiology)
EISENACH, J. E., Obstetric Anaesthesiology
ELSTER, A. D., Radiological Sciences (Radiology)
ERNEST, III, J. M., Obstetrics and Gynaecology (Maternal/Fetal Medicine)
ESPELAND, M. A., Public Health Sciences (Biostatistics)
FELDMAN, S. R., Pathology
FERRARIO, C. M., Surgical Sciences (General)
FERREE, C. R., Radiation Oncology
FLEISCHER, A. B., JR, Dermatology
FRANKEL, A. E., Cancer Biology, Internal Medicine (Haematology/Oncology)

FURBERG, C. D., Public Health Sciences
GARRISON, R. S., Dentistry
GARVIN, A. J., Pathology
GEISINGER, K. R., Pathology
GELFAND, D. W., Radiological Sciences (Radiology)
GIVNER, L. G., Paediatrics
GMEINER, W. H., Biochemistry
GOOD, D. C., Neurology
GREVEN, C. M., Surgical Sciences (Orthopaedics)
GREVEN, K. M., Radiation Oncology
HALL, M., Public Health Sciences (Social Sciences and Health Policy)
HAMMON, J. W., JR, Surgical Sciences (Cardiothoracic)
HANSEN, K. J., Surgical Sciences (General)
HARLE, T. S., Radiological Sciences (Radiology)
HARRIS, M. B., Surgical Sciences (Orthopaedics)
HENKEL, C. K., Neurobiology and Anatomy
HERRINGTON, D. M., Internal Medicine (Cardiology)
HILL, I. D., Paediatrics
HUDSPETH, A. S., Surgical Sciences (Cardiothoracic)
HURD, D. D., Internal Medicine (Haematology/Oncology)
HUTSON, S. M., Biochemistry
JANEWAY, R., Neurology
JOHNSON, C. A., Paediatrics
JORIZZO, J. L., Dermatology
KAMMER, G. M., Internal Medicine (Rheumatology)
KAPLAN, J. R., Comparative Medicine, Anthropology
KELLEY, A. E., Psychiatry and Behavioural Medicine (Child/Adolescent Psychiatry)
KELLY, D. L., JR, Surgical Sciences (Ophthalmology)
KOMAN, L. A., Surgical Sciences (Orthopaedics)
KON, N., Surgical Sciences (Cardiothoracic)
KOUFMAN, J. A., Surgical Sciences (Otolaryngology)
KREMKAU, F. W., Medical Ultrasound
KROWCHUK, D. P., Paediatrics, Dermatology
KUCERA, L. S., Microbiology and Immunology
LAWLESS, M. R., Paediatrics
LICHSTEIN, P. R., Internal Medicine
LINK, K. M., Radiological Sciences (Radiology)
LITTLE, W. C., Internal Medicine (Cardiology)
LIVELY, M. O., III, Biochemistry
LONGINO, C. F., JR, Public Health Sciences (Epidemiology)
LORENTZ, W. B., Paediatrics
LYLES, D. S., Microbiology and Immunology
McCALL, C. E., Microbiology and Immunology, Internal Medicine (Infectious Diseases)
McCALL, W. V., Psychiatry and Behavioural Medicine
McCULLOUGH, D. L., Surgical Sciences (Urology)
McGUIRT, W. F., SR, Surgical Sciences (Otolaryngology)
MACH, R. H., Radiological Sciences (Radiology), Physiology and Pharmacology
McPHAIL, L. C., Biochemistry
MARKS, M. W., Surgical Sciences (Plastic/Reconstructive)
MAYNARD, C. D., Radiological Sciences (Radiology)
MEIS, P. J., Obstetrics and Gynaecology (Maternal/Fetal Medicine), Family and Community Medicine
MEREDITH, J. Q., Surgical Sciences (General)
MEYERS, D. A., Paediatrics

MICHIELUTTE, R. L., Family and Community Medicine
MILLER, A. A., Internal Medicine (Haematology/Oncology)
MILLER, M. E., Public Health Sciences (Biostatistics)
MIZEL, S. B., Microbiology and Immunology
MOODY, D. M., Radiological Sciences (Radiology)
MORGAN, T. M., Public Health Sciences (Biostatistics)
MORTON, K. A., Radiological Sciences (Radiology)
MOSKOVITZ, J., Public Health Sciences
MUELLER-HEUBACH, E., Obstetrics and Gynaecology
NELSON, L. H., III, Obstetrics and Gynaecology (Maternal/Foetal Medicine)
NELSON, T. E., Anaesthesiology
OBER, K. P., Internal Medicine (Endocrinology/Metabolism)
O'FLAHERTY, J. T., Internal Medicine (Haematology/Oncology)
OPPENHEIM, R., Neurobiology and Anatomy
O'SHEA, T. M. D., Paediatrics
OTT, D. J., Radiological Sciences (Radiology)
OWEN, J., Internal Medicine (Haematology/Oncology)
PARKS, J. S., Comparative Medicine
PAUCA, A. L., Anaesthesiology
PEACOCK, J. E., JR, Internal Medicine (Haematology/Oncology)
PEGRAM, P. S., Internal Medicine (Haematology/Oncology)
PENNELL, T. C., Surgical Sciences (General)
PETROZZA, P. H., Anaesthesiology
POEHLING, G. G., Surgical Sciences (Orthopaedics)
PONS, T., Surgical Sciences (Neurosurgery), Physiology and Pharmacology
POWELL, B. L., Internal Medicine (Haematology/Oncology)
PRIELIPP, R. C., Anaesthesiology
PRINEAS, R. J., Public Health Sciences (Epidemiology)
QUANDT, S. A., Public Health Sciences (Epidemiology)
RAPP, S. R., Psychiatry and Behavioural Medicine (Geriatric Medicine)
RAUTAHARJU, P. M., Public Health Sciences
REIFLER, B. V., Psychiatry and Behavioural Medicine
RICH, S. S., Public Health Sciences
RILEY, W. A., Neurology
ROGERS, L. F., Radiological Sciences (Radiology)
ROHR, M. S., Surgical Sciences (General)
ROSE, J. C., Obstetrics and Gynaecology (Maternal/Fetal Medicine)
ROUFAIL, W. M., Internal Medicine (Gastroenterology)
ROY, R. C., Anaesthesiology
ROYSTER, R. L., Anaesthesiology
RUBIN, B. K., Paediatrics, Physiology and Pharmacology
RUDEL, L. L., Comparative Medicine, Biochemistry
ST CLAIR, R. W., Pathology
SANGÜEZA, O. P., Pathology
SARTIANO, G. P., Internal Medicine (Haematology/Oncology)
SCUDERI, P. E., Anaesthesiology
SHAW, E. G., Radiation Oncology
SHERERTZ, R. J., Internal Medicine (Infectious Diseases), Microbiology and Immunology
SHIHABI, Z. K., Pathology
SHIVELY, C. A., Comparative Medicine
SHUMAKER, S. A., Public Health Sciences (Social Sciences and Health Policy)
SIMON, J. L., Paediatrics
SINAL, S. H., Paediatrics, Family and Community Medicine

SLUSHER, M. M., Surgical Sciences (Ophthalmology)
SMITH, J. E., Physiology and Pharmacology
SMITH, P. B., Biochemistry
STEIN, B. E., Neurobiology and Anatomy
STRANDHOY, J. W., Physiology and Pharmacology
SUMNER, T. E., Radiological Sciences (Radiology)
TEGELER, C. H., IV, Neurology
THOMAS, M. J., Biochemistry
THOMPSON, J. N., Surgical Sciences (Otolaryngology)
TOOLE, J. F., Neurology
TORTI, F. M., Cancer Biology, Internal Medicine (Haematology/Oncology)
TROOST, B. T., Neurology
TYTELL, M., Neurobiology and Anatomy
VAN DE RIJN, I., Microbiology and Immunology
VEILLE, J.-C., Obstetrics and Gynaecology (Maternal/Fetal Medicine)
VELEZ, R., Internal Medicine
WAGNER, W. D., Comparative Medicine
WALKER, F. O., Neurology (Neuromuscular Diseases)
WARD, W. G., Surgical Sciences (Orthopaedics)
WASILAUSKAS, B. L., Pathology
WEBB, L. X., Surgical Sciences (Otolaryngology)
WEBBER, R. L., Radiological Sciences (Medical Engineering), Dentistry
WEINBERG, R. B., Internal Medicine (Gastroenterology)
WHEELER, K. T., JR, Radiological Sciences (Radiology)
WILLIAMS, J. K., Comparative Medicine
WILLINGHAM, M. C., Pathology
WOOD, F. B., Neurology (Neuropsychology)
WOODWARD, D. J., Physiology and Pharmacology
WYKLE, R. L., Biochemistry
ZAGORIA, R. J., Radiological Sciences (Radiology)
ZAMKOFF, K. W., Internal Medicine (Haematology/Oncology)

Divinity School:
KIMBALL, C. A., Religion
LEONARD, W. J., Church History
TRIBLE, P., Religion
TUPPER, E. F., Theology

WARREN WILSON COLLEGE

POB 9000, Asheville, NC 28815-9000
701 Warren Wilson Rd, Swannanoa, NC 28778
Telephone: (828) 298-3325
Fax: (828) 298-1440
E-mail: admit@warren-wilson.edu
Internet: www.warren-wilson.edu
Founded 1894 as Asheville Farm School
Private control
Academic year: August to May

Areas of study incl. art, Appalachian studies, biology, business, chemistry, creative writing, English, environmental studies, global studies, history and political science, integrative studies, mathematics, modern languages, music and archaeology, philosophy, psychology, religious studies, social work, sociology and anthropology, sustainable business, theatre

Pres.: Dr WILLIAM SANBORN PFEIFFER
Vice-Pres. for Academic Affairs and Dean of College: Dr PAULA GARRETT
Vice-Pres. for Admin. and Finance: JONATHAN EHRLICH
Vice-Pres. for Advancement, Admission and Marketing: RICHARD BLOMGREN
Dean of Students: DEBORAH MYERS
Registrar: CHRISTA BRIDGMAN
Library Dir: CHRISTINE RICHERT NUGENT

Library of 100,000 vols
Number of teachers: 70
Number of students: 1,000

WINGATE UNIVERSITY

POB 159, Wingate, NC 28174-9905
Telephone: (704) 233-8000
Fax: (704) 233-8110
E-mail: admit@wingate.edu
Internet: www.wingate.edu
Founded 1896, present status 1995
Private control
Academic year: August to May
Pres.: Dr JERRY E. MCGEE
Sr Vice-Pres. for Academic Affairs: Dr MARTHA S. ASTI
Vice-Pres. for Business and Chief Financial Officer: WILLIAM H. DURHAM
Vice-Pres. for Graduate and Professional Programmes: Dr ROBERT B. SUPERNAW
Vice-Pres. for Resource Devt: VINT TILSON
Vice-Pres. for Student Life and Enrolment Services: T. RHETT BROWN
Dir of Admissions: LINDSAY KREIS
Registrar: NICCI C. BROWN
Library Dir: AMEE ODOM

Library of 102,000 vols
Number of teachers: 107
Number of students: 2,529

DEANS

Charles A. Cannon College of Arts and Sciences: Prof. Dr H. DONALD MERRILL
Lloyd and Georgia Thayer School of Education: Dr SARAH HARRISON-BURNS
Porter B. Byrum School of Business: Prof. JOSEPH M. GRAHAM
School of Pharmacy: Prof. Dr ROBERT B. SUPERNAW
School of Sport Sciences: Dr MICHAEL R. JUDD

NORTH DAKOTA

FORT BERTHOLD COMMUNITY COLLEGE

POB 490, 220 Eighth Ave N, New Town, ND 58763
Telephone: (701) 627-4738
Fax: (701) 627-3609
Internet: www.fortbertholdcc.bia.edu
Founded 1973
Tribal control
Academic year: August to May

Offers Bachelor of science in education and environmental science; Bachelor of arts in Native American studies

Pres.: RUSSELL D. MASON, JR
Vice-Pres. for Academics: Dr CLARICE BAKER-BIG BACK
Vice-Pres. for Native Studies: ALYCE SPOTTED BEAR
Dean for Students: ROZ ST CLAIRE
Library Dir: QUINCEE BAKER

Library of 19,000 vols, 200 periodicals.

JAMESTOWN COLLEGE

6000 College Lane, Jamestown, ND 58405
Telephone: (701) 252-3467
Fax: (701) 253-4318
E-mail: admissions@jc.edu
Internet: www.jc.edu
Founded 1883
Private control
Academic year: August to May

Depts of biology, business, accounting and economics, chemistry, communication, computer science and technology, criminal justice, English, fine arts, foreign language, health and physical education, history, math-

ematics, music, nursing, psychology, religion and philosophy, teacher education, theatre
Pres.: Dr ROBERT S. BADAL
Vice-Pres. and Dean for Academic Services: Dr GARY WATTS
Vice-Pres. for Institutional Advancement: POLLY PETERSON
Dean for Enrolment Management: TENA LAWRENCE
Dean for Students: GARY VAN ZINDEREN
Registrar: MICHAEL WOODLEY
Dir for Library: PHYLLIS BRATTON
Library of 150,000 vols
Number of teachers: 60
Number of students: 1,000

MEDCENTER ONE COLLEGE OF NURSING

512 N Seventh St, Bismarck, ND 58501
Telephone: (701) 323-6271
Internet: medcenterone.com/collegeofnursing
Founded 1988
Private control
Academic year: August to May (2 semesters)
Provost and Dean: Dr KAREN LATHAM
Library Dir: TRAVIS SCHULZ.

NORTH DAKOTA UNIVERSITY SYSTEM

Dept 215, 10th Fl., State Capitol, 600 E Boulevard Ave, Bismarck, ND 58505-0230
Telephone: (701) 328-2960
Fax: (701) 328-2961
E-mail: ndus.office@ndus.edu
Internet: www.ndus.edu
Founded 1990
Sate control
Chancellor: WILLIAM G. GOETZ
Vice-Chancellor for Academic and Student Affairs: MICHEL HILLMAN
Vice-Chancellor for Administrative Affairs: LAURA GLATT
Vice-Chancellor for Strategic Planning: MARSHA KROTSENG
Dean for Libraries: JAMES COUNCIL
Number of teachers: 4,000
Number of students: 36,020 (f. t. e.).

CONSTITUENT UNIVERSITIES

Dickinson State University

291 Campus Dr., Dickinson, ND 58601-4896
Telephone: (701) 483-2507
Fax: (701) 483-2006
E-mail: dsu.hawk@dickinsonstate.edu
Internet: www.dickinsonstate.edu
Founded 1918
Pres.: Dr D. C. COSTON (acting)
Vice-Pres. for Academic Affairs: Dr JON BRUDVIG
Vice-Pres. for Business Affairs: ALVIN BINSTOCK
Vice-Pres. for Student Devt: HAL HAYNES
Registrar: MARSHALL MELBYE
Dir for Library Services: RITA ENNEN
Library of 164,000 vols, 21,000 periodicals, 10,000 e-books
Number of teachers: 234 (141 part-time, 93 full-time)
Number of students: 2,650

DEANS

College of Arts and Sciences: Dr JON BRUDVIG
College of Education, Business and Applied Sciences: Dr DOUGLAS A. LAPLANTE

Mayville State University

330 Third St, NE, Mayville, ND 58257-1299
Telephone: (701) 786-2301
Fax: (701) 788-4818

E-mail: askmsu@mayvillestate.edu
Internet: www.mayvillestate.edu
Founded 1889, present name 1987
Academic year: August to May
Divs of business and computer information systems, education and psychology, health, liberal arts, physical education and recreation, science and mathematics
Pres.: GARY HAGEN
Vice-Pres. for Academic Affairs: Dr KEITH STENEHJEM
Vice-Pres. for Student Affairs and Institutional Research: Dr RAYMOND GERSZEWSKI
Registrar: PAM BRAATEN
Dir for Library Services: KELLY KORNKVEN
Library of 83,964 vols
Number of teachers: 76
Number of students: 929
Publication: *MSU Today* (1 a year).

Minot State University

500 University Ave, W, Minot, ND 58707-0001
Telephone: (701) 858-3000
E-mail: msu@minotstateu.edu
Internet: www.minotstateu.edu
Founded 1913
Pres.: Dr DAVID FULLER
Vice-Pres. for Academic Affairs: Dr LENORE M. KOCZON
Vice-Pres. for Admin. and Finance: BRIAN FOISY
Vice-Pres. for Advancement: MARV SEMRAU
Vice-Pres. for Student Affairs: Dr RICHARD R. JENKINS
Registrar: REBECCA PORTER
Library Dir: SARAH HENDERSON
Library of 500,000 vols
Number of teachers: 220
Number of students: 3,866

DEANS

Center for Extended Learning: Dr KRIS WARMOTH
College of Arts and Sciences: Dr CONRAD DAVIDSON
College of Business: Dr JOANN LINRUD
College of Education and Health Sciences: Dr NEIL NORDQUIST
Graduate School: Dr LINDA CRESAP

North Dakota State University

POB 6050, Fargo, ND 58108-6050
1340 Administration Ave, Fargo, ND 58102
Telephone: (701) 231-8011
Fax: (701) 231-8802
E-mail: ndsu.admission@ndsu.edu
Internet: www.ndsu.edu
Founded 1890
Pres.: Dr DEAN L. BRESCIANI
Provost: Dr J. BRUCE RAFERT
Vice-Pres. for Finance and Admin.: BRUCE BOLLINGER
Vice-Pres. for Information Technology: BONNIE NEAS
Vice-Pres. for Research, Creative Activities and Technology Transfer: PHILIP BOUDJOUK
Vice-Pres. for Student Affairs: PRAKASH C. MATHEW
Asst Vice-Pres. for Univ. Relations: LAURA McDANIEL
Registrar: KRISTI WOLD-McCORMICK
Dean for Libraries: MICHELE M. REID
Library: see Libraries and Archives
Number of teachers: 684
Number of students: 14,399

DEANS

College of Agriculture, Food Systems and Natural Resources: KEN GRAFTON
College of Arts, Humanities and Social Sciences: Dr KENT SANDSTROM

College of Business: RONALD D. JOHNSON
College of Engineering and Architecture: GARY R. SMITH
College of Human Development and Education: VIRGINIA CLARK JOHNSON
College of Pharmacy, Nursing and Allied Sciences: CHARLES D. PETERSON
College of Science and Mathematics: Dr KEVIN McCAUL

University of North Dakota

University Station, Grand Forks, ND 58202
Telephone: (701) 777-3000
Fax: (701) 777-3650
E-mail: und.info@email.und.edu
Internet: www.und.edu
Founded 1883
Academic year: August to May
Pres.: Dr ROBERT O. KELLEY
Provost and Vice-Pres. for Academic Affairs: PAUL LEBEL
Vice-Pres. for Finance and Operations: ALICE BREKKE
Vice-Pres. for Research and Economic Devt: PHYLLIS E. JOHNSON
Vice-Pres. for Student Affairs: LORI REESOR
Dir for Libraries: WILBUR STOLT
Library: see Libraries and Archives
Number of teachers: 610
Number of students: 14,697

DEANS

College of Arts and Sciences: KATHLEEN TIEMANN
College of Business and Public Administration: DENNIS J. ELBERT
College of Education and Human Devt: DAN RICE
College of Nursing: DENISE KORNIEWICZ
Graduate School: WAYNE SWISHER
John D. Odegard School of Aerospace Sciences: BRUCE A. SMITH
School of Engineering and Mines: HESHAM EL-REWINI
School of Law: KATHRYN RAND
School of Medicine and Health Sciences: JOSHUA WYNNE

Valley City State University

101 College St, SW, Valley City, ND 58072
Telephone: (701) 845-7990
Fax: (701) 845-7245
Internet: www.vcsu.edu
Founded 1890
Divs of business and information technology, communication arts and social science, education and graduate studies, fine arts, mathematics, physical education, science and health
Pres.: Dr STEVEN W. SHIRLEY
Vice-Pres. for Academic Affairs: Dr MARGARET DAHLBERG
Vice-Pres. for Student Affairs: VITALIANO FIGUEROA
Registrar: JODY KLIER
Library Dir: DONNA JAMES
Library of 80,000 vols
Number of teachers: 56
Number of students: 1,384

DEANS

School of Education and Graduate Studies: GARY THOMPSON

There are five two-year colleges offering associate and trade/technical degrees.

SITTING BULL COLLEGE

9299 Highway 24, Fort Yates, ND 58538
Telephone: (701) 854-8000
Fax: (701) 854-3403

E-mail: info@sbci.edu

Internet: www.sittingbull.edu

Founded 1973 as Standing Rock Community College, present name 1996

Tribal control

Offers Bachelor of science in business administration, education, early childhood education, elementary education, environmental science, general studies, secondary science education; campuses at McLaughlin and Mobridge (South Dakota)

Pres.: Dr LAUREL VERMILLION

Vice-Pres. for Academics: Dr KOREEN RESSLER

Vice-Pres. for Finance: LEONICA ALKIRE

Librarian: MARK HOLMAN

Library of 20,000 vols

Number of teachers: 20

Number of students: 315

TRINITY BIBLE COLLEGE

50 Sixth Ave, S, Ellendale, ND 58436

Telephone: (701) 349-3621

Fax: (701) 349-5786

E-mail: president@trinitybiblecollege.edu

Internet: www.trinitybiblecollege.edu

Founded 1948 as Lakewood Park Bible School, present name 1983

Private control

Academic year: August to May

Areas of study: biblical studies, Christian leadership, elementary education, general studies, intercultural studies, physical education

Pres.: JACK STROM

Sr Vice-Pres. and Dean for the College: Dr MICHAEL L. DUSING

Vice-Pres. for Academic Affairs: Dr DAYTON KINGSRITER

Dir for Enrolment: JAN DRESSANDER

Registrar: RACHELLE SPRINGER

Dir for Library: DIANE OLSON

Library of 90,000 vols, 11,700 e-books

Number of teachers: 25

Number of students: 280

TURTLE MOUNTAIN COMMUNITY COLLEGE

POB 340, Belcourt, ND 58316

10145 BIA Rd 7, Belcourt, ND 58316

Telephone: (701) 477-7862

Fax: (701) 477-7807

Internet: www.tm.edu

Founded 1972

Tribal control

Academic year: August to July

Offers Bachelor of science degrees in elementary education and secondary science

Pres.: Dr JIM DAVIS

Academic Dean: LARRY HENRY

Dean for Student Services: WANDA LADUCER

Registrar: ANGEL GLADUE

Library Dir: KATHE JO ZASTE-PELTIER

Library of 26,278 vols.

UNITED TRIBES TECHNICAL COLLEGE

3315 University Dr., Bismarck, ND 58504

Telephone: (701) 255-3285

Fax: (701) 530-0605

Internet: www.uttc.edu

Founded 1969 as United Tribes of North Dakota Devt Corpn, present name 1987

Tribal control

Areas of study: business administration, criminal justice, elementary education

Pres.: Dr DAVID M. GIPP

Vice-Pres. for Academic, Career and Technical Education: PHIL BAIRD

Vice-Pres. for Student and Campus Services: RUSSELL SWAGGER

Assoc. Vice-Pres. for Enrolment Management: NATHAN STRATTON

Registrar: JOETTA MCLEOD

Librarian: CHARLENE WEIS

Library of 7,500 vols, 100 magazines and journals, 40 newspapers

Number of students: 647

UNIVERSITY OF MARY

7500 University Dr., Bismarck, ND 58504

Telephone: (701) 255-7500

Fax: (701) 255-7687

E-mail: admissions@umary.edu

Internet: www.umary.edu

Founded 1955 as Mary College, present name and status 1986

Private control

Academic year: August to May

Pres.: Fr JAMES P. SHEA

Vice-Pres. for Academic Affairs: Dr DIANE FLADELAND

Vice-Pres. for Enrolment Services: BRENDA KASPARI

Vice-Pres. for Public Affairs: NEAL KALBERER

Vice-Pres. for Student Devt: Dr TIM SEAWORTH

Library Dir: CHERYL BAILEY

Library of 70,000 vols, 600 periodicals, 5,000 multimedia items

Number of teachers: 101

Number of students: 3,000

DEANS

Gary Tharaldson School of Business: Dr. SHANDA TRAISER

School of Arts and Sciences: Dr. DAVID FLEISCHACKER

School of Education and Behavioral Sciences: Dr. ROD A. JONAS

School of Health Sciences: Dr. JODI ROLLER

OHIO

AIR FORCE INSTITUTE OF TECHNOLOGY

2950 Hobson Way, Wright-Patterson Air Force Base, OH 45433-7765

Telephone: (937) 255-3636

Fax: (937) 656-7600

E-mail: pa@afit.edu

Internet: www.afit.edu

Founded 1919 as Air School of Application, present name and status 1947

State control

Commandant: Col Dr TIMOTHY J. LAWRENCE

Vice-Commandant: TIMOTHY J. DUENING

Dir forAdmissions: EDWARD HART

Library Dir: JAMES T. HELLING

Library of 120,000 vols

Number of teachers: 280

DEANS

Civil Engineering School: Col RODGER G. SCHULD

Graduate School of Engineering and Management: Dr MARLIN U. THOMAS

School of Systems and Logistics: Col TIMOTHY J. FENNELL

ANTIOCH UNIVERSITY

900 Dayton St, Yellow Springs, OH 45387

Telephone: (937) 769-1340

Fax: (937) 769-1350

Internet: www.antioch.edu

Founded 1852

Private control

Academic year: July to June

Areas of study: arts, education, environmental studies and sustainability, health and human development, humanities, liberal studies, management and leadership, psychology; campuses in Los Angeles and Santa Barbara (California), Midwest (Ohio), New England (New Hampshire), and Seattle (Washington)

Chancellor: Dr TONI A. MURDOCH

Vice-Chancellor for Univ. Academic Affairs: Dr LAURIEN ALEXANDRE

Vice-Chancellor for Univ. Advancement: GRADY JONES

Registrar: VICKIE NIGHSWANDER

Number of teachers: 273

Number of students: 5,023

ART ACADEMY OF CINCINNATI

1212 Jackson St, Cincinnati, OH 45202

Telephone: (513) 562-6262

Fax: (513) 562-8778

E-mail: admissions@artacademy.edu

Internet: www.artacademy.edu

Founded 1869 as McMicken School of Design, present name 1887

Private control

Academic year: August to May

Offers BA in art history, communication arts, fine arts; MA in education

Pres. and Academic Dean: DIANE K. SMITH

Vice-Pres. for Enrolment Management: Dr GREGORY STEWART

Dir for Admissions: JOHN WADDELL

Dir for Student Life: LIZ NEAL

Registrar: SUE HUTCHENS

Number of teachers: 38 (14 full-time, 24 adjunct)

Number of students: 220 (200 undergraduate, 20 graduate)

ASHLAND UNIVERSITY

401 College Ave, Ashland, OH 44805

Telephone: (419) 289-4142

Fax: (419) 289-5999

E-mail: enrollme@ashland.edu

Internet: www.ashland.edu

Founded 1878 as Ashland College, present name 1989

Private control

Academic year: August to May

Pres.: Dr FREDERICK J. FINKS

Provost: Prof. Dr FRANK E. PETTIGREW

Vice-Pres. and Pres. for the Seminary: Dr JOHN C. SHULTZ

Vice-Pres. for Devt and Institutional Advancement: RON HUIATT

Vice-Pres. for Enrolment Management and Marketing: SCOTT VAN LOO

Vice-Pres. for Student Affairs and Dean for Students: B. SUE HEIMANN

Registrar: KATHLEEN HALL

Dir for Libraries: ED KRAKORA

Library of 280,000 vols

Number of teachers: 205

Number of students: 6,459

Publications: *Accent Magazine*, *American Secondary Education* (3 a year), *Executive Eagle*, *River Teeth* (2 a year)

DEANS

College of Arts and Sciences: Dr DAWN WEBER

Dwight Schar College of Education: Dr JAMES P. VAN KEUREN

Dwight Schar College of Nursing: FAYE GRUND

Founders School of Continuing Education: Dr DWIGHT L. MCELFRESH

Graduate School: Dr W. GREGORY GERRICK

Richard E and Sandra J. Dauch School of Business and Economics: Dr JEFFREY E. RUSSELL

ATHENAEUM OF OHIO

6616 Beechmont Ave, Cincinnati, OH 45230
Telephone: (513) 231-2223
Fax: (513) 231-3254
E-mail: ath@mtsm.org
Internet: www.mtsm.org

Founded 1829, present name and status 1928
Private control
Academic year: September to June

Offers Master's degrees in biblical studies, pastoral counselling, theology

Pres. and Rector: Rev. EDWARD P. SMITH
Vice-Pres. for Finance and Admin.: DENNIS K. EAGAN
Dean: Rev. EARL FERNANDES
Dean of Spec. Studies: Dr TERRANCE D. CALLAN
Registrar: MICHAEL E. SWEENEY
Dir for Library: CONNIE SONG

Library of 111,000 vols; spec. colln of 9,000 books, incl. 35 MSS and 22 incunabula
Number of teachers: 58
Number of students: 252

Publication: *Athenaeum Magazine*.

BALDWIN-WALLACE COLLEGE

275 Eastland Rd, Berea, OH 44017-2005
Telephone: (440) 826-2900
E-mail: info@bw.edu
Internet: www.bw.edu

Founded 1845
Private control

Divs of business administration, education, health and physical education, humanities, conservatory, science and mathematics, social sciences

Pres.: RICHARD W. DURST
Sr Vice-Pres.: RICHARD L. FLETCHER
Vice-Pres. for Academic Affairs and Dean for College: Dr MARY LOU HIGGERSON
Vice-Pres. for Enrolment Management: SUSAN DILENO
Vice-Pres. for Finance and Admin.: WILLIAM M. RENIFF
Vice-Pres. for Student Affairs: Dr TRINA DOBBERSTEIN
Vice-Pres. for Univ. Advancement: WILLIAM J. SPIKER
Dir for Libraries: Dr PATRICK SCANLAN

Library of 210,000 vols
Number of teachers: 165 (full-time)
Number of students: 4,081

BLUFFTON UNIVERSITY

1 University Dr., Bluffton, OH 45817-2104
Telephone: (419) 358-3000
Fax: (419) 358-3323
E-mail: admissions@bluffton.edu
Internet: www.bluffton.edu

Founded 1899 as Bluffton College, present name and status 2004
Private control
Academic year: August to May

Divs of business studies, communication and fine arts, education and sport science, humanities, natural sciences, social and behavioural sciences

Pres.: JAMES M. HARDER
Vice-Pres. and Academic Dean: SALLY WEAVER SOMMER
Vice-Pres. for Enrolment Management and Student Life: ERIC FULCOMER
Vice-Pres. for Institutional Advancement: HANS HOUSHOWER
Dir for Admissions: CHRIS JEBSEN

Registrar: IRIS NEUFELD
Dir for libraries: MARY JEAN JOHNSON
Library of 160,000 vols
Number of teachers: 112 (63 full-time, 49 part-time)
Number of students: 1,229 (1,115 undergraduate, 114 graduate)

BOWLING GREEN STATE UNIVERSITY

Bowling Green, OH 43403-0001
Telephone: (419) 372-2531
Internet: www.bgsu.edu

Founded 1910, present status 1935
State control
Academic year: August to May

Pres.: Dr MARY ELLEN MAZEY
Provost and Sr Vice-Pres. for Academic Affairs: Dr RODNEY ROGERS
Vice-Pres. for Enrolment Management: ALBERT COLOM
Vice-Pres. for Finance and Admin.: SHERIDEEN S. STOLL
Vice-Pres. for Research and Economic Devt: Dr MICHAEL OGAWA
Vice-Pres. for Univ. Advancement: THOMAS HILES
Dean for Students: JILL CARR
Registrar: CHRISTOPHER PHILIP COX
Dean for Univ. Libraries: SARA BUSHONG

Library of 2,884,569 vols, 74,411 e-books, 57,592 e-journals, 2,373,898 microform units, 2,437 periodicals
Number of teachers: 800 (full-time)
Number of students: 21,000

Publications: *BGSU Magazine*, *Dimensions Magazine*, *Journal of Popular Culture* (4 a year, online (www.msu.edu/~tjpc)), *Mid-American Review*, *Philosopher's Index* (4 a year)

DEANS

College of Arts and Sciences: Dr SIMON MORGAN-RUSSELL
College of Business Administration: Dr B. MADHU RAO
College of Education and Human Development: Dr BRAD COLWELL
College of Health and Human Services: Dr LINDA PETROSINO
College of Musical Arts: Dr JEFFREY SHOWELL
College of Technology: Dr FARIS MALHAS
Firelands College: Dr WILLIAM K. BALZER
Graduate College: Dr MICHAEL OGAWA

CAPITAL UNIVERSITY

1 College and Main, Columbus, OH 43209-2394
Telephone: (614) 236-6011
Fax: (614) 236-6147
Internet: www.capital.edu

Founded 1830
Private control
Academic year: August to May (2 terms)

Schools of communications, conservatory of music, humanities, management and leadership, natural sciences, nursing and health, social sciences and education

Pres.: Dr DENVY A. BOWMAN
Provost and Vice-Pres. for Academic and Student Affairs: RICHARD M. ASHBROOK
Vice-Pres. for Business and Finance: SUSAN TATE
Exec. Vice-Pres. for Planning and Advancement: KEVIN W. SAYERS
Dir for Admission: AMANDA L. STEINER
Dean for the College: CEDRIC ADDERLEY
Registrar: BRENT A. KOERBER
Dir for Library: BELEN FERNANDEZ

Number of teachers: 400 (200 full-time, 200 part-time)

Number of students: 3,550

CASE WESTERN RESERVE UNIVERSITY

10900 Euclid Ave, Cleveland, OH 44106
Telephone: (216) 368-2000
Fax: (216) 368-4325
Internet: www.case.edu

Founded 1967 by merger of Western Reserve Univ. (f. 1826 as College) with Case Institute of Technology (f. 1880 as Case School of Applied Science)
Private control
Academic year: August to May

Pres.: BARBARA R. SNYDER
Provost and Exec. Vice-Pres.: WILLIAM A. BAESLACK, III
Sr Vice-Pres. for Admin.: JOHN WHEELER
Sr Vice-Pres. for Univ. Relations and Devt: BRUCE LOESSIN
Vice-Pres. for Enrolment: RICK BISCHOFF
Vice-Pres. for Govt Relations: DAVID BELL
Vice-Pres. for Inclusion, Diversity and Equal Opportunity: MARILYN SANDERS MOBLEY
Vice-Pres. for Information Technology Services and Chief Information Officer: LEV S. GONICK
Vice-Pres. for Student Affairs: GLENN NICHOLLS
Vice-Pres. for Univ. Planning: CHRISTINE ASH
Gen. Counsel: COLLEEN TREML
Registrar: AMY S. HAMMETT
Univ. Librarian: ARNOLD HIRSHON

Library: see Libraries and Archives
Number of teachers: 2,745 (full-time)
Number of students: 9,837 (4,227 undergraduate, 5,610 graduate and professional)

Publication: *Think* (2 a year, online (www.case.edu/magazine))

DEANS

Case School of Engineering: NORMAN TIEN
College of Arts and Sciences: CYRUS TAYLOR
Frances Payne Bolton School of Nursing: MARY E. KERR
Mandel School of Applied Social Sciences: GROVER GILMORE
School of Dental Medicine: JEROLD GOLDBERG
School of Graduate Studies: CHARLES ROZEK
School of Law: LAWRENCE MITCHELL
School of Medicine: PAMELA BOWES DAVIS
Weatherhead School of Management: MOHAN REDDY
Undergraduate Studies: JEFFREY WOLCOWITZ

PROFESSORS

Case School of Engineering (tel. (216) 368-4436; internet www.engineering.case.edu):
ADAMS, M. L., Mechanical and Aerospace Engineering
ALEXANDER, J. I. D., Mechanical and Aerospace Engineering
BAER, E., Macromolecular Science and Engineering
BALLARINI, R., Engineering Mechanics
BEER, R., Electrical Engineering and Computer Science
BLACKWELL, J., Macromolecular Science and Engineering
CAWLEY, J. D., Materials Science and Engineering
CRAGO, P. E., Biomedical Engineering
DAVY, D. T., Mechanical and Aerospace Engineering
DURAND, D. M., Biomedical Engineering
EDWARDS, R. V., Chemical Engineering
ERNST, F., Materials Science and Engineering
FEKE, D. L., Chemical Engineering
GASPARINI, D. A., Structural Engineering
GREBER, I., Mechanical and Aerospace Engineering

HEUER, A. H., Materials Science and Engineering
HILTNER, A., Macromolecular Science and Engineering
ISHIDA, H., Macromolecular Science and Engineering
JAMIESON, A. M., Macromolecular Science and Engineering
JENNINGS, A. A., Environmental Engineering
KADAMBI, J. R., Mechanical and Aerospace Engineering
KAMOTANI, Y., Mechanical and Aerospace Engineering
LACKS, D. J., Chemical Engineering
LANDAU, U., Chemical Engineering
LANDO, J. B., Macromolecular Science and Engineering
LEWANDOWSKI, J. J., Materials Science and Engineering
LITT, M., Macromolecular Science and Engineering
LIU, C.-C., Chemical Engineering
LOPARO, K. A., Electrical Engineering and Computer Science
MALAKOOTI, B., Electrical Engineering and Computer Science
MANAS-ZLOCZOWER, I., Macromolecular Science and Engineering
MANN, J. A., Jr, Chemical Engineering
MANSOUR, J. M., Mechanical and Aerospace Engineering
MARCHANT, R. E., Biomedical Engineering
MEHREGANY, M., Electrical Engineering and Computer Science
MESAROVIC, M. D., Electrical Engineering and Computer Science
MICHAL, G. M., Materials Science and Engineering
MULLEN, R. L., Engineering Mechanics
NEWMAN, W. S., Electrical Engineering and Computer Science
OSTRACH, S., Mechanical and Aerospace Engineering
OZSOYOGLU, G., Electrical Engineering and Computer Science
OZSOYOGLU, Z. M., Electrical Engineering and Computer Science
PAPACHRISTOU, C. A., Electrical Engineering and Computer Science
PAYER, J. H., Materials Science and Engineering
PECKHAM, P. H., Biomedical Engineering
PINTAURO, P. N., Chemical Engineering
PIROUZ, P., Materials Science and Engineering
PRAHL, J. M., Mechanical and Aerospace Engineering
QUINN, R. D., Mechanical and Aerospace Engineering
QUTUBUDDIN, S., Chemical Engineering
SAADA, A. S., Geotechnical Engineering
SAIDEL, G. M., Biomedical Engineering
SAVINELL, R. F., Chemical Engineering
TABIB-AZAR, M., Electrical Engineering and Computer Science
T'IEN, J. S., Mechanical and Aerospace Engineering
WELSCH, G. E., Materials Science and Engineering
WHITE, L., Electrical Engineering and Computer Science
WILSON, D., Biomedical Engineering
ZAWODZINSKI, T., Chemical Engineering

College of Arts and Sciences (tel. (216) 368-4413; internet www.case.edu/artsci):

ADAMS, H., Art History and Art
AKERIB, D., Physics
ALEXANDER, J., Mathematics
ANDERSON, A. B., Chemistry
BARKLEY, M. D., Chemistry
BEAL, T., Religion
BEALL, C. M., Anthropology
BROWN, R., Physics
BURKE, M., Biology

CALVETTI, D., Mathematics
CAPLAN, A. I., Biology
CARRIER, D., Art History and Art
CHIEL, H. J., Biology
CHOTTINER, G. S., Physics
CULLIS, C. A., Biology
DANNEFER, W. D., Sociology
DEACOSTA, A. D., Mathematics
DEIMLING, G. T., Sociology
DETTERMAN, D. K., Psychology
DUFFIN, R. W., Music
DUNBAR, R. C., Chemistry
FAGAN, J. F., JR, Psychology
FARRELL, D. E., Physics
GAINES, A. D., Anthropology
GARNER, P. P., Chemistry
GILMORE, G. C., Psychology
GOLDSTEIN, M. C., Anthropology
GREENE, R. L., Psychology
GREKSA, L. P., Anthropology
GRUNDY, K. W., Political Science
GUP, T. S., English
GURARIE, D., Mathematics
HAAS, P. J., Religion
HAMMACK, D. C., History
HEFLING, S. E., Music
HELZE, M., Classics
HURLEY, M. G., Mathematics
IKELS, C., Anthropology
JENKINS, J. H., Anthropology
KAHANA, E., Sociology
KASH, K., Physics
KENNEY, M. E., Chemistry
KIM, C.-T., Philosophy
KOONCE, J. F., Biology
KORBIN, J. E., Anthropology
KOTELENEZ, P., Mathematics
KOWALSKI, K. L., Physics
KRAUSS, L. M., Physics
LAMBRECHT, W., Physics
LANDAU, E. G., Art History and Art
LANGER, J., Mathematics
LATHERS, M., Modern Languages and Literature
LEE, D. H., Mathematics
LEITMAN, M. J., Mathematics
LOADER, C., Statistics
LUCK, R. E., Astronomy
MCCALL, P. L., Geological Sciences
MCHALE, V. E., Political Science
MARLING, W. H., English
MATEESCU, G. D., Chemistry
MATISOFF, G., Geological Sciences
NEILS, J., Art History and Art
OLSZEWSKI, E. J., Art History and Art
ORLOCK, J. M., Theatre Arts
OVERHOLSER, J. C., Psychology
PEARSON, A. J., Chemistry
PETSCHEK, R. G., Physics
PROTASIEWICZ, J., Chemistry
RITZMANN, R. E., Biology
ROCKE, A. J., History
ROSENBLATT, C. S., Physics
RUHL, J. E., Physics
RUSS, S. W., Psychology
SALOMON, R. G., Chemistry
SAVIN, S. M., Geological Sciences
SAYRE, L. M., Chemistry
SCHERSON, D. A., Chemistry
SCHUELE, D. E., Physics
SEDRANSK, J., Statistics
SETTERSTEN, R., JR, Sociology
SIEBENSCHUH, W. R., English
SINGER, D. A., Mathematics
SINGER, K. D., Physics
STARKMAN, G. D., Physics
STEINBERG, T. L., History
STOLLER, E. P., Sociology
STONUM, G. L., English
STRAUSS, M. E., Psychology
STUEHR, J. E., Chemistry
SUN, J., Statistics
SZAREK, S. J., Mathematics
TAYLOR, C. C., Physics
TAYLOR, P., Physics
TURNER, M., Cognitive Science

URBACH, F. L., Chemistry
VACHASPATI, T., Physics
WERNER, E., Mathematics
WHITBECK, C., Philosophy
WHITE, J., Political Science
WILSON, R. G., Theatre Arts
WOODMANSEE, M. A., English
WOYCZYNSKI, W. A., Statistics
WU, T.-S., Mathematics
ZULL, J. E., Biology

Frances Payne Bolton School of Nursing (tel. (216) 368-4700; internet fpb.case.edu):

ANDERSON, G., Nursing
ANDREWS, C., Nursing
FITZPATRICK, J. J., Nursing
GARY, F. A., Nursing
GOOD, M., Nursing
LUDINGTON, S. M., Paediatric Nursing
MOORE, S., Nursing
ROBERTS, B. L., Gerontological Nursing
WYKLE, M. L., Gerontological Nursing

Mandel School of Applied Social Sciences (tel. (216) 368-2290; internet msass.case.edu):

BIEGEL, D. E., Social Work Practice, Psychiatry and Sociology
CHATTERJEE, P., Social Work
COULTON, C. J., Social Work and Urban Poverty
FLEISHER, M., Violence Prevention, Research and Education
GINGERICH, W. J., Social Work
GROZA, V., Social Work
HOKENSTAD, M. C., Jr, International Social Work
MAHONEY, G., Families and Communities
SINGER, M. I., Social Work, Youth Violence
WELLS, K., Social Work, Child Welfare
YOUNG, D. R., Non-profit Management

School of Dentistry (tel. (216) 368-3200; internet dental.case.edu):

BISSADA, N., Periodontics
GOLDBERG, J. S., Oral and Maxillofacial Surgery
OCCHIONERO, R. L., Dentistry
SAWYER, D. R., Oral Diagnosis and Radiology
WOTMAN, S., Community Dentistry

School of Law (11075 East Blvd, Cleveland, OH 44106; tel. (216) 368-3600; fax (216) 368-1042; e-mail lawadmissions@case.edu; internet law.case.edu):

AUSTIN, A. D., II
CHISOLM, L. B.
CHODOSH, H. E.
COFFEY, R. J.
DENT, G. W., Jr
DURCHSLAG, M. R.
ENTIN, J. L.
GABINET, L.
GERHART, P. M.
GIANNELLI, P. C.
HESSLER, K.
JENSEN, E. M.
KATZ, L. R.
KING, H. T., Jr
KORNGOLD, G.
KOSTRITSKY, J. P.
KU, R. S. R.
LAWRY, R. P.
LEATHERBERRY, W. C.
LIPTON, J. P.
MCKINNEY, L. W.
MCMUNIGAL, K. C.
MARGOLIS, K. R.
MEHLMAN, M. J.
MORRISS, A. P.
NANCE, D. A.
NARD, C. A.
NETH, S.
SCHARF, M. P.
SHANKER, M. G.
SHARPE, C. W.
SOUTHWORTH, A.
STRASSFELD, R. N.

School of Medicine (tel. (216) 368-2820; e-mail casemed@case.edu; internet casemed .case.edu):

AACH, R. D., Medicine
ABDUL-KARIM, F., Pathology
ADLER, D., Cardiology
AGARWAL, A., Surgery
AGICH, G. J., Medicine
AGLE, D., Psychiatry
ALTHOF, S., Urology
ALTOSE, M. D., Medicine
ANDERSON, J. M., Pathology
ANDERSON, V., Biochemistry and Chemistry
ARAFAH, B., Molecular Endocrinology
ARNOLD, J. E., Otolaryngology
ARON, D. C., Endocrinology and Hypertension
ARROLIGA, A., Medicine
ASKARI, A. D., Medicine
ATAYA, K., Reproductive Biology
BAHLER, R. C., Medicine
BALEY, J. E., Paediatrics
BANERJEE, A., Virology
BARNETT, G., Surgery
BERGER, M., Paediatrics
BERGER, N., Medicine, Biochemistry
BERMAN, B., Paediatrics
BINDER, L. S., Emergency Medicine
BINSTOCK, R. H., Bioethics, Ageing, Health and Society
BLUMER, J. L., Paediatrics and Pharmacology
BODNAR, D., Urology
BOHLMAN, H., Orthopaedics
BOOM, W. H., Infectious Disease
BOOTHMAN, D. A., Radiation Oncology
BORDEN, E., Molecular Medicine
BROUHARD, B. H., Paediatrics
BROZOVICH, F. V., Medicine and Physiology
BRUNENGRABER, H., Nutrition
BUCKLEY, P., Psychiatry
BUDD, G., Medicine
BUKOWSKI, R., Medicine
BURNEY, E., Ophthalmology
CALABRASE, J. R., Psychiatry
CAMPBELL, J., Family Medicine
CAREY, P., Biochemistry
CAREY, W. D., Medicine
CARLIN, C., Physiology and Biophysics
CARLSON, M. D., Cardiology
CARTER, S. G., Medicine
CASCORBI, H. F., Anaesthesiology
CATALANO, P. M., Reproductive Biology
CATHCART, M., Molecular Medicine
CAVANAUGH, P., Molecular Medicine
CEBUL, R. D., Medicine
CHAO, J., Family Medicine
CHISHOLM, G., Molecular Medicine
CHWALS, W. J., Surgery
CLARK, G. S., Medicine
COHEN, A. R., Neurosurgery
COHEN, M. L., Pathology
COLE-KELLY, K., Family Medicine
CONNORS, A., Medicine
COOPER, K. D., Dermatology
COOPERMAN, D. R., Orthopaedics
CRABB, J. W., Molecular Medicine
CROMER, B. A., Paediatrics
CULP, L. A., Molecular Biology and Microbiology
CUTTLER, L., Paediatrics and Pharmacology
CZINN, S. J., Paediatrics
DAHMS, B. B., Pathology
DAHMS, W., Paediatrics
DAROFF, R., Neurology
DAVIS, B. R., Dermatology
DAVIS, P. B., Paediatrics, Physiology and Biophysics, Molecular Biology and Microbiology
DAWSON, N. V., Medicine
DEARBORN, D., Paediatrics
DEBANNE, S., Epidemiology and Biostatistics

DEHASETH, P., Biochemistry
DELANEY, C., Surgery
DELGARDO, P. L., Psychiatry
DELL'OSSO, L., Neurology
DENERIS, E., Neuroscience
DENNIS, V. W., Medicine
DEVEREAUX, M., Neurology
DICORLETO, P. E., Physiology and Biophysics
DIMARCO, A. F., Physiology and Biophysics
DIERKER, L. J., Reproductive Biology
DISTELHORST, C. W., Haematology, Oncology
DOERSCHUK, C., Paediatrics
DRAKE, R., Surgery
DREICER, R., Medicine
DRISCOLL, D., Molecular Medicine
DROTAR, D., Paediatrics
DUBYAK, G. R., Physiology, Biophysics
DUERK, J. L., Radiology
ECKERT, R., Physiology
ELDER, J. S., Urology
ELLIS, S., Medicine
ELSTON, R. C., Epidemiology and Biostatistics
EMANCIPATOR, S. N., Pathology
EMERMAN, C. L., Emergency Medicine
ERNHART, C., Psychiatry
ERZURUM, S. C., Medicine
ESCLAMADO, R., Surgery
ESTAFANOUS, F., Anaesthesiology
EVANS, H., Radiation Oncology
FAIRCHILD, R. L., Surgery
FALCONE, T., Surgery
FANAROFF, A. A., Paediatrics
FARAH, M. G., Cardiology
FINDLING, R., Psychiatry
FINKE, J., Molecular Medicine
FIOCCHI, C., Gastroenterology Medicine
FOX, J. E. B., Physiology and Biophysics
FOX, P., Molecular Medicine
FRANCIS, G., Medicine
FRATIANNE, R. B., Surgery
FRIEDLAND, R., Neurology
GAMBETTI, P., Pathology
GANAPATHI, R., Medicine
GENUTH, S. M., Endocrinology and Hypertension
GERSON, S. L., Haematology and Oncology
GHANNOUM, M. A., Dermatology
GILL, I., Surgery
GOLDBERG, V. M., Orthopaedics
GOLDBLUM, J., Pathology
GOLDING, L., Molecular Medicine
GOLDSTONE, J., Surgery
GORDON, N. H., Bioethics
GORODESKI, G. I., Reproductive Biology
GRAHAM, A. V., Family Medicine
GRAHAM, L., Surgery
GRAHAM, R. C., Medicine
GREENFIELD, E., Orthopaedics
GREENSPAN, N. S., Pathology
GUDKOV, A. V., Biochemistry
HAAGA, J. R., Radiology
HACK, M., Paediatrics
HALL, G., Pathology
HAMILTON, T., Molecular Medicine
HAMPEL, N., Surgery
HANSON, R. W., Biochemistry
HAQQI, T. M., Medicine
HARDING, C. V., III, Pathology
HARDY, R. W., Neurosurgery
HART, W. R., Pathology
HARTE, P., Genetics
HASCALL, V. C., Biochemistry
HATZOGLOU, M., Nutrition
HAUGHEL-DE-MOUZON, S., Reproductive Biology
HAXHIU, M., Paediatrics
HAZEN, S., Molecular Medicine
HENDERSON, J. M., Surgery
HENSON, L., Anaesthesiology
HERRUP, K., Alzheimer Centre
HESTON, W., Molecular Medicine
HINES, J. D., Medicine
HODGSON, J., Medicine

HOFFMAN, G. S., Medicine
HOIT, B., Cardiology
HOLLYFIELD, J., Molecular Medicine
HOPFER, U., Physiology and Biophysics
HOPPEL, C. H., Pharmacology
HORWITZ, R. I., Medicine
HORWITZ, S. M., Psychiatry
HOSKINS, L. C., Gastroenterology Medicine
HOWE, P., Physiology and Biophysics
HRICIK, D. E., Nephrology Medicine
HUANG, S., Ophthalmology
HUGHES, G., Surgery
HUNDERT, E., Bioethics
ISMAIL-BEIGI, F., Endocrinology, Hypertension
JACOBBERGER, J. W., Cancer Research Center
JACOBS, M. R., Pathology
JACOBSEN, D., Molecular Medicine
JENTOFT, J. E., Biochemistry
JONES, S. W., Physiology
JUNIGRO, D., Molecular Medicine
KAISERMAN-ABRAMOF, I., Anatomy
KALHAN, S. C., Paediatrics
KAMINSKI, H. J., Neurology
KAPLAN, D. R., Pathology
KARN, J., Molecular Biology and Microbiology
KARNIK, S., Molecular Medicine
KASHANI, J. H., Psychiatry
KASS, L., Pathology
KATIRJI, M. B., Neurology
KATZ, D. M., Neurosciences
KAZURA, J. W., International Health
KEITH, M. W., Orthopaedics
KERCSMAR, C. M., Paediatrics
KERN, J. A., Pulmonary and Critical Care
KERN, T. S., Clinical and Molecular Endocrinology
KERR, D., Paediatrics
KHAN, M. A., Medicine
KIKANO, G. E., Family Medicine
KINSELLA, T. J., Radiation Oncology
KLEIN, A., Medicine
KLEIN, E., Paediatrics
KODISH, E., Surgery
KOWAL, J., Geriatric Medicine
KUMAR, M. L., Paediatrics
KUNZE, D. L., Neurosciences
KURSH, E., Surgery
KUSHNER, I., Medicine
LAMANNA, J. C., Anatomy
LAMM, M. E., Pathology
LANDAU, B. R., Endocrinology and Hypertension
LANDIS, D. M., Neurology and Neurosciences
LANDMESSER, L., Neurosciences
LANDRETH, G., Neurology and Neurosciences
LANZIERI, C. F., Radiology
LARNER, A., Molecular Medicine
LASEK, R. J., Bio-architectonics
LASS, J. H., Ophthalmology
LATSON, L. A., Paediatrics
LAUER, M. S., Medicine
LAVERTU, P., Otolaryngology
LAZARUS, H., Haematology and Oncology
LEDERMAN, M., Infectious Disease
LEHMANN, P. V., Pathology
LEIGH, R. J., Neurology
LEVIN, K., Medicine
LEVINE, A. D., Gastroenterology Medicine
LEVITAN, N., Haematology and Oncology
LEWIS, H., Surgery
LIEBERMAN, I., Surgery
LIEBMAN, J., Paediatrics
LIEDKE, C. M., Paediatrics
LINCOFF, A., Medicine
LIU, J., Reproductive Biology
LOUE, S., Epidemiology and Biostatistics
LOWE, J., Pathology
LÜDERS, H. O., Medicine
LUSE, D., Biochemistry
LUST, W. D., Neurological Surgery
MACIUNAS, R. J., Neurosurgery

McCULLOUGH, A. J., Medicine
McFADDEN, E. R., Jr, Pulmonary and Critical Care
McHENRY, C. R., Surgery
McLAIN, R., Surgery
MACKLIN, W. B., Neurosciences
MACKNIN, R. J., Paediatrics
MACLIS, R., Medicine
MAGUIRE, M. E., Pharmacology
MALANGOLI, M., Surgery
MALEMUD, C. J., Rheumatology Medicine
MANSOUR, E. G., Surgery
MARCHANT, K., Pathology
MARCUS, R. E., Orthopaedics
MARKOWITZ, S., Haematology, Oncology
MARSOLAIS, E. B., Orthopaedics
MARTIN, P. J., Physiology and Biophysics
MARTIN, R. J., Paediatrics
MASARYK, T. J., Radiology
MAVISSAKALIAN, M., Psychiatry
MAYBERG, M. R., Surgery
MEDOF, M. E., Pathology
MENON, M., Urology
MERCER, B. M., Reproductive Medicine
MERRICK, W. C., Biochemistry
MIEYAL, J. J., Pharmacology
MILLER, C., Surgery
MILLER, R., Neurosciences
MILLER, R. T., Medicine
MODIC, M., Radiology
MONNIER, V. M., Pathology
MONTAGUE, D., Surgery
MONTENEGRO, H. D., Pulmonary and Critical Care
MOORE, J. J., Paediatrics
MORGAN, P. G., Anaesthesiology
MOSKOWITZ, R. W., Rheumatology Medicine
MULLEN, K. D., Medicine
MURRAY, P., Anaesthesiology
MUSCHLER, G., Surgery
NADEAU, J. H., Genetics
NAGARAJ, R., Ophthalmology
NAGY, L., Nutrition
NAIR, R., Cardiology
NEARMAN, H. S., Anaesthesiology
NEDRUD, J. G., Pathology
NEUHAUSER, D., Epidemiology and Biostatistics
NEWMAN, C., Surgery
NILSEN, T. W., Molecular Biology
NILSON, J. H., Pharmacology
NOSEK, T., Physiology and Biophysics
NOVIC, A. C., Surgery
O'HARA, P., Surgery
OLEINICK, N., Radiation Oncology
OLNESS, K. N., Paediatrics
OURIEL, K., Surgery
PEACHEY, N., Molecular Medicine
PEARLMAN, E., Ophthalmology
PELLETT, P., Molecular Medicine
PERRY, G., Pathology
PETOT, G., Nutrition
PILAR, G., Neurosciences
PIÑA, I. L., Medicine
PLOW, E. F., Molecular Medicine
PONSKY, J. L., Surgery
POST, S. G., Bioethics
PRABHAKAR, N. R., Physiology and Biophysics
PRAYSON, R. A., Pathology
PRESTON, D. C., Neurology
PRETLOW, T. G., II, Pathology
PRETLOW, T. P., Pathology
QIN, J., Pharmacology
RANSOHOFF, R., Molecular Medicine
RATCHESON, R. A., Neurosurgery
REDLINE, R. W., Pathology
REDLINE, S., Paediatrics
REED, M. D., Paediatrics
REINHART, W., Ophthalmology
REMICK, S. C., Medicine
RESNICK, M. I., Urology
RESNICK, P., Psychiatry
RICANATI, E. S., Medicine
RICE, L. B., Infectious Disease
RICE, T., Surgery

RIMM, A. A., Epidemiology and Biostatistics
RONIS, R., Psychiatry
ROSE, P. G., Reproductive Biology
ROSS, J., Radiology
ROTE, N. S., Reproductive Biology
ROTH, B. L., Biochemistry
RUDICK, R. A., Medicine
RUFF, R., Neurology
SAGAR, S., Neurology
SAHGAL, V., Medicine
SALATA, R. A., Infectious Disease
SALZ, H., Genetics
SAMOLS, D., Biochemistry
SCARPA, A., Physiology and Biophysics
SCHER, M., Paediatric Neurology
SCHILLING, W. P., Physiology and Biophysics
SCHLUCHTER, M. D., Paediatrics
SCHUBERT, A., Anaesthesiology
SCHULAK, J. A., Surgery
SCHWARTZ, S., Genetics
SEDENSKY, M. M., Anaesthesiology
SEDOR, J. R., Medicine
SEDWICK, W. D., Haematology and Oncology
SEFTEL, A., Urology
SEGRAVES, R. T., Psychiatry
SELMAN, W. R., Neurosurgery
SEN, G. C., Physiology and Biophysics
SEN, S., Molecular Medicine
SHAFFER, J. W., Orthopaedics
SHU, S., Surgery
SHUCK, J., Anatomy, Surgery
SCHURIN, S., Paediatrics
SIEGEL, R. E., Pharmacology
SILVER, J., Neurosciences
SILVERMAN, R. H., Biochemistry
SILVERSTEIN, R., Molecular Medicine
SIMINOFF, L. A., Bioethics
SINGER, L. T., Paediatrics
SIVAK, M. V., Gastroenterology Medicine
SIVIT, C. J., Radiology
SMITH, C. E., Anaesthesiology
SMITH, C. K., Family Medicine
SMITH, J., Molecular Medicine
SMITH, M. A., Pathology
SMITH, M. C., Nephrology Medicine
SODEE, D. B., Radiology
SPIRNAK, J. P., Surgery
STANCIN, T., Paediatrics
STANGE, K. C., Family Medicine
STANLEY, W., Physiology and Biophysics
STANTON-HICKS, M., Anaesthesiology
STARK, G. R., Genetics
STAVNEZER, E., Biochemistry
STELLATO, T. A., Surgery
STERN, R., Paediatrics
STOLLER, J. K., Medicine
STORK, E. K., Paediatrics
STRAUSS, M., Otolaryngology
STROHL, K. P., Anatomy, Pulmonary and Critical Care
STROME, M., Surgery
SUPER, D. M., Paediatrics
SUREWICZ, W. K., Physiology and Biophysics
SY, M.-S., Pathology
TAKAOKA, Y., Surgery
TARR, R. W., Radiology
TARTAKOFF, A. M., Pathology
TAVILL, A. S., Medicine
TAYLOR, H. G., Paediatrics
TETZLAFF, W., Anaesthesiology
THOMPSON, G. H., Orthopaedics
TOMASHEFSKI, J. F., Pathology
TOOSSI, Z., Infectious Disease
TOPOL, E. J., Medicine
TRAPP, B., Neurosciences
TUBBS, R. R., Pathology
TUCKER, H. M., Otolaryngology
TUOHY, V., Molecular Medicine
VERTES, V., Medicine
WALDO, A. L., Cardiology
WALSH, R. A., Medicine
WALSH-SUKYS, M. C., Paediatrics

WEBER, P., Surgery
WEISS, M., Biochemistry
WEISS, M. F., Medicine
WESSELS, B. W., Radiation Oncology
WHITE, R. J., Surgery
WHITEHOUSE, F. W., Medicine
WHITEHOUSE, P. J., Bioethics, Neurology, Neuroscience, and Psychiatry
WILBER, J. H., Orthopaedics
WILKOFF, B., Medicine
WILLIAMS, B. R. G., Genetics
WISE, J., Molecular Biology and Microbiology
WISH, J. B., Nephrology Medicine
WISNIESKI, J., Medicine
WOLPAW, D., General Internal Medicine
WRIGHT, J., Hypertension Medicine
YANG, Y.-C., Pharmacology
YEN-LIEBERMAN, B., Pathology
YOMTOVIAN, R. A., Pathology
YOUNG, J., Medicine
YOUNGNER, S. J., Bioethics
ZAHKA, K. G., Paediatrics
ZIGMOND, R. E., Neurosciences
ZINS, J., Surgery
ZOLLINGER, R. M., Surgery
ZYZANSKI, S. J., Family Medicine

Weatherhead School of Management (tel. (216) 368-2030; internet weatherhead.case.edu):

ANVARI, M., Finance
ARAM, J. D., Management Policy
BALLOU, R. H., Operations
BOLAND, R., Information Systems
BOYATZIS, R. E., Organizational Behaviour
BRICKER, R., Accountancy
CARLSSON, B., Economics
CHATTERJEE, S., Management Policy
COLLOPY, F., Information Systems
COOPERRIDER, D., Organizational Behaviour
ERDILEK, A., Economics
FINE, S., Banking and Finance
FOGARTY, T., Accountancy
GERHART, P. F., Labour and Human Resource Policy
HELPER, S., Economics
HISRICH, R. D., Entrepreneurial Studies
KOLB, D. A., Organizational Behaviour
LYNN, J., Management Policy
LYYTINEN, K., Information Systems
NEILSEN, E. H., Organizational Behaviour
OSBORNE, R. L., Practice of Management
PEARSON, D., Practice of Accountancy
POZA, E. J., Practice of Family Business
PREVITS, G. J., Accountancy
REBITZER, J. B., Economics
RITCHKEN, P. H., Banking and Finance
ROOMKIN, M., Labour and Human Resource Policy
SALIPANTE, P. F., Jr, Labour and Human Resource Policy
SALKIN, H. M., Operations
SHANE, S. A., Economics
SILVERS, J. B., Banking and Finance
SINGH, J., Marketing
SOBEL, M. J., Operations
VANDENBOSCH, B., Information Systems
VONK, T., Labour and Human Resource Policy

CEDARVILLE UNIVERSITY

251 N Main St, Cedarville, OH 45314
Telephone: (937) 766-7700
Fax: (937) 766-7575
E-mail: admissions@cedarville.edu
Internet: www.cedarville.edu

Founded 1887 as Cedarville College, present name and status 2000
Private control
Academic year: August to May
Pres.: Dr WILLIAM E. BROWN
Chancellor: Dr PAUL H. DIXON

Provost: Dr JOHN S. GREDY
Academic Vice-Pres. and Chief Academic Officer: Dr THOMAS CORNMAN
Vice-Pres. for Advancement: WILLIAM L. BIGHAM
Vice-Pres. for Business and Chief Financial Officer: CHRISTOPHER SOHN
Vice-Pres. for Christian Ministries: ROBERT K. ROHM
Vice-Pres. for Enrolment Management: JANICE L. SUPPLEE
Vice-Pres. for Operations: RODNEY S. JOHNSON
Vice-Pres. for Student Life: Dr CARL A. RUBY
Registrar: FRAN CAMPBELL
Dean for Library Services: LYNN A. BROCK
Library of 285,000 vols, 9,000 e-journal subscriptions, 47,000 e-books
Number of teachers: 226 (215 full-time, 11 part-time)
Number of students: 3,299
Publications: *Inspire* (3 a year), *Journal of Biblical Integration in Business* (1 a year), *Torch* (2 a year)

DEANS

College of Arts and Sciences: Dr STEVEN WINTEREGG
College of Extended Learning: Dr ANDREW RUNYAN
College of Health Professions: Dr PAMELA DIEHL JOHNSON
College of Professions: Dr MARK MCCLAIN
Graduate Studies: Dr ANDY RUNYAN
School of Pharmacy: Prof. Dr MARC SWEENEY

CENTRAL STATE UNIVERSITY

1400 Brush Row Rd, Wilberforce, OH 45384
Telephone: (937) 376-6011
Fax: (937) 376-6141
E-mail: info@centralstate.edu
Internet: www.centralstate.edu
Founded 1887 as Combined Normal and Industrial Dept at Wilberforce Univ., present name and status 1965
State control
Pres.: JOHN W. GARLAND
Provost and Vice-Pres. for Academic Affairs: Dr JULIETTE B. BELL
Vice-Pres. for Admin.: COLETTE PIERCE BURNETTE
Vice-Pres. for Information Technology: Dr DONALD STEWARD
Vice-Pres. for Institutional Advancement: ANTHONY FAIRBANKS
Vice-Pres. for Student Affairs: Dr JERRYL BRIGGS
Registrar: LATONYA BRANHAM
Library Dir: JOHNNY W. JACKSON
Library of 223,745 vols, 846,190 units of microfiche and microfilm, 383 periodicals, 28,400 vols of periodicals, 21,000 e-books, 41,000 e-journals
Number of teachers: 80
Number of students: 2,171

DEANS

College of Business: Dr CHARLES H. SHOWELL
College of Education: Dr REGINALD NNAZOR
College of Humanities, Arts and Social Sciences: Dr LOVETTE CHINWAH-ADEGBOLA
College of Science and Engineering: Dr SUBRAMANIA I. SRITHARAN

CHANCELLOR UNIVERSITY

6000 Lombardo Center Dr., Suite 200, Seven Hills, OH 44131
Telephone: (216) 391-6937
Fax: (216) 426-9296
E-mail: cuadmissions@chancelloru.edu
Internet: www.chancelloru.edu

Founded 1848 as Folsom's Business College, present name and status 2008
Private control
Pres.: Dr ROBERT C. DAUGHERTY
Provost and Exec. Vice-Pres.: Dr STEVEN KERR
Sr Dir for Admissions and Devt: KEVAN FORD
Sr Dir for Student Services: BETHANY BATEMAN
Library Dir: RICHARD BRHEL
Number of teachers: 15
Number of students: 1,150

DEANS

College of Liberal Arts and Sciences: Dr THERESA HUEFTLE
College of Professional Studies: Dr DARIUS NAVRAN

CINCINNATI CHRISTIAN UNIVERSITY

POB 04320, 2700 Glenway Ave, Cincinnati, OH 45204
Telephone: (513) 244-8100
Fax: (513) 244-8140
E-mail: info@ccuniversity.edu
Internet: www.ccuniversity.edu
Founded 1924 as Cincinnati Bible Seminary by merger of McGarvey Bible College (f. 1923) with Cincinnati Bible Institute (f. 1923), present name and status 2004
Private control
Academic year: August to May
3 Colleges: Bible college, college of adult learning, Bible seminary
Pres.: Dr DAVID FAUST
Vice-Pres. for Advancement: BARBARA RENDEL
Academic Dean for College and Vice-Pres. for Academic Affairs: Dr JON A. WEATHERLY
Academic Dean for Seminary: JOHNNY G. PRESSLEY
Dean for Students: KRIS MERRILL
Dir for Admissions: ALEX EDDY
Registrar: DON THOMASON
Dir for Libraries: JAMES H. LLOYD
Library of 150,000 vols
Number of teachers: 89 (34 full-time, 55 adjunct)
Number of students: 995

CINCINNATI COLLEGE OF MORTUARY SCIENCE

645 W North Bend Rd, Cincinnati, OH 45224-1462
Telephone: (513) 761-2020
Fax: (513) 761-3333
E-mail: info@ccms.edu
Internet: www.ccms.edu
Founded 1882 as Cincinnati School of Embalming, present name 1966
Private control
Pres.: KAREN GILES
Academic Dean: Dr JULIE GILL
Exec. Dir for Enrolment Management and Registrar: PATRICIA SULLIVAN
Dir for Library and Information Technology: MICHAEL WELLS
Library of 2,000 vols
Number of teachers: 6
Number of students: 120

CLEVELAND INSTITUTE OF ART

11141 East Blvd, Cleveland, OH 44106-1710
Telephone: (216) 421-7000
Fax: (216) 421-7438
E-mail: admissions@cia.edu
Internet: www.cia.edu
Founded 1882, present name and status 1949
Private control

Academic year: August to May
Areas of study: craft and material culture, design, foundation art, integrated media, liberal arts, visual arts and technologies
Pres. and CEO: GRAFTON J. NUNES
Sr Vice-Pres. for Institutional Advancement: R. MICHAEL COLE
Vice-Pres. for Academic and Faculty Affairs: CHRIS WHITTEY
Vice-Pres. for Business Affairs: ALMUT ZVOSEC
Exec. Dir for Enrolment and Financial Aid: ROBERT BORDEN
Dean for Student Affairs: NANCY NEVILLE
Registrar: KAREN HUDY
Library Dir: CRISTINE C. ROM
Library of 45,000 vols, 145 periodical subscriptions, 125,000 art and architecture slides, 1,600 sound recordings, 600 video cassettes, DVDs and films
Number of teachers: 90 (50 full-time, 40 adjunct)
Number of students: 500

CLEVELAND INSTITUTE OF MUSIC

11021 East Blvd, Cleveland, OH 44106
Telephone: (216) 791-5000
Fax: (216) 791-3063
E-mail: info@cim.edu
Internet: www.cim.edu
Founded 1920
Private control
Academic year: August to May
Pres.: JOEL SMIRNOFF
Dean: ADRIAN DALY
Dir for Admissions: WILLIAM FAY
Dir for Devt: CHRIS DUNWORTH
Registrar: HALLIE MOORE
Library Dir: JEAN TOOMBS
Library of 52,000 vols, 23,000 audiovisual materials
Number of teachers: 100
Number of students: 400

CLEVELAND STATE UNIVERSITY

2121 Euclid Ave, Cleveland, OH 44115-2214
Telephone: (216) 687-2000
Fax: (216) 687-9366
E-mail: admissions@csuohio.edu
Internet: www.csuohio.edu
Founded 1964
State control
Pres.: Dr RONALD M. BERKMAN
Provost and Sr Vice-Pres. for Academic Affairs: GEOFFREY S. MEARNS
Vice-Pres. for Enrolment Services and Student Affairs: CARMEN A. BROWN
Vice-Pres. for Institutional Diversity: Dr NJERI NURU-HOLM
Vice-Pres. for Research and Graduate Studies: Dr GEORGE E. WALKER
Vice-Pres. for Univ. Advancement: BERINTHIA LEVINE
Dir for Libraries: GLENDA THORNTON
Library of 856,978 vols, 4,005 periodicals, 625,191 microforms
Number of teachers: 575 (full-time)
Number of students: 16,000
Publications: *Perspective*, *Whiskey Island*

DEANS

College of Education and Human Sciences: Dr SAJIT ZACHARIAH
College of Graduate Studies: Dr CRYSTAL M. WEYMAN
College of Liberal Arts and Social Sciences: Dr GREGORY M. SADLEK
College of Sciences and Health Professions: Dr MEREDITH BOND
Cleveland-Marshall College of Law: CRAIG M. BOISE

Fenn College of Engineering: Dr CHIN Y. KUO
Maxine Goodman Levin College of Urban Affairs: Dr EDWARD HILL
Monte Ahuja College of Business: Dr ROBERT F. SCHERER

COLLEGE OF MOUNT ST JOSEPH

5701 Delhi Rd, Cincinnati, OH 45233-1670
Telephone: (513) 244-4200
Fax: (513) 244-4601
E-mail: info@mail.msj.edu
Internet: www.msj.edu

Founded 1920
Private control

Pres.: Dr ANTHONY ARETZ
Vice-Pres. for Institutional Advancement: (vacant)
Chief Academic Officer and Dean for the Faculty: Dr ALAN DeCOURCY
Chief Information Officer: KEITH WEBER
Dir for Admissions: PEGGY MINNICH
Dean for Students: Dr DOUGLAS K. FRIZZELL
Registrar: PATSY J. KENNER
Dir for Library Services: PAUL JENKINS

Library of 96,000 vols
Number of teachers: 123 (full-time)
Number of students: 2,324

DEANS

Division of Arts and Humanities: Dr MARGE KLOOS
Division of Behavioural and Natural Sciences: Dr DIANA DAVIS
Division of Business: Dr CHARLES KRONCKE
Division of Education: Dr MARY WEST
Division of Health Sciences: Dr SUSAN JOHNSON

COLLEGE OF WOOSTER

1189 Beall Ave, Wooster, OH 44691
Telephone: (330) 263-2000
Fax: (330) 263-2427
E-mail: admissions@wooster.edu
Internet: www.wooster.edu

Founded 1866
Private control
Academic year: August to May
Liberal arts college

Pres.: GRANT H. CORNWELL
Provost: CAROLYN NEWTON
Vice-Pres. for Devt: LAURIE K. HOUCK
Vice-Pres. for Enrolment and College Relations: SCOTT FRIEDHOFF
Vice-Pres. for Finance and Business: LAURIE STICKELMAIER
Dean for Admissions: JENNIFER D. WINGE
Dean for Students: KURT C. HOLMES
Registrar: SUZANNE BATES
Dir for Libraries: MARK CHRISTEL

Library of 1,269,829 vols
Number of teachers: 171 (full-time)
Number of students: 1,982

COLUMBUS COLLEGE OF ART AND DESIGN

60 Cleveland Ave, Columbus, OH 43215
Telephone: (614) 224-9101
Fax: (614) 222-4040
Internet: www.ccad.edu

Founded 1879 as Columbus Art School, present name 1959
Private control
Academic year: August to August

Pres.: DENNISON W. GRIFFITH
Vice-Pres. for Academic Affairs: KEVIN J. CONLON
Vice-Pres. for Enrolment Management: JONATHAN W. LINDSAY
Vice-Pres. for Institutional Advancement: LAURIE BETH SWEENEY

Vice-Pres. for Student Affairs and Dean for Students: DWAYNE TODD
Dean for Faculty: CHAR NORMAN
Registrar: MICHELE KIBLER
Dir for Library: GAIL STORER

Library of 50,000 vols, 275 periodicals
Number of teachers: 193
Number of students: 1,300

Publication: *IMAGE Magazine* (2 a year)

DEANS

Fine Arts: Prof. JULIE TAGGART
Industrial and Interior Design: Prof. CARL GARANT
Liberal Arts: Prof. Dr EDWARD LATHY
Media Studies: Prof. RON SAKS
Visual Communications: Prof. RICHARD ASCHENBRAND

DEFIANCE COLLEGE

701 N Clinton St, Defiance, OH 43512
Telephone: (419) 784-4010
E-mail: admissions@defiance.edu
Internet: www.defiance.edu

Founded 1850 as Defiance Female Seminary, present name 1903
Private control

Divs of arts and humanities, behavioural and applied social sciences, business and allied health, education, science and mathematics

Pres.: MARK C. GORDON
Provost and Vice-Pres. for Academic Affairs: Dr BARBARA R. SCHIRMER
Vice-Pres. for Enrolment Management: MIKE SUZO
Vice-Pres. for Institutional Advancement: RICH PEJEAU
Vice-Pres. for Student Engagement and Dean for Students: Dr KENNETH WETSTEIN
Dir for Admissions: BRAD HARSHA
Registrar: MARIAH ORZOLEK
Dir for Library and Informational Resources: ANDREW WHITIS

Library of 90,000 vols
Number of teachers: 86
Number of students: 1,100

Publication: *The Magazine*.

DENISON UNIVERSITY

100 W College St, Granville, OH 43023-0603
Telephone: (740) 587-0810
Fax: (740) 587-6417
E-mail: admissions@denison.edu
Internet: www.denison.edu

Founded 1831
Private control
Academic year: September to May
Liberal arts

Pres.: DALE T. KNOBEL
Provost: BRADLEY W. BATEMAN
Vice-Pres. and Dir for Admissions: PERRY ROBINSON
Vice-Pres. for Student Devt: LAUREL KENNEDY
Vice-Pres. for Institutional Advancement: JULIA HOUPT
Dean for Students: LAURA NEFF
Registrar: YADIGAR COLLINS
Library Dir: MARY PROPHET

Library of 462,409 vols, 360,324 documents, 963 periodicals, 35,147 audiovisual material, 127,645 microforms, 762 linear ft archives
Number of teachers: 212 (full-time)
Number of students: 2,162

Publications: *Collage: A Magazine for Language & the Arts*, *Denison Journal of Biological Science* (1 a year), *Denison Journal of Geosciences* (1 a year), *Denison Journal of Religion* (1 a year), *Denison

Magazine (4 a year), *Ephemeris* (1 a year), *Episteme*, *Prologue* (1 a year).

FRANCISCAN UNIVERSITY OF STEUBENVILLE

1235 University Blvd, Steubenville, OH 43952
Telephone: (740) 283-3771
Fax: (740) 284-7225
E-mail: admissions@franciscan.edu
Internet: www.franciscan.edu

Founded 1946
Private control
Academic year: August to May

Pres.: Rev. TERENCE HENRY
Chancellor: Rev. MICHAEL SCANLAN
Exec. Vice-Pres.: Dr ROBERT FILBY
Vice-Pres. for Academic Affairs: THOMAS WILSON
Vice-Pres. for Advancement: MICHAEL HERNON
Vice-Pres. for Enrolment: JOEL RECZNIK
Vice-Pres. for Student Life: DAVID SCHMIESING
Dir for Admissions: MARGARET WEBER
Library Dir: WILLIAM JAKUB

Library of 232,156 vols, 250,968 microfiche, 5,400 e-journals
Number of teachers: 222 (115 full-time, 107 part-time)
Number of students: 2,548 (2,125 undergraduate, 423 graduate)

Publications: *Fides Quaerens Intellectum* (4 a year), *Franciscan Way Magazine*.

FRANKLIN UNIVERSITY

201 S Grant Ave, Columbus, OH 43215
Telephone: (614) 797-4700
Fax: (614) 356-6729
E-mail: info@franklin.edu
Internet: www.franklin.edu

Founded 1902 as YMCA School of Commerce, present name 1933
Private control

Campuses at Delaware, Dublin, Westerville (Ohio) and Indianapolis (Indiana); online degree programmes

Pres.: Dr DAVID R. DECKER
Provost and Sr Vice-Pres. for Academic Affairs: Dr CHRISTOPHER WASHINGTON
Sr Vice-Pres. for Admin.: JANE ROBINSON
Sr Vice-Pres. for Univ. Advancement and Strategic Relations: BONNIE SMITH QUIST
Exec. Dir for Enrolment Management: SCOTT BOOTH
Dean for Students: Dr WILLIAM MOLASSO
Dir for Library Services: JOHN CANTER
Number of students: 11,000

Publication: *CLOCKTOWER*

DEANS

College of Arts, Sciences and Technology: Dr KEITH GROFF
College of Business: Dr ROSS WIRTH
College of Health and Public Administration: ROBERT CURTIS

HEIDELBERG UNIVERSITY

310 E Market St, Tiffin, OH 44883-2462
Telephone: (419) 448-2000
Fax: (419) 448-2124
E-mail: adminfo@heidelberg.edu
Internet: www.heidelberg.edu

Founded 1850, present name and status 2009
Private control
Academic year: August to May

Pres.: Dr ROBERT H. HUNTINGTON
Provost and Vice-Pres. for Academic Affairs: Dr DAVID A. WEININGER

Vice-Pres. for Enrolment Management: LINDSAY SOOY
Vice-Pres. for Institutional Advancement and Univ. Relations: Dr JAMES A. TROHA
Dean for Students: DUSTIN BRENTLINGER
Registrar: CYNTHIA SUTER
Dir for Library Services: NANCY RUBENSTEIN
Library of 432,509 vols, 119,517 books, 8,556 audiovisual materials, 162,336 govt documents, 68,000 e-books
Number of teachers: 150 (63 full-time, 87 part-time)
Number of students: 1,200
Publication: *Morpheus*

DEANS

School of Business: Dr HASEEB AHMED
Undergraduate Faculty: Dr VICKI B. OHL

HIRAM COLLEGE

POB 67, Hiram, OH 44234
11715 Garfield Rd, Hiram, OH 44234
Telephone: (330) 569-3211
Fax: (330) 569-5944
E-mail: admission@hiram.edu
Internet: www.hiram.edu
Founded 1850 as Western Reserve Eclectic Institute, present name and status 1867
Private control
Academic year: August to May
Liberal arts college
Pres.: THOMAS V. CHEMA
Vice-Pres. and Dean for the College: (vacant)
Vice-Pres. and Dean for Students: ERIC R. RIEDEL
Dir for Admission: SHERMAN DEAN
Registrar: VIRGINIA TAYLOR
Library Dir: DAVID EVERETT
Library of 200,000 vols, 425 periodicals, 10,000 CDs, 2,500 video cassettes, 65,000 e-books, 50,000 periodicals
Number of teachers: 73 (full-time)
Number of students: 1,354 (1,334 undergraduate, 20 graduate)
Publication: *Hiram Poetry Review* (2 a year).

JOHN CARROLL UNIVERSITY

Telephone: (216) 397-1886
Fax: (216) 397-4256
Internet: www.jcu.edu
Founded 1886, present name 1923
Private control
Academic year: September to May
Pres.: Rev. ROBERT L. NIEHOFF
Provost and Academic Vice-Pres.: Dr JOHN T. DAY
Vice-Pres. for Enrolment: BRIAN G. WILLIAMS
Vice-Pres. for Finance and Admin. Services: RICHARD F. MAUSSER
Vice-Pres. for Student Affairs: Dr MARK D. MCCARTHY
Vice-Pres. for Univ. Advancement: DOREEN KNAPP RILEY
Registrar: KATHLEEN DI FRANCO
Dir for Library: Dr JEANNE SOMERS
Library of 778,287 vols, 850 periodical subscriptions, 701,253 microforms, 9,985 audiovisual materials, 11,159 e-journals, 76,346 e-books
Number of teachers: 374 (204 full-time, 170 part-time)
Number of students: 3,709 (3,001 undergraduate, 708 graduate)
Publication: *John Carroll magazine* (online (sites.jcu.edu/magazine))

DEANS

Boler School of Business: Dr KAREN SCHUELE

College of Arts and Sciences: Dr JEANNE COLLERAN

KENT STATE UNIVERSITY

Kent, OH 44242
Telephone: (330) 672-3000
Internet: www.kent.edu
Founded 1910
State control
Academic year: July to June
7 Regional campuses in Ashtabula, East Liverpool, Geauga, Salem, Stark, Trumbull, Tuscarawas (Ohio)
Pres.: Dr LESTER A. LEFTON
Provost and Sr Vice-Pres. for Academic Affairs: ROBERT G. FRANK
Vice-Pres. for Diversity, Equity and Inclusion: ALFREDA BROWN
Vice-Pres. for Enrolment Management and Student Affairs: GREG JARVIE
Vice-Pres. for Finance and Admin.: GREGG S. FLOYD
Vice-Pres. for Information Services: EDWARD G. MAHON
Vice-Pres. for Institutional Advancement: EUGENE J. FINN
Vice-Pres. for Research: W. GRANT MCGIMPSEY
Vice-Pres. for Univ. Relations: IRIS HARVEY
Registrar: GLENN DAVIS
Dean for Univ. Libraries: JAMES BRACKEN
Library: 2.3m. vols
Number of teachers: 2,521
Number of students: 42,185

DEANS

College of Architecture and Environmental Design: DOUGLAS STEIDL
College of Arts: JOHN CRAWFORD
College of Arts and Sciences: TIMOTHY MOERLAND
College of Business Administration: Dr KATHRYN WILSON
College of Communication and Information: STANLEY WEARDEN
College of Education, Health and Human Services: DAN MAHONY
College of Nursing: Dr LAURA COX DZUREC
College of Public Health: SONIA ALEMAGNO
College of Technology: JACK GRAHAM
Graduate Studies: MARY ANN STEPHENS
Honors College: DON WILLIAMS
Undergraduate Studies: (vacant)

KENYON COLLEGE

Gambier, OH 43022-9623
Telephone: (740) 427-5000
Fax: (740) 427-5770
E-mail: admissions@kenyon.edu
Internet: www.kenyon.edu
Founded 1824
Private control
Academic year: August to May
Depts of fine arts, humanities, natural sciences, social sciences
Pres.: S. GEORGIA NUGENT
Provost: NAYEF SAMHAT
Vice-Pres. for College Relations: SARAH H. KAHRL
Vice-Pres. for Finance: JOSEPH G. NELSON
Dir for Admissions: C. DARRYL UY
Dean for Admissions and Financial Aid: JENNIFER DELAHUNTY BRITZ
Dean for Students: HENRY P. TOUTAIN
Registrar: ELLEN K. HARBOURT
Vice-Pres. for Library and Information Services: RONALD K. GRIGGS
Library: 1m. vols, 1,000 periodical subscriptions, 330,000 e-books, 7,300 e-journals
Number of teachers: 200
Number of students: 1,600

Publication: *Kenyon College Alumni Bulletin* (online (bulletin.kenyon.edu)).

KETTERING COLLEGE OF MEDICAL ARTS

3737 Southern Blvd, Kettering, OH 45429
Telephone: (937) 395-8601
Fax: (937) 395-8338
E-mail: information@kc.edu
Internet: www.kc.edu
Founded 1967
Private control
Divs of allied health, arts and sciences, graduate studies, nursing
Pres.: Dr CHARLES SCRIVEN
Dean for Academic Affairs: Dr WILLIAM NELSON
Dean for Enrolment Management: VICTOR BROWN
Dir for Admissions: BECKY MCDONALD
Registrar: ROBIN VANDERBILT
Dir for Library: BEV COBB (acting)
Library of 25,000 vols, 250 journal subscriptions, 1,500 audiovisual items.

LAKE ERIE COLLEGE

391 W Washington St, Painesville, OH 44077
Telephone: (440) 296-1856
Fax: (440) 375-7005
E-mail: admissions@lec.edu
Internet: www.lec.edu
Founded 1856
Private control
Academic year: August to May
Pres.: MICHAEL T. VICTOR
Vice-Pres. for Academic Affairs and Chief Academic Officer: Dr JANA HOLWICK
Vice-Pres. for Admin. and Finance: RICK EPLAWY
Vice-Pres. for Enrolment Management and Student Affairs: ROBIN MCDERMOTT
Vice-Pres. for Institutional Advancement: SCOTT EVANS
Dean for Admissions and Financial Aid: CHRISTOPHER HARRIS
Registrar: BARBARA ARILSON
Library Dir: CHRISTOPHER BENNETT
Library of 100,000 vols
Number of teachers: 46 (full-time)
Number of students: 1,200

DEANS

School of Arts, Humanities and Social Science: Dr MIMI PIPINO
School of Business: Prof. ROBERT TREBAR
School of Equine Studies: Prof. ELISABETH GIEDT
School of Natural Science and Mathematics: Dr STEVEN REYNOLDS, JR
School of Professional and Continuing Education: JOHN MEEHL

LAURA AND ALVIN SIEGAL COLLEGE OF JUDAIC STUDIES

26500 Shaker Blvd, Cleveland, OH 44122
Telephone: (216) 464-4050
Fax: (216) 464-5827
E-mail: info@siegalcollege.edu
Internet: www.siegalcollege.edu
Founded 1947 as Cleveland Institute of Jewish Studies, present name 2002
Private control
Languages of instruction: English, Hebrew
Pres.: Dr SEYMOUR KOPELOWITZ
Provost: Dr BRIAN AMKRAUT
Library Dir: JEAN LETTOFSKY
Library of 40,000 vols, 160 periodicals
Number of teachers: 20
Number of students: 30

LOURDES UNIVERSITY

6832 Convent Blvd, Sylvania, OH 43560
Telephone: (419) 885-5291
Fax: (419) 824-3916
E-mail: admissionslcadmits@lourdes.edu
Internet: www.lourdes.edu

Founded 1958 as Lourdes Junior College, present name and status 2011
Private control

Pres.: Dr ROBERT HELMER
Provost: Dr JANET ROBINSON
Vice-Pres. for Finance and Admin.: MICHAEL KILLIAN
Vice-Pres. for Institutional Advancement: MARY ARQUETTE
Vice-Pres. for Student Services: ROSANNE GILL-JACOBSON
Dean for Enrolment: AMY L. MERGEN
Dir for Admissions: AMY MERGEN
Registrar: MICHELLE RABLE
Dir for Library: SANDRA RUTKOWSKI

Library of 60,000 vols, 200 periodicals
Number of students: 2,655

DEANS

College of Arts and Sciences: Dr GEOFFREY J. GRUBB
College of Business and Leadership: Dr DEAN C. LUDWIG
College of Education and Human Services: Dr MICHAEL J. SMITH
College of Nursing: Dr JUDY DIDION

MALONE UNIVERSITY

2600 Cleveland Ave, NW, Canton, OH 44709
Telephone: (330) 471-8100
Fax: (330) 471-8478
E-mail: admissions@malone.edu
Internet: www.malone.edu

Founded 1892, present name and status 2008
Private control

Pres.: Dr DAVID A. KING
Provost: Dr DONALD L. TUCKER
Vice-Pres. for Advancement: HOWARD E. TAYLOR
Vice-Pres. for Enrolment Management: Dr BROCK C. SCHROEDER
Vice-Pres. for Student Devt: Dr CHRISTOPHER T. ABRAMS
Dir for Admissions: DAVID L. KLEFFMAN
Registrar: GARY L. PHELPS
Dir for Library Services: STANFORD TERHUNE

Library of 969,436 vols
Number of teachers: 89 (full-time)
Number of students: 2,201 (f.t.e.)

Publications: *Malone Magazine*, *Sightlines* (online (www.sightlinesmag.org))

DEANS

College of Theology, Arts and Sciences: Dr D. NATHAN PHINNEY
School of Business and Leadership: MARJORIE F. CARLSON HURST
School of Education and Human Development: Dr RHODA C. SOMMERS
School of Nursing and Health Sciences: DEBRA LEE

MARIETTA COLLEGE

215 Fifth St, Marietta, OH 45750
Telephone: (740) 376-4643
Fax: (740) 376-4896
E-mail: admit@marietta.edu
Internet: www.marietta.edu

Founded 1797 as Muskingum Acad., present name and status 1835
Private control
Academic year: August to May

Areas of study: Asian and international studies, computer science, economics, environmental science, fine arts, international business, liberal arts and sciences, management and accounting, petroleum engineering, sports medicine

Pres.: Dr JEAN A. SCOTT
Provost and Dean for Faculty: Prof. GAMA PERRUCI
Vice-Pres. for Admin. and Finance: DAN BRYANT
Vice-Pres. for Advancement: LORI LEWIS
Vice-Pres. for Enrolment Management: DAVID RHODES
Vice-Pres. for Student Life and Dean for Students: Dr ROBERT PASTOOR
Dir for Admission: JASON TURLEY
Dir for Library: DOUGLAS ANDERSON

Library of 250,000 vols, 450 print, 4,000 online periodicals
Number of teachers: 103
Number of students: 1,400

MERCY COLLEGE OF OHIO

2221 Madison Ave, Toledo, OH 43604
Telephone: (419) 251-1313
Internet: www.mercycollege.edu

Founded 1918, present name 2011
Private control

Offers BSc in health care administration and nursing

Pres.: JOHN F. HAYWARD
Vice-Pres. for Academic Affairs and Dean for Faculty: Dr ANNE LOOCHTAN
Vice-Pres. for Admin. Services and Dean for Students: JAMES L. HARTER
Dir for Admissions: AIMEE BISHOP-STUART
Registrar: HEATHER HOPPE
Library Man.: DEBORAH L. JOHNSON

Library of 10,000 vols.

METHODIST THEOLOGICAL SCHOOL IN OHIO

3081 Columbus Pike, Delaware, OH 43015
Telephone: (740) 363-1146
Fax: (740) 362-3133
E-mail: admit@mtso.edu
Internet: www.mtso.edu

Founded 1958
Private control
Academic year: August to May

Pres.: JAY RUNDELL
Vice-Pres. for Admin. Services: JON JUMP
Academic Dean: RANDY LITCHFIELD
Dir for Admissions: APRIL CASPERSON
Dir for Student Life: LESLIE TAYLOR
Registrar: SUSAN LAMPHERE
Library Dir: PAUL BURNAM

Library of 130,000 vols
Number of teachers: 32 (17 full-time, 15 part-time)
Number of students: 224

Publication: *The Story*.

MIAMI UNIVERSITY

501 E High St, Oxford, OH 45056
Telephone: (513) 529-1809
Fax: (513) 529-3841
E-mail: info@muohio.edu
Internet: www.miami.muohio.edu

Founded 1809
State control
Academic year: August to May (2 semesters)

Pres.: Dr DAVID C. HODGE
Provost and Exec. Vice-Pres. for Academic Affairs: CONRADO M. GEMPESAW
Vice-Pres. for Information Technology: DEBRA ALLISON
Vice-Pres. for Student Affairs: BARBARA JONES
Vice-Pres. for Univ. Advancement: JAYNE E. WHITEHEAD
Dean for Students: Dr SUSAN MOSLEY-HOWARD
Registrar: DAVE SAUTER
Dean and Univ. Librarian: JUDITH SESSIONS

Library of 4,111,957 vols, 23,060 video cassettes, 572,506 e-books
Number of teachers: 849 (full-time)
Number of students: 23,239

DEANS

College of Arts and Science: Dr PHYLLIS CALLAHAN
Farmer School of Business: ROGER L. JENKINS
Graduate School: JIM ORIS
School of Education, Health and Society: CARINE M. FEYTEN
School of Engineering and Applied Science: Prof. MAREK DOLLÁR
School of Fine Arts: Dr JAMES LENTINI

MOUNT CARMEL COLLEGE OF NURSING

127 S Davis Ave, Columbus, OH 43222
Telephone: (614) 234-5800
Fax: (614) 234-2875
E-mail: admissions@mccn.edu
Internet: www.mccn.edu

Founded 1903 as Mount Carmel School of Nursing, present name and status 1990
Private control
Academic year: August to May (2 semesters)
Campus in Lancaster

Pres. and Dean: Dr ANN SCHIELE
Library Dir: STEVO ROKSANDIC
Number of students: 914

MOUNT VERNON NAZARENE UNIVERSITY

800 Martinsburg Rd, Mount Vernon, OH 43050
Telephone: (740) 392-6868
Fax: (740) 397-2769
Internet: www.mvnu.edu

Founded 1968
Private control

Pres.: Dr DANIEL J. MARTIN
Provost and Chief Academic Officer: Dr HENRY SPAULDING, II
Vice-Pres. for Enrolment Devt and Marketing: DOUG BANBURY
Vice-Pres. for Student Life: Dr LANETTE SESSINK
Dir for Admissions and Student Recruitment: JAMES W. SMITH
Registrar: R. MERRILL SEVERNS
Dir for Library: DAVID E. TIPTON

Number of teachers: 241 (full-time)
Number of students: 2,574

DEANS

Jetter School of Business: Dr ROBERT ROLLER
School of Arts and Humanities: Dr BARNEY COCHRAN
School of Education and Professional Studies: Dr SONJA SMITH
School of Natural and Social Sciences: Dr RICHARD L. SUTHERLAND
School of Nursing and Health Sciences: Dr TERESA L. WOOD
School of Theology and Philosophy: Dr C. JEANNE SERRÃO

MUSKINGUM UNIVERSITY

163 Stormont St, New Concord, OH 43762
Telephone: (740) 826-8211
Fax: (740) 826-8196
Internet: www.muskingum.edu

Founded 1837

Private control
Pres.: (vacant)
Vice-Pres. for Academic Affairs: PAUL F. REICHARDT
Vice-Pres. for Enrolment: JEFF ZELLERS
Vice-Pres. for Institutional Advancement: JOHN SHORROCK
Vice-Pres. for Student Affairs and Dean of Students: JANET HEETER-BASS
Registrar: DANIEL WILSON
Librarian: SHEILA ELLENBERGER
Library of 215,000 vols, 600 periodicals, 140,000 microforms
Number of teachers: 82
Number of students: 1,700

NORTHEAST OHIO MEDICAL UNIVERSITY

4209 State Route 44, Rootstown, OH 44272-0095

Telephone: (330) 325-6600
E-mail: admission@neomed.edu
Internet: www.neomed.edu
Founded 1973, present name 2011
State control
Academic year: July to June
Pres.: Dr JAY A. GERSHEN
Vice-Pres. for Admin. and Finance: JOHN WRAY
Vice-Pres. for External Affairs: KATHLEEN RUFF
Vice-Pres. for Research: Dr WALTER E. HORTON, JR
Chief Student Affairs Officer: Dr SANDRA M. EMERICK
General Counsel: MARIA SCHIMER
Registrar: MICHELLE C. COLLINS
Dir for Library: BETH A. LAYTON
Library of 100,588 vols
Number of teachers: 73
Number of students: 750
Publication: *Ignite*

DEANS

College of Graduate Studies: Dr WALTER E. HORTON, JR
College of Medicine: JEFFREY L. SUSMAN
College of Pharmacy: Dr RICHARD J. KASMER

NOTRE DAME COLLEGE

4545 College Rd, South Euclid, OH 44121-4293

Telephone: (216) 381-1680
Fax: (216) 373-5278
E-mail: admissions@ndc.edu
Internet: www.notredamecollege.edu
Founded 1922
Private control
Academic year: September to May
Divs of arts and humanities, business administration, education, nursing, science and mathematics
Pres.: Dr ANDREW P. ROTH
Provost: Dr MARY B. BRECKENRIDGE
Sr Vice-Pres. for Finance and Admin.: JOHN PHILLIPS
Vice-Pres. for Devt: DAVID ARMSTRONG
Dean for Admissions and Financial Aid: BETH FORD
Dean for Student Affairs: BRIAN J. EMERSON
Registrar: JAMEKA WINDHAM
Dir for Library: KAREN ZOLLER
Library of 877,773 vols
Number of teachers: 61 (full-time)
Number of students: 2,156

OBERLIN COLLEGE

101 N Professor St, Oberlin, OH 44074
Telephone: (440) 775-8121
Internet: www.oberlin.edu

Founded 1833 as Oberlin Collegiate Institute, present name 1850
Private control
Academic year: September to May
Pres.: MARVIN KRISLOV
Vice-Pres. for Devt and Alumni Affairs: WILLIAM BARLOW
Dean for Admissions and Financial Aid: DEBRA CHERMONTE
Dean for Students: ERIC ESTES
Dean for Studies: KATHRYN STUART
Registrar: ELIZABETH CLERKIN
Dir for Libraries: RAY ENGLISH
Library: 1.3m. vols
Number of teachers: 250
Number of students: 2,800

DEANS

College of Arts and Sciences: Prof. SEAN DECATUR
Conservatory of Music: Prof. DAVID STULL

OHIO CHRISTIAN UNIVERSITY

1476 Lancaster Pike, Circleville, OH 43113
Telephone: (740) 474-8669
Fax: (740) 477-7755
E-mail: enroll@ohiochristian.edu
Internet: www.ohiochristian.edu
Founded 1948 as Circleville Bible College
Private control
Academic year: September to May
Pres.: Dr MARK A. SMITH
Provost: Dr HANK KELLY
Exec. Vice-Pres.: HENRY F. KELLY
Vice-Pres. for Academic Affairs: Dr JOE C. BROWN
Vice-Pres. for Enrolment: MIKE EGENREIDER
Vice-Pres. for Student Devt and Athletics: RICK CHRISTMAN
Vice-Pres. for Univ. Advancement: MARK TAYLOR
Registrar: RODNEY SONES
Library Dir: BARBARA MEISTER
Library of 62,000 vols
Number of teachers: 25
Number of students: 2,400

OHIO COLLEGE OF PODIATRIC MEDICINE

6000 Rockside Woods Blvd, Independence, OH 44131
Telephone: (216) 231-3300
Fax: (216) 231-0453
Internet: www.ocpm.edu
Founded 1916 as Ohio College of Chiropody, present name 1974
Private control
Academic year: August to May
Depts of basic sciences, general medicine, podiatric biomechanics and orthopedics, podiatric medicine, podiatric surgery
Pres.: THOMAS V. MELILLO
Exec. Vice-Pres.: Dr DAVID R. NICOLANTI
Vice-Pres. and Dean of Academic Affairs: Dr VINCENT J. HETHERINGTON
Dean for Student Affairs and Admissions: LOIS LOTT
Registrar: DAVID PUTMAN
Dir for Library Services: DONNA PERZESKI
Library of 15,000 vols
Number of students: 375
Publication: *Footsteps*.

OHIO DOMINICAN UNIVERSITY

1216 Sunbury Rd, Columbus, OH 43219
Telephone: (614) 251-4500
Fax: (614) 252-0776
E-mail: admissions@ohiodominican.edu
Internet: www.ohiodominican.edu

Founded 1911 as College of St Mary of the Springs, present name and status 2002
Private control
Academic year: September to May (2 terms and a summer session)
Divs of arts and letters, business, education, mathematics, computer and natural sciences, social and behavioural sciences
Pres.: Dr PETER CIMBOLIC
Vice-Pres. for Academic Affairs and Dean for the Faculty: Dr ALISON MEARNS BENDERS
Vice-Pres. for Advancement: MURLEY MILLER
Vice-Pres. for Finance and Admin.: DAVID KOSANOVIĆ
Vice-Pres. for Student Devt: JAMES CARIDI
Dir for Admission: NICOLE EVANS
Registrar: SHIRLEY McBRAYER
Dir for Library Services: JIM LADEN
Library of 115,000 vols
Number of teachers: 130
Number of students: 3,097

Publication: *ODU Magazine* (2 a year).

OHIO NORTHERN UNIVERSITY

525 S Main St, Ada, OH 45810
Telephone: (419) 772-2000
Fax: (419) 772-1932
Internet: www.onu.edu
Founded 1871 as Northwestern Ohio Normal School, present name 1885
Private control
Academic year: September to May
Pres.: Dr DANIEL A. DiBIASIO
Vice-Pres. for Academic Affairs: Dr DAVID C. CRAGO
Vice-Pres. for Enrolment Management: LAWRENCE LESICK
Vice-Pres. for Financial Affairs: Dr ROGER YOUTH
Vice-Pres. and Dean for Student Affairs: ADRIANE THOMPSON-BRADSHAW
Vice-Pres. for Univ. Advancement: KENNETH BLOCK
Registrar: TAMELA BASH
Dir for Library: PAUL LOGSDON
Library of 500,000 vols
Number of teachers: 225
Number of students: 3,356

DEANS

College of Arts and Sciences: Dr CATHERINE ALBRECHT
College of Business: Dr JAMES W. FENTON, JR
College of Engineering: Dr ERIC T. BAUMGARTNER
College of Law: Dr DAVID C. CRAGO
College of Pharmacy: Dr JON E. SPRAGUE

OHIO STATE UNIVERSITY

Enarson Hall, 154 W 12th Ave, Columbus, OH 43210
Telephone: (614) 292-4373
Fax: (614) 292-1885
Internet: www.osu.edu
Founded 1870
State control
Campuses at Lima, Mansfield, Marion and Newark in Ohio
Pres.: Dr E. GORDON GEE
Provost and Exec. Vice-Pres.: Dr JOSEPH A. ALUTTO
Sr Vice-Pres. for Admin. and Planning: JAY KASEY
Sr Vice-Pres. for Devt: JEFF KAPLAN
Sr Vice-Pres. for Outreach and Engagement: JOYCE BEATTY
Sr Vice-Pres. for Univ. Communications: TOM KATZENMEYER
Sr Vice-Pres. and Gen. Counsel: CHRISTOPHER M. CULLEY
Vice-Pres. for Research: CAROLINE WHITACRE

Vice-Pres. for Student Life: Dr JAVAUNE ADAMS-GASTON
Chief Information Officer: KATHLEEN STARK-OFF
Registrar: BRAD A. MYERS
Dir for Univ. Libraries: CAROL DIEDRICHS
Library: see Libraries and Archives
Number of teachers: 5,292 (f.t.e.)
Number of students: 64,435

Publications: *American Periodicals: A Journal of History, Criticism and Bibliography* (2 a year, online (www.amperiodicals.org)), *EHE Inspire* (1 a year), *Journal of Higher Education* (6 a year, online (ohiostatepress.org/index.htm?journals/jhe/jhe-main.htm)), *Journal of Money, Credit and Banking* (6 a year, online (jmcb.osu.edu)), *Narrative* (3 a year), *Ohio State Alumni Magazine*, *Ohio State Engineer* (4 a year, online (osemagazine.org.ohio-state.edu)), *Ohio State Journal of Criminal Law* (2 a year, online (moritzlaw.osu.edu/osjcl)), *Ohio State Journal on Dispute Resolution* (4 a year, online (moritzlaw.osu.edu/jdr)), *Ohio State Law Journal* (6 a year, online (moritzlaw.osu.edu/lawjournal)), *The Leibniz Review* (Mansfield Campus, 1 a year), *Theory into Practice* (4 a year, online (ehe.osu.edu/publications/tip))

DEANS

College of Arts and Sciences: JOSEPH E. STEINMETZ (Exec. Dean)
College of Dentistry: PATRICK M. LLOYD
College of Education and Human Ecology: CHERYL L. ACHTERBERG
College of Engineering: DAVID B. WILLIAMS
College of Food, Agricultural and Environmental Sciences: BOBBY D. MOSER
College of Medicine: CHARLES J. CHARLES J. LOCKWOOD
College of Nursing: BERNADETTE MELNYK
College of Optometry: MELVIN D. SHIPP
College of Pharmacy: ROBERT W. BRUEGGEMEIER
College of Public Health: STANLEY A. LEMESHOW
College of Social Work: TOM GREGOIRE
College of Veterinary Medicine: LONNIE KING
Graduate School: PATRICK S. OSMER
Max M. Fisher College of Business: CHRISTINE A. POON (acting)
Moritz College of Law: ALAN C. MICHAELS

OHIO UNIVERSITY

Athens, OH 45701
Telephone: (740) 593-1000
Fax: (614) 593-4229
Internet: www.ohio.edu

Founded 1804
State control
Academic year: September to June

Regional campuses at Chillicothe, Ironton, Lancaster, St Clairsville, Zanesville

Pres.: Dr RODERICK J. McDAVIS
Provost and Exec. Vice-Pres.: Dr PAMELA J. BENOIT
Vice-Provost for Enrolment Management: CRAIG CORNELL
Vice-Pres. for Finance and Admin.: STEPHEN T. GOLDING
Vice-Pres. for Research and Creative Activity: Dr JOSEPH SHIELDS
Vice-Pres. for Student Affairs: Dr KENT J. SMITH, JR
Vice-Pres. for Univ. Advancement: J. BRYAN BENCHOFF
Registrar: DEBRA M. BENTON
Dean for Univ. Libraries: SCOTT SEAMAN
Library of 2,979,370 vols
Number of teachers: 1,903 (1,113 full-time, 790 part-time)
Number of students: 35,324

Publications: *New Ohio Review* (online (www.ohio.edu/nor)), *Ohio Research and Clinical Review*, *Perspective* (2 a year), *Quarter After Eight* (1 a year, online (www.quarteraftereight.org)), *Sphere*

DEANS

College of Arts and Sciences: Dr HOWARD DEWALD
College of Business: Dr HUGH SHERMAN
College of Fine Arts: CHARLES McWEENY
College of Health Sciences and Professions: Dr RANDY LEITE
Graduate College: Dr JOSEPH SHIELDS
Heritage College of Osteopathic Medicine: JOHN BROSE
Honors Tutorial College: Dr JEREMY WEBSTER
Patton College of Education and Human Services: Dr RENÉE MIDDLETON
Russ College of Engineering and Technology: Dr DENNIS IRWIN
Scripps College of Communications: Dr SCOTT TITSWORTH
University College: Dr DAVID DESCUTNER

OHIO WESLEYAN UNIVERSITY

61 S Sandusky St, Delaware, OH 43015
Telephone: (740) 368-2000
Fax: (740) 368-3374
E-mail: owupr@owu.edu
Internet: www.owu.edu

Founded 1842
Private control
Academic year: August to May

Depts of ancient, medieval, and renaissance studies, Black World studies, botany-microbiology, chemistry, E Asian studies, economics, education, English, environmental studies, fine arts, geology and geography, health professions advising, history, humanities-classics, international studies, journalism, Latin American studies, mathematics and computer science, modern foreign languages, music, neuroscience, philosophy, physical education, physics and astronomy, politics and government, psychology, religion, sociology-anthropology, theatre and dance, urban studies, women's and gender studies, zoology

Pres.: ROCK JONES
Provost: DAVID O. ROBBINS
Vice-Pres. for Finance and Admin.: ERIC ALGOE
Vice-Pres. for Student Affairs: CRAIG ULLOM
Vice-Pres. for Univ. Enrolment and Strategic Communication: REBECCA ECKSTEIN
Vice-Pres. for Univ. Relations: COLLEEN GARLAND
Registrar: SHELLY A. McMAHON
Dir for Libraries: CATHERINE CARDWELL
Library of 550,000 vols
Number of teachers: 137 (full-time)
Number of students: 1,850

Publications: *Civic Arts Review* (4 a year, online (car.owu.edu)), *Ohio Wesleyan Magazine* (online (magazine.owu.edu)), *Zumari: a Journal of Black World Studies* (2 a year).

OTTERBEIN UNIVERSITY

1 S Grove St, Westerville, OH 43081-2006
Telephone: (614) 890-3000
Fax: (614) 823-1200
E-mail: uotterb@otterbein.edu
Internet: www.otterbein.edu

Founded 1847
Private control
Academic year: September to August

Pres.: Dr KATHY KRENDL
Provost and Vice-Pres. for Academic Affairs: Dr VICTORIA McGILLIN

Vice-Pres. for Enrolment Management: JEFFERSON BLACKBURN-SMITH
Vice-Pres. for Institutional Advancement: HEIDI TRACY
Vice-Pres. for Student Affairs and Dean for Students: ROBERT M. GATTI
Registrar: DONALD W. FOSTER
Library Dir: LOIS SZUDY
Library of 200,000 vols
Number of teachers: 140
Number of students: 3,000

Publications: *Aegis: The Otterbein Humanities Journal* (1 a year), *Journal of Teacher Initiated Research* (1 a year), *Towers Magazine*

DEANS

Graduate School and Research: Dr BARBARA H. SCHAFFNER
School of Arts and Sciences: Prof. Dr PAUL EISENSTEIN
School of Professional Studies: Dr BARBARA H. SCHAFFNER

PONTIFICAL COLLEGE JOSEPHINUM

7625 N High St, Columbus, OH 43235
Telephone: (614) 885-5585
Fax: (614) 885-2307
Internet: www.pcj.edu

Founded 1888, present status 1892
Private control
College of liberal arts and school of theology

Rector and Pres.: Prof. Rev. JAMES A. WEHNER
Exec. Vice-Pres.: Prof. Dr CHRISTOPHER J. SCHRECK
Academic Dean: Dr MICHAEL D. ROSS
Registrar: BARBARA COUTS
Dir for Library: PETER G. VERACKA

Publication: *Josephinum Journal of Theology* (2 a year, online (www.pcj.edu/journal)).

SAINT MARY SEMINARY AND GRADUATE SCHOOL OF THEOLOGY

28700 Euclid Ave, Wickliffe, OH 44092-2585
Telephone: (440) 943-7600
Fax: (440) 943-7577
E-mail: mal@dioceseofcleveland.org
Internet: www.stmarysem.edu

Founded 1848 as a diocesan seminary, present name 1968
Private control
Academic year: August to May

Pres.-Rector: Rev. Dr THOMAS W. TIFFT
Vice-Pres., Vice-Rector, Academic Dean and Dean for Students: Rev. MARK A. LATCOVICH
Registrar: BRENDON ZAJAC
Librarian: ALAN K. ROME
Library of 60,000 vols, 340 periodicals, 1,000 audio and video cassettes
Number of teachers: 20
Number of students: 130

SHAWNEE STATE UNIVERSITY

940 Second St, Portsmouth, OH 45662-4344
Telephone: (740) 351-4778
Fax: (740) 351-3416
E-mail: info@shawnee.edu
Internet: www.shawnee.edu

Founded 1986
State control
Academic year: September to June

Pres.: Dr RITA RICE MORRIS
Provost and Vice-Pres. for Academic Affairs: Dr DAVID TODT
Vice-Pres. for Finance and Admin.: Dr ELINDA C. BOYLES

Vice-Pres. for Student Affairs: Dr MARY
OLING-SISAY
Dir for Admissions: BOB TRUSZ
Registrar: MARK MOORE
Library Dir: CONNIE SALYERS STONER
Library of 160,000 vols
Number of teachers: 300
Number of students: 4,200

DEANS

College of Arts and Sciences: Dr TIMOTHY E.
SCHEURER
College of Professional Studies: Dr JAMES R.
KADEL

TIFFIN UNIVERSITY

155 Miami St, Tiffin, OH 44883

Telephone: (419) 447-6443
Fax: (419) 443-5006
E-mail: info@tiffin.edu
Internet: www.tiffin.edu

Founded 1888
Private control
Academic year: August to May
12 Regional campuses

Pres.: Dr PAUL MARION
Vice-Pres. for Academic Affairs: Dr CHARLES
CHRISTENSEN
Vice-Pres. for Devt: Dr MICHAEL GRANDILLO
Vice-Pres. for Enrolment Management: RON
SCHUMACHER
Vice-Pres. for Finance and Admin.: JAMES
WHITE
Dean for Students: LISA KIRCHNER
Registrar: ALICE NICHOLS
Library Dir: FRANCES A. FLEET
Number of teachers: 133
Number of students: 4,900

Publications: Challenge Magazine (2 a year),
TU Review (online (www.tiffin.edu/ture-
view))

DEANS

Graduate Studies: Dr BONNIE TIELL
School of Arts and Sciences: Dr GENE CRUT-
SINGER
School of Business: Dr LILLIAN SCHUMACHER
School of Criminal Justice and Social Sci-
ences: ROBERT JAMES ORR, III

TRINITY LUTHERAN SEMINARY

2199 E Main St, Columbus, OH 43209-2334

Telephone: (614) 235-4136
Internet: www.tlsohio.edu

Founded 1830 as Evangelical Lutheran
Theological Seminary, present name 1978
Private control
Academic year: September to May

Pres.: MARK R. RAMSETH
Academic Dean: Dr BRAD A. BINAU
Dir for Admissions: SHARI L. AYERS
Registrar: CAROL M. DIXON
Dir for Library: RAY A. OLSON

Library of 140,000 vols, 6,000 audiovisual
items
Number of teachers: 20
Number of students: 250

Publications: Te Deum, Trinity Seminary
Review (2 a year).

UNION INSTITUTE & UNIVERSITY

440 E McMillan St, Cincinnati, OH 45206-
1925

Telephone: (513) 861-6400
Fax: (513) 861-4887
E-mail: admissions@myunion.edu
Internet: www.myunion.edu

Founded 1964
Private control

Offers doctoral degrees in interdisciplinary
studies, psychology and education; academic
centres in Cincinnati (Ohio), North Miami
Beach (Florida), Los Angeles (California),
Sacramento (California), Brattleboro (Vermont), Montpelier (Vermont)

Pres.: Dr ROGER H. SUBLETT
Provost: Dr RICHARD HANSEN
Vice-Pres. for Enrolment Management: JON
MAYS
Vice-Pres. for Devt and Univ. Relations:
KRISTINE HOWLAND
Registrar: LEW RITA MOORE
Library Dir: MATTHEW PAPPATHAN

Library of 50,000 vols, 2,000 periodicals,
60,000 online monographs
Number of teachers: 400
Number of students: 2,000

Publication: InsideUnion (4 a year, online
(magazine.myunion.edu)).

UNITED THEOLOGICAL SEMINARY

4501 Denlinger Rd, Trotwood, OH 45426

Telephone: (937) 529-2201
Fax: (937) 529-2292
E-mail: utscom@united.edu
Internet: www.united.edu

Founded 1954 by merger of Bonebrake Theological Seminary with Evangelical School
of Theology
Private control

Offers doctoral degrees in ministry and
missiology; campuses at Dayton and Buffalo
(New York)

Pres.: Dr WENDY J. DEICHMANN
Vice-Pres. for Academic Affairs and Aca-
demic Dean: Dr DAVID F. WATSON
Vice-Pres. for Enrolment: Dr HAROLD HUD-
SON
Registrar: MARTHA M. ANDERSON
Dir for Library and Information Services:
SARAH D. BROOKS BLAIR

Library of 150,000 vols
Number of teachers: 12
Number of students: 170 (full-time)

UNIVERSITY OF AKRON

302 Buchtel Common, Akron, OH 44325-
3101

Telephone: (330) 972-7111
Fax: (330) 972-8604
E-mail: international@uakron.edu
Internet: www.uakron.edu

Founded 1870 as Buchtel College, present
status 1967
State control
Academic year: August to May

Pres.: Dr LUIS M. PROENZA
Sr Vice-Pres. and Provost and Chief Operat-
ing Officer: Dr WILLIAM M. SHERMAN
Vice-Pres. and Chief of Staff: CANDACE CAMP-
BELL-JACKSON
Vice-Pres. and Gen. Counsel: TED A. MALLO
Vice-Pres. for Finance and Admin.: DAVID J.
CUMMINS
Vice-Pres. for Information Technology: JIM
SAGE
Vice-Pres. for Research: Dr GEORGE R. NEW-
KOME
Vice-Pres. for Student Engagement and Suc-
cess: Dr CHARLES J. FEY
Dean for Univ. Libraries: CHERYL KERN-
SIMIRENKO

Library: 2.9m. vols
Number of teachers: 2,555
Number of students: 29,000

Publications: Akron Magazine (3 a year,
online (www.uakron.edu/alumni-friends/
akron-magazine.dot)), International Journal of Strategic Cost Management (4 a
year), The Akron Intellectual Property

Journal (2 a year), The Akron Tax Journal
(1 a year)

DEANS

Buchtel College of Arts and Sciences: Prof.
CHAND K. MIDHA
College of Business Administration: Prof.
RAVI KROVI
College of Creative and Professional Arts: Dr
CHAND K. MIDHA
College of Education: MARK D. SHERMIS
College of Engineering: Prof. Dr GEORGE K.
HARITOS
College of Health Sciences and Human Ser-
vices: Dr ROBERTA DEPOMPEI
College of Nursing: Dr ROBERTA DEPOMPEI
College of Polymer Science and Polymer
Engineering: Prof. Dr STEPHEN Z. CHENG
Graduate School: Dr GEORGE R. NEWKOME
Honors College: Dr DALE H. MUGLER
School of Law: Prof. MARTIN H. BELSKY
Summit College: STANLEY B. SILVERMAN
University College: STANLEY B. SILVERMAN
Wayne College: NEIL SAPIENZA

UNIVERSITY OF CINCINNATI

2624 Clifton Ave, Cincinnati, OH 45221

Telephone: (513) 556-6000
Fax: (513) 556-2340
Internet: www.uc.edu

Founded 1819 as Cincinnati College, present
status 1977
State control
Academic year: September to June

Pres.: GREGORY H. WILLIAMS
Provost and Sr Vice-Pres. for Academic
Affairs: Prof. Dr SANTA J. ONO
Sr Vice-Pres. for Admin. and Finance:
ROBERT F. AMBACH
Exec. Vice-Pres.: KAREN K. FAABORG
Vice-Pres. for Devt and Alumni Relations:
STEVE WILSON
Vice-Pres. for Finance: JAMES D. PLUMMER
Vice-Pres. for Governmental Relations and
Univ. Communications: GREGORY J. VEHR
Vice-Pres. for Information Technology and
Chief Information Officer: MIKE LIEBERMAN
Vice-Pres. for Research: WILLIAM BALL
Vice-Pres. for Student Affairs and Services:
Dr MITCHEL D. LIVINGSTON
Registrar: Dr DOUGLAS K. BURGESS
Dean and Univ. Librarian: Dr VICTORIA
MONTAVON

Library: see Libraries and Archives
Number of teachers: 4,373 (2,272 full-time,
2,101 part-time)
Number of students: 42,421 (31,985 undergraduate, 9,376 postgraduate, 1,060 professional)

Publications: Freedom Center Journal (1 a
year), Journal of Crime and Justice (2 a
year), The Cincinnati Review (online
(www.cincinnatireview.com)), UC Magazine (3 a year, print and online (magazi-
ne.uc.edu))

DEANS

Blue Ash College: Dr CADY SHORT-THOMPSON
Carl H. Lindner College of Business: DAVID
M. SZYMANSKI
Clermont College: Dr GREGORY S. SOJKA
College-Conservatory of Music: PETER LANDG-
REN
College of Allied Health Sciences: Dr ELIZA-
BETH C. KING
College of Design, Architecture, Art and
Planning: ROBERT PROBST
College of Education, Criminal Justice and
Human Services: Dr LAWRENCE J. JOHNSON
College of Engineering and Applied Science:
Dr CARLO D. MONTEMAGNO
College of Law: LOUIS D. BILLIONIS
College of Medicine: THOMAS F. BOAT

College of Nursing: Dr GREER GLAZER
Graduate School: Dr ROBERT ZIEROLF
James L. Winkle College of Pharmacy: Dr WILLIAM K. FANT
Lindner College of Business: DAVID SZYMANSKI
McMicken College of Arts and Sciences: VALERIE GRAY HARDCASTLE

UNIVERSITY OF DAYTON

300 College Park, Dayton, OH 45469
Telephone: (937) 229-1000
E-mail: info@udayton.edu
Internet: www.udayton.edu
Founded 1850 as St. Mary's School for Boys, present name and status 1920
Private control
Academic year: August to May
Pres.: Dr DANIEL J. CURRAN
Provost: Dr JOSEPH E. SALIBA
Vice-Pres. for Finance and Admin. Services: THOMAS E. BURKHARDT
Vice-Pres. for Enrolment Management: SUNDAR KUMARASAMY
Vice-Pres. for Research: Dr MICKEY MCCABE
Vice-Pres. for Student Devt: WILLIAM FISCHER
Vice-Pres. for Univ. Advancement: DAVID HARPER
Registrar: THOMAS J. WESTENDORF
Dean for Libraries: KATHLEEN M. WEBB
Library: 1m. vols, 295,000 vols of printed legal materials and microfilms
Number of teachers: 864 (542 full-time, 322 part-time)
Number of students: 11,063
Publications: *Law Review* (3 a year), *Orpheus* (2 a year), *UD Magazine* (online (udquickly.udayton.edu/category/udmagazine))

DEANS

College of Arts and Sciences: Dr PAUL H. BENSON
Graduate, Professional and Continuing Education: Dr PAUL VANDERBURGH
School of Business Administration: Dr JOSEPH CASTELLANO
School of Education and Allied Professions: Dr KEVIN R. KELLY
School of Engineering: Dr TONY E. SALIBA
School of Law: PAUL E. MCGREAL

UNIVERSITY OF FINDLAY

1000 N Main St, Findlay, OH 45840
Telephone: (419) 422-8313
Fax: (419) 424-4822
Internet: www.findlay.edu
Founded 1882, present name 1989
Private control
Pres.: Dr KATHERINE ROWE FELL
Vice-Pres. for Academic Affairs: Dr DANIEL J. MAY
Vice-Pres. for Devt: DAVID P. FERGUSON
Vice-Pres. for Student Services: DAVID W. EMSWELLER
Vice-Pres. for Univ. Advancement: Dr JOHN W. MOSSER
Registrar: TONY G. GOEDDE
Dir for Library: MARGARET HIRSCHY
Library of 127,000 vols
Number of teachers: 340
Number of students: 3,700
Publication: *Findlay Magazine* (2 a year)

DEANS

College of Business: Dr PAUL SEARS
College of Education: Dr JULIE MCINTOSH
College of Health Professions: Dr ANDREA W. KOEPKE
College of Liberal Arts: Dr GARY JOHNSON
College of Pharmacy: Dr DONALD STANSLOSKI

College of Sciences: Prof. Dr TERRY D. SCHWANER

UNIVERSITY OF MOUNT UNION

1972 Clark Ave, Alliance, OH 44601
Telephone: (330) 821-5320
Fax: (330) 829-2811
E-mail: info@mountunion.edu
Internet: www.mountunion.edu
Founded 1846, present name and status 2010
Private control
Pres.: Dr RICHARD F. GIESE
Vice-Pres. for Academic Affairs and Dean for Univ.: Dr PATRICIA DRAVES
Vice-Pres. for Enrolment Services: AMY A. TOMKO
Vice-Pres. for Student Affairs and Dean for Students: JOHN FRAZIER
Vice-Pres. for Univ. Advancement: GREGORY KING
Dir for Admission: GRACE CHALKER
Registrar: KAREN MORIARTY
Library Dir: ROBERT R. GARLAND
Number of teachers: 90 (full-time)
Number of students: 2,257 (2,200 undergraduate, 57 graduate)

DEANS

Arts and Humanities: Dr ANDREW PRICE
Math and Sciences: Dr JONATHAN SCOTT
Professional Studies: Dr PATRICIA MATTHEWS
Social Sciences: Dr RICHARD DUTSON

UNIVERSITY OF NORTHWESTERN OHIO

1441 N Cable Rd, Lima, OH 45805
Telephone: (419) 998-3120
Fax: (419) 998-3139
E-mail: info@unoh.edu
Internet: www.unoh.edu
Founded 1920
Private control
Pres.: Dr JEFFREY A. JARVIS
Provost and Vice-Pres. for Academic Affairs: Dr CHERYL MUELLER
Vice-Pres. for Devt: STEVE FARMER
Vice-Pres. for Enrolment Management: RICK MORRISON
Vice-Pres. for Student Life: ROBERT FRICKE
Registrar: STACIA BURGOON
Dir for Library: GEORGENA NANSON

DEANS

College of Applied Technologies: THOMAS GROTHOUS
College of Business: DEAN HOBLER

UNIVERSITY OF RIO GRANDE

218 N College Ave, Rio Grande, OH 45674-3131
Telephone: (740) 245-5353
E-mail: info@rio.edu
Internet: www.rio.edu
Founded 1876
Private control
Academic year: August to May
Pres.: Dr BARBARA GELLMAN-DANLEY
Provost and Vice-Pres. for Academic Affairs: Dr KENNETH J. PORADA
Vice-Pres. for Admin. Services and Student Services: PAUL HARRISON
Dean for Enrolment Management: MARK F. ABELL
Dean for Student Services: AARON QUINN
Library Dir: J. DAVID MAUER
Library of 94,197 vols, 230 periodicals, 446,409 microforms, 2,412 audiovisual materials, 30,000 govt documents
Number of teachers: 85
Number of students: 2,400

DEANS

College of Liberal Arts and Sciences: Dr KENNETH PORADA
College of Professional Studies: Prof. DAVID LAWRENCE

UNIVERSITY OF TOLEDO

2801 W Bancroft, Toledo, OH 43606-3390
Telephone: (419) 530-4636
Fax: (419) 530-4504
Internet: www.utoledo.edu
Founded 1872 as Toledo Univ. of Arts and Trades, present status 1967
State control
Pres.: Dr LLOYD A. JACOBS
Chancellor: Dr JEFFREY P. GOLD
Provost and Exec. Vice-Pres. for Academic Affairs: Dr WILLIAM MCMILLEN
Vice-Pres. for Admin.: CHARLES LEHNERT
Vice-Pres. for Govt Relations: Dr WILLIAM MCMILLEN
Vice-Pres. for Institutional Advancement: C. VERNON SNYDER
Vice-Pres. for Research and Economic Devt: Dr FRANK J. CALZONETTI
Vice-Pres. for Student Affairs: KAYE PATTEN WALLACE
Registrar: SHERRI ARMSTRONG
Dean for Libraries: JOHN GABOURY
Library: 1m. vols
Number of teachers: 1,702
Number of students: 22,610
Publication: *UT Alumni Magazine*

DEANS

College of Adult and Lifelong Learning: Dr DENNIS LETTMAN
College of Business and Innovation: Dr THOMAS GUTTERIDGE
College of Engineering: Prof. Dr NAGI G. NAGANATHAN
College of Graduate Studies: Dr PATRICIA KOMUNIECKI
College of Languages, Literature and Social Sciences: Dr JAMIE BARLOWE
College of Law: Prof. DANIEL J. STEINBOCK
College of Medicine: JEFFREY P. GOLD
College of Natural Sciences and Mathematics: Dr KAREN BJORKMAN
College of Nursing: Prof. Dr TIMONTHY GASPAR
College of Pharmacy and Pharmaceutical Sciences: Prof. Dr JOHNNIE EARLY, II
College of Visual and Performing Arts: DEBRA A. DAVIS
Judith Herb College of Education, Health Science and Human Service: Dr BEVERLY J. SCHMOLL

URBANA UNIVERSITY

579 College Way, Urbana, OH 43078
Telephone: (937) 484-1400
E-mail: admissions@urbana.edu
Internet: www.urbana.edu
Founded 1850 as Urbana Seminary, present name and status 1985
Private control
Pres.: Dr STEPHEN JONES
Sr Vice-Pres. for Academic Affairs and Dean for the Faculty: Dr KIRK PETERSON
Vice-Pres. for Admin. Services: BARBARA STEWART
Vice-Pres. for Student and Enrolment Services and Dean for Students: Dr JAMES WEISGERBER
Vice-Pres. for Institutional Advancement: JAMES THORNTON
Dir for Admissions: MARY ANNE BARR
Registrar: KATHY YODER
Library Dir: BARBARA MACKE
Library of 71,000 vols, 800 periodicals

Number of teachers: 52 (full-time)
Number of students: 1,505 (1,332 under-graduate, 173 graduate)

DEANS

College of Arts and Sciences: Prof. Dr CHERYL FENNO
College of Business: Dr HERSCHEL PURDUE
College of Education and Sports Studies: LUCINDA LEUGERS
College of Nursing and Allied Health: Prof. Dr NANCY SWEENEY
College of Social and Behavioral Sciences: Prof. Dr ALICE E. SIDDLE
School of Adult and Continuing Education: WILLIAM D. BLIZZARD

URSULINE COLLEGE

2550 Lander Rd, Pepper Pike, Cleveland, OH 44124
Telephone: (440) 449-4200
Fax: (440) 646-8318
E-mail: info@ursuline.edu
Internet: www.ursuline.edu
Founded 1871
Private control
Academic year: August to May
Pres.: Dr DIANA STANO
Vice-Pres. for Academic Affairs: Dr JOANNE PODIS
Vice-Pres. for Institutional Advancement: KEVIN GLADSTONE
Vice-Pres. for Student Affairs: DEANNE HURLEY
Registrar: LEAH SULLIVAN
Library Dir: BETSEY BELKIN
Library of 120,000 vols
Number of teachers: 146
Number of students: 1,488

Publication: *Voices*

DEANS

Breen School of Nursing: Dr CHRISTINE WYND
Graduate and Professional Studies: DEBRA L. FLEMING
School of Arts and Sciences: BETH KAVRAN

WALSH UNIVERSITY

2020 E Maple St, NW, North Canton, OH 44720
Telephone: (330) 490-7090
Internet: www.walsh.edu
Founded 1960 as Walsh College
Private control
Campuses at North Canton, Akron, Medina (Ohio)
Pres.: RICHARD JUSSEAUME
Provost and Vice-Pres. for Academic Affairs: Dr LAURENCE F. BOVE
Vice-Pres. for Academic Projects: NANCY BLACKFORD
Vice-Pres. for Business and Finance: PHILIP DANIELS
Vice-Pres. for Enrolment Management: BRETT FRESHOUR
Vice-Pres. for Advancement and Univ. Relations: BRIDGETTE NEISEL
Dean for Students: AMY K. MALASKA
Registrar: EDNA MCCULLOH
Library Dir: DANIEL SUVAK
Library of 141,000 vols, 90,000 e-books, 3,000 audiovisual items
Number of teachers: 124 (full-time)
Number of students: 2,982

Publication: *Walsh Times* (3 a year)

DEANS

DeVille School of Business: Dr CAROLE C. MOUNT
School of Nursing: Dr LINDA LINC

WILBERFORCE UNIVERSITY

Telephone: (937) 376-2911
Fax: (937) 376-2627
E-mail: admission@wilberforce.edu
Internet: www.wilberforce.edu
Founded 1856
Private control
Academic year: August to May
Pres.: Dr PATRICIA LOFTON HARDAWAY
Vice-Pres. for Academic Affairs: Dr MURIEL WRIGHT-BRAILEY
Vice-Pres. for Admin. and Financial Affairs: TIJUANA HUDSON
Dir for Admissions: JUAN ALEXANDER
Dean for Students: PARRIS CARTER
Registrar: GAIL D. LASH
Dir for Library: Dr WILLETTE STINSON
Library of 62,000 vols, 500 journal and magazine subscriptions
Number of teachers: 75 (55 full-time, 20 part-time)
Number of students: 850

Publications: *The Wilberforcean*, *The Yard*

DEANS

Arts and Sciences: Dr EUGENIA SHITTU
Engineering and Computing: Dr EDWARD ASIKELE

WILMINGTON COLLEGE

1870 Quaker Way, Wilmington, OH 45177
Telephone: (937) 382-6661
Fax: (937) 382-7077
E-mail: admission@wilmington.edu
Internet: www.wilmington.edu
Founded 1870
Private control
Academic year: August to May
Programmes in accounting, agriculture, art, athletic training, biology, business administration, chemistry and physics, communication arts, criminal justice, education, English, environmental science, equine studies, history, mathematics, music, psychology, religion and philosophy, social and political studies, social work, Spanish, sports management and health/PE, theatre; campus at Blue Ash and on-site programmes at Cincinnati State Technical and Community College
Pres.: JIM REYNOLDS
Vice-Pres. for Academic Affairs and Dean for Faculty: Dr ERIKA GOODWIN
Vice-Pres. for College Advancement: ROBERT C. HARROD
Vice-Pres. for Enrolment Management: MARK DENNISTON
Vice-Pres. for External Programmes: IRIS KELSON
Vice-Pres. for Student Affairs and Dean for Students: SIGRID B. SOLOMON
Registrar: KAREN M. GARMAN
Dir for Library: JEAN MULHERN
Library of 110,000 vols
Number of teachers: 65 (full-time)
Number of students: 1,508

WINEBRENNER THEOLOGICAL SEMINARY

950 N Main St, Findlay, OH 45840
Telephone: (419) 434-4200
Fax: (419) 434-4267
E-mail: admissions@winebrenner.edu
Internet: www.winebrenner.edu
Founded 1942, present name and status 1961
Private control
Academic year: August to May
Pres.: Dr DAVID E. DRAPER
Vice-Pres. for Academic Advancement: Prof. JOEL W. COCKLIN

Vice-Pres. for Institutional Advancement: JIM SMARKEL
Registrar: SHARI BRANDEBERRY
Dir for Library Services: MARGARET HIRSCHY
Library of 38,000 vols, 145 periodicals
Number of teachers: 17
Number of students: 117

WITTENBERG UNIVERSITY

POB 720, 200 W Ward St, Springfield, OH 45501-0720
Telephone: (937) 327-6231
Fax: (937) 327-6340
E-mail: admission@wittenberg.edu
Internet: www.wittenberg.edu
Founded 1845
Private control
Academic year: August to May
Programmes in Africana studies, American studies, art, biochemistry and molecular biology, biology, chemistry, communication, community education, computer science, dance, East Asian studies, economics, education, engineering, English, environmental studies, forestry, geography, geology, global studies, health/fitness/sport, history, languages, management, marine biology, mathematics, music, nursing, occupational therapy, philosophy, physics, political science, pre-law, pre-medicine, psychology, religion, Russian area studies, sociology, theatre and dance, urban studies, women's studies
Pres.: Dr MARK H. ERICKSON
Provost: Prof. CHRISTOPHER M. DUNCAN
Vice-Pres. for Enrolment Management and Dean for Students: SARAH M. KELLY
Vice-Pres. for Univ. Advancement: JIM GEIGER
Dir for Admissions: KAREN HUNT
Registrar: JACK CAMPBELL
Dir for Library: DOUGLAS LEHMAN
Library of 367,000 vols, 1,500 periodicals
Number of teachers: 180 (full-time)
Number of students: 1,900

Publications: *East Asian Studies Journal* (1 a year), *History Journal* (1 a year), *Journal of Political Science* (1 a year), *Pholeos* (2 a year), *Spectrum* (1 a year), *Wittenberg Review of Literature and Art*.

WRIGHT STATE UNIVERSITY

3640 Colonel Glenn Highway, Dayton, OH 45435
Telephone: (937) 775-3333
Fax: (937) 775-3301
E-mail: registrar@wright.edu
Internet: www.wright.edu
Founded 1967
State control
Campus at Celina (Ohio)
Pres.: Dr DAVID R. HOPKINS
Provost: Dr STEVEN R. ANGLE
Vice-Pres. for Advancement: REBECCA COLE
Vice-Pres. for Enrolment Management: Dr JACQUELINE MCMILLAN
Vice-Pres. for Research and Graduate Studies: Dr ROBERT E. W. FYFFE
Vice-Pres. for Student Affairs: Dr DAN ABRAHAMOWICZ
Registrar: MARIAN BRAINERD
Dean for Libraries: Dr STEPHEN FOSTER
Library of 696,000 vols
Number of teachers: 860 (full-time)
Number of students: 19,721

Publications: *The Grand Lake Review* (online (www.wright.edu/~martin.kich/glr/glrIndex.htm)), *Wright State University Magazine* (2 a year)

DEANS

Boonshoft School of Medicine: HOWARD M. PART
College of Education and Human Services: Dr CHARLOTTE HARRIS
College of Engineering and Computer Science: Dr S. NARAYANAN
College of Liberal Arts: Dr CHARLES S. TAYLOR
College of Nursing and Health: Dr ROSALIE O'DELL MAINOUS
College of Science and Mathematics: Dr YI LI
Graduate School: Dr ANDREW T. HSU
Raj Soin College of Business: Dr BERKWOOD M. FARMER
School of Professional Psychology: Dr LARRY C. JAMES

XAVIER UNIVERSITY

3800 Victory Parkway, Cincinnati, OH 45207
Telephone: (513) 745-3000
Fax: (513) 745-4223
Internet: www.xavier.edu
Founded 1831
Private control
Academic year: August to May
Pres.: Rev. MICHAEL J. GRAHAM
Provost and Chief Academic Officer: Dr SCOTT A. CHADWICK
Vice-Pres. for Admin.: Dr JOHN F. KUCIA
Vice-Pres. for Financial Admin.: MARIBETH AMYOT
Vice-Pres. for Information Resources and Chief Information Officer: DAVID DODD
Vice-Pres. for Student Enrolment: TERRY RICHARDS
Vice-Pres. for Univ. Relations: GARY R. MASSA
Registrar: MARY ALYCE ORAHOOD
Dir for Library and Information Management: ANNETTE MARKSBERRY
Library of 374,000 vols
Number of teachers: 341
Number of students: 6,945
Publication: *Xavier Magazine* (online (www.xavier.edu/magazine))

DEANS

College of Arts and Sciences: Dr JANICE B. WALKER
College of Social Science, Health and Education: Dr MARK MEYERS
Williams College of Business: Dr R. STAFFORD JOHNSON

YOUNGSTOWN STATE UNIVERSITY

1 University Plaza, Youngstown, OH 44555
Telephone: (330) 941-3000
Fax: (330) 742-1998
Internet: web.ysu.edu
Founded 1908
State control
Academic year: September to August (4 terms)
Pres.: Dr CYNTHIA E. ANDERSON
Provost and Vice-Pres. for Academic Affairs: Dr IKRAM KHAWAJA
Vice-Pres. for Finance and Admin.: EUGENE P. GRILLI
Vice-Pres. for Student Affairs: JACK P. FAHEY
Vice-Pres. for Univ. Advancement: (vacant)
Registrar: JEANNE HERMAN
Exec. Dir for Library: PAUL J. KOBULNICKY
Library of 700,000 vols, 300,000 govt documents, 800,000 microforms
Number of teachers: 457 (full-time)
Number of students: 15,194
Publication: *YSU Magazine*

DEANS

Beeghly College of Education: Dr MARY LOU DIPILLO
Bitonte College of Health and Human Services: Dr JOSEPH L. MOSCA
College of Fine and Performing Arts: Dr BRYAN DEPOY
College of Liberal Arts and Social Sciences: Dr SHEARLE FURNISH
College of Science, Technology, Engineering and Mathematics: Dr MARTIN ABRAHAM
School of Graduate Studies and Research: Dr PETER J. KASVINSKY
Williamson College of Business Administration: Dr BETTY JO LICATA

OKLAHOMA

BACONE COLLEGE

2299 Old Bacone Rd, Muskogee, OK 74403
Telephone: (918) 683-4581
Fax: (918) 781-7416
E-mail: admissionsoffice@bacone.edu
Internet: www.bacone.edu
Founded 1880, present name 1910
Private control
Divs of adult education, arts and sciences, business, education, general studies, health sciences
Pres.: Rev. Dr ROBERT J. DUNCAN, JR
Exec. Vice-Pres. and Dean for Faculty: ROBERT BROWN
Asst Vice-Pres. for Institutional Advancement: EUGENE G. BLANKENSHIP
Asst Vice-Pres. for Student Life: SHELLI HOPKINS
Dir for Admissions: MIKE JACKSON
Dir for Enrolment Management: KATHYE WATSON
Registrar: VIRGINIA THOMPSON.

CAMERON UNIVERSITY

2800 W Gore Blvd, Lawton, OK 73505-6377
Telephone: (580) 581-2200
Fax: (580) 581-2421
E-mail: admissions@cameron.edu
Internet: www.cameron.edu
Founded 1909
State control
Academic year: June to August
Pres.: CINDY ROSS
Provost: Dr JOHN M. MCARTHUR
Vice-Pres. for Student Services: JENNIFER HOLLAND
Vice-Pres. for Univ. Advancement: ALBERT JOHNSON, JR
Assoc. Vice-Pres. for Enrolment Management: JAMIE GLOVER
Dir for Library: SHERRY YOUNG
Number of teachers: 73
Number of students: 6,000
Publications: *The Oklahoma Review* (2 a year, online (www.cameron.edu/okreview)), *The Southwest Business & Economics Journal*

DEANS

School of Business: Dr ORIS L. ODOM, II
School of Education and Behavioural Sciences: Prof. RONNA VANDERSLICE
School of Liberal Arts: VON UNDERWOOD
School of Science and Technology: Dr REZA KAMALI

EAST CENTRAL UNIVERSITY

1100 E 14th St, Ada, OK 74820
Telephone: (580) 332-8000
Fax: (580) 559-5432
E-mail: parmstro@ecok.edu

Internet: www.ecok.edu
Founded 1909, present name 1985
State control
Pres.: Dr JOHN R. HARGRAVE
Provost and Vice-Pres. for Academic Affairs: Dr DUANE C. ANDERSON
Vice-Pres. for Admin. and Finance: STEVE TURNER
Vice-Pres. for Student Devt: JERRY FORBES
Dir for Enrolment Management: BONITA BLACKBURN
Dean for Student Affairs: BRONSON WARREN
Registrar: PAMLA ARMSTRONG
Dir for Library: ADRIANNA LANCASTER
Library of 275,000 vols
Number of teachers: 267 (168 full-time, 99 part-time)
Number of students: 5,727

DEANS

College of Education and Psychology: BRENDA WALLING
College of Health and Sciences: Dr BRUCE WEEMS
College of Liberal Arts and Social Sciences: Prof. Dr MARK HOLLINGSWORTH (acting)
School of Business: WENDELL GODWIN
School of Graduate Studies: Dr RICK WETHERILL

LANGSTON UNIVERSITY

POB 1500, Langston, OK 73050
Telephone: (405) 466-3428
Fax: (405) 466-3391
E-mail: admissions@lunet.edu
Internet: www.lunet.edu
Founded 1897
State control
Academic year: August to May
Campuses at Tulsa and Oklahoma City in Oklahoma
Pres.: Dr HENRY PONDER
Vice-Pres. for Academic Affairs: Dr CLYDE MONTGOMERY, JR
Vice-Pres. for Fiscal and Admin. Affairs: ANGELA R. WATSON
Vice-Pres. for Institutional Advancement and Devt: MISTY WAKEFIELD
Vice-Pres. for Student Affairs and Enrolment Management: Dr ANGELIA YOUNG JONES
Registrar: KATHY SIMMONS
Dir for Univ. Libraries: BETTYE BLACK (acting)
Number of teachers: 143
Number of students: 3,482
Publication: *Greatness Magazine*

DEANS

Physical Therapy: Dr MILAGROS JORGE
School of Agriculture and Applied Sciences: Dr MARVIN BURNS
School of Arts and Sciences: Dr CLARENCE A. HEDGE (acting)
School of Business: Dr SOLOMON S. SMITH
School of Education and Behavioral Sciences: Dr JOE HORNBEAK
School of Nursing and Health Professions: Dr CAROLYN T. KORNEGAY

MID-AMERICA CHRISTIAN UNIVERSITY

3500 SW 119th St, Oklahoma City, OK 73170
Telephone: (405) 691-3800
E-mail: info@macu.edu
Internet: www.macu.edu
Founded 1953 as South Texas Bible Institute, present name 2003
Private control
Academic year: August to May

Schools of business, behavioural science, general education, mathematics and science, ministry, music, teacher education
Pres. and CEO: Dr JOHN D. FOZARD
Vice-Pres. for Academic Affairs: Dr KATHALEEN REID-MARTINEZ
Vice-Pres. for Enrolment Management: MAURICE SHOE
Vice-Pres. for Strategic Initiatives: Dr ERIC ANTHONY JOSEPH
Chief Admin. Officer: SEVIER OWEN
Dir for Admissions: DUSTIN ROWTON
Dir for Student Services: DIANE CLEARY
Dean for College of Adult and Graduate Studies: Dr SHIRLEY RODDY
Univ. Registrar: BOBBIE SPURGEON-HARRIS
Library Dir: MICHAEL FOOTE
Library Dir: ELISSA PATADAL
Number of teachers: 59
Number of students: 1,447

NORTHEASTERN STATE UNIVERSITY

600 N Grand Ave, Tahlequah, OK 74464-2399
Telephone: (918) 456-5511
Fax: (918) 458-2015
E-mail: nsuinfo@nsuok.edu
Internet: www.nsuok.edu
Founded 1846 as Cherokee Nat. Female Seminary, present name 1985
State control
Academic year: August to July
Campuses at Broken Arrow and Muskogee in Oklahoma
Pres.: Dr DON BETZ
Provost and Vice-Pres. for Academic Affairs: Dr MARTIN TADLOCK
Vice-Pres. for Admin. and Finance: DAVID KOEHN
Vice-Pres. for Operations: TIM FOUTCH
Vice-Pres. for Teaching and Learning: Dr CHARLES ZIEHR
Vice-Pres. for Univ. Relations: MARK KINDERS
Exec. Dir for Enrolment Management: JERRETT PHILLIPS
Dean for Graduate Studies and Research: Dr THOMAS JACKSON
Dean for Broken Arrow Campus: Dr CHRISTEE JENLINK
Dean for Muskogee Campus: Dr TIM McELROY
Registrar: JULIE SAWYER
Exec. Dir for Libraries: PAULA SETTOON
Library of 424,278 vols, 5,749 current serial titles, 758,474 microforms, 71,985 audiovisual materials, 43,030 e-books
Number of teachers: 504 (348 full-time, 156 part-time)
Number of students: 9,261

DEANS

College of Business and Technology: Dr ROGER COLLIER
College of Education: Dr KAY GRANT
College of Extended Learning: Dr CHRISTEE JENLINK
College of Liberal Arts: Dr PAUL WESTBROOK
College of Optometry: Dr DOUGLAS K. PENISTEN
College of Science and Health Professions: Dr MARTIN VENNEMAN
Graduate College: Dr THOMAS JACKSON

NORTHWESTERN OKLAHOMA STATE UNIVERSITY

709 Oklahoma Blvd, Alva, OK 73717-2799
Telephone: (580) 327-1700
Fax: (580) 327-8413
E-mail: recruit@nwosu.edu
Internet: www.nwosu.edu
Founded 1897, present name 1974
State control

Academic year: August to May
Campuses at Enid and Woodward in Oklahoma
Pres.: Dr JANET CUNNINGHAM
Exec. Vice-Pres.: Dr STEVE LOHMANN
Vice-Pres. for Admin.: DAVID PECHA
Vice-Pres. for Student Affairs and Enrolment Management: BRAD FRANZ
Dean for Enid Campus: Dr CHERYL EVANS
Dean for Woodward Campus: Dr DEENA FISHER
Registrar: SHERI LAHR
Dir for Libraries: SUSAN K. JEFFRIES
Library of 500,000 vols (incl. microforms)
Number of teachers: 168
Number of students: 2,233

DEANS

School of Arts and Sciences: Dr MIKE KNEDLER
School of Professional Studies: Dr JAMES BROWN

OKLAHOMA BAPTIST UNIVERSITY

500 W University, Shawnee, OK 74804
Telephone: (405) 275-2850
Fax: (405) 878-2069
E-mail: info@okbu.edu
Internet: www.okbu.edu
Founded 1910
Private control
Academic year: August to May
Pres.: Dr DAVID W. WHITLOCK
Provost and Exec. Vice-Pres. for Campus Life: Dr R. STANTON NORMAN
Sr Vice-Pres. for Academic Services: Dr DEBBIE BLUE
Exec. Vice-Pres. for Business and Admin. Services: RANDY L. SMITH
Vice-Pres. for Univ. Advancement: WILL SMALLWOOD
Dean for Enrolment Management: BRUCE PERKINS
Dean for Students: BRANDON SKAGGS
Dir for Graduate Studies: Dr SCOTT HARRIS
Dean for Library Services: Dr RICHARD CHEEK
Library of 220,000 vols, 310,000 microforms
Number of teachers: 115
Number of students: 1,871
Publication: OBU Magazine

DEANS

College of Arts and Humanities: Dr PAM ROBINSON
College of Business: Dr DAVID C. HOUGHTON
College of Fine Arts: Dr KEN GABRIELSE
College of Humanities and Social Sciences: Dr PAM ROBINSON
College of Nursing: Dr LANA BOLHOUSE
College of Science and Mathematics: Dr DEBORAH BLUE
College of Theology and Ministry: Dr MARK McCLELLAN

OKLAHOMA CHRISTIAN UNIVERSITY

POB 11000, Oklahoma City, OK 73136
2501E Memorial Rd, Edmond, OK 73013
Telephone: (405) 425-5000
Fax: (405) 425-5090
E-mail: info@oc.edu
Internet: www.oc.edu
Founded 1950 as Central Christian College, present name 1997
Private control
Academic year: August to April
Pres.: Dr MIKE E. O'NEAL
Exec. Vice-Pres.: BILL GOAD
Sr Vice-Pres. for Academic Affairs: Dr ALLISON D. GARRETT

Sr Vice-Pres. for Advancement: Dr JOHN DESTEIGUER
Vice-Pres. and Dean for Students: NEIL ARTER
Vice-Pres. for Enrolment Management: RISA FORRESTER
Vice-Pres. for Finance: JEFF BINGHAM
Vice-Pres. for Univ. and Marketing Communications: RON FROST
Dir for Admissions: DARCI THOMPSON
Registrar: MICKEY D. BANISTER
Library Dir: TAMIE WILLIS
Library of 110,000 vols and media, 30,000 e-books, access to 8,000 periodicals in electronic or print format
Number of teachers: 105
Number of students: 2,161
Publication: View magazine

DEANS

College of Arts and Sciences: Dr DAVID LOWRY
College of Biblical Studies: Dr ALAN MARTIN
College of Professional Studies: Dr PHIL LEWIS

OKLAHOMA CITY UNIVERSITY

2501 N Blackwelder, Oklahoma City, OK 73106-1493
Telephone: (405) 208-5000
Fax: (405) 521-5264
Internet: www.okcu.edu
Founded 1904 as Epworth Univ., present name 1924
Private control
Academic year: August to July
Chancellor: TOM McDANIEL
Pres.: Dr ROBERT HENRY
Provost and Vice-Pres. for Academic Affairs: Dr SUSAN BARBER (acting)
Assoc. Provost: Dr THOMAS L. BROWN (acting)
Vice-Pres. for Enrolment Services: EDUARDO PRIETO
Vice-Pres. for Student Affairs: Dr RICHARD E. HALL
Vice-Pres. for Univ. Advancement: JOHN HILLIS
Vice-Pres. for Univ. and Church Relations: Rev. MARGARET A. BALL
Dean for Students: JOHN RIGGS
Registrar: CHARLES L. MONNOT
Dir for Library: Dr VICTORIA SWINNEY
Library of 520,953 vols, 975,580 microfilms, 12,000 video and audio items, 200,379 monographs, 528 serial subscriptions, 21,199 bound periodical vols
Number of teachers: 342
Number of students: 3,546
Publications: Oklahoma City University Law Review (3 a year), Scarab (1 a year), Stellar (1 a year)

DEANS

Ann Lacy School of American Dance and Arts Management: JOHN BEDFORD
Kramer School of Nursing: Dr MARVEL L. WILLIAMSON
Meinders School of Business: Dr STEVE C. AGEE
Petree College of Arts and Sciences: Dr MARK Y. A. DAVIES
School of Adult and Continuing Education: Dr LEO WERNEKE
School of Law: ERIC T. LAITY
School of Religion: Dr SHARON BETSWORTH
School of Theatre: MARK E. PARKER
Wanda L. Bass School of Music: MARK E. PARKER

OKLAHOMA PANHANDLE STATE UNIVERSITY

POB 430, Goodwell, OK 73939

Telephone: (580) 349-2611
Fax: (580) 349-2302
E-mail: opsu@opsu.edu
Internet: www.opsu.edu

Founded 1909 as Pan-Handle Agricultural Institute, present name 1974
State control
Academic year: August to May (2 semesters)

Pres.: DAVID A. BRYANT
Vice-Pres. for Academic Affairs and Outreach: WAYNE E. MANNING
Vice-Pres. for Fiscal Affairs: LARRY PETERS
Dir for Student Services and Activities: JESSICA LOFLAND
Dir for Univ. College: CAROLYN MCCARGISH
Registrar and Dir for Admissions: BOBBY JENKINS
Dir for Library: TONY HARDMAN

Library of 91,000 vols, 33,000 e-books
Number of teachers: 69
Number of students: 1,400

DEANS

Agriculture: Prof. Dr PETER CAMFIELD
Business and Technology: Prof. DIANE MURPHEY
Development Studies: CAROLYN MCCARGISH
Education: Prof. R. WAYNE STEWART
Liberal Arts: Prof. Dr SARAH JANE RICHTER
Science, Mathematics and Nursing: Prof. Dr JUSTIN K. COLLINS

PROFESSORS

CAMFIELD, P., Animal Science
COLLINS, J. K., Biology
MURPHEY, D. M., Computer Information Systems
RICHTER, S. J., English
SHAFER, L., Education
STEWART, R. W., Education
THATCHER, R. M., Education
TOWNSEND, J., Agriculture

OKLAHOMA STATE UNIVERSITY

Stillwater, OK 74078

Telephone: (405) 744-5000
Fax: (405) 744-5285
E-mail: admit@okstate.edu
Internet: osu.okstate.edu

Founded 1890
State control
Academic year: August to May

Pres.: BURNS HARGIS
Provost, Sr Vice-Pres. and Vice-Pres. for Academic Affairs: Dr ROBERT J. STERNBERG
Vice-Pres. for Admin. and Finance: JOE WEAVER
Vice-Pres. for Enrolment Management: KYLE WRAY
Vice-Pres. for Research and Technology Transfer: Dr STEPHEN W. MCKEEVER
Vice-Pres. for Student Affairs: Dr LEE E. BIRD
Vice-Pres. for Univ. Relations: GARY C. CLARK
Assoc. Vice-Pres. for Institutional Diversity: Dr JASON KIRKSEY
Registrar: Dr K. CELESTE CAMPBELL
Dean for Libraries: SHEILA G. JOHNSON

Library: see Libraries and Archives
Number of teachers: 1,060
Number of students: 30,500

Publications: *International Fire Service Journal of Leadership and Management* (4 a year), *Journal of Computer Information Systems* (4 a year), *The Review of Regional Studies* (3 a year)

DEANS

Center for Veterinary Health Sciences: JEAN E. SANDER
College of Agricultural Sciences and Natural Resources: Dr ROBERT E. WHITSON
College of Arts and Sciences: Dr PETER M. A. SHERWOOD
College of Education: Dr C. ROBERT DAVIS
College of Engineering, Architecture and Technology: Dr KHALED A. M. GASEM
College of Human Sciences: Dr STEPHAN M. WILSON
Graduate College: Dr SHERYL TUCKER
Spears School of Business: Dr LAWRENCE A. CROSBY

OKLAHOMA STATE UNIVERSITY INSTITUTE OF TECHNOLOGY— OKMULGEE

1801 E Fourth St, Okmulgee, OK 74447

Telephone: (918) 293-4680
Fax: (918) 293-4643
E-mail: information@okstate.edu
Internet: www.osuit.edu
State control
Academic year: May to February

Divs of allied health science, arts and sciences, automotive service technologies, construction technology, culinary arts, engineering technologies, heavy equipment and vehicle institute, information technologies

Pres. and Provost: Dr DAVID BOSSERMAN
Exec. Vice-Pres. for Academic Affairs: Dr LINDA AVANT
Vice-Pres. for Enrolment Management: INA AGNEW
Vice-Pres. for Univ. and External Relations: ANITA GORDY-WATKINS
Dir for Library: JENNY DUNCAN
Number of students: 3,018 (2,113 full-time, 905 part-time)

OKLAHOMA WESLEYAN UNIVERSITY

2201 Silver Lake Rd, Bartlesville, OK 74006

Telephone: (918) 335-6200
Fax: (918) 335-6229
E-mail: info@okwu.edu
Internet: www.okwu.edu

Founded 1910 as Colorado Springs Bible College, present name 2001
Private control
Academic year: August to July

Pres.: Dr EVERETT PIPER
Exec. Vice-Pres. and Academic Dean: Dr ROBERT M. MEYERS
Vice-Pres. for Academic Programme Devt: Dr BRETT ANDREWS
Vice-Pres. for Adult and Graduate Studies: Dr PAULITA BROOKER
Vice-Pres. for Devt: Dr RANDY THOMPSON
Vice-Pres. for Enrolment: JOHN MEANS
Vice-Pres. for Student Life: KYLE WHITE
Registrar: CINDY RIFFE
Library Dir: WENDELL THOMPSON

Library of 80,000 vols
Number of teachers: 70
Number of students: 960

DEANS

School of Arts and Sciences: GAIL RICHARDSON
School of Business: Prof. Dr BRETT ANDREWS
School of Education: Dr SHELDON BUXTON
School of Nursing: BECKY LE
School of Religion and Philosophy: Prof. Dr MARK WEETER

ORAL ROBERTS UNIVERSITY

7777 S Lewis Ave, Tulsa, OK 74171

Telephone: (918) 495-6161
Fax: (918) 495-6222
E-mail: admissions@oru.edu
Internet: www.oru.edu

Founded 1965
Private control
Academic year: August to May

Pres.: Dr MARK RUTLAND
Provost: Dr RALPH FAGIN
Exec. Vice-Pres.: TIM PHILLEY
Exec. Vice-Pres. and Chief Financial Officer: MICHELLE FINLEY
Vice-Pres. for Academic Affairs: Dr DEBBIE SOWELL
Vice-Pres. for Enrolment Management: Dr NANCY BRAINARD
Vice-Pres. for Sponsored Programmes and Admin. Affairs: KELLY BAILEY
Vice-Pres. and Gen. Counsel: TERRY KOLLMORGEN
Registrar: DAVID FULMER
Dean for Learning Resources: Dr WILLIAM JERNIGAN

Library: 1m. vols
Number of teachers: 275
Number of students: 3,259

DEANS

College of Arts and Cultural Sciences: Dr WENDY SHIRK
College of Business: Dr STEVE GREENE
College of Education: Dr KIM BOYD
College of Nursing: Dr KENDA JEZEK
College of Science and Engineering: Dr DOMINIC HALSMER
College of Theology and Ministry: Dr THOMSON MATHEW

PHILLIPS THEOLOGICAL SEMINARY

901 N Mingo Rd, Tulsa, OK 74116

Telephone: (918) 610-8303
Fax: (918) 610-8404
Internet: www.ptstulsa.edu

Founded 1906 as College of the Bible, present name 1995
Private control

Pres.: GARY PELUSO-VERDEND
Vice-Pres. for Academic Affairs and Dean: Dr DON A. PITTMAN
Vice-Pres. for Admin.: LORA CONGER
Registrar: TONI WINE IMBLER
Library Dir: SANDY SHAPOVAL

Library of 90,000 vols, 80,000 monographs, 750 journals
Number of teachers: 15
Number of students: 200

ROGERS STATE UNIVERSITY

1701 W Will Rogers Blvd, Claremore, OK 74017

Telephone: (918) 343-7777
Fax: (918) 343-7550
Internet: www.rsu.edu

Founded 1909 as Eastern Univ. Preparatory School, present name 1999
State control

Campuses at Bartlesville and Pryor

Pres.: Dr LARRY RICE
Provost: BILL R. BEIERSCHMITT
Exec. Vice-Pres. for Admin. and Finance: THOMAS VOLTURO
Vice-Pres. for Academic Affairs: Dr RICHARD A. BECK
Vice-Pres. for Student Affairs: Dr TOBIE TITSWORTH
Dir for Library: ALAN LAWLESS

Library of 76,000 vols, 46,000 e-books, 40,000 e-journals, 225 periodical subscriptions, 1,200 DVDs, 1,200 CDs
Number of students: 4,300

Publication: *Cooweescoowee* (1 a year)

DEANS

School of Business and Technology: Prof. Dr BRUCE GARRISON
School of Liberal Arts: Dr FRANK ELWELL
School of Mathematics, Science and Health Sciences: Prof. Dr KEITH W. MARTIN

SAINT GREGORY'S UNIVERSITY

1900 W MacArthur St, Shawnee, OK 74804

Telephone: (405) 878-5100
Fax: (405) 878-5198
E-mail: info@stgregorys.edu
Internet: www.stgregorys.edu

Founded 1875
Private control
Academic year: August to June

Divs of business, humanities, natural science, social science, theology
Chancellor: Rt Rev. LAWRENCE STASYSZEN
Pres.: D. GREGORY MAIN
Provost: Dr RON FAULK
Exec. Vice-Pres.: TERRY McCULLAR
Assoc. Vice-Pres. for Enrolment: RONALD G. BROWN
Dean for Students: JOSHUA CLARY
Registrar and Assoc. Dean for Academic Services: KAY K. STITH
Library Dir: ANITA M. SEMTNER
Number of students: 744

DEANS

College for Working Adults: Dr JEAN THORN-BRUGH
College of Arts and Sciences: DANY DOUGHAN

SOUTHEASTERN OKLAHOMA STATE UNIVERSITY

1405 N Fourth St, Durant, OK 74701

Telephone: (580) 745-2000
Internet: www.se.edu

Founded 1909 as Southeastern State Normal School, present name 1974
State control
Academic year: August to May (and summer session)
Pres.: Dr LARRY MINKS
Vice-Pres. for Academic Affairs, Educational Outreach and Project Devt: Dr DOUGLAS N. McMILLAN
Vice-Pres. for Student Affairs: SHARON ROBINSON
Dean for Enrolment Management: ELIZABETH McCRAW
Registrar: KRISTIE LUKE
Library Dir: Dr SHARON MORRISON
Library of 191,240 vols, 513,852 microforms, 981 current periodicals, 231,527 govt documents, 14,381 Oklahoma documents, 9,400 e-books
Number of students: 4,075

DEANS

John Massey School of Business: Dr WALTER GASTER
School of Arts and Sciences: Dr LUCRETIA SCOUFOS
School of Education and Behavioral Sciences: Dr WILLIAM T. MAWER
School of Graduate and University Studies: Dr BRYON CLARK

SOUTHERN NAZARENE UNIVERSITY

6729 NW 39th Expressway, Bethany, OK 73008-2605

Telephone: (405) 789-6400
Fax: (405) 491-6381
E-mail: admissions@snu.edu
Internet: www.snu.edu

Founded 1899
Private control

Academic year: August to June (2 summer sessions and 2 terms)
Pres.: Dr LOREN P. GRESHAM
Provost: Dr MARY JONES
Vice-Pres. for Business and Financial Affairs: Dr DONNA NANCE
Vice-Pres. for Enrolment Management: Dr MIKE REDWINE
Vice-Pres. for Student Devt: SCOTT STRAWN
Vice-Pres. for Univ. Advancement and Church Relations: Dr TERRY N. TOLER
Dir for Admissions: Dr LINDA CANTWELL
Registrar: CHARLES S. CHITWOOD
Library Dir: Dr ARLITA HARRIS
Library of 105,000 vols, 13,000 periodicals, 339,000 microform items
Number of teachers: 120
Number of students: 2,100

DEANS

College of Business, Education and Kinesiology: Dr MARY JONES (acting)
College of Humanities: Dr MELANY KYZER
College of Natural, Social and Health Sciences: Dr DENNIS WILLIAMS
College of Professional and Graduate Studies: Dr W. DAVIS BERRYMAN
College of Teaching and Learning: Dr DENNIS WILLIAMS

SOUTHWESTERN CHRISTIAN UNIVERSITY

7210 NW 39th Expressway, Bethany, OK 73008

Telephone: (405) 789-7661
Fax: (405) 495-0078
E-mail: admissions@swcu.edu
Internet: www.swcu.edu

Founded 1946 as Southwestern Bible College, present name 2001
Private control
Pres.: Dr ED HUCKEBY
Provost and Vice-Pres. for Academic Affairs: Dr REGGIES WENYIKA
Vice-Pres. for Institutional Advancement: JON R. CHASTEEN
Vice-Pres. for Student Affairs and Dean for Students: DAVID CHISSOE
Vice-Pres. for Student Devt: JEFF KEENEY
Dir for Admissions and Enrolment Management: CHAD PUGH
Registrar: JEAN PERDUE
Library Dir: MARILYN A. HUDSON
Library of 25,000 vols
Number of teachers: 24
Number of students: 150

DEANS

School of Adult and Graduate Studies: Dr TERRY TRAMEL
School of Arts and Sciences: Dr DONNA McCOY
School of Professional Studies: ADRIAN HINKLE

SOUTHWESTERN OKLAHOMA STATE UNIVERSITY

100 Campus Dr., Weatherford, OK 73096

Telephone: (580) 772-6611
Fax: (580) 774-3795
E-mail: admissions@swosu.edu
Internet: www.swosu.edu

Founded 1901 as Southwestern Normal School, present name 1974
State control
Academic year: July to June
Pres.: Dr RANDY BEUTLER
Provost and Sr Vice-Pres.: Dr BLAKE SONOBE
Vice-Pres. for Admin. and Finance: TOM FAGAN
Assoc. Provost and Vice-Pres. for Student Affairs: Dr CYNTHIA FOUST

Dean for Students and Dir for Student Activities: CINDY DOUGHERTY
Registrar: DANIEL ARCHER
Dir for Libraries: JON SPARKS
Library of 242,406 vols
Number of teachers: 210
Number of students: 4,571 (f. t. e.)

DEANS

College of Arts and Sciences: Dr JAMES SOUTH
College of Pharmacy: Dr DENNIS THOMPSON
College of Professional and Graduate Studies: Dr KEN ROSE

UNIVERSITY OF CENTRAL OKLAHOMA

100 N University Dr., Edmond, OK 73034

Telephone: (405) 974-2000
Fax: (405) 359-5841
Internet: www.uco.edu

Founded 1890, present name 1990
State control
Pres.: Dr DON BETZ
Provost and Vice-Pres. for Academic Affairs: Dr WILLIAM J. RADKE
Exec. Vice-Pres. for Admin.: STEVE KREIDLER
Vice-Pres. for Devt: ANNE HOLZBERLEIN
Vice-Pres. for Enrolment Management: Dr MYRON L. POPE
Vice-Pres. for Student Affairs: Dr KATHRYN GAGE
Exec. Dir for Univ. Library: Dr BONNIE McNEELY
Library of 706,000 vols
Number of teachers: 450 (full-time)
Number of students: 17,000

DEANS

College of Business Administration: Dr MICKEY HEPNER (acting)
College of Education and Professional Studies: Dr JAMES MACHELL
College of Fine Arts and Design: Dr JOHN CLINTON
College of Liberal Arts: Dr PAMELA WASHINGTON
College of Mathematics and Science: Dr JOHN BARTHELL
Dr Joe C. Jackson College of Graduate Studies: Dr RICHARD BERNARD

UNIVERSITY OF OKLAHOMA

660 Parrington Oval, Norman, OK 73019-0390

Telephone: (405) 325-0311
E-mail: publicaffairs@ou.edu
Internet: www.ou.edu

Founded 1890
State control
Academic year: August to May (summer session June and July)
Campuses at Norman, Oklahoma City and Tulsa in Oklahoma
Pres.: DAVID L. BOREN
Sr Vice-Pres. and Provost: Dr NANCY L. MERGLER
Sr Vice-Pres. and Provost: DEWAYNE ANDREWS
Exec. Vice-Pres. and Vice-Pres. for Admin. and Finance: NICHOLAS S. HATHAWAY
Vice-Pres.: ANIL GOLLAHALLI
Vice-Pres. for Enrolment and Student Financial Services and Registrar: MATTHEW HAMILTON
Vice-Pres. for Information Technology and Chief Information Officer: LORETTA EARLY
Vice-Pres. for Research: Dr KELVIN DROEGEMEIER
Vice-Pres. for Student Affairs and Dean for Students: CLARKE STROUD
Vice-Pres. for Univ. Devt: TRIPP HALL (acting)

Vice-Pres. for Univ. Governance: Dr CHRIS A. PURCELL
Dean for Univ. Libraries: SUL H. LEE
Library: see Libraries and Archives
Number of teachers: 1,708 (1,431 full-time, 277 part-time)
Number of students: 30,591
Publications: *American Indian Law Review* (2 a year), *Genre: Forms of Discourse and Culture* (4 a year), *Oklahoma Law Review* (4 a year), *Papers on Anthropology* (2 a year), *World Literature Today* (4 a year)

DEANS

College of Architecture: Dr CHARLES GRAHAM
College of Arts and Sciences: Dr PAUL B. BELL
College of Atmospheric and Geographic Sciences: Dr BERRIEN MOORE
College of Engineering: THOMAS L. LANDERS
College of Law: JOSEPH HARROZ
College of Liberal Studies: JAMES P. PAPPAS
Gaylord College of Journalism and Mass Communication: Prof. JOE FOOTE
Graduate College: Dr T. H. LEE WILLIAMS
Jeannine Rainbolt College of Education: Dr GREGG A. GARN
Joe C. and Carole Kerr McClendon Honors College: Dr DAVID RAY
Mewbourne College of Earth and Energy: Dr LARRY GRILLOT
Michael F. Price College of Business: Dr KENNETH R. EVANS
Tulsa Graduate College: Dr WILLIAMS RAY
University College: Dr DOUGLAS GAFFIN
Weitzenhoffer Family College of Fine Arts: RICHARD C TAYLOR

CAMPUSES

University of Oklahoma Health Sciences Center

POB 26901, Oklahoma City, OK 73126-0901
1000 Stanton L. Young Blvd, Oklahoma City, OK 73117-1208
Telephone: (405) 271-4000
Fax: (405) 271-3151
Internet: www.ouhsc.edu
Founded 1900
Academic year: June to May
Sr Vice-Pres. and Provost: M. DEWAYNE ANDREWS
Vice-Provost for Academic Affairs and Faculty Devt: Dr VALERIE N. WILLIAMS
Vice-Pres. for Admin. and Finance: KENNETH D. ROWE
Vice-Pres. for Research: Dr JOHN J. IANDOLO
Number of teachers: 1,318 (1,051 full-time, 265 part-time)
Number of students: 4,229 (f.t.e.)

DEANS

College of Allied Health: KEVIN RUDEEN
College of Dentistry: STEPHEN K. YOUNG
College of Medicine: DEWAYNE ANDREWS
College of Nursing: Dr LAZELLE BENEFIELD
College of Pharmacy: Dr JOLAINE REIERSON DRAUGALIS
College of Public Health: GARY RASKOB
Graduate College: JAMES J. TOMASEK

University of Oklahoma—Tulsa Schusterman Center

4502 E 41st St, Tulsa, OK 74135-2515
Telephone: (918) 660-3000
Internet: www.ou.edu/tulsa
Pres.: GERARD P. CLANCY
Library Dir: STEWART M. BROWER
Library of 18,000 vols, 500 print journals

DEANS

Graduate College: WILLIAM O. RAY

School of Community Medicine: F. DANIEL DUFFY

UNIVERSITY OF SCIENCE AND ARTS OF OKLAHOMA

1727 W Alabama, Chickasha, OK 73018-5322
Telephone: (405) 224-3140
Fax: (405) 574-1220
Internet: www.usao.edu
Founded 1908, present name 1973
State control
Divs of arts and humanities, business and social sciences, education and speech language pathology, mathematics, science and physical education, teacher education programme
Pres.: JOHN FEAVER
Vice-Pres. for Academic Affairs: Dr JOHN D. MARBLE
Vice-Pres. for Business and Finance: MICHAEL COPONITI
Vice-Pres. for Enrolment Management and Student Affairs: MONICA TREVINO
Vice-Pres. for Information Services and Technology: J. LYNN BOYCE
Vice-Pres. for Univ. Advancement: Dr MICHAEL NEALEIGH
Dir for Admissions: KELLEE JOHNSON
Dean for Students: NANCY HUGHES
Registrar: JOE EVANS
Librarian: KELLY BROWN
Library of 97,000 vols
Number of teachers: 55
Number of students: 1,050

UNIVERSITY OF TULSA

800 S Tucker Dr., Tulsa, OK 74104-9700
Telephone: (918) 631-2000
Fax: (918) 631-5003
E-mail: admission@utulsa.edu
Internet: www.utulsa.edu
Founded 1894 as Henry Kendall College, reorganized and present name 1920
Private control
Academic year: August to May
Pres.: Dr STEADMAN UPHAM
Provost and Vice-Pres. for Academic Affairs: ROGER N. BLAIS
Exec. Vice-Pres.: KEVAN C. BUCK
Vice-Pres. for Enrolment and Student Services: ROGER W. SOROCHTY
Vice-Pres. for Research: ALLEN ROBERT SOLTOW
Dean for Students: YOLANDA D. TAYLOR
Registrar: GINNA LANGSTON
Dean for Libraries: ADRIAN W. ALEXANDER
Library: 3m. vols (incl. 29,000 e-journals, 2,000 print journals, 30,000 e-books), 128,000 rare books, 3,500 linear ft of literary and historical MSS
Number of teachers: 306
Number of students: 4,187
Publications: *James Joyce Quarterly, Nimrod International Journal, Tulsa Studies in Women's Literature*

DEANS

College of Engineering and Natural Sciences: STEVEN J. BELLOVICH
College of Law: JANET KOVEN LEVIT
Collins College of Business: A. GALE SULLENBERGER
Graduate School: Dr JANET A. HAGGERTY
Henry Kendall College of Arts and Sciences: Dr D. THOMAS BENEDIKTSON

PROFESSORS

ADAMS, C. W., Law
ALLISON, G. D., Law
ARNOLD, M. T., Law
ASHENAYI, K., Electrical Engineering

BAILEY, G. A., Anthropology
BELSKY, M. H., Law
BENEDIKTSON, D. T., Languages
BERRY, J. O., Psychology
BEY, R. P., Finance
BLAIR, D. M., Law
BRADLEY, J. C., History
BROWN, C. R., Biological Sciences
BUCHOLTZ, B. K., Law
BUCKLEY, T. H., History
BURGESS, R. C., Finance
BURSTEIN, A. M., History
CAGLEY, J. W., Management and Marketing
CAIRNS, T. W., Mathematics and Computer Science
CHIANG, W. C., Operations Management
COLLIER, G. E., Biological Science
COLLINS, J. M., Finance
CONSTANDA, C., Mathematics and Computer Science
COOK, D. B., Theatre
CRAVENS, K. S., Accounting
CULLEM, C. M., Law
DE ALMEIDA, H. B., English
DIAZ, J. C., Mathematics and Computer Science
DONALDSON, R. H., Political Science
DOTY, D. R., Mathematics and Computer Science
DUGGER, W. M., Economics
DURHAM, M. O., Electrical Engineering
EISENACH, E. J., Political Science
FINKELMAN, P., Law
GAMBLE, R. F., Computer Science
GASTON, S. K., Nursing
GILPIN, G. H., English
HAGGERTY, J. A., Geosciences
HANSSON, R. O., Psychology
HENNESSEE, P. A., Accounting
HENRY, D. O., Anthropology
HENSHAW, J. M., Mechanical Engineering
HICKS, J. F., Law
HIPSHER, W. L., Education
HITTINGER, F. R., Philosophy and Religion
HOLLAND, T. L., Law
HOLLINGSWORTH, W. G., Law
HORNE, T. A., Political Science
HOWARD, R. E., Chemistry
HOWLAND, J. A., Philosophy
HUIE, M. C., Law
HYATTE, R. L., Languages
JENSEN, J. K., Communication
KANE, G. R., Electrical Engineering
KELKAR, B. G., Petroleum Engineering
KESTNER, J. A., English
KRAIGER, K., Psychology
LACEY, L. J., Law
LAIRD, H. A., English
LAMPTON, J. D., Art
LANGENKAMP, R. D., Law
LAWLESS, R. W., Mathematical Sciences and Quantitative Methods
LEVETIN, E. A., Biological Science
LEWICKI, P., Psychology
LIMAS, V. J., Law
LINDSTROM, L. C., Anthropology
LUKS, K. D., Chemical Engineering
MANNING, F. S., Chemical Engineering
MANSFIELD, M. E., NELPI, Law
MARTIN, B. C., Nursing
MICHAEL, P. J., Geosciences
MILLER, G. P., Physics
MISKA, S. Z., Petroleum Engineering
MONCRIEF, D. L., Communication
MONROE, R. J., Finance
NEIDELL, L. A., Management and Marketing
NORBERG, A. H., Music
ODELL, G. H., Anthropology
PARKER, J. C., Law
PRICE, G. L., Chemical Engineering
RAHE, P. A., History
REDNER, R. A., Mathematics and Computer Science
REEDER, R. L., Biological Science
REYNOLDS, A. C., Petroleum Engineering
RONDA, J. P., History

ROYSTER, J. V., Law
RUSSELL, R. A., Management Information Systems
RYBICKI, E. F., Mechanical Engineering
SAMIEE, S., Management and Marketing
SARICA, C., Petroleum Engineering
SCHOENEFELD, D. A., Mathematics and Computer Science
SEN, S., Computer Science
SHADLEY, J. R., Mechanical Engineering
SHENOI, S., Mathematics and Computer Science
SHIRAZI, S. A., Mechanical Engineering
SHOHAM, O., Petroleum Engineering
SMITH, P. C., Management
SOREM, J. R., Mechanical Engineering
STEIB, S., Economics
SUBLETTE, K. L., Chemical Engineering
SULLENBERGER, A. G., Management Information Systems and Operations Management
TAI, H. M., Electrical Engineering
TAKACH, N. E., Chemistry
TATUM, M. L., Law
TAYLOR, G. O., English
TEETERS, D. C., Chemistry
THOMAS, J. C., Law
TIPTON, S. M., Mechanical Engineering
TOMLINS, C. B., Art
URBAN, T. L., Operations Management
VOZIKIS, G. S., Bovaird Chair
WAINWRIGHT, R. L., Mathematics and Computer Science
WAITS, K., Law
WATSON, J. G., English
WHALEN, M. E., Anthropology
WILSON, L. C., Theatre
YASSER, R. L., Law
YEVTUSHENKO, Y. A., English
ZEDALIS, R. J., NELPI

OREGON

ART INSTITUTE OF PORTLAND

1122 NW Davis St, Portland, OR 97209-2911
Telephone: (503) 228-6528
Fax: (503) 228-4227
E-mail: aipdadm@aii.edu
Internet: www.artinstitutes.edu

Founded 1963, fmrly Bassist College
Private control
Academic year: October to September

Liberal education and professional education

Pres.: TIMOTHY MOSCATO
Dean for Student Affairs: JASON CLARY
Dir for Admin.: ANGELA BOSTOCK
Dir for Learning Resources: NANCY THURSTON
Library Dir: TRICIA JUETTEMEYER
Registrar: ROBERT TUFTS

Number of teachers: 33 full-time, 60 adjunct per quarter
Number of students: 1,538

CONCORDIA UNIVERSITY

2811 NE Holman St, Portland, OR 97211
Telephone: (503) 288-9371
E-mail: registrar@cu-portland.edu
Internet: www.cu-portland.edu

Founded 1905 as a 4-year acad., present name and status 1995
Private control
Academic year: August to May

Pres.: Dr CHARLES E. SCHLIMPERT
Provost and Chief Operating Officer: Dr MARK WAHLERS
Dean for Admission: BOBI SWAN
Dean for Students: Dr STEVE DEKLOTZ
Dir of Enrolment Services: JIM CULLEN
Registrar: PAUL RÉVER
Librarian: BRENT MAI

Number of teachers: 60
Number of students: 2,500

DEANS

College of Education: Dr JOSEPH MANNION
College of Health and Human Services: Dr MARK D. JAGER
College of Theology, Arts and Sciences: Dr CHARLES J. KUNERT
School of Law: Dr CATHY R. SILAK

CORBAN UNIVERSITY

5000 Deer Park Dr., SE, Salem, OR 97317-9392
Telephone: (503) 581-8600
Fax: (503) 585-4316
E-mail: president@corban.edu
Internet: www.corban.edu

Founded 1935 as Bible Institute, Western Baptist College 1946, present name 2005
Private control
Academic year: August to April

Pres.: Dr RENO R. HOFF
Provost and Exec. Vice-Pres.: MATT LUCAS
Vice-Pres. for Advancement: MICHAEL BATES
Vice-Pres. for Business: KEVIN BRUBAKER
Vice-Pres. for Marketing: J. STEVEN HUNT
Vice-Pres. for Student Life: NANCY HEDBERG
Vice-Pres. for Enrolment Management: MARTIN ZIESEMER
Dean of Students: JANINE ALLEN
Registrar: CHRIS VETTER

Library of 115,000 vols, 600 periodicals
Number of teachers: 60
Number of students: 1,175

DEANS

Education Programme: Dr JANINE ALLEN
Human Performance Programme: Dr DAVID B. BALE
School of Ministry: Dr GREG TRULL

EASTERN OREGON UNIVERSITY

One Univ. Blvd, La Grande, OR 97850-2807
Telephone: (541) 962-3672
Fax: (541) 962-3023
E-mail: admissions@eou.edu
Internet: www.eou.edu

Founded 1929
Academic year: July to June

Pres.: BOB DAVIES
Provost and Vice-Pres. for Academic Affairs: STEVE ADKISON
Vice-Pres. for Finance and Admin.: LON WHITAKER
Vice-Pres. for Student Affairs: Dr CAMILLE CONSOLVO
Dir for Libraries: KAREN CLAY

Library of 153,000 vols, 1,300 periodicals
Number of teachers: 120 full-time, 26 part-time
Number of students: 4,137

Publication: Eastern Oregon Science Journal

DEANS

College of Arts and Sciences: SARAH WITTE (acting)
College of Business: DAN MIELKE
College of Education: DAN MIELKE

GEORGE FOX UNIVERSITY

414 N Meridian St, Newberg, OR 97132-2697
Telephone: (503) 538-8383
Fax: (503) 537-3830
E-mail: president@georgefox.edu
Internet: www.georgefox.edu

Founded 1891 as Pacific College, present name 1996
Private control
Academic year: September to April

Pres.: Dr ROBIN E. BAKER
Provost: PATRICK ALLEN

Exec. Vice-Pres. for Enrolment and Marketing: ROB WESTERVELT
Exec. Vice-Pres. for Finance and Operations: TED ALLEN
Exec. Vice-Pres. for Univ. Advancement and Integrated Marketing: BRIAN GARDNER
Vice-Pres. for Student Life: BRAD LAU
Univ. Librarian: MERRILL JOHNSON

Library of 200,000 vols
Number of teachers: 388
Number of students: 3,519

Publication: George Fox Journal (3 a year)

DEANS

George Fox Evangelical Seminary: CHUCK CONNIRY
School of Arts and Sciences: HANK HELSABECK
School of Behavioral and Health Sciences: JIM FOSTER
School of Business: DIRK BARRAM
School of Education: LINDA SAMEK

LEWIS AND CLARK COLLEGE

0615 SW Palatine Hill Rd, Portland, OR 97219
Telephone: (503) 768-7000
Fax: (503) 768-7055
E-mail: wwwadmin@lclark.edu
Internet: www.lclark.edu

Founded 1867 as Albany Collegiate Institute, present status 1966
Private control

Pres.: BARRY GLASSNER
Provost and Vice-Pres.: JANE MONNIG ATKINSON
Vice-Pres., Sec. and Gen. Counsel: DAVID ELLIS
Vice-Pres. for Business and Finance: CARL B. VANCE
Vice-Pres. for Institutional Advancement: GREGORY VOLK
Dean for Students: LATRICIA BRAND
Dean for Admissions: LISA MEYER
Registrar: JUDY C. FINCH
Dir of Library: JAMES KOPP

Library of 477,010 vols
Number of teachers: 191
Number of students: 3,500

Publication: Journal

DEANS

College of Arts and Sciences: TUAJUANDA JORDAN
Graduate School of Education and Counseling: SCOTT FLETCHER
Law School: ROBERT KLONOFF

MARYLHURST UNIVERSITY

POB 261, 17600 Pacific Highway, Marylhurst, OR 97036-0261
Telephone: (503) 636-8141
Fax: (503) 636-9526
E-mail: admissions@marylhurst.edu
Internet: www.marylhurst.edu

Founded 1893 as St. Mary's Acad. and College, present name 1998
Private control

Pres.: Dr JUDITH JOHANSEN
Provost: Dr DAVID PLOTKIN
Exec. Vice-Pres. and Chief Financial Officer: MICHAEL LAMMERS
Vice-Pres. for Human Resources and Org. Excellence: CELINA RATLIFF
Vice-Pres. for Enrolment Management: BETH WOODWARD
Vice-Pres. for Information Technology: ETHAN BENATAN
Vice-Pres. for Univ. Advancement: LYNN MAWE

Library of 100,000 vols, 2,500 videos, 1,700 CDs, 200 print periodical subscriptions

Number of teachers: 506 (52 full-time, 454 part-time)
Number of students: 1,917 (985 graduates, 932 undergraduates)

MULTNOMAH UNIVERSITY

8435 NE Glisan St, Portland, OR 97220
Telephone: (503) 255-0332
Fax: (503) 254-1268
E-mail: admiss@multnomah.edu
Internet: www.multnomah.edu
Founded 1936 as Multnomah School of the Bible, present name 2008
Private control
Academic year: August to May
Multnomah Bible College and Multnomah Biblical Seminary
Pres.: Dr DANIEL R. LOCKWOOD
Academic Dean and Vice-Pres.: Dr WAYNE STRICKLAND
Vice-Pres. and Dir of Information Systems: Dr JOE WONG
Dean of Student Services: MATTHEW RYGG
Registrar: Prof. AMY STEPHENS
Dir of Library: Dr PHILIP JOHNSON
Library of 500,000 vols
Number of teachers: 106 (incl. full-time and part-time)
Number of students: 929

NEW HOPE CHRISTIAN COLLEGE

2155 Bailey Hill Rd, Eugene, OR 97405
Telephone: (541) 485-1780
Fax: (541) 343-5801
E-mail: admissions@newhope.edu
Internet: www.newhope.edu
Founded 1925
Private control
Academic year: August to May (3 semesters)
Works towards devt of Christian leaders with a focus on theology, ministry skills and character
Chancellor and Pres.: Dr WAYNE CORDEIRO
Vice-Pres.: GUY HIGASHI
Academic Dean: Dr LARRY R. BURKE
Dir for Student Ministry: LONNY R. BURKE
Registrar: Dr JAMES WICK
Librarian: JANET L. KELLEY
Number of teachers: 15
Number of students: 200

NORTHWEST CHRISTIAN UNIVERSITY

828 E 11th Ave, Eugene, OR 97401
Telephone: (541) 343-1641
Fax: (541) 343-9159
E-mail: admissions@nwcc.edu
Internet: www.nwcu.edu
Founded 1895 as Eugene Divinity School, present name 2008
Academic year: September to June
Pres.: Dr JOSEPH WOMACK
Vice-Pres. for Finance and Admin.: LISA CASTLEBURY
Vice-Pres. for Enrolment and Student Devt: MICHAEL FULLER
Vice-Pres. for Academic Affairs: Prof. Dr DENNIS LINDSAY
Vice-Pres. for Advancement: GREG STRAUSBAUGH
Library Dir: STEVE SILVER
Registrar: AARON PRUITT
Library of 74,000 vols
Number of teachers: 30
Number of students: 625

OREGON HEALTH & SCIENCE UNIVERSITY

3181 SW Sam Jackson Park Rd, Portland, OR 97239-3098
Telephone: (503) 494-8311
Internet: www.ohsu.edu
Founded 1887 as Univ. of Oregon Dept of Medicine, present name 1981
Pres.: Dr PETER O. KOHLER
Provost: Dr JEANETTE MLADENOVIĆ
Vice-Provost for Academic and Student Affairs: ROBERT L. VIEIRA
Chief Financial Officer: LAWRENCE J. FURNSTAHL
Exec. Vice-Pres.: STEVEN D. STADUM
Library of 90,809 vols, 16,267 e-books, 2,008 journals, 12,634 e-journals with electronic access
Number of students: 3,400

DEANS

College of Pharmacy: MARK ZABRISKIE
School of Dentistry: Dr GARY CHIODO
School of Medicine: Dr MARK A. RICHARDSON
School of Nursing: MICHAEL BLEICH

OREGON STATE UNIVERSITY

Corvallis, OR 97331
Telephone: (541) 737-1000
Fax: (541) 737-2400
E-mail: osuadmit@oregonstate.edu
Internet: oregonstate.edu
Founded 1868 as Corvallis College
State control
Academic year: September to June
Pres.: Dr EDWARD J. RAY
Provost and Exec. Vice-Pres.: SABAH U. RANDHAWA
Vice-Pres. for Finance and Admin.: MARK E. MCCAMBRIDGE
Vice-Pres. for Research: RICK SPINRAD
Vice-Pres. for Univ. Relations and Marketing: STEVE CLARK
Vice-Provost for Academic Affairs: LARRY ROPER
Vice-Provost for Student Affairs: REBECCA L. WARNER
Registrar: BARBARA S. BALZ
Univ. Librarian: FAYE CHADWELL
Library: 2m. vols, 1,905,093 microfilms
Number of teachers: 3,481
Number of students: 24,977
Publications: Beaver (1 a year), Oregon Agricultural Progress (3 a year), Oregon Stater (3 a year), Prism (literary magazine, 1 a year), Research OSU (1 a year)

DEANS

College of Agricultural Sciences: SONNY RAMASWAMY
College of Business: Dr ILLENE K. KLEINSORGE
College of Education: LARRY FLICK
College of Engineering: SCOTT ASHFORD
College of Forestry: HAL SALWASSER
College of Liberal Arts: LARRY RODGERS
College of Oceanic and Atmospheric Sciences: Prof. Dr MARK R. ABBOTT
College of Pharmacy: Prof. Dr MARK ZABRISKIE
College of Public Health and Human Sciences: TAMMY M. BRAY
College of Science: Prof. SHERMAN H. BLOOMER
College of Veterinary Medicine: CYRIL R. CLARKE
Graduate School: BRENDA MCCOMB
Univ. Honors College: DAN ARP

PACIFIC NORTHWEST COLLEGE OF ART

1241 NW Johnson St, Portland, OR 97209
Telephone: (503) 226-4391
Fax: (503) 226-3587
E-mail: admissions@pnca.edu
Internet: www.pnca.edu
Founded 1909
Private control
Academic year: September to May
Offers Bachelors and Masters in fine arts, applied craft and design, collaborative design and visual studies
Pres.: Dr THOMAS MANLEY
Vice-Pres. for Academic Affairs: GREG WARE
Vice-Pres. for Finance and Admin.: NANCY BARROWS
Dir for Advancement: SUZANNE HASHIM
Registrar: JENNIFER DEKALB
Library Dir: RACHEL MENDEZ
Number of teachers: 99 (29 full-time, 70 part-time)
Number of students: 621 (undergraduates and graduates)

PACIFIC UNIVERSITY

1411 SW Morrison St, Suite 201, Portland, OR 97205
Telephone: (503) 352-6151
Internet: www.pacificu.edu
Founded 1849
Pres.: Dr LESLEY M. HALLICK
Provost and Vice-Pres. for Academic Affairs: Dr JOHN MILLER
Vice-Pres. for Student Affairs and Dean of Students: EVA C. KREBS
Vice-Pres. for Finance and Admin.: MIKE MALLERY
Co-Vice Pres. for Univ. Advancement: JAN STRICKLIN
Co-Vice-Pres. for Univ. Advancement: TAMMY SPENCER
Assoc. Dir of Admissions: TANIA M. HAND
Library Management Team Coordinator: ALEX TOTH
Library of 100,000 vols, 2,500 newspapers, magazines and journals and 4,000 reference resources
Number of teachers: 79 (full-time)
Number of students: 1,750 (full-time)
Publication: Pacific Magazine

DEANS

College of Arts and Sciences: Dr JOHN HAYES
College of Education: Dr MARK E. ANKENY
College of Health Professions: Dr ANN BARR
College of Optometry: Dr JENNIFER SMYTHE
School of Pharmacy: Dr SUSAN STEIN
School of Professional Psychology: Dr JAMES LANE

PORTLAND STATE UNIVERSITY

POB 751, Portland, OR 97207-0751
1825 SW Broadway, Portland, OR 97201
Telephone: (503) 725-3000
Fax: (503) 725-4882
E-mail: admissions@pdx.edu
Internet: www.pdx.edu
Founded 1946
Academic year: September to June
Pres.: Prof. MICHAEL REARDON
Provost and Vice-Pres. for Academic Affairs: ROY KOCH
Vice-Pres. for Enrolment Management and Student Affairs: JACKIE BALZE
Vice-Pres. for Finance and Admin.: LINDSAY DESROCHERS
Vice-Provost and Dean of Extended Studies: MICHAEL BURTON

Vice-Provost for Graduate Studies and Research: WILLIAM FEYERHERM
Vice-Provost for Student Affairs: DAN FORTMILLER
Dean for Student Life: MICHELE TOPPE
Dir for Financial Aid: PHILLIP RODGERS
Dir for Institutional Research and Planning: KATHI KETCHESON
Assoc. Vice-Pres. for Information Technology: MARK GREGORY
Univ. Dir for Library: LYNN K. CHMELIR
Library of 1,805,336 vols
Number of teachers: 1,260
Number of students: 29,703
Publication: *Portland State Magazine*

DEANS

College of Liberal Arts and Sciences: SUSAN BEATTY
College of Urban and Public Affairs: LAWRENCE WALLACK
Graduate School of Education: Dr RANDY HITZ
Maseeh College of Engineering and Computer Science: Dr RENJENG SU
School of Business Administration: Dr SCOTT DAWSON
School of Extended Studies: MICHAEL BURTON
School of Fine and Performing Arts: BARBARA SESTAK
School of Social Work: Prof. Dr NANCY KOROLOFF

REED COLLEGE

3203 SE Woodstock Blvd, Portland, OR 97202-8199
Telephone: (503) 771-1112
Fax: (503) 777-7769
Internet: www.reed.edu
Founded 1908
Private control
Academic year: August to May
Pres.: COLIN S. DIVER
Vice-Pres. and Treas.: EDWIN O. MCFARLANE
Vice-Pres. and Dean of Student Services: MICHAEL BRODY
Vice-Pres. for College Relations: HUGH PORTER
Registrar: NORA MCLAUGHLIN
Dean of Admissions: KEITH TODD
Dean for the Faculty: PATRICK G. MCDOUGAL (acting)
Dean for Institutional Diversity: CRYSTAL ANN WILLIAMS
Dir for Devt: JAN KURTZ
Dir for Institutional Research: MICHAEL TAMADA
Librarian: DENA HUTTO
Library of 490,000 vols, 10,000 journals
Number of teachers: 135
Number of students: 1,400
Publication: *Reed Magazine* (4 a year).

SOUTHERN OREGON UNIVERSITY

1250 Siskiyou Blvd, Ashland, OR 97520
Telephone: (541) 552-7672
Fax: (541) 552-6337
Internet: www.sou.edu
Founded 1926
State control
Academic year: September to June
3 Campuses: Ashland and the Rogue Valley campus, Ashland campus and Medford campus
Pres.: MARY CULLINAN
Provost and Vice-Pres. for Academic Affairs: JAMES M. KLEIN
Registrar: MATT STILLMAN
Dean for Library: PAUL ADALIAN
Library of 335,371 vols, 302,340 govt documents, 803,548, microfilms, 3,571 period-

ical subscriptions, 10,492 audiovisual holdings, 43,829 e-books
Number of teachers: 288
Number of students: 6,745

DEANS

College of Arts and Sciences: ALISSA ARP
School of Business: RAJ PARIKH
School of Education: GEOFF MILLS

UNIVERSITY OF OREGON

POB 3237 Eugene, OR 97403-0237
Telephone: (541) 346-1000
Fax: (541) 346-3017
E-mail: pres@uoregon.edu
Internet: www.uoregon.edu
Founded 1872
State control
Academic year: September to June
Pres.: ROBERT M. BERDAHL
Sr Vice-Pres. and Provost: LORRAINE DAVIS (acting)
Vice-Pres. for Academic Affairs: RUSSELL S. TOMLIN
Vice-Pres. for Devt: MICHAEL ANDREASEN
Vice-Pres. for Finance and Admin.: FRANCES DYKE
Vice-Pres. for Univ. Relations: MICHAEL REDDING
Vice-Pres. for Public and Govt Affairs: MICHAEL REDDING
Vice-Pres. for Research and Innovation: KIMBERLY ANDREWS ESPY
Vice-Pres. for Student Affairs: ROBIN HOLMES
Registrar: HERBERT R. CHERECK
Dean of Libraries: DEBORAH A. CARVER
Library: see Libraries
Number of teachers: 1,168
Number of students: 24,447 (part-time and full-time)
Publications: *Bulletin of the Museum of Natural History, Comparative Literature, Governmental Research Bulletins, Imprint Oregon, Northwest Review, Oregon Business Review* (4 a year), *Oregon Law Review*

DEANS

College of Arts and Sciences: Dr SCOTT COLTRANE
College of Education: MICHAEL BULLIS
Graduate School: KIMBERLY ANDREWS ESPY
Lundquist College of Business: CORNELIS A. DE KLUYVER
Robert D. Clark Honors College: DAVID A. FRANK
School of Architecture and Allied Arts: FRANCES BRONET
School of Journalism and Communication: TIMOTHY GLEASON
School of Law: MICHAEL MOFFITT
School of Music and Dance: BRAD FOLEY

PROFESSORS

ACRES, A. J., Art History
AGUIRRE, C. A., History
AIKENS, C. M., Anthropology
ALBAUM, G. S., Business
ALBERTGALTIER, A., Romance Languages
ALLEY, H. M., Honours College
ALPERT, L. J., Fine Arts
ALTMANN, B., Romance Languages
ANDERSON, F. W., Mathematics
ANDERSON, M. C., Psychology
ANDERSON, S. C., German
ANDERSON-INMAN, L., Education Policy and Management
AOKI, K., Law
ARIOLA, Z., Computer and Information Science
ASH, A. D., Political Science
AXLINE, M. D., Law
AYRES, W. S., Anthropology
BALDWIN, D. A., Psychology

BALDWIN, J. H., Planning Public Policy Management
BAMBURY, J. E., Architecture
BARACCHI, C., Philsophy
BARKAN, A., Biology
BARNES, B. A., Mathematics
BARNHARD, R. J., Chemistry
BARR, S. A., Dance
BARTLEIN, P., Geography
BARTON, R. F., Theatre Arts
BAUGH, W. H., Political Science
BAUMGOLD, D. J., Political Science
BAYLESS, M. J., English
BELITZ, D., Physics
BENDER, S. W., Law
BENGSTON, M. C., Fine Arts
BENNETT, R. W., Music
BENZ, M. R., Education Policy and Management
BERK, G. P., Political Science
BEST, R. J., Business
BEUDERT, M. C., Music
BIERSACK, A., Anthropology
BIRN, R. F., History
BIVINS, T. H., Journalism
BJERRE, C., Law
BLANDY, D. E., Arts and Admin.
BLONIGEN, B. A., Economics
BOGEL, C. J., Art History
BOLTON, C. R., Recreation and Tourist Management
BONDS, A. B., Theatre Arts
BONINE, J. E., Law
BOREN, J. L., English
BOROVSKY, Z. P., German
BOSS, J. F., III, Music
BOTHUN, G. D., Physics
BOTVINNIK, B., Mathematics
BOUSH, D. M., Business
BOWDITCH, P. L., Classics
BOWERMAN, B. A., Biology
BOYNTON, S. L., Music
BRADSHAW, W. E., Biology
BRANCHAUD, B. P., Chemistry
BRAU, J. E., Physics
BRICK, H., History
BRICKER, D. D., Special Education
BRODIE, D. W., Law
BROKAW, C. J., History
BROWN, G. Z., Architecture
BROWN, S. T., East Asian Languages
BROWN, W. B., Business
BROX, R. M., Romance Languages
BULLIS, M. D., Education Policy and Management
BURRIS, V. L., Sociology
BUSTAMANTE, C. J., Chemistry
BYBEE, C. R., Journalism
BYRD, B. K., Labour Education Center
CALHOON, K. S., German
CALIN, F. G., Romance Languages
CAMPBELL, E. A., Music
CAPALDI, R. A., Biology
CARMICHAEL, H. J., Physics
CARNINE, D. W., Education Policy and Management
CARPENTER, G. M., Recreation and Tourism Management
CARPENTER, K. L., Linguistics
CARROLL, G. C., Biology
CARTER, L. R., Sociology
CARTIER, C. L., Geography
CARTWRIGHT, V., Architecture
CASHMAN, K. V., Geological Sciences
CASTENHOLZ, R. W., Biology
CASTILLO, D., Romance Languages
CHALMERS, J. M., Business
CHANDLER, V. L., Biology
CHANEY, R. P., Anthropology
CHATFIELD, S. J., Dance
CHENG, N. YEN-WEN, Architecture
CINA, J., Chemistry
CLARK, R., Music
CLARK, S., English
COGAN, F. B., Honours College
COHEN, J. D., Physics

COHEN, S. E., Geography
COLEMAN, E. L., II, English
COLLIN, R. M., Law
COLLINS, P. F., Psychology
CONERY, J. S., Computer and Information Science
CONLEY, D. T., Education Policy and Management
CORNER, D. B., Architecture
CRAIG, J. P., Dance
CROSSWHITE, J. R., English
CRUMB, D. R., Music
CRUZ, J., Romance Languages
CSONKA, P. L., Physics
CUNY, J., Computer and Information Science
DAHLQUIST, F. W., Chemistry
DANN, L. Y., Business
DARST, R. G., Political Science
DAVIE, W. E., Philosophy
DAVIES, P. H., Creative Writing
DAVIS, H., Architecture
DAVIS, R. L., Romance Languages
DAWSON, J. I., Political Science
DEGGE, R. M., Arts and Admin.
DELANCEY, S. C., Linguistics
DELGUERCIO, D. G., Business
DENNIS, M., History
DESCUTNER, J. W., Dance
DESHPANDE, N. G., Physics
DEVRIES, P. J., Biology
DIAMOND, I., Political Science
DICKMAN, A. W., Biology
DIETHELM, J. K., Landscape Architecture
DISHION, T. J., Special Education
DOERKSEN, D. P., Music
DOERKSEN, P. F., Music
DOLEZAL, M.-L., Art History
DORSEY, R. J., Geological Science
DOUGLAS, S. A., Computer and Information Science
DOWD, C. R., Music
DOWNES, B. T., Planning Public Policy Management
DOXSEE, K. M., Chemistry
DREILING, M. C., Sociology
DUFEK, J. S., Exercise and Movement Sciences
DUFF, S. F., Architecture
DUGAW, D. M., English
DUNCAN, I. H., English
DURRANT, S., East Asian Languages
DYER, M. N., Mathematics
DYKE, T. R., Chemistry
EARL, J. W., English
EDSON, C. H., Education Policy and Management
EISEN, J. S., Biology
ELLIS, C. J., Economics
EMLET, R. B., Biology
ENGELKING, P. C., Chemistry
EPPLE, J. A., Romance Languages
EPPS, G., Law
EPSTEIN, M., East Asian Languages
ERLANDSON, J. M., Anthropology
ETTINGER, L. F., Arts and Admin.
EVANS, G. W., Economics
EXTON, D., Chemistry
FAGOT, B. I., Psychology
FAIR, L. J., History
FANG, Y., Business
FARLEY, A. M., Computer and Information Science
FARWELL, M. R., English
FICKAS, S. F., Computer and Information Science
FIGLIO, D. N., Economics
FISHLEN, M. B., East Asian Languages
FLYNN, G. C., Chemistry
FORD, K. J., English
FORELL, C. A., Law
FOSTER, J. B., Sociology
FRACCHIA, J. G., Honours College
FRANK, D. A., Honours College
FRANKLIN, J. D., Journalism
FRAZIER, G. V., Business
FREINKEL, L. A., English

FREY, R. E., Physics
FREYD, J. J., Psychology
FRIESTAD, M. S., Business
FRISHKOFF, P., Business
FRY, G., International Studies
FUJII, N., East Asian Languages
FULLER, L. O., Sociology
GAGE, J. T., English
GALE, M. K., Planning Public Policy Management
GALL, M. D., Education Policy and Management
GARCIA-PABON, L., Romance Languages
GARY, S. N., Law
GASSAMA, I. J., Law
GAST, W. G., Architecture
GENASCI, D. B., Architecture
GEORGE, K. M., Anthropology
GEORGE, O., English
GERBER, T. P., Sociology
GERNON, H., Business
GERSTEN, R. M., Special Education
GILKEY, P. B., Mathematics
GILLAND, W. G., Architecture
GIRLING, C. L., Landscape Architecture
GIVON, T., Linguistics
GLADHART, A., Romance Languages
GLASER, S. R., Business
GLEASON-RICKER, M. M., Education Policy and Management
GLOVER, E., Special Education
GOBLE, A. E., History
GOLDMAN, M. S., Sociology
GOLDMAN, P., Education Policy and Management
GOLDRICH, D., Political Science
GOLDSCHMIDT, S. M., Education Policy and Management
GOLES, G. G., Geological Sciences
GOOD, R. H., III, Special Education
GOODMAN, B., History
GORDON-LICKEY, B., Psychology
GORDON-LICKEY, M., Psychology
GOULD, E., Romance Languages
GRAFF, R. J., Fine Arts
GRAY, J., Biology
GRAY, J. A., Economics
GREENE, F. D., Law
GREENE, R. A., Comparative Literature
GREENLAND, D. E., Geography
GREGORY, S., Physics
GRIFFITH, O. H., Chemistry
GROSENICK, J. K., Education Policy and Management
GRUDIN, R., English
GWARTNEY, P., Sociology
HACKMAN, R. M., Academic Affairs
HALEY, M. M., Chemistry
HANES, J. E., History
HARBAUGH, W. T., Economics
HARFORD, W. T., Business
HARRIS, L. J., Law
HARVEY, S. M., Anthropology
HASKETT, R. S., History
HATON, D. S., Music
HAUSHALTER, G. D., Business
HAWKINS, D. I., Business
HAWLEY, D. K., Chemistry
HAWN, A. W., Architecture
HAYDOCK, R., Physics
HAYNES, S. E., Economics
HECKER, S. F., Labour Education Center
HELPHAND, K. I., Landscape Architecture
HERRICK, D. R., Chemistry
HESSLER, J. M., History
HIBBARD, J., Planning Public Policy Management
HIBBARD, M. J., Planning Public Policy Management
HICKMAN, R. C., Fine Arts
HILDRETH, R. G., Law
HINTZMAN, D. L., Psychology
HO, S., Architecture
HODGES, S. D., Psychology
HOKANSON, K. E., Comparative Literature
HOLCOMB, J. M., Fine Arts

HOLLAND, M. J., Law
HOLLANDER, J. A., Sociology
HONGO, G. K., Creative Writing
HORNER, R. H., Center on Human Devt
HOSAGRAHAR, J., Architecture
HOUSWORTH, E. A., Mathematics
HOWARD, D. R., Business
HUDSON, B. S., Chemistry
HUHNDORF, S. M., English
HULSE, D. W., Landscape Architecture
HUMMER, T. R., Creative Writing
HUMPHREYS, E. D., Geological Sciences
HURWIT, J. M., Art History
HURWITZ, R., Music
HUTCHINSON, J., Chemistry
HYMAN, R., Psychology
IMAMURA, J. N., Physics
ISENBERG, J., Mathematics
JACOBS, D., Political Science
JACOBSON, J. L., Law
JACOBSON-TEPFER, E., Art History
JAEGER, M. K., Classics
JEWETT, W. J., Architecture
JOHNSON, B. R., Landscape Architecture
JOHNSON, D. C., Chemistry
JOHNSON, L. B., Fine Arts
JOHNSON, L. T., Architecture
JOHNSON, M. L., Philosophy
JOHNSTON, A. D., Geological Sciences
JONES, B. J. K., Arts and Admin.
JONES, S. I., Landscape Architecture
KAHLE, L. R., Business
KAMEENUI, E. J., Education Policy and Management
KANAGY, R., East Asian Languages
KANTOR, W. M., Mathematics
KARLYN, K., English
KATAOKA, H. C., East Asian Languages
KAYS, M. A., Geological Sciences
KEANA, J. F. W., Chemistry
KELLETT, R. W., Architecture
KELLMAN, M. E., Chemistry
KELSKY, K. L., Anthropology
KEMPNER, K. M., Education Policy and Management
KESSLER, L. J., Journalism
KEVAN, S. D., Physics
KEYES, P. A., Architecture
KIMBALL, R. A., History
KIMBLE, D. P., Psychology
KIMMEL, C. B., Biology
KING, R. D., Business
KINTZ, L. C., English
KIRKPATRICK, L. C., Law
KLESHCHEV, A., Mathematics
KLOPPENBERG, L. A., Law
KLUG, G. A., Exercise and Movement Sciences
KOCH, R. M., Mathematics
KOHL, S. W., East Asian Languages
KOKIS, G., Fine Arts
KOLPIN, V. W., Economics
KOREISHA, S. G., Business
KRAMER, D. F., Music
KRAUS, R. C., Political Science
KRUSOE, S., Fine Arts
KYR, R. H., Music
LAFER, G. C., Labour Education
LANDE, R., Biology
LARSON, S., Music
LARSON, S. J., English
LARSON, W. A., East Asian Languages
LASKAYA, C. A., English
LAUX, D. L., Creative Writing
LAVERY, R. M., Journalism
LAWRENCE, M. S., Law
LEAHY, J. V., Mathematics
LEE, C.-R., Creative Writing
LEES, C. A., English
LEFEVRE, H. W., Physics
LEONG, A., Russian
LESAGE, J. L., English
LEVI, D. S., Philosophy
LIBERMAN, K. B., Sociology
LIBESKIND, S., Mathematics
LIN, H., Mathematics

LIVELYBROOKS, D. W., Physics
LO, V. M., Computer and Information Science
LOCKERY, S. R., Biology
LONERGAN, M., Chemistry
LONG, J. W., Chemistry
LOVINGER, R. J., Landscape Architecture
LOWENSTAM, S. D., Classics
LUCKTENBERG, K., Music
LUEBKE, D. M., History
LUKACS, J. R., Anthropology
LUKS, E. M., Computer and Information Science
LYNCH, M. R., Biology
LYONS, R. M., Creative Writing
LYSAKER, J. T., Philosophy
McCOLE, J. J., History
McDOWELL, P. F., Geography
McGOWEN, R. E., History
McKERNIE, G., Theatre Arts
McLAUCHLAN, G., Sociology
McWHIRTER, B. T., Behaviour and Communication Sciences
McWHIRTER, E. H., Behaviour and Communication Sciences
MADDEX, J. P., Jr, History
MADRIGAL, R., Business
MAITLAND-GHOLSON, J. C., Arts and Admin.
MALLE, B. F., Psychology
MALLINCKRODT, B. S., Counselling Psychology
MALONY, A., Computer and Information Science
MALSCH, D. L., Linguistics
MANCE, A. M., English
MANGA, M., Geological Sciences
MARCUS, A. H., Chemistry
MARROCCO, R. T., Psychology
MARTIN, G. M., Music
MARTINS, E., Biology
MATE, M., History
MATHAS, A., German
MATSUNAGA, S. R., Business
MATTHEWS, B. W., Physics
MATTHEWS, K. M., Architecture
MAURO, R., Psychology
MAVES, L. C., Jr, Music
MAXWELL, A., Journalism
MAY, B. D., Romance Languages
MAY, G. A., History
MEDLER, J. F., Political Science
MEEKS-WAGNER, D. R., Biology
MELONE, N. P., Business
MERSKIN, D. L., Journalism
MEYER, A. D., Business
MEYER, G. W., Computer and Information Science
MIKKELSON, W. H., Business
MILLS, P. K., Business
MITCHELL, R. B., Political Science
MOHR, J. C., History
MONROE, S. M., Psychology
MOONEY, R. J., Law
MOORE, J. R., Music
MOORE, R. S., Music
MORENO-BLACK, G., Anthropology
MORGEN, S. L., Sociology
MORROGH, A., Art History
MORSE, D. C., Business
MOSES, L., Psychology
MOSS, M. L., Anthropology
MOSSBERG, T. W., Physics
MOURSUND, D. G., Education Policy and Management
MOURSUND, J. P., Counselling Psychology
MOWDAY, R. T., Business
MOYE, G. W., Architecture
MURPHY, A. B., Geography
MYAGKOV, M. G., Political Science
NATELLA, D. C., Fine Arts
NEAL, L. L., Recreation and Tourism Management
NEVILLE, H., Psychology
NICHOLSON, K., Art History
NICOLS, J., History
NIPPOLD, M. A., Special Education
NOVKOV, J. L., Political Science

O'BRIEN, R. M., Sociology
O'CONNELL, K. R., Fine Arts
O'FALLON, J. M., Law
O'KEEFE, T., Business
ORBELL, J. M., Political Science
OSTERNIG, L. R., Exercise and Movement Sciences
OSTLER, J., History
OVERLEY, J. C., Physics
OWEN, H. J., Music
OWEN, S. W., Music
PAGE, C. J., Chemistry
PAINTER, R. W., Law
PALMER, T. W., Mathematics
PAN, Y., Business
PARIS, M. L., Law
PARK, K., Physics
PARTCH, M. M., Business
PASCOE, P. A., History
PAUL, K. H., Fine Arts
PAYNE, D. L., Linguistics
PENA, R. B., Architecture
PEPPIS, P. W., English
PETING, D. L., Architecture
PETTINARI, J. A., Architecture
PHILLIPS, N. C., Mathematics
PICKETT, B. S., Fine Arts
PIELE, P. K., Education Policy and Management
POLOGE, S., Music
PONDER, S. E., Journalism
PONTO, R. D., Music
POPE, B. C., Women's Studies
POPE, D. A., History
POSNER, M. I., Psychology
POSTLETHWAIT, J. H., Biology
POVEY, D. C., Planning Public Policy Management
POWELL, D. T., Fine Arts
PRATT, S. L., Philosophy
PRENTICE, M. H., Fine Arts
PROSKUROWSKI, A., Computer and Information Science
PROUDFOOT, R. C., International Studies
PSAKI, F. R., Romance Languages
PYLE, F. B., III, English
RACETTE, G. A., Business
RAISKIN, J. L., Women's Studies
RAMIREZ, E. C., Theatre Arts
RAMSING, K. D., Business
RAVITS, M. A., Women's Studies
RAYFIELD, G. W., Physics
RAYMER, M. G., Physics
RECKER, G. W., Music
REED, M. H., Geological Sciences
REMINGTON, S. J., Physics
RETALLACK, G. J., Geological Sciences
REYNOLDS, J. S., Architecture
RIBE, R. G., Landscape Architecture
RICE, J. L., Russian
RICE, J. M., Geological Sciences
RICE, K. S., Physical Education and Recreation Services
RICHARDS, L. E., Business
RICHMOND, G. L., Chemistry
ROBERTS, W. M., Biology
ROBINSON, D. M., Journalism
ROCHA, E., Planning Public Policy Management
ROCKETT, G. W., English
RONDEAU, J. F., History
ROSE, J., Theatre Arts
ROSS, K. A., Mathematics
ROSSI, W. J., English
ROTH, L. M., Art History
ROTHBART, M., Psychology
ROTHBART, M. K., Psychology
ROWE, G. E., English
ROWELL, J., Architecture
RUSH, K. L., Behaviour and Communication Sciences
RUSSIAL, J. T., Journalism
RUSSO, M. V., Business
RYAN, C. C., Philosophy
RYAN, W. E., II, Journalism

SABRY, A., Computer and Information Science
SADOFSKY, H., Mathematics
SANG, T., East Asian Languages
SARANPA, K., German
SAUCIER, G. T., Psychology
SAYRE, G. M., English
SCHACHTER, J., Linguistics
SCHOMBERT, J. M., Physics
SCHULTZ, K. L., German
SCHUMAN, D., Law
SCHWARZ, I. E., Special Education
SEGALL, Z., Computer and Information Science
SEITZ, G. M., Mathematics
SELKER, E. U., Biology
SERCEL, P. C., Physics
SHANKMAN, S., English
SHANKS, A. L., Institute of Marine Biology
SHAO, Q. M., Mathematics
SHAPIRO, L., Biology
SHELTON, B. S., Mathematics
SHERER, P. D., Business
SHERIDAN, G. J., Jr, History
SHERMAN, S. R., English
SHINN, M. R., Special Education
SHURTZ, N. E., Law
SIERADSKI, A. J., Mathematics
SILVA, E. C., Economics
SILVERMAN, C. T., Anthropology
SIMMONS, D. C., Education Policy and Management
SIMMONS, W. S., Art History
SIMONDS, P. E., Anthropology
SIMONS, A. D., Psychology
SIMONSEN, W. S., Planning Public Policy Management
SINGELL, L. D., Jr, Economics
SISLEY, B. L., Physical Education and Recreation Services
SKALNES, L., Political Science
SLOVIC, P., Psychology
SMITH, J. R., Business
SMITH, M. E., Music
SOHLBERG, M. M., Behavioural and Communication Sciences
SOHLICH, W. F., Romance Languages
SOKOLOFF, D. R., Physics
SOPER, D. E., Physics
SOUTHWELL, P., Political Science
SPALTENSTEIN, J. N., Mathematics
SPRAGUE, G. F., Jr, Biology
SPRAGUE, K. U., Biology
STAHL, F. W., Biology
STAVITSKY, A. G., Journalism
STEEVES, H. L., Journalism
STEIN, A. J., Sociology
STEIN, R. L., English
STEINHARDT, V., Music
STEVENS, K. A., Computer and Information Science
STEVENS, T. H., Chemistry
STEVENSON, R. C., English
STOCKARD, A. J., Sociology
STOLET, J., Dance
STONE, J. A., Economics
STORMSHAK, E. A., Behaviour and Communication Sciences
STRAKA, L. M., Music
STROM, D. M., Physics
SUGAI, G. M., Education Policy and Management
SUNDT, R. A., Art History
SUTTMEIER, R. P., Political Science
SWAN, P. N., Law
SZURMUK, M., Romance Languages
TAKAHASHI, T. T., Biology
TAN, Y., Fine Arts
TAYLOR, M. E., Psychology
TAYLOR, Q., Jr, History
TEDARDS, A. B., Music
TEICH, N., English
TERBORG, J. R., Business
TERWILLIGER, N. B., Biology
THALLON, R., Architecture
THEODOROPOULOS, C., Architecture

THOMA, M. A., Economics
THOMAS, S., Mathematics
THOMPSON, A. C., Religious Studies
TICE, J. T., Architecture
TINDAL, G., Education Policy and Management
TIRAS, S. L., Business
TOKUNO, K., Religious Studies
TOMLIN, R., Linguistics
TONER, J., Physics
TOOMEY, D. R., Geological Sciences
TROMBLEY, R., Music
TUAN, M. H. C., Sociology
TUANA, N., Philosophy
TUBLITZ, N. J., Biology
TUCKER, D. M., Psychology
TYLER, D. R., Chemistry
UDOVIC, J. D., Biology
UNGSON, G. R., Business
UPSHAW, J. R., Journalism
UTSEY, G. F., Architecture
UTSEY, M. D., Architecture
VAKARELIYSKA, C., Russian
VANDENNOUWELAND, A., Economics
VANHEECKEREN, J., Business
VAN HOUTEN, D. R., Sociology
VAN SCHEEUWIJCK, M., Music
VARGAS, M., Music
VERSACE, G. T., Music
VETRI, D. R., Law
VITULLI, M. A., Mathematics
VLATTEN, A., German
VONHIPPEL, P. H., Chemistry
WACHTER, C. L., Music
WAFF, H. S., Geological Sciences
WAGLE, K. E., Fine Arts
WALKER, H. M., Center on Human Devt
WALKER, P. A., Geography
WANG, H., Physics
WANTA, W. M., Journalism
WARPINSKI, T. L., Fine Arts
WASKO, J., Journalism
WATSON, J. C., Theatre Arts
WEEKS, E. C., Planning Public Policy Management
WEEKS, J. C., Biology
WEINSTEIN, M. G., Business
WEISS, A. M., International Studies
WEISS, J., Romance Languages
WEISS, M. R., Exercise and Movement Sciences
WEISS, R. L., Psychology
WELCH, M. C., Architecture
WELDON, R. J., Geological Sciences
WELKE, B. Y., History
WESTERFIELD, M., Biology
WESTLING, L. H., English
WESTLING, W. T., Law
WESTON, J. A., Biology
WHEELER, T. H., Journalism
WHITELAW, W. E., Economics
WHITLOCK, C. L., Geography
WIDENOR, M. R., Labour Education Center
WILLIAMS, J. P., Music
WILLIAMS, J. R., Theatre Arts
WILLIS, J. H., III, Biology
WILSON, C. B., Computer and Information Science
WILSON, M. C., Classics
WILSON, W. W., Economics
WIXMAN, R., Geography
WOJCIK, D. N., English
WOLFE, A. S., East Asian Languages
WOLFE, J. M., Mathematics
WONHAM, H. B., English
WOOD, A. M., Biology
WOOD, M. C., Law
WOOD, M. E., English
WOOLLACOTT, M. H., Exercise and Movement Sciences
WRIGHT, C. R. B., Mathematics
WRIGHT, P. L., Business
WYBOURNE, M. N., Physics
XU, D., Mathematics
XU, Y., Mathematics
YOUNG, J. E., Architecture

YOUNG, M. T., Computer Science
YOUNG, P. D., Anthropology
YUZVINSKY, S., Mathematics
ZILIAK, J. P., Economics
ZIMMER, L. K., Architecture
ZIMMERMAN, R. L., Physics
ZINBARG, R., Psychology
ZUCK, O. V., German

UNIVERSITY OF PORTLAND

5000 N Willamette Blvd, Portland, OR 97203-5798
Telephone: (503) 943-8000
Fax: (503) 943-7399
Internet: www.up.edu
Founded 1901 as Columbia Univ., present name 1930
Private control
Language of instruction: English
Academic year: August to May
Pres.: Rev. E. WILLIAM BEAUCHAMP
Provost: Dr DONALD J. STABROWSKI
Exec. Vice-Pres.: Rev. MARK POORMAN
Vice-Pres. for Financial Affairs: ALAN P. TIMMINS
Vice-Pres. for Student Affairs: Rev. GERRY OLINGER
Vice-Pres. for Univ. Operations: JIM RAVELLI
Vice-Pres. for Univ. Relations: JAMES LYONS
Registrar: BOBBI LINDAHL
Dean of the Library: DREW HARRINGTON
Library of 248,000 vols, 17,000 audio-visual resources, over 1,200 journals
Number of teachers: 320 (full-time and part-time)
Number of students: 3,800

DEANS

College of Arts and Sciences: Rev. Dr STEPHEN C. ROWAN
Graduate School: Dr THOMAS GREENE
Pamplin School of Business: ROBIN D. ANDERSON
School of Education: Prof. JOHN L. WATZKE
School of Nursing: Prof. JOANNE WARNER
Shiley School of Engineering: Dr SHARON A. JONES

PROFESSORS

ADRANGI, B., Business Admin.
ALBRIGHT, R. J., Engineering
ARWOOD, E., Education
ASARNOW, H., English and Foreign Languages
ASKAY, R., Philosophy
BAILLIE, J., Philosophy
BOWEN, E., Drama
DOYLE, R. O., Music
DRAKE, B. H., Business Admin.
DUFF, R., Psychology and Social Science
FALLER, T., Philosophy
FAVERO, T., Biology
FREED, E., Business Admin.
GAYLE, B., Communication Studies
GRITTA, P. R., Business Admin.
HODDICK, J. P., Theatre
HOSINSKI, T., Theology
HOUCK, B., Biology
INAN, A., Engineering
KHAN, K. H., Engineering
KLESYNSKI, K., Music
KOLMES, S., Biology
LINCOLN, S., Chemistry
LUM, L., Mathematics and Computer Science
MALE, J., Engineering
MASSON, L., English
MONTO, M., Sociology
MURTY, D., Engineering
RUTHERFORD, H. R., Theology
SHANK, T., Business
SHERRER, C., English and Foreign Languages
SNOW, M., Physics
UTLAUT, M., Physics
WYNNE, A., Nursing

UNIVERSITY OF WESTERN STATES

2900 NE 132nd Ave, Portland, OR 97230-3099
Telephone: (503) 256-3180
Fax: (503) 251-5723
E-mail: info@uws.edu
Internet: www.uws.edu
Founded 1904 as Marshes' School and Cure, present name and status 2010
Private control
Academic year: September to June
Pres.: Dr JOSEPH E. BRIMHALL
Vice-Pres. for Academic Affairs:: GARY SCHULTZ
Vice-Pres. for Clinics: JOSEPH PFEIFER
Vice-Pres. for Enrolment and Student Services: Dr PATRICK BROWNE
Vice-Pres. for Finance and Admin.: ERIC BLUMENTHAL
Univ. Librarian: JANET TAPPER
Number of teachers: 35
Number of students: 400

WARNER PACIFIC COLLEGE

2219 SE 68th Ave, Portland, OR 97215
Telephone: (503) 517-1020
Fax: (503) 517-1350
E-mail: admiss@warnerpacific.edu
Internet: www.warnerpacific.edu
Founded 1937 as as Pacific Bible College, present name 1959
Private control
Academic year: August to May
Pres.: Dr ANDREA P. COOK
Vice-Pres. for Academic Affairs and Dean of Faculty: Dr COLE P. DAWSON
Vice-Pres. for Institutional Advancement and External Relations: KEVIN BRYANT
Vice-Pres. for Operations: STEVE STENBERG
Dir. for Institutional Research: GALE ROID
Dean for the Adult Degree Program: TONI PAULS
Registrar: TORI CUMMINGS
Gen. Library Admin.: ALICE KIENBERGER
Library of 53,000 vols
Number of teachers: 35 (incl. 29 full time)
Number of students: 1,680

WESTERN OREGON UNIVERSITY

345 N Monmouth Ave, Monmouth, OR 97361
Telephone: (503) 838-8000
Fax: (503) 838-8067
E-mail: president@wou.edu
Internet: www.wou.edu
Founded 1856 as Monmouth Univ., present name 1997
Academic year: September to June
Pres.: MARK D. WEISS
Provost and Vice-Pres. for Academic Affairs: Dr KENT NEELY
Vice-Pres. for Student Affairs: Dr GARY L. DUKES
Dean for the Library: Dr ALLEN W. McKIEL
Registrar: MARIA L. MARTINEZ
Number of teachers: 150
Number of students: 6,600 (undergraduates and graduates)
Publication: *The WOU Magazine*

DEANS

College of Education: Dr HILDA ROSSELLI
College of Liberal Arts and Sciences: Dr STEPHEN H. SCHECK

WESTERN SEMINARY

5511 SE Hawthorne Blvd, Portland, OR 97215
Telephone: (503) 517-1800
Fax: (503) 517-1801

E-mail: western@westernseminary.edu
Internet: www.westernseminary.edu

Founded 1927 as Western Baptist Theological Seminary

Private control

Academic year: September to April

Campuses at Portland (Oregon), San Jose
and Sacramento (California)

Pres.: Dr RANDY. ROBERTS
Academic Dean and Provost: Dr RANDAL R.
ROBERTS
Vice-Pres. for Advancement: DUANE STOREY
Dean for Student Devt and Registrar: Dr
ROBERT W. WIGGINS
Library Dir: Dr ROBERT A. KRUPP

Number of teachers: 40
Number of students: 886

Publication: *Western Magazine* (2 a year).

WILLAMETTE UNIVERSITY

900 State St, Salem, OR 97301

Telephone: (503) 370-6300
E-mail: communications@willamette.edu
Internet: www.willamette.edu

Founded 1842
Private control

Pres.: STEPHEN E. THORSETT
Vice-Pres.: KRISTEN GRAINGER
Vice-Pres. for Administrative Services: JAMES
R. BAUER
Vice-Pres. for Admission and Financial Aid:
MADELEINE E. RHYNEER
Vice-Pres. for Devt and Alumni Relations:
DENISE CALLAHAN
Vice-Pres. for Enrolment Management:
MADELEINE E. RHYNEER
Vice-Pres. for Financial Affairs: WILLIAM A.
YASINSKI
Dean for Campus Life: DAVID A. DOUGLASS
Registrar: THOMAS H. HIBBARD
Dir for Library: RICHARD BREEN

Library of 285,000 vols, 1,355 periodicals
Number of teachers: 374
Number of students: 2,827

Publications: *Willamette College of Law
Journal, Willamette Scene*

DEANS

College of Law: PETER V. LETSOU
College of Liberal Arts: MARLENE MOORE
George H. Atkinson Graduate School of
Management: DEBRA J. RINGOLD
Graduate School of Education: JULIE GESS-
NEWSOME

PENNSYLVANIA

ALBRIGHT COLLEGE

POB 15234, 13th and Bern Sts, Reading, PA
19612-5234
1621 N, 13th St, Reading, PA 19604

Telephone: (610) 921-2381
Fax: (610) 921-7258
E-mail: transcripts@alb.edu
Internet: www.albright.edu

Founded 1856 as Union Seminary, present
name 1898
Private control
Academic year: May to May

Liberal arts college

Pres.: Dr LEX O. MCMILLAN, III
Provost and Vice-Pres. for Academic Affairs:
Dr ANDREA CHAPDELAINE
Vice-Pres. for Advancement: Dr TIMOTHY A.
MCELWEE
Vice-Pres. for Admin. and Financial Services:
WILLIAM W. WOOD
Vice-Pres. for Enrolment Management and
Dean for Admission: GREGORY E. EICHHORN

Vice-Pres. for Student Affairs and Dean for
Students: Dr GINA-LYN CRANCE
Library Dir: ROSEMARY DEEGAN

Library of 240,000 vols
Number of teachers: 118 (full-time)
Number of students: 1,660

Publications: *Albright Reporter, The Low-
down.*

ALLEGHENY COLLEGE

520 N Main St, Meadville, PA 16335

Telephone: (814) 332-3100
E-mail: admissions@allegheny.edu
Internet: www.allegheny.edu

Founded 1815
Private control
Academic year: September to May

Pres.: JAMES H. MULLEN, JR
Provost and Dean for College: LINDA C.
DEMERITT
Exec. Vice-Pres. and Treas.: DAVID MCINALLY
Vice-Pres. for Devt and Alumni Affairs:
MARJORIE KLEIN
Vice-Pres. for Enrolment and Communica-
tions: BRIAN DALTON
Chief Information Officer: RICHARD HOLMG-
REN
Registrar: ANN SHEFFIELD
Dean for Students: JOSEPH J. DICHRISTINA
Dir for Library: LINDA BILLS

Library of 956,133 vols, 35,000 journals,
5,000 videos and DVDs
Number of teachers: 164 (full-time)
Number of students: 2,123 (undergraduates
on campus)

Publications: *Allegheny Magazine* (3 a year),
Allegheny Review (1 a year), *Film Criti-
cism* (3 a year), *Kaldron* (1 a year), *The
Soapbox* (1 a year)

PROFESSORS

BARRY, MICHAEL J., Mathematics
BENSEL, TERRENCE, Environment Science
BOWDEN, RICHARD D., Environmental Science
BUCK, SUE, Art
BULMAN, JAMES C., English
BYWATER, WILLIAM G., JR, Philosophy and
Religious Studies
CASLER, STEPHEN D., Economics
CHIEN, ALEC F.-L., Music
CROSS, JEFFREY D., Psychology
CUPPER, ROBERT D., Computer Science
D'AMICO, DIANE, English
DELAMARTER, WILLIAM A., Psychology
DODGE, COURTENAY B., Modern and Classical
Languages
ENSBERG, PETER, Modern and Classical Lan-
guages
GEFFEN, AMARA B., Art
GOLDSTEIN, DONALD, Economics
HEPLER, LOWELL E., Music
HEUCHERT, J. W. P., Psychology
HOLLAND, GLENN S., Philosophy and Reli-
gious Studies
JAMISON, WARD M., Music
KEELEY, MICHAEL N., Communication Arts/
Theatre
LO BELLO, ANTHONY J., Mathematics
LYONS, STEPHEN M., History
MANIATES, MICHAEL F., Political Science
MICHAELS, LLOYD, English
MILLER, DAVID C., English
MUMME, RONALD L., Biology
NESSET, KIRK, English
OLSON, CARL, Philosophy and Religious Stud-
ies
OSTROFSKY, MILTON L., Biology
OZORAK, ELIZABETH W., Psychology
PALLANT, ERIC. T., Environmental Science
QUINN, LAURA, English
RAHMAN, SHAFIQUR M., Physics
RANKIN, SUSAN M., Biology

RICHTER, JOCHEN H., Modern and Classical
Languages
ROLAND, GEORGE S., Art
SCHWARTZ, ROBERT K., Geology
SEDDIG, ROBERT G., Political Science
SERRA, MARTIN J., Chemistry
SHAPIRO, BARRY M., History
SHEA, DANIEL M., Political Science
SHEFFIELD, ANN E., Chemistry
SMITH, BRUCE J., Political Science
STATMAN, DAVID, Physics
TAMASHIRO, HOWARD, Political Science
TRECKEL, PAULA A., History
WILLEY, DANIEL R., Physics
WISSINGER, SCOTT A., Biology
WOLFE, PHILLIP J., Modern and Classical
Languages

ALVERNIA UNIVERSITY

400 St Bernardine St, Reading, PA 19607-
1799

Telephone: (610) 796-8228
Fax: (610) 796-8367
E-mail: admissions@alvernia.edu
Internet: www.alvernia.edu

Founded 1926 as Teacher's Seminarium,
present name and status 2008
Private control
Academic year: August to May

Pres.: Dr THOMAS F. FLYNN
Provost: Dr SHIRLEY J. WILLIAMS
Vice-Pres. for Advancement: J. MICHAEL
PRESSIMONE
Vice-Pres. for Enrolment Management: JOHN
MCCLOSKEY, JR
Vice-Pres. for Finance and Admin.: DOUGLAS
F. SMITH
Vice-Pres. for Marketing and Communica-
tions: BRAD DREXLER
Vice-Pres. for Mission: Sis. ROSEMARY STETS
Vice-Pres. for Univ. Life and Dean for Stu-
dents: Dr JOSEPH J. CICALA
Registrar: BEKI STEIN
Library Dir: SHARON A. NEAL

Library of 92,464 vols, 900 periodicals
Number of teachers: 85
Number of students: 2,242

DEANS

College of Arts and Sciences: Dr JAMES
FOSTER
College of Professional Programmes: Dr
KAREN THACKER

AMERICAN COLLEGE

270 S Bryn Mawr Ave, Bryn Mawr, PA 19010

Telephone: (610) 526-1000
Fax: (610) 526-1465
E-mail: graduate.school@theamericancollege
.edu
Internet: www.theamericancollege.edu

Founded 1927
Private control

Distance-education instn; professional diplomas and designations; graduate degrees in
the financial sciences and management

Pres. and CEO: Dr LAURENCE BARTON
Sr Vice-Pres.: STEPHEN D. TARR
Sr Vice-Pres. for Advancement: CHARLES
CRONIN, III
Vice-Pres. for Academics and Dean: Dr WALT
J. WOERHEIDE
Vice-Pres. for Information Technology:
EDWARD M. MCEVOY
Chief Operating Officer: NEAL R. FEGELY
Exec. Dir for Online Learning: BILLY L.
WILLIAMS
Librarian: JUDITH L. HILL

Library of 8,000 vols, 500 journals
Number of teachers: 20
Number of students: 35,000

ARCADIA UNIVERSITY

450 S Easton Rd, Glenside, PA 19038-3295
Telephone: (215) 572-2900
Fax: (215) 572-0240
E-mail: admiss@arcadia.edu
Internet: www.arcadia.edu
Founded 1853, present name and status 2000
Academic year: September to May
Pres.: Dr CARL OXHOLM, III
Provost and Vice-Pres. for Academic Affairs: Dr STEVE O. MICHAEL
Vice-Pres. for Enrolment Management: MARK LAPREZIOSA
Vice-Pres. for Finance and Treas.: MICHAEL COVENEY
Vice-Pres. for Technology and Chief Information Officer, Library and Technology: STEVE ALTER
Vice-Pres. for Univ. Advancement: NICK COSTA
Gen. Counsel: MICHAEL J. KOROLISHIN
Dir for Library Services: JEANNE BUCKLEY
Registrar: BILL ELNICK
Library of 140,000 vols, 97,000 titles, 56,940 microforms
Number of teachers: 125 (full-time)
Number of students: 4,078 (2,228 undergraduate, 1,850 graduate)
Publication: *Arcadia Magazine*

DEANS

College of Arts and Sciences: Dr BARBARA NODINE
College of Global Studies: Dr DENNIS DUTSCHKE
College of Health Sciences: Dr ARCHIE J. VOMACHKA
School of Business: Dr N. J. DELENER
School of Continuing Studies: Dr ERIK NELSON

ART INSTITUTE OF PITTSBURGH

420 Blvd of the Allies, Pittsburgh, PA 15219-1301
Telephone: (412) 263-6600
Fax: (412) 263-6667
E-mail: admissions-aip@aii.edu
Internet: www.artinstitutes.edu/pittsburgh
Founded 1921, present location 2001
Private control
Academic year: July to June
Courses in advertising, culinary management, entertainment design, fashion and retail management, fashion design, hotel and restaurant management, industrial design and interior design
Pres.: GEORGE W. SEBOLT
Vice-Pres. for Academic Affairs: Dr DANIEL J. GARLAND
Vice-Pres. for Admissions: LEE COLKER
Vice-Pres. and Dir for Admin. and Financial Services: JANICE M. VUCIĆ
Vice-Pres. and Dir for Human Resources: MALINDA A. HALLET
Vice-Pres. and Dean for Student Affairs: NADINE W. JOSEPHS
Dir for Library Services: KATHLEEN S. OBER
Number of teachers: 158
Number of students: 2,200

BAPTIST BIBLE COLLEGE AND SEMINARY

538 Venard Rd, Clarks Summit, PA 18411
Telephone: (570) 586-2400
Fax: (570) 586-1753
E-mail: info@bbc.edu
Internet: www.bbc.edu
Founded 1932
Private control
Academic year: August to May
Pres.: JAMES JEFFERY
Provost and Vice-Pres.: Dr JAMES LYTLE
Seminary Dean and Vice-Pres. for Seminary Academics: Dr MICHAEL D. STALLARD
Vice-Pres. for Alumni Services and Church Relations: MEL WALKER
Vice-Pres. for Business and Finance: HAL CROSS
Vice-Pres. for College Academics: Dr BARRY PHILLIPS
Vice-Pres. for Enrolment Management and Marketing Services: KENNETH M. SHEPARD
Vice-Pres. for Institutional Advancement: DONALD PATTEN
Dean for Students: MATT POLLOCK
Registrar: ALLEN DREYER
Library Dir: JOSHUA MICHAEL
Library of 100,000 vols
Number of teachers: 45
Number of students: 1,053 (672 college, 174 graduates, 207 seminary)
Publications: *Journal of Ministry & Theology*, *Paraklesis* (3 a year), *Summit Magazine*.

BIBLICAL SEMINARY

200 N Main St, Hatfield, PA 19440
Telephone: (215) 368-5000
Fax: (215) 368-4913
E-mail: admissions@biblical.edu
Internet: www.biblical.edu
Founded 1971 as Biblical School of Theology
Private control
Campus in Philadelphia
Pres.: Dr DAVID G. DUNBAR
Vice-Pres. for Student Advancement: PAM SMITH
Dean for Faculty and Academic Advancement: R. TODD MANGUM
Dir for Library Services: DANIEL LaVALLA
Library of 52,000 vols, 400 periodicals
Number of teachers: 29 (13 full-time, 16 adjunct)
Number of students: 319
Publication: *Missional Journal* (irregular).

BRYN ATHYN COLLEGE

POB 462, 2945 College Dr., Bryn Athyn, PA 19009-0717
Telephone: (267) 502-2400
Fax: (267) 502-2658
E-mail: admissions@brynathyn.edu
Internet: www.brynathyn.edu
Founded 1877
Private control
Academic year: August to May
Pres.: Dr KRISTIN KING
Chief Financial Officer: DANIEL T. ALLEN
Dean for Academics and Faculty: Dr ALLEN J. BEDFORD
Dean for Students: KIRI K. ROGERS
Library Dir: CARROLL C. ODHNER
Library of 118,000 vols
Number of teachers: 39
Number of students: 230
Publications: *The Academy Journal*, *The Lion's Pride*

DEANS

Theological School: The Rev. Dr ANDREW M. T. DIBB

BRYN MAWR COLLEGE

101 N Merion Ave, Bryn Mawr, PA 19010-2899
Telephone: (610) 526-5000
Fax: (610) 526-6525
E-mail: info@brynmawr.edu
Internet: www.brynmawr.edu
Founded 1885
Private control
Academic year: September to May
Pres.: JANE DAMMEN MCAULIFFE
Provost: KIMBERLY E. CASSIDY
Chief Admin. Officer: JERRY BERENSON
Chief Enrolment and Communications Officer: JENNIFER RICKARD
Chief Financial Officer and Treas.: JOHN GRIFFITH
Dean for Undergraduate College: MICHELE RASMUSSEN
Dir for Libraries: ELLIOTT SHORE
Library: 1m. vols
Number of teachers: 156 (full-time)
Number of students: 1,300 (undergraduate)
Publications: *Bryn Mawr Classical Review* (online), *Bryn Mawr Review of Comparative Literature* (1 a year)

DEANS

Graduate School of Arts and Sciences: MARY OSIRIM
Graduate School of Social Work and Social Research: DARLYNE BAILEY

BUCKNELL UNIVERSITY

Telephone: (570) 577-2000
Fax: (570) 577-3760
E-mail: admisssions@bucknell.edu
Internet: www.bucknell.edu
Founded 1846 as Univ. at Lewisburg, present name 1886
Private control
Academic year: August to May
Pres.: Dr JOHN C. BRAVMAN
Provost: MICHAEL SMYER
Vice-Pres. for Devt: SCOTT ROSEVEAR
Vice-Pres. for Finance and Admin.: DAVID SURGALA
Vice-Pres. for Enrolment Management: KURT THIEDE
Dean for Graduate Studies: JAMES RICE
Dean for Students: SUSAN LITTLE LANTZ
Dir for Information Services and Resources: PARAM BEDI
Gen. Counsel: WAYNE BROMFIELD
Library of 818,837 vols
Number of teachers: 379 (358 full-time, 21 part-time)
Number of students: 3,635 (3,530 undergraduate, 78 graduate, 27 part-time)
Publication: *Aperçus*

DEANS

College of Arts and Sciences: Dr GEORGE C. SHIELDS
College of Engineering: Dr KEITH BUFFINTON

CABRINI COLLEGE

610 King of Prussia Rd, Radnor, PA 19087-3698
Telephone: (610) 902-8100
Fax: (610) 902-8539
E-mail: admit@cabrini.edu
Internet: www.cabrini.edu
Founded 1957
Private control
Academic year: August to May
Pres.: Dr MARIE ANGELELLA GEORGE
Provost and Vice-Pres. for Academic Affairs: Dr ANNE A. SKLEDER
Vice-Pres. for Enrolment Management: DENNIS KELLY
Vice-Pres. for Finance and Admin.: STEVEN FELD
Vice-Pres. for Marketing and Communications and Interim Vice-Pres. for Institutional Advancement: GENE CASTELLANO

Vice-Pres. for Student Devt: Dr CHRISTINE LYSIONEK
Dean for Graduate and Professional Studies: Dr DENNIS DOUGHTERY
Dir for Admissions: CHARLES SPENCER
Library Dir: Dr ROBERTA JACQUET
Library of 112,500 vols, 7,215 periodicals
Number of teachers: 194 (56 full-time, 138 part-time)
Number of students: 3,225 (1,300 undergraduate, 1,925 graduate)

CARLOW UNIVERSITY

3333 Fifth Ave, Pittsburgh, PA 15213
Telephone: (412) 578-6000
E-mail: admissions@carlow.edu
Internet: www.carlow.edu
Founded 1929 as Mount Mercy College, present name and status 2004
Private control
Academic year: August to May
Pres.: Dr MARY HINES
Provost and Vice-Pres. for Academic Affairs: Dr MARGARET MCLAUGHLIN
Vice-Pres. for Univ. Advancement: Dr KAREN GALENTINE
Vice-Pres. for Finance and Operations: TYLER KELSCH
Vice-Pres. for Institutional Relations: ANN RAGO
Vice-Pres. for Student Affairs: Dr CAROL A. GRUBER
Vice-Pres. for Univ. Communications and External Relations: LOUISE CAVANAUGH SCIANNAMEO
Dir of Admissions: SUSAN WINSTEL
Dir of Graduate and Adult Admissions: SUSAN SHUTTER
Registrar: JASON KRALL
Librarian: ELAINE MISKO
Library of 109,600 vols, 15,000 print and e-journals, 820 video cassettes and DVDs
Number of teachers: 280 (92 full-time, 188 part-time)
Number of students: 2,346 (1,446 undergraduate, 900 graduate)
Publications: *Accent on Progress, The Carlow Journal, The Carlow Sun* (24 a year)

DEANS

College of Arts and Science: Dr KARYN Z. SPROLES
College of Professional Studies and Graduate School: Dr M. CYNTHIA ROTHENBERGER

CARNEGIE MELLON UNIVERSITY

5000 Forbes Ave, Pittsburgh, PA 15213
Telephone: (412) 268-2000
Fax: (412) 268-7838
Internet: www.cmu.edu
Founded 1900 as Carnegie Technical Schools, present name and status 1967
Private control
Academic year: August to May
Pres.: JARED L. COHON
Provost: Dr MARK S. KAMLET
Vice-Pres. of Finance and Chief Financial Officer: DEBORAH MOON
Vice-Pres. of Univ. Advancement: ROBBEE BAKER KOSAK
Vice-Pres. for Campus Affairs: MICHAEL MURPHY
Vice-Pres. for Research: RICHARD MCCULLOUGH
Dean for Univ. Libraries: GLORIANA ST CLAIR
Library of 961,507 vols
Number of teachers: 1,316
Number of students: 11,530 (6,020 undergraduate, 5,510 graduate)
Publications: *Carnegie Mellon Today, Gigapan Magazine* (online (www.gigapanmaga-zine.org)), *Huntia, Journal of Field Robotics*

DEANS

Carnegie Institute of Technology: PRADEEP KHOSLA
College of Fine Arts: DAN MARTIN
Dietrich College of Humanities and Social Sciences: JOHN LEHOCZKY
H. John Heinz III College: RAMAYYA KRISHNAN
Mellon College of Science: FRED GILMAN
School of Computer Science: RANDAL BRYANT
Tepper School of Business: Dr ROBERT M. DAMMON

PROFESSORS

Carnegie Institute of Technology (tel. (412) 268-2481; fax (412) 268-6421; internet www .cit.cmu.edu):
AKAY, A., Mechanical Engineering
AMON, C., Mechanical Engineering
ANDERSON, J., Chemical Engineering
BAUMANN, D. M. B., Mechanical Engineering
BHAGAVATULA, V., Electrical and Computer Engineering
BIEGLER, L. T., Chemical Engineering
BIELAK, J., Civil Engineering
CAGAN, J., Mechanical Engineering
CARLEY, L. R., Electrical and Computer Engineering
CASASENT, D., Electrical and Computer Engineering
CHIGIER, N. A., Mechanical Engineering
CRAMB, A., Materials Science Engineering
DAVIDSON, C., Civil Engineering
DOMACH, M., Chemical Engineering
DZOMBAK, D. A., Civil Engineering
FRUEHAN, R. J., Materials Science Engineering
GABRIEL, K. S., Electrical and Computer Engineering
GARRETT, J. H., Civil Engineering
GARRISON, W. M., Jr, Materials Science Engineering
GELLMAN, A., Chemical Engineering
GREVE, D. W., Electrical and Computer Engineering
GRIFFIN, J. H., Mechanical Engineering
GROSSMANN, I. E., Chemical Engineering
HENDRICKSON, C. T., Civil Engineering
HOBURG, J. F., Electrical and Computer Engineering
JHON, M. S., Chemical Engineering
KHOSLA, P., Electrical and Computer Engineering
KIM, H. S., Electrical and Computer Engineering
KROGH, B., Electrical and Computer Engineering
KRYDER, M. H., Electrical and Computer Engineering
KUMTA, P., Materials Science Engineering
LAMBETH, D. N., Electrical and Computer Engineering
LAUGHLIN, D. E., Materials Science Engineering
MCHENRY, M., Materials Science Engineering
MCMICHAEL, F. C., Civil Engineering
MALY, W., Electrical and Computer Engineering
MORGAN, M. G., Engineering and Public Policy
MOURA, J. M., Electrical and Computer Engineering
NEUMAN, C. P., Electrical and Computer Engineering
OPPENHEIM, I. J., Civil Engineering
PIEHLER, H. R., Materials Science Engineering
PILEGGI, L., Electrical and Computer Engineering
POWERS, G., Chemical Engineering

PRIEVE, D. G., Chemical Engineering
REHAK, D. R., Civil Engineering
ROHRER, G., Materials Science Engineering
ROLLETT, T., Materials Science Engineering
RUBIN, E. S., Engineering and Public Policy
RUTENBAR, R., Electrical and Computer Engineering
SAIGAL, S., Civil Engineering
SCHLESINGER, E., Electrical and Computer Engineering
SHEN, J., Electrical and Computer Engineering
SIDES, P. J., Chemical Engineering
SINCLAIR, G. B., Mechanical Engineering
SIRBU, M. A., Engineering and Public Policy
SKOWRONSKI, M., Materials Science Engineering
SMALL, M. J., Civil Engineering
STANCIL, D. D., Electrical and Computer Engineering
STEIF, P. S., Mechanical Engineering
STERN, R., Electrical and Computer Engineering
STROJWAS, A., Electrical and Computer Engineering
TALUKDAR, S., Electrical and Computer Engineering
THOMAS, D. E., Jr, Electrical and Computer Engineering
WESTERBERG, A. W., Chemical Engineering
WHITE, L. R., Chemical Engineering
WHITE, R., Electrical and Computer Engineering
WICKERT, J., Mechanical Engineering
WYNBLATT, P., Materials Science Engineering
YAO, S.-C., Mechanical Engineering
YDSTIE, B. E., Chemical Engineering
ZHU, J., Electrical and Computer Engineering

College of Fine Arts (tel. (412) 268-2349; internet www.cmu.edu/cfa):
AKIN, O., Architecture
ANDERSON, B. J. B., Drama
ANDERSON, C. R., Drama
BALADA, L. I., Music
BALLAY, J. M., Design
BAXTRESSER, J., Music
BECKLEY, J., Art
BELLAN-GILLEN, P., Art
BENNETT, R., Art
BOYARSKI, D., Design
BUCHANAN, R., Design
BURGESS, L., Art
CARDENES, A., Music
COOPER, W. D., Architecture
FLEMMING, U., Architecture
FRISCH, P., Drama
HARTKOPF, V., Architecture
IZQUIERDO, J.-P., Music
JOHNSTON, B., Drama
JOSEPH, A., Music
KEELING, K., Sr, Music
KING, E., Art
KRISHNAMURTI, R., Architecture
KUMATA, C., Art
LEE, S., Architecture
LEHANE, G., Drama
LOFTNESS, V., Architecture
MAHDAVI, A., Architecture
MAIER, J., Art
MARINELLI, D., Drama
MENTZER, M., Design
MIDANI, A., Drama
OLDS, H. T., Art
PREKOP, M., Art
SLAVICK, S., Art
STITT, M., Drama
SWINEHART, R. O., Design
THOMAS, M., Music
VOGEL, C. M., Design
WADSWORTH, D. H., Drama
WEIDNER, M., Art

Dietrich College of Humanities and Social Sciences (tel. (412) 268-2830; internet hss.cmu.edu):

ANDERSON, J. R., Psychology
BALAS, E., History
BICCHIERI, C., Philosophy
CARLEY, K. M., Social and Decision Sciences
CARPENTER, J., Psychology
CARRIER, D. S., Philosophy
CLARK, M., Psychology
COHEN, S. A., Psychology
COHEN, W., Social and Decision Sciences
COSTANZO, G., English
DANIELS, J., English
DAVIS, O. A., Social and Decision Sciences
DAWES, R., Social and Decision Sciences
EDDY, W. F., Statistics
FEINBERG, S. E., Statistics
FISCHHOFF, B., Social and Decision Sciences
FLOWER, L. S., English
FREED, B. F., Modern Languages
GLYMOUR, C., Philosophy
GREENHOUSE, J., Statistics
HAYES, A. L., English
HAYES, J. R., Psychology
HOPPER, P., English
HOUNSHELL, D. A., History and Social and Decision Sciences
JOHNSTONE, B., English
JUST, M. A., Psychology
KADANE, J. B., Statistics
KASS, R. E., Statistics
KAUFER, D., English
KEECH, W., Social and Decision Sciences
KELLY, K. T., Philosophy
KENNEDY, A., English
KLAHR, D., Psychology
KLATZKY, R., Psychology
KLEPPER, S., Social and Decision Sciences
KNAPP, P., English
KOTOVSKY, K., Psychology
LEHOCZKY, J. P., Statistics
LINDEMANN, M., History
LOEWENSTEIN, G., Social and Decision Sciences
LYNCH, K., History
McCLELLAND, J., Psychology
MacWHINNEY, B., Psychology
MASTERS, H., English
MILLER, D. W., History
MILLER, J. H., Social and Decision Sciences
MODELL, J., History
REDER, L., Psychology
RESNICK, D. P., History
ROEDER, K., Statistics
SCHEIER, M. F., Psychology
SCHERVISH, M., Statistics
SCHLOSSMAN, B. F., Modern Languages
SCHLOSSMAN, S., History
SEIDENFELD, T., Philosophy
SHUMWAY, D., English
SIEG, W., Philosophy
SIEGLER, R. S., Psychology
SPIRTES, P. L., Philosophy
STEINBERG, E. R., English
SUTTON, D., History
TARR, J. A., History
TROTTER, J., History
TUCKER, G. R., Modern Languages
WASSERMAN, L., Statistics

H. John Heinz III College (tel. (412) 268-2159; fax (412) 268-7036; e-mail hnzadmit@andrew.cmu.edu; internet www.heinz.cmu.edu):

BABCOCK, L. C., Economics
BLUMSTEIN, A., Urban Systems and Operations Research
CAULKINS, J. P., Operations Research
DUNCAN, G., Statistics
FLORIDA, R., Public Policy and Management
GAYNOR, M. S., Economics and Health Policy

GORR, W., Public Policy and Management Information Systems
KRACKHARDT, D. M., Organizations and Public Policy
KRISHNAN, R., Management Science and Information Systems
LARKEY, P. D., Public Policy and Decision-making
NAGIN, D., Management
ROUSSEAU, D., Organization Behaviour
STEWMAN, S., Sociology and Demography
STRAUSS, R. P., Economics and Public Policy
TAYLOR, L., Economics and Public Policy

Mellon College of Science (tel. (412) 268-7699; fax (412) 268-3268; e-mail mcsdean@andrew.cmu.edu; internet www.cmu.edu/mcs):

ANDREWS, P. B., Mathematical Sciences
BERRY, G. C., Chemistry
BROWN, W. E., Biology
COLLINS, T., Chemistry
FEENSTRA, R., Physics
FERGUSON, T., Physics
FONSECA, I., Mathematical Sciences
FRANKLIN, G. B., Physics
FRIEZE, A., Physics
GAROFF, S., Physics
GILMAN, F., Physics
GREENBERG, J., Mathematical Sciences
GRIFFITHS, R. B., Physics
GRIFFITHS, R. E., Physics
GURTIN, M. E., Mathematical Sciences
HACKNEY, D., Biology
HEATH, D. C., Mathematical Sciences
HO, C., Biology
HOLLINGER, J. O., Biology
HOLMAN, R. F., Physics
HRUSA, W. J., Mathematical Sciences
JONES, E. W., Biology
KAPLAN, M., Chemistry
KAROL, P., Chemistry
KINDERLEHRER, D., Mathematical Sciences
KISSLINGER, L. S., Physics
KRAEMER, R. W., Physics
LEVINE, M. J., Physics
LI, L.-F., Physics
LLINÁS, M., Chemistry
McCLURE, W. R., Biology
McCULLOUGH, R., Chemistry
MAJETICH, S., Physics
MATYJASZEWSKI, K., Chemistry
MIZEL, V. J., Mathematical Sciences
MÜNCK, E., Chemistry
NAGLE, J. F., Physics
NICOLAIDES, R. A., Mathematical Sciences
OWEN, D. R., Mathematical Sciences
PATTERSON, G. D., Chemistry
RUSS, J. S., Physics
SCHÄFFER, J. W., Mathematical Sciences
SCHUMACHER, R. A., Physics
SEKERKA, R. F., Physics
SHREVE, S. E., Mathematical Sciences
STALEY, S. W., Chemistry
STATMAN, R., Mathematical Sciences
STEWART, R. F., Chemistry
SUTER, R., Physics
SWENDSEN, R. H., Physics
TA'ASAN, S., Mathematical Sciences
TARTAR, L., Mathematical Sciences
VOGEL, H., Physics
WAGGONER, A., Biology
WALKINGTON, N. J., Mathematical Sciences
WIDOM, M., Physics
WILLIAMS, J. F., Biology
WILLIAMS, W. O., Mathematical Sciences
WOOLFORD, J., Biology
YOUNG, H., Physics

School of Computer Science (tel. (412) 268-8525; fax (412) 268-5576; internet www.cs.cmu.edu):

BLELLOCH, G. E., Computer Science
BRYANT, R. E., Computer Science
CARBONELL, J. G., Computer Science
CLARK, E. M., Jr, Computer Science

FALOUTSOS, C. N., Computer Science
HARPER, R. W., Computer Science
HERBERT, M., Robotics
KANADE, T., Robotics
KIESLER, S., Human–Computer Interaction
KRAUT, R. E., Human–Computer Interaction
LEE, P., Computer Science
MASON, M. T., Computer Science
MILLER, G. L., Computer Science
MITCHELL, T. M., Computer Science
MORRIS, J., Computer Science
PAUSCH, R. F., Human–Computer Interaction
REDDY, R., Computer Science
REYNOLDS, J. C., Computer Science
SATYANARAYANEN, M., Computer Science
SCOTT, D. F., Computer Science, Mathematics and Philosophy
SHAW, M., Computer Science
SIEWIOREK, D., Human–Computer Interaction
SLEATOR, D. D., Computer Science
WAIBEL, A., Language Technologies
WING, J., Computer Science

Tepper School of Business (tel. 412-268-2268; internet www.gsia.cmu.edu):

ARGOTE, L., Organizational Behaviour
BALAS, E., Industrial Admin. and Mathematics
BAYBARS, I., Industrial Admin.
CORNUEJOLS, G. P., Operations Research and Mathematics
DUNN, D., Industrial Admin. and Statistics
EPPLE, D., Economics
GOODMAN, P. S., Industrial Admin. and Psychology
GREEN, R. C., Financial Economics
HOOKER, J., Jr, Industrial Admin.
IJIRI, Y., Industrial Admin.
KEKRE, S., Industrial Admin.
KYDLAND, F. E., Economics
LAVE, L. B., Economics
McCALLUM, B. T., Economics
MELTZER, A. H., Economics, Industrial Admin. and Public Policy
MILLER, R., Economics
MUKHOPADHYAY, T., Information Systems
SHAW, K., Economics
SPATT, C. S., Economics and Finance
SPEAR, S., Economics
SRINIVASAN, K., Industrial Admin.
SRIVASTAVA, S., Economics and Finance
TAYUR, S.
THOMPSON, G. L., Industrial Admin. and Mathematics
WILLIAMS, J., Industrial Admin.
ZIN, S., Economics and Finance

CEDAR CREST COLLEGE

100 College Dr., Allentown, PA 18104
Telephone: (610) 437-4471
Fax: (610) 437-5955
E-mail: admissions@cedarcrest.edu
Internet: www.cedarcrest.edu
Founded 1867
Private control
Academic year: August to May

Liberal arts college for women; courses in art, business and management, education and nursing; certificate course in child welfare

Pres.: CARMEN TWILLIE AMBAR
Provost: Dr ELIZABETH M. MEADE (acting)
Sr Exec. Vice-Pres. for Enrolment Management and Student Affairs: KIMBERLY OWENS
Vice-Pres. for Institutional Advancement: PATRICIA MORAN
Chief Financial Officer and Treas.: AUDRA J. KAHR
Library Dir: KYLE CRIMI

Library of 144,037 vols, 1,705 e-books, 15,053 current serials titles, 14,637 microform units, 19,329 audiovisual material
Number of teachers: 92 (full-time)
Number of students: 1,400
Publications: *Alumnae Magazine*, *Exchange* (4 a year), *Pitch*.

CENTRAL PENN COLLEGE

POB 309, 600 Valley Rd, Summerdale, PA 17093-0309
Telephone: (717) 732-0702
E-mail: admissions@centralpenn.edu
Internet: www.centralpenn.edu
Founded 1881 as Pennsylvania Business College, present status 2000
Private control
Academic year: July to September,October to December,January to March,April to June (4 terms)
Campuses in Summerdale, Lancaster and Lehigh Valley
Pres.: TODD A. MILANO
Provost: JANICE MOORE
Vice-Pres. and Chief Academic Officer: Dr MELISSA M. VAYDA
Dean for Academic Affairs: KATHY ANDERSEN
Dean for Student Services: ED LIESCH
Registrar: JEN CORRELL
Library Dir: DIANE PORTERFIELD
Number of teachers: 275
Number of students: 1,283
Publication: *PennDulum*.

CHATHAM UNIVERSITY

Woodland Rd, Pittsburgh, PA 15232
Telephone: (412) 365-1100
Fax: (412) 365-1609
E-mail: admissions@chatham.edu
Internet: www.chatham.edu
Founded 1869 as Pennsylvania Female College, present name and status 2007
Private control
Academic year: August to May
Campuses: Eden Hall campus, Eastside campus and Shadyside campus
Pres.: Dr ESTHER L. BARAZZONE
Vice-Pres. for Academic Affairs: Dr LAURA ARMESTO
Vice-Pres. for Enrolment Management: WENDY BECKEMEYER
Vice-Pres. for Finance and Admin.: WALT FOWLER
Vice-Pres. for University Advancement: RICHARD DONOVAN
Vice-Pres for Student Affairs and Dean for Students: Dr ZAUYAH WAITE
Library Dir: JILL AUSEL
Library of 117,078 vols, 970 CDs, 526 DVDs
Number of teachers: 294 (101 full-time)
Number of students: 2,220 (903 undergraduate, 1,317 graduate)

DEANS

Chatham College for Women: Dr KAROL E. DEAN
College for Graduate Studies: Dr DAVID DONNELLY
School of Sustainability and Environment: Dr DAVID HASSENZAHL

CHESTNUT HILL COLLEGE

9601 Germantown Ave, Philadelphia, PA 19118
Telephone: (215) 248-7000
Fax: (215) 248-7056
E-mail: admissions@chc.edu
Internet: www.chc.edu
Founded 1924

Private control
Pres.: Dr CAROL JEAN VALE
Provost: Dr JOHN FLYNN
Sr Vice-Pres. and Vice-Pres. for Academic Affairs: KENNETH J. SOPRANO
Vice-Pres. for Academic Affairs: Dr KENNETH J. SOPRANO
Vice-Pres. for Enrolment Management: JODIE K. SMITH
Vice-Pres. for Financial Affairs: LAURI STRIMKOVSKY
Vice-Pres. for Information Technology: Dr GEORGE P. MCKENNA
Vice-Pres. for Institutional Advancement: KENNETH M. HICKS
Vice-Pres. for Student Life: Dr LYNN ORTALE
Registrar: DEBORAH EBBERT
Dean for Library: MARY JOSEPHINE LARKIN
Library of 135,554 vols
Number of teachers: 120
Number of students: 1,543
Publication: *Chestnut Hill Magazine*

DEANS

School of Continuing and Professional Studies: Dr ELAINE R. GREEN
School of Graduate Studies: Dr STEVEN GUERRIERO
School of Undergraduate Studies: Dr CECELIA J. CAVANAUGH

MISERICORDIA UNIVERSITY

301 Lake St, Dallas, PA 18612
Telephone: (570) 674-6400
E-mail: admiss@misericordia.edu
Internet: www.misericordia.edu
Founded 1924 as College Misericordia, present name and status 2007
Private control
Academic year: August to May
Pres.: Dr MICHAEL A. MACDOWELL
Vice-Pres. for Academic Affairs: MARI P. KING
Vice-Pres. for Finance and Admin.: JOHN RISBOSKIN
Vice-Pres. for Planning, Assessment and Research: Dr BARBARA SAMUEL LOFTUS
Vice-Pres. for Student Affairs: JEAN MESSAROS
Vice-Pres. for Univ. Advancement: SUSAN M. HELWIG
Dean for Students: KIT FOLEY
Registrar: JOSEPH REDINGTON
Library Dir: MARTHA STEVENSON
Library of 71,546 vols, 2,832 video cassettes
Number of teachers: 109 (full-time)
Number of students: 2,830 (1,719 full-time, 707 part-time, 404 graduate)

DEANS

College of Arts and Sciences: Dr RUSS POTTLE
College of Health Sciences: Dr JEAN A. DYER
College of Professional Studies and Social Sciences: FRED J. CROOP

CURTIS INSTITUTE OF MUSIC

1726 Locust St, Philadelphia, PA 19103
Telephone: (215) 893-5252
Fax: (215) 893-9065
E-mail: info@curtis.edu
Internet: www.curtis.edu
Founded 1924
Private control
Academic year: September to May
Areas of study: composition conducting keyboard instruments (piano, organ, harpsichord); orchestral instruments (strings, harp, woodwinds, brass, timpani, percussion); vocal studies (voice, opera); guitar
Pres.: ROBERTO DÍAZ
Exec. Vice-Pres. for Finance and Admin.: ELIZABETH WARSHAWER

Vice-Pres. for Devt: ELIZABETH A. WRIGHT
Vice-Pres. and Dean: Dr JOHN R. MANGAN
Registrar: PAUL BRYAN
Dir of Library and Information Resources: ELIZABETH WALKER
Library of 65,000 vols incl. musical scores and books, 33,000 recordings
Number of teachers: 108
Number of students: 165
Publication: *Overtones* (2 a year).

DELAWARE VALLEY COLLEGE

Doylestown, PA 18901
Telephone: (215) 345-1500
Fax: (215) 345-8916
E-mail: info@delval.edu
Internet: www.delval.edu
Founded 1896 as Nat. Farm School, present name 1989
Private control
Academic year: August to May
Pres.: Dr JOSEPH S. BROSNAN
Vice-Pres for Academic Affairs and Dean for Faculty: Dr BASHAR W. HANNA
Vice-Pres. for Institutional Advancement: JASON KETTER
Vice-Pres. for Student Affairs: JOHN BROWN
Registrar: ROBERT P. MORAN
Library Dir: PETER KUPERSMITH
Library of 73,600 vols
Number of teachers: 81
Number of students: 2,000 (1,600 undergraduate)

DEANS

Agriculture and Environmental Sciences: RUSSELL REDDING
Business, Education, Arts and Sciences: Dr BENJAMIN E. RUSILOSKI

DESALES UNIVERSITY

2755 Station Ave, Center Valley, PA 18034-9568
Telephone: (610) 282-1100
Fax: (610) 282-2206
E-mail: admiss@desales.edu
Internet: www.desales.edu
Founded 1964 as Allentown College of St Francis de Sales, present name and status 2001
Private control
Academic year: August to May
Campuses in Bethlehem, Center Valley and Lansdale
Pres.: Fr BERNARD F. O'CONNOR
Provost and Vice-Pres. for Academic Affairs: Dr KAREN DOYLE WALTON
Vice-Pres. for Admin., Finance and Campus Environment: ROBERT SNYDER
Vice-Pres. for Institutional Advancement: THOMAS L. CAMPBELL
Vice-Pres. for Student Life: Dr GERARD JOYCE
Dean for Enrolment Management: MARY BIRKHEAD
Dean for Undergraduate Studies: Dr ROBERT BLUMENSTEIN
Dean for Students: LINDA ZERBE
Registrar: THOMAS MANTONI
Library Dir: DEBORAH MALONE
Library of 161,900 vols, 5,000 videos
Number of teachers: 521 (312 full-time and 209 part-time)
Number of students: 3,171 (2,376 undergraduate, 795 graduate)
Publication: *DeSales University Magazine* (2 a year).

DICKINSON COLLEGE

POB 1773, Carlisle, PA 17013-2896
Telephone: (717) 243-5121

Fax: (717) 245-1899
Internet: www.dickinson.edu
Founded 1783
Private control
Academic year: August to May
Global campuses: Australia, Cameroon, China, England, France, Germany, Italy, Japan, Republic of Korea, Mexico, Russia and Spain
Pres.: WILLIAM G. DURDEN
Provost: NEIL WEISSMAN
Vice-Pres. for College Advancement: CAROLYN YEAGER
Vice-Pres. for Enrolment, Marketing and Communications and Dean for Admissions: STEPHANIE BALMER
Vice-Pres. for Finance and Admin. and Treas.: THOMAS A. K. QUEENAN
Vice-Pres. for Student Devt: APRIL VARI
Gen. Counsel: DANA SCADUTO
Dean for Students: LEONARD BROWN, JR
Registrar: KAREN WEIKEL
Dir for Library: ELEANOR MITCHELL
Library of 510,000 vols, 1,600 periodical subscriptions
Number of teachers: 210
Number of students: 2,365
Publications: *Dickinson Magazine*, *The Dickinson Review* (1 a year), *Frontiers* (1 a year).

DREXEL UNIVERSITY

3141 Chestnut St, Philadelphia, PA 19104
Telephone: (215) 895-2000
Fax: (215) 895-1414
E-mail: univrel@drexel.edu
Internet: www.drexel.edu
Founded 1891 as Drexel Institute of Art, Science and Industry, present name and status 1970
Private control
Academic year: September to August
Pres.: JOHN A. FRY
Provost and Sr Vice-Pres. for Academic Affairs: Dr MARK GREENBERG
Vice-Provost for Institutional Research: Dr CRAIG N. BACH
Sr Vice-Pres. for Enrolment Management: JOAN T. MCDONALD
Sr Vice-Pres. for Finance and Treas.: HELEN Y. BOWMAN
Sr Vice-Pres. for Institutional Advancement: Dr ELIZABETH A. DALE
Sr Vice-Pres. for Student Life and Admin. Services: JAMES R. TUCKER
Sr Vice-Pres. for Univ. Communications: LORI N. DOYLE
Sr Vice-Pres. and Exec. Dir: BRIAN T. KEECH
Sr Vice-Pres. and General Counsel: MICHAEL J. EXLER
Vice-Pres. for Govt and Community Relations: DAVID E. WILSON
Vice-Pres. for Information Resources and Technology: Dr JOHN A. BIELEC
Vice-Pres. for Univ. Facilities: ROBERT FRANCIS
Vice-Pres. and Comptroller: SUSAN WILMER
Dean for Students: Dr DAVID A. RUTH
Dean for Libraries: Dr DANUTA NITECKI
Library of 611,143 vols
Number of teachers: 1,760 (1,044 full-time, 716 part-time)
Number of students: 23,500
Publications: *BMa: The Sonia Sanchez Literary Review*, *Drexel Law Review*, *Drexel Med Journal*, *Journal of Culture and Retail* (irregular), *Maya Literary Magazine*, *The Smart Set*

DEANS

Antoinette Westphal College of Media Arts and Design: ALLEN SABINSON

Bennett S. LeBow College of Business: Dr GEORGE P. TSETSEKOS
College of Arts and Sciences: Dr DONNA MURASKO
College of Engineering: Dr JOSEPH HUGHES
College of Information Science and Technology: Dr DAVID E. FENSKE
College of Nursing and Health Professions: Dr GLORIA F. DONNELLY
Drexel Univ. College of Medicine: Dr DANIEL V. SCHIDLOW
Earle Mack School of Law: Dr ROGER J. DENNIS
Goodwin College—School of Technology and Professional Studies: Dr WILLIAM F. LYNCH
Pennoni Honors College: Dr D. B. JONES
School of Public Health: Dr MARLA J. GOLD

DUQUESNE UNIVERSITY

600 Forbes Ave, Pittsburgh, PA 15282
Telephone: (412) 396-6000
E-mail: admissions@duq.edu
Internet: www.duq.edu
Founded 1878 as Pittsburgh Catholic College
Private control
Academic year: August to May
Pres.: Dr CHARLES J. DOUGHERTY
Provost and Academic Vice-Pres.: Dr RALPH L. PEARSON
Exec. Vice-Pres. for Student Life: Rev. SEAN M. HOGAN
Vice-Pres. for Univ. Advancement: JOHN PLANTE
Vice-Pres. for Legal Affairs, Gen. Counsel and Univ. Sec.: Dr LINDA DRAGO
Vice-Pres. for Management and Business: STEPHEN A. SCHILLO
Registrar: PATRICIA JAKUB
Librarian: Dr LAVERNA SAUNDERS
Library of 723,919 vols, 328,312 microforms
Number of teachers: 991 (480 full-time, 511 part-time)
Number of students: 10,011 (5,751 undergraduate, 3,620 graduate, 640 law)
Publications: *Classical World* (4 a year), *Duquesne Business Law Journal*, *Duquesne Criminal Law Journal* (2 a year), *Duquesne Law Review* (4 a year), *Duquesne University Magazine*

DEANS

Bayer School of Natural and Environmental Sciences: Dr DAVID W. SEYBERT
Mary Pappert School of Music: Dr EDWARD KOCHER
McAnulty College and Graduate School of Liberal Arts: Dr JAMES C. SWINDAL (acting)
Mylan School of Pharmacy: Dr J. DOUGLAS BRICKER
Palumbo Donahue School of Business: Dr ALAN R. MICIAK
Rangos School of Health Sciences: Dr GREGORY H. FRAZER
School of Education: Dr OLGA M. WELCH
School of Law: KEN GORMLEY
School of Leadership and Professional Advancement: Dr DOROTHY BASSETT
School of Nursing: Dr EILEEN ZUNGOLO

EASTERN UNIVERSITY

1300 Eagle Rd, St Davids, PA 19087-3696
Telephone: (610) 341-5800
Fax: (610) 341-1377
Internet: www.eastern.edu
Founded 1932 as dept of Eastern Baptist Theological Seminary, present name and status 2001
Private control
Academic year: August to May
Chancellor and Dean of Palmer Seminary: Dr CHRISTOPHER HALL
Pres.: Dr DAVID R. BLACK

Provost and Chief Academic Officer: Dr KENTON SPARKS
Sr Vice-Pres.: Dr M. THOMAS RIDINGTON
Vice-Pres. for Admin. and Univ. Registrar: DIANA BACCI
Vice-Pres. for Devt: DEREK RITCHIE
Vice-Pres. for Education: Rev. Dr ELIZABETH CONDE-FRAZIER
Vice-Pres. for Finance and Operations: J. PERNELL JONES
Vice-Pres. for Int. Relations: STEPHANIE MAC-TAVISH
Vice-Pres. for Student Devt: Dr BETTIE ANN BRIGHAM
Dir for Library: JAMES L. SAUER
Library of 500,000 vols (incl. e-books), 65,429 online periodicals
Number of teachers: 512 (145 full-time, 367 part-time)
Number of students: 4,464
Publication: *Spirit Magazine*

DEANS

Campolo College of Graduate and Professional Studies: Dr DEBRA HEATH-THORNTON
College of Arts and Sciences: Dr BETH MACLAY DORIANI
Esperanza College: Dr ELIZABETH CONDE-FRAZIER
Palmer Theological Seminary: Dr CHRISTOPHER HALL
Templeton Honors College: Dr JONATHAN YONAN

ELIZABETHTOWN COLLEGE

One Alpha Dr., Elizabethtown, PA 17022-2290
Telephone: (717) 361-1000
E-mail: admissions@etown.edu
Internet: www.etown.edu
Founded 1899
Private control
Academic year: August to May
Pres.: CARL J. STRIKWERDA
Provost and Sr Vice-Pres.: Dr SUSAN TRAVERSO
Vice-Pres. for Admin.: DAVID DENTLER
Vice-Pres. for Enrolment: PAUL CRAMER
Vice-Pres. for Financial Services and Treas.: RICHARD L. BAILEY
Vice-Pres. for Institutional Advancement and Community Relations: DAVID C. BEIDLEMAN
Dean for Faculty: FLETCHER MCCLELLAN
Dean for Students: MARIANNE CALENDA
Dir for Library: BETH ANN ZAMBELLA
Library of 256,000 vols
Number of teachers: 123 (full-time)
Number of students: 1,900
Publications: *The Business & Economics Digest*, *The Oyster* (2 a year).

EVANGELICAL SEMINARY

121 S College St, Myerstown, PA 17067-1299
Telephone: (717) 866-5775
Fax: (717) 866-4667
E-mail: info@evangelical.edu
Internet: www.evangelical.edu
Founded 1953 as Evangelical Congregational School of Theology, present name 2011
Private control
Academic year: 2 semesters
Pres.: Dr ANTHONY L. BLAIR
Vice-Pres. for Finance and Operations: KEVIN C. HENRY
Vice-Pres. for Institutional Advancement: ANN E. STEEL
Dean for Academic Programmes: LAURIE A. MELLINGER
Dean for Admissions: TOM M. MAIELLO
Registrar: ELLIS I. KIRK

Head Librarian: TERRY M. HEISEY
Library of 75,000 vols; 550 periodical titles
Number of teachers: 15
Number of students: 200

Publication: *The Evangelical Journal* (2 a year).

FRANKLIN & MARSHALL COLLEGE

POB 3003, Lancaster, PA 17604-3003
415 Harrisburg Ave, Lancaster, PA 17603
Telephone: (717) 291-3911
Fax: (717)-291-4183
Internet: www.fandm.edu

Founded 1787, present name and status 1853
Private control
Academic year: August to May

Pres.: DAN POTERFIELD
Provost: Dr ANN STEINER
Vice-Pres. for College Advancement: LEWIS E. THAYNE
Dean: Dr KENT TRACHTE
Registrar: CHRISTINE D. ALEXANDER
Librarian: PAMELA SNELSON

Library of 523,323 vols, 29,096 periodicals
Number of teachers: 217
Number of students: 2,228

Publication: *The Liberal Arts Review*.

GANNON UNIVERSITY

109 University Sq., Erie, PA 16541-0001
Telephone: (814) 871-7000
Internet: www.gannon.edu

Founded 1925
Private control
Academic year: 2 semesters

Pres.: Dr KEITH TAYLOR
Provost and Vice-Pres. for Academic Affairs: Dr LINDA FLEMING
Vice-Pres. for Enrolment: WILLIAM R. EDMONDSON
Vice-Pres. for Finance and Admin.: LINDA WAGNER
Vice-Pres. for Mission: Rev. GEORGE STROH-MEYER
Vice-Pres. for Univ. Advancement: JACK H. SIMS
Dean for Students: WARD MCCRACKEN
Registrar: MARILYN MOORE
Library Dir: KEN BRUNDAGE

Library of 265,000 vols, 4000 audiovisual items
Number of teachers: 291 (197 full-time, 144 adjunct)
Number of students: 4,076 (2,925 undergraduate, 1,151 graduate)

DEANS

College of Engineering and Business: Dr MELANIE L. HATCH
College of Humanities, Education and Social Sciences: Prof. JOHN YOUNG
Morosky College of Health Professions and Sciences: Dr CAROLYNN B. MASTERS

GENEVA COLLEGE

3200 College Ave, Beaver Falls, PA 15010
Telephone: (724) 846-5100
Fax: (724) 847-6687
E-mail: admissions@geneva.edu
Internet: www.geneva.edu

Founded 1848
Private control
Academic year: August to May

Depts: Bible, Christian ministries and philosophy; biology; business; chemistry; communication; computer science, mathematics and physics; education; engineering; English; history, political science and sociology; languages and cultures; music; psychology,

counselling and human services; physical education

Pres.: Dr KENNETH A. SMITH
Provost: KEN CARSON
Exec. Vice-Pres.: LARRY GRIFFITH
Vice-Pres. for Advancement: JEFF JONES
Chief Financial Officer: MIKE FOX
Dean for Academic Programmes: Dr MELINDA STEPHENS
Dean for Faculty and Admin.: Dr TERRI WILLIAMS
Registrar: ANDREA KORCAN-BUZZA
College Librarian: JOHN DONCEVIĆ

Library of 167,206 vols, 879 periodicals, 198,624 units of micro texts and instructional media
Number of teachers: 96 (full-time)
Number of students: 1,879

GETTYSBURG COLLEGE

300 N Washington St, Gettysburg, PA 17325
Telephone: (717) 337-6300
Fax: (717) 337-6008
E-mail: admiss@gettysburg.edu
Internet: www.gettysburg.edu

Founded 1832 as Pennsylvania College, present name 1921
Private control
Academic year: August to May

Pres.: JANET MORGAN RIGGS
Provost: CHRISTOPHER ZAPPE
Exec. Vice-Pres.: JANE NORTH
Vice-Pres. for College Life and Dean for Students: JULIE L. RAMSEY
Dir for Admissions: GAIL SWEEZEY
Library Dir: ROBIN WAGNER

Library of 425,000 vols, 11,000 sound recordings, 19,000 DVDs and videos, 3,400 linear ft of MSS and archives, 9,000 music scores, 70,800 microforms
Number of teachers: 174
Number of students: 2,600

Publication: *Gettysburg Review*.

GRATZ COLLEGE

7605 Old York Rd, Melrose Park, PA 19027
Telephone: (215) 635-7300
Fax: (215) 635-1046
E-mail: enroll@gratz.edu
Internet: www.gratzcollege.edu

Founded 1856 as Hebrew Teacher's College
Private control
Academic year: September to May

Courses in Jewish communal service, Jewish early childhood education, Jewish education, Jewish music, Jewish non-profit management, Jewish studies

Pres. and Chief Operating Officer: Dr JOY W. GOLDSTEIN
Dean for Academic Affairs: Dr JERRY M. KUTNICK
Library Dir: ELIEZER M. WISE

Library of 125,000 vols
Number of teachers: 15
Number of students: 150

GROVE CITY COLLEGE

100 Campus Dr., Grove City, PA 16127
Telephone: (724) 458-2000
Fax: (724) 458-2190
E-mail: admissions@gcc.edu
Internet: www.gcc.edu

Founded 1876
Private control
Academic year: August to May

Pres.: Dr RICHARD G. JEWELL
Provost and Vice-Pres. for Academic Affairs: Dr WILLIAM P. ANDERSON

Vice-Pres. for Financial Affairs: ROGER K. TOWLE
Vice-Pres. for Institutional Advancement: JEFFREY PROKOVICH
Vice-Pres. for Operations: THOMAS W. GREGG
Vice-Pres. for Student Life and Learning: LARRY HARDESTY
Dean for Int. Studies, Graduate Advancement and Faculty Devt: Dr CHARLES W. DUNN
Registrar: JOHN G. INMAN
Library Dir: DIANE H. GRUNDY

Number of teachers: 115
Number of students: 2,530

DEANS

Albert A. Hopeman, Jr., School of Science, Engineering and Mathematics: Dr STACY BIRMINGHAM,
Alva J. Calderwood School of Arts and Letters: Dr JOHN A. SPARKS

GWYNEDD-MERCY COLLEGE

POB 901, 1325 Sumneytown Pike, Gwynedd Valley, PA 19437-0901
Telephone: (215) 646-7300
E-mail: admissions@gmc.edu
Internet: www.gmc.edu

Founded 1948 as Gwynedd-Mercy Junior College, present name 1963
Private control
Academic year: August to December

Campuses at Bensalem, Gwynedd Valley and East Norriton

Pres.: Dr KATHLEEN OWENS
Vice-Pres. for Academic Affairs: Dr ROBERT N. FUNK
Vice-Pres. for Enrolment Management: JAMES ABBUHL
Vice-Pres. for Finance and Admin.: KEVIN O'FLAHERTY
Vice-Pres. for Institutional Advancement: GERALD MCLAUGHLIN
Vice-Pres. for Student Services: Dr CHERYL LYNN HORSEY
Registrar: THERESA ANDERSON
Library Dir: DANIEL SCHABERT

Number of teachers: 81 (full-time)
Number of students: 2,700 (1,260 undergraduate)

Publications: *The Griffin, Today*

DEANS

School of Allied Health Professions: LINDA REILLY
School of Arts and Sciences: LISA MCGARRY
School of Business and Center for Lifelong Learning: Dr MOHAMED LATIB
School of Education: Dr SANDRA D. MANGANO
School of Nursing: ANDREA HOLLINGSWORTH

HAVERFORD COLLEGE

370 Lancaster Ave, Haverford, PA 19041-1392
Telephone: (610) 896-1000
Fax: (610) 896-1224
E-mail: admission@haverford.edu
Internet: www.haverford.edu

Founded 1833 as Haverford School
Private control
Academic year: September to May

Liberal arts college

Pres.: Dr JOANNE V. CREIGHTON
Provost: LINDA BELL
Vice-Pres. for Admin. and Finance and Treas.: G. RICHARD WYNN
Vice-Pres. for Institutional Advancement: MICHAEL KIEFER
Dean for Admissions and Financial Aid: JESS H. LORD
Dean for College: MARTHA DENNEY

Registrar: LEE WATKINS
Librarian: TERRY SNYDER
Library of 595,522 vols
Number of teachers: 139 (119 full-time, 20 part-time)
Number of students: 1,177
Publication: *Haverford Magazine* (3 a year).

HOLY FAMILY UNIVERSITY

9801 Frankford Ave, Philadelphia, PA 19114
Telephone: (215) 637-7700
Fax: (215) 281-1022
E-mail: admissions@holyfamily.edu
Internet: www.holyfamily.edu
Founded 1954
Private control
Academic year: October to May (two semesters)
Campuses in Northeast Philadelphia, Newtown and Bensalem
Pres.: Sis. Dr FRANCESCA ONLEY
Vice-Pres. for Academic Affairs: Sis. Dr MAUREEN MCGARRITY
Vice-Pres. for Finance and Admin.: JOHN JASZCZAK
Vice-Pres. for Institutional Advancement: MARGARET S. KELLY
Vice-Pres. for Student Services: Sis. Dr MARCELLA BINKOWSKI
Exec. Dir for Admissions: LAUREN CAMPBELL
Dir for Library Services: LORI A. SCHWABEN-BAUER
Library of 106,000 vols
Number of teachers: 256
Number of students: 3,184 (1,971 undergraduate, 910 graduate, 22 doctoral, 281 accelerated)
Publications: *Familogue* (1 a year), *Folio, Mosaic, The Family Tree*

DEANS

School of Arts and Sciences: Dr MICHAEL MARKOWITZ
School of Business Administration: Dr JACK V. KIRNAN
School of Education: Dr LEONARD G. SOROKA
School of Nursing and Allied Health Professions: Dr CHRISTINE ROSNER

IMMACULATA UNIVERSITY

1145 King Rd, Immaculata, PA 19345
Telephone: (610) 647-4400
Fax: (610) 251-1668
Internet: www.immaculata.edu
Founded 1920 as Villa Maria College, present name and status 2002
Private control
Pres.: Sis. Dr R. PATRICIA FADDEN
Vice-Pres. for Academic Affairs: Sis. Dr ANN M. HEATH
Vice-Pres. for Finance and Admin.: JENNIFER M. SAUER
Vice-Pres. for Student Devt and Engagement: Dr BARBARA W. WILLIAMS
Vice-Pres. for Univ. Advancement: Dr STEPHEN J. PUGLIESE
Vice-Pres. for Univ. Communications: ROBERT D. COLE
Registrar: JANICE BATES
Dir for Admissions: NICOLA DiFRONZO-HEITZER
Library Dir: JEFFREY ROLLISON
Library of 115,000 vols
Number of teachers: 164
Number of students: 4,400 (3,200 undergraduate, 1,200 graduate and doctoral)

DEANS

College of Graduate Studies: Dr JANET KANE
College of LifeLong Learning: Dr SAMUEL WRIGHTSON

College of Undergraduate Studies: Sis. Dr ELAINE GLANZ

JUNIATA COLLEGE

1700 Moore St, Huntingdon, PA 16652
Telephone: (814) 641-3000
Fax: (814) 641-3199
E-mail: info@juniata.edu
Internet: www.juniata.edu
Founded 1876
Private control
Academic year: August to May
Depts: accounting, business, and economics; art; biology; chemistry; communication; environmental sciences; education; English; geology; health professions; history; information technology, computer science, and digital media; international education; international studies; mathematics; music; peace and conflict studies; philosophy; physics and engineering physics; politics; psychology; religious studies; sociology, anthropology, and social work; theatre; world languages and cultures
Pres.: Dr THOMAS R. KEPPLE, JR
Provost and Exec. Vice-Pres. for Student Devt: JAMES LAKSO
Exec. Vice-Pres. for Enrolment and Retention: JOHN HILLE
Vice-Pres. for Advancement and Marketing: GABE WELSCH
Vice-Pres. for Finance and Operations: ROB YELNOSKY
Assoc. Vice-Pres. and Chief Information Officer: DAVE FUSCO
Dean for Students: KRIS CLARKSON
Registrar: ATHENA FREDERICK
Library Dir: JOHN MUMFORD
Number of teachers: 147
Number of students: 1,619 (full-time)

KEYSTONE COLLEGE

POB 50, One College Green, La Plume, PA 18440-0200
Telephone: (570) 945-8000
Fax: (570) 945-7916
E-mail: admissions@keystone.edu
Internet: www.keystone.edu
Founded 1868 as Keystone Acad., present name 1995
Private control
Divs: business, management and technology; communication arts and humanities; education; fine arts; natural sciences and mathematics; social and behavioural sciences
Pres.: Dr EDWARD G. BOEHM, JR
Vice-Pres. for Academic Affairs and Dean for College: THEA A. HARRINGTON
Vice-Pres. for Enrolment: SARAH KEATING
Vice-Pres. for Finance and Admin.: KEVIN WILSON
Vice-Pres. for Student Affairs and Dean for Students: Dr ROBERT J. PERKINS
Registrar: KATE OWENS
Dir for Admissions: KATHRYN REILLY
Library Dir: MARI FLYNN
Number of students: 1,773

KING'S COLLEGE

133 N River St, Wilkes-Barre, PA 18711
Telephone: (570) 208-5900
Fax: (570) 825-9049
E-mail: admissions@kings.edu
Internet: www.kings.edu
Founded 1946
Private control
Academic year: August to May
Pres.: Rev. Dr JOHN RYAN
Vice-Pres for Academic Affairs: NICHOLAS A. HOLODICK

Vice-Pres for Business Affairs and Treas.: LISA MARIE MCCAULEY
Vice-Pres. for Institutional Advancement: FREDERICK A. PETTIT
Vice-Pres. for Student Affairs: JANET E. MERCINCAVAGE
Assoc. Vice-Pres. for Enrolment and Academic Services: TERESA PECK
Dean of Students: ROBERT B. MCGONIGLE
Registrar: DANIEL CEBRICK
Library Dir: Dr TERRENCE MECH
Library of 185,614 vols
Number of teachers: 235 (132 full-time, 103 part-time)
Number of students: 2,296

LA ROCHE COLLEGE

9000 Babcock Blvd, Pittsburgh, PA 15237-5898
Telephone: (412) 367-9300
E-mail: admsns@laroche.edu
Internet: www.laroche.edu
Founded 1963
Private control
Pres.: Sis. Dr CANDACE INTROCASO
Vice-Pres. for Academic Affairs and Academic Dean: Dr HOWARD J. ISHIYAMA
Vice-Pres. for Administrative Services: GEORGE ZAFFUTO
Vice-Pres. for Finance and Chief Financial Officer: ROBERT VOGEL
Vice-Pres. for Enrolment Management and Marketing: WILLIAM H. FIRMAN, JR
Vice-Pres. for Institutional Advancement: MICHAEL ANDREOLA
Vice-Pres. for Student Life and Dean of Students: COLLEEN RUEFLE
Dir for Admissions: STEPHEN STEPPE
Gen. Counsel: Dr MARY BETH FETCHKO
Registrar: JOAN CUTONE
Library Dir: LaVERNE P. COLLINS
Number of teachers: 155
Number of students: 1,356 (984 undergraduate)

LA SALLE UNIVERSITY

1900 W Olney Ave, Philadelphia, PA 19141
Telephone: (215) 951-1000
Fax: (215) 951-1892
Internet: www.lasalle.edu
Founded 1863
Private control
Academic year: August to May
Pres.: Bro. MICHAEL J. MCGINNISS
Provost: Dr JOSEPH R. MARBACH
Vice-Pres. for Univ. Adavncement: BRIAN ELDERTON
Vice-Pres. for Finance and Admin.: MATTHEW S. MCMANNESS
Vice-Pres. for Student Affairs and Dean for Students: JAMES E. MOORE
Exec. Dir for Admissions: JIM PLUNKETT
Library Dir: JOHN BAKY
Library of 375,000 vols
Number of teachers: 210 (full-time)
Number of students: 7,331 (3,359 full-time undergraduate, 1,314 part-time undergraduate and 2,658 graduate)
Publications: *Four Quarters* (4 a year), *La Salle Bulletin* (4 a year), *La Salle Magazine* (4 a year)

DEANS

College of Professional and Continuing Studies: JOSEPH Y. UGRAS
School of Arts and Sciences: Dr THOMAS A. KEAGY
School of Business: PAUL R. BRAZINA
School of Nursing and Health Sciences: Dr ZANE ROBINSON WOLF

LAFAYETTE COLLEGE

Quad Dr., Easton, PA 18042
Telephone: (610) 330-5100
E-mail: admissions@lafayette.edu
Internet: www.lafayette.edu

Founded 1826
Private control
Academic year: August to May

Pres.: DANIEL H. WEISS
Provost and Dean for Faculty: WENDY L. HILL
Registrar: FRANCIS A. BENGINIA
Dean for College: HANNAH W. STEWART-GAMBINO
Dean for Libraries: NEIL J. MCELROY

Library of 502,603 vols
Number of teachers: 213 (full-time)
Number of students: 2,360

LAKE ERIE COLLEGE OF OSTEOPATHIC MEDICINE

1858 W Grandview Blvd, Erie, PA 16509-1025
Telephone: (814) 866-6641
Fax: (814) 866-8123
Internet: www.lecom.edu

Founded 1993
Private control
Academic year: August to May

Campuses: Greensburg and Seton Hill, Pennsylvania; Bradenton, Florida

Pres. and CEO: Dr JOHN M. FERRETT
Provost, Sr Vice-Pres. and Dean for Academic Affairs: SILVIA M. FERRETTI
Vice-Pres. for Academic Affairs: Dr HERSHEY BELL
Vice-Pres. for Fiscal Affairs and Chief Financial Officer: RICHARD P. OLINGER
Dir for Student Affairs: RONALD SHIVELY

DEANS

School of Pharmacy: Dr HERSHEY BELL

LANCASTER BIBLE COLLEGE

901 Eden Rd, Lancaster, PA 17601
Telephone: (717) 569-7071
E-mail: admissions@lbc.edu
Internet: www.lbc.edu

Founded 1933
Private control

Depts: arts and sciences, Bible and theology, Church and min. leadership, counselling and social work, education, health and physical education, worship and performing arts

Pres.: Dr PETER W. TEAGUE
Exec. Vice-Pres.: RICHARD A. WILSON
Vice-Pres. for Academic Affairs: Dr PHILIP E. DEARBORN
Vice-Pres. for Enrolment Management: JOSHUA BEERS
Dean for Undergraduate Education: G. GORDON GREGORY, JR
Library Dir: GERALD E. LINCOLN

Library of 201,051 vols
Number of teachers: 106 (54 full-time, 52 part-time)
Number of students: 1,113 (955 undergraduate, 158 graduate)

LANCASTER GENERAL COLLEGE OF NURSING & HEALTH SCIENCES

410 N Lime St, Lancaster, PA 17602
Telephone: (717) 544-4912
E-mail: lgc_admissions@lancastergeneral.org
Internet: www.lancastergeneralcollege.edu

Founded 1903 as Lancaster Gen. Hospital School of Nursing, present name and status 2001
Private control

Academic year: August to May

Pres.: SIMCOX MARY GRACE
Vice-Pres. for Academic Affairs: PENNI ATEN LONGENECKER
Vice-Pres. for Finance and Admin.: THOMAS HULSTINE
Vice-Pres. for Learning Devt: DONNA WILLIAMSON
Dean for Enrolment Management: SANDRA ZERBY
Dir of Admissions: LYN LONGENECKER
Registrar: GERALDINE MAY
Library Dir: CYNTHIA MCCLELLAN

Library of 8,000 vols, incl. 400 print journals

Publication: *Destiny* (3 a year)

DEANS

Division of General Education: Dr PEGGY ROSARIO
Division of Health Sciences: CONSTANCE CORRIGAN
Division of Nursing: CHERYL GRAB

LANCASTER THEOLOGICAL SEMINARY

555 W James St, Lancaster, PA 17603
Telephone: (717) 393-0654
Fax: (717) 393-4254
E-mail: seminary@lancasterseminary.edu
Internet: www.lts.org

Founded 1825 as Seminary of the Reformed Church
Private control

Pres.: Dr CAROL E. LYTCH
Vice-Pres. for Academic Affairs and Acting Dean: Dr DAVID M. MELLOTT
Vice-Pres. for Business and Finance: VALERIE A. CALHOUN
Vice-Pres. for Advancement and Communications: CRYSTAL MILLS
Library Dir: RICHARD BERG

Library of 150,000 vols
Number of teachers: 12
Number of students: 150

LEBANON VALLEY COLLEGE

101 N College Ave, Annville, PA 17003-1400
Telephone: (717) 867-6100
Fax: (717) 867-6018
E-mail: admission@lvc.edu
Internet: www.lvc.edu

Founded 1866
Private control
Academic year: August to May

Courses in physical therapy, business administration, music education and science education

Pres.: STEPHEN C. MACDONALD
Vice-Pres. for Academic Affairs and Dean for Faculty: MICHAEL R. GREEN (acting)
Vice-Pres. for Admin. and Information Technology: ROBERT A. RILEY
Vice-Pres. for Advancement: ANNE M. BERRY
Vice-Pres. for Enrolment: WILLIAM J. BROWN
Vice-Pres. for Finance: DEBORAH R. FULLAM
Vice-Pres. for Student Affairs: GREGORY H. KRIKORIAN
Registrar: JEREMY A. MAISTO
Dir for Library: FRANK MOLS

Library of 225,000 vols, 3,000 print and e-journal subscriptions
Number of teachers: 102 (full-time)
Number of students: 2,102 (1,630 full-time undergraduate, 155 part-time undergraduate, 317 graduate)

Publication: *The Valley Magazine*.

LEHIGH UNIVERSITY

27 Memorial Dr., W, Bethlehem, PA 18015-3089
Telephone: (610) 758-3000
Fax: (610) 758-3154
Internet: www.lehigh.edu

Founded 1865
Private control
Academic year: August to May

Pres.: ALICE P. GAST
Provost and Vice-Pres. for Academic Affairs: PATRICK V. FARRELL
Vice-Provost for Institutional Research: J. GARY LUTZ
Vice-Provost for Library and Technology Services: BRUCE M. TAGGART
Vice-Provost for Student Affairs: JOHN W. SMEATON
Vice-Pres. for Advancement: JOSEPH KENDER
Vice-Pres. for Communications and Public Affairs: FREDERICK J. MCGRAIL
Vice-Pres. for Finance and Admin.: MARGARET F. PLYMPTON
Vice-Pres. for Int. Affairs: MOHAMED EL-AASSER
Gen. Counsel: FRANK ROTH
Registrar: EMIL GNASSO

Library of 1,324,500 vols, 25,000 periodicals, 100,000 e-books
Number of teachers: 666 (463 full-time)
Number of students: 7,036 (4,766 undergraduate, 2,270 graduate)

DEANS

College of Arts and Sciences: Dr DONALD E. HALL
College of Business and Economics: PAUL R. BROWN
College of Education: SASSO GARY
P. C. Rossin College of Engineering and Applied Science: S. DAVID WU

PROFESSORS

College of Arts and Sciences (tel. (610) 758-3300):

ABEL, J. H., Biological Sciences
ALHADEFF, J., Chemistry
BARKEY, H., Int. Relations
BAYLOR, M., History
BEARN, G., Philosophy
BEHE, M., Biological Sciences
BEIDLER, P., English
BICKHARD, M., Psychology
BORSE, G., Physics
BROSS, A., English
CARRELL-SMITH, K., History
CARSON, R., Earth and Environmental Sciences
CHABUT, M.-H., Modern Languages and Literature
COLON, F., Political Science
CUNDALL, D., Biological Sciences
DAVIS, D., Mathematics
DELEO, G., Physics
DOBRIC, V., Mathematics
DOTY, A., English
DUFFY, I., History
EISENBERG, B., Mathematics
EVENSON, E., Earth and Environmental Sciences
FERGUS, J., English
FIFER, E., English
FOLK, R., Physics
FRIEDMAN, S., Journalism
GALLAGHER, E., English
GANS, L., Art and Architecture
GATEWOOD, J., Sociology and Anthropology
GHOSH, B. K., Mathematics
GIRARDOT, N., Religion
GOLDMAN, S., Philosophy
GORNEY, C., Journalism
GUNTON, J., Physics
HEINDEL, N. D., Chemistry

HERRENKOHL, R., Sociology and Anthropology
HICKMAN, P., Physics
HUANG, W.-M., Mathematics
HUENNEKENS, J., Physics
HYLAND, D., Psychology
ITZKOWITZ, M., Biological Sciences
KANOFSKY, A., Physics
KHABBAZ, S., Mathematics
KIM, Y., Physics
KING, J. P., Mathematics
KLIER, K., Chemistry
KODAMA, K., Earth and Environmental Sciences
KRAFT, K., Religion
KRAWIEC, S., Biological Sciences
KRITZ, A., Physics
KROLL, B., English
LARSEN, J., Chemistry
LASKER, J., Sociology and Anthropology
LULE, J. F., Journalism
McCLUSKEY, G. E., Mathematics
McINTOSH, J., Sociology and Anthropology
MALT, B., Psychology
MARKLEY, N. G., Mathematics
MASON, D., Art and Architecture
MATTHEWS, R., Political Science
MELTZER, A. S., Earth and Environmental Sciences
MENON, M. R., International Relations
MILET, J., Theatre
MOON, B., International Relations
MORGAN, E., Political Science
MUNDHENK, R., English
MYERS, P. B., Earth and Environmental Sciences
NYBY, J. G., Biological Sciences
OLSON, L., Political Science
OU-YANG, D., Physics
PANKENIER, D., Modern Languages and Literature
PETERS, T., Art and Architecture
PHILLIPS, C. R., History
RAPOSA, M., Religion
REGEN, S. L., Chemistry
RICHTER, M., Psychology
RIPA, A., Theatre
ROSENWEIN, R., Sociology and Anthropology
SAEGER, J. S., History
SALATHE, E., Mathematics
SALERNI, P., Music
SAMETZ, S., Music
SANDS, J., Biological Sciences
SCHRAY, K., Chemistry
SCOTT, W. R., History
SILBERSTEIN, L., Religion
SIMMONS, G. W., Chemistry
SIMON, N., Biological Sciences
SIMON, R., History
SINE, N., Music
SMALL, D., Sociology and Anthropology
SMOLANSKY, O., International Relations
SODERLUND, J., History
STANLEY, L., Mathematics
STAVOLA, M., Physics
STEFFEN, L., Religion
STENGLE, G. A., Mathematics
STEWART-GAMBINO, H., Political Science
TANNENBAUM, N., Sociology and Anthropology
TOULOUSE, J., Physics
TRAISTER, B., English
USSLER, C., Art and Architecture
VIERA, R., Art and Architecture
WEINTRAUB, S. H., Mathematics
WEISS, R., Philosophy
WEISSLER, L. E. C., Religion
WILLIAMSON, C., Earth and Environmental Sciences
WOLFGANG, L., Modern Languages and Literature
WRIGHT, B., Religion
WYLIE, R., International Relations
YUKICH, J., Mathematics
ZAKNIC, I., Art and Architecture

ZEITLER, P., Earth and Environmental Sciences
ZEROKA, D., Chemistry

College of Business and Economics (tel. (610) 758-3400):
ARONSON, J. R., Business and Economics
BARSNESS, R. W., Management
BUELL, S. G., Finance
DEARDEN, J. A., Economics
DURAND, R. M., Management and Marketing
FALCINELLI, D. F., Marketing and Management
HYCLAK, T. J., Economics
KING, A. E., Economics
KISH, R. J., Finance
KOLCHIN, M. G., Management
KUCHTA, R., Management and Marketing
LARGAY, J. A., III, Accounting
MUNLEY, V. G., Economics
NATION, G. A., III, Law and Business
NAYAR, N., Finance
O'BRIEN, A. P., Economics
PAUL, J. W., Accounting
SHERER, S. A., Management and Technology
SINCLAIR, K. P., Accounting
SIVAKUMAR, K., International Marketing and Logistics
SMACKEY, B. M., Marketing and Manufacturing Systems Engineering
STEVENS, J. E., Management
TAYLOR, L. W., Economics
THORNTON, R. J., Economics
ZIRKEL, P. A., Education and Law

College of Education (tel. (610) 758-3225):
BAMBARA, L. M., Special Education
CATES, W. M., Instructional Design and Devt
COLE, C., Psychology
DuPAUL, G., Psychology
JITENDRA, A., Special Education
MILLER, D. N., Psychology
SHAPIRO, E., Psychology
ZIRKEL, P., Education and Law

P. C. Rossin College of Engineering and Applied Science (tel. (610) 758-4025):
BLYTHE, P. A., Chemical Engineering, Mechanical Engineering and Mechanics
BOULT, T. E., Computer Science and Engineering
BROWN, F. T., Mechanical Engineering and Mechanics
CARAM, H. S., Chemical Engineering
CARGILL, G. S., III, Materials Science and Engineering
CHAN, H. M., Materials Science and Engineering
CHARLES, M., Chemical Engineering
CHAUDHURY, M. K., Chemical Engineering
CHEN, J. C., Chemical Engineering
CHRISTODOULIDES, D., Electrical and Computer Engineering
COULTER, J. P., Mechanical Engineering and Mechanics
DECKER, D. R., Electrical and Computer Engineering
DELPH, T. J., Mechanical Engineering and Mechanics
EADES, J. A., Materials Science and Engineering
EL-AASSER, M. S., Chemical Engineering
FARRINGTON, G. C., Chemical Engineering
FISHER, J. W., Civil and Environmental Engineering
FREY, D. R., Electrical and Computer Engineering
FRITCHMAN, B. D., Electrical and Computer Engineering
GARDINER, K. M., Industrial and Systems Engineering
GROOVER, M. P., Industrial and Systems Engineering

GULDEN, S. L., Computer Science and Engineering
HARLOW, D. G., Mechanical Engineering and Mechanics
HARMER, M. P., Materials Science and Engineering
HARTRANFT, R. J., Mechanical Engineering and Mechanics
HATALIS, M., Electrical and Computer Engineering
HEINDEL, N. D., Chemistry
HERTZBERG, R. W., Materials Science and Engineering
HILLMAN, D. J., Computer Science and Engineering
HSU, J. T., Chemical Engineering
HWANG, J. C. M., Electrical and Computer Engineering
JAIN, H., Materials Science and Engineering
JOHNSON, S. H., Mechanical Engineering and Mechanics
KALNINS, A., Mechanical Engineering and Mechanics
KAY, E. J., Computer Science and Engineering
KAZAKIA, J. Y., Mechanical Engineering and Mechanics
KLEIN, A., Chemical Engineering
KORTH, H., Computer Science and Engineering
KOSTEM, C. N., Civil and Environmental Engineering
LARSEN, J. W., Chemistry
LENNON, G. P., Civil and Environmental Engineering
LEVY, E. K., Mechanical Engineering and Mechanics
LU, L.-W., Civil and Environmental Engineering
LUCAS, R. A., Mechanical Engineering and Mechanics
LUYBEN, W. L., Chemical Engineering
McAULAY, A. D., Electrical and Computer Engineering
McHUGH, A., Chemical Engineering
MACPHERSON, A. K., Mechanical Engineering and Mechanics
MARDER, A. R., Materials Science and Engineering
NAGEL, R. N., Computer Science and Engineering
NETI, S., Mechanical Engineering and Mechanics
NIED, H. F., Mechanical Engineering and Mechanics
NOTIS, M. R., Materials Science and Engineering
OCHS, J. B., Mechanical Engineering and Mechanics
ODREY, N. G., Industrial and Systems Engineering
OU-YANG, H. D., Physics
REGEN, S. L., Chemistry
ROBERTS, R., Mechanical Engineering and Mechanics
ROCKWELL, D. O., Mechanical Engineering and Mechanics
SAWYERS, K. N., Mechanical Engineering and Mechanics
SCHIESSER, W. E., Chemical Engineering
SCHRAY, K. J., Chemistry
SENGUPTA, A. K., Chemical Engineering, Civil and Environmental Engineering
SILEBI, C. A., Chemical Engineering
SIMMONS, G. W., Chemistry
SMITH, C. R., Mechanical Engineering and Mechanics
SORENSEN, R. M., Civil and Environmental Engineering
SPERLING, L. H., Chemical Engineering, Materials Science and Engineering
STENGER, H. G., Jr, Chemical Engineering
TARBY, S. K., Materials Science and Engineering

TZENG, K. K., Electrical and Computer Engineering
VARLEY, E., Mechanical Engineering and Mechanics
VOLOSHIN, A. S., Mechanical Engineering and Mechanics
WACHS, I. E., Chemical Engineering
WALKER, J. D. A., Mechanical Engineering and Mechanics
WEI, R. P., Mechanical Engineering and Mechanics
WEISMAN, R. N., Civil and Environmental Engineering
WHITE, M. H., Electrical and Computer Engineering
WILLIAMS, D. B., Materials Science and Engineering
WILSON, J. L., Civil and Environmental Engineering
WU, S. D., Industrial and Systems Engineering
ZIMMERS, E. W., Jr, Industrial and Systems Engineering

LINCOLN UNIVERSITY OF THE COMMONWEALTH OF PENNSYLVANIA

POB 179, 1570 Baltimore Pike, PA, 19352
Telephone: (484) 365-8000
Fax: (484) 365-8109
E-mail: admiss@lu.lincoln.edu
Internet: www.lincoln.edu
Founded 1854 as Ashmun Institute
Academic year: August to April
Pres.: Dr ROBERT R. JENNINGS
Provost and Sr Vice-Pres. for Academic Affairs: Dr GRANT VENERABLE, II
Exec. Vice-Pres.: MICHAEL B. HILL
Exec. Vice-Pres. for Devt, Relations and Services: MICHAEL HILL
Vice-Pres. for External Affairs: REGAN FARLEY
Vice-Pres. for Fiscal Affairs and Admin.: JAMES T. LEWIS
Vice-Pres. for Institutional Advancement: ANDRE DIXON
Vice-Pres. for Student Affairs: F. CARL WALTON
Dean for Enrolment Services: THELMA ROSS
Dean for Students: JERRYL BRIGGS
Registrar: CATHERINE RUTLEDGE
Library Dir: NEAL CARSON
Library of 159,007 vols
Number of teachers: 108 (full-time)
Number of students: 2,240

DEANS

School of Humanities and Graduate Studies: (vacant)
School of Natural Sciences and Mathematics: JOHN O. CHIKWEM
School of Social Sciences and Behavioural Studies: Dr PATRICIA A. JOSEPH

LUTHERAN THEOLOGICAL SEMINARY AT GETTYSBURG

61 Seminary Ridge, Gettysburg, PA 17325-1795
Telephone: (717) 334-6286
Fax: (717) 334-3469
E-mail: info@ltsg.edu
Internet: www.ltsg.edu
Founded 1826, present location 1832
Private control
Academic year: September to May
Pres.: Rev. MICHAEL L. COOPER-WHITE
Dean: Rev. Dr ROBIN J. STEINKE
Registrar: Rev. Dr MARTY STEVENS
Treas.: LARRY WEBBER
Library Dir: BRIANT BOHLEKE
Library of 190,000 vols
Number of teachers: 21

Number of students: 228
Publication: *Seminary Ridge Review* (2 a year).

LUTHERAN THEOLOGICAL SEMINARY AT PHILADELPHIA

7301 Germantown Ave, Philadelphia, PA 19119-1794
Telephone: (215) 248-4616
Fax: (215) 248-4577
E-mail: admissions@ltsp.edu
Internet: www.ltsp.edu
Founded 1864
Private control
Pres.: Rev. Dr PHILIP D. W. KREY
Vice-Pres. for Advancement: Rev. JOHN V. PUOTINEN
Dean: PAUL RAJASHEKAR
Dir for Admissions: Rev. LOUISE N. JOHNSON
Registrar: RENÉ DIEMER
Library Dir: KARL KRUEGER
Library of 200,000 vols
Number of teachers: 35
Number of students: 220 (full-time)
Publication: *PS Magazine*.

LYCOMING COLLEGE

700 College Pl., Williamsport, PA 17701
Telephone: (717) 321-4000
Fax: (717) 321-4337
E-mail: admissions@lycoming.edu
Internet: www.lycoming.edu
Founded 1812 as Williamsport Acad. for the Education of Youth in the English and other Languages, in the Useful Arts, Science and Literature, present name 1948
Private control
Areas of study: liberal arts and sciences, health care administration, actuarial mathematics and environmental sustainability
Pres.: Dr JAMES E. DOUTHAT
Provost and Dean: Dr PHILIP SPRUNGER
Vice-Pres. for Admin. and Planning: SUE S. GAYLOR
Vice-Pres. for College Advancement: CHIP EDMONDS
Vice-Pres. for Admissions and Financial Aid: JAMES D. SPENCER
Dean for Student Affairs: Dr DANIEL P. MILLER
Registrar: MARY SAVOY
Dir for Library Services: JANET MCNEIL HURLBERT
Library of 187,722 vols, 1,200 periodicals
Number of teachers: 90 (full-time)
Number of students: 1,400
Publication: *Lycoming Magazine*.

MARYWOOD UNIVERSITY

2300 Adams Ave, Scranton, PA 18509-1598
Telephone: (570) 348-6211
Fax: (570) 961-4763
E-mail: yourfuture@marywood.edu
Internet: www.marywood.edu
Founded 1915 as Marywood College
Private control
Pres.: Sis. Dr ANNE MUNLEY
Vice-Pres. for Academic Affairs: Dr ALAN M. LEVINE
Vice-Pres. for Business Affairs and Treas.: JOSEPH X. GARVEY
Vice-Pres. for Student Life: Dr RAYMOND P. HEATH
Vice-Pres. for Univ. Advancement: CLAYTON N. PHEASANT
Dir for Library: CATHY SCHAPPERT
Library of 216,191 vols
Number of teachers: 400 (151 full-time)
Number of students: 3,400

DEANS

College of Health and Human Services: Dr MARK E. RODGERS
College of Liberal Arts and Sciences: Dr MICHAEL A. FOLEY
Insalaco College of Creative and Performing Arts: COLLIER A. PARKER
Reap College of Education and Human Development: Dr MARY ANNE FEDRICK
School of Architecture: GREGORY K. HUNT

MERCYHURST COLLEGE

501 E 38th St, Erie, PA 16546-0001
Telephone: (814) 824-2000
Internet: www.mercyhurst.edu
Founded 1926
Private control
Academic year: September to May
Pres.: Dr THOMAS J. GAMBLE
Provost: Dr JAMES M. ADOVASIO
Exec. Vice-Pres.: Dr GARY M. BROWN
Vice-Pres. for Academic Affairs: Dr PHILLIP J. BELFIORE
Vice-Pres. for Enrolment Management: Dr GERAD TOBIN
Vice-Pres. for Finance and Treas.: JANE M. KELSEY
Vice-Pres. for Advancement: Dr DAVID LIVINGSTON
Registrar: Sis. PATRICIA WHALEN
Dir for Libraries: DARCI JONES
Number of teachers: 149 (full-time)
Number of students: 3,077

MESSIAH COLLEGE

One College Ave, Grantham, PA 17027
Telephone: (717) 766-2511
Fax: (717) 691-6025
E-mail: admiss@messiah.edu
Internet: www.messiah.edu
Founded 1909
Private control
Satellite campuses: Philadelphia and Harrisburg
Academic year: September to May
Pres.: Dr KIM S. PHIPPS
Provost: Dr RANDALL G. BASINGER
Vice-Pres. for Advancement: BARRY G. GOODLING
Vice-Pres. for Finances: Dr LOIS J. VOIGT
Vice-Pres. for Operations: KATHRYNNE G. SHAFER
Vice-Pres. of Enrolment Management: JOHN CHOPKA
Vice-Provost and Dean for Students: Dr KRISTIN M. HANSEN-KIEFFER
Registrar: JAMES J. SOTHERDEN
Dir for Library: JONATHAN D. LAUER
Library of 292,272 vols, 103,550 microforms and 20,328 audiovisual materials
Number of teachers: 288 (177 full-time, 111 part-time)
Number of students: 2,976 (2,805 undergraduate, 171 graduate)
Publication: *The Bridge*

DEANS

School of Arts: Dr RICHARD E. ROBERSON
School of Business, Education and Social Sciences: Dr SUSAN S. HASSELER
School of Humanities: Dr PETER K. POWERS
School of Science, Engineering and Health: Dr W. RAY NORMAN

MOORE COLLEGE OF ART AND DESIGN

20th Sst and The Parkway, Philadelphia, PA 19103-1179
Telephone: (215) 568-4000
Fax: (215) 568-8017

E-mail: info@moore.edu
Internet: www.moore.edu

Founded 1848 as the Philadelphia School of Design for Women, present name 1989
Private control
Academic year: August to May

Pres.: Dr HAPPY CRAVEN FERNANDEZ
Vice-Pres. for Finance and Admin.: WILLIAM L. HILL, II
Academic Dean: DONA LANTZ
Dean for Students: RUTH ROBBINS
Registrar: DIANNE SARIDAKIS
Library Dir: SHARON WATSON-MAURO

Number of teachers: 135
Number of students: 582 (527 undergraduate, 55 graduate and postgraduate)

MORAVIAN COLLEGE

1200 Main St, Bethlehem, PA 18018
Telephone: (610) 861-1300
Fax: (610) 861-1445
E-mail: admissions@moravian.edu
Internet: www.moravian.edu

Founded 1742, present name and status 1954
Private control
Academic year: August to May

Pres.: Dr CHRISTOPHER M. THOMFORDE
Vice-Pres. for Academic Affairs and Dean for Faculty: GORDON WEIL
Vice-Pres. for Admin.: MARK REED
Vice-Pres. for Enrolment Management: KEN HUUS
Vice-Pres. for Institutional Advancement: GARY CARNEY
Vice-Pres. for Student Affairs: BEVERLY J. KOCHARD
Dean for Student Life: NICOLE LOYD
Registrar: MARY MARGARET GROS
Library Dir: DAVID SCHAPPERT

Library of 256,000 vols
Number of teachers: 120 (full-time)
Number of students: 1,564

Publication: *Moravian College Magazine.*

MOUNT ALOYSIUS COLLEGE

7373 Admiral Peary Highway, Cresson, PA 16630-1999
Telephone: (814) 886-4131
Internet: www.mtaloy.edu

Founded 1853
Private control

Offers courses in arts and sciences; business administration; community counselling; criminal justice management and psychology

Pres.: Dr THOMAS P. FOLEY
Sr Vice-Pres. for Academic Affairs and Dean for Faculty: Dr TIMOTHY FULOP
Vice-Pres. for Enrolment Management and Dean for Undergraduate and Graduate Admissions: FRANCIS C. CROUSE, JR
Vice-Pres. for Student Affairs: Dr JANE M. GRASSADONIA
Registrar: Dr CHRISTOPHER LOVETT
Dir for Library: Dr BRANDI PORTER

Library of 100,000 vols, 15,000 current print and e-journals
Number of teachers: 175
Number of students: 2,500 (1,300 full-time undergraduate, 1,200 part-time undergraduate, graduate and continuing education)

MUHLENBERG COLLEGE

2400 W Chew St, Allentown, PA 18104-5586
Telephone: (484) 664-3100
Fax: (484) 664-3234
E-mail: admissions@muhlenberg.edu
Internet: www.muhlenberg.edu

Founded 1848, present name 1867

Private control
Liberal arts and pre-professional studies

Pres.: PEYTON RANDOLPH HELM
Provost: Dr JOHN RAMSAY
Vice-Pres. for Devt and Alumni Relations: REBEKKAH L. BROWN
Dean for Academic Life: Dr SHINER WILSON
Dean for Admissions and Financial Aid: CHRIS HOOKER-HARING
Dean for Students: KAREN GREEN
Library Dir: TINA HERTEL

Library of 310,000 vols, 360,000 microforms, 29,000 print and e-journals
Number of teachers: 285 (170 full-time, 115 part-time)
Number of students: 2,225

NEUMANN UNIVERSITY

One Neumann Dr., Aston, PA 19014-1298
Telephone: (610) 459-0905
Fax: (610) 459-1370
E-mail: neumann@neumann.edu
Internet: www.neumann.edu

Founded 1965 as Our Lady of Angels College, present name and status 2009
Private control
Academic year: August to May

Pres.: Dr ROSALIE M. MIRENDA
Vice-Pres. for Academic Affairs: Dr GERALD P. O'SULLIVAN
Vice-Pres. for Enrolment Management and Student Affairs: DENNIS MURPHY
Vice-Pres. for Finance and Admin.: JOSEPH GORMAN
Vice-Pres. for Institutional Advancement and College Relations: HENRY A. SUMNER
Vice-Pres. for Mission and Min. Affairs: Sr MARGUERITE O'BEIRNE
Vice-Pres. and Gen. Counsel: JONATHAN PERI
Dean of Students: Sr Dr PEGGY EGAN
Registrar: LARRY S. FRIEDMAN
Library Dir: TIFFANY McGREGOR

Number of teachers: 321 (97 full-time, 224 part-time)
Number of students: 3,087 (2,617 undergraduate, 470 graduate)

Publications: *Accent Magazine* (2 a year), *Journal of Neumann's First-Year Knight Writers*, *The Neumann Business Review* (1 a year), *Viewbook*

DEANS

Division of Arts and Sciences: Dr MAC GIVEN
Division of Business and Information Management: JANET MASSEY
Division of Continuing Adult and Professional Studies: Dr TISH SZYMURSKI
Division of Education and Human Services: Dr JOSEPH E. GILLESPIE
Division of Nursing and Health Sciences: Dr KATHLEEN GEIGER HOOVER

PEIRCE COLLEGE

1420 Pine St, Philadelphia, PA 19102
Telephone: (215) 545-6400
Fax: (215) 546-5996
E-mail: info@peirce.edu
Internet: www.peirce.edu

Founded 1865
Private control
Academic year: September to May

Areas of study incl. business, healthcare, information technology and paralegal studies

Pres. and CEO: JAMES J. MERGIOTTI
Provost and Sr Vice-Pres. for Academic Advancement and: Dr PATRICIA A. RUCKER
Sr Vice-Pres. for Finance and Admin.: JAMES M. VITALE
Vice-Pres. for Institutional Advancement: CHARLES A. WRIGHT, III

Dean for Enrolment Management: NADINE M. MAHER
Dean for Students: Dr RITA J. TOLIVER-ROBERTS.

PENNSYLVANIA COLLEGE OF ART & DESIGN

POB 59, 204 N Prince St, Lancaster, PA 17608-0059
Telephone: (717) 396-7833
Fax: (717) 396-1339
E-mail: bwitmer@pcad.edu
Internet: www.pcad.edu

Founded 1982 as Pennsylvania School of the Arts, present name 2003
Private control
Academic year: August to May

Pres.: MARY COLLEEN HEIL
Vice-Pres. for Finance and Operations: PATRICIA ERNST
Dean for Academic Affairs: MARC TORICK
Dean for Students: PAMELA RICHARDSON
Registrar: FAITH GADDIE
Dir for Admissions: NATALIE A. LASCEK-SPEAKMAN
Library Dir: KAREN HUTCHISON.

PENNSYLVANIA STATE SYSTEM OF HIGHER EDUCATION

Office of the Chancellor, Dixon Univ. Center, 2986 N Second St, Harrisburg, PA 17110
Telephone: (717) 720-4000
Fax: (717) 720-4011
E-mail: feedback@passhe.edu
Internet: www.passhe.edu

Chancellor: Dr JOHN C. CAVANAUGH
Exec. Vice-Chancellor: Dr PETER GARLAND
Vice-Chancellor for Admin. and Finance: JAMES DILLON
Chief Counsel: LEONIDAS PANDELADIS
Number of students: 120,000.

CONSTITUENT INSTITUTIONS

Bloomsburg University of Pennsylvania

400 E Second St, Bloomsburg, PA 17815-1301
Telephone: (570) 389-4000
E-mail: buadmiss@bloomu.edu.edu
Internet: www.bloomu.edu

Founded 1839, present name and status 1983

Pres.: Dr DAVID L. SOLTZ
Provost and Sr Vice-Pres.: Dr IRA BLAKE
Vice-Pres. for Admin. and Finance: RICHARD RUGEN
Registrar: JOSEPH KISSELL

Library of 493,467 vols, 2,136,712 micro-text, 13,558 non-print holdings
Number of teachers: 520
Number of students: 9,512

Publication: *Bloomsburg: The University Magazine*

DEANS

College of Business: MICHAEL TIDWELL
College of Education: ELIZABETH K. MAUCH
College of Liberal Arts: JAMES BROWN
College of Science and Technology: ROBERT MARANDE

California University of Pennsylvania

250 University Ave, California, PA 15419-1394
Telephone: (724) 938-4000
Internet: www.calu.edu

Founded 1852

Pres.: GERALDINE M. JONES (acting)
Vice-Pres. for Admin. and Finance: ROBERT THORN

Vice-Pres. for Marketing and Univ. Relations: CRAIG BUTZINE
Vice-Pres. for Student Affairs: Dr LENORA ANGELONE
Vice-Pres. for Univ. Devt and Alumni Relations: SHARON NAVONEY
Dean for Admissions: WILLIAM A. EDMONDS
Dean for Library Services: DOUGLAS A. HOOVER

Library of 260,485 vols, 901,363 microforms
Number of teachers: 257
Number of students: 8,809

Publication: *Inkwell*

DEANS

College of Education and Human Services: Dr KEVIN KOURY
College of Liberal Arts: Dr MOHAMED YAMBA
Eberly College of Science and Technology: Dr LEONARD COLELL
School of Graduate Studies and Research: Dr JOHN R. CENCICH

Cheyney University of Pennsylvania

POB 200, 1837 University Circle, Cheyney, PA 19319-0200
Telephone: (610) 399-2275
Fax: (610) 399-2099
E-mail: admissions@cheyney.edu
Internet: www.cheyney.edu
Founded 1837 as Institute for Colored Youth, present name and status 1983
Academic year: August to May
Pres.: Dr MICHELLE R. HOWARD-VITAL
Provost and Vice-Pres. for Academic Affairs: Dr IVAN BANKS
Vice-Pres. for Finance and Admin.: GERALD COLEMAN
Vice-Pres. for Institutional Devt: LAWRENCE GREEN
Vice-Pres. for Student Affairs and Student Life: Dr SUZANNE D. PHILLIPS
Dir of Enrolment Management: MICHAEL TAYLOR
Librarian: LUT NERO
Library of 238,699 vols
Number of teachers: 102
Number of students: 2,000
Publication: *Cheyney Magazine*

DEANS

School of Arts and Sciences: Dr BERNADETTE CARTER
School of Education and Professional Studies: Dr LARNELL FLANNAGAN

Clarion University

840 Wood St, Clarion, PA 16214-1232
Telephone: (814) 393-2000
E-mail: info@clarion.edu
Internet: www.clarion.edu
Founded 1867
Academic year: August to May
Pres.: Dr KAREN M. WHITNEY
Provost and Vice-Pres. for Academic Affairs: Dr RONALD NOWACZYK
Vice-Pres. for Finance and Admin.: W. PAUL BYLASKA
Vice-Pres. for Student and Univ. Affairs: HARRY E. TRIPP
Dir for Admissions: WILLIAM D. BAILEY
Dean for Libraries: TERRY LATOUR
Library of 454,580 vols
Number of teachers: 390
Number of students: 7,315 (6,225 undergraduate, 1,090 graduate)

DEANS

College of Arts and Sciences: Dr RACHELLE C. PRIOLEAU
College of Business Administration: Dr JAMES G. PESEK

College of Education and Human Services: Dr JOHN GROVES

East Stroudsburg University

200 Prospect St, East Stroudsburg, PA 183301-2999
Telephone: (570) 422-3532
Fax: (570) 422-3846
E-mail: undergrads@po-box.esu.edu
Internet: www.esu.edu
Founded 1893 as East Stroudsburg Normal School, present name 1983
Academic year: August to May
Pres.: Dr ROBERT J. DILLMAN
Provost and Vice-Pres. for Academic Affairs: Dr VAN A. REIDHEAD
Vice-Pres. for Economic Devt and Research Support: MARY FRANCES POSTUPACK
Vice-Pres. for Enrolment Management: Dr VICTORIA L. SANDERS
Vice-Pres. for Finance and Admin.: RICHARD A. STANESKI
Vice-Pres. for Student Affairs: DOREEN TOBIN
Registrar: KIZZY MORRIS
Dean for Library and Univ. Collns: EDWARD OWUSU-ANSAH
Library of 361,410 vols, 28,600 print and e-periodicals, 91,600 govt documents, 1.4m. microform items
Number of teachers: 326
Number of students: 7,387 (6,372 undergraduate, 1,015 graduate)

DEANS

College of Arts and Sciences: Dr PETER HAWKES
College of Business and Management: Dr ALLA L. WILSON
College of Education: Dr PAMELA KRAMER ERTEL
College of Health Sciences: Dr MARK J. KILKER
Graduate College: Dr MARILYN J. WELLS

Edinboro University

219 Meadville St, Edinboro, PA 16444
Telephone: (814) 732-2000
Fax: (814) 732-2880
E-mail: eup_admissions@edinboro.edu
Internet: www.edinboro.edu
Founded 1857
Academic year: August to May
Pres.: Dr JULIE WOLLMAN
Provost and Vice-Pres. for Academic Affairs: Dr PHILIP E. GINNETTI
Vice-Pres. for Finance and Admin.: GORDON J. HERBST
Vice-Pres. for Student Affairs and Student Success: Dr KAHAN SABLO
Vice-Pres. for Univ. Advancement: TINA MENGINE
Registrar: TIM PILEWSKI
Dir for Admissions: CRAIG GROOMS
Assoc. Vice-Pres. for Univ. Libraries: Dr DONALD DILMORE
Library of 503,349 vols
Number of teachers: 404
Number of students: 8,700

DEANS

School of Arts and Sciences: Dr TERRY L. SMITH
School of Business: Dr MICHAEL HANNAN
School of Education: Dr NOMSA GELETA
School of Graduate Studies and Research: Dr ALAN BIEL

Indiana University of Pennsylvania

1011 S Dr., Indiana, PA 15705
Telephone: (724) 357-2100
E-mail: graduate-admissions@iup.edu
Internet: www.iup.edu

Founded 1875 as Indiana State Normal School
Academic year: September to May (two sessions)
Pres.: Dr DAVID WERNER
Provost and Vice-Pres. for Academic Affairs: Dr GERALD W. INTEMANN
Vice-Pres. for Admin. and Finance: Dr CORNELIUS WOOTEN
Vice-Pres. for Enrolment Management and Communications: JAMES BEGANY
Vice-Pres. for Student Affairs: Dr RHONDA LUCKEY
Vice-Pres. for Univ. Relations: ROBERT O. DAVIES
Dean for Graduate Studies and Research: Dr TIMOTHY MACK
Dean for Libraries: Dr LUIS J. GONZALEZ
Library of 800,000 vols, 50,000 audiovisual items, 16,000 journals
Number of teachers: 754
Number of students: 15,126
Publication: *IUP Magazine* (4 a year)

DEANS

College of Education and Educational Technology: Dr A. KEITH DILS
College of Fine Arts: Dr MICHAEL HOOD
College of Health and Human Services: Dr MARY SWINKER
College of Humanities and Social Sciences: Dr YAW A. ASAMOAH
College of Natural Sciences and Mathematics: Dr DEANNE L. SNAVELY
Eberly College of Business and Information Technology: Dr ROBERT C. CAMP
School of Graduate Studies and Research: Dr TIMOTHY P. MACK
School of Continuing Education: Dr NICHOLAS E. KOLB

Kutztown University

POB 730, 15200 Kutztown Rd, Kutztown, PA 19530
Telephone: (610) 683-4000
Fax: (610) 683-4693
E-mail: admission@kutztown.edu
Internet: www.kutztown.edu
Founded 1866 as Keystone State Normal School, present name and status 1983
Academic year: September to May
Pres.: Dr FRANCISCO JAVIER CEVALLOS
Provost and Vice-Pres. for Academic and Student Affairs: Dr CARLOS VARGAS-ABURTO
Vice-Pres. for Admin. and Finance: GERALD L. SILBERMAN
Dir for Admissions: Dr VALERIE REIDOUT
Registrar: MICHELLE HUGHES
Dean for Library Services: Dr BARBARA DARDEN
Library of 555,000 vols, 56,000 print and e-periodical subscriptions
Number of teachers: 365
Number of students: 10,283

DEANS

College of Business: Dr WILLIAM DEMPSEY
College of Education: Dr DARRELL GARBER (acting)
College of Liberal Arts and Sciences: Dr ANNE ZAYAITZ (acting)
College of Visual and Performing Arts: Dr WILLIAM MOWDER

Lock Haven University

401 N Fairview St, Lock Haven, PA 17745
Telephone: (570) 484-2011
Fax: (717) 893-2432
E-mail: admissions@lhup.edu
Internet: www.lhup.edu
Founded 1870 as the Central State Normal School, present status 1983

Academic year: August to May
Pres.: Dr MICHAEL FIORENTINO, JR
Provost and Vice-Pres. for Academic Affairs: Dr DAVID WHITE
Vice-Pres. for Finance and Admin.: WILLIAM HANELLY
Vice-Pres. for Student Affairs: Dr LINDA D. KOCH
Registrar: JILL R. MITCHLEY
Dir for Admissions: ROBIN ROCKEY
Dir of Library Services: BRENDA CORMAN
Library of 352,369 vols
Number of teachers: 270
Number of students: 5,040
Publications: *Lock Haven International Review* (1 a year), *The Haven magazine*

DEANS

College of Arts and Sciences: Dr ZAKIR HOSSAIN
College of Education and Human Services: MARY L. ROSE-COLLEY

Mansfield University

Mansfield, PA 16933
Telephone: (570) 662-4000
Fax: (570) 662-4121
E-mail: admissions@mansfield.edu
Internet: www.mansfield.edu
Founded 1857 as Mansfield Classical Seminary
Academic year: September to May
Pres.: Dr ALLAN GOLDEN
Provost and Vice-Pres. for Academic Affairs: Dr PETER KELLER
Vice-Pres. for Finance and Admin.: Dr DANIEL DoBELL
Vice-Pres. for Student Affairs: BILL MALLOY
Registrar: LORI CASS
Dir for Admissions: CHRISTINE BELL
Dir for Library Information Resources: SCOTT DiMARCO
Library of 222,650 vols
Number of teachers: 213 (148 full-time)
Number of students: 3,411

Millersville University

POB 1002, One S George St, Millersville, PA 17551-0302
Telephone: (717) 872-3011
Fax: (717) 871-2147
E-mail: admissions@millersville.edu
Internet: www.millersville.edu
Founded 1855 as Lancaster Co Normal School, present name and status 1983
Academic year: September to August
Pres.: Dr FRANCINE G. McNAIRY
Provost and Vice-Pres. for Academic Affairs: VILAS A. PRABHU
Vice-Pres. for Finance and Admin.: ROGER V. BRUSZEWSKI
Vice-Pres. for Information Resources: ROBERT F. GERMAN, JR
Vice-Pres. for Student Affairs: AMINTA HAWKINS BREAUX
Vice-Pres. for Univ. Advancement: GERALD C. ECKERT
Registrar: CANDACE A. DEEN
Dir for Univ. Library: Dr MAJORIE WARMKESSEL
Library of 1,106,025 vols
Number of teachers: 328 (full-time)
Number of students: 8,729 (7,604 undergraduate, 1,125 graduate)

DEANS

College of Graduate and Professional Studies: Dr VICTOR S. DESANTIS
School of Education: Dr JANE S. BRAY
School of Humanities and Social Sciences: Dr DIANE ZIMMERMAN UMBLE

School of Science and Mathematics: Dr ROBERT T. SMITH

Shippensburg University of Pennsylvania

1871 Old Main Dr., Shippensburg, PA 17257-2299
Telephone: (717) 477-7447
Fax: (717) 477-1273
E-mail: admiss@ship.edu
Internet: www.ship.edu
Founded 1871 as Cumberland Valley State Normal School, present name and status 1983
Academic year: August to May
Pres.: Dr WILLIAM N. RUUD
Provost and Sr Vice-Pres. for Academic Affairs: Dr BARBARA G. LYMAN
Vice-Pres. for Admin. and Finance: DENNY E. TERRELL
Vice-Pres. for Student Affairs: Dr ROGER L. SERR
Dean for Admissions: JOSEPH CRETELLA
Dean for Library and Media Services: Dr MARIAN B. SCHULTZ
Registrar: CATHY SPRENGER
Library: 2m. vols
Number of teachers: 324 (full-time)
Number of students: 8,300 (7,200 undergraduate and 1,200 graduate)
Publication: *Proteus: A Journal of Ideas* (2 a year)

DEANS

College of Arts and Sciences: Dr JAMES H. MIKE
College of Education and Human Services: Dr JAMES R. JOHNSON
John L. Grove College of Business: Dr JOHN G. KOOTI
School of Extended Studies: Dr CHRISTINA M. SAX
School of Graduate Studies: Dr TRACY SCHOOLCRAFT

Slippery Rock University

One Morrow Way, Slippery Rock, PA 16057
Telephone: (724) 738-9000
Fax: (724) 738-2098
E-mail: asktherock@sru.edu
Internet: www.sru.edu
Founded 1889 as Slippery Rock State Normal School, present name and status 1983
Academic year: June to May
Pres.: Dr CHARLES CURRY (acting)
Provost and Vice-Pres. for Academic Affairs: Dr WILLIAM F. WILLIAMS
Vice-Pres. for Student Life: Dr CONSTANCE FOLEY
Vice-Pres. for Univ. Advancement: BARBARA ENDER
Dir for Admissions: W. C. VANCE
Dir for Library Services: PHILIP TRAMDACK
Library of 500,000 vols, 10,000 online full text journals, magazines and newspapers
Number of teachers: 442 (381 full-time, 61 part-time)
Number of students: 8,852
Publications: *Ginger Hill* (1 a year), *Saxigena* (1 a year), *The Rock* (4 a year)

DEANS

College of Business, Information and Social Sciences: Dr KURT E. SCHIMMEL
College of Education: Dr KATHLEEN STRICKLAND
College of Health, Environment and Sciences: Dr SUSAN HANNAM
College of Humanities, Fine and Performing Arts: Dr EVA TSUQUIASHI-DADDESIO

West Chester University of Pennsylvania

700 S High St, West Chester, PA 19383
Telephone: (610) 436-1000
E-mail: ugadmiss@wcupa.edu
Internet: www.wcupa.edu
Founded 1871
Pres.: Dr GREG R. WEISENSTEIN
Provost and Vice-Pres. for Academic Affairs: Dr LINDA L. LAMWERS
Vice-Pres. for Finance and Admin.: MARK P. MIXNER
Vice-Pres. for Information Services: ADEL BARIMANI
Vice-Pres. for Student Affairs: Dr MATTHEW BRICKETTO
Dir for Admissions: Ms MARSHA HAUG
Dir for Library Services: RICHARD SWAIN
Registrar: JOSEPH SANTIVASCI
Library: 4.8m. vols
Number of teachers: 840 (571 full-time, 269 part-time)
Number of students: 15,100
Publications: *College Literature: A Journal of Critical Literary Studies*, *West Chester University Magazine* (3 a year)

DEANS

College of Arts and Sciences: LORI A. VERMEULEN
College of Business and Public Affairs: Dr CHRISTOPHER M. FIORENTINO
College of Education: Dr KENNETH D. WITMER, JR
College of Health Sciences: Dr DONALD E. BARR
College of Visual and Performing Arts: Dr TIMOTHY V. BLAIR

PENNSYLVANIA STATE UNIVERSITY

University Park, PA 16802
Telephone: (814) 865-4700
Internet: www.psu.edu
Founded 1855 as Agricultural College of Pennsylvania, present name 1953
Academic year: August to May
Campuses: Abington, Altoona, Beaver, Berks, Brandywine, DuBois, Erie (Behrend College), Fayette, Greater Allegheny, Harrisburg, Hazleton, Lehigh Valley, Mont Alto, New Kensington, Schuylkill, Shenango, University Park, Wilkes-Barre, Worthington Scranton and York
Pres.: Dr RODNEY A. ERICKSON
Exec. Vice-Pres. and Provost: ROBERT N. PANGBORN
Sr Vice-Pres. for Devt and Alumni Relations: RODNEY P. KIRSCH
Sr Vice-Pres. for Finance and Business and Treas.: DAVID J. GRAY
Sr Vice-Pres. for Health Affairs: HAROLD L. PAZ
Vice-Pres. and Dean for Undergraduate Education: ROBERT N. PANGBORN
Vice-Provost for Academic Affairs: BLANNIE BOWEN
Vice-Pres. for Admin.: THOMAS G. POOLE
Vice-Pres. for Commonwealth Campuses: MADLYN L. HANES
Vice-Pres. for Educational Equity: W. TERRELL JONES
Vice-Pres. for Outreach: CRAIG D. WEIDEMANN
Vice-Pres. for Research and Dean for Graduate School: HENRY C. FOLEY
Vice-Pres. for Student Affairs: DAMON SIMS
Vice-Pres. for Univ. Relations: WILLIAM M. MAHON, III
Vice-Pres. and Gen. Counsel: CYNTHIA BALDWIN
Dean for Libraries and Scholarly Communications: BARBARA I. DEWEY

Library: see under Libraries and Archives
Number of teachers: 41,144 (24,459 full-time, 16,685 part-time)
Number of students: 81,813 (all locations)
Publications: *iConnect, Research Penn State, Science Journal, Smeal Report*

DEANS

College of Agricultural Sciences: BRUCE MCPHERON
College of Arts and Architecture: BARBARA O. KORNER
College of Communications: DOUGLAS A. ANDERSON
College of Earth and Mineral Sciences: WILLIAM E. EASTERLING
College of Education: DAVID H. MONK
College of Engineering: DAVID N. WORMLEY
College of Health and Human Development: ANN C. CROUTER
College of Information Sciences and Technology: DAVID HALL
College of Medicine: Dr HAROLD L. PAZ
College of the Liberal Arts: SUSAN WELCH
Dickinson School of Law: PHILIP J. MCCON-NAUGHAY
Eberly College of Science: DANIEL J. LARSON
Graduate School: Dr HENRY C. FOLEY
School of Nursing: Dr PAULA MILONE-NUZZO
Schreyer Honors College: CHRISTIAN BRADY
Smeal College of Business: JAMES B. THOMAS

PROFESSORS

(Some professors serve in more than one department)

College of Agricultural Sciences (201 Agricultural Admin. Bldg, University Park, PA 16802; tel. (814) 865-2541; internet www.cas.psu.edu):

Agricultural and Biological Engineering:

BUFFINGTON, D. E., Agricultural Engineering
ELLIOT, H. A., Agricultural Engineering
GRAVES, R. E.
HEINEMANN, P. H., Systems Modelling
JARRETT, A. R.
MANBECK, H. B.
MURPHY, D. J., Agricultural Engineering
PURI, V. M., Agricultural Engineering
WALKER, P. N.
YOUNG, R. E.

Agricultural Economics and Rural Sociology:

ABLER, D. G., Agricultural, Environmental and Regional Economics and Demography
ALTER, T. R., Agricultural Economics
BAILEY, K. W., Agricultural Economics
BECKER, J. C., Agricultural Economics
BEIERLEIN, J. G., Agricultural Economics
BLANDFORD, D., Agricultural Economics
DUNN, J. W., Agricultural Economics
EPP, D. J., Agricultural Economics
FISHER, A. N. P., Agricultural and Environmental Economics
HANSON, G. D., Agricultural Economics
HARPER, J. K., Agricultural and Environmental Economics
HYMAN, D. W., Public Policy and Community Systems
JENSEN, L. I., Rural Sociology and Demography
LULOFF, A. E., Rural Sociology
MOORE, H. L., Agricultural Economics
SACHS, C., Rural Sociology
SHORTLE, J. S., Agricultural Economics
SMITH, S. M., Agricultural Economics
STEFANOU, S. E., Agricultural Economics
STOKES, C. S., Rural Sociology
VAN HORN, J. E., Rural Sociology
WEAVER, R. D., Agricultural Economics
WILLITS, F. K., Rural Sociology
ZOUMAS, B., Agribusiness

Agricultural and Extension Education:

BOWEN, B. E., Agricultural and Extension Education
CAREY, H. A., Extension Information
FLANAGAN, C. A., Agricultural and Extension Education
LEWIS, R. B., 4-H Youth
SCANLON, D. C., Agricultural and Extension Education
THOMSON, J. S., Agricultural Communications
YODER, E. P., Agricultural and Extension Education

Crop and Soil Sciences:

BEEGLE, D. B., Agronomy
CIOLKOSZ, E. J., Soil Genesis and Morphology
CURRAN, W. S., Weed Science
FRITTON, D. D., Soil Physics
HALL, M. H., Agronomy
HATLEY, O. E., Agronomy
KOMARNENI, S., Clay Mineralogy
KRUEGER, C. R., Agronomy
LANYON, L. E., Soil Science and Management
PENNYBACKER, B. W., Agronomy
PETERSEN, G. W., Soil and Land Resources
SYLVIA, D., Soil Microbiology
TURGEON, A. J., Turfgrass Management
WATSCHKE, T. L., Turfgrass Science

Dairy and Animal Science:

BAUMRUCKER, C. R., Animal Nutrition-Physiology
CASH, E. H., Animal Science
ETHERTON, T. D., Animal Nutrition
HAGEN, D. R., Animal Science
HEALD, C. W., Dairy Science
HEINRICHS, A. J., Dairy and Animal Science
HENNING, W. R., Animal Science
KEPHART, K. B., Animal Science
KILLIAN, G. J., Reproductive Physiology
MULLER, L. D., Dairy Science
O'CONNOR, M. L., Dairy Science
VARGA, G. A., Animal Science
VASILATOS-YOUNKEN, R., Endocrine Physiology and Nutrition

Entomology:

CALVIN, D.
FELTON, G.
FRAZIER, J. L.
HELLER, P. R.
HULL, L. A.
KIM, K. C.
MCPHERON, B.
MULLIN, C. A.
SCHULTZ, J. C.

Food Science:

ANANTHESWARAN, R. C., Food Science
BEELMAN, R. B., Food Science
FLOROS, J. D., Food Science
HOOD, L. F., Food Science
MARETZKI, A. N., Food Science and Nutrition
THOMPSON, D. B., Food Science

Horticulture:

ARTECA, R. N., Horticultural Physiology
BROWN (EVENSON), K. M., Post-harvest Physiology
CRAIG, R., Plant Breeding
CRASSWELLER, R. M., Tree Fruit
EISSENSTAT, D. M., Woody Plant Physiology
FERRETTI, P. A., Vegetable Crops
GUILTINAN, M. J., Plant Molecular Biology
HEUSER, C. W., Horticultural Physiology
HOLCOMB, E. J., Floriculture
KOIDE, R. T., Horticultural Ecology
KUHNS, L. J., Ornamental Horticulture
ORZOLEK, M. D., Horticulture

Plant Pathology:

AYERS, J. E.
CHRIST, B. J., Potato Breeding and Diseases

COLE, H., Jr, Agricultural Sciences
DAVIS, D. D.
GILDOW, F. E., Virus-vector Biology
FLORES, H. E.
LUKEZIC, F. L.
MACNAB, A. A.
MOORMAN, G. W., Plant Pathology
PELL, E. J., Agriculture
ROMAINE, C. P., Plant Viruses
ROYSE, D. J., Plant Pathology
SKELLY, J. M.
STEWART, E. L., Plant Pathology
TRAVIS, J. W.

Poultry Science:

ELKIN, R. G., Nutritional Biochemistry
LEACH, R. M., Jr, Poultry Science
VASILATOS-YOUNKEN, R., Metabolic Endocrinology

School of Forest Resources:

ABRAMS, M. D., Forestry
BLANKENHORN, P. R., Wood Technology
BOWERSOX, T. W., Silviculture
BROOKS, R. P., Wildlife and Wetlands
DEWALLE, D. R., Forest Hydrology
GERHOLD, H. D., Forest Genetics
LYNCH, J. A., Forest Hydrology
MCCORMICK, L. H., Forest Resources
MCKINSTRY, R. B., Forestry and Environmental Resource Management
SAN JULIAN, G., Wildlife Resources
SHARPE, W. E., Forest Resources
SMITH, P. M., Wood Products Marketing
STAUFFER, J. R., Ichthyology
STEINER, K. C., Forest Biology
YAHNER, R. H., Wildlife Management

Veterinary Science:

GRIEL, L. C., Jr
HUTCHINSON, L. J.
OMIECINSKI, C.
PERDEW, G. H.
REDDY, C. C.
SHAW, D. P.
SORDILLO, L. M.
WOJCHOWSKI, D. M.

College of Arts and Architecture (Office of the Dean, 124 Borland Bldg, University Park, PA 16802; tel. (814) 865-2591; fax (814) 865-7140; e-mail aqs2@psu.edu; internet www.artsandarchitecture.psu.edu):

Architecture:

HAIDER, J.
KALISPERIS, L. N.
LUCAS, J. P.

Art History:

CUTLER, A.

Integrative Arts:

HAMPTON, G., Art Education and Integrative Arts
LANG, G., Art and Integrative Arts

Landscape Architecture:

DICKIE, G.
JONES, D. R.
ORLAND, B.

School of Music:

ARMSTRONG, D. C., Music
BROYLES, M., Music and American History
CARR, M. A., Music
DOSSE, M., Music
SMITH, S. H., Music
THOMPSON, K. P., Music Education
TRINKLEY, W. B., Music
WILLIAMS, E. V., Music
YODER, M. D., Music

School of Theatre:

CARTER, D. H.
GIBSON, A. A.
LEONARD, R. E.
NICHOLS, R.

School of Visual Arts:

AMATEAU, M., Art and Women's Studies

GRAVES, K., Art
HAMPTON, G., Art and Art Education
LANG, G., Art
LEUPP, L. G., Art
MADDOX, J., Art
PORTER, S., Art
SOMMESE, L. B., Art
STEPHENSON, J. E., Art
WILSON, B. G., Art Education

College of Communications (Dean's Office, 201 Carnegie Bldg, University Park, PA 16802; tel. (814) 865-1503; internet www .comm.psu.edu):

Advertising and Public Relations:

BAUKUS, R. A., Communications (non-professorial Head)

Film/Video and Media Studies:

BARTON, R. L., Media Studies
COHEN, J., Communications
DAVIS, D., Communications
NICHOLS, J. S., Communications

Journalism:

BERNER, R. T., Journalism and American Studies
CURLEY, J., Communications
FOREMAN, G., Communications
RICHARDS, R. D., Journalism and Law

Telecommunications:

FRIEDEN, R. M., Cable Telecommunications
SCHEMENT, J. R., Telecommunications
TAYLOR, R. D., Telecommunications Studies and Law

College of Earth and Mineral Sciences (; tel. (814) 865-6546; fax (814) 863-7708; e-mail contact@ems.psu.edu; internet www.ems.psu .edu):

Energy and Geo-Environmental Engineering:

ADEWUMI, M., Petroleum and Natural Gas Engineering
BISE, C. J., Mining Engineering and Industrial Health and Safety
CHANDER, S., Mineral Processing and Geo-Environmental Engineering
ELSWORTH, D., Energy and Geo-Environmental Engineering
ERTEKIN, T., Petroleum and Natural Gas Engineering
GRADER, A., Petroleum and Natural Gas Engineering
OSSEO-ASARE, K., Metals Science and Engineering and Geo-Environmental Engineering
PARIZEK, R., Geosciences and Geo-Environmental Engineering
SCARONI, A., Energy and Geo-Environmental Engineering
SCHOBERT, H. H., Fuel Science
WYNGAARD, J. C., Meteorology, Mechanical Engineering, and Geo-Environmental Engineering
YOUNG, G., Meteorology and Geo-Environmental Engineering

Geography:

CARLETON, A. M.
DOWNS, R. M.
ERICKSON, R. A., Geography and Business Admin.
GLASMEIER, A. K., Geography and Regional Planning
HOLDSWORTH, D. W.
KNIGHT, C. G.
MACEACHREN, A. M.
PEUQUET, D. J.
YARNAL, B. M.

Geosciences:

ALEXANDER, S. S., Geophysics
ALLEY, R. B., Geosciences
ARTHUR, M. A., Geosciences
BARRON, E. J., Geosciences
BRANTLEY, S. L., Geosciences
CUFFEY, R. J., Palaeontology

DEINES, P., Geochemistry
EGGLER, D. H., Petrology
ENGELDER, T. E., Geosciences
FURLONG, K. P., Geosciences
GRAHAM, E. K., Geophysics
KASTING, J. F., Geosciences and Meteorology
KERRICK, D. M., Petrology
KUMP, L. R., Geosciences
OHMOTO, H., Geochemistry
PARIZEK, R. R., Geology
SLINGERLAND, R. L., Geology
VOIGHT, B., Geology
WHITE, W. B., Geochemistry

Materials Science and Engineering:

ADAIR, J. H., Materials Science and Engineering
ALLARA, D. L., Polymer Science and Chemistry
BROWN, P., Ceramic Science and Engineering
CHEN, L.-Q., Materials Science and Engineering
CHUNG, T.-C., Polymer Science
COLBY, R. H., Polymer Science
COLEMAN, M. M., Polymer Science
DEBROY, T., Metallurgy
GREEN, D. J., Ceramic Science and Engineering
HARRISON, I. R., Polymer Science
HOWELL, P. R., Metallurgy
KOSS, D. A., Metallurgy
KUMAR, S. K., Materials Science and Engineering
LANAGAN, M., Materials Science and Engineering
MacDONALD, D. D., Materials Science and Engineering
MESSING, G. L., Ceramic Science and Engineering
OSSEO-ASARE, K., Metallurgy
PAINTER, P. C., Polymer Science
PANTANO, C. G., Materials Science and Engineering
PICKERING, H. W., Metallurgy
RUNT, J. P., Polymer Science
RUZYLLO, J., Electrical Engineering and Materials Science
SCHLOM, D. G., Materials Science and Engineering
SINGH, J., Materials Science and Engineering
SPEAR, K. E., Ceramic Science
TRESSLER, R. E., Materials Science and Engineering
TROLIER-McKINSTRY, S., Ceramic Science

Meteorology:

BANNON, P.
BRUNE, W. H.
CAHIR, J. J.
CARLSON, T. N.
DUTTON, J. A.
FRANK, W. M.
FRITSCH, J. M.
KASTING, J. F., Geosciences and Meteorology
KLEIT, A. N., Economics
LAMB, D.
THOMSON, D. W.
WYNGAARD, J. C.
YOUNG, G. S., Meteorology and Geo-environmental Engineering

College of Education (228 Chambers Bldg, University Park, PA 16802; tel. (814) 865-0488; e-mail coed@psu.edu; internet www.ed .psu.edu):

Adult Education, Instructional Systems, and Workforce Education and Development:

ASKOV, E. N., Education
DWYER, F., Instructional Systems
GRAY, K. C., Education
PASSMORE, D. L., Education
ROTHWELL, W. J., Workforce Education and Devt

Counsellor Education, Counselling Psychology, and Rehabilitation Services:

HERBERT, J. T., Counsellor Education
HERR, E. L., Education
KEAT, D. B., II, Education and Counselling Psychology
NILES, S. G., Counsellor Education
SLANEY, R. B., Counselling Psychology

Curriculum and Instruction:

BLUME, G. W., Mathematics Education
CARLSEN, W. S., Science Education
GIROUX, H.
HEID, M. K., Mathematics Education
JOHNSON, J. E.
NELSON, M. R., Education and American Studies
NOLAN, J. F., Jr, Curriculum and Supervision
RUBBA, P. A., Jr
SHANNON, P.
SIMON, M. A., Mathematics Education
SOTO, L., Language and Literacy
YAWKEY, T. C.

Education Policy Studies:

BAKER, D. P., Education
BOYD, W. L., Educational Admin.
EVENSEN, D., Education
GEIGER, R., Education
HARTMAN, W., Education
HENDRICKSON, R. M., Education
NICELY, R., Jr, Education
PRAKASH, M. S., Education
STEFKOVICH, J. A., Education
TERENZIN, P., Education
TIPPECONNIC, J., III, Education
VOLKWEIN, J. F., Education

Educational and School Psychology and Special Education:

GAJAR, A. H., Special Education
HALE, R. L., Education
HUGHES, C. A., Education
MEYER, B. J. F., Educational Psychology
ROBERTS, D. M., Educational Psychology
RUHL, K. L., Special Education
SALVIA, J. A., Special Education
SUEN, H. K., Educational Psychology
WATKINS, M., Education (School Psychology)

College of Engineering (101 Hammond Bldg, University Park, PA 16802; internet www .engr.psu.edu):

Acoustics:

ATCHLEY, A. A.
BLOOD, I. M., Communication Disorders
BRENTNER, K. S., Aerospace Engineering
FRANK, T. A., Communication Disorders
GARRETT, S. L.
HETTCHE, L. R., Engineering Research
KOOPMANN, G. H., Mechanical Engineering
LAMANCUSA, J. S., Mechanical Engineering
LAUCHLE, G. C.
LESIEUTRE, G. A., Aerospace Engineering
LONG, L. N., Aerospace Engineering
McLAUGHLIN, D. K., Aerospace Engineering
MAYNARD, J. D., Physics
MORRIS, P. J., Aerospace Engineering
SHUNG, K. K., Bioengineering
STERN, R., Applied Science and Mechanics
THOMSON, D. W., Meteorology
TITTMANN, B. R., Engineering Science and Mechanics

Aerospace Engineering:

CAMCI, C., Aerospace Engineering
LESIEUTRE, G. A., Aerospace Engineering
LONG, L.
McLAUGHLIN, D. K.
MAUGHMER, M. D., Aerospace Engineering
MELTON, R. G., Aerospace Engineering
MICCI, M. M.
MORRIS, P. J.

Agricultural and Biological Engineering:
BUFFINGTON, D. E., Agricultural Engineering
ELLIOT, H. A., Agricultural Engineering
GRAVES, R. E.
HEINEMANN, P. H., Systems Modelling
JARRETT, A. R.
MANBECK, H. B.
MURPHY, D. J., Agricultural Engineering
PURI, V. M., Agricultural Engineering
WALKER, P. N.
YOUNG, R. E.

Architectural Engineering:
BEHR, R. A.
BURNETT, E. F. P., Architectural and Civil Engineering
GESCHWINDER, L. F.
MUMMA, S. A.

Bioengineering:
ALLCOCK, H. R., Chemistry
BROWN, P. W., Materials Science and Engineering
CURTIS, W. R., Chemical Engineering
FREIVALDS, A., Industrial and Manufacturing Engineering
GESELOWITZ, D. B., Bioengineering
HIGGINS, W. E., Electrical and Computer Engineering
KENNEY, E. S., Nuclear Engineering
LIPOWSKY, H. H., Bioengineering and Engineering Science
ROSE, J. L., Engineering Design and Manufacturing
ROSENBERG, G., Bioengineering and Surgery
RUNT, J. P., Polymer Sciences
SNYDER, A. J., Surgery and Bioengineering
TARBELL, J. M., Chemical Engineering and Bioengineering
ULTMAN, J. S., Chemical Engineering
ZELIS, R., Medicine and Cellular and Molecular Physiology

Chemical Engineering:
BEN-JEBRIA, A.
BORHAN, A.
CURTIS, W.
DANNER, R. P.
DUDA, J. L.
FICHTHORN, K.
FOLEY, H. C.
NAGARAJAN, R.
NEDWICK, R.
TARBELL, J. M.
ULTMAN, J. S.
VANNICE, M. A.
VRENTAS, J. S.
ZYDNEY, A. L.

Civil and Environmental Engineering:
ANDERSON, D. A.
BURNETT, E. F. P., Architectural and Civil Engineering
GOULIAS, K. G.
JOVANIS, P. P.
KILARESKI, W. P.
KRAUTHAMMER, T.
LOGAN, B. E.
MATSON, J. V.
MILLER, A. C.
REGAN, R. W., Sr
SCANLON, A.
THOMAS, H. R.
WANG, M. C.

Computer Science and Engineering
(joint department with the Eberly College of Science)

ACHARYA, R.
BARLOW, J.
DAS, C.
FENG, T.-Y.
GILES, C. L.
HIGGINS, W.

HURSON, A. R.
IRWIN, M. J.
KASTURI, R.
KUMARA, S.
LA PORTA, T.
LONG, L. N.
METZNER, J. J.
MILLER, D. A.
MILLER, W. C.
PALAMIDESSI, C.
SARASWAT, V. A.
YEN, J.

Electrical Engineering:
AYDIN, K.
BOSE, N. K.
BREAKALL, J. K.
BURTON, L. C., Electrical and Computer Engineering
CROSKEY, C. L.
CROSS, L. E.
FERRARO, A. J.
GILDENBLAT, G.
HALL, D. L.
HIGGINS, W.
JACKSON, T. N.
JENKINS, K.
KAVEHRAD, M.
KHOO, I. C.
KURTZ, S. K.
LEE, K. Y.
LUEBBERS, R. J.
MATHEWS, J. D.
METZNER, J.
MILLER, D. L.
MITCHELL, J. D.
MITTRA, R.
PHILBRICK, C. R.
PHOHA, S., Electrical and Computer Engineering
RUSSELL, D.
RUZYLLO, J., Electrical Engineering and Materials Science and Engineering
SZNAIER, M.
UCHINO, K.
WRONSKI, C. R., Microelectronic Materials and Devices
YU, F. T. S.
ZHANG, Q.

Engineering Science and Mechanics:
AMATEAU, M. F., Engineering Science and Mechanics
ASHOK, S., Engineering Science
AWADLEKARIM, O. O., Engineering Science and Mechanics
BAKIS, C. E.
CONWAY, J. C., Engineering Mechanics
ENGEL, R. S.
FONASH, S. J., Engineering Science
GERMAN, R. M., Materials
HAYEK, S. I., Engineering Mechanics
LAKHTAKIA, A.
LENAHAN, P. M., Engineering Science and Mechanics
McGRATH, R. T.
McNITT, R. P., Engineering Science and Mechanics
MESSIER, R. F., Engineering Science and Mechanics
PANGBORN, R. N., Engineering Mechanics
QUEENEY, R. A., Engineering Mechanics
ROSE, J. L., Engineering Design and Manufacturing
SALAMON, N. L., Engineering Science and Mechanics
TITTMANN, B. R., Engineering
TODD, J. A., Engineering Science and Mechanics
URQUIDI-MACDONALD, M.
VARADAN, V. K., Engineering Science and Mechanics
VARADAN, V. V., Engineering Science and Mechanics, and Electrical Engineering
VENTSEL, E. S., Engineering Science
WRONSKI, C. R., Microelectronic Devices and Materials

Industrial and Manufacturing Engineering:
CAVALIER, T. M.
CHANDRA, M. J.
COHEN, P. H.
ENSCORE, E. E.
FREIVALDS, A.
JOSHI, S. B.
KUMARA, S.
RAVINDRAN, A.
RUUD, C. O.
VENTURA, J. A.
VOIGHT, R. C.
WYSK, R. A.

Mechanical and Nuclear Engineering:
BARATTA, A. J.
BELEGUNDU, A. D.
BRASSEUR, J. G.
CATCHEN, G. L.
CHEUNG, F. B.
CIMBALA, J. M.
HARRIS, T. A.
HOCHREITER, L.
JESTER, W. A.
KOOPMAN, G. H.
KULAKOWSKI, B. T.
KULKARNI, A. K.
KUO, K. K.
LAMANCUSA, J. S.
LITZINGER, T. A.
MODEST, M. F.
PEREZ-BLANCO, H.
RAY, A.
SANTAVICA, D. A.
SANTORO, R. J.
SETTLES, G. S.
SINHA, A.
SOMMER, H. J., III
THYNELL, S. T.
TRETHEWY, M. W.
TURNS, S. R.
WEBB, R. L.
YANG, V.
YAVUZKURT, S.

School of Engineering Technology and Commonwealth Engineering:
HAGER, W. R.

College of Health and Human Development (Office of the Dean, 201 Henderson Bldg, University Park, PA 16802-6501; tel. (814) 865-1428; fax (814) 865-3282; e-mail healthhd@psu.edu; internet www.hhdev.psu.edu):

Biobehavioural Health:
AHERN, F. M.
AIRHIHENBUWA, C. O., Biobehavioural Health
BEARD, J. L., Nutrition Science
BECHTEL, L. J., Biobehavioural Health
CAVANAGH, P. R., Locomotion Studies, Biobehavioural Health, Medicine and Orthopaedics
FINKELSTEIN, J. W.
GRAHAM, J. W., Biobehavioural Health and Human Devt
GRANGER, D. A., Biobehavioural Health, Human Devt and Family Studies
JONES, B. C., Biobehavioural Health and Pharmacology
KOZLOWSKI, L. T.
McCLEARN, G. E., Biobehavioural Health and Psychology
NEWELL, K. M., Biobehavioural Health and Kinesiology
NICHOLSON, M. E., Health Education and Biobehavioural Health
ROLLS, B. J., Biobehavioural Health
SUSMAN, E. J., Biobehavioural Health, Human Devt and Nursing
VICARY, J. R.
VOGLER, G. P., Biobehavioural Health

Communication Disorders:
BLOOD, G. W.
BLOOD, I. M.

FRANK, T. A.
LIGHT, J. C.
PROSEK, R. A.

Health Policy and Administration:

BRANNON, D.
KEMPER, P.
SHEA, D. G.
SHORT, P. F.
YESALIS, C. E.
YU, L. C.

Hotel, Restaurant and Recreational Management:

CALDWELL, L., Leisure Studies
CHICK, G., Hotel, Restaurant and Recreation Management (Leisure Studies)
GODBEY, G. C., Leisure Studies
LEE, R. D., Public Admin.
SHAFER, E. L., Environmental Management and Tourism

Human Development and Family Studies:

BARRY, K., Human Devt
BIRCH, L. L.
BURGESS, R. L.
BURTON, L. M., Sociology and Human Devt
COLLINS, L. M.
CROUTER, A. C., Human Devt
D'AUGELLI, A. R., Human Devt
EDELBROCK, C. S., Behavioural Health
GREENBERG, M. T.
MCHALE, S. M., Human Development
SCHAIE, K. W., Human Devt and Psychology
STIFTER, C. A.
VONDRACEK, F. W.
WILLIS, S. L.
ZARIT, S. H., Human Devt

Kinesiology:

BUCKLEY, W. E., Exercise and Sport Science and Health Education
CAVANAUGH, P. R., Locomotion Studies
ECKHARDT, R. B., Kinesiology
FARRELL, P. A., Physiology
GRAHAM, G. M., Kinesiology
KENNEY, W. L., Physiology and Kinesiology
KRETCHMAR, R. S., Exercise and Sport Science
LARSSON, L. G., Physiology and Clinical Neurophysiology
LATASH, M. L., Kinesiology
MARTIN, P. E., Kinesiology
NEWELL, K. M., Kinesiology and Biobehavioural Health
ZATSIORSKY, V., Kinesiology

Nursing:

BROWN, R.
PRESTON, D.

Nutrition:

ACHTERBERG, C. L.
BAUMRUCKER, C. R., Animal Nutrition, Physiology
BEARD, J. L.
BERLIN, C. M., Jr, Paediatrics, Pharmacology
BIRCH, L. L.
CONNOR, J. R.
ETHERTON, T. D., Animal Nutrition
GREEN, M. H., Nutrition Science
JEFFERSON, L. S., Jr
KRIS-ETHERTON, P. M., Nutrition Science
LEACH, R. M., Jr
MARETZKI, A. N., Food Science and Nutrition
MASTRO, A. M., Microbiology and Cell Biology
REDDY, C. C.
ROLLS, B. J., Nutrition and Biobehavioural Health
ROSS, A. C., Nutrition and Veterinary Science
SMICIKLAS-WRIGHT, H.
THOMPSON, D. B.
VASILATOS-YOUNKEN, R.
YEH, Y.-Y.

College of Information Sciences and Technology (332 Information Sciences and Technology Bldg, University Park, PA 16802-6823; tel. (814) 865-3528; fax (814) 865-5604; internet ist.psu.edu):

BAGBY, J. W., Information Sciences and Technology
GILES, C. L., Information Sciences and Technology, Computer Science and Engineering
TRAUTH, E. M., Information Sciences and Technology
YEN, J., Information Sciences and Technology, Computer Science and Engineering

College of Medicine (500 Univ. Dr., Hershey, PA 17033; tel. (717) 531-8521; internet www.pennstatehershey.org/web/college):

Behavioural Science:

JONES, M. B.
NORGREN, R.

Biochemistry and Molecular Biology:

BHAVANANDAN, V. P.
BOND, J. S.
GOWDA, D. C.
HOPPER, A. K.
HOPPER, J. E.
SCHENGRUND, C.-L.

Cellular and Molecular Physiology:

FLOROS, J.
JEFFERSON, L. S., Jr
LANG, C. H.
LANOUE, K. F.
PEGG, A. E.
QUINN, P. G.
RANNELS, D. E.
VARY, T. C.

Comparative Medicine:

GRIFFITH, J. W.
LANG, C. M.

Health Evaluation Sciences:

CHINCHILLI, V. M.
LLOYD, T.
ORKIN, F. K.
YOUNG, M. J.

Humanities:

BALLARD, J. O., Medicine and Humanities
HAWKINS, A. H., Humanities
HUFFORD, D., Humanities, Behavioural Science and Family and Community Medicine

Microbiology and Immunology:

CHORNEY, M. J., Microbiology and Immunology, Paediatrics
COURTNEY, R. J.
HOWETT, M. K.
ISOM, H. C.
MEYERS, C. M.
SUN, S.-C.
TEVETHIA, M. J.
TEVETHIA, S. S.
WIGDAHL, B.
WILLS, J. W.

Neuroscience and Anatomy:

CONNOR, J. R.
MILNER, R. J.
SIMPSON, I. A.
ZAGON, I. S.

Ophthalmology:

AMINLARI, A., Clinical Ophthalmology
GARDNER, T. W., Ophthalmology, Cellular and Molecular Physiology
SASSANI, J. W., Ophthalmology and Pathology

Pharmacology:

BERLIN, C. M., Jr, Paediatrics and Pharmacology
BILLINGSLEY, M. L., Pharmacology
BURKHART, K. K., Emergency Medicine and Pharmacology

JONES, B. C., Biobehavioural Health and Pharmacology
KESTER, M., Pharmacology
LAKOSKI, J. M., Pharmacology and Anaesthesiology
LEVENSON, R., Pharmacology
LLOYD, T. A., Health Evaluation Sciences
MULDER, K. M., Pharmacology
NAIDES, S. J., Medicine, Microbiology and Immunology, Pharmacology
PEGG, A. E., Cellular and Molecular Physiology and Pharmacology
SMITH, C. D., Pharmacology
SUMMY-LONG, J. Y., Pharmacology
VESELL, E. S., Pharmacology, Medicine, Genetics

College of the Liberal Arts (111 Sparks Bldg, University Park, PA 16802; tel. (814) 865-7691; fax (814) 863-2085; internet www.la.psu.edu):

African and African-American Studies:

MCBRIDE, D., African-American History
MENGISTEAB, K.
SPENCER, R. C., African-American History

American Studies:

CLARKE, D. C.

Anthropology:

DURRENBERGER, E.
HIRTH, K. G.
MILNER, G. R.
RICHTSMEIER, J. T.
SANDERS, W. T.
SNOW, D. R.
WALKER, A.
WEBSTER, D. L.
WEISS, K. M., Anthropology and Genetics
WOOD, J. W.

Classics and Ancient Mediterranean Studies:

BALDI, P. H., Linguistics and Classics
HALPERN, B., Ancient History and Religious Studies
KNOPPERS, G.
PETERSEN, W., Religious Studies
REDFORD, D. B.

Communication Arts and Sciences (Speech Communication):

BENSON, T. W.
BROWNE, S. H.
GOURAN, D. S.
HECHT, M.
HOGAN, J.
NUSSBAUM, J. F.
PARROTT, R. L.

Comparative Literature:

BEEBEE, T. O., Comparative Literature and German
BEGNAL, M., English and Comparative Literature
CHENEY, P., English and Comparative Literature
ECKHARDT, C. D., English and Comparative Literature
EDWARDS, R. R., English and Comparative Literature
GROSSMAN, K., French
HALE, T. A., African, French, and Comparative Literature
KADIR, D., Comparative Literature
LIMA, R. F., Spanish and Comparative Literature
MAKWARD, C. P., French and Women's Studies
STOEKL, A., French and Comparative Literature
STRASSER, G. F., German and Comparative Literature

Crime, Law and Justice:

AUSTIN, R. L., Theory of Crime and Deviancy
BERNARD, T. J.
BLOCK, A. A.
FELSON, R., Crime

KRAMER, J. H., Sociology and Admin. of Justice
MILLER, L. L.
OSGOOD, D. W.
RUBACK, R. B.
SILVER, E.
STEFFENSMEIER, D., Sociology and Crime, Law and Justice
ULMER, J. T.

Economics:

BIERENS, H. J.
BOND, E. W.
CHATTERJEE, K., Economics and Management Science
FELLER, I.
ICKES, B. W.
JORDAN, J. S.
KLEIN, P. A.
KRISHNA, K.
KRISHNA, V.
LOMBRA, R. E.
MARSHALL, R. C.
NELSON, J. P.
ROBERTS, B.-Y.
ROBERTS, M. J.
SHAPIRO, D., Economics and Women's Studies
SJÖSTRÖM, J. T.
TYBOUT, J. R.
WALLACE, N.

English:

BECKER, R., English and Women's Studies
BEGNAL, M. H., English and Comparative Literature
BELL, B.
BIALOSTOSKY, D.
BUCKALEW, R.
CHENEY, P., English and Comparative Literature
CLAUSEN, C.
ECKHARDT, C. D., English and Comparative Literature
EDWARDS, R., English and Comparative Literature
GANNON, R.,
GILYARD, K.
HARRIS, S. K.
HUME, K.
HUME, R. D.
NEALON, J.
SELZER, J. L.
SQUIER, S. M., Women's Studies and English
WEST, J. L. W., III
WOODBRIDGE, L.

French:

BRAGGER, J. D.
GREENBERG, W. N.
GROSSMAN, K. M.
HALE, T. A., African, French and Comparative Literature
LACY, N. J.
MAKWARD, C. P., French and Women's Studies
STOEKL, A., French and Comparative Literature

Germanic and Slavic Languages and Literature:

BEEBEE, O. B., Comparative Literature and German
GENTRY, F. G.
NAYDAN, M. M.
SCHURER, E.
STRASSER, G. F., German and Comparative Literature

History and Religious Studies:

CROSS, G. S., Modern European History
DERICKSON, A., Labour History
FINKE, R., Sociology and Religious Studies
HALPERN, B., Ancient History and Jewish Studies
HSIA, R., History and Religious Studies
JENKINS, P., Religious Studies and History

KNOPPERS, G., Religious Studies
LANDES, J. B., Women's Studies and History
McMURRY, S. A., American History
MOSES, W. J., American History
NEELY, M. E., American Civil War
PENCAK, W. A., American History
PETERSEN, W., Religious Studies
PREBISH, C., Religious Studies
PROCTOR, R. N., History of Science
ROEBER, A. G., Early Modern History and Religious Studies
ROSE, A. C., American History and Religious Studies
ROSE, P. L., European History, Jewish Studies
RUGGIERO, G., Renaissance History
SCHIEBINGER, L. L., History of Science
SWEENEY, J. R., Medieval European History

Jewish Studies:

BLOCK, A., Admin. of Justice
HALPERN, B., Ancient History and Religious Studies
KNOPPERS, G., Religious Studies
ROSE, P. L., European History, Jewish Studies

Labour Studies and Industrial Relations:

CLARK, P. F.
DERICKSON, A., Labour Studies and History
DRAGO, R.
GOURAN, D. S., Communications Arts and Sciences
FILIPPELI, R. L.
ROGERS, J. K.
STEWART, J. B.

Latin American Studies:

GONZALEZ-PEREZ, A., Spanish
HIRTH, K., Anthropology
LIMA, R., Spanish and Comparative Literature
NICHOLS, J. S., Communications
PEAVLER, T. J., Spanish
SNOW, D., Anthropology
WEBSTER, D., Anthropology

Linguistics and Applied Language Studies:

BALDI, P. H., Linguistics and Classics
GOLOMBEK, P., English as a Second Language
JOHNSON, K. E., Applied Linguistics
KROLL, J., Psychology and Applied Linguistics
LANTOLF, J. P., Spanish and Applied Linguistics
SAVIGNON, S. J., Applied Linguistics

Philosophy:

COLAPIETRO, V.
CONWAY, D. W.
GROSHOLZ, E. R.
JACQUETTE, D. L.
SALLIS, J.
SCOTT, C. E.
STUHR, J. J.
TUANA, N.

Political Science:

BAUMGARTNER, F.
BREMER, S.
EISENSTEIN, J.
HARKAVY, R. E.
LAPORTE, R., Jr, Public Admin. and Political Science
WELCH, S.

Psychology:

BERENBAUM, S.
BIERMAN, K. L.
BORKOVEC, T. D.
CARLSON, R.
CLEVELAND, J. N.
COLE, P. M.
CRNIC, K. A.
FARR, J. L.
JACOBS, R. R.

JOHNSON, E.
KROLL, J. F.
LIBEN, L. S.
MARK, M. M.
MURPHY, K. R.
NELSON, K. E.
RAY, W. J.
ROSENBAUM, D. A.
SHIELDS, S. A., Women's Studies and Psychology
STERN, R. M.
THOMAS, H.

Sociology:

BAKER, D. P., Education and Sociology
BOOTH, A.
BURTON, L., Human Devt and Sociology
CLEMENTE, F. A.
DE JONG, G. F.
FARKAS, G., Sociology and Demography
FELSON, R., Crime, Law, Justice and Sociology
FINKE, R., Sociology and Religious Studies
FIREBAUGH, G.
HAYWARD, M. D.
JOHNSON, D. R., Sociology and Human Devt and Family Studies
KRAMER, J., Sociology, Crime, Law and Justice
LANDALE, N. S., Sociology and Demography
LEE, B. A.
McCARTHY, J. D.
MORRIS, M. W.
NELSEN, H. M.
OSGOOD, D. W., Crime, Law, Justice and Sociology
RUBACK, R. B., Crime, Law, Justice and Sociology
SCHOEN, R., Family Sociology and Demography
SICA, A.
STEFFENSMEIER, D. J., Sociology and Crime, Law and Justice

Spanish, Italian and Portuguese:

GONZALEZ-PEREZ, A., Spanish
LANTOLF, J., Spanish and Applied Linguistics
LIPSKI, J. M., Spanish and Linguistics

Women's Studies:

LANDES, J. B., Women's Studies and History
MANSFIELD, P. K., Women's Studies and Health Education
SQUIER, S. M., Women's Studies and English

Commonwealth Campuses (111 Old Main, University Park, PA 16802-1501; tel. (814) 863-0327; fax (814) 865-3692; internet www.cwc.psu.edu):

Arts and Humanities Division:

CLEMENT, P., History
GINSBERG, R., Philosophy
PLUHAR, E., Philosophy

Business and Economics Division:

KUCUKEMIROGLU, O., Accounting

Engineering Division:

WALTERS, R.
WEED, M.

English Division:

COLLISON, G.
FRUSHELL, R.
JARRETT, J.
McCARTHY, W.
PRICE, R. A.
SORKIN, A.

Mathematics Division:

BARSHINGER, R.
DAWSON, J.
GOMEZ-CALDERON, J.
HELOU, C.
HORWITZ, A.
IVANOV, A.

NOURI, M.
ZEMYAN, S.

Science Division:

BITTNER, E., Chemistry
BLACK, R., Biology
BURSEY, C., Biology
CAMARDA, H., Physics
DE ROSA, M., Chemistry
FEHLNER, J., Chemistry
HARRISON, E., Chemistry
HOULIHAN, J., Physics
KHAN, A., Chemistry
MARICONDI, C., Chemistry
MILLER, D., Physics
MONROE, J., Physics
OBERMYER, R., Physics
SARAFIAN, H., Physics
SUBRAMANIAM, G., Chemistry
VISWANATHAN, N., Chemistry
WINTER, T., Physics
WOLFE, C., Biology

Social Sciences and Education Division:

BALL, R., AOJ
CIMBALA, S., Political Science
GERGEN, M., Psychology
GRESSON, A., Curriculum and Instruction
JOHNSON, J., Psychology

Dickinson School of Law (Lewis Katz Bldg, University Park, PA 16802; tel. (814) 865-8900; fax (814) 863-7274; e-mail psulaw_admit@law.psu.edu; internet www.law.psu.edu):

ACKERMAN, R. M.
ALEXANDER, P. C.
BACKER, L. C.
BARKER, W. B.
DEL DUCA, L. F.
FARMER, S. B.
FARRIOR, S. T.
FELDMAN, H. A.
FOX, J. R.
GILDIN, G. S.
GLENN, P. G.
HAUGHNEY, E. W.
KEATING, W. J.
KELLETT, C. H.
MACRAE, L. M.
MARION, C.
MOGILL, M. A.
MOOTZ, F. J., III
MULLER-PETERSON, J.
NAIDES, P. H.
NAVIN, M. J.
PEARSON, K.
PLACE, T. M.
POLACHEK, M. K.
RAINS, R. E.
RIGLER, J.
ROMERO, V.
SCOTT, G. R.
TERRY, L. S.

Eberly College of Science (Office of Public Information, 517 Thomas Bldg, University Park, PA 16802-2112; tel. (814) 865-9591; fax (814) 863-0491; e-mail sciencedean@psu.edu; internet www.science.psu.edu):

Astronomy and Astrophysics:

BEATTY, J. J.
FEIGELSON, E. D.
GARMIRE, G. P.
LAGUNA, P.
MESZAROS, P. I.
RAMSEY, L. W.
RICHARDS, M.
SCHNEIDER, D. P.
WOLSZCZAN, A.

Biochemistry and Molecular Biology:

BRENCHLEY, J. E., Microbiology and Biotechnology
BRYANT, D. A., Biotechnology
FERRY, J. G., Biochemistry and Molecular Biology
FRISQUE, R. J., Molecular Virology

GAY, C. V., Cell Biology and Poultry Science
GOLBECK, J. H., Biochemistry and Biophysics
HARDISON, R. C., Biochemistry
KAO, T.-H., Biochemistry and Molecular Biology
MASTRO, A. M., Microbiology and Cell Biology
SCHLEGEL, R. A., Biochemistry and Molecular Biology
SIMPSON, R. T., Biochemistry and Molecular Biology
TIEN, M., Biochemistry
TU, C.-P. D., Biochemistry and Molecular Biology

Biology:

ASSMANN, S. M.
CAVENER, D. R.
COSGROVE, D. J.
CYR, R. J.
FEDOROFF, N. V.
FISHER, C. R.
HEDGES, B.
MA, H.
MITCHELL, R. B.
NEI, M.
STEPHENSON, A. G.
UHL, C.
WALKER, A., Anthropology and Biology

Chemistry:

ALLARA, D. L., Polymer Science and Chemistry
ALLCOCK, H. R.
ANDERSON, J. B.
BENKOVIC, S. J.
CASTLEMAN, A. W., Jr
ERNST, W. E., Physics and Chemistry
EWING, A. G.
FELDMAN, K.
FUNK, R. L.
GARRISON, B. J.
JURS, P. C.
MALLOUK, T. E.
MARONCELLI, M.
MERZ, K. M., Jr
SEN, A.
WEINREB, S. M., Natural Products Chemistry
WEISS, P. S.
WINOGRAD, N.

Mathematics:

ANDERSON, J. H.
ANDREWS, G. E.
BANYAGA, A.
BAUM, P.
BROWNAWELL, D.
DU, Q.
FORMANEK, E.
HAMMACK, J.
HUNTER, R. P.
JAMES, D. G.
KATOK, A.
KATOK, S.
LALLEMENT, G. J.
LEVI, M.
LI, W.-C.
MULLEN, G. L.
NISTOR, V.
NOURI, M.
OCNEANU, A.
PESIN, Y. B.
ROE, J.
SIMPSON, S.
SWIATEK, G.
VASERSTEIN, L.
VAUGHAN, R.
WARE, R. P.
WATERHOUSE, W. C.
XU, J.
ZARHIN, Y.
ZHENG, Y.

Physics:

BANAVAR, J. R.

CASTLEMAN, W., Jr
CHAN, M. H. W.
COLE, M. W.
COLLINS, J. C.
COLLINS, R. W.
DIEHL, R.
ERNST, W. E.
FREED, N.
GUNAYDIN, M.
JAIN, J.
MAYNARD, J. D.
OH, B.
SOKOL, P. E.
STRIKMAN, M.
WEISS, D. S.
WHITMORE, J. J.

Statistics:

AKRITAS, M. G.
ARNOLD, S. F.
BABU, G. J.
CHINCHILLI, V., Biostatistics
FONG, D., Management Science and Statistics
HARKNESS, W. L.
HETTMANSPERGER, T. P.
LIN, D. K. J., Management Science and Statistics
LINDSAY, B. G.
PATIL, G. P.
RAO, C. R.
ROSENBERGER, J. L.
TEMPELMAN, A.

Penn State Abington (1600 Woodland Rd, Abington, PA 19001-3918; tel. (215) 881-7300; fax (215) 881-7412; internet www.abington.psu.edu):

Division of Arts and Humanities:

KLIGER, H., Communications and Jewish Studies
MILLER, L., English
MUSTAZZA, L., English and American Studies
SMITH, J. F., English and American Studies
STUTMAN, S., English

Division of Science and Engineering:

AYOUB, A., Mathematics
JOHNSON, K., Mathematics
MOORE, G., Chemistry
REDLIN, L., Mathematics
SCHUSTER, I., Chemistry

Division of Social and Behavioural Sciences:

SMITH, J., English and American Studies

Penn State Altoona (3000 Ivyside Park, Altoona, PA 16601; tel. (814) 949-5000; internet www.aa.psu.edu):

Division of Arts and Humanities:

MARSHALL, I. S., English
MOORE, D. W., English
WOLFE, M., History

Division of Education, Human Development and Social Sciences:

BECHTEL, L. J., Biobehavioural Health

Penn State Berks, Penn State Lehigh Valley (Berks campus: Tulpehocken Rd, POB 7009, Reading, PA 19610-6009
Lehigh Valley campus: 2809 Saucon Valley Rd, Center Valley, PA 18034-8447; tel. (610) 396-6000 (Berks), (610) 285-5000 (Lehigh Valley); fax (610) 285-5220 (Lehigh Valley); internet www.bk.psu.edu):

BARTKOWIAK, R. A., Engineering
FIFER, K., English
GREENBERG, W., French
LITVIN, D. B., Physics
LODWICK, K. L., History
MILAKOFSKY, L., Chemistry
RILEY, M., English

Penn State Erie, the Behrend College (4701 College Dr., Erie, PA 16563; tel. (814) 898-6000; e-mail behrend.admissions@psu.edu; internet psbehrend.psu.edu):

School of Business:

PATTERSON, R., Accountancy
VOSS, J. A., Accountancy

School of Humanities and Social Sciences:

BALDWIN, D., English
FERNANDEZ-JIMENEZ, J., Spanish
FRANKFORTER, A. D., European History
GAMBLE, J. K., Political Science and International Law
GEORGE, D. H., English and Women's Studies
MORRIS, G. L., American Literature
PORAC, C., Psychology
WOLFE, K., French
WOLFORD, C., English, Business

School of Science:

LARSON, R., Mathematics (Calculus)

Penn State Schuylkill, Penn State Harrisburg (*Harrisburg campus*: 777 W Harrisburg Pike, Middletown, PA 17057-4846
Schuylkill campus: 200 University Dr., Schuylkill Haven, PA 17972-2208; tel. (717) 948-6250 (Harrisburg), (570) 385-6000 (Schuylkill); fax (570) 385-3672 (Schuylkill); internet www.cl.psu.edu):

ANSARY, O., Engineering
ASWAD, A., Engineering
BLUMBERG, M., Management
BRONNER, S. J., American Studies and Folklore
CARDAMONE, M. J., Physics
CHEN, Y. F., Civil Engineering
CHISHOLM, R. F., Management
CIGLER, B. A., Public Policy and Admin.
COLE, C. A., Engineering
COUCH, S. R., Sociology
CULPAN, R., Management
DISHNER, E. K., Education
FOXX, R., Psychology
HANES, M. L., Education
KAYNAK, E., Marketing
MAHAR, W. J., Humanities and Music
MILLS, P., Business Admin.
PETERSON, S. A., Public Affairs
PLANT, J. F., Public Policy and Admin.
RABIN, J. M., Public Admin. and Public Policy
RAY, G., Engineering
RICHMAN, I., American Studies and History
SACHS, H. G., Biology
STEPHENS, J. L., Speech Communications
YAVERBAUM, G. J., Information Systems
ZIEGENFUSS, J. T., Management and Health Care Systems

School of Graduate Professional Studies (30 E Swedesford Rd, Malvern, PA 19355-1443; tel. (610) 648-3200; e-mail gvinfo@psu.edu; internet www.gv.psu.edu):

Education:

MILHEIM, W.

Engineering:

McCOOL, J., Systems Engineering
RUSSELL, D., Electrical Engineering

Information Sciences:

RUSSELL, D., Electrical Engineering

Management:

FRITZSCHE, D. J., Management and Organization

Smeal College of Business (Dean's Office, 801 H Business Admin. Bldg, University Park, PA 16802-3009; tel. (814) 867-0448; fax (814) 865-7064; e-mail deansoffice@smeal.psu.edu; internet www.smeal.psu.edu):

Accounting:

DIRSMITH, M. W.
GIVOLY, D.
McKEOWN, J. C.
SMITH, C. H.

Business Logistics:

SPYCHALSKI, J. C.

STENGER, A. J.
TYWORTH, J. E.

Finance:

EZZELL, J. R.
GHADAR, F.
KRACAW, W. A.
MILES, J. A.
MUSCARELLA, C.
WOOLRIDGE, J. R.

Insurance and Real Estate:

BAGBY, J. W., Business Law
JAFFE, A. J., Business Admin.
LUSHT, K. M., Business Admin.
SHAPIRO, A. F., Business Admin.
YAVAS, A., Business Admin.

Management and Organization:

GIOIA, D. A., Organizational Behaviour
GRAY, B. L., Organizational Behaviour
HAMBRICK, D., Management
HARRISON, D. A., Management
KILDUFF, M., Organizational Behaviour
SNOW, C. C., Business Admin.
STEVENS, J. M.
SUSMAN, G. I., Management
TREVINO, L. K., Management

Management Science and Information Systems:

BALAKRISHNAN, A.
BARTON, R., Management Science
BHARGAVA, H., Management Information Systems
BOLTON, G. E., Management Science
CHATTERJEE, K., Management Science
FONG, D. K. H., Management Science and Statistics
HARRISON, T. P., Management Science
KELTON, W. D., Management Science and Information Systems
LILIEN, G. L., Management Science
LIN, D. K., Management Science
XU, S., Management Science

Marketing:

BAUMGARTNER, J.
DESARBO, W. S.
GOLDBERG, M. E.
OLIVA, R. A.
OLSON, J. C.
RANGASWANY, A.

PHILADELPHIA BIBLICAL UNIVERSITY

200 Manor Ave, Langhorne, PA 19047
Telephone: (215) 752-5800
E-mail: admissions@pbu.edu
Internet: www.pbu.edu

Founded 1913 as Bible Institute of Pennsylvania, present name and status 2000
Private control
Academic year: August to May
Pres.: Dr TODD J. WILLIAMS
Sr Vice-Pres. for Finance and Admin.: JAN M. HAAS
Provost: Dr BRIAN TOEWS
Sr Vice-Pres. for Univ. Advancement: SCOTT A. KEATING
Vice-Pres. for Research and Planning: MAE E. STEWART
Vice-Pres. and Dir for Learning Resources: TIMOTHY HUI
Library of 132,778 vols
Number of teachers: 135
Number of students: 1,227

DEANS

School of Arts and Sciences: Dr JEAN MINTO
School of Bible and Ministry: Dr HERB HIRT
School of Business and Leadership: RON FERNER
School of Education: Dr DEB MacCULLOUGH
School of Music and Performing Arts: PAUL ISENSEE

PHILADELPHIA COLLEGE OF OSTEOPATHIC MEDICINE

4170 City Ave, Philadelphia, PA 19131
Telephone: (215) 871-6100
E-mail: admissions@pcom.edu
Internet: www.pcom.edu

Founded 1899, present name 1921
Private control
2 Campuses: Philadelphia and Georgia
Pres. and CEO: Dr MATTHEW SCHURE
Provost and Sr Vice-Pres. for Academic Affairs and Dean: Dr KENNETH J. VEIT
Vice-Pres. for Alumni Relations and Devt: FLORENCE D. ZELLER
Vice-Pres. for Finance and Chief Financial Officer: PETER DOULIS
Vice-Pres. for Graduate Programmes and Academic Planning: Dr ROBERT G. CUZZOLINO
Registrar: DEBORAH A. CASTELLANO
Number of students: 1,410
Publication: *Digest*.

PHILADELPHIA UNIVERSITY

4201 Henry Ave, Philadelphia, PA 19144-5497
Telephone: (215) 951-2700
Fax: (215) 951-2615
E-mail: pr@philau.edu
Internet: www.philau.edu

Founded 1884 as Philadelphia Textile School, present name and status 1999
Private control
Academic year: September to August
Pres.: Dr STEPHEN SPINELLI, JR
Provost and Dean for Faculty: RANDY SWEARER
Vice-Pres. for Academic Affairs: CAROL S. FIXMAN
Vice-Pres. for Devt and Alumni Relations: JESSE R. SHAFER
Vice-Pres. for Finance and Admin.: RANDALL D. GENTZLER
Vice-Pres. for Enrolment and Student Affairs: JANE H. ANTHEIL
Dean for Students: MARK GOVONI
Registrar: JULIA AGGREH
Library Dir: KAREN ALBERT
Library of 88,000 vols, 16,000 periodicals, 5,500 microforms
Number of teachers: 400
Number of students: 3,200
Publication: *Innovator Magazine*

DEANS

College of Architecture and the Built Environment: L. PADULO
College of Design, Engineering and Commerce: (vacant)
College of Science, Health and the Liberal Arts: MATT DANE BAKER

PITTSBURGH THEOLOGICAL SEMINARY

616 N Highland Ave, Pittsburgh, PA 15206-2525
Telephone: (412) 362-5610
Fax: (412) 363-3260
Internet: www.pts.edu

Founded 1794
Private control
Academic year: September to May
Pres.: Rev. Dr WILLIAM CARL, III
Vice-Pres. for Academic Affairs and Dean for Faculty: BYRON JACKSON
Vice-Pres. for Business and Admin.: ANN GETKIN
Vice-Pres. for Planning and Institutional Effectiveness: JIM DOWNEY

Vice-Pres. for Strategic Advancement: THOMAS PAPPALARDO
Vice-Pres. for Student Services and Dean for Students: JOHN WELCH
Registrar: ANNE MALONE
Library Dir: SHARON TAYLOR
Library of 400,000 vols, incl. 296,000 books
Number of teachers: 24
Number of students: 307 (251 full-time, 56 part-time)

POINT PARK UNIVERSITY

201 Wood St, Pittsburgh, PA 15222
Telephone: (412) 391-4100
Fax: (412) 392-6164
E-mail: ptenroll@pointpark.edu
Internet: www.pointpark.edu
Founded 1933, present name and status 2003
Private control
Academic year: August to May
Pres.: Dr PAUL HENNIGAN
Sr Vice-Pres. for Academic and Student Affairs and Dean for Faculty: Dr KAREN S. MCINTYRE
Sr Vice-Pres. for Finance and Operations: BRIDGET MANCOSH
Vice-Pres. for Devt and Alumni Affairs: RICK HASKINS
Vice-Pres. for External Affairs: MARIANN K. GEYER
Registrar: JENNIFER FEDELE
Library Dir: LIZ EVANS
Number of teachers: 1,507
Number of students: 3,920

DEANS

Conservatory of Performing Arts: FRED JOHNSON
School of Arts and Sciences: Dr ROBERT K. FESSLER (acting)
School of Business: Dr ANGELA ISAAC
School of Communication: RONALD ALLAN-LINDBLOM (acting)

RECONSTRUCTIONIST RABBINICAL COLLEGE

1299 Church Rd, Wyncote, PA 19095
Telephone: (215) 576-0800
Fax: (215) 576-6143
E-mail: info@rrc.edu
Internet: www.rrc.edu
Founded 1968, present location 1982
Private control
Pres.: DAN EHRENKRANTZ
Vice-Pres. for Admin.: JENNIFER ABRAHAM
Vice-Pres. for Academic Affairs: Dr S. TAMAR KAMIONKOWSKI
Vice-Pres. for Governance: Dr DEBORAH WAXMAN
Asst Vice-Pres. for Devt: BARBARA G. LISSY
Library Dir: DEBORAH STERN
Number of teachers: 38 (full-time, adjunct)
Number of students: 80

ROBERT MORRIS UNIVERSITY

6001 University Blvd, Moon Township, PA 15108
Telephone: (412) 397-5200
Fax: (412) 397-2425
E-mail: admissionsoffice@rmu.edu
Internet: www.rmu.edu
Founded 1921 as Pittsburgh School of Accountancy, present name and status 2002
Private control
Academic year: August to May
Pres.: Dr GREGORY G. DELL'OMO
Provost and Sr Vice-Pres. for Academic Affairs: DAVID L. JAMISON

Sr Vice-Pres. for Business Affairs: DAN KIENER
Sr Vice-Pres. for Institutional Advancement: JAY T. CARSON
Vice-Pres. and Gen. Counsel: SIDNEY ZONN
Vice-Pres. for Enrolment and Financial Aid: MIKE FRANTZ
Vice-Pres. for Financial Operations: JEFFREY A. LISTWAK
Registrar: FRANCIS E. PERRY
Dean of Libraries: Dr FRANCES J. CAPLAN
Library of 115,350 vols
Number of teachers: 409 (200 full-time)
Number of students: 4,984
Publications: *Foundations Magazine*, *Sentry*

DEANS

School of Business: Dr PAT LITZINGER
School of Communications and Information Systems: Dr BARBARA J. LEVINE
School of Education and Social Sciences: Dr MARY ANN RAFOTH
School of Engineering, Mathematics and Science: Dr MARIA V. KALEVITCH
School of Nursing and Health Sciences: Dr LYNDA J. DAVIDSON

ROSEMONT COLLEGE

1400 Montgomery Ave, Rosemont, PA 19010
Telephone: (610) 527-0200
Fax: (610) 527-1041
E-mail: admissions@rosemont.edu
Internet: www.rosemont.edu
Founded 1921
Private control
Pres.: Dr SHARON LATCHAW HIRSH
Provost and Vice-Pres. for Academic and Student Affairs: Dr B. CHRISTOPHER DOUGHERTY
Vice-Pres. for Institutional Advancement: MADONNA MARION-LANDAIS
Registrar: JOSEPH T. ROGERS
Exec. Dir for Library Services: CATHERINE LAWLOR FENNELL
Library of 157,000 vols
Number of teachers: 141
Number of students: 903 (518 undergraduate, 385 graduate)

DEANS

Schools of Graduate and Professional Studies: DENNIS DOUGHERTY
Undergraduate College: PAULETTE HUTCHINSON

SAINT CHARLES BORROMEO SEMINARY

100 E Wynnewood Rd, Wynnewood, PA 19096
Telephone: (610) 667-3394
Fax: (610) 617-9267
E-mail: developmentscs@adphila.org
Internet: www.scs.edu
Founded 1838
Private control
Academic year: September to May
Rector: Rev. SHAUN L. MAHONEY
Vice-Rector: Rev. JOSEPH BONGARD
Vice-Pres. for Finance and Operations: ELAINE K. RICE
Registrar: LAWRENCE A. HEYMAN
Library Dir: CAIT KOKOLUS
Library of 148,000 vols, 500 periodicals
Number of teachers: 32
Number of students: 140 (full-time)
Publications: *The Brook*, *The Fact Book*

DEANS

Graduate School of Theology and Program of Catholic Studies: Dr KELLY BOWRING

SAINT FRANCIS UNIVERSITY

POB 600, 117 Evergreen Dr., Loretto, PA 15940
Telephone: (814) 472-3000
E-mail: admissions@francis.edu
Internet: www.francis.edu
Founded 1847
Academic year: August to May
Pres.: Rev. GABRIEL J. ZEIS
Provost: Dr WAYNE POWEL
Vice-Pres. for Academic Affairs: Rev. ANTHONY DE CONCILIIS
Vice-Pres. for Advancement: ROBERT CRUSCIEL
Vice-Pres. for Enrolment Management: ERIN MCCLOSKEY
Vice-Pres. for Finance: ROBERT DATSKO
Vice-Pres. for Student Devt: Dr FRANK MONTECALVO
Dir for Devt: RAYMOND PONCHIONE
Dir for Library: SANDRA A. BALOUGH
Library of 120,800 vols, 6,200 microforms, 30,000 journals
Number of teachers: 113 (full-time)
Number of students: 2,449 (1,832 undergraduate, 617 graduate)

DEANS

School of Arts and Letters: Dr TIMOTHY WHISLER
School of Business: Dr RANDY L. FRYE
School of Health Sciences: Dr DOUGLAS R. SOUTHARD
School of Sciences: Dr CHARLES MACVEAN

SAINT JOSEPH'S UNIVERSITY

5600 City Ave, Philadelphia, PA 19131-1395
Telephone: (610) 660-1000
Fax: (610) 660-3300
E-mail: admit@sju.edu
Internet: www.sju.edu
Founded 1851
Private control
Pres.: JOHN SMITHSON
Provost: Dr BRICE WACHTERHAUSER
Vice-Pres. for Financial Affairs: LOUIS J. MAYER
Vice-Pres. for Planning: Dr KATHLEEN D. GAVAL
Gen. Counsel: MARIANNE SCHIMELFENIG
Registrar: GERARD DONAHUE
Librarian: EVELYN MINICK
Library of 354,850 vols, 57,000 e-journals, 4,700 e-books, 863,500 microforms, 4,850 audiovisual materials
Number of teachers: 300 (full-time)
Number of students: 8,950
Publication: *SJU Magazine*

DEANS

College of Arts and Sciences: Dr WILLIAM MADGES
College of Professional and Liberal Studies: Dr PAUL L. DEVITO
Erivan K. Haub School of Business: Dr JOSEPH A. DIANGELO

SAINT VINCENT COLLEGE

300 Fraser Purchase Rd, Latrobe, PA 15650-2690
Telephone: (724) 532-6600
Fax: (724) 532-5083
E-mail: admission@stvincent.edu
Internet: www.stvincent.edu
Founded 1846 as St Vincent Archabbey and College
Pres.: Bro. NORMAN HIPPS
Vice-Pres. for Academic Affairs and Academic Dean: Dr JOHN SMETANKA

Vice-Pres. for Finance and Admin.: DENNIS BRANSON (acting)
Vice-Pres. for Institutional Advancement: TRACY H. TAYLOR
Vice-Pres. for Student Affairs: MARY COLLINS
Registrar: CELINE R. HAAS
Librarian: Rev. CHRYSOSTOM V. SCHLIMM
Library of 340,000 vols
Number of teachers: 100
Number of students: 1,937 (1,693 undergraduate, 244 graduate)
Publication: *Saint Vincent Magazine* (4 a year)

DEANS

Alex G. McKenna School of Business, Economics and Government: Dr GARY M. QUINLIVAN
Herbert W. Boyer School of Natural Sciences, Mathematics and Computing: STEPHEN M. JODIS
School of Humanities and Fine Arts: Fr RENE M. KOLLAR
School of Social Sciences, Communication and Education: Dr MARY BETH SPORE

SALUS UNIVERSITY

8360 Old York Rd, Elkins Park, PA 19027-1516
Telephone: (215) 780-1400
Fax: (215) 780-1336
E-mail: admissions@salus.edu
Internet: www.salus.edu
Founded 1919
Academic year: August to May
Pres.: Dr THOMAS L. LEWIS
Vice-Pres. for Academic Affairs: ANTHONY F. DI STEFANO
Vice-Pres. and Dean for Student Affairs: ROBERT E. HORNE
Assoc. Vice-Pres. for Finance: DONALD C. KATES
Dir for Devt: LYNNE C. CORBOY
Dir for Library: KEITH LAMMERS
Library of 21,000 vols, 160 video cassettes, 9,650 audio cassettes and 100 slide sets
Number of teachers: 70 (46 full-time, 24 part-time)
Number of students: 1,800

DEANS

College of Education and Rehabilitation: Dr AUDREY J. SMITH
College of Health Sciences: Dr ANTHONY F. DI STEFANO
George S. Osborne College of Audiology: Dr VICTOR H. BRAY
Pennsylvania College of Optometry: Dr LINDA CASSER

SETON HILL UNIVERSITY

One Seton Hill Dr., Greensburg, PA 15601
Telephone: (724) 834-2200
Fax: (724) 830-1294
E-mail: admit@setonhill.edu
Internet: www.setonhill.edu
Founded 1885, present name and status 2002
Private control
Academic year: August to May
5 Academic divs: education, humanities, natural and health sciences, social sciences, visual and performing arts
Pres.: Dr JOANNE W. BOYLE
Provost and Dean for Faculty: Dr MARY ANN GAWELEK
Vice-Pres. for Advancement: CHRISTINE M. MUESELER
Vice-Pres. for Finance and Admin.: PAUL T. ROMAN
Vice-Pres. for Enrolment Services: BARBARA HINKLE

Vice-Pres. for Mission and Student Life: Sis. Dr LOIS SCULCO
Dir for Library: DAVID STANLEY
Library of 119,000 vols
Number of teachers: 114 (58 full-time, 56 part-time)
Number of students: 2,145

SUSQUEHANNA UNIVERSITY

51 University Ave, Selinsgrove, PA 17870
Telephone: (574) 374-0101
Fax: (574) 372-4040
E-mail: suadmiss@susqu.edu
Internet: www.susqu.edu
Founded 1858
Pres.: Dr L. JAY LEMONS
Provost and Dean for Faculty: Dr CARL O. MOSES
Exec. Vice-Pres. for Admin. and Planning: SARA G. KIRKLAND
Vice-Pres. for Enrolment Management: DEBORAH C. STIEFFEL
Vice-Pres. for Finance and Treas.: MICHAEL A. COYNE
Vice-Pres. for Student Life and Dean for Students: Dr PHILIP E. WINGER
Vice-Pres. for Univ. Relations: RONALD A. COHEN
Registrar: MIMI ARCURI
Dir for Library: KATHLEEN GUNNING
Library of 341,000 vols, 67,000 e-books, 50,000 journals, 8,680 DVDs, video cassettes and audio CDs, 4,750 printed scores, 8,300 pieces of sheet music
Number of teachers: 123
Number of students: 2,300
Publications: *Susquehanna Currents* (3 a year), *Ventures* (2 a year)

DEANS

School of Arts, Humanities and Communications: VALERIE G. MARTIN
School of Natural and Social Sciences: Dr LUCIEN T. WINEGAR
Sigmund Weis School of Business: Dr ALICIA J. JACKSON

SWARTHMORE COLLEGE

500 College Ave, Swarthmore, PA 19081-1397
Telephone: (610) 328-8000
Fax: (610) 328-8673
E-mail: admissions@swarthmore.edu
Internet: www.swarthmore.edu
Founded 1864
Private control
Academic year: September to May
Pres.: REBECCA CHOPP
Provost: THOMAS STEPHENSON
Vice-Pres. and Dean for Admissions: JAMES L. BOCK
Vice-Pres. for College and Community Relations: MAURICE G. ELDRIDGE
Vice-Pres. for Devt and Alumni Relations: KARL CLAUSS
Vice-Pres. for Facilities and Services: C. STUART HAIN
Vice-Pres. for Finance and Treas.: SUZANNE P. WELSH
Registrar: MARTIN O. WARNER
Dean for Admissions and Financial Aid: JAMES L. BOCK
Dean for Students: H. ELIZABETH BRAUN
Librarian: PEGGY SEIDEN
Library of 900,000 vols, 15,164 online journals, 501,811 e-books
Number of teachers: 166
Number of students: 1,545
Publication: *Swarthmore College Bulletin*.

TEMPLE UNIVERSITY

1801 N Broad St, Philadelphia, PA 19122
Telephone: (215) 204-7000
E-mail: askanowl@temple.edu
Internet: www.temple.edu
Founded 1884 as Temple College, present name 1907
State control
4 Regional campuses; int. campuses in Rome, Itlay and Japan
Pres.: Dr ANN WEAVER HART
Provost and Sr Vice-Pres. for Academic Affairs: Dr RICHARD ENGLERT
Vice-Provost for Faculty Affairs: Dr DIANE C. MALESON (acting)
Sr Vice-Pres. for Govt, Community and Public Affairs: KENNETH LAWRENCE
Sr Vice-Pres. for Institutional Advancement: DAVID UNRUH
Sr Vice-Provost for Int. Affairs: Dr HAI-LUNG DAI
Sr Vice-Pres. for Univ. Counsel: GEORGE MOORE
Exec. Vice-Pres. for Financial Affairs, Chief Financial Officer and Treas.: ANTHONY WAGNER
Vice-Pres. for Research and Graduate Studies: Dr KENNETH SOPRANO
Vice-Pres. for Univ. College: Dr VICKI LEWIS MCGARVEY
Dean for Libraries: CAROL LANG
Library of 4,060,061 vols, 80,484 current serials, 10m. photographs and other graphic images
Number of teachers: 2,600
Number of students: 37,696
Publications: *HSR: Health Services Research* (6 a year), *Journal of Economics and Business* (6 a year), *Journal of Information Technology & Tourism, Journal of International Management, Journal of Management, Spirituality and Religion, Journal of Product Innovation Management, Journal of Risk Finance, Law Quarterly, Risk Management and Insurance Review, Temple Review, The American Journal of Legal History, The Asia-Pacific Journal of Risk and Insurance*

DEANS

Beasley School of Law: JOANNE EPPS
Boyer College of Music and Dance: ROBERT STROKER
College of Education: JAMES EARL DAVIS
College of Engineering: KEYA SADEGHIPOUR
College of Health Professions and Social Work: MICHAEL SITLER
College of Liberal Arts: TERESA SOUFAS
College of Science and Technology: HAI-LUNG DAI (acting)
Fox School of Business and Management: MOSHE PORAT
Maurice H. Kornberg School of Dentistry: AMID ISMAIL
School of Communications and Theatre: THOMAS JACOBSON
School of Education: JAMES EARL DAVIS
School of Environmental Design: TERESA SOUFAS
School of Medicine: LARRY KAISER
School of Pharmacy: PETER DOUKAS
School of Podiatric Medicine: JOHN MATTIACCI
School of Tourism and Hospitality Management: MOSHE PORAT
Temple Rome: KIM STROMMEN
Temple Univ. Japan: BRUCE STRONACH
Tyler School of Art: ROBERT STROKER

THIEL COLLEGE

75 College Ave, Greenville, PA 16125
Telephone: (412) 589-2000
E-mail: admissions@thiel.edu
Internet: www.thiel.edu

Founded 1866
Private control
Academic year: August to May
Pres.: Dr TROY D. VANAKEN
Vice-Pres. for Academic Affairs and Dean for College: Dr LYNN FRANKEN
Vice-Pres. for College Advancement: DAVID J. GROBER
Vice-Pres. for Finance and Management: DOUG KELLAR
Dir for Library: ALLEN S. MORRILL
Dean for Enrolment: AMY BECHER
Dean for Faculty: MERVIN E. NEWTON
Dean for Students: MICHAEL McKINNEY
Library of 135,000 vols
Number of teachers: 113
Number of students: 1,109
Publications: *Endymion*, *The Bell*.

THOMAS JEFFERSON UNIVERSITY

1020 Walnut St, Philadelphia, PA 19107
Telephone: (215) 955-6000
Fax: (215) 503-9920
E-mail: jcgs-info@jefferson.edu
Internet: www.jefferson.edu
Founded 1824 as Jefferson Medical College, present name and status 1969
Pres.: Dr ROBERT L. BARCHI
Sr Vice-Pres. for Strategic Initiatives: JUDITH L. BACHMAN
Vice-Pres. and Univ. Counsel: CRISTINA G. CAVALLERI
Vice-Pres. for Finance: RICHARD SCHMLD
Vice-Pres. for Research: Dr STEVEN E. McKENZIE
Librarian: EDWARD N. TAWYEA
Library of 167,504 vols
Number of teachers: 761
Number of students: 2,600
Publications: *American Journal of Medical Quality—Official Journal of the American College of Medical Quality, Biotechology Healthcare—Official Journal of the Biologic Finance and Access Council, P&T (Pharmacy and Therapeutics), Population Health Management*

DEANS

Jefferson College of Graduate Studies: GERALD B. GRUNWALD
Jefferson Medical College: Dr MARK L. TYKOCINSKI
Jefferson School of Health Professions: Dr JANICE P. BURKE
Jefferson School of Pharmacy: Dr REBECCA S. FINLEY
Jefferson School of Population Health: Dr DAVID B. NASH

TRINITY SCHOOL FOR MINISTRY

311 11th St, Ambridge, PA 15003
Telephone: (724) 266-3838
Fax: (724) 266-4617
E-mail: info@tsm.edu
Internet: www.tsm.edu
Founded 1975
Private control
Pres. and Dean: Rev. Dr JUSTYN TERRY
Academic Dean: Dr MARK STEVENSON
Dean for Students and Dir for Admissions: Rev. TINA LOCKETT
Registrar: Rev. BILL STARKE
Library Dir: SUSANAH HANSON
Library of 80,000 vols, 400 periodicals
Number of teachers: 40
Number of students: 110 (full-time)
Publication: *Trinity Journal for Theology & Ministry* (2 a year).

UNIVERSITY OF PENNSYLVANIA

3451 Walnut St, Philadelphia, PA 19104
Telephone: (215) 898-5000
E-mail: info@admissions.upenn.edu
Internet: www.upenn.edu
Founded 1740 as Acad. and Charitable School in the Province of Pennsylvania
Private control
Academic year: September to May, and two six-week summer terms
Pres.: Dr AMY GUTMANN
Provost: VINCENT PRICE
Vice-Provost and Dir for Libraries: CARTON ROGERS, III
Exec. Vice-Pres.: CRAIG CARNAROLI
Exec. Vice-Pres. for Univ. of Pennsylvania Health System: J. LARRY JAMESON
Sr Vice-Pres. and Gen. Counsel: WENDY WHITE
Vice-Pres. and Chief of Staff: GREGORY S. ROST
Vice-Pres. and Sec.: LESLIE LAIRD KRUHLY
Vice-Pres. for Business Services: MARIE WITT
Vice-Pres. for Devt and Alumni Relations: JOHN H. ZELLER
Vice-Pres. for Finance and Treas.: STEPHEN D. GOLDING
Vice-Pres. for Govt and Community Affairs: JEFFREY COOPER
Vice-Pres. for Human Resources: JOHN J. HEUER
Vice-Pres. for Information Systems and Computing: ROBIN BECK
Vice-Pres. for Institutional Affairs: JOANN MITCHELL
Vice-Pres. for Univ. Communications: STEPHEN J. MacCARTHY
CEO for Univ. of Pennsylvania Health System: RALPH W. MULLER
Registrar: MICHELLE H. BROWN-NEVERS
Dean for Admissions: ERIC J. FURDA
Library: see Libraries and Archives
Number of teachers: 4,246
Number of students: 24,832 (21,329 full-time, 3,503 part-time)
Publications: *Arts at Penn, Red and Blue, Research at PENN* (online)

DEANS

Annenberg School for Communication: Dr MICHAEL X. DELLI CARPINI
Graduate School of Education: Dr ANDREW C. PORTER
Raymond and Ruth Perelman School of Medicine: Dr J. LARRY JAMESON
School of Arts and Sciences: Dr REBECCA BUSHNELL
School of Dental Medicine: DENIS F. KINANE
School of Design: MARILYN JORDAN TAYLOR
School of Engineering and Applied Science: Dr EDUARDO GLANDT
School of Law: MICHALE A. FITTS
School of Nursing: AFAF I. MELEIS
School of Social Policy and Practice: Dr RICHARD GELLES
School of Veterinary Medicine: Dr JOAN C. HENDRICKS
Wharton School: Dr THOMAS S. ROBERTSON

PROFESSORS

Annenberg School for Communication
Communications:
CAPPELLA, J.
DELLI CARPINI, M.
FISHBEIN, M.
GANDY, O. H.
GROSS, L.
HORNIK, R.
JAMIESON, K. H.
JEMMOTT, J.
KATZ, E.
KRIPPENDORFF, K.
LINEBARGER, D.

MARVIN, C.
MESSARIS, P.
PRICE, V.
TUROW, J.
ZELIZER, B.

Wharton School
Accounting:
BAIMAN, S.
GONEDES, N.
HOLTHAUSEN, R.
ITTNER, C.
LAMBERT, R. A.
LARCKER, D.
VERRECCHIA, R.

Business and Public Policy:
ALLEN, W. B.
BAILEY, E.
FAULHABER, G.
PACK, H.
PACK, J.
WALDFOGEL, J.

Finance:
ABEL, A.
ALLEN, H. F.
BLUME, M.
GIBBONS, M.
GORTON, G.
HERRING, R.
INMAN, R.
KEIM, D.
KIHLSTROM, R.
LEWIS, K. K.
MACKINLAY, A. C.
MARSTON, R.
RAMASWAMY, K.
SIEGEL, J.
STAMBAUGH, R.

Health Care Systems:
BURNS, L.
DANZON, P.
HARRINGTON, S.
PAULY, M.

Insurance and Risk Management:
BABBEL, D.
CUMMINS, J. D.
DOHERTY, N.
LEMAIRE, J.
MITCHELL, O.
ROSENBLOOM, J.

Legal Studies:
BELLACE, J.
DONALDSON, T.
DUNFEE, T.
ORTS, E.
ROSOFF, A.
SHELL, G. R.
SHROPSHIRE, K.

Management:
AMIT, R.
CAPPELI, P.
GERRITY, T.
GULLEN, M.
HAMILTON, W. F.
HOUSE, R.
KIMBERLY, J.
KLEIN, K.
KOBRIN, S.
LEVINTHAL, D.
MACMILLAN, I.
MEYER, M.
PENNINGS, J.
SINGH, H.
SINGH, J.
USEEM, M.
WEIGELT, K.
WINTER, S.

Marketing:
ARMSTRONG, J. S.
DAY, G.
ELIASHBERG, J.
FADER, P.

HOCH, S.
HUTCHISON, J.
IANOBUCCI, D.
KAHN, B.
LODISH, L.
MEYER, R.
RAJU, J. S.
REIBSTEIN, D.
SCHMITTLEIN, D.
WARD, S.
WIND, Y.

Operations and Information Management:

CLEMONS, E.
COHEN, M.
FISHER, M.
GUIGNARD-SPIELBERG, M.
HARKER, P.
HERSHEY, J.
KIMBROUGH, S.
KLEINDORFER, P.
KUNREUTHER, H.
ULRICH, K.
ZHENG, Y.

Real Estate:

GYOURKO, J.
LINNEMAN, P.
POINDEXTER, G.
WACHTER, S.

Statistics:

BROWN, L.
BUJA, A.
GEORGE, E.
KRIEGER, A.
LOW, M.
ROSENBAUM, P.
SHAMAN, P.
STEELE, J. M.
STINE, R.

Raymond and Ruth Perelman School of Medicine (295 John Morgan, Philadelphia, PA 19104-6055; internet www.med.upenn .edu):

Anaesthesia:

DEUTSCHMANN, C.
ECKENDOFF, R.
FLEISHER, L.
LONGNECKER, D.

Biochemistry and Biophysics:

DEGRADO, W.
DREYFUSS, G.
DUTTON, P. L.
ENGLANDER, S. W.
KALLEN, R.
LEMMON, M.
LEWIS, M.
LIEBMAN, P.
MATSCHINSKY, F.
OHNISHI, T.
VAN DUYNE, G.
VANDERKOOI, J.
WAND, A. J.
WILSON, D.
YONETANI, T.

Biostatistics and Epidemiology:

HEITJAN, D.
KUMANYIKA, S.
LANDIS, J. R.
LEE, H.
REBBECK, T.
STROM, B.
TEN HAVE, T.

Cancer Biology:

ALWINE, J.

Cell and Developmental Biology:

DiNARDO, S.
FRANZINI-ARMSTRONG, C.
SANGER, J.
SIMON, M.
WEISEL, J.

Dermatology:

ROOK, A.

STANLEY, J.

Emergency Medicine:

BAXT, W. G.
THORN, S.

Family Practice and Community Medicine:

BOWMAN, M.

Genetics:

BUCAN, M.
GASSER, D.
KADESCH, T.
KAZAZIAN, H.
LIEBHABER, S.
SPIELMAN, R.

Medical Ethics:

CAPLAN, A.

Medicine:

ALBELDA, S.
ASCH, D.
BENNETT, J.
BIRNBAUM, M.
BLUMBERG, B.
BRASS, L.
COHEN, P.
COLLMAN, R.
COOKE, N.
DANIELE, R.
EISENBERG, R.
EMERSON, S. G.
EPSTEIN, J.
FELDMAN, H.
FITZGERALD, G.
FRIEDMAN, H. M.
GEWIRTZ, A.
GLICK, J.
HILLMAN, A.
HOXIE, J.
KELLEY, W.
LAZAR, M.
LEVINSON, A.
MACGREGOR, R. R.
MADAIO, M.
PACK, A.
PANETTIERI, R.
PARMACEK, M.
PHILLIPS, S.
PYERITZ, R.
RUBENSTEIN, A.
RUBIN, H.
RUSTGI, A.
SCHAFER, A.
SCHREIBER, A.
SCHUMACHER, H.
SCHWARTZ, J.
SNYDER, P.
TANNEN, R.
THOMPSON, C.
TURKA, L.
TURNER, B.
WEBER, B.
WILSON, J.
ZIYADEH, F.

Microbiology:

BOETTIGER, D.
BUSHMAN, F.
DAVIES, H. C.
FRANKEL, F.
FRASER, N.
GOLDFINE, H.
KAJI, A.
PATERSON, Y.
ROSS, S.
WEISS, S.

Neurology:

BARCHI, R.
BERMAN, P.
BROWN, M.
COSLETT, H. B.
DICHTER, M.
GONZALEZ-SCARANO, F.
PLEASURE, D.
SCHERER, S.
SELZER, M.

TENNEKOON, G. I.

Neuroscience:

HAYDON, P.
LEVITAN, I.
LINDSTROM, J.
NUSBAUM, M.
PALMER, L.
RAPER, J.
ROSENQUIST, A.
SALZBERG, B.
SEHGAL FIELD, A.
STERLING, P.

Neurosurgery:

GRADY, M. S.
WELSH, F.

Obstetrics and Gynaecology:

HECHT, N.
MASTROIANNI, L.
MENNUTI, M.
RUBIN, S.
STRAUSS, J.

Ophthalmology:

BENNETT, J.
FINE, S.
JACOBSON, S.
LATIES, A.
PUGH, E.
STONE, R.

Orthopaedic Surgery:

FITZGERALD, R.
HEPPENSTALL, R.
KAPLAN, F.
SOSLOWSKY, L.

Otorhinolaryngology:

DOTY, R.
KENNEDY, D.
O'MALLEY, B.
SAUNDERS, J.

Paediatrics:

ASAKURA, T.
BALLARD, P. L.
BRODEUR, G.
DOUGLAS, S.
EMANUEL, B.
FOX, W.
GRUNSTEIN, M.
HIGH, K.
HONIG, P.
HOYER, J.
JOHNSON, P.
LEVY, R.
OFFIT, P.
PONCZ, M.
SEGAL, S.
SILBER, J.
YUDKOFF, M.

Pathology and Laboratory Medicine:

ARGON, Y.
CANCRO, M.
CHOI, Y.
CINES, D.
DAVIES, P.
DOMS, R.
GAULTON, G.
GONATAS, N.
GREENE, M.
HANCOCK, W.
JARETT, L.
JUNE, C. H.
KAMOUN, M.
KORETZKY, G. A.
LAMBRIS, J.
LEE, V. M.-Y.
LIVOLSI, V.
MONROE, J.
MUSCHEL, R.
NOWELL, P.
SCHLAEPFER, W.
SHAW, L.
TROJANOWSKI, J.
TYKOCINSKI, M.
WOLF, B.

YOUNG, D.

Pharmacology:

ASSOIAN, R.
BLAIR, I.
EBERWINE, J.
MANNING, D.
PENNING, T.
PITTMAN, R.
WHITEHEAD, A. S.

Physiology:

BAYLOR, S. M.
CIVAN, M.
COBURN, R.
DE WEER, P.
DEUTSCH, C.
FISHER, A.
FOSKETT, J. K.
GOLDMAN, Y.
HOLZBAUR-HOWARD, E.
JAMMEY, P.
LAHIRI, S.
LU, Z.
SWEENEY, H. L.
WINEGRAD, S.

Psychiatry:

ASTON-JONES, G.
BERRETTINI, W.
COYNE, J.
CRITS-CHRISTOPH, P.
DINGES, D. F.
EVANS, D.
FOA, E.
GUR, R.
KATZ, I.
LERMAN, C.
LUCKI, I.
NICHOLLS, R.
O'BRIEN, C.
PRICE, R.
RICKELS, K.
WADDEN, T.
WELLER, E.

Radiation Oncology:

BIAGLOW, J.
BLOCH, P.
GLATSTEIN, E.
KENNEDY, A.
KOCH, C.
MCKENNA, W.

Radiology:

BAUM, S.
BRYAN, R. N.
JOSEPH, P.
KARP, J.
KUNG, H.
LEIGH, J.
SCHNALL, M.
UDUPA, J.
WEHRLI, F.

Surgery:

ADZICK, N. S.
BARKER, C. F.
DREBIN, J.
EDMUNDS, L.
FLAKE, A.
KAISER, L.
NAJI, A.
NUSBAUM, M.
ROMBEAU, J.
ROSATO, E.
SHAKED, A.
SPRAY, T.
WEIN, A.
WHITAKER, L.

School of Arts and Sciences

Anthropology:

DIBBLE, H. L.
KOPYTOFF, I.
LEVENTHAL, R.
POSSEHL, G.
SABLOFF, J.
SANDAY, P.

SHARER, R.
SILVERSTEIN, M.
SPOONER, B.
URBAN, G.

Biology:

BINNS, A.
CASHMORE, A.
CASPER, B.
CEBRA, J.
CHENEY, D.
DALDAL, M. F.
DUNHAM, A. E.
EWENS, W.
GUILD, G.
JANZEN, D.
KIM, J.
PETRAITIS, P.
POETHIG, R. S.
REA, P. A.
ROME, L.
ROOS, D. S.
SCHULTZ, R.
WALDRON, I.
WEINBERG, E.
ZIGMOND, S.

Chemistry:

BERRY, D.
BLASIE, J. K.
CHRISTIANSON, D.
COOPERMAN, B.
DAI, H.-L.
FITTS, D.
HOCHSTRASSER, R.
JOULLIE, M.
KLEIN, M.
LESTER, M. I.
LU, P.
MACDIARMID, A.
MOLANDER, G.
PERCEC, V.
SMITH, A. B.
SNEDDON, L.
THERIEN, M.
THORNTON, E.
TOPP, M. R.
WAYLAND, B.
WINKLER, J.

Classical Studies:

COPELAND, R.
FARRELL, J., Jr
MURNAGHAN, S.
ROSEN, R.

Criminology:

SHERMAN, L.

Earth and Environmental Science:

GIEGENGACK, R.
JOHNSON, A.
PFEFFERKORN, H.
SCATENA, F.

East Asian Languages and Civilizations:

HURST, G.
LAFLEUR, W.
MAIR, V.
STEINHARDT, N.

Economics:

BEHRMAN, J. R.
BURDETT, K.
CASS, D.
DIEBOLD, F.
ETHIER, W.
LEVINE, H.
MAILATH, G.
MATTHEWS, S.
MERLO, A.
POSTLEWAITE, A.
RIOS-RULL, J.-V.
ROB, R.
WOLPIN, K.
WRIGHT, R.

English:

AUERBACH, N.
BERNSTEIN, C.

BUSHNELL, R.
CONN, P.
CORRIGAN, T.
CURRAN, S.
DAVIS, T.
DE GRAZIA, M.
ENGLISH, J.
FILREIS, A.
KAPLAN, A.
KAUL, S.
LOOMBA, A.
MAHAFFEY, V.
PERELMAN, R.
QUILLIGAN, M.
RABATE, J.
RICHETTI, J.
STALLYBRASS, P.
STEINER, W.
STEWART, S.
WALLACE, D.

Germanic Languages and Literatures:

TROMMLER, F.
WEISSBERG, L.

History:

BEEMAN, R.
BERRY, M. F.
CHILDERS, T.
ENGS, R. F.
FARRISS, N.
HACKNEY, S.
HAHN, S.
KATZ, M.
KORS, A.
KUKLICK, B.
LEES, L. H.
LICHT, W.
LUDDEN, D.
MCDOUGALL, W.
PEISS, K.
PETERS, E.
RICHTER, D.
RUDERMAN, D.
SAVAGE, B.
STEINBERG, J.
SUGRUE, T. J.
TODD, M.
WALDRON, A.
ZUCKERMAN, M.

History and Sociology of Science:

COWAN, R.
FEIERMAN, S.
KOHLER, R.
KUKLICK, H.
LINDEE, M.
SIVIN, N.

History of Art:

BROWNLEE, D.
HOLOD, R.
MEISTER, M.
PITTMAN, H.
SILVER, L.

Linguistics:

CARDONA, G.
KROCH, A.
LABOV, W.
LIBERMAN, M
PRINCE, E.
RINGE, D.
SANKOFF, G.

Mathematics:

CHAI, C.
CHINBURG, T.
CROKE, C.
DETURCK, D.
DONAGI, R.
EPSTEIN, C.
FREYD, P.
GERSTENHABER, M.
GLUCK, H.
HARBATER, D.
KADISON, R. V.
KAZDAN, J.
KIRILLOV, A.

MINSKY, Y.
PEMANTLE, R.
PIMSNER, M.
POP, F.
PORTER, G.
POWERS, R.
SCEDROV, A.
SHANESON, J.
SHATZ, S.
WILF, H.
ZILLER, W.

Music:

BERNSTEIN, L.
KALLBERG, J.
NARMOUR, E.
PRIMOSCH, J.
REISE, J.
TOMLINSON, G.

Near Eastern Languages and Civilizations:

ALLEN, R.
BEN-AMOS, D.
SILVERMAN, D.
STERN, D.
TIGAY, J. H.

Philosophy:

BICCHIERI, C.
DOMOTOR, Z.
FREEMAN, S.
GUYER, P.
HATFIELD, G.
KAHN, C.
ROSS, J.
WEINSTEIN, S.

Physics and Astronomy:

BALAMUTH, D.
BEIER, E.
CVETIC, M.
DURIAN, D.
FORTUNE, H.
HEINEY, P.
HOLLEBEEK, R.
KAMIEN, R.
LANDE, K.
LANGACKER, P. G.
LIU, A.
LOCKYER, N.
LUBENSKY, T.
MELE, E.
NELSON, P.
OVRUT, B.
SEGRE, G.
SOVEN, P.
WILLIAMS, H.
YODH, A.

Political Science:

CALLAGHY, T.
DIIULIO, J.
FRANKEL, F.
GOLDSTEIN, A.
GUMANN, A.
KENNEDY, E.
KETTI, D.
LUSTICK, I. S.
MANSFIELD, E.
MUTZ, D.
NAGEL, J.
NORTON, A.
O'LEARY, B.
REED, A.
SMITH, R.
TEUNE, H.

Psychology:

BARON, J.
BRAINARD, D.
CHAMBLESS, D.
DERUBEIS, R.
FARAH, M.
GRILL, H.
KAHANA, M.
NORMAN, M. F.
RESCORLA, R.
RICHARDS, V.
RODIN, J.

ROZIN, P.
SABINI, J. P.
SELIGMAN, M.
SEYFARTH, R.

Religious Studies:

DUNNING, S.
DYSON, M.
MATTER, E. A.

Romance Languages:

ALONSO, C.
BROWNLEE, K.
DEJEAN, J.
DONALDSON-EVANS, L.
KIRKHAM, V.
LOPEZ, I.
MARCUS, M.
PRINCE, G.

Slavic Languages:

STEINER, P.

Sociology:

ALLISON, P.
ANDERSON, E.
BERG, I.
BIELBY, W.
BOSK, C.
COLLINS, R.
ENGLAND, P.
FURSTENBERG, F.
JACOBS, J.
MADDEN, J. F.
PRESTON, S.
SMITH, H.
WATKINS, S.
ZUBERI, T.

South Asian Regional Studies:

ROCHER, R.
SCHIFFMAN, H.

School of Dental Medicine

Anatomy/Cell Biology:

MACARAK, E.
GIBSON, C.

Biochemistry:

ADAMS, S.
GOLUB, E. E.
LEBOY, P.
MALAMUD, D.

Endodontics:

KIM, S.

Microbiology:

COHEN, G.
DIRIENZO, J.
RICCIARDI, R.

Oral Medicine:

GREENBERG, M.

Oral Surgery:

FONSECA, R.
HERSH, E.
QUINN, P.

Orthodontics:

KATZ, S.
VANARSDALL, R.

Pathology:

LALLY, E.
SHENKER, B.

Periodontics:

EVIANS, C.
JEFFCOAT, M.
POLSON, A.

School of Education:

BOE, E.
BORUCH, R.
FANTUZZO, J.
FUHRMAN, S.
GOERTZ, M.
GOODMAN, J.
HORNBERGER, N.
INGERSOLL, R.
KURILOFF, P.

LAZERSON, M.
MCDERMOTT, P.
MAYNARD, R.
PICA, T.
SLAUGHTER-DEFOE, D.
SPENCER, M. B.
WAGNER, D.
WORTHAM, S.
ZEMSKY, R. M.

School of Engineering and Applied Science:

ALUR, R.
AYYASWAMY, P.
BADLER, N.
BASSANI, J.
BAU, H.
BONNELL, D.
BORDOGNA, J.
BUCHSBAUM, G.
CASSEL, T.
CHEN, I.-W.
COHEN, I.
DAVIDSON, S.
DAVIES, P.
DIAMOND, S.
DUCHEYNE, P.
EGAMI, T.
ENGHETA, N.
FARHAT, N.
FINKEL, L.
FISCHER, J.
FOSTER, K.
GALLIER, J. H.
GIRIFALCO, L.
GLANDT, E.
GORTE, R.
GRAHAM, W.
GUERIN, R.
HAMMER, D.
JAGGARD, D.
JOSHI, A.
KANNAN, S.
KASSAM, S.
KEARNS, M.
KEENAN, J.
KUMAR, V.
LAIRD, C.
LAKER, K.
LEE, I.
LIOR, N.
LUZZI, D.
MACARAK, E.
MARCUS, M. P.
MARGULIES, S.
MEANEY, D.
MINTZ, M.
PEREIRA, F.
PIERCE, B.
PONTE-CASTANEDA, P.
POPE, D.
RABII, S.
SCHERER, P.
SEIDER, W.
SHIEH, W.
SILVERMAN, B.
SMITH, J. M.
SMITH, T.
SOSLOWSKY, L.
TANNEN, V. B.
ULRICH, K.
VAN DER SPEIGEL, J.
VITEK, V.
VOHS, J.
VUCHIC, V.

School of Law:

ADLER, M.
ALLEN-CASTELLITO, A.
AUSTIN, R.
BAKER, C. E.
BURBANK, S.
CHANG, H.
DELISLE, J.
EWALD, W.
FINKELSTEIN, C.
FITTS, M.
GOODMAN, F.

GORDON, S.
JOHNSTON, J.
KATZ, L.
KNOLL, M.
KREIMER, S.
KUBLER, F.
LESNICK, H.
MANN, B.
MOONEY, C.
MORSE, S.
PARCHOMOVSKY, G.
PERRY, S.
REITZ, C.
ROBINSON, P.
ROCK, E.
RUBIN, E.
SANCHIRICO, C.
SCHEPPLE, K. L.
SHULDINER, R.
SKEEL, D.
WACHTER, M.
WAX, A.

School of Nursing:
AIKEN, L.
BARNSTEINER, J.
BROWN, L. P.
BUHLER-WILKERSON, K.
EVANS, L.
GENNARO, S.
JEMMOTT, L.
LANG, N.
McCAULEY, L.
MEDOFF-COOPER, B.
MELEIS, A.
NAYLOR, M.
O'SULLIVAN, A.
STRUMPF, N.

School of Social Work
  Social Work:
CNAAN, R.
ESTES, R.
SANDS, R.
SELTZER, V.
SOLOMON, P.
SPIGNER, C.
STERN, M.

School of Veterinary Medicine:
AQUIRRE, G.
ATCHISON, M.
AVADHANI, N.
BEECH, J.
BELLO, L.
BENSON, C.
BOSTON, R.
BRINSTER, R.
CHACKO, S.
CHALUPA, W.
DAVIES, R.
DODSON, P.
DROBATZ, K.
EISENBERG, R.
FARRELL, J.
FERGUSON, J.
FERRER, J.
FLUHARTY, S.
GIGER, U.
GOLDSCHMIDT, M. H.
HARVEY, C.
HASKINS, M.
HENDRICKS, J. C.
KELLY, A.
KING, L.
KLIDE, A.
LASTER, L.
MISELIS, R.
NEWTON, C.
NUNAMAKER, D.
RAMBERG, C.
REEF, V.
RICHARDSON, D.
ROSS, M.
ROZMIAREK, H.
SCHAD, G.
SCOTT, P.

SERPELL, J.
SHAPIRO, B.
SMITH, G.
SOMA, L.
SPEAR, J.
SWEENEY, C.
WEBER, W.
WEISS, L.
WOLFE, J. H.

PennDesign:
GYOURKO, J.
LINNEMAN, P.
POINDEXTER, G.
RYBCZYNSKI, W.
SAGALYN, L.

UNIVERSITY OF PITTSBURGH

Pittsburgh, PA 15260
Telephone: (412) 624-4141
Internet: www.pitt.edu

Founded 1787 as Pittsburgh Acad., present
  name 1908, present status 1966
State control
Academic year: August to April (2 semesters)
Chancellor: MARK A. NORDENBERG
Provost and Sr Vice-Chancellor: PATRICIA E.
  BEESON
Assoc. Chancellor: VIJAI SINGH
Exec. Vice-Chancellor and Gen. Counsel:
  JEROME COCHRAN
Sr Vice-Chancellor for Health Sciences: Dr
  ARTHUR S. LEVINE
Chief Financial Officer: ARTHUR G. RAMICONE
Vice-Chancellor for Community Initiatives
  and Chief of Staff: G. REYNOLDS CLARK
Vice-Chancellor for Govt Relations: PAUL
  SUPOWITZ
Vice-Chancellor for Health Sciences Devt:
  CLYDE B. JONES, III
Vice-Chancellor for Institutional Advance-
  ment: ALBERT J. NOVAK, JR
Vice-Chancellor for Public Affairs: ROBERT
  HILL
Vice-Chancellor for Research Conduct and
  Compliance: RANDY JUHL
Vice-Provost and Dean for Students: KATHY
  W. HUMPHREY
Univ. Registrar: RALPH E. HERTEL
Dir for Univ. Library System: RUSH G.
  MILLER

Library: see under Libraries and Archives
Number of teachers: 4,938
Number of students: 28,766

Publications: *Pitt Magazine* (4 a year), *Pitt
  Med* (4 a year), *Pittsburgh Economic Quarterly*, *The Original* (2 a year)

DEANS

College of General Studies: N. JOHN COOPER
Dietrich School of Arts and Sciences: N. JOHN
  COOPER
Graduate School of Public and International
  Affairs: JOHN T. S. KEELER
Graduate School of Public Health: Dr
  DONALD S. BURKE
Joseph M. Katz Graduate School of Business
  and College of Business Admin.: JOHN T.
  DELANEY
School of Dental Medicine: THOMAS W. BRAUN
School of Education: ALAN LESGOLD
School of Health and Rehabilitation Sciences:
  CLIFFORD E. BRUBAKER
School of Information Sciences: RONALD L.
  LARSEN
School of Law: WILLIAM M. CARTER
School of Medicine: Dr ARTHUR S. LEVINE
School of Nursing: Dr JACQUELINE DUNBAR-
  JACOB
School of Pharmacy: PATRICIA DOWLEY KRO-
  BOTH
School of Social Work: LARRY E. DAVIS
Swanson School of Engineering: GERALD D.
  HOLDER

Univ. Honors College: EDWARD M. STRICKER

REGIONAL CAMPUSES

University of Pittsburgh at Bradford:
300 Campus Dr., Bradford, PA 16701; tel.
(814) 362-7500; fax (814) 362-7588; internet
www.upb.pitt.edu; f. 1963, present status
1979; academic year August to April; 5
academic divs: behavioral and social sciences; biological and health sciences; communication and the arts; management and
education; physical and computational sciences; Pres. Dr LIVINGSTON ALEXANDER; Vice-
Pres. and Dean for Academic Affairs STEVE
HARDIN; Registrar JAMES L. BALDWIN; library
of 97,963 vols, 3,782 audiovisual materials,
1,055 microform items, 50,000 e-journals,
300,000 e-books; 137 (78 full-time, 59 part-
time) teachers; 1,564 students.

University of Pittsburgh at Greensburg:
150 Finoli Dr., Greensburg, PA 15601; tel.
(724) 837-7040; internet www.greensburg
.pitt.edu; f. 1963, present status 1988; academic year August to April; Pres. SHARON P.
SMITH; Vice-Pres. for Academic Affairs Dr J.
WESLEY JAMISON; Registrar LINDA SMITH;
library of 78,000 vols; 92 teachers; 1,803
students.

University of Pittsburgh at Johnstown:
450 Schoolhouse Rd, Johnstown, PA 15904;
tel. (814) 269-7000; fax (814) 269-7044;
e-mail upjadmit@pitt.edu; internet www.upj
.pitt.edu; f. 1927; academic year August to
April; Divs: education; engineering technology; humanities; natural science; nursing
and health sciences; social science; Pres. Dr
JEM M. SPECTAR; Vice-Pres. for Academic
Affairs Dr JANET L. GRADY; Vice-Pres. for
Enrolment Services and Planning Dr JAMES
F. GYURE; Vice-Pres. for Finance and Admin.
Dr KELLY M. AUSTIN; Vice-Pres. for Student
Affairs JONATHAN D. WESCOTT; library of
230,000 vols; 253 (141 full-time, 112 part-
time) teachers; 3,000 students.

University of Pittsburgh at Titusville:
504 E Main St, Titusville, PA 16354; tel.
(814) 827-4400; internet www.upt.pitt.edu; f.
1963; academic year August to April; Pres.
Dr WILLIAM A. SHIELDS; Vice-Pres. for Academic Affairs Dr DAVID E. FITZ; Vice-Pres. for
Business Affairs DENISE McCLOSKEY; Vice-
Pres. for Student Affairs Dr CHECKA LEIN-
WALL; Registrar CHRISTOPHER COAT; library of
40,000 vols; 65 teachers; 514 students; publ.
Panther Print.

UNIVERSITY OF SCRANTON

800 Linden St, Scranton, PA 18510-4699
Telephone: (570) 941-7400
Fax: (570) 941-5928
E-mail: info@scranton.edu
Internet: www.scranton.edu

Founded 1888 as St Thomas College, present
  status 1938
Private control
Academic year: August to May
Pres.: Rev. Dr KEVIN QUINN
Provost and Vice-Pres. for Academic Affairs:
  Dr HAROLD W. BAILLIE
Exec. Vice-Pres.: PATRICK LEAHY
Vice-Pres. for Alumni and Public Relations:
  GERALD C. ZABOSKI
Vice-Pres. for Finance and Treas.: EDWARD J.
  STEINMETZ
Vice-Pres. for Student Affairs: Dr VINCENT
  CARILLI
Registrar: HELEN H. STAGER
Gen. Counsel: ROBERT B. FARRELL
Dean for Library: CHARLES E. KRATZ

Library of 514,915 vols, 17,498 non-print
  item, 48,201 journals print and online
Number of teachers: 287 (full-time)
Number of students: 6,034

Publications: *Diakonia, The Scranton Journal* (4 a year), *Windhover* (1 a year)

DEANS

Arthur J. Kania School of Management: Dr MICHAEL O. MENSAH

College of Arts and Sciences: Dr BRIAN P. CONIFF

College of Graduate and Continuing Education: Dr WILLIAM JEFFREY WELSH

Panuska College of Professional Studies: Dr DEBRA A. PELLIGRINO

UNIVERSITY OF THE ARTS

320 S Broad St, Philadelphia, PA 19102

Telephone: (215) 717-6030

Fax: (215) 717-6045

E-mail: admissions@uarts.edu

Internet: www.uarts.edu

Founded 1985 by merger of Philadelphia College of Art (f. 1876) with Philadelphia College of the Performing Arts (f. 1870), present name and status 1984

Private control

Academic year: September to May

Pres.: SEAN T. BUFFINGTON

Provost: Dr KIRK E. PILLOW

Vice-Pres. for Advancement: LUCIE HUGHES

Vice-Pres. for Enrolment, Retention and Student Affairs: R. ALAN LEFFERS

Vice-Pres. for Facilities Management and Operations: PHILLIP VAN CLEAVE

Vice-Pres. for Finance and Admin.: STEPHEN J. LIGHTCAP

Vice-Pres. for Technology and Information Services: THOMAS H. CARNWATH

Vice-Pres. for Univ. Communications: PAUL F. HEALY

Dean for Admissions: SUSAN GANDY

Dean for Students: ALLEN LEFFERS

Dir for Libraries: CAROL GRANEY

Number of teachers: 546 (126 full-time, 420 part-time)

Number of students: 2,200

DEANS

College of Art, Media and Design: CHRISTOPHER SHARROCK

Division of Continuing Studies: ERIN ELMAN

Division of Liberal Arts: PETER STAMBLER

UNIVERSITY OF THE SCIENCES

600 S 43rd St, Philadelphia, PA 19104-4495

Telephone: (215) 596-8800

E-mail: admit@usciences.edu

Internet: www.usciences.edu

Founded 1821 as Philadelphia College of Pharmacy

Private control

Academic year: August to May

Pres.: Dr MARVIN SAMSON

Provost and Sr Vice-Pres. for Academic Affairs: Dr RUSSELL J. DiGATE

Sr Vice-Pres. for Finance and Treas.: JOSEPH G. TRAINOR

Sr Vice-Pres. for Operations and Chief Operations Officer: SARA M. CAMPBELL

Vice-Pres. for External Affairs: WILLIAM L. ASHTON

Vice-Pres. for Institutional Effectiveness: Dr PETER MILLER

Dean for Students: Dr WILLIAM CUNNINGHAM

Registrar: M. THERESE SCANLON

Dir for Library and Information Services: CHARLES J. MYERS

Library of 76,000 vols

Number of teachers: 161 (full-time)

Number of students: 2,970 (2,600 undergraduate, 370 graduate)

Publication: *The Bulletin*

DEANS

College of Graduate Studies: Dr RODNEY J. WIGENT

Mayes College of Healthcare Business and Policy: ANDREW PETERSON

Misher College of Arts and Sciences: Dr SUZANNE MURPHY

Philadelphia College of Pharmacy: Dr LISA LAWSON

Samson College of Health Sciences: Dr LAURIE SHERWEN

URSINUS COLLEGE

POB 1000, 601 E Main St, Collegeville, PA 19426-1000

Telephone: (610) 409-3000

Fax: (610) 409-3197

E-mail: admissions@ursinus.edu

Internet: www.ursinus.edu

Founded 1869

Private control

Pres.: Dr BOBBY FONG

Sr Vice-Pres. for Advancement: JILL MARSTELLER

Vice-Pres. for Academic Affairs: JUDITH T. LEVY

Vice-Pres. for Enrolment: RICK DiFELICIANTONIO

Vice-Pres. for Finance and Admin.: WINFIELD GUILMETTE

Dean for Student Affairs: DEBORAH NOLAN

Registrar: BARBARA BORIS

Library Dir: CHARLIE JAMISON

Library of 420,000 vols

Number of teachers: 165

Number of students: 1,750

Publication: *The Lantern* (2 a year).

VALLEY FORGE CHRISTIAN COLLEGE

1401 Charlestown Rd, Phoenixville, PA 19460

Telephone: (610) 935-0450

Fax: (610) 917-2069

E-mail: admissions@vfcc.edu

Internet: www.vfcc.edu

Founded 1931 as Maranatha Summer Bible School, present name 1977

Private control

Academic year: August to May

Pres.: Dr DONALD G. MEYER

Provost and Vice-Pres. for Academic Affairs: Dr PHILIP MCLEOD

Vice-Pres. for Finance: RICK DUNHAM

Vice-Pres. for Institutional Advancement: CHARLES COLES

Vice-Pres. for Student Life: JENNIFER GALE

Registrar: RUSSELL CAMBRIA

Dir for Library: PAUL MATHIAS

Number of teachers: 75

Number of students: 856

VILLANOVA UNIVERSITY

800 E Lancaster Ave, Villanova, PA 19085-1603

Telephone: (610) 519-4500

Fax: (610) 519-6450

E-mail: gotovu@villanova.edu

Internet: www.villanova.edu

Founded 1842

Academic year: August to May

Private control

Pres.: Rev. Dr PETER M. DONOHUE

Vice-Pres. and Gen. Counsel: DOROTHY MALLOY

Vice-Pres. for Academic Affairs: Rev. Dr KAIL C. ELLIS

Vice-Pres. for Admin. and Finance: Rev. KENNETH G. VALOSKY

Vice-Pres. for Institutional Advancement: JOHN M. ELIZANDRO

Vice-Pres. for Student Life: Rev. JOHN P. STACK

Registrar: PAMELA J. BRAXTON

Librarian: JOSEPH LUCIA

Library of 1,010,421 vols, 2,998 periodicals, 1,789,816 microforms

Number of teachers: 820 (511 full-time, 309 part-time)

Number of students: 10,467

Publication: *Villanova Magazine*

DEANS

College of Engineering: Dr GARY A. GABRIELE

College of Liberal Arts and Science: Dr JEAN ANN LINNEY

College of Nursing: Dr M. LOUISE FITZPATRICK

School of Law: JOHN Y. GOTANDA

Villanova School of Business: Dr KEVIN D. CLARK

WASHINGTON & JEFFERSON COLLEGE

60 S Lincoln St, Washington, PA 15301

Telephone: (724) 222-4400

Fax: (724) 223-6534

E-mail: info@washjeff.edu

Internet: www.washjeff.edu

Founded 1781

Private control

Academic year: September to May

Pres.: Dr TORI HARING-SMITH

Vice-Pres. for Academic Affairs and Dean for Faculty: JOHN ZIMMERMAN

Vice-Pres. for Business and Finance and Chief Financial Officer: DENNIS MCMASTER

Vice-Pres. for Devt and Alumni Relations: MICHAEL GRZESIAK

Vice-Pres. for Enrolment: ALTON E. NEWELL

Vice-Pres. and Dean for Student Life: BYRON MCCRAE

Dir for Admissions: ROBERT ADKINS

Dir for Financial Aid: MICHELLE ANDERSON

Dir for Library Services: ALEXIS RITTENBERGER

Registrar: LESLIE MAXIN

Library of 186,925 vols, 15,532 microforms, 10,217 audiovisual materials, 3,958 e-books, 34,679 current serial subscriptions and periodicals

Number of teachers: 160 (113 full-time, 47 part-time)

Number of students: 1,457 (1,436 full-time, 21 part-time)

Publications: *Follow the Leader, Topic, Washington & Jefferson College Review* (1 a year), *Wooden Tooth Review* (1 a year)

PROFESSORS

BENZE, J., Jr, Political Science

BRLETIC, P., Chemistry

CAMERON, W., Theatre and Communications

CAVOTI, N., Psychology

CRABTREE, M., Psychology

DiSARRO, J., Political Science

DODGE, R., History

DREW-BEAR, A., English

DRYDEN, R., Biology

EASTON, R., English

GORMLY, J., History

GREB, E., Sociology

GREGOR, J., Economics and Business

KUHN, S., Economics and Business

KYLER, C., English

LEE, A., Biology

LIST, V., History

LONGO, J., Education

MAINWARING, W., History

MALONEY, P., Art

MILLER, S., Sociology

MORROW, D., Mathematics

MYERS, S., Psychology

ROBISON, K., Economics and Business
SCOTT, J., Jr, Modern Languages
SHEERS, W., Physics
STATON, V., Physical Education
TRELKA, D., Biology
TROOST, L., English
VAN DE KAPPELLE, R., Religion
WEST, J., Economics and Business
WOLTERMANN, M., Mathematics
WONG, R., Mathematics
WOODARD, S., Music

WAYNESBURG UNIVERSITY

51 W College St, Waynesburg, PA 15370
Telephone: (724) 627-8191
E-mail: admissions@waynesburg.edu
Internet: www.waynesburg.edu
Founded 1849 as Waynesburg College
Private control
Academic year: August to May
Pres.: TIMOTHY R. THYREEN
Provost: Dr ROBERT GRAHAM
Sr Vice-Pres. for Enrolment and Marketing: ROBIN L. KING
Sr Vice-Pres. for Institutional Planning, Research and Educational Services: RICHARD L. NOFTZGER, Jr
Exec. Vice-Pres. for Institutional Advancement: DOUG LEE
Vice-Pres. for Business and Finance: ROY R. BARNHART
Vice-Pres. of Student Devt: GERALD WOOD
Dir for Admissions: SARAH E. ZWINGER
Dir for Univ. Relations: BETHANY DOYLE
Registrar: VICKI WILSON
Library Dir: REA REDD
Library of 100,000 vols
Number of teachers: 128
Number of students: 2,500 (1,500 under-graduate, 900 graduate and professional adults)
Publication: *The Lamp*.

WESTMINSTER COLLEGE

319 S Market St, New Wilmington, PA 16172-0001
Telephone: (724) 946-8761
Fax: (724) 946-7171
Internet: www.westminster.edu
Founded 1852
Private control
Academic year: August to May
Pres.: Dr RICHARD H. DORMAN
Vice-Pres. for Academic Affairs and Dean for College: JESSE T. MANN
Vice-Pres. for Enrolment: BRADLEY P. TOKAR
Vice-Pres. for Finance and Management Services: KENNETH J. ROMIG
Vice-Pres. for Institutional Advancement: GLORIA C. CAGIGAS
Vice-Pres. for Student Affairs and Dean of Students: NEAL A. EDMAN
Registrar: JUNE G. PIERCE
Head Librarian: MOLLY P. SPINNEY
Library of 224,000 vols
Number of teachers: 100
Number of students: 1,550
Publications: *Scrawl, Westminster Magazine* (4 a year).

WESTMINSTER THEOLOGICAL SEMINARY

POB 27009, Philadelphia, PA 19118
2960 W Church Rd, Glenside, PA 19038
Telephone: (215) 887-5511
Fax: (215) 887-5404
E-mail: admissions@wts.edu
Internet: www.wts.edu
Founded 1929
Private control

Academic year: June to May
4 Campuses: Philadelphia, Dallas, New York and London, United Kingdom
Pres.: Dr PETER A. LILLBACK
Provost: Dr CARL TRUEMAN
Chief Administrative Officer: STEVEN CARTER
Chief Financial Officer: MARK WILSON
Chief Operating Officer: A. D. DABNEY
Vice-Pres. for Academic Affairs: Dr CARL R. TRUEMAN
Vice-Pres. and Dean of Texas Campus: STEVEN T. VANDERHILL
Vice-Pres. for Devt: WILLIAM BROWN VINCENT, JR
Vice-Pres. for Institutional Partnerships: Dr DAVID B. GARNER
Dean for Students: GREG HOBAUGH
Registrar and Dir for Financial Aid: MELINDA E. G. DUGAN
Library Dir: ALEXANDER FINLAYSON
Library of 140,000 vols, 700 current periodical titles
Number of teachers: 50
Number of students: 450 (full-time)

WIDENER UNIVERSITY

One University Pl., Chester, PA 19013-5792
Telephone: (610) 499-4000
Fax: (610) 876-9751
E-mail: presoffc@widener.edu
Internet: www.widener.edu
Founded 1821, fmrly Widener College, present name and status 1979
Private control
Campuses in Delaware, Exton and Harrisburg
Pres: Dr JAMES T. HARRIS, III
Provost and Sr Vice-Pres. for Academic Affairs: Dr STEPHEN C. WILHITE
Sr Vice-Pres. for Admin. and Finance: JOSEPH J. BAKER
Sr Vice-Pres. for Univ. Advancement: LINDA S. DURANT
Dean for Student Services: DENISE GIFFORD
Library Dir: ROBERT DANFORD
Library of 845,762 vols
Number of teachers: 720 (326 full-time, 394 part-time)
Number of students: 6,464 (3,823 full-time, 3,532 part-time)
Publications: *Corporate Law Journal, Law Review, Widener Law Symposium Journal*

DEANS

College of Arts and Sciences: Dr MATTHEW POSLUSNY
School of Business Administration: Dr SAVAS ÖZATALAY
School of Engineering: Dr FRED A. AKL
School of Hospitality Management: NICHOLAS J. HADGIS
School of Human Service Professions: Dr PAULA T. SILVER (acting)
School of Nursing: Dr DEBORAH R. GARRISON
University College: Dr DON DEVILBISS

WILKES UNIVERSITY

84 W S St, Wilkes-Barre, PA 18766
Telephone: (570) 408-5000
Fax: (570) 408-7800
E-mail: info@wilkes.edu
Internet: www.wilkes.edu
Founded 1933 as Bucknell Univ. Jr College, present name and status 1990
Private control
Academic year: August to May
Pres.: PATRICK F. LEAHY
Provost: REYNOLD VERRET
Vice-Pres. for Advancement: MICHAEL WOOD
Vice-Pres. for Devt: MARTY WILLIAMS

Vice-Pres. for Enrolment: MELANIE MICKELSON
Vice-Pres. for Finance and Gen. Counsel: LOREN D. PRESCOTT, JR
Vice-Pres. for Human Resources: MAGGIE LUND
Vice-Pres. for Student Affairs: PAUL S. ADAMS
Registrar: SUSAN A. HRITZAK
Dean for Library: JOHN STACHACZ
Library of 200,000 vols, 800,000 microforms, 400 current journals
Number of teachers: 122 (full-time)
Number of students: 2,000 (full-time)

DEANS

College of Arts, Humanities and Social Sciences: Dr LINDA A. WINKLER
College of Graduate and Professional Studies: MICHAEL SPEZIALE
College of Science and Engineering: Dr DALE A. BURNS
Jay S. Sidhu School of Business and Leadership: Dr JEFFREY R. ALVES
Nesbit College of Pharmacy of Nursing: Dr BERNARD W. GRAHAM
School of Education: MICHAEL SPEZIALE

WILSON COLLEGE

1015 Philadelphia Ave, Chambersburg, PA 17201-1285
Telephone: (717) 264-4141
Fax: (717) 264-1578
E-mail: admissions@wilson.edu
Internet: www.wilson.edu
Founded 1869
Private control
Academic year: August to May
Liberal arts college for women
Pres.: Dr BARBARA K. MISTICK
Vice-Pres. for Academic Affairs and Dean for Faculty: MARY HENDRICKSON
Vice-Pres. for Enrolment: MARY ANN NASO
Vice-Pres. for Finance and Admin.: LORI TOSTEN
Vice-Pres. for College Advancement: JEFF ZUFELT
Registrar: JEAN HOOVER
Library Dir: KATHLEEN MURPHY
Library of 177,491 vols, 450 periodicals
Number of teachers: 77 (38 full-time, 39 part-time)
Number of students: 800

WON INSTITUTE OF GRADUATE STUDIES

137 S Easton Rd, Glenside, PA 19038
Telephone: (215) 884-8942
Fax: (215) 884-9002
E-mail: administration@woninstitute.edu
Internet: www.woninstitute.edu
Courses in acupuncture studies, applied meditation studies and Won Buddhist studies
Private control
Pres.: Dr BOKIN KIM
Chief Academic Officer: COLLEEN O'CONNELL
Chief Finance Officer: MARIA PERRY
Academic Dean: Dr LINDA LELII.

YORK COLLEGE OF PENNSYLVANIA

441 Country Club Rd, York, PA 17403-3651
Telephone: (717) 846-7788
Fax: (717) 846-1607
E-mail: admissions@ycp.edu
Internet: www.ycp.edu
Founded 1787 as York County Acad., present name 1968
Private control
Academic year: August to May

Courses in behavioural sciences; biological sciences; business; education; English and humanities; history and political science; hospitality, recreation and sport management; music, art and communication; nursing; physical sciences

Pres.: Dr GEORGE W. WALDNER
Dean for Academic Services: Dr DEBORAH RICKER (acting)
Dean for College Advancement: DANIEL HELWIG
Dean for Student Affairs: JOSEPH F. MERKLE
Registrar: REBECCA LINK
Library Dir: SUSAN M. CAMPBELL
Number of teachers: 162 (full-time)
Number of students: 4,900 (4,600 full-time undergraduate, 300 graduate)

Publication: *Past and Present*.

RHODE ISLAND

BROWN UNIVERSITY

Providence, RI 02912
Telephone: (401) 863-1000
Fax: (401) 863-9300
E-mail: president@brown.edu
Internet: www.brown.edu
Founded 1764 as College of Rhode Island
Private control
Academic year: September to May
Chancellor: THOMAS J. TISCH
Pres. and CEO: RUTH J. SIMMONS
Provost: MARK S. SCHLISSEL
Sr Vice-Pres. for Corporation Affairs and Governance: RUSSELL CAREY
Sr Vice-Pres. for Univ. Advancement: STEVEN KING
Exec. Vice-Pres. for Finance and Admin.: ELIZABETH HUIDEKOPER
Exec. Vice-Pres. for Planning: RICHARD R. SPIES
Vice-Pres. and Chief Investment Officer: CYNTHIA E. FROST
Vice-Pres. and Gen. Counsel: BEVERLY E. LEDBETTER
Vice-Pres. for Campus Life and Student Services: MARGARET KLAWUNN
Vice-Pres. for Computing and Information Services: MICHAEL PICKETT (acting)
Vice-Pres. for Devt: (vacant)
Vice-Pres. for Facilities Management: STEPHEN MAIORISI
Vice-Pres. for Int. Affairs: MATTHEW GUTMANN
Vice-Pres. for Public Affairs and Univ. Relations: MARISA QUINN
Vice-Pres. for Research: CLYDE BRIANT
Vice-Pres. and Chief Information Officer: MICHAEL PICKETT
Dean for College: KATHERINE BERGERON
Dean for Admission: JAMES MILLER
Dean for Faculty: KEVIN MCLAUGHLIN
Univ. Registrar: ROBERT F. FITZGERALD
Univ. Librarian: EDWARD WIDMER
Library: 6.8m. vols
Number of teachers: 688
Number of students: 8,454 (6,118 undergraduate, 1,919 graduate, 417 medical)

Publications: *Brown Alumni Magazine* (2 a year), *Somos* (2 a year), *Visions* (1 a year)

DEANS

Continuing Education: KAREN SIBLEY
Division of Biology and Medicine: Dr EDWARD J. WING
Graduate School: Prof. PETER M. WEBER
School of Engineering: LAWRENCE LARSON

BRYANT UNIVERSITY

1150 Douglas Pike, Smithfield, RI 02917-1284
Telephone: (401) 232-6000
Fax: (401) 232-6319
E-mail: admission@bryant.edu
Internet: www.bryant.edu
Founded 1863 as Bryant and Stratton Nat. Business College, present name 2004
Private control
Academic year: September to August
Pres.: RONALD K. MACHTLEY
Vice-Pres. for Academic Affairs: Dr JOSÉ-MARIE GRIFFITHS
Vice-Pres. for Business Affairs: BARRY MORRISON
Vice-Pres. for Enrolment Management: LORNA J. HUNTER
Vice-Pres. for Information Services: CHUCK LOCURTO
Vice-Pres. for Student Affairs: J. THOMAS EAKIN
Vice-Pres. for Univ. Advancement: JAMES DAMRON
Dir for Library Services: MARY F. MORONEY
Library: over 150,000 vols, 25,000 journals
Number of students: 3,614 (3,370 undergraduate, 244 graduate)

Publication: *Bryant magazine* (3 a year)

DEANS

College of Arts and Sciences: DAVID LUX
College of Business: MICHAEL COOPER

JOHNSON & WALES UNIVERSITY

8 Abbott Park Pl., Providence, RI 02903
Telephone: (401) 598-1000
Fax: (401) 598-2880
E-mail: admissions@jwu.edu
Internet: www.jwu.edu
Founded 1914 as business school, present name 1988, present status 1992
Private control
Academic year: September to August
Campuses in Charleston (South Carolina), Denver (Colorado), North Miami (Florida)
Chancellor: Dr JOHN J. BOWEN
Vice-Chancellor: THOMAS L. G. DWYER
Provost: Dr VEERA S. GAUL
Chief Financial Officer and Treas.: WILLIAM F. MCARDLE
Sr Vice-Pres. and Gen. Counsel: Dr WAYNE M. KEZIRIAN
Sr Vice-Pres. for Enrolment Management: KENNETH F. DISAIA
Sr Vice-Pres. for Student Services: MARIE BERNARDO-SOUSA
Vice-Pres. for Academic Affairs: Dr JEFFREY SENESE
Vice-Pres. for Finance: JOSEPH J. GREENE
Vice-Pres. for Student Affairs: Dr RONALD L. MARTEL
Registrar: TAMMY HARRIGAN
Dean for Libraries: Dr HELENA RODRIGUES
Number of students: 17,230

Publication: *JWU Magazine* (4 a year)

DEANS

Alan Shawn Feinstein Graduate School: Dr FRANK PONTARELLI
College of Business: Dr DAVID M. MITCHELL
College of Culinary Arts: Dr KARL J. GUGGENMOS
Hospitality College: RICHARD L. BRUSH
John Hazen White School of Arts and Sciences: Dr ANGELA R. RENAUD
School of Technology: FRANCIS X. TWEEDIE

NEW ENGLAND INSTITUTE OF TECHNOLOGY

1 New England Tech Blvd, East Greenwich, RI 02818-1205
Telephone: (401) 467-7744
Fax: (401) 738-8990
E-mail: info@neit.edu
Internet: www.neit.edu
Founded 1940 as New England Technical Institute, present name 1977, present status 1984
Private control
Areas of study: criminal justice technology, interior design, software engineering technology
Pres.: RICHARD I. GOUSE
Provost and Sr Vice-Pres.: Dr THOMAS F. WYLIE
Sr Vice-Pres. for Financial Affairs: CHERYL C. CONNORS
Exec. Vice-Pres.: SETH A. KURN
Vice-Pres. and Gen. Counsel: PHILIP G. PARSONS
Vice-Pres. for Devt and Alumni Relations: ALLAN A. LANGER
Vice-Pres. for Student Support Services: CATHERINE KENNEDY
Dir for Admissions: MARK BLONDIN
Registrar: DOREEN LASIEWSKI
Library Dir: SHARON J. CHARETTE
Number of students: 3,200

PROVIDENCE COLLEGE

1 Cunningham Sq., Providence, RI 02918-0001
Telephone: (401) 865-1000
Fax: (401) 865-2826
E-mail: pcadmiss@providence.edu
Internet: www.providence.edu
Founded 1917
Private control
Academic year: September to May
Pres.: Rev. BRIAN J. SHANLEY
Provost and Sr Vice-Pres. for Academic Affairs: Dr HUGH LENA
Sr Vice-Pres. and Chief Financial Officer: JOHN SWEENEY
Sr Vice-Pres. for Institutional Advancement: DAVID WEGRZYN
Exec. Vice-Pres. and Treas.: Rev. KENNETH SICARD
Vice-Pres. and Gen. Counsel: MARIFRANCES McGINN
Vice-Pres. for Academic Affairs: Dr HUGH LENA
Vice-Pres. for College Relations and Planning: EDWARD J. CARON
Vice-Pres. for Finance and Business: MICHAEL FRAZIER
Vice-Pres. for Student Affairs: KRISTINE GOODWIN
Dean for Admission: RAÚL A. FONTS
Librarian: Dr RUSSELL BAILEY
Library: 375,000 vols, 240,000 e-books, 38,000 e-journals
Number of teachers: 310 (276 full-time, 34 part-time)
Number of students: 4,500

DEANS

International Studies: ADRIAN G. BEAULIEU
Multicultural Affairs: Dr EDWARD TWYMAN
School of Arts and Sciences: Dr SHEILA ADAMUS LIOTTA
School of Business: Dr MARY JANE LENON
School of Continuing Education: JANET L. CASTLEMAN
School of Professional Studies: Dr BRIAN M. McCADDEN

RHODE ISLAND COLLEGE

600 Mount Pleasant Ave, Providence, RI 02908-1991

Telephone: (401) 456-8000
Fax: (401) 456-8379
E-mail: graduatestudies@ric.edu
Internet: www.ric.edu

Founded 1854 as Rhode Island State Normal School, present name 1959
State control
Academic year: August to August (2 semesters)

Pres.: NANCY CARRIUOLO
Vice-Pres. for Academic Affairs: RONALD E. PITT
Vice-Pres. for Admin. and Finance: WILLIAM H. GEARHART
Vice-Pres. for College Advancement: JAMES SALMO
Vice-Pres. for Student Affairs: GARY M. PENFIELD
Dir for Admissions: LUCILLE RIOS SAUNDERS
Library Dir: HEDI BENAICHA
Library of 654,000 vols, 2,600 print and e-periodicals, 1m. microforms
Number of teachers: 375
Number of students: 9,044

DEANS

Faculty of Arts and Sciences: EARL SIMSON
Feinstein School of Education and Human Development: ALEXANDER SIDORKIN
School of Management: DAVID BLANCHETTE
School of Nursing: JANE WILLIAMS
School of Social Work: SUE PEARLMUTTER

RHODE ISLAND SCHOOL OF DESIGN

2 College St, Providence, RI 02903-2784

Telephone: (401) 454-6100
Fax: (401) 454-6420
E-mail: admissions@risd.edu
Internet: www.risd.edu

Founded 1877
Private control
Academic year: September to May

Pres.: Dr JOHN MAIDA
Provost: ROSANNE SOMERSON
Sr Vice-Pres. for Enrolment and Students Services: JEAN C. EDDY
Exec. Vice-Pres. for Finance and Admin.: WILLIAM DECATUR
Vice-Pres. for Institutional Engagement: ERIC GRAAGE
Dir for Admissions: EDWARD NEWHALL
Dir for Institutional Research: JENNIFER DUNSEATH
Dir for Library Services: CAROL TERRY
Library of 140,667 vols, 400 periodicals
Number of teachers: 542
Number of students: 2,396

DEANS

Architecture and Design: WILLIAM NEWKIRK
Fine Arts: Prof. ANAIS A. MISSAKIAN
Foundation Studies: Prof. JOANNE STRYKER
Graduate Studies: BRIAN GOLDBERG
Liberal Arts: Dr BARBARA VON ECKARDT

ROGER WILLIAMS UNIVERSITY

1 Old Ferry Rd, Bristol, RI 02809

Telephone: (401) 253-1040
Fax: (401) 254-3557
E-mail: admit@rwu.edu
Internet: www.rwu.edu

Founded 1919 as br. of Northeastern Univ., present name and status 1992
Private control
Academic year: September to May

Pres.: Dr DONALD J. FARISH
Provost: Dr ROBERT A. POTTER

Sr Vice-Pres. for Enrolment Management: LYNN M. FAWTHROP
Sr Vice-Pres. for Legal Affairs and Gen. Counsel: ROBERT H. AVERY
Vice-Pres. and Chief Information Officer: JOSEPH PANGBORN
Exec. Vice-Pres. for Finance and Admin.: JEROME F. WILLIAMS
Vice-Pres. for Student Affairs: Dr JOHN J. KING
Vice-Pres. for Univ. Advancement: ROBERT L. WEST
Registrar: ANNIE RUSSELL (acting)
Dean for Libraries: PETER DEEKLE
Number of teachers: 315
Number of students: 5,169 (3,840 full-time undergraduate, 823 postgraduate and professional, 506 continuing studies)
Publications: *RWU Law, RWU: The Magazine of Roger Williams University* (2 a year)

DEANS

Feinstein College of Arts and Sciences: Dr ROBERT A. COLE
Mario J. Gabelli School of Business: JERRY DAUTERIVE
School of Architecture, Art and Historic Preservation: STEPHEN WHITE
School of Education: Dr ROBERT A. COLE
School of Engineering, Computing and Construction Management: Dr ROBERT A. POTTER
School of Graduate and Continuing Studies: Dr ROBERT W. ROBERTSON
School of Justice Studies: Dr STEPHANIE PICOLO MANZI
School of Law: Prof. DAVID A. LOGAN

SALVE REGINA UNIVERSITY

100 Ochre Point Ave, Newport, RI 02840-4192

Telephone: (401) 847-6650
Fax: (401) 341-2916
E-mail: sruadmis@salve.edu
Internet: www.salve.edu

Founded 1947 as Salve Regina College, present name and status 1991
Private control
Academic year: September to August (2 semesters)

Pres.: Dr JANE GERETY
Chancellor: Dr M. THERESE ANTONE
Provost and Dean for Faculty: Dr DEAN DE LA MOTTE
Vice-Pres. for Academic Affairs: Dr DEAN DE LA MOTTE
Vice-Pres. for Admin. and Chief Financial Officer: WILLIAM B. HALL
Vice-Pres. for Enrolment: Dr LAURA MCPHIE OLIVEIRA
Vice-Pres. for Student Affairs: Dr MARGARET HIGGINS
Vice-Pres. for Student Life: JOHN J. ROK
Vice-Pres. for Univ. Relations and Advancement: MICHAEL SEMENZA
Dean for Students: JOHN F. QUINN
Registrar: Dr JAMES H. TERRY
Dir for Library Services: KATHLEEN BOYD
Library of 125,000 vols
Number of teachers: 110 (full-time)
Number of students: 2,604 (2,028 undergraduate, 576 graduate)

DEANS

Arts and Sciences: Dr LAURA O'TOOLE
Professional Studies: Dr TRACI WARRINGTON

US NAVAL WAR COLLEGE

686 Cushing Rd, Newport, RI 02841-1207
Telephone: (401) 841-3089
Fax: (401) 841-1297
Internet: www.usnwc.edu

Founded 1884
State control
Pres.: JOHN N. CHRISTENSON
Provost: MARY ANN PETERS
Dean for Academic Affairs: Prof. Dr JOHN GAROFANO
Dean for Students: RAY KELEDEI
Library Dir: Prof. TERRY METZ
Library of 290,000 vols, 450,000 microfiches, 1,000 MSS, 1,700 periodical titles
Number of teachers: 165

DEANS

College of Naval Warfare: Prof. ROBERT RUBEL
College of Operational and Strategic Leadership: JAMIE KELLY
International Programmes: Prof. THOMAS MANGOLD

UNIVERSITY OF RHODE ISLAND

Kingston, RI 02881

Telephone: (401) 874-1000
Fax: (401) 874-5491
E-mail: admissions@uri.edu
Internet: www.uri.edu

Founded 1888 as State Agricultural School, present name 1951
State control
Academic year: September to May (2 semesters)
Campuses in Providence, Narragansett Bay, West Greenwich

Pres.: Dr DAVID M. DOOLEY
Provost and Vice-Pres. for Academic Affairs: Dr DONALD H. DEHAYES
Vice-Pres. for Admin. and Finance: ROBERT A. WEYGAND
Vice-Pres. for Research and Economic Devt: Dr PETER ALFONSO
Vice-Pres. for Student Affairs: Dr THOMAS R. DOUGAN
Vice-Pres. for Univ. Advancement: ROBERT L. BEAGLE
Chief Information Officer: GARRY BOZYLINSKY
Dean for Graduate School: Dr NASSER H. ZAWIA
Registrar: ROBERT STROBEL
Dean for Univ. Libraries: DAVID MASLYN
Library: 1.5m. vols, 27,000 periodical subscriptions, 2.3m. items of govt documents, audiovisual materials, computer files, MSS, archives, maps, nautical charts, microforms
Number of teachers: 721
Number of students: 16,000 (13,000 undergraduate, 3,000 graduate)
Publication: *Maritimes* (4 a year)

DEANS

College of Arts and Sciences: WINIFRED E. BROWNELL
College of Business Administration: Prof. Dr MARK HIGGINS
College of Engineering: Dr RAYMOND M. WRIGHT
College of Environment and Life Sciences: Dr JOHN KIRBY
College of Human Science and Services: Dr W. LYNN MCKINNEY
College of Nursing: Dr DAYLE H. JOSEPH
College of Pharmacy: Dr RONALD P. JORDAN
Graduate School of Oceanography: STEVEN L. D'HONDT
University College: Dr JAYNE RICHMOND

SOUTH CAROLINA

ALLEN UNIVERSITY

1530 Harden St, Columbia, SC 29204
Telephone: (803) 376-5700

Fax: (803) 376-5733
E-mail: admissions@allenuniversity.edu
Internet: www.allenuniversity.edu
Founded 1870
Private control
Academic year: August to May (2 semesters)
Divs of business administration, humanities, mathematics and natural sciences, religion
Pres.: Dr PAMELA M. WILSON
Exec. Vice-Pres.: Dr WILLIE L. PARSON
Vice-Pres. for Academic Affairs: Dr JUNE HUBBARD-COLE
Vice-Pres. for Fiscal Affairs: THOMAS POITIER
Vice-Pres. for Planning, Research and Sponsored Programmes: MARCUS V. BELL
Vice-Pres. for Student Affairs: Dr ORLANDO W. LEWIS
Gen. Counsel: RENARDO L. HICKS
Library of 50,000 vols
Number of teachers: 35
Number of students: 800

ANDERSON UNIVERSITY

316 Blvd, Anderson, SC 29621-40350
Telephone: (864) 231-2000
Fax: (864) 231-2033
E-mail: admissions@andersonuniversity.edu
Internet: www.andersonuniversity.edu
Founded 1911 as Anderson College, present name and status 2006
Private control
Academic year: August to May
Pres.: Dr EVANS P. WHITAKER
Provost: Dr DANNY M. PARKER
Vice-Pres. for Enrolment Management: OMAR RASHED
Vice-Pres. for Finance and Operations: JAMES A. WRIGHT, JR
Vice-Pres. for Institutional Advancement: R. DEAN WOODS
Vice-Pres. for Student Devt: Dr BOB L. HANLEY
Registrar: KENDRA B. WOODSON
Library Dir: KENT MILLWOOD
Library of 100,000 vols, 41,000 e-books
Number of teachers: 151
Number of students: 2,279

DEANS

College of Adult and Professional Studies: Dr W. DAVID SHIRLEY
College of Arts and Sciences: (vacant)
College of Business: Prof. Dr CAROL L. KARNES
College of Education: Dr RAYMOND S. LOCY
College of Visual and Performing Arts: Prof. Dr DAVID W. LARSON
Graduate, Online and Non-Traditional Programmes: Prof. Dr SANDRA M. MANCUSO
School of Interior Design: E. ANNE MARTIN
School of Nursing: Dr PAMELA BINNS-TURNER

BENEDICT COLLEGE

1600 Harden St, Columbia, SC 29204
Telephone: (803) 253-5000
Fax: (803) 705-4840
Internet: www.benedict.edu
Founded 1870 as Benedict Institute, present name 1894
Private control
Academic year: August to May
Pres.: Dr DAVID HOLMES SWINTON
Exec. Vice-Pres.: Dr RUBY W. WATTS
Vice-Pres. for Academic Affairs: Dr JANEEN P. WITTY
Vice-Pres. for Business and Finance: BRENDA WALKER
Vice-Pres. for Community Devt: JABARI SIMAMA
Vice-Pres. for Institutional Advancement: BARBARA C. MOORE (acting)

Vice-Pres. for Institutional Effectiveness: Dr GAYLA B. THOMAS
Vice-Pres. for Student Affairs: GARY E. KNIGHT
Registrar: WANDA SCOTT-KINNEY
Library Dir: DARLENE ZINNERMAN-BETHEA
Library of 100,000 vols, 300 journals, 1,600 govt publs
Number of teachers: 159 (126 full-time, 33 part-time)
Number of students: 3,135

DEANS

School of Business and Economics: GERALD H. SMALLS
School of Continuing Education: Dr BURNETT JOINER
School of Education: Dr ALLEN J. COLES
School of Honors: Dr WARREN ROBINSON
School of Humanities, Arts and Social Sciences: Dr CHARLES P. AUSTIN, SR
School of Science, Technology, Engineering and Mathematics: Dr SAMIR S. RAYCHOUDHURY

CHARLESTON SOUTHERN UNIVERSITY

9200 University Blvd, Charleston, SC 29406
Telephone: (843) 863-7000
Fax: (843) 863-7533
Internet: www.csuniv.edu
Founded 1964
Private control
Academic year: August to April
Pres.: Dr JAIRY C. HUNTER, JR
Provost: Dr A. KENNERLEY BONNETTE
Vice-Pres. for Advancement: DAVE BAGGS
Vice-Pres. for Business Affairs: LUKE BLACKMON
Vice-Pres. for Enrolment Management: DEBRA B. WILLIAMSON
Vice-Pres. for Student Affairs: Dr RICK BREWER
Registrar: AMANDA SISSON
Library Dir: SANDRA H. HUGHES
Library of 250,000 vols
Number of teachers: 141 (full-time)
Number of students: 3,298 (2,921 undergraduate, 377 graduate)
Publication: CSU Magazine (3 a year)

DEANS

College of Distance and Continuing Education: Dr JAMES H. JONES
College of Humanities and Social Sciences: Dr DONALD L. MARTIN, JR
College of Science and Mathematics: Prof. Dr JERYL W. JOHNSON
School of Business: Prof. Dr JOHN B. DUNCAN
School of Education: Dr NORMA HARPER
School of Nursing: Prof. Dr TARA HULSEY

CITADEL

171 Moultrie St, Charleston, SC 29409
Telephone: (843) 225-3294
Fax: (703) 742-4239
E-mail: admissions@citadel.edu
Internet: www.citadel.edu
Founded 1842
State control
Academic year: August to May
Pres.: Lt-Gen. JOHN W. ROSA
Provost and Dean for College: Dr SAMUEL M. HINES, JR
Exec. Vice-Pres. for Finance, Admin. and Operations: Brig. Gen. THOMAS J. ELZEY
Vice-Pres. for External Affairs: Dr JEFF PEREZ
Commandant of Cadets: Col LEO A. MERCADO
Registrar: SYLVIA L. NESMITH (acting)
Dir for Library Services: ELIZABETH CONNOR

Library of 1,128,798 vols, 449,390 microfilms
Number of teachers: 244 (163 full-time, 53 part-time, 28 ROTC)
Number of students: 3,256 (2,162 undergraduate, 1,094 graduate)
Publications: Citadel Review, Le Gaulois Litteraire (1 a year), The Art of Good Taste, The Brigadier, The Guidon, The Citadel (1 a year), The Gold Star Journal (1 a year), The Shako (1 a year), The Sphinx

DEANS

Graduate College: STEVE A. NIDA
School of Business Administration: Dr RONALD F. GREEN
School of Education: Dr TONY W. JOHNSON
School of Engineering: Dr RONALD W. WELCH
School of Humanities and Social Sciences: Dr WINFRED B. MOORE, JR
School of Science and Mathematics: Dr ISAAC S. METTS, JR

CLAFLIN UNIVERSITY

400 Magnolia St, Orangeburg, SC 29115
Telephone: (803) 535-5000
Fax: (803) 535-5402
E-mail: admissions@claflin.edu
Internet: www.claflin.edu
Founded 1869
Private control
Academic year: August to May (2 semesters)
Pres.: Dr HENRY N. TISDALE
Exec. Vice-Pres.: DREXEL B. BALL
Vice-Pres. for Academic Affairs: Dr HOWARD D. HILL
Vice-Pres. for Devt and Alumni Affaris: Rev. WHITTAKER V. MIDDLETON
Vice-Pres. for Planning, Assessment and Information Services: Dr ZIA HASAN
Vice-Pres. for Student Devt and Services: Dr LEROY A. DURANT
Dir for Admissions: Dr MICHAEL ZEIGLER
Registrar: ROE B. HUNT
Library Dir: MARILYN PRINGLE
Library of 162,000 vols, 445 periodicals, 17,000 e-periodicals, 47,000 e-books, 1,200 audiovisual materials
Number of teachers: 50
Number of students: 965

DEANS

School of Business: Dr HARPAL S. GREWAL
School of Education: Dr VALERIE E. HARRISON
School of Humanities and Social Science: Dr PEGGY STEVENSON RATLIFF
School of Natural Science and Mathematics: Prof. Dr VERLIE A. TISDALE

CLEMSON UNIVERSITY

Clemson, SC 29634
Telephone: (864) 656-3311
Fax: (864) 656-4676
E-mail: graduate_school@clemson.edu
Internet: www.clemson.edu
Founded 1889 as Clemson Agricultural College, present name 1964
State control
Academic year: August to May (2 semesters)
Pres.: JAMES F. BARKER
Provost and Vice-Pres. for Academic Affairs: DORIS R. HELMS
Vice-Pres. for Advancement: A. NEILL CAMERON, JR
Vice-Pres. for Agriculture, Public Service and Economic Devt: JOHN W. KELLY, JR
Vice-Pres. for Finance and Operations: BRETT A. DALTON
Vice-Pres. for Research: GERALD SONNENFELD
Vice-Pres. for Student Affairs: Dr GAIL A. DISABATINO
Gen. Counsel: CHIP HOOD
Registrar: STAN SMITH

Dean for Libraries: KAY WALL
Library: 1.8m. vols
Number of teachers: 1,204 (1,057 full-time, 147 part-time)
Number of students: 19,453

DEANS

College of Agriculture, Forestry and Life Sciences: Dr THOMAS R. SCOTT
College of Architecture, Arts and Humanities: Dr RICHARD E. GOODSTEIN
College of Business and Behavioral Science: Dr CLAUDE C. LILLY
College of Engineering and Science: Dr R. LARRY DOOLEY
College of Health, Education and Human Development: Dr LAWRENCE R. ALLEN
Graduate School: Dr KAREN BURG

COASTAL CAROLINA UNIVERSITY

POB 261954, Conway, SC 29528-6054
Telephone: (843) 347-3161
Fax: (843) 349-2914
E-mail: admissions@coastal.edu
Internet: www.coastal.edu
Founded 1954 as Coastal Carolina Jr College, present name and status 1993
State control
Academic year: August to May (2 semesters)
Pres.: Dr DAVID A. DeCENZO
Provost and Sr Vice-Pres. for Academic and Student Affairs: Dr ROBERT SHEEHAN
Exec. Vice-Pres. and Chief Operating Officer: EDGAR DYER
Vice-Pres. for Enrolment Services: Dr JUDY VOGT
Vice-Pres. for Finance and Admin.: STACIE BOWIE
Vice-Pres. for Student Affairs and Dean for Students: HAVEN L. HART
Registrar: DANIEL LAWLESS
Dean for Library Services: BARBARA BURD
Number of teachers: 346 (full-time)
Number of students: 9,084
Publications: Archarios (1 a year), Coastal Carolina (1 a year), Tempo (1 a year)

DEANS

College of Business Administration: Dr J. RALPH BYINGTON
College of Education: EDWARD JADALLAH
College of Science: Dr MICHAEL H. ROBERTS
Thomas W. and Robin W. Edwards College of Humanities and Fine Art: Prof. Dr DANIEL ENNIS
University College: Dr NELLJEAN M. RICE

COKER COLLEGE

300 E College Ave, Hartsville, SC 29550
Telephone: (843) 383-8000
Fax: (843) 383-8033
E-mail: admissions@coker.edu
Internet: www.coker.edu
Founded 1894 as Welsh Neck High School, present name 1969
Private control
Academic year: September to May (2 semesters)
Areas of study: art, behavioural and social science, business administration, communication, language and literature, dance, music and theatre, education, history, philosophy and religion, physical education and sport studies, science and mathematics, social work
Pres.: Dr ROBERT L. WYATT
Provost: Dr TRACY PARKINSON
Vice-Pres. for Business Operations: GERALD O. SILVER
Vice-Pres. for Institutional Advancement: THOMAS W. GIFFIN

Vice-Pres. for Student and Enrolment Services: Dr STEPHEN B. TERRY
Registrar: STACY ATKINSON
Dir for Library: ALEXA E. BARTEL
Library of 170,000 vols, 105,000 e-books
Number of teachers: 68 (full-time)
Number of students: 1,107

COLLEGE OF CHARLESTON

66 George St, Charleston, SC 29424
Telephone: (843) 805-5507
Fax: (843) 953-5811
E-mail: admissions@cofc.edu
Internet: www.cofc.edu
Founded 1770
State control
Academic year: August to July (2 semesters)
Pres.: Dr P. GEORGE BENSON
Provost and Sr Vice-Pres. for Academic Affairs: GEORGE W. HYND
Exec. Vice-Pres. for Business Affairs: STEPHEN C. OSBORNE
Exec. Vice-Pres. for External Relations: MICHAEL R. HASKINS
Exec. Vice-Pres. for Student Affairs: VICTOR K. WILSON
Exec. Vice-Pres. for Institutional Advancement: GEORGE P. WATT, JR
Vice-Pres. for Legal Affairs and Gen. Counsel: TOM TRIMBOLI
Registrar: CATHERINE C. BOYD
Dean for Libraries: DAVID J. COHEN
Library of 817,658 vols
Number of teachers: 542 (full-time)
Number of students: 11,649 (10,461 undergraduate, 1,188 graduate)
Publications: Chrestomathy (1 a year), College of Charleston Magazine (3 a year), Crazyhorse (2 a year), Illuminations (1 a year), Polyphony (1 a year)

DEANS

Graduate School: Dr AMY T. McCANDLESS
School of Arts: VALERIE B. MORRIS
School of Business: Prof. Dr ALAN T. SHAO
School of Education, Health and Human Performance: Dr FRANCES C. WELCH
School of Humanities and Social Sciences: Dr CYNTHIA J. LOWENTHAL
School of Languages, Cultures and World Affairs: Dr DAVID J. COHEN
School of Sciences and Mathematics: Dr MICHAEL AUERBACH

COLUMBIA COLLEGE

1301 Columbia College Dr., Columbia, SC 29203
Telephone: (803) 786-3871
Fax: (803) 786-3674
E-mail: admissions@columbiasc.edu
Internet: www.columbiasc.edu
Founded 1854
Private control
Academic year: August to May (2 semesters)
Divs of arts and communication studies, behavioural studies and human inquiry, business, mathematics and sciences, education, languages and literatures
Pres.: Dr CAROLINE WHITSON
Provost and Vice-Pres. for Academic Affairs: Dr LAURIE B. HOPKINS
Vice-Pres. for Advancement: BARBARA PARKS
Vice-Pres. for Enrolment Management: Dr RONALD G. WHITE
Vice-Pres. for Finance: JOHN D. JONES
Dean of Students: Dr LaNaé BRIGGS BUDDEN
Registrar: Dr SCOTT A. SMITH
Dir for Library and Information Technology Services: DAN MURPHY
Library of 177,000 vols, 400 journals and magazines, 30,000 media items

Number of teachers: 163 (81 full-time, 82 part-time)
Number of students: 1,300

COLUMBIA INTERNATIONAL UNIVERSITY

7435 Monticello Rd, Columbia, SC 29203
Telephone: (803) 754-4100
Fax: (803) 786-4209
E-mail: yesciu@ciu.edu
Internet: www.ciu.edu
Founded 1923 as Columbia Bible School, present name 1994
Private control
Academic year: August to May (2 semesters)
Pres.: Dr WILLIAM H. JONES
Chancellor: Dr GEORGE W. MURRAY
Provost and Sr Vice-Pres. for Academic and Student Affairs: Dr JAMES LANPHER
Vice-Pres. for Devt and Operations: KEITH MARION
Vice-Pres. for Enrolment Management and Corporate Communications: MIKE BLACKWELL
Vice-Pres. for Institutional Assessment: BOB KALLGREN
Registrar: KATHY KROLL
Dean for Student Life: RICK SWIFT
Library Dir: JO ANN RHODES
Library of 122,551 vols
Number of teachers: 75
Number of students: 980
Publications: Connection (2 a year), President's Letter (3 a year), Upward (3 a year)

DEANS

College of Arts and Sciences: Dr BRYAN E. BEYER
College of Counseling: HARVEY PAYNE
College of Education: Dr CONNIE MITCHELL
College of Intercultural Studies: Dr MIKE BARNETT
Seminary and School of Ministry: JOHN D. HARVEY

CONVERSE COLLEGE

580 E Main St, Spartanburg, SC 29302
Telephone: (864) 596-9000
Fax: (864) 596-9225
E-mail: admission@converse.edu
Internet: www.converse.edu
Founded 1889
Private control
Academic year: September to May
Pres.: Dr ELIZABETH A. FLEMING
Sr Vice-Pres.: THOMAS McDANIEL
Vice-Pres. for Academic Affairs: JEFFREY BARKER
Vice-Pres. for Enrolment and Marketing: SALLY HAMMOND
Vice-Pres. for Finance and Admin.: SUSAN STEVENSON
Vice-Pres. for Institutional Advancement: BOBBY STEWART
Vice-Pres. for Student Life and Dean for Students: MOLLY DUESTERHAUS
Dir for Admissions: APRIL LEWIS
Registrar: MARY BROWN
Librarian: WADE WOODWARD
Library of 155,000 vols, 87,000 microforms, 500 periodicals
Number of teachers: 85
Number of students: 1,200

DEANS

School of Education and Graduate Studies: Dr KATHY GOOD
School of Humanities and Sciences: Prof. Dr JEFFREY BARKER
School of the Arts: RICHARD HIGGS

ERSKINE COLLEGE

POB 338, Due West, SC 29639
2 Washington St, Due West, SC 29639
Telephone: (864) 379-2131
Fax: (864) 379-2167
E-mail: admissions@erskine.edu
Internet: www.erskine.edu

Founded 1839
Academic year: August to May (2 semesters)
Depts of art, athletic training, bible, biology, business administration, chemistry, education, English, health and human performance, history and politics, mathematics, modern languages, music, physics, psychology, religion and philosophy
Pres.: Dr DAVID A. NORMAN
Vice-Pres. and Dean for College: BRAD CHRISTIE
Vice-Pres. for Advancement: DAVID EARLE
Vice-Pres. for Erskine Theological Seminary: STEVE LOWE
Vice-Pres. for Finance and Operations: GREG HASELDEN
Vice-Pres. for Student Services: ROBYN AGNEW
Dir for Admissions: TOBE R. FRIERSON
Registrar: TRACY SPIRES
Library Dir: JOHN F. KENNERLY, JR
Library of 155,000 vols, 20,000 periodical, 57,000 microforms, 1,500 audiovisual, media and multimedia items, 15,000 archives and spec, colln items, 7,000 e-journals
Number of teachers: 62
Number of students: 600
Publication: *Inside Erskine* (2 a year).

FRANCIS MARION UNIVERSITY

POB 100547, Florence, SC 29502-0547
Telephone: (843) 661-1231
Fax: (843) 661-4635
E-mail: admissions@fmarion.edu
Internet: www.fmarion.edu

Founded 1970, present name and status 1992
State control
Academic year: August to May (2 semesters)
Pres.: Dr LUTHER F. CARTER
Provost and Dean for College: Dr RICHARD N. CHAPMAN
Vice-Pres. for Admin.: Dr CHARLENE WAGES
Vice-Pres. for Business Affairs: JOHN J. KISPERT
Vice-Pres. for Devt: JOHN P. DOWD, III
Vice-Pres. for Student Affairs and Dean for Students: TERESA JOHNSON RAMEY
Dir for Admissions: PERRY T. WILSON
Registrar: DOLLIE J. NEWHOUSE
Dean for Library: JOYCE M. DURANT
Library of 410,000 vols, 1,100 journals, 21,000 e-journals, 27,500 e-books
Number of teachers: 262
Number of students: 4,187 (3,876 undergraduate, 311 graduate)
Publication: *View Magazine* (2 a year)

DEANS

College of Liberal Arts: Dr RICHARD N. CHAPMAN
School of Business: Dr M. BARRY O'BRIEN
School of Education: Dr JAMES RON FAULKENBERRY

FURMAN UNIVERSITY

3300 Poinsett Highway, Greenville, SC 29613
Telephone: (864) 294-2000
Fax: (864) 294-3949
E-mail: admission@furman.edu
Internet: www.furman.edu

Founded 1826, present name and status 1850
Private control

Academic year: August to May (2 semesters)
Depts of arts, Asian studies, business, education, humanities, military science, neuroscience, sciences and mathematics, social sciences, sustainability science
Pres.: Dr RODNEY ALAN SMOLLA
Vice-Pres. for Academic Affairs and Dean: JOHN STEPHEN BECKFORD
Vice-Pres. for Admin. and Finance: MARY LOU MERKT
Vice-Pres. for Devt: MICHAEL D. GATCHELL
Vice-Pres. for Student Life: CONNIE L. CARSON
Registrar: BRAD E. BARRON
Dir for Library: JANIS BANDELIN
Library: 1.3m. items incl. 450,000 vols, 15,000 print and online journals, 140,000 govt documents and maps, 800,000 microforms
Number of teachers: 238
Number of students: 2,907 (2,704 undergraduate, 203 graduate)
Publications: *ConBrio, Engage, Furman Magazine* (4 a year), *Humanities Review* (1 a year), *The Echo* (2 a year).

LANDER UNIVERSITY

320 Stanley Ave, Greenwood, SC 29649-2099
Telephone: (864) 388-8000
Fax: (864) 388-8890
E-mail: admissions@lander.edu
Internet: www.lander.edu

Founded 1872 as Williamston Female College, present name 1992
State control
Academic year: August to April (2 semesters)
Pres.: Dr DANIEL W. BALL
Provost and Vice-Pres. for Academic Affairs: DANNY L. MCKENZIE
Vice-Pres. for Business and Admin.: GLENDA E. RIDGELY
Vice-Pres. for Student Affairs: HUEY RANDALL BOUKNIGHT
Vice-Pres. for Univ. Advancement: RALPH E. PATTERSON
Dir for Admissions: JENNIFER M. MATHIS
Registrar: MAC KIRKPATRICK
Dean for Library Services: SAMUEL D. MASH
Library of 275,000 vols
Number of teachers: 137 (full-time)
Number of students: 3,000

DEANS

College of Arts and Humanities: Prof. ALICE TAYLOR-COLBERT
College of Business and Public Affairs: DOUG GRIDER
College of Education: JUDITH A. NEUFELD
College of Science and Mathematics: Prof. DAVID A. SLIMMER

LIMESTONE COLLEGE

1115 College Dr., Gaffney, SC 29340-3799
Telephone: (864) 489-7151
Fax: (864) 487-8706
E-mail: admiss@limestone.edu
Internet: www.limestone.edu

Founded 1845
Private control
Academic year: August to May (2 semesters)
Campuses in Aiken, Charleston, Columbia, Florence, Greer, Kingstree and Yemassee; depts of arts and letters, natural science, professional studies, social and behavioural science, interdisciplinary studies
Pres.: Dr WALT GRIFFIN
Vice-Pres. for Academic Affairs: Dr KAREN W. GAINEY
Vice-Pres. for Enrolment Services: CHRISTOPHER N. PHENICIE

Vice-Pres. for Financial Affairs: DAVID S. RILLING
Vice-Pres. for Institutional Advancement: Dr WILLIAM H. BAKER
Vice-Pres. for Student Services: ROBERT OVERTON
Registrar: BRENDA WATKINS
Dir for Library: LORI HETRICK
Library of 151,677 vols, 2,873 microforms, 2,900 audio and video cassettes, 91,000 e-books
Number of teachers: 80 (full-time)
Number of students: 3,625
Publication: *Limestone Today* (2 a year).

LUTHERAN THEOLOGICAL SOUTHERN SEMINARY

4201 Main St, Columbia, SC 29203-5898
Telephone: (803) 786-5150
Fax: (803) 786-6499
E-mail: admissions@ltss.edu
Internet: www.ltss.edu

Founded 1830
Private control
Academic year: August to May
Pres.: Rev. Dr MARCUS J. MILLER
Vice-Pres. for Academic Affairs: Rev. Dr VIRGINIA BARFIELD
Vice-Pres. for Devt and Seminary Relations: RON WALRATH
Dir for Admin. and Finance: ANDY SMITH
Library Dir: Dr LYNN A. FEIDER
Library of 100,000 vols, 400 journal subscriptions
Number of teachers: 17
Number of students: 152
Publication: *Taproot*.

MEDICAL UNIVERSITY OF SOUTH CAROLINA

171 Ashley Ave, Charleston, SC 29425
Telephone: (843) 792-1414
Fax: (803) 792-0392
E-mail: oes-web@musc.edu
Internet: www.musc.edu

Founded 1824
State control
Academic year: August to August
Pres.: Dr RAYMOND S. GREENBERG
Provost and Vice-Pres. for Academic Affairs and: Dr MARK SOTHMANN
Vice-Pres. for Devt: JIM FISHER
Vice-Pres. for Finance and Admin.: LISA MONTGOMERY
Vice-Pres. for Information Technology: Dr FRANK C. CLARK
Vice-Pres. for Medical Affairs: Dr ETTA PISANO
Dir for Libraries: Prof. THOMAS G. BASLER
Number of teachers: 1,281
Number of students: 2,339
Publication: *Humanitas* (1 a year)

DEANS

College of Dental Medicine: Prof. Dr JOHN J. SANDERS
College of Graduate Studies: Dr PERRY V. HALUSHKA
College of Health Professions: Prof. Dr LISA S. SALADIN
College of Medicine: Dr ETTA D. PISANO
College of Nursing: Prof. Dr GAIL W. STUART

MORRIS COLLEGE

100 W College St, Sumter, SC 29150-3599
Telephone: (803) 934-3200
Fax: (803) 773-3687
Internet: www.morris.edu

Founded 1908

Private control
Academic year: August to May (2 semesters)
Divs of business administration, education, general studies, natural sciences and mathematics, religion and humanities, social sciences
Pres.: LUNS C. RICHARDSON
Academic Dean: Prof. LEROY STAGGERS
Dean for Student Affairs: ELIZA E. BLACK
Dir for Admissions and Records: DEBORAH C. CALHOUN
Dir for Institutional Advancement: MELVIN MACK
Number of teachers: 70
Number of students: 880

NEWBERRY COLLEGE

2100 College St, Newberry, SC 29108
Telephone: (803) 276-5010
Fax: (803) 321-5526
E-mail: admissions@newberry.edu
Internet: www.newberry.edu
Founded 1856, present location 1911
Private control
Academic year: August to May
Areas of study: arts and communications, business, behavioural and social sciences, education, humanities, music, nursing, sciences and mathematics, military science
Pres.: JOHN H. HUDGENS, II (acting)
Exec. Vice-Pres. for Academic Affairs and Dean for College: TIMOTHY ELSTON
Vice-Pres. for Admin. Affairs and Chief Financial Officer: RON MATTHIAS
Dean for Enrolment Management: SHEILA M. WENDELN
Dean for Students: KAY BANKS
Registrar: CAROL BICKLEY
Dir for Library Services: LAWRENCE ELLIS
Library of 80,000 vols, 146 magazines, scholarly journals, newspapers
Number of teachers: 62 (full-time)
Number of students: 1,155
Publication: *Dimensions* (2 a year).

NORTH GREENVILLE UNIVERSITY

POB 1892, Tigerville, SC 29688
7801 N Tigerville Rd, Tigerville, SC 29688
Telephone: (864) 977-7000
Fax: (864) 977-7021
E-mail: admissions@ngu.edu
Internet: www.ngu.edu
Founded 1892 as North Greenville High School
Private control
Academic year: August to May (2 semesters)
Pres.: Dr JAMES B. EPTING
Vice-Pres. and Dean for Graduate Studies: J. SAMUEL ISGETT, JR
Vice-Pres. for Academic Affairs: Dr RANDALL J. PANNELL
Vice-Pres. for Admissions and Financial Planning: KELI SEWELL
Vice-Pres. for Business Affairs: MICHELLE SABOU
Vice-Pres. for Campus Ministries: STEPHEN G. CROUSE
Vice-Pres. for Student Services: TONY BEAM
Vice-Pres. for Univ. Advancement: ALEXANDER A. MILLER
Registrar: PAMELA FARMER
Dir for Library: CARLA C. MCMAHAN
Library of 60,000 vols, 536 periodicals, 1,168 video materials, 1,600 audio items
Number of teachers: 35
Number of students: 1,300

DEANS

College of Business and Sport Professions: Dr RALPH JOHNSON

College of Christian Studies: Dr WALTER JOHNSON
College of Education: Dr ROBIN JOHNSON
College of Fine Arts: Dr JACQUELYN H. GRIFFIN
College of Humanities: Dr CATHERINE SEPKO
College of Science and Mathematics: Dr THOMAS C. ALLEN
Graduate School of Business: Dr TRACY R. KRAMER
Graduate School of Christian Ministry: LARRY S. MCDONALD
Graduate School of Education: Dr VIVIAN R. DUGLE

PRESBYTERIAN COLLEGE

503 S Broad St, Clinton, SC 29325
Telephone: (864) 833-2820
Fax: (864) 833-8481
E-mail: admissions@presby.edu
Internet: www.presby.edu
Founded 1880 as Clinton College
Private control
Academic year: August to May (2 semesters)
Pres.: Dr JOHN VINCENT GRIFFITH
Provost: Dr ANITA OLSON GUSTAFSON
Exec. Vice-Pres. for Finance and Admin.: MORRIS M. GALLOWAY, JR
Vice-Pres. for Advancement: RAYMOND E. CARNLEY
Vice-Pres. for Enrolment Management: DEBORAH J. THOMPSON
Dean for Students: LINDA C. JAMEISON
Dir for Admissions: BRIAN J. FORTMAN
Registrar: KEITH KARRIKER
Dir for Library: DAVID W. CHATHAM
Library of 166,110 vols
Number of teachers: 84 (full-time)
Number of students: 1,200

DEANS

School of Pharmacy: Dr RICHARD E. STULL

SHERMAN COLLEGE OF CHIROPRACTIC

POB 1452, Spartanburg, SC 29304
2020 Springfield Rd, Boiling Springs, SC 29316
Telephone: (864) 578-8770
Fax: (864) 599-4860
E-mail: admissions@sherman.edu
Internet: www.sherman.edu
Founded 1973
Private control
Academic year: January to December
Pres.: Dr JON SCHWARTZBAUER
Vice-Pres. for Academic Affairs: Dr ROBERT IRWIN
Vice-Pres. for Business and Finance: TIMOTHY D. REVELS
Vice-Pres. for Enrolment Services: KELLEY JONES ASHCRAFT
Dean for Student Affairs: LaSHANDA HUTTO-HARRIS
Registrar: MELODY SABIN
Dir for Learning Resources: CRISSY LEWIS
Publication: *Sherman*

DEANS

Basic Sciences: Dr PENGJU LUO
Clinical Sciences: Dr JOSEPH J. DONOFRIO
Clinics: KEITH HENRY

SOUTH CAROLINA COLLEGE OF PHARMACY

Medical University of South Carolina Campus: 274 Calhoun St, MSC 141, Charleston, SC 29425-1410
Telephone: (843) 792-3740
Fax: (843) 792-9081

University of South Carolina: Coker Life Science Bldg, 715 Sumter St, Columbia, SC 29208
Telephone: (803) 777-4151
Fax: (803) 777-2775
E-mail: office@sccp.sc.edu
Internet: www.sccp.sc.edu
Founded 2004; attached to Medical Univ. of South Carolina and Univ. of South Carolina
State control
Depts of clinical pharmacy and outcome sciences, pharmaceutical and biomedical sciences
Exec. Dean: Dr JOSEPH T. DiPIRO
Medical Univ. of South Carolina Campus Dean: Dr PHILIP D. HALL
Univ. of South Carolina Campus Dean: Dr RANDALL C. ROWEN
Number of teachers: 74 (full-time)
Number of students: 190
Publication: *PharmSC* (4 a year).

SOUTH CAROLINA STATE UNIVERSITY

300 College St, NE, Orangeburg, SC 29117
Telephone: (803) 536-7000
Fax: (803) 533-3622
E-mail: registrar@scsu.edu
Internet: www.scsu.edu
Founded 1896 as Normal, Industrial, Agricultural and Mechanical College, present name 1992
State control
Academic year: August to May
Pres.: Dr RITA JACKSON TEAL (acting)
Vice-Pres. for Finance and Facilities: JOSEPH M. PEARMAN
Vice-Pres. for Institutional Advancement: Dr ANTHONY L. HOLLOMAN
Vice-Pres. for Research and Economic Devt and Public Service: Dr G. DALE WESSON
Vice-Pres. for Student Affairs: Dr VALERIE FIELDS
Registrar: ANNIE BELTON
Dean for Library and Information Services: ADRIENNE C. WEBBER
Library of 302,768 vols, 1,028,132 microforms, 974 journal and magazine subscriptions
Number of teachers: 311
Number of students: 5,000

DEANS

College of Business and Applied Professional Sciences: Dr ORA SPANN
College of Education, Humanities and Social Sciences: Dr RONALD E. SPEIGHT
College of Science, Mathematics and Engineering Technology: Dr KENNETH D. LEWIS
Honors College: Dr HARRIET A. ROLAND
School of Graduate Studies: Dr FREDERICK M. G. EVANS

SOUTHERN WESLEYAN UNIVERSITY

POB 1020, 907 Wesleyan Dr., Central, SC 29630-1020
Telephone: (864) 644-5557
Fax: (864) 644-5914
E-mail: president@swu.edu
Internet: www.swu.edu
Founded 1906 as Wesleyan Methodist Bible Institute, present name 1995
Private control
Academic year: August to May
Pres.: Dr TODD S. VOSS
Provost and Academic Vice-Pres.: Dr KEITH IDDINGS
Sr Vice-Pres. for Finance: MARTY ATCHESON
Vice-Pres. for Admin. and Programme Operations: GARY CARR

Vice-Pres. for Devt: Rev. JAMES WIGGINS
Vice-Pres. for Student Life: Dr JOE BROCK-INTON
Dir for Admissions and Enrolment Management: AMANDA YOUNG
Registrar: ROCK McCASKILL
Dir for Library Services: ROBERT E. SEARS
Library of 115,000 vols
Number of teachers: 130
Number of students: 2,414 (1,694 undergraduate, 720 graduate)

DEANS

College of Arts and Sciences: Dr WALT SINNAMON
School of Business: Prof. Dr ROYCE CAINES
School of Education: Dr PAUL SHOTSBERGER

UNIVERSITY OF SOUTH CAROLINA

Columbia, SC 29208
Telephone: (803) 777-7000
Fax: (803) 777-0101
E-mail: info@sc.edu
Internet: www.sc.edu
Founded 1801 as South Carolina College, present name 1866
State control
Academic year: August to May (2 semesters)
Campuses in Aiken, Allendale, Beaufort, Lancaster, Spartanburg, Sumter, Union
Pres.: Dr HARRIS PASTIDES
Provost and Exec. Vice-Pres. for Academic Affairs: Dr MICHAEL D. AMIRIDIS
Vice-Provost for Academic Affairs and Dean for Undergraduate Studies: Dr HELEN I. DOERPINGHAUS
Vice-Pres. for Research: Dr PRAKASH NAGARKATTI
Vice-Pres. for Student Affairs: Dr DENNIS A. PRUITT
Vice-Provost for System Affairs and Exec. Dean for Extended Univ.: Dr CHRIS P. PLYLER
Registrar: Dr AARON MARTERER
Chancellor of USC Aiken: Dr THOMAS L. HALLMAN
Chancellor of USC Beaufort: Dr JANE T. UPSHAW
Chancellor of USC Upstate: THOMAS F. MOORE
Dean for Libraries: Dr TOM McNALLY
Library: 9m. vols
Number of teachers: 2,184 (full-time; all campuses)
Number of students: 45,774 (all campuses)
Publications: *Journal of Law & Education* (4 a year), *Real Property, Trust & Estate Law Journal* (4 a year), *South Carolina Journal of International Law and Business* (2 a year), *South Carolina Law Review* (1 a year), *Southeastern Environmental Law Journal* (2 a year)

DEANS

Arnold School of Public Health: Dr G. THOMAS CHANDLER
College of Arts and Sciences: Dr MARY ANNE FITZPATRICK
College of Education: Dr LEMUEL WATSON (acting)
College of Engineering and Computing: Dr ANTHONY AMBLER
College of Hospitality, Retail and Sport Management: Dr BRIAN J. MIHALIK (acting)
College of Mass Communications and Information Studies: CHARLES BIERBAUER
College of Nursing: Dr PEGGY HEWLETT
College of Social Work: Prof. Dr ANNA SCHEYETT
Graduate School: Dr LACY FORD
Moore School of Business: Dr HILDY J. TEEGEN
School of Law: ROBERT M. WILCOX

School of Medicine: Dr RICHARD A. HOPPMANN
School of Music: Dr TAYLOE HARDING
South Carolina Honors College: Dr STEVEN LYNN

VOORHEES COLLEGE

POB 678, Denmark, SC 29042
Telephone: (803) 780-1234
Fax: (803) 780-1038
E-mail: info@voorhees.edu
Internet: www.voorhees.edu
Founded 1897 as Denmark Industrial School, present name and status 1962
Private control
Academic year: August to May
Pres. and CEO: Dr CLEVELAND L. SELLERS, JR
Exec. Vice-Pres. for Academic Affairs: Dr PAUL BAKER
Vice-Pres. for Fiscal and Admin. Affairs and Chief Financial Officer: V. DIANE O'BERRY
Vice-Pres. for Institutional Advancement: COURTNEY L. DAVENPORT
Vice-Pres. for Planning, Information Management and Technology: SAMUEL BLACKWELL
Vice-Pres. for Student Affairs: WILLIE JEFFERSON
Registrar: MELIKA JACKSON
Library Dir: Dr MARIE MARTIN
Number of teachers: 42 (full-time)
Number of students: 642 (undergraduate)

DEANS

Division of Arts and Sciences: Dr DORIS J. WARD
Division of Business and Professional Studies: Dr BERNARD MOSES
Division of General Studies: LUGENIA ROCHELLE

WINTHROP UNIVERSITY

701 Oakland Ave, Rock Hill, SC 29733
Telephone: (803) 323-2191
Fax: (803) 323-4600
E-mail: admissions@winthrop.edu
Internet: www.winthrop.edu
Founded 1886, present name and status 1992
State control
Academic year: August to May (2 semesters)
Pres.: Dr ANTHONY J. DiGIORGIO
Vice-Pres. for Academic Affairs and Dean of Faculty: Dr DEBRA C. BOYD
Vice-Pres. for Finance and Business: J. P. McKEE
Vice-Pres. for Student Life: Dr FRANK P. ARDAIOLO
Vice-Pres. for Univ. Advancement: Dr KATHRYN HOLTEN
Registrar: GINA G. JONES
Dir for Admissions: DEBI BARBER
Dean for Library Services: Dr MARK Y. HERRING
Library of 357,110 vols
Number of teachers: 401
Number of students: 5,913 (4,859 undergraduate, 1,054 graduate)
Publications: *The Johnsonian* (52 a year), *The Tatler, The Winthrop Anthology* (1 a year)

DEANS

College of Arts and Sciences: Dr PETER JUDGE
College of Business Administration: ROGER D. WEIKLE
College of Visual and Performing Arts: DAVID WOHL
Graduate School: Dr DEBRA BOYD
Richard W. Riley College of Education: JENNIE RAKESTRAW
University College: GLORIA G. JONES

WOFFORD COLLEGE

429 N Church St, Spartanburg, SC 29303-3663
Telephone: (864) 597-4000
Fax: (864) 597-4019
E-mail: admission@wofford.edu
Internet: www.wofford.edu
Founded 1854
Private control
Academic year: September to May (2 semesters)
Liberal arts college
Pres.: Dr BENJAMIN BERNARD DUNLAP
Sr Vice-Pres. for Academic Affairs and Dean for College: DAVID SHIEL WOOD
Sr Vice-Pres. for Devt and College Relations: MARION B. PEAVEY
Sr Vice-Pres. for Operations and Finance: ROBERT L. KEASLER
Vice-Pres.: B. G. STEPHENS
Vice-Pres.: LARRY McGEHEE
Vice-Pres. for Academic Admin. and Planning: BOYCE M. LAWTON, III
Vice-Pres. for Admin.: DAVID M. BEACHAM
Vice Pres. for Enrolment: BRAND R. STILLE
Vice-Pres. for Student Affairs and Dean for Students: ROBERTA HURLEY BIGGER
Dean for Int. Programmes: Dr ANA MARIÁ WISEMAN
Registrar: JENNIFER R. ALLISON
Dean for Library: OAKLEY HERMAN COBURN
Library of 250,000 vols, 135,000 e-books, 39,000 e-journals
Number of teachers: 126 (full-time)
Number of students: 1,536

SOUTH DAKOTA

AUGUSTANA COLLEGE

2001 S Summit Ave, Sioux Falls, SD 57197
Telephone: (605) 274-0770
Fax: (605) 274-5299
E-mail: admission@augie.edu
Internet: www.augie.edu
Founded 1860
Private control

Depts of art/anthropology, biology, business administration, chemistry, communication, computer science, economics, education, English, government and international affairs, health, history, international studies, mathematics, modern foreign languages, music, nursing, philosophy and classics, physical education and recreation, physics, psychology, religion, sociology, theatre
Pres.: ROBERT C. OLIVER
Vice-Pres. for Academic Affairs and Dean for the College: Dr SUSAN HASSELER
Vice-Pres. for Devt: JON HENKES
Vice-Pres. for Enrolment: NANCY DAVIDSON
Vice-Pres. for Finance and Admin.: THOMAS M. MEYER
Vice-Pres. for Marketing and Communications: ROBERT PRELOGER
Vice-Pres. for Student Services and Dean for Students: Dr JAMES BIES
Registrar: JONI KRUEGER
Dir for Mikkelsen Library: RONELLE THOMPSON
Library of 228,000 vols
Number of teachers: 138
Number of students: 1,790

BLACK HILLS STATE UNIVERSITY

1200 University St, Spearfish, SD 57799-9502
Telephone: (605) 642-6088
Fax: (605) 642-6254
E-mail: admissions@bhsu.edu
Internet: www.bhsu.edu

Founded 1883 as Dakota Territorial Normal School
State control
Academic year: August to May
Pres.: Dr KAY SCHALLENKAMP
Provost and Vice-Pres. for Academic Affairs: Dr RODNEY CUSTER
Vice-Pres. for Finance and Admin.: KATHY JOHNSON
Vice-Pres. for Institutional Advancement: STEVE MEEKER
Vice-Pres. for Student Life: LOIS FLAGSTAD
Chief Information Officer: WARREN WILSON
Dir for Admissions: BETH AZEVEDO
Dean for Libraries: RAJEEV BUKRALIA
Library of 235,000 vols, 70,000 govt documents, 635,000 vols of additional resource materials, 2,225 vols of state, co and local histories, 7,000 vols on history of English literature
Number of teachers: 183
Number of students: 4,415
Publication: *BHSU Alumni Magazine*

DEANS

College of Business and Natural Sciences: Dr PRISCILLA ROMKEMA
College of Education and Behavioral Sciences: PATRICIA SIMPSON
College of Liberal Arts: Dr CURTIS CARD

DAKOTA STATE UNIVERSITY

Madison, SD 57042
820 N Washington Ave, Madison, SD 57042-1799
Telephone: (605) 256-5111
Fax: (605) 256-5316
E-mail: dsuinfo@pluto.dsu.edu
Internet: www.dsu.edu
Founded 1881
State control
Academic year: September to May
Pres.: Dr DOUGLAS D. KNOWLTON
Vice-Pres. and Dean for Student Affairs: JESSE WISE
Vice-Pres. for Academic Affairs: Dr CECELIA M. WITTMAYER
Vice-Pres. for Business and Admin. Services: STACY KRUSEMARK
Vice-Pres. for Univ. Advancement: JUDY PAYNE
Registrar: SANDRA A. ANDERSON
Dean for Graduate Studies and Research: OMAR EL-GAYAR
Dir for Admissions: AMY CRISSINGER
Dir for Library: Prof. ETHELLE BEAN
Library of 133,371 vols
Number of teachers: 110
Number of students: 2,800
Publication: *Dakota State Magazine* (1 a year)

DEANS

College of Arts and Sciences: Dr KARI FORBES-BOYTE
College of Business and Information Systems: Dr TOM HALVERSON
College of Education: Dr JUDY DITTMAN

DAKOTA WESLEYAN UNIVERSITY

1200 W University Ave, Mitchell, SD 57301
Telephone: (605) 995-2600
Fax: (605) 995-2699
E-mail: admissions@dwu.edu
Internet: www.dwu.edu
Founded 1885
Private control
Pres.: Dr ROBERT G. DUFFETT
Provost and Exec. Vice-Pres.: AMY C. NOVAK
Vice-Pres. for Business and Institutional Advancement: THERESA KRIESE

Vice-Pres. for Univ. Relations: LORI ESSIG
Registrar: KAREN KNOELL
Dir for Learning Resources: KEVIN KENKEL
Library of 65,000 vols, 400 current magazine subscriptions
Number of teachers: 49
Number of students: 780

DEANS

College of Arts and Humanities: Dr VINCE REDDER
College of Healthcare, Fitness and Sciences: Dr ROCHELLE VON EYE
College of Leadership and Public Service: Dr DONALD C. SIMMONS

PROFESSORS

ALMJELD, P., Music
CATALANO, M., Mathematics
DITTA, J., English
FARNEY, M. N., Mathematics
McGREEVY, M. J., Criminal Justice
MILLER, M. H., Religion and Philosophy
MITCHELL, D. B., Business Administration and Economics
MULLICAN, T. R., Biology
NIELSON, G. E., Sociology
TATINA, R. E., Biology

MOUNT MARTY COLLEGE

1105 W Eighth St, Yankton, SD 57078-3725
Telephone: (605) 668-1545
Fax: (605) 668-1508
E-mail: mmcadmit@mtmc.edu
Internet: www.mtmc.edu
Founded 1936
Private control (Benedictine)
Academic year: August to May (2 semesters)
Areas of study: business and social sciences, humanities, natural sciences, nursing, teacher education; campuses at Sioux Falls, Watertown and Yankton in South Dakota
Pres.: Dr JOSEPH N. BENOIT
Vice-Pres. and Dean for Academic Affairs: ROBERT TERESHINSKI
Vice-Pres. and Dean for Student Affairs: SARAH CARDA
Vice-Pres. for Enrolment Management: BRANDI DeFRIES
Vice-Pres. for Finance and Admin.: DAISY HALVORSON
Vice-Pres. for Institutional Advancement: DEREK WESLEY
Registrar: JONNA SUPURGECI
Dir for Library: SANDRA BROWN
Library of 75,000 vols
Number of teachers: 65
Number of students: 1,100

NATIONAL AMERICAN UNIVERSITY

5301 S Highway 16, Suite 200, Rapid City, SD 57701
Telephone: (605) 721-5200
Fax: (605) 721-5241
Internet: www.national.edu
Founded 1941 as Nat. School of Business
Private control
Academic year: September to August
Areas of study: communications, humanities, information technology, mathematics, science, social and behavioural sciences; campuses in Centennial, Denver and Colorado Springs (Colorado), Albuquerque and Rio Rancho (New Mexico), Lee's Summit, Independence and Kansas City (Missouri), Bloomington, Brooklyn Center, Minnetonka, and Minneapolis (Minnesota), Allen and Austin (Texas), Overland Park and Wichita (Kansas) and Sioux Falls (South Dakota)
Univ. Pres.: JERRY L. GALLENTINE
CEO: RONALD SHAPE

Provost and Gen. Counsel: SAMUEL D. KERR
Assoc. Provost and System Vice-Pres. for Curriculum and Instruction: MARILYN HOLMGREN
System Vice-Pres. for Graduate Studies and Dean for the Graduate School: PHYLLIS OKREPKIE
System Vice-Pres. for Academic Operations and Learner Services: JASON WARR
Chief Information Officer: JOHN BUXTON
Registrar: TOM MAHON
System Librarian: PAT HAMILTON.

NORTHERN STATE UNIVERSITY

1200 S Jay St, Aberdeen, SD 57401
Telephone: (605) 626-3011
Fax: (605) 626-3022
E-mail: info@northern.edu
Internet: www.northern.edu
Founded 1901 as Northern Normal and Industrial School, present name and status 1989
State control
Pres.: Dr JAMES SMITH
Provost and Vice-Pres. for Academic Affairs: Dr TOM HAWLEY
Vice-Pres. for Finance and Admin.: DON ERLENBUSCH
Vice-Pres. for Student Affairs: RHODA SMITH
Dir for Univ. College: STEVE RASMUSSEN
Dir for Univ. Relations: BRENDA DREYER
Registrar: PEGGY HALLSTROM
Dir for Libraries: ROBERT RUSSELL
Library of 250,000 vols
Number of teachers: 150
Number of students: 2,698

DEANS

College of Arts and Sciences: Dr CELESTINO MENDEZ
School of Business: Dr WILLARD BROUCEK
School of Education: CONSTANCE GEIER
School of Fine Arts: Dr ALAN D. LaFAVE

OGLALA LAKOTA COLLEGE

3 Mile Creek Rd, POB 490, Kyle, SD 57752-0490
Telephone: (605) 455-6000
Fax: (605) 455-2787
Internet: www.olc.edu
Founded 1971, present name 1983
Tribal control
Academic year: August to May
Areas of study: liberal arts and information technology; centres at Allen (Pass Creek College Center), Batesland (East Wakpamni College Center), Eagle Butte (OLC Cheyenne River College Center), Kyle (Pejuta Haka College Center), Manderson (Wounded Knee College Center), Martin (LaCreek College Center), Oglala (White Clay College Center), Pine Ridge (Pine Ridge College Center), Porcupine (Pahin Sinte College Center), Rapid City (He Sapa Center) and Wanblee (Eagle Nest College Center)
Pres.: THOMAS SHORTBULL
Vice-Pres. for Business: ARLENE QUIST
Vice-Pres. for Instruction: Dr GERALD GIRAUD
Registrar: LESLIE MESTETH
Library Dir: LaVERA ROSE
Library of 20,000 vols
Number of teachers: 15
Number of students: 1,400 (full-time)

PRESENTATION COLLEGE

1500 N Main St, Aberdeen, SD 57401
Telephone: (605) 229-8505
Fax: (605) 229-8518
E-mail: admit@presentation.edu
Internet: www.presentation.edu

Founded 1922 as Notre Dame Junior College; present name 1965

Private control

Academic year: August to May (2 semesters)

Depts of allied health, arts and sciences, business, education, nursing, social work; campuses at Aberdeen and Eagle Butte (South Dakota), and Fairmont (Minnesota)

Pres.: VIRGINIA TOBIN

Vice-Pres. for Advancement: LORI HARMEL

Vice-Pres. for Enrolment: JOELLEN LINDNER

Vice-Pres. for Finance: CATHY HALL

Vice-Pres. for Student Services: BOB SCHU-CHARDT

Registrar: MAUREEN SCHUCHARDT

Dir for Libraries: LEA BRIGGS

Number of teachers: 47

Number of students: 642

SINTE GLESKA UNIVERSITY

POB 105, Mission, SD 57555

Telephone: (605) 856-8100

Fax: (605) 856-4135

E-mail: admin@sinte.edu

Internet: www.sintegleska.edu

Founded 1970 as Sinte Gleska College, present name 1992

Tribal control

Academic year: August to May

Depts of art and sciences, business administration and management, education, human services

Pres.: LIONEL R. BORDEAUX

Vice-Pres. for Academic Affairs: CHERYL MEDEARIS

Vice-Pres. for Education: MIKE BENGE

Vice-Pres. for Institutional Relations and Resource Devt: GEORGIA HACKETT

Vice-Pres. for Student Services: MIKE BENGE

Registrar: JACK HERMAN

Library Dir: RACHEL LINDVALL

Number of teachers: 36

Number of students: 1,080 (960 undergraduate, 120 postgraduate)

SIOUX FALLS SEMINARY

2100 S Summit Ave, Sioux Falls, SD 57105

Telephone: (605) 336-6588

Fax: (605) 335-9090

E-mail: info@sfseminary.edu

Internet: www.sfseminary.edu

Founded 1949

Private control

Academic year: September to May

Areas of study: Christian leadership, counselling, marriage and family therapy, ministry, theological studies

Pres.: Dr G. MICHAEL HAGAN

Academic Vice-Pres. and Dean: Dr RONALD D. SISK

Dir for Enrolment: NATE HELLING

Registrar: BRENDA MEDALEN

Library of 72,500 vols, 300 periodicals

Number of teachers: 13

Number of students: 250

SOUTH DAKOTA SCHOOL OF MINES AND TECHNOLOGY

501 E St Joseph St, Rapid City, SD 57701

Telephone: (605) 394-2511

Fax: (605) 394-3388

E-mail: info@sdsmt.edu

Internet: www.sdsmt.edu

Founded 1885

State control

Academic year: September to May

Depts of atmospheric sciences, chemical and biological engineering, chemistry, civil and environmental engineering, electrical and computer engineering, geology and geological engineering, humanities, industrial engineering, materials and metallurgical engineering, mathematics and computer science, mechanical engineering, military science, mining engineering, physical education, physics, social sciences

Pres.: ROBERT A. WHARTON

Provost and Vice-Pres. for Academic Affairs: DUANE HRNCIR

Vice-Pres. for Finance and Admin.: TIMOTHY G. HENDERSON

Vice-Pres. for Research: RONALD WHITE

Vice-Pres. for Student Affairs and Dean for Students: PATRICIA G. MAHON

Vice-Pres. for Univ. Relations: CHRISTY A. HORN

Dir for Library: PATRICIA M. ANDERSEN

Library of 220,224 vols

Number of teachers: 130 (full-time)

Number of students: 2,313

Publication: *Hardrock Magazine*.

SOUTH DAKOTA STATE UNIVERSITY

POB 2201, Brookings, SD 57007

Telephone: (605) 688-4121

Fax: (605) 688-6891

E-mail: sdsu.admissions@sdstate.edu

Internet: www.sdstate.edu

Founded 1881 as Dakota Agricultural College, univ. status in 1964

State control

Academic year: August to May

Pres.: Dr DAVID L. CHICOINE

Provost and Vice-Pres. for Academic Affairs: Dr LAURIE NICHOLS

Vice-Pres. for Admin.: Dr MICHAEL REGER

Vice-Pres. for Information Technology: Dr MICHAEL F. ADELAINE

Vice-Pres. for Research: Dr KEVIN D. KEPHART

Vice-Pres. for Student Affairs: Dr MARYSZ RAMES

Dean for Libraries: DAVID GLEIM

Library: see Libraries and Archives

Number of teachers: 657 (515 full-time, 142 part-time)

Number of students: 12,816

DEANS

College of Agriculture and Biological Sciences: Dr BARRY DUNN

College of Arts and Sciences: (vacant)

College of Education and Human Sciences: JILL THORNGREN

College of Engineering: Dr LEWIS F. BROWN

College of Nursing: Dr ROBERTA K. OLSON

College of Pharmacy: DENNIS D. HEDGE

Graduate School: (vacant)

University College: Dr KEITH CORBETT

UNIVERSITY OF SIOUX FALLS

1101 W 22nd St, Sioux Falls, SD 57105

Telephone: (605) 331-5000

Fax: (605) 331-6615

E-mail: admissions@usiouxfalls.edu

Internet: www.usiouxfalls.edu

Founded 1883 as Dakota Collegiate Institute, present name 1995

Private control

Academic year: September to August

Areas of study: information sciences, liberal arts, music, philosophy, social work, theology

Pres.: MARK BENEDETTO

Provost and Vice-Pres. for Academic Affairs: BRETT BRADFIELD

Vice-Pres. for Business and Finance: Dr MARSHA DENNISTON

Vice-Pres. for Institutional Advancement: JON HIATT

Vice-Pres. for Student Devt and Enrolment Management: AIMEE VANDERFEEN

Assoc. Vice-Pres. for Student Devt and Dean for Students: KAREN SUMNER

Registrar: ANNA HECKENLAIBLE

Dir for Library Services: RACHEL CROWLEY

Library of 84,354 vols

Number of teachers: 184 (63 full-time; 121 part-time)

Number of students: 1,488 (1,165 undergraduate, 323 graduate)

UNIVERSITY OF SOUTH DAKOTA

414 E Clark St, Vermillion, SD 57069

Telephone: (605) 677-5011

Fax: (605) 677-5073

E-mail: admissions@usd.edu

Internet: www.usd.edu

Founded 1862

State control

Academic year: August to May

Pres.: JAMES W. ABBOTT (acting)

Provost and Vice-Pres. for Academic Affairs: CHUCK STABEN (acting)

Vice-Pres. for Admin. and Technology: ROBERTA AMBUR

Vice-Pres. for Finance: SHEILA GESTRING

Vice-Pres. for Marketing, Enrolment and Student Services: JEFFREY BAYLOR

Vice-Pres. for Research: LAURA JENSKI

Registrar: KURT HACKEMER

Dean for Univ. Libraries: ANNE COOPER MOORE

Library: see Libraries and Archives

Number of teachers: 423

Number of students: 9,970

Publications: *Business Connections* (1 a year), *South Dakotan Lawyer* (1 a year), *South Dakotan MD* (2 a year), *The South Dakotan* (2 a year), *USD Nursing* (1 a year)

DEANS

Beacom School of Business: MICHAEL J. KELLER

College of Arts and Sciences: Dr MATTHEW C. MOEN

College of Fine Arts: Dr LARRY SCHOU

Graduate School: Dr LAURIE BECVAR

Sanford School of Medicine: (vacant)

School of Education: Dr RICK MELMER

School of Health Sciences: Prof. Dr MICHAEL J. LAWLER

School of Law: Prof. THOMAS E. GEU

TENNESSEE

AMERICAN BAPTIST COLLEGE

1800 Baptist World Centre Dr., Nashville, TN 37207-4952

Telephone: (615) 256-1463

Fax: (615) 226-7855

E-mail: mspring@abcnash.edu

Internet: www.abcnash.edu

Founded 1924 as American Baptist Theological Seminary

Private control

Academic year: August to May (2 semesters)

Degree programmes in arts, pastoral studies, theology

Pres. and CEO: Dr FORREST ELLIOTT HARRIS, SR

Vice-Pres. for Academic Affairs: Dr RENITA WEEMS

Chief Financial Officer: CLARA A. WILLIAMS

Chief of Campus Operations: JOYCE ACKLEN

Dir for Enrolment Management: Dr RENITA WEEMS

Admissions and Registrar Administrator: PAM TABOR

Dir of Library Services: Dr CHERISNA JEAN-MARIE

Library of 20,000 vols, 170 periodicals.

AQUINAS COLLEGE

4210 Harding Pike, Nashville, TN 37205
Telephone: (615) 297-7545
Fax: (615) 279-3892
E-mail: admissions@aquinascollege.edu
Internet: www.aquinascollege.edu
Founded 1928 as St Cecilia Normal School, present name and status 1994
Private control
Academic year: August to May (2 semesters)
Areas of study incl. business, liberal arts, nursing, teacher education
Pres.: Sis. MARY SARAH
Vice-Pres. for Academic Affairs: Sis. ELIZABETH ANNE
Vice-Pres. for Admin. Affairs: Sis. MARY CECILIA
Vice-Pres. for Institutional Advancement: TIM STRANSKY
Chief Financial Officer: ROGER MUEHE
Dir of Admissions: CONNIE HANSOM
Dir of Student Affairs: SUZETTE TELLI
Registrar: ETTA MASON
Head Librarian: J. MARK HALL
Library of 70,000 vols
Publication: *Aquinas College Magazine* (2 a year)

DEANS

Nursing: Bro. IGNATIUS

AUSTIN PEAY STATE UNIVERSITY

601 College St, Clarksville, TN 37044
Telephone: (931) 221-7011
Fax: (931) 221-7297
E-mail: gov@apsu.edu
Internet: www.apsu.edu
Founded 1927 as Austin Peay Normal School, present status 1967, present name 1943
State control
Academic year: August to May
Campuses in Dickson, Fort Campbell in KY, Springfield in TN
Pres.: Dr TIMOTHY L. HALL
Provost and Vice-Pres. for Academic Affairs: Dr TRISTAN DENLEY
Vice-Pres. for Admin. and Finance: MITCH ROBINSON
Vice-Pres. for Student Affairs: Dr SHERYL A. BYRD
Dean of Students: GREGORY R. SINGLETON
Exec. Dir of Univ. Advancement: ROY GREGORY
Dir of Admissions: AMY DEATON
Registrar: TELAINA WRIGLEY
Dir of Library: JOSEPH E. WEBER
Library of 222,219 vols, 55,135 e-books, 52,950 bound periodicals, 695 journals, 34,204 e-journal titles, 674,316, microforms, 6,685 audiovisual items, 91,786 govt publs, 2,040 maps
Number of teachers: 626
Number of students: 10,873

DEANS

College of Arts and Letters: Dr DIXIE WEBB
College of Behavioral and Health Sciences: Dr DAVID DENTON
College of Business: Dr WILLIAM RUPP
College of Education: Dr CARLETTE HARDIN
College of Graduate Studies: Dr DIXIE DENNIS
College of Science and Mathematics: Dr JAIME R. TAYLOR
Extended and Distance Education: DANA WILLETT

BAPTIST COLLEGE OF HEALTH SCIENCES

1003 Monroe Ave, Memphis, TN 38104
Telephone: (901) 575-2247
Fax: (901) 572-2461
E-mail: admissions@bchs.edu
Internet: www.bchs.edu
Founded 1912 as Baptist Memorial Hospital, present name 1994
Private control
Pres.: BETTY SUE MCGARVEY
Provost: Dr WILLIAM J. SOBOTOR
Vice-Pres. for Business and Financial Services: LEANNE SMITH
Dean of Student Services: NANCY REED
Dir of Admissions: LISSA MORGAN
Registrar: JANA D. TURNER
Number of students: 975

DEANS

Div. of Allied Health: Dr LINDA REED
Div. of General and Health Studies: Dr BARRY SCHULTZ
Div. of Nursing: Dr ANNE PLUMB

BELMONT UNIVERSITY

1900 Belmont Blvd, Nashville, TN 37212-3757
Telephone: (615) 460-6000
Fax: (615) 460-5434
E-mail: admissions@belmont.edu
Internet: www.belmont.edu
Founded 1890 as Belmont College, present name 1991
Private control
Academic year: August to May (2 semesters)
Pres.: Dr ROBERT C. FISHER
Chancellor: Dr HERBERT GABHART
Provost: Dr THOMAS BURNS
Vice-Pres.: Dr SUSAN H. WEST
Vice-Pres. for Admin. and Univ. Counsel: Dr JASON B. ROGERS
Vice-Pres. for Finance and Operations: STEVEN T. LASLEY
Vice-Pres. for Univ. Advancement: Dr BETHEL E. THOMAS, JR
Dean of Enrolment Services: DAVID MEE
Dean of Students and Assoc. Provost: Dr ANDREW J. JOHNSTON
Registrar: STEVEN REED
Library Dir: Dr ERNEST WILLIAM HEARD, JR
Library of 335,000 vols, 1,000 periodicals
Number of teachers: 657 (316 full-time, 341 part-time)
Number of students: 6,365 (4,974 undergraduate, 1,391 graduate)
Publications: *Belmont Circle* (4 a year), *Explore* (1 a year), *The Tower* (1 a year)

DEANS

College of Arts and Sciences: Dr BRYCE F. SULLIVAN
College of Business Admin.: Dr J. PATRICK RAINES
College of Law: JEFF KINSLER
College of Visual and Performing Arts: Dr CYNTHIA R. CURTIS
Gordon E. Inman College of Health Sciences and Nursing: Dr CATHY R. TAYLOR
Mike Curb College of Entertainment and Music Business: Dr WESLEY A. BULLA
School of Pharmacy: Dr PHIL JOHNSTON
School of Religion: Dr DARRELL GWALTNEY
Univ. College: Dr JIMMY T. DAVIS

BETHEL UNIVERSITY

325 Cherry Ave, McKenzie, TN 38201
Telephone: (731) 352-4000
Fax: (731) 352-4069
E-mail: admissions@bethelu.edu
Internet: www.bethelu.edu

Founded 1842 as Bethel Seminary, present name and status 2009
Private control
Academic year: August to May (2 semesters)
Pres.: Dr ROBERT PROSSER
Vice-Pres. for Univ. Devt: MIKE PARKER
Chief Financial Officer: SANDY ASHLEY
Dean of Enrolment Services: TINA HODGES
Registrar: BECKY HAMES
Dir of Library: JILL WHITFILL
Library of 43,000 vols, 48 periodicals, 100,000 e-periodicals
Number of teachers: 36
Number of students: 4,673
Publications: *Bethel Beacon* (52 a year), *Bethel Captions* (4 a year), *Log Cabin* (1 a year)

DEANS

College of Graduate Studies: Dr DOROTHY BLACK
College of Liberal Arts: CINDY MALLARD
College of Professional Studies: LISA VAUGHN

BRYAN COLLEGE

POB 7000, Dayton, TN 37321-7000
721 Bryan Dr., Dayton, TN 37321-7000
Telephone: (423) 775-2041
Fax: (423) 775-7330
E-mail: info@bryan.edu
Internet: www.bryan.edu
Founded 1930 as William Jennings Bryan Univ., present name 1993
Private control
Academic year: August to May
Areas of study incl. Biblical studies, biology, business administration, Christian ministry, Christian leadership, Christian thought, communication studies, creative writing, criminal justice, education, English, environmental science, exercise and health science, history, liberal arts, mathematics, music, politics and government, nursing, psychology, Spanish, theatre
Pres.: Dr STEPHEN LIVESAY
Academic Vice-Pres.: Dr BRADFORD SAMPLE
Vice-Pres. for Advancement: BLAKE HUDSON
Vice-Pres. for Enrolment Management: MICHAEL SAPIENZA
Vice-Pres. for Finance: VANCE BERGER
Vice-Pres. for Operations: TIM HOSTETLER
Registrar: JANET M. PIATT
Library Dir: Dr GARY FITSIMMONS
Library of 181,220 vols, 30,299 periodicals, 71 microforms
Number of teachers: 44 (full-time)
Number of students: 1,400
Publications: *Bryan Life* (4 a year), *Illumine*

DEANS

School of Adult and Graduate Studies: Dr MICHAEL CHASE

CARSON-NEWMAN COLLEGE

2130 Branner Ave, Jefferson City, TN 37760
Telephone: (865) 471-2000
Fax: (865) 471-4817
E-mail: admitme@cn.edu
Internet: www.cn.edu
Founded 1851 as Mossy Creek Missionary Baptist Seminary, present name 1889
Private control
Academic year: August to May (2 semesters)
Pres.: Prof. Dr J. RANDALL O'BRIEN
Provost: Dr KINA MALLARD
Vice-Pres. for Advancement: Dr WILLIAM DANNY NICHOLSON
Vice-Pres. for Student Affairs: Dr ROSS BRUMMETT
Chief Financial Officer: MARTHA H. CHAMBERS

Dean of Enrolment Services and Registrar: SHERYL M. GRAY
Dean of Library Service: BRUCE G. KOCOUR
Library of 200,000 vols, 166,000 e-books, 8,000 periodicals
Number of teachers: 129 (full-time)
Number of students: 2,065
Publications: *Baptist History and Heritage, CN Studies, JOURNEY Magazine, Mossy Creek Reader, NUA—Studies in Contemporary Irish Writing*

DEANS

School of Business: Prof. Dr CLYDE E. HERRING
School of Education: Prof. Dr SHARON TEETS
School of Family and Consumer Sciences: Prof. Dr KITTY ROBERTS COFFEY
School of Fine Arts: Dr MARK HUSSUNG
School of Humanities: Dr MARY E. BALDRIDGE
School of Natural Sciences and Mathematics: Prof. Dr CAREY R. HERRING
School of Nursing and Behavioral Health: Dr GREGORY CASALENUOVO
School of Religion: Prof. Dr DAVID E. CRUTCHLEY
School of Social Sciences: Prof. Dr LAURA R. WADLINGTON

CHRISTIAN BROTHERS UNIVERSITY

650 E Parkway, S, Memphis, TN 38104
Telephone: (901) 321-3000
Fax: (901) 321-3257
E-mail: admissions@cbu.edu
Internet: www.cbu.edu

Founded 1871 as Christian Brothers College, present name 1990; attached to De La Salle Christian Brothers (Brothers of the Christian Schools)
Private control
Academic year: August to May
Pres.: Dr JOHN SMARRELLI, JR
Vice-Pres. for Academic Affairs: Dr FRANK BUSCHER
Vice-Pres. for Advancement: ANDREW PRISLOVSKY
Vice-Pres. for Enrolment Management: JAMES SCHLIMMER
Vice-Pres. for Finance and Admin.: C. DANIEL WORTHAM
Vice-Pres. for Student Life: Bro. DOMINIC EHRMANTRAUT
Dean of Admissions: Dr ANNE KENWORTHY
Registrar: MELODY NABORS
Librarian: KAY CUNNINGHAM
Library of 97,000 vols, 300 print periodicals, 60,000 e-books, 1,800 DVDs, CDs and video cassettes
Number of teachers: 106 (full-time)
Number of students: 1,641 (f.t.e.)

DEANS

Graduate and Professional Studies: Dr MICHAEL R. RYAN
School of Arts: Dr PAUL HAUGHT
School of Business: Dr JOHN HARGETT
School of Engineering: Dr ERIC B. WELCH
School of Sciences: Dr JOHNNY B. HOLMES

CUMBERLAND UNIVERSITY

1 Cumberland Sq., Lebanon, TN 37087-3408
Telephone: (615) 444-2562
Fax: (615) 444-2569
E-mail: admissions@cumberland.edu
Internet: www.cumberland.edu
Founded 1842
Private control
Academic year: August to May (2 semesters)
Pres.: Dr HARVILL C. EATON
Exec. Vice-Pres.: EDDIE PAWLAWSKI
Vice-Pres. for Academic Affairs and Registrar: Dr WILBUR PETERSON

Vice-Pres. for Admin.: JOE GRAY
Vice-Pres. for Advancement: RUSTY RICHARDSON
Vice-Pres. for Business and Finance: JUDY JORDAN
Dir of Enrolment Services: BEATRICE LA CHANCE
Dir of Library: ELOISE HITCHCOCK
Library of 35,000 vols, 40,000 e-books, 300 periodicals, 1,300 audiovideo materials
Number of teachers: 127
Number of students: 1,491 (1,135 full-time, 356 part-time)

DEANS

Jeanette C. Rudy School of Nursing: Dr CAROLE ANN BACH
Labry School of Business and Technology: Dr PAUL STUMB
School of Education and Public Service: Dr K. CHARLES COLLIER
School of Liberal Arts and Sciences: Dr LAURIE P. DISHMAN
School of Music and the Arts: TED CHARLES ROSE

EAST TENNESSEE STATE UNIVERSITY

807 University Pkwy, POB 70267, Johnson City, TN 37614-1700
Telephone: (423) 439-1000
Fax: (423) 439-6604
E-mail: pittsm@etsu.edu
Internet: www.etsu.edu

Founded 1911 as East Tennessee State Normal School, present name and status 1963
State control
Academic year: August to May (2 semesters)
Pres.: Dr BRIAN NOLAND
Provost and Vice-Pres. for Academic Affairs: Dr BERT C. BACH
Vice-Pres. for Admin. and Finance: Dr DAVID D. COLLINS
Vice-Pres. for Univ. Advancement: Dr RICHARD A. MANAHAN
Vice-Provost and Dean of Students: Dr JOE H. SHERLIN, JR
Registrar: SHERYL BURNETTE
Dean of Univ. Libraries: Dr JEAN FLANIGAN
Library of 467,613 vols, 80,000 e-books, 272 journals, 22,755 audiovisual materials, 19,685 e-journals
Number of teachers: 650
Number of students: 15,000
Publications: *Aethlon: Journal of Sport Literature* (2 a year), *ETSU Today Magazine* (2 a year), *Science Educator* (2 a year), *Storytelling World* (2 a year), *The Tennessee Reading Educator* (2 a year)

DEANS

Claudius G. Clemmer College of Education: Dr W. HAL KNIGHT
College of Arts and Sciences: Dr GORDON ANDERSON
College of Business and Technology: Dr LINDA R. GARCEAU
College of Clinical and Rehabilitative Health Sciences: Dr NANCY J. SCHERER
College of Nursing: Dr WENDY NEHRING
College of Public Health: Dr RANDY WYKOFF
Gatton College of Pharmacy: Prof. Dr LARRY D. CALHOUN
Honors College: Dr REBECCA A. PYLES
James H. Quillen College of Medicine: Dr PHILIP C. BAGNELL
School of Continuing Studies and Academic Outreach: Dr RICK OSBORN
School of Graduate Studies: Dr CECILIA MCINTOSH

EMMANUEL CHRISTIAN SEMINARY

One Walker Dr., Johnson City, TN 37601
Telephone: (423) 926-1186
Fax: (423) 926-6198
E-mail: admissions@ecs.edu
Internet: www.ecs.edu
Founded 1965
Private control
Academic year: August to May (2 semesters)
Offers Masters degree in arts, divinity, religion
Pres.: MICHAEL L. SWEENEY
Chancellor: C. ROBERT WETZEL
Exec. Dir of Devt: DAN R. LAWSON
Dir of Admissions and Recruitment: ERIN LAYTON
Dir of Finance: DAVID MARSHALL
Dean and Registrar: JACK HOLLAND
Librarian: JOHN MARK WADE
Library of 171,000 vols.

FISK UNIVERSITY

1000 17th Ave, N, Nashville, TN 37208-3051
Telephone: (615) 329-8500
Fax: (615) 329-8576
E-mail: admit@fisk.edu
Internet: www.fisk.edu
Founded 1866 as Fisk School, present name and status 1867
Private control
Academic year: August to May
Pres.: Dr HAZEL R. O'LEARY
Provost and Exec. Vice-Pres.: Dr M. PRINCILLA EVANS MORRIS
Vice-Pres. for Finance and Chief Financial Officer: CLANCY ROBERTS
Vice-Pres. for Institutional Assessment: Dr MICHAEL K. FLEMING
Dean of Admissions: KEITH CHANDLER
Dean of Student Engagement: LAMETRIUS DANIELS
Dir of Student Affairs: LYNWOOD BERRY
Dean of Library: JESSIE CARNEY SMITH
Library of 210,000 vols
Number of teachers: 53 (full-time)
Number of students: 477
Publications: *Fisk Focus* (6 a year), *Fisk News* (1 a year)

DEANS

School of Humanities and Social Sciences: Prof. Dr REAVIS L. MITCHELL, JR
School of Natural Sciences, Mathematics and Business: Prof. Dr LEE E. LIMBIRD

FREE WILL BAPTIST BIBLE COLLEGE

3606 West End Ave, Nashville, TN 37205
Telephone: (615) 844-5000
Fax: (615) 269-6028
Internet: www.fwbbc.edu
Founded 1942
Private control
Academic year: August to May (2 semesters)
Areas of study incl. accounting, biblical and ministry studies, business administration, child development and learning, history, languages, music, pastoral studies, psychology, science
Pres.: Dr J. MATHEW PINSON
Chancellor: Dr TOM MALONE
Provost: Dr GREG KETTEMAN
Vice-Pres. for Financial Affairs: CRAIG MAHLER
Vice-Pres. for Institutional Advancement: DAVID WILLIFORD
Vice-Pres. for Institutional Planning: Dr MILTON FIELDS
Vice-Pres. for Student Services and Dean of Students: Dr JON FORLINES

Dir of Enrolment Services: RUSTY CAMPBELL
Librarian: CAROL REID (acting)
Library of 60,000 vols
Number of students: 350

FREED-HARDEMAN UNIVERSITY

158 E Main St, Henderson, TN 38340-2399
Telephone: (731) 989-6648
Fax: (731) 989-6650
Internet: www.fhu.edu
Founded 1869 as Private High School and College, present name 1919, present status 1990
Private control
Academic year: August to May (2 semesters)
Pres.: Dr JOE A. WILEY
Exec. Vice-Pres. and Chief Financial Officer: Dr DWAYNE H. WILSON
Vice-Pres. for Academics and Enrolment Management: Dr CHARLES J. VIRES
Vice-Pres. for Student Services and Dean of Students: Dr E. WAYNE SCOTT
Vice-Pres. for Univ. Advancement: DAVID A. CLOUSE
Registrar: LARRY OLDHAM
Library Dir: HOPE SHULL
Library of 153,276 vols, 126,310 e-books, 34,696 periodicals, 48,500 audiovisual items
Number of students: 1,992

DEANS

Honors College: Dr JENNIFER S. JOHNSON
School of Arts and Humanities: Dr W. STEPHEN JOHNSON
School of Biblical Studies: Dr WILLIAM R. SMITH
School of Business: Prof. Dr KEITH W. SMITH
School of Education: Dr SHAREN L. CYPRESS
School of Sciences and Mathematics: Dr LEANN SELF-DAVIS

HARDING SCHOOL OF THEOLOGY

1000 Cherry Rd, Memphis, TN 38117-5499
Telephone: (901) 761-1350
Fax: (901) 761-1358
E-mail: hstadmissions@hst.edu
Internet: hst.edu
Founded 1952 as Harding Univ. Graduate School of Religion, present name 2011; attached to Harding Univ. in Searcy, Ark
Private control
Pres.: Dr DAVID B. BURKS
Vice-Pres. and Dean: Dr EVERTT W. HUFFARD
Dir of Admissions: MATT CARTER
Dir of Advancement: LARRY ARICK
Librarian: DON L. MEREDITH
Library of 140,000 vols, 590 periodicals.

HIWASSEE COLLEGE

225 Hiwassee College Dr., Madisonville, TN 37354
Telephone: (423) 442-2001
Fax: (423) 442-8521
E-mail: enroll@hiwassee.edu
Internet: www.hiwassee.edu
Founded 1826 as Tullagalla Acad., present name 1849, present status 1980
Private control
Academic year: August to May (2 semesters)
Bachelors degree in arts, science
Pres.: Dr ROBIN J. TRICOLI
Vice-Pres. for Academic and Student Affairs and Academic Dean: Dr BETH R. SCRUGGS
Vice-Pres. for Admissions and Financial Aid: J. RON HEMPHILL
Vice-Pres. for Business Affairs and Treas.: WALTON LIPSCOMB
Vice-Pres. for Financial Aid: RON HEMPHILL

Vice-Pres. for Institutional Advancement: D. MARK ELAM
Dean of Students: MARK JOHNSON
Registrar: JANE DYE
Dir of Library Services: Dr CURTIS CHAPMAN
Library of 30,000 vols, 300 periodicals, 110 magazines and newspapers.

JOHNSON UNIVERSITY

7900 Johnson Dr., Knoxville, TN 37998
Telephone: (865) 573-4517
Fax: (865) 251-2337
E-mail: johnsonu@johnsonu.edu
Internet: www.johnsonu.edu
Founded 1893 as School of the Evangelists, present name and status 2011
Private control
Academic year: August to May (2 semesters)
Academic programmes incl. arts, biblical studies, intercultural studies, music, science
Pres.: Dr GARY E. WEEDMAN
Vice-Pres. for Academics and Academic Dean: Dr RICHARD K. BEAM
Vice-Pres. for Business and Finance: CHRISTOPHER R. ROLPH
Vice-Pres. for Devt: PHILIP A. EUBANKS
Vice-Pres. for Student Services and Dean of Students: DAVID A. LEGG
Registrar: SANDRA BLEVINS
Library Dir: CARRIE BETH LOWE
Library of 111,000 vols, 80,000 ebooks
Number of teachers: 55
Number of students: 845 (725 undergraduate, 120 graduate)
Publication: *Johnson* (3 a year).

KING COLLEGE

1350 King College Rd, Bristol, TN 37620
Telephone: (423) 652-4861
Fax: (423) 652-6040
E-mail: admissions@king.edu
Internet: www.king.edu
Founded 1867
Private control
Academic year: August to May (2 semesters)
Pres.: Dr GREGORY D. JORDAN
Provost and Vice-Pres. for Academic Affairs: Dr PAUL M. PERCY
Vice-Pres. for Business Operations and Chief Financial Officer: JAMES P. DONAHUE
Vice-Pres. for Institutional Advancement: WILLIAM M. McELROY
Vice-Pres. for Student Affairs: Dr ROBERT A. LITTLETON
Registrar: SARAH L. DILLOW
Dean of Library Services: ERIKA BRAMMER
Library of 140,000 vols incl. books, periodicals, microforms, audiovisual items, govt documents
Number of teachers: 70
Number of students: 1,515
Publications: *The Descant, Tornado*

DEANS

Peeke School of Mission: FRED FOY STRANG
School of Arts and Sciences: Prof. Dr KATHERINE VANDE BRAKE
School of Business: Prof. Dr TODD H. ERICKSON
School of Education: Prof. Dr CARA E. ANDERSON
School of Nursing: Dr JOHANNE A. QUINN

LANE COLLEGE

545 Lane Ave, Jackson, TN 38301-4598
Telephone: (731) 426-7500
Fax: (731) 427-3987
E-mail: admissions@lanecollege.edu
Internet: www.lanecollege.edu

Founded 1882 as C. M. E. High School, present name 1896
Private control
Academic year: August to June
Offers Bachelor of arts, science
Pres.: Dr WESLEY CORNELIUS McCLURE
Exec. Vice-Pres.: SHARRON TAYLOR BURNETT
Vice-Pres. for Academic Affairs: Dr LORA BATTLE BAILEY
Vice-Pres. for Business and Finance: MELVIN ROSS HAMLETT
Vice-Pres. for Institutional Advancement: RICHARD HULON DONNELL
Vice-Pres. for Student Affairs: SHERRILL BERRY SCOTT
Registrar: TERRY BLACKMON
Head Librarian: LAN WANG
Library of 154,000 vols
Number of teachers: 102
Number of students: 2,200

LEE UNIVERSITY

1120 N Ocoee St, Cleveland, TN 37320-3450
Telephone: (423) 614-8000
E-mail: admissions@leeuniversity.edu
Internet: www.leeuniversity.edu
Founded 1918 as Bible Institute, present status 1997
Private control
Pres.: Dr CHARLES PAUL CONN
Vice-Pres. for Academic Affairs: Dr CAROLYN DIRKSEN
Vice-Pres. for Admin.: WALTER C. MAULDIN
Vice-Pres. for Business and Finance: CHRIS CONINE
Vice-Pres. for Enrolment Management: PHIL COOK
Vice-Pres. for Information Services: Dr JAYSON VAN HOOK
Vice-Pres. for Student Devt: Dr MIKE HAYES
Vice-Pres. for Univ. Relations: Dr JEROME HAMMOND
Dir of Library Services: BARBARA McCULLOUGH
Library of 150,000 vols, 400 periodicals, 32,000 e-journals, 110,000 e-books
Number of students: 4,411

DEANS

College of Arts and Sciences: Dr J. MATTHEW MELTON
Helen DeVos College of Education: Dr DEBORAH MURRAY
School of Music: WILLIAM GREEN
School of Religion: Prof. Dr TERRY L. CROSS

LEMOYNE—OWEN COLLEGE

807 Walker Ave, Memphis, TN 38126
Telephone: (901) 435-1000
Fax: (901) 435-1724
E-mail: contact@nile.loc.edu
Internet: www.loc.edu
Founded 1968 by merger of LeMoyne College (f. 1862) with Owen College (f. 1947)
Private control
Academic year: July to May
Divs of business and economic development, education, liberal arts and humanities, natural and mathematical sciences, social and behavioural sciences
Pres.: JOHNNIE B. WATSON
Vice-Pres. for Academic Affairs and Chief Academic Officer: Dr BARBARA FRANKLE
Vice-Pres. for Finance and Chief Financial Officer: JIM DUGGER
Dean of Students: EDYTHE COBB
Dir of Admin. Services: JESSE CHATMAN
Registrar: ADDIE HARVEY
Dir of Library: ANNETTE HUNT
Library of 117,000 vols, 375 periodicals
Number of teachers: 41

Number of students: 1,212

LINCOLN MEMORIAL UNIVERSITY

6965 Cumberland Gap Parkway, Harrogate, TN 37752

Telephone: (423) 869-3611
Fax: (423) 869-6444
E-mail: admissions@lmunet.edu
Internet: www.lmunet.edu

Founded 1897
Private control
Academic year: August to May (2 semesters)
Pres.: Dr B. JAMES DAWSON
Vice-Pres.: Dr RAY E. STOWERS
Vice-Pres. for Academic Affairs: Dr CLAYTON HESS
Vice-Pres. for Finance: RANDY ELDRIDGE
Vice-Pres. for Univ. Advancement: CYNTHIA WHITT
Dean for Admin.: LISA BLAIR-COX
Dean for Enrolment Management: SHERRY MCCREARY
Dean ofor Students: FRANK SMITH
Dir for Admissions: SHERRY MCCREARY
Registrar: HELEN BAILEY
Dir for Library Services: GABRIEL MORLEY
Library of 326,800 vols e-books, e-journals, periodicals, microfilm, audiovisual materials
Number of teachers: 275 (169 full-time, 84 part-time)
Number of students: 4,550 (1,753 graduate, 1,858 undergraduate, 939 professional)
Publication: *The Lincoln Herald* (4 a year)

DEANS

Carter and Moyers School of Education: Dr MICHAEL CLYBURN
Caylor School of Nursing: Prof. Dr MARY ANNE MODRCIN
DeBusk College of Osteopathic Medicine: Dr RAY E. STOWERS
Duncan School of Law: SYDNEY BECKMAN
Paul V. Hamilton School of Arts and Sciences: Dr AMIEL JARSTFER
School of Allied Health: Prof. RANDALL K. EVANS
School of Business: Dr JACK T. MCCANN

LIPSCOMB UNIVERSITY

One University Park Dr., Nashville, TN 37204-3951
3901 Granny White Pike, Nashville, TN 37204-3951

Telephone: (615) 269-1000
Fax: (615) 966-1808
E-mail: registrar@lipscomb.edu
Internet: www.lipscomb.edu

Founded 1891 as Nashville Bible School, present name 1994
Private control
Academic year: August to May (2 semesters)
Pres.: Prof. Dr L. RANDOLPH LOWRY, III
Provost: Dr W. CRAIG BLEDSOE
Sr Vice-Pres. for Finance and Admin.: DANNY H. TAYLOR
Vice-Pres.: Dr MIKE HAMMOND
Vice-Pres. and Chief Information Officer: MIKE GREEN
Vice-Pres. for Devt and Alumni Relations: Dr BENNIE HARRIS
Vice-Pres. for Student Devt and Dean of Campus Life: Dr SCOTT MCDOWELL
Vice-Pres. for Univ. Relations: WALT LEAVER
Registrar: JANET CATES
Library Dir: CAROLYN T. WILSON
Library of 400,000 vols incl. books, periodicals, microforms
Number of teachers: 300
Number of students: 4,195
Publication: *Lipscomb Now*

DEANS

College of Arts and Sciences: Dr NORMA BURGESS
College of Bible and Ministry: Dr TERRY BRILEY
College of Business: TURNEY STEVENS
College of Education: Prof. Dr CANDICE MCQUEEN
College of Pharmacy and Health Sciences: Dr ROGER L. DAVIS
Raymond B. Jones College of Engineering: GREG G. NORDSTROM

MARTIN METHODIST COLLEGE

433 W Madison St, Pulaski, TN 38478-2799

Telephone: (931) 363-9800
Fax: (931) 363-9818
E-mail: info@martinmethodist.edu
Internet: www.martinmethodist.edu

Founded 1870 as Martin Female College, present name 1986
Private control
Academic year: July to May (2 semesters)
Liberal arts college; academic divs incl. business, education, humanities, mathematics and science, nursing, social science
Pres.: Dr TED BROWN
Vice-Pres. for Academic Affairs: JAMES T. MURRELL
Vice-Pres. for Enrolment and Campus Life: ROBBY SHELTON
Vice-Pres. for Finance and Admin.: DAVID STEPHENS
Vice-Pres. for Planning and Effectiveness: Dr DENNIS HASKINS
Registrar: ANDREW B. BROWN
Library Dir: RICHARD MADDEN
Library of 100,000 vols incl. print and e-books, 2,000 print and e-journals.

MARYVILLE COLLEGE

502 E Lamar Alexander Parkway, Maryville, TN 37804

Telephone: (865) 981-8000
Fax: (865) 981-8136
E-mail: campusvisit@maryvillecollege.edu
Internet: www.maryvillecollege.edu

Founded 1819 as Southern and Western Theological Seminary, present name 1842
Private control
Academic year: August to May (2 semesters)
Academic divs incl. behavioural sciences, education, fine arts, humanities, languages and literature, mathematics and computer science, natural sciences, social sciences
Pres.: Dr WILLIAM TOM BOGART
Vice-Pres. and Dean for College: Dr BARBARA WELLS
Vice-Pres. and Dean for Students: VANDY KEMP
Vice-Pres. and Treas.: DANA SMITH
Vice-Pres. for Advancement and Community Relations: HOLLY JACKSON-SULLIVAN
Vice-Pres. for Enrolment: Dr DOLPHUS HENRY
Registrar: KATHI WILSON
Library Dir: ANGELA QUICK
Library of 132,000 vols, 144,000 e-books, 20,000 journal titles
Number of teachers: 112 (72 full-time, 40 part-time)
Number of students: 1,103
Publications: *Impressions* (2 a year), *Laurels* (2 a year).

MEHARRY MEDICAL COLLEGE

1005 Dr D. B. Todd, Jr Blvd, Nashville, TN 37208

Telephone: (615) 327-6000
Fax: (615) 327-6228
E-mail: recordsdepartment@mmc.edu

Internet: www.mmc.edu
Founded 1876 as medical dept of Central Tennessee College, present status 1915
Private control
Academic year: August to July
Pres.: Prof. Dr WAYNE J. RILEY
Provost and Exec. Vice-Pres.: Dr ANGELA L. FRANKLIN
Sr Vice-Pres., Gen. Counsel and Corporate Sec.: BENJAMIN RAWLINS
Sr Vice-Pres. for Finance: LAMEL BANDY-NEAL
Sr Vice-Pres. for Institutional Advancement: ROBERT POOLE
Vice-Pres. for Research: Dr RUSSELL POLAND
Vice-Pres. for Student and Academic Affairs: PAMELA WILLIAMS
Registrar: SHANITA BROWN
Library Dir: FATIMA MNCUBE-BARNES
Library of 66,104 vols, 4,165 e-journals, 1,264 e-books
Number of teachers: 218 (full-time)
Number of students: 781

DEANS

School of Dentistry: Dr JANET H. SOUTHERLAND (acting)
School of Graduate Studies and Research: Dr MARIA DE FATIMA LIMA
School of Medicine: Dr CHARLES P. MOUTON

MEMPHIS COLLEGE OF ART

Overton Park, 1930 Poplar Ave, Memphis, TN 38104-2764

Telephone: (901) 272-5100
Fax: (901) 272-5104
E-mail: info@mca.edu
Internet: www.mca.edu

Founded 1936
Private control
Academic year: August to May (2 semesters)
Areas of study incl. animation, liberal studies, digital media, drawing, graphic design, illustration, painting, photography, printmaking, sculpture
Pres.: Dr RON JONES
Dean: REMY MILLER
Vice-Pres. for Academic Affairs: KEN STRICKLAND
Vice-Pres. for College Advancement: KIM WILLIAMS
Vice-Pres. for Finance and Admin.: SHERRY YELVINGTON
Vice-Pres. for Student Affairs: SUSAN MILLER
Dean for Admissions: ANNETTE JAMES MOORE
Director for Student Life: CARLA RUFFER
Registrar: ELESHA NEWBERRY
Librarian: LESLIE HOLLAND
Library of 19,000 vols
Number of teachers: 59
Number of students: 297

MEMPHIS THEOLOGICAL SEMINARY

168 East Parkway, S, Memphis, TN 38104

Telephone: (901) 458-8232
Fax: (901) 452-4051
E-mail: admissions@memphisseminary.edu
Internet: www.memphisseminary.edu

Founded 1908 as Theological Seminary by merger of Cumberland Presbyterians with Presbyterian Church, present name 1964
Private control
Academic year: August to May (2 semesters)
Pres.: Prof. Dr DANIEL J. EARHEART-BROWN
Vice-Pres. for Academic Affairs and Dean: Dr ROBERT S. WOOD
Vice-Pres. for Advancement: CATHI JOHNSON
Vice-Pres. for Operations and Chief Financial Officer: CASSANDRA PRICE-PERRY
Registrar: GAIL D. ROBINSON
Library Dir: STEVEN R. EDSCORN

Library of 87,000 vols, 382 periodicals, microfilm, microfiche, audiovideo items
Number of students: 312

MID-AMERICA BAPTIST THEOLOGICAL SEMINARY

2095 Appling Rd, Cordova, TN 38016
Telephone: (901) 751-8453
Fax: (901) 751-8454
E-mail: info@mabts.edu
Internet: www.mabts.edu
Founded 1971 as School of the Prophets, present name 1972
Private control
Academic year: August to July (2 semesters)
Campus in Albany, NY
Pres.: Dr MICHAEL R. SPRADLIN
Exec. Vice-Pres.: Dr BRADLEY C. THOMPSON
Academic Vice-Pres.: Dr TIMOTHY SEAL
Vice-Pres. for Finance and Operations: RANDY REDD
Vice-Pres. for Institutional Advancement: Dr GARY REDDING
Vice-Pres. for Institutional Assessment: Dr SOO GEUN SONG
Registrar: CARY BETH DUFFEL
Dir of Library Services: TERRENCE NEAL BROWN
Library of 163,000 vols
Publications: *The Journal of Evangelism and Missions*, *The Messenger* (3 a year).

MIDDLE TENNESSEE SCHOOL OF ANESTHESIA

POB 417, Madison, TN 37116
315 Hospital Dr., Madison, TN 37115
Telephone: (615) 732-7662
Fax: (615) 868-9885
E-mail: info@mtsa.edu
Internet: www.mtsa.edu
Founded 1950 as Madison Hospital School of Anesthesia, present name 1980
Private control
Areas of study incl. nurse anaesthesia
Pres.: Dr KENNETH L. SCHWAB
Vice-Pres. and Dean: Dr MARY E. DEVASHER
Vice-Pres. for Advancement and Alumni: JAMES B. CLOSSER
Dir of Learning Resource Centre and Dir of Information Systems Support: Dr AMY C. GIDEON
Library of 400 vols.

MIDDLE TENNESSEE STATE UNIVERSITY

1301 East Main St, Murfreesboro, TN 37132-0001
Telephone: (615) 898-2300
Fax: (615) 898-5906
E-mail: admissions@mtsu.edu
Internet: www.mtsu.edu
Founded 1911 as Middle Tennessee State Normal School, present name and status 1965
State control
Academic year: August to May (2 semesters)
Pres.: Prof. Dr SIDNEY A. MCPHEE
Provost and Exec. Vice-Pres.: Prof. Dr BRAD BARTEL
Sr Vice-Pres. for Business and Finance: Dr JOHN W. COTHERN
Vice-Pres. for Devt and Univ. Relations: WILLIAM J. BALES
Vice-Pres. for Finance and Admin.: DUANE STUCKY
Vice-Pres. for Student Affairs and Vice-Provost for Enrolment and Academic Services: Dr DEBRA SELLS
Registrar: CATHY KIRCHNER

Dean of Library: DON OMACHONU (acting)
Library of 1,000,000 vols
Number of teachers: 900
Number of students: 26,000

DEANS
College of Basic and Applied Sciences: Dr TOM CHEATHAM
College of Behavioral and Health Sciences: Dr HAROLD D. WHITESIDE
College of Education: Dr LANA C. SEIVERS
College of Liberal Arts: Dr MARK BYRNES
College of Mass Communication: Prof. Dr ROY L. MOORE
Graduate Studies: Dr MICHAEL D. ALLEN
Honors College: Prof. Dr JOHN R. VILE
Jennings A. Jones College of Business: Prof. Dr E. JAMES BURTON
Univ. College: Dr MIKE BOYLE

MILLIGAN COLLEGE

POB 500, Milligan College, TN 37682
Telephone: (423) 461-8700
Fax: (423) 461-8716
E-mail: admissions@milligan.edu
Internet: www.milligan.edu
Founded 1866 as Buffalo Male and Female Institute, present name 1881
Private control
Academic year: August to May (2 semesters)
Academic programmes incl. accounting, allied health, art, Bible, biology, business administration, chemistry, communications, economics, education history, legal studies, management, nursing, pharmacy, Psychology, Spanish, sports management, theatre
Pres.: Dr WILLIAM B. GREER
Vice-Pres. for Academic Affairs and Dean: Dr GARLAND YOUNG
Vice-Pres. for Business and Finance: JACQUI STEADMAN
Vice-Pres. for Enrolment Management and Marketing: Dr LEE FIERBAUGH
Vice-Pres. for Institutional Advancement: JACK SIMPSON
Vice-Pres. for Student Devt and Dean of Students: MARK FOX
Registrar: SUE SKIDMORE
Dir of Library Service: GARY F. DAUGHT
Library of 108,500 vols
Number of teachers: 75 (full-time)
Number of students: 1,200

O'MORE COLLEGE OF DESIGN

423 S Margin St, Franklin, TN 37064
Telephone: (615) 794-4254
Fax: (615) 790-1662
E-mail: admissions@omorecollege.edu
Internet: www.omorecollege.edu
Founded 1970
Private control
Academic year: August to May (2 semesters)
Areas of study incl. fashion design, fine art, interior design, liberal arts, visual communications
Pres.: Dr K. MARK HILLIARD
Vice-Pres. for Academic Affairs: SHARI FOX
Vice-Pres. for Student Affairs: AMY SHELTON
Dir of Admissions: MELINDA DABBS
Librarian: ALLISON CRAWFORD.

PENTECOSTAL THEOLOGICAL SEMINARY

POB 3330, Cleveland, TN 37320-3330
Telephone: (423) 478-1131
Fax: (423) 478-7711
E-mail: president@ptseminary.edu
Internet: www.ptseminary.edu
Founded 1975
Private control

Academic year: July to August
Areas of study incl. Christian formation, Church ministries, counselling and discipleship, divinity
Pres.: Prof. Dr STEVEN JACK LAND
Vice-Pres. for Academics: Prof. Dr SANG-EHIL HAN
Vice-Pres. for Finance: ROBERT BUXTON
Vice-Pres. for Institutional Advancement: Dr KENNETH R. DAVIS
Dir of Admin. Services: ALANNA HENRY
Registrar and Dir of Admissions: ANITA BLEVINS
Library Dir: BARBARA MCCULLOUGH
Library of 150,000 vols, 400 periodicals, 70,000 e-books.

RHODES COLLEGE

2000 N Parkway, Memphis, TN 38112-1690
Telephone: (901) 843-3000
Fax: (901) 843-3718
E-mail: adminfo@rhodes.edu
Internet: www.rhodes.edu
Founded 1848
Private control
Academic year: August to May
Liberal arts college; academic depts incl. anthropology and sociology, art, biology, chemistry, commerce and business, economics, education, English, Greek and Roman studies, history, int. studies
Pres.: WILLIAM E. TROUTT
Provost: CHARLOTTE G. BORST
Vice-Pres. for Academic Affairs and Dean of Faculty: Dr MICHAEL R. DROMPP
Vice-Pres. for College Relations: RUSSELL T. WIGGINTON
Vice-Pres. for Devt: JENNA GOODLOE WADE
Vice-Pres. for Enrolment and Communications and Dean of Admissions: CAREY THOMPSON
Vice-Pres. for Finance and Business Affairs: JAMES ALLEN BOONE, JR
Vice-Pres. for Information Services: ROBERT M. JOHNSON, JR
Dean of Students: CAROL E. CASEY
Registrar: DEANNA ADAMS
Dir of Library: DARLENE BROOKS
Library of 338,950 vols incl. 287,950 print publs, 51,000 e-books
Number of teachers: 167 full-time
Number of students: 1,712
Publication: *Rhodes Magazine* (3 a year).

RICHMONT GRADUATE UNIVERSITY

1815 McCallie Ave, Chattanooga, GA 37404-3026
Telephone: (423) 266-4574
Fax: (423) 265-7375
E-mail: admissions@richmont.edu
Internet: richmont.edu
Founded 2000 by merger of Chattanooga Bible Institute (f. 1933) with Psychological Studies Institute; present name and status 2003
Private control
Academic year: August to August
Campus in Atlanta
Pres.: Dr C. JEFFREY TERRELL
Academic Dean: Dr PHILIP A. COYLE
Exec. Vice-Pres.: BOB RODGERS
Vice-Pres. for Advancement: GEORGE DEMPSEY
Chief Financial Officer: WILLIAM J. MUELLER
Dean of Students: Dr DEANNE TERRELL
Dir of Admissions: NOVELL BLAIN
Dir of Libraries: JOHN L. HUGHES
Library of 37,000 vols, 15,000 e-books

DEANS

Clinical Affairs: Dr EVALIN RHODES HANSHEW
School of Counseling: Dr KENY FELIX
School of Ministry: Dr LELAND ELIASON

SOUTH COLLEGE

3904 Lonas Dr., Knoxville, TN 37909
Telephone: (865) 251-1800
Internet: www.southcollegetn.edu

Founded 1882 as br. of Nashville Business
College, present name 2001
Private control
Academic year: September to June

Masters degree in health science; Bachelors
degree in business administration, science

Pres.: STEPHEN A. SOUTH
Exec. Vice-Pres.: Dr KIMBERELY B. HALL
Vice-Pres. for Admin. and Regulatory Compliance: STEVE WOODFORD
Vice-Pres. for Business Operations: KEVIN SPARKS
Vice-Pres. for Enrolment Management: WALTER HOSEA
Vice-Pres. for Institutional Effectiveness and Student Services: BARBARA BRIMI
Dean for Student Services: CAROLYN HILLEGAS
Dir for Admissions: CARRIE MAJOR
Registrar: KIM WOOD
Head Librarian: MEL McHUGH.

SOUTHERN ADVENTIST UNIVERSITY

POB 370, Collegedale, TN 37315-0370
5010 University Dr., Collegedale, TN 37315
Telephone: (423) 238-2111
Fax: (423) 238-3001
E-mail: postmaster@southern.edu
Internet: www.southern.edu

Founded 1892 as Graysville Acad., present
name and status 1996
Private control
Academic year: August to May

Pres.: GORDON BIETZ
Sr Vice-Pres. for Academic Admin.: ROBERT YOUNG
Sr Vice-Pres. for Financial Admin.: TOM VERRILL
Vice-Pres. for Advancement: CHRIS CAREY
Vice-Pres. for Enrolment Services: MARC GRUNDY
Vice-Pres. for Student Services: BILL WOHLERS
Registrar: JONI ZIER
Dir of Libraries: Dr JOSIP MOCNIK
Library of 175,000 vols, 11,163 periodical
subscriptions, 587,809 microforms
Number of teachers: 111 (108 full-time, 3
part-time)
Number of students: 3,000
Publication: *Columns*

DEANS

Graduate Studies: CARL SWAFFORD
School of Business and Management: Dr DON VAN ORNAM
School of Nursing: Prof. BARBARA JAMES
School of Religion: Prof. Dr GREG A. KING
School of Social Work: Dr RENÉ DRUMM
School of Visual Art and Design: RANDY CRAVEN

SOUTHERN COLLEGE OF OPTOMETRY

1245 Madison Ave, Memphis, TN 38104-2222
Telephone: (901) 722-3200
Fax: (901) 722-3328
E-mail: informationservices@sco.edu
Internet: www.sco.edu

Founded 1932
Private control

Academic year: August to May (2 semesters)
Offers doctorate degree in optometry

Pres.: Dr RICHARD W. PHILLIPS
Vice-Pres. for Academic Affairs: Dr LEWIS N. REICH
Vice-Pres. for Clinical Programmes: JAMES E. VENABLE
Vice-Pres. for Finance and Admin.: DAVID WEST
Vice-Pres. for Institutional Advancement: KRISTIN K. ANDERSON
Vice-Pres. for Student Services: JOSEPH H. HAUSER
Dir of Admissions and Enrolment Services: MICHAEL N. ROBERTSON
Dir of Library Services: Dr SHARON E. TABACHNICK
Number of teachers: 60

TENNESSEE STATE UNIVERSITY

POB 9609, Nashville, TN 37209
3500 John A. Merritt Blvd, Nashville, TN 37209-1561
Telephone: (615) 963-5000
Fax: (615) 963-2930
E-mail: admissions@tnstate.edu
Internet: www.tnstate.edu

Founded 1912, present name 1968, merger of
former Univ. of Tennessee at Nashville
with Tennessee State Univ. 1979
State control
Academic year: August to May (2 semesters)

Pres.: Dr PORTIA HOLMES SHIELDS
Provost and Exec. Vice-Pres. for Academic Affairs: Dr MILLICENT LOWNES-JACKSON
Vice-Pres. for Academic Affairs for Research and Sponsored Programmes: Dr MICHAEL BUSBY
Vice-Pres. for Business and Finance: CYNTHIA BROOKS
Vice-Pres. for Student Affairs: Dr ADRIAN DEXTER SAMUELS
Vice-Pres. for Univ. Relations and Devt: WILLIAM NELSEN
Dean of Students: PEGGY EARNEST
Registrar: THELRIA HARDAWAY
Dean of Libraries and Media Centres: Dr YILDIZ BINKLEY
Library of 442,802 vols, 1,386 periodicals
subscriptions, 93,597 bound periodicals,
15,202 microfilms, 888,562 microfiche
Number of teachers: 450
Number of students: 9,165 (7,105 undergraduate, 2,060 graduate)
Publication: *Alumni Life Magazine* (1 a year)

DEANS

College of Agriculture, Human and Natural Sciences: Prof. Dr CHANDRA REDDY
College of Business: Dr TILDEN CURRY
College of Education: Dr PETER E. MILLET
College of Engineering, Technology and Computer Science: Prof. Dr S. KEITH HARGROVE
College of Health Sciences: KATHLEEN McENERNEY
College of Liberal Arts: Dr GLORIA C. JOHNSON
College of Public Service and Urban Affairs: Dr BRUCE ROGERS
School of Graduate Studies and Research: Dr ALEX SEKWAT
School of Nursing: Prof. Dr KATHY MARTIN

TENNESSEE TECH UNIVERSITY

1 William L. Jones Dr., Cookeville, TN 38505
Telephone: (931) 372-3888
Fax: (931) 372-6250
E-mail: admissions@tntech.edu
Internet: www.tntech.edu

Founded 1912 as Dixie College

State control
Academic year: August to May

Pres. and CEO: Dr ROBERT R. BELL
Provost and Vice-Pres. for Academic Affairs: Dr MARK STEPHENS
Vice-Pres. for Business and Fiscal Affairs: Dr CLAIRE STINSON
Vice-Pres. for Extended Programmes and Regional Devt: Dr SUSAN ELKINS
Vice-Pres. for Student Affairs: MARC BURNETT
Vice-Pres. for Univ. Advancement: MARK HUTCHINS
Registrar: ELIZABETH ROGERS
Dean of Library and Learning Assistance: Dr DOUGLAS BATES
Library of 353,000 vols, 27,000 e-books, 1.5m.
microforms, 3,050 magazines, journals and
newspapers
Number of teachers: 400
Number of students: 11,768 (9,920 undergraduate, 1,848 graduate)

DEANS

College of Agricultural and Human Sciences: Prof. PAT BAGLEY
College of Arts and Sciences: Dr PAUL SEMMES
College of Business: JAMES JORDAN-WAGNER
College of Education: MATTHEW R. SMITH
College of Engineering: Prof. Dr JOSEPH J. RENCIS
School of Interdisciplinary Studies: Dr SUSAN ELKINS

TENNESSEE TEMPLE UNIVERSITY

1815 Union Ave, Chattanooga, TN 37404-3587
Telephone: (423) 493-4100
Fax: (423) 493-4497
E-mail: ttuinfo@tntemple.edu
Internet: www.tntemple.edu

Founded 1946 as Tennessee Temple College,
present name and status 1979
Private control
Academic year: August to May

Dept of Bible and Christian ministries, business administration; divs of arts and sciences, education

Chancellor: Dr DAVID E. BOULER
Pres.: Dr D. JAMES O'NEILL
Vice-Pres. for Academic Services: Dr SUSAN LOVETT
Chief Operating Officer: Dr JEFF RECTOR
Dir of Student Services Centre and Admissions: Dr PAM FREJOSKI
Registrar: RICHARD D. VAUPEL
Dir of Library Services: KEVIN WOODRUFF
Library of 154,000 vols, 9,000 periodicals.

TENNESSEE WESLEYAN COLLEGE

204 E College St, Athens, TN 37303
Telephone: (423) 745-7504
Fax: (423) 744-9968
E-mail: admissions@twcnet.edu
Internet: www.twcnet.edu

Founded 1857 as Athens Female College,
present name 1954
Private control
Academic year: August to May (2 semesters)

Programmes of study incl. arts, applied science, chemistry, Church vocations, criminal justice, English, exercise and sports sciences, general science, history, music education, science, science in nursing

Pres.: Dr HARLEY KNOWLES
Sr Vice-Pres.: LARRY WALLACE
Vice-Pres. for Academic Affairs: Dr SUZANNE HINE
Vice-Pres. for Enrolment Services: STAN HARRISON

Vice-Pres. for Financial Affairs: GAIL HARRIS
Vice-Pres. for Student Life: Dr SCOTT MASH-BURN
Chief Advancement Officer: RANDY NELSON
Registrar: JULIE MCCASLIN
Assoc. Dir of Library: JULIE E. ADAMS
Library of 57,251 vols, 1,173 periodicals, 8,260 microforms, 146,129 e-books
Number of teachers: 101 (53 full-time, 48 part-time)
Number of students: 1,103
Publication: *ARCHES Magazine* (2 a year).

TREVECCA NAZARENE UNIVERSITY

333 Murfreesboro Rd, Nashville, TN 37210
Telephone: (615) 248-1200
Fax: (615) 248-1432
E-mail: admissions@trevecca.edu
Internet: www.trevecca.edu
Founded 1901 as Literary and Bible Training School for Christian Workers, present name 1995
Private control
Academic year: August to May (2 semesters)
Pres.: Prof. Dr DAN BOONE
Provost: Prof. Dr STEPHEN M. PUSEY
Exec. Vice-Pres. for Finance and Admin.: DAVID CALDWELL
Vice-Pres. for External Relations: PEGGY COONING
Dean of Academic Affairs and Assoc. Provost: CAROL MAXSON
Dean of Enrolment Management and Assoc. Provost: KATHRYN BAUGHER
Dean of Student Devt and Assoc. Provost: STEPHEN HARRIS
Registrar: BECKY NIECE
Dir of Library Services: RUTH KINNERSLEY
Library of 103,571 vols, 507 print periodicals, 3,632 audiovisual items, 295,265 microforms, e-periodicals
Number of teachers: 100 (full-time)
Number of students: 2,478 (2,048 full-time, 430 part-time)

DEANS

College of Lifelong Learning: DAVID PHILLIPS
Millard Reed School of Religion: Dr TIMOTHY GREEN
School of Arts and Sciences: Dr LENA HEGI WELCH
School of Business and Technology: Dr JAMES HIATT
School of Education: Dr ESTHER SWINK

TUSCULUM COLLEGE

POB 5093, Greeneville, TN 37743
60 Shiloh Rd, Greeneville, TN 37743
Telephone: (423) 636-7300
Fax: (423) 638-7166
E-mail: admissions@tusculum.edu
Internet: www.tusculum.edu
Founded 1794
Private control
Academic year: August to May (2 semesters)
Centres in Knoxville, Morristown, Tri-Cities; areas of study incl. computer information systems, film and broadcasting, history, museum studies, religious studies
Pres.: Dr NANCY B. MOODY
Provost and Vice-Pres. for Academic Affairs: Prof. Dr MELINDA DUKES
Vice-Pres. and Chief Financial Officer: STEPHEN GEHRET
Vice-Pres. for Admin.: MARK A. STOKES
Vice-Pres. for Enrolment Management: Dr THOMAS STEIN
Vice-Pres. for Institutional Advancement: HEATHER PATCHETT
Dean of Students: Dr DAVID MCMAHAN
Registrar: BOBBIE CLARKSTON

Library Dir: MYRON J. SMITH, JR
Library of 192,000 vols
Number of teachers: 130
Number of students: 2,203

UNION UNIVERSITY

1050 Union University Dr., Jackson, TN 38305
Telephone: (731) 668-1818
Fax: (901) 661-5187
E-mail: info@uu.edu
Internet: www.uu.edu
Founded 1823 as Jackson Male Acad., present name 1907
Private control
Academic year: September to May
Campuses in Germantown, Hendersonville
Pres.: Prof. Dr DAVID S. DOCKERY
Provost and Exec. Vice-Pres.: Prof. Dr CARLA D. SANDERSON
Sr Vice-Pres. for Business and Financial Services: GARY L. CARTER
Sr Vice-Pres. for Enrolment Services: RICH GRIMM
Sr Vice-Pres. for Univ. Relations: Dr JERRY N. TIDWELL
Vice-Pres. for Academic Admin.: GENE FANT
Vice-Pres. for Regional Campuses: JIMMY DAVIS
Vice-Pres. for Student Services and Dean of Students: Dr KIMBERLY C. THORNBURY
Registrar: BARBARA MCMILLIN (acting)
Dir of Library and Assoc. Vice-Pres. for Academic Resources: ANNA BETH MORGAN
Library of 225,319 vols, 76,918 e-books
Number of teachers: 197
Number of students: 4,050

DEANS

College of Arts and Sciences: Prof. Dr GENE FANT
College of Education and Human Studies: Prof. Dr THOMAS R. ROSEBROUGH
McAfee School of Business Administration: Prof. Dr R. KEITH ABSHER
School of Nursing: Prof. Dr TIMOTHY L. SMITH
School of Pharmacy: Dr SHEILA L. MITCHELL
School of Theology and Missions: Prof. Dr GREGORY A. THORNBURY

UNIVERSITY OF MEMPHIS

Memphis, TN 38152
Telephone: (901) 678-2000
Fax: (901) 678-3299
E-mail: admissions@memphis.edu
Internet: www.memphis.edu
Founded 1912 as West Tennessee State Normal School, present status 1957, present name 1994
State control
Academic year: August to May
Pres.: Dr SHIRLEY C. RAINES
Provost: Dr RALPH J. FAUDREE
Vice-Pres. for Advancement: JULIE A. JOHNSON
Vice-Pres. for Business and Finance: DAVID ZETTERGREN
Vice-Pres. for Information Systems and Chief Information Officer: Dr DOUGLAS E. HURLEY
Vice-Pres. for Student Affairs: Dr ROSIE PHILLIPS BINGHAM
Registrar: DONNA VAN CANNEYT
Dean of Univ. Libraries: Dr SYLVERNA V. FORD
Library of 1,200,795 vols, 64,339 e-books, 592,140 govt documents, 9,728,360 MSS, 60,728 maps, 760,582 photographs, 3,512,244 microfiche
Number of teachers: 930 (full-time)
Number of students: 22,725

Publications: *Law Review, Mid-South Business Journal, Memphis Economy, The Southern Journal of Philosophy* (4 a year), *The University of Memphis Magazine* (4 a year)

DEANS

Cecil C. Humphreys School of Law: Prof. Dr KEVIN H. SMITH
College of Arts and Sciences: Dr HENRY A. KURTZ
College of Communication and Fine Arts: Dr RICHARD R. RANTA
College of Education, Health and Human Sciences: Dr DONALD I. WAGNER
Fogelman College of Business And Economics: Prof. Dr RAJIV GROVER
Herff College of Engineering: Dr RICHARD C. WARDER, JR
Loewenberg School of Nursing: Prof. Dr LIN ZHAN
School of Audiology And Speech Language Pathology: Dr MAURICE I. MENDEL
School of Public Health: Dr LISA M. KLESGES
Univ. College: Dr DAN L. LATTIMORE

UNIVERSITY OF TENNESSEE SYSTEM

Knoxville, TN 37996
Telephone: (615) 974-1000
Fax: (865) 974-3753
Internet: www.tennessee.edu
Founded 1968 as Blount College, present name and status 1968
State control
Academic year: September to August
Pres.: Dr JOSEPH A. DIPIETRO
Exec. Vice-Pres. and Vice-Pres. for Research and Economic Devt: Dr DAVID MILLHORN
Sr Vice-Pres. and Chief Financial Officer: Dr GARY W. ROGERS
Vice-Pres. for Academic Affairs and Student Success: Dr KATIE HIGH
Vice-Pres. for Agriculture: Dr JOSEPH A. DIPIETRO
Vice-Pres. for Devt and Alumni Affairs: JOHNNIE RAY
Vice-Pres for Public and Govt Relations: HANK DYE, HANK DYE
Gen. Counsel and Sec.: CATHERINE S. MIZELL
Library: see under Libraries and Archives
Number of teachers: 3,034
Number of students: 49,597
Publications: *Extension Series* (4 to 6 a year), *Horizons* (4 a year), *Tennessee Alumnus* (4 a year), *The University Record.*

MAJOR CAMPUSES

University of Tennessee at Chattanooga
615 McCallie Ave, Chattanooga, TN 37403-2598
Telephone: (423) 425-4111
Fax: (423) 425-2172
E-mail: utcmocs@utc.edu
Internet: www.utc.edu
Founded 1886 as Chattanooga Univ., present name and status 1969
Academic year: August to May
Chancellor: Dr ROGER G. BROWN
Provost and Vice-Chancellor for Academic Affairs: Dr PHILIP B. OLDHAM
Sr Vice-Chancellor for Advancement: BOB LYON
Sr Vice-Chancellor for Finance, Operations and Information Technology and Chief Financial Officer: Dr RICHARD BROWN
Vice-Chancellor for Student Devt: Dr JOHN DELANEY
Registrar: LINDA ORTH
Dean of Libraries: THERESA LIEDTKA

Library of 510,890 vols, 20,982 audiovisual materials, 344 microforms, 1,991 e-journal
Number of students: 11,438 (9,891 undergraduate, 1,547 graduate)
Number of teachers: 762 (454 full-time, 308 part-time)

DEANS

College of Arts and Sciences: Dr HERBERT BURHENN
College of Business: Dr ROBERT S. DOOLEY
College of Engineering and Computer Science: Dr WILLIAM SUTTON
College of Health, Education and Professional Studies: Dr MARY TANNER (acting)

University of Tennessee Health Science Center

920 Madison Ave, Memphis, TN 38163
Telephone: (902) 448-5500
Fax: (901) 448-7772
E-mail: uthscadmit@thsc.edu
Internet: www.uthsc.edu
Founded 1911
Campuses in Chattanooga, Knoxville
Academic year: August to July (3 semesters)
Chancellor: Dr STEVE J. SCHWAB
Exec. Vice-Chancellor and Chief Operations Officer: Dr KENNARD D. BROWN
Vice-Chancellor for Academic, Faculty and Student Affairs: Dr CHERYL R. SCHEID
Vice-Chancellor for Finance and Operations: ANTHONY A. FERRARA
Vice-Chancellor for Devt and Alumni Affairs: BETHANY GOOLSBY
Vice-Pres. and Gen. Counsel: CATHERINE MIZELL
Registrar and Dir of Academic Records: Dr GLENDA K. ALEXANDER
Library of 260,000 vols, 150 current periodical titles, 2,800 e-journal titles
Number of students: 2,815

DEANS

College of Allied Health Sciences: Prof. Dr NOMA BENNETT ANDERSON
College of Dentistry: TIMOTHY L. HOTTEL
College of Graduate Health Sciences: Dr CHERYL R. SCHEID
College of Medicine: DAVID M. STERN
College of Nursing: NAURA TALBOT
College of Pharmacy: MARIE CHISHOLM-BURNS

University of Tennessee at Knoxville

Knoxville, TN 37996
Telephone: (615) 974-1000
Fax: (865) 974-2606
E-mail: chancellor@utk.edu
Internet: www.utk.edu
Founded 1794 as Blount College, present name 1879
Academic year: August to August (3 semesters)
Chancellor: Dr JIMMY G. CHEEK
Provost and Sr Vice-Chancellor for Academic Affairs: Dr SUSAN MARTIN
Vice-Chancellor for Devt and Alumni Affairs: SCOTT RABENOLD
Vice-Chancellor for Finance and Admin.: CHRIS CIMINO
Vice-Chancellor for Research and Engagement: LEE RIEDINGER
Vice-Chancellor for Student Life: W. TIMOTHY ROGERS
Registrar and Assoc. Dean of Enrolment: MONIQUE ANDERSON
Dean of Libraries: Dr STEVEN SMITH
Library: 2.3m. vols
Number of teachers: 1,309
Number of students: 27,523 (21,308 undergraduate, 6,215 graduate)

DEANS

College of Agricultural Sciences and Natural Resources: Dr CAULA BEYL
College of Architecture and Design: SCOTT POOLE
College of Arts and Sciences: Dr THERESA M. LEE
College of Business Administration: Dr JAN WILLIAMS
College of Communications and Information: Dr MICHAEL WIRTH
College of Education, Health and Human Sciences: Dr ROBERT RIDER
College of Engineering: Dr WAYNE T. DAVIS
College of Law: DOUGLAS A. BLAZE
College of Nursing: Dr VICTORIA NIEDERHAUSER
College of Social Work: Dr KAREN SOWERS
College of Veterinary Medicine: Dr JAMES THOMPSON
Graduate School: Dr CAROLYN R. HODGES
Graduate School of Medicine: Dr JAMES J. NEUTENS
Tennessee Agricultural Experiment Station: Dr WILLIAM F. BROWN
UT Extension, Univ. Outreach and Continuing Education: Dr TIM CROSS

PROFESSORS

Center for Assessment Research:
   McGLASSON, N.

College of Agriculture:
   ALLEN, F. L., Plant and Soil Science
   ASHBURN, E. L., Plant and Soil Science
   BERNARD, E. C., Entomology and Plant Pathology
   BLEDSOE, B. L., Agricultural Engineering
   BOST, S. C., Entomology and Plant Pathology
   BREKKE, C. J., Food Science and Technology
   BROOKER, J. R., Agricultural Economics
   BUCKNER, E. R., Forestry
   BURGESS, E. E., Entomology and Plant Pathology
   CALLAHAN, L. M., Ornamental Horticulture and Landscape Design
   CARTER, C. E., Jr, Agricultural Extension Education
   CHAMBERS, A. Y., Entomology and Plant Pathology
   CLELAND, C. L., Agricultural Economics
   COFFEY, D. L., Plant and Soil Science
   COLLINS, J. L., Food Technology and Science
   CONATSER, G. E., Animal Science
   CONGER, B. V., Plant and Soil Science
   COOK, O. F., Four-H Club
   CRATER, G. D., Ornamental Horticulture and Landscape Design
   DALY, R. T., Home Economics
   DEARDEN, B. L., Forestry
   DIMMICK, R. W., Forestry
   DRAUGHON, F. A., Food Science and Technology
   EASTWOOD, D. B., Agricultural Economics
   ENGLISH, B. C., Agricultural Economics
   FARMER, C. M., Agricultural Economics
   FLINCHUM, W. T., Plant and Soil Science
   FOSS, J. E., Plant and Soil Science
   FRIBOURG, H. A., Plant and Soil Science
   GARLAND, C. D., Agricultural Economics
   GERHARDT, R. R., Entomology and Plant Pathology
   GILL, W. W., Animal Science
   GOAN, H. C., Animal Science
   GODKIN, J. D., Animal Science
   GRAHAM, E. T., Ornamental Horticulture and Landscape Design
   GRAVES, C. R., Plant and Soil Science
   GRESSHOFF, P. M., Ornamental Horticulture, Center of Excellence
   HADDEN, C. H., Entomology and Plant Pathology

   HALL, R. F., Extension Veterinary Medicine
   HAYES, R. M., Plant and Soil Science
   HENRY, Z. A., Agricultural Engineering
   HILL, T. K., Forestry
   HOPPER, G. M., Forestry
   HOWARD, D. D., Plant and Soil Science
   HUNTER, D. L., Agricultural Economics
   JENKINS, R. P., Agricultural Economics
   KIRKPATRICK, F. D., Animal Science
   LAMBDIN, P. L., Entomology and Plant Pathology
   LANE, JR, C. D., Animal Science
   LESSLY, R. R., Agricultural Extension Education
   LEUTHOLD, F. O., Agricultural Economics
   LITTLE, R. L., Forestry
   LOCKWOOD, D. W., Plant and Soil Science
   McDANIEL, G. L., Ornamental Horticulture and Landscape Design
   McLEMORE, D. L., Agricultural Economics
   MAYS, G. C., Communication
   MEADOWS, D. G., Animal Science (Beef)
   MELTON, C. C., Food Technology
   MELTON, S. L., Food Technology and Science
   MILLER, J. K., Animal Science
   MILLER, R. D., Plant and Soil Science
   MONTGOMERY, M. J., Animal Science
   MORRIS, W. C., Food Science and Technology
   MOTE, C. R., Agricultural Engineering
   MULLINS, C. A., Plant and Soil Science
   MUNDY, S. D., Agricultural Economics
   NEEL, J. B., Animal Science
   NEWMAN, M. A., Entomology and Plant Pathology
   OLIVER, S. P., Animal Science
   OSTERMEIER, D. M., Forestry
   PARK, W. M., Agricultural Economics
   PATRICK, C. R., Entomology and Plant Pathology
   PELTON, M. R., Forestry
   PENFIELD, M. P., Food Technology and Science
   PLESS, C. D., Entomology and Plant Pathology
   POWELL, B. T., Four-H
   RAWLS, E. L., Agricultural Economics
   RAY, D. E., Agricultural Economics
   REINHARDT, C. A., Communication
   RENNIE, J. C., Forestry
   REYNOLDS, J. H., Plant and Soil Science
   ROBBINS, K. R., Animal Science
   ROBERTS, R. K., Agricultural Economics
   RUTLEDGE, A. D., Plant and Soil
   SAMS, C. E., Plant and Soil Science
   SAMS, D. W., Plant and Soil Science
   SANDERS, W. L., Statistics
   SAXTON, A. M., Statistics
   SIMMS, R. H., Animal Science
   SMITH, G. F., Agricultural Economics
   SOUTHARDS, C. J., Entomology and Plant Pathology
   STRANGE, R. J., Forestry
   TODD, J. D., Agricultural Extension and Education
   TYLER, D. D., Plant and Soil Science
   WEST, D. R., Plant and Soil Science
   WESTBROOK, E. M., Home Economics and Family Economy
   WILHELM, L. R., Agricultural Engineering
   WILLIAMS, D. B., Ornamental Horticulture and Landscape Design
   WILLIAMSON, H., Agricultural Economics
   WILLS, J. B., Agricultural Engineering
   WILSON, J. L., Forestry

College of Business Administration:
   BARNABY, D. J., Marketing and Transportation
   BLACK, H. A., Finance
   BOEHM, T. P., Finance
   BOHM, R. A., Economics
   BOWLBY, R. L., Economics

CADOTTE, E. R., Marketing and Transportation
CARROLL, S. L., Economics
CHANG, H., Economics
CLARK, D. P., Economics
COLE, W. E., Economics
DAVIDSON, P., Economics
DAVIS, F. W., Jr, Marketing and Transportation
DEWHIRST, H. D., Management
DICER, G. N., Marketing and Transportation
FISHER, B. D., Accounting
FOX, W. F., Economics
GARRISON, C. B., Economics
HERRING, H. C., Accounting
HERZOG, H. W., Economics
JAMES, L. R., Management
KIGER, J. E., Accounting
LANGLEY, JR, C. J., Marketing and Transportation
LEE, F.-Y., Economics
MAYHEW, A., Economics
MAYO, J. W., Economics
MENTZER, J. T., Marketing Logistics and Transportation
MUNDY, R. A., Marketing and Transportation
PARR, W. C., Statistics
PATTON, E. P., Marketing and Transportation
PHILIPPATOS, G. C., Finance
PHILPOT, J. W., Statistics
REEVE, J. M., Accounting
ROTH, H. P., Accounting
RUSH, M. C., Management
SANDERS, R. D., Statistics
SCHLOTTMANN, A., Economics
SHRIEVES, R. E., Finance
STAHL, M. J., Business Admin.
STANGA, K. G., Accounting
SYLWESTER, D. L., Statistics
WACHOWICZ, J. M., Finance
WANSLEY, J. W., Finance
WILLIAMS, J. R., Accounting
WOODRUFF, R. B., Marketing Logistics and Transportation

College of Communications:

ASHDOWN, P. G., Journalism
BOWLES, D. A., Journalism
CROOK, J. A., Journalism
EVERETT, G. A., Journalism
HOWARD, H. H., Broadcasting
LITTMANN, M. E., Journalism
MILLER, M. M., Journalism
MOORE, B. A., Broadcasting
SINGLETARY, M. W., Journalism
SMYSER, R. D., Journalism
STANKEY, M. J., Advertising
SWAN, N. R., Jr, Broadcasting
TAYLOR, R. E., Advertising

College of Education:

ALEXANDER, J. E., Holistic Teaching and Learning
ALLISON, C. B., Cultural Studies in Education
BENNER, S. M., Inclusive Early Childhood Education
BLANK, K. J., Inclusive Early Childhood Education
BOGUE, E. G., Leadership Studies
BUTEFISH, W. L., Education in Science and Mathematics
CAMERON, W., Psychoeducational Studies
COLEMAN, L. J., Inclusive Early Childhood Education
DAVIS, A. R., Holistic Teaching and Learning
DAVIS, K. L., Counselor Education and Counseling Psychology
DESSART, D. J., Curriculum and Instruction
DICKINSON, D. J., Education in Science and Mathematics
DOAK, E. D., Education in Science and Mathematics

FRENCH, R. L., Education in Science and Mathematics
GEORGE, T. W., Educational Administration
HARGIS, C. H., Holistic Teaching and Learning
HARRIS, G., Leadership Studies
HECTOR, M. A., Counselor Education and Counseling Psychology
HIPPLE, T. W., Holistic Teaching and Learning
HOWLEY, E. T., Exercise Science
HUCK, S. W., Counselor Education and Counseling Psychology
HUFF, P. E., Holistic Teaching and Learning
HULL, H. N., Language Communication and Humanities Education
JOST, K. J., Holistic Teaching and Learning
KASWORM, C. E., Bureau of Educational Research and Services
KNIGHT, L. N., Holistic Teaching and Learning
KOZAR, A. J., Exercise Science
KRONICK, R. F., Holistic Teaching and Learning
LIEMOHN, W. P., Exercise Science
MCCALLUM, R. S., Psychoeducational Studies
MCINTYRE, L. D., Education in Science and Mathematics
MALIK, A., Cultural Studies in Education
MEAD, B. J., Cultural Studies in Education
MERTZ, N. T., Leadership Studies
MILLER, J. H., Rehabilitation and Deafness Programs
MORGAN, W. J., Cultural Studies in Education
MYER, JR, M. E., Education in Science and Mathematics
PAUL, M. J., Cultural Studies in Education
PETERS, J. M., Psychoeducational Studies
PETERSON, M. P., Counselor Education and Counseling Psychology
POPPEN, W. A., Counselor Education and Counseling Psychology
RAY, J. R., Education in Science and Mathematics
ROCKETT, I. R. H., Exercise Science
ROESKE, C. E., Education in Science and Mathematics
ROWELL, C. G., Educational Administration
SCHINDLER, W. J., Holistic Teaching and Learning
THOMPSON, C. L., Counselor Education and Counseling Psychology
TURNER, T. N., Holistic Teaching and Learning
UBBEN, G. C., Leadership Studies
WELCH, O. M., Rehabilitation and Deafness Programs
WILEY, P. D., Language Communication and Humanities Education
WILLIAMS, R. L., Psychoeducational Studies
WOODRICK, W. E., Rehabilitation and Deafness Programmes
WRISBERG, C. A., Cultural Studies in Education

College of Engineering:

ALEXEFF, I., Electrical Engineering
ARIMILLI, R. V., Mechanical and Aerospace Engineering
BAILEY, J. M., Electrical Engineering
BAKER, A. J., Engineering Science and Mechanics
BENNETT, R. M., Civil and Environmental Engineering
BIENKOWSKI, P. R., Chemical Engineering
BIRDWELL, J. D., Electrical Engineering
BISHOP, A. O., Jr, Electrical Engineering
BLALOCK, T. V., Electrical Engineering
BODENHEIMER, R. E., Electrical Engineering
BOGUE, D. C., Chemical Engineering
BONTADELLI, J. A., Industrial Engineering

BOSE, B. K., Electrical Engineering
BOULDIN, D. W., Electrical Engineering
BROOKS, JR, C. R., Materials Science and Engineering
BUCHANAN, R. A., Materials Science and Engineering
BURDETTE, E. G., Civil and Environmental Engineering
CARLEY, T. G., Engineering Science and Mechanics
CHATTERJEE, A., Civil and Environmental Engineering
CLARK, E. S., Materials Science and Engineering
CLAYCOMBE, W. W., Industrial Engineering
COUNCE, R. M., Chemical Engineering
CUMMINGS, P. T., Chemical Engineering
DAVIS, W. T., Civil and Environmental Engineering
DEPORTER, E. L., Industrial Engineering
DODDS, H. L., Nuclear Engineering
DRUMM, E. C., Civil and Environmental Engineering
EDMONDSON, A. J., Mechanical and Aerospace Engineering
FELLERS, J. F., Materials Science and Engineering
FORRESTER, J. H., Engineering Science and Mechanics
FRAZIER, G. C., Chemical Engineering
GHOSH, M. M., Civil and Environmental Engineering
GONZALEZ, R. C., Electrical Engineering
GOODPASTURE, D. W., Civil and Environmental Engineering
GREEN, W. L., Electrical Engineering
HANSEN, M. G., Chemical Engineering
HODGSON, J. W., Mechanical and Aerospace Engineering
HOFFMAN, G. W., Electrical Engineering
HUNG, J. C., Electrical Engineering
JENDRUCKO, R. J., Engineering Science and Mechanics
JOHNSON, W. S., Mechanical and Aerospace Engineering
KENNEDY, E. J., Electrical Engineering
KERLIN, T. W., Jr, Nuclear Engineering
KIM, K. H., Engineering Science and Mechanics
KRANE, R. J., Mechanical and Aerospace Engineering
KRIEG, R. D., Engineering Science and Mechanics
LANDES, J. D., Engineering Science and Mechanics
LAWLER, J. S., Electrical Engineering
LIAW, P. K., Materials Science and Engineering
LUNDIN, C. D., Materials Science and Engineering
MILLER, L. F., Nuclear Engineering
MILLER, W. A., Civil and Environmental Engineering
MILLIGAN, M. W., Mechanical and Aerospace Engineering
MOORE, C. F., Chemical Engineering
NEFF, JR, H. P., Electrical Engineering
OLIVER, B. F., Materials Science and Engineering
PACE, M. O., Electrical Engineering
PARANG, M., Mechanical and Aerospace Engineering
PARSONS, J. R., Mechanical and Aerospace Engineering
PEDRAZA, A. J., Materials Science and Engineering
PERONA, J. J., Chemical Engineering
PHILLIPS, P. J., Materials Science and Engineering
PITTS, D. R., Engineering—Admin.
PRADOS, J. W., Chemical Engineering
REED, G. D., Civil and Environmental Engineering
ROBERTS, M. J., Electrical Engineering
ROBINSON, R. B., Civil and Environmental Engineering

ROTH, J. R., Electrical Engineering
SCHMITT, H. W., Industrial Engineering
SCOTT, W. E., Engineering Science and Mechanics
SHANNON, T. E., Nuclear Engineering
SMITH, G. V., Mechanical and Aerospace Engineering
SNIDER, J. N., Industrial Engineering
SOLIMAN, O., Engineering Science and Mechanics
SPECKHART, F. H., Mechanical and Aerospace Engineering
SPRUIELL, J. E., Materials Science and Engineering
SYMONDS, F. W., Electrical Engineering
TOMPKINS, F. D., Engineering Academic
TRIVEDI, M. M., Electrical Engineering
TSCHANTZ, B. A., Civil and Environmental Engineering
UHRIG, R. E., Nuclear Engineering
UPADHYAYA, B. R., Nuclear Engineering
WASSERMAN, J. F., Engineering Science and Mechanics
WEGMANN, F. J., Civil and Environmental Engineering
WEITSMAN, Y. J., Center of Excellence
WILKERSON, H. J., Mechanical and Aerospace Engineering
WILSON, C. C., Mechanical and Aerospace Engineering

College of Human Ecology:
BLANTON, P. W., Child and Family Studies
CAMPBELL, C. P., Human Resources Devt
CARRUTH, B. R., Nutrition
CHEEK, G. D., Human Resources Devt
COAXLEY, C. B., Human Resources Devt
CRAIG, D. G., Human Resources Devt
CUNNINGHAM, J. L., Child and Family Studies
DELONG, A. J., Textiles, Retailing and Interior Design
DRAKE, M. F., Textiles, Retailing and Interior Design
DUCKETT, K. E., Textiles, Retailing and Interior Design
FOX, G. L., Child and Family Studies
GORSKI, J. D., Health, Leisure and Safety Sciences
HAMILTON, C. B., Health, Leisure and Safety Sciences
HANSON, R. R., Human Resources Devt
HASKELL, R. W., Human Resources Devt
HAYES, G. A., Health, Leisure and Safety Sciences
KIRK, R. H., Health, Leisure and Safety Sciences
MORAN, J. D., Admin.
NORDQUIST, V. M., Child and Family Studies
SACHAN, D. S., Nutrition
SKINNER, J. D., Nutrition
STEELE, C., Child and Family Studies
TWARDOSZ, S. L., Child and Family Studies
WADSWORTH, L. C., Textiles, Retailing and Interior Design
WALLACE, B. C., Health, Leisure and Safety Sciences
ZEMEL, M. B., Nutrition

College of Law:
BLAZE, D. A.
COHEN, N. P.
COOK, J. G.
DESSEM, R. L.
HARDIN, P.
HESS, A. M.
KING, JR, J. H.
LECLERQ, F. S.
LLOYD, R. M.
PHILLIPS, J. J.
RIVKIN, D. H.
SOBIESKI, JR, J. L.

College of Liberal Arts:
ADCOCK, J. L., Chemistry
AIKEN, C. S., Geography

ALEXANDRATOS, S. D., Chemistry
ALEXIADES, V., Mathematics
ALIKAKOS, N., Mathematics
ANDERSON, D. F., Mathematics
AQUILA, R. E., Philosophy
ASP, C. W., Audiology and Speech Pathology
BAGBY, R. M., Zoology
BAKER, D. C., Chemistry
BAKER, G. A., Mathematics
BALL, C. H., Music
BARRETTE, P., Romance and Asian Languages
BARTMESS, J. E., Chemistry
BECKER, J. M., Microbiology
BELL, T. L., Geography
BERGERON, P. H., History
BETZ, M., Sociology
BINGHAM, C. R., Physics
BITZAS, G. C., Music
BLACK, J. A., Sociology
BLAIN, S. J., Arts
BLASS, W. E., Physics
BRADY, P. S., Romance and Asian Languages
BRAKKE, P. M., Arts
BRATTON, E. W., English
BREINIG, M., Physics
BRENKERT, G. G., Philosophy
BROADHEAD, T., Geological Sciences
BROCK, JR, J. P., Music
BUGG, W. M., Physics
BUHITE, R. D., History
BULL, W. E., Chemistry
BUNTING, D. L., II, Ecology
BURGDOERFER, J. E., Physics
BURGHARDT, G. M., Psychology
BURSTEIN, A. G., Psychology
CALHOUN, W. H., Psychology
CALLCOTT, T. A., Physics
CAPONETTI, J. D., Botany
CARNEY, P. J., Audiology and Speech Pathology
CARROLL, D. A., English
CARRUTH, J. H., Mathematics
CEBIK, L. B., Philosophy
CHAMBERS, J. Q., Chemistry
CHEN, T. T., Zoology
CHILDERS, R. W., Physics
CHMIELEWSKI, E. V., History
CHURCHICH, J. E., Biochemistry
CLARK, C. E., Mathematics
COBB, C. W., Romance and Asian Languages
COBB, J. C., History
COHEN, C. P., Psychology
COHN, H. O., Physics
COKER, J., Music
COMBS, F. M., Music
CONDO, G. T., Physics
CONWAY, J. B., Mathematics
COOK, K. D., Chemistry
COOKE, T. P., Theatre
COTHRAN, JR, R. M., Theatre
COX, D. R., English
CUNNINGHAM, R. B., Political Science
CUSTER, M., Theatre
CUTLER, E. W., History
DAEHNERT, R. H., Arts
DAVERMAN, R. J., Mathematics
DOBBS, D. E., Mathematics
DONGARRA, J., Computer Science
DRAKE, JR, R. Y., English
DUNGAN, D. L., Religious Studies
DYDAK, J., Mathematics
ECHTERNACHT, A. C., Zoology
EDWARDS, R. B., Philosophy
EGUILUZ, A. G., Physics
ELSTON, S. B., Physics
ENSOR, A. R., English
ETNIER, D. A., Zoology
FALSETTI, J. S., Arts
FARRIS, W. W., History
FAULKNER, C. H., Anthropology
FIELD, R. C., Theatre
FINGER, J. R., History

FINNERAN, R. J., English
FITZGERALD, M. R., Political Science
FORESTA, R., Geography
FOX, K., Physics
FRANDSEN, H., Mathematics
GANT, M. M., Political Science
GEORGHIOU, S., Physics
GESELL, G. C., Classics
GOLDENSTEIN, M. B., Arts
GORMAN, R., Political Science
GRABER, G. C., Philosophy
GRIMM, F. A., Chemistry
GROSS, L. J., Mathematics
GUIDRY, M. W., Physics
GUIOCHON, G. A., Chemistry
HAAS, A. G., History
HALLAM, T. G., Mathematics
HANDEL, M. A., Zoology
HANDEL, S. J., Psychology
HANDELSMAN, M. H., Romance and Asian Languages
HANDLER, L., Psychology
HANDLER, T., Physics
HAO, YEN-PING, History
HARRIS, W. F., Biology
HART, E. L., Physics
HASTINGS, D. W., Sociology
HATCHER, R. D., Zoology
HEFFERNAN, T. J., English
HEFLIN, W. H., Romance and Asian Languages
HICKOK, L. G., Botany
HINTON, D. B., Mathematics
HOLTON, R. W., Botany
HOOD, T. C., Sociology
HUGHES, K. W., Botany
HUSCH, L. S., Mathematics
JACKSON, C. O., Admin.
JACOBS, K. A., Music
JACOBSON, H. C., Admin.
JANTZ, R. L., Anthropology
JEON, K. W., Zoology
JOHANNSON, K., Mathematics
JONES, W. H., Psychology
JORDAN, G. S., Mathematics
JOSHI, J. G., Biochemistry
JOY, D. C., Zoology
JUMPER, S. R., Geography
KABALKA, G. W., Chemistry
KALLET, M., English
KAMYCHKOV, I. A., Physics
KARAKASHIAN, O., Mathematics
KEELING, K. A., Music
KEENE, M. L., English
KELLY, R. M., English
KENNEDY, J. R., Zoology
KENNEDY, W. C., Arts
KLEINFELTER, D. C., Chemistry
KLIPPEL, W. E., Anthropology
KOPP, O. C., Geology
KOVAC, J. D., Chemistry
LABOTKA, T. C., Geological Sciences
LANGSTON, M. A., Computer Science
LAWLER, J. E., Psychology
LAWLER, K., Psychology
LEE, B. S., Arts
LEGGETT, B. J., English
LEKI, I., English
LELAND, W. E., Arts
LENHART, S. M., Mathematics
LESTER, L. W., Admin.
LEVY, K. D., Romance and Asian Languages
LINGE, D. E., Religious Studies
LIVINGSTON, P. R., Arts
LOFARO, M. A., English
LUBAR, J., Psychology
LYONS, W., Political Science
MacCABE, J. A., Zoology
McCLELLAND, D. K., Music
McCONNEL, R. M., Mathematics
McCORMICK, J. F., Ecology
McCRACKEN, G. F., Zoology
MACEK, J. H., Physics
McSWEEN, H. Y., Geological Sciences

MAGDEN, N. E., Arts
MAGID, L. J., Chemistry
MAGID, R. M., Chemistry
MAHAN, G. D., Physics
MALAND, C., English
MALONE, JR, J. C., Psychology
MARSH, F. H., Arts
MARTINSON, F. H., Arts
MASHBURN, R. R., Speech and Theatre
MATHEWS, H. T., Mathematics
MISRA, K. C., Geology
MONTIE, T. C., Microbiology
MONTY, K. J., Biochemistry
MOORE, M. C., Music
MOORE, R. N., Microbiology
MOSER, H. D., History
MULLIN, B. C., Botany
NABELEK, A. K., Audiology and Speech Pathology
NAZAREWICZ, W., Physics
NORMAN, R. V., Religious Studies
NORTHINGTON, D. B., Music
PAGNI, R. M., Chemistry
PAINTER, L. R., Physics
PEACOCK, D., Arts
PEDERSON, D. M., Music
PEGG, D. J., Physics
PENNER, A. R., English
PETERSEN, R. H., Botany
PETERSON, H. A., Audiology and Speech Pathology
PETERSON, J. R., Chemistry
PIMM, S. L., Zoology
PLAAS, H., Political Science
PLOCH, D. R., Sociology
PLUMMER, E. W., Physics
POLLIO, H. R., Psychology
POORE, J. H., Computer Science
POSTOW, B. C., Philosophy
PULSIPHER, L. M., Geography
QUINN, J. J., Physics
RAJPUT, B. S., Mathematics
RALSTON, B. A., Geography
REESE, J. E., English
REYNOLDS, C. H., Religious Studies
RIECHERT, S. E., Zoology
RIESING, T. J., Arts
RIGGSBY, W. S., Microbiology
RIVERA-RODAS, O., Romance and Asian Languages
ROMEISER, J. B., Romance and Asian Languages
ROSINSKI, J., Mathematics
ROTH, L. E., Zoology
RUTLEDGE, H. C., Classics
SAMEJIMA, F., Psychology
SANDERS, N. J., English
SAUDARGAS, R. S., Psychology
SAVAGE, D. C., Psychology
SAYLER, G. S., Microbiology
SCHAEFER, P. W., Mathematics
SCHEB, J. M., Political Science
SCHILLING, E., Botany
SCHMUDDE, T. H., Geography
SCHWEITZER, G. K., Chemistry
SCURA, D. M., English
SELLIN, I. A., Physics
SEPANIAK, M. J., Chemistry
SERBIN, S. M., Mathematics
SHIH, C. C., Physics
SHIVERS, C. A., Zoology
SHOVER, N. E., Sociology
SHURR, W. H., English
SILVERSTEIN, B., Audiology and Speech Pathology
SIMPSON, H. C., Mathematics
SMITH, T. A., Political Science
SMITH, W. O., Botany
SONI, K., Mathematics
SONI, R. P., Mathematics
SORENSEN, S. P., Physics
STACEY, G., Microbiology
STEPHENS, JR, O. H., Political Science
STEPHENSON, K., Mathematics
STEWART, F. C., Arts
STUTZENBERGER, D. R., Music

SUNDBERG, C., Mathematics
SUNDELL, S. E., Physics
SUNDSTROM, E. D., Psychology
TAYLOR, L. A., Geology
THISTLETHWAITE, M. B., Mathematics
THOMAS, J. C., English
THOMASON, M. G., Computer Science
THOMPSON, JR, J. R., Physics
THONNARD, N., Science Alliance
TIPPS, A. W., Music
TRAHERN, J. B., English
TRAVIS, C. B., Psychology
UNGS, T. D., Political Science
VAN DE VATE, JR, D., Philosophy
VANHOOK, A., Chemistry
VAUGHN, G. L., Zoology
WADE, W. R., II, Mathematics
WAGNER, C. G., Mathematics
WAHLER, R. G., Psychology
WALKER, K. R., Geology
WALLACE, S. E., Sociology
WALNE, P. L., Botany
WARD, B. F. L., Physics
WARD, R. C., Computer Science
WASHBURN, Y. M., Romance and Asian Languages
WEHRY, E. L., Chemistry
WEIR, A., English
WELBORN, D. M., Political Science
WHEELER, T. V., English
WHEELER, W. B., History
WHITE, D. C., Microbiology
WHITSON, G. L., Zoology
WICKS, W. D., Biochemistry
WILLIAMS, T. F., Chemistry
WOODS, C., Chemistry
WUNDERLICH, B., Chemistry
YATES, S. A., Arts
ZAK, T., Mathematics
ZHANG, J. Y., Physics

College of Veterinary Medicine:
BRACE, J. J., Administration
BRIAN, D. A., Microbiology and Veterinary Medicine
BRIGHT, R. M., Small Animal Clinical Sciences
DORN, A. S., Small Animal Clinical Sciences
EDWARDS, D. F., Pathology
FARKAS, W. R., Comparative Medicine
GREEN, E. M., Large Animal Clinical Sciences
HENRY, R. W., Animal Science
HOPKINS, F. M., Large Animal Clinical Sciences
KRAHWINKEL, D. J., Jr, Small Animal Clinical Sciences
LEGENDRE, A. M., Small Animal Clinical Sciences
McCORD, S. P., Comparative Medicine
McDONALD, T. P., Animal Science and Veterinary Medicine
McGAVIN, M. D., Pathology
OLIVER, J. W., Comparative Medicine
PATTON, C. S., Pathology
POTGIETER, L. N. D., Comparative Medicine
ROUSE, B. T., Microbiology and Veterinary Medicine
SCHULLER, H. M., Pathology
SHULL, R. M., Pathology
SHULTZ, T. W., Animal Science and Veterinary Medicine
SIMS, M. H., Animal Science and Veterinary Medicine
SLAUSON, D. O., Pathology

Energy, Environment and Resources Center:
COLGLAZIER, E. M.

Graduate School of Biomedical Sciences:
OLINS, A. L.
OLINS, D. E.
POPP, R. A.

Graduate School of Library and Information Science:
ESTES, G. E.

TENOPIR, C.

Graduate School of Planning:
JOHNSON, D. A.
PROCHASKA, J. M.
SPENCER, J. A.

Graduate School of Social Work:
CETINGOK, M.
FAVER, C. A.
GLISSON, C. A.
HIRAYAMA, H.
NOOE, R. M.
RUBINSTEIN, H.

Learning Research Center:
HUMPHREYS, WALTER L.

Library:
BAYNE, P. S.
BEST, R. A., Law
CRAWFORD, M. F.
FELDER-HOEHNE, F. H.
GRADY, A. M.
LECLERCQ, A. W.
PHILLIPS, L. L.
PIQUET, D. C., Law
RADER, J. C.

School of Architecture:
ANDERSON, G.
GRIEGER, F.
KELSO, R. M.
KERSAVAGE, J. A.
KINZY, S. A.
LAUER, W. J.
LESTER, A. J.
LIZON, P.
ROBINSON, M. A.
RUDD, J. W.
SHELL, W. S.
WATSON, J. S.
WODEHOUSE, L. M.

School of Nursing:
ALLIGOOD, M. R.
GOODFELLOW, D. H.
MOZINGO, J.
THOMAS, S. P.

Space Institute:
ANTAR, B. N.
COLLINS, F. G.
CRATER, H. W.
CRAWFORD, L. W.
CRAWFORD, R. A.
FLANDRO, G. A.
GARRISON, G. W.
KEEFER, D. R.
KUPERSCHMIDT, B. A.
LEWIS, J. W.
LO, C.
McCAY, M. H.
PALUDAN, C. T. N.
PETERS, C. E.
PUJOL, A.
SCHULZ, R. J.
SHAHROKHI, F.
SHETH, A. C.
WU, J. M.

University of Tennessee at Martin

Martin, TN 38328
Telephone: (731) 881-7000
Fax: (731) 881-7019
E-mail: chancellor@utm.edu
Internet: www.utm.edu

Founded 1900 as Hall-Moody Institute, present name 1967
Academic year: August to August

Chancellor: Dr THOMAS A. RAKES
Provost and Vice-Chancellor for Academic Affairs: Dr E. JERALD OGG, JR
Exec. Vice-Chancellor and Vice-Chancellor for Admin. and Devt: NICK DUNAGAN
Vice-Chancellor for Finance and Admin.: NANCY YARBROUGH

Vice-Chancellor for Student Affairs: Dr MARGARET Y. TOSTON
Vice-Chancellor for Univ. Advancement: LENORA P. SOLOMONS
Registrar: BRANDY D. CARTMELL
Library Dir: MARY VAUGHAN CARPENTER
Library of 371,877 vols, 688,273 microfiche, 20,231 microfilms, 107,772 govt documents, 1,080 periodicals
Number of students: 7,913 (7500 undergraduate, 413 graduate)

DEANS

College of Agriculture and Applied Sciences: Dr JERRY GRESHAM
College of Business and Global Affairs: Prof. Dr ERNEST R. MOSER
College of Education, Health and Behavioural Sciences: Dr MARY LEE HALL
College of Engineering and Natural Sciences: Dr RICHARD J. HELGESON
College of Humanities and Fine Arts: Prof. Dr LYNN M. ALEXANDER
Dept of Agriculture, Geosciences and Natural Resources: Prof. Dr JERRY D. GRESHAM
Graduate Studies: Prof. Dr VICTORIA S. SENG

UNIVERSITY OF THE SOUTH

735 University Ave, Sewanee, TN 37383-1000
Telephone: (931) 598-1000
Fax: (931) 598-3248
E-mail: admiss@sewanee.edu
Internet: www.sewanee.edu
Founded 1858
Private control
Academic year: August to May
Pres. and Vice-Chancellor: Dr JOHN M. MCCARDELL, JR
Provost: Dr JOHN R. SWALLOW
Vice-Pres. for Univ. Relations: JAY FISHER
Treasurer: JERRY FORSTER
Dean of College: JOHN J. GATTA, JR
Dean of Students: ERIC HARTMAN
Dean of Admission and Financial Aid: LEE ANN M. AFTON-BACKLUND
Registrar: PAUL G. WILEY, II
Univ. Librarian and Assoc. Provost for Information Technology Services: Dr VICKI SELLS
Library of 749,105 vols
Number of teachers: 172 (137 full-time, 35 part-time)
Number of students: 1,544 (1,470 undergraduate, 80 graduate)
Publications: Sewanee Review, Sewanee Theological Review

DEANS

College of Arts and Sciences: Dr JOHN J. GATTA
School of Theology: Rev. Dr WILLIAM S. STAFFORD

VANDERBILT UNIVERSITY

211 Kirkland Hall, Nashville, TN 37240
Telephone: (615) 322-7311
Fax: (615) 343-7765
E-mail: admissions@vanderbilt.edu
Internet: www.vanderbilt.edu
Founded 1873
Private control
Academic year: August to April
Chancellor: Prof. NICHOLAS ZEPPOS
Provost and Vice-Chancellor for Academic Affairs: RICHARD MCCARTY
Vice-Chancellor for Admin.: JERRY FIFE
Vice-Chancellor for Devt and Alumni Relations: SUSIE STALCUP
Vice-Chancellor for Finance and Chief Financial Officer: BRETT SWEET

Vice-Chancellor for Health Affairs: JEFFREY BALSER
Vice-Chancellor for Univ. Affairs and Athletics, Gen. Counsel and Sec. of the Univ.: DAVID WILLIAMS, II
Vice-Provost for Enrolment and Dean of Admissions: DOUGLAS L. CHRISTIANSEN
Dean of Libraries: CONNIE VINITA DOWELL
Library of 2,607,058 vols (incl. books and serial backfiles), 78,041 serial subscriptions, 69,255 audio visual items
Number of teachers: 3,990 (3,551 full-time, 439 part-time)
Number of students: 12,859 (6,817 undergraduate, 6,042 graduate and professional)
Publications: Acorn Chronicle (online (www.vanderbilt.edu/magazines/acorn-chronicle)), Alumniexclusive (online (www.vanderbilt.edu/alumni/alumni-exclusive)), Arts and Science (online (www.vanderbilt.edu/magazines/arts-and-science)), Peabody Reflector (2 a year, online (www.vanderbilt.edu/magazines/peabody-reflector)), The Spire (online (www.vanderbilt.edu/alumni/magazines/spire)), Vanderbilt Business (online (www.vanderbilt.edu/magazines/vanderbilt-business)), Vanderbilt Engineering (online (www.vanderbilt.edu/magazines/vanderbilt-engineering)), Vanderbilt Lawyer (online (law.vanderbilt.edu/alumni/alumni-publications/index.aspx)), Vanderbilt Magazine, Vanderbilt Medicine (online (www.mc.vanderbilt.edu/vanderbiltmedicine)), Vanderbilt Nurse (online (www.vanderbilt.edu/vanderbiltnurse))

DEANS

Blair School of Music: Prof. Dr MARK WAIT
College of Arts and Science: Dr CAROLYN DENVER
Divinity School: Prof. Dr JAMES HUDNUT-BEUMLER
George Peabody College: Dr CAMILLA P. BENBOW
Graduate School: DENNIS G. HALL
Ingram Commons: FRANK WCISLO
Law School: Prof. Dr CHRIS GUTHRIE
Owen Graduate School of Management: Prof. Dr JAMES BRADFORD
School of Engineering: Prof. Dr KENNETH F. GALLOWAY
School of Medicine: Dr JEFFREY R. BALSER
School of Nursing: Prof. Dr COLLEEN CONWAY-WELCH

PROFESSORS

ABKOWITZ, M. D., Civil and Environmental Engineering
ABUMRAD, N. N., Surgery
AHNER, J., Mathematics
ALBRIDGE, R. G., Physics and Astronomy
ALDROUBI, A., Mathematics
ALLEN, G. S., Neurological Surgery
ARMSTRONG, R. N., Biochemistry
ARTEAGA, C. L., Medicine
ATACK, J., Economics
ATKINSON, III, J. B., Pathology
AURBACH, M. L., Art and Art History
AVISON, M. J., Radiology and Radiological Sciences
BADER, D. M., Medicine
BALDWIN, H. S., Pediatrics
BALDWIN, L. V., Religious Studies
BALL, C. A., Management
BALLARD, D. W., Microbiology and Immunology
BALSER, J. R., Anaesthesiology
BARRY, B., Management
BARSKY, R. F., French and Italian
BASU, P. K., Civil and Environmental Engineering
BEAUCHAMP, R. D., Surgery
BELL, V. M., English
BELTON, R., Law

BENBOW, C. P., Psychology and Human Devt
BERNARD, G. R., Medicine
BESS, F. H., Hearing and Speech Sciences
BETH, A. H., Molecular Physiology and Biophysics
BIAGGIONI, I. O., Medicine
BICKMAN, L., Psychology and Human Devt
BISCH, D., Mathematics
BLACKBURN, J. O., Management
BLACKETT, R., History
BLAKE, R., Psychology
BLAKELY, R. D., Pharmacology
BLANNING, R. W., Management
BLOCH, F. S., Law
BOEHM, F. H., Obstetrics and Gynaecology
BÖER, G. B., Management
BOLTON, R., Management
BOND, E., Economics
BONDS, III, A. B., Electrical Engineering and Computer Science
BOOTH, W. J., Political Science
BORNHOP, D. J., Chemistry
BOYD, S. B., Oral and Maxillofacial Surgery
BRANDON, M. E., Law
BRANDT, S. J., Medicine
BRASH, A. R., Pharmacology
BRAU, C. A., Physics and Astronomy
BRAXTON, J., Leadership, Policy and Organizations
BRESSMAN, L. S., Law
BREYER, M. D., Medicine
BROADIE, K., Biological Sciences
BROWN, R. L., Law
BRUCE, J. W., Law
BUERHAUS, P. I., Nursing
BURK, R. F., Medicine
BURNETT, L. S., Obstetrics and Gynaecology
BURNS, J. P., Divinity
BURR, I. M., Paediatrics
BYRD, III, B. F., Medicine
CADZOW, J. A., Electrical Engineering and Computer Science
CAMARATA, S. M., Hearing and Speech Sciences
CAPDEVILA, J. H., Medicine
CAPRIOLI, R. M., Biochemistry
CARBONE, D. P., Medicine
CARPENTER, G. F., Biochemistry
CARROLL, JR, F. E., Radiology and Radiological Sciences
CARTER, C. E., Biological Sciences
CASAGRANDE, V. A., Cell Biology
CHALKLEY, G. R., Molecular Physiology and Biophysics
CHANEY, P. K., Management
CHAZIN, W. J., Biochemistry
CHERRINGTON, A. D., Molecular Physiology and Biophysics
CHRISTIE, W. G., Management
CHRISTMAN, J. W., Medicine
CHURCHILL, L. R., Medicine
CLAYTON, E., Pediatrics
CLAYTON, J. B., English
COBB, P. A., Teaching and Learning
COFFEY, R. J., Jr, Medicine
COLE, D. A., Psychology and Human Devt
COLLINS, R. D., Pathology
COMPAS, B., Psychology and Human Devt
CONLEY, J., Economics
CONN, P. J., Pharmacology
CONTURE, E. G., Hearing and Speech Sciences
CONWAY-WELCH, C. M., Nursing
COOK, G. E., Electrical Engineering and Computer Science
CORBIN, J. D., Molecular Physiology and Biophysics
CORDRAY, D. S., Psychology and Human Devt
CORN, A. L., Special Education
CORNFIELD, D. B., Sociology
COTTON, R. B., Paediatrics
COVINGTON, R. N., Law
CROOKE, III, P. S., Mathematics
CROWSON, R., Leadership, Policy and Organizations
CUMMINGS, P., Chemical Engineering

D'AQUILA, R. T., Medicine
DAFT, R. L., Management
DALLEY, A. F., Cell Biology
DAMON, W. W., Economics
DANZO, B. J., Obstetrics and Gynaecology
DAUGHETY, A. F., Economics
DAVIDSON, J. L., Electrical Engineering and Computer Science
DAVIDSON, J. M., Pathology
DAVIS, S. N., Medicine
DAVIS, T. M., English
DeFELICE, L. J., Pharmacology
DELBEKE, D., Radiology and Radiation Sciences
DEMAREST, A. A., Anthropology
DERMODY, T. S., Pediatrics
DESHPANDE, J. K., Pediatrics
DesPREZ, R. M., Nursing
DEUTCH, A. Y., Psychiatry
DEY, S. K., Pediatrics
DiBENEDETTO, E., Mathematics
DICKERSON, D. C., History
DILLEHAY, T. D., Anthropology
DILTS, D., Electrical Engineering and Computer Science
DITTUS, R. S., Medicine
DOKECKI, P. R., Human and Organizational Devt
DOWDY, L. W., Electrical Engineering and Computer Science
DOWNING, J. W., Anaesthesiology
DOYLE, D. H., History
DREWS, R., Classical Studies
DRINKWATER, JR, D. C., Cardiac and Thoracic Surgery
DRISKILL, R. A., Economics
DuBOIS, JR, R. N., Medicine
DUNCAVAGE, J. A., Otolaryngology
DUPONT, W. D., Preventative Medicine
DYKENS, E. A., Psychology and Human Devt
EAKIN, M. C., History
EBNER, F. F., Psychology
EDELMAN, P. H., Mathematics
EDEN, B., Economics
EDWARDS, K. M., Pediatrics
ELLEDGE, W. P., English
ELLIOTT, S. N., Special Education
ELY, J. W., History
ELY, J. W., Law
ENTERLINE, L., English
ENTMAN, S. S., Obstetrics and Gynaecology
EPSTEIN, J. A., History
ERNST, D. J., Physics and Astronomy
EXTON, J. H., Molecular Physiology and Biophysics
FAN, Y., Economics
FANNING, E. H., Biological Sciences
FARRAN, D., Teaching and Learning
FAZIO, S., Medicine
FELZMAN, L. C., Physics and Astronomy
FENICHEL, G. M., Neurology
FITZ, E. E., Spanish and Portuguese
FITZPATRICK, J. M., Electrical Engineering and Computer Science
FLEETWOOD, D. M., Electrical Engineering and Computer Science
FLEISCHER, A. C., Radiology and Radiological Sciences
FLEXNER, J. M., Medicine
FOGO, A. B., Pathology
FOLGARAIT, L., Art and Art History
FOSTER, J. E., Economics
FOX, R., Psychology
FRANKS, J. J., Psychology
FREEMAN, M. L., Radiation Oncology
FREEMON, F. R., Neurology
FRIEDMAN, E. H., Spanish and Portuguese
FRIEDMAN, R. A., Management
FROMENT-MEURICE, M., French and Italian
FRYD, V. G., Art and Art History
FUCHS, D. H., Special Education
FUCHS, L. S., Special Education
FURBISH, D. J., Geology
GABBE, S. G., Obstetrics and Gynaecology
GAFFNEY, F. A., Medical Admin.

GALLOWAY, K. F., Electrical Engineering and Computer Science
GALLOWAY, JR, R. L., Biomedical Engineering
GARBER, J., Psychology and Human Devt
GAY, V. P., Religious Studies
GEE, E. G., Law
GEER, J., Political Science
GEORGE, JR, A. L., Medicine
GIRGUS, S. B., English
GIUSE, N. B., Biomedical Informatics
GOLDBERG, J. C., Law
GOLDENRING, J. R., Surgery
GOLDRING, E., Leadership, Policy and Organizations
GOODMAN, L. E., Philosophy
GORDON, J., Nursing
GORE, J. C., Radiology and Radiological Sciences
GOTTFRIED, R. K., English
GOULD, K. L., Cell and Developmental Biology
GOULD, M. I., Mathematics
GRAHAM, JR, G. J., Political Science
GRAHAM, JR, T. P., Paediatrics
GRANNER, D. K., Molecular Physiology and Biophysics
GRANTHAM, D. W., Hearing and Speech Sciences
GREEN, N. E., Orthopaedics and Rehabilitation
GREENE, J. W., Pediatrics
GREER, J. P., Medicine
GREGOR, T. A., Anthropology
GRIFFIN, L. J., Sociology and Political Science
GRIFFIN, M. R., Preventive Medicine
GUENGERICH, F. P., Biochemistry
GUTHRIE, C. P., Law
GUTHRIE, J. W., Leadership, Policy and Organizations
HAGLUND, R. F., Physics and Astronomy
HAHN, B., German and Slavic Language
HAINES, J. L., Molecular Physiology and Biophysics
HALL, D., Physics and Astronomy
HALL, D. J., Law
HALL, R., Teaching and Learning
HALLAHAN, D., Radiation Oncology
HALPERIN, J., English
HAMILTON, J. H., Physics and Astronomy
HAMM, H. E., Pharmacology
HANCOCK, M. D., Political Science
HANDE, K. R., Medicine
HANKS, S. K., Cell Biology
HANN, S. R., Cell Biology
HARRIS, JR, R. C., Medicine
HARRIS, T. R., Biomedical Engineering
HAWIGER, J., Microbiology and Immunology
HAZINSKI, T. A., Paediatrics
HEAD, D. R., Pathology
HEARN, J., Leadership, Policy and Organizations
HELDERMAN, J. H., Medicine
HELFER, L. R., Law School
HELLER, JR, R. M., Radiology and Radiological Sciences
HELLERQVIST, C. G., Biochemistry
HERCULES, D. M., Chemistry
HERNANZ-SCHULMAN, M., Radiology and Radiological Sciences
HESS, JR, B. A., Chemistry
HETCHER, S. A., Law
HEYNEMAN, S., Leadership, Policy and Organizations
HICKSON, G. B., Pediatrics
HIEBERT, S. W., Biochemistry
HILL, G. C., Medical Admin.
HODAPP, R., Special Education
HODGES, M., Philosophy
HOFFMAN, D. L., Management
HOGGE, J. H., Psychology and Human Devt
HOLLON, S. D., Psychology
HOOVER, R. L., Pathology
HUDNET-BEUMLER, J., Divinity
HUDSON, B. G., Medicine
HUFFMAN, G. W., Economics
HUGHES, C. B., Mathematics

ICHIKAWA, I., Paediatrics
INAGAMI, T., Biochemistry
ISAAC, L. W., Sociology
JACOBSON, G. P., Hearing and Speech Sciences
JACOBSON, H. R., Medicine
JARMAN, M. F., English
JENSEN, G. F., Sociology
JENSEN, R. M., Divinity
JOHNS, C. M. S., Art and Art History
JOHNSON, C. H., Biological Sciences
JOHNSON, D. A., Divinity
JOHNSON, D. H., Nursing
JONES, III, H. W., Obstetrics and Gynaecology
JRADE, C. L., Spanish and Portuguese
KAAS, J. H., Psychology
KAISER, A. B., Medicine
KAISER, A. P., Special Education
KANG, W. P., Electrical Engineering and Computer Science
KASPAROV, G., Mathematics
KAWAMURA, K., Electrical Engineering and Computer Science
KAYE, J. J., Radiology and Radiological Sciences
KESSLER, R. M., Radiology and Radiological Sciences
KING, JR, L. E., Medicine
KING, N. J., Law
KINSER, D. L., Mechanical Engineering
KIRSHNER, H. S., Neurology
KNIGHT, D. A., Divinity
KOSSON, D. S., Civil and Environmental Engineering
KOURY, M. J., Medicine
KOVACS, W. J., Medicine
KREYLING, M. P., English
KUTZINSKI, V. M., Dean's Office
LACHS, J., Philosophy
LAMB, J., English
LaMONTAGNE, L. L., Nursing
LANCASTER, L. E., Nursing
LAPPIN, J. S., Psychology
LAWTON, III, A. R., Paediatrics
LEBLANC, L. J., Management
LEGAN, H. L., Oral and Maxillofacial Surgery
LEHRER, R., Teaching and Learning
LeSTOURGEON, W. M., Biological Sciences
LeVAN, D. M., Chemical Engineering
LEVINE, A.-J., Divinity
LEVITT, P. R., Pharmacology
LEWIS, J. G., Medicine
LIEBLER, D. C., Biochemistry
LIGHT, R. W., Medicine
LIMBIRD, L. E., Pharmacology
LINTON, M. F., Medicine
LOGAN, G. D., Psychology
LOOSEN, P. T., Psychiatry
LORENZI, N. M., Biomedical Informatics
LOYD, J. E., Medicine
LUBINSKI, D., Psychology and Human Devt
LUIS, W., Spanish and Portuguese
LUKEHART, C. M., Chemistry
LYBRAND, T. P., Chemistry
McCARTHY, J. A., German and Slavic Languages
McCARTY, R., Psychology
McCAULEY, D. E., Biological Sciences
McCLURE, J. S., Divinity
McCOY, T. R., Law
MACDONALD, R. L., Neurology
McKENNA, S. J., Oral and Maxillofacial Surgery
McKENZIE, R. N., Mathematics
McLOED, R., Nursing
McMAHON, D. G., Biological Sciences
McNAMARA, T. P., Psychology
McWILLIAM, R. A., Paediatrics
MAGNUSON, M. A., Molecular Physiology and Biophysics
MAGUIRE, C. F., Physics and Astronomy
MAHADEVAN, S., Civil and Environmental Engineering
MAIER, H. G., Law
MANESCHI, A. E., Economics

MARCH, S. T., Management
MARCUS, L. S., English
MARGO, R. A., Economics
MARNETT, L. J., Biochemistry
MARTIN, P. R., Psychiatry
MASSENGILL, L.W., Electrical Engineering and Computer Science
MASULIS, R. W., Management
MATRISIAN, L. M., Cancer Biology
MATUSIK, R. J., Urologic Surgery
MAY, J. M., Medicine
MEEKS, M. D., Divinity
MEGIBBEN, C. K., Mathematics
MELLOR, A. M., Mechanical Engineering
MELNER, M. H., Obstetrics and Gynaecology
MELTZER, H. Y., Psychiatry
MEYRICK-CLARRY, B. O., Pathology
MIHALIK, M. L., Mathematics
MILLER, C. F., Geology
MILLER, G. G., Medicine
MILLER, M. F., Geology
MILLER, R. A., Biomedical Informatics
MILLER-MCLEMORE, B. J., Divinity
MITCHELL, W. M., Pathology
MONGA, L., French and Italian
MOORE, R. A., Nursing
MORAN, B. I., Law
MORRIS, JR, J. A., Surgery
MORROW, J. D., Medicine
MOSES, H. L., Cancer Biology
MURPHY, J. F., Leadership and Organizations
MURPHY, M. L., Art and Art History
NAGAREDA, R. A., Law
NANNEY, L. B., Plastic Surgery
NEILSON, E. G., Medicine
NELSON, D., Dean's Office
NETTERVILLE, J. L., Otolaryngology
NEWBROUGH, J. R., Human and Organization Devt
NEWMAN, J. H., Medicine
NORDEN, J. J., Cell and Devt Biology
NOVAK, T. P., Management
OATES, J. A., Medicine
OBERACKER, V. E., Physics and Astronomy
O'DAY, D. M., Ophthalmology and Visual Sciences
O'HARA, E. A., Law
OHDE, R. N., Hearing and Speech Sciences
OLIVER, K., Philosophy
OLIVER, R. L., Management
OLSEN, N. J., Medicine
OLSON, G. E., Cell and Developmental Biology
ONG, D. E., Biochemistry
OPPENHEIMER, B. I., Political Science
ORGEBIN-CRIST, M. C., Obstetrics and Gynaecology
OSHEROFF, N., Biochemistry
OSSOFF, R. H., Otolaryngology
OSTEEN, K. G., Obstetrics and Gynaecology
OUTLAW, L. T., Philosophy
OVERHOLSER, K. A., Biomedical Engineering
OZBOLT, J. G., Nursing
PACE, J., Nursing
PAGE, D. L., Pathology
PAGE, T. L., Biological Sciences
PANTELIDES, S. T., Physics and Astronomy
PARK, J. H., Molecular Physiology and Biophysics
PARKER, F. L., Civil and Environmental Engineering
PARL, F. F., Pathology
PARTAIN, C. L., Radiology and Radiological Sciences
PARTRIDGE, W., Human and Organizational Devt
PATTE, D. M., Religious Studies
PATTON, J. A., Radiology and Radiological Sciences
PENN, J. S., Ophthalmology and Visual Sciences
PHILLIPS, J. A., III, Paediatrics
PIETENPOL, J. A., Biochemistry
PILON, B. A., Nursing
PINCUS, T., Medicine

PISTON, D. W., Molecular Physiology and Biophysics
PITZ, R. W., Mechanical Engineering
PLUMMER, J. F., English
PLUMMER, M. D., Mathematics
POLAVARAPU, P. L., Chemistry
PORTER, A. C., Leadership and Organizations
PORTER, N. A., Chemistry
PRICE, R. R., Radiology and Radiological Sciences
PRIETO, R., Spanish and Portuguese
PRILLELTENSKY, I., Human and Organizational Devt
PUTNAM, JR, J. B., Thoracic Surgery
QUARANTA, V., Cancer Biology
RAMAYYA, A. V., Physics and Astronomy
RASCH, R. F. R., Nursing
RASICO, P. D., Spanish and Portuguese
RASMUSSEN, R. K., Law
RATCLIFFE, J. G., Mathematics
RAY, J. L., Political Science
RAY, W. A., Preventive Medicine
REINGANUM, J. F., Economics
RESCHLY, D. J., Special Education
REYNOLDS, A. B., Cancer Biology
RICHARDS, W. O., Surgery
RICHMOND, J. A., Cancer Biology
RIESER, J. J., Psychology and Human Devt
RISKO, V. J., Teaching and Learning
ROBACK, H. B., Psychiatry
ROBERTS, L. J., II, Pharmacology
ROBERTSON, D. H., Medicine
ROBERTSON, R. M., Medicine
RODEN, D. M., Medicine
ROSELLI, R. J., Biomedical Engineering
ROTH, B. J., Medicine
ROTH, J. A., Chemical Engineering
ROTHENBERG, M. L., Medicine
RUBIN, C. A., Mechanical Engineering
RUBIN, D. H., Medicine
RULEY, H. E., Microbiology and Immunology
SAFF, E. B., Mathematics
SANDERS-BUSH, E., Pharmacology
SANDLER, H. M., Psychology and Human Devt
SANDLER, M. P., Radiology and Radiological Sciences
SAPIR, M., Mathematics
SASSON, J., Divinity
SCHAFFNER, W., Preventative Medicine
SCHALL, J. D., Psychology
SCHAUBLE, L., Teaching and Learning
SCHERRER, R. J., Physics and Astronomy
SCHLUNK, H. J., Law
SCHMIDT, D., Electrical Engineering and Computer Science
SCHNELLE, K. B., Chemical Engineering
SCHOENBLUM, J. A., Law
SCHRIMPF, R., Electrical Engineering and Computer Science
SCHUENING, F. G., Medicine
SCHULMAN, G., Medicine
SCHUMAKER, L. L., Mathematics
SCHWARTZ, H. S., Orthopedics and Rehabilitation
SCHWARTZ, T. A., History
SCUDDER, G. D., Management
SEGOVIA, F. F., Divinity
SELIGSON, M. A., Political Science
SERGENT, J. S., Medicine
SEVIN, D. H. O., German and Slavic Languages
SHACK, R. B., Plastic Surgery
SHELTON, R. C., Psychiatry
SHENAI, J., Pediatrics
SHEPHERD, V. L., Pathology
SHERRY, S., Law
SHIAVI, R. G., Biomedical Engineering
SHU, X. O., Medicine
SHYR, Y., Preventative Medicine
SIAMI, G., Medicine
SIEGFRIED, J. J., Economics
SINGLETON, C. K., Biological Sciences
SLOVIS, C. M., Emergency Medicine
SMITH, H. W., History
SMITH, JR, J. A., Urologic Surgery

SMITH, W. P., Psychology
SNELL, JR, J. D., Medicine
SODERQUIST, L. D., Law
SOSMAN, J. A., Medicine
SPENGLER, D. M., Orthopedics and Rehabilitation
SPICKARD, JR, W. A., Medicine
SPINDLER, K. P., Orthopedics and Rehabilitation
SRIRAM, S., Neurology
STAHLMAN, M. T., Pediatrics
STEAD, W. W., Medicine
STEIGER, J. H., Psychology and Human Devt
STEIN, R. W., Molecular Physiology and Biophysics
STEINBERG, R., Sociology
STERNBERG, P., Ophthalmology and Visual Sciences
STOLL, H. R., Management
STONE, M. P., Chemistry
STONE, W. J., Medicine
STONE, W. L., Pediatrics
STRANGE, K., Anaesthesiology
STRAUSS, A. M., Mechanical Engineering
STRAUSS, A. W., Pediatrics
STRICKLIN, G. P., Medicine
STUBBS, G. J., Biological Sciences
STUHR, J. J., Philosophy
SUNDELL, H. W., Pediatrics
SWAIN, C. M., Law
SWIFT, L. L., Pathology
SYVERUD, J., Electrical Engineering and Computer Science
SZTIPANOVITS, J., Electrical and Computer Engineering
TAM, J. P., Microbiology and Immunology
TANNER, R. D., Chemical Engineering
TATE, C. N., Political Science
TELLINGHUISEN, J., Chemistry
TELOH, H. A., Philosophy
THOITS, P. A., Sociology
THOMAS, J. W., II, Medicine
THOMAS, R. S., Law
THOMPSON, P. W., Teaching and Learning
THOMPSON, R. B., Law
TICHI, C., English
TOLK, N. H., Physics and Astronomy
TRANGENSTEIN, P., Nursing
TULIPAN, N. B., Neurological Surgery
UMAR, S. A., Physics and Astronomy
USNER, D. H., History
VAN KAER, L., Microbiology and Immunology
VAUGHAN, D. E., Medicine
VICTOR, B., Management
WAGNER, C., Biochemistry
WALDEN, T. A., Psychology and Human Devt
WALKER, L. S., Pediatrics
WALLER, N., Psychology and Human Devt
WALLSTON, K. A., Nursing
WANG, P., Economics
WANG, T. G., Mechanical Engineering
WARD, P. A., French and Italian
WASHINGTON, M. K., Pathology
WASSERMAN, D. H., Molecular Physiology and Biophysics
WASSERSTEIN, D. J., History
WATERMAN, M. R., Biochemistry
WEBB, G. F., Mathematics
WEBSTER, M. S., Physics and Astronomy
WEIL, P. A., Molecular Physiology and Biophysics
WEILER, T. J., Physics and Astronomy
WEINER, E. E., Nursing
WELLER, R. A., Electrical Engineering and Computer Science
WENTE, S. R., Cell and Devt Biology
WEYMARK, J. A., Economics
WIKSWO, J. P., Physics and Astronomy, Molecular Physiology and Biophysics
WILEY, R. G., Neurology
WILKINSON, G. R., Pharmacology
WILSON, J. R., Medicine
WILTSHIRE, S. F., Classical Studies
WOLERY, M., Special Education
WONG, K. K., Leadership, Policy and Organizations

Wood, A. J., Medicine
Wood, D. C., Philosophy
Wrenn, K. D., Emergency Medicine
Wright, C. V., Cell and Developmental Biology
Wright, P. F., Pediatrics
Xia, D., Mathematics
Yoder, P. J., Special Education
Yu, G., Mathematics
Zeppos, N. S., Jr, Law
Zheng, W., Medicine
Zutter, M. M., Pathology

VICTORY UNIVERSITY

255 N Highland St, Memphis, TN 38111
Telephone: (901) 320-9777
Fax: (901) 320-9791
E-mail: admissions@victory.edu
Internet: www.victory.edu

Founded 1944 as Mid-South Bible Center, present status 1958, present name 2010
Private control
Academic year: August to August

Depts of arts and sciences, behavioural sciences, bible and theology, business, education

Pres.: Dr Shirley Robinson Pippins
Provost: Dr Sheryl Weems
Vice-Pres. for Academic and Student Affairs: Bill Alexander
Vice-Pres. for Financial Affairs: Troy R. Graham
Vice-Pres. for Student Enrollment: Darrel Hanbury
Dir of Student Devt: Brian Duffy
Registrar: Sean Scott
Library Dir: Pam B. Walker

Library of 56,000 vols (incl. books, bound journals, videos, DVDs, tapes, CDs, microfiche), 64 periodicals
Number of teachers: 63 (35 full-time, 28 adjunct)
Number of students: 1,095

TEXAS

ABILENE CHRISTIAN UNIVERSITY

ACU Box 29100, Abilene, TX 79699-9100
Telephone: (325) 674-2000
Fax: (325) 674-2958
E-mail: info@admissions.acu.edu
Internet: www.acu.edu

Founded 1906 as Childers Classical Institute, present name 1976
Private control
Academic year: August to May

Pres.: Dr Phil Schubert
Chancellor: Dr Royce Money
Provost: Dr Gregory Straughn
Vice-Pres.: Dr Gary McCaleb
Vice-Pres. for Advancement: Robert Rhodes
Vice-Pres. for Student Life and Dean for Students: Dr Jean-Noel Thompson
Chief Enrolment Officer: Kevin Campbell
Registrar and Dir for Academic Records: Bart Herridge
Dean for Library and Information Resources: Dr John Weaver

Library of 541,024 vols, 535 periodical titles, 76,224 e-books
Number of teachers: 282
Number of students: 4,558
Publication: ACU Today Magazine

DEANS

College of Arts and Sciences: Dr Greg Straughn
College of Biblical Studies: Dr Ken Cukrowski
College of Business Administration: Dr Rick Lytle

College of Education and Human Services: Dr Lloyd Goldsmith
Graduate School: Dr Carley Dodd
Honors College: Dr Stephen Johnson

ARLINGTON BAPTIST COLLEGE

3001 W Division St, Arlington, TX 76012
Telephone: (817) 461-8741
Fax: (817) 274-1138
E-mail: info@abconline.org
Internet: www.abconline.org

Founded 1927 as Fundamental Bible Institute, present name and location 1955
Private control
Academic year: August to May

Divs incl. biblical/theological studies, general studies, professional studies

Pres.: Dr D. L. Moody
Academic Dean: Dr Helen Sullivan
Dean for Students: Emil Balliet
Registrar: Janie Taylor

Library of 30,000 vols.

ART INSTITUTE OF HOUSTON

4140 Southwest Freeway, Houston, TX 77027
Telephone: (713) 623-2040
Fax: (713) 966-2797
E-mail: aihadm@aii.edu
Internet: www.artinstitutes.edu/houston

Founded 1965 as Houston School of Commercial Art, present name 1978
Private control
Academic year: October to September

Part of art institutes system of schools; areas of study: culinary, design, fashion, general education, media arts

Pres: Larry Horn
Dean for Academic Affairs: Kenneth Pascal
Dean for Student Affairs: John Willis
Sr Dir for Admissions: Bobbi Rabine
Dir for Admin. and Student Financial Services: Thomas Kuper
Dir for Institutional Effectiveness and Research: Charles Lartey
Registrar: Kimberly Joyner
Dir for Library: Elene Gedevanishvili

Library of 30,916 vols, 160 periodicals
Number of students: 2,000

AUSTIN COLLEGE

900 N Grand Ave, Sherman, TX 75090-4400
Telephone: (903) 813-2000
Fax: (903) 813-3199
E-mail: admission@austincollege.edu
Internet: www.austincollege.edu

Founded 1849
Private control
Academic year: September to June

Pres.: Dr Marjorie Hass
Vice-Pres. for Academic Affairs and Dean for the Faculty: Michael A. Imhoff
Vice-Pres. for Business Affairs: Heidi Ellis
Vice-Pres. for Institutional Advancement: Brooks Hull
Vice-Pres. for Institutional Enrolment: Nan Davis
Vice-Pres. for Student Affairs and Athletics: Timothy P. Millerick
Dean for Student Services: Dr Rose Rothmeier
Registrar: Tex Ruegg
Library Dir: John West

Library of 200,000 vols, 4,000 media items
Number of teachers: 122 (92 full-time, 30 part-time)
Number of students: 1,300

DEANS

Humanities Division: Prof. Dr Patrick Duffey
Sciences Division: Dr Steve Goldsmith
Social Sciences Division: Prof. Dr Jerry Johnson

AUSTIN GRADUATE SCHOOL OF THEOLOGY

7640 Guadalupe St, Austin, TX 78752-1333
Telephone: (512) 476-2772
Fax: (512) 476-3919
E-mail: info@austingrad.edu
Internet: www.austingrad.edu

Founded 1917 as Bible Chair at Univ. of Texas, present name 2001
Private control
Academic year: August to August

Chancellor: David Worley
Vice-Chancellor: Jack Wright
Pres.: Stanley G. Reid
Vice-Pres.: Dave Arthur
Dir for Devt: Neil Haney
Dean for Students: R. Mark Shipp
Registrar: Celeste Scarborough
Dir for Library: M. Todd Hall

Library of 30,000 vols, 135 journal subscriptions
Number of students: 99
Publication: Christian Studies.

AUSTIN PRESBYTERIAN THEOLOGICAL SEMINARY

100 E 27th St, Austin, TX 78705-5711
Telephone: (512) 404-4800
Fax: (512) 479-0738
Internet: www.austinseminary.edu

Founded 1902
Private control
Academic year: January to May

Pres.: Rev. Theodore J. Wardlaw
Vice-Pres. for Admissions: John H. Barden
Vice-Pres. for Business Affairs: Kurt A. Gabbard
Vice-Pres. for Institutional Advancement: Donna G. Scott
Vice-Pres. for Student Affairs and Vocation: Jacquline L. Saxon
Academic Dean: Allan Hugh Cole, Jr
Registrar: Jacqueline D. Hefley
Dir for Library: Timothy D. Lincoln

Library of 160,000 vols
Publications: Communitas (1 a year), Horizons in Biblical Theology (2 a year), Insights (2 a year), Windows.

BAPTIST MISSIONARY ASSOCIATION THEOLOGICAL SEMINARY

POB 670, 1530 E Pine St, Jacksonville, TX 75766-5407
Telephone: (903) 586-2501
Fax: (903) 586-0378
E-mail: bmatsem@bmats.edu
Internet: www.bmats.edu

Founded 1957
Private control
Academic year: August to May

Pres.: Dr Charley Holmes
Dean and Registrar: Dr Philip Attebery
Dir for Student Services: Ronie Jeff Johnson
Dir for Library: Dr James C. Blaylock

Library of 128,000 vols.

BAYLOR COLLEGE OF MEDICINE

1 Baylor Plaza, Houston, TX 77030
Telephone and fax (713) 798-4951
E-mail: admissions@bcm.edu

Internet: www.bcm.edu
Founded 1900 as Univ. of Dallas Medical Dept, present name and status 1969
Private control
Academic year: July to June
Pres. and CEO: Dr PAUL KLOTMAN
Vice-Pres. and Chief Technology Officer, Information Technology: ALEXANDER IZA-GUIRRE
Vice-Pres., Gen. Counsel and Corporate Sec.: ROBERT F. CORRIGAN, JR
Vice-Pres. for Communications and Marketing: CLAIRE M. BASSETT
Vice-Pres. for Devt: KRISTI SHERWOOD COOPER
Vice-Pres. for Facilities: ROCK MORILLE
Vice-Pres. for Research: Dr ADAM KUSPA
Chief Academic Officer: LORIE TABAK
Registrar and Sr Dir for Student Affairs: JOHN RAPP
Number of teachers: 2,217 (1,790 full-time, 427 part-time)
Number of students: 329
Publication: *Solutions*

DEANS

Graduate School of Biomedical Sciences: Dr HIRAM F. GILBERT
Medical School: Dr STEPHEN B. GREENBERG
National School of Tropical Medicine: Dr PETER J. HOTEZ
School of Allied Health Sciences: Dr J. DAVID HOLCOMB

BAYLOR UNIVERSITY

1 Bear Place, Waco, TX 76798
Telephone: (254) 710-1011
Fax: (254) 710-2233
E-mail: registrar@baylor.edu
Internet: www.baylor.edu
Founded 1845
Private control
Academic year: August to May
Pres.: Dr KENNETH WINSTON STARR
Provost and Exec. Vice-Pres.: ELIZABETH DAVIS
Vice-Pres. for Finance and Admin.: REAGAN RAMSOWER
Vice-Pres. for Student Life: KEVIN JACKSON
Vice-Pres. for Univ. Devt: JERRY HAAG
Dean for Univ. Libraries and Vice-Pres. for Information Technology: Dr PATTIE ORR
Library of 2,521,216 vols, 73,204 serials, 394,559 e-books, 68,607 e-journals, 2,213,631 microforms, 128,845 audiovisual items
Number of teachers: 775
Number of students: 15,029 (12,575 undergraduate, 2,454 graduate/professional)
Publications: *Baylor Business Review, Baylor Geological Studies, Baylor Line, Baylor Magazine* (6 a year), *Baylor News, Journal of Church and State, Law Review, The Lariat*

DEANS

College of Arts and Sciences: Dr LEE NORDT
George W. Truett Theological Seminary: Dr DAVID E. GARLAND
Graduate School: Dr LARRY LYON
Hankamer School of Business: Dr TERRY S. MANESS
Honors College: Prof. Dr THOMAS S. HIBBS
Law School: BRAD TOBEN
Louise Herrington School of Nursing: Prof. Dr SHELLEY F. CONROY
School of Education: Dr JON M. ENGELHARDT
School of Engineering and Computer Science: Dr BENJAMIN S. KELLEY
School of Music: WILLIAM V. MAY
School of Social Work: DIANA R. GARLAND

BRAZOSPORT COLLEGE

500 College Dr., Lake Jackson, TX 77566
Telephone: (979) 230-3000
Fax: (979) 230-3376
Internet: www.brazosport.edu
Founded 1968 as Brazosport Jr College, present name 1970
State control
Academic year: August to May (2 semesters)
Pres.: Dr MILLICENT M. VALEK
Provost and Dean for Academic and Student Affairs: KEN TASA
Exec. Dir for Institutional Advancement: SERENA ANDREWS
Dean for Admin. Services and Chief Financial Officer: FRED SCOTT
Dean for Students: PAMELA DAVENPORT
Dir for College Services: GARY DICKS
Dir for Information Technology: RON PARKER
Librarian: JO ANNE ALCORN
Library of 70,000 vols, 43,000 e-books
Number of teachers: 88
Number of students: 15,405

FISHER MORE COLLEGE

3020 Lubbock Ave, Fort Worth, TX 76109
Telephone: (817) 923-8459
Fax: (817) 394-2340
E-mail: admissions@cstm.edu
Internet: www.fishermore.edu
Founded 1981 as Saint Thomas More Institute, present name 2012
Private control
Academic year: September to May
Liberal arts college
Pres.: Dr MICHAEL G. KING
Dean for College: Dr RYAN DOUGLAS MADISON
Dir for Admissions and Financial Aid: JUSTIN NELSON
Dir for Devt: Dr RAYMOND PFANG
Dir for Enrolment Management: PETER CAPANI
Dir for Student Life: SHANTI GUY
Registrar: JOHN HEITZENRATER
Library of 14,451 vol, 543 audiovisual items.

CONCORDIA UNIVERSITY TEXAS

11400 Concordia Univ. Dr., Austin, TX 78726
Telephone: (512) 313-3000
Fax: (512) 313-3999
E-mail: admissions@concordia.edu
Internet: www.concordia.edu
Founded 1926, present name and status 1995
Private control
Academic year: July to June
Pres.: Dr THOMAS CEDEL
Provost: ALAN RUNGE
Vice-Pres. for Academic Services: JOEL HECK
Vice-Pres. for Advancement: JOHN SCHOEDEL
Vice-Pres. for Business Services: PAMELA LEE
Vice-Pres. for External Relations: DON ADAM
Vice-Pres. for Student Services: WILLIAM DRISKILL
Vice-Pres. for Univ. Services: Dr DAVID L. KLUTH
Dir for Library Services: MIKAIL MCINTOSH-DOTY
Registrar: CONNIE BERAN
Number of students: 2,500
Publication: *Concordia University Texas Magazine* (4 a year)

DEANS

College of Business: Dr DONALD CHRISTIAN
College of Education: Dr JIM MCCONNELL
College of Liberal Arts: Dr KEN SCHMIDT
College of Science: Dr MICHAEL MOYER

CRISWELL COLLEGE

4010 Gaston Ave, Dallas, TX 75246
Telephone: (214) 821-5433
Fax: (214) 370-0497
E-mail: admission@criswell.edu
Internet: www.criswell.edu
Founded 1970
Private control
Academic year: August to July
Areas of study: biblical languages, Christian leadership, counselling ministry, education ministry, evangelism/missions, humanities, Jewish studies, pastoral ministry, philosophy, preaching, student ministry
Pres.: Dr JERRY A. JOHNSON
Provost and Exec. Vice-Pres.: LAMAR E. COOPER, SR
Vice-Pres. for Business and Chief Financial Officer: MICHAEL W. RODGERS
Vice-Pres. for Devt: KATE FINLEY
Dean for Students: JOE THOMAS
Dir for Admissions: JOSEPH F. THOMAS
Registrar: RON LOWERY
Dir for Library Services: PHILLIP NOTT
Library of 75,000 vols, 500 periodical titles
Number of teachers: 17 (full-time)
Number of students: 460
Publication: *Criswell Theological Review* (2 a year).

DALLAS BAPTIST UNIVERSITY

3000 Mountain Creek Parkway, Dallas, TX 75211-9299
Telephone: (214) 333-7100
Fax: (214) 333-5447
E-mail: admiss@dbu.edu
Internet: www.dbu.edu
Founded 1898, fmrly Decatur Baptist College, present name 1985
Private control
Pres.: Dr GARY COOK
Provost: Dr GAIL LINAM
Exec. Vice-Pres.: Dr J. BLAIR BLACKBURN
Vice-Pres. for Advancement: Dr ADAM WRIGHT
Vice-Pres. for External Affairs: Dr CORY HINES
Vice-Pres. for Financial Affairs: ERIC BRUNTMYER
Vice-Pres. for Graduate and Corporate Affairs and Sr Assoc. Provost: Dr DENNIS DOWD
Vice-Pres. for Technology: MATT MURRAH
Library Dir: DEBRA Y. COLLINS
Library of 810,447 vols, 1,119 periodicals
Number of teachers: 127 (full-time)
Number of students: 5,545

DEANS

College of Business: Dr CHARLENE CONNER
College of Fine Arts: RONALD BOWLES
College of Humanities and Social Sciences: Dr JACK GOODYEAR
College of Natural Sciences and Mathematics: Dr BEVERLY GILTNER
College of Professional Studies: Dr DONOVAN FREDRICKSEN
Dorothy M. Bush College of Education: Dr CHARLES CARONA
Gary Cook Graduate School of Leadership: Dr DENNIS DOWD (acting)
Mary C. Crowley College of Christian Faith: Dr STEVE MULLEN
Online Education: Dr JEKABS BIKIS

DALLAS CHRISTIAN COLLEGE

2700 Christian Parkway, Dallas, TX 75234-7299
Telephone: (972) 241-3371
Fax: (972) 241-8021
E-mail: admissions@dallas.edu

Internet: www.dallas.edu

Founded 1950

Private control

Academic year: August to May

Depts of arts and sciences, Bible, business administration, education, psychology

Pres.: DUSTIN D. RUBECK

Vice-Pres. for Academic Affairs: Dr PAUL KISSLING

Vice-Pres. for Institutional Effectiveness: Dr RON RIFE

Dir for Student Life: ERIC HINTON

Registrar: CRYSTAL LAIDACKER

Dir for Library: JANE REYNOLDS

Library of 35,000 vols, 17,000 e-books, 250 periodicals, 3,000 e-journals.

DALLAS THEOLOGICAL SEMINARY

3909 Swiss Ave, Dallas, TX 75204

Telephone: (214) 824-3094

Fax: (214) 841-3664

E-mail: registrar@dts.edu

Internet: www.dts.edu

Founded 1924 as Evangelical Theological College, present name 1969

Private control

Campuses in Atlanta, Austin, Guatemala, Houston, Knoxville, Philadelphia, San Antonio, Tampa, Washington; depts of biblical counselling, biblical exposition, Christian education, ministry, New Testament studies, Old Testament studies, pastoral ministries, philosophy, spiritual formation and leadership, theological studies, world missions, and intercultural studies

Pres.: Dr MARK L. BAILEY

Vice-Pres. for Academic Affairs and Academic Dean: Dr JOHN GRASSMICK

Vice-Pres. for Advancement: KIMBERLY TILL

Vice-Pres. for Business and Finance: DALE LARSON

Vice-Pres. for Operations: ROBERT RIGGS

Vice-Pres. for Student Services and Dean for Students: Dr ROBERT GARIPPA

Dir for Admissions: JOSHUA BLEEKER

Dir for Library: MARVIN HUNN

Library of 303,000 vols (incl. 215,000 print vols, 59,000 microforms, 29,000 audiovisual items)

Number of students: 2,024

Publications: *Bibliotheca Sacra*, *Kindred Spirit* (3 a year), *Veritas* (5 a year).

EAST TEXAS BAPTIST UNIVERSITY

1 Tiger Dr., Marshall, TX 75670-1498

Telephone: (903) 935-7963

Fax: (903) 923-2001

E-mail: admissions@etbu.edu

Internet: www.etbu.edu

Founded 1912 as College of Marshall, present name and status 1984

Private control

Academic year: August to May

Pres.: Dr SAMUEL W. OLIVER

Provost and Vice-Pres. for Academic Affairs: Dr SHERILYN EMBERTON

Vice-Pres. for Admin. and Finance: NED CALVERT

Vice-Pres. for Enrolment Management and Marketing: VINCE BLANKENSHIP

Vice-Pres. for Student Affairs: Dr DENNIS ROBERTSON

Vice-Pres. for Univ. Advancement: CATHERINE A. CRAWFORD

Registrar: CHRIS WOOD

Librarian: Dr CYNTHIA L. PETERSON

Library of 96,393 vols, 97,806 e-books, 15,175 serials, 22,458 e-journals, 41,458 audiovisual items

Number of teachers: 55

Number of students: 1,200

DEANS

School of Business: Dr SCOTT RAY

School of Christian Studies: Dr JOHN L. HARRIS

School of Education: Dr DONNA HARRELL LUBCKER

School of Fine Arts: Dr THOMAS R. WEBSTER

School of Humanities: Dr JERRY L. SUMMERS

School of Natural and Social Science: Dr LYNN NEW

School of Nursing: Dr ELLEN FINEOUT-OVERHOLT

FISHER MORE COLLEGE

3020 Lubbock Ave, Fort Worth, TX 76109

Telephone: (817) 923-8459

Fax: (817) 394-2340

E-mail: admissions@cstm.edu

Internet: www.fishermore.edu

Founded 1981 as Saint Thomas More Institute, present name 2012

Private control

Academic year: September to May

Liberal arts college

Pres.: Dr MICHAEL G. KING

Dean for College: Dr RYAN DOUGLAS MADISON

Dir for Admissions and Financial Aid: JUSTIN NELSON

Dir for Devt: Dr RAYMOND PFANG

Dir for Enrolment Management: PETER CAPANI

Dir for Student Life: SHANTI GUY

Registrar: JOHN HEITZENRATER

Library of 14,451 vol, 543 audiovisual items.

GRADUATE INSTITUTE OF APPLIED LINGUISTICS (GIAL)

7500 W Camp, Wisdom Rd, Dallas, TX 75236

Telephone: (972) 708-7340

Fax: (972) 708-7292

E-mail: info@gial.edu

Internet: www.gial.edu

Founded 1998

Private control

Academic year: July to June

Pres.: Dr DAVID A. ROSS

Vice-Pres. for Finance: DOUGLAS W. MADDOCKS

Dean for Academic Affairs: Dr DOUG TIFFIN

Dean for Students: RUTH E. SCHILBERG

Dir for Admissions: MAGGIE JOHNSON

Dir for Devt: ROD BROWN

Chief Financial Officer: ROD JENKINS

Registrar: LYNNE M. LAMIMAN

Dir for Library: FERNE WEIMER

Library of 49,000 vols

Publication: *GIALens: Electronic Notes Series* (3 a year).

HARDIN-SIMMONS UNIVERSITY

2200 Hickory, Abilene, TX 79698

Telephone: (325) 670-1000

Fax: (325) 671-2157

Internet: www.hsutx.edu

Founded 1891 as Simmons College, present name 1934

Private control

Academic year: August to May (2 semesters)

Pres.: LANNY HALL

Provost and Chief Academic Officer: Dr THOMAS BRISCO

Sr Vice-Pres. for Finance and Management: HAROLD R. PRESTON

Sr Vice-Pres. for Student Devt: Dr MIKE WHITEHORN

Vice-Pres. for Enrolment Management and Marketing Management: Dr SHANE DAVIDSON

Vice-Pres. for Institutional Advancement: MIKE HAMMACK

Registrar: KACEY HIGGINS

Dean for Univ. Libraries: ALICE W. SPECHT

Library of 337,596 vols

Number of teachers: 202 (138 full-time, 64 part-time)

Number of students: 2,358 (1,891 undergraduate, 467 graduate)

Publications: *Range Rider* (2 a year), *The Bronco* (1 a year)

DEANS

Cynthia Ann Parker College of Liberal Arts: Prof. Dr ALAN STAFFORD

Holland School of Sciences and Mathematics: Prof. Dr CHRISTOPHER L. MCNAIR

Irvin School of Education: Dr PAMELA K. WILLIFORD

Kelley College of Business: Dr MICHAEL L. MONHOLLON

Logsdon School of Theology: Dr DON WILLIFORD

Logsdon Seminary: Dr DONALD D. WILLIFORD

School of Music and Fine Arts: Dr ROBERT BROOKS

HOUSTON BAPTIST UNIVERSITY

7502 Fondren Rd, Houston, TX 77074-3298

Telephone: (281) 649-3000

Fax: (281) 649-3701

E-mail: admissions@hbu.edu

Internet: www.hbu.edu

Founded 1960 as Houston Baptist College, present name 1973

Private control

Academic year: August to May

Pres.: Dr ROBERT B. SLOAN, JR

Provost: Dr ROBERT STACEY

Vice-Pres. for Advancement: CHARLES BACARISSE

Vice-Pres. for Enrolment Management: JAMES STEEN

Vice-Pres. for Financial Operations: SANDY MOONEY

Vice-Pres. for Univ. Communications: R. KIMBERLY GAYNOR

Vice-Pres. for Univ. Relations: SHARON SAUNDERS

Dir for Student Life: WHITTINGTON GOODWIN

Registrar: ERINN HUGHES

Dean for Library: ANN NOBLE

Library of 300,000 vols, 100,000 e-books, 60,000 e-journals

Number of teachers: 227

Number of students: 2,597

DEANS

College of Arts and Humanities: Dr CHRISTOPHER HAMMONS

College of Science and Mathematics: Dr DORIS WARREN

Graduate School: Dr MOHAN KURUVILLA

Honors College: Dr ROBERT STACEY

School of Business: Dr MOHAN KURUVILLA

School of Education: Dr D. R. WILSON (acting)

School of Nursing and Allied Health: Dr MARGARET UGALDE

HOWARD PAYNE UNIVERSITY

1000 Fisk St, Brownwood, TX 76801

Telephone: (325) 649-8020

Fax: (325) 649-8901

E-mail: enroll@hputx.edu

Internet: www.hputx.edu

Founded 1889 as Howard Payne College, present name 1974

Private control

Academic year: August to May

Pres.: Dr WILLIAM N. ELLIS

Provost and Chief Academic Officer: Dr WILLIAM MARK TEW

Sr Vice-Pres. for Finance and Admin.: BRENDA J. MCLENDON
Sr Vice-Pres. for Institutional Advancement: Dr BRAD JOHNSON
Vice-Pres. for Devt: PAUL A. DUNNE
Vice-Pres. for Student Life and Dean for Students: Dr BRENT A. MARSH
Registrar: LANA WAGNER
Dean for Libraries: NANCY ANDERSON

Library of 116,667 vols
Number of teachers: 123
Number of students: 1,400

DEANS

Advising and General Education: Dr WENDY MCNEELEY
School of Business: Dr LESLIE PLAGENS
School of Christian Studies: Dr DONNIE AUVENSHINE
School of Education: Dr MICHAEL ROSATO
School of Humanities: Dr JUSTIN MURPHY
School of Music and Fine Arts and Extended Education: Dr ROBERT TUCKER
School of Science and Mathematics: Dr LYNN LITTLE

HUSTON-TILLOTSON UNIVERSITY

900 Chicon St, Austin, TX 78702-2795
Telephone: (512) 505-3000
Fax: (512) 505-3190
E-mail: admission@htu.edu
Internet: www.htu.edu
Founded 1952 by merger of Samuel Huston College (f. 1876) with Tillotson College (f. 1875), present name 2005
Private control
Academic year: July to June
Pres.: Dr LARRY L. EARVIN
Provost and Vice-Pres. for Academic and Student Affairs: Dr VICKI VERNON LOTT
Vice-Pres. for Admin. and Finance: VALERIE D. HILL
Vice-Pres. for Institutional Advancement: Dr RODERICK L. SMOTHERS
Dean for Enrolment Management: Dr B. SHERRANCE RUSSELL
Dean for Student Affairs: EDMUND GRAHAM
Registrar: EARNESTINE STRICKLAND
Dir for Library and Media Services: PATRICIA WILKINS

Library of 97,000 vols
Number of teachers: 81
Number of students: 950

DEANS

College of Arts and Sciences: Dr MICHAEL HIRSCH
School of Business and Technology: Dr STEVEN EDMOND

JARVIS CHRISTIAN COLLEGE

POB 1470, Highway 80E, Private Rd 7631, Hawkins, TX 75765-1470
Telephone: (903) 730-4890
Fax: (903) 730-4893
Internet: www.jarvis.edu
Founded 1912 as Jarvis Christian Institute, present name 1950
Private control
Academic year: August to May
Areas of study: art, biology, business administration, chemistry, computer information systems, criminal justice, English, environmental science, history, kinesiology, mathematics, music, professional education/teacher certification, psychology, religion, social work, sociology, Spanish, speech
Pres.: Dr LESTER C. NEWMAN
Vice-Pres. for Academic Affairs: Dr MARTIN YALE
Vice-Pres. for Admin. and Finance: REGINALD DICKENS

Dir for Library: RODNEY ATKINS
Registrar: AUTRY ACREY.

LETOURNEAU UNIVERSITY

POB 7001, Longview, TX 75607
2100 S Mobberly Ave, Longview, TX 75602
Telephone: (903) 233-4300
Fax: (903) 233-4301
E-mail: admissions@letu.edu
Internet: www.letu.edu
Founded 1946 as LeTourneau Technical Institute, present name and status 1989
Private control
Academic year: August to May
Campuses in Austin, Bedford, Dallas, Houston, Tyler
Pres.: Dr DALE A. LUNSFORD
Provost and Exec. Vice-Pres.: Dr PHILIP A. COYLE
Exec. Vice-Pres. for External Relations: (vacant)
Vice-Pres. for Devt: BEN Y. MARCH
Vice-Pres. for Enrolment Services: Dr STEPHEN M. CONDON
Vice-Pres. for Finance and Admin.: MIKE S. HOOD
Vice-Pres. for the School of Graduate and Professional Studies: Dr CAROL C. GREEN
Dean for Faculty and Assoc. Provost: Dr STEVEN D. MASON
Dean for Students: COREY R. ROSS
Registrar: GINGER MOORE
Dir for Library: LINDA PRICE

Library of 76,495 vols, 52,058 e-books, 13,017 e-periodical titles, 688 microform titles, 181 serial subscriptions
Number of students: 76 (full-time)
Number of students: 2,950

DEANS

School of Aeronautical Science: Prof. Dr FRED RITCHEY, JR
School of Arts and Sciences: Dr LARRY J. FRAZIER
School of Business: Prof. Dr BOB WHARTON
School of Education: Dr WAYNE J. JACOBS
School of Engineering and Engineering Technology: Dr RONALD A. DELAP

LUBBOCK CHRISTIAN UNIVERSITY

5601 19th St, Lubbock, TX 79407
Telephone: (806) 720-7151
Fax: (806) 720-7162
E-mail: admissions@lcu.edu
Internet: www.lcu.edu
Founded 1957 as Lubbock Christian College, present name and status 1987
Private control
Academic year: August to May
Pres.: Dr L. KEN JONES
Provost and Chief Academic Officer: Dr ROD BLACKWOOD
Exec. Vice-Pres.: Dr BRIAN STARR
Vice-Pres. for Facilities: KEVIN ELMORE
Vice-Pres. for Financial Affairs: TIA CLARY
Vice-Pres. for Univ. Advancement: JOHN KING
Chief Financial Officer: TIA CLARY
Dir for Admissions: CHARLIE WEBB
Registrar: JANICE STONE
Dir for Library: REBECCA VICKERS

Library of 121,889 vols, 50,575 e-books

DEANS

B. Ward Lane College of Professional Studies: Dr STEVE GERMAN
College of Biblical Studies and Behavioral Sciences: Dr JESSE LONG
J. E. and Eileen Hancock College of Liberal Arts and Education: Dr SUSAN BLASSINGAME

McMURRY UNIVERSITY

POB 278, 1 McMurry Station, Abilene, TX 79697
Telephone: (325) 793-3800
E-mail: admissions@mcm.edu
Internet: www.mcm.edu
Founded 1923 as McMurry College, present name 1990
Private control
Academic year: August to May
Pres.: Dr JOHN H. RUSSELL
Vice-Pres. for Academic Affairs: Dr PAUL FABRIZIO
Vice-Pres. for Devt: DEBRA HULSE
Vice-Pres. for Financial Affairs: LISA WILLIAMS
Vice-Pres. for Information and Support Services: BRAD POORMAN
Vice-Pres. for Institutional Advancement: STEVE CRISMAN
Dean for Students: VANESSA ROBERTS
Registrar: CAROLYN CALVERT
Dir for Library: TERRY YOUNG

Library of 150,000 vols, 240 journals, magazines and newspapers
Number of teachers: 119
Number of students: 1,400

DEANS

School of Arts and Letters: Dr CHRISTINA H. WILSON
School of Business: Dr K. O. LONG
School of Education: Dr PERRY KAY HALEY BROWN
School of Natural and Computational Sciences: Dr ALICIA WYATT
School of Social Sciences and Religion: Dr PHILIP LEMASTERS

MIDLAND COLLEGE

3600 N Garfield, Midland, TX 79705
Telephone: (432) 685-4500
Fax: (432) 685-6401
E-mail: president@midland.edu
Internet: www.midland.edu
Founded 1969
State control
Academic year: August to May (2 semesters)
Pres.: Dr STEVE THOMAS
Exec. Vice-Pres.: RICHARD JOLLY
Vice-Pres. for Administrative Services: RICK BENDER
Vice-Pres. for Information Technology and Facilities: DENNIS SEVER
Vice-Pres. for Instruction: REX PEEBLES
Vice-Pres. for Student Services: RITA NELL DIFFIE
Dean for Enrolment Management: MICHAEL CHAVEZ
Registrar: ANGELA BALCH

Library of 62,000 vols, 300 magazine, journal and newspaper subscriptions
Number of teachers: 154 (full-time)
Number of students: 7,425

Publication: *Chaparral* (1 a year)

DEANS

Adult and Developmental Education: LYNDA WEBB
Business Studies: GAVIN FRANTZ
Distance Learning and Continuing Education: DALE BEIKIRCH
Fine Arts and Communications: WILLIAM FEELER
Health Sciences: BECKY HAMMACK
Mathematics and Sciences: MARGARET WADE
Social and Behavioral Sciences and Education Studies: WILLIAM MORRIS
Technical Studies: CURT PERVIER

MIDWESTERN STATE UNIVERSITY

3410 Taft Blvd, Wichita Falls, TX 76308
Telephone: (940) 397-4000
Fax: (940) 397-4672
E-mail: admissions@mwsu.edu
Internet: www.mwsu.edu
Founded 1922 as Wichita Falls Jr College, present name 1975
State control
Academic year: August to May (2 semesters)
Pres.: Dr JESSE W. ROGERS
Provost: ALISA R. WHITE
Vice-Pres. for Admin. and Finance: JUAN SANDOVAL
Vice-Pres. for Admin. and Institutional Effectiveness: Dr ROBERT E. CLARK
Vice-Pres. for Business Affairs and Finance: JUAN SANDOVAL
Vice-Pres. for Student Affairs and Enrolment Management: Dr KEITH LAMB
Vice-Pres. for Univ. Advancement and Public Affairs: Dr HOWARD FARRELL
Dean for Students: DAIL NEELY
Dir for Admissions: BARBARA MERKLE
Registrar: DARLA INGLISH
Librarian: CLARA LATHAM
Library of 900,000 vols
Number of teachers: 229 (full-time)
Number of students: 6,182 (5,465 undergraduate, 717 graduate)
Publications: *Faculty Forum Papers* (1 a year), *The Wai-Kun* (1 a year), *The Wichitan* (52 a year), *Voices* (1 a year)

DEANS

College of Health Sciences and Human Services: Dr PATTI HAMILTON
College of Science and Mathematics: Dr LYNN LITTLE
Dillard College of Business Administration: Dr BARBARA NEMECEK
Gordon T. and Ellen West College of Education: MATTHEW CAPPS
Graduate School: DEVAH SCHOLL
Lamar D. Fain College of Fine Arts: Prof. RON FISCHLI
Prothro-Yeager College of Humanities and Social Sciences: SAMUEL WATSON, III

OBLATE SCHOOL OF THEOLOGY

285 Oblate Dr., San Antonio, TX 78216-6693
Telephone: (210) 341-1366
Fax: (210) 341-4519
E-mail: info@ost.edu
Internet: www.ost.edu
Founded 1903 as San Antonio Philosophical and Theological Seminary
Private control
Pres.: Fr RONALD ROLHEISER
Academic Dean: Dr R. SCOTT WOODWARD
Exec. Vice-Pres.: Rev. WARREN BROWN
Vice-Pres. for Admin. Affairs: Rev. DAVID KALERT
Vice-Pres. for Finance: RENE ESPINOSA
Vice-Pres. for Institutional Advancement: LEA KOCHANEK
Registrar and Dir for Admissions: JAMES OBERHAUSEN
Dir for Library: MARIA M. GARCIA.

OUR LADY OF THE LAKE UNIVERSITY

411 SW 24th St, San Antonio, TX 78207
Telephone: (210) 434-6711
Fax: (210) 431-4036
E-mail: registrar@lake.ollusa.edu
Internet: www.ollusa.edu
Founded 1895
Private control
Academic year: August to May
Campuses in Harlingen, Houston

Pres.: Dr TESSA MARTINEZ POLLACK
Exec. Vice-Pres.: Dr DAVID C. ESTES
Vice-Pres. for Academic Affairs: Dr HELEN J. STREUBERT
Vice-Pres. for Enrolment Management: MICHAEL ACOSTA
Vice-Pres. for Finance and Facilities: ALLEN KLAUS
Vice-Pres. for Institutional Advancement: DAN YOXALL
Vice-Pres. for Student Life: JACK HANK
Dean for Library: JUDY LARSON
Library of 254,419 vols
Number of teachers: 114 (full-time)
Number of students: 2,660 (1,595 undergraduate, 1,065 graduate)

DEANS

College of Arts and Sciences: Dr ROGER V. BENNETT
School of Business and Leadership: Dr ROBERT BISKING
School of Professional Studies: Dr ROBERT BISKING

PARKER UNIVERSITY

2540 Walnut Hill Lane, Dallas, TX 75229
Telephone: (972) 438-6932
Fax: (214) 902-2413
E-mail: future@parker.edu
Internet: www.parker.edu
Founded 1982 as Parker College of Chiropractic, present name 2011
Private control
Academic year: January to December
Areas of study: anatomy, chiropractic, health and wellness
Pres.: Dr FABRIZIO MANCINI
Provost: Dr GERY HOCHANADEL
Vice-Pres. for Academics: Dr KENNETH C. THOMAS
Vice-Pres. for Business Affairs: DAVID GARAFOLA
Vice-Pres. for Devt: JOLYNNE JENSEN
Vice-Pres. for Finance: DAVID GARAFOLA
Vice-Pres. for Research, Wellness Centres, Seminars and Continuing Education: Dr GILLES LAMARCHE
Dean for Enrolment Services: LYNN NASATO
Dean for Student Affairs: VICTOR BALLESTEROS
Registrar: JUDITH VERGARA
Library of 16,000 vols, 33,000 e-books
Number of students: 847

PATTY HANKS SHELTON SCHOOL OF NURSING

2149 Hickory St, Abilene, TX 79601
Telephone: (325) 671-2399
Fax: (325) 671-2386
Internet: www.phssn.edu; attached to Abilene Christian Univ., Hardin-Simmons Univ. and McMurry Univ.
Private control
Offers Bachelor and Master of science in family nurse practitioner, nursing
Dean: Dr NINA OUIMETTE
Graduate Dir: Prof. Dr AMY TOONE
Undergraduate Dir: Dr INDIRA D. TYLER.

PAUL QUINN COLLEGE

3837 Simpson-Stuart Rd, Dallas, TX 75241
Telephone: (214) 376-1000
Fax: (214) 379-5516
E-mail: admissions@pqc.edu
Internet: www.pqc.edu
Founded 1872
Private control
Academic year: August to May

Depts of business and legal studies, education, general education, science and technology
Pres.: MICHAEL J. SORRELL
Exec. Vice-Pres.: Dr HOMERO LOPEZ
Vice-Pres. for Academic Affairs: Dr KIZU-WANDA GRANT
Chief Operating Officer: ANTWANE OWENS
Dean for Students: KELSEL THOMPSON
Dir for Enrolment Management: EDDIE FRANCIS
Registrar: BEVERLY SMITH
Dir for Library: CLARICE P. MEDLEY-WEEKS
Library of 51,000 vols
Number of teachers: 48
Number of students: 780
Publication: *Paul Quinn Gazette*.

RICE UNIVERSITY

POB 1892, Houston, TX 77251-1892
6100 Main St, Houston, TX 77005-1827
Telephone: (713) 348-0000
Fax: (713) 348-5010
E-mail: info@rice.edu
Internet: www.rice.edu
Founded 1891 as The Rice Institute
Private control
Pres.: DAVID W. LEEBRON
Provost: GEORGE L. McLENDON
Vice-Pres. and Gen. Counsel: RICHARD A. ZANSITIS
Vice-Pres. for Admin.: KEVIN E. KIRBY
Vice-Pres. for Enrolment: CHRIS MUÑOZ
Vice-Pres. for Finance: KATHY COLLINS
Vice-Pres. for Public Affairs: LINDA L. THRANE
Vice-Pres. for Resource Devt: DARROW ZEIDENSTEIN
Registrar: DAVID TENNEY
Vice-Provost and Univ. Librarian: SARA LOWMAN
Library of 2,570,000 vols, 68,000 e-books, 72,000 journal subscriptions, 3,276,000 units of microform
Number of teachers: 1,112 (670 full-time, 108 part-time, 334 adjunct)
Number of students: 6,082 (3,708 undergraduate, 2,374 graduate)
Publications: *Close Up, Baker Institute Report, Environmental Toxicology and Chemistry, Feminist Economics, Houston Area Survey* (1 a year), *Jones Journal* (2 a year), *Journal of Southern History* (4 a year), *Macrocosm, Rice Magazine, Rice University Studies* (4 a year), *Studies in English Literature 1500–1900* (4 a year), *The Sarmatian Review* (3 a year)

DEANS

George R. Brown School of Engineering: NED THOMAS
Graduate and Postdoctoral Studies: Dr PAULA SANDERS
Jesse H. Jones Graduate School of Management: WILLIAM GLICK
School of Architecture: SARAH WHITING
School of Humanities: NICOLAS SHUMWAY
School of Social Sciences: LYN RAGSDALE
Shepherd School of Music: ROBERT YEKOVICH
Susanne M. Glasscock School of Continuing Studies: Dr MARY B. McINTIRE
Undergraduate Education: Dr JOHN S. HUTCHINSON
Wiess School of Natural Sciences: DANIEL D. CARSON

PROFESSORS

AAZHANG, B., Electrical and Computer Engineering
AKIN, J. E., Mechanical Engineering
ALCOVER, M., French
ALFORD, J. R., Political Science
AMBLER, J. S., Political Science

ANDERSON, J. B., Earth Science
ANTOULAS, A. C., Electrical and Computer Engineering
ARESU, B., French Studies
ARMENIADES, C. D., Chemical Engineering
ATHANASIOU, A., Bioengineering
AVE-LALLEMANT, H. G., Earth Science
BAGOZZI, R., Management
BAKER, S. D., Physics and Astronomy
BARRON, A., Chemistry
BAYAZITOGLU, Y., Mechanical Engineering and Materials Science
BECKINGHAM, K., Biochemistry and Cell Biology
BEDIENT, P. B., Civil and Environmental Engineering
BENNETT, G., Biochemistry and Cell Biology
BILLUPS, W. E., Chemistry
BLACK, E., Political Science
BOLES, J. B., History
BONNER, B. E., Physics and Astronomy
BOSHERNITZAN, M., Mathematics
BRACE, P., Political Science
BRITO, D. L., Economics
BRODY, B. A., Philosophy
BROKER, K. L., Art and Art History
BROOKS, P. R., Chemistry
BROWN, B. W., Economics and Statistics
BROWN, J. N., Economics
BRYANT, J., Economics
BURRUS, C. S., Electrical and Computer Engineering
BUYSE, L., Music
CAMFIELD, W. A., Art and Art History
CANNADY, W. T., Architecture
CARROLL, M. M., Computational and Applied Mathematics
CARTWRIGHT, R. S., Computer Science
CASBARIAN, J. J., Architecture
CASTAÑEDA, J. A., Hispanic and Classical Studies
CHANCE, J., English
CHAPMAN, W. G., Chemical Engineering
CITRON, M., Music
CLARK, J. W., Jr, Electrical and Computer Engineering
CLOUTIER, P. A., Physics and Astronomy
COCHRAN, T., Mathematics
COOPER, K. D., Computer Science
CORCORAN, M., Physics and Astronomy
COX, D., Statistics
COX, S. G., Philosophy
COX, S. J., Computational and Applied Mathematics
CROWELL, S. G., Philosophy
CURL, R. F., Jr, Chemistry
CUTHBERTSON, G. M., Political Science
DAVIDSON, C., Sociology
DAVIS, P. W., Linguistics
DHARAN, B. G., Management
DIPBOYE, R., Psychology
DOODY, T., English
DRISKILL, L., English
DUCK, I., Physics and Astronomy
DUFOUR, R. J., Physics and Astronomy
DUNHAM, J. F., Music
DUNNING, F. B., Physics and Astronomy
DURRANI, A. J., Civil and Environmental Engineering
EIFLER, M., German and Slavic Studies
EL-GAMAL, M., Economics
ELLISON, P., Music
ENGEL, P. S., Chemistry
ENGELHARDT, T., Philosophy
ENSOR, K. B., Statistics
FARWELL, J., Music
FELLEISEN, M., Computer Science
FEW, A., Physics and Astronomy
FISCHER, N., Music
FISHER, F. M., Jr, Ecology and Evolutionary Biology
FORMAN, R., Mathematics
GEORGE, J., Management
GLANTZ, R. M., Biochemistry and Cell Biology
GLASS, G. P., Chemistry
GOLDMAN, R. N., Computer Science

GOLDSMITH, K., Music
GOMER, R. H., Biochemistry and Cell Biology
GONZÁLEZ-STEPHEN, B., Hispanic and Classical Studies
GORDON, R., Earth Science
GORRY, G. A., Management
GOTTSCHALK, A. W., Music
GOUX, J., French
GRANDY, R. E., Philosophy
GROB, A., English
GRUBER, I. D., History
HALAS, N., Electrical and Computer Engineering
HAMM, K. E., Political Science
HANNON, J. P., Physics and Astronomy
HARCOMBE, P., Ecology and Environmental Biology
HARDT, R. M., Mathematics
HARTLEY, P. R., Economics
HARVEY, F. R., Mathematics
HASKELL, T., History
HEMPEL, J., Mathematics
HIGHTOWER, J. W., Chemical Engineering
HILL, T. W., Physics and Astronomy
HIRASAKI, G., Chemical Engineering
HOLLOWAY, C., Music
HUANG, H. W., Physics and Astronomy
HUFFER, L., French Studies
HUGHES, J. B., Civil and Environmental Engineering
HULET, R., Physics and Astronomy
HUSTON, J. D., English
HUTCHINSON, J. S., Chemistry
IAMMARINO, N., Kinesiology
ISLE, W., English
JOHNSON, D. H., Electrical and Computer Engineering
JONES, B. F., Mathematics
JUMP, J. R., Electrical and Computer Engineering
KANATAS, G., Administrative Science
KAUN, K., Music
KELBER, W. H., Religious Studies
KENNEDY, K. W., Jr, Computer Science
KIMMEL, M., Statistics
KINSEY, J. L., Chemistry
KLEIN, A., Religious Studies
KLINEBERG, S. L., Sociology
KONISKY, J., Biochemistry and Cell Biology
KULSTAD, M., Philosophy
LANE, N., Physics and Astronomy
LEE, B., Anthropology
LEEMAN, W. P., Earth Science
LEVANDA, R. A., Music
LEVANDER, A. R., Earth Science
LIANG, E., Physics and Astronomy
LUCA, S., Music
MCINTIRE, L. V., Chemical Engineering
MCINTOSH, R. J., Anthropology
MCINTOSH, S. K., Anthropology
MCLELLAN, R. B., Materials Science
MANCA, J., Art and Art History
MARCUS, G. E., Anthropology
MARGRAVE, J. L., Chemistry
MARTIN, R. C., Psychology
MARTIN, W. C., Sociology
MATUSOW, A., History
MICHIE, H., English
MIESZKOWSKI, P., Economics
MIETTINEN, H. E., Physics and Astronomy
MIKOS, A., Bioengineering
MILLER, C. A., Chemical Engineering
MORGAN, T. C., Political Science
MORRIS, W. A., English
MORRISON, D. R., Philosophy
MOULIN, H. M., Economics
MUTCHLER, G. S., Physics and Astronomy
NAPIER, H. A., Management
NELSON, D., French Studies
NORDLANDER, P., Physics and Astronomy
ODHIAMBO, A., History
OLSON, J. S., Biochemistry
ORCHARD, M. T., Electrical and Computer Engineering
OSHERSON, D., Psychology
PARKER, J. K., Music

PARRY, R. J., Chemistry
PATTEN, R. L., English
POLKING, J. C., Mathematics
POULOS, B., Art and Art History
QUELLER, D. C., Ecology and Evolutionary Biology
RACHLEFF, L., Music
RAU, C., Physics and Astronomy
REIFF, P., Physics and Astronomy
ROBERT, M., Chemical Engineering
ROBERTS, J. B., Physics and Astronomy
ROJO, J., Statistics
ROUX, R., Music
RUDOLPH, F. B., Biochemistry and Cell Biology
SAN, K. Y., Bioengineering
SASS, R. L., Ecology and Evolutionary Biology
SAWYER, D., Earth Science
SCHNEIDER, D. J., Psychology
SCHNOEBELEN, A. M., Music
SCOTT, D. W., Statistics
SCUSERIA, G., Chemistry
SEED, P., History
SEMMES, S. W., Mathematics
SHER, G., Philosophy
SHIBATANI, M., Linguistics
SICKLES, R., Economics
SKURA, M., English
SMALLEY, R. E., Chemistry
SMITH, G., Art and Art History
SMITH, G. W., Economics
SMITH, R. J., History
SNOW, E. A., English
SOLIGO, R., Economics
SORENSEN, D. C., Computational and Applied Mathematics
SPANOS, P. D., Mechanical Engineering and Materials Science
SPENCE, D. W., Kinesiology
STEIN, R., Political Science
STEVENSON, P. M., Physics and Astronomy
STEWART, C. R., Biochemistry and Cell Biology
STOKES, G., History
STOLL, R. J., Political Science
STRASSMAN, J., Ecology and Evolutionary Biology
STRONG, R., Mathematics
STROUP, J. M., Religious Studies
SYMES, W. W., Computational and Applied Mathematics
TALWANI, M., Earth Science
TAPIA, R. A., Computational and Applied Mathematics
TAYLOR, J., Anthropology
TAYLOR, R. N., Management
TEZDUYAR, T. E., Mechanical Engineering and Materials Science
THOMPSON, E. M., German and Slavic Studies
THOMPSON, J. R., Statistics
TITTEL, F., Electrical and Computer Engineering
TOMSON, M. B., Civil and Environmental Engineering
TOUR, J., Chemistry
TYLER, S. A., Anthropology
UECKER, W. C., Management
VARDI, M. Y., Computer Science
VEECH, W. A., Mathematics
VELETSOS, A. S., Civil and Environmental Engineering
WARD, C. H., Civil and Environmental Engineering
WARREN, J. D., Computer Science
WATKINS, M. J., Psychology
WEISMAN, R. B., Chemistry
WEISSENBERGER, K. H., German and Slavic Studies
WESTBROOK, R. A., Management
WHITAKER, G., Management
WHITMIRE, K. H., Chemistry
WIENER, M. J., History
WIESNER, M., Civil and Environmental Engineering
WILLIAMS, E. E., Management
WILSON, L. J., Chemistry

WILSON, R. K., Political Science
WILSON, W. L., Electrical and Computer Engineering
WINDSOR, D., Management
WINKLER, K., Music
WINNINGHAM, G. L., Art and Art History
WITTENBERG, G., Architecture
WOLF, M., Mathematics
WOLF, R. A., Physics and Astronomy
WOOD, S., English
WYSCHOGROD, E., Religious Studies
YOUNG, J. F., Electrical and Computer Engineering
YUNIS, H., Hispanic and Classical Studies
ZAMMITO, J. H., History
ZEFF, S. A., Management
ZODROW, G., Economics
ZWAENEPOEL, W., Computer Science
ZYGOURAKIS, K., Chemical Engineering

SCHREINER UNIVERSITY

2100 Memorial Blvd, Kerrville, TX 78028
Telephone: (830) 896-5411
Fax: (830) 792-7226
E-mail: admissions@schreiner.edu
Internet: www.schreiner.edu

Founded 1923 as Schreiner College, present name 2001
Private control
Academic year: August to May
Pres.: Dr TIM SUMMERLIN
Provost and Vice-Pres. for Academic Affairs: Dr CHARLIE McCORMICK
Vice-Pres. for Admin. and Finance: BILL MUSE
Vice-Pres. for Advancement and Public Affairs: MARK TUSCHAK
Vice-Pres. for Enrolment and Student Services: PEG LAYTON
Dean for Admissions and Financial Aid: SANDY SPEED
Registrar: DARLENE BANNISTER
Dir for Library: Dr CANDICE SCOTT
Library of 83,000 vols, 200 periodical subscriptions, 10,000 e-journals, 30,000 e-books
Number of teachers: 117
Number of students: 1,117
Publication: *Scene* (2 a year)

DEANS

Cailloux School of Professional Studies: Dr DAVID SMITH
School of Liberal Arts: Dr WILLIAM WOODS
Trull School of Sciences and Math: Dr DIANA COMUZZIE

SEMINARY OF THE SOUTHWEST

POB 2247, Austin, TX 78768
501 East 32nd, Austin, TX 78705
Telephone: (512) 472-4133
Fax: (512) 472-3098
E-mail: seminary@ssw.edu
Internet: www.ssw.edu

Founded 1951 as Episcopal Theological Seminary, present name 2008
Private control
Academic year: August to May
Pres. and Dean: Very Rev. Dr DOUGLAS TRAVIS
Exec. Vice-Pres. of Admin. and Finance: JOHN BENNET WATERS
Vice-Pres. for Advancement: TARA HOLLEY (acting)
Vice-Pres. of Devt: NANCY SPRINGER-BALDWIN
Academic Dean: CYNTHIA BRIGGS KITTREDGE
Exec. Dir for Enrolment: JENNIELLE STROTHER
Registrar: MADELYN SNODGRASS
Dir for Library: Dr DONALD E. KEENEY
Library of 100,000 vols, 1,000 periodicals, 10,000 e-serial titles

Number of students: 117

SOUTH TEXAS COLLEGE

POB 9701, McAllen, TX 78502-9701
3201 W Pecan, McAllen, TX 78501
Telephone: (956) 872-8311
Fax: (956) 872-6461
Internet: www.southtexascollege.edu

Founded 1993
State control
Academic year: August to May
Campuses in Weslaco and Rio Grande City
Pres.: Dr SHIRLEY A. REED
Vice-Pres. for Academic Affairs: JUAN E. MEJIA
Vice-Pres. for Finance and Admin. Services: DIANA A. PENA
Vice-Pres. for Student Affairs and Enrollment Management: Dr WILLIAM SERRATA
Dir for Admissions and Registrar: MATTHEW HEBBARD
Dean for Library Services and Instructional Technologies: NOEMI GARZA
Library of 140,000 vols
Number of students: 28,000

DEANS

Division of Business and Technology: MARIO REYNA
Division of Liberal Arts and Social Sciences: Dr MARGARETHA E. BISCHOFF
Division of Math and Science: Dr ALI ESMAEILI
Division of Nursing Allied Health: Dr MELBA TREVINO

SOUTH TEXAS COLLEGE OF LAW

1303 San Jacinto St, Houston, TX 77002-7000
Telephone: (713) 659-8040
Fax: (713) 646-2909
E-mail: admissions@stcl.edu
Internet: www.stcl.edu

Founded 1923 as South Texas School of Law, present name 1945
Private control
Academic year: August to May
Pres. and Dean: DONALD J. GUTER
Exec. Vice-Pres.: Prof. HELEN BISHOP JENKINS
Sr Vice-Pres. and Chief Financial Officer: GREGORY A. BROTHERS
Vice-Pres. and Assoc. Dean for Academic Admin.: Prof. BRUCE A. McGOVERN
Vice-Pres. and Assoc. Dean for Academic Affairs: Prof. JOHN J. WORLEY
Vice-Pres. for Devt and Alumni Relations: KIM PARKER
Vice-Pres. for Strategic Planning and Institutional Research: Prof. JEFFREY L. RENSBERGER
Dir for Library Services and Vice-Pres.: Prof. DAVID G. COWAN
Library of 500,000 vols
Number of teachers: 55 (full-time)
Number of students: 1,305
Publications: *Construction Law Journal, Currents International Trade Law Journal, Law Review, Texas Journal of Business Law.*

SOUTHERN METHODIST UNIVERSITY

6425 Boaz, Dallas, TX 75205
Telephone: (214) 768-2000
Fax: (214) 768-1001
E-mail: enrol_serv@mail.smu.edu
Internet: www.smu.edu

Founded 1911
Private control
Academic year: August to May

Campuses in Plano (Texas) and Ranchos de Taos (New Mexico)
Pres.: Dr R. GERALD TURNER
Provost and Vice-Pres. for Academic Affairs: Dr PAUL W. LUDDEN
Vice-Pres. for Business and Finance: CHRISTINE C. REGIS
Vice-Pres. for Devt and External Affairs: BRAD E. CHEVES
Vice-Pres. for Exec. Affairs: Dr THOMAS E. BARRY
Vice-Pres. for Legal Affairs and Govt Relations, Gen. Counsel and Univ. Sec.: PAUL WARD
Vice-Pres. for Student Affairs: LORI S. WHITE
Registrar and Exec. Dir for Enrolment Services: JOHN HALL
Dean for Central Univ. Libraries: GILLIAN M. McCOMBS
Library: 3m. vols
Number of teachers: 668 (full-time)
Number of students: 10,938 (6,192 undergraduate, 3,372 graduate)
Publications: *Journal of Air Law and Commerce* (4 a year), *Law and Business Review of the Americas* (4 a year), *SMU Law Review* (4 a year), *SMU Magazine* (2 a year), *SMU Science and Technology Law Review* (3 a year), *Southwest Review* (4 a year), *The International Lawyer* (4 a year)

DEANS

Annette Caldwell Simmons School of Education and Human Development: DAVID J. CHARD
Dedman College of Humanities and Sciences: Dr WILLIAM M. TSUTSUI
Dedman School of Law: JOHN B. ATTANASIO
Edwin L. Cox School of Business: Dr ALBERT W. NIEMI, JR
Lyle School of Engineering: Dr GEOFFREY C. ORSAK
Meadows School of the Arts: Dr JOSÉ ANTONIO BOWEN
Perkins School of Theology: Dr WILLIAM B. LAWRENCE
Research and Graduate Studies: JAMES E. QUICK

SOUTHWESTERN ADVENTIST UNIVERSITY

POB 567, Keene, TX 76059-0567
100 W Hillcrest, Keene, TX 76059
Telephone: (817) 202-6794
Fax: (817) 202-6744
E-mail: enroll@swau.edu
Internet: www.swau.edu

Founded 1893 as Keene Industrial Acad., present name 1996
Private control
Areas of study: biology and geology, business administration, communication, computer science, education, English, history and social sciences, kinesiology, mathematics and physical science, modern languages, music, nursing, psychology, religion
Pres.: ERIC ANDERSON
Vice-Pres. for Academic Admin.: BENJAMIN McARTHUR
Vice-Pres. for Enrolment: ENGA ALMEIDA
Vice-Pres. for Financial Admin.: LARRY GARRETT
Vice-Pres. for Student Services: JAMES
Vice-Pres. for Univ. Advancement: GARY TEMPLE
Registrar: BOB GARDNER
Univ. Librarian: CRISTINA THOMSEN
Library of 100,000 vols, 450 journals and magazines, 27,000 e-books
Number of students: 790

SOUTHWESTERN ASSEMBLIES OF GOD UNIVERSITY (SAGU)

1200 Sycamore St, Waxahachie, TX 75165

Telephone: (972) 937-4010
Fax: (972) 923-0488
E-mail: info@sagu.edu
Internet: www.sagu.edu

Founded 1941 by merger of Southwestern Bible School (f. 1927), Shield of Faith Bible Institute (f. 1931) and Southern Bible College (f. 1931), fmrly as Southwestern Bible Institute, present name 1994
Private control

Pres.: Dr KERMIT S. BRIDGES
Vice-Pres. for Academics: PAUL BROOKS
Vice-Pres. for Advancement: IRBY MCKNIGHT
Vice-Pres. for Business and Finance: JAY TREWERN
Vice-Pres. for Enrolment and Retention: EDDIE DAVIS
Vice-Pres. for Student Services: TERRY PHIPPS
Registrar: HEATHER FRANCIS
Dir for Library: EUGENE HOLDER

Library of 110,000 vols
Number of students: 2,064

DEANS

College of Arts and Professions: LARRY GOOD-RICH
College of Bible and Church Ministries: LEROY BARTEL

SOUTHWESTERN BAPTIST THEOLOGICAL SEMINARY

POB 22000, Fort Worth, TX 76122
2001 W Seminary Dr., Fort Worth, TX 76115

Telephone: (817) 923-1921
Fax: (817) 921-8761
E-mail: presidentsoffice@swbts.edu
Internet: www.swbts.edu

Founded 1901 as part of theological dept at Baylor Univ., present name 1907
Private control
Academic year: August to August (4 semesters)

Pres.: Dr PAIGE PATTERSON
Provost and Exec. Vice-Pres.: CRAIG BLAISING
Vice-Pres. for Business Admin.: KEVIN ENS-LEY
Vice-Pres. for Institutional Advancement: MIKE HUGHES
Vice-Pres. for Student Services and Communications: THOMAS WHITE
Dean for Libraries: BERRY DRIVER

Library of 1,068,877 vols, 35,000 audiovisual items, 2,200 periodical subscriptions
Number of teachers: 117 (full-time)
Number of students: 3,246
Publications: Southwestern Journal of Theology (4 a year), Southwestern News (4 a year)

DEANS

College at Southwestern: Dr STEVEN SMITH
Jack D. Terry, Jr, School of Church and Family Ministries: Dr WAYLAN OWENS
J. Dalton Havard School for Theological Studies: Prof. Dr DENNY AUTREY
Roy Fish School of Evangelism and Missions: Prof. Dr KEITH EITEL
School of Church Music: Dr STEPHEN JOHN-SON
School of Theology: Prof. Dr DAVID L. ALLEN
Southwestern Centre for Extension Education: DERON BILES
William R. Marshall Centre for Theological Studies: RUDY GONZÁLEZ

SOUTHWESTERN CHRISTIAN COLLEGE

POB 10, Terrell, TX 75160

Telephone: (972) 524-3341
Fax: (972) 563-7133
Internet: www.swcc.edu

Founded 1948 as Southern Bible Institute, present name 1949
Private control
Academic year: August to May (2 semesters)
Offers BSc degrees

Pres.: Dr JACK EVANS, SR
Vice-Pres. for Academic Affairs: ZOAANN TURNER
Vice-Pres. for Fiscal Affairs: DOUGLAS HOWIE
Vice-Pres. for Institutional Expansion: Dr JAMES MAXWELL
Vice-Pres. for Student Affairs: Dr BEN FOS-TER
Dir for Admissions: WALTER PRICE
Librarian: DORIS JOHNSON

Library of 26,000 vols, 190 magazines, journals and newspapers
Number of teachers: 21
Number of students: 220

SOUTHWESTERN UNIVERSITY

Telephone: (512) 863-6511
Fax: (512) 863-9601
E-mail: admission@southwestern.edu
Internet: www.southwestern.edu

Founded 1840
Private control
Academic year: August to May

Pres.: JAKE B. SCHRUM
Provost and Dean for the Faculty: Dr JAMES W. HUNT
Vice-Pres. for Enrolment Services: DAVID J. VOSKUIL
Vice-Pres. for Fiscal Affairs: RICHARD L. ANDERSON
Vice-Pres. for Institutional Advancement and Univ. Relations: C. RICHARD MCKEL-VEY
Vice-Pres. for Student Life: Dr GERALD D. BRODY
Registrar: DAVID STONES
Dean for Library Services: LYNNE BRODY

Library of 300,000 vols
Number of teachers: 116
Number of students: 1,372
Publications: The Megaphone (52 a year), Southwestern Magazine (4 a year), The Sou' Wester (1 a year)

DEANS

Brown College of Arts and Sciences: Dr G. BENJAMIN OLIVER
Sarofin School of Fine Arts: Dr PAUL J. GAFFNEY

ST EDWARD'S UNIVERSITY

3001 South Congress Ave, Austin, TX 78704-6489

Telephone: (512) 448-8400
Fax: (512) 448-8492
E-mail: seu.admit@stedwards.edu
Internet: www.stedwards.edu

Founded 1885, present name 1925
Private control
Academic year: August to May
Campus in Angers (France)

Pres.: Dr GEORGE E. MARTIN
Provost and Exec. Vice-Pres.: DONNA M. JURICK
Vice-Pres. for Academic Affairs: Dr BRENDA VALLANCE
Vice-Pres. for Financial Affairs: RHONDA CARTWRIGHT

Vice-Pres. for Information Technology: DAVID WALDRON
Vice-Pres. for Marketing and Enrolment Management: PAIGE BOOTH
Vice-Pres. for Student Affairs: Dr SANDRA PACHECO
Vice-Pres. for Univ. Advancement: MICHAEL F. LARKIN
Dean for Academic Standing: Dr MOLLY E. MINUS
Dean for Admissions: TRACY MANIER
Dean for Graduate and Adult Services: Dr THOMAS M. EVANS
Dir for Campus Min.: Fr RICHARD WILKINSON
Registrar: Dr LANCE R. HAYES
Dir for Library: THOMAS SENNYEY

Library of 215,912 vols
Number of teachers: 497
Number of students: 5,330
Publications: Directions, St. Edward's University Magazine

DEANS

New College: Dr HELENE CAUDILL
School of Behavioural and Social Sciences: RUSSELL FROHARDT
School of Education: Dr GRANT W. SIMPSON, JR
School of Humanities: SHARON NELL
School of Management and Business: Dr MARSHA C. KELLIHER
School of Natural Sciences: Dr THOMAS MITZEL

ST MARY'S UNIVERSITY

1 Camino Santa Maria, San Antonio, TX 78228-8572

Telephone: (210) 436-3011
Fax: (210) 436-3500
E-mail: uadm@stmarytx.edu
Internet: www.stmarytx.edu

Founded 1852
Private control
Academic year: August to May

Pres.: Dr CHARLES L. COTRELL
Provost and Vice-Pres. for Academic Affairs: Dr ANDRÉ HAMPTON (acting)
Vice-Pres. for Admin. and Finance: REBECKAH J. DAY
Vice-Pres. for Enrolment Management: SUZANNE M. PETRUSCH
Vice-Pres. for Student Devt: KATHERINE M. SISOIAN
Vice-Pres. for Univ. Advancement: Dr PAUL T. KETTERING, III
Dean for Students: Dr TIM BESSLER
Registrar: CHRISTINA F. VILLANUEVA
Librarian: H. PALMER HALL

Library of 500,000 vols
Number of teachers: 192 (full-time)
Number of students: 4,105
Publications: St. Mary's Journal on Legal Malpractice and Ethics, St. Mary's Law Journal (4 a year)

DEANS

Bill Greehey School of Business: Dr TANUJA SINGH (acting)
Graduate School: Dr HENRY FLORES
School of Humanities and Social Sciences: Dr JANET B. DIZINNO
School of Law: Dr CHARLES E. CANTÚ
School of Science, Engineering and Technology: Prof. Dr WINSTON EREVELLES

STEPHEN F. AUSTIN STATE UNIVERSITY

1936 North St, Nacogdoches, TX 75962
Telephone: (936) 468-3401
Fax: (936) 468-3849
E-mail: admissions@sfasu.edu
Internet: www.sfasu.edu

Founded 1923 as Stephen F. Austin State Teachers College, present name and status 1969

State control

Academic year: August to May

Pres.: Dr BAKER PATTILLO

Provost and Vice-Pres. for Academic Affairs: Dr RICHARD BERRY

Vice-Pres. for Devt: Dr SID WALKER

Vice-Pres. for Finance and Admin.: DANNY R. GALLANT

Vice-Pres. for Univ. Affairs: Dr STEVE WESTBROOK

Dir of Library: SHIRLEY DICKERSON

Library of 1,465,322 vols

Number of teachers: 743

Number of students: 12,903

DEANS

James I. Perkins College of Education: Dr JUDY A. ABBOTT

College of Fine Arts: Dr A. C. HIMES

Arthur Temple College of Forestry and Agriculture: Dr STEVEN H. BULLARD

College of Liberal and Applied Arts: Dr BRIAN MURPHY (acting)

College of Sciences and Mathematics: Dr KIMBERLY CHILDS

Graduate School: JAMES STANDLEY

Nelson Rusche College of Business: Dr DANNY R. ARNOLD

TEXAS A&M UNIVERSITY SYSTEM

301 Tarrow St, College Station, TX 77840

Telephone: (979) 458-7700

Fax: (979) 458-6025

E-mail: syscomm@tamu.edu

Internet: www.tamus.edu

Founded 1948

Academic year: September to August

Chancellor: Dr JOHN SHARP

Deputy Chancellor for Academic Institutions and Agencies: Dr LEO SAYAVEDRA

Chief Financial Officer and Treas.: GREGORY R. ANDERSON

Vice-Chancellor for Academic Affairs: JAMES HALLMARK

Vice-Chancellor for Agriculture: Dr EDWARD HILER

Vice-Chancellor for Business Services: TOM KALE

Vice-Chancellor for Engineering: Dr C. ROLAND HADEN

Vice-Chancellor for Facilities Planning and Construction: Gen. WESLEY PEEL

Vice-Chancellor for Fed. and State Relations: Dr GUY DIEDRICH

Vice-Chancellor for Research, Planning and Continuing Education: Dr J. CHARLES LEE

Number of students: 120,379.

CONSTITUENT UNIVERSITIES

Prairie View A&M University

POB 519, Prairie View, TX 77446-0519

FM 1098 Rd and University Dr., Prairie View, TX 77446

Telephone: (936) 261-3311

Fax: (409) 857-3928

E-mail: ire@pvamu.edu

Internet: www.pvamu.edu

Founded 1876 as Alta Vista Agriculture and Mechanical College of Texas for Colored Youths, present name and status 1973

Academic year: August to May

Pres.: GEORGE C. WRIGHT

Provost and Sr Vice-Pres. for Academic Affairs: E. JOAHANNE THOMAS-SMITH

Sr Vice-Pres. for Business Affairs: COREY S. BRADFORD

Vice-Pres. for Admin. and Auxiliary Services: FRED E. WASHINGTON

Vice-Pres. for Research: WILLIE F. TROTTY

Vice-Pres. for Student Affairs and Institutional Advancement: LAURETTA F. BYARS

Dir for Devt: NELSON BOWMAN

Registrar: DEBORAH DUNGEY

Dir for Library: Dr ROSIE L. ALBRITTON

Library of 370,000 vols, 700 periodicals, 42,000 e-periodicals, over 30,000 e-books

Number of teachers: 501

Number of students: 8,781

DEANS

College of Agriculture and Human Sciences: Dr FREDDIE L. RICHARDS, SR

College of Business: Dr MUNIR QUDDUS

College of Juvenile Justice and Psychology: Dr DENNIS E. DANIELS

College of Nursing: Dr BETTY N. ADAMS

Graduate School: Dr WILLIE F. TROTTY

Marvin D. and June Samuel Brailsford College of Arts and Sciences: Dr DANNY R. KELLEY

Roy G. Perry College of Engineering and Architecture: Dr KENDALL T. HARRIS

Northwest Houston Center: Dr MICHAEL McFRAZIER

School of Architecture: Dr IKHLAS SABOUNI

Whitlowe R. Green College of Education: Prof. Dr LUCIAN YATES, III

Tarleton State University

POB T-0001, Stephenville, TX 76402

333 W Washington, Stephenville, TX 76402

Telephone: (254) 968-9000

Fax: (254) 968-9920

E-mail: uadm@tarleton.edu

Internet: www.tarleton.edu

Founded 1899 as John Tarleton College, present status 1917, present name 1973

Academic year: September to August

Pres.: Dr F. DOMINIC DOTTAVIO

Provost and Exec. Vice-Pres. for Academic Affairs: Dr KAREN MURRAY

Vice-Pres. for Finance and Admin.: JERRY GRAHAM

Vice-Pres. for Enrolment and Information Management: Dr BRAD CHILTON

Vice-Pres. for Institutional Advancement: Dr RICK RICHARDSON

Vice-Pres. for Student Life and Dean for Students: RUSTY JERGINS

Registrar: DENISE GROVES

Librarian: DONNA SAVAGE

Library: 1m. items

Number of teachers: 942

Number of students: 9,465

DEANS

College of Agricultural and Environmental Sciences: Dr DON CAWTHON

College of Business Administration: Dr ADOLFO BENEVIDAS

College of Education: Dr JILL BURK

College of Graduate Studies: Dr LINDA JONES

College of Liberal and Fine Arts: Dr KELLI STYRON

College of Science and Technology: Dr JAMES PIERCE

Texas A&M Health Science Center (TAMHSC)

8441 State Highway 47, 1 Clinical Bldg , Suite 3100, Bryan, TX 77807

Telephone: (979) 436-9100

Fax: (979) 436-0072

E-mail: registrar@tamhsc.edu

Internet: www.tamhsc.edu

Founded 1999

Academic year: August to May (2 semesters)

Pres.: Dr NANCY W. DICKEY

Exec. Vice-Pres.: Dr ELVIN E. SMITH

Vice-Pres. for Academic Affairs: Dr RODERICK E. McCALLUM

Vice-Pres. for Finance and Admin.: Dr BARRY C. NELSON

Vice-Pres. for Governmental Affairs: Dr JENNY E. JONES

Vice-Pres. for Institutional Advancement and Communications: Dr RUSS GIBBS

Vice-Pres. for Research: Dr DAVID S. CARLSON

Registrar: DANA PENCE

Dir for Medical Sciences Library: GUADALUPE REYES

Library of 32,000 vols, 6,000 e-journals

Number of students: 1,312

DEANS

Baylor College of Dentistry: Dr LAWRENCE WOLINSKY

College of Medicine: Dr THOMAS SHOMAKER

College of Nursing: Dr SHARON WILKERSON

Irma Lerma Rangel College of Pharmacy: Dr INDRA K. REDDY

School of Graduate Studies: Dr CHRISTOPHER COLENDA

School of Rural Public Health: Dr CRAIG H. BLAKELY

Texas A&M International University

5201 University Blvd, Laredo, TX 78041-1900

Telephone: (956) 326-2001

Fax: (956) 326-2346

Internet: www.tamiu.edu

Founded 1970, present status 1989, present name 1993

Languages of instruction: English, Spanish

Academic year: August to August (3 semesters)

Pres.: Dr RAY M. KECK, III

Provost and Vice-Pres. for Academic Affairs: Dr PABLO ARENAZ

Vice-Pres. for Finance and Admin.: JUAN J. CASTILLO, JR

Vice-Pres. for Institutional Advancement: CANDY HEIN

Dean of Graduate Studies and Research: JEFFREY M. BROWN

Dean of Student Affairs: Dr GERARDO ALVA

Dir for Admissions: ROSIE A. DICKINSON

Registrar: OSCAR E. REYNA

Dir of Library: DOUGLAS M. FERRIER

Library of 259,086 vols, 1,079,218 microfiche and microfilm, over 51,298 state and fed. documents, 1,464 print subscriptions, approx. 28,895 e-journals, 46,000 e-books

Number of teachers: 307

Number of students: 7,037

Publications: *International Trade Journal, Journal of Border Education Research, Journal of Social and Ecological Boundaries, Western Hemispheric Trade Digest*

DEANS

A. R. Sanchez, Jr School of Business Administration: Dr R. STEPHEN SEARS

College of Arts and Sciences: Dr THOMAS R. MITCHELL

College of Education: Dr CATHERYN J. WEITMAN

College of Nursing and Health Sciences: Dr REGINA C. AUNE

Texas A&M University

College Station, TX 77843-1246

Telephone: (979) 845-3211

E-mail: admissions@tamu.edu

Internet: www.tamu.edu

Founded 1876 as a college, present name and status 1963

Academic year: August to August (2 semesters)

Br. campuses in Galveston, Qatar

Pres.: Dr R. BOWEN LOFTIN

Provost and Exec. Vice-Pres. for Academic Affairs: Dr KARAN L. WATSON

Vice-Pres. and Assoc. Provost for Diversity:
Dr CHRISTINE A. STANLEY
Vice-Pres. for Admin.: Dr RODNEY P.
MCCLENDON
Vice-Pres. for Finance and Chief Financial
Officer: B. J. CRAIN
Vice-Pres. for Research: Dr JEFFREY R.
SEEMANN
Vice-Pres. for Student Affairs: Lt-Gen.
JOSEPH F. WEBER
Registrar: VENESA A. HEIDICK
Dean for Univ. Libraries: Dr CHARLES GIL-
REATH

Library of 4,577,598 vols, 936,270 e-books,
108,064 serials, 5,714,052 microforms
Number of teachers: 2,900
Number of students: 50,000

DEANS

Bush School of Government and Public Ser-
vice: ANDREW H. CARD, JR (acting)
College of Agriculture and Life Sciences: Dr
MARK A. HUSSEY
College of Architecture: Prof. JORGE VANEGAS
College of Education and Human Develop-
ment: Dr DOUGLAS J. PALMER
College of Geosciences: Dr KATE C. MILLER
College of Liberal Arts: Dr JOSÉ LUIS BERMÚ-
DEZ
College of Medicine: Dr T. SAM SHOMAKER
College of Science: Dr H. JOSEPH NEWTON
College of Veterinary Medicine and Biomedi-
cal Sciences: Dr ELEANOR M. GREEN
Dwight Look College of Engineering: Dr M.
KATHERINE BANKS
Mays Business School: Dr JERRY R. STRAWSER

Texas A&M University—Central Texas

1001 Leadership Pl., Killeen, TX 76549
Telephone: (254) 519-5400
Fax: (254) 519-5482
E-mail: info@ct.tamus.edu
Internet: www.ct.tamus.edu

Founded 1999 as Tarleton-Central Texas,
present name and status 2009
Academic year: August to May

Schools of arts and sciences, business admin-
istration, education; div. of graduate studies
Pres.: Dr MARC A. NIGLIAZZO
Provost and Vice-Pres. for Academic and
Student Affairs: Dr PEG GRAY-VICKREY
Vice-Pres. for Finance and Admin.: GAYLENE
NUNN
Registrar: DAWN KHOURY
Dir for Library Services: MARK HARRIS

Library of 120,000 vols, 25,800 periodicals
and govt documents
Number of teachers: 61
Number of students: 2,553

Texas A&M University—Commerce

POB 3011, Commerce, TX 75429
2600 S Neal St, Commerce, TX 75428
Telephone: (903) 886-5014
Fax: (903) 886-5888
E-mail: admissions@tamu-commerce.edu
Internet: www.tamu-commerce.edu

Founded 1889, present status 1996
Academic year: August to May

Pres. and CEO: Dr DAN JONES
Provost and Vice-Pres. for Academic Affairs:
Dr LARRY F. LEMANSKI
Vice-Pres. for Business and Admin.: BOB
BROWN
Vice-Pres. for Institutional Advancement:
RANDY VAN DEVEN
Registrar: PAIGE BUSSELL
Dir for Libraries: GREG MITCHELL

Library: 1m. vols
Number of teachers: 450 (full-time)
Number of students: 8,900
Publication: *PRIDE*

DEANS

College of Business and Entrepreneurship:
Dr HAL LANGFORD
College of Education and Human Services:
Prof. Dr BRENT MANGUS
College of Humanities, Social Sciences and
Arts: Prof. Dr SALVATORE ATTARDO
College of Science, Engineering and Agricul-
ture: Prof. Dr GRADY PRICE BLOUNT

Texas A&M University—Corpus Christi

6300 Ocean Dr., Corpus Christi, TX 78412
Telephone: (361) 825-5700
Fax: (361) 825-5810
E-mail: admiss@tamucc.edu
Internet: www.tamucc.edu

Founded 1947 as Univ. of Corpus Christi,
present status 1989, present name 1993
Academic year: August to August

Pres.: Dr FLAVIUS C. KILLEBREW
Provost and Vice-Pres. for Academic Affairs:
Dr CHRIS MARKWOOD
Exec. Vice-Pres. for Finance and Admin.:
KATHRYN FUNK-BAXTER
Vice-Pres. for Institutional Advancement: Dr
S. TRENT HILL
Vice-Pres. for Research, Commercialization
and Outreach: Dr LUIS CIFUENTES
Vice-Pres. for Student Affairs: Dr ELIOT
CHENAUX
Registrar: MICHAEL RENDON
Library Dir and Asst Vice-Pres.: CHRISTINE
SHUPALA

Library: 1.1 m. vols
Number of teachers: 335
Number of students: 10,000

DEANS

College of Business: Dr MOUSTAFA H. ABDEL-
SAMAD
College of Education: Dr ARTHUR HERNANDEZ
College of Liberal Arts: Dr KELLY QUINTA-
NILLA
College of Nursing and Health Sciences: Dr
MARY JANE HAMILTON
College of Science and Engineering: Dr
FRANK L. PEZOLD, III
Community Outreach: Dr JAMES NEEDHAM
Graduate Studies: Dr JoANN CANALES
Teacher Education: ART HERNANDEZ

Texas A&M University—Kingsville

700 University Blvd, MSC 101, Kingsville,
TX 78363-8202
Telephone: (361) 593-2111
Fax: (361) 593-2195
E-mail: registrar@tamuk.edu
Internet: www.tamuk.edu

Founded 1917 as South Texas Normal
School, present status 1989, present name
1993
Academic year: August to May (2 semesters)
Pres.: STEVEN H. TALLANT
Provost and Vice-Pres. for Academic Affairs:
REX GANDY
Sr Vice-Pres. for Fiscal and Student Affairs:
TERISA RILEY
Vice-Pres. for Enrolment Management: MAN-
UEL LUJAN
Vice-Pres. for Finance and Admin.: MARILYN
FOWLÉ
Vice-Pres. for Institutional Advancement: D.
SCOTT GINES
Dean for Students: KIRSTEN COMPARY
Registrar: GEORGE WEIR
Library Dir: BRUCE R. SCHUENEMAN

Library of 2,742,941 vols, 2,122 periodicals,
853 journals, 40,501 e-books, 654,007
microforms, 9,722 audiovisual items
Number of teachers: 387
Number of students: 6,200

DEANS

College of Arts and Sciences: Dr MICHAEL S.
HOUF
College of Business Administration: Dr V.
THOMAS DOCK
College of Education and Human Perform-
ance: Dr ALBERTO RUIZ
Dick and Mary Lewis Kleberg College of
Agriculture, Natural Resources and
Human Sciences: Dr G. ALLEN RASMUSSEN
Frank H. Dotterweich Engineering: Dr STE-
PHAN NIX
College of Graduate Studies: Dr MOHAMED
ABDELRAHMAN
Honors College: Dr DOLORES GUERRERO

Texas A&M University—San Antonio

1 University Way, San Antonio, TX 78224
Telephone: (210) 784-1000
E-mail: ir@tamusa.tamu.edu
Internet: www.tamusa.tamus.edu

Founded 2000

Schools of arts and sciences, business, edu-
cation and kinesiology, graduate studies
Pres.: Dr MARIA HERNANDEZ FERRIER
Provost and Vice-Pres. for Academic Affairs:
Dr BRENT MARRIOTT SNOW
Vice-Pres. for Finance and Admin. and Chief
Financial Officer: KEN MITTS
Vice-Pres. for Strategic Initiatives, Institu-
tional Advancement and Military Affairs:
Dr CHARLES RODRIGUEZ
Univ. Librarian: STEFANIE WITTENBACH
Number of teachers: 161
Number of students: 3,120 (2,324 under-
graduate, 796 graduate)

Texas A&M University—Texarkana

7101 University Ave, Texarkana, TX 75503
Telephone: (903) 223-3000
Fax: (903) 223-3140
E-mail: admissions@tamut.edu
Internet: tamut.edu

Founded 1971 as E Texas State Univ. at
Texarkana, present status 1996
Academic year: August to May
Pres.: Dr CARLISLE B. RATHBURN, III
Provost and Sr Vice-Pres. for Academic Affairs:
ROSANNE STRIPLING
Vice-Pres. for Finance and Admin. and Chief
Financial Officer: RANDY RIKEL
Vice-Pres. for Student Engagement and Suc-
cess: DANIEL KENT KELSO

Number of teachers: 53 (full-time)
Number of students: 1,738

DEANS

College of Business: Dr LARRY DAVIS
College of Education and Liberal Arts: Dr
GLENDA BALLARD
College of Science, Technology, Engineering
and Mathematics: Dr ARTHUR E. LINKINS

West Texas A&M University

2501 Fourth Ave, Canyon, TX 79016-0001
2403 Russell Long Blvd, Canyon, TX 79015
Telephone: (806) 651-0000
Fax: (806) 651-2126
E-mail: cbarnes@wtamu.edu
Internet: wtamu.edu

Founded 1910 as West Texas State Normal
College, present name 1993
Academic year: August to May
Pres. and CEO: Dr J. PATRICK O'BRIEN
Provost and Vice-Pres. for Academic Affairs:
Dr WADE SCHAEFFER
Vice-Pres. for Business and Finance: GARY
BARNES
Vice-Pres. for Enrolment Management: DAN
D. GARCIA
Vice-Pres. for Institutional Advancement: Dr
NEAL R. WEAVER

Vice-Pres. for Student Affairs: Dr Don D. Albrecht
Chief Information Officer: James D. Webb
Dir of Information and Library Resources: Shawna Kennedy-Witthar
Library of 350,000 vols, 650,000 govt documents
Number of teachers: 252 (full-time)
Number of students: 7,902 (6,619 undergraduate, 1,283 graduate)

DEANS

College of Agriculture, Science and Engineering: Dr Don R. Topliff
College of Business: Dr Neil Terry
College of Education and Social Sciences: Dr Eddie Henderson
College of Nursing and Health Sciences: Dr J. Dirk Nelson
Graduate School and Research: Angela Spaulding
Sybil B. Harrington College of Fine Arts and Humanities: Dr Jessica Mallard

TEXAS CHIROPRACTIC COLLEGE

5912 Spencer Highway, Pasadena, TX 77505-1699
Telephone: (281) 487-1170
Fax: (281) 991-4871
E-mail: admissions@txchiro.edu
Internet: www.txchiro.edu
Founded 1908
Private control
Academic year: September to August
Pres.: Dr Richard G. Brassard
Provost and Sr Vice-Pres.: Dr Clay McDonald
Vice-Pres. for Academic and Program Devt: Al Adams
Vice-Pres. for Administrative Affairs: Dr Stephen L. Haslund
Vice-Pres. for Enrolment Management: Dr Fred Zuker
Vice-Pres. for Student Affairs: Dr Stephen Haslund
Chief Fiscal Officer: William S. Quinn
Dean for Academic Affairs: John Mrozek
Library of 18,135 vols, 1,148 audiovisual items, 182 journals
Number of teachers: 27
Number of students: 400

TEXAS CHRISTIAN UNIVERSITY

POB 297020, Fort Worth, TX 76129
2800 S University Dr., Fort Worth, TX 76129
Telephone: (817) 257-7000
Fax: (817) 257-7333
E-mail: frogmail@tcu.edu
Internet: www.tcu.edu
Founded 1873 as Addran Male and Female College, present name 1902
Private control
Academic year: August to May
Chancellor: Victor J. Boschini, Jr
Provost and Vice-Chancellor for Academic Affairs: R. Nowell Donovan
Vice-Chancellor for Finance and Admin.: Brian G. Gutierrez
Vice-Chancellor for Govt Affairs: Larry D. Lauer
Vice-Chancellor for Student Affairs: Kathy Cavins-Tull
Vice-Chancellor for Univ. Advancement: Donald J. Whelan, Jr
Registrar: Patrick Miller
Dean for Library: Dr June Koelker
Library of 2,179,178 vols incl. 79,353 periodicals titles
Number of teachers: 637
Number of students: 9,518

Publications: *Image Magazine, Neeley Magazine, TCU Magazine* (4 a year)

DEANS

Addran College of Liberal Arts: Dr Andrew Schoolmaster
College of Communication: Dr David Whillock
College of Education: Mary M. Patton
College of Fine Arts: Dr Scott A. Sullivan
College of Science and Engineering: Demitris Kouris
Harris College of Nursing and Health Sciences: Dr Paulette Burns
John V. Roach Honors College: Peggy W. Watson
Neeley School of Business: O. Homer Erekson

TEXAS COLLEGE

2404 N Grand Ave, Tyler, TX 75702
Telephone: (903) 593-8311
Fax: (903) 526-4426
Internet: www.texascollege.edu
Founded 1894
Private control
Academic year: August to May (2 semesters)
Divs of business and social sciences, education, general studies and humanities, natural and computational sciences
Pres.: Dr Dwight J. Fennell
Vice-Pres. for Academic Affairs: Cynthia Marshall-Biggins
Vice-Pres. for Business and Finance: James Harris
Vice-Pres. for Institutional Advancement: Johnnye Jones
Vice-Pres. for Student Affairs: Calvin Green
Dean for Student Affairs: Anthony Meyers
Registrar: John Roberts
Dir for Library Services: Joyce Arps
Number of teachers: 63
Number of students: 740

TEXAS LUTHERAN UNIVERSITY

1000 W Court St, Seguin, TX 78155
Telephone: (830) 372-8000
Fax: (830) 372-8096
E-mail: admissions@tlu.edu
Internet: www.tlu.edu
Founded 1891
Private control
Academic year: August to May
Offers courses in accountancy, arts, business administration, music, science
Pres.: Dr Stuart Dorsey
Vice-Pres. and Dean of Student Life and Learning: Kristi Quiros
Vice-Pres. for Academic Affairs: Dr John McClusky
Vice-Pres. for Devt and Alumni Relations: Steve Anderson (acting)
Vice-Pres. for Enrolment Services: Tom Oliver
Vice-Pres. for Finance and Admin.: Andrew Nelson
Registrar: Glenn Yockey
Univ. Librarian: Prof. Martha Rinn
Library of 135,000 vols, 27,786 e-books
Number of teachers: 77 (full-time)
Number of students: 1,400

TEXAS SOUTHERN UNIVERSITY

3100 Cleburne Ave, Houston, TX 77004
Telephone: (713) 313-7011
Fax: (713) 313-7851
E-mail: admissions@tsu.edu
Internet: www.tsu.edu
Founded 1947 as Texas State Univ. for Negroes, present name 1951

State control
Academic year: September to August
Pres.: Dr John M. Rudley
Provost and Vice-Pres. for Academic Affairs and Research: Dr Sunny E. Ohia
Sr Vice-Pres. for Admin.: Bruce Wilson
Vice-Pres. for Academic Services and Dean for Students: Willie Marshall
Vice-Pres. for Finance and Chief Financial Officer: Jim C. McShan
Vice-Pres. for Univ. Advancement: Wendy H. Adair
Registrar: Marilynn Square
Dir for Libraries: Dr Norma Bean
Library of 261,506 vols, 504,149 microforms, 1,462 govt documents, 1,774 periodicals
Number of teachers: 588
Number of students: 9,500
Publications: *Ex-Press* (4 a year), *Inside TSU* (12 a year), *Urban Notebook* (4 a year)

DEANS

Barbara Jordan-Mickey Leland School of Public Affairs: Dr Robert D. Bullard
College of Continuing Education: Dr Irvine Epps
College of Education: Dr Lillian B. Poats
College of Liberal Arts and Behavioral Sciences: Dr Danille K. Taylor
College of Pharmacy and Health Sciences: Dr Shirlette G. Milton
College of Science and Technology: Prof. Dr Lei Yu
Graduate School: Dr Gregory H. Maddox
Jesse H. Jones School of Business: Dr Ronald A. Johnson
School of Communication: Dr James W. Ward
Thomas F. Freeman Honors College: Dr Humphrey A. Regis
Thurgood Marshall School of Law: Prof. Dannye Holley

TEXAS STATE UNIVERSITY SYSTEM

Thomas J. Rusk Bldg, 208 E 10th St, Suite 600, Austin, TX 78701-2407
Telephone: (512) 463-1808
Fax: (512) 463-1816
E-mail: chancellor@tsus.edu
Internet: www.tsus.edu
Founded 1911 as State Normal School Board of Regents, present name 1975
Chancellor: Dr Brian McCall
Vice-Chancellor and Gen. Counsel: Dr Fernando Gomez
Vice-Chancellor for Academic Affairs: Dr Perry Moore
Vice-Chancellor for Contract Administration: Dr Peter Graves
Vice-Chancellor for Finance: Dr Roland Smith
Vice-Chancellor for Governmental Relations: Dr Sean Cunningham
Number of students: 70,000 (at 9 univs and colleges).

CONSTITUENT UNIVERSITIES

Lamar University

4400 MLK Blvd, POB 10009, Beaumont, TX 77710
Telephone: (409) 880-7011
Fax: (409) 880-8404
E-mail: records@lamar.edu
Internet: www.lamar.edu
Founded 1923 as South Park Jr College, present name 1971
Academic year: August to May
Pres.: Dr James M. Simmons
Provost and Vice-Pres.: Dr Stephen Doblin
Vice-Pres. for Finance and Operations: Dr Gregg Lassen

Vice-Pres. for Student Affairs: NORMAN BEL-
LARD
Vice-Pres. for Univ. Advancement: CAMILLE
MOUTON
Registrar: DAVID SHORT
Dir of Library Services: DAVID CARROLL
Library: 1m. vols, 1,000 periodicals
Number of teachers: 507
Number of students: 14,388

DEANS

College of Arts and Sciences: Dr BRENDA
NICHOLS
College of Business: Dr ENRIQUE R. VENTA
College of Education and Human Devt: Dr
HOLLIS LOWERY-MOORE
College of Engineering: Dr JACK R. HOPPER
College of Fine Arts and Communications: Dr
RUSS A. SCHULTZ
College of Graduate Studies: Dr VICTOR A.
ZALOOM

Sam Houston State University

POB 2026, Huntsville, TX 77341
Telephone: (409) 294-1013
E-mail: adm_smm@shsu.edu
Internet: www.shsu.edu

Founded 1879 as Sam Houston Normal
Institute, present name 1969
Academic year: August to May

Pres.: Dr DANA L. GIBSON
Provost and Vice-Pres. for Academic Affairs:
Dr JAIMIE HEBERT
Vice-Pres. for Enrolment Management: Dr
HEATHER THIELEMANN
Vice-Pres. for Finance and Operations: ALVIN
G. HOOTEN
Vice-Pres. for Student Services: FRANK PAR-
KER
Vice-Pres. for Univ. Advancement: FRANK R.
HOLMES
Dean of Students: JOHN YARABECK
Registrar: JOELLEN TIPTON
Dir of Libraries: ANN HOLDER

Library of 1,379,682 vols, 3,556 periodicals,
1,379,682 microforms, 629,489 records and
tapes
Number of teachers: 819
Number of students: 17,618

Publications: *Advancing Women in Leader-
ship, Crime and Justice International, Ed
Leadership Review, Heritage Magazine* (2 a
year), *Journal of Business Strategies,
Texas Review* (2 a year), *The Texas Crime
Pole*

DEANS

College of Business Administration: Dr
MITCHELL J. MUEHSAM
College of Criminal Justice: Dr VINCENT J.
WEBB
College of Education: Prof. Dr GENEVIEVE
BROWN
College of Fine Arts and Mass Communica-
tion: Dr MARY ROBBINS
College of Humanities and Social Sciences:
Dr JOHN DE CASTRO
College of Sciences: Dr JERRY COOK
Graduate Studies: Dr KANDI TAYEBI

Sul Ross State University

POB C-114, Alpine, TX 79832
Telephone: (432) 837-8011
Fax: (432) 837-8334
Internet: www.sulross.edu

Founded 1917 as Sul Ross State Normal
College, present name and status 1969
Academic year: September to August

Pres.: Dr RICARDO MAESTAS
Provost and Vice-Pres. for Academic and
Student Affairs: Dr JIM CASE
Vice-Pres. for Enrolment Management:
DENISE GROVES

Vice-Pres. for Finance and Operations:
CESARIO VALENZUELA
Registrar: ROBERT CULLINS
Dean of Library: DON DOWDEY
Library of 760,700 vols
Number of teachers: 117
Number of students: 5,187

DEANS

School of Agricultural and Natural Resource
Sciences: Dr ROBERT KINUCAN
School of Arts and Sciences: Dr CHRISTOPHER
RITZI
School of Professional Studies: Dr MELANIE
A. CROY

ATTACHED COLLEGE

Rio Grande College: 205 Wildcat Dr., Del
Rio, TX 78840; tel. (830) 703-4808; fax (830)
279-3014; internet rgc.sulross.edu; f. 1985 as
Sul Ross State Univ. Study Center, present
name 1995; campuses at Eagle Pass, Uvalde;
offers Bachelors degree in biology, chemistry,
criminal justice, English, general business,
history, interdisciplinary studies, mathematics, psychology, social science, Spanish; offers
Masters degree in business administration,
education; 1,100 students; Dean and Assoc.
Provost Dr J. PAUL SORRELS; Dir of Admissions and Records CLAUDIA R. WRIGHT.

Texas State University—San Marcos

601 University Dr., JCK 883, San Marcos, TX
78666

Telephone: (512) 245-2111
Fax: (512) 245-8446
E-mail: registrar@txstate.edu
Internet: www.txstate.edu

Founded 1899 as Southwest Texas State
Normal School, present name and status
2003
Academic year: August to May

Pres.: Dr DENISE M. TRAUTH
Provost and Vice-Pres. for Academic Affairs:
Dr EUGENE J. BOURGEOIS
Vice-Pres. for Finance and Support Services:
WILLIAM A. NANCE
Vice-Pres. for Student Affairs: Dr JOANNE
SMITH (acting)
Vice-Pres. for Univ. Advancement: Dr BAR-
BARA BREIER (acting)
Registrar: LLOYDEAN ECKLEY
Assoc. Vice-Pres. for Univ. Library: JOAN
HEATH

Library of 1,569,028 vols, 99,700 e-journals,
1,892,327 microforms, 14,764 serials,
276,124 audiovisual items, 491,291 e-books
Number of teachers: 1,588
Number of students: 34,087

Publications: *Electronic Journal of Differential Equations, Persona* (1 a year), *Southwestern American Literature* (2 a year),
Texas Books in Review (4 a year), *The
Journal of Texas Music History* (2 a year)

DEANS

College of Applied Arts: Dr T. JAIME CHAHIN
College of Education: Dr STAN CARPENTER
College of Fine Arts and Communication: Dr
TIMOTHY MOTTET
College of Health Professions: Dr RUTH B.
WELBORN
College of Liberal Arts: Dr MICHAEL HEN-
NESSY
College of Science and Engineering: Dr
STEPHEN SEIDMAN
Emmett and Miriam McCoy College of Busi-
ness Administration: Dr DENISE SMART
Graduate College: Dr J. MICHAEL WIL-
LOUGHBY
Honors College: Dr HEATHER GALLOWAY
Univ. College: Dr DANIEL BROWN

PROFESSORS

ABBASIAN, R., Mathematics
ALI, M., Computer Science
ALLEN, J., Consumer Science
ANDREWS, G., History
ANGIRASSA, A., Agribusiness
ARCHER, R., Psychology
ARON, G., Biology
AUGUSTIN, B., Geography
BACCUS, J., Biology
BALANOFF, H., Political Science
BANDY, C., Mathematics
BECK, J., Education Administration
BEEBE, S., Communication Studies
BELL, J., Management
BELL-METEREAU, R., English
BIBLE, J., Business Law
BLAIR, J., English
BLANCHARD-BOEHM, D., Geography
BLANDA, M., Chemistry and Biochemistry
BLANKMEYER, E., Economics
BOEHM, R., Geography
BOONE, M., Education Administration
BURKE, G., Health Administration
BUTLER, D., Geography
BYNUM, V., History
CASSIDY, P., Chemistry and Biochemistry
CAVERLY, D., Curriculum and Instruction
CHAMPION, J., Spanish
CHATFIELD, J., Mathematics
CHAVKIN, A., English
CHAVKIN, N., Social Work
CHIODO, B., Management
COHEN, P., English
COOK, R., Computer Information Systems
DAVIS, J., Psychology
DAVIS, W., Computer Science
DAY, F., Geography
DAY, S., Sociology
DE LA TEJA, J., History
DIX, J., Mathematics
DOLEZAL, C., Curriculum and Instruction
DONNELLY, D., Physics
ECHEVERRIA, M., Spanish
EDGELL, J., Mathematics
EIKNER, E., Accounting
ESTAVILLE, L., Geography
FITE, K., Curriculum and Instruction
FLAHERTY, D., Accounting
FLAMMANG, R., Economics
FLING, S., Psychology
FORREST, J., French
FRIEDMAN, B. J., Nutrition and Foods
FULMER, G., Philosophy
FURNEY, S., Health Education
GARBER, J., Anthropology
GAROFALO, C., Political Science
GEURAS, D., Philosophy
GILLIS, M., Curriculum and Instruction
GINSBURG, H., Psychology
GLASSMAN, D., Anthropology
GORDAN, S., Educational Administration
GORDON, J., Philosophy
GORMAN, R., Political Science
GOWENS, P., Economics
GRASSO, K., Political Science
GRAYSON, N., English
GREEN, D., Respiratory Care
GROSS, D., English
GU, W., Mathematics
GUTIERREZ, C., Physics
HABINGREITHER, R., Technology
HATCHER, B., Curriculum and Instruction
HAWKINS, C., Social Work
HAZELWOOD, D., Mathematics
HEABERLIN, D., English
HENNESSY, M., English
HILL, J., English
HOFER, M., Political Science
HOLT, E., English
HORNE, F., Biology
HUFFMAN, D., Biology
HULING, L., Curriculum and Instruction
HUMPHREY, J., Accounting
HUNNICUTT, G., Management

HUSTON, M., Biology
HUTCHESON, P., Philosophy
INGRAM, A., English
JAFFE, C., Spanish
JAGER, R., History
JAMES, S. G., Health Education
JAMIESON, J., Criminal Justice
JIA, X.-D., Mathematics
JOHNSON, M., Physical Education
JOHNSTON, W., Computer Information Systems
JORGENSON, C., School Psychology
JOY, G., Philosophy
KENS, P., Political Science
KISHAN, R., Economics
KOKE, J., Biology
LAIRD, E., English
LARSEN, R., Geography
LEDER, P., English
LEMKE, D., Biology
LOCHMAN, D., English
LONGLEY, G., Biology
McGEE, JOHN, Business Law
McGEE, JON, Anthropology
MANDZIUK, R., Communication Studies
MARGERISON, K., History
MARTIN, G., Curriculum and Instruction
MARTIN, R., Computer Information Systems
MEIXNER, W., Accounting
MELZER, B., Physical Therapy
MENDEZ, R., Psychology
MICHALK, V., Physics
MIDDLEBROOK, B., Management
MIJARES, T., Criminal Justice
MINIFIE, J., Management
MOGAB, J., Economics
MONROE, D., English
MONTODON, L., Accounting
MURRAY, T., Physical Education
NEELY, J., Music
NELSON, D., Mass Communication
NEWSOM, R., Sociology
NIELSON, E., Art and Design
NOWICKI, M., Health Administration
OGLETREE, S., Psychology
OLNEY, R., Management
OLSON, D., Physics
OLSON, M., English
OPHEIM, C., Political Science
PAESE, P., Physical Education
PANKEY, R., Physical Education
PARKIN, D., English
PASCOE, C., Theatre
PASSTY, G., Mathematics
PEIRCE, K., Mass Communication
PETERSEN, J., Geography
PETOFF, P., Respiratory Care
PINO, D., Music
POHL, J., History
POLLOCK, J., Criminal Justice
RAHE, H., Agriculture
RANSOME, J., Physical Education
RENFRO, P., Mass Communication
RIEPE, R., Music
RONAN, C., English
ROSSMO, K., Criminal Justice
RUDZINSKI, W., Chemistry and Biochemistry
SALEM, P., Communication Studies
SHAH, V., Computer Information Systems
SINGH, S., Mathematics
SKERPAN-WHEELER, E., English
SMITH, B., Mass Communication
SODDERS, R., Theatre
SPELLMANN, J., Mathematics
STEA, D., Geography
STEPHENSON, S., Quantitative Methods
STIMMEL, D., Psychology
STONE, W., Criminal Justice
STOUFFER, W., Political Science
STUTTS, M., Marketing
STUTZMAN, J., Finance
SULLIVAN, A., Political Science
SUMMERS, J., Health Administration
TAYLOR, R., Marketing
THICKSTUN, T., Mathematics
THOMAS, N., Music

TORREJON, R., Mathematics
UGALDE, S., Spanish
WAITE, D., Educational Administration
WALTER, R., Chemistry and Biochemistry
WANG, C. J., Computer Science
WARMS, R., Anthropology
WARSHAUER, M., Mathematics
WATKINS, T., Social Work
WAYMAN, M., Criminal Justice
WEBBER, J. A., Curriculum and Instruction
WEINBERGER, G., Political Science
WELSH, S., Mathematics
WHEELER, L., Curriculum and Instruction
WHEELER, R., Psychology
WILLIAMS, M. L., Communication Studies
WILLIAMSON, P., Biology
WILSON, J., History
WINEK, G., Technology
WINKING, K., Music
WOOSLEY, T., Music
WRIGHT, L., Psychology
YAGER, B., Chemistry and Biochemistry
YICK, J., History

Other constituent institutions awarding Associate-level degrees include: Lamar Institute of Technology, Lamar State College-Orange and Lamar State College-Port Arthur.

TEXAS TECH UNIVERSITY SYSTEM

Lubbock, TX 79409-2005
Telephone: (806) 742-0012
Fax: (806) 742-8050
E-mail: chancellor@ttu.edu
Internet: www.texastech.edu
Founded 1996
State control
Academic year: August to May
Chancellor: Dr KENT R. HANCE
Vice-Chancellor: Dr TIM HUDSON
Vice-Chancellor and Gen. Counsel: JOHN T. HUFFAKER
Vice-Chancellor and Chief Financial Officer: JIM BRUNJES
Vice-Chancellor for Academic Affairs: Dr JOSEPH C. RALLO
Vice-Chancellor for Facilities Planning and Construction: MICHAEL MOLINA
Vice-Chancellor for Governmental Relations: MIKE SANDERS
Vice-Chancellor for Institutional Advancement: Dr KELLY OVERLEY
Vice-Chancellor for Policy and Planning: Dr JOHN OPPERMAN
Vice-Chancellor for Research and Commercialization: JODEY ARRINGTON.

CONSTITUENT UNIVERSITIES

Angelo State University

c/o Office of Admissions, ASU Station 11014, San Angelo, TX 76909-1014
2601 West Ave N, San Angelo, TX 76909
Telephone: (325) 942-2041
Fax: (325) 942-2078
E-mail: admissions@angelo.edu
Internet: www.angelo.edu
Founded 1928 as San Angelo Jr College, present name 1965
Academic year: September to August
Pres.: Dr JOSEPH C. RALLO
Provost and Vice-Pres. for Academic Affairs: Dr BRIAN J. MAY
Vice-Pres. for Devt and Public Relations: Dr JASON C. PENRY
Vice-Pres. for Finance and Admin.: MICHAEL REID
Vice-Pres. for Student Affairs and Enrolment Management: Dr JAVIER FLORES
Dir of Admissions and Recruitment Services: MICHAEL LOEHRING

Registrar: CYNTHIA D. WEEAKS
Library Exec. Dir: Dr MAURICE G. FORTIN
Library of 1,705,900 items
Number of teachers: 332
Number of students: 7,084

DEANS

College of Arts and Sciences: Dr PAUL K. SWETS
College of Business: Dr CORBETT F. GAULDEN, JR
College of Education: Dr JOHN J. MIAZGA, JR
College of Graduate Studies: Dr BRIAN J. MAY
College of Health and Human Services: Prof. Dr LESLIE M. MAYRAND

Texas Tech University

2500 Broadway, Lubbock, TX 79409-2005
Telephone: (806) 742-2011
Fax: (806) 742-2138
E-mail: admissions@ttu.edu
Internet: www.ttu.edu
Founded 1923 as Texas Technological College, present name 1969
Academic year: August to May
Pres.: Dr GUY BAILEY
Provost and Sr Vice-Pres.: Dr BOB SMITH
Sr Vice-Pres. for Research: TAYLOR EIGHMY
Vice-Pres. for Admin. and Finance and Chief Financial Officer: KYLE CLARK
Vice-Pres. for Research: TAYLOR EIGHMY
Registrar: BOBBIE BROWN
Dean of Libraries: DON DYAL
Library of 1,700,000 vols
Number of teachers: 1,574
Number of students: 31,637
Publications: *Engineering Our Future* (2 a year), *Envision* (1 a year), *Estate Planning and Community Property Law Journal* (2 a year), *Texas Tech Administrative Law Journal* (2 a year), *Texas Tech Law Review* (4 a year)

DEANS

College of Agricultural Sciences and Natural Resources: Dr MICHAEL GALYEAN
College of Architecture: Prof. ANDREW VERNOOY
College of Arts and Sciences: Dr LAWRENCE SCHOVANEC
College of Education: Dr SCOTT RIDLEY
College of Human Sciences: Dr LINDA C. HOOVER
College of Mass Communication: JERRY HUDSON
College of Visual and Performing Arts: Dr CAROL EDWARDS
Edward E. Whitacre College of Engineering: Dr AL SACCO, JR
Graduate School: Dr PEGGY GORDON MILLER
Honors College: Dr STEPHEN E. FRITZ
Rawls College of Business Admin.: Dr ALLEN T. McINNES
School of Law: Prof. Dr DARBY DICKERSON
Univ. College: Dr VALERIE PATON

Texas Tech University Health Sciences Center

3601 Fourth St, Lubbock, TX 79430
Telephone: (806) 743-1000
Internet: www.ttuhsc.edu
Founded 1969 as Texas Tech University School of Medicine, present name and status 1979
Campuses in Abilene, Amarillo, Dallas Fort Worth, El Paso, Permian Basin
Pres.: Dr TEDD MITCHELL
Exec. Vice-Pres. and Provost and Vice-Pres. for Medical Affairs: Dr STEVEN L. BERK
Exec. Vice-Pres. for Finance and Admin.: ELMO CAVIN
Exec. Vice-Pres. for Research: Dr DOUGLAS M. STOCCO

Sr Vice-Pres. for Academic Affairs: Dr RIAL ROLFE

Library of 54,500 vols, 23,000 e-journals, 50,000 e-books

Number of teachers: 861 (full-time)

Number of students: 4,094

DEANS

Anita Perry School of Nursing: Dr MICHAEL EVANS

Gayle Greve Hunt School of Nursing: Dr JOSEFINA LUJAN

Graduate School of Biomedical Sciences: Dr DOUGLAS M. STOCCO

Paul L. Foster School of Medicine: Dr JOSE MANUEL DE LA ROSA

School of Allied Health Sciences: Dr PAUL P. BROOKE, JR

School of Medicine: Dr STEVEN LEE BERK

School of Nursing: Dr MICHAEL EVANS

School of Pharmacy: Dr ARTHUR A. NELSON, JR

TEXAS WESLEYAN UNIVERSITY

1201 Wesleyan St, Fort Worth, TX 76105-1536

Telephone: (817) 531-4444

Fax: (817) 531-7515

E-mail: info@txwesleyan.edu

Internet: www.txwes.edu

Founded 1890 as Polytechnic College, present name 1989

Private control

Academic year: September to May

Pres.: Prof. FREDERICK G. SLABACH

Provost and Sr Vice-Pres.: Dr ALLEN H. HENDERSON

Vice-Pres. for Advancement: JOAN CANTY

Vice-Pres. for Enrolment and Student Services: PATI ALEXANDER

Vice-Pres. for Finance and Admin.: KAREN MONTGOMERY

Registrar: KAHLA VAN TOORN

Univ. Librarian: CINDY SWIGGER

Library of 219,053 vols

Number of teachers: 168 (full-time)

Number of students: 3,181

Publication: *Wesleyan Magazine* (2 a year)

DEANS

School of Arts and Letters: Dr STEVEN DANIELL

School of Business Administration: Dr HECTOR QUINTANILLA

School of Education: Dr CARLOS MARTINEZ

School of Natural and Social Sciences: Dr TREVOR MORRIS

Texas Wesleyan School of Law: FREDERIC WHITE

TEXAS WOMAN'S UNIVERSITY

POB 425589, 304 Administration Dr., Denton, TX 76204

Telephone: (940) 898-2000

Fax: (940) 898-3081

E-mail: admissions@twu.edu

Internet: www.twu.edu

Founded 1901 as Girls Industrial College, present name 1957

State control

Academic year: August to May

Chancellor and Pres.: Dr ANN STUART

Provost and Vice-Pres. for Academic Affairs: Dr ROBERT NEELY

Vice-Pres. for Finance and Admin.: Dr BRENDA FLOYD

Vice-Pres. for Information Services: BILL PALMERTREE

Vice-Pres. for Institutional Advancement: (vacant)

Vice-Pres. for Student Life: Dr RICHARD NICHOLAS

Dean for Libraries: SHERILYN BIRD

Library of 788,271 vols

Number of teachers: 989

Number of students: 14,180

DEANS

College of Arts and Sciences: Dr ANN Q. STATON

College of Health Sciences: Dr JIMMY H. ISHEE

College of Nursing: PATRICIA HOLDEN-HUCHTON

College of Professional Education: Dr L. NAN RESTINE

Graduate School: Dr JENNIFER MARTIN

TRINITY UNIVERSITY

1 Trinity Pl., San Antonio, TX 78212-7200

Telephone: (210) 999-8401

Fax: (210) 999-7696

E-mail: admissions@trinity.edu

Internet: www.trinity.edu

Founded 1869

Private control

Academic year: August to May

Liberal arts and sciences

Pres.: Dr DENNIS A. AHLBURG

Vice-Pres. for Faculty and Student Affairs: Dr MICHAEL FISCHER

Vice-Pres. for Finance and Admin.: MARK A. DETTERICK

Vice-Pres. for Information Resources: CHARLES B. WHITE

Dean for Admissions: CHRISTOPHER ELLERTSON

Dean for Students and Assoc. Vice-Pres. for Student Affairs: DAVID M. TUTTLE

Registrar: ALFRED RODRIGUEZ

Librarian: DIANE GRAVES

Library: 1m. vols

Number of teachers: 246 (full-time)

Number of students: 2,417

UNIVERSITY OF DALLAS

1845 E Northgate Dr., Irving, TX 75062-4736

Telephone: (972) 721-5000

Fax: (972) 721-5017

E-mail: admiss@gsm.udallas.edu

Internet: www.udallas.edu

Founded 1956

Private control

Academic year: August to May

Pres.: THOMAS W. KEEFE

Provost and Exec. Vice-Pres.: Dr J. WILLIAM BERRY

Exec. Vice-Pres.: ROBERT M. GALECKE

Vice-Pres. and Dean for Enrolment: Dr JOHN G. PLOTTS

Vice-Pres. for Univ. Advancement: Dr AMANDA RAINEY

Dean for Student Life: JOSEPH CASSIDY

Registrar: JANET BURK

Dir for Library and Univ. Research: ROBERT S. DUPREE

Library of 370,493 vols

Number of teachers: 132

Number of students: 2,843

DEANS

Braniff Graduate School of Liberal Arts: Dr DAVID R. SWEET

College of Business: Dr ROBERT SCHERER

Constantin College of Liberal Arts: Dr CHARLES W. EAKER

School of Ministry: Dr MARK GOODWIN

UNIVERSITY OF HOUSTON SYSTEM

4800 Calhoun, Houston, TX 77004-2018

Telephone: (713) 743-8189

Fax: (713) 743-0946

Internet: www.uhsa.uh.edu

Chancellor: Dr RENU KHATOR

Number of students: 65,000.

CONSTITUENT INSTITUTIONS

University of Houston

4800 Calhoun Rd, Houston, TX 77004

Telephone: (713) 743-1000

Fax: (713) 743-8342

E-mail: president@uh.edu

Internet: www.uh.edu

Founded 1927, present status 1977

Academic year: September to August

Pres.: Dr RENU KHATOR

Provost and Sr Vice-Pres. for Academic Affairs: Dr JOHN J. ANTEL

Exec. Vice-Pres. for Admin. and Finance: Dr CARL CARLUCCI

Vice-Pres. for Community Relations and Institutional Access: Dr ELWYN C. LEE

Vice-Pres. for Governmental Relations: GROVER CAMPBELL

Vice-Pres. for Legal Affairs and Gen. Counsel: Dr DONA HAMILTON CORNELL

Vice-Pres. for Research and Technology Transfer: Dr RATHINDRA N. BOSE

Vice-Pres. for Student Affairs: Dr J. RICHARD WALKER

Vice-Pres. for Univ. Advancement: ELOISE DUNN STUHR

Dean of Students: Dr WILLIAM F. MUNSON

Dean of Libraries: DANA C. ROOKS

Library: 2.7m. vols, 76,000 journals

Number of teachers: 3,446

Number of students: 39,820

Publications: *Experts Directory*, *UHouston*

DEANS

College of Education: Dr ROBERT McPHERSON

College of Liberal Arts and Social Sciences: JOHN W. ROBERTS

College of Natural Sciences and Mathematics: Dr MARK A. SMITH

College of Optometry: Prof. Dr EARL L. SMITH, III

College of Pharmacy: F. LAMAR PRITCHARD

College of Technology: Dr WILLIAM E. FITZGIBBON, III

Conrad N. Hilton College of Hotel and Restaurant Management: Dr JOHN T. BOWEN

C. T. Bauer College of Business Administration: Prof. Dr LATHA RAMCHAND

Cullen College of Engineering: Prof. Dr JOSEPH W. TEDESCO

Gerald D. Hines College of Architecture: PATRICIA BELTON OLIVER

Graduate College of Social Work: Prof. Dr IRA C. COLBY

Honors College: Prof. Dr WILLIAM MONROE

Law Center: Prof. RAYMOND T. NIMMER

University of Houston–Clear Lake

2700 Bay Area Blvd, Houston, TX 77058-1098

Telephone: (281) 283-7600

Fax: (281) 283-2010

E-mail: president@cl.uh.edu

Internet: www.uhcl.edu

Founded 1974

Academic year: September to August

Pres.: Prof. Dr WILLIAM A. STAPLES

Sr Vice-Pres. for Academic Affairs and Provost: CARL A. STOCKTON

Vice-Pres. for Admin. and Finance: MICHELLE DOTTER

Dean of Students: DAVID RACHITA

Registrar (vacant)

Exec. Dir: KAREN WEILHORSKI

Library of 2,222,020 vols

Number of teachers: 744

Number of students: 8,099

DEANS

School of Business: Dr WILLIAM THEODORE CUMMINGS
School of Education: Dr DENNIS W. SPUCK
School of Human Sciences and Humanities: Dr RICK SHORT
School of Science and Computer Engineering: Dr ZBIGNIEW CZAJKIEWICZ

University of Houston—Downtown

1 Main St, Houston, TX 77002
Telephone: (713) 221-8000
Fax: (713) 221-8157
E-mail: uhdinfo@uhd.edu
Internet: www.uhd.edu
Founded 1974 as Univ. of Houston-Downtown College, present name 1983
Academic year: August to July
Pres.: Dr WILLIAM V. FLORES
Provost and Sr Vice-Pres. for Academic Affairs: Dr BRIAN CHAPMAN
Vice-Pres. for Admin. and Finance: DAVID BRADLEY
Vice-Pres. for Advancement and External Relations: JOHANNA WOLFE
Vice-Pres. for Operations and Employment Services: IVONNE MONTALBANO
Vice-Pres. for Student Success and Enrolment Management: LISA MONTGOMERY
Dir of Institutional Advancement: CAROL TUCKER
Dean of Student Affairs (vacant)
Registrar: CYNTHIA SANTOS
Exec. Dir of Library Services: PAT ENSOR

Library of 301,428 vols, 167,640 e-books, 478 journals, 72,250 e-journals, 3,133 audiovisual items, 28,174 e-audiovisual items
Number of teachers: 642
Number of students: 12,918

DEANS

College of Business: DONALD BATES
College of Humanities and Social Sciences: ROBERT JARRETT
College of Public Service: Dr BETH PELZ
College of Sciences and Technology: Prof. Dr AKIF UZMAN
Univ. College: Dr CHRIS BIRCHAK

University of Houston—Victoria

3007 N Ben Wilson, Victoria, TX 77901
Telephone: (361) 570-4848
Fax: (361) 570-4339
E-mail: webmaster@uhv.edu
Internet: www.uhv.edu
Founded 1973 as Univ. of Houston Victoria Center, present name and status 1983
Academic year: August to May (2 semesters)
Pres.: Dr PHIL CASTILLE
Provost and Vice-Pres. for Academic Affairs: Dr DON SMITH
Vice-Pres. for Admin. and Finance: WAYNE B. BERAN
Registrar: TRUDY WORTHAM
Sr Dir for Libraries: Dr JOE DAHLSTROM

Library of 250,000 vols, 45,000 e-books, 23,293 microforms, 23,293 audiovisual materials
Number of teachers: 208
Number of students: 4,330

Publications: *American Book Review* (6 a year), *Symplokē*

DEANS

School of Arts and Sciences: Prof. Dr JEFFREY R. DiLEO
School of Business Administration: Dr FARHANG NIROOMAND
School of Education and Human Devt: Dr DIANE PRINCE
School of Nursing: Dr KATHRYN TART

UNIVERSITY OF MARY HARDIN-BAYLOR

900 College St, Belton, TX 76513
Telephone: (254) 295-8642
Fax: (254) 295-4535
E-mail: registrar@umhb.edu
Internet: www.umhb.edu
Founded 1845, present name 1978
Private control
Academic year: August to May (2 semesters)
Pres.: Dr RANDY G. O'REAR
Provost and Sr Vice-Pres. for Academic Affairs: Dr STEVE L. OLDHAM
Dir for Admissions: BRENT BURKS
Registrar: AMY MCGILVRAY
Dir for Learning Resources and Librarian: DENISE KARIMKHANI

Library of 202,229 vols, 26,760 e-books, 878 journals, 74,000 e-journals, 6,869 audiovisual items, 1,944 CDs, 13,712 microforms
Number of teachers: 320 (full-time)
Number of students: 3,137

DEANS

College of Business: Dr JAMES R. KING, JR
College of Christian Studies: Prof. Dr TIMOTHY G. CRAWFORD
College of Education: Dr MARLENE ZIPPERLEN
College of Humanities: Dr DANIEL S. MYNATT
College of Nursing: Dr SHARON SOUTER
College of Sciences: Dr DARRELL G. WATSON
College of Visual and Performing Arts: Prof. TED BARNES
Graduate School: Dr COLIN WILBORN

UNIVERSITY OF NORTH TEXAS SYSTEM

UNT System Bldg, 1901 Main St, Dallas, TX 75201
Telephone: (214) 752-8585
Fax: (214) 752-8827
E-mail: untsystem@untsystem.edu
Internet: untsystem.edu
State control
Chancellor: LEE F. JACKSON
Vice-Chancellor for Academic Affairs and Student Success: ROSEMARY R. HAGGETT
Vice-Chancellor for Administrative Services: RAYNARD O. KEARBEY
Vice-Chancellor for Finance: TERRY PANKRATZ
Vice-Chancellor for Government Relations: JACK MORTON
Vice-Chancellor for Strategic Partnerships: WILLIAM H. LIVELY.

CONSTITUENT UNIVERSITIES

University of North Texas at Dallas

7300 University Hills Blvd, Dallas, TX 75241
Telephone: (972) 780-3600
Fax: (972) 780-3636
E-mail: untdallas@unt.edu
Founded 1999
Pres.: Dr JOHN ELLIS PRICE
Provost and Vice-Pres.: Dr JOHN BEEHLER
Vice-Pres. for Finance and Admin: WAYNE USRY
Vice-Pres. for Univ. Advancement: J. DOUGLAS SMITH
Head Librarian: BRENDA ROBERTSON

DEANS

Division of Education and Human Services: Dr SHERYL SANTOS-HATCHETT
Division of Liberal Arts and Life Sciences: Dr GERARD RAMBALLY
Division of Urban and Professional Studies: Dr JEHAD YASIN

University of North Texas at Denton

1155 Union Circle 311277, Denton, TX 76203-5017
Telephone: (940) 565-2000
E-mail: undergrad@unt.edu
Internet: www.unt.edu
Founded 1890 as Texas Normal College and Teacher Training Institute, present name 1988
State control
Academic year: August to May
Pres.: Dr V. LANE RAWLINS
Provost and Vice-Pres. for Academic Affairs: Dr WARREN BURGGREN
Vice-Pres. and Gen. Counsel: Dr RICHARD RAFES
Vice-Pres. for Admin. and Finance: ANDREW M. HARRIS
Vice-Pres. for Advancement: LISA BIRLEY BARONIO
Vice-Pres. for External Affairs: WALTER E. PARKER
Vice-Pres. for Institutional Equity and Diversity: Dr GILDA GARCIA
Vice-Pres. for Research and Economic Devt: Dr GEOFF GAMBLE
Vice-Pres. for Student Affairs: Dr ELIZABETH WITH
Vice-Pres. for Univ. and Community Affairs: Dr HERMAN TOTTEN
Vice-Pres. for Univ. Relations, Communications and Marketing: DEBORAH LELIAERT
Dir for Admissions: MARCILLA COLLINSWORTH
Registrar: JONEEL J. HARRIS
Dean for Libraries: Dr MARTIN HALBERT

Library: 6m. vols
Number of teachers: 1,044 (full-time)
Number of students: 33,431 (26,305 undergraduate, 7,126 graduate)

University of North Texas Health Science Center at Fort Worth

3500 Camp Bowie Blvd, Fort Worth, TX 76107
Telephone: (817) 735-2000
Fax: (817) 735-2419
Internet: www.hsc.unt.edu
Founded 1970 as Texas College of Osteopathic Medicine, present status 1999
Pres.: Dr SCOTT B. RANSOM
Provost and Exec. Vice-Pres. for Academic Affairs: Dr THOMAS YORIO
Exec. Vice-Pres.: Dr KATHLEEN FORBES
Vice-Pres. and Chief Financial Officer: JOHN A. HARMAN
Vice-Pres. and Chief Medical Officer: ROBERT C. ADAMS
Vice-Pres. for Admin. and Chief of Staff: JENNIFER M TREVIÑO
Vice-Pres. for Devt and Institutional Advancement: GARY GRANT
Vice-Pres. for Financial Services: MICHAEL MUELLER
Vice-Pres. for Governmental Affairs: DANIEL M. JENSEN
Vice-Pres. for Research: Dr GLENN DILLON
Vice-Pres. for Student Affairs: Dr THOMAS MOORMAN

Library of 27,000 vols, 16,000 e-journals
Number of teachers: 400
Number of students: 1,760

DEANS

College of Pharmacy: Dr MYRON K. JACOBSON
Graduate School of Biomedical Sciences: Dr JAMBOOR VISHWANATHA
School of Health Professions: Dr J. WARREN ANDERSON
School of Public Health: Dr RICHARD KURZ
Texas College of Osteopathic Medicine: Dr DON PESKA

UNIVERSITY OF ST THOMAS

3800 Montrose, Houston, TX 77006-4626

Telephone: (713) 522-7911
Fax: (713) 525-6968
E-mail: admissions@stthom.edu
Internet: www.stthom.edu

Founded 1947
Private control
Academic year: August to May
Pres.: Dr ROBERT R. IVANY
Vice-Pres. for Academic Affairs: Dr DOMINIC A. AQUILA
Vice-Pres. for Finance: JAMES M. BOOTH
Vice-Pres. for Institutional Advancement: CYNTHIA COLBERT RILEY
Vice-Pres. for Marketing Communications and Enrolment Management: VICKIE ALLEMAN
Vice-Pres. for Planning and Technology: GARY MCCORMACK
Vice-Pres. for Student Affairs and Dean for Students: PATRICIA MCKINLEY
Registrar: KIMBERLY SANDERS
Dean for Univ. Libraries: JAMES PICCININNI
Library of 247,533 vols, 48,000 periodicals
Number of teachers: 333
Number of students: 3,754
Publications: *St Thomas Magazine* (3 a year), *The Summa* (8 a year), *UST Insider* (3 a year)

DEANS

Cameron School of Business: Dr BARRY WILBRATTE
Extended Programs: Dr RAVI SRINIVAS
School of Arts and Sciences: Rev. JOSEPH PILSNER
School of Education: Dr NORA HUTTO
School of Nursing: Dr POLDI TSCHIRCH
School of Theology: Dr SANDRA MAGIE

UNIVERSITY OF TEXAS SYSTEM

601 Colorado St, Austin, TX 78701-2982

Telephone: (512) 499-4200
Fax: (512) 499-4215
Internet: www.utsystem.edu

Founded 1883
Chancellor: Dr FRANCISCO GONZALEZ CIGARROA
Exec. Vice-Chancellor for Academic Affairs: Dr PEDRO REYES
Exec. Vice-Chancellor for Business Affairs: SCOTT C. KELLEY
Vice-Chancellor for Admin.: TONYA MOTEN BROWN
Vice-Chancellor for Community and Business Relations: JOHN DE LA GARZA, JR
Vice-Chancellor for External Relations: RANDA S. SAFADY
Vice-Chancellor for Fed. Relations: WILLIAM H. SHUTE
Vice-Chancellor for Governmental Relations: BARRY R. MCBEE
Vice-Chancellor and Gen. Counsel: BARRY D. BURGDORF
Number of teachers: 18,893
Number of students: 211,213.

CONSTITUENT INSTITUTIONS

University of Texas at Austin

1 University Station, Austin, TX 78712

Telephone: (512) 471-3434
Fax: (512) 475-7478
E-mail: president@po.utexas.edu
Internet: www.utexas.edu

Founded 1883 as Univ. of Texas, present name 1967
Academic year: September to May (2 terms)
Pres.: WILLIAM POWERS, JR
Provost and Exec. Vice-Pres.: STEVEN LESLIE

Vice-Pres. and Chief Financial Officer: KEVIN P. HEGARTY
Vice-Pres. for Research: JUAN M. SANCHEZ
Vice-Pres. for Student Affairs: JUAN C. GONZÁLEZ
Vice-Pres. for Univ. Operations: PATRICIA L. CLUBB
Chief Information Officer and Assoc. Vice-Pres.: BRAD ENGLERT
Dean of Students and Sr Assoc. Vice-Pres. for Student Affairs: Dr SONCIA REAGINS-LILLY
Vice-Provost and Registrar: SHELBY STANFIELD
Vice-Provost and Dir of Libraries: FRED M. HEATH
Library: see under Libraries and Archives
Number of teachers: 3,271
Number of students: 51,195

DEANS

Cockrell College of Engineering: Dr GREGORY L. FENVES
College of Communication: RODERICK P. HART
College of Education: Prof. Dr MANUEL J. JUSTIZ
College of Fine Arts: DOUGLAS DEMPSTER
College of Liberal Arts: Dr RANDY L. DIEHL
College of Natural Sciences: Prof. Dr LINDA HICKE
College of Pharmacy: Dr M. LYNN CRISMON
Graduate School: Dr JUDITH H. LANGLOIS
Jackson School of Geosciences: Dr SHARON MOSHER
LBJ School of Public Affairs: Dr ROBERT HUTCHINGS
McCombs School of Business: Dr THOMAS W. GILLIGAN
School of Architecture: Dr FREDERICK R. STEINER
School of Information: Prof. Dr ANDREW P. DILLON
School of Law: WARD FARNSWORTH
School of Nursing: Prof. Dr ALEXA K. STUIFBERGEN
School of Social Work: Prof. Dr LUIS H. ZAYAS
School of Undergraduate Studies: Prof. PAUL WOODRUFF

PROFESSORS

School of Architecture:
ALOFSIN, A.
ARUMI, F. N.
ATKINSON, S. D.
BENEDIKT, M. L.
BLACK, J. S.
GARRISON, M. L.
KAHN, T. D.
KWALLEK, N. P.
LEIDING, G.
SPECK, L. W.
SWALLOW, R. P.
WILSON, P. A.

School of Information:
DAVIS, D. G., Jr
GRACY, II, D. B.
HALLMARK, J.
HARMON, E. G.
IMMROTH, B. F.
LUKENBILL, W. B.
MIKSA, F. L.
ROY, L.

School of Law:
ANDERSON, D. A.
ASCHER, M. L.
BAKER, L. A.
BERMAN, M. N.
BLACK, B. S.
BLAIS, L. E.
BOBBITT, P. C.
CARSON, II, L. C.
CHURGIN, M. J.
CLEVELAND, S. H.
COHEN, J. M.
DAWSON, R. O.

DIX, G. E.
DZIENKOWSKI, J. S.
ENGLE, K. L.
FORBATH, W. E.
GERGEN, M. P.
GETMAN, J. G.
GOODE, S. J.
GRAGLIA, L. A.
HANSEN, P. I.
HU, H. T. C.
JOHANSON, S. M.
JOHNSON, C. H.
KLEIN, S. R.
LAYCOCK, H. D.
LEITER, B. R.
LEVINSON, S. V.
MCGARITY, T. O.
MANN, R. J.
MARKESINIS, B. S.
MARKOVITS, I.
MARKOVITS, R. S.
MULLENIX, L. S.
PERONI, R. J.
POWE, L. A., JR
RABBAN, D. M.
RAU, A. S.
REESE, R. A.
ROBERTSON, D. W.
ROBERTSON, J. A.
SAGER, L.
SAMPSON, J. J.
SHARLOT, M. M.
SILVER, C. M.
SMITH, E. E.
STEIKER, J. M.
STURLEY, M. F.
TORRES, G.
WAGNER, W. E.
WEINBERG, L.
WELLBORN, O. G.
WESTBROOK, J. L.
WOOLLEY, P.
YOUNG, E. A.

School of Nursing:
GROBE, S. J.
HOUSTON, L. S.
PENTICUFF, J. H.
REW, D. L.
STUIFBERGEN, A. M.
WALKER, L. O.

School of Social Work:
CHOI, N.
DINITTO, D. M.
FONG, R.
FRANKLIN, C. G. S.
GREENE, R. R.
LAUDERDALE, M. L.
LEIN, L.
MCROY, R. G.
POOLE, D. L.
RUBIN, A.
SCHWAB, A. J., Jr
SHORKEY, C. T.
STREETER, C. L.

LBJ School of Public Affairs:
APFEL, K. S.
AUERBACH, R. D.
BOSKE, L. B.
EATON, D. J.
FLAMM, K.
GALBRAITH, J. K.
HAMILTON, D. S.
INMAN, B. R.
RHODES, L.
SCHOTT, R. L.
SPELMAN, W. G.
WARNER, D. C.
WILSON, R. H.

McCombs School of Business:
ALLISON, J. R., Management Science and Information Systems
ALPERT, M. I., Marketing Admin.
ANDERSON, U. L., Accounting
ATIASE, R., Accounting

BAGCHI, U., Management
BALAKRISHNAN, A., Management Science and Information Systems
BARUA, A., Management Science and Information Systems
BROCKETT, P. L., Management Science and Information Systems
BRONIARCZYK, S. M., Marketing Admin.
BROWN, K. C., Finance
BUTLER, J. S., Management
COX III, E. P., Marketing Admin.
CROSS, F. B., Management Science and Information Systems
CUNNINGHAM, W. H., Marketing Admin.
DAMIEN, P., Management Science and Information Systems
DAVIS-BLAKE, A., Management
DEITRICK, J. W., Accounting
DUKERICH, J. M., Management
DYER, J. S., Management Science and Information Systems
FITZSIMMONS, J. A., Management
FREDRICKSON, J. W., Management
FREEMAN, R. N., Accounting
GOLDEN, L. L., Marketing Admin.
GRANOF, M. H., Accounting
HENION, II, K. E., Marketing Admin.
HIRST, D. E., Accounting
HOYER, W. D., Marketing Admin.
HUBER, G. P., Management
HUFF, D. L., Marketing Admin.
JARVENPAA, S. L., Management Science and Information Systems
JEMISON, D. B., Management
JENNINGS, R. G., Accounting
KACHELMEIER, S. J., Accounting
KINNEY, W. R., Jr, Accounting
KOEHLER, J. J., Management Science and Information Systems
KOONCE, L. L., Accounting
LASDON, L. S., Management Science and Information Systems
LIMBERG, S. T., Accounting
MCALISTER, L. M., Marketing Admin.
MCDANIEL, R. R., JR, Management Science and Information Systems
MAGEE, S. P., Finance
MAHAJAN, V., Marketing Admin.
MAY, R. G., Accounting
METTLEN, R. D., Finance
MORRICE, D. J., Management
MURRAY, P. C., Management Science and Information Systems
NEWMAN, D. P., Accounting
PETERSON, R. A., Marketing Admin.
PRENTICE, R. A., Management Science and Information Systems
RAO, R. K. S., Finance
ROBINSON, J. R., Accounting
RONN, E. I., Finance
RUEFLI, T. W., Management Science and Information Systems
SAGER, T. W., Management Science and Information Systems
SALBU, S. R., Management Science and Information Systems
SHAW, B. M., Management Science and Information Systems
SHIVELY, T. S., Management Science and Information Systems
SPELLMAN, L. J., Finance
STARKS, L. T., Finance
TITMAN, S., Finance
WESTPHAL, J. D., Management
WHINSTON, A. B., Management Science and Information Systems
YU, G., Management Science and Information Systems

College of Communication:

ALVES, R. C., Journalism
BERG, C. E., Radio, Television, Film
BRANHAM, L. E., Journalism
BROWNING, L. D., Communication Studies
BRUMMETT, B., Communication Studies
BURNS, N. M., Advertising

CHAMPLIN, C. A., Communication Sciences and Disorders
CHERWITZ, R. A., Communication Studies
CUNNINGHAM, I. C., Advertising
DALY, J. A., Communication Studies
DARLING, D. C., Journalism
DAVIS, B. L., Communication Sciences and Disorders
GILLAM, R. B., Communication Sciences and Disorders
KNAPP, M. L., Communication Studies
LECKENBY, J. D., Advertising
MCCOMBS, M. E., Journalism
MARQUARDT, T. P., Communication Sciences and Disorders
MARTIN, F. N., Communication Sciences and Disorders
MAXWELL, M. M., Communication Studies
MORRISON, D. K., Advertising
MURPHY, J. H., Advertising
OLASKY, M. N., Journalism
REESE, S. D., Journalism
RICHARDS, J. I., Advertising
SCHATZ, T. G., Radio-Television-Film
STAIGER, J., Radio-Television-Film
STEKLER, P. J., Radio-Television-Film
STOUT, P. A., Advertising
STRAUBHAAR, J., Radio-Television-Film
STROVER, S. L., Radio-Television-Film
TODD, R. G., Journalism
VANGELISTI, A. L., Communication Studies
WILCOX, G. B., Advertising
WILLIAMS, J. D., Advertising

College of Education:

ABRAHAM, L. D., Curriculum and Instruction
AINSLIE, R. C., Educational Psychology
BARUFALDI, J. P., Curriculum and Instruction
BETHEL, L. J., Curriculum and Instruction
BORICH, G. D., Educational Psychology
BRYANT, D. P., Special Education
CANTU, N. V., Educational Admin.
CARLSON, C. I., Educational Psychology
CHALIP, L. H., Kinesiology and Health Education
COYLE, E. F., Kinesiology and Health Education
DAVIS, O. L., JR, Curriculum and Instruction
DODD, B. G., Educational Psychology
DUNCAN, J. P., Educational Adminstration
EMMER, E. T., Educational Psychology
FALBO, T. L., Educational Psychology
FARRAR, R. P., Kinesiology and Health Education
FIELD, S. L., Curriculum and Instruction
FOLEY, D. E., Curriculum and Instruction
GOTTLIEB, N. H., Kinesiology and Health Education
GUSZAK, F. J., Curriculum and Instruction
HOFFMAN, J. V., Curriculum and Instruction
HOLAHAN, C. K., Kinesiology and Health Education
HORWITZ, E. K., Curriculum and Instruction
IVY, J. L., Kinesiology and Health Education
KAMEEN, M. C., Educational Admin.
KEITH, T. Z., Educational Psychology
KOCH, W. R., Educational Psychology
LASHER, W. F., Educational Adminstration
MANASTER, G. J., Educational Psychology
MOORE, W., Educational Admin.
ORTIZ, A. A., Special Education
OVANDO, M. N., Educational Admin.
PARKER, R. M., Special Education
REIFEL, S., Curriculum and Instruction
RESTA, P. E., Curriculum and Instruction
RICHARDSON, F. C., Educational Psychology
RIETH, H. J., Special Education
ROSER, N. L., Curriculum and Instruction
ROUECHE, J. E., JR, Educational Admin.
SCHALLERT, D. L., Educational Psychology

SCRIBNER, J. D., Educational Admin.
SEMRUD-CLIKEMAN, M., Educational Psychology
SIGAFOOS, J., Special Education
SPIRDUSO, W. W., Kinesiology and Health Education
STARK, K. D., Educational Psychology
STARNES, J. W., Kinesiology and Health Education
STEINHARDT, M. A., Kinesiology and Health Education
THOMAS, M. P., JR, Educational Admin.
VALENCIA, R., Educational Psychology
VAUGHN, S., Special Education
WEINSTEIN, C. E., Educational Psychology
WICKER, F. W., Educational Psychology
YATES, J. R., Educational Admin.

College of Engineering:

ABRAHAM, J. A., Electrical and Computer Engineering
AGGARWAL, J. K., Electrical and Computer Engineering
ALLEN, D. T., Chemical Engineering
AMBLER, A. P., Electrical and Computer Engineering
ARAPOSTATHIS, A., Electrical and Computer Engineering
BABUSKA, I. M., Aerospace Engineering
BALDICK, R., Electrical and Computer Engineering
BANERJEE, S. K., Electrical and Computer Engineering
BARBER, K. S., Electrical and Computer Engineering
BARD, J. F., Mechanical Engineering
BARNES, J. W., Mechanical Engineering
BARR, R. E., Mechanical Engineering
BEAMAN, J. J., JR, Mechanical Engineering
BECKER, E. B., Aerospace Engineering
BECKER, M. F., Electrical and Computer Engineering
BENNIGHOF, J. K., Aerospace Engineering
BISHOP, R. H., Aerospace Engineering
BOGARD, D. G., Mechanical Engineering
BONNECAZE, R. T., Chemical Engineering
BOSTICK, F. X., JR, Electrical and Computer Engineering
BOURELL, D. L., Mechanical Engineering
BOVIK, A. C., Electrical and Computer Engineering
BREEN, J. E., Civil Engineering
BRYANT, M. D., Mechanical Engineering
BUCKMAN, A. B., Electrical and Computer Engineering
CAMPBELL, J. C., Electrical and Computer Engineering
CAREY, G. F., Aerospace Engineering
CHARBENEAU, R. J., Civil Engineering
CHEN, R. T., Electrical and Computer Engineering
COGDELL, J. R., Electrical and Computer Engineering
CORSI, R. L., Civil Engineering
CRAWFORD, M. E., Mechanical Engineering
CRAWFORD, M. M., Mechanical Engineering
CRAWFORD, R. H., Mechanical Engineering
DAWSON, C. N., Aerospace Engineering
DE VECIANA, G. A., Electrical and Computer Engineering
DEMKOWICZ, L. F., Aerospace Engineering
DEPPE, D. G., Electrical and Computer Engineering
DILLER, K. R., Biomedical Engineering
DODABALAPUR, A., Electrical and Computer Engineering
DOLLING, D. S., Aerospace Engineering
DRIGA, M. D., Electrical and Computer Engineering
EDGAR, T. F., Chemical Engineering
EKERDT, J. G., Chemical Engineering
ELLZEY, J. L., Mechanical Engineering
ENGELHARDT, M. D., Civil Engineering
FAHRENTHOLD, E. P., Mechanical Engineering

FLAKE, R. H., Electrical and Computer Engineering
FOWLER, D. W., Civil Engineering
FOWLER, W. T., Aerospace Engineering
FRANK, K. H., Civil Engineering
FREEMAN, B. D., Chemical Engineering
GARG, V. K., Electrical and Computer Engineering
GEORGIOU, G., Chemical Engineering
GHOSH, J., Electrical and Computer Engineering
GIBSON, G. E., Jr, Civil Engineering
GOODENOUGH, J. B., Mechanical Engineering
GRADY, W. M., Electrical and Computer Engineering
GRAY, K. E., Petroleum and Geosystems Engineering
GREEN, P. F., Chemical Engineering
HAAS, C. T., Civil Engineering
HALL, M. J., Mechanical Engineering
HALLOCK, G. A., Electrical and Computer Engineering
HAMILTON, M. F., Mechanical Engineering
HAYES, L. J., Aerospace Engineering
HO, P. S., Mechanical Engineering
HOWELL, J. R., Mechanical Engineering
HUGHES, T. J., Aerospace Engineering
HULL, D. G., Aerospace Engineering
JIRSA, J. O., Civil Engineering
JOHNSTON, K. P., Chemical Engineering
JOSE-YACAMAN, M., Chemical Engineering
KINNAS, S. A., Civil Engineering
KLINGNER, R. E., Civil Engineering
KOEN, B. V., Mechanical Engineering
KWONG, D.-L., Electrical and Computer Engineering
KYRIAKIDES, S., Aerospace Engineering
LAKE, L. W., Petroleum and Geosystems Engineering
LANDSBERGER, S., Mechanical Engineering
LAWLER, D. F., Civil Engineering
LEE, J. C., Electrical and Computer Engineering
LIECHTI, K. M., Aerospace Engineering
LILJESTRAND, H. M., Civil Engineering
LING, H., Electrical and Computer Engineering
LIPOVSKI, G. J., Electrical and Computer Engineering
LLOYD, D. R., Chemical Engineering
MACHEMEHL, R. B., Civil Engineering
MCKINNEY, D. C., Civil Engineering
MAIDMENT, D. R., Civil Engineering
MALINA, J. F., JR, Civil Engineering
MANTHIRAM, A., Mechanical Engineering
MARK, H. M., Aerospace Engineering
MASADA, G. Y., Mechanical Engineering
MATTHEWS, R. D., Mechanical Engineering
MEAR, M. E., Aerospace Engineering
MOON, T. J., Mechanical Engineering
MULLINS, C. B., Chemical Engineering
NEIKIRK, D. P., Electrical and Computer Engineering
NICHOLS, S. P., Mechanical Engineering
O'CONNOR, J. T., Civil Engineering
ODEN, J. T., Aerospace Engineering
PANDY, M. G., Biomedical Engineering
PANTON, R. L., Mechanical Engineering
PATT, Y. N., Electrical and Computer Engineering
PAUL, D. R., Chemical Engineering
PEARCE, J. A., Electrical and Computer Engineering
PEPPAS, N. A., Biomedical Engineering
PERRY, D. E., Electrical and Computer Engineering
PETERS, E. J., Petroleum and Geosystems Engineering
POPE, G. A., Petroleum and Geosystems Engineering
POWERS, E. J., JR, Electrical and Computer Engineering
QIN, S. Z. J., Chemical Engineering
RALLS, K. M., Mechanical Engineering

RAPPAPORT, T. S., Electrical and Computer Engineering
RAVI-CHANDAR, K. A., Aerospace Engineering
REIBLE, D. D., Civil Engineering
RICHARDS KORTUM, R. R., Biomedical Engineering
ROCHELLE, G. T., Chemical Engineering
RODIN, G. J., Aerospace Engineering
ROSSEN, W. R., Petroleum and Geosystems Engineering
RYLANDER III, H. G., Biomedical Engineering
SANCHEZ, I. C., Chemical Engineering
SANDBERG, I. W., Electrical and Computer Engineering
SCHMIDT, P. S., Mechanical Engineering
SCHUTZ, B. E., Aerospace Engineering
SEPEHRNOORI, K., Petroleum and Geosystems Engineering
SHARMA, M. M., Petroleum and Geosystems Engineering
SORBER, C. A., Civil Engineering
SPEITEL, G. E., JR, Civil Engineering
STEARMAN, R. O., Aerospace Engineering
STOKOE II, K. H., Civil Engineering
SWARTZLANDER, E. E., JR, Electrical and Computer Engineering
TAPLEY, B. D., Aerospace Engineering
TASSOULAS, J. L., Civil Engineering
TESAR, D., Mechanical Engineering
VALVANO, J. W., Electrical and Computer Engineering
VANRENSBURG, W. C. J., Petroleum and Geosystems Engineering
VARGHESE, P. L., Aerospace Engineering
VLIET, G. C., Mechanical Engineering
WAGNER, T. J., Electrical and Computer Engineering
WALSER, R. M., Electrical and Computer Engineering
WALTON, C. M., Civil Engineering
WELCH, A. J., Biomedical Engineering
WHEELER, M. F., Aerospace Engineering
WILLSON, C. G., Chemical Engineering
WOMACK, B. F., Electrical and Computer Engineering
WOOD, K. L., Mechanical Engineering
WOOD, S. L., Civil Engineering
WRIGHT, S. G., Civil Engineering
YURA, J. A., Civil Engineering

College of Fine Arts:
ALLEN, G. D., Music
ANTOKELETZ, E. M., Music
BALTZER, R. A., Music
BARNITZ, J. E., Art and Art History
BEHAGUE, G. H., Music
BLOOM, M., Theatre and Dance
BOLIN, P. E., Art and Art History
BRICKENS, N. O., Music
BROCKETT, O. G., Theatre and Dance
BROOKS, R. L., Art and Art History
CHANDLER, B. G., Music
CLARKE, J. R., Art and Art History
COLES, T. R., Art and Art History
DALY, S. J., Art and Art History
DEMPSTER, D. J., Theatre and Dance
DESIMONE, R. A., Music
DOLAN, J. S., Theatre and Dance
DORN, F., Theatre and Dance
DUKE, R. A., Music
ERLMANN, V. F., Music
GARRETT, N. B., Music
GLAVAN, J. J., Theatre and Dance
GOODMAN, M. K., Art and Art History
GRANTHAM, D. J., Music
GUERRA, L. A., Music
HALE, K. J., Art and Art History
HELLMER, J. L., Music
HENDERSON, L. D., Art and Art History
HILLEY, M. F., Music
HOLLADAY, J. A., Art and Art History
HOLZMAN, A., Music
ISACKES, R. M., Theatre and Dance
JELLISON, J. A., Music

JENNINGS, C. A., Theatre and Dance
JUNKIN, J. F., Music
LEWIS, W. L., Music
LUCERO, A. L., Theatre and Dance
LUNDBERG, W. A., Art and Art History
McFARLAND, L. D., Art and Art History
MARCH, H. C., Music
MARIANI, V. A., Art and Art History
MILLER, L. C., Theatre and Dance
MILLIKEN, G., Art and Art History
NEL, A., Music
NEUBERT, B. D., Music
NEUMEYER, D. P., Music
PINKSTON, R. F., Music
PITTEL, H. C., Music
RICHTER, G. A., Music
SASAKI, R. K., Music
SAWYER, M. L., Art and Art History
SCHMIDT, R. N., Theatre and Dance
SHIFF, R. A., Art and Art History
SLAWEK, S. M., Music
SMITH, J. C., Art and Art History
STUART, D. S., Art and Art History
TAYLOR, R. A., Music
TUSA, M. C., Music
ULBRICHT, J. W., Art and Art History
WELCHER, D. E., Music
WILEY, D. C., Music
WIMAN, L. R., Art and Art History
YOUNG, P. C., Music
ZEDER, S. L., Theatre and Dance

College of Liberal Arts:
ABBOUD, P. F., Middle Eastern Studies
ABZUG, R. H., History
ALBRECHT, D. G., Psychology
ALLAIRE, E. B., Philosophy
ANGEL, R. J., Sociology
ANGELELLI, I. A., Philosophy
ARENS, K. M., Germanic Studies
ARMSTRONG, D., Classics
ASHER, N. M., Philosophy
AYRES, J. B., English
BAKER, M.-F. J., French and Italian
BAR-ADON, A., Middle Eastern Studies
BARANY, Z. D., Government
BARNOUW, J., English
BEALER, G., Philosophy
BERNUCCI, L. M., Spanish and Portuguese
BERTELSEN, L., English
BINI, D., French and Italian
BIOW, D. G., French and Italian
BIRDSONG, D. P., French and Italian
BLOCKLEY, M. E., English
BONEVAC, D. A., Philosophy
BRAYBROOKE, D., Government
BRONARS, S. G., Economics
BROW, J. B., Anthropology
BROWN, J. C., History
BROWN, N. D., History
BUCHANAN, II, B., Government
BUDZISZEWSKI, J., Government
BUMP, J. F., English
BUSS, A. H., Psychology
BUSS, D. M., Psychology
BUTZER, K. W., Geography
CABLE, T. M., English
CARLSON, C. L., Psychology
CARTER, J. C., Classics
CARTON, E. B., English
CARVER, L. D., English
CAUSEY, R. L., Philosophy
CAUVIN, J.-P. B., French and Italian
CHANG, S.-S., Asian Studies
CHARNEY, D. H., Rhetoric and Composition
COHEN, L. B., Psychology
COOPER, R. W., Economics
CORBAE, P. D., Economics
CREW, D. F., History
CULLINGFORD, E., English
CVETKOVICH, A., English
DACY, D. C., Economics
DAVIES, C. S., Geography
DAWSON, R. L., French and Italian
DEIGH, J., Philosophy
DIEHL, R. L., Psychology

DIETZ, H. A., Government
DOMJAN, M. P., Psychology
DONAHUE, F. E., Germanic Studies
DONALD, S., Economics
DOOLITTLE, W., Geography
DOUGHTY, R. W., Geography
DULLES, J. W. F., American Studies
DUSANSKY, R., Economics
EDLUND-BERRY, I. M., Classics
EDWARDS, D. V., Government
ELLISON, C. G., Sociology
ENELOW, J. M., Government
ENGLAND, N. C., Linguistics
FAIGLEY, L. L., English
FALOLA, O. O., History
FARRELL, J. P., English
FLORES, R. R., Anthropology
FREEMAN, G. P., Government
FRIEDMAN, A. W., English
FRISBIE, W. P., Sociology
FULLERTON, D., Economics
FURMAN, L. J., English
GAGARIN, M., Classics
GALINSKY, G. K., Classics
GALLE, O. R., Sociology
GARRISON, J. D., English
GEISLER, III, W. S., Psychology
GERACI, V. J., Economics
GHANOONPARVAR, M., Middle Eastern Studies
GHOSE, Z. A., English
GILDEN, D. L., Psychology
GLADE, W. P., Economics
GLENN, N. D., Sociology
GOETZMANN, W. H., History
GONZALEZ-GERTH, M., Spanish and Portuguese
GONZALEZ-LIMA, F., Psychology
GRAHAM, D. B., English
HAKE, S., Germanic Studies
HAMERMESH, D. S., Economics
HANCOCK, I. F., Linguistics
HANKINSON, R. J., Philosophy
HANSEN, K. G., Asian Studies
HARLOW, B. J., English
HARMS, R. T., Linguistics
HEINZELMAN, K. O., English
HELMREICH, R. L., Psychology
HENDRICKS, K., Economics
HENRY, C. M., Government
HENSEY, F. G., Spanish and Portuguese
HIGGINS, K. M., Philosophy
HIGLEY, J. C., Government
HILFER, A. C., English
HILLMANN, M. C., Middle Eastern Studies
HINICH, M. J., Government
HINOJOSASMITH, R., English
HOBERMAN, J. M., Germanic Studies
HOCHBERG, H. I., Philosophy
HOLAHAN, C. J., Psychology
HOLDEN, G. W., Psychology
HOPKINS, A. G., History
HORN, J. M., Psychology
HUBBARD, T. K., Classics
HUMMER, R. A., Sociology
JACOBSOHN, G. J., Government
KALLET, L., Classics
KANE, R. H., Philosophy
KAPPELMAN, J. W., Jr, Anthropology
KAULBACH, E. N., English
KELLY, W. R., Sociology
KENDRICK, D. A., Economics
KING, R. D., Linguistics
KOLSTI, J. S., Slavic Languages and Literatures
KOONS, R. C., Philosophy
KROLL, J. H., Classics
KRONZ, F. M., Philosophy
KRUPPA, J. E., English
KURTZ, L. R., Sociology
LAMBRECHT, K. P., French and Italian
LAMPHEAR, J. E., History
LANGLOIS, J. H., Psychology
LaSALLE, P. N., English
LEVACK, B. P., History
LIEBOWITZ, H. A., Middle Eastern Studies

LIMON, J. E., English
LINDSTROM, N. E., Spanish and Portuguese
LIPPMANN, J. N., French and Italian
LITVAK, L., Spanish and Portuguese
LOUIS, W. R., History
LUJAN, M. E., Spanish and Portuguese
McFADDEN, D., Psychology
MACKAY, C. H., English
MacNEILAGE, P. F., Psychology
MAGNUSON, J. L., English
MANNERS, I. R., Geography
MARKMAN, A. B., Psychology
MARSHALL, S. E., Sociology
MARTINICH, A. P., Philosophy
MEIER, R. P., Linguistics
MEIKLE, J. L., American Studies
MENCHACA, M., Anthropology
MINAULT, G., History
MIROWSKY, J., Sociology
MONTREUIL, J.-P., French and Italian
MORGAN, M. G., Classics
MOURELATOS, A., Philosophy
MULLIN, J. A., Rhetoric and Composition
NAPIER, S. J., Asian Studies
NETHERCUT, W. R., Classics
NEWTON, A. Z., English
NORMAN, A. L., Economics
OLIVELLE, J. P., Asian Studies
OSHINSKY, D. A., History
PALAIMA, T. G., Classics
PANGLE, T. L., Government
PARKER, D. S., Classics
PELLS, R. H., History
PENNEBAKER, J. W., Psychology
PEREZ, F. L., Geography
PHILLIPS, S. H., Philosophy
POTTER, J. E., Sociology
PRINDLE, D. F., Government
PULLUM, T. W., Sociology
RAMIREZ III, M., Psychology
RAPPAPORT, G. C., Slavic Languages and Literature
REBHORN, W. A., JR, English
RENWICK, R. D., English
ROBERTS, B. E., Government
ROBERTS, B. R., Sociology
ROSS, C. E., Sociology
ROSSMAN, C. R., English
RUMRICH, J. P., English
RUSZKIEWICZ, J. J., Rhetoric and Composition
SAINSBURY, R. M., Philosophy
SARKAR, S., Philosophy
SCHALLERT, T. J., Psychology
SCHEICK, W. J., English
SEUNG, T. K., Philosophy
SHELMERDINE, C. W., Classics
SHERZER, D. M., French and Italian
SHERZER, J. F., Anthropology
SHUMWAY, N., Spanish and Portuguese
SINGH, D., Psychology
SJOBERG, G. A., Sociology
SLESNICK, D. T., Economics
SMITH, C. S., Linguistics
SOLE, C. A., Spanish and Portuguese
SOLOMON, R. C., Philosophy
STAFFORD, M. C., Sociology
STAHL, II, D. O., Economics
STINCHCOMBE, M. B., Economics
STROSS, B. M., Anthropology
SUSSMAN, H. M., Linguistics
SWAFFAR, J. K., Germanic Studies
SWANN, W. B., Jr, Psychology
TELCH, M. J., Psychology
TRIMBLE, J. R., English
TULLY, W. A., History
TWINAM, A., History
TYE, M., Philosophy
TYLER, R. C., History
UMBERSON, D. J., Sociology
VAN OLPHEN, H. H., Asian Studies
WAGNER, R. H., Government
WALKER, J., Rhetoric and Composition
WALKER, J. E., History
WALKER, S. S., Anthropology
WALTERS, S. K., Linguistics

WARD, P., Sociology
WARR, E. M., Sociology
WEINSTOCK, J. M., Germanic Studies
WEVILL, D. A., English
WEYLAND, K. G., Government
WHIGHAM, F. F., JR, English
WHITBREAD, T. B., English
WHITE, L. M., Classics
WILCZYNSKI, W., Psychology
WILLIAMS, C. L., Sociology
WILSON, P. W., Economics
WILSON, S. M., Anthropology
WINSHIP, M. B., English
WOLITZ, S. L., French and Italian
WOODBURY, A. C., Linguistics
WOODRUFF, P. B., Philosophy
ZIMIC, S., Spanish and Portuguese
ZONN, L. E., Geography

College of Natural Sciences:

ANSLYN, E. V., Chemistry and Biochemistry
ANTONIEWICZ, P. R., Physics
APPLING, D. R., Chemistry and Biochemistry
ARBOGAST, T. J., Mathematics
ARMENDARIZ, E. P., Mathematics
ARTZT, K. J., Molecular Genetics and Microbiology
BAJAJ, C. L., Computer Sciences
BANNER, J. L., Geological Sciences
BARBARA, P. F., Chemistry and Biochemistry
BARD, A. J., Chemistry and Biochemistry
BASH, F. N., Astronomy
BATORY, D. S., Computer Sciences
BAULD, N. L., Chemistry and Biochemistry
BECKNER, W., Mathematics
BENGTSON, R. D., Physics
BENNETT, P. C., Geological Sciences
BERK, H. L., Physics
BICHTELER, K. R., Mathematics
BITTNER, G. D., Neurobiology
BOHM, A. R., Physics
BOSE, H. R., Molecular Genetics and Microbiology
BOYER, R. S., Computer Sciences
BRAND, J. J., Molecular Cell and Development Biology
BRILEY, M. E., Human Ecology
BRODBELT, J. S., Chemistry and Biochemistry
BRONSON, F. H., Integrative Biology
BROWN, R. M., JR, Molecular Genetics and Microbiology
BROWNE, J. C., Computer Sciences
BULL, J. J., Integrative Biology
BUSKEY, E. J., Marine Science
CAFFARELLI, L. A., Mathematics
CAMPION, A., Chemistry and Biochemistry
CARLSON, W. D., Geological Sciences
CHENEY, E. W., Mathematics
CHIU, C. B., Physics
CLINE, A. K., Computer Sciences
CLOOS, M. P., Geological Sciences
COKER, W. R., Physics
COWLEY, A. H., Chemistry and Biochemistry
CREWS, D. P., Integrative Biology
DANIEL, J. W., Mathematics
DAVIS, R. E., Chemistry and Biochemistry
DE LA LLAVE, R., Mathematics
DE LOZANNE, A. L., Physics
DICUS, D. A., Physics
DINERSTEIN, H. L., Astronomy
DISTLER, J., Physics
DOWNER, M. W., Physics
DRUMMOND, W. E., Physics
DUDLEY, J. P., Molecular Genetics and Microbiology
DUNTON, K. H., Marine Science
DURBIN, J. R., Mathematics
EARHART, C. F., Molecular Genetics and Microbiology
ELLINGTON, A., Chemistry and Biochemistry

EMERSON, II, E. A., Computer Sciences
ENGQUIST, B., Mathematics
ERSKINE, J. L., Physics
EVANS, II, N. J., Astronomy
FINK, M., Physics
FISCHLER, W., Physics
FISHER, W. L., Geological Sciences
FOWLER, N. L., Integrative Biology
FREED, D. S., Mathematics
FREELAND, J. H., Human Ecology
FREEMAN, G. L., Integrative Biology
FROMMHOLD, L. W., Physics
FUSSELL, D. S., Computer Sciences
GAMBA, I. M., Mathematics
GARDNER, W. S., Marine Science
GENTLE, K. W., Physics
GERTH III, F. E., Mathematics
GILBERT, J. C., Chemistry and Biochemistry
GILBERT, J. E., Mathematics
GILBERT, L. E., Integrative Biology
GLEESON, A. M., Physics
GOMPF, R. E., Mathematics
GORDON, C. M., Mathematics
GOUDA, M. G., Computer Sciences
GRAND, S. P., Geological Sciences
GUY, W. T., JR, Mathematics
HACKERT, M. L., Chemistry and Biochemistry
HAMRICK, G. C., Mathematics
HARRIS, R. A., Neurobiology
HARSHEY, R. M., Molecular Genetics and Microbiology
HARVEY, P. M., Astronomy
HAZELTINE, R. D., Physics
HEINZEN, D. J., Physics
HEITMANN, R. C., Mathematics
HERRIN, D. L., Molecular Cell and Development Biology
HILLIS, D. M., Integrative Biology
HOFFMANN, G. W., Physics
HOLCOMBE, J. A., Chemistry and Biochemistry
HORTON, C. W., Jr, Physics
HUNT, W. A., JR, Computer Sciences
HUSTON, A. C., Human Ecology
HUSTON, T. L., Human Ecology
IVERSON, B. L., Chemistry and Biochemistry
JACOBVITZ, D. B., Human Ecology
JAFFE, D. T., Astronomy
JANSEN, R. K., Integrative Biology
JAYARAM, M., Molecular Genetics and Microbiology
JOHNSON, K., Chemistry and Biochemistry
JOHNSTON, D., Neurobiology
JONES, R. A., Chemistry and Biochemistry
KALTHOFF, K. O., Molecular Cell and Development Biology
KAPLUNOVSKY, V., Physics
KEEL, S. M., Mathematics
KETO, J. W., Physics
KIRKPATRICK, M. A., Integrative Biology
KITTO, G. B., Chemistry and Biochemistry
KLEINMAN, L., Physics
KLINE, K., Human Ecology
KOCH, H. A., Mathematics
KOCUREK, G. A., Geological Sciences
KORMENDY, J., Astronomy
KRISCHE, M. J., Chemistry and Biochemistry
KRUG, R. M., Molecular Genetics and Microbiology
KUIPERS, B. J., Computer Sciences
KUMAR, P., Astronomy
KYLE, J. R., Geological Sciences
LA CLAIRE, II, J. W., Molecular Cell and Development Biology
LACY, J. H., Astronomy
LAGOW, R. J., Chemistry and Biochemistry
LAGOWSKI, J. J., Chemistry and Biochemistry
LAGOWSKI, J. M., Neurobiology
LAM, S. S., Computer Sciences
LAMBOWITZ, A., Molecular Genetics and Microbiology

LANG, K., Physics
LARIMER, J. L., Neurobiology
LAUDE, D. A., Chemistry and Biochemistry
LEVIN, D. A., Integrative Biology
LIFSCHITZ, V., Computer Sciences
LONG, L. E., Geological Sciences
LOOP, R., Human Ecology
LUECKE, J. E., Mathematics
MABRY, T. J., Molecular Cell and Development Biology
MCADAM, S. J., Mathematics
MCBRIDE, E. F., Geological Sciences
MCDEVITT, J. T., Chemistry and Biochemistry
MACDONALD, A. H., Physics
MACDONALD, P. M., Molecular Cell and Development Biology
MAGNUS, P. D., Chemistry and Biochemistry
MARDER, M. P., Physics
MARKERT, J. T., Physics
MARTIN, S. F., Chemistry and Biochemistry
MATZNER, R. A., Physics
MAUSETH, J. D., Integrative Biology
MEYER, R. J., Molecular Genetics and Microbiology
MIIKKULAINEN, R. P., Computer Sciences
MISRA, J., Computer Sciences
MOK, A. K., Computer Sciences
MOLINEUX, I. J., Molecular Genetics and Microbiology
MONTAGNA, P. A., Marine Science
MOONEY, R. J., Computer Sciences
MOORE, C. F., Physics
MOORE, II, J. S., Computer Sciences
MORRISON, P. J., Physics
MOSHER, S., Geological Sciences
NAKAMURA, Y., Geological Sciences
NIU, Q., Physics
NOVAK, G. S., JR, Computer Sciences
OAKES, M. E. L., Physics
ODELL, E. W., Mathematics
PALKA, B. P., Mathematics
PAYNE, S. M., Molecular Genetics and Microbiology
PIANKA, E. R., Integrative Biology
PLAXTON, C. G., Computer Sciences
POLLAK, G. D., Neurobiology
PORTER, B. W., Computer Sciences
RADIN, C. L., Mathematics
RAIZEN, M. G., Physics
RAMACHANDRAN, V., Computer Sciences
REICHL, L. E., Physics
REID, A. W., Mathematics
RICHARDSON, R. H., Integrative Biology
RIGGS, II, A. F., Neurobiology
RILEY, P. J., Physics
RITCHIE, J. L., Physics
ROBERTUS, J. D., Chemistry and Biochemistry
ROBINSON, E. L., Astronomy
ROSENTHAL, H. P., Mathematics
ROSSKY, P. J., Chemistry and Biochemistry
ROUX, S. J., JR, Molecular Cell and Development Biology
ROWE, T. B., Geological Sciences
RYAN, H. M. J., Integrative Biology
SADUN, L. A., Mathematics
SALTMAN, D. J., Mathematics
SANDERS, B. G., Molecular Genetics and Microbiology
SCALO, J. M., Astronomy
SCHIEVE, W. C., Physics
SCHWITTERS, R. F., Physics
SEN, M. K., Geological Sciences
SESSLER, J. L., Chemistry and Biochemistry
SHANKLAND, S. M., Molecular, Cellular and Developmental Biology
SHAPIRO, P. R., Astronomy
SHARP, J. M., JR, Geological Sciences
SHIELDS, G. A., Astronomy
SHIH, C.-K., Physics
SIMPSON, B. B., Integrative Biology
SINGER, M. C., Integrative Biology
SITZ, G. O., Physics

SMITH, M. K., Mathematics
SNEDEN, C. A., Astronomy
SOUGDANIDIS, P. E., Mathematics
SPRINKLE, J. T., Geological Sciences
STANTON, J. F., Chemistry and Biochemistry
STARBIRD, M. P., Mathematics
STEEL, R. J., Geological Sciences
SUDARSHAN, G., Physics
SURRA, C. A., Human Ecology
SWIFT, J. B., Physics
SWINNEY, H. L., Physics
SZANISZLO, P. J., Molecular Genetics and Microbiology
TATE, J. T., Mathematics
TATHAM, R. H., Geological Sciences
THOMAS, P., Marine Science
THOMPSON, W. J., Neurobiology
TREISMAN, P. U., Mathematics
TUCKER, P. W., Molecular Genetics and Microbiology
UDAGAWA, T., Physics
UHLENBECK, K., Mathematics
VAALER, J. D., Mathematics
VAN DE GEIJN, R. A., Computer Sciences
VIN, H. M., Computer Sciences
VISHIK, M. M., Mathematics
VOLOCH, J. F., Mathematics
WALKER, J. R., Molecular Genetics and Microbiology
WARNOW, T., Computer Sciences
WEBBER, S. E., Chemistry and Biochemistry
WEINBERG, S., Physics
WHEELER, J. C., Astronomy
WHITE, J. M., Chemistry and Biochemistry
WILLIS, R. A., Human Ecology
WILLS, D., Astronomy
WILSON, C. R., Geological Sciences
WINGET, D. E., Astronomy
WYATT, R. E., Chemistry and Biochemistry
XIN, J., Mathematics
XU, B., Human Ecology
ZAKON, H. H., Neurobiology
ZARIPHOPOULOU, T., Mathematics
ZUCKERMAN, D. I., Computer Sciences

College of Pharmacy:
ABELL, C. W.
BUSSEY, H. I.
COMBS, A. B.
CRISMON, M. L.
DAVIS, P. J.
ERICKSON, C. K.
GONZALES, R. A.
KEHRER, J. P.
KOELLER, J. M.
KUHN, J. G.
LITTLEFIELD, L. C.
LIU, H.-W.
MCGINITY, J. W.
PEARLMAN, R.
RASCATI, K. L.
SHEPHERD, M. D.
STAVCHANSKY, S. A.
TALBERT, R. L., JR
WHITMAN, C. P.
WILCOX, R. E.

University of Texas at Arlington
701 S Nedderman Dr., Arlington, TX 76019
Telephone: (817) 272-2011
Fax: (817) 272-5656
E-mail: records@uta.edu
Internet: www.uta.edu

Founded 1895 as Arlington College, present name 1965
Academic year: August to May

Pres.: Dr JAMES D. SPANIOLO
Provost and Vice-Pres. for Academic Affairs: Dr RONALD L. ELSENBAUMER
Sr Vice-Pres. for Finance and Admin.: M. DAN WILLIAMS
Vice-Pres. for Admin. and Campus Operations: JOHN D. HALL

Vice-Pres. for Devt: JIM LEWIS
Vice-Pres. for Research: Dr CAROLYN L. CASON
Vice-Pres. for Student Affairs: Dr FRANK LAMAS
Dean of Library: JULIE ALEXANDER
Library of 1,204,064 vols, 275,606 e-books, 34,160 print e-serial titles, 38,231 e-serial titles, 1,486,429 microforms, 9,033 video items, 3,141 audio items, 34,722 maps
Number of teachers: 997
Number of students: 33,439 (25,419 undergraduate, 8,020 graduate)
Publication: *Research* (1 a year)

DEANS

College of Business: Prof. Dr DAVID A. GRAY
College of Education and Health Professions: Dr JEANNE MARCUM GERLACH
College of Engineering: Dr JEAN-PIERRE BARDET
College of Liberal Arts: Dr BETH WRIGHT (acting)
College of Nursing: Prof. Dr ELIZABETH C. POSTER
College of Science: Dr PAMELA JANSMA
Graduate School: Dr PHILIP COHEN
School of Architecture: Prof. DONALD F. GATZKE
School of Social Work: Dr SCOTT D. RYAN
School of Urban and Public Affairs: Dr BARBARA BECKER

University of Texas at Brownsville and Texas Southmost College

80 Fort Brown, Brownsville, TX 78520
Telephone: (956) 8828200
Fax: (956) 5448832
E-mail: admissions@utb.edu
Internet: www.utb.edu
Founded 1991
Languages of instruction: English, Spanish
Academic year: August to December
Pres.: Dr JULIET V. GARCÍA
Provost: Dr ALAN F. J. ARTIBISE
Vice-Pres. for Business Affairs: ROSEMARY MARTÍNEZ
Vice-Pres. for Economic Devt and Community Services: IRVINE DOWNING
Vice-Pres. for External Affairs: Dr TONY ZAVALETA
Vice-Pres. for Institutional Advancement: Dr MELONEY LINDER
Vice-Pres. for Partnership Affairs: Dr DAVID PEARSON
Vice-Pres. for Research: Dr LUIS COLOM
Vice-Pres. for Student Affairs: Dr HILDA SILVA
Registrar: AL BARREDA
Univ. Librarian: ANNABEL TREVINO
Library of 300,000 vols
Number of teachers: 598
Number of students: 13,836

DEANS

College of Biomedical Sciences and Health Professions: Dr ELDON NELSON
College of Education: Dr MIGUEL ANGEL ESCOTET
College of Liberal Arts: Dr DANIEL HEIMMERMANN
College of Nursing: Dr EDNA GARZA-ESCOBEDO
College of Science, Mathematics and Technology: Dr MIKHAIL BOUNIAEV
Graduate Studies: Dr CHARLES LACKEY
School of Business: Dr MARK KROLL
School of Health Sciences: Dr ELDON NELSON
Univ. College: Dr TERRY OVERTON

University of Texas at Dallas

800 W Campbell Rd, Richardson, TX 75080-3021
Telephone: (972) 883-2111
Fax: (972) 883-2237
E-mail: utdallas@utdallas.edu
Internet: www.utdallas.edu
Founded 1961 as Graduate Research Center of the Southwest, present name 1969
Academic year: September to August
Pres.: Dr DAVID E. DANIEL
Provost and Exec. Vice-Pres.: Dr B. HOBSON WILDENTHAL
Vice-Pres. for Admin.: Dr CALVIN JAMISON
Vice-Pres. for Budget and Finance: WANDA MIZUTOWICZ (acting)
Vice-Pres. for Business Affairs: Dr CALVIN JAMISON
Vice-Pres. for Devt and Alumni Relations: Dr AARON CONLEY
Vice-Pres. for Research: Dr. BRUCE GNADE
Vice-Pres. for Student Affairs: Dr DARRELENE RACHAVONG
Vice-Pres. for Enrolment Management: CURT ELY
Registrar: Dr KAREN JARRELL
Dir of Libraries: Dr ELLEN SAFLEY
Library of 2,504,906 vols, 1,829,754 titles, 2,860,567 microform units, 14,590 audiovisual items, 28,263 maps, 981,074 e-books, 63,256 e-journals, 212,157 govt documents
Number of teachers: 924
Number of students: 18,864
Publications: *The Exley, Issues in Science and Technology* (4 a year), *Political Research Quarterly, Public Administration Review* (6 a year), *Translation Review* (3 a year)

DEANS

Erik Jonsson School of Engineering and Computer Science: Dr MARK W. SPONG
Graduate Studies: Dr AUSTIN J. CUNNINGHAM
Naveen Jindal School of Management: Dr HASAN PIRKUL
School of Arts and Humanities: Dr DENNIS M. KRATZ
School of Behavioral and Brain Sciences: Dr BERT S. MOORE
School of Economic, Political and Policy Sciences: Dr JAMES W. MARQUART
School of Interdisciplinary Studies: Dr GEORGE W. FAIR
School of Natural Sciences and Mathematics: Dr BRUCE NOVAK
Undergraduate Education: Dr SHEILA AMIN GUTIERREZ DE PINERES

PROFESSORS

ABDI, H.
AIKEN, C.
ALI, A.
AMMANN, L.
ARGYROS, A.
ASSMANN, P.
BALKUS, K.
BALSARA, P.
BAMBACH, C.
BARON, M.
BARTLETT, J.
BASTANI, F.
BAUGHMAN, R.
BERON, K.
BLANCHARD, A.
BOWER, T.
BRETTELL, R.
BRIGGS, R.
BUHRMESTER, D.
BULLA, L.
BUTTS, T.
CALDWELL, R.
CANTRELL, C.
CHAMPAGNE, A.

CHANDRASEKARAN, R.
CHANEY, R.
CHANNELL, D.
CHAPMAN, S.
CLARKE, H.
COHEN, M.
COLLINS, C.
CREADY, W.
CURCHACK, F.
DAY, T.
DESS, G.
D'MELLO, S.
DOLLAGHAN, C.
DOWLING, W.
DRAPER, R.
DUMAS, L.
ECKEL, C.
EDMUNDS, R.
EFROMOVICH, S.
ELLIOTT, E.
ENTHOVEN, A.
FARAGO, A.
FENYVES, E.
FERRARIS, J.
FONSEKA, J.
FORD, D.
FRENSLEY, W.
FUMAGALLI, A.
GLOSSER, R.
GNADE, B.
GOLDEN, R.
GOODMAN, S.
GRAY, D.
GRIFFITH, D.
GUPTA, G.
HAMBLY, G.
HANSEN, J.
HARPHAM, E.
HEELIS, R.
HICKS, D.
HOFFMAN, J.
HOOSHYAR, M.
HULSE, R.
HUNT, L.
HUYNH, D.
IZEN, J.
JACOB, V.
JERGER, S.
KEHTARNAVAZ, N.
KEMPF-LEONARD, K.
KIASALEH, K.
KIEL, L.
KIM, M.
KONSTANS, C.
LEAF, M.
LEE, G.
LIEBOWITZ, S.
LINEHAN, T.
LOIZOU, P.
LOU, X.
LOWRY, R.
MACFARLANE, D.
MCMECHAN, G.
MADRIGUERA, E.
MAJUMDAR, S.
MANTON, W.
MARQUART, J.
MELTON, L.
MOLDOVAN, D.
MOLLER, A.
MOOKERJEE, V.
NADIN, M.
NIU, S.
NTAFOS, S.
OBER, R.
O'TOOLE, A.
OVERZET, L.
OWEN, M.
OZSVATH, I.
OZSVATH, Z.
PACE, B.
PENG, M.
PERVIN, W.
PRAGER, K.
RABE, S.
RADHAKRISHNAN, S.

RAGHAVACHARI, B.
RAO, R.
REDLINGER, L.
REDMAN, T.
REITZER, L.
REYNOLDS, R.
RICCIO, T.
RINDLER, W.
RODRIGUEZ, R.
ROESER, R.
SANDLER, T.
SANTROCK, J.
SARKAR, S.
SCHULTE, R.
SCOTCH, R.
SELDON, B.
SERFLING, R.
SETHI, S.
SHA, H.
SHERRY, A.
SRISKANDARAJAH, C.
STECKE, K.
STERN, R.
STEWART, M.
STILLMAN, R.
SUDBOROUGH, I.
TAMIL, L.
THIBODEAU, L.
THURAISINGHAM, B.
TINSLEY, B.
TOBEY, E.
TRACY, P.
TRUEMPER, K.
TURI, J.
TURNER, F.
ULATOWSKA, H.
UNDERWOOD, M.
VAN KLEECK, A.
VIJVERBERG, W.
WATSON, D.
WIORKOWSKI, J.
ZAKHIDOV, A.
ZHANG, K.
ZHENG, S.
ZHOU, D.

University of Texas at El Paso

500 W University Ave, El Paso, TX 79968-0500

Telephone: (915) 747-5000
Fax: (915) 747-8893
E-mail: uc@utep.edu
Internet: www.utep.edu

Founded 1914 as Texas School of Mines and Metallurgy, present name 1967
Academic year: August to August

Pres.: Prof. Dr DIANA NATALICIO
Sr Exec. Vice-Pres.: HAWARD C. DAUDISTEL
Exec. Vice-Pres.: RICARDO ADAUTO, III
Provost and Vice-Pres. for Academic Affairs: Dr JUNIUS GONZALES
Vice-Pres. for Business Affairs: CYNTHIA VIZCAINO VILLA
Vice-Pres. for Information Resources and Planning: STEPHEN RITER
Vice-Pres. for Research: Dr ROBERTO A. OSEGUEDA
Vice-Pres. for Student Affairs: GARY EDENS
Dean of Students: Dr WILLIAM SCHAFER
Exec. Dir of Admissions: LUISA M. HAVENS
Library Dir and Assoc. Vice-Pres.: ROBERT L. STAKES

Library: see under Libraries and Archives
Number of teachers: 1,241
Number of students: 22,640

Publications: *Nova* (9 a year), *Minero* (2 a year), *Rio Grande Review*, *Shangri-La*, *Southwestern Studies* (irregular), *Southwest Journal of Business and Economics* (irregular), *The Prospector*

DEANS

College of Business Administration: Dr ROBERT NACHTMANN

College of Education: Dr JOSEFINA V. TINAJERO
College of Engineering: Dr RICHARD SCHOEPHOERSTER
College of Health Sciences: Dr KATHLEEN A. CURTIS
College of Liberal Arts: Dr PATRICIA WITHERSPOON
College of Sciences: Dr ANNY MORROBEL-SOSA
Graduate School: Dr BENJAMIN FLORES
School of Nursing: Dr PROVENCIO-VASQUEZ

University of Texas at San Antonio

1 UTSA Circle, San Antonio, TX 78249

Telephone: (210) 4584011
Fax: (210) 4584117
E-mail: registrar@utsa.edu
Internet: www.utsa.edu

Founded 1969

Pres.: Prof. Dr RICARDO ROMO
Provost and Vice-Pres. for Academic Affairs and Interim Vice-Pres. for Research: Dr JOHN FREDERICK
Vice-Pres. for Business Affairs: KERRY L. KENNEDY
Vice-Pres. for Extended Services: Dr JUDE VALDEZ
Vice-Pres. for Research: ROBERT GRACY
Vice-Pres. for Student Affairs: GAGE PAINE
Vice-Pres. for Univ. Advancement: MARJIE FRENCH
Asst Vice-Pres. and Univ. Registrar: JOE DECRISTOFORO
Dean of Libraries: Dr KRISELLEN MALONEY

Library of 1,747,099 vols, 3,215,276 microforms, 422,000 e-books, 34,500 e-journals, 3,556,960 audiovisual items
Number of teachers: 622
Number of students: 30,300

DEANS

College of Architecture: Dr JOHN D. MURPHY, JR
College of Business: Dr LYNDA Y. DE LA VIÑA
College of Education and Human Devt: Dr BETTY MERCHANT
College of Engineering: Prof. Dr C. MAULI AGRAWAL
College of Liberal and Fine Arts: Dr DANIEL J. GELO
College of Public Policy: Dr ROGELIO SAENZ
College of Sciences: Dr GEORGE PERRY
Graduate School: Dr DOROTHY FLANAGAN
Honors College: Dr RICHARD A. DIEM

University of Texas at Tyler

3900 University Blvd, Tyler, TX 75799

Telephone: (903) 5667203
Fax: (903) 5667068
E-mail: enroll@uttyler.edu
Internet: www.uttyler.edu

Founded 1971 as Tyler State College, present name 1979
Academic year: August to May

Br. campuses in Longview, Palestine

Pres.: Dr RODNEY H. MABRY
Provost and Vice-Pres. for Academic Affairs: Dr DONNA DICKERSON
Vice-Pres. for Business Affairs: Dr RANDALL POWELL
Vice-Pres. for Univ. Advancement: JERRE IVERSEN
Registrar: SONJA MORALE
Library Dir: JEANNE STANDLEY

Library of 215,000 vols
Number of teachers: 388
Number of students: 6,699 (5,117 undergraduate, 1,582 graduate)

Publication: *UT Tyler Magazine* (2 a year)

DEANS

College of Arts and Sciences: Prof. Dr MARTIN SLANN

College of Business and Technology: Prof. Dr D. HAROLD DOTY
College of Education and Psychology: Prof. Dr WILLIAM L. GEIGER
College of Engineering and Computer Science: Prof. Dr JAMES K. NELSON, JR
College of Nursing and Health Sciences: Dr LINDA KLOTZ

University of Texas of the Permian Basin

4901 E Univ., Odessa, TX 79762

Telephone: (915) 552-2020
Fax: (432) 552-2109
E-mail: president@utpb.edu
Internet: www.utpb.edu

Founded 1969

Pres.: W. DAVID WATTS
Provost and Vice-Pres. for Academic Affairs: Dr BILL FANNIN
Vice-Pres. for Business Affairs: CHRISTOPHER R. FORREST
Vice-Pres. for Student Services: Dr SUSAN LARA
Dir of Institutional Research, Planning and Effectiveness: DENISE WATTS
Univ. Registrar: HECTOR A. GOVEA
Dir of Library (vacant)

Library of 763,000 vols
Number of teachers: 184
Number of students: 2,409

DEANS

College of Arts and Sciences: Dr MYLAN REDFERN
School of Business: Dr JACK D. LADD
School of Education: Dr RACHEL JUAREZ-TORRES

University of Texas—Pan American

1201 W University Dr., Edinburg, TX 78539-2999

Telephone: (956) 665-8872
Fax: (956) 381-2150
E-mail: info@panam.edu
Internet: www.utpa.edu

Founded 1927 as Edinburg College, present name and status 1989
Academic year: September to August

Pres.: Dr ROBERT S. NELSEN
Provost and Vice-Pres. for Academic Affairs: Dr HAVIDÁN RODRÍGUEZ
Vice-Pres. for Business Affairs: MARTIN V. BAYLOR
Vice-Pres. for Student Affairs: Dr MARTHA A. CANTU (acting)
Vice-Pres. for Univ. Advancement (vacant)
Dean of Admissions and Enrolment Services and Assoc. Vice-Pres.: Dr MAGDALENA HINOJOSA
Dean of Univ. of Libraries: FARZANEH RAZZAGHI

Library of 655,000 vols, 159,000 govt documents, 30,000 print and e-journals
Number of teachers: 797
Number of students: 19,034 (16,631 undergraduate, 2,403 graduate)

DEANS

College of Arts and Humanities: Dr DAHLIA GUERRA
College of Business Admin.: Dr TEOFILO OZUNA, JR
College of Education: Dr SALVADOR HECTOR OCHOA
College of Health Sciences and Human Services: Dr JOHN RONNAU
College of Engineering and Computer Science: Dr DAVID H. ALLEN
College of Science and Mathematics: Dr JOHN M. TRANT
College of Social and Behavioral Sciences: Dr WALTER DÍAZ

University of Texas Southwestern Medical Center

5323 Harry Hines Blvd, Dallas, TX 75390

Telephone: (214) 648-3111
Fax: (214) 648-3289
E-mail: admissions@utsouthwestern.edu
Internet: www.utsouthwestern.edu

Founded 1943 as Southwestern Medical School, present name 1987
Academic year: July to June
Pres.: Dr DANIEL K. PODOLSKY
Provost and Exec. Vice-Pres. for Academic Affairs: Prof. Dr J. GREGORY FITZ
Exec. Vice-Pres. for Business Affairs: ARNIM E. DONTES
Exec. Vice-Pres. for Clinical Operations: Dr JOHN DOUGLAS RUTHERFORD
Vice-Pres. and Chief of Staff: Dr ROBIN M. JACOBY
Vice-Pres. for External Relations: CYNTHIA BASSEL
Vice-Pres. for Financial Affairs: MICHAEL SERBER
Vice-Pres. for Devt: Dr RANDY L. FARMER
Vice-Pres. for Student and Alumni Affairs: Prof. WES NORRED
Asst Vice-Pres. for Library Services: LAURIE THOMPSON
Library of 259,000 vols, 62,685 e-journals
Number of teachers: 4,056
Number of students: 4,590

DEANS

Southwestern Graduate School of Biomedical Sciences: Prof. Dr MICHAEL ROTH
Southwestern Medical School: Prof. Dr J. GREGORY FITZ
Southwestern School of Health Professions: Dr RAUL CAETANO

University of Texas Medical Branch at Galveston

301 University Blvd, Galveston, TX 77555-0144
Suite 6, 100 Admin, Bldg, Galveston, TX 77555-0144

Telephone: (409) 772-1011
Fax: (409) 772-5064
E-mail: public.affairs@utmb.edu
Internet: www.utmb.edu

Founded 1891 as Univ. of Texas Medical Dept, present name 1919
Pres.: Dr DAVID L. CALLENDER
Exec. Vice-Pres. and Provost: Dr CARY W. COOPER
Exec. Vice-Pres. and CEO: DONNA K. SOLLENBERGER
Exec. Vice-Pres. and Chief Business and Finance Officer: WILLIAM R. ELGER
Sr Vice-Pres. and Gen. Counsel: Dr CAROLEE KING
Vice-Pres.: Dr ELIZABETH J. PROTAS
Vice-Pres. and Chief of Staff: Dr KATRINA M. LAMBRECHT
Vice-Pres. for Education: PAMELA G. WATSON
Assoc. Vice-Pres. for Academic Resources and Dir of Library: Dr BRETT A. KIRKPATRICK
Number of teachers: 1,215
Number of students: 2,825 (2,534 f.t.e.)

DEANS

Graduate School of Biomedical Sciences: Dr CARY W. COOPER
School of Health Professions: Dr ELIZABETH J. PROTAS
School of Medicine: Dr DONALD S. PROUGH
School of Nursing: Dr PAMELA G. WATSON

University of Texas Health Science Center at Houston

7000 Fannin, Suite 1200, Houston, TX 77030
Telephone: (713) 500-4472

Fax: (713) 500-3026
E-mail: info@uth.tmc.edu
Internet: www.uthouston.edu
Founded 1972
Academic year: August to August (3 semesters)
Pres.: Dr GIUSEPPE N. COLASURDO
Sr Exec. Vice-Pres., Chief Operating and Financial Officer: KEVIN DILLON
Exec. Vice-Pres. for Academic and Research Affairs: Dr GEORGE M. STANCEL
Sr Vice-Pres. for Finance and Business Services: MICHAEL TRAMONTE
Vice-Pres. for Advancement (vacant)
Vice-Pres. and Chief Human Resources Officer: ERIC FERNETTE
Registrar: ROBERT JENKINS
Number of teachers: 1,538 (1,272 full-time, 266 part-time)
Number of students: 4,600

DEANS

Graduate School of Biomedical Sciences: Prof. Dr GEORGE M. STANCEL
Medical School: Prof. Dr GIUSEPPE N. COLASURDO
School of Biomedical Informatics: Prof. Dr JIAJIE ZHANG
School of Dentistry: Prof. Dr JOHN A. VALENZA
School of Nursing: Prof. Dr PATRICIA LEE STARCK
School of Public Health: Dr ROBERTA B. NESS

University of Texas Health Science Center at San Antonio

7703 Floyd Curl Dr., San Antonio, TX 78229
Telephone: (210) 567-7000
Fax: (210) 567-2685
E-mail: registrars@uthscsa.edu
Internet: www.uthscsa.edu
Founded 1959 as South Texas Medical School, present name 1972
Academic year: July to August
Pres.: Dr WILLIAM L. HENRICH
Sr Exec. Vice-Pres. and Chief Operating Officer: MICHAEL E. BLACK
Vice-Pres. and Chief Communications Officer: A. JEROME YORK
Vice-Pres. for Academic, Faculty and Student Affairs: Dr DENISE WILBUR
Vice-Pres. for Business Affairs and Chief Financial Officer: ANDREA MARKS
Vice-Pres. for Devt and Chief Devt Officer: DEBORAH H. MORRILL
Vice-Pres. for Governmental Relations: ARMANDO DIAZ
Vice-Pres. for Institutional Advancement and Chief Devt Officer: DEBORAH H. MORRILL
Vice-Pres. for Research: Dr DAVID S. WEISS
Vice-Pres. for South Texas Programmes: Dr JOSEPH B. MCCORMICK
Registrar: BLANCA GUERRA
Exec. Dir of Libraries: RAJIA TOBIA
Library of 192,576 vols
Number of students: 3,270

DEANS

Dental School: Dr KENNETH L. KALKWARF
Graduate School of Biomedical Sciences: Dr DAVID S. WEISS
School of Health Professions: Dr JUANITA S. WALLACE
School of Medicine: Dr FRANCISCO GONZÁLEZ-SCARANO
School of Nursing: Prof. Dr EILEEN T. BRESLIN

University of Texas Health Science Center at Tyler

11937 US Highway 271, Tyler, TX 75708-3154

Telephone: (903) 877-7777
Fax: (903) 877-8839
E-mail: library@uthct.edu
Internet: www.uthct.edu

Founded 1948 as East Texas Tuberculosis Sanatorium; present status 1977
Schools of medical biological sciences, community health and health professions
Pres.: Dr KIRK A. CALHOUN
Exec. Vice-Pres. and Chief of Staff: Dr JOSEPH WOELKERS
Vice-Pres. for Clinical and Academic Affairs: Dr DAVID COULTAS
Vice-Pres. for Research and Post-Graduate Education: Dr STEVEN IDELL
Library of 3,000 vols, 5000 periodicals.

University of Texas MD Anderson Cancer Center

1515 Holcombe Blvd, Houston, TX 77030

Telephone: (713) 7922121
Internet: www.mdanderson.org

Founded 1941
Academic year: August to July
Pres.: Dr RONALD DEPINHO
Provost and Exec. Vice-Pres.: Dr RAYMOND DUBOIS
Exec. Vice-Pres. and Physician-in-Chief: Dr THOMAS BURKE
Exec. Vice-Pres. and Chief Business Officer: Dr LEON J. LEACH
Sr Vice-Pres. for Academic Affairs: Dr OLIVER BOGLER
Exec. Vice-Pres. for Operations: ADRIENNE LANG
Exec. Dir of Library: STEPHANIE FULTON
Library of 27,197 bound journal vols, 7,439 e-books, 844 audiovisual items, 25,248 microform units
Number of teachers: 1,500
Number of students: 6,869

DEANS

Graduate School of Biomedical Sciences: Dr GEORGE STANCEL
School of Health Professions: Dr MICHAEL AHEARN

UNIVERSITY OF THE INCARNATE WORD

4301 Broadway, San Antonio, TX 78209-6397

Telephone: (210) 829-6000
Fax: (210) 829-6096
E-mail: admis@uiwtx.edu
Internet: www.uiw.edu

Founded 1881 as Acad. of the Incarnate Word, present status 1996
Private control
Academic year: August to May
Chancellor: Dr HELENA MONAHAN
Pres.: Dr LOUIS J. AGNESE, JR
Provost: Dr DENISE DOYLE
Vice-Pres. for Business and Finance: Dr DOUGLAS B. ENDLSEY
Vice-Pres. for Enrolment Management and Student Services: Dr DAVID JURENOVICH
Vice-Pres. for Extended Academic Programmes: Dr CYNDI WILSON-PORTER
Vice-Pres. for Institutional Advancement: Sis. KATHLEEN COUGHLIN
Vice-Pres. for Int. Affairs: Dr MARCOS FRAGOSO
Gen. Counsel: CYNTHIA ESCAMILLA
Registrar: Dr BOBBYE G. FRY
Dean for Library Services: Dr CHERYL ANDERSON

Library of 273,468 vols, 70,017 current serial subscriptions, 301,272 microforms, 11,350 audiovisual items
Number of teachers: 499
Number of students: 8,455

Publications: *Illuminatus, Journal of the Life and Culture of San Antonio, Quirk-Student Journal of Collegiate Inquiry and Debate, Verbum Incarnatum*

DEANS

College of Humanities, Arts and Social Sciences: Dr ROBERT CONNELLY
Dreeben School of Education: Dr DENISE STAUDT
Feik School of Pharmacy: Dr ARCELIA JOHNSON-FANNIN
H. E. B. School of Business and Administration: Dr SHAWN P. DALY
Ila Faye Miller School of Nursing and Health Professions: Dr KATHI LIGHT
Rosenberg School of Optometry: Dr ANDREW BUZZELLI
School of Graduate Studies and Research: Dr KEVIN B. VICHCALES
School of Mathematics, Science and Engineering: Dr GLENN JAMES
School of Media and Design: Dr SHARON WELKEY

WADE COLLEGE

1950 N Stemmons Freeway, Suite 4080, LB 562, Dallas, TX 75207
Telephone: (214) 637-3530
Fax: (214) 637-0827
Internet: www.wadecollege.edu
Founded 1962
Academic year: October to September
Private control
Areas of study: art, design, business, computers, liberal arts
Pres.: HARRY DAVROS
Vice-Pres. for Education: JOHN CONTE
Exec. Dir: SUE WADE
Dir for Academic and Student Affairs: MITZI MORRIS
Dir for Admissions and Marketing: JULIA ANDALMAN
Dir for Financial Services: LISA HOOVER
Dir for Student Services: RUSTY BELL
Registrar and Dir for Institutional Support: KIMBERLY PARKER
Dir for Library: BOBBIE BAUMGARTEN
Library of 5,100 vols, 131 periodicals, 400 audiovisual items
Publication: *D&M Magazine.*

WAYLAND BAPTIST UNIVERSITY

1900 W Seventh St, Plainview, TX 79072
Telephone: (806) 291-1000
Fax: (806) 291-1960
E-mail: admityou@wbu.edu
Internet: www.wbu.edu
Founded 1908 as Wayland Literary and Technical Institute, chartered 1908, present name and status 1981
Private control
Academic year: June to May
Campuses in Albuquerque (NM), Altus (OK), Amarillo (TX), Anchorage (AK), Clovis (NM), Fairbanks (AK), Lubbock (TX), Mililani (HI), Phoenix (AZ), San Antonio (TX), Sierra Vista (AZ), Tucson (AZ), Wichita Falls (TX), Vance AFB, Kenya (Africa)
Pres.: Dr PAUL ARMES
Provost and Exec. Vice-Pres.: Dr BOBBY HALL
Vice-Pres. for Enrolment Management: Dr CLAUDE LUSK
Vice-Pres. for External Campuses and Graduate Services: Dr ELANE SEEBO
Chief Financial Officer: JAMES SMITH

Dean for Students: TOM HALL
Registrar: JULIE BOWEN
Dir for Libraries: Dr POLLY LACKEY
Library of 129,646 vols
Number of teachers: 95
Number of students: 1,725
Publication: *Footprints* (24 a year)

DEANS

Don Williams School of Education and Exercise and Sport Science: Dr JAMES TODD
School of Behavioral and Social Sciences: Dr ESTELLE OWENS
School of Business: Dr OTTO B. SCHACHT
School of Fine Arts: Dr MARTI RUNNELS
School of Languages and Literature: Dr CINDY McCLENAGAN
School of Math and Sciences: Dr HERBERT GROVER
School of Music: Dr ANN B. STUTES
School of Nursing: Dr DIANE FRAZOR
School of Religion and Philosophy: Dr PAUL SADLER

WILEY COLLEGE

711 Wiley Ave, Marshall, TX 75670
Telephone: (903) 927-3300
Fax: (903) 938-8100
Internet: www.wileyc.edu
Founded 1873
Private control
Academic year: August to May
Pres. and CEO: Dr HAYWOOD L. STRICKLAND
Provost and Exec. Vice-Pres.: Dr GLENDA F. CARTER
Vice-Pres. for Academic Affairs: Dr ERNEST PLATA
Vice-Pres. for Business and Finance: WILLIE HUGHEY
Vice-Pres. for Student Affairs and Enrolment Services: Dr JOSEPH L. MORALE
Dir for Admissions and Recruitment: ASHLEY L. BENNETT
Dir for Devt: Dr PRINCE BROWN
Registrar: VANESSA VALENTINE
Dir for Library: ALMA RAVENELL
Library of 98,000 vols (incl. 27,000 e-books and 350 periodicals)
Number of teachers: 72
Number of students: 1,351

DEANS

Division of Business and Technology: Prof. Dr ABDALLA F. HAGEN
Division of Sciences: Dr WALTER SHUMATE
Division of Social Sciences and Humanities: Dr SHERLYNN H. BYRD

UTAH

BRIGHAM YOUNG UNIVERSITY

A-41 ASB, Provo, UT 84602
Telephone: (801) 378-4636
E-mail: admissions@byu.edu
Internet: home.byu.edu/home
Founded 1875 as Brigham Young Acad., present name 1903
Private control
Academic year: August to April
Pres.: CECIL O. SAMUELSON
Chief Financial Officer and Vice-Pres. for Admin.: BRIAN K. EVANS
Vice-Pres. for Academic Affairs: BRENT W. WEBB
Vice-Pres. for Advancement: KEVIN J. WORTHEN
Vice-Pres. for Student Life: JANET S. SCHARMAN
Gen. Counsel and Asst to the Pres.: MICHAEL R. ORME

Dean for Admissions and Records: ERLEND D. PETERSON
Dean for Students: VERNON L. HEPERI
Univ. Librarian: H. JULENE. BUTLER
Library: 8m. vols (incl. 3.3m. books, 27,000 journals, 250,000 maps, 1m. photographs and a colln of videos)
Number of teachers: 1,500
Number of students: 39,577

DEANS

College of Family, Home and Social Sciences: BENJAMIN M. OGLES
College of Fine Arts and Communications: STEPHEN M. JONES
College of Humanities: JOHN R. ROSENBERG
College of Life Sciences: RODNEY T. BROWN
College of Nursing: BETH V. COLE
College of Physical and Mathematical Sciences: SCOTT D. SUMMERFELDT
College of Religious Education: TERRY BALL
Continuing Education: WAYNE J. LOTT
David McKay School of Education: K. RICHARD YOUNG
Ira A. Fulton College of Engineering and Technology: ALAN R. PARKINSON
J. Reuben Clark Law School: JAMES R. RASBAND
Marriott School of Management: GARY C. CORNIA
Religious Education: TERRY B. BALL

DIXIE STATE COLLEGE OF UTAH

225 S 700E, St. George, UT 84770
Telephone: (435) 652-7500
E-mail: jointhestorm@dixie.edu
Internet: www.dixie.edu
Founded 1935
State control
Academic year: August to May (2 semesters)
Pres: Dr STEPHEN D. NADAULD
Vice-Pres. for Admin. Services: STAN PLEW
Exec. Dir Campus Services: SHERRY RUESCH
Exec. Dir Business Services: SCOTT TALBOT
Dean and Dir for the Library: DAPHNE SELBERT
Number of teachers: 175
Number of students: 10,000

DEANS

School of Arts and Letters: DONALD R. HINTON
School of Education: Dr BRENDA SABEY
School of Nursing and Allied Health: Dr CAROLE GRADY
School of Science and Technology: Dr VICTOR HASFURTHER
Udvar-Hazy School of Business: Dr WILLIAM J. CHRISTENSEN

ITT TECHNICAL INSTITUTE

920 W LeVoy Dr., Murray, UT 84123
Telephone: (801) 263-3313
Fax: (801) 263-3497
Internet: www.itt-tech.edu
Founded 1969
Private control
Breckinridge School of Nursing; School of Business; School of Criminal Justice; School of Drafting and Design; School of Electronics Technology; School of Health Sciences; School of Information Technology
Exec. Sec.: NORMA JEAN SEGER
Number of students: 80,000

UNIVERSITY OF UTAH

201 President's Circle, Room 201, Salt Lake City, UT 84112-9009
Telephone: (801) 581-7200
Fax: (801) 581-3007

Internet: www.utah.edu

Founded 1850 as Univ. of Deseret, present name 1892

Academic year: August to May

Pres.: Dr A. LORRIS BETZ

Sr Vice-Pres. for Academic Affairs: DAVID W. PERSHING

Sr Vice-Pres. for Health Sciences: A. LORRIS BETZ

Vice-Pres. for Admin. Services: ARNOLD B. COMBE

Vice-Pres. for Human Resources: LORETTA F. HARPER

Vice-Pres. for Institutional Advancement: FRED C. ESPLIN

Vice-Pres. for Research: THOMAS N. PARKS

Vice-Pres. for Student Affairs: BARBARA H. SNYDER

Exec. Asst to the Pres.: LIZ MCCOY

Gen. Counsel: JOHN K. MORRIS

Registrar: TIM EBNER

Dir for Library: JOYCE L. OGBURN

Number of teachers: 3,274

Number of students: 31,000

Publications: *Hinckley Journal of Politics, Journal of Land Resources and Environmental Law, Journal of Law and Family Studies, Political Research Quarterly, Quarterly West* (creative writing journal), *Tanner Lectures on Human Values* (cumulative volume of transcripts), *Undergraduate Research Abstracts, Utah Foreign Language Abstracts, Utah Law Review* (4 a year), *Western Humanities* (4 a year)

DEANS

College of Architecture and Planning: BRENDA CASE SCHEER

College of Education: MICHAEL L. HARDMAN

College of Engineering: RICHARD B. BROWN

College of Fine Arts: RAYMOND TYMAS-JONES

College of Health: Dr JAMES E. GRAVES

College of Humanities: ROBERT NEWMAN

College of Mines and Earth Sciences: FRANCIS H. BROWN

College of Nursing: Dr MAUREEN R. KEEFE

College of Pharmacy: Dr CHRIS M. IRELAND

College of Science: Dr PIERRE V. SOKOLSKY

College of Social and Behavioral Science: M. DAVID RUDD

College of Social Work: JANNAH MATHER

Continuing Education: CHUCK WIGHT

David Eccles School of Business: TAYLOR RANDALL

Graduate School: Dr CHARLES A. WIGHT

Honors College: Dr SYLVIA TORTI

School of Medicine: Dr VIVIAN S. LEE

S. J. Quinney College of Law: HIRAM E. CHODOSH

UTAH STATE UNIVERSITY

Office of the Pres., 1400 Old Main Hill, Logan, UT 84322-1400

Telephone: (435) 797-1000

Fax: (435) 797-1680

E-mail: prm@usu.edu

Internet: www.usu.edu

Founded 1888 as Agricultural College of Utah, present name 1957

Academic year: January to December

Pres.: STAN L. ALBRECHT

Exec. Vice-Pres. and Provost: RAYMOND T. COWARD

Exec. Sr Vice-Provost: LAURENS H. SMITH

Vice-Pres. for Business and Finance: DAVE COWLEY

Vice-Pres. for Extension and Agriculture: NOELLE COCKETT

Chief Information Officer: ERIC HAWLEY

Vice-Pres. for Research and Dean of Graduate Studies: MARK R. MCLELLAN

Vice-Pres. for Student Services: JAMES D. MORALES

Chief Operating Officer for Univ. Advancement: ANNETTE HARDNER

Library of 1,505,000 vols (incl. 620,800 books, 300,370 govt documents, over 100,000 maps, 12,760 current serial subscriptions)

Number of teachers: 880

Number of students: 28,401

Publications: *Outlook* (6 a year), *Outreach* (12 a year), *Utah Science* (4 a year), *Western American Literary Journal* (4 a year), *Western Historical Quarterly*

DEANS

Caine College of the Arts: CRAIG JESSOP

College of Agriculture: GARY STRAQUADINE

College of Engineering: H. SCOTT HINTON

College of Humanities and Social Sciences: JOHN C. ALLEN

College of Natural Resources: Dr CHRIS LUECKE

College of Science: JIM MACMAHON

Emma Eccles Jones College of Education and Human Services: BETH FOLEY

Jon M. Huntsman School of Business: DOUGLAS D. ANDERSON

School of Graduate Studies: MARK R. MCLELLAN

UTAH VALLEY UNIVERSITY

800 W Univ. Parkway, Orem, UT 84058

Telephone: (801) 863-8000

E-mail: instantinfo@uvu.edu

Internet: www.uvu.edu

Founded 1941 as Central Utah Vocational School, present name 2008

State control

Academic year: January to December

Pres.: Dr MATTHEW S. HOLLAND

Vice-Pres. for Academic Affairs: IAN WILSON

Vice-Pres. for Admin. and Legislative Affairs: VAL L. PETERSON

Vice-Pres. for Advancement: MARC ARCHAMBAULT

Vice-Pres. for Devt and Alumni: MARC ARCHAMBAULT

Vice-Pres. for Student Affairs: CORY DUCKWORTH

Vice-Pres. for Univ. Relations: VAL HALE

Library of 61,000 vols, 184,106 books, 12,222 ebooks, 2,742 maps, 19,364 videos, 5,132 audio CDs, 1,571 archival materials

Number of students: 28,765

DEANS

College of Humanities and Social Sciences: DAVID P. YELLS

College of Science and Health: SAM RUSHFORTH

College of Technology and Computing: ERNEST CAREY

School of Education: BRIANT J. FARNSWORTH

School of the Arts: PATRICK M. JONES

University College: K. D. TAYLOR

Woodbury School of Business: NORMAN S. WRIGHT

WEBER STATE UNIVERSITY

3848 Harrison Blvd, Ogden, UT 84408

Telephone: (801) 626-6000

Fax: (801) 626-8021

E-mail: mediarelations@weber.edu

Internet: www.weber.edu

Founded 1889 as Weber Stake Acad., present name 1991

Public control

Academic year: August to August

Pres.: F. ANN MILLNER

Provost: MICHAEL B. VAUGHAN

Vice-Pres. for Admin. Services: NORMAN TARBOX

Vice-Pres. for Student Affairs: Dr JAN WINNIFORD

Vice-Pres. for Information Technology: BRET R. ELLIS

Vice-Pres. for Univ. Advancement: BRAD MORTENSEN

Registrar: Dr WINSLOW L. HURST

Dir for Library: JOAN G. HUBBARD

Library of 458,115 vols, 90,628 electronic resources

Number of teachers: 442

Number of students: 25,000

Publications: *Metaphor* (1 a year), *WSU Viewbook, Weber State University Magazine* (2 a year, online), *Weber Studies* (4 a year)

DEANS

College of Applied Science and Technology: DAVID FERRO

College of Science: DAVID MATTY

College of Social and Behavioral Sciences: FRANCIS B. HARROLD

Dr Ezekiel R. Dumke College of Health Professions: Dr YASMEN SIMONIAN

Jerry and Vickie Moyes College of Education: Dr JACK RASMUSSEN

John B. Goddard School of Business and Economics: JEFF STEAGALL

Telitha E. Lindquist College of Arts and Humanities: MADONNE MINER

WESTMINSTER COLLEGE

1840 S 1300 E St, Salt Lake City, UT 84105

Telephone: (801) 484-7651

Fax: (801) 466-6916

E-mail: admissions@wcslc.edu

Internet: www.wcslc.edu

Founded 1875 as Salt Lake Collegiate Institute, present name 1902

Private control

Pres.: Dr MICHAEL S. BASSIS

Provost and Vice-Pres. for Academic Affairs: JAMES E. SEIDELMAN

Exec. Vice-Pres. and Treas.: STEPHEN MORGAN

Dean of the Faculty: Dr STEPHEN R. BAAR

Vice-Pres. for Information Technology: Dr SHERYL PHILLIPS

Vice-Pres. for Advancement and Alumni Relations: NANCY MICHAEKO

Vice-Pres. for Enrolment Services: JOEL BAUMAN

Vice-Pres. for Finance and Admin.: CURTIS R. RYAN

Dean for Students: MARK FERNE

Library Dir: DIANE VANDERPOL

Library of 84,000 vols

Number of teachers: 327 (136 full-time, 191 part-time)

Number of students: 3,000 (graduate and undergraduate)

DEANS

Bill and Vieve Gore School of Business: Dr JIN WANG

Division of New Learning: ARIC KRAUSE

School of Arts and Sciences: Dr MARY JANE CHASE

School of Education: Dr ROBERT SHAW

School of Nursing and Health Sciences: SHERYL STEADMAN

VERMONT

BENNINGTON COLLEGE

1 College Dr., Bennington, VT 05201-6003

Telephone: (802) 442-5401

Fax: (802) 442-4320

E-mail: admissions@bennington.edu

Internet: www.bennington.edu

Founded 1932

Private control

Academic year: September to June

Areas of study: acting, animation, anthropology, architecture, art history, astronomy, biology, ceramics, chemistry, Chinese, computer science, conflict resolution, dance, design, digital arts, directing, drama, drawing, economics, education, environmental science, film and video, French, history, int. relations, Italian, Japanese, literature, mathematics, music, painting, philosophy, photography, physics, playwriting, political science, printmaking, psychology, religion, sculpture, Spanish, teaching, theatre, visual arts, writing

Pres.: ELIZABETH COLEMAN

Vice-Pres. and Chief Financial Officer: LAURA KRAUSE

Vice-Pres. for External Relations: PAIGE BARTELS

Vice-Pres. for Planning and Admin.: DAVID REES

Vice-Pres. for Planning and Spec. Projects: JOAN GOODRICH

Dean for Admissions and Financial Aid: KEN HIMMELMAN

Dean for College: ISABEL ROCHE

Dean for Students: EVA CHATTERJEE-SUTTON

Registrar: KATHY POSEY

Dir for Library and Information Services: OCEANA WILSON

Library of 108,000 vols

Number of teachers: 70

Number of students: 822 (686 undergraduate, 136 graduate)

BURLINGTON COLLEGE

351 North Ave, Burlington, VT 05401

Telephone: (802) 862-9616

Fax: (802) 660-4331

E-mail: admissions@burlington.edu

Internet: www.burlington.edu

Founded 1972 as Vermont Institute of Community Involvement, present name 1979

Private control

Areas of study: expressive arts, graphic design, humanities, hospitality and event management, photography, social sciences, woodworking, writing, literature

Pres.: (vacant)

Vice-Pres. for Academic and Student Affairs: ARTHUR HESSLER

Vice-Pres. for Admin. and Finance: CHRISTINE PLUNKETT

Vice-Pres. for Institutional Advancement: MICHAEL LUCK

Dir for Admissions: GILLIAN HOMSTED

Dir for Devt: SARAH JUDD

Dir for Library and Information Services: JESSICA ALLARD

Registrar: MELISSA HOWANITZ

Library of 13,000 vols, 1,000 video cassettes, 500 sound recordings

Number of teachers: 76

Number of students: 193

CASTLETON STATE COLLEGE

86 Seminary St, Castleton, VT 05735

Telephone: (802) 468-5611

Fax: (802) 468-6470

E-mail: info@castleton.edu

Internet: www.csc.vsc.edu

Founded 1787 as Rutland County Grammar School , present status 1962

State control

Academic year: August to May

Depts of art, business administration, communication, criminal justice, economics and politics, education, English, geography, geology, health science, history, mathematics, music, natural science, nursing, physical education, psychology, sociology, social

work, sports administration, Spanish, theatre arts

Pres.: DAVID S. WOLK

Dean for Academics: Dr JOSEPH T. MARK

Dean for Admin.: SCOTT DIKEMAN

Dean for Education: HONORÉE FLEMING

Dean for Enrolment: MAURICE OUIMET

Dean for Students: DENNIS PROULX

Dir for Communications: ENNIS DULING

Dir for Devt: GEORGE MCGURL

Registrar: LORI ARNER

Dir for Library: SANDRA DULING

Library of 208,454 vols, 49,974 print and e-journal subscriptions

Number of teachers: 94 (full-time)

Number of students: 2,192

CHAMPLAIN COLLEGE

246 S Willard St, Burlington, VT 05401

Telephone: (802) 860-2700

Fax: (802) 862-2772

E-mail: admission@champlain.edu

Internet: www.champlain.edu

Founded 1878 as Burlington Business School, present name 1958

Private control

Academic year: August to May

Pres.: Dr DAVID F. FINNY

Provost and Chief Academic Officer: Dr ROBIN ABRAMSON

Sr Vice-Pres. for Finance and Admin.: DAVID PROVOST

Vice-Pres. for Advancement: SHELLEY RICHARDSON

Vice-Pres. for Devt and Alumni Affairs: SHELLEY RICHARDSON

Vice-Pres. Enrolment Management: IAN MORTIMER

Registrar: BECKY PETERSON

Library Dir: JANET COTTRELL

Number of teachers: 112

Number of students: 2,000

DEANS

Core Division: Dr ELIZABETH BEAULIEU

Division of Business: Prof. DAVID STRUBLER

Division of Communication and Creative Media: Prof. JEFF RUTENBECK

Division of Continuing Professional Studies: CHUCK MANISCALCO

Division of Education and Human Studies: Prof. SUE ROWLEY

Division of Information Technology and Sciences: Dr ALI RAFIEYMEHR

COLLEGE OF ST. JOSEPH

71 Clement Rd, Rutland, VT 05701

Telephone: (802) 773-5900

E-mail: admissions@csj.edu

Internet: www.csj.edu

Founded 1956 as St Joseph's Teacher's College, present name 1983

Language of instruction: English

Private control

Academic year: September to May

Divs of arts and sciences, business, criminal justice, education, psychology and human services

Pres.: FRANK G. MIGLORIE

Vice-Pres. for External Affairs: SUSAN ENGLESE

Academic Dean: NANCY J. KLINE

Dean for Admissions: JOEL WINCOWSKI

Dean for Students: ROBERT LUKASKIEWICZ

Registrar: PATRICIA C. MIGLORIE

Librarian: DOREEN J. MCCULLOUGH

Library of 140,000 vols, 3,000 periodicals

Number of students: 425

GODDARD COLLEGE

123 Pitkin Rd, Plainfield, VT 05667

Telephone: (802) 454-8311

Fax: (802) 454-1029

E-mail: admissions@goddard.edu

Internet: www.goddard.edu

Founded 1863 as Green Mountain Central Institute, present location 1938

Private control

Areas of study: creative writing, education and licensure, health arts and sciences, psychology and counselling

Pres.: BARBARA VACARR

Vice-Pres. for Academic Affairs: MARIANNE REIFF

Chief Finance and Admin. Officer: FAITH BROWN

Dean for Enrolment Management: PETER BURNS

Registrar: JOSH CASTLE

Dir for Information Access: CLARA BRUNS

Library of 72,000 vols, 39,000 e-books

Number of teachers: 104

Number of students: 500

GREEN MOUNTAIN COLLEGE

1 Brennan Circle, Poultney, VT 05764

Telephone: (802) 287-8000

Fax: (802) 287-8099

E-mail: admiss@greenmtn.edu

Internet: www.greenmtn.edu

Founded 1834 as Troy Conf. Acad., present name 1957

Private control

Academic year: August to May (2 semesters)

Depts of business and economics, education, English and communications, environmental liberal arts, environmental studies, liberal studies, natural and mathematical sciences, natural resource management, philosophy, recreation and outdoor studies, resort and hospitality management, social and behavioural science, visual and performing arts

Pres.: Dr PAUL J. FONTEYN

Provost and Vice-Pres. for Academic Affairs: Prof. Dr WILLIAM THROPP

Vice-Pres. for Finance and Admin.: JOSEPH MANNING, III

Vice-Pres. for Student Life: E. JOSEPH PETRICK

Dir for Admissions: MAIA HANRON-SANFORD

Dir for Devt: MARY LOU WILLITS

Dean for Faculty: THOMAS J. MAUHS-PUGH

Registrar: SHARON L. HOFFMAN

Dir for Library, IT Services and Learning Support: PAUL MILLETTE

Library of 72,000 vols, 46,000 e-books, 27,250 e-journals, 300 journals

Number of teachers: 45 (full-time)

Number of students: 750

JOHNSON STATE COLLEGE

337 College Hill, Johnson, VT 05656-9464

Telephone: (802) 635-2356

Fax: (802) 635-1230

E-mail: jscadmissions@jsc.edu

Internet: www.jsc.edu

Founded 1828, present name 1962

State control

Academic year: August to May

Depts of behavioural sciences, business and economics, education, environmental and health sciences, fine and performing arts, humanities, mathematics, writing and literature

Pres.: BARBARA E. MURPHY

Academic Dean: DANIEL REGAN

Dean for Admin.: SHARRON SCOTT

Dean for Students: DAVID BERGH

Registrar: DOUGLAS EASTMAN

Faculty Librarian: JOSEPH FARARA

Library of 111,000 vols, 6,500 e-books, 36,000 e-journals, 384 journals

Number of teachers: 143 (55 full-time, 88 part-time)

Number of students: 2,000

LYNDON STATE COLLEGE

POB 919, Lyndonville, VT 05851

Telephone: (802) 626-6413

Fax: (802) 626-6335

E-mail: admissions@lyndonstate.edu

Internet: www.lyndonstate.edu

Founded 1911, present name and status 1961

State control

Academic year: August to May

College of liberal arts and professional programmes; depts of arts, atmospheric sciences, business administration, education, electronic journalism arts, English, exercise science, film studies, general studies, liberal studies, music and performing arts, mountain recreation management, mathematics and computer science, natural sciences, philosophy, psychology, social sciences, visual arts

Pres.: Dr STEVE GOLD

Dean for Academic and Student Affairs: DONNA DALTON

Dean for Admin.: WAYNE T. HAMILTON

Dean for Institutional Advancement: ROBERT E. WHITTAKER

Library Dir: GARET NELSON

Library of 113,000 vols

Number of teachers: 151 (58 full-time, 93 part-time)

Number of students: 1,429

MARLBORO COLLEGE

POB A, Marlboro, VT 05344-0300

2582 South Rd, Marlboro, VT 05344

Telephone: (802) 257-4333

Fax: (802) 451-7555

E-mail: admissions@marlboro.edu

Internet: www.marlboro.edu

Founded 1946

Private control

Academic year: August to May

Areas of study: arts, humanities, liberal studies, natural sciences, social sciences, world studies

Pres.: ELLEN MCCULLOCH-LOVELL

Chief Advancement Officer: LISA CHRISTENSEN

Dean for Admissions: NICOLE CURVIN

Dean for Faculty and Graduate Education: RICHARD GLEJZER

Dean for Students: KEN SCHNECK

Registrar: TOBIAS GELSTON

Library Dir: EMILY ALLING

Library of 75,000 vols, 17,000 periodicals

Number of teachers: 40 (full-time)

Number of students: 330

MIDDLEBURY COLLEGE

Middlebury, VT 05753

Telephone: (802) 443-5000

Fax: (802) 443-2056

E-mail: presoff@middlebury.edu

Internet: www.middlebury.edu

Founded 1800

Private control

Academic year: September to May (2 semesters)

Depts of history of art and architecture, international politics and economics, literary studies, molecular biology and biochemistry, political science, studio art, writing programmes

Pres.: Prof. RONALD D. LIEBOWITZ

Provost and Exec. Vice-Pres.: ALISON BYERLY

Sr Vice-Pres.: MICHAEL D. SCHOENFELD

Vice-Pres. for Academic Affairs: Prof. TIM SPEARS

Vice-Pres. for Admin.: TIMOTHY SPEARS

Vice-Pres. for College Advancement: JAMES R. KEYES

Vice-Pres. for Finance and Treas.: PATRICK NORTON

Vice-Pres. for Language Schools, Schools Abroad and Graduate Programmes: MICHAEL GEISLER

Vice-Pres. for Planning and Assessment: Prof. SUSAN CAMPBELL BALDRIDGE

Dean for Admissions: GREGORY B. BUCKLES

Dean for College and Chief Diversity Officer: SHIRLEY M. COLLADO

Dean for Faculty: JAMES RALPH

Dean for Library and Information Services: MARY BACKUS

Library of 1,000,000 vols

Number of teachers: 280

Number of students: 2,450 (undergraduate)

Publications: *Middlebury Magazine* (4 a year), *New England Review* (4 a year).

NORWICH UNIVERSITY

158 Harmon Dr., Northfield, VT 05663

Telephone: (802) 485-2000

Fax: (802) 485-2032

E-mail: nuadm@norwich.edu

Internet: www.norwich.edu

Founded 1819 as private military college

Private control

Academic year: August to May

Pres.: Dr RICHARD W. SCHNEIDER

Sr Vice-Pres. for Academic Affairs and Dean for Faculty: Dr GUIYOU HUANG

Vice-Pres. for Devt and Alumni Relations: DAVID J. WHALEY

Vice-Pres. for Enrolment and Communication: KAREN P. MCGRATH

Vice-Pres. for Student Affairs and Commandant of Corps of Cadets: MICHAEL B. KELLEY

Chief Admin. Officer: DAVID MAGIDA

Chief Financial Officer and Treas.: LAUREN D. WOBBY

Library Dir: ELLEN HALL

Library of 240,000 vols and microfilms; military history colln

Number of teachers: 112 (full-time)

Number of students: 2,300

Publication: *The Record* (4 a year)

DEANS

David Crawford School of Engineering: Dr SAEED MOAVENI

School of Architecture and Art: ARON P. TEMKIN

School of Business and Management: Dr FRANK THOMAS VANECEK

School of Graduate and Continuing Studies: Dr WILLIAM CLEMENTS

School of Humanities: ANDREW KNAUF

School of Mathematics and Science: Prof. CATHY M. FREY

School of Social Sciences: Dr THOMAS FRANK TAYLOR

SAINT MICHAEL'S COLLEGE

POB 7, 1 Winooski Park, Colchester, VT 05439

Telephone: (802) 654-3000

Fax: (802) 654-2906

E-mail: admission@smcvt.edu

Internet: www.smcvt.edu

Founded 1904 as St Michael's Institute

Private control

Majors in accounting, American studies, art, biochemistry, biology, business, chemistry,

classics, computer science, East Asian studies, economics, education, engineering, English, environmental science, environmental studies, finance, fine arts, French, gender/women's studies, geography, global studies, history, information systems, int. business, Italian, journalism and mass communication, language and linguistics, management, marketing, mathematics, medieval studies, modern languages and literature, music, peace and justice, philosophy, physical science, physics, political science, psychology, religious studies, sociology/anthropology, Spanish, theatre

Academic year: August to May

Pres.: Dr JACK J. NEUHAUSER

Provost and Vice-Pres. of Academic Affairs: Dr KAREN A. TALENTINO

Vice-Pres. for Enrolment: JERRY E. FLANAGAN

Vice-Pres. for Finance and Treas.: NEAL E. ROBINSON

Vice-Pres. for Instn Advancement: PATRICK J. GALLIVAN

Vice-Pres. for Student Life: MICHAEL D. SAMARA

Dean for College: Dr JEFFREY A. TRUMBOWER

Registrar: JOHN D. SHEEHEY

Dir for Library and Information Services: JOHN K. PAYNE

Library of 270,000 vols, 60,000 e-journals, 7,000 videos

Number of teachers: 150 (full-time)

Number of students: 2,800 (1,900 undergraduate, 650 graduate, 250 int.)

SIT GRADUATE INSTITUTE

POB 676, 1 Kipling Rd, Brattleboro, VT 05302-0676

Telephone: (802) 257-7751

Fax: (802) 258-3428

E-mail: info@sit.edu

Internet: www.sit.edu

Founded as School for International Training, present name 2007

Private control

Academic year: August to June

Areas of study: conflict transformation, international education, intercultural service, leadership and management, sustainable development

Pres. and CEO: Dr ADAM S WEINBERG

Sr Vice-Pres. for Academic Programmes: JOHN LUCAS

Dean for Academic Admin. and Assessment: ELLEN HOLMES

Dean for External Relations and Strategic Enrolment Management: LAURIE BLACK

Dean: Dr PREETI SHROFF-MEHTA

Dean for Student Affairs: MICHAEL SMALLIS

Registrar: GINNY NELLIS

Dir for Libraries and Academic Resources: PAMELA CONTAKOS.

SOUTHERN VERMONT COLLEGE

982 Mansion Dr., Bennington, VT 05201-6002

Telephone: (802) 442-4000

Fax: (802) 447-4695

E-mail: registrar@svc.edu

Internet: www.svc.edu

Founded 1926 as St Joseph College, present name 1974

Private control

Academic year: August to May

Divs of business, humanities, nursing, science and technology, social sciences

Pres.: KAREN GROSS

Provost: ALBERT DECICCIO

Chief Financial Officer: JAMES BECKWITH

Dean for Academics: REBECCA M. DILIDDO

Dean for Advancement: KAREN TRUBRITT

Dean for Enrolment: JOEL WINCOWSKI
Dean for Students: ANNE HOPKINS GROSS
Registrar: JAMES FREDERICK
Dir for Library: SARAH K. SANFILIPPO
Number of teachers: 40
Number of students: 550

STERLING COLLEGE

POB 72, Craftsbury Common, VT 05827
16 Sterling Dr., Craftsbury Common, VT 05827
Telephone: (802) 586-7711
Fax: (802) 586-2596
E-mail: admissions@sterlingcollege.edu
Internet: www.sterlingcollege.edu
Founded 1958
Academic year: September to August (3 semesters)
Areas of study: conservation ecology, environmental humanities, natural history, northern studies, outdoor education, sustainable agriculture
Pres.: WILLIAM R. WOOTTON
Exec. Vice-Pres.: NED HOUSTON
Dean for Academics: PAVEL CENKL
Dir for Advancement: TIM PATTERSON
Dean for Students: JILL FINEIS
Dir for Admissions: LYNNE A. BIRDSALL
Registrar: LAURIE LAGGNER
Librarian: PETRA VOGEL
Library of 3,000 vols, 100 journal titles
Number of students: 125
Publication: *Common Voice* (2 a year).

UNIVERSITY OF VERMONT

Burlington, VT 05405
Telephone: (802) 656-3131
Fax: (802) 656-9220
E-mail: admissions@uvm.edu
Internet: www.uvm.edu
Founded 1791, present status 1862
State control
Academic year: September to May
Pres.: E. THOMAS SULLIVAN
Sr Vice-Pres. and Provost: JANE E. KNODELL
Vice-Pres. for Enrolment Management: CHRISTOPHER H. LUCIER
Vice-Pres. for Finance and Admin.: RICHARD CATE
Vice-Pres. for Legal Affairs and Gen. Counsel: FRANCINE T. BAZLUKE
Vice-Pres. for Research and Dean for Graduate Studies: DOMENICO GRASSO
Vice-Pres. for State and Fed. Relations: KAREN M. MEYER
Vice-Pres. for Univ. Relations and Campus Life: THOMAS J. GUSTAFSON
Registrar: KEITH P. WILLIAMS
Dean for Libraries: MARA R. SAULE
Library of 2,994,391 vols, 55,449 serial titles, 2,041,225 microforms, 47,810 audiovisual materials, 312,736 e-books
Number of teachers: 1,471 (1,183 full-time, 288 part-time)
Number of students: 13,478 (11,482 undergraduate, 1,996 graduate)

DEANS

College of Agriculture and Life Sciences: Dr THOMAS C. VOGELMANN
College of Arts and Sciences: Dr JOEL GOLDBERG
College of Education and Social Services: Dr FAYNEESE MILLER
College of Engineering and Mathematical Sciences: Dr BERNARD F. COLE
College of Medicine: Dr FREDERICK C. MORIN, III
College of Nursing and Health Sciences: Dr PATRICIA A. PRELOCK
Continuing Education: CYNTHIA L. BELLIVEAU

Graduate College: Dr DOMENICO GRASSO
Honors College: Dr S. ABU RIZVI
Rubenstein School of Environment and Natural Resources: Dr MARY WATZIN
School of Business Administration: SANJAY SHARMA

VERMONT LAW SCHOOL

POB 96, 164 Chelsea St, South Royalton, VT 05068
Telephone: (802) 831-1000
Fax: (802) 763-2663
E-mail: admiss@vermontlaw.edu
Internet: www.vermontlaw.edu
Founded 1972
Private control
Academic year: August to May (2 semesters)
Pres. and Dean: Prof. GEOFFREY B. SHIELDS
Vice-Dean for Academic Affairs: Prof. GIL KUJOVICH
Vice-Pres. for Finance and Admin.: LORRAINE ATWOOD
Vice-Pres. for Operations: DENNIS STERN
Exec. Dir for Institutional Advancement: MATTHEW RIZZO
Registrar: KATHY MAIELI
Dir for Library: CARL A. YIRKA
Library of 349,000 vols, 149,000 titles
Number of teachers: 107 (55 full-time, 9 visiting, 43 adjunct)
Number of students: 206
Publications: *Vermont Journal of Environmental Law* (online), *Vermont Law Review* (4 a year).

VERMONT TECHNICAL COLLEGE

POB 500, Randolph Center, VT 05061-0500
Telephone: (802) 728-1000
Fax: (802) 728-1597
E-mail: admissions@vtc.edu
Internet: www.vtc.edu
Founded 1866 as Randolph State Normal School, present name 1962
State control
Academic year: August to May
Areas of study: architectural engineering technology, aviation, business technology and management, computer engineering technology, computer information technology, computer software engineering, construction practice and management, dental hygiene, diversified agriculture, electrical engineering technology, electromechanical engineering technology, equine studies, sustainable design and technology
Pres.: Dr PHILIP A. CONROY, JR
Dean for Academic Affairs: PATRICIA MENCHINI
Dean for Admin.: G. GEOFFREY LINDEMER
Dean for College: MICHAEL VAN DYKE
Registrar: MICHAEL DEMPSEY
Library Dir: DAVID STURGES
Number of students: 1,453

VIRGINIA

AVERETT UNIVERSITY

420 W Main St, Danville, VA 24541
Telephone: (434) 791-5600
E-mail: admit@averett.edu
Internet: www.averett.edu
Founded 1859 as Union Female College, present name 2001
Private control
Academic year: July to June
Pres.: Dr TIFFANY MCKILLIP FRANKS
Exec. Vice-Pres.: CHARLES HARRIS
Vice-Pres. and Chief Financial Officer: THOM DAVIS

Vice-Pres. for Academic Affairs: Dr JANET LAUGHLIN
Vice-Pres. for Admin. and Finance: PEGGY C. WRIGHT
Vice-Pres. for Enrolment Management: Dr STUART JONES
Vice-Pres. for Institutional Advancement: BUDDY RAWLEY
Vice-Pres. for Student Services: CHARLES HARRIS
Dean for Students: WILLIAM WOODWARD
Dir for Admissions: JOEL NESTER
Registrar: JANET ROBERSON
Dir for Library: ELAINE L. DAY
Library of 162,878 vols, , 36,957 current serial subscriptions, 101,773 microforms, 749 sheets or reels, 688 audiovisual materials
Number of teachers: 124 (59 full-time, 65 part-time)
Number of students: 901
Publications: *Averett Journal* (1 a year), *Averett TODAY Magazine* (1 a year)

DEANS

Graduate and Professional Studies: A. KENDALL CARTER

BAPTIST THEOLOGICAL SEMINARY AT RICHMOND

3400 Brook Rd, Richmond, VA 23227
Telephone: (804) 355-8135
Fax: (804) 355-8182
E-mail: admissions@btsr.edu
Internet: www.btsr.edu
Founded 1991
Private control
Academic year: September to May
Pres.: RONALD CRAWFORD
Vice-Pres. for Institutional Advancement: TIMOTHY BRUCE HEILMAN
Academic Dean: Prof. ISRAEL GALINDO
Dir for Admissions and Recruitment: TIFFANY KELLOGG PITTMAN
Dir for Business Affairs: JAMES F. PEAK, JR
Registrar and Dir for Financial Aid: IDA MAE HAYS
Dir for Library: MILTON COALTER
Library of 300,000 vols, 1,300 periodical subscriptions, 6,000 e-journals
Number of teachers: 12
Number of students: 133

BLUEFIELD COLLEGE

3000 College Dr., Bluefield, VA 24605
Telephone: (276) 326-3682
Fax: (276) 326-4288
E-mail: bluefield@bluefield.edu
Internet: www.bluefield.edu
Founded 1922
Private control
Academic year: August to August
Divs of business, Christian studies, education, exercise sports science, fine arts, language, literature and communications, science and mathematics, social science
Pres.: DAVID W. OLIVE
Vice-Pres. for Academic Affairs: ROBERT SHIPPEY
Vice-Pres. for Advancement: RUTH BLANKENSHIP
Vice-Pres. for Enrolment Management: TRENT ARGO
Vice-Pres. for Finance and Admin.: SARAH BEAMER
Vice-Pres. for Institutional Advancement: RUTH BLANKENSHIP
Vice-Pres. for Student Devt and Exec. Dir for Faith Formation and Church Relations: DAVID TAYLOR
Dir for Admissions: MARK HIPES

Dir for Library Services: NORA LOCKETT
Registrar: AMANDA PARKS
Library of 40,000 vols, 63,000 e-books, 16,000 magazines and journals.

BRIDGEWATER COLLEGE

402 E College St, Bridgewater, VA 22812
Telephone: (540) 828-8000
Fax: (540) 828-5481
E-mail: admissions@bridgewater.edu
Internet: www.bridgewater.edu
Founded 1880
Private control
Academic year: August to May

Depts of art, biology, chemistry, communication studies and theatre, economics and business administration, education, English, family and consumer sciences, foreign languages, health and exercise science, history and political science, mathematics and computer science, music, philosophy and religion, physics, psychology, sociology
Pres.: Dr ROY W. FERGUSON, JR
Exec. Vice-Pres.: ROY W. FERGUSON, JR
Vice-Pres. and Dean of Academic Affairs: Dr CAROL A. SCHEPPARD
Vice-Pres. for Enrolment Management: REGGIE A. WEBB
Vice-Pres. for Finance: ANNE B. KEELER
Vice-Pres. for Institutional Advancement: BRUCE D. SMITH
Dean for the College: ART HESSLER
Dean for Students: Dr WILLIAM D. MIRACLE
Registrar: CYNTHIA K. HOWDYSHELL
Dir for Library: ANDREW PEARSON
Library of 174,000 vols, 35,000 e-journals
Number of teachers: 141 (106 full-time, 35 part-time)
Number of students: 1,648
Publication: *The Philomathean* (1 a year).

CHRISTENDOM COLLEGE

134 Christendom Dr., Front Royal, VA 22630-6534
Telephone: (540) 636-2900
Fax: (540) 636-1655
E-mail: info@christendom.edu
Internet: www.christendom.edu
Founded 1977
Private control
Academic year: August to May
Liberal arts college
Pres.: Dr TIMOTHY T. O'DONNELL
Vice-Pres. for Academic Affairs: Dr STEVEN C. SNYDER
Vice-Pres. for Advancement: JOHN F. CISKANIK
Academic Dean: Dr PATRICK KEATS
Dean for Student Life: JESSE DORMAN
Dir for Admissions: TOM MCFADDEN
Registrar: WALTER JANARO
Dir for Library: ANDREW ARMSTONG
Library of 90,000 vols, 5,000 audiovisual items, 30,000 periodicals
Number of students: 407

CHRISTOPHER NEWPORT UNIVERSITY

1 University Place, Newport News, VA 23606-3072
Telephone: (757) 594-7000
Fax: (757) 594-7864
E-mail: admit@cnu.edu
Internet: www.cnu.edu
Founded 1960 as 2-year br. of College of William and Mary, present name and status 1992
State control
Academic year: August to May (2 semesters)

Pres.: PAUL S. TRIBLE, JR
Provost: Dr MARK W. PADILLA
Vice-Provost: Dr LAURA DEIULIO
Dean for Enrolment Services and Univ. Registrar: LISA DUNCAN RAINES
Dean for Students: Dr KEVIN HUGHES
Univ. Librarian: MARY SELLEN
Library of 207,932 vols, 46,400 periodicals (print and electronic)
Number of students: 4,800
Publication: *Currents* (1 a year)

DEANS

College of Arts and Humanities: STEVEN BREESE
College of Natural and Behavioral Sciences: Dr DAVID DOUGHTY
College of Social Sciences: Dr ROBERT E. COLVIN

COLLEGE OF WILLIAM & MARY

POB 8795, Williamsburg, VA 23187-8795
Telephone: (757) 221-4000
Fax: (757) 221-2151
E-mail: admiss@wm.edu
Internet: www.wm.edu
Founded 1693
State control
Academic year: September to May
Campuses in Gloucester Point (Virginia) and Dupont Circle (Washington, DC)
Pres.: W. TAYLOR REVELEY, III
Provost and Chief Academic Officer: MICHAEL R. HALLERAN
Vice-Pres. for Admin.: ANNA MARTIN
Vice-Pres. for Devt: SEAN PIERI
Vice-Pres. for Finance: SAMUEL E. JONES
Vice-Pres. for Strategic Initiatives: JAMES GOLDEN
Vice-Pres. for Student Affairs: VIRGINIA AMBLER
Registrar: SARA L. MARCHELLO
Dean for Libraries: CARRIE L. COOPER
Library: 2m. vols
Number of teachers: 591 (full-time)
Number of students: 8,200 (6,071 undergraduate, 2,129 graduate)
Publications: *Business Review* (1 a year), *James Blair Historical Review* (1 a year), *William & Mary Magazine*, *William and Mary Environmental Law and Policy Review*, *William and Mary Law Review*, *The Monitor*, *The William and Mary Quarterly*

DEANS

Arts and Sciences: EUGENE R. TRACY
Law School: DAVISON M. DOUGLAS
Mason School of Business: LAWRENCE B. PULLEY
School of Education: Dr VIRGINIA L. MCLAUGHLIN
School of Marine Science: Dr JOHN T. WELLS

EASTERN MENNONITE UNIVERSITY

1200 Park Rd, Harrisonburg, VA 22802-2462
Telephone: (540) 432-4000
Fax: (540) 432-4444
E-mail: admiss@emu.edu
Internet: www.emu.edu
Founded 1917 as Eastern Mennonite School, present name 1994
Private control
Academic year: August to May (2 semesters)
Liberal arts college, with emphasis on international education; campus at Lancaster (Pennsylvania)
Pres.: LOREN SWARTZENDRUBER
Provost: Dr FRED KNISS
Vice-Pres. and Seminary Dean: MICHAEL A. KING

Vice-Pres. and Undergraduate Academic Dean: NANCY HEISEY
Vice-Pres. for Advancement: KIRK L. SHISLER
Vice-Pres. for Enrolment: LUKE HARTMAN
Vice-Pres. for Finance: DARYL W. BERT
Vice-Pres. for Student Life: KEN L. NAFZIGER
Graduate Dean: P. DAVID GLANZER
Dir for Admissions: DON YODER
Registrar: DAVE DETROW
Dir for Library: BERYL BRUBAKER
Library of 149,000 vols
Number of teachers: 90
Number of students: 1,500
Publications: *Crossroads Magazine* (3 a year), *Peacebuilder* (2 a year).

EASTERN VIRGINIA MEDICAL SCHOOL

POB 1980, Norfolk, VA 23501-1980
714 Woodis Ave, Norfolk, VA 23501
Telephone: (757) 446-5600
Fax: (757) 446-8946
Internet: www.evms.edu
Founded 1973
Private control
Pres.: HARRY T. LESTER
Provost and Dean: Dr RICHARD V. HOMAN
Vice-Pres. for Admin. and Finance: MARK BABASHANIAN
Asst Dean for Admissions and Enrolment: Dr DONALD MEYER
Asst Dean for Student Affairs: Dr ANN E. CAMPBELL
Registrar: JENNIFER GRAY
Assoc. Dean for Library and Learning: JUDITH ROBINSON MERCER
Number of teachers: 1,604
Publication: *EVMS Magazine* (3 a year)

DEANS

School of Health Professions: Dr C. DONALD COMBS

ECPI UNIVERSITY

5555 Greenwich Rd, Virginia Beach, VA 23462
Telephone: (757) 490-9090
Internet: www.ecpi.edu
Private control
Schools of business and criminal justice, culinary arts, health science, technology; campuses at Newport News and Richmond (Virginia), Raleigh and Charlotte (North Carolina).

EMORY & HENRY COLLEGE

POB 947, Emory, VA 24327
Telephone: (276) 944-4121
E-mail: ehadmiss@ehc.edu
Internet: www.ehc.edu
Founded 1836
Private control
Academic year: August to May (2 semesters)
Areas of study: art, biology, business administration, chemistry, economics, English, geography, history, languages, mass communications, mathematics, music, philosophy, physical education, physics, political science, psychology, religion, sociology, theatre
Pres.: Dr ROSALIND REICHARD
Vice-Pres. for Academic Affairs and Dean for Faculty: LINDA HARRIS DOBKINS
Vice-Pres. for Business and Finance: DIRK WILMOTH
Vice-Pres. for Enrolment Management: DAVID HAWSEY
Vice-Pres. for Institutional Advancement: JOSEPH TAYLOR
Vice-Pres. for Student Life and Dean for Students: PAMELA GOURLEY

Dir for Institutional Research and Institutional Effectiveness: KEVORK HORRISSIAN
Registrar: TAMMY SHEETS (acting)
Dir for Library and Information Services: LORRAINE N. ABRAHAM
Library of 350,000 vols, 400 journal subscriptions
Number of teachers: 69 (full-time)
Number of students: 982 (939 undergraduate, 43 graduate)

FERRUM COLLEGE

POB 1000, Ferrum, VA 24088
Telephone: (540) 365-2121
Fax: (540) 365-4266
E-mail: admissions@ferrum.edu
Internet: www.ferrum.edu
Founded 1913
Private control
Academic year: August to May (2 semesters)
Pres.: Dr JENNIFER L. BRAATEN
Provost and Exec. Vice-Pres.: Dr LESLIE LAMBERT
Assoc. Provost and Chief Information Officer: CHRISTINE H. STINSON
Dir for Int. Programmes: SASHA A. SAARI
Dir for Professional Studies: DAVID R. SULZEN
Dean for Academic Planning and Programmes: GAIL L. SUMMER
Registrar: YVONNE S. WALKER
Dir for Library: GEORGE LOVELAND
Library of 210,000 vols
Number of students: 1,484

DEANS

School of Arts and Humanities: Dr JOHN W. BRUTON
School of Natural Science and Mathematics: Dr JASON POWELL
School of Social Sciences and Professional Studies: Dr KEVIN REILLY

GEORGE MASON UNIVERSITY

4400 University Dr., Fairfax, VA 22030-4444
Telephone: (703) 993-1000
Fax: (703) 993-4668
E-mail: registrar@gmu.edu
Internet: www.gmu.edu
Founded 1957 as N Virginia br. of Univ. of Virginia, present name and status 1972
State control
Academic year: August to May (2 semesters)
Campuses at Arlington, Manassas and Sterling
Pres.: Dr ALAN G. MERTEN
Provost: Dr PETER N. STEARNS
Sr Vice-Pres. for Finance and Planning: Dr MAURICE W. SCHERRENS
Vice-Pres. for Enrolment Services and Vice-Provost for Academic Affairs: LINDA A. SCHWARTZSTEIN
Vice-Pres. for Global Strategies: ANNE SCHILLER
Vice-Pres. for Research and Economic Devt: ROGER STOUGH
Vice-Pres. for Univ. Devt and Alumni Affairs: MARC BRODERICK
Vice-Pres. for Univ. Life: Dr SANDRA SCHERRENS
Vice-Pres. for Univ. Relations: PAUL LIBERTY
Univ. Registrar: SUSAN H. JONES
Univ. Librarian: JOHN ZENELIS
Library of 2,846,733 vols
Number of teachers: 1,658 (965 full-time, 693 part-time)
Number of students: 33,320
Publications: *Faculty Bibliography* (1 a year), *Mason Research* (1 a year)

DEANS

College of Education and Human Development: MARK GINSBERG
College of Humanities and Social Sciences: JACK CENSER
College of Health and Human Services: SHIRLEY S. TRAVIS
College of Science: VIKAS CHANDHOKE
College of Visual and Performing Arts: WILLIAM REEDER
Honors College: ZOFIA BURR
School of Law: DANIEL POLSBY
School of Management: JORGE HADDOCK
School of Public Policy: EDWARD RHODES
Volgeneau School of Engineering: LLOYD GRIFFITHS

HAMPDEN-SYDNEY COLLEGE

POB 859 Hampden-Sydney, VA 23943
Telephone: (434) 223-6000
Fax: (434) 223-6346
E-mail: info@hsc.edu
Internet: www.hsc.edu
Founded 1775
Private control
Academic year: August to May
Men's college of liberal arts and sciences
Pres.: Dr CHRISTOPHER B. HOWARD
Vice-Pres. for Admin., Strategy and Board Affairs: Dr DALE JONES
Vice-Pres. for Business Affairs and Finance and Treas.: W. GLENN CULLEY, JR
Vice-Pres. for Institutional Advancement: Dr LEE KING
Dean for Admissions: ANITA H. GARLAND
Dean for the Faculty: ROBERT T. HERDEGEN, III
Dean for Students: DAVID A. KLEIN
Registrar: DAWN L. CONGLETON
Dir for Library and Academic Information Services: CYRUS I. DILLON, III
Library of 250,000 vols
Number of teachers: 96 (full-time)
Number of students: 1,100

HAMPTON UNIVERSITY

100 E Queen St, Hampton, VA 23668
Telephone: (757) 727-5000
Fax: (757) 727-5746
Internet: www.hamptonu.edu
Founded 1868 Hampton Normal and Agricultural Institute, present name 1984
Private control
Academic year: August to May (2 semesters)
Pres.: Dr WILLIAM R. HARVEY
Provost: Dr PAMELA V. HAMMOND
Exec. Vice-Pres.: Dr JoANN W. HAYSBERT
Vice-Pres. and Gen. Counsel: FAYE HARDY-LUCAS
Vice-Pres. for Admin. Services: Dr RODNEY D. SMITH
Vice-Pres. for Business Affairs and Treas.: DORETHA J. SPELLS
Vice-Pres. for Devt: LARON J. CLARK
Vice-Pres. for Student Affairs: Dr BARBARA INMAN
Dir for Admissions: ANGELA BOYD
Registrar: JORSENE S. COOPER
Library of 331,727 vols
Number of teachers: 467 (333 full-time, 134 part-time)
Number of students: 5,402 (4,565 undergraduate, 770 graduate)

DEANS

College of Education and Continuing Studies: Dr CASSANDRA HERRING
Graduate College: Dr WILLIAM I. YOUNG, JR
School of Business: Dr SID HOWARD CREDLE
School of Engineering and Technology: Dr ERIC JAMES SHEPPARD
School of Liberal Arts: Dr MAMIE E. LOCKE
School of Nursing: Dr DEBORAH E. JONES
School of Pharmacy: Dr WAYNE T. HARRIS
School of Science: Dr ROBERT DIXON
Scripps Howard School of Journalism and Communication: Prof. ROSALYNNE WHITAKER-HECK

HOLLINS UNIVERSITY

POB 9707, Roanoke, VA 24020-1707
Telephone: (540) 362-6000
Fax: (540) 362-6642
E-mail: huadm@hollins.edu
Internet: www.hollins.edu
Founded 1842 as Valley Union Seminary, present name 1998
Private control
Academic year: August to August
Liberal arts college; undergraduate programme for women, selected graduate programmes or both men and women
Pres.: NANCY OLIVER GRAY (acting)
Provost: L. WAYNE MARKERT
Vice-Pres. for Academic Affairs: JEANINE STEWART
Vice-Pres. for Enrolment: STEFANIE NILES
Vice-Pres. for External Relations: MARK JONES
Vice-Pres. for Finance and Admin.: KERRY EDMONDS
Dean for Students: PATRICIA O'TOOLE
Dir for Admissions: NICOLE L. WILLIAMS
Dir for Scholarships and Financial Assistance: MARY JEAN CORRISS
Univ. Registrar and Exec. Dir for Institutional Research: ANNA K. GOODWIN
Univ. Librarian: JOAN D. RUELLE
Library of 212,000 vols
Number of teachers: 99 (71 full-time, 28 part-time)
Number of students: 1,008 (759 undergraduate, 249 graduate)
Publications: *Hollins Magazine* (3 a year), *The Hollins Critic* (4 a year).

INSTITUTE FOR THE PSYCHOLOGICAL SCIENCES

2001 Jefferson Davis Highway, Suite 511, Arlington, VA 22202
Telephone: (703) 416-1441
Fax: (703) 416-8588
Internet: ipsciences.edu
Founded 1997 as Institute for Faith and Psychological Sciences, present name 1999
Private control
Academic year: August to August
Pres.: Rev. Dr CHARLES SIKORSKY
Academic Dean: Dr GLADYS M. SWEENEY
Vice-Pres. of Finance and Admin.: ROBERTO PARTARRIEU
Vice-Pres. for Institutional Effectiveness, Research and Planning: Dr MARY ANN LaFLEUR
Dean for Students: Dr G. ALEXANDER ROSS
Dir for Admissions and Marketing: ANNE-MARIE D. MINNIS
Dir for Enrolment Services and Registrar: JENNIFER KARNS
Dir for Library: JEFFREY ELLIOTT
Library of 10,000 vols.

JAMES MADISON UNIVERSITY

800 S Main St, Harrisonburg, VA 22807-0001
Telephone: (540) 568-6211
Fax: (540) 568-3634
E-mail: admissions@jmu.edu
Internet: www.jmu.edu
Founded 1908 as State Normal and Industrial School for Women, present name 1977
State control

Academic year: August to May (2 semesters)
Pres.: Dr LINWOOD H. ROSE
Exec. Vice-Pres.: (vacant)
Interim Provost and Sr Vice-Pres. for Academic Affairs: Dr A. JERRY BENSON
Sr Vice-Pres. for Admin. and Finance: CHARLES KING
Sr Vice-Pres. for Student Affairs and Univ. Planning: Dr MARK WARNER
Vice-Pres. for Univ. Advancement: Dr NICK LANGRIDGE (acting)
Univ. Registrar: MICHELE WHITE
Dean for Libraries and Educational Technologies: RALPH ALBERICO

Library of 700,000 vols, 13,000 journals
Number of teachers: 1,266 (906 full-time, 360 part-time)
Number of students: 19,722 (17,900 undergraduate, 1,822 graduate)

DEANS

College of Arts and Letters: DAVID K. JEFFREY
College of Business: Dr IRVINE CLARKE, III
College of Education: Dr PHIL WISHON
College of Integrated Science and Technology: Dr SHARON LOVELL
College of Science and Mathematics: Dr DAVID BRAKKE
College of Visual and Performing Arts: Dr GEORGE E. SPARKS
The Graduate School: Dr REID LINN
University Studies: LINDA CABE HALPERN

JEFFERSON COLLEGE OF HEALTH SCIENCES

101 Elm Ave, SE, Roanoke, VA 24013
Telephone: (540) 985-8483
Fax: (540) 224-6703
E-mail: admissions@jchs.edu
Internet: www.jchs.edu
Founded 1914 as Jefferson Hospital School of Nursing, present name 2003
Private control
Academic year: August to August (3 semesters)
Areas of study: health psychology, humanities and social sciences, nursing, occupational therapy
Pres.: Dr NATHANIEL L. BISHOP
Dean for Academic Affairs: Prof. Dr LISA ALLISON-JONES
Dean for Admin. Services: ANNA MILLIRONS
Dir for Admissions: JUDITH MCKEON
Dean for Student Affairs: SCOTT HILL
Registrar: LINDA WILLIAMS
Dir for Library Services: MONA THISS

Library of 5,140 vols, 424 audiovisual items
Number of teachers: 70 (full-time)
Number of students: 1,032
Publication: Jefferson Chronicle (2 a year).

LIBERTY UNIVERSITY

1971 University Blvd, Lynchburg, VA 24502
Telephone: (434) 582-2000
Fax: (434) 582-2304
E-mail: admissions@liberty.edu
Internet: www.liberty.edu
Founded 1971
Private control
Academic year: August to May (2 semesters)
Chancellor and Pres.: JERRY FALWELL, JR
Provost and Sr Vice-Pres. for Academic Affairs: RONALD S. GODWIN
Vice-Provost: Dr RONALD E. HAWKINS
Exec. Vice-Pres.: NEAL A. ASKEW
Sr Vice-Pres. for Enrolment Management: CHRIS E. JOHNSON
Sr Vice-Pres. for Student Affairs: MARK HINE
Vice-Pres. for Admin.: SHARON J. HARTLESS
Vice-Pres. for Devt: TOM ARNOLD

Vice-Pres. for Investment Management and Chief Financial Officer: DON MOON
Vice-Pres. for Outreach and Strategic Partnerships: BARRY N. MOORE
Vice-Pres. for Student Leadership: Dr TODD CAMPO
Registrar and Vice-Pres. for Admin. Information Management: LAWRENCE SHACKLETON
Dean for Integrated Learning Resource Center: CARL MERAT

Library of 315,000 vols, 1,31,000 e-books, 67,000 e-journals
Number of teachers: 2,000
Number of students: 82,500 (12,500 residential, 70,000 online)

DEANS

Center for Academic Support and Advising Services: Dr BRIAN C. YATES
College of Arts and Sciences: Dr ROGER SCHULTZ
College of General Studies: Dr EMILY HEADY
Graduate School: Dr KEVIN CORSINI
Helms School of Government: SHAWN D. AKERS
Liberty Baptist Theological Seminary: ELMER L. TOWNS
School of Aeronautics: DAVID L. YOUNG
School of Business: SCOTT HICKS
School of Communication: Dr CECIL V. KRAMER
School of Education: Dr KAREN L. PARKER
School of Engineering and Computational Sciences: Prof. Dr RON SONES
School of Law: MATHEW D. STAVER
School of Religion: ELMER TOWNS

LONGWOOD UNIVERSITY

201 High St, Farmville, VA 23909
Telephone: (434) 395-2000
Fax: (434) 395-2635
E-mail: admit@longwood.edu
Internet: www.longwood.edu
Founded 1839 as Farmville Female Seminary, present name 2002
State control
Academic year: August to May (2 semesters)
Pres.: Dr PATRICK FINNEGAN
Vice-Pres. for Academic Affairs: KENNETH B. PERKINS
Vice-Pres. for Admin. and Finance: KATHY S. WORSTER
Vice-Pres. for Facilities Management: RICHARD W. BRATCHER
Vice-Pres. for Student Affairs: Dr TIM J. PIERSON
Vice-Pres. for Univ. Advancement: Dr BRYAN K. ROWLAND
Dir for Financial Aid: KAREN SCHINABECK
Registrar: CYNTHIA ERICKSON
Dean for Library: SUZY SZASZ PALMER

Library of 288,175 vols
Number of teachers: 214 (full-time)
Number of students: 4,800

DEANS

College of Business and Economics: Dr PAUL T. BARRETT
College of Education and Human Services: Dr DENEESE L. JONES
College of Graduate and Professional Studies: Dr JEANNINE R. PERRY
Cook-Cole College of Arts and Sciences: Dr CHARLES D. ROSS
Cormier Honors College: Dr ALIX FINK

LYNCHBURG COLLEGE

1501 Lakeside Dr., Lynchburg, VA 24501-3113
Telephone: (434) 544-8100
Fax: (434) 544-8220

E-mail: president@lynchburg.edu
Internet: www.lynchburg.edu
Founded 1903
Private control
Academic year: August to May (2 semesters)
Pres.: Dr KENNETH R. GARREN
Vice-Pres. and Dean for Academic Affairs: Dr JULIUS SIGLER
Vice-Pres. and Dean for Student Devt: JOHN ECCLES
Vice-Pres. for Advancement: DENISE MCDONALD
Vice-Pres. for Business and Finance: STEPHEN E. BRIGHT
Vice-Pres. for Enrolment Management: RITA DETWILER
Dean for the College: Dr RICHARD C. BURKE
Dir for Admissions: SHARON WALTERS-BOWER
Registrar: JAY K. WEBB
Dir for Library: CHRISTOPHER MILLSON-MARTULA

Library of 243,300 vols
Number of teachers: 171 (full-time)
Number of students: 2,830 (2,280 undergraduate, 550 graduate)
Publication: Lynchburg College Magazine (2 a year)

DEANS

School of Business and Economics: Dr JOSEPH H. TUREK
School of Communication and the Arts: Dr OEIDA M. HATCHER
School of Education and Human Development: Dr JAN S. STENNETTE
School of Health Sciences and Human Performance: Dr LINDA ANDREWS
School of Humanities and Social Sciences: Dr KIMBERLY MCCABE
School of Sciences: Dr BARRY LOBB

MARINE CORPS UNIVERSITY

2076 South St, Quantico, VA 22134-5068
Telephone: (703) 784-6837
Fax: (703)-784-6838
E-mail: mcu_web_inquiries@usmc.mil
Internet: www.mcu.usmc.mil
Founded 1989
State control
Academic year: July to June

Comprises College of Distance Education and Training, Command and Staff College, Enlisted Professional Military Education, Expeditionary Warfare School, Lejeune Leadership Institute, Marine Corps War College, School of Advanced War Fighting
Pres.: Major Gen THOMAS M. MURRAY
Vice-Pres. for Academic Affairs: Dr Col JERRE WILSON
Vice-Pres. for Instructional and Research Support: Col Dr KURT A. SANFTLEBEN
Vice-Pres. for Student Affairs and Business Operations: DARRELL BROWNING
Registrar: STEFAN ROHAL
Dir for Library: CAROL E. RAMKEY

Library of 150,000 vols, 400 periodicals, 120,000 microforms
Number of teachers: 207
Number of students: 7,642
Publication: Marine Corps University Journal (2 a year).

MARY BALDWIN COLLEGE

POB 1500, Staunton, VA 24402
318 Prospect St, Staunton, VA 24401
Telephone: (540) 887-7019
Fax: (540) 887-7292
E-mail: info@mbc.edu
Internet: www.mbc.edu
Founded 1842 as Augusta Female Seminary, present name 1923

Private control
Academic year: August to May

Schools of arts, humanities and renaissance studies; education, health and social work; science; social sciences, business and global studies

Pres.: PAMELA FOX
Sr Vice-Pres. for Business and Finance: DAVID MOWEN
Sr Vice-Pres. for Enrolment and Admin. and Dean for Students: BRENDA BRYANT
Vice-Pres. for Academic Affairs and Dean for the College: CATHARINE O'CONNELL
Vice-Pres. for Institutional Advancement: DAVID ATCHLEY
Registrar, Assoc. Dean for the College and Dir for Institutional Research: LEWIS D. ASKEGAARD
Dir for Library: CAROL CREAGER

Library of 150,205 vols, 61,761 microforms, 7,907 audiovisual items, 19,000 print and online journal subscriptions, 25,848 e-books
Number of teachers: 138
Number of students: 2,341 (797 undergraduate, 273 graduate, 1,271 adult degree)

MARYMOUNT UNIVERSITY

2807 N Glebe Rd, Arlington, VA 22207-4299
Telephone: (703) 284-1500
Fax: (703) 522-0349
E-mail: admissions@marymount.edu
Internet: www.marymount.edu

Founded 1950 as Marymount College, present name 1986
Private control
Academic year: August to May (2 semesters)

Pres.: Dr MATTHEW D. SHANK
Provost and Vice-Pres. for Academic Affairs: SHERRI HUGHES
Vice-Pres. for Enrolment and Student Services: CHRIS DOMES
Vice-Pres. for Financial Affairs and Treas.: RALPH KIDDER
Vice-Pres. for Univ. Devt: EMILY MAHONY
Dir for Student Services: ALISON MALLOY
Univ. Registrar: SCOTT SPENCER
Dean for Library: ZARY MOSTASHARI

Library of 236,000 vols, 37,000 journals (print and electronic)
Number of teachers: 346 (145 full-time, 201 part-time)
Number of students: 3,572

DEANS

Malek School of Health Professions: Dr THERESA CAPPELLO
School of Arts and Sciences: Dr GEORGE CHEATHAM
School of Business Administration: JAMES RYERSON
School of Education and Human Services: Dr WAYNE LESKO

NORFOLK STATE UNIVERSITY

700 Park Ave, Norfolk, VA 23504
Telephone: (757) 823-8600
Fax: (757) 823-2342
E-mail: president@nsu.edu
Internet: www.nsu.edu

Founded 1935 as Norfolk unit of Virginia Union Univ., present name and status 1979
State control
Academic year: August to May (2 semesters)

Pres.: Dr TONY ATWATER
Provost and Vice-Pres. for Academic Affairs: Dr SANDRA J. DELOATCH
Vice-Pres. for Finance and Admin.: REGINA V. K. WILLIAMS

Vice-Pres. for Research and Economic Devt: Dr JOSEPH C. HALL
Vice-Pres. for Student Affairs: SHARON B. LOWE
Vice-Pres. for Univ. Advancement: PHILLIP ADAMS
Exec. Dir for Enrolment Management: TERRICITA SASS
Registrar: REGINA BYNUM
Dir for Library: Dr TOMMY L. BOGGER

Library of 348,953 vols, 59,542 periodicals, 25,633 microforms, 18,294 e-journals, 48,601 e-books
Number of teachers: 269
Number of students: 7,091 (6,264 undergraduate, 827 graduate)

DEANS

College of Liberal Arts: Dr BELINDA C. ANDERSON
College of Science, Engineering and Technology: Dr SANDRA DELOATCH (acting)
Graduate School: Dr MILDRED K. FULLER
Honors College: Dr PAGE LAWS
School of Business: Dr STEVEN PAPAMARCOS
School of Education: Dr JEAN BRAXTON
School of Extended Learning: Dr MARGARET MASSEY
School of Social Work: Dr DOROTHY C. BROWNE

OLD DOMINION UNIVERSITY

5155 Hampton Blvd, Norfolk, VA 23529
Telephone: (757) 683-3000
Fax: (757) 683-4505
E-mail: admissions@odu.edu
Internet: www.odu.edu

Founded 1930 as Norfolk Div. of The College of William and Mary, present name and status 1969
Private control

Pres.: JOHN R. BRODERICK
Provost and Vice-Pres. for Academic Affairs: CAROL SIMPSON
Vice-Provost for Planning and Institutional Effectiveness: MARTHA SMITH SHARPE
Vice-Pres. for Admin. and Finance: ROBERT L. FENNING
Vice-Pres. for Research: MOHAMMAD A. KARIM
Vice-Pres. for Student Engagement and Enrolment Services: ELLEN NEUFELDT
Vice-Pres. for Univ. Advancement: ALONZO C. BRANDON
Registrar: MARY SWARTZ
Librarian: VIRGINIA S. O'HERRON (acting)

Library: 3.2m. items (incl. 20,000 journals, 2m. microforms, 68,000 maps and audiovisual items)
Number of teachers: 1,224 (722 full-time, 502 part-time)
Number of students: 24,466 (18,965 undergraduate, 5,501 graduate)
Publication: Monarch

DEANS

College of Arts and Letters: Dr CHARLES E. WILSON, JR
College of Business and Public Administration: GILBERT YOCHUM
College of Health Sciences: Dr DEANNE SHUMAN
College of Sciences: Dr CHRIS D. PLATSOUCAS
Darden College of Education: Dr LINDA IRWIN-DEVITIS
Frank Batten College of Engineering and Technology: Dr OKTAY BAYSAL
Honors College: Dr DAVID METZGER

RADFORD UNIVERSITY

East Main St, Radford, VA 24142
Telephone: (540) 831-5000
Fax: (540) 831-5142

E-mail: admissions@radford.edu
Internet: www.radford.edu

Founded 1910 as State Normal and Industrial School for Women, present name and status 1979
State control
Academic year: August to May (2 semesters)

Pres.: Dr PENELOPE W. KYLE
Provost and Vice-Pres. for Academic Affairs: Dr SAM MINNER
Vice-Provost for Enrolment Planning and Management: JAMES PENNIX
Vice-Pres. for Finance and Admin. and Chief Financial Officer: RICHARD ALVAREZ
Vice-Pres. for Information Technology: DANNY M. KEMP
Vice-Pres. for Student Affairs: Dr MARK SHANLEY
Vice-Pres. for Univ. Advancement: Dr DEBORAH J. ROBINSON
Dean for Students: DON APPIARIUS
Registrar: MATTHEW BRUNNER
Dean for the Library: STEVEN HELM

Library of 552,687 vols
Number of teachers: 623 (406 full-time, 217 part-time)
Number of students: 9,370
Publications: Gaelic, The Beehive (1 a year)

DEANS

College of Business and Economics: Dr FAYE W. GILBERT
College of Education and Human Development: Dr PATRICIA SHOEMAKER
College of Graduate and Professional Studies: Dr DENNIS GRADY
College of Humanities and Behavioral Sciences: Dr KATHERINE HAWKINS
College of Science and Technology: Dr J. ORION ROGERS
College of Visual and Performing Arts: Dr JOSEPH SCARTELLI
Waldron College of Health and Human Services: RAYMOND LINVILLE

RANDOLPH-MACON COLLEGE

POB 5005, Ashland, VA 23005-5505
Telephone: (804) 752-7200
Fax: (804) 752-4707
E-mail: admissions@rmc.edu
Internet: www.rmc.edu

Founded 1830
Private control
Academic year: September to May
Liberal arts college

Pres.: Dr ROBERT R. LINDGREN
Treas.: JOHN A. AHLADAS
Provost and Vice-Pres. for Academic Affairs: Dr WILLIAM T. FRANZ
Vice-Pres. for Advancement: DIANE M. LOWDER
Dean for Admissions and Financial Aid: DAVID L. LESESNE
Dean for Students: Dr GRANT L. AZDELL
Dir for Institutional Research: Dr TIM MERRILL
Registrar: ALANA R. DAVIS
Dir for Library: Dr GINGER YOUNG

Library of 182,368 vols
Number of teachers: 93 (full-time)
Number of students: 1,240

RANDOLPH COLLEGE

2500 Rivermont Ave, Lynchburg, VA 24503-1526
Telephone: (434) 947-8000
Fax: (434) 947-8138
E-mail: admissions@randolphcollege.edu
Internet: www.randolphcollege.edu

Founded 1891 as Randolph-Macon Woman's College, present name 2007

Private control
Academic year: August to May
Liberal arts college
Pres.: JOHN E. KLEIN
Vice-Pres. for Academic Affairs and Dean for the College: DENNIS STEVENS
Vice-Pres. for Enrolment Management: Dr SANDRA C. BARTHOLOMEW
Vice-Pres. for Finance and Admin.: CHRISTOPHER L. BURNLEY
Vice-Pres. for Institutional Advancement: JAN Y. MERIWETHER
Vice-Pres. for Student Affairs and Dean for Students: Dr SARAH L. SWAGER
Dir for Devt: LEE MAYHALL
Dean for Students and Dir for Residence Life: TERRY BODINE
Registrar: BARBARA THRASHER
Librarian: THEODORE JON HOSTETLER
Library of 200,000 vols, 300 print periodical subscriptions and 70,000 e-periodical subscriptions
Number of teachers: 96
Number of students: 764
Publications: *Hail, Muse!* (1 a year), *Randolph* (3 a year).

REGENT UNIVERSITY

1000 Regent University Dr., Virginia Beach, VA 23464

Telephone: (757) 352-4127
Fax: (757) 352-4033
E-mail: admissions@regent.edu
Internet: www.regent.edu

Founded 1978
Private control
Academic year: August to July

Chancellor and Founder: Dr PAT ROBERTSON
Pres.: Dr CARLOS CAMPO
Exec. Vice-Pres.: PAUL BONICELLI
Vice-Pres. and Gen. Counsel: LOUIS ISAKOFF
Vice-Pres. for Academic Affairs: Dr FRED ROVAI
Vice-Pres. for Advancement: ANN LeBLANC
Vice-Pres. for Devt and Communications: MAUREEN McDONNELL
Vice-Pres. for Enrolment Management and Information Technology: TRACY STEWART
Vice-Pres. for Finance: DEAN WOOTEN
Vice-Pres. for Student Services: Dr JEFF PITTMAN
Registrar: ALTHEA KIMES
Dean for Library: Dr SARA BARON
Library of 304,000 vols, 593,000 microforms, 14,000 audiovisual items, 156,000 e-books, 98,900 journal titles
Number of teachers: 511
Number of students: 5,915
Publications: *Christian Leader*, *Emerging Leadership Journeys* (2 a year), *Faith and Therapy* (12 a year), *Inner Resources for Leaders* (3 a year), *International Journal of Leadership Studies*, *Journal of Biblical Perspectives in Leadership* (2 a year), *Journal of Practical Consulting*, *Journal of Strategic Leadership*, *Journal of Virtues & Leadership*, *Law Review* (2 a year), *Leadership Advance Online*, *Regent Global Business Review* (6 a year), *Regent Journal of International Law* (2 a year), *Regent Journal of Law & Public Policy*, *Regent University Law Review*, *The Journal of Virtues & Leadership*

DEANS

Robertson School of Government: Dr GARY ROBERTS
School of Education: Dr ALAN ARROYO
School of Communication and the Arts: Dr MITCH LAND
School of Divinity: Dr MICHAEL PALMER

School of Global Leadership and Entrepreneurship: Dr BRUCE WINSTON
School of Law: Dr JEFF BRAUCH
School of Psychology and Counseling: Dr WILLIAM HATHAWAY
School of Undergraduate Studies: Dr GERSON MORENO-RIANO

ROANOKE COLLEGE

221 College Lane, Salem, VA 24153

Telephone: (540) 375-2500
Fax: (540) 375-2267
E-mail: admissions@roanoke.edu
Internet: roanoke.edu

Founded 1842 as Virginia Institute, present name 1853
Private control
Academic year: August to May
Liberal arts college

Pres.: MICHAEL CREED MAXEY
Vice-Pres. and Dean for the College: Prof. Dr RICHARD A. SMITH
Vice-Pres. for Business Affairs: MARK P. NOFTSINGER
Vice-Pres. for Enrolment and Dean for Admissions and Financial Aid: BRENDA PORTER POGGENDORF
Vice-Pres. for Resource Devt: CONNIE CARMACK
Vice-Pres. For Student Affairs and Dean for Students: EUGENE L. ZDZIARSKI, II
Assoc. Dean and Registrar: LEAH L. RUSSELL
Dir for Library: STANLEY F. UMBERGER
Library of 400,000 vols, 1,000 DVDs
Number of teachers: 125
Number of students: 2,057
Publications: *Roanoke* (3 a year), *Teacher-Scholar* (1 a year).

SAINT PAUL'S COLLEGE

115 College Dr., Lawrenceville, VA 23868

Telephone: (434) 848-3111
Internet: saintpaulsnet.com

Founded 1888 as St Paul Normal and Industrial School, present name 1957
Private control
Liberal arts college

Pres. and CEO: Dr EDDIE N. MOORE, JR
Provost and Vice-Pres. for Academic and Student Affairs: Dr RAYMOND HOLMES
Vice-Pres. for Financial Affairs and Comptroller: GERALDINE JONES
Vice-Pres. for Institutional Advancement: KIMBERLY TETLOW
Registrar: HELEN JACKSON
Dir for Library Services: MARC L. FINNEY.

SHENANDOAH UNIVERSITY

1460 University Dr., Winchester, VA 22601

Telephone: (540) 665-4500
Fax: (540) 665-4627
E-mail: admit@su.edu
Internet: www.su.edu

Founded 1875 as Shenandoah Seminary, present name and status 1991
Private control
Academic year: August to May (2 semesters)

Pres.: Dr TRACY FITZSIMMONS
Sr Vice-Pres. and Vice-Pres. for Academic Affairs: Dr BRYON L. GRIGSBY
Vice-Pres. for Admin. and Finance: RICHARD C. SHICKLE
Vice-Pres. for Advancement: MITCHELL L. MOORE
Vice-Pres. for Enrolment Management and Student Success: CLARRESA MOORE MORTON
Vice-Pres. for Student Life: Rev. Dr RHONDA VanDYKE
Registrar: MELANIE WINTER
Dir for Univ. Libraries: CHRISTOPHER BEAN

Library of 275,000 vols (incl. 131,000 books and journals), 13,000 audio items, 16,000 scores, 1,500 video cassettes, 32,000 print and e-journals, 115,000 ERIC documents
Number of teachers: 436
Number of students: 4,052

DEANS

Bernard J. Dunn School of Pharmacy: Dr ALAN B. McKAY
College of Arts and Sciences: Dr CALVIN H. ALLEN, JR
Conservatory: MICHAEL J. STEPNIAK
Harry F. Byrd, Jr, School of Business: W. RANDY BOXX
School of Health Professions: (vacant)

STRATFORD UNIVERSITY

7777 Leesburg Pike, Falls Church, VA 22043

Telephone: (703) 821-8570
E-mail: registrar@stratford.edu
Internet: www.stratford.edu

Founded 1976
Private control
Academic year: January to December

Campuses in Baltimore (Maryland); Newport News, Richmond and Woodbridge (Virginia); int. campus in New Delhi (India)

Pres. and CEO: Dr RICHARD R. SHURTZ, II
Exec. Vice-Pres.: MARY ANN SHURTZ
Vice-Pres. for Human Resources: SHIRLEY DIAZ
Vice-Pres. for Int. Programmes: FEROZE KHAN
Chief Financial Officer: JOHN DOVI
Dir for Admissions: CARL SIEBECKER
Registrar: HEATHER RICHARDS

DEANS

School of Computer Information Systems: (vacant)
School of Culinary Arts and Hospitality Management: JORDAN LICHMAN
School of Health Sciences: Dr BENNETT SOLBERG
School of Nursing: Dr SHARRON GUILLETT

STRAYER UNIVERSITY

Suite 300, 1133 15th St, NW, Washington, DC 20005

Telephone: (202) 408-2400
Fax: (202) 289-1831
E-mail: washington@strayer.edu
Internet: www.strayer.edu

Founded 1892 as Strayer Business College, present name 1998
Private control
Academic year: September to September

Pres. and CEO: ROBERT S. SILBERMAN
Provost and Academic Dean: Dr J. CHRIS TOE
Campus Man.: ED DOBSON
Library of 32,000 vols
Number of teachers: 575 (125 full-time, 450 adjunct)
Number of students: 16,500

DEANS

Jack Welch Management Institute: Dr DANNY SZPIRO
School of Arts and Sciences: Dr MARILYN BROADUS-GAY
School of Business: Dr WENDY HOWARD
School of Education: Dr VANESSA P. ESLINGER-BROWN
School of Information Systems and Technology: Dr BILL DAFNIS

SWEET BRIAR COLLEGE

134 Chapel Rd, Sweet Briar, VA 24595

Telephone: (804) 381-6100
Fax: (804) 381-6484

E-mail: info@sbc.edu
Internet: www.sbc.edu
Founded 1901
Private control
Academic year: August to May
Areas of study: arts management, biochemistry and molecular biology, biology, business, chemistry, classics, creative writing, dance, economics, education, science
Pres.: Dr Jo Ellen Parker
Vice-Pres. and Chief of Staff: Louise Swiecki Zingaro
Vice-Pres. for Academic Affairs and Dean for the Faculty: Dr Amy Jessen-Marshall
Vice-Pres. for Alumnae and Devt: Heidi Hansen McCrory
Vice-Pres. for Finance and Admin.: Scott C. Shank
Vice-Pres. for Student Affairs and Dean for Co-Curricular Life: Dr Cheryl L. Steele
Dean for Admissions: Gretchen Gravley-Tucker
Registrar: Deborah L. Powell
Dir for Libraries and Integrated Learning Resources: John G. Jaffe
Library of 250,000 vols, 375,000 microforms, 1,000 periodicals, 6,500 audiovisual items
Number of teachers: 126 (77 full-time, 49 part-time)
Number of students: 760
Publication: *Alumnae Magazine* (3 a year).

UNION PRESBYTERIAN SEMINARY

3401 Brook Rd, Richmond, VA 23227
Telephone: (804) 355-0671
Fax: (804) 355-3919
E-mail: admissions@upsem.edu
Internet: www.upsem.edu
Founded 1812 as Union Theological Seminary, present name 2010
Private control
Academic year: September to June
Campus at Charlotte (North Carolina)
Pres.: Dr Brian K. Blount
Vice-Pres. for Finance and Admin.: Michael B. Cashwell
Vice-Pres. for Institutional Advancement: Richard Wong
Dean for Union Presbyterian Seminary (Richmond Campus): Stanley H. Skreslet
Dean for Union Presbyterian Seminary (Charlotte Campus): Thomas W. Currie
Dean for Students and Chaplain: Edna Jacobs Banes
Assoc. Dean for Academic Programmes: E. Carson Brisson
Dir for Admissions: Kate Fiedler Boswell
Dir for Enrolment Management: Michelle Walker
Dir for Student Services: Elsie P. Hackett
Registrar: J. Stanley Hargraves
Dir for Library and Institutional Effectiveness: Milton J. Coalter
Library of 315,000 vols, 600 print periodical subscriptions, 6,000 e-journal subcsriptions
Number of teachers: 32
Number of students: 139

UNIVERSITY OF MARY WASHINGTON

1301 College Ave, Fredericksburg, VA 22401-5300
Telephone: (540) 654-1000
Fax: (540) 654-1857
E-mail: admit@umw.edu
Internet: www.umw.edu
Founded 1908 as Fredericksburg's State Normal and Industrial School for Women, present name 2004
State control
Academic year: August to July

Pres.: Richard V. Hurley
Provost: Dr Ian D. C. Newbould
Vice-Pres. for Admin. and Finance: Richard R. Pearce
Vice-Pres. for Advancement and Univ. Relations: Salvatore M. Meringolo
Vice-Pres. for Student Affairs: Douglas N. Searcy
Registrar: Rita F. Dunston
Univ. Librarian: Rosemary Huff Arneson
Library of 367,000 vols
Number of teachers: 177
Number of students: 5,000 (4,000 undergraduate, 1,000 graduate)

DEANS

College of Arts and Sciences: Dr Richard Finklestein
College of Business: Dr Lynne D. Richardson
College of Education: Dr Mary Gendernalik-Cooper

UNIVERSITY OF RICHMOND

28 Westhampton Way, University of Richmond, VA 23173
Telephone: (804) 289-8000
Fax: (804) 287-6540
E-mail: admissions@richmond.edu
Internet: www.richmond.edu
Founded 1830 as Richmond College, present name 1920
Private control
Academic year: August to May
Pres.: Dr Edward L. Ayers
Chancellor: Dr E. Bruce Heilman
Chancellor: Dr Richard L. Morrill
Provost and Vice-Pres.: Dr Stephen Allred
Vice-Pres. for Advancement: Thomas C. Gutenberger
Vice-Pres. for Business and Finance and Treas.: Dr Hossein Sadid
Vice-Pres. for Student Devt: Dr Stephen Damian Bisese
Asst Vice-Pres. and Dean for Admission: Gil Villanueva
Registrar: Susan Denman Breeden
Univ. Librarian: Kevin Butterfield
Library of 500,000 vols, 100,000 bound periodicals and e-resources, 10,000 video titles, 1,500 audiobooks, 500 audio cassettes, 16,000 scores, 9,100 CDs
Number of teachers: 558 (379 full-time, 179 part-time)
Number of students: 4,405
Publications: *Richmond Alumni Magazine* (4 a year), *Richmond International* (1 a year)

DEANS

International Education: Dr Uliana Gabara
Jepson School of Leadership Studies: Dr Sandra J. Peart
Richmond College: Dr Joseph R. Boehman
Robins School of Business: Dr Nancy A. Bagranoff
School of Arts and Sciences: Dr Kathleen Roberts Skerrett
School of Law: Wendy Collins Perdue
School of Professional and Continuing Studies: Prof. Dr James L. Narduzzi
Westhampton College: Dr Juliette L. Landphair

UNIVERSITY OF VIRGINIA

POB 400229, Charlottesville, VA 22904-4229
Telephone: (434) 924-0311
Fax: (434) 924-0938
E-mail: undergradadmission@virginia.edu
Internet: www.virginia.edu
Founded 1819
State control
Academic year: September to May
Pres.: Teresa A. Sullivan

Provost and Exec. Vice-Pres.: John D. Simon
Sr Vice-Pres. for Devt and Public Affairs: Robert D. Sweeney
Exec. Vice-Pres. and Chief Operating Officer: Michael Strine
Vice-Pres.: Dr Steven T. DeKosky
Vice-Pres. and CEO for Health System: R. Edward Howell
Vice-Pres. and Chief Financial Officer: Yoke San L. Reynolds
Vice-Pres. and Chief Human Resources Officer: Susan A. Carkeek
Vice-Pres. and Chief Information Officer: James L. Hilton
Vice-Pres. and Chief Student Affairs Officer: Dr Patricia M. Lampkin
Vice-Pres. for Management and Budget: Colette Sheehy
Vice-Pres. for Research: Thomas C. Skalak
Dean for Admissions (Undergraduate): Gregory W. Roberts
Dean for Students: Allen Groves
Univ. Librarian: Karin Wittenborg
Library: see under Libraries and Archives
Number of teachers: 1,296
Number of students: 24,297
Publications: *Virginia Law Review*, *Virginia Law Weekly*, *Virginia Quarterly Review*

DEANS

College and Graduate School of Arts and Sciences: Dr Meredith Jung-En Woo
Curry School of Education: Robert C. Pianta
Darden School of Business: Robert F. Bruner
Frank Batten School of Leadership and Public Policy: Harry Harding
McIntire School of Commerce: Carl P. Zeithaml
School of Architecture: Kim Tanzer
School of Continuing and Professional Studies: Billy Cannaday, Jr
School of Engineering and Applied Science: Prof. James H. Aylor
School of Law: Paul G. Mahoney
School of Medicine: Dr Steven T. DeKosky
School of Nursing: Dr Dorrie Fontaine

PROFESSORS

Curry School of Education (POB 400260, Charlottesville, VA 22904-4260; tel. (434) 924-3334; fax (434) 924-0747; e-mail curry@virginia.edu; internet curry.edschool.virginia.edu):
  Bredo, E., Leadership, Foundations and Policy Studies
  Breneman, D., Education
  Bull, G., Leadership, Foundations and Policy Studies
  Burbach, H., Leadership, Foundations and Policy Studies
  Butler, A., Leadership, Foundations and Policy Studies
  Callahan, C., Leadership, Foundations and Policy Studies
  Cohen, S., Curriculum, Instruction and Special Education
  Cornell, D., Human Services
  Duke, D., Leadership, Foundations and Policy Studies
  Fan, X., Leadership, Foundations and Policy Studies
  Gaesser, G., Human Services
  Gansneder, B., Leadership, Foundations and Policy Studies
  Hallahan, D., Curriculum, Instruction and Special Education
  Hansen, J., Education
  Ingersoll, C., Human Services
  Invernizzi, M., Curriculum, Instruction and Special Education
  Kelly, L., Human Services
  Kneedler, R., Education
  Lawrence, E., Human Services
  Lloyd, J., Education

LOPER, A., Human Services
MCKENNA, M., Curriculum, Instruction and Special Education
MCNERGNEY, J., Education
MCNERGNEY, R., Leadership, Foundations and Policy Studies
MILLER, M., Leadership, Foundations and Policy Studies
PATE, R., Education
REEVE, R., Human Services
RICHARDS, H., Leadership, Foundations and Policy Studies
SHERAS, P., Human Services
SHORT, J., Leadership, Foundations and Policy Studies
SMOLKIN, L., Curriculum, Instruction and Special Education
SNELL, M., Curriculum, Instruction and Special Education
STRANG, H., Leadership, Foundations and Policy Studies
TOMLINSON, C., Leadership, Foundations and Policy Studies
WELTMAN, A., Human Services

Darden School (Graduate School of Business Administration) (POB 400321, Charlottesville, VA 22904-4321; tel. (434) 924-3900; fax (434) 924-4859; internet www.darden.edu):

ALLEN, B.
BECKENSTEIN, A.
BODILY, S.
BOURGEOIS, L.
BROWNLEE, E.
CHAPLINSKY, S.
CHEN, M.
CLAWSON, J.
COLLEY, J.
DAVIS, E.
DOYLE, J.
EADES, K.
EAKER, M.
FARRIS, P.
FREEMAN, R.
FREY, S.
GLYNN, J.
HARRIS, R.
HASKINS, M.
HESS, E.
HORNIMAN, A.
LANDEL, R.
LIEDTKA, J.
MOORE, M.
PFEIFER, P.
SIHLER, W.
SNELL, S.
SPEKMAN, R.
VENKATARAMAN, S.
WEISS, E.
WERHANE, P.

McIntire School of Commerce (POB 400173, Charlottesville, VA 22904-4173; tel. (434) 924-3257; internet www.commerce.virginia.edu):

ATCHISON, M.
BATEMAN, T.
BROOME, O.
DE MONG, R.
KEHOE, W.
KEMP, R.
LINDGREN, J.
MALONEY, D.
MARSTON, F.
MICK, D.
NELSON, R.
NETEMEYER, R.
OVERSTREET, G.
SMITH, D.
WEBB, R.
WILHELM, W.
WILLIAMS, S.

School of Architecture (POB 400122, Charlottesville, VA 22904-4122; tel. (434) 924-

3715; fax (434) 982-2678; internet www.virginia.edu/arch):

BEATLEY, T., Planning
BEDNAR, M., Architecture
BOESCHENSTEIN, W., Architecture
CLARK, W., Architecture
DRIPPS, R., Architecture
FORD, E., Architecture
LUCY, W., Planning
MORRISH, W., Architecture
SCHWARTZ, K., Architecture
SPAIN, D., Planning
WALDMAN, P., Architecture
WILSON, R., Architectural History

School of Arts and Sciences (POB 400772, Charlottesville, VA 22904-4772; tel. (434) 924-3389; fax (434) 924-1317; e-mail grad-a-s@virginia.edu; internet artsandsciences.virginia.edu):

ADLER, P., Biology
ALLEN, J., Psychology
ALLEN, R., Chemistry
ANDERSON, A., Spanish, Italian and Portuguese
ANDERSON, S., Economics
ANDREWS, L., Chemistry
ANTONOVICS, J., Biology
ARNOLD, A., French Literature and General Linguistics
ARNOLD, K., Music
ARNOLD, P., Physics
ARON, M., History
ARRAS, J., Philosophy
BAKER, P., English
BAROLSKY, P., Art
BEATTIE, A., Creative Writing
BELANGER, T., Book Arts Press
BELL, M., Art
BENNETT, B., German Literature
BERLANSTEIN, L., History
BEST, T., German Literature
BLACK, D., Sociology
BLOOM, G., Biology
BLOOMFIELD, L., Physics
BLUMBERG, R., Sociology
BOND, H., History
BOOTH, A., English
BRADEN, G., English
BRODIE, E., Biology
BRUNJES, P., Psychology
BRYANT, R., Chemistry
BURNETT, R., Chemistry
BURTON, E., Economics
CAFISO, D., Chemistry
CANTOR, P., English
CARGILE, J., Philosophy
CASEY, J., Creative Writing
CATES, G., Physics
CEASER, J., Government and Foreign Affairs
CHANG, T., Statistics
CHAPEL, R., Drama Operations
CHASE LEVENSON, K., English
CHEN, J., History
CHEVALIER, R., Astronomy
CHILDRESS, J., Religious Studies
CLAY, J., Classics
CLORE, G., Psychology
COLOMB, G., English
CONETTI, S., Physics
CONFINO, A., History
CONNOLLY, J., Slavic Languages and Literature
CONTINI-MORAVA, E., Anthropology
COX, B., Physics
CRABB, D., Nuclear and Particle Physics
CRACKEL, T., Editing Wash Papers
CRAWFORD, J., Classics
CRONMILLER, C., Biology
CROSBY, E., History
CROZIER, R., Art
CUSHMAN, S., English
DAMON, F., Anthropology
DASS, D., Art
DAVIS, R., Environmental Sciences

DAY, D., Nuclear and Particle Physics
DEAVER, B., Physics
DELLA COLETTA, C., Spanish, Italian and Portuguese
DELOACHE, J., Psychology
DEMAS, J., Chemistry
DEVEREUX, D., Philosophy
DOBBINS, J., Art
DOLAN, R., Environmental Sciences
DOVE, R., Creative Writing
DRUCKER, J., Media Studies
DUKES, E., Physics
EDMUNDSON, M., English
EISENBERG, D., Creative Writing
ELSON, M., Slavic Languages and Literature
ELZINGA, K., Economics
EMERY, R., Psychology
ENGERS, M., Economics
FATTON, R., Government and Foreign Affairs
FELDMAN, J., English
FELSKI, R., English
FENDLEY, P., Physics
FERREIRA, M., Religious Studies
FISHBANE, P., Physics
FOGARTY, G., Religious Studies
FOWLER, M., Physics
FRAIMAN, S., English
FRASER, C., Chemistry
FREEMAN, J., Psychology
FRICK, J., Drama Operations
FRIESEN, W., Biology
FUCHS, S., Sociology
FUENTES, J., Environmental Sciences
GALLAGHER, G., History
GALLAGHER, T., Physics
GALLOWAY, J., Environmental Sciences
GAMBLE, H., Religious Studies
GARRETT, R., Biology
GEIGER, P., Art
GERLI, E., Spanish, Italian and Portuguese
GERRANS, G., Chemistry
GEYSEN, H., Chemistry
GIES, D., Spanish, Italian and Portuguese
GOEDDE, L., Art
GRAINGER, R., Biology
GREEN, C., Biology
GRISHAM, C., Chemistry
GRONER, P., Religious Studies
GUTERBOCK, T., Sociology
HABERLY, D., Spanish, Italian and Portuguese
HANDLER, R., Anthropology
HARMAN, W., Chemistry
HARRISON, A., Chemistry
HART, K., Religious Studies
HAWLEY, J., Astronomy
HAYDEN, B., Environmental Sciences
HECHT, S., Chemistry
HERBST, I., Mathematics
HERMAN, J., Environmental Sciences
HESS, G., Physics
HILL, D., Psychology
HILL, R., Spanish, Italian and Portuguese
HIRSH, J., Biology
HOH, L., Drama Operations
HOLSINGER, B., Music
HOLT, C., Economics
HOLT, M., History
HORNBERGER, G., Environmental Sciences
HOWARD, A., Environmental Sciences
HUECKSTEDT, R., Middle Eastern and South Asian Languages and Culture
HUMPHREYS, P., Philosophy
HUNT, D., Chemistry
HUNTER, J., English
HUNTER, J., Sociology
IMBRIE, J., Mathematics
JAMES, J., Economics
JOHNSON, W., Economics
JONES, R., Physics
JORDAN, D., Government and Foreign Affairs
JOST, W., English
KAWASAKI, M., Biology

KEEN, R., Psychology
KEENAN, D., Statistics
KEENE, W., Environmental Sciences
KELLER, R., Biology
KETT, J., History
KHARE, R., Anthropology
KINGSTON, P., Sociology
KINNEY, A., East Asian Languages, Literature and Cultures
KINNEY, J., English
KLOSKO, G., Government and Foreign Affairs
KOVACS, P., Classics
KRETSINGER, R., Biology
KRIETE, T., Mathematics
KUBOVY, M., Psychology
KUHN, N., Mathematics
KUMAR, J., Sociology
LAGOS, M., Spanish, Italian and Portuguese
LANDERS, J., Chemistry
LANE, A., History
LANG, K., Religious Studies
LASIECKA, I., Mathematics
LEFFLER, M., History
LEFFLER, P., History
LEGRO, J., Government and Foreign Affairs
LEHMANN, K., Chemistry
LENDON, J., History
LERDAU, M., Environmental Sciences
LEVENSON, M., English
LILLARD, A., Psychology
LINDGREN, R., Nuclear and Particle Physics
LLEWELLYN, P., Psychology
LOMASKY, L., Philosophy
LOTT, E., English
LYNCH, A., Government and Foreign Affairs
LYONS, J., French Literature and General Linguistics
MACCLUER, B., Mathematics
MCCRIMMON, K., Mathematics
MCCURDY, C., History
MACDONALD, T., Chemistry
MCDONALD, W., German Literature
MCDOWELL, D., English
MCGANN, J., English
MCKINLEY, M., French Literature and General Linguistics
MCKINNON, S., Anthropology
MCLAREN, J., Economics
MACKO, S., Environmental Sciences
MAJEWSKI, S., Astronomy
MARLATT, M., Art
MARSH, C., Religious Studies
MARSHALL, J., Chemistry
MARTENS, L., German Literature
MATTERN, D., Editing Madison Papers
MAUS, K., English
MEGILL, A., History
MELLON, D., Biology
MENAKER, M., Biology
MERRICKS, T., Philosophy
METCALF, P., Anthropology
MICHAELS, P., Environmental Sciences
MIDELFORT, H., History
MIKALSON, J., Classics
MILANI, F., Middle Eastern and South Asian Languages and Culture
MILKIS, S., Government and Foreign Affairs
MILLER, J., Classics
MILLER, J., History
MILLS, A., Environmental Sciences
MILLS, D., Economics
MIRMAN, L., Economics
MOST, R., Undergraduate College Operations
NELSON, R., English
NESSELROADE, J., Psychology
NIMA, T., Religious Studies
NOCK, S., Sociology
NOHRNBERG, J., English
NOLAN, B., English
NORUM, B., Physics

O'BRIEN, D., Government and Foreign Affairs
O'CONNELL, R., Astronomy
OCHS, P., Religious Studies
OLICK, J., Sociology
OLSEN, E., Economics
ONUF, P., History
OPERE, F., Spanish, Italian and Portuguese
ORR, G., Creative Writing
OSHEIM, D., History
PAPOVICH, J., Undergraduate College Operations
PARKER, D., Spanish, Italian and Portuguese
PARSHALL, B., Mathematics
PARSHALL, K., Mathematics
PATE, B., Chemistry
PATTERSON, C., Psychology
PERIASAMY, A., Biology
PERKOWSKI, J., Slavic Languages and Literature
PHAM, H., Physics
PLOG, S., Anthropology
POCANIC, D., Physics
POON, J., Physics
POPE, R., Spanish, Italian and Portuguese
PRESS, A., Sociology
PROFFITT, D., Psychology
PU, L., Chemistry
QUANDT, W., Government and Foreign Affairs
RAILTON, S., English
RAMAZANI, R., English
RAMIREZ, D., Mathematics
RAPINCHUK, A., Mathematics
RAY, B., Religious Studies
REPPUCCI, N., Psychology
REYNOLDS, B., Economics
RHOADS, S., Government and Foreign Affairs
RINI, J., Spanish, Italian and Portuguese
ROBERTS, M., Art
ROGER, P., French Literature and General Linguistics
ROOD, R., Astronomy
ROSS, M., English
SACHEDINA, A., Religious Studies
SALTHOUSE, T., Psychology
SARAZIN, C., Astronomy
SASLAW, W., Astronomy
SAVAGE, J., Government and Foreign Affairs
SAWAIE, M., Middle Eastern and South Asian Language and Culture
SCHOPPA, L., Government and Foreign Affairs
SCHUKER, S., History
SCHWARTZ, H., Government and Foreign Affairs
SCOTT, D., Philosophy
SCOTT, L., Mathematics
SENEVIRATNE, H., Anthropology
SHATIN, J., Music
SHAW, D., Spanish, Italian and Portuguese
SHUGART, H., Environmental Sciences
SIMMONS, A., Philosophy
SKRUTSKIE, M., Astronomy
SMITH, D., Environmental Sciences
SPEARING, A., English
SPELLMAN, B., Psychology
STAGG, J., Editing Madison Papers
STERN, S., Economics
STEWART, G., Undergraduate College Options
SUMMERS, J., Art
SUNDBERG, R., Chemistry
TAYLOR, D., Biology
THACKER, H., Physics
THOMAS, L., Mathematics
THOMAS, M., History
THOMPSON, A., Religious Studies
THORNTON, S., Physics
THUAN, T., Astronomy
TILGHMAN, C., Creative Writing
TIMKO, M., Biology
TOLBERT, C., Astronomy

TRIGGIANI, R., Mathematics
TRINDLE, C., Chemistry
TUCKER, H., English
TURKHEIMER, E., Psychology
TURNER, E., Art
UPTON, D., Art
VAN WINCOOP, E., Economics
VANDER MEULEN, D., English
VORIS, R., German Literature
WAGNER, R., Anthropology
WALKER, K., Psychology
WALL, C., English
WANG, W., Mathematics
WARNER, R., Drama Operations
WEBER, A., Spanish, Italian and Portuguese
WEST, G., Drama Operations
WHITE, S., Government and Foreign Affairs
WHITTLE, D., Astronomy
WIBERG, P., Environmental Sciences
WICKE, J., English
WILBUR, H., Biology
WILKEN, R., Religious Studies
WILLIAMS, B., Sociology
WILLINGHAM, D., Psychology
WILSON, M., East Asian Languages, Literature and Cultures
WILSON, M., Psychology
WILSON, T., Psychology
WOMACK, B., Government and Foreign Affairs
WOODMAN, A., Classics
WRIGHT, C., Creative Writing
ZELIKOW, P., History
ZIEMAN, J., Environmental Sciences
ZUNZ, O., History

School of Continuing and Professional Studies:

ABOUZEID, M., TEMPO Reading Programme
HARRISON, E., N Virginia Center
ROBERSON, S., Lynchburg Center

School of Engineering and Applied Science (POB 400246, Charlottesville, VA 22904-4246; tel. (434) 924-3072; fax (434) 924-3555; internet www.seas.virginia.edu):

ACTON, S., Electrical and Computer Engineering
ALLAIRE, P., Mechanical and Aerospace Engineering
BAILEY, M., Computer Science
BARAGIOLA, R., Materials Science and Engineering
BARRETT, L., Mechanical and Aerospace Engineering
BEAN, J., Electrical and Computer Engineering
BERGER, T., Electrical and Computer Engineering
BROWN, D., Systems and Information Engineering
CAHEN, G., Materials Science and Engineering
CAMPBELL, J., Electrical and Computer Engineering
CARLSON, W., Science, Technology and Society
CARTA, G., Chemical Engineering
CRANDALL, J., Mechanical and Aerospace Engineering
DAVIDSON, J., Computer Science
DAVIS, R., Chemical Engineering
DEMETSKY, M., Civil and Environmental Engineering
DORNING, J., Materials Science and Engineering
DUGAN, J., Electrical and Computer Engineering
FERNANDEZ, E., Chemical Engineering
FORD, R., Chemical Engineering
GANGLOFF, R., Materials Science and Engineering
GARBER, N., Civil and Environmental Engineering

GILLIES, G., Mechanical and Aerospace Engineering
GORMAN, M., Science, Technology and Society
GRIMSHAW, A., Computer Science
GUPTA, M., Electrical and Computer Engineering
HAIMES, Y., Systems and Information Engineering
HAJ-HARIRI, H., Mechanical and Aerospace Engineering
HARRIOTT, L., Electrical and Computer Engineering
HOEL, L., Civil and Environmental Engineering
HOLMES, A., Electrical and Computer Engineering
HORGAN, C., Civil and Environmental Engineering
HOROWITZ, B., Systems and Information Engineering
HOWE, J., Materials Science and Engineering
HUDSON, J., Chemical Engineering
HULL, R., Materials Science and Engineering
HUMPHREY, J., Mechanical and Aerospace Engineering
HUMPHREY, M., Computer Science
IWASAKI, T., Mechanical and Aerospace Engineering
JESSER, W., Materials Science and Engineering
JOHNSON, B., Electrical and Computer Engineering
JOHNSON, D., Science, Technology and Society
JOHNSON, R., Materials Science and Engineering
JOHNSON, W., Materials Science and Engineering
JONES, A., Computer Science
KELLY, R., Materials Science and Engineering
KENT, R., Mechanical and Aerospace Engineering
KING, M., Chemical Engineering
KIRWAN, D., Chemical Engineering
KNIGHT, J., Computer Science
KRZYSZTOFOWICZ, R., Systems and Information Engineering
LIN, Z., Electrical and Computer Engineering
LUNG, W., Civil and Environmental Engineering
MCDANIEL, J., Mechanical and Aerospace Engineering
MARSHALL, P., Electrical and Computer Engineering
MASLEN, E., Mechanical and Aerospace Engineering
MIKSAD, R., Civil and Environmental Engineering
NEUROCK, M., Chemical Engineering
NORRIS, P., Mechanical and Aerospace Engineering
O'CONNELL, J., Chemical Engineering
PINDERA, M., Civil and Environmental Engineering
REED, M., Electrical and Computer Engineering
REYNOLDS, P., Computer Science
RICHARDS, L., Mechanical and Aerospace Engineering
ROBERTS, W., Mechanical and Aerospace Engineering
ROBINS, G., Computer Science
SCHERER, W., Systems and Information Engineering
SCULLY, J., Materials Science and Engineering
SHIFLET, G., Materials Science and Engineering
SKALAK, T., Biomedical Engineering Department

SMITH, J., Civil and Environmental Engineering
SOFFA, M., Computer Science
SOFFA, W., Materials Science and Engineering
SON, S., Computer Science
STANKOVIC, J., Computer Science
STARKE, E., Materials Science and Engineering
TAO, G., Electrical and Computer Engineering
THACKER, J., Mechanical and Aerospace Engineering
THORNTON, K., Science, Technology and Society
TOWNSEND, I., Science, Technology and Society
VEERARAGHAVAN, M., Electrical and Computer Engineering
WADLEY, H., Materials Science and Engineering
WEAVER, A., Computer Science
WEIKLE, R., Electrical and Computer Engineering
WHITE, K., Systems and Information Engineering
WILSON, S., Electrical and Computer Engineering
WOLF, S., Materials Science and Engineering
WOOD, H., Mechanical and Aerospace Engineering
WULF, W., Computer Science

School of Law (POB 400405, Charlottesville, VA 22904-4405; tel. (434) 924-7354; fax (434) 924-7536; internet www.law.virginia.edu):

ABRAHAM, K.
ARMACOST, B.
BAGLEY, M.
BALNAVE, R.
BEVIER, L.
BLASI, V.
BONNIE, R.
BROWN, D.
BROWN-NAGIN, T.
BUCK, D.
CANNON, J.
COHEN, G.
COLLINS, M.
COUGHLIN, A.
CUSHMAN, B.
DOOLEY, M.
DUDLEY, E.
FORDE-MAZRUI, K.
GOLUBOFF, R.
HARRISON, J.
HOWARD, A.
HYNES, R.
IBBEKEN, D.
JOHNSON, A.
KITCH, E.
KLARMAN, M.
KORDANA, K.
KRAUS, J.
LESLIE, D.
LOW, P.
MAGILL, M.
MAHONEY, J.
MAHONEY, P.
MARTIN, D.
MITCHELL, P.
MONAHAN, J.
MOORE, J.
NACHBAR, T.
NELSON, C.
O'CONNELL, J.
ORTIZ, D.
RILEY, M.
ROBINSON, G.
ROBINSON, M.
RUTHERGLEN, G.
RYAN, J.
SAYLER, R.
SCHRAGGER, R.
SETEAR, J.

SINCLAIR, K.
SMITH, S.
STEPHAN, P.
TURNER, R.
VERKERKE, J.
WALKER, W.
WALT, S.
WHITE, G.
WHITE, T.
WOOLHANDLER, N.
YIN, G.

School of Medicine (POB 800793, Charlottesville, VA 22908-0793; tel. (434) 924-5118; internet www.healthsystem.virginia.edu/internet/som/home.cfm):

ABEL, M., Paediatric Orthotics
ALFORD, B., Musculoskeletal Medicine
APPREY, M., Psychiatry
ARLET, V., Orthopaedics (Spine)
AYERS, C., Cardiovascular Medicine
BALIAN, G., Orthopedic Research
BARRETT, E., Endocrinology
BARRETT, P., Pharmacology
BARTH, J., Psychiatry
BAUM, V., Anaesthesiology
BAYLISS, D., Pharmacology
BECKER, D., Medicine
BELLER, G., Cardiovascular Medicine
BENDER, T., Microbiology
BENNETT, J., Neurology
BERGIN, J., Cardiovascular Medicine
BERTRAM, E., Neurology
BEYER, A., Microbiology
BLOODGOOD, R., Cell Biology
BOLTON, W., Nephrology
BORISH, L., Allergy
BOUTON, A., Microbiology
BRADDOCK, S., Genetics
BRADY, W., Emergency Medicine
BRANT, W., Thoracoabdominal Radiology
BRAUTIGAN, D., Cell Signalling
BROOKEMAN, J., Radiological Research
BROWN, J., Microbiology
BURKE, D., Biochemistry and Molecular Genetics
BUSHWELLER, J., Molecular Physics and Biophysics
CANTERBURY, R., Psychiatry
CAREY, R., Endocrinology
CASANOVA, J., Cell Biology
CASTLE, J., Cell Biology
CHIRGWIN, J., Endocrinology
CLAYTON, A., Psychiatry
COHEN, M., Breast Imaging
COMINELLI, F., Gastroenterology
CONCANNON, P., Biochemistry and Molecular Genetics
CONNELLY, J., Medicine
CONWAY, B., Ophthalmology
CORBETT, E., Medicine
CORWIN, J., Neuroscience
COUSAR, J., Clinical Pathology
COX, D., Psychiatry
CREUTZ, C., Pharmacology
DALKIN, A., Endocrinology
DEREWENDA, Z., Molecular Physics and Biophysics
DESIMONE, D., Cell Biology
DIDUCH, D., Sports Medicine
DIMARCO, J., Cardiovascular Medicine
DONOWITZ, G., Infectious Diseases
DULING, B., Molecular Physics and Biophysics
DURBIN, C., Anaesthesiology
DURIEUX, M., Anaesthesiology
DUTTA, A., Biochemistry and Molecular Genetics
EGELMAN, E., Biochemistry and Molecular Genetics
ENGELHARD, V., Microbiology
ERNST, P., Gastroenterology
EVANS, W., Endocrinology
FOX, J., Microbiology
FRACASSO, P., Haematology and Oncology
FRYSINGER, R., Multiple Neuralgia

Fu, S., Rheumatology
Gal, T., Anaesthesiology
Galazka, S., Family Medicine
Garrison, J., Pharmacology
Gaskin, F., Psychiatry
Gear, A., Biochemistry and Molecular Genetics
Gibson, R., Cardiovascular Medicine
Gimple, L., Cardiovascular Medicine
Goldberg, J., Microbiology
Greer, K., Dermatology
Greyson, C., Psychiatry
Guerrant, R., Infectious Diseases
Guise, T., Endocrinology
Gumbiner, B., Cell Biology
Guyenet, P., Pharmacology
Hackett, J., Molecular Physics and Biophysics
Hagspiel, K., Radiology
Haley, E., Neurology
Hamlin, J., Biochemistry and Molecular Genetics
Hammarskjold, M., Microbiology
Harrison, M., Neurology
Harvey, J., Breast Imaging
Hayden, F., Epidemiology
Herr, J., Cell Biology
Hess, C., Haematology and Oncology
Hewlett, E., Clinical Pharmacy
Hinton, B., Cell Biology
Hoffman, P., Infectious Diseases
Holroyd, S., Psychiatry
Horwitz, A., Cell Biology
Howards, S., Urology
Jagger, J., Infectious Diseases
Jevtović-Todorović, V., Anaesthesiology
Johnson, B., Psychiatry
Johnson, M., Pharmacology
Johnston, K., Neurology
Ju, S., Rheumatology
Kapur, J., Neurology
Kassell, N., Cardiovascular Disease
Kerrigan, D., Physical Medicine and Rehabilitation
Kim, Y., Biomedical Engineering
Koenig, S., Pulmonary Medicine
Kramer, C., Radiological Research
Kutchai, H., Molecular Physics and Biophysics
Larner, J., Radiation Oncology
Laurencin, C., Sports Medicine
Lee, K., Neuroscience
Ley, K., Biomedical Engineering
Li, M., Psychiatry
Lin, K., Plastic Surgery
Linden, J., Cardiovascular Medicine
Login, I., Neurology
Lynch, C., Anaesthesiology
Lynch, K., Pharmacology
McCall, A., Endocrinology
McDuffie, M., Microbiology
McNamara, C., Cardiovascular Medicine
Macara, I., Cell Signalling
Marshall, J., Endocrinology
Martin, M., Emergency Medicine
Miller, M., Sports Medicine
Minor, W., Molecular Physics and Biophysics
Moenter, S., Endocrinology
Moorman, J., Cardiovascular Medicine
Morgan, R., Plastic Surgery
Mugler, J., Radiological Research
Nadler, J., Endocrinology
Nakamoto, R., Molecular Physics and Biophysics
Newman, S., Ophthalmology
Obrig, T., Nephrology
O'Connor, R., Emergency Medicine
Okusa, M., Nephrology
Oldfield, E., Neuroendocrinology
Owens, G., Molecular Physics and Biophysics
Parker, W., Neurology
Parsons, J., Microbiology
Parsons, S., Microbiology
Pearson, R., Geographic Medicine

Pearson, W., Biochemistry and Molecular Genetics
Perez-Reyes, E., Pharmacology
Peters, C., Urology
Petri, W., Infectious Diseases
Peura, D., Gastroenterology
Philbrick, J., Medicine
Phillips, L., Neurology
Platts-Mills, T., Allergy
Porterfield, P., Psychiatry
Powers, R., Medicine
Ravichandran, K., Microbiology
Rein, M., Infectious Diseases
Rekosh, D., Microbiology
Rembold, C., Cardiovascular Medicine
Reynolds, P., Medicine
Rich, G., Anaesthesiology
Rich, T., Radiation Oncology
Rissman, E., Biochemistry and Molecular Genetics
Rodeheaver, G., Plastic Surgery
Rose, C., Pulmonary Medicine
Rowlingson, J., Anaesthesiology
Rust, R., Neurology
Saleh, K., Adult Reconstruction
Saller, D., Maternal Fetal Medicine
Sando, J., Anaesthesiology
Santen, R., Endocrinology
Scheld, W., Infectious Diseases
Schiff, D., Neurology
Schlager, T., Emergency Medicine
Schorling, J., Medicine
Schwartz, M., Microbiology
Shaffrey, C., Neuro-Oncology
Shaffrey, M., Neuro-Oncology
Shao, Z., Molecular Physics and Biophysics
Shupnik, M., Endocrinology
Silverman, L., Clinical Pathology
Sinkin, R., Neonatology
Siragy, H., Endocrinology
Slawson, D., Family Medicine
Smith, M., Microbiology
Somlyo, A., Molecular Physics and Biophysics
Steers, W., Urology
Steiner, L., Gamma Knife
Stoler, M., Surgical Pathology
Stovall, D., Reproductive Endocrinology and Infertility
Sturgill, T., Pharmacology
Suratt, P., Pulmonary Medicine
Sutherland, W., Cell Biology
Syverud, S., Emergency Medicine
Szabo, G., Molecular Physics and Biophysics
Tamm, L., Molecular Physics and Biophysics
Taylor, R., Biochemistry and Molecular Genetics
Theodorescu, D., Urology
Thisse, B., Cell Biology
Thisse, C., Cell Biology
Thorner, M., Endocrinology
Tiedeman, J., Ophthalmology
Truwit, J., Pulmonary Medicine
Turner, T., Urology
Tuttle, J., Neuroscience
Vance, M., Endocrinology
Warren, J., Psychiatry
Waters, D., Family Medicine
Watson, D., Radiological Research
Weber, M., Microbiology
Weiss, G., Haematology and Oncology
White, C., Cell Biology
Whitehill, R., Orthopaedics (Spine)
Williams, M., Haematology and Oncology
Williams, M., Medicine
Williamson, R., Nuclear Medicine
Wispelwey, B., Infectious Diseases
Wooten, G., Neurology
Yeager, M., Molecular Physics and Biophysics

School of Nursing (POB 800782, Charlottesville, VA 22908-0782; tel. (434) 924-0141;

e-mail nur-osa@virginia.edu; internet www.nursing.virginia.edu):

Brashers, V.
Hauenstein, E.
Hollen, P.
Keeling, A.
Lyder, C.
Merwin, E.
Parker, B.
Steeves, R.
Taylor, A.

AFFILIATED COLLEGE

University of Virginia's College at Wise: 1 College Ave, Wise, VA 24293; tel. (276) 328-0100; fax (276) 376-1012; e-mail info@uvawise.edu; f. 1954; academic year August to May; liberal arts college; Chancellor David J. Prior; Provost Sanders Huguenin; Vice-Chancellor for Devt and College Relations Tami Ely; Vice-Chancellor for Enrolment Management Russell D. Necessary; Vice-Chancellor for Finance and Admin. Simeon E. Ewing; Vice-Chancellor for Information Technology and Chief Information Officer J. Keith Fowlkes; Dean for Students Jewell Worley; Registrar Narda Porter; Dir for Library Services Robin Benke; 140 teachers; 2,067 students

PROFESSORS

Achua, C.
Adams-Ramsey, K.
Cantrell, R.
Costa, T.
Daniel, V.
Din, F.
Kendall, D.
Richardson, S.
Rouse, D.
Sheldon, G.
Tucker, M.
Turner, C.
Wheatley, F.
Wills, B.
Zylawy, R.

VIRGINIA COMMONWEALTH UNIVERSITY

910 W Franklin St, Richmond, VA 23284

Telephone: (804) 828-0100

Fax: (804) 828-1899

E-mail: ugrad@vcu.edu

Internet: www.vcu.edu

Founded 1838 as Hampden-Sydney College, present status 1968

State control

Academic year: August to May

Campuses at Northern Virginia, Doha (Qatar), Charles City County (Virginia)

Pres.: Dr Michael Rao

Provost and Vice-Pres. for Academic Affairs: Dr Beverly J. Warren

Vice-Provost for Student Affairs and Enrolment Services: Henry G. Rhone

Vice-Pres. for Devt and Alumni Relations: John I. Blohm

Vice-Pres. for Finance and Admin.: David Hanson

Vice-Pres. for Health Sciences and CEO of the VCU Health System: Dr Sheldon M. Retchin

Vice-Pres. for Research: Dr Francis L. Macrina

Vice-Pres. for Univ. Outreach: Sue A. Messmer

Asst. Vice-Pres. for Advancement Services: Lauren L. Shiver

Exec. Dir for Govt Relations: Mark E. Rubin

Registrar: Natasha Williams

Univ. Librarian: John E. Ulmschneider

Library of 1,680,393 vols, 3,007,035 microforms, 9,188 printed journals, 17,441 electronic journals
Number of teachers: 1,660 (full-time)
Number of students: 31,899

DEANS

College of the Humanities and Sciences: JAMES S. COLEMAN
Graduate School: F. DOUGLAS BOUDINOT
Honors College: Dr TIMOTHY L. HULSEY
School of Allied Health Professions: Dr CECIL B. DRAIN
School of the Arts: JOSEPH H. SEIPEL
School of Business: ED GRIER
School of Dentistry: Dr DAVID C. SARRETT
School of Education: Dr MICHAEL D. DAVIS
School of Engineering: Dr J. CHARLES JENNETT
School of Medicine: JEROME F. STRAUSS, III
School of Nursing: Dr NANCY F. LANGSTON
School of Pharmacy: Dr VICTOR A. YANCHICK
School of Social Work: Dr JAMES E. HINTERLONG
University College: JOSEPH A. MAROLLA

VIRGINIA INTERMONT COLLEGE

1013 Moore St, Bristol, VA 24201
Telephone: (276) 466-7867
Fax: (540) 669-5763
E-mail: viadmit@vic.edu
Internet: vic.edu
Founded 1884 as Southwest Virginia Institute, present name 1891
Private control
Academic year: August to May
Divs of arts and sciences, fine arts, professional studies
Pres.: Dr E. CLORISA PHILLIPS
Provost: Dr MARK A. ROBERTS
Vice-Pres. for Admin.: CONNY W. SAULS
Vice-Pres. for Business and Finance: LINDA C. MORGAN
Vice-Pres. for Institutional Advancement: MARY ANNE HOLBROOK
Dean for Student Devt: RONDA K. COLE
Dir for Admission: ROBIN BROOKS
Registrar: PAM HAMMOND
Library Dir: JONATHAN TALLMAN
Library of 160,000 vols, 97,000 e-books
Number of teachers: 73
Number of students: 583

VIRGINIA MILITARY INSTITUTE

Lexington, VA 24450
Telephone: (540) 464-7207
Fax: (540) 464-7726
E-mail: registrar@vmi.edu
Internet: www.vmi.edu
Founded 1839
State control
Academic year: August to May
Divs of arts and humanities, engineering, leadership, natural science and mathematics, social science
Superintendent: Gen. J. H. BINFORD PEAY, III
Deputy Supt. for Academics and Dean for the Faculty: Brig. Gen. R. WANE SCHNEITER
Deputy Supt. for Finance, Admin. and Support: Brig. Gen. ROBERT L. GREEN
Business Exec.: Brig. Gen. ROBERT GREEN
Commandant: Col THOMAS H. TRUMPS
Treas.: Col GARY R. KNICK
Registrar: Col JANET M. BATTAGLIA
Head Librarian: Col DONALD H. SAMDAHL, Jr
Library of 300,000 vols, 200,000 govt documents, 60,000 e-journals, 300 periodicals
Number of teachers: 206 (119 full-time, 61 part-time, 26 military)
Number of students: 1,500

VIRGINIA POLYTECHNIC INSTITUTE AND STATE UNIVERSITY

Blacksburg, VA 24061-0002
Telephone: (540) 231-6000
Fax: (540) 231-3242
E-mail: vtadmiss@vt.edu
Internet: www.vt.edu
Founded 1872 as Virginia Agricultural and Mechanical College, present name 1896
State control
Academic year: August to May
Pres.: Dr CHARLES W. STEGER
Provost and Sr Vice-Pres.: MARK G. McNAMEE
Vice-Provost for Academic Affairs: DAVID FORD
Exec. Vice-Pres. and Chief Operating Officer: JAMES HYATT
Vice-Pres. for Admin. Services: SHERWOOD G. WILSON
Vice-Pres. for Devt and Univ. Relations: ELIZABETH A. FLANAGAN
Vice-Pres. for Finance and Chief Financial Officer: M. DWIGHT SHELTON, JR
Vice-Pres. for Information Technology: EARVING L. BLYTHE
Vice-Pres. for Research: ROBERT WALTERS
Vice-Pres. for Student Affairs: EDWARD F. D. SPENCER
Univ. Treas. and Chief Operating Officer for Virginia Tech Foundation: RAYMOND D. SMOOT, JR
Dir for Admissions: NORRINE BAILEY SPENCER
Registrar: WANDA HANKINS DEAN
Dean for Univ. Libraries: TYLER WALTERS
Library of 2,686,659 vols, 6,330,610 microforms, 148,411 maps, 399,525 govt documents, 13528 audio items, 40,922 journals
Number of teachers: 1,306 (full-time)
Number of students: 30,936
Publications: *Research Magazine*, *Virginia Tech Magazine*

DEANS

College of Agriculture and Life Sciences: ALAN GRANT
College of Architecture and Urban Studies: A. JACK DAVIS
College of Engineering: RICHARD BENSON
College of Liberal Arts and Human Sciences: SUE OTT ROWLANDS
College of Natural Resources and Environment: PAUL M. WINISTORFER
College of Science: LAY NAM CHANG
Graduate School: KAREN P. DePAUW
Pamplin College of Business: RICHARD E. SORENSEN
Virginia-Maryland Regional College of Veterinary Medicine: GERHARDT SCHURIG
Virginia Tech Carilion School of Medicine: CYNDA A. JOHNSON

VIRGINIA STATE UNIVERSITY

1 Hayden Dr., Petersburg, VA 23806
Telephone: (804) 524-5000
Fax: (804) 524-6505
E-mail: admiss@vsu.edu
Internet: www.vsu.edu
Founded 1882 as Virginia Normal and Collegiate Institute, present name 1979
State control
Academic year: August to May
Pres.: Dr KEITH T. MILLER
Provost and Vice-Pres. for Academic Affairs: Dr W. WELDON HILL
Vice-Provost and Graduate Dean: Dr JAMES E. HUNTER
Vice-Pres. for Admin. and Finance: DAVID J. MEADOWS
Vice-Pres. for Student Affairs: Dr MICHAEL SHACKLEFORD

Vice-Pres. for Devt and Univ. Relations: ROBERT L. TURNER, JR
Registrar: DEBERA S. BONNER
Dean for Library: Dr ELSIE WEATHERINGTON
Library of 245,731 vols
Number of teachers: 191
Number of students: 5,890

DEANS

Reginald F. Lewis School of Business: Dr MIRTA M. MARTIN
School of Agriculture: JEWEL HAIRSTON
School of Engineering, Science and Technology: Dr KEITH M. WILLIAMSON
School of Graduate Studies, Research and Outreach: Dr JAMES E. HUNTER
School of Liberal Arts and Education: Dr ANDREW KANU

VIRGINIA THEOLOGICAL SEMINARY

3737 Seminary Rd, Alexandria, VA 22304
Telephone: (703) 370-6600
Fax: (703) 370-6234
E-mail: admissions@vts.edu
Internet: www.vts.edu
Founded 1823
Private control
Academic year: September to May
Dean and Pres.: Very Rev. Dr IAN S. MARKHAM
Vice-Pres. and Assoc. Dean for Academic Affairs: Dr TIMOTHY F. SEDGWICK
Vice-Pres. for Admin. and Finance: HEATHER ZDANCEWICZ
Vice-Pres. for Institutional Advancement: Rev. Dr J. BARNEY HAWKINS, IV
Registrar: TAMI SHEPHERD
Head Librarian: Prof. Dr MITZI JARRETT BUDDE
Library of 185,000 vols, 6,800 microforms, 1,050 journals, periodicals and newspaper subscriptions, 600 music CDs
Number of students: 232
Publications: *Episcopal Teacher* (4 a year), *The Journal of Episcopal Church Canon Law* (2 a year), *The Virginia Seminary Journal* (2 a year).

VIRGINIA UNION UNIVERSITY

1500 N Lombardy St, Richmond, VA 23220
Telephone: (804) 257-5600
Fax: (804) 257-5818
E-mail: visitus@vuu.edu
Internet: www.vuu.edu
Founded 1865
Private control
Academic year: August to July (3 semesters)
Pres. and CEO: Dr CLAUDE G. PERKINS
Sr Vice-Pres.: Dr JOSEPH F. JOHNSON
Vice-Pres. for Academic Affairs: Dr W. FRANKLIN EVANS
Vice-Pres. for Enrolment Management and Student Affairs: (vacant)
Vice-Pres. for Financial Affairs: GREGORY LEWIS
Vice-Pres. for Institutional Advancement: Dr ANTHONY THOMPSON
Vice-Pres. for Research, Planning and Special Programmes: Dr JOY GOODRICH
Vice-Pres. for Student Affairs: Dr JOSEPH JOHNSON
Dir for Univ. Services: GILBERT L. CARTER
Registrar: MARILYN A. BROOKS
Dir for Library: Dr DELORES PRETLOW
Library of 562,000 vols
Number of teachers: 105 (85 full-time, 20 part-time)
Number of students: 1,500

DEANS

Evelyn Reid Syphax School of Education, Psychology and Interdisciplinary Studies: Dr MARSHA TAYLOR HORTON

Samuel DeWitt Proctor School of Theology: Dr JOHN W. KINNEY

School of Humanities and Social Sciences: Dr LINDA SCHLICHTING

School of Mathematics, Science and Technology: Dr PHILLIP W. ARCHER

Sydney Lewis School of Business: Dr ADELAJA O. ODUTOLA

VIRGINIA WESLEYAN COLLEGE

1584 Wesleyan Dr., Norfolk, VA 23502-5599

Telephone: (757) 455-3200

Fax: (757) 461-5238

E-mail: admissions@vwc.edu

Internet: www.vwc.edu

Founded 1961

Private control

Academic year: August to May (2 semesters)

Divs of humanities, natural sciences and mathematics, social sciences

Pres.: WILLIAM T. GREER, JR

Vice-Pres. for Academic Affairs and Kenneth R. Perry Dean for the College: Dr TIMOTHY G. O'ROURKE

Vice-Pres. for College Advancement: MARGUERITE K. VAIL

Vice-Pres. for Finance: CARY A. SAWYER

Vice-Pres. for Operations: BRUCE VAUGHAN

Vice-Pres. for Student Affairs and Dean for Enrolment Services: DAVID E. BUCKINGHAM

Assoc. Vice-Pres. for Institutional Research and Effectiveness and Dir for Strategic Planning: R. BRYAN PRICE

Dean for Admissions: PATTY PATTEN

Registrar: BOBBIS S. ADAMS

Dir for Library: JAN PACE

Library of 132,514 vols, 59,354 e-books, 231 journals, 37,416 e-journals, 15,953 microfilms, 3,599 audiovisual items

Number of teachers: 132 (87 full-time, 45 part-time)

Number of students: 1,404

WASHINGTON AND LEE UNIVERSITY

204 W Washington St, Lexington, VA 24450-2116

Telephone: (540) 458-8400

Fax: (540) 458-8945

E-mail: admissions@wlu.edu

Internet: www.wlu.edu

Founded 1749 as Augusta Acad., present name 1870

Private control

Academic year: September to June

Pres.: Dr KENNETH P. RUSCIO

Provost: Dr ROBERT A. STRONG

Vice-Pres. for Finance and Treas.: STEVEN G. MCALLISTER

Vice-Pres. for Student Affairs and Dean for Students: SIDNEY SPRINGFIELD EVANS

Vice-Pres. for Univ. Advancement: DENNIS W. CROSS

Dean for Student Life: DAVID M. LEONARD

Registrar: D. SCOTT DITTMAN

Univ. Librarian: TERRANCE J. METZ

Library of 956,354 vols, 10,362 paper, microforms and e-periodical subscriptions, 17,300 audiovisual items; law library incl. 428,517 vols

Number of teachers: 233 (208 full-time, 25 adjunct)

Number of students: 2,153

Publications: *Journal of Science, Political Review, Shenandoah* (4 a year), *Washington and Lee Law Review*

DEANS

Ernest Williams II School of Commerce, Economics and Politics: Dr LARRY C. PEPPERS

School of Law: Dr MARK H. GRUNEWALD

The College: Dr HOWARD DOBIN

WASHINGTON

ART INSTITUTE OF SEATTLE

2323 Elliott Ave, Seattle, WA 98121-1642

Telephone: (206) 448-6600

Fax: (206) 448-2501

E-mail: aisadm@aii.edu

Internet: www.artinstitutes.edu/seattle

Founded 1946 as the Burnley School for Professional Art, present name and status 1982

Private control

Culinary, design, fashion, liberal arts, media arts

Pres.: ELDEN MONDAY

Dir for Admin. and Financial Services: GREG WOODARD

Sr Dir for Admissions: LIANE SOOHOO

Dean for Academic Affairs: SCOTT CARNZ

Dean for Student Affairs: MEGAN KIJEWSKI

Dir for Human Resources: NATASHA OILAR

Dir for Library Services: ANDREW HARBISON

Number of students: 2,300

BASTYR UNIVERSITY

14500 Juanita Dr., NE, Kenmore, WA 98028-4966

Telephone: (425) 823-1300

Fax: (425) 823-6222

E-mail: admissions@bastyr.edu

Internet: www.bastyr.edu

Founded 1978 as John Bastyr College of Naturopathic Medicine

Natural health, arts and sciences

Pres.: Dr DANIEL K. CHURCH

Library of 19,000 vols

Number of teachers: 172 (53 full-time, 119 part-time)

Number of students: 1,018

DEANS

School of Naturopathic Medicine: Dr JANE GUILTINAN

CENTRAL WASHINGTON UNIVERSITY

400 E Univ. Way, Ellensburg, WA 98926

Telephone: (509) 963-2111

Internet: www.cwu.edu

Founded 1891 as Washington State Normal School, present name 1977

Pres.: JAMES L. GAUDINO

Provost and Vice-Pres. for Academic Affairs: Dr MARILYN LEVINE

Vice-Pres. for Business and Financial Affairs: GEORGE CLARK

Vice-Pres. for Student Affairs and Enrollment Management: CHARLOTTE TULLOS

Vice-Pres. for Univ. Advancement: (vacant)

Registrar: TRACY

Dean for Library Services: PATRICIA CUTRIGHT

Library of 485,417 vols

Number of teachers: 370

Number of students: 10,750

DEANS

College of Arts and Humanities: MARJI MORGAN

College of Business: Dr ROY SAVOIAN

College of Education and Professional Studies: Dr CONNIE LAMBERT

College of the Sciences: KIRK A. JOHNSON

Graduate Studies: WAYNE QUIRK

CITY UNIVERSITY OF SEATTLE

11900 NE First St, Bellevue, WA 98005

150–120th Ave, NE, Bellevue, WA 98005

Telephone: (425) 637-1010

Fax: (425) 637-9689

E-mail: info@cityu.edu

Internet: www.cityu.edu

Founded 1973 as City College, present name 1982

Private control

Sites in states of Washington and California, and in Australia, Bulgaria, Canada, China, Czech Republic, Greece, Mexico, Romania, Slovakia and Switzerland

Pres.: LEE GORSUCH

Provost: Dr STEVEN OLSWANG

Exec. Vice-Pres. for Academic Affairs: Dr FERNANDO LEON GARCIA

Exec. Vice-Pres. for Finance and Admin. and Chief Financial Officer: BRUCE BRYANT

Vice-Pres. for Academic and Institutional Assessment: CHRIS J. RIGOS

Vice-Pres. for Admissions and Student Services and Registrar: Dr MELISSA MECHAM

Vice-Pres. for the Business Office and Controller: MARIETA C. JOHNSON

Vice-Pres. for European Operations: Ing. JAN REBRO

Vice-Pres. for External Relations: Dr WINSTON C. ADDIS

Vice-Pres. for Univ. Advancement: CHRISTOPHER ROSS

Dir. for Human Resources: TIMOTHY SPRAKE

Dir for Library Affairs: MARY MARA

Number of teachers: 1,300

Number of students: 6,840 worldwide

DEANS

Gordon Albright School of Education: Dr CRAIG SCHEIBER

School of Management: Dr KURT KIRSTEIN

CLARK COLLEGE

1933 Fort, Vancouver Way, Vancouver, WA 98663

Telephone: (360) 699-6398

Internet: www.clark.edu

Founded 1933

State control

Dental hygiene, social work and technology

Pres.: ROBERT K. KNIGHT

Vice-Pres. for Instruction: Dr TIM COOK

Vice-Pres. for Admin. Services: BOB WILLIAMSON

Vice-Pres. for Student Affairs: WILLIAM BELDEN

Dean for Libraries: MICHELLE BAGLEY

Number of students: 16,000

Publications: *Clark 24/7* (24 a year), *Clark College Connections* (4 a year), *The Clark Journal* (12 a year).

CORNISH COLLEGE OF THE ARTS

1000 Lenora St, Seattle, WA 98121

Telephone: (206) 726-5016

E-mail: provostoffice@cornish.edu

Internet: www.cornish.edu

Founded 1914

Offers Baccalaureate studies in the performing and visual arts; major fields of study: art, dance, design, music, performance production and theatre

Pres.: Dr NANCY J. USCHER

Provost and Vice-Pres. for Academic Affairs: Dr LOIS HARRIS

Vice-Pres. for Finance and Admin.: JEFF RIDDELL
Vice-Pres. for Institutional Advancement: JANE EWING
Dean for Enrolment Management: GARY CRAIG
Dir for Library Services: HOLLIS NEAR
Registrar: ADRIENNE M. BOLYARD
Number of teachers: 145
Number of students: 800

EASTERN WASHINGTON UNIVERSITY

Office of Academic Affairs, 220 Showalter Hall, Cheney, WA 99004
Telephone: (509) 359-7900
Fax: (509) 359-2248
E-mail: universityre@ewu.edu
Internet: www.ewu.edu
Founded 1882, present name and status 1978
State control
Language of instruction: English
Academic year: September to June
Pres.: Dr RODOLFO ARÉVALO
Provost and Vice-Pres. for Academic Affairs: Dr REX FULLER
Vice-Pres. for Student Affairs: Dr STACEY MORGAN FOSTER
Registrar: ERIN MORGAN
Assoc. Vice-Pres. for Enrolment Management: Dr LAWRENCE BRIGGS
Dean for Libraries: Dr RICHARD WILSON
Library of 1,113,167 vols, 750,000 books, 3,100 e-books, 903 current periodicals, 43 periodical microforms
Number of teachers: 365
Number of students: 10,750

DEANS

College of Arts, Letters and Education: Dr LYNN BRIGGS
College of Business and Public Admin.: Dr ELIZABETH TIPTON
College of Science, Health and Engineering: Dr JUDD A. CASE
College of Social and Behavioral Sciences and Social Work: Dr VICKIE RUTLEDGE SHIELDS

EVERGREEN STATE COLLEGE

2700 Evergreen Parkway, NW, Olympia, WA 98505
Telephone: (360) 867-6000
Fax: (360) 867-6745
E-mail: admissions@evergreen.edu
Internet: www.evergreen.edu
Founded 1971
State control
Liberal arts college; 3 campuses: Grays Harbor, Olympia and Tacoma
Pres.: Dr THOMAS LES PURCE
Provost and Vice-Pres. for Academic Affairs: KEN TABBUTT
Vice-Pres. for College Advancement: D. LEE HOEMANN
Vice-Pres. for Finance and Admin.: JOHN HURLEY
Vice-Pres. for Student Affairs: ART COSTANTINO
Exec. Dir for Tacoma Campus: Dr ARTEE F. YOUNG
Dean for the Library and Media Service: BILL BRUNER
Library of 35,000 journals, spec. collns, rare books, archival material and govt docs
Number of teachers: 247
Number of students: 4,900
Publication: *Evergreen Magazine.*

GONZAGA UNIVERSITY

502 E. Boone Ave, Spokane, WA 99258-0102
Telephone: (509) 328-4220
Fax: (509) 313-5780
Internet: www.gonzaga.edu
Founded 1881 as Gonzaga College
Private control
Academic year: August to May, and summer session
Chancellor: BERNARD J. COUGHLIN
Pres.: Dr THAYNE M. McCULLOH
Exec. Vice-Pres.: EARL F. MARTIN
Vice-Pres. for Academic Affairs: Dr PATRICIA O'CONNELL KILLEN
Vice-Pres. for Admin. and Planning: HARRY H. SLADICH
Vice-Pres. for Finance: CHARLES J. MURPHY
Vice-Pres. for Student Life: Dr SUE WEITZ
Vice-Pres. for Univ. Relations: MARGOT J. STANFIELD (acting)
Dean for Admissions: PHILLIP BALLINGER
Librarian: EILEEN BELL-GARRISON
Library of 425,000 vols
Number of teachers: 364
Number of students: 7,837
Publications: *Charter* (1 a year), *Gonzaga Magazine* (12 a year), *Reflections* (1 a year), *Report of the President* (1 a year), *Spires Yearbook* (1 a year)

DEANS

College of Arts and Sciences: MARC MANGANARO
College of Business Administration: Dr CLARENCE H. BARNES
School of Education: Dr JON D. SUNDERLAND
School of Engineering and Applied Science: DENNIS R. HORN
School of Law: JANE KORN
School of Professional Studies: Dr MICHAEL R. L. CAREY

HERITAGE UNIVERSITY

3240 Fort Rd, Toppenish, WA 98948
Telephone: (888) 272-6190
Fax: (509) 865-7976
E-mail: admissions@heritage.edu
Internet: www.heritage.edu
Founded 1907 as Spokane's Fort Wright College, univ. status 2004
Private control
Academic year: August to June
Liberal arts univ.; 3 regional sites in Moses Lake, Tri-Cities and South Seattle
Pres.: Dr JOHN BASSETT
Provost and Vice-Pres. for Academic Affairs: Dr SNEH B. VEENA
Vice-Pres. for Advancement: MICHAEL P. MOORE
Vice-Pres. for Support Services and Chief Financial Officer: RICK R. GAGNIER
Dir for Admissions and Recruitment: MIGUEL PUENTE
Dean for Students: MELISSA FILKOWSKI
Dean for Enrolment Management Services: NORBERTO T. ESPINDOLA
Library Dir: BILL McCAY
Library of 70,000 vols (in print), 45,000 vols (electronic)
Number of teachers: 170 (45 full-time, 125 part-time)
Number of students: 1,355

DEANS

Arts and Sciences: KAZUHIRO SONODA
Education and Psychology: Dr ROBERT LYNN SMART

NORTHWEST UNIVERSITY

POB 579, Kirkland, WA 98083-0579
5520 108th Ave, NE, Kirkland, WA 98033
Telephone: (425) 822-8266
Fax: (425) 889-5224
E-mail: recpt@northwestu.edu
Internet: www.northwestu.edu
Founded 1934 as Northwest Bible Institute, present name 2005
Private control
Language of instruction: English
Academic year: August to May
Pres.: Dr JOSEPH CASTLEBERRY
Chancellor: Dr DON ARGUE
Exec. Vice-Pres.: DAN NEARY
Provost: JIM HEUGEL
Sr Vice-Pres. for Finance: DAN SCHIMELPFENIG
Vice-Pres. for Advancement: JASON MILES
Vice-Pres. for Campus Ministries: PHIL RASMUSSEN
Vice-Pres. for Student Devt: PAUL BANAS
Asst Vice-Pres. for Devt: JEFF LOCKHART
Asst Vice-Pres. for Enrolment: ROSE-MARY SMITH
Assoc. Vice-Pres. for Marketing: MERLIN QUIGGLE
Dir for Library: ADAM EPP
Library of 88,794 vols, 12,458 periodicals
Number of teachers: 53
Number of students: 11,736

DEANS

College of Arts and Sciences: Prof. DARREL HOBSON
College of Ministry: Prof. WAYDE GOODALL
College of Social and Behavioral Sciences: Dr MATT NELSON
School of Business and Management: TERESA GILLESPIE
School of Education: GARY NEWBILL
School of Nursing: Dr CARL CHRISTENSEN

PROFESSORS

CHARETTE, BLAINE, Bible, Greek
HARRIS, MOSES, Education, Modern Languages
JOHNSON, LEROY, History, Interdisciplinary Studies, Political Science
JUNGJIN, DOO, Chemistry
LEACH, KEVIN, Psychology
KOWALSKI, WALDEMAR, Bible, Theology
KRESS, PAUL, Education
MESTRE, MICHEL, Business
STALLMAN, ROBERT, Bible, Hebrew
THOMPSON, MICHAEL, Christian Education, Youth Ministries

PACIFIC LUTHERAN UNIVERSITY

12180 Park St S, Tacoma, WA 98447-0003
Telephone: (206) 531-6900
Fax: (253) 536-5136
E-mail: admission@plu.edu
Internet: www.plu.edu
Founded 1890
Private control
Pres.: Dr LOREN J. ANDERSON
Provost: Dr STEVEN P. STARKOVICH
Vice-Pres. for Admission and Enrolment Services: KARL STUMO
Vice-Pres. for Devt and Univ. Relations: STEPHEN J. OLSON
Vice-Pres. for Finance and Operations: Dr SHERI TONN
Vice-Pres. for Student Life: Dr LAURA F. MAJOVSKI
Dean for Information Resources: CHRIS D. FERGUSON
Library of 363,580 vols
Number of teachers: 283 (246 full-time, 37 part-time)
Number of students: 3,461

SAINT MARTIN'S COLLEGE

5000 Abbey Way, SE, Lacey, WA 98503-7500
Telephone: (206) 491-4700
Fax: (206) 459-4124
E-mail: information@stmartin.edu
Internet: www.stmartin.edu

Founded 1895 as Saint Martin's College, present name 2005
Academic year: September to May

Chancellor: ABBOT NEAL ROTH
Pres.: Dr ROY F. HEYNDERICKX
Provost and Vice-Pres. for Academic Affairs: Dr JOSEPH D. BESSIE
Vice-Pres. for Finance: SUSAN HELTSLEY
Vice-Pres. for Institutional Advancement: ROSANNE A. NICHOLS
Vice-Pres. Int. Programmes and Devt: JOSEPHINE YUNG
Dean for Students: MELANIE RICHARDSON
Registrar: MARY LAW
Librarian: DALIA HAGAN

Library of 85,000 vols
Number of teachers: 70
Number of students: 978

DEANS

College of Arts and Sciences: Dr ERIC APFELSTADT
College of Education and Professional Psychology: Dr JOYCE V. S. WESTGARD
School of Business: Dr RICHARD BEER
School of Engineering: Dr ZELLA L. KAHN-JETTER

SEATTLE PACIFIC UNIVERSITY

3307 Third Ave W, Seattle, WA 98119-1997
Telephone: (206) 281-2000
Fax: (206) 281-2115
Internet: www.spu.edu

Founded 1891
Private control
Academic year: September to June

Pres.: PHILIP W. EATON
Sr Vice-Pres. for Admin. and Univ. Relations: MARJORIE R. JOHNSON
Sr Vice-Pres. for Business and Planning: DONALD W. MORTENSON
Vice-Pres. for Academic Affairs: BRUCE CONGDON
Vice-Pres. and Dean for Student Life: JEFFREY C. JORDAN
Vice-Pres. for Univ. Advancement: THOMAS W. BOX
Assoc. Vice-Pres. for Information and Data Management: JANET L. WARD
Dir for Student Academic Services and Univ. Registrar: RUTH L. RUTH L. ADAMS
Univ. Librarian: MICHAEL PAULUS

Library of 200,000 vols, 1,300 journals and database
Number of teachers: 363
Number of students: 4,167

DEANS

College of Arts and Sciences: Prof. BRUCE D. CONGDON
School of Business and Economics: Dr JEFFREY VAN DUZER
School of Education: Dr RICK EIGENBROOD
School of Health Sciences: Dr LUCILLE M. KELLEY
School of Psychology, Family and Community: Dr MÍCHEÁL D. ROE
School of Theology: Dr DOUG STRONG

SEATTLE UNIVERSITY

POB 222000, 901 12th Ave, Seattle, WA 98122-1090
Telephone: (206) 296-6000
Fax: (206) 296-2012
E-mail: admissions@seattleu.edu

Internet: www.seattleu.edu

Founded 1891 as Seattle College, present name 1948
Private control
Academic year: October to July

Pres.: STEPHEN V. SUNDBORG
Provost: ISIAAH CRAWFORD
Exec. Vice-Pres.: TIMOTHY P. LEARY
Vice-Pres. for Enrolment Management: MARILYN CRONE
Vice-Pres. for Finance: JAMES ADOLPHSON
Vice-Pres. for Human Resources and Univ. Services: JERRY HUFFMAN
Vice-Pres. for Mission and Ministry: PETER ELY
Vice-Pres. for Student Devt: JACOB DIAZ
Vice-Pres. for Univ. Advancement: MARY KAY MCFADDEN
Vice-Pres. for Univ. Planning and Vice-Provost: ROBERT J. DULLEA
Dean for Admissions: MICHAEL MCKEON
Univ. Librarian: JOHN POPKO

Library of 234,978 vols
Number of teachers: 440
Number of students: 7,900

DEANS

Albers School of Business and Economics: Dr JOSEPH M. PHILLIPS
College of Arts and Sciences: DAVID V. POWERS
College of Education: SUE SCHMITT
College of Nursing: Dr AZITA EMAMI
College of Science and Engineering: Dr MICHAEL J. QUINN
Matteo Ricci College: Dr JODI KELLY
School of Law: Dr MARK NILES
School of Theology and Ministry: Dr MARK S. MARKULY

TRINITY LUTHERAN COLLEGE

2802 Wetmore Ave, Everett, WA 98201
Telephone: (425) 249-4800
Fax: (425) 249-4801
E-mail: info@tlc.edu
Internet: tlc.edu

Founded 1944 as Lutheran Bible Institute of Seattle, present name 1998
Private control

Pres.: JOHN REED
Academic Dean: Dr JEFF MALLINSON
Registrar: CHUCK NELSON.

UNIVERSITY OF PUGET SOUND

1500 N Warner, Tacoma, WA 98416
Telephone and fax (253) 879-3419
E-mail: mediarelations@pugetsound.edu
Internet: www.pugetsound.edu

Founded 1888
Private control

Pres.: RONALD R. THOMAS
Vice-Pres. for Academics and Dean for the Univ.: KRISTINE M. BARTANEN
Vice-Pres. for Enrolment: GEORGE H. MILLS
Vice-Pres. for Finance and Admin.: SHERRY MONDOU
Vice-Pres. for Student Affairs and Dean for Students: MICHAEL SEGAWA
Vice-Pres. for Univ. Relations: DAVID R. BEERS
Registrar: JOHN FINNEY
Library Dir: JANE A. CARLIN

Library of 580,000 vols
Number of teachers: 219
Number of students: 2,600 full-time

UNIVERSITY OF WASHINGTON

POB 351270, Seattle, WA 98195-1270
Telephone: (206) 543-2100
Fax: (206) 221-4622

E-mail: uwvic@u.washington.edu
Internet: www.washington.edu

Founded 1861
State control

Pres.: MICHAEL YOUNG
Provost: Dr ANA MARI CAUCE
Sr Vice-Pres. for Finance and Facilities: V'ELLA WARREN
Vice-Pres. for External Affairs: RANDY HODGINS
Vice-Pres. for Human Resources: MINDY KORNBERG
Vice-Pres. for Minority Affairs and Diversity: SHEILA EDWARDS LANGE (acting)
Vice-Pres. for Student Life: ERIC GODFREY
Vice-Pres. for Univ. Advancement: CONNIE KRAVAS
Exec. Vice-Provost: DOUG WADDEN (acting)
Vice-Provost for Academic Personnel: CHERYL A. CAMERON (acting)
Vice-Provost for Educational Outreach: DAVID SZATMARY
Vice-Provost for Global Affairs: STEPHEN E. HANSON
Vice-Provost for the Graduate School: GERALD BALDASTY
Vice-Provost for Minority Affairs and Diversity: SHEILA EDWARDS LANGE
Vice-Provost for Planning and Budgeting: PAUL JENNY
Vice-Provost for Research: MARY LIDSTROM
Vice-Provost for Special Programs: GUS K. J. KRAVAS
Vice-Provost for Undergraduate Academic Affairs: ED TAYLOR
Dir of Fed. Relations: CHRISTY GUILLION
Dir of State Relations: MARGARET SHEPHERD
Dir of Libraries: LIZABETH WILSON

Library: see Libraries
Number of teachers: 4,000
Number of students: 48,022

Publications: *American Journal of Human Genetics, Biochemistry, Journal of Financial and Quantitative Analysis, Journal of Limnology and Oceanography, Modern Language Quarterly, Pacific Northwest Quarterly, Papers of Regional Science Association, Poetry Northwest, Trends in Engineering, Washington Law Review*

DEANS

College of Arts and Sciences: ROBERT STACEY
College of Built Environments: Dr DANIEL S. FRIEDMAN
College of Education: TOM STRITIKUS
College of Engineering: MATTHEW O'DONNELL (acting)
College of the Environment: LISA GRAUMLICH (acting)
College of Ocean and Fishery Sciences: ARTHUR NOWELL
Evans School of Public Affairs: SANDRA O. ARCHIBALD
Graduate School: GERALD BALDASTY (acting)
Information School: HARRY BRUCE
Michael G. Foster School of Business: JAMES JIAMBALVO (acting)
School of Dentistry: (vacant)
School of Law: KELLYE TESTY
School of Medicine: PAUL G. RAMSEY
School of Nursing: MARLA E. SALMON
School of Pharmacy: THOMAS A. BAILLIE
School of Public Health: Dr HOWARD FRUMKIN
School of Social Work: Dr EDWINA UEHARA (acting)

PROFESSORS

College of Architecture and Urban Planning (Box 355726, Seattle, WA 98195; tel. (206) 543-7679; fax (206) 543-2463; internet www.caup.washington.edu):

BADANES, S. P., Architecture
BLANCO, H. J., Urban Design and Planning
CHING, F. D. K., Architecture

DANIALI, S., Construction Management
FINROW, J. V., Architecture
MILLER, D. E., Architecture
MILLER, D. H., Urban Design and Planning
MUGERAUER, R., Architecture
OCHSNER, J. K., Architecture
PYATOK, M., Architecture
STREATFIELD, D. C., Landscape Architecture
SUTTON, S. E., Architecture
VERNEZ-MOUDON, A., Urban Design and Planning

College of Arts and Sciences (50 Communications #353765, Univ. of Washington, Seattle, WA 98195-3765; tel. (206) 543-5340; fax (206) 543-5462; internet www.artsci .washington.edu):
ADELBERGER, E. G., Physics
ALEXANDER, E., English
ALLEN, C., English
AMMERLAHN, H., German
AMMIRATI, J. F., Biology
ANDERSEN, N. H., Chemistry
ANDERSON, S., Astronomy
BACHMAN, D. M., International Studies
BALDASTY, G. J., Communication
BALICK, B., Astronomy
BARASH, D. P., Psychology
BARDEEN, J. M., Physics
BARLOW, T. E., Women Studies
BARRACK, C. M., German
BARZEL, Y., Economics
BATTISTI, D. S., Atmospheric Science
BEECHER, M. D., Psychology
BEHLER, D. I., German
BEHLMER, G. K., History
BENDICH, A. K., Biology
BENNETT, W. L., Political Science
BERGANTZ, G. W., Earth and Space Sciences
BERGER, P. E., Art
BERNARD, J. W., Music
BERNSTEIN, I. L., Psychology
BERTSCH, G. F., Physics
BESAG, J. E., Statistics
BEYERS, W. B., Geography
BIERDS, L. L., English
BLAKE, K., English
BLAU, H., English
BLIQUEZ, L. J., Classics
BLONDELL, R., Classics
BOARCH-JACOBSEN, M., Comparative Literature
BOERSMA, P. D., Biology
BOLTZ, W., Asian Languages and Literatures
BONJOUR, L. A., Philosophy
BOOKER, J. R., Earth and Space Sciences
BORDEN, W. T., Chemistry
BOULWARE, D. G., Physics
BOURGEOIS, J., Earth and Space Sciences
BOYNTON, P., Physics
BOZARTH, G. S., Music
BRADSHAW, H. D., Biology
BRAME, M. K., Linguistics
BRAVMANN, R. A., Art
BRENOWITZ, E. A., Psychology
BRETHERTON, C. S., Atmospheric Science
BROWN, J. K., German
BROWN, J. M., Earth and Space Sciences
BROWN, M. J., English
BROWNLEE, D. E., Astronomy
BRUCE, N., Economics
BUBE, K. P., Mathematics
BUCK, S. L., Psychology
BULGAC, A., Physics
BURDZY, K., Mathematics
BURKE, J. V., Mathematics
BURNETT, T. H., Physics
BURSTEIN, P., Sociology
BUTLER, J. E., American Ethnic Studies
CALLIS, J. B., Chemistry
CAMPBELL, C. T., Chemistry
CAMPBELL, P. S., Music
CAPORASO, J. A., Political Science

CASTERAS, S. P., Art
CATTOLICO, R. A., Biology
CAUCE, A. M., Psychology
CHALOUPKA, V., Physics
CHAN, K. W., Geography
CHEN, Z., Mathematics
CHENEY, E. S., Earth and Space Sciences
CHIROT, D., International Studies
CIRTAUTAS, I. D., Near Eastern Languages and Literatures
CLATTERBAUGH, K. C., Philosophy
CLAUSEN, M. L., Art
CLAUSS, J. J., Classics
CLOSE, A. E., Anthropology
COBURN, R. C., Philosophy
COHEN, S. M., Philosophy
COLDEWEY, J. C., English
COLLINGWOOD, D., Mathematics
COMAI, L., Biology
COVEY, E., Psychology
COWAN, D. S., Earth and Space Sciences
COX, C. D., Asian Languages and Literatures
CRAMER, J. G., Jr, Physics
CREAGER, K. C., Earth and Space Sciences
CRIMINALE, W. O., Jr, Applied Mathematics
CRUTCHFIELD, R. D., Sociology
CURTIS, E. B., Mathematics
DAHLSTROM, R. A., Drama
DALTON, L. R., Chemistry
DANIEL, T. L., Sociology
DAWSON, G., Psychology
DEL MORAL, R., Biology
DEN NIJS, M. P., Physics
DIAZ, F. L., Psychology
DILLON, G. L., English
DOVICHI, N. J., Chemistry
DROBNY, G. P., Chemistry
DUCHAMP, T. E., Mathematics
DUNN, R. J., English
DURAND, J., Music
DURRAN, D. R., Atmospheric Science
EBREY, P. B., History
ELLINGSON, T. J., Music
ELLIS, J. M., Geography
ELLIS, S. D., Physics
ENGEL, T., Chemistry
EPIOTIS, N., Chemistry
ERICKSON, K. B., Mathematics
EROS, P. S., Music
FAILING, P. A., Art
FAIN, S. C., Physics
FINDLEY, J. M., History
FINE, A. I., Philosophy
FLORES, L. H., American Ethnic Studies
FOLLAND, G. B., Mathematics
FOLSOM, R. C., Speech and Hearing Sciences
FORTSON, E. N., II, Physics
FREY, C. H., English
GAMMON, R. H., Chemistry
GARCIA, A., Physics
GATES, S. N., Drama
GEIST, A. L., Romance Languages and Literatures
GELB, M. H., Chemistry
GHOSE, S., Earth and Space Sciences
GIFFARD, C. A., Communications
GOLDE, H., Computer Science
GOLDSTEIN, A. A., Mathematics
GORE, W. J., Political Science
GOTTMAN, J. M., Psychology
GOUTERMAN, M. P., Chemistry
GRAYSON, D. K., Anthropology
GREENBERG, R., Mathematics
GREENWALD, A. G., Psychology
GREGORY, N. W., Chemistry
GROSSMAN, A. J., Music
GRUNBAUM, B., Mathematics
GUARRERA, F. P., Music
GUEST, A. M., Sociology
GURALNIK, M. J., Psychology and Pediatrics
HALL, B. D., Genetics
HALLET, B., Geological Sciences
HALPERIN, C. S., Botany
HALPERN, I., Physics

HALSEY, G. D., Jr, Chemistry
HALVORSEN, R., Economics
HANEY, J. V., Slavic Languages and Literatures and International Studies
HANKINS, T. L., History
HANLEY, S. B., International Studies
HARMON, D. P., Classics and Comparative Literature
HARRELL, C. S., Anthropology and International Studies
HARTMANN, D., Atmospheric Sciences
HARTWELL, L. H., Genetics
HASKINS, E. F., Botany
HEER, N. L., Near Eastern Languages and Literature
HELLER, E. J., Chemistry and Physics
HELLMANN, D. C., Political Science and School of International Studies
HENLEY, E. M., Physics
HERTLING, G. H., Germanics
HILDEBRAND, G., Art History and Architecture
HIRSCHMAN, C., Sociology
HIXSON, W. J., Art
HOBBS, P. V., Atmospheric Sciences
HODGE, P. W., Astronomy
HOLTON, J. R., Atmospheric Sciences
HOSTETLER, P. S., Drama
HOUZE, R. A., Atmospheric Physics
HU, M., Art
HUEY, R. B., Zoology
HUNN, E. S., Anthropology
HUNT, E. B., Psychology
HUTTON, R. S., Psychology
INGALLS, R. L., Physics
IRVING, R., Mathematics
JACKSON, W. A. D., Geography and School of International Studies
JACOBSON, N., Psychology
JAEGER, C. S., German
JANS, J. P., Mathematics
JOHNSON, C. R., English
JONES, R. C., Art
KAPETANIC, D., Slavic Languages and Literature, and International Studies
KAPLAN, A., Music
KARTIGANER, D. M., English
KENAGY, G. J., Zoology
KEYES, C. F., Anthropology
KEYT, D., Philosophy
KINGSBURY, M., Art History
KLAUSENBURGER, J., Romance Languages and Literature
KLEE, V. M., Jr, Mathematics
KNAPP, J. S., Dance
KNECHTGES, D. R., Asian Languages and Literature
KOBLITZ, N., Mathematics
KOHN, A. J., Zoology
KORG, J., English
KOTTLER, H. W., Art
KOTTWITZ, R., Mathematics
KOWALSKI, B. R., Chemistry
KRUMME, G., Geography
KUHL, P. K., Speech and Hearing
KWIRAM, A. L., Chemistry
LADNER, R. E., Computer Science
LAIRD, C. D., Zoology
LANG, G. E., Communications, Political Science and Sociology
LANG, K., Communications
LARDY, N., International Studies
LAZOWSKA, E., Computer Science
LEGTERS, L. H., School of International Studies
LEOPOLD, E. B., Botany and Forest Resources
LEOVY, C. B., Atmospheric Sciences and Geophysics
LEV, D. S., Political Science
LEVI, M. A., Political Science
LEVY, F. J., History
LEWIS, B., Geophysics and Oceanography
LIND, D. A., Mathematics
LISTER, C. R. B., Geophysics and Oceanography

LOCKARD, J. S., Psychology and Neurosurgery
LOCKWOOD, T. F., English
LOFTUS, E. J., Psychology
LOFTUS, G. R., Psychology
LOPER, R. B., Drama
LORD, J. J., Physics
LUBATTI, H. J., Physics
LUJAN, H. D., Political Science
LUNDIN, N. K., Art
LUNDQUIST, B. R., Music
LUNNEBORG, C., Psychology and Statistics
MCCALLUM, I. S., Geological Sciences
MCCOLL, W. D., Music
MCCRACKEN, J. D., English
MCCRONE, D. J., Political Science
MCDERMOTT, L. C., Physics
MCDERMOTT, M. N., Physics
MCELROY, C. W., English
MCGEE, J. S., Economics
MCHUGH, H., English
MACKAY, P. A., Classics, Comparative Literature, Near Eastern Language and Civilization
MARGON, B., Astronomy
MARKS, C. E., Philosophy
MARLATT, G. A., Psychology
MARSHALL, D., Mathematics
MARSHALL, J. C., Art
MARTIN, R. D., Statistics
MATTHEWS, D. R., Political Science
MAYER, J., Geography
MELTZOFF, A., Psychology
MERRILL, R. T., Geophysics and Geological Sciences
MICHAEL, E. A., Mathematics
MICKLESEN, L. R., Slavic Languages and Literature, Linguistics and International Studies
MIGDAL, J. S., International Studies
MILLER, G., Physics
MILLER, R. A., Asian Languages and Literature
MINIFIE, F. D., Speech and Hearing Sciences
MITCHELL, T. R., Management and Organization and Psychology
MODELSKI, G., Political Science
MODIANO, R., English and Comparative Literature
MORRILL, R. L., Geography and Environmental Studies
MORROW, J. A., Mathematics
MOSELEY, S., Art
NAMIOKA, I., Mathematics
NASON, J. D., Anthropology
NELSON, C. R., Economics
NELSON, T. O., Psychology
NEUMAN, D. M., Art
NEWELL, L. L., Anthropology
NEWMEYER, F. J., Linguistics
NOE, J. D., Computer Science
NORMAN, J. G., Chemistry
NORMAN, J. L., Asian Languages and Literatures
NUNKE, R. J., Mathematics
NUTE, P. E., Anthropology
ODELL, G. M., Zoology
O'DOAN, N. D., Music
OLSON, D. J., Political Science
OPPERMAN, H. N., Art
ORIANS, G. H., Zoology and Environmental Studies
OSBORNE, M. S., Mathematics
OTTENBERG, S., Anthropology
PAINE, R. T., Jr, Zoology
PALAIS, J. B., International Studies and History
PALKA, J. M., Zoology
PALMER, J. M., Prosthodontics and Speech and Hearing Sciences
PARKS, G. K., Geophysics
PARKS, R. W., Economics
PASCAL, P., Classics
PEASE, O. A., History
PEMBER, D. R., Communication

PERLMAN, M. D., Statistics
PERRY, E., International Studies
PETERS, P. C., Physics
PHELPS, R. R., Mathematics
PIZZUTO, E., Art
POCKER, Y., Chemistry
PORTER, S. C., Geological Sciences
POTTER, K. H., International Studies and Philosophy
PRINS, D., Speech and Hearing Sciences
PUFF, R. D., Physics
PUNDT, G. H., Art and Architecture
PYKE, R., Mathematics
PYLE, K. B., International Studies and History
RAGOZIN, D., Mathematics
RAHN, J., Music
RAYMOND, C. F., Geophysics
REED, R., Atmospheric Sciences
REHR, J. J., Physics
REID, B. R., Chemistry
REINERT, O., English and Comparative Literature
RENSBERGER, J. M., Geological Sciences
RESHETAR, J. S., Jr, Political Science
RICHMAN, R. J., Philosophy
RIDDIFORD, L. M., Zoology
RIEDEL, E. K., Physics
ROCKAFELLAR, R. T., Mathematics
ROHWER, S. A., Zoology
RORABAUGH, W. J., History
ROSE, N. J., Chemistry
ROSSEL, S. H., Scandinavian Languages and Literatures
ROTHBERG, J. E., Physics
RUBIN, J., Asian Languages and Literatures
RUSS, J., English
RUTHERFOORD, J. P., Physics
RUZICKA, J., Chemistry
SACKETT, G. P., Psychology
SALE, R. H., English
SAPORTA, S., Linguistics and Romance Languages
SARASON, I. G., Psychology
SARASON, L., Mathematics
SAUM, L. O., History
SAX, G., Education
SCHEIDEL, T. M., Speech
SCHEINGOLD, S. A., Political Science
SCHICK, M., Physics
SCHIFFMAN, H. F., Asian Languages and Literatures
SCHMITT, D. R., Sociology
SCHOMAKER, V., Chemistry
SCHUBERT, W. M., Chemistry
SCHUBIGER, G. A., Zoology
SCHURR, J. M., Chemistry
SCHWARTZ, P., Sociology
SCOTT, J. W., American Ethnic Studies, Sociology
SEGAL, J., Mathematics
SHAW, A. C., Computer Science
SHORACK, G. R., Statistics
SHULMAN, R., English
SIKI, B., Music
SILBERBERG, E., Economics
SILBERGELD, J. L., Art
SIMONSON, H. P., English
SIMPSON, J. B., Psychology
SKOWRONEK, F. E., Music
SLUTSKY, L. J., Chemistry
SMITH, C. W., Art
SMITH, J. D., Oceanography, Geophysics and Geological Sciences
SMITH, R. E., Psychology
SMITH, S. W., Geophysics
SMITH, W. O., Music
SNYDER, L., Computer Science
SNYDER, R., Zoology
SPAFFORD, M. C., Art
STADLER, D. R., Genetics
STAMM, K., Communications
STARK, R., Sociology
STARYK, S. S., Music
STEELE, C. M., Psychology

STEENE, B., Scandinavian Languages and Literature and Comparative Literature
STERN, E. A., Physics
STEVICK, R. D., English
STORCH, L., Music
STOUT, E. L., Mathematics
STRATHMANN, R. R., Zoology
STREITBERGER, W., English
STUIVER, M., Geological Sciences
SUGAR, P. F., History and International Studies
SULLIVAN, J. B., Mathematics
SULLIVAN, W., Astronomy
SWINDLER, D. R., Anthropology
TANIMOTO, S. L., Computer Science
TAYLOR, M. J., Political Science
TELLER, D. Y., Psychology and Physiology
THOMAS, C. S., History
THOMAS, M. D., Geography
THOMPSON, E. A., Statistics
THOMPSON, G., Speech and Hearing Sciences
THORNTON, J., Economics
THOULESS, D. J., Physics
TOWNSEND, J. R., International Studies and Political Science
TREADGOLD, D. W., International Studies and History
TRUMAN, J. W., Zoology
TSUKADA, M., Botany
TUFTS, P. D., Music
UHLMANN, G. A., Mathematics
ULLMAN, J. C., History
UNTERSTEINER, N., Atmospheric Sciences and Geophysics
VAN DEN BERGHE, P. L., Sociology
VANDENBOSCH, R., Chemistry
VANDYCK, R. S., Physics
VELIKONJA, J., Geography
VILCHES, O. E., Physics
VOYLES, J. B., Germanics
WAALAND, J. R., Botany
WADDEN, D. J., Art
WAGER, L. W., Sociology
WAGONER, D. R., English
WALLACE, J. M., Atmospheric Sciences
WALLERSTEIN, G., Astronomy
WAN, F. Y., Applied Mathematics
WANG, C. H., Asian Languages and Literature and Comparative Literature
WARASHINA, P. B., Art
WARD, P., Geological Sciences
WARFIELD, R. B., Mathematics
WARNER, G. W., Jr, Mathematics
WATTS, R. O., Chemistry
WEBB, E., International Studies and Comparative Literature
WEIS, J. G., Sociology
WELLNER, J. A., Statistics
WESTWATER, M. J., Mathematics
WHISLER, H. C., Botany
WHITEHILL-WARD, J., Art
WILETS, L., Physics
WILEY, H., Dance
WILLEFORD, W., English and Comparative Literature
WILLIAMS, R. W., Physics
WILLOWS, A. O. D., Zoology
WILSON, W. R., Speech and Hearing Sciences
WINANS, E. V., Anthropology
WINGFIELD, J., Zoology
WITHERSPOON, G., Anthropology
WOODS, S. C., Psychology
YAMAMURA, K., International Studies
YANTIS, P. A., Speech and Hearing Sciences
YOUNG, K. K., Physics
YOUNG, P. R., Computer Science
ZOLLER, W. H., Chemistry

College of Education (POB 353600, Seattle, WA 98195-3600; e-mail coe@u.washington.edu; internet education.washington.edu):

ABBOTT, R. D.
AFFLECK, J. Q.
ANDERSON, R.

ANDREWS, R. L.
BANKS, J. A.
BILLINGSLEY, F. F.
BOLTON, D. L.
BRAMMER, L. M.
BURGESS, C. O.
BUTTERFIELD, E. C.
DOI, J. I.
EDGAR, E. B.
EVANS, E. D.
GOODLAD, J. I.
HARING, N. G.
HUNKINS, F. P.
JENKINS, J. R.
KALTSOUNIS, T.
KERR, D. H.
KERR, S. T.
KLOCKARS, A. J.
LIEBERMAN, A.
LOVITT, T. C.
LOWENBRAUN, S.
MCCARTIN, R. E.
MADSEN, D. L.
MORISHIMA, J. K.
NEEL, R. S.
OLSTAD, R. G.
PECKHAM, P. D.
RYCKMAN, D. B.
SAX, G.
SCHILL, W. J.
SEBESTA, S. L.
THOMPSON, M. D.
TOSTBERG, R. E.
WHITE, O.
WINN, W. D.

College of Engineering (371 Loew Hall, Box 352180, Seattle, WA 98195-2180; tel. (206) 543-0340; fax (206) 685-0666; e-mail coeinfo@u.washington.edu; internet www.engr.washington.edu):

AKSAY, I. A., Materials Science Engineering
ALBRECHT, R. W., Electrical and Nuclear Engineering
ALEXANDER, D. E., Mechanical Engineering
ALEXANDRO, F., Electrical Engineering
ALLAN, G. G., Forest Resources and Chemical Engineering
ANDERSEN, J., Electrical Engineering
ARCHBOLD, T. F., Mining, Metallurgical and Ceramic Engineering
BABB, A. L., Chemical and Nuclear Engineering
BALISE, P. L., Mechanical Engineering
BEREANO, P., Interdepartmental Curricular Programme
BERG, J. C., Chemical Engineering
BOGAN, R. H., Civil Engineering
BOLLARD, R. J. H., Aeronautics and Astronautics
BOWEN, J. R., Chemical Engineering
BRADT, R. C., Mining, Metallurgical and Ceramic Engineering
BROWN, C. B., Civil Engineering
BURGES, S. J., Civil Engineering
CHALUPNIK, J. D., Mechanical Engineering
CHEUNG, P. W., Electrical Engineering and Bioengineering
CHRISTIANSEN, W. H., Aeronautics and Astronautics
CLARK, R. N., Electrical Engineering
COLCORD, J. E., Civil Engineering
CORLETT, R. C., Mechanical Engineering
DALY, C. H., Mechanical Engineering
DAVIS, E. J., Chemical Engineering
DECHER, R., Aeronautics and Astronautics
DEPEW, C. A., Mechanical Engineering
DOW, D. G., Electrical Engineering
ELIAS, Z. M., Civil Engineering
EMERY, A. F., Mechanical Engineering
EVANS, R. J., Civil Engineering
FERGUSON, J. F., Civil Engineering
FINLAYSON, B. A., Chemical Engineering
FISCHBACH, D. B., Materials Science and Engineering

FYFE, I. M., Aeronautics and Astronautics
GARLID, K. L., Chemical and Nuclear Engineering
GESSNER, F., Mechanical Engineering
HARALICK, R. M., Electrical Engineering
HAWKINS, N. M., Civil Engineering
HEIDEGER, W. J., Chemical Engineering
HERTZBERG, A., Aeronautics and Astronautics
HOFFMAN, A. S., Chemical Engineering and Bioengineering
HOLDEN, A., Electrical Engineering
HOLSAPPLE, K. A., Aeronautics and Astronautics
HSU, C.-C., Electrical Engineering
ISHIMARU, A., Electrical Engineering
JOHNSON, D. E., Bioengineering
JOHNSON, D. L., Electrical Engineering
JOPPA, R. G., Aeronautics and Astronautics
JORGENSEN, J. E., Mechanical Engineering
KEVORKIAN, J. K., Aeronautics and Astronautics
KIPPENHAM, C. J., Mechanical Engineering
KOBAYASHI, A. S., Mechanical Engineering
KOSALY, G., Nuclear and Mechanical Engineering
KUROSAKA, M., Aeronautics and Astronautics
LAURITZEN, P. O., Electrical Engineering
LYTLE, D. W., Electrical Engineering
MCCORMICK, N. J., Nuclear Engineering
MCKEAN, W. T., Chemical Engineering and Forest Resources
MALTE, P. C., Mechanical Engineering
MAR, B. W., Civil Engineering
MARKS, R. J., Electrical Engineering
MATTOCK, A. H., Civil Engineering
MEDITCH, J. S., Electrical Engineering
MONTGOMERY, D. C., Industrial Engineering
MORITZ, W. E., Electrical Engineering
NECE, R. E., Civil Engineering
NIHAN, N. L., Civil Engineering
NOGES, E., Electrical Engineering
PARMETER, R. R., Aeronautics and Astronautics
PEARSON, C. E., Aeronautics and Astronautics, Applied Mathematics
PEDEN, I., Electrical Engineering
PILAT, M. J., Civil Engineering
PINTER, R. E., Electrical Engineering
POLONIS, D. H., Mining, Metallurgical and Ceramic Engineering
PORTER, R. P., Electrical Engineering
PRATT, D. T., Mechanical Engineering
RAO, Y. K., Mining, Metallurgical and Ceramics Engineering
RATNER, B., Bioengineering and Chemical Engineering
RIBE, F. L., Nuclear Engineering
RILEY, J., Mechanical Engineering
ROBKIN, M. A., Nuclear Engineering
ROEDER, C. W., Civil Engineering
RUSSELL, D. A., Aeronautics and Astronautics
SCHNEIDER, J. B., Urban Planning and Civil Engineering
SCOTT, W. D., Mining, Metallurgical and Ceramic Engineering
SEFERIS, J. C., Chemical Engineering
SIGELMANN, R. A., Electrical Engineering
SLEICHER, C. A., Jr, Chemical Engineering
SPINDEL, R. C., Electrical Engineering
STEAR, E. B., Electrical Engineering
STENSEL, H. D., Civil Engineering
STOEBE, T. G., Mining, Metallurgical and Ceramic Engineering
TAGGART, R., Mechanical Engineering
TSANG, L., Electrical Engineering
VAGNERS, J., Aeronautics and Astronautics
VENKATA, S. S., Electrical Engineering
VERESS, S. A., Civil Engineering
VESPER, K. H., Mechanical Engineering and Management and Organization, Marine Studies
VLASES, G. C., Nuclear Engineering

WELCH, E. B., Civil Engineering
WOLAK, J., Mechanical Engineering
WOODRUFF, G. L., Nuclear Engineering
YEE, S. S., Electrical Engineering
ZICK, G. L., Electrical Engineering

College of Forest Resources:

ADAMS, D. M.
AGEE, J. K.
ALLAN, G. G., Forest Resources and Chemical Engineering
BARE, B. B.
BETHEL, J. S.
BRUBAKER, L. B.
COLE, D. W.
DOWDLE, B.
EDMONDS, R. L.
FIELD, D. R.
FRITSCHEN, L. J.
GARA, R. I.
HATHEWAY, W. H.
HINCKLEY, T. M.
HRUTFIORD, B. F.
LEE, R. G.
MANUWAL, D. A.
OLIVER, C.
PICKFORD, S. G.
SARKENEN, K., Forest Resources and Chemical Engineering
SCHREUDER, G. F.
SHARPE, G. W.
STETTLER, R. F.
THORUD, D. B.
TUKEY, H. B.
UGOLINI, F. C.
WAGGENER, T. R.
WOTT, J. A.

College of Ocean and Fishery Science
School of Oceanography:

BANSE, K.
CARPENTER, R.
COACHMAN, L.
CREAGER, H. S.
DELANEY, J.
EMERSON, S.
ERIKSEN, C.
FROST, B. W.
HEATH, G. R.
HEDGES, J.
HERSHMAN, M. J.
JUMARS, P. A.
LEWIS, B.
LISTER, C. R. B.
MCMANUS, D. A.
MERRILL, R. T.
MILES, E. L.
MURPHY, S. R.
MURRAY, J.
NOWELL, A. R. M.
RHINES, P. B.
RICHARDS, F. A.
SMITH, J. D.
STERNBERG, R. W.
WELANDER, P.
WINTER, D. R.
WOOSTER, W. S.

School of Fisheries:

BRANNON, E. L.
BROWN, G. W.
CHEW, K. K.
FORD, E. D.
FRANCIS, R. C.
GALLUCCI, V. F.
HALVER, J. D.
HILBORN, R. W.
LANDOLT, M.
LISTON, J.
MATCHES, J. R.
MATHEWS, S. B.
MILLER, B. S.
PIETSCH, T. W.
PIGOTT, G. M.
SCHELL, W. R.
SMITH, L. S.
STICKNEY, R. R.

TAUB, F.
WHITNEY, R. R.

Graduate School of Library and Information Science:
CHISHOLM, M. E.

Graduate School of Public Affairs:
DENNY, B. C.
KROLL, M., Public Affairs and Political Science
LOCKE, H. G.
LYDEN, F. J.
WILLIAMS, W.
ZERBE, R. O.

School of Business:
ALBERTS, W. W., Finance, Business Economics and Quantitative Methods
BOURQUE, P. J., Finance, Business Economics and Quantitative Methods
CHIU, J. S. Y., Management Science
D'AMBROSIO, C. A., Finance, Business Economics
DUKES, R. E., Accounting
ETCHESON, W. W., Marketing
FAALAND, B. H., Finance, Business Economics and Quantitative Methods
FROST, P. A., Finance, Business Economics and Quantitative Methods
HALEY, C. W., Finance, Business Economics and Quantitative Methods
HEATH, L. C., Accounting
HENNING, D. A., Management and Organization
HESS, A. C., Finance, Business Economics and Quantitative Methods
HIGGINS, R. C., Finance, Business Economics and Quantitative Methods
INGENE, C., Marketing and International Business
JACOB, N. L., Finance, Business Economics and Quantitative Methods
JIAMBALVO, J., Accounting
JOHANSSON, J. K., Marketing, Transportation, and International Business
JOHNSON, D. W., Finance, Business Economics and Quantitative Methods
KLASTORIN, T., Management Science
KNUDSON, H. R., Management and Organization
LATHAM, G., Management and Organization
MACLACHLAN, D. L., Marketing
MITCHELL, T. R., Management and Organization
MOINPOUR, R., Marketing, Transportation and International Business
MUELLER, G. G., Accounting
NARVER, J. C., Marketing, Transportation and International Business
NEWELL, W. T., Management and Organization, Management Science
NOREEN, E. W., Accounting
PAGE, A. N., Finance, Business Economics and Quantitative Methods
PETERSON, R. B., Finance, Business Economics and Quantitative Methods
RAMANATHAN, K. V., Accounting
ROLEY, V. V., Finance and Business Economics
SAXBERG, B. O., Management and Organization
SCHALL, L. D., Finance, Business Economics and Quantitative Methods
SCOTT, W. G., Management and Organization
SPRATLEN, T. H., Marketing, Transportation and International Business
SUMMER, C. E., Management and Organization
SUNDEM, G. L., Accounting
WHEATLEY, J. J., Marketing, Transportation and International Business
YALCH, R., Marketing

School of Dentistry (D322 Health Sciences Bldg, Box 356365, , WA 98195-6365; internet www.dental.washington.edu):
AMMONS, W. F., Periodontics
BOLENDER, C. L., Prosthodontics
BRUDVIK, J. S., Prosthodontics
CANFIELD, R. C., Restorative Dentistry
CLAGETT, J. A., Periodontics and Microbiology
CONRAD, D. A., Dental Public Health Sciences and Health Services
DERONEN, T. A., Dental Public Health Services, Biostatistics
DWORKIN, S. F., Oral Surgery
ENGEL, D., Periodontics
FRANK, R. P., Prosthodontics
GEHRIG, J. D., Oral Surgery
HARRINGTON, G. W., Endodontics
JOHNSON, R. H., Periodontics
KOKICH, V., Orthodontics
LEWIS, T. M., Restorative Dentistry
LITTLE, R. M., Orthodontics
MILGROM, P. M., Dental Public Health Services
MOFFETT, B. C., Orthodontics
MYALL, R. W., Oral Surgery
NATKIN, E., Endodontics
NICHOLLS, J. I., Restorative Dentistry
OMNELL, K.-A., Oral Medicine
PAGE, R. C., Pathology and Periodontics
PALMER, J. M., Speech and Hearing Sciences and Prosthodontics
ROBINOVITCH, M. R., Oral Biology
SHAPIRO, P., Orthodontics
SMITH, D. E., Prosthodontics
TAMARIN, A., Oral Biology
WARNICK, M. E., Restorative Dentistry
WORTHINGTON, P., Oral and Maxillofacial Surgery
YUODELIS, R. A., Restorative Dentistry

School of Law (William H. Gates Hall, Box 353020, Seattle, WA 98195-3020; tel. (206) 543-2100; e-mail lawadm@uw.edu; internet www.law.washington.edu):
ANDERSON, W. R.
ARONSON, R. H.
BURKE, W. T.
CHISUM, D. S.
FITZPATRICK, J. F.
FLETCHER, R. L.
HALEY, J. O.
HARDISTY, J. H.
HAZELTON, P. A.
HENDERSON, D. F.
HJORTH, R. L.
HUME, L. S.
HUSTON, J. C.
JAY, S. M.
JOHNSON, R. W.
JUNKER, J. M.
KUMMERT, R. O.
LOH, W. D.
MORRIS, A.
PECK, C. J.
PRICE, J. R.
PROSTERMAN, R. L.
RODDIS, R. S.
RODGERS, W. H.
ROMBAUER, M.
SMITH, F. W., Jr
STOEBUCK, W. B.
TRAUTMAN, P. A.

School of Medicine (325 Ninth Ave, Seattle, WA 98104-2499; tel. (206) 744-3000; internet uwmedicine.washington.edu):
ABELSON, H. T., Pediatrics
ABRASS, I., Medicine
ADAMSON, J. W., Medicine
ALBERT, R., Medicine
ALMERS, W., Physiology and Biophysics
ALVORD, E. C., Pathology
ANDERSON, M. E., Rehabilitation Medicine and Physiology
ANSELL, J. S., Urology

APPELBAUM, F., Medicine
BARNES, G. W., Urology
BASSINGTHWAIGHTE, J. B., Bioengineering
BEAVO, J., Pharmacology
BECKER, J., Psychiatry, Psychology
BELKNAP, B. H., Medicine
BENEDETTI, T. J., Obstetrics and Gynaecology
BEN-MENACHEM, Y., Radiology
BERGER, A. J., Physiology and Biophysics
BERGMAN, A. B., Pediatrics
BERNSTEIN, I. D., Pediatrics
BIERMAN, E. L., Medicine
BINDER, M., Physiology and Biophysics
BIRD, T., Medicine
BLACKMON, J. R., Medicine
BLAGG, C. R., Medicine
BLEYER, W. A., Pediatrics
BORNSTEIN, P., Medicine and Biochemistry
BOWDEN, D. M., Psychiatry
BREMNER, W. J., Medicine
BRENGELMANN, G., Physiology and Biophysics
BROWN, B. G., Medicine
BRUNZELL, J. D., Medicine
BUCHANAN, T. M., Medicine and Pathobiology
BUCKNER, C. D., Medicine
BUNT-MILAM, A. H., Ophthalmology
BUTLER, J., Medicine
BYERS, P., Medicine and Pathology
CARR, J. E., Psychiatry and Psychology
CARRICO, C. J., Surgery
CATTERALL, W. A., Pharmacology
CHAIT, A., Medicine
CHAMPOUX, J. J., Microbiology
CHAPMAN, C. R., Anaesthesiology and Psychiatry
CHAPMAN, W. H., Urology
CHATRIAN, G. E., Laboratory Medicine and Neurological Surgery
CHEEVER, M. A., Medicine
CHENEY, F. W., Anaesthesiology
CHESNUT, C. H., Radiology and Medicine
CLARREN, S., Pediatrics
COBB, L. A., Medicine
COPASS, M. K., Medicine
COREY, L., Laboratory Medicine and Microbiology
COUNTS, G. W., Medicine
COUSER, W. G., Medicine
CRILL, W. E., Medicine, Physiology and Biophysics
CROAKE, J. S., Psychiatry
CULLEN, B. F., Anaesthesiology
CUMMINGS, C. W., Otolaryngology
DALE, D. C., Medicine
DAVIE, E. W., Biochemistry
DEISHER, R. W., Pediatrics
DELATEUR, B. J., Rehabilitation Medicine
DETTER, J. C., Laboratory Medicine
DETWILER, P., Physiology and Biophysics
DILLARD, D. H., Surgery
DOBIE, R. A., Otolaryngology
DODGE, H. T., Medicine
DODRILL, C. B., Neurological Surgery
DOERR, H. O., Psychiatry and Psychology
DOHNER, C. W., Medicine and Education
DONALDSON, J. A., Otolaryngology
DUNNER, D. L., Psychiatry
EISENBERG, M., Medicine
EMANUEL, I., Epidemiology and International Health and Pediatrics
ENSINCK, J. W., Medicine
ESCHENBACH, D., Obstetrics and Gynaecology
EYRE, D. R., Orthopaedics
FARRELL, D. F., Pediatrics
FEFER, A., Medicine
FEIGL, E., Physiology and Biophysics
FETZ, E. E., Physiology and Biophysics
FIALKOW, P. J., Medicine and Genetics
FIGGE, D. C., Obstetrics and Gynaecology
FIGLEY, M. M., Radiology
FISCHER, E. H., Biochemistry
FRENCH, J. W., Pediatrics

FUCHS, A., Physiology and Biophysics
FUJIMOTO, W. Y., Medicine
GARTLER, S. M., Medicine and Genetics
GEYMAN, J. P., Family Medicine
GILLILAND, B., Laboratory Medicine and Medicine
GLOMSET, J. A., Medicine and Biochemistry
GODWIN, J. D., Radiology
GOLDMAN, M. L., Radiology
GOODNER, C. J., Medicine
GORDON, A. M., Physiology and Biophysics
GORDON, M., Biochemistry
GRAHAM, C. B., Radiology and Pediatrics
GREENBERG, P., Medicine
GREENE, H. L., Medicine
GREER, B. E., Obstetrics and Gynaecology
GRIFFIN, T. W., Radiation Oncology
GROMAN, N. B., Microbiology
GROUDINE, M., Radiation Oncology
GUNTHEROTH, W. G., Pediatrics
GUY, A., Rehabilitation Medicine and Bioengineering
HAGGITT, R. C., Pathology
HAKOMORI, S., Pathobiology and Microbiology
HALAR, E. M., Rehabilitation Medicine
HANDSFIELD, H. H., Medicine
HANSEN, J. A., Medicine
HANSEN, S., Orthopaedics
HARLEY, J. D., Radiology
HARRIS, A. B., Neurological Surgery
HAUSCHKA, S. D., Biochemistry
HAYDEN, P., Pediatrics
HEIMAN, J., Psychiatry and Behavioural Sciences
HEIMBACH, D. M., Surgery
HELLSTROM, I. E., Microbiology
HELLSTROM, K. E., Pathology
HENDERSON, M., Medicine and Epidemiology
HENDRICKSON, A. E., Ophthalmology and Biological Structure
HERMAN, C. M., Surgery
HILDEBRANDT, J., Physiology and Medicine
HILLE, B., Physiology and Biophysics
HLASTALA, M. P., Physiology and Biophysics and Medicine
HODSON, W. A., Pediatrics
HOLBROOK, K. A., Biological Structure
HOLMES, K. K., Medicine
HORITA, A., Pharmacology
HORNBEIN, T. F., Anaesthesiology, Physiology and Biophysics
HUDSON, L. D., Medicine
HUNTSMAN, L. L., Bioengineering
INUI, T. S., Medicine and Health Services
IVEY, T. D., Surgery
JOHANSEN, K. H., Surgery
JOHNSON, M. H., Psychiatry
JONES, R. F., Surgery
JONSEN, A. R., Medical History and Ethics
JUCHAU, M. R., Pharmacology
KALINA, R. E., Ophthalmology
KEHL, T. H., Physiology, Biophysics and Computer Science
KELLY, W. A., Neurological Surgery
KENNEDY, J. W., Medicine
KENNY, M. A., Laboratory Medicine
KLEBANOFF, S. J., Medicine
KNOPP, R. H., Medicine
KOEHLER, J. K., Biological Structure
KOERKER, D. J., Physiology and Biophysics and Medicine
KRAFT, G. H., Rehabilitation Medicine
KREBS, E. G., Pharmacology and Biochemistry
KROHN, K., Radiology
LABBE, R. F., Laboratory Medicine
LAKSHMINARAYAN, S., Medicine
LANDESMAN, S., Psychiatry
LARAMORE, G., Radiation Oncology
LARSON, E., Medicine
LEHMANN, J. F., Rehabilitation Medicine
LEIN, J. N., Obstetrics and Gynaecology
LEMIRE, R. J., Pediatrics
LIVINGSTON, R. B., Medicine

LOCKARD, J. S., Neurological Surgery
LOEB, L. A., Pathology
LOESER, J. B., Neurological Surgery
LOGERFO, J. P., Medicine and Health Services
LOOP, J. W., Radiology
LUFT, J. H., Biological Structure
MCARTHUR, J. R., Medicine
MCDONALD, G. B., Medicine
MACK, L. A., Radiology
MACKLER, B., Pediatrics
MANNIK, M., Medicine
MARAVILLA, K. R., Radiology and Neurological Surgery
MARCHIORO, T. L., Surgery
MARTIN, G. M., Pathology
MARTIN, J. C., Psychiatry
MATSEN, F. A., Orthopaedics
MAYO, M. E., Urology
MEYERS, J., Medicine
MILLS, R. P., Ophthalmology
MONSEN, E. R., Medicine
MORRIS, D. E., Biochemistry
MOSS, A. A., Radiology
MOTTET, N. K., Pathology and Environmental Health
MOTULSKY, A., Genetics and Medicine
MURPHY, T. M., Anaesthesiology
NEFF, J. M., Pediatrics
NEIMAN, P. E., Medicine
NELP, W. B., Medicine and Radiology
NELSON, J. A., Radiology
NESTER, E. W., Microbiology
NORWOOD, T., Pathology
NOVACK, A. H., Pediatrics
OCHS, H. D., Pediatrics
ODLAND, G. F., Medicine, Biological Structure
OJEMANN, G. A., Neurological Surgery
OMENN, G. S., Medicine and Environmental Health
PAGE, R. C., Pathology and Periodontics
PALMER, J., Medicine
PALMITER, R. D., Biochemistry
PAPAYANNOPOULOU, T., Medicine
PARSON, W. W., Biochemistry
PAULSEN, C. A., Medicine
PETRA, P. H., Obstetrics and Gynaecology and Biochemistry
PHILLIPS, T. J., Family Medicine
PIERSON, D., Medicine
PIOUS, D. A., Pediatrics
PLORDE, J. J., Laboratory Medicine
POLLACK, G. H., Bioengineering
POPE, C. E., Medicine
PORTE, D., Medicine
PRESTON, T. A., Medicine
PRINZ, P., Psychiatry
RAISYS, V., Laboratory Medicine
RASEY, J. S., Radiation Oncology
RASKIND, M. A., Psychiatry
RAUSCH, R. L., Animal Medicine and Pathobiology
REICHENBACH, D. D., Pathology
REICHLER, R. J., Psychiatry
REID, B. R., Biochemistry and Chemistry
RICE, C. L., Surgery
RITCHIE, J. L., Medicine
ROBERTS, T. S., Neurological Surgery
ROBERTSON, W. O., Pediatrics
ROBINSON, N. L., Surgery
RODIECK, R. W., Ophthalmology
ROHRMAN, C. A., Radiology
ROOS, B. A., Medicine
ROSENBLATT, R. A., Family Medicine
ROSS, R., Pathology
ROSSE, C., Biological Structure
ROWELL, L. B., Physiology and Biophysics
RUBELL, E. W., Otolaryngology
RUBIN, C. E., Medicine
RUVALCABA, R., Pediatrics
SAARI, J. C., Ophthalmology and Biochemistry
SALE, G., Pathology
SAUNDERS, D. R., Medicine
SCHER, A. M., Physiology and Biophysics

SCHMER, G., Laboratory Medicine
SCHOENKNECHT, F. D., Laboratory Medicine and Microbiology
SCHUFFLER, M., Medicine
SCHWARTZ, S. M., Pathology
SCHWARTZKROIN, P., Neurological Surgery and Physiology, Biophysics
SCHWINDT, P. C., Physiology and Biophysics
SCOTT, C. R., Pediatrics
SCRIBNER, B. H., Medicine
SELLS, C. J., Pediatrics
SHAPIRO, B. M., Biochemistry
SHAW, C., Pathology
SHEPARD, T. H., Pediatrics
SHERRARD, D. J., Medicine
SHERRIS, J. C., Microbiology
SHURTLEFF, D. B., Pediatrics
SILVERSTEIN, F., Medicine
SIMKIN, P. A., Medicine
SINGER, J., Medicine
SLICHTER, S., Medicine
SMITH, A. L., Pediatrics
SMITH, O. A. Jr, Physiology and Biophysics
SNYDER, J. M., Otolaryngology
SOULES, M. R., Obstetrics and Gynaecology
SPADONI, L. R., Obstetrics and Gynaecology
SPENCE, A. M., Medicine
STAHELI, L. T., Orthopaedics
STAHL, W., Medicine, Physiology and Biophysics
STALEY, J. T., Microbiology
STAMATOYANNOPOULOS, G., Medicine
STAMM, W., Medicine
STEINER, R., Obstetrics and Gynaecology, Physiology and Biophysics
STENCHEVER, M. A., Obstetrics and Gynaecology
STEVENSON, J. G., Pediatrics
STIRLING, C. E., Physiology and Biophysics
STOLOV, W. C., Rehabilitation Medicine
STORM, D. R., Pharmacology
STRANDJORD, P. E., Laboratory Medicine
STRANDNESS, D. E., Surgery
STREISSGUTH, A. P., Psychiatry
SUMI, S. M., Medicine and Pathology
SWANSON, P. D., Medicine
TAPPER, D., Surgery
TELLER, D. C., Biochemistry
TELLER, D. Y., Physiology and Psychology
THOMAS, E. D., Medicine
THOMPSON, A. R., Medicine
TOWE, A. L., Physiology and Biophysics
TOWNES, B. D., Psychiatry
TRIER, W. C., Surgery
TRUOG, W. E., Pediatrics
TUCKER, G. J., Psychiatry
TURCK, M., Medicine
VANARSDEL, P. P., Medicine
VANCITTERS, R. L., Physiology and Biophysics, Medicine
VANHOOSIER, G. L., Animal Medicine
VESTAL, R., Medicine
VINCENZI, F. F., Pharmacology
VONTVER, L., Obstetrics and Gynaecology
VRACKO, R., Pathology
WALKER, R. D., Psychiatry and Behavioural Science
WALLACE, J. F., Medicine
WALSH, K. A., Biochemistry
WARD, R. J., Anaesthesiology
WEDGWOOD, R. J., Pediatrics
WESTRUM, L. E., Neurological Surgery and Biological Structure
WEYMULLER, E. A., Otolaryngology
WHITELEY, H. R., Microbiology
WHORTON, J. C., Biomedical History
WIGHT, T., Pathology
WINN, H. R., Neurological Surgery
WINTERSCHEID, L. C., Surgery
WOODRUM, D. E., Pediatrics
WOOTON, P., Radiation Oncology
YOUNG, E. T., Biochemistry
ZAGER, R., Medicine

School of Nursing (Box 357260, Seattle, WA 98195; tel. (206) 543-8736; fax (206) 685-1613; internet nursing.uw.edu):

BARNARD, K. E., Parent and Child Nursing
BATEY, M. V., Community Health Care Systems
BENOLIEL, J. Q., Community Health Care Systems
CHRISMAN, N. J., Community Health Care Systems
DE TORNYAY, R., Community Health Care Systems
EYRES, S. J., Parent and Child Nursing
GALLUCCI, B. J., Physiological Nursing
GOERTZEN, I. E., Community Health Care Systems
HORN, B. J., Community Health Care Systems
HEGYVARY, S. T., Community Health Care Systems
KOGAN, H., Psychosocial Nursing
KURAMOTO, A., Physiological Nursing
LEWIS, F. M., Community Health Care Systems
MITCHELL, P. H., Physiological Nursing
OSBORNE, O. H., Psychosocial Nursing
PATRICK, M. I., Physiological Nursing
ROSE, M. H., Parent and Child Nursing
WOLF-WILETS, V. C., Psychosocial Nursing
WOODS, N. A., Physiological Nursing

School of Pharmacy (Box 357631, H362 Health Sciences Bldg, Seattle, WA 98195-7631; tel. (206) 543-6100; e-mail pharminf@uw.edu; internet sop.washington.edu):

BAILLIE, T., Medicinal Chemistry
BRADY, L. R., Medicinal Chemistry
CAMPBELL, W. H., Pharmacy Practice
GIBALDI, M., Pharmaceutics
KRADJAN, W., Pharmacy Practice
LEVY, R. H., Pharmaceutics
NELSON, S. D., Medicinal Chemistry
NELSON, W. L., Medicinal Chemistry
PLEIN, J. B., Pharmacy Practice
TRAGER, W. F., Medicinal Chemistry

School of Public Health and Community Medicine (Box 357230, Seattle, WA 98195; tel. (206) 543-1144; fax (206) 543-3813; e-mail publichealth@uw.edu; internet sph.washington.edu):

BRESLOW, N. E., Biostatistics
BUCHANAN, T. L., Pathobiology and Medicine
CROWLEY, J. J., Biostatistics
DALING, J. R., Epidemiology
DAVIS, K. A., Biostatistics
DAY, R. W., Health Services
DE ROUEN, T., Biostatistics
DIEHR, P. K., Biostatistics
EMANUEL, I., Epidemiology and Pediatrics
FEIGL, P., Biostatistics
FISHER, L. D., Biostatistics
FLEMING, T. R., Biostatistics
FOY, H. M., Epidemiology
GALE, J. I., Epidemiology
GRAYSTON, J. T., Epidemiology
HAKOMORI, S., Pathobiology and Microbiology
HENDERSON, M. M., Epidemiology and Medicine
INUI, T. S., Health Services and Medicine
JACKSON, K. L., Environmental Health
KENNY, G. E., Pathobiology
KOEPSELL, T., Health Services, Epidemiology
KRONMAL, R. A., Biostatistics
KUO, C.-C., Pathobiology
LEE, J. A., Environmental Health
LOGERFO, J. P., Health Services and Medicine
MARTIN, D. C., Biostatistics
MOOLGAVKAR, S. H., Epidemiology
MOTTET, N. K., Environmental Health and Pathology
MURPHY, S. D., Environmental Health

OMENN, G. S., Environmental Health and Medicine
PATRICK, D. L., Health Services
PERINE, P. L., Epidemiology
PERRIN, E. B., Health Services
PETERSON, A. V., Biostatistics
PRENTICE, R. L., Biostatistics
RAUSCH, R. L., Pathobiology
ROBKIN, M. A., Environmental Health and Nuclear Engineering
THOMAS, D. B., Epidemiology
VAN BELLE, G., Biostatistics
WAGNER, E. H., Health Services
WAHL, P. W., Biostatistics
WANG, S., Pathobiology
WEISS, N. S., Epidemiology
WILSON, J. T., Environmental Health
WORTHINGTON-ROBERTS, B., Epidemiology

School of Social Work (Box 354900, Seattle, WA 98195-4900; tel. (206) 543-5640; fax (206) 543-1228; internet socialwork.uw.edu):

BRIAR, S.
GOTTLIEB, N. R.
HAWKINS, J. D.
JAFFEE, B.
LEVY, R. L.
PATTI, R. J.
RESNICK, H.
TAKAGI, C. Y.
WHITTAKER, J. K.

WALLA WALLA UNIVERSITY

204 S College Ave, College Place, WA 99324
Telephone: (509) 527-2615
Fax: (509) 527-2253
E-mail: info@wallawalla.edu
Internet: www.wallawalla.edu
Founded 1892 as Walla Walla College, present name 2007
Private control
Academic year: September to June
Campuses at Anacortes (WA), Billings, Missoula (MT), Portland (OR)
Pres.: JOHN K. McVAY
Vice-Pres. for Academic Admin.: GINGER KETTING-WELLER
Vice-Pres. for Marketing and Enrolment Services: JODI WAGNER
Vice-Pres. for Univ. Advancement: PATSY WAGNER
Vice-Pres. for Financial Admin.: STEVE ROSE
Vice-Pres. for Student Life and Mission: KEN ROGERS
Registrar: CAROLYN DENNEY
Dir for Libraries: CAROLYN GASKELL
Library of 190,000 vols, 3,000 current periodicals
Number of teachers: 207 (112 full-time, 95 part-time)
Number of students: 1,865

WASHINGTON STATE UNIVERSITY

POB 641227, Pullman, WA 99164-5910
Telephone: (509) 335-3564
E-mail: presidentsoffice@wsu.edu
Internet: www.wsu.edu
Founded 1890 as Washington Agricultural College and School of Science, univ. status 1959
Public control
Academic year: August to May
Pres.: Dr ELSON S. FLOYD
Provost and Exec. Vice-Pres.: WARWICK M. BAYLY
Vice-Pres. for Business and Finance: ROGER PATTERSON
Vice-Pres. for Information Services and Chief Information Officer: VIJI MURALI
Vice-Pres. for Student Affairs and Enrolment Management: JOHN FRAIRE

Chancellor for Spokane Campus: BRIAN PITCHER
Chancellor for Tri-Cities Campus: VICKY CARWEIN
Chancellor for Vancouver Campus: HAROLD DENGERINK
Registrar: JULIA POMERENK
Dean for Libraries: JAY STARRATT
Library of 2,178,040 vols
Number of teachers: 1,650
Number of students: 27,327
Publications: ESQ: A Journal of the American Renaissance (3 a year), LandEscapes, Western Journal of Black Studies (4 a year)

DEANS

College of Agriculture, Human and Natural Resource Sciences: DANIEL I. BERNARDO
College of Business: Dr ERIC SPANGENBERG
College of Education: A. G. RUD
College of Engineering and Architecture: CANDIS CLAIBORN
College of Liberal Arts: DOUGLAS EPPERSON
College of Nursing: PATRICIA BUTTERFIELD
College of Pharmacy: GARY M. POLLACK
College of Sciences: Dr DARYLL B. DEWALD
College of Veterinary Medicine: BRYAN K. SLINKER
Edward R. Murrow College of Communication: LAWRENCE PINTAK
Graduate School: HOWARD D. GRIMES
Honors College: Dr LIBBY WALKER

WESTERN WASHINGTON UNIVERSITY

516 High St, Bellingham, WA 98225
Telephone: (360) 650-3000
E-mail: admit@cc.wwu.edu
Internet: www.wwu.edu
Founded 1893 as Bellingham Normal School, present name 1977
Academic year: September to June
Pres.: BRUCE SHEPARD
Provost and Vice-Pres. for Academic Affairs: Dr CATHERINE A. RIORDAN
Vice-Pres. for Business and Financial Affairs: Dr RICHARD VAN DEN HUL
Vice-Pres. for Enrolment and Student Services: Dr EILEEN V. COUGHLIN
Vice-Pres. for External Affairs: ROBERT EDIE
Vice-Pres. for Univ. Advancement: STEPHANIE BOWERS
Dean for Libraries: CHRISTOPHER COX
Library: 1.4m. vols
Number of teachers: 615
Number of students: 14,979
Publications: Bellingham Review (literary, 2 a year), Journal of Cross-Cultural Psychology (int., 1 a year), Journal of Rural Sociology (1 a year), Northwest Journal of Business and Economics (1 a year), Studies in American Indian Literature (4 a year)

DEANS

College of Business and Economics: Dr BRIAN K. BURTON
College of Fine and Performing Arts: DAN GUYETTE
College of Humanities and Social Sciences: Dr BRENT CARBAJAL
College of Sciences and Technology: JEFF WRIGHT
Fairhaven College of Interdisciplinary Studies: Prof. ROGER GILMAN
Huxley College of the Environment: Dr BRADLEY F. SMITH
Woodring College of Education: Dr FRANCISCO RIOS

WHITMAN COLLEGE

345 Boyer Ave, Walla Walla, WA 99362
Telephone: (509) 527-5111

E-mail: communication@whitman.edu
Internet: www.whitman.edu
Founded 1882
Private control
Academic year: August to May (2 semesters)
Pres.: Dr GEORGE BRIDGES
Provost and Dean for Faculty: TIMOTHY KAUFMAN-OSBORN
Vice-Pres. for Devt and College Relations: JOHN W. BOGLEY
Dean for Admission and Financial Aid: TONY CABASCO
Dean for Students: CHARLES E. CLEVELAND
Registrar: RONALD F. URBAN
College Librarian: DALIA CORKRUM
Library of 400,000 vols (incl. 3,500 linear ft archival and MSS and over 5,000 rare books), 21,000 journals
Number of teachers: 101 full-time
Number of students: 1,596

WHITWORTH UNIVERSITY

300 W Hawthorne Rd, Spokane, WA 99251
Telephone: (509) 777-1000
Fax: (509) 777-4763
Internet: www.whitworth.edu
Founded 1890
Private control
Pres.: Dr BECK A. TAYLOR
Vice-Pres. for Academic Affairs: Dr MICHAEL K. LEROY
Dir for Admissions: MARIANNE HANSEN
Library Dir: Dr HANS BYNAGLE
Library of 176,000 vols
Number of teachers: 156 full-time
Number of students: 3,000

WEST VIRGINIA

ALDERSON-BROADDUS COLLEGE

101 College Hill Dr., Philippi, WV 26416
Telephone: (304) 457-1700
Fax: (304) 457-6239
Internet: www.ab.edu
Founded 1932 by merger of Broaddus College (f. 1871) with Alderson Acad. and Junior College (f. 1901)
Private control
Divs of education and special programmes, humanities, natural sciences and social sciences
Pres.: RICK CREEHAN
Provost and Exec. Vice-Pres. for Academic Affairs: Dr JOAN PROPST
Vice-Pres. for Business and Finance: MARSHA DENNISTON
Vice-Pres. for Enrolment Management: TANYA SHELTON
Vice-Pres. for Institutional Advancement: J. NIKKY LUNA
Dir for Marketing and Communications: ASHLEY MITTELMEIER
Dir for Devt: ANNETTE FETTY
Dir for Financial Aid: BRIAN WEINGART
Dean for Student Affairs: SARAH WARD
Registrar: SAUNDRA HOXIE
Librarian: DAVID E. HOXIE
Library of 90,000 vols, 1,600 audiovisual items, 11,000 full text journals, magazines and newspapers, 65,000 music CDs
Number of teachers: 76 (60 full-time, 16 part-time)
Number of students: 780

AMERICAN PUBLIC UNIVERSITY SYSTEM

111 W Congress St, Charles Town, WV 25414
Telephone: (877) 777-9081
Fax: (304) 724-3788

Internet: www.apus.edu
Founded 1991 as American Military Univ., present name and students 2002
Private control
2 Online univs: American Public Univ. and American Military Univ.
Pres. and CEO: Dr WALLACE E. BOSTON
Provost and Exec. Vice-Pres.: Dr KARAN POWELL
Exec. Vice-Pres. and Chief Financial Officer: HARRY T. WILKINS
Exec. Vice-Pres. and Chief Operations Officer: Dr SHARON VAN WYK
Sr Vice-Pres. and Chief Admin. Officer: PETER W. GIBBONS
Sr Vice-Pres. and Chief Information Officer: W. DALE YOUNG
Vice-Pres. and Dean for Libraries and Course Materials: Dr FRED STIELOW
Vice-Pres. for Enrolment Management: TERRY GRANT
Vice-Pres. for Research and Devt: Dr PHIL ICE
Vice-Pres. for Student Services: LYN GEER
Vice-Pres. for Student Services: Dr RONALD KOVACH
Library of 100,000 vols, 30,000 scholarly journals
Number of teachers: 1,600
Number of students: 100,000

DEANS

School of Arts and Humanities: Dr LINDA MOYNIHAN
School of Business: Dr CHAD PATRIZI
School of Education: Dr HENRY G. BRZYCKI
School of Management: Dr SHAWN BLACK
School of Public Safety and Health: Dr MICHAEL JACKSON
School of Science and Technology: DAN BENJAMIN
School of Security and Global Studies: Dr ELENA MASTORS

APPALACHIAN BIBLE COLLEGE

161 College Dr., Mount Hope, WV 25880
Telephone: (304) 877-6428
Fax: (304) 877-5082
E-mail: abc@abc.edu
Internet: www.abc.edu
Founded 1950, present name 1978
Private control
Areas of study: Bible and theology, elementary education, music, ministries
Pres.: Dr DANIEL L. ANDERSON
Vice-Pres. for Academics: DANIEL HANSHEW
Vice-Pres. for Business: KEN LILLY
Vice-Pres. for Devt: Dr JONATHAN RINKER
Vice-Pres. for Student Services: DAVID CHILDS
Library of 52,000 vols
Number of students: 300

BETHANY COLLEGE

Main St, Bethany, WV 26032
Telephone: (304) 829-7000
Fax: (304) 829-7108
Internet: www.bethanywv.edu
Founded 1840
Private control
Academic year: August to May (2 semesters)
Pres.: Dr SCOTT D. MILLER
Assoc. Provost: Dr WALLACE B. NEEL
Exec. Vice-Pres. and Gen. Counsel: WILLIAM R. KIEFER
Vice-Pres. for Academic Affairs and Dean for Faculty: Dr DARIN E. FIELDS
Vice-Pres. for Institutional Advancement: SVEN DE JONG
Dean for Students: GERALD STEBBINS
Registrar: JoANN SUSAN DOTY

Dir for Libraries: HEATHER MAY-RICCIUTI
Library of 200,000 vols, 50,000 e-books, 2,000 periodical subscriptions, 100,000 microforms
Number of teachers: 65 (56 full-time, 9 part-time)
Number of students: 1,030
Publication: *Bethany Today* (2 a year)

PROFESSORS
BURNS, J., Biology
CSAPLAR, JR, W., Economics
FARWELL, J., Religious Studies and Philosophy
HULL, E., English
HULL, J., Psychology
LOVANO, J., World Languages and Cultures
MAFFETT, C., Political Science
MCGOWAN, J., Physical Education and Sports Studies
MENZ, H., World Languages and Cultures
MORGAN, K., Fine Arts
PAYSEN, R., Chemistry
RAMJEE, A., Business
RICCIUTI, H., Learning Resources
SAWTARIE, F., Computer Science
SHELEK-FURBEE, K., Social Work
SUTHERLAND, P., Communications
WEAVER, H., Fine Arts

BLUEFIELD STATE COLLEGE

219 Rock St, Bluefield, WV 24701-2198
Telephone: (304) 327-4000
Fax: (304) 325-7747
E-mail: bscadmit@bluefieldstate.edu
Internet: www.bluefieldstate.edu
Founded 1895 as Bluefield Colored Institute, present name 1943
State control
Academic year: August to May
Pres.: Dr THOMAS E. BLEVINS
Provost, Vice-Pres. for Academic Affairs and Dean for Academic Affairs: Dr LEWIS L. JONES
Vice-Pres. for Financial and Admin. Affairs: SHELIA D. JOHNSON
Vice-Pres. for Student Affairs and Enrolment Management: JOHN C. CARDWELL
Dir for Admissions: KENNY MANDEVILLE
Dir for Library Services: JOANNA THOMPSON
Library of 75,700 vols
Number of teachers: 90
Number of students: 3,600

DEANS

School of Arts and Sciences: Dr DAVID HAUS
School of Education: Dr ELISABETH M. STEEN-KEN
School of Engineering Technology and Computer Science: E. FRANK HART
School of Nursing and Allied Health: ANGELA M. LAMBERT
W. Paul Core, Jr, School of Business: Dr GLEN STEVE BOURNE

CONCORD UNIVERSITY

POB 1000, Vermillion St, Athens, WV 24712-1000
Telephone: (304) 384-5249
Fax: (304) 384-3218
E-mail: info@concord.edu
Internet: www.concord.edu
Founded 1872 as Concord State Normal School, present name 2004
State control
Academic year: September to May
Areas of study: arts, history, language and literature, mathematics and sciences, philosophy
Pres.: Dr GREGORY F. ALOIA

Vice-Pres. and Academic Dean: Dr KENDRA
  BOGGESS
Vice-Pres. for Admin.: RICK DILLON
Vice-Pres. for Advancement: ALICIA BESENYEI
Vice-Pres. for Business and Finance: Dr
  CHUCK BECKER
Vice-Pres. for Student Affairs, Dean for
  Students and Dir for Retention: Dr MARJIE
  FLANIGAN
Dir for Enrolment: KENT J. GAMBLE
Dir for Library: Dr STEPHEN D. ROWE
Library of 200,000 vols, 5,000 periodicals
Number of teachers: 110
Number of students: 2,797

DAVIS AND ELKINS COLLEGE

100 Campus Dr., Elkins, WV 26241
Telephone: (304) 637-1900
Internet: www.dewv.edu
Founded 1904
Private control
Academic year: August to May

Depts of biology and environmental science,
business administration. and economics,
chemistry, communications and foreign languages, computer science and physics, education, English, fine and performing arts,
health, history and political science, math-
ematics, nursing, psychology and human
services, religion and philosophy, sociology
and criminology, sport and movement sci-
ences
Pres.: Dr G. T. BUCK SMITH
Provost: MICHAEL P. MIHALYO, JR
Exec. Vice-Pres.: KEVIN WILSON
Vice-Pres. for Academic Affairs and Dean for
  the Faculty: Dr LAURENCE B. MCARTHUR
Vice-Pres. for College Advancement: PATRICIA
  J. SCHUMANN
Vice-Pres. for Student Affairs: SCOTT D.
  GODDARD
Registrar: Prof. Dr STEPHANIE E. HAYNES
Dir for the Library: JACKIE SCHNEIDER
Library of 116,000 vols
Number of teachers: 45 (full-time)
Number of students: 751

FAIRMONT STATE UNIVERSITY

1201 Locust Ave, Fairmont, WV 26554
Telephone: (304) 367-4892
Fax: (304) 366-4789
E-mail: admit@fairmontstate.edu
Internet: www.fairmontstate.edu
Founded 1865 as West Virginia Normal
  School, present name 2004
State control
Pres.: Dr MARIA C. BENNETT ROSE
Provost and Vice-Pres. for Academic Affairs:
  CHRISTINA LAVORATA
Sr Vice-Pres. for Enrolment and Student
  Services: MICHAEL BELMEAR
Vice-Pres. for Admin. and Fiscal Affairs:
  ENRICO PORTO
Vice-Pres. and Chief Information Officer:
  DAVID TAMM
Vice-Pres. for Institutional Advancement:
  DEVANNA CORLEY
Dean for Graduate Studies: Dr VAN DEMPSEY
Dir for Communications: SARAH HENSLEY
Dir for Library Services: THELMA HUTCHINS
Library of 265,000 vols, 50,000 e-books
Number of teachers: 190
Number of students: 7,450

DEANS

College of Liberal Arts: Prof. Dr DEANNA
  SHIELDS
College of Science and Technology: Prof. Dr
  ANTHONY F. GILBERTI
School of Business: Dr RICHARD HARVEY

School of Education, Health and Human
  Performance: Prof. Dr VAN DEMPSEY
School of Fine Arts: PETER LACH
School of Human Services: Prof. Dr BETH
  NEWCOME

GLENVILLE STATE COLLEGE

200 High St, Glenville, WV 26351
Telephone: (304) 462-7361
E-mail: admissions@glenville.edu
Internet: www.glenville.edu
Founded 1872
State control
Academic year: August to May
Depts of business, criminal justice, English,
fine arts, land resources, science and math-
ematics, social science, teacher education
Pres.: Dr PETER B. BARR
Provost and Sr Vice-Pres.: M. KATHERINE
  BUTLER
Exec. Vice-Pres.: ROBERT O. HARDMAN
Sr Vice-Pres. for External Relations: Dr
  WILLIAM D. NICHOLSON
Vice-Pres. for College Advancement: DENNIS
  J. POUNDS
Vice-Pres. for Enrolment Management: D.
  DUANE CHAPMAN
Dean for Student Affairs: JERRY L. BURKHAM-
  MER
Library Dir: GAIL WESTBROOK
Library of 110,000 vols, 483,000 microforms,
  625 hard-copy periodical titles, 18 news-
  paper titles
Number of teachers: 86 (59 full-time, 27
  part-time)
Number of students: 1,443

MARSHALL UNIVERSITY

1 John Marshall Dr., Huntington, WV 25755
Telephone: (304) 696-3646
Fax: (304) 696-3135
E-mail: admissions@marshall.edu
Internet: www.marshall.edu
Founded 1837 as Marshall Acad.
State control
Academic year: August to May
Extended campus sites: South Charleston,
Point Pleasant, Beckley, Logan and Gilbert
Pres.: Dr STEPHEN J. KOPP
Chief of Staff: MATTHEW TURNER
Provost and Sr Vice-Pres. for Academic
  Affairs: Dr GAYLE L. ORMISTON
Gen. Counsel and Sr Vice-Pres. for Exec.
  Affairs: LAYTON COTTRILL
Sr Vice-Pres. for Finance and Admin.: Dr
  KAREN KIRTLEY
Vice-Pres. for Multicultural Affairs: Dr SHARI
  CLARKE
Vice-Pres. for Research: Dr JOHN MAHER
Dir for Admissions: Dr TAMMY R. JOHNSON
Univ. Librarian and Dir for Libraries Oper-
  ations: JINGPING ZHANG
Library of 1,411,480 vols
Number of teachers: 666 (full-time)
Number of students: 14,196

DEANS

College of Education: Dr ROBERT BOOKWAL-
  TER
College of Fine Arts: DONALD VAN HORN
College of Health Professions: Dr MICHAEL
  PREWITT
College of Information Technology and
  Engineering: Dr WAEL ZATAR
College of Liberal Arts: Dr DAVID PITTENGER
College of Science: CHARLES SOMERVILLE
Graduate College: Dr DONNA J. SPINDEL
Graduate School of Education and Profes-
  sional Devt: TERESA EAGLE
Honors College: Dr MARY TODD

Joan C. Edwards School of Medicine: ROBERT
  C. NERHOOD JR
Lewis College of Business: Dr CHONG W. KIM
W. Page Pitt School of Journalism and Mass
  Communications: Dr CORLEY DENNISON

OHIO VALLEY UNIVERSITY

1 Campus View Dr., Vienna, WV 26105-8000
Telephone: (304) 865-6000
Fax: (304) 865-6001
E-mail: admissions@ovu.edu
Internet: www.ovu.edu
Founded 1958
Private control
Chancellor: Dr E. KEITH STOTTS
Pres.: Dr HAROLD SHANK
Exec. Vice-Pres.: DENVER LUCKY
Vice-Pres. for Academic Affairs: Dr JAMES
  BULLOCK
Vice-Pres. for Advancement: Dr SUSIE BUL-
  LOCK
Vice-Pres. for Enrolment: LARRY LYONS
Vice-Pres. for Marketing and Financial Aid:
  DENNIS COX
Dean for Student Services: KATHY MULLER
Dir for Admissions: AMY BORTELL
Library Dir: RODNEY WOOTEN
Library of 34,000 vols, 142 print periodical
  subscriptions, 60,203 microforms, 6,779
  audio visual materials, 30 electronic data-
  bases for periodicals, reference sources and
  93,763 e-book titles
Number of students: 501

DEANS

College of Arts and Sciences: Prof. Dr STEVEN
  HARDY
College of Biblical Studies and Behavioral
  Sciences: Dr MICHAEL MOSS
College of Business: Dr JOY JONES
College of Education: JO PENNINGTON

SALEM INTERNATIONAL UNIVERSITY

223 W Main St, Salem, WV 26426
Telephone: (304) 326-1109
Fax: (304) 782-5395
E-mail: admissions@salemu.edu
Internet: www.salemu.edu
Founded 1888 as Salem College, present
  name 2000
Private control
Areas of study: arts and sciences, business,
criminal justice, education, information tech-
nology, nursing
Chancellor and CEO: J. WILLIAM BROOKS
Pres.: JOHN A. LUOTTO
Provost and Chief Academic Officer: Dr
  DEBRA HARRISON
Exec. Vice-Pres.: C. ERIC KIRKLAND
Vice-Pres. for Admissions and Enrolment
  Management: ANDREW ANDERSON
Vice-Pres. for Business Affairs and Chief
  Financial Officer: DAN NELANT
Vice-Pres. for Information Technology and
  Chief Information Officer: PIETER BRESLER
Registrar: REBECCA HALL
Dean for Library Services: Dr PHYLLIS D.
  FREEDMAN
Library of 74,000 vols, 84 periodicals, 5
  newspapers, 2,765 e-journals, 300,000
  microfiche
Number of teachers: 55
Number of students: 810

SHEPHERD UNIVERSITY

POB 3210, Shepherdstown, WV 25443-3210
Telephone: (304) 876-5000
Fax: (304) 876-3101
Internet: www.shepherd.edu

Founded 1871, present name and status 2004
State control
Academic year: August to May
Areas of study: business administration, liberal arts, natural sciences, social sciences, teacher education
Pres.: Dr SUZANNE SHIPLEY
Vice-Pres. for Academic Affairs: Dr RICHARD J. HELLDOBLER
Vice-Pres. for Admin. and Finance: RICK STAISLOFF (acting)
Vice-Pres. for Advancement: Dr DIANE MELBY
Vice-Pres. for Enrolment Management: KIMBERLY SCRANAGE
Vice-Pres. for Student Affairs: Dr THOMAS C. SEGAR
Dean for Graduate and Continuing Education: Dr SCOTT BEARD
Dean for the Library: ANN WATSON
Library of 500,000 vols, 6,000 periodicals
Number of teachers: 327 (119 full-time, 208 part-time)
Number of students: 4,185
Publication: *Shepherd University Magazine* (3 a year)

DEANS

School of Arts and Humanities: DOW BENEDICT, IV
School of Business and Social Sciences: Dr ANN LEGREID
School of Education and Professional Studies: Dr VIRGINIA HICKS
School of Natural Sciences and Mathematics: Dr COLLEEN NOLAN

UNIVERSITY OF CHARLESTON

2300 MacCorkle Ave, SE, Charleston, WV 25304
Telephone: (304) 357-4800
Fax: (304) 357-4781
E-mail: admissions@ucwv.edu
Internet: www.ucwv.edu
Founded 1888 as Barboursville Seminary, present name 1978
Private control
Academic year: August to April
Areas of study: business administration, forensic accounting, nursing, pharmacy
Pres.: Dr EDWIN H. WELCH
Vice-Pres. for Academic Affairs and Dean for the Faculty: Dr LETHA ZOOK
Vice-Pres. for Admin. and Finance: CLETA M. HARLESS
Vice-Pres. for Communications: JENNIE O. FERRETTI
Vice-Pres. for Devt: BEN BEAKES
Dir for Library Services: JOHN ADKINS
Library of 120,000 vols, 250 print journals and magazines
Number of teachers: 65 (full-time)
Number of students: 1,399

DEANS

School of Business: Dr CHARLES F. STEBBINS
School of Pharmacy: Dr MICHELLE EASTON

WEST LIBERTY UNIVERSITY

POB 295, 208 University Dr., West Liberty, WV 26074
101 Faculty Dr., West Liberty, WV 26074-0295
Telephone: (304) 336-5000
Fax: (304) 336-8403
E-mail: admissions@westliberty.edu
Internet: westliberty.edu
Founded 1837 as West Liberty Acad.
State control
Academic year: August to May (2 semesters)
Pres.: Prof. ROBIN C. CAPEHART
Provost: Dr ANTHONY KOYZIS

Exec. Vice-Pres. and Chief Financial Officer: JOHN WRIGHT, III
Exec. Vice-Pres. and Gen. Counsel: JOHN L. DAVIS
Vice-Pres. for Institutional Advancement: JASON KOEGLER
Dir for Admissions and Recruitment: BRENDA KING
Dir for Institutional Research and Assessment: PAULA TOMASIK
Dean for Students and Registrar: SCOTT A. COOK
Library Dir: CHERYL R. HARSHMAN
Library of 200,000 vols
Number of teachers: 197 (119 full-time, 78 part-time)
Number of students: 2,611 (f.t.e.)

DEANS

College of Arts and Communication: Dr WILLIAM BARONAK
College of Education: Dr KEELY CAMDEN
College of Liberal Arts: BRIAN CRAWFORD
College of Sciences: Dr ROBERT KREISBERG
Gary E. West College of Business: Dr LOREN A. WENZEL
School of Professional Studies: Dr THOMAS MICHAUD

WEST VIRGINIA SCHOOL OF OSTEOPATHIC MEDICINE

400 N Lee St, Lewisburg, WV 24901
Telephone: (304) 647-6238
E-mail: dgetson@osteo.wvsom.edu
Internet: www.wvsom.edu
Founded 1972
State control
Academic year: August to May
Areas of study: biomedical sciences, clinical sciences, osteopathic medical education
Pres.: Dr MICHAEL ADELMAN
Vice-Pres. for Academic Affairs and Dean: LORENZO L. PENCE
Vice-Pres. for Admin. and External Relations: Dr JAMES W. NEMITZ
Vice-Pres. for Finance and Facilities: LARRY WARE
Dir for Admissions: DONNA VARNEY
Registrar: JENNIFER D. SEAMS
Dir for Library: ANNIE McMILLION
Library of 17,000 vols (incl. 450 print journals), 2,000 multimedia titles, 8,000 full-text e-journals, 23,000 osteopathic articles
Number of teachers: 55 (full-time)
Number of students: 800
Publication: *WVSOM Magazine* (4 a year).

WEST VIRGINIA STATE UNIVERSITY

POB 1000, Institute, WV 25112-1000
Telephone: (304) 766-3000
E-mail: admissions@wvstateu.edu
Internet: www.wvstateu.edu
Founded 1891 as West Virginia Collegiate Institute, present name and status 2004
State control
Pres.: Dr HAZO W. CARTER, JR
Provost and Vice-Pres. for Academic Affairs: Dr R. CHARLES BYERS
Vice-Pres. for Admin. Services: Dr CASSANDRA B. WHYTE
Vice-Pres. for Business and Finance: MELVIN JONES
Vice-Pres. for Planning and Advancement: Dr JOHN M. BERRY
Vice-Pres. for Student Affairs: S. BRYCE CASTO
Dir for Library: DAVID CLENDINNING
Library of 200,000 vols, 300 periodical subscriptions, 9,000 bound periodical vols, 200,000 items in microfilm and microfiche

Number of teachers: 253 (137 full-time, 16 part-time)
Number of students: 3,750

DEANS

College of Arts and Humanities: Dr BARBARA LADNER
College of Business and Social Sciences: Dr ABAINESH MITIKU
College of Natural Science and Mathematics: Dr KATHERINE HARPER
College of Professional Studies: Dr ROBERT L. HARRISON, JR

WEST VIRGINIA UNIVERSITY

POB 6201, Morgantown, WV 26506-6201
Telephone: (304) 293-0111
Fax: (304) 293-3080
E-mail: wvuadmissions@mail.wvu.edu
Internet: www.wvu.edu
Founded 1867
State control
Academic year: August to May
Pres.: Dr JAMES P. CLEMENTS
Provost and Vice-Pres.: Dr MICHELE G. WHEATLY
Campus Provost of WVU Institute of Technology: Dr CAROLYN LONG
Provost of Potomac State College of WVU: Dr KERRY S. ODELL
Chancellor for Robert C. Byrd Health Sciences Center: CHRISTOPHER C. COLENDA
Vice-Pres. for Admin. and Finance: NARVEL G. WEESE, JR
Vice-Pres. for Human Resources: MARGARET R. PHILLIPS
Vice-Pres. for Legal Affairs: WILLIAM HUTCHENS
Vice-Pres. for Research and Economic Devt: Dr FRED KING
Vice-Pres. for Student Affairs: KENNETH D. GRAY
Vice-Pres. for Univ. Relations: CHRISTINE MARTIN
Library: see Libraries and Archives
Number of teachers: 2,239
Number of students: 29,306

DEANS

Benjamin M. Statler College of Engineering and Mineral Resources: Dr EUGENE V. CILENTO
College of Business and Economics: Dr JOSE SARTARELLI
College of Creative Arts: Dr PAUL K. KREIDER
College of Human Resources and Education: Dr ELIZABETH DOOLEY
College of Law: JOYCE E. McCONNELL
College of Physical Activity and Sport Sciences: Dr DANA D. BROOKS
Davis College of Agriculture, Natural Resources and Design: Dr RUDOLPH P. ALMASY
Eberly College of Arts and Sciences: Dr ROBERT JONES
Perley Isaac Reed School of Journalism: MARYANNE REED
School of Dentistry: Dr DAVID A. FELTON
School of Medicine: Dr ARTHUR ROSS
School of Nursing: GEORGIA L. NARSAVAGE
School of Pharmacy: PATRICIA A. CHASE

WEST VIRGINIA UNIVERSITY AT PARKERSBURG

300 Campus Dr., Parkersburg, WV 26104-8647
Telephone: (304) 424-8000
Fax: (304) 424-8315
E-mail: wvupinfo@mail.wvu.edu
Internet: www.wvup.edu

Founded 1961 as Parkersburg Br. of West Virginia Univ., present name and status 1989

State control

Areas of study: business, economics, education and humanities, health sciences, languages, mathematics, science and technology, social sciences; technical college affiliated with West Virginia Univ.

Pres.: Dr MARIE FOSTER GNAGE

Sr Vice-Pres. for Academic Affairs: Dr RHONDA TRACY

Vice-Pres. for Student Services: ANTHONY UNDERWOOD

Vice-Pres. for Workforce and Community Education: MARY BETH BUSCH

Registrar: LESLIE SIMS

Library Dir: STEPHEN HUPP

Number of students: 4,300

WEST VIRGINIA WESLEYAN COLLEGE

59 College Ave, Buckhannon, WV 26201

Telephone: (304) 473-8000

Fax: (304) 473-8187

Internet: www.wvwc.edu

Founded 1890

Private control

Offers degrees in arts, athletic training, business administration, education, fine arts—creative writing, music education, science, science in nursing

Pres.: PAMELA BALCH

Vice-Pres. for Academic Affairs and Dean for the College: Dr LARRY R. PARSONS

Vice-Pres. for Admin. and Finance: Dr BARRY R. PRITTS

Vice-Pres. for Information Technology: R. DUWANE SQUIRES

Vice-Pres. for Institutional Advancement: BRENT A. BUSH

Vice-Pres. for Student Affairs and Enrolment Management: JULIA A. KEEHNER

Dir for Admin. Services: KEITH NICHOLS

Dir for Marketing and Communication: ROBERT N. SKINNER, II

Dir for Admission: JOHN R. WALTZ

Dean for Graduate Studies and Extended Learning: Dr KATHLEEN M. LONG

Dir for Library Services: PAULA L. MCGREW

Library of 149,085 vols

Number of teachers: 171 (77 full-time, 94 part-time)

Number of students: 1,405 (undergraduate)

WHEELING JESUIT UNIVERSITY

316 Washington Ave, Wheeling, WV 26003-6295

Telephone: (304) 243-2000

Fax: (304) 243-2243

E-mail: news@wju.edu

Internet: www.wju.edu

Founded 1954 as Wheeling College

Private control

Academic year: August to May

Areas of study: biology, business chemistry, communications and fine arts, computer science, English, history, mathematics, modern languages, nuclear medicine, nursing, philosophy, physical therapy, physics, professional education, psychology, respiratory therapy, social science, theology

Pres.: RICHARD ALLEN BEYER

Univ. Vice-Pres. and Chief of Staff: Fr JAMES FLEMING

Vice-Pres. for Academic Affairs and Dean for the Faculty: Dr STEPHEN STAHL

Vice-Pres. for Enrolment Management: LARRY VALLAR

Vice-Pres. for Institutional Advancement: JAMES HOLT

Dean for Student Devt: Dr CHRISTINE OHL-GIGLIOTTI

Dir for Admissions: JAY DEFRUSCIO (acting)

Registrar: MARK ULSETH

Dir for Library: KELLY MUMMERT (acting)

Library of 139,000 vols

Number of teachers: 97

Number of students: 1,500

WISCONSIN

ALVERNO COLLEGE

POB 343922, 3400 S 43rd St, Milwaukee, WI 53234-3922

Telephone: (414) 382-6000

Fax: (414) 382-6167

E-mail: admissions@alverno.edu

Internet: www.alverno.edu

Founded 1887

Private control

Academic year: August to May

Bachelor of arts, music, science, science in nursing; Master of arts, business administration, science in nursing; Master of science in community psychology

Chair.: MAURICE J. MCSWEENEY

Pres.: Dr MARY J. MEEHAN

Sr Vice-Pres. for Academic Affairs: Dr KATHLEEN O'BRIEN

Sr Vice-Pres. for Finance and Management Services: JAMES K. OPPERMANN

Vice-Pres. for Marketing and Enrolment Management: SUSAN M. SMITH

Registrar: PATRICIA HARTMAN

Dir for Library: CAROL BRILL

Library of 82,416 vols, 1,382 periodicals, 287,726 microforms, 15,728 audiovisual items

Number of teachers: 118 (full-time)

Number of students: 2,759

Publication: *Alverno Magazine*.

BELLIN COLLEGE

3201 Eaton Rd, Green Bay, WI 54311

Telephone: (920) 433-6699

Fax: (920) 433-1922

Internet: www.bellincollege.edu

Founded 1909 as Deaconess Sanitarium Training School, present name 2009

Private control

Offers BSc in nursing and radiologic sciences; MSc in nursing

Pres. and CEO: Dr CONNIE J. BOERST

Vice-Pres. for Academic Affairs: Dr CONNIE J. BOERST

Vice-Pres. for Business and Finance: JOSEPH KEEBAUGH

Vice-Pres. for Devt and Public Relations: MATT RENTMEESTER

Vice-Pres. for Student Services: JOANN WOELFEL

Dir for Admissions: KATIE KLAUS

Registrar: VICKY SCHAULAND

Librarian: CINDY REINL

Number of teachers: 19

Number of students: 290

BELOIT COLLEGE

700 College St, Beloit, WI 53511

Telephone: (608) 363-2000

Fax: (608) 363-2075

E-mail: admiss@beloit.edu

Internet: www.beloit.edu

Founded 1846

Private control

Academic year: August to May

Pres.: SCOTT BIERMAN

Provost and Dean for the College: ANN DAVIES

Vice-Pres. for Admin. and Treas.: JOHN M. NICHOLAS

Vice-Pres. for Enrolment Services: NANCY MONNICH

Dean for Students: CHRISTINA KLAWITTER

Dir for Admissions: JIM ZIELINSKI

Registrar: MARY BOROS-KAZAI

Dir for Library and Archives: LISA VIEZBICKE

Library of 268,000 vols, 31,726 periodical and newspaper titles

Number of teachers: 127

Number of students: 1,275

Publications: *Avatar* (1 a year), *Beloit Magazine* (3 a year), *The Round Table* (36 a year).

CARDINAL STRITCH UNIVERSITY

6801 N Yates Rd, Milwaukee, WI 53217

Telephone: (414) 410-4000

Fax: (414) 410-4088

Internet: www.stritch.edu

Founded 1937, present name and status 1997

Private control

Academic year: April to August

Chancellor: Dr M. CAMILLE KLIEBHAN

Pres.: Dr JAMES P. LOFTUS

Exec. Vice-Pres. and Chief Operating Officer: DAVID WEINBERG-KINSEY

Exec. Vice-Pres. for Academic Affairs: Dr TIA BOJAR

Exec. Vice-Pres. for Admin. and Chief Financial Officer: THOMAS W. VANHIMBERGEN

Vice-Pres. and Chief Information Officer: THOMAS J. RAINS

Vice-Pres. for Enrolment Services: JOHN MUELLER

Vice-Pres. for Student Devt and Dean for Students: CHRISTINE ROBINSON

Vice-Pres. for Univ. Advancement: MICHAEL J. BRAUER

Registrar: CHRISTINE L. GLYNN

Dir for Library and Learning Services: DAVID WEINBERG-KINSEY

Library of 139,000 vols

Number of teachers: 98

Number of students: 6,093

Publication: *Stritch Magazine* (2 a year, online (www.stritch.edu/magazine))

DEANS

College of Arts and Sciences: Dr DANIEL SCHOLZ

College of Business and Management: Dr PETER J. HOLBROOK

College of Education and Leadership: Dr FREDA RUSSELL

Ruth S. Coleman College of Nursing: Dr RUTH M. WAITE

CARROLL UNIVERSITY

100 N East Ave, Waukesha, WI 53186

Telephone: (414) 547-1211

Fax: (414) 524-7139

E-mail: info@carrollu.edu

Internet: www.carrollu.edu

Founded 1846 as Carroll College, present name and status 2008

Bachelors in arts, science, science in nursing, music education, masters in education, software engineering, business admin., physician assistant studies and doctor of physical therapy degrees

Academic year: August to July (2 semesters)

Pres.: Dr DOUGLAS N. HASTAD

Provost and Vice-Pres. for Academic Affairs: Dr JOANNE PASSARO

Dean of Students: Dr THERESA BARRY

Library Dir: LELAN E. MCLEMORE

Library of 196,000 vols, 140,000 journals

Number of teachers: 125 full-time
Number of students: 3,535 full-time

DEANS

College of Humanities and Social Sciences: CHARLES A. BYLER
College of Natural Sciences, Health Sciences and Business: JANE F. HOPP

CARTHAGE COLLEGE

2001 Alford Park Dr., Kenosha, WI 53140
Telephone: (262) 551-8500
Fax: (262) 551-5762
E-mail: admissions@carthage.edu
Internet: www.carthage.edu
Founded 1847, present name 1870
Private control

4 Year courses in liberal arts and sciences; academic divs: education, fine arts, humanities, interdisciplinary studies, natural science, social science
Pres.: Dr F. GREGORY CAMPBELL
Provost: Prof. JULIO RIVERA
Assoc. Provost: DAVID STEEGE
Sr Vice-Pres. for Academic Resources: BRAD ANDREWS
Sr Vice-Pres. for Admin. and Business: WILLIAM ABT
Vice-Pres. for Library and Information Services: TODD KELLEY
Assoc. Vice-Pres. for Communications: ROBERT ROSEN
Dean for Students: LOUISE PASKEY
Number of teachers: 150
Number of students: 3,400

COLLEGE OF MENOMINEE NATION

N 172 Hwy 47/55, POB 1179, Keshena, WI 54135
Telephone: (715) 799-5600
Internet: www.menominee.edu
Tribal control
Academic year: August to July
Areas of study: arts and sciences, applied science, nursing, science, technical; campus at Green Bay
Pres.: Dr S. VERNA FOWLER
Vice-Pres. for Academic Affairs: DONNA POWLESS
Vice-Pres. for Finance: LAURIE REITER
Vice-Pres. for Student Services: GARY BESAW
Vice-Pres. for Oneida Campus: NORBERT HILL JR
Vice-Pres. for Planning and Operations: RONALD JURGENS
Library of 154,336 vols
Number of teachers: 51 (28 full-time, 23 part-time)
Number of students: 634 (356 full-time, 278 part-time)

COLUMBIA COLLEGE OF NURSING, INC.

4425 N Port Washington Rd, Glendale, WI 53212
Telephone: (414) 326-2330
Fax: (414) 326-2331
E-mail: cconinformation@ccon.edu
Internet: www.ccon.edu
Founded 1901, present name 1909
Private control
Academic year: August to May (2 semesters)
Areas of study: medical sonography and radiologic technology
Dean and CEO: Prof. Dr JILL WINTERS
Registrar: HALEY JO GEIGER
Man. for Library Services: SHARON WOCHOS.

CONCORDIA UNIVERSITY WISCONSIN

12800 N Lake Shore Dr., Mequon, WI 53097-2418
Telephone: (262) 243-5700
Fax: (262) 243-4351
E-mail: admissions@cuw.edu
Internet: www.cuw.edu
Founded 1881 as Concordia College, present name and status 1989
Pres.: Rev. Dr PATRICK T. FERRY
Exec. Vice-Pres. and Chief Operating Officer: ALLEN J. PROCHNOW
Vice-Pres. for Academic Operations: Dr MICHAEL BESCH
Vice-Pres. for Student Affairs: Dr ANDREW LUPTAK
Dir for Library Services: CHRISTIAN R. HIMSEL
Library of 114,000 vols, 600 print periodical subscriptions, 20,000 e-periodicals
Number of teachers: 277 (128 full-time, 149 part-time)
Number of students: 7,485 (3,610 full-time, 3,875 part-time)

DEANS

School of Arts and Sciences: Dr GAYLUND K. STONE
School of Business and Legal Studies: Dr DAVID BORST
School of Education: Dr MICHAEL UDEN
School of Human Services: Dr RUTH GRESLEY
School of Pharmacy: Dr DEAN L. ARNESON

EDGEWOOD COLLEGE

1000 Edgewood College Dr., Madison, WI 53711-1997
Telephone: (608) 663-4861
Fax: (608) 663-3291
E-mail: admissions@edgewood.edu
Internet: www.edgewood.edu
Founded 1927
Private control
Academic year: September to May
Pres.: Dr DANIEL J. CAREY
Vice-Pres. for Academic Affairs and Academic Dean: MARY KELLY-POWELL
Vice-Pres. for Student Devt and Dean for Students: Dr MAGGIE BALISTRERI-CLARKE
Registrar: ELLEN FEHRING
Dir for Library: SYLVIA CONTRERAS
Library of 125,000 vols
Number of teachers: 159 (72 full-time, 87 part-time)
Number of students: 2,650

DEANS

School of Arts and Sciences: Dr BRANDON CLAYCOMB
School of Business: Prof. MARTIN A. PREIZLER
School of Education: Dr JANE BELMORE
School of Integrative Studies: DEAN A. PRIBBENOW
School of Nursing: Dr MARGARET C. NOREUIL

HERZING UNIVERSITY

5218 E Terrace Dr., Madison, WI 53718
Telephone: (608) 249-6611
Fax: (608) 249-8593
E-mail: info@msn.herzing.edu
Internet: www.herzing.edu
Founded 1965, present name and status 2009
Private control
Academic year: January to December (3 semesters)
11 Campuses in 8 states: Birmingham (Alabama), Winter Park (Florida), Atlanta (Georgia), Kenner (Los Angeles), Crystal (Minnesota), Omaha (Nebraska), Akron (Ohio), Toledo (Ohio); areas of study: business management, electronics, graphic design and public safety, health care
Pres.: RENÉE HERZING
Vice-Pres. for Finance and Chief Financial Officer: RYAN O'DESKY
Vice-Pres. for Information Technology: CHRISTY CRUTE
Chief Academic Officer: Dr BILL GETTER.

LAKELAND COLLEGE

POB 359, Sheboygan, WI 53082-0359
Telephone: (414) 565-2166
Fax: (414) 565-1515
Internet: www.lakeland.edu
Founded 1862 as Missionshaus, present name 1956
Areas of study: business administration, creative arts, education, general. studies, humanities, natural sciences, social sciences; 7 campuses in Wisconsin and 1 campus in Tokyo; distance education programmes
Private control
Pres.: Dr STEPHEN A. GOULD
Sr Vice-Pres. for Admin.: DANIEL W. ECK
Vice-Pres. for Academic Affairs and Dean for the College: Dr MARGARET ALBRINCK
Vice-Pres. for Advancement: KEN D. STRMISKA
Vice-Pres. for Finance: JOSEPH D. BOTANA, II
Vice-Pres. for Int. Programmes and Gen. Counsel: E. ANTHONY FESSLER
Vice-Pres. for Student Devt: NATHAN D. DEHNE
Dean for Students: SANDRA GIBBONS-VOLLBRECHT
Dir for Library Services: ANN PENKE
Library of 65,000 vols, 300 periodicals
Number of teachers: 41
Number of students: 4,000
Publication: Lakeland (3 a year).

LAWRENCE UNIVERSITY

711 E Boldt Way, SPC 29 Appleton, WI 54911
115 S Drew St, Appleton, WI 54911
Telephone: (920) 832-7000
Fax: (920) 832-6782
E-mail: excel@lawrence.edu
Internet: www.lawrence.edu
Founded 1847, present name and status 1964
Private control
Academic year: September to June
Language of instruction: English, French, German, Japanese, Russian, Spanish
College of liberal arts and sciences with conservatory of music
Pres.: Dr JILL BECK
Provost and Dean for the Faculty: DAVID BURROWS
Vice-Pres. for Alumni, Devt and Communications: CALVIN HUSMANN
Vice-Pres. for Student Affairs and Dean for Students: NANCY D. TRUESDELL
Dean for Admissions and Financial Aid: KEN ANSELMENT
Registrar: ANNE S. NORMAN
Library Dir: PETER GILBERT
Library of 394,383 vols, 344,118 govt documents, 2,478 current periodical subscriptions, 17,786 music scores, and 143,083 video cassettes, recordings and microform items, 3,400 rare book colln
Number of teachers: 156 (full-time)
Number of students: 1,566
Publication: Lawrence Today (4 a year).

MARANATHA BAPTIST BIBLE COLLEGE

745 West Main St, Watertown, WI 53094

Telephone: (920) 261-9300
Fax: (920) 261-9109
E-mail: admissions@mbbc.edu
Internet: www.mbbc.edu

Founded 1968
Private control
Academic year: September to May

Areas of study: applied science, Bible and church ministries, business, humanities, music, nursing, teacher education

Pres.: Dr S. MARTIN MARRIOTT
Vice-Pres. for Academic Affairs: Dr JOHN BROCK
Vice-Pres. for Business Affairs: MARK STEVENS
Vice-Pres. for Institutional Advancement: Dr JIM HARRISON
Dean for Students: DOUG RICHARDS
Registrar: DAVID HERSHBERGER

Library of 124,000 vols
Number of teachers: 40
Number of students: 862

MARIAN UNIVERSITY

45 S National Ave, Fond du Lac, WI 54935-4699

Telephone: (920) 923-7600
Fax: (920) 923-7154
Internet: www.marianuniversity.edu

Founded 1936 as Marian College, present name and status 2008
Private control
Academic year: August to May

Campuses at Appleton, West Allis, Green Bay, Kenosha, Madison, Watertown, Wausau and West Bend

Pres.: Dr STEVEN DiSALVO
Exec. Vice-Pres. for Academic and Student Affairs: Dr EDWARD H. OGLE
Vice-Pres. for Academic Affairs: Dr JIM VAN DYKE
Vice-Pres. for Advancement: PAUL NEUBERGER
Vice-Pres. for Mission and Retention: KATE CANDEE
Dean for Students: KERRY STRUPP
Registrar: CHERYL TEICHMILLER
Dir for Libraries: MARY ELLEN GORMICAN

Library of 92,000 vols
Number of teachers: 96 (93 full-time, 3 part-time)
Number of students: 2,903 (full-time)

Publication: *Marian University Magazine*

DEANS

School of Arts, Humanities and Letters: Dr JAMES VAN DYKE
School of Business: Dr JEFFREY G. REED
School of Criminal Justice: Dr MICHELLE MAJEWSKI
School of Education: Dr SUE STODDART
School of Math and Natural Science: Dr LANCE URVEN
School of Nursing: Dr JULIE LUETSCHWAGER
School of Social and Behavioral Science: Dr LARRY REYNOLDS

MARQUETTE UNIVERSITY

POB 1881, Milwaukee, WI 53201-1881
1250 W Wisconsin Ave, Milwaukee, WI 53233

Telephone: (414) 288-7250
Fax: (414) 288-7197
E-mail: admissions@marquette.edu
Internet: www.marquette.edu

Founded 1881 as Marquette College, chartered as univ. in 1907

Private control

Pres.: Rev. SCOTT R. PILARZ
Provost: Dr JOHN J. PAULY
Provost: Dr GARY MEYER
Vice-Provost for Research and Dean for the Graduate School: Dr JEANNE HOSSENLOPP
Assoc. Sr Vice-Pres.: Dr THOMAS J. PETERS
Assoc. Sr Vice-Pres.: ANNE O'BRIEN
Vice-Pres. and Gen. Counsel: CYNTHIA M. BAUER
Vice-Pres. for Admin.: ARTHUR F. SCHEUBER
Vice-Pres. for Finance: JOHN C. LAMB
Vice-Pres. for Marketing and Communication: TRICIA GERAGHTY
Vice-Pres. for Mission and Ministry: STEPHANIE RUSSELL
Vice-Pres. for Public Affairs: RANA H. ALTENBURG
Vice-Pres. for Student Affairs: Dr L. CHRISTOPHER MILLER
Vice-Pres. for Univ. Advancement: JULIE TOLAN
Dean for Undergraduate Admissions and Enrollment Planning: ROBY BLUST
Dean for Univ. Libraries: JANICE SIMMONS-WELBURN

Library of 4,000,000 vols
Number of teachers: 1,100
Number of students: 12,002 (8,387 undergraduate, 3,615 professional)

DEANS

College of Business Administration and Graduate School of Management: Dr LINDA M. SALCHENBERGER
College of Education: WILLIAM A. HENK
College of Engineering: Dr ROBERT H. BISHOP
College of Health Sciences: Dr WILLIAM E. CULLINAN
College of Nursing: Dr MARGARET FAUT-CALLAHAN
College of Professional Studies: Dr ROBERT J. DEAHL
Helen Way Klingler College of Arts and Sciences: PHILIP J. ROSSI
J. William and Mary Diederich College of Communication: Dr LORI BERGEN
Law School: JOSEPH D. KEARNEY
School of Dentistry: Dr WILLIAM K. LOBB
The Graduate School: Dr JEANNE HOSSENLOPP

MEDICAL COLLEGE OF WISCONSIN

8701 Watertown Plank Rd, Milwaukee, WI 53226

Telephone: (414) 955-8296
Fax: (414) 955-6550
E-mail: officeofthepresident@mcw.edu
Internet: www.mcw.edu

Founded 1893 as Wisconsin College of Physicians and Surgeons, present name 1970
Private control

Offers degrees in basic and translational research, biochemistry, biophysics, biostatistics, cell biology, neurobiology and anatomy, micro biology and molecular genetics, pharmacology and toxicology, physiology, public and community health and functional imaging

Pres. and CEO: JOHN R. RAYMOND, SR
Exec. Vice-Pres. and Dean for Medical School: Dr JOSEPH E. KERSCHNER
Sr Vice-Pres. for Finance and Admin.: GLENN ALLEN BOLTON, JR
Assoc. Dean for Student Affairs: Dr RICHARD HOLLOWAY

Library of 252,000 vols, 6,000 online journals, 3,400 e-books
Number of teachers: 1,590
Number of students: 1,265

MILWAUKEE INSTITUTE OF ART AND DESIGN

273 E Erie St, Milwaukee, WI 53202

Telephone: (414) 847-3200
Fax: (414) 291-8077
E-mail: miadadm@miad.edu
Internet: www.miad.edu

Founded 1920, present name and status 1974
Private control

Areas of study: advertising, animation, art history, business, communication design, drawing, illustration, industrial design, integrated studio arts, interior architecture and design, multidisciplinary fine arts, painting, photography, printmaking, sculpture, time-based media, video, writing

Pres.: NEIL HOFFMAN
Provost and Vice-Pres. for Academic Affairs: DAVID MARTIN (acting)
Vice-Pres. for Enrolment Management: MARY SCHOPP
Assoc. Vice-Pres. for Academic Planning and Assessment: CYNTHIA LYNCH
Dean for Students: TONY NOWAK
Registrar: JEAN WEIMER

Library of 500,000 vols, 2,000 video cassettes
Number of students: 700
Number of teachers: 200

MILWAUKEE SCHOOL OF ENGINEERING

1025 N Broadway, Milwaukee, WI 53202-3109

Telephone: (414) 277-6763
Fax: (414) 277-7475
E-mail: explore@msoe.edu
Internet: www.msoe.edu

Founded 1903
Private control
Academic year: September to May

Int. programmes in Lübeck, Germany, Prague, Czech Republic, India

Pres.: Dr HERMANN VIETS
Vice-Pres. for Academics: Dr FREDERICK BERRY
Vice-Pres. for Devt: FRANK HABIB
Vice-Pres. for Enrolment Management: TIM VALLEY
Vice-Pres. for Finance and Chief Financial Officer: ARMUND JANTO
Vice-Pres. for Student Life and Dean for Students: PATRICK J. COFFEY
Library Dir: GARY SHIMEK

Library of 45,000 vols, 300 print journals, 100,000 e-books and 90,000 e-journals
Number of teachers: 133 (full-time)
Number of students: 2,486

Publication: *Dimensions* (3 a year).

MOUNT MARY COLLEGE

2900 N Menomonee River Parkway, Milwaukee, WI 53222-4597

Telephone: (414) 258-4810
E-mail: mccrediw@mtmary.edu
Internet: www.mtmary.edu

Founded as St. Mary's Institute, present name and status 1913
Private control

Areas of study: art and design, business administration., education and mathematics, health and sciences, language, literature and communication, philosophy and theology, social sciences

Pres.: Dr EILEEN SCHWALBACH
Vice-Pres. for Academic and Student Affairs: Dr DAVID NIXON
Vice-Pres. for Enrolment Services: DAVE WEGENER

Vice-Pres. for External Relations: DONNA GASTEVICH
Vice-Pres. for Finance and Admin.: REYES GONZALEZ
Vice-Pres. for Mission and Identity: Dr JOAN PENZENSTADLER
Library Dir: JULIE KAMIKAWA
Library of 111,000 vols
Number of teachers: 144
Number of students: 1,963

NASHOTAH HOUSE

2777 Mission Rd, Nashotah, WI 53058
Telephone: (262) 646-6500
E-mail: nashotah@nashotah.edu
Internet: www.nashotah.edu
Founded 1842, chartered in 1847
Private control
Academic year: July to June
Seminary of the Episcopal Church in the Anglican Communion of Churches; areas of study: Anglican studies, arts, divinity and ministry, theological studies
Pres. and Dean: Rt Rev. EDWARD L. SALMON, JR
Provost: Rev. Dr RICHARD LONGABAUGH
Assoc. Dean for Academic Affairs: Rev. Dr STEVEN PEAY
Dir for Admissions: Dr CAROL KLUKAS
Dir for Library: DAVID SHERWOOD
Library of 100,000 vols, 280 current periodicals
Number of teachers: 11
Number of students: 126
Publication: *The Missioner*.

NORTHLAND COLLEGE

1411 Ellis Ave, Ashland, WI 54806-3999
Telephone: (715) 682-1699
Fax: (715) 682-1308
E-mail: admit@northland.edu
Internet: www.northland.edu
Founded 1892, present name and status 1906
Private control
Academic year: September to May
Language of instruction: English
Pres.: MICHAEL A. MILLER
Vice-Pres. for Academic Affairs and Academic Dean: ALAN BREW
Vice-Pres. for Enrolment Management: RICK J. SMITH
Vice-Pres. for Finance and Admin.: ROBERT JACKSON
Vice-Pres. for Institutional Advancement: KRISTY LIPHART
Vice-Pres. for Marketing: DAVID WAHLBERG
Dean for Student Life: MICHELE MEYER
Dir for Sigurd Olson Environmental Institute: MARK LEACH
Registrar: KATHY TRAYNOR
Library Dir: JULIA WAGGONER
Library of 76,640 vols, 250 print periodical subscriptions
Number of teachers: 45 (full-time)
Number of students: 700
Publications: *Eco-Vision* (1 a year), *Northland College Magazine* (2 a year), *The Drifts* (student paper, print and online)

PROFESSORS

ALLDRITT, L., Religion
DAMRELL, J., Sociology and Anthropology
DILLENSCHNEIDER, C., Outdoor Education
GLICKMAN, J., Music
GOETZ, B., Geoscience
GORMAN, W., Biology
GOYKE, A., Biology
JOYAL, R., Business Administration and Economics
KIM, Y., Mathematics and Computer Information Systems

SMALL, M., English and Modern Languages

RIPON COLLEGE

POB 248, Ripon, WI 54971
Telephone: (920) 748-8115
Fax: (920) 748-8335
E-mail: adminfo@ripon.edu
Internet: www.ripon.edu
Founded 1851, present status 1863
Private control
Academic year: August to June (2 semesters)
Liberal arts and sciences college
Pres.: Rev. Dr DAVID C. JOYCE
Vice-Pres. and Dean for Faculty: GERALD SEAMAN
Vice-Pres. and Dean for Students: CHRISTOPHER M. OGLE
Vice-Pres. for Advancement: WAYNE WEBSTER
Vice-Pres. for Finance: MARY deREGNIER
Dean for Admissions: LEIGH MLODZIK
Dean for Faculty and Registrar: MICHELE WITTLER
Chair. for Library Dept: ANDREW PRELLWITZ
Library of 150,000 vols
Number of teachers: 75
Number of students: 1,057

SACRED HEART SCHOOL OF THEOLOGY

POB 429, 7335 S Highway 100, Hales Corners, WI 53130-0429
Telephone: (414) 425-8300
Fax: (414) 529-6999
Internet: www.shst.edu
Founded 1932, present name 1972
Private control
Academic year: August to June
Language of instruction: English
Pres. and Rector: Very Rev. JAN DE JONG
Vice-Rector and Vice-Pres. for External Affairs: Rev. THOMAS L. KNOEBEL
Vice-Pres. for Academic Affairs and Academic Dean: Rev. RAÚL GÓMEZ RUIZ
Vice-Pres. for Finance: SALLY A. SMITS
Vice-Pres. for Human and Spiritual Formation: Rev. PETER SCHUESSLER
Academic Dean: Rev. RAUL GOMEZ
Dir for Pastoral Education: Rev. ROBERT SCHIAVONE
Registrar: ROSE KOPENEC
Dir for Library: SUSANNA PATHAK
Library of 100,000 vols, 450 periodicals
Number of teachers: 39
Number of students: 174

ST NORBERT COLLEGE

100 Grant St, De Pere, WI 54115-2099
Telephone: (920) 403-3005
Fax: (920) 403-4072
E-mail: admit@snc.edu
Internet: www.snc.edu
Founded 1898
Private control
Language of instruction: English, French, German, Japanese, Spanish
Academic year: August to May
Areas of study: humanities and fine arts, natural sciences, social sciences
Pres.: THOMAS KUNKEL
Vice-Pres. for Business and Finance: EILEEN M. JAHNKE
Vice-Pres. for College Advancement: PHIL OSWALD
Vice-Pres. for Enrolment Management and Communications: BRIDGET KRAGE O'CONNOR
Vice-Pres. for Mission and Student Affairs: Rev. Dr JAY FOSTNER
Dean for the College and Academic Vice-Pres.: Dr JEFFREY FRICK

Registrar: RICHARD GUILD
Dir for Library: SALLY L. HANSEN
Library of 247,000 vols
Number of teachers: 197 (139 full-time, 58 part-time)
Number of students: 2,225 (2174 undergraduate, 51 graduate)
Publications: *St. Norbert College Magazine* (3 a year), *The Chronicle* (online).

SILVER LAKE COLLEGE OF THE HOLY FAMILY

2406 S Alverno Rd, Manitowoc, WI 54220-9319
Telephone: (920) 684-6691
Fax: (920) 684-7082
E-mail: admslc@sl.edu
Internet: www.sl.edu
Founded 1935, present name 1972
Private control
Academic year: May to August
Depts of art, English and world languages, history, mathematics and computer sciences, music, natural science, nursing, psychology, religious studies and philosophy, social science, studio art
Pres.: Dr GEORGE ARNOLD
Vice-Pres. for Advancement and External Relations: JAKE CZARNIK-NEIMEYER
Academic Dean: Dr JULIE MAYROSE
Dean for Students: Dr GEORGE GRINDE
Registrar: JANICE STINGLE
Dir for Library Services: RITA ROSE STAHL
Library of 60,000 vols, 250 current print periodicals and newspapers
Number of teachers: 122 (42 full-time, 80 part-time)
Number of students: 1,000
Publications: *Silver Reflections* (1 a year), *SLC Update* (52 a year).

UNIVERSITY OF WISCONSIN SYSTEM

1720 Van Hise Hall, 1220 Linden Dr., Madison, WI 53706-1559
Telephone: (608) 262-2321
Fax: (608) 262-3985
Internet: www.wisconsin.edu
Founded 1848 as Univ. of Wisconsin, merged with the Wisconsin State Univs system 1971
State control
13 Instns offering 4-year courses (constituent univs), and 2 other instns offering 2-year courses (other constituent institutions)
Pres.: KEVIN P. REILLY
Sr Vice-Pres. for Admin. and Fiscal Affairs: MICHAEL MORGAN
Sr Vice-Pres. for Academic Affairs: MARK NOOK
Vice-Pres. for Finance: DEBORAH A. DURCAN
Assoc. Vice-Pres. for Academic and Faculty Programs: STEPHEN KOLISON
Assoc. Vice-Pres. for Budget and Planning: FREDA HARRIS
Assoc. Vice-Pres. for Equity, Diversity and Inclusion: VICKI WASHINGTON
Assoc. Vice-Pres. for Human Resources: ALAN CRIST
Gen. Counsel: TOMAS STAFFORD
Number of teachers: 32,000
Number of students: 182,000 (26 campuses).

CONSTITUENT UNIVERSITIES

University of Wisconsin—Eau Claire
POB 4004, 105 Garfield Ave, Eau Claire, WI 54702-4004
Telephone: (715) 836-2637
Fax: (715) 836-2902
Internet: www.uwec.edu

Founded 1916 as Eau Claire State Normal School, present status 1971
Academic year: September to May
Chancellor: Dr BRIAN LEVIN-STANKEVICH
Provost and Vice-Chancellor for Academic Affairs: PATRICIA A. KLEINE
Vice-Chancellor for Student Affairs: BETH A. HELLWIG
Dean for Students: BRIAN CARLISLE
Registrar: JIM BARRETT
Dir for Libraries: JOHN POLITZ

Library of 1,680,588 vols, 162,756 govt documents, 27,085 Wisconsin documents, 1,066,446 microfilms and microfiches, 36,768 periodical and newspaper subscriptions, 12,152 audiovisual materials, 61,087 maps
Number of teachers: 796
Number of students: 11,233

DEANS

College of Arts and Sciences: MARTY WOOD
College of Business: DIANE HOADLEY
College of Education and Human Sciences: GAIL SCUKANEC
College of Nursing and Health Sciences: Prof. Dr LINDA K. YOUNG

University of Wisconsin—Green Bay

2420 Nicolet Dr., Green Bay, WI 54311-7001
Telephone: (920) 465-2000
Fax: (920) 465-2032
E-mail: uwgb@uwgb.edu
Internet: www.uwgb.edu
Founded 1965
Academic year: September to May
Chancellor: Dr THOMAS HARDEN
Provost and Vice-Chancellor for Academic Affairs: Dr JULIA E. WALLACE
Vice-Chancellor for Business and Finance (vacant)
Vice-Chancellor for Planning and Budget: Dr DEAN RODEHEAVER
Dean for Students: BRENDA AMENSON-HILL
Registrar: AMANDA HRUSKA
Library Dir: PAULA GANYARD

Library of 285,000 vols, 1m. bibliographic items, 50,000 maps, 2,000 music scores
Number of teachers: 356
Number of students: 6,636

DEANS

College of Liberal Arts and Sciences: SCOTT R. FURLONG
College of Professional Studies: Dr SUE J. MATTISON

University of Wisconsin—La Crosse

1725 State St, La Crosse, WI 54601
Telephone: (608) 785-8000
Fax: (608) 785-8809
Internet: www.uwlax.edu
Founded 1909 as La Crosse Normal School
Chancellor: JOE GOW
Provost and Vice-Chancellor for Academic Affairs: KATHLEEN ENZ FINKEN
Vice-Chancellor for Admin. and Finance: BOB HETZEL
Asst Chancellor and Dean for Students: Dr PAULA M. KNUDSON
Dean for Student Devt and Academic Services: Dr PAULA M. KNUDSON
Dir for Library: ANITA EVANS

Library of 500,370 vols, 209,745 e-books, 10,697 current serial titles, 581,624 microforms, 14,372 audiovisual material, 120,0331 govt documents
Number of teachers: 612
Number of students: 10,135

DEANS

College of Business Administration: Dr BILL COLCLOUGH

College of Liberal Studies: RUTHANN E. BENSON
College of Science and Health: BRUCE RILEY

University of Wisconsin—Madison

Madison, WI 53706
Telephone: (608) 263-2400
Fax: (608) 262-8333
Internet: www.wisc.edu
Founded 1848, present status 1904
Academic year: September to May
Chancellor: DAVID WARD
Provost and Vice-Chancellor for Academic Affairs: PAUL M. DeLUCA, JR
Vice-Chancellor for Admin. and Budget: DARRELL BAZZELL
Vice-Chancellor for Medical Affairs: ROBERT N. GOLDEN
Vice-Chancellor for Research and Dean for Graduate School: MARTIN T. CADWALLADER
Vice-Chancellor for Univ. Relations: VINCE SWEENEY
Dean for Students: LORI BERQUAM
Registrar: SCOTT OWCZAREK
Dir for Admissions: ADELE C. BRUMIELD
Dir-Gen. for Library System: KENNETH FRAZIER

Library: see Libraries and Archives
Number of teachers: 2,177
Number of students: 42,595

DEANS

College of Agricultural and Life Sciences: KATHRYN VANDENBOSCH
College of Engineering: PAUL S. PEERCY
College of Letters and Science: GARY SANDEFUR
Division of Continuing Studies: JEFFREY RUSSELL
Division of Int. Studies: GILLES BOUSQUET
Law School: MARGARET RAYMOND
School of Education: JULIE UNDERWOOD
School of Human Ecology: ROBIN A. DOUTHITT
School of Medicine and Public Health: Dr ROBERT N. GOLDEN
School of Nursing: Prof. KATHARYN A. MAY
School of Pharmacy: JEANETTE ROBERTS
School of Veterinary Medicine: Dr DARYL D. BUSS
Wisconsin School of Business: FRANÇOIS ORTALO-MAGNÉ

PROFESSORS

Some professors serve in more than one college or school

College of Agriculture and Life Sciences (116 Agricultural Hall, 1450 Linden Dr., Madison, WI 53706; tel. (608) 262-3003; fax (608) 265-5905; e-mail info@cals.wisc.edu; internet www.cals.wisc.edu):

ALANEN, A. R., Landscape Architecture
ALBRECHT, K. A., Agronomy
ALBRECHT, R. M., Animal Science
AMASINO, R. M., Biochemistry
ANDERSON, P., Genetics
ANDREWS, J. H., Plant Pathology
ARMENTANO, L. E., Dairy Science
ATKINSON, R. L., Nutritional Sciences, Medicine
ATTIE, A. D., Biochemistry
BALKE, N. E., Agronomy
BARHAM, B. L., Program on Agricultural Technology Studies
BISHOP, J. R., Food Science
BISHOP, R. C., Agricultural and Applied Economics
BLAND, W. L., Soil Science
BLATTNER, F. R., Genetics
BLEAM, W. F., Soil Science
BOCKHEIM, J. G., Soil Science
BOERBOOM, C. M., Agronomy
BOHNHOFF, D. R., Biological Systems Engineering

BROMLEY, D. W., Agricultural and Applied Economics
BROWN, M. R., Life Sciences Communication
BUEGE, D. R., Animal Science
BUNDY, L. G., Soil Science
BUONGIORNO, J., Forest Ecology and Management
BUTTEL, F. H., Rural Sociology
CAMPBELL, G. R., Agricultural and Applied Economics
CARROLL, S. B., Genetics
CARTER, M. R., Agricultural and Applied Economics
CHAMBLISS, G. H., Bacteriology
CHENOWETH, R. E., Urban and Regional Planning
CLAGETT-DAME, M., Biochemistry
CLAYTON, M. K., Statistics
CLELAND, W. W., Biochemistry
COLLINS, J. L., Rural Sociology, Women's Studies Program
COMBS, D. K., Dairy Science
CONVERSE, J. C., Biological Systems Engineering
COOK, M. E., Animal Science
COORS, J. G., Agronomy
COX, M. M., Biochemistry
COX, T. L., Agricultural and Applied Economics
COXHEAD, I. A., Agricultural and Applied Economics
CRAIG, E. A., Biochemistry
CRAVEN, S. R., Wildlife Ecology
CRENSHAW, T. D., Animal Science
DAMODARAN, S., Food Science
DELLER, S. C., Agricultural and Applied Economics
DeLUCA, H. F., Biochemistry
DOEBLEY, J., Genetics
DOLL, J. D., Agronomy
DONOHUE, T. J., Bacteriology
DOWNS, D. M., Bacteriology
DUKE, S. H., Agronomy
EIDE, D. J., Nutritional Sciences
ENGELS, W. R., Genetics
ESCALANTE, J. C., Bacteriology
ETZEL, M. R., Food Science
FIELD, D. R., Forest Ecology and Management
FILUTOWICZ, M. S., Bacteriology
FIRST, N. L., Animal Science
FOX, B. G., Biochemistry, Enzyme Institute
FREY, P. A., Biochemistry
FRIESEN, P. D., Biochemistry, Institute for Molecular Virology
GANETZKY, B. S., Genetics
GERMAN, T. L., Entomology
GIANOLA, D., Animal Science
GILBERT, J. C., Rural Sociology
GOLDMAN, I. L., Horticulture
GOODMAN, R. M., Plant Pathology
GOODMAN, W. G., Entomology
GOURSE, R. L., Bacteriology
GOWER, S. T., Forest Ecology and Management
GRAU, C. R., Plant Pathology
GREASER, M. L., Animal Science
GREEN, G. P., Rural Sociology
GRUMMER, R. R., Dairy Science
GUNASEKARAN, S., Biological Systems Engineering
GUNTHER, A. C., Life Sciences Communication
GURIES, R. P., Forest Ecology and Management
HANDELSMAN, J., Plant Pathology
HARRINGTON, J. A., Landscape Architecture
HARRIS, P. E., Agricultural and Applied Economics
HARTEL, R. W., Food Science
HAYES, C. E., Biochemistry
HELMKE, P. A., Soil Science
HICKEY, W. J., Soil Science
HITCHON, J. C., Life Sciences Communication

HOLDEN, H. M., Biochemistry
HOLMES, B. J., Biological Systems Engineering
HOWELL, E. A., Landscape Architecture
INGHAM, S. C., Food Science
INMAN, R. B., Biochemistry
INMAN, R. B., Institute for Molecular Virology
JEANNE, R. L., Entomology
JESSE, E. V., Agricultural and Applied Economics
JIANG, J., Horticulture
JOHNSON, E. A., Food Microbiology and Toxicology
JOHNSON, M. B., Agricultural and Applied Economics
JONES, B. L., Agricultural Database for Decision Support
KAEPPLER, S. M., Agronomy
KAMMEL, D. W., Biological Systems Engineering
KARASOV, W. H., Wildlife Ecology
KASPAR, C. W., Food Microbiology and Toxicology
KELLER, N. P., Food Microbiology and Toxicology, Plant Pathology
KIMBLE, J. E., Biochemistry
KIRKPATRICK, B. W., Animal Science
KLOPPENBURG, J. R., Rural Sociology
KRUGER, E. L., Forest Ecology and Management
KUNG, C., Genetics, Molecular Biology
KUNG, K.-J. S., Soil Science
KUSSOW, W. R., Soil Science
LAGRO, J. A., Jr, Urban and Regional Planning
LANDICK, R. C., Bacteriology
LAUER, J. G., Agronomy
LAUGHON, A. S., Genetics
LINDROTH, R. L., Entomology
LINDSAY, R. C., Food Science
LORIMER, C. G., Forest Ecology and Management
LOWERY, B., Soil Science
MCCLAIN, W. H., Bacteriology
MCCOWN, B. H., Horticulture
MACGUIDWIN, A. E., Plant Pathology
MADISON, F. W., Soil Science
MAHR, D. L., Entomology
MANSFIELD, J. M., Bacteriology
MARKLEY, J. L., Biochemistry
MARTIN, T. F. J., Biochemistry
MASSON, P. H., Genetics
MENON, A. K., Biochemistry
MLADENOFF, D. J., Forest Ecology and Management, Statistics
NELSON, D. L., Biochemistry
NEY, D. M., Nutritional Sciences
NIENHUIS, J., Horticulture
NITZKE, S. A., Nutritional Sciences
NORBACK, J. P., Food Science
NORDHEIM, E. V., Statistics
NORMAN, J. M., Soil Science
NOWAK, P., Soil and Water Conservation
NTAMBI, J. M., Biochemistry, Nutritional Sciences
OSBORN, T. C., Agronomy
PALMENBERG, A. C., Biochemistry
PALTA, J. P., Horticulture
PARIZA, M. W., Food Microbiology and Toxicology
PARKIN, K. L., Food Science
PARRISH, J. J., Animal Science
PASKEWITZ, S. M., Entomology
PETERSON, J. O., Environmental Resources Center
PHILLIPS, G. N., Jr, Biochemistry
PIKE, J. W., Biochemistry
PINGREE, S., Life Sciences Communication
POSNER, J. L., Agronomy
RAFFA, K. F., Entomology
RAINES, R. T., Biochemistry
RAYMENT, I., Biochemistry, Enzyme Institute
REED, G. H., Biochemistry

REINEMANN, D. J., Biological Systems Engineering
REZNIKOFF, W. S., Biochemistry
ROBERTS, G. P., Bacteriology
ROPER, T. R., Horticulture
ROUSE, D. I., Plant Pathology
RUTLEDGE, J. J., Animal Science
SCHAEFER, D. M., Animal Science
SCHOELLER, D. A., Nutritional Sciences
SCHULER, R. T., Biological Systems Engineering
SHAVER, R. D., Dairy Science
SHEFFIELD, L. G., Dairy Science
SHINNERS, K. J., Biological Systems Engineering
SHOOK, G. E., Dairy Science
SMITH, S. M., Nutritional Sciences
STANOSZ, G. R., Plant Pathology
STEELE, J. L., Food Science
STEVENSON, W. R., Plant Pathology
STIER, J. C., Forest Ecology and Management
STIMART, D. P., Horticulture
STOLTENBERG, D. E., Agronomy
SUNDE, R. A., Nutritional Sciences
SUSSMAN, M. R., Biochemistry
TEMPLE, S. A., Wildlife Ecology
THOMAS, D. L., Animal Science
TIGGES, L. M., Rural Sociology
TRACY, W. F., Agronomy
TYLER, E. J., Small-scale Waste, Soil Science
UNDERSANDER, D. J., Agronomy
VIERSTRA, R. D., Genetics
VOSS, P. R., Rural Sociology
WALSH, P. W., Biological Systems Engineering
WENDORFF, W. J., Food Science
WENTWORTH, B. C., Animal Science
WICKENS, M. P., Biochemistry
WILTBANK, M. C., Dairy Science
WONG, A. C., Food Microbiology and Toxicology
WYMAN, J. A., Entomology
YOUNG, D. K., Entomology

College of Engineering (2640 Engineering Hall, 1415 Engineering Dr., Madison, WI 53706; tel. (608) 262-3484; e-mail contact-us@engr.wisc.edu; internet www.engr.wisc.edu):

ABBOTT, N. L., Chemical Engineering
ADAMS, T. M., Civil and Environmental Engineering
ANDERSON, D. T., Electrical and Computer Engineering
ANDERSON, M. A., Civil and Environmental Engineering
ARMSTRONG, D. E., Civil and Environmental Engineering
BABCOCK, S. E., Materials Science and Engineering
BANK, L., Civil and Environmental Engineering
BARMISH, B. R., Electrical and Computer Engineering
BENSON, C. H., Civil and Environmental Engineering
BIER, V. M., Industrial Engineering
BISOGNANO, J. J., Synchrotron Radiation Center
BLANCHARD, J. P., Engineering Physics
BOOSKE, J. H., Electrical and Computer Engineering
BOSSCHER, P. J., Civil and Environmental Engineering
BOTEZ, D., Electrical and Computer Engineering
BUCKLEW, J. A., Electrical and Computer Engineering
CARAYON, P., Industrial Engineering
CERRINA, F., Electrical and Computer Engineering
CHANG, Y. A., Materials Science and Engineering
CORRADINI, M. L., Engineering Physics

CRAMER, S. M., Civil and Environmental Engineering
DAVIS, J. L., Engineering Outreach Technical Japanese, Technical Communications
DEMARCO, C., Electrical and Computer Engineering
DEPABLO, J. J., Chemical Engineering
DEVRIES, M. F., Mechanical Engineering
DOBSON, I., Electrical and Computer Engineering
DRUGAN, W. J., Engineering Physics
DUFFIE, N. A., Mechanical Engineering
DUMESIC, J. A., Chemical Engineering
EDIL, T. B., Civil and Environmental Engineering
ENGELSTAD, R. L., Mechanical Engineering
EOM, C.-B., Materials Science and Engineering
FARRELL, P. V., Mechanical Engineering
FONCK, R. J., Engineering Physics
FOSTER, D. E., Mechanical Engineering
FRONCZAK, F. J., Mechanical Engineering
GIACOMIN, A. J., Mechanical Engineering
GRAHAM, M. D., Chemical Engineering
HAIMSON, B. C., Materials Science and Engineering
HANNA, A. S., Civil and Environmental Engineering
HELLSTROM, E. E., Materials Science and Engineering
HENDERSON, D. L., Engineering Physics
HERSHKOWITZ, N., Engineering Physics
HILL, C. G., Jr, Chemical Engineering
HITCHON, W. N., Electrical and Computer Engineering
HOOPES, J. A., Civil and Environmental Engineering
HU, Y. H., Electrical and Computer Engineering
JAHNS, T., Electrical and Computer Engineering
KAMMER, D. C., Engineering Physics
KLEIN, S. A., Mechanical Engineering
KOU, S., Materials Science and Engineering
KUECH, T. F., Chemical Engineering
LAGALLY, M. G., Materials Science and Engineering
LAKES, R. C., Engineering Physics
LARBALESTIER, D. C., Materials Science and Engineering
LIPO, T. A., Electrical and Computer Engineering
LORENZ, R. D., Mechanical Engineering
LOVELL, E. G., Mechanical Engineering
LUMELSKY, V. J., Mechanical Engineering
MCCAUGHAN, L., Electrical and Computer Engineering
MARTIN, J. K., Mechanical Engineering
MOSES, G. A., Engineering Physics
MOSKWA, J. J., Mechanical Engineering
MURPHY, R. M., Chemical Engineering
OLEARY, P. R., Engineering Professional Devt
OSSWALD, T. A., Mechanical Engineering
PARK, J. K., Civil and Environmental Engineering
PEREPEZKO, J. H., Materials Science and Engineering
PLESHA, M. E., Engineering Physics
POTTER, K. W., Civil and Environmental Engineering
RADWIN, R. G., Biomedical Engineering
RAMANATHAN, P., Electrical and Computer Engineering
RAWLINGS, J. B., Chemical Engineering
REITZ, R. D., Mechanical Engineering
ROBINSON, S. M., Industrial Engineering
ROWLANDS, R. E., Mechanical Engineering
RUSSELL, J. S., Civil and Environmental Engineering
RUTLAND, C. J., Mechanical Engineering
SALUJA, K. K., Electrical and Computer Engineering

SCHARER, J. E., Electrical and Computer Engineering
SETHARES, W. A., Electrical and Computer Engineering
SHAPIRO, V., Mechanical Engineering
SHI, L., Industrial Engineering
SHOHET, J. L., Electrical and Computer Engineering
SMITH, J. E., Electrical and Computer Engineering
SMITH, M. J., Industrial Engineering
STEUDEL, H. J., Industrial Engineering
SURI, R., Industrial Engineering, Manufacturing Systems Engineering
TOMPKINS, W. J., Biomedical Engineering
UICKER, J. J., Jr, Mechanical Engineering
VANDERHEIDEN, G. C., Industrial Engineering
VANDERWEIDE, D. W., Electrical and Computer Engineering
VAN VEEN, B. D., Electrical and Computer Engineering
VEERAMANI, D., Industrial Engineering
VONDEROHE, A. P., Civil and Environmental Engineering
WENDT, A. E., Electrical and Computer Engineering
YIN, J., Chemical Engineering
ZIMMERMANN, D. R., Industrial Engineering

College of Letters and Science (5Suite 155, 1305 Linden Dr., Madison, WI 53706-1523; tel. (608) 262-5858; fax (608) 262-5093; internet www.ls.wisc.edu):

ABRAMSON, L. Y., Psychology
ACKERMAN, S. A., Space Science and Engineering Center
ADELL, S. A., Afro-American Studies
ADEM, A., Mathematics
ADLER, H., German
AHERN, P. R., Mathematics
ALBUQUERQUE, S. J., Spanish and Portuguese
ALEY, J. E., School of Music
ALIBALI, M. W., Psychology
ALLEN, T. F., Botany
ANDERSON, L. A., School of Music
ANDERSON, M. P., Geology and Geophysics
ANDREONI, J., Economics
ANGENENT, S. B., Mathematics
ARCHDEACON, T. J., History
ASSADI, A. H., Mathematics
ATIS, S. G., Languages and Cultures of Asia
BACH, C. E., Computer Sciences
BAHR, J. M., Geology and Geophysics
BAKER, T. B., Gen. Internal Medicine
BALANTEKIN, A. B., Physics
BARGER, V. D., Physics
BARTLEY, L. L., School of Music
BATES, D. M., Statistics
BAUGHMAN, J. L., Journalism and Mass Communication
BAUM, D. A., Botany
BECK, A., Mathematics
BECKER, D. E., School of Music
BEISSINGER, M., Political Science
BENDER, T. K., English
BENKART, G. M., Mathematics
BERG, W. J., French and Italian
BERGHAHN, K. L., German
BERNARD-DONALS, M. F., English
BERNAULT, F., History
BERNSTEIN, S. D., English
BERRIDGE, C. W., Psychology
BERRY, P. E., Botany
BETHEA, D. M., Slavic Languages
BICKNER, R. J., Languages and Cultures of Asia
BILBIJA, K., Spanish and Portuguese
BLAIR, S. S., Zoology
BLANCO, A., Spanish and Portuguese
BLEECKER, A. B., Botany
BLESS, D. M., Communicative Disorders

BLUM, D. L., Journalism and Mass Communication
BOLOTIN, S. V., Mathematics
BORN, S. M., Urban and Regional Planning
BOSTON, N., Mathematics
BOWIE, K. A., Anthropology
BOYDSTON, J., History
BOYETTE, P. J., Theatre and Drama
BRANDT, D. L., English
BRANTLY, S. C., Scandinavian Studies
BRENNER, R. F., Hebrew and Semitic Studies
BRIGHOUSE, M. H., Philosophy
BROCK, W. A., Economics
BROWER, A. M., Social Work
BROWN, P. E., Geology and Geophysics
BRUALDI, R. A., Mathematics
BRUCH, L. W., Physics
BUCCINI, S., French and Italian
BUENGER, B. C., Art History
BÜHNEMANN, G., Languages and Cultures of Asia
BUNKER, S. G., Sociology
BUNN, H. T., Anthropology
BURKE, S. D., Chemistry
BURSTYN, J. N., Chemistry
BURT, J. E., Geography
BUSBY, K. R., French and Italian
BYERS, C. W., Geology and Geophysics
CAI, J.-Y., Computer Sciences
CALDERON, J. F., School of Music
CAMIC, C., Sociology
CANCIAN, M., Institute for Research on Poverty
CANON, D. T., Political Science
CARD, C. F., Philosophy
CARLSMITH, D. L., Physics
CARPENTER, S. R., Zoology
CARROLL, A. R., Geology and Geophysics
CARROLL, N., Philosophy
CASEY, C. P., Chemistry
CASPI, A., Psychology
CASSINELLI, J. P., Astronomy
CASTRONOVO, R., English
CAULKINS, J. H., French and Italian
CHAPPELL, R. J., Biostatistics and Medical Informatics
CHAVEZ, M. M. T., German
CHE, Y.-K., Economics
CHENG, T. F., East Asian Languages and Literature
CHIAL, M. R., Communicative Disorders
CHINN, M. D., Economics
CHISHOLM, S. L., School of Music
CHUBUKOV, A. V., Physics
CHURCHWELL, E. B., Astronomy
COE, C. L., Psychology
COHEN, C. L., History
COHEN, L. K., Comparative Literature
COLEMAN, J. J., Political Science
COOK, S. C., School of Music
COOPER, J. M., Jr, History
COPPERSMITH, S. N., Physics
CORFIS, I. A., Spanish and Portuguese
CORN, R. M., Chemistry
CORTEZ, E. M., Library and Information Studies
COURTENAY, W. J., History
COWELL, D. C., African Languages and Literature
COX, D. P., Physics
CRAVENS, T. D., French and Italian
CRIM, F. F., Jr, Chemistry
CRONON, W., History
CROOK, D., School of Music
CURTIN, M. J., Communication Arts
CUTTER, R. J., East Asian Languages and Literature
D'ACCI, J., Communication Arts
DAHL, L. F., Chemistry
DANNEMILLER, J. L., Psychology
DAVIDSON, R. J., Psychology
DAVIS, R., School of Music
DE STASIO, G., Physics
DEBAISIEUX, M. M., French and Italian
DELAMATER, J. D., Sociology

DEMBSKI, S., School of Music
DEMETS, D. C., Geology and Geophysics
DENECKERE, R. J., Economics
DESAN, S. M., History
DESAUTELS, E. J., Computer Sciences
DEVINE, P. G., Psychology
DEWITT, D. J., Computer Sciences
DICKEY, L. W., History
DICKEY, R. W., Mathematics
DILL, C. W., School of Music
DOANE, A. N., English
DODSON, S. I., Zoology
DOKSUM, K. A., Statistics
DOLININ, A. A., Slavic Languages
DONNELLY, J. S., Jr, History
DORN, D. L., Theatre and Drama
DOWNS, D. A., Political Science
DRAINE, B., English
DRECHSEL, R. E., Journalism and Mass Communication
DRESANG, D. L., Political Science
DREWAL, H. J., Art History
DUBOIS, T. A., Scandinavian Studies
DUBROW, H., English
DUNLAVY, C. A., History
DUNWOODY, S. L., Journalism and Mass Communication
DURAND, B., Physics
DURLAUF, S. N., Economics
DYER, C. R., Computer Sciences
EARP, L. M., School of Music
EDIGER, M. D., Chemistry
EELLS, E. T., Philosophy
ELDER, J. W., Languages and Cultures of Asia
ELLIS, A. B., Chemistry
ELLIS WEISMER, S., Communicative Disorders
ENC, M., Linguistics
ENGEL, C. M., Economics
ERWIN, A. R., Physics
ESSIG, L., Theatre and Drama
FAIR, J. E., Journalism and Mass Communication
FERNANDEZ, D. E., Botany
FERREE, M. M., Sociology
FERRIS, M. C., Computer Sciences
FILIPOWICZ, H., Slavic Languages
FINK, M. D., School of Music
FISCHER, C. N., Computer Sciences
FITZPATRICK, M. A., Communication Arts
FOLEY, J. A., Sustainability and Global Environment
FORD, C. E., English
FORSTER, M. R., Philosophy
FOWLER, C. G., Communicative Disorders
FOX, M. V., Hebrew and Semitic Studies
FRANKLIN, C. H., Political Science
FRIEDLAND, L. A., Journalism and Mass Communication
FRIEDMAN, E., Political Science
FRIEDMAN, S. S., English
FUJIMURA, J., Sociology
FULMER, M. K., School of Music
GALLAGHER, J. S., III, Astronomy
GAMORAN, A., Center for Education Research
GEARY, D. H., Geology and Geophysics
GEIGER, G. L., Art History
GELLMAN, S. H., Chemistry
GEORGE, K. M., Anthropology
GERNSBACHER, M. A., Psychology
GIVNISH, T. J., Botany
GLENBERG, A. M., Psychology
GOLDSMITH, H. H., Psychology
GOLDSTEIN, K. M., Political Science
GOODKIN, R. E., French and Italian
GOODMAN, J. R., Computer Sciences
GORSKI, P. S., Sociology
GOTTLIEB, P. L., Philosophy
GRAHAM, L. K., Botany
GREENBERG, J., Social Work
GREIVE, T. D., School of Music
GRIFFEATH, D. S., Mathematics
GROSS, S. D., German
GUERIN GONZALES, C., Chicano Studies

HAEBERLI, W., Physics
HALZEN, F. L., Physics
HAMERS, R. J., Chemistry
HAN, T., Physics
HANSEN, B. E., Economics
HARACKIEWICZ, J. M., Psychology
HARDIN, J. D., Zoology
HARRIS, R. A., Spanish and Portuguese
HAUSER, R. M., Sociology
HAUSMAN, D., Philosophy
HAWKINS, R. P., Journalism and Mass Communication
HENDEL, I. E., Economics
HILDNER, D. J., Spanish and Portuguese
HILL, D. D., School of Music
HILL, M. D., Computer Sciences
HILL, R. J., English
HILMES, M., Communication Arts
HILTS, V. L, History of Science
HIMPSEL, F. J., Physics
HINDEN, M. C., English
HITCHMAN, M. H., Atmospheric and Oceanic Sciences
HOESSEL, J. G., Astronomy
HORWITZ, S. B., Computer Sciences
HOWELL, R. B., German
HUBER, D. L., Physics
HUDDLESTON, J. R., Urban and Regional Planning
HUNT, L. H., Philosophy
HUNTER, L., African Languages and Literature
HUTCHINSON, S. E., Anthropology
HUTCHISON, J. C., Art History
HUTCHINSON, S., Spanish and Portuguese
HYDE, J. S., Women's Studies Research Center
HYER, B., School of Music
IONEL, E.-N., Mathematics
ISAACS, I. M., Mathematics
IVES, A. R., Zoology
JACOBS, H. M., Urban and Regional Planning
JACOBS, L., Communication Arts
JAMES, C. J., German
JAMES, S. M., Afro-American Studies
JENISON, R. L., Psychology
JENSEN, J. L., School of Music
JIN, S., Mathematics
JOHNSON, A. A., Mathematics
JOHNSON, C. M., Geology and Geophysics
JOHNSON, R. A., Statistics
JOYNT, R. J., Physics
KAISER, N. A., German
KAISER, N. A., Women's Studies Program
KAISER, R. J., Geography
KARP, P. D., School of Music
KAUTSKY, C. C., School of Music
KEENE, N., Communication Arts
KELLER, L., English
KELLEY, T. M., English
KENNAN, J. F., Economics
KENOYER, J. M., Anthropology
KENT, R. D., Waisman Center for Mentally Retarded People and Human Devt
KEPLEY, V. I., Communication Arts
KERCHEVAL, J. L., English
KHAZANOV, A., Anthropology
KIESSLING, L. L., Biochemistry
KIRSCH, J. A. W., Zoology
KITCHELL, J. F., Zoology
KLEINHENZ, C., French and Italian
KLUENDER, K. R., Psychology
KLUGE, C. L., German
KNOWLES, R. A. J., English
KNOX, J. C., Geography
KNUTSON, L. D., Physics
KOSHAR, R. J., History
KOSOROK, M. R., Biostatistics and Medical Informatics
KRAVETZ, D., Social Work
KRITZER, H. M., Political Science
KUELBS, J. D., Mathematics
KUNEN, K., Mathematics
KURTZ, T. G., Mathematics
KURTZ, T. G., Statistics

LANDIS, C. R., Chemistry
LANGER, U. G., French and Italian
LAWLER, J. E., Physics
LAYOUN, M. N., Comparative Literature
LEARY, J. P., Folklore
LECKRONE, M. E., School of Music
LEE, J. B., History
LEMPP, S., Mathematics
LEPOWSKY, M. A., Anthropology
LEZRA, J., English
LI, Y., Linguistics
LIN, C. C., Physics
LINDSTROM, D. L., History
LIU, Z.-U., Atmospheric and Oceanic Sciences
LIVNY, M., Computer Sciences
LOEWENSTEIN, D. A., English
LOH, W.-Y., Statistics
LONGINOVIC, T., Slavic Languages
LOUDEN, M. L., German
LUCAS, S. E., Communication Arts
LUNDIN, A. H., Library and Information Studies
LUTFI, R. A., Communicative Disorders
MACAULAY, M. A., Linguistics
McCAMMON, D., Physics
McCLINTOCK, A. P., English
McCLURE, L. K., Integrated Liberal Studies
McCOY, A. W., History
McDONALD, D. M., History
MACDONALD, M. C., Psychology
McGLOIN, N. H., East Asian Languages and Literature
McKAY, N. Y., Afro-American Studies
McKAY, N. Y., English
McKEOWN, J. C., Classics
McLEOD, D. M., Journalism and Mass Communication
McMAHON, R. J., Chemistry
MACKEN, M. A., Linguistics
MAGNAN, S. S., French and Italian
MALLON, F. E., History
MANION, M., Political Science
MANOOGIAN, V. I., School of Music
MANUELLI, R. E., Economics
MARCOUILLER, D. W., Urban and Regional Planning
MARLER, C. A., Psychology
MARQUEZ, B., Political Science
MARTIN, J. E., Atmospheric and Oceanic Sciences
MATHIEU, R. D., Astronomy
MAYER, K. R., Political Science
MAYNARD, D. W., Sociology
MAZZAOUI, M. F., History
MEMON, M. U., Languages and Cultures of Asia
MENOCAL, N. G., Art History
MEYER, D. R., Social Work
MEYER, R. R., Computer Sciences
MICKELSON, D. M., Geology and Geophysics
MIERNOWSKI, J., French and Italian
MILEWSKI, P. A., Mathematics
MILLER, A. W., Mathematics
MILLER, B. P., Computer Sciences
MILLER, J. F., Communicative Disorders
MITMAN, G. A., History of Science
MOFFITT, T. E., Psychology
MOORE, C. F., Psychology
MOORE, J. W., Chemistry
MOORE, M. L., English
MORAHG, G., Hebrew and Semitic Studies
MORGAN, D. O., Institute for Humanities Research
MORSE, R. M., Physics
MORTENSEN, C. D., Communication Arts
MURPHY, J. J., Communication Arts
MURRAY, J. K., Art History
NADLER, S. M., Philosophy
NARAYAN, K., Anthropology
NATHANSON, G. M., Chemistry
NAUGHTON, J. F., Computer Sciences
NELSEN, S. F., Chemistry
NEWLANDS, C., Classics
NEWMAN, J. P., Psychology

NICHOLS, D. A., Lafollette School of Public Affairs
NIENHAUSER, W. H., East Asian Languages and Literature
NILES, J. D., English, Institute for Humanities Research
NIXON, R. D., English
NORDSIECK, K. H., Astronomy
NYSTRAND, P. M., English
OGELMAN, H. B., Physics
OH, Y.-G., Mathematics
OHNUKI-TIERNEY, E., Anthropology
OLANIYAN, T., African Languages and Literature
OLIVER, P. E., Sociology
OLSSON, M. G., Physics
ONELLION, M. F., Physics
ONO, K., Mathematics
ORLIK, P. P., Mathematics
OSTERGREN, R. C., Geography
PALLONI, A., Sociology
PAN, Z., Communication Arts
PASSMAN, D. S., Mathematics
PAWLEY, J. B., Zoology
PAYNE, L. A., Political Science
PAYNE, S. G., History
PECK, J. A., Geography
PERRY, D., School of Music
PETTY, G. W., Atmospheric and Oceanic Sciences
PHILLIPS, Q. E., Art History
PILIAVIN, J. A., Sociology
PLUMMER, B. G., Afro-American Studies
PODESTA, G. A., Spanish and Portuguese
PONDROM, C. N., English
PONDROM, L. G., Physics
PORTER, W. P., Zoology
POWELL, B. B., Classics
PRAGER, S. C., Physics
PREPOST, R., Physics
PRICE, T. D., Anthropology
RABINOWITZ, P. H., Mathematics
RADANO, R. M., School of Music
RAFFERTY, E. M., Languages and Cultures of Asia
RAM, A., Mathematics
RAMAKRISHNAN, R., Computer Sciences
RAND, N. T., French and Italian
RAO, V. N., Languages and Cultures of Asia
REAMES, S. L., English
RECORD, M. T., Jr, Biochemistry
REEDER, D. D., Physics
REICH, H. J., Chemistry
REPS, T. W., Computer Sciences
RESCHOVSKY, A. M., Lafollette School of Public Affairs
REYNOLDS, A. J., Waisman Center for Mentally Retarded People and Human Devt
REYNOLDS, R. J., Astronomy
RICHARDSON, N. R., Political Science
RICHARDSON, W. W., Music
RIFKIN, B., Slavic Languages
RILEY, P. T., Political Science
RISLEY, W. R., Spanish and Portuguese
ROBBIN, J. W., Mathematics
ROBBINS, L. S., Library and Information Studies
ROBERTS, M. L., History
ROESLER, F. L., Physics
RON, A., Computer Sciences
ROSAY, J.-P., Mathematics
ROSENMEYER, P., Classics
ROTHSTEIN, E., English
RUAN, Y., Mathematics
RZCHOWSKI, M. S., Physics
SACK, R. D., Geography
SAIZ, P., Comparative Literature
SALMONS, J. C., German
SALOMON, F. L., Anthropology
SAMUELSON, L. W., Economics
SAPIRO, V., Academic Affairs
SAVAGE, B. D., Astronomy
SCARANO, F. A., History
SCHAEFFER, N. C., Sociology

SCHAFER, B. E., Political Science
SCHAFER-LANDAU, R. S., Philosophy
SCHAFFER, J. W., School of Music
SCHAMILOGLU, U., Languages and Cultures of Asia
SCHAPIRO, L. A., Philosophy
SCHATZBERG, M. G., Political Science
SCHAUB, T. H., English
SCHEUB, H. E., African Languages and Literature
SCHEUFELE, D. A., Journalism and Mass Communication
SCHLEICHER, A. Y., African Languages and Literature
SCHOLZ, J. K., Economics
SCHULTZ, S. K., History
SCHWARTZ, D. C., Chemistry
SEEGER, A., Mathematics
SEIDENBERG, M. S., Psychology
SEIDMAN, G. W., Sociology
SHAH, D. V., Journalism and Mass Communication
SHAH, H. G., Journalism and Mass Communication
SHAKHASHIRI, B. Z., Chemistry
SHANK, M. H., History of Science
SHAO, J., Statistics
SHARKEY, T. D., Botany
SHARPLESS, J. B., History
SHAVLIK, J. W., Computer Sciences
SHCHEGLOV, Y. K., Slavic Languages
SIBERT, E. L., Chemistry
SIDELLE, A. G., Philosophy
SILBERMAN, M. D., German
SIMO, J. A., Geology and Geophysics
SKINNER, J. L., Chemistry
SKLOOT, R., Theatre and Drama
SLEMROD, M., Mathematics
SMITH, J. R., School of Music
SMITH, LESLIE M., Mathematics
SMITH, LLOYD M., Chemistry
SMITH, W. H., Physics
SNOWDON, C. T., Psychology
SOBER, E. R., Philosophy
SOHI, G. S., Computer Sciences
SOLL, A. I., Philosophy
SOLOMON, M. H., Computer Sciences
SOMMERVILLE, J. P., History
SORKIN, D. J., Institute for Humanities Research
SPALDING, E. P., Botany
SPARKE, L. S., Astronomy
SPROTT, J. C., Physics
STAIGER, R. W., Economics
STAMPE, D. W., Philosophy
STEAKLEY, J. D., German
STEELE, J. A., English
STERN, S. J., History
STEUDEL, K. L., Zoology
STEVENS, J. D., School of Music
STOWE, J. C., School of Music
STRETTON, A. O., Zoology
STRIER, K. B., Anthropology
STRIKWERDA, J. C., Computer Sciences
SUCHMAN, M. C., Sociology
SUTTON, R. A., School of Music
SWACK, J. R., School of Music
SWEENEY, S. R., Theatre and Drama
SYTSMA, K. J., Botany
TAYLOR, M. S., Economics
TEMPRANO, J. C., Spanish and Portuguese
TERRY, P. W., Physics
TERWILLIGER, P. M., Mathematics
TESFAGIORGIS, F. H. W., Afro-American Studies
THIMMIG, L. L., School of Music
THOMSON, E. J., Sociology
THORNTON, M. C., Afro-American Studies
THURBER, C. H., Geology and Geophysics
TIMBIE, P. T., Physics
TREICHEL, P. M., Chemistry
TRIPOLI, A., Political Science
TRIPP, G. J., Atmospheric and Oceanic Sciences
TSUI, K.-W., Statistics
TURNER, M. G., Zoology

TZAVARAS, A., Mathematics
UHLENBROCK, D., Mathematics
VALLEY, J. W., Geology and Geophysics
VAN DEBURG, W. L., Afro-American Studies
VANDENHEUVEL, M. J., Theatre and Drama
VARDI, U., School of Music
VAUGHN, S. L., Journalism and Mass Communication
VERNON, M. K., Computer Sciences
WAHBA, G. G., Statistics
WAINGER, S., Mathematics
WALEFFE, F., Mathematics
WALKER, J. R., Economics
WALKER, T. G., Physics
WALLACE, R. W., English
WALLER, D. M., Botany
WANDEL, L. P., History
WANDEL, L. P., Institute for Humanities Research
WANG, P.-K., Atmospheric and Oceanic Sciences
WARDROP, R. L., Statistics
WEIMER, D., Political Science
WEINBROT, H. D., English
WEINHOLD, F. A., Chemistry
WEISMER, G. G., Communicative Disorders
WEISSHAAR, J. C., Chemistry
WELBOURNE, T. G., School of Music
WERNER, C., Afro-American Studies
WEST, K. D., Economics
WHITEHEAD, N. L., Anthropology
WHITLOCK, H. W., Jr, Chemistry
WILSON, F. D., Sociology
WILSON, G. K., Political Science
WILSON, R. L., Mathematics
WINICHAKUL, T., History
WINK, A., History
WINOKUR, M. J., Physics
WINSPUR, S., French and Italian
WITTE, J. F., Political Science
WOFFORD, S., English
WOLF, K., Scandinavian Studies
WOOD, D. A., Computer Sciences
WOODS, R. C., Chemistry
WORCESTER, N. A., Women's Studies Program
WRIGHT, E. O., Sociology
WRIGHT, J. C., Chemistry
WRIGHT, S. J., Computer Science
WU, S. L. Y., Physics
YANDELL, K. E., Philosophy
YETHIRAJ, A., Chemistry
YOUNG, J. A., Atmospheric and Oceanic Sciences
YOUNG, R. F., English
ZAMORA, M. M., Spanish and Portuguese
ZEDLER, J. B., Arboretum: Tours
ZEDLER, J. B., Botany
ZEITLIN, J., Sociology
ZEPPENFELD, D., Physics
ZIMMERER, K. S., Geography
ZIMMERMAN, H. E., Chemistry
ZUENGLER, J., English
ZWEIBEL, E. G., Physics

Law School (975 Bascom Hall, Madison, WI 53706; tel. (608) 262-2240; fax (608) 262-5485; e-mail deansoffice@law.wisc.edu; internet www.law.wisc.edu):

ALTHOUSE, A.
BRITO, T. L.
CARSTENSEN, P. C.
CHARO, R. A.
CHURCH, W. L.
CLAUSS, C. A.
DICKEY, W. J.
ERLANGER, H. S.
GREENE, L. S.
IRISH, C. R.
KAPLAN, L. V.
KIDWELL, J. A.
KLUG, H. J.
KOMESAR, N. K.
LARSON, J. E.
MACAULAY, S.
MCEVOY, A. F.

MERTZ, E. E.
MORAN, B. I.
NOURSE, V. F.
PALAY, T. M.
SCHACTER, J. S.
SCHULTZ, D. E.
SHAFFER, G. C.
SMITH, D. G.
SMITH, M. E.
THOMPSON, C. F.
TRUBEK, D. M.

School of Education (Dean's Office, 377 Education Bldg, 1000 Bascom Hall, Madison, WI 53706; tel. (608) 262-1763; fax (608) 265-3284; e-mail easinfo@education.wisc.edu; internet www.education.wisc.edu):

ABBEDUTO, L. J., Educational Psychology
APPLE, M. W., Curriculum and Instruction
BECKER, D. H., Art
BERVEN, N. L., Rehabilitation Psychology and Spec. Education
BLOCH, M., Curriculum and Instruction
BRECKENRIDGE, B. M., Art
BREDESON, P. V., Gen. Education
BROWN, B. B., Educational Psychology
CABRERA, A. F., Gen. Education
CAPPER, C. A., Gen. Education
CHAN, F., Rehabilitation Psychology and Spec. Education
COLEMAN, H. L. K., Counseling Psychology
CONRAD, C. F., Gen. Education
DAMER, J. F., Art
DERRY, S. J., Educational Psychology
ENRIGHT, R. D., Educational Psychology
ESCALANTE, J. A., Art
FENNELL, P., Art
FENSTER, F., Art
FEREN, S. F., Art
FULTZ, M., Educational Policy Studies
GEE, J. P., Curriculum and Instruction
GETTINGER, M., Educational Psychology
GLORIA, A. M., Counseling Psychology
GOMEZ, M. L., Curriculum and Instruction
GRANT, C. A., Curriculum and Instruction
GRAUE, M. E., Center for Education Research
HANLEY-MAXWELL, C. D., Rehabilitation Psychology and Spec. Education
HAYES, E. R., Curriculum and Instruction
HEWSON, P. W., Curriculum and Instruction
JI, L.-L., Kinesiology
KALISH, C. W., Educational Psychology
KAZAMIAS, A. M., Educational Policy Studies
KETCHUM, C. G., Art
KNOX, A. B., Gen. Education
KOYKKAR, J. N., Dance
KOZA, J. E., Curriculum and Instruction
KRATOCHWILL, T. R., Center for Education Research, Educational Psychology
LADSON-BILLINGS, G. J., Curriculum and Instruction
LEE, S. J., Educational Policy Studies
LI, C.-P., Dance
LOCKWOOD, A. L., Curriculum and Instruction
LOESER, T., Art
LONG, R. L., Art
LOWE, T. T., Art
LYNCH, R. T., Rehabilitation Psychology and Spec. Education
MARSCHALEK, D. G., Art
MELROSE, C. A., Dance
METZ, M. H., Educational Policy Studies
MORGAN, W. P., Kinesiology
MYERS, F. J., Art
ODDEN, A. R., Center for Education Research
OLNECK, M. R., Educational Policy Studies
PEKARSKY, D. N., Educational Policy Studies
PETERSON, K. D., Gen. Education
PHELPS, L. A., Center on Education and Work

POPKEWITZ, T. S., Curriculum and Instruction
PRICE, G. G., Curriculum and Instruction
PYLANT, C. S., Art
QUINTANA, S. M., Counseling Psychology
REESE, W. J., Educational Policy Studies
RIEBEN, J. R., Art
SCHEER, J. M., Art
SCHNEIDER, M. L., Kinesiology
SCHRAG, F. K., Educational Policy Studies
SERLIN, R. C., Educational Psychology
STEWART, J. H., Curriculum and Instruction
STREIBEL, M. J., Curriculum and Instruction
SUBKOVIAK, M. J., Educational Psychology
TARVER, S. G., Rehabilitation Psychology and Spec. Education
TOCHON, F. V., Curriculum and Instruction
VANDELL, D. L., Educational Psychology
WAMPOLD, B. E., Counseling Psychology
ZEICHNER, K. M., Curriculum and Instruction

School of Human Ecology (Third Fl., 1305 Linden Dr., Madison, WI 53706; tel. (608) 262-2608; fax (608) 265-4969; e-mail csdept@ mail.sohe.wisc.edu; internet www.sohe.wisc .edu):

APPLE, R. D., Consumer Science
AQUILINO, W. S., Human Devt and Family Studies
BOGENSCHNEIDER, K. P., Human Devt and Family Studies
BOYD, V. T., Environment, Textiles and Design
DOHR, J. H., Environment, Textiles and Design
DONG, W., Environment, Textiles and Design
GOEBEL, K. P., Consumer Science
GORDON, B., Environment, Textiles and Design
HOLDEN, K. C., Lafollette School of Public Affairs
HOYT, A. A., Consumer Science
HUNT, M. E., Environment, Textiles and Design
JASPER, C. R., Consumer Science
MARKS, N. F., Human Devt and Family Studies
RILEY, D. A., Human Devt and Family Studies
ROSSING, B. E., Interdisciplinary Studies
SARMADI, M., Environment, Textiles and Design
SHEEHAN, D., Environment, Textiles and Design
SMALL, S. A., Human Devt and Family Studies
WAY, W. L., Gen. Science
ZEPEDA, L., Consumer Science

School of Medicine and Public Health (750 University Ave, Madison, WI 53705; tel. (608) 263-8668; fax (608) 262-2327; internet www.med.wisc.edu):

ABBOTT, D. H., Primate Research Center
ABBS, J. H., Neurology
ALBANESE, M. A., Population Health Sciences
ALBERT, D. M., Ophthalmology and Visual Sciences
ALLEN-HOFFMANN, B. L., Anatomic Pathology
ANDERSON, R. A., Pharmacology
ANDERSON, W. H., History of Medicine
BACH-Y-RITA, P., Rehabilitation Medicine
BANGS, J. D., Medical Microbiology
BENCA, R. M., Psychiatry
BENTZ, M. L., Dental and Plastic Surgery
BERSU, E. T., Anatomy
BERTICS, P. J., Biomolecular Chemistry
BIANCO, J. A., Nuclear Medicine
BIRD, I. M., Obstetrics and Gynaecology
BRADFIELD, C. A., Oncology

BRANDT, C. R., Ophthalmology and Visual Sciences
BRESNICK, E. H., Pharmacology
BROOKS, B. R., Neurology
BROW, D. A., Biomolecular Chemistry
BRUSKEWITZ, R. C., Urology
BURGESS, R. R., Oncology
CARNES, M. L., Geriatrics and Adult Devt
CHIU, S.-Y., Physiology
COMPTON, T., Oncology
CORONADO, R., Physiology
CRAIG, W. A., Infectious Disease
CRUICKSHANKS, K. J., Ophthalmology and Visual Sciences
DAHL, J. L., Pharmacology
DAHLBERG, J. E., Biomolecular Chemistry
DALESSANDRO, A., Transplant Research and Devt
DEJESUS, O. T., Medical Physics
DELUCA, P. M., Jr, Medical Physics
DEMETS, D. L., Biostatistics and Medical Informatics
DEMPSEY, J. A., Population Health Sciences
DEMPSEY, R. J., Neurological Surgery
DENNISTON, C., Genetics
DESMET, A. A., Diagnostic
DIAMOND, R. J., Psychiatry
DOVE, W. F., Sr, Oncology
DREZNER, M. K., Endocrinology
DRINKWATER, N. R., Oncology
EHRMEYER, S. L., Clinical Laboratory Science Programme
EPSTEIN, M. L., Anatomy
ERVASTI, J. M., Physiology
FAHL, W. E., Oncology
FALLON, J. F., Anatomy
FETTIPLACE, R., Physiology
FILLINGAME, R. H., Biomolecular Chemistry
FIORE, M. C., Gen. Internal Medicine
FLEMING, J. O., Neurology
FLEMING, M. F., Research Grants
FOLTS, J. D., Cardiology
FORD, C. N., Otolaryngology
FOST, N. C., Pediatrics
FREY, J. J., Family Medicine
FRYBACK, D. G., Population Health Sciences
GENTRY, L. R., Diagnostic
GERN, J. E., Pediatrics
GJERDE, C. L., Education Research and Devt
GLASSROTH, J. L., Medicine
GOLOS, T. G., Obstetrics and Gynaecology
GOULD, M. N., Oncology
GRAZIANO, F. M., Rheumatology
GREENSPAN, D. S., Anatomic Pathology
GREER, F. R., Pediatrics
GRIEP, A. E., Anatomy
GRIST, T. M., Diagnostic
GURMAN, A. S., Psychiatry
GUSTAFSON, J. P., Psychiatry
HABERLY, L. B., Anatomy
HACKNEY, C. M., Anatomy
HALL, T. J., Medical Physics
HARMS, B. A., Gen. Surgery
HART, M. N., Anatomic Pathology
HARTING, J. K., Anatomy
HAUGHTON, V. M., Diagnostic
HERMANN, B. P., Neurology
HOFFMANN, F. M., Oncology
HOLDEN, J. E., Medical Physics
JACKSON, M. B., Physiology
JANUARY, C. T., Cardiology
JARJOUR, N. N., Pulmonary Medicine
JEFCOATE, C. R., Pharmacology
KAHAN, L., Biomolecular Chemistry
KALAYOGLU, M., Transplant Research and Devt
KALIL, K., Anatomy
KALIL, R. E., Center for Neuroscience
KALIN, N. H., Psychiatry
KANAREK, M. S., Population Health Sciences
KAUFMAN, P. L., Ophthalmology and Visual Sciences

KEENE, J. S., Orthopedics
KELLEY, A. E., Psychiatry
KILEY, P. J., Biomolecular Medicine
KIM, K.-M., Biostatistics and Medical Informatics
KLEIN, B. E. K., Ophthalmology and Visual Sciences
KLEIN, B. S., Pediatrics
KLEIN, M. H., Psychiatry
KLEIN, R., Ophthalmology and Visual Sciences
KLIEWER, M. A., Diagnostic
KNECHTLE, M. J., Transplant Research and Devt
KUDSK, K. A., Gen. Surgery
KUHLMAN, J. E., Diagnostic
LALLEY, P. M., Physiology
LAMBERT, P. F., Oncology
LAUBE, D. W., Obstetrics and Gynaecology
LEAVITT, J. W., History of Medicine
LEAVITT, L. A., Pediatrics
LEMANSKE, R. F., Pediatrics
LINZER, M., Gen. Internal Medicine
LIPTON, P., Physiology
LOEB, D. D., Oncology
LONGLEY, B. J., Dept of Dermatology
LOVE, R. R., Clinical Oncology
LUCEY, M. R., Gastroenterology
MCBRIDE, P. E., Cardiology
MACDONALD, M. J., Pediatrics
MACK, E. A., Gen. Surgery
MACKIE, T. R., Medical Physics
MAGNESS, R. R., Obstetrics and Gynaecology
MAKI, D. G., Infectious Disease
MAKIELSKI, J. C., Cardiology
MALKOVSKY, M., Medical Microbiology
MALTER, J. S., Anatomic Pathology
MARES, J. A., Ophthalmology and Visual Sciences
MARSHALL, J. R., Psychiatry
MEHTA, M. P., Human Oncology
MEISNER, L. F., Population Health Sciences
MERTZ, J. E., Oncology
MEYER, K. C., Pulmonary Medicine
MISTRETTA, C. A., Medical Physics
MONTERO, V. M., Physiology
MOSHER, D. F., Hematology
MOSS, R. L., Physiology
MUKHTAR, H., Dept of Dermatology
MULLAHY, J., Population Health Sciences
NICKLES, R. J., Medical Physics
NIEDERHUBER, J. E., Comprehensive Cancer Center
NIETO, F. J., Population Health Sciences
NUMBERS, R. L., History of Medicine
OBERLEY, T. D., Anatomic Pathology, Medicine
OERTEL, D., Physiology
OLIVE, D. L., Obstetrics and Gynaecology
PALIWAL, B. R., Human Oncology
PALTA, M., Population Health Sciences
PAULI, R. M., Genetics
PAULNOCK, D. M., Medical Microbiology
PEARCE, R. A., Anesthesiology
PROCTOR, R. A., Infectious Disease, Medical Microbiology
RAPRAEGER, A. C., Anatomic Pathology
REMINGTON, P. L., Population Health Sciences
RHODE, W. S., Physiology
RIKKERS, L., Dept of Surgery
ROBBINS, J., Gastroenterology
ROBINS, H. I., Clinical Oncology
ROSS, J., Oncology
RUOHO, A. E., Pharmacology
RUTECKI, P. A., Neurology
SANDOR, M., Anatomic Pathology
SCHILLER, J. H., Clinical Oncology
SCHULTZ, E., Anatomy
SKATRUD, J. B., Pulmonary Medicine
SKOCHELAK, S. E., Family Medicine
SOBKOWICZ, H. M., Neurology
SOLLINGER, H. W., Transplant Research and Devt
SONDEL, P. M., Pediatrics

SONZOGNI, W. C., Environmental Health Admin.
STAFSTROM, C. E., Neurology
STARLING, J. R., Gen. Surgery
STEELE, T. H., Nephrology
SUGDEN, W. M., Oncology
SUTULA, T. P., Neurology
SVENDSEN, C. N., Anatomy
TERASAWA-GRILLEY, E. I., Primate Research Center
THOMSON, J. A., Anatomy
TONONI, G., Psychiatry
TURNIPSEED, W. D., Gen. Surgery
TURSKI, P. A., Diagnostic
UEHLING, D. T., Urology
VALDIVIA, H. H., Physiology
VANDERBY, R., Jr, Orthopedics
VERMA, A. K., Human Oncology
WAKAI, R. T., Medical Physics
WALKER, J. W., Physiology
WATKINS, D. I., Anatomic Pathology
WEIDANZ, W. P., Medical Microbiology
WEINDRUCH, R. H., Geriatrics and Adult Devt
WEISBLUM, B., Pharmacology
WELCH, R. A., Medical Microbiology
WESTGARD, J. O., Anatomic Pathology
WHITE, J. G., Molecular Biology
WOLFE, B. L., Population Health Sciences
WOLFF, J. A., Pediatrics
WOOD, G. S., Dept of Dermatology
YIN, T. C. T., Physiology
YOUNG, J. A. T., Oncology
YOUNG, T. B., Population Health Sciences
ZAGZEBSKI, J. A., Medical Physics
ZDEBLICK, T. A., Orthopedics
ZISKIND-CONHAIM, L., Physiology

School of Nursing (K6/287 Clinical Science Center, 600 Highland Ave, Madison, WI 53792-2455; tel. (608) 263-5200; fax (608) 263-5323; e-mail clangsdo@facstaff.wisc.edu; internet www.son.wisc.edu):

BAUMANN, L. J.
BOWERS, B. J.
BRENNAN, P.
BROWN, R. L.
DIEKELMANN, N. L.
DIEMER, G. A.
ESSER-ANDERSON, J. J.
GALAROWICZ, L. R. B.
KIRCHHOFF, K.
LASKY, P. A.
LITTLEFIELD, V. M.
MCCARTHY, D. O.
MCCUBBIN, M. A.
MAY, K. A.
OWEN, B. D.
RATHER, M. L.
RIESCH, S.
WARD, S. E.
WELLS, T.

School of Pharmacy (Renn & Bohm Hall, 777 Highland Ave, Madison, WI 53705-2222; tel. (608) 262-6234; fax (608) 262-3943; internet www.pharmacy.wisc.edu):

DEMUTH, J. E., Pharmacy Outreach
HANSON, A. L., Pharmacy Outreach
HEIDEMAN, W.
HORNEMANN, U.
KRELING, D. H.
MELLON, W. S.
NORTHROP, D. B.
PETERSON, R. E.
RICH, D. H.
ROBINSON, J. R.
RUDY, T. A.
SCARBOROUGH, J.
SHEN, B.
THORSON, J. S.

School of Veterinary Medicine (2015 Linden Dr., Madison, WI 53706-1102; tel. (608) 263-2525; e-mail oaa@vetmed.wisc.edu; internet www.vetmed.wisc.edu):

AIKEN, J. M.

BEHAN, M., Comparative Biosciences
BJORLING, D. E., Surgical Sciences
BOSU, W. T., Medical Sciences
CAREY, H. V., Comparative Biosciences
CHRISTENSEN, B. M.
COLLINS, M.
CZUPRYNSKI, C. J
DUBIELZIG, R. R.
DUNCAN, I. D., Medical Sciences
ELFARRA, A. A., Comparative Biosciences
GINTHER, O. J.
HELLEKANT, G.
KAWAOKA, Y.
MCGUIRK, S. M., Medical Sciences
MACWILLIAMS, P. S.
MANLEY, P. A., Surgical Sciences
MARKEL, M. D., Medical Sciences
MESSING, A.
MILETIC, V., Comparative Biosciences
MITCHELL, G. S., Comparative Biosciences
MURPHY, C. J., Surgical Sciences
OAKS, J. A., Comparative Biosciences
OLSEN, C. W.
SCHULER, L. A., Comparative Biosciences
SCHULTZ, R. D.
SPLITTER, G. A.
WILSMAN, N. J., Comparative Biosciences
YOSHINO, T. P.

Division of Continuing Studies (tel. (608) 262-1156; fax (608) 265-4555; e-mail info@dcs .wisc.edu; internet www.dcs.wisc.edu):

AUERBACH, E. K., Liberal Studies and the Arts
CAMPBELL, J. A., Professional Devt and Applied Studies
COOK, M. J., Liberal Studies and the Arts
KESSEL, R., Professional Devt and Applied Studies
NELSON, L. J., Liberal Studies and the Arts
ORTON, B. M., Professional Devt and Applied Studies
PADDOCK, S. C., Professional Devt and Applied Studies
SCHULENBURG, J. A., Liberal Studies and the Arts
WILLIAMS, R. T., Professional Devt and Applied Studies

Nelson Institute for Environmental Studies, The (122 Science Hall, 550 N Park St, Madison, WI 53706-1491; tel. (608) 265-5296; fax (608) 262-0014; internet www.ies .wisc.edu):

ADAMS, M. S., Botany
ALANEN, A. R., Landscape Architecture
ALBRECHT, K. A., Agronomy
ALLEN, T. F., Botany, Integrated Liberal Studies
ALVARADO, F. L., Electrical and Computer Engineering
ANDERSON, D. R., Business
ANDERSON, M. P., Geology and Geophysics
ANDREN, A. W., Civil and Environmental Engineering
ANDREWS, J. H., Plant Pathology
ARMSTRONG, D. E., Civil and Environmental Engineering
BAHR, J. M., Geology and Geophysics, Geological Engineering
BARROWS, R. L., Agricultural and Applied Economics
BAYLIS, J. R., Zoology
BERRY, P. E., Botany
BISHOP, R. C., Agricultural and Applied Economics
BLEAM, W. F., Soil Science
BOCKHEIM, J. G., Soil Science
BORN, S. M., Urban and Regional Planning
BRETHERTON, F. P., Atmospheric and Oceanic Sciences
BRINKMANN, W. A. R., Geography
BROWN, M. R., Agricultural Journalism
BUBENZER, G. D., Biological Systems Engineering
BUONGIORNO, J., Forest Ecology and Management

BUTTEL, F. H., Rural Sociology
CAMPBELL, G. R., Agricultural and Applied Economics
CARD, C. F., Philosophy, Women's Studies
CARPENTER, S. R., Zoology
CHENOWETH, R. E., Urban and Regional Planning
COLLINS, J. L., Sociology, Women's Studies
COMPTON, J. L., Forest Ecology and Management
CONVERSE, J. C., Biological Systems Engineering
CORRADINI, M. L., Engineering Physics, Mechanical Engineering
CRONON, W., History, Geography
DEWITT, C. B., Environmental Studies
DODSON, S., Zoology
DUNWOODY, S. L., Journalism and Mass Communication
ELDER, J. W., Sociology, Languages and Cultures of Asia
FELSTEHAUSEN, H. H., Urban and Regional Planning
FELTSKOG, E. N., English
FIELD, D. R., Forest Ecology and Management, Rural Sociology
FREUDENBURG, W. R., Rural Sociology
FRIEDMAN, E., Political Science
GIVNISH, T. J., Botany
GOODMAN, R. M., Plant Pathology
GRAHAM, L. K., Botany
GURIES, R. P., Forest Ecology and Management
HAMERS, R. J., Chemistry
HARRINGTON, J. A., Landscape Architecture
HAVEMAN, R. H., Economics
HEBERLEIN, T. A., Rural Sociology
HILL, R. J., English, American Indian Studies
HOOPES, J. A., Civil and Environmental Engineering
HOWELL, E. A., Landscape Architecture
HUDDLESTON, J. R., Urban and Regional Planning
IRISH, C. R., Law
JACOBS, H. M., Urban and Regional Planning
JEANNE, R. L., Entomology
JEFFRIES, T. W., Bacteriology
JOERES, E. F., Civil and Environmental Engineering
KANAREK, M. S., Preventive Medicine
KARASOV, W. H., Wildlife Ecology, Zoology
KITCHELL, J. F., Zoology
KNOX, J. C., Geography
KOEGEL, R. C., Biological Systems Engineering, Mechanical Engineering
KULCINSKI, G. L., Engineering Physics
KUTZBACH, J. E., Atmospheric and Oceanic Sciences
LEPOWSKY, M., Anthropology, Women's Studies
LILLESAND, T. M., Forest Ecology and Management, Civil and Environmental Engineering
LINDROTH, R. L., Entomology
LONG, W. F., Electrical and Computer Engineering
LOWERY, B., Soil Science
MCCOWN, B. H., Horticulture
MCEVOY, A. F., Law, History
MCSWEENEY, K., Soil Science
MADISON, F. W., Soil Science
MARIEN, E. J., Business
MICKELSON, D. M., Geology and Geophysics
MITCHELL, J. W., Mechanical Engineering
MOERMOND, T. C., Zoology
NIEMANN, B. J., Jr, Urban and Regional Planning
NORMAN, J. M., Soil Science, Atmospheric and Oceanic Sciences
NOWAK, P., Rural Sociology
O'KEEFE, G. J., Life Sciences Communication
O'LEARY, P. R., Biological Systems Engineering

PALLONI, A., Sociology
PINGREE, S., Life Sciences Communication, Human Ecology
PORTER, W. P., Zoology
POSNER, J. L., Agronomy
POTTER, K. W., Civil and Environmental Engineering
RAY, R. O., Forest Ecology and Management
REED, J. D., Animal Sciences, Dairy Science
RICHARDSON, N. R., Political Science
RUTLEDGE, J. J., Animal Sciences, Genetics
SCARPACE, F. L., Civil and Environmental Engineering
SCHMIT, J. T., Business
SCHULER, R. T., Biological Systems Engineering
SNOWDON, C. T., Psychology, Zoology
SONZOGNI, W. C., Civil and Environmental Engineering
STEVENSON, R. E., Business
STEVENSON, W. R., Plant Pathology
STEWART, J. H., Curriculum and Instruction
STIER, J. C., Forest Ecology and Management
STRAUB, R. J., Biological Systems Engineering
STRIER, K. B., Anthropology, Zoology
TAYLOR, M. S., Economics
TEMPLE, S. A., Wildlife Ecology
TISHLER, W. H., Landscape Architecture
TRIPLETT, E. W., Agronomy
VALE, T. R., Geography
VANDELL, K. D., Business
VENTURA, S. J., Soil Science
VONDEROHE, A. P., Civil and Environmental Engineering
WALLER, D. M., Botany
WANG, P. K., Atmospheric and Oceanic Sciences
YANDELL, B. S., Statistics, Horticulture
YUILL, T. M., Animal Health and Biomedical Sciences, Pathobiological Sciences, Wildlife Ecology
ZEDLER, J. B., Botany, Arboretum
ZEDLER, P. H., Arboretum
ZIMMERER, K. S., Geography

Wisconsin School of Business (2265 Grainger Hall, 975 University Ave, Madison, WI 53706; tel. (608) 262-1550; fax (608) 265-6041; e-mail busundergrads@bus.wisc.edu; internet www.bus.wisc.edu):

ALDAG, R. J.
ANDERSON, D. R.
ANTONIONI, D. T.
BROWN, D. P.
BROWNE, M. J.
COVALESKI, M. A.
DAVIS, J. S.
DUNHAM, R. B.
EICHENSEHER, J. W.
FREES, E. W.
GERHART, B. A.
HARMATUCK, D. J.
HAUSCH, D. B.
HEIDE, J. B.
HODDER, J. E.
JOHANNES, J. M.
KRAINER, R. E.
MALPEZZI, S.
MARIEN, E. J.
MILLER, R. B.
MINER, A. S.
MORRIS, J. G.
NAIR, R. D.
NEVIN, J. R.
PETER, J. P.
RIDDIOUGH, T. J.
RITTENBERG, L. E.
SCHMIT, J. T.
SHILLING, J. D., Real Estate
STEVENSON, R. E.
THOMPSON, J. C., Marketing

VANDELL, K. D.
WEMMERLÖV, U.
WEYGANDT, J. J.
WILD, J. J.

University of Wisconsin—Milwaukee

2200 E Kenwood Blvd, POB 413, Milwaukee, WI 53201-0413

Telephone: (414) 229-1122
Internet: www4.uwm.edu

Founded 1885
Academic year: September to May

Chancellor: MICHAEL R. LOVELL
Provost and Vice-Chancellor for Academic Affairs: JOHANNES J. BRITZ
Vice-Chancellor for Devt and Alumni Relations: PAT BORGER
Vice-Chancellor for Finance and Admin. Affairs: CHRISTY L. BROWN
Vice-Chancellor for Student Affairs: MICHAEL R. LALIBERTE
Vice-Chancellor for Univ. Relations: TOM LULJAK
Dir of Libraries: EWA BARCZYK
Library: 5.2m. vols, 450,000 photographs
Number of teachers: 1,007
Number of students: 30,502

DEANS

College of Engineering and Applied Science: Prof. TIEN-CHIEN JEN
College of Health Sciences: CHUKUKA S. ENWEMEKA
College of Letters and Science: RODNEY A. SWAIN
College of Nursing: Dr SALLY P. LUNDEEN
Graduate School: DAVID YU
Helen Bader School of Social Welfare: Dr STAN STOJKOVIĆ
Peck School of the Arts: WADE HOBGOOD
School of Architecture and Urban Planning: SHARADHA NATRAJ
School of Continuing Education: Dr PATRICIA ARREDONDO
School of Education: CAROL COLBECK
School of Information Studies: DIETMAR WOLFRAM
Sheldon B. Lubar School of Business: TIMOTHY L. SMUNT

CHAIRS OF DEPARTMENT

College of Engineering and Applied Science (POB 784, Milwaukee, WI 53201-0784 3200 N Cramer St, Milwaukee, WI 53211; tel. (414) 229-4768; fax (414) 229-6958; e-mail ceas-adv@uwm.edu; internet www.uwm.edu/ceas):

Civil Engineering and Mechanics: HECTOR BRAVO
Computer Science: HOSSEIN HOSSEINI
Electrical Engineering: GEORGE HANSON
Industrial and Manufacturing Engineering: ARUN GARG
Materials Engineering: NIDAL ABU-ZAHRA
Mechanical Engineering: ANOOP DHINGRA

College of Health Sciences (POB 413, Milwaukee, WI 53201-0413; tel. (414) 229-2758; fax (414) 906-3920; e-mail chs-info@uwm.edu; internet www4.uwm.edu/chs):

Communication Sciences and Disorders: Dr MARYLOU GELFER
Health Informatics and Admin.: Dr TIMOTHY PATRICK
Health Sciences: Dr JERI-ANNE LYONS
Human Movement Sciences: Dr BARBARA MEYER
Occupational Science and Technology: Dr GINNY STOFFEL

College of Letters and Science (142 Holton Hall, 2442 E Hartford Ave, POB 413, Milwaukee, WI 53201; tel. (414) 229-4654; fax (414) 229-6827; e-mail let-sci@uwm.edu; internet www.uwm.edu/letsci):

Africology: JOYCE KIRK
Anthropology: THOMAS MALABY
Art History: KENNETH BENDINER
Biological Sciences: DAAD SAFFARINI
Chemistry and Biochemistry: PETER GEISSINGER
Communication: WILLIAM KEITH
Economics: MOHSEN BAHMANI
English: LIAM CALLANAN
Foreign Languages and Literature: KEVIN MUSE
French, Italian and Comparative Literature: PETER PAIK
Geography: MARK SCHWARTZ
Geosciences: JOHN ISBELL
History: MERRY WIESNER-HANKS
Journalism, Advertising and Media Studies: DAVID ALLEN
Linguistics: HAMID OUALI
Mathematical Sciences: RICHARD STOCKBRIDGE
Philosophy: RICHARD TIERNEY
Physics: ALAN WISEMAN
Political Science: THOMAS HOLBROOK
Psychology: JAMES MOYER
Sociology: KENT REDDING
Spanish and Portuguese: R. JOHN MCCAW

College of Nursing (1921 E Hartford Ave, POB 413, Milwaukee, WI 53201; tel. (414) 229-4801; fax (414) 229-6474; e-mail asknursing@uwm.edu; internet www.umw.edu/dept/nursing):

Foundations of Nursing: BETH ROGERS
Health Maintenance: EILEN SHEIL
Health Restoration: MARY WIERENGA

School of Architecture and Urban Planning (POB 413, Milwaukee, WI 53201; tel. (414) 229-4014; fax (414) 229-6976; e-mail sarup-advising@uwm.edu; internet www.uwm.edu/sarup):

Architecture: LISA DiSALVO
Urban Planning: LINDA SCUNCIO

School of Education (POB 413, Milwaukee, WI 53201-0413
Enderis Hall, 2400 E Hartford Ave, Milwaukee, WI 53211; tel. (414) 229-4721; fax (414) 229-6548; e-mail soedean@uwm.edu; internet www.uwm.edu/soe):

Admin. Leadership: BARB DALEY
Curriculum and Instruction: Dr HOPE LONGWELL-GRICE
Educational Policy and Community Studies: AARON SCHUTZ
Educational Psychology: NADYA FOUAD
Exceptional Education: AMY OTIS-WILBORN

Peck School of the Arts (POB 413, Milwaukee, WI 53201; tel. (414) 229-4762; fax (414) 229-6154; internet www.uwm.edu/soa):

Art and Design: LEE ANN GARRISON
Dance: Assoc. Prof. SIMONE FERRO
Film: ROB YEO
Music: Dr JON WELSTEAD
Theatre: LEROY STONER

University of Wisconsin—Oshkosh

800 Algoma Blvd, Oshkosh, WI 54901

Telephone: (920) 424-1234
Fax: (920) 424-7317
Internet: www.uwosh.edu

Founded 1871, present name and status 1971

Chancellor: RICHARD H. WELLS
Provost and Vice-Chancellor for Academic Affairs: Dr LANE EARNS
Vice-Chancellor for Student Affairs: PETRA ROTA
Vice-Chancellor for Admin. Services: TOM SONNLEITNER
Dean of Students: SHARON KIPETZ
Dir of Library: PATRICK WILKINSON

Library of 448,751 vols, 12,812 e-books , 96,046 bound periodical vols, 1,183 current periodical subscriptions, 133,282 vols govt

documents, 1.4m. microforms, 34,000 maps and 2,400 linear ft of archival material
Number of teachers: 281
Number of students: 13,002

DEANS

College of Business: Dr WILLIAM TALLON
College of Education and Human Services: Dr FREDERICK YEO
College of Letters and Science: Dr JOHN KOKER
College of Nursing: Dr ROSEMARY SMITH

University of Wisconsin—Parkside

900 Wood Rd, POB 2000, Kenosha, WI 53141-2000
Telephone: (262) 595-2345
Internet: www.uwp.edu
Founded 1968
Academic year: September to May
Chancellor: Dr DEBORAH FORD
Provost and Vice-Chancellor: Dr TERRY BROWN
Assoc. Provost for Academic Affairs: DENNIS ROME
Vice-Chancellor and Dean of Students: STEVE McLAUGHLIN
Vice-Chancellor for Univ. Relations and Advancement: KAREN COY-ROMANO
Vice-Chancellor for Admin. and Fiscal Affairs: WILLIAM STREETER
Vice-Chancellor for Institutional Effectiveness: ANN ZANZIG
Registrar: RHONDA KIMMEL
Library Dir: VANAJA MENON
Library of 400,000 vols
Number of teachers: 125 full-time
Number of students: 5,300

DEANS

College of Arts and Sciences: Prof. Dr DEAN YOHNK
School of Business and Technology: Prof. Dr FRED EBEID

University of Wisconsin—Platteville

1 University Plaza, Platteville, WI 53818
Telephone: (608) 342-1491
Fax: (608) 342-1232
Internet: www.uwplatt.edu
Founded 1866 as Platteville Normal School, present name 1966, present status 1971
Chancellor: DENNIS J. SHIELDS
Provost and Vice-Chancellor for Academic Affairs: MITTIE NIMOCKS
Assoc. Vice-Chancellor: DAVID VAN BUREN
Asst Chancellor for Admission and Enrolment Services: ANGELA UDELHOFEN
Asst Chancellor for Admin. Services: ROBERT CRAMER
Asst Chancellor for Student Affairs: JOANNE WILSON
Asst Chancellor for Univ. Advancement: DENNIS COOLEY
Library Dir: ZORA SAMPSON
Library of 195,000 vols
Number of teachers: 264
Number of students: 7,928

DEANS

College of Business, Industry, Life Science and Agriculture: WAYNE WEBER
College of Engineering, Mathematics and Science: BILL HUDSON
College of Liberal Arts and Education: LAURA ANDERSON

University of Wisconsin—River Falls

410 S Third St, River Falls, WI 54022
Telephone: (715) 425-3911
Fax: (715) 425-4487
Internet: www.uwrf.edu

Founded 1874 as State Normal School, present name and status 1971
Academic year: August to May
Chancellor: Dr DEAN VAN GALEN
Provost and Vice-Chancellor for Academic Affairs: Dr FERNANDO P. DELGADO
Vice-Chancellor for Admin. and Finance: JOSEPH HARBOUK
Assoc. Vice-Chancellor for Student Affairs: GREGG HEINSELMAN
Library Dir: VALERIE MALZACHER
Library of 220,500 vols
Number of teachers: 222
Number of students: 6,600

DEANS

College of Agriculture, Food and Environmental Sciences: DALE GALLENBERG
College of Arts and Sciences: BRAD CASKEY
College of Business and Economics: GLENN POTTS
College of Education and Professional Studies: LARRY SOLBERG
Outreach and Graduate Studies: Dr DOUG JOHNSON

University of Wisconsin—Stevens Point

2100 Main St, Stevens Point, WI 54481-3897
Telephone: (715) 346-0123
Fax: (715) 346-2561
Internet: www.uwsp.edu
Founded 1894
Academic year: September to May
Chancellor: Dr BERNIE L. PATTERSON
Provost and Vice-Chancellor for Academic Affairs: GREGORY SUMMERS
Vice-Chancellor for Business Affairs: GREGORY M. DIEMER
Vice-Chancellor for Student Affairs: ALFRED THOMPSON
Library Dir: KATHY DAVIS
Library of 1,925,000 vol items
Number of teachers: 400
Number of students: 9,500
Publication: *Issues in Writing* (2 a year)

DEANS

College of Fine Arts and Communication: JEFFREY W. MORIN
College of Letters and Science: CHRISTOPHER CIRMO
College of Natural Resources: CHRISTINE THOMAS
College of Professional Studies: Dr MARTIN J. LOY

University of Wisconsin—Stout

Menomonie, WI 54751
Telephone: (715) 232-1122
Fax: (715) 232-1667
Internet: www.uwstout.edu
Founded 1891, present name and status 1971
Academic year: September to May
Chancellor: Dr CHARLES W. SORENSON
Provost and Vice-Chancellor for Academic and Student Affairs: Dr MARY HOPKINS-BEST
Vice-Chancellor for Admin. and Student Life Services: ED NIESKES
Vice-Chancellor for Univ. Advancement and Marketing: MARK PARSONS
Dean of Students: JOAN THOMAS
Assoc. Vice-Chancellor: JACKIE WEISSENBURGER
Dir for Univ. Library: WILLIAM JOHNSTON
Library of 256,544 vols
Number of teachers: 450
Number of students: 9,339
Publication: *Stoutonia* (14 a year)

DEANS

College of Arts, Humanities, and Social Sciences: MARIA ALM
College of Education, Health and Human Sciences: Dr ROBERT PETERS
College of Management: ABEL ADEKOLA
College of Science, Technology, Engineering and Mathematics: JEFFREY ANDERSON

University of Wisconsin—Superior

Belknap and Catlin, POB 2000, Superior, WI 54880-4500
Telephone: (715) 394-8101
Fax: (715) 394-8588
E-mail: relations@uwsuper.edu
Internet: www.uwsuper.edu
Founded 1893, present name and status 1971
Chancellor: Dr RENÉE WACHTER
Provost, Interim Vice-Chancellor for Academic Affairs and Dean of Faculties: Dr FAITH HENSRUD
Vice-Chancellor for Admin. and Finance: JANET HANSON
Vice-Chancellor for Univ. Advancement: JEANNE THOMPSON
Registrar: DIANE DOUGLAS
Dir of Library Services: DEBRA NORDGREN
Library of 240,000 vols
Number of teachers: 268 (112 full time, 56 part time)
Number of students: 2,867

University of Wisconsin—Whitewater

800 W Main St, Whitewater, WI 53190-1790
Telephone: (262) 472-1234
Fax: (262) 472-1518
Internet: www.uww.edu
Founded 1868
Academic year: August to May
Chancellor: RICHARD J. TELFER
Provost and Vice-Chancellor for Academic Affairs: BEVERLY KOPPER
Vice-Chancellor for Admin. Affairs: JEFF ARNOLD
Vice-Chancellor for Student Affairs: THOMAS RIOS
Vice-Chancellor for Univ. Advancement: JON ENSLIN
Library Dir: MYRNA McCALLISTER
Library of 1,873,561 vols (incl. books, serial backfiles and govt documents), 1,153,073 microforms and 12,197 audio visual items, 7,030 current serial subscriptions, 57,165 e-books, 15,000 print and e-journals
Number of teachers: 565
Number of students: 11,643

DEANS

College of Arts and Communication: MARK McPHAIL
College of Business and Economics: Dr CHRISTINE CLEMENTS
College of Education and Professional Studies: KATY HEYNING
College of Letters and Sciences: MARY PINKERTON
School of Graduate Studies and Continuing Education: JOHN STONE.

OTHER CONSTITUENT INSTITUTIONS

University of Wisconsin Colleges

Central Administrative Offices, 780 Regent St, Suite 130, Madison, WI 53715-2635
Telephone: (608) 262-1783
Internet: www.uwc.edu

Colleges at Barron Co, Baraboo/Sauk Co, Fox Valley, Fond du Lac, Manitowoc, Marathon Co, Marshfield/Wood Co, Marinette, Richland, Rock Co, Sheboygan, Washington Co, Waukesha; 2-year courses at all colleges
Chancellor: RAY CROSS

Provost and Vice Chancellor: GREG HUTCHINS
Provost and Vice-Chancellor for Academic Affairs: GREG LAMPE
Vice-Chancellor for Admin. Services: STEVEN WILDECK
Registrar: LARRY GRAVES
Number of students: 14,385 at 13 campuses

University of Wisconsin Extension

432 N Lake St, Madison, WI 53706
Telephone: (608) 262-3786
Internet: www.uwex.edu
Works in partnership with 26 Univ. of Wisconsin System campuses, 72 Wisconsin counties, 3 tribal govts and public and private orgs; provides online distance programmes, spec. programmes and distance learning programmes
Chancellor: RAY CROSS
Provost and Vice-Chancellor: GREGORY HUTCHINS
Vice-Chancellor for Admin. and Financial Services: STEVE WILDECK.

VITERBO UNIVERSITY

900 Viterbo Dr., La Crosse, WI 54601
Telephone: (608) 796-3000
E-mail: communication@viterbo.edu
Internet: www.viterbo.edu

Founded 1890, present name and status 2000
Private control
Academic year: August to May
Pres.: Dr RICHARD B. ARTMAN
Vice-Pres. for Academic Affairs: BARBARA GAYLE
Vice-Pres. for Admin. and Finance: TODD ERICSON
Vice-Pres. for Admission: ROLAND NELSON
Vice-Pres. for Communications and Marketing: PATRICK KERRIGAN
Vice-Pres. for Institutional Advancement: GARY KLEIN
Vice-Pres. for Mission and Ministry: Fr TOM O'NEILL
Vice-Pres. for Student Devt: DIANE BRIMMER
Dean for Admission: ROBERT FORGET
Registrar: AMY GLEASON
Library Dir: GRETEL STOCK-KUPPERMAN
Library of 90,000 vols
Number of teachers: 176 (92 full-time, 84 part-time)

Number of students: 3,192

DEANS

Dahl School of Business: THOMAS E. KNOTHE
School of Education: SUE BATELL
School of Fine Arts: TIMOTHY SCHORR
School of Letters and Sciences: GLENA G. TEMPLE
School of Nursing: Dr SILVANA F. RICHARDSON

WISCONSIN LUTHERAN COLLEGE

8800 W Bluemound Rd, Milwaukee, WI 53226
Telephone: (414) 443-8800
Fax: (414) 443-8514
E-mail: admissions@wlc.edu
Internet: www.wlc.edu
Founded 1973
Private control
Pres.: Dr DANIEL W. JOHNSON
Provost: Dr JOHN KOLANDER
Vice-Pres. for Adult and Graduate Studies: JIM BRANDT
Vice-Pres. for Devt: CRAIG RUSSOW
Vice-Pres. for Finance: GARY SCHMID
Vice-Pres. for Student Affairs: Dr DENNIS MILLER
Assoc. Vice-Pres. for Marketing and Communication: VICKI HARTIG
Registrar: CAROL KOELPIN
Dir for Library Services: STARLA SIEGMANN
Number of students: 1,022

DEANS

College of Adult and Graduate Studies: JOYCE S. NATZKE
College of Arts and Sciences: JARROD ERBE
College of Professional Studies: DAVID BRIGHTSMAN

WISCONSIN SCHOOL OF PROFESSIONAL PSYCHOLOGY

9120 W Hampton Ave 212, Milwaukee, WI 53225-4960
Telephone: (414) 464-9777
Fax: (414) 358-5590
E-mail: admissions@wspp.edu
Internet: www.wspp.edu
Founded 1978
Private control

Pres.: Dr KATHLEEN M. RUSCH
Dean: Dr DALE BASPALEC
Library of 100 vols.

WYOMING

UNIVERSITY OF WYOMING

POB 3314, Laramie, WY 82071
1000 E University Ave, Laramie, WY 82071
Telephone: (307) 766-1121
Fax: (307) 766-2606
Internet: www.uwyo.edu
Founded 1886
State control
Language of instruction: English
Academic year: September to May
Pres.: Dr THOMAS BUCHANAN
Provost and Vice-Pres. for Academic Affairs: MYRON ALLEN
Assoc. Provost: NICOLE BALLENGER
Assoc. Provost: ANDREW HANSEN
Assoc. Provost and Dean for the Outreach School: MAGGI MURDOCK
Vice-Pres. for Admin.: DOUGLAS H. VINZANT
Vice-Pres. for Information Technology: ROBERT AYLWARD
Vice-Pres. for Institutional Advancement: BEN BLALOCK
Vice-Pres. for Research and Economic Devt: WILLIAM GERN
Vice-Pres. for Student Affairs: SARA AXELSON
Dean for Univ. Libraries: MAGGIE FARREL
Library: see Libraries and Archives
Number of teachers: 685
Number of students: 13,476
Publication: UWYO Magazine (3 a year)

DEANS

College of Agriculture and Natural Resources: FRANK GALEY
College of Arts and Sciences: B. OLIVER WALTER
College of Business: BRENT HATHAWAY
College of Education: KAY PERSICHITTE
College of Engineering and Applied Science: ROB ETTEMA
College of Health Sciences: JOE STEINER
College of Law: STEVE EASTON
Graduate School: DON ROTH
Outreach School: Dr MAGGI MURDOCK

GUAM

The Higher Education System

Higher education in the unincorporated US territory of Guam is principally provided by the University of Guam (founded in 1952; present name and status adopted 1968 and 1984, respectively) and Guam Community College (founded in 1977), the latter of which provides vocational training programmes, which grant direct access to employment or transfer to a four-year college or university degree elsewhere. Enrolment at both institutions, which are accredited by the USA's Western Association of Schools and Colleges, has expanded in recent years, with 10,268 students enrolled at the Guam Community College in 2005/06 and 3,387 students enrolled at the University of Guam in 2008/09. Mangilao is home to the main campus of the Pacific Islands University (founded in 1976 as the Micronesian Institute of Biblical Studies on the island of Tol in Chuuk; present name and status adopted 2009); the Christian liberal arts institution is accredited by the USA's Transnational Association of Christian Colleges and Schools, and had a total enrolment of 99 students (of whom 62 were full-time and 37 were part-time) in 2010/11.

Regulatory Body

GOVERNMENT

Department of Chamorro Affairs: POB 2950, Hagatna, GU 96910; 238 Archbishop Felixberto C. Flores St, DNA Bldg, Fourth Fl., Suite 408, Hagatna, GU 96910; tel. (671) 475-4278; fax (671) 475-4227; internet www .dca.guam.gov; Chair. JOHN MAFNAS; Pres. JOSEPH CAMERON.

Guam Department of Education: POB DE, Hagåtña, GU 96932; Manuel F. Leon Guerrero Admin. Bldg, 312 Aspinall Ave, Hagåtña, GU 96932; tel. (671) 475-0462; fax (671) 472-5003; e-mail geis@teleguam.net; internet www.gdoe.net; Superintendent NERISSA BRETANIA UNDERWOOD.

Department of Youth Affairs/Depåttamenton Asunton Manhoben: POB 23672, GMF, GU 96921; 169 San Isidro St, Mangilao, GU 96923; tel. (671) 735-5010; fax (671) 734-7536; internet dya.guam.gov; f. 1978; Dir ADONIS J. MENDIOLA.

Guam Historic Resources Division: 490 Chalan Palasyo, Agana Heights, GU 96910; tel. (671) 475-6294; fax (671) 477-2822; internet historicguam.org; attached to Dept of Parks and Recreation; also known as the State Historic Preservation Office (SHPO); implements projects and activities that help engage in comprehensive historic preservation programmes that promote the use, conservation, preservation and presentation of historic properties; Guam State Historic Preservation Officer LYNDA BORDALLO-AGUON.

FUNDING

Guam Council on the Arts and Humanities/Kahan I Kutturan Guahan: POB 2950, Hagatna, GU 96932; Terlaje Professional Bldg, First Fl., 194 Hernan Cortez Ave, Hagatna, GU; tel. (671) 475-3661; fax (671) 477-2786; e-mail info@caha.guam.gov; internet www.guamcaha.org; f. 1967 as Insular Arts Council; assures issuance of grants to individuals and organizations for the perpetuation of arts and culture of Guam; Dir. JOSEPH ARTERO-CAMERON.

Learned Societies

BIBLIOGRAPHY, LIBRARY SCIENCE AND MUSEOLOGY

Guam Library Association: POB 210, Hagatna, GU 96932; tel. (671) 475-4753; fax (671) 477-9777; e-mail guam.library .association@gmail.com; internet sites.google .com/site/guamlibraryassociation/home; promotes knowledge; develops and improves library services, resources on the island; provides continuing library-related education; Pres. CYNTHIA PRUSKI; Vice-Pres. for Membership PATRIA SABLAN; Vice-Pres. for Programmes (vacant); Sec. OMAIRA BRUNAL-PERRY; Treas. MARIA OVALLES.

Guam Museum Foundation, Inc: POB 518, Hagatna, GU 96932; tel. (671) 475-4634; fax (671) 475-4636; internet www .guammuseum.com; promotes cultural and historical activities; helps organize non-profit foundations under the laws of Guam; works closely with all govt entities, educational and religious instns, public and private orgs to maximize public benefits and opportunities.

ECONOMICS, LAW AND POLITICS

Guam Chamber of Commerce: 173 Aspinall Ave, Suite 101, Ada Plaza Center, Hagåtña, GU 96910; tel. (671) 472-6311; fax (671) 472-6202; internet www.guamchamber .com.gu; develops, encourages, promotes and protects commercial, professional, financial, and gen. business interests of the Territory of Guam; extends and promotes trade and commerce, and fosters, develops and protects the industry of the Territory; procures laws and regulations desirable for the benefit of business in gen.; Chair. MARK J. SABLAN; Pres. DAVID P. LEDDY; Sec. and Treas. JOE ARNETT.

FINE AND PERFORMING ARTS

Guam Preservation Trust/Inangokkon Inadahi Guahan: POB 3036, Hagåtña, GU 96932; Historic Lujan House, 167, Padre Palomo St, Hagåtña, GU 96910; tel. (671) 472-9439; fax (671) 477-2047; e-mail jqpreservation@guam.net; internet www .guampreservationtrust.com; f. 1990; acquires titles for preservation threatened historical sites; supports activities related to public appreciation of historic places; awards grants for property documentation, protection through stabilization, rehabilitation, reconstruction and restoration; archival and archaeological research; Chief Programme Officer JOSEPH E. QUINATA; Programme Officer ROSANNA BARCINAS.

Guam Symphony Society: POB 4069, Hagåtña, GU 96932; tel. (671) 477-1959; e-mail guamsymphonysociety@gmail.com; internet www.guamsymphony.com; f. 1967; non-profit org.; promotes classical music; develops local musical talent; conducts spec. orchestral performances; 50 volunteer musicians; 44 mems; Dir for Music and Conductor STEPHEN C. BEDNARZYK; Pres. CLIFFORD A. GUZMAN; Vice-Pres. JOHN ROBERTSON; Sec. APRIL BRIGGS; Treas. MONICA PIDO.

MEDICINE

Guam Medical Association: tel. (671) 483-6600; e-mail guammedicalassociation@gmail .com; internet www.gma-assn.org; non-profit org.; promotes art and science of medicine; advocates for community and public health issues; Pres. Dr PATRICK SANTOS; Pres.-Elect Dr THOMAS SHIEH; Exec. Dir PRAM SULLIVAN; Sec. Dr BEVAN GESLANI; Treas. Dr CHRIS BIELING; publ. *GMA Medical Journal*.

Research Institutes

HISTORY, GEOGRAPHY AND ARCHAEOLOGY

WERI–Water and Environmental Research Institute of the Western Pacific: UOG Station, Mangilao, GU 96923; tel. (671) 735-2690; fax (671) 734-8890; internet www.weriguam.org; f. 1975, fmrly the Water and Energy Research Institute of the Western Pacific, present name 1998; attached to Univ. of Guam; research on water problems and water-related phenomena, incl. engineering, environmental chemistry, environmental toxicology, geology, geohydrology, hydrology, mapping and modelling, meteorology; production, distribution and management of freshwater resources; teaching and outreach programmes; Dir Prof. Dr GARY DENTON; Sec. NORMA C. BLAS.

LANGUAGE AND LITERATURE

Richard F. Taitano Micronesia Area Research Center (MARC): UOG Station, Mangilao, GU 96923; tel. (671) 735-2150; fax (671) 734-7403; internet www.uog.edu/marc; attached to Univ. of Guam; preserves and provides access to collns of archival maps, photographs, texts and cultural materials related to the Micronesian geographical region; offers a programme in archaeological studies; instns: Micronesian Language Institute, Chamorro Language and Culture Centre; 200 titles in separate series; library of 40,000 vols on Guam, Micronesia and the Pacific; 800 dissertations and theses, news clippings and brochures; Dir Dr JOHN A. PETERSON; Dir for Chamorro Language and Culture Centre Dr MARILYN SALAS (acting).

MEDICINE

Cancer Research Center: UOG Station, Mangilao, GU 96923; tel. (671) 735-3036; fax

(671) 734-3636; e-mail u54@uguam.uog.edu; internet www.guamcancerresearch.org; f. 2004; attached to Univ. of Guam; promotes improvement in cancer research capabilities; undergraduate and postgraduate education and training; Principal Investigator Dr HELEN WHIPPY.

NATURAL SCIENCES

Western Pacific Tropical Research Center: UOG Station, Mangilao, GU 96923; tel. (671) 735-2684; fax (671) 734-0485; internet www.wptrc.org; attached to Univ. of Guam; research in agricultural profitability, economic devt using natural resources, improvement in quality and safety of food products, protection of environment; offers Masters programmes in biology and environmental science; field stations in Ija, Inarajan and Yigo; soil testing laboratory; Dean and Dir Dr LEE S. YUDIN; Assoc. Dir Dr GREG WIECKO; Assoc. Dean Dr HENRY TAIJERON; publ. *WPTRC Impact Report* (1 a year).

Libraries and Archives

Hagåtña

Guam Law Library: 141 San Ramon St, Hagåtña, GU 96910-4333; tel. (671) 477-7623; fax (671) 472-1246; e-mail gll@teleguam.net; internet www.guamlawlibrary.org; f. 1978; maintains the Judicial Centre br. libraries serving judges and law clerks of the Guam Supreme and Superior courts; serves as depository for all public laws, exec. orders, legislative materials and decisions of the courts; 55,623 vols; Pres. VERNON PEREZ; Vice-Pres. BRIDGET ANN KEITH; Sec. JUDITH HATTORI; Treas. MITCHELL THOMPSON; Exec. Dir and Librarian GERALDINE A. CEPEDA.

Guam Public Library System: 254 Martyr St, Hagåtña, GU 96910-5141; tel. (671) 475-4751; fax (671) 477-9777; e-mail gpls@gpls.guam.gov; internet gpls.guam.gov; f. 1949; promotes literacy and lifelong learning; maintains materials of cultural significance on the island; cooperates with libraries on other islands; local govt document depository; br. libraries in Barrigada, Dededo, Yona; 1 bookmobile; Dir and Acting Territorial Librarian TERESITA KENNIMER; Sec. BERTHA GUERRERO.

Branch Libraries:

Barrigada Public Library: 177 San Roque Dr., Barrigada; tel. (671) 734-5007; fax (671) 734-5008.

Dededo Public Library: 283 W Santa Barbara Ave, Dededo; tel. (671) 632-5503; fax (671) 632-1046.

Yona Public Library: 265 Sister Mary Eucharita Dr., Yona; tel. (671) 789-5010; fax ((671)477-9777.

Mangilao

University of Guam, Robert F. Kennedy Memorial Library: Tan Siu Lin Bldg, UOG Station, Mangilao, GU 96923; tel. (671) 735-2331; fax (671) 734-6882; e-mail csctsmth@uguam.uog.edu; internet www.uog.edu/dynamicdata/libraryhome.aspx; f. 1963; central library facility at the Univ. of Guam; 124,977 vols, 98,059 print titles, 925,650 microfilm and microfiche units, 1,527 serial titles, 5,289 audiovisual items, 28,845 e-journals; Dir CHRISTINE K. SCOTT-SMITH.

Museums and Art Galleries

Agana

Marianas Military Museum: POB 455, 152 FPO AP, GU 96540-1000; tel. (617) 339-3319; fax (671) 339-8194; e-mail milmuseum@kuentos.guam.net; internet www.guam.net/pub/milmuseum; f. 1999; non-profit corpn; helps explore the history of the relationship between the United States military, the Japanese military and island people of the W Pacific during the years of the Second World War; collns consist of American liberator and Japanese defender history and artefacts.

Jeff's Seaside Museum: 111 S Chalan Antigo, Ipan Talofofo, Agana, GU 96915-3708; tel. (671) 789-2683; fax (671) 789-1741; e-mail info@jeffspiratescove.com; internet www.jeffspiratescove.com/museum.htm; f. 2000; displays unique artifacts, glass fish floats, stone tools, ifit wood sculptures, rare seashells, pottery, fine oil paintings, black coral and floating rock, actual wheel from the USS Battleship Oregon of 1893; CEO and Gen. Man. JEFFREY E. PLEADWELL.

Hagåtña

Guam Gallery of Arts: POB 362, Chamorro Village, Hagåtña, GU 96932; tel. (671) 472-9659; e-mail guamarts@ite.net; f. 1994; displays and sells original artwork and reproductions by local artists; seasonal exhibits and art events; Dir FILAMORE PALOMO ALCON.

Guam Museum of Culture, Art and History: POB 518, Hagåtña, GU 96932; 238 Archbishop Felixberto Flores St, DNA Bldg, 4th Fl., Suite 405, A, Hagåtña, GU 96910; tel. (671) 475-4634; fax (671) 475-4636; e-mail leona@guammuseum.com; internet www.guammuseum.com; attached to Guam Museum Foundation Inc.; represents Guam and Chamorro cultures; holds artefacts and remnants destroyed during the Second World War; Dir ANTHONY RAMIREZ (acting).

Kahan i Kutturan Guahan—The Gallery: c/o Guam Ccl on Arts and Humanities Agency, POB 2950, Hagåtña GU 96932; Dos Amantes Complex, Two Lovers' Leap, Tamuning; tel. (671) 475-2781; fax (671) 477-2786; e-mail info@caha.guam.gov; internet www.guamcaha.org; f. 1972 as the Insular Arts Ccl Gallery; attached to Guam Ccl on the Arts and Humanities Agency; local art exhibits; fellowship programmes; grants and services to local artists; Chair. MONICA GUZMAN; Dir PATRICK BAMBA.

National Museum of the Dulce Nombre de Maria Cathedral Basilica: Cathedral-Basilica Pastoral Centre, 207 Archbishop Felixberto C. Flores St, Hagåtña, GU 96910; tel. (671) 472-6201; fax (671) 472-1729; e-mail info@aganacathedral.org; internet aganacathedral.org; f. 2006; attached to Dulce Nombre de Maria Cathedral Basilica; displays frame views of the *Plaza de España*; inspirational art by local artists; Rector Mgr JAMES LEON GUERRERO BENAVENTE.

Pacific War Museum: POB 2037, Hagåtña, GU 96932; tel. (671) 477-8355; fax (671) 472-6070; internet www.guammuseum.com/pacific-war.htm; f. 2008; dedicated to the USA and Japanese armed forces who fought during the liberation of Guam; displays 15 military vehicles and 3 motorcycles; Chair. JOHN GERBER; Admin. Dir MELA L. GOMEZ.

War in the Pacific National Historical Park: 135 Murray Blvd, Suite 100, Hagåtña, GU 96910; tel. (671) 477-7278; fax (671) 477-7281; internet www.nps.gov/wapa; attached to Nat. Park Service (USA); battlefields, gun emplacements, trenches and historic structures recreate life in Guam during the Second World War; Memorial Wall: displays 16,142 names of Chamorro and US casualties; Liberator's Memorial: honours the armed forces of the 1944 landing on Guam; tropical resources incl. 3,500 marine species and 200 coral species.

Mangilao

Isla Center for the Arts: House 15, Dean's Circle, Univ. of Guam, Mangilao, GU 96923; tel. (671) 735-2965; fax (671) 735-2967; e-mail islacenter@gmail.com; internet www.uog.edu/isla; f. 1980; attached to Univ. of Guam; conducts exhibitions, workshops, lectures; promotes appreciation and awareness of cultures of the W Pacific; permanent colln: indigenous arts and crafts from Micronesia, Europe and Philippines, items of contemporary W fine art, sculpture and Pre-Columbian art; Isla colln: 492 2-D and 3-D objects of folk art (produced for decorative purposes), ceremonial art (used by specific cultures in ceremonies and rituals), utilitarian crafts; other 2-D and 3-Dd works produced in Asian or Western cultures; Dir Dr VELMA YAMASHITA.

Universities

PACIFIC ISLANDS UNIVERSITY

POB 22619 GMF, Mangilao, GU 96921-2619
172 Kinney's Rd, Mangilao, GU 96913

Telephone: (671) 734-1812
Fax: (671) 734-1813
E-mail: guamcampus@piu.edu
Internet: www.piu.edu

Founded 1976 as Micronesian Institute of Biblical Studies, present name and status 2009
Private control
Academic year: July to June

Christian liberal arts education; comprises Pacific Islands Bible College, Pacific Islands Evangelical Seminary, Pacific Islands Christian College

Chair.: HOWARD MERRELL
Sec.: SISKA HUTAPEA
Pres.: Dr DAVID L. OWEN
Provost and Academic Vice-Pres.: CHRISTEL WOOK (acting)
Vice-Pres. for Advancement: LISA COLLINS
Dir for Finance: CELIA ATOIGUE
Dir for Operations: CELIA ATOIGUE
Vice-Pres. for Student Life: ROBERT WATT
Registrar and Dir for Enrolment Management: URTE SCHERER
Dir for Library: LISA COLLINS

Library of 13,500 vols
Number of teachers: 30
Number of students: 164 (160 undergraduate, 4 graduate)

UNIVERSITY OF GUAM/ UNIBETSEDÅT GUAHAN

UOG Station, Mangilao, GU 96923

Telephone: (671) 735-2990
Fax: (671) 734-2296
E-mail: admitme@uguam.uog.edu
Internet: www.uog.edu

Founded 1952 as the Territorial College of Guam, present campus 1960, accredited 1963 and 1965, present name 1968, present status 1984
Public control
Language of instruction: English
Academic year: August to May

Pres.: Dr ROBERT A. UNDERWOOD
Sr Vice-Pres. for Academic and Student Affairs: Dr HELEN J. D. WHIPPY

Vice-Pres. for Admin. and Finance: DAVID M.
O'BRIEN
Dean for Enrolment Management and Stu-
dent Services: Dr JULIE ULLOA-HEATH
Registrar: REMY B. CRISTOBAL
Library: see Libraries and Archives
Number of teachers: 260
Number of students: 3,639

Publications: *Impact* (1 a year), *Isla* (2 a
year), *Micronesian Educator* (1 a year),
Micronesica (2 a year), *Storyboard: A
Journal of Pacific Imagery*, *University
Magazine* (1 a year)

DEANS

College of Liberal Arts and Social Sciences:
Dr JAMES D. SELLMANN

College of Natural and Applied Sciences: Dr
LEE S. YUDIN
School of Business and Public Administra-
tion: Dr ANITA BORJA-ENRIQUEZ
School of Education: Dr ELIZABETH
HAWTHORNE
School of Nursing and Health Sciences: Dr
MARIA SALOMON

PUERTO RICO

The Higher Education System

The Universidad de Puerto Rico (founded in 1903) is the oldest
institution of higher education in the Commonwealth of Puerto
Rico. The US unincorporated territory has both public and
private higher education institutions, some of which are
sizeable with a number of branch campuses dispersed throughout the island. In 2009/10 a total of 249,372 students were
enrolled within higher education, of which 177,803 were
enrolled at private institutions and 71,569 were enrolled at
public institutions. A strong US influence is evident within the
Puerto Rican education system as a whole, and the higher
education sector is no different.

Responsibility for the provision of higher education within
Puerto Rico lies with the Consejo de Educación de Puerto Rico
(Puerto Rico Council on Education). Quality assurance and
accreditation is the responsibility of the Council's División de
Licenciamiento y Acreditación (Division of Licensing and
Accreditation). A number of institutions are concurrently
accredited by the USA's Middle States Association of Colleges
and Schools.

Admission to degree-level education requires students to hold
the High School Graduation Diploma and to sit an entrance
examination. Some programmes at certain institutions may

have additional entrance requirements. The Grado Asociado
(Associate degree), which allows specialization in either the
arts or the sciences, requires at least two years' study and can
lead to further study or grant direct access to employment. The
Grado de Bachillerato (Bachelors degree) can last between
three and six years, depending on the course and grant access
to postgraduate programmes of study. The main postgraduate
qualification is the Grado de Maestría (Masters degree), which
requires an additional one to three years of study following the
Grado de Bachillerato. Certificado Profesional Post Bachillerato (Professional Postgraduate Certificate) and Certificado Post
Maestría (Post-Masters Certificate) programmes are also available, and require one or two semesters of study following the
Grado de Bachillerato or the Grado de Maestría, respectively.
The Doctorado (Doctorate) is the highest academic qualification
and requires a further five years of study following the Grado
de Bachillerato or four years following the Grado de Maestría.

Technical and vocational education is offered by technical
colleges, which offer two-year Certificate courses and two-year
Associate degrees, as well as university bridging courses. A
number of vocational courses are also provided by the Department of Education, some of which lead to specific careers and
others of which are more general in nature.

Regulatory and Representative Bodies

GOVERNMENT

Consejo de Educación de Puerto Rico:
POB 19900, San Juan, PR 00910-1900; Ave
Ponce de León 268, Edif. Hato Rey Centre,
Suite 1500, San Juan, PR 00918; tel. (787)
641-7100; fax (787) 641-2573; e-mail info@cge
.gobierno.pr; internet www.ce.pr.gov; f. 2010,
by merger of Consejo de Educación Superior
de Puerto Rico (CESPR) with Consejo Gen-
eral de Educación (CGE); 9 mems; Pres. Dr
RICARDO APONTE PARSI; Dir. Dr CARMEN LUZ
BERRIOS RIVERA.
Department of Education: POB 190759,
San Juan, PR 00917-0759; Avda Teniente
César González, esq. Calle Juan Calaf, Urb.
Industrial Tres Monjitas, San Juan, PR
00919-0759; tel. (787) 759-2000; fax (787)
250-0275; internet www.de.gobierno.pr; Sec.
EDWARD MORENO ALONSO.

Learned Societies

GENERAL

Ateneo de Ponce: POB 32144, Ponce, PR
00732-2144; e-mail ateneodeponce@yahoo

.com; internet www.pucpr.edu/alianzas/
ateneodeponce; f. 1956; lectures, competitions, confs and concerts; publs; 5 divs of
fine arts, history, literature, moral and political sciences, physics, natural science and
mathematics; Pres. Dr JOSÉ R. ESCABÍ; Vice-
Pres. Prof. ADA HILDA MARTÍNEZ DE ALICEA;
Sec. Prof. MARÍA ISABEL CHAPARRO DE ESCABÍ;
publ. *Primera Antología de Poesía.*

Ateneo Puertorriqueño: Apdo 9021180,
San Juan PR 00902-1180; Parada 1, Ave
Constitución, Puerta de Tierra San Juan PR
00902; tel. (787) 721-3877; fax (787) 725-
3873; e-mail ateneopr@caribe.net; internet
www.puertadetierra.info/edificios/ateneo/
ateneo.htm; f. 1876; promotes science, literature and fine arts; art gallery: holds 450
works of art; 600 mems; library of 30,000
vols, periodicals, old newspapers and microfiche; Pres. Lic. EDUARDO MORALES COLL;
Vice-Pres. Dr JOSÉ MILTON SOLTERO; Sec. Dr
INÉS QUILES; publ. *Revista* (2 a year).

**Fundación Puertorriqueña de las
Humanidades** (Puerto Rican Endowment
for the Humanities): POB 9023920, San
Juan, PR 00902-3920; 109 San José St, Third
Fl., Old San Juan, PR; tel. (787) 721-2087;
fax (787) 721-2684; e-mail contacto@fphpr
.org; internet www.fphpr.org; f. 1977;
attached to Nat. Endowment for the Human-

ities; promotes appreciation of Puerto Rican
culture; stimulates exchange of ideas and
diffusion of humanistic knowledge in soc.;
sponsors humanities projects; develops educational programmes, educational instns,
public and private entities, cultural centres
around Puerto Rico; Exec. Dir Dr JUAN M.
GONZÁLEZ LAMELA.

BIBLIOGRAPHY, LIBRARY SCIENCE AND MUSEOLOGY

**Sociedad de Bibliotecarios de Puerto
Rico:** Apdo 22898, San Juan, PR 00931-
2898; tel. (787) 764-0000; fax (787) 764-5205;
e-mail sbpr1961@gmail.com; internet www
.sociedadbibliotecarios.org; f. 1961; attached
to Dept of State of Puerto Rico; protects,
nurtures and educates its mems in information services; mems incl. academic librarians,
scholars, specialists, archivists, librarians,
booksellers, publishers and other professionals in the field of information; organizes
confs, continuing education activities; promotes Library Week; 280 mems; Pres. Dr
SNEJANKA PENKOVA; Vice-Pres. JUAN VARGAS;
Sec. NYDIA HERNANDE REVERON; publ. *Acce-
so:Revista Puertorriqueña de Bibliotecología
y Documentación* (1 a year).

FINE AND PERFORMING ARTS

Fundación Nacional para la Cultura Popular: Apdo 9023971, San Juan, PR 00902-3971; Calle Fortaleza 56, Viejo San Juan, PR 00901; tel. (787) 724-7165; fax (787) 725-2498; e-mail info@prpop.org; internet www.prpop.org; f. 1996; attached to Dept of State of Puerto Rico; promotes popular culture, classical and folk music; Dir JAVIER SANTIAGO.

Instituto de Cultura Puertorriqueña (Institute of Puerto Rican Culture): POB 9024184, San Juan, PR 00902-4184; tel. (787) 724-0700; fax (787) 724-8393; e-mail webicp@icp.gobierno.pr; internet www.icp .gobierno.pr; f. 1955; studies and preserves Puerto Rican historical and cultural patrimony; promotes study of Puerto Rican culture; Exec. Dir MERCEDES GÓMEZ MARRERO; Dir HECTOR FIGUEROA CRUZ.

Sociedad Mayagüezana Pro Bellas Artes: POB 5004, Mayagüez, PR 00709; f. 1977; ballet, opera, concerts, lectures, symphonies, art and sculpture exhibitions; 300 mems; Pres. Dr LUIS E. BACÓ RODRÍGUEZ.

HISTORY, GEOGRAPHY AND ARCHAEOLOGY

Academia Puertorriqueña de la Historia: Apdo 1447, San Juan; Del Cristo 52, San Juan, PR 00901-1308; tel. (787) 721-5200; f. 1932; 40 mems; Pres. LUIS E. GONZÁLEZ VALES.

LANGUAGE AND LITERATURE

Academia Puertorriqueña de la Lengua Española: Apdo 36 4008, San Juan, PR 00936-4008; Cuartel de Ballajá, 3er Piso, Viejo San Juan, PR 00906; tel. (787) 721-6070; fax (787) 724-6463; e-mail info@ academiapr.org; internet www.academiapr .org; f. 1955; attached to Asociación de Academias de la Lengua Española; promotes, conserves and studies Spanish; represents Puerto Rico internationally; conducts research and ensures representation of Spanish in all academic publs; 28 mems; Dir Dr JOSÉ LUIS VEGA; Deputy Dir LUCE LÓPEZ BARALT; Sec. EDUARDO FORASTIERI (acting); publ. *DILO* (2 a year).

PEN Club de Puerto Rico: 6 Mariano Ramírez Bages, Apt 4B, San Juan, PR 00907; tel. (787) 645-9533; internet www .pen-international.org/centres/puerto-rican-centre; f. 1966; promotes literature and defends freedom of expression; 40 mems; Pres. MAIRYM CRUZ-BERNALL; Sec. ANA MARÍA FUSTER.

MEDICINE

Sociedad Puertorriqueña de Endocrinología y Diabetología: POB 364208, San Juan, PR 00936-4208; tel. (787)309-3707; e-mail sped.endos@gmail.com; internet www .spedpr.org; f. 1977; promotes clinical endocrinology, diabetology; Pres. Dr HARRY JIMÉNEZ; Pres.-Elect Dr ANGEL L. COMULADA; Sec. Dra MYRNA LYZETTE LÓPEZ; publ. *Revista Diabetes*.

NATURAL SCIENCES

General

Sociedad de Historia Natural de Puerto Rico (Natural History Society of Puerto Rico): POB 361036, San Juan, PR 00936-1036; internet www.shnpr.org; f. 1960; promotes, studies, conserves environment and natural resources; incl. monthly confs and field trips; Pres. GLORIA MEDINA; Vice-Pres. ROBERTO PARÉS; Sec. CARMEN MEDINA.

Biological Sciences

Heliconia Society of Puerto Rico, Inc.: Urb. Atlantic View, 44 Calle Venus, Carolina, PR 00979-4806; tel. (787) 396-6544; fax (240) 238-7366; internet www.heliconiasocietypr .org; f. 1996; promotes understanding of Heliconia and related plants of the order of Zingiberales through education, research and communication; interacts with Heliconia Soc. Int; 60 mems; Pres. HÉCTOR MÉNDEZ CARATINI; Sec. YVETTE RIVERA.

Research Institutes

AGRICULTURE, FISHERIES AND VETERINARY SCIENCE

International Institute of Tropical Forestry: USDA Forest Service, Jardín Botánico Sur, 1201 Calle Ceiba, San Juan, PR 00926-1119; tel. (787) 766-5335; fax (787) 766-6302; internet www.fs.fed.us/global/iitf; f. 1939; attached to US Dept of Agriculture, Forest Service; research in tropical American forests, timber management, tropical ecosystem, plantation forestry, wildlife management, watershed management and global change research; cooperative assistance to state and private forest landowners, timber processors; cooperative research with univs and US and foreign governmental agencies; trains foreign forestry students in cooperation with FAO and USAID; library of 15,000 vols; Dir Dr ARIEL E. LUGO.

Tropical Agriculture Research Station: 2200 Pedro Albizu Campos Ave, Suite 201, Mayagüez, PR 00680-5470; tel. (787) 831-3435; fax (787) 831-3386; internet www.ars .usda.gov/saa/tars; f. 1901; attached to Agricultural Research Service, US Dept of Agriculture; conducts research to develop solutions to agricultural problems of high nat. priority; protects human health and environment; Coordinator Dr RICARDO GOENAGA; Sec. MARIBEL ROLDÁN.

MEDICINE

Puerto Rico Health Services Research Institute: POB 365067, Univ. of Puerto Rico, Medical Sciences Campus, San Juan, PR 00936; tel. (787) 758-2525; internet prhsri .rcm.upr.edu; f. 2003; attached to Univ. of Puerto Rico, Medical Sciences Campus; develops research-based knowledge to help decision-makers in evaluating health policy options; Dir Prof. Dr ROBERTO E. TORRES ZENO.

NATURAL SCIENCES

Biological Sciences

Institute for Tropical Ecosystem Studies: POB 70377, San Juan, PR 00936-8377; 207 Anexo Facundo Bueso, Ponce de León Ave, Univ. of Puerto Rico, Río Piedras campus, San Juan, PR 00931; tel. (787) 764-0000; fax (787) 772-1481; e-mail admisionesgrad@ uprrp.edu.; internet www.ites.upr.edu; f. 1957 as PR Nuclear Center; attached to Univ. of Puerto Rico; research and devt of tropical terrestrial ecological studies; graduate-level research and training centre in basic ecological principles, primarily for minorities; increases public awareness on the importance of natural ecosystems to human welfare; field station in Rio Grande; Dir Dr NICHOLAS BROKAW; Sec. EVA CORTES.

Puerto Rico Water Resources and Environmental Research Institute: POB 9000, Mayagüez, PR 00681-9000; tel. (787) 833-0300; fax (787) 833-3985; e-mail prwreri@uprm.edu; internet prwreri.uprm .edu; attached to Univ. of Puerto Rico, Mayagüez Campus; conducts basic and applied research to solve water and environmental problems of Puerto Rico, the Caribbean, and Latin America; trains scientists and engineers through hands-on participa-

tion in research; Dir Dr JORGE RIVERA SANTOS; Assoc. Dir Dr WALTER SILVA ARAYA.

Physical Sciences

Arecibo Observatory: HC-3, POB 53995, Arecibo, PR 00612; tel. (787) 878-2612; fax (787) 878-1861; e-mail prcz@naic.edu; internet www.naic.edu; f. 1960; attached to Nat. Astronomy and Ionosphere Centre; provides observing time, electronics, computer, travel and logistic support to scientists from all over the world; 1,000-ft diameter fixed spherical reflector with movable feeds; for use in the radar study of planets and the properties of the earth's upper atmosphere and reception of natural radio emissions from celestial objects incl. pulsars and quasars; reflector surface upgraded to work at higher frequencies; library of 2,300 vols, 845 periodicals; Dir Dr ROBERT KERR.

RELIGION, SOCIOLOGY AND ANTHROPOLOGY

Instituto de Estudios del Caribe: Apdo 23361, San Juan, PR 00931-3361; tel. (787)764-0000; fax (787)764-3099; e-mail iec@upracd.upr.clu.edu; internet graduados .uprrp.edu/icaribe/i_caribe.htm; f. 1958; attached to Faculty of Social Sciences, Univ. of Puerto Rico; research and outreach programmes on topics of the Greater Caribbean; Dir PEDRO J. RIVERA GUZMÁN; Sec. VIVIAN IGLESIAS; Sec. MILDRED SANTIAGO.

Libraries and Archives

Bayamón

Biblioteca Municipal de Bayamón Dra. Pilar Barbosa: POB 1588, Bayamón, PR 00960; tel. (787) 787-5074; fax (787) 785-2763; f. 2000; attached to Dept of Municipal Education; provides information services for digital print, process devt research and education; Dir GLADYS GALLARDO JANER.

Mayagüez

Biblioteca General Recinto Universitario de Mayagüez (General Library Mayagüez Campus): POB 9000, Univ. of Puerto Rico, Mayagüez Campus, Mayagüez, PR 00681; tel. (787) 265-3810; fax (787) 265-5483; e-mail library@uprm.edu; internet www.uprm.edu/library; f. 1911; main library and 1 spec. departmental colln; subject areas incl. agriculture, animal industries, energy, engineering, marine and environmental sciences, natural and applied sciences, technology; 164,068 vols, 5,259 journals, 263,982 microfiches, 12,719 micro cards, 19,486 microfilms, 561,641 govt documents, 949 films, 8,149 maps, 8,458 sound recordings, 606 musical scores, 917 sound magnetic tapes, 24,810 slides, 4,550 video cassettes, 687 film strips, 3,585 theses and dissertations, 7m. US patents and 3m. US issues trademarks; Dir Prof. NORMA I. SOJO (acting); publs *Bibliorum* (4 a year), *Conoce Tu Biblioteca* (1 a year).

Ponce

Biblioteca Encarnación Valdés (Encarnación Valdés Library): Ponce, PR 00717-0777; tel. (787) 841-2000; fax (787) 651-2665; internet www.pucpr.edu/biblioteca; f. 1969; attached to Pontifical Catholic Univ. of Puerto Rico; spec. collns: Puerto Rican materials, Murga Colln; 269,000 vols, 46,000 periodicals, 4,600 microfilms, 5,000 records, 358 classical music CDs and 363 cassettes of classical and popular music, spec. colln incl. 6,000 vols of Puerto Rican journals; Dir MAGDA I. VARGAS RODRÍGUEZ; Exec. Sec. CECILIA LUGO CASIANO.

Centro de Información e Investigación Jurídica: 2250 Avda Las Américas, Suite 544, Ponce, PR 00717-9997; tel. (787) 841-2000; fax (787) 841-5354; e-mail bib-derecho@pucpr.edu; internet www.pucpr.edu/derecho/nbiblioteca/index.html; f. 1961; attached to Law School, Pontifical Catholic Univ. of Puerto Rico; spec. collns: UN and US fed. documents; 207,095 vols; Dir NOELIA PADUA; Sec. PEREZ SOLMARIE; publ. *Revista de Derecho Puertorriqueño* (4 a year).

Ponce Public Library: POB 7477, Ponce, PR 00732; Calle Reina, Esquina Fogos, Ponce, PR 00731; f. 1937; 20,000 vols; Librarian M. MADERA.

San Juan

Archivo General de Puerto Rico: Instituto de Cultura Puertorriqueña, Apdo 9024184, San Juan, PR 00902-4184; Avda Ponce de León 500, Puerta de Tierra, San Juan, PR 00902-4184; tel. (787) 725-1060; fax (787) 725-1685; e-mail archivogeneral@icp.gobierno.pr; internet www.icp.gobierno.pr/agp; f. 1955; attached to Instituto de Cultura Puertorriqueña; 80,000 cubic ft of documents, incl. text, graphics (drawings, maps), print (newspapers, journals), films and recordings in various formats; Dir and Archivist JOSÉ A. FLORES.

Biblioteca del Departamento de Justicia: GPOB 9020192, San Juan, PR 00902-0192; Calle Olimpo, Esquina Axtmayer, Pda. 11, Miramar, San Juan, PR; tel. (787) 724-6869; fax (787) 729-2059; e-mail webmail@justicia.gobierno.pr; internet www.justicia.gobierno.pr/rs_template/v2/secauxase/secauxase_biblo.html; f. 1950; attached to Dept of Justice of Puerto Rico; provides and manages bibliographic and reference services required by the Office of the Atty Gen.; allocates library resources to lawyers and specialized divs of the Dept of Justice; incl. dictionaries, encyclopedias, treatises, Puerto Rican colln files, legislative histories, fed. and state collns, texts by subject, colln of Spanish jurisprudence, magazines and annual reports of public agencies; 75,000 vols; Dir of the Law Library Atty SHEILA MIRANDA RIVERA; publs *Anuario Estadístico*, *Informe Anual del Secretario de Justicia de Puerto Rico*, *Opiniones del Secretario de Justicia de Puerto Rico*.

Biblioteca del Tribunal Supremo (Library of the Supreme Court): Apdo 9022392, San Juan, PR 00902-2392; tel. (787) 723-3550; fax (787) 724-5090; internet www.ramajudicial.pr/sistema/supremo/biblioteca.htm; f. 1953; attached to Dept of Justice of Puerto Rico; non-lending library for general public; spec. collns: Law reviews, US statutes and cases, rare 19th-century law books, Puerto Rican law, common and Spanish civil law; 80,000 vols; Head Librarian IVETTE TORRES ALVAREZ; Sec. CECILIA SANTANA GONZALEZ; publ. *Nuevas Adquisiciones* (12 a year).

Biblioteca Madre María Teresa Guevara: Apdo 12383, San Juan, PR 00914-12383; tel. (787) 728-1515; fax (787) 268-8868; internet biblioteca.sagrado.edu; f. 1935; attached to Univ. del Sagrado Corazón; incl. historical archives of reports, catalogues, directories, maps, correspondence, photographs, posters and magazines of the univ.; Puerto Rican colln of journals and brochures published by govt agencies; 130,000 vols, 1,375 periodicals, 17,000 reference materials incl. dictionaries, encyclopedias, handbooks; Dir SONIA DÍAZ LATORRE.

Biblioteca Nacional: Instituto de Cultura Puertorriqueña, Apdo 9024184, San Juan, PR 00902-4184; Ave Ponce de León 500, Puerta de Tierra, San Juan, PR 00902-4184; tel. (787) 725-1060; fax (787) 723-5006; e-mail biblioteca@icp.gobierno.pr; internet www.icp.gobierno.pr/bge; f. 2003; attached to Instituto de Cultura Puertorriqueña; acquires, preserves and disseminates the literature written and published in Puerto Rico; incl. rare and general books on Puerto Rico, Van Deussen library of Puerto Rico, Puerto Rican colln, Eugenio Maria de Hostos, Jose S. Joy, John Smith Hood and Dr. Concha Meléndez in the house library of Concha Meléndez; 66,000 vols incl. Puerto Rican colln, colln of Eugenio Maria de Hostos, rare books; Dir JOSEFINA GÓMEZ DE HILLYER.

Biblioteca Regional del Caribe y de Estudios Latinoamericanos: Edif. José M. Lázaro, 1er piso, Ala Oeste, San Juan, PR 00931-1927; tel. (787) 764-0000; fax (787) 763-5685; e-mail afigueroa@uprrp.edu; internet biblioteca.uprrp.edu/caribe.htm; f. 1946 in Trinidad, present location 1975; attached to Univ. of Puerto Rico, Río Piedras campus; research library, specializes in all topics related to Latin America and Caribbean; resources available in Dutch, English, French, Spanish; 50,000 vols; spec. colln of Caribbean Comm. documents; Librarian Prof. ALMALUCES FIGUEROA ORTIZ.

Carnegie Public Library: 7 Avda Ponce de León, Puerta de Tierra, San Juan, PR 00901-2010; tel. (787) 722-4753; fax (787) 725-0261; f. 1903 as Island Library, present name and bldg 1918; attached to Dept of Education of Puerto Rico; 50,000 vols; Dir MARY JEAN HAVER.

Programa de Servicios Bibliotecarios y de Información (Programme Library and Information Services): POB 190759, San Juan, PR 00919-0759; tel. (787) 759-2000; attached to Dept of Education of Puerto Rico; 1,500,000 vols; Dir MARIA LUGO.

University of Puerto Rico School of Law Library: Univ. of Puerto Rico, POB 23310, San Juan. PR 00931-3310; tel. (787) 999-9684; fax (787) 999-9680; internet www.law.upr.edu; f. 1913; Caribbean Basin legal colln; spec. colln incl books on foreign laws, colln of int. law incl. int. agreements, int. law theory and Int. Military Tribunal; rare book colln; Puerto Rico legal colln incl. primary and secondary sources of Puerto Rican law; archival colln of retired judges of the Supreme Court of Puerto Rico; 400,000 vols, 4,000 serials; Dir Dr MARÍA M. OTERO DE LEÓN; Archivist JOSEPH H. MORALES CARDONA; Sec. ARLENE I. AGOSTO GARCÍA.

Museums and Art Galleries

Ponce

Museo de Arte de Ponce: 2325 Ave Las Américas, Ponce, PR 00717-0776; tel. (787) 848-0505; fax (787) 841-7309; e-mail info@museoarteponce.org; internet www.museoarteponce.org; f. 1959; European, American and Hispanic American paintings and sculptures; western art from the Renaissance to the 19th century; permanent colln consists of 4,500 paintings, sculptures, decorative arts, ceramics, 3D objects, photographs, prints, drawings, cassettes and sound art installations; library of 7,000 vols; Exec. Dir AGUSTÍN ARTEAGA; Chief Curator CHERYL HARTUP; Sec. ETIENNE TOTTI.

Museo de la Historia de Ponce: Calle 53 Isabel, Ponce, PR; tel. (787) 844-7071; fax (787) 812-3053; e-mail museodelahistoriadeponce@yahoo.com; f. 1992; promotes research and preservation of Ponce's heritage for the devt of the Puerto Rican culture; 10 galleries display colln of 3,000 Ponce historical relics, photos and documents.

Museo de la Música Puertorriqueña: Calle Isabel, esquina Salud, Ponce, PR; tel. (787) 290-6617; e-mail museosyparques@icp.gobierno.pr; internet www.icp.gobierno.pr/myp/museos/m15.htm; f. 1990; attached to Museos y Parques, Instituto de Cultura Puertorriqueña; neoclassical residence that displays the history of indigenous Puerto Rican music from pre-Columbian times to the present; Dir NICOLE PIETRI.

San Germán

Museo de Arte Religioso Santo Domingo de Porta Coeli: Apdo 1160, San Germán, PR 00683; Frente a la Plaza Santo Domingo, San Germán, PR; tel. (787) 892-5845; e-mail museosyparques@icp.gobierno.pr; internet www.icp.gobierno.pr/myp/museos/m12.htm; attached to Museos y Parques, Instituto de Cultura Puertorriqueña; 17th-century church of Porta Coeli; constructed as a chapel for convent of Dominican Friars in San Germán; restored and converted into museum of religious art (paintings, pictures, sculptures, ornaments and ritual objects) in 1960; Admin. GUIDO BARLETTA.

San Juan

La Casa del Libro: Amigos de Calle del Cristo 255, POB 9023544, San Juan, PR 00902-3544; 319 Calle Fortaleza Esq, Chapel Alley, San Juan, PR; tel. and fax (787) 723-0354; e-mail lcdl@prw.net; internet www.lacasadellibro.org; f. 1955; permanent bldg closed for renovation; devoted to the art and history of the book; library of 7,000 vols (incl. MSS, incunabula and works in areas relating to the arts of the book); Dir MARIA TERESA ARRARÁS; Librarian JOSE M. ESTRADA-BOLIVAR.

Museo de Arte Contemporáneo de Puerto Rico (Puerto Rico Museum of Contemporary Art): POB 362377, San Juan, PR 00936-2377; Edif. Histórico Rafael M. de Labra, Ave Juan Ponce de León, esquina Ave Roberto H. Todd, Parada 18, Santurce, San Juan, PR; tel. (787) 977-4030; fax (787) 977-4036; e-mail adm1@museocontemporaneopr.org; internet www.museocontemporaneopr.org; f. 1984; collects, preserves, documents and disseminates art produced in Puerto Rico, the Caribbean and Latin America from the 1940s to present; library of 32,000 vols; Pres. SALVADOR ALEMAÑY; Vice-Pres. Ing. WILLIAM DÍAZ; Sec. HÉCTOR SALDAÑA EGOZCUE; Exec. Dir MARIANNE RAMÍREZ APONTE; Curator Dr LILLIANA RAMOS-COLLADO; publs *25 años del Museo de Arte Contemporáneo de Puerto Rico* (25 Years of the Puerto Rico Museum of Contemporary Art), *Arnaldo Roche Rabell: Azul, David LaChapelle. NosOtros: La humanidad al borde* (David LaChapelle. NosOtros: Humanity on the Edge).

Museo de Arte de Puerto Rico (Museum of Art of Puerto Rico): Ave De Diego 299, Santurce, San Juan, PR 00909; tel. (787) 977-6277; fax (787) 977-4446; e-mail info@mapr.org; internet www.mapr.org; f. 2000; colln of Puerto Rican fine art from 17th century to present; 1,100 works of art incl. drawings, prints, photography, sculpture and new media; Pres. ARTURO GARCIA-SOLA (acting); Exec. Dir Dr LOURDES RAMOS; Sec. DIEGO R. FIGUEROA (acting).

Museo de Arte e Historia de San Juan (Museum of Art and History in San Juan): Calle Norzagaray 150, San Juan, PR; tel. (787) 724-1875; f. 1979; museum bldg reflects Spanish colonial architecture; showcases history of San Juan from 1521 to the present; displays artworks by local artists.

Museo de Historia Militar: c/o Instituto de Cultura Puertorriqueña, POB 9024184, San Juan, PR 00902-4184; tel. (787) 723-7837; e-mail info@icp.gobierno.pr; internet www .icp.gobierno.pr; small Spanish fort from 16th century.

Universities

AMERICAN UNIVERSITY OF PUERTO RICO

POB 2037, Bayamón, PR 00960
Carr. 2 KM, 14 Hato Tejas, Bayamón, PR 00960-2037

Telephone: (787) 620-2040
Fax: (787) 785-7377
Internet: www.aupr.edu

Founded 1963 as American Business College
Depts of arts and sciences, business administration, education and technology
Private control

Pres.: JUAN B. NAZARIO NEGRÓN
Rector: JOSEPHINE RESTO OLIVO
Vice-Pres. for Academic and Student Affairs: CONSUELO CASTRO MELÉNDEZ
Vice-Pres. for Admin. and Finance: JUAN CARLOS NAZARIO TORRES
Vice-Pres. for Enrolment Management: JAIME GONZÁLEZ RIVERA
Dir of Admissions: KEREN LLANOS FIGUEROA
Registrar: MARÍA A. RODRÍGUEZ-PAZ
Dir of Library: DORIS ROBLES TOLEDO
Number of teachers: 112 (21 full-time, 91 part-time)
Number of students: 1,453 (1,347 undergraduate, 106 graduate)

CARIBBEAN UNIVERSITY

POB 493, Bayamón, PR 00960-0493
Telephone: (787) 780-0070
Fax: (787) 999-8252
E-mail: registraduria@caribbean.edu
Internet: www.caribbean.edu

Founded 1969 as Caribbean Jr College, present name 1978
Private control
Campuses in Carolina, Ponce, Vega Baja
Pres.: Dr ANNE E. CUCURELLA-ADORNO
Registrar: KENDRA M. ORTIZ RIVERA.

COLUMBIA CENTRO UNIVERSITARIO

POB 8517, Caguas, PR 00725
Telephone: (787) 743-4041
Fax: (787) 744-7031
E-mail: info@columbiaco.edu
Internet: www.columbiaco.edu

Founded 1966

Campus in Yauco; divs of administration, arts, health, technology
Private control
Academic year: September to August
Pres.: ALEX A. DE JORGE
Vice-Pres. for Academic Affairs: CARMEN J. LÓPEZ
Vice-Pres. of Admin.: DARITZA MULERO
Vice-Pres. for Operations: CARMEN M. RIVERA
Vice-Pres. for Student Affairs: BRENDALIZ ZAYAS
Dean of Academic Affairs: MYRNA TORRES
Registar: WILMARIE TORRES
Librarian: LUZ Z. NEGRÓN.

PONTIFICAL CATHOLIC UNIVERSITY OF PUERTO RICO

2250 Ave Las Americas, Ponce, PR 00717-0777
Telephone: (787) 841-2000
Fax: (787) 840-4295

Internet: www.pucpr.edu
Founded 1948 as Santa María
Languages of instruction: English, Spanish
Private control
Academic year: August to May (2 semesters and 2 summer sessions)
Campuses at Arecibo, Mayagüez
Chancellor: Most Rev. RICARDO SURIÑACH
Pres.: Prof. JORGE IVÁN VÉLEZ AROCHO (acting)
Vice-Pres. for Academic Affairs: Dr LEANDRO A. COLÓN ALICEA
Vice-Pres. for Finance and Admin.: Prof. IRMA RODRÍGUEZ
Vice-Pres. for Student Affairs: Prof. FREDDIE MARTINEZ SOTOMAYOR
Rector for Arecibo Campus: Dr EDWIN HERNÁNDEZ VERA
Rector for Mayagüez Campus: Prof. MEI-LING VELÁZQUEZ SEPÚLVEDA
Dir of Admissions: Dr ANA O. BONILLA DE SÁNCHEZ
Registrar: Prof. IVÁN E. DÁVILA
Dir of Libraries: MAGDA VARGAS RODRÍGUEZ
Library: 1m. vols
Number of teachers: 702
Number of students: 8,203 (5,750 undergraduate, 2,453 graduate)
Publications: *Horizontes*, *Revista Collage* (2 a year), *Revista de Derecho Puertorriqueño*

DEANS

College of Arts and Humanities: Prof. ALFONSO SANTIAGO CRUZ
College of Business Administration: Dr JAIME L. SANTIAGO CANET
College of Education: Dr LILLIAN NEGRÓN COLON
College of Graduate Studies in Behavioural Sciences and Community Affairs: Dr HERNÁN A. VERA RODRÍGUEZ
College of Science: Prof. CARMEN C. VELÁZQUEZ
School of Architecture: ABEL MISLA VILLALBA
School of Law: ANGEL GONZÁLEZ ROMÁN

SISTEMA UNIVERSITARIO ANA G. MENDEZ

POB 21345, San Juan, PR 00928-1345
Telephone: (787) 751-0178
Fax: (787) 766-1706
Internet: www.suagm.edu
Founded 1941 as Puerto Rico High School of Commerce, present name 1993
Private control
Pres.: JOSÉ F. MÉNDEZ
Vice-Pres. for Admin. Affairs: JESÚS A. DÍAZ
Vice-Pres. for Financial Affairs: (vacant)
Vice-Pres. for Human Resources: VICTORIA DE JESÚS
Vice-Pres. for Planning, Academic Affairs and Research: JORGE L. CRESPO ARMAIZ
Vice-Pres. for Marketing and Student Affairs: FRANCISCO J. BARTOLOMEI
Number of students: 34,302 students

DEANS

School of Continuing Education: YANAIRA VÁZQUEZ
School of Professional Studies: MILDRED Y. RIVERA
School of Technical Studies: JOSÉ R. DEL VALLE

CAMPUSES
Universidad del Este
(Eastern University)

POB 2010, Carolina, PR 00984-2010
Ave Principal Sabana, Carr. 190, Barrio Sabana Abajo, Carolina, PR 00983
Telephone: (787) 257-7373
Fax: (787) 752-0070

Internet: www.suagm.edu/une
Founded 1949 present status 2001
Univ. centres in Barceloneta, Cabo Rojo, Santa Isabel, Utuado, Yauco
Chancellor: ALBERTO MALDONADO RUIZ
Vice-Chancellor: MILDRED HUERTAS SOLÁ
Vice-Chancellor for Information Resources and Telecommunications: CARMEN ORTEGA
Vice-Chancellor for Student Affairs: GEORGINA LEÓN DE RIVERA
Registrar: EIGNA I. DE JESÚS MOLINARI
Dir of Library: ELSA MARIANI
Library of 224,979 vols
Number of teachers: 643 (108 full-time, 535 part-time)
Number of students: 13,317

DEANS

José A. (Tony) Santana International School of Hospitality and Culinary Arts: OMAR J. PAGÁN
School of Business Administration: Dr MARITZA I. ESPINA
School of Continuing Education: YANAIRA VÁZQUEZ CRUZ
School of Education: MARÍA G. VÉAZ MORALES
School of Health Sciences: Dr JESÚS IRIZARRY MORA
School of Sciences and Technology: Dr WILFREDO COLÓN GUASP
School of Social and Human Sciences: Dr JHON J. SANABRIA RODRÍGUEZ

Universidad del Turabo
(University of Turabo)

POB 3030, Gurabo, PR 00778-3030
Telephone: (787) 743-7979
Internet: www.suagm.edu/turabo
Founded 1972
Centres in Barceloneta, Cayey, Isabela, Naguabo, Ponce and Yabucoa
Chancellor: DENNIS ALICEA
Vice-Chancellor: ROBERTO LORÁN
Vice-Chancellor for Admin. Affairs: GLADYS BETANCOURT
Vice-Chancellor for External Resources: JACQUELINE MULLEN-HUNT
Vice-Chancellor for Int. Affairs: DAVID MÉNDEZ
Vice-Chancellor for Student Affairs: ANA ORTEGA
Dir of Library: LUISA TORRES
Registrar: ZORAIDA ORTIZ
Number of teachers: 176 full-time
Number of students: 15,000

DEANS

Int. School of Design: AURORISA MATEO
School of Business and Entrepreneurship: MARCELINO RIVERA
School of Education: ANGELA CANDELARIO
School of Engineering: JACK T. ALLISON
School of Health Sciences: ÁNGEL L. RIVERA
School of Professional Studies: MILDRED Y. RIVERA
School of Science and Technology: TERESA LIPSETT-RUIZ (acting)
School of Social and Human Sciences: MARCO A. GIL DE LAMADRID

Universidad Metropolitana
(Metropolitan University)

POB 21150, San Juan, PR 00928-1150
1399 Ave Ana G Méndez, San Juan, PR 00926-2602

Telephone: (787) 766-1717
Internet: www.suagm.edu/umet
Founded 1967 as Cupey campus of Puerto Rico Jr College, present name and status 1985
Univ. centers in Aguadilla, Bayamón, Jayuya
Chancellor: Dr FEDERICO MATHEU

Vice-Chancellor: OMAR PONCE RIVERA
Vice-Chancellor for Admin. Affairs: MARÍA DE
  P. CHARNECO
Vice-Chancellor for Information Resources:
  CARLOS FUENTES (acting)
Vice-Chancellor for Student Affairs: CARMEN
  ROSADO LEÓN
Dir of Admissions: YADIRA RIVERA LUGO
Dir of Library: MARÍA DE LOS ÁNGELES LUGO
Number of students: 12,622

Publications: *Panorama, Revista Cupey*

DEANS

School of Business Administration: JUAN
  OTERO SERRANO
School of Education: Dr JUDITH A. GONZÁLEZ
School of Environmental Affairs: Dr CARLOS
  M. PADÍN BIBILONI
School of Health Sciences: Dra LOURDES
  MALDONADO
School of Science and Technology: KAREN
  GONZÁLEZ PARRILLA
School of Social Sciences, Humanities and
  Communications: Dr ELOISA GORDON
School of Professional Studies: MILDRED Y.
  RIVERA CORDERO

UNIVERSIDAD ADVENTISTA DE LAS ANTILLAS

POB 118, Mayagüez, PR 00681
Telephone: (787) 834-9595
Fax: (787) 834.9597
E-mail: admissions@uaa.edu
Internet: www.uaa.edu

Founded 1957 as Mayagüez Puerto Rican
  Adventist College, present name 1989
Dept of science and technology
Private control
Pres.: OBED JIMÉNEZ
Vice Pres. for Academic Affairs: JOSÉ DAVID
  GÓMEZ
Vice Pres. for Financial Affairs: MISAEL
  JIMÉNEZ
Vice Pres. for Institutional Advancement: Dr
  AUREA ARAÚJO
Vice-Pres. for Student Affairs: ROSA M. DEL
  VALLE
Dir of Admissions: YOLANDA FERRER
Registrar: ANA D. TORRES
Dir of Library: AIXA VEGA
Library of 85,000 vols, 6,000 journals, 7,000
  e-books
Number of teachers: 93 (42 full-time, 51
  part-time)
Number of students: 1,174

UNIVERSIDAD CENTRAL DE BAYAMÓN

POB 1725, Bayamón, PR 00960-1725
Urb. La Milagrosa, Ave Zaya Verde, Baya-
  món, PR 00960
Telephone: (787) 786-3030
Fax: (787) 740-2200
E-mail: info@ucb.edu.pr
Internet: www.ucb.edu.pr

Founded 1961 as an extension of Catholic
  Univ. of Puerto Rico, present name and
  status 1970
Private control
Language of instruction: Spanish
Academic year: August to May
Pres.: Dr LILLIAN NEGRÓN COLÓN
Academic Dean: Dra PURA ECHANDI
Dean of Finance and Admin.: ROSIMAR FER-
  RER
Dean of Student Affairs: Prof. NIZA ZAYAS
Dir of Admissions: CHRISTINE HERNANDEZ
  CORTIELLA
Registrar: VICTOR COLÓN-RODRÍGUEZ
Library Dir: ANNETTE VALENTÍN
Library of 51,011 vols

Number of teachers: 57 (full-time)
Number of students: 3,228

Publications: *Cruz Ansata* (1 a year), *Familia
  y Escuela* (12 a year), *Revista Halcón,
  President's Letter* (4 a year)

DEANS

College of Business and Technology Develop-
  ment: Dra NIDIA COLÓN QUINTANA
College of Education and Professional Con-
  duct: Dra PURA ECHANDI
College of Liberal Arts, Sciences and Health
  Professions: Dr LUIS A. SÁNCHEZ GÓMEZ

UNIVERSIDAD CENTRAL DEL CARIBE

POB 60327, Bayamón, PR 00960-6032
Ave Laurel 100, Santa Juanita, Bayamón,
  PR 00956
Telephone: (787) 798-3001
Fax: (787) 269-7550
E-mail: ucc@uccaribe.edu
Internet: www.uccaribe.edu

Founded 1976 as Cayey School of Medicine,
  present name 1978
Graduate programmes incl. medical imaging
technology, biomedical science and substance
abuse counselling; postgraduate programme
offered by School of Medicine
Private control
Pres.: Dr JOSE GINEL RODRIGUEZ
Dean of Academic Affairs: Dr ARÍSTIDES CRUZ
Dean of Admin. Affairs: EMILIA SOTO
Dean of Admissions and Student Affairs: Dr
  NEREIDA DÍAZ
Dir of Library: MILDRED I. RIVERA VAZQUEZ
Number of teachers: 36 (full-time)
Number of students: 485 (177 undergradu-
  ate, 308 graduate)

UNIVERSIDAD DE PUERTO RICO

POB 364984, San Juan, PR 00936-4984
Telephone: (787) 250-0000
Fax: (787) 759-6917
Internet: www.upr.edu

Founded 1903, present status 1998
State control
Languages of instruction: Spanish, English
Academic year: August to May
Pres.: Dr ANTONIO GARCÍA PADILLA (acting)
Vice-Pres. for Academic Affairs: IBIS L.
  APONTE-AVELLANET
Vice-Pres. for Research and Technology: JOSÉ
  A. LASALDE DOMINICCI
Dir for Communications: IVÁN RÍOS HERNÁN-
  DEZ
Dir for Enrolment Management: SANDRA
  TORRES CLEMENTE
Dir for Finance: MARIA VARGAS CAPRÍLES
  (acting)
Dir for Financial Aid: HERNÁN VAZQUEZTELL
Dir for Information Systems: ALINA M. DÍAZ
  MÉNDEZ (acting)
Dir for Planning and Devt: IRVING JIMÉNEZ
  (acting)
Number of teachers: 5,287
Number of students: 61,967

Publications: *Diálogo* (12 a year), *La Torre,
  RIE* (4 a year).

ATTACHED CAMPUSES

Recinto de Ciencias Médicas: Apdo
365067, San Juan, PR 00936-5067; tel. (787)
758-2525; fax (787) 758-2556; e-mail
juntaadmin.rcm@upr.edu; internet www.upr
.edu/frames/rcm/index.htm; f. 1926; promotes education integrated with practice
and experimentation; offers multiple programmes of study in the health field incl.
assoc. degrees, BA degrees, post-baccalaureate certificates, MA, doctoral, residences,

post-doctoral degrees; library of 125,000 vols;
826 (632 full-time, 194 part-time) teachers;
2,371 (530 undergraduate, 1,841 graduate)
students; Chancellor RAFAEL RODRÍGUEZ-
MERCADO (acting); Dean of Academic Affairs
Dra ILKA C. RIÓS REYES; Dean of Admin.
ELEUTERIO POMALES (acting); Dean of Student
Affairs Dra MARÍA M. HERNÁNDEZ MALDO-
NADO; Registrar REINALDO POMALES; Library
Dir Dra IRMA QUIÑONES-MAURÁS; publ.
Buhití, Puerto Rico Health Science Journal.

**Universidad de Puerto Rico en Agua-
dilla:** POB 6150, Aguadilla, PR 00604-6150;
tel. (787) 890-2681; fax (787) 891-3455;
e-mail administracion.uprag@upr.edu;
internet www.uprag.edu; f. 1972 as Colegio
Regional de Aguadilla, present status 1997;
programmes in biology with an emphasis on
bioinformatics, biomedical quality systems
assessment process industries, environmental technology, education (concentration on
English) and multimedia technology, quality
control in manufacturing; 153 (116 full-time,
37 part-time) teachers; 2,932 students; Chancellor Prof. IVELICE CARDONA; Exec. Sec.
CRISTINA DÍAZ VEGA; Dean for Academic
Affairs Dra SONIA RIVERA GONZALEZ; Dean of
Admin. SR HÉCTOR M. VÉLEZ RODRÍGUEZ
(acting); Library Dir Prof. CANDE GÓMEZ.

Universidad de Puerto Rico en Arecibo:
POB 4010, Arecibo, PR 00614-4010; tel. (787)
815-0000; fax (787) 880-4972; internet www
.upra.edu; f. 1967 as Arecibo Regional College, present status 1998; depts of biology,
business administration, chemical physics,
computer science, counselling and guidance,
education, English, humanities, mathematics, nursing, social sciences, Spanish, tele-
radio communication; 274 teachers; 4,000
students; Chancellor Prof. JUAN RAMÍREZ-
SILVA; Dean of Academic Affairs Dr MANUEL
SAPONARA CURRUTO; Dean of Admin. Affairs
Prof. JUAN PÉREZ GONZÁLEZ; Dean of Student
Affairs Prof. DIÓMEDES PAGÁN NAVARETTE;
Dir of Admissions MAGALY MÉNDEZ CARDONA;
Registrar MILAGROS PITRE NIEVES; Library
Dir VICTOR MALDONADO MALDONADO (acting);
publ. *Cuarto Propio: Revista Literaria* (Span-
ish, online (cuartopropio.upra.edu)).

**Universidad de Puerto Rico en Baya-
món:** 170 Industrial Minillas Carr 174,
Bayamón, PR 00959-1919; tel. (787) 993-
0000; fax (787) 993-8929; e-mail admisiones
.bayamon@upr.edu; internet www.uprb.edu;
f. 1971, present status 1998; depts of early
childhood education, electronics, materials
engineering, natural science, physical education; 263 (164 full-time, 99 part-time) teachers; 4,992 students; Chancellor Dr IRMA
SCHMIDT SOLTERO (acting); Dean of Academic
Affairs Dr HÉCTOR DE JESÚS CARDONA; Dean
of Admin. Affairs JOSÉ RODRÍGUEZ VICENTY;
Dean of Student Affairs Prof. EVANGELINE
MEDINA GUARCH (acting); Dir of Admissions
CARMEN I. MONTES BURGOS; Registrar CAR-
MEN M. CINTRON OTERO; publ. *Milenio.*

**Universidad de Puerto Rico en Caro-
lina:** Apdo 4800, Carolina, PR 00984-4800;
tel. (787) 257-0000; fax (787) 750-7940;
internet www.uprc.edu; f. 1974; programmes
in automotive technology, cultural tourism,
hotel and restaurant administration, industrial automation, interior design, mechanical
engineering, physical education and recreation for people with disabilities; 213 (110
full-time, 103 part-time) teachers; 4,004 students; Rector Prof TRINIDAD FERNÁNDEZ-MIR-
ANDA; Dean of Academic Affairs Dr LUIS D.
TORRES TORRES; Dean of Admin. Affairs
EFRAÍN BENJAMÍN FIGUEROA; Dean of Student Affairs Prof JAVIER LASSO VALENCIA;
Library Dir STANLEY PORTELA VALENTÍN.

Universidad de Puerto Rico en Cayey:
Antonio R. Barceló 205, Cayey, PR 00736; tel.

(787) 738-2161; internet www.cayey.upr.edu; f. 1967; programmes in business administration, biology, chemistry, humanities, Hispanic studies, mathematics and physics, natural sciences, social sciences, pedagogy; promotes student participation in scientific research in univ. laboratories outside Puerto Rico; attached centres: Environmental Education Centre, Institute for Interdisciplinary Research; 224 teachers; 3,626 students; Chancellor RAFAEL RIVERA-LEHMAN; Registrar ANGEL L. MATOS; publ. *Revista Identidades*.

Universidad de Puerto Rico en Humacao: POB 860, Humacao, PR 00792; tel. (787) 850-0000; e-mail rectoria.uprh@upr.edu; internet www.uprh.edu; f. 1962, present status 1973; programmes in applied physical electronics, business administration, coastal marine biology, computational mathematics, education, industrial chemistry, microbiology and general biology, nursing sciences, social sciences, social work, wildlife management; 281 (242 full-time, 39 part-time) teachers; 4,314 students; Rector Dra CARMEN J. HERNÁNDEZ CRUZ (acting); Dean of Academic Affairs Dr ERNESTO ESTEBAN AVILA (acting); Dean of Admin. LUIS LIZARDI SANTANA; Dean of Students Prof. CARRIÓN ANGEL TAVAREZ; Dir of Admissions ELIZABETH GERENA; Registrar JORGE ACEVEDO; Library Dir Prof. FELIX NERIS BAEZ; publ. *Cuaderno Internacional de Estudios Humanísticos y Literatura.*

Universidad de Puerto Rico en Ponce: POB 7186, Ponce, PR 00732-7186; tel. (787) 844-8181; fax (787) 840-8679; internet www.uprp.edu; f. 1970 as Regional College of Ponce, present name and status 2000; programmes in civil engineering (architectural delineation and technology construction), industrial engineering, natural science (biodiversity assessment, biotechnology, coastal marine environment assessment), physical therapy; 163 (108 full-time, 55 part-time) teachers; 3,233 students; Chancellor Prof. JAIME C. MARRERO VÁZQUEZ; Dean of Academic Affairs Prof. LIZZETTE A. ROIG LAMA; Dean of Admin. Affairs Dr DRIANFEL VÁZQUEZ TORRES (acting); Dean of Student Affairs Prof. ROSA MARGARITA LÓPEZ; Registrar HARRY BENGOCHEA VÁZQUEZ; Library Dir SAULO COTTO FRANCOIS; publ. *Ceiba* (1 a year).

Universidad de Puerto Rico en Río Piedras: POB 23301, San Juan, PR 00931-3301; tel. (787) 764-0000; fax (787) 764-3680; e-mail amaortiz@uprrp.edu; internet www.uprrp.edu; f. 1903; colleges and schools of architecture, business administration, communication, education, general studies, humanities, law, natural sciences, planning, school of sciences and information technology, social sciences; system of 29 libraries; 1,237 (957 full-time, 280 part-time) teachers; 17,539 (14,072 undergraduate, 3,467 graduate) students; Chancellor Dra ANA R. GUADALUPE; Dean for Academic Affairs ASTRID CUBANO IGUINA; Dean for Admin. ALBERT FELICIANO NIEVES; Dean of Graduate Studies and Research Dr HAYDEE SEIJO; Dean of Students Dr MAYRA CHARRIEZ; publ. *Análisis, Caribbean Studies, Centro de Investigaciones Comerciales e Iniciativas Académicas* (online (cicia.uprrp.edu/forum.html)), *Contornos Caribeños, Psychiko, Revista de Administración Pública, Revista de Ciencias Sociales, Sargasso, Tonguas* (1 a year).

Universidad de Puerto Rico Recinto de Mayagüez: Apdo 5000, Mayagüez, PR 00709-5000; tel. (787) 832-4040; fax (787) 834-3031; e-mail rectoria@uprm.edu; internet www.uprm.edu; f. 1911 as College of Agriculture at Mayagüez, present status 1966; colleges of agricultural sciences, arts and sciences, business administration, engin-

eering; library of 542,534 vols; 884 teachers; 13,221 (12,165 undergraduate, 1,056 graduate) students; Pres. Dr JORGE I. RIVERA SANTOS; Dean of Academic Affairs DARNYD W ORTIZ SEDA; Dean of Admin. ÁNGEL L. MATOS; Dean of Student Affairs WILMA SANTIAGO GABRIELINI (acting); Library Dir Prof. WANDA PÉREZ; publ. *Atenea* (2 a year, English and Spanish), *Caribbean Journal of Science* (3 a year), *Ceteris Paribus: The Puerto Rico Economic Review* (2 a year), *Journal of Agriculture of the University of Puerto Rico* (2 a year), *LACJEE* (2 a year, online), *Revista Internacional de Desastres Naturales, Accidentes e Infraestructura Civil* (2 a year).

UNIVERSIDAD DEL SAGRADO CORAZON

POB 12383, San Juan, PR 00914-0383

Telephone: (787) 728-1515

Fax: (787) 728-1692

E-mail: admision@sagrado.edu

Internet: www.sagrado.edu

Founded 1880, present name 1976

Depts of business administration, communication, education, humanities and social sciences, natural sciences

Private control

Language of instruction: Spanish

Academic year: August to May

Pres.: Dr JOSÉ JAIME RIVERA

Dir of Enrollment Planning and Management: LILLIA PLANELL HERNÁNDEZ

Dir of Finance: MAYRA I. RODRÍGUEZ MELÉNDEZ (acting)

Dean of Academic and Student Affairs: Dr LYDIA E. ESPINET DE JESÚS

Dean of Admin.: JOSÉ L. RICCI

Dean of Devt Affairs: ADLÍN RÍOS RIGAU

Library Dir: SONIA DÍAZ LATORRE

Number of teachers: 360 (100 full-time and 260 part-time)

Number of students: 6,095 (5,083 undergraduate, 1,012 graduate)

UNIVERSIDAD INTERAMERICANA DE PUERTO RICO
(Inter American University of Puerto Rico)

POB 363255, San Juan, PR 00936-3255

Telephone: (787) 766-1912

Fax: (787) 296-0452

Internet: www.inter.edu

Founded 1912 as Polytechnic Institute of Puerto Rico

Private control

Languages of instruction: English, Spanish

Academic year: August to May (2 semesters)

Pres.: Dr JOSÉ M. FERNÓS

Vice-Pres. for Academic and Student Affairs and Systemic Planning: AGUSTÍN ECHEVARRÍA SANTIAGO

Vice-Pres. for Financial Affairs, Admin. and Services: LUIS R. ESQUILÍN HERNÁNDEZ

Vice-Pres. for Religious Affairs: Rev. Fr NORBERTO DOMÍNGUEZ

Number of teachers: 2,548

Number of students: 43,000

Publication: *Homines.*

UNIVERSIDAD POLITÉCNICA DE PUERTO RICO
(Polytechnic University Campus)

POB 192017, San Juan, PR 00919-2017

377 Ponce de León Ave, Hato Rey, PR 00918

Telephone: (787) 622-8000

E-mail: admisiones@pupr.edu

Internet: www.pupr.edu

Founded 1966

Campuses in Miami and Orlando in the US; schools of architecture, engineering, management

Private control

Academic year: August to May

Pres.: ERNESTO VÁZQUEZ-BARQUET

Vice-Pres. for Academic Affairs: Dr MIGUEL RIESTRA

Vice-Pres. of Admin. and Finance: ERNESTO VÁZQUEZ-MARTINEZ

Dir of Admission: TERESA CARDONA

Registrar: MAYRA LÓPEZ

Dir of Library: MARITZA GRAJALES

Library of 140,000 vols

Number of teachers: 309 (157 full-time, 152 part-time)

Number of students: 5,941 (5,216 undergraduate, 725 graduate)

Colleges

Centro de Estudios Avanzados de Puerto Rico y El Caribe: Apdo 9023970, San Juan, PR 00902-3970; Calle Cristo 52, Viejo San Juan, PR; tel. (787) 723-4481; fax (787) 723-4810; e-mail centro@ceaprc.org; internet www.ceaprc.edu; f. 1832; offers MA of arts and doctoral degrees in history of Puerto Rico and the Caribbean; library: 17,000 vols; Rector MIGUEL RODRÍGUEZ LÓPEZ; Dean of Academic Affairs Dra ELIZABETH CRESPO KEBLER; Dean of Admin. Affairs LIZZETTE CARRILLO; Dir of Library Prof. FRANCIS JAVIER MOJICA GARCÍA; Registrar MAYRA RAMÍREZ VALDEJULLI.

Colegio Universitario de San Juan: Apdo 70179, San Juan, PR 00936; tel. (787) 480-2400; fax (787) 753-5649; internet www.cunisanjuan.edu; f. 1972; BA degree in accounting, arts in criminal justice, information systems, nursing; Rector DEBORAH D. DRAHUS CAPÓ; Dean of Academic Affairs MERCY FALERO SOTO; Dean of Admin. Affairs CRUZ CORRALIZA TORRES; Dean of Student Affairs VIRGEN PAGÁN.

Conservatorio de Música de Puerto Rico (Conservatory of Music of Puerto Rico): 951 Ave Ponce de León, Miramar, San Juan, PR 00907-3373; tel. (787) 751-0160; fax (787) 766-1216; e-mail info@cmpr.edu; internet www.cmpr.edu; f. 1959; performance, composition, jazz and teacher training; offers BA and MA degree in music; library: 50,000 vols; 140 teachers; 1,600 students; Pres. MARIA CRISTINA FIRPI; Vice-Pres. RAFAEL IRIZARRY CUEBAS; Rector MARÍA DEL CARMEN GIL; Dean of Academic Affairs MELANIE SANTANA-SANTANA; Dean of Admin. and Finance JUAN CARLOS HERNÁNDEZ; Dean of Students Affairs MICHAEL RAJABALLEY; Dir of Admissions ILSAMAR HERNÁNDEZ; Registrar JOSÉ A. MATOS; Library Dir DAMARIS CORDERO.

EDP College of Puerto Rico, Inc.: POB 192303, San Juan, PR 00919-2303; 560 Ave. Ponce de León, Hato Rey, PR 00918; tel. (787) 765-3560; fax (787) 777-0025; e-mail info@edpcollege.edu; internet www.eduedp.net; f. 1969; campus in San Sebastian; BA degrees in business administration with majors in management and accounting, computer programming, digital imaging, information systems with majors in networks, computer programming, technological office administration; MA degrees in fraud investigation, information systems, information technology for education; Pres. GLADYS NIEVES VÁZQUEZ; Vice-Pres. for Academic Planning and Institutional Devt Dr ROSA ALICEA; Vice-Pres. for Finance LUIS RIVERA; Vice-Pres. for Institutional and Int. Relations Dr MARILYN PASTRANA; Vice-Pres. for Technology and Distance Education Prof. MAYRA RIVERA.

Escuela de Artes Plásticas de Puerto Rico: POB 9021112, San Juan, PR 00902-1112; Campo del Morro, Barrio Ballajá, Viejo San Juan, PR; tel. (787) 725-8120; fax (787) 721-3798; e-mail info@eap.edu; internet www.eap.edu; f. 1966; BA degree in art education, fashion design, image and design, industrial design, painting, sculpture; library: 30,000 vols; 480 students; Chancellor MARIMAR BENÍTEZ; Dean of Admin. EDUARDO BERRÍOS; Dean of Academic and Student Affairs MARINÉS LÓPEZ-LÓPEZ.

Facultad de Derecho: POB 70351, San Juan, PR 00936-8351; Calle Federico Costa 170, Hato Rey, San Juan, PR; tel. (787) 751-1912; fax (787) 751-2975; internet www.derecho.inter.edu; f. 1961; attached to Inter American Univ. of Puerto Rico; language of instruction: Spanish; library: 200,000 vols; 875 students; 78 (28 full-time, 50 part-time) teachers; Dean Prof. LUIS MARIANO NEGRÓN PORTILLO; Dir of Admissions ANGELA R. TORRES; Dir of Library HECTOR R. SÁNCHEZ FERNÁNDEZ; publ. *Law Review* (3 a year).

Humacao Community College: POB 9139, Calle Georgetti 69, Humacao, PR 00792; tel. (787) 852-1430; fax (787) 850-1577; internet hccpr.edu; f. 1978; offers BA in business administration with specialization in accounting, management and information systems; Pres. JORGE E. MOJICA; Vice-Pres. Prof. AIDA E. RODRÍGUEZ; Dean of Student and Academic Affairs Prof. GLADYS E. FLECHA DELGADO; Dir of Centre for Educational Resources Prof. LOURDES ELIZA; Registrar VIVIAN E. TORRES MILLÁN.

Ponce School of Medicine & Health Sciences: POB 7004, Ponce, PR 00732-7004; 388 Zona Ind Reparada 2, Ponce, PR 00716-2347; tel. (787) 840-2575; fax (787) 840-2317; e-mail info@psm.edu; internet www.psm.edu; f. 1980, present status 1980; grants doctorate of medicine; graduate programmes in biomedical sciences; psychology and public health programmes; 456 (162 full-time, 294 part-time) teachers; 607 students; Pres. and Dean Dr OLGA RODRÍGUEZ DE ARZOLA; Sr Vice-Pres. and Exec. Dean for Admin. and Finance REINALDO DÍAZ; Provost for Research Dr YASUHIRO YAMAMURA (acting); Dean for Health Science and Academic Affairs Dr OLGA RODRIGUEZ DE ARZOLA; Dir of Admissions Dr WANDA VELEZ; Dir of Library CARMEN MALAVET; Registrar SEGUNDINA C. DE TORRES.

Recinto de Aguadilla: POB 20000, Aguadilla, PR 00605-2000; tel. (787) 891-0925; fax (787) 882-3020; internet www.aguadilla.inter.edu; f. 1957, present status 1991; attached to Inter American Univ. of Puerto Rico; graduate-level programmes; promotes social commitment, cultural appreciation, environmental awareness, critical thinking, handling of multi-manner communication skills; library: 70,596 vols, incl. 59, 608 gen. colln, 10,271 audiovisual materials, 460 microforms and 257 CDs and DVDs; 276 (77 full-time, 199 part-time) teachers; 4,722 (4,423 undergraduate, 299 graduate) students; Pres. Dr ELIE AGÉSILAS; Dean of Admin. ISRAEL AYALA; Dean of Students ANA C. MELÓN; Dean of Studies Prof. NILSA ROMÁN; Dir of Admissions DORIS PÉREZ; Registrar MARÍA PÉREZ.

Recinto de Arecibo: POB 4050, Arecibo, PR 00614-4050; tel. (787) 878-5475; fax (787) 880-1624; internet www.arecibo.inter.edu; f. 1957; attached to Inter American Univ. of Puerto Rico; non-univ. post-secondary academic programmes; undergraduate and graduate studies; research; 308 (93 full-time, 215 part-time) teachers; 4,700 students; Pres. Dr RAFAEL RAMIREZ RIVERA; Dean of Academic Affairs Dr ANNETTE VEGA;

Dean of Admin. WANDA I. PÉREZ RAMÍREZ; Dean of Student Affairs Prof. ILVIS AGUIRRE FRANCO; Dean of Studies VÍCTOR CONCEPCIÓN SANTIAGO; Dir of Admissions PROVI MONTALVO BONILLA; Dir of Library SARA ABREU; Registrar CARMEN L. RODRÍGUEZ MARTÍNEZ; publ. *Prism.*

Recinto de Barranquitas: POB 517, Barranquitas, PR 00794; tel. (787) 857-3600; fax (787) 857-2244; internet www.br.inter.edu; f. 1957; attached to Inter American Univ. of Puerto Rico; Depts incl. business administration, education, health sciences, science and technology; 177 (42 full-time, 135 part-time) teachers; 2,422 (2,316 undergraduate, 106 graduate) students; Rector Dra IRENE FERNÁNDEZ; Dean of Admin. JOSÉ E. ORTIZ; Dean of Students ARAMILDA CARTAGENA SANTIAGO; Dean of Studies Dr PATRICIA ÁLVAREZ SWIHART; Dir of Admission EDGARDO CINTRÓN VEGA; Registrar SANDRA MORALES RODRÍGUEZ; Library Dir Dr RODRIGUEZ RIVERA CLARIBETTE.

Recinto de Bayamón: 500 Carretera Dr John Will Harris, Bayamón, PR 00957-6257; tel. (787) 279-1912; fax (787) 279-2205; e-mail interbcinfo@bc.inter.edu; internet bc.inter.edu; f. 1956, present name and status 1991; attached to Inter American Univ. of Puerto Rico; programmes with emphasis on technology, engineering, aviation, computing, communications, science and business administration; 331 (111 full-time, 220 part-time) teachers; 5,148 (5,034 undergraduate, 114 graduate) students; Pres. Prof. JUAN MARTÍNEZ RODRÍGUEZ; Dean of Admin. LUIS M. CRUZ; Dean of Students GEMA C. TORRES SÁNCHEZ; Dean of Studies Dr CARLOS J. OLIVARES PACHECO; Registrar EDDIE AYALA MÉNDEZ.

Recinto de Fajardo: POB 70003, Fajardo, PR 00738-7003; tel. (787) 863-2390; fax (787) 860-3470; internet www.fajardo.inter.edu; f. 1960; attached to Inter American Univ. of Puerto Rico; BA and MA degree in business administration, education, science and technology; 143 (38 full-time, 105 part-time) teachers; 2,357 (2,299 undergraduate, 58 graduate) students; Pres. ISMAEL SUÁREZ; Dean of Admin. LYDIA E. SANTIAGO ROSADO; Dean of Students Affairs HILDA VELÁZQUEZ DIAZ; Dean of Studies Dr PAULA SAGARDÍA OLIVERAS; Dir of Admissions ADA CARABALLO CARMONA; Registrar ABIGAÍL RIVERA.

Recinto de Guayama: POB 10004, Guayama, PR 00784-4004; tel. (787) 864-2222; fax (787) 866-1176; internet www.guayama.inter.edu; f. 1956 present status 1993; attached to Inter American Univ. of Puerto Rico; depts of business administration, education and social sciences, health sciences, humanities, natural and applied sciences; 187 (48 full-time, 139 part-time) teachers; 2,393 (2,315 undergraduate, 78 graduate) students; Rector CARLOS E. COLÓN RAMOS; Dean of Admin. NESTOR LEBRÓN; Dean of Students Dr ROSA J. MARTÍNEZ RAMOS; Dean of Studies ÁNGELA DE JESÚS ALICEA; Dir of Admissions LAURA E. FERRER SÁNCHEZ; Registrar LUIS A. SOTO RIVERA.

Recinto de Ponce: 104 Turpeaux Ind Park, Ponce, PR 00715-1602; tel. (787) 284-1912; fax (787) 841-0103; internet ponce.inter.edu; f. 1962; attached to Inter American Univ. of Puerto Rico; depts of business administration, graduate studies, health sciences, humanistic studies, pedagogical studies, science and technology, social and behavioural sciences; 343 (100 full-time, 243 part-time) teachers; 6,460 (6,089 undergraduate, 371 graduate) students; Rector Dra VILMA E. COLÓN ACOSTA; Dean of Admin. VÍCTOR ALEJANDRO FELIBERTY-RUBERTÉ; Dean of Students EDDA R. COSTAS VÁZQUEZ; Dean of

Studies Dr JACQUELINE ÁLVAREZ; Dir of Admissions FRANCO L. DÍAZ; Registrar MARÍA DEL C. PÉREZ.

Recinto de San Germán: POB 5100, San Germán, PR 00683; tel. (787) 264-1912; fax (787) 892-6350; e-mail eberroca@sg.inter.edu; internet www.sg.inter.edu; f. 1912 as Puerto Rico Polytechnic Institute; attached to Inter American Univ. of Puerto Rico; depts of biology, chemistry and environmental sciences, business and management, education and physical education, fine arts, health sciences, languages and literature, mathematics and applied sciences, social sciences and liberal arts; library: 159,279 vols, 18,547 e-books. 2,211 video cassettes; 343 (129 full-time, 214 part-time) teachers; 5,408 (4,602 undergraduate, 806 graduate) students; Rector Prof. AGNES MOJICA; Dean of Admin. FRANCES CARABALLO; Dean of Student Affairs EFRAÍN ANGLERÓ; Dean of Studies Dr NYVIA ALVARADO; Dir of Admissions MILDRED CAMACHO; Registrar ARLEEN SANTANA.

Recinto Metro: Apdo 191293, San Juan, PR 00919-1293; tel. (787) 250-1912; fax (787) 250-0782; internet www.metro.inter.edu; f. 1912; attached to Inter American Univ. of Puerto Rico; faculties of economics and administrative sciences, education and professional conduct, humanistic studies, science and technology; 626 teachers; 10,681 (7,357 undergraduate, 3,324 graduate) students; Pres. MANUEL J. FERNÓS; Rector Prof. MARILINA LUCCA WAYLAND; Dean of Admin. JIMMY CANCEL; Dean of Studies Dr CARMEN A. OQUENDO; Dir of Admissions JANIES OLIVIERI CAMPOS; Registrar LISETTE RIVERA ORTIZ.

San Juan Bautista School of Medicine: POB 4968, Caguas, PR 00726-4968; Luis A. Ferré Highway, Rd 172, Caguas to Cidra, Turabo Gardens, Caguas, PR 00725; tel. (787) 743-3038; fax (787) 746-3093; e-mail admissions@sanjuanbautista.edu; internet www.sanjuanbautista.edu; f. 1978; MA degree in public health and physical assistance; postgraduate programme in basic sciences; depts of biomedical sciences, clinical sciences; 61 teachers; 272 students; Pres. and Dean Prof. Dr YOCASTA BRUGAL-MENA; Dean of Admin. and Human Resources CARLOS FCO. ABREU; Dir of Library CARLOS A. ALTAMIRANO; Registrar LISSETTE TORRES.

School of Optometry: 500 John Will Harris Ave, Rd 830, Bayamón, PR 00957-6257; tel. (787) 765-1915; fax (787) 756-7351; e-mail admissions@inter.edu; internet www.optonet.inter.edu; f. 1981, present status 1992; attached to Inter American Univ. of Puerto Rico; languages of instruction: English, Spanish; offers 4-year professional programme leading to the degree of doctorate of Optometry; 39 (18 full-time, 21 part-time)teachers; 220 students; Dean Dr ANDRÉS PAGÁN; Dean of Admin. Dr FRANCISCO RIVERA MEDINA; Dir of Library WILMA MARRERO ORTIZ.

Seminario Evangélico de Puerto Rico: 776 Ponce de León, San Juan, PR 00925; tel. (787) 763-6700; fax (787) 751-0847; e-mail registro@se-pr.edu; internet www.se-pr.edu; f. 1919 by merger of Portorricense Theological Seminary (Presbyterian), Mayagüez, Grace Institute Conaway (Baptist), Rio Piedras, Institute Robinson (Methodist), Hatillo and Institute Disciples of Christ in Bayamón; MA in divinity and arts in religion; doctoral degrees in ministry; library: 70,000 vols, 365 journals; Pres. Dr SERGIO OJEDA-CÁRCAMO; Dean of Academic Affairs Dr JOSÉ IRIZARRY MERCADO; Dir of Admin. MYRNA E. PÉREZ LÓPEZ; Dir of Library Prof. SONIA ARRILLAGA MONTALVO; Registrar MARI LILLIAN RIVERA.

UNITED STATES VIRGIN ISLANDS

The Higher Education System

The Virgin Islands' Department of Education is responsible for the provision of higher education within the US unincorporated territory, serving as both a local education agency and a state-level agency. The University of the Virgin Islands (founded in 1962 as the College of the Virgin Islands; present name and status adopted 1986) has two campuses—one on St Croix and the other on St Thomas—at which it offers Associate, Bachelors and Masters degree programmes. The University also offers Certificate and training courses through its Community Engagement and Lifelong Learning Center. In 2009 there were a total of 2,602 students enrolled at the University, which is accredited by the USA's Middle States Association of Colleges and Schools.

Regulatory Body

GOVERNMENT

Department of Education: 1834 Kongens Gade, St Thomas, VI 00802; tel. (340) 774-0100; fax (340) 715-3460; e-mail teachusvi@doe.vi; internet www.doe.vi; Commr Dr LaVerne Terry.

Department of Planning & Natural Resources: Cyril E. King Airport, Terminal Bldg, Second Fl., Suite 6, 8100 Lindberg Bay, St Thomas, VI 00802; tel. (340) 774-3320; fax (340) 775-5706; internet www.dpnr.gov.vi; Dir David Alvaro Simon.

Department of Sports, Parks & Recreation: Property and Procurement Bldg 1, Sub Base, Second Fl., Room 206, Charlotte Amalie, St Thomas, VI 00802; tel. (340) 774-0255; fax (340) 774-4600; e-mail info@dspr.vi; internet www.dspr.vi; f. 1954; Commr Claire N. Williams.

Learned Societies

GENERAL

Virgin Islands Humanities Council: 1829 Kongens Gade, St Thomas, VI 00802; tel. (340) 776-4044; fax (340) 774-3972; e-mail info@vihumanities.org; internet www.vihumanities.org; f. 1984; non-profit org.; supports research, education and promotion of public projects in humanities; Exec. Dir Ayesha Morris; Chair Opal Palmer Adisa; Sec. Charlene A. Matthew; Treas. Celestina Nkechi Lapenna.

BIBLIOGRAPHY, LIBRARY SCIENCE AND MUSEOLOGY

Virgin Islands Library Association: POB 446, Kingshill, VI 00851-0446; tel. (340) 692-4132; fax (340) 692-4135.

HISTORY, GEOGRAPHY AND ARCHAEOLOGY

St Croix Landmarks Society: 52 Estate Whim, Frederiksted, St Croix, VI 00840; tel. (340) 772-0598; fax (340) 772-9446; e-mail info@stcroixlandmarks.org; internet www.stcroixlandmarks.org; f. 1948; advances understanding and appreciation of historical and cultural legacy of St Croix through preservation, research and education; attached museums: Apothecary Hall Museum, Estate Whim Museum and Lawaetz Family Museum; library of 6,000 vols; holdings incl. traditional research resources such as artwork, collns of photographs, maps and MSS, drawings of the Virgin Islands by Henry Morton (1843–44) and Dr Allen Voorhees Lesley (1856), extensive photographic colln from Axel Ovesen (1902–72), street scenes from Christiansted and Frederiksted and images of bldgs from both the towns and country estates in the 19th and 20th centuries; Exec. Dir Sonia Jacobs Dow; Chair Hans Lawaetz.

St John Historical Society: POB 1256, St John, VI 00831; e-mail contactus@stjohnhistoricalsociety.org; internet www.stjohnhistoricalsociety.org; f. 1974; promotes appreciation and deeper understanding of history and cultural heritage of the island of St John; Pres. David W. Knight; Sec. Mary Andrews; Treas. Margie Labrenz.

St Thomas Historical Trust: POB 6707, Charlotte Amalie, St Thomas, VI 00804; tel. (340) 774-5541; e-mail execdirector@stthomashistoricaltrust.org; internet www.stthomashistoricaltrust.org; f. 1965; advocacy and education; identifies, protects and preserves historical sites, structures and cultural heritage of St Thomas; Pres. Ronald S. Lockhart; Vice-Pres. Bernice Turnbull; Sec. Lisa Chamley-Aqui; Treas. Frank McConnell.

MEDICINE

US Virgin Islands Medical Society (VIMS): POB 5986, Sunny Isle, St Croix, VI; tel. (340) 712-2402; fax (340) 712-2449; e-mail vimedicalsociety@hotmail.com; internet www.viqio.org/links/vims.html; f. 1955; represents physicians of the Virgin Islands; elevates and makes effective the opinions of the profession in all scientific, legislative, public health, material and social affairs, to the end that medical science may be advanced and the profession receives respect and support within its own ranks and from the community; affiliated to American Medical Asscn and Nat. Medical Asscn; Pres. Dr Ronald C. Nimmo; Pres.-Elect Dr Raymond Cintron; Exec. Sec. and Treas. Dr Cora L. E. Christian; Sec. Dr Gilbert Commissiong; Treas. Dr Alfred O. Heath.

NATURAL SCIENCES

Biological Sciences

Island Resources Foundation: 6292 Estate Nazareth 100, Red Hook, St Thomas, VI 00802; tel. (340) 775-6225; fax (340) 779-2022; e-mail irf@irf.org; internet www.irf.org; f. 1972; not-for-profit org.; assists small islands to meet the challenges of social, economic and institutional growth while protecting and enhancing their environments; library of 10,000 vols; Pres. Bruce Potter; Vice-Pres. Dr Barbara J. Lausche; Sec. and Treas. Judith A. Towle.

St Croix Environmental Association: 5032 Anchor Way, Suite 3, Christiansted, St Croix, VI 00820; tel. (340) 773-1989; fax (340) 773-7545; e-mail info.atsea@gmail.com; internet www.stxenvironmental.org; f. 1986; advocacy, research and programmes in conservation and education for a sustainable environment; 500 mems; Chair. Dr Ken Haines; Vice-Chair. Michael Baron; Sec. Melanie Feltmate; Treas. Theo T. Broodie; Exec. Dir Paul Chakroff; Programme Dir Carol Cramer-Burke.

Research Institutes

GENERAL

Virgin Islands Experimental Program to Stimulate Competitive Research (VI-EPSCoR): Univ. of the Virgin Islands, 2 John Brewer's Bay, St Thomas, VI 00802-9990; tel. (340) 693-1428; fax (340) 693-1425; e-mail viepscor@uvi.edu; internet epscor.uvi.edu; attached to Univ. of the Virgin Islands; conducts research on areas of scientific inquiry linked to the Territory's economic devt; improves research infrastructure to strengthen competitiveness; increases participation of students in science and technology in order to build a skilled workforce; builds partnerships between govt, non-governmental orgs, and private sector to create a foundation of research and devt for economic growth.; Asst Dir Nick Drayton.

AGRICULTURE, FISHERIES AND VETERINARY SCIENCE

Agricultural Experiment Station: RR 1, POB 10,000, Kingshill, St Croix, VI 00850; tel. (340) 692-4020; fax (340) 692-4035; internet www.uvi.edu; attached to Univ. of the Virgin Islands; conducts basic and applied research to meet the needs of the local agricultural community in increasing production, improving efficiency, developing new enterprises, preserving and propagating germplasm unique to the Virgin Islands, and protecting the natural resource base; Dir Robert W. Godfrey.

Cooperative Extension Service: Univ. of the Virgin Islands, 2 John Brewer's Bay, St Thomas, VI 00802-9990; tel. (340) 693-2083; fax (340) 693-1085; internet www.uvi.edu; attached to Univ. of the Virgin Islands; delivers programmes in areas of agriculture and natural resources, 4-H, family and consumer science, and communications, technology and distance education; State Dir Kwame Garcia.

Virgin Islands Sustainable Farm Institute (VISFI): POB 2903, Frederiksted, St Croix, VI 00841; tel. (340) 220-0466; internet www.visfi.org; f. 2003; community education in environmental sustainability; promotes agroecology and creation of sustainable life systems; Co-Founder Ben Jones; Dir Nate Olive.

ECONOMICS, LAW AND POLITICS

Eastern Caribbean Center: Univ. of the Virgin Islands, St Thomas Campus, 2 John Brewer's Bay, St Thomas, VI 00802-9990; tel. (340) 693-102; internet www.uvi.edu; attached to Univ. of the Virgin Islands; compiles and analyzes demographic, social and economic data, and disseminates this data into various forums and formats; conducts scientific surveys to measure the Territory's population and housing characteristics; provides training in geographic information systems; Dir FRANK MILLS.

MEDICINE

Caribbean Exploratory NIMHD Research Center: Univ. of the Virgin Islands, St Thomas Campus, 2 John Brewer's Bay, St Thomas, VI 00802-9990; tel. (340) 693-1178; internet cercuvi.com; attached to School of Nursing, Univ. of the Virgin Islands; research in diabetes, cancer, obesity and HIV/AIDS; Dir Dr GLORIA B. CALLWOOD.

Virgin Islands Medical Institute, Inc.: POB 5989, 1AD Diamond Ruby, Sunny Isle, Christiansted, VI 00823-5989; tel. (340) 712-2400; fax (340) 712-2449; e-mail askvimi@viqio.sdps.org; internet www.viqio.org; f. 1977; researches and documents areas of devt and improvement in health care; monitors the quality of the health care system on the Islands; non-profit org.; Pres. Dr ALFRED O. HEATH; Vice-Pres. Dr EMMANUEL GRAHAM; Sec. LEONARD W. BONELLI, SR; Treas. JOYCE L. CHRISTIAN; Medical Dir Dr CORA L. E. CHRISTIAN; publ. *Medicare Watch* (1 a year).

NATURAL SCIENCES

General

Caribbean Green Technology Center: Univ. of the Virgin Islands, St Thomas Campus, 2 John Brewer's Bay, St Thomas, VI 00802-9990; tel. (340) 693-1158; internet cgtc.uvi.edu; attached to College of Science and Mathematics, Univ. of the Virgin Islands; fosters research, education and public service on sustainability; advances interdisciplinary investigations and learning; collaborates with governmental agencies and industry partners; researches, develops, demonstrates and monitors green technology; Dir Dr WAYNE ARCHIBALD.

Biological Sciences

Center for Marine and Environmental Studies: Univ. of the Virgin Islands, RR1 10,000, Kingshill, St Croix, VI 00850-9781; tel. (340) 693-1380; internet www.uvi.edu; f. 1999; attached to Univ. of the Virgin Islands; research areas incl. evolutionary and ecological patterns and processes, ocean and coastal processes and environmental analysis and management; Dir Dr KONSTANTINOS T. ALEXANDRIDIS (acting).

Water Resources Research Institute: 2 John Brewers Bay, St Thomas, VI 00802-9990; tel. (340) 693-1062; fax (340) 693-1065; internet www.uvi.edu/sites/uvi/pages/wrri-home.aspx; f. 1973; attached to Univ. of the Virgin Islands; research, information dissemination and training on water resources and related areas; Dir Dr HENRY H. SMITH.

Libraries and Archives

St Croix

St George Village Botanical Library: 127 Estate St George, Frederiksted, St Croix, VI 00840; tel. (340) 692-2874; fax (340) 692-6154; e-mail infoatthegarden@gmail.com; internet www.sgvbg.org/library; historical, horticultural and botanical information; 500 vols; Exec. Dir DAVID HAMADA.

Virgin Islands Public Library System: Div. of Libraries, Archives and Museums, 1122 King St, Christiansted, St Croix, VI 00820; tel. (340) 773-5715; fax (340) 773-5327 23 Dronningens Gade, St Thomas, VI 00802; tel. (340) 774-3407; fax (340) 775-1887; e-mail dlmdir@vipowernet.net; internet www.virginislandspubliclibraries.org; attached to Div. of Libraries, Archives and Museums, Dept of Planning and Natural Resources; depository of govt records; preserves historical and public records; spec. collns: Von Scholten Colln, Caribbean Colln; houses books, MSS, pamphlets; newspapers on microfilm; church records incl. birth and death certificates, other archival materials; Territorial Dir Dr INGRID A. BOUGH; Asst Dir DONALD G. COLE.

Public Libraries:

> **Athalie McFarlane Petersen Public Library:** Strand St, Frederiksted, St Croix, VI 00840; tel. (340) 772-0315.

> **Elaine I. Sprauve Public Library:** POB 30, Enighed Estate, St John, VI 00831; tel. (340) 776-6359; f. 1980; temporarily closed for renovation; Head Librarian CAROL MCGUINNESS.

> **Enid M. Baa Public Library:** 20 Dronningens Gade, St. Thomas, VI 00802; tel. (340) 774-0630; f. 1920 fmrly St Thomas library, present name 1978.

> **Florence Williams Public Library:** 1122 King St, Christiansted, St Croix, VI 00820; tel. (340) 773-5715; fax (340) 773-5327; f. 1920; 30,000 vols.

> **VI Regional Library for the Blind & Physically Handicapped (Talking Books Library):** 3012 Golden Rock, Christiansted, St Croix, VI 00820; tel. ((340) 718-2250; fax (340) 718-3545; e-mail reglib@vipowernet.net; Head Librarian LETITIA GITTENS.

Museums and Art Galleries

St Croix

Fort Frederik–Frederiksfort: Waterfront, Frederiksted, St Croix, VI 00840; tel. (340) 772-2021; named after Frederik V of Denmark; deep red rubble and masonry fort represents classic Danish military architecture of the period; indoor exhibits display colonial military life; listed in the Nat. Register for Historic Places in 1996 and Nat. Historic Landmark in 1997.

St George Village Museum: 127 Estate St George, Frederiksted, St Croix, VI 00840; tel. (340) 692-2874; fax (340) 692-6154; e-mail infoatthegarden@gmail.com; internet www.sgvbg.org/museum; attached to St George Village Botanical Gdn; display of artefacts of early Amerindian settlers; Exec. Dir DAVID HAMADA; Sec. CAROLYN FORNO; Treas. SANDRA J. RADCZENKO.

St John

Bajo el Sol Gallery: Mongoose Junction, Cruz Bay, St John, VI; tel. (340) 693-7070; fax (340) 715-4841; e-mail bajoelsol@pennswoods.net; internet www.bajoelsolgallery.com; f. 1993; ceramics, jewellery, painting, sculpture and works by local artists.

Galeria del Mar: Wharfside Village, Cruz Bay, St John, VI; tel. (340) 693-9399; fax (340) 693-9599; Caribbean fine arts and crafts gallery; original works and ltd edn prints by local artists, glasswork, pottery and wood sculptures.

Ivan Jadan Museum: 251 Contant, POB 84, Cruz Bay, St John, VI 00831; tel. (340) 776-6423; fax (340) 779-4323; e-mail ijadan@islands.vi; internet www.ijadan.vi; 5,000 artefacts relating to the life of Russian tenor Ivan Jadan; collns incl. books, historical documents, photographs, CDs and videos; Curator DORIS JADAN.

St Thomas

American Caribbean Historical Museum: 32 Raadets Gade, Charlotte Amalie, St Thomas, VI; tel. (340) 714-5150; history of the Virgin Islands since 15th century; exhibits incl. artefacts, documents, historic costumes and photographs.

Fort Christian and Virgin Islands Museum: Waterfront, Charlotte Amalie, St Thomas, VI; tel. (340) 776-8605; historic museum housed within Fort Christian, the oldest standing structure in St Thomas (built in 1672); exhibits incl. antique maps, handmade W Indian furnishings, military hardware, natural history colln, period furniture; attached art gallery; added to Nat. Register of Historic Places in 1977.

University

UNIVERSITY OF THE VIRGIN ISLANDS

St Croix Campus: RR1 POB 10,000, Kingshill, St Croix, VI 00850-9781

Telephone: (340) 692-4158

St Thomas Campus: 2 John Brewer's Bay, St Thomas, VI 00802-9990

Telephone: (340) 693-1160 (St Thomas)
E-mail: admissions@uvi.edu
Internet: www.uvi.edu

Founded 1962 as College of the Virgin Islands, present name 1986
State control
Academic year: August to DecemberJanuary to May (2 semesters)
Pres.: Dr DAVID HALL
Provost: Dr KARL S. WRIGHT
Vice-Pres. for Admin. and Finance: SHIRLEY LAKE-KING
Vice-Pres. for Institutional Advancement: Dr DIONNE V. JACKSON
Vice-Provost for Access and Enrolment: Dr JUDITH EDWIN
Vice-Provost for Research and Public Service: Dr HENRY H. SMITH
Chief Information Officer: TINA M. KOOPMANS
Library: St Croix Campus: 53,000 vols, 167 periodicals; spec. colln incl. VI govt documents and ERIC documents; St Thomas campus: 80,500 vols, 690 periodicals, 590,000 microforms, 15,000 US govt documents, 20,000 other items; spec. collns: Virgin Islands Digital colln, Ralph D. DeChabert spec. colln, Caspar Holstein Colln, Charles William Taussig Memorial colln and Caribbean colln
Number of teachers: 615 (390 full-time, 225 part-time)
Number of students: 2,602
Publications: *The Caribbean Writer* (1 a year), *UVI Magazine* (1 a year)

DEANS

College of Liberal Arts and Social Sciences: Dr GEORGE LORD
College of Science and Mathematics: Dr CAMILLE MCKAYLE
School of Business: Dr CHARLES WILLIAMS
School of Education: Dr LINDA V. THOMAS
School of Nursing: Dr CHERYL FRANKLIN

URUGUAY

The Higher Education System

Institutions of higher education date from after Uruguay's independence from Spain in 1825, the oldest being Universidad de la República, which was founded in 1849 and is the sole public university. The next oldest institution is Universidad del Trabajo de Uruguay, which was founded in 1878. All education, including university tuition, is provided free of charge. Higher education is provided by universidades públicas (public universities), universidades privadas (private universities), institutos universitarios (university institutes), institutos terciarios no universitario públicos (public non-university higher institutions) and institutos terciarios no universitario privados (private non-university higher institutions). There were six public universities and their equivalents in 2005 with 72,100 students. In 2006 there were four private universities, 11 university institutes (private), 12 public non-university institutes and five private non-university institutes.

The main requirement for admission to higher education is the Bachillerato Diversificado, the main secondary school award, with specialization depending on the degree applied for. Carreras intermedios (intermediate degrees) last two-and-a-half to three years and often culminate with the award of a professional title; students may then graduate to full undergraduate degrees. Carreras de grado (undergraduate degrees) last a minimum of four years and lead to the award of Título de Licenciado (Bachelors) in the subject studied. Some professional degrees, such as Licenciado en Enfermería (nursing), Licenciado en Nutrición (nutrition) and Licenciado en Psicolo-

gía (psychology) last upwards of four-and-a-half years. Until 2006 medical degrees were available only at Universidad de la República and lasted eight years, with students receiving the title Doctor en Medicina. Since 2006 a six-year medicine programme accredited by El Mecanismo Experimental de Acreditación de Carreras del Mercosur (see below) has been available at Centro Latinoamericano de Economi Humana. The first postgraduate degree is the especialización (specialist course), which lasts for a minimum of one year and leads to award of the Título de Especialista or Título de Diplomado. The Título de Maestría (Masters) lasts a minimum of two years; students are required to submit a thesis in the second year to complete the degree. Finally, the highest level of postgraduate study is at doctoral level, where students work for a minimum of three years to achieve the Doctorado (Doctorate).

The Consejo de Educación Técnico y Professional—Universidad del Trabajo is responsible for providing post-secondary technical and vocational education (although, despite what its name might suggest, it does not offer degree-level qualifications). The primary qualification awarded at this level is the Título Técnico in the subject studied.

Uruguay is a member of Mercado Común del Sur (Mercosur—Southern Common Market) and therefore participates in El Mecanismo Experimental de Acreditación de Carreras del Mercosur, which has so far accredited programmes in agronomy, medicine and engineering. However, Uruguay is the only member of Mercosur that does not have a national accreditation or quality assurance agency.

Regulatory Body

GOVERNMENT

Ministry of Education and Culture: Reconquista 535, 11000 Montevideo; tel. and fax 2916 1016; e-mail rpi@mec.gub.uy; internet www.mec.gub.uy; Min. RICARDO EHRLICH; Gen. Dir Dr JAIME RUBEN SAPOLINSKI.

Learned Societies

AGRICULTURE, FISHERIES AND VETERINARY SCIENCE

Asociación Rural del Uruguay (Rural Association): Avda Uruguay 864, Montevideo; tel. 2902 0484; fax 2902 0489; internet www.aru.org.uy; f. 1871; 3,000 mems; library of 3,000 vols; Pres. Ing. JOSÉ BONICA HENDERSON; Librarian Lic. ISABEL MA. TRIAY; publ. *Revista* (12 a year).

ARCHITECTURE AND TOWN PLANNING

Sociedad de Arquitectos del Uruguay (Society of Architects): Gonzalo Ramírez 2030, 11200 Montevideo; tel. 2419 3463; e-mail sau@sau.org.uy; internet www.sau.org.uy; f. 1914; 2,000 mems; library of 2,000 vols; Pres. Arq. JOSÉ OLIVER; Exec. Sec. Arq. GRICELDA BARRIOS; publ. *Boletín de Arquitectura* (6 a year).

BIBLIOGRAPHY, LIBRARY SCIENCE AND MUSEOLOGY

Agrupación Bibliotecológica del Uruguay (Library Association): Cerro Largo 1666, 11200 Montevideo; tel. 2400 5740; f.

1960; activities incl. library science, archives, documentation, bibliography, history and numismatics; 238 mems; Pres. LUIS ALBERTO MUSSO; publs *Anales del Senado del Uruguay-Cronología* (2nd edition), *Aportes para la historia de la bibliotecología en el Uruguay*, *Archivos del Uruguay*, *Artigas en la medalla Inventario de una colección*, *Bibliografía básica de la historia de la República Oriental del Uruguay*, *Bibliografía bibliográfica y bibliotecología*, *Bibliografía de Bibliografías uruguayas*, *Bibliografía de Luis Alberto Musso*, *Bibliografía del Poder Legislativo desde sus comienzos hasta el año 1965*, *Bibliografía Uruguaya sobre Brasil*, *Bibliografía Uruguaya sobre Historia Argentina*, *Bibliografía y documentación en el Uruguay*, *Breves apuntes para la historia del microfilm*, *Canarios en el Uruguay*, *Colonización canaria en la Banda Oriental*, *De Libros y Lectores*, *Documentalistas Uruguayos*, *El Río de la Plata en el Archivo de Indias*, *Fernández Saldaña. Obra bibliográfica*, *Historiografía y Bibliografía sobre los canarios en el Uruguay*, *Indice de la Revista Jurídica 'La Revista Nueva*, *Indice de la Revista Jurídica 'Los Debates'*, *Indice Suplemento Diario 'El Día'*, *La Estrella del Sur*, *La Revista Nueva*, *Legislación Uruguaya sobre Brasil*, *Los cabildantes canarios de Montevideo*, *Uruguay, Brasil y sus Medallas*.

Asociación de Bibliotecólogos del Uruguay (Uruguayan Librarians' Association): Eduardo V. Haedo 2255, 11200 Montevideo; tel. and fax 2409 9989; e-mail abu@adinet.com.uy; f. 1978; 300 mems; Pres. Lic. ALICIA OCASO FERREIRA; publ. *Panel de Noticias*.

HISTORY, GEOGRAPHY AND ARCHAEOLOGY

Instituto Histórico y Geográfico del Uruguay: Río Negro 1495/a. 202, Montevideo; e-mail histogeo@adinet.com.uy; f. 1843; 40 academicians; Pres. Prof. EDMUNDO M. NARANCIO; publ. *Revista*.

LANGUAGE AND LITERATURE

Academia Nacional de Letras (National Academy of Literature): Ituzaingó 1255, 11000 Montevideo; tel. 2915 2374; fax 2916 7460; e-mail academia@montevideo.com.uy; internet www.mec.gub.uy/academiadeletras; f. 1943; researches in Spanish language, mainly lexicography, especially Uruguayan spoken Spanish; also Uruguayan literature; organizes lectures, readings of Uruguayan literature, workshops; contributes to comprehensive works elaborated within the ASALE (Asociación de Academias de la Lengua Española) such as the Nueva Gramática de la lengua española, Diccionario de Americanismos, Ortografía de la lengua española, etc.; 19 mems, 33 corresp. mems; Pres. Dr WILFREDO PENCO; Sec. Dr ADOLFO ELIZAINCÍN; publs *Boletín*, *Ensayos Literarios*, *Revista de la Academia Nacional de Letras*.

Alliance Française: Bulevar Artigas 1229, Montevideo; tel. and fax 2400 0505; e-mail info@alliancefrancaise.edu.uy; internet www.alliancefrancaise.edu.uy; f. 1923; offers courses and examinations in French language and culture and promotes cultural exchange with France; attached teaching centres in Artigas, Colonia, Florida, Maldonado, Melo, Mercedes, Montevideo, Paysandú, Rocha, Salto, San José, Tacuarembó and Trinidad; Pres. PEDRO NICOLÁS BARIDON; Dir YVES MAHÉ.

Goethe-Institut: Canelones 1524, 11200 Montevideo; tel. 2410 5813; fax 2410 4432; e-mail info@montevideo.goethe.org; internet www.goethe.de/montevideo; offers courses and examinations in German language and culture and promotes cultural exchange with Germany; library of 8,000 vols, 23 periodicals; Dir MIKKO FRITZE.

MEDICINE

Academia Nacional de Medicina del Uruguay: 18 de Julio 2175, 5° piso, Montevideo; tel. 2408 4103; fax 2401 6058; e-mail academiamed@adinet.com.uy; f. 1976; 26 mems; Dir Dr ROBERTO DE BELLIS; publ. *Boletín* (1 a year).

Asociación Odontológica Uruguaya (Odontological Association): Avda Durazno 937-39, Montevideo; tel. and fax 2900 1572; e-mail aou@adinet.com.uy; internet www.aou.org.uy; f. 1946; 3,000 mems; comprises 8 depts and 6 sections; museum; library of 6,000 vols; Sec. Dr ALVARO RODA; Sec. Dr RAFAEL PÉREZ; publs *Boletín Informativo* (12 a year), *Odontología Uruguaya* (2 a year).

Sociedad de Cirugía del Uruguay (Surgical Society): Canelones 2280, Montevideo CP 11200; tel. 2402 6820; fax 2403 0532; e-mail scu@cirugia-uy.com; internet cirugia-uy.com; f. 1920; scientific sessions, meetings, continuous education, annual Uruguayan congress of surgery; 443 mems; library of 2,800 vols; Pres. Dr MARIO BOUNOUS; Vice-Pres. Dr MARIO BURGER; Sec.-Gen. Dra MONICA CARABALLO; publ. *Cirugía del Uruguay* (3 a year).

Sociedad de Radiología e Imagenología del Uruguay: Julio César 1460 bis, Montevideo; tel. and fax 2481 1714; e-mail sriu@adinet.com.uy; internet www.sriu.org.uy; f. 1923; scientific activity linked to the Médicos Imagenólogos; holds confs and seminars; 150 mems; Pres. Dr IVONNE MARTINEZ; Sec. Dr LUIS DIBARBOURE; publ. *Revista de Imagenología del Uruguay.*

Attached Institutes:

Gremial Uruguaya de Médicos Radiólogos: Montevideo; f. 1972; 70 mems; Pres. Dr ERNESTO H. CIBILS.

Sociedad Uruguaya de Historia de la Medicina: Casilla de Correo 157, Montevideo; tel. 2401 4701; fax 2409 1603; e-mail histmed@fmed.edu.uy; f. 1971; research on history of medicine and allied sciences; 80 mems; Pres. Prof. Dr FERNANDO MAÑÉ GARZÓN; Sec. Dr JUAN I. GIL; publ. *Sesiones de la Sociedad Uruguaya* (1 a year).

Sociedad Uruguaya de Pediatría (Paediatrics Society): Centro Hospitalario Pereira Rossell, Bulevar Artigas 1550, Montevideo; tel. 2709 1801; fax 2708 5213; e-mail pedsoc@adinet.com.uy; internet www.sup.org.uy; f. 1915; 500 mems; affiliated to the Asociación Latino Americana de Pediatría; library of 3,500 vols, 6,500 periodicals; Pres. Dr ÁLVARO GALIANA; Sec. Dr DANIEL BORBONET; publ. *Archivos de Pediatría del Uruguay* (4 a year).

NATURAL SCIENCES
Biological Sciences

Sociedad Malacológica del Uruguay (Malacological Society): Casilla 1401, 11000 Montevideo; e-mail smu@adinet.com.uy; internet moluscos.net/smu; f. 1957; 210 mems; Pres. JORGE BROGGI; Sec. JUAN CARLOS ZAFFARONI; publ. *Comunicaciones* (2 a year).

Sociedad Zoológica del Uruguay: Casilla 10739, 11200, Montevideo; tel. 2525 8618; fax 2525 8617; internet www.serpentario.edu.uy/szu; f. 1961; 200 mems; Pres. RAÚL MANEYRO; Sec. FEDERICO ACHAVAL; publ. *Boletín* (irregular, online).

TECHNOLOGY

Academia Nacional de Ingeniería: Cuareim 1492, Montevideo; tel. 2901 1762; fax 2900 8951; e-mail cutinella@redfacil.com.uy; internet www.artech.com.uy/aniu; f. 1965; 40 full mems; Pres. Ing. ALVARO CUTINELLA; Sec. Ing. EDISON GARCÍA REGUEIRO.

Asociación de Ingenieros del Uruguay (Association of Uruguayan Engineers): Cuareim 1492, Montevideo; tel. 2901 1762; fax 2900 8951; e-mail asocing@adinet.com.uy; internet www.aiu.org.uy; f. 1905; affiliated to the Unión Panamericana de Asociaciones de Ingenieros; 1,400 mems, also hon. and corresp. mems abroad; library of 2,000 vols; Pres. Ing. EDUARDO ALVAREZ MAZZA; Sec. Ing. CARLOS MALCUORI; publ. *Revista de Ingeniería.*

Research Institutes
GENERAL

Dirección Nacional de Ciencia, Tecnología y Innovación (DINACYT): Paraguay 1470, Piso 2, 11100 Montevideo; tel. 2901 4285; fax 2902 4870; e-mail webmaster@dicyt.gub.uy; internet www.dicyt.gub.uy; f. 1961 to encourage research in all branches of knowledge, especially scientific, technological and innovation policies; fmrly Consejo Nacional de Investigaciones Científicas y Técnicas (CONICYT); 14 council mems; library of 7,000 vols, 275 periodicals; Gen. Dir Dr AMILCAR DAVYT; publs *Boletín electrónico* (52 a year), *Claro Que Se Puede* (irregular), *El Proceso de Innovación en la Industria Uruguaya* (every 2 years), *Indicadores de Ciencia y Tecnología* (irregular).

UNESCO Office Montevideo and Regional Office for Science in Latin America and the Caribbean: Casilla de correo 859, Montevideo; Edificio del MERCOSUR (ex Parque Hotel), Calle Dr Luis Piera 1992 (2° piso), 11200 Montevideo; tel. 2413 2075; fax 2413 2094; e-mail montevideo@unesco.org.uy; internet www.unesco.org.uy; f. 1949; designated Cluster Office for Argentina, Brazil, Paraguay, Uruguay; coordinates UNESCO's programmes in the region, particularly: basic sciences, environmental and water sciences, science, technology and society, earth sciences and natural hazards, marine sciences, information and communication, education, culture and world heritage; Dir JORGE GRANDI.

AGRICULTURE, FISHERIES AND VETERINARY SCIENCE

Centro de Investigaciones Pesqueras y Piscicultura (Fisheries and Fish-farming Research Institute): c/o DINARA, Villa Constitución, Salto; internet www.dinara.gub.uy; attached to State Office for Aquatic Resources; Nat. Dir for Aquatic Resources DANIEL MONTIEL.

Instituto Nacional de Investigación Agropecuaria (National Agricultural Research Institute): Andes 1365, Piso 12 CP, 11100 Montevideo; tel. 2902 0550; fax 2902 3633; internet www.inia.org.uy; f. 1914; library of 12,000 vols, 1,000 periodicals; Dir MARIO ALLEGRI; publs *Boletín de Divulgación, Hojas de Divulgación, Serie Actividades de Difusión, Serie Técnica.*

ECONOMICS, LAW AND POLITICS

Centro de Estadísticas Nacionales y Comercio Internacional del Uruguay (CENCI Uruguay): Juncal 1327D, Oficina 1603, Montevideo; tel. 2915 2930; fax 2915 4578; e-mail cenci@cenci.com.uy; internet www.cenci.com.uy; f. 1956; provides eco-

nomic and statistical information on all American countries; operates computer programmes handling the import tariffs on commodities; library of 900 vols; Dir KENNETH BRUNNER; publs *Anuario estadístico sobre el intercambio comercial* (1 a year), *Dictámenes de Clasificación Arancelaria—MERCOSUR, Estudios del Mercado, Industrias por sectores de actividad, Manual práctico Aduanero* (12 a year), *Manual práctico del Contribuyente* (12 a year), *Manual práctico del Exportador* (12 a year), *Manual práctico del Importador* (12 a year), *Régimen de Origen—ALADI y MERCOSUR.*

Instituto Nacional de Estadística (Statistical Office): Río Negro 1520, 11100 Montevideo; tel. 2902 7303; fax 2903 2881; e-mail difusion@ine.gub.uy; internet www.ine.gub.uy; f. 1852; library of 4,000 vols; Technical Dir Ec. ALICIA MELGAR; publs *Anuario Estadístico, Boletín Trimestral* (4 a year), *Encuesta Continua de Hogares, Síntesis Estadística.*

HISTORY, GEOGRAPHY AND ARCHAEOLOGY

Servicio Geográfico Militar (Military Geographical Institute): Avda 8 de Octubre 3255, 11600 Montevideo; tel. 2487 1810; fax 2487 0868; e-mail sgm@iau.gub.uy; f. 1913; cartography, geodesy, geophysics, photogrammetry; library of 3,500 vols; Dir Col ARTIGAS P. BACCI; publs *Boletín*, scale aeronautic and aerial maps.

MEDICINE

Instituto Nacional del Cáncer: Av. 8 de Octubre 3265 y Abreu, Montevideo; tel. 2481 3625; f. 1960; Dir Dr ALBERTO VIOLA.

Liga Uruguaya contra la Tuberculosis (Anti-Tuberculosis League): Magallanes 1320, 11200 Montevideo; tel. 2408 3570; fax 2400 5575; e-mail ligatub@adinet.com.uy; f. 1902; specializes in combating tuberculosis in children and the elderly; library of 3,000 vols; Pres. MÁXIMO A. SAAVEDRA; Sec. Dr LORENZO PÍRIZ LOSTAO.

NATURAL SCIENCES
Biological Sciences

Instituto de Investigaciones Biológicas Clemente Estable: Avda Italia 3318, 11600 Montevideo; tel. 2487 1616; fax 2487 5548; e-mail asistentes@iibce.edu.uy; internet www.iibce.edu.uy; f. 1927; 12 divs, 3 depts; biological research; library of 12,000 vols; Pres. Dr GUSTAVO FOLLE.

Physical Sciences

Dirección Nacional de Meteorología del Uruguay (National Meteorological Directorate): Javier Barrios Amorín 1488, Casilla de Correo 64, 11200 Montevideo; tel. 2400 5655; fax 2409 7391; e-mail dnm25255@adinet.com.uy; internet www.meteorologia.com.uy; f. 1895; library of 6,000 vols, 13,800 documents; Dir RAUL MICHELINI; publs *Anuario Climatológico, Boletín Agrometeorológico, Boletín Pluviométrico, Notas Técnicas.*

Observatorio Astronómico de Montevideo (Montevideo Astronomical Observatory): Liceo No. 35 IAVA, J. E. Rodó y E. Acevedo, Montevideo; tel. 2408 5825; f. 1927; library of 5,000 vols; Dir (vacant).

RELIGION, SOCIOLOGY AND ANTHROPOLOGY

Instituto Interamericano del Niño (Inter-American Children's Institute): Avda 8 de Octubre 2904, 11600 Montevideo; tel. 2487 2150; fax 2487 3242; e-mail iin@oas.org; internet www.iin.oea.org; f. 1927; specialized institute of the Organization of American

States (OAS); library: specialized library of 50,000 vols, open to the public; computerized information centre; Pres. CARMEN BERGÉS DE AMARO; Dir-Gen. ALEJANDRO BONASSO; publ. *Boletín*.

TECHNOLOGY

Dirección Nacional de Minería y Geología: Calle Hervidero 2861, CP 11800, Montevideo; tel. 2200 1951; fax 2209 4905; e-mail secretaria@dinamige.miem.gub.uy; internet www.dinamige.gub.uy; f. 1912; library of 3,000 vols; Nat. Dir Prof. PIER ROSSI; publ. *Industria Extractiva del Uruguay* (1 a year).

Dirección Nacional de Tecnología Nuclear: Mercedes 1041, 11100 Montevideo; tel. 2900 6919; fax 2902 1619; f. 1955 as Comisión Nacional de Energía Atómica; controls activities involving the use of radioactive materials or equipment producing ionizing radiation; prepares technical and safety rules for activities involving nuclear technology; liaises with national and international institutions on procedural aspects of nuclear technology; library of 3,500 vols; collection of microfiches; Dir ROSARIO ODINO; publs *Memoria* (1 a year), *Revista* (1 a year).

Instituto Uruguayo de Normas Técnicas (Uruguayan Standards Institution): Plaza Independencia 812, (2°piso), Montevideo; tel. 2901 2048; fax 2902 1681; e-mail unit-iso@unit.org.uy; internet www.unit.org .uy; f. 1939; standardization, certification, information on standards, training in high-level management; library of 250,000 vols; Dir Eng. PABLO BENIA; publ. *UNIT Standards*.

Libraries and Archives
Florida
Biblioteca Municipal: C/Barreiro 420, 94000 Florida; tel. and fax 3522 102; f. 1889; 42,000 vols; Dir FERNANDO GABRIEL GIORDANO FOLIGNO.

Montevideo
Archivo General de la Nación (National Archives): Calle Convención 1474, Montevideo; tel. 2900 7232; fax 2908 1330; e-mail agn@adinet.com.uy; internet www.mec.gub .uy/agn; f. 1926; 14,000 vols; Dir ABELARDO MANUAL GARCIA VIERA; publ. *Revista*.

Biblioteca Central de Educación Secundaria: Eduardo Acevedo 1427, 11200 Montevideo; tel. 2408 4273; fax 2408 1252; e-mail biblos@adinet.com.uy; internet www.ces.edu .uy/bibliotecacentral/bicentral.htm; f. 1885; books for higher education; collns incl. ancient and rare books section (from 16th-century editions); 74,000 vols; Librarian MARIANELA FALERO.

Biblioteca del Museo Histórico Nacional (Library of the National Historical Museum): Rincón 437, 1000, Montevideo; f. 1940; specialization in the history of America and history of art; iconography, engravings, maps, numismatics; the entire library and Uruguayan collns of Dr Pablo Blanco Acevedo; 150,000 vols, 4,000 vols of MSS; Dir ELISA SILVA CAZET.

Biblioteca del Palacio Legislativo: Avda Libertador Brigadier Gral Lavalleja y Avda Gral Flores, Montevideo; f. 1929; legal deposit library in conjunction with National Library; 322,000 vols; specializes in jurisprudence; Dir LUIS H. BOIONS POMBO; publs *Bibliografía Uruguaya*, *Boletín Bibliográfico* (12 a year).

Biblioteca Municipal 'Dr Francisco Albero Schinca': 8 de Octubre 4210, Mon-

tevideo; tel. 2508 8152; f. 1929; 14,000 vols; Dir GRACIELA NAVARRO.

Biblioteca Municipal 'Joaquín de Salterain': Solis 1456 e/ 25 de Mayo y Cerrito, Montevideo; tel. 2915 6282; 36,000 vols; incl. a slide library; Librarian GRACIELA FERNÁNDEZ RIBEIRO.

Biblioteca Nacional del Uruguay (National Library): Avda 18 de Julio 1790, Montevideo; tel. 2400 6385; fax 2409 6902; e-mail bibna@adinet.com.uy; internet www .bibna.gub.uy; f. 1816; 900,000 vols, 20,000 periodicals; comprises reference service, copyright office, legal deposit, Uruguayan and special materials, restoration of printed works, National Information System project, cultural extension; Dir-Gen. RAÚL RICARDO VALLARINO; publ. *Revista de la Biblioteca Nacional*.

Attached Institute:

    Centro Nacional de Documentación Científica, Técnica y Económica: 18 de Julio 1790, Montevideo; tel. 2408 4172; fax 2409 6902; f. 1953; part of National Library; Dir ELENA CASTRO.

Biblioteca Pedagógica Central 'Mtro. Sebastián Morey Otero' (Pedagogic Library): Plaza de Cagancha 1175, Montevideo; tel. 2902 0915; fax 2908 4131; e-mail bepece@adinet.com.uy; f. 1889; 120,000 vols; Dir ANAIR MARTINOL; publs *Bibliografía Uruguaya sobre Educación, Información Bibliográfica* (2 a year), *Temas, Traducciones*.

Museums and Art Galleries
Montevideo
Museo de Descubrimiento: Zabala 1583 y Piedras, 11000 Montevideo; evokes the journeys of Cristóbal Colón, the meeting of the two worlds; maps, dioramas and photographs.

Museo Histórico Nacional (National Historical Museum): Casa Rivera, Calle Rincón 437, 11000 Montevideo; tel. 2915 1051; fax 2915 6863; e-mail mhistoricnac@mixmail .com; f. 1900; sectional collns of local Indian cultures (prehistoric, colonial epoch, development and political history of the country); portraits, relics, arms, documents, coins, medals, etc., relating to the Wars of Independence, British invasion, early revolutions, etc.; Dir Prof. ENRIQUE MENA SAGARRA; publ. *Revista Histórica*.

Museo Municipal de Bellas Artes 'Juan Manuel Blanes': Avda Millán 4015, 11700 Montevideo; tel. 2336 2248; fax 2336 7134; e-mail blanes@internet.com.uy; internet www.montevideo.gub.uy/museoblanes; f. 1928; paintings, drawings, wood-carvings, sculptures; Coordinator Arq. GABRIEL PELUFFO.

Museo Nacional de Artes Visuales (National Museum of Visual Arts): Tomás Giribaldi 2283 esq. Julio Herrera y Reissig-Parque Rodó, 11300 Montevideo; tel. 2711 6124; fax 2711 6127; e-mail secretaria@mnav .gub.uy; internet www.mnav.gub.uy; f. 1911; 6,200 paintings, engravings, drawings, sculptures, ceramics; library of 11,000 vols; Dir ENRIQUE AGUERRE.

Museo Nacional de Historia Natural y Antropología (National Museum of Natural History and Anthropology): Casilla 399, 11000 Montevideo; tel. 2916 0908; fax 2917 0213; e-mail mnhn@internet.com.uy; internet www.mec.gub.uy/natura; f. 1837 as National Museum; archaeology, botany, ethnography, history of natural sciences,

zoology, palaeontology; library of 250,000 vols; Dir ALVARO MONES; publs *Anales* (irregular), *Comunicaciones Antropológicas* (irregular), *Comunicaciones Botánicas* (irregular), *Comunicaciones Paleontológicas* (irregular), *Comunicaciones Zoológicas* (irregular), *Publicación Extra* (irregular).

Museo Pedagógico 'José Pedro Varela' (Pedagogic Museum): Plaza Cagancha 1175, Montevideo; tel. 2900 4744; fax 2908 4131; e-mail museopedagogico@gmail.com; internet www.cep.edu.uy; f. 1888; contains 5,000 exhibits, 2,000 photographs; library of 6,500 vols and periodicals; Dir SUSANA LUZARDO BRIANO; publ. *Boletín* (52 a year).

Museo y Archivo Histórico Municipal: Palacio del Cabildo, Calle Juan Carlos Gómez 1362, 11100 Montevideo; tel. and fax 2915 9685; e-mail museocabildo@correo.imm.gub .uy; f. 1915; permanent exhibition of the history of Montevideo from 1726; furniture, icons, paintings, jewellery and maps; library of 9,000 vols; Hon. Dir JORGE R. DELUCCHI; publ. *Anales*.

Museo y Jardin Botánico de Montevideo 'Prof. Atilio Lombardo': Avda 19 de Abril 1181, 11700 Montevideo; tel. 2336 4005; fax 2336 6488; e-mail botanico@adinet.com.uy; f. 1902; Dir Ing. Agr. PABLO B. ROSS.

Museo Zoológico 'Dámaso Antonio Larrañaga': Rambla República de Chile 4215, Montevideo; tel. 2622 0258; f. 1956; instruction on nat. and exotic fauna; library of 2,000 specialized vols; 2,000 species of fauna and molluscs, etc.; Dir JUAN PABLO CUELLO.

San José de Mayo
Museo de Bellas Artes Departamental de San José: Calle Dr Julián Becerro de Bengoa 493, 80000 San José de Mayo; tel. 3642; f. 1947; school of art; paintings, drawings, sculptures, ceramics; library of 3,000 vols; Dir CÉSAR BERNESCONI; publ. *Notimuseo* (12 a year).

Tacuarembó
Museo del Indio y del Gaucho: General Artigas 256, Tacuarembó; affilated to the Museo Histórico de Montevideo; large colln representing ancient native crafts, weapons and other implements of the aboriginal Indians and gauchos; Founder and Dir WASHINGTON ESCOBAR.

Universities
UNIVERSIDAD CATÓLICA DEL URUGUAY

Avda 8 de Octubre 2738, 11600 Montevideo
Telephone: 2487 2717
Fax: 2480 8124
E-mail: relinter@ucu.edu.uy
Internet: www.ucu.edu.uy

Founded 1985
Private control
Academic year: March to November

Chancellor: Mgr NICOLÁS COTUGNO
Vice-Chancellor: Fr JOSÉ LUIS MOSCA
Rector: Fr EDUARDO CASAROTTI
Vice-Pres. for Academic Affairs: Dr ARIEL CUADRO
Vice-Pres. for Administrative Affairs: Cr. AUGUSTO BAYLEY
Vice-Pres. for Devt: Fr MARCELO COPPETTI
Vice-Pres. for Univ. Environment: Fr MARCELO COPPETTI
Librarian: Dra. SUSANA MONREAL

Number of teachers: 607
Number of students: 5,000

Publications: *Cuadernos de Negocios Internacionales e Integración, Prisma, Rela-*

ciones Laborales en el Uruguay, Revista de Derecho, Revista FCE (Facultad de Ciencias Empresariales), Revista Lazos, Revista Págines del Área Educación

DEANS

Faculty of Business Administration: JOHN
Faculty of Dentistry: Dr WALTER LIEBER
Faculty of Engineering and Technology: Ing. OMAR PAGANINI
Faculty of Human Sciences: ADRIANA ARISTIMUÑO
Faculty of Law: Dr CARLOS BARBÉ
Faculty of Psychology: Mag. MARA GONZÁLEZ
Postgraduate Centre: Dr CARONLINA GREISING (Dir)

UNIVERSIDAD DE LA REPÚBLICA

Avda 18 de Julio 1968 (2° piso), 11200 Montevideo
Telephone: 2408 4901
Fax: 2408 0303
E-mail: secretar@oce.edu.uy
Internet: www.universidad.edu.uy
Founded 1849
State control
Language of instruction: Spanish
Academic year: March to December

Rector: Dr RODRIGO AROCENA
Vice-Rector: Dr ÁLVARO MAGLIA

Pro-Rector for Academic Affairs: Dr LUIS CALEGARI
Pro-Rector for Admin. Management: Dr RICARDO ROCA
Pro-Rector for Extension: Dr HUMBERTO TOMMASINO
Pro-Rector for Research: Dr GREGORY RANDALL
Sec.: MANUEL FLORES
Library: 1m. vols
Number of teachers: 6,130
Number of students: 81,774

DEANS

Faculty of Agronomy: Ing. Agr. FERNANDO GARCÍA PRÉCHAC
Faculty of Architecture: Arq. GUSTAVO SCHEPS
Faculty of Chemistry: Dr EDUARDO MANTA
Faculty of Dentistry: Dr HUGO CALABRIA
Faculty of Economics and Administration: Cr. WALTER ROSSI
Faculty of Engineering: Ing. ISMAEL PIEDRA CUEVA
Faculty of Humanities and Education: Prof. Dr JOSÉ SEOANE
Faculty of Law: DORA BAGDASSARIAN
Faculty of Medicine: Dr FELIPE SCHELOTTO
Faculty of Nursing: Prof. Mag. ALICIA CABRERA
Faculty of Psychology: Prof. Lic. LUIS LEOPOLD

Faculty of Science: Dr JULIO FERNÁNDEZ
Faculty of Social Sciences: Mag. DIEGO PIÑEIRO
Faculty of Veterinary Medicine: Dra PERLA A. CABRERA

Colleges

Escuela Universitaria de Bibliotecología y Ciencias Afines 'Ing. Federico E. Capurro': Emilio Frugoni 1427, 11200 Montevideo; tel. and fax 2400 5810; e-mail eubca@adinet.com.uy; f. 1945; attached to Univ. de la República; 4-year courses in library and information science, 3-year courses in archive studies; library: 13,150 books and monographs, 200 periodicals; 50 teachers; 500 students; Dir Lic. MARÍA GLADYS CERETTA; publ. *Informatio* (1 a year).

Universidad del Trabajo del Uruguay: Calle San Salvador 1674, Montevideo; e-mail web.utu@anep.edu.uy; internet www.utu.edu.uy; f. 1878; offers 220 different courses at 81 colleges in agriculture, handicrafts, industry and commerce; lower- and intermediate-level education and training; 4,500 full-time teachers; 50,000 students; Dir Prof. WILSON NETTO MARTURET; publs *Boletín UTU* (irregular), *Serie Estadística* (1 a year, online).

UZBEKISTAN

The Higher Education System

Institutions of higher education predate Uzbekistan (formerly Uzbek SSR)'s independence from the USSR in 1991, the oldest being the National University of Uzbekistan named after Mirzo Ulugbek, Tashkent State Medical Institute and Tashkent Institute of Irrigation and Melioration. In 1997 major reforms of the education system at all levels commenced under the National Programme for Personnel Training (NPPT). Reforms specific to the higher education sector include the remodelling of the degree system, particularly the abolition of the old-style Soviet-era degrees and introduction of two-tier Bachelors and Masters degrees; institutional restructuring; strengthening of links between universities and industries; and improvements to part-time and distance education programmes. In 2004 higher education was provided in 63 institutes, which had a combined enrolment of 263,600 students. There are also two foreign universities operating in Uzbekistan: the Tashkent branches of the Westminster International University and the Russian Academy of Economics.

The main laws governing education in Uzbekistan are the Law on Education (1990) and the Law on Education (1997). Higher education is mostly the responsibility of the Ministry of Higher and Specialized Secondary Education although other ministries administer the relevant specialist schools. The Monitoring Department of the Ministry of Higher and Specialized Secondary Education is responsible for accreditation and quality assurance at the tertiary level, standards for which are defined by the Ministry.

The main requirements for admission to higher education are the O'rta Ma'lumot To'g'risida Shahodatnoma (Diploma of Specialized Secondary Education) and results achieved in a national university entrance examination, the Kirish Imtakhoni, which is administered by the Devlet Test Markazi (State Testing Centre). The old-style Soviet degree system consisted primarily of a single five-year Specialist Diploma followed by doctoral-level studies. Since the implementation of the NPPT students are required to gain both the Bakalavr Diplomi and Magistr Diplomi (Bachelors and Masters degrees) before pursuing doctoral studies. The Bakalavr Diplomi typically lasts four years divided into two phases of two years each, although programmes in some (usually professional) fields of study last longer—for example, dentistry, medicine and veterinary medicine (which last five or six years). In the first phase students undertake a general programme of study before, in the second phase, focusing on a 'major' subject. Graduates who have been awarded the Bakalavr Diplomi are eligible for the Magistr Diplomi, which is a two-year course, often in the same subject as the undergraduate degree. At the doctoral level, the Soviet distinction between the titles of Candidate of Science and Doctor of Science has been retained, albeit under their Uzbek names of, respectively, Fanlari Nomzodi and Fanlari Doctori. The Fanlari Nomzodi is a three-year period of study consisting of independent research leading to the submission of a thesis. Students intending to pursue a career in research or academia then work towards the Fanlari Doctori, which is awarded after an unspecified period of study and research and is the highest academic award available in Uzbekistan.

Post-secondary technical and vocational education takes the form of two- to four-year courses in 260 areas of specialization, resulting in the award of the O'rta Maxsus Ta'lim To'g'risidagi Diplom (Diploma of Post Secondary Vocational Education).

Regulatory Bodies

GOVERNMENT

Ministry of Culture and Sport Affairs: Mustakillik Sq. 5, Tashkent 100159; tel. (71) 239-83-31; fax (71) 239-46-11; e-mail minister@mcs.uz; internet www.mcs.uz; Minister TURSUNALI KUZIYEV.

Ministry of Higher and Specialized Secondary Education: Apt 96, 2-Chimbay str., Tashkent 100095; tel. and fax (71) 246-01-95; e-mail mhsse@edu.uz; internet www.edu.uz; Minister B. Y. XODIEV.

Ministry of Public Education: 5 Mustakillik Sq., Tashkent 100095; tel. (71) 239-17-35; fax (71) 239-42-14; e-mail devonxona@mno.uz; internet www.uzedu.uz; Min. TEMIR SHIRINOV.

Learned Societies

GENERAL

UNESCO Office in Tashkent: 9 Ergashev St, Tashkent 100084; tel. (71) 120-71-16; fax (71) 120-71-59; e-mail tashkent@unesco.org; internet www.tashkent.unesco.org; f. 1996; contributes to bldg of peace, alleviation of poverty, sustainable devt and intercultural dialogue through education, sciences, culture, communication and information; Head JORGE IVAN ESPINAL.

Uzbekistan Academy of Sciences: Ya Gulomov Str. 70, Tashkent 100047; tel. (71) 233-68-47; fax (71) 233-74-82; e-mail academy@uznet.net; internet www.academy.uz; f. 1943; divs of natural sciences, physical-mathematical and technical sciences, social and humanitarian sciences; 2 regional brs and 33 attached research institutes: see under Research Institutes; library: see under Libraries and Archives; 156 mems (71 ordinary, 85 corresp.); Pres. Acad. SHAVKAT SALIKHOV; Sec.-Gen. Prof. Dr BAKHTIER IBRAGIMOV; publs *Chemistry of Natural Compounds*, *Doklady* (Reports), *Geliotechnica*, *Obshchestvennye Nauki v Uzbekistane* (Social Sciences in Uzbekistan), *Science and Life*, *Uzbek Geological Journal*, *Uzbekskii Fizicheskii Zhurnal* (Uzbek Journal of Physics), *Uzbekskii Khimicheskii Zhurnal* (Uzbek Chemical Journal), *Uzbekskii Matematicheskii Zhurnal* (Uzbek Journal of Mathematics), *Uzbekskii Zhurnal—Problemy Informatiki i Energetiki* (Uzbek Journal—Problems in Informatics and Energetics), *Uzbekskii Zhurnal—Problemy Mekhaniki* (Uzbek Journal—Problems in Mechanics), *Uzbeksky Biologichesky Zhurnal* (Uzbek Biological Journal), *Uzbeksky Yazik i Literatura* (Uzbek Language and Literature).

LANGUAGE AND LITERATURE

Alliance Française: Ul. Baraka 26, Samarqand 140104; tel. and fax (66) 33-66-27; offers courses and examinations in French language and culture; promotes cultural exchange with France.

British Council: 13th Fl., Block A, Int. Business Centre, 107A Amir Temur St, Tashkent 100084; tel. (71) 140-06-60; fax (71) 140-06-67; e-mail bc-tashkent@britishcouncil.uz; internet www.britishcouncil.org/uzbekistan; f. 1996; offers courses and examinations in English language and British culture; promotes cultural exchange with the UK; library of 5,000 vols; Dir STEVE MCNULTY.

Goethe-Institut: Amir Timur ko'chasi 42, Tashkent 100000; tel. (71) 140-14-70; fax (71) 140-14-71; e-mail info@taschkent.goethe.org; internet www.goethe.de/taschkent; offers courses and examinations in German language and culture; promotes cultural exchange with Germany; Dir Dr JOHANNES DAHL.

Research Institutes

GENERAL

Buxoro Scientific Centre: Naqshbandi 153, Buxoro 200109; tel. (65) 225-02-41; fax (65) 225-42-30; e-mail alexz@uzpak.uz; attached to Uzbekistan Acad. of Sciences; Dir I. SAFAROV.

Karakalpak Branch of the Uzbek Academy of Sciences: Berdakh gazari 41, Nukus, Qoraqalpog'iston 230100; tel. (61) 222-17-44; fax (61) 222-17-56; e-mail nukus@aknuk.uzsci.net; internet www.aknuk.uzsci.net; Pres. AIMBETOV NAGMET KALLIEVICH.

Khorezm Mamun Academy: Markaz-1, Khiva 220900; tel. (62) 375-70-01; fax (62) 375-51-43; e-mail mamun1000@mail.ru; internet www.mamun.uz; f. 1997; attached to Uzbekistan Acad. of Sciences; promotes historical sciences, protection of architectural monuments, ecological and agricultural problems of Khorezm; library of 16,400 vols; Dir Dr RUZUMBOY ESHCHANOV.

Research Institute of Regional Problems: Temur Malik 3, Samarqand 140100; tel. (662) 33-19-94; fax (662) 31-00-39; e-mail samacdem@online.ru; attached to Uzbekistan Acad. of Sciences; Dir B. KHUJAYOROV.

Samarqand Branch of the Uzbek Academy of Sciences: Temur Malik 3, Samarqand 140100; tel. (662) 33-39-50; fax (662) 31-00-39; e-mail samacdem@online.ru; Chair. T. SHIRINOV.

AGRICULTURE, FISHERIES AND VETERINARY SCIENCE

Research Institute of Karakul Sheep Breeding and Ecology of Deserts: Mirzo Ulugbek ko'chasi 47, Samarqand 140100; tel. (662) 33-32-79; fax (662) 33-34-81; e-mail ecokar@rol.uz; f. 1930; library of 56,000 vols; Dir Dr SURATBEK YUNUSOVICH YUSUPOV; publ. *Collection of Contributions Concerning Karakul Sheep Breeding and Arid Fodder Production* (every 2 years).

State Research Institute of Soil Science and Agrochemistry: Kamarniso ko'chasi 3, Tashkent 100179; tel. (71) 246-09-50; fax (71) 246-76-00; e-mail gosniipa@rambler.ru; Dir D. S. SATTAROV.

ECONOMICS, LAW AND POLITICS

Abu Rayhan Biruni Institute of Oriental Studies: 81 Mirzo Ulugbek str., Tashkent 100170; tel. (71) 262-54-61; fax (71) 262-52-77; e-mail beruni@globalnet.uz; f. 1943; attached to Uzbekistan Acad. of Sciences; research activity in the sphere of medieval oriental MSS and in the field of medieval and modern history of Central Asia; library of 39,300 vols, 25,261 MSS; Dir B. A. ABDUKHALIMOV; publ. *Sharqshunoslik* (1 a year).

Institute of Economics: Borovskogo ko'chasi 5, Tashkent 100060; tel. and fax (71) 133-14-78; e-mail econ@uzsci.net; f. 1943; attached to Uzbekistan Acad. of Sciences; Dir O. KHIKMATOV.

Muminov, I., Institute of Philosophy and Law: Muminov ko'chasi 9, Tashkent 100170; tel. (71) 262-38-87; e-mail ifpanuz@yahoo.com; attached to Uzbekistan Acad. of Sciences; Dir Prof. R. D. RUZIEV.

EDUCATION

Scientific-Training Centre 'Fanum': Muminov ko'chasi 9, Tashkent 100170; tel. (71) 289-13-78; fax (71) 269-13-78; e-mail fanum@uznet.net; attached to Uzbekistan Acad. of. Sciences; conducts lessons for postgraduate students and research workers with scientific degrees on programmes est. by VAK (Higher Appraisal Commission) under the Cabinet of the Ministries of the Republic of Uzbekistan; organizes translation activities; promotes public education; Dir Prof. N. Y. TURAEV; publ. *Uzbek Physics Journal*.

HISTORY, GEOGRAPHY AND ARCHAEOLOGY

Institute of Archaeology: Abdullayev ko'chasi 3, Samarqand 140151; tel. (662) 32-15-13; fax (662) 31-12-90; e-mail archaeo@online.ru; f. 1970; attached to Uzbekistan Acad. of Sciences; Dir T. SHIRINOV.

Institute of History: Muminov ko'chasi 9, Tashkent 100170; tel. (71) 162-38-73; fax (71) 162-93-51; e-mail tarih@uzsci.net; internet www.history.uzsci.net; f. 1943; attached to Uzbekistan Acad. of Sciences; Dir DILOROM

AGZAMOVNA ALIMOVA; publ. *Uzbekiston Tarihi* (4 a year).

Institute of History, Archaeology and Ethnography: Amir Temur 179A, Nukus, Qoraqalpog'iston 230100; tel. (61) 224-05-98; fax (61) 217-72-28; e-mail vyagodin@online .ru; attached to Uzbekistan Acad. of Sciences; Dir V. YAGODIN.

LANGUAGE AND LITERATURE

Institute of Language and Literature: Amir Temur 199A, Nukus, Qoraqalpog'iston 230100; tel. (61) 217-21-61; attached to Uzbekistan Acad. of Sciences; Dir S. BAHADIROVA.

Institute of Language and Literature named after Alisher Navoi: Muminov ko'chasi 9, Tashkent 100170; tel. (71) 162-42-64; attached to Uzbekistan Acad. of Sciences; Dir T. M. MIRZAEV.

MEDICINE

Institute for Dermatology and Venereology: Farabi 3, Tashkent 100109; tel. (71) 246-08-07; f. 1932; attached to Min. of Health; library of 14,000 vols; Dir Prof. V. A. AKOVBAYAN; publ. *Pathogenesis and Therapy for Skin and Venereal Diseases* (1 a year).

Institute of Haematology and Blood Transfusion: Druzhba Narodov 42, Tashkent 100059; tel. (71) 279-79-35; fax (71) 279-95-26.

Institute of Immunology: Ya. Gulamov 74, Tashkent 100060; tel. (71) 133-08-05; fax (71) 133-08-55; e-mail immuno@uzsci.net; attached to Uzbekistan Acad. of Sciences; Dir R. RUZIBAKIYEV.

Institute of Vaccines and Sera: Abdurashidov 37, Tashkent 100084; tel. (71) 243-79-53; fax (71) 234-77-22; Dir B. A. SHEVCHENKO.

L. M. Isaev Research Institute of Medical Parasitology: Isaeva 38, Samarqand 140105; tel. (662) 37-42-42; f. 1923; library of 45,000 vols; Dir SH. A. RAZAKOV; publ. *Current Problems in Medical Parasitology* (1 a year).

Republic Specialized Centre of Cardiology: Osio 4, Tashkent 100052; tel. (71) 236-08-16; e-mail cardio@sarkor.com; f. 1976; library of 30,000 vols; Dir Prof. RAVSHANBEK DAVLETOVICH KURBANOV.

Research Institute of Clinical and Experimental Medicine: M. Gorkogo ko'chasi 185, Nukus, Qoraqalpog'iston 230100; tel. (612) 24-50-41.

Research Institute of Epidemiology, Microbiology and Infectious Diseases: Reshetova 2, Tashkent 100133; tel. (71) 243-36-05; e-mail akhodiev@gmail.com; f. 1961; Dir SH. SH. SHAVAKHABOV.

Uzbek Institute of Rehabilitation and Physiotherapy (Semashko Institute): Khurshida 4, Tashkent 100084; tel. (71) 234-55-00; fax (71) 235-30-63; f. 1919; physiotherapy in cardiology, arthropology, neurology and pulmonology, oriental medicine, phytotherapy; library of 16,210 vols; Dir Prof. KARIM U. ULDASHEV; publ. *Collection of Scientific Works* (1 a year).

Uzbek Research Institute of Traumatology and Orthopaedics: Pakhlavon Makhmud str. 78, Tashkent 100047; tel. (371) 233-10-30; f. 1932; library of 30,000 vols; Dir Prof. M. AZIMOV.

NATURAL SCIENCES
General

Institute for Natural Sciences: Berdakh gazari 41, Nukus, Qoraqalpog'istan 230100; tel. (612) 22-17-45; fax (612) 22-17-45; f.

1996; attached to Uzbekistan Acad. of Sciences; Dir BAKHYT NARYMBETOV.

Biological Sciences

Acad. A. Sadikov Institute of Bioorganic Chemistry: Abdullayev ko'chasi 83, Tashkent 100143; tel. (71) 262-35-40; fax (71) 262-70-63; e-mail ibchem@uzsci.net; f. 1977; attached to Uzbekistan Acad. of Sciences; bioorganic chemistry, chemistry of natural physiologic active compounds; Dir Prof. ABBOSKHON S. TURAEV.

Institute of Biochemistry: Abdullayev ko'chasi 56, Tashkent 100143; tel. (71) 162-25-66; fax (71) 162-24-41; e-mail saatov@uzsci.net; attached to Uzbekistan Acad. of Sciences; Dir T. S. SAATOV.

Institute of Bioecology: Berdakh gazari 1, Nukus, Qoraqalpog'istan 230100; tel. (612) 17-17-13; fax (612) 17-72-28; e-mail ecol@online.ru; attached to Uzbekistan Acad. of Sciences; Dir A. BAKHIYEV.

Institute of Botany: Khodzhayev ko'chasi 32, Tashkent 100143; tel. (71) 162-70-65; fax (71) 162-79-38; e-mail botany@uzsci.net; attached to Uzbekistan Acad. of Sciences; Dir Prof. Dr OZODBEK A. ASHURMETOV.

Institute of Genetics and Plant Experimental Biology: Kibrai Dist., Yukori-Yuz, Tashkent 702151; tel. (71) 112-32-71; fax (71) 264-22-30; e-mail inst@gen.org.uz; internet genetics.uzsci.net; attached to Uzbekistan Acad. of Sciences; Dir A. ABDUKARIMOV.

Institute of Microbiology: Abdulla Kadiri gazari 7B, Tashkent 100128; tel. (71) 144-25-19; fax (71) 144-25-82; e-mail imbasru@uzsci.net; f. 1965; attached to Uzbekistan Acad. of Sciences; Dir K. DAVRANOV; publ. *Uzbeksky Biologichesky Zhurnal*.

Institute of Physiology and Biophysics: A. Niyazov str. 1, Tashkent 100095; tel. (71) 246-95-17; fax (71) 246-92-54; e-mail pusman@uzsci.net; internet biophys.fan.uz; f. 1975; attached to Uzbekistan Acad. of Sciences; Dir Prof. PULAT B. USMANOV.

Institute of the Chemistry of Plant Substances: Mirzo Ulugbek St 77, Tashkent 100170; tel. (71) 262-70-00; fax (71) 262-74-76; e-mail shakhidoyatov@yahoo.com; attached to Uzbekistan Acad. of Sciences; organic synthesis, nature chemistry, physical chemistry; Dir Prof. Dr KHUSNUTDIN SHAKHIDOYATOV; publ. *Chemistry of Natural Compounds*.

Institute of Zoology: 1 A. Niyazov St, Tashkent 100095; tel. (71) 246-07-18; fax (71) 120-67-91; e-mail zool-uz@uzsci.net; f. 1950; attached to Uzbekistan Acad. of Sciences; Dir DJALOLIDDIN AZIMOV.

Mathematical Sciences

Institute of Mathematics and Information Technologies: Akademgorodok, Dormon Yoli 29, Tashkent 100125; tel. (71) 262-56-94; fax (71) 262-73-57; e-mail mathinst@uznet.net; f. 1943, fmrly Romanovsky, V. I., Institute of Mathematics, present name and status 2007; attached to Uzbekistan Acad. of Sciences; research in pure and applied mathematics, mathematical modelling, informatics; library of 112,000 vols; Dir Prof. Acad. SHAVKAT AYUPOV; publ. *Uzbek Mathematical Journal* (4 a year).

Physical Sciences

G. Mavlynov Institute of Seismology: 3 Zulfiyakhonim str., Tashkent 700128; tel. (712) 135-75-34; fax (71) 137-75-31; e-mail tashkent@seismo.org.uz; internet www.seismos.uz; f. 1966, present name 1990; attached to Uzbekistan Acad. of Sciences; research on problems of seismic zoning, earthquakes risk management, earthquakes prediction, physics of earthquake sources;

library of 43,000 vols; Dir Prof. KAKHARBAY NASIRBEKOVICH ABDULLABEKOV; publ. *Uzbek Geological Journal* (6 a year).

Heat Physics Department of the Uzbek Academy of Sciences: 28 Katartal St, Tashkent 100135; tel. (71) 276-44-57; fax (71) 276-26-68; e-mail hpd@uzsci.net; f. 1977; Dir PULAT KHABIBULLAYEV.

Institute of General and Inorganic Chemistry: Amir Temur ko'chasi 77A, Tashkent 100170; tel. (71) 162-56-60; fax (71) 162-79-90; e-mail ionxanruz@mail.ru; internet www.igic.uzsci.net; f. 1933; attached to Uzbekistan Acad. of Sciences; researches colloidal, inorganic and petroleum chemistry, involved in localization of new fertilizers, defoliants for agriculture, materials of construction, flocculating agents, oil additives, depressors, corrosion inhibitors for domestic industry; library of 50,000 vols; Dir Prof. ZAKIRJAN SALIMOV; Deputy Dir Prof. BAHTYER ZAKIROV; publs *Reports of Uzbekistan Academy of Sciences—Joint Academic Institutes Journal* (6 a year), *Uzbekistan Journal of Chemistry* (6 a year).

Institute of Mineral Resources: T. Shevchenko St 11A, Tashkent 100060; tel. (71) 256-13-49; fax (71) 140-08-12; e-mail gpniimr@evo.uz; internet www.gpniimr.uz; f. 1957; Dir M. U. ISOKOV; publ. *Geology and Mineral Resources* (6 a year).

Institute of Nuclear Physics: Ulugbek, Tashkent 100214; tel. (71) 150-30-70; fax (71) 150-30-80; e-mail info@inp.uz; internet www.inp.uz; f. 1956; attached to Uzbekistan Acad. of Sciences; research areas incl. activation analysis, nuclear physics, radiochemistry and radioisotope production, research works automation, solid-state radiation physics, radiation material science and instrumentation devt; library of 221,215 vols; Dir Prof. UMAR SAGITOVICH SALIKHBAEV.

Institute of Polymer Chemistry and Physics: 7B A. Kadyri str., Tashkent 700128; tel. (71) 142-85-94; fax (71) 144-26-61; e-mail carbon@uzsci.net; f. 1979; attached to Uzbekistan Acad. of Sciences; research fields incl. chemistry, native polymers, physics and technology of synthetics; Dir SAYERA RASHIDOVA.

Kh. M. Abdullaev Institute of Geology and Geophysics: 49 Khodjibaeva str., Tashkent 100041; tel. (71) 262-65-16; fax (71) 262-63-81; e-mail ingeo@ingeo.uz; internet www.ingeo.uz; f. 1939; attached to Uzbekistan Acad. of Sciences; study of the structure, composition, and evolution of the lithosphere; devt of the fundamentals of expansion of mineral raw materials in Uzbekistan and effective exploitation of mineral deposits; research areas incl. geology, petrology, mineralogy, geochemistry, ecology, geophysics, mathematical geology, oil geology and history of geology; Dir Dr SABIT KHAMIDOVICH MAKSUDOV; publ. *Geology and Mineral Resources* (6 a year).

Physical–Technical Institute: G. Mavlyanova 2B, Tashkent 700084; tel. (71) 233-12-71; fax (71) 235-42-91; e-mail lutp@physic.uzsci.net; internet fti.fan.uz; f. 1943; attached to Uzbekistan Acad. of Sciences; research and devt of high technology products; Dir S. LUTPULLAYEV; publ. *Applied Solar Engineering*.

Ulugh Beg Astronomical Institute: 33 Astronomiya, Tashkent 100052; tel. (71) 235-81-02; fax (71) 234-48-67; e-mail admin@astrin.uz; internet www.astrin.uz; f. 1873 as Tashkent Astronomical Observatory, present name and status 1966; attached to Uzbekistan Acad. of Sciences; research divs incl. extraterrestrial astronomy, galactic astronomy and cosmology, solar-terrestrial physics, stellar astrophysics, theoretical

astrophysics; Dir Prof. SHUHRAT A. EHGAMBERDIEV.

RELIGION, SOCIOLOGY AND ANTHROPOLOGY

Institute for Socio-Economic Problems of the Aral Sea Region: 179A Amir Temur St, Nukus, Qoraqalpog'istan 742000; tel. (61) 224-22-09; fax (61) 217-72-28; e-mail nagmet@aknuk.uzsci.net; internet www.aknuk.uzsci.net; attached to Uzbekistan Acad. of Sciences; Dir NAGMET AIMBETOV.

TECHNOLOGY

Institute of Cybernetics: 34 F. Khodjaev St, Tashkent 700125; tel. (71) 262-72-47; fax (71) 262-73-21; e-mail uzkiber@cyber.ccc.uz; f. 1966; attached to Uzbekistan Acad. of Sciences; library of 100,000 vols; Dir FAZILOV SHAVKAT; publs *Algoritmy* (3 a year), *Problemy Informatiki i Energetiki* (6 a year), *Voprosy Kibernetiki* (3 a year), *Voprosy Modelirovaniya i Informatizatsii Ekonomiki* (3 a year), *Voprosy Vychislitelnoi i Prikladnoi Matematiki* (3 a year).

Institute of Electronics named after U. A. Arifov: F. Khodjaev str. 33, Tashkent 100125; tel. (71) 262-79-40; fax (71) 262-87-67; e-mail ae@aie.uz; internet www.aie.uz; f. 1967; attached to Uzbekistan Acad. of Sciences; Dir KHATAM R. ASHUROV.

Institute of Hydrogeology and Engineering Geology: Olimlar St 64, Tashkent 100041; tel. and fax (71) 262-75-90; e-mail hydrouz@rambler.ru; f. 1960; attached to Int. Consortium of Landslides, Int. Union of Geological Sciences; research into hydrogeology, petroleum, geoecology, landslides and remote-sensing; library of 18,000 vols; Dir Dr ASLON A. MAVLONOV; publs *Geology and Mineral Resources* (6 a year), *Hydrogeology and Engineering Geology Problems in Uzbekistan* (1 a year).

Institute of Materials Science: Bodomzor yoli 2B, Tashkent 100084; tel. (71) 235-75-06; fax (71) 233-95-64; e-mail jabbar@uzsci.net; attached to Uzbekistan Acad. of Sciences; Dir Dr ABDUJABBAR ABDURAKHMANOV.

Institute of Mechanics and Seismic Stability of Structures: Akademia Shaharchasi, Dormon yoli 31, Tashkent 100125; tel. (71) 162-72-97; fax (71) 162-71-52; e-mail instmech@uzsci.net; internet www.instmech.fan.uz; f. 1959; attached to Uzbekistan Acad. of Sciences; Dir Prof. ANVAR ABDULLAEVICH RIZAEV; publ. *Problems in Mechanics* (6 a year).

Institute of Power Engineering and Automation: Akademgorodok, Tashkent 100143; tel. (71) 262-05-22; fax (71) 262-09-19; e-mail ipea@uzsci.net; f. 1941; attached to Uzbekistan Acad. of Sciences; Dir TIMUR SALIKHOV.

Institute of Water Problems: 25A Khodjayev St, Tashkent 100187; tel. and fax (71) 269-12-70; e-mail root@pwater.tashkent.su; f. 1992; attached to Uzbekistan Acad. of Sciences; Dir ERNAZAR J. MAKHMUDOV.

Scientific and Production Association 'Akadempribor': Akademia Shaharchasi, Tashkent 100125; tel. (71) 262-72-73; fax (71) 269-01-24; e-mail bahramov@mail.ru; f. 1962; attached to Uzbekistan Acad. of Sciences; research, design and production of the instruments and equipment for scientific orgs, agriculture, medicine and industry; Dir-Gen. Prof. SAGDILLA A. BAKHRAMOV.

Scientific Production Centre 'Modern Information Technologies': 34 F. Hodjaev St, Tashkent 700143; tel. (71) 262-72-47; fax (71) 162-73-12; e-mail shavkat@cyber.ccc.uz; attached to Uzbekistan Acad. of Sciences; Dir OZOD NABIEV.

Uzbek Research Institute of Sericulture: Jar-Arik, Zangyata, Tashkent 111812; f. 1927; attached to Min. of Agriculture and Water; Dir SH. YULDASHEV; publ. *Silk*.

UzLITIneftgaz/Uzbekistan Research and Design Institute of the Gas and Oil Industry: T. Shevchenko ko'chasi 2, Tashkent 100170; tel. (71) 256-74-17; fax (71) 256-66-48; Dir U. S. NAZAROV; publ. *Uzbek Journal of Oil and Gas* (4 a year).

Libraries and Archives
Samarqand

Samarqand State University Central Library: Pl. Navoi 15, Samarqand 140100; tel. (662) 35-19-38; fax (662) 35-64-90; e-mail soleev@samuni.silk.org; 1,632,000 vols; spec. collns incl. ancient oriental literature; Dir R. KHOLMURODOV.

Tashkent

Central State Archive: Chilonzar ko'chasi 2, Tashkent 700043; tel. (71) 277-04-80; e-mail csa@archive.uz; internet central.archive.uz; Dir SHUHRATBAY KHODJIBAEV.

Foundation Library of the Uzbekistan Academy of Sciences: Muminov str. 13, Tashkent 100170; tel. (71) 262-74-56; fax (71) 262-74-58; e-mail acadlib@acadlib.uzsci.net; internet www.acadlib.uzsci.net; f. 1934; Uzbekistan Acad. of Sciences library system incl. 24 other research institute libraries; 5,000,000 vols; Dir ZUHRA SH. BERDIEVA.

Library of the National University of Uzbekistan named after Mirzo Ulugbek: Vozgorodok, Universitet ko'chasi 95, Tashkent 100095; tel. (371) 2466771; fax (371) 2460222; e-mail info@nuu.uz; 18 hrs; 350,000 vols, 45,000 journals, 2,600 govt documents, 4,000 maps; Dir IRINA LVOVNA KISLITSINA.

National Library of Uzbekistan named after Alisher Navoi: Milliy kutubxonasi, Xorazm ko'chasi 51, Tashkent 100047; tel. (71) 2392-83-92; fax (71) 233-09-08; e-mail navoi@natlib.uz; internet natlib.webmaster.uz; f. 1870, incorporates Republican Library for Science and Technology since 2002; 10,720,000 vols; Dir KHODJAYEV ASAD AZADBEKOVICH.

Museums and Art Galleries
Nukus

Botanical Garden: Chimbay St, Nukus, Qoraqalpog'istan 142004; tel. (61) 222-30-47; fax (61) 217-72-28; attached to Uzbekistan Acad. of Sciences; Dir TULEGEN OTENOV.

Karakalpak Historical Museum: Rakhmatov ko'chasi 3, Nukus, Qoraqalpog'istan 230100; illustrates the part played by the Uzbek people in the October Socialist Revolution, the Civil War and the Second World War.

Karakalpak State Museum of Arts named after I. V. Savitsky: K. Rzaev St, Nukus, Qoraqalpog'istan 230100; tel. and fax (61) 222-25-56; e-mail museum_savitsky@mail.ru; internet museum.kr.uz; f. 1966; archaeology of ancient Khorezym, Karakalpak folk art, Russian and Central Asian avant-garde art 1910–1935; library of 10,500 vols; Dir MARINIKA BABANAZAROVA; Chief Curator VALENTINA SYCHEVA.

Samarqand

Samarqand State United Historical–Architectural and Art Museum Preserve: Registan ko'chasi 1, Samarqand 140100; tel. (66) 35-38-96; f. 1982; comprises 9 museums in Samarqand city and Viloyat, containing more than 182,000 exhibits in total.

Tashkent

Alisher Navoi State Museum of Literature: Navoi str. 69, Tashkent 100011; tel. (71) 241-02-75; fax (71) 244-00-61; e-mail a_navoi@uzsci.net; internet www.navoimuseum.uz; f. 1936; attached to Uzbekistan Acad. of Sciences; collects, investigates, maintains and displays the history of Uzbek literature, incl. MSS, documents, pictures, archives and photographic materials; Dir Prof. SAIDBEK KHASANOV; publ. *Adabiyot kozgusi* (12 a year).

Museum of Applied Art: 15 Rakatboshi St, Tashkent 100031; tel. (71) 256-40-42; fax (71) 252-13-67; e-mail artmuzey@mail.ru; internet www.artmuseum.uz; f. 1927, fmrly Permanent Exhibition of Applied Art of Uzbekistan, present name and status 1997; displays 7000 rare works of applied art.

Museum of Uzbek History: Sharaf Rashidov ko'chasi 3, Tashkent 100000; tel. (71) 139-10-83; f. 1992 by merger of the Museum of the History of the People of Uzbekistan and the Lenin Central Museums; more than 300,000 exhibits; Dir G. R. RASHIDOV.

Oibek, M. T., Historical Museum of Uzbekistan: Sh. Rashidov ko'chasi 3, Tashkent 100047; tel. (71) 139-10-83; fax (71) 139-44-25; attached to Uzbekistan Acad. of Sciences; Dir K. INOYATOV.

State Museum of Arts: 16, Amir Temur pr, Tashkent 100060; tel. (71) 236-74-36; fax (71) 236-77-40; e-mail info@fineartmuzeum.uz; internet fineartmuzeum.uz; f. 1918; attached to Min. of Cultural and Sports Affairs; colln incl. works of arts of Uzbekistan, East, Russian and West-Europe; library of 22,700 vols; Dir D. S. RUSIBAYEV.

State Museum of Timurid History: Amir Temur 1, Tashkent 700000; tel. and fax (71) 132-02-13; e-mail timurid@uzsci.net; attached to Uzbekistan Acad. of Sciences; Dir N. KHABIBULLAYEV.

Universities

ACADEMY OF STATE AND SOCIAL CONSTRUCTION

45 Uzbekistan St, Tashkent 100029
Telephone: (71) 232-60-60
Fax: (71) 232-60-66
E-mail: info@assc.uz
Founded 1995
State control
Languages of instruction: Uzbek, Russian
Rector: NAZAROV KIYOM NORMIRZAEVICH

Courses incl. bases and principles of market economy, interstate relations and foreign economic relations, retraining and professional devt, state and social construction.

ANDIJAN STATE UNIVERSITY

Bldg 129, 170020 Andijon
Telephone: (74) 225-05-09
Fax: (74) 222-18-63
E-mail: adu@andijon.uz
Founded 1939
State control
Languages of instruction: Russian, Uzbek
Academic year: September to June

Rector: Prof. Dr T. A. MADUMAROV
Library of 320,314 vols
Number of teachers: 434
Number of students: 5,021

DEANS

Faculty of Biology: ALIJON DADAMIRZAYEV
Faculty of Chemistry: MIRAHMAD KHOJIMATOV
Faculty of History: ZOKIR KUTIBOYEV
Faculty of Mathematics: ABDUVAHOB MILADJONOV
Faculty of Philology: DILMUROD QURONOV
Faculty of Physical Education: DEHQONBOY MAMATISAQOV
Faculty of Physical Training: NOIB YULDASHEV
Faculty of Physics: ABDULQAHOR ORTIQOV
Faculty of Teacher Training: MUHTOR VOHIDOV

BRANCH OF THE RUSSIAN ECONOMIC UNIVERSITY AFTER G. V. PLEKHANOV IN TASHKENT

49 Uzbekistan St, Seventh bldg, Third Fl., Tashkent 100003
Telephone: (71) 232-60-23
Fax: (71) 232-60-22
E-mail: rea@rea.uz
Internet: rea.uz
State control; attached to Russian Economic Univ. after G. V. Plekhanov

Economy of firm and br. markets; finance and credit; financial economy; labour economy

Dir: K. KH. ABDURAKHMANOV.

BUXORO DAVLAT UNIVERSITETI (Bukhara State University)

Muhammad Ikbol str. 11, Bukhara 200100
Telephone: (65) 223-23-14
Fax: (65) 223-12-54
E-mail: bsu_info@edu.uz
Internet: www.buxdu.uz
Founded 1930
State control
Languages of instruction: Russian, Uzbek
Academic year: September to June
Rector: Prof. Dr ZOKIRKHODJA TADJIKHODJAEV
Vice-Rector for Educational Affairs: Dr DURDIMUROD DURDIEV
Vice-Rector for Scientific Affairs: Prof. Dr SIDDIK KAHHAROV
Library of 700,000
Number of teachers: 501
Number of students: 7,700
Publications: *Marifat Nuri* (12 a year), *Pedagogical Competence* (4 a year), *Psychology* (4 a year), *University Review* (12 a year)

DEANS

Faculty of Chemistry and Biology: Dr HAFIZA ORTIKOVA
Faculty of History: Dr SOHIB RAUPOV
Faculty of Pedagogics: Prof. Dr SHARIF BAROTOV
Faculty of Philology: Dr RAMAZON BOBOKALONOV
Faculty of Physics and Mathematics: Prof. Dr SHAVKAT MIRZAEV
Military Faculty: Dr MIRZOJAMOL GAFUROV
Social-Economical Faculty: Dr MAHMUD ORIPOV
Sports Faculty: Dr BAHODIR MAMUROV

FARG'ONA DALVAT UNIVERSITETI (Ferghana State University)

19 Murabbiylar str., Ferghana 150100
Telephone: (73) 224-28-71
Fax: (73) 224-35-32
E-mail: frsu_info@edu.uz

Founded 1991
State control
Languages of instruction: Uzbek, Russian, English
Rector: MADAMINBEK KHOTAMOVICH AKHMEDOV
Library of 757,461 vols
Number of teachers: 459
Number of students: 5,639

GULISTAN DAVLAT UNIVERSITETI (Gulistan State University)

Microraion 4, Gulistan 120100
Telephone: (672) 25-02-75
Fax: (672) 25-40-42
E-mail: gdu@intal.uz
Internet: www.guldu.uz
Founded 1992
State control
Languages of instruction: Russian, Uzbek

Faculties of economics and engineering, education, foreign languages, history and Uzbek philology, Kazakh philology, natural sciences, physics and mathematics

Rector: EMINOV ASHRAP MAMUROVICH
Pro-rector for Science and Informational Technologies: KUSHIEV KHABIB HOJIBOBOEVICH
Pro-Rector for Scientific Works: KARSHIBAEV KHAZRATKUL KILICHOVICH
Pro-Rector for Spiritual and Moral Education: MAKHMUDOV RAVSHANBEK JALILOVICH
Library of 195,000 vols
Number of teachers: 400
Number of students: 4,217

KARAKALPAK STATE UNIVERSITY

Ch. Abidov 1, Nukus, Qoraqalpog'istan 742000
Telephone: (61) 223-60-47
Fax: (61) 223-60-78
E-mail: karsu(@)karsu.uz
Internet: www.karsu.uz
Founded 1979
State control

Faculties of agriculture, chemistry, construction, engineering, economics, law and history, natural sciences, philology, physics and mathematics

Rector: Prof. Dr MATCHANOV AZAT TAUBALDIEVICH
Number of students: 7,000

KARSHI STATE UNIVERSITY

Kuchabog 17, Karshi 140103
Telephone: (752) 25-34-13
Fax: (752) 25-57-01
E-mail: kardu@mail.ru
Internet: www.kasu.uz
Founded 1956
State control
Languages of instruction: Uzbek, Russian
Academic year: September to June
Rector: Prof. MURADULLA NORMURADOV
Library of 10,000 vols.

NAMANGAN STATE UNIVERSITY

Uychi 316, Namangan 160119
Telephone: (692) 26-55-01
Fax: (692) 26-61-07
E-mail: pulathon2001@yahoo.com
Internet: www.namsu.uz
Founded 1942
Public control
Languages of instruction: Uzbek, Russian, English
Academic year: September to June
Rector: Dr YULDOSHALI RAHIMOV

Library of 1,000,000 vols
Number of teachers: 420
Number of students: 7,500

Publication: *Periodical of Namangan State University*

DEANS

Faculty of Art and Drawing: BOTIRSHER JABBOROV
Faculty of Biology and Chemistry: YOLDOSHALI TOSHMATOV
Faculty of Education: MUNOJATHON MIRABDULLAYEVA
Faculty of Geography and Economics: MUHAMMADSOLI MUMINOV
Faculty of Graduate Studies: SHAVKAT ABDULLAYEV
Faculty of History: RUZIMAT JURAYEV
Faculty of Law: YULDOSHALI RHIMOV
Faculty of Mathematics: SOBIRJON ALIHANOV
Faculty of Physical Education and Sport: SOBITHON AZIZOV
Faculty of Physics and Labour Education: TOSHKINBOY UMARALIYEV
Faculty of Uzbek Philology: TOHIRJON RAHMONOV
Faculty of World Languages: SAIDUMOR SAIDALIYEV

NATIONAL UNIVERSITY OF UZBEKISTAN NAMED AFTER MIRZO ULUGBEK

Vozgorodok, Tashkent 100174
Telephone: (71) 227-12-24
Fax: (71) 246-53-21
E-mail: rector@nuu.uz
Internet: www.nuu.uz
Founded 1918 as Muslim People's Univ., present name and status 2000
State control
Languages of instruction: Russian, Uzbek
Academic year: September to June

Faculties of biology and soil science, chemistry, economics, foreign philology, geography, geology, history, journalism, law, mechanics and mathematics, philosophy, physics, Uzbek philology

Rector: Prof. Dr GAFURDJAN ISRAILOVICH MUXAMEDOV
Pro-Rector: Q. Q. KURANBOEV
Library Dir: I. L. KISLITSINA

Library of 3,000,000 vols
Number of teachers: 990
Number of students: 8,504

Publication: *ACTA NUUz.*

NIZOMIY NOMIDAGI TOSHKENT DAVLAT PEDAGOGIKA UNIVERSITETI
(Tashkent State Pedagogical University named after Nizami)

Yu. X. Xadijb 103, 700100 Tashkent
Telephone: (71) 254-92-02
Fax: (71) 152-73-92
E-mail: tdpu@yandex.ru
Internet: www.tdpu.uz
Founded 1935
State control
Languages of instruction: Uzbek, Russian, Kazakh, Korean, German, English
Academic year: September to June
Rector: INOYATOV ULUG'BEK ILYOSOVICH
Pro-Rector: DILSHOD ERGASHEVICH UNAROV

Number of teachers: 932
Number of students: 10,380

DEANS

Faculty of Applied Physiologists Training: FAZLIDDIN KHAYDAROV
Faculty of Arts: S. ABDURASULOV

Faculty of Drawing and Applied Art: BOTOR BOYMETOV
Faculty of Elementary Education: D. H. SHODMONKULOVA
Faculty of Foreign Languages: A. KURBONOV
Faculty of Handicrafts Education: NARZULLA MUSLIMOV
Faculty of History: O. MANSUROV
Faculty of Military Physical Training: ILHOM IKROMOV
Faculty of Music: HAMIDULLA NURMATOV
Faculty of Natural Sciences: FARIDA MIRXAMIDOVA
Faculty of Pedagogics and Psychology: N. S. SAFAYEV
Faculty of Physics and Mathematics: K. JUMANIYAZOV
Faculty of Professional Training: O. AVAZBOYEV
Faculty of Russian and Korean Philology: RUSTAM KOBILOV
Faculty of Teaching Skills Enhancement: NURIDDIN DOSANOV
Faculty of Uzbek Language and Literature: I. AZIMOV

SAMARQAND DAVLAT UNIVERSITETI
(Samarqand State University)

Universitet ko'chasi 15, Samarqand 140104
Telephone: (66) 235-16-02
Fax: (66) 235-19-38
E-mail: support@samdu.uz
Internet: www.samdu.uz
Founded 1927
State control
Languages of instruction: Uzbek, Russian, Tajik
Academic year: September to June
Rector: Dr T. SH. SHIRINOV
Vice-Rector: Prof. M. K. MHIDDINOV

Faculties of applied mathematics, biology, chemistry, economics, foreign languages, geography, history, law, management, mathematics, musical education, physical training, physics, pre-school and primary education, sociology, Uzbek, Tajik and Russian philology

Number of teachers: 800
Number of students: 13,000

Publication: *Samarqand Davlat Universiteti* (52 a year).

TOSHKENT DAVLAT IQTISODIYOT UNIVERSITETI
(Tashkent State University of Economics)

Uzbekistanskaya 49, Tashkent 100003
Telephone: (71) 132-64-21
Fax: (71) 139-41-23
E-mail: info@tdiu.uz
Internet: www.tdiu.uz
Founded 1931
Rector: Prof. NODIR JUMAEV

Faculties of accounting, agricultural economics, economic cybernetics, economic planning, financial economics, trade economics; campus. in Andijon

Library of 300,000 vols
Number of teachers: 600
Number of students: 11,000

TOSHKENT ISLOM UNIVERSITETI
(Tashkent Islamic University)

Abdullah Qodiriy 11, Tashkent 100006
Telephone: (71) 139-52-15
Fax: (71) 139-82-15
Internet: www.tiu.uz
Founded 1999
State control
Languages of instruction: Uzbek, Arabic

Academic year: September to June
Rector: Prof. RAVSHAN ABDULLAEV

Faculties of advanced training, Islamic history and philosophy, Islamic law, economy and natural sciences
Number of students: 100

TERMIZ DAVLAT UNIVERSITETI
(Termez State University)

F. Hodjaev 43, Termiz 190111
Telephone and fax (762) 22-87-16
Internet: www.terdu.uz
Founded 1992
State control
Languages of instruction: Uzbek, Russian
Academic year: September to June
Rector: Prof. KHAYDAROV MAMAT
Pro-Rector: XURRAMOV SHUKUR XURRAMOVICH
Pro-Rector: BAKIROV POYAN URALOVICH

Faculties of economics, history, natural sciences and geography, pedagogy, philology, physical education, physics and mathematics, professional education, technics and chemistry

Library of 250,000
Number of teachers: 495
Number of students: 7,000

URGANCH DAVLAT UNIVERSITETI
(Urgench State University named after Al—Khorezmi)

H. Olimjon St, Urgench 220100
Telephone: (62) 226-61-66
Fax: (62) 226-35-44
E-mail: xabursu@mail.ru
Internet: www.urgenchsu.narod.ru
Founded 1992
State control
Languages of instruction: Russian, Uzbek
Academic year: September to June
Rector: Prof. Dr RUZUMBOY ESHCHANOV
Library of 360,000 vols
Number of teachers: 500
Number of students: 7,000

Publication: *Ilm sarchashmasi*

DEANS

Faculty of Natural Science and Geography: Dr IKRAM ABDULLAEV

WESTMINSTER INTERNATIONAL UNIVERSITY IN TASHKENT

12 Istiqbol St, Tashkent 100047
Telephone: (71) 238-74-17
Fax: (71) 238-74-00
E-mail: info@wiut.uz
Internet: www.wiut.uz
Founded 2002; attached to Univ. of Westminster, the UK

Faculties of business development, human resources and management, economics, English, finance and accounting, information technology and computing, law, marketing and quantitative analysis

Rector: Dr ABDUMALIK DJUMANOV
Deputy Rector for Academic Affairs: ALAN FRANCE.

Other Higher Educational Institutes

Academy of Arts of Uzbekistan: Sharif Rashidov gazari 40, Tashkent 100029; tel. (71) 256-50-47; fax (71) 256-50-46; e-mail acart@umid.uz; internet www.arts-academy .uz; f. 1997 by merger of existing instns;

190 teachers; 900 students; Rector TURSUNALI KUZIYEV.

Ajiniyaz Nomidagi Nukus Davlat Pedagogika Instituti (Nukus State Teacher—Training Institute named after Ajiniyaz): 104 A. Dosnazarov St, Nukus, Qoraqalpog'istan 230100; tel. (61) 222-65-10; fax (61) 222-65-46; e-mail nkspi_info@edu.uz; internet www.ndpi.uz; f. 1934, present name and status 1992; attached to Min. of Public Education; faculties of history, Karakalpak language and literature, natural sciences, pedagogy, primary education, philology, physical training, physics and mathematics; Rector MURAT KARLIBAEVICH BERDIMURATOV; Vice-Rector for Academic Affairs MAMAN KTAYBEKOVICH SARIBAEV; publ. *Science and Society*.

Andijon Cotton Institute: Selo Kuigan-Yar, Andijon 170600; tel. (74) 224-54-34.

Andijon Davlat Tibbiyot Instituti (Andijan State Medical Institute): Atabekova 1, Andijon 170100; tel. (74) 237-93-53; fax (74) 222-19-41; e-mail rector@andmi.uz; internet www.andmi.uz; f. 1955; faculties of curative science, medical pedagogies, nurses training, pediatrics; library: 286,000 vols; Rector Prof. Dr SHODMONOV ALISHER KAYUMOVICH; Pro-Rector for Academic Affairs Prof. Dr MADAZIMOV MADAMIN MUMINOVICH; Pro-Rector for Scientific Affairs Prof. Dr KHAJIMATOV GULOMJON MINHODJIEVICH.

Andijon State Pedagogical Institute of Languages: Babur ko'chasi 5, Andijon 170111; tel. (74) 224-75-15; fax (74) 224-75-26; e-mail adtpi@online.ru; f. 1966; faculties of Russian language and literature, foreign languages (English, German, French); Rector RAHMONOV TOJIDDIN YAKUBOVICH; publ. *Scientific Proceedings*.

Buxoro State Medical Institute: Navoi ko'chasi 1, Buxoro 200118; tel. (65) 223-00-50; fax (65) 223-49-43; e-mail buhme@rambler.ru; internet www.buhmi.uz; f. 1990; library: 90,000 vols; 240 teachers; 1,728 students; Rector Prof. RAKHMAT M. AKHMEDOV.

Buxoro Technological Institute of Food and Light Industry: K. Murtazoyev 15, Buxoro 200117; tel. (65) 223-61-97; fax (65) 223-78-84; e-mail javlonbek@intal.uz; f. 1976; faculties of business and management, food technology, light industry, mechanical engineering, oil and gas, professional education; 320 teachers; 4,800 students; Rector Prof. INOBAT HIKMATOVA.

Farg'ona Polytechnic Institute: Ferganskaya ko'chasi 86, Farg'ona 150100; tel. (732) 22-13-50; fax (732) 22-13-33; e-mail monitoring@farpi.uz; internet www.farpi.uz; f. 1967; faculties of chemical technology, construction, economics, mechanics, power; device building centre; library: 290,000 vols; 234 teachers; 3,239 students; Rector RASUL J. TOJIYEV; publ. *Scientific-Technical Journal* (4 a year).

Samarqand Agricultural Institute: M. Ulugbek 77, Samarqand 140103; tel. (662) 34-33-20; fax (662) 34-07-86; e-mail samsi@uzpak.uz; f. 1929; faculties of agro-engineering, agronomics, animal husbandry, economics and accounting, karakul (sheepbreeding), veterinary science, zootechnics; library: 533,777 vols; 274 teachers; 3,500 students (2,000 full-time, 1,500 correspondence); Rector Prof. ABDI-KADIR ERGASHEV.

Samarqand Cooperative Institute: A. Temur 9, Samarqand 140100; tel. (662) 33-38-72; fax (662) 31-12-53; e-mail samki@intal.uz; f. 1931; faculties of accounting, engineering technology, trade, trade economics; library: 205,718 vols; 210 teachers; 7,000 students; Rector AKBARALI N. JABRIYEV.

Samarqand Davlat Chet Tillar Instituti (Samarqand State Institute of Foreign Languages): Akhunbabayev str. 93, Samarqand 140104; tel. and fax (66) 233-78-43; e-mail ssifl_info@mail.ru; internet samdchti.uz; f. 1994; faculties of English philology, Roman and German Philology, translation; library: 91,000 vols; 225 teachers; 2,165 students (1,387 undergraduate, 778 postgraduate); Rector Prof. SHAHRIYOR SAFAROV.

Samarqand State Architectural and Civil Engineering Institute: Lolazor 70, Samarqand 140147; tel. (662) 37-15-93; fax (662) 31-04-52; e-mail unesco_aliance@rambler.ru; f. 1966; depts of architecture, building, building engineering and ecology, building technology, economics, engineering, machine construction and land cadastre, professional education; library: 400,000 vols; 266 teachers; 2,000 students; Rector SOBIR M. BOBOEV.

Samarqand State Medical Institute: Amir Temur 18, Samarqand 140100; tel. and fax (662) 33-54-21; e-mail info@sammi .samuni.silk.org; f. 1930; faculties of general practice and paediatrics; library: 330,000 vols; Rector B. U. SOBIROV.

State Conservatory of Uzbekistan: B. Zakirova St 1, Tashkent 700027; tel. (71) 144-53-20; fax (71) 144-95-08; e-mail uzkonservatory@mail.ru; internet www .konservatoriya.uz; f. 1936; choral conducting, composition, orchestral, musicology, piano, singing, sound production Uzbek folk instruments; library: 243,000 vols; 188 teachers; 1,000 students; Rector Prof. DILORA MURADOVA.

Tashkent Abu Reihan Beruni State Technical University: Universitetskaya 2, Tashkent 100095; tel. (71) 246-46-00; fax (71) 229-48-96; e-mail intdep@online.ru; internet www.tstu.re.uz; f. 1929; faculties of automation and computer hardware, electronics, humanities, mechanical engineering and machine building, mining and geology, oil and gas, power engineering; 2,000 teachers; 20,000 students; Rector KAKHRAMON R. ALLAYEV.

Tashkent Institute of Architecture and Construction: Navoi 13, Tashkent 100011; tel. (71) 241-10-84; fax (71) 241-80-00; e-mail otvtasi@uzsci.net; internet www.tasi.uzsci .net; faculties of architecture, construction of buildings, construction management, engineering and construction; 200 teachers; 2,400 students; Rector MIRAKHMEROV MAKHAMADJON MIRAKHMEDOVICH.

Tashkent Institute of Irrigation and Melioration: 39 Qori-Niyoziy St, Tashkent 100000; tel. and fax (71) 237-38-79; e-mail admin@tiim.uz; internet www.tiim.uz; f. 1934 as Tashkent Institute of Irrigation and Agricultural Mechanization Engineers, present name 2004; faculties of agricultural mechanization, economics, education science, electrical energetic of agriculture and water management, hydromelioration, irrigation and land improvement of hydromeliorative works, land management, magistracy, management and marketing, natural resources management; library: 864,000 vols; 484 teachers; 5,371 students; Rector Prof. UKTAM PARDAYEVICH UMURZAKOV (acting).

Tashkent Institute of Railway Transport Engineers: Adilkhodjayeva 1, Tashkent 100167; tel. (71) 191-14-40; fax (71) 191-10-73; f. 1931; faculties of automation, engineering, construction, economics, industrial and civil construction, telemechanics and communication, traffic management; library: 500,000 vols; 400 teachers; 12,000 students; Rector FERUZA FUZAILOVNA KARIMOVA (acting); Pro-Rector BATIR ZAKIROV.

Tashkent Institute of Textile and Light Industry: Shohjahon St 5, Yakkasaroy Dist., Tashkent 100100; tel. (71) 253-06-06; fax (71) 253-36-17; e-mail rector@titli.uz; internet titli.uz; f. 1932; faculties of chemical technology, cotton technology, engineering economics, mechanical technology, technology for light industry; library: 644,000 vols; 242 teachers; 2,214 students; Rector Prof. Dr JUMANIYAZOV KADAM JUMANIYAZOVICH; Vice-Rector for Academic Affairs Prof. Dr KAMILOVA XOLIDA XAFIZOVNA; Vice-Rector for Science BAZAROV ORIFJAN SHADIEVICH.

Tashkent Paediatric Medical Institute: Obidova 223, Tashkent 100140; tel. and fax (71) 262-34-22; e-mail tpmiim@gmail.com; internet tashpmi.uz; f. 1972; fmrly Middle Asian Paediatric Medical Institute; offers education in emergency, health economics, management and marketing in medicine, medical law, preventive medicine; 3,453 students; Rector Prof. B. T. DAMINOV.

Tashkent Pharmaceutical Institute: Oybek str. 45, Tashkent 100015; tel. (71) 256-37-38; fax (71) 256-45-04; e-mail pharmi@bcc.com.uz; internet www.pharmi .uz; f. 1937; faculties of improvement in industrial pharmacy, pharmacists' skills, pharmacy; library: 423,420 vols; 212 teachers; 1,323 students; Rector Prof. Dr AKHMADKHODJA NIGMANOVICH YUNUSKHOJAYEV; Pro-Rector ZOKIRJON ABIDOVICH YULDASHEV (acting); publ. *Pharmaceutical Journal*.

Tashkent State Agrarian University: Universitetskaya 5, Kibray Dist., Tashkent 100140; tel. and fax (71) 263-76-00; e-mail gulumov@atabah.silk.org; f. 1930; depts of accounting, agrochemistry and soil science, agronomy, economics and management, forestry, fruit and vegetable growing, plant protection, silkworm breeding, viticulture; library: 196,000 vols; 320 teachers; 7,200 students; Rector H. C. H. BURIYEV.

Toshkent Avtomobil-yo'llar Instituti (Tashkent Automobile and Road Construction Institute): Mavoraunnakhr 20A, Tashkent 100060; tel. (71) 232-14-39; fax (71) 233-08-27; e-mail tadi_info@edu.uz; internet www.tayi.uz; f. 1972; faculties of automobile mechanics, management of transport and transport communications, road construction, road transport; br. in Termez; 142 teachers; 4,000 students; Rector IKRAMOV MURAT AKRAMOVICH.

Toshkent Davlat Yuridik Instituti (Tashkent Law Institute): Sayilgokh 3, Tashkent 100047; tel. (71) 133-41-09; fax (71) 133-37-46; e-mail rektor@tsil.uz; internet www.tsil.uz; 3 faculties of law; 221 teachers; 2,182 students; Rector Prof. Dr MIRZAYUSUF HAKIMOVICH RUSTAMBAYEV; Pro-Rector for Academic Work RUSTAM AKHMEDOVICH ZUFAROV.

Toshkent Moliya Instituti (Tashkent Financial Institute): Asomova 7, Tashkent 100084; tel. (71) 234-53-34; fax (71) 235-77-04; e-mail rektor@tfi.uz; internet www.tfi.uz; f. 1991; offers courses in areas of auditing and accounting, banking, finance, insurance, projects financing, securities, stock exchange, taxation; 350 teachers; 4,200 students; Rector Prof. Dr ALISHER V. VAKHABOV; publ. *Moliya*.

Tashkent State Institute of Culture named after Abdulla Qadiri: Yalangach St 127A, Tashkent 100164; tel. (71) 262-03-23; fax (71) 262-12-35; e-mail tdmi@uzsci.net; f. 1974; librarianship, educational and cultural work; br. in Namangan; 170 teachers; 1,500 students; Rector Prof. AZIZ APPAKOVICH TURAEV; First Pro-Rector Prof. Dr ABDUKHALIL ABDULKHAEVICH MAVRULOV; Pro-Rector for Educational Work and Information Technologies ANVAR SHOMURADOVICH NORBEKOV.

Tashkent State Medical Institute: 103 Musahanov St, Tashkent 700048; tel. (71) 267-63-05; fax (71) 233-62-26; e-mail tashmi@mail.ru; f. 1920; trains general practitioners and stomatologists; library: 600,000 vols; 450 teachers; 3,000 students; Rector Prof. T. A. DAMINOV.

Tashkent University of Information Technology: Amir Temur 108, Tashkent 100084; tel. (71) 138-64-20; fax (71) 135-10-40; e-mail teic@uzpak.uz; f. 1955 as Tashkent Electrotechnical Institute of Communication, present name and status 2002; faculties of economics, radio communication, special communication, telecommunication networks and switching systems, telecommunication transmission systems, television and broadcasting; library: 500,000 vols; 400 teachers; 8,500 students; Rector Prof. Dr MADJID KARIMOV.

University of World Economics and Diplomacy: Buyuk Ipak yuli 54, Tashkent 100045; tel. (71) 267-67-69; fax (71) 267-09-13; e-mail uwed@list.ru; internet www.uwed.uz; f. 1992; 350 teachers; 1,200 students; Rector ABDUJABBAR ABDUVAKHITOV.

Uzbek State World Languages University: 21A Kichik halqa yuli str., Uchtepa Dist., Tashkent 100138; tel. (71) 275-97-95; fax (71) 275-55-47; e-mail usuw_info@edu.uz; internet www.uzswlu.uz; f. 1992 by merger of Tashkent State Pedagogical Institute of Foreign Languages and Republican Russian Language and Literature Pedagogic Institute; faculties of English, German, French, Spanish, Chinese and Russian philology, int. journalism, theory and practice of translation; 587 teachers; 7,073 students; Rector A. ISMAILOV; Vice-Rector for Academic Affairs N. ARTIKOV; Vice-Rector for Scientific Affairs G. BAKIYEVA.

VANUATU

The Higher Education System

Higher education in Vanuatu is limited, the only institution being a campus of the University of the South Pacific, which opened in 1989 and which offers courses leading to certificates, diplomas, degrees and postgraduate qualifications. The campus in Port Vila, known as the Emalus Campus, houses the University's law school. Students from Vanuatu may also receive higher education at the University's principal faculties (in Suva, Fiji), or at higher education institutions in Papua New Guinea, Australia or New Zealand, while those from Vanuatu's French schools may attend institutions in New Caledonia or French Polynesia. In 2002 there were 2,124 students enrolled in tertiary education. Gross enrolment at tertiary level was just 5% in 2005.

Admission to the University of the South Pacific is primarily via the Pacific Senior Secondary Certificate and completion of preparatory Preliminary and/or Foundation Programmes, which are designed to bridge the gap between secondary and tertiary education. The Bachelors degree typically lasts three years, although some courses may last longer—for example, medicine, which is a four-year programme of study. The Masters degree lasts between one and two years upon completion of the Bachelors. The Doctorate, which is the highest academic award available, requires a minimum of two additional years of study and research following award of the Masters.

Regulatory Body

GOVERNMENT

Ministry of Education: PMB 028, Port Vila; tel. 22309; fax 24569; Minister CHARLOT SALWAI.

Learned Societies

BIBLIOGRAPHY, LIBRARY SCIENCE AND MUSEOLOGY

Pacific Islands Museums Association (PIMA): Vanuatu Cultural Centre, Port Vila; tel. 28063; fax 26590; e-mail pimasg@gmail.com; f. 1994; preserves, celebrates and nurtures the heritage of the peoples of the Pacific Islands; Sec.-Gen. TARISI VUNIDILO.

Vanuatu Library Association/Vanuatu Laebri Asosiesen/Association Des Bibliothèques Vanuatuanes: Port Vila; tel. 22888; fax 24494; internet www.vanuatu.usp .ac.fj/library/vla; develops and improves library services; supports and encourages devt of libraries, archives and associated professions; Pres. SYLVIE TAPASEI; Sec. PAULINE KALO; Treas. KYM FRERICKS.

Research Institute

NATURAL SCIENCES

Biological Sciences

Environment Unit: Pompidou Complex, Port Vila; e-mail environ@vanuatu.com.vu; internet www.biodiversity.com.vu; provides technical advice and organizes programmes for devt, conservation and management of natural resources; Head ERNEST BANI.

Libraries and Archives

Port Vila

National Library: Nat. Museum Bldg, Port Vila; tel. 22129; fax 26590; e-mail nasonal .laebri@vanuatuculture.org; internet www .vanuatuculture.org/site-bm2/library; 2 spec. collns, Pacific and Vanuatu in English, French and Bislama; linguistics section on the 113 vernacular languages; anthropological and archaeological materials, art and arts references, autobiographical records and biographies, large section of works on the languages of Vanuatu, mission histories, oral traditions, cultural, historical and political records; Chief Librarian ANNE NAUPA; Librarian JUNE NORMAN.

National Photo, Film and Sound Archive: POB 184, Port Vila; tel. 23197; fax 26590; e-mail filmandaudio@vanuatuculture .org; internet www.vanuatuculture.org/ site-bm2/film-sound; preserves information about custom, culture and tradition; 3,000 hours of footage (8mm films, Video 8 and VHS ½-inch video) and photographs of oral traditions and rituals.

Port Vila Public Library: Cultural Centre Bldg, Port Vila; tel. (678) 23837; fax (678) 27837; e-mail pablik.laebri@vanuatu.com.vu; internet www.vanuatuculture.org/site-bm2/ library/050517_publiclibrary.shtml; f. 1960; only public library in Vanuatu; Librarian NAOMI ANIEL.

Museum

Port Vila

Vanuatu Cultural Centre and National Museum/Vanuatu Kaljoral Senta: POB 184, Port Vila; tel. 23197; fax 26590; e-mail vks@vanuatu.com.vu; internet www .vanuatuculture.org; f. 1960 as Port Vila Library, Museum opened in 1995; incl. Malakula Cultural Centre in Lakatoro; houses Vanuatu Cultural and Historic Sites Survey (VCHSS), Young People's Project, Women's Cultural Project; supports and encourages preservation, protection and devt of cultural heritage; collns of canoe paraphernalia, photographs, informational text, identification labels and DVDs on story of canoes; archaeological items; traditional artefacts (masks, slit gongs, outrigger canoes); historical and contemporary art; Dir of Vanuatu Cultural Centre MARCELLIN ABONG.

University

UNIVERSITY OF THE SOUTH PACIFIC, EMALUS CAMPUS

PMB 9072, Port Vila
Telephone: 22748
Fax: 22633
E-mail: ngwele_a@vanuatu.usp.ac.fj
Internet: www.vanuatu.usp.ac.fj
Pacific Languages Unit, School of Early Childhood Education, School of Law
Dir: JEAN PIERRE NIRUA
Librarian: MARGARET AUSTRAI-KAILO
Library of 15,596 vols (incl. Emalus Campus, Santo Centre and Tanna Centre)
Number of students: 930

VATICAN CITY

The Higher Education System

The State of the Vatican City is situated entirely within the Italian capital, Rome. In 1929 the Lateran Treaty was concluded between the Italian Government and the Holy See (a term designating the papacy, i.e. the office of the Pope, and thus the central governing body of the Roman Catholic Church). Higher education principally consists of Pontifical universities, colleges and institutes offering training for the priesthood and conducting research relating to the Roman Catholic Church, the oldest being the Pontificia Universitas Gregoriana, which was founded in 1553. The majority of institutions are located in Rome outside the boundaries of the Vatican City itself. Many of the institutions award graduate degrees, including doctorates.

Regulatory and Representative Bodies

GOVERNMENT

Congregation for Catholic Education: Palazzo delle Congregazioni, Piazza Pio XII 3, 00193 Rome; tel. (6) 69884167; fax (6) 69884172; e-mail cec@cec.va; f. 1588; concerned with the direction, temporal admin. and studies of Catholic univs, seminaries, schools and colleges; Prefect Cardinal ZENON GROCHOLEWSKI; Sec. Most Rev. JEAN-LOUIS BRUGUÈS.

Pontifical Commission for the Cultural Patrimony of the Church: Via della Conciliazione 5, 00193 Rome; Città del Vaticano, 00120 Rome; tel. (6) 69885640; fax (6) 69884621; e-mail beniculturali@beniculturali.va; f. 1988; acts as curator for the artistic and historical patrimony of the whole Church; library of 6,500 vols; Pres. GIANFRANCO CARD RAVASI.

ACCREDITATION

ENIC/NARIC Holy See: Congregation for Catholic Education, 00120 Vatican City; tel. (6) 69884167; fax (6) 69884172; e-mail educatt@ccatheduc.va; internet www.vatican.va; Contact Rev. PASCALE IDE.

Learned Societies

GENERAL

Pontificia Academia Sancti Thomae Aquinatis (Pontifical Academy of St Thomas Aquinas): 00120 Vatican City 00120; tel. (6) 69881441; fax (6) 69885218; e-mail past@past.va; internet www.past.va; f. 1879; theological, philosophical and juridico-economic sections; 54 mems; Pres. Prof. LLUÍS CLAVELL; Sec. Prof. HE MARCELO SÁNCHEZ SORONDO; publ. *Doctor Communis* (irregular).

ECONOMICS, LAW AND POLITICS

Pontificia Accademia delle Scienze Sociali (Pontifical Academy of Social Sciences): Casina Pio IV, 00120 Vatican City; tel. (6) 69881441; fax (6) 69885218; e-mail pass@pass.va; internet www.pass.va; f. 1994; social, economic, political and juridical sciences; 37 mems; Pres. Prof. MARY ANN GLENDON; Chancellor Prof. HE MARCELO SÁNCHEZ SORONDO; publs *Acta*, *Miscellanea*.

FINE AND PERFORMING ARTS

Pontificia Insigne Accademia di Belle Arti e Lettere dei Virtuosi al Pantheon: Via della Conciliazione, 5, 00193 Rome, Italy; tel. (6) 69882232; f. 1542; 90 mems; Pres. Dott. VITALIANO TIBERIA; Sec. Dott. VITTORIO DI GIACOMO; publ. *Annali* (1 a year).

HISTORY, GEOGRAPHY AND ARCHAEOLOGY

Pontificia Accademia Romana di Archeologia (Pontifical Roman Academy of Archaeology): Via della Conciliazione 5, 00193 Rome, Italy; f. 1810; 109 mems; Pres. MARCO BUONOCORE; Sec. PAOLO LIVERANI; publs *Memorie*, *Rendiconti*.

NATURAL SCIENCES

General

Pontificia Academia Scientiarum (Pontifical Academy of Sciences): Casina Pio IV, 00120 Vatican City; tel. (6) 69883451; fax (6) 69885218; e-mail pas@pas.va; internet www.pas.va; f. 1603; promotes the mathematical, physical and natural sciences and the study of related epistemological problems; 80 mems; Pres. Prof. WERNER ARBER; Chancellor Prof. Mgr MARCELO SÁNCHEZ SORONDO; publs *Acta*, *Commentari*, *Documenta*, *Scripta Varia*.

RELIGION, SOCIOLOGY AND ANTHROPOLOGY

Collegium Cultorum Martyrum: Via Napoleone III 1, 00185 Rome, Italy; f. 1879; 750 mems; Master Mgr EMANUELE CLARIZIO; Sec. LUIGI CIOTTI.

Pontificia Academia Mariana Internationalis (Pontifical International Marian Academy): Via Merulana 124, 00185 Rome, Italy; premises in Vatican City; tel. (6) 70373235; fax (6) 70373234; e-mail pami@pami.info; internet www.pami.info; f. 1946, Pontifical since 1959; studies on Our Lady; 80 mems, 155 corresp. mems, 134 hon. mems; Pres. VINCENZO BATTAGLIA; Sec. STEFANO CECCHIN; publ. *Scientific collections*.

Pontificia Accademia dell'Immacolata (Academy of the Immaculate Conception): Via del Serafico 1, 00142 Rome, Italy; f. 1835; 15 mems; promotes Marian studies and culture, especially the doctrine of the Immaculate Conception in the fields of theology, literature and art; Pres. Cardinal ANDREA M. DESKUR; Sec. and Archivist Fr ZDZISLAW J. KIJAS.

Pontificia Accademia di Teologia: Piazza St Giovanni in Laterano 4, 00120 Vatican City; tel. 06-69895513; e-mail path@pul.it; f. 1718; 7 emeritus mems; 39 ordinary mems; 25 normally resident in Rome, 6 in the rest of Italy and 8 in other countries; 16 corresp. mems; Pres. MARCELLO BORDONI; Sec. Prof. PIERO CODA; publ. *PATH*.

Research Institute

NATURAL SCIENCES

Physical Sciences

Vatican Observatory: 00120 Vatican City; tel. (6) 69885266; f. 1889; carries out research into dark matter and energy in the cosmos, the acceleration of the universe, quasars, globular clusters; library of 33,000 vols; Dir Fr JOSÉ GABRIEL FUNES.

Attached Centre:

Vatican Observatory Research Group (VORG): see entry for Mount Graham International Observatory in USA chapter.

Libraries and Archives

Vatican City

Archivio Segreto Vaticano (Papal Archives): 00120 Vatican City; internet asv.vatican.va; f. 1611; attached school: see Schools; Prefect HE SERGIO PAGANO; publs *Collectanea Archivi Vaticani*, *Varia*.

Biblioteca Apostolica Vaticana (Vatican Library): 00120 Vatican City; tel. (6) 69879400; fax (6) 69885327; e-mail bav@vatlib.it; internet www.vaticanlibrary.va; f. 1451 as a public library by Pope Nicholas V, and provided with staff and a structure by Sixtus IV in 1475; at the present time it contains 75,000 MSS, 80,000 archival files, 1.6m. engravings, 8,000 incunabula, and 1m. other vols; collns incl. those of the Dukes of Urbino (1657), of Queen Christina of Sweden (1690), of the Florentine Marquis Capponi (1745), of Barberini (1902), of Chigi (1923), and the Borghese colln, which included many items housed in the Papal Library at Avignon; the Sistine Chapel colln is of importance to historians of music; the Library holds a 4th–century Greek Bible, Vergils from the 4th–6th centuries, a 4th–5th century palimpsest of Cicero's *Republic*, autographs of St Thomas Aquinas, Tasso, Petrarch, Boccaccio, Poliziano, Michelangelo, and Luther; houses numismatic colln; attached museums: see Museums and Art Galleries; attached school: see Schools; Protector Cardinal RAFAELLE FARINA; Prefect CEASARE PASINI; Vice-Prefect Dr AMBROGIO M. PIAZZONI.

Museums and Art Galleries

Vatican City

Museo Profano: Vatican City; f. 1767 by Pope Clement XIII; administered by Vatican

Apostolic Library; bronze sculptures and minor arts of the classical era; Curator Dr GIOVANNI MORELLO.

Museo Sacro (o Cristiano): Vatican City; f. 1756 by Pope Benedict XIV; contains objects of liturgical art, historical relics and curios from the Lateran; objects of palaeolithic, medieval and Renaissance minor arts, paintings of the Roman era; Curator Dr GUIDO CORNINI.

Vatican Museums: 00120 Vatican City; tel. (6) 69883333; fax (6) 69885061; internet www .museivaticani.va; Dir-Gen. Prof. ANTONIO PAOLUCCI; Admin. PAOLO NICOLINI; Sec. Dr ARNOLD NESSELRATH; publs *Bollettino dei Monumenti, Musei e Gallerie Pontificie.*

Constituent Museums:

Collezione d'Arte Religiosa Moderna (Collection of Modern Religious Art): 00120 Vatican City; f. 1973 by Pope Paul VI; paintings, sculptures and drawings offered to the Pope by over 200 artists and donors; Curator Dott. MICOL FORTI.

Museo Chiaramonti e Braccio Nuovo (Chiaramonti Museum and 'New Side'): 00120 Vatican City; f. by Pope Pius VII at the beginning of the 19th century; house the many new findings excavated in the 19th century; exhibits incl. the statues of the Nile, of Demosthenes and of the Augustus 'of Prima Porta'; Curator Dott. GIANDOMENICO SPINOLA.

Museo Gregoriano Egizio (Gregorian Egyptian Museum): 00120 Vatican City; internet mv.vatican.va/3_en/pages/mez/ mez_main.html; f. 1839 by Pope Gregory XVI; contains artefacts from Ancient Egypt; 9 exhibition rooms dating from 2600BC to 8th century AD incl. hieroglyphic stelae and statues, finds from Ancient Mesopotamia and Syria–Palestine, Hellenistic and Roman Egypt; Curator Dr ALESSIA AMENTA.

Museo Gregoriano Etrusco (Gregorian Etruscan Museum): 00120 Vatican City; tel. (6) 69883041; fax (6) 69885061; e-mail aei.musei@scv.va; internet mv.vatican.va/ 3_en/pages/mge/mge_main.html; f. 1837 by Pope Gregory XVI; artefacts from the early Iron Age to the end of the Roman Empire; jewellery, bronzes, terracottas, glasses, Etruscan sculptures and reliefs; figured vases (Greek, Etruscan and Italiote) from Etruria and Magna Graecia; grave goods from the Tomba Regolini Galassi of Cerveteri, the Mars of Todi, the amphora by Exekias; Curator Dott. MAURIZIO SANNIBALE.

Museo Gregoriano Profano (Gregorian Museum of Profane Art): 00120 Vatican City; f. by Gregory XVI in 1844 and housed in the Lateran Palace; transferred from fmr site in the Vatican and opened to the public in 1970; Roman sculptures from the Pontifical States; portrait-statue of Sophocles, the Marsyas of the Myronian group of Athena and Marsyas, the Flavian reliefs from the Palace of the Apostolic Chancery; Curator Dott. GIANDOMENICO SPINOLA.

Museo Missionario Etnologico (Ethnological Missionary Museum): 00120 Vatican City; internet mv.vatican.va/3_en/ pages/met/met_main.html; f. by Pius XI in 1926 and housed in the Lateran Palace; transferred from that site in the Vatican and opened to the public in 1973; ethnographical collns from all over the world; Curator Rev. NICOLA MAPELLI.

Museo Pio Clementino (Museum of Popes Clement XIV and Pius VI): 00120 Vatican City; f. by Pope Clement XIV (1769–74), and enlarged by his successor, Pius VI (1775–1799); exhibits include the

Apollo of Belvedere, Roman copies of the Apoxyomenos by Lysippus, of the Meleager by Skopas and of the Apollo Sauroktonous by Praxiteles; the original Vatican Colln was begun with the Apollo—already in possession of Pope Julius II when he was still a Cardinal, at the end of the 15th century—and the Laocoon Group, found in 1506; Curator Dott. GIANDOMENICO SPINOLA.

Museo Pio Cristiano Lapidario Cristiano Lapidario Ebraico (Early Christian Art Museum—Christian and Jewish Lapidaries): 00120 Vatican City; tel. (6) 69881349; fax (6) 69885061; e-mail ap .musei@scv.va; f. 1854 by Pius IX, housed in the Lateran Palace; transferred from fmr site in the Vatican and opened to the public in 1970; largest colln in the world of early Christian sarcophagi; Latin and Greek inscriptions from Christian cemeteries and basilicas; the Good Shepherd; inscriptions from Jewish catacombs; Curator Prof. Dr UMBERTO UTRO.

Padiglione delle Carrozze (Carriage Pavilion): 00120 Vatican City; f. 1973 by Pope Paul VI; located in the Vatican gardens, containing carriages, berlins and the first cars used by the Popes; Dir Asst Mons. PIETRO AMATO.

Pinacoteca Vaticana (Vatican Picture Gallery): 00120 Vatican City; internet mv .vatican.va/3_en/pages/pin/pin_main.html; inaugurated by Pope Pius XI in 1932; incl. paintings by Giotto, Fra Angelico, Raphael, Leonardo da Vinci, Titian and Caravaggio, and the Raphael Tapestries; Curator Dott. ARNOLD NESSELRATH.

Vatican Palaces: 00120 Vatican City; Nicoline Chapel decorated by Beato Angelico (1448–1450); Sistine Chapel restructured by Sixtus IV (1477–1483): frescoes by Perugino, Botticelli, Cosimo Rosselli, Ghirlandaio, Luca Signorelli, Michelangelo; Borgia Apartment: decorated by Pinturicchio and his workshop; Chapel of Urban VIII (1631–1635); Raphael Stanze and loggias decorated by Raphael and his assistants; Gallery of Maps (1580–83), Gallery of Tapestries, etc.; Curator Dott. ARNOLD NESSELRATH.

Universities

PONTIFICIA UNIVERSITÀ DELLA SANTA CROCE
(Pontifical University of the Holy Cross)

Piazza di Sant'Apollinare 49, 00186 Rome

Telephone: (6) 681641
Fax: (6) 68164400
E-mail: santacroce@pusc.it
Internet: www.pusc.it

Founded 1984; univ. status 1998
Private control (erected by the Holy See)

Chancellor: Rev. Bishop JAVIER ECHEVARRÍA
Vice-Chancellor: Mgr Prof. FERNANDO OCÁRIZ
Rector: Mgr. Prof. LUIS ROMERA
Vice-Rector: Rev. Prof. HÉCTOR FRANCESCHI
Gen.-Sec.: Rev. MANUEL MIEDES
Dir of Academic Affairs: Rev. Prof. FRANCISCO FERNÁNDEZ
Dir of Communications: Prof. NORBERTO GONZÁLEZ GAITANO
Dir of Devt: Dr JOAQUÍN GÓMEZ-BLANES
Librarian: Dott. JUAN DIEGO RAMÍREZ
Number of teachers: 163 ((126 permanent profs, 28 visiting profs in four faculties); 46 permanent profs, 8 visiting professors in the Higher Institute for Religious Studies)

Number of students: 1,470 (1003 students in the 4 faculties; 467 students in the Higher Institute for Religious Studies)
Publications: *International Canon Law journal:* 'IUS Ecclesiae', *International Philosophy journal:* 'Acta Philosophica', *International Theology journal:* 'Annales Theologici'.

AFFILIATED INSTITUTE

Institut de formation théologique de Montréal: 2065, rue Sherbrooke Ouest, Montréal, QC H3H 1G6, Canada; tel. (514)-935-1169; fax (514)-935-5497; e-mail info@ iftm.ca; internet www.iftm.ca; Private Control; language of instruction: French; academic year September to May; library of 140,000 monographs, 175 periodicals; Rector Prof. CHARLES LANGLOIS; Dean of Studies Prof. PETER KRASUSKI; publ. *L'entre deux tours* (online, (www.iftm.ca/iftm_bulletin.php))

DEANS

Department of Canon Law: Prof. ERNEST CAPARROS
Department of Pastoral Theology: Prof. GUY GUINDON
Department of Philosophy: Prof. TÉLESPHORE GAGNON
Department of Theology: Prof. JAROSLAW KAUFMANN

PROFESSORS

Faculty of Church Communications:
ARASA, D.
BAILLY-BAILLIÉRE, A.
BARILLARI, A.
BÜHREN, R. V.
CALOGERO, F.
CANTONI, L.
CARROGGIO, M.
CONTRERAS, D.
DE LA CIERVA, Y.
DOLZ, M.
ESPOZ., C.
FUSTER, E.
GAGLIARDI, F.
GARCÍA-NOBLEJAS, J. J.
GONZÁLEZ GAITANO, N.
GRAZIANI, N.
GRONOWSKI, D.
JIMÉNEZ, A.
JIMÉNEZ CATAÑO, R.
LA PORTE, J. M.
MACCARINI, A.
MASTROIANNI, B.
MILÁN, J.
MORA, J. M.
PILAVAKIS, M.
POLENGHI, G.
ROMOLO, R.
RUIZ LUCIO, A.
RUSSO, M.
SHAW, R.
TAPIA, S.
TRIDENTE, G.
WAUCK, J.

Faculty of Theology:
AGULLES, P.
AREITIO, J. R.
ARROYO, J. M.
BELDA, M.
BOSCH, V.
CHACÓN, A.
COLOM, E.
DE SALIS AMARAL, M.
DE VIRGILIO, G.
DÍAZ DORRONSORO, R.
DIÉGUEZ, J.
DUCAY, A.
ESTRADA, B.
FABBRI, M. V.
GALVÁN, J. M.
GARCÍA IBÁÑEZ, A.

GONZÁLEZ, E.
GOYRET, P.
GRANADOS, A.
GROHE, J.
JÓDAR, C.
LAMERI, A.
LEAL, J.
LIMBURG, K.
LÓPEZ DÍAZ, J.
MARTÍNEZ-FERRER, L.
MASPERO, G.
MIRA, M.
MIRALLES, A.
NIN, M.
O'CALLAGHAN, P.
OSSANDÓN, J. C.
PIOPPI, C.
PORRAS, A.
REALE, V.
REQUENA, F.
REQUENA, P.
RIESTRA, J. A.
RIO GARCÍA, M.
RODRÍGUEZ LUÑO, A.
ROSSI ESPAGNET, C.
SANZ, S.
SCHLAG, M.
SILVESTRE, J. J.
TÁBET, M.
TANZELLA-NITTI, G.
TORRES, E.
TOUZE, L.
VIAL, W.
WIELOCKX, R.

School Of Canon Law:

ÁLVAREZ DE LAS ASTURIAS, N.
ARAÑA, J. A.
ARRIETA, J. I.
BACCARI, M. P.
BAURA, E.
CANOSA, J.
CITO, D.
DEL POZZO, M.
EISENRING, G.
ERRÁZURIZ M., C. J.
FRANCESCHI, H.
GEFAELL, P.
GÓMEZ-IGLESIAS, V.
GUTIÉRREZ, J. L.
LLOBELL, J.
MARTÍN DE AGAR, J. T.
MIÑAMBRES, J.
NAVARRO, L.
ORTIZ, M. A.
PUIG, F.
SÁNCHEZ-GIL, A. S.
SCHOUPPE, J.-P.

School Of Philosophy:

ACERBI, A.
AIELLO, A.
BERGAMINO, F.
BROCK, S. L.
CHIRINOS, M. A.
CLAVELL, L.
DALLEUR, P.
D'AVENIA, M.
FARO, G.
FERNÁNDEZ LABASTIDA, F.
FERRARI, M. A.
GAHL, R. A.
IPPOLITO, B.
ITURBE, M.
LOMBO, J. A.
MALO, A.
MARTÍNEZ, R.
MERCADO, J. A.
PÉREZ DE LABORDA, M.
PORTA, M.
QUINTILIANI, M.
REYES, C.
RHONHEIMER, M.
ROMERA, L.
RUSSO, F.
SANGUINETI, J. J.

VITORIA, M. A.
YARZA, I.

PONTIFICIA UNIVERSITÀ SAN TOMMASO D'AQUINO
(St Thomas Aquinas Pontifical University)

Largo Angelicum 1, 00184 Rome, Italy
Telephone: (6) 67021
Fax: (6) 6790407
E-mail: segreteria@pust.urbe.it
Internet: www.angelicum.org
Founded 1580 as college, became Univ. 1909; present title conferred 1963
Languages of instruction: Italian, English
Academic year: October to June
Grand Chancellor: Rev. CARLOS AZPIROZ COSTA
Rector Magnificus: Rev. CHARLES MOREROD
Administrator: Rev. VIRGILIO AMBROSINI
Sec.-Gen.: Rev. GLENN MORRIS
Librarian: Rev. MIGUEL ITZA
Library of 200,000 vols
Number of teachers: 125
Number of students: 1,300
Publications: *Angelicum, Istituto S. Tommaso: Studi, Oikonomia* (ethics and social sciences, 3 a year), *Rassegna di Letteratura Tomistica, Studia Univ. S. Thomae In Urbe*

DEANS

Faculty of Canon Law: Rev. MIROSLAV KONSTANC ADAM
Faculty of Philosophy: Rev. PHILIPPE-ANDRE HOLZER
Faculty of Social Sciences: Rev. Sr HELEN ALFORD
Faculty of Theology: JOSEPH PHANTAN THAN

DIRECTORS

Institute of St Thomas: Rev. WALTER SENNER
Institute of Spirituality: Rev. PAUL MURRAY
'Mater Ecclesiae' Institute: S. JURIC

PONTIFICIA UNIVERSITAS GREGORIANA
(Pontifical Gregorian University)

Piazza della Pilotta 4, 00187 Rome, Italy
Telephone: (6) 67011
Fax: (6) 67015413
E-mail: segreteria@unigre.it
Internet: www.unigre.it
Founded by St Ignatius Loyola and St Francis Borgia, and constituted by Pope Julius III in 1553; confirmed and established by Pope Gregory XIII in 1582
The central university for ecclesiastical studies is under the direction of the Jesuit Order; Pontificium Institutum Biblicum and Pontificium Institutum Orientalium Studiorum are autonomous colleges associated with the Univ.
Languages of instruction: Italian, English, German, French, Spanish, Portuguese
Academic year: October to June (2 terms)
Grand Chancellor: HE Card. ZENON GROCHOLEWSKI
Vice-Grand Chancellor: Rev. PETER-HANS KOLVENBACH
Rector Magnificus: Rev. GIANFRANCO GHIRLANDA
Vice-Rector: Rev. FRANCISCO J. EGAÑA
Academic Vice-Rector: Rev. SERGIO BASTIANEL
Admin. Vice-Rector: Rev. VITALE SAVIO
Sec.-Gen.: LUIGI ALLENA
Librarian: Dr MARTA GIORGI DEBANNE
Library of 900,000 vols
Number of teachers: 423
Number of students: 2,949

Publications: *Acta Nuntiaturae Gallicae, Analecta Gregoriana, Archivum Historiae Pontificiae, Documenta Missionalia, Gregorianum, Inculturation, Miscellanea Historiae Pontificiae, Periodica de re morali canonica liturgica, Saggi ISR, Studia Missionalia, Studia Socialia, Tesi Gregoriana*

DEANS AND DIRECTORS

Cultural Heritage of the Church: J. JANSSENS
Faculty of Canon Law: M. HILBERT
Faculty of Ecclesiastical History: M. INGLOT
Faculty of Missionary Work: A. WOLANIN
Faculty of Philosophy: K. FLANNERY
Faculty of Social Sciences: J. JELENIC
Faculty of Theology: L. LADÁRIA
Institute of Psychology: T. HEALY
Institute of Religious Sciences: S. BARLONE
Institute of Spirituality: M. SZENTMÁRTONI
Interdisciplinary Centre of Social Communication: J. SRAMPICKAL

PROFESSORS

Cultural Heritage of the Church (tel. (6) 67015114; e-mail segrbcc@unigre.it):

JANSSENS, J., Church History
PFEIFFER, H., Art History

Faculty of Canon Law (tel. 6 67015123; e-mail hilbert@unigre.it):

ASTIGUETA, D., Text of Canon Law
CONN, J., Text of Canon Law
GHIRLANDA, G., Canon Law and Theology of Church Law
HILBERT, M., Text of Canon Law
KOWAL, J., Canon Law and Sacraments
SUGAWARA, Y., Text of Canon Law

Faculty of Ecclesiastical History (tel. (6) 67015410; e-mail inglot@unigre.it):

BENITEZ, J. M., Modern Church History
DE LASALA CLAVER, F., History of the Roman Curia
GUTIERREZ, A., Church History of Latin America
INGLOT, M., History of the Roman Curia
JANSSENS, J., Christian Archaeology—Historical Methodology
MEZZADRI, L., Modern Church History
PFEIFFER, H., Christian Art

Faculty of Missionary Work (tel. (6) 67015240; e-mail wolanin@unigre.it):

FARAHIAN, E., Missionary Biblical Theology
FUSS, M., Buddhism
SHELKE, C., Comparative Study of Religions
WOLANIN, A., Mission Dogmatics

Faculty of Philosophy (tel. and fax (6) 67015441; e-mail filosofia@unigre.it):

BABOLIN, S., Aesthetics and Philosophy of Human Culture
CARUANA, L., Philosophy of Science and Nature
DI MAIO, A., Medieval Philosophy
FLANNERY, K., Greek Philosophy
GILBERT, P., Metaphysics
GORCZYCA, J., Ethics
LECLERC, M., History of Modern Philosophy
LUCAS, R., Philosophical Anthropology
NKERAMIHIGO, T., Philosophy of Theology
PANGALLO, M., History of Medieval Philosophy

Faculty of Social Sciences (tel. (6) 67015316; e-mail scienzesoc@unigre.it):

BAUGH, L., Film and Television Language
JELENIC, J., Social Sciences
SCARVAGLIERI, G., General Religious Sociology

Faculty of Theology (tel. and fax (6) 67015262; e-mail teologia@unigre.it):

ATTARD, M., Moral Theology
BASTIANEL, S., Moral Theology
CALDUCH BENAGES, N., Old Testament Exegesis

CHAPPIN, M., Church History
CONROY, C., Old Testament Exegesis
COSTACURTA, B., Exegesis
FARRUGIA, M., Dogmatic Theology
GALLAGHER, M. P., Fundamental Theology
GRILLI, M., New Testament Exegesis
HENN, W., Dogmatic Theology
LADÁRIA, L., Dogmatic Theology
MEYNET, R., New Testament Exegesis
MILLÁS, J. M., Dogmatic Theology
PASTOR, F., Dogmatic Theology
PECKLERS, K., Liturgy
SCHMITZ, P., Moral Theology
TANNER, N., Patristic Theology
VITALI, D., Dogmatic Theology

Institute of Psychology (tel. (6) 67015299; e-mail psicologia@unigre.it):

HEALY, T., Psychology and Statistics
IMODA, F., Psychology
KIELY, B., Psychopathology
VERSALDI, G., Psychology and Psychotherapy

Institute of Religious Sciences (tel. and fax (6) 67015405; e-mail segrsr@unigre.it):

BARLONE, S., Fundamental Theology
FINAMORE, R., Education
SALATIELLO, G., Anthropology

Institute of Spirituality (tel. (6) 67015532; e-mail szentmartoni@unigre.it):

COSTA, M., Spiritual Theology
GARCÍA MATEO, R., Spiritual Theology
SECONDIN, B., Pastoral Theology
SZENTMÁRTONI, M., Pastoral Psychology

Interdisciplinary Centre of Social Communication (tel. (6) 67015393; fax (6) 67015124; e-mail comunicazione@unigre.it):

BABOLIN, S., Symbology
BAUGH, L., Film and Television Language

AFFILIATED INSTITUTES

Filozofsko-Teološki Institut Družbe Isusove: Jordanovac 110, 41001 Zagreb, Croatia; Dir M. STEINER.

Institut de Philosophie St Pierre Canisius: Kimwenza, BP 3724, Kinshasa-Gombe, Democratic Republic of the Congo; Rector R. DE HAES; Sec. E. STIENNON.

Instituto Superior de Direito Canônico do Brasil: Rua Benjamin Constant 23, 20241 Rio de Janeiro, Brazil; Dir L. MADERO LOPEZ.

Istituto Superiore per i Formatori: Seminario Vescovile, c/o Almo Collegio Capranica 98, 00186 Rome, Italy; Dir A. RAVAGLIOLI.

Istituto Superiore di Scienze Religiose 'Giuseppe Toniolo': Via S. Benedetto da Norcia 2, 65127 Pescara, Italy; Pres. G. CILLI.

Istituto di Filosofia 'Aloisianum': Via Donatello 24, 35123 Padua, Italy; Dir S. BONGIOVANNI.

Jesuit School of Philosophy and Theology 'Arrupe College': POB MP320, Mount Pleasant, Harare, Zimbabwe; Pres. A. L. SHIRIMA.

Pontificio Istituto 'Regina Mundi': Lungotevere Tor di Nona 7, 00186 Rome, Italy; Rector C. MCGOVERN.

Priesterseminar Redemptoris Mater des Erzbistum Berlin: Fortunaallee 29, 12683 Berlin, Germany; Rector S. LATINI.

PONTIFICIA UNIVERSITAS LATERANENSIS
(Pontifical Lateran University)

Piazza S. Giovanni in Laterano, 400120 Vatican City
Telephone: (6) 69895599
Fax: (6) 69886508
E-mail: segreteria.generale@pul.it
Internet: www.pul.it

Founded 1773
Language of instruction: Italian
Academic year: October to June
Grand Chancellor: HE Card. AGOSTINO VALLINI
Rector: HE Bishop ENRICO DAL COVOLO
Vice Rector: Rev. Mgr PATRICK VALDRINI
Gen. Sec. and Registrar: Dr ULDERICO CONTI
Chief Bursar: Ing. FLAMINIA SACERDOTI
Library of 600,000 vols
Number of teachers: 142
Number of students: 3,903
Publications: *Apollinaris* (Questions in Canon and Comparative Law, 2 a year), *Aquinas* (Philosophy, 4 a year), *Lateranum* (Theology, 4 a year), *Studia et Documenta Historiae et Iuris* (Roman Law, 1 a year)

DEANS

Faculty of Canon Law: Rev. Prof. LUIS BOMBIN BOMBIN
Faculty of Civil Law: Prof. VINCENZO BUONOMO
Faculty of Philosophy: Rev. Prof. GIANFRANCO BASTI
Faculty of Theology: Rev. Prof. RENZO GERARDI

INCORPORATED INSTITUTES

Istituto Patristico 'Augustinianum': Via Paolo VI 25, 00193 Rome, Italy; Pres. Rev. Fr ROBERT J. DODARO.

Istituto Superiore di Teologia Morale 'Accademia Alfonsiana': Via Merulana 31, 00185 Rome, Italy; Pres. Rev. Fr MARTIN MCKEEVER.

Istituto di Teologia della Vita Consacrata 'Claretianum': Largo Lorenzo Mossa 4, 00165 Rome, Italy; Pres. Fr JOSU MIRENA ALDAY.

AGGREGATED INSTITUTES

Institut de Formation Théologique de Montréal Département de Philosophie: 2065, Rue Sherbrooke Ouest, Montréal, QC H3H 1G6, Canada; tel. (4) 935-1169; fax (4) 935-5497; e-mail info@iftm.ca; internet www .iftm.ca; Private control; language of instruction: French; academic year September to May; Rector Prof. . CHARLES LANGLOIS; Dean of Studies Prof. PETER KRASUSKI; library: 140,00 monographies and 175 periodicals; publ. *L'etre deux tours* (online (www.iftm.ca/ iftm_bulletin.php))

DEANS

Department of Philosophy: Prof. TÉLESPHORE GAGNON

Instituto di Direito Canônico 'Pe. Dr Giuseppe Beinto Pegoraro': Av. Nazaré 993, Ipiranga, 04263-100 São Paulo, Brazil; Dir Mgr MARTIN SEGÚ GIRONA.

Instituto Diocesano de Estudios Canónicos: C/ Corona 34, 46003 Valencia, Spain; Pres. Rev. ANTONIO CORBÍ COPOVÍ.

Istituto Superiore per l'Insegnamento del Diritto 'Université St Paul la Sagesse' de Beyrouth: POB 50-501, Furn El Chebbak, Baada 1011 2050, Lebanon; teaching of law; Pres. Mgr JOSEPH MERHEJ.

Istituto Teologico di Assisi: Piazza S. Francesco 2, 06081 Assisi Santuario, Italy; Pres. Mgr GIOVANNI CAPPELLI.

Istituto Teologico Marchigiano: Via Monte Dago 87, 60131 Ancona, Italy; Pres. Mgr MARIO FLORIO.

AFFILIATED INSTITUTES

Istituto Filosofico della Facoltá di Teologia di Lugano: Via Buffi 13, CP 4663, 69004 Lugano, Switzerland; Rector Prof. LIBERO GEROSA.

Istituto Teologico Abruzzese-Molisano di Chieti: Via Nicoletto Vernia 1, 66100 Chieti, Italy; Prefect of Studies Rev. GIOVANNI GIORGIO.

Istituto Teologico-Cattolico per l'Oceania 'Blessed Diego Luis de San Vitores' di Guam: Catholic Theological Institute for Oceania, 130 Chalan Seminariu, Yona, 96915 Guam, USA; Prefect of Studies Mgr DAVID C. QUITUGUA.

Istituto Teologico della Comunità 'Saint Martin': BP 34, 41120 Candé sur Beuvron, France; Prefect of Studies Rev. Fr FRANÇOIS-REGIS MOREAU.

Istituto Teologico del Seminario di Alba Iulia: Str. Bibliotecii 3, 510009 Alba Iulia, Romania; Prefect of Studies Fr ZSOLT F. KOVACS.

Istituto Teologico del Seminario di Denver: St John Vianney Theological Seminary, 1300 S Steele St, Denver, CO 80210-2599, USA; Prefect of Studies Dr ANTHONY LILLES.

Istituto Teologico del Seminario di Guadalajara: Seminario Mayor, Santo Domingo 1120, Col. Chapalita, 45040 Guadalajara, Jal., Mexico; Prefect of Studies Rev. FRANCISCO GARCÍA VELARDE.

Istituto Teologico del Seminario di Györ: R. K. Hittudományi Főiskola, Káptalandomb 7, 9021 Györ, Hungary; Prefect of Studies Rev. GÁBOR NÉMETH.

Istituto Teologico del Seminario di Iaşi: Str. Vâscâuteanu 6, 700462 Iaşi, Romania; Prefect of Studies Rev. MIHAI PATRASCU.

Istituto Teologico del Seminario di Kamyanets-Podilskyi 'Seminarium Maius S. Spiritus': Provulok O. Wanagsa 14, 32000 Gorodok, Khmelnystka obl., Ukraine; Prefect of Studies Rev. JERZY KURCEK.

Istituto Teologico del Seminario di Rīga: Rigas Teologijas Instituts, Katolu iela 16, 1003 Rīga, Latvia; Pro-Prefect of Studies Rev. EDGAR CAKULS.

Istituto Teologico del Seminario Roermond: Groot-Seminarie Rolduc, Heyendallaan 82, 6464 EP Kerkrade, Netherlands; tel. (45) 5466999; e-mail info@rolduc.nl; internet www.rolduc.nl/seminarie; Rector Dr JAN VRIES; Prefect of Studies Dr LAMBERT HENDRIKS.

Istituto Teologico del Seminario San Giuseppe di Vilnius: Juozapo Kunigu Seminarija, Kalvariju 325, 2021 Vilnius, Latvia; Prefect of Studies Rev. HANS FRIEDRICH FISCHER.

Istituto Teologico 'Josephinum' di Columbus: Pontifical College Josephinum, 7625 N High St, Columbus, OH 80210-2599, USA; Prefect of Studies Rev. Fr MICHAEL ROSS.

Istituto Teologico 'St Giovanni Crisostomo' del Seminario di St Pietroburgo: Vysshaya Dukhovnaya Seminariya 'Maria-Tsaritsa Apostolov', Ul. 1-aya Krasnoarmeiskaya 11, 198005 St Petersburg, Russia; Prefect of Studies Rev. JAKUB BLASZCZYSZYN.

Istituto Teologico 'Willibrordhuis' della Diocesi di Haarlem: Willibrordhuis, Zilkerduinweg 375, 2114 Vogelenzang, Netherlands; Prefect of Studies Fr J. MANUEL TERCERO SIMÓN.

Studio Filosofico dell' 'Oratorio di San Filippo Neri': 1372 King St, W, Toronto, ON MGK 1H3, Canada.

Studio Filosofico del Seminario Patriarcale Latino di Gerusalemme: Séminaire Patriarchal Latin, POB 14152, Jerusalem, Israel; tel. (2) 2742612; fax (2) 2742885; e-mail adibz@latinseminary.org; Rector Fr ADIB ZOOMOT.

Studio Teologico del Seminario di Gerusalemme: Séminaire Patriarcal Latin, POB 14152, Jerusalem, Israel; tel. (2) 2742612; fax (2) 2742885; e-mail adibz@latinseminary.org; Rector Fr ADIB ZOOMOT; Prefect of Studies JAMAL KHADER.

Studio Teologico 'Studium Theologicum': CP 153, 80001-970 Curitiba, PR, Brazil;Ave. Presidente Getúlio Vargas 1193, 80250-180 Curitiba, PR, Brazil; Dir Rev. Fr JAIME SANCHEZ BOSCH.

INSTITUTES WITHIN THE PREMISES

Pontifical John Paul II Institute for Studies on Marriage and Family: Pres. HE Bishop RINO FISICHELLA.

Pontifical Pastoral Institute 'Redemptor Hominis': Piazza St Giovanni in Laterano 4, 00120 Rome, Italy; Pres. Mgr DARIO E. VIGANÒ.

PONTIFICIA UNIVERSITAS URBANIANA
(Pontifical Urbanian University)

Via Urbano VIII 16, 00165 Rome, Italy
Telephone: (6) 69889611
Fax: (6) 69881871
E-mail: segreteria@urbaniana.edu
Internet: www.urbaniana.edu
Founded 1627 by Pope Urban VIII
Language of instruction: Italian
Academic year: October to June
Chancellor: Cardinal FERNANDO FILONI
Vice-Chancellor: Mgr SAVIO HON TAI-FAI
Rector Magnificus: Rev. ALBERTO TREVISIOL
Vice-Rector: Rev. L. GODFREY ONAH
Sec.-Gen.: Rev. DON ROBERTO CHERUBINI
Librarian: Rev. Fr MAREK ROSTKOWSKI
Library of 400,000 vols
Number of teachers: 160 (incl. 50 full-time)
Number of students: 1,450
Publications: *Annales*, *Bibliografia Missionaria*, *Euntes Docete*, *IUS Missionale*, *Urbaniana*

DEANS

Faculty of Canon Law: Rev. Prof. ANDREA D'AURIA
Faculty of Missiology: Rev. Prof. BENEDICT KANAKAPALLY
Faculty of Philosophy: Rev. Prof. GUIDO MAZZOTTA
Faculty of Theology: Rev. Prof. FRANCESCO CICCIMARRA

PROFESSORS

Faculty of Canon Law:
  D'AURIA, A., General Norms
  MOSCA, V., Matrimony and Canon Law
  PAPALE, C., Oriental Canon Law
  SABBARESE, L., Matrimony and Canon Law
Faculty of Missiology:
  BARREDA, J., Ecumenism
  COLZANI, G., Missionary Systematic Theology
  DOTOLO, C., History and Phenomenology of Religions
  MAZZOLINI, S., Ecclesiology
  SCAIOLA, D., Scriptures
  TREVISIOL, A., History of Missions
Faculty of Philosophy:
  CONGIUNTI, L., Hermeneutics
  MAZZOTTA, G., Metaphysics
  NORECA, A., Logic, Philosophy of Knowledge
  ONAH, I. G., Methodology, Anthropology
  VENDEMIATI, A., General Ethics

Faculty of Theology:
  BIGUZZI, G., New Testament Exegesis
  CICCIMARRA, F., Canon Law
  DEIANA, G., Biblical Languages and Scriptures
  GONZALEZ FERNANDEZ, F., Church History
  PIRC, J., Ecclesiology
  RIZZI, G., Old Testament Exegesis
  ZUCCARO, C., Moral Theology

DIRECTORS

Affiliated Institutes: Rev. P. GIUSEPPE IULIANO
Chinese Study Centre: Rev. P. ALESSANDRO DELL'ORTO
Dept of Languages: Rev. FRANCESCO COCCO
Dept of Social Communication: LUCA PANDOLFI
Institute for Missionary Catechesis and Spirituality: Fr POMBO KYPOI
Institute for the Study of Atheism: Prof. ARDIAN NDRECA

UNIVERSITÀ PONTIFICIA SALESIANA
(Salesian Pontifical University)

Piazza Ateneo Salesiano 1, 00139 Rome, Italy
Telephone: (6) 872901
Fax: (6) 87290318
E-mail: segreteria@unisal.it
Internet: www.unisal.it
Founded 1940, univ. status granted by Pope Paul VI 1973
Language of instruction: Italian
Academic year: October to June (2 semesters)
Chancellor: Very Rev. PASCUAL CHÁVEZ VILLANUEVA
Rector: Very Rev. CARLO NANNI
Vice-Rector: Very Rev. GIANFRANCO COFFELE
Vice-Rector: Very Rev. MAURO MANTOVANI
Vice-Rector: Very Rev. VITO ORLANDO
Admin.: Very Rev. TULLIO ORLER
Sec.-Gen.: Very Rev. JAROSŁAW ROCHOWIAK
Librarian: Very Rev. GIUSEPPE TABARELLI
Library of 750,000 vols
Number of teachers: 284
Number of students: 4,218
Publications: *Orientamenti Pedagogici* (6 a year), *Salesianum* (4 a year)

DEANS

Department of Youth, Pastoral Theology and Catechetics: Very Rev. UBALDO MONTISCI
Faculty of Canon Law: Very Rev. JESU PUDUMAI DOSS
Faculty of Education: Very Rev. PAOLO GAMBINI
Faculty of Letters (Christian and Classics): Very Rev. MANLIO SODI
Faculty of Philosophy: Very Rev. LUIS ROSON GALACHE
Faculty of Social Communication Sciences: Very Rev. MAURO MANTOVANI
Faculty of Theology: Very Rev. ANTONIO CASTELLANO
Postgraduate School of Clinical Psychology: Prof. CARLA DE NITTO

PROFESSORS

Faculty of Canon Law (tel. (6) 87290639; fax (6) 87290258; e-mail diritto@unisal.it):
  ARDITO, S., Text of Canon Law
  GRAULICH, M., Foundation and History of Canon Law
  PUDUMAI DOSS, M. J., Canon Law
  URÍA, J., Text of Canon Law
Faculty of Education (tel. (6) 87290426; fax (6) 87290656; e-mail fse@unisal.it):
  BAY, M., Methodology of Research
  CANGIÀ, C., Pedagogy of Communication
  CASELLA, F., History of Pedagogy
  COLASANTI, A., Psychology

COMOGLIO, M., Didactics
CURSI, G., Sociology of Deviance
DE LUCA, M., Psychopathology
DE NITTO, C., Psychology
DE SOUZA, C., Anthropology and Catechesis
DELLAGIULIA, A., Developmental Psychology
DESBOUTS, C., Didactics
FORMELLA, Z., Psychology of Education
GAHUNGU, M., Pedagogic Methodology
GAMBINI, P., General Psychology
GRZADZIEL, D., General Pedagogy
LLANOS, M., Pedagogic Methodology
MASTROMARINO, R., Psychology
MESSANA, C., Psychology
MONTISCI, U., Theology of Education
MORAL DE LA PARTE, J., Religious Pedagogy
NANNI, C., Philosophy of Education
ORLANDO, V., Social Pedagogy
PASTORE, C., Bible and Catechesis
QUINZI, G., Pedagogical Methodology
ROGGIA, G., Pedagogical Methodology
SCHIETROMA, S., Psychology
TOGNACCI, S., Psychobiology and Physiological Psychology
VALLABARAJ, J., Catechesis
VETTORATO, G., Sociology of Deviance
WIERZBICKI, M., Religious Pedagogy
ZANNI, N., Didactics

Faculty of Letters (Christian and Classics) (tel. (6) 87290304; fax (6) 87290641; e-mail lettere@ups.urbe.it):
  BOLOGNA, O., Ancient Greek Literature
  BRACCHI, R., History of the Greek And Latin Language
  FILACCHIONE, P., Archeology
  SAJOVIC, M., Ancient Christian Latin Literature
  SODI, M., Medieval Latin Literature
  SPATARO, R., Ancient Christian Greek Literature

Faculty of Philosophy (tel. (6) 87290625; fax (6) 87290640; e-mail filosofia@unisal.it):
  ABBÀ, G., Ethics
  ALESSI, A., Metaphysics
  FRENI, C., Linguistics and Rhetoric
  KUREETHADAM, J., Philosophy of Science
  KURUVACHIRA, J., Philosophical Anthropology
  MANTOVANI, M., Metaphysics
  MARIN, M., History of Ancient Philosophy
  ROSON GALACHE, L., Philosophical Anthropology
  THURUTHIYIL, S., History of Modern Philosophy

Faculty of Social Communication Sciences (tel. (6) 87290331; fax (6) 87290536; e-mail fsc@unisal.it; internet fscs.ups.urbe.it):
  ALVATI, C., Theory and Technics of Media
  CASSANELLI, E., Theory and Technics of Media
  CEPEDA, E., Theory and Research of Social Communication
  DEVADOSS, J., Theory of Social Communication
  GONSALVES, P., Theory and History of Social Communication
  LEVER, F., Theory and Technics of Television
  LEWICKI, T., Theory and Technics of Theatre
  PASQUALETTI, F., Theory and Technics of Radio
  PRESERN, V., Theory and Research of Social Communication

Faculty of Theology (tel. (6) 87290297; fax (6) 87290556; e-mail teologia@unisal.it):
  ANTHONY, F., Pastoral Theology
  ARNAULD, D., History of the Church
  BALDACCI, A., Liturgy
  BESSO, C., Patrology
  BIANCARDI, G., Catechesis
  BOZZOLO, A., Dogmatics
  CABANAS, V., Old Testament

CAPUTA, G., Fundamental Theology
CARELLI, R., Dogmatics
CARLOTTI, P., Moral Theology
CASTELLANO, A., Dogmatics
CHUNKAPURA, J., Missiology
COFFELE, G., Fundamental Theology
ESCUDERO CABELLO, A., Dogmatics
FERNANDO, R., Canon Law
FERNANDO, S., Moral Theology
FISSORE, M., Spiritual Theology
FRIGATO, S., Moral Theology
GARCÍA, J., Spiritual Theology
GIANAZZA, P., Dogmatics
GIRAUDO, A., Spiritual Theology
GRACH, P., Dogmatics
KRASON, F., Liturgy
MARCHIS, M., Canon Law
MARITANO, M., Ancient Church History and
    Patristics
MEDEIROS DE SANTOS, D., Liturgy
MERLO, P., Moral Theology
MULE STAGNO, A., Liturgy
MUSONI, A., Ecclesiology and Ecumenism
ONI, S., History of the Church
PALOMBELLA, M., Dogmatics
PLASCENCIA, J., Dogmatics
PULIANMACKAL, B., Moral Theology
ROSSETTI, M., New Testament
RUSSELL POLLOCK, W., Dogmatics
SARBINOWSKI, M., Fundamental Theology
VICENT, R., Old Testament
WYCKOFF, E., New Testament

SALESIAN HOUSE THEOLOGICAL STUDIES, VIETNAM

Centre Saint-Augustin: Villa Contiguë au
Village S.O.S., BP 15222, Dakar-Fann, Senegal; Dean Very Rev. CHRISTIAN CARLIER.

**Département de Philosophie de l'Insti-
tut Catholique de l'Afrique Centrale:** BP
11628, Yaoundé, Cameroon; Dean Rev.
KIZITO FORBI.

**Departamento de Filosofía del Instituto
de Teología para Religiosos:** 3A Avda con
6A Transversal (H. B. Pinto), Apdo 68865
Altamira, Caracas 1062-A, Venezuela; Dean
Rev. CARLOS LUIS SUÁREZ CODORNIÚ.

**Institut de Philosophie 'Saint-Joseph-
Mukasa':** Nkol-Bisson, BP 185, Yaoundé,
Cameroon; Dean Rev. KRZYSZTOF ZIELENDA.

**Institut de Theologie Saint François de
Sales Lubumbashi:** Congo; tel. and fax
(243) 970-176-94; e-mail theosdb_lubum@
yahoo.com; Pres. Prof. JEAN-LUC VANDE KER-
KHOVE.

Instituto 'Santo Tomás de Aquino': Rua
Itutinga 300-B, Minas Brasil, 30535-640 Belo
Horizonte, MG, Brazil; Dean Very Rev.
PAULO ROBERTO GOMES.

**Instituto Superior de Ciencias Reli-
gioses 'Don Bosco':** Avda Card. Vidal i
Barraquer 1, 08035 Barcelona, Spain; Dean
Very Rev. JORDI LA TORRE I CASTILLO.

**Instituto Superior de Estudios Teologi-
cos 'Cristo Buen Pastor' (ISET):** Hipólito
Yrigoyen 3951, 1208 Buenos Aires, Argenti-
nia; Dir Very Rev. JUAN PICCA.

**Instituto de Teología para Religiosos–
ITER:** 3A Avda con 6A Transversal (H. B.
Pinto), Apdo 68865 Altamira, Caracas 1062-
A, Venezuela; Dean Rev. CARLOS LUIS SUÁREZ
CODORNIÚ.

Instituto Teológico Pio XI: Rua Pio XI,
1100–Alto da Lapa, 05060-001 São Paulo,
Brazil; tel. (11) 364-902-00; fax (11) 383-185-
74; e-mail secretaria@institutoteologico.org
.br; Pres. Prof. RONALDO ZACHARIAS.

**Instituto Teológico Salesiano 'Cristo
Resucitado' Tlaquepaque:** Apdo. POB 66,
45500, San Pedro Tlaquepaque, Messico; tel.
(3) 657-45-55; fax (3) 635-54-54; e-mail
teologia_its@yahoo.com.mx; Pres. SERGIO DE
LA CRUZ LOERA.

**Instituto Universitario Salesiano 'Padre
Ojeda':** Avda El Liceo, Apdo 43, Los Teques,
1201-A Venezuela; Dean Very Rev. JULIÁN
RODRÍGUEZ V.

**Philosophische-Theologische
Hochschule der Salesianer:** Don Bosco-
Str. 1, 83671 Benediktbeuern, Germany;
Rector Very Rev. LOTHAR BILY.

**Salesian House Philosophical Studies,
Nave:** Centro di Studi 'Paolo VI', Via S.
Giovanni Bosco 1, 25075 Nave, Italy; Dean
Very Rev. PAOLO ZINI.

**Salesian House Philosophical Studies,
Santiago:** Avda Lo Cañas 3636, Casilla 53,
La Florida, Santiago, Chile; Dean Very Rev.
NILO DAMIÁN ZÁRATE LÓPEZ.

**Salesian House Theological Studies,
Bangalore:** Kristu Jyoti College, Bosco
Nagar, Krishnarajapuram, Bangalore
560036, India; Dean Very Rev. ANTON PAUL
PADINJARATHALA.

**Salesian House Theological Studies
'Don Bosco', Manila:** POB 8206, CPO
1700, Parañaque City, Metro Manila, Philippines; Dean Very Rev. RAFAEL DELA CRUZ.

**Salesian House Theological Studies,
Guatemala:** 20 Avda 13–45, Zona 11, Gua-
temala City, Guatemala 01011, CA; Dean
Very Rev. FÉLIX VALLEJOS.

**Salesian House Theological Studies,
Meghalaya:** Sacred Heart Theological Col-
lege, Mawlai, Shillong 793008, Meghalaya,
India; Dean Very Rev. JOSEPH PUYKUNNEL.

**Salesian House Theological Studies,
'Saints Peter and Paul', Jerusalem:** St
Paul, 26 Rehov Shmuel Hanagid St, POB
7336, 91072 Jerusalem, Israel; Dean Very
Rev. ROBERTO SPATARO.

**Salesian House for Theological Studies
'S. Tommaso d'Aquino', Messina:** Via del
Pozzo 43–CP 28, 98121 Messina, Italy; Dean
Very Rev. GIOVANNI RUSSO.

Salesian Institute of Philosophy: Divya
Daan, Don Bosco Marg, College Rd, Nasik
422005, India; Dean Very Rev. ROBERT PEN.

Colleges

ATHENAEUM PONTIFICIUM REGINA APOSTOLORUM

Via degli Aldobrandeschi 190, 00163 Rome,
    Italy
Telephone: (6) 66527800
Fax: (6) 66527814
E-mail: segreteria@upra.org
Internet: www.upra.org
Founded 1993

Rector: Fr PAOLO SCARAFONI
Sec.-Gen.: Fr LUCA MARIA GALLIZIA

DEANS

Faculty of Bioethics: Fr GONZALO MIRANDA
Faculty of Philosophy: Fr MICHAEL RYAN
Faculty of Theology: Fr THOMAS WILLIAMS

PONTIFICIA FACOLTÀ DI SCIENZE DELL'EDUCAZIONE 'AUXILIUM'

Via Cremolino 141, 00166 Rome, Italy
Telephone: (6) 6157201
Fax: (6) 61564640
E-mail: segreteria@pfse-auxilium.org
Internet: www.pfse-auxilium.org
Founded 1954
Language of instruction: Italian
Academic year: October to July
Grand Chancellor: Dr PASCUAL CHAVEZ VIL-
    LANUEVA
Vice-Grand Chancellor: YVONNE REUNGOAT

Decan: GIUSEPPINA DEL CORE
Sec.-Gen.: M. GIOVANNA CERUTI
Librarian: MARIA ANTONIETTA VALENTINO
Library of 110,000 vols, 1,000 periodicals of
    which 574 are currently active
Number of teachers: 59
Number of students: 430

Publication: *Rivista di Scienze dell' Educa-
    zione* (3 a year).

PONTIFICIA FACOLTÀ TEOLOGICA SAN BONAVENTURA

Via del Serafico 1, 00142 Rome, Italy
Telephone: (6) 5192007
Fax: (6) 5192067
E-mail: segreteria@seraphicum.org
Internet: www.seraphicum.org
Founded 1587, re-founded 1905
Grand Chancellor: Most Rev. MARCO TASCA
Pres.: Rev. Fr DOMENICO PAOLETTI
Vice-Pres.: Rev. Fr GERMANO SCAGLIONI
Sec.: Rev. Fr JUAN MIGUEL VICENTE
Librarian: Rev. Fr EMIL KUMKA
Library of 250,000 vols
Number of teachers: 51
Number of students: 289

Publication: *Miscellanea Francescana* (2 a
    year).

PONTIFICIA FACOLTÀ TEOLOGICA 'MARIANUM'

Viale Trenta Aprile 6, 00153 Rome, Italy
Telephone: (6) 58391601
Fax: (6) 5880292
E-mail: marianum@marianum.it
Internet: www.marianum.it
Founded 1950
Academic year: October to July
Grand Chancellor: Rev. Fr ÁNGEL M. RUIZ
    GARNICA
Pres.: Rev. Fr SALVATORE M. PERRELLA
Sec.: Sis. ORNELLA DI ANGELO
Library of 110,000 vols on Mariological stud-
    ies
Number of teachers: 45
Number of students: 205

Publication: *Marianum* (2 a year).

PONTIFICIA FACOLTÀ TEOLOGICA TERESIANUM

Piazza San Pancrazio 5A, 00152 Rome, Italy
Telephone: (6) 58540248
Fax: (6) 58540243
E-mail: segreteria@teresianum.org
Internet: www.teresianum.org
Founded 1935
Academic year: October to June
Grand Chancellor: Most Rev. Fr LUIS AROS-
    TEGUI GAMBOA
Pres.: Fr VIRGILIO PASQUETTO
Sec.-Gen.: Fr ADRIAN ATTARD
Librarian: Fr ARTURO BELTRAN
Library of 500,000 vols (open to the public)
Number of teachers: 51
Number of students: 450

Publications: *Bibliographia Internationalis
    Spiritualitatis, Studia Theologica, Teresia-
    num* (specialist review, 2 a year).

ATTACHED INSTITUTE

Pontificio Istituto di Spiritualità: f. 1957;
30 teachers; 300 students; centre for bibliographical research in field of spiritual theology; Moderator Fr BENITO GOYA.

PONTIFICIO ATENEO ST ANSELMO

Piazza Cavalieri di Malta 5, 00153 Rome, Italy

Telephone: (6) 5791401
Fax: (6) 5791402
E-mail: segreteria@santanselmo.org
Internet: www.santanselmo.org
Founded 1687
Language of instruction: Italian
Academic year: October to June
Grand Chancellor: Most Rev. Fr NOTKER WOLF
Rector Magnificus: Rev. Fr MARK SHERIDAN
Registrar: Rev. Fr STEFANO VISINTIN
Librarian: Rev. Fr JAMES LEACHMAN
Treas.: Rev. Fr GERARDO GAREGNANI

Library of 131,000 vols
Number of teachers: 78
Number of students: 423

Publications: *Corpus Consuetudinum Monasticarum*, *Ecclesia Orans* (Liturgical Inst. Review), *Rerum Ecclesiasticarum Documenta* (Critical Editions of Liturgical Texts), *Studia Anselmiana*

DEANS

Faculty of Philosophy: Rev. Mons. ANICETO MOLINARO
Faculty of Theology: Rev. Fr DANIEL HOMBERGEN
Pontifical Liturgical Institute: Rev. Fr JUAN JAVIER FLORES ARCAS

PONTIFICIO ATENEO ANTONIA

Via Merulana 124, 00185 Rome, Italy

Telephone: (6) 70373502
Fax: (6) 70373604
E-mail: segreteriapaa@ofm.org
Internet: www.antonianum.ofm.org
Founded 1933
Franciscan Int. Univ.
Grand Chancellor: Most Rev. J. RODRÍGUEZ CARBALLO
Rector Magnificus: Rev. Fr JOHANNES B. FREYER
Vice-Rector: Rev. P. MANUEL BLANCO
Sec.-Gen.: Rev. Fr JORGE HORTA
Librarian: Rev. Fr MARCELLO SARDELLI

Library of 500,000 vols

Number of professors: 145

Publication: *Antonianum*

DEANS

Faculty of Biblical Science and Archaeology: Rev. Fr GIOVANNI C. BOTTINI
Faculty of Canon Law: Rev. Fr PRIAMO ETZI
Faculty of Philosophy: Rev. Fr STÉPHANE OPPES
Faculty of Theology: Rev. Fr VINCENZO BATTAGLIA

DIRECTORS

Higher Institute of Religious Studies: Sr M. MELONE
Higher School of Medieval and Franciscan Studies: Rev. Fr A. CACCIOTTI
Institute of Ecumenical Studies: Rev. Fr R. GIRALDO
Institute of Spirituality: Rev. Fr P. MARTINELLI

PONTIFICIO ISTITUTO DI ARCHEOLOGIA CRISTIANA

Via Napoleone III 1, 00185 Rome, Italy

Telephone: (6) 4465574
Fax: (6) 4469197
E-mail: piac@piac.it
Internet: www.piac.it
Founded 1925 by Pope Pius XI
Academic year: November to May

Grand Chancellor: Bishop ZENON GROCHOLEWSKI
Rector: Prof. VINCENZO FIOCCHI NICOLAI
Sec.: Dr OLOF BRANDT
Librarian and Prefect of Collns: Dr GIORGIO NESTORI

Library of 60,000 vols
Number of teachers: 8
Number of students: 80

Publications: *Inscriptiones Christianae Urbis Romae*, *Monumenti di Antichità Cristiana*, *Rivista di Archeologia Cristiana*, *Roma Sotterranea Cristiana*, *Studi di Antichità Cristiana*, *Sussidi allo Studio delle Antichità Cristiane*

PROFESSORS

BISCONTI, F., Christian Iconography
DATTRINO, L., Patristics
FIOCCHI NICOLAI, V., Christian Cemeteries and Topography of Ancient Rome
GUIDOBALDI, F., Ancient Sacred Architecture
HEID, S., Hagiography and Liturgy of the Early Church
MAZZOLENI, D., Classical and Christian Epigraphy
PERGOLA, PH., 'Orbis Christianus' and Classical Topography
RAMIERI, A. M., Art History
SPERA, L., Christian Topography of Rome

PONTIFICIO ISTITUTO DI MUSICA SACRA

Via di Torre Rossa 21, 00165 Rome, Italy

Telephone: (6) 6638792
Fax: (6) 6622453
E-mail: pims@musica-sacra.va
Internet: www.vatican.va
Founded 1911 by Pope Pius X
Language of instruction: Italian
Academic year: October to June
Grand Chancellor: HE Rev. Mgr ZENON GROCHOLEWSKI
Pres.: Mgr VALENTINO MISERACHS GRAU
Sec.: Dott. GIUSEPPE MORETTI
Librarian: Dott. ANTONIO ADDAMIANO

Library of 40,000 vols
Number of teachers: 18
Number of students: 141

Publication: *Calendar* (1 a year).

PONTIFICIO ISTITUTO ORIENTALE (Pontifical Oriental Institute)

Piazza Santa Maria Maggiore 7, 00185 Rome, Italy

Telephone: (6) 4474170
Fax: (6) 4465576
E-mail: piosgr@pio.urbe.it
Internet: www.pio.urbe.it
Founded 1917 by Pope Benedict XV for the benefit of Eastern and Western scholars both Catholic and non-Catholic, interested in Oriental ecclesiastical questions
Associated with the Pontifical Gregorian University (see above)
Rector: Rev. Prof. JAMES M. MCCANN
Gen. Sec.: MAURIZIO DOMENICUCCI
Librarian: Rev. FRANÇOIS GICK

Library of 185,000 vols
Number of teachers: 77
Number of students: 372

Publications: *Anaphorae Orientales*, *Kanonika*, *Orientalia Christiana Analecta*, *Orientalia Christiana Periodica*

DEANS

Faculty of Oriental Canon Law: Rev. Prof. MICHAEL J. KUCHERA
Faculty of Oriental Ecclesiastical Studies: Rev. Prof. JAMES M. MCCANN

PROFESSORS

ARRANZ, L. M., Oriental Liturgy
CECCARELLI MOROLLI, D., Oriental Canon Law
FARRUGIA, E., Oriental Theology
GARGANO, G., Oriental Patrology
GIRAUDO, C., Liturgy and Dogmatic Theology
LUISIER, P., Coptic Patrology and Language
NEDUNGATT, G., Oriental Canon Law
RUGGERI, V., Byzantine History and Archaeology
SENYK, S., Ukrainian Church History
SIMON, C., Slavic History
TAFT, R., Byzantine Liturgy
VALL VILARDELL, H., Ecumenism
VASIL, C., Oriental Canon Law
YOUSSIF, P., Syriac Patrology
ŽUŽEK, I., Oriental Canon Law

PONTIFICIO ISTITUTO DI STUDI ARABI E D'ISLAMISTICA

Viale di Trastevere 89, 00153 Rome, Italy

Telephone: (6) 58392611
Fax: (6) 5882595
E-mail: info@pisai.it
Founded 1949
Academic year: October to June
Dir: Fr MIGUEL ÁNGEL AYUSO GUIXOT
Librarian: Fr PIET HORSTEN

Library of 32,500 vols
Number of teachers: 10
Number of students: 52

Publications: *Encounter* (Documents for Christian–Muslim Understanding, 10 a year), *Etudes Arabes* (1 a year), *Islamochristiana* (1 a year).

PONTIFICIUM INSTITUTUM BIBLICUM

Via della Pilotta 25, 00187 Rome, Italy

Telephone: (6) 695261
Fax: (6) 695266211
E-mail: pibsegr@biblico.it
Internet: www.biblico.it
Founded 1909 by Pope Pius X for scriptural studies, Faculty of Ancient Oriental Studies added 1932, Pontifical Biblical Institute of Jerusalem (f. 1927), br. of Roman Institute
Associated with the Pontifical Gregorian Univ. (see above)
Languages of instruction: Italian, English
Academic year: October to June
Rector: Rev. JOSÉ MARIA ABREGO DE LACY
Sec.: CARLO VALENTINO
Librarian: Rev. J. JANSSENS

Number of teachers: 40
Number of students: 300

Library of 165,000 vols

Publications: *Acta Pont. Inst. Biblici* (1 a year), *Analecta Biblica*, *Analecta Orientalia*, *Biblica* (4 a year), *Biblica et Orientalia*, *Elenchus of Biblica* (1 a year), *Orientalia* (4 a year), *Studia Pohl*, *Subsidia Biblica*

DEANS

Faculty of Ancient Oriental Studies: Rev. A. GIANTO
Faculty of Biblical Studies: Rev. S. PISANO

PROFESSORS

Faculty of Ancient Oriental Studies:
ALTHANN, R., Languages and Literature of Ancient Israel
GIANTO, A., Semitic Philology and Linguistics
MAYER, W., Accadian Language and Literature
MORRISON, C., Syriac and Targumic-Aramaic Languages

Faculty of Biblical Studies:

ALETTI, J.-N., New Testament Exegesis
BARBIERO, G., Old Testament Exegesis
BECHARD, D., New Testament Exegesis
BOVATI, P., Old Testament Exegesis
LUZARRAGA, J., New Testament Exegesis
NEUDECKER, R., Rabbinic Literature
PISANO, S., Textual Criticism
SIEVERS, J., History and Literature of the
Intertestamental Period

SKA, J. L., Old Testament Exegesis

Schools

Scuola Vaticana di Biblioteconomia
(Vatican School of Library Services): 00120
Vatican City; tel. (6) 69879526; fax (6)
69879525; e-mail scuola@vatlib.it; internet
www-urbs.vatlib.it/scuola; f. 1934; attached

to Vatican Apostolic Library; 6 teachers; 48
students a year; Dir Prof. Don RAFFAELE
FARINA.

Scuola Vaticana di Paleografia, Diplomatica e Archivistica (Vatican School of
Paleography, Diplomacy and Archive Science): 00120 Vatican City; tel. (6) 69883595;
fax (6) 69881377; e-mail asv@asv.va;
attached to Papal Archives; Dir SERGIO
PAGANO; publ. *Littera Antiqua*.

VENEZUELA

The Higher Education System

Institutions of higher education predate Venezuela's independence from Spain in 1830, the oldest being Universidad Central de Venezuela, which was founded in 1721. The next oldest institution is Universidad de los Andes, which was founded in 1785 (current status 1810). The Ministry of Higher Education has supreme authority over higher education, which consists of public and private universities, polytechnic institutes and an 'open' university (for distance-learning and continuing education). In 2003/04 there were 48 universities with 626,837 students. In the same year there were an estimated 120 other higher education institutions, with an estimated combined enrolment of 447,513 students. Legislation approved in December 2010 that would have increased government control over several key areas of the public and private university systems was rescinded in January 2011 following widespread popular criticism over the perceived challenge to universities' autonomy. Much of the criticism levelled against the legislation centred on its proposed concentration of power in the Minister of Higher Education.

The main requirement for admission to higher education is the Bachillerato, the secondary school certificate. In 2009 the government passed a law to establish a national standardized university entrance examination system, replacing public universities' internal entrance examinations. However, some universities have rejected the new system. There are two levels of undergraduate qualifications: carreras cortas (short-cycle degrees) and carreras largas (long-cycle degrees). The former last between two and three years and lead to award of the Título de Técnico Superior Universitario (Title of Higher University Technician). Long-cycle degrees typically last five years, although a few programmes, including medicine, last upwards of six years, and lead to award of the Licenciatura or a professional title. Following this, graduates may study for a further year for the Título de Especialista, which indicates specialization in a particular area or subject. Alternatively, graduates may study for the Maestría (Masters) degree, a two-year course of study culminating with the submission of a thesis. Finally, the highest university degree is the Doctorado (Doctorate), a research-based degree usually lasting three years following the award of either the Maestría or Especialización.

The Instituto Nacional de Cooperación Educativa, an autonomous agency under the Ministry of Education, is the national agency responsible for the provision of technical and vocational education. Post-secondary technical and vocational education is offered by institutos universitarios de tecnología (technological institutes) and colegios universitarios (university colleges), but the qualifications are regarded as sub-degree level. The main qualification is the Técnico Superior, a three-year course comprising mostly of practical study.

There is currently no external agency that accredits undergraduate programmes, although the Consejo Nacional de Universidades (National Council of Universities) maintains a register of authorized degree programmes. All postgraduate programmes are subject to accreditation by the Consejo Consultivo Nacional de Postgrado (National Graduate Advisory Council), an independent accreditation body established by the Ministry of Education.

Regulatory and Representative Bodies

GOVERNMENT

Ministry of Culture: Edif. Archivo General de la Nación, Avda Panteón, Foro Libertador, Caracas; tel. (212) 509-56-00; e-mail mppc@ministeriodelacultura.gob.ve; internet www.ministeriodelacultura.gob.ve; Minister FRANCISCO SESTO.

Ministry of Education: Edif. Ministerio de Educación, Mezzanina, esq. de Salas, Parroquia Altagracia, Caracas, 1010; tel. (212) 506-8211; e-mail atencion_al_publico@me.gob.ve; internet www.me.gov.ve; Minister HÉCTOR NAVARRO.

Ministry of Higher Education: Torre MCT, 6°, Avda Universidad, esq. el Chorro, Caracas 1010; tel. (212) 596-5293; e-mail enlacesmes@mes.gov.ve; internet www.mes.gov.ve; Minister LUIS AUGUSTO ACUÑA CEDEÑO.

NATIONAL BODIES

Asociación Venezolana de Rectores Universitarios (AVERU) (Venezuelan Association of University Rectors): Avda Santa Fe Sur, Edif. 'Araucaria', Piso 4°-43, Urb. Santa Fe, Caracas; tel. (212) 975-14-62; fax (212) 979-92-63; Pres. RITA AÑEZ.

Consejo Nacional de Universidades (National Council of Universities): Avda La Salle, Centro Capriles P. B., Caracas; tel. (212) 709-1200; e-mail webmaster@cnu.gov.ve; internet www.cnu.gov.ve/informacion/cnu.php; f. 1946; consists of staff and student reps of all univs and reps from the Ministry of Finance and the Science Council; coordinates academic relations within the higher education system and fosters links between the univs and the remainder of the nat. educational system; establishes academic, cultural and scientific policies in the higher education sector and stipulates its devt; suggests to the Nat. Exec. regulations concerning the recognition of studies and qualifications; proposes to the Nat. Exec. the annual univ. budget and distributes funding to nat. univs; library of 2,000 vols; Pres. THE MINISTER OF HIGHER EDUCATION; Perm. Sec. ASALIA VENEGAS SIMANCAS; publ. *Boletín Informativo* (4 a year).

Learned Societies

GENERAL

Academia Venezolana de la Lengua (Venezuelian Academy of Language): Apdo 1421, Caracas; Palacio de las Academias, Av. Universidad, Caracas 1010-A; tel. (212) 481-2890; fax (212) 481-2890; e-mail acadlengv@cantv.net; f. 1883; corresp. of the Real Academia Española (Madrid, Spain); 24 mems; library: see Libraries and Archives; Pres. OSCAR SAMBRANO URDANETA; Sec. HORACIO BIORD CASTILLO; publs *Boletín* (4 a year), *Clásicos Venezolanos*.

ARCHITECTURE AND TOWN PLANNING

Asociación de Agrimensores de Venezuela (Surveyors' Association): c/o Colegio de Ingenieros de Venezuela, Apdo 2006, Bosque Los Caobos, Caracas 1010; Pres. Agm. GERMÁN AÑEZ OTERO; Sec. Agm. RAFAEL ELSTER NODA.

Colegio de Arquitectos de Venezuela (Venezuela Architects' Association): C. C. Casa Mall en Los Naranjos, El Cafetal, Caracas; tel. (212) 988-1331; internet cav.org.ve; f. 1945 as Sociedad Venezolana de Arquitectos; 3,600 mems; Pres. Arq. ITALO BALBI; Sec. Arq. HENRY SAAD; publ. *Revista del CAV*.

BIBLIOGRAPHY, LIBRARY SCIENCE AND MUSEOLOGY

Colegio de Bibliotecólogos y Archivólogos de Venezuela (Venezuelan Librarians' and Archivists' Association): Parroquia Altagracia, Avda Panteón, Foro Libertador, Biblioteca Nacional, Cuerpo 2, S1, Caracas; tel. (212) 564-1203; fax (212) 564-1203; e-mail cbiarchiv@hotmail.com; internet personales.com/venezuela/caracas/cbav; f. 1989; 419 mems; Pres. Lic. ELSI JIMENEZ DE DÍAZ; Vice-Pres. Lic. FLOR MARINA LUNA; publs *AB Te Informa* (4 a year), *CBActualidad* (irregular).

ECONOMICS, LAW AND POLITICS

Academia de Ciencias Políticas y Sociales (Academy of Political and Social Sciences): Palacio de las Academias, Bolsa a San Francisco, Caracas 1010; tel. (212) 481-6035; fax (212) 483-2674; e-mail acienpol@cantv.net; internet www.acienpol.org.ve; f. 1915; 35 mems; library of 12 vols; Pres. Dr ENRIQUE LAGRANGE; Sec. GABRIEL RUAN SANTOS; Chief Librarian BEATRIZ MARTÍNEZ; publ. *Boletín de la Academia*.

Colegio de Abogados del Distrito Capital (Lawyers' Association): Apdo Postal 1060, Caracas; Av. Veracruz, Edif. Keope, Piso 1, Of. 15-B, Las Mercedes, Caracas; tel. (212) 991-98-45; e-mail secretaria@justicia .net; internet www.justicia.net; f. 1788; 2,000 mems; Pres. Abog. RAFAEL VELOZ GARCIA; Sec. Abog. ROSAURA SÁNCHEZ; publ. *Revista*.

EDUCATION

Grupo Universitario Latinoamericano de Estudio para la Reforma y el Perfeccionamiento de la Educación (GULERPE) (Latin American University Group for Reform and Improvement in Education): Residencias Araucaria, Apdo 43, Santa Fe Sur, Caracas 1080-150; Piso 4, Avda Santa Fe Sur, Santa Fe, Caracas 1080-150; tel. (212) 979-9263; fax (212) 979-9263; internet www.universitas2000.usb.ve; f. 1965; higher education, research, and educational policy, administration and planning; 150 mems; Pres. Dra ELIZABETH Y. DE CALDERA; Exec. Sec. Prof. FELIPE BEZARA; publ. *Universitas 2000* (in single or double editions, 4 a year).

FINE AND PERFORMING ARTS

Asociación Venezolana Amigos del Arte Colonial (Venezuelan Association of Friends of Colonial Art): Museo de Arte Colonial, Quinta de 'Anauco', Avda Panteón, San Bernardino, Caracas 1011; tel. (212) 551-8517; fax (212) 551-8517; e-mail artecolonialanauco@cantv.net; internet www .quintadeanauco.org.ve; f. 1942; preservation and collection of architectural forms, bronze, ceramics, glass, iron, music, period furniture, paintings, porcelain, silver, sculpture, textiles from the 16th–18th centuries; Pres. JUAN CARLOS SOSA; Dir CARLOS F. DUARTE; publ. *Revista*.

Consejo Nacional de la Cultura (CONAC) (National Cultural Council): Torre Norte, Pisos 12–16, Centro Simón Bolívar, Apdo 50995, Caracas; tel. (212) 483-4980; e-mail directorgeneral@conac.gov.ve; internet www.conac.gov.ve; f. 1990 for the planning, promotion, dissemination and formation of human resources in the fields of cinema and folklore music, dancing, historic and artistic resources, literature, libraries, museums, plastic arts, theatre; Pres. Dr FRANCISCO SESTO NOVAS; Dir-Gen. SILVIA DÍAZ ALVARADO; Sec. GUSTAVO ARNSTEIN; publs *Revista de Cine 'ENCUADRE'* (4 a year), *Revista 'IMAGEN'* (12 a year), *Revista Nacional de Cultura* (4 a year).

Attached Foundation:

Fundación de Etnomusicología y Folklore del CONAC (Foundation for Ethnomusicology and Folklore): Apdo 81015, Caracas 1080; f. 1990; consists of: Instituto Nacional de Folklore (INAF, f. 1950), Instituto Interamericano de Etnomusicología y Folklore (INIDEF, f. 1970), Museo Nacional de Folklore (f. 1971), Centro Interamericano de Etnomusicología y Folklore (CIDEF, f. 1973) for the OAS Regional Development Programme; aims to preserve and protect the American cultural heritage; annual courses in ethnomusicology, folklore, handicrafts, ethnohistory, anthropolinguistic studies; PRA/OAS scholarships; archive of ethnomusic, slides and photographs; library of 2,700 vols, 308 periodicals; Dir Dra ISABEL ARETZ; publ. *Anuario FUNDEF*.

Instituto Zuliano de la Cultura 'Andrés E. Blanco': Gobernación del Estado Zulia, Academia de Bellas Artes 'Neptali Rincón', Maracaibo; f. 1972; administers all the cultural institutes in the state; Dir CARMEN DELGADO PEÑA; Administrator DOMINGO GUZMÁN RAMOS.

HISTORY, GEOGRAPHY AND ARCHAEOLOGY

Academia de Historia del Táchira: Casa Bolivariana, Calle 4 entre carreras 3 y 4, San Cristóbal, Estado Táchira; f. 1942; Pres. Dr ROBERTO ESTEBAN AVENDAÑO; Sec. Lic. JOSÉ ERNESTO BECERRA GOLINDANO; publ. *Boletín*.

Academia de Historia del Zulia: Calle 95 esquina con Av. 5, Sector Plaza Bolívar, al lado del Palacio de Gobierno del Zulia, Maracaibo, Estado Zulia; tel. (261) 725-1194; e-mail academiadehistoriadelzulia@ gmail.com; internet www .academiahistoriazulia.com; f. 1940; 25 mems; Pres. ALFREDO RINCÓN RINCÓN; Vice-Pres. JESÚS A. SEMPRÚN PARRA; Sec. ANTONIO MÁRQUEZ MORALES; Librarian NEVI ORTÍN DE MEDINA.

Academia Nacional de la Historia (National Academy of History): Palacio de las Academias, Bolsa a San Francisco, Caracas 1010; tel. (212) 482-6720; fax (212) 482-6720; e-mail anhistoria@cantv.net; internet www.acadnachistoria.org; f. 1888; library: see Libraries and Archives; Dir RAFAEL FERNÁNDEZ HERES; Sec. MARIANELA PONCE; publs *Boletín*, *Memorias*.

Centro de Historia Larense (Lara Historical Centre): Carrera 17 frente a la Plaza Lara, Barquisimeto, Distrito Iribarren; f. 1941; 12 mems; library of 1,000 vols; publ. *Boletín*.

Centro Histórico Sucrense (Historical Centre): Cumaná; f. 1945; 24 national and 14 foreign corresp. mems; Dir R. P. Fray CAYETANO DE CARROCERA; Sec.-Gen. Br. ALBERTO SANABRIA; publ. *Boletín*.

Junta Nacional Protectora y Conservadora del Patrimonio Histórico y Artístico de la Nación (Commission for the Protection and Preservation of the Historical and Artistic Heritage of the Nation): Palacio de Miraflores, Avda Urdaneta, Caracas; there is a subsidiary office in each State; authorizes exploration and excavation of sites; mems are nominated by the Government for 5-year terms, and may be re-elected; Dir Dr RAFAEL ARMANDO ROJAS.

Sociedad Bolivariana de Venezuela (Bolivar Society): San Jacinto a Traposos, Urb. Catedral, Caracas; tel. (212) 545-7271; f. 1938; to promote by all available media the knowledge of Simón Bolívar's life and works, as well as his political, cultural and social ideas; publishes about 15,000 volumes of historical works per year; 300 mems; library of 6,000 vols; Pres. Gral CANDIDO PEREZ MENDEZ; Sec. Gral ADOLFO ROMERO LUENGO; publ. *Revista*.

LANGUAGE AND LITERATURE

Alliance Française: Av. Mohedano entre 1A y 2A Transversal, Quinta Wilmarú, Urb La Castellana, Caracas; tel. (212) 264-4611; fax (212) 267-3470; e-mail castellana@afcaracas .org; internet www.afcaracas.org; offers courses and exams in French language and culture and promotes cultural exchange with France; attached teaching centres in Barquisimeto, Maracaibo, Margarita, Mérida and Valencia.

British Council: Torre Credicard, Piso 3, Avda Principal de El Bosque, Chacaíto, Caracas 1050; tel. (212) 952-9965; fax (212) 952-9691; e-mail information@britishcouncil .org.ve; internet www.britishcouncil.org/es/ venezuela; teaching centre; offers courses and exams in English language and British culture and promotes cultural exchange with the UK; Dir BARBARA WICKHAM.

Goethe-Institut: Avda Juan Germán Roscio, cruce con Avda Jorge Washington, Qta. 'Asociación Cultural Humboldt', San Bernardino, Apdo 60501, Caracas 1060; tel. (212) 552-6445; fax (212) 552-5621; e-mail sekr@ caracas.goethe.org; internet www.goethe.de/ hn/car; offers courses and exams in German language and culture and promotes cultural exchange with Germany; library of 4,000 vols; Dir Dr ULRICH GMÜNDER.

MEDICINE

Academia de Medicina del Zulia: Apdo 1725, Maracaibo, Zulia 4001A; tel. (61) 42-34-42; fax (61) 42-34-42; f. 1927; 150 mems; library of 950 vols; Pres. Dr GILBERTO OLIVARES; Sec. Dr JOSÉ A. COLINA-CHOURIO; publ. *Revista*.

Academia Nacional de Medicina (National Academy of Medicine): Bolsa a San Francisco, Apdo 804, Caracas 1010; tel. (212) 42-18-68; internet www.anm.org.ve; f. 1904; 40 mems; 50 nat. corresp. mems; 30 foreign corresp. mems; library: see Libraries and Archives; Pres. Dr AUGUSTO LEÓN C.; Sec. Dr JULIAN MORALES R.; publs *Boletín*, *Gaceta Médica de Caracas* (4 a year).

Colegio de Farmacéuticos del Distrito Federal y Estado Miranda (Association of Pharmacists): Urbanización Las Mercedes, Caracas 1060; deals with all aspects of the pharmaceutical industry; 1,200 mems; library of 600 vols; Pres. Dr PEDRO RODRÍGUEZ MURILLO; Sec. Dra ESTHER VALERA DE PÉREZ B.; Librarian Dra CARMEN ELENA GARCIA; publ. *Revista 'Colfar'*.

Colegio de Médicos del Distrito Metropolitano de Caracas (Doctors' Association): Plaza de Bellas Artes, Avda Bellas Artes, Los Chaguaramos, Caracas; tel. (212) 979-9846; fax (212) 979-2986; e-mail presidencia@ cmdmc.com.ve; internet www.cmdmc.com.ve; f. 1942; 2,800 mems; Pres. Dr FERNANDO JOSE BIANCO COLMENARES; Sec. Dra TAHIRI MARIÑEZ; publ. *Acta Médica Venezolana*.

Colegio de Médicos del Estado Miranda (Doctors' Association): Av. El Golf, Qta La Setentiseis, Urb. El Bosque, Caracas 1041-A; f. 1944; 3,100 mems; professional and scientific association; Pres. Dr HERNÁN VÁSQUEZ RIGUAL; Gen. Sec. Dr RUBEN HERNÁNDEZ SERRANO; publ. *Cuadernos Medicos*.

Instituto J. I. Baldó: El Algodonal, Antímano, Caracas; f. 1937; lung diseases; Pres. Dr MANUEL ADRIANZA.

Sociedad de Obstetricia y Ginecología de Venezuela (Society of Obstetrics and Gynaecology): Maternidad Concepción Palacios, Avda San Martín, Apdo 20081, Caracas 1020-A; tel. (212) 451-0895; fax (212) 451-0895; e-mail sogvzla01@gmail.com; internet www.sogvzla.org; f. 1940; 1,200 mems; Pres. Dr ROGELIO PEREZ D'GREGORIO; publ. *Revista de Obstetricia y Ginecología de Venezuela* (4 a year).

Sociedad Venezolana de Anestesiología (Society of Anaesthesiology): Final Av. Guaicaipuro, Edificio Edicentro, Piso 4, Oficina 4-B, diagonal a la entrada principal del Centro Médico de Caracas, Urb. San Bernardino, Caracas; tel. (212) 552-8788; fax (212) 552-8520; e-mail svanestesiologia@cantv.net; internet www.sva.org.ve; f. 1954; Pres. OSCAR LOYNAZ-REVERÓN.

Sociedad Venezolana de Cardiología (Society of Cardiology): Oficina B-1, Piso 2, Torre Colegio de Médicos, Av. José María Vargas, Urb. Santa Fe Norte, Caracas 1080; tel. (212) 263-5787; e-mail editorweb@ svcardiologia.org; internet www .svcardiologia.org; f. 1954; 196 mems; Pres. Dr JOSÉ ANTONIO CANDADO R.; Sec.-Gen. Dr GUILLERMO VILLORIA.

Sociedad Venezolana de Cirugía (Society of Surgery): Av. Sucre, Los Dos Caminos, Edif. Centro, Parque Boyacá, Torre Centro, Piso 17, Oficina 173, Caracas; tel. (212) 286-8106; e-mail sv_cirugia@cantv.net; internet www.sociedadvenezolanadecirugia.org; f. 1945; Pres. Dr AUGUSTO DIEZ; Sec.-Gen. Dr ISMAEL J. SALAS M.

Sociedad Venezolana de Cirugía Ortopédica y Traumatología (Society of Orthopaedics and Traumatological Surgery): Av. José María Vargas, Torre Colegio de Médicos, Piso 3 Oficina N° 3, Santa Fe Norte, Caracas; e-mail info@svcot.web.ve; internet www.svcot.web.ve; f. 1949; 197 mems; Pres. Dr RAFAEL HERRERA; publ. *Boletín de Ortopedia y Traumatología* (4 a year).

Sociedad Venezolana de Dermatología y Cirugía Dermatología (Society of Dermatology and Dermatological Surgery): Avda. Francisco de Miranda, Edif. Menegrande, Piso 6, Ofic. 6-4, Los Palos Grandes, Caracas 1080; tel. (212) 285-5284; fax (212) 285-0896; e-mail derma@svdcd.org.ve; internet www.svdcd.org.ve; f. 1946; promotes dermatological education and dermatological science in Venezuela; organizes monthly meetings, annual journals and congress; Pres. Dr ELDA GIANSANTE DE MARINUCCI; Vice-Pres. Dr NAHIR LOYO; Gen. Sec. Dr ROSANELLY ROYE.

Sociedad Venezolana de Gastroenterología (Venezuelan Society of Gastroenterology): Paseo Enrique Eraso, Torre La Noria, piso 5, Oficina 5-B3, Urb. Las Mercedes, Caracas 1061; tel. (212) 991-2660; fax (212) 992-7879; e-mail paginawebsovegastro@gmail.com; internet www.sovegastro.com; f. 1945; 606 mems; Pres. Dr SATURNINO FERNÁNDEZ; Sec. Dra MARIA LUISA CLAVO; publ. *GEN* (4 a year).

Sociedad Venezolana de Hematología (Society of Haematology): Avda José María Vargas, Edif. Torre del Colegio, Piso 2, Local E–2 Urb. Santa Fe Norte, Caracas 1080; tel. (212) 979-5664; f. 1959; library of 527 vols, 14 periodicals; Pres. Dr CARLOS GOLDSTEIN.

Sociedad Venezolana de Historia de la Medicina (History of Medicine Society): Palacio de las Academias, Bolsa a San Francisco, Caracas 1010; tel. (212) 483-4361; fax (212) 483-4361; e-mail migongue@yahoo.com; f. 1944; 75 mems; Pres. Dr MIGUEL GONZÁLEZ GUERRA; publ. *Revista* (2 a year).

Sociedad Venezolana de Medicina Interna (Society of Internal Medicine): Av. Francisco de Miranda, Edificio Mene Grande, Piso 6, Oficina 6-4, Los Palos Grandes, Caracas 1010; tel. (212) 285-0237; fax (212) 285-4026; e-mail socvmi@cantv.net; internet www.svmi.web.ve; f. 1956; Pres. Dr MARIO PATIÑO TORRES; Gen. Sec. Dra MARÍA EVELYN MONSALVE.

Sociedad Venezolana de Oftalmología (Society of Ophthalmology): Avda Principal de Los Ruices, Centro Empresarial Los Ruices (Piso 05, Oficina 507), Caracas; tel. (212) 239-8127; fax (212) 239-4384; e-mail svo@reacciun.ve; internet www.svo.org.ve; f. 1953; 600 mems; Pres. Dra SILVIA SALINAS; Sec.-Gen. Dr ROSEADO CASTELLANOS; publ. *Revista Oftalmológica Venezolana* (4 a year).

Sociedad Venezolana de Otorrinolaringología (Society of Otorhinolaryngology): Av. Principal de Santa Fe (Av. José María Vargas), Edificio Colegio de Médicos del Distrito Capital, Piso 2, Oficina 10, Santa Fe Norte, Caracas; tel. (212) 978-3311; internet www.svorl.org.ve; Pres. Dr FRANÇOIS CONDE JAHN; Sec. Dr GERMÁN TOVAR BUSTAMANTE; publ. *Acta Venezolana de ORL* (1 a year).

Sociedad Venezolana de Psiquiatría (Society of Psychiatry): Apdo 3380, Caracas 1010A; tel. (212) 731-2024; fax (212) 731-2024; f. 1942; 600 mems; library of 1,650 vols; Pres. Dr MANUEL MATUTE; Sec.-Gen. Dr EDGARD BELFORT; publ. *Archivos Venezolanos de Psiquiatría y Neurología* (2 a year).

Sociedad Venezolana de Puericultura y Pediatría (Society of Puericulture and Paediatrics): Apdo 3122, Caracas 1010A; Urb. La Castellana, Av. San Felipe, entre 2da Transversal y Calle José Angel Lamas, Centro Coinasa, Mezzanina 6, Caracas; tel. (212) 263-7378; fax (212) 267-6078; internet www.pediatria.org; Pres. Dra MICHELLE LÓPEZ.

Sociedad Venezolana de Radiología y Diagnóstico por Imágenes (Society of Radiology and Diagnostic Imaging): Hospital de Clínicas Caracas, Av. Panteón, San Bernardino, Caracas; tel. (212) 574-8210; fax (212) 575-2310; e-mail uribvictor@gmail.com; internet www.soveradi.org.ve; Pres. Dr RODRIGO SOCARRAS; Pres. Dr ANIBAL RIVERO.

NATURAL SCIENCES
General

Academia de Ciencias Físicas, Matemáticas y Naturales (Academy of Physical, Mathematical and Natural Sciences): Bolsa a San Francisco, Avda Universidad, Apdo 1421, Caracas 1010; tel. (212) 482-2954; fax (212) 484-6611; e-mail acfiman@cantv.net; internet www.acfiman.org.ve; f. 1917; 80 mems (30 ordinary, 20 Venezuelan corresp., 30 foreign corresp.); Pres. LUIS MANUEL CARBONELL; Sec. JOSÉ M. CARRILLO; publ. *Boletín* (4 a year).

Asociación Venezolana para el Avance de la Ciencia (ASOVAC) (Venezuelan Association for the Advancement of Science): Edificio Fundavac–Asovac, Calle Neverí, Colinas de Bello Monte, Caracas; internet www.asovac.org.ve; f. 1950; 3,000 mems; Pres. FRANCISCO EMIRO DURÁN; Sec.-Gen. YOLANDA SEVILLA; publ. *Acta Científica Venezolana* (6 a year).

Fundación La Salle de Ciencias Naturales (La Salle Foundation of Natural Sciences): Edificio Fundación La Salle, Avda Boyacá, Apdo 1930, Caracas 1010-A; tel. (212) 709-5811; fax (212) 793-7493; internet www.fundacionlasalle.org.ve; f. 1957; agronomy, anthropology, aquaculture, limnology, mining and forestry, oceanography; runs stations for marine, agricultural and hydrobiological research, the *Instituto Universitario de Tecnología del Mar* on the island of Margarita, *Instituto de Tecnología Agropecuaria* at San Carlos and at Boconó, *Instituto de Tecnología Industrial* at San Félix, *Instituto Universitario de Technología* at Tumeremo and *Instituto Universitario de Technología Amazonas* in Amazonas State; library: (see under Libraries); 1,300 mems; Pres. Hno. GINÉS; publs *Antropológica* (review, 4 a year), *Memoria* (oceanography and natural science studies, 2 a year), *Natura* (3 a year).

Biological Sciences

Sociedad de Ciencias Naturales 'La Salle' ('La Salle' Society of Natural Sciences): Edificio Fundación La Salle, Avda Boyacá, Apdo 1930, Caracas 1010A; tel. (212) 21-76-53; fax (212) 22-48-12; f. 1940; 504 mems; 17 hon., 42 national and 30 foreign corresps, 500 associates; comprises 3 depts: botany, publications, zoology; the Museum contains more than 100,000 exhibits; Dir Lic. JESÚS HOYOS; Pres. Dr LUIS RIVAS L.; Sec. Dr CARLOS ACEVEDO; publs *Memoria* (2 a year), *Natura* (4 a year).

Sociedad Venezolana de Ciencias Naturales (Venezuelan Society of Natural Sciences): Calle Arichuna y Cumaco, El Marqués, Apdo 1521, Caracas 1010A; tel. (212) 21-76-53; fax (212) 22-48-12; f. 1931; 1,100 mems; library of 12,000 vols, 400 periodicals; annual exhibitions, lectures, films on nature conservation; department of speleology for study and exploration of caves throughout the country; biological station for research on flora and fauna, soil science and crop studies, ecology of neo-tropical savannas; dept for education on environmental protection; depts for the study of tropical orchids, bromeliads and astronomy; studies in environmental pollution; Pres. R. AVELEDO HOSTOS; Gen. Sec. Dr RICARDO MUÑOZ TÉBAR; publs *Boletín de la SVCN, Boletín Informativo*.

Physical Sciences

Sociedad Venezolana de Geólogos (Venezuelan Geological Society): Apdo 17493, Parque Central, Caracas, 1015-A; located at: Avda A, Quinta Mercedes 13-10, Urbanización, La Carlota, Caracas; tel. (212) 234-4085; fax (212) 234-0716; e-mail svg@mailser .reacciun.ve; internet www.socvengeo.org; f. 1955; 1,050 mems; Pres. DANIEL LOUREIRO; Sec. FRANCISCO BARRIOS; publs *Boletín* (3 a year), *Geologia de Venezuela*.

TECHNOLOGY

Asociación Venezolana de Ingeniería Sanitaria y Ambiental (Sanitary and Environmental Engineering Association): El Trigal Centro, Calle Pocaterra 88-20, Quinta los Corales, Valencia 2002, Carabobo; tel. (41) 421-435; fax (41) 428-028; e-mail avisa@eldish.net; Pres. Ing. RAFAEL DAUTANT.

Colegio de Ingenieros de Venezuela (Engineers' Association): Av. Principal de Quebrada Honda, Los Caobos, Caracas 1050; tel. (212) 575-3532; internet www.civ .net.ve; f. 1861; 7,000 mems; library of 4,000 vols; Pres. DARÍO BRILLEMBOURG; Sec. JULIO URBINA; publ. *Boletín* (12 a year).

Sociedad Venezolana de Ingeniería Hidráulica (Society of Hydraulic Engineering): c/o Colegio de Ingenieros de Venezuela, Los Caobos, Caracas; tel. (414) 868-2570; internet www.svihvenezuela.org.ve; f. 1960; Pres. ARTURO MARCANO.

Sociedad Venezolana de Ingenieros Agrónomos (Society of Agricultural Engineers): c/o Colegio de Ingenieros de Venezuela, Av. Principal de Quebrada Honda, Los Caobos, Caracas 1050; f. 1944; Pres. Ing. Agr. HUMBERTO FONTANA.

Sociedad Venezolana de Ingenieros Civiles (Society of Civil Engineers): c/o Colegio de Ingenieros de Venezuela, v. Principal de Quebrada Honda, Los Caobos, Caracas 1050; tel. (212) 368-6077; e-mail sovinciv@sovinciv.com; internet www .sovinciv.com; f. 1995; Pres. MANUEL FERNANDO MEJÍAS.

Sociedad Venezolana de Ingenieros de Petróleo (Society of Petroleum Engineers): Calle Negrín con calle Las Flores, Torre Negrín, piso 5, oficina 5A, Sabana Grande, Caracas 1050; tel. (212) 761-4497; fax (212) 761-4223; e-mail soveip@cantv.net; internet www.svip.org; f. 1958; Pres. FERNANDO SÁNCHEZ.

Sociedad Venezolana de Ingenieros Forestales (Society of Forestry Engineers): c/o Colegio de Ingenieros de Venezuela, Av. Principal de Quebrada Honda, Los Caobos, Caracas 1050; internet www.civ.net.ve; f. 1960; 1,122 mems; library of 8,000 vols; Pres. Ing. For. LOURDES ALTUVE; Sec. Ing. For. SONIA RIVAS; publ. *Revista Forestal* (4 a year).

Sociedad Venezolana de Ingenieros Químicos (Society of Chemical Engineers): c/o Colegio de Ingenieros de Venezuela; Av. Principal de Quebrada Honda, Los Caobos, Caracas 1050; f. 1958 to promote the chemical engineering profession and exchange information with similar orgs in Venezuela and abroad; 1,000 mems; Exec. Dir YOLANDA DE OSORIO; publ. *Boletín* (4 a year).

Research Institutes

GENERAL

Consejo Nacional de Investigaciones Científicas y Tecnológicas (CONICIT) (National Council for Scientific and Technological Research): Apdo 70617, Los Ruices, Caracas; fax (212) 239-8677; f. 1967 for the promotion of scientific and technological research, and for coordinating the activities of organizations involved in the science and technology sector, and of organizations of the national executive; Pres. Dr IGNACIO AVALOS GUTIERREZ; Vice-Pres. Dr MICHAEL SUAREZ F.

Instituto Venezolano de Investigaciones Científicas (IVIC) (Venezuelan Scientific Research Institute): Apdo 21827, Caracas 1020A; tel. (212) 504-1122; fax (212) 504-1428; e-mail webmaster@ivic.ve; internet www.ivic.ve; f. 1959; research in anthropology, archaeology, atomic research, biology, chemistry, mathematics and technology, medicine, physics, sociology of science; postgraduate studies; library: see Libraries and Archives; Dir MAXIMO GARCIO SUCRE.

AGRICULTURE, FISHERIES AND VETERINARY SCIENCE

Centro Nacional de Investigaciones Agropecuarias (Agricultural Research Centre): Avda Casanova Godoy, Maracay 2103, Estado Aragua; tel. (243) 245-3075; fax (243) 245-4320; internet www.ceniap.gov.ve; f. 1937; attached to the Instituto Nacional de Investigaciones Agricolas de Venezuela; Dir Dra SUSMIRA GODOY; publs *Agronomía Tropical*, *Veterinaria Tropical*, *Zootecnia Tropical*.

Estación Experimental Táchira: Bramón, Rubio 6070, Edo Táchira; tel. (76) 66783; f. 1953; agricultural research; library of 1,100 vols; Dir JOSÉ ROSARIO MANRIQUE.

Instituto de Investigaciones Veterinarias (Veterinary Research Institute): Apdo 70, Maracay, Estado Aragua; Av. Las Delicias, Maracay, Estado Aragua; tel. (243) 414-365; f. 1940; small specialized library; 55 mems; Dir Dr CLAUDIO FUENMAYOR F.

Instituto Nacional de Investigaciones Agrícolas de Venezuela (National Institute for Agricultural Research): Via El Limon, Maracay, Estado Aragua; fax (243) 283-6978; e-mail ger_inia@impsat.com.ve; internet www.inia.gov.ve; f. 1961 as Fondo Nacional de Investigaciones Agropecuarias, 2000 re-named; centres and experimental stations: Amazonas, Anzoátegui, Apure, Barinas, CENIAP, Delta Amacuro, Falcón, Guárico, Lara, Mérida, Miranda, Monagas, Portuguesa, Sucre, Táchira, Trujillo, Yaracuy, Zulia; Pres. PRUDENCIO CHACÓN; Gen.-Man. ALICIA LEÓN.

Instituto Nacional de Tierras (National Land Institute): Calle San Carlos, Urb. Vista Alegre, Qta. La Barranca, Caracas; internet www.inti.gob.ve; f. 1949; concerned with agrarian reform activities; Pres. JUAN CARLOS LOYO; publ. *Memoria y Cuenta*.

ARCHITECTURE AND TOWN PLANNING

Dirección General de Ordenación del Territorio Urbanístico del Ministerio del Poder Popular para las Obras Públicas y Vivienda (Bureau of Urban Development of the Ministry for Public Works and Housing): Av. Francisco de Miranda, Torre Minfra, Piso 10, Chacao, Caracas; f. 1946; 350 mems; library of 20,000 vols; Dir MARIBEL CHELLINI AROCHA.

ECONOMICS, LAW AND POLITICS

Centro de Estudios del Desarrollo Universidad Central de Venezuela (Centre for Development Studies): Av. Neverì, Edif. Fundavac-Asovac, Colinas de Bello Monte, POB 47604, Caracas 1041; tel. (212) 753-3475; fax (212) 751-2691; e-mail cendesdir@ucv.ve; internet www.cendes-ucv.edu.ve; f. 1961; centre for research and graduate studies on problems relating to economic, social, educational, regional, political, ecological, environmental and scientific-technological devt of Venezuela and Latin America; library of 12,011 vols, 35,141 documents, 915 periodicals and 578 thesis; Dir Dr CARLOS WALTER; publs *Cuadernos del CENDES* (3 a year), *Revista Cuadernos del CENDES*.

Instituto Iberoamericano de Derecho Agrario y Reforma Agraria: Facultad de Ciencias Jurídicas y Políticas, Universidad de los Andes, Mérida; tel. (275) 402646; fax (275) 402644; f. 1973; 12 mem. countries; training and research in agrarian law, agricultural economics, rural sociology; postgraduate courses; library of 4,000 vols; Pres. RAMÓN VICENTE CASANOVA; publ. *Revista de Derecho Agrario y Reforma Agraria*.

Oficina Central de Estadística e Informática (Central Office of Statistics and Informatics): Apdo 4593, Caracas 1010; tel. (212) 782-1133; e-mail ocei@platino.gov.ve; internet www.ocei.gov.ve; f. 1978; Dir Dr GUSTAVO MÉNDEZ; publs *Anuario del Comercio Exterior de Venezuela*, *Anuario Estadístico de Venezuela*.

EDUCATION

Instituto Latinoamericano de Investigaciones Científicas en Educación a Distancia (Latin American Institute of Scientific Research on Distance Education): Calle California, Qta. Las Churrucas, Apdo 69680, Las Mercedes 1060A, Caracas; f. 1980; research, teaching and planning in distance and open education; library of 8,000 vols; Pres. MIGUEL A. ESCOTET.

HISTORY, GEOGRAPHY AND ARCHAEOLOGY

Centro de Historia del Estado Carabobo: Valencia, Edo de Carabobo; f. 1979 to conduct research into national and regional history, preserve and improve regional archives, conserve monuments, encourage and publicize celebrations of national historic events, and establish cultural relations with similar Venezuelan and foreign organizations; 24 mems; Pres. Lic. LUIS CUBILLÁN; Sec. Dr MARCO TULIO MÉRIDA; publ. *Boletín*.

Instituto de Geografía y Conservación de Recursos Naturales (Institute of Geography and Conservation of Natural Resources): Vía Chorros de Milla, Mérida; tel. and fax (274) 2401603; e-mail intgeogr@ula.ve; internet www.forest.ula.ve/geografiayconservacion; f. 1959; library of 20,236 vols and 44,555 periodicals; research in theoretical geography, applied geography and geographical techniques; committees for research and teaching technical coordination; documentation and informa-

tion; Dir Prof. JUAN CARLOS RIVERO; publs *Cuadernos Geográficos* (irregular), *Revista Geográfica Venezolana* (2 a year).

Ministerio del Ambiente y de los Recursos Naturales Renovables, Servicio Autónomo del Geografía y Cartografía Nacional: Avda Este 6, Esquina de Camejo, Edificio Camejo (Piso 2-220), Centro Simón Bolívar, Caracas; tel. (212) 482-2218; fax (212) 542-0374; f. 1935; Dir-Gen. Lic. ALICIA MOREAU D.

MEDICINE

Instituto de Medicina Experimental (Institute of Experimental Medicine): Apdo 50587, Sabana Grande, Ciudad Universitaria, Caracas 1051; tel. (212) 693-1862; fax (212) 693-1260; f. 1940; research in biochemistry, general and applied pathology, neurology, pharmacology, physiology; 130 staff; library of 30,176 vols, 4,100 periodicals; Dir Dra ITALA LIPPO DE BECEMBERG; Librarian Lic. TRINA YANES DE RAMÍREZ; publ. *Boletín Informativo Sistema Nacional de Documentación e Información Biomédica*; (see also under the Universidad Central de Venezuela).

Instituto Nacional de Nutrición (Institute of Nutrition): Av. Baralt, Esquina El Carmen, Edif. INN, Quinta Crespo, Municipio Libertador, Caracas; tel. (212) 483-3378; e-mail amogollon@inn.gob.ve; internet www.inn.gob.ve; f. 1949; library of 10,000 vols; Dir Dr LUIS BERMÚDEZ CHAURIO; publ. *Archivos Latinoamericanos de Nutrición*.

NATURAL SCIENCES

General

Estación de Investigaciones Marinas (EDIMAR): Apdo 144, Porlamar, Punta de Piedras, Isla de Margarita, Edo Nueva Esparta; tel. (295) 239-8051; fax (295) 239-8051; e-mail marllano@edimar.org; internet www.edimar.org; affiliated to the Fundación La Salle de Ciencias Naturales (see under Learned Societies); f. 1958; aquaculture, fisheries, marine biology, marine geology, marine food processing, oceanography; library: 'H. Ginés' of 18,000 vols, 1,200 periodicals; Dir Dr MARTÍN LLANO GARCÍA; publ. *Memoria de la Sociedad La Salle de Ciencias Naturales*.

Biological Sciences

Estación Biológica de los Llanos (Biological Station): Calabozo, Estado Guárico; f. 1961; library of 3,200 vols; Dirs F. TAMAYO, R. A. HOSTOS, L. ARISTEGUIETA.

Fundación Instituto Botánico de Venezuela (Botanical Institute): Apdo 2156, Jardín Botánico de Caracas, Avda Salvador Allende, Caracas 1010-A; tel. (212) 605-3989; fax (212) 605-3994; e-mail unidad.educacion.fibv@gmail.com; internet www.fibv.org.ve; f. 1991; library of 14,000 vols, 1,300 periodicals; Pres. Dr ANÍBAL CASTILLO SUÁREZ; publs *Acta Botanica Venezuelica* (2 a year), *Flora de Venezuela*.

Physical Sciences

Dirección de Geología del Ministerio de Energía y Minas (Department of Geology of the Ministry of Energy and Mines): Torre Oeste, 4° piso, Parque Central, Caracas 1010; f. 1936; conducts national geological surveys, and research in geotechnics, marine geology and mineralogy; library of 120,000 vols; Dir SIMÓN E. RODRIGUEZ; publs *Boletín de Geología* (2 a year), *Boletín Informativo del Centro de Análisis de Información Geológica-Minera (CAIGEOMIN)* (2 a year), *Cuadernos Geológicos* (3 a year), research bulletins, statistical and other data (1 a year).

Estación Meteorológica (Meteorological Station): Ciudad Bolívar; f. 1940; undertakes meteorological research and hydrographical surveys of the River Orinoco and its tributaries; Dir E. SIFONTES; numerous publications on meteorology and climatology of Venezuela.

Observatorio Naval 'Juan Manuel Cagigal' (Juan Manuel Cagigal Naval Observatory): Apdo 6745, La Planicie, 23 Enero, Caracas; tel. (212) 481-2266; fax (212) 483-5878; e-mail dhn@truevision.net; f. 1888; astronomy, hydrography, meteorology, oceanography, planetarium; Dir GREGORIO PÉREZ MORENO; publs *Almanaque Astronómico Venezolano*, *Boletín Avisos a los Navegantes*, *Boletín Climatológico Anual*, *Boletín Meteorologico* (1 a year).

RELIGION, SOCIOLOGY AND ANTHROPOLOGY

Fundación Lisandro Alvarado: Casa de Los Celis, Av. Soublette c/o Calle Comercio, Valencia; tel. (41) 421245; e-mail casacelis@ cantv.net; internet mipagina.cantv.net/ casacelis; f. 1965; museums of art, history, anthropology, historical archives; brs in Maracay (archaeological and historical research; museums of history and anthropology; specialized library (in preparation)) and Puerto Cabello (museum of art and history); 40 mems; Pres. Dra HENRIQUETA PEÑALVER GÓMEZ; Dir Tec. CESAR A. VARELA H.

Instituto Caribe de Antropología y Sociología: Av. Boyacá (Cota Mil) con Maripérez, al lado de la Estación del Teleférico 'Avila Mágica', Caracas; tel. (212) 709-5845; e-mail info@fundacionlasalle.org.ve; internet www.fundacionlasalle.org.ve; f. 1962; anthropological research and devt programmes among Indian populations of Venezuela; dept of the Fundación La Salle de Ciencias Naturales (see under Learned Societies); library of 40,000 vols; Pres. JUAN BOSCO CHACON; Dir MIGUEL ANGEL PERERA; publ. *Antropológica* (2 a year).

TECHNOLOGY

Dirección de Minas del Ministerio de Minas e Hidrocarburos (Department of Mining of the Ministry of Mines and Hydrocarbons): Torre Norte, 20° piso, Caracas 101; f. 1936; Dir BRÍGIDO R. NATERA.

PDUSA-INTEVEP, Centro de Investigación y Apoyo Tecnológico: Apdo 76343, Caracas 1070A; tel. (212) 908-6111; fax (212) 908-6447; f. 1974; research and development branch of Petróleos de Venezuela, concerned with hydrocarbons and petrochemicals; Information Centre of 30,000 publs, 1,600 periodicals, connected to int. online systems; Pres. FRANCISCO PRADAS; publ. *Visión Tecnológica* (2 a year).

Libraries and Archives

Barquisimeto

Biblioteca Pública 'Pio Tamayo' (Public Library): Calle 26, entre Carreras 20 y 21, Barquisimeto; f. 1911; 21,943 vols; Librarian GERMÁN HURTADO REYES.

Biblioteca Técnica Científica Centralizada 'Froilan Alvarez Yepez' (Central Scientific and Technical Library): Apdo 254, Barquisimeto; fax (251) 544394; f. 1966; specializes in social sciences, economic development and technology; 50,000 vols, 800 periodicals; Librarian Lic. CECILIA VEGA F.; publ. *Indice Bibliográfico de los estudios de FUDECO*.

Caracas

Archivo de Música Colonial Venezolano (Archives of Colonial Music): Escuela Superior de Música, esquinas de Veroes a Santa Capilla de la Av. Urdaneta, Caracas; Librarian GARCÍA LAZO.

Archivo General de la Nación (National Archives): Av. Panteón, Foro Libertador, Edif. Archivo General de la Nación, Caracas 1010; tel. (212) 509-5600; e-mail mppc@ ministeriodelacultura.gob.ve; f. 1910; sections: La Colonia (1498–1810), La Revolución (1810–21), La Gran Colombia (1821–30), La República (1830 to present day); comprises Seminario de Investigación Archivística and courses on palaeography; Dir CARMEN ALIDA SOTO; publs *Biblioteca Venezolana de Historia* (2 a year), *Boletín* (2 a year).

Biblioteca Central de la Universidad Católica 'Andrés Bello' (Central Library of the 'Andrés Bello' Catholic University): Edificio de Biblioteca, piso 1, Urb. Montalbán, La Vega, Caracas; tel. (212) 407-4172; fax (212) 471-3307; e-mail tbalza@ucab.edu .ve; f. 1953; 111,558 vols; Librarian TAIDÉ BALZA; publ. *Montalbán*.

Biblioteca Central de la Universidad Central de Venezuela (Central University Library): Apdo 1050, Caracas; Edif. Biblioteca Central, Ciudad Universitaria, Los Chaguaramos, Caracas; tel. (212) 605-4190; fax (212) 605-0861; internet www.sicht.ucv .ve:8080/bc; f. 1850; sections on social science, the humanities, pure science and technology; official publications; reference section; 280,000 vols; 3,500 periodicals; Dir Prof. MANUEL RODRIGUEZ CAMPOS.

Biblioteca Central del Ministerio de Agricultura y Cría (Library of the Ministry of Agriculture): Avda Lecuna, Parque Central, Torre Este, 1° piso, Caracas; f. 1936; 70,000 vols; Librarian TUSNELDA CRESPO PIETRI.

Biblioteca Central del Ministerio del Trabajo (Library of the Ministry of Labour): Centro Simón Bolívar, Edificio Sur, 5° piso, Caracas; f. 1988; 3,200 vols; Librarian MARCELA GARCÍA JORDAN; publ. *Boletín Legislativo*.

Biblioteca de la Academia Nacional de la Historia (Library of the National Academy of History): Palacio de las Academias, Avda Universidad, Bolsa a San Francisco, Caracas; tel. (212) 482-3849; fax (212) 482-6720; f. 1888; 120,000 vols; Dir Dr RAFAEL FERNÁNDEZ HERES; publ. *Boletín de la Academia Nacional de la Historia*.

Biblioteca de la Academia Nacional de Medicina (Library of the National Academy of Medicine): Apdo 1121-A, Caracas; Palacio de las Academias, Av. Universidad, Bolsa a San Francisco, Caracas; tel. (212) 481-8939; fax (212) 481-8939; e-mail bibliotanm@yahoo .es; internet www.msinfo.info/default/anm; f. 1893; 4,000 vols; Librarian Dr TULIO BRICEÑO MAAZ; publ. *Gaceta Médica de Caracas*.

Biblioteca de la Academia Venezolana de la Lengua (Library of the Venezuelan Academy of Language): Apdo 1421, Caracas; Palacio de las Academias, Av. Universidad, Caracas 1010-A; e-mail acadlengv@cantv .net; f. 1883; 25,000 vols; special collections: Venezuelan classics, dictionaries, Ayacucho collection, 'El Coyo Ilustrado'; Librarian FRANCISCO JAVIER PÉREZ.

Biblioteca del Ministerio de Fomento (Library of the Ministry of Development): Centro Simón Bolívar, Edificio Sur, 5° piso, Oficina 535, Caracas; f. 1953; 6,000 vols; Librarian ROSARIO BARNOLA.

Biblioteca del Ministerio de Obras Públicas (Library of the Ministry of Public Works): Centro Simón Bolívar, Edificio

Camejo, Mezzanina, Caracas; f. 1948; 4,312 vols; Dir CARLOS A. ARREAZA F.

Biblioteca del Ministerio de Relaciones Interiores (Library of the Ministry of the Interior): Esquina de Carmelitas, 2° piso, Caracas; 3,585 vols; Librarian Dr RUIZ LANDER.

Biblioteca del Ministerio de Sanidad y Asistencia Social (Library of the Ministry of Health): c/o Ministerio de Salud y Desarrollo Social, Parque Central, Torre Oeste Piso 30-41 Distrito Federal, Caracas; f. 1936; 9,411 vols; Librarian ESPERANZA REYES BAENA; publs *Memorias del MSAS*, *Revista Venezolana de Sanidad y Asistencia Social*.

Biblioteca del Ministerio del Poder Popular para Relaciones Exteriores (Library of the Ministry of Foreign Affairs): Av. Urdaneta, Torre MRE, al lado del Correo de Carmelitas, Caracas; e-mail dgab .divisionbiblioteca@mre.gob.ve; 7,450 items; specializes in international law; Librarian Lic. MIGUEL ABELLO.

Biblioteca del Tribunal Supremo de Justicia (Library of the Supreme Tribunal of Justice): Edificio del Tribunal Supremo de Justicia, Mezzanina, final de la Av. Baralt, esquina dos pilitas, Caracas; tel. (212) 801-9051; e-mail biblioteca@tsj.gov.ve; internet www.tsj.gov.ve/index.shtml; f. 1942; 4,500 vols; Dir Br FERNANDO ARAUJO M.

Biblioteca 'Dr M. A. Sánchez Carvajal' de la Sociedad de Obstetricia y Ginecología de Venezuela (Dr M. A. Sánchez Carvajal Library of the Society for Obstetrics and Gynaecology of Venezuela): Maternidad Concepción Palacios, Avda San Martín, Apdo 20081, Caracas 1020A; tel. (212) 451-0895; fax (212) 451-0895; e-mail sogvzla@cantv.net; internet www.sogvzla.org; f. 1940; 8,500 vols, 113 periodicals, also MSS and medical history collection; Librarian Dra FANNY FLEITAS.

Biblioteca Ernesto Peltzer del Banco Central de Venezuela: Apdo 2017, Caracas; Esquina de Mijares, Plaza Juan Pedro López, Mezzanina 2, Altagracia, Caracas 1010; tel. (212) 801-8617; fax (212) 861-0048; internet www.bcv.org.ve//biblioteca/ biblioep.htm; f. 1940; economics and finance; 100,000 vols, 862 periodicals; Dir SILVIO CASTELLANOS.

Biblioteca Juan Pablo Pérez Alfonzo (Library of the Ministry of Energy and Petroleum): Av. Lecuna, Parque Central, Torre Oeste, 2° piso, Caracas; tel. (212) 507-5206; fax (212) 575-4386; f. 1950; specializes in mines, petroleum, gas, geology, refinement, petrochemicals; 20,000 vols; Librarian Lic. SILVIA PERNIA C.; publs *Anuario Estadísticos Mineros*, *Boletín de Geología*, *Carta Semanal*, *Compendia Estadística del Sector Eléctrico*, *Memoria y Cuenta del Ministerio de Energía y Minas*, *Petróleo y otros Datos Estadísticos*.

Biblioteca Luís Beltrán Prieto Figueroa (Library of the National Assembly): Monjas a San Francisco, Palacio Federal Legislativo, El Silencio, Caracas; internet www .bibliotecalbpf.an.gob.ve; f. 1915; 9,000 vols; Librarian Lic. LUÍS PÉREZ PESCADOR.

Biblioteca 'Marcel Roche' del Instituto Venezolano de Investigaciones Científicas (Library of the Venezuelan Institute of Scientific Research): Altos de Pipe, Km 11, Carretera Panamericana, Apdo 21827, Caracas 1020A; tel. (212) 504-1515; fax (212) 504-1423; internet www.zeus.ivic.ve/biblioteca; f. 1959; 500,000 vols, 5,817 periodicals; Dir Dr EGIDIO ROMANO; Librarian XIOMARA JAYARO Y.

Biblioteca Nacional de Venezuela (National Library of Venezuela): Parroquia Altagracia, Final Avda Panteón, Esquina Fe a Remedios, Caracas 1010; tel. (212) 505-9254; fax (212) 505-9175; internet www .bibliotecanacional.bib.ve; f. 1883; 6.5m. books, newspapers, MSS and audiovisual items, 2.5m. records on database; Dir SAÉL IBÁÑEZ; publ. *Revista Bibliotecas Públicas* (4 a year).

Biblioteca Pública Mariano Picón Salas (Public Library): Av. Andrés Bello, cruce con Av. Principal de Maripérez, Parque Arístides Rojas, Maripérez, Caracas; f. 1965; 23,689 vols; Dir Lic. ROMULO NAVEA SOTO.

Centro de Documentación e Información Fundación La Salle de Ciencias Naturales (Documentation and Information Centre, 'La Salle' Foundation for Natural Sciences): Avda Boyacá, Cota Mil., Edif. Fundación La Salle, Apdo 1930, Caracas 1010A; tel. (212)709-5845; fax (212) 793-7493; f. 1942; 40,000 vols; spec. colln: botany, cultural anthropology, local languages, natural resources contamination, zoology, Venezuelan Indians; Librarian MIREYA VILORIA.

Cumaná

Biblioteca General de la Universidad de Oriente (General Library of the Universidad de Oriente): Ave Universidad, Cerro Colorado, 6101 Cumaná; tel. (293) 4008158; fax (293) 4008358; e-mail bashiru@udo.edu.ve; internet biblioteca.udo.edu.ve; f. 1958; 500,000 vols; Librarian Lic. ROSA GONZÁLEZ DE LÓPEZ; publs *Boletín del Instituto Oceanografico* (2 a year), *Saber* (2 a year).

Maracaibo

Biblioteca Central 'General Rafael Urdaneta': Apartado Postal 526, Maracaibo 4001-A; tel. (261) 759-6700; fax (261) 759-6703; e-mail bibcentral.serbi@luz.edu.ve; internet www1.serbi.luz.edu.ve; f. 1946; 19,000 vols; Librarian Lic. EGLA ORTEGA.

Biblioteca Pública del Estado Zulia: Maracaibo; administered by the Instituto Zuliano de la Cultura (*q.v.*); Dir FERNANDO GUERRERO MATHEUS.

Maracay

Biblioteca Central del Centro Nacional de Investigaciones Agropecuarias (Library of the National Agricultural Research Centre): Av. Casanova Godoy, Zona Universitaria, Maracay 2103, Estado Aragua; tel. (243) 245-2491; fax (243) 245-4320; f. 1937; 200,000 vols; Library Asst NANCY GARCÉS DE HERNÁNDEZ.

Mérida

Servicios Bibliotecarios Universidad de los Andes (Los Andes University Library Services): Edificio Administrativo de la Universidad de los Andes, 2° piso, Mérida 5101; tel. (275) 402731; fax (275) 402507; f. 1889; 250,000 vols, 7,817 periodical titles; reference books for all subjects taught in the University; small collection of 16th- and 17th-century books; Coordinator Lic. MARÍA E. CHÁVEZ DE BURGOS.

Trujillo

Biblioteca '24 de Julio' (Public Library): Trujillo; f. 1930; 12,000 vols; Librarian ITALA BRICEÑO RUMBOS.

Valencia

Biblioteca Central de la Universidad de Carabobo: Urb. Prebo, Av. Andrés Eloy Blanco c/o 137-20, Edif. Centro Escorpio, pisos 2 y 3, Valencia; tel. (241) 822-2606; fax (241) 821-2121; internet www.cid.uc.edu .ve; 11,000 vols; Librarian ANTONIETA PINTO DE KATZ.

Museums and Art Galleries

Caracas

Casa Natal del Libertador Simón Bolívar (Simón Bolívar's Birthplace): San Jacinto a Traposos, Caracas; tel. (212) 541-2563; murals by Tito Salas depicting the life of Bolívar and events of the Independence Movement; Curator JOSEFINA DE SANDOVAL.

Colección Ornitológica Phelps (Phelps Ornithological Collection): c/o Robin Restall, POB 025304, Miami, FL 33102-5304, USA; located at: Blvd Sabana Grande, Edif. Gran Sabana, 3° piso, Apdo 2009, Caracas, 1001A; tel. (212) 719-238; fax (212) 762-5921; f. 1938; library of 10,000 vols; Pres. KATHLEEN PHELPS; Curator M. LENTINO R.

Fundación Museo de Ciencias: Avda Mexico, Plaza de los Museos, Parque Los Caobos, Apdo Postal 5883, Caracas 1010; tel. (212) 577-5094; fax (212) 571-1265; e-mail mciencia@reacciun.ve; internet www .museo-de-ciencias.org; f. 1875 as Museo Nacional, subsequently Museo de Ciencias Naturales; anthropology, archaeology, entomology, ethnology, geology, palaeontology, zoology; library of 2,100 vols; Pres. Ing. SERGIO ANTILLANO ARMAS.

Galería de Arte Nacional: Plaza de los Museos, Los Caobos, Apdo 6729, Caracas 1010; tel. (212) 578-1818; fax (212) 578-1661; e-mail prensafmn1@gmail.com; internet www.wtfe.com/gan; f. 1976; Venezuelan visual art from pre-Hispanic time to the present; Pres. CLEMENTINA VAAMONDE B.; Exec. Dir RAFAEL SANTANA.

Museo Bolivariano (Bolívar Museum): Esquina San Jacinto a Traposos, Caracas; f. 1911 and inaugurated in present building 1960; contains 1,546 exhibits; mementos, portraits, personal relics and historical paintings of Simón Bolívar and his fellow-workers in the Independence Movement; library of 1,200 vols; Dir ANITA TAPIAS.

Museo de Arte Colonial (Museum of Colonial Art): Quinta de Anauco, Avda Panteón, San Bernardino, Caracas 1011; tel. (212) 551-8650; fax (212) 551-8517; e-mail artecolonialanauco@cantv.net; internet www .quintadeanauco.org.ve; f. 1942; painting, sculpture, decorative arts; library; under the supervision of the Asociación Venezolana de Amigos del Arte Colonial (*q.v.*); Dir CARLOS F. DUARTE.

Museo de Arte Contemporáneo de Caracas Sofía Imber (Sofía Imber Museum of Contemporary Art in Caracas): Zona Cultural, Parque Central, Apdo 17093, Caracas 1010; tel. (212) 577-0075; fax (212) 577-1883; internet www.maccsi.org.ve; f. 1973; incl. works by Picasso, Braque, Chagall, Bacon, Matisse, Kandinsky and Miró; Dir RITA SALVESTRINI.

Museo de Bellas Artes de Caracas (Museum of Fine Arts): Plaza Morelos, Parque Los Caobos, Caracas 105; tel. (212) 578-2197; fax (212) 571-0169; e-mail fmba@ reacciun.ve; internet www .museodebellasartes.org; f. 1917; paintings and sculpture by national and foreign artists; library of 6,000 vols; Dir MARÍA ELENA RAMOS.

Ciudad Bolívar

Museo 'Talavera: Quinta San Isidro, Ciudad Bolívar; f. 1940; pre-Columbian and Colonial period exhibits, religious art, natural science, numismatics; Dir Dr J. GABRIEL MACHADO; publ. *Museo Talavera*.

El Tocuyo

Museo Colonial (Historical Museum): El Tocuyo; f. 1945.

Maracaibo

Museo Histórico 'General Rafael Urdaneta' (Museum of Military History): Calle 91A No. 7A-70, Sector Veritas, Maracaibo; tel. (261) 721-3414; f. 1936; collns of art, arms, sculpture, numismatic and philatelic items, photographs; Dir Prof. J. C. BORGES ROSALES.

Trujillo

Museo 'Cristóbal Mendoza' (Historical Museum): Trujillo.

Universities

UNIVERSIDAD DE CARABOBO

Av. Bolívar Norte, Sede del Rectorado U.C., Valencia, Edo. Carabobo

Telephone: (241) 821-5044

E-mail: di@uc.edu.ve

Internet: www.uc.edu.ve

Founded 1852

State control

Academic year: September to February, March to July

Rector: Dr GUSTAVO HIDALGO-VITALE

Academic Vice-Rector: Dr ELIS MERCADO MATUTE

Admin. Vice-Rector: Ing. JOSÉ BOTELLO WILSON

Sec.: Dr RUBÉN BALLESTEROS

Librarian: ANTONIETA PINTO DE KATZ

Library: see Libraries and Archives

Number of teachers: 2,585

Number of students: 44,654

Publications: *Boletín Universitario*, *Utopia y Praxis*

DEANS

Faculty of Economics and Social Sciences: Econ. LIONEL AGUDO

Faculty of Education: Lic. CARLOS HERRERA

Faculty of Engineering: Ing. GIOVANNI NANI

Faculty of Health Sciences: Dr CLAUDIO ROMANO

Faculty of Law: Abog. ELOY RUTMAN CISNEROS

Postgraduate Studies: Dr ALEJANDRO SUE MACHADO

UNIVERSIDAD CATÓLICA 'ANDRÉS BELLO'

Urb. Montalbán, La Vega, Apdo 1020, Caracas 1020

Telephone: (212) 407-4444

Fax: (212) 407-4349

E-mail: webmaster@ucab.edu.ve

Internet: www.ucab.edu.ve

Founded 1953

Private control (Society of Jesus)

Academic year: October to July

Campuses in San Cristóbal, Táchira

Chancellor: Rev. Fr PEDRO NICOLÁS BERMÚDEZ

Vice-Chancellor: Rev. Fr JESUS MARÍA ORBEGOZO EGUIGUREN

Rector: Rev. Fr LUIS UGALDE

Academic Vice-Rector: Dra MIRIAM LÓPEZ DE VALDIVIESO

Admin. Vice-Rector: Ing. LORENZO CALDENTEY LUQUE

Dean of Student Devt: Dr RUBÉN ANGEL PEÑALVER GODINES

Sec.-Gen.: Rev. Fr GUSTAVO SUCRE

Librarian: Lic. EMILIO PÍRIZ PÉREZ

Library: see Libraries and Archives

Number of teachers: 1,225

Number of students: 14,131

Publications: *Analogías del Comportamiento, Cuadernos Venezolanos de Filosofía, Encuentro EAC y Cuadernos UCAB-Educación, Espacios, Pensamiento Agustiniano, Revista de la Facultad de Derecho, Revista Montalbán, Revista de Relaciones Industriales y Laborales, Revista Tekhne de la Facultad de Ingeniería, Temas de Comunicación Social, Temas de Coyuntura*

DEANS

Faculty of Engineering: Ing. RAFAEL HERNÁNDEZ SÁNCHEZ-OCAÑA
Faculty of Humanities and Education: Dra SILVANA CAMPAGNARO
Faculty of Law: Dr JESÚS MARÍA CASAL
Faculty of Social and Economic Sciences: Dr EDUARDO OTIZ
Faculty of Theology: Rev. Fr GIAN PAOLO PERÓN

DIRECTORS

School of Business Administration and Accounting: Lic. FREDDY MARTÍN
School of Civil Engineering: Ing. JOSÉ OCHOA ITURBE
School of Economics: Econ. MARÍA ISABEL MARTÍNEZ ABAL
School of Education: Dra MARÍA ELENA FEBRES-CORDERO BRICEÑO
School of Engineering: Ing. MILAGROS BOSCHETTI
School of Industrial Engineering: Ing. VICENTE NAPOLITANO CASTALDO
School of Informatics: Ing. SUSANA GARCÍA MARTÍNEZ
School of Law: Abga AURA JANESKY LEHMANN
School of Letters: Lic. MARÍA DE LOS ANGELES PEÑA
School of Philosophy: Lic. JESÚS HERNÁEZ
School of Psychology: Dr GUSTAVO PEÑA
School of Social Sciences: Lic. INGRID OCHOA DE PÉREZ
School of Telecommunications Engineering: Ing. MAYRA NARVÁEZ
School of Theology: Rev. Fr RAFAEL SERRANO
Institute of Economic and Social Research: Lic. LUIS PEDRO ESPAÑA NAVARRO
Institute of Historical Research: Dr ELÍAS PINO ITURRIETA
Centre of Advice and Human Development: Lic. ALCIRA TEXEIRA DE CERRADA
Centre of Behavioural Studies: Dra SILVANA CAMPAGNARO
Centre of Communication Research: Lic. ERCILIA VÁSQUEZ
Centre of Engineering Research: Ing. LOURDES ORTIZ
Centre of Human Rights: Abga LIGIA BOLÍVAR
Centre of Legal Research: Dra MARÍA GRACIA MORAIS DIAZ
Centre of Philosophical Studies: Dra SILVANA CAMPAGNARO
Centre of Religious Studies: Dra SILVANA CAMPAGNARO
Engineering Laboratories: Ing. FRANCISCO MORERA

UNIVERSIDAD CATÓLICA DEL TÁCHIRA

Barrio Obrero, Calle 14 con Carrera 14, San Cristóbal, Edo. Táchira

Telephone: (276) 342-1614
E-mail: asosa@ucat.edu.ve
Internet: www.ucat.edu.ve

Founded 1982

Rector: Dr ARTURO SOSA ABASCAL
Vice-Rector: ASTRID RICO DE MÉNDEZ
Chief Admin. Officer: FÉLIDA ROA DE ROA
Librarian: EMILIO J. URBINA MENDOZA

Number of teachers: 336
Number of students: 5,000

Publications: *Paramillo* (1 a year), *Revista Tachirense de Derecho* (1 a year), *Siglo XXI* (1 a year), *Tributum* (1 a year)

DEANS

Faculty of Economics and Social Sciences: MARINÉS SÁNCHEZ
Faculty of Humanities and Education: EDUARDO FAJARDO RUEDA
Faculty of Law and Political Science: JESÚS ALBERTO LABRADOR SUÁREZ
Faculty of Religion: EDUARDO FAJARDO RUEDA

UNIVERSIDAD CENTRAL DE VENEZUELA

Apdo Postal 1050, Ciudad Universitaria, Los Chaguaramos, Caracas 1051

Telephone: (212) 605-4050
Fax: (212) 605-4086
Internet: www.ucv.ve

Founded 1721
State control
Language of instruction: Spanish
Academic year: January to December

Rector: GIUSEPPE GIANNETTO
Academic Vice-Rector: ERNESTO GONZÁLEZ
Admin. Vice-Rector: MANUEL MARIÑA
Registrar: Dr ANTONIO DEL NOGAL
Gen. Coordinator: JEANETTE BLANCO DE MÉNDEZ
Sec.: ELIZABETH MARVAL
Librarian: Dr EUDIS BORRA

Number of teachers: 6,987
Number of students: 45,000

Publications: *Acta Odontologica, Akademos* (2 a year), *Aula Magna, Boletín del Archivo Histórico, Boletín de Lingüística, Correo Ucevista, Gaceta Universitaria, Revista Alcance 57* (organic soil science, 2 a year), *Revista del Centro de Información y Documentación* (6 a year), *Revista Escuela de Metalurgia, Revista de la Facultad de Agronomía* (2 a year), *Revista de la Facultad de Ciencias Jurídicas y Políticas* (4 a year), *Revista de la Facultad de Ciencias Veterinarias, Revista de la Facultad de Farmacia* (4 a year), *Revista de la Facultad de Ingeniería* (6 a year), *Revista de la Facultad de Medicina, Revista Latinoamericana de Estudios Avanzados, Revista Tecnología y Construcción* (3 a year), *Revista Tharsis, Revista Urbana* (town planning, 2 a year), *Revista Venezolana de Economía y Ciencias Sociales, Revista Venezolana de Estudios Internacionales*

DEANS

Faculty of Agriculture: FRANKLÍN CHACÍN LUGO
Faculty of Architecture and Town Planning: ABNER COLMENARES
Faculty of Dentistry: CECILIA GARCÍA AROCHA
Faculty of Economic and Social Sciences: VÍCTOR RAGO
Faculty of Engineering: RAFAEL ROCA
Faculty of Humanities and Education: BENJAMÍN SÁNCHEZ
Faculty of Law and Political Science: PEDRO GUEVARA
Faculty of Medicine: MIGUEL REQUENA
Faculty of Pharmacy: ORLANDO VIZCARRONDO
Faculty of Science: MASSIMO CANESTRARI
Faculty of Veterinary Science: RAFAEL INFANTES

UNIVERSIDAD CENTRO-OCCIDENTAL 'LISANDRO ALVARADO'

Apdo 400, Barquisimeto, Lara

Telephone: (251) 259-1061
Fax: (251) 259-1064
Internet: www.ucla.edu.ve

Founded 1963 as Experimental Centre of Higher Education; univ. status 1968
State control
Language of instruction: Spanish
Academic year: January to December

Rector: Dr RICARDO GARCÍA DE LONGORIA
Academic Vice-Rector: Dra GADRA SÁNCHEZ DE PÉREZ
Admin. Vice-Rector: Dr GUÉDEZ CORTEZ
Sec.-Gen.: Dr RICARDO GÁSPERI MAGO
Librarian: Lic. MORELLA BARRANCOS

Number of teachers: 930
Number of students: 9,665

Publications: *Boletín Científico, Boletín Informativo, El Veterinario* (12 a year), *Escuela de Administración, Escuela de Agronomía, Memoria y Cuenta* (1 a year), *Tarea Común* (4 a year)

DEANS

Faculty of Administration and Accountancy: Lic. CÉSAR MORENO
Faculty of Agronomy: Ing. JOSÉ PASTOR GUTIÉRREZ
Faculty of Civil Engineering: Ing. HERMES ESPINOZA
Faculty of Medicine: Dr RÉGULO CARPIO
Faculty of Sciences: Dr JOSÉ BETHELMY
Faculty of Veterinary Medicine: Dr RAMÓN SALCEDO

ATTACHED INSTITUTES

Consejo Asesor de Investigación y Servicios (Advisory Council on Research and Services): assessment and consultation on the planning of research; Pres. Dr FRANCISCO MONTES DE OCA.

Instituto de la Uva (Institute for Research on Grapes): research on grape cultivation and advisory service to wine growers; Dir MARIA LUISA DE PIRE.

UNIVERSIDAD DE LOS ANDES

Avda 3, Independencia, Edif. Rectorado, Mérida 5101

Telephone: (275) 240-1111
Fax: (275) 240-1998
E-mail: dsia@ula.ve
Internet: www.ula.ve

Founded 1785 as the Real Colegio Seminario de San Buenaventura de Mérida, became Univ. 1810

Campuses at Trujillo and Táchira
State control
Language of instruction: Spanish
Academic year: January to December

Rector: GENRY VARGAS
Academic Vice-Rector: MANUEL HERNÁNDEZ
Admin. Vice-Rector: JULIO FLORES MENESINI
Sec.: GLADYS BECERRA DEPABLOS
Registrar: (vacant)
Librarian: NILZA GONZÁLEZ DE GUTIÉRREZ

Library: see Libraries and Archives
Number of teachers: 2,947
Number of students: 34,294

DEANS

Faculty of Architecture: Arq. INÉS BENAVIDES
Faculty of Economic and Social Sciences: MANUEL ARANGUREN
Faculty of Engineering: Ing. RUBÉN AÑEZ
Faculty of Forestry: Prof. CERES BOADA
Faculty of Humanities and Education: FRANCISCO GAVIDIA
Faculty of Law and Political Science: ANDREY GROMIKO URDANETA
Faculty of Medicine: Dr JOSÉ FREYTEZ O'CALLAGHAN
Faculty of Odontology: Dr PATRICIO JARPA
Faculty of Pharmacy: Dr ALFREDO CARABOT CUERVO
Faculty of Sciences: CARLOS ALVAREZ

Rafael Rangel Campus: Dr CONRADO DABOÍN VÁSQUEZ

Táchira Campus: Dr RAMÓN GONZÁLEZ E.

UNIVERSIDAD METROPOLITANA

Apdo 76819, Caracas 1070

Telephone: (212) 242-2958

Fax: (212) 242-5450

E-mail: cvicentini@unimet.edu.ve

Internet: www.unimet.edu.ve

Founded 1970

Private control

Language of instruction: Spanish

Academic year: October to September

Pres.: Ing. HERNAN ANZOLA

Rector: Ing. JOSÉ IGNACIO MORENO LEÓN

Academic Vice-Rector: Ing. JOSÉ ROBERTO BELLO

Admin. Vice-Rector: Ing. ANTINIO IZSAK

Registrar: Prof. MARÍA DE LOURDES ACEDO DE SUCRE

Librarian: Dr ELEIDA GARCÍA

Number of teachers: 438

Number of students: 4,670

Publications: *Anales de la Universidad Metropolitana* (2 a year), *Revista UNIMET* (12 a year)

DEANS

Arts and Sciences: Prof. JAVIER RÍOS

Economics and Social Sciences: Prof. JOSÉ ANGEL VELÁZQUEZ

Engineering: Ing. MARIA BLANCA FERNÁNDEZ

UNIVERSIDAD NACIONAL ABIERTA
(Open University)

Apdo 2096, Caracas 1010A

Telephone: (212) 574-1322

Fax: (212) 574-4075

E-mail: mromero@reacciun.ve

Internet: www.una.edu.ve

Founded 1977 on the 'open university' principle, using modern methods of communication and educational technology. One national centre in Caracas and 20 regional centres

State control

Language of instruction: Spanish

Academic year: October to July

Rector: Dr MANUEL CASTRO PEREIRA

Academic Vice-Rector: Dr NÉSTOR LEAL ORTIZ

Admin. Vice-Rector: Prof. ARNALDO ESCALONA PEÑUELA

Sec.: Prof. ARELIS COROMOTO SAAVEDRA

Librarian: Lic. CARMEN IBARRA

Number of teachers: 831

Number of students: 61,648

Publications: *Informe de Investigaciones Educativas, Una Documenta*

COURSE COORDINATORS

Academic Areas and Courses: Prof. MARÍA J. BERMÚDEZ

Academic Coordinator: Dr MANUEL CASTRO PEREIRA

Academic Evaluation: Prof. ISALIV MATHEUS

Accountancy: Prof. FRANCISCO EGAÑEZ

Administration and Accountancy: Dr PEDRO RUIZ

Education: Dra ERICKA NAVEDA

General Studies: Dra MARÍA CLARA SALAS

Industrial Engineering: Prof. MARTHA URBINA

Mathematics: Prof. SERGIO RIVAS

Planning and Evaluation: Dra ARLETTE URGELLES

Regional and Local Centres: Prof. MIRIAM PÉREZ

Student Services: Prof. OMAIRA CORDERO

Systems Engineering: Prof. JUDIT CARVALLO

University Extension: Prof. TERESITA PÉREZ DE MAZA

LOCAL CENTRES

Anzoátegui: Dir Prof. LUIS RIVAS.

Apure: Dir Prof. JOSÉ GREGORIO FIGUEROA.

Aragua: Dir Prof. NELSON GUARDIA.

Barinas: Dir Prof. RAMÓN CHACÓN.

Bolivar: Dir Prof. ELMES PÉREZ.

Carabobo: Dir Prof. LUCILA CABRICES.

Cojedes: Dir (vacant).

Falcón: Dir Prof. NOÉ JIMENEZ.

Guárico: Dir Prof. DUNIA SISO.

Lara: Dir Prof. MILAGROS BARTOLOMÉ.

Mérida: Dir Prof. NAPOLEÓN SÁNCHEZ.

Metropolitano: Dir Prof. OSCAR ODÓN.

Monagas: Dir Prof. LUIS BALBAS.

Nueva Esparta: Dir Prof. AQUILES ROJAS.

Portuguesa: Dir Prof. NANCY CONTRERAS.

Sucre: Dir Prof. FREDDY PÉREZ.

Táchira: Dir MARÍA LOURDES RINCÓN.

T. F. Delta Amacuro: Dir Prof. JUANA LUGO.

Trujillo: Dir Prof. EVELYN HACKETT.

Yaracuy: Dir Prof. JORGE MILLA.

Zulia: Dir Prof. ANA YSOLINA SOTO.

UNIVERSIDAD NACIONAL EXPERIMENTAL FRANCISCO DE MIRANDA

Edif. Rectorado, Calle Norte, Santa Ana de Coro, Estado Falcón

Telephone: (293) 250-2406

Fax: (293) 250-2429

E-mail: webmaster@unefm.edu.ve

Internet: www.unefm.edu.ve

Founded 1977

Academic year: January to December (two semesters)

Chancellor: SIMON ALBERTO CONSALVI

Rector: Dr PEDRO BORREGALES P.

Academic Vice-Rector: Dr OSCAR ABREU

Admin. Vice-Rector: Dr JULIO LÓPEZ P.

Administrator: Lic. CESAR VELÁSQUEZ

Librarian: Lic. NIDYA PETIT DE MOTTA

Number of teachers: 350

Number of students: 3,000

Publications: *Boletín* (52 a year), *Cultura Falconiana* (4 a year), *Gaceta Universitaria* (4 a year)

DEANS

Faculty of Civil and Industrial Engineering: Ing. ORANGEL NUÑEZ

Faculty of Medicine: Dr ROBERTO GRAND L.

Faculty of Veterinary Medicine and Agriculture: Dr DIOGENES RODRÍGUEZ

UNIVERSIDAD NACIONAL EXPERIMENTAL DE GUAYANA

Avda Las Américas, Edificio General de Seguros, Puerto Ordaz, Estado Bolívar

Telephone: (286) 923-2423

Fax: (286) 922-5673

E-mail: secretaria@uneg.edu.ve

Internet: www.uneg.edu.ve

Founded 1982

State control

Rector: JOSÉ TARAZONA

Vice-Rector for Academic Affairs: Dr LUIS ALEXIS VELÁSQUEZ

Vice-Rector for Admin.: Dra MARÍA ELENA LATUFF

Sec.-Gen.: Dra MYRIAN ARLENY ZAMBRANO DE GUERRERO

Publications: *Copérnico, Gaceta Universitaria* (12 a year), *Kaleidoscopio* (4 a year)

Depts of education, humanities and arts, man and the environment, management and science and technology.

UNIVERSIDAD NACIONAL EXPERIMENTAL DE LOS LLANOS CENTRALES 'ROMULO GALLEGOS'

Ciudad Universitaria, Avenida Universitaria, vía El Castrero, San Juan de los Morros, Estado Guárico

Telephone: (246) 431-0584

Fax: (246) 431-2670

E-mail: webmaster@unerg.edu.ve

Internet: www.unerg.edu.ve

Founded 1977

State control

Language of instruction: Spanish

Academic year: March to December (2 semesters)

Pres. and Rector: Ing. GIOVANNI NANI R.

Academic Vice-Rector: Ing. ENRIQUE MUJICA ALVÁREZ

Admin. Vice-Rector: Lic. GHENRY J. NAVARRO U.

Librarian: Lic. RHAIZA MARQUEZ

Number of teachers: 367

Number of students: 5,306

Publication: *Horizontes Universitarios*

DEANS

Continuing Education: Lic. YOLANDA VILLAS-MIL

Faculty of Economics: Lic. CARLOS HERRERA

Faculty of Education: Lic. CECILIA REQUENA R.

Faculty of Engineering: Ing. NELSON MARTE

Faculty of Health: Dra MARTHA CANTAVELLA

Faculty of Odontology: Dr OMAR SCOVINO

Faculty of Veterinary Medicine: Méd. Vet. SALVADOR DE J. PÉREZ ALEMÁN

Postgraduate Studies: Lic. GLADYS MORENO V.

Research and Extension: Prof. GEOMAIRA MONTENEGRO

ATTACHED INSTITUTE

Centre for Legal Studies: Dir Abog. GLADYS BOYER.

UNIVERSIDAD NACIONAL EXPERIMENTAL DE LOS LLANOS OCCIDENTALES 'EZEQUIEL ZAMORA'

Av. 23 de Enero, Redoma de Punto Fresco, Barinas

Telephone: (73) 41201

Fax: (73) 41858

Internet: www.unellez.edu.ve

Founded 1975

Language of instruction: Spanish

Academic year: January to December (2 semesters)

Rector: Prof. MIGUEL ÁNGEL HENRÍQUEZ MARCANO

Vice-Rector: Dr JOSÉ ALFREDO GUERRERO SOSA

Sec.: Dr LUIS A. SUÁREZ CORDERO

Librarian: Dra MIGDALIA DE LARA

Number of teachers: 600

Number of students: 8,000

Publications: *Biollania, Revista UNELLEZ de Ciencia y Tecnología*

Experimental govt-sponsored institute of higher education, serving the Los Llanos Occidentales region, and the States of Apure, Barinas, Cojedes and Portuguesa

Courses in agriculture and mechanization, economics, social development, regional planning, human ecology.

UNIVERSIDAD NACIONAL EXPERIMENTAL MARÍTIMA DEL CARIBE

Calle El Ejército, Catia La Mar, Vargas, Caracas

Telephone: (212) 351-0834
Fax: (212) 351-0834
Internet: www.umc.edu.ve

Founded 2000
State control

Rector: MIGUEL LÓPEZ
Vice-Rector (for Academic Affairs: REYNALDO MONTES DE OCA
Vice-Rector for Admin.: MANUEL PÉREZ ALVAREZ.

UNIVERSIDAD NACIONAL EXPERIMENTAL POLITECNICA 'ANTONIO JOSÉ DE SUCRE'

Apdo Postal 539, Barquisimeto, Edo Lara

Telephone: (251) 420133
Fax: (251) 413880
Internet: www.unellez.edu.ve

Founded 1962
Private control

Rector: Dr IVÁN OLAIZOLA D'ALESSANDRO
Vice-Rector for Secretariat: Dr RAMÓN VIELMA
Vice-Rector for Barquisimeto Campus: Ing. AMAEL CASTELLANO
Vice-Rector for Caracas Campus: Ing. ILDELFONSO MEJÍA ZAMBRANO
Vice-Rector for Ordaz Campus: Ing. LUIS CÁRDENAS CASTILLO
Academic Admin. Coordinator: Ing. EDUARDO CABRÉ TRUJILLO
Coordinator: Lic. XIOMARA DE BARRA

Library of 19,200 vols, 9,000 periodicals
Number of teachers: 900
Number of students: 10,000

Publications: *Avance Universitario* (2 a year), *Boletín Bibliográfico de Publicaciones Recibidas* (2 a year), *Información General de la Universidad* (1 a year)

Faculties of chemistry and industrial engineering, electrical engineering, electronic engineering, mechanical engineering, metallurgy, systems.

UNIVERSIDAD NACIONAL EXPERIMENTAL RAFAEL MARÍA BARALT

Avda El Rosario, Parroquia Carmen Herrera, Cabimas, Estado Zulia

Telephone: (264) 241-5306
E-mail: rectorado@unermb.edu.ve
Internet: www.unermb.edu.ve

Founded 1982
State control

Rector: Dr VICTOR HUGO MERIÑO CÓRDOBA
Vice-Rector for Academic Affairs: BOLÍVAR SÁENZ TRAÑA
Vice-Rector for Admin.: AÍDA CÓRTES DE VERBEL
Sec.-Gen.: ODA GONZÁLEZ RINCÓN.

UNIVERSIDAD NACIONAL EXPERIMENTAL SIMÓN RODRÍGUEZ

Calle 1, Zona Industrial Urb. Palo Verde, Caracas

Telephone: (212) 251-3684
Internet: www.unesr.edu.ve

Founded 1974

Regional centres in 13 towns

Pres.: Dr GUSTAVO GONZÁLEZ ERASO
Rector: Dr MANUEL MARIÑAS
Academic Vice-Rector: JUDITH SOSA DE VÁZQUEZ

Admin. Vice-Rector: ASDRÚBAL LOZANO FERNÁNDEZ
Sec.: MARÍA SILVA VIVANCO

Number of teachers: 387
Number of students: 12,859

Publications: *Gaceta Universitaria* (4 a year), *Memoria y Cuenta de la Universidad* (1 a year), *Revista de Cultura* (4 a year)

Faculties of administration, education and food technology.

UNIVERSIDAD NACIONAL EXPERIMENTAL DEL TÁCHIRA

Apdo 436, Avda Universidad, Paramillo, San Cristóbal, Táchira

Telephone: (276) 353-0422
Fax: (276) 353-2896
E-mail: rectorad@unet.edu.ve
Internet: www.unet.edu.ve

Founded 1974
State control
Language of instruction: Spanish
Academic year: February to December

Rector: Lic. JOSÉ VICENTE SÁNCHEZ FRANK
Academic Vice-Rector: Ing. CARLOS CHACÓN LABRADOR
Admin. Vice-Rector: Ing. MARTÍN PAZ
Sec.: Arq. OSCAR MEDINA HERNÁNDEZ
Dean of Extension: Ing. SALVADOR GALEANO
Dean of Graduate Studies: Ing. JESÚS WILFREDO BOLÍVAR
Dean of Research: Ing. RAÚL CASANOVA
Dean of Teaching: Ing. JOSÉ BECERRA
Dean of Undergraduate Studies: Ing. LUIS VERGARA
Librarian: Ing. ERLAND MARTÍNEZ

Number of teachers: 530
Number of students: 10,500 (6,000 undergraduate, 1,500 propaedeutic, 3,000 graduate)

Publications: *Aleph sub cero*, *Boletín*, *Boletín Estadístico*, *Gaceta*, *Revista Científica UNET*, *Vocero Universitario*.

UNIVERSIDAD NACIONAL EXPERIMENTAL DEL YARACUY

Zona Industrial Agustín Rivero, Edificio Fundación CIEPE, San Felipe, Estado Yaracuy

Telephone: (254) 232-2441
Fax: (254) 232-1351
E-mail: rectorado@uney.edu.ve
Internet: www.uney.edu.ve

Founded 1999
State control

Rector: Dr FREDDY CASTILLO CASTELLANOS
Vice-Rector: Ing. JOSÉ LUIS NAJUL SALDIVIA
Sec.-Gen.: Ing. RAMÓN G. SÁNCHEZ SIVIRA

Courses in food science and sport.

UNIVERSIDAD DE ORIENTE

Edificio Rectorado, Apdo 094, Cumaná, Estado Sucre

Telephone: (93) 23366
Internet: www.udo.edu.ve

Founded 1958
State control
Academic year: February to December

Rector: Dr ANDRÉS PASTRANA VÁSQUEZ
Academic Vice-Rector: Dr OSWALDO BETANCOURT
Admin. Vice-Rector: Dr DIOGENES FIGUEROA LUGO
Sec.-Gen.: Dr CESAR A. BOADA SALAZAR

Library: see Libraries and Archives
Number of teachers: 1,382
Number of students: 23,084

Publications: *Boletín del Instituto Oceanográfico*, *Catálogo de la UDO* (1 a year),

Directorio del Personal Docente e Investigación (1 a year), *Lagena*, *La UDO Investiga*, *Oriente Agropecuario*, *Oriente Universitario* (12 a year, bulletin).

CONSTITUENT CAMPUSES

Universidad de Oriente, Nucleo Anzoátegui

Apdo postal 4327, Puerto La Cruz, Anzoátegui

Telephone: (281) 420-3402
Internet: www.anz.udo.edu.ve

Founded 1965

Dean: Prof. MANUEL LÓPEZ FARÍAS
Number of teachers: 418
Number of students: 9,000

HEADS OF SCHOOLS

Administrative Sciences: Prof. JUAN D. GUAICAIN
Basic Courses: Prof. PEDRO JIMÉNEZ
Engineering and Applied Science: Prof. RUBÉN AULAR

Universidad de Oriente, Nucleo Bolívar

La Sabanita, Ciudad Bolívar
Internet: www.bolivar.udo.edu.ve

Dean: Dr ARTURO RAUL LARA ROJAS

DIRECTORS

Basic Courses: Prof. MARGOTH SISO DE SAN MARTIN
Geology and Mines: Prof. OSCAR GARCÍA CACHAZO
Medicine: Prof. VICTOR ESPINOZA LEÓN

Universidad de Oriente, Nucleo de Monagas

Avda Universidad, Maturín, Edo Monagas
Internet: www.monagas.udo.edu.ve

Founded 1961

Dean: Dr JOSÉ JIMÉNEZ TIAMO
Academic Coordinator: Ing. LUIS ARISMENDI
Admin. Coordinator: Ing. MARCIAL VIÑAS DE LA HOZ
Librarian: Lic. RAMÓN JOSÉ NÚÑEZ

Publication: *Oriente Agropecuario* (2 a year)

HEADS OF SCHOOLS

Basic Courses: Prof. JOSÉ VICENTE ANDÉRICO
Programme of Administrative Science: Prof. ARNALDO ROJAS
Programme of Human Resources: Prof. LUIS MÁRQUEZ
School of Agricultural Engineering: NILDA ALCORCES DE GUERRA

Universidad de Oriente, Nucleo Nueva Esparta

Apdo Postal 147, Guatamare, Nueva Esparta

Telephone: (95) 610131
Fax: (95) 610131
Internet: www.ne.udo.edu.ve

Founded 1958
State control

Dean: Ing. CASTO GONZÁLEZ M.
Academic Coordinator: Prof. JOSÉ G. MARCANO
Admin. Coordinator: Ing. LUIS MARCANO

HEADS OF SCHOOLS

Applied Ocean Sciences: Prof. JOSÉ LUIS FUENTES
Basic Courses: Prof. ESTEBAN OBANDO
Hotel and Tourism: Prof. JOSÉ M. VELÁSQUEZ

Universidad de Oriente, Nucleo de Sucre

Cumaná
Internet: www.sucre.udo.edu.ve

Dean: Prof. FRANCIA PADILLA DE KORCHOFF

HEADS OF SCHOOLS

Administration and Accountancy: Prof. JOSÉ ANTONIO ARISTIMUÑO
Basic Courses: Prof. FORTUNATO MALAN
Humanities and Education: Prof. EZEQUIEL SALAZAR
Sciences: Prof. ELSIE ROMERO DE BELLORIN
Social Sciences: Prof. MARÍA ELENA ZAJÍA

UNIVERSIDAD PEDAGÓGICA EXPERIMENTAL LIBERTADOR

Avda Sucre, Parque del Oeste, Catia, 1030 Caracas

Telephone: (212) 864-7511
Fax: (212) 864-7977
Internet: www.upel.edu.ve

Founded 1983
State control
Academic year: September to July

Rector: Prof. ÁNGEL ARÍSTIDES HERNÁNDEZ ABREU
Vice-Rector for Extension: Prof. LUIS MARÍN
Vice-Rector for Research and Postgraduate Studies: Prof. MAXIMILIANO BEZADA
Vice-Rector for Teaching: Prof. JESÚS RODRÍGUEZ
Sec.: Prof. FRANCIA CELIS.

CONSTITUENT INSTITUTES

Instituto de Mejoramiento Profesional del Magisterio

Avda Rómulo Gallegos, Segunda Transversal de Montecristo, Caracas 1071

Telephone: (212) 234-6640
Fax: (212) 234-6608
E-mail: pontivero@impm.upel.edu.ve
Internet: www.impm.upel.edu.ve.

Institutio Pedagógico de Barquisimeto

Avda Los Horcones con Calle 64, Barquisimeto, Estado Lara

Telephone: (251) 442-5333
Fax: (251) 423-887
E-mail: r.valera@ipb.upel.edu.ve
Internet: www.ipb.upel.edu.ve
Dir: RAFAEL VALERA.

Instituto Pedagógico de Caracas

Avda Páez, El Paraíso, Caracas 1020

Telephone: (212) 461-6121
Fax: (212) 462-2760
E-mail: webmaster@ipc.upel.edu.ve
Internet: www.ipc.upel.edu.ve

Founded 1936 as Instituto Pedagógico Nacional; present status 1987
Academic year: May to February (2 semesters)

Dir: Prof. CRISTIAN SÁNCHEZ
Sub-Dir for Extension: Prof. ÁNGEL FLORES
Sub-Dir for Research and Postgraduate Studies: Prof. SILVANA MESSORI DE NEGRETE
Sub-Dir for Teaching: Prof. HEAGDLINE ARIAS
Librarian: Lic. MELVIS PIRE

Publications: Candidus Infantil (4 a year), Lingvo & Internacia Komunikado, Revista de Investigación, Tiempo y Espacio.

Instituto Pedagógico de Maturín

Carretera Sur, Maturín 6263, Estado Monagas

Telephone: (291) 641-6863
Fax: (291) 641-7750
E-mail: carzolay@ipm.upel.edu.ve
Internet: www.ipm.upel.edu.ve
Dir: COSME ALZOLAY.

Instituto Pedagógico de Miranda

Calle 6, Edificio Papeca Modulo 2, Urbanización La Urbina, Caracas 1070

Telephone: (212) 461-6472
Fax: (212) 462-2760
E-mail: nbarreto@ipmjmsm.upel.edu.ve
Internet: www.ipmjmsm.upel.edu.ve
Dir: NANCY BARRETO.

Instituto Pedagógico Rural 'El Mácaro'

Carretera Nacional Maracay/Turmero, Maracay 2115, Estado Aragua

Telephone: (244) 631294
Fax: (244) 61380
E-mail: aperales@iprm.upel.edu.ve
Internet: www.iprm.upel.edu.ve
Dir: AURA DÍAZ DE PERALES.

Instituto Pedagógico Rural 'Gervasio Rubio'

Final Avda Dr 'Manuel Pulido Méndez', Vía Bramón, Rubio, Estado Táchira

Telephone: (276) 762-1746
Fax: (276) 762-4041
E-mail: fespinel@iprgr.upel.edu.ve
Internet: www.iprgr.upel.edu.ve
Dir: FRANCISCO ESPINEL.

UNIVERSIDAD SIMÓN BOLÍVAR

Carretera Hoyo de la Puerta, Valle de Sartenejas Baruta Estado Miranda

Telephone: (212) 906-3111
Fax: (212) 962-1615
Internet: www.usb.ve

Founded 1970
State control
Language of instruction: Spanish
Academic year: September to July

Rector: Ing. PEDRO ASO
Academic Vice-Rector: Dr OSMAR ISSA
Admin. Vice-Rector: Ing. JUAN LEON
Gen.-Sec.: Dr PEDRO MARÍA ASO
Librarian: Dra ROSARIO GASSOL DE HOROWITZ

Number of teachers: 850
Number of students: 10,000

Publications: Argos, Atlántida, Perfiles

DEANS

General Studies: JUAN CARLOS RODRÍGUEZ
Postgraduate Studies: CARLOS PÉREZ
Professional Studies: RAUL GONCALVES
Research: BENJAMÍN SCHARIFKER

DIVISION DIRECTORS

Biological Sciences: DAISY PÉREZ DE ACOSTA
Humanities and Social Sciences: ANA MARÍA RAJKAY
Physics and Mathematics: ROBERTO RÉQUIZ
Technological Studies (Núcleo Universitario del Litoral): ENRIQUE LÓPEZ CONTRERAS

UNIVERSIDAD DEL ZULIA

Av. 16 con calle 67B, Maracaibo, Estado Zulia

Telephone: (261) 759-8441
E-mail: webmaster@luz.edu.ve
Internet: www.luz.edu.ve

Founded 1891, closed 1904, reopened 1946
State control
Academic year: September to July

Rector: Dr ANGEL LOMBARDI LOMBARDI
Academic Vice-Rector: Lic. ANTONIO CASTEJÓN
Admin. Vice-Rector: Econ. NEURO VILLALOBOS
Sec.: Ing. ANGEL LARREAL
Librarian: Lic. EGLA ORTEGA

Library: see Libraries and Archives
Number of teachers: 3,652
Number of students: 47,590

Publications: Gaceta (4 a year), Memoria y Cuenta de LUZ (1 a year), Publicaciones de la Unidad de Estadísticas

DEANS

Faculty of Agriculture: Prof. ALONSO FERNÁNDEZ
Faculty of Architecture: Prof. IGNACIO DE OTEIZA
Faculty of Dentistry: Prof. EXEQUIADES PAZ A.
Faculty of Economic and Social Sciences: Prof. JULIANA FERRER
Faculty of Engineering: Prof. NELSON MOLERO
Faculty of Experimental Sciences: Prof. TERESITA ALVAREZ DE FERNANDEZ
Faculty of Humanities and Education: Prof. NERÍO VÍLCHEZ
Faculty of Law: Dr HERMANN PETZOLD PERNÍA
Faculty of Medicine: Dr RAFAEL MARTÍNEZ
Faculty of Veterinary Sciences: Prof. GUSTAVO SOTO

Polytechnic Institute

INSTITUTO UNIVERSITARIO POLITÉCNICO 'LUIS CABALLERO MEJÍAS'

Apdo 20955, San Martin, Caracas 1020A
Telephone: (212) 498917

Founded 1974

Dir: Ing. RAFAEL DUQUE SALINAS
Deputy Dir of Academic Affairs: Ing. IDELFONSO MEJÍAS
Deputy Dir of Admin. Affairs: Lic. RAMÓN PELLES
Librarian: Lic. MYRIAM LÓPEZ ACOSTA

Number of teachers: 216
Number of students: 2,017

College

Instituto de Estudios Superiores de Administración (IESA) (Institute for Advanced Studies in Administration): Edificio IESA, Avda IESA, San Bernardino, Caracas 1010; tel. (212) 552-2055; e-mail relinsti@iesa.edu.ve; internet www.iesa.edu.ve; f. 1965; private non-profit business school; Pres. RAMÓN PIÑANGO.

Schools of Art and Music

Centro de Bellas Artes (Centre for Fine Arts): Avenida 3F Nº 67-217, Colonia Bella Vista, Sector La Lago, Maracaibo; tel. (261) 912950; fax (261) 912239; e-mail centrobellasartes@iamnet.com; f. 1954 to promote cultural activities; theatre, 2 art galleries, school of ballet and modern dance, Maracaibo Contemporary Dance Troupe, Maracaibo Symphony Orchestra, National Youth Theatre, Goajiro Indian workshop, Colegio Bellas Artes, library; Dir OSCAR D'EMPAIRE.

Conservatorio de Música José Luis Paz: Av. 2 El Milagro, Edif. Secretaría de Cultura, 2° piso, Maracaibo; tel. (261) 808-6231; internet conservatoriojlp.com.ve; f. 1943; Dir Prof. OSCAR FACCIO.

Escuela de Artes Visuales 'Cristóbal Rojas' (Cristóbal Rojas School of Visual Arts): Esquina No Pastor, frente a la Plaza Parque Carabobo, La Candelaria, Caracas 1010; tel. (212) 621-0940; f. 1936; Dir EMILY HERNÁNDEZ DE VILLAROEL.

Escuela Superior de Arte 'Neptali Rincón': Centro Vocacional Dr O. Hernández, Avda El Milagro Diagonal al Hospital Central, Maracaibo; tel. (261) 223868; f. 1957; courses in painting, sculpture, ceramics, etc.; 12 teachers; 300 students; Dir CONSUELO BUSTOS.

Escuela Superior de Música 'José Angel Lamas' (Lamas High School of Music): Av. Urdaneta, Esq. de Santa Capilla, Caracas; tel. (212) 864-1618; f. 1887; Dir VICENTE EMILIO SOJO.

Fundación Teresa Carreño: Teatro Teresa Carreño, Final Paseo Colón, Caracas; tel. (212) 574-9122; e-mail webmaster@teatroteresacarreno.com; internet www.teatroteresacarreno.com; f. 1983; concerts, opera, ballet, master classes and courses for opera singers; Dir-Gen. BEATRICE RANGEL MANTILLA.

VIET NAM

The Higher Education System

Institutions of higher education predate Viet Nam's partition in 1954 (it was reunified as the Socialist Republic of Viet Nam in 1976), the oldest being Hanoi Medical University, which was founded in 1902 when Viet Nam was under French colonial rule. Over 30 institutions were founded during the period of partition (1954–76), including major universities in Hanoi and Ho Chi Minh City (formerly Saigon). In 1989 Viet Nam's first private college since 1954 was opened in Hanoi; Thang Long College was to cater for university students. The presence of foreign universities is increasing with universities such as Royal Melbourne Institute of Technology and University of Hawaii offering degrees in fields such as business, English as a Second Language and Information Technology. According to preliminary estimates, in 2010/11 there were 414 universities and colleges of higher education, with a total enrolment of 2.0m. students.

The Ministry of Education and Training is responsible for higher education, with the exception of technical and vocational education, which is the responsibility of the Ministry of Labour, Invalids and Social Affairs , and institutions of health education and military or security training, which come under the appropriate ministries. The National Council for Education Accreditation, which was established in October 2008, is responsible for accreditation and quality assurance within the higher education sector.

Since the 2002/03 academic year a national university entrance examination has been the determining factor in university admissions; students sit examinations in one of four subject streams, depending on the course of study for which the student has applied. A credit-based degree system is being introduced and was expected to have been fully implemented by 2012/13. The Tot Nghiep Dai Hoc (College Diploma or Associate degree) is a three-year course that can be upgraded to a Bang tot nghiep dai hoc (Bachelors degree) after one year. The Bachelors is the main undergraduate qualification and often lasts four years, although degrees in veterinary medicine (five years) and medicine (six years) are longer in duration. Graduates who have been awarded the Bachelors degree are eligible to sit the entrance examination for admission to the Thac si (Masters degree), a two-year taught or research-based course. The Tien si (Doctorate) is open to students who hold either the Bachelors or the Masters degree and admission is again based on competitive examination. However, students with Bachelors degrees must study for four to five years to gain the Doctorate (and usually earn a Masters 'in passing') while students with the Masters are awarded the Doctorate after two or three years. Technical and vocational education at the post-secondary level is offered by colleges, universities, training centres, agencies, social organizations and private companies and leads to award of the Vocational Education Graduation Diploma, which requires one to two years of study following completion of secondary school education, or the Junior College Graduation Diploma, which has a practical focus and typically lasts three years.

In 2009 the World Bank approved a US \$50m. loan for its higher education development policy programme in Viet Nam; in return, the bank is expecting a 40% increase in student enrolments by 2020. Meanwhile, the Vietnamese Government initiated the Higher Education Reform Agenda for the period 2006–20 with a view to improving the quality, efficiency and governance of the higher education system, increasing the enrolment rate at universities, and strengthening the quality of teaching and research at universities and other higher education institutions.

Regulatory Bodies

GOVERNMENT

Ministry of Culture, Sports and Tourism: 51–53 Ngo Quyen, Hoan Kiem District, Hanoi; tel. (4) 9438231; fax (4) 9439009; internet www.cinet.gov.vn; Minister of Culture, Sports and Tourism Hoang Tuan Anh.

Ministry of Education and Training: 49 Dai Co Viet, Hai Ba Trung District, Hanoi; tel. (4) 8694904; fax (4) 8694085; e-mail intlaff@iupui.edu; internet www.edu.net.vn; Minister Nguyen Thien Nhan.

Learned Societies

GENERAL

UNESCO Office Hanoi: 23 Cao Ba Quat St, Hanoi; tel. (4) 7470275; fax (4) 7470274; e-mail registry@unesco.org.vn; internet www.unesco.org.vn; gender equality, HIV/AIDS prevention, youth devt, and poverty reduction; Dir Dung Doan Thi.

Viet Nam Union of Literary and Arts Associations: 51 Tran Hung Dao St, Hanoi; tel. (4) 8682608; fax (4) 9437431; f. 1957; 10 mem. orgs (assocs of writers, cinematographers, fine arts, composers and musicologists, theatre artists, photographers, folklorists, dancers, architects, and minority writers and artists), with a total of 10,000 mems; Pres. Nguyen Dinh Thi; Sec.-Gen. Thanh To Ngoc; publ. *Dien dan van nghe Viet Nam* (Forum of Vietnamese Literature and Arts, 4 a year).

Viet Nam Union of Science and Technology Associations: 53 Nguyen Du St, Hanoi; tel. (4) 9432206; fax (4) 8227593; e-mail thongtin@vusta.vn; internet www.vusta.org.vn; f. 1983; 114 mem. socs; Chair. Prof. Dr Ho Uy Liem (acting).

AGRICULTURE, FISHERIES AND VETERINARY SCIENCE

National Association of Vietnamese Gardeners: 15 Thanh Cong St, Hanoi; tel. (4) 8345216; f. 1985; Pres Nguyen Ngoc Triu.

Viet Nam Forestry Association: 114 Hoang Quoc Viet St, Cau Giay District, Hanoi; tel. (4) 7541311; Pres. Nguyen Ngoc Lung; Sec.-Gen. Ngo Duc Minh.

ARCHITECTURE AND TOWN PLANNING

Builders' Association: 34 Hang Chuoi St, Hanoi; Pres. Vu Khoa.

ECONOMICS, LAW AND POLITICS

Economics Association: 1B Cam Hoi St, Hai Ba Trung Dist., Hanoi; tel. (4) 9712899; e-mail vie-lam@fpt.vn; f. 1974, recognized by Govt. 1975; attached to ASEAN Federation of Economics Associations, International Economics Association, , Viet Nam Union of Science and Technology Associations (VUSTA),; 2,000 mems.

Viet Nam Lawyers Association: A2-261 Thuy Khue St, Tay Ho District, Hanoi; tel. (4) 8474826; fax (4) 8474831; e-mail vla@fpt.vn; attached to ASEAN Law Association; Sec.-Gen. (vacant).

HISTORY, GEOGRAPHY AND ARCHAEOLOGY

Vietnamese Association of Historians: 25 Tong Dan St, Hanoi; tel. (4) 8256588; Pres. Phan Huy Le; Sec.-Gen. Duong Trung Quoc.

LANGUAGE AND LITERATURE

British Council: 40 Cat Linh St, Dong Da District, Hanoi; tel. (4) 8436780; fax (4) 8434962; e-mail bchanoi@britishcouncil.org.vn; internet www.britishcouncil.org/vietnam; f. 1993; offers courses and exams in English language and British culture and promotes cultural exchange with the UK; attached teaching centre in Ho Chi Minh City; Dir Keith Davies; Training Centre Man. Tim Hood.

Goethe-Institut: Nguyen Thai Hoc St 56–58, Ba Dinh District, Hanoi; tel. (4) 7342251; fax (4) 7342254; e-mail gihanoi-il@fpt.vn; internet www.goethe.de/so/han/deindex.htm; offers courses and exams in German language and culture and promotes cultural exchange with Germany; Dir Franz Xaver Augustin.

MEDICINE

Traditional Medicine Association of Viet Nam: 19 Tong Dan St, Hanoi; tel. (4) 8253006; Pres. NGUYEN XUAN HUONG.

Viet Nam General Association: 68A Ba Trieu St, Hanoi; tel. and fax (4) 39439323; e-mail vgamp@hn.vnn.vn; internet tonghoiyhoc.org.vn; f. 1955; 21 mem. socs; Pres. Prof. PHAM SONG; Sec.-Gen. TRAN HUU THANG; publ. *Y hoc Viet Nam* (magazine).

NATURAL SCIENCES

Biological Sciences

Viet Nam Association of Biological Science Societies: Biological Experiment Centre, Ha Noi Pedagogical Institute, Hanoi; tel. (4) 8347654; Pres. VU TUYEN HOANG; Sec.-Gen. NGUYEN LAN HUNG.

Mathematical Sciences

Viet Nam Mathematical Society: 46 Lieu Giai St, Hanoi; tel. (4) 8682414; President DO LONG VAN; Sec.-Gen. TONG DINH QUY.

Physical Sciences

Geological Society of Viet Nam: 6 Pham Ngu Lao St, Hanoi; tel. (4) 8260752; fax (4) 8254734; e-mail gsv@hn.vnn.vn; f. 1983; 5,000 mems; Sec.-Gen. NGUYEN TIEN THANH.

Viet Nam Physical Society: P104-46 Nguyen Van Ngoc St, Hanoi; tel. (4) 8349209; fax (4) 8349050; Pres. PHAN HONG KHOI.

TECHNOLOGY

Mining Association: 54 Hai Ba Trung St, Hanoi; tel. (4) 9342723; fax (4) 5654995; Pres. NGUYEN VAN LONG; Sec.-Gen. DINH NGOC DANG.

Viet Nam Foundry and Metallurgical Association: 54 Hai Ba Trung St, Hanoi; tel. (4) 8262052; Pres. PHAN TU PHUNG.

Vietnamese Association of Mechanics: 264 Doi Can, Badinh, Hanoi; tel. (4) 7625804; fax (4) 8683280; e-mail phong@mail.hut.edu .vn; internet www.cohocvietnam.org.vn; Pres. NGUYEN HOA THINH; Sec.-Gen. DINH VAN PHONG.

Research Institutes

GENERAL

Viet Nam Institute of Culture and Arts: 32 Pho Hao Nam, La Thanh, Phuong O Cho Dua, Quan Dong Da, Hanoi; tel. (4) 8569160; fax (4) 8516415; e-mail vncvhnt@fpt.vn; f. 1971; attached to Min. of Culture, Sports and Tourism; 50 staff; study of Vietnamese culture in all its aspects and relations with other countries; library of 5,000 vols; Dir-Gen. Prof. NGUYEN CHI BEN; publ. *Culture Research Information*.

AGRICULTURE, FISHERIES AND VETERINARY SCIENCE

Centre for Applied Research in Agricultural Engineering: 10A Tran Nhat Duat St, 1st District, Ho Chi Minh City; tel. (8) 8442947; fax (8) 8438842; f. 1976; 100 mems; library of 3,000 vols; Head of Administration PHAM VAN TAN; publ. *Agricultural Engineering* (1 a year).

Food Crops Research Institute: Lien Hong, Gia Loc, Hai Duong Province; tel. (320) 3716463; fax (320) 3716385; e-mail vcltctp@fpt.vn; f. 1968; research on varietal and technological improvement of rice, root and tuber crops, legumes, vegetables and fruit-tree crops; library of 1,950 vols, 170 journals; Dir Prof. Dr HOAN NGUEN TRI (acting); publ. *Research Bulletin of Field Crops* (every 2–3 years).

Forest Science Institute of Viet Nam (FSIV): Chem, Tu Liem District, Hanoi; tel. (4) 8389031; fax (4) 8389722; internet www .fsiv.org.vn; f. 1988; Dir-Gen. Prof. Dr TRIEU VAN HUNG; publ. *Vietnam Forestry Review* (4 a year).

Fruits and Vegetables Research Institute: Thi Tran Trau Quy, Huyen Gia Lam, Thanh Pho, Hanoi; tel. (4) 8276254; fax (4) 8276148; e-mail vrqhnvn@hn.vnn.vn; f. 1969; attached to Viet Nam Acad. of Agricultural Sciences; responsible for scientific research and technology transfer on vegetables, fruits, flowers, landscape plants, mulberry silk.

Institute of Agricultural Science of South Viet Nam: 121 Nguyen Binh Khiem St, 1st District, Ho Chi Minh City; tel. (8) 38291746; fax (8) 38297650; e-mail iasvn@ vnn.vn; internet iasvn.org; f. 1925; research on pedology, crop sciences and animal sciences, agricultural systems, agricultural and development economics; library of 10,000 vols; collection of insects; Dir Prof. BUI CHI BUU.

Institute of Soil and Fertilizer Research: East Ngac, Tu Liem Dist., Hanoi; tel. (4) 8362379; fax (4) 8389924; e-mail khkh_tnnh@hn.vnn.vn; f. 1968; attached to Viet Nam Acad. of Agricultural Sciences; Dir Dr. BUI HUY HIEN.

National Institute of Animal Husbandry: Chem Thuy Phuong, Hanoi; tel. (4) 385022; fax (4) 389775; f. 1969; research on domestic animals; extension service; Dir Dr LE VIET LY; publ. *Scientific and Technical Journal on Animal Husbandry*.

National Institute of Veterinary Research: 86 Truong Chinh Rd, Dong Da Precinct, Hanoi; tel. (4) 8686817; fax (4) 8686615; e-mail longlinh5@yahoo.com; f. 1968.

Plant Protection Research Institute: Dongngac, Tu Liem District, Hanoi; tel. (4) 38389724; fax (4) 38363563; e-mail nipp-tonghop@hn.vnn.vn; internet www .vaas.org.vn; f. 1968; attached to Viet Nam Acad. of Agricultural Sciences; plant protection research and development with emphasis on biological and genetic control, integrated pest management of food and vegetable and specific tropical crops; library of 700 vols; Dir Dr NGO VINH VIEN; publ. *Plant Protection Bulletin* (6 a year).

Research Institute for Aquaculture: Dinh Bang, Tu Son, Bac Ninh; tel. (4) 271368; fax (4) 273070; e-mail vanphong@ ria1.org; internet www.ria1.org; f. 1975.

Research Institute of Marine Fisheries: 170 Le Lai St, Haiphong; tel. (31) 3836656; fax (31) 3836812; e-mail vhs@rimf.org.vn; f. 1961; study, training and research in fisheries biology, stock assessment, brackish water aquaculture, mariculture, oceanography, technology of fishing and processing; library of 12,000 vols; Dir Prof. Dr DO VAN KHUONG; publs *Aquaculture, Aquaculture Asia, Aquaculture International, Aquaculture Research, Infofish International, Journal of Fish Disease, World Fishing*.

Rubber Research Institute of Viet Nam: 177 Hai Ba Trung St, Ho Chi Minh City; tel. (8) 8294139; fax (8) 8298599; e-mail rriv@ hcm.vnn.vn; f. 1975; library of 3,000 vols; Gen. Dir MAI VAN SON.

Viet Nam Institute of Agricultural Engineering: A2 Phuong Mai, Dong Da, Hanoi; tel. (4) 8523187; fax (4) 8521131; f. 1968; research machinery for agricultural production and food processing; library of 3,000 vols; Dir Prof. Dr PHAM VAN LANG; publ.

Agricultural and Food Industries (12 a year, in Vietnamese with a summary in English).

Viet Nam Institute of Agricultural Science and Technology: Thanh Tri District, Hanoi; f. 1978; Dir Prof. DAO THE TUAN.

ECONOMICS, LAW AND POLITICS

Central Institute of Economic Management: 68 Phan Dinh Phung, Ba Dinh, Hanoi; tel. (4) 7338930; fax (4) 7338930; internet www.ciem.org.vn; f. 1978.

Institute of Economics: 27 Tran Xuan Soan St, Hanoi; tel. (4) 8261633; fax (4) 8261632; f. 1960; library of 16,000 vols; attached to Viet Nam National Centre for Social Sciences and Humanities; Dir DO HOAI NAM; publs *Nghien Cuu Kinh Te* (Economic Studies Review, 12 a year in Vietnamese), *Viet Nam's Socio-Economic Development* (4 a year).

Institute of Finance: 7 Ly Thuong Kiet St, Hoan Kiem District, Hanoi; tel. (4) 9331872; fax (4) 9331865; e-mail hvtc@hn.vnn.vn; f. 1961.

Institute for International Relations: 69 Chua Lang St, Dong Da District, Hanoi; tel. (4) 8344540; fax (4) 8343543; e-mail iirmofa@ hn.vnn.vn; f. 1959; library of 25,000 vols; publ. *International Studies* (6 a year in Vietnamese, 2 a year in English).

Institute of Labour Science and Social Affairs: 2 Dinh Le St, Hanoi; tel. (4) 8258801; fax (4) 8269733; f. 1978; labour relations, working conditions, wages and living standards, levels of skill, social security; Dir Dr DO MINH CUONG.

Institute of Social Sciences: 49 Nguyen Thi Minh Khai St, District 1, Ho Chi Minh City; tel. (8) 8223995; fax (8) 8223735; f. 1978; Dir Dr NGUYEN THE NGHIA; publ. *Journal of Social Sciences* (6 a year).

Institute of State and Law: 27 Tran Xuan Soan St, Hai Ba Trung, Hanoi; tel. (4) 39784637; fax (4) 39713136; f. 1960; attached to Viet Nam Acad. of Social Sciences; Dep. Dir NGUYEN NHU THE.

Institute of Statistical Science: 48A Lang Trung, Dong Da, Hanoi; tel. (4) 8244234; fax (4) 8243763; f. 1976; library of 3,700 vols (2,600 foreign books, 1,100 Vietnamese); spec. colln in field of statistics; Dir NGUYEN VIET CUONG; publs *Bulletin of Statistical Science*, selection of information dissemination periodicals.

Research Institute of Trade: 46 Ngo Quyen St, Hoan Kiem District, Hanoi; tel. (4) 8262720; fax (4) 8248279; f. 1995 following merger of Research Institute for Foreign Economic Relations and Institute of Economic and Technological Research on Trade.

EDUCATION

Centre for Information and Library Educational Science: 101 Tran Hung Dao St, Hanoi; tel. (4) 8220911; fax (4) 8223213; e-mail dinhphuong@bdvn.vnmail.vnd.net; f. 1961 as National Institute for Educational Science; library of 5,000 vols and 1,500 periodicals; Dir Assoc. Prof. Dr DANG THANH HUNG; publ. *Information on Educational Sciences* (6 a year).

Research Centre for Vocational and Higher Education: 101 Tran Hung Dao St, Hanoi; tel. (4) 9423108; fax (4) 8221521; e-mail vkhgd.qhqt@bdvn.vnd.net; f. 1977; attached to National Institute for Education Strategy and Curriculum Development; Dir Assoc. Prof. Dr NGUYEN HUU CHAU.

Viet Nam Sports Science Institute: 141 Nguyen Thai Hoc St, Ba Dinh, Hanoi; tel. (4) 7330286; e-mail vkh-tt@fpt.vn; f. 1979; 5,000 mems; library of 10,000 vols on sports science; publ. *Bulletin* (16 a year).

FINE AND PERFORMING ARTS

Ha Noi Institute of Stage and Cinematography: Tu Liem, Hanoi; tel. (4) 8243397; f. 1978.

Vietnamese Institute for Musicology: 32 Nguyen Thai Hoc St, Ba Dinh District, Hanoi; tel. (4) 8457368; fax (4) 8434953; e-mail musicology@hn.vnn.vn; f. 1976; research in the national heritage of music, song, dance; Dir Prof. NGUYEN PHUC LINH; publ. *Bulletin* (in English and Vietnamese, 3 a year).

HISTORY, GEOGRAPHY AND ARCHAEOLOGY

Institute of Archaeology: 61 Phan Chu Trinh, Quan Hoan Kiem, Hanoi; tel. (4) 8255449; fax (4) 9331607; f. 1968; Dir and Editor-in-Chief HA VAN TAN; Dep. Dirs HA VAN PHUNG, TONG TRUNG TIN.

Institute of History: 38 Hang Chuoi, Quan Hai Ba Trung, Hanoi; tel. (4) 9711682; fax (4) 9717615; f. 1960; attached to Viet Nam Acad. of Social Sciences; library of 70,000 vols from fmr library of Ecole Français d'Extrême-Orient; Dir NGUYEN VAN NHAT; publ. *Nghien cuu Lich su (Historical Studies) Review*.

Viet Nam Research Institute of Land Administration: Hoang Quoc Viet St, Cau Giay, Hanoi; tel. (4) 7561154; fax (4) 7540186; e-mail vgcr@hn.vnn.vn; internet www.virila.ac.vn; f. 1994; attached to Min. of Natural Resources and the Environment; scientific research and technological development in geodesy, cartography, and land administration; dependent centres: GIS and databases, geodynamics, spatial images and aerial photography; 240 staff; Dir Dr NGUYEN DUNG TIEN.

LANGUAGE AND LITERATURE

Institute of Linguistics: 36 Hang Chuoi St, Hanoi; tel. (4) 9710968; fax (4) 9712247; e-mail lytoanthang@yahoo.com; f. 1968; library of 12,000 vols; Dir Dr LY TOAN CHANG; publ. *Ngon Ngu* (4 a year).

Institute of Literary Studies: 20 Ly Thai To St, Hanoi; tel. (4) 8253548; fax (4) 8250385; f. 1959; library of 150,000 vols; Dir Prof. Dr PHAN TRONG THUONG; publ. *Tap chi Nghien cuu Van hoc* (Literary Studies Review, 12 a year).

Institute of Research on Chinese and Demotic Characters: 26 Ly Thuong Kiet St, Hanoi; f. 1970.

MEDICINE

Central Institute of Ophthalmology: 85 Ba Trieu St, Hanoi; tel. and fax (4) 9438004; e-mail tonthi.kimthanh@hn.vnn.vn; f. 1957.

Ho Chi Minh City Institute of Hygiene and Epidemiology: 167 Nguyen Thi Minh Khai St, Ho Chi Minh City; f. 1977.

Ho Chi Minh City Institute of Hygiene and Public Health: 159 Hung Phu St, District 8, Ho Chi Minh City; tel. (8) 8559503; fax (8) 8563164; e-mail vienvsytcc@hcm.vnn.vn; f. 1977; Dir Prof. LE THE THU.

Institute for the Protection of the Mother and Newborn Child: 43 Trang Thi St, 08-4 Hanoi; tel. (4) 8252161; fax (4) 8254638; e-mail ipmn@hn.vnn.vn; f. 1966; obstetrics, gynaecology, care of the newborn child and family planning, in vitro fertilization; library of 5,000 vols; Dir Dr NGUYEN DUC VY; publs *Nôi san Sản Phu Khoa* (internal journal of obstetrics and gynaecology, 1 a year), *Tông kêt công trinh nghiên cúu*

khoa hoc (review of scientific studies, 1 a year).

Institute of Malariology, Parasitology and Entomology: Luong The Vinh St, Hanoi; tel. (4) 8543035; fax (4) 8543015; e-mail nimpe@netnam.org.vn; f. 1957.

Institute of Traditional Medicine in Ho Chi Minh City: 273 Nam Ky Khoi Nghia St, Phu Nhuan Dist., Ho Chi Minh City; tel. (8) 38443047; fax (8) 38444769; e-mail v.ydhdt@tphcm.gov.vn; internet www.vienydhdt.com.vn; f. 1975; short-term courses in health: acupuncture, acupressure, massage (foot and body), yoga.

Institute of Vaccines and Medical Biologicals: 9 Pasteur St, Nha Trang, Khanh Hoa; e-mail ivac@dng.vnn.vn; f. 1979.

National Hospital of Odonto—Stomatology/Benh Vien Rang Ham Mat Trung uong Hanoi: 40B Trang Thi St, Hoan Kiem Dist., Hanoi; tel. (4) 8269723; e-mail ranghammat@hotmail.com; internet www.ranghammat.vn; f. 2002 by merger of Odonto-Maxillofacial dept of Hanoi Medical University and Hanoi Odonto-Maxillo-Facial Institute; attached to Min. of Health; treats patients with dental and facial diseases; does research and trains the provinces hospital staffs; provides a practical centre for Hanoi Medical Univ.; Dir Assoc. Prof. Dr TRINH DINH HAI.

National Institute of Drug Quality Control: 48 Hai Ba Trung St, Hoan Kiem Dist., Hanoi; tel. (4) 38255742; fax (4) 38256911; e-mail dc_son@yahoo.com; f. 1957 as Drug Quality Control Laboratory; drug quality control analysis and specification evaluation, devt of standards and reference substances, scientific research and training, participating in devt of Vietnamese pharmacopoeia; library of 1,450 vols; Dir Prof. Dr THAO NGUYEN THI PHUONG; publ. *Journal of Drug Quality Control* (4 a year).

National Institute of Hygiene and Epidemiology: 1 Yersin St, 10000 Hanoi; tel. (4) 8212416; fax (4) 9723130; e-mail nihe@netnam.org.vn; f. 1924; epidemiology of communicable diseases, vaccine development; library of 12,000 vols; Dir Prof. NGUYEN TRAN HIEN; publ. *Tap Chi Ve Sinh Phong Dich* (Journal, in Vietnamese with abstract in English, 4 a year).

National Institute of Medicinal Materials: 3B Quang Trung St, Hoan Kiem District, Hanoi; tel. (4) 8252644; fax (4) 9349072; e-mail htqt-mm@hn.vnn.vn; internet www.nimm.org.vn; f. 1961; multidisciplinary research on pharmaceutical materials, mainly medicinal plants; postgraduate training; library of 6,000 vols; Dir Prof. NGUYEN GIA CHAN; publ. *Materia Medica Bulletin* (4 a year).

National Institute of Nutrition: 48B Tang Bat Ho St, Hanoi; tel. (4) 39717090; fax (4) 39717885; e-mail ninvietnam@viendinhduong.vn; internet www.viendinhduong.vn; f. 1980; depts of basic nutrition, community nutrition, applied nutrition, clinical nutrition, food science, food safety, dietetics, experiment workshop, library; Dir Assoc. Prof. LE THI HOP; publs *Journal of Food and Nutrition Sciences, Nutrition, Health and Life*.

National Institute of Occupational and Environmental Health Research: c/o Ministry of Health, Ib pho Yersin, Hanoi; tel. (4) 9713649; fax (4) 8212894; e-mail byt@moh.gov.vn; Dir Prof. Dr LE VAN TRUNG.

National Institute of Otolaryngology: Bachmai Hospital Centre, 78 Giai Phong St, Phuong Mai, Hanoi; tel. (4) 8693731; fax (4) 8691607; f. 1969; 200 staff; library of 1,000 vols; Dir Prof. LUONG SY CAN; publs *Noi San*

Tai Mui Hong (1 a year), *Thong Tin Tai Mui Hong* (1 a year).

National Institute of Paediatrics: 18/8779 La Thanh, Dong Da, Hanoi; tel. (4) 8343700; fax (4) 7754448; e-mail nip@hn.vnn.vn; internet www.benhviennhitu.org.vn; f. 1969 as the Institute of Child Care, renamed Viet Nam—Sweden Children's Hospital and the Olof Palme Paediatric Institute, present name since 1997; Dir Assoc. Prof NGUYEN THANH LIEM.

National Institute of Traditional Medicine: The National Hospital of Traditional Medicine, 29 Nguyen Binh Khiem, Hanoi; tel. (4) 9432442; fax (4) 8229353; e-mail yhcotruyen@hn.vnn.vn; internet www.natiotradimedhos.org.vn; f. 1957; traditional medicine; library of 19,343 vols, special collection of books on Chinese medicine and medicine in Viet Nam since 15th century; Dir Prof. Dr CHU QUOC TRUONG; publ. *Journal of Research in Vietnamese Traditional Medicine and Pharmacy* (4 a year).

National Institute of Tuberculosis and Respiratory Diseases: 120 Hoang Hoa Tham St, Hanoi; tel. (4) 8326249; fax (4) 8326162; f. 1957; research on asthma, chronic bronchitis, lung cancer, occupational lung diseases, tuberculosis; operates two national programmes: Acute Respiratory Infections in Children, National Tuberculosis Control Programme; library of 10,000 vols; Dir Prof. N. V. Co; publ. *Lao và bênh phôi* (4 a year).

Nha Trang Institute of Hygiene and Epidemiology: 10 Tran Phu St, Nha Trang, Phu Khanh Province; f. 1976.

Tay Nguyen Institute of Hygiene and Epidemiology: Buon Ma Thuoc, Dak Lak Province; f. 1976; Man. for Planning and Science HAU VAN PHAM; Vice-Man. HAU PHAM VAN.

NATURAL SCIENCES

General

National Centre for Scientific Research of Viet Nam, Ho Chi Minh City Branch: 1 Mac Dinh Chi St, Dist. 1, Ho Chi Minh City; tel. (8) 222246; fax (8) 222068; f. 1975; chemistry, fundamental and applied research in biology, geoscience, mathematics, physics; Pres. Prof. Dr HO SI THOANG; Sec. Prof. Dr NGUYEN VAN TRONG.

Biological Sciences

Dalat Institute of Biology: 116 Xo Viet Nghe Tinh, Dalat, Lam Dong; tel. (63) 822078; fax (63) 831028; e-mail sdhl@vnn.vn; internet www.vast.ac.vn; f. 1975; attached to Viet Nam Acad. of Science and Technology; biochemistry and molecular biology of nitrogen fixation; plant genetics; Dir Prof. LE XUAN TU; publ. *Journal of Biology*.

Mathematical Sciences

Institute of Mathematics: Vietnamese Acad. of Science and Technology, 18 Hoang Quoc Viet, 10307 Hanoi; tel. (4) 7563474; fax (4) 7564303; e-mail vientruong@math.ac.vn; internet www.math.ac.vn; f. 1969; attached to Vietnamese Acad. of Science and Technology; algebra, dynamic systems, discrete mathematics, functional analysis, geometry and topology, methods of mathematical physics, numerical analysis, operations research, optimal control theory, partial differential equations, probability and mathematical statistics; library of 12,000 vols, 350 periodicals; Dir Prof. HA HUY KHOAI, Prof. Dr NGO VIET TRUNG; publ. *Acta Mathematica Vietnamica* (3 a year).

Physical Sciences

Institute of Chemistry: 18 Hoang Quoc Viet Rd, Cau Giay District, Hanoi; tel. (4) 7564312; fax (4) 8361283; e-mail info@vienhoahoc.ac.vn; internet www.vienhoahoc.ac.vn; f. 1978; attached to Vietnamese Acad. of Science and Technology; basic and applied research and engineering in organic, inorganic, physicochemical and analytical chemistry; chemistry of natural products and polymers; library of 6,000 vols; Dir Prof. Dr TRAN VAN SUNG; publs *Collection of Selected Scientific Works* (1 a year), *Tap chí Hóa hoc* (Journal of Chemistry, 6 a year).

Institute of Geological Sciences: 84 Chua Lang St, Dong Da, Hanoi; tel. (4) 37754798; fax (4) 37754797; e-mail info@igsvn.ac.vn; internet www.igsvn.ac.vn; f. 1967; Dir Dr TRONG-HUE TRAN.

Institute of Meteorology and Hydrology: Gate 62/5, Nguyen Chi Thanh, Dong Da, Hanoi; tel. (4) 7733090; fax (4) 8355993; e-mail mandt@vkttv.edu.vn; internet www.imh.ac.vn; f. 1977; Dir Dr TRAN THUC.

Institute of Oceanography: 01 Cau Da, Nha Trang, Khanh Hoa Province; tel. (58) 590036; fax (58) 590034; e-mail haiduong@dng.vnn.vn; internet www.vnio.org.vn; f. 1923; library of 60,000 vols; incorporates National Oceanographic Museum and Aquarium; Dir Dr NGUYEN TAC AN; publs *Collection of Marine Research Works* (1 a year), *Journal of Marine Science and Technology* (4 a year).

Institute of Physics: 10 Dao Tan, Thu Le, Ba Dinh, Hanoi; tel. (4) 22123631; fax (4) 37669050; e-mail office@iop.vast.ac.vn; internet iop.vast.ac.vn; f. 1969; attached to Viet Nam Acad. of Science and Technology; Deputy Dir Assoc. Prof. Dr NGUYEN HONG QUANG.

Viet Nam Institute of Geosciences and Mineral Resources: Ministry of Natural Resources and Environment, Thanh Xuan, Hanoi; tel. (4) 8547335; fax (4) 8542125; e-mail van@vigmr.vn; f. 1976; Dir Assoc. Prof. NGUYEN XUAN KHIEN; publ. *Geology and Mineral Resources* (irregular).

PHILOSOPHY AND PSYCHOLOGY

Institute of Philosophy: 59 Lang Ha St, Ba Dinh District, Hanoi; tel. (4) 5143338; fax (4) 5141935; e-mail ducphilosophy@yahoo.com; internet www.vientriethoc.com.vn; f. 1962; research on theoretical and practical issues of the devt of Viet Nam; scientific foundation for the planning of the Party and govt's policies and guidelines in Viet Nam; research on philosophical issues and practice of devt of philosophy in Viet Nam, devts and achievements of philosophical research both in Viet Nam and abroad; other research and teaching activities incl. training MA and PhD students, organizing nat. and int. seminars and conferences; library of 50,000 vols; Dir Prof. PHAM VAN DUC; publ. *Philosophy* (12 a year, in Vietnamese; English edn 4 a year).

RELIGION, SOCIOLOGY AND ANTHROPOLOGY

Institute of Ethnology: 27 Tran Xuan Soan, Quan Hai Ba Trung, Hanoi; tel. (4) 9784867; fax (4) 9711435; e-mail khongdienvdt@hn.vnn.vn; f. 1968; research in cultural history and social structure of the nationalities in Viet Nam and Southeast Asia; 62 staff; library of 10,000 vols; attached to Viet Nam Acad. of Social Sciences; Dir PHAM QUANG HOAN; publ. *Ethnographical Studies* (4 a year).

TECHNOLOGY

Broadcast Research and Application Center: 171 Ly Chinh Thang St, Dist. 3, Ho Chi Minh City; tel. (8) 8298427; fax (8) 8293487; f. 1978; 150 staff; library of 3,000 vols; Dir Prof. NGUYEN KIM SACH.

Food Industry Research Institute: Km. 8 Nguyen Trai Rd, Thanh Xuan, Hanoi; tel. (4) 8584318; fax (4) 8584554; e-mail vu@fii.ac.vn; f. 1967; carries out research in biotechnology, food processing technology using local raw materials, and other areas connected with food; Dir Prof. Dr LE DUC MANH.

Hydraulic Engineering Consultants Corporation No. 1: 95/2 Chùa Bôc, Dong Da, Hanoi; tel. (4) 8534162; fax (4) 5632169; e-mail hec1@hn.vnn.vn; f. 1956; library of 9,000 vols; Dir-Gen. HOANG MINH DZUNG; publ. *Hydraulic Engineering* (1 a year).

Institute for Building Science and Technology: Tran Cung St, Nghia Tan Ward, Cau Giay District, Hanoi; tel. (4) 7544196; fax (4) 8361197; e-mail ibst_vn@fpt.vn; internet www.ibst.vn; f. 1963; concrete and concrete technology, construction chemistry, corrosive research and structural protection, construction technology, environmental engineering, fire safety for houses and engineering works, geotechnical and foundation engineering, geodesy and engineering surveying, structural engineering, structural testing, water supply and drainage technology; 370 mems; library of 22,000 vols; Dir Assoc. Prof. Dr CAO DUY TIEN; publ. *Building Science and Technology Journal* (4 a year).

Institute for Standardization in Construction: 303 Doi Can St, Hanoi; tel. 343689; f. 1979; library of 5,000 vols; Dir Dr PHAM KINH CUONG; publs *National Typification Design in Construction, Vietnamese Standards* (TCVN).

Institute for Tropical Technology: 18 Hoang Quoc Viet, Cau Giay, Hanoi; tel. (4) 8360376; fax (4) 7564696; e-mail hien-vktnd@hn.vnn.vn; f. 1980; corrosion testing and metal protection, concrete protection, testing of non-metallic materials, their resistance to tropical climates and lifetime prediction, development of new materials, new coatings (organic and inorganic), tropic-proofing of electrical and electronic equipment; small library; Dir Dr LE XUAN HIEN.

Institute of Cybernetics and Computing Technology: Tu Liem District, Hanoi; f. 1976.

Institute of Electronics, Informatics and Automation: 156A, Quan Thanh St, Hanoi; tel. (4) 37164855; fax (4) 37164842; e-mail vielina@hn.vnn.vn; internet www.vielina.com.vn; f. 1985 as Viet Nam Institute of Research and Development in Electronics; informatics and automation, research and application of new technologies, techniques and products concerned with electronics; centeres and laboratories: Automatic Control Centre, High-Tech Centre, Hydrodynamics and Automation, Information Technology Centre, Information Technology Support Centre, Quality Measurement Centre, Robotics Laboratory, High Quality Printed Circuit Laboratory, Special Laboratory of PLC; 81 researchers and employees; Dir Prof. Dr NGUYEN XUAN QUYNH.

Branch Office:

Branch Institute of Electronics, Informatics and Automation: 138 To Thien Thanh St, 10th District, Ho Chi Minh City; tel. (8) 8652126; fax (8) 8652126; juridicial basics.

Institute of Energy: Ton That Tung St, Khuong Thuong, Dong Da, Hanoi; tel. (4) 8523741; fax (4) 8523311; f. 1988; research, programmes and projects concerning energy development in Viet Nam; departments: cience and technology; nuclear, thermal power and the environment; electrical design; computers; electrical power systems development; energy demand forecasting and management; energy economics; high voltage electrical techniques; Gia Sang Research Station for the Protection of Electrical Lines from Lightning; hydropower; electrical network planning; biogas energy; rural energy planning and fuel; solar and wind energy; basic construction projects; production; 193 staff; Dir Dr TRAN QUOC CUONG.

Institute of Industrial Chemistry: 2 Pham Ngu Lao St, Hoan Kiem District, Hanoi; tel. (4) 8253930; fax (4) 8257383; e-mail vienhoacn@hn.vnn.vn; internet www.vinachem.com.vn/english/companydetail.asp?comid=43; f. 1959; Dir Prof. Dr MAI NGOC CHUC.

Institute of Machinery and Industrial Instruments: 34 Lang Ha St, Dong Da Dist., Hanoi; tel. (4) 8344372; fax (4) 8344975; f. 1973; library of 10,000 vols; Dir Dr TRAN VIET HUNG.

Institute of Mechanics: 264 Doi Can St, Ba Dinh, Hanoi; tel. (4) 8325541; fax (4) 8333039; f. 1979; basic and applied research in the fields of fluids, deformable solids and vibration mechanics; library of 14,182 vols; Dir Prof. NGUYEN TIEN KHIEM; publ. *Journal of Mechanics* (4 a year).

Institute of Mining Science and Technology: Phuong Lien St, Dong Da Dist, Hanoi; tel. (4) 8642024; fax (4) 8641564; e-mail ttthan@hn.vnn.vn; f. 1979; research on underground and opencast mining, mine development and construction, excavating and tunnelling, environmental mine safety, ventilation, electro-mechanization, transport, coal preparation and processing; library of 9,000 vols; Dir Dr PHUNG MANH DAC; publs *Mining Management* (12 a year), *Mining Technology Information* (6 a year), *Works Collection* (every 5 years).

Institute of Paper and Cellulose Research: Thanh Xuan District, Hanoi, Vinh Phu Province; tel. (4) 8581072; fax (4) 8581070; f. 1970.

Institute of Transport Science and Technology: 80 Tran Hung Dao St, Hoan Kiem, Hanoi; tel. (4) 38224464; fax (4) 38222979; e-mail itc-mot@mt.gov.vn; f. 1978; attached to Ministry of Transport.

National Institute for Urban and Rural Planning: 37 Le Dai Hanh St, Hanoi; tel. (4) 9760691; fax (4) 9764339; f. 1956, current name 1990; research and establishment of construction planning projects, and environmental and landscape organization in the territorial regions, urban and rural settlements; 8 research, design and planning divisions, 4 administrative divisions; centres: Centre for Research on Urban and Rural Environmental Planning, Centre for Rural Planning and Development, Centre for Urban and Rural Planning in the Middle Regions; 290 staff; Dir Prof. Dr LE HONG KE.

National Research Institute for Mechanical Engineering: Thang Long St, Caugiay, Hanoi; tel. (4) 8344225; fax (4) 8347883; f. 1962 as the Institute of Mechanical Design and Manufacture; 4 professional depts: administration and personnel, economic planning, finance, scientific management,; research depts: 'cold' welding, dynamics, hydromechanical and hydroelectrical heavy mechanics, mechanical design, technology; 265 staff; Dir Prof. Dr HAN DUC KIM.

National Research Institute of Mining and Metallurgy: 30B Doan Thi Diem St, Hanoi; tel. (4) 8233775; fax (4) 8456983;

e-mail vimluki@netnam.org.vn; f. 1967; library of 10,000 vols; Dir Dr NGUYEN ANH.

Research Institute for Agricultural Machinery: Km 9 Nguyen Trai St, Thanh Xuan, Dong Da, Hanoi; tel. (4) 8544429; fax (4) 8547366; f. 1970; research, machinery design; library of 5,500 vols; Dir NGUYEN VAN HOI.

Research Institute of Posts and Telecommunications: 122 Hoang Quoc Viet Rd, Nghia Tan, Cau Giay Dist., Hanoi; tel. (4) 7562037; fax (4) 7562036; e-mail vkhktbdld@hn.vnn.vn; internet www.ptit.edu.vn/ptit_english.asp; Dir Prof. Dr NGUYEN CANH TUAN; publ. *Ket Qua Nghien Cuu Khoa Hoc* (1 a year).

Scientific and Technological Institute for Communications and Transport: 80 Tran Hung Dao St, Hoan Kiem, Hanoi; tel. (4) 38224464; fax (4) 38222979; e-mail vukhcn@mt.gov.vn; internet khcn.mt.gov.vn; f. 1956.

Shipbuilding Science and Technology Institute—SHIPSCITECH: 80B Tran Hung Dao St, Hanoi; tel. (4) 8257070; fax (4) 8258672; f. 1983; development and application of new technologies in shipbuilding, design, building and modernization of marine facilities, consultancy services, training of staff and development of standards; units and facilities: professional design department, Centre for Research and Testing of Models, pilot production workshops, testing tank; Dir Dr NGO CAN (acting).

Textile Research Institute: 478 Minhkhai St, Hanoi; tel. (4) 8624025; fax (4) 8622867; e-mail viendetmay@hn.vnn.vn; f. 1969; research in material technology, machinery for spinning, weaving and finishing; inspection of quality of material and finished products, fashion design; library of 3,500 vols; Dir Dr NGUYEN VAN THONG; publs *Textiles Magazine* (6 a year), *Textile Research Journal* (1 a year).

Viet Nam Atomic Energy Commission: 59 Ly Thuong Kiet St, Hanoi; tel. (4) 9423479; fax (4) 9424133; e-mail hg.vaec@hn.vn.vnn; internet www.vaec.gov.vn; f. 1979; nuclear science and technology; Chair. TRAN HUU PHAT; publ. *Nuclear Science and Technology.*

Viet Nam Institute for Building Materials: 235 Nguyen Trai St, Thanh Xuan, Hanoi; tel. (4) 8581111; fax (4) 8581112; e-mail vienvlxd@hn.vnnn.vn; internet www .vibm.vn; f. 1975; Pres. THAI DUY SAM.

Viet Nam Institute of Water Conservation: 299 Tayson St, Dong Da District, Hanoi; tel. (4) 8522086; fax (4) 8536290; f. 1959; units: Centre for Termite Prevention, Centre for Irrigation, Centre for Water Treatment and Environmental Research, Centre for Research in River and Marine Dynamics, Centre for Hydraulic Research, Centre for Structures and Materials, Centre for Small-Scale Hydroelectric Research, Geotechnics Division, Hydraulic Research Division, Irrigation Systems Management Division, Pump Research Division; 236 staff; Dir Dr NGUYEN TUAN ANH.

Libraries and Archives
Hanoi

Central Health Information and Technology Institute: 15 Le Thanh Tong, Hoan Kiem and valley 135 Nui Truc, Ba Dinh, Hanoi; tel. (4) 37368315; fax (4) 37368319; e-mail cimsi@cimsi.org.vn; internet www .cimsi.org.vn; f. 1979 by merger of Central Library for Medical Sciences (2001) and Central Institute for Medical Sciences Infor-

mation (1979); attached to Min. of Health of Socialist Republic of Viet Nam; specialized in medical information and technology services to all orgs of health sector in Viet Nam; 7,000 vols; Gen. Dir Dr LUONG CHI THANH; publs *Health Newsweek from Internet* (48 a year), *Medical and Pharmaceutical Information Journal* (12 a year).

Central Library for Science and Technology: 24 Lý Thuòng Kiêt, Hanoi; tel. (4) 9349111; fax (4) 8246325; e-mail thutt@vista .gov.vn; internet www.clst.ac.vn; f. 1960; attached to the National Centre for Scientific and Technological Information and Documentation; 230,000 vols, 4,500 periodicals; Dir VU VAN SON.

Institute of Social Sciences Information—National Social Sciences Library: 26 Ly Thuong Kiet, Hanoi; tel. and fax (4) 8253074; f. 1975 by amalgamation of Dept. of Social Sciences Information and Central Social Sciences Library; attached to Viet Nam Academy of Social Sciences; 1m. vols; Dir Prof. HO SI QUY; publs *Bibliography of Social Sciences* (1 a year), *Review of Social Sciences Information* (12 a year).

National Centre for Scientific and Technical Information: 24 Ly Thuong Kiet St, Hanoi; tel. (4) 9342945; fax (4) 8249874; e-mail techmart@vista.gov.vn; internet vista .gov.vn; f. 1990 by merger of the Central Institute for Scientific and Technical Information and the Central Library; formulation and implementation of Science and Technology programmes; national databank, documentation sources and publications; publs *Information and Documentation* (4 a year), *KCM—S&T Information* (12 a year), *Vietnam S&T Abstracts* (6 a year).

National Library of Viet Nam: 31 Trang Thi, 10000 Hanoi; tel. (4) 8253040; fax (4) 8253357; e-mail ptkhang@nlv.gov.vn; f. 1917; attached to Ministry of Culture and Information; 1.2m. vols, 8,000 periodical titles; Dir PHAM THE KHANG; publs *Information on Culture and Arts, Library and Bibliographical Work* (4 a year), *Library Magazine* (4 a year), *National Bibliography* (12 a year and 1 a year).

Ho Chi Minh City

General Sciences Library of Ho Chi Minh City: 69 Ly Tu Trong, Dist. 1, Ho Chi Minh City; tel. (8) 8225055; fax (8) 8299318; e-mail gsl.hcmc@hcm.vnn.vn; internet www.gslhcm.org.vn; f. 1976; attached to Service of Culture, Sports and Tourism of Ho Chi Minh City; 700,000 vols, 4,500 periodical titles, databases; Dir BUI XUAN DUC.

Social Sciences Library: 49 Nguyen Thi Minh Khai, Dist. 3, Ho Chi Minh City; tel. (8) 8228934; fax (8) 8223735; e-mail siss@hcm .vnn.vn; f. 1975; attached to Institute of Social Sciences; the collections of the fmr Archaeological Research Institute have been added to the library; provides facilities for research in archaeology, economics, ethnology, history, law, literature, linguistics, philosophy, sociology; 145,000 vols; Dir TRAN MINH DUC.

Museums and Art Galleries
Haiphong

Haiphong Museum: c/o Dept. of Tourism, 44 Lach Tray, Haiphong; 65 Dien Bien Phu St, Haiphong; tel. (31) 852720; f. 1919; local history.

Hanoi

Bao tàng Cách mang Viêt Nam (National Museum of Vietnamese Revolution): 25 Tong Dan St, 216 Tran Quang Khai, Hoan Kiem District, Hanoi; tel. (4) 8254323; fax (4) 9342064; e-mail baotangcmvn@hn.vnn.vn; internet www.baotangcm.gov.vn; f. 1959; study of revolutionary history of Viet Nam; library of 21,000 vols and historical documents, 17,900 documentary photographs; Dir Prof. Dr TRIEU VAN HIEN.

Ho Chi Minh Museum: 19 Ngoc Ha St, Ba Dinh Dist., Hanoi; tel. (4) 8463572; fax (4) 8439837; f. 1990 1977; study of Ho Chi Minh's life and work; Dir HA HUY GIAP.

Viet Nam Fine Arts Museum: 66 Nguyên Thai Hoduc St, Ba Dinh Dist, Hanoi; tel. (4) 38233084; fax (4) 37341427; e-mail binhtruong451@hn.vnn.vn; f. 1966; preservation and presentation of nat. cultural heritage; research on ancient and modern fine arts, ceramics, handicrafts, folk arts; exhibitions of foreign art; library of 1,100 vols; Dir TRUONG QUOC BINH.

Viet Nam History Museum: 1 Trang Tien, Hanoi; tel. (4) 8253518; fax (4) 8252853; f. 1958; research and conservation, history of Viet Nam from palaeolithic period to 1945; Dir Dr PHAM QUOC QUÂN; publ. *Bulletin* (1 a year).

Viet Nam Military History Museum: 28A Dien Bien Phu St, Ba Dinh, Hanoi; tel. (4) 7334682; fax (4) 7334692; e-mail btqsvn@bt .vnn.vn; internet www.btlsqsvn.org.vn; f. 1959; fmrly People's Army Museum; exhibits Viet Nam's military history since the founding of the country to the Ho Chi Minh era; 4,000 of 160,000 objects on display; Dir LE CHIEU.

Ho Chi Minh City

Ho Chi Minh City Museum: 65 Ly Tu Trong, Ward Dist. 1 Ho Chi Minh City; tel. (8) 8299741; fax (8) 8298250; e-mail bttphcm@hcm.vnn.vn; internet www .hcmc-museum.edu.vn; f. 1977; 2 sections: 1 devoted to the revolution, the other to ancient arts.

Hue

Hue Royal Antiquities Museum: 3 Le Truc St, Hue; tel. (54) 3524429; fax (54) 3522879; e-mail hueroyalmuseum@yahoo .com.vn; f. 1923; history of the old capital; administered by the Hue Monuments Conservation Centre; library of 1,345 vols; Man. NGUYEN PHUOC HAI TRUNG; Head of Exhibition Dept HOANG NGOC SON; publ. *Hue Royal Antiquities Museum.*

Thai Nguyen

Museum of the Cultures of Ethnic Groups in Viet Nam: Doi Can Rd, Thai Nguyen 84, Thai Nguyen province; tel. (280) 855781; fax (280) 752940; e-mail baotangvh@ hn.vnn.vn; f. 1960; conserves and publicizes the cultural heritage of Viet Nam's ethnic groups; Dir HA THI NU.

Vinh

Nghe-Tinh Museum: 10 Dao Tan, Khoi 3, Cong Vien Thanh Co, Phuong Cua Nam, Thanh Pho Vinh, Nghe Tinh Province; tel. (38) 841890; f. 1960; study of the Nghe-Tinh 'Soviet' Uprising, 1930–31; artefacts on view incl. photographs and documents related to the uprising, weapons and equipment used, including the personal possessions of leading revolutionaries Nguyen Phong Sac, Nguyen Tiem and Nguyen Chau; Man. PHAN XUAN THANH.

Universities

CAN THO UNIVERSITY

3/2 Street, Cantho City, Cantho Province
Telephone: (710) 3838237
Fax: (710) 3838474
E-mail: ductri@ctu.edu.vn
Internet: www.ctu.edu.vn

Founded 1966
State control
Academic year: September to July

Rector: TRAN THUONG TUAN
Vice-Rectors: CHAU VAN LUC, Dr LE QUANG MINH

Library of 30,000 vols
Number of teachers: 752
Number of students: 14,000

Publication: annual scientific and technology reports

DEANS

College of Information Technology: VO VAN CHIN
School of Agriculture: Prof. TRAN THUONG TUAN
School of Economics and Business Administration: NGUYEN TAN NHAN
School of Education: Dr LE PHUOC LOC
School of Law: Dr NGUYEN NGOC DIEN
School of Medicine, Dentistry and Pharmacy: PHAM HUNG LUC
School of Sciences: NGUYEN XUAN TRANH
School of Technology: LE QUANG MINH

DA NANG UNIVERSITY OF TECHNOLOGY

54 Nguyen Luong Bang Hoa Khanh, Lien Chieu, Da Nang City
Telephone: (511) 842308
Fax: (511) 842771
E-mail: dhbk@ud.edu.vn
Internet: www.dut.edu.vn

Founded 1975, fmrly Univ. Polytechnic Da Nang.

DUY TAN UNIVERSITY

184 Nguyen Van Linh St, Thank Khe Dist., Da Nang City
Telephone: (511) 3650403
Fax: (511) 3650443
E-mail: webmaster@dtu.edu.vn
Internet: www.dtu.edu.vn

Founded 1994

Pres.: LE CONG CO

Faculties of accountancy and finance, business, engineering, languages, technology.

FOREIGN TRADE UNIVERSITY

91 Chua Lang, Lang Thuong, Dong Da, Hanoi
Telephone: (4) 32595168
Fax: (4) 38343605
E-mail: qhqt@ftu.edu.vn
Internet: www.ftu.edu.vn

Founded 1960

Chair. of Board of Trustees: Prof. Dr VU CHI LOC
Pres.: Prof. Dr HOANG VAN CHAU
Vice-Pres.: Prof. Dr BUI NGOC SON
Vice-Pres.: Assoc. Prof. Dr DAO THI THU GIANG
Vice-Pres.: Assoc. Prof. Dr NGUYEN DINH THO
Vice-Pres.: Prof. Dr NGUYEN VAN HONG
Rector: Prof. Dr NGUYEN THI MO
Vice-Rectors: Prof. Dr HOANG VAN CHAU, Prof. Dr HOANG NGOC THIET, Prof. Dr NGUYEN PHUC KHANH
Number of teachers: 193
Number of students: 10,720

Publication: External Economics Review (4 a year)

DEANS

Faculty of Basic and Fundamental Studies: Prof. Dr LE THANH CUONG
Faculty of Business Administration: Dr BU NGOC SON
Faculty of Business English: Dr NGUYEN DUC HOAT
Faculty of Foreign Trade Economics: Dr VU SY TUAN
Faculty of In-Service Training: NGUYEN THI MO
Faculty of Marxism and Leninism Studies: Dr DOAN VAN KHAI
Faculty of Postgraduate Studies: Prof. Dr VU CHI LOC

HAIPHONG UNIVERSITY OF MEDICINE

213 Tran Quoc Toan (Lach Tray), Ngo Quyen, Haiphong
Telephone: (31) 731907
Fax: (31) 731224
E-mail: dhyhp@hn.vnn.vn

Rector: HUU CHINH NGUYEN.

HANOI AGRICULTURAL UNIVERSITY

Trau Quy, Gia Lam, Hanoi
Telephone: (4) 62617586
Fax: (4) 38276554
E-mail: raico@hua.edu.vn
Internet: www.hau.edu.vn/en

Founded 1956
Public control
Languages of instruction: English, Vietnamese
Academic year: August to June

Faculties of agronomy and agricultural resources environment management, animal husbandry and veterinary medicine, economics and rural development, farm engineering and rural electricity, land resources and environment, post-harvest technology and food processing, postgraduate studies and technical teachers training; Institute of Agricultural Biology; Experimental and Demonstration Station, Viet Nam Agricultural College Training, Research and Development Centre, Center for Sustainable Agriculture Research and Development, Professional Dogs Research Centre, Botanical Garden and Germplasm Conservation, Centre for Agricultural Research and Environmental Studies, Cadastral Centre

Rector: DUC VIEN TRAN

Number of teachers: 850
Number of students: 12,900

Publication: Journal of Scientific Development.

HANOI ARCHITECTURAL UNIVERSITY

Km 10, Nguyen Trai Rd, Thanh Xuan, Hanoi
Telephone: (4) 8544346
Fax: (4) 8541616
E-mail: pth@hn.vnn.vn
Internet: www.hau.edu.vn

Founded 1969

Rector: Prof. Dr Arch. TRONG HAN TRAN
Vice-Rectors: Prof. Dr Arch. CHE DINH HOANG, Dr. DO DINH DUC, Prof. Dr Arch. DO HAU
Dir for Centre of Information and Library: PHAM VAN THRNH

DEANS

Dept of Political Theory: PHAM KHOAN
Faculty of Architecture: Dr Arch. LE QUAN

Faculty of Civil Engineering: Asst Prof. Dr NGUYEN TAI TRUNG
Faculty of Infrastructure Techniques and Urban Environment: Asst Prof. HOANG VAN HUE
Faculty of Rural and Urban Planning: Asst Prof. Dr Arch. LE DUC THANG
Faculty of Urban Management: Asst Prof. Dr Arch. NGUYEN TO LANG
In-Service Faculty: Asst Prof. Dr VUONG VAN THANH
Postgraduate Faculty: Asst Prof. Dr Arch. DANG DUC QUANG

HANOI LAW UNIVERSITY

87 Nguyen Chi Thanh, Duong Lang, Hanoi
Telephone: (4) 8352630
Fax: (4) 8343226
E-mail: info@hlu.edu.vn
Internet: www.hlu.edu.vn

Founded 1979

Rector: LE MINH TAM

Faculties of administrative and state law, economic law, international law, justice, part-time learning, postgraduate training.

HANOI MEDICAL UNIVERSITY

1 Ton That Tung St, Dong Da, Hanoi
Telephone: (4) 38523798
Fax: (4) 38525115
E-mail: daihocyhn@hmu.edu.vn
Internet: www.hmu.edu.vn

Founded 1902
Academic year: September to June

Dir.: Prof. NGUYEN LAN VIET
Rector: Prof. NGUYEN DUC HINH
Vice-Rector: Dr LUU NGOC HOAT
Vice-Rector for Finance: DOAN NGOC XUAN
Vice-Rector for Postgraduate Training: TA THANH VAN
Vice-Rector for Scientific Research: TA THANH VAN
Vice-Rector for Undergraduate Training: NGUYEN HUU TU
Number of teachers: 508
Number of students: 6,000

Publication: Journal of Medical Research (1 a year).

HANOI NATIONAL ECONOMICS UNIVERSITY

207 Duong Giai Phong, Quan Hai Ba Trung, Hanoi
Telephone: (4) 36280280
E-mail: nghind@neu.edu.vn
Internet: www.neu.edu.vn

Founded 1956
Languages of instruction: English, French
Number of teachers: 1,000
Number of students: 32,000

Publication: Economics and Development Review (12 a year)

Faculties of accountancy and auditing, agricultural economics, banking and finance, industrial economics, labour economics, planning and statistics.

HANOI NATIONAL UNIVERSITY OF EDUCATION

136 Duong Xuan Thuy, Quan Hoa Cau Giay, Tu Liem, Hanoi
Telephone: (4) 7547823
Fax: (4) 7547971
E-mail: p.qhqt@hnue.edu.vn
Internet: www.hnue.edu.vn

Founded 1951

Faculties of foreign languages education, teacher training.

HANOI OPEN UNIVERSITY

Nha B-101 Phuong Bach Khoa, Quan Hai Ba
   Trung, Hanoi
Telephone: (4) 8694821
Fax: (4) 8691587
E-mail: dhm-hou@hn.vnn.vn
Internet: www.hou.edu.vn

Founded 1990, univ. status since 1993
Language of instruction: Vietnamese
Academic year: August to June

Number of teachers: 470
Number of students: 19,000

Faculties of biological technology, education
and training, foreign languages, industrial
design, information systems, law, management training, telecommunication technology; multimedia centre; research centre of
distance education.

HANOI UNIVERSITY OF CIVIL ENGINEERING

5 Giai Phong Rd, Hanoi
Telephone: (4) 8691302
Fax: (4) 8691684
E-mail: dngoaidhxd@hn.vnn.vn
Internet: www.dhxd.edu.vn

Founded 1956, univ. status since 1966
Language of instruction: Vietnamese
Academic year: August to June

Number of teachers: 700
Number of students: 14,000

Publication: *Science-Technology*

Rector: LE NINH NGUYEN

Faculties of architecture, civil and industrial
engineering, construction engineering, environmental engineering, highway and bridge
construction, hydraulic engineering, industrial economics, information technology,
mechanical engineering, postgraduate studies; institute of offshore engineering; centre
for continuing education.

HANOI UNIVERSITY OF CULTURE

418 De La Thanh, Dong Da Dist., Hanoi
Telephone: (4) 8511971
Fax: (4) 5141629
E-mail: daihocvanhoahanoi@gmail.com
Internet: www.huc.edu.vn

Founded 1977

Number of teachers: 125
Number of students: 2,514

Rector: Prof. Dr TRAN DUC NGON

Faculty of cultural studies, library and information, tourism, postgraduate training.

HANOI UNIVERSITY OF FINE ARTS

42 Yet kien, Quan Hoan Kiem, Hanoi
Telephone: (4) 8224013
Fax: (4) 8226418
E-mail: dhmythuathn@hn.vnn.vn

Founded 1957 as the Hanoi College of Fine
   Art, univ. status 1981

Dir: NGUYEN LUONG TIEU BACH
Dept Dir: LE ANH VAN

Offers 5-year BFA programmes, 2- and 3-
year full and part-time MA programmes in
painting, graphic art, sculpture.

HANOI UNIVERSITY OF FOREIGN STUDIES

Km 9, Nguyen Trai St, Thanh Xuan, Hanoi
Telephone: (4) 38544338
Fax: (4) 38544550
E-mail: hanu@hanu.vn
Internet: www.hunu.edu.vn

Founded 1959

Depts of accountancy, business, commerce,
economics, human resource management,
international studies, languages and tourism
Pres.: NGUYEN DINH LUAN.

HANOI UNIVERSITY OF FOREIGN TRADE

91 Chua Lang St, Dong Da Dist., Hanoi
Telephone: (4) 8356800
Fax: (4) 8343605
E-mail: qhqt@ftu.edu.vn
Internet: www.ftu.edu.vn

Founded 1965

Pres: Prof. Dr HOANG VAN CHAU
Rector: Prof Dr THI MO NGUYEN
Vice-Rectors: Prof. Dr NGUYEN HONG DAM,
   HOANG NGOC THIET

Faculties of international business, business
administration, commercial english.

HANOI UNIVERSITY OF INDUSTRIAL FINE ARTS

360 La Thanh, O Cho Dua, Dong Da, Hanoi
Telephone: (4) 8517364
Fax: (4) 8517390
E-mail: pkhmtcn@fpt.vn

Founded 1965

Rector: LE HUYEN

Dept of industrial art.

HANOI UNIVERSITY OF MINING AND GEOLOGY

Dong Ngac Commune, Tu Liem Dist., Hanoi
Telephone: (4) 8389633
Fax: (4) 8389633
E-mail: thdn@hn.vnn.vn
Internet: www.humg.edu.vn

Founded 1966

Prin.: Dr TRAN DINH KIEN
Deputy-Prins: Dr NGUYEN PHU VU, Dr
   NGUYEN XUAN TRUONG, Dr TA DUC THINH
Dir of Univ. Library: PHAM MINH KHOI

Library of 100,000 vols, 900 periodicals
Number of students: 5,338

DEANS

Dept of Defence Education: Col DO KIM
   CHIEN
Dept of General Education: NGUYEN MINH
   MAN
Dept of Graduate and Postgraduate Train-
   ing: TRAN HONG HAI
Dept of Open Science: VO TRONG HUNG
Dept of Science and Technology: NGUYEN
   QUANG LUAT
Faculty of Economics and Business Admin-
   istration: DO HUU TUNG
Faculty of Electrical Engineering: NGUYEN
   CHI TINH
Faculty of Geodesy: NAM DANG CHINH
Faculty of Geology: NGUYEN VAN LAM
Faculty of Information Technology: NGUYEN
   TRUONG XUAN
Faculty of Oil: LE HAI AN
Faculty of Political Theory: NGUYEN BINH
   YEN

HANOI UNIVERSITY OF TECHNOLOGY

1 Dai Co Viet Rd, Hanoi
Telephone: (4) 8693796
Fax: (4) 8696720
E-mail: qhqt@mail.hut.edu.vn
Internet: www.hut.edu.vn

Founded 1956
Language of instruction: Vietnamese
Academic year: August to July

Rector: QUOC THANG TRAN

Vice-Rectors: Prof. Dr CONG HOA LE
Chief Admin. Officer: DUONG VAN NGHI
Librarian: GIAN HUU CAN

Library of 700,000 vols
Number of teachers: 1,500
Number of students: 35,650

Publication: *Sciences et Techniques* (4 a year)

DEANS

Applied Mathematics: Dr NGUYEN CANH
   LUONG
Chemical Technology: Dr VU DAO THANG
Economics and Management: Dr TRAN VAN
   BINH
Electronics and Telecommunications: Dr
   PHAM MINH VIET
Engineering Education: Prof. NGUYEN HOA
   TOAN
Foreign Languages: DO VAN MOC
General Chemistry: LE CONG HOA
Hydraulic Machinery and Automation:
   NGUYEN PHU VINH
Industrial Management: NGUYEN MINH DUE
Information Technology: Prof. NGUYEN THUC
   HAI
Mechanical Engineering: Prof. TANG HUY
Metallurgy and Materials Technology: Prof.
   DO MINH NGHIEP
Physical Education: LE VAN LINH
Social Sciences: Prof. NGO MINH KHANG
Textile Engineering: Dr TRAN MINH NAM

HANOI WATER RESOURCES UNIVERSITY

175 Tay Son St, Dong Da, Hanoi
Telephone: (4) 8522201
Fax: (4) 5633351
E-mail: wru@wru.edu.vn
Internet: www.wru.edu.vn

Founded 1959

Rectors: Assoc. Prof. Dr DO VAN HUA, Prof.
   Dr LE KIM TRUYEN
Vice-Rectors: Prof. Dr DAO XUAN HOC, Assoc.
   Prof. Dr PHAM NGOC QUY
Chief Librarian: Dr NGUYEN HUU THAI

Number of teachers: 520
Number of students: 6,930

DEANS

Department of Foreign Languages: LE VAN
   KHANG (Head)
Department of Marxist-Leninist Philosophy
   and Sociology: Dr NGUYEN QUOC LUAT
   (Head)
Department of Military and Physical Educa-
   tion: Sr Lt-Col NGUYEN SY HOI (Head)
Faculty of Hydraulic Construction: Assoc. Dr
   NGUYEN VAN MAO
Faculty of Hydraulic Machinery and Equip-
   ment: Dr NGUYEN DANG CUONG
Faculty of Hydrology and Environment:
   Assoc. Prof. Dr DO TAT TUC
Faculty of Hydrology Power: Assoc. Prof. Dr
   HO SY DU
Faculty of Information Technology: Prof. Dr
   NGUYEN VAN LE
Faculty of In-Service Training: TRAN NGU
   PHUC
Faculty of Planning and Management of
   Water Resources Systems: Dr PHAM NGOC
   HAI
Faculty of Postgraduate Studies: Assoc. Prof.
   Dr DUONG VAN TIEN
Faculty of Water Resources Economics: Dr
   NGUYEN XUAN PHU

HO CHI MINH CITY OPEN UNIVERSITY

97 Vo Van Tan, Ward 6, Dist. 3, Ho Chi Minh
   City
Telephone: (8) 9300210
Fax: (8) 9300085

E-mail: international@ou.edu.vn
Internet: www.ou.edu.vn

Founded 1990, univ. status since 1993
Language of instruction: Vietnamese
Academic year: September to July

Rector: Assoc. Prof. Dr LE BAO DONG
Vice-Rector: Dr NGUYEN THUAN

Library of 12,000
Number of teachers: 530
Number of students: 14,000

Faculties of biotechnology, computer science, economics and business administration, engineering and technology, foreign languages, southeast asian studies and sociology; centres of applied computer science, distance training, foreign languages and overseas studies, professional accounting.

HO CHI MINH CITY UNIVERSITY OF ARCHITECTURE

196 rue Pasteur, Q. 3, Ho Chi Minh City
Telephone: (83) 8222748
Fax: (83) 8244678
E-mail: vuvietanh@hcmuarc.edu.vn
Internet: www.hcmuarc.edu.vn

Founded 1976
State control
Languages of instruction: Vietnamese, English(for Urban Design programme only)

Rector: Dr PHAM TU
Vice-Rector: Dr LE QUANG QUY
Vice-Rector: Dr LE VAN THUONG
Vice-Rector: TRUONG NGOC AN
Librarian: NGUYEN THI THANH THUY

Number of teachers: 450
Number of students: 8,000

DEANS

Architecture: Dr TRINH DUY ANH
Civil Engineering: Dr CHUNG BAC AI
Industrial Art: Dr NGO THI THU TRANG
Interior Architecture: Dr LE THANH SON
Interior Design: (vacant)
Urban Infrastructure: Dr PHAM ANH DUNG
Urban Planning: Dr NGUYEN THANH HA

HO CHI MINH CITY UNIVERSITY OF ECONOMICS

59C, Nguyen Dinh Chieu, Dist. 3, Ho Chi Minh City
Telephone: (8) 8295299
Fax: (8) 8241186
E-mail: tchc@ueh.edu.vn
Internet: www.ueh.edu.vn

Founded 1976
Public control
Languages of instruction: Vietnamese, English, French
Academic year: January to December

Rector: PHAM VAN NANG
Vice-Rector: Prof. Dr MINH DUONG THI BINH
Vice-Rector: Assoc. Prof. Dr TE NGUYEN QUOC
Vice-Rector: Assoc. Prof. Dr NGUYEN VIET
Vice-Rector: Prof. Dr. PHONG NGUYEN DONG
Vice-Rector: Assoc. Prof. Dr. DINH NGUYEN NGOC
Vice-Rector: Assoc. Prof. Dr. NGAN TRAN HOANG
Dir of Univ. Library: THUY DOAN THI

Library of 60,000 vols
Number of teachers: 700
Number of students: 50,000

Publication: *Economic Development Review* (12 a year)

DEANS

Dept of Foreign Languages: Prof. PHUOC VO DINH
Dept of Political Studies: Dr TUAN NGUYEN MINH

Faculty of Accounting and Auditing: Assoc. Prof. Dr DUOC PHAM VAN
Faculty of Business Administration: Assoc. Prof. Dr DUNG HO TIEN
Faculty of Commerce, Tourism and Marketing: Dr BUU LE TAN
Faculty of Corporate Finance: Prof. Dr THO TRAN NGOC
Faculty of Development Economics: Assoc. Prof. Dr HOAI TRONG HOAI
Faculty of Economical Mathematics and Statistics: Dr TRUNG BUI PHUC
Faculty of Economics Law: Dr HUNG LE VAN
Faculty of Management Information System: HUONG VU THI LIEN
Faculty of Public Finance: Assoc. Prof. Dr THANH SU DINH

ATTACHED INSTITUTES

Centre for Economic Studies and Application (CESAIS): 59C Nguyen Dinh Chieu, Dist. 3, Ho Chi Minh; tel. (8) 8223408.

Centre for Excellence in Management Development: 196 Tran Quang Khai St, Dist. 1, Ho Chi Minh City; tel. (8) 38483107; fax (8) 38483252; e-mail cemd@ueh.edu.vn; internet www.cemd.ueh.edu.vn.

Institute of Development Economics Research: 279 Nguyen Tri Phuong, Dist. 10, Ho Chi Minh City; tel. and fax (8) 8561250; e-mail vnckt@idr.edu.vn; internet www.idr.edu.vn; Dir Ho DUC HUNG.

International Centre for Informatics Training (KOVIT): 279 Nguyen Tri Phuong, Dist. 10, Ho Chi Minh City; tel. (8) 8549352.

International Commerce Training Centre: 54 Nguyen Van Thu, Dist 1, Ho Chi Minh City; tel. (8) 8297233; fax (8) 8221210; e-mail ict@ueh.edu.vn; internet www.ueh.edu.vn/ict/default.htm; Dir DONG NGUYEN PHONG.

HO CHI MINH CITY UNIVERSITY OF FINE ARTS

5 Phan Dang Luu, Ho Chi Minh City
Telephone: (8) 84126010
Fax: (8) 8412695
E-mail: dhmt@hcm.vnn.vn

Founded 1913
Dir: Prof. NGUYEN HUY LONG

Number of teachers: 58
Number of students: 700

Publication: *Fine Arts Information*

Courses taught incl. graphic arts and graphic design, painting, sculpture; depts of applied arts, basic knowledge, fine arts pedagogy, fine arts critique, fine art higher education.

HO CHI MINH CITY UNIVERSITY OF FOREIGN LANGUAGES AND INFORMATION TECHNOLOGY

155 Su Van Hanh St (Extension), Ward 13, Dist. 10, Ho Chi Minh City
Telephone: (8) 8632052
Fax: (8) 8650991
E-mail: daotaohuflit@hcm.vnn.vn
Internet: www.huflit.vnn.vn

Founded 1994
Chair.: HUYNH THE CUOC

Number of teachers: 100
Number of students: 1,200

Schools of computer sciences and eastern cultures and languages, foreign languages.

HO CHI MINH CITY UNIVERSITY OF LAW

2 Nguyen tat Thanh, Phuong 12, Q4, Ho Chi Minh City
Telephone: (8) 9400989
Fax: (8) 8265291
E-mail: quantrimang@hcmulaw.edu.vn
Internet: www.hcmulaw.edu.vn

Founded 1996

Rector: VAN LUYEN NGUYEN

Faculties of administrative and state law, business law, civil law, criminal law, international law, part-time training, postgraduate training.

HO CHI MINH CITY UNIVERSITY OF MEDICINE AND PHARMACY

217 Hong Bang, Q. 5, Ho Chi Minh City
Telephone: (8) 8558411
Fax: (8) 8552304
E-mail: info@yds.edu.vn
Internet: www.yds.edu.vn

Founded 1947 as Saigon Univ. of Medicine and Pharmacy, present name since 1976

Rector: DINH HOI NGUYEN

Number of teachers: 982
Number of students: 7,966

Library of 30,000 vols, 700 periodicals

Publication: *Journal of Medicine of Ho Chi Minh City* (4 a year)

Faculties of fundamental sciences, medicine, odonto-stomatology, traditional medicine, pharmacy, nursing medical techniques, public health; University medical centre; advanced medical technology centre; biomedical laboratory; pharma technology centre, medical skills lab unit.

HO CHI MINH CITY UNIVERSITY OF PEDAGOGY

280 An Duong Vuong, Quan 5, Ho Chi Minh City
Telephone: (8) 8352020
Fax: (8) 8398946
E-mail: nttrac@vol.vnn.vn
Internet: www.hcmupeda.edu.vn

Founded 1976

Rector: MANH NHI BUI

Faculties of education, teacher training.

HO CHI MINH CITY UNIVERSITY OF TRANSPORT

2 D3 St, Binh Thanh District M, Ho Chi Minh City
Telephone: (8) 8992862
Fax: (8) 8980456
E-mail: ird@hcmutrans.edu.vn
Internet: www.hcmutrans.edu.vn

Founded 1962 as part of Viet Nam Maritime Univ., ind. status since 2001

Faculties of construction, information technology, marine electrical, marine engineering and electronic engineering, mechanics and transport economics, naval architecture and floating construction, navigation; departments of basic education, foreign languages, in-service training, political reasoning education, postgraduate studies; Centre of Foreign Languages and Information Technology; Merchant Marine Training Centre; Training Centre of Transport Vocation

Rector: CANH VINH TRAN
Vice-Rectors: HUU KHUONG NGUYEN, VAN THU NGUYEN

Number of teachers: 298
Number of students: 8,062

HO CHI MINH UNIVERSITY OF TECHNICAL EDUCATION

1 Vo Van Ngan St, Thu Duc, Ho Chi Minh City
Telephone: (8) 37221223
Fax: (8) 38964922
E-mail: webmaster@hcmute.edu.vn
Internet: www.hcmute.edu.vn

Founded 1962 as Ho Chi Minh City Pedagogical Univ. of Technology; became College of Technical Teacher Training 1996; present name and status 2002
State control
Languages of instruction: Vietnamese, English
Academic year: September to May

Pres.: Assoc. Prof. Dr THAI BA CAN
Vice-Pres.: Assoc. Prof. Dr DO VAN DUNG
Vice-Pres.: Dr LAM MAI LONG
Vice-Pres.: NGUYEN VAN MINH
Librarian: VU TRONG LUAT

Library of 298,332 vols, 227 articles and journals
Number of teachers: 700
Number of students: 26,344

Publication: *Tap san Su Pham Ky Thuat* (4 a year)

DEANS

Faculty of Automotive Engineering: NGUYEN TAN QUOC
Faculty of Chemical and Food Technology: Assoc. Prof. Dr NGUYEN VAN SUC
Faculty of Civil Engineering and Applied Mechanics: Assoc. Prof. Dr NGUYEN HOAI SON
Faculty of Economics: Dr TRAN DANG THINH
Faculty of Electrical and Electronic Engineering: Assoc. Prof. Dr QUYEN HUY ANN
Faculty of Foreign Languages: Dr NGUYEN DINH THU
Faculty of Foundation Sciences: Dr VO THANH TAN
Faculty of Garment Technology and Fashion Design: VU MINH HANH
Faculty of Graphic Arts and Media: Dr NGO ANH TUAN
Faculty of Information Technology: Dr DANG TRUONG SON
Faculty of Marxism-Leninism and Ho Chi Minh's Ideology: Assoc. Prof. DOAN DUC HIEU
Faculty of Mechanical Engineering: Dr NGUYEN NGOC PHUONG
Faculty of Technical Education: Dr NGUYEN VAN TUAN

HONG DUC UNIVERSITY

307 Duong Le Lai Rd, Phuong Dong Son, Thanh Hoa City
Telephone: (37) 910222
Fax: (37) 910475
Internet: www.hdu.edu.vn

Founded 1977 by amalgamation of 3 colleges

DEANS

Department of Foreign Languages: PHAM VAN CHU
Faculty of Agriculture and Forestry: Dr LE HUU CAN
Faculty of Economics and Business Administration: Dr NGUYEN HUU DIEN
Faculty of Medicine: NGUYEN THI TRUONG
Faculty of Natural Science: Dr DUONG DINH HOAN
Faculty of Nursery Teacher Training: NGUYEN THI TRUONG
Faculty of Primary Teacher Training: Dr NGUYEN DINH MAI
Faculty of Social Science: Dr NGUYEN VAN TRUONG
Faculty of Technology: Dr NGUYEN MANH AN

HUE UNIVERSITY

3 Le Loi, Hue City, Thua Thien Hue
Telephone: (54) 845658
Fax: (54) 845658
E-mail: bantin_dhh@hueuni.edu.vn
Internet: www.hueuni.edu.vn

Founded 1957
Language of instruction: Vietnamese
Academic year: November to July

Rector: VIEN THO NGUYEN

Library of 30,000
Number of teachers: 1,316
Number of students: 16,181 full-time, 19,387 part-time

Colleges of agriculture and forestry, economics, medicine, pedagogy, sciences.

HUE UNIVERSITY OF AGRICULTURE AND FORESTRY

102 Phung Hung, Hue
Telephone: (54) 3522535
Fax: (54) 3524923
E-mail: admin@huaf.edu.vn
Internet: www.huaf.edu.vn

Founded 1967
State control
Languages of instruction: English, Vietnamese
Academic year: September to July

Rector: Prof. Dr NGUYEN MINH HIEU
Vice-Rector: Assoc. Prof. Dr LE DUC NGOAN
Vice-Rector: Assoc. Prof. Dr LE THANH BON
Vice-Rector: Assoc. Prof. Dr LE VAN AN

Library of 200,000
Number of teachers: 411
Number of students: 6,800

DEANS

Central Research and Development in Agro-Forestry Technology: Dr HOANG MANH QUAN (Dir)
Centre for Rural Development: Assoc. Prof. Dr LE VAN AN (Dir)
Department of Sciences and International Relations: PHUNG THANG LONG (Dir)
Faculty of Agricultural Engineering and Post-Harvest Technology: LE THANH LONG
Faculty of Agronomy: Dr TRAN DANG HOA
Faculty of Animal Sciences: Dr DAM VAN TIEN
Faculty of Forestry: DANG THAI DUONG

NHA TRANG UNIVERSITY

2 Nguyen Dinh Chieu, Nha Trang City, Khan Hoa Province
Telephone: (58) 831149
Fax: (58) 831147
E-mail: censtrad@ntu.edu.vn
Internet: www.ntu.edu.vn

Founded 1959

Rector: Assoc. Prof. Dr QUAC DINH LIEN
Vice-Rectors: Dr THAI VAN NGAN, Assoc. Prof. Dr TRAN THI LUYEN, VU VAN THUNG

Library of 18,000 vols, 500 periodicals
Number of teachers: 300
Number of students: 7,000

Publications: *Fisheries Journal* (4 a year), *Journal of Science and Technology* (4 a year)

Faculties of aquaculture, basic sciences, fishery economics, marine mechanics, marine products processing, navigation and marine exploitation,.

NONG LAM UNIVERSITY

Khu Pho 6, Linh Trung Ward, Thu Duc Dist., Ho Chi Minh City
Telephone: (8) 8960711
Fax: (8) 8960713

E-mail: vp@hcmuaf.edu.vn
Internet: www.hcmuaf.edu.vn

Founded 1955, as Univ. of Forestry and Agriculture
Language of instruction: Vietnamese
Academic year: September to July

Rector: Dr BUI CACH TUYEN

Library of 60,000
Number of teachers: 400
Number of students: 11,000

Publication: *University Journal of Agricultural Sciences and Technology* (4 a year)

Faculties of agricultural energy and machinery research centre; agronomy, animal science and veterinary medicine, biotechnological research centre; fruit and vegetable processing research centre; centre for research and application of cadastral science and technology; chemical and biological analysis and experiment centre; computer centre; continuing education and placement service economics, engineering, fishery, environmental technology and management centre; environmental technology, experimental research and technology transfer centre; food science and technology, foreign language centre; foreign languages, forestry, industrial crops centre; information technology; science, technology research centre and veterinary clinic wood science.

RMIT INTERNATIONAL UNIVERSITY VIET NAM

702 Nguyen Van Linh Blvd, Tan Phong Ward, Dist. 7, Ho Chi Minh City
Telephone: (8) 37761300
Fax: (8) 37761399
E-mail: enquiries@rmit.edu.vn
Internet: www.rmit.edu.vn

Founded 2001
Private Control
Language of instruction: English'
Academic year: February to January

Undergraduate programmes: univ. preparation, BSc (applied science in software engineering, commerce, information technology for business, information technology and multimedia,); Postgraduate programmes: CELTA courses, English programmes; Graduate Diploma in Tertiary Teaching and Learning, MBA and Management, MEd Leadership;

Pres.: Prof. MERILYN LIDDELL
Vice-Pres. for Academic Affairs: Prof. RON EDWARDS
Exec. Dir for Students: STEVE PARIS
Exec. Dir for Operations and Planning: MATTHEW SUKUMARAN
Head of Hanoi campus: JOHN CROOK

Number of teachers: 350
Number of students: 6,000

THAI BINH MEDICAL UNIVERSITY

373 Ly Bon St, Thai Binh
Telephone: (36) 838545
Fax: (36) 847509
E-mail: dhytb@hn.vnn.vn
Internet: www.tbmc.edu.vn

Founded 1968
State control

Rector: Assoc. Prof. LUONG XUAN HIEN
Vice-Rectors: NGUYEN VAN SAI, Assoc. Prof. TRAN QUOC KHAM

Library of 30,000
Number of teachers: 305
Number of students: 2,500

DEANS

Faculty of Biology: LUONG XUAN HIEN
Faculty of Public Health: PHAM VAM TRONG

Faculty of Traditional Medicine: BUI THI NGUYET

THAI NGUYEN UNIVERSITY

Luong Ngoc Quyen St, Tan Thinh Ward, Thai Nguyen
Telephone: (280) 751681
Fax: (280) 852665
E-mail: bancntt@tnu.edu.vn
Internet: www.tnu.edu.vn
Founded 1994
State control
Academic year: September to June
Pres.: LE CAO THANG
Number of teachers: 1,400
Number of students: 39,000 (incl. 23,000 full-time)

DEANS

Faculty of Foreign Languages: (vacant)
Faculty of Information Technology: PHAM VIET BINH
Faculty of Natural and Social Sciences: (vacant)
Vocational School of Economics and Techniques: (vacant)

Learning Resource Centre: Tan Thinh Ward, Thai Nguyen; tel. (280) 3656600; e-mail vyhong@lrc-tnu.edu.vn; internet www.lrc-tnu.edu.vn; Librarian VU THI YEN HONG.

UNIVERSITY COLLEGES

College of Agriculture and Forestry

Telephone: (280) 855564
Fax: (280) 852921
E-mail: aitc@tuaf.edu.vn
Internet: www.tuaf.edu.vn
Rector: Assoc. Prof. DANG KIM VUI
Vice-Rectors: Assoc. Prof. NGUYEN QUANG TUYEN, Assoc. Prof. NGUYEN THI KIM LAN, Assoc. Prof. TRAN NGOC NGOAN

DEANS

Faculty of Agricultural Extension and Rural Development: Assoc. Prof. Dr NGUYEN DUY HOAN
Faculty of Agricultural Pedagogy: Dr NGUYEN THI LIEN
Faculty of Agricultural Sciences: Assoc. Prof. Dr LUAN THI DEP
Faculty of Animal Husbandry: Dr NGUYEN VAN QUANG
Faculty of Forestry: Dr. LE SY TRUNG
Faculty of Natural Resources and Environment Agriculture: Assoc. Prof. Dr NGUYEN NGOC NONG

College of Economics and Business Administration

Km 9, Duong 3/2 Tich Luong, Thai Nguyen
Telephone: (280) 647685
Fax: (280) 647684
E-mail: tueba@tueba.edu.vn
Internet: www.tueba.edu.vn
Rector: Assoc. Prof. Dr TRAN CHI THIEN

DEANS

Faculty of Accounting: Dr NGUYEN THI MINH THO
Faculty of Basic Science: Assoc. Prof. NGUYEN THI THU HUONG
Faculty of Business Administration: Assoc. Prof TRAN QUANG HUY
Faculty of Economics: Dr DO QUANG QUY
Postgraduate Studies: Dr TRAN DINH TUAN

College of Education

Duong Luong, Ngoc Quyen, Thai Nguyen
Telephone: (280) 856886
Fax: (280) 859521
E-mail: dhsupham.edu@hn.vnn.vn
Internet: www.dhsptn.edu.vn
Rector: NGUYEN VAN LOC
Vice-Rectors: PHAM HONG QUANG, PHAM HIEN BANG, DUONG DUY HUNG, PHAM VIET DUC

DEANS

Faculty of Chemistry: LE HUU THIENG
Faculty of Foreign Languages: NGUYEN VINH QUANG
Faculty of History: DAM THI UYEN
Faculty of Languages: NGUYEN HANG PHUONG
Faculty of Marxist-Leninist Political Theory: DONG VAN QUAN
Faculty of Mathematics: PHAM VIET DUC
Faculty of Physical Education: NGUYEN VAN LUC
Faculty of Physics: PHAM THAI CUONG
Faculty of Psychology: NGUYEN THI TINH

College of Industrial Technology

3–2 St, Thai Nguyen
Telephone: (2) 80847145
Fax: (2) 80847904
E-mail: tnut_office@tnut.edu
Internet: www.tnut.edu.vn
Rector: Dr NGUYEN DANG BINH
Vice-Rectors: Assoc. Prof NGUYEN NHU HIEN, Assoc. Prof NGUYEN DANG HOE, Assoc. Prof. PHAN QUANG THE

DEANS

Faculty of Basic Science: NGUYEN VAN TUAN
Faculty of Electrical Engineering: TRAN XUAN MINH
Faculty of Electronics: NGUYEN HUU CONG
Faculty of Management & Industrial Environment: MAI VAN GU
Faculty of Mechanical Engineering: VU QUY DUC
Faculty of Pedagogy: DUONG PHUC TY

College of Medicine and Pharmacy

284 Duong Luong Ngoc, Quyen Thanh, Thai Nguyen
Telephone: (280) 852671
Fax: (280) 855710
E-mail: dhyktn@hn.vnn.vn
Internet: www.tnmc.edu.vn
Founded 1968
Rector: Assoc. Prof. Dr NGUYEN THANH TRUNG.

THAI NGUYEN UNIVERSITY OF AGRICULTURE AND FORESTRY

Quyet Thinhdan Commune, Thai Nguyen City, Thai Nguyen
Telephone: (280) 3855564
Fax: (280) 3852921
E-mail: tuaf@hn.vnn.vn
Internet: www.tuaf.edu.vn
Founded 1970
Faculties of agricultural economics, agricultural technology, agronomy, animal husbandry and veterinary science, forestry, graduate studies, land management, pedagogy; agro-forestry research and development centre for northern mountainous regions of Viet Nam; centre for mountainous natural resources and environment; experimental farm; life science research institute; centre for agricultural experiment and practices; mountainous resources and environment centre; centre for foreign language studies; centre for applied information technologies; centre for international training cooperation and consultancy

Rector: Prof. Dr DANG KIM VUI
Number of teachers: 300
Number of students: 10,000

UNIVERSITY OF DALAT

01 Phu Dong Thien, Vuong, Dalat, Lamdong
Telephone: (63) 3822246
Fax: (63) 3823380
E-mail: irdept@dlu.edu.vn
Internet: www.dlu.edu.vn
Founded 1958
State control
Languages of instruction: Vietnamese, English
Academic year: September to June
Faculties: agronomy, biology, business administration, chemistry, environmental studies, foreign languages, graduate studies history, information technology, law, mathematics, oriental philology, physics, social work and community development, studies, teacher training, tourism
Rector: Assoc. Prof. Dr LE BA DUNG
Vice-Rector: Dr NGUYEN DUC HOA
Vice-Rector: Dr MAI XUAN TRUNG
Vice-Rector: Dr NGUYEN DINH HAO
Number of teachers: 500
Number of students: 13,000
Publication: *Scientific Journal* (1 a year).

UNIVERSITY OF DANANG

41 Le Duan St, Da Nang
Telephone: (511) 822041
Fax: (511) 823683
E-mail: relint@dng.vnn.vn
Internet: www.ud.edu.vn
Founded 1994
State control
Library of 25,000 vols, 250 periodicals
Number of teachers: 889
Number of students: 35,000
President: Prof. Dr PHAN QUANG XUNG
Vice-Presidents: Prof. Dr BUI VAN GA, Dr LE THE GIOI

DIRECTORS

College of Economics and Business Administration: Dr VO XUAN TIEN
College of Education: NGUYEN KHAC SINH
College of Technology: Prof. Dr PHAM PHU LY
School of Technology: DANG VAN SON

VAN LANG UNIVERSITY

45 Nguyen Khac Nhu, Q 1, Ho Chi Minh City
Telephone: (8) 38367933
Fax: (8) 38369716
E-mail: tuyensinh@vanlangunni.edu.vn
Internet: www.vanlanguni.edu.vn
Rector: DUNG NGUYEN
Faculty of Foreign Languages.

VIET NAM FORESTRY UNIVERSITY

Main Campus, Xuan Mai, Chuong My, Hanoi
Second Campus, Trang Bom, Trang Bom, Dong Na
Telephone: (4) 33840441
Fax: (4) 33840540
E-mail: vfuhtqt@hn.vnn.vn
Internet: www.vfu.edu.vn
Founded 1964
Academic year: August to June
Rector: TRAN HUU VIEN
Library of 29,302 books, 15,696 periodicals
Number of teachers: 320
Number of students: 11,761
Research and production units: centre for experimental research and forest industry

technology transfer, consulting company for forestry investment and development, institute for forest ecology and environment

Publications: *Forest Science and Technology Newsletter* (4 a year), *Scientific Research Periodical* (4 a year)

DEANS

Faculty of Economics and Business Administration: TRAN HUU DAO
Faculty of Engineering: LE TAN QUYNH
Faculty of Forest Products Technology: VU HUY DAI
Faculty of Forest Resources and Environmental Management: NGUYEN THE NHA
Faculty of Marx-Lenin: DOAN VAN HANH
Faculty of Postgraduate Training: NGUYEN PHAN THIET
Faculty of Silviculture: NGUYEN TRONG BINH
High School for Ethnic Students: NGUYEN QUANG CHUNG

PROFESSORS

HINH, V.
HUU VIEN, T.
PHAN THIET, N.
VAN CHU, T.
VAN CHUONG, P.
VAN TUAN, N.
XUAN HOAN, P.

VIET NAM MARITIME UNIVERSITY

19B/260, Thuy Khue, Tay Ho, Hanoi
Telephone: (4) 8470279
E-mail: duyluat@bigwall.com
Internet: www.vimaru.edu.vn

Founded 1956
Academic year: August to May

Rector: Dr DANG VAN UY
Vice-Rectors: Dr LUONG CONG NHO, Prof. Dr PHAM TIEN TINH, Prof. Dr PHAM VAN CUONG
Librarian: TRAN THI YEN

Number of teachers: 800
Number of students: 15,000

DEANS

Department of Postgraduate Studies: LE VIET LUONG
Faculty of Information Technology: LE QUOC DINH
Faculty of Marine Electrical and Electronic Engineering: PHAM NGOC TIEP
Faculty of Marine Engineering: NGUYEN DAI AN
Faculty of Navigation: DINH XUAN MANH
Faculty of Sea-Transport Economics: PHAM VAN CUONG
Faculty of Shipbuilding: NGUYEN VINH PHAT
Faculty of Waterway Construction: NGUYEN VAN NGOC

VIET NAM NATIONAL UNIVERSITY, HANOI

144 Xuan Thuy Rd, Cau Giay, Hanoi
Telephone: (4) 8332015
Fax: (4) 7680429
E-mail: vandao@vnu.ac.vn
Internet: www.vnu.edu.vn

Founded 1993 by amalgamation of Univ. of Hanoi and other instns of higher education in Hanoi
State control
Academic year: September to July

Faculties of general education, foreign languages, science, social sciences and humanities, teacher training; colleges of foreign languages, science, social sciences, humanities; school of business; institute of information technology training; centres of biotechnology, cooperation in mechanics training, education quality assurance and research development, natural resources management and environmental studies, systems development, teachers of political theory, Vietnamese and intercultural studies and women's studies; research centres in applied microbiology and Asian studies

Rector: Prof. Dr DAO TRONG THI
Vice-Rector: Prof. NGUYEN DUC CHINH
Librarian: NGUYEN HUY CHUONG
Library of 800,000 vols, 3,000 periodicals
Number of teachers: 1,320
Number of students: 22,761

Publication: *Tap Chí Khoa Hoc* (Scientific Journal).

VIET NAM NATIONAL UNIVERSITY, HO CHI MINH CITY

KP6, Linh-Trung, Thu Duc Dist., Ho Chi Minh City
Telephone: (84) 87242160
Fax: (84) 87242057
E-mail: hopthu_tuyensinh@vnuhcm.edu.vn
Internet: www.vnuhcm.edu.vn

Founded 1954, present structure since 1995
Dir: Dr PHAN THANH BÌNH.

CONSTITUENT UNIVERSITIES

University of Natural Sciences

227 Nguyen Van Cu, Dist. 5, Ho Chi Minh City
Telephone: (8) 8353193
Fax: (8) 8350096
Internet: www.hcmuns.edu.vn

Founded as a div. of the Indochina College of Sciences, Hanoi 1942, became Faculty of Sciences of Univ. of Saigon 1956; part of Ho Chi Minh Univ. 1977; current status since 1996

Rector: Assoc. Prof. Dr DUONG AI PHUONG
Vice-Rector: Assoc. Prof. Dr DONG THI BICH THUY
Vice-Rector: NGUYEN THANH HUONG
Vice-Rector: Assoc. Prof. Dr PHAM DINH HUNG
Library Dir: NGUYEN MINH HIEP
Library of 50,000 vols, 392 periodicals

DEANS

Department of Foreign Languages: NGUYEN HOANG TUAN (Head)
Department of Material Science: Prof. Dr LE KHAC BINH (Head)
Department of Physical Education: NGUYEN VAN HUNG
Faculty of Biology: Assoc. Prof. Dr TRAN LINH THUOC
Faculty of Chemistry: Assoc. Prof. Dr HA THUC HUY
Faculty of Environmental Science: Assoc. Prof. Dr LE MANH TAN
Faculty of Geology: TRAN PHU HUNG
Faculty of Information Technology: Dr DUONG ANH DUC
Faculty of Mathematics and Informatics: Dr TO ANH DUNG
Faculty of Physics: Dr DAV VAN LIET

University of Social Sciences and Humanities

10–12 Dinh Tien Hoang St, Ho Chi Minh City
E-mail: nckhhtqt@hcmc.netnam.vn
Internet: www.hcmussh.edu.vn

Founded 1996
Language of instruction: Vietnamese
Academic year: October to June

Faculties of Chinese linguistics and literature, English linguistics and literature, French linguistics and literature, geography, German linguistics and literature, history, linguistics and journalism, literature, oriental studies, philosophy, Russian linguistics and literature, sociology, Viet Nam studies and Vietnamese for foreigners; sections of anthropology, culture studies and physical education;; centre for foreign languages;; centre for informatics technology; centre for overseas studies; centre for research in social development and poverty reduction; Vietnamese and southeast asian research centre

Rector: VAN LE NGO
Librarian: Dr BUI LOAN THUY
Library of 87,784 vols, 375 periodicals.

Ho Chi Minh City University of Technology

268 Ly Thuong Kiet St, Dist. 10, Ho Chi Minh City
Telephone: (8) 38652442
Fax: (8) 38653823
E-mail: inter@hcmut.edu.vn
Internet: www.hcmut.edu.vn
State control
Academic year: September to July

Training and research; 11 faculties of applied sciences, chemical technology, civil engineering, computer science and engineering, electrical and electronic engineering, environment, geology and petroleum, industrial management, information technology, material technology, mechanical engineering, transportation engineering; school of industrial management

Rector: Assoc. Prof. Dr THANH VU DINH.

VIET NAM UNIVERSITY OF COMMERCE

Mai Dich, Cau Giay, Hanoi
Telephone: (4) 7643219
Fax: (4) 7643228
E-mail: dhtm@vcu.edu.vn
Internet: www.vcu.edu.vn

Founded 1965

Rector: Prof. Dr PHAM VU LUAN
Vice-Rectors: NGUYEN THIEN DAT, Assoc. Prof. Dr TRAN THI DUNG, Assoc. Prof. Dr NGUYEN BACH KHOA
Library Dir: VU THI HUE

Library of 100,000 vols
Number of teachers: 267
Number of students: 7,600

DEANS

Faculty of Business Administration: VU THUY DUONG
Faculty of Economics: Dr THAN DANH PHUC
Faculty of Finance and Accounting: Dr DO MINH THANH
Faculty of Hospitality and Tourism: Dr BUI XUAN NHAN
Faculty of International Trade: Dr NGUYEN VAN THANH
Faculty of Part-Time Training: Assoc. Prof. Dr NGUYEN THI MINH NGUYET
Faculty of Postgraduate Training: Dr NGUYEN VAN MINH
Faculty of Trading Business: Dr DO THI NGOC
Section of Environment Economics: NGUYEN QUOC TIEN (Head)
Section of Foreign Languages: NGUYEN DUC CHAU (Head)
Section of the History of Viet Nam's Communist Party and Socialism: NGO XUAN DAU (Head)
Section of Mathematics: Dr HOANG VAN LAM (Head)
Section of Philosophy: Dr PHUONG KY SON (Head)
Section of Physical and Military Training: NGUYEN VAN KHANH (Head)
Section of Political Economy: Dr DINH THI THUY (Head)

VINH UNIVERSITY

182 Le Duan St, Vinh
Telephone: (38) 3855452
Fax: (38) 3855269
E-mail: lprvvinh@hn.vnn.vn
Rector: NGUYEN DINH HUAN
Vice-Rectors: NGUYEN NGOC HOI, TRAN NGOC GIAO
Number of students: 10,000

Colleges

ART AND SOCIAL ARTS AND CONSERVATOIRES

College of Law: Thuong Tin, Lang Ha Hanoi, Son Binh Province; tel. (4) 8343251.

Dong Nai College of Decorative Arts: 368 Quoc Lo 1, Thanh Pho Bien Hoa, Tinh Dong Nai; tel. (61) 822042; fax (61) 816170; e-mail mythuat.tung@gmail.com; internet dongnaiart.edu.vn; f. 1965; administered directly by the Min. of Culture, Sports and Tourism; specializes in art, ceramics, bronze-casting and natural and artificial stone sculpturing.

Hanoi College of Fine Arts: 42 Yet Kieu St, Hanoi; there are 3 faculties.

Hanoi Cultural College: 103 De La Thanh St, Hanoi; tel. (4) 8512606; there are 4 faculties.

Hanoi National Conservatory of Music: 77 Hao Nam, O Cho Dua, Dong Da Hanoi; fax (4) 8513545; e-mail nhacvienhn@netnam.vn; internet www.nhacvienhanoi.vn; Dir NGO THANH VAN.

Hanoi University of Drama and Cinematography: Mai Dich, Cau Giay, Hanoi; tel. (4) 7643397; fax (4) 8348732; e-mail skda@fpt.vn; f. 1980; undergraduate and postgraduate degrees in , cinematography, screen writing and theatre direction; Dir Prof. Dr NGUYEN MANH LAN.

Ho Chi Minh City College of Performing Arts and Cinema: 125 Cong Quynh St, Ho Chi Minh City; tel. (8) 8393658; f. 1995; costume design, film and cinematography, pantomime and mime, radio and television, theatre.

Ho Chi Minh City Conservatory: 112 Nguyen Du St, Dist. 1, Thanh Po Ho Chi Minh City; tel. (8) 8225841; fax (8) 8220916; e-mail nhacvienhcm@hcm.vnn.vn; f. 1956; composition, conducting, electric instruments, singing, national and orchestral instruments, theory; 136 teachers; 758 students; Dir Prof. HOANG CUONG.

ECONOMICS AND PLANNING

Academy of Finance: 7 Ly Thuong Kiet St, Hoan Kiem Dist., Hanoi; tel. (4) 9331853; fax (4) 9331865; e-mail hvtc@hn.vnn.vn; internet www.hvtc.edu.vn; f. 2001; faculties of accounting, banking and insurance, business administration, continuing education, corporate finance, customs taxation, economic information systems, foundation studies, international finance, marx-lenin-ho chi minh ideology, postgraduate training, public finance; institutes of financial science, and for market and price research; library: 157,000 vols (16,500 titles), 162 current periodicals, 2,100 other publications; 350 teachers; 13,274 students; Dir-Gen. CHI NGO THE; publs *Finance and Accounting Research* (12 a year), *Financial Bulletin* (2 a month), *International Economics and Finance News* (52 a year), *Market Bulletin* (online, 365 a year), *Market and Price Bulletin* (in English, 52 a year), *Monography* (5 a year), *News for Leaders* (24 a year), *Scientific Research* (10 a year).

College of Commerce: Mai Dich, Tu Liem Dist., Hanoi; tel. (4) 8343207; there are 5 faculties.

College of Economics: 144, Xuan Thuy St, Hanoi; tel. (4) 7547506; fax (4) 7546765; e-mail kinhte@vnu.edu.vn; internet www .economics.vnu.edu.vn; attached to Viet Nam National Univ.; there are 12 faculties.

Ho Chi Minh City College of Finance and Accountancy: College Library, 279 Nguyen Tri Phuong St, Dist. 10, Ho Chi Minh City; tel. (8) 8550783; there are 3 faculties.

MEDICINE, PHYSICAL EDUCATION AND SPORTS

College of Physical Training and Sports: Tu Son Dist., Bac Ninh Province; tel. (241) 831609; fax (241) 832550; f. 1959; there are 6 faculties; 215 teachers; 2,500 students; Dir Prof. Dr TRAN DUC DUNG.

Hanoi College of Pharmacy: 13–15 Le Thanh Tong St, Hanoi; tel. (4) 8254539; fax (4) 9332332; e-mail dhduochn@netnam.org .vn; f. 1961; 160 teachers; 780 students; library: 20,000 vols; Dean Prof. Dr NGUYEN THANH DO.

TECHNICAL AND INDUSTRIAL

College of Water Conservancy: Dong Da Precinct, Hanoi; there are 6 faculties.

Posts and Telecommunications Training Centre No. 1: 10 Km, Nguyen Trai Rd, Hadong, Hatay, Hanoi; tel. (4) 8547795; fax (4) 5540587; e-mail pttci@hn.vnn.vn; internet www.ptit.edu.vn; f. 1953; library: 7,000 vols; Dir Dr CHU QUANG TOAN.

Road and Rail Transport College: Tu Liem Dist., Hanoi; there are 5 faculties.

YEMEN

The Higher Education System

Institutions of higher education predate Yemen's formation from a merger of the Yemen Arab Republic and the People's Democratic Republic of Yemen in 1990, the oldest being San'a University, which was founded in 1970. In 1975 the University of Aden was founded and these remained the principal institutions of higher education until the 1990s. In 2008/09 a total of 256,125 students was enrolled at institutions of higher education, which numbered 16 in 2004/05. In 2010 the World Bank signed a US $13m. credit agreement intended to assist with the enactment of university reforms, curriculum development and the introduction of new academic programmes, together with the development of a higher education committee to oversee academic curricula and standards. A further six agreements, collectively worth $5.8m., were signed between the Yemeni Government and the World Bank in February 2011, which were intended to upgrade facilities and launch science-based programmes at the public universities in Taiz, Aden, Ibb, Dhamar and Amran.

The most recent legislation pertaining to higher education is the Law on Private Universities (No. 13, 2005) and the Universities, Colleges and Institutions of Higher Education Law (No. 14, 2005). The Ministry of Higher Education and Scientific Research is split into two main departments. The first is the University Affairs division, which is responsible for qualifications and certificates, equivalency, approval and recognition, with responsibility for both public and private universities. The second department is the National Accreditation Committee (NAC), which in 2011 was not yet fully established; however it was implementing partial accreditation procedures and processes with regards to the monitoring of public and private universities, and as such its work was largely limited to determining whether or not institutions should have the legal right to operate; this is reflected in the Law on Private Universities, which gave the ministry the power to shut down deficient programmes and courses. The NAC was also working towards the development of strategies for the accreditation of programmes offered at universities and this remains one of the Council's highest priorities. The Ministry of Technical Education and Vocational Training, which was established in 2001, is the national body responsible for technical and vocational education in Yemen.

The Thanawiya (General Secondary Education Certificate) is the principal requirement for admission to both public and private higher education. In 2001 the pass mark in the Thanawiya for entry to all undergraduate degrees was set at 70%; additionally, applicants to popular programmes such as engineering or medicine may have to sit a university entrance examination and attend a personal interview. Universities offer two-year, sub-degree Diplomas in professional and technical fields from which students can progress onto advanced degree programmes. Bachelors degrees must last at least four years, and students are required to accumulate a minimum of 132 'credits' for graduation. (The Bachelors of Medicine is a six-year programme of study.) Traditionally, Yemeni graduate students travelled abroad to study for postgraduate degrees, however in recent years Yemeni institutions have begun awarding postgraduate degrees (although the range is still quite limited). The first postgraduate qualification is the postgraduate Diploma (referred to variously as the Higher Diploma, the Specialist Diploma, the Graduate Diploma or the Preparatory Diploma), which is a one-year course that is also regarded as a preparatory course for the Masters degree, which lasts two years and is now available at both public and private universities. Finally, although Doctorates are now being offered by universities on an 'in-house' basis, there is no uniform system for their award.

Post-secondary technical and vocational education is offered by a range of different professional and vocational institutes and is divided into Regular (or General), Parallel and Further (or Continuing) Education and Training. The Certificate in Technical Education is awarded after a two-year course at technical institutes and is open to students with either the Thanawiya or the Certificate of Vocational Training. US-style 'community' colleges have been established and they specialize in three-year Diploma courses, admission to which requires the Thanawiya.

Regulatory Bodies

GOVERNMENT

Ministry of Culture and Tourism: POB 129, San'a; tel. (1) 235461; fax (1) 251557; e-mail moc@y.net.ye; internet www.mocyemen.com; Minister of Culture ABDULLAH AUBAL MANDHOUQ; Minister of Tourism QASIM SALLAM.

Ministry of Education: San'a; tel. (1) 274548; fax (1) 274555; e-mail moetele@yemen.net.ye; internet www.moe.gov.ye; Minister of Education ABD AL-RAZZAQ YAHYA AL-ASHWAL; Minister of Higher Education and Scientific Research YAHYA AL-SHU'AIBI.

Learned Society

LANGUAGE AND LITERATURE

British Council: 3rd Fl., Administrative Tower, San'a Trade Centre, Algiers St, POB 2157, San'a; tel. (1) 448356; fax (1) 448360; e-mail information@ye.britishcouncil.org; internet www.britishcouncil.org/me-yemen.htm; offers courses and exams in English language and British culture and promotes cultural exchange with the UK; Asst Dir, Resources AZIZ AL-BAAR.

Libraries and Archives

Aden

Miswat Library: Aden; previously called Lake Library; administered by Aden Municipality; 30,000 vols, in English, Arabic and Urdu.

Teachers' Club Library: Aden; over 2,000 vols.

Travelling Library: Aden; ancillary to Miswat Library; administered by Aden Municipality; 9,500 vols, in English and Arabic.

San'a

British Council Library: Al-Sanabani Roundabout, Al Jame'a St, San'a; tel. (1) 373248; e-mail h.jailan@ust.edu.ye; internet www.britishcouncil.org/me-yemen-learning--centre-membership-details.htm; 10,000 vols, 36 periodicals; Dir RAJA'A BAZARA.

Library of the Great Mosque of San'a: San'a; f. 1925; the colln of 10,000 MSS and printed vols is not at present accessible to the public; Librarian ZAID BIN ALI ENAN.

Universities

UNIVERSITY OF ADEN

POB 6312, Khormaksar, Aden

Telephone: (2) 234428

Fax: (2) 234426

E-mail: rector@adenuniversity.edu.ye

Internet: www.adenuniversity.edu.ye

Founded 1975

State control

Languages of instruction: Arabic, English

Academic year: September to June

Rector: Prof. Dr ABDUL WAHAB RAWEH

Vice-Rector for Academic Affairs: Assoc. Prof. Dr SAEED ABDO GABALI

Vice-Rector for Scientific Research and Postgraduate Studies: Assoc. Prof. Dr AHMED ALI AL-HAMDANI

Vice-Rector for Students' Affairs: Asst Prof. Dr NASSER A. NASSER

Sec.-Gen.: Assoc. Prof. Dr AHMED SALEH MUNASSER

Number of teachers: 1,482

Number of students: 22,761

Publications: *Al-Tawassul* (2 a year), *Al-Yemen* (2 a year), *Journal of Natural and Applied Sciences* (2 a year), *Journal of Social Sciences and Humanities* (2 a year), *Saba* (2 a year), *Yemen Engineer* (3 a year), *Yemeni Journal for Agricultural Research* (2 a year)

DEANS

Faculty of Administration: Assoc. Prof. FUAD RASHED ABDO

Faculty of Agricultural Sciences: Assoc. Prof. Dr ABBAS BAWAZIR

Faculty of Arts: Assoc. Prof. Dr SULAIMAN FARAJ BIN AZOON

Faculty of Economics: Prof. Dr MOHAMED A. WARET

Faculty of Education (Aden): Asst Prof. Dr YACOOB A. KASSEM

Faculty of Education (Dalea): Asst Prof. Dr MOHD S. OBADI

Faculty of Education (Loder): Asst Prof. Dr SALEH A. AL BORKANI

Faculty of Education (Radfan): Asst Prof. Dr ABDULLA MOHAMMED

Faculty of Education (Sabr): Assoc. Prof. Dr ALI QASEM AKLAN

Faculty of Education (Shabwa): Assoc. Prof. Dr NASER SALEH. HABTOOR

Faculty of Education (Tur Al-Baha): Asst Prof. Dr HAMID ABDUL MAGEED QUBATI

Faculty of Education (Yafai): Assoc. Prof. Dr ABDUL RAHMAN AL-WALI

Faculty of Education (Zingibar): Assoc. Prof. Dr MOHAMMED A. HOSEEN

Faculty of Engineering: Assoc. Prof. Dr ABDUL WALI HADI

Faculty of Law: Assoc. Prof Dr SAAD M. SAAD

Faculty of Medicine: Assoc. Prof. Dr ABDULLA SAEED HATAB

Faculty of Oil and Minerals: Asst Prof. Dr KHALED ALI. AL SHAMSI

UNIVERSITY OF DHAMAR

POB 87246, Dhamar

Telephone: (6) 509554

Fax: (6) 509556

Internet: www.thuniv.edu.ye

Founded 1996

Rector: AHMED AL-HADHRANI

Faculties of admin. sciences, art, dentistry, education, engineering, law, medicine, nursing, physical sciences, tourism, veterinary medicine.

HADHRAMOUT UNIVERSITY OF SCIENCE AND TECHNOLOGY

POB 50512–50511, Mukalla-Hadhramout Governate

Telephone: (5) 360865

Fax: (5) 360864

E-mail: hadhramout_univ@y.net.ye

Internet: www.hust.edu.ye

Founded 1993

State control

Vice-Rector: SALEM AWAD RAMODHA

Faculties of admin. sciences, applied science, arts, engineering and technology, environment science and marine biology, nursing; College for Women, College of Education.

HODEIDAH UNIVERSITY

POB 3114, Hodeidah

Telephone: (3) 222703

Fax: (3) 222703

E-mail: info@hoduniv.edu.ye

Internet: www.hoduniv.edu.ye

State control

Chair.: Dr MOHAMMAD QASIM BERT

Faculties of education, management systems, marine sciences.

IBB UNIVERSITY

POB 70270, Ibb

Telephone: (4) 408069

Fax: (4) 408068

E-mail: ibbunv@yemen.net.ye

Internet: www.ibbunv.com.ye

Founded 1996

State control

Rector: Prof. Dr AHMED M. SHUQ'A ALDEEN

Faculties of agriculture and veterinary science, arts, dentistry, economics and management, education, engineering and architecture and science; centres for agricultural and environmental consultancy, educational technology and engineering consultancy.

QUEEN ARWA UNIVERSITY

Asteen St-Fajj Attan, Sana'a

Telephone: (1) 445991

Fax: (1) 445996

E-mail: arwauniversity@y.net.ye

Internet: www.arwauniversity.org

Founded 1996

Private control

Languages of instruction: Arabic, English

Academic year: September to June

Colleges of arts and human science, economics and administration, engineering and computer science, law, medicine and pharmacy

Vice-Rector: MUHAMMED A. ALKHAYYAT

Dean of Student Affairs: Dr HAZZA ABDO SALEM AL-HOMAIDI

Library of 30,000 vols

Number of teachers: 150

Number of students: 3,000

Publication: *Queen Arwa University Magazine* (2 a year).

SAN'A UNIVERSITY

POB 1247, San'a

Telephone: (1) 464483

Fax: (1) 464483

E-mail: info@suye.ac

Internet: www.new.suye.ac/en

Founded 1970

State control; financial support from Kuwait

Languages of instruction: Arabic, English

Academic year: October to June

Pres.: Dr KHALID ABDULLAH TAMEM

Number of teachers: 332

Number of students: 10,715

Publication: Faculty research journals

DEANS

Faculty of Agriculture: Dr NASSER AULAQI (acting)

Faculty of Arts: Dr AHMED AL SAYDI

Faculty of Commerce and Economics: Dr NASSER AULAQI

Faculty of Education: Dr MOHAMED AL KHADER

Faculty of Engineering: Dr AWAD SALEH

Faculty of Law and Sharia: Dr ABDUL MUNIM AL BADRAWI

Faculty of Medicine and Health Sciences: Dr ABDALLAH AL-HURAYBI

Faculty of Science: Dr ALI AL SHUKAI

TAIZ UNIVERSITY

POB 6803, Taiz

Telephone: (4) 221378

Fax: (4) 221381

Internet: www.taiz university.net

Founded 1995

State control

Languages of instruction: Arabic, English

Pres.: Prof. MOHAMED AL-SOOFI

Dean of Libraries: ABDULLAH AHMAD ALTHAIFANY

Library of 95,139 vols, 5700 periodicals

Number of teachers: 790

Number of students: 29,000

Publications: *Journal of Educational and Academic Development* (1 a year), *Journal of Educational Sciences and Psychology* (1 a year), *Journal of the Faculty of Arts* (1 a year), *Taiz University Journal* (1 a year), *Taiz University Research Journal* (1 a year)

DEANS

Faculty of Administrative Science: Prof. MAHFOUZ ALHADAITHY

Faculty of Applied Sciences: Prof. ADAM AL SHAMIRY

Faculty of Arts: Assoc. Prof. HAMOOD SHARAF AL-DEEN

Faculty of Education: Prof. NABEEL SUFIAN

Faculty of Education in Turba: Assoc. Prof. ABDULQAWI ALHUSAINY

Faculty of Engineering and IT: Assoc. Prof. ABDUL GHANY AHMAD

Faculty of Languages and Translation: Prof. WAHBIYA MOHARRAM

Faculty of Law: Prof. AHMAD MOHAMED ALHUMAIDY

Faculty of Medicine: Prof. ABDUL MALIK AL MORTAZA

Faculty of Science: Prof. ABDULRAHMAN ALZOBIRI

PROFESSORS

ABDULKARIM MOHARRAM, W., English Language Teaching

ABDULLAH ALSOOFI, M., Social Psychology in Education

ABDURRAHMAN ALZOBIRI, Microbiology

AHMAD ALTHAIFANY, A., Foundation of Education

AL HAKIMY, A. H., Science Education

AL SAYAGHI, K., Psychology (Especial Education)

AL SHAMIRY, A., Microbiology

ALI KAHTAN, M., Planning Management of National Economy

ALMEKHLAFY, S., Educational Management

ALSOOFI, M., Socio-Psychology in Education

ALZOBIRI, A., Microbiology

HAIDER, A., Teaching Methods of Science

MALIK ANAM, A., Morphology and Syntax (Arabic Language)

MOHAMED ALHAKIMY, A., Plant Physiology

MOHAMED TRBUSH, K., General Law

NASIR ALI, A., Geography

SAEED ALSHOAYBY, M., General International Law

SALEH SUFIAN, N., Psychology

SHARAF GHALEB, A., Geology (Minerals)

SOSWAH, A., Linguistics

TARESH, M., Educational Planning

TALIB, A., Science Education

College

High College of Koran Kareem: POB 11229, Riyadh Av., San'a; tel. (1) 216865; fax (1) 216869; e-mail high-kuraan@y.net; Sharia and Islamic Studies.

ZAMBIA

The Higher Education System

Institutions of higher education predate the independence of the Republic of Zambia (formerly Northern Rhodesia) from the United Kingdom in 1964, the oldest being Zambia College of Agriculture, which was founded in 1947. In 1965 the University of Zambia was founded and it remained the only university-level institution until the foundation of Copperbelt University in 1987, which offers degrees in professional fields only; in 2010 a total of 16,655 students were enrolled at these two universities. In 2008 the National College of Management and Development Studies was converted into Mulungushi University by the Government in a public–private partnership with Konkola Copper Mines There are also a number of technical, vocational and teacher-training colleges. In 1999/2000 there were an estimated 24,553 students enrolled in tertiary education, which is administered by the Ministry of Education. Affirmative action programmes, including the creation of bursaries for academically gifted female students who could otherwise not afford to pay for tertiary education, have significantly reduced gender disparities within higher education in recent years. The Government's Sixth National Development Plan for the period 2011–15, which was launched in February 2011, had a strong focus on higher education, particularly on improving access to and participation in university education and on expanding research activities; the plans included proposals to establish a quality assurance mechanism by which to regulate university-level education and to establish a student loan scheme. In October of that year the newly elected President, Michael Sata, announced plans to reform the higher education sector, including the establishment of three new universities, the opening of new technical colleges in each of Zambia's nine provinces, and the upgrading and updating of the country's existing institutions.

The standard administrative structure consists of the Chancellor, Vice-Chancellor, Registrar, Bursar, University Council, Senate, Boards of Studies, Deans and Heads of Department. The Chancellor is appointed by the Head of State while the Vice-Chancellors are appointed by the Minister of Education, who also appoints the University Council; the University Council in turn appoints the Registrar and Bursar. Other than the state budget, the main source of university funding is students' tuition fees.

Students are required to obtain five credit-level passes on the Zambian School Certificate (Grade 12) for admission to university. The Bachelors is the main undergraduate degree and is generally four years in duration, although degrees in professional fields may last longer, including agriculture, architecture, engineering (five years), veterinary science (six years) and medicine (seven years). Postgraduate Certificate and Diploma programmes, which typically last between one and two years, are offered in a wide range of subjects. The Masters degree is open to students who have been awarded the Bachelors and is a two- to four-year programme of study. The PhD is the highest university degree in Zambia but is only available in a limited number of specialized subjects; it requires up to four years of study.

The Ministry of Science, Technology and Vocational Training is responsible for providing post-secondary vocational and technical education. Within the Ministry, the Department of Technical Education and Vocational Training administers 11 institutions and 90 technical courses. The principal qualifications are (in ascending order) the Craft Certificate, Certificate, Advanced Certificate and Diploma.

Regulatory Bodies

GOVERNMENT

Ministry of Education: 15102 Ridgeway, POB RW50093, Lusaka; tel. (1) 227636; fax (1) 222396; Minister GEOFFREY LUNGWANGWA.

Ministry of Science, Technology and Vocational Training: POB 50464, Lusaka; tel. (1) 229673; fax (1) 252951; Minister PETER DAKA.

Learned Societies

BIBLIOGRAPHY, LIBRARY SCIENCE AND MUSEOLOGY

Zambia Library Association: POB 38636, Lusaka 10101; internet www.zla.co.zm; Chair. BENSON NJOBVU; Hon. Sec. MUTINTA NABUYANDA; publ. *Journal* (4 a year).

LANGUAGE AND LITERATURE

Alliance Française: Plot 22725, Alick Nkhata Ave, Longacres, POB 30948, 10101 Lusaka; tel. (1) 253467; fax (1) 254735; e-mail afl@microlink.zm; offers courses and exams in French language and culture and promotes cultural exchange with France; attached teaching centres in Kabwe, Kitwe, Livingstone and Ndola.

British Council: Heroes Place, Cairo Rd, POB 34571, Lusaka; tel. (1) 223602; fax (1) 224122; e-mail info@britishcouncil.org.zm; internet www.britishcouncil.org/zambia; offers courses and exams in English language and British culture and promotes cultural exchange with the UK; Dir JOHN MITCHELL.

MEDICINE

Zambia Medical Association: POB RW 148, Lusaka; Chair. Dr S. SIKANETA; Sec. Dr D. LEVITT; publ. *Medical Journal of Zambia* (6 a year).

NATURAL SCIENCES

Biological Sciences

Wildlife and Environmental Conservation Society of Zambia: POB 30255, Lusaka; tel. (1) 251630; fax (1) 251630; e-mail wecsz@zamnet.zm; internet www .conservationzambia.org; f. 1953; dedicated to promoting wildlife and natural resource conservation, environmental education; 2,000 mems; Pres. ADAM JONATHAN POPE; Programme Coordinator PATRICK SHAWA; publs *Black Lechwe* (4 a month), *Chongololo Magazine and Guide* (24 a year), *Chipembele Magazine and Guide* (24 a year).

TECHNOLOGY

Engineering Institution of Zambia: POB 34730, Lusaka; f. 1955; 2,600 mems; Pres. G. K. CHIBUYE; Vice-Pres. Dr K. AKAPELWA; publ. *Journal* (4 a year).

Research Institutes

GENERAL

National Institute for Scientific and Industrial Research: POB 310158, International Airport Rd, 15302 Lusaka; tel. (1) 281082; fax (1) 283533; e-mail directorate@ nisir.org.zm; internet www.nisir.org.zm; f. 1967; statutory body to conduct scientific and industrial research and to collect and disseminate scientific information; incorporates Building and Industrial Minerals Research Unit, Food Technology Research Unit, Information Services Unit, Livestock and Pest Research Centre, Material Testing Unit, Radioisotopes Research Unit, Tree Improvement Research Centre, Technical Services Unit , Water Resources Research Unit; library of 9,200 vols, 100 periodicals; Exec. Dir Dr MWANANYANDA MBIKUSITA LEWANIKA; publs *Sci-Tech Newsletter* (4 a year), *Zambia Journal of Science and Technology* (irregular), *Zambia Science Abstracts* (1 a year).

AGRICULTURE, FISHERIES AND VETERINARY SCIENCE

Central Fisheries Research Institute: POB 350100, Chilanga; tel. (1) 278597; fax (1) 278173; e-mail piscator@zamnet.zm; f. 1965; hydrobiological research directed towards increasing fish production, co-management research directed towards sustainable fisheries management, fish-stock assessment, social and economic studies in fishing regions; library of 4,700 vols; Deputy Dir C. K. KAPASA; Chief Fisheries Research Officer P. NGALANDE; publs *Fisheries Statistics*, *Project Reports* (irregular).

Central Veterinary Research Station: POB 33980, Lusaka; tel. (1) 233444; e-mail cvri@zamnet.zm; f. 1926; directed by the Ministry of Lands and Agriculture; general veterinary diagnosis and research; Prin. Veterinary Research Officer Dr S. H. KABILIKA.

Division of Forest Products Research: POB 20388, Kitwe; tel. (2) 227088; f. 1963; controls research into wood utilization, timber properties preservation, engineering, forest products and wood composite studies; Chief Officer S. M. MUTEMWA; publ. *Records* (irregular).

Division of Forest Research: POB 22099, Kitwe; tel. (2) 220456; fax (2) 224110; f. 1956; ecological and botanical studies; soil and site assessment investigations; silvicultural research, exotic plantations and indigenous forests and woodlands; mensurational studies of plantation growth; tree breeding and selection; agroforestry and fuelwood projects; forest pathology and entomology; seed collection, processing, testing and low-temperature storage; staff of 24; library of 7,800 vols, 150 periodicals and 100 serials; Chief Forest Research Officer F. M. MALAYA; publs *Research Bulletins*, *Research Newsletter*, *Research Notes*, *Research Pamphlets*.

International Red Locust Control Organization for Central and Southern Africa: POB 240252, Ndola; tel. (2) 651251; fax (2) 650117; e-mail locust@zamnet.zm; f. 1970; to prevent plagues of red locust by controlling incipient outbreaks, to assist mem. countries in the management of army worm and grain-eating birds and to carry out research and training; member countries: Kenya, Malawi, Mozambique, Tanzania, Zambia, Zimbabwe; library of 3,000 vols, 35 periodicals; Dir A. D. GADABU; publ. *Scientific Papers*.

Mount Makulu Agricultural Research Station: Zambia Agriculture Research Institute, Private Bag 7, Chilanga; tel. and fax (1) 278130; internet www.zari.gov.zm/makuluresearchtest.php; f. 1952; Headquarters of Department of Research and Specialist Services, Ministry of Agriculture, Food and Fisheries, and 11 regional and specialist research stations; research on soils, soil classification, vegetation types and land classification; agronomy; chemistry; ecology; entomology; pasture research; phytosanitary services; plant breeding; plant pathology; Seeds Control and Certification Institute; stored products entomology; cotton entomology; main crops under investigation: beans, cotton, groundnuts, maize, pastures and pasture legumes, sorghum, soyabeans, tobacco, wheat; library of 30,000 vols, 20,000 reports, 15,000 reprints; Prin. Agricultural Research Officer BERNADETTE LUBOZUYA; publs *Accessions List* (6 a year), *Production Farming in Zambia* (12 a year), *Reprints of Articles by Staff Members*, *Research Branch Memoranda* (irregular).

ECONOMICS, LAW AND POLITICS

Pan-African Institute for Development, East and Southern Africa: POB 80448, Kabwe; tel. (5) 223651; fax (5) 223451; e-mail paidesa@zamnet.zm; f. 1979; training, research, surveys, follow-up action; library of 8,000 vols; Dir Dr LUTHER BANGA; publ. *Current Contents: Development Studies* (4 a year).

MEDICINE

National Food and Nutrition Commission: POB 32669, 10101 Lusaka; tel. (1) 227803; fax (1) 221426; e-mail nfnc@zamnet.zm; f. 1967; statutory body to improve the nutritional status of the people of Zambia; 98 mems; Chair. CRESTA KALUBA; Exec. Dir PRISCILLA N. LIKWASI.

Occupational Health Safety and Research Bureau: Independence Ave, POB 20205, Kitwe; tel. (2) 228977; fax (2) 222823; e-mail ohmb@zamnet.zm; internet www.geocities.com/ohsrb; f. 1950; research on pneumoconiosis and related chest diseases, assessment and advice on control of hazardous conditions in industrial workplaces; library of 300 vols; Dir Dr C. M. MUSOWE.

Tropical Diseases Research Centre: POB 71769, Ndola; tel. and fax (2) 620737; e-mail info@tdrc.org.zm; internet www.tdrc.org.zm; f. 1976; research in communicable diseases, support for disease control and primary health care programmes; trains Zambian scientists in the field of biomedical research, serves as int. research and training centre; epidemiological research, clinical trials, research in malaria, schistosomiasis, trypanosomiasis, diarrhoeal diseases, etc.; 28 researchers, 76 support staff; library of 3,300 vols, 219 periodicals; Dir Dr EMMANUEL KAFWEMBE.

NATURAL SCIENCES

Physical Sciences

Geological Survey of Zambia (Ministry of Mines and Minerals Development): POB 50135, Lusaka; tel. (1) 250174; fax (1) 250174; e-mail gsd@zamnet.zm; f. 1951; statutory depository for all mining and prospecting records and reports; responsible for assisting the public on mineral matters and advising the Ministry on all mineral and geological matters, economic mineral investigations, geological mapping; library of 89,346 vols; Dir D. MULELA; publs *Annotated Bibliography and Index of the Geology of Zambia*, *Economic Reports*, *Memoirs*, *Occasional Papers*, *Records*, *Reports*, and maps.

Libraries and Archives

Kitwe

Hammarskjöld Memorial Library: POB 21493, Kitwe; tel. (2) 211488; fax (2) 211001; e-mail daglib@zamnet.zm; internet www.mindolo.org/dml; f. 1963; 26,000 vols; colln of films, filmstrips, slides, microfiche, video cassettes, tape-recordings on local history; rare book colln on the history of central Africa; specializes in social sciences; research library and archives of the Mindolo Ecumenical Foundation; colln on American society and culture; Librarian DUNSTAN CHIKONKA.

Kitwe Public Library: POB 20070, Kaunda Sq., Kitwe; tel. 213685; f. 1954; 33,000 vols; 1 br. library.

Lusaka

Lusaka City Libraries: POB 31304, Katondo Rd, Lusaka; tel. (1) 227282; f. 1943; 3 br. libraries and a mobile library; 145,000 vols, 200 periodicals, 320 maps; Librarian J. C. NKOLE; publ. *Library Bulletin* (4 a year).

National Archives of Zambia: POB 50010, Lusaka; tel. (1) 254081; fax (1) 254080; e-mail naz@zamnet.zm; f. 1947; covers national literature from 1890 to the present day in the forms of national archives, historical MSS, microfilms, cartographic, philatelic, currency, pictorial and printed publication collns; 18,000 linear metres of records; depository and reference library of 17,000 vols and 11,000 periodicals; the National Archives Library is a reference and legal deposit library for all printed publications published in Zambia; Dir CRISPIN HAMOOYA; Senior Archivist T. M. SUUYA; Senior Librarian H. K. NYENDWA; publs *Annual National Bibliography*, *Calendars of District Note Books, Vols I and IV, Information About the National Archives of Zambia*, *List of Periodicals*.

Zambia Library Service: c/o Ministry of Education, POB 50093, Civic Center Area Plot 82, cnr Mogadishu and Chimanga Rd, 10101 Lusaka; tel. (1) 250855; fax (1) 250760; internet www.moe.gov.zm; f. 1962; 6 regional libraries, 18 branch libraries and a central library of 500,000 vols; aims to provide a countrywide free public library service; Chief Librarian ETHEL N. TEMBO; publ. *Zambia Library Service Newsletter* (irregular).

Ndola

Ndola Public Library: POB 70388, Independence Way, Ndola; tel. (2) 617173; f. 1934; 90,000 vols, 140 periodicals; public library services in Lusaka serving Ndola City Council Community; central library, 4 brs, 2 prison library centres; centre for American Circulating Library from American Cultural Center; Librarian Dr K. MUMBA CHISAKA; publ. *Copperbelt Library Bulletin* (irregular).

Museums and Art Galleries

Livingstone

Livingstone Museum: Mosi-oa-Tunya Rd, POB 60498, Livingstone; tel. (3) 321204; fax (3) 320991; e-mail livmus@zamnet.zm; f. 1934; ethnology of the peoples of Zambia; prehistory, history and natural history of Zambia; autograph, letters and relics of David Livingstone; library of 20,000 vols, 200 periodicals, including special collection of 2,000 vols on prehistory, history, ethnography and Africana; supporting depts of taxidermy, conservation and education; Dir V. K. KATANEKWA; publs *The Livingstone Museum Newsletter*, *Zambia Museum Journal*.

Mbala

Moto Moto Museum: POB 420230, Mbala; tel. and fax (4) 450243; e-mail motomoto@zamtel.zm; f. 1974; research in ethnography, prehistory and history; educational and exhibition programmes; library of 5,000 vols; Dir NKOLE E. SOSALA; publ. *Zambia Museums Journal* (irregular).

Ndola

Copperbelt Museum: 911 Buteko Ave, POB 71444, Ndola; tel. (2) 613591; fax (2) 617450; e-mail cbmus@zamnet.zm; f. 1962; colln, conservation, preservation, documentation and exhibit of geological and historical items, ethnography and natural history; Dir STANFORD MUDENDA SIACHOONO.

Universities

COPPERBELT UNIVERSITY

POB 21692, Kitwe
Telephone: (2) 225155
Fax: (2) 222469
E-mail: registrar@cbu.ac.zm
Internet: www.cbu.edu.zm

Founded 1979 as Ndola Campus of Univ. of Zambia, present status 1987
State control
Language of instruction: English
Academic year: March to December (3 terms)
Chancellor: Prof. MUYUNDA MWANALUSHI
Vice-Chancellor: Prof. NAISON NGOMA (acting)
Deputy Vice-Chancellor: Dr SHADRECK CHAMA (acting)
Registrar: ALLAN M. ILLUNGA
Librarian: CHARLES B. M. LUNGU
Number of teachers: 774
Number of students: 10,276
Publication: *Journal of Business* (4 a year)

DEANS

Academic Development Centre: Prof. ADELE PATRICK PHIRI
School of Built Environment: Dr ROY CHILESHE
School of Business: Dr SUMBYE KAPENA
School of Engineering: CHARLES MHANGO (acting)
School of Graduate Studies: Dr THOMAS K. TAYLOR
School of Mathematics and Natural Sciences: Prof. FRANK TAILOKA
School of Medicine: Prof. KASONDE BOWA
School of Mines and Mineral Sciences: Prof. GLASWELL NKONDE
School of Natural Resources: Dr EXHILDAH CHISHA-KASUMU
School of Technology: Dr I. S. SINGH

PROFESSORS

KASONDE, B., School of Medicine
LUNGU, J., School of Business
MASEKA, K., School of Mathematics and Natural Sciences
NKONDE, G., School of Mines and Mineral Sciences
PHIRI, A., Academic Development Centre
SHUMBA, O., School of Mathematics and Natural Sciences
SIULAPWA, J., School of Medicine
SIZIYA, P., School of Medicine
TAILOKA, F., School of Mathematics and Natural Sciences
TEMBO, J., School of Business

CONSTITUENT SCHOOLS

School of Built Environment: tel. (2) 225086; e-mail deansbe@cbu.ac.zm.

School of Business: tel. (2) 227946; fax (2) 228346; e-mail deansb@cbu.ac.zm.

School of Natural Resources: tel. (2) 227946; e-mail forestry@cbu.ac.zm.

School of Technology: tel. (2) 228212; fax (2) 228212; e-mail deanst@cbu.ac.zm.

ATTACHED INSTITUTES

Centre for Lifelong Education: Dir Col (rtd) LLOYD MWILA.

Institute of Environmental Management: Dir M. NABUYANDA.

UNIVERSITY OF ZAMBIA

POB 32379, Lusaka
Telephone: (1) 291777
Fax: (1) 253952
E-mail: registrar@unza.zm
Internet: www.unza.zm
Founded 1965
State control
Language of instruction: English
Academic year: July to May
Chancellor: Dr JACOB M. MWANZA
Vice-Chancellor: Prof. STEPHEN SIMUKANGA
Deputy Vice-Chancellor: Dr WILSON MWENYA
Registrar: Dr ALVERT N'GANDU
Librarian: Dr V. CHIFWEPA

Number of teachers: 535
Number of students: 13,500

Publications: *African Social Research, Journal of Humanities, Journal of Medicine, Journal of Sciences and Technology, Zambia Law Journal, Zambian Papers, Zango*

DEANS

Agricultural Sciences: Dr MIKE MWALA
Distance Education: CHISHIMBA NKOSHA (Dir)
Education: W. CHAKANIKA
Engineering: Dr ZEBEDIAH PHIRI
Humanities and Social Sciences: Dr SIAMWIZA BENARD
Law: Dr M. MUNALULA
Medicine: Dr F. GOMA
Mines: Dr O. SIKAZWE
Natural Sciences: Dr HENRY M. SICHINGABULA
Research and Graduate Studies: Prof. S. NYAMBE (Dir)
Veterinary Medicine: Dr AARON MWEENE

PROFESSORS

BANDA, G. P. A., Geography
BANDA, S. F., Chemistry
BANDA, S. S., Medical Education
BHAT, G. J., Paediatrics and Child Health
CHAKANIKA, W., Adult Education and Extension Studies
CHISHIMBA, C. P., In-Service Education and Advisory Science Education
CHITAMBO, H., Paraclinical Studies
DILLON-MALONE, C., Philosophy
ERZINGATSIAN, K., Surgery
HAMBOKOMA, C., Mathematics and Science Education
HAWORTH, A., Psychiatry
KAELA, L. C. W., Political and Administrative Studies
KAFUMUKACHE, E. B., Anatomy
KAILE, T., Pathology and Microbiology
KALINDA, T., Agricultural Economics and Extension Education
KAMBANI, S., Mining Engineering
KASEBA, C., Obstetrics and Gynaecology
KWENDAKWEMA, N. J., Agricultural Engineering
LAMBWE, E., Post-Basic Nursing
LEMBA, M., Social Development Studies
LIPALITE, M., Development Studies
LUNGU, I. O., Soil Science
LUSWILI, J., Mathematics and Statistics
MANAKOV, A. K., Physiological Sciences
MATONDO, P., Internal Medicine
MILIMO, M. C., Gender Studies
MSANGO, H. J., Educational Administration and Policy Studies
MULENGA, F. E., History
MULENGA, M. N., Civil Engineering
MWALA, M. S., Crop Science
MWEENE, H. V., Physics
MWIKISA, C. N., Economics
NAMBOTA, A., Disease Control
NG'ANDU, A. N., Mechanical Engineering
NGANDU, S. K., Educational Psychology, Sociology and Special Education
NKHUWA, C. W., Geology
NSOMBO, P., Surveying
NYIRENDA, L. D., Electrical and Electronic Engineering
PHIRI, I. K., Clinical Studies
SIAKALIMA, D. (acting), Psychology
SIKULUMBA, J. K., Literature and Languages
SIULAPWA, J. N., Biomedical Sciences
SIZIYA, S., Community Medicine
TAMBULUKANI, G. (acting), Language and Social Sciences Education
WACHINGA, D. M., Biological Sciences
WITIKA, L. K., Metallurgy and Mineral Processing
YAMBAYAMBA, E. S. K., Animal Sciences
ZULU, S., Library and Information Studies

Colleges

Evelyn Hone College of Applied Arts and Commerce: POB 30029, Lusaka; tel. (1) 235344; fax (1) 225127; e-mail ehcbs@zamnet.zm; f. 1963; library: 14,000 vols; 145 teachers; 3,000 students (1,600 full-time, 1,400 part-time); Prin. MICHAEL TANDEO; Librarian SEBASTIAN NGWIRA.

National Institute of Public Administration: POB 31990, 10101 Lusaka; tel. (1) 228802; fax (1) 227213; e-mail nipa@zamnet.zm; f. 1963; trains govt administrators and accounting personnel for central and local govt; offers training and consultancy in the private sector in management, secretarial work, purchasing and supplies, and law and information technology; library: 28,000 vols; 50 teachers; 1,316 students; Exec. Dir Dr M. C. BWALYA; Registrar PAUL SIMUKOKO; Librarian N. MTANGA.

Natural Resources Development College: POB 310099, Lusaka; tel. (1) 284639; fax (1) 281941; f. 1964; 3-year diploma courses in agriculture, agricultural education and engineering, nutrition, fisheries, water engineering; library: 32,000 vols; 48 teachers; 430 students; Prin. T. F. F. MALUZA; Librarian M. M. MISENGO.

Northern Technical College: POB 250093, Ndola; tel. (2) 680141; fax (2) 680423; e-mail nortec@zamnet.zm; f. 1960; automotive, electrical, heavy duty and mechanical engineering, business studies and communication skills, refrigeration and air-conditioning; library: 20,000 vols; 96 teachers (68 full-time, 28 part-time); 1,300 students (800 full-time, 500 part-time); Prin. (vacant); Librarian NABOMBE PUMULO.

Zambia College of Agriculture: POB 660053, Monze; f. 1947; 2-year certificate course; 42 staff; library: 3,000 vols; 240 students; Prin. D. H. McCLEERY.

ZIMBABWE

The Higher Education System

Institutions of higher education predate the independence of Zimbabwe (formerly Southern Rhodesia) from the United Kingdom in 1980, the oldest being Esigodini Agricultural Institute, which was founded in 1921. The oldest university-level institution is the University of Zimbabwe (formerly the University College of Rhodesia), which was founded in 1955 (present status since 1970 and present name since 1980) and is one of two state-run universities, the other being the University of Science and Technology at Bulawayo. There are also several private universities including Africa University in Mutare and Solusi University in Figtree. In 2008/09 a total of 49,645 students were enrolled at institutions of higher education. A national higher education plan for the period 2011–15 was launched in July 2011, the stated objective of which was to reverse an alarming decline in higher education standards precipitated by political and economic instability during the post-independence era, particularly from the early 2000s, and to transform Zimbabwe into a regional leader for higher education.

The Ministry of Higher and Tertiary Education is the national agency responsible for the provision of higher education in Zimbabwe. The national President serves as the Chancellor of the public universities, the day-to-day administration of which is overseen by a Vice-Chancellor. Both public and private universities are governed by University Councils. In 2008 a new law replacing the National Council for Higher Education Act was enacted amid much criticism. According to the Minister of Higher and Tertiary Education, the act had been promulgated to register and accredit institutions of higher education and to regulate quality assurance in them. Critics of President Robert Mugabe's Government contested that it was an attempt to politicize education since the board that would exert control over institutions under the legislation would be appointed by the Government.

The minimum requirement for admission to undergraduate studies is two grade 'E' passes at GCE A-level; however, the strength of competition has effectively raised the bar for admission to grade 'C' in at least three subjects. Admission is also granted to applicants who hold the National Diploma. The principal undergraduate degree is the Bachelors, which may be classified either 'General' or 'Honours' (the distinction lies in the content rather than the length of the course). On average, the Bachelors lasts three to four years, but in some subjects the period of study is longer, such as the Bachelors of Medicine and Bachelors of Surgery (both five years). Masters degrees are the first postgraduate-level qualifications, and vary in length from one to three years; they are usually a composite of coursework and research for a dissertation, but the MPhil, which lasts two to three years, is usually a purely research-based degree. The main doctoral-level degree is the DPhil, which is three to four years in duration.

In 1990 the Government initiated wide-ranging reforms of technical and vocational education owing to the failure of the secondary and higher education sectors to match the expectations of both students and employers. Colleges, polytechnics and technical colleges, universities and university colleges all offer vocational training combining class-work and workplace experience. Vocational training centres were first established in 1998 to provide for a Government initiative known as the Skills Training programme. The principal post-secondary technical and vocational awards are as follows: National Certificate, National Diploma and Higher National Diploma. Apprenticeships are also available, and are offered in about 80 trade areas. Apprenticeships typically last between three and four years, and comprise a mixture of practical and theoretical work, with 'on the job' training constituting around 80% of the programme.

Regulatory and Representative Bodies

GOVERNMENT

Ministry of Education, Sports and Culture: Ambassador House, Union Ave, POB CY 121, Causeway, Harare; tel. (4) 734051; fax (4) 707599; internet www.moesc.gov.zw; Minister AENEAS CHIGWEDERE.

Ministry of Higher Education and Technology: Government Composite Bldg, cnr Fourth St and Samora Machel Ave, Union Ave, POB UA 275, Harare; tel. (4) 796440; fax (4) 790923; e-mail thesecretary@mhet.ac .zw; internet www.mhet.ac.zw; Minister of Higher and Tertiary Education I. STANISLAUS GORERAZVO MUDENGE.

NATIONAL BODIES

Zimbabwe National Association for Distance and Open Learning: POB 2713, Harare; fax (4) 737640; e-mail college@ speciss.co.zw; internet www.saide.org.za/ worldbank/countries/zimbabwe/zinadol.htm; f. 1997; Chair. NARAN KALA; Sec. EVISON MUTI.

Learned Societies

GENERAL

UNESCO Office Harare: POB HG 435, Highlands, Harare; located at: 8 Kenilworth Rd, Newlands, Harare; tel. (4) 332222; fax (4) 332344; internet www.zimaids.co.zw/hae; designated Cluster Office for Botswana, Malawi, Mozambique, Zambia and Zimbabwe; Dir KO-CHIH TUNG.

AGRICULTURE, FISHERIES AND VETERINARY SCIENCE

Crop Science Society of Zimbabwe: POB UA 409, Union Ave, Harare; f. 1970; 200 mems.

Zimbabwe Agricultural Society: POB 442, Harare; tel. (4) 705641; fax (4) 705644; f. 1895; 3,500 mems; Gen. Man. J. R. PEARCE.

Zimbabwe Veterinary Association: POB 8397, Causeway, Harare; tel. (4) 303574; fax (4) 307349; f. 1920; 175 mems; Pres. Dr G. GELDART; publ. *Zimbabwe Veterinary Journal* (2 a year).

BIBLIOGRAPHY, LIBRARY SCIENCE AND MUSEOLOGY

Zimbabwe Library Association: POB 3133, Harare; tel. (4) 792641; fax (4) 703050; e-mail harare.docu-center@unesco .org; f. 1959; 254 mems; Chair. DRIDEN KUNAKA; Sec. ALBERT MASHEKA; publ. *Zimbabwe Librarian*.

HISTORY, GEOGRAPHY AND ARCHAEOLOGY

Geographical Association of Zimbabwe: c/o Dept of Geography and Environmental Science, University of Zimbabwe, Box MP 167, Mount Pleasant, Harare; tel. (4) 303211; fax (4) 883264; e-mail cumming@arts.uz.ac .zw; f. 1967; 500 mems; Chair. T. ZINYANDU; Sec. A. CHIKANDA; publs *Geographical Education Magazine* (2 a year), *Geographical Journal of Zimbabwe* (1 a year).

Prehistory Society of Zimbabwe: POB 876, Harare; tel. (4) 300516; f. 1958; promotion of the study of early history, prehistory and archaeology in Africa, with particular reference to Zimbabwe; 100 mems; library of 1,000 vols; Chair. (vacant); publ. *Zimbabwean Prehistory* (every 2 years).

LANGUAGE AND LITERATURE

Alliance Française: 328 Herbert Chitepo Ave, POB 2515, Harare; tel. (4) 704801; e-mail afharare@telco.co.zw; internet www .afzim.org/afharare/hre.html; offers courses and exams in French language and culture and promotes cultural exchange with France; attached teaching centre in Bulawayo.

British Council: Corner House, Samora Michel Ave, POB 664, Harare; tel. (4) 775313; fax (4) 756661; e-mail general .enquiries@britishcouncil.org.zw; internet www.britishcouncil.org.zw; offers courses and exams in English language and British culture and promotes cultural exchange with the UK; attached office in Bulawayo; Regional Dir, Central Africa DAVID MARTIN; Dir Operations, Zimbabwe RAJIV BENDRE.

Zimbabwe Writers Union: Gloag High School, POB 61, Turk Mine; Pres. CONT MHLANGA; Sec.-Gen. PATHISA NYATHI.

MEDICINE

Pharmaceutical Society of Zimbabwe: POB 1476, Harare; tel. (4) 706967; fax (4) 706967; Pres. G. N. MAHLANGY; Sec. Dr F. CHINYANGANYA.

Zimbabwe Dental Association: 1 Thorton Ave, POB 1268, Bulawayo; tel. (9) 72194; fax (9) 634589; e-mail musiyaw@netconnect.co.zw; f. 1939; affiliated to World Dental Fed.; 130 mems; Pres. Dr WEBSTER MUSIYA.

Zimbabwe Medical Association: POB 3671, Harare; tel. (4) 720731; Pres. B. G. MAUCHAZA; Sec. E. VUSHE.

NATURAL SCIENCES

General

Zimbabwe Scientific Association: POB 978, Harare; fax (4) 335143; f. 1899; 380 mems; Pres. Dr L. MHLANGA; Sec. Dr J. HUSSEIN; publs *Transactions* (1 a year), *Zimbabwe Science News* (2 a year).

Biological Sciences

BirdLife Zimbabwe: POB RV 100, Runiville, Harare; tel. (4) 481496; fax (4) 490208; e-mail birds@zol.co.zw; internet www.birdlifezimbabwe.co.zw; f. 1951; 480 mems; Dir CHIPANGURA CHIRARA; publs *Babbler* (6 a year), *Honeyguide* (2 a year).

Botanical Society of Zimbabwe: POB 461, Harare; tel. (4) 735163; f. 1934; Hon. Sec. J. R. JAMES.

Kirk Biological Society: Dept of Biological Sciences, University of Zimbabwe, POB MP 167, Mount Pleasant, Harare; tel. (4) 303211; fax (4) 333407; e-mail jmugodo@yahoo.com; f. 1969; botany, zoology, ecology, microbiology; Chair. JAMES MUGODO.

Lowveld Natural History Branch, Wildlife and Environment Zimbabwe: POB 81, Chiredzi; f. 1968; promotion of conservation and natural history education; 186 mems; Chair. G. DABBS; Sec. S. DE ROBILLARD; publs *Newsletter* (12 a year), *The Hartebeest* (1 a year).

Wildlife and Environment Zimbabwe: POB HG 996, Highlands, Harare; tel. (4) 747500/684; fax (4) 747174; e-mail zimwild@mweb.co.zw; internet www.zimwild.co.zw; f. 1927; all aspects of wildlife conservation and environmental awareness; 2,500 mems; Pres. ISAIAH NYAKUSENDWA; Dir Dr WILLIE K. NDUKU; publ. *Zimbabwe Wildlife* (4 a year, online).

Physical Sciences

Geological Society of Zimbabwe: POB CY 1719, Causeway, Harare; internet www.mining.co.zw/gsz.htm; f. 1981; 320 mems; Chair. M. L. VINYU; Sec. H. A. JELSMA.

Mennell Society: Dept of Geology, University of Zimbabwe, POB MP 167, Mount Pleasant, Harare; f. 1964; to promote the understanding of earth sciences through lectures, films, field trips; 40 mems; Pres. H. MUNYANYIWA; Chair. W. MOYCE; publ. *Detritus*.

TECHNOLOGY

Institution of Materials, Minerals and Mining (Zimbabwe Section): POB MP 791, Mount Pleasant, Harare; e-mail kirmir@zol.co.zw; f. 1931; Chair. J. L. NIXON; Hon. Sec. M. R. RICHARDSON.

Survey Institute of Zimbabwe: POB 3869, Harare; f. 1967; 80 mems; voluntary asscn of surveyors in the fields of land, engineering, topographical and mine surveying; Pres. S. Z. ZHOU; Hon. Sec. J. BIRKETT.

Zimbabwe Institution of Engineers: POB 660, Harare; tel. (4) 746821; fax (4) 746652; e-mail zie@zarnet.ac.zw; internet www.zie.org.zw; f. 1944; 2,568 mems; Pres. Eng. DANIEL MACKENZIE NCUBE; Deputy Pres. Eng. D. Z. MAREYA; publs *Proceedings* (2 a year), *Zimbabwe Engineer* (12 a year).

Research Institutes

GENERAL

Research Council of Zimbabwe: POB CY 294, Causeway, Harare; tel. (4) 727562; fax (4) 726860; e-mail secretariat@zarnet.ac.zw; internet www.rcz.ac.zw; f. 1964, reconstituted 1984; advisory body to the Government on general scientific policy and official channel for exchange of national and international scientific and technical information; Chair. Dr F. P. GUDJANGA; Sec. S. MUZITE; publs *Directory of Organizations concerned with Scientific Research and Services in Zimbabwe* (every 2 years), *Zimbabwe Research Index* (1 a year), *Symposium Proceedings* (every 2 years).

AGRICULTURE, FISHERIES AND VETERINARY SCIENCE

Agricultural Research Council of Zimbabwe: POB CY 594, Causeway, Harare; internet www.arc.co.zw; f. 1970; advises on agricultural research policy and programmes in Zimbabwe; administers regional research institutes and stations through the Department of Research and Specialist Services (Dir Dr N. R. GATA); Chair. Prof. M. RUKUNI; publs *Kirkia—Journal of Botany of Zimbabwe* (1 a year), *Zimbabwe Agricultural Journal* (6 a year), *Zimbabwe Journal of Agricultural Research* (2 a year).

Research Institutes and Stations:

Agronomy Research Institute: POB CY 550, Causeway, Harare; tel. (4) 704531; fax (4) 728317; e-mail bmavankeni@gmail.com; f. 1975; research into crop agronomy, crop ecology and crop production; Head BUSISO MAVANKENI (acting).

Chemistry and Soil Research Institute: POB CY 550, Causeway, Harare; tel. (4) 704531; fax (4) 728317; f. 1905; research and advisory work on soils and agricultural chemistry; registration and regulation of fertilizers and foodstuffs; crop nutrition, chemistry, pedology, soil physics and soil productivity research sections; Head C. F. MUSHAMBI.

Coffee Research Station: POB 61, Chipinge; tel. (27) 2400; fax (27) 2951; f. 1964; research into all aspects of coffee management, growth, pest and disease control; tea research projects; Officer-in-Charge D. KUTYWAYO.

Cotton Research Institute: PMB 765, Kadoma; tel. (68) 23994; fax (68) 23996; e-mail zimcott@africaonline.co.zw; f. 1925; all aspects of cotton agronomy, breeding, pest and disease research; Head L. T. GONO (acting).

Crop Breeding Institute: POB CY 550, Causeway, Harare; tel. (4) 704531; fax (4) 728317; f. 1948; responsible for breeding programmes on maize, soya beans, groundnuts, wheat, barley, potatoes, sunflowers, cowpen, bambara, groundnut and foodbean; Head Dr A. MASHIRIGWANI.

Department of Research & Specialist Services, Division of Research Services: Fifth St Ext., POB Cy 550, Causeway, Harare; tel. (4) 704531; fax (4) 731133; e-mail rjkangai_biometrics@drss.org.zw; internet www.drss.gov.zw; f. 1967; attached to Biometrics Bureau; undertakes applied biometrical research, provides professional advice and training on experimental design, statistical problems and computer services for research workers; Head JOSEPHINE R. KANGAI.

Farming Systems Research Unit: POB 550, Causeway, Harare; f. 1983; responsible for adapting, developing and testing on farms improved crop and livestock production technologies and systems, and a model for farm systems research acceptable to the Department of Research and Specialist Services and suitable for wide-scale application in Zimbabwe; Team Leader B. MOMBESHORA.

Grasslands Research Station: PMB 3701, Marondera; tel. (79) 23526; fax (79) 23198; f. 1930; research on pasture, animal and crop production for the high-rainfall sandveld area; selection and testing of Rhizobium strains and commercial production of legume inoculants; Head G. MANYAN.

Henderson Research Station: PMB 2004, Mazowe; tel. (75) 2281; fax (75) 2284; f. 1948; pasture work on the introduction and screening of grasses and legumes for suitability as fertilized pastures; research in ruminant nutrition; herbicide and weed control research; Head Mr SCHAKEREDZA (acting).

Horticultural Research Centre: Grasslands Research Station, POB 810, Marondera; tel. (79) 24122; fax (79) 23198; f. 1975; responsible for all aspects of horticultural research; Officer-in-Charge N. NENGUWO.

Lowveld Research Station: POB 97, Chiredzi; tel. (31) 2397; f. 1967; research in irrigation agronomy in South-Eastern Lowveld; subtropical horticulture and vegetable crops; Head Dr P. NYAMUDEZA.

Makoholi Experiment Station: PMB 9182, Masvingo; f. 1962; research into problems of animal and crop production for sandveld and medium rainfall districts of Zimbabwe; crop agronomy, cattle production (indigenous breeds) and natural grazing management; Head I. CHIGAMBA.

Matopos Research Station: PMB K 5137, Bulawayo; tel. (83) 8212; fax (83) 8289; f. 1903; research in veld management, ecology of regional soil types, bush encroachment, cattle breeding, and beef production; Head Dr S. MAYO.

Nyanga Experimental Station: POB 2061, Nyanga; fax (31) 2739; f. 1911; Pome fruit research; Officer-in-Charge N. NAUBE.

Plant Protection Research Institute: POB CY 550, Causeway, Harare; tel. (4) 704531; fax (4) 728317; e-mail plantpro@ecoweb.co.zw; f. 1964; research and advisory work on plant pests and diseases; biological control, entomology, pathology and nematology sections; Head Dr S. Z. SITHOLE.

Agricultural Research Trust: POB MP 84, Mount Pleasant, Harare; tel. and fax (4) 2930359; e-mail artfarm@mweb.co.zw; internet www.artfarm.co.zw; f. 1980; research into cereals, grains, oilseed and horticultural crops and the provision of research field sites for crop breeders, agronomists and the crop chemical industry; Dir

NICK BROOKE; Research Man. LANGTON T. MUTEMERI; Financial Man. GORDON A. LIND.

Department of Veterinary Services; Tsetse Control Branch: POB CY 52, Causeway, Harare; tel. (4) 707381; fax (4) 722684; f. 1909; attached to Ministry of Agriculture, Mechanisation and Irrigation Devt; for the control of the tsetse fly population and the investigation of methods of control; laboratory at Harare and research station in the Zambezi Valley; Chief Research Officer W. SHERENI.

Attached Laboratory:

Central Veterinary Laboratory: POB CY 551, Causeway, Harare; tel. (4) 705885; fax (4) 707952; e-mail vetlabs@africaonline .co.zw; f. 1906; diagnostic centre and research institute for animal diseases; 35 mems; library of 1,500 vols; Head of Veterinary Diagnostics and Research Branch Dr P. V. HAKAYA.

Forestry Commission: POB HG 139, Highlands, Harare; tel. (4) 498439; fax (4) 497070; f. 1954; state forest authority, responsible for formulating forest policy in Zimbabwe; engaged in large-scale plantation operations; research and advisory services, forestry extension and wildlife utilization.

Attached Centre:

Forest Research Centre: POB HG 595, Highlands, Harare; tel. (4) 498816; fax (4) 497070; conducts research into many aspects of forestry, principally high-yielding plantations, with special emphasis on tree genetics and the production of progressively improved pine and eucalypt seed, wood quality, general plantation management and fertilizer research; screening of multi-purpose tree species for use in fuelwood plantations and social forestry; Deputy Gen. Man. C. M. GUMBIE; publ. *Format* (4 a year).

Tobacco Research Board: POB 1909, Harare; tel. (4) 575289; fax (4) 575288; e-mail tobres@kutsaga.co.zw; f. 1950; conducts research into all types of tobacco, agronomy, breeding, engineering and pest control; operates 3 research stations; board mems, appointed by the Minister of Agriculture, represent growers, buyers, and Ministry of Agriculture, Mechanisation and Irrigation Devt; library of 12,000 vols, 250 periodicals; Chair. Dr R. M. MUPAWOSE; Dir A. J. MASUKA.

ECONOMICS, LAW AND POLITICS

Central Statistical Office: POB CY 342, Causeway, Harare; tel. (4) 703971; fax (4) 728529; f. 1927; coordinated statistical service for the Government; staff of 400; Dir L. MACHIROVI.

Institute of Development Studies: University of Zimbabwe, POB MP 167, Harare; tel. (4) 333341; fax (4) 333345; f. 1982 to undertake policy-oriented research, consultancy and training; three research departments: Agrarian and Labour Studies, Economics and Technology Studies and International Relations and Social Development Studies; Poverty Reduction Forum; library of 17,500 vols, 24,000 documents; Dir Dr DONALD P. CHIMANIKIRE.

MEDICINE

Public Health Laboratory: Box CY 430, Causeway, Harare; tel. and fax (4) 720746; e-mail maxhove@yahoo.com; f. 1909; Dir Dr M. G. M. HOVE; Pathologist Dr D. MADZIWA; Chief Medical Technologist L. ZAWAIRA; Chief Medical Technologist Dr O. MAYO.

NATURAL SCIENCES
Physical Sciences

Geological Survey of Zimbabwe: POB CY 210, Causeway, Harare; tel. (4) 726342; fax (4) 739601; e-mail zimgeosv@africaonline.co .zw; internet www.geosurvey.co.zw; f. 1910; geological mapping and survey of mineral resources; library of 1,400 vols, 800 symposia, 11,900 periodicals, 2,600 technical files; museum displaying Zimbabwean geology and economic minerals; Dir W. MAGALELA; publs *Bulletins*, *Mineral Resources Series* (irregular), short reports and maps.

Meteorological Service: POB BE 150, Belvedere, Harare; tel. (4) 778173; fax (4) 778161; e-mail jchifuna@weather.utande.co .zw; internet www.weather.utande.co.zw; f. 1897; part of the Ministry of Transport and Communications; Dir RUNGANO P. KARIMANZIRA; publs *Agromet Bulletin* (October–March), *Climate Handbook Supplements*, *Monthly Meteorological Summaries*, *Rainfall Handbook Supplements*, daily weather reports and forecasts, weekly rainfall maps during rainy season November–March.

Affiliated Institute:

Goetz Observatory: POB AC 65, Ascot, Bulawayo; tel. (9) 66197; fax (9) 77811; e-mail goetz@harare.iafrica.com; also seismology; publs *Agricultural Meteorological Bulletin* (12 a year), *Seismological Bulletin*.

TECHNOLOGY

Department of Metallurgy: Ministry of Mines, POB 1375, Causeway, Harare; tel. (4) 726629; fax (4) 793065; f. 1962; 88 staff; library of 280 vols; conducts investigations on methods of economic extraction from precious, base-metal and non-metallic ores and industrial minerals evaluation, also on physical metallurgy, e.g. non-destructive testing, impact testing, etc.; Dir T. I. NYATSANGA; publ. *Testwork Reports*.

Standards Association of Zimbabwe: POB 2259, Harare; tel. (4) 885511; fax (4) 882020; internet www.saz.org.zw; f. 1957; laboratory facilities for testing raw materials and manufactured goods and operates certification mark schemes; prepares and publishes Zimbabwean nat. standards; provides information service on standards and a WTO/ Technical Barriers to Trade enquiry point on standards and conformity assessment; provides training on standards; Chair. TRUST CHIKOHORA; Dir-Gen. EVE CHRISTINE GADZIKWA; publs *Catalogue of Zimbabwe Standards*, *Fulcrum* (official bulletin).

Libraries and Archives
Bulawayo

Bulawayo Public Library: 100 Fort St, Bulawayo; tel. (9) 60965; fax (9) 60966; e-mail bpl@graffiti.net; internet www .angelfire.com/ky/bpl; f. 1896; reference, lending, junior library; mobile library; postal service to rural readers; braille collection; African and Zimbabwe collections; Zimbabwe map collection; legal deposit library for Zimbabwe; video and audio cassette collns; 16,000 mems; 100,000 vols; Librarian and Sec. ROBIN WILLIAM DOUST.

National Library and Documentation Service, National Free Library of Zimbabwe: POB 1773, Bulawayo; tel. (9) 62359; fax (9) 77662; f. 1943 as national lending library for educational, scientific and technical books; national centre for inter-library loans; maintains National Union Catalogue; 100,000 vols; Librarian H. R. NCUBE.

Harare

Harare City Library: POB 1087, Harare; tel. (4) 751834; e-mail hararecitylibrary@ yahoo.com; f. 1902; 150,000 vols; Public Subscription Library; Librarian and Sec. TRYMORE SIMANGO.

National Archives of Zimbabwe: Private Bag 7729, Causeway, Harare; tel. (4) 792741; fax (4) 792398; f. 1935 as the Government Archives of Southern Rhodesia; Dir. I. MURAMBIWA; incorp. archives of Northern Rhodesia and Nyasaland and designated the Central African Archives 1947; became National Archives of Rhodesia and Nyasaland 1958–63; reverted January 1964 to Rhodesian Government and responsibility for Northern Rhodesia and Nyasaland archives ceased; also serves Zimbabwean municipalities and some parastatal bodies and holds archives of Federation of Rhodesia and Nyasaland; comprises sections of Records Management, Research (Public Archives, Historical Manuscripts), Library (nat. historical reference colln, incl. photographic and map collns, legal deposit, depository for UNESCO publications) and Technical (Reprographic Unit, Conservation Unit, Oral History, Automation, Audio-Visual Archives Unit); exhibition gallery; four provincial records centres; Dir. I. MURAMBIWA; publs *Bibliographical Series*, *Current Periodicals*, *Directory of Libraries*, *Guide to the Historical Manuscripts in the National Archives*, *Guide to the Public Archives of Rhodesia, Vol. 1, 1890–1923*, *Oppenheimer Series*, *Report of the Director* (1 a year), *Zimbabwe National Bibliography* (1 a year).

Parliament of Zimbabwe Library: POB CY 298, Causeway, Harare; tel. (4) 252936 ext. 2187; fax (4) 252935; e-mail munatsir@ parliament.gov.zw; internet www.parlzim .gov.zw; f. 1923; parliamentary and govt documents from Zimbabwe Parliament and from several Commonwealth countries; gen. colln specializing in political science, history, political biography, economics, sociology, public admin. and management, education, foreign relations; separate law colln, separate archival and reference colln and Zimbabwean publs; 116,000 vols; Prin. Librarian RONALD MUNATSI.

University of Zimbabwe Library: POB MP 45, Mount Pleasant, Harare; tel. (4) 303211; fax (4) 335383; e-mail librarian@ uzlib.uz.ac.zw; internet www.uz.ac.zw/ library; f. 1956; c. 700,000 vols; more than 10,000 periodicals; Africana (Zimbabweana) colln; Education library; colln of African languages; Institute of Devt Studies Library; Lake Kariba Research Station library; Law library; Map library; Medical library; Mpilo Hospital library; Veterinary library; U. Z. Theses Colln; Librarian A. CHIKONZO; publ. *Newsletter* (12 a year).

Zimbabwe National Library and Documentation Service: POB 758, Harare; tel. (4) 774943; f. 1972; co-ordinates all libraries in govt depts, colleges of education, agriculture and technology, public libraries; combined stock (100 libraries): 1m. vols; Dir S. R. DUBE; publs *Directory of Zimbabwean Libraries*, *Government Library Service Newsletter*.

Mutare

City of Mutare Public Libraries: POB 48, Mutare; tel. (20) 63412; fax (20) 67785; e-mail dmandowo@mutare.mweb.co.zw; f. 1902; incorporates Sakubva Public Library (f. 1972, 27,000 vols), Dangamvura Public Library (f. 1988, 18,000 vols), Turner Memorial Library (f. 1902, 40,000 vols), Chikanga Public Library (f. 2004, 5,000 vols); Head of Library Services D. MANDOWO.

Museums and Art Galleries

Bulawayo

Natural History Museum of Zimbabwe: Leopold Takawira Ave and Park Rd, POB 240, Bulawayo; tel. (9) 230046; fax (9) 234019; e-mail natmuse@acacia.samara.co.zw; f. 1901; entomological, geological, palaeontological, zoological; study collections and exhibits covering Ethiopian region, with special reference to southern Africa; historical, ethnographical and prehistorical exhibits appertaining to Zimbabwe and adjacent regions; Dir A. KUMIRAI; Curator of Arachnology M. FITZPATRICK; Curator of Entomology R. SITHOLE; Curator of Herpetology R. L. CHIDAVAENZI; Curator of Ichthyology P. MAKONI; Curator of Mammals F. P. D. COTTERILL; Curator of Ornithology A. MSIMANGA; Curator of Palaeontology D. MUNYIKWA; publs *Arnoldia (Zimbabwe)*, *Syntarsus*.

Gweru

Military Museum of Zimbabwe: Lobengula Ave, POB 1300, Gweru; tel. (54) 22816; fax (54) 20321; e-mail museum@harare.iafrica.com; f. 1972; history of Zimbabwe Midlands and military history of Zimbabwe; Dir T. TSOMONDO.

Harare

National Gallery of Zimbabwe: 20 Julius Nyerere Way, POB CY 848, Causeway, Harare; tel. (4) 704666; fax (4) 704668; e-mail info@nationalgallery.co.zw; internet www.nationalgallery.co.zw; f. 1957; nat. colln of sculpture, paintings, drawings, prints, ceramics and artefacts by Zimbabwean and other Southern African artists; incl. European works of art dating from 16th century, and traditional and contemporary African art; regular exhibition programme; education programme; Visual Art Studios for emerging young artists; library of 6,500 vols; Exec. Dir DOREEN J. SIBANDA; Librarian NICOLETY MWABAYA.

National Herbarium and Botanic Garden: POB A 889, Avondale, Harare; tel. (4) 744170; fax (4) 708938; internet www.nationalherbarium.co.zw; f. 1909; attached to Department of Agricultural Research and Extension (AREX); maintains a comprehensive collection of 500,000 specimens, provides an identification service for workers in agriculture and related fields and contributes to knowledge of the flora of South-Central Africa; taxonomic and ecological research, and research on medicinal and poisonous plants; library of 544 vols; Head NOZIPO NOBANDA; publ. *Kirkia* (1 a year).

Zimbabwe Museum of Human Sciences: Civic Centre, POB CY 33, Causeway, Harare; tel. (4) 751797; fax (4) 774207; e-mail nmmz@pci.co.zw; internet www.zimheritage.co.zw/site/nr_museum.htm; f. 1902; zoological, ethnographical, archaeological and historical exhibits, study collections of archaeological and ethnographical material, and rock art appertaining to Zimbabwe and adjacent areas; Dir T. MASONA; publs *Cookeia*, *Zimbabwea*.

Masvingo

Great Zimbabwe National Monument: PB 1060, Masvingo; tel. (39) 62080; fax (39) 63310; e-mail greatzim@mweb.co.zw; internet www.zimheritage.co.zw; ruins of medieval dry-stone buildings representing the Zimbabwe culture; history and development of Great Zimbabwe shown in site museum; world heritage site; Dir E. MATENGA.

Mutare

Mutare Museum: Aerodrome Rd, POB 920, Mutare; tel. (20) 63672; fax (20) 61100; e-mail mutarmus@comone.co.zw; internet www.zimheritage.co.zw; f. 1959; archaeological, zoological and historical exhibits, appertaining to the Eastern Districts in particular; national collection of road transport and firearms; aviary with 200 birds of 24 species; Dir Dr PAUL MUPIRA; publs *Cookeia*, *Syntarsus*, *Zimbabwea*.

Universities

BINDURA UNIVERSITY OF SCIENCE EDUCATION

Private Bag 1020, Bindura, Mashonaland Central

Telephone: (271) 7531

Fax: (271) 7616

E-mail: info@buse.ac.zw

Internet: www.buse.ac.zw

Founded 1996 as part of Univ. of Zimbabwe, present status 2000

State control

Language of instruction: English

Academic year: August to July

Vice-Chancellor: Prof. EDIAS MWENJE (acting)

Pro-Vice-Chancellor: CUTHBERT A. T. KATSVANGA

Registrar: TARIRO F. RUMHUMA

Librarian: AUDREY MHALANGA

Library of 24,507 vols, 54,000 e-books and 3,000 e-journals

Number of teachers: 247

Number of students: 4,494

Publication: *Southern Africa Journal of Science and Technology* (2 a year)

DEANS

Faculty of Agriculture and Environmental Science: CUTHBERT A. T. KATSVANGA

Faculty of Commerce: LANGTON RUNYOWA

Faculty of Science: (vacant)

Faculty of Science Education: A. ZENGAYA

MIDLANDS STATE UNIVERSITY

PMB 9055, Gweru

Telephone: (54) 260409

Fax: (54) 260233

E-mail: registrar@msu.ac.zw

Internet: www.msu.ac.zw

Founded 1999 by Act of Parliament

State control

Academic year: March to December

Vice-Chancellor: Prof. NGWABI BHEBE

Pro-Vice-Chancellor: Prof. RUNGANO J. ZVOBGO

Registrar: G. T. GUNIRA

Library of 50,850 vols

Number of teachers: 229

Number of students: 8,979

Publications: *Southern African Journal of Science and Agriculture and Technology* (4 a year), *The Dyke* (social sciences, 4 a year)

DEANS

Faculty of Arts: Prof. CAROLINE HARFORD

Faculty of Commerce: KATAZO C. MBETU

Faculty of Education: Dr O. P. NDAWI

Faculty of Natural Resources Management and Agriculture: FRANCIS MUGABE

Faculty of Science: A. CHAWANDA

Faculty of Social Sciences: C. N. GWATIDZO

NATIONAL UNIVERSITY OF SCIENCE AND TECHNOLOGY

POB AC 939, Ascot, Bulawayo

Telephone: (9) 282842

Fax: (9) 289057

E-mail: mtkariwo@nust.ac.zw

Internet: www.nust.ac.zw

Founded 1990

State control

Language of instruction: English

Academic year: August to May

Chancellor: Pres. of Zimbabwe R. G. MUGABE

Vice-Chancellor: (vacant)

Pro Vice-Chancellor: Prof. L. R. NDLOVU

Registrar: M. T. KARIWO

Librarian: K. MATSIKA

Number of teachers: 150 full-time

Number of students: 2,800

DEANS

Faculty of Applied Sciences: Dr M. M. BHALA

Faculty of Architecture and Quantity Surveying: Prof. S. IK-UMENNE

Faculty of Commerce: R. TADU

Faculty of Communication and Information Science: Prof. S. M. MADE

Faculty of Industrial Technology: Dr P. K. KUIPA

Depts of accounting, applied biology, applied chemistry, applied mathematics, applied physics, architecture, banking, business management, chemical engineering, civil and water engineering, computer science, electronic engineering, finance, industrial and manufacturing engineering, insurance and actuarial science, textile technology, business school, quantity surveying, environmental science and health, journalism and media studies, technical teacher education, sports science and coaching, and library, information science and archives; centre for continuing education, forestry resources and wildlife management; medical school

PROFESSORS

Faculty of Applied Sciences:

GHOLAP, A. V.

MUNDY, P.J.

READ, J. S.

Faculty of Architecture and Quantity Surveying:

HYLAND, A. D. C.

Faculty of Communication and Information Science:

MADE, S. M.

UNIVERSITY OF ZIMBABWE

POB MP 167, Mount Pleasant, Harare

Telephone: (4) 303212

Fax: (4) 333407

Internet: www.uz.ac.zw

Founded 1955 as Univ. College of Rhodesia; became Univ. of Rhodesia in 1970, present name 1980

Language of instruction: English

Academic year: August to June

Chancellor: HE THE PRES. OF THE REPUBLIC OF ZIMBABWE

Vice-Chancellor: Prof. LEVI NYAGURA

Registrar: SERGEANT CHEVO

Librarian: A. C. CHIKONZO

Number of teachers: 834

Number of students: 12,500

Publications: *Central African Journal of Medicine* (12 a year), *Journal of Applied Science in Southern Africa* (2 a year), *Zambezia* (2 a year)

DEANS

Faculty of Agriculture: Dr C. MUTISI
Faculty of Arts: Prof. P. MASHIRI
Faculty of Commerce: Dr I. CHANETA
Faculty of Education: Prof. R. MOYANA
Faculty of Engineering: W. NYEMBA
Faculty of Law: E. MAGADE
Faculty of Medicine: Prof. M. M. CHIDZONGA
Faculty of Science: Dr M. MUCHUWETI
Faculty of Social Studies: Prof. R. GAIDZANWA
Faculty of Veterinary Science: Prof. T. HOVE

ZIMBABWE OPEN UNIVERSITY

POB MP 1119, Mt Pleasant, Harare
Telephone: (4) 333452
Fax: (4) 303151
E-mail: kdzvimbo@icon.co.zw
Founded 1999
State control
Language of instruction: English
Chancellor: The President of the Republic of Zimbabwe
Vice-Chancellor: Prof. K. P. DZVIMBO
Registrar: R. E. MHASVI
Librarian: L. MAENZANISE

Library of 16,214 books, 16 periodicals
Number of teachers: 78 full-time
Number of students: 13,877 (13,443 undergraduate, 434 postgraduate)

DEANS

Faculty of Commerce and Law: C. J. MUROMBEDZI

Faculty of Education and the Humanities: Prof. M. IZUAGIE
Faculty of Science and the Social Sciences: Dr R. CHIMEDZA

Colleges

Bulawayo Polytechnic: Park Rd, 12th Ave, POB 1392, Bulawayo; tel. (9) 63181; f. 1927; tertiary education in technical, commercial, scientific, design and catering fields; library: 37,170 vols; 360 teachers (210 full-time, 150 part-time); 5,448 students; Prin. A. MWADIWA.

Chibero College of Agriculture: Private Bag 901, Norton; tel. (62) 2238; f. 1960; 2-year national diploma in agriculture; library: 6,000 vols; 15 teachers; 120 students; Prin. M. E. NYAMANGARA; publ. *Agricultural Education.*

Esigodini Agricultural Institute: Private Bag 5808, Esigodini; tel. (88) 297; fax (88) 296; f. 1921; 18 teachers; 120 students; Prin. DAVID THEMBA MGUNI.

Gwebi College of Agriculture: Private Bag 376B, Harare; tel. (4) 304515; fax (4) 333850; e-mail gwebiagric@gta.gov.zw; f. 1950; 3-year diploma in agriculture, 15-month higher national diploma in horticulture; library: 2,300 vols; 15 teachers; 120 students; Prin. W. MATIZHA.

Harare Polytechnic: POB CY 407, Causeway, Harare; tel. (4) 752311; fax (4) 720955; f. 1927; full-time and sandwich courses for technicians and craftsmen; courses in printing and adult education; full-time and part-time courses in automotive engineering, business studies, civil construction, computer studies, library and information science, mass communication, mechanical engineering, science and technology, secretarial studies; library: 68,000 vols; 500 teachers (incl. part-time); 9,000 students; Prin. S. RAZA.

Kushinga-Phikelela National Farmer Training Centre: Private Bag 3705, Marondera; tel. (79) 24329; fax (79) 23916; e-mail kushinga@africaonline.co.zw; f. 1982; 3-year certificate courses in commercial farming; short courses in animal production, crop production, farm machinery and farm and agri-business; library: 3,100 vols; 13 teachers; 120 students; Prin. B. NLEYA.

Mlezu Institute of Agriculture: POB 8062, Kwekwe; f. 1982; 2-year course; Prin. J. K. D. MARIPFONDE (acting).

School of Social Work: University of Zimbabwe, Private Bag 66022, Kopje, Harare; tel. (4) 752965; fax (4) 751903; e-mail sswprinc@samara.co.zw; f. 1964; first degrees, certificate, Masters degree and diploma courses; library: 19,870 vols; 13 teachers; 250 students; Dir Prof. E. KASEKE.

Zimbabwe College of Music: Box 66352, Kopje, Harare; tel. and fax (4) 749077; e-mail zcmlib@zol.co.zw; f. 1948; library: 3,000 vols; 35 teachers; 500 students; Chair. BEN ZULU; Dir CHRISTOPHER TIMBE; Registrar FRIDAY MBIRIMI; Librarian PRISCILLA CHIDOHWE.

INDEX OF INSTITUTIONS

Accreditation, Certification and Quality Assurance Institute, Bayreuth, 818

Accreditation Commission on Colleges of Medicine (ACCM), 1129

Accreditation Commission, Prague, 628

Accreditation Committee of Cambodia, Phnom-Penh, 357

Accreditation Council, Bonn, 819

Accreditation Council for Business Schools & Programs, 2393

Accreditation Council for Universities of Applied Sciences, 172

Accreditation Council of Trinidad and Tobago (ACTT), Port-of-Spain, 2151

Accreditation Organisation of the Netherlands and Flanders, 1527

Accreditation Service for International Colleges (ASIC), Stockton-on-Tees, 2224

Accrediting Agency of Chartered Colleges and Universities in the Philippines, Inc. (AACCUP), Quezon City, 1688

Accrediting Commission of Career Schools and Colleges (ACCSC), 2393

Accrediting Council for Independent Colleges and Schools (ACICS), 2394

Accrington and Rossendale College, 2359

ACE Denmark—Accreditation Agency, 649

ACE Denmark—Akkrediteringsinstitutionen, 649

Acelin Institute of Business, Adelaide, 169

Acharya N. G. Ranga Agricultural University, 1023

Acharya Nagarjuna University, 1023

Acharya Narendra Dev Pustakalaya, 1021

Ackland Art Museum, 2490

Acoustical Society of America, 2412

Acoustical Society of China, 464

Acoustical Society of Finland, 717

Acoustics Research Institute, Vienna, 181

Acropolis Museum, Athens, 948

Acton Public Library, 2433

Acuario Nacional de Cuba, 618

ACUM (Society of Authors, Composers and Music Publishers in Israel), 1141

Ada Community Library, 2438

Adair County Public Library, 2447

Adam Mickiewicz University in Poznań, 1730

Adam Smith College, 2380

Adams County Library, 2453

Adams County Library System, Gettysburg, 2456

Adams National Historical Park, 2480

Adams State College, 2551

Adamson University, 1692

Adamson University Library, 1690

Adams-Pratt Oakland County Law Library, 2445

Adana Bölge Müzesi, 2162

Addis Ababa University, 707

Addis Ababa University Libraries, 707

Addison Gallery of American Art, 2480

Adelaide Central School of Art, 169

Adelaide College of Divinity, 169

Adelaide College of Ministries, 169

Adelhausermuseum, Freiburg im Breisgau, 852

Adelphi University, 2768

Adhesion Institute, Delft, 1532

Adler Graduate School, 2715

Adler Museum of Medicine, Johannesburg, 1979

Adler Planetarium, Chicago, 2474

Adler School of Professional Psychology, 2605

Administración Nacional de Laboratorios e Institutos de Salud 'Dr Carlos G. Malbran', Buenos Aires, 107

Administration of State Castles and Gardens, 850

Administrative Bibliotek, Copenhagen, 655

Administrative Staff College of India, 1079

Admiral Makarov State Maritime Academy, St Petersburg, 1898

Adnan Malki Museum, Damascus, 2116

Adnan Menderes Üniversitesi, Aydin, 2163

Adrian College, 2694

Adriatic Institute, Zagreb, 608

Adriatic Society of Sciences, 1167

Adult Education Association of Guyana Inc. M.S., 966

Adult Learning Australia Inc, 130

Advance Material and Process Research Institute, Bhopal, 1012

Advanced Centre for Technical Development of Punjabi Language, Literature and Culture, 1015

Advanced Centre for Treatment, Research and Education in Cancer (ACTREC), Mumbai, 1015

Advanced School for Computing and Imaging, 1543

Advanced Science and Technology Institute, Manila, 1689

Advanced Virtual Reality Research Centre, Loughborough, 2262

Advisory Centre for Education (ACE) Ltd, London, 2231

Advokatska Komora Bosne i Hercegovine, 288

Advokatska-Odvjetnicka Komora Federacije Bosne i Hercegovine, 288

Adyar Library and Research Centre, 1021

Adygea Agricultural Research Institute, 1830

Adyghe State University, Maykop, 1863

AECL Research, Chalk River Laboratories, 373

AECL Research, Whiteshell Laboratories, 373

Aegean University, 2168

AEI-NOOSR, Canberra, 129

Aeronautical Society of India, 1010

Aeronautical Society of South Africa (AeSSA), 1975

Aeroseum, 2063

Aerospace Medical Association, Alexandria, 2406

Afanasev, V. A., Research Institute of Fur-Bearing Animals and Rabbits, Moscow, 1830

Afet İşleri Genel Müdürlüğü Deprem Araştırma Dairesi, Ankara, 2160

Afghan Cultural House, 80

Afghan Institute of Archaeology, 80

Afghan Rectors' Conference, 79

Afghanistan Institute in Switzerland, 2094

Afghanistan Research and Evaluation Unit (AREU), 80

Afghanistan Technical Vocational Institute, 82

Afonso Chaves Society, 1766

Africa Centre, 910

Africa Institute of South Africa, 1975

Africa Nazarene University, Nairobi, 1353

Africa Rice Centre (WARDA), 42

African Academy of Sciences, 69

African American Heritage Center, Inc, 2478

African and Asian Studies Centre, Lisbon, 1763

African and Malagasy Council for Higher Education, 51

African Art Museum, Tenafly, 2486

African Association for the Advancement of Science and Technology, 69

African Centre for Applied Research and Training in Social Development (ACARTSOD), Tripoli, 1417

African Medical and Research Foundation, 64

African Network of Scientific and Technological Institutions (ANSTI), Nairobi, 1351

African Organization for Cartography and Remote Sensing, 686

African Regional Centre for Technology, Dakar, 1918

African Society, Cairo, 686

African Studies Association of the United Kingdom, 2243

African Studies Association, Piscataway, 2414

African Training and Research Centre in Administration for Development, 48

African Virtual University, Nairobi, 1354

Africana Museum, Monrovia, 1413

Africana Studies and Research Center, Ithaca, 2426

AFRO Health Sciences Library and Documentation Centre, 597

AFW Wirtschaftsakademie Bad Harzburg GmbH, 821

Afyon Kocatepe Üniversitesi, 2163

Aga Khan University, 1644

Agence de la Francophonie, Paris, 739

Agence pour l'Evaluation de la Qualité de l'Enseignement Supérieur, 248

Agence Universitaire de la Francophonie, 52

Agencia Española de Cooperación Internacional para el Desarrollo (AECID), 1996

Agencia Estatal de Meteorología, Madrid, 2005

Agencia Nacional de Evaluación de la Calidad y Acreditación, Madrid, 1995

Agencia Nacional de Evaluación y Acreditación de la Educación Superior (ANEAES), Asunción, 1674

Agencija za Statistiku Bosne i Hercegovine, 289

Agencija za znanost i visoko obrazovanje, 606

Agency for Higher Education Quality Assurance and Career Development (AQA), Moscow, 1826

Agency for Science and Higher Education, Zagreb, 606

Agency for Science, Innovation and Technology, Vilnius, 1420

Agency for Statistics of Bosnia and Herzegovina, 289

Agenţia Română de Asigurare a Calităţii în Învăţământul Superior (ARACIS), 1782

Agentur für Qualitätssicherung durch Akkreditierung von Studiengängen, 819

Agenzia Nazionale per le Nuove Tecnologie, l'Energia e lo Sviluppo Economico Sostenibile (ENEA), Rome, 1175

AGH University of Science and Technology, 1747

Agnes Scott College, 2591

Agraren Universitet Plovdiv, 344

Agrarian Economists Association of Romania, 1783

Agrarian Institute, Moscow, 1830

Agrarian Law Society, Utrecht, 1529

Agrarian Society, Valletta, 1457

Agrarsoziale Gesellschaft eV (ASG), Göttingen, 820

AgResearch, 1575

Agricultural Association of China, Taipei, 2118

Agricultural Biotechnology Research Institute of Iran (ABRII), Karaj, 1107

Agricultural Chemical Research Institute, Pyongyang, 1359

Agricultural Cooperative College, 1386

Agricultural Department Library, Zanzibar, 2131

Agricultural Economics Research Centre, 1063

Agricultural Economics Research Institute, Giza, 687

Agricultural Economics Research Institute, Ulan Bator, 1497

Agricultural Economics Society, Uckfield, 2227

Agricultural Engineering Research Institute, Giza, 687

Agricultural Engineering Research, Vihti, 718

Agricultural Experiment Station, 2977

Agricultural Experiment Station, Paramaribo, 2051

Agricultural Extension and Rural Development Research Institute, Giza, 687

Agricultural Genetic Engineering Research Institute, 687

Agricultural History Society, Washington, 2398

Agricultural Information Centre, Ras Al Khaimah, 2218

Agricultural Institute, Barcelona, 1997

Agricultural Institute of Canada, 368

Agricultural Institute of Slovenia, 1964

Agricultural Institute, Shumen, 335

Agricultural Irrigation Research Institute, Onchon County, 1359

Agricultural Mechanization Research Institute, Pyongyang, 1359

Agricultural Museum, 1230

Agricultural Museum, Cairo, 690

Agricultural Museum, Damascus, 2116

Agricultural Research and Extension Trust, Lilongwe, 1441

Agricultural Research Centre Library, Tripoli, 1416

Agricultural Research Centre, Ministry of Agriculture, Giza, 687

Agricultural Research Corporation, Central Library, Wad Medani, 2048

Agricultural Research Corporation, Wad Medani, 2047

Agricultural Research Council, 1172

Agricultural Research Council of Zimbabwe, 3028

Agricultural Research Council, Pretoria, 1975

Agricultural Research Institute, Baku, 203

Agricultural Research Institute for the Central Areas of the Non-Black Soil (Nechernozem) Zone, 1830

Agricultural Research Institute, Khovd, 1497

Agricultural Research Institute (Mlingano), 2130

Agricultural Research Institute of Rwanda–Ruhande Station, 1902

Agricultural Research Institute, Reykjavík, 1002

Agricultural Research Institute, Washington, 2418

Agricultural Research Organization, Bet-Dagan, 1142

Agricultural Research Trust, Harare, 3028

Agricultural Science Information Centre, Taipei, 2120

Agricultural Society of Kenya, 1352

Agricultural Society of Trinidad and Tobago, 2151

Agricultural Technology and Production Studies Centre, Lisbon, 1763

Agricultural Technology Science, Technology and Production Corporation, Ulan Bator, 1498

Agricultural University of Iceland, 1003

Agricultural University of Tiranë, 86

Agricultural University Plovdiv, 344

Agriculture and Food Development Authority, 1132

Agriculture and Water Resources Research Centre, Baghdad, 1123

Agriculture and Water Resources Research Centre, Fudhailiyah, 1123

Agriculture Technologies Transfer Centre (ATTC), Shkodër, 84

Agri-Food and Biosciences Institute, 2249

AgriFood Economics Centre, 2058

Agri-Horticultural Society of India, 1005

Agri-Horticultural Society of Madras, 1005

Agrimetrics Institute, Pretoria, 1975

Agro-Economic Research Centre, Santiniketan, 1012

Agronomists Society, Bucharest, 1783

Agronomy Research Institute, Harare, 3028

Agronomy Society of New Zealand, 1573

AgroParisTech, 790

Agrophysical Research Institute, St Petersburg, 1830

Agroscope, 2091

Al-Isra Private University, 1335
Albjóóamálastofnun, 1001
Al-Jouf Museum, 1911
Al-Khair University, 1645
Al-Khawarizmi International College, 2221
Al-Khozam Palace Museum, 1911
All India Association for Educational Research, Bhubaneswar, 1006
All India Bar Association, 1006
All India Council for Technical Education (AICTE), 1005
All India Fine Arts and Crafts Society, 1006
All India Institute of Hygiene and Public Health, 1080
All India Ophthalmological Society, 1007
All Nations Christian College, 2366
All Pakistan Educational Conference Library, 1642
All Souls College, Oxford, 2348
Allahabad Mathematical Society, 1009
Allahabad Public Library, 1021
Allama I. I. Kazi Central Library, 1642
Allama Iqbal Open University, 1645
Allama Iqbal Open University Central Library, Islamabad, 1642
Allameh Tabataba'i University, 1109
Allard Pierson Museum, 1548
Állattenyésztési és Takarmányozási Kutatóintézet, Herceghalom, 975
Allegany County Library System, Cumberland, 2443
Allegany Museum, Cumberland, 2479
Allegheny College, 2850
Allen College, 2633
Allen County Library, Fort Wayne, IN, 2439
Allen County Public Library, Scottsville, KY, 2441
Allen Memorial Art Museum, 2491
Allen Parish Libraries, 2442
Allen University, 2881
Allergen State Unitary Enterprise, Stavropol, 1835
Allerød Biblioteker, 654
Allerød Libraries, 654
Allgemeine Bibliotheken der Gesellschaft für das Gute und Gemeinnützige, Basel, 2093
Alliance Française, Abu Dhabi, 2218
Alliance Française, Accra, 939
Alliance Française, Addis Ababa, 706
Alliance Française, Agadez, Niger, 1587
Alliance Française, Andorra la Vella, 97
Alliance Française, Antananarivo, 1437
Alliance Française, Asmara, 700
Alliance Française, Asunción, 1674
Alliance Française, Bali, 1083
Alliance Française, Bangkok, 2136
Alliance Française, Bangui, 443
Alliance Française, Beijing, 463
Alliance Française, Bergen, 1615
Alliance Française, Bethlehem, 1663
Alliance Française, Bitola, 1432
Alliance Française, Bogatá, 578
Alliance Française, Bratislava, 1950
Alliance Française, Brunei, 331
Alliance Française, Bucharest, 1784
Alliance Française, Buenos Aires, 103
Alliance Française, Canberra, 132
Alliance Française, Caracas, 3000
Alliance Française, Castries, 1905
Alliance Française, Chişinău, 1491
Alliance Française, Coimbra, 1762
Alliance Française, Copenhagen, 651
Alliance Française d'Islamabad, 1637
Alliance Française, Dakar, 1917
Alliance Française, Dar es Salaam, 2130
Alliance Française de Bichkek, 1393
Alliance Française de Bruxelles-Europe, 250
Alliance Française de Colombo, 2040
Alliance Française de Dhaka, 213
Alliance Française de Katmandou, 1524
Alliance Française de Kuala Lumpur, 1444
Alliance Française de Lima, Lima, 1678
Alliance Française de Zurich, 2088
Alliance Française, Djibouti, 669
Alliance Française, Dublin, 1131
Alliance Française, El Jadida, 1506
Alliance Française, El Obeid, 2047

Alliance Française, Freetown, 1941
Alliance Française, Gaborone, 294
Alliance Française, Georgetown, 966
Alliance Française, Guatemala City, 960
Alliance Française, Harare, 3027
Alliance Française, Havana, 615
Alliance Française in India, 1007
Alliance française in Kathmandu, 1524
Alliance Française, Johannesburg, 1974
Alliance Française, Kampala, 2191
Alliance Française, Kingston, Jamaica, 1213
Alliance Française, Kingstown, 1906
Alliance Française, Kinshasa, 593
Alliance Française, La Paz, 282
Alliance Française, Lagos, 1590
Alliance Française, Limassol, 622
Alliance Française, London, 2235
Alliance Française, Luanda, 99
Alliance Française, Lusaka, 3024
Alliance Française, Macao, 574
Alliance Française, Madrid, 1998
Alliance Française, Managua, 1585
Alliance Française, Manama, 209
Alliance Française, Manila, 1689
Alliance Française, Maseru, 1411
Alliance Française, Mbabane, 2052
Alliance Française, Miami, 2405
Alliance Française, Mindelo, Cape Verde, 442
Alliance Française, Monrovia, 1413
Alliance Française, Monte Carlo, 1495
Alliance Française, Montevideo, 2979
Alliance Française, Nairobi, 1352
Alliance Française, Nassau, 208
Alliance Française, Ngaoundéré, 363
Alliance Française, Nouakchott, 1460
Alliance Française, Osaka, 1219
Alliance Française, Ottawa, 370
Alliance Française, Panamá, 1668
Alliance Française, Paramaribo, 2051
Alliance Française Paris Ile-de-France, 739
Alliance Française, Plovdiv, 334
Alliance Française, Port Gentil, Gabon, 808
Alliance Française, Port Louis, 1462
Alliance Française, Port Moresby, 1671
Alliance Française, Port Saïd, 686
Alliance Française, Port-au-Prince, 968
Alliance Française, Port-of-Spain, 2151
Alliance Française, Prague, 629
Alliance Française, Quito, 677
Alliance Française, Riga, 1403
Alliance Française, Rio De Janeiro, 298
Alliance Française, Rome, 1166
Alliance Française, Roseau, 670
Alliance Française, St John's, 101
Alliance Française, St Kitts and Nevis, 1904
Alliance Française, St Michael, Barbados, 236
Alliance Française, St Petersburg, 1828
Alliance Française, Samarqand, 2983
Alliance Française, San José, Costa Rica, 598
Alliance Française, San Marino, 1908
Alliance Française, San Salvador, 696
Alliance Française, Santiago, Chile, 448
Alliance Française, Santo Domingo, 671
Alliance Française, São Tomé E Principe, 1909
Alliance Française, Seoul, 1363
Alliance Française, Singapore, 1943
Alliance Française, Stockholm, 2056
Alliance Française, Suva, 710
Alliance Française, Szeged, 973
Alliance Française, Tallinn, 701
Alliance Française, Tegucigalpa, 970
Alliance Française, Tiranë, 84
Alliance Française, Utrecht, 1530
Alliance Française, Victoria, Seychelles, 1940
Alliance Française, Vilnius, 1421
Alliance Française, Wan Chai, 566
Alliance Française, Warsaw, 1708
Alliance Française, Wellington, 1574
Alliance Française, Yamoussoukro, 603
Alliance Française, Yerevan, 125
Alliance Française, Zagreb, 607
Alliance Française—Alianza Francesa México, 1466

Alliance Franco-Gambienne, Banjul, 810
Alliance of Literary Societies, Havant, 2235
Alliance of Sector Skills Councils (SSCs), London, 2225
Alliant International University, 2519
All-India Institute of Medical Sciences, 1069
All-Russia Antibiotics Research Institute, 1835
All-Russia Electrotechnical Institute (VEI), 1846
All-Russia Geological Oil Research Institute (VNIGNI), Moscow, 1842
All-Russia Horticulture Institute for Breeding, Agrotechnology and Nursery, 1830
All-Russia Institute of Plant Protection, 1830
All-Russia Legumes and Pulse Crops Research Institute, 1830
All-Russia Logachev Scientific Research Institute of Exploration Geophysics (VIRG-Rudgeofizika), St Petersburg, 1846
All-Russia Maize Research Institute, 1830
All-Russia Meat Research Institute, 1830
All-Russia Oil Geological Prospecting Institute, 1846
'All-Russia Patent and Technical Library' of Federal Institute of Industrial Property of Federal Service for Intellectual Property, Patents and Trademarks (Rospatent), 1853
All-Russia Potato Research Institute, 1830
All-Russia Poultry Research and Technology Institute, 1830
All-Russia Railway Transport Research Institute, 1846
All-Russia Research and Design Institute for Atomic Power Station Equipment, 1846
All-Russia Research and Design Institute for Problems of the Development of Oil and Gas Resources on the Continental Shelf, 1846
All-Russia Research and Design Institute of Electroceramics, 1846
All-Russia Research and Design Institute of Metallurgical Engineering, 1846
All-Russia Research and Design Institute of the Oil-Refining and Petrochemical Industry, 1846
All-Russia Research and Design Institute of the Statistical Information System, 1833
All-Russia Research and Technological Institute for Chemical Land Reclamation, 1830
All-Russia Research and Technological Institute for Chemicalization in Agriculture, 1830
All-Russia Research and Technological Institute for Mechanization in Livestock Raising, 1830
All-Russia Research, Design and Technological Institute of Lighting Technology, 1846
All-Russia Research Institute for Agricultural Biotechnology, 1830
All-Russia Research Institute for Agricultural Economics and Standards and Norms, 1830
All-Russia Research Institute for Beef Cattle Breeding and Production, 1830
All-Russia Research Institute for Biological Control, 1830
All-Russia Research Institute for Cybernetics in the Agro-industrial Complex, 1830
All-Russia Research Institute for Economics, Labour and Management in Agriculture, 1830
All-Russia Research Institute for Electrification in Agriculture, 1830

All-Russia Research Institute for Farm Animal Genetics and Breeding, 1830
All-Russia Research Institute for Floriculture and Subtropical Crops, 1830
All-Russia Research Institute for Horse Breeding, 1830
All-Russia Research Institute for Irrigated Arable Farming, 1830
All-Russia Research Institute for Irrigated Horticulture and Vegetable Crops Production, 1830
All-Russia Research Institute for Mechanization in Agriculture, 1830
All-Russia Research Institute for Nature Conservation, 1840
All-Russia Research Institute for Nuclear Power Plant Operation, 1846
All-Russia Research Institute for Oil Refining JSC, 1846
All-Russia Research Institute for Sheep and Goat Breeding, 1830
All-Russia Research Institute for the Agricultural Use of Reclaimed and Improved Land, 1831
All-Russia Research Institute for the Biosynthesis of Protein Substances, 1831
All-Russia Research Institute for the Canned and Vegetable Dry Products Industry, 1846
All-Russia Research Institute for the Dairy Industry, 1846
All-Russia Research Institute for the Geology and Mineral Resources of the World's Oceans, St Petersburg, 1842
All-Russia Research Institute for the Protection of Metals from Corrosion, 1846
All-Russia Research Institute for the Refrigeration Industry, 1847
All-Russia Research Institute for Vegetable Breeding and Seed Production, 1831
All-Russia Research Institute for Veterinary Sanitation, Hygiene and Ecology, 1831
All-Russia Research Institute of Agricultural Microbiology, 1831
All-Russia Research Institute of Animal Husbandry, 1831
All-Russia Research Institute of Applied Microbiology, 1840
All-Russia Research Institute of Arable Farming and Soil Erosion Control, 1831
All-Russia Research Institute of Chemical Technology, 1842
All-Russia Research Institute of Economic Problems in Development of Science and Technology, 1833
All-Russia Research Institute of Economics in Agriculture, 1831
All-Russia Research Institute of Electrical Insulating Materials and Foiled Dielectrics, 1847
All-Russia Research Institute of Electromechanics (VNIIEM), 1847
All-Russia Research Institute of Exploration Geophysics, 1847
All-Russia Research Institute of Eye Diseases, 1835
All-Russia Research Institute of Fibre-Optic Systems of Communication and Data Processing, 1847
All-Russia Research Institute of Food Biotechnology, 1847
All-Russia Research Institute of Fuel and Energy Problems (VNIIKTEP), 1847
All-Russia Research Institute of Helium Technology, 1847
All-Russia Research Institute of Hydrolysis, 1842
All-Russia Research Institute of Information, Technological and Economic Research on the Agro-Industrial Complex, 1831
All-Russia Research Institute of Marine Fisheries and Oceanography, 1831

American Pharmacists Association, 2413

American Philological Association, 2405

American Philosophical Association, 2414

American Philosophical Society, 2397

American Philosophical Society Library, Philadelphia, 2456

American Philosophical Society Museum, Philadelphia, 2494

American Physical Society, 2413

American Physical Therapy Association, 2407

American Physiological Society, 2408

American Phytopathological Society, 2410

American Planning Association, 2399

American Political Science Association, 2401

American Psychiatric Association, 2408

American Psychological Association, 2414

American Public Health Association, 2408

American Public University System, 2951

American Research Center in Egypt (ARCE), San Antonio, 2426

American Roentgen Ray Society, Reston, 2408

American School of Classical Studies at Athens, 957

American Schools of Oriental Research, Boston, 2426

American Society for Aesthetics, 2403

American Society for Biochemistry and Molecular Biology, 2413

American Society for Clinical Laboratory Science, 2408

American Society for Clinical Pathology, 2408

American Society for Eighteenth-Century Studies, 2404

American Society for Engineering Education, 2416

American Society for Ethnohistory, 2414

American Society for Horticultural Science, 2398

American Society for Information Science and Technology (ASIS&T), 2399

American Society for Investigative Pathology, 2408

American Society for Microbiology, 2408

American Society for Nutritional Sciences, 2408

American Society for Pharmacology and Experimental Therapeutics, 2408

American Society for Photobiology, 2410

American Society for Photogrammetry and Remote Sensing, 2416

American Society for Political and Legal Philosophy, 48

American Society for Psychical Research, Inc., 2426

American Society for Public Administration, 2401

American Society for Theatre Research, 2403

American Society of Agricultural and Biological Engineers, 2398

American Society of Agronomy, 2398

American Society of Animal Science, 2398

American Society of Church History, 2404

American Society of Civil Engineers, 2416

American Society of Clinical Hypnosis, 2408

American Society of Composers, Authors and Publishers (ASCAP), 2403

American Society of Heating, Refrigerating and Air-Conditioning Engineers, 2416

American Society of Human Genetics, 2411

American Society of Ichthyologists and Herpetologists, 2411

American Society of International Law, 2401

American Society of Limnology and Oceanography, 2409

American Society of Mammalogists, 2411

American Society of Mechanical Engineers, 2416

American Society of Naturalists, 2411

American Society of Naval Engineers, 2416

American Society of Parasitologists, 2411

American Society of Tropical Medicine and Hygiene, 2408

American Sociological Association, 2414

American Speech-Language-Hearing Association, 2408

American Statistical Association, 2401

American Studies Institute, 1665

American Surgical Association, 2408

American Swedish Historical Museum, Philadelphia, 2494

American Theological Library Association, 2399

American University in Bulgaria, 344

American University in Cairo, 691

American University in Cairo Library, 689

American University in Dubai, 2219

American University in Kosovo (AUK), Prishtinë, 1388

American University in the Emirates, 2219

American University Museum, Beirut, 1407

American University of Afghanistan, 81

American University of Beirut, 1407

American University of Beirut Libraries, 1407

American University of Central Asia, 1395

American University of Kuwait, 1391

American University of Paris, 795

American University of Puerto Rico, 2973

American University of Rome, 1207

American University of Sharjah, 2219

American University of the Caribbean School of Medicine, Cupecoy, 1571

American University, Washington, 2571

American Urological Association, 2408

American Veterinary Medical Association, 2399

American Welding Society, 2416

Americanos College, 627

Americans for the Arts, 2403

Amerièka visoka škola za management i tehnologiju, 614

Amerikanski Universitet v Bulgaria, 344

Ames Research Center, Moffet Field, 2428

Amgueddfa Cymru, 2283

Amgueddfa Cymru—National Museum Wales Library, 2267

Amherst Center for Russian Culture, 2444

Amherst College, 2665

Amherst Libraries, 2444

Amherst Town Library, 2449

Amics de la Cultura, Escaldes-Engordany, 97

Amics dels Museus de Catalunya, 1997

Amirkabir University of Technology, Tehran, Tehran, 1109

Amity Law School, 1080

Amman University College for Applied Engineering, 1337

Ammattikorkeoulujen rehtorineuvosto, Helsinki, 713

Amon Carter Museum of American Art, 2497

Amos Anderson Art Museum, 721

Amos Andersonin taidemuseo, 721

Amoud University, 1970

Amridge University, 2503

Amrita Vishwa Vidyapeetham, 1072

Amsterdam Business School (ABS), 1532

Amsterdam Center for Career Research (ACCR), 1532

Amsterdam Center for Entrepreneurship, 1535

Amsterdam Center for Entrepreneurship at VU, 1532

Amsterdam Center for Finance and Insurance, 1535

Amsterdam Center for Law & Economics (ACLE), 1535

Amsterdam Centre for Child Studies, 1541

Amsterdam Centre for Corporate Finance (ACCF), 1535

Amsterdam Centre for Environmental Law and Sustainability (ACELS), 1535

Amsterdam Centre for International Law (ACIL), 1535

Amsterdam Centre for Language and Communication (ACLC), 1538

Amsterdam Centre for Research in International Finance (CIFRA), 1535

Amsterdam Centre for Service Innovation (AMSI), 1535

Amsterdam Historical Museum, 1548

Amsterdam Institute for Advanced Labour Studies, 1535

Amsterdam Institute for Business and Economic Research Foundation (AMBER), 1535

Amsterdam Institute for International Development (AIID), 1532

Amsterdam Institute for Social Science Research, 1542

Amsterdam Public Library, 1545

Amsterdam School for Cultural Analysis, 1542

Amsterdam School of Real Estate, 1560

Amsterdam School of the Arts, 1565

Amsterdams Historisch Museum, 1548

Amsterdams Instituut voor ArbeidsStudies (AIAS), 1535

Amsterdamse Hogeschool voor de Kunsten, 1565

Amtsbókasafnið á Akureyri, 1002

Amur Complex Research Institute, 1842

Amur State University, 1864

Amuri Museum of Workers' Housing, 722

Amurin Työläismuseokortteli, 722

Anacortes Museum, 2500

Anadarko Community Library, 2455

Anadolu Medeniyetleri Müzesi, 2162

Anadolu Üniversitesi, 2164

Anadolu University, 2164

Anastasie Fătu Botanical Garden of Alexandru Ioan Cuza University of Iaşi, 1785

Anatomical Society, Erlaugen, 823

Anatomical Society, London, 2237

Anatomische Gesellschaft, Lübeck, 823

Anchorage Museum, 2463

Ancient House Museum, Thetford, 2290

Ancient Iran Cultural Society, Tehran, 1106

Ancient Monuments Society, London, 2233

Ancient Orient Museum, Tokyo, 1232

Andalusian School of Public Health, 2037

Anderson County Library System, 2457

Anderson County Museum, 2495

Anderson Museum of Contemporary Art, 2487

Anderson Park Art Gallery (Inc.), 1578

Anderson University, Anderson, IN, 2624

Anderson University, Anderson, SC, 2882

Andhra Pradesh State Museum, 1021

Andhra University, 1024

Andijan State Medical Institute, 2988

Andijan State University, 2986

Andijon Cotton Institute, 2988

Andijon Davlat Tibbiyot Instituti, 2988

Andijon State Pedagogical Institute of Languages, 2988

Andong Institute of Information and Technology, 1386

Andong National University, 1366

Andongsoju and Traditional Food Museum, 1366

Andorra Postal Museum, 98

Andorra Scientific Society, 97

Andorran Model Museum, Escaldes-Engordany, 98

Andover Newton Theological School, 2665

Andras Keve Library for Ornithology and Nature Conservation, 979

Andrássy Gyula Budapesti Német Nyelvö Egyetem, 998

Andrea Palladio International Centre for the Study of Architecture, 1164

Andreev Acoustics Institute, Michigan, 1842

Andreev Leonid, House Museum, Orel, 1859

Andrei Saguna University of Constanţa, 1800

Andrews University, 2694

Andronikashvili Institute of Physics, Tbilisi, 814

Angeles University Foundation, Angeles City, 1692

Angkor City Institute, 360

Angkor University, 360

Anglia Ruskin University, 2292

Anglia Ruskin University Library, 2268

Anglo–European College of Chiropractic, 2364

Angono Petroglyphs Site Museum, 1691

Angra do Heroísmo Museum, 1769

Angus L. Macdonald Library, Antigonish, 375

Anhalt Library of Dessau, 841

Anhalt University of Applied Sciences, 936

Anhaltische Landesbücherei Dessau, 841

Anhui Provincial Library, 471

Anhui University, 472

Animal Health and Veterinary Laboratories Agency, Addlestone, 2249

Animal Health and Welfare, Belfast, 2249

Animal Health Research Centre, Entebbe, 2192

Animal Health Research Institute, Dokki, 687

Animal Health Trust, Kentford, 2249

Animal Husbandry Research Institute, Comilla, 214

Animal Improvement Institute, Irene, 1975

Animal Nutrition and Animal Products Institute, Irene, 1975

Animal Production Corporation, Research Division, Khartoum, 2047

Animal Production Research Institute, Dokki, 687

Animal Production Research, Jokioinen, 718

Animal Reproduction Research Institute, Giza, 687

Animal Research Institute, Achimota, 939

Animation Research Centre, Farnham, 2262

Anjuman Taraqqi-e-Urdu Pakistan, 1637

Anjuman-i-Islam Urdu Research Association, Mumbai, 1018

Anjuman-i-Islam Urdu Research Institute, 1015

Ankara Üniversitesi, 2164

Ankara Üniversitesi, Kütüphane ve Dokümantasyon Daire Başkanlığı, 2161

Ankara University Libraries and Documentation Centre, 2161

Ann Arbor District Library System, 2445

Anna Freud Centre, London, 2261

Anna Maria College, Paxton, 2665

Anna University, 1024

Annaba Study and Research Centre for Regional Development, Algiers, 90

An-Najah National University, 1665

Annamalai University, 1024

Annapolis Maritime Museum, 2479

Anne Frank Museum, Amsterdam, 1548

Annmary Brown Memorial, 2495

Annonciade, Musée de St-Tropez, 761

Anokhin, P. K., Institute of Normal Physiology, Moscow, 1835

Anotati Scholi Kalon Technon, 949

Ansan College of Technology, 1386

Ansan Fishing Village Folk Museum, 1365

Ansonia Library, 2433

Arquivo da Universidade de Coimbra, 1767
Arquivo Distrital de Braga, 1767
Arquivo Distrital de Bragança, 1767
Arquivo Distrital de Leiria, 1768
Arquivo Distrital de Setúbal, 1769
Arquivo Distrital de Vila Real, 1769
Arquivo Distrital de Viseu, 1769
Arquivo Distrital do Porto, 1769
Arquivo do Arco do Cego, Lisbon, 1768
Arquivo do Estado de São Paulo, 305
Arquivo do Reino de Galicia, 2006
Arquivo Fotográfico, Lisbon, 1768
Arquivo Histórico de Macau, 575
Arquivo Histórico de Moçambique, 1511
Arquivo Histórico de São Tomé e Príncipe, 1909
Arquivo Histórico, Lisbon, 1768
Arquivo Histórico Militar, 1768
Arquivo Histórico Municipal do Porto, 1769
Arquivo Histórico Nacional, Luanda, 99
Arquivo Histórico Parlamentar, 1768
Arquivo Intermédio, Lisbon, 1768
Arquivo Municipal de Lisboa, 1768
Arquivo Municipal de Sintra/Arquivo Histórico, 1769
Arquivo Nacional, Rio de Janeiro, 304
Arquivo Público do Estado do Pará, 303
Arquivo Público Estadual do Espírito Santo, Vitória, 306
Arquivo Regional da Madeira, 1768
ARRB Group Ltd, 138
Ars Aevi—Museum of Contemporary Art Sarajevo, 291
Arsip Nasional Republik Indonesia, 1086
Art Academy of Cincinnati, 2825
Art and Design Research Institute, 2253
Art and Museum Library of the City of Cologne, 841
Art Center College of Design, Pasadena, 2520
Art Centre Silkeborg Bad, 658
Art Complex Museum, Duxbury, 2481
Art Gallery of Alberta, 377
Art Gallery of Bosnia and Herzegovina, 291
Art Gallery of Hamilton, 378
Art Gallery of Matica Srpska, 1923
Art Gallery of New South Wales, 141
Art Gallery of Nova Scotia, 378
Art Gallery of Ontario, 378
Art Gallery of South Australia, 141
Art Gallery of Western Australia, 142
Art Gallery, Skopje, 1434
Art Gallery Split, 610
Art History Institute in Florence—Max Planck Institute, 828
Art History Society, Vienna, 174
Art Institute of Atlanta, 2592
Art Institute of Chicago, 2474
Art Institute of Houston, 2903
Art Institute of Pittsburgh, 2851
Art Institute of Portland, 2844
Art Institute of Seattle, 2942
Art Libraries Society of North America (ARLIS/NA), 2400
Art Libraries Society of United Kingdom and Ireland, 2228
Art Library of Calouste Gulbenkian Foundation, 1768
Art Museum at the University of Kentucky, 2478
Art Museum, Brașov, 1794
Art Museum, Constanța, 1795
Art Museum, DeKalb, 2474
Art Museum, New Territories, 567
Art Museum of Bayreuth, 848
Art Museum of Estonia, 703
Art Museum of Greater Lafayette, 2475
Art Museum of Southeast Texas, 2497
Art Museum of the Americas, Washington, 2470
Art Museum of University of Memphis (AMUM), 2497
Art Museum, Târgu Jiu, 1798
Art Museum, Târgu Mureș, 1798
Art Palace Museum (incorporating the Art Academy Collection and Hentrich Glass Museum), 852
Art Photographers Association, Oradea, 1783
Art School of Porto, 1779

Art Society of India, 1006
Arte Music Academy, 627
Artesis Hogeschool Antwerpen, 270
Arteveldehogeschool, 270
ArtEZ Academie voor Art & Design, Enschede, 1565
ArtEZ Academy of Art & Design, 1565
ArtEZ Hogeschool voor de Kunsten, 1565
ArtEZ Institute of the Arts, 1565
Arthritis Research UK, Chesterfield, 2254
Arthur M. Sackler Gallery, Washington, 2469
Arthur M. Sackler Museum of Art and Archaeology, Beijing, 472
Arti et Amicitiae, Amsterdam, 1529
Artists Association of Bucharest, 1783
Artists' Association of Finland, 715
Artists' Association of the 18th November, Copenhagen, 650
Artists' Society, Nuuk, 667
Arts & Science Center, Pine Bluff, 2465
Arts and Crafts Centre, Aiwo, 1523
Arts and Humanities Research Council (AHRC), Swindon, 2224
Arts and Humanities Research Council, Bristol, 2254
Arts and Industries Building, Washington, 2470
Arts and Letters Circle, Escaldes-Engordany, 97
Arts Centre, Helsingborg, 2064
Arts Council, Dublin, 1130
Arts Council Norway, 1615
Arts Council of England, 2231
Arts Council of Northern Ireland, 2231
Arts Council of Pakistan, 1637
Arts Council of Sri Lanka, 2040
Arts Council of Wales, 2231
Arts Educational Schools London, 2365
Arts University College at Bournemouth, 2359
Aruba Numismatic Museum, 1568
Arubaanse Muziekschool, 1568
Aruban Historical Museum, 1568
Aruban Model Trains Museum, 1568
Aruban School of Music, 1568
Arusha Declaration Museum, 2131
Arusha Natural History Museum, 2131
Arxiu del Regne de Mallorca, 2007
Arxiu Diocesà de Barcelona, 2006
Arxiu Històric de la Ciutat de Barcelona, 1998
Arxiu Històric de Lleida, 2007
Arxiu Històric de Sabadell, 2007
Arxiu Nacional d'Andorra, 97
ASA University Bangladesh, 217
Asahikawa Medical College, 1233
Asamblea Nacional de Rectores, Lima, 1677
Asbury Theological Seminary, 2643
Asbury University, Wilmore, 2643
Ascension Parish Library, 2442
Asheville Art Museum, 2490
Ashford University, Clinton, 2633
Ashland University, 2825
Ashmolean Museum, University of Oxford, 2290
Ashridge Business School, 2363
Ashton Sixth Form College, 2359
Ashtown Food Research Centre, Dublin, 1132
Asia Euro University, Phnom Penh, 360
Asia Foundation, San Francisco, 2397
Asia Pacific Accreditation and Certification Commission (APACC), 57
Asia Pacific Institute, Phnom Penh, 360
Asia Pacific International College, North Sydney, 167
Asia Research Centre, London, 2248
Asia Society Museum, New York, 2488
Asia University, Tokyo, 1308
Asian and Pacific Development Centre, Kuala Lumpur, 1445
Asian Art Museum, 2465
Asian Art Museum, Berlin, 849
Asian Association of Open Universities, 52
Asian Institute of Management, 1705

Asian Institute of Management, Knowledge Resource Centre Library, Makati City, 1690
Asian Institute of Technology, Bangkok, 2137
Asian Institute of Technology Library, Pathumthani, 2136
Asian Media Information and Communication Centre, Singapore, 1944
Asian Medical Institute, Kant, 1399
Asian University, Chonburi, 2137
Asian University for Women, Chittagong, 217
Asian University of Bangladesh, 217
Asia–Pacific Cultural Centre for UNESCO (ACCU), Tokyo, 1219
Asia-Pacific Quality Network (APQN), 57
Asiatic Society, Kolkata, 1009
Asiatic Society of Bangladesh, 213
Asiatic Society of Mumbai, 1009
ASÍS—The Icelandic Centre for Asian Studies, 1002
Âsiyan Museum, Istanbul, 2162
Askeri Müze ve Kültür Sitesi Komutanlığı, Istanbul, 2162
Askham Bryan College, York, 2362
Aslib (The Association for Information Management), London, 2228
Aslib-IMI Information and Library Service, 2271
ASM International, 2416
Asmara Public Library, 700
Asociace hudebních umělců a vědců, Prague, 629
Asociación Argentina Amigos de la Astronomía, 105
Asociación Argentina de Astronomía, 105
Asociación Argentina de Bibliotecas y Centros de Información Científicos y Técnicos, 103
Asociación Argentina de Biología y Medicina Nuclear, 104
Asociación Argentina de Ciencias Naturales, 105
Asociación Argentina de Cirugía, 104
Asociación Argentina de Estudios Americanos, 105
Asociación Argentina de Farmacia y Bioquímica Industrial, 104
Asociación Argentina de Geofísicos y Geodestas, 105
Asociación Argentina de la Ciencia del Suelo, 103
Asociación Argentina de Micología, Buenos Aires, 105
Asociación Argentina de Ortopedia y Traumatología, 104
Asociación Argentina del Frío, 105
Asociación Argentina para el Progreso de las Ciencias, 105
Asociación Bernardino Rivadavia—Biblioteca Popular, 110
Asociación Bioquímica Argentina, 105
Asociación Chilena de Astronomía y Astronáutica, 449
Asociación Chilena de Sismología e Ingeniería Antisísmica, 449
Asociación Científica y Técnica de Chile, 449
Asociación Colombiana de Bibliotecarios (ASCOLBI), 578
Asociación Colombiana de Facultades de Medicina—ASCOFAME, 579
Asociación Colombiana de Fisioterapia, 579
Asociación Colombiana de Industrias Gráficas—ANDIGRAF, 579
Asociación Colombiana de Informática y Comunicaciones, 579
Asociación Colombiana de Psiquiatría, 579
Asociación Colombiana de Sociedades Científicas, 579
Asociación Colombiana de Universidades, 577
Asociación Costarricense de Cardiología, 598
Asociación Costarricense de Cirugía, 598
Asociación Costarricense de Medicina Interna, 598

Asociación Costarricense de Pediatría, 598
Asociación de Agrimensores de Venezuela, 2999
Asociación de Artistas Aficionados, Lima, 1677
Asociación de Bibliotecarios Graduados de la República Argentina (ABGRA), 103
Asociación de Bibliotecarios y Archivistas de Honduras, 970
Asociación de Bibliotecólogos del Uruguay, 2979
Asociación de Escritores y Artistas Españoles, 1998
Asociación de Ingenieros Civiles del Perú, 1678
Asociación de Ingenieros del Uruguay, 2980
Asociación de Ingenieros y Arquitectos de México, 1466
Asociación de Ingenieros y Geólogos de Yacimientos Petrolíferos Fiscales Bolivianos (AIG—YPFB), 282
Asociación de Lingüística y Filología de América Latina, 45
Asociación de Médicas Mexicanas, AC, 1467
Asociación de Obstetricia y Ginecología de Costa Rica, 598
Asociación de Universidades Amazónicas, 52
Asociación Dominicana de Bibliotecarios, Inc., Santo Domingo, 671
Asociación Dominicana de Rectores de Universidades, 671
Asociación Electrotécnica Argentina, 105
Asociación Electrotécnica Peruana, 1678
Asociación Española de Entomología, 1999
Asociación Española de Pintores y Escultores, 1997
Asociación Geológica Argentina, 105
Asociación Guatemalteca de Historia Natural, 960
Asociación Iberoamericana de Educación Superior a Distancia, 1995
Asociación Iberoamericana de Educación Superior a Distancia (AIESAD), 52
Asociación Indigenista del Paraguay, Asunción, 1674
Asociación Interamericana de Ingeniería Sanitaria y Ambiental, Santiago, 450
Asociación Internacional de Arqueología del Caribe, 45
Asociación Internacional de Hidatidología, 65
Asociación Latinoamericana de Análisis y Modificación del Comportamiento, 64
Asociación Médica Argentina, 104
Asociación Médica de Santiago, Santiago de los Caballeros, 671
Asociación Médica Dominicana, 671
Asociación Médica Peruana, 1678
Asociación Mexicana de Bibliotecarios, AC, 1466
Asociación Mexicana de Facultades y Escuelas de Medicina, 1467
Asociación Mexicana de Geólogos Petroleros, 1468
Asociación Mexicana de Microbiología, AC, 1467
Asociación Mundial de Ciencias de la Educación (AMCE), 57
Asociación Musical Manuel M. Ponce, AC, 1466
Asociación Nacional de Educadoras Sampedranas, Lima, 1677
Asociación Nacional de Químicos de España, 1999
Asociación Nacional de Universidades e Instituciones de Educación Superior (ANUIES), México, 1465
Asociación Nicaragüense de Bibliotecarios y Profesionales afines, 1585
Asociación Odontológica Argentina, 104

Biggs Museum of American Art, Dover, 2469
Bihar Research Society, 1014
Bihar Secretariat Library, 1020
Bijutsu-shi Gakkai, Tokyo, 1219
Bila Tserkva State Agrarian University, 2203
Bilbao Museum of Fine Arts, 2009
Bildmuseet, 2068
Bilkent Üniversitesi, 2165
Bilkent University, 2165
Bill Douglas Centre for History of Cinema and Popular Culture, 2248
Bill Memorial Library, 2433
Billedkunstnernes Forbund, 650
Billy Blue College of Design, North Sydney, 167
Bina Nusantara University, 1099
Bindura University of Science Education, Bindura, 3030
Binghamton University, 2800
Binghamton University Art Museum, 2488
Bioanthropology Research Institute, Hamden, 2422
Biochemical, Biophysical and Microbiological Society of Finland, 716
Biochemical Society, London, 2240
Biochemical Society, Moscow, 1829
Biocomposites Centre, Bangor, 2258
Bioengineering Center, Detroit, 2420
Bioengineering Research Centre, Moscow, 1840
Bio-Farming and Forestry Information Centre, 111
Biofizikai Intézet, Szeged, 977
Biofyzikální ústav AV ČR, Brno, 631
Biogeographical Society of Japan, 1219
Bioinformatics Centre, Copenhagen, 653
Bioinformatics Centre, Srinagar, 1019
Bioinformatik-Centret, 653
Biokémiai Intézet, Szeged, 977
Bioko Biodiversity Protection Program, Malabo, 699
Biola University, La Mirada, 2520
Biological Institute Helgoland, 836
Biological Museum, Stockholm, 2066
Biological Research Centre, Jadiriya, 1123
Biological Research Centre of the Hungarian Academy of Sciences, 977
Biological Research Institute of Cluj-Napoca, 1788
Biological Station Neusiedler See, Illmitz, 180
Biologické centrum AV ČR, v.v.i., Entomologický ústav, 632
Biologische Anstalt Helgoland, 836
Biologische Station Neusiedler See, 180
Biologisk Institut, 653
Biologiska Museet, 2066
Biology Centre AS CR v.v.i., Institute of Entomology, 632
Biološki inštitut Jovana Hadžija ZRC SAZU, 1965
Bio-Medical Engineering Centre, Dhaka, 214
Biomedical Engineering Institute, Tianjing, 466
Biomedical Research Institute, Diepenbeek, 254
Biomedical Sciences Research Institute, 2258
Biomedical/Clinical Engineering Association of Ireland, 1132
Biomedisch Onderzoeksinstituut, 254
Biophysical Society of China, 463
Biophysical Society, Rockville, 2411
BIOS, London, 2258
Biosciences Federation, London, 2240
Biosciences Graduate Research School, Birmingham, 2258
Biotech Research & Innovation Centre, Copenhagen, 654
Biotechnical Research Institute, Moscow, 1840
Biotechnologia JSC, Moscow, 1840
Biotechnology and Biological Sciences Research Council, Swindon, 2249
Biotechnology Research Center, 1118

Biotechnology Scientific Technological Centre, Ashgabat, 2188
Biotechnology Society, Moscow, 1829
Biotechnology Society of Nepal, 1524
Bioterra University of Bucharest, 1801
Bioversity International, 43
Biozentrum Klein Flottbek, Hamburg, 836
Birbal Sahni Institute of Palaeobotany, 1016
Bird College—Dance, Music and Theatre Performance, 2365
BirdLife Australia, 134
Birdlife Finland, 716
BirdLife International, 69
BirdLife South Africa, 1974
BirdLife Zimbabwe, 3028
BIREME—Centro Latino-Americano e do Caribe de Informação em Ciências da Saúde, São Paulo, 305
Birger Sandzén Memorial Gallery, 2477
Birla Industrial and Technological Museum, 1023
Birla Institute of Technology and Science, Pilani, 1073
Birla Institute of Technology and Science, Pilani—Dubai, 2221
Birla Institute of Technology, Ranchi, 1073
Birla Research Institute for Applied Sciences, 1019
Birmingham City University, 2292
Birmingham Civil Rights Institute, 2463
Birmingham Library Services, 2265
Birmingham Museum of Art, 2463
Birmingham Museums and Art Gallery, 2282
Birmingham Public Library, Birmingham, AL, 2429
Birmingham School of Acting, 2365
Birmingham—Southern College, 2503
Birsa Agricultural University, 1027
Birzeit University, 1666
Bischöfliche Zentralbibliothek, Regensburg, 846
Bishkek Academy of Finance and Economics, 1399
Bishkek branch of International Slavic University, 1399
Bishkek branch of Moscow Institute of Business and Law, 1399
Bishkek Higher Military College named after K. Usenbekov, 1396
Bishkek Humanities University named after K. Karasaev, 1396
Bishkek Institute of Moscow State University of Economics, Statistics and Informatics, 1399
Bishkek State Institute of Economics and Commerce, 1396
Bishop Burton College, 2360
Bishop Grosseteste University College, Lincoln, 2359
Bishop Museum, Honolulu, 2473
Bishop Museum's Library and Archives, 2437
Bishop's Stortford Museum, 2282
Bishop's University, Lennoxville, 380
Bistrița County Museum, 1794
Bistrița-Năsăud District Library, 1791
Bjärnum Museum and Local Historical Collections, 2064
Bjärnum Museum och Hembygdssamlingar, 2064
Black Hills State University, 2886
Blackburn College, Carlinville, 2605
Blackburn Museum and Art Gallery, 2282
Blackburn with Darwen Library and Information Services, 2265
Blackfriars, Oxford, 2348
Blackpool and The Fylde College, 2360
Blackpool Library Service, 2265
Blackwell, The Arts & Crafts House, Bowness-on-Windermere, 2285
Blaenau Gwent Libraries, 2268
Blagoevgrad Regional History Museum, 342
Blagonravov, A. A., Institute of Machine Science, Moscow, 1847
Blagoveshchensk State Medical Academy, 1897

Blagoveshchensk State Pedagogical University, 1882
Blaine County Museum, 2484
Blanco Renaissance Museum, 1087
Blanden Art Museum, 2476
Blanton Museum of Art, 2497
Blekinge Institute of Technology, 2082
Blekinge Institute of Technology Library, 2061
Blekinge Museum, 2064
Blekinge Tekniska Högskola, 2082
Blekinge Tekniska Högskola Library, 2061
Blessed John XXIII National Seminary, 2667
Blokhin, N. N., Cancer Research Center, Moscow, 1835
Blood Transfusion Institute, Sichuan, 466
Blood Transfusion Research Institute, Moscow, 1836
Bloomfield College, 2757
Blue Mountain College, 2733
Blue Mountains International Hotel Management School, Sydney South, 167
Blue Nile University, Damazeen, 2048
Bluefield College, 2930
Bluefield State College, 2951
Bluffton University, 2826
BMLFUW Abteilung VII/3– Wasserhaushalt, Vienna, 180
BMT Group Ltd, 2262
Bændasamtök Íslands, 1000
Board of the Swiss Federal Institutes of Technology, 2085
Board on Infrastructure and the Constructed Environment, Washington, 2428
Boaz Public Library, 2429
Bob Campbell Geology Museum, 2495
Bob Jones University Museum and Gallery, 2495
Bobojon Gafurov Khujand State University, 2127
Boca Raton Museum of Art, 2471
Bochvar, A. A., All-Russia Research Institute of Inorganic Materials, Moscow, 1842
Bodensee-Naturmuseum, Konstanz, 854
Bodleian Library, Oxford, 2278
Bodø University College, 1631
Bodrum Sualtı Arkeoloji Müzesi, 2162
Boekmanstichting Bibliotheek, 1545
Boğaziçi Üniversitesi, Istanbul, 2166
Boğaziçi University, 2166
Boğaziçi University Library, Istanbul, 2161
Bogdan-Vodă University of Cluj-Napoca, 1801
Bogolyubov Institute for Theoretical Physics, Kyiv, 2199
Bogor Agricultural University, 1088
Bogor Agricultural University Library, 1087
Bogor Botanical Gardens, 1085
Bogyoke Aung San Museum, 1514
Bohdan and Varvara Khanenko Museum of Arts, Kyiv, 2203
Boise Art Museum, 2473
Boise Bible College, 2603
Boise Public Library, 2438
Boise State University, 2604
Bókasafn Hafnarfjarðar, 1002
Bókasafn Ísafjarðar, 1002
Bolan Medical College, 1660
Bolinao Branch Museum, 1691
Bolivar County Library System, 2447
Bolivian National Academy of Sciences, 282
Bolivian National Scientific and Technological Documentation Centre, 283
Bologna Center of the Johns Hopkins University Paul H. Nitze School of Advanced International Studies (SAIS), 1207
Bolyai János Matematikai Társulat, Budapest, 974
Bombay Art Society, 1007
Bombay Medical Union, 1008
Bombay Natural History Society (BNHS), 1009

Bombay Textile Research Association, 1019
Bonaire National Marine Park, 1566
Bonanzaville, 2491
Bond University, Queensland, 151
Bone and Joint Research Unit, London, 2255
Bone Creek Museum of Agrarian Art, 2485
Bonn City Archive and Historical Library, 840
Bonnefantenmuseum, 1551
Bonner Springs City Library, 2440
Book Research Institute, Moscow, 1833
Booker Washington Institute, Kakata, 1414
Booktrust, London, 2229
Boone County Library, 2431
Boonslick Regional Library, 2447
Booth Museum of Natural History, 2282
Booth Western Art Museum, 2472
Boothbay Harbor Memorial Library, 2442
Bőr-, Cipő-, és Bőrfeldolgozóipari Tudományos Egyesület, Budapest, 975
Borås City Library, 2061
Borås stadsbibliotek, 2061
Boreskov Institute of Catalysis, Novosibirsk, 1842
Borgarbókasafn Reykjavíkur, 1002
Borgo e Rocca Medioevale, Turin, 1189
Boricua College, 2769
Borissiak Palaeontological Institute of Russian (PIN RAS), Moscow, 1840
Borneo University, 1099
Borno State Library Board, 1593
Borochov Library, Haifa, 1144
Borodino State War and History Museum, 1856
Borough of Poole Libraries, 2279
Borstel Research Centre for Medicine and Biological Sciences, 836
Bose Institute, 1016
Bosnia and Herzegovina Small Animal Veterinary Association, 288
Bosniak Institute—Adil Zulfikarpasic Foundation, 288
Bošnjački Institut—Fondacija Adila Zulfikarpašića, 288
Bosscha Observatory, 1085
Boston Architectural College, 2667
Boston Athenaeum, 2444
Boston College, 2667
Boston College School of Theology and Ministry, 2668
Boston Conservatory, 2668
Boston Graduate School of Psychoanalysis, 2669
Boston Public Library, 2444
Boston University, 2669
Boston University Institute for Dental Research and Education, 2221
Boston University Libraries, 2444
Botanic Garden and Botanical Museum Berlin-Dahlem, 848
Botanic Garden, Copenhagen, 656
Botanical Garden and Botanical Museum, Oslo, 1619
Botanical Garden, Baku, 203
Botanical Garden FEB RAS, Vladivostok, 1861
Botanical Garden Institute of the Academy of Sciences of Moldova, Chişinău, 1491
Botanical Garden named after Gareev A. Z., Bishkek, 1395
Botanical Garden, Nukus, 2985
Botanical Garden, Ulan Bator, 1499
Botanical Gardens, Kingstown, 1906
Botanical Gardens, Lisbon, 1766
Botanical Information Agency of Bavaria, 824
Botanical Institute and Garden of the University of Belgrade, 1922
Botanical Institute, Coimbra, 1766
Botanical Institute, São Paulo, 302
Botanical Museum, 112
Botanical Museum, Helsinki, 721
Botanical Museum, Lund, 2064
Botanical Museum, St Petersburg, 1859
Botanical Society, Coimbra, 1762
Botanical Society of America, 2411
Botanical Society of China, 463

British Institute in Eastern Africa, Nairobi, 1352
British Institute of Florence, 1173
British Institute of International and Comparative Law, 2229
British Institute of Persian Studies, Tehran, 1106
British Institute of Professional Photography, Ware, 2231
British Institute of Radiology, 2237
British Institute of Technology and E-Commerce, 2366
British Interplanetary Society, 2242
British Library, 2271
British Library, Ljubljana, 1965
British Library of Political and Economic Science, 2272
British Medical Association, 2237
British Medical Association Library, 2272
British Museum, 2286
British Mycological Society, 2241
British Nuclear Energy Society, 2242
British Numismatic Society, 2233
British Nutrition Foundation, 2237
British Ornithologists' Union, 2241
British Orthodontic Society, 2237
British Orthopaedic Association, 2237
British Pharmacological Society, 2237
British Postal Museum & Archive, London, 2287
British Psychoanalytical Society, 2238
British Psychological Society, 2243
British Records Association, 2233
British School at Athens, 958
British School at Rome, 1173
British Science Association, 2240
British Society for Middle Eastern Studies, 2244
British Society for Plant Pathology, 2241
British Society for Research on Ageing, 2238
British Society for Rheumatology, 2238
British Society for the History of Mathematics, 2242
British Society for the History of Science, 2240
British Society of Aesthetics, 2243
British Society of Animal Science, 2227
British Society of Gastroenterology, 2238
British Society of Painters, Ilkley, 2232
British Society of Rheology, 2244
British Society of Soil Science, 2227
British Sociological Association, 2244
British Textile Technology Group (BTTG), 2262
British Trust for Ornithology, 2241
British University in Dubai, 2219
British Veterinary Association, 2227
British Watercolour Society, 2232
Brlić House (Ivana Brlić-Mažuranić Memorial), Slavonski Brod, 609
Brno University of Technology, 645
Broadcast Research and Application Center, Ho Chi Minh City, 3013
Brock University, St Catharines, Ontario, 381
Brockway Library, 2436
Bromley College of Further and Higher Education, 2360
Bromley Libraries, 2272
Brontë Society, Haworth, 2236
Bronx Museum, 2489
Brookhaven National Laboratory, Long Island, 2428
Brookings Public Library, 2458
Brookings, Washington, 2418
Brooklands Museum, Weybridge, 2291
Brooklyn Botanic Garden, 2489
Brooklyn College, New York, 2770
Brooklyn Historical Society, 2404
Brooklyn Law School, 2769
Brooklyn Museum, 2489
Brooklyn Public Library, 2451
Brooks Institute, Santa Barbara, 2520
Brooksby Melton College, 2362
Broom's Barn Research Centre, Bury St Edmunds, 2250
Broward College, 2581
Broward County Division of Libraries, 2436
Brown University, 2880

Brown University Library, Providence, 2457
Brownsville Public Library System, 2458
Bruce Museum, 2468
Brücke-Museum, Berlin, 848
Brüder Grimm-Museum Kassel, 854
Bruggemuseum, 261
Brukenthal National Museum, 1797
Brunei Agricultural Research Centre, Department of Agriculture, Brunei, 331
Brunei Darussalam National Accreditation Council, Berakas, 331
Brunei History Centre, 331
Brunei Museum, 331
Brunel University, 2293
Bruning Archaeological Museum, 1680
Brussels Royal Academy of Fine Arts, 273
Brussels Society for Latin Studies, 251
Bryan College, 2889
Bryansk State Agricultural Academy, 1895
Bryansk State Museum of Soviet Fine Arts, 1856
Bryansk State Technical University, 1884
Bryansk State University, 1865
Bryansk Technological Institute, 1899
Bryant & Stratton College, 2769
Bryant University, 2880
Bryn Athyn College, 2851
Bryn Mawr College, 2851
BSI Group (British Standards Institution), 2245
Bu-Ali Sina University, Hamadan, Hamadan, 1109
Bucerius Law School, 935
Bucharest Metropolitan Library, 1791
Bucharest Municipality Museum, 1794
Bucharest Technical University of Civil Engineering, 1822
Bucheon Museum of Bow, 1365
Büchereien Wien, 185
Buckinghamshire County Library, 2264
Buckinghamshire New University, 2293
Bucknell University, 2851
Bucovina National Museum, 1797
Budapest Főváros Levéltára, 978
Budapest University of Technology and Economics, 986
Budapesti Corvinus Egyetem, 985
Budapesti Corvinus Egyetem Entz Ferenc Könyvtár és Levéltár, Budapest, 979
Budapesti Corvinus Egyetem Központi Könyvtár, 979
Budapesti Gazdasági Főiskola, 998
Budapesti Kommunikációs és Üzleti Főiskola, Budapest, 998
Budapesti Műszaki és Gazdaságtudományi Egyetem, 986
Budapesti Műszaki és Gazdaságtudományi Egyetem Országos Műszaki Információs Központ és Könyvtár (BME OMIKK), 979
Budapesti Műszaki Főiskola, 999
Budapesti Tanárképző Intézet, 990
Budapesti Történeti Múzeum, 981
Budavári Mátyás-Templom Egyházművészeti Gyüjteménye, Budapest, 981
Buddhist Academy of Ceylon, 2040
Buddhist Association, Phnom-Penh, 357
Buddhist Institute, Phnom Penh, 358
Buddhist Research Centre, Bangkok, 2136
Budnikov, P. P., All-Russia Research Institute of Construction Materials and Structures, Moscow, 1847
Buena Vista University, 2634
Buffalo and Erie County Public Library System, 2451
Buffalo Bill Historical Center, 2501
Buffalo City Municipal Library Service, 1977
Buffalo Museum of Science, 2489
Buffalo Nations Museum, Banff, 377
Buffalo Society of Natural Sciences, 2410
Build Bright University, 360
Builders' Association, Hanoi, 3010

Building and Road Research Institute, Kumasi, 939
Building Centre, 652
Building Institute, Ulan Bator, 1497
Building Research Centre, Jadiriya, 1123
Building Research Establishment (BRE), Watford, 2262
Building Research Institute, Tsukuba, 1227
Built Environment Research Institute, 2251
Bukbu Library, 1364
Bukhara State University, 2986
Bukkyo University, 1308
Bukovinian State Medical University, Chernivtsi, 2210
Bukura Agricultural College, 1356
Bulacan State University, Malolos, 1694
Bulawayo Polytechnic, 3031
Bulawayo Public Library, Bulawayo, 3029
Bulgarian Academy of Sciences, 333
Bulgarian Association of Criminology, 334
Bulgarian Association of International Law, 334
Bulgarian Astronautical Society, 335
Bulgarian Botanical Society, 334
Bulgarian Comparative Education Society, 333
Bulgarian Geographical Society, 334
Bulgarian Geological Society, 335
Bulgarian Pedagogical Society, 335
Bulgarian Philologists' Society, 334
Bulgarian Philosophical Association, 335
Bulgarian Rectors' Conference, 333
Bulgarian Society for Parasitology, 334
Bulgarian Society of Natural History, 334
Bulgarian Society of Neurosciences, 334
Bulgarian Society of Sports Medicine and Kinesitherapy, 334
Bulgarian Sociological Association, 335
Bulgaria–Romania Interuniversity Europe Centre, 351
Bund Schweizer Architekten, 2085
Bunda College of Agriculture, 1441
Bundelkhand University, 1027
Bundesamt für Landwirtschaft, Bern, 2091
Bundesamt für Meteorologie und Klimatologie (MeteoSchweiz), Zürich, 2090
Bundesamt für Seeschiffahrt und Hydrographie, Hamburg, 836
Bundesamt und Forschungszentrum für Landwirtschaft, Wien, 177
Bundesamt und Forschungszentrum für Wald, 178
Bundesamts für Bauwesen und Raumordnung, Wissenschaftliche Bibliothek, Bad Godesberg, 840
Bundesanstalt für Agrarwirtschaft, 178
Bundesanstalt für Alpenländische Landwirtschaft, Gumpenstein, 178
Bundesanstalt für Geowissenschaften und Rohstoffe (BGR), 836
Bundesanstalt für Materialforschung und -Prüfung, Berlin, 838
Bundesarchiv, Koblenz, 844
Bundesdenkmalamt, Vienna, 173
Bundesforschungsinstitut für Kulturpflanzen Informationszentrum und Bibliothek, Brunswick, 840
Bundesinstitut für Bevölkerungsforschung, Wiesbaden, 837
Bundesstaatliche Paedagogische Bibliothek beim Landesschulrat für Niederösterreich, 184
Bündner Kunstmuseum, Chur, 2096
Buniatian, H., Institute of Biochemistry, 125
Bunin Museum, Orel, 1859
Bunkyo University, Tokyo, 1233
Burapha University, Muang Chonburi, 2138
Burden Neurological Institute, Bristol, 2255
Burdenko Neurosurgical Institute, Moscow, 1836

Bureau Canadien de l'Education Internationale, 368
Bureau de Normalisation (NBN), Brussels, 252
Bureau de Recherches et de Participations Minières (BRPM), Rabat, 1506
Bureau de Recherches Géologiques et Minières (BRGM), Abidjan, 604
Bureau de Recherches Géologiques et Minières (BRGM), Antananarivo, 1438
Bureau de Recherches Géologiques et Minières (BRGM), Dakar, 1918
Bureau de Recherches Géologiques et Minières (BRGM), Jeddah, 1911
Bureau de Recherches Géologiques et Minières (BRGM), Kinshasa, 594
Bureau de Recherches Géologiques et Minières (BRGM), Libreville, 809
Bureau de Recherches Géologiques et Minières (BRGM), Niamey, 1587
Bureau de Recherches Géologiques et Minières (BRGM), Orléans, 748
Bureau de Recherches Géologiques et Minières (BRGM), Ouagadougou, 353
Bureau des Longitudes, Paris, 748
Bureau for Nature Conservation, Zagreb, 608
Bureau international des poids et pesures, 72
Bureau National d'Ethnologie, Port-au-Prince, 968
Bureau of Educational and Cultural Affairs (ECA), Washington, 2394
Bureau of Indian Standards (BIS), 1019
Bureau of International Cultural and Educational Relations, Taipei, 2118
Bureau of Plant Industry, Manila, 1690
Burenie Scientific and Production Co., Krasnodar, 1847
Burg Giebichenstein Kunsthochschule Halle, 936
Burg Giebichenstein University of Art and Design Halle, 936
Burg Museum of Frankenberg, 848
Burgas Free University, 344
Burgas Prof. Assen Zlatarov University, 344
Burgaski Svoboden Universitet, 344
Burgenland Provincial Archives, 183
Burgenland Provincial Library, Eisenstadt, 183
Burgenland Provincial Museum, Eisenstadt, 186
Burgenländische Landesbibliothek, 183
Burgenländisches Landesarchiv, 183
Burgenländisches Landesmuseum, 186
Burgerbibliothek Bern, 2093
Burke County Public Library, 2453
Burke Theological Library, New York, 2452
Burlington College, 2928
Burlington Public Library, 2444
Burnley College, 2360
Burns Cottage and Museum, Ayr, 2281
Burrell Collection, Glasgow, 2284
Burren College of Art, 1139
Bursa Arkeoloji Müzesi, 2162
Bursa Türk ve İslâm Eserleri Müzesi, 2162
Buryat State Agricultural Academy, 1895
Buryat State University, Ulan-Ude, 1865
Busan Digital University, 1385
Busan Gyeongsang College, 1386
Busan Museum, 1365
Busan Museum of Modern Art, 1365
Busan Women's College, 1386
Business History Unit, London, 2253
Business School, Madrid, 2037
Business School Netherlands, 1560
Business School Notenboom—Institute for Business, Hotel and Leisure Management, 1560
Busra Museum, 2116
Bustarfell Museum, 1002
Butler County Law Library, 2454
Butler Institute of American Art, 2491
Butler Public Library, 2449
Butler University, 2625
Butsuri Tansa Gakkai, Tokyo, 1222

Butuan Branch Museum, 1691
Buxoro Davlat Universiteti, 2986
Buxoro Scientific Centre, 2983
Buxoro State Medical Institute, 2988
Buxoro Technological Institute of Food and Light Industry, 2988
Buzău County Museum, 1795
Buzău 'V. Voiculescu' District Library, 1792
Bvumbwe Agricultural Research Station, 1441
Býarbókasavnið, 665
Bydgoskie Towarzystwo Naukowe, 1707
Bydgoszcz Dr W. Bełza Voivodship and Public Municipal Library, 1721
Byggecentrum, Middelfart, 652
Byrd Polar Research Center at the Ohio State University, 2424
BYU Museum of Art, 2498
BYU Museum of Paleontology, 2498
Byurakan Astrophysical Observatory, 125
Byzantine and Christian Museum, Athens, 948

C

C. & O. Vogt-Institut für Hirnforschung, Universität Düsseldorf, 835
C. E. Weldon Public Library, 2458
C. G. Jung Institute Zürich, 2113
C. I. Parhon Institute of Endocrinology, 1787
C. M. Russell Museum, 2484
C. S. Nicolaescu-Plopsor Institute for Research in Social and Human Sciences, 1790
Ca' Rezzonico, Venice, 1190
CAB International (CABI), 42
Cabarrus College of Health Sciences, 2806
Cabell County Public Library, 2461
Cabinet d'Arts Graphiques, Geneva, 2096
Cabinet for Architecture and Urban Planning, Zagreb, 607
Cabinet of Prints and Drawings, 851
Cabinet Office Library, Kampala, 2192
Cabrini College, 2851
Caerphilly Library Service, 2279
Çağ Üniversitesi, 2166
Cagayan de Oro City Public Library, 1690
Cagayan State University, 1694
Cagsawa Branch, 1691
Cahoon Museum of American Art, 2481
CAIJ—Montréal, 377
Cairnmillar Institute—School of Psychology Counselling and Psychotherapy, Camberwell, 170
Cairo Geological Museum, 690
Cairo Museum of Hygiene, 690
Cairo Polytechnic Institute, 694
Cairo University, 691
Cairo University Library, 689
Călăraşi 'Al. Odobescu' District Library, 1792
Calcutta Mathematical Society, 1009
Caldwell College, 2757
Calgary Public Library, 374
California Academy of Sciences, 2410
California African American Museum, 2465
California Baptist University, 2520
California College of the Arts, 2521
California Historical Society, 2404
California Institute of Integral Studies, 2521
California Institute of Technology, 2521
California Institute of the Arts, 2522
California Library Association, 2400
California Lutheran University, 2522
California Maritime Academy, 2522
California Pacific Medical Center Research Institute, 2420
California Palace of the Legion of Honor, 2466
California Polytechnic State University, 2523
California School Library Association, 2400
California State Library, 2431

California State Polytechnic University, Pomona, 2523
California State University, Bakersfield, 2523
California State University, Chico, 2523
California State University, Dominguez Hills, 2523
California State University, East Bay, 2523
California State University, Fresno, 2524
California State University, Fullerton, 2524
California State University, Long Beach, 2524
California State University, Los Angeles, 2524
California State University, Monterey Bay, 2524
California State University, Northridge, 2524
California State University, Sacramento, 2525
California State University, San Bernardino, 2525
California State University, San Marcos, 2525
California State University, Stanislaus, 2525
California State University System, 2523
California University of Pennsylvania, Pennsylvania, 2861
Callatis Archaeological Museum of Mangalia, 1796
Calumet College of St Joseph, 2625
Calvary Bible College and Theological Seminary, Kansas City, 2736
Calvin Center for Christian Scholarship, 2427
Calvin College, 2695
Calvin Theological Seminary, 2695
Cámara de Comercio y Producción de Santo Domingo, Centro de Información y Documentación Comercial, Santo Domingo, 672
'Cámara Pestana' Bacteriological Institute, 1765
Cambodia Development Resource Institute, 357
Cambodian Institute for Cooperation and Peace, 358
Cambodian Institute of Human Rights, 358
Cambodian Mekong University, 360
Cambodian Society of Agriculture, 357
Cambodian University for Specialties, 360
Camborne School of Mines, 2366
Cambrian Archaeological Association, 2233
Cambridge Bibliographical Society, 2229
Cambridge College, 2669
Cambridge International College, Australia, 170
Cambridge Philosophical Society, 2240
Cambridge Programme for Sustainability Leadership, 2248
Cambridge Public Library, 2444
Cambridge Theological Federation, 2366
Cambridge University Botanic Garden, 2258
Cambridge University Institute of Astronomy, 2259
Cambridge University Library, 2266
Cambridgeshire Libraries, Archives and Information, 2267
Camden County Library System, Voorhees, 2450
Camden Leisure and Community Services (Libraries, Arts and Tourism), 2272
Cameron University, 2839
Camões - Institute of Cooperation and Language, I. P., 1761
Camões—Instituto da Cooperação e da Língua, I. P., 1761
Camp Olden Civil War Round Table & Museum, Inc., 2486
Campaign to Protect Rural England (CPRE), 2228

Campbell County Public Library System, 2462
Campbell University, 2806
Campbellsville University, 2643
Campion College, 167
Campion College, Regina, 424
Campion Hall, Oxford, 2348
Campo Agrícola Experimental Río Bravo, 1468
Campo de Santana, Rio de Janeiro, 302
Câmpulung Zonal Museum, 1795
CAMPUS 02 Fachhochschule der Wirtschaft, 199
CAMPUS 02 University for Applied Sciences, 199
Campus Library in Varberg, 2063
Campusbiblioteket i Varberg, 2063
Can Tho University, 3015
Canada Centre for Inland Waters, 374
Canada Council for the Arts, 369
Canada Institute for Scientific and Technical Information, 375
Canada Science and Technology Museum Corporation, Ottawa, 378
Canadian Academic Centre in Italy, 1173
Canadian Academy of Engineering, 372
Canadian Aeronautics and Space Institute, 372
Canadian Agriculture Library, Ottawa, 375
Canadian Association for Anatomy, Neurobiology and Cell Biology, 370
Canadian Association for Latin American and Caribbean Studies, 371
Canadian Association of African Studies, 371
Canadian Association of Geographers, 369
Canadian Association of Law Libraries, 368
Canadian Association of Optometrists, 370
Canadian Association of Physicists, 371
Canadian Authors Association, 370
Canadian Bar Association, 369
Canadian Bureau for International Education, Ottawa, 368
Canadian Cancer Society Research Institute, 373
Canadian Centre for Architecture, 379
Canadian Council for International Co-operation, 368
Canadian Council of Professional Engineers, 372
Canadian Dental Association, 370
Canadian Economics Association, 369
Canadian Education and Training Accreditation Commission (CETAC), Toronto, 367
Canadian Education Association, 369
Canadian Electricity Association, 372
Canadian Federation for the Humanities and Social Sciences, 373
Canadian Film Institute, 369
Canadian Forest Service, 372
Canadian Forestry Association, 368
Canadian Historical Association, 369
Canadian Information Centre for International Credentials (CICIC), 367
Canadian Institute of Chartered Accountants, 369
Canadian Institute of International Affairs, 369
Canadian Institute of Mining, Metallurgy and Petroleum, 372
Canadian Institutes of Health Research, 372
Canadian Library Association, 369
Canadian Linguistic Association, 2236
Canadian Lung Association, 370
Canadian Mathematical Society, 371
Canadian Medical Association, 370
Canadian Meteorological and Oceanographic Society, 371
Canadian Museum of Civilization, 379
Canadian Museum of Nature, 378
Canadian Museums Association, 369
Canadian Music Centre, 369
Canadian Network for Innovation in Education (CNIE), Ottawa, 368

Canadian Paediatric Society, 370
Canadian Pharmacists Association, 370
Canadian Philosophical Association, 371
Canadian Physiological Society, 370
Canadian Phytopathological Society, 370
Canadian Political Science Association, 369
Canadian Psychiatric Association, 370
Canadian Psychological Association, 371
Canadian Public Health Association, 370
Canadian Society for Cellular and Molecular Biology, 370
Canadian Society for Immunology, 371
Canadian Society for Nutritional Sciences, 370
Canadian Society for the Study of Education, 369
Canadian Society of Animal Science, 368
Canadian Society of Biblical Studies, 372
Canadian Society of Biochemistry, Molecular and Cellular Biology, 371
Canadian Society of Landscape Architects, 368
Canadian Society of Microbiologists, 371
Canadian Society of Petroleum Geologists, 371
Canadian University of Dubai, 2219
Canadian Veterinary Medical Association, 368
Çanakkale Onsekiz Mart Üniversitesi, 2166
Canarian Museum, 2009
Canaries Institute of Astrophysics, 2005
Canberra Campus, 144
Canberra Institute of Technology, 167
Cancer Care Ontario, 373
Cancer Institute and Hospital, Beijing, 466
Cancer Institute, Japanese Foundation for Cancer Research, 1226
Cancer Research Center, Mangilao, 2968
Cancer Research Institute, Bratislava, 1951
Cancer Research Institute, Karachi, 1640
Cancer Research Institute, Tomsk, 1839
Cancer Research UK, 2255
Cancer Research UK Beatson Institute for Cancer Research, 2255
Cancer Research UK Jersey, 2391
Cancer Society of Finland, 716
Canillo Community Library, 98
Canisius College, 2769
Çankaya Üniversitesi, 2166
Canning House Library, London, 2272
Cantacuzino Institute, 1787
Canterbury and York Society, 2233
Canterbury Cathedral Archives and Library, 2267
Canterbury Christ Church University, 2294
Canterbury Medical Research Foundation, 1576
Canterbury Museum, Christchurch, 1577
Canton Museum of Art, 2491
Cantonal and County Archive, Travnik, 290
CAP Art Centre and President Osmeña Memorabilia, Cebu City, 1691
CAPC Musée d'Art Contemporain de Bordeaux, 756
Cape Breton University, Sydney, 381
Cape Coast Castle Museum, 940
Cape Fear Museum of History and Science, 2490
Cape Peninsula University of Technology, 1980
Cape Town City Libraries, 1977
Capella University, 2716
Capital City Public Library, Brussels, 258
Capital Library, Beijing, 470
Capital Medical University, Beijing, 480
Capital Normal University, Beijing, 480
Capital University, Columbus, 2826
Capitan Public Library, 2450

Central Agricultural Library of Michał Oczapowski, 1723

Central Agricultural Library, Prague, 635

Central Agricultural Library, Sofia, 341

Central Agricultural Research Institute, Suakoko, 1413

Central Agricultural University, Imphal, Imphal, 1027

Central American Technical Institute, Santa Tecla, 698

Central and Eastern European Network of Quality Assurance Agencies in Higher Education (CEENQA), 57

Central Applications Office, Galway, 1130

Central Archaeological Library, New Delhi, 1020

Central Archive of Modern Records, Warsaw, 1722

Central Archive of the Ministry of Labour and Immigration, 2007

Central Archive of the Teutonic Order, Vienna, 185

Central Archives for the History of the Jewish People, Jerusalem, 1145

Central Archives of China, 470

Central Arid Zone Research Institute, Jodhpur, 1012

Central Army Museum, Yogyakarta, 1088

Central Asian Plague Prevention Research Institute, Almaty, 1340

Central Baptist College, Conway, 2516

Central Baptist Theological Seminary, 2639

Central Bedfordshire Libraries, 2265

Central Bible College, Springfield, 2736

Central Biomedical Library, Yangon, 1514

Central Boiler and Turbine Institute, St Petersburg, 1847

Central Botanical Garden, Ashgabat, 2188

Central Botanical Garden, Minsk, 240

Central Building Research Institute, Roorkee, 1010

Central Bureau for Genealogy, The Hague, 1529

Central Bureau of Statistics, The Hague, 1535

Central Caribbean Marine Institute, Grand Cayman, 2387

Central Catholic Library, Dublin, 1133

Central Chabad Lubavitch Library and Archive Center, 2451

Central China Normal University (Huazhong Normal University), 483

Central China Teachers' University Library, 472

Central Christian College of Kansas, 2639

Central Christian College of the Bible, Moberly, 2736

Central City Library named after M. Auezov, 1341

Central College, Pella, 2634

Central Connecticut State University, 2556

Central Conservatory of Music, Beijing, 484

Central Cotton Research Institute, Sindh, 1639

Central Design and Research Institute of the Standard and Experimental Design of Livestock Units for the Production of Milk, Beef and Pork, Moscow, 1847

Central Diesels Research and Development Institute, St Petersburg, 1847

Central Documentation and Library of the Ministry of Information, Jakarta, 1086

Central Drug Research Institute, Lucknow, 1010

Central Economic Library, Ljubljana, 1965

Central Economics and Mathematics Institute, Moscow, 1833

Central Economics Research Institute, Moscow, 1833

Central Electrochemical Research Institute, Karaikudi, 1010

Central Electronics Engineering Research Institute, Pilani, 1011

Central Electronics Research Institute, Moscow, 1847

Central European University, 998

Central Fisheries Research Institute, Chilanga, 3024

Central Food Technological Research Institute, Mysore, 1011

Central Forest Library, Peshawar, 1643

Central Geological Survey, Taipei, 2120

Central Glass and Ceramic Research Institute, Kolkata, 1011

Central Health Information and Technology Institute, Hanoi, 3014

Central Health Laboratories, Cairo, 688

Central Hindi Directorate, 1007

Central Inland Fisheries Research Institute, Barrackpore, 1012

Central Institute for Labour Protection—National Research Institute, 1718

Central Institute for Leprosy Research, Jakarta, 1085

Central Institute for Meteorology and Geodynamics, Vienna, 181

Central Institute for Research on Cotton Technology, Mumbai, 1019

Central Institute for the Restoration and Conservation of Archives and Libraries, 1164

Central Institute of Advanced Qualification of Teachers, Dushanbe, 2128

Central Institute of Aviation Engines, Moscow, 1847

Central Institute of Civil Service, 1517

Central Institute of Economic Management, Hanoi, 3011

Central Institute of Experimental Analysis, Pyongsong, 1360

Central Institute of Fisheries Education, Mumbai, 1073

Central Institute of Higher Tibetan Studies, Varanasi, 1073

Central Institute of Indian Languages, Mysore, 1080

Central Institute of Medicinal and Aromatic Plants, Lucknow, 1011

Central Institute of Mining and Fuel Research, Dhanbad, 1011

Central Institute of Ophthalmology, Hanoi, 3012

Central Institute of Technology, Upper Hutt, 1584

Central Institute of the Union Catalogue of Italian Libraries and Bibliographical Information, 1181

Central Institute of Traumatology and Orthopaedics, Moscow, 1836

Central Kazakhstan Scientific and Research Institute of Agriculture, 1339

Central Laboratory of Applied Physics, Plovdiv, 340

Central Laboratory of Geodesy, Sofia, 339

Central Laboratory of Mechatronics and Instrumentation, Sofia, 340

Central Laboratory of Molecular Biology, Preparatory Office, Taipei, 2119

Central Laboratory of Optical Storage and the Processing of Information, Sofia, 339

Central Laboratory of Photoprocesses 'Acad. Jordan Malinowski', 339

Central Laboratory of Physico-Chemical Mechanics, Sofia, 340

Central Laboratory of Seismic Mechanics and Earthquake Engineering, Sofia, 341

Central Laboratory of Socio-Economic Measurements, Moscow, 1833

Central Laboratory of Solar Energy & New Energy Sources, Sofia, 339

Central Leather Research Institute, Chennai, 1011

Central Leprosy Teaching and Research Institute, Chengalpattu, 1015

Central Library, 1792

Central Library and Archive of the Leibniz Institute for Regional Geography, 844

Central Library and Archives of the University of West Hungary, 980

Central Library and Documentation Centre of Shahid Beheshti University, 1108

Central Library and Documentation Centre of University of Tehran, 1108

Central Library, Bahawalpur, 1642

Central Library, Bandung Institute of Technology, 1086

Central Library for Science and Technology, Hanoi, 3014

Central Library for the County of North Jutland, 654

Central Library Leisure and Culture Dundee, 2268

Central Library of Cantabria, 2007

Central Library of Labour and Social Security, Warsaw, 1723

Central Library of Petroleum-Gas University of Ploiești, 1793

Central Library of Politehnica University of Bucharest, 1791

Central Library of St Lucia, 1905

Central Library of Semmelweis University, 980

Central Library of Silesian University of Technology, 1721

Central Library of the Academy of Economic Studies, Bucharest, 1791

Central Library of the Academy of Medical Sciences, Moscow, 1853

Central Library of the Azerbaijan Academy of Sciences, 204

Central Library of the Bulgarian Academy of Sciences, Sofia, 341

Central Library of the Diocese of Regensburg, 846

Central Library of the European Commission, 258

Central Library of the Georgian Academy of Sciences, 815

Central Library of the Gheorghe Ionescu-Șișești Academy of Agricultural and Forestry Sciences, 1791

Central Library of the Gr. T. Popa University of Medicine and Pharmacy in Iași, 1792

Central Library of the Ministry of Economy and Finance, Madrid, 2007

Central Library of the Palace of Justice, Vienna, 185

Central Library of Trinidad and Tobago, 2152

Central Library, Vadodara, 1020

Central Library—Chapingo Autonomous University, 1470

Central Library—University of Peshawar, 1643

Central Luzon State University, 1694

Central Marine Research and Design Institute Ltd (CNIIMF), St Petersburg, 1847

Central Mechanical Engineering Research Institute, Durgapur, 1011

Central Medical Library, 1723

Central Medical Library, Bowshar, 1634

Central Medical Library, Faculty of Medicine, Ljubljana, 1965

Central Medical Library, Lagos, 1593

Central Medical Library—MU Sofia, Sofia, 341

Central Medical Veterinary Research Institute, Sofia, 335

Central Metallurgical Research and Development Institute, Cairo, 688

Central Methodist University, Fayette, 2737

Central Michigan University, 2695

Central Military Library, Bandung, 1087

Central Military Library, Madrid, 2007

Central Mindanao University, 1694

Central Mississippi Regional Library System, 2447

Central Municipal Library, Lisbon, 1768

Central Museum, Nagpur, 1022

Central Museum of Armed Forces, Moscow, 1857

Central Museum of Aviation and Cosmonautics, Moscow, 1857

Central Museum of Railway Transport of Russia, 1859

Central Museum of Textiles, 1724

Central National Library of Montenegro, 1503

Central Naval Library, Madrid, 2007

Central Naval Museum, St Petersburg, 1859

Central Ostrobothnia Polytechnic, 736

Central Paper Research Institute, Pravdinsky, 1847

Central Penn College, 2854

Central Philippine University, 1695

Central Public Library Dhaka, 216

Central Research and Design Institute of Dwellings, Moscow, 1832

Central Research and Design Institute of Fuel Apparatus and Vehicle and Tractor Engines and Stationary Engines, St Petersburg, 1847

Central Research and Design Institute of Town Planning, Moscow, 1832

Central Research Institute for Animal Sciences Research and Development, Bogor, 1084

Central Research Institute for Machine Building, Korolev, 1847

Central Research Institute for the Evaluation of Working Capacity and Vocational Assistance to Disabled Persons, Moscow, 1836

Central Research Institute of Coating Materials and Artificial Leathers, Moscow, 1847

Central Research Institute of Dermatology and Venereal Diseases, Moscow, 1836

Central Research Institute of Engineering Technology, Moscow, 1847

Central Research Institute of Epidemiology, Moscow, 1836

Central Research Institute of Gastroenterology, Moscow, 1836

Central Research Institute of Geological Prospecting for Base and Precious Metals, Moscow, 1847

Central Research Institute of Roentgenology and Radiology, St Petersburg, 1836

Central Research Institute of Telecommunications, Moscow, 1847

Central Research Institute of the Ministry of Defence, Bolshevo, 1847

Central Research Institute, Solan, 1015

Central Research Laboratory for the Introduction of Personal Computers, Moscow, 1847

Central Research Library of the National Academy of Sciences of the Kyrgyz Republic, 1395

Central Research Station for Plant Cultivation on Sand, Dolj, 1785

Central Research Station for Tobacco Growing and Industrialization, Bucharest, 1786

Central Rice Research Institute, Cuttack, 1013

Central Road Research Institute, New Delhi, 1011

Central Roman-German Museum–Research Museum for Prehistory and Early History, 855

Central Saint Martins College of Art and Design, London, 2355

Central Salt and Marine Chemicals Research Institute, Bhavnagar, 1011

Central School of Speech and Drama, London, 2365

Central Scientific Agricultural Library of the Russian Academy of Agricultural Sciences, 1853

Central Scientific Archive of the National Academy of Sciences of Belarus, Minsk, 242

Central Scientific Instruments Organization, Chandigarh, 1011

Central Scientific Library 'Andrei Lupan' of the Academy of Sciences of Moldova, 1492

Centre for Applied Research in Agricultural Engineering, Ho Chi Minh City, 3011

Centre for Applied Research in Educational Technologies (CARET), Cambridge, 2252

Centre for Arab Unity Studies, Beirut, 1407

Centre for Archaeological Research of Montenegro, 1503

Centre for Architectural Studies, Sofia, 337

Centre for Arid Zone Studies, Bangor, 2259

Centre for Art Studies, 84

Centre for ASEAN Studies, 254

Centre for Asia Minor Studies, Athens, 946

Centre for Asian and African Studies, México, 1468

Centre for Asian Documentation, Kolkata, 1021

Centre for Astronomy of Heidelberg University, 898

Centre for Atmospheric Science, Cambridge, 2248

Centre for Attention Perception and Motor Control, Bangor, 2261

Centre for Automotive Management, Loughborough, 2262

Centre for Aviation and Aerospace, Hsinchu, 2120

Centre for Basic Research, Kampala, 2192

Centre for Bhutan Studies, 279

Centre for Biblical Studies, Exeter, 2261

Centre for Biomedical Imaging, 2092

Centre for Brain Ageing and Vitality, 2255

Centre for Business Research, Cambridge, 2248

Centre for Cellular and Molecular Biology, Hyderabad, 1011

Centre for Chemical and Biological Analysis, 1665

Centre for Chemistry and Petrochemistry Research and Development, Buenos Aires, 110

Centre for Child and Family Research, Loughborough, 2255

Centre for City and Regional Studies, Hull, 2253

Centre for Civil Society, London, 2248

Centre for Climate Change, Environment, Energy and Sustainable Development (CEESD), 710

Centre for Cognitive Ageing and Cognitive Epidemiology, 2255

Centre for Comparative Criminology and Criminal Justice, Bangor, 2251

Centre for Computational Chemistry, Bangor, 2262

Centre for Conflict and Peace Studies, Kabul, 80

Centre for Construction Materials, State Material-Testing Foundation-Faculty and Institute of Material Science, 839

Centre for Construction Research and Development, Buenos Aires, 110

Centre for Contemporary British History, London, 2253

Centre for Crime and Justice Studies (ISTD), London, 2261

Centre for Dance Research, London, 2253

Centre for Defence Studies, London, 2327

Centre for Democracy and Development, London and Abuja, 48

Centre for Development in Primary Health Care, 1665

Centre for Development Information, Colombo, 2041

Centre for Development Innovation, Wageningen, 1534

Centre for Development Studies, Caracas, 3002

Centre for Development Studies (CDS), 1532

Centre for Documentation and Information, Chamber of Deputies, Brazil, 304

Centre for Documentation and Information, Chinese Academy of Social Sciences, Beijing, 470

Centre for Documentation and Research, Abu Dhabi, 2218

Centre for Drug Research, Craiova, 1787

Centre for Dungan Studies, Bishkek, 1394

Centre for Early Modern Studies, Exeter, 2248

Centre for Ecological and Evolutionary Studies (CEES), Haren, 1541

Centre for Ecological–Noosphere Studies, Yerevan, 125

Centre for Ecology & Hydrology, Crowmarsh Gifford, 2258

Centre for Economic and Social Research, 1172

Centre for Economic Development Studies, 579

Centre for Economic Performance, London, 2251

Centre for Economic Studies, México, 1468

Centre for Economic Study of Innovation and Technology, 257

Centre for Educational and Psychological Research, Baghdad, 1123

Centre for Educational Research and Development, Lincoln, 2253

Centre for Educational Research and Documentation, Madrid, 2004

Centre for Educational Research, London, 2253

Centre for Educational Studies, Hull, 2253

Centre for Educational Studies, México, 1468

Centre for Elections, Media and Parties (CEMaP), 2251

Centre for Electrical Power Engineering, Glasgow, 2262

Centre for Electromagnetic Materials Research (CEMR), Exeter, 2259

Centre for Electronics and Computer Science Research and Development, Buenos Aires, 109

Centre for Electroplating and Superficial Processes Research and Development, Buenos Aires, 110

Centre for Energy and Environment, Exeter, 2260

Centre for Energy, Environmental and Technological Research, Madrid, 2005

Centre for Energy Studies, Dhaka, 215

Centre for Engineering and Design Education, Loughborough, 2262

Centre for English Language Studies, Birmingham, 2254

Centre for Enterprise and Regional Development, Bangor, 2248

Centre for Entrepreneurship Development and Consultancy Services, Moratuwa, 2042

Centre for Environmental and Resource Management, Dhaka, 215

Centre for Environmental Engineering Research and Development, Buenos Aires, 109

Centre for Environmental Management of Degraded Ecosystem, 1063

Centre for Environmental Sciences, Diepenbeek, 255

Centre for Environmental Studies, Loughborough, 2260

Centre for Ethics, Antwerp, 256

Centre for European and International Business Education and Research, 254

Centre for European Governance, Exeter, 2251

Centre for European Legal Studies, Exeter, 2251

Centre for European Policy Studies, Brussels, 253

Centre for European Studies (CES), Enschede, 1537

Centre for European Studies, Sofia, 342

Centre for Experimental Consumer Psychology, Bangor, 2261

Centre for Flexible Education (U-Vett), 1616

Centre for Food Crops Research and Development, 1084

Centre for Gender and Development Studies, 237

Centre for Genetic Engineering and Biotechnology of Cuba, 616

Centre for Genomics and Biotechnology, 1766

Centre for Geographical Research, Tiranë, 85

Centre for Geological Survey, Bandung, 1086

Centre for GIS, 1781

Centre for Grammar, Cognition and Typology, Antwerp, 254

Centre for Gymnastics Research, Loughborough, 2248

Centre for Hazard & Risk Management, Loughborough, 2260

Centre for Health Studies, Nuuk, 668

Centre for Healthcare Operations Improvement & Research (CHOIR), Enschede, 1538

Centre for Higher Education Policy Studies (CHEPS), Enschede, 1537

Centre for Historical and Ethnological Studies, Ferreira do Zêzere, 1765

Centre for Historical Research and Documentation on War and Contemporary Society, 258

Centre for History and European Civilization, Iaşi, 1787

Centre for Human Rights and Humanitarian Law, 1665

Centre for Industrial Information and Statistics, 111

Centre for Industrial Safety and Health Technology, Hsinchu, 2120

Centre for Information and Library Educational Science, Hanoi, 3011

Centre for Information on Natural Resources, Santiago, 450

Centre for Innovation Research, Tilburg, 1532

Centre for Innovative and Collaborative Construction Engineering, Loughborough, 2262

Centre for Integrative Medicine—Centre for Advanced Studies in Health Sciences, Lisbon, 1766

Centre for Interdisciplinary Studies of Mountain and Hill Environment (CISMHE), 1063

Centre for International Cooperation, Amsterdam, 1537

Centre for International Cooperation (CIS), Amsterdam, 1535

Centre for International Economics and Shipping, 1618

Centre for International Education and Research, Birmingham, 2253

Centre for International Forestry Research (CIFOR), Sindangbarang, 43

Centre for International Management and Development, 253

Centre for International Mobility, Helsinki, 713

Centre for International Studies, London, 2253

Centre for Internet Computing, Hull, 2262

Centre for Islamic Architecture, 289

Centre for Islamic Studies, 2160

Centre for Jerusalem Studies, 1665

Centre for Language Studies, Nijmegen, 1538

Centre for Latin American Research and Documentation, 1545

Centre for Law, Administration and Society, Groningen, 1536

Centre for Leadership Studies, Exeter, 2248

Centre for Learning Development, Hull, 2253

Centre for Leather Research and Development, Buenos Aires, 109

Centre for Leather, Rubber and Plastic (CLRP), Yoogyakarta, 1086

Centre for Legal History Research, Exeter, 2251

Centre for Legal Procedure and Litigation, Tilburg, 1535

Centre for Linguistic and Literary Studies, 1469

Centre for Lower Alentejo Studies, 1764

Centre for Magnetic Resonance Investigations, Hull, 2262

Centre for Management Development, Ikeja, 1592

Centre for Manuscript Genetics, Antwerp, 254

Centre for Manx Studies, 2390

Centre for Marine and Environmental Research, Faro, 1765

Centre for Maritime Historical Studies, Exeter, 2260

Centre for Mathematical and Scientific Instruction, 910

Centre for Mathematics, 1766

Centre for Mathematics and Computer Science, Amsterdam, 1540

Centre for Measurement Standards, Hsinchu, 2120

Centre for Meat Research and Development, Buenos Aires, 109

Centre for Mechanics Research and Development, Buenos Aires, 110

Centre for Mechanisms of Human Toxicity, Leicester, 2255

Centre for Medical Education (CME), Dhaka, 214

Centre for Medical History, Exeter, 2255

Centre for Medieval Studies, Exeter, 2254

Centre for Mediterranean Studies, Exeter, 2253

Centre for Metaphysics and Culture, 256

Centre for Methods and Techniques Research and Development for Small and Medium-Size Industries, Buenos Aires, 109

Centre for Metrology and Accreditation, 719

Centre for Migration and Intercultural Studies, 253

Centre for Mobile Communications Research, Loughborough, 2262

Centre for Modern Art—Calouste Gulbenkian Foundation, 1770

Centre for Molecular Biology of Heidelberg University, 898

Centre for Molecular Genetics, Karachi, 1640

Centre for National Culture, Accra, 938

Centre for National Economic Studies, 960

Centre for Natural Resources and the Environment, Lisboa, 1766

Centre for Neuroscience and Cell Biology, Coimbra, 1765

Centre for New Electronic Architecture, Bucharest, 1786

Centre for North-East Asian Studies, Ulan Bator, 1497

Centre for Oceanographic and Fisheries Research, Algiers, 90

Centre for Olympic Studies & Research, Loughborough, 2248

Centre for Optical Research, La Plata, 107

Centre for Packaging Research and Development, Buenos Aires, 109

Centre for Particle Characterization and Analysis, Paisley, 2263

Centre for Pathology and Pathobiology, Chişinău, 1491

Centre for Patristic Research, 1542

Centre for Pavement Engineering Education Inc., Box Hill North, 170

Centre for Peace Studies, 1616

Centre for Petrology and Geochemistry, Lisboa, 1765

Centre for Pharmacological Studies and Botany, Buenos Aires, 107

Centre for Philosophical Psychology, Antwerp, 256

Centre for Philosophical Research, Sarajevo, 289

Centre for Philosophy of Natural and Social Science, London, 2260

Centre for Philosophy of Technology and Engineering Science, 1542

Centre for Physics Research and Development, Buenos Aires, 110

Centre for Plant Ecophysiology, Buenos Aires, 107

Centre for Plasma Physics and Radiation Technology, Eindhoven, 1543

Centre for Political and Constitutional Studies, Madrid, 1997

Centre for Pollution Control Technology, Hsinchu, 2120

Centre for Population Biology, Ascot, 2258

Centre for Population Studies, Sofia, 337

Centre for Prehistoric Studies, 1173

Centre for Pre-School Education, Moscow, 1834

Centre for Professional Legal Studies, Glasgow, 2251

Centre for Quality Assessment in Higher Education—CQAHE, 1421

Centre for Quality Assurance and Accreditation for Higher Education and Training Institutions, 1415

Centre for Radiation Science and Technology, 1665

Centre for Regional Cooperation for Adult Education in Latin America and the Caribbean, 1465

Centre for Renewable Energy Systems Technology, Loughborough, 2260

Centre for Research and Advanced Studies, National Polytechnic Institute, 1469

Centre for Research and Development for the Rational Use of Energy, Buenos Aires, 110

Centre for Research and Technical Assistance to Food Processing Industry, Villa Regina, 109

Centre for Research and Technological Development of the Plastics Industry, Buenos Aires, 109

Centre for Research and Technological Development of the Rubber Industry, Buenos Aires, 110

Centre for Research for National Regulations on Civil Work Safety, Buenos Aires, 109

Centre for Research in Applied Economics for Development, Algiers, 90

Centre for Research in Architecture and Town Planning, Algiers, 90

Centre for Research in Ecology, London, 2260

Centre for Research in Environmental History, Stirling, 2260

Centre for Research in Evolutionary Anthropology, London, 2261

Centre for Research in Film and Audiovisual Cultures, London, 2253

Centre for Research in Finance and Management, 253

Centre for Research in Greek Philosophy, Athens, 947

Centre for Research in History and Theory, London, 2254

Centre for Research in Human Rights, London, 2248

Centre for Research in Islamic Education, Mecca, 1911

Centre for Research in Philosophical and Cultural Anthropology, Buenos Aires, 107

Centre for Research in Plant Sciences in Agriculture, 1153

Centre for Research in Polish History, Stirling, 2254

Centre for Research in Psychology and Sociology, Havana, 617

Centre for Research in Renaissance Studies, London, 2254

Centre for Research in Science and Engineering Geology, Caparica, 1765

Centre for Research in Social and Environmental Accounting, 2005

Centre for Research in Social Policy, Loughborough, 2261

Centre for Research in the Arts, Social Sciences and Humanities, Cambridge, 2253

Centre for Research in the History of Greek Law, 946

Centre for Research into Controlling Harmful Organisms, San Miguel de Tucumán, 107

Centre for Research into Economics and Finance in Southern Africa, London, 2251

Centre for Research into Geological Resources, Buenos Aires, 107

Centre for Research into Solar Energy, Santiago de Cuba, 617

Centre for Research on Biological Resources of the Land, Algiers, 90

Centre for Research on Technologies for the Industrialization of Food Production, Buenos Aires, 109

Centre for Research on Technologies for the Industrialization of Grain Production, Buenos Aires, 109

Centre for Research on the Elderly, 1617

Centre for Research on the Epidemiology of Disasters, 255

Centre for Rural Policy Research, Exeter, 2250

Centre for Russian and East European Studies, Birmingham, 2253

Centre for Sami Health Research, 1616

Centre for Scientific and Technical Information and Documentation, Tiranë, 85

Centre for Scientific and Technical Information and for Technological Transfer, Algiers, 90

Centre for Scientific Information in the Social Sciences, Chişinău, 1492

Centre for Scottish Cultural Studies, Glasgow, 2254

Centre For Service Research, Exeter, 2248

Centre for Social Development, Phnom-Penh, 358

Centre for Social Investment, 898

Centre for Social Pedagogics, Moscow, 1834

Centre for Social Policy Research and Development, Bangor, 2255

Centre for Social Studies, Coimbra, 1764

Centre for Socio-Economic Documentation and Publications, Tehran, 1108

Centre for Sociology of Law, 256

Centre for South Asian Studies, Lahore, 1639

Centre for South West Writing, 2254

Centre for South-Western Historical Studies, Exeter, 2254

Centre for Special Pollutants Research and Development, Buenos Aires, 110

Centre for Strategic and International Studies, Jakarta, 1085

Centre for Studies and Research in International Law and International Relations, The Hague, 61

Centre for Studies in Languages, Linguistics and Literature, 1765

Centre for Studies in Photosynthesis and Biochemistry, Rosario, 107

Centre for Studies in Security and Diplomacy, Birmingham, 2251

Centre for Studies on Technologies in Distributed Intelligence Systems (TeDIS), 1172

Centre for Studies on the Archaeological Heritage of Prehistory, 2005

Centre for Sustainable Design, Farnham, 2260

Centre for Swedish Folk Music and Jazz Research, 2063

Centre for Synthetic Biology, Groningen, 1540

Centre for Technical Geoscience, Delft, 1537

Centre for Technical Studies and Research, Gipuzkoa, 2005

Centre for Telematics and Information Technology, 1543

Centre for Textile Research and Development, Buenos Aires, 110

Centre for the Advanced Study of Religion in Wales, Bangor, 2261

Centre for the Albanian Encyclopedical Dictionary, 85

Centre for the Chemistry of Drugs—All-Russia Chemical and Pharmaceutical Research Institute, Moscow, 1836

Centre for the Coordination of Studies and Research on the Infrastructure and Facilities of the Ministry of Higher Education and Scientific Research, Algiers, 90

Centre for the Development of Scientific Equipment and Instruments, Havana, 617

Centre for the Economics of Education, London, 2253

Centre for the Environment, Fisheries and Aquaculture Science (CEFAS), Lowestoft, 2250

Centre for the Evaluation of Vaccination, Antwerpen-Wilrijk, 254

Centre for the Industrial and Service Economy, Bucharest, 1786

Centre for the Preservation of Historical Documentary Collections, Moscow, 1853

Centre for the Preservation of the Reserve Collection, Yalutorovsk, 1855

Centre for the Research and Technology of Agro-Environmental and Biological Sciences, 1764

Centre for the Research of Greek and Latin Literature, Athens, 947

Centre for the Standardisation of Terminology, Bangor, 2254

Centre for the Study of 15th-Century Painting in the Southern Netherlands and the Principality of Liège, 254

Centre for the Study of Democracy (CSD), Enschede, 1535

Centre for the Study of Human Rights, London, 2248

Centre for the Study of International Relations, Stockholm, 2055

Centre for the Study of Law and Governance, New Delhi, 1013

Centre for the Study of Marketing Problems, Chişinău, 1491

Centre for the Study of Migration, London, 2261

Centre for the Study of Nationality Problems, Moscow, 1833

Centre for the Study of Public Policy, Glasgow, 2251

Centre for the Study of the Christian Church, Exeter, 2261

Centre for the Study of the History of Jews in Romania, 1787

Centre for the Study of War, State and Society, Exeter, 2248

Centre for the Understanding of Pyrenean Culture, 97

Centre for the Wood Industry and Related Research and Development, Hurlingham, 109

Centre for Thematic Environmental Networks (TEN), 1172

Centre for Theoretical and Computational Chemistry, 1617

Centre for Theoretical Physics, Groningen, 1540

Centre for Theoretical Study at Charles University, 633

Centre for Transboundary Legal Development, Tilburg, 1535

Centre for Transport Studies, Enschede, 1544

Centre for Volcanology and Geological Risk Assessment, Ponta Delgada, 1765

Centre for Water Systems (CWS), Exeter, 2260

Centre for Women's and Gender Research, 1617

Centre for Youth Ministry, Swindon, 2366

Centre Français de Droit Comparé, Paris, 791

Centre Historique des Archives Nationales, Paris, 752

Centre IFREMER de Brest, 749

Centre IFREMER de Nantes, 749

Centre IFREMER de Toulon, 749

Centre IFREMER du Pacifique, 801

Centre IFREMER Océanologique du Pacifique, 749

Centre Interdisciplinaire d'étude des Religions et de la Laïcité, 256

Centre Interfacultaire Bernoulli, 2093

Centre Interfacultaire de Gérontologie, 2092

Centre International d'Etudes Monétaires et Bancaires, 49

Centre International d'Etudes Pédagogiques de Sèvres, 747

Centre International d'Etudes Romanes, Tournus, 741

Centre International de Formation de l'OIT, 48

Centre International de Hautes Etudes Agronomiques Méditerranéennes, 44

Centre International de Recherche en Aménagement Linguistique, 373

Centre International de Recherche sur le Cancer, 65

Centre International de Recherches Médicales de Franceville, 808

Centre International du Film pour l'Enfance et la Jeunesse, 45

Centre International pour la Formation et les Echanges en Géosciences (CIFEG), Orléans, 748

Centre Interuniversitaire de Mécanique (UNIMECA), 763

Centre IRD d'Orléans, 748

Centre IRD de Bondy, 748

Centre IRD de Bretagne, 748

Centre IRD de Montpellier, 748

Centre IRD de Sète, 748

Centre Ivoirien de Recherches et d'Etudes Juridiques, 603

Centre Mondial de la Paix, des Libertés et des Droits de l'Homme, Verdun, 761

Centre National d'Astronomie, d'Astrophysique et de Géophysique (CNAAG), Algiers, 90

Centre National d'Education, Yaoundé, 364

Centre National d'Etudes et de Recherches pour l'Aménagement du Territoire (CNERAT), Algiers, 90

Centre National d'Etudes Spatiales (CNES), Paris, 750

Centre National d'Hydrométéorologie, Bujumbura, 355

Centre National de Documentation et de Recherche en Pédagogie (CNDRP), Algiers, 90

Centre National de Documentation et de Recherche Scientifique (CNDRS), 592

Centre National de Documentation, Rabat, 1506

Centre National de Documentation Scientifique et Technique (CNDST), Dakar, 1918

Centre National de la Recherche Scientifique (CNRS), Paris, 746

Centre National de la Recherche Scientifique et Technologique, Bamako, 1455

Centre National de la Recherche Scientifique et Technologique (CENAREST), Libreville, 808

Centre National de la Recherche Scientifique et Technologique, Ouagadougou, 353

Centre National de l'Informatique, Tunis, 2155

Centre National de Littérature, Mersch, 1430

Centre National de Recherche Agronomique (CNRA), Abidjan, 603

Centre National de Recherche Appliquée au Développement Rural (CENRADERU), Antananarivo, 1438

Centre National de Recherche sur les Zones Arides (CNRZA), Algiers, 90

Centre National de Recherches Agronomiques (CNRA), Bambey, 1918

Centre National de Recherches et d'Application des Géosciences (CRAG), Algiers, 90

Centre National de Recherches Fruitières, Bamako, 1455

Centre National de Recherches Météorologiques, Toulouse, 748

Centre National de Recherches Préhistoriques Anthropologiques et Historiques, Algiers, 90

Centre National de Recherches Zootechniques, Bamako, 1455

Centre National de Traduction et de Terminologie Arabe (CNTTA), Algiers, 90

Centre National des Archives, Ouagadougou, 353

Centre National du Livre, Paris, 742

Centre National du Microfilm, St-Gilles-du-Gard, 752

Centre National pour la Recherche Scientifique et Technique, Rabat, 1506

Centre of Advanced International Studies, Exeter, 2253

Centre of African Studies, Cambridge, 2253

Centre of Behavioural and Cognitive Sciences, Allahabad, 1018

Centre of Biomedical Magnetic Resonance, Lucknow, 1019

Centre of Biotechnology and Microbiology, Peshawar, 1640

Centre of Central Asian Studies, Srinagar, 1018

Centre of Coastal Applied Ecology, Corrientes, 107

Centre of Commonwealth Studies, 2248

Centre of Documentation and Studies on Ancient Egypt, Cairo, 689

Centre of Documentation and Studies on the History of Madrid, 2004

Centre of Economic Information and Documentation, Bucharest, 1792

Centre of Endocrinological Research, Buenos Aires, 107

Centre of Environmental and Waste Management, Paisley, 2260

Centre of Excellence for Women's Studies, Karachi, 1641

Centre of Excellence in Marine Biology, Karachi, 1640

Centre of Experimental Seismology, Central Station, Chişinău, 1492

Centre of Financial and Monetary Research 'Victor Slăvescu', 1786

Centre of Geographical Studies of the University of Lisbon, 1764

Centre of Hydraulic Research, Tiranë, 85

Centre of International and European Economic Law, Thessaloniki, 946

Centre of Labour Study and Research, Buenos Aires, 107

Centre of Latin American Studies, Cambridge, 2253

Centre of Medical Genetics, Yerevan, 125

Centre of Natural Sciences, Kabul, 80

Centre of Physiotherapy and Rehabilitation, Sofia, 338

Centre of Planning and Economic Research, Athens, 946

Centre of Polymer and Carbon Materials PAS, Zabrze, 1717

Centre of Research on Psychology in Somatic Diseases (CoRPS), Tilburg, 1538

Centre of Rock Art, Kratovo, 1434

Centre of Science Methodology and Social Research, Bishkek, 1394

Centre of Seismology and Geomagnetism, Ulan Bator, 1498

Centre of South Asian Studies, Cambridge, 2253

Centre of Traumatology, Orthopaedics, Burns and Radiology, 125

Centre PEN Suisse Romand, 2088

Centre pour le Développement de l'Horticulture (CDH), Dakar, 1918

Centre Régional Africain de Technologie, 1918

Centre Régional de Recherche et de Documentation pour le Développement Culturel (CREDEC), Dakar, 1918

Centre Régional de Recherche et de Documentation sur les Traditions Orales et pour le Développement des Langues Africaines (CERDOTOLA), Yaoundé, 364

Centre Régional de Recherche Sud-Bénin, 277

Centre Saint-Augustin, Dakar, 2996

Centre Scientifique de Monaco, 1495

Centre Social et Éducatif, Bujumbura, 356

Centre Technique Forestier Tropical, Antananarivo, 1438

Centre Technique Forestier Tropical, Section Gabon, 808

Centre Universitaire d'Ecologie Humaine et des Sciences de l'Environnement, Carouge, 2093

Centre Universitaire d'El-Tarf, 94

Centre Universitaire de Bordj Bou Arréridj, 94

Centre Universitaire de Bouira, 94

Centre Universitaire de Formation et de Recherche Jean-François Champollion, 762

Centre Universitaire de Ghardaia, 94

Centre Universitaire de Khenchela, 94

Centre Universitaire de Recherches, d'Etudes et de Réalisations (CURER), Constantine, 90

Centre Universitaire de Souk-Ahras, 95

Centre Universitaire d'El Oued, 94

Centre Universitaire Khemis Miliana, 95

Centre Wallon de Recherches Agronomiques, 253

Centres de Recherche Rizicole, Kankan, 1455

Centro Agronómico Tropical de Investigación y Enseñanza (CATIE), Turrialba, 599

Centro Amazónico de Antropología y Aplicación Práctica (CAAAP), Lima, 1678

Centro Aquicola do Rio Ave, 1767

Centro Argentino de Datos Oceanográficos (CEADO), 107

Centro Argentino de Espeleología, 105

Centro Argentino de Etnología Americana (CAEA), 107

Centro Argentino de Información Científica y Tecnológica (CAICYT), 110

Centro Argentino de Ingenieros, 105

Centro Argentino de Primates (CAPRIM), 107

Centro Austral de Investigaciones Científicas (CADIC-CONICET), Ushuaia, 107

Centro Brasileiro de Pesquisas Físicas, 302

Centro Camuno di Studi Preistorici, 1173

Centro Ciência Viva de Amadora, 1769

Centro Co-ordinador y Difusor de Estudios Latinoamericanos, México, 1469

Centro Cultural Hispano-Guineano, Malabo, 699

Centro de Ambiente e Ciências da Terra do Instituto de Investigação Científica Tropical, 1763

Centro de Antropobiologia do Instituto de Investigação Científica Tropical, 1763

Centro de Antropología, 617

Centro de Antropologia Cultural e Social do Instituto de Investigação Científica Tropical, 1763

Centro de Arte Moderna—Fundação Calouste Gulbenkian, 1770

Centro de Astronomia e Astrofísica da Universidade de Lisboa, 1767

Centro de Bellas Artes, Maracaibo, 3008

Centro de Botânica do Instituto de Investigação Científica Tropical, 1763

Centro de Cartografia do Instituto de Investigação Científica Tropical, 1763

Centro de Ciência Animal e Veterinária (CECAV), 1764

Centro de Ciências, Letras e Artes, Campinas, 301

Centro de Cooperación Regional para la Educación de Adultos en América Latina y el Caribe (CREFAL), Pátzcuaro, 1465

Centro de Cristalografia e Mineralogia do Instituto de Investigação Científica Tropical, 1763

Centro de Dados Geológico-Mineiro Alfragide, 1767

Centro de Desarrollo Científico de Montañas, Guantanamo, 617

Centro de Desarrollo de Equipos e Instrumentos Científicos (CEDEIC), Havana, 617

Centro de Desenvolvimento da Tecnologia Nuclear (CDTN), 302

Centro de Desenvolvimento Global do Instituto de Investigação Científica Tropical, 1763

Centro de Detecção Remota para o Desenvolvimento do Instituto de Investigação Científica Tropical, 1763

Centro de Diagnóstico e Investigaciones Veterinarias Formosa (CEDIVEF), 107

Centro de Diseño de Sistemas Automatizados de Computación (CEDISAC), Havana, 617

Centro de Documentação e Informação da Câmara dos Deputados do Brasil, Brasília, 304

Centro de Documentação Técnica e Científica, São Tomé, 1909

Centro de Documentación Bibliotecológica, Bahía Blanca, 106

Centro de Documentación de la Oficialía Mayor de la Secretaría de Economía, México, 1471

Centro de Documentación e Información Fundación La Salle de Ciencias Naturales, 3004

Centro de Documentación e Información Internacional, Buenos Aires, 111

Centro de Documentación Regional 'Juan Bautista Vázquez' de la Universidad de Cuenca, 678

Centro de Documentación y Biblioteca, México, 1471

Centro de Documentación y Estudios para la Historia de Madrid, 2004

Centro de Ecofisiología Vegetal (CEVEG), Buenos Aires, 107

Centro de Ecofisiologia, Bioquímica e Biotecnologia Vegetal do Instituto de Investigação Científica Tropical, 1763

Centro de Ecología Aplicada del Litoral (CECOAL), Corrientes, 107

Centro de Energia Nuclear na Agricultura (CENA), Piracicaba, 299

Centro de Ensino Unificado de Brasília, 328

Centro de Estadísticas Nacionales y Comercio Internacional del Uruguay (CENCI Uruguay), 2980

Centro de Estatística e Informações, Salvador, 301

Centro de Estudios Antropológicos de la Universidad Católica, Asunción, 1674

Centro de Estudios Avanzados de Puerto Rico y El Caribe, 2975

Centro de Estudios Conservacionistas, Guatemala City, 961

Centro de Estudios de Asia y África, México, 1468

Centro de Estudios de Población y Desarrollo (CEPDE), Havana, 616

Centro de Estudios del Desarrollo Universidad Central de Venezuela, 3002

Centro de Estudios del Patrimonio Arqueológico de la Prehistoria, 2005

Centro de Estudios Demográficos, Urbanos y Ambientales, México, 1468

Centro de Estudios e Investigaciones Laborales (CEIL), Buenos Aires, 107

Centro de Estudios e Investigaciones Técnicas de Gipuzkoa, 2005

Centro de Estudios Económicos, 1468

Centro de Estudios Educativos, AC, México, 1468

Centro de Estudios Farmacológicos y Botanicos (CEFYBO), Buenos Aires, 107

Centro de Estudios Fotosintéticos y Bioquímicos (CEFOBI), Rosario, 107

Centro de Estudios Histórico-Militares del Perú, 1678

Centro de Estudios Históricos, México, 1468

Centro de Estudios Internacionales, México, 1468

Centro de Estudios Lingüísticos y Literarios, México, 1469

Centro de Estudios Políticos y Constitucionales, Madrid, 1997

Centro de Estudios sobre Desarrollo Económico, Bogotá, 579

Centro de Estudios Sociológicos, México, 1470

Centro de Estudos Africanos e Asiáticos do Instituto de Investigação Científica Tropical, 1763

Centro de Estudos da Guiné-Bissau, 965

Centro de Estudos de Fitossanidade do Armazenamento do Instituto de Investigação Científica Tropical, 1763

Centro de Estudos de História e Cartografia Antiga do Instituto de Investigação Científica Tropical, 1763

Centro de Estudos de Pedologia do Instituto de Investigação Científica Tropical, 1763

Centro de Estudos de Produção e Tecnologia Agrícolas do Instituto de Investigação Científica Tropical, 1763

Centro de Estudos de Vectores e Doenças Infecciosas Doutor Francisco Cambournac, 1765

Centro de Estudos do Baixo Alentejo, 1764

Centro de Estudos do Território, Cultura e Desenvolvimento, 1763

Centro de Estudos em Letras, 1765

Centro de Estudos Geográficos da Universidade de Lisboa, 1764

Centro de Estudos Geológicos e Mineiros de Beja, 1767

Centro de Estudos Históricos e Etnológicos, 1765

Centro de Estudos Sociais da Faculdade de Economia da Universidade de Coimbra, 1764

Centro de Estudos Transdisciplinares para o Desenvolvimento (CETRAD), 1763

Centro de Etnologia Ultramarina do Instituto de Investigação Científica Tropical, 1763

Centro de Fotogrametria do Instituto de Investigação Científica Tropical, 1764

Centro de Genómica e Biotecnologia (CGB), 1766

Centro de Geodesia do Instituto de Investigação Científica Tropical, 1764

Centro de Geografia do Instituto de Investigação Científica Tropical, 1764

Centro de Geologia da Universidade do Porto, 1765

Centro de Geologia do Instituto de Investigação Científica Tropical, 1764

Centro de Historia del Estado Carabobo, 3002

Centro de Historia Larense, 3000

Centro de Informação e Biblioteca em Educação, Brasília, 304

Chase Home Museum of Utah Folk Arts, 2498
Château d'Azay-le-Ferron, 761
Château de Fontainebleau, 756
Château de Langeais, 756
Château de Maisons-Laffitte, Maisons-Laffitte, 757
Château Musée, Saumur, 761
Château Ramezay Museum, 369
Chateau Slavkov—Austerlitz, 637
Chatham County Public Libraries, 2453
Chatham Historical Museum, 2490
Chatham University, 2854
Chatrapati Shahu Ji Maharaj University, Kanpur, 1028
Chattagram International Dental College, 234
Chattahoochee Valley Libraries, 2437
Chatterley Whitfield Mining Museum, 2291
Chaudhary Charan Singh Haryana Agricultural University, 1028
Chaudhary Charan Singh University, 1028
Chaudhary Devi Lal University, 1028
Chaudhary Sarwan Kumar Himachal Pradesh Agricultural University, 1028
Chaudhary Sarwan Kumar Himachal Pradesh Krishi Vishvavidyalaya, 1028
Chazen Museum of Art, 2501
Chea Sim University of Kamchaymear, 358
Cheaha Regional Library, 2429
Chechen State University, 1865
Chechen State University Library, 1852
Chehel Sotun Museum, Isfahan, 1108
Cheju Tourism College, 1386
Chekhov, A. P., House-Museum, Moscow, 1857
Chekhov, A. P., Museum, Taganrog, 1861
Chekhov, A. P. State Literature and Memorial Museum-Reserve, 1856
Chelmsford Public Library, 2445
Chelsea College of Art and Design, London, 2355
Chelsea District Library, 2445
Chelsea Physic Garden, 2258
Chelyabinsk Agricultural Research Institute, 1831
Chelyabinsk State Agro-Engineering University, 1862
Chelyabinsk State Institute of Art and Culture, 1900
Chelyabinsk State Medical Academy, 1897
Chelyabinsk State Picture Gallery, 1856
Chelyabinsk State University, 1865
Chemical Industry and Engineering Society of China, 464
Chemical Institute of Canada, 371
Chemical Processing and Forest Products Utilization Research Institute, Nanjing, 469
Chemical Research Centre of the Hungarian Academy of Sciences, 978
Chemical Society of Japan, 1223
Chemical Society, Taipei, 2119
Chemical-Metallurgical Institute, Karaganda, 1340
Chemisch-Physikalische Gesellschaft in Wien, 176
Chemistry and Soil Research Institute, Harare, 3028
Chemistry Centre—Vila Real, 1766
Chemnitz University of Technology, 899
Chemotherapeutisches Forschungsinstitut Georg-Speyer-Haus, 835
Chengdu Institute of Geology and Mineral Resources, 468
Chengdu University of Technology, 489
Chengdu University of Traditional Chinese Medicine, 490
Cheongju National University of Education, 1384
Cheongju University, 1373
Cherepovets State University, 1865
Chernihiv Literary Museum 'Mikhailo Kotsyubinsky', 2202

Chernivtsi Memorial Museum 'Yu. A. Fedkovych', 2202
Chernivtsi National University 'Yuriy Fedkovych', 2205
Chernyshevsky Memorial Museum, Saratov, 1861
Cherokee County History & Arts Museum, 2496
Cherokee Strip Museum, 2492
Cherokee Strip Regional Heritage Center, 2492
Cherry Hill Public Library, 2450
Cheshire Libraries, 2268
Cheshire Public Library, 2433
Chestatee Regional Library System, 2437
Chester Beatty Library, 1133
Chester College of New England, 2752
Chester County Library System, Exton, 2456
Chesterfield College, 2360
Chestnut Hill College, 2854
Chetco Community Public Library, 2455
Chetham's Library, 2277
Cheyenne Frontier Days Old West Museum, 2502
Cheyney University of Pennsylvania, 2862
Chhatrapati Shivaji Maharaj Vastu Sangrahalay, 1022
Chiado Museum, 1771
Chiang Mai University, 2138
Chiapas State University of Arts and Sciences, 1478
Chiba Prefectural Central Library, 1228
Chiba University, 1233
Chibero College of Agriculture, 3031
Chicago Academy of Sciences, 2410
Chicago Public Library, 2438
Chicago School of Professional Psychology, 2606
Chicago State University, 2606
Chicago Theological Seminary, 2606
Chickasaw Regional (Public) Library System, 2455
Chief Dull Knife College, 2746
Chifley Business School, Melbourne, 170
Chigaku Dantai Kenkyu-Kai, 1222
Chikobava, A. S., Institute of Linguistics, 813
Chikushi Jogakuen University, 1309
Chikyu-Denjiki Chikyu-Wakuseiken Gakkai, 1222
Child Institute, 1665
Children's Health and Exercise Research Centre, 2255
Chilean Academy of Fine Arts, 447
Chilean Academy of History, 448
Chilean Academy of Language, 448
Chilean Academy of Medicine, 448
Chilean Academy of Sciences, 448
Chilean Academy of Social, Political and Moral Sciences, 448
Chilean Association of Seismology and Earthquake Engineering, 449
Chilean College of Architects, 448
Chilean International Plastic Arts Association, 448
Chilean Maritime League, 449
Chilean Public Health Institute, 450
Chilean Society of Food Technology, 450
Chilean Wildlife Society, 449
China Academy of Traditional Chinese Medicine, 463
China Academy, Yang Ming Shan, 2118
China Agricultural University, 490
China Art Gallery, Beijing, 472
China Association for Science and Technology (CAST), 463
China Association of Traditional Chinese Medicine, 463
China Association of Zhenjiu (Acupuncture and Moxibustion), 463
China Central Institute of Fine Arts, Beijing, 491
China Central Radio and Television University, 495
China Coal Research Institute, 469
China Coal Society, 465
China Computer Federation, 465

China Education Association for International Exchange, Beijing, 461
China Electrotechnical Society, 465
China Energy Research Society, 465
China Engineering Graphics Society, 465
China Fire Protection Association, 465
China Foreign Affairs University, 492
China Law Society, 462
China Medical College, Taichung, 2125
China Medical University, 492
China National Association of Literature and the Arts, Taipei, 2118
China National Space Administration, 469
China Pharmaceutical University, 494
China Railway Society, 465
China Scholarship Council, Beijing, 461
China Society for Scientific and Technical Information, 465
China Society of Fisheries, 462
China Society, Taipei, 2118
China State Bureau of Technical Supervision (CSBTS), 469
China University of Geosciences (Wuhan), 492
China University of Mining and Technology, 493
China University of Petroleum, 493
China University of Political Science and Law, 494
China Zoological Society, 463
Chinese Abacus Association, 465
Chinese Academy of Agricultural Sciences, 462
Chinese Academy of Engineering (CAE), 465
Chinese Academy of Forestry, 462
Chinese Academy of Medical Sciences and Peking Union Medical College, 463
Chinese Academy of Meteorological Sciences, 464
Chinese Academy of Sciences, 461
Chinese Academy of Social Sciences, 461
Chinese Academy of Space Technology, 465
Chinese Academy of Surveying and Mapping, National Bureau of Surveying and Mapping, Beijing, 466
Chinese Aerodynamics Research Society, 464
Chinese Agricultural Economics Society, 462
Chinese American Museum, 2466
Chinese Anti-Cancer Association, 463
Chinese Anti-Tuberculosis Society, 463
Chinese Archives Society, 462
Chinese Association for European Studies, 462
Chinese Association for Folklore, Taipei, 2119
Chinese Association for Mental Health, 463
Chinese Association for Physiological Sciences, 463
Chinese Association of Agricultural Science Societies, 462
Chinese Association of Animal Science and Veterinary Medicine, 463
Chinese Association of Automation, 465
Chinese Association of Integrated Medicine, 463
Chinese Association of Natural Science Museums, 462
Chinese Association of Political Science, 462
Chinese Astronomical Society, 464
Chinese Ceramic Society, 465
Chinese Chemical Society, 464
Chinese Civil Engineering Society, 465
Chinese Culture University, Taipei, 2121
Chinese Education Society, 462
Chinese Forestry Association, Taipei, 2118
Chinese Geological Society, 464
Chinese Geological Survey, 464
Chinese Geophysical Society, 464
Chinese High-Energy Physics Society, 464

Chinese Historical Society, 462
Chinese Hydraulic Engineering Society, 465
Chinese Institute of Atomic Energy, Beijing, 468
Chinese Institute of Civil and Hydraulic Engineering, Taipei, 2119
Chinese Institute of Engineers, Taipei, 2119
Chinese Language Society, Taipei, 2119
Chinese Legal History Society, 462
Chinese Light Industry Society, 465
Chinese Literature Institute, Beijing, 466
Chinese Mathematical Society, 464
Chinese Mechanical Engineering Society, 465
Chinese Medical Association, Beijing, 463
Chinese Medical Association, Taipei, 2119
Chinese Meteorological Society, 464
Chinese National Foreign Relations Association, Taipei, 2119
Chinese Nuclear Physics Society, 464
Chinese Nuclear Society, 464
Chinese Nursing Association, 463
Chinese Nutrition Society, 463
Chinese Petroleum Society, 465
Chinese Pharmaceutical Association, 463
Chinese Pharmacological Society, 463
Chinese Physical Society, 464
Chinese Postal Museum, Taipei, 2121
Chinese Psychological Society, 464
Chinese Research Institute of the Wood Industry, Beijing, 465
Chinese Research Society for the Modernization of Management, 462
Chinese Sericulture Society, 462
Chinese Society for Anatomical Sciences, 463
Chinese Society for Future Studies, 462
Chinese Society for Horticultural Science, 462
Chinese Society for Metals, 465
Chinese Society for Microbiology, 463
Chinese Society for Mineralogy, Petrology and Geochemistry, 464
Chinese Society for Oceanology and Limnology, 463
Chinese Society for Rock Mechanics and Engineering, 464
Chinese Society for Urban Studies, 462
Chinese Society of Aeronautics and Astronautics, 464
Chinese Society of Agricultural Machinery, 462
Chinese Society of Astronautics (CSA), 465
Chinese Society of Biochemistry and Molecular Biology, 464
Chinese Society of Electrical Engineering, 465
Chinese Society of Engineering Thermophysics, 465
Chinese Society of Environmental Sciences, 464
Chinese Society of Forestry, 462
Chinese Society of Geodesy, Photogrammetry and Cartography, 462
Chinese Society of Library Science, 462
Chinese Society of Naval Architects and Marine Engineers, 465
Chinese Society of Oceanography, 462
Chinese Society of Plant Physiology, 464
Chinese Society of Space Research, 464
Chinese Society of the History of International Relations, 462
Chinese Society of the History of Science and Technology, 463
Chinese Society of Theoretical and Applied Mechanics (CSTAM), 465
Chinese Society of Tropical Crops, 462
Chinese Sociological Research Society, 464
Chinese Statistical Association, Taipei, 2119
Chinese Study of Religion Society, 464
Chinese Textile Engineering Society, 465
Chinese Traditional Opera College, 495
Chinese University of Hong Kong, 568

Codrington Library (All Souls College), Oxford, 2278
Coe College, 2634
Coeur d'Alene Public Library, 2438
Coffee Research Foundation, Ruiru, 1352
Coffee Research Station, Chipinge, 3028
Coffee Rusts Research Centre, Oeiras, 1764
Cogswell Polytechnical College, 2526
Cohn-Haddow Center for Judaic Studies, 2419
Coimbra Branch, 1767
Coimbra Public Library, 1768
Coimbra Univ. Astronomical Observatory, 1766
Coimbra University School of Arts, 1779
Coin Cabinet, 851
Coin Cabinet, Gotha, 853
Coin Collection, Mainz, 855
Coker College, 2883
Coláiste Mhuire, Marino, 1137
Colburn Earth Science Museum, 2490
Colby College, 2654
Colby College Museum of Art, 2479
Colby-Sawyer College, 2752
Colchester Institute, 2360
Colchester Museums, 2283
Cold and Arid Regions Environmental and Engineering Research Institute, Lanzhou, 468
Cold Spring Harbor Laboratory, 2423
Colección Carlos Alberto Pusineri Scala, Asunción, 1675
Colección Ornitológica Phelps, 3004
Colectia de arta plastica Alexandru Balintescu, 1797
Coleg Gwent, 2385
Coleg Llandrillo Cymru, 2385
Coleg Menai, 2385
Coleg Morgannwg, 2385
Coleg Sir Gâr, 2385
Colegio de Abogados de la Ciudad de Buenos Aires, 103
Colegio de Abogados del Distrito Capital, 3000
Colegio de Arquitectos de Bolivia, 282
Colegio de Arquitectos de Chile, 448
Colegio de Arquitectos de Honduras, 970
Colegio de Arquitectos de Venezuela, 2999
Colegio de Arquitectos del Perú, 1677
Colegio de Bibliotecarios de Chile, AG, 448
Colegio de Bibliotecólogos del Perú, 1677
Colegio de Bibliotecólogos y Archivólogos de Venezuela, 2999
Colegio de Farmacéuticos del Distrito Federal y Estado Miranda, 3000
Colegio de Géologos de Bolivia, 282
Colegio de Ingenieros de Chile, AG, 450
Colegio de Ingenieros de Guatemala, 960
Colegio de Ingenieros de Venezuela, 3001
Colegio de Ingenieros Forestales de Chile A.G., Santiago, 448
Colegio de la Frontera Sur, San Cristóbal de las Casas, 1486
Colegio de Médicos del Distrito Metropolitano de Caracas, Caracas, 3000
Colegio de Médicos del Estado Miranda, 3000
Colegio de Médicos y Cirujanos de Costa Rica, San José, 598
Colegio de México, 1486
Colegio de Químico-Farmacéuticos y Bioquímicos de Chile, 448
Colegio Médico de El Salvador, 696
Colegio Militar de la Nación, Buenos Aires, 122
Colegio Nacional, México, 1465
Colegio Universitario de San Juan, 2975
Coleman University, 2526
Colgate Rochester Crozer Divinity School, 2772
Colgate University, 2772
Collaborative Antwerp Psychiatric Research Institute, 255

Collection of Classical Antiquities at the Pergamon Museum and the Old Museum, 849
Collection of Prints and Drawings of ETH Zurich, 2098
Collections and Swedish National Portrait Gallery, University of Stockholm, 2058
Collections Artistiques de l'Université de Liège, 262
College Art Association, New York, 2403
College Board, New York, 2396
Collège d'Enseignement Technique Agricole, Sibiti, 597
Collège de France, 790
Collège d'Europe, Bruges, 270
College for Creative Studies, Detroit, 2695
College for Financial Planning, 2552
Collège International de Chirurgiens, 63
Collège International pour la Recherche en Productique, 58
Collège Libre des Sciences Sociales et Economiques, Paris, 797
Collège Médical, Luxembourg, 1429
College of African Wildlife Management, Mweka, 2134
College of Agricultural and Environmental Education Vienna, 201
College of Agriculture at Križevci, 614
College of Agriculture, Darkhan, 1501
College of Agriculture, Food and Rural Enterprise, 2369
College of Agriculture, Science and Education, Port Antonio, 1215
College of Arms, London, 2272
College of Banking and Financial Studies, 1634
College of Basic Education, Adailiya, 1392
College of Business Administration, 1915
College of Business Education, Dar es Salaam, 2134
College of Business Studies, Hawalli, 1392
College of Catalan Notaries, 1997
College of Central Florida, 2581
College of Charleston, 2883
College of Coastal Georgia, 2593
College of Commerce, Hanoi, 3021
College of Economics, 3021
College of Economics and Administration, Plovdiv, 351
College of Economics and Business Administration, 3019
College of Education, 3019
College of Estate Management, Reading, 2361
College of Europe, Bruges, 270
College of Health Sciences, Bahrain, 211
College of Health Sciences, Faiha, 1392
College of Idaho, 2604
College of Industrial Technology, 3019
College of Integrated Chinese Medicine, 2364
College of Islamic Studies, Malé, 1454
College of Law, Guildford, 2359
College of Law, St Leonards, 167
College of Law, Thuong Tin, 3021
College of Medical and Dental Sciences, Birmingham, 2364
College of Medicine and Pharmacy, 3019
College of Medicine, Blantyre, 1442
College of Menominee Nation, 2955
College of Micronesia, 1489
College of Micronesia Learning Resources Center, 1489
College of Mount St Joseph, 2831
College of Mount Saint Vincent, 2772
College of Natural Resources, Punakha Dzongkhag, 280
College of New Jersey, Ewing, 2758
College of New Rochelle, 2772
College of Nursing, Burwood, 167
College of Optometrists, London, 2238
College of Osteopaths, Borehamwood, 2364
College of Physical Training and Sports, Tu Son, 3021
College of Physicians and Surgeons Pakistan, 1638

College of Physicians of Philadelphia, 2409
College of Saint Benedict, 2716
College of Saint Elizabeth, Morristown, 2758
College of St Hild and St Bede, Durham, 2312
College of St. Joseph, Rutland, 2928
College of Saint Mary, Omaha, 2748
College of Saint Rose, 2772
College of St Scholastica, 2716
College of Science and Technology, 280
College of Social and Political Science, Masohi, 1105
College of Staten Island, 2770
College of Surveying, Tehran, 1121
College of Teachers, Epping, 2225
College of Technological Studies, Shuwaikh, 1392
College of Technology London, 2366
College of the Atlantic, 2654
College of the Bahamas, 208
College of the Bahamas–Libraries and Instructional Media Services, 208
College of the Holy Cross, Worcester, 2670
College of the North Atlantic-Qatar, 1781
College of the North Atlantic-Qatar Campus Library System, 1780
College of the Ozarks, 2737
College of the Resurrection, 2366
College of Tourism and Hotel Management, 627
College of Tourism, Burgas, 351
College of Visual Arts, St Paul, 2716
College of Water Conservancy, Hanoi, 3021
College of West Anglia, 2360
College of Westchester, 2772
College of William & Mary, 2931
College of Wooster, 2831
Collège Rural d'Ambatobe, 1439
Collège Technique, Commercial et Industriel de Brazzaville (et Centre d'Apprentissage), 597
Colleges Northern Ireland, 2226
Colleges of Medicine of South Africa, 1974
Col·legi d'Arquitectes de Catalunya, 1997
Col·legi de Notaris de Catalunya, 1997
Col·legi Oficial d'Enginyers Industrials de Catalunya, 2000
Collegium Basilea, 2092
Collegium Cultorum Martyrum, Rome, 2991
Collegium Medicum Uniwersytetu Jagiellońskiego, 1758
Collegium Romanicum, Neuchâtel, 2088
Colleish Ellan Vannin, Douglas, 2390
Collezione d'Arte Religiosa Moderna, Vatican City, 2992
Collezioni del Novecento, 1183
Collingwood College, Durham, 2312
Collingwood Museum, 379
Colombia Free University, 590
Colombian Academy of History, 578
Colombian Academy of Jurisprudence, 578
Colombian Association of Librarians, 578
Colombian Association of Medical Faculties, 578
Colombian Farmers' Society, 578
Colombian Institute for Educational Loans and Advanced Studies Abroad, 577
Colombian Institute for the Promotion of Higher Education, 578
Colombian National Academy of Medicine, 578
Colombian Universities Association, 577
Colombo Dutch Period Museum, 2042
Colombo National Museum, 2042
Colombo National Museum Library, 2041
Colombo Public Library, 2042
Colonial Williamsburg, 2499
Colonial Williamsburg Foundation, 2499
Colorado Christian University, 2552
Colorado College, 2552
Colorado Mesa University, 2552

Colorado Mountain College, 2552
Colorado School of Mines, 2552
Colorado Springs Fine Arts Center, 2467
Colorado Springs Pioneers Museum, 2467
Colorado State Archives, 2433
Colorado State Library, 2433
Colorado State University, 2552
Colorado State University Libraries, 2433
Colorado State University—Pueblo, 2553
Colorado Supreme Court Library, 2433
Colorado Technical University, 2553
Columbia Centro Universitario, Caguas, 2973
Columbia College, 2737
Columbia College Chicago, 2606
Columbia College Hollywood, 2526
Columbia College of Nursing, Inc., 2955
Columbia College, South Carolina, 2883
Columbia County Library, 2431
Columbia International University, 2883
Columbia Museum of Art, 2496
Columbia Theological Seminary, 2593
Columbia University, 2772
Columbia University Libraries, New York, 2451
Columbus College of Art and Design, 2831
Columbus Metropolitan Library, 2454
Columbus Museum, 2472
Columbus Museum of Art, 2492
Columbus Palace, Santo Domingo, 673
Columbus State University, 2593
Combustion Institute, Pittsburgh, 2428
Comenius Museum, 1551
Comenius University in Bratislava, 1958
Comilla University, 220
Comisión Chilena de Energía Nuclear, 449
Comisión de Acreditación de la Calidad de la Educación Superior, San Salvador, 696
Comisión de Energía Atómica de Costa Rica, 599
Comisión Ecuatoriana de Energía Atómica, Quito, 678
Comisión Nacional de Acreditación, Santiago, 447
Comisión Nacional de Actividades Espaciales (CONAE), Buenos Aires, 109
Comisión Nacional de Energía Atómica, Buenos Aires, 109
Comisión Nacional de Evaluación y Acreditación Universitaria (CONEAU), Buenos Aires, 102
Comisión Nacional de Investigación Científica y Tecnológica (CONICYT), 451
Comisión Nacional de Museos y de Monumentos y Lugares Históricos, Buenos Aires, 103
Comisión Nacional para el Desarrollo de los Pueblos Indígenas, México, 1470
Comisión Nacional Protectora de Bibliotecas Populares, Buenos Aires, 103
Comisión Salvadoreña de Energía Nuclear (COSEN), 696
Comissão Nacional de Arte Sacra e do Património Cultural da Igreja, 1767
Comissão Nacional de Energia Nuclear (CNEN), 302
Comissão Nacional de Folclore, Rio de Janeiro, 299
Comitato Elettrotecnico Italiano (CEI), 1168
Comitato Glaciologico Italiano, 1175
Comitato Nazionale per la Valutazione del Sistema Universitario, Rome, 1162
Comitato Termotecnico Italiano (CTI), 1168
Comité Culturel National, Tunis, 2154
Comité des Travaux Historiques et Scientifiques, Paris, 739
Comité Ejecutivo de la Universidad Boliviana (CEUB), La Paz, 281

DEEWR Library, Department of Education, Employment and Workplace Relations, Canberra, 139
Defence Academy, Ulan Bator, 1501
Defence Institute of Advanced Technology, Pune, 1073
Defence Library, Copenhagen, 655
Defence Research and Development Institute, 2160
Defence Science and Technology Laboratory (DSTL), Porton Down, 2263
Defence Science and Technology Organisation, Canberra, 138
Defence Science and Technology Organisation, Fishermens Bend, 138
Defence Services Academy, Mandalay, 1517
Defence Services Technological Academy, Mandalay, 1517
Defiance College, 2831
Deichmanske Bibliotek, 1618
Deir ez-Zor Museum, 2116
DeKalb County Public Library, 2437
Delaware Agricultural Museum & Village, Dover, 2469
Delaware Art Museum, Wilmington, 2469
Delaware County Library System, Media, 2456
Delaware Division of Libraries, 2434
Delaware History Museum, Wilmington, 2469
Delaware Museum of Natural History, 2469
Delaware Public Archives, 2434
Delaware State Police Museum, Dover, 2469
Delaware State University, 2568
Delaware Valley College, 2854
DELETE Groningen Research Institute for the Study of Culture (ICOG), 1542
DELETE Maui Arts & Cultural Center, Kahului, 2473
Delft Centre for Aviation, 1543
Delft Centre for Engineering Design, 1543
Delft Institute for Earth-Oriented Space Research, 1543
Delft Institute for Information Technology in Service Engineering, 1543
Delft Institute of Microsystems and Nanoelectronics (Dimes), 1543
Delft University of Technology, 1554
Delft University Research Centre of Intelligent Sensor Microsystems, 1543
Delft University Wind Energy Research Institute, 1543
Delhi Public Library, 1020
Delmon University for Science and Technology, Manama, 210
Delphi Public Library, 2439
Delray Beach Public Library, 2436
Delta Community Library, 2430
Delta State University, 2733
Dementia Services Development Centre, Stirling, 2255
Demeure Historique, Paris, 741
'Demokritos' National Centre for Scientific Research, Athens, 947
'Demokritos' University of Thrace, 950
Demopolis Public Library, 2429
Den Grønlandske Forfatterforening, 667
Den Norske Forfatterforening, 1615
Denbighshire Library Service, 2280
Denison University, 2831
Denki Gakkai, 1224
Denmark-America Foundation, 650
Dennos Museum Center, 2482
Denshi Joho Tsushin Gakkai, 1224
Dental Association of Bosnia and Herzegovina, 288
Dental Council, Dublin, 1131
Dentistry Canada Fund, 373
Denver Art Museum, 2467
Denver Museum of Nature and Science, 2467
Denver Public Library, 2433
Denver Seminary, 2553

Departamento Administrativo Nacional de Estadística, Bogotá, 579
Departamento de Antropología e Historia de Nayarit, 1466
Departamento de Bibliotecas, Universidad de Antioquia, 581
Departamento de Bibliotecas, Universidad del Cauca, 581
Departamento de Estudios Etnográficos y Coloniales, Santa Fé, 109
Departamento de Estudios Históricos Navales, Buenos Aires, 106
Departamento de Filosofía del Instituto de Teología para Religiosos, Caracas, 2996
Departamento de Servicios Bibliotecarios, Documentación e Información de la Asamblea Legislativa, San José, 599
Departamento Nacional da Produção Mineral, Brasília, 302
Département d'Amélioration des Méthodes pour l'Innovation Scientifique (CIRAD-AMIS), Montpellier, 746
Département d'Élevage et de Médecine Vétérinaire (CIRAD-EMVT), Montpellier, 746
Département de la Guadeloupe Archives Départementales, 802
Département de Philosophie de l'Institut Catholique de l'Afrique Centrale, 2996
Département de Recherches Agronomiques de la République Malgache, 1438
Département des Cultures Annuelles (CIRAD-CA), Montpellier, 746
Département des Cultures Pérennes (CIRAD-CP), Montpellier, 746
Département des Études de Population à l'Union Douanière et Économique de l'Afrique Centrale, Bangui, 443
Département des Territoires, Environnement et Acteurs (CIRAD-TERA), Montpellier, 746
Département des Traditions Orales, du Centre Polynésien des Sciences Humaines 'Te Anavaharau', 801
Département Environnement Technologie et Société (DENTES), 763
Département Forestier (CIRAD-Forêt), Montpellier, 746
Département Métiers de l'Image et du Son (SATIS), 763
Departement Moleculaire Genetica, 255
Department for Business, Innovation and Skills, London, 2224
Department for Children, Education, Lifelong Learning and Skills, Cardiff, 2224
Department for Children, Schools and Family Library, London, 2272
Department for Culture, Media and Sport, London, 2224
Department for Education, Cheshire, 2224
Department for Education, Sport and Culture, St Helier, 2391
Department for Employment and Learning, Belfast, 2224
Department for Innovation and Curricular Development, Lisbon, 1760
Department of Agricultural Research, Maseru, 1411
Department of Agricultural Sciences of the National Academy of Sciences of Belarus, 238
Department of Agriculture, Fisheries & Forestry Information Centre, Pretoria, 1978
Department of Agriculture, Kuala Lumpur, 1444
Department of Alternative Energy Development and Efficiency, Bangkok, 2136
Department of Anthropology and History in Nayarit, 1466
Department of Antiquities and Museums, Safat, 1391
Department of Antiquities, Shahat (Cyrene), 1416

Department of Antiquities, Tripoli, 1416
Department of Archaeology and Museums, Islamabad, 1637
Department of Archives, Nassau, 208
Department of Archives, St James, 236
Department of Art Research and Inventory of the Federal Office for the Protection of Monuments, Vienna, 179
Department of Arts, Culture, Science and Technology Library, Pretoria, 1978
Department of Atomic Energy, Yangon, 1513
Department of Biological Sciences of the National Academy of Sciences of Belarus, 239
Department of Bitola, 1434
Department of Chamorro Affairs, Hagatna, 2968
Department of Chemistry and Earth Sciences of the National Academy of Sciences of Belarus, 239
Department of Cultural and Customary Affairs, Nouméa, 805
Department of Culture, Arts and Leisure, Belfast, 2224
Department of Earth and Atmospheric Sciences Museum, University of Alberta, 377
Department of Education, 1566
Department of Education and Children, 2390
Department of Education and Skills, Dublin, 1129
Department of Education, Bangor, 2224
Department of Education, Culture and Sports, Oranjestad, 1567
Department of Education, Employment and Workplace Relations, Canberra, 129
Department of Education Library, Pretoria, 1978
Department of Education, Nouméa, 805
Department of Education, Palikir, 1489
Department of Education, Pasig City, 1688
Department of Education, St Thomas, 2977
Department of Education, San Juan, 2970
Department of Education, Waigani, 1671
Department of Education, Washington, 2393
Department of Embryology, Baltimore, 2422
Department of Environmental Protection, Bermuda, 2386
Department of Ethnographical and Colonial Studies, 109
Department of Geography, National Institute of Geophysics, Geodesy and Geography, Sofia, 337
Department of Geology and Mineral Survey, Kabul, 80
Department of Geology of the Ministry of Energy and Mines, 3002
Department of Global Ecology, Stanford, 2422
Department of Health Library, London, 2272
Department of Higher Education and Recognition of Diplomas, Tiranë, 83
Department of Higher Education Institution Accreditation, 1490
Department of Higher Education, Ministry of Human Resource Development, New Delhi, 1004
Department of Humanitarian Sciences and Arts of the National Academy of Sciences of Belarus, 238
Department of Kumanovo, 1434
Department of Libraries, Archives and Documentation Services, Kingstown, 1906
Department of Medical Research (Lower Myanmar), Yangon, 1513
Department of Medical Sciences of the National Academy of Sciences of Belarus, 239
Department of Metallurgy, Harare, 3029

Department of Meteorology, Colombo, 2041
Department of Mineral Resources, Bangkok, 2136
Department of National Archives, Colombo, 2042
Department of Naval History Studies, Buenos Aires, 106
Department of Occupational Standards, Thimphu, 279
Department of Ohrid, 1434
Department of Physical and Engineering Sciences of the National Academy of Sciences of Belarus, 239
Department of Physics, Mathematics and Informatics of the National Academy of Sciences of Belarus, 239
Department of Planning & Infrastructure, Sydney, 136
Department of Planning & Natural Resources, St Thomas, 2977
Department of Plant Biology, Stanford, 2423
Department of Plant Protection, Karachi, 1640
Department of Prilep, 1434
Department of Prints and Drawings, Zagreb, 610
Department of Public Libraries, Dhaka, 216
Department of Quality Control in Education of the Ministry of Education, 238
Department of Records and Information Services, New York, 2451
Department of Religious Affairs, Yangon, 1513
Department of Research & Specialist Services, Division of Research Services, Harare, 3028
Department of Science Service, Bangkok, 2136
Department of Scientific and Industrial Research, Baghdad, 1123
Department of Skopje, 1434
Department of Social and Biological Communication, Bratislava, 1952
Department of Sports, Parks & Recreation, St Thomas, 2977
Department of Stip, 1434
Department of Strumica, 1434
Department of Terrestrial Magnetism, Washington, 2423
Department of Tetovo, 1434
Department of the Art and Museum Book Collections of the State Russian Museum, 1854
Department of the Treasury Library, Washington, 2435
Department of Tourism, Culture and Sport, Dublin, 1129
Department of Veles, 1434
Department of Veterans Affairs, Headquarters Library, Washington, 2435
Department of Veterinary Services; Tsetse Control Branch, Harare, 3029
Department of Vocational Training, Nouméa, 805
Department of Wild Life Conservation, Colombo, 2041
Department of Youth Affairs, Hagatna, 2968
Department und Sammlungen für Geschichte der Medizin, 187
Departmental Library, Indian and Northern Affairs Canada, 375
DePaul University, 2606
Depauw University, 2625
Dept of Ethnography and Folk Art Orăştie, 1796
DeQuincy Railroad Museum, 2478
Derby City Libraries, 2268
Derbyshire County Council, Cultural and Community Services, Libraries and Heritage Division, 2277
Déri Múzeum, 982
Dermatology Institute, Jiangsu, 466
Dermatovenereological Research Institute of the Committee for Health, Almaty, 1340
Derna University, 1416

Diaconia University of Applied Sciences, 735

Diakonia-Ammattikorkeakoulu, Helsinki, 735

Diamond and Precious Metal Geology Institute of the Siberian Branch of the Russian Academy of Sciences (DPMGI SB RAS), Yakutsk, 1843

Dibrugarh University, 1029

Dickens Fellowship, London, 2236

Dickinson Area Public Library, 2453

Dickinson College, 2854

Dickinson Museum Center, 2491

Dickson Mounds Museum, 2474

Dicle Üniversitesi, 2167

Dictionary Research Centre, Birmingham, 2254

Didrichsen Art Museum, 721

Didrichsen Taidemuseo, 721

Die Internationale Vereinigung der Musikbibliotheken, Musikarchive und Musikdokumentationszentren, 47

Die Ständige Konferenz der Kultusminister der Länder in der Bundesrepublik Deutschland, Bonn, 818

Dietitians NZ, 1574

DigiPen Institute of Technology—Singapore, 1947

Dillard University, 2648

Dilliraman—Kalyani Regmi Memorial Library, 1525

Dimitr Blagoev Museum, 343

'Dimitrie Cantemir' Christian University, 1802

Dimitrie Cantemir University of Târgu Mureş, 1804

Dimitrie Gusti Institute of Sociology, 1790

Dimokriteio Panepistimio Thrakis, 950

DIN Deutsches Institut für Normung eV, 828

Dinajpur Medical College, 234

Dinas Geodesi, Jawatan Topografi TNI-AD, 1085

Dinas Hidro-Oseanografi, Jakarta, 1086

Dinas Intelijen Medan & Geografi Jawatan Topografi TNI-AD, 1085

Diné College, 2508

Diocesan Archives, Barcelona, 2006

Diözesanarchiv Wien, 185

Dipartimento di Ingegneria Nucleare, Centro Studi Nucleari Enrico Fermi (CESNEF), Milan, 1175

Diplomatic Academy of the Ministry of Foreign Affairs of the Kyrgyz Republic, 1396

Diplomatic Academy of Vienna, Vienna, 201

Diplomatische Akademie Wien, 201

Diponegoro University, 1091

Direcção Nacional de Geologia, Centro de Documentação, Maputo, 1511

Direcção Nacional de Geologia, Maputo, 1511

Direcção Provincial dos Serviços de Geologia e Minas de Angola, 99

Direcção-Geral de Inovação e de Desenvolvimento Curricular (DGIDC), 1760

Dirección de Bibliotecas—Sede Bogotá, Universidad Nacional de Colombia, 580

Dirección de Geología del Ministerio de Energía y Minas, Caracas, 3002

Dirección de Minas del Ministerio de Minas e Hidrocarburos, Caracas, 3003

Dirección del Sistema de Bibliotecas de la Universidad de Santiago de Chile, 451

Dirección General de Bellas Artes, Santo Domingo, 676

Dirección General de Bibliotecas, 1466

Dirección General de Bibliotecas Municipales, 111

Dirección General de Educación Superior, Asunción, 1674

Dirección General de Energía Nuclear, Guatemala City, 961

Dirección General de Estadística y Censos, San Salvador, 696

Dirección General de Hidrocarburos, Quito, 678

Dirección General de Meteorología del Perú, 1679

Dirección General de Ordenación del Territorio Urbanístico del Ministerio del Poder Popular para las Obras Públicas y Vivienda, Caracas, 3002

Dirección General de Relaciones Culturales y Científicas, Madrid, 1996

Dirección General de Relaciones Educativas, Científicas y Culturales, México, 1465

Dirección Meteorológica de Chile, 451

Dirección Nacional de Ciencia, Tecnología y Innovación (DINACYT), Montevideo, 2980

Dirección Nacional de Meteorología del Uruguay, 2980

Dirección Nacional de Minería y Geología, Montevideo, 2981

Dirección Nacional de Tecnología Nuclear, Montevideo, 2981

Dirección Nacional del Antártico, Buenos Aires, 106

Dirección Nacional del Patrimonio Histórico, Panamá, 1669

Direction de la Géologie, Rabat, 1506

Direction de la Médecine Préventive, Brazzaville, 596

Direction de la Météorologie Nationale, Douala, 364

Direction de l'Epidémiologie et de Lutte Contre les Maladies, Rabat, 1506

Direction des Mines et de la Géologie, Kigali, 1902

Direction des Mines et de la Géologie, Nouakchott, 1460

Direction des Musées de Nice, 758

Direction des Recherches sur les Productions Forestières, Dakar-Hann, 1914

Direction des Services d'Archives de Paris, 754

Direction du Musée National, des Sites et Monuments, Lomé, 2148

Direction du Patrimoine Culturel, Algiers, 91

Direction Générale de la Géologie et des Mines, Bujumbura, 355

Direction Générale de la Recherche Scientifique et Technique, Brazzaville, 596

Direction Générale des Archives Nationales, de la Bibliothèque Nationale et de la Documentation Gabonaise (DGABD), 809

Direction Nationale de la Météorologie, Bamako, 1455

Direction Nationale de la Recherche Scientifique et Technique, Conakry, 963

Directorate for Cultural Heritage, 1614

Directorate for the Protection and Development of the Historical and Archaeological Heritage, Jakarta, 1085

Directorate General for the Portuguese Archives, 1768

Directorate General Statistics and Economic Information, 255

Directorate of Archives and Archival Museum, Lahore, 1644

Directorate of Archives and Libraries, Dhaka, 216

Directorate of Continuing Education, Dhaka, 214

Directorate of Metrology, Bandung, 1086

Directorate of National Education, Youth and Sports, Monaco, 1495

Directorate of Water Resources Research, Muscat, 1634

Directorate-General of Higher Education, Jakarta, 1083

Direktorat Jenderal Pendidikan Tinggi, 1083

Direktorat Metrologi, 1086

Direktorat Perlindungan dan Pembinaan Peninggalan Sejarah dan Purbakala, Jakarta, 1085

Discoteca Oneyda Alvarenga, São Paulo, 305

Discover Stamford—Heritage at your library, 2271

DiscoverSea Shipwreck Museum, Fenwick Island, 2469

Discovery Center of Idaho, 2474

Discovery Museum and Planetarium, Bridgeport, 2468

Discovery Museum, Newcastle upon Tyne, 2289

Dishman Art Museum, 2498

Distance Education and Training Council (DETC), 2394

Distance Education Association of New Zealand, 1572

Distance Learning University, Brig, 2112

Distance-Learning University in Hagen, 867

District Archives Leiria, 1768

District Archives of Setúbal, 1769

District Archives, Porto, 1769

District Historical Museum, Berat, 86

District Historical Museum, Fier, 86

District Historical Museum, Vlorë, 86

District Museum for Art and Culture, Bremen, 850

District Museum of History, Galaţi, 1796

District of Columbia Public Library, Washington, 2435

Ditsong National Museum of Natural History, Pretoria, 1980

DIU Medunarodno sveučilište, 611

Divadelní ústav, Prague, 629

Divine Word College, Epworth, 2635

Divine Word University, Madang, 1672

División de Documentación e Información Educativa, Ministerio de Educación Nacional, Bogotá, 580

Division of Forest Products Research, Kitwe, 3025

Division of Forest Research, Kitwe, 3025

Divisional Government Public Library, Chittagong, 215

Dixie Regional Library System, 2447

Dixie State College of Utah, 2926

Dixon Gallery & Gardens, 2497

DLO–Research Institute for Plant Protection, 1540

Dniprodzerzhynsk Museum of Town History, 2202

Dniprodzerzhynsk State Technical University, 2211

Dnipropetrovsk Historical Museum 'D. I. Yavornystkiy', 2202

Dnipropetrovsk National Technical University of Railway Transport 'V. Lazaryan', 2211

Dnipropetrovsk National University, 2205

Dnipropetrovsk National University Library 'O. Gonchar', 2202

Dnipropetrovs'k State Agrarian University, 2204

Dnipropetrovsk State Art Museum, 2203

Dnipropetrovsk State Medical Academy, 2215

Doane College, 2749

Dobó István Vármúzeum, 982

Doboku-Gakkai, 1224

Dobroliubov Arkhangelsk Regional Research Library, 1852

Dobrudzha Agricultural Institute, 336

DOC Boulder Laboratories Library, 2433

Doctor John Garang De Mabior Memorial University of Science and Technology, 1994

Documenta Archiv, Kassel, 844

Documentary Library of the History of Medicine, Bucharest, 1791

Documentary Library of the National Archives, Bucharest, 1791

Documentation and Information Centre, 'La Salle' Foundation for Natural Sciences, 3004

Documentation Centre, 1906

Documentation Centre, Caribbean Community Secretariat, Georgetown, 966

Documentation Centre of Cambodia, 358

Documentation Centre of the Ministry of Foreign Affairs, 1618

Documentation Research and Training Centre, Bengaluru, 1013

Doge's Palace, 1190

Dogus University, 2167

Doha International Institute for Family Studies and Development, 1780

Dohto University, 1309

Dokkyo University, 1309

Dokuchaev Central Soil Museum, 1860

Dokuz Eylul University, Izmir, 2168

Dollezhal, N. A. Research and Development Institute of Power Engineering, Moscow, 1848

Dolnośląska Biblioteka Publiczna im. Tadeusza Mikulskiego we Wrocławiu, 1723

Dom Bosco Regional Museum, 306

Dominica Museum, 670

Dominican Academy, 671

Dominican Academy of History, 671

Dominican Association of University Presidents, 671

Dominican College, 2784

Dominican College of Philosophy and of Theology, Ottawa, 384

Dominican Medical Association, 671

Dominican School of Philosophy & Theology, 2527

Dominican Sugar Institute, 671

Dominican University, 2607

Dominican University of California, 2527

Dominion Arboretum, Ottawa, 372

Dominion Astrophysical Observatory, Victoria, 373

Domus Aurea, 1188

Don Juan Institute of Valencia, 2009

Don Mariano Marcos Memorial State University, Bacnotan, 1695

Don State Agrarian University, 1862

Don State Technical University, Rostov-on-Don, 1884

Don Zone Agricultural Research Institute, 1831

Donald F. and Mildred Topp Othmer Library of Chemical History, Philadelphia, 2456

Donald W. Reynolds Library, 2431

Donbass State Academy of Civil Engineering and Architecture, 2216

Donbass State Engineering Academy, 2216

Donbass State Technical University, Alchevsk, 2211

Doncaster College, 2360

Doncaster Museum and Art Gallery, 2283

Donders Institute for Brain, Cognition and Behaviour, 1540

Donetsk Art Museum, 2203

Donetsk Botanical Gardens, 2203

Donetsk Institute for Physics and Engineering 'O. O. Galkin', 2200

Donetsk Musical-Pedagogical Institute, 2216

Donetsk National Technical University, 2212

Donetsk National University, 2205

Donetsk National University of Economics and Trade 'M. Tuhan-Baranovskiy', Donetsk, 2205

Donetsk Scientific Research Institute of Traumatology and Orthopaedics, 2198

Dong Nai College of Decorative Arts, Hanoi, 3021

Dong Yang University, 1374

Dong-a University, 1373

Dongbei University of Finance and Economics, 496

Dongbu Library, 1364

Dongduk Women's University, 1374

Dong-Eui University, 1374

Dong-Eui University Central Library, 1364

Dongguk University, 1374

Dongguk University Library, 1365

Donghua University, 496

Dongseo University, 1374

Dongshin University, 1374

Donnelly College, 2640
Donner Institute for Research in Religious and Cultural History/ Steiner Memorial Library, 719
Door County Maritime Museum, 2501
Dordrechts Museum, 1550
Dordt College, 2635
Dorodnicyn Computing Centre of the Russian Academy of Sciences (CC RAS), 1848
Dorset County Library, 2268
Dorset County Museum and Dorset Natural History and Archaeological Society, 2283
Dorset Historical Society, 2499
Dortmund Museum of Art and Cultural History, 851
Doshisha University, 1310
Doshisha Women's College of Liberal Arts, 1310
Dostoevsky, F. M., Museum, Moscow, 1857
Dostoevsky Memorial Museum, St Petersburg, 1860
Douglas County Libraries, 2433
Dove Cottage and the Wordsworth Museum, 2285
Dover Public Library, Dover, DE, 2434
Dover Public Library, Dover, NH, 2449
Dow University of Health Sciences, 1646
Dowling College, 2784
Downing College, Cambridge, 2310
Downing College: The Maitland Robinson Library, 2266
Dozenal Society of America, 2412
Dr B. R. Ambedkar Centre For Biomedical Research (ACBR), 1063
Dr B. R. Ambedkar National Institute of Technology, 1073
Dr B. R. Ambedkar Open University, 1030
Dr B. R. Ambedkar University, 1030
Dr Babasaheb Ambedkar Marathwada University, 1030
Dr Babasaheb Ambedkar Open University, 1030
Dr Babasaheb Ambedkar Technological University, 1030
Dr Balasaheb Sawant Konkan Krishi Vidyapeeth, 1031
Dr Bhau Daji Lad Mumbai City Museum, Mumbai, 1022
Dr Cecil Cyrus Museum, Kingstown, 1906
Dr Francisco Cambournac Centre for the Study of Vectors and Infectious Diseases, 1765
Dr Harisingh Gour University, 1030
Dr Harisingh Gour Vishwavidyalaya, 1030
'Dr José Evaristo Uriburu' Numismatics Museum, 112
Dr Karl Kummer Institut für Sozialreform, Sozial- und Wirtschaftspolitik, 179
'Dr Luis E. Betetta' Allergy Research Institute, 1679
Dr M. G. R. University, 1073
Dr Mahmud Husain Library, 1643
Dr. Martin Luther King Jr. Library, 2431
Dr N. T. R. University Of Health Sciences, Andhra Pradesh, 1031
Dr Panjabrao Deshmukh Krishi Vidyapeeth, 1031
Dr Ram Manohar Lohia Avadh University, 1031
Dr Raziuddin Siddiqi Memorial Library, 1642
Dr Remeis-Sternwarte Bamberg, 836
Dr Sarvepalli Radhakrishnan Rajasthan Ayurveda University, 1031
Dr Soliman Fakeeh College for Nursing and Medical Science, 1915
Dr Sun Yat-sen Library, Taipei, 2120
Dr Sun Yat-sen Museum, 568
Dr Tjipto Mangunkusumo Hospital Library, 1086
Dr Williams's Library, 2272
Dr Yashwant Singh Parmar University of Horticulture & Forestry, 1031

Dragan European University of Lugoj, 1809
Drake University, 2635
Drama School attached to the E. B. Vakhtangov State Theatre 'B. V. Shchukin', 1901
Drama School attached to the Maly Theatre 'M. S. Shchepkin', 1901
Dramatiki Scholi, Athens, 958
Dramatiska Institutet, 2082
Drammen Library, 1618
Drammens Museum–Fylkesmuseum for Buskerud, 1619
Drammensbiblioteket, 1618
Dravidian University, Kuppam, 1032
Drenthe Archive, 1545
Drents Archief, 1545
Drents Museum, Assen, 1549
Dresden City Museum, 851
Dresden Museum of Zoology, 851
Dresden Public Libraries, 842
Drew University, Madison, 2758
Drexel University, 2855
Driestar Hogeschool, 1561
Druk Gyyelzin Tshula Lopdhey, 280
Drum Barracks Civil War Museum, 2466
Drury University, 2738
Drustva sudija Srbije, 1920
Društvo Arhivskih Radnika Bosne i Hercegovine, 288
Društvo Bibliotekara BiH, 288
Društvo Fizičara u BiH, 288
Društvo Istoričara BiH, 288
Društvo Ljekara BiH, 288
Društvo Matematičara Republike Srpske, 288
Društvo matematikov, fizikov in astronomov Slovenije, 1964
Društvo na Fizičarite na Republika Makedonija, 1432
Društvo na Istoričarite na Umetnosta od Makedonija, 1432
Društvo na Likovnite Umetnici na Makedonija, 1432
Društvo na Literaturnite Preveduvači na Makedonija, 1432
Društvo na Muzejskite Rabotnici na Makedonija, 1432
Društvo na Pisatelite na Makedonija, 1432
Društvo Pisaca BiH, 288
Društvo Psihologa BiH, 288
Društvo Psihologa Republike Srpske, 288
Društvo slovenskih skladateljev, 1963
Društvo Urbanista Bosne i Hercegovine, 288
Društvo za Filozofija, Sociologija i Politikologija na Makedonija, 1432
Društvo za Proučavanje i Unapredenje Pomorstva, Rijeka, 606
Društvo za Srpski Jezik i Književnost, 1921
Družbenomedicinski inštitut ZRC SAZU, 1965
Dryden Flight Research Center, Edwards, 2428
Državen Arhiv na Republika Makedonija, 1434
Državni arhiv Crne Gore, 1503
Državni hidrometeorološki zavod, 608
Državni univerzitet u Novom Pazaru, 1924
Državniot Univerzitet vo Tetovo, 1434
DTU Aqua, 654
DTU Fødevareinstituttet, 652
DTU Veterinærinstituttet, 653
Dubai Aerospace Enterprise Flight Academy, 2221
Dubai Medical College for Girls, 2221
Dubai Municipality Public Libraries, 2219
Dubai Pharmacy College, 2221
Dubai Police Academy, 2221
Dubai School of Government, 2221
Dublin City Gallery, The Hugh Lane, 1134
Dublin City Public Libraries, 1133
Dublin City University, 1134
Dublin Institute for Advanced Studies, 1137
Dublin Institute of Technology, 1138

Dublin University Biological Association, 1131
Dublin Writers Museum, 1134
Dublin Zoo, 1131
Dubrovacki muzeji, 609
Dubrovnik International University, 611
Dubrovnik Museums, 609
Dubuque Museum of Art, 2476
Duchesne College, 169
Duke University, 2807
Duke University Library, 2453
Duksung Women's University, 1374
Duluth Public Library, 2446
Dulwich Picture Gallery, 2287
Dumbarton Oaks Research Library and Collection, Washington, 2435
Dumfries Museums, 2283
Dumlupınar Üniversitesi, 2168
Dun Laoghaire Institute of Art, Design and Technology, 1138
Dunaújvárosi Főiskola, 999
Duncan Public Library, 2455
Dundalk Institute of Technology, 1138
Dundurn Castle, Hamilton, 379
Dunedin Public Art Gallery, 1578
Dunedin Public Libraries, 1576
Dunkers Kulturhus, 2064
Dunklin County Library, 2447
Dunn-Seiler Geology Museum, 2483
Dunsink Observatory, 1132
Dunwoody College of Technology, 2717
Duquesne University, 2855
Durban Museums, 1979
Durban University of Technology, 1981
Durham Arts, Libraries and Museums Department, 2268
Durham Public Library, 2449
Durham University, Oriental Museum, 2283
Durmishidze Institute of Plant Biochemistry, 814
Durrës Public Library, 85
Duryu Public Library, 1364
Dutch Association for Aesthetics, 1531
Dutch House of Representatives; Library Department and Documentation Department, 1548
Dutch Institute of Agricultural History, 1534
Dutch Institute of Systems and Control, 1543
Dutch Mycological Society, 1531
Dutch National Research School Combination Catalysis Controlled by Chemical Design (NRSC-Catalysis), 1543
Dutch Ornithological Union, 1531
Dutch Society for Philosophy of Science, 1532
Dutch Society of Educational Psychologists, 1527
Dutch Tile Museum, 1551
Duy Tan University, 3015
'Dvir Bialik' Municipal Central Public Library, 1145
Dwight D. Eisenhower Presidential Library and Museum, 2440
Dwight Foster Public Library, 2461
Dyal Singh Trust Library, 1643
Dzanelidze, A. I., Geological Institute, 814
Džemal Bijedić University of Mostar, 292
Dzhambul University, 1344

E

E. R. Burrowes School of Art, Georgetown, 967
'Eagle' Heraldry and Genealogy Society, 174
Eagle Public Library, 2438
Ealing Libraries, 2272
Earlham College, 2625
Early Childhood Research Centre, London, 2248
Early Christian Art Museum— Christian and Jewish Lapidaries, 2992
Early English Text Society, Oxford, 2236

Earth and Mineral Sciences Museum and Art Gallery, University Park, 2494
Earth Sciences Information Centre, Ottawa, 376
Earth Sciences Museum, National Department of Mineral Production at the Ministry of Mines and Energy, 307
Earth Sciences Research Administration, Jerusalem, 1143
East Africa Law Society, Arusha, 2130
East African Wildlife Society, Nairobi, 1352
East Asian Institute (EAI), Singapore, 1944
East Baton Rouge Parish Library, 2442
East Carolina University, 2814
East Central Georgia Regional Library, 2437
East Central Regional Library, Cambridge, 2446
East Central University, Ada, 2839
East China Normal University, 497
East China Normal University Library, 471
East China University of Science and Technology, 497
East Delta University, 221
East Hartford Public Library System, 2433
East Kazakhstan Scientific and Research Institute of Agriculture, 1339
East London Museum, 1979
East Longmeadow Public Library, 2445
East Lyme Public Library, 2434
East Riding College, 2360
East Stroudsburg University, 2862
East Sussex Library and Information Service, 2271
East Tennessee State University, 2890
East Texas Baptist University, 2905
East University named after Mahmud Kashgari-Barskani, 1396
East West Medical College, 234
East West University, Dhaka, 221
Eastern African Centre for Research on Oral Traditions and African National Languages (EACROTANAL), Zanzibar, 2131
Eastern and Southern African Management Institute, Arusha, 2134
Eastern Caribbean Center, St Thomas, 2978
Eastern Connecticut State University, 2556
Eastern Illinois University, 2607
Eastern Kentucky University, 2644
Eastern Mediterranean University, 624
Eastern Mennonite University, 2931
Eastern Michigan University, 2696
Eastern Mining and Metallurgical Research Institute for Non-ferrous Metals, Ust-Kamenogorsk, 1341
Eastern Nazarene College, 2670
Eastern New Mexico University, 2764
Eastern Oregon University, 2844
Eastern Siberian Research Centre, 1836
Eastern Siberian State Institute of Culture, 1900
Eastern Siberian State University of Technology, 1884
Eastern Southland Gallery (Inc.), 1578
Eastern University, 2973
Eastern University, Chenkaladi, 2042
Eastern University, St Davids, 2855
Eastern Virginia Medical School, 2931
Eastern Washington University, 2943
East-West Center, Honolulu, 2418
East-West University, Chicago, 2607
EAU Plant Biotechnological Research Centre EVIKA, 702
Eberhard-Karls-Universität Tübingen, 865
Ebonyi State University, 1607
EBS Universität für Wirtschaft und Recht, Tübingen, 866
Ecclesiastical History Society, Glasgow, 2233
Ecclesiological Society, London, 2244
Eckerd College, 2581

Escuela Nacional de Danzas, Buenos Aires, 123

Escuela Nacional de Danzas, Panama, 1670

Escuela Nacional de Educación Técnica 'Gral Ing. Enrique Mosconi', Plaza Huincul, 123

Escuela Nacional de Medicina del Trabajo, Madrid, 2005

Escuela Nacional de Teatro, Panama, 1670

Escuela Nacional Superior Autónoma de Bellas Artes del Perú, Lima, 1687

Escuela Politécnica Del Ejercito, Sangolquí, 679

Escuela Politécnica Nacional, 679

Escuela Regional de Bellas Artes 'Diego Quispe Tito', 1687

Escuela Regional de Música de Huánuco, 1687

Escuela Superior De Administración Pública, Bogotá, 581

Escuela Superior de Arte Dramático de Murcia, 2038

Escuela Superior de Arte 'Neptali Rincón', Maracaibo, 3009

Escuela Superior de Bellas Artes de San Carlos, 2038

Escuela Superior de Bellas Artes 'Ernesto de la Cárcova', Buenos Aires, 123

Escuela Superior de Bellas Artes 'Hernando Siles', 286

Escuela Superior de Formación Artística 'Mario Urteaga', 1687

Escuela Superior de Guerra, Buenos Aires, 122

Escuela Superior de Música 'Condorcunca', 1687

Escuela Superior de Música 'José Angel Lamas', Caracas, 3009

Escuela Superior de Música 'José María Valle Riestra', 1687

Escuela Superior de Música 'Luis Duncker Lavalle', 1687

Escuela Superior de Música Reina Sofía, 2038

Escuela Superior Politécnica Agropecuaria De Manabí, Calceta, 679

Escuela Superior Politécnica De Chimborazo, 680

Escuela Superior Politécnica Del Litoral, 680

Escuela Superior Pública de Arte Carlos Baca Flor, 1687

Escuela Superior Pública de Formación Artística 'Francisco Lase', 1687

Escuela Superior Técnica, Buenos Aires, 122

Escuela Técnica Superior de Arquitectura de Sevilla, 2038

Escuela Técnica Superior de Ingenieros Industriales, Madrid, 2037

Escuela Universitaria de Bibliotecología y Ciencias Afines 'Ing. Federico E. Capurro', 2982

ESIDEC – Ecole Supérieure Internationale de Commerce de Metz, 796

Esie Museum, 1593

ESIEE Paris, Noisy-le-Grand, 798

Esigodini Agricultural Institute, 3031

Esitpa – Ecole d'Ingénieurs en Agriculture, Val de Reuil, 796

Eskilstuna Municipal and County Library, 2061

Eskilstuna stads- och länsbibliotek, 2061

Eskişehir Arkeoloji Müzesi, 2162

Eskitis Institute for Cell and Molecular Therapies, 136

ESME Sudria, 798

Espace Maritime et Portuaire du Havre, 757

Española Public Library, 2450

ESPEME Nice, 795

Espéranto-Jeunes (JEFO), 742

Espoo City Library/Regional Central Library, 719

Espírito Santo Historical and Geographical Institute, 298

ESS Jean Piaget, 1778

ESSEC Business School, 1948

Essener Kolleg für Geschlechterforschung, 915

Essex Biomedical Sciences Institute, 2255

Essex County Council Libraries, 2268

Estação Agronómica Nacional, 1764

Estación Biológica de los Llanos, 3002

Estación de Investigaciones Marinas (EDIMAR), Isla de Margarita, 3002

Estación Experimental Agro-Industrial 'Obispo Colombres', 106

Estación Experimental Apícola, La Lisa, 616

Estación Experimental 'Las Vegas' de la Sociedad Nacional de Agricultura, Santiago, 450

Estación Experimental Táchira, Bramón, 3002

Estación Experimental Vista Florida, 1679

Estación Hidrobiológica, Puerto Quequén, 108

Estación Meteorológica, Ciudad Bolívar, 3003

Esterházy Castle Museum, Fertőd, 983

Estonian Academy of Arts, 705

Estonian Academy of Music, 705

Estonian Academy of Sciences, 701

Estonian Agrobiocentre, 702

Estonian Biocentre, 702

Estonian Energy Research Institute, Tallinn, 703

Estonian Geographical Society, 701

Estonian History Museum, 703

Estonian Institute for Futures Studies, 702

Estonian Institute of Agricultural Engineering, 702

Estonian Institute of Economic Research, 702

Estonian Institute of Economics at Tallinn University of Technology, 702

Estonian Interuniversity Population Research Centre, 703

Estonian Literary Museum, 703

Estonian Marine Institute, 702

Estonian Meteorological and Hydrological Institute, 702

Estonian Mother Tongue Society, 702

Estonian National Museum, 703

Estonian Naturalists' Society, 702

Estonian Open Air Museum, 703

Estonian Rectors' Conference, 701

Estonian Research Institute of Agriculture, 702

Estonian Theatre and Music Museum, 703

Estonian Union of the History and Philosophy of Science, 702

Estonian University of Life Sciences, 703

Estorick Collection of Modern Italian Art, London, 2287

Estyn, Cardiff, 2226

Etablissement Communal d'Enseignement Supérieur Artistique 'Le 75', 273

Etaireia Kypriakon Spoudon, 622

Etairia Ellinon Logotechnon, Athens, 945

Etairia Ellinon Theatricon Syngrapheon, Athens, 945

ETEA—Institución Universitaria de la Compañía de Jesús, 2037

Etelä-Karjalan Ammattikorkeakoulu, Lappeenranta, 735

EThames Graduate School, London, 2360

ETH-Bibliothek, Zürich, 2095

eThekwini Municipal Library Service, 1977

Ethiopia National Archives and Library Agency, 707

Ethiopian Institute of Agricultural Research, Addis Ababa, 707

Ethiopian Library and Information Association, 706

Ethiopian Mapping Agency, 707

Ethiopian Medical Association, 707

Ethiopian Public Health Association, 707

Ethniko Kentro Pistopoiisis (EKEPIS), Athens, 944

Ethniko Metsovio Polytechneio, Athens, 952

Ethnikon Idryma Erevnon, Athens, 945

Ethnikon Kai Kapodistriakon Panepistimion Athinon, 952

Ethnographic and Folk Culture Society, Lucknow, 1018

Ethnographic Collection, Lübeck, 855

Ethnographic Institute and Museum, Sofia, 340

Ethnographic institute of the Serbian Academy of Sciences and Arts, 1921

Ethnographic Museum, 86

Ethnographic Museum of Moldavia, 1796

Ethnographic Museum of Veliko Tărnovo, Veliko Tărnovo, 344

Ethnographic Museum, Plovdiv, 343

Ethnographic Museum, Vlorë, 86

Ethnographic Museum Zagreb, 610

Ethnographical Museum, Ankara, 2162

Ethnographical Museum, Arkhangai, 1499

Ethnographical Museum, Brașov, 1794

Ethnographical Museum Dresden, 854

Ethnographical Museum Herrnhut, 854

Ethnographical Museum in Leipzig, 854

Ethnographical Museum, Khartoum, 2048

Ethnographical Museum, Khentii, 1499

Ethnographical Museum of Belgrade, 1923

Ethnographical Museum of Split, 610

Ethnological Missionary Museum, 2992

Ethnological Museum, 849

Ethnological Museum of Geographical Society of Lisbon, Lisbon, 1771

Ethnological Museum of Porto, 1771

Ethnologisches Museum, Berlin, 849

Ethnology Society of Romania, 1784

Ethnomusicology Research and Studies Centre, 1665

Ethnos—Suomen Kansatieteilijöiden Yhdistys, 715

Ethnos—The Association of Finnish Ethnologists, 715

Etnografisch Museum, 260

Etnografiska Museet, 2066

Etnografski muzej Split, 610

Etnografski muzej u Beogradu, Belgrade, 1923

Etnografski muzej Zagreb, 610

Etnologický ústav AV ČR, v.v.i., 633

Eton College Library, 2269

Etpison Museum, 1662

Etruria Industrial Museum, Stoke on Trent, 2291

Etruscan Academy, 1163

Eugene Public Library, 2455

Eugenides Foundation Library, Athens, 947

Euler Institute for Discrete Mathematics and its Applications, 1540

Euler, L., International Institute of Mathematics, 1842

Eunice Kennedy Shriver National Institute of Child Health and Human Development, Bethesda, 2421

Euphrates University, 2170

Eurandom, 1540

Eureka College, 2607

EuroArab Management School (EAMS), Granada, 2037

EuroAsian Universities Association, 53

Europa Nostra, 45

Europacentrum Jean Monnet, 253

Europäische Bibliotheken für Theologie, 47

Europäische Gesellschaft für Ingenieur-Ausbildung, 59

Europa-Universität Viadrina, 866

European Academy of Anaesthesiology, 64

European Association for Health Information and Libraries, 47

European Association for International Education, 53

European Association for Population Studies, 49

European Association for Quality Assurance in Higher Education (ENQA), Helsinki, 57

European Association for the Education of Adults, 54

European Association of Distance Teaching Universities, 54

European Association of Institutions in Higher Education (EURASHE), 54

European Atomic Energy Community (Euratom), 69

European Banking Centre, Tilburg, 1533

European Business School London, 2363

European Centre for Advanced Research in Economics and Statistics, 253

European Centre for Medium-Range Weather Forecasts, 69

European Centre for Social Welfare Policy and Research, 49

European College of Business and Management, London, 2363

European College of Economics and Management, 351

European Consortium for Accreditation in Higher Education (ECA), The Hague, 57

European Construction Institute, Loughborough, 2248

European Cooperation in Science and Technology (COST), 257

European Cultural Centre, Bucharest, 1783

European Cultural Foundation, 45

European Distance and E-Learning Network (EDEN), 54

European Economic Association, 49

European Federation of Internal Medicine, 64

European Festivals Association, 68

European Foundation for Management Development (EFMD), 49

European Geosciences Union, 70

European Institute, London, 2248

European Institute of Education and Social Policy, 54

European Institute of Environmental Medicine, 70

European Institute of Public Administration, Maastricht, 1564

European Institute of Retailing and Services Studies (EIRASS), Eindhoven, 1533

European Institute of Technology, Paris, 798

European Journalism Observatory, Lugano, 2091

European Molecular Biology Laboratory, 70

European Molecular Biology Organization (EMBO), 70

European Movement, 2230

European Muslim Research Centre, 2261

European Network for Housing Research, 2058

European Organization for Civil Aviation Equipment (EUROCAE), 59

European Organization for Nuclear Research (CERN), 70

European Physical Society, 70

European Policies Research Centre, Glasgow, 2252

European Research Council, 70

European Research Institute, Birmingham, 2248

European Research Institute in Service Science (ERISS), Tilburg, 1533

European School of Economics, 2363

European School of Osteopathy, 2364

European Science Foundation, 70

European Society of Cardiology, 65

European Southern Observatory (ESO), Santiago, 451

European Southern Observatory, Garching, 70

European Space Agency (ESA), 70

European University Association, 54

European University College Brussels, 2221

European University Institute, Florence, 1207

European University of Lefke, 624

European Values Study (EVS), Tilburg, 1533
European Vision University, 1388
EuroPort Business School, 1561
Euskal Herriko Unibertsitatea, 2027
Euskaltzaindia, Bilbao, 739
Eustis Memorial Library, 2436
Evaluation and Accreditation Commission, Khartoum, 2047
Evangel University, Springfield, 2738
Evangelical Academy in Vienna, 177
Evangelical Press Society of Bavaria, 845
Evangelical Seminary, Myerstown, 2855
Evangelical-Lutheran Theological University, 998
Evangélikus Hittudományi Egyetem, Budapest, 998
Evangelische Akademie Wien, 177
Evangelischer Presseverband für Bayern eV, Munich, 845
Evansville Museum of Arts, History & Science, 2475
Evelyn Hone College of Applied Arts and Commerce, Lusaka, 3026
Everest College Phoenix, 2508
Everest University, 2582
Everett Public Library, 2460
Evergreen Museum & Library, 2480
Evergreen State College, Olympia, 2943
Everhart Museum of Natural History, Science and Art, 2494
Everson Museum of Art, 2489
Evolução Litosférica e Meio Ambiente Superficial, 1765
Evolutionsmuseet, 2068
Évora Public Library, 1768
Ewell Sale Stewart Library and Archives of the Academy of Natural Sciences, Philadelphia, 2456
Ewha Woman's University Library, 1365
Ewha Women's University, 1374
Ewing Memorial Library, 1643
Excelsior College, 2784
Executive Committee of the Bolivian University, 281
Exeter Biocatalysis Centre, 2260
Exeter Cathedral Library and Archives, 2269
Exeter Centre for Ethno-Political Studies (EXCEPS), 2252
Exeter Centre for Strategic Processes and Operations (XSPO), 2249
Exeter Centre for the Study of Esotericism (EXESESO), 2261
Exeter College, 2360
Exeter College Library, Oxford, 2278
Exeter College, Oxford, 2348
Exeter Historical Society, 2486
Exeter Interdisciplinary Institute (EII), 2249
Exeter Turkish Studies, 2261
Experimental and Research Centre for Leather, Ulan Bator, 1498
Experimental and Research Centre for Wool, Ulan Bator, 1498
Experimental Centre for Low-Cost Housing, Córdoba, 107
Experimental Factory for Analytical Instrumentation, St Petersburg, 1848
Experimental Factory for Scientific Instrumentation, Chernogolovka, 1848
Experimental Institute of Agricultural Zoology, Florence, 1172
Experimental Natural Philosophy Society, Rotterdam, 1532
Experimental Psychology Society, Bristol, 2243
Experimental Research Institute of Metal-Cutting Machine Tools, Moscow, 1848
Experimental Station of the Research Institute for Arable Farming, Korçë, 84
Expertise Centrum Hoger Onderwijs, 254
Exposition Permanente du Débarquement, Arromanches, 756
EXPres, 1533

F

F. Brooke Whiting House & Museum, 2480
Faaborg Museum, 657
Fabian Society, London, 2230
Fachbereichsbibliothek Rechtswissenschaften, Vienna, 185
Fachgebiet Wasserwirtschaft und Hydrosystemmodellierung, 828
Fachhochschule IMC Krems, 200
Fachhochschule Nordwestschweiz, 2112
Fachhochschule Technikum Kärnten, 200
Fachhochschule Technikum Wien, 200
Fachhochschule Vorarlberg, 200
Fachhochschule Westschweiz, 2112
Fachhochschulrat (FHR), 172
Fachhochschul-Studiengang Bauingenieurwesen-Baumanagement, 199
Fachhochschul-Studiengang Burgenland GmbH, Eisenstadt, 200
Fachhochschul-Studiengang Oberösterreich, Graz, 200
Fachhochschul-Studiengang Salzburg, 200
Fachhochschul-Studiengänge bfi Wien, 200
Fachhochschul-Studiengänge Campus Wien, 200
Fachhochschul-Studiengänge der Wiener Neustadt, 200
Fachhochschul-Studiengänge Kufstein, 200
Fachhochschul-Studiengänge St Pölten, 200
Fachhochschul-Studiengänge Technikum Joanneum, Graz, 200
Fachhochschul-Studiengänge WIFI Steiermark, Graz, 200
Facoltà Di Teologia Di Lugano, 2113
Faculdade de Belas Artes de São Paulo, 330
Faculdade de Ciências de Barretos, 329
Faculdade de Ciências Políticas e Econômicas de Cruz Alta, 328
Faculdade de Ciências Sociais Aplicadas do Sul de Minas Gerais, 328
Faculdade de Direito Cândido Mendes, Rio de Janeiro, 329
Faculdade de Direito da Guiné-Bissau, 965
Faculdade de Direito de São Bernardo do Campo, 329
Faculdade de Direito de Sorocaba, 329
Faculdade de Engenharia de Barretos, 329
Faculdade de Medicina do Triângulo Mineiro, 329
Faculdade Estadual de Ciências Econômicas de Apucarana, 329
Faculdade Santa Marcelina (FASM), Perdizes, 330
Faculdades ASMEC, 328
Faculdades Integradas Hebraico Brasileira Renascença, 328
Faculdades Oswaldo Cruz, 328
Facultad de Derecho, San Juan, 2976
Facultad de Teología de Granada (Institución Universitaria de la Compañía de Jesús), Granada, 2029
Facultad Latinoamericana de Ciencias Sociales (FLACSO), Santiago, 460
Faculté de Droit et Science Politique, 767
Faculté de Langues, Littératures et Civilisations Étrangères, 789
Faculté de Médecine, de Pharmacie et d'Odonto-Stomatologie, Bamako, 1456
Faculté de Psychologie, 789
Faculté d'Économie, Gestion et AES, 767
Faculté des Lettres et Sciences Sociales, Brest, 797
Faculté des Sciences, Espaces, Sociétés, 789
Faculté des Sciences Juridiques et Economiques, Bamako, 1456
Faculté d'Histoire, Arts et Archéologie, 789

Faculté Libre de Théologie Protestante de Paris, 797
Faculté Polytechnique de Mons, 267
Faculteit Katholieke Theologie te Utrecht, 1561
Faculteit voor Vergelijkende Godsdienstwetenschappen, Antwerp, 270
Facultés Universitaires Catholiques de Mons, 268
Facultés Universitaires Notre-Dame de la Paix, 268
Facultés Universitaires Saint-Louis, 269
Faculty Centre of Biodiversity at University of Vienna, Vienna, 180
Faculty for Comparative Study of Religions, Antwerp, 270
Faculty Library of Legal Studies, Vienna, 185
Faculty of Advocates, Edinburgh, 2230
Faculty of Agricultural Sciences, Tjele, 653
Faculty of Geo-Information Science and Earth Organization Library, 1546
Faculty of Hygiene and Environmental Studies, Khartoum, 2050
Faculty of Islamic Call, 1417
Faculty of Law, Economics and Business, 778
Faculty of Life Sciences Library, Frederiksberg, 655
Faculty of Protestant Theology, Brussels, 268
Faculty of Royal Designers for Industry, London, 2245
Faculty of Theology in Paderborn, 936
Failaka Island Archaeological Museum, 1391
Failaka Island Ethnographic Museum, 1391
Faipari Tudományos Egyesület, Budapest, 975
Fairbanks Community Museum, 2464
Fairbanks Museum and Planetarium, 2499
Fairfax County Public Library, 2460
Fairfield Museum and History Center, 2468
Fairfield University, 2556
Fairhope Public Library, 2429
Fairleigh Dickinson University, Teaneck, 2758
Fairmont State University, 2952
Faith Baptist Bible College and Theological Seminary, Ankeny, 2635
Fakir Mohan University, 1032
Fakultätszentrum für Biodiversität an der Universität Wien, 180
FALCK NUTEC—Norwegian Underwater Technology Centre, 1617
Falcon College of Hotel Management and Tourism, 2221
Falkirk Council Library Services, 2269
Falmouth Memorial Library, 2442
Falmouth Public Library, 2445
Family and Education Institute, Moscow, 1834
Family Assessment and Support Unit, Hull, 2261
Family History Library of the Church of Jesus Christ of Latter-day Saints, Salt Lake City, 2459
Far East State Agrarian University, 1862
Far Eastern Institute of Geology, Vladivostok, 1843
Far Eastern Institute of Trade, Vladivostok, 1899
Far Eastern Library — Library of the Museum of Far Eastern Antiquities, Stockholm, 2062
Far Eastern National Technical University, Vladivostok, 1884
Far Eastern Research Institute of Mineral Raw Materials, Khabarovsk, 1848
Far Eastern Scientific Center of Physiology and Pathology of Respiration, 1836
Far Eastern State Marine Reserve, Vladivostok, 1861

Far Eastern State Technical Fisheries University, Vladivostok, 1884
Far Eastern State Transport University, Khabarovsk, 1885
Far Eastern State University Central Library, Vladivostok, 1855
Far Eastern State University, Vladivostok, 1866
Far Eastern University Library, Manila, 1690
Far Eastern University, Manila, 1695
Faraday Centre, Napier, 1578
Farah Provincial Library, 80
Fare Vana'a, 800
Far-Eastern State Academy of Arts, Vladivostok, 1900
Far-Eastern State Maritime Academy, Vladivostok, 1898
Farga Rossell, 98
Färgfabriken Contemporary Art Gallery, 2066
Fargo Air Museum, 2491
Farg'ona Dalvat Universiteti, 2986
Farg'ona Polytechnic Institute, 2988
Faridpur Medical College, 234
Farmaceutiska Föreningen i Finland, 716
Farmaceutsko Društvo na Makedonija, 1432
Farmaceutsko društvo Republike Srpske, 288
Farmakologický ústav AV ČR, 631
Farmers' Association of Iceland, 1000
Farming Systems Research Unit, Harare, 3028
Farmington Public Library, 2443
Farnborough College of Technology, 2366
Farnsworth Art Museum, 2479
Faro Municipal Museum, 1770
Faroe Marine Research Institute, 665
Faroe-British Museum, 666
Faroese Archaeological Society, 665
Faroese Food and Veterinary Agency, 665
Faroese Society of Science and Letters, 665
Faroese Writers' Association, 665
Faryab Higher Education Institution, 82
Faryab Provincial Library, Andkhoi, 80
Faryab Provincial Library, Maymana, 80
Fashion and Textile Museum, London, 2287
Fashion Business Academy 'Symbat', 1350
Fashion Institute of Technology, New York, 2784
Fatih Üniversitesi, 2170
Fatima Jinnah Women University, 1646
Faulkner University, 2503
Fauna & Flora International, Cambridge, 2241
Fauquier County Public Library, 2460
Fayette Community Library, 2440
Fayetteville Public Library, 2431
Fayetteville State University, 2814
Fazl-i-Omar Research Institute, 1640
FDI World Dental Federation, 62
Federação Brasileira de Associações de Bibliotecários, Cientistas da Informação e Instituições (FEBAB), 297
Federación Argentina de Asociaciones de Anestesia, Analgesia y Reanimación, 104
Federación de Instituciones Mexicanas Particulares de Educación Superior, México, 1465
Federación Española de Asociaciones de Archiveros, Bibliotecarios, Arqueólogos, Museólogos y Documentalistas, 1997
Federación Internacional de Mujeres de Negocios y Profesionales, 50
Federación Internacional de Universidades Católicas, 55
Federación Lanera Argentina, 106
Federación Médica Colombiana, 579
Federación Médica Ecuatoriana, Quito, 678
Federación Médica Peruana, Lima, 1678

Federación Mexicana de Ginecología y Obstetricia, 1467

Federación Mundial de Sociedades de Anestesiólogos, 68

Federacja Stowarzyszeń Naukowo-Technicznych–Naczelna Organizacja Techniczna (FSNT-NOT), Warsaw, 1712

Federal Agency for Education, Moscow, 1827

Federal Agency for Postgraduate Education, Brasília, 296

Federal Archival Agency, 1853

Federal Archives, Koblenz, 844

Federal Bar Association, Washington, 2402

Federal Bureau for Medical and Social Expertise, Moscow, 1836

Federal Bureau of Statistics, Islamabad, 1639

Federal College of Agriculture, Akure, 1613

Federal College of Agriculture, Ibadan, 1613

Federal College of Forestry, Ibadan, 1613

Federal Council on the Arts and the Humanities, Washington, 2397

Federal G. G. Devyatykh Institute of the Chemistry of High-Purity Substances, Nizhny Novgorod, 1843

Federal Hydrometeorological Institute, 289

Federal Institute for Geosciences and Natural Resources, Hanover, 836

Federal Institute for Materials Research and Testing, 838

Federal Institute for Population Research, 837

Federal Institute for Serums and Biomedicines, 835

Federal Institute of Agricultural Economics, Vienna, 178

Federal Institute of Industrial Research (FIIRO), Lagos, 1592

Federal Maritime and Hydrographic Agency, 836

Federal Ministry of Agriculture, Forestry, Environment and Water Management Sub-Dept VII/3–Water Balance, Vienna, 180

Federal Ministry of Education and Research, Berlin, 818

Federal Ministry of Education, Arts and Culture, Vienna, 172

Federal Ministry of Science and Research, Vienna, 172

Federal Ministry of Science and Technology, Library and Documentation Centre, Ibadan, 1593

Federal Office and Research Centre for Agriculture, Vienna, Vienna, 177

Federal Office and Research Centre for Forests, 178

Federal Office for Agriculture, 2091

Federal Office for the Care and Protection of Monuments, Vienna, 173

Federal Office of Meteorology and Climatology (MeteoSwiss), 2090

Federal Planning Bureau, Brussels, 254

Federal Polytechnic, Ado-Ekiti, 1611

Federal Polytechnic, Auchi, 1611

Federal Polytechnic, Bauchi, 1611

Federal Polytechnic, Bida, 1611

Federal Polytechnic, Ede, 1612

Federal Polytechnic, Idah, 1612

Federal Polytechnic, Ilaro, 1612

Federal Polytechnic, Kaura Namoda, 1612

Federal Polytechnic, Mubi, 1613

Federal Polytechnic, Nasarawa, 1613

Federal Polytechnic, Nekede, 1613

Federal Polytechnic, Offa, 1613

Federal Polytechnic, Oko, 1613

Federal Research Centre for Cultivated Plants Information Centre and Library, 840

Federal Research Institute for Agriculture in Alpine Regions, Gumpenstein, 178

Federal Research Institute for Health Education and Health Promotion, Moscow, 1836

Federal Research Institute for Rural Areas, Forestry and Fisheries, 831

Federal Research Institute of Paediatric Gastroenterology, Nizhnii Novgorod, 1836

Federal School of Dental Hygiene, Lagos, 1613

Federal Service for Supervision in Education and Science, Moscow, 1826

Federal Service of State Statistics, 1833

Federal State Library of Upper Austria, 184

Federal State Unitary Enterprise Central Scientific Research Automobile and Engine Institute of the Russian Federation, Moscow, 1848

Federal Statistical Office, Neuchatel, 2086

Federal Statistical Office, Wiesbaden, 833

Federal Trust for Education and Research, London, 2230

Federal University of Technology, Akure, 1597

Federal University of Technology, Minna, 1597

Federal University of Technology, Owerri, 1597

Federal University of Technology, Yola, 1598

Federal Urdu University of Arts, Science and Technology, Karachi, 1646

Federalni Meteorološki Zavod, Sarajevo, 289

Federalni Zavod za Statistiku, Sarajevo, 289

Federasie van Afrikaanse Kultuurvereniginge, 1973

Federaţia Filatelică Română, 1783

Federatie BelastingAcademie BV, 1561

Fédération Dentaire Internationale (FDI), 62

Fédération des Architectes Suisses, 2085

Fédération des Gynécologues et Obstétriciens de Langue Française, Paris, 743

Fédération Française de Spéléologie, 742

Fédération Française des Sociétés de Sciences Naturelles, 744

Fédération Française pour les sciences de la Chimie, Paris, 745

Fédération International des Producteurs Agricoles, 44

Fédération Internationale d'Astronautique, 72

Fédération Internationale d'Education Physique (FIEP), 66

Fédération Internationale de Biologie Cellulaire, 72

Fédération Internationale de Gynécologie et d'Obstétrique, 66

Fédération Internationale de Laiterie, 44

Fédération Internationale de l'Automatique, 58

Fédération Internationale de Neurophysiologie Clinique, 63

Fédération Internationale des Archives du Film, 48

Fédération Internationale des Associations d'Anatomistes, 66

Fédération Internationale des Associations d'Etudes Classiques, 40

Fédération Internationale des Associations de Bibliothécaires et des Bibliothèques, 48

Fédération Internationale des Collèges de Chirurgie, 63

Fédération Internationale des Ecrivains de Langue Française (FIDELF), 45

Fédération Internationale des Femmes Diplômées des Universités, 55

Fédération Internationale des Géomètres, 60

Fédération Internationale des Hôpitaux, 66

Fédération Internationale des Langues et Littératures Modernes, 39

Fédération Internationale des Musiciens, 68

Fédération Internationale des Organisations de Science Sociale, 40

Fédération Internationale des Professeurs de Français, 54

Fédération Internationale des Sociétés d'Ingénieurs des Techniques de l'Automobile (FISITA), 60

Fédération Internationale des Sociétés de Microscopie, 72

Fédération Internationale des Sociétés de Philosophie, 39

Fédération Internationale des Sociétés Oto-rhino-laryngologiques, 63

Fédération Internationale des Universités Catholiques (FIUC), 55

Fédération Internationale du Diabète, 63

Fédération Internationale du Génie Médical et Biologique, 66

Fédération Internationale pour la Recherche Théâtrale, 46

Fédération Internationale pour le Droit Européen (FIDE), 62

Fédération Internationale pour l'Habitation, l'Urbanisme et l'Aménagement des Territoires (FIHUAT), 60

Fédération Interuniversitaire de l'Enseignement à Distance (FIED), Paris, 739

Fédération Mondiale des Concours Internationaux de Musique, 68

Fédération Mondiale des Sociétés de Neurochirurgie, 68

Fédération Mondiale pour la Santé Mentale, 41

Fédération Nationale des Costumes Suisses, Burgdorf, 2090

Fédération Nationale des Médecins Radiologues, Paris, 743

Federation of Accrediting Agencies of the Philippines (FAAP), Quezon City, 1688

Federation of American Societies for Experimental Biology, 2411

Federation of Anaesthesiologists and Reanimatologists, Moscow, 1828

Federation of Arab Scientific Research Councils, 70

Federation of Arab Scientific Research Councils, Baghdad, 1123

Federation of Asian Scientific Academies and Societies (FASAS), 70

Federation of Astronomical and Geophysical Data Analysis Services, 39

Federation of Australian Scientific and Technological Societies, 133

Federation of British Artists, London, 2232

Federation of Finnish Learned Societies, 713

Federation of Mexican Higher Education Institutions, 1465

Federation of Obstetric and Gynaecological Societies of India, 1008

Federation of Technical and Scientific Associations, 828

Federation of the Scientific-Technical Unions in Bulgaria, 335

Federation of the Universities of the Islamic World (FUIW), 54

Fédération Royale des Sociétés d'Architectes de Belgique, 249

Fédération Suisse des Avocats, 2086

Fédération Suisse des Notaires, 2086

Fédération Universelle des Associations Chrétiennes d'Etudiants, 57

Fédération Wallonne de l'Agriculture, 249

Federazione delle Associazioni Scientifiche e Tecniche, Milan, 1167

Federazione Italiana di Elettrotecnica, Elettronica, Automazione, Informatica e Telecomunicazioni (AEIT), 1168

Federazione Svizzera degli Avvocati, 2086

Federazione Svizzera dei Notai, 2086

Fedorov, E. K., Institute of Applied Geophysics, 1848

Feijoo Institute of Eighteenth-Century Studies, 2005

Fejér Megyei Múzeumok Igazgatósága—Intercisa Múzeum, Dunaújváros, 982

Félag Íslenzkra Leikara, 1001

Félag Íslenzkra Listdansara, 1001

Félag Íslenzkra Tónlistarmanna, 1001

Félag Kvikmyndagerðarmanna, 1001

Félag Leikstjóra á Íslandi, 1001

Felician College, Lodi, 2758

Felicja Blumental Music Center and Library, 1146

FelixArchief/Stadsarchief, Antwerp, 257

Fellowship of Australian Writers NSW Inc., 132

Felsőoktatási és Tudományos Tanács, Budapest, 972

Felsőoktatási Konferenciák Szövetsége, Budapest, 972

Felsőoktatási Kutatóintézet, Budapest, 976

Feng Chia University, Taichung, 2121

Ferdinand Postma Library, North-West University, 1978

Ferdinand Tavadze Institute of Metallurgy and Materials Science, 814

Ferdowsi University of Mashhad, 1109

Ferdowsi University of Mashhad Information Centre and Central Library, 1107

Ferenc Hopp Museum of Eastern Asiatic Arts, 981

Ferenc Liszt Academy of Music, 990

Ferenc Liszt Academy of Music, Budapest, 973

Ferenc Liszt Memorial Museum and Research Centre, 981

Ferenczy Múzeum, 984

Ferghana State University, 2986

Fergusson College, Pune, 1079

Fermilab, Washington, 2425

Fernando Ortiz Library of the Institute of Literature and Linguistics, Havana, 617

Fernbank Museum of Natural History, 2472

Fernuniversität In Hagen, 867

Ferris State University, 2696

Ferrous Metallurgy Society, Moscow, 1829

Ferrum College, 2932

Fersman Mineralogical Museum, 1857

Fertilizers Research Institute, Puławy, 1713

Fesenkov Astrophysical Institute, 1340

FH Gesundheitsberufe OÖ GmbH, 200

FHG—Centre for Health Sciences, Tirol GmBH, 200

FHG—Zentrum für Gesundheitsberufe Tirol GmBH, 200

FH—Wien University of Applied Sciences, 200

FH—Wien-Studiengänge der WKW, 200

FIDM Museum & Galleries, 2466

Field Crops Institute, Chirpan, 336

Field Crops Research Institute, Giza, 687

Field Museum, 2474

Field Naturalists Club of Victoria, 134

Field Studies Council, Shrewsbury, 2240

Fielding Graduate University, 2527

Fife Council Libraries and Museums, 2270

Figge Art Museum, 2476

Fiji Higher Education Commission, 710

Fiji Medical Association, 710

Fiji Museum, 711

Fiji National University, 711

Filatov Institute for Eye Diseases and Tissue Therapy, Odesa, 2198

Filipinas Heritage Library, 1690

Filmakademie Baden-Württemberg, 935

Filozofický ústav Akademie věd České republiky, Prague, 630

Filozofický ústav AV ČR, 633

Filozofski inštitut ZRC SAZU, 1965
Filozofsko-Teološki Institut Družbe Isusove, Zagreb, 2994
Finance Academy under the Government of the Russian Federation, 1896
Finance and Taxation Institute, 834
'Financial Academy' JSC, Astana, 1350
Financial Markets Group, London, 2252
Financial Research Institute, Moscow, 1833
Fine Art and Ceramic Museum, West Jakarta, 1087
Fine Art Museum, Cullowhee, 2490
Fine Arts Council, Santo Domingo, 676
Finger Lakes Library System, Ithaca, 2451
Finlandia University, 2696
Finlands biblioteksförening, 714
Finlands museiförbund, 714
Finlands Nationalmuseum, 721
Finlands svenska författareförening, 715
Finlands Tonsättare rf, 715
Finlandsinstitutet, 2055
Finnish Academy of Science and Letters, 713
Finnish Academy of Technology, 718
Finnish Adult Education Association, 713
Finnish Air Pollution Prevention Society, 717
Finnish Anthropological Society, 717
Finnish Antiquarian Society, 715
Finnish Art Society, 715
Finnish Artificial Intelligence Society, 718
Finnish Association for Administrative Studies, 714
Finnish Association for Aerosol Research, 718
Finnish Association for Mass Communication Research, 713
Finnish Association for Nature Conservation, 717
Finnish Association for Structural Mechanics, 718
Finnish Association of Architects, 713
Finnish Association of Civil Engineers, 713
Finnish Association of Criminologists, 714
Finnish Astronomical Society, 713
Finnish Bryological Society, 717
Finnish Cardiac Society, 716
Finnish Chemical Society, 717
Finnish Conference of Polytechnic Rectors, 713
Finnish Cultural Centre, Stockholm, 2055
Finnish Demographic Society, 714
Finnish Dental Society Apollonia, 716
Finnish Dramatists' Union, 715
Finnish Economic Association, 714
Finnish Economic History Association, 714
Finnish Educational Research Association, 719
Finnish Environment Institute, 719
Finnish Folklore Society, 717
Finnish Food Safety Authority—Evira, 718
Finnish Forest History Society, 715
Finnish Forest Research Institute, 718
Finnish Funding Agency for Technology and Innovation, 713
Finnish Game and Fisheries Research Institute, 718
Finnish Geodetic Institute, 719
Finnish Higher Education Evaluation Council, 713
Finnish Historical Society, 715
Finnish Institute of Marine Research, 719
Finnish Lawyers' Society, 714
Finnish Legal Society, 714
Finnish Library Association, 714
Finnish Limnological Society, 717
Finnish Literary Research Society, 715
Finnish Literature Society, 716
Finnish Mathematical Society, 717
Finnish Medical Society Duodecim, 716
Finnish Meteorological Institute, 719

Finnish Museum of Natural History, 721
Finnish Museum of Photography, 721
Finnish Museums Association, 714
Finnish Musicological Society, 715
Finnish National Board of Education, 713
Finnish National Gallery, 721
Finnish Nuclear Society, 718
Finnish Nurses Association, 716
Finnish Operations Research Society, 718
Finnish Oriental Society, 717
Finnish Peatland Society, 714
Finnish Pharmaceutical Society, 716
Finnish Pharmacological Society, 716
Finnish Political Science Association, 714
Finnish Psychiatric Association, 717
Finnish Psychological Society, 717
Finnish Railway Museum, 721
Finnish Research Library Association, 714
Finnish Society for Aesthetics, 717
Finnish Society for Computer Science, 718
Finnish Society for Dairy Science, 713
Finnish Society for Environmental Sciences, 717
Finnish Society for Ethnomusicology, 715
Finnish Society for Tribology, 718
Finnish Society for Urban Studies, 713
Finnish Society of Automation, 718
Finnish Society of Chemical Engineers, 717
Finnish Society of Chemistry, 717
Finnish Society of Church History, 715
Finnish Society of Environmental Law, 714
Finnish Society of Food Science and Technology, 713
Finnish Society of Forestry Science, 714
Finnish Society of International Law, 714
Finnish Society of Nuclear Medicine, 716
Finnish Society of Sciences and Letters, 713
Finnish Society of Sport Sciences, 713
Finnish Society of Surveying Sciences, 717
Finnish Society of Toxicology, 716
Finnish Statistical Society, 714
Finnish Theological Literature Society, 717
Finnish Veterinary Association, 713
Finno-Ugrian Society, 716
Finsen Laboratory, Copenhagen, 653
Finska Fornminnesföreningen, 715
Finska Historiska Samfundet, 715
Finska Kyrkohistoriska Samfundet, 715
Finska Läkaresällskapet, 716
Finska Litteratursällskapet, Helsinki, 716
Firat Üniversitesi, 2170
Firdavsi Tajik National Library, 2127
First Historical Archives of China, 470
First Nations University of Canada, 424
Fiscaal Instituut Tilburg (FIT), 1536
Fiscal—Legal Institute, Dushanbe, 2128
Fisher College, 2671
Fisher More College, 2904-2905
Fisheries and Fish-farming Research Institute, 2980
Fisheries and Nautical Training Centre, Majuro, 1459
Fisheries Industry Institute, Burgas, 336
Fisheries Research Centre, 616
Fisheries Research Station, Monkey Bay, 1441
Fisheries Society of Nigeria, 1589
Fishery Research Institute, 450
Fishery Technological Development Division, Bangkok, 2136
Fishing and Maritime Museum, 2068
Fisk University, 2890
Fiske- och sjöfartsmuseet, 2068
Fitchburg Art Museum, 2481
Fitchburg State University, 2671
Fitzwilliam College, Cambridge, 2310
Fitzwilliam College Library, 2266

Fitzwilliam Museum, Cambridge, 2282
Five Branches University, 2527
Five Towns College, 2785
Flagler College, 2582
Flagler County Public Library System, 2436
Flagstaff City-Coconino County Public Library, 2430
Flax Research Institute, Torzhok, 1831
Fleischmann Planetarium & Science Center, 2485
Flemish Council of University Colleges, 249
Flemish Interuniversity Council, 249
Flemish Ministry of Education and Training, 248
Flemish Museums Association, 250
Flinders Petrie Library, Khartoum, 2048
Flinders University, 156
Flinders University Library, 140
Flint Institute of Arts, 2482
Flintshire Library and Information Service, 2277
Florence County Library System, 2457
Florence Griswold Museum, 2468
Florence Museum of Art, Science and History, 2496
Florence-Lauderdale Public Library, 2429
Florentino Ameghino Provincial Museum of Natural History, 113
Florida Agricultural and Mechanical University, 2582
Florida Atlantic University, 2583
Florida Christian College, 2583
Florida College, 2583
Florida Gulf Coast University, 2583
Florida Hospital College of Health Sciences, 2583
Florida Institute of Technology, 2583
Florida International University, 2584
Florida Memorial University, 2584
Florida National College, 2584
Florida Southern College, 2584
Florida State College at Jacksonville, 2584
Florida State University, 2584
Florida State University Libraries, 2436
Főapátsági Könyvtár Pannonhalma, 980
FOBID Netherlands Library Forum, 1528
Focke-Museum, Bremen, 850
FOI Swedish Defence Research Agency, 2060
FOI Totalförsvarets Forskningsinstitut, 2060
Folger Shakespeare Library, Washington, 2435
Folk Art Museum, Constanța, 1795
Folk Literature Research Institute, Ulan Bator, 1497
Folk Music House, 2065
Folk Research Centre, Castries, 1905
Folkeuniversitetet I Danmark, 649
Folkhögskolornas informationstjänst, Stockholm, 2054
Folklore Archives of the Finnish Literature Society, 720
Folklore Museum, Amman, 1334
Folklore Museum in Schleswig, 857
Folklore Museum, Tournai, 263
Folklore of Ireland Society, 1131
Folklore Society, London, 2244
Folkmusikens hus, 2065
FOM Institute of Atomic and Molecular Physics (AMOLF), 1541
FOM—Dutch Institute for Fundamental Energy Research (DIFFER), 1541
FOM—Instituut voor Atoom- en Molecuulfysica, Amsterdam, 1541
FON University, 1434
FON Univerzitet, 1434
Fondacionin e Kosovës për Shoqëri të Hapur, 1387
Fondation Baur, Musée des Arts d'Extrême-Orient, Geneva, 2096
Fondation Bibliotheca Afghanica, 2094
Fondation Biermans-Lapôtre, 741
Fondation Emile Blémont, 743
Fondation et Institut Charles de Gaulle, Paris, 747

Fondation Européenne de la Culture, 45
Fondation internationale des stations scientifiques du Jungfraujoch et du Gornergrat, 73
Fondation Maeght, 761
Fondation Maison des Sciences de l'Homme, Paris, 749
Fondation Nationale des Sciences Politiques, Paris, 740
Fondation pour la Recherche de Base dans les Sciences de l'Homme, 2092
Fondation 'Pour la Science', Centre international de Synthèse, 70
Fondation Saint-John Perse, Aix-en-Provence, 742
Fondation Suisse pour l'Energie, 2089
Fondation Suisse pour Recherches Alpines, 2089
Fondazione Archivio del Moderno, Medrisio, 2091
Fondazione Brescia Musei, Brescia, 1182
Fondazione Centro Italiano di Studi sull'Alto Medioevo, 1173
Fondazione di Ricerca 'Istituto Carlo Cattaneo', Bologna, 1175
Fondazione Giangiacomo Feltrinelli, 1172
Fondazione Guglielmo Marconi, 1176
Fondazione Internazionale Premio E. Balzan—'Premio', Milan, 1163
Fondazione ISI, Turin, 1174
Fondazione Istituto Italiano per la Storia della Musica, 1165
Fondazione Luigi Villa, Milan, 1166
Fondazione Marco Besso, Rome, 1168
Fondazione Rui, Rome, 1162
Fondazione Salvatore Romano, 1183
Fondazione Scientifica Querini-Stampalia, Venice, 1182
Fondazione Torino Musei, 1189
Fondo Del Sol Visual Arts Center, 2470
Fondo Nacional de las Artes, Buenos Aires, 103
Fonds national suisse de la Recherche scientifique, Bern, 2085
Fonds Quetelet Library, Brussels, 258
Fonds zur Förderung der wissenschaftlichen Forschung, Vienna, 172
Fontbonne University, 2738
Fontys Bestuursacademie—Instituut voor Bestuurlijke Innovatie, 1561
Fontys Hogescholen, 1553
Fontys University of Applied Sciences, 1553
Food & Biobased Research, Wageningen, 1534
Food and Agriculture Organization of the United Nations, 42
Food and Environment Research Agency (FERA), Sand Hutton, 2250
Food and Nutrition Research Institute, Manila, 1690
Food Crops Research Institute, Gialoc, 3011
Food Industry Research Institute, Hanoi, 3013
Food Research and Development Institute, Plovdiv, 336
Food Research Institute, Accra, 939
Food Research Institute, Tiranë, 85
Food Technology Research Institute, Giza, 687
Forage Research Institute, Fushë-Krujë, 84
Ford Green Hall, Stoke on Trent, 2291
Fordham University, 2785
Foreign Language Centre, Exeter, 2254
Foreign Literature Institute, Beijing, 466
Foreign Policy and United Nations Association of Austria, 173
Foreign Policy Association, New York, 2402
Foreign Trade University, Hanoi, 3015
Foreningen af Mejerilledere og Funktionærer, Odense, 649
Föreningen för konsthistoria ry, Helsinki, Helsinki, 715
Föreningen Svenska Tonsättare, 2055
Forest and Forest Products Research Institute, Ibaraki, 1225

Geneva University of Art and Design, 2113

Genghis Khan World Academy, 1497

Génie Industriel, Grenoble, 762

Gennadius Library, Athens, 948

Genomics Research Centre, 137

Genootschap Architectura et Amicitia, 1528

Genootschap ter bevordering van Natuur-, Genees- en Heelkunde, 1530

Gentofte Bibliotekerne, 655

Geochemical Society, St Louis, 2413

Geodesic and Geological Engineering Institute, Ulan Bator, 1498

Geodesy Centre, Lisbon, 1764

Geodetic and Research Branch, Survey of India, 1017

Geodetic Institute of Bosnia and Herzegovina, 289

Geodetic Section, Army Topographic Service, Bandung, 1085

Geodetic Society of Japan, 1223

Geodetical and Geophysical Research Institute of the Hungarian Academy of Sciences, 978

Geodetiska Institutet, Masala, 719

Geodetski Zavod Bosne i Hercegovine, 289

Geodezijos Institutas, Vilnius, 1422

Geofysiska Sällskapet, Helsinki, 717

Geofyzikální ústav AV ČR, 632

Geografija, 607

Geografiska Sällskapet i Finland, 715

Geografski inštitut Antona Melika ZRC SAZU, Ljubljana, 1964

Geografsko Društvo BiH, 288

Geografsko Društvo na R. Makedonija, 1432

Geografsko Društvo Republike Srpske, 288

Geographical and Historical Academy of Guatemala, 960

Geographical Association of Zimbabwe, 3027

Geographical Association, Sheffield, 2234

Geographical Institute, jakarta, 1085

Geographical Institute 'Jovan Cvijić', 1922

Geographical Museum of the Anton Melik Geographical Institute at ZRC SAZU, 1966

Geographical Research Institute, Hungarian Academy of Sciences, 976

Geographical Society of Berlin, 822

Geographical Society of Bosnia and Herzegovina, 288

Geographical Society of China, 462

Geographical Society of Finland, 715

Geographical Society of India, 1007

Geographical Society of Ireland, 1131

Geographical Society of Macedonia, 1432

Geographical Society of Moldova, 1491

Geographical Society of New South Wales Inc., 132

Geographische Gesellschaft Bern, 2087

Geographisch-Ethnographische Gesellschaft Zürich, 2087

Geographisch-Ethnologische Gesellschaft Basel, 2087

Geography Centre, Lisbon, 1764

Geologica Belgica, Brussels, 252

Geological and Mining Data Centre, Alfragide, 1767

Geological and Mining Studies Centre, Beja, 1767

Geological and Palaeontological Institute and Museum, Hamburg, 837

Geological Association, 826

Geological Association of Canada, 371

Geological Institute of Kola Science Centre, 1843

Geological Institute, São Paulo, 297

Geological Institute 'Strashimir Dimitrov', Sofia, 339

Geological Institute, Ulan-Ude, 1843

Geological, Mining and Metallurgical Society of India, 1010

Geological, Mining and Metallurgical Society of Liberia, 1413

Geological Mining Service, Paramaribo, 2051

Geological Museum, Copenhagen, 656

Geological Museum, Helsinki, 721

Geological Museum of Barcelona Seminary, 2008

Geological Museum of China, Beijing, 472

Geological Museum of Portugal, Lisbon, 1771

Geological Museum of the Institute of Geology, Yerevan, 126

Geological Museum, Oslo, 1619

Geological Museum, Seoul, 1365

Geological Research Authority, Khartoum, 2048

Geological Research Authority of the Sudan Library, Khartoum, 2048

Geological Research Institute, Tiranë, 85

Geological Society of America, 2413

Geological Society of Australia, 135

Geological Society of Belgium, 252

Geological Society of Denmark, 652

Geological Society of Finland, 717

Geological Society of Japan, 1223

Geological Society of London, Library, 2272

Geological Society of London, 2242

Geological Society of Norway, 1616

Geological Society of Romania, 1784

Geological Society of South Africa, 1975

Geological Society of Spain, 1999

Geological Society of Sweden, 2057

Geological Society of Trinidad and Tobago, 2152

Geological Society of Viet Nam, 3011

Geological Society of Zimbabwe, 3028

Geological Survey and Mines Bureau, Dehiwala, 2041

Geological Survey and Mines Department, Entebbe, 2192

Geological Survey and Mines Department, Mbabane, 2052

Geological Survey Department, Maseru, 1411

Geological Survey Department, Mogadishu, 1970

Geological Survey Division, Freetown, 1941

Geological Survey Museum and Documentation Centre, Entebbe, 2192

Geological Survey of Austria, Vienna, 180

Geological Survey of Bangladesh, 215

Geological Survey of Botswana, 294

Geological Survey of Canada, 373

Geological Survey of Denmark and Greenland, 654

Geological Survey of Estonia, 702

Geological Survey of Ethiopia, 707

Geological Survey of Finland, 719

Geological Survey of Ghana, 940

Geological Survey of India, 1017

Geological Survey of Israel, 1143

Geological Survey of Malawi, 1441

Geological Survey of New South Wales, 138

Geological Survey of Nigeria, 1590

Geological Survey of Norway, 1617

Geological Survey of Slovenia, 1965

Geological Survey of Sweden, 2060

Geological Survey of Tanzania, Dodoma, 2131

Geological Survey of Western Australia, 138

Geological Survey of Zambia (Ministry of Mines and Minerals Development), 3025

Geological Survey of Zimbabwe, 3029

Geological Surveying Oil Research Institute, Atyrau, 1340

Geologický ústav AV ČR, v.v.i., 632

Geologisch Mijnbouwkundige Dienst, 2051

Geologische Bundesanstalt, Vienna, 180

Geologische Vereinigung e.V., Mendig, 826

Geologisch-Paläontologisches Institut und Museum, Universität Hamburg, 837

Geologisk Museum, Copenhagen, 656

Geologisk museum, Oslo, 1619

Geologiska Föreningen, Stockholm, 2057

Geologiska Forskningscentralen, Espoo, 719

Geologiska Museet, Helsinki, 721

Geologiska Sällskapet i Finland, 717

Geologists' Association, London, 2242

Geology Centre, Lisbon, 1764

Geology Centre of the University of Porto, Porto, 1765

Geology Institute, Skopje, 1433

Geološki Zavod, Skopje, 1433

Geološki Zavod Slovenije, 1965

Geomedical Research Office of the Heidelberg Academy of Sciences, 835

Geomedizinische Forschungsstelle der Heidelberger Akademie der Wissenschaften, 835

Geophysical Institute, Coimbra, 1765

Geophysical Institute of Israel, Holon, 1143

Geophysical Laboratory, Washington, 2423

Geophysical Observatory, Addis Ababa, 707

Geophysical Observatory, Tihany, 978

Geophysical Society of Finland, 717

Geoponiko Panepistimio Athinon, 953

Georg-Agricola Gesellschaft zur Förderung der Geschichte der Naturwissenschaften und der Technik eV, 824

Georg-August-Universität Göttingen, 867

George A. Smathers Libraries, 2437

George Bacovia University of Bacău, 1810

'George Bariţiu' County Library Braşov, 1791

George Bush Presidential Library and Museum, 2459

George C. Marshall Space Flight Center, Alabama, 2428

'George Enescu' National Museum, 1795

George Fox University, 2844

George Hail Free Library, 2457

George Mason University, 2932

George Padmore Research Library on African Affairs, Accra, 940

George R. Gardiner Museum of Ceramic Art, 379

George Washington University, 2572

George Washington University Libraries, 2435

Georgetown College, 2644

Georgetown University, 2577

Georgetown University Library, 2435

Georgi Dimitrov National Museum, 343

Georgi Nadjakov Institute of Solid State Physics, 339

Georgia College and State University, 2597

Georgia Health Sciences University, 2597

Georgia Institute of Technology, 2597

Georgia Museum of Art, 2472

Georgia O'Keeffe Museum, 2487

Georgia Southern University, 2597

Georgia Southwestern State University, 2597

Georgia State University, 2597

Georgian Academy of Physical Education, Tbilisi, 815

Georgian Academy of Sciences, 812

Georgian Bio-Medico-Technical Society, 812

Georgian Botanical Society, 813

Georgian Court University, Lakewood, 2758

Georgian Geographical Society, 812

Georgian Geological Society, 813

Georgian History Society, 812

Georgian National Museum, 815

Georgian National Museum—National Gallery, Tbilisi, 815

Georgian National Speleological Society, 813

Georgian Neuroscience Association, Tbilisi, 812

Georgian Philosophy Society, 813

Georgian 'S. Rustaveli' State Institute of Theatre and Cinematography, 817

Georgian Scientific Research Institute of Industrial Hygiene and Occupational Diseases, 813

Georgian Society of Biochemists, 813

Georgian Society of Geneticists and Selectionists, 813

Georgian Society of Parasitologists, 813

Georgian Society of Patho-Anatomists, 813

Georgian Society of Psychologists, 813

Georgian State Academy of Animal Husbandry and Veterinary Medicine, Tbilisi, 815

Georgian State Agrarian University, 817

Georgian State Art Museum, 815

Georgian State Institute of Subtropical Agriculture, 817

Georgian State Museum of Oriental Art, 815

Georgian Technical University, 815

Geoscience Australia (GA), Canberra, 138

Geoscience Society of New Zealand, 1575

GeoScience Victoria, 138

Geospatial Information Authority of Japan, Ibaraki, 1226

Gépipari Tudományos Egyesület (GTE), Budapest, 975

Gerald R. Ford Presidential Library & Museum, 2446

Gereformeerde Hogeschool, 1561

Germa Museum, 1416

German Academic Exchange Service, 819

German Academy for Regional Geography of Germany, 822

German Academy for Urban and Regional Spatial Planning, 832

German Adult Education Association, 819

German Aerospace Centre, 838

German Agricultural Society, 820

German Archaeological Institute, 834

German Archaeological Institute, Cairo, 688

German Archaeological Institute in Athens, 958

German Archaeological Institute, Madrid, 1998

German Architecture Museum, 852

German Association for Asian Studies, 826

German Association for East European Studies, 821

German Association for Materials Research and Testing, 828

German Association for Psychiatry and Psychotherapy, 824

German Association for Research on Sexuality, 835

German Association of Mining Surveyors, 827

German Association of University Professors and Lecturers, 819

German Bible Archive, 843

German Book Museum, 854

German Botanical Society, Berlin, 824

German Bunsen Society for Physical Chemistry, 825

German Cancer Society, 835

German Cardiac Society, 835

German Cartographic Society, 822

German Centre for Productivity and Innovation, 828

German Ceramic Society, 827

German Chemical Society, 826

German Composers' Association, 822

German Concrete Association, 827

German Council of Science and Humanities, Cologne, 824

German Council on Foreign Relations, 821

German Dermatologic Society, 823

German Federation for Housing and Planning, 821

German Film and Television Academy, Berlin GmbH, 934

German Film Museum, 852

German Folksong Archive, Research Centre for Song and Popular Culture, 842

German Forestry Council, 820

German Forum on Nuclear Energy, 826
German Foundrymen's Association, 828
German Freemasons' Museum in Bayreuth, 848
German Gemmological Association, 827
German Geographical Society, 822
German Geological Society, 826
German Geophysical Society, 825
German Historical Institute in Rome, 1174
German Historical Institute, London, 2254
German Historical Museum, 849
German Institute for Economic Research, 832
German Institute for International and Security Affairs, 834
German Institute for International Educational Research, 834
German Institute for Standardization, 828
German Institute of Global and Area Studies (GIGA), 834
German Institute of Navigation, 822
German Institute of Science and Technology—TUM Asia (GIST—TUM Asia), Singapore, 1947
German Library, Helsinki, 719
German Linguistic Society, 823
German Mathematical Society, 825
German Meteorological Service, 836
German Meteorological Service National Meteorological Library, 846
German Meteorological Society, 826
German Mineralogical Society, 826
German Mozart Society, 822
German Museum in Bonn, 855
German Museum in Flugwerft Schleissheim, 855
German Museum of Scientific and Technological Masterpieces, 855
German Museums Association, 821
German Museum—Transport Centre, 855
German National Library, 842
German National Library of Economics—Leibniz Information Centre for Economics, 844
German National Library of Medicine, 841
German National Library of Science and Technology and University Library Hanover, 843
German Nautical Association of 1868, 822
German Oriental Society, 826
German Patent and Trademark Office, 845
German Peat Society, 836
German PEN Centre, 823
German Phytomedical Society, 825
German Political Science Association, 821
German Psychological Society, 826
German Rectors' Conference, 819
German Refrigeration Association, 827
German Research Centre for Environmental Health, 835
German Research Institute for Food Chemistry, 838
German Society for Aeronautics and Astronautics, 827
German Society for Animal Production, 824
German Society for Applied Optics, 823
German Society for Constructional Engineering, 827
German Society for Dental, Oral and Craniomandibular Sciences, 824
German Society for European Ethnology and Folklore Studies, 827
German Society for General and Applied Entomology, 824
German Society for Gynaecology and Birth Support, 823
German Society for Internal Medicine, 823
German Society for Non-Destructive Testing, 827
German Society for Operations Research, 825

German Society for Otorhinolaryngology, Head and Neck Surgery, 823
German Society for Photogrammetry, Remote Sensing and Geoinformation, 827
German Society for Photography, 822
German Society for Plastic and Reconstructive Surgery, 823
German Society for Social Medicine and Prevention, 824
German Society for Studies in Art History, 822
German Society for Wood Research, 831
German Society of Glass Technology, 827
German Society of Legal Medicine, 824
German Society of Pediatrics and Adolescent Medicine, 823
German Society of Physiology, 824
German Sociological Association, 826
German Sport University Cologne, 864
German Surgical Society, 823
German Technical and Scientific Association for Gas and Water, 828
German Technical-Scientific Society for Light and Lighting, 827
German University of Technology in Oman, 1634
German Veterinary Medical Society, 820
German Welding Society, 828
German Wool Research Institute, 892
German Zoological Society, 825
Germanisches Nationalmuseum, Nuremberg, 856
Germany Archive of the Nobility, 845
Gerontological Society of America, 2409
Gerontology and Geriatrics Society, Kyiv, 2196
Gerontology Institute, Atlanta, 2421
Gerrit Rietveld Academie, 1561
Gesamtverein der Deutschen Geschichts- und Altertumsvereine eV, 822
Geschichtsverein für Kärnten, 174
Gesellschaft der Ärzte in Wien, 175
Gesellschaft der Chirurgen in Wien, 175
Gesellschaft der Musikfreunde in Wien, 173
Gesellschaft Deutscher Chemiker, 826
Gesellschaft Deutscher Naturforscher und Ärzte eV, 824
Gesellschaft für Angewandte Mathematik und Mechanik, Dresden, 825
Gesellschaft für Anthropologie, Bremen, 827
Gesellschaft für antike Philosophie eV, 826
Gesellschaft für Biochemie und Molekularbiologie, Tutzing, 825
Gesellschaft für deutsche Sprache eV, Wiesbaden, 823
Gesellschaft für deutsche Sprache und Literatur in Zürich, 2089
Gesellschaft für Deutschlandforschung eV, Berlin, 833
Gesellschaft für die Geschichte des Protestantismus in Österreich, 177
Gesellschaft für Erdkunde zu Berlin, 822
Gesellschaft für Evangelische Theologie, Bamberg, 827
Gesellschaft für Geistesgeschichte, Potsdam, 826
Gesellschaft für Hopfenforschung eV, 831
Gesellschaft für Informatik eV, Bonn, 828
Gesellschaft für Klassische Philologie in Innsbruck, 175
Gesellschaft für Landeskunde von Oberösterreich, 173
Gesellschaft für Musikforschung, Kassel, 834
Gesellschaft für Naturkunde in Württemberg, 825
Gesellschaft für Öffentliche Wirtschaft, Berlin, 821
Gesellschaft für Operations Research eV (GOR), Bochum, 825
Gesellschaft für Pädagogik und Information eV, Berlin, 834

Gesellschaft für Rechtsvergleichung e.V., Freiburg, 821
Gesellschaft für Schweizerische Kunstgeschichte, 2086
Gesellschaft für Sozial- und Wirtschaftsgeschichte, Bamberg, 821
Gesellschaft für vergleichende Kunstforschung, Vienna, 179
Gesellschaft für Wissenschaftliche Gerichts- und Rechtspsychologie, 826
Gesellschaft Österreichischer Chemiker, 176
Gesellschaft Schweizer Tierärztinnen und Tierärzte, 2085
Gesellschaft zur Förderung Pädagogischer Forschung eV, Frankfurt, 834
Gesellschaft zur Förderung Slawistischer Studien, Vienna, 175
GESIS-Leibniz-Institut für Sozialwissenschaften, Mannheim, 838
GESIS-Leibniz-Institute for the Social Sciences, 838
Gestalt Therapy Brisbane, Holland Park, 169
Getica Cultural Scientific Society, 1783
Getty Conservation Institute, 2418
Getty Research Institute, 2417
Getty Villa, Malibu, 2466
Gettysburg College, 2856
Gezira Research Station Library, 2048
GfK Association, Nuremberg, 832
GfK Verein, 832
Ghana Academy of Arts and Sciences, 938
Ghana Association of Writers, 939
Ghana Bar Association, 939
Ghana Geographical Association, 939
Ghana Institute of Architects, 938
Ghana Institute of Management and Public Administration, 943
Ghana Institution of Engineers, 939
Ghana Library Association, 938
Ghana Library Board, 940
Ghana Meteorological Agency, 940
Ghana National Museum, 940
Ghana Science Association, 939
Ghana Sociological Association, 939
Ghazni Museum, 81
Ghazni Provincial Library, 80
Ghent Museum of Fine Arts, 262
Ghent University, 266
'Gheorghe Asachi' Technical University of Iaşi, 1823
Gheorghe Cristea Romanian University of Sciences and Arts, 1811
Gheorghe Mihoc-Caius Iacob Institute of Mathematical Statistics and Applied Mathematics, 1788
'Gheorghe Şincai' Bihor Oradea District Library, 1793
'Gheorghe Şincai' Institute for Social Sciences and Humanities, 1790
Gheorghe Zane Institute for Economic Research, 1786
Ghulam Ishaq Khan Institute of Engineering Sciences and Technology, 1647
Gibbes Museum of Art, 2496
Gibraltar Archives, 2388
Gibraltar Garrison Library, 2388
Gibraltar Museum, 2388
Gibraltar Ornithological & Natural History Society, 2388
Gidan Makama Museum, 1594
GIFT University, 1647
Gifu Pharmaceutical University, 1304
Gifu University, 1237
GIGA German Institute of Global and Area Studies, 827
Gilbert Public Library, 2446
Gilbert White's House and Garden and the Oates Museum, 2291
Giovale Library, 2459
Gipsformerei, Berlin, 849
Girne American University, 624
Girton College, Cambridge, 2310
Giurgiu District 'I. A. Bassarabescu' Library, 1792
Giurgiu District Museum, 1796
Gjirokastër Public Library, 85

GL STRAND Gallery of Modern and Contemporary Art, 650
Gladstone Pottery Museum, Stoke on Trent, 2291
Gladstone's Library, 2270
Glafo, 2060
Glasbenonarodopisni Inštitut ZRC SAZU, 1964
Glasgow Caledonian University, 2370
Glasgow Caledonian University Library, 2269
Glasgow Libraries, 2269
Glasgow Museums, 2284
Glasgow School of Art, 2381
Glasmuseet Ebeltoft, 657
Glass Museum Ebeltoft, 657
Glenbow Library and Archives, 374
Glenbow Museum, Calgary, 377
Glendale Public Library, 2430
Glenn L. Martin Maryland Aviation Museum, 2480
Glenn Research Center, Cleveland, Ohio, 2428
Glenville State College, 2952
'Glinka, M. I.', State Central Museum of Musical Culture, 1857
Global College, 627
Global Development Centre, Lisbon, 1763
Global University, Springfield, 2738
Globus Competence Centre for Globalization and Sustainable Development, 1542
Gloucester Folk Museum, 2285
Gloucestershire Libraries and Information HQ, 2270
Główna Biblioteka Lekarska, Warsaw, 1723
Główna Biblioteka Pracy i Zabezpieczenia Społecznego, Warsaw, 1723
Główny Instytut Górnictwa, Katowice, 1718
Glyptothèque HAZU, Zagreb, 610
GNS Science, Lower Hutt, 1576
Goa University, 1033
Gobabeb Training and Research Centre, 1521
Goce Delcev University of Stip, 1435
Göcseji Falumúzeum, 985
Goddard College, 2928
Goddard Space Flight Center, Greenbelt, Maryland, 2428
Goethe Institut Jordanien, 1334
Goethe-Gedenkstätte (im Inspektorhaus des Botanischen Gartens), Jena, 853
Goethe-Gesellschaft in Weimar eV, 820
Goethe-Informationszentrum, Pyongyang, 1359
Goethe-Institut, Abidjan, 603
Goethe-Institut, Addis Ababa, 707
Goethe-Institut, Almaty, 1338
Goethe-Institut, Amsterdam, 1530
Goethe-Institut, Ankara, 2159
Goethe-Institut, Athens, 945
Goethe-Institut, Bangkok, 2136
Goethe-Institut, Beijing, 463
Goethe-Institut, Beirut, 1406
Goethe-Institut, Belgrade, 1921
Goethe-Institut, Bogotá, 578
Goethe-Institut, Bratislava, 1950
Goethe-Institut, Brussels, 251
Goethe-Institut, Bucharest, 1784
Goethe-Institut, Budapest, 973
Goethe-Institut, Buenos Aires, 104
Goethe-Institut, Cairo, 686
Goethe-Institut, Caracas, 3000
Goethe-Institut, Chişinău, 1491
Goethe-Institut, Colombo, 2040
Goethe-Institut, Copenhagen, 651
Goethe-Institut, Dakar, 1917
Goethe-Institut, Damascus, 2115
Goethe-Institut, Dhaka, 213
Goethe-Institut, Dublin, 1131
Goethe-Institut, Ghana, 939
Goethe-Institut, Hanoi, 3010
Goethe-Institut, Helsinki, 715
Goethe-Institut, Jakarta, 1084
Goethe-Institut, Jerusalem, 1141
Goethe-Institut, Johannesburg, 1974
Goethe-Institut, Kabul, 80
Goethe-Institut, Karachi, 1637
Goethe-Institut, Kuala Lumpur, 1444

Groupe ENI (Ecoles Nationales d'Ingénieurs), 793
Groupe ESA – Ecole Supérieure d'Agriculture d'Angers, Angers, 796
Groupe ESC Clermont, Clermont-Ferrand, 790
Groupe ESC Lille – Ecole Supérieure de Commerce de Lille, 796
Groupe ESCEM Campus Poitiers, 796
Groupe IPAC, 795
Grove City College, 2856
Growth and Bloom, Zoetermeer, 1528
Grozny State Oil Institute, 1899
Grünes Gewölbe, Dresden, 851
Grupo Argentino del Color, 105
Grupo Universitario Latinoamericano de Estudio para la Reforma y el Perfeccionamiento de la Educación (GULERPE), Caracas, 3000
Gruppo Interdisciplinare per la Ricerca Sociale, Rome, 1168
GSI Helmholtz Centre for Heavy Ion Research GmbH, 838
GSI Helmholtzzentrum für Schwerionenforschung GmbH, Darmstadt, 838
G.Tsulukidze Mining Institute, 814
Guadalajara Regional Museum, 1471
Guam Chamber of Commerce, Hagåtña, 2968
Guam Council on the Arts and Humanities, 2968
Guam Department of Education, 2968
Guam Gallery of Arts, 2969
Guam Historic Resources Division, 2968
Guam Law Library, 2969
Guam Library Association, 2968
Guam Medical Association, 2968
Guam Museum Foundation, Inc, Hagatna, 2968
Guam Museum of Culture, Art and History, 2969
Guam Preservation Trust, 2968
Guam Public Library System, 2969
Guam Symphony Society, 2968
Guangdong College of Medicine and Pharmacy, 499
Guangxi Normal University, 499
Guangxi Traditional Chinese Medical University, 500
Guangxi University, 500
Guangxi Zhuang Autonomous Region Library, 471
Guangzhou Institute of Chemistry, 468
Guangzhou University, 500
Guangzhou University of Traditional Chinese Medicine, 500
Guardian News and Media Archive, 2272
Guatemala Academy of Letters, 960
Gubkin, Acad. I. M., Petroleum and Gas Society, Moscow, 1829
Gubkin Russian State University of Oil and Gas, 1848, 1885
Guernsey Museums & Galleries, 2389
Guggenheim Bilbao Museoa, 2009
Guggenheim Museum, Bilbao, 2009
Gugushvili, P. V., Institute of Economics, 813
GUIDE—Research Institute for Chronic Diseases and Drug Innovation, 1538
Guild of Church Musicians, Blechingley, 2232
Guild of Icelandic Film Directors, 1001
Guildford College, 2361
Guildford School of Acting, 2365
Guildhall Library, City of London, 2272
Guildhall School of Music and Drama, 2365
GuildHE, London, 2225
Guilford College, 2810
Guilin Library of Guangxi Zhuang Autonomous Region, 471
Guille Allès Library, 2389
Guizhou Provincial Library, 471
Guizhou University, 501
Guizhou University of Technology, 501
Gujarat Ayurved University, 1033
Gujarat Research Society, 1015
Gujarat University, 1033
Gujarat Vidyapeeth Granthalaya, 1020
Gujarat Vidyapith, 1074
Gukje Digital University, 1385
Gulbarga University, 1033

Gulbenkian Library, Jerusalem, 1145
Gulf Arab States Educational Research Centre, Shamia, 1390
Gulf Coast State College, 2585
Gulf College of Hospitality and Tourism, Muharraq, 211
Gulf Cooperation Council Folklore Centre, Doha, 1780
Gulf Medical University, 2220
Gulf University for Science and Technology, 1391
Gulf University, Sanad, 211
Gulisashvili, V. Z., Institute of Mountain Forestry, Tbilisi, 813
Gulistan Davlat Universiteti, 2986
Gulistan State University, 2986
Guliyev, A.M., Institute of Additive Chemistry, Baku, 204
Gulu University, 2192
Gunma University, 1237
Gurakuqi, Luigi, House-Museum, Shkodër, 86
Gurkha Memorial Museum, Pokhara, 1526
Guru Ghasidas Vishwavidyalaya, 1033
Guru Gobind Singh Indraprastha University, 1033
Guru Jambeshwar University of Science & Technology, 1034
Guru Nanak Dev University, 1034
Gurukul Kangri Vishwavidyalaya, 1074
Gustav III's Antikmuseum, 2066
Gustav III's Museum of Antiquities, 2066
Gustavus Adolphus College, 2717
Gutenberg-Museum, Mainz, 855
Guyana Industrial Training Centre, 967
Guyana Institute of International Affairs, 966
Guyana Library Association, 966
Guyana Medical Science Library, 966
Guyana Museum, 967
Guyana School of Agriculture Corporation, 967
Guyana Zoological Park, National Parks Commission, 967
Gwacheon Provincial Library of Gyeonggi, 1364
Gwangju Museum of Art, 1365
Gwangju National Museum, 1365
Gwebi College of Agriculture, 3031
Gwynedd Library and Information Service, 2266
Gwynedd Museum and Art Gallery, Bangor, 2281
Gwynedd-Mercy College, 2856
Gyeonggi Museum of Modern Art, 1365
Gyeonggi Provincial Museum, 1365
Gyeongju National Museum, 1366
Gyeongsang National University, 1367
Gyeongsangbuk-do Forest Science Museum, 1366
Gymnastik- och Idrottshögskolan, 2082
Györffy István Nagykun Múzeum, 983
Győr-Moson-Sopron Megyei Múzeumok Igazgatósága Soproni Múzeum, 984
Gyumri M. Nalbandian State Pedagogical Institute, 127

H

H. E. J. Research Institute of Chemistry, 1641
H. H. Meeter Center for Calvin Studies, 2420
H. M. Government of Gibraltar Ministry of Education, Gibraltar, 2388
H. R. MacMillan Space Centre, Vancouver, 377
'H. S. Skovoroda' Institute of Philosophy, Kyiv, 2200
Ha Noi Institute of Stage and Cinematography, Hanoi, 3012
HAAGA-HELIA Ammattikorkeakoulu, 735
Hacettepe Üniversitesi, 2171
Hachinohe Institute of Technology, 1304
Hackney Library Services, 2272
Hadassah College, 1160
Hadhramout University of Science and Technology, Mukalla, 3023
Hadlow College, 2362

Hadtörténeti Könyvtár és Térképtár, Budapest, 979
Haegang Ceramics Museum, 1366
Haeju Historical Museum, 1361
Haematological Research Centre, Moscow, 1836
Haematology Institute, Tianjing, 466
Haematology Oncology Research Center, 1118
HafenCity University Hamburg— University of the Built Environment and Metropolitan Development, 870
Haffenreffer Museum of Anthropology, 2495
Haffkine Institute for Training, Research and Testing, 1015
Hafnarfjörður Public Library, 1002
Hafrannsóknastofnunin, 1002
Haggerty Museum of Art, 2501
Hagley Museum and Library, Wilmington, 2469
Hagstofa Íslands, 1001
Hague Academy of International Law, 61
Hague Conference on Private International Law, 61
Hahoe Mask Museum, 1366
Haifa AMLI Library of Music, 1144
Haifa Museum of Art, 1146
Haigazian University, Beirut, 1410
Haines Borough Public Library, 2430
Haiphong Museum, 3014
Haiphong University of Medicine, 3015
Hajdúsági Múzeum, 983
Hajee Mohammad Danesh University Of Science And Technology, Dinajpur, 221
Hajvery University, 1647
Hakluyt Society, London, 2234
Hakodate City Library, 1228
Hakodate City Museum, 1230
Hakodate University, 1311
Hakone Museum of Art, 1230
Hakuoh University, 1304
Hakutsuru Bijitsukan, 1231
Haliç Üniversitesi, 2174
Haliç University, 2174
Halifax Regional Library, 375
Halil Hamit Paşa Library, 2161
Hall County Library System, 2437
Hall of State, Dallas, 2498
Halle Institute for Economic Research, 833
Hallepoort, 261
Hallwylska Museet, 2066
Hallym University, 1375
Halmstad City Library, 2061
Halmstad University College, 2081
Halmstads Stadsbibliotek, 2061
Halton Borough Libraries, 2280
Hama Museum, 2116
Hamamatsu University School of Medicine, 1304
Hamburg Institute of International Economics (HWWI), 832
Hamburg Museum of Art and Industry, 853
Hamburg Observatory, 837
Hamburg University of Music and Theatre, 935
Hamburg University of Technology, 903
Hamburger Bahnhof–Museum für Gegenwart—Berlin, 849
Hamburger Kunsthalle, 853
Hamburger Sternwarte, 837
Hamburgisches WeltWirtschaftsInstitut gemeinnützige GmbH (HWWI), 832
Hamdan Bin Mohammed e-University, 2220
Hamdard Foundation Pakistan, Karachi, 1639
Hamdard University, Karachi, 1648
Hamden Public Library, 2434
Häme Museum, 722
Häme Polytechnic, 735
Hämeen Ammattikorkeakoulu, Hämeenlinna, 735
Hämeen Museo, Tampere, 722
Hamhung Historical Museum, 1361
Hamilton and Sinclair Libraries, 2438
Hamilton College, 2785
Hamilton County Law Library, 2454
Hamilton Public Library, 376

Hamilton-Wenham Public Library, 2445
Hamline University, 2717
Hammarskjöld Memorial Library, Kitwe, 3025
Hammer Museum, Haines, AK, 2464
Hammer Museum, Los Angeles, CA, 2466
Hammersmith and Fulham Public Libraries, 2273
Hammonds House Museum, 2473
Hampden-Sydney College, 2932
Hampshire College, 2672
Hampshire County Public Library, 2461
Hampshire Library and Information Service, 2281
Hampton Court Palace, 2287
Hampton Public Library, 2460
Hampton University, 2932
Hampton University Museum, 2499
Hamptonne Country Life Museum, 2391
Han Nam University, 1375
Hanbat Library, 1364
Hancock County Library System, 2447
Hancock County Public Library, 2439
Handels- og Søfartsmuseet, Elsinore, 657
Handelshochschule Leipzig (HHL), 934
Handelshögskolan i Stockholm, 2082
Handelshögskolans i Stockholm— Bibliotek, 2062
Handelshøjskolen i København, 661
Handelshøjskolens Bibliotek, Århus, 654
Handelshøyskolen BI, 1631
Hango Agricultural College, 2150
Hangzhou University of Commerce, 501
Hanken School of Economics, 732
Hanken Svenska Handelshögskolans Bibliotek, Helsinki, 720
Hankuk Aviation University, 1384
Hankuk University of Foreign Studies, 1375
Hankyong National University, 1384
Hanlyo University, 1385
Hannah Research Institute, 2250
Hannan University, 1304
Hannibal-LaGrange University, 2738
Hanoi Agricultural University, 3015
Hanoi Architectural University, 3015
Hanoi College of Fine Arts, 3021
Hanoi College of Pharmacy, 3021
Hanoi Cultural College, 3021
Hanoi Law University, 3015
Hanoi Medical University, 3015
Hanoi National Conservatory of Music, 3021
Hanoi National Economics University, 3015
Hanoi National University of Education, 3015
Hanoi Open University, 3016
Hanoi University Of Civil Engineering, 3016
Hanoi University of Culture, 3016
Hanoi University of Drama and Cinematography, Hanoi, 3021
Hanoi University of Fine Arts, 3016
Hanoi University of Foreign Studies, 3016
Hanoi University of Foreign Trade, 3016
Hanoi University of Industrial Fine Arts, 3016
Hanoi University of Mining and Geology, 3016
Hanoi University of Technology, 3016
Hanoi Water Resources University, 3016
Hanover College, 2626
Hanover Medical School, 884
Hanover Society of Natural History, 825
Hanover State Museum, 853
Hans Christian Andersen Museum, 658
Hans Christian Andersens Hus, 658
Hans Raj College, 1079
Hansági Múzeum, 983
Hansard Society, 2230
Hanseo University, 1375
Hanshin University, 1375
Hansung University, 1375
Hanyang University, 1376
Hanze University Groningen, University of Applied Sciences, 1561

Indian Chemical Society, 1009
Indian Council for Cultural Relations (ICCR), 1005
Indian Council of Agricultural Research (ICAR), 1013
Indian Council of Forestry Research and Education, 1013
Indian Council of Historical Research, 1014
Indian Council of Medical Research, 1015
Indian Council of Social Science Research (ICSSR), 1018
Indian Council of World Affairs, 1006
Indian Council of World Affairs Library, 1020
Indian Cultural Centre, Kathmandu, 1525
Indian Dairy Association, 1005
Indian Economic Association, 1006
Indian Institute of Advanced Study, Shimla, 1014
Indian Institute of Architects, 1006
Indian Institute of Astrophysics, 1017
Indian Institute of Chemical Biology, Kolkata, 1011
Indian Institute of Chemical Technology, Hyderabad, 1011
Indian Institute of Foreign Trade, 1074
Indian Institute of Geomagnetism, 1017
Indian Institute of Information Technology, 1074
Indian Institute of Integrative Medicine, 1012
Indian Institute of Management, Ahmedabad, 1079
Indian Institute of Management, Bangalore, 1079
Indian Institute of Management, Calcutta, 1079
Indian Institute of Management, Indore, 1079
Indian Institute of Management, Kozhikode, 1079
Indian Institute of Management, Lucknow, 1079
Indian Institute of Metals, 1010
Indian Institute of Natural Resins & Gums, 1019
Indian Institute of Petroleum, Dehradun, 1011
Indian Institute of Public Administration, 1013
Indian Institute of Science, 1074
Indian Institute of Technology, Bombay, 1070
Indian Institute of Technology, Delhi, 1070
Indian Institute of Technology, Guwahati, 1070
Indian Institute of Technology, Kanpur, 1070
Indian Institute of Technology, Kharagpur, 1071
Indian Institute of Technology, Madras, 1071
Indian Institute of Technology Madras Central Library, 1021
Indian Institute of Technology, Roorkee, 1071
Indian Institute of Toxicology Research, Lucknow, 1011
Indian Institute of World Culture, 1005
Indian Law Institute, 1074
Indian Library Association, 1006
Indian Mathematical Society, 1009
Indian Medical Association, 1008
Indian Museum, Kolkata, 1023
Indian National Academy of Engineering (INAE), 1010
Indian National Science Academy, 1008
Indian Pharmaceutical Association, 1008
Indian Phytopathological Society, 1009
Indian Plywood Industries Research and Training Institute, 1013
Indian Psychometric and Educational Research Association, 1014
Indian Public Health Association, 1008
Indian Pueblo Cultural Center, 2487
Indian River State College, 2585
Indian Rubber Manufacturers Research Association, 1019
Indian School of Mines University, 1074

Indian Science Congress Association, 1008
Indian Society for Afro-Asian Studies, 1010
Indian Society for Medical Statistics, 1008
Indian Society of Agricultural Economics, Mumbai, 1005
Indian Society of Anaesthesiologists, 1008
Indian Society of Genetics and Plant Breeding, 1009
Indian Society of Mechanical Engineers (ISME), 1010
Indian Society of Oriental Art (Calcutta), 1007
Indian Society of Soil Science, 1006
Indian Space Research Organization (ISRO), 1017
Indian Statistical Institute, 1013
Indian Statistical Institute, Kolkata, 1071
Indian Veterinary Research Deemed Institute, 1074
Indiana Institute of Technology, 2626
Indiana State Archives, 2439
Indiana State Library, 2439
Indiana State Museum, 2476
Indiana State University, 2626
Indiana Supreme Court Law Library, 2439
Indiana University, 2627
Indiana University Art Museum, 2476
Indiana University Bloomington Libraries, 2439
Indiana University East, 2627
Indiana University Kokomo, 2627
Indiana University Northwest, 2627
Indiana University of Pennsylvania, 2862
Indiana University South Bend, 2628
Indiana University Southeast, 2628
Indiana University—Purdue University at Fort Wayne, 2627
Indiana University—Purdue University at Indianapolis, 2627
Indiana Wesleyan University, Marion, 2628
Indianapolis Museum of Art, 2476
Indianapolis-Marion County Public Library, 2439
Indigenous Film Archive, Kathmandu, 1524
Indira Gandhi Agricultural University, 1035
Indira Gandhi Centre for Atomic Research, 1017
Indira Gandhi Cultural Centre, Dhaka, 212
Indira Gandhi Institute of Development Research, 1074
Indira Gandhi Krishi Vishwavidyalaya, 1035
Indira Gandhi National Centre for the Arts, 1020
Indira Gandhi National Open University, 1035
Indira Kala Sangit Vishwavidyalaya, 1035
Indonesia Institute of the Arts Surakarta, 1088
Indonesia Institute of the Arts Yogyakarta, 1088
Indonesian Biotechnology Research Institute for Estate Crops, 1084
Indonesian Centre for Agricultural Library and Technology Dissemination, 1087
Indonesian Centre for Horticulture Research and Development (ICHORD), 1084
Indonesian Institute of Engineers, 1084
Indonesian Institute of Sciences, 1084
Indonesian Institute of World Affairs, 1085
Indonesian Library Association, 1083
Indonesian Medical Association, 1084
Indonesian Museum Association, 1083
Indonesian Oil Palm Research Institute, 1084
Indonesian Open Learning University, 1097
Indonesian Research Centre for Veterinary Science (IRCVS),

Indonesian Agency for Agricultural Research and Development (IAARD), Ministry of Agriculture, 1084
Indonesian Scientific Knowledge Centre, 1086
Indonesian Standards Institution, 1086
Indonesian Sugar Research Institute, 1085
Indonesian Tropical Fruit Research Institute, 1084
Indus Institute of Higher Education, 1648
Indus Valley School of Art and Architecture, 1648
Industrial and Commercial Museum, Lahore, 1644
Industrial Control Centre, Glasgow, 2263
Industrial Designers Society of America, 2416
Industrial Economics Institute, Beijing, 466
Industrial Health Foundation, Inc, Pittsburgh, 2409
Industrial Information Centre and Extension Services (FIIRO Indices), 1593
Industrial Medicine Institute, Hamhung, 1360
Industrial Property Office, Prague, 634
Industrial Research and Consultancy Centre, Khartoum, 2048
Industrial Research Institute, Arlington, 2428
Industrial Technology Development Institute, Manila, 1690
Industrial Technology Institute, Colombo, 2041
Industrial Technology Institute Information Services Centre, Colombo, 2042
Industrial Technology Research Institute, Hsinchu, 2120
Industrial Training Institute, 1392
Infante D. Henrique Nautical School, 1777
'Infante D. Luis' Geophysical Institute, 1765
Informatics Institute, Ulan Bator, 1498
Informatie Expertise Centrum/Bibliotheek Technische Universiteit Eindhoven, 1546
Information and Documentation Service, Lisbon, 1762
Information, Documentation and Electronic Information Service of the Gheorghe Ionescu-Şişeşti Academy of Agricultural and Forestry Sciences, 1792
Information Expertise Centre/Library of the Eindhoven University of Technology, 1546
Information Processing Society of Japan, 1218
Information Science and Technology Association, 1218
Information Service of the Swedish Folk High Schools, 2054
Information Technology Science, Technology and Production Corporation, Ulan Bator, 1498
Information Technology Society within VDE, 828
Informationstechnische Gesellschaft im VDE (ITG), Frankfurt, 828
Information—The Icelandic Library and Information Science Association, 1001
Infoterra Ltd, Farnborough, 2263
Infraproject Consulting SH.p.K., 85
Ingeniørforeningen i Danmark (IDA), 652
Ingeniørhøjskolen i Århus, 664
Ingeniørhøjskolen i København, 664
Ingush State University, 1868
Inha Technical College, 1386
Inha University, 1376
Inholland Select Studies, 1562
Inholland University of Applied Sciences Library, 1546
Inje University, 1376
Inland Fisheries Station, Vila do Conde, 1767

Inner Mongolia Agricultural University, 511
Inner Mongolia Autonomous Region Library, 471
Inner Mongolia University, 511
Inner Mongolia University for Nationalities, 512
Inner Temple Library, 2273
Innis College, Toronto, 432
InNOVAcorp, 372
Innovation Centre of Phytotechnology, Bishkek, 1395
Innovative Manufacturing and Construction Research Centre, Loughborough, 2251
Innovative University of Eurasia, 1344
Innovatory Scientific Institute of Special Structures 'Kompozitas', 1421
Innsbruck University, 190
Innventia AB, Stockholm, 2060
Inokashira Onshi Koen Shizen Bunkaen, 1232
İnönü Üniversitesi, 2174
Inovacinis Specialiųjų Konstrukcijų ir Statinių Mokslo Institutas 'Kompozitas', 1421
INRA Antilles-Guyane, 802
INRS-Institut Armand-Frappier, 402
INSAN Centre for Gender and Women's Studies, 1665
INSEAD, 1948
INSEAD, Fontainebleau, 797
Insectarium de Montréal, 379
In—Service Training Institute, Peradeniya, 2045
Institiúid Teangeolaíochta Éireann, 1132
Institouton Geologikon kai Metalleutikon Ereunon, Athens, 947
Institución 'Fernando el Católico', Excma Diputación Provincial de Zaragoza, 2000
Institut Africain d'Informatique, Libreville, 809
Institut Africain de Développement Economique et de Planification des Nations Unies, 1918
Institut Africain et Mauricien de Statistique et d'Economie Appliquée, Kigali, 1903
Institut Africain International, 49
Institut Agrícola, Barcelona, 1997
Institut Agronomique et Vétérinaire Hassan II, Rabat, 1509
Institut Agronomique néo-Calédonien, 805
Institut Alfred-Fournier, Paris, 747
Institut Amatller d'Art Hispànic, 1998
Institut Archéologique du Luxembourg, Arlon, 250
Institut Archéologique Liégeois, 250
Institut Arthur-Vernes, Paris, 747
Institut Bahasa Melayu Malaysia, Kuala Lumpur, 1452
Institut Belge des Hautes Etudes Chinoises, Brussels, 252
Institut Catholique d'Arts et Métiers (ICAM), Lille, 795
Institut Catholique de Paris, 794
Institut Catholique de Toulouse, 794
Institut Catholique des Hautes Études Commerciales, Brussels, 272
Institut Congolais pour la Conservation de la Nature, Kinshasa, 594
Institut Cooremans, Brussels, 272
Institut Culturel d'Expression Française (ICEF), Malabo, 699
Institut Curie, Paris, 749
Institut d'Administration des Entreprises, Yaoundé, 366
Institut d'Agro-Développement International, Cergy, 794
Institut d'Astronomie et d'Astrophysique, 256
Institut d'Économie Quantitative, Tunis, 2157
Institut d'Economie Scientifique et de Gestion (IESEG), Lille, 795
Institut d'Égypte, 686
Institut d'Elevage et de Médecine Vétérinaire des Pays Tropicaux, Antananarivo, 1438

Institute for Geothermal Research, Makhachkala, 1843

Institute for Heart Research, Bratislava, 1951

Institute for High Energy Physics, Amsterdam, 1540

Institute for High-Energy Physics, Protvino, 1843

Institute for High-performance Computing and Networking, 1170

Institute for Historical, Literary and Cultural Studies, 1542

Institute for Human Rights, 653

Institute for Humanities and Cultural Studies (IHCS), Tehran, 1107

Institute for Hydraulic Engineering and Calibration of Hydrometrical Current-Meters, Vienna, 182

Institute for Hydrochemistry and Chemical Balneology at the Technical University of Munich, 835

Institute for Ibero-American Co-operation, Madrid, 1996

Institute for Informatics and Telematics, 1170

Institute for Information Law, Amsterdam, 1536

Institute for Information Recording, Kyiv, 2201

Institute for Innovation and Governance Studies (IGS), Enschede, 1536

Institute for Integrated Sensor Systems, 182

Institute for International and Intercultural Studies, Bellaterra, 2004

Institute for International Economic and Political Studies, Moscow, 1833

Institute for International Economic Studies, 2058

Institute for International Legal Studies, 1169

Institute for International Relations, Hanoi, 3011

Institute for International Relations, Zagreb, 608

Institute for International Studies, Leiden, 1537

Institute for Islands Development, Kuressaare, 702

Institute for Land Reclamation, 239

Institute for Language and Folklore, 2059

Institute for Legal Studies of the Hungarian Academy of Sciences, 976

Institute for Legal Studies, Sofia, 337

Institute for Legislation and Comparative Law, Moscow, 1833

Institute for Lexicography of Austrian Dialects and Names, Vienna, 180

Institute for Limnology, Mondsee, 180

Institute for Linguistic Studies, St Petersburg, 1835

Institute for Linguistics and Semiotics, Lugano, 2092

Institute for Literature, Sofia, 337

Institute for Liturgical and Ritual Studies, Tilburg, 1542

Institute for Logic, Language and Computation, 1543

Institute for Macromolecular Studies of CNR, 1172

Institute for Management of Architectural and Archaeological Heritage, Lisbon, 1761

Institute for Management Research, Nijmegen, 1536

Institute for Market Analysis and Agricultural Trade Policy, Brunswick, 833

Institute for Materials Research, 910

Institute for Mathematics, Astrophysics and Particle Physics, 1540

Institute for Mechanization of Animal Husbandry, Zaporizhzhya, 2197

Institute for Media and Journalism, Lugano, 2091

Institute for Medical Research, 1154

Institute for Medical Research and Occupational Health, Zagreb, 608

Institute for Medical Research and Training, Nairobi, 1353

Institute for Medical Research (IMR), Kuala Lumpur, 1445

Institute for Medical Technology Assessment (iMTA), 1544

Institute for Medieval and Early Modern Material Culture, Krems an der Donau, 180

Institute for Mediterranean Affairs, Inc., Washington, 2402

Institute for Mediterranean Agriculture and Forest Systems, 1169

Institute for Membrane Technology, 1172

Institute for Metallurgical Studies and Designs, Elbasan, 85

Institute for Metals Superplasticity Problems of RAS, Ufa, 1843

Institute for Microeconomics and Public Economics, Lugano, 2091

Institute for Microelectronics and Microsystems, 1171

Institute for Microtechnology, Mainz, 875

Institute for Migration and Ethnic Studies, Amsterdam, 1542

Institute for Molecules and Materials (IMM), Nijmegen, 1541

Institute for Multidisciplinary Research in Quantitative Modelling and Analysis, Louvain-la-Neuve, 254

Institute for Musicology of the Hungarian Academy of Sciences, 976

Institute for Natural Sciences, Nukus, 2984

Institute for Nature Conservation and Biodiversity, Lisboa, 1766

Institute for Nature Management, Minsk, 240

Institute for Neohellenic Research, Athens, 945

Institute for Nuclear Sciences and Alternative Energy, 580

Institute for Occupational Health, Kyiv, 2198

Institute for Operations Research and the Management Sciences, Hanover, 2402

Institute for Organic Syntheses and Photoreactivity, 1171

Institute for Petroleum Research, 838

Institute for Photonics and Nanotechnologies, 1170

Institute for Physical Research, Ashtarak, 126

Institute for Plant Genetic Resources 'K. Malkov', Sadovo, 336

Institute for Plant Protection and the Environment, Belgrade, 1921

Institute for Plasma and Nuclear Fusion, Lisboa, 1766

Institute for Plasma Physics, 1170

Institute for Plasma Research, Gandhinagar, 1017

Institute for Plastics Technology, Aachen, 892

Institute for Policy Research and Development, Kathmandu, 1525

Institute for Political and International Studies (IPIS), Tehran, 1107

Institute for Political and International Studies Library and Documentation Centre, Tehran, 1108

Institute for Political Science of the Hungarian Academy of Sciences, 976

Institute for Prevention and Occupational Medicine of the German Social Accident Insurance, 835

Institute for Problems of Cryobiology and Cryomedicine, Kharkiv, 2198

Institute for Process and Application Technology in Ceramics, Aachen, 892

Institute for Programming Research and Algorithmics, 1540

Institute for Psychosocial Intervention and Communication Research, 201

Institute for Public Policy, Bishkek, 1394

Institute for Quantum Optics and Quantum Information, 182

Institute for Reference Materials and Measurements, 257

Institute for Relations between Italy and the Countries of Africa, Latin America and the Middle and Far East, 1173

Institute for Research, Analysis and Organic Synthesis of Natural Products, Santa Fe, 108

Institute for Research and Information in the Geosciences, Mining, the Environment and Nuclear Physics, Bogotá, 580

Institute for Research in Fundamental Sciences, 1107

Institute for Research in Health Sciences, Palma, 2005

Institute for Research in Humanities Library, Kyoto, 1228

Institute for Research in Mathematics Education, Cayenne, 799

Institute for Research in Rationalization, Aachen, 892

Institute for Research into Dangerous Substances, 837

Institute for Research of Crimes Against Humanity and International Law, 289

Institute for Research of Eretz Israel, Jerusalem, 1144

Institute for Research on Combustion, 1170

Institute for Research on Judicial Systems, 1169

Institute for Research on Population and Social Policies, 1169

Institute for Retail Studies, Stirling, 2249

Institute for School Development in Siberia, the Far East and the North, Tomsk, 1834

Institute for Science and Art, Vienna, 180

Institute for Science, Innovation and Society (ISIS), 1544

Institute for Science of Labour, 1226

Institute for Scientific and Artistic Work in Split, 607

Institute for Scientific Information on the Social Sciences of the Russian Academy of Sciences, 1853

Institute for Security and Development Policy, Nacka, 2058

Institute for Security Policy at Kiel University (ISPK), 864

Institute for Security, Technology, and Society, Hanover, 2428

Institute for Serbian Language SASA, 1922

Institute for Service Industry Research, 1169

Institute for Social and Economic Change, Bengaluru, 1014

Institute for Social and Economic Research, Colchester, 2252

Institute for Social and Environmental Research—Nepal, 1525

Institute for Social Reform and Social Politics, Vienna, 179

Institute for Social Research, Vilnius, 1421

Institute for Social Research Zagreb, 608

Institute for Socio-Economic Problems of the Aral Sea Region, Nukus, 2985

Institute for Socio-Economic Studies of Population, St Petersburg, 1833

Institute for Soil, Climate and Water, Pretoria, 1976

Institute for Solar Physics of the Royal Swedish Academy of Sciences, 2059

Institute for Sorption and Endoecology Problems, Kyiv, 2199

Institute for Spatial Design, 178

Institute for Sport & Leisure, Enschede, 1533

Institute for Standardization in Construction, Hanoi, 3013

Institute for Standardization of Bosnia and Herzegovina, 289

Institute for State and Law, Minsk, 240

Institute for Steel Structures and Shell Structures, Graz, 182

Institute for Structural Analysis, 182

Institute for Studies and Design of Oil and Gas Geology, Fier, 85

Institute for Studies and Design of Oil and Gas Technology, Tiranë, 85

Institute for Studies and Technology of Minerals, Tiranë, 85

Institute for Studies in Social Sciences and Humanities from Sibiu, 1790

Institute for Superconductors, Innovative Materials and Devices, 1171

Institute for Superhard Materials, Kyiv, 2201

Institute for Surface Chemistry, Stockholm, 2060

Institute for Sustainable Development, Msida, 1458

Institute for Systems Analysis and Computer Science, 1170

Institute for Systems Analysis, Moscow, 1848

Institute for Technologies Applied to Cultural Heritage, 1169

Institute for Technology and the Storage of Agricultural Products, Bet-Dagan, 1142

Institute for Technology of Nuclear and Other Mineral Raw Materials, 1922

Institute for Textile Technology and Process Engineering Denkendorf, 838

Institute for the Advancement of Animal Husbandry of Macedonia, 1433

Institute for the Advancement of Viticulture of Macedonia, 1433

Institute for the Application of Remote Sensing Information, Changsha, 468

Institute for the Arts and Humanities, University Park, 2418

Institute for the Bulgarian Language, Sofia, 338

Institute for the Coastal Marine Environment, 1170

Institute for the Conservation and Valorization of Cultural Heritage, Sesto Fiorentino, 1169

Institute for the Contemporary Urban Project, Medrisio, 2091

Institute for the Control of Foot and Mouth Disease and Dangerous Infections, Sliven, 336

Institute for the Cultural and Intellectual History of Asia, Vienna, 181

Institute for the Danube Region and Central Europe, 54

Institute for the Dynamics of Environmental Processes, 1170

Institute for the Encouragement of Scientific Research and Innovation of Brussels, 249

Institute for the European Intellectual Lexicon and the History of Ideas, 1169

Institute for the History and Philosophy of Science in Zagreb, 607

Institute for the History of Art in Florence, 1165

Institute for the History of Philosophical and Scientific Thought in the Modern Age, 1169

Institute for the History of Science and Technology—St Petersburg Branch, 1840

Institute for the History of the Italian Revival, 1165

Institute for the Integration of Latin America and the Caribbean, 106

Institute for the Occupational Training of Youth, Moscow, 1834

Institute for the Philosophy of Science, Salzburg, 180

Institute for the Preparation of Serums and Vaccines, Mogadishu, 1970

Institute for the Protection of Cultural Monuments of Serbia, 1921

Institute for the Protection of the Cultural, Historical and Natural Heritage of Bosnia and Herzegovina, 289

Institute for the Protection of the Cultural, Historical and Natural

Heritage of the Canton of Sarajevo, 289

Institute for the Protection of the Mother and Newborn Child, Hanoi, 3012

Institute for the Psychological Sciences, 2932

Institute for the Structure of Matter, 1171

Institute for the Study of Ancient Culture, 180

Institute for the Study of International Aspects of Competition, Kingston, 2419

Institute for the Study of International Politics, Milan, 1172

Institute for the study of Judaism, Brussels, 256

Institute for the Study of Labour, 833

Institute for the Study of Mankind in Africa, Johannesburg, 1976

Institute for the Study of Regionalism, Federalism and Self-Government, 1169

Institute for the Study of Societies and Knowledge, Sofia, 340

Institute for the Study of the Americas, London, 2335

Institute for the Study of the Italic and Ancient Mediterranean Civilizations, Monterotondo, 1169

Institute for the Training and Development of Human Resources, 1668

Institute for Theological and Leadership Philosophy Jaffray, 1105

Institute for Theoretical Physics, Amsterdam, 1540

Institute for Tourism Studies, Macao, 576

Institute for Trade Studies and Research, Tehran, 1107

Institute for Transport and Maritime Management Antwerp, 257

Institute for Tropical Ecosystem Studies, San Juan, 2971

Institute for Tropical Technology, Hanoi, 3013

Institute for University Co-operation, 1162

Institute for Urban and Regional Research, Vienna, 181

Institute for Urban History (City Archives), Frankfurt, 842

Institute for Urbanism, 178

Institute for Veterinary Research, Lubango, 99

Institute for Water and Environmental Problems, Barnaul, 1841

Institute for Wetland and Water Research (IWWR), 1541

Institute of Acoustics and Sensors, 1172

Institute of Acoustics, Beijing, 468

Institute of Acoustics, St Albans, 2242

Institute of Actuaries, London, 2230

Institute of Administration, Baghdad, 1128

Institute of Administration, Karkh (Baghdad), 1128

Institute of Advanced Business Studies (IESE), Barcelona, 2024

Institute of Advanced Legal Studies Library, London, 2273

Institute of Advanced Studies in Education Deemed University, 1074

Institute of Advanced Study, Basel, 2092

Institute of African Studies, Freetown, 1941

Institute of Agricultural and Environmental Engineering, Wageningen, 1544

Institute of Agricultural and Food Information, Prague, 635

Institute of Agricultural Architecture, Ulan Bator, 1497

Institute of Agricultural Biology and Biotechnology, 1168

Institute of Agricultural Economics, Kyiv, 2197

Institute of Agricultural Economics, Minsk, 239

Institute of Agricultural Economics, Sofia, 336

Institute of Agricultural Engineering, Bet-Dagan, 1142

Institute of Agricultural Information (with Central Agricultural Library), Sofia, 342

Institute of Agricultural Meteorology, Beijing, 466

Institute of Agricultural Research and Training (IART), Ibadan, 1591

Institute of Agricultural Science of South Viet Nam, 3011

Institute of Agriculture, Akademija, 1421

Institute of Agriculture, Chabani, 2197

Institute of Agriculture, Kabul, 82

Institute of Agriculture, Kyustendil, 336

Institute of Agriculture, Skopje, 1433

Institute of Agro-environmental and Forest Biology, 1169

Institute of American Indian and Alaska Native Culture and Arts Development, 2764

Institute of American Studies, Beijing, 466

Institute of Analytical Chemistry AS CR, 632

Institute of Analytical Chemistry, Hamhung, 1360

Institute of Analytical Instrumentation, St Petersburg, 1848

Institute of Andean Biology, 1679

Institute of Andorran Studies, 97

Institute of Animal Biochemistry and Genetics, Ivanka pri Dunaji, 1952

Institute of Animal Husbandry Research, Tiranë, 84

Institute of Animal Physiology, Košice, 1952

Institute of Animal Production, 239

Institute of Animal Science, Bet-Dagan, 1142

Institute of Animal Science, Kostinbrod, 336

Institute of Anthropological and Spatial Studies ZRC SAZU, 1964

Institute of Anthropology, University of Iceland, 1002

Institute of Applied Arts, Baghdad, 1128

Institute of Applied Astronomy, St Petersburg, 1843

Institute of Applied Botany at Hamburg University, 836

Institute of Applied Ecology, Shenyang, 467

Institute of Applied Geosciences, Graz, 179

Institute of Applied Manpower Research, Delhi, 1018

Institute of Applied Mathematics and Information Technology, 1170

Institute of Applied Mathematics and Mechanics, Donetsk, 2201

Institute of Applied Mathematics, Beijing, 467

Institute of Applied Mathematics, Vladivostok, 1848

Institute of Applied Mechanics, 178

Institute of Applied Mechanics, Bahía Blanca, 108

Institute of Applied Mechanics, Izhevsk, 1848

Institute of Applied Mechanics, Moscow, 1848

Institute of Applied Optics, Mogilev, 241

Institute of Applied Physics, 1170

Institute of Applied Physics, Chişinău, 1492

Institute of Applied Physics, Minsk, 241

Institute of Applied Physics, Nizhnii Novgorod, 1843

Institute of Applied Problems of Physics, Yerevan, 126

Institute of Applied Social Studies, Birmingham, 2261

Institute of Appropriate Technology, Dhaka, 215

Institute of Aquaculture, 946

Institute of Arab and Islamic Studies, Exeter, 2261

Institute of Arab Music, Cairo, 686

Institute of Arab Research and Studies, Cairo, 688

Institute of Arabic and Religious Study, Kabul, 82

Institute of Archaeological Heritage—Monuments and Sites, Lecce, 1169

Institute of Archaeology, 1665

Institute of Archaeology and Ancient History, Chişinău, 1491

Institute of Archaeology and Ethnography, Baku, 203

Institute of Archaeology and Ethnography, Yerevan, 125

Institute of Archaeology and Ethnology of the Polish Academy of Sciences, 1715

Institute of Archaeology and History of Art of the Romanian Academy, 1787

Institute of Archaeology and Museum Studies, Jos, 1592

Institute of Archaeology at ZRC SAZU, 1964

Institute of Archaeology, Delhi, 1014

Institute of Archaeology, Hanoi, 3012

Institute of Archaeology, Iaşi, 1787

Institute of Archaeology, Iceland, 1001

Institute of Archaeology, Kyiv, 2197

Institute of Archaeology, Moscow, 1834

Institute of Archaeology, Nitra, 1951

Institute of Archaeology, Pyongyang, 1360

Institute of Archaeology, Samarqand, 2984

Institute of Archaeology, Tiranë, 84

Institute of Archaeology, Ulan Bator, 1497

Institute of Architectural Theory, History of Art and Cultural Studies, Graz, 178

Institute of Architectural Typologies, Graz, 178

Institute of Architecture and Art, Baku, 203

Institute of Architecture and Building Engineering, Pyongyang, 1360

Institute of Architecture and Landscape, Graz, 178

Institute of Architecture and Media, Graz, 178

Institute of Architecture and Town Planning, Ulan Bator, 1497

Institute of Architecture Technology, Graz, 178

Institute of Architecture, Vilnius, 1421

Institute of Arctic Studies, Hanover, 2423

Institute of Area Studies, 1665

Institute of Art, Folklore Studies and Ethnography 'M. T. Rylsky', Kyiv, 2200

Institute of Art History AS CR, v. v. i., 631

Institute of Art History, Bratislava, 1951

Institute of Art Studies, Sofia, 337

Institute of Arts, Ethnography and Folklore, Minsk, 241

Institute of Astro- and Particle Physics, University of Innsbruck, Innsbruck, 181

Institute of Astrology, Ulan Bator, 1498

Institute of Astronomy and Astrophysics, 256

Institute of Astronomy, Bucharest, 1789

Institute of Astronomy, México, 1469

Institute of Astronomy, Moscow, 1843

Institute of Astronomy of the University of Latvia, 1403

Institute of Astrophysics, Dushanbe, 2127

Institute of Astrophysics, Göttingen, 837

Institute of Asturian Studies, Oviedo, 2000

Institute of Atmospheric Optics, Tomsk, 1843

Institute of Atmospheric Physics AS CR, v.v.i., 633

Institute of Atmospheric Physics, Beijing, 468

Institute of Atmospheric Physics, Moscow, 1843

Institute of Atmospheric Sciences and Climate, 1170

Institute of Atmospheric Sounding, Beijing, 468

Institute of Atomic and Molecular Sciences, Preparatory Office, Taipei, 2120

Institute of Automatics and Information Technology, Bishkek, 1395

Institute of Automation and Control Processes, Vladivostok, 1848

Institute of Automation and Electrometry, Novosibirsk, 1848

Institute of Automation, Beijing, 469

Institute of Avian Research 'Vogelwarte Helgoland', 836

Institute of Aviation, 1719

Institute of Bangladesh Studies, Rajshahi, 215

Institute of Bankers in South Africa, 1973

Institute of Banking Studies, 1392

Institute of Basic Medical Sciences, Beijing, 466

Institute of Beekeeping, P. I. Prokopovych, Kyiv, 2197

Institute of Biochemistry, Bucharest, 1788

Institute of Biochemistry, Grodno, 240

Institute of Biochemistry, Molecular Biology and Biotechnology, Colombo, 2046

Institute of Biochemistry, Szeged, 977

Institute of Biochemistry, Tashkent, 2984

Institute of Biochemistry, Vilnius, 1422

Institute of Biocomputation and Physics of Complex Systems, 2006

Institute of Biocybernetics and Biomedical Engineering, 1715

Institute of Biodiversity and Ecosystem Research, Sofia, 338

Institute of Biodiversity Conservation and Research, Addis Ababa, 707

Institute of Bioecology, Nukus, 2984

Institute of Bioelectronic and Molecular Microsystems, Bangor, 2263

Institute of Biological Chemistry, Taipei, 2119

Institute of Biological, Environmental and Rural Sciences, 2385

Institute of Biological, Environmental and Rural Sciences - IBERS, Aberystwyth University, Aberystwyth, 2249

Institute of Biological, Environmental and Rural Sciences (IBERS) - Gogerddan Research Centre, 2250

Institute of Biological Instrumentation, Moscow, 1848

Institute of Biological Problems of the North, Magadan, 1840

Institute of Biological Research and Biotechnology, Athens, 945

Institute of Biological Sciences, Rajshahi, 214

Institute of Biology and Experimental Medicine, 107

Institute of Biology and Immunology of Reproduction 'Acad. K. Bratanov', 338

Institute of Biology and Soil Science, Vladivostok, 1840

Institute of Biology and Soil Sciences, Bishkek, 1394

Institute of Biology, Bucharest, 1788

Institute of Biology, Medicine and Agriculture, 359

Institute of Biology, Novosibirsk, 1840

Institute of Biology, Odense, 653

Institute of Biology of Southern Seas, Sevastopol, 2199

Institute of Biology, Petrozavodsk, 1840

Institute of Biology, Salaspils, 1403

Institute of Biology, Syktyvkar, 1840

Institute of Biology, Ufa, 1840

Institute of Biology, Ulan Bator, 1498

Institute of Biology, Ulan-Ude, 1840

Institute of Biology, Yakutsk, 1840

Institute of Biomedical Chemistry, Moscow, 1837

Institute of Biomedical Engineering, 1171

Institute of Biomedical Problems, Moscow, 1837

Institute of Biomedical Research and Therapy, Moscow, 1837

Institute of Geophysics, Ekaterinburg, 1844

Institute of Geophysics, Kyiv, 2200

Institute of Geosciences and Earth Resources, 1169

Institute of Geotechnical Mechanics, Dnipropetrovsk, 2201

Institute of Geotechnics, Košice, 1952

Institute of Geotectonics, Changsha, 468

Institute of Germanic and Romance Studies, London, 2335

Institute of Gerontology, Detroit, 2421

Institute of Gerontology, Kyiv, 2198

Institute of Glass and Ceramic Research and Testing, 214

Institute of Global Climate and Ecology, Moscow, 1840

Institute of Grains and Feed Industry, Sofia, 336

Institute of Grassland and Environmental Research—Bronydd Mawr Research Centre, Brecon, 2250

Institute of Greek and Roman Antiquity, Athens, 945

Institute of Haematology and Blood Transfusion, Tashkent, 2984

Institute of Health, 301

Institute of Health Economics, Dhaka, 214

Institute of Health Policy & Management, Rotterdam, 1538

Institute of Health Science of Royal Cambodian Armed Forces, 358

Institute of Health Sciences, Ruwi, 1635

Institute of Health Sciences-North, 1779

Institute of Heraldic and Genealogical Studies, Canterbury, 2234

Institute of High Current Electronics, Tomsk, 1849

Institute of High Energy Physics, Beijing, 468

Institute of High Energy Physics, Vienna, 181

Institute of High Pressure Physics, 1717

Institute of High-Altitude Physiology and Experimental Pathology of High Rocks, Bishkek, 1394

Institute of Higher Education, Jowzjan, 82

Institute of Higher Education, Moscow, 1834

Institute of Higher Education of Guyana, 799

Institute of Higher Nervous Activity and Neurophysiology, Moscow, 1841

Institute of High-Pressure Physics, Troitsk, 1844

Institute of High-Temperature Electrochemistry, Ekaterinburg, 1844

Institute of High-Temperature Physics, Moscow, 1844

Institute of Highway Engineering and Transport Planning, Graz, 178

Institute of Himalayan Bioresource Technology, 1011

Institute of Historical Research Library, London, 2273

Institute of Historical Research, London, 2335

Institute of Historical Studies, Bratislava, 1951

Institute of Historical Studies, Sofia, 337

Institute of History and Archaeology, Ekaterinburg, 1835

Institute of History and Cultural Heritage, Bishkek, 1394

Institute of History and Philology, Taipei, 2119

Institute of History, Archaeology and Ethnography named after A. Donish, Dushanbe, 2127

Institute of History, Archaeology and Ethnography, Nukus, 2984

Institute of History AS CR, 631

Institute of History, Ashgabat, 2187

Institute of History, Baku, 203

Institute of History, Chişinău, 1491

Institute of History, Hanoi, 3012

Institute of History, Language and Literature, Ufa, 1835

Institute of History, Minsk, 240

Institute of History of Latvia, Rīga, 1403

Institute of History, Philology and Philosophy, Novosibirsk, 1835

Institute of History, Pyongyang, 1360

Institute of History, Sarajevo, 289

Institute of History, Tallinn, 702

Institute of History, Tashkent, 2984

Institute of History, Tiranë, 84

Institute of History, Ulan Bator, 1497

Institute of History, Warsaw, 1715

Institute of History, Yerevan, 125

Institute of Horticulture, Babtai, 1421

Institute of Housing, Real Estate, Urban and Regional Development Ltd, Bochum, 832

Institute of Human and Animal Physiology, Almaty, 1340

Institute of Human Genetics, Moscow, 1838

Institute of Human Morphology, Moscow, 1837

Institute of Human Resource Advancement, Colombo, 2046

Institute of Humanities and Social Sciences, 359

Institute of Humanities, Khorog, 2127

Institute of Hydraulic Engineering and Water Resources Management, Graz, 178

Institute of Hydraulic Engineering, Pyongyang, 1361

Institute of Hydraulic Studies and Design, Tiranë, 85

Institute of Hydraulics and Hydrology, Chingleput, 1019

Institute of Hydrobiology, Kyiv, 2199

Institute of Hydrobiology, Wuhan, 467

Institute of Hydrodynamics, Novosibirsk, 1844

Institute of Hydrogeology and Engineering Geology, Tashkent, 2985

Institute of Hydrogeology and Engineering Geology, Tbilisi, 814

Institute of Hydrogeology and Engineering Geology, Zhengding, 469

Institute of Hydrology, Bratislava, 1952

Institute of Hydromechanics, Kyiv, 2201

Institute of Hydrometeorology, Tbilisi, 814

Institute of Hydrometeorology, Tiranë, 85

Institute of Hydroponics Problems, Yerevan, 125

Institute of Hygiene, Epidemiology and Microbiology, Ulan Bator, 1497

Institute of Hygiene, Vilnius, 1422

Institute of Immunology, Moscow, 1837

Institute of Immunology, Tashkent, 2984

Institute of Indigenous Medicine, 2041

Institute of Industrial Biology, Pyongsong, 1361

Institute of Industrial Biotechnology, Lahore, 1640

Institute of Industrial Chemistry, Hanoi, 3013

Institute of Industrial Economics, Donetsk, 2197

Institute of Industrial Electronics Engineering, Karachi, 1641

Institute of Industrial Engineers, Norcross, 2417

Institute of Industrial Medicine and Human Ecology, Angarsk, 1836

Institute of Industrial Organic Chemistry, 1720

Institute of Industrial Science, 1224

Institute of Industrial Technologies and Automation, 1172

Institute of Influenza, St Petersburg, 1837

Institute of Informatics and Applied Mathematics, Tiranë, 85

Institute of Informatics and Control Problems, Almaty, 1341

Institute of Informatics and Mathematical Modelling of Technological Processes, Apatity, 1849

Institute of Informatics, Bratislava, 1953

Institute of Informatics Problems of the Russian Academy of Sciences (IPIRAN), 1849

Institute of Information and Communication Technology, Dhaka, 215

Institute of Information and Prognoses of Education, 1951

Institute of Information Science and Automation, St Petersburg, 1849

Institute of Information Science and Technology 'Alessandro Faedo', 1170

Institute of Information Science, Taipei, 2120

Institute of Information Technologies, Sofia, 341

Institute of Information Technology, Baku, 204

Institute of Information Technology, Dhaka, 215

Institute of Information Transmission Problems (Kharkevich Institute), Moscow, 1849

Institute of Inland Waters, 946

Institute of Inorganic and Surface Chemistry, 1171

Institute of Inorganic Chemistry and Electrochemistry, Tbilisi, 814

Institute of Inorganic Chemistry AS CR, v.v.i., 632

Institute of Inorganic Chemistry, Bratislava, 1952

Institute of Inorganic Chemistry, Hamhung, 1360

Institute of Inorganic Chemistry, Salaspils, 1403

Institute of Inorganic Methodologies and Plasmas, 1171

Institute of Integrated Development Studies, Kathmandu, 1525

Institute of Intelligent Systems for Automation, 1172

Institute of Internal Medicine, Novosibirsk, 1837

Institute of International Affairs, Pyongyang, 1360

Institute of International Affairs, Reykjavík, 1001

Institute of International Affairs, Rome, 1172

Institute of International and Comparative Agricultural Law, 1168

Institute of International and Social Studies, Tallinn, 703

Institute of International Business, Atlanta, 2419

Institute of International Education, New York, 2396

Institute of International Law, Founex, 61

Institute of International Politics and Economics, Belgrade, 1921

Institute of International Public Law and International Relations, Thessaloniki, 946

Institute of International Relations, 84

Institute of International Sociology, 2060

Institute of International Studies, Ulan Bator, 1497

Institute of Ionized Gas, 1170

Institute of Ionosphere, Almaty, 1340

Institute of Ionosphere, Kharkiv, 2200

Institute of Irrigation and Drainage Studies and Designs, Tiranë, 84

Institute of Islamic Culture, Lahore, 1638

Institute of Ismaili Studies, 2261

Institute of Isotope Geochronology and Geology, Buenos Aires, 108

Institute of Jamaica, 1213

Institute of Jewish Studies, Antwerp, 254

Institute of Juche Literature, Pyongyang, 1360

Institute of Judicial Administration, Birmingham, 2252

Institute of Judicial Research of the Academy Andrei Rădulescu, 1786

Institute of Judicial Studies, Cayenne, 799

Institute of Justice, 1714

Institute of Karst Geology, Guilin, 468

Institute of Kiswahili Research, Dar es Salaam, 2131

Institute of Kyrgyz Language and Literature named after Ch. Aitmatov, 1394

Institute of Laboratory Animal Science, Beijing, 466

Institute of Labour Science and Social Affairs, Hanoi, 3011

Institute of Landscape Ecology, Bratislava, 1952

Institute of Language and Literature named after Alisher Navoi, 2984

Institute of Language and Literature, Nukus, 2984

Institute of Language and Literature, Sarajevo, 289

Institute of Language, Literature and Arts, Makhachkala, 1835

Institute of Language, Literature and History, Syktyvkar, 1835

Institute of Language, Literature, Oriental Studies and Written Heritage named after Rudaki, 2126

Institute of Language, Literature, Oriental Studies and Written Heritage named after Rudaki, Dushanbe, 2127

Institute of Languages and Literature, Kabul, 80

Institute of Laser and Information Technology, Shatura, 1849

Institute of Laser Research, 1875

Institute of Laser Technology, Sofia, 341

Institute of Latin American Studies, 867

Institute of Latin American Studies, Beijing, 466

Institute of Law, Birzeit, 1664

Institute of Law, Lugano, 2091

Institute of Law, Pyongyang, 1360

Institute of Law, University of Iceland, 1001

Institute of Legal Information Theory and Techniques, 1169

Institute of Lexicology and Lexicography of the Portuguese Language, 1765

Institute of Library Economics and Documentation, 90

Institute of Limnology, St Petersburg, 1840

Institute of Linguistics and Literature, 85

Institute of Linguistics, Beijing, 466

Institute of Linguistics, Bishkek, 1394

Institute of Linguistics, Chişinău, 1491

Institute of Linguistics, Hanoi, 3012

Institute of Linguistics, Literature and History, Petrozavodsk, 1835

Institute of Linguistics, Moscow, 1835

Institute of Linguistics, Msida, 1458

Institute of Linguistics 'O. O. Potebni', Kyiv, 2198

Institute of Linguistics, Pyongyang, 1360

Institute of Linguistics 'Ya. Kolas', Minsk, 240

Institute of Literary Studies, Hanoi, 3012

Institute of Literature and Folklore, Chişinău, 1491

Institute of Literature, Folklore and Art, Riga, 1403

Institute of Literature, Minsk, 240

Institute of Literature 'Shevchenko, T. G.', Kyiv, 2198

Institute of Lithuanian History, Vilnius, 1422

Institute of Lithuanian Language, Vilnius, 1422

Institute of Lithuanian Literature and Folklore, Vilnius, 1422

Institute of Low Temperature and Structure Research PAS, Wrocław, 1718

Institute of Macedonian Literature, 1433

Institute of Machine Mechanics and Reliability, Minsk, 241

Institute of Machine Mechanics, Tbilisi, 814

Institute of Machinery and Industrial Instruments, Hanoi, 3013

Institute of Machinery Sciences, Bishkek, 1395

Institute of Macromolecular Chemistry, Hamhung, 1360

Institute of Macro-Molecular Compounds, St Petersburg, 1844

Institute of Malariology, Parasitology and Entomology, Hanoi, 3012

Institute of Management and Development, Pursat, 361

Institute of Management and Technology, Enugu, 1612

Institute of Management Development, Ulan Bator, 1497

Institute of Management Science, Kompong Cham, 361

Institute of Management, Lugano, 2091

Institute of Management Sciences, 1648

Institute of Management Sciences, Peshawar, 1648

Institute of Management Services, Enfield, 2246

Institute of Management Technology, 2221

Institute of Marine Biological Resources, 946

Institute of Marine Biology and Oceanography, Freetown, 1941

Institute of Marine Biology, Kotor, 1503

Institute of Marine Biology, Petropavlovsk-Kamchatskii, 1841

Institute of Marine Biology, Vladivostok, 1841

Institute of Marine Biology/Genetics, 946

Institute of Marine Engineering, Science and Technology (IMarEST), London, 2246

Institute of Marine Geology and Geophysics, Yuzhno-Sakhalinsk, 1844

Institute of Marine Research, 1617

Institute of Marine Science, Karachi, 1641

Institute of Marine Sciences, 1170

Institute of Marine Technology, 1517

Institute of Marine Technology, Boca del Río, 1469

Institute of Market Studies, Ulan Bator, 1497

Institute of Marketing and Communication Management, Lugano, 2091

Institute of Material Culture of the Middle Ages and Early Modern Period, 181

Institute of Materials and Machine Mechanics, Bratislava, 1953

Institute of Materials for Electronics and Magnetism, Parma, 1172

Institute of Materials, Minerals and Mining, London, 2246

Institute of Materials Research, Košice, 1952

Institute of Materials Science, Tashkent, 2985

Institute of Materials Workshop, 1171

Institute of Mathematical Sciences, Chennai, 1017

Institute of Mathematical Statistics, Hayward, 70

Institute of Mathematics, 1717

Institute of Mathematics, Almaty, 1340

Institute of Mathematics and Computer Science, Chişinău, 1492

Institute of Mathematics and Informatics, Sofia, 339

Institute of Mathematics and Informatics, Vilnius, 1422

Institute of Mathematics and Information Technologies, Tashkent, 2984

Institute of Mathematics and its Applications, Southend, 2242

Institute of Mathematics and Mechanics, Ashgabat, 2188

Institute of Mathematics and Mechanics, Baku, 203

Institute of Mathematics and Mechanics, Ekaterinburg, 1849

Institute of Mathematics AS CR, 632

Institute of Mathematics, Beijing, 468

Institute of Mathematics, Bratislava, 1952

Institute of Mathematics, Dushanbe, 2127

Institute of Mathematics, Hanoi, 3012

Institute of Mathematics, Kyiv, 2199

Institute of Mathematics, Minsk, 241

Institute of Mathematics, Physics and Mechanics, Ljubljana, 1965

Institute of Mathematics, Pyongsong, 1360

Institute of Mathematics, Taipei, 2120

Institute of Mathematics, Ufa, 1842

Institute of Mathematics, Ulan Bator, 1498

Institute of Mathematics, Yerevan, 125

Institute of Measurement and Control, London, 2246

Institute of Measurement Science, Bratislava, 1952

Institute of Mechanical Engineering, Pyongsong, 1361

Institute of Mechanical Technology Studies and Design, Tiranë, 85

Institute of Mechanics and Seismic Stability of Structures, Tashkent, 2985

Institute of Mechanics, Beijing, 469

Institute of Mechanics, Hanoi, 3013

Institute of Mechanics, Sofia, 339

Institute of Mechanics, Yerevan, 126

Institute of Medical and Biological Cybernetics, Novosibirsk, 1837

Institute of Medical and Social Care Research, Bangor, 2255

Institute of Medical Biotechnology, Tbilisi, 813

Institute of Medical Climatology and Rehabilitation, Vladivostok, 1837

Institute of Medical Genetics, Tomsk, 1839

Institute of Medical Information, Beijing, 470

Institute of Medical Instrument Making, Moscow, 1849

Institute of Medical Problems of the North, Krasnoyarsk, 1837

Institute of Medical Problems, Osh, 1394

Institute of Medicine, Washington, 2397

Institute of Mediterranean European History, 1169

Institute of Mesoscale Meteorology, Beijing, 468

Institute of Metal Physics, Ekaterinburg, 1844

Institute of Metal Research, Shenyang, 468

Institute of Metal Science, Equipment and Technologies with Hydroaerodynamics Centre 'Acad. A. Balevski', Sofia, 341

Institute of Metallo-organic Chemistry, Nizhnii Novgorod, 1844

Institute of Metallurgy and Ore Enrichment, Almaty, 1341

Institute of Metallurgy, Ekaterinburg, 1844

Institute of Meteorological Instrument Calibration, Beijing, 469

Institute of Meteorological, Scientific and Technical Information, Beijing, 470

Institute of Meteorology and Hydrology, Hanoi, 3013

Institute of Meteorology and Hydrology, Ulan Bator, 1498

Institute of Meteorology, Havana, 617

Institute of Meteorology, Lisbon, 1766

Institute of Meteorology, Sarajevo, 289

Institute of Methodologies for Environmental Analysis, 1169

Institute of Metrology named after D. I. Mendeleyev (VNIIM), St Petersburg, 1844

Institute of Microbial Technology, Chandigarh, 1011

Institute of Microbiology, Abovian, 125

Institute of Microbiology and Biotechnology, Chişinău, 1491

Institute of Microbiology and Virology, Almaty, 1340

Institute of Microbiology, Baku, 203

Institute of Microbiology, Beijing, 467

Institute of Microbiology, Epidemiology and Infectious Diseases, Almaty, 1340

Institute of Microbiology, Minsk, 240

Institute of Microbiology, Moscow, 1841

Institute of Microbiology, Tashkent, 2984

Institute of Microcirculation, Beijing, 467

Institute of Microelectronics Technology and High-purity Materials, Moscow, 1850

Institute of Military History, Moscow, 1835

Institute of Mineral Deposits, Beijing, 468

Institute of Mineral Resources, Tashkent, 2985

Institute of Mineralogy and Crystallography 'Acad. Ivan Kostov', Sofia, 341

Institute of Mineralogy, Miass, 1844

Institute of Minerals and Materials Technology, Bhubaneswar, 1011

Institute of Mining and the Chemical Industry, Lviv, 2201

Institute of Mining, Khabarovsk, Khabarovsk, 1849

Institute of Mining, Novosibirsk, Novosibirsk, 1849

Institute of Mining of the North, Yakutsk, 1849

Institute of Mining, Perm, 1849

Institute of Mining Science and Technology, Hanoi, 3013

Institute of Modern History, Taipei, 2119

Institute of Modern Languages, Dhaka, 214

Institute of Modern Media, 1665

Institute of Molecular and Atomic Physics, Minsk, 241

Institute of Molecular and Cell Biology, Porto, 1765

Institute of Molecular Bioimaging and Physiology, 1171

Institute of Molecular Biology and Biological Physics, Tbilisi, 814

Institute of Molecular Biology and Genetics, Kyiv, 2199

Institute of Molecular Biology and Pathology, Rome, 1170

Institute of Molecular Biology, Bratislava, 1952

Institute of Molecular Biology of the Gene, Moscow, 1841

Institute of Molecular Biology, Pyongyang, 1360

Institute of Molecular Biology 'Roumen Tsanev', Sofia, 338

Institute of Molecular Biology, Yerevan, 125

Institute of Molecular Biotechnology, Salzburg, 180

Institute of Molecular Genetics, 1171

Institute of Molecular Genetics, Antwerpen, 255

Institute of Molecular Genetics AS CR, v.v.i., 632

Institute of Molecular Genetics, Moscow, 1841

Institute of Molecular Medicine, Lisbon, 1765

Institute of Molecular Pathology and Immunology of the University of Porto, 1766

Institute of Molecular Physiology and Genetics, Bratislava, 1952

Institute of Molecular Science and Technologies, 1171

Institute of Mongol Studies, Ulan Bator, 1497

Institute of Mongolian Language and Literature, Ulan Bator, 1497

Institute of Monitoring of Climatic and Ecological Systems, Tomsk, 1849

Institute of Moralogy, 1223

Institute of Mountain Research: Man and Environment, Innsbruck, 180

Institute of Museum and Library Services, Washington, 2395

Institute of Musical Research, London, 2335

Institute of Musicology at ZRC SAZU, 1964

Institute of Musicology, Bratislava, 1951

Institute of Musicology of the Serbian Academy of Sciences and Arts, 1921

Institute of Nanostructured Materials, 1172

Institute of National Affairs, Port Moresby, 1671

Institute of National Development, Ulan Bator, 1497

Institute of National Economic Forecasting, Moscow, 1833

Institute of National Economy, Bucharest, 1787

Institute of National Economy, Kyiv, 2216

Institute of National History, Skopje, 1433

Institute of National Language, 359

Institute of National Minorities Studies, Chişinău, 1492

Institute of National Planning, Cairo, 688

Institute of National Problems of Education, Moscow, 1834

Institute of Natural Resources named after Djamanbaev A. S., 1395

Institute of Natural Sciences, Bogotá, 580

Institute of Natural Sciences, Ulan-Ude, 1840

Institute of Naval History and Culture, Madrid, 1998

Institute of Neurobiology and Molecular Medicine, 1171

Institute of Neurobiology, Košice, 1951

Institute of Neurogenetics and Neuropharmacology, 1171

Institute of Neurological Sciences, 1171

Institute of Neurology and Psychiatry, Bucharest, 1788

Institute of Neurology, London, 2255

Institute of New Chemical Problems, Chernogolovka, 1844

Institute of New Technologies, Osh, 1395

Institute of Non-ferrous Metals, Gliwice, 1719

Institute of Non-Ferrous Metals, Nampo, 1360

Institute of Normal and Pathological Physiology, Bratislava, 1951

Institute of North American Studies, Barcelona, 1996

Institute of Nuclear Chemistry and Technology, Warsaw, 1719

Institute of Nuclear Energy Research, Lung-Tan, 2120

Institute of Nuclear Physics, Almaty, 1340

Institute of Nuclear Physics, Novosibirsk, 1844

Institute of Nuclear Physics, Tashkent, 2985

Institute of Nuclear Physics, Tiranë, 85

Institute of Nuclear Research and Nuclear Energy, Sofia, 339

Institute of Nuclear Research, Kyiv, 2200

Institute of Nuclear Research, Moscow, 1844

Institute of Nuclear Research of the Hungarian Academy of Sciences, 978

Institute of Nuclear Studies applied to Agriculture, 1168

Institute of Nursing Research, 2255

Institute of Nutrition, Almaty, 1340

Institute of Nutrition and Food Sciences, Dhaka, 215

Institute of Nutrition, Moscow, 1837

Institute of Nutrition of Central America and Panama, 961

Institute of Obstetrics and Gynaecology, Sofia, 338

Institute of Occupational Health, Moscow, 1837

Institute of Oceanography, 946

Institute of Oceanography and Fisheries, Cairo, 687

Institute of Oceanography and Fisheries, Split, 607

Institute of Transport Economics, Oslo, 1618

Institute of Transport Science and Technology, Hanoi, 3013

Institute of Traumatology and Orthopaedics, Irkutsk, 1836

Institute of Tropical and Subtropical Crops, Nelspruit, 1976

Institute of Tropical Geography, Havana, 616

Institute of Tropical Medicine, Antwerp, 272

Institute of Turkology Library, Istanbul, 2161

Institute of Urban Planning and Design, Tiranë, 84

Institute of Urban Water Management and Landscape Water Engineering, 182

Institute of USA and Canada Studies, Moscow, 1834

Institute of Vaccines and Medical Biologicals, Nha Trang, 3012

Institute of Vaccines and Sera, Tashkent, 2984

Institute of Vegetable Crops, 239

Institute of Vegetables and Potatoes, Tiranë, 84

Institute of Vertebrate Biology AS CR, v.v.i, 632

Institute of Vertebrate Palaeontology and Palaeo-Anthropology, Beijing, 467

Institute of Veterinary Research of the Ukrainian Academy of Agricultural Sciences, Kyiv, 2197

Institute of Veterinary Research, Tiranë, 84

Institute of Veterinary Research, Ulan Bator, 1497

Institute of Viral Preparations, Moscow, 1837

Institute of Virology, Bratislava, 1951

Institute of Viticulture and Oenology, Pleven, 336

Institute of Vocational Education, St Petersburg, 1834

Institute of Volcanology and Seismology, Petropavlovsk-Kamchatskii, 1845

Institute of Water and Ecological Problems, Khabarovsk, 1841

Institute of Water and Flood Management, Dhaka, 215

Institute of Water Problems and Hydropower, Bishkek, 1395

Institute of Water Problems, Hydropower and Ecology, Dushanbe, 2127

Institute of Water Problems, Moscow, 1845

Institute of Water Problems of the North, Petrozavodsk, 1845

Institute of Water Problems, Sofia, 336

Institute of Water Problems, Tashkent, 2985

Institute of Weather Modification, Beijing, 468

Institute of Welding, Gliwice, 1720

Institute of Welding, Nampo, 1361

Institute of West Asian and African Studies, Beijing, 466

Institute of Women's Studies, Birzeit, 1664

Institute of World Economics and International Relations, Moscow, 1834

Institute of World Economy and International Relations, Kyiv, 2197

Institute of World Economy 'Costin Murgescu', 1786

Institute of World History, Moscow, 1835

Institute of World Literature, Bratislava, 1951

Institute of World Politics, Washington, 2579

Institute of World Religions, Beijing, 469

Institute of Youth Sport, Loughborough, 2249

Institute of Zoology, Almaty, 1340

Institute of Zoology and Botany, Tartu, 702

Institute of Zoology and Parasitology named after E. N. Pavlovskii, Dushanbe, 2127

Institute of Zoology, Ashgabat, 2188

Institute of Zoology, Baku, 203

Institute of Zoology, Beijing, 467

Institute of Zoology, Bratislava, 1952

Institute of Zoology, Chişinău, 1491

Institute of Zoology, London, 2259

Institute of Zoology, Minsk, 240

Institute of Zoology, Pyongyang, 1360

Institute of Zoology, Sofia, 339

Institute of Zoology, Taipei, 2120

Institute of Zoology, Tashkent, 2984

Institute of Zoology, Tbilisi, 814

Institute of Zoology, Yerevan, 125

Institute–Museum of Genocide, Yerevan, 125

Institutes for Applied Research, Ben-Gurion University of the Negev, 1144

Institutet för Näringslivsforskning, 2058

Institutet för rymdfysik, 2059

Institutet för Social Forskning, 2060

Institutet för Språk och Folkminnen, Uppsala, 2059

Instituti i Arkeologjisë, 84

Instituti i Duhanit, Cërrik, 84

Instituti i Energjetikës, 85

Instituti i Fizikës Bërthamore, 85

Instituti i Gjuhësisë dhe i Letërsisë, Tiranë, 85

Instituti i Hidrometeorologjisë, 85

Instituti i Historisë, Tiranë, 84

Instituti i Informatikës dhe i Matematikës së Aplikuar, 85

Instituti i Kërkimeve Biologjike, Tiranë, 85

Instituti i Kërkimeve Bujqësore Lushnje, 84

Instituti i Kërkimeve Pyjore dhe Kullotave, 84

Instituti i Kërkimeve të Foragjere, 84

Instituti i Kërkimeve të Pemëve Frutore dhe Vreshtave, Tiranë, 84

Instituti i Kërkimeve të Ushqimit, 85

Instituti i Kërkimeve të Zooteknisë, 84

Instituti i Kërkimeve Veterinare, 84

Instituti i Kerkimit te Bimeve te Arave, Stacioni Eksperimental, 84

Instituti i Kulturës Popullore, 85

Instituti i Mbrojtjes Bimeve, 84

Instituti i Mjekësisë Popullore, 85

Instituti i Monumenteve të Kulturës, 84

Instituti i Perimeve dhe i Patates, 84

Instituti i Shëndetit Publik, 85

Instituti i Sizmologjise, 85

Instituti i Studimeve dhe i Projektimeve Gjeologjike të Naftës e të Gazit, 85

Instituti i Studimeve dhe i Projektimeve të Hidrocentraleve, 85

Instituti i Studimeve dhe i Projektimeve të Metalurgjise, 85

Instituti i Studimeve dhe i Projektimeve të Minierave, 85

Instituti i Studimeve dhe i Projektimeve të Teknologjisë Kimike, 85

Instituti i Studimeve dhe i Projektimeve të Teknologjisë Mekanike, 85

Instituti i Studimeve dhe i Projektimeve të Veprave të Kullimit dhe Ujitjes, 84

Instituti i Studimeve dhe i Projektimeve Teknologjike të Mineraleve, 85

Instituti i Studimeve dhe i Projektimeve Teknologjike të Naftës e të Gazit, 85

Instituti i Studimeve dhe i Teknologjisë Ndërtimit, 85

Instituti i Studimeve dhe Projektimeve Mekanike, 85

Instituti i Studimeve dhe Projektimeve të Gjeologjise, 85

Instituti i Studimeve e Projektimeve Urbanistikë, 84

Instituti i Studimeve Pedagogjike, 84

Instituti i Studimeve të Marrëdhënieve Ndërkombëtare, Tiranë, 84

Instituti i Studimeve të Tokave, 84

Instituti i Ullirit dhe i Agrumeve, 84

Instituti Kombëtar i Shëndetësise Publike te Kosoves, 1388

Instituti Kosovar për Kërkime dhe Zhvillime të Politikave, 1388

Institutio Pedagógico de Barquisimeto, 3008

Institution for Research of Materials and Development of New Technologies, 1433

Institution för Spanska. Portugisiska och Latinamerika Studier, 2058

Institution of Agricultural Engineers (IAgrE), Bedford, 2227

Institution of Certificated Mechanical and Electrical Engineers, South Africa, 1975

Institution of Chemical Engineers, Rugby, 2246

Institution of Civil Engineers, London, 2246

Institution of Civil Engineers (Republic of Ireland Division), 1132

Institution of Electrical and Electronics Engineers Pakistan (IEEEP), 1639

Institution of Electronics and Telecommunication Engineers (IETE), New Delhi, 1010

Institution of Electronics, Spital, 2246

Institution of Engineering and Technology Library and Archives, London, 2273

Institution of Engineering and Technology, London, 2246

Institution of Engineering and Technology (Republic of Ireland Division), 1132

Institution of Engineering Designers, Westbury, 2246

Institution of Engineers and Shipbuilders in Scotland, 2246

Institution of Engineers, Australia trading as Engineers Australia, 136

Institution of Engineers, Bangladesh, 213

Institution of Engineers (India), 1010

Institution of Engineers of Kenya, 1352

Institution of Engineers (Pakistan), 1639

Institution of Engineers, Sri Lanka, 2040

Institution of Environmental Sciences, Bourne, 2240

Institution of Ferdinando the Catholic, 2000

Institution of Fire Engineers, Leicester, 2246

Institution of Gas Engineers and Managers, London, 2247

Institution of Highways and Transportation, London, 2247

Institution of Lighting Engineers, Rugby, 2247

Institution of Marine Research, Coimbra, 1766

Institution of Materials, Minerals and Mining (Zimbabwe Section), 3028

Institution of Mechanical Engineers, London, 2247

Institution of Nuclear Engineers, London, 2247

Institution of Professional Engineers New Zealand, 1575

Institution of Russian Academy of Education Ushinsky State Pedagogical Library, Moscow, 1854

Institution of Structural Engineers, London, 2247

Institution Saint Jude, Lille, 795

Instituto Açoriano de Cultura, 1761

Instituto 'Adolfo Lutz', São Paulo, 301

Instituto Agrario Argentino de Cultura Rural, 106

Instituto Agrícola Metodista 'El Vergel', 460

Instituto Agronômico, Campinas, 301

Instituto Antártico Argentino, 107

Instituto Antártico Chileno, 451

Instituto Argentino de Investigaciones de las Zonas Aridas (IADIZA), 108

Instituto Argentino de Nivología, Glaciología y Ciencias Ambientales (IANIGLA), 108

Instituto Argentino de Normalización (IRAM), 109

Instituto Argentino de Oceanografía (IADO), 108

Instituto Argentino de Radioastronomía (IAR), 108

Instituto Arqueológico, Histórico e Geográfico Pernambucano, 297

Instituto Azucarero Dominicano, 671

Instituto 'Benjamin Constant', Urca, 301

Instituto Biológico, São Paulo, 302

Instituto Boliviano de Ciencia y Tecnología Nuclear, 283

Instituto Boliviano del Petróleo (IBP), 283

Instituto Bonaerense de Numismática y Antigüedades, 103

Instituto Botânico 'Dr Júlio Henriques', 1766

Instituto Brasileiro de Economia, 297

Instituto Brasileiro de Educação, Ciência e Cultura (IBECC), Rio de Janeiro, 297

Instituto Brasileiro de Estudos e Pesquisas de Gastroenterologia (IBEPEGE), 301

Instituto Brasileiro de Informação em Ciência e Tecnologia (IBICT), 304

Instituto Brasileiro de Petróleo, 303

Instituto Brasileiro do Meio Ambiente e dos Recursos Naturais Renováveis (IBAMA), 301

Instituto Butantan, 301

Instituto Caribe de Antropología y Sociología, Caracas, 3003

Instituto Caro y Cuervo, Bogotá, 578

Instituto Cartográfico Militar de las Fuerzas Armadas, Santo Domingo, 671

Instituto Centroamericano de Administración de Empresas (INCAE), Managua, 1586

Instituto Centroamericano de Administración Pública (ICAP), San José, 601

Instituto Centroamericano de Investigación y Tecnología Industrial (ICAITI), Guatemala City, 961

Instituto Cervantes, Algiers, 89

Instituto Cervantes, Amman, 1334

Instituto Cervantes, Athens, 945

Instituto Cervantes, Beirut, 1406

Instituto Cervantes, Berlin, 823

Instituto Cervantes, Brussels, 251

Instituto Cervantes, Bucharest, 1784

Instituto Cervantes, Budapest, 973

Instituto Cervantes, Cairo, 686

Instituto Cervantes, Damascus, 2115

Instituto Cervantes de Lisboa, 1762

Instituto Cervantes, Dublin, 1131

Instituto Cervantes, Istanbul, 2159

Instituto Cervantes, London, 2236

Instituto Cervantes, Madrid, 1996

Instituto Cervantes, Manila, 1689

Instituto Cervantes, Moscow, 1828

Instituto Cervantes, New York, 2406

Instituto Cervantes, Paris, 743

Instituto Cervantes, Rabat, 1506

Instituto Cervantes, Rio de Janeiro, 298

Instituto Cervantes, Rome, 1166

Instituto Cervantes, Stockholm, 2056

Instituto Cervantes, Tel Aviv, 1141

Instituto Cervantes, Tunis, 2155

Instituto Cervantes, Utrecht, 1530

Instituto Cervantes, Vienna, 175

Instituto Cervantes, Warsaw, 1709

Instituto CEU de Humanidades Ángel Ayala, 2004

Instituto Científico y Tecnológico de Navarra, 2006

Instituto Colombiano Agropecuario, 579

Instituto Colombiano de Antropología e Historia, 580

Instituto Colombiano de Crédito Educativo y Estudios Técnicos en el Exterior (ICETEX), 577

Instituto Colombiano de Geología y Mineria (INGEOMINAS), 580

Instituto Colombiano de Normas Técnicas y Certificación (ICONTEC), 580

Instituto Colombiano del Petróleo, 580

Instituto Colombiano para el Desarrollo de la Ciencia y la Tecnología 'Francisco José de Caldas' (Colciencias), 579

Instituto Colombiano para el Fomento de la Educación Superior, 579

Instituto Colombiano para el Fomento de la Educación Superior (ICFES), Bogotá, 578

Instituto Conmemorativo Gorgas de Estudios de la Salud, Panamá, 1668

Instituto Costarricense de Investigación y Enseñanza en Nutrición y Salud, 599

Instituto Cubano de Investigaciones de los Derivados de la Caña de Azúcar (ICIDCA), 616

Instituto Cultural do Governo da R. A. E. de Macau, 577

Instituto da Conservação da Natureza e da Biodiversidade, 1766

Instituto de Algodão de Moçambique, 1511

Instituto de Altos Estudos, 1763

Instituto de Antropología e Historia, Guatemala City, 960

Instituto de Arte Peruano 'José Sabogal', 1677

Instituto de Astrofísica de Canarias (IAC), 2005

Instituto de Astronomía, México, 1469

Instituto de Bibliografía del Ministerio de Educación de la Provincia de Buenos Aires, 106

Instituto de Biocomputación y Física de Sistemas Complejos, 2006

Instituto de Biología Andina, Lima, 1679

Instituto de Biología y Medicina Experimental, Buenos Aires, 107

Instituto de Biologia Molecular e Celular, 1765

Instituto de Botánica 'Carlos Spegazzini', Buenos Aires, 108

Instituto de Botánica 'Darwinion', 108

Instituto de Botánica del Nordeste (IBONE), Corrientes, 108

Instituto de Botânica, São Paulo, 302

Instituto de Cancerología 'Cupertino Arteaga', 282

Instituto de Chile, 447

Instituto de Cibernética, Matemática y Física (ICIMAF), Havana, 617

Instituto de Ciências Biomédicas de Abel Salazar, 1765

Instituto de Ciencias Naturales, Bogotá, 580

Instituto de Ciencias Nucleares, Quito, 678

Instituto de Ciencias Nucleares y Energías Alternativas, Bogotá, 580

Instituto de Ciências Sociais, 1767

Instituto de Cooperación con el Mundo Arabe, Mediterráneo y Países en Desarrollo, 1996

Instituto de Cooperación Iberoamericana, Madrid, 1996

Instituto de Cultura Alimentaria Birchner-Benner, 1679

Instituto de Cultura Dominicana, 671

Instituto de Cultura Puertorriqueña, 2971

Instituto de Desarrollo Económico y Social, Buenos Aires, 106

Instituto de Desarrollo Tecnológico para la Industria Química (INTEC), Santa Fé, 108

Instituto de Ecología, AC, Xalapa, 1469

Instituto de Economia Agrícola, São Paulo, 301

Instituto de Edafología Agrícola, Buenos Aires, 106

Instituto de Empresa, Madrid, 2037

Instituto de Engenharia Nuclear (IEN), Rio de Janeiro, 302

Instituto de Enseñanza Superior del Ejército, Buenos Aires, 122

Instituto de España, Madrid, 1996

Instituto de Estudios de la Democracia, 2004

Instituto de Estudios del Caribe, San Juan, 2971

Instituto de Estudios Etnológicos, 1678

Instituto de Estudios Fiscales, Madrid, 2004

Instituto de Estudios Islámicos, Lima, 1678

Instituto de Estudios Para El Desarrollo, 1533

Instituto de Estudios Superiores de Administración (IESA), Caracas, 3008

Instituto de Estudos Clássicos, 1765

Instituto de Filosofía, Havana, 617

Instituto de Fomento Pesquero, Valparaíso, 450

Instituto de Formação Turística, 576

Instituto de Geocronología y Geología Isotópica (INGEIS), Buenos Aires, 108

Instituto de Geofísica y Astronomía, 617

Instituto de Geografía Tropical, Havana, 616

Instituto de Geografía y Conservación de Recursos Naturales, Mérida, 3002

Instituto De Gestão Do Património Arquitectónico e Arqueológico, 1761

Instituto de Historia y Cultura Naval, Madrid, 1998

Instituto de Información Científica y Tecnológica (IDICT), 617

Instituto de Ingenieros de Chile, 450

Instituto de Ingenieros de Minas de Chile, 450

Instituto de Investigação Agronómica, Huambo, 99

Instituto de Investigação Científica 'Bento da Rocha Cabral', 1766

Instituto de Investigação Científica Tropical, 1763

Instituto de Investigação das Pescas e do Mar (INRB), 1766

Instituto de Investigação Veterinária, 99

Instituto de Investigación Agropecuaria de Panamá, Panama City, 1668

Instituto de Investigación de Productos Naturales, de Análisis y de Síntesis Orgánica (IPNAYS), Santa Fé, 108

Instituto de Investigación en Ingeniería de Aragón, 2006

Instituto de Investigación Médica 'Mercedes y Martín Ferreyra' (INIMEC), 108

Instituto de Investigaciones Agropecuarias 'Jorge Dimitrov', 616

Instituto de Investigaciones Agropecuarias, Santiago, 450

Instituto de Investigaciones Alérgicas 'Dr Luis E. Betetta', San Miguel, 1679

Instituto de Investigaciones Arqueológicas y Museo 'R.P. Gustavo Le Paige, S.J.', 450

Instituto de Investigaciones Avícolas, Havana, 616

Instituto de Investigaciones Bibliográficas, México, 1468

Instituto de Investigaciones Biológicas Clemente Estable, 2980

Instituto de Investigaciones Bioquímicas (INIBIBB), Bahía Blanca, 108

Instituto de Investigaciones de Sanidad Vegetal, Havana, 616

Instituto de Investigaciones Eléctricas, Cuernavaca, 1470

Instituto de Investigaciones en Catálisis y Petroquímica (INCAPE), Santa Fé, 108

Instituto de Investigaciones en Viandas Tropicales, Santo Domingo, 616

Instituto de Investigaciones Estadísticas (INIE), Tucumán, 108

Instituto de Investigaciones Farmacológicas (ININFA), Buenos Aires, 108

Instituto de Investigaciones Forestales, Havana, 616

Instituto de Investigaciones Fundamentales en Agricultura Tropical 'Alejandro de Humboldt', 616

Instituto de Investigaciones Geohistóricas (IIGHI), Resistencia, 108

Instituto de Investigaciones Marinas y Costeras 'José Benito Vives de Andréis' (INVEMAR), 580

Instituto de Investigaciones Médicas 'Alfredo Lanari', Buenos Aires, 107

Instituto de Investigaciones Porcinas, Bauta, 616

Instituto de Investigaciones Veterinarias, Maracay, 3002

Instituto de Investigaciones y Ensayes de Materiales (IDIEM), Universidad de Chile, 451

Instituto de la Ingeniería de España, 2000

Instituto de la Patagonia, Punta Arenas, 455

Instituto de Lexicologia e Lexicografia da Língua Portuguesa, 1765

Instituto de Limnología 'Dr Raul A. Ringuelet' (ILPLA), 108

Instituto de Literatura y Lingüística 'José Antonio Portuondo Valdor', Havana, 616

Instituto de Matemática de Bahía Blanca (INMABB), Bahía Blanca, 108

Instituto de Matemáticas, México, 1469

Instituto de Mecánica Aplicada (IMA), Bahía Blanca, 108

Instituto de Mecánica Aplicada y Estructuras, Santa Fé, 109

Instituto de Medicina Experimental, Caracas, 3002

Instituto de Medicina Experimental del Servicio Nacional de Salud, Santiago, 450

Instituto de Medicina Molecular, 1765

Instituto de Meteorología (INSMET), 617

Instituto de Meteorologia, 1766

Instituto de Neurobiología (IDNEU), Buenos Aires, 108

Instituto de Nutrición de Centro América y Panamá (INCAP), Guatemala City, 961

Instituto de Oceanología, Havana, 616

Instituto de Orientação Profissional, 1764

Instituto de Patalogia e Imunologia da Universidade do Porto, 1766

Instituto de Pesquisas do Jardim Botânico do Rio de Janeiro, 302

Instituto de Pesquisas Energéticas e Nucleares (IPEN), São Paulo, 303

Instituto de Pesquisas Tecnológicas do Estado de São Paulo S.A. (IPT), 303

Instituto de Planeamiento Regional y Urbano (IPRU), Buenos Aires, 106

Instituto de Plasmas e Fusão Nuclear, 1766

Instituto de Radioproteção e Dosimetria (IRD), Rio de Janeiro, 303

Instituto de Relaciones Europeo-Latinoamericanas (IRELA), Madrid, 2004

Instituto de Robótica, 2006

Instituto de Salud Pública de Chile, 450

Instituto de Saúde, São Paulo, 301

Instituto de Sociología Boliviana (ISBO), 282

Instituto de Tecnologia do Paraná, 303

Instituto de Teología para Religiosos–ITER, Caracas, 2996

Instituto de Valencia de Don Juan, 2009

Instituto de Zootecnia, Nova Odessa, 301

Instituto del Mar del Perú (IMARPE), 1679

Instituto del Patrimonio Cultural de España, 2004

Instituto do Ceará, 297

Instituto dos Advogados Brasileiros, 297

Instituto Ecuatoriano de Antropología y Geografía, Quito, 678

Instituto Egipcio de Estudios Islámicos, Madrid, 1996

Instituto Español de Enseñanza Secundaria 'Severo Ochoa', 1510

Instituto Español de Oceanografía, 2005

Instituto Estadual do Ambiente (INEA), Rio de Janeiro, 302

Instituto Evandro Chagas (MS-Fundação Nacional de Saúde), Belém, 301

Instituto Experimental de Educación Primaria No. 1, Lima, 1679

Instituto Feijoo del Siglo XVIII, 2005

Instituto Florestal (Estado de São Paulo), 301

Instituto Forestal, 450

Instituto Genealógico Brasileiro, 297

Instituto Geofísico, 1765

Instituto Geofísico del Perú, 1679

Instituto Geográfico 'Agustín Codazzi', Bogotá, 580

Instituto Geográfico e Histórico da Bahia, 297

Instituto Geográfico e Histórico do Amazonas (IGHA), 297

Instituto Geográfico Militar, 678

Instituto Geográfico Militar, Asunción, 1674

Instituto Geográfico Militar, Buenos Aires, 107

Instituto Geográfico Militar, La Paz, 282

Instituto Geográfico Militar, Santiago, 448

Instituto Geográfico Nacional (IGN), Tegucigalpa, 970

Instituto Geográfico Nacional 'Ing. Alfredo Obiols Gómez', Guatemala City, 961

Instituto Geográfico Nacional, Lima, 1678

Instituto Geográfico Nacional, Madrid, 1998

Instituto Geográfico Nacional, San José, 599

Instituto Geográfico Português, 1761

Instituto Geológico, Minero y Metalúrgico, Lima, 1679

Instituto Geológico, São Paulo, 297

Instituto Geológico y Minero de España, 2006

Instituto Gregoriano de Lisboa, 1761

Instituto Gulbenkian de Ciência, 1766

Instituto Hidrográfico, 1767

Instituto Histórico da Ilha Terceira (IHIT), 1761

Instituto Histórico e Geográfico Brasileiro, 297

Instituto Histórico e Geográfico de Alagoas, 297

Instituto Histórico e Geográfico de Goiás, 297

Instituto Histórico e Geográfico de Santa Catarina, 298

Instituto Histórico e Geográfico de São Paulo, 298

Instituto Histórico e Geográfico de Sergipe, 298

Instituto Histórico e Geográfico do Espírito Santo, 298

Instituto Histórico e Geográfico do Maranhão, 298

Instituto Histórico e Geográfico do Pará, 298

Instituto Histórico e Geográfico do Paraná, 298

Instituto Histórico e Geográfico do Rio Grande do Norte, 298

Instituto Histórico e Geográfico do Rio Grande do Sul, 298

Instituto Histórico e Geográfico Paraíbano, 298

Instituto Histórico y Geográfico del Uruguay, 2979

Instituto Hondureño de Antropología e Historia, 970

Instituto Hondureño de Cultura Interamericana (IHCI), 970

Instituto Hondureño del Café, 970

Instituto Iberoamericano de Derecho Agrario y Reforma Agraria, Mérida, 3002

Instituto Indigenista Interamericano, México, 1470

Instituto Indigenista Peruano, 1678

Instituto Interamericano de Cooperación para la Agricultura, 43

Instituto Interamericano de Estadística, 49

Instituto Interamericano del Niño, 2980

Instituto Internacional de la UNESCO para la Educación en América Latina y el Caribe, 56

Instituto Internacional para la Educación Superior en América Latina y el Caribe (IESALC), 54

Instituto Interuniversitario de Estudios de Iberoamérica y Portugal, 2004

Instituto Isaac Newton, Santiago, 451

Instituto J. I. Baldó, Caracas, 3000

Instituto Universitario de Seguridad Marítima, Buenos Aires, 123

Instituto Universitario Nacional del Arte, Buenos Aires, 123

Instituto Universitario Naval, Buenos Aires, 123

Instituto Universitario Politécnico 'Luis Caballero Mejías', Caracas, 3008

Instituto Universitario Salesiano 'Padre Ojeda', Los Teques, 2996

Instituto Universitario sobre Modelización y Simulación en Fluidodinámica, Nanociencia y Matemática Industrial 'Gregorio Millán Barbany', 2014

Instituto Uruguayo de Normas Técnicas, 2981

Instituto Valenciano de Investigaciones Económicas, 2004

Instituto Venezolano de Investigaciones Científicas (IVIC), 3002

Instituto Vizcardo de Estudios Históricos, Miraflores, 1678

Instituto Zuliano de la Cultura 'Andrés E. Blanco', 3000

Institutot za Životna Sredina i Zdravje, 1432

Instituts du Ministère de l'Enseignement Supérieur, Yaoundé, 363

Instituts für Niederrheinische Kulturgeschichte und Regionalenwicklung, 915

Institutt for Energiteknikk, Kjeller, 1617

Instituttet for Sammenlignende Kulturforskning, Oslo, 1617

Institutul Astronomic, 1789

Institutul Biblic și de Misiune al Bisericii Ortodoxe Române, 1784

Institutul Cantacuzino, 1787

Institutul Cultural Român, 1783

Institutul de Antropologie Francisc I. Rainer, 1790

Institutul de Arheologie, 1787

Institutul de Arheologie și Istoria Artei al Academiei Române, 1787

Institutul de Arheologie 'Vasile Pârvan', 1787

Institutul de Biochimie, 1788

Institutul de Biologie, 1788

Institutul de Biologie și Patologie Celulară 'Nicolae Simionescu', 1788

Institutul de Cercetare Dezvoltare pentru Ecologie Acvatica, Pescuit si Acvacultura, 1785

Institutul de Cercetare Dezvoltare pentru Pomicultura, 1785

Institutul de Cercetare și Dezvoltare pentru Bovine, 1785

Institutul de Cercetare și Dezvoltare pentru Valorificarea Produselor Horticole, 1785

Institutul de Cercetare și Inginerie Tehnologică pentru Irigații și Drenaje, 1785

Institutul de Cercetare și Producție pentru Creșterea Ovinelor și Caprinelor, 1785

Institutul de Cercetare și Producție pentru Creșterea Păsărilor și Animalelor Mici, 1785

Institutul de Cercetare-Dezvoltare pentru Apicultură, 1785

Institutul de Cercetare-Dezvoltare pentru Cultura și Industrializarea Sfeclei de Zahăr și Substanțelor Dulci, 1785

Institutul de Cercetare—Dezvoltare pentru Pajisti, 1785

Institutul de Cercetare—Dezvoltare pentru Protecția Plantelor, 1785

Institutul de Cercetări Biologice Cluj-Napoca, 1788

Institutul de Cercetări Biologice Iași, 1788

Institutul de Cercetări Chimice, 1789

Institutul de Cercetări Dezvoltare pentru Legumicultură și Floricultură, 1785

Institutul de Cercetări Eco-Muzeale Tulcea, 1788

Institutul de Cercetări Juridice 'Acad. Andrei Rădulescu', 1786

Institutul de Cercetări pentru Cereale și Plante Tehnice, 1785

Institutul de Cercetări pentru Inteligență Artificială, 1787

Institutul de Cercetări pentru Viticultură și Vinificație, 1785

Institutul de Cercetări și Amenajări Silvice, 1785

Institutul de Cercetări Socio-Umane 'C. S. Nicolaescu-Plopsor', 1790

Institutul de Cercetări Socio-Umane din Sibiu, 1790

Institutul de Cercetări Socio-Umane 'Gheorghe Șincai' al Academiei Române, 1790

Institutul de Chimie Alimentară, 1786

Institutul de Chimie Fizică 'Ilie Murgulescu', 1789

Institutul de Chimie Macromoleculară 'Petru Poni' al Academiei Romane, 1789

Institutul de Chimie Organică 'Costin D. Nenițescu', 1789

Institutul de Chimie Timișoara, 1789

Institutul de Economie Mondială 'Costin Murgescu', 1786

Institutul de Economie Națională, 1787

Institutul de Endocrinologie 'C.I. Parhon', 1787

Institutul de Etnografie și Folclor 'Constantin Brăiloiu', 1790

Institutul de Filologie Română 'Al. Philippide', 1787

Institutul de Filosofie si Psihologie 'Constantin Rădulescu-Motru', 1789

Institutul de Fiziologie Normală și Patologică 'D. Danielopolu', 1788

Institutul de Fonoaudiologie și Chirurgie Funcțională ORL 'Prof. Dr. D. Hociotă', 1788

Institutul de Geodinamică 'Sabba S. Ștefănescu', 1789

Institutul de Geografie, 1787

Institutul de Informatică Teoretică, 1790

Institutul de Istoria Artei 'G. Oprescu', 1787

Institutul de Istorie 'A. D. Xenopol', 1787

Institutul de Istorie 'Nicolae Iorga', 1787

Institutul de Istorie și Teorie Literară 'G. Călinescu', 1787

Institutul de Lingvistica 'Iorgu Iordan–Al. Rosetti', 1787

Institutul de Matematică 'Octav Mayer', 1788

Institutul de Matematică 'Simion Stoilow', 1788

Institutul de Mecanica Solidelor, 1790

Institutul de Medicină Internă 'Nicolae Gh. Lupu', 1788

Institutul de Neurologie și Psihiatrie, 1788

Institutul de Patologie și Genetică Medicală 'V. Babeș', 1788

Institutul de Prognoză Economică, 1787

Institutul de Relații Internaționale din Moldova, 1494

Institutul de Sănătate Publică, București, 1788

Institutul de Sănătate Publică 'Prof. Dr Iuliu Moldovan', 1788

Institutul de Sănătate Publică 'Prof. Dr Leonida Georgescu', Timișoara, 1788

Institutul de Sociologie 'Dimitrie Gusti', 1790

Institutul de Speologie 'Emil Racoviță', 1789

Institutul de Statistică Matematică și Matematică Aplicată 'Gheorghe Mihoc-Caius Iacob', 1788

Institutul de Științe Politice și Relații Internaționale, 1790

Institutul de Științe Socio-Umane, 1790

Institutul de Studii Banatice 'Titu Maiorescu', 1790

Institutul de Virusologie 'Ștefan S. Nicolau' (IVN), 1788

Institutul Geologic al României, 1789

Institutul 'Gheorghe Zane' de Cercetări Economice și Sociale, 1786

Institutul Național de Cercetare Dezvoltare pentru Cartof si Sfeclă de Zahar, 1786

Institutul Național de Cercetare Dezvoltare pentru Chimie si Petrochimie, 1789

Institutul National de Cercetare Dezvoltare pentru Metale Neferoase Și Rare, 1790

Institutul Național de Cercetare-Dezvoltare 'Delta Dunarii', 1789

Institutul Național de Cercetare—Dezvoltare Marină 'Grigore Antipa', 1786

Institutul Național de Cercetare-Dezvoltare în Construcții, Urbanism și Dezvoltare Teritorială Durabilă URBAN-INCERC, 1786

Institutul Național de Cercetare-Dezvoltare pentru Biologie si Nutriție Animala, 1786

Institutul Național de Cercetare-Dezvoltare pentru Fizică Tehnică—IFT Iași, 1789

Institutul Național de Cercetare-Dezvoltare pentru Pedologie, Agrochimie și Protecția Mediului—ICPA București, 1786

Institutul Național de Cercetare-Dezvoltare pentru Protecția Mediului (ICIM București), 1790

Institutul Național de Cercetare-Dezvoltare pentru Științe Biologice, 1788

Institutul Național de Cercetări Economice 'Costin C. Kirițescu', 1786

Institutul Național de Cercetări-Dezvoltare pentru Protectia Mediului, 1786

Institutul Național de Educație Fizică și Sport, Chișinău, 1494

Institutul Național de Informare și Documentare, 1790

Institutul Național de Medicină Legală 'Mina Minovici', 1788

Institutul Național de Medicină Veterinară Pasteur, 1786

Institutul Național de Meteorologie și Hidrologie, 1789

Institutul Național de Metrologie, 1789

Institutul Național pentru Fizică și Inginerie Nucleară 'Horia Hulubei', 1789

Institutul Oncologic 'Al. Trestioreanu', 1788

Institutul pentru Controlul de Stat al Medicamentului și Cercetări Farmaceutice 'Petre Ionescu-Stoian', 1788

Institutul Teologic Baptist din București, 1825

Institutul Teologic Protestant Cluj, 1825

Institutul Teologic Romano-Catolic 'Sf. Losif' Iași, 1825

Institutum Romanum Finlandiae, Rome, 1174

Instituut Beleid & Management Gezondheidszorg (iBMG), 1538

Instituut ter Bevordering van het Wetenschappelijk Onderzoek en de Innovatie van Brussel, 249

Instituut voor Bedrijfs- en Industriële Statistiek (IBIS), 1533

Instituut voor Biodiversiteit en Ecosysteem Dynamica, 1541

Instituut voor de Studie van de Letterkunde in de Nederlanden, 254

Instituut voor Fundamentele en Klinische Bewegingswetenschappen, 1538

Instituut voor Hoge Energie Fysica (IHEF), 1540

Instituut voor Informatierecht, 1536

Instituut voor Internationale Studien, 1537

Instituut voor Joodse Studies, 254

Instituut voor Liturgische en Rituele Studies (ILRS), 1542

Instituut voor Milieu & Duurzame Ontwikkeling, 256

Instituut voor Milieu en Agritechniek (IMAG-DLO), 1544

Instituut voor Milieuvraagstukken (IVM), 1537

Instituut voor Mobiliteit, 257

Instituut voor Natuur- en Bosonderzoek, 256

Instituut voor Onderwijs- en Informatiewetenschappen, 254

Instituut voor Ontwikkelingsbeleid en-beheer, 253

Instituut voor Plantenziektenkundig Onderzoek (IPO–DLO), Wageningen, 1540

Instituut voor Programmatuurkunde en Algoritmiek, Eindhoven, 1540

Instituut voor Psychosynthese, 1562

Instituut voor Samenwerking tussen Universiteit en Arbeidersbeweging, 253

Instituut voor Theoretische Fysica, 1540

Instytut Agrofizyki im. Bohdana Dobrzańskiego PAN, Lublin, 1712

Instytut Archeologii i Etnologii PAN, 1715

Instytut Automatyki Systemów Energetycznych, Wrocław, 1719

Instytut Badań Edukacyjnych, Warsaw, 1714

Instytut Badań Literackich PAN, 1715

Instytut Badań Rynku, Konsumpcji i Koniunktur, Warsaw, 1714

Instytut Badań Systemowych PAN, Warsaw, 1719

Instytut Badawczy Dróg i Mostów, Warsaw, 1719

Instytut Badawczy Leśnictwa, Warsaw, 1712

Instytut Biochemii i Biofizyki PAN, 1716

Instytut Biocybernetyki i Inżynierii Biomedycznej PAN, Warsaw, 1715

Instytut Biologii Doświadczalnej im M. Nenckiego, 1716

Instytut Biopolimerów i Włókien Chemicznych, Łódź, 1716

Instytut Biotechnologii Przemysłu Rolno-Spożywczego, Warsaw, 1712

Instytut Botaniki im. Władysława Szafera PAN, 1716

Instytut Budownictwa, Mechanizacji i Elektryfikacji Rolnictwa, Warsaw, 1712

Instytut Budownictwa Wodnego PAN, 1719

Instytut Chemii Bioorganicznej PAN, 1717

Instytut Chemii Fizycznej PAN, Warsaw, 1717

Instytut Chemii i Techniki Jądrowej, Warsaw, 1719

Instytut Chemii Nieorganicznej, Gliwice, 1719

Instytut Chemii Organicznej PAN, Warsaw, 1717

Instytut Chemii Przemysłowej, Warsaw, 1719

Instytut Dendrologii PAN, 1717

Instytut Ekonomiki Rolnictwa i Gospodarki Żywnościowej, Warsaw, 1713

Instytut Ekspertyz Sądowych, Cracow, 1714

Instytut Elektrotechniki, Warsaw, 1719

Instytut Energetyki, Warsaw, 1719

Instytut Energii Atomowej, Otwock-Świerk, 1719

Instytut Farmaceutyczny, Warsaw, 1715

Instytut Farmakologii PAN, Cracow, 1715

Instytut Filozofii i Socjologii PAN, 1718

Instytut Fizjologii i Żywienia Zwierząt im. Jana Kielanowskiego PAN, 1713

Instytut Fizjologii Roślin im. Franciszka Górskiego PAN, 1713

Instytut Fizyki Jądrowej im. Henryka Niewodniczańskiego Polskiej Akademii Nauk, 1718

Instytut Fizyki Molekularnej PAN, 1718

Instytut Fizyki PAN, 1718

Instytut Fizyki Plazmy i Laserowej Mikrosyntezy im. Sylwestra Kaliskiego, 1718

Instytut Genetyki Człowieka PAN, 1716

Instytut Genetyki i Hodowli Zwierząt PAN, 1713
Instytut Genetyki Roślin PAN, 1713
Instytut Geodezji i Kartografii, Warsaw, 1715
Instytut Geofizyki PAN, 1718
Instytut Geografii i Przestrzennego Zagospodarowania im. S. Leszczyckiego PAN, 1715
Instytut Gospodarki Mieszkaniowej, Filtrowa, 1714
Instytut Gospodarki Przestrzennej i Mieszkalictwa, Warsaw, 1714
Instytut Hematologii i Transfuzjologii, Warsaw, 1716
Instytut Historii im. Tadeusza Manteuffla PAN, 1715
Instytut Historii Nauki PAN, 1716
Instytut Immunologii i Terapii Doświadczalnej im. Ludwika Hirszfelda PAN, 1716
Instytut Informatyki Teoretycznej i Stosowanej PAN, 1719
Instytut Inżynierii Chemicznej PAN, 1719
Instytut Języka Polskiego PAN, 1715
Instytut Kardiologii im. Prymasa Tysiąclecia Stefana Kardynała Wyszyńskiego, Warsaw, 1716
Instytut Katalizy i Fizykochemii Powierzchni PAN, 1718
Instytut Kształcenia Zawodowego, Warsaw, 1715
Instytut Kultury, Warsaw, 1712
Instytut Łączności, Warsaw, 1719
Instytut Lotnictwa, Warsaw, 1719
Instytut Maszyn Matematycznych, Warsaw, 1719
Instytut Maszyn Przepływowych im. R. Szewalskiego PAN, 1719
Instytut Maszyn Spożywczych, Warsaw, 1719
Instytut Matematyczny PAN, 1717
Instytut Matki i Dziecka, Warsaw, 1716
Instytut Mędycyny Doświadczalnej i Klinicznej im. M. J. Mossakowskiego PAN, Warsaw, 1716
Instytut Mędycyny Pracy i Zdrowia Środowiskowego, Sosnowiec, 1716
Instytut Mędycyny Pracy im. prof. dra med. Jerzego Nofera, Łódź, 1716
Instytut Mędycyny Wsi im. Witolda Chodźki, 1716
Instytut Mechaniki Górotworu PAN, 1718
Instytut Mechanizacji Budownictwa i Górnictwa Skalnego, Warsaw, 1719
Instytut Medycyny Morskiej i Tropikalnej, Gdynia, 1716
Instytut Metali Niezelaznych, Gliwice, 1719
Instytut Metalurgii i Inżynierii Materiałowej im. Aleksandra Krupkowskiego PAN, 1720
Instytut Metalurgii Żelaza im. Stanisława Staszica, Gliwice, 1720
Instytut Meteorologii i Gospodarki Wodnej, Warsaw, 1713
Instytut Mineralnych Materiałów Budowlanych, Opole, 1720
Instytut Morski, Gdańsk, 1720
Instytut Nafty i Gazu, Cracow, 1720
Instytut Nauk Ekonomicznych PAN, Warsaw, 1714
Instytut Nauk Geologicznych PAN, 1718
Instytut Nauk Prawnych PAN, 1714
Instytut Nawozów Sztucznych, Puławy, 1713
Instytut Niskich Temperatur i Badań Strukturalnych PAN, Wrocław, 1718
Instytut Obróbki Plastycznej, Poznań, 1720
Instytut Oceanologii PAN, 1716
Instytut Ochrony Przyrody PAN, 1717
Instytut Odlewnictwa, Cracow, 1720
Instytut Ogrodnictwa, Skierniewice, 1713
Instytut Organizacji i Zarządzania w Przemyśle 'ORGMASZ', Warsaw, 1714

Instytut Paleobiologii im. Romana Kozłowskiego PAN, 1717
Instytut Parazytologii im Witolda Stefańskiego PAN, 1717
Instytut Podstaw Informatyki Polskiej Akademii Nauk, 1720
Instytut Podstaw Inżynierii Środowiska PAN, 1712
Instytut Podstawowych Problemów Techniki PAN, 1720
Instytut Pracy i Spraw Socjalnych, Warsaw, 1714
Instytut Problemów Jądrowych im. Andrzeja Sołtana, 1718
Instytut Przedsiębiorstwa, Warsaw, 1714
Instytut Przemysłu Cukrowniczego, Warsaw, 1713
Instytut Przemysłu Gumowego 'Stomil', 1720
Instytut Przemysłu Organicznego, Warsaw, 1720
Instytut Psychiatrii i Neurologii, Warsaw, 1716
Instytut Psychologii PAN, 1718
Instytut Roślin i Przetworów Zielarskich, Poznań, 1713
Instytut Rozwoju Wsi i Rolnictwa PAN, 1713
Instytut Rybactwa Śródlądowego im. Stanisława Sakowicza, Olsztyn-Kortowo, 1713
Instytut Slawistyki PAN, 1712
Instytut Spawalnictwa, 1720
Instytut Sportu, Warsaw, 1712
Instytut Środowiska Rolniczego i Leśnego PAN, Poznań, 1713
Instytut Studiow Politycznych PAN, Warsaw, 1714
Instytut Systematyki i Ewolucji Zwierząt PAN, 1717
Instytut Systemów Sterowania, Chorzów, 1720
Instytut Szkła, Ceramiki, Materiałów Ogniotrwałych i Budowlanych w Warszawie, Warsaw, 1720
Instytut Sztuki PAN, 1715
Instytut Techniki Budowlanej, Warsaw, 1714
Instytut Technologiczno-Przyrodniczy, Raszyn, 1713
Instytut Technologii Drewna, 1713
Instytut Technologii Elektronowej, Warsaw, 1720
Instytut Technologii Materiałów Elektronicznych, Warsaw, 1720
Instytut Technologii Nafty im. Prof. Stanisława Pilata, Cracow, 1720
Instytut Transportu Samochodowego, Warsaw, 1720
Instytut Turystyki, Warsaw, 1714
Instytut Uprawy, Nawożenia i Gleboznawstwa—Państwowy Instytut Badawczy, Puławy, 1713
Instytut Warzywnictwa, Skierniewice, 1713
Instytut Włókien Naturalnych, Poznań, 1720
Instytut Włókiennictwa, 1721
Instytut Wymiaru Sprawiedliwości, Warsaw, 1714
Instytut Wzornictwa Przemysłowego, Warsaw, 1721
Instytut Zachodni im. Zygmunta Wojciechowskiego, Poznań, 1714
Instytut Zdrowia Publicznego, Warsaw, 1716
Instytut Zootechniki, Balice, 1713
Instytut Żywności i Żywienia, Warsaw, 1716
Instytut-Centrum Badań Molekularnych i Makromolekularnych PAN, 1717
Insubria Centre on International Security (ICIS), Como, 1172
Inter American University of Puerto Rico, 2975
Interactive Science Centre of Amadora, 1769
Interafrican Bureau for Animal Resources, Nairobi, 1352
Interafrican Electrical Engineering College, 605

Inter-American Children's Institute, 2980
Inter-American Distance Education Consortium, 53
Inter-American Institute for Cooperation on Agriculture, 43
Inter-American Institute for Cooperation on Agriculture (IICA), 966
Inter-American Organization for Higher Education, 54
Inter-American Statistical Institute, 49
InterCollege Business School, The Hague, 1562
Intercollege (International College), Nicosia, 627
Inter-Continental University of the Caribbean (ICUC), 1570
Interdenominational Theological Center, Atlanta, 2598
Interdisciplinair Instituut voor Breedband Technologie, 257
Interdisciplinary Centre for Neuroscience, Heidelberg, 898
Interdisciplinary Centre for Scientific Computing, Heidelberg, 898
Interdisciplinary Institute for Broadband Technology, 257
Interdisciplinary Institute of Management, London, 2249
Interdisciplinary Research Centre in Biomedical Materials, London, 2259
Interdisciplinary Research Centre in Materials Processing, Birmingham, 2263
Intered Institute, Phnom Penh, 361
Interfaculty Centre for Gerontology, Acacias, 2092
Intergovernmental Committee of the Universal Copyright Convention, 61
Intergovernmental Oceanographic Commission (IOC) of UNESCO, 70
Internationaal Instituut voor Sociale Geschiedenis, 1529
Internationaal Juridisch Instituut, 1529
International Academy for Production Engineering, 58
International Academy of Astronautics (IAA), 71
International Academy of Business, Almaty, 1344
International Academy of Indian Culture, New Delhi, 1015
International Academy of Management, Law, Finance and Business, Bishkek, 1396
International Academy of Portuguese Culture, 1762
International African Institute (IAI), 49
International Agency for Research on Cancer, 65
International Agency for the Prevention of Blindness, 65
International Akademie für Philosophie im Fürstentum Liechtenstein, 1419
International Amateur Theatre Association—Organization for Understanding and Education through Theatre, 45
International Association for Child and Adolescent Psychiatry and Allied Professions, 65
International Association for Educational and Vocational Guidance, 54
International Association for Humanitarian Medicine (IAHM), Bogis-Bossey, 65
International Association for Hydro-Environment Engineering and Research, 58
International Association for Mass Communication Research, 47
International Association for Mathematics and Computers in Simulation, 71
International Association for Penal Law, 61
International Association for Philosophy of Law and Social Philosophy (IVR), 61
International Association for Plant Physiology (IAPP), 71

International Association for Plant Taxonomy, 71
International Association for Radiation Research, 65
International Association for South-East European Studies, 49
International Association for South-East European Studies, Bucharest, 1790
International Association for the Exchange of Students for Technical Experience (IAESTE), London, 54
International Association for the History of Religions, 39
International Association for the Physical Sciences of the Ocean (IAPSO), 71
International Association for the Study of Insurance Economics, 49
International Association for the Study of the Liver, 62
International Association for Vegetation Science, 71
International Association of Agricultural Economists, 43
International Association of Agricultural Information Specialists, 47
International Association of Agricultural Medicine and Rural Health, 65
International Association of Applied Linguistics, 45
International Association of Applied Mathematics and Mechanics, Dresden, 825
International Association of Applied Psychology, 65
International Association of Art, 45
International Association of Art Critics, 45
International Association of Asthmology, 65
International Association of Bibliophiles, 47
International Association of Biological Oceanography, 71
International Association of Democratic Lawyers (IADL), 61
International Association of Dental Students, 54
International Association of Environmental Mutagen Societies, 65
International Association of Geodesy, 71
International Association of Geomagnetism and Aeronomy (IAGA), 71
International Association of Gerontology and Geriatrics (IAGG), 65
International Association of Horticultural Producers, 44
International Association of Hydatidology, 65
International Association of Hydrological Sciences, 71
International Association of Jewish Lawyers and Jurists, 1141
International Association of Law Libraries (IALL), 47
International Association of Lawyers, 61
International Association of Legal Sciences, 40
International Association of Literary Critics, 45
International Association of Meteorology and Atmospheric Sciences (IAMAS), 71
International Association of Music Libraries, Archives and Documentation Centres—IAML, 821
International Association of Oral and Maxillofacial Surgeons, 65
International Association of Schools of Social Work (IASSW), 49
International Association of Sedimentologists, 71
International Association of Technological University Libraries (IATUL), 47

Istituto di Genetica e Biofisica 'Adriano Buzzati Traverso', 1170
Istituto di Genetica Molecolare, 1171
Istituto di Genetica Vegetale, 1168
Istituto di Geologia Ambientale e Geoingegneria, 1169
Istituto di Geoscienze e Georisorse, 1169
Istituto di Informatica e Telematica, 1170
Istituto di Ingegneria Biomedica, 1171
Istituto di Linguistica Computazionale 'Antonio Zampolli', 1169
Istituto di Marketing e Comunicazione Aziendale, Lugano, 2091
Istituto di Matematica Applicata e Tecnologie Informatiche, 1171
Istituto di Metodologie Chimiche, 1171
Istituto di Metodologie Inorganiche e dei Plasmi, 1171
Istituto di Metodologie per l'Analisi Ambientale, 1169
Istituto di Neurobiologia e Medicina Molecolare, 1171
Istituto di Neurogenetica e Neurofarmacologia, 1171
Istituto di Neuroscienze, 1171
Istituto di Norvegia in Roma, 1174
Istituto di Ricerca per il Progetto Urbano Contemporaneo, Medrisio, 2091
Istituto di Ricerca per la Protezione Idrogeologica, 1170
Istituto di Ricerca sui Sistemi Giudiziari, 1169
Istituto di Ricerca sulle Acque, 1170
Istituto di Ricerca sull'Impresa e lo Sviluppo, 1169
Istituto di Ricerche Economiche, Lugano, 2092
Istituto di Ricerche Farmacologiche 'Mario Negri', 1174
Istituto di Ricerche sulla Combustione, 1170
Istituto di Ricerche sulla Popolazione e le Politiche Sociali, 1169
Istituto di Ricerche sulle Attività Terziarie, 1169
Istituto di Scienza dell'Alimentazione, 1168
Istituto di Scienza e Tecnologia dei Materiali Ceramici, 1172
Istituto di Scienza e Tecnologie dell'Informazione 'Alessandro Faedo', 1170
Istituto di Scienze dell'Atmosfera e del Clima, 1170
Istituto di Scienze delle Produzioni Alimentari, 1169
Istituto di Scienze e Tecnologie della Cognizione, 1169
Istituto di Scienze e Tecnologie Molecolari, 1171
Istituto di Scienze Marine, 1170
Istituto di Scienze Neurologiche, 1171
Istituto di Storia dell'Arte di Firenze, 1165
Istituto di Storia dell'Europa Mediterranea, 1169
Istituto di Struttura della Materia, 1171
Istituto di Studi Europei 'Alcide De Gasperi', Rome, 1172
Istituto di Studi Filosofici 'Enrico Castelli', Rome, 1175
Istituto di Studi Giuridici Internazionali, 1169
Istituto di Studi Italiani, Lugano, 2092
Istituto di Studi Nucleari per l'Agricoltura (ISNA), Rome, 1168
Istituto di Studi sui Sistemi Intelligenti per l'Automazione, 1172
Istituto di Studi sui Sistemi Regionali Federali e sulle Autonomie 'Massimo Severo Giannini', 1169
Istituto di Studi sulle Civiltà dell'Egeo e del Vicino Oriente, 1169
Istituto di Studi sulle Civiltà Italiche e del Mediterraneo Antico, 1169
Istituto di Studi sulle Società del Mediterraneo, 1169
Istituto di Tecnologie Avanzate per l'Energia 'Nicola Giordano', 1170
Istituto di Tecnologie Biomediche, 1171
Istituto di Tecnologie Industriali e Automazione, 1172

Istituto di Teoria e Tecniche dell'Informazione Giuridica, 1169
Istituto di Virologia Vegetale, 1169
Istituto Ellenico di Studi Bizantini e Postbizantini di Venezia, 1174
Istituto Gemmologico Italiano, 1175
Istituto Geografico Militare, Florence, 1165
Istituto Idrografico della Marina, Genoa, 1175
Istituto Internazionale di Studi Liguri, 50
Istituto Internazionale per la Ricerca Teatrale, Venice, 1173
Istituto Italiano del Marchio di Qualità (IMQ), 1168
Istituto Italiano della Saldatura, 1168
Istituto Italiano di Antropologia, 1175
Istituto Italiano di Numismatica, 1165
Istituto Italiano di Paleontologia Umana, 1165
Istituto Italiano di Scienze Umane (SUM), 1208
Istituto Italiano di Speleologia, 1175
Istituto Italiano di Studi Germanici, 1174
Istituto Italiano di Studi Legislativi, 1172
Istituto Italiano per gli Studi Storici, 1174
Istituto Italiano per la Storia Antica, 1165
Istituto Italiano per l'Africa e l'Oriente (IsIAO), 1165
Istituto Italo-Latino Americano, 50
Istituto Linguistico-Semiotico, Lugano, 2092
Istituto Lombardo Accademia di Scienze e Lettere, 1163
Istituto Luigi Sturzo, Rome, 1175
Istituto Media e Giornalismo, Lugano, 2091
Istituto Motori, 1170
Istituto Nanoscienze, 1171
Istituto Nazionale di Alta Matematica Francesco Severi, Rome, 1174
Istituto Nazionale di Archeologia e Storia dell'Arte, Rome, 1165
Istituto Nazionale di Architettura (IN-ARCH), Rome, 1164
Istituto Nazionale di Astrofisica, Rome, 1175
Istituto Nazionale di Fisica Nucleare (INFN), Frascati, 1175
Istituto Nazionale di Geofisica e Vulcanologia, Rome, 1175
Istituto Nazionale di Oceanografia e di Geofisico Sperimentale, Trieste, 1175
Istituto Nazionale di Ottica (INO), 1171
Istituto Nazionale di Ricerca per gli Alimenti e la Nutrizione, Rome, 1174
Istituto Nazionale di Statistica, Rome, 1172
Istituto Nazionale di Studi Etruschi ed Italici, Florence, 1165
Istituto Nazionale di Studi Romani, Rome, 1174
Istituto Nazionale di Studi sul Rinascimento, Florence, 1174
Istituto Nazionale di Studi Verdiani, Parma, 1165
Istituto Nazionale di Urbanistica (INU), Rome, 1164
Istituto Nazionale per la Grafica, Rome, 1187
Istituto Nazionale per la Ricerca sul Cancro, Genoa, 1174
Istituto Nazionale per la Valutazione del Sistema Educativo di Istruzione e di Formazione, Rome, 1162
Istituto Nazionale per Studi ed Esperienze di Architettura Navale, 1176
Istituto Officina dei Materiali, 1171
Istituto Opera del Vocabolario Italiano, 1169
Istituto Papirologico 'Girolamo Vitelli', 1174
Istituto per gli Studi di Politica Internazionale, 1169
Istituto per i Beni Archeologici e Monumentali, 1169

Istituto per i Materiali Compositi e Biomedici, 1171
Istituto per i Processi Chimico-Fisici, 1171
Istituto per i Sistemi Agricoli e Forestali del Mediterraneo, 1169
Istituto per i Trapianti d'Organo e Immunocitologia, 1171
Istituto per il Lessico Intellettuale Europeo e la Storia delle Idee, 1169
Istituto per il Rilevamento Elettromagnetico dell'Ambiente, 1170
Istituto per il Sistema Produzione Animale in Ambiente Mediterraneo, 1169
Istituto per la Conservazione e Valorizzazione dei Beni Culturali, 1169
Istituto per la Cooperazione Universitaria Onlus, Rome, 1162
Istituto per la Dinamica dei Processi Ambientali, 1170
Istituto per la Microelettronica e Microsistemi, 1171
Istituto per la Protezione delle Piante, 1169
Istituto per la Sintesi Organica e la Fotoreattività, 1171
Istituto per la Storia del Pensiero Filosofico e Scientifico Moderno, 1169
Istituto per la Storia del Risorgimento Italiano, 1165
Istituto per la Tecnologia delle Membrane, 1171
Istituto per la Valorizzazione del Legno e delle Specie Arboree, 1170
Istituto per l'Ambiente Marino Costiero, 1170
Istituto per le Applicazioni del Calcolo 'Mauro Picone', 1171
Istituto per le Macchine Agricole e Movimento Terra, 1172
Istituto per le Relazioni tra l'Italia e i Paesi dell'Africa, America Latina, Medio ed Estremo Oriente (IPALMO), Rome, 1173
Istituto per le Tecnologie Applicate ai Beni Culturali, 1169
Istituto per le Tecnologie della Costruzione, 1172
Istituto per le Tecnologie Didattiche, 1169
Istituto per l'Endocrinologia e l'Oncologia 'Gaetano Salvatore', 1170
Istituto per l'Energetica e le Interfasi, 1170
Istituto per lo Studio degli Ecosistemi, 1170
Istituto per lo Studio dei Materiali Nanostrutturati, 1172
Istituto per lo Studio delle Macromolecole del CNR, 1172
Istituto per l'Oriente C. A. Nallino, Rome, 1175
Istituto per Ricerche ed Attività Educative, 1173
Istituto Regionale di Studi e Ricerca Sociale, Trento, 1208
Istituto Siciliano di Studi Bizantini e Neoellenici 'B. Lavagnini', 1174
Istituto Sperimentale per la Zoologia Agraria, 1172
Istituto Statale d'Arte 'Enrico e Umberto Nordio', Trieste, 1212
Istituto Statale d'Arte 'Filippo Figari', Sassari, 1212
Istituto Statale d'Arte 'G. Ballardini', Faenza, 1212
Istituto Statale d'Arte, Urbino, 1212
Istituto Storico Austriaco Roma, 1174
Istituto Storico Italiano per il Medio Evo, 1165
Istituto Storico Italiano per l'Età Moderna e Contemporanea, 1165
Istituto sull'Inquinamento Atmosferico, 1170
Istituto Superconduttori, Materiali Innovativi e Dispositivi, 1171
Istituto Superiore di Sanità, 1174
Istituto Superiore di Scienze Religiose 'Giuseppe Toniolo', 2994

Istituto Superiore per i Formatori, Rome, 2994
Istituto Superiore per la Conservazione ed il Restauro, 1173
Istituto Svizzero di Diritto Comparato, 2091
Istituto Universitario di Studi Europei (IUSE), Turin, Turin, 1208
Istituto Universitario di Studi Superiori (IUSS), 1208
Istituto Universitario Federale per la Formazione Professionale, 2113
Istituto Universitario Olandese di Storia dell'Arte, Florence, 1165
Istituto Veneto di Scienze, Lettere ed Arti, 1163
Istituzione Biblioteca Classense, Ravenna, 1179
Istituzione Biblioteca Malatestiana, Cesena, 1176
Istorijski institut Crne Gore, 1502
Istorijski muzej Srbije, 1923
Italia Conti Academy of Theatre Arts, 2365
Italia Nostra—Associazione Nazionale per la Tutela del Patrimonio Storico, Artistico e Naturale della Nazione, 1164
Italia Nostra—National Association for the Preservation of the Historical, Artistic and Natural Heritage of the Nation, 1164
Italian Academy of Forest Sciences, 1164
Italian Agrarian Economics Society, 1164
Italian Association of Aeronautical and Space Sciences, 1168
Italian Astronomical Society, 1167
Italian Authors' and Publishers' Society, 1166
Italian Botanical Society Onlus, 1167
Italian Chemical Society, 1167
Italian Dante Society, 1166
Italian Ecological Society, 1167
Italian Economists' Society, 1164
Italian Entomological Society, 1167
Italian Federation for Electrotechnology, Electronics, Automation, Information Technology and Telecommunications, 1168
Italian Geophysical Association, 1167
Italian Glaciological Committee, 1175
Italian Institute for Africa and the East, 1175
Italian Institute for Ancient History, 1165
Italian Institute for Germanic Studies, 1174
Italian Institute for Historical Studies, 1174
Italian Institute for Legislative Studies, 1172
Italian Institute for the History of Music, 1165
Italian Institute of Anthropology, 1175
Italian Institute of Human Palaeontology, 1165
Italian Institute of the Quality Mark, 1168
Italian Library Association, 1164
Italian Metallurgical Association, 1168
Italian Microbiological Society, 1167
Italian Musicological Society, 1165
Italian National Standards Association, 1168
Italian Numismatics Institute, 1165
Italian Pharmacological Society, 1166
Italian Philosophical Society, 1168
Italian Physics Society, 1168
Italian School of Archaeology at Athens, Athens, 958
Italian Society for Gynaecology and Obstetrics, 1166
Italian Society for Internal Medicine, 1166
Italian Society for Odontostomatology and Maxillofacial Surgery, 1166
Italian Society for Orthopaedics and Traumatology, 1166
Italian Society for Rheumatology, 1167
Italian Society for Road Accident Traumatology, 1167

J

Japanese Society of Applied Entomology and Zoology, 1222
Japanese Society of Applied Glycoscience, 1217
Japanese Society of Cultural Anthropology, 1224
Japanese Society of Developmental Biologists, 1222
Japanese Society of Fisheries Science, 1217
Japanese Society of Gastroenterology, 1220
Japanese Society of German Literature, 1219
Japanese Society of Haematology, 1221
Japanese Society of Internal Medicine, 1220
Japanese Society of Irrigation, Drainage and Reclamation Engineering, 1224
Japanese Society of Medical Entomology and Zoology, 1222
Japanese Society of Microscopy, 1222
Japanese Society of Naval Architects and Ocean Engineers, 1217
Japanese Society of Neurology, 1221
Japanese Society of Nuclear Medicine, 1220
Japanese Society of Oral and Maxillofacial Surgeons, 1220
Japanese Society of Parasitology, 1221
Japanese Society of Pathology, 1221
Japanese Society of Pharmacognosy, 1220
Japanese Society of Physical Education, Health and Sport Sciences, 1219
Japanese Society of Plant Physiologists, 1222
Japanese Society of Psychiatry and Neurology, 1220
Japanese Society of Sericultural Science, 1217
Japanese Society of Snow and Ice, 1223
Japanese Society of Soil Science and Plant Nutrition, 1217
Japanese Society of Tribologists, 1224
Japanese Society of Veterinary Science, 1217
Japanese Society of Western History, 1219
Japanese Sociological Society, 1224
Japanese Stomatological Society, 1220
Japanese Studies Institute, Beijing, 466
Jardim Botânico, 1766
Jardim e Museu Agrícola Tropical do Instituto de Investigação Científica Tropical, 1770
Jardin Botanique de Montréal, 373
Jardín Botánico de Bogotá 'José Celestino Mutis', 581
Jardín Botánico Nacional de Cuba, Havana, 618
Jardín Botánico y Museo de Historia Natural, Asunción, 1675
Jarvis Christian College, 2906
Jász Múzeum, 983
Jatiya Kabi Kazi Nazrul Islam University, 223
Javanese Culture and Art Museum, 1088
Javna Biblioteka Unsko-sanskog Kantona, 290
Jawaharlal Institute of Postgraduate Medical Education and Research, 1081
Jawaharlal Nehru Centre for Advanced Scientific Research, 1075
Jawaharlal Nehru Krishi Vishwavidyalaya, Jabalpur, 1037
Jawaharlal Nehru Technological University, 1037
Jawaharlal Nehru University, 1037
Jay C. Byers Memorial Library, 2455
Jaypee University of Information Technology, 1037
Jazan Museum, 1911
Jazan University, 1912
Jazz Music Institute, Brisbane, 169
Jean and Alexander Heard Library, 2458
Jeddah College of Technology, 1915
Jeddah Health Institute, 1915
Jednota českých matematiků a fyziků, 630

Jednota slovenských matematikov a fyzikov, Bratislava, 1950
Jefferson College of Health Sciences, 2933
Jefferson County Library, High Ridge, MO, 2447
Jefferson County Library, Madras, OR, 2455
Jefferson Davis Parish Library, 2442
Jefferson Patterson Park and Museum, State Museum of Archaeology, 2480
Jefferson-Madison Regional Library, 2460
Jeff's Seaside Museum, 2969
Jefri Bolkiah College of Engineering, Kuala Belait, 332
Jeju National University, 1367
Jenkins Law Library, Philadelphia, 2456
Jeonju National Museum, 1366
Jeonju University, 1376
Jerez Archaeological Museum Town Library, 2006
Jericho Local Urban Observatory Centre, 1665
Jersey Archive, 2391
Jersey Heritage, 2391
Jersey Library, 2391
Jersey Museum and Art Gallery, St Helier, 2391
Jersey War Tunnels, 2391
Jerusalem Academy of Music and Dance, 1160
Jerusalem Artists' House, 1146
Jerusalem City (Public) Library, 1145
Jerusalem College of Technology, 1160
Jerusalem Institute for Israel Studies, 1143
Jerusalem University College, 1160
Jerusalemer Institut der Görres-Gesellschaft, Jerusalem, 1141
Jessamine County Public Library, 2441
Jesuit School of Philosophy and Theology 'Arrupe College', 2994
Jesus College, Cambridge, 2310
Jesus College Library, Oxford, 2278
Jesus College Old Library, Cambridge, 2266
Jesus College, Oxford, 2348
Jet Propulsion Laboratory, Pasadena, 2428
Jeunesse Ouvrière Chrétienne Internationale, 55
Jeunesses Musicales de France, 741
Jeunesses Musicales International (JMI), 68
Jeunesses Musicales of Sarajevo, 288
Jewish Historical Cultural Museum, 1569
Jewish Historical Museum, Amsterdam, 1548
Jewish Historical Society of Delaware Archives, 2434
Jewish Historical Society of England, 2234
Jewish History Museum, Tucson, 2464
Jewish Museum, 857
Jewish Museum, New York, 2489
Jewish Museum of Bosnia and Herzegovina, 291
Jewish Museum, Stockholm, 2066
Jewish Theological Seminary Library, New York, 2451
Jewish Theological Seminary, New York, 2786
Jiangnan University, 512
Jiangsu University, 513
Jiangxi Agricultural University, 513
Jiangxi Provincial Library, 471
Jigme Namgyel Polytechnic, 280
Jihočeská Univerzita v Českých Budějovicích, 641
Jihočeské muzeum v Českých Budějovicích, 635
Jikei University, 1313
Jilin Provincial Library, 470
Jilin University, 513
Jilin University Library, 470
Jill Dando Institute for Crime Science, London, 2252
Jim Gatchell Memorial Museum, 2502
Jimma University, 708
Jimmy Carter Library & Museum, 2437
Jinan University, 514

Jingu Bunko, 1228
Jingu Chokokan, 1230
Jingu Historical Museum, 1230
Jingu Nogyokan, 1230
Jinju National University, 1384
Jinnah Postgraduate Medical Centre, 1660
Jinnah University for Women, 1649
Jishoji (Ginkakuji), 1231
Jiwaji University, 1037
JMC Academy, Surry Hills, 168
João José da Graça—Horta Public Library and Regional Archive, 1768
Jôchi Daigaku, 1329
Jodrell Bank Observatory, 2260
Joe Alon Centre for Regional and Folklore Studies, D N Negel, 1143
Joensuu Regional Library—Central Library of North Karelia, 720
Joensuun seutukirjasto—Pohjois-Karjalan maakuntakirjasto, 720
Jõgeva Plant Breeding Institute, 702
Johann Bernoulli Institute of Mathematics and Computing Science (JBI), 1540
Johänn Heinrich von Thünen Institute, Hamburg, 831
Johann Radon Institute for Computational and Applied Mathematics, 182
Johann Strauss Society of Vienna, 174
Johann Strauss-Gesellschaft Wien, 174
Johanna Museet, 2065
Johannes Gutenberg University Mainz, 873
Johannes Kepler Universität Linz, 189
Johannes Kepler University, Linz, 189
Johannesburg Art Gallery, 1980
John A. Hartford Foundation, New York, 2409
John and Mable Ringling Museum of Art, 2471
John Brown University, 2517
John Cabot University, Rome, 1208
John Carroll University, 2832
John Carter Brown Library, 2457
John Crerar Library of the University of Chicago, 2438
John Eugene Derrickson Memorial Library, Wilmington, 2434
John F. Kennedy Presidential Library and Museum, 2445
John F. Kennedy Space Center, Cape Canaveral, 2428
John F. Kennedy University, 2529
John G. McCullough Free Library, 2459
John G. Shedd Aquarium, 2474
John Innes Centre, Norwich, 2250
John Jay College of Criminal Justice, 2771
John Logie Baird Centre for Research in Television and Film, Glasgow, 2263
John Mackintosh Hall Library, 2388
John Marshall Law School, 2609
John Paul II Catholic University of Lublin, 1726
John Paul II Institute for Marriage & Family, East Melbourne, 170
John Paul II Library, National University of Ireland, Maynooth, 1134
John Rylands University Library, University of Manchester, 2277
John Snow College, Stockton, 2312
John W. Graham Library, University of Trinity College, 376
John Young Museum of Art, 2473
Johns Hopkins Archaeological Museum, Baltimore, 2480
Johns Hopkins University, Baltimore, 2657
Johns Hopkins University Libraries, Baltimore, 2443
Johnson & Wales University, 2880
Johnson C. Smith University, 2811
Johnson City Public Library, 2458
Johnson County Kansas Law Library, 2440
Johnson County Library System, 2462
Johnson State College, 2928
Johnson University, 2891
Joho Kagaku Gijutsu Kyokai, 1218
Joho-Jigyo, Kagaku-Gijutsu Shinko Kiko, 1218

Joint Art Library of the Nationalmuseum and the Museum of Modern Art, Stockholm, 2062
Joint Institute for Nuclear Research, Dubna, 1845
Joint Laboratory of Solid State Chemistry of the Institute of Macromolecular Chemistry AS CR and Pardubice University, 632
Joint Library of the Hellenic and Roman Societies, London, 2273
Joint Russian-Vietnamese Tropical Research and Technological Centre, Leninsky, 1850
Joint Science Conference, Bonn, 818
Jöklarannsóknafélag Íslands, 1001
Jolo Branch Museum, 1692
Þjóðminjasafn Íslands, 1002
Jomo Kenyatta University of Agriculture and Technology, 1354
Jones College, 2585
Jones International University, 2553
Jones Memorial Library, 2460
Jönköping city library, 2061
Jönköping International Business School, 2082
Jönköping University College, 2082
Joods Historisch Museum, Amsterdam, 1548
Jordan Archaeological Museum, 1334
Jordan Historical Museum of the Twenty, 379
Jordan Library and Information Association, 1334
Jordan Schnitzer Museum of Art, 2493
Jordan Statistical Training Centre, 1337
Jordan University of Science and Technology (JUST), 1335
Jordbrugsakademikernes Forbund (JA), Klampenborg, 649
Jorge B. Vargas Museum and Filipiniana Research Centre, 1692
Jorvik Viking Centre, 2291
Jósa András Múzeum, 984
José A. Negri Library of the College of Notaries, 110
José Antonio Portuondo Valdor Institute of Literature and Linguistics, 616
Josep Pallach Institute of Education, 2004
Joseph Conrad Society, 2236
Joseph Haydn Conservatory of Burgenland, 201
Joseph Haydn Konservatorium des Landes Burgenland, 201
Joseph P. Horner Memorial Library, Philadelphia, 2456
Josephine Butler College, Stockton, 2312
Josip Bepo Benković, 1503
Josip Jurja Strossmayer University of Osijek, 611
Þjóðskjalasafn Íslands, 1002
Joslyn Art Museum, 2485
Journalism Institute, Beijing, 466
Journey Museum, Rapid City, 2496
Jovan Hadži Institute of Biology at ZRC SAZU, 1965
Jowzjan Provincial Library, 80
Joyce K. Carver Soldotna Public Library, 2430
JSC Bekturov Institute of Chemical Sciences, 1340
JTI—Institutet för jordbruks- och miljöteknik, 2058
JTI—Swedish Institute of Agricultural and Environmental Engineering, 2058
Juan B. Ambrosetti Ethnographical Museum, 112
Juan Bautista Vázquez Regional Documentation Centre, 678
Juan Cornelio Moyano Museum of Anthropology and Natural Sciences, 112
Juan Manuel Cagigal Naval Observatory, 3003
Jubail Industrial College, 1915
Jubilee Library, Brighton, 2266
Judges' Association of Serbia, 1920
Jüdisches Museum Rendsburg, Schleswig, 857

Kazakh Scientific and Research Institute of Feeding-stuff Production and Pasture, 1339

Kazakh Scientific and Research Institute of Forestry JSC KazAgroInnovation, Shchuchinsk, 1339

Kazakh Scientific and Research Institute of Fruit Growing and Viticulture, 1339

Kazakh Scientific and Research Institute of Grain and Processed Grain Products, 1339

Kazakh Scientific and Research Institute of Mechanization and Electrification in Agriculture, 1339

Kazakh Scientific and Research Institute of Poultry, 1339

Kazakh Scientific and Research Institute of the Fishing Industry, 1339

Kazakh Scientific and Research Institute of the Food Industry, 1339

Kazakh Scientific and Research Institute of Water Management, 1339

Kazakh Scientific and Research Technological Institute of Exploitation and Maintenance of Agricultural Machinery, 1339

Kazakh Scientific, Research and Design Institute of the Meat and Milk Industry, 1339

Kazakh State University of Agriculture, 1346

Kazakh State Women's Pedagogical Institute, 1346

Kazakh University of Communications, 1346

Kazakh University of Economics, Finance and International Trade, 1346

Kazakh Veterinary Scientific and Research Institute, 1339

Kazakh—American Free University, 1345

Kazakh—American University, 1345

Kazakh—British Technical University, 1345

Kazakh—German University, 1344

Kazakh—Russian University, 1346

Kazakhstan Engineering—Technological University, 1346

Kazakhstan Institute for Strategic Studies under the President of the Republic of Kazakhstan, 1339

Kazakhstan Institute of Management, Economics and Strategic Research (KIMEP), 1350

Kazan Federal University N. I. Lobachevsky Library, 1853

Kazan Finance and Economics Institute, 1899

Kazan Institute of Biology, 1841

Kazan Institute of Epidemiology, Microbiology and Hygiene, 1837

Kazan Physical-Technical Institute, 1850

Kazan State A. M. Gorky Memorial Museum, 1856

Kazan State Academy of Veterinary Medicine 'N. E. Bauman', 1895

Kazan State Agricultural Academy, 1895

Kazan State Conservatoire, 1900

Kazan State Institute of Culture, 1900

Kazan State Institute of Orthopaedics and Traumatology, 1837

Kazan State Medical University, 1881

Kazan State Technical University 'A. N. Tupolev', 1885

Kazan State Technological University, 1885

Kazan State University of Architecture and Civil Engineering, 1885

Kazan (Volga Region) Federal University, 1869

KDI School of Public Policy and Management, 1386

KDU College, 1452

Kean University, 2758

Keats-Shelley House, 1187

Keble College Library, Oxford, 2278

Keble College, Oxford, 2348

Kecskeméti Főiskola, Kecskemet, 999

Kedah State Public Library Corporation, 1445

Keeler Tavern Museum & Garden House, 2468

Keene Public Library, 2449

Keene State College, New Hampshire, 2756

Kegoayah Kozga Library, 2430

Keikinzoku Gakkai, 1224

Keimyung University, 1377

Keio University, 1316

Keio University Media Center, 1229

Keiser University, 2585

Keisoku Jidouseigyo Gakkai SICE, 1224

Keith B. Mather Library, 2430

Keizai Chiri Gakkai, 1219

Keizai Riron Gakkai, 1218

Keizaigaku-shi Gakkai, 1218

Kekayon Puppet Museum Yogyakarta, 1088

Kekelidze, K. S., Institute of Manuscripts, 813

Kekkaku Yobo Kai Kekkaku Kenkyujo, 1226

Kelantan Public Library Corporation, 1445

Keldysh, M.V., Institute of Applied Mathematics, Moscow, 1850

Kelham Island Museum, 2291

Kelley Library, 2449

Kellogg College, Oxford, 2348

Kellogg-Hubbard Library, 2459

Kelsey Museum of Archaeology, 2482

Kelvingrove Art Gallery and Museum, Glasgow, 2284

Kemal Kapetanović Metallurgical Institute, 289

Kemerovo Institute of Food Science and Technology, 1899

Kemerovo State Academy of Culture and Arts, 1900

Kemerovo State Medical Academy, 1897

Kemerovo State University, 1869

Kemerovo State University Library, 1853

Kemisk Forening, 652

Kemiska Sällskapet i Finland, 717

Kemisktekniska Forening ry, Helsinki, 717

Kemi-Tornio Polytechnic, 735

Kemi-Tornion Ammattikorkeakoulu, 735

Kemper Museum of Contemporary Art, 2484

Kendal Museum of Natural History and Archaeology, 2285

Kendall College, 2609

Kendriya Hindi Nideshalaya, 1007

Keninklik Frysk Genoatskip foar Skiednis en Kultuer, 1529

Kennedy Center, 653

Kennedy Centret, 653

Kennedy Museum of Art, 2492

Kennesaw State University, 2598

Kenneth Dike Library, University of Ibadan, 1593

Kenosha Public Library, 2462

Kenosha Public Museum, 2501

Kenrick-Glennon Seminary, 2739

Kensington and Chelsea Library Service, 2273

Kensington College of Business, 2364

Kent Institute of Business and Technology, Sydney, 168

Kent Libraries, Registration and Archives, 2277

Kent State University, 2832

Kent State University Museum, 2492

Kenton County Public Library, 2441

Kentro Erevnas Byzantinis kai Metabyzantinis Technis, 946

Kentron Epistemonikōn Erevnōn, 622

Kentron Ereunes Hellenikes kai Latinikes Grammateias, Athens, 947

Kentron Ereunes Historias Hellenikou Dikaiou, Athens, 946

Kentron Erevnis Archaiotitos, Athens, 946

Kentron Erevnis Ellinikis Kinonias, Athens, 947

Kentron Erevnis Ellinikis Philosophias, Athens, 947

Kentron Erevnis Messeonikou kai Neou Ellinismou, Athens, 946

Kentron Erevnis Neoterou Ellinismou, Athens, 946

Kentron Erevnis Phissikistis Atmospheras kai Climatologias, Athens, 947

Kentucky Christian University, 2644

Kentucky Department for Libraries and Archives, 2441

Kentucky Historical Society, 2478

Kentucky Mountain Bible College, 2645

Kentucky Museum, 2478

Kentucky State University, 2645

Kentucky Wesleyan College, 2645

Kenya Agricultural Research Institute, 1352

Kenya Agricultural Research Institute Library, 1353

Kenya Astronomical Society, Nairobi, 1352

Kenya Conservatoire of Music, 1356

Kenya Industrial Research and Development Institute, 1353

Kenya Institute of Administration, 1356

Kenya Library Association, 1352

Kenya Medical Association, 1352

Kenya Medical Research Institute (KEMRI), 1353

Kenya Medical Training College, Nairobi, 1356

Kenya Methodist University, 1354

Kenya National Academy of Sciences, 1351

Kenya National Archives and Documentation Service, 1353

Kenya National Library Services, 1353

Kenya Polytechnic, 1357

Kenya School of Law, 1357

Kenyatta University, 1355

Kenyon College, 2832

Kenyon Institute, 1143

Kerala Agricultural University, 1039

Kerala State Central Library, 1021

Keramiekmuseum Princessehof, 1551

Kerch State Archaeological Museum, 2203

Keresztény Múzeum, Esztergom, 983

Kermanshah University of Medical Sciences, 1112

Kern County Library, 2432

Kernfysisch Versneller Instituut (KVI), 1540

KES College, 627

Kestnergesellschaft, Hanover, 822

Ketchikan Campus Library, 2430

Ketchikan Public Library, 2430

Ketskhoveli, N., Institute of Botany, 814

Kettering College of Medical Arts, 2832

Kettering University, 2697

Keuka College, 2787

Keve András Madártani és Természetvédelmi Szakkönyvtár, 979

Keystone College, 2857

Kfar Giladi Library, 1145

KFKI Atomic Energy Research Institute of the Hungarian Academy of Sciences, 978

Kh. M. Abdullaev Institute of Geology and Geophysics, Tashkent, 2985

Khabarovsk Research Institute of Epidemiology and Microbiology of Rospotrebnadzor, 1837

Khabarovsk State Academy of Economics and Law, 1896

Khabarovsk State Institute of Culture, 1900

Khabarovsk State Pharmaceutical Institute, 1899

Khadim Ali Shah Bukhari Institute of Technology (KASBIT), 1650

Khakassia State University 'N. F. Katanov', Abakan, 1869

Khalifa University of Science, Technology and Research, 2220

Khalifa's House, Omdurman, 2048

Khalikdina Hall Library Association, 1643

'Khalkha Juram' Higher School of Law, 1501

Khan-Uul Higher School, 1501

Kharkiv Institute of Agricultural Mechanization and Electrification, 2217

Kharkiv Institute of Industrial and Applied Arts, 2217

Kharkiv National Automobile and Highways University, 2212

Kharkiv National Medical University, 2210

Kharkiv National Pedagogical University 'H. S. Skovoroda', 2211

Kharkiv National University of Economics, 2205

Kharkiv National University of Radioelectronics, 2212

Kharkiv State Academy of Culture, 2217

Kharkiv State Academy of Railway Transport, 2216

Kharkiv State Academy of Zooveterinary Science, 2216

Kharkiv State Agrarian University 'V. V. Dokuchayev', 2204

Kharkiv State Art Museum, 2203

Kharkiv State Historical Museum, 2203

Kharkiv State Institute of Arts, 2217

Kharkiv State Municipal Academy, 2216

Kharkiv State Technical University of Civil Engineering and Architecture, 2212

Kharkiv V. N. Karazin National University Central Scientific Library, 2202

Khartoum Nursing College, 2050

Khatlon Scientific Centre, Kulob, 2126

Khazar University, 206

Khemarak University, 361

Kherson A. D. Tsuryupa Agricultural Institute, 2217

Kherson National Technical University, 2212

Khlopin, V. G., Radium Institute, St Petersburg, 1845

Khmelnytsky State University, 2205

Khmer University of Technology and Management, 361

Khon Kaen University, 2140

Khorezm Mamun Academy, 2983

Khorog Institute of Social Sciences, 2128

Khorog State University, 2128

Khost University, 82

Khuda Bakhsh Oriental Public Library, 1020

Khujand Scientific Centre, 2126

Khulna University, 223

Khulna University of Engineering and Technology, 223

Khwaja Yunus Ali Medical College, 234

Khyber Medical University, 1650

Khyber Pakhtunkhwa Agricultural University, 1650

Kiambu Institute of Science and Technology, 1357

Kiangan Branch, 1692

Kiasma—Museum of Contemporary Art, 721

Kie—Associação Conhecimento, Inovação e Educaçã, 1764

Kie—Association of Knowledge, Innovation and Education, Lisbon, 1764

Kiel University Library, 844

Kielce University of Technology, 1753

Kieleckie Towarzystwo Naukowe, 1707

Kiepenheuer-Institut für Sonnenphysik, Freiburg, 837

Kigali Institute of Science, Technology and Management (KIST), 1903

Kihara Institute for Biological Research, 1227

KIIT University, 1075

Kildalton College of Agriculture, 1132

Kilgore Memorial Library, 2448

Killhope, the North of England Lead Mining Museum, 2283

Kim Chaek University of Technology, 1361

Kim Hyong-Jik University of Education, Pyongyang, 1361

Kim Il Sung University, 1361

Kimbell Art Museum, 2498

Kimberley Public Library, 1978

Mechanical Engineering Society, Moscow, 1830
Mechanical Industry Research Laboratories, Hsinchu, 2120
Mechanics Research Institute, Tiranë, 85
Mechnikov I. I., Institute of Vaccines and Sera, 1838
Medaille College, 2788
Medcenter One College of Nursing, 2824
Medelhavsmuseet, Stockholm, 2066
Medgar Evers College, 2771
Media Museum, Odense, 658
Media Plan Institute, Sarajevo, 289
Mediaş Municipal Museum, 1796
Mediathek Wallis (Kantonsbibliothek), 2095
Médiathèque Ceccano, Avignon, 750
Médiathèque Centrale d'Agglomération Emile Zola, Montpellier, 752
Médiathèque d'Orléans, 752
Médiathèque de l'Agglomération Troyenne, Troyes, 755
Médiathèque de l'Institut Français de Madagascar, Antananarivo, 1438
Médiathèque François-Mitterrand, 754
Médiathèque Michel Crépeau, La Rochelle, 751
Médiathèque Pierre Amalric, Albi, 750
Médiathèque Publique et Universitaire, Valence, 755
Médiathèque Raphaël Barquissau, 807
Médiathèque Valais (Bibliothèque Cantonale), 2095
Medical Academy of São Paulo, 299
Medical Association of Jamaica, 1213
Medical Association of Malawi, 1440
Medical Association of Thailand, 2136
Medical Biology Institute, Kunming, 467
Medical Biotechnological Institute, Minsk, 241
Medical Biotechnology Institute, Beijing, 467
Medical College, Burgas, 351
Medical College for Women, Dhaka, 234
Medical College of Wisconsin, 2956
Medical Council, Dublin, 1131
Medical Council of India, 1008
Medical Institute, Sucre, 282
Medical Library Association, Chicago, 2400
Medical Library, Beijing, 470
Medical Library, Boroko, 1672
Medical Research Centre, 1665
Medical Research Centre for Preventive Medicine and the Protection of the Health of Industrial Workers, Ekaterinburg, 1838
Medical Research Council Dunn Nutrition Unit, Keneba, 810
Medical Research Council, Fajara, 810
Medical Research Council Laboratories, Mona, 1214
Medical Research Council (MRC), London, 2255
Medical Research Institute, Colombo, 2041
Medical Research Institute, Ulan Bator, 1498
Medical Research Library of Brooklyn, 2451
Medical Society of Copenhagen, 651
Medical Society of Finland, 716
Medical Society of London, 2238
Medical Society of the State of New York, 2409
Medical University, Innsbruck, Innsbruck, 192
Medical University of Graz, Graz, 191
Medical University of Łódź, 1737
Medical University of Plovdiv, 345
Medical University of South Carolina, 2884
Medical University of the Americas, Charlestown, Nevis, 1904
Medical University Pleven, 345
Medical University 'Prof. Dr Paraskev Stoyanov', 346
Medical University Sofia, 346
Medical University, Vienna, Vienna, 192
Medical Women's International Association (MWIA), Burnaby, 63

Medicinal Plant Development Institute, Beijing, 467
Medicine Hat Museum and Art Gallery, 377
Medicine Shield College Program— American Indian Association of Illinois, Chicago, 2611
Medicinske Selskab i København, 651
Medicinski Universitet Pleven, 345
Medicinski Universitet Plovdiv, 345
Medicinski Universitet 'Prof. Dr Paraskev Stoyanov', 346
Medicinski Universitet Sofia, 346
Medico-Legal Society of Japan, 1221
Mediemuseum, 658
Medieval Academy of America, 2404
Medina County District Library, 2454
Medinaceli Archives, 2008
Mediterranean Agronomic Institute of Bari, 44
Mediterranean Agronomic Institute of Chania, 44
Mediterranean Agronomic Institute of Montpellier, 44
Mediterranean Agronomic Institute of Zaragoza, 44
Mediterranean Institute of Management, Nicosia, 627
Mediterranean University, Podgorica, 1503
Medizinische Akademie Erfurt, 935
Medizinische Hochschule Hannover, 884
Medizinische Universität Graz, 191
Medizinische Universität Innsbruck, 192
Medizinische Universität Wien, 192
Medjunarodna Galerija Portreta Tuzla, 291
Mednarodni Grafični Likovni Center (MGLC), 1966
Međunarodna diplomska škola za poslovno upravljanje Zagreb, 614
Medway Council, 2279
Meenakshi Academy of Higher Education and Research, 1075
Meenakshi University, 1075
Meertens Instituut, 1542
Megatrend University, 1924
Megatrend Univerzitet, 1924
Megunaroden Balkanski Univerzitet, 1435
Meguro Parasitological Museum, 1232
Meharry Medical College, 2892
Mehedinţi 'I. G. Bibicescu' District Library, 1792
Mehmet Paşa Library, 2161
Mehran University of Engineering & Technology, 1651
Mehran University of Engineering & Technology Library, 1642
Meijeritieteellinen Seura ry, Helsinki, 713
Meiji Gakuin University, 1318
Meiji Jingu Homotsuden, 1232
Meiji University, 1318
Meijo University, 1319
Meiktila Institute of Economics, 1517
Meisei University, 1319
Mejiro University, 1319
Melbourne Institute of Technology (MIT), 171
Melbourne Museum, 142
Melikishvili, P. G., Institute of Physical and Organic Chemistry, 814
Melitopol Institute of Agricultural Mechanization, 2217
Mellemfolkeligt Samvirke, Copenhagen, 650
Melnikov Permafrost Institute, Yakutsk, 1845
Memorial Institute for Ophthalmic Research, Cairo, 688
Memorial Museum named after K. I. Satpayev, 1342
Memorial Museum of the War of Liberation, Pyongyang, 1361
Memorial Museum of Victims of Political Persecution, Ulan Bator, 1499
Memorial Sloan-Kettering Cancer Center, New York, 2421
Memorial University of Newfoundland, 388

Memphis Brooks Museum of Art, 2497
Memphis College of Art, 2892
Memphis Public Library & Information Center, 2458
Memphis Theological Seminary, 2892
Mendel Art Gallery and Civic Conservatory (Saskatoon Gallery and Conservatory Corporation), 380
Mendel University in Brno, 642
Mendeleev, D. I., Chemical Society, Moscow, 1829
Mendelova Univerzita v Brně, 642
Menéndez Pelayo Library, 2007
Menia University, 692
Menil Collection, 2498
Menlo College, 2530
Mennell Society, Harare, 3028
Mennello Museum of American Art, 2472
Menninger, Houston, 2421
Menno Simons College, Winnipeg, 438
Menominee Tribal/County Library, 2462
Mental Health America, Alexandria, 2409
Mental Health Foundation, Cay Hill, 1571
Mental Health Research Institute, Parkville, 137
Mental Health Research Institute, Tomsk, 1839
Mercedes and Martín Ferreyra Medical Research Institute, 108
Mercer County Library System, Lawrenceville, 2450
Mercer University, 2599
Mercy College, 2788
Mercy College of Health Sciences, 2637
Mercy College of Ohio, 2833
Mercyhurst College, 2860
Meredith College, 2811
Merentutkimuslaitos, Helsinki, 719
Méréstechnikai és Automatizálási Tudományos Egyesület, Budapest, 975
Meridian Lauderdale County Public Library, 2447
Meridian Museum of Art, 2483
Meritxell Sanctuary, 98
Merowe Museum, 2048
Merrimack College, 2686
Merrimack Public Library, 2449
Merseyside Maritime Museum, 2286
Mersin Üniversitesi, 2179
Merthyr Tydfil County Borough Library, 2277
Merton College Library, Oxford, 2279
Merton College, Oxford, 2348
Merton Libraries and Heritage Service, 2274
Mesa County Libraries, 2433
MESA+ Institute for Nanotechnology, 1544
Messiah College, 2860
Mestna knjižnica Ljubljana, 1966
Mestni muzej Ljubljana, 1966
Městská knihovna v Praze, 634
Městská knižnica Bratislava, 1953
Městské muzeum Mariánské Lázně, 636
Mestské muzeum v Bratislave, 1953
Met Office, Bracknell, 2260
Metal Forming Institute, 1720
Metal Polymer Research Institute 'V. A. Belyi', Gomel, 241
Metals Industry Research and Development Centre, Taguig, 1690
Metals Science Society, Prague, 630
Metalurški Institut 'Kemal Kapetanović', 289
Metanoia Institute, 2364
Metaphysical Society of America, 2414
Météo-France, Paris, 749
Meteorological and Ecological Centre, Rome, 1172
Meteorological and Hydrological Service, 608
Meteorological Bureau, Santiago, 451
Meteorological Department Curaçao, 1569
Meteorological Museum of the Central Geophysical Observatory, Voeikovo, 1861
Meteorological Research Institute, Tsukuba, 1227

Meteorological Service, Harare, 3029
Meteorological Society of Japan, 1223
Meteorological Society of New Zealand, 1575
Meteorologiska Institutet, Helsinki, 719
Meteorologiske Institutt, 1617
Meteorology, Climatology and Geophysics Agency, Jakarta, 1085
Meteorološka opservatorija Beograd, 1922
Methodist College of Nursing, 2611
Methodist Theological School in Ohio, 2833
Methodist University, Fayetteville, 2812
Methodology Institute, London, 2262
Metropolitan College of New York, 2788
Metropolitan Libraries Section, 48
Metropolitan Museum of Art, New York, 2489
Metropolitan Museum of Manila, 1691
Metropolitan State College of Denver, 2553
Metropolitan State University, 2718
Metropolitan University, 2973
Metropolitan University, Sylhet, 223
Metsähistorian Seura, 715
Metsäntutkimuslaitos (Metla), 718
Metz, Musées de La Cour d'Or, 757
Mevlâna Museum, Konya, 2163
Mexican Academy of Dermatology, 1467
Mexican Academy of Letters, 1466
Mexican Academy of Sciences, 1467
Mexican Anthropological Society, 1468
Mexican Association of Petroleum Geologists, 1468
Mexican Botanical Society, 1467
Mexican Cardiological Society, 1467
Mexican National Academy of Medicine, 1467
Mexican Parasitological Society, 1467
Mexican Petroleum Institute, 1470
Mexican Society for Nutrition and Endocrinology, 1467
Mexican Society of Geography and Statistics, 1466
Mexican Society of Mycology, 1467
Mexican Society of Plant Genetics, 1467
MF Norwegian School of Theology, 1632
MGH Institute of Health Professions, 2686
MHATEM 'N.I. Pirogov', 338
Miami Art Museum, 2472
Miami Dade College, 2586
Miami International University of Art & Design, 2586
Miami Public Library, 2455
Miami University Art Museum, 2492
Miami University, Oxford, OH, 2833
Miami-Dade Public Library System, 2436
MIC Norsk Musikkinformasjon, 1615
Michael C. Carlos Museum, 2473
Michael Okpara University of Agriculture, Umudike, 1602
Michigan Jewish Institute, 2698
Michigan School of Professional Psychology, 2698
Michigan State University, 2698
Michigan State University – Dubai, 2222
Michigan State University Libraries, 2446
Michigan State University Museum, 2482
Michigan Technological University, 2704
Michurin, I. V., All-Russia Research Institute for Genetics and Breeding in Horticulture, 1832
Michurin, I. V., All-Russia Research Institute for Horticulture, 1832
Michurinsk State Agrarian University, 1862
Micro and Trace Analysis Centre, 257
Microbiological Society of Moldova, 1491
Microelectronics Institute, Yaroslavl, 1850
Micronesia Conservation Trust, 1489
Microscopy Society of America, 2413
Mid Sweden University, 2075
Mid-America Baptist Theological Seminary, 2893

Ministry of Culture, Youth and Sports, Juba, Juba, 1994
Ministry of Culture, Youth and Sports, Nouakchott, 1460
Ministry of Culture, Youth and Sports, Prishtina, 1387
Ministry of Culture, Zagreb, 606
Ministry of Defence, Information Services, 2274
Ministry of Economic Affairs, Social Affairs and Culture, Oranjestad, 1568
Ministry of Education, Abu Dhabi, 2218
Ministry of Education, Abuja, 1589
Ministry of Education, Accra, 938
Ministry of Education, Addis Ababa, 706
Ministry of Education, Amman, 1333
Ministry of Education and Community Development, Paramaribo, 2051
Ministry of Education and Culture, Asunción, 1674
Ministry of Education and Culture, Budapest, 972
Ministry of Education and Culture, Castries, 1905
Ministry of Education and Culture, Helsinki, 712
Ministry of Education and Culture, Montevideo, 2979
Ministry of Education and Culture, Nicosia, 622
Ministry of Education and Higher Education, Beirut, 1406
Ministry of Education and Higher Education, Doha, 1780
Ministry of Education and Higher Education, Praia, 442
Ministry of Education and Higher Education, Ramallah, 1663
Ministry of Education and Human Resource Development, Roseau, 670
Ministry of Education and Human Resource Development, St George's, 959
Ministry of Education and Human Resource Development, St Michael, 236
Ministry of Education and Human Resources Development, Honiara, 1969
Ministry of Education and Human Resources, Phoenix, 1462
Ministry of Education and Research, Oslo, 1614
Ministry of Education and Research, Stockholm, 2054
Ministry of Education and Research, Tartu, 701
Ministry of Education and Science, and Youth and Sport, Kyiv, 2195
Ministry of Education and Science, Bishkek, 1393
Ministry of Education and Science, Moscow, 1826
Ministry of Education and Science, Mostar, 287
Ministry of Education and Science of the Republic of Kazakhstan, 1338
Ministry of Education and Science, Podgorica, 1502
Ministry of Education and Science, Rīga, 1402
Ministry of Education and Science, Skopje, 1431
Ministry of Education and Science, Tbilisi, 812
Ministry of Education and Science, Tiranë, 83
Ministry of Education and Science, Vilnius, 1420
Ministry of Education and Science, Yerevan, 124
Ministry of Education and Skills Development, Gaborone, 294
Ministry of Education and Sports, Kampala, 2191
Ministry of Education and Sports, Vientiane, 1400
Ministry of Education and Training, Hanoi, 3010
Ministry of Education and Training, Maseru, 1411
Ministry of Education and Vocational Training, Dar es Salaam, 2130

Ministry of Education and Vocational Training, Port-au-Prince, 968
Ministry of Education and Youth, Belmopan, 275
Ministry of Education and Youth, Chişinău, 1490
Ministry of Education, Ashgabat, 2187
Ministry of Education, Asmara, 700
Ministry of Education, Baghdad, 1122
Ministry of Education, Baku, 202
Ministry of Education, Bandar Seri Begawan, 331
Ministry of Education, Bangkok, 2135
Ministry of Education, Basseterre, 1904
Ministry of Education, Beijing, 461
Ministry of Education, Belgrade, 1920
Ministry of Education, Brasilia, 296
Ministry of Education, Bratislava, 1949
Ministry of Education, Buenos Aires, 102
Ministry of Education, Cairo, 685
Ministry of Education, Caracas, 2999
Ministry of Education, Colombo, 2039
Ministry of Education, Culture and Science, The Hague, 1527
Ministry of Education, Culture and Science, Ulan Bator, 1496
Ministry of Education, Culture and Vocational Training, São Tomé, 1909
Ministry of Education, Culture, Sports, Science and Technology, Tokyo, 1216
Ministry of Education, Culture, Youth and Sport, Dili, 2147
Ministry of Education, Culture, Youth and Sports Affairs, Philipsburg, 1570
Ministry of Education, Dakar, 1917
Ministry of Education, Damascus, 2115
Ministry of Education, Department for Education and Science Policy, Helsinki, 712
Ministry of Education, Dhaka, 212
Ministry of Education, Dushanbe, 2126
Ministry of Education, Employment and the Family, Valletta, 1457
Ministry of Education, Georgetown, 966
Ministry of Education, Guatemala City, 960
Ministry of Education, Hamilton, 2386
Ministry of Education, Havana, 615
Ministry of Education, Higher Education and Research, Papeete, 800
Ministry of Education, Islamabad, 1636
Ministry of Education, Jerusalem, 1140
Ministry of Education, Kabul, 79
Ministry of Education, Kathmandu, 1524
Ministry of Education, Khartoum, 2047
Ministry of Education, Kigali, 1902
Ministry of Education, Kingston, 1213
Ministry of Education, Kingstown, 1906
Ministry of Education, Koror, 1662
Ministry of Education, La Paz, 281
Ministry of Education Library, Kabul, 80
Ministry of Education, Lifelong Learning and Religion, Athens, 944
Ministry of Education, Lima, 1677
Ministry of Education, Lisbon, 1760
Ministry of Education, Luanda, 99
Ministry of Education, Lusaka, 3024
Ministry of Education, Madrid, 1995
Ministry of Education, Majuro, 1459
Ministry of Education, Malé, 1453
Ministry of Education, Managua, 1585
Ministry of Education, Manama, 209
Ministry of Education, Maputo, 1511
Ministry of Education, Mbabane, 2052
Ministry of Education, Minsk, 238
Ministry of Education, Monrovia, 1413
Ministry of Education, Mont Fleuri, 1940
Ministry of Education, Muscat, 1633
Ministry of Education, Nay Pyi Taw, 1513
Ministry of Education, Panamá, 1668
Ministry of Education, Port Vila, 2990
Ministry of Education, Pretoria, 1972
Ministry of Education, Putrajaya, 1443
Ministry of Education, Pyongyang, 1359
Ministry of Education, Quito, 677

Ministry of Education, Research and Nordic Cooperation, 666
Ministry of Education, Research, Youth and Sport, Bucharest, 1782
Ministry of Education, Riyadh, 1910
Ministry of Education, Safat, 1390
Ministry of Education, St Clair, 2151
Ministry of Education, San Salvador, 696
Ministry of Education, San'a, 3022
Ministry of Education, Santiago, 447
Ministry of Education, Science and Culture, Reykjavík, 1000
Ministry of Education, Science and Sports, Malabo, 699
Ministry of Education, Science and Technology, Freetown, 1941
Ministry of Education, Science and Technology, Lilongwe, 1440
Ministry of Education, Science and Technology, Nassau, 208
Ministry of Education, Science and Technology, Prishtina, 1387
Ministry of Education, Science and Technology, Seoul, 1363
Ministry of Education, Science, Culture and Sports, Willemstad, 1569
Ministry of Education, Singapore, 1943
Ministry of Education, Sport, Culture and Science, Ljubljana, 1963
Ministry of Education, Sports and Culture, Apia, 1907
Ministry of Education, Sports and Culture, Harare, 3027
Ministry of Education, Sports and Culture, Vaiaku, 2190
Ministry of Education, Sports, Youth and Gender Affairs, St Johns, 101
Ministry of Education, Suva, 710
Ministry of Education, Taipei, 2118
Ministry of Education, Tegucigalpa, 970
Ministry of Education, Tehran, 1106
Ministry of Education, Thimphu, 279
Ministry of Education, Training and Employment, George Town, 2387
Ministry of Education, Tunis, 2154
Ministry of Education, Universities and Research, Rome, 1162
Ministry of Education, Wellington, 1572
Ministry of Education, Windhoek, 1521
Ministry of Education, Women Affairs and Culture Library, Nukualofa, 2150
Ministry of Education, Women's Affairs and Culture, Nuku'alofa, 2150
Ministry of Education, Yaren, 1523
Ministry of Education, Youth and Science, Sofia, 333
Ministry of Education, Youth and Sport Development, Bikenibeu, 1358
Ministry of Education, Youth and Sport, Phnom-Penh, 357
Ministry of Education, Youth and Sport, Prague, 628
Ministry of Education, Youth and Sport, Sant Julià de Lòria, 97
Ministry of Foreign Affairs Library, Tokyo, 1229
Ministry of Health, Environment, Youth, Sports and Culture, George Town, 2387
Ministry of Heritage and Culture, Muscat, 1633
Ministry of Higher and Specialized Secondary Education, Tashkent, 2983
Ministry of Higher and University Education, Kinshasa, 593
Ministry of Higher Education and Research, Lomé, 2148
Ministry of Higher Education and Research, Paris, 738
Ministry of Higher Education and Scientific Research, Abidjan, 603
Ministry of Higher Education and Scientific Research, Abu Dhabi, 2218
Ministry of Higher Education and Scientific Research, Algiers, 89
Ministry of Higher Education and Scientific Research, Amman, 1333
Ministry of Higher Education and Scientific Research, Baghdad, 1122

Ministry of Higher Education and Scientific Research, Bamako, 1455
Ministry of Higher Education and Scientific Research, Bujumbura, 355
Ministry of Higher Education and Scientific Research, Cairo, 685
Ministry of Higher Education and Scientific Research, Conakry, 963
Ministry of Higher Education and Scientific Research, Cotonou, 277
Ministry of Higher Education and Scientific Research, Tunis, 2154
Ministry of Higher Education and Technology, Harare, 3027
Ministry of Higher Education, Brazzaville, 596
Ministry of Higher Education, Caracas, 2999
Ministry of Higher Education, Colombo, 2039
Ministry of Higher Education, Damascus, 2115
Ministry of Higher Education, Havana, 615
Ministry of Higher Education, Kabul, 79
Ministry of Higher Education, Putrajaya, 1443
Ministry of Higher Education, Research, Science and Technology, Banjul, 810
Ministry of Higher Education, Riyadh, 1910
Ministry of Higher Education, Ruwi, 1633
Ministry of Higher Education, Safat, 1390
Ministry of Higher Education, Science and Technology, Juba, 1994
Ministry of Higher Education, Science and Technology, Ljubljana, 1963
Ministry of Higher Education, Science and Technology, Nairobi, 1351
Ministry of Higher Education, Scientific Research and Professional Training, N'Djamena, 445
Ministry of Higher Education, Staff Training and Scientific Research, Rabat, 1505
Ministry of Higher Education, Yaoundé, 363
Ministry of Home and Cultural Affairs, Thimphu, 279
Ministry of Human Resource Development, New Delhi, 1004
Ministry of Human Resources, Youth and Sports, Malé, 1453
Ministry of Information and Culture, Conakry, 963
Ministry of Information and Culture, Kabul, 79
Ministry of Information, Culture and Sports, Dar es Salaam, 2130
Ministry of Information, Culture and Tourism, Malabo, 699
Ministry of Information, Culture and Tourism, Monrovia, 1413
Ministry of Information, Culture and Tourism, Vientiane, 1400
Ministry of Information, Culture, Youth and Sports, Kingston, 1213
Ministry of Justice and Education, Oranjestad, 1568
Ministry of Justice Library, Tokyo, 1229
Ministry of Labour and Social Solidarity, Lisbon, 1760
Ministry of Livestock Development, Department of Veterinary Services, Nairobi, 1352
Ministry of National Development, Investment and Culture, Belmopan, 275
Ministry of National Education, Algiers, 89
Ministry of National Education and Professional Training, Djibouti, 669
Ministry of National Education and Scientific Research, Antananarivo, 1437
Ministry of National Education and Vocational Training, Luxembourg, 1429
Ministry of National Education, Ankara, 2158

Ministry of National Education, Bangui, 443

Ministry of National Education, Bogotá, 577

Ministry of National Education, Culture and Science, Bissau, 965

Ministry of National Education, Higher Education and Scientific Research, Nouakchott, 1460

Ministry of National Education, Higher Education, Scientific Research and Innovation and Culture, Libreville, 808

Ministry of National Education, Jakarta, 1083

Ministry of National Education, Warsaw, 1706

Ministry of National Education, Youth and Community Life, Paris, 738

Ministry of National Security, Public Administration, Information, Information Communications Technology, Legal Affairs and Culture, St George's, 959

Ministry of Public Education, San José, 598

Ministry of Public Education, Tashkent, 2983

Ministry of Research, Science and Technology, Wellington, 1572

Ministry of Science and Higher Education, Warsaw, 1706

Ministry of Science and Innovation, Madrid, 1995

Ministry of Science and Technology, 1636

Ministry of Science and Technology, Jerusalem, 1140

Ministry of Science and Technology, Luanda, 99

Ministry of Science, Education and Sports, Zagreb, 606

Ministry of Science, Innovation and Higher Education, Copenhagen, 648

Ministry of Science, Technology and Higher Education, Lisbon, 1760

Ministry of Science, Technology and Tertiary Education, St James, 2151

Ministry of Science, Technology and Vocational Training, Lusaka, 3024

Ministry of Scientific Research and Innovation, Yaoundé, 363

Ministry of Scientific Research and Technical Innovation, Brazzaville, 596

Ministry of Secondary and Higher Education, Ouagadougou, 353

Ministry of Secondary and Higher Education, Research and Technology, Niamey, 1587

Ministry of Sports, Culture and Leisure, Antananarivo, 1437

Ministry of Technical Education and Vocational Training, Brazzaville, 596

Ministry of the Arts and Multiculturalism, Port-of-Spain, 2151

Ministry of the French-speaking Community, Office for Education and Social Promotion, 248

Ministry of the French-speaking Community, Office for Higher Education, Brussels, 248

Ministry of the German-speaking Community, Department of Education, Vocational Training and Employment, Eupen, 248

Ministry of the Interior Academy, 351

Ministry of Tourism and Civil Aviation, Kathmandu, 1524

Ministry of Tourism and Cultural Affairs, Freetown, 1941

Ministry of Tourism and Culture, Banjul, 810

Ministry of Tourism, Arts and Culture, Malé, 1453

Ministry of Tourism, Civil Aviation, Culture and the Environment, St Johns, 101

Ministry of Tourism, Culture and Sport, Basseterre, 1904

Ministry of Tourism, Culture, Youth and Sports, Tiranë, 83

Ministry of Tourism, Environment and Culture, Maseru, 1411

Ministry of Training and Vocational Education, Algiers, 89

Ministry of Unity, Arts, Culture and Heritage, Kuala Lumpur, 1443

Ministry of Urban Development, Labour, Culture and Electoral Matters, Kingstown, 1906

Ministry of Youth and Sports, Kathmandu, 1524

Ministry of Youth, National Service, Sport and Culture, Windhoek, 1521

Ministry of Youth, Sports and Culture, Bujumbura, 355

Ministry of Youth, Sports and Culture, Gaborone, 294

Ministry of Youth, Sports and Culture, Kigali, 1902

Ministry of Youth, Sports and Culture, Nassau, 1525

Minneapolis College of Art and Design, 2718

Minneapolis Institute of Arts, 2483

Minnesota Historical Society, 2404

Minnesota Historical Society Library, 2446

Minnesota Lakes Maritime Museum, 2483

Minnesota Museum of American Art, 2483

Minnesota State Archives, 2446

Minnesota State Colleges and Universities, 2718

Minnesota State Law Library, 2446

Minnesota State Library Services, 2400

Minnesota State University Library, 2446

Minnesota State University, Mankato, 2718

Minnesota State University Moorhead, 2718

Minno-Geoložki Universitet 'Sv. Ivan Rilski', 346

Minobusan Homotsukan, 1231

Minot State University, 2824

Minsk Institute of Management, 247

Minsk State Higher Education College of Civil Aviation, 247

Minsk State Linguistic University, 245

Mint Museum, 2491

MINTEK, Randburg, 1976

Mints, Acad. A. L., Institute of Radio Technology JSC, 1850

Minufiya University, 693

Mio, V., House-Museum, Korçë, 86

Miramichi Natural History Museum, 378

'Miran Jarc' Regional Public Library, 1966

Miras University, 1347

'Miroslav Krleža' Lexicographic Institute, 608

Mirpur University of Science & Technology, 1651

Miryang National University, 1384

Misericordia University, 2854

Miskolci Egyetem, 990

Miskolci Egyetem Könyvtár, Levéltár, Múzeum, 980

Misr University for Science and Technology (MUST), 693

Mission Pédologique, Rabat, 1506

Mission Sociologique Du Haut-Oubangui, 443

Missionary Museum, King William's Town, 1980

Mississippi Armed Forces Museum, 2483

Mississippi College, 2734

Mississippi Museum of Art, 2483

Mississippi Museum of Natural Science, 2483

Mississippi State University, 2734

Mississippi University for Women, 2734

Mississippi Valley State University, 2734

Missoula Public Library, 2448

Missouri Baptist University, 2740

Missouri Botanical Garden, 2423

Missouri Southern State University, 2740

Missouri State Archives, 2448

Missouri State Library, 2448

Missouri State University, 2740

Missouri University of Science and Technology, 2745

Missouri Valley College, 2740

Missouri Western State University, 2740

Miswat Library, Aden, 3022

Mitchell College, 2557

Mitchell Library, 2269

Mitre Museum, 112

Mittag-Leffler Institute, 2059

Mittatekniikan Keskus, 719

Mittuniversitetet, 2075

Mixteca Technological University, 1485

Miyagi Gakuin Women's College, 1319

Miyake Medical Institute, Takamatsu City, 1226

Mizoram University, 1046

Mlezu Institute of Agriculture, 3031

MLibrary University of Michigan, 2446

M-Museum Leuven, 262

MOA Museum of Art, Atami, 1230

Mobile Life Centre, 2060

Modern Art Museum of Fort Worth, 2498

Modern Art Oxford, 2290

Modern Church, 2244

Modern College of Business and Science, 1635

Modern History Research Association, 834

Modern Humanitarian University, Khujand, 2128

Modern Humanities Research Association, Bath, 2254

Modern Hungarian Gallery II, 1955–2001, 984

Modern Language Association, New York, 2406

Modern Language Society, 716

Modern Magyar Képtár I, 984

Modern Magyar Képtár II, 984

Moderna galerija, 1966

Moderna Galerija, Zagreb, 610

Moderna Museet, 2066

MODUL University Vienna, 192

Mody Institute of Technology & Science, 1075

Moesgård Museum, 657

Mogilev Oblast Library 'V. I. Lenin', 242

Mogilev State Foodstuffs University, 245

Mogilev State University 'A. A. Kuleshov', 246

Mohammad Ali Jinnah University, 1651

Mohan Lal Sukhadia University, 1046

Mohi-ud-Din Islamic University, Nerian Sharif, 1651

Moholy-Nagy Müvészeti Egyetem, 991

Moholy-Nagy University of Arts, 991

Mohyla míru, Prace u Brna, 636

Moi University, 1355

Mokpo National Maritime University, 1371

Mokpo National University, 1371

Mokpo Natural History Museum, 1366

Mokslo, Inovacijų ir Technologijų Agentūra, 1420

Mokwon University, 1379

'Moldova' Iaşi National Museum Complex, 1796

Moldova State University, 1493

Moldova State University Library, 1492

Moldovan Sociological Association, 1491

Moldovan State Agrarian University, 1492

Molecular Infection Medicine Sweden, 2059

Molecular Medicine Ireland, 1132

Molloy College, Rockville Centre, 2789

Mombasa Polytechnic, 1357

Mommsen-Gesellschaft eV, 823

Momoyama Gakuin University, Osaka, 1319

Mon State Museum, Mon, 1514

Monash University, 160

Monash University Library, 140

Monasterio de las Descalzas Reales, 2010

Monasterio de Santa Maria la Real de las Huelgas, 2010

Monasterio de Yuste, 2011

Mondragon Unibertsitatea, 2012

Mondriaanhuis, 1553

Money Museum, Utrecht, 1552

Mong Ha Library, 575

'Mongol' Higher School, 1501

Mongolian Academy of Sciences, 1496

Mongolian Business Institute, 1501

Mongolian Civil Engineers' Association, 1497

Mongolian Development Research Centre, 1497

Mongolian Muslims' Society, Ulan Bator, 1497

Mongolian National Council for Education Accreditation, Ulan Bator, 1496

Mongolian National Gallery of Modern Art, Ulan Bator, 1499

Mongolian National Higher School, Ulan Bator, 1501

Mongolian National Mining Association, Ulan Bator, 1497

Mongolian National Water Association, 1497

Mongolian State Education University, 1499

Mongolian State University of Agriculture, 1499

Mongolian State University of Arts and Culture, Ulan Bator, 1499

Mongolian University of Science and Technology, 1500

Mongui Maduro Library, 1569

Monkwearmouth Station Museum, 2289

Monmouth College, 2612

Monmouth County Historical Association Museum & Library, 2487

Monmouth University, West Long Branch, 2759

Monmouthshire Libraries and Information Service, 2268

'Monos' Higher School of Medicine, Ulan Bator, 1501

Monroe College, 2789

Monroe County Library System, 2446

Monroe County Library System, Rochester, 2452

Monroe County Public Library, 2461

Montana Cowboy Hall of Fame, 2484

Montana Historical Society Museum, 2484

Montana State Library, 2448

Montana State University, 2746

Montana State University—Billings, 2747

Montana State University—Great Falls College of Technology, 2747

Montana State University—Northern, 2747

Montana Tech, Butte, 2747

Montanuniversität Leoben, 192

Montclair Art Museum, 2487

Montclair State University, 2759

Montclair State University Art Gallery, 2487

Montenegrin Academy of Sciences and Arts, 1502

Montenegrin PEN Centre, 1502

Montenegro Business School, 1504

Montenegro Council of Higher Education, 1502

Montenegro Tourism School, 1504

Monterey Institute of International Studies: A Graduate School of Middlebury College, 2530

Montevideo Astronomical Observatory, 2980

Montgomery City-County Public Library, 2430

Montgomery Museum of Fine Arts, 2463

Montomery County Law Library, 2454

Montpellier SupAgro, 791

Montréal Biodôme, 379

Montreal Diocesan Theological College, Montréal, 385

Montréal Museum of Fine Arts, Montreal, 379

Montreat College, 2812

Montserrat College of Art, 2686

Monumen Perjuangan Rakyat (MONPERA) Sumatera Bagian Selatan, 1087

Monumenta Germaniae Historica, Munich, 822

Museo de la Educación Gabriela Mistral, Santiago, 453

Museo de la Familia Dominicana Siglo XIX, 673

Museo de la Farmacia Hispana, 2010

Museo de la Fortaleza de San Fernando de Omoa, Cortés, 971

Museo de la Historia de Ponce, 2972

Museo de la Música Puertorriqueña, 2972

Museo de la Paeria, 2009

Museo de la Patagonia 'Dr Francisco P. Moreno', 113

Museo de La Plata, 112

Museo de la Policía Federal Argentina, 112

Museo de la Real Academia de Bellas Artes de San Fernando, 2010

Museo de las Americas, 2468

Museo de las Atarazanas Reales, 672

Museo de las Bellas Artes, Toluca, 1473

Museo de las Casas Reales, Santo Domingo, 672

Museo de las Culturas de Oaxaca, 1472

Museo de los Concilios y de la Cultura Visigoda, Toledo, 2012

Museo de los Orígenes, Casa de San Isidro, 2010

Museo de Mallorca, 2011

Museo de Metales Preciosos Precolombinos, La Paz, 283

Museo de Pontevedra, 2011

Museo de Prehistoria y Arqueología de Cantabria, 2011

Museo de Remedios 'José Maria Espinosa', 618

Museo de Santa Cruz, 2012

Museo de Sitio San Andrés, 697

Museo de Valladolid, 2012

Museo de Zamora, 2012

Museo de Zaragoza, 2012

Museo de Zoología, San José, 600

Museo degli Affreschi 'Giovanni Battista Cavalcaselle' alla Tomba di Giulietta, Verona, 1190

Museo degli Argenti, Florence, 1183

Museo del Ejército del Perú, Callao, 1680

Museo del Ejército, Madrid, 2010

Museo del Estado de Jalisco, Guadalajara, 1471

Museo del Ferrocarril de Madrid, Madrid, 2010

Museo del Fin del Mundo, Ushuaia, 113

Museo del Greco, 2012

Museo del Hombre Dominicano, 672

Museo del Indio y del Gaucho, Tacuarembó, 2981

Museo del Limari, 452

Museo del Merletto, Venice, 1190

Museo del Oro, 581

Museo del Palacio de Bellas Artes, México, 1472

Museo del Risorgimento, 1185

Museo del Risorgimento 'A. Saffi', 1184

Museo del Risorgimento, Brescia, 1182

Museo del Risorgimento e della Resistenza, Vicenza, 1190

Museo del Risorgimento e Istituto Mazziniano, Genoa, 1184

Museo del Risorgimento e Sacrario Oberdan, Trieste, 1189

Museo del Romanticismo, Madrid, 2010

Museo del Tesoro della Basilica di S. Francesco in Assisi, Assisi, 1182

Museo del Tesoro della Cattedrale di San Lorenzo, Genoa, 1185

Museo del Vetro, 1190

Museo del Virreinato, Lima, 1680

Museo dell' Opera di Santa Maria del Fiore, Florence, 1183

Museo della Casa Buonarroti, Florence, 1183

Museo della Civiltà Romana, 1187

Museo della Fondazione Querini Stampalia, Venice, 1190

Museo della Risiera di San Sabba—Monumento Nazionale, Trieste, 1189

Museo della Via Ostiense, 1188

Museo delle Armi 'Luigi Marzoli', 1182

Museo delle Curiosità, 1908

Museo delle Porcellane, Florence, 1183

Museo di Antichità, Turin, 1189

Museo di Archeologia Ligure, Genoa, 1184

Museo di Castelvecchio, Verona, 1190

Museo di Milano, 1185

Museo di Palazzo Davanzati (Antica Casa Fiorentina), Florence, 1183

Museo di Palazzo Vecchio, Florence, 1183

Museo di Palazzo Venezia, Rome, 1187

Museo di Roma, 1187

Museo di San Francesco, 1908

Museo di San Marco, Florence, 1183

Museo di Santa Maria Novella, 1183

Museo di Sant'Agostino, Genoa, 1184

Museo di Stato, San Marino, 1908

Museo di Storia Naturale, Venice, 1190

Museo Dillman S. Bullock, Angol, 452

Museo Diocesano, Brescia, 1182

Museo Diocesano d'Arte Sacra, Volterra, 1190

Museo Doctor Francia, Yaguarón, 1675

Museo 'Duca di Martina' alla Floridiana, Naples, 1186

Museo e Gallerie Nazionali di Capodimonte, 1186

Museo e Pinacoteca Nazionale di Palazzo Mansi, Lucca, 1185

Museo Egizio, Turin, 1189

Museo Emilio Bacardi Moreau, Santiago, 618

Museo Ernest Hemingway, Havana, 618

Museo Estudio Diego Rivera, México, 1472

Museo Etnográfico 'Andrés Barbero', Asunción, 1675

Museo Etnográfico 'Juan B. Ambrosetti', Buenos Aires, 112

Museo Etnografico Romagnolo 'B. Pergoli', 1184

Museo Etnográfico y Arqueológico, Tzintzuntzan, 1473

Museo Etrusco Guarnacci, Volterra, 1190

Museo Faro a Colón, 672

Museo Ferroviario di Trieste Campo Marzio, Trieste, 1189

Museo Filatélico del Banco de la República, Medellín, 581

Museo Firenze com'era, 1183

Museo Folklórico Araucano de Cañete 'Juan A. Ríos M.', 452

Museo Fortuny, 1190

Museo Gabriela Mistral de Vicuña, 453

Museo Galileo—Istituto e Museo di Storia della Scienza, Florence, 1183

Museo Geológico de la Universidad Nacional de Ingeniería del Perú, Lima, 1680

Museo 'Giannettino Luxoro', Genoa, 1184

Museo Gregoriano Egizio, 2992

Museo Gregoriano Etrusco, 2992

Museo Gregoriano Profano, 2992

Museo Hendrik Christian Andersen, 1187

Museo Historico Arubano, 1568

Museo Histórico Buenos Aires 'Cornelio de Saavedra', Buenos Aires, 112

Museo Histórico Cultural Juan Santamaría, 600

Museo Histórico de Corrientes, 112

Museo Histórico de Entre Rios 'Martiniano Leguizamón', 112

Museo Histórico 'General Rafael Urdaneta', 3004

Museo Histórico Militar, 1675

Museo Histórico Nacional, Buenos Aires, 112

Museo Histórico Nacional, Montevideo, 2981

Museo Histórico Nacional, Santiago, 453

Museo Histórico Provincial de Rosario 'Dr Julio Marc', 112

Museo Histórico Provincial de Santa Fe, 113

Museo Histórico Regional de Ayacucho, 1680

Museo Histórico Regional del Cusco, 1680

Museo Histórico Sarmiento, Buenos Aires, 112

Museo Histórico y Antropológico 'Mauricio Van de Maele', 453

Museo Horne, Florence, 1183

Museo Ignacio Agramonte, 618

Museo Indígeno, San José, 600

Museo Internazionale delle Ceramiche, Faenza, 1183

Museo Jacinto Jijón y Caamaño, 679

Museo Joyce, Trieste, 1189

Museo Lapidario Estense, Modena, 1186

Museo Lapidario Maffeiano, Verona, 1190

Museo Larco, Lima, 1680

Museo Marino Marini, 1184

Museo Mario Praz, 1187

Museo 'Martín Gusinde', Puerto Williams, 452

Museo Misional de Nuestra Señora de Regla, 2009

Museo Missionario Etnologico, Vatican City, 2992

Museo Mitre, Buenos Aires, 112

Museo Monográfico Municipal de Carteia, 2011

Museo Monográfico y Necrópolis del Puig des Molins, 2009

Museo Municipal de Arte Decorativo 'Firma y Odilo Estevez', 112

Museo Municipal de Arte e Historia 'Alberto Mena Caamaño', Quito, 679

Museo Municipal de Bellas Artes de Tandil, 113

Museo Municipal de Bellas Artes 'Juan B. Castagnino', 112

Museo Municipal de Bellas Artes 'Juan Manuel Blanes', Montevideo, 2981

Museo Municipal de Guanabacoa, 618

Museo Municipal, Guayaquil, 679

Museo Municipal 'Oscar M. de Rojas', Cárdenas, 618

Museo Nacional, Bogotá, 581

Museo Nacional Centro de Arte Reina Sofía, 2010

Museo Nacional Colegio de San Gregorio, 2012

Museo Nacional 'David J. Guzmán', San Salvador, 697

Museo Nacional de Aeronáutica, Morón, 112

Museo Nacional de Antropología, 581

Museo Nacional de Antropología, Madrid, 2010

Museo Nacional de Antropología, México, 1472

Museo Nacional de Arqueología, Antropología e Historia del Perú, Lima, 1680

Museo Nacional de Arqueología, La Paz, 283

Museo Nacional de Arqueología y Etnología de Guatemala, Guatemala City, 961

Museo Nacional de Arquitectura, México, 1472

Museo Nacional de Arte Decorativo, Buenos Aires, 112

Museo Nacional de Arte, La Paz, 283

Museo Nacional de Arte, México, 1472

Museo Nacional de Arte Moderno, Guatemala City, 961

Museo Nacional de Arte Oriental, Buenos Aires, 112

Museo Nacional de Arte Romano, 2011

Museo Nacional de Artes Decorativas, 2010

Museo Nacional de Artes e Industrias Populares del Instituto Nacional Indigenista, México, 1472

Museo Nacional de Artes Visuales, Montevideo, 2981

Museo Nacional de Bellas Artes, 453

Museo Nacional de Bellas Artes, Asunción, 1675

Museo Nacional de Bellas Artes, Buenos Aires, 112

Museo Nacional de Cerámica 'González Marti', 2012

Museo Nacional de Ciencia y Tecnología, Madrid, 2010

Museo Nacional de Ciencias Naturales, Madrid, 2010

Museo Nacional de Costa Rica, 600

Museo Nacional de Historia, Guatemala City, 961

Museo Nacional de Historia, México, 1472

Museo Nacional de Historia Natural 'Jorge A. Ibarra', Guatemala City, 961

Museo Nacional de Historia Natural, Santiago, 453

Museo Nacional de Historia Natural, Santo Domingo, 672

Museo Nacional de Historia Natural y Antropología, Montevideo, 2981

Museo Nacional de Historia y Geografía, Santo Domingo, 672

Museo Nacional de la Cultura Peruana, Lima, 1680

Museo Nacional de la Dirección Cultural del Banco Central del Ecuador, 679

Museo Nacional de la Estampa, México, 1472

Museo Nacional de las Culturas, México, 1472

Museo Nacional de las Intervenciones, México, 1472

Museo Nacional de Nicaragua, 1586

Museo Nacional de Reproducciones Artísticas, 2010

Museo Nacional de San Carlos, México, 1472

Museo Nacional del Prado, 2010

Museo Nacional del Virreinato, Tepotzotlán, 1473

Museo Nacional y Palacio de Bellas Artes, Havana, 618

Museo Napoleonico di Villa S. Martino, Portoferraio, 1187

Museo Napoleónico, Havana, 618

Museo Naturalistico Archeologico, Vicenza, 1190

Museo Naval, 2010

Museo Naval de la Nación, Buenos Aires, 112

Museo Naval del Perú, Callao, 1680

Museo Navale, Genoa, 1184

Museo Nazionale Archeologico Etnografico 'G. A. Sanna', Sassari, 1188

Museo Nazionale d'Abruzzo, L'Aquila, 1185

Museo Nazionale d'Arte Orientale, Rome, 1187

Museo Nazionale D. Ridola, Matera, 1185

Museo Nazionale del Bargello, 1184

Museo Nazionale della Scienza e della Tecnologia 'Leonardo da Vinci', 1185

Museo Nazionale dell'Alto Medioevo, 1188

Museo Nazionale di Castel Sant'Angelo, 1187

Museo Nazionale di Ravenna, 1187

Museo Nazionale di San Martino, Naples, 1186

Museo Nazionale di San Matteo, Pisa, 1187

Museo Nazionale di Villa Giulia, Rome, 1187

Museo Nazionale di Villa Guinigi, Lucca, 1185

Museo Nazionale Preistorico Etnografico 'Luigi Pigorini', 1187

Museo Nazionale, Reggio Calabria, 1187

Museo Nazionale Romano, 2011

Museo ng Arkidiyosesis ng Maynila (MANA), 1691

Museo ng Kalinangang Pilipino, 1692

Museo Numantino, Soria, 2011

Museo Numismatico Aruba, 1568

Museo Numismático 'Dr José Evaristo Uriburu', Buenos Aires, 112

Museo Numismático, Havana, 618

Museo O'Higginiano y de Bellas Artes de Talca, 453

Museo Omar Rayo, Roldanillo, 581

Museo Pablo Gargallo, 2012

Museo Paleocristiano, Aquileia, 1182

Museo Pedagógico 'José Pedro Varela', Montevideo, 2981

Museo Petrarchesco Piccolomineo, Trieste, 1189

Museo Pio Clementino, 2992

Museo Pio Cristiano Lapidario Cristiano Lapidario Ebraico, 2992

Museo Poldi Pezzoli, Milan, 1185

N

National Centre for Epidemiology, Budapest, 977

National Centre for Genetic Resources and Biotechnology (NACGRAB), Ibadan, 1591

National Centre for Geoscientific Research and Application, Algiers, 90

National Centre for Information and Documentation (at the Ministry of Education, Youth and Science), Sofia, 342

National Centre for Information Technology, Malé, 1453

National Centre for Linguistic and Historical Research, Malé, 1454

National Centre for 'Manas' Studies and Fine Arts, Bishkek, 1394

National Centre for Policy Research, Kabul, 80

National Centre for Radiation Research and Technology (NCRRT), Cairo, 689

National Centre for Regional Development and Housing Policy, Sofia, 337

National Centre for Research in Children's Literature, London, 2254

National Centre for Research, Khartoum, 2047

National Centre for Research on Arid Zones, Algiers, 90

National Centre for Scientific and Technical Information, Hanoi, 3014

National Centre for Scientific Research of Viet Nam, Ho Chi Minh City Branch, 3012

National Centre for Seismological Research, Santiago de Cuba, 617

National Centre for Sensor Research, 1132

National Centre for Studies and Research in National and Regional Development, Algiers, 90

National Centre for Technology in Education, 1130

National Centre for the Arts, Malé, 1454

National Centre for Training and Education in Prosthetics and Orthotics, Glasgow, 2257

National Centre for Tuberculosis Problems, Almaty, 1340

National Centre for Vocational Education Research (NCVER), Adelaide, 136

National Centre of Astronomy, Astrophysics and Geophysics, Algiers, 90

National Centre of Excellence in Geology, Peshawar, 1640

National Centre of Excellence in Physical Chemistry, Peshawar, 1641

National Centre of Experimental Mineralogy and Petrology, Allahabad, 1017

National Centre of Geodesy, Cartography, Photogrammetry and Remote-Sensing, Bucharest, 1785

National Centre of Haematology and Transfusiology, Sofia, 338

National Centre of Health Informatics, Sofia, 333

National Centre of Innovation and Entrepreneurship, 126

National Centre of Labour Hygiene and Occupational Diseases, Karaganda, 1340

National Centre of Preventive Medicine, Chişinău, 1491

National Centre of Public Health Protection, Sofia, 338

National Centre of Radiobiology and Radiation Protection, Sofia, 338

National Centre of Rural Medicine, Tromsø, 1616

National Centre of Social Research (EKKE), Athens, 947

National Cereals Research Institute (NCRI), Badeggi, 1591

National Chemical Laboratories Library, Khartoum, 2048

National Chemical Laboratory, Pune, 1012

National Cheng Kung University Library, 2120

National Cheng Kung University, Tainan, 2122

National Chengchi University, Taipei, 2122

National Chiao Tung University, 2122

National Chung Hsing University, 2122

National Civil Engineering Laboratory, Lisbon, 1767

National Coach Museum, Lisbon, 1771

National Coal Mining Museum for England, 2290

National College, México, 1465

National College of Arts, Lahore, 1651

National College of Business Administration & Economics, Lahore, 1651

National College of Ireland, Dublin, 1138

National College of the Arts, Mahé, 1940

National Commission for Academic Accreditation and Assessment, Riyadh, 1910

National Commission for Culture and the Arts, Santiago, 447

National Commission for Scientific and Technological Research, Santiago, 451

National Commission for University Evaluation and Accreditation, 102

National Commission on Space Activities, 109

National Committee for Historical Sciences, Bucharest, 1783

National Committee for Sacred Art and the Cultural Heritage of the Church, Fátima, 1767

National Communication Association, Washington, 2406

National Computing Centre Education, Manchester, 2366

National Computing Centre, Manchester, 2259

National Conference of University Policy, Madrid, 1995

National Conference of University Professors, Swansea, 2225

National Conservatoire, México, 1488

National Conservatory, Athens, 958

National Conservatory of Music, 1687

National Conservatory of Music, Bogotá, 591

National Conservatory of the Arts and Crafts, Nouméa, 806

National Consumer Research Centre, Helsinki, 718

National Council for Accreditation and Attestation, 1490

National Council for Accreditation of Teacher Education (NCATE), 2394

National Council for Cement and Building Materials, Ballabgarh, 1019

National Council for Culture, Arts and Letters, Safat, 1390

National Council for Education, Lisbon, 1760

National Council for Higher Education, Kampala, 2191

National Council for Science and Technology, Nairobi, 1352

National Council for Special Education, 1130

National Council for Tertiary Education, Accra, 938

National Council of Applied Economic Research, New Delhi, 1014

National Council of Education, Santiago, 447

National Council of Educational Research and Training (NCERT), New Delhi, 1005

National Council of Official Colleges of Doctors and Licentiates in Arts and Science, 1995

National Council of Scientific and Technical Research, Buenos Aires, 107

National Council of Universities, 2999

National Council on the Arts, Washington, 2397

National Council on the Humanities, Washington, 2397

National Cowboy & Western Heritage Museum, 2493

National Cryptologic Museum, Meade, 2480

National Cultural Council, 3000

National Cultural History Museum, Sunnyside, 1980

National Dairy Products Research Centre, Fermoy, 1132

National Dairy Research Institute, Karnal, 1013, 1076

National Defence Headquarters Library, Ottawa, 376

National Defence University, Islamabad, 1651

National Defense University, Akmola, 1347

National Defense University, Washington, 2579

National Diet Library, Tokyo, 1229

National Documentation and Research Centre for Education, Algiers, 90

National Drug Institute, Sofia, 338

National Dutch Graduate Research School of Polymer Science and Technology (PTN), 1544

National Dutch Graduate School of Polymer Science and Technology (PTN), 1544

National Education Association, 2396

National Education Society of Sri Lanka, 2040

National Educational Library and Museum, Budapest, 980

National Einar Jónsson Museum, 1002

National Endowment for the Arts, Washington, 2397

National Endowment for the Humanities, Washington, 2397

National English Literary Museum, Grahamstown, 1977

National Environmental Engineering Research Institute, Nagpur, 1012

National Environmental Research Institute, Roskilde, 667

National Ethnographic Museum, Kruja, 86

National Ethnographical Museum, Bissau, 965

National Ethnographical Museum, Sofia, 343

National Ethnological Museum, Lisbon, 1771

National Evaluation and Accreditation Agency, Sofia, 333

National Eye Centre, Kaduna, 1613

National Eye Institute, Bethesda, 2421

National Federation of Advanced Information Services (NFAIS), Philadelphia, 2418

National Fibre Research Centre, Kibos, 1353

National Film and Television Institute (NAFTI), Accra, 943

National Film and Television School, Beaconsfield, 2366

National Film Archives, Kabul, 80

National Fine Arts Gallery, Santo Domingo, 672

National Fine Arts Museum of Algiers, 91

National Fisheries University of Busan, 1371

National Fishery Institute, Guayaquil, 678

National Folk Museum at Cregneash, 2390

National Food Administration, Uppsala, 2059

National Food and Nutrition Commission, Lusaka, 3025

National Food Institute, Søborg, 652

National Food Research Institute, Ibaraki, 1225

National Forensic Research Centre, Ulan Bator, 1498

National Foundation for Educational Research, 2253

National Foundation on the Arts and the Humanities, Washington, 2397

National Galleries of Scotland, 2284

National Gallery, 1966

National Gallery, London, 2288

National Gallery of Armenia, 126

National Gallery of Art, Washington, 2470

National Gallery of Australia, 141

National Gallery of Canada, 379

National Gallery of Decorative Arts, Sofia, 343

National Gallery of Denmark, 657

National Gallery of Ireland, 1134

National Gallery of Modern Art, New Delhi, 1022

National Gallery of Scotland, 2284

National Gallery of the Cayman Islands, 2388

National Gallery of the Komi Republic, 1861

National Gallery of Victoria, Melbourne, 142

National Gallery of Zimbabwe, 3030

National Gandhi Museum, 1022

National Geographic Institute, 1678

National Geographic Society Library, Washington, 2435

National Geographic Society, Washington, 2404

National Geographical, Geodetic and Geophysical Committee, 451

National Geographical Institute, Madrid, 1998

National Geophysical Research Institute, Hyderabad, 1012

National Glass Museum—The Glass Factory, 1550

National Graduate School of Quality Management, Falmouth, 2686

National Handicrafts & Handlooms Museum, New Delhi, 1022

National Health and Medical Research Council, Canberra, 137

National Health Laboratories, Yangon, 1513

National Health Laboratory Service, Johannesburg, 1976

National Heart Hospital, Sofia, 338

National Heart, Lung and Blood Institute, Bethesda, 2421

National Hellenic Research Foundation, 945

National Hepatology and Tropical Medicine Research Institute, Cairo, 688

National Herbarium, Addis Ababa, 707

National Herbarium and Botanic Garden, Harare, 3030

National Herbarium of the Netherlands, 1540

National Heritage Board, Amersfoort, 1528

National Heritage Board, Singapore, 1944

National Heritage, Madrid, 2010

National Heritage, Mahé, 1940

National Heritage Museum, Lexington, 2481

National High School of Marine Sciences and Coastal Management, 95

National Historic Museum, Tiranë, 86

National Historical Archives, Madrid, 2007

National Historical Archives, Quito, 679

National Historical Library of Ukraine, Kyiv, 2202

National Historical Museum, Rio de Janeiro, 2981

National Historical Museum, Montevideo, 2981

National Historical Museum of Greece, 948

National History Museum, Ciudad Autónoma de Buenos Aires, 112

National History Museum of Latvia, 1404

National History Museum of Romania, 1795

National History Museum of the Republic of Belarus, Minsk, 242

National History Museum of Transylvania, 1795

National Horticultural Research Centre, Thika, 1352

National Horticultural Research Institute (NIHORT), Ibadan, 1591

National Hospital of Odonto—Stomatology, Hanoi, 3012

National Human Genome Research Institute (NHGRI), 2421

National Humanities Centre, Research Triangle Park, 2418

National Immunological Society, Moscow, 1828

National Infantry Museum & Soldier Center, Colombus, 2473

National Institute for Administration, 1667

National Institute for Agricultural Technology, 106

National Institute for Biological Standards and Control—A Centre of the HPA, Potters Bar, 2259

National Institute for Biomedical Imaging and Bioengineering (NIBIB), 2421

National Institute for Bioprocessing Research and Training, 1132

National Institute for Cellular Biotechnology, 1133

National Institute for Compilation and Translation, Taipei, 2119

National Institute for Education – Centre For Higher Education Research, Sofia, 337

National Institute for Educational Policy Research, 1226

National Institute for Etruscan and Italic Studies, 1165

National Institute for Food and Agricultural Research and Technology, Madrid, 2004

National Institute for Freshwater Fisheries Research (NIFFR), New Bussa, 1591

National Institute for Health and Welfare, Helsinki, 719

National Institute for Health Development, 702

National Institute for Higher Education, Minsk, 238

National Institute for Information and Documentation, Bucharest, 1790

National Institute for Interdisciplinary Science and Technology, Thiruvananthapuram, 1012

National Institute for Japanese Language, 1226

National Institute for Marine Research and Development 'Grigore Antipa', 1786

National Institute for Materials Science, Tsukuba, 1227

National Institute for Medical Research, London, 2257

National Institute for Medical Research, Mwanza Centre, 2131

National Institute for Medical Research (NIMR), 2131

National Institute for Psychobiology in Israel, 1143

National Institute for Public Administration, Oeiras, 1778

National Institute for Research and Development in Constructions, Urbanism and Sustainable Spatial Development URBAN-INCERC, 1786

National Institute for Research and Development of Environmental Protection, Bucharest, 1786

National Institute for Rural Engineering, Tsukuba, 1225

National Institute for Scientific and Industrial Research, Lusaka, 3024

National Institute for Space Research, São José dos Campos, 303

National Institute for Standards, Giza, 689

National Institute for Strategic Health Research Health Policy Library, 979

National Institute for Subatomic Physics, Amsterdam, 1541

National Institute for Technology, 1667

National Institute for the Assessment of the Educational System, Frascati, 1162

National Institute for the Physical Sciences of Matter, 1171

National Institute for the Study of Theatre, Buenos Aires, 106

National Institute for Training of Educational Administrators, Seoul, 1364

National Institute for Urban and Rural Planning, Hanoi, 3013

National Institute for Viticulture and Vinification, Codru, 1491

National Institute of Administration, Tripoli, 1417

National Institute of Adult Continuing Education (England and Wales), 2225

National Institute of Advanced Industrial Science and Technology, Tokyo, 1228

National Institute of Agricultural Botany, Cambridge, 2250

National Institute of Agrobiological Sciences (NIAS), Tsukuba, 1225

National Institute of Allergy and Infectious Diseases, Bethesda, 2421

National Institute of Animal Health, Ibaraki, 1225

National Institute of Animal Husbandry, Hanoi, 3011

National Institute of Anthropology and History, México, 1470

National Institute of Applied Optics, 1171

National Institute of Aquatic Resources, Charlottenlund, 654

National Institute of Archaeology and History of Art, Rome, 1165

National Institute of Archaeology and Museum, Sofia, 337

National Institute of Arthritis and Musculoskeletal and Skin Diseases, Bethesda, 2422

National Institute of Aviation Technology, Moscow, 1850

National Institute of Biological Resources IP, 1764

National Institute of Business, Phnom Penh, 358

National Institute of Chemical Physics and Biophysics, Tallinn, 702

National Institute of Conductive Education, 2364

National Institute of Crop Science, Ibaraki, 1225

National Institute of Dental and Craniofacial Research, Bethesda, 2422

National Institute of Deserts, Flora and Fauna, Ashgabat, 2187

National Institute of Design, Ahmedabad, 1014

National Institute of Development Administration, Bangkok, 2142

National Institute of Diabetes and Digestive and Kidney Diseases, Bethesda, 2422

National Institute of Dramatic Art, Sydney, 168

National Institute of Drug Quality Control, Hanoi, 3012

National Institute of Economic and Social Research, London, 2252

National Institute of Economic Research 'Costin C. Kiritescu', 1786

National Institute of Education, Maharagama, 2041

National Institute of Education, Minsk, 240

National Institute of Education, Phnom Penh, 358

National Institute of Educational Planning and Administration, New Delhi, 1076

National Institute of Environmental Health Sciences, Bethesda, 2422

National Institute of Epidemiological Diagnosis and Reference, México, 1469

National Institute of Fashion Technology, New Delhi, 1081

National Institute of Fine Arts and Literature, 1466

National Institute of Fine Arts and Literature (Art Education and Research), México, 1471

National Institute of Folk and Traditional Heritage, 1637

National Institute of Fruit Tree Science, Ibaraki, 1225

National Institute of General Medical Sciences, Bethesda, 2422

National Institute of Genetics, Mishima City, 1226

National Institute of Geophysics and Volcanology, 1175

National Institute of Health, 580

National Institute of Health and Family Welfare (NIHFW), New Delhi, 1081

National Institute of Health and Nutrition, Tokyo, 1226

National Institute of Health Dr. Ricardo Jorge, 1766

National Institute of Health, Lima, 1679

National Institute of Health Sciences, Tokyo, 1226

National Institute of Historical and Cultural Research, Islamabad, 1640

National Institute of Hydrology, Roorkee, 1019

National Institute of Hygiene and Epidemiology, Hanoi, 3012

National Institute of Hygiene, Guayaquil, 678

National Institute of Industrial Technology, Buenos Aires, 109

National Institute of Infectious Diseases, Tokyo, 1226

National Institute of Japanese Literature, 1226

National Institute of Japanese Literature Library, Tokyo, 1229

National Institute of Legal Medicine and Forensic Sciences, 579

National Institute of Legal Medicine, Coimbra, 1766

National Institute of Library and Information Science, Colombo, 2046

National Institute of Limnology, 109

National Institute of Livestock and Grassland Science, Tsukuba, 1225

National Institute of Medical Herbalists, Exeter, 2364

National Institute of Medicinal Materials, Hanoi, 3012

National Institute of Medicine, Ulan Bator, 1498

National Institute of Mental Health and Neurosciences, Bengaluru, 1076

National Institute of Mental Health, National Center of Neurology and Psychiatry, Ichikawa, 1227

National Institute of Mental Health (NIMH), 2422

National Institute of Meteorology and Hydrology, Bucharest, 1789

National Institute of Meteorology and Hydrology (NIMH), Sofia, 340

National Institute of Meteorology, Brasília, 302

National Institute of Metrology, Bucharest, 1789

National Institute of Naval Architecture Studies and Experiments, Rome, 1176

National Institute of Neurological Disorders and Stroke, Bethesda, 2422

National Institute of Nuclear Research, Ocoyoacac, 1469

National Institute of Nuclear Science and Technology, 750

National Institute of Nursing Research, Bethesda, 2422

National Institute of Nutrition, Hanoi, 3012

National Institute of Nutrition, Hyderabad, 1016

National Institute of Occupational and Environmental Health Research, Hanoi, 3012

National Institute of Occupational Safety and Health, Kawasaki City, 1226

National Institute of Oceanography, Panaji, 1012

National Institute of Otolaryngology, Hanoi, 3012

National Institute of Paediatrics, Hanoi, 3012

National Institute of Pharmaceutical Education and Research, Mohali, Mohali, 1071

National Institute of Pharmaceutical Research and Development (NIPRD), Idu, 1592

National Institute of Polar Research, 1227

National Institute of Population and Social Security Research, Tokyo, 1225

National Institute of Public Administration, Jakarta, 1085

National Institute of Public Administration, Lahore, 1639

National Institute of Public Administration, Lusaka, 3026

National Institute of Public Administration, Madrid, 1997

National Institute of Public Health, Cuernavaca, 1469

National Institute of Public Health Library, Cuernavaca, 1470

National Institute of Public Health of Kosovo, 1388

National Institute of Public Health, Phnom-Penh, 358

National Institute of Public Health, Tokyo, 1226

National Institute of Renaissance Studies, Florence, 1174

National Institute of Research and Development for Biological Sciences, Bucharest, 1788

National Institute of Research and Development for Chemistry and Petrochemistry, Bucharest, 1789

National Institute of Research And Development for Non-Ferrous and Rare Metals, Pantaleon, 1790

National Institute of Research and Development for Technical Physics, Iaşi, 1789

National Institute of Rock Mechanics, Kolar Gold Fields, 1017

National Institute of Roman Studies, 1174

National Institute of Rural Development, Rajendranagar, 1018

National Institute of Science Communication and Information Resources, 1020

National Institute of Science, Technology and Development Studies, New Delhi, 1012

National Institute of Seismology, Vulcanology, Meteorology and Hydrology, 961

National Institute of Social Sciences, New York, 2415

National Institute of Standardization, Santiago, 451

National Institute of Standards and Technology, Gaithersburg, 2428

National Institute of Standards and Technology Research Library, Gaithersburg, 2444

National Institute of Statistics, 1172

National Institute of Statistics and Censuses, Buenos Aires, 106

National Institute of Statistics and Economic Studies–Regional Directorate of Réunion, 806

National Institute of Statistics and Geography, Aguascalientes, 1466

National Institute of Statistics, La Paz, 282

National Institute of Statistics, Lima, 1678

National Institute of Studies and Research, Bissau, 965

National Institute of Technology, Agartala, 1076

National Institute of Technology, Bandung, 1105

National Institute of Technology, Calicut, 1076

National Institute of Technology, Durgapur, 1076

National Institute of Technology, Hamirpur, 1076

National Institute of Technology, Jamshedpur, 1076

National Statistics and Census Institute, Quito, 678

National Struggle Museum, 623

National Sugar Institute, Kanpur, 1013

National Survey and Cadastre, 654

National Swedish Museums of Military History, 2067

National Széchényi Library, 980

National Széchényi Library, Hungarian Library Institute, 980

National Szekler Museum, 1797

National Taiwan Arts Education Centre, 2119

National Taiwan College of Arts, 2125

National Taiwan Museum, 2121

National Taiwan Museum of Fine Arts, 2121

National Taiwan Normal University, 2123

National Taiwan Ocean University, 2123

National Taiwan Science Education Centre, 2121

National Taiwan University, 2123

National Taiwan University of Science and Technology, 2124

National Taras Shevchenko Museum, Kyiv, 2203

National Technical Museum, Prague, 636

National Technical Training Institute, Phnom Penh, 359

National Technical University 'Kharkiv Polytechnic Institute', 2214

National Technical University of Athens, 952

National Technical University of Athens Central Library, 948

National Textile University, Faisalabad, 1652

National Theatre Conservatory, Denver, 2554

National Theatre Museum, Lisboa, 1771

National Tile Museum, Lisboa, 1771

National Transport University, Kyiv, 2214

National Trust for Historic Preservation, Washington, 2399

National Trust for Places of Historic Interest or Natural Beauty, London, 2228

National Trust for Scotland, 2228

National Trust for the Cayman Islands, 2387

National Trust, Hughenden Manor, 2285

National Tsing Hua University, Hsinchu, 2124

National Tuberculosis Institute, Bengaluru, 1016

National Union of Architects of Ukraine, 2196

National Union of Cinematographers of Ukraine, 2196

National Universities Commission, Abuja, 1589

National University, Gazipur, 224

National University, La Jolla, 2530

National University, Manila, 1697

National University of Arts Bucharest, 1810

National University of Computer and Emerging Sciences, Islamabad, 1652

National University of East Timor, 2147

National University of Educational Planning and Administration, 1077

National University of Food Technologies, Kyiv, 2214

National University of Health Sciences, Lombard, 2612

National University of Ireland, Maynooth, 1135

National University of Ireland (NUI), 1135

National University of Kyiv-Mohyla Academy, 2206

National University of Laos, 1400

National University of Laos Central Library, 1400

National University of Lesotho, 1411

National University of Lviv 'Ivan Franko', 2206

National University of Malaysia, 1447

National University of Management, Phnom Penh, 359

National University of Modern Languages, Islamabad, 1652

National University of Mongolia, 1500

National University of Pharmacy, Kharkiv, 2211

National University of Physical Education and Sport, Bucharest, 1810

National University of Physical Education and Sports of Ukraine, 2211

National University of Samoa, 1907

National University of Science and Technology, Bulawayo, 3030

National University of Sciences and Technology, Rawalpindi, 1652

National University of Singapore, 1945

National University of Singapore Libraries, 1944

National University of Somalia, 1970

National University of Timor Lorosa'e Library, Dili, 2147

National University of Uzbekistan named after Mirzo Ulugbek, 2987

National University of Water Management and Nature Resources Use, Rivne, 2214

National Veterans Art Museum, Chicago, 2475

National Veterinary Institute DTU, Copenhagen, 653

National Veterinary Institute, Uppsala, 2058

National Veterinary Research Centre (MUGUGA), Kikuyu, 1352

National Veterinary Research Institute (NVRI), Vom, 1591

National Village Museum 'Dimitrie Gusti', 1794

National Vine Growing and Wine Producing Institute, 106

National Vision Research Institute of Australia, 137

National War College Library, Taipei, 2120

National War Museum of Scotland, 2284

National Water Research Institute, Burlington, Ontario, 374

National Waterfront Museum, Cardiff, 2283

National Wildlife Federation, Reston, 2411

National Wool Museum, Drefach Felindre, 2283

National Workshop for Handmade Paper 'St. Kliment Ohridski', 1434

National World War I Museum at Liberty Memorial, Kansas City, 2484

National Writers' Union of Ukraine, 2196

National Zoological Garden, Havana, 618

National Zoological Gardens of South Africa, Pretoria, 1976

Nationale Forskningscenter for Arbejdsmiljø, 652

Nationale Plantentuin van België, 255

Nationalekonomisk Forening, Copenhagen, 650

Nationalekonomiska Föreningen, 2055

Nationalhistoriske museum paa Frederiksborg Slot, 657

Nationalities Studies Institute, Beijing, 469

Nationalities Youth Resource Development Degree College, 1518

Nationalmuseet, Copenhagen, 656

Nationalmuseum, Stockholm, 2066

Nationalökonomische Gesellschaft, 173

Natishvili, A. N., Institute of Experimental Morphology, 813

Native American Educational Services, 2611

NATO Multimedia Library, Public Diplomacy Division, 259

Natrona County Public Library, 2462

Natsagdorj Museum, 1499

Náttúrufræðistofnun Íslands, 1002

Natura Artis Magistra, 1531

Natural Environment Research Council (NERC), Swindon, 2258

Natural Freezing and Food Technology Institute, Ulan Bator, 1498

Natural History and Historical Society for the Lippe Region, 825

Natural History Museum, 855

Natural History Museum Alfredo Dugès Guanajuato University, 1471

Natural History Museum, Ankara, 2162

Natural History Museum, Århus, 656

Natural History Museum Belgrade, 1923

Natural History Museum, Berlin, 849

Natural History Museum, Campinas, 306

Natural History Museum Complex, Constanţa, 1795

Natural History Museum, Kathmandu, 1526

Natural History Museum, Library and Archives, London, 2274

Natural History Museum, London, 2288

Natural History Museum, Obafemi Awolowo University, 1593

Natural History Museum of Barcelona, 2008

Natural History Museum of Barcelona, Geology Building, 2008

Natural History Museum of Los Angeles County, 2467

Natural History Museum of Montenegro, 1503

Natural History Museum of the National University of San Marcos, 1680

Natural History Museum of the University of Basrah, 1124

Natural History Museum of Zimbabwe, Bulawayo, 3030

Natural History Museum, Prague, 636

Natural History Museum Rijeka, 609

Natural History Museum, Salzburg, 186

Natural History Museum, Santiago, 453

Natural History Museum, Tórshavn, 666

Natural History Museum, Ulan Bator, 1499

Natural History Museum, University of Kansas, 2477

Natural History Museum, University of Oslo, 1619

Natural History Museum, Vienna, 187

Natural History Society for Bielefeld and the Region, 824

Natural History Society of Hamburg, 825

Natural History Society of Lower Lusatia, 825

Natural History Society of Oulu, 716

Natural History Society of Puerto Rico, 2971

Natural History Society of Schwäbisch Gmünd, 825

Natural History Society of Slovenia, 1964

Natural Resources Canada, Headquarters Library, 376

Natural Resources Development College, Lusaka, 3026

Natural Resources Institute, Chatham Maritime, 2263

Natural Science Museum Complex, Galaţi, 1796

Natural Science Museum, Madrid, 2010

Natural Science Museum of the Ilmen State Reserve, 1856

Natural Science Museum, Plovdiv, 343

Natural Science Museum, Tiranë, 86

Natural Sciences and Engineering Research Council of Canada (NSERC), 373

Nature and Agriculture Museum, 575

Nature Conservancy, Arlington, 2411

Nature Foundation St Maarten, 1571

Nature Kenya, the East Africa Natural History Society, Nairobi, 1352

Nature Research Centre, Vilnius, 1422

Nature Reserves Federation, 825

Naturforschende Gesellschaft Bamberg eV, 836

Naturforschende Gesellschaft in Basel, 2089

Naturforschende Gesellschaft in Bern, 2089

Naturforschende Gesellschaft zu Freiburg im Breisgau, 836

Naturhistorische Gesellschaft Hannover, 825

Naturhistorisches Museum, Bern, 2096

Naturhistorisches Museum Mainz, 855

Naturhistorisches Museum, Vienna, 187

Naturhistorisk Museum, 656

Naturhistorisk museum, Universitetet i Oslo, 1619

Naturhistoriska Centralmuseet, Helsinki, 721

Naturhistoriska Riksmuseet, 2067

Naturkunde-Museum Bamberg, 856

Naturkundeverein Schwäbisch Gmünd eV, 825

Naturmuseum St Gallen, 2097

Naturskyddsföreningen, 2057

Naturwissenschaftliche Gesellschaft Winterthur, 2089

Naturwissenschaftlicher und Historischer Verein für das Land Lippe eV, 825

Naturwissenschaftlicher Verein der Niederlausitz eV, 825

Naturwissenschaftlicher Verein für Bielefeld und Umgegend eV, 824

Naturwissenschaftlicher Verein für Kärnten, 176

Naturwissenschaftlicher Verein in Hamburg, 825

Naturwissenschaftlicher Verein zu Bremen, 825

Natuurhistorisch Museum Maastricht, 1551

Natuurmonumenten, 's-Graveland, 1530

Nauru Phosphate Corporation Museum, Aiwo, 1523

Nautical Museum, Castletown, 2390

Nava Nalanda Mahavihara, 1077

Navajo Technical College, 2765

Naval Aerospace Medical Institute, Pensacola, 2422

Naval College, 2222

Naval Hydro-Oceanographic Office, Jakarta, 1086

Naval Institute, Aktau, 1350

Naval Institute of Technology, Naval, 1705

Naval Library, Lisbon, 1768

Naval Museum, 2067

Naval Museum, Madrid, 2010

Naval Postgraduate School, Monterey, 2531

Navitas College of Public Safety, 171

Navy Department Library, Washington, 2435

Nazarbayev University, 1347

Nazarene Bible College, 2554

Nazarene Theological Seminary, 2740

Nazareth College, 2789

Nazo Annah Library, 81

NBS—Múzeum mincí a medailí, Kremnica, 1954

NCB Naturalis, 1551

NCB Naturalis Library, 1547

Ndejje University, 2194

Ndola Public Library, 3025

Neamţ District Museums Complex, 1796

Neamţ 'G. T. Kirileanu' District Library, 1793

Neanderthal-Museum, 855

Neapolitan Society of Italian History, 1165

Near East School of Theology, Beirut, 1410

Near East School of Theology Library, Beirut, 1407

Near East University, 627

Neath Port Talbot College, 2385

Neath Port Talbot Library and Information Service, 2279

Nebraska Christian College, 2749

Nebraska Methodist College of Nursing and Allied Health, 2749

Nebraska State Historical Society, 2485

Nebraska State Historical Society Library and Archives, Lincoln, 2448

Nebraska State Library, Lincoln, 2448

Nebraska Wesleyan University, 2750
NECSA (South African Nuclear Energy Corporation), Pretoria, 1976
NED University of Engineering and Technology, 1652
NED University of Engineering and Technology Central Library, 1643
Nederlands Agronomisch-Historisch Instituut, 1534
Nederlands Architectuur Instituut, 1528
Nederlands Architectuurinstituut, 1552
Nederlands Cultuurhistorisch Instituut, Pretoria, 1973
Nederlands Fotomuseum, 1552
Nederlands Genootschap voor Esthetica, 1531
Nederlands Institute of Ecology, 1541
Nederlands Instituut voor Ecologie, 1541
Nederlands Instituut voor Internationale Betrekkingen 'Clingendael', 1536
Nederlands Instituut voor Neurowetenschappen, 1538
Nederlands Instituut voor Onderzoek in de Katalyse, 1540
Nederlands Interdisciplinair Demografisch Instituut (NIDI-KNAW), 1536
Nederlands Openluchtmuseum, 1549
Nederlands Psychoanalytisch Genootschap, 1532
Nederlands Scheepvaartmuseum Amsterdam, 1549
Nederlands Studiecentrum Criminaliteit en Rechtshandhaving (NCSR), 1536
Nederlands Tegelmuseum, 1551
Nederlandsch Economisch-Historisch Archief (NEHA), 1529
Nederlandse Entomologische Vereniging, 1531
Nederlandse Museumvereniging, 1528
Nederlandse Mycologische Vereniging, 1531
Nederlandse Natuurkundige Vereniging, 1531
Nederlandse Onderzoekschool voor Theologie en Religiewetenschap (NOSTER), 1542
Nederlandse Organisatie voor Toegepast—Natuurwetenschappelijk Onderzoek (TNO), 1539
Nederlandse Organisatie voor Wetenschappelijk Onderzoek (NWO), 1539
Nederlandse Ornithologische Unie, 1531
Nederlandse Tuinbouwraad, 1528
Nederlandse Vereniging van Pedagogen en Onderwijskundigen (NVO), 1527
Nederlandse Vereniging voor Beroepsbeoefenaren in de bibliotheek-, informatie- en kennissector (NVB), 1528
Nederlandse Vereniging voor Godsdienstwijsbegeerte, 1531
Nederlandse Vereniging voor Heelkunde, 1530
Nederlandse Vereniging voor Internationaal Recht, 1529
Nederlandse Vereniging voor Logica en Wijsbegeerte der Exacte Wetenschappen, 1532
Nederlandse Vereniging voor Neurologie, 1530
Nederlandse Vereniging voor Orthodontische Studie, 1530
Nederlandse Vereniging voor Parasitologie, 1531
Nederlandse Vereniging voor Psychiatrie, 1530
Nederlandse Vereniging voor Tropische Geneeskunde en Internationale Gezondheidszorg, 1530
Nederlandse Vereniging voor Wetenschapsfilosofie, 1532
Nederlandse Zoötechnische Vereniging, 1531
Nederlands-Vlaamse Accreditatieorganisatie, 1527
Needham Research Institute, 2267

Negev Museum, Be'ersheva, 1146
Negev Nuclear Research Centre, 1144
Nehemia Levzion Centre for Islamic Studies, 1154
Nehru Memorial Museum & Library, 1020
Nei Monggol Autonomous Region Library, 471
Neilson Hays Library, Bangkok, 2136
Neiraku Museum, 1232
Neka Art Museum, 1087
Nekrasov Apartment Museum, St Petersburg, 1860
Nelson A. Rockefeller Center at Dartmouth College, 2419
Nelson County Public Library, 2441
Nelson Mandela Metropolitan Art Museum, Port Elizabeth, 1980
Nelson Mandela Metropolitan Libraries, 1978
Nelson Mandela Metropolitan University Library and Information Services, 1978
Nelson Mandela Metropolitan University, Port Elizabeth, 1981
Nelson Marlborough Institute of Technology, 1584
Nelson Memorial Public Library, Apia, 1907
Nelson Provincial Museum, 1578
Nelson-Atkins Museum of Art, 2484
Nemirovich-Danchenko, V., Flat-Museum, 1857
NEMO, Amsterdam, 1549
Neo-Pythagorean Institute, Curitiba, 302
Nepal Academy, 1524
Nepal Academy of Science and Technology, 1524
Nepal Agricultural Research Council, 1525
Nepal Bharat Library, 1525
Nepal Development Research Institute, 1525
Nepal Institute for Policy Studies, 1525
Nepal Institute of Development Studies, 1525
Nepal Institute of Peace, 1524
Nepal National Library, 1525
Nepal Olympic Museum, 1526
Nepal Pragya Pratisthan, 1524
Nepal Sanskrit University, 1526
Néprajzi Múzeum, Budapest, 982
Nerman Museum of Contemporary Art, 2477
Nesmeyanov, A. N., Institute of Elementary Organic Compounds, Moscow, 1845
Netaji Subhas Open University, 1047
Netherlands Architecture Institute, 1528
Netherlands Association for Animal Husbandry, 1531
Netherlands Association for Library, Information and Knowledge Professionals, 1528
Netherlands Association of Universities of Applied Sciences, 1527
Netherlands Branch of International Law Association, 1529
Netherlands Cancer Institute—Antoni van Leeuwenhoek Hospital, 1538
Netherlands Centre for Biodiversity Naturalis, 1551
Netherlands Centre of the International PEN, 1530
Netherlands Economic-Historical Archives Society, 1529
Netherlands Entomological Society, 1531
Netherlands Graduate Research School of Science, Technology and Modern Culture (WTMC), 1539
Netherlands Graduate School of Urban and Regional Research, 1534
Netherlands Horticultural Council, 1528
Netherlands Institute for Advanced Study in the Humanities and Social Sciences (NIAS), 1542
Netherlands Institute for Art History, 1529
Netherlands Institute for Catalysis Research, 1540

Netherlands Institute for Neuroscience, 1538
Netherlands Institute for the Study of Crime and Law Enforcement, 1536
Netherlands Institute in Turkey, 2160
Netherlands Institute of Applied Geoscience TNO—National Geological Survey, 1541
Netherlands Institute of International Relations 'Clingendael', 1536
Netherlands Interdisciplinary Demographic Institute, 1536
Netherlands Maritime Museum Amsterdam, 1549
Netherlands Museums Association, 1528
Netherlands Open Air Museum, 1549
Netherlands Organization for Applied Scientific Research, 1539
Netherlands Organization for Scientific Research, 1539
Netherlands Orthodontics Society, 1530
Netherlands Physical Society, 1531
Netherlands Psychiatric Association, 1530
Netherlands Psychoanalytical Association, 1532
Netherlands Public Library Association, 1529
Netherlands Research School in Process Technology, 1539
Netherlands School for Advanced Studies in Theology and Religion, 1542
Netherlands Society for Neurology, 1530
Netherlands Society for Parasitology, 1531
Netherlands Society for Statistics and Operations Research, 1531
Netherlands Society for Tropical Medicine and International Health, 1530
Netherlands Society of Public Health and Science, 1530
Netherlands Theatre Institute, 1529
Netspar, Network for Studies on Pensions, Ageing and Retirement, 1533
Network for Religion in Public Life, Exeter, 2262
Neue Galerie, Kassel, 854
Neue Galerie, New York, 2490
Neue Nationalgalerie, Berlin, 850
Neue Sammlung–Staatliches Museum für Angewandte Kunst, Munich, 855
Neumann János Számitógéptudományi Társaság, Budapest, 975
Neumann University, 2861
Neurobiology Institute, Buenos Aires, 108
Neuropathogenesis Unit, Edinburgh, 2249
Neuropsychiatric Research Institute, Tokyo, 1227
Neuroscience Institute, 1171
Nevada Museum of Art, 2486
Nevada State College, 2751
Nevada State Museum and Historical Society, 2486
Nevada System of Higher Education, 2751
Neville Public Museum, 2501
Nevis Historical and Conservation Society, 1904
Nevis Public Library, 1904
New Amsterdam Technical Institute, 967
New Asia College, 573
New Britain Museum of American Art, 2468
New Brunswick Museum, 378
New Brunswick Theological Seminary, 2759
New Bulgarian University, 346
New Caledonia Archive Service, 805
New Caledonia Centre for Pedagogic Documentation, 805
New Caledonia Society for Historical Studies, 805
New Caledonian Agronomic Institute, 805
New Carlsberg Foundation, 650

New Castle Historical Society, 2469
New College Durham, 2361
New College, Edinburgh, 2376
New College Library, Oxford, 2279
New College Nottingham, 2361
New College of Florida, 2586
New College, Oxford, 2348
New College, Toronto, 432
New England Aquarium, 2424
New England Association of Schools and Colleges: Commission on Institutions of Higher Education (NEASC—CIHE), Bedford, 2394
New England College, 2756
New England College of Business and Finance, 2686
New England College of Optometry, 2686
New England Conservatory of Music, 2687
New England Institute of Art, 2687
New England Institute of Technology, 2880
New England Law—Boston, 2687
New English Art Club, 2232
New Hampshire Law Library, 2449
New Hampshire State Library, 2449
New Hope Christian College, 2845
New Jersey City University, 2759
New Jersey Institute of Technology, Newark, 2759
New Jersey Maritime Museum, 2487
New Jersey State Library, Trenton, 2450
New Jersey State Museum, 2487
New Masters Gallery, 851
New Mexico Archives and Historical Services Division, 2450
New Mexico Bureau of Geology and Mineral Resources, 2428
New Mexico Highlands University, 2765
New Mexico Museum of Art, 2488
New Mexico Museum of Natural History and Science, 2488
New Mexico Space Grant Consortium, 2429
New Mexico State Library, 2450
New Mexico State Monuments, 2488
New Mexico State University, 2765
New Mexico State University Museum, 2488
New Mexico Tech, 2765
New Mexico Water Resources Research Institute, 2424
New National Gallery, 850
New Orleans Baptist Theological Seminary, 2650
New Orleans Museum of Art, 2478
New Orleans Public Library, 2442
New Plymouth Astronomical Society, 1576
New School, 2789
New South Wales and Institute of Psychiatry, Parramatta BC, 168
New University of Lisbon, 1777
New York Academy of Medicine, 2409
New York Academy of Medicine Library, 2452
New York Academy of Sciences, 2397
New York Botanical Garden, 2424
New York Chiropractic College, 2789
New York City College of Technology (CUNY), 2771
New York College of Podiatric Medicine, 2790
New York Historical Society, 2404
New York Institute of Technology, Abu Dhabi, 2222
New York Institute of Technology, Old Westbury, NY, 2790
New York Law Institute Library, 2452
New York Law School, 2790
New York Medical College, 2790
New York Public Library, 2452
New York School of Interior Design, 2790
New York State Archives, Albany, 2452
New York State Library, 2452
New York Theological Seminary, 2790
New York University, 2790
New York University Libraries, 2452
New York University Tisch School of Arts Asia, 1948

New Zealand Academy of Fine Arts, 1578
New Zealand Archaeological Association (Inc.), 1574
New Zealand Association of Scientists, 1574
New Zealand Book Council, 1573
New Zealand Cartographic Society (Inc.), 1574
New Zealand Computer Society (Inc.), 1575
New Zealand Council for Educational Research, 1575
New Zealand Ecological Society (Inc.), 1574
New Zealand Educational Institute, 1572
New Zealand Freshwater Sciences Society (Inc.), 1574
New Zealand Geographical Society Inc., Auckland, 1574
New Zealand Historic Places Trust, 1574
New Zealand Historical Association, 1574
New Zealand Hydrological Society, 1575
New Zealand Institute for Industrial Research and Development (Industrial Research Ltd), 1576
New Zealand Institute of Agricultural and Horticultural Science, 1573
New Zealand Institute of Architects, 1573
New Zealand Institute of Chemistry (Inc.), 1575
New Zealand Institute of Economic Research, 1575
New Zealand Institute of Food Science and Technology (Inc.), 1575
New Zealand Institute of Forestry, 1573
New Zealand Institute of International Affairs, 1573
New Zealand Institute of Physics, 1575
New Zealand Institute of Surveyors, 1573
New Zealand Law Society, 1573
New Zealand Law Society Library, Otago Branch, 1577
New Zealand Library Association (Inc.), 1573
New Zealand Maori Arts and Crafts Institute, 1573
New Zealand Marine Sciences Society, 1574
New Zealand Mathematical Society, 1575
New Zealand Medical Association, 1574
New Zealand Microbiological Society (Inc.), 1574
New Zealand Psychological Society (Inc.), 1575
New Zealand Qualifications Authority, Wellington, 1572
New Zealand Society for Biochemistry and Molecular Biology (Inc.), 1575
New Zealand Society for Earthquake Engineering, 1575
New Zealand Society for Parasitology Inc., 1574
New Zealand Society of Animal Production Inc., 1573
New Zealand Society of Authors (PEN NZ Inc.), 1574
New Zealand Society of Plant Biologists, 1574
New Zealand Society of Soil Science Inc., 1573
New Zealand Statistical Association (Inc.), 1575
New Zealand Veterinary Association (Inc.), Wellington, 1573
Newark Museum, 2487
Newark Public Library, 2450
Newberry College, 2885
Newberry Library, 2438
Newbold College of Higher Education, 2361
Newbury College, 2687
Newcastle Libraries and Information Service, 2277
Newcastle Region Library, 139
Newcastle University, 2298
Newcastle University The Robinson Library, 2277

Newcomen Society for the Study of the History of Engineering and Technology, 2247
Newfoundland and Labrador Public Libraries, St John's, 375
Newham College, 2361
Newham Public Libraries, 2274
Newman Grove Public Library, 2448
Newman University, 2641
Newman University College, 2359
Newnham College, Cambridge, 2310
Newnham College Library, 2266
Newport Art Museum & Art Association, 2495
Newport Community Learning and Libraries, 2277
Newport Museum and Art Gallery, 2290
Newports Institute of Communications and Economics, 1652
Newton County Library System, 2437
Newton Thilay University, 361
Nexus Institute, 1533
Nexus Instituut, 1533
Nez Perce National Historical Park, Spalding, 2474
Nezu Institute, 1232
Ngee Ann Polytechnic, Singapore, 1947
Nghe-Tinh Museum, 3014
Nha Trang Institute of Hygiene and Epidemiology, 3012
Nha Trang University, Nhatrang City, 3018
NHL Hogeschool, 1563
NHL University, 1563
NHTV Breda University of Applied Sciences, 1563
NHTV Internationaal Hoger Onderwijs Breda, 1563
NI Institute and Museum Bitola, 1434
N.I. Vavilov All Russian Research Institute of the Plant Industry, St Petersburg, 1832
NIAB, Cambridge, 2250
Niagara University, 2796
Nichibei Hougakukai, 1218
Nicholas Copernicus University of Toruń, 1737
Nicholas County Public Library, 2441
Nicholls State University, 2652
Nichols College, 2687
Nicholson Museum, Sydney, 141
Nicolaï Siadristy's Microminiature Museum, 98
Nicolae Gh. Lupu Institute of Internal Medicine, 1788
Nicolae Iorga Institute of History, 1787
'Nicolae Iorga' Library, 1793
'Nicolae Testemiţanu' State Medical and Pharmaceutical University, 1493
Nicolae Titulescu University of Bucharest, 1810
Nicolaysen Art Museum, 2502
Niederösterreichische Landesbibliothek, 184
Niederösterreichisches Landesarchiv, 184
Niederösterreichisches Landesmuseum, 187
Niedersächsische Institut für Wirtschaftsforschung (NIW), 833
Niedersächsische Staats- und Universitätsbibliothek Göttingen, 843
Niedersächsisches Landesarchiv, 843
Niedersächsisches Landesarchiv, Staatsarchiv Bückeburg, 841
Niedersächsisches Landesarchiv—Staatsarchiv Osnabrück, Osnabrück, 846
Niedersächsisches Landesmuseum Hannover, 853
Niedersächsisches Staatsarchiv Aurich, 839
Niedersächsisches Staatsarchiv in Oldenburg, 846
Niedersächsisches Staatsarchiv, Wolfenbüttel, 848
Niels Bohr Institutet, Copenhagen, 654
NiĞde Üniversitesi, 2179
Niger Delta State University, 1609
Nigerian Academy of Science, 1590
Nigerian Bar Association, 1590
Nigerian Building and Road Research Institute (NBRRI), 1592

Nigerian Dental Association, 1590
Nigerian Educational Research Council, 1592
Nigerian Geographical Association, 1590
Nigerian Institute for Oceanography and Marine Research (NIOMR), 1592
Nigerian Institute for Oil Palm Research (NIFOR), 1591
Nigerian Institute for Trypanosomiasis Research (NITR), 1592
Nigerian Institute of Architects, 1590
Nigerian Institute of International Affairs, 1590
Nigerian Institute of Management, 1590
Nigerian Institute of Medical Research (NIMR), Lagos, 1592
Nigerian Institute of Social and Economic Research, 1592
Nigerian Library Association, 1590
Nigerian Medical Association, 1590
Nigerian Political Science Association (NPSA), 1590
Nigerian Society for Microbiology, 1590
Nigerian Society of Engineers, 1591
Nigerian Stored Products Research Institute (NSPRI), 1592
Nigerian Veterinary Medical Association, 1589
Nihon Boeki Shinkokiko, Ajia Keizai Kenkyusho, 1225
Nihon Bunseki Kagaku-Kai, 1222
Nihon Dobutsu Gakkai, 1222
Nihon Dokubungakkai, 1219
Nihon Eibungakkai, 1220
Nihon Eisei Gakkai, 1220
Nihon Engeki Gakkai, 1219
Nihon Esperanto Gakkai, 1220
Nihon Gakko-hoken Gakkai, 1219
Nihon Gakujutsu Kaigi, 1217
Nihon Gakujutsu Shinko-kai, 1217
Nihon Gengogakkai, 1220
Nihon Genshiryoku Gakkai, 1224
Nihon Hakubutsukan Kyokai, 1218
Nihon Hassei Seibutsu Gakkai, Sendai, 1222
Nihon Hikaku Kyoiku Gakkai, 1219
Nihon Hinyokika Gakkai, 1220
Nihon Hotetsu Shika Gakkai, 1220
Nihon Ikushu Gakkai, 1217
Nihon Indogaku Bukkyôgakukai, 1224
Nihon Ishi-Kai, 1220
Nihon Ju-í Gakkai, 1217
Nihon Junkanki Gakkai, 1220
Nihon Kagakushi Gakkai, 1222
Nihon Kairui Gakkai, 1222
Nihon Kakuigakukai, 1220
Nihon Kasai Gakkai, 1224
Nihon Keizai Gakkai, 1218
Nihon Keizai Kenkyu Center, 1225
Nihon Kikai Gakkai, 1224
Nihon Kinyu Gakkai, 1218
Nihon Kobutsu Kagaku Kai, 1222
Nihon Koho Gakkai, 1218
Nihon Kokogakkai, 1219
Nihon Koku Eisei Gakkai, 1220
Nihon Koku Geka Gakkai, 1220
Nihon Kokuka Gakkai, 1220
Nihon Kontyû Gakkai, 1222
Nihon Kyoiku Gakkai, 1219
Nihon Kyoiku-shakai Gakkai, 1219
Nihon Kyoiku-shinri Gakkai, 1219
Nihon Kyosei Shikagakkai, 1220
Nihon Masuika Gakkai, 1220
Nihon Mendel Kyokai, 1222
Nihon Minji Soshoho Gakkai, 1218
Nihon Naika Gakkai, 1220
Nihon Nensho Gakkai, 1223
Nihon Nogyo-Kisho Gakkai, 1223
Nihon No-Shinkei Geka Gakkai, 1220
Nihon Oyo Toshitsu Kagaku Kai, 1217
Nihon Rinrigakukai, 1223
Nihon Ronen Igakukai, 1220
Nihon Sanshi Gakkai, 1217
Nihon Seishin Shinkei Gakkai, 1220
Nihon Seitai Gakkai, 1222
Nihon Seppyo Gakkai, 1223
Nihon Shika Hoshasen Gakkai, 1220
Nihon Shika Igakkai, 1220
Nihon Shinringakkai, 1217
Nihon Shiritsu Daigaku Kyokai, Tokyo, 1217

Nihon Shokaki-byo Gakkai, 1220
Nihon Shokubutsu Bunrui Gakkai, 1222
Nihon Shonika Gakkai, 1220
Nihon Shūkyō Gakkai, 1224
Nihon Sugaku Kai, 1222
Nihon Syoyakugakkai, 1220
Nihon Teii Kinou Shinkei Geka Gakkai, 1220
Nihon Tokei Gakkai, 1218
Nihon Toshokan Kyokai, 1218
Nihon University, 1320
Nihon Yakuri Gakkai, 1220
Nihon Zoen Gakkai, 1217
Nihon Zosen Gakkai, 1217
Niigata Prefectural Library, 1229
Niigata University, 1272
Niigata University Library, 1229
Nijkerk Library, 1547
Nijmeegs Instituut voor Sociaal en Cultureel Onderzoek (NISCO), 1542
Nijmegen Centre for Evidence Based Practice (NCEBP), 1538
Nijmegen Centre for Molecular Life Sciences (NCMLS), 1540
Nijmegen Institute for Social and Cultural Research, 1542
Nijmegen Intitute for Infection, Inflammation and Immunity, 1539
Nikita Botanical Gardens, Yalta, 2203
Nikola Tesla Museum, 1923
Nikola Tesla Society, 1921
Nikolaev Institute of Inorganic Chemistry, Novosibirsk, 1845
Nikolai Rubinstein Museum, 1857
Nikos—Dutch Institute for Knowledge Intensive Entrepreneurship, 1533
Nile Valley University, 2049
Nimba Research Laboratory, 1413
Nimitz Library, 2444
Ningxia Library, 472
Ningxia Medical College, 527
Ninnaji Reihôden, 1231
Ninth September University, Izmir, 2168
NIOD Institute for War, Holocaust and Genocide Studies, 1537
NIOD Instituut voor Oorlogs-, Holocaust- en Genocide Studies, 1537
NIOZ Koninklijk Nederlands Instituut voor Zeeonderzoek, 1541
NIOZ Royal Netherlands Institute for Sea Research, 1541
Nipissing University, 390
Nippon Bitamin Gakkai, 1221
Nippon Bunko Gakkai, 1223
Nippon Butsuri Gakkai, 1223
Nippon Byorigakkai, 1221
Nippon Chikusan Gakkai, 1217
Nippon Chishitsu Gakkai, 1223
Nippon Chô Gakkai, 1222
Nippon Dai-Yonki Gakkai, 1223
Nippon Dental University, 1321
Nippon Dobutsu Shinri Gakkai, 1223
Nippon Dojo-Hiryo Gakkai, 1217
Nippon Dokyo Gakkai, 1224
Nippon Eisei-Dobutu Gakkai, 1222
Nippon Gakushiin, 1217
Nippon Gan Gakkai, 1221
Nippon Ganka Gakkai, 1221
Nippon Geka Gakkai, 1221
Nippon Hifu-ka Gakkai, 1221
Nippon Hoi Gakkai, 1221
Nippon Hoshakai Gakkai, 1218
Nippon Hoshasen Eikyo Gakkai, 1221
Nippon Hotetsu-Gakkai, 1218
Nippon Iden Gakkai, 1222
Nippon Igaku Hôshasen Gakkai, 1221
Nippon Jibi-Inkoka Gakkai, 1221
Nippon Jinruigaku Kai, 1224
Nippon Kagaku Kyoiku Gakkai, 1219
Nippon Kagakukai, 1223
Nippon Kaibo Gakkai, 1221
Nippon Kaisui Gakkai, 1223
Nippon Kaiyo Gakkai, 1223
Nippon Kansenshoh Gakkai, 1221
Nippon Kazan Gakkai, 1223
Nippon Keidanren, 1225
Nippon Keiei Gakkai, 1218
Nippon Keiho Gakkai, 1218
Nippon Keizai Seisaku Gakkai, 1218
Nippon Kekkaku-byo Gakkai, 1221
Nippon Kessho Gakkai, 1223

Nippon Ketsueki Gakkai, 1221
Nippon Kin Gakkai, 1222
Nippon Kinzoku Gakkai, 1224
Nippon Kisei-chu Gakkai, 1221
Nippon Kisho Gakkai, 1223
Nippon Kogakukai, 1224
Nippon Kokai Gakkai, 1223
Nippon Kokogaku Kyokai, 1219
Nippon Koku Ūchu Gakkai, 1224
Nippon Koseibutsu Gakkai, 1223
Nippon Koshu-Eisei Kyokai, 1221
Nippon Kumo Gakkai, 1222
Nippon Mingeikan, 1232
Nippon Nougei Kagaku Kai, 1217
Nippon Ongaku Gakkai, 1219
Nippon Onkyo Gakkai, 1223
Nippon Onsei Gakkai, 1220
Nippon Oriento Gakkai, 1219
Nippon Oyo-Dobutsu-Konchu Gakkai,
    1222
Nippon Rai Gakkai, 1221
Nippon Research Center Ltd, 1225
Nippon Rikusui Gakkai, 1222
Nippon Saikingakkai, 1221
Nippon Sakumotsu Gakkai, 1217
Nippon Sanka-Fujinka Gakkai, 1221
Nippon Seibutsuchiri Gakkai, 1219
Nippon Seibutsu-Kogaku Kai, 1217
Nippon Seikei Geka Gakkai, 1221
Nippon Seiri Gakkai, 1221
Nippon Seiyo Koten Gakkai, 1220
Nippon Seiyoshigakukai, 1219
Nippon Seizi Gakkai, 1218
Nippon Seramikusu Kyoukai, 1224
Nippon Shakai Gakkai, 1224
Nippon Shakai Shinri Gakkai, 1223
Nippon Shashin Gakkai, 1224
Nippon Shika Hozon Gakkai, 1221
Nippon Shinkei Gakkai, 1221
Nippon Shinkeikagaku Gakkai, 1221
Nippon Shinri Gakkai, 1223
Nippon Shogyo Gakkai, 1219
Nippon Shokubutsu Gakkai, 1222
Nippon Shokubutsu Seiri Gakkai, 1222
Nippon Shokubutsu-Byori Gakkai, 1217
Nippon Sokuchi Gakkai, 1223
Nippon Sport Science University, 1321
Nippon Sugaku Kyoiku Gakkai, 1219
Nippon Suisan Gakkai, 1217
Nippon Taiiku Gakkai, 1219
Nippon Tekko Kyoukai, 1224
Nippon Temmon Gakkai, 1223
Nippon Tonyo-byo Gakkai, 1221
Nippon Toshi Keikaku Gakkai, 1218
Nippon Toshokan Joho Gakkai, 1218
Nippon Tribologi Gakkai, 1224
Nippon Uirusu Gakkai, 1221
Nippon Yakugaku-Kai, 1221
Nippon Yukagaku Kai, 1223
Nippon Yuketsu Gakkai, 1221
Nirma University of Science and
    Technology, 1048
Nivaagaard Picture Gallery, 658
Nivaagaards Malerisamling, 658
NIVA—Norsk Institutt for
    Vannforskning, 1617
NIVA—Norwegian Institute for Water
    Research, 1617
Nixon Presidential Library and
    Museum, 2432
Nizami Gandjavi State Museum of
    Azerbaijan Literature, 204
Nizami Institute of Literature, 203
Nizamiah and Japal-Rangapur
    Observatories and Centre of
    Advanced Study in Astronomy, 1017
Nizam's Institute of Medical Sciences,
    1048
Nizhne-Volzhsky Agricultural Research
    Institute, 1832
Nizhnii Novgorod Historical Museum,
    1858
Nizhnii Novgorod Institute for Skin and
    Venereal Diseases, 1838
Nizhnii Novgorod Institute of Industrial
    Hygiene and Occupational Diseases,
    1838
Nizhnii Novgorod N. I. Lobachevsky
    State University Central Library,
    1854
Nizhnii Novgorod Research Institute of
    Traumatology and Orthopaedics,
    1838

Nizhnii Novgorod State Agricultural
    Academy, 1896
Nizhnii Novgorod State Conservatoire
    'M. I. Glinka', 1900
Nizhnii Novgorod State Linguistics
    University 'N. A. Dobrolyubov',
    1883
Nizhnii Novgorod State Medical
    Academy, 1897
Nizhnii Novgorod State Museum of Art,
    1858
Nizhnii Novgorod State Technical
    University, 1889
Nizhnii Novgorod State University 'N. I.
    Lobachevsky', 1872
Nizhnii Novgorod State University of
    Architecture and Civil Engineering,
    1889
Nizomiy Nomidagi Toshkent Davlat
    Pedagogika Universiteti, 2987
Nnamdi Azikiwe University, 1603
Noakhali Science and Technology
    University, 224
Nobel Library of the Swedish Academy,
    2062
Nobel Museum, 2067
Nobelmuseet, 2067
Nobelmuseet i Karlskoga, 2064
Noble Maritime Collection, Staten
    Island, 2490
Nodibināӣums Augstākās izglītības
    kvalitātes novrtšanas centrs, Rīga,
    1402
Noginsk Research Centre, Moscow,
    1845
Nógrádi Történeti Múzeum, 984
Noguchi Institute, Tokyo, 1228
Nogyo-Doboku Gakkai, 1224
Nogyokikai Gakkai, 1217
Nonferrous Metals Society of China, 465
Nong Lam University, 3018
Non-Traditional Energetics and
    Energy-Saving Scientific and
    Engineering Centre, Minsk, 241
Noordbrabants Museum, 1552
Noordelijk Scheepvaartmuseum, 1550
Noord-Hollands Archief, 1546
Nord Anglia Education, Burton-upon-
    Trent, 2225
Nordenfjeldske Kunstindustrimuseum,
    1620
Nordens Institut i Grønland, 666
Nordens Institut på Åland, 737
Nordic Africa Institute, Uppsala, 2058
Nordic Centre for Spatial Development,
    Stockholm, 2058
Nordic Institute for Theoretical Physics,
    2060
Nordic Institute of Asian Studies,
    Copenhagen, 50
Nordic Institute on Åland, 737
Nordic Library at Athens, 948
Nordic Museum, Stockholm, 2067
Nordic Watercolour Museum, 2068
Nordisk Institut for Asienstudier, 50
Nordiska Afrikainstitutet, 2058
Nordiska Akvarellmuseet, 2068
Nordiska museet, 2067
Nordita, 2060
NORDITA (Nordic Institute for
    Theoretical Physics), Stockholm, 74
Nordland Research Institute, 1616
Nordlandsforskning, 1616
Nordregio, 2058
Nordrhein-Westfälische Akademie der
    Wissenschaften und der Künste,
    820
Norfolk Library and Information
    Service, 2278
Norfolk Museums and Archaeology
    Service, 2290
Norfolk Public Library, 2460
Norfolk State University, 2934
Norges Forskningsråd, 1614
Norges Geologiske Undersøkelse, 1617
Norges Geotekniske Institutt (NGI),
    1617
Norges Handelshøyskole, 1631
Norges Idrettshøgskole, 1632
Norges Musikkhøgskole, 1632
Norges Tekniske Vitenskapsakademi,
    1616
Norges Teknisk-Naturvitenskapelige
    Universitet (NTNU), 1620

Norges Veterinærhøgskole, 1632
Norilsk Industrial Institute, 1899
Norin Suisansho Toshokan, 1230
Norman Rockwell Museum, 2481
Norrköping Art Museum, 2065
Norrköping City Library, 2061
Norrköpings Konstmuseum, 2065
Norrköpings Stadsbibliotek, 2061
NORSAR, 1617
Norsk Arkeologisk Selskap, 1615
Norsk Bibliotekforening, 1615
Norsk Botanisk Forening, 1616
Norsk Farmasøytisk Selskap, 1615
Norsk Folkemuseum, 1620
Norsk Forbund for Fjernundervisning
    og Fleksibel Utdanning (NFF), 1614
Norsk Forening for Internasjonal Rett,
    1615
Norsk Geologisk Forening, 1616
Norsk Institutt for By- Og
    Regionforskning, 1617
Norsk Institutt for Luftforskning, 1617
Norsk Kirurgisk Forening, 1615
Norsk Kjemisk Selskap, 1616
Norsk Lokalhistorisk Institutt, 1615
Norsk Luftfartsmuseum, 1619
Norsk Maritimt Museum, 1620
Norsk PEN, 1615
Norsk Polarinstitutt, 1617
Norsk Regnesentral, 1617
Norsk Samfunnsvitenskapelig
    Datatjeneste (NSD), 1616
Norsk Slektshistorisk Forening, 1615
Norsk Teknisk Museum, 1620
Norsk Utenrikspolitisk Institutt, 1616
Norsk Utvandrermuseum, Hamar, 1619
Norske Arkitekters Landsforbund
    (NAL), 1615
Norske Billedkunstnere, 1615
Norske Historiske Forening, 1615
Norske Laegeforening, 1615
Norske Nobelinstitutt, 1616
Norske Tannlegeforening (NTF), 1615
Norske Videnskaps-Akademi, 1614
North American Spanish Language
    Academy, 2397
North Bohemian Gallery of Fine Art in
    Litoměřice, 636
North Bohemian Museum in Liberec,
    636
North Bohemian Research Library, 635
North Brabant Museum, 1552
North Carolina Agricultural and
    Technical State University, 2814
North Carolina Central University,
    2814
North Carolina Museum of Art, 2491
North Carolina Museum of History,
    2491
North Carolina Museum of Natural
    Sciences, 2491
North Carolina State University, 2815
North Carolina Wesleyan College, 2812
North Caucasus Institute of Mining
    and Metallurgical (State
    Technological University),
    Vladikavkaz, 1889
North Caucasian State Technical
    University, Stavropol, 1889
North Caucasus Mountains and
    Foothills Agricultural Research
    Institute, 1832
North Caucasus Research Institute for
    Horticulture and Viticulture, 1832
North Central College, Naperville, 2612
North Central University, 2719
North China Electric Power University,
    527
North Dakota Museum of Art, 2491
North Dakota State Library, 2454
North Dakota State University, 2824
North Dakota State University
    Libraries, Fargo, 2454
North Dakota University System, 2824
North East Medical College, Sylhet, 234
North Eastern Education and Library
    Board, 2264
North Georgia College and State
    University, 2599
North Greenville University, 2885
North Hamgyong Provincial Library,
    1361
North Hertfordshire College, 2361
North Holland Archives, 1546

North Hwanghae Provincial Library,
    1361
North Karelia Polytechnic, 736
North Kazakhstan State University
    named after Manash Kozybaev,
    1347
North Kingstown Free Library, 2457
North Lindsey College, 2361
North Maharashtra University, 1048
North Olympic Library System (NOLS),
    2461
North Orissa University, 1048
North Ossetia State Medical Academy,
    1897
North Ossetian State University, 1872
North Park University, Chicago, 2612
North Platte Public Library, 2448
North Pyongan Provincial Library, 1361
North Rhine-Westphalia Art Collection,
    852
North Rhine-Westphalia State Agency
    for Nature, Environment and
    Consumer Protection, 838
North Scituate Public Library, 2457
North South University, Dhaka, 224
North South University Library, 216
North University of Baia Mare, 1802
North West Kent College, 2361
North West Regional College, 2369
North Yorkshire County Library, 2277
Northamptonshire Libraries and
    Information Service, 2278
Northcentral University, Prescott
    Valley, 2509
Northeast Forestry University, Harbin,
    527
North-East Institute of Science and
    Technology, Jorhat, 1012
North-East Interdisciplinary Scientific
    Research Institute FEB RAS, 1840
Northeast Normal University Library,
    Changchun, 470
Northeast Ohio Medical University,
    2834
North-Eastern Federal University,
    Yakutsk, 1872
North-Eastern Hill University, 1048
Northeastern Illinois University, 2613
Northeastern Institute of Botany,
    Corrientes, 108
Northeastern State University,
    Tahlequah, 2840
Northeastern University, Boston, 2687
Northeastern University, Shenyang,
    528
Northern Arizona University, 2509
Northern Arizona University Art
    Museum, 2464
Northern Forestry Centre, Edmonton,
    372
Northern Illinois University, 2613
Northern International University,
    Magadan, 1872
Northern Ireland Association for Mental
    Health, 2238
Northern Ireland Foundation, 2227
Northern Kazakhstan Research
    Institute of Animal Breeding and
    Veterinary Science, 1339
Northern Kentucky University, 2646
Northern Maritime Museum,
    Groningen, 1550
Northern Michigan University, 2704
Northern New Mexico College, 2765
Northern Ostrobothnia Museum, 722
Northern Regional College, 2369
Northern Research Station, Roslin,
    2250
Northern School of Contemporary
    Dance, Leeds, 2365
Northern Seminary, 2613
Northern State Medical University,
    Arkhangelsk, 1882
Northern State University, Aberdeen,
    2887
Northern Technical College, Ndola,
    3026
Northern Technical Institute,
    Chiangmai, 2146
Northern Territory Library, 139
Northern University Bangladesh, 224
Northern University, Nowshera, 1652
Northern University of Malaysia, 1452
Northland College, 2957

North-Ossetian K. L. Khetagurov Memorial Museum, 1861
North-Ossetian State University Library, 1855
Northrhine-Westphalia Academy of Sciences and Humanities, 820
North-South Institute, Ottawa, 372
Northumberland County Library, 2277
Northumbria University, 2298
Northville District Library, 2446
Northwest Christian University, Eugene, 2845
Northwest Commission on Colleges and Universities, Redmond, 2394
Northwest Florida State College, 2586
Northwest Missouri State University, 2740
Northwest Nazarene University, 2604
North-West Provincial Library Services, Mmabatho, 1978
North-West State Technical University, 1889
North-West University, 1981
Northwest University, Kirkland, 2943
Northwest University, Xian, 528
Northwestern College, Orange City, 2637
Northwestern College, St Paul, 2719
Northwestern Health Sciences University, 2719
Northwestern Oklahoma State University, 2840
Northwestern Polytechnical University, Xi'an, 528
Northwestern State University of Louisiana, 2652
Northwestern University, Evanston, 2613
Northwestern University in Qatar, 1781
Northwestern University Libraries, Evanston, 2439
Northwood University, 2704
Norton Museum of Art, 2472
Norton University, 361
Norwegian Academy for Language and Literature, 1615
Norwegian Academy of Music, 1632
Norwegian Academy of Science, 1614
Norwegian Academy of Technological Sciences, 1616
Norwegian Archaeological Society, 1615
Norwegian Association for Distance Education and Flexible Education, 1614
Norwegian Authors' Union, 1615
Norwegian Botanical Association, 1616
Norwegian Centre for International Cooperation in Higher Education, 1614
Norwegian Centre of International PEN, 1615
Norwegian Chemical Society, 1616
Norwegian College of Surgeons, 1615
Norwegian Computing Centre, 1617
Norwegian Dental Association, 1615
Norwegian Emigrant Museum, 1619
Norwegian Genealogical Society, 1615
Norwegian Geotechnical Institute, 1617
Norwegian Industrial Property Office, 1618
Norwegian Institute for Air Research, 1617
Norwegian Institute for Urban and Regional Research, 1617
Norwegian Institute in Rome, 1174
Norwegian Institute of International Affairs, 1616
Norwegian Library Association, 1615
Norwegian Marine Technology Research Institute (MARINTEK), 1617
Norwegian Maritime Museum, 1620
Norwegian Medical Association, 1615
Norwegian Medical Society, 1615
Norwegian Meteorological Institute, 1617
Norwegian Museum of Cultural History, 1620
Norwegian Museum of Science and Technology, 1620
Norwegian Nobel Institute, 1616
Norwegian Pharmaceutical Society, 1615
Norwegian Polar Institute, 1617

Norwegian School of Economics and Business Administration, 1631
Norwegian School of Sport Sciences, 1632
Norwegian School of Veterinary Science, 1632
Norwegian Social Science Data Services, 1616
Norwegian Society of Chartered Technical and Scientific Professionals (Tekna), 1616
Norwegian Structural Biology Centre (NorStruct), 1617
Norwegian University of Life Sciences, 1623
Norwegian University of Life Sciences, Library, 1618
Norwegian University of Science and Technology, 1620
Norwich Castle Museum and Art Gallery, Norwich, 2290
Norwich Cathedral Library, 2278
Norwich School of Art and Design, 2363
Norwich University, 2929
Norwich University College of the Arts, 2359
Notre Dame College, 2834
Notre Dame College, Dhaka, 234
Notre Dame de Namur University, Belmont, 2531
Notre Dame of Maryland University, Baltimore, 2662
Notre Dame Seminary, 2650
Notre Dame University, Fremantle, 165
Notre Dame University Louaize, 1408
Nottingham Castle Museum, 2290
Nottingham City Libraries and Information Service, 2278
Nottingham Natural History Museum, 2290
Nottingham Trent University, 2298
Nouveau Musée National de Monaco Villa Sauber/Villa Paloma, 1495
Nov Bulgarki Universitet, 346
Nova Scotia Agricultural College, 390
Nova Scotia Archives, 375
Nova Scotia College of Art and Design (NSCAD), 390
Nova Scotia Legislative Library, 375
Nova Scotia Museum of Natural History, 378
Nova Scotian Institute of Science, 370
Nova Southeastern University, 2586
Novgorod State University, 1873
Novia Polytechnic, 735
Novia Yrkeshögskolan, Vaasa, 735
Novocherkassk Institute of Engineering Amelioration, 1899
Novocherkassk Museum of the History of the Don Cossacks, 1858
Novodevichii Monastery Museum, 1857
Novorossiisk State Maritime Academy, 1898
Novosibirsk Architectural Institute, 1898
Novosibirsk Institute of Commerce, 1899
Novosibirsk Institute of National Economy, 1899
Novosibirsk Institute of Tuberculosis, 1838
Novosibirsk State Academy of Water Transport, 1898
Novosibirsk State Agrarian University, 1863
Novosibirsk State Conservatoire 'M. I. Glinka', 1900
Novosibirsk State Medical Academy, 1897
Novosibirsk State Technical University, 1889
Novosibirsk State University, 1873
Novosibirsk State University Library, 1854
Novosibirsk State University of Architecture and Civil Engineering, 1889
Noxubee County Public Library, 2447
NTNU library, 1618
NTNU Vitenskapsmuseet, 1620
NU Zavod i Muzej Bitola, 1434
Nubia Museum, 690
Nuclear and Radiation Safety Agency, Dushanbe, 2127

Nuclear Engineering Institute, Rio de Janeiro, 302
Nuclear Institute, Majuro, 1459
Nuclear Physics Accelerator Institute, Groningen, 1540
Nuclear Physics Institute AS CR, 633
Nuclear Research Centre, Baghdad, 1123
Nuclear Research Centre (NRC), Inshas, 689
Nuclear Research Centre, Rīgas rajons, 1403
Nuclear Research Institute Řež, 633
Nuclear Technology Development Centre, Belo Horizonte, 302
Nuclear-Physics Accelerator Institute, Groningen, 1541
Núcleo de Monitoramento Ambiental de Recursos Naturais por Satélite, Campinas, 300
Núcleo Museológico do Posto de Comando do Movimento das Forças Armadas, Odivelas, 1771
Nueva Ecija University of Science and Technology, Cabanatuan City, 1697
Nuffield College Library, Oxford, 2279
Nuffield College, Oxford, 2348
Nukada Institute for Medical and Biological Research, Chiba, 1227
Nukus State Teacher—Training Institute named after Ajiniyaz, 2988
Numismatic Collection, 849
Numismatic Museum, Willemstad, 1569
Nunavut Public Library Services, Iqaluit, 375
Nunavut Research Institute, Iqaluit, 372
Nuremberg Art Museum, 856
Nurses Association of Macao, 574
Nursing Institute, 1392
Nursing School of Coimbra, 1777
Nuruosmaniye Library, Istanbul, 2161
Nusa Cendana University, 1095
Nushi Brothers Museum, Vlorë, 86
NUTEC—Norsk Undervannsteknologisk Senter A/S, 1617
Nutrition Institute, Jakarta, 1085
Nutrition Society, London, 2238
Nutrition Society of Nigeria, 1590
Nutrition Society of Southern Africa, 1974
Nuuk Artmuseum, 667
Nuup Katersugaasivii, 667
NWFP University of Engineering and Technology, 1652
Ny Carlsberg Glyptotek, Copenhagen, 657
Ny Carlsbergfondet, 650
Nyack College, 2796
Nyala University, Nyala, 2049
Nyanga Experimental Station, 3028
Nydahl Collection, 2067
Nyenrode Business Universiteit, 1553
Nyenrode Business Universiteit Library, 1546
Nyenrode Business University, 1553
Nyíregyházi Főiskola, Nyiregyhaza, 999
NYU Abu Dhabi, 2220
Nyugat-Magyarországi Egyetem, 991
Nyugat-Magyarországi Egyetem Központi Könyvtár es Leveltar, 980
NZEI Te Riu Roa, 1572

O

'O. O. Bohomolets' Institute of Physiology, Kyiv, 2199
'O. Tleikhan' Building College, Ulan Bator, 1501
Oak Hills Christian College, 2719
Oak Institute for the Study of International Human Rights, 2427
Oak Ridge Associated Universities, 2413
Oakland City University, 2629
Oakland Public Library, 2432
Oakland University, 2704
Oakwood University, 2504
Obafemi Awolowo University, 1604
Obalne Galerije Piran, 1966
Obec architektů, Prague, 628
Obec spisovatelů, 629

Oberhessisches Museum und Gailsche Sammlungen der Stadt Giessen, 853
Oberlausitzische Bibliothek der Wissenschaften Görlitz, 843
Oberlin College, 2834
Oberösterreichische Landesbibliothek, Linz, 184
Oberösterreichische Landesmuseen, 186
Oberösterreichisches Landesarchiv, 184
Obihiro University of Agriculture and Veterinary Medicine, 1272
Obirin University, 1321
'Obispo Colombres' Agro-Industrial Experimental Research Station, 106
Oblastní galerie v Liberci, 636
Oblate School of Theology, 2907
Obninsk State Technical University for Nuclear Power Engineering (Technical University), 1889
'Obraztsov Chiflik' Institute of Agriculture and Seed Science, 336
Obraztsov Puppet Museum of the Central State Academic Puppet Theatre, 1857
Observatoire Astronomique de l'Université de Genève, 2093
Observatoire Astronomique de Marseille–Provence, 749
Observatoire Astronomique de Marseille-Provence (OAMP), 763
Observatoire Astronomique de Strasbourg, 749
Observatoire de Bordeaux, 749
Observatoire de la Côte d'Azur, 749
Observatoire de Lyon, 749
Observatoire de Paris, 749
Observatoire de Paris, Site de Meudon, 749
Observatoire de Physique du Globe de Clermont-Ferrand, 749
Observatoire des Sciences de l'Univers de Besançon, 749
Observatoire Midi-Pyrénées, 749
Observatoriemuseet, 2067
Observatories of the Carnegie Institution, 2423
Observatorio Astronómico, Córdoba, Argentina, 109
Observatório Astronómico da Universidade de Coimbra, 1766
Observatório Astronómico de Lisboa, 1767
Observatorio Astronómico de Montevideo, 2980
Observatorio Astronómico de Quito, 678
Observatorio Astronómico, La Plata, 109
Observatorio Astronómico Nacional, Bogotá, 580
Observatorio Astronómico Nacional, Madrid, 2005
Observatorio Astronómico Nacional, Santiago, 451
Observatório de Medicina Integrativa—Centro de Estudos Avançados em Ciências da Saúde, 1766
Observatorio del Roque de los Muchachos, 2005
Observatorio del Teide, 2005
Observatorio Fabra, 2005
Observatorio Geofísico, Managua, 1585
Observatorio Interamericano de Cerro Tololo, 451
Observatório Nacional—Brazil, 302
Observatorio Naval 'Juan Manuel Cagigal', Caracas, 3003
Observatorio San Calixto, La Paz, 282
Observatorium Bosscha, 1085
Observatory museum, 2067
Obstetrics and Gynaecology Association, San José, 598
Obuvnické muzeum, Zlín, 637
OC Public Libraries, 2432
Occidental College, Los Angeles, 2531
Occupation Tapestry Gallery, St Helier, 2391
Occupational Health Safety and Research Bureau, Kitwe, 3025
Ocean City Free Public Library, 2450
Oceanarium of the Pacific Research Fisheries Centre, Vladivostok, 1861
Oceania Polytechnic Institute of Education, Melbourne, 171

Rannsoknamidstod Íslands, 1001
Rannsóknastofnun landbúnadarins, 1002
Raoul Wallenberg Institute of Human Rights and Humanitarian Law, 2058
Rapid City Public Libraries, 2458
Rapides Parish Library, 2442
Ras al-Khaimah Medical and Health Sciences University, 2220
Rashtrasant Tukadoji Maharaj Nagpur University, 1053
Rashtriya Sanskrit Sansthan, New Delhi, 1077
Rashtriya Sanskrit Vidyapeetha, Tirupati, 1077
Rasmussen College, 2719
Ráth György Múzeum, Budapest, 981
Rathausbücherei der Landeshauptstadt Stuttgart, 847
Rathenau Institute, 1534
Rathenau Instituut, 1534
Ratio Institute, 2058
Ratnapura National Museum, 2042
Rautenstrauch-Joest-Museum, 850
Ravensbourne College of Design and Communication, 2363
Raw Materials Research and Development Council (RMRDC), Abuja, 1592
Rawalpindi Government College of Technology, 1661
Ray Society, London, 2241
Rayat London College, 2364
Razi University, 1113
Razi Vaccine and Serum Research Institute, 1107
REA College, 627
Reactor Institute Delft, 1544
Reading Borough Libraries, 2279
Reading Public Museum, 2495
Real Academia de Bellas Artes de la Purísima Concepción, Valladolid, 1998
Real Academia de Bellas Artes de San Fernando, 1996
Real Academia de Bellas Artes de San Telmo, 1998
Real Academia de Bellas Artes de Santa Isabel de Hungría, 1998
Real Academia de Bellas Artes y Ciencias Históricas de Toledo, 1997
Real Academia de Ciencias Exactas, Físicas, Químicas y Naturales de Zaragoza, 1999
Real Academia de Ciencias Exactas, Físicas y Naturales, 1996
Real Academia de Ciencias Morales y Políticas, Madrid, 1996
Real Academia de Ciencias Veterinarias, Madrid, 1997
Real Academia de Ciencias y Artes de Barcelona, 1997
Real Academia de Doctores, Madrid, 1997
Real Academia de España en Roma, 1165
Real Academia de Jurisprudencia y Legislación, Madrid, 1996
Real Academia de la Historia, Madrid, 1996
Real Academia de la Lengua Vasca, Bilbao, 1998
Real Academia de Medicina y Cirugía de Palma de Mallorca, 1999
Real Academia de Nobles y Bellas Artes de San Luis, 1998
Real Academia Española, 1996
Real Academia Galega, 1997
Real Academia Hispano-Americana, 1997
Real Academia Nacional de Farmacia, Madrid, 1996
Real Academia Nacional de Medicina, Madrid, 1996
Real Academia Sevillana de Buenas Letras, 1998
Real Biblioteca del Monasterio de San Lorenzo de El Escorial, 2007
Real Biblioteca, Madrid, 2007
Real Centro Universitario 'Escorial—María Cristina', 2037

Real Conservatorio Profesional de Música 'Manuel de Falla', 2038
Real Conservatorio Superior de Música de Madrid, 2038
Real Escuela Superior de Arte Dramático, Madrid, 2038
Real Instituto Arqueológico de Portugal, 1762
Real Instituto de Estudios Asturianos, Oviedo, 2000
Real Instituto y Observatorio de la Armada, Cádiz, 2005
Real Jardín Botánico, Madrid, 2011
Real Monasterio de la Encarnación, 2011
Real Monasterio de Santa Clara de Tordesillas, 2011
Real Monasterio de Santa Isabel, 2011
Real Sociedad Bascongada de los Amigos del País, 2000
Real Sociedad Económica de Amigos del País de Tenerife, 1997
Real Sociedad Española de Física, 1999
Real Sociedad Española de Historia Natural, 1999
Real Sociedad Española de Química, 1999
Real Sociedad Fotográfica, Madrid, 1998
Real Sociedad Geográfica, Madrid, 1998
Real Sociedad Matemática Española, 1999
Real Sociedade Arqueológica Lusitana, 1762
Reale Istituto Neerlandese a Roma, 1174
Reaseheath College, 2362
Recinto de Aguadilla, 2976
Recinto de Arecibo, 2976
Recinto de Barranquitas, 2976
Recinto de Bayamón, 2976
Recinto de Ciencias Médicas, 2974
Recinto de Fajardo, 2976
Recinto de Guayama, 2976
Recinto de Ponce, 2976
Recinto de San Germán, 2976
Recinto Metro, 2976
Recklinghausen City Museums, 856
Reconstructionist Rabbinical College, Wyncote, 2871
Record Office Kampen, 1546
Recreational Cultural House, Gaza, 1664
Rectoren College, Utrecht, 1528
Rectors' Conference of Thailand, 2135
Rectors' Conference of the French-speaking Community of Belgium, 249
Rectors' Conference of the Netherlands, 1528
Rectors' Conference of the Swiss Universities, 2085
Rectors' Conference, Zagreb, 606
Red Crescent Society of Tajikistan, 2126
Red Iberoamericana para la Acreditación de la Calidad de la Educación Superior (RIACES), 58
Red Sea University, Port Sudan, 2049
Redbridge College, Romford, 2361
Redcliffe College, Gloucester, 2366
Redeemer University College, Ancaster, 392
Redpath Museum, 380
Reece Museum, 2497
Reed College, 2846
Reed Research Institute, Haeju, 1360
Reference Centre for Lactobacillus, San Miguel de Tucumán, 107
Referentiecentrum voor Biologische Merkers van Geheugenstoornissen, 255
Reformed Church Center, New Brunswick, 2427
Reformed Theological Seminary, Jackson, 2734
Rega Institute for Medical Research, 255
Rega-Instituut, 255
Regent College, Vancouver, 411
Regent University, 2935
Regent's Business School London, 2364
Regent's Park College, Oxford, 2348
Regents Theological College, West Malvern, 2366

Regeringskansliet Utrikesdepartementets Bibliotek, 2062
Reghin Ethnographic Museum, 1797
Regierungsgebäude, Vaduz, 1418
Regina Public Library, 377
Reginald F. Lewis Museum of Maryland African American History & Culture, 2480
Regionaal Archief Alkmaar, 1545
Regionaal Historisch Centrum Groninger Archieven, 1546
Regionaal Historisch Centrum Limburg, 1547
Regional Archaeological Museum, 854
Regional Archive of Lower Saxony, 843
Regional Bureau for Education in Latin America and the Caribbean, 448
Regional Center of Public Health Iaşi, Iaşi, 1787
Regional Centre for Adult Education (ASFEC), Menoufia, 694
Regional Centre for the Promotion of Books in Latin America and the Caribbean, 578
Regional Council of Hautes Écoles, Brussels, 249
Regional Historic Centre Limburg, 1547
Regional Historical Museum, Burgas, 342
Regional Historical Museum, Pleven, 343
Regional History and Local Lore Museum, Akmola, 1341
Regional History and Local Lore Museum, Atyrau, 1342
Regional History and Local Lore Museum, South Kazakhstan, 1342
Regional History and Local Lore Museum, Zhambyl, 1342
Regional Institute for the Protection of Historic Monuments, Split, 608
Regional Library 'Mihalacky Gergiev', 342
Regional Library of Palatinate, 846
Regional Library, Stara Zagora, 342
Regional Library, Yogyakarta, 1087
Regional Museum, Brežice, 1966
Regional Museum in Kristianstad, 2064
Regional Museum of Anthropology, Mérida, 1472
Regional Museum of History – Shumen, 343
Regional Museum of History – Veliko Tărnovo, 344
Regional Museum of History, Dobrich, 342
Regional Museum of History, Haskovo, 342
Regional Museum of History, Lovech, 343
Regional Museum of History, Montana, 343
Regional Museum of History, Pazardzhik, 343
Regional Museum of History, Pernik, 343
Regional Museum of History, Ruse, 343
Regional Museum of History, Stara Zagora, 344
Regional Museum of History, Vratsa, 344
Regional Museum of History—Varna, 344
Regional Museum of Maribor, 1966
Regional Museum of Oltenia, 1795
Regional Museum, Travnik, 291
Regional Museum—Reserve 'Khan Ordaly Saraishyk', 1342
Regional Record Office Alkmaar, Alkmaar, 1545
Regional State Archives, 1618
Regional Studies Association, Seaford, 2235
Regional Universal-Scientific Library named after L. N. Tolstoy, 1341
Regional Veterinary Institute, Plovdiv, 336
Regional Veterinary Institute, Veliko Tărnovo, 336
Regional Veterinary Research Institute and Centre, Stara Zagora, 336
Regionální muzeum v Kolíně, 635
Regionální muzeum v Teplicích, 637

Regionalni Muzej Doboj, 291
Regionalni zavod za zaštitu spomenika kulture, Split, 608
Regionmuseet Kristianstad, 2064
Regis College, Toronto, 432
Regis College, Weston, 2688
Regis University, 2554
Reguly Antal Historic Library, 980
Rehabilitation International—International Society for Rehabilitation of the Disabled, 64
Reial Acadèmia Catalana de Belles Arts de Sant Jordi, 2006
Reial Acadèmia de Bones Lletres, Barcelona, 1999
Reial Societat Arqueològica Tarraconense, 1998
Reims Management School, 797
Reina Sofia Higher School of Music, 2038
Reinhardt University, 2600
Reiss-Engelhorn-Museen Mannheim, 855
Rektorite Nõukogu, Tartu, 701
Rektorski zbor, Zagreb, 606
Religious Research Association, Galva, 2415
Rembrand House Museum, 1549
Rembrandthuis Museum, Amsterdam, 1549
Remote Sensing and Photogrammetry Society, Nottingham, 2247
Remote Sensing for Development Centre, Lisbon, 1763
Renaissance Society of America, 2405
Renewable Energy Development Centre, Algiers, 90
Renewable Energy Science, Technology and Production Corporation, Ulan Bator, 1498
Renfrewshire Libraries, 2279
Rengeoin (Sanjusangendo), 1231
Renison University College, Waterloo, 434
Renmin University of China, 531
Renmin University of China Library, 470
Rensselaer at Hartford, 2557
Rensselaer Polytechnic Institute, 2797
Representative Church Body Library, Dublin, 1133
Republic Engineering-Technical Centre for the Restoration and Strengthening of Components of Machines and Mechanisms, Tomsk, 1850
Republic Institute for the Protection of Cultural Monuments of Montenegro, 1502
Republic of Srpska Association of Judges, 288
Republic of the Marshall Islands Environmental Protection Authority (RMIEPA), 1459
Republic Polytechnic, Singapore, 1947
Republic Specialized Centre of Cardiology, Tashkent, 2984
Republic University, Sivas, 2167
Republican Institute of Advanced Teachers' Studies, Dushanbe, 2128
Republican Library for Science and Technology of Belarus, 242
Republican Library for the Blind and Visually Impaired Citizens of the Republic of Kazakhstan, 1341
Republican Literary Memorial Museum Complex named after S. Mukanov and G. Musrepov, 1342
Republican Museum of Book, Almaty, 1342
Republican Museum of Folk Musical Instruments named after Ykylas, 1342
Republican Research and Practical Centre for Epidemiology and Microbiology, 240
Republican Scientific and Engineering Centre for Environmental Remote Sensing 'Ecomir', Minsk, 241
Republican Scientific and Technical Library, 1341
Republican Scientific Medical Library, 242

Royal Academy of Fine Arts, San Telmo, 1998
Royal Academy of Fine Arts, Santa Isabel de Hungría, 1998
Royal Academy of Fine Arts, Valladolid, 1998
Royal Academy of French Language and Literature, Brussels, 250
Royal Academy of History, Madrid, 1996
Royal Academy of Jurisprudence and Law, Madrid, 1996
Royal Academy of Medicine and Surgery, Palma de Mallorca, 1999
Royal Academy of Medicine in Ireland, 1131
Royal Academy of Medicine of Belgium, 251
Royal Academy of Moral and Political Sciences, Madrid, 1996
Royal Academy of Music, Århus, 664
Royal Academy of Music Library, London, 2274
Royal Academy of Music, London, 2330
Royal Academy of Music, Madrid, 2038
Royal Academy of Noble and Fine Arts of San Luis, 1998
Royal Academy of Science, Letters and Fine Arts of Belgium, 249
Royal Academy of the Basque Language, Bilbao, 1998
Royal Academy of Veterinary Sciences, Madrid, 1997
Royal Academy Schools, London, 2363
Royal Aeronautical Society, Australian Division, 136
Royal Aeronautical Society, London, 2247
Royal African Society, London, 2244
Royal Agricultural College, Cirencester, 2359
Royal Agricultural Society of England, 2227
Royal Agricultural Society of New Zealand (Inc.), 1573
Royal Air Force Museum London, 2288
Royal Alberta Museum, 377
Royal Angkor Foundation, Budapest, 357
Royal Anthropological Institute of Great Britain and Ireland, 2244
Royal Archaeological Institute, London, 2254
Royal Archaeological Institute of Portugal, 1762
Royal Archaeological Society in Tarragona, 1998
Royal Architectural Institute of Canada, 368
Royal Archives of Aragon, 2006
Royal Armouries, London, 2288
Royal Armouries Museum, Leeds, 2286
Royal Armoury, Stockholm, Stockholm, 2066
Royal Art Society of New South Wales, 131
Royal Asiatic Society Hong Kong Branch, 566
Royal Asiatic Society, Korea Branch, 1363
Royal Asiatic Society Library, London, 2275
Royal Asiatic Society, Malaysian Branch, 1444
Royal Asiatic Society of Great Britain and Ireland, 2244
Royal Asiatic Society of Sri Lanka, Colombo, 2039
Royal Association for Disability and Rehabilitation, London, 2238
Royal Association for Historic Buildings, Brussels, 249
Royal Association of Medical Scientific Societies of Belgium, 251
Royal Astronomical Society Library and Archives, London, 2275
Royal Astronomical Society, London, 2242
Royal Astronomical Society of Antwerp, 252
Royal Astronomical Society of Canada, 371
Royal Astronomical Society of New Zealand (Inc.), 1575

Royal Australasian College of Dental Surgeons, 133
Royal Australasian College of Physicians, 133
Royal Australasian College of Surgeons, 133
Royal Australian and New Zealand College of Ophthalmologists, 133
Royal Australian and New Zealand College of Psychiatrists, 133
Royal Australian and New Zealand College of Radiologists, 133
Royal Australian Chemical Institute, 135
Royal Australian College of General Practitioners, 133
Royal Australian Historical Society, 132
Royal Belgian Entomological Society, 252
Royal Belgian Institute of Natural Sciences, 255
Royal Belgian Overseas Union, 250
Royal Belgian Society of Anthropology and Prehistory, 252
Royal Belgian Society of Political Economy, 250
Royal Belgian Zoological Society, 252
Royal Borough of Windsor and Maidenhead Libraries, 2277
Royal Botanic Garden, Edinburgh, 2259
Royal Botanic Garden Library, Edinburgh, 2269
Royal Botanic Gardens, Kew, 2259
Royal Botanic Gardens, Kew, Library, Art & Archives, 2275
Royal Botanic Gardens Melbourne, 137
Royal Botanic Gardens, Peradeniya, 2042
Royal Botanic Gardens, Sydney, 137
Royal Botanical Garden, Madrid, 2011
Royal Botanical Society of Belgium, 252
Royal Botanical Society of the Netherlands, 1531
Royal British Columbia Museum, 378
Royal British Society of Sculptors, 2232
Royal Cambrian Academy of Art, 2232
Royal Canadian Academy of Arts, 368
Royal Canadian College of Organists, 441
Royal Canadian Geographical Society, 369
Royal Canadian Institute for the Advancement of Science, 368
Royal Catalan Academy of Fine Arts, Sant Jordi, 2006
Royal Coin Cabinet—National Museum of Economy, 2066
Royal College of Anaesthetists, London, 2238
Royal College of Applied Science and Technology, 2222
Royal College of Art Library, London, 2275
Royal College of Art, London, 2363
Royal College of General Practitioners, London, 2238
Royal College of Music in Stockholm, 2083
Royal College of Music Library, London, 2275
Royal College of Music, London, 2365
Royal College of Music Museum of Instruments, London, 2288
Royal College of Nursing, Australia, 133
Royal College of Nursing of the United Kingdom, 2238
Royal College of Obstetricians and Gynaecologists, London, 2238
Royal College of Ophthalmologists, London, 2238
Royal College of Paediatrics and Child Health, London, 2238
Royal College of Pathologists, London, 2238
Royal College of Pathologists of Australasia, 133
Royal College of Physicians and Surgeons of Canada, 370
Royal College of Physicians and Surgeons of Glasgow, 2239
Royal College of Physicians and Surgeons of Glasgow Library, 2270

Royal College of Physicians' Library Archive and Museum Services, London, 2275
Royal College of Physicians, London, 2238
Royal College of Physicians of Edinburgh, 2239
Royal College of Physicians of Edinburgh Library, 2269
Royal College of Physicians of Ireland, 1138
Royal College of Psychiatrists, London, 2239
Royal College of Radiologists, London, 2239
Royal College of Surgeons in Ireland Library (The Mercer Library), 1133
Royal College of Surgeons in Ireland Medical University of Bahrain, Adliya, 211
Royal College of Surgeons in Ireland Museum, 1134
Royal College of Surgeons of Edinburgh, 2239
Royal College of Surgeons of Edinburgh Library and Archive, 2269
Royal College of Surgeons of England, 2239
Royal College of Surgeons of England Library and Lumley Study Centre, 2275
Royal College of Veterinary Surgeons, London, 2227
Royal College of Veterinary Surgeons Trust Library, 2275
Royal Commonwealth Society, 2244
Royal Conservatoire of Antwerp, 273
Royal Conservatoire of Scotland, 2371
Royal Conservatory of Music, Toronto, 441
Royal Danish Academy of Fine Arts Library, 655
Royal Danish Academy of Fine Arts, School of Architecture, 664
Royal Danish Academy of Fine Arts, School of Conservation, 664
Royal Danish Academy of Music, 664
Royal Danish Academy of Science and Letters, 649
Royal Danish Agricultural Society, 649
Royal Danish Geographical Society, 651
Royal Danish Society for National History, 651
Royal Dublin Society, 1130
Royal Dublin Society Library (RDS Library), 1133
Royal Dutch Antiquarian Society, 1529
Royal Dutch Association for the Advancement of Pharmacy, 1530
Royal Dutch Forestry Association, 1528
Royal Dutch Geographical Society, 1529
Royal Dutch Mathematical Society, 1531
Royal Dutch Medical Association, 1530
Royal Dutch Musician's Union, 1529
Royal Dutch Society for Meteorology and Astronomy, 1531
Royal Dutch Society for Natural History, 1530
Royal Dutch Zoological Society, 1531
Royal Economic Society, London, 2231
Royal Economic Society of Friends of Tenerife, 1997
Royal Entomological Society, 2241
Royal Faculty of Procurators in Glasgow, 2231
Royal Fine Art Commission for Scotland, 2232
Royal Flemish Academy of Belgium for Science and the Arts, 249
Royal Flemish Association of Engineers, 253
Royal Forestry Society, 2227
Royal Frisian Society for History and Culture, 1529
Royal Galician Academy, 1997
Royal Geographic Society, Madrid, 1998
Royal Geographical Society of Queensland Inc., 132
Royal Geographical Society (with the Institute of British Geographers), 2235

Royal Geographical Society (with the Institute of British Geographers) Library, London, 2275
Royal Geological and Mining Society of the Netherlands, 1531
Royal Gustavus Adolphus Academy for Swedish Folk Culture, 2057
Royal Hibernian Academy, 1131
Royal Highland and Agricultural Society of Scotland, 2227
Royal Historical Commission, Brussels, 249
Royal Historical Society, London, 2235
Royal Historical Society of Queensland, 132
Royal Historical Society of Victoria, 132
Royal Holland Society of Sciences and Humanities, 1528
Royal Holloway, University of London, 2330
Royal Horticultural Society, London, 2227
Royal Horticultural Society of Ireland, 1130
Royal Incorporation of Architects in Scotland, 2228
Royal Institute, Bangkok, 2135
Royal Institute for International Relations, Brussels, 254
Royal Institute for Tourism and Hospitality, Thimphu, 280
Royal Institute of Art, Stockholm, 2082
Royal Institute of British Architects, 2228
Royal Institute of Dutch Architects, 1528
Royal Institute of Engineers (KIVI NIRIA), 1532
Royal Institute of Health Sciences, Thimphu, 280
Royal Institute of International Affairs Library, London, 2275
Royal Institute of International Affairs, London, 2231
Royal Institute of Management, Thimphu, 280
Royal Institute of Oil Painters, London, 2232
Royal Institute of Painters in Water Colours, London, 2232
Royal Institute of Philosophy, London, 2243
Royal Institute of Public Health, London, 2239
Royal Institute of Technology Library, Stockholm, 2062
Royal Institute of Technology, Stockholm, 2083
Royal Institute of the Architects of Ireland, 1130
Royal Institution of Chartered Surveyors, London, 2228
Royal Institution of Great Britain, 2240
Royal Institution of Great Britain Archives, 2275
Royal Institution of Great Britain Michael Faraday Museum, 2288
Royal Institution of Naval Architects, London, 2247
Royal Irish Academy, 1130
Royal Irish Academy of Music, 1139
Royal Jersey Agricultural & Horticultural Society, 2391
Royal Library, Copenhagen, 655
Royal Library, Madrid, 2007
Royal Library of Belgium, 258
Royal Library of the Monastery of San Lorenzo de El Escorial, 2007
Royal Lusitanian Archaeological Society, 1762
Royal Marine Conservation Society of Jordan, 1334
Royal Medical Society, Edinburgh, 2239
Royal Melbourne Institute of Technology, 162
Royal Meteorological Institute of Belgium, 256
Royal Meteorological Society, Reading, 2242
Royal Microscopical Society, Oxford, 2243
Royal Military College of Canada, 392
Royal Museum, Edinburgh, 2284
Royal Museum for Central Africa, 261

St Petersburg Institute of Painting, Sculpture and Architecture 'I. E. Repin', 1901

St Petersburg Institute of Phthisiopulmonology, 1839

St Petersburg Institute of Trade and Economics, 1899

St Petersburg Institute of Tuberculosis, 1839

St Petersburg Institute of Vaccines and Sera, 1839

St Petersburg M. Gorky House of Scientists, 1829

St Petersburg Pasteur Institute of Epidemiology and Microbiology, 1839

St Petersburg Petrov, N. N., Research Institute of Oncology, 1839

St Petersburg Research Institute of Industrial Hygiene and Occupational Diseases, 1839

St Petersburg State Academy of Aerospace Instrumentation, 1898

St Petersburg State Academy of Engineering and Economics, 1896

St Petersburg State Academy of Paediatric Medicine, 1897

St Petersburg State Academy of Refrigeration and Food Technology, 1898

St Petersburg State Agrarian University, 1863

St Petersburg State Chemical-Pharmaceutical Academy, 1897

St Petersburg State Conservatoire 'N. A. Rimsky-Korsakov', 1900

St Petersburg State Institute of Culture, 1901

St Petersburg State Marine Technical University, 1891

St Petersburg State Medical Academy 'I. I. Mechnikov', 1897

St Petersburg State Medical University 'Acad. I. P. Pavlov', 1882

St Petersburg State Mining Institute (Technical University), 1891

St Petersburg State Museum of Theatre and Music, 1860

St Petersburg State Polytechnical University, 1891

St Petersburg State Technological University of Plant Polymers, 1891

St Petersburg State Theatre Arts Academy, 1901

St Petersburg State University, 1875

St Petersburg State University M. Gorky Scientific Library, 1855

St Petersburg State University of Architecture and Civil Engineering, 1891

St Petersburg State University of Cinema and Television, 1875

St Petersburg State University of Economics and Finance, 1875

St Petersburg State University of Information Technology, Mechanics and Optics, 1891

St Petersburg State University of Refrigeration and Food Engineering, 1891

St Petersburg State University of Technology and Design, 1891

St Petersburg State University of Telecommunications 'Prof. M. A. Bonch-Bruyev', 1891

Saint Petersburg State University of Waterway Communications, 1891

St Petersburg Theatrical Library, 1855

St Petersburg Veterinary Institute, 1899

St Philip's Fortress, Santo Domingo, 673

St Scholastica's College, Manila, 1705

St Sophia of Kiev National Conservation Area, 2203

St Stephen's College, Delhi, 1080

St Stephen's House, 2349

St. Tammany Parish Library, 2442

St Thomas Aquinas College, Sparkill, 2799

St Thomas Aquinas Pontifical University, 2993

St Thomas Historical Trust, 2977

St Thomas University, Fredericton, 421

St Thomas University, Miami, 2588

Saint Vincent and the Grenadines National Trust, 1906

Saint Vincent and the Grenadines Visual Arts Society, Kingstown, 1906

Saint Vincent College, Latrobe, 2871

St Vincent de Paul Regional Seminary, 2588

St Vincent's College, 2558

St Vladimir's Orthodox Theological Seminary, Yonkers, 2799

Saint Xavier University, Chicago, 2615

St Xavier's College, Ahmedabad, 1080

St Xavier's College, Kolkata, 1080

St Xavier's College, Mumbai, 1080

Saitama University, 1281

Sakarya Üniversitesi, 2184

Sakhalin State University, Yuzhno-Sakhalinsk, 1875

Sala de Arte Prehispánico, Santo Domingo, 673

Sălaj District Museum of History and Art, 1798

Sălaj 'Ioniţă Scipione Bădescu' District Library, 1793

Salalah College of Technology, 1635

Salar Jung Museum, 1021

Salem College, 2813

Salem International University, 2952

Salem State University, 2688

Salem-South Lyon District Library, 2446

Salesian House for Theological Studies 'S. Tommaso d'Aquino', Messina, 2996

Salesian House Philosophical Studies, Nave, 2996

Salesian House Philosophical Studies, Santiago, 2996

Salesian House Theological Studies, Bangalore, 2996

Salesian House Theological Studies 'Don Bosco', Manila, 2996

Salesian House Theological Studies, Guatemala, 2996

Salesian House Theological Studies, Meghalaya, 2996

Salesian House Theological Studies, 'Saints Peter and Paul', Jerusalem, 2996

Salesian Institute of Philosophy, Nasik, 2996

Salesian Museum 'Maggiorino Borgatello', 452

Salesian Pontifical University, 2995

Salina Public Library, 2441

Salisbury and South Wiltshire Museum, 2291

Salisbury Cathedral Library, 2280

Salisbury Public Library, 2445

Salisbury University, 2663

Salish Kootenai College, 2747

Salk Institute for Biological Studies, La Jolla, 2424

Sällskapet för Förvaltningsforskning, Tampere, 714

Salten Museum, 1619

Saltire Society, Edinburgh, 2227

Salus University, 2872

Salve Regina University, 2881

Salzburg Museum, 187

Salzburg Provincial Archives, Salzburg, 184

Salzburg University, 196

Salzburg University Library, Salzburg, 184

Salzburger Landesarchiv, 184

Sam Cohen Library, 1521

Sam Higginbottom Institute of Agriculture, Technology & Sciences, 1077

Sam Houston State University, 2914

Sam Noble Museum, 2493

Samara A. M. Gorky Memorial Museum, 1861

Samara Agricultural Institute, 1899

Samara Art Museum, 1861

Samara Institute of Epidemiology, Microbiology and Hygiene, 1839

Samara Institute of Railway Engineers, 1900

Samara State Academy of Economics, 1897

Samara State Aerospace University 'S. P. Korolev', 1892

Samara State Institute of Culture, 1901

Samara State Medical University, 1882

Samara State Technical University, 1892

Samara State University, 1875

Samara State University Library, 1855

Samara State University of Architecture and Civil Engineering, 1892

Samarqand Agricultural Institute, 2988

Samarqand Branch of the Uzbek Academy of Sciences, 2984

Samarqand Cooperative Institute, 2988

Samarqand Davlat Chet Tillar Instituti, 2988

Samarqand Davlat Universiteti, 2987

Samarqand State Architectural and Civil Engineering Institute, 2988

Samarqand State Institute of Foreign Languages, 2988

Samarqand State Medical Institute, 2988

Samarqand State United Historical–Architectural and Art Museum Preserve, 2986

Samarqand State University, 2987

Samarqand State University Central Library, 2985

Samarra Museum, 1124

Şamaxı Astro-Physical Observatory, 204

Sambalpur University, 1053

Samband Íslenzkra Myndlistarmanna, 1001

Samchok National University, 1384

Samford University, 2504

Samfundet de Nio, 2056

Samfundet for Dansk Genealogi og Personalhistorie, 651

Samfundet för Pedagogisk Forskning, Jyväskylä, 719

Sammenslutningen af Danske Kunstforeninger, 650

Sammenslutningen af museer i Grønland, 667

Samoilov, Ya. V., Research Institute of Fertilizers and Insectofungicides, 1832

Sampurnanand Sanskrit University, 1054

Sampurnanand Sanskrit Vishvavidyalaya, 1054

Samra University of Oriental Medicine, Los Angeles, 2534

Samstarfsnefnd háskólastigsins, 1000

Samtök Kvikmundaleikstjóra, 1001

Samtse College of Education, 280

Samuel Jackman Prescod Polytechnic, St Michael, 237

Samuel Merritt University, Oakland, 2534

Samuel Neaman Institute for Advanced Studies in Science and Technology, 1142

San Agustín Museum, 1692

San Angelo Museum of Fine Arts, 2498

San Antonio Museum of Art, 2498

San Beda College, 1705

San Carlos School of Fine Arts, 2038

San Diego Christian College, 2534

San Diego County Public Law Library, 2432

San Diego Museum of Art, 2467

San Diego Natural History Museum, 2467

San Diego Public Library, 2432

San Diego State University, 2534

San Fernando Carnegie Free Library, 2152

San Fernando Royal Academy of Fine Arts, 1996

San Francisco Art Institute, 2534

San Francisco Conservatory of Music, 2534

San Francisco Law Library, 2432

San Francisco Museum of Modern Art, 2467

San Francisco Public Library, 2432

San Francisco State University, 2534

San Francisco Theological Seminary, San Anselmo, 2535

San Jacinto Museum of History, 2498

San José State University, 2535

San Juan Bautista School of Medicine, 2976

San Marcos National University General Library, 1680

San Telmo Museoa, 2011

San'a University, 3023

Sandberg Instituut, 1566

Sangeet Natak Akademi, New Delhi, 1007

Sangji University, 1379

Sangju National University, 1384

Sangkha College, 1401

Sangmyung University, 1379

Sanibel Public Library, 2436

Sanjay Gandhi Postgraduate Institute of Medical Sciences, 1072

Sanno Institute of Management, 1328

Sant Jordi Iconography and Christianity Museum, 98

Sant Julià de Lòria Community Library, 98

Santa Catarina Historical and Geographical Institute, 298

Santa Clara University, 2535

Santa Cruz County Law Library, 2432

Santa Fe Public Library, 2451

Santa Fe University of Art and Design, 2765

Santa Giulia–Museo della Città, 1182

Santiago Medical Association, 671

Santiago Medical Society, 449

São Miguel de Odrinhas Archaeological Museum, 1772

São Paulo University Museum, 307

Sapienza Università di Roma, 1191

Sapparo Dental College, 235

Sapporo Gakuin University, 1328

Sapporo Medical University, 1306

Sapporo University, 1328

Sara Hildén Art Museum, 722

Sara Hildénin Taidemuseo, 722

Sarabhai Foundation—Calico Museum of Textiles, Ahmedabad, 1022

Sarah Lawrence College, 2800

Sarajevo City Library, 290

Sarajevo Historical Archives, 290

Saratov A. N. Radishchev State Art Museum, 1861

Saratov Animal Husbandry and Veterinary Institute, 1899

Saratov Institute of Agricultural Engineering, 1899

Saratov Institute of Economics, 1899

Saratov Institute of Restorative Surgery, Traumatology and Orthopaedics, 1839

Saratov State Academy of Law, 1897

Saratov State Agrarian University, N. I. Vavilov, 1863

Saratov State Conservatoire 'L. V. Sobinov', 1900

Saratov State Medical University, 1882

Saratov State University 'N. G. Chernyshevsky', 1876

Sarawak Museum, 1446

Sarawak State Library, 1446

Sarayköy Nuclear Research and Training Centre, 2161

Sarayköy Nükleer Araştırma ve Eğitim Merkezi, 2161

Sarbajanik Vidyabhawan Library, 1525

Sardar Bahadur Khan Women's University, 1654

Sardar Patel University, 1054

Sardar Vallabh Bhai Patel University of Agriculture and Technology, 1054

Sardar Vallabhbhai National Institute of Technology, 1078

Sargent Memorial Library, 2445

Sarhad University of Science & Information Technology, 1654

Sarjeant Gallery, Wanganui, 1578

Sárospataki Református Kollégium Tudományos Gyűjteményei Nagykönyvtára, 980

Sarpay Beikman Public Library, Yangon, 1514

Sarrià Institute of Chemistry, 2037

Sarsen Amanzholov East Kazakhstan State University, 1348

Saskatchewan Legislative Library, 377

Saskatchewan Provincial Library and Literacy Office, 377

Society of Instrument and Control Engineers, 1224
Society of Irish Foresters, 1130
Society of Japanese Virologists, 1221
Society of Jurists of Slovenia, 1963
Society of Liberian Authors, 1413
Society of Light Industry, Moscow, 1830
Society of Literary Translators of Macedonia, 1432
Society of Malawi, 1440
Society of Manufacturing Engineers, Dearborn, 2417
Society of Mathematicians of Macedonia, 1432
Society of Mathematicians of Republika Srpska, 288
Society of Mathematicians of Serbia, 1921
Society of Mathematicians, Physicists and Astronomers of Slovenia, 1964
Society of Medical Jurisprudence, New York, 2409
Society of Miniaturists, Ilkley, 2232
Society of Mongolian Surgeons, 1497
Society of Naval Architects & Marine Engineers, Jersey City, 2417
Society of Netherlands Literature, 1530
Society of Non-Ferrous Metallurgy, Moscow, 1829
Society of Obstetrics and Gynaecology, Caracas, 3000
Society of Occupational Medicine, London, 2239
Society of Operations Engineers, London, 2248
Society of Ophthalmology, 3001
Society of Oriental Researches, 1219
Society of Ornithologists, Moscow, 1829
Society of Orthopaedics and Traumatological Surgery, 3001
Society of Otorhinolaryngology, 3001
Society of Petroleum Engineers, Richardson, 2417
Society of Physicians and Naturalists in Iaşi, 1784
Society of Physicists of Macedonia, 1432
Society of Plant Physiology and Biochemistry of Moldova, 1491
Society of Polish Surgeons, 1710
Society of Polish Town Planners, 1708
Society of Polymer Science, Japan, 1222
Society of Protozoologists, St Petersburg, 1829
Society of Psychologists, Moscow, 1829
Society of Radiology and Diagnostic Imaging, Caracas, 3001
Society of Rheology, Madison, 2417
Society of Scribes & Illuminators, London, 2233
Society of Serbian Language and Literature, 1921
Society of Slovene Composers, 1963
Society of South African Geographers, 1973
Society of Swedish Authors in Finland, 715
Society of Swedish Composers, 2055
Society of Swedish Literature in Finland, 716
Society of the Food Industry, Moscow, 1830
Society of the Friends of History, Helsinki, 715
Society of the History of Sciences and Technology, 630
Society of the Instrument Manufacturing Industry and Metrologists, Moscow, 1830
Society of the Timber and Forestry Industry, Moscow, 1827
Society of Town Planning of Bosnia and Herzegovina, 288
Society of Vertebrate Paleontology, Deerfield, 2411
Society of Wildlife Artists, London, 2232
Socio—Economic Research Institute, Kolkata, 1014
Socio-Economics Centre, Lisbon, 1764
Sociological Association of Ukraine, 2196
Sociologický ústav AV ČR, 633
Sociology Institute, Beijing, 469
Sociomedical Institute at ZRC SAZU, 1965

Sodertorn University College, 2082
Södertörns Högskola, 2082
SOD-Opleidingen, Woerden, 1563
Sofia City Art Gallery, 344
Sofia City Library, 342
Sofia Museum of History, 344
Sofia University 'St Kliment Ohridski', 347
Sofiiski Universitet 'Sveti Kliment Ohridski', 347
Sogang University, 1380
Sogo Kenkyu Kaihatsu Kiko, 1225
Söguélag, 1001
Sohar University, 1634
Soil and Agricultural Climate Research Centre, 1085
Soil Research Institute, Kumasi, 939
Soil Resources Agency, Sofia, 334
Soil Science Research Institute, Pyongyang, 1360
Soil Science Society, Moscow, 1827
Soil Science Society of America, 2399
Soil Science Society of China, 462
Soil, Water and Environment Research Institute, Giza, 687
Sojourner-Douglass College, 2662
Sojuz na društvata na arhivskite rabotnici na Makedonija, 1432
Sojuz na Društvata na Veterinarnite Lekari i Tehničari na Makedonija, 1431
Sojuz na Društvata za Makedonski Jazik i Literatura, 1432
Sojuz na Ekonomistite na Makedonija, 1432
Sojuz na Inženeri i Tehničari na Makedonija, 1432
Sojuz na Inženeri i Tehničari po Sumarstvo i Industrija za Prerabotka na Drvo na Makedonija, 1431
Sojuz na Istoricarite na Republika Makedonija, 1432
Sojuz na Kompozitorite na Makedonija, 1432
Sojuz na Matematičari na Makedonija, 1432
Sojuz na Združenijata na Pravnicite na Makedonija, 1432
Soka University, 1329
Sokhumi Botanical Garden, 815
Sokoine National Agricultural Library, Morogoro, 2131
Sokoine University of Agriculture, 2132
Solar Energy Research Centre, Jadiriya, 1123
Solar-Terrestrial Influences Laboratory, Sofia, 340
Solomon Islands College of Higher Education, 1969
Solomon Islands College of Higher Education Library, 1969
Solomon Islands National Archives, 1969
Solomon Islands National Library, 1969
Solomon Islands National Museum and Cultural Centre, 1969
Solomon R. Guggenheim Museum, New York, 2489
SOM Research Institute, 1536
Somali Institute of Public Administration Library, 1970
Somali National Museum, 1970
Somerset College, 2363
Somerset County Council, Library Service, 2265
Somerset County Library System, Princess Anne, 2444
Somerville College, Oxford, 2348
Somogy Megyei Múzeumok Igazgatósága, Kaposvár, 983
Somogyi Library, Szeged, 981
Somogyi-könyvtár, Szeged, 981
Sonoma State University, 2535
Soochow University, 545
Soochow University, Taipei, 2124
Sookmyung Women's University, 1381
Soongsil University, 1381
Sophia (Jōchi) University Library, 1230
Sophia University, 1329
Sophiahemmet Högskola, 2082
Sophiahemmet University College, 2082

Soprintendenza alla Galleria Nazionale d'Arte Moderna e Contemporanea, Rome, 1187
Soprintendenza per i Beni Archeologici della Liguria, Genoa, 1185
Soprintendenza Speciale per i Beni Archeologici di Roma, 1187
Soreq Nuclear Research Centre, 1144
SORIN Biomedica SpA, Saluggia, 1176
Sörmlands museum, 2065
Sorolla Museum, Madrid, 2010
Sorprintendza Speciale Per I Beni Archeologici Di Napoli E Pompei, 1186
Sosiaalilääketieteen Yhdistys ry, 716
Sotamuseo, 721
Sotheby's Institute of Art, London, 2363
Sourasky Central Library, Tel-Aviv University, 1146
Sous-Direction de l'Archéologie, Paris, 747
South Africa House, Amsterdam, 1528
South African Academy for Science and Arts, 1973
South African Archaeological Society, 1973
South African Astronomical Observatory, 1976
South African Brain Research Institute, 1976
South African Bureau of Standards, Pretoria, 1977
South African Chemical Institute, 1975
South African Institute of Agricultural Engineers, 1975
South African Institute of Architects, 1973
South African Institute of Electrical Engineers, 1975
South African Institute of International Affairs, 1973
South African Institute of Mining and Metallurgy, 1975
South African Institute of Physics, 1975
South African Institute of Race Relations, 1975
South African Institution of Civil Engineering (SAICE), 1975
South African Institution of Mechanical Engineering, 1975
South African Library, 1977
South African Medical Association, 1974
South African Medical Research Council, Tygerberg, 1976
South African Museums Association, 1973
South African National Association for the Visual Arts (SANAVA), 1973
South African National Biodiversity Institute, Claremont, 1974
South African PEN Centre, 1974
South African Pharmacology Society, 1974
South African Society for Animal Science, 1973
South African Society for Microbiology, 1974
South African Society of Biochemistry and Molecular Biology, 1974
South African Society of Dairy Technology, 1973
South African Society of Obstetricians and Gynaecologists, 1974
South Asia Institute, Heidelberg, 898
South Asian Institute of Technology and Medicine, 2046
South Australian Museum, 142
South Berwick Public Library, 2443
South Bohemian Museum in České Budějovice, 635
South Carolina College of Pharmacy, 2885
South Carolina Confederate Relic Room & Military Museum, 2496
South Carolina State Library, 2457
South Carolina State Museum, 2496
South Carolina State University, 2885
South Cheshire College, 2361
South China Agricultural University, 546
South China Botanical Garden, 467
South China Normal University, 546
South China Sea Institute of Oceanology, Guangzhou, 467

South China Teachers' University Library, 471
South China University of Technology, 547
South College, Knoxville, 2894
South Dakota Agricultural Heritage Museum, 2496
South Dakota Art Museum, 2496
South Dakota School of Mines and Technology, 2888
South Dakota State Archives, 2458
South Dakota State Library, 2458
South Dakota State University, 2888
South Dakota State University Library, 2458
South East European University, 1435
South Eastern Education and Library Board, 2265
South Eastern Regional College, 2369
South Eastern University of Sri Lanka, 2043
South Essex College, 2361
South Hamgyong Provincial Library, 1361
South Hwanghae Provincial Library, 1361
South Karelia Polytechnic, 735
South Kazakhstan Scientific and Research Institute of Agriculture, 1339
South Kazakhstan Technical University, 1350
South London Gallery, 2288
South Nottingham College, 2361
South Pyongan Provincial Library, 1361
South Russia State Technical University (Novocherkassk Polytechnic Institute), 1893
South St Landry Community Library, 2442
South Shields Museum and Art Gallery, 2289
South Texas College, 2909
South Texas College of Law, 2909
South Thames College, 2362
South Tyneside College, 2362
South University, Savannah, 2601
South Ural State University, 1876
South Urals Agricultural Research Institute, 1832
South Valley University, Kena, 693
South Wales Institute of Engineers Educational Trust, 2248
South West College, 2369
South Western University of Finance and Economics, 548
Southampton City Art Gallery, 2291
Southampton City Libraries, 2280
Southampton Solent University, Southampton, 2299
Southbank Institute of Technology, South Brisbane, 169
South-East Agricultural Research Institute, Saratov, 1832
South-East Asia University, 2144
Southeast Asian Ministers of Education Organization Regional Center for Educational Innovation and Technology (SEAMEO INNOTECH), Quezon City, 1690
Southeast Asian Ministers of Education Organization (SEAMEO), 56
Southeast Missouri State University, 2743
Southeast University, Dhaka, 226
Southeast University, Nanjing, 547
Southeastern Baptist College, 2735
Southeastern Baptist Theological Seminary, Wake Forest, 2813
Southeastern Bible College, 2505
Southeastern Louisiana University, 2652
Southeastern Oklahoma State University, 2842
Southeastern University, Lakeland, 2589
Southend on Sea Borough Libraries Department, 2280
Southern Adventist University, 2894
Southern Africa Association for the Advancement of Science, 1974
Southern African Institute of Forestry, 1973

Stowarzyszenie Miłośników Dawnej Broni i Barwy, Cracow, 1708
Stowarzyszenie Neuropatologów Polskich, 1710
Stowe Free Library, 2459
St-Patrick's International College, London, 2362
Stradiņ Museum of the History of Medicine, 1404
Strake Jesuit Art Museum, 2498
Strålsäkerhetscentralen, Helsinki, 719
Strangeways Research Laboratory, 2258
Stranmillis University College, 2369
Strategic Air & Space Museum, 2485
Stratford University, 2935
Strathclyde Fermentation Centre, Glasgow, 2260
Strathclyde Institute for Drug Research, Glasgow, 2258
Strathmore University, 1355
Stratingh Institute for Chemistry, 1539
Strayer University, 2935
Stredoslovenské múzeum, 1953
Strindberg Museum, 2067
Strindbergsmuseet, 2067
Stroke Association, London, 2239
Strokestown Park House Garden and Famine Museum, Strokestown, 1134
Strossmayerova galerija starih majstora, 611
Strossmayers' Gallery of Old Masters, Zagreb, 611
Stroud College, 2362
Structural Engineering Research Centre, Chennai, 1012
Structural Engineering Research Centre, Ghaziabad, 1012
Sts Cyril and Methodius University in Skopje, 1435
Studie Centrum voor Onderneming en Beurs, 254
Studie- en Documentatiecentrum Hugo Claus, 254
Studiecentrum voor de 15de-Eeuwse Schilderkunst in de Zuidelijke Nederlanden en het Prinsbisdom Luik, 254
Studiecentrum voor Kernenergie, 255
Studies and Design Institute for Public Works, Bucharest, 1786
Studijų kokybės vertinimo centras, 1421
Studijní a vědecká knihovna, Hradec Králové, 634
Studijní a vědecká knihovna Plzeňského kraje, Plzeň, 634
Studio-School of the Moscow Arts Theatre 'V. I. Nemirovich-Danchenko', 1901
Studium Biblicum Franciscanum, Jerusalem, 1161
Study and Research Centre for Human and Animal Biology, Algiers, 90
Stuhr Museum of the Prairie Pioneer, 2485
Stuttgart Art Museum, 857
Stuttgart Institute of Management and Technology, 935
Stuttgart State Academy of Art and Design, 934
Styrelsen for Bibliotek og Medier, Copenhagen, 649
Styrelsen för Internationellt Utvecklingssamarbete, 2054
Styrelsen for Statens Uddannelsesstøtte, Copenhagen, 649
Styrian Federal State Library, Graz, 183
Styrian Historical Association, 174
Styrian Provincial Archives, Graz, 183
'Submicron' Research Institute, 1852
Sub-Tropical Forestry Research Institute, Fuyang, 466
Sudan Academy for Administrative Sciences, Khartoum, 2047
Sudan Medical Research Laboratories, Khartoum, 2047
Sudan Medical Research Laboratories Library, 2048
Sudan National Museum, 2048
Sudan Natural History Museum, 2048

Sudan University Of Science And Technology, 2049
Sudley House, 2286
Südtiroler Archäologiemuseum, Bolzano, Bolzano, 1182
Suermondt-Ludwig-Museum, Aachen, 848
Suez Canal University, 693
Suffolk County Council—Libraries, Archives and Information, 2270
Suffolk University, 2689
Sugar Beet Research Institute, Kyiv, 2197
Sugar Crops Research Institute, Giza, 687
Sugar Industry Research Institute, Mandeville, 1214
Sugar Manufacture Association of Trinidad and Tobago, 2151
Sugar Research Institute of Fiji, 710
Suid-Afrikaanse Akademie vir Wetenskap en Kuns, 1973
Suid-Afrikaanse Instituut van Landbou-Ingenieurs, 1975
Suid-Afrikaanse Vereniging vir Veekunde, 1973
Suider-Afrikaanse Instituut van Boswese, 1973
Sukhothai Thammathirat Open University, 2144
Sukhumi I. N. Vekua Institute of Physics and Technology, 814
Sukkur Institute of Business Administration, 1655
Sul Ross State University, 2914
Süleyman Demirel Üniversitesi, 2184
Suleyman Demirel University, 1348
Süleymaniye Kütüphanesi, Istanbul, 2161
Sullivan Family Library, 2438
Sullivan University, 2647
Sultan Abdul Samad Library, 1446
Sultan Ali Dinar Museum, 2048
Sultan Idris Education University, 1449
Sultan Qaboos University, 1634
Sultan Saiful Rijal Technical College, Brunei, 332
Summer Garden and Museum Palace of Peter the Great, 1861
Sumy Art Museum 'Nukanor Onatsky', 2203
Sun Yat-sen Institute for Social Sciences and Philosophy, Taipei, 2120
Sun Yat-Sen University, 550
Sun Yat-Sen University of Medical Sciences, 550
Sunchon National University, 1372
Sunderland Museum and Winter Gardens, 2290
Sunds Bibliotek, 737
Sungkyul Christian University, 1381
Sungkyunkwan University, 1381
Sungshin Women's University, 1382
Suntory and Toyota International Centres for Economics and Related Disciplines, London, 2252
SUNY Downstate Medical Center, 2803
Sunyani Polytechnic, 943
Suomalainen Lääkäriseura Duodecim, 716
Suomalainen Lakimiesyhdistys ry, 714
Suomalainen Teologinen Kirjallisuusseura, 717
Suomalainen Tiedeakatemia, 713
Suomalaisen Kirjallisuuden Seuran Kirjallisuusarkisto, 720
Suomalaisen Kirjallisuuden Seuran Kirjasto, 720
Suomalaisten Kemistien Seura, 717
Suomalais-Ugrilainen Seura, Helsinki, 716
Suomen Aerosolitutkimusseura ry, 718
Suomen Akatemia, 718
Suomen Aktuaariyhdistys ry, 713
Suomen Arkeologinen Seura ry, 715
Suomen Arkkitehtiliiton, 713
Suomen arkkitehtuurimuseo, 721
Suomen Automaatioseura ry, 718
Suomen Biologian Seura Vanamo, 716
Suomen Eläinlääkäriliitto, 713
Suomen Englanninopettajat ry, 716
Suomen Estetiikan Seura ry, 717

Suomen Etnomusikologinen Seura ry, 715
Suomen Farmakologiyhdistys, 716
Suomen Filosofinen Yhdistys, 717
Suomen Hammaslääkäriseura Apollonia, 716
Suomen Hyönteistieteellinen Seura, 716
Suomen Itämainen Seura, 717
Suomen Kansantietouden Tutkijain Seura ry, 717
Suomen Kardiologinen Seura, 716
Suomen Kartografinen Seura, 715
Suomen Kaupunkitutkimuksen Seuran, 713
Suomen Kemistiseura, 717
Suomen Kirjailijaliitto, 716
Suomen Kriminalistiyhdistys, 714
Suomen Limnologinen yhdistys, 717
Suomen Luonnonsuojeluliitto, 717
Suomen Maataloustieteellinen Seura ry, 714
Suomen Matemaattinen Yhdistys, 717
Suomen Metsätieteellinen Seura, 714
Suomen Naistutkimuksen Seura, 713
Suomen Näytelmäkirjailijat ja Käsikirjoittajat—Finlands Dramatiker och Manusförfattare ry, 715
Suomen Operaatiotutkimusseura, 718
Suomen Psykiatriyhdistys, 717
Suomen Psykologinen Seura ry, 717
Suomen Rakennusinsinöörien Liitto, 713
Suomen Rautatiemuseo, 721
Suomen Sairaanhoitajaliitto ry, 716
Suomen Sammalseura ry, 717
Suomen Tähtitieteilijäseura ry, 713
Suomen Taideyhdistys, 715
Suomen Tekoälyseura, 718
Suomen Tiedeseura, 713
Suomen Tieteellinen Kirjastoseura, 714
Suomen Toksikologiyhdistys, 716
Suomen Tribologiayhdistys ry, 718
Suomen Väestötieteen Yhdistys, 714
Suomen Valokuvataiteen Museo, 721
Suomen Vesiyhdistys, 714
Suomen yliopistot UNIFI ry, 713
Suomen Ympäristökeskus, 719
Suoseura ry, 714
Supélec—Ecole Supérieure d'Electricité, Gif sur Yvette, 798
Superintendence of Cultural Heritage, Valletta, 1458
Superior Court Law Library, 2431
Superior Group of Colleges, 1655
SUPINFO – Ecole Supérieure d'Informatique, Montreuil, 798
Supméca Paris—Institut Supérieur de Mécanique de Paris, St Ouen, 794
Supméca Toulon—Institut Supérieur de Mécanique de Toulon, 794
Supreme Council of Antiquities, Cairo, 686
Supreme Council of Universities, Giza, 685
Supreme Court Library, Jerusalem, 1145
Supreme Court Library, London, 2276
Supreme Court Library, Tokyo, 1230
Supreme Court of Canada Library, 376
Supreme Court of Queensland Library, Brisbane, 140
Sur University College, 1635
Suranaree University of Technology, 2145
Surgical Society, Montevideo, 2980
Surgut State University, 1877
Surrey Libraries, 2270
Sursock Museum, 1407
Surtsey Research Society, 1002
Surtseyjarfélagið, 1002
Survey Institute of Zimbabwe, 3028
Survey of India, 1014
Survey Technique and Applied Research (STAR) Centre of the Institute of Sociology, Moscow, 1834
Surveying and Spatial Sciences Institute, 136
Suseong Library, 1364
Susini College, 627
Susquehanna University, 2872
Sussex County Library System, Newton, 2450

Sustainable Development Study Centre, Lahore, 1641
Sutton Library Service, 2276
Suva City Library, 711
Suvirinimo ir Medžiagotyros Problemų Institutas, Vilnius, 1423
Suvorov Museum, 1856
Suwon University, 1372
Suzanne H. Arnold Art Gallery, 2495
Svaneholm Castle Museum, 2065
Svaneholms Slottsmuseum, 2065
Sven Lovén Centre for Marine Sciences, 2059
Sven Lovén Centrum för Marina Vetenskaper, 2059
Svensk Form, 2056
Svenska Akademien, 2056
Svenska Akademiens Nobelbibliotek, 2062
Svenska Bioenergiföreningen (Svebio), 2057
Svenska Fysikersamfundet, 2057
Svenska Geotekniska Föreningen, 2057
Svenska Handelshögskolan, Helsinki, 732
Svenska institutet, 2054
Svenska institutet i Athen, 958
Svenska Institutet i Rom, 1174
Svenska Läkaresällskapet, 2056
Svenska Linnésällskapet, 2057
Svenska Litteratursällskapet i Finland, 716
Svenska litteratursällskapet i Finland, arkiv och bibliotek, 720
Svenska Matematikersamfundet, 2057
Svenska Museiföreningen, 2056
Svenska PEN, 2056
Svenska Sällskapet för Antropologi och Geografi, 2056
Svenska Samfundet för Musikforskning, 2056
Svenska Skidmuseet, 2068
Svenska Statistikfrämjandet, 2057
Svenska Teknik & Designföretagen, 2055
Svenska Tekniska Vetenskapsakademien i Finland, 718
Svenska Vitterhetssamfundet, 2056
Svenskt Visarkiv, 2063
Sveriges Allmänna Konstförening, 2056
Sveriges Författarförbund, 2056
Sveriges Geologiska Undersökning, 2060
Sveriges Ingenjörer, 2057
Sveriges Järnvägsmuseum, 2063
Sveriges Lantbruksuniversitet, 2077
Sveriges lantbruksuniversitets—Bibliotek, 2063
Sveriges Radio Förvaltings AB, 2063
Sveriges universitets- och högskoleförbund (SUHF), 2054
Sveučilišna knjižnica Rijeka, 609
Sveučilišna knjižnica u Puli, 608
Sveučilišna knjižnica u Splitu, 609
Sveučilište Josipa Jurja Strossmayera u Osijeku, 611
Sveučilište Jurja Dobrile u Puli, 612
Sveučilište u Dubrovniku, 613
Sveučilište u Mostaru, 291
Sveučilište u Rijeci, 612
Sveučilište u Splitu, 612
Sveučilište u Zadru, 613
Sveučilište u Zagrebu, 613
Svrzina Kuća, 291
Svrzo House, 291
SVUSS Praha, s. r. o., Prague, 633
S-VYASA, 1078
Swami Keshwanand Rajasthan Agricultural University, Bikaner, 1056
Swami Ramanand Teerth Marathwada University, 1057
Swami Vivekananda Yoga Anusandhana Samsthana, 1078
Swammerdam Institute for Life Sciences, 1540
Swansea Metropolitan University, 2384
Swansea University, 2384
Swansea University Library, 2280
Swarthmore College, 2872
Swaziland Art Society, 2052
Swaziland College of Technology, 2053

Swaziland Institute of Management and Public Administration, 2053
Swaziland Library Association, 2052
Swaziland National Archives, 2052
Swaziland National Library Service, 2052
Swaziland National Museum, 2052
Swedenborg Society, 2244
Swedish Academy, 2056
Swedish Academy of Engineering Sciences in Finland, 718
Swedish Art Music Society, 2056
Swedish Arts Council, 2056
Swedish Association of Graduate Engineers, 2057
Swedish Bioenergy Association (Svebio), 2057
Swedish Cartographic Society, 2056
Swedish Cement and Concrete Research Institute, 2060
Swedish Collegium for Advanced Study (SCAS), 2059
Swedish Council for Humanities and Social Sciences, 2058
Swedish Economic Association, 2055
Swedish Federation of Consulting Engineers and Architects, 2055
Swedish General Art Association, 2056
Swedish Geotechnical Institute, 2060
Swedish Geotechnical Society, 2057
Swedish Glass Research Institute, 2060
Swedish ICT, 2060
Swedish Institute, 2054
Swedish Institute at Athens, 958
Swedish Institute for Social Research, 2060
Swedish Institute of Classical Studies in Rome, 1174
Swedish Institute of International Affairs, 2055
Swedish Institute of Space Physics, 2059
Swedish Institute of Steel Construction, 2060
Swedish International Development Cooperation Agency, 2054
Swedish Linnaeus Society, 2057
Swedish Mathematical Society, 2057
Swedish Meteorological and Hydrological Institute, 2060
Swedish Museum of Architecture, 2066
Swedish Museum of Natural History, 2067
Swedish Museums Association, 2056
Swedish National Agency for Education, 2054
Swedish National Agency for Higher Vocational Education, 2054
Swedish National Institute of Public Health, 2059
Swedish National Portrait Gallery, 2065
Swedish PEN, 2056
Swedish Physical Society, 2057
Swedish Railway Museum, 2063
Swedish Research Council, 2058
Swedish Research Council Formas, 2057
Swedish School of Sport and Health Sciences, 2082
Swedish Ski Museum, 2068
Swedish Society for Anthropology and Geography, 2056
Swedish Society for Musicology, 2056
Swedish Society for Nature Conservation, 2057
Swedish Society of Crafts and Design, 2056
Swedish Society of Medicine, 2056
Swedish Statistics Promotion, 2057
Swedish University of Agricultural Sciences, 2077
Swedish Writers' Union, 2056
Swedish–Pakistani Institute of Technology, Gujrat, 1661
Sweet Briar College, 2935
Sweida Museum, 2116
Swerea Corrosion and Metals Research Institute AB, 2060
Swerea IVF AB, 2060
Swerea KIMAB AB, 2060
Swerea MEFOS, 2060
Swerea SICOMP, 2060
Swerea SWECAST, 2060

Swinburne University of Technology, 162
Swindon Borough Libraries, 2281
Swindon College, 2362
Swiss Academy of Engineering Sciences, 2085
Swiss Academy of Humanities and Social Sciences, 2085
Swiss Academy of Medical Sciences, 2089
Swiss Academy of Sciences, 2085
Swiss Arts Council, 2087
Swiss Association of Geomatics, 2090
Swiss Astronomical Society, 2090
Swiss Bar Association, 2086
Swiss Center of Accreditation and Quality Assurance in Higher Education, 2084
Swiss Conference of Cantonal Ministers of Education, 2085
Swiss Economic Archives, 2093
Swiss Energy Foundation, 2089
Swiss Engineering–STV, 2091
Swiss ENIC—Naric, Bern, 2084
Swiss Federal Archives, 2094
Swiss Federal Institute for Forest, Snow and Landscape Research, 2093
Swiss Federal Institute for Vocational Education and Training, 2113
Swiss Federal Institute of Technology, 2100
Swiss Federation of Automatic Control, 2090
Swiss Foundation for Alpine Research, 2089
Swiss Geological Society, 2090
Swiss Graduate School of Public Administration, 2112
Swiss Heritage Society, 2085
Swiss Institute for Art Research, 2087
Swiss Institute of Allergy and Asthma Research, 2092
Swiss Institute of Comparative Law, 2091
Swiss Institute of International Studies, 2092
Swiss Mathematical Society, 2090
Swiss National Association of Libraries and Librarians, 2086
Swiss National Costume Association, 2090
Swiss National Library, 2093
Swiss National Museum, 2098
Swiss National Science Foundation, 2085
Swiss Numismatic Society, 2088
Swiss Palaeontological Society, 2090
Swiss Physical Society, 2090
Swiss Science and Technology Council, 2085
Swiss Society for Astrophysics and Astronomy, 2093
Swiss Society for the History of Medicine and Sciences, 2089
Swiss Society of Cartography, 2088
Swiss Society of Economics and Statistics, 2086
Swiss Society of General Internal Medicine, 2089
Swiss Society of Writers, 2088
Swiss Sociological Association, 2090
Swiss Transport Museum, 2097
Swiss Tropical and Public Health Institute, 2092
Swiss University Conference, 2084
Swiss University Teachers' Association, 2085
Swiss Water Association, 2091
Swiss Windband Association, 2087
Swope Art Museum, 2476
Syddansk Musikkonservatorium & Skuespillerskole, 664
Syddansk Universitet, 663
Syddansk Universitetsbibliotek, 655
Sydney College of Divinity, North Ryde, 168
Sydney Medical School Foundation, Sydney, 133
Syktyvkar State University, 1878
Syktyvkar State University Library, 1855
Sylhet Agricultural University, 226
Sylhet International University, 226
Sylhet Women's Medical College, 235

Syllogos pros Diadosin ton Hellenikon Grammaton, Athens, 945
Symbiosis College of Arts and Commerce, Pune, 1080
Symbiosis International University, 1078
Symbiosis Law School, 1080
Syndesmos Ellinidon Epistimonon (SEE), 945
Synodos Prytaneon Ellinikon Panepistimion, Athens, 945
Synthetic & Art Silk Mills' Research Association, Mumbai, 1019
Syracuse University, 2803
Syracuse University Library, 2452
Syscoms College, 2222
Sysin, A. N., Institute of Human Ecology and Environmental Hygiene, Moscow, 1839
Systematics Association, Egham, 2241
Systems Engineering Innovation Centre, Loughborough, 2264
Systems Engineering Society of China, 465
Systems Research Institute, Warsaw, 1719
Systems Society of India, 1010
Sytenko Institute of Spine and Joint Pathology, Kharkiv, 2199
Szabadtéri Néprajzi Múzeum, Szentendre, 984
Szatmári Múzeum, 983
Szczecin University, 1741
Széchenyi Academy of Letters and Arts, 973
Széchenyi Irodalmi és Művészeti Akadémia, 973
Széchenyi István Egyetem, 995
Széchenyi István Emlékmúzeum, 984
Széchenyi István Memorial Museum, 984
Széchenyi István University, 995
Szegedi Tudományegyetem, 995
Szegedi Tudományegyetem Egyetemi Könyvtár, 981
Szekler Museum of Ciuc, 1796
Szent István Egyetem, 997
Szent István Egyetem Állatorvostudományi Könyvtár, Levéltár és Múzeum, Budapest, 980
Szent István Egyetem Gödöllői Tudományos Könyvtár, 980
Szent István Király Múzeum, 984
Szent István University, 997
Szépművészeti Múzeum, Budapest, 982
Szervezési és Vezetési Tudományos Társaság, Budapest, 975
Szilikátipari Központi Kutató és Tervező Intézet, Budapest, 978
Szilikátipari Tudományos Egyesület, Budapest, 975
Szinház- és Filmművészeti Egyetem, Budapest, 998
Szkoła Główna Gospodarstwa Wiejskiego W Warszawie, 1726
Szkoła Główna Handlowa, Warsaw, 1758
Szkoła Wyzsza Psychologii Społecznej, Warsaw, 1758
Szőlészeti és Borászati Kutató Intézet, Kecskemét, 976
Szórakaténusz Játékmúzeum és Műhely, Kecskemet, 983

T

T. A. Marryshow Community College (TAMCC), St George's, 959
T. Chałubiński Tatra Museum, 1725
Tabon Cave Complex, 1692
Tabor Adelaide, 170
Tabor College, 2641
Tabor College Tasmania, 170
Tabor College Victoria, 171
Tabriz Public Library, 1107
Tabriz University of Medical Sciences, 1118
Tacoma Public Library, 2461
Taekyeung College, 1386
Taft Museum of Art, 2492
Taganrog Institute of Technology, 1877
Tai Sophia Institute, Laurel, 2662
Taibah University, 1915

Taipei Astronomical Museum, 2121
Taipei City Library, 2120
Taipei Fine Arts Museum, 2121
Taipei Institute of Technology, 2125
Taipei Medical University, 2125
Taipei National University of the Arts, 2124
Tairawhiti Museum, 1578
Tairunnessa Memorial Medical College, 235
Taiten Kinen Kyoto Shokubutsuen, 1231
Taiwan Agricultural Research Institute, 2119
Taiwan Branch Library, National Central Library, 2120
Taiwan Fisheries Research Institute, 2119
Taiwan Forestry Research Institute, 2119
Taiwan Studies Institute, Beijing, 466
Taiwan Sugar Research Institute, 2119
Taiyuan University of Technology, 550
Taiz University, 3023
Tajik Agrarian University named after Shirinsho Shotemur, 2128
Tajik Institute of Management, 2128
Tajik Islamic University, 2128
Tajik Open University, 2128
Tajik State Historical Museum, 2127
Tajik State Institute of Fine Arts, 2128
Tajik State Institute of Languages, 2129
Tajik State National University, 2129
Tajik State Pedagogical University named after S. Aini, 2129
Tajik State University Library, 2127
Tajik State University of Commerce, 2129
Tajik State University of Law, Business and Politics, 2129
Tajik Technical University named after Academician M. Osimi, 2129
Tajikistan Association of Professional Social Workers, 2126
Tajoura Nuclear Research Center, 1415
Takhar Provincial Library, 81
Takhar University, 82
Takoradi Polytechnic, 943
Takushoku University, 1329
Talaba Qabulu üzre Dövlat Komissiyasi (TQDK), Baku, 202
Talas State University, 1399
Taldykorgan Agricultural Research Institute, 1339
Tallinn City Museum, 703
Tallinn University, 703
Tallinn University of Technology, 703
Taloustieteellinen Yhdistys, 714
Taloustutkimus, 718
Tama Art University, 1332
Tamagawa University, 1329
Tambov Picture Gallery, 1861
Tambov State Technical University, 1893
Tambov State University 'G. R. Derzhavin', 1878
Tameside Metropolitan Borough Council Libraries and Customer Services Department, 2264
Tamil Language Society, Kuala Lumpur, 1444
Tamil Nadu Agricultural University, 1057
Tamil Nadu Dr Ambedkar Law University, 1057
Tamil Nadu Dr M. G. R. Medical University, 1057
Tamil Nadu Veterinary and Animal Sciences University, 1058
Tamil University, 1058
Tamkang University, Taipei, 2124
Tampa Museum of Art, 2472
Tampere Art Museum, 722
Tampere City Library—Pirkanmaa Regional Library, 721
Tampere Museums, 722
Tampere University Library, 721
Tampere University of Applied Sciences, 736
Tampere University of Technology, 733
Tampere University of Technology Library, 721
Tampereen Ammattikorkeakoulu, 736

Tobago District Agricultural Society, 2151
Tobolsk Picture Gallery, 1861
Toccoa Falls College, 2601
Tochigi Prefectural Library, 1230
Todaiji, 1232
Togliatti State University, 1878
Tōhō Gakkai, 1224
Toho Gakuen School of Music, 1332
Tohoku Gakuin University, 1330
Tohoku University, 1282
Tohoku University Library, 1229
Tokai University Educational System, 1330
Tokiwa University, 1330
Tokyo Biochemical Research Institute, 1227
Tokyo Bunkazai Kenkyu-jo, 1226
Tokyo Chigaku Kyokai, 1219
Tokyo College of Music, 1332
Tokyo Daigaku Keizai Gakkai, 1219
Tokyo Daigaku Rigaku Kenkyu-ka Fuzoku Shokubutsuen, 1233
Tokyo Denki Daigaku, 1330
Tokyo Denki University, 1330
Tokyo Dental College, 1330
Tokyo Geijutsu Daigaku Toshokan, 1230
Tokyo Geographical Society, 1219
Tokyo Institute of Technology, 1289
Tokyo Keizai University, 1330
Tokyo Kokuritsu Hakubutsukan, 1233
Tokyo Medical and Dental University, 1292
Tokyo Metropolitan Art Museum, 1233
Tokyo Metropolitan Central Library, 1230
Tokyo Metropolitan Institute of Medical Science, 1227
Tokyo Metropolitan University, 1306
Tokyo National Museum, 1233
Tokyo National Research Institute of Cultural Properties, 1226
Tokyo National University of Fine Arts and Music, 1292
Tokyo University of Agriculture, 1331
Tokyo University of Agriculture and Technology, 1299
Tokyo University of Fisheries, 1299
Tokyo University of Foreign Studies, 1299
Tokyo University of Foreign Studies Library, 1230
Tokyo University of Marine Science and Technology Library, 1230
Tokyo University of Mercantile Marine, 1300
Tokyo University of Pharmacy and Life Sciences, 1330
Tokyo University of Science, 1331
Tokyo University of the Arts Library, 1230
Tokyo Women's Christian University, 1331
Tokyo Women's Medical University, 1331
Tokyo-to Bijutsukan, 1233
Toledo Museum of Art, 2492
Toledo Royal Academy of Fine Arts and Historical Sciences, 1997
Toledo-Lucas County Public Library, 2455
Tolhouse Museum, Great Yarmouth, 2290
Tolson Memorial Museum, 2285
Tolstoy Residence Museum, 1858
Tom Thomson Memorial Art Gallery, 379
Tomas Bata University in Zlín, 643
Tomsk Institute of Physiotherapy and Spa Treatment, 1839
Tomsk Polytechnic University, 1893
Tomsk Research Centre, 1839
Tomsk State Academy of Civil Engineering, 1895
Tomsk State University, 1878
Tomsk State University Library, 1855
Tomsk State University of Control Systems and Radioelectronics, 1893
Tonga Institute of Science and Technology, 2150
Tonga Library Association, 2150
Tonga National Qualifications and Accreditation Board, 2150

Tonga Wildlife Centre, 2150
Tongass Historical Museum, 2464
Tongji Medical University, 553
Tongji University, 553
Tónlistarfélagið, 1001
Tønsberg and Nøtterøy Public Library, 1618
Tønsberg og Nøtterøy Bibliotek, 1618
Tónskáldafélag Íslands, 1001
Top Education Institute, Sydney, 168
Top Institute for Evidence Based Education Research (TIER), Amsterdam, 1537
Topchiev, A. V., Institute of Petro-Chemical Synthesis, Moscow, 1852
Topeka and Shawnee County Public Library, 2441
Topkapı Palace Museum, 2162
Toraigyrov Oblast Universal Scientific Library, 1341
Torbay Libraries, 2281
Torfaen Libraries, 2279
Tornquist Library, 110
Tornyai Janos Museum and Cultural Centre, 983
Tornyai János Múzeum és Közművelődési Központ, 983
Toronto Biomedical NMR Centre, 373
Toronto Public Library, 376
Torre Civica di Mestre, Venice, 1190
Torre dell'Orologio, Venice, 1190
Toshkent Avtomobil-yo'llar Instituti, 2988
Toshkent Davlat Iqtisodiyot Universiteti, 2987
Toshkent Davlat Yuridik Instituti, 2988
Toshkent Islom Universiteti, 2987
Toshkent Moliya Instituti, 2988
Totem Heritage Center, 2464
Tottori University, 1300
Tougaloo College, 2735
Touro College, 2803
Towarzystwo Chirurgów Polskich, 1710
Towarzystwo im. Fryderyka Chopina, Warsaw, 1708
Towarzystwo Internistów Polskich, 1710
Towarzystwo Literackie im. Adama Mickiewicza, Warsaw, 1709
Towarzystwo Miłośników Historii i Zabytków Krakowa, 1708
Towarzystwo Naukowe Organizacji i Kierownictwa, Warsaw, 1712
Towarzystwo Naukowe Płockie, 1707
Towarzystwo Naukowe w Toruniu, 1707
Towarzystwo Naukowe Warszawskie, 1707
Towarzystwo Przyjaciół Nauk w Przemyślu, 1707
Towarzystwo Urbanistów Polskich, 1708
Towarzystwo Wiedzy Powszechnej, Warsaw, 1707
Towarzystwo Wolnej Wszechnicy Polskiej, 1707
Tower Hamlets Idea Stores and Libraries, 2276
Town and Country Planning Association, London, 2228
Town Hall Library of the State Capital of Stuttgart, 847
Town Hall Museum Vierschaar, 1553
Town House, King's Lynn, 2290
Town Library, Tórshavn, 665
Town Museum, Bayan-Ölgii, 1499
Town of Chapel Hill Public Library, 2453
Towneley Hall Art Gallery and Museums, 2282
Towson University, 2663
Toy Museum and Workshop, Kecskemet, 983
Toyama University, 1300
Toyo Bunko, Tokyo, 1230
Tōyō Ongaku Gakkai, 1226
Toyo University, 1331
Toyohashi University of Technology, 1300
Toyokuni Jinja Hómotsuden, 1231
Toyoshi-Kenkyu-Kai, 1219
Tractor Research and Development Institute, Moscow, 1852
Trade, Finance and Material Supply Institute, Beijing, 466

Trade Society Romsuintest Periş SA, 1786
Traditional Medicine Association of Viet Nam, Hanoi, 3011
Traditional Medicine Science, Technology and Production Corporation, Ulan Bator, 1498
Trafford Centre for Medical Research, Brighton, 2258
Trafford College, Manchester, 2362
Tragor Ignác Múzeum, 985
Trakai Historical Museum, 1423
Trakia University, 349
Trakiyski Universitet, Stara Zagora, 349
Trakya Üniversitesi, 2184
Tram Museum, Porto, 1771
Trammell & Margaret Crow Collection of Asian Art, 2498
Transcaucasian Hydrometeorological Research Institute, 814
Transdisciplinary Studies Centre for Development, Vila Real, 1763
Transfer Group Rotterdam, 1564
Transfergroep Rotterdam, 1564
Transitional Justice Institute, 2252
Transnationale Universiteit Limburg, 1565
Transport and Telecommunication Institute, Rīga, 1405
Transport Infrastructure and Logistics (TRAIL) Research School, 1534
Transport Library, Seoul, 1365
Transport Museum Dresden, 852
Transport Research and Production Corporation, Ulan Bator, 1498
Transport Research Institute, 1423
Transport Research Institute, Inc., Žilina, 1953
Transporto Institutas, Vilnius, 1423
Transportøkonomisk Institutt, Oslo, 1618
Transvaal Education Department, Education Media Service, 1978
Transylvania County Library, 2453
Transylvania University, 2647
Transylvania University of Braşov Central Library, 1791
Transylvanian Museum of Ethnography, 1795
Tranzo—Scientific Centre for Care and Welfare, 1534
Trapholt, 658
Travelling Library, Aden, 3022
Treasure Hall of the Oyamazumi Shrine, 1232
Treasury and Cabinet Office Library, London, 2276
Tree and Timber Institute, 1170
Trenčianska Univerzita Alexandra Dubčeka, 1958
Trent University, 396
Trenton City Museum, 2487
Tresham College of Further and Higher Education, Corby, 2362
TRESOAR Fries Historisch en Letterkundig Centrum, 1547
TRESOAR Frisian Historical and Literary Centre, 1547
Trevecca Nazarene University, 2895
Trevelyan College, Durham, 2312
TRI Princeton, 2429
Tribhuvan University, 1526
Tribhuvan University Central Library, 1525
Trine University, 2630
Trinidad and Tobago Institute of Architects, 2151
Trinidad Music Association, 2151
Trinity Bible College, 2825
Trinity Christian College, 2616
Trinity College, Cambridge, 2310
Trinity College Dublin, The University of Dublin, 1137
Trinity College, Hartford, 2558
Trinity College Library, Cambridge, 2267
Trinity College Library, Dublin, 1133
Trinity College Library, Oxford, 2279
Trinity College of Nursing & Health Sciences, 2616
Trinity College, Oxford, 2348
Trinity Evangelical Divinity School, Deerfield, 2617

Trinity Graduate School, Deerfield, 2617
Trinity Hall, Cambridge, 2310
Trinity Hall Library, 2267
Trinity International University, Deerfield, 2616
Trinity Laban Conservatoire of Music and Dance, London, 2365
Trinity Lutheran College, 2944
Trinity Lutheran Seminary, 2836
Trinity School for Ministry, 2873
Trinity University, San Antonio, 2916
Trinity Washington University, Washington, 2579
Trinity Western University, 397
Tripura University, 1058
TRL Ltd, Wokingham, 2264
Trnava University, 1958
Trnavská Univerzita, 1958
Troitsk Research Centre, 1846
Tromsø Museum (Universitetetsmuseet), 1620
Trondheim Academy of Fine Art, Norwegian University of Science and Technology, 1632
Tropenmuseum, 1549
Tropical Agriculture Research Station, Mayaguez, 2971
Tropical Botanic Garden and Research Institute, Thiruvananthapuram, 1016
Tropical Diseases Research Centre, Ndola, 3025
Tropical Forestry Research Institute, Guangzhou, 466
Tropical Pesticides Research Institute, Arusha, 2131
Tropical Science Centre, San José, 599
Tropical Science Research Institute, Lisbon, 1763
Trout Museum of Art, 2501
Troy University, 2505
Troy University ITS Sharjah Campus, 2222
Troy University, Montgomery, 2505
Troy University, Phenix City, 2505
Truett McConnell College, 2601
Truman State University, 2744
Truva Müzesi, 2162
Tsarskoe Selo State Museum, 1859
Tselinny Scientific and Research Institute of Mechanization and Electrification in Agriculture, 1339
Tsereteli, G. V., Institute of Oriental Studies, 813
Tsereteli Institute of Philosophy, Tbilisi, 814
Tshwane University of Technology, 1983
Tsinghua University, 553
Tsinghua University Library, 470
Tsiolkovsky, K. E., State Museum of the History of Cosmonautics, 1856
Tskhinvali Pedagogical Institute–Georgian Sector, Gori, 817
Tsubouchi Memorial Theatre Museum, Waseda University, 1233
Tsuda College, 1331
Tšuj University, 1399
Tsuru University, 1332
TU Delft Library, 1546
Tuberculosis and Lung Disease Center, 1118
TÜBiTAK Marmara Araştırma Merkezi Gen Mühendisliği ve Biyoteknoloji Araştırma Enstitüsü, 2160
TÜBiTAK Marmara Research Centre Genetic Engineering and Biotechnology Institute, 2160
TUBITAK Space Technologies Research Institute, 2160
TÜBiTAK Uzay Teknolojileri Araştırma Enstitüsü, 2160
Tubman Centre of African Cultures, 1413
Tucker House Museum, 2386
Tucson Museum of Art and Historic Block, 2465
Tudományos Ismeretterjesztő Társulat, Budapest, 974
Tufts University, 2689
Tuguegarao Branch, 1692
Tula Agricultural Research Institute, 1832

Universidad del Ejército y Fuerza Aérea, México, 1480

Universidad del Golfo, 1481

Universidad del Istmo, 1670

Universidad del Magdalena, 584

Universidad del Mar, Puerto Ángel, 1481

Universidad del Museo Social Argentino, 122

Universidad del Norte, Asunción, 1676

Universidad del Norte, Barranquilla, 589

Universidad del Norte Santo Tomás De Aquino, 122

Universidad del Pacífico, Asunción, 1676

Universidad Del Pacífico, Buenaventura, 584

Universidad del Pacifico, Lima, 1686

Universidad del Quindío, 584

Universidad del Rosario – Colegio Mayor de Nuestra Señora del Rosario, 589

Universidad del Sagrado Corazón, 2975

Universidad del Salvador, Buenos Aires, 122

Universidad del Tolima, 584

Universidad del Trabajo del Uruguay, 2982

Universidad del Turabo, 2973

Universidad del Valle, Cali, 584

Universidad del Valle de Guatemala, 962

Universidad del Valle de México, 1481

Universidad del Zulia, 3008

Universidad di Aruba, 1568

Universidad Diego Portales, 459

Universidad Distrital 'Francisco José De Caldas', 584

Universidad Dominicana O&M, Santo Domingo, 674

Universidad 'Dr José Matías Delgado', 698

Universidad Eafit, Medellín, 589

Universidad Empresarial de Costa Rica, 600

Universidad Empresarial Mateo Kuljis, Santa Cruz, Santa Cruz, 284

Universidad Esan, Lima, 1686

Universidad Especializada de las Americas, Panamá, 1669

Universidad Estatal a Distancia, San José, 601

Universidad Estatal de Bolívar, 681

Universidad Estatal de Estudios Pedagógicos, Mexicali, 1481

Universidad Estatal de Milagro, Los Rios, 681

Universidad Estatal del sur de Manabí, Jipijapa, 681

Universidad Estatal del Valle de Ecatepec, 1481

Universidad Estatal Península de Santa Elena, La Libertad, 681

Universidad Eugenio María de Hostos, 674

Universidad Europea de Madrid (CEES), 2027

Universidad Evangélica del Paraguay, Asunción, 1676

Universidad Experimental 'Felix Adam', Santo Domingo, 674

Universidad Externado de Colombia, 589

Universidad Federico Henríquez y Carvajal, 674

Universidad Femenina de México, 1481

Universidad Femenina del Sagrado Corazón, 1685

Universidad Fidelitas, 601

Universidad Francisco de Paula Santander, 584

Universidad Francisco Marroquin, Guatemala City, 962

Universidad Gabriela Mistral, 459

Universidad Galileo, Guatemala, 962

Universidad IberoAmericana, México, 1482

Universidad Iberoamericana, Santo Domingo, 675

Universidad Iberoamericana—Puebla, 1482

Universidad Iberoamericana—Tijuana, 1482

Universidad Iberoamericana—Torreón, 1482

Universidad ICESI, Cali, 590

Universidad Inca Garcilaso de la Vega, 1685

Universidad Incca de Colombia, 590

Universidad Industrial de Santander, 584

Universidad Interamericana de Panamá, 1670

Universidad Interamericana de Puerto Rico, 2975

Universidad Interamericana, Santo Domingo, 675

Universidad Intercontinental, México, 1482

Universidad Internacional de Andalucía, 2027

Universidad Internacional de las Americas, 601

Universidad Internacional Menéndez Pelayo, 2037

Universidad Jaume I de Castellón, 2027

Universidad Juárez Autónoma de Tabasco, 1482

Universidad Juárez del Estado de Durango, 1483

Universidad la Gran Colombia, 590

Universidad la Salle, 1483

Universidad Laica 'Vicente Rocafuerte' De Guayaquil, 683

Universidad Latina de Costa Rica, 601

Universidad Latina de Panamá, 1670

Universidad Latinoamericana de Ciencia y Tecnologia (ULACIT), 601

Universidad Libre de Colombia, 590

Universidad Libre, Seccional de Pereira, 590

Universidad Mariano Gálvez de Guatemala, 962

Universidad Mayor de San Andrés, 284

Universidad Mayor de San Simón, Cochabamba, Cochabamba, 285

Universidad Mayor, Real y Pontificia de San Francisco Xavier de Chuquisaca, 285

Universidad Metropolitana, 2973

Universidad Metropolitana, Caracas, 3006

Universidad Metropolitana de Ciencias de la Educación, Santiago, 457

Universidad Michoacana de San Nicolás de Hidalgo, 1483

Universidad Miguel Hernández de Elche, 2028

Universidad Militar Nueva Granada, Bogotá, 585

Universidad Motolinia AC, 1483

Universidad Nacional Abierta, 3006

Universidad Nacional Abierta y a Distancia, Bogotá, 585

Universidad Nacional Agraria de la Selva, 1681

Universidad Nacional Agraria la Molina, 1681

Universidad Nacional Agraria, Managua, 1586

Universidad Nacional Autónoma de Honduras, 971

Universidad Nacional Autónoma de México, 1483

Universidad Nacional Autónoma de Nicaragua, 1586

Universidad Nacional Daniel Alcides Carrión, 1682

Universidad Nacional de Ancash 'Santiago Antúnez de Mayolo', 1681

Universidad Nacional de Asunción, 1676

Universidad Nacional de Cajamarca, 1681

Universidad Nacional de Catamarca, 113

Universidad Nacional de Chimborazo, Riobamba, 681

Universidad Nacional de Colombia, 585

Universidad Nacional de Córdoba, 114

Universidad Nacional de Cuyo, 114

Universidad Nacional de Educación a Distancia, Madrid, Madrid, 2028

Universidad Nacional de Educación a Distancia (UNED), Equatorial Guinea Branch, Malabo, 699

Universidad Nacional de Educación 'Enrique Guzmán y Valle', 1682

Universidad Nacional de Entre Ríos, Concepción del Uruguay, Concepción del Uruguay, 114

Universidad Nacional de Formosa, Formosa, 114

Universidad Nacional de General San Martín, 114

Universidad Nacional de General Sarmiento, Los Polvorines, 115

Universidad Nacional de Guinea Ecuatorial (UNGE), Malabo, 699

Universidad Nacional de Huancavélica, 1682

Universidad Nacional de Ingeniería, Lima, 1683

Universidad Nacional de Ingeniería, Managua, 1586

Universidad Nacional de Jujuy, 115

Universidad Nacional de la Amazonía Peruana, 1681

Universidad Nacional De La Matanza, San Justo, San Justo, 115

Universidad Nacional de la Pampa, 115

Universidad Nacional de la Patagonia Austral, Rio Gallegos, 115

Universidad Nacional de la Patagonia San Juan Bosco, 115

Universidad Nacional de la Plata, 115

Universidad Nacional de la Rioja, 116

Universidad Nacional de Lanús, 116

Universidad Nacional De Loja, 681

Universidad Nacional de Lomas de Zamora, 116

Universidad Nacional de Luján, 116

Universidad Nacional de Mar del Plata, 116

Universidad Nacional de Misiones, 117

Universidad Nacional de Piura, 1683

Universidad Nacional de Quilmes, Bernal, 117

Universidad Nacional de Río Cuarto, 117

Universidad Nacional de Rosario, 117

Universidad Nacional de Salta, 117

Universidad Nacional de San Agustín de Arequipa, 1684

Universidad Nacional de San Antonio Abad del Cusco, 1684

Universidad Nacional de san Cristóbal de Huamanga, 1684

Universidad Nacional de San Juan, 117

Universidad Nacional de San Luis, 118

Universidad Nacional de San Martín, 1684

Universidad Nacional de Santiago del Estero, 118

Universidad Nacional de Tres de Febrero, Caseros, Caseros, 118

Universidad Nacional de Trujillo, 1684

Universidad Nacional de Tucumán, 118

Universidad Nacional de Tumbes, 1685

Universidad Nacional de Ucayali, 1685

Universidad Nacional de Villa María, 118

Universidad Nacional del Altiplano, 1681

Universidad Nacional del Callao, 1682

Universidad Nacional del Centro de la Provincia de Buenos Aires, 113

Universidad Nacional del Centro del Perú, 1682

Universidad Nacional del Comahue, 113

Universidad Nacional del Este, Ciudad del Este, 1676

Universidad Nacional del Litoral, Santa Fé, 116

Universidad Nacional del Nordeste, Corrientes, 117

Universidad Nacional del Santa, Chimbote, 1684

Universidad Nacional del Sur, Bahía Blanca, 118

Universidad Nacional Evangélica, 675

Universidad Nacional Experimental De Guayana, Puerto Ordaz, 3006

Universidad Nacional Experimental de los Llanos Centrales 'Romulo Gallegos', 3006

Universidad Nacional Experimental de los Llanos Occidentales 'Ezequiel Zamora', 3006

Universidad Nacional Experimental del Táchira, 3007

Universidad Nacional Experimental del Yaracuy, San Felipe, 3007

Universidad Nacional Experimental Francisco de Miranda, Coro, Coro, 3006

Universidad Nacional Experimental Marítima Del Caribe, Caracas, 3007

Universidad Nacional Experimental Politecnica 'Antonio José De Sucre', 3007

Universidad Nacional Experimental Rafael María Baralt, Cabimas, 3007

Universidad Nacional Experimental Simón Rodríguez, Caracas, 3007

Universidad Nacional Federico Villarreal, 1682

Universidad Nacional, Heredia, 601

Universidad Nacional Hermilio Valdizán, 1683

Universidad Nacional Jorge Basadre Grohmann, 1683

Universidad Nacional José Faustino Sánchez Carrión, Huacho, 1683

Universidad Nacional Mayor de San Marcos, 1683

Universidad Nacional Micaela Bastidas de Apurimac, Abancay, 1683

Universidad Nacional 'Pedro Henríquez Ureña', 675

Universidad Nacional Pedro Ruiz Gallo, Lambayeque, 1683

Universidad Nacional San Luis Gonzaga de Ica, 1684

Universidad Nacional 'Siglo XX', 285

Universidad Nacional Tecnológica, 675

Universidad Notarial Argentina, 122

Universidad Odontológica Dominicana, 675

Universidad Pablo De Olavide, 2028

Universidad PanAmericana, 1484

Universidad Panamericana de El Salvador, San Salvador, 698

Universidad PanAmericana de Nuevo Laredo, 1484

Universidad Pedagógica de Durango, Durango, 1484

Universidad Pedagógica Experimental Libertador, Caracas, 3008

Universidad Pedagógica Nacional, Bogotá, Bogotá, 585

Universidad Pedagógica Nacional 'Francisco Morazán', Tegucigalpa, 971

Universidad Pedagógica Nacional, Tlalpan, 1484

Universidad Pedagógica Veracruzana, Xalapa, 1484

Universidad Pedagógica y Tecnológica de Colombia, 585

Universidad Pedagógica y Tecnológica de Colombia, Biblioteca Central, Tunja, 581

Universidad Perez Rosales, Santiago, 459

Universidad Peruana Cayetano Heredia, 1686

Universidad Politécnica de Cartagena, 2034

Universidad Politécnica de Madrid, 2036

Universidad Politécnica de Nicaragua, 1586

Universidad Politécnica de Puerto Rico, 2975

Universidad Politécnica de San Luis Potosí, 1485

Universidad Politécnica de Valencia, 2036

Universidad Politécnica de Zacatecas, Guadalupe, 1485

Universidad Pontificia Bolivariana, 590

Universidad Pontificia 'Comillas', 2028

Universidad Pontificia De Salamanca, 2029

Universidad Popular Autónoma del Estado de Puebla, 1485

Universidad Popular de la Chontalpa, 1485

Universidad Popular del César, Valledupar, 586

Universidad Psicología Industrial Dominicana, 675

University of Puget Sound, 2944
University of Pune, 1066
University of Puthisastra, 362
University of Qatar, 1781
University of Queensland, 153
University of Queensland Library, 140
University of Quintana Roo, 1480
University of Rajasthan, 1066
University of Rajshahi, 231
University of Reading, 2349
University of Reading Library, 2279
University of Redlands, 2548
University of Regina, 423
University of Reykjavík, 1003
University of Rhode Island, 2881
University of Richmond, 2936
University of Rijeka, 612
University of Rio Grande, 2837
University of Rizal System, Tanay, 1701
University of Rochester, 2804
University of Rochester Libraries, 2453
University of Ruhuna, 2045
University of St Andrews, 2378
University of St Andrews Library, 2280
University of Saint Francis, Fort Wayne, 2632
University of St Francis, Joliet, 2623
University of St Gallen, 2103
University of Saint Joseph, West Hartford, 2562
University of St Martin, 1571
University of Saint Mary of the Lake—Mundelein Seminary, 2623
University of St Michael's College, Toronto, 432
University of St Thomas, Houston, 2918
University of St Thomas, St Paul, 2732
University of Saints Cyril and Methodius in Trnava, 1961
University of Salahaddin, 1127
University of Salahaddin Central Library, 1123
University of Salford, 2350
University of Salford Information Services Division, 2280
University of San Agustín, 1701
University of San Carlos, 1702
University of San Carlos Library, 1690
University of San Carlos Museum, Cebu City, 1691
University of San Diego, 2548
University of San Francisco, 2548
University of San Jose-Recoletos, 1702
University of Santo Tomás, 1702
University of Santo Tomás Library, 1691
University of Santo Tomas Museum(UST Museum), 1692
University of Sarajevo, 292
University of Sargodha, 1659
University of Saskatchewan Libraries, 377
University of Saskatchewan, Saskatoon, Saskatoon, 424
University of Science and Arts of Oklahoma, 2843
University of Science and Technology, Bannu, 1659
University of Science and Technology Beijing, 554
University of Science and Technology Chittagong, 233
University of Science and Technology of China, 554
University of Science, Malaysia, 1450
University of Scranton, 2877
University of Seoul, 1385
University of Sharjah, 2220
University of Sheffield, 2351
University of Sheffield Library, 2280
University of Shkodra 'Luigj Gurakuqi', 87
University of Sierra Leone, 1942
University of Silesia in Katowice, 1739
University of Sindh, 1659
University of Sint Eustatius School of Medicine, 1567
University of Sioux Falls, 2888
University of Sirt, 1119
University of Sistan and Baluchistan, 1119
University of Social Sciences and Humanities, Ho Chi Minh City, 3020

University of South Africa, 1987
University of South Africa Library, 1978
University of South Alabama, 2507
University of South Asia, Dhaka, 233
University of South Asia, Lahore, 1659
University Of South Australia, 158
University of South Australia Library, 140
University of South Bohemia in České Budějovice, 641
University of South Carolina, 2886
University of South Dakota, 2888
University of South Dakota Libraries, 2458
University of South East Asia, 362
University of South Florida, 2590
University of South Florida Contemporary Art Museum, Tampa, 2472
University of South Florida St. Petersburg, 2590
University of Southampton, 2353
University of Southampton Library, 2280
University of Southeastern Philippines, Davao City, 1702
University of Southern California, 2548
University of Southern California Libraries, 2432
University of Southern Denmark, 663
University of Southern Indiana, 2633
University of Southern Maine, 2656
University of Southern Mindanao, 1702
University of Southern Mississippi, 2735
University of Southern Philippines, 1702
University of Southern Queensland, 156
University of Split, 612
University of Sri Jayewardenepura, 2045
University of Stavanger, 1629
University of Stellenbosch, 1989
University of Stirling, 2379
University of Stirling Library, 2280
University of Strathclyde, Glasgow, 2379
University of Strathclyde Library, 2270
University of Stuttgart, 927
University of Sudbury, 385
University of Sulaimaniya, 1127
University of Sumatera Utara, 1097
University of Sunderland, 2353
University of Surrey, 2353
University of Surrey Library, 2270
University of Sussex, 2354
University of Sussex Library, 2266
University of Swaziland, 2052
University of Sydney, 147
University of Sydney Library, 139
University of Szeged, 995
University of Tabriz, 1119
University of Tabriz Central Library and Documentation Centre, 1107
University of Tampa, 2591
University of Tampere, 733
University of Tartu, 704
University of Tartu Art Museum, 703
University of Tasmania, 158
University of Tasmania Library, 140
University of Technology, Baghdad, 1127
University of Technology, Jamaica, 1214
University of Technology Malaysia, 1451
University of Technology, Mauritius, Pointe-aux-Sables, 1463
University of Technology, Sydney, 149
University of Tehran, 1120
University of Tennessee at Knoxville, 2896
University of Tennessee at Martin, 2899
University of Tennessee Health Science Center, 2896
University of Tennessee, Knoxville Libraries, 2458
University of Tennessee System, 2895
University of Texas at Arlington, 2922
University of Texas at Brownsville and Texas Southmost College, 2923
University of Texas at Dallas, 2923
University of Texas at El Paso, 2924

University of Texas at San Antonio, 2924
University of Texas at Tyler, 2924
University of Texas Health Science Center at Houston, 2925
University of Texas Health Science Center at San Antonio, 2925
University of Texas Health Science Center at Tyler, 2925
University of Texas Libraries, 2459
University of Texas MD Anderson Cancer Center, 2925
University of Texas Medical Branch at Galveston, 2925
University of Texas of the Permian Basin, 2924
University of Texas Southwestern Medical Center, 2925
University of Texas System, 2918
University of Texas—Pan American, 2924
University of the Aegean, 954
University of the Arctic, 57
University of the Argentine Museum of Sociology, 122
University of the Arts Bremen, 934
University of the Arts London, London, 2355
University of the Arts, Philadelphia, 2878
University of the Arts, The Hague, 1565
University of the Azores, 1776
University of the Basque Country, 2027
University of the City of Manila, 1697
University of the Cumberlands, Williamsburg, 2648
University of the District of Columbia, 2580
University of the Dutch Caribbean, 1570
University of the East Library, Manila, 1691
University of the East, Manila, 1703
University of the Faroe Islands, 666
University of the Federal Armed Forces, Hamburg, 872
University of the Free State, 1990
University of the Free State Library and Information Services, 1977
University of The Gambia, 811
University of the Humanities, Ulan Bator, 1500
University of the Incarnate Word, 2925
University of the Merchant Navy, 121
University of the Ozarks, 2519
University of the Pacific, Stockton, 2550
University of the Peloponnese, 957
University of the Philippines Diliman University Library, 1691
University of the Philippines Manila, University Library, 1691
University of the Philippines System, 1703
University of the Punjab, 1659
University of the Punjab Library, Lahore, 1643
University of the Rockies, 2555
University of the Ryukyus, 1279
University of the Sacred Heart, Tokyo, 1328
University of the Saviour, 122
University of the Sciences, Philadelphia, 2878
University of the Sea, Puerto Ángel, 1481
University of the South Pacific, Alafua Campus, 1907
University of the South Pacific, Emalus Campus, Port Vila, 2990
University of the South Pacific, Kiribati Campus, 1358
University of the South Pacific, Marshall Islands Campus, 1459
University of the South Pacific, Nauru Campus, 1523
University of the South Pacific Solomon Islands Centre, 1969
University of the South Pacific, Suva, 711
University of the South Pacific, Tonga Campus Library, 2150
University of the South Pacific, Tonga Centre, 2150

University of the South Pacific, Tuvalu Centre, Funafuti, 2190
University of the South, Sewanee, 2900
University of the Southwest, Hobbs, 2768
University of the Sunshine Coast, 156
University of the Thai Chamber of Commerce, 2146
University of the Virgin Islands, 2978
University of the Visayas, 1704
University of the Visual & Performing Arts, Colombo, 2045
University of the West Indies (Bahamas Office), 208
University of the West Indies Branch, Basseterre, 1904
University of the West Indies, Dominica Centre, Roseau, 670
University of the West Indies Library, Kingston, 1214
University of the West Indies Main Library, Bridgetown, 236
University of the West Indies, Main Library, St Augustine, 2152
University of the West Indies, Mona Campus, 1214
University of the West Indies, St Augustine Campus, 2152
University of the West Indies School of Continuing Studies (Antigua and Barbuda), 101
University of the West Indies School of Continuing Studies, Belize City, 276
University of the West Indies, School of Continuing Studies, Castries, 1905
University of the West Indies School of Continuing Studies, St George's, 959
University of the West of England (UWE), 2356
University of the West of Scotland, 2380
University of the Western Cape, 1990
University of the Witwatersrand, Johannesburg, 1990
University of the Witwatersrand Library, 1977
University of Thessaly, 957
University of Thessaly Central Library, Volos, 948
University of Thi-Qar, 1127
University of Tikrit, 1127
University of Tiranë, 87
University of Tokushima, 1288
University of Tokyo, 1292
University of Tokyo Library System, 1230
University of Toledo, 2837
University of Toronto Libraries, 376
University of Toronto, Saskatoon, 426
University of Transport 'Todor Kableshkov', 350
University of Trás-os-Montes and Alto Douro, 1775
University of Trinidad and Tobago (UTT), 2152
University of Trinity College, Toronto, 432
University of Tromsø, 1629
University of Tsukuba, 1300
University of Tulsa, 2843
University of Turabo, 2973
University of Turku, 733
University of Twente, 1555
University of Twente Library and Archive, 1546
University of Ulsan, 1382
University of Ulster, 2368
University of Ulster Learning Resource Centre, 2277
University of Utah, 2926
University of Uyo, 1606
University of Vaasa, 735
University of Vechta, 930
University of Venda for Science and Technology, 1991
University of Vermont, 2930
University of Vermont Libraries, 2460
University of Veterinary and Animal Sciences, Lahore, 1660
University of Veterinary and Pharmaceutical Sciences Brno, 643
University of Veterinary Medicine and Pharmacy in Košice, 1961

Voronezh State Technical University, 1895

Voronezh State Technological Academy, 1898

Voronezh State University, 1881

Voronezh State University of Architecture and Civil Engineering, 1895

Vorres Museum of Contemporary Greek Art and Folk Art, Paiania, 949

Vrancea 'Duiliu Zamfirescu' District Library, 1792

Vratsa College of Education, 352

Vrije Universiteit, Amsterdam, 1559

Vrije Universiteit Brussel, 267

Vrije Universiteit Brussel, Universiteitsbibliotheek, 259

Vísindafélag Íslendinga, 1001

vTI Johann Heinrich von Thünen-Institut, 833

VTT Technical Research Centre of Finland, Espoo, 719

VU Medisch Centrum, 1539

VU University Medical Center, 1539

Vúje Trnava Inc., 1953

VÚTS Liberec a.s., 633

VUZF University, Sofia, 351

Vyatka State Agricultural Academy, 1896

Vyatka State Technical University, 1895

Východočeské muzeum v Pardubicich, 636

Východoslovenské múzeum, 1954

Vysoká Škola BáŇská – Technická Univerzita Ostrava, 644

Vysoká Škola Chemicko-Technologická v Praze, 644

Vysoká Škola Ekonomická v Praze, Prague, 645

Vysoká Škola Múzických Umení, Bratislava, 1962

Vysoká Škola Umĕleckoprůmyslová, Prague, 647

Vysoká škola výtvarných umení v Bratislave, Bratislava, 1962

Vysoké UČení Technické v Brnĕ, 645

Vytautas Magnus University, 1427

Vytautas the Great War Museum, 1423

Vytauto Didžiojo Universitetas, 1427

Výzkumný ústav geodetický, topografický a kartografický (VUGTK), Zdiby, 631

W

W. Chodźko Institute of Agricultural Medicine, 1716

W. F. Albright Institute of Archaeological Research, 1143

W. H. Over Museum of Natural and Cultural History, 2497

W. J. Kolff Institute for Biomedical Engineering and Materials Science, 1539

W. Kahn Institute of Theoretical Psychiatry and Neuroscience, 1539

W. M. Keck Earth Science and Mineral Engineering Museum, 2486

Wabash College, 2633

Wadden Sea Station Sylt, 836

Wade College, 2926

Wadham College Library, Oxford, 2279

Wadham College, Oxford, 2348

Wadleigh Memorial Library, 2449

Wadsworth Atheneum Museum of Art, 2468

Wageningen Universiteit, 1559

Wageningen University, 1559

Wageningen UR Library, 1548

Wagner College, 2805

Wagner Society Netherlands, 1529

Wagnergenootschap Nederland, 1529

Waikato Institute of Technology, 1584

Wäinö Aaltonen Museum of Art, 722

Wäinö Aaltosen Museo, 722

Waitangi Treaty Grounds, 1578

Wakayama Medical University, 1307

Wakayama University, 1301

Wake County Public Libraries, 2453

Wake Forest University, 2821

Wakefield College, 2362

Wakefield Metropolitan District Council Access and Culture—Libraries and Museums, 2291

Walailak University, 2146

Walden University, 2732

Waldorf College, 2638

Waljat Colleges of Applied Sciences, 1635

Walker African American Museum, 2486

Walker Art Center, 2483

Walker Art Gallery, 2286

Walla Walla University, 2950

Wallace Collection, 2289

Wallace District Mining Museum, 2474

Wallenberg Wood Science Centre, 2058

Wallenfels'sches Haus, Giessen, 853

Walloon Agricultural Research Centre, 253

Wallraf-Richartz-Museum & Fondation Corboud, 850

Walsh College of Accountancy and Business Administration, 2712

Walsh University, 2838

Walter and Eliza Hall Institute of Medical Research, 137

Walter Anderson Museum of Art, 2484

Walter Eucken Institut, 833

Walter Sisulu University for Technology and Science, Eastern Cape, 1992

Walters Art Museum, 2480

Waltham Forest Public Libraries, 2276

Waltham Public Library, 2445

Wandsworth Public Libraries, 2276

Wapiti Regional Library, 377

War in the Pacific National Historical Park, 2969

War Museum, Cairo, 690

Warburg Institute Library, 2276

Warburg Institute, London, 2336

Warner Pacific College, 2849

Warner University, 2591

Warren and Reba Lummis Library, 2450

Warren County-Vicksburg Public Library, 2447

Warren Wilson College, 2823

Warren-Trumbull County Public Library, 2455

Warrington Borough Libraries, 2281

Warsaw University of Life Sciences–SGGW(WULS-SGGW), 1726

Warsaw University of Technology, 1754

Warszawski Uniwersytet Medyczny, 1746

Warszawskie Towarzystwo Muzyczne, 1708

Wartburg College, 2638

Wartburg Theological Seminary, 2639

Warwickshire Library and Information Service, 2281

Waseda Daigaku Tsubouchi Hakase Kinen Engeki Hakubutsukan, 1233

Waseda University Library, 1230

Waseda University, Tokyo, 1332

Washburn University, Leavenworth, 2642

Washington & Jefferson College, 2878

Washington Adventist University, Takoma Park, 2665

Washington And Lee University, 2942

Washington Bible College/Capital Bible Seminary/Equip Institute, Lanham, 2665

Washington College, Chestertown, 2665

Washington County Law Library, 2447

Washington County Library System, 2447

Washington County Museum of Fine Arts, 2480

Washington County Public Library, 2430

Washington County Public Library System, 2460

Washington State History Museum, 2500

Washington State Library, 2461

Washington State University, 2950

Washington Theological Union, 2580

Washington University in Saint Louis, 2746

Washoe County Law Library, 2449

Washoe County Library, 2449

Wasilla Meta-Rose Public Library, 2430

Wat Si Saket, Vientiane, 1400

Watauga Regional Library, 2458

Water Association Finland, 714

Water Management Institute of Georgian Technical University, Tbilisi, 813

Water Policy Research Institute, Ulan Bator, 1498

Water Research Institute, 1170

Water Research Institute, Accra, 939

Water Resources Research Institute, St Thomas, 2978

Water Transport Society, Moscow, 1830

Waterford City Council Central Library, 1134

Waterford County Library Headquarters, 1134

Waterford County Museum, 1134

Waterford Institute of Technology, 1138

Waterford Public Library, 2453

Waterloo Center for the Arts, 2477

Waterloo Historical Society, Kitchener, 370

Waterloo Public Library, 2440

Watertown Regional Library, 2458

Wattis Institute for Contemporary Arts, 2521

Waukesha Public Library, 2462

Waupaca Area Public Library, 2462

Wayamba University of Sri Lanka, 2045

Wayland Baptist University, 2926

Wayne Public Library, 2448

Wayne State College, 2751

Wayne State University, 2712

Wayne State University Libraries, 2446

Waynesboro-Wayne County Library System, 2447

Waynesburg University, 2879

WB National University of Juridical Sciences, 1068

Weald and Downland Open Air Museum, 2291

Weatherford Public Library, 2459

Weatherspoon Art Museum, 2491

Webb Institute, 2805

Webber International University, 2591

Weber State University, 2927

Weber-Museum, Dresden, 852

Webster University, 2746

Webster University Leiden, 1564

Webster University, Vienna, 199

Weill Cornell Medical College in Qatar, 1781

Weingarten University of Education, 887

WEINSTADT Museum, Krems, 186

Weisman Art Museum, 2483

Weitz Center for Development Studies, Rehovot, 1143

Weizmann Archives, Rehovot, 1145

Weizmann Institute of Science, 1159

Weizmann Institute of Science Libraries, 1145

Wellcome Library, 2276

Wellcome Trust/Cancer Research UK Gurdon Institute, Cambridge, 2258

Wellesley College, 2692

Wellington City Libraries, 1577

Wellington Institute of Technology, 1584

Wellington Medical Research Foundation, 1576

Wells College, 2805

Wells, H. G., Society, Bottesford, 2237

Wells Public Library, 2443

Welsh Academy, The, 2235

Welsh National Centre for Religious Education, 2262

Weltkulturen Museum, Frankfurt, 852

Weltverband der Anaesthesisten-Gesellschaften, 68

Wenner-Gren Foundation, New York, 2427

Wenner-Gren Foundations, 2057

Wenner-Gren Stiftelserna, 2057

Wentworth Institute of Technology, 2693

Wereldmuseum Rotterdam, 1552

WERI–Water and Environmental Research Institute of the Western Pacific, 2968

Werkbund Suisse, 2087

Wesley College, Belize City, 276

Wesley College, Bristol, 2362

Wesley College, Dover, 2570

Wesley Historical Society, 2235

Wesley Institute, 168

Wesley Study Centre, Durham, 2366

Wesley Theological Seminary, Washington, 2580

Wesleyan College, Macon, 2602

Wesleyan University, Middletown, 2562

WESSA—Wildlife and Environment Society of South Africa, 1974

West Africa Computer Science Institute, Accra, 943

West African Association of Agricultural Economics, Ibadan, 1590

West African Examinations Council, Accra, 939

West African Health Organisation (WAHO), 67

West African Science Association, Legon, 939

West Baton Rouge Museum, 2479

West Bengal University of Animal and Fishery Sciences, 1068

West Bengal University of Technology, 1068

West Berkshire Libraries, 2277

West Cheshire College, Chester, 2362

West Chester University of Pennsylvania, 2863

West China Centre of Medical Sciences, 554

West Coast Historical Museum, Hokitika, 1578

West Fargo Public Library, 2454

West Java Research Institute for Agricultural Technology, 1105

West Kazakhstan Government Medical University of M. Ospanov, 1349

West Kazakhstan State University named after M. Utemisov, 1349

West Liberty University, 2953

West London College, 2362

West Norway Museum of Decorative Art, 1619

West Pomeranian University of Technology, Szczecin, 1757

West Sussex County Council Library and Information Service, 2268

West Tennessee Regional Art Center, 2497

West Texas A&M University, 2912

West Thames College, 2362

West University of Timişoara, 1803

West Valley Art Museum, 2465

West Virginia School of Osteopathic Medicine, 2953

West Virginia State Archives, 2461

West Virginia State Museum at the Cultural Center, 2501

West Virginia State University, 2953

West Virginia University, 2953

West Virginia University at Parkersburg, 2953

West Virginia University Libraries, 2461

West Virginia Wesleyan College, 2954

West Visayas State University, Iloilo City, 1704

West Yangon Technological University, 1517

Westchester Library System, 2453

Western Association of Schools and Colleges: Accrediting Commission for Senior Colleges and Universities, Alameda, 2394

Western Australian Museum, 142

Western Cape Education Library and Information Service (EDULIS), 1977

Western Cape Provincial Library Service, 1977

Western Carolina University, 2820

Western Connecticut State University, 2563

Western Education & Library Board, Omagh, 2278

Western Illinois University, 2623

Western International University, Phoenix, 2515

Western Kazakhstan Agrarian—Technical University named after Zhangir Khan, 1349

Western Kentucky University, 2648

Western Michigan University, 2715

Western Mindanao State University, 1704
Western Nevada College, 2752
Western New England University, 2693
Western New Mexico University, 2768
Western Oregon University, 2849
Western Pacific Tropical Research Center, 2969
Western Regional Library, Lautoka, 710
Western Regional Library, Sekondi, 940
Western Reserve Historical Society, 2405
Western Seminary, Portland, 2849
Western State College of Colorado, 2555
Western State University College of Law, Fullerton, 2551
Western Theological Seminary, 2715
Western University College of Science and Technology, Kakamega, 1357
Western University of Health Sciences, Pomona, 2551
Western University, Phnom Penh, 362
Western Washington University, 2950
Westfälische Wilhelms—Universität Münster, 933
Westfield Athenaeum Library, 2445
Westfield State University, 2693
Westford Public Library, 2460
Westfries Museum, 1550
Westminster Abbey Library and Muniment Room, 2276
Westminster College, 2879
Westminster College, Fulton, 2746
Westminster College, Salt Lake City, 2927
Westminster International University in Tashkent, 2987
Westminster Music Library, 2272
Westminster Reference Library, 2272
Westminster Seminary California, 2551
Westminster Theological Seminary, 2879
Westmoreland Museum of American Art, 2495
Weston Park Museum, 2291
Westphalian Museum of Art and Cultural History, 856
Westsächsische Hochschule Zwickau – University of Applied Sciences, 937
Wetenschappelijk Instituut Volksgezondheid., 255
Wetland Archaeology and Environments Research Centre, Hull, 2254
Wetlands International, 74
Whanganui Regional Museum, 1578
Wheaton College, 2624
Wheaton College, Norton, 2693
Wheeling Jesuit University, 2954
Wheelock College, 2693
Wheelwright Museum of the American Indian, 2488
White Cube, 2289
Whitechapel Gallery, 2289
Whitehouse Institute of Design, Surry Hills, 168
Whitman College, 2950
Whitney Museum of American Art, 2490
Whittier College, Whittier, 2551
Whitworth University, 2951
WHO Library, Yangon, 1514
WHU—Otto Beisheim School of Management, 933
Wichita Art Museum, 2477
Wichita State University, 2642
Wicomico Public Library, 2444
Widener University, 2879
Widener University Art Gallery, 2495
Widener University School of Law, Wilmington, 2571
Wien Museum, 187
Wiener Beethoven Gesellschaft, 174
Wiener Gesellschaft für Theaterforschung, 179
Wiener Humanistische Gesellschaft, 175
Wiener Institut für Internationalen Dialog und Zusammenarbeit, 51
Wiener Juristische Gesellschaft, 173
Wiener Katholische Akademie, 177
Wiener Konzerthausgesellschaft, 174
Wiener Medizinische Akademie für Ärztliche Fortbildung und Forschung, 176

Wiener Psychoanalytische Vereinigung, 177
Wiener Secession, 174
Wiener Sprachgesellschaft, 175
Wiener Stadt- und Landesarchiv, 185
Wiener Stadt- und Landesbibliothek, 185
Wijsgerige Vereniging Thomas van Aquino, 1532
Wikinger Museum Haithabu–Stiftung Schleswig-Holsteinische Landesmuseen Schloss Gottorf, 857
Wilberforce University, 2838
Wilderness Coast Public Libraries, 2437
Wildfowl & Wetlands Trust, Slimbridge, 2259
Wildlife and Environment Zimbabwe, Harare, 3028
Wildlife and Environmental Conservation Society of Zambia, 3024
Wildlife Conservation Society, Bronx, 2412
Wildlife Management Institute, Gardners, 2412
Wildlife Museum, Ulan Bator, 1499
Wildlife Preservation Society of Australia Limited, 134
Wildlife Society, Bethesda, 2412
Wildlife Trusts, Newark, 2240
Wiley College, 2838
Wilfrid Israel Museum of Oriental Art and Studies, Hazorea, 1146
Wilfrid Laurier University, 438
Wilhelm Johannsen Centre for Functional Genome Research, 653
Wilkes University, 2879
Willamette University, 2850
Willem de Kooning Academie, 1566
Willem de Kooning Academy, 1566
William Angliss Institute, Melbourne, 171
William Blue College of Hospitality Management, North Sydney, 168
William Breman Jewish Heritage & Holocaust Museum, 2473
William C. Jason Library, 2434
William Carey University, 2735
William F. Harrah College of Hotel Administration, 1948
William F. Laman Public Library System, 2431
William Fogg Public Library, 2443
William J. Clinton Presidential Library & Museum, 2431
William Jessup University, 2551
William Jewell College, 2746
William Mitchell College of Law, 2732
William Morris Society, London, 2243
William Paterson University of New Jersey, Wayne, 2764
William Penn University, 2639
William S. Richardson School of Law Library, 2438
William T. Cozby Public Library, 2459
William V. S. Tubman College of Technology, Monrovia, 1414
William Woods University, 2746
Williams Baptist College, 2519
Williams College, 2693
Williams College, London, 2364
Williams College Museum of Art, 2482
Williamsburg Regional Library, 2460
Wilmington College, 2838
Wilmington University, 2571
Wilson College, 2879
Wilsonville Public Library, 2456
Wiltshire College, Chippenham, 2362
Wiltshire Heritage Museum, 2283
Wiltshire Libraries and Heritage and Arts, 2281
Wimbledon College of Art, 2355
Winchester Public Library, 2462
Windham Public Library, 2443
Windhoek Public Library, 1522
Wine and Spirits Research Institute of Bulgaria, Sofia, 337
Winebrenner Theological Seminary, 2838
Wingate University, 2823
Winnipeg Art Gallery, 378
Winona State University, 2719
Winston-Salem State University, 2820

Winterthur Museum, Garden & Library, 2469
Winthrop University, 2886
Wiros Lokh Institute, Colombo, 2041
Wirtschafts- und Sozialwissenschaftliches Institut in der Hans-Böckler-Stiftung, Düsseldorf, 833
Wirtschaftsuniversität Wien, 199
Wirtz Labor Library, Washington, 2436
Wisconsin Historical Museum, 2501
Wisconsin Historical Society, 2405
Wisconsin Lutheran College, 2967
Wisconsin Maritime Museum, 2501
Wisconsin School of Professional Psychology, 2967
Wisconsin State Law Library, 2462
Wisconsin Veterans Museum, 2501
Wissenschaftliche Gesellschaft für Theologie eV, Berlin, 827
Wissenschaftliche Stadtbibliothek, Mainz, 844
Wissenschaftskolleg zu Berlin, 934
Wissenschaftsrat, Cologne, 824
Wissenschaftszentrum Berlin für Sozialforschung, 834
Wistar Institute of Anatomy and Biology, 2422
Witte de With Centre for Contemporary Art, Rotterdam, 1552
Wittenberg University, 2838
Witten/Herdecke University, 930
Woburn Experimental Station (Lawes Agricultural Trust), 2251
Wofford College, 2886
Wojewódzka Biblioteka Publiczna – Książnica Kopernikańska w Toruniu, 1722
Wojewódzka Biblioteka Publiczna w Krakowie, 1721
Wojewódzka i Miejska Biblioteka Publiczna im. dr. Witolda Bełzy w Bydgoszczy, 1721
Wojewódzka i Miejska Biblioteka Publiczna im. Hieronima Łopacińskiego, 1722
Wojewódzka i Miejska Biblioteka Publiczna im. Marszałka Józefa Piłsudskiego w Łodzi, 1722
Wolfson College, Cambridge, 2310
Wolfson College, Oxford, 2348
Wolfsonian—Florida International University, 2472
Woljeon Museum of Art, 1366
Wolverhampton Art Gallery and Museums, 2291
Women's Library and Information Center Foundation, Istanbul, 2161
Women's Library, London Metropolitan University, London, 2276
Women's Study Development Centre, 1063
Women's University, 1056
Won Institute of Graduate Studies, 2879
Won Kwang University, 1382
Wonkwang Digital University, 1385
Wonsan Historical Museum, 1361
Wood Research Austria, Vienna, 182
Wood Technology Institute, Poznan, 1713
Woodbury University, Burbank, 2551
Wooden Art Museum, Câmpulung Moldovenesc, 1795
Woodford County Library, 2442
Woodman Institute Museum, 2486
Woodmere Art Museum, 2495
Woodrow Wilson International Center for Scholars, 2395
Woods Hole Oceanographic Institution, 2426
Woodstock Historical Society, 2499
Woodsworth College, Toronto, 432
Woosong University, 1385
Worcester Art Museum, 2482
Worcester College Library, Oxford, 2279
Worcester College, Oxford, 2348
Worcester Foundation for Biomedical Research, 2422
Worcester Polytechnic Institute, 2694
Worcester Public Library, MA, 2445
Worcester State University, 2694
Worcestershire Libraries and Learning Service, 2281
Workers' College Library, Yangon, 1514

Workers' College, Yangon, 1518
Workers' Educational Association (WEA), London, 2231
World Academy of Art and Science, 74
World Agroforestry Centre, 43
World Allergy Organization (WAO), 63
World Association for Animal Production, 45
World Association for Public Opinion Research, 41
World Association of Center Associates (WACA), 62
World Association of Judges (WAJ), 62
World Association of Law Professors (WALP), 62
World Association of Lawyers (WAL), 62
World Association of Societies of (Anatomic and Clinical) Pathology, 68
World Association of Veterinary Microbiologists, Immunologists and Specialists in Infectious Diseases, 68
World Bank Institute, 51
World Buddhism Association for Development, Cambodia Regional Center, 358
World Confederation for Physical Therapy, 68
World Council of Optometry, 68
World Crafts Council, 47
World Economy and Politics Institute, Beijing, 466
World Education Fellowship-International (WEF), 57
World Energy Council (WEC), 58
World Federation for Medical Education, 63
World Federation for Mental Health, 41
World Federation of Associations of Paediatric Surgeons, 63
World Federation of International Music Competitions, 68
World Federation of Neurology, 63
World Federation of Neurosurgical Societies, 68
World Foundrymen Organization, 59
World Future Society, Bethesda, 2410
World Gastroenterology Organisation, 63
World Health Organization, 62
World Health Organization Library and Information Networks for Knowledge, Geneva, 2094
World Heart Federation, 64
World Intellectual Property Organization (WIPO), 51
World Jewish Bible Center, 1144
World Jurist Association (WJA), 62
World Maritime University, 57
World Medical Association, 64
World Meteorological Organization, 74
World Museum Liverpool, 2286
World Museum of Mining, Butte, 2485
World Organisation of Systems and Cybernetics, 75
World Peace Foundation, Somerville, 2402
World Resources Institute, Washington, 2423
World Road Association, 59
World Society for Ekistics, 51
World Student Christian Federation (WSCF), 57
World Union of Jewish Students, 57
World University of Bangladesh, 233
World Veterinary Association, 45
World Wide Web Consortium (W3C), 61
WorldFish Centre, 43
Worldview Centre for Intercultural Studies, St Leonards, 170
Worms City Museum, 858
Wosinsky Mór Megyei Múzeum, 984
WOTRO Science for Global Development, 1539
WRc PLC, 2264
Wrexham County Borough Council, Library and Information Service, 2281
Wright Institute, Berkeley, 2551
Wright Museum of Art, 2501
Wright Museum of WWII History, 2486
Wright State University, Dayton, 2838
Writers' Association of Macedonia, 1432

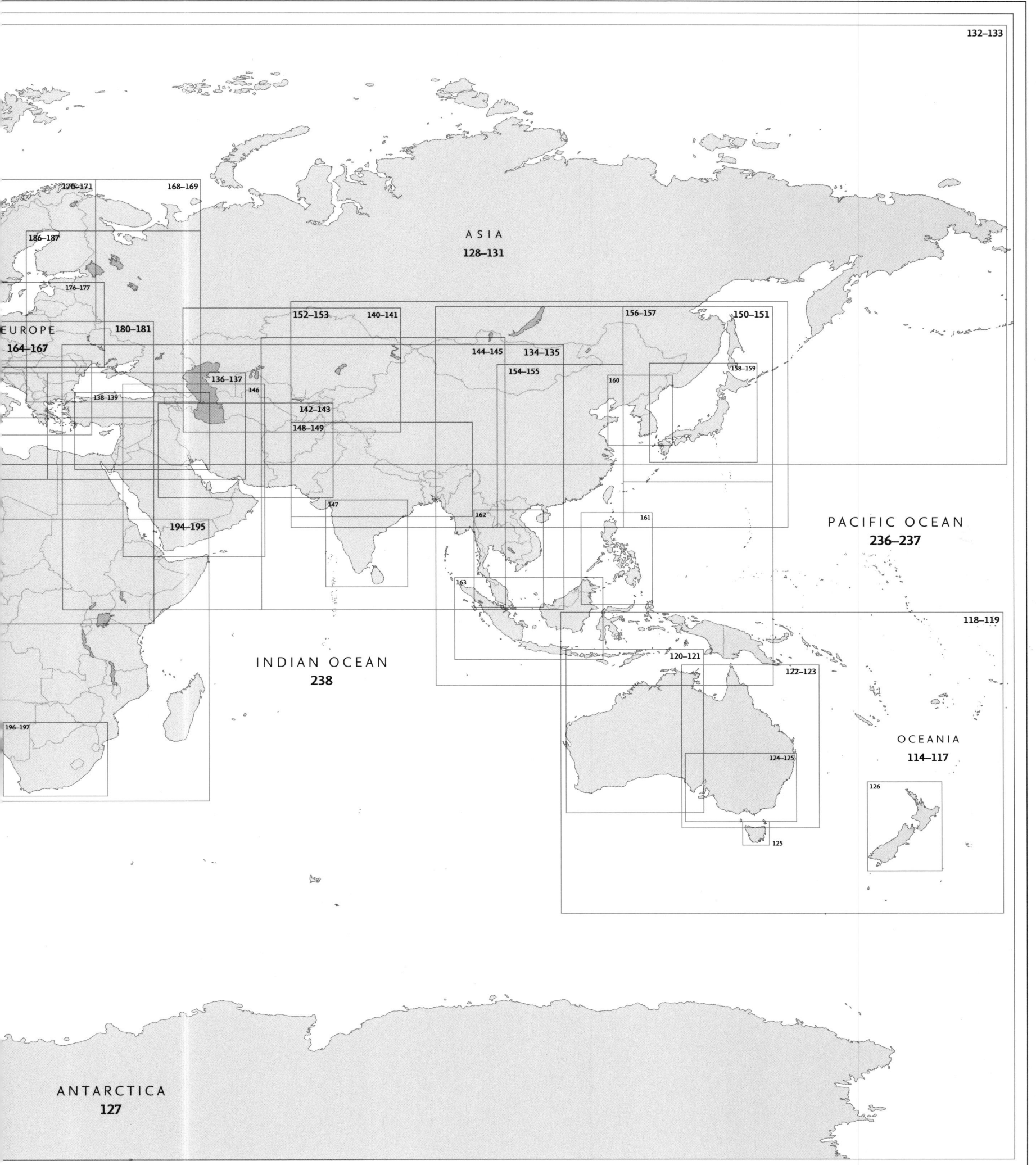

132–133

176–171   168–169

186–187

176–177

EUROPE   180–181
164–167

152–153   140–141   156–157   150–151

144–145   134–135

136–137   154–155   158–159

146   160

138–139

142–143

148–149

ASIA
128–131

147

194–195

162   161

PACIFIC OCEAN
236–237

163

118–119

INDIAN OCEAN
238

120–121   122–123

196–197   OCEANIA
114–117

124–125

126

125

ANTARCTICA
127

World Atlas

Collins World Atlas

Collins

An imprint of HarperCollins Publishers

77-85 Fulham Palace Road London W6 8JB

First Published 2010

Printed in Thailand by Imago

British Library Cataloguing in Publication Data
A catalogue record for this book is available from the British Library

ISBN 978 0 00 787345 6

Imp 001

All mapping in this atlas is generated from
Collins Bartholomew digital databases.

Collins Bartholomew, the UK's leading independent geographical
information supplier, can provide a digital, custom,
and premium mapping service to a variety of markets.
For further information:
Tel: +44 (0) 141 306 3752

e-mail: collinsbartholomew@harpercollins.co.uk
or visit our website at: www.collinsbartholomew.com

Cover image: Planetary Visions
www.planetaryvisions.com

More mapping online at
www.collinsmaps.com

Collins
World Atlas

DISCOVER THE WORLD THROUGH MAPS

Contents

Oceania

The continent of Oceania comprises Australia, New Guinea, New Zealand and the islands of the Pacific Ocean. The main Pacific island groups of Melanesia, Micronesia and Polynesia sit among the complex of ridges and troughs which make up the Pacific sea floor. Notable among these, and visible extending northwards from New Zealand, are the Kermadec and Tonga trenches – the latter reaching a depth of 10 800 m at Horizon Deep. Australia itself appears largely dry and barren, its vast interior consisting of several deserts, with brighter salt lakes in the low artesian basin of the east central area. The east coast of Australia, separated from the interior by the Great Dividing Range – the source of the continent's longest rivers the Murray and the Darling – is more densely vegetated. New Guinea is covered by dense tropical forest, while New Zealand displays a great variety of land cover types, most prominent being the snow-capped Southern Alps on South Island.

Ring of Fire

This image shows the western portion of the 'Ring of Fire' – the 35 000 km boundary between the Pacific oceanic crustal plate and its neighbouring continental plates which is characterized by the frequent occurrence of earthquakes and volcanoes. Approximately 70 per cent of historically recorded active volcanoes have occurred within this belt. The ocean floor topography reveals the plate boundaries running north from New Zealand, through the islands of the West Pacific, eastern Indonesia, the Philippines and Japan. In the far northeast of the image, the remarkable Hawaiian-Emperor chain of volcanic islands is visible. Over 5800 km long, this chain of islands has formed over the last 70 million years as the Pacific plate has moved across an area of high volcanic activity known as a hotspot. This has created a chain of volcanoes which get progressively younger and higher in elevation towards the southeast. The island of Hawaii is the most recent addition to the chain with active volcanoes Mauna Loa and Kilauea.

Australian Deserts

Australia is the driest inhabited continent on earth, 70 per cent of it is arid or semi-arid. Deserts occupy 30 per cent of land, mainly on the western plateau and the interior lowlands. The orange area near the centre of the country is the Simpson Desert where the world's longest parallel sand dunes run for hundreds of kilometres. The light yellow area to the southeast of this is the inhospitable area of the Tirari, Strzelecki and Sturt Stony Deserts. Salt lakes occur in many lowland areas. The largest is Lake Eyre, its dry lake bed appearing white on the image. Until recently, Lake Eyre was thought to be permanently dry. In the last forty years, however, it has been spectacularly filled several times, becoming, temporarily, Australia's largest lake.

7

Asia

This vast continent – the world's largest – covers an enormous area and contains a great variety of landscapes, evident on this image. It stretches from the Mediterranean Sea in the west to the far east of the Russian Federation and Japan, and from arctic Siberia in the north to the tropical islands of Indonesia. The Caspian Sea – the world's largest lake – is prominent in the west. The snow-capped Caucasus mountains stretching from the Caspian Sea to the Black Sea clearly mark the divide between Asia and Europe. Just east of the Caspian Sea lies the complex shape of the Aral Sea. This was once the world's fourth largest lake, but is now drastically reduced in size because of climate change and the extraction of water for irrigation.

The Himalaya

The great Asian mountain system of the Himalaya can be seen as a snow-covered arc on the image as it stretches for over 2000 km in a series of parallel ridges from the Ganges basin in the east to the Plateau of Tibet in the west. Formed 25–70 million years ago, as the earth's crust folded due to the northward push of the Indian subcontinent, the system is still growing and is subject to severe earthquakes. All fourteen of the world's peaks above 8000 m are found in the Himalaya and adjoining ranges. The main range, in which the highest peaks are found, is permanently snow-covered and there are extensive glaciers which give rise to the Indian subcontinent's major rivers. The image clearly shows the contrast between the aridity of the Plateau of Tibet and the Tarim Basin to the north, shown in yellow tones in this image, and the more vegetated land to the south, appearing green-brown. This is a result of the interception of the moisture-laden monsoon weather system by the south-facing slopes of the Himalaya.

Rivers of Bangladesh

The courses and confluence of the Ganges and Brahmaputra Rivers can be seen in the centre of the image. Bangladesh, the country in which they meet, is dominated by rivers and, as most of the country lies less than 110 m above sea level, is prone to flooding. Many of India's largest cities lie in the valley of the Ganges where its flood plains support over 8 per cent of the world's population. The Ganges, considered sacred by Hindus, discharges into the Bay of Bengal, nearly 2500 km downstream from its source in the Gangotri Glacier in the Himalaya. It carries with it 2 billion tons of sediment every year which has led to the formation of the world's largest river delta. Dense wetland forests, known as the Sundarbans, grow along the coast and appear as a dark green strip on this image.

9

Europe

The generally densely vegetated continent of Europe contains some dramatic geographical features. The complex coastlines of Iceland, Scandinavia and northwestern Russian Federation mark its northern and western limits, while the British Isles sit on the flat, wide continental shelf. Europe's mountain ranges divide the continent – in the southwest, the Pyrenees separate France from the drier Iberian Peninsula; the wide arc of the Alps separates Italy from the rest of western Europe; the Carpathian Mountains, appearing as a dark curve between the Alps and the Black Sea, mark the edge of the vast European plains; and the Caucasus, stretching between the Black Sea and the Caspian Sea, create a prominent barrier between Europe and Asia. Two of Europe's greatest rivers are also clearly visible on this image – the Volga, Europe's longest river, flowing south from the Ural Mountains into the Caspian Sea and the Dnieper flowing across the plains into the northern Black Sea.

The Alps

Highlighted by snow cover on this image, this 800-km-long mountain system in south central Europe has been formed in the last 55 million years by the northward movement of the African landmass crumpling up the rocks of the Eurasian landmass. This squeezing action formed huge folds in the rock many kilometres in size. The folds would often break and slide over one another to form huge thrust faults as they pushed northwards. The resultant mountain range has Mont Blanc (4808 m) as its highest peak, and is the source of several of Europe's major rivers, including the Rhine, the Rhone and the Po. The highest peaks are permanently snow-capped and there are numerous glaciers. Glaciation was more extensive in the past and carved a unique Alpine mountain landscape characterized by U-shaped valleys and long, moraine-blocked lakes, several of which appear black on this image.

Caspian Sea

Seen near the eastern edge of this image is the Caspian Sea – the world's largest body of inland water. Like the much smaller Aral Sea, to its northeast, the Caspian Sea was once connected to the Mediterranean before falling sea levels during the ice age cut it off. The Volga river supplies over 75 per cent of its inflow. Water levels have fluctuated greatly as a result of dam construction and water extraction from the Volga. Rapid lowering of its level was seen between 1929 and 1978 but since then levels have risen by 2.5 m, pushing the Volga delta (the dark area on the northwest shore of the sea) 100 km inland. The Caspian Sea has no outflow and salinity levels vary across it. Highest levels of 20 per cent are found in the very shallow Garabogazköl Aýlagy – the prominent grey inlet on the eastern shoreline – which is exploited for salt.

Africa

This image of Africa clearly shows the change in vegetation through the equatorial regions from the vast, dry Sahara desert covering much of the north of the continent, through the rich forests of the Congo basin – the second largest drainage basin in the world – to the high plateau of southern Africa. Lake Victoria dominates central east Africa and the Nile and its delta create a distinctive feature in the desert in the northeast. The path of the Great Rift Valley can be traced by the pattern of linear lakes in east Africa, to Ethiopia, and along the Red Sea. The small, dark fan-shaped feature in central southern Africa is the Okavango Delta in Botswana – one of the world's most ecologically sensitive areas. To the east of the continent lies Madagascar, and in the Indian Ocean northeast of this is the Mascarene Ridge sea feature stretching from the Seychelles in the north to Mauritius and Réunion in the south.

East Africa Rift Valley

More than 6700 km long, the East African Rift was formed 30 million years ago when the African and Arabian continental plates separated. The two branches of the Rift, each of which is about 50 km wide, are visible on this image. The western branch is dominated by larger lakes, including Lake Albert in the north and Lake Tanganyika in the south, while the eastern branch is dotted with smaller lakes including Lake Natron. The land here is mostly 1000 m above sea level, and drier and less densely vegetated than west Africa. Lake Victoria, the third largest lake in the world, lies on the equatorial plain between the two branches of the Rift. One of the main headwater reservoirs of the River Nile, its lake basin is heavily populated and intensely cultivated. Mount Kilimanjaro and Mount Kenya – the two highest mountains in Africa – lie to the east of Lake Victoria.

Sahel

The Sahel is a thin band of dry savanna grassland stretching 5000 km from Senegal and Mauritania in northwest Africa to the Red Sea coast of Sudan and Eritrea in the northeast. It appears on this image as a light green and tan strip running across the continent between the yellow desert sands of the Sahara, and the dark green densely vegetated area of equatorial Africa. The Sahel region is one of Africa's most productive crop areas but it has a history of famine due to highly erratic rainfall. A dry period from the early 1970s to the mid 1990s left many wondering if the Sahara was creeping south. Satellite images are being used to study the area over time and, although the area is not becoming a desert on a large scale, areas of land degradation are being identified.

13

North America

Many well-known geographical features are identifiable on this image of North America, which also illustrates the contrasts in landscapes across the continent. Greenland – the world's largest island – sits off the northeast coast while the dramatic chain of the Aleutian Islands in the northwest stretches from Alaska across the Bering Sea to the Kamchatka Peninsula in the Russian Federation. Further south in the Pacific Ocean, at the far left of the image, lie the Hawai'ian Islands and their very distinctive ocean ridge. There is a strong west-east contrast across the continent. The west is dominated by the Rocky Mountains which give way to the Great Plains. In the east, the Great Lakes, the largest of which, Lake Superior, is second in size only to the Caspian Sea in Asia, the valley of the Mississippi and the Coastal Plain are prominent. In the southeast the complex floor of the Caribbean Sea is visible, particularly the dramatic Cayman Trench, stretching from the Gulf of Honduras to southern Cuba.

Great Lakes

During a succession of ice ages in the last 2 million years, much of Canada was covered by a vast ice sheet. When it melted, a huge volume of water was released southwards and some of this remains trapped in the glacier-carved lake basins of the Great Lakes and numerous smaller lakes on the Canadian Shield – a plateau in eastern Canada and the northeast USA. Four of the five Great Lakes mark the boundary between the USA and Canada. The lakes are connected by canals and short rivers creating a 1867 km waterway from the western end of Lake Superior to the St Lawrence river outflow at the eastern end of Lake Ontario. The St Lawrence Seaway, opened in 1959, allowed deep-draught shipping direct access to the lakes from the Atlantic Ocean. The height above sea level of the lake surfaces varies. The greatest height difference, of 51 m, occurs between Lakes Erie and Ontario at Niagara Falls.

Greenland Ice sheet

The ice sheet which covers more than 80 per cent of Greenland is the northern hemisphere's largest remaining relic of the last ice age. The ice sheet has shrunk noticeably since 1978. Studies of satellite data reveal that it has lost 20 per cent more mass than it received in recent years due to melting and iceberg calving. There are fears that the rate of melting is increasing due to global warming, and that this could have serious implications for world sea levels, ocean currents and weather patterns. If the Greenland ice sheet were to melt completely, the sea level would rise by more than 7 m. In 2007, a new island Uunartoq Qeqertoq (Warming Island) was discovered. This was previously thought to be part of mainland Greenland, but as ice melted it was revealed as an island.

15

South America

The Andes mountains stretch along the whole length of the west coast of South America, widening into the high plains of the Altiplano in Bolivia and Peru in the centre of the continent. Lake Titicaca, the world's highest large navigable lake, lies on the Altiplano, straddling the Bolivia-Peru border. Running parallel to the Andes, just off the west coast, is the Peru-Chile Trench which marks the active boundary between the Nazca and South American tectonic plates. Movement between these plates gives rise to numerous volcanoes in the Andes. The Amazon river runs across almost the whole width of the continent in the north, meeting the Atlantic Ocean in its wide delta on the northeast coast. The vast Amazon basin is one of the most ecologically diverse areas of the Earth. In the south, the wide continental shelf stretches eastwards from the tip of the continent to the Falkland Islands and South Georgia on the bottom edge of the image.

Amazon

The world's second longest river, the 6516 km long Amazon, discharges one-fifth of the total fresh water entering the world's oceans. The enormous Amazon Basin covers most of northern Brazil, as well as parts of five other South American countries and supports the world's largest rainforest, its rich plant life shown in dark green tones on this image. The Andes define the western rim of the Basin and supply the headwaters of many of the Amazon's 500 tributaries. The confluence of the Rio Negro (appearing black on the image) and the Amazon (appearing yellow) is visible near the centre of the Basin. The difference in appearance between the rivers is a result of the low sediment content of the Rio Negro. In contrast, the Amazon empties approximately 1.3 million tons of sediment into the Atlantic Ocean every day. The vast delta which has formed from this sediment is seen as a bright yellow area on the image.

Andes

The world's longest mountain range, the Andes, stretches more than 8000 km from Venezuela to Chile. Higher than any other mountains, with the exception of the Himalaya, they are home to many areas of volcanic activity. Earthquakes, mudflows and landslides present additional hazards. The bright area in the centre of the image, near the west coast of the continent, is the driest place on earth – the Atacama Desert. This is a large area of saltpans and bare rock, some parts of which have not had rain for more than a century. Other, smaller salt flats are also visible as light areas. These are remnants of a vast inland sea which once covered the area. White areas on the southern part of the image are glaciers in the southern Andes.

17

Antarctica

Protected by the Antarctic Treaty, implemented in 1959, from commercial exploitation and from the realization of territorial claims, Antarctica is perhaps the world's greatest unspoilt, and relatively unexplored, wilderness. This image combines bathymetric data (incomplete in some black areas) with satellite images to show the extent of the continental ice sheet in an austral summer. Floating sea ice is not shown. The Antarctic Peninsula – home to numerous scientific research stations – in the top left of the image reaching towards South America, the huge Ronne and Ross ice shelves, and the Transantarctic Mountains – dividing the continent into West and East Antarctica – are the dominant physical features.

Antarctica Ice Sheet Under Threat

The largest mass of ice on earth, the Antarctic ice sheet contains over 70 per cent of the earth's fresh water. On Antarctica's high inland plateau the ice sheet is up to 4.5 km thick and feeds massive ice shelves which float out onto the surrounding seas. This particular image does not show floating sea ice but the analysis of satellite images (commonly known as the science of remote sensing) provides valuable data for scientists studying the extent and characteristics of the ice. The stability of the ice sheet is being threatened by global warming and in the 1990s it was predicted that the ice shelves that surround Antarctica were in danger of becoming unstable.

Studies of the extent of seven ice shelves along the Antarctic Peninsula, in the top left of this image, reveal a decline of 13 500 sq km since 1974. In 1998, over only thirty-one days, the Larsen B ice shelf disintegrated into thousands of icebergs and it is now a mere 40 per cent of its previous extent. After analyzing twenty years of satellite data of the continent as a whole, scientists have concluded that persistent melting of the ice has been occurring further inland and at higher altitudes over the past two decades. These changes are attributed to a steady warming of the climate in the region. The rate of warming is approximately 0.5 Centigrade degrees (C°) per decade and the trend has been present since the late 1940s.

McMurdo Dry Valleys

A few parts of Antarctica have little or no snow or ice cover and the 4800 sq km McMurdo Dry Valleys, near the bottom of the image at the southern end of the Transantarctic Mountains, is the largest of these areas. The bare rock here is representative of the ancient rocky continent beneath the continental ice sheet. Valley floors are covered with gravel and the 19-km-long Onyx River flows during the brief summer. Endolithic plants – plants growing within rocks – have been found here but the area is extremely barren and is described as one of the world's most extreme deserts.

The Earth

Before the end of the 19th century, earth scientists had no way of discovering the composition of the interior of the Earth. Ideas about the internal structure were therefore based almost entirely on speculation. The only evidence related to phenomena apparent at the Earth's surface, but which seemed to arise from within. These consisted of earthquakes, volcanoes, and geysers. To early thinkers, earthquakes indicated that the Earth could not be made entirely of solid rock, but might contain underground caverns full of air. Geysers and springs also suggested that the interior of the Earth was partly, or largely, made up of water. On the other hand, volcanic eruptions seemed to indicate that fire existed underground. For a long time, debate continued between the neptunists who favoured a watery interior and the volcanists favouring a fiery one. With the development of instrumental seismology and worldwide seismic monitoring, starting around 1900, a more soundly based answer began to appear. Careful study of the time differences of different earthquake waves showed that features of the Earth's structure could be deduced by analysing the way in which waves travel through it. Boundaries between different layers within the Earth were identified by the way waves were reflected or refracted by them. It was also possible to tell which parts of the Earth's interior must be liquid, since some types of wave can only travel through solid regions. As a result, the basic internal structure of the Earth became known.

The Himalaya can be clearly seen in this image. They are being formed as the Indian continental plate to the south collides with the Asian plate to the north. This is an example of a continental destructive plate boundary.

Plate Tectonics

Over the course of geological time the Earth's crust has broken up into large fragments, which are known as lithospheric or tectonic plates. These plates are slowly moving relative to one another at rates of a few centimetres per year. This process – originally described as continental drift, a term coined by the meteorologist Alfred Wegener who first proposed the idea in the 1920s – is known as plate tectonics. The interaction of plates along their boundaries causes volcanic and seismic activity. The fact that the shapes of South America and Africa dovetail neatly into one another was noticed as early as the 17th century, and this has proved to be no coincidence.

The Earth's Internal Structure

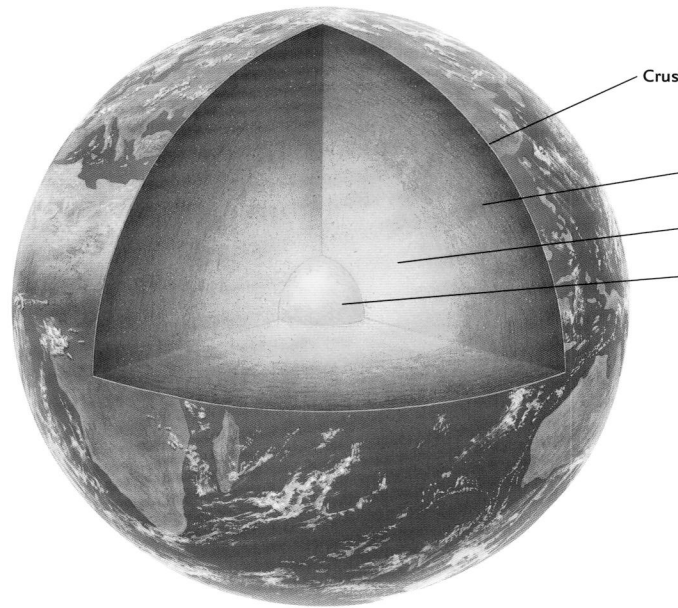

The interior of the Earth can be divided into three principal regions. The outermost region is the crust which is extremely thin compared to the Earth as a whole. The next layer down is known as the mantle. This is about 2850 km thick and is believed to consist mostly of the minerals olivine, pyroxene and garnet. Below the mantle is the Earth's core, which is about 3470 km in radius, and is mainly made up of iron. The greater part of the core is completely liquid. However, there is an inner core which is solid, and about 1220 km in radius.

Mass	5.974 x 10^{21} tonnes
Total area	509 450 000 sq km / 196 698 645 sq miles
Land area	149 450 000 sq km / 57 702 645 sq miles
Water area	360 000 000 sq km / 138 996 000 sq miles
Volume	1 083 207 x 10^6 cubic km / 259 911 x 10^6 cubic miles
Equatorial diameter	12 756 km / 7 927 miles
Polar diameter	12 714 km / 7 901 miles
Equatorial circumference	40 075 km / 24 903 miles
Meridional circumference	40 008 km / 24 861 miles

Plate Tectonics

The Earth looked very different 200 million years ago. All the continents were at one time joined together in a great landmass called Pangaea.

By 100 million years ago Africa had split away from the Americas, Antarctica and Australia then broke away from Africa and subsequently from each other.

About 165 million years ago this super-continent began to break up.

Around 50 million years ago, North America and Europe separated, and India, which was formerly attached to Antarctica, moved northwards to collide with Asia.

Types of Plate Boundary

A constructive (or divergent) plate boundary occurs where two plates are moving away from each other, with new crust being formed along the ridge between them. One place where such a boundary occurs on land is in Iceland. Here the mid-Atlantic ridge creates a dramatic rift in the landscape at Thingvellir, the site of the old Icelandic parliament.

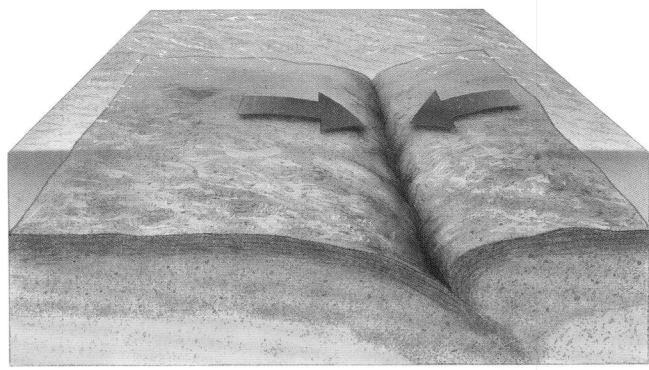

With a destructive (or convergent), boundary two plates are colliding. When an oceanic crust meets another piece of oceanic crust it sinks under it, creating a subduction zone (usually accompanied by a deep ocean trench) as it does so.

In some places, two plates slide past one another, with neither being destroyed. This is known as a conservative (or transform) boundary. The classic example is in California, where the Pacific Plate is sliding northwest relative to the North American Plate, along the line of the San Andreas Fault.

Occasionally, with a destructive (or convergent) boundary a continental crust meets another continental crust, and the two crumple up, one eventually being forced under the other. This is what is happening between India and Asia, with the Himalaya being formed as a result.

Tectonic Plate Boundaries

EURASIAN PLATE

NORTH AMERICAN PLATE

1.0

2.3

2.5

ARABIAN PLATE

PHILIPPINE PLATE

PACIFIC PLATE

CARIBBEAN PLATE

8.6 COCOS PLATE

AFRICAN

5.0

SOUTH AMERICAN PLATE

PLATE

3.0

15.1

SOUTH 3.5

4.4

INDO-AUSTRALIAN

NAZCA PLATE

AMERICAN

1.4

PLATE

15.1

PLATE 3.5

1.4

9.4 5.9

1.4

7.2

7.5

SCOTIA PLATE

ANTARCTIC PLATE

SCOTIA PLATE

Constructive boundary - mid ocean ridge
▲▲▲▲ Destructive boundary
Conservative boundary
→ 7.2 Rate of movement (cm per year)

Earthquakes and Volcanoes

Any map showing the distribution of earthquakes and volcanoes will inevitably look very similar to a map showing the boundaries of the tectonic plates. This is because both phenomena are largely controlled by the processes of plate tectonics. The vast majority of the world's earthquakes occur at plate boundaries as a result of one plate pushing past, or under, another. Even those earthquakes which occur away from plate margins are still mostly due to stresses in the rocks which result indirectly from plate movements.

Tsunamis

Earthquakes can sometimes give rise to another phenomenon which can cause even more destruction and loss of life – the tsunami. Tsunami is a Japanese word, meaning 'harbour wave', and is used today in preference to the expression 'tidal wave' (tides are not involved). When an earthquake occurs offshore, it may cause a sudden change in the shape of the ocean floor, as a result of submarine landslides or vertical fault movement. This causes a massive displacement of water, which in turn produces a powerful wave or series of waves, able to travel over huge distances.

This satellite image of Lhoknga near the provincial capital of Banda Aceh, Sumatra was taken in January 2003 and shows lush and well-cultivated land, with woodland and several villages. The darker area in the centre is water. The coast has sandy beaches, some with barrier islands or reefs protecting them.

Three days after the tsunami of 26 December 2004 the extent of the destructive force of the waves can be seen. The coastal area has been stripped bare of vegetation and buildings. Inland, the low-lying areas are now filled with salt water and it is only the slightly higher level of the roads which keeps them visible.

Deadliest Earthquakes 1900–2008

Year	Location	Deaths
1905	**Kangra**, India	19 000
1907	west of **Dushanbe**, Tajikistan	12 000
1908	**Messina**, Italy	110 000
1915	**Abruzzo**, Italy	35 000
1917	**Bali**, Indonesia	15 000
1920	**Ningxia Province**, China	200 000
1923	**Tōkyō**, Japan	142 807
1927	**Qinghai Province**, China	200 000
1932	**Gansu Province**, China	70 000
1933	**Sichuan Province**, China	10 000
1934	**Nepal/India**	10 700
1935	**Quetta**, Pakistan	30 000
1939	**Chillán**, Chile	28 000
1939	**Erzincan**, Turkey	32 700
1948	**Aşgabat**, Turkmenistan	19 800
1962	northwest **Iran**	12 225
1970	**Huánuco Province**, Peru	66 794
1974	**Yunnan** and **Sichuan Provinces**, China	20 000
1975	**Liaoning Province**, China	10 000
1976	central **Guatemala**	22 778
1976	**Tangshan**, Hebei Province, China	255 000
1978	**Khorāsān Province**, Iran	20 000
1980	**Chlef**, Algeria	11 000
1988	**Spitak**, Armenia	25 000
1990	**Manjil**, Iran	50 000
1999	**İzmit (Kocaeli)**, Turkey	17 000
2001	**Gujarat**, India	20 000
2003	**Bam**, Iran	26 271
2004	**Sumatra**, Indonesia/Indian Ocean	>225 000
2005	northwest **Pakistan**	74 648
2008	**Sichuan Province**, China	>40 000

Distribution of Earthquakes and Volcanoes

- ● Deadliest earthquake
- ● Earthquake of magnitude >=7.5
- · Earthquake of magnitude 5.5 – 7.5
- ▲ Major volcano
- ▲ Other volcano

Richter Scale

The scale measures the energy released by an earthquake. The scale is logarithmic – a quake measuring 4 is 30 times more powerful than one measuring 3, and a quake measuring 6 is 27 000 times more powerful than one measuring 3.

Not recorded
Recorded, tremor felt
Quake easily felt, local damage caused
Destructive earthquake
Major earthquake
Most powerful earthquake recorded – 8.9

Winkel Tripel Projection
scale approximately 1:109 000 000

EURASIAN PLATE

NORTH AMERICAN PLATE

PACIFIC PLATE

COCOS PLATE

CARIBBEAN PLATE

NAZCA PLATE

SOUTH AMERICAN PLATE

AFRICAN PLATE

ARABIAN PLATE

SCOTIA PLATE

ANTARCTIC PLATE

Arctic Circle

Tropic of Cancer

Equator

Tropic of Capricorn

Antarctic Circle

Hekla
Mt St Helens
Kilauea
El Chichónal
Guatemala
Soufrière Hills
Nevado del Ruiz
Volcán Galeras
Huánuco
Chillan
Volcán Llaima
Mount Etna
Chlef
Messina
Izmit (Kocaeli)
Erzincan
Spitak
Monjil
NW Iran
Dushanbe
Aşgabat
NW Pakistan
Khorāsān
Kangra
Bam
Quetta
Gujarat
Nepal/India
Nyiragongo

Major Volcanic Eruptions 1980–2007

Year	Volcano	Country
1980	**Mt St Helens**	USA
1982	**El Chichónal**	Mexico
1982	**Gunung Galunggung**	Indonesia
1983	**Kilauea**	Hawaii, USA
1983	**Ō-yama**	Japan
1985	**Nevado del Ruiz**	Colombia
1991	**Mt Pinatubo**	Philippines
1991	**Unzen-dake**	Japan
1993	**Mayon**	Philippines
1993	**Volcán Galeras**	Colombia
1994	**Volcán Llaima**	Chile
1994	**Rabaul**	Papua New Guinea
1997	**Soufrière Hills**	Montserrat
2000	**Hekla**	Iceland
2001	**Mount Etna**	Italy
2002	**Nyiragongo**	Democratic Republic of the Congo

Mount Bromo, Java, Indonesia, is one of the many active volcanoes that have formed around the edge of the Pacific Ocean. It is unique in having seven eruptive centres in the caldera and is also a great location to see spectacular sunrises.

Climate

The climate classification shown on the main map is a simplified version of the system developed by W. Köppen. It is based on the relationship between temperature and precipitation data, and on vegetation characteristics. Extremes of climate, particularly tropical storms and tornadoes, are significant because of their destructive power. Increasing knowledge of these phenomena – particularly through the use of satellite imagery – will help in their prediction and will allow action to minimize their destructive effects.

Tornadoes

A tornado is a violent rotating column of air extending from a thunderstorm to the ground. The most violent tornadoes can cause massive destruction with wind speeds of 400 km per hr (249 miles per hr) or more. Although tornadoes occur in many parts of the world, they are found most frequently in the USA east of the Rocky Mountains and west of the Appalachian Mountains. They occur during the spring and summer months. In the USA in an average year 800 tornadoes are reported.

In April 2007 intense storms in northeast USA created a powerful tornado which touched down in southern Maryland destroying the historic centre of La Plata before moving east, flattening vegetation as it passed.

Tropical Storms

Tropical storms have different names in different parts of the world: hurricanes in the north Atlantic and east Pacific; typhoons in the northwest Pacific; and cyclones in the Indian Ocean region. There are also many other local names for these often catastrophic events. Tropical storms are among the most powerful and destructive weather systems on Earth. Of the eighty to one hundred which develop annually over the tropical oceans, many make landfall and cause considerable damage to property and loss of life as a result of high winds and heavy rain.

Major Climatic Regions and Ocean Surface Currents

Polar
- Ice cap
- Tundra

Cooler humid
- Subarctic
- Continental cool summer
- Continental warm summer

Warmer humid
- Temperate
- Humid subtropical
- Mediterranean

Dry
- Steppe
- Desert

Tropical humid
- Savanna
- Rain forest

- • Weather extreme location
- → Warm current
- → Cold current
- → Seasonal drift during northern winter

Tracks of Tropical Storms

- ⇒ Cyclone track
- → Typhoon track
- → Hurricane track
- Source area of tropical cyclones
- Tornado high risk areas
- • Major tropical storm (1994–2008)

World Weather Extremes

	Location
Highest shade temperature	57.8°C / 136°F Al 'Azīzīyah, Libya (13th September 1922)
Hottest place – Annual mean	34.4°C / 93.9°F Dalol, Ethiopia
Driest place – Annual mean	0.1 mm / 0.004 inches Atacama Desert, Chile
Most sunshine – Annual mean	90% Yuma, Arizona, USA (over 4 000 hours)
Lowest screen temperature	-89.2°C / -128.6°F Vostok Station, Antarctica (21st July 1983)
Coldest place – Annual mean	-56.6°C / -69.9°F Plateau Station, Antarctica
Wettest place – Annual mean	11 873 mm / 467.4 inches Meghalaya, India
Most rainy days	Up to 350 per year Mount Waialeale, Hawaii, USA
Windiest place	322 km per hour / 200 miles per hour in gales, Commonwealth Bay, Antarctica
Highest surface wind speed	512 km per hour / 318 miles per hour in a tornado, Oklahoma City, Oklahoma, USA (3rd May 1999)
Greatest snowfall	31 102 mm / 1 224.5 inches Mount Rainier, Washington, USA (19th February 1971 – 18th February 1972)
Highest barometric pressure	1 083.8 mb Agata, Siberia, Russian Federation (31st December 1968)
Lowest barometric pressure	870 mb 483 km / 300 miles west of Guam, Pacific Ocean (12th October 1979)

Tropical Cyclone Nargis, reached Category 4 status with winds of 210 km per hr (130 miles per hr), while crossing the Bay of Bengal. By the time this image was taken on 3 May 2008, it had weakened to tropical storm strength, but the path of the cyclone took it over the coastal plains of Myanmar and almost directly over the city of Rangoon. There was extensive flooding and many thousands of people were killed.

Climate Change

The global average temperature can be established for approximately the last 150 years from the worldwide network of weather stations on land and observations made on board ships. Eleven of the last twelve years rank among the twelve warmest years on record, so the world has been warmer over the last decade than at any time since measurements began. This warming is observed over the oceans as well as over land, suggesting that it is a truly global phenomenon and not a conglomeration of 'local' increases in temperature caused by some small-scale process such as the urban heat island effect.

Observing Climate Change

Changes have also been seen in various areas of the climate system. Snow cover and mountain glaciers have shrunk, and some melting of the Greenland and Antarctic ice sheets has been measured. Global average sea level rose by approximately 17 cm through the 20th century, partly because of the additional water in the ocean basins resulting from the melting of ice on land, and partly because water expands when it heats up. Patterns of precipitation (rainfall and snowfall) have also changed, with parts of North and South America, Europe and northern and central Asia becoming wetter while the Sahel region of central Africa, southern Africa, the Mediterranean and southern Asia have become drier. Intense rainfall events have become more frequent. In Europe, Asia and North America, growing seasons have extended, with flowers emerging and trees coming into leaf several days earlier in the year than in the mid-twentieth century.

Male, the capital of the Maldives, is approximately 2 m above the sea, but its reclaimed land is lower leaving it very vulnerable to a sustained rise in sea level.

The Causes of Climate Change

Climate can change naturally, but over the last century the industrial and agricultural activities of humans have become additional causes of climate change. Changes in the concentration of 'greenhouse gases' can also result in climate change. The most important greenhouse gas is water vapour, followed by carbon dioxide. While many of these gases occur naturally in the atmosphere, humans are responsible for increasing the concentration of many of them through the burning of fossil fuels, deforestation and other industrial and agricultural processes. We have also introduced new greenhouse gases, the 'halocarbons' such as chlorofluorocarbons (CFCs) which have damaged the ozone layer in the stratosphere.

The McCarty Glacier in the Kenai Peninsula in Alaska is a tidewater glacier which has retreated around 16 km between 1909 (top) and 2004 (bottom).

Projection of Global Temperatures 2090–2099

Based on IPCC scenario A1B. Change relative to 1980–1999.

© IPCC (2007)

| 0.5 | 1 | 1.5 | 2 | 2.5 | 3 | 3.5 | 4 | 4.5 | 5 | 5.5 | 6 | 6.5 | 7 | 7.5 |

Change in average surface temperature (C°)

Faster warming is expected near the poles, as the melting snow and sea ice exposes the darker underlying land and ocean surfaces which then absorb more of the sun's radiation instead of reflecting it back to space in the way that brighter ice and snow do.

Threat of Rising Sea Level

It has been suggested that further global warming of between 1.0 and 6.4 C° may occur by the end of the 21st century. Sea level is projected to rise by between 28 cm and 58 cm, threatening a number of coastal cities, low-lying deltas and small islands. Larger rises are predicted in some locations than others.

Areas at Risk of Submersion

○ Major cities

▭ Coastal areas at greatest risk

▬ Islands and archipelagos

▬ Areas of low-lying islands

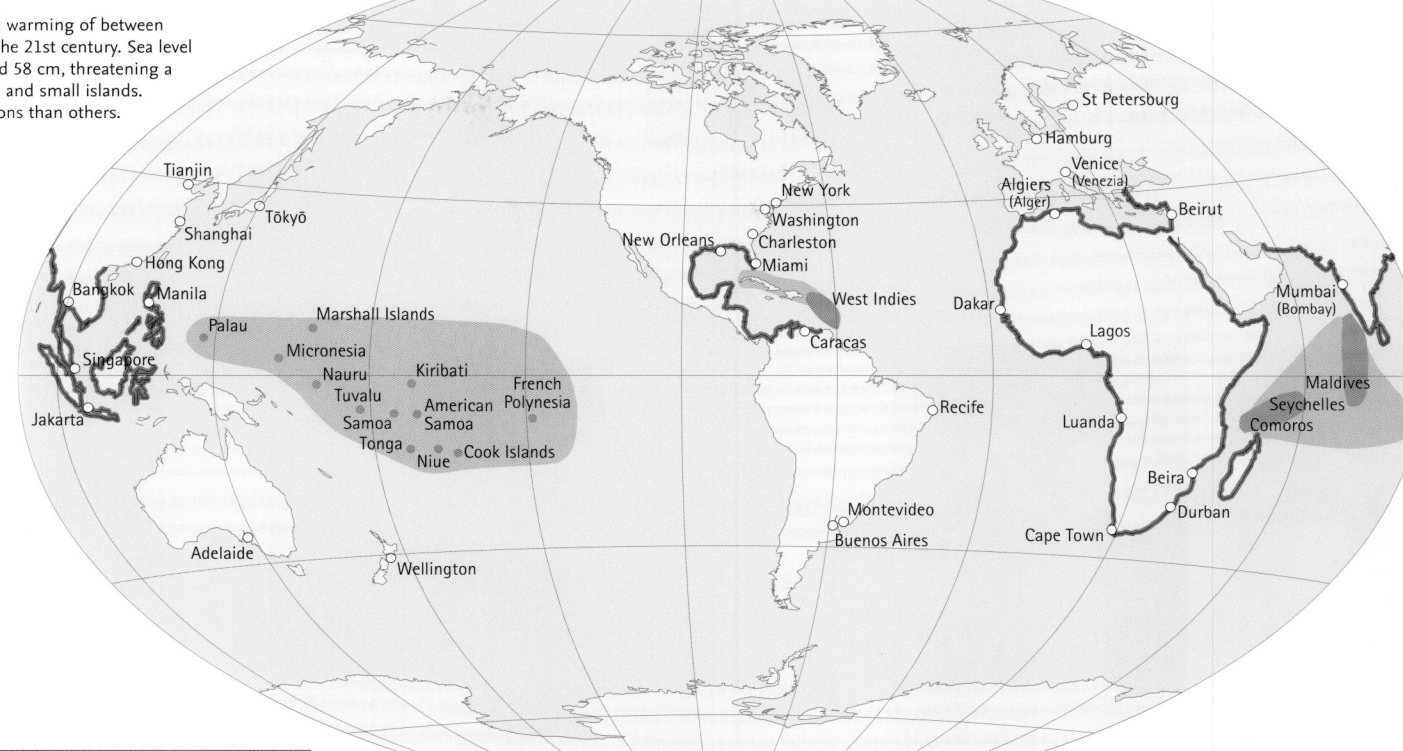

Lowest Pacific Islands

Location	Maximum height above sea level	Land area sq km	Land area sq miles	Population
Kingman Reef	1 m (3 ft)	1	0.4	0
Palmyra Atoll	2 m (7 ft)	12	5	0
Ashmore and Cartier Islands	3 m (10 ft)	5	2	0
Howland Island	3 m (10 ft)	2	1	0
Johnston Atoll	5 m (16 ft)	3	1	0
Tokelau	5 m (16 ft)	10	4	1 000
Tuvalu	5 m (16 ft)	25	10	10 000
Coral Sea Islands Territory	6 m (20 ft)	22	8	0
Wake Island	6 m (20 ft)	7	3	0
Jarvis Island	7 m (23 ft)	5	2	0

Projection of Global Precipitation 2090–2099

Based on IPCC scenario A1B. Change relative to 1980–1999.

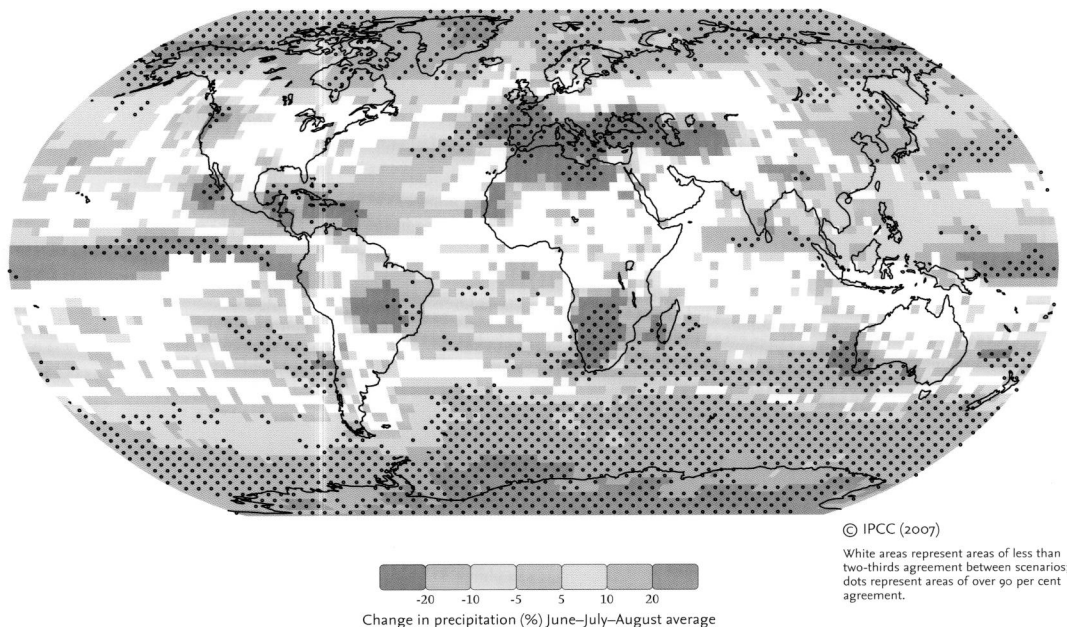

© IPCC (2007)

White areas represent areas of less than two-thirds agreement between scenarios; dots represent areas of over 90 per cent agreement.

-20 -10 -5 5 10 20

Change in precipitation (%) June–July–August average

In the high-latitude regions (central and northern Europe, Asia and North America) the year-round average precipitation is projected to increase, while in most sub-tropical land regions it is projected to decrease by as much as 20 per cent. This would increase the risk of drought and, in combination with higher temperatures, threaten agricultural productivity.

Historical Climate Records

Changes relative to 1961–1990 averages

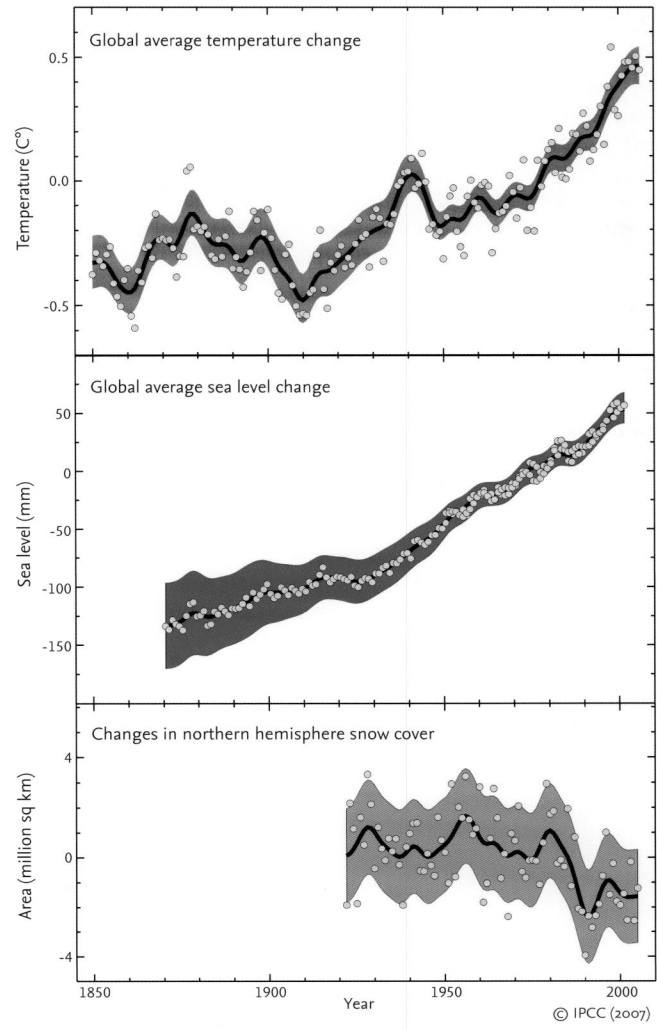

Global average temperature change

Global average sea level change

Changes in northern hemisphere snow cover

© IPCC (2007)

Curves represent decadal averages; circles are yearly values; shaded areas are uncertainty intervals.

Environment and Biodiversity

Throughout history people have altered the natural environment, influencing landscapes, land cover, biodiversity, and the chemical composition of air, land, and water. The rate of change has accelerated dramatically since the industrial revolution, as a result of advances in technology, changing lifestyles and associated patterns of production and consumption, and the rapidly growing global population. As the human population has increased, so too has demand for the Earth's natural resources, leading in many areas to environmental degradation which has had significant impacts on people's lives in many parts of the world.

For many thousands of years the Hamoun wetlands have been a major source of food and shelter in the middle of vast arid plains in central Asia. From the mid 1990s however, the Helmand river was increasingly used for irrigation and diverted into dams leaving the area vulnerable to a prolonged drought. These false colour images of 1976 and 2001 show the extent of the devastation.

Environmental Change

Land cover has changed more over the past fifty years than at any time in human history. Much of this change has been due to the conversion of natural ecosystems to agricultural land to help meet demand for food production. Wetlands and other freshwater environments have been dramatically affected by changes in land cover and use. It is speculated that approximately one-third of all mangroves and half of all inland wetlands were converted during the 20th century. Fragmentation and the modification of river flow have resulted from the construction of dams and other structures along rivers, affecting almost 60 per cent of the large river systems in the world.

Biodiversity

Biodiversity, derived from the term 'biological diversity', is the name given to the variety and processes of all life on Earth, including individual living organisms, their genes, and the habitats or ecosystems of which they are part, whether terrestrial, freshwater or marine. The diversity of life is not evenly distributed around the world, and based on the number of species in a location, or 'species richness', a general pattern emerges of considerably more biodiversity in the tropics than at higher latitudes. To date approximately two million species have been identified and described.

Ecological Footprint

Humanity's ecological footprint by component 1961–2003.

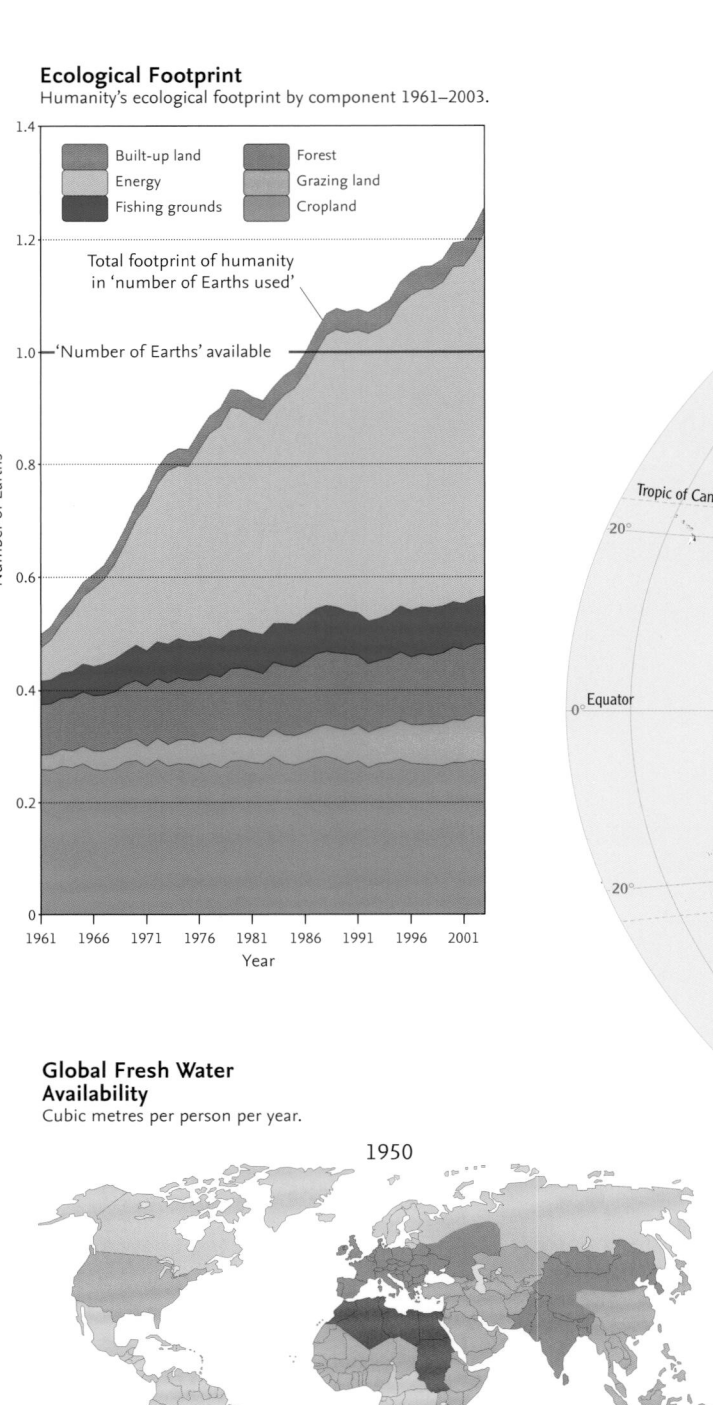

Global Fresh Water Availability

Cubic metres per person per year.

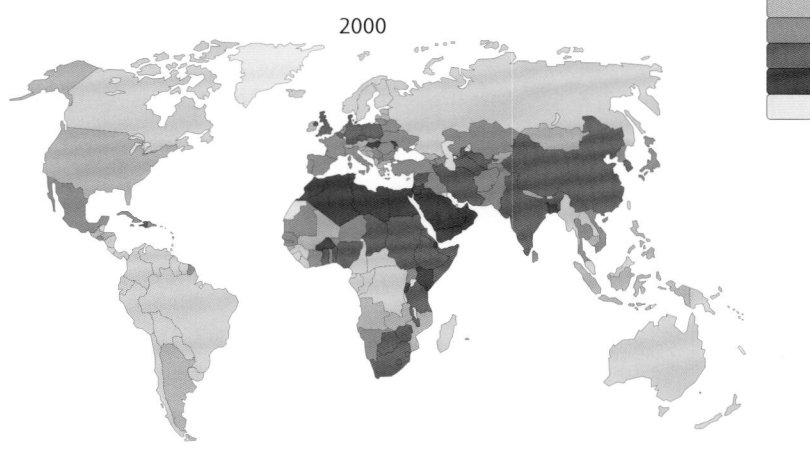

- >15 000
- 5 000–15 000
- 2 500–5 000
- 1 000–2 500 (Water deficiency)
- 0–1 000 (Acute shortage)
- no data

World Land Cover

Winkel Tripel Projection
scale approximately 1:112 000 000

Evergreen needleleaf forest
Evergreen broadleaf forest
Deciduous needleleaf forest
Deciduous broadleaf forest
Mixed forest
Closed shrublands
Open shrublands
Woody savannas
Savannas
Grasslands
Permanent wetlands
Croplands
Urban and built-up
Cropland/Natural vegetation mos:
Snow and Ice
Barren or sparsely vegetated
Water bodies

Arctic Circle
Tropic of Cancer
Equator
Tropic of Capricorn
Antarctic Circle

Living Planet Index
Trends in population of terrestrial, freshwater and marine species 1970–2003.

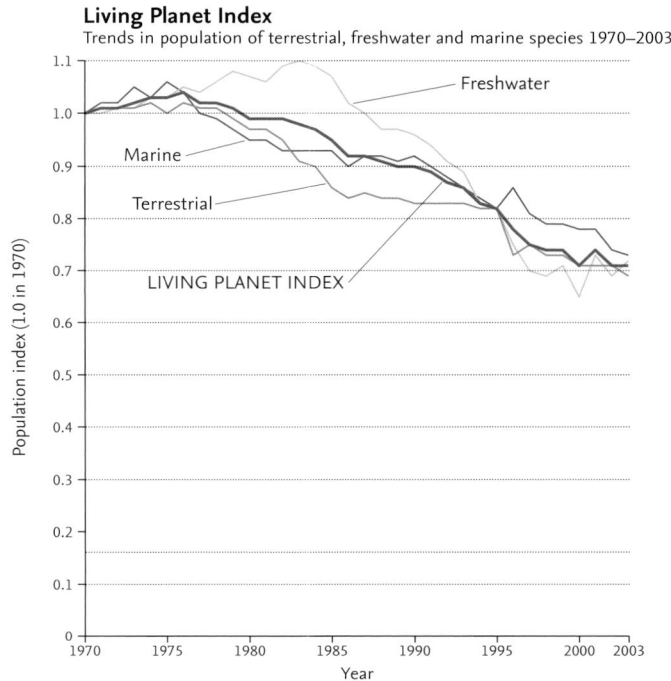

Freshwater
Marine
Terrestrial
LIVING PLANET INDEX

Population index (1.0 in 1970)

Year

Protected Areas of the World
Proportion of large marine ecosystems and terrestrial ecoregions under protection.

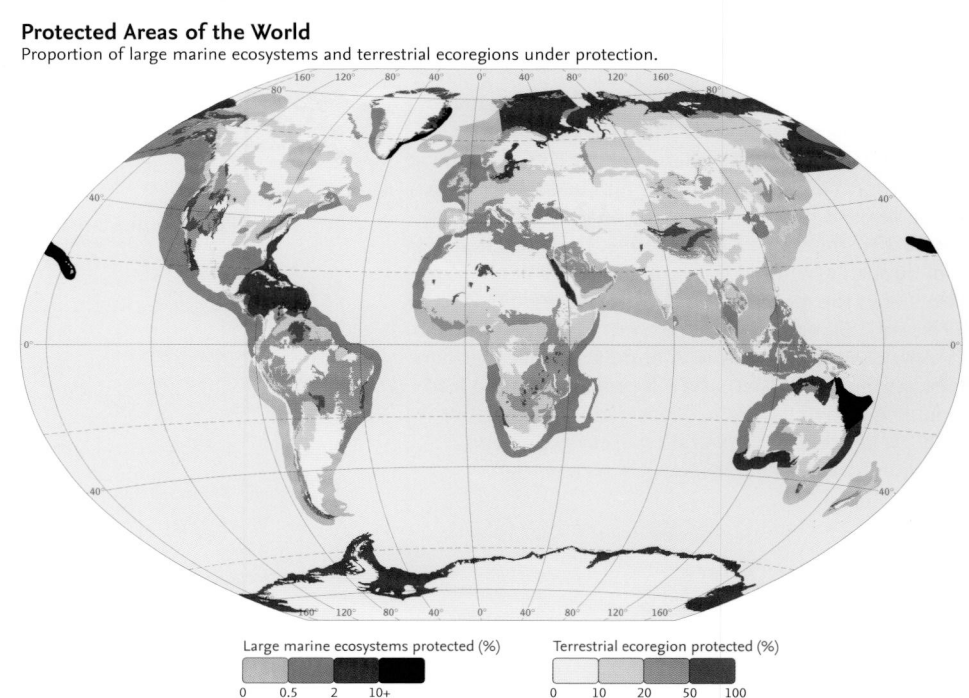

Large marine ecosystems protected (%)
0   0.5   2   10+

Terrestrial ecoregion protected (%)
0   10   20   50   100

Population

World population is currently undergoing the biggest transformation that it has ever seen, but this process is impacting very unevenly. While overall numbers have been growing extremely rapidly since 1950, almost nine-tenths of the increase has taken place in the less developed regions, especially southern and eastern Asia, while Europe's population is now estimated to be in overall decline and ageing rapidly. India and China alone are responsible for over one-third of current growth, but most of the highest percentage rates of growth are to be found in Sub-Saharan Africa, where the demographic transition process is still at a relatively early stage.

Population growth in the 20th century was rapid and continued growth could carry the world's population past seven billion by 2015.

Population Distribution

People are distributed very unevenly over the face of the planet, even after allowing for the two-thirds that is covered by water. As shown on the main map, over a quarter of the land area is uninhabited or has extremely low population density, notably the polar regions, the Amazon basin and the dry deserts of Saharan Africa, southwest and central Asia, and Australia.

Population Growth

Over the past half century world population has been growing faster than it has ever done before. While world population did not pass the one billion mark until 1804 and took another 123 years to reach two billion, it then added the third billion in 33 years, the fourth in 14 years and the fifth in 13 years, with the addition of the 6 billionth person being celebrated by the UN 12 years after this on 12 October 1999. The latest trends in population growth at country level emphasize the continuing contrast between the more and less developed regions. Annual growth rates of 1.5 per cent or more remain common in Latin America, Africa and southern Asia. A number of countries have rates in excess of 3.0 per cent, which if continued would lead to the doubling of population in 23 years or less. Ten countries account for 60 per cent of the world's current population growth, with India and China responsible for over half.

Top Twenty Countries by Population and Population Density 2007

Total population	Country	Rank	Country*	Inhabitants per sq mile	Inhabitants per sq km
1 313 437 000	China	1	Bangladesh	2 854	1 102
1 169 016 000	India	2	Taiwan	1 638	632
305 826 000	United States of America	3	South Korea	1 258	486
231 627 000	Indonesia	4	Netherlands	1 024	395
191 791 000	Brazil	5	India	988	381
163 902 000	Pakistan	6	Belgium	887	343
158 665 000	Bangladesh	7	Japan	877	339
148 093 000	Nigeria	8	Sri Lanka	762	294
142 499 000	Russian Federation	9	Philippines	759	293
127 967 000	Japan	10	Vietnam	687	265
106 535 000	Mexico	11	United Kingdom	646	249
87 960 000	Philippines	12	Germany	599	231
87 375 000	Vietnam	13	Pakistan	528	204
83 099 000	Ethiopia	14	North Korea	511	197
82 599 000	Germany	15	Italy	506	195
75 498 000	Egypt	16	Nepal	496	192
74 877 000	Turkey	17	Nigeria	415	160
71 208 000	Iran	18	China	355	137
63 884 000	Thailand	19	Czech Republic	335	129
62 636 000	Democratic Republic of the Congo	20	Uganda	332	128

*Only countries with a population of over 10 million are considered.

Age Pyramids

World population by five-year age group and sex.

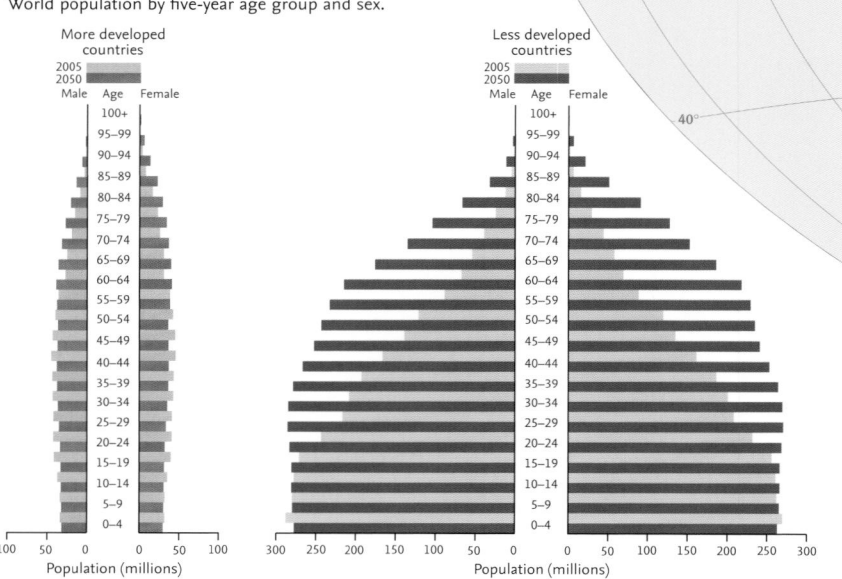

Key Population Statistics for Major Regions

	Population 2007 (millions)	Growth (per cent)	Infant mortality rate	Total fertility rate	Life expectancy (years)	% aged 60 and over 2005	% aged 60 and over 2050
World	6 671	1.2	49	2.6	67	10	22
More developed regions[1]	1 223	0.3	7	1.6	77	20	33
Less developed regions[2]	5 448	1.4	54	2.8	65	8	20
Africa	965	2.3	87	4.7	53	5	10
Asia	4 030	1.1	43	2.3	69	9	24
Europe[3]	731	0.0	8	1.5	75	21	35
Latin America and the Caribbean[4]	572	1.2	22	2.4	73	9	24
North America	339	1.0	6	2	79	17	27
Oceania	34	1.2	26	2.3	75	14	25

Except for population and % aged 60 and over figures, the data are annual averages projected for the period 2005–2010.

1. Europe, North America, Australia, New Zealand and Japan.
2. Africa, Asia (excluding Japan), Latin America and the Caribbean, and Oceania (excluding Australia and New Zealand).
3. Includes Russian Federation.
4. South America, Central America (including Mexico) and all Caribbean Islands.

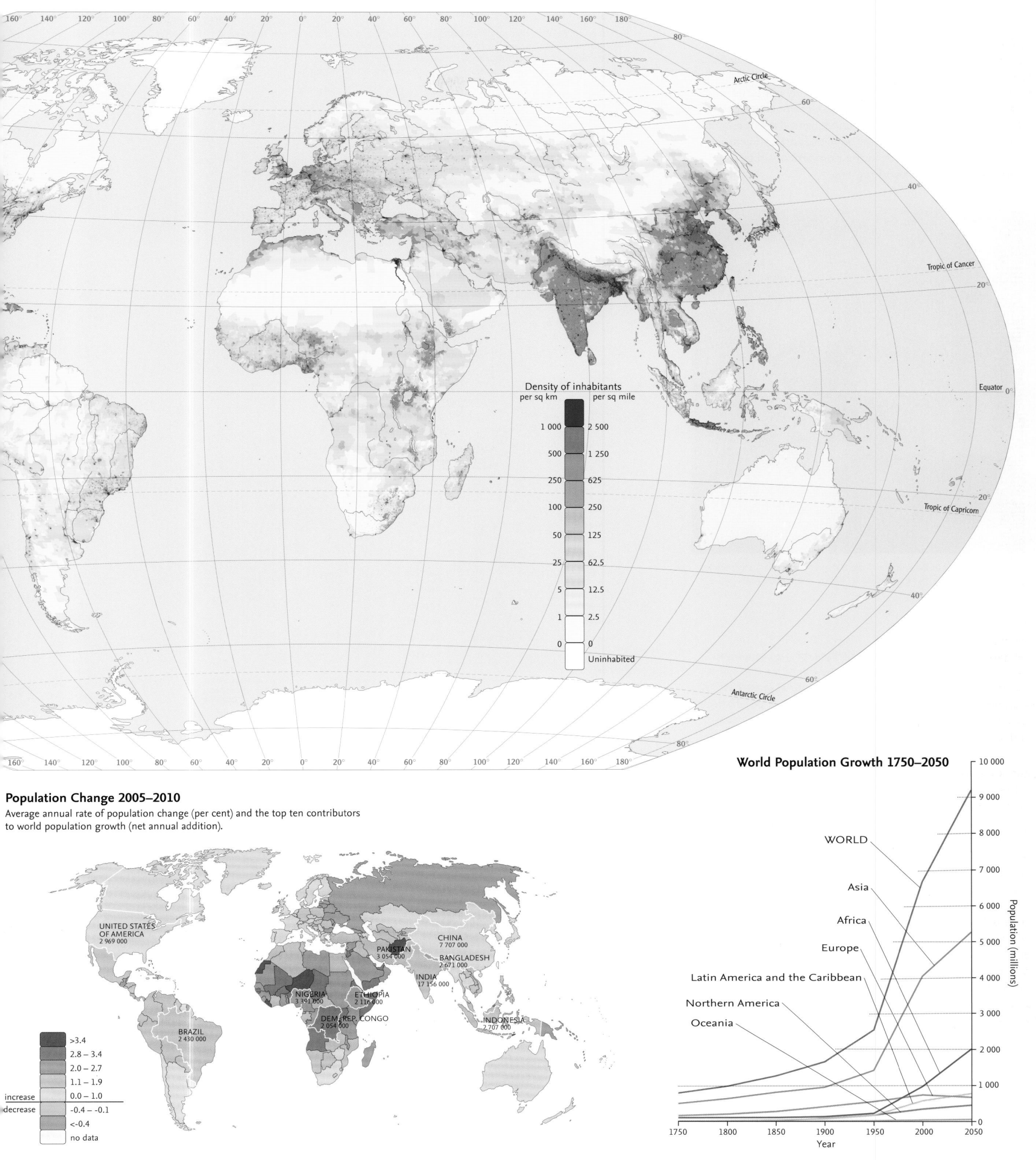

Density of inhabitants

per sq km	per sq mile
1 000	2 500
500	1 250
250	625
100	250
50	125
25	62.5
5	12.5
1	2.5
0	0
	Uninhabited

Population Change 2005–2010

Average annual rate of population change (per cent) and the top ten contributors to world population growth (net annual addition).

UNITED STATES
OF AMERICA
2 969 000

PAKISTAN
3 054 000

CHINA
7 707 000

BANGLADESH
2 671 000

INDIA
17 156 000

NIGERIA
3 391 000

ETHIOPIA
2 116 000

DEM. REP. CONGO
2 054 000

INDONESIA
7 707 000

BRAZIL
2 430 000

	>3.4
	2.8 – 3.4
	2.0 – 2.7
	1.1 – 1.9
increase	0.0 – 1.0
decrease	-0.4 – -0.1
	<-0.4
	no data

World Population Growth 1750–2050

WORLD

Asia

Africa

Europe

Latin America and the Caribbean

Northern America

Oceania

Population (millions)

10 000
9 000
8 000
7 000
6 000
5 000
4 000
3 000
2 000
1 000
0

1750   1800   1850   1900   1950   2000   2050

Year

Urbanization

World population is urbanizing rapidly and, in this respect, 2008 is a momentous point in world history. In 2008, for the first time urban dwellers will outnumber those living in traditionally rural areas. But the current level of urbanization varies greatly across the world, as too does its rate of increase. In the hundred years up to 1950 the greatest changes took place in Europe and North America. Relatively few large cities developed elsewhere and most of these were in coastal locations with good trading connections with the imperial and industrial nations. The main feature of the past half century has been the massive growth in the numbers of urban dwellers in the less developed regions.

Tōkyō is the largest city in the world and more than a quarter of the population of Japan live here. The city was established in 1603 and has been growing steadily ever since then.

Towards an Urbanized World

The annual rise in the percentage of the world's population living in cities has been accelerating steadily since the 1970s and it will be running at very high levels until at least 2030. As a result, by then, 3 in 5 people (59.9 per cent) will be urbanites compared to 35.9 per cent in 1970 and 50.8 per cent in 2010. In absolute terms, the global urban population more than doubled between 1970 and 2000, adding 1.5 billion to its 1970 total of 1.33 billion, and it is expected to grow by a further 2.07 billion by 2030. There is a broad contrast in the level of urbanization between the more and less developed regions, but also a great deal of variation within them. In the more developed regions as a whole, three-quarters of the population now live in urban areas.

The Growth of Large Cities

Alongside the rise in the world's urban population has occurred a massive increase in the number and size of cities, especially of the very large cities or 'megacities'. In 1950, New York was the only agglomeration with over 10 million inhabitants, and there were still only three cities of this size by 1975 – New York, Tōkyō and Mexico City. By 2000, there were eighteen and there are expected to be twenty-two by 2015. Urban areas are also becoming more diffuse and polycentric, making the task of defining separate cities on the ground even more difficult.

World's Largest Cities 2010

Figures are for the urban agglomeration, defined as the population contained within the contours of a contiguous territory inhabited at urban levels without regard to administrative boundaries. They incorporate the population within a city plus the suburban fringe lying outside of, but adjacent to, the city boundaries.

City	Country	Population
Tōkyō	Japan	35 467 000
Mexico City	Mexico	20 688 000
Mumbai	India	20 036 000
São Paulo	Brazil	19 582 000
New York	USA	19 388 000
Delhi	India	16 983 000
Shanghai	China	15 790 000
Kolkata	India	15 548 000
Jakarta	Indonesia	15 206 000
Dhaka	Bangladesh	14 625 000
Lagos	Nigeria	13 717 000
Karachi	Pakistan	13 252 000
Buenos Aires	Argentina	13 067 000
Los Angeles	USA	12 738 000
Rio de Janeiro	Brazil	12 170 000
Cairo	Egypt	12 041 000
Manila	Philippines	11 799 000
Beijing	China	11 741 000
Ōsaka	Japan	11 305 000
Moscow	Russian Federation	10 967 000
İstanbul	Turkey	10 546 000
Paris	France	9 856 000
Seoul	South Korea	9 554 000
Guangzhou	China	9 447 000
Chicago	USA	9 186 000
London	United Kingdom	8 607 000
Bogotá	Colombia	8 416 000
Shenzhen	China	8 114 000
Tehrān	Iran	7 807 000
Lima	Peru	7 590 000
Chennai	India	7 545 000
Wuhan	China	7 542 000
Kinshasa	Dem. Rep. Congo	7 526 000
Tianjin	China	7 468 000
Hong Kong	China	7 416 000
Bangalore	India	7 216 000
Lahore	Pakistan	7 201 000
Bangkok	Thailand	6 963 000
Hyderabad	India	6 749 000
Chongqing	China	6 690 000
Baghdād	Iraq	6 593 000

World's Major Cities

Urban agglomerations with over 2.5 million inhabitants.

- 2.5 million - 5 million
- 5 million - 10 million
- 10 million - 20 million
- over 20 million

Level of Urbanization

Percentage of total population living in urban areas 2005. The world's urban population is expected to reach 50 per cent of the total population during 2008.

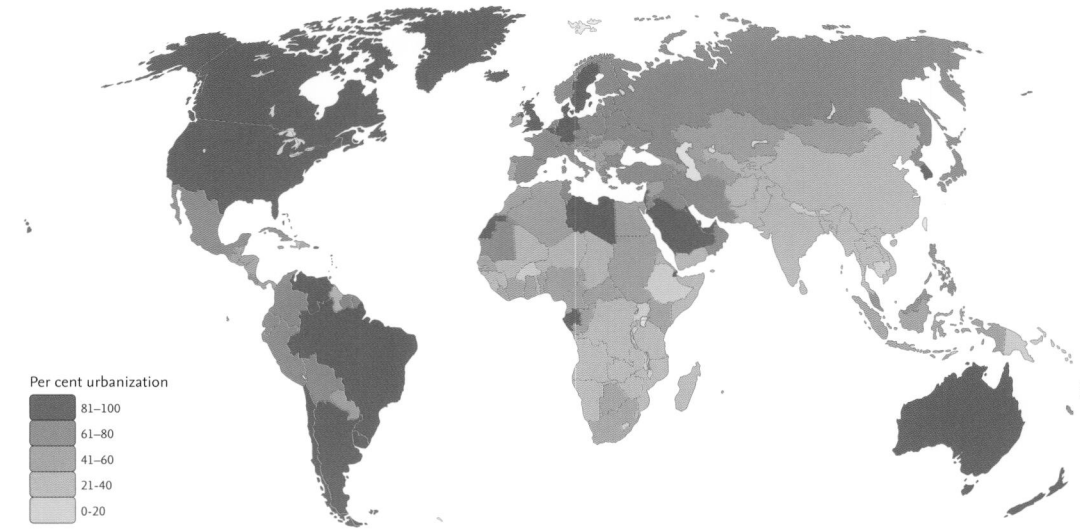

Per cent urbanization
- 81–100
- 61–80
- 41–60
- 21–40
- 0-20

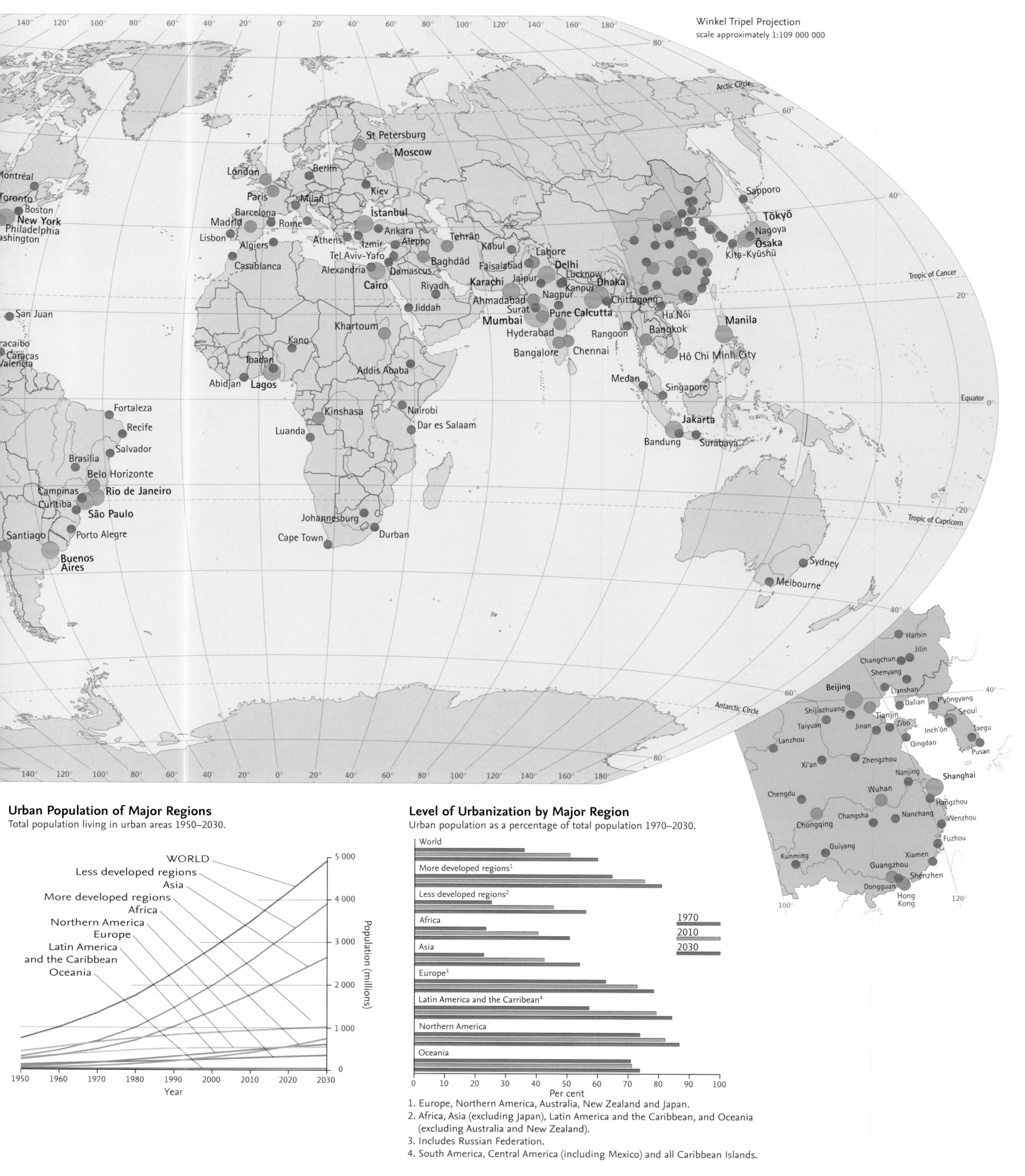

Winkel Tripel Projection
scale approximately 1:109 000 000

Urban Population of Major Regions
Total population living in urban areas 1950–2030.

WORLD
Less developed regions
Asia
More developed regions
Africa
Northern America
Europe
Latin America
and the Caribbean
Oceania

Population (millions)

Year

Level of Urbanization by Major Region
Urban population as a percentage of total population 1970–2030.

World
More developed regions[1]
Less developed regions[2]
Africa
Asia
Europe[3]
Latin America and the Carribean[4]
Northern America
Oceania

1970
2010
2030

Per cent

1. Europe, Northern America, Australia, New Zealand and Japan.
2. Africa, Asia (excluding Japan), Latin America and the Caribbean, and Oceania
   (excluding Australia and New Zealand).
3. Includes Russian Federation.
4. South America, Central America (including Mexico) and all Caribbean Islands.

Wealth, Poverty and Trade

The globalization of the economy is making the world appear a smaller place. However, this shrinkage is an uneven process. Countries are being included and excluded to differing degrees in the global economy. The world economy remains divided between the richer (core) and relatively poorer (peripheral) countries. A common method of defining these groups uses Gross National Income (GNI) per capita as a measure of average income in each country. The fates of core and peripheral countries are closely related. Economic success and prosperity for one country can often be at the expense of others. Some newly industrializing countries have attempted to grow fast enough to cross the divide between core and periphery. Economic inequalities exist between and within countries, as well as between and within social groups in countries. These inequalities are evident in terms of wealth, growth, and debt. Increasingly large and dominant transnational corporations are driving and, in turn, being driven by the process of globalization.

Poverty, hunger, and environmental degradation are problems experienced in areas such as this in Freetown, capital of Sierra Leone, one of the world's poorest countries.

Trade, Debt and Aid

Different countries and regions are participating in the global economy to different degrees. The value of merchandise exports, for instance, illustrates the extent to which countries are engaged in cross-border trading. Global trade is concentrated among the developed countries, in particular North America, the European Union, and the Asia-Pacific region. The USA, Germany, and Japan stand out as the world's largest exporters. Since exports earn hard currency, it is no coincidence that the weakest exporters are among the world's poorest countries, including Burundi and the Democratic Republic of the Congo in Africa. The developed countries with the higher values of exports are more closely integrated into the core of the global economy. The weak exporters remain reliant upon imports and stay on the periphery of the global trading system. Foreign direct investment (FDI) is another motor of the global economy. FDI inflows in 2004 were dominated by the developed countries, in particular western Europe, and, to a lesser degree, the Asia-Pacific region among the developing nations.

Globalization means the poorest countries find it particularly hard to develop and attract economic activity, resulting in an inability to repay loans or stimulate their own economies. Therefore their debts become greater and more loans are taken out to cover them. International efforts are ongoing in trying to suspend or write off some of these debts but meanwhile overseas aid is essential for the survival of some of the poorest countries.

Inequalities in Wealth Distribution
Gross National Income (GNI) per capita, 2005 and Gini Index (latest available figures).

The Gini Index reveals the degree of inequality in the internal distribution of income . When the figure is higher, national income is more concentrated in the hands of fewer people.

Gini Index

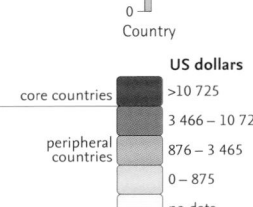

US dollars

core countries	>10 725
	3 466 – 10 725
peripheral countries	876 – 3 465
	0 – 875
	no data

Foreign Direct Investment
Host Economies 2004

	Country	US$ (millions)
Developed countries	United States	106 831
	Luxembourg	78 678
	United Kingdom	72 561
	Australia	42 469
	Belgium	40 080
Developing countries	China	54 937
	Hong Kong	34 035
	Brazil	18 166
	Mexico	17 377
	Singapore	16 032

Debt Service Ratio
Debt as a percentage of GNI and top 5 total debt service, 2004.

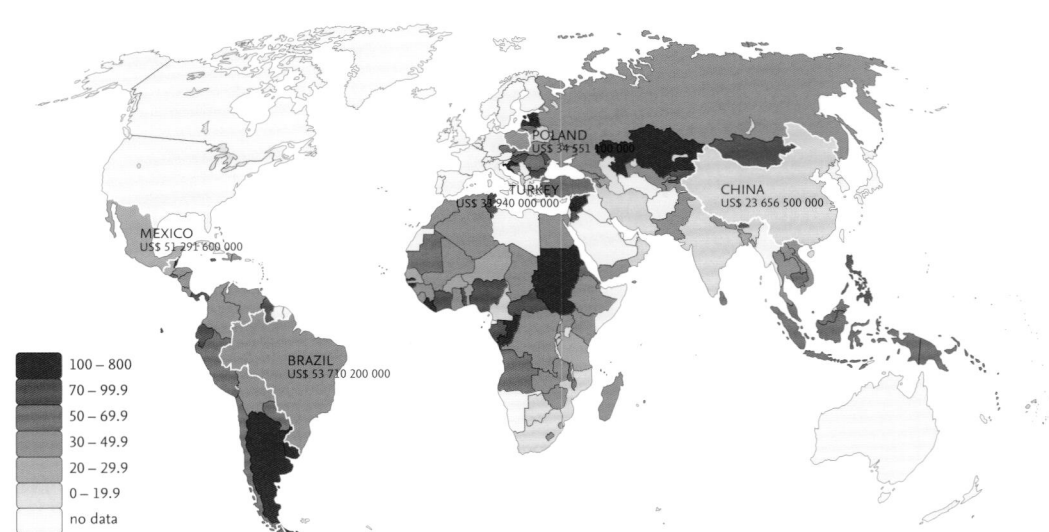

	100 – 800
	70 – 99.9
	50 – 69.9
	30 – 49.9
	20 – 29.9
	0 – 19.9
	no data

Winkel Tripel Projection
scale 1 : 107 000 000

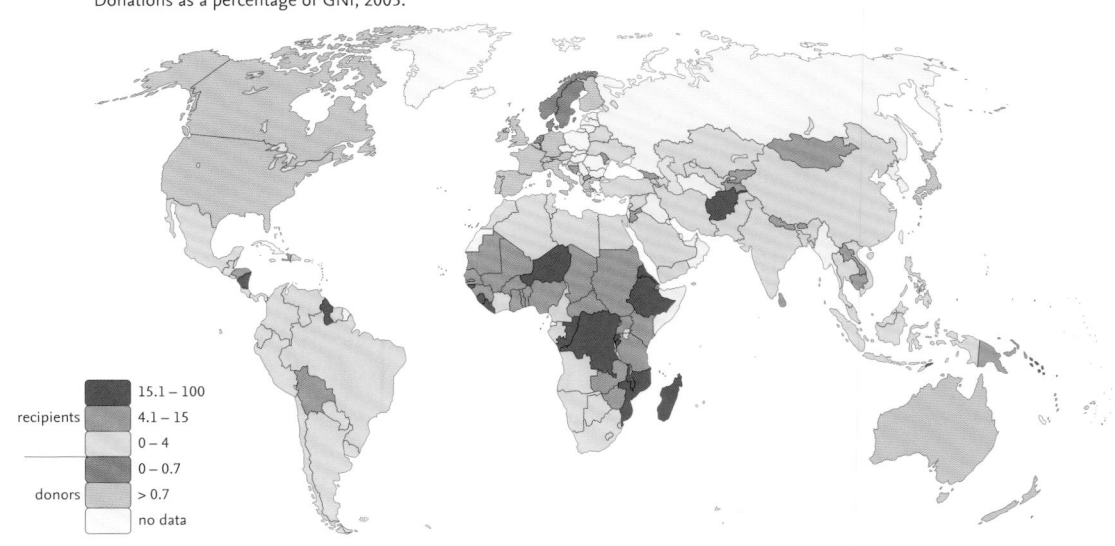

Map labels (bar chart values on map):

39.9 Russian Federation
25.8
36.0
29.7
25.8 Norway
Belarus
United Kingdom
Slovakia
34.4
61.3
43.7
47.0 Guinea-Bissau
Egypt
42.5
Nigeria
Central African Republic
Kenya
57.8
South Africa
58.0
Brazil
30.6 Pakistan
32.5 India
44.7 China
46.1 Philippines
35.2 Australia

Arctic Circle
Tropic of Cancer
Equator
Tropic of Capricorn
Antarctic Circle

Overseas Aid

Donations as a percentage of GNI, 2005.

recipients	
15.1 – 100	
4.1 – 15	
0 – 4	
0 – 0.7	
donors	> 0.7
no data	

Value of Exports 2004

	US$ (millions)
World	9 145 028
Developed Countries	6 138 451
Developing Countries	2 837 539
High Income Countries	6 490 100
Low Income Countries	212 769
Middle Income Countries	2 259 406
Asia (excluding Middle East)	2 374 267
Central America and Caribbean	223 513
Europe	4 197 378
Middle East and North Africa	534 350
North America	1 135 732
Oceania	111 638
South America	241 703
Sub-Saharan Africa	143 693

Communications

The rapid growth of the telecommunications industry over the last two decades, has contributed to the 'death of distance' by linking different parts of the world ever more cheaply and reliably due to improvements in technology. This process has meant that millions of virtual places, identified by telephone numbers, e-mail addresses, and World Wide Web sites, have become an essential part of the world's social and economic landscape. The huge demand for mobile and satellite telephones has contributed to satellite demand and to the building of ground stations. The parallel demand for electronic addresses has also triggered a building boom for international submarine cables as well as adding to the demand for satellites. Initially, most of these networks served an information belt running from western Europe across North America to eastern Asia, but now the rest of the world is gradually becoming connected.

Internet Communications

Internet users have been increasing rapidly, especially in the last ten years. However, access levels vary, with approximately thirty countries still with less than 1 per cent internet penetration. In the G8 countries, with 15 per cent of the world's population, there are almost 50 per cent of total internet users while the entire continent of Africa, with over fifty countries, has fewer internet users than France. Constraints include the high costs of international bandwidth to developing countries if they have to pay for a link to a hub in a developed country. International bandwidth is a critical part of the infrastructure as it is the most important factor in the speed of access to websites in other countries.

Satellite Communications

Communications satellites are important for person-to-person communication, including cellular telephones, and for broadcasting. Unlike submarine cables, which must connect at fixed points, satellites can transmit information between Earth stations located anywhere within a satellite's radio beam, or 'footprint'. Geostationary satellites, which orbit at 36 000 kilometres (22 370 miles) above the Earth may have footprints spanning over 1000 kilometres (620 miles), thus providing a broad service area for point-to-multi-point voice, video and data communications. The positions of communications satellites are critical to their use, and reflect the demand for such communications in each part of the world. While satellites are historically most important for international telephone calls they have since developed for the provision of television, radio and to provide broadband internet services.

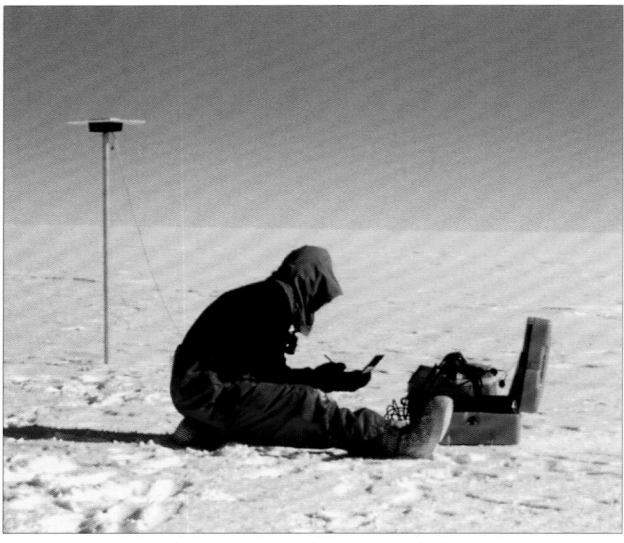

Communications satellites are placed in 'geostationary' orbit above the equator. This means that they move at the same speed as the earth and remain fixed above a single point on the earth's surface. The Global Positioning System (GPS) – seen in use here in Antarctica for monitoring glacier movement – allows accurate position fixing and navigation. Originally developed by the US military, the signals from the satellites now serve hand-held personal and in-car navigation uses, as well as more sophisticated surveying and mapping applications.

World Communication Equipment 1991–2006

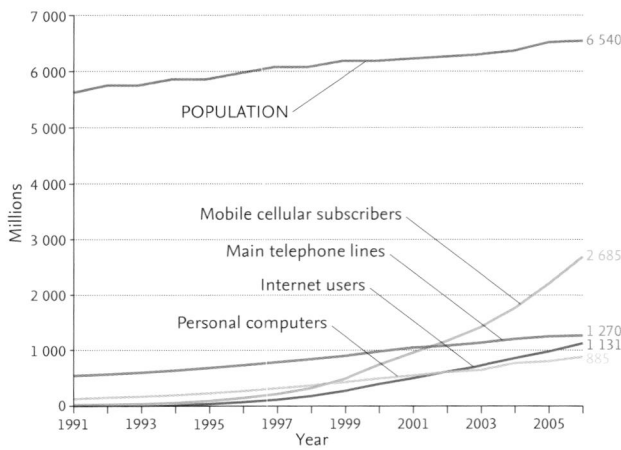

International Telecommunications Indicators by Region 2006

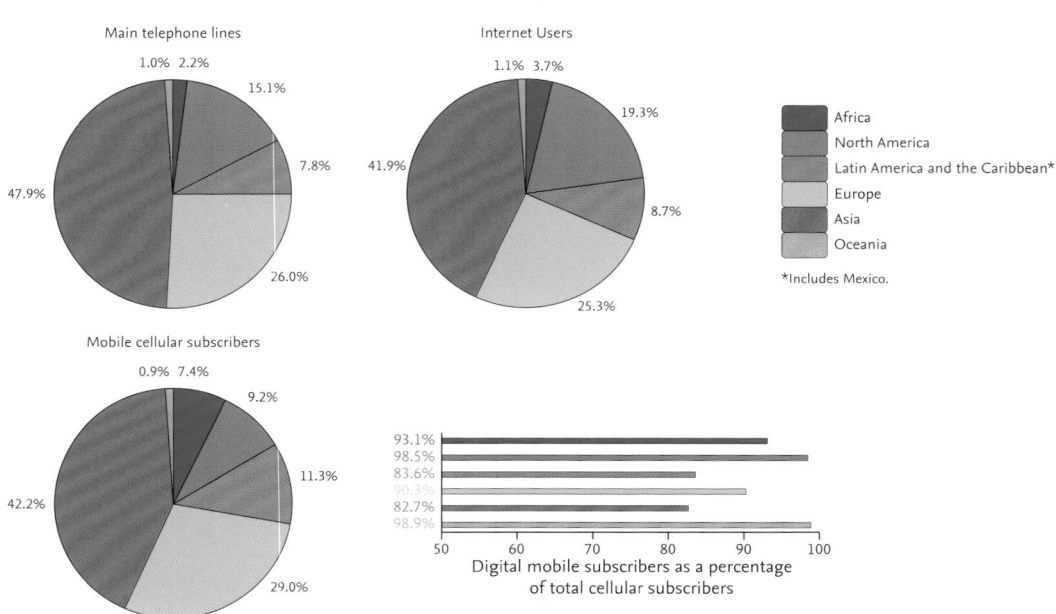

Internet Users and Capacity

International Telecommunications Traffic 2006

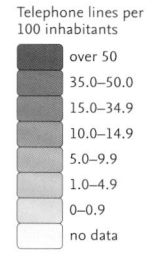

Telephone lines per
100 inhabitants

- over 50
- 35.0–50.0
- 15.0–34.9
- 10.0–14.9
- 5.0–9.9
- 1.0–4.9
- 0–0.9
- no data

Millions of minutes of
telecommunications traffic

15 000   7 500   2 500

Each band is proportional to the total annual TDM (Time
Division Multiplexed) traffic on the public telephone network
in both directions between each pair of countries.

The main projection depicts
inter-continental flows greater than 100
Mbps.

The area of each circle is
proportional to the volume of the
total annual outgoing TDM traffic
from each country.

- 10 001 – 20 000
- 5 001 – 10 000
- 1 001 – 5 000
- 101–1000
- >100

© TeleGeography Research
www.telegeography.com

Geostationary Communications Satellites and Cellular Mobile Subscribers

Geostationary
communication
satellites

- In service
- Inclined orbit
- Planned

Cellular mobile subscribers
per 100 inhabitants 2006

- over 100
- 80–100
- 60–79.9
- 40–59.9
- 20–39.9
- 0–19.9
- no data

Physical Features

The images below illustrate some of the major physical features of Australasia, Asia, Europe and Africa.

Australasia

Lake Eyre, South Australia

The island of New Guinea

Asia

The island of Borneo

Mt Everest, China/Nepal

Europe

The river Volga, Russian Federation

The Caspian Sea

Africa

The island of Madagascar

Kilimanjaro, Tanzania

Australasia Total Land Area 8 844 516 sq km / 3 414 887 sq miles (includes New Guinea and Pacific Island nations)

HIGHEST MOUNTAINS	metres	feet
Puncak Jaya, Indonesia	5 030	16 502
Puncak Trikora, Indonesia	4 730	15 518
Puncak Mandala, Indonesia	4 700	15 420
Puncak Yamin, Indonesia	4 595	15 075
Mt Wilhelm, Papua New Guinea	4 509	14 793
Mt Kubor, Papua New Guinea	4 359	14 301

LARGEST ISLANDS	sq km	sq miles
New Guinea	808 510	312 167
South Island, New Zealand	151 215	58 384
North Island, New Zealand	115 777	44 701
Tasmania	67 800	26 178

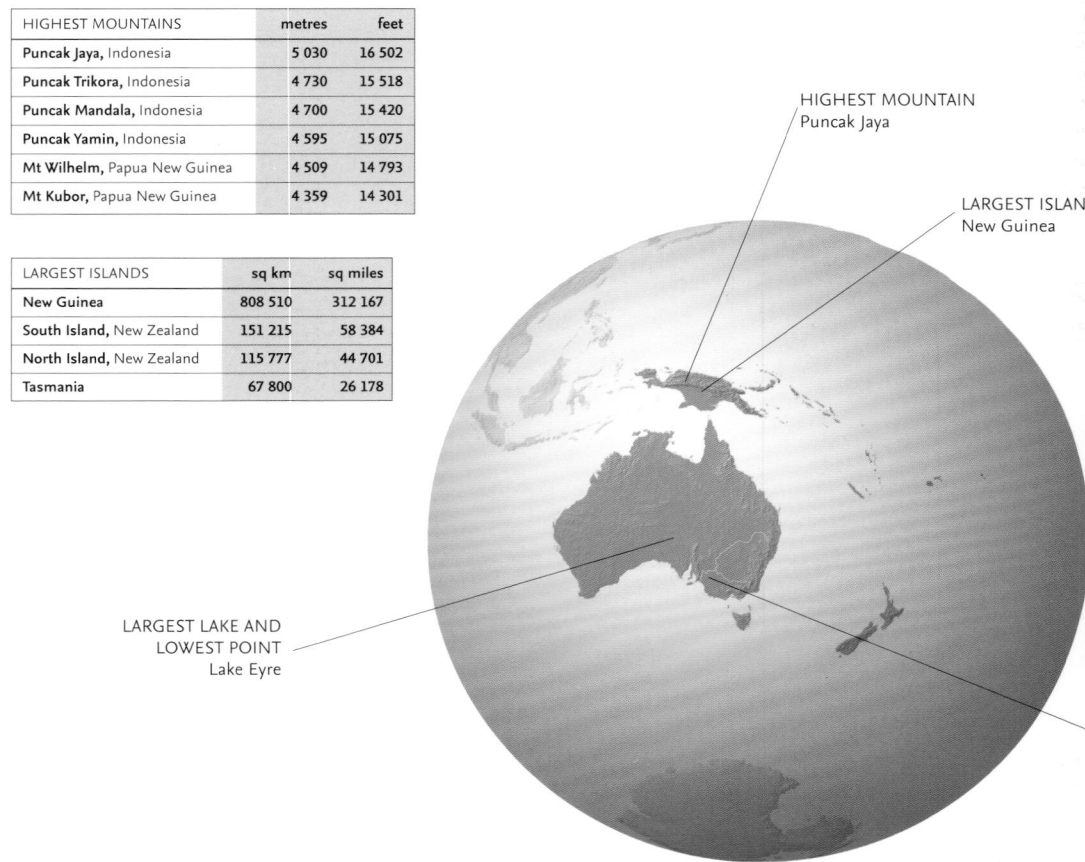

HIGHEST MOUNTAIN
Puncak Jaya

LARGEST ISLAND
New Guinea

LARGEST LAKE AND
LOWEST POINT
Lake Eyre

Asia Total Land Area 45 036 492 sq km / 17 388 686 sq miles

HIGHEST MOUNTAINS	metres	feet
Mt Everest (Sagarmatha/ Qomolangma Feng), China/Nepal	8 848	29 028
K2 (Qogir Feng), China/Pakistan	8 611	28 251
Kangchenjunga, India/Nepal	8 586	28 169
Lhotse, China/Nepal	8 516	27 939
Makalu, China/Nepal	8 463	27 765
Cho Oyu, China/Nepal	8 201	26 906

LARGEST ISLANDS	sq km	sq miles
Borneo	745 561	287 861
Sumatra (Sumatera)	473 606	182 859
Honshū	227 414	87 805
Celebes (Sulawesi)	189 216	73 056
Java (Jawa)	132 188	51 038
Luzon	104 690	40 421

LARGEST LAKE
Caspian Sea

LARGEST DRAINAGE
BASIN
Ob'-Irtysh

LOWEST POINT
Dead Sea

HIGHEST MOUNTAIN
Mt Everest

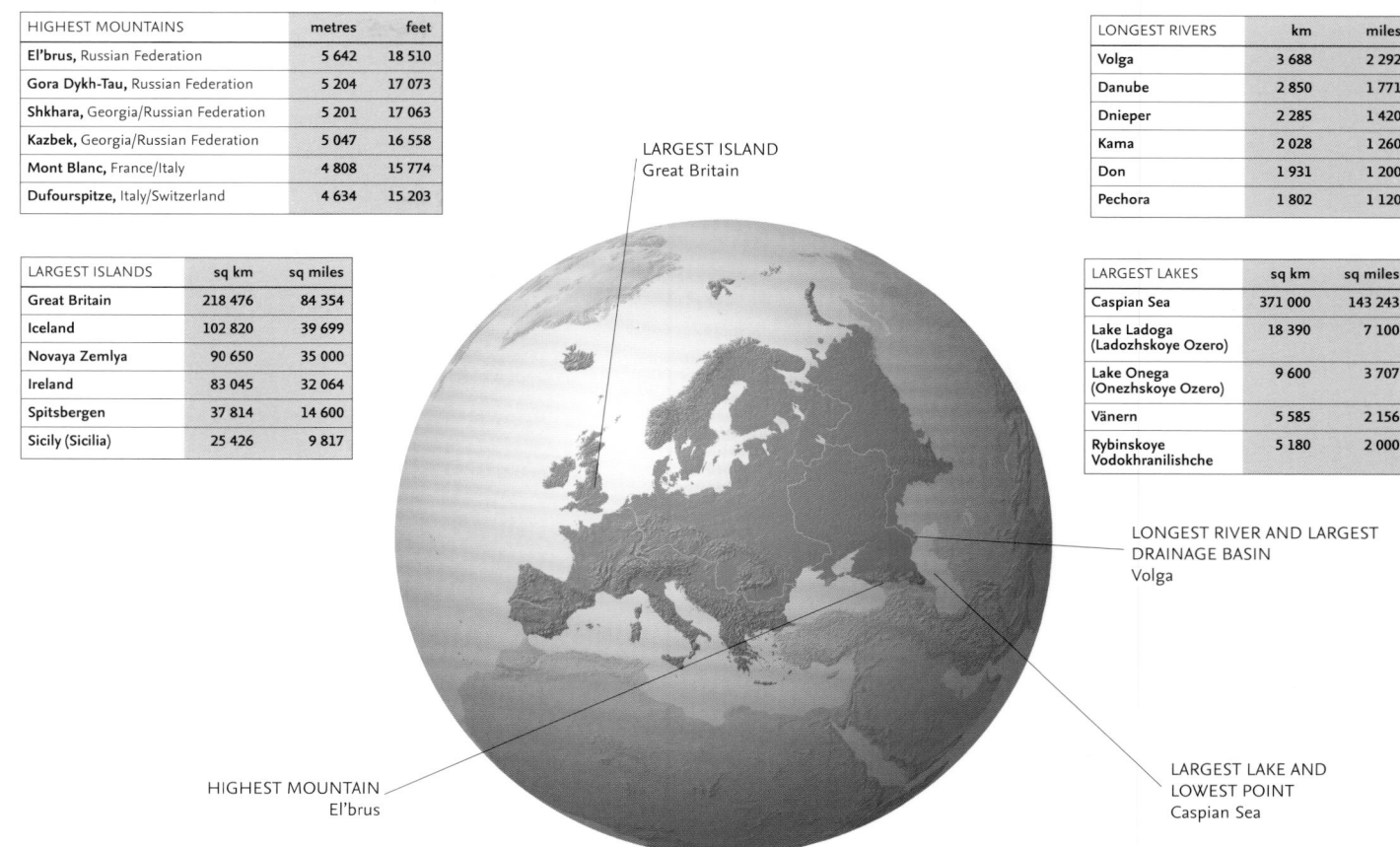

Europe Total Land Area 9 908 599 sq km / 3 825 731 sq miles

LONGEST RIVERS	km	miles
Murray-Darling	3 750	2 330
Darling	2 739	1 702
Murray	2 589	1 609
Murrumbidgee	1 690	1 050
Lachlan	1 480	920
Macquarie	950	590

LARGEST LAKES	sq km	sq miles
Lake Eyre	0–8 900	0–3 436
Lake Torrens	0–5 780	0–2 232

LONGEST RIVER AND LARGEST
DRAINAGE BASIN
Murray-Darling

HIGHEST MOUNTAINS	metres	feet
El'brus, Russian Federation	5 642	18 510
Gora Dykh-Tau, Russian Federation	5 204	17 073
Shkhara, Georgia/Russian Federation	5 201	17 063
Kazbek, Georgia/Russian Federation	5 047	16 558
Mont Blanc, France/Italy	4 808	15 774
Dufourspitze, Italy/Switzerland	4 634	15 203

LARGEST ISLANDS	sq km	sq miles
Great Britain	218 476	84 354
Iceland	102 820	39 699
Novaya Zemlya	90 650	35 000
Ireland	83 045	32 064
Spitsbergen	37 814	14 600
Sicily (Sicilia)	25 426	9 817

LONGEST RIVERS	km	miles
Volga	3 688	2 292
Danube	2 850	1 771
Dnieper	2 285	1 420
Kama	2 028	1 260
Don	1 931	1 200
Pechora	1 802	1 120

LARGEST LAKES	sq km	sq miles
Caspian Sea	371 000	143 243
Lake Ladoga (Ladozhskoye Ozero)	18 390	7 100
Lake Onega (Onezhskoye Ozero)	9 600	3 707
Vänern	5 585	2 156
Rybinskoye Vodokhranilishche	5 180	2 000

LARGEST ISLAND
Great Britain

LONGEST RIVER AND LARGEST
DRAINAGE BASIN
Volga

LARGEST LAKE AND
LOWEST POINT
Caspian Sea

HIGHEST MOUNTAIN
El'brus

Africa Total Land Area 30 343 578 sq km / 11 715 721 sq miles

LONGEST RIVERS	km	miles
Yangtze (Chang Jiang)	6 380	3 965
Ob'-Irtysh	5 568	3 460
Yenisey-Angara-Selenga	5 550	3 449
Yellow (Huang He)	5 464	3 395
Irtysh	4 440	2 759
Mekong	4 425	2 750

LARGEST LAKES	sq km	sq miles
Caspian Sea	371 000	143 243
Lake Baikal (Ozero Baykal)	30 500	11 776
Lake Balkhash (Ozero Balkhash)	17 400	6 718
Aral Sea (Aral'skoye More)	17 158	6 625
Ysyk-Köl	6 200	2 394

LONGEST RIVER
Yangtze
(Chang Jiang)

LARGEST ISLAND
Borneo

HIGHEST MOUNTAINS	metres	feet
Kilimanjaro, Tanzania	5 892	19 330
Mt Kenya (Kirinyaga), Kenya	5 199	17 057
Margherita Peak, Democratic Republic of the Congo/Uganda	5 110	16 765
Meru, Tanzania	4 565	14 977
Ras Dejen, Ethiopia	4 533	14 872
Mt Karisimbi, Rwanda	4 510	14 796

LARGEST LAKES	sq km	sq miles
Lake Victoria	68 870	26 591
Lake Tanganyika	32 600	12 587
Lake Nyasa (Lake Malawi)	29 500	11 390
Lake Volta	8 482	3 275
Lake Turkana	6 500	2 510
Lake Albert	5 600	2 162

LONGEST RIVERS	km	miles
Nile	6 695	4 160
Congo	4 667	2 900
Niger	4 184	2 600
Zambezi	2 736	1 700
Webi Shabeelle	2 490	1 547
Ubangi	2 250	1 398

LARGEST ISLANDS	sq km	sq miles
Madagascar	587 040	226 656

LONGEST RIVER
Nile

LOWEST POINT
Lake Assal

LARGEST DRAINAGE BASIN
Congo

HIGHEST MOUNTAIN
Kilimanjaro

LARGEST LAKE
Lake Victoria

LARGEST ISLAND
Madagascar

Physical Features

The images below illustrate some of the major physical features of North America, South America, and Antarctica.

North America

Mississippi-Missouri,
United States of America

The island of Greenland

Mt McKinley, United States of America

South America

Lake Titicaca, Bolivia/Peru

Cerro Aconcagua,
Argentina

The river Amazon

Antarctica

Vinson Massif, West Antarctica

North America Total Land Area 24 680 331 sq km / 9 529 129 sq miles (including Hawaiian Islands)

HIGHEST MOUNTAINS	metres	feet
Mt McKinley, USA	6 194	20 321
Mt Logan, Canada	5 959	19 550
Pico de Orizaba, Mexico	5 610	18 405
Mt St Elias, USA	5 489	18 008
Volcán Popocatépetl, Mexico	5 452	17 887
Mt Foraker, USA	5 303	17 398

LARGEST ISLANDS	sq km	sq miles
Greenland	2 175 600	839 999
Baffin Island	507 451	195 927
Victoria Island	217 291	83 896
Ellesmere Island	196 236	75 767
Cuba	110 860	42 803
Newfoundland	108 860	42 031
Hispaniola	76 192	29 418

HIGHEST MOUNTAIN
Mt McKinley

LARGEST ISLAND
Greenland

LOWEST POINT
Death Valley

South America Total Land Area 17 815 420 sq km / 6 878 572 sq miles

HIGHEST MOUNTAINS	metres	feet
Cerro Aconcagua, Argentina	6 959	22 831
Nevado Ojos del Salado, Argentina/Chile	6 908	22 664
Cerro Bonete, Argentina	6 872	22 546
Cerro Pissis, Argentina	6 858	22 500
Cerro Tupungato, Argentina/Chile	6 800	22 309
Cerro Mercedario, Argentina	6 770	22 211

LARGEST ISLANDS	sq km	sq miles
Isla Grande de Tierra del Fuego	47 000	18 147
Isla de Chiloé	8 394	3 241
East Falkland	6 760	2 610
West Falkland	5 413	2 090

LONGEST RIVER AND
LARGEST DRAINAGE BASIN
Amazon (Amazonas)

LARGEST LAKE
Lake Titicaca

HIGHEST MOUNTAIN
Cerro Aconcagua

LONGEST RIVERS	km	miles
Mississippi-Missouri	5 969	3 709
Mackenzie-Peace-Finlay	4 241	2 635
Missouri	4 086	2 539
Mississippi	3 765	2 340
Yukon	3 185	1 979
Rio Grande (Río Bravo del Norte)	3 057	1 900

LARGEST LAKES	sq km	sq miles
Lake Superior	82 100	31 699
Lake Huron	59 600	23 012
Lake Michigan	57 800	22 317
Great Bear Lake	31 328	12 096
Great Slave Lake	28 568	11 030
Lake Erie	25 700	9 923
Lake Winnipeg	24 387	9 416
Lake Ontario	18 960	7 320

LARGEST LAKE
Lake Superior

LONGEST RIVER AND
LARGEST DRAINAGE BASIN
Mississippi-Missouri

LONGEST RIVERS	km	miles
Amazon (Amazonas)	6 516	4 049
Río de la Plata-Paraná	4 500	2 796
Purus	3 218	2 000
Madeira	3 200	1 988
São Francisco	2 900	1 802
Tocantins	2 750	1 709

LARGEST LAKES	sq km	sq miles
Lake Titicaca	8 340	3 220

LOWEST POINT
Laguna del Carbón

LARGEST ISLAND
Isla Grande de Tierra del Fuego

HIGHEST MOUNTAIN
Vinson Massif

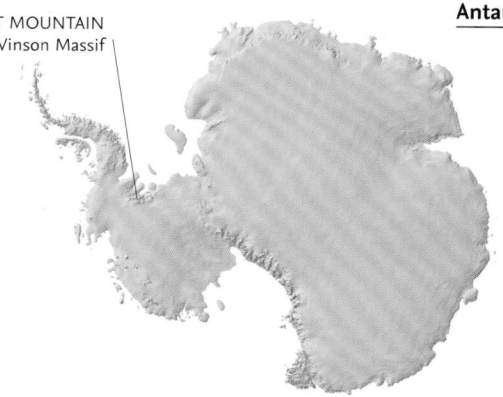

Antarctica Total Land Area 12 093 000 sq km / 4 669 133 sq miles (excluding ice shelves)

HIGHEST MOUNTAINS	metres	feet
Vinson Massif	4 897	16 066
Mt Tyree	4 852	15 918
Mt Kirkpatrick	4 528	14 855
Mt Markham	4 351	14 275
Mt Jackson	4 190	13 747
Mt Sidley	4 181	13 717

Atlantic Ocean Total Area 86 557 000 sq km / 33 420 000 sq miles

ATLANTIC OCEAN	Area square km	square miles	Deepest Point metres	feet
Extent	86 557 000	33 420 000	8 605	28 231
Arctic Ocean	9 485 000	3 662 000	5 450	17 880
Caribbean Sea	2 512 000	970 000	7 680	25 196
Mediterranean Sea	2 510 000	969 000	5 121	16 800
Gulf of Mexico	1 544 000	596 000	3 504	11 495
Hudson Bay	1 233 000	476 000	259	849
North Sea	575 000	222 000	661	2 168
Black Sea	508 000	196 000	2 245	7 365
Baltic Sea	382 000	147 000	460	1 509

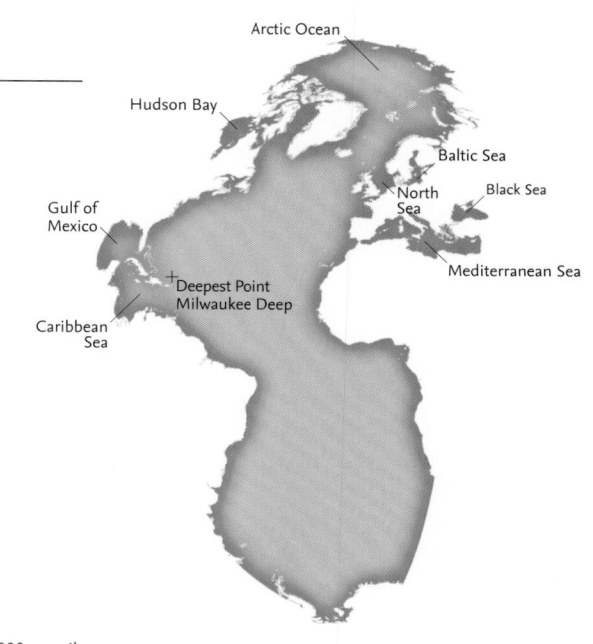

Arctic Ocean
Hudson Bay
Baltic Sea
Black Sea
North Sea
Gulf of Mexico
Deepest Point Milwaukee Deep
Caribbean Sea
Mediterranean Sea

Red Sea
The Gulf
Bay of Bengal

Indian Ocean Total Area 73 427 000 sq km / 28 350 000 sq miles

Deepest Point
Java Trench

INDIAN OCEAN	Area square km	square miles	Deepest Point metres	feet
Extent	73 427 000	28 350 000	7 125	23 376
Bay of Bengal	2 172 000	839 000	4 500	14 763
Red Sea	453 000	175 000	3 040	9 973
The Gulf	238 000	92 000	73	239

Pacific Ocean Total Area 166 241 000 sq km / 64 186 000 sq miles

PACIFIC OCEAN	Area square km	square miles	Deepest Point metres	feet
Extent	166 241 000	64 186 000	10 920	35 826
South China Sea	2 590 000	1 000 000	5 514	18 090
Bering Sea	2 261 000	873 000	4 150	13 615
Sea of Okhotsk	1 392 000	537 000	3 363	11 033
Sea of Japan (East Sea)	1 013 000	391 000	3 743	12 280
East China Sea and Yellow Sea	1 202 000	464 000	2 717	8 913

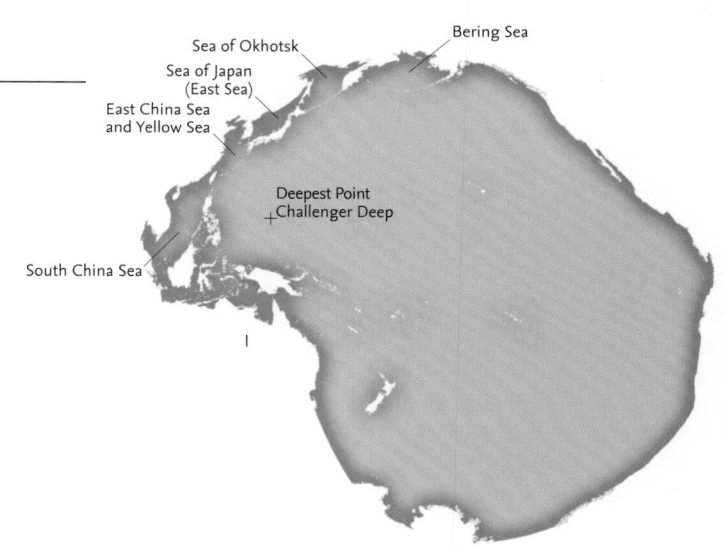

Sea of Okhotsk
Bering Sea
Sea of Japan (East Sea)
East China Sea and Yellow Sea
Deepest Point Challenger Deep
South China Sea

World Tourism

The growth of low-cost air transport opened up the world for global tourism, making air travel accessible to an increasing share of the world's population. More recently, the widespread use of the Internet has accelerated the direct selling of travel and accommodation options, broadening the possibilities for researching and booking holidays, and increasing the scope to search for discounted deals. Since the early 1990s world tourism, measured by international tourist arrivals, has nearly doubled.

Global economic difficulties combined with an increasing awareness of the environmental cost of long distance destinations has led to a slight decline in this upward trend in more recent years, but the general forecast is still for growth. Global policies increasingly support the sustainable development of tourism, and the individual is finding ways to reconcile and adapt beliefs and circumstances with the irresistible longing to experience the wonders of our world.

Europe and the Americas retain a long-standing and steady attraction to tourists but emerging destinations in Asia, the Pacific, Africa and the Middle East are showing the greatest increase in tourism. Speciality travel is also emerging as a growth industry, fulfilling such needs as the ecological and social consciousness of ecotourism and the adrenaline rush of extreme tourism. Yet, remaining at the heart of world tourism is a desire to see and experience lands and cultures outside the realm of our everyday life, and so the world's great natural wonders and iconic landmarks remain in the list of the world's most visited places.

Niagara Falls, Canada/USA (page 53)

Times Square, New York, USA (page 52)

Sacré Coeur, Paris, France (page 48)

Rio de Janeiro, Brazil (page 54)

Los Glaciares National Park, Argentina (page 55)

● **Highlighted tourist sites (page numbers)**

44 Sydney, Australia
45 Fiordland, New Zealand
46 Beijing, China
47 Bali, Indonesia
48 Sacré Coeur, Paris, France
49 Colosseum, Rome, Italy
50 Luxor, Egypt
51 Masai Mara, Kenya
52 Times Square, New York, USA
53 Niagara Falls, Canada/USA
54 Rio de Janeiro, Brazil
55 Los Glaciares National Park, Argentina

● **Top 50 tourist attractions**

1 Times Square, New York, USA
2 National Mall & Memorial Parks, Washington D.C., USA
3 Disney World's Magic Kingdom, Florida, USA
4 Trafalgar Square, London, UK
5 Disneyland Park, California, USA
6 Niagara Falls, Canada/USA
7 Fisherman's Wharf/Golden Gate National Recreation Area, San Francisco,
8 Tokyo Disneyland/Disney Sea, Tokyo, Japan

9 Notre Dame de Paris, Paris, France
10 Disneyland Paris, France
11 The Great Wall, China
12 The Great Smoky Mountain National Park, USA
13 Universal Studios Japan, Osaka, Japan
14 Basilique du Sacré Coeur de Montmartre, Paris, France
15 Musée du Louvre, Paris, France
16 Everland, South Korea
17 The Forbidden City/Tiananmen Square, Beijing, China

18 Eiffel Tower, Paris, France
19 Universal Studios/Islands of Adventure, Florida, USA
20 Sea World Florida, Florida, USA
21 Pleasure Beach, Blackpool, UK
22 Lotte World, Seoul, South Korea
23 Yokohama Hakkeijima Sea Paradise, Japan
24 Hong Kong Disneyland, China
25 Centre Pompidou, Paris, France
26 Tate Modern, London, UK
27 British Museum, London, UK

Top 50 tourist attraction visitor numbers (millions) in 2007

Beijing, China (page 46)

Luxor, Egypt (page 50)

Masai Mara, Kenya (page 51)

Bali, Indonesia (page 47)

Sydney, Australia (page 44)

Fiordland, New Zealand (page 45)

28 Universal Studios, Los Angeles, USA
29 National Gallery, London, UK
30 Metropolitan Museum, New York, USA
31 Grand Canyon, USA
32 Tivoli Gardens, Copenhagen, Denmark
33 Ocean Park, Hong Kong, China
34 Busch Gardens, Florida, USA
35 Sea World California, San Diego, USA
36 Statue of Liberty, New York, USA
37 The Vatican and its museums, Rome, Italy

38 Sydney Opera House, Australia
39 The Colosseum, Rome, Italy
40 The American Museum of Natural History, New York, USA
41 Grauman's Chinese Theater, California, Hollywood, USA
42 Empire State Building, New York, USA
43 Natural History Museum, London, UK
44 The London Eye, London, UK
45 Palace of Versailles, France

46 Yosemite National Park, USA
47 Pyramids of Giza, Egypt
48 Pompeii, Italy
49 Hermitage Museum, St Petersburg, Russia
50 Taj Mahal, India
Source: Forbes Magazine, 2007

Sydney – AUSTRALIA

Situated on the southeast coast of Australia and containing within its harbour area two of the world's most iconic structures – Sydney Opera House and the Harbour Bridge – Sydney is one of the world's most popular tourist destinations.

From beaches to national parks, museums to water-side restaurants and boat trips, the city offers a superb and diverse range of activities for the tourist.

Away from the harbour area are shopping areas, parks, gardens, museums and galleries. The famous Bondi Beach is only a short distance from the city centre yet offers locals and tourists alike the opportunity to relax away from the frenetic pace of city life with some sunbathing or surfing.

44

Fiordland – NEW ZEALAND

Fiordland, on the southwest corner of New Zealand's South Island, is an area of spectacular scenery. In 1990 it achieved World Heritage status due to its unique flora and fauna which are representative of the ancient southern supercontinent of Gondwanaland.

Aoraki (Mount Cook), New Zealand's highest mountain, steep-sided fiords such as Milford and Doubtful Sounds, high waterfalls and deep lakes are all characteristic of the region.

The focal point of the area is the town of Te Anau from where it is possible to take trips to many of the best-known locations, such as Milford Sound and Lake Manapouri. A wide range of activities is available to the tourist: trekking; diving; fishing and hunting; boat trips and visits to farms or glowworm caves.

Beijing – CHINA

Beijing, capital of the People's Republic of China, is the main port of entry into the country. With its ancient past and having opened its doors to foreign visitors it is now one of the world's foremost tourist destinations.

The Forbidden City, home of the Ming and Qing dynasty emperors, is a vast palace complex lying at the heart of the city, and contains the Palace Museum which houses collections of Chinese art. Tianamen Square lies just outside the Forbidden City and since its creation in the early 20th century has been the location for many political events.

Parks, gardens and imposing buildings such as the Great Hall of the People and the National Museum of China surround the Forbidden City. Within the city and on its outskirts are a number of World Heritage sites, including the Peking Man site at Zhoukoudian.

Bali – INDONESIA

The island of Bali, lying between the islands of Java and Lombok, has long been a popular tourist destination in Indonesia. Surrounded by coral reefs and white and black sand beaches and with its mountainous volcanic interior it offers a wide range of activities for the visitor.

Kuta, close to the island's capital of Denpasar, is the prime beach resort, while Ubud to the north of the capital is the cultural centre. The coral reefs afford excellent diving and there are trekking opportunities in the mountains. For the less active tourist there are sightseeing trips to the rice terraces and villages, where local craftsmen produce a wide range of handicrafts such as batik, carvings and silverware.

Basilica of Sacré Coeur – Paris, FRANCE

On the hill of Montmartre ('mount of martrys'), in the north of Paris, the Basilica of Sacré Coeur dominates the skyline. Work started in 1875 and was completed in 1914, but it was not consecrated until 1919, after the end of the First World War.

It was designed by architect Paul Abadie, who died in 1884, but five other architects continued with the work. Built of travertine stone, the basilica remains white despite pollution and weathering, and is a major tourist attraction for visitors to Paris. The complex also includes a garden and fountain, and the dome of the basilica, open to the public, affords panoramic views to the south over much of the city.

The Colosseum – Rome, ITALY

Probably the world's greatest ancient amphitheatre, the Colosseum (Amphithetrum Flavium) was built almost 2000 years ago. Regarded by many as one of the greatest works of Roman architecture and engineering, it occupies a site to the east of the Forum and was completed in AD 80.

Games were held in the amphitheatre – the most popular being hunts and gladiatorial games – and it is estimated that many thousands of people and animals were killed in these games over five centuries.

It continued to be used for entertainment up to the Middle Ages, and although now partially ruined, as a result of stone removal, it remains an iconic symbol of Imperial Rome.

It is one of the main tourist sites in Rome, attracting four million visitors annually, and although it cannot now house large events it is often used as the backdrop for concerts.

Luxor – EGYPT

Described as "the world's greatest open-air museum", the area around Luxor on the river Nile in southern Egypt has been a tourist destination since ancient times. Today, visitors come to see the many historic sites of Luxor, Karnak and Thebes.

Since the discovery of Tutankhamun's tomb by Howard Carter, Luxor has been regarded as a destination that simply cannot be missed during a trip to Egypt.

On the east bank of the Nile are the Temple of Luxor, the Mummification Museum, Luxor Museum and the Temple of Karnak. A short boat trip across the river allows access to the Valley of the Kings, the Valley of the Queens, the Temple of Seti I, the Temples of Mentuhetep I, Hatshepsut and Thutmose III, and the famous Ramesseum (memorial temple of Rammesses II), as well as many other historic sites.

Masai Mara – KENYA

The Masai Mara game reserve in southwest Kenya is an area of rolling hills and open grassland that is a continuation of the Serengeti National Park in Tanzania. Covering over 1500 km^2 the reserve is the destination of wildebeest, zebra and Thomson's gazelle migrating from the Seregeti.

Within easy reach from Nairobi, the Mara is a popular attraction, with lodges and tented camps for tourists who come to the reserve to see the 'Big Five' – lion, African elephant, Cape buffalo, leopard and black rhinoceros. There are, however, many other animal species in abundance – cheetah, giraffe, hippopotamus, zebra, antelope, monkey, baboon and crocodile.

Recently, balloon safaris, which afford a bird's eye view of the animals and the landscape, have become popular.

Times Square – New York, USA

In 2007, Times Square, New York, was the No. 1 location in the Forbes Magazine list of the Top 50 Most Visited Tourist Attractions in the world.

Formerly known as Longacre Square, and named after the Times Building, which was the former headquarters of The New York Times, it lies at the intersection of Broadway and Seventh Avenue and has achieved iconic status throughout the world as a symbol of New York. It is a major cultural centre of the city, with many Broadway theatres, nightspots and shops catering for New Yorkers and tourists alike. The Square is at its spectacular best in the hours of darkness when the animated, digital advertisements light up the area.

On New Year's Eve the square is thronged with over one million people who gather to watch, along with a worldwide TV audience, the 'New Year's Eve ball drop' when a crystal ball is lowered to welcome in the New Year.

Niagara Falls – CANADA/USA

Niagara Falls has been a tourist destination since the early 19th century but it was the advent of the motor car that made the area easily accessible. As a result, a thriving tourist industry developed and the Falls remain one of the world's top tourist attractions with over 20 million visitors a year.

The Falls are made up of the American Falls and the Horseshoe Falls, both of which were formed by the rushing waters of the Niagara river flowing through a gorge from Lake Erie to Lake Ontario after the last Ice Age.

Although used for hydroelectric power generation the flow of the Niagara river is controlled by agreement between the US and Canada to ensure that during the tourist season the spectacle of the Falls is preserved.

Cable cars, helicopter trips, balloon trips, boat trips, observation platforms and underground walkways offer different ways of viewing the Falls.

Rio de Janeiro – BRAZIL

Brazil's second largest city, Rio is the prime tourist destination in the southern hemisphere, attracting nearly three million tourists every year.

Known also as *cidade maravilhos* (marvellous city), it is famous for its carnival, beaches such as Copacobana and Ipanema, and its landmarks of Christ the Redeemer which stands on Corcovado mountain overlooking the city, and Sugarloaf mountain.

The carnival, held in the summer, attracts visitors from all over the globe, with the Samba School Parade taking place at the permanent Sambódromo (Sambadrome), a grandstand-lined parade avenue.

The city also boasts one of the largest football stadiums in the world, the Maracanã, and in 2016 will host the Olympic Games.

Los Glaciares National Park – ARGENTINA

Designated a World Heritage site in 1981, Los Glaciares National Park in southern Argentina is an area of exceptional natural beauty, with rugged, towering mountains and numerous glacial lakes. It is a popular tourist attraction with visitors able to witness glaciers in action and to see the impressive wildlife, especially birds such as swans, ducks, geese, flamingos and huge Andean condors.

For the more active visitor there are opportunities for climbing and trekking, especially around Mount Fitzroy and Cerro Torre, two of the most imposing peaks in the Park, as well as horse riding, fishing and white-water rafting.

World Heritage and UNESCO's World Heritage Mission

A visit to a World Heritage site is often an activity in a tourist's itinerary. On the reference maps in this atlas the locations of World Heritage sites are shown, and in the following pages selected ones are described in detail. The sites are those submitted by various countries to the UNESCO World Heritage Committee and approved by it for inclusion on the World Heritage List. To be accepted for inclusion various criteria, as explained below, have to be met.

Heritage is our legacy from the past, what we live with today, and what we pass on to future generations. Our cultural and natural heritage are both irreplaceable sources of life and inspiration. Places as unique and diverse as the wilds of East Africa's Serengeti, the Pyramids of Egypt, the Great Barrier Reef in Australia and the Baroque cathedrals of Latin America make up our world's heritage.

The United Nations Educational, Scientific and Cultural Organization (UNESCO) seeks to encourage the identification, protection and preservation of cultural and natural heritage around the world considered to be of outstanding universal value to humanity. This is embodied in a unique international treaty, called the Convention Concerning the Protection of the World Cultural and Natural Heritage adopted by UNESCO in 1972 (see http://whc.unesco.org/en/conventiontext).

One of the world's most successful conservation instruments, the World Heritage Convention is exceptional in that it links together in a single document the concepts of nature conservation and the preservation of cultural properties. It is also significant in its universal application – World Heritage sites belong to all the peoples of the world, irrespective of the territory on which they are located. By regarding heritage as both cultural and natural, the Convention recognizes the ways in which people interact with nature, and of the fundamental need to preserve the balance between the two.

UNESCO's World Heritage mission is to:
- encourage countries to sign the World Heritage Convention and to ensure the protection of their natural and cultural heritage;
- encourage States Parties to the Convention to nominate sites within their national territory for inclusion on the World Heritage List;
- encourage States Parties to establish management plans and set up reporting systems on the state of conservation of their World Heritage sites;
- help States Parties safeguard World Heritage properties by providing technical assistance and professional training;
- provide emergency assistance for World Heritage sites in immediate danger;
- support States Parties' public awareness-building activities for World Heritage conservation;
- encourage participation of the local population in the preservation of their cultural and natural heritage;
- encourage international cooperation in the conservation of our world's cultural and natural heritage.

THE CRITERIA FOR SELECTION
The World Heritage Convention stipulates the creation of a World Heritage List. In a detailed process, properties are inscribed by an intergovernmental twenty-one member elected Committee, only after a preselection, nomination, and evaluation process. Two leading international Non-Governmental Organizations, the International Union for the Conservation of Nature (IUCN) and the International Council on Monuments and Sites (ICOMOS), review and advise on the natural and cultural nominations respectively. The International Centre for the Study of the Preservation and Restoration of Cultural Property provides the Committee with expert advice on conservation of cultural sites. To be included, sites must be of outstanding universal value and meet at least one out of ten selection criteria:

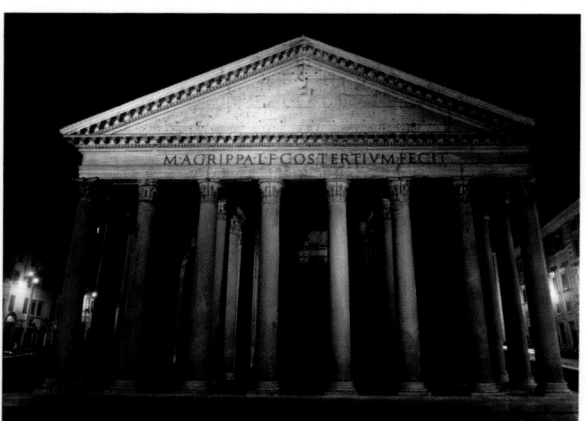

Historic Centre of Rome, Italy

Human creative genius
i. to represent a masterpiece of human creative genius;

Interchange of values
ii. to exhibit an important interchange of human values, over a span of time or within a cultural area of the world, on developments in architecture or technology, monumental arts, town-planning or landscape design;

Site of Palmyra, Syria

Testimony to cultural tradition
iii. to bear a unique or at least exceptional testimony to a cultural tradition or to a civilization which is living or which has disappeared;

Rapa Nui National Park, Chile

Brasilia, Brazil

Significance in human history
iv. to be an outstanding example of a type of building, architectural or technological ensemble or landscape which illustrates (a) significant stage(s) in human history;

Traditional human settlement
v. to be an outstanding example of a traditional human settlement, land-use, or sea-use which is representative of a culture (or cultures), or human interaction with the environment especially when it has become vulnerable under the impact of irreversible change;

Venice and its Lagoon, Italy

Auschwitz Birkenau, Poland

Heritage associated with events of universal significance
vi. to be directly or tangibly associated with events or living traditions, with ideas, or with beliefs, with artistic and literary works of outstanding universal significance. (The Committee considers that this criterion should preferably be used in conjunction with other criteria);

Natural phenomena or beauty
vii. to contain superlative natural phenomena or areas of exceptional natural beauty and aesthetic importance;

Kilimanjaro National Park, Tanzania

Emerald Lake, Yoho National Park, Canada

Major stages of Earth's history
viii. to be outstanding examples representing major stages of Earth's history, including the record of life, significant on-going geological processes in the development of landforms, or significant geomorphic or physiographic features;

Significant ecological and biological processes
ix. to be outstanding examples representing significant on-going ecological and biological processes in the evolution and development of terrestrial, fresh water, coastal and marine ecosystems and communities of plants and animals;

Everglades National Park, USA

Virunga National Park, Dem. Rep. of the Congo

Significant natural habitat for biodiversity
x. to contain the most important and significant natural habitats for in-situ conservation of biological diversity, including those containing threatened species of outstanding universal value from the point of view of science or conservation.

UNESCO World Heritage Sites – Oceania

The sites in this continent cover a huge range in both time and type. In New Zealand the Tongariro site is of great cultural and religious significance to the Maori. There are ancient fossil sites in Australia along with the native peoples' sites such as Uluru, associated with the Anangu, one of the ancient Australian Aboriginal peoples. The world famous Great Barrier Reef is a site of great ecological significance and the iconic Sydney Opera House is a landmark feature in the city.

PALAU

FEDERATED STATES
OF MICRONESIA

A S I A

22

PAPUA NEW
GUINEA

Coral
Sea

7

16

10

1

4

INDIAN

OCEAN

A U S T R A L I A

2

15

12

3

8

17

5

13

1

11

Tasman
Sea

14

**Heard and McDonald
Islands** (Australia)

6

9

MARSHALL
ISLANDS

NAURU

PACIFIC

KIRIBATI

SOLOMON
ISLANDS

TUVALU

VANUATU

25

18

New
Caledonia
(France)

FIJI

SAMOA

Niue
(N.Z.)

TONGA

OCEAN

Cook
Islands
(N.Z.)

Australia
1. Australian Fossil Mammal Sites
   (Riversleigh/Naracoorte)
2. Fraser Island
3. Gondwana Rainforests of Australia
4. Great Barrier Reef
5. Greater Blue Mountains Area
6. Heard and McDonald Islands
7. Kakadu National Park
8. Lord Howe Island Group
9. Macquarie Island
10. Purnululu National Park
11. Royal Exhibition Building and Carlton
    Gardens
12. Shark Bay, Western Australia
13. Sydney Opera House
14. Tasmanian Wilderness
15. Uluru-Kata Tjuta National Park
16. Wet Tropics of Queensland
17. Willandra Lakes Region

New Caledonia
18. Lagoons of New Caledonia:
    Reef Diversity and Associated Ecosystems
    (France)

New Zealand
19. New Zealand Sub-Antarctic Islands
20. Te Wahipounamu – South West
    New Zealand
21. Tongariro National Park

Papua New Guinea
22. Kuk Early Agricultural Site

Pitcairn Islands
23. Henderson Island (U.K.)

Solomon Islands
24. East Rennell

Vanuatu
25. Chief Roi Mata's Domain

Pitcairn Islands (U.K.)

23

NEW
ZEALAND

21

20
20
20

20
20

19

19

19

19

59

Great Barrier Reef – AUSTRALIA

Inscribed 1981 – Natural phenomena or
beauty; Major stages of Earth's history;
Significant ecological and biological processes;
Significant natural habitat for biodiversity.

The Great Barrier Reef is a site of remarkable variety
and beauty on the northeast coast of Australia.
It is the world's most extensive stretch of coral reefs.
The great diversity of its fauna reflects the maturity
of an ecosystem that has evolved over millions of
years on the northeast continental shelf of Australia.

The site contains a huge range of species including
over 1 500 species of fish, about 360 species of hard
coral and 5 000 species of mollusc, plus a great
diversity of sponges, sea anemones, marine worms
and crustaceans. About 215 species of birds are
found in its islands and cays. Extending to Papua
New Guinea, the reef system comprises some 2 900
individual reefs covering more than 20 000 km^2,
including 760 fringing reefs. The reefs range in size
from under 0.01 km^2 to over 100 km^2 and vary in
shape to provide the most spectacular marine
scenery on Earth. There are approximately 600
continental islands including many with towering
forests and freshwater streams, and some 300 coral
cays and unvegetated sand cays. A rich variety of
landscapes and seascapes, including rugged
mountains with dense and diverse vegetation,
provide spectacular scenery.

The form and structure of the individual reefs show
great variety. There are two main classes: platform
or patch reefs, resulting from radial growth; and
wall reefs, resulting from elongated growth, often
in areas of strong currents. There are also the
many fringing reefs where growth is established
on subtidal rock of the mainland coast or
continental islands.

The site includes major feeding grounds for the
endangered dugong and nesting grounds of
world significance for four species of marine turtle
including the endangered loggerhead turtle.
Given the severe pressures on these species
elsewhere, the Great Barrier Reef may be a last
stronghold. It is also an important breeding area
for humpback and other whale species.

A wide range of fleshy algae occurs, often small
and inconspicuous but highly productive
and heavily grazed by turtles, fish, molluscs and sea
urchins. In addition, calcareous algae are an
important component of reef building processes.
Fifteen species of seagrass grow throughout the
area, forming over 3 000 km^2 of seagrass meadows
and providing an important food source for grazing
animals, such as dugongs and turtles.

The Great Barrier Reef is important in the historic
and contemporary culture of the Aboriginal and
Torres Strait Islander groups of the coastal areas of
northeast Australia. The contemporary use of and
association with the Marine Park plays an important
role in the maintenance of their cultures and there is
a strong spiritual connection with the ocean and its
inhabitants. New species continue to be discovered
throughout the Great Barrier Reef. A new species of
dolphin, the Australian snub-nose dolphin, was
discovered in 2005 within inshore areas.

Uluru-Kata Tjuta National Park – AUSTRALIA

Inscribed 1987 – Traditional human settlement; Heritage associated with events of universal significance; Natural phenomena or beauty; Major stages of Earth's history.

Uluru-Kata Tjuta National Park is included on the World Heritage List for both its natural and cultural values. Formerly called Ayers Rock – Mount Olga National Park, it is located in Australia's Red Centre. It lies in the traditional lands of the Western Desert Aboriginal people, locally known as Anangu. Anangu are part of one of the oldest human societies in the world.

The huge rock formations of Uluru and Kata Tjuta and the surrounding country are part of an important cultural landscape. For Anangu these features are physical evidence of the actions, artefacts and bodies of the ancestral beings (tjukuritja) who travelled the Earth in the creation time. These ancestors, who combined the attributes of humans and animals, journeyed across the landscape creating not only its features, but also Tjukurpa (the law) – the code of behaviour followed by Anangu today.

Uluru and the rock domes of Kata Tjuta dominate the vast red plain, dwarfing the desert oak and spinifex grass of central Australia. Uluru is composed of hard red sandstone, exposed as a result of the folding, faulting and erosion of the surrounding rock. It is 9.4 km in circumference and rises to a relatively flat top that is more than 340 m above the shallow, red sandy dunes around it. Rock art in the caves around its base provides further evidence of the enduring cultural traditions of Anangu.

The thirty-six steep-sided rock domes of Kata Tjuta, lying about 32 kilometres to the west of Uluru, are made up of gently dipping Mount Currie conglomerate. The undulating domes are interspersed with moisture-rich gullies and rocky valleys that are home to rare plants and desert animals. Like Uluru, Kata Tjuta's domes are the visible tips of huge rock slabs that extend far beneath the ground.

The park is home to twenty-one native mammals including the rare hairy-footed dunnart, the sandhill dunnart and the mulgara. More than 170 bird species, 73 species of reptile and at least 7 species of bat have been recorded in the park.

UNESCO World Heritage Sites – Asia

This vast continent contains some of the world's most spectacular sites. The Great Wall of China, the terracotta warriors in the Tomb of the First Qin Emperor, the temple of Angkor and the Taj Mahal are all well known, but smaller yet equally important sites are also on the World Heritage List.

● Cultural site   ● Natural site   ● Mixed site

Afghanistan
1. Cultural Landscape and Archaeological Remains of the Bamiyan Valley
2. Minaret and Archaeological Remains of Jam

Armenia
3. Cathedral and Churches of Echmiatsin and the Archaeological Site of Zvartnots
4. Monasteries of Haghpat and Sanahin
5. Monastery of Geghard and the Upper Azat Valley

Azerbaijan
6. Gobustan Rock Art Cultural Landscape
7. Walled City of Baku with the Shirvanshah's Palace and Maiden Tower

Bahrain
8. Qal'at al-Bahrain – Ancient Harbour and Capital of Dilmun

Bangladesh
9. Historic Mosque City of Bagerhat
10. Ruins of the Buddhist Vihara at Paharpur
11. The Sundarbans

Cambodia
12. Angkor
13. Temple of Preah Vihear

China
14. Ancient Building Complex in the Wudang Mountains

15. Ancient City of Ping Yao
16. Ancient Villages in Southern Anhui – Xidi and Hongcun
17. Capital Cities and Tombs of the Ancient Koguryo Kingdom
18. Classical Gardens of Suzhou
19. Dazu Rock Carvings
20. Fujian Tulou
21. Historic Centre of Macao
22. Historic Ensemble of the Potala Palace, Lhasa
23. Huanglong Scenic and Historic Interest Area
24. Imperial Palaces of the Ming and Qing Dynasties in Beijing and Shenyang
25. Imperial Tombs of the Ming and Qing Dynasties
26. Jiuzhaigou Valley Scenic and Historic Interest Area
27. Kaiping Diaolou and Villages
28. Longmen Grottoes
29. Lushan National Park
30. Mausoleum of the First Qin Emperor
31. Mogao Caves
32. Mount Emei Scenic Area, including Leshan Giant Buddha Scenic Area
33. Mount Huangshan
34. Mount Qingcheng and the Dujiangyan Irrigation System
35. Mount Sanqingshan National Park

62

36. Mount Taishan
37. Mount Wutai
38. Mount Wuyi
39. Mountain Resort and its Outlying Temples, Chengde
40. Old Town of Lijiang
41. Peking Man Site at Zhoukoudian
42. Sichuan Giant Panda Sanctuaries – Wolong, Mt Siguniang and Jiajin Mountains
43. South China Karst
44. Summer Palace and Imperial Garden in Beijing
45. Temple and Cemetery of Confucius and the Kong Family Mansion in Qufu
46. Temple of Heaven: an Imperial Sacrificial Altar in Beijing
47. The Great Wall
48. Three Parallel Rivers of Yunnan Protected Areas
49. Wulingyuan Scenic and Historic Interest Area
50. Yin Xu
51. Yungang Grottoes

Cyprus
52. Choirokoitia
53. Painted Churches in the Troodos Region
54. Paphos

Georgia
55. Bagrati Cathedral and Gelati Monastery
56. Historical Monuments of Mtskheta
57. Upper Svaneti

India
58. Agra Fort
59. Ajanta Caves
60. Buddhist Monuments at Sanchi
61. Champaner-Pavagadh Archaeological Park
62. Chhatrapati Shivaji Terminus (formerly Victoria Terminus)
63. Churches and Convents of Goa
64. Elephanta Caves
65. Ellora Caves
66. Fatehpur Sikri
67. Great Living Chola Temples
68. Group of Monuments at Hampi
69. Group of Monuments at Mahabalipuram
70. Group of Monuments at Pattadakal
71. Humayun's Tomb, Delhi
72. Kaziranga National Park
73. Keoladeo National Park
74. Khajuraho Group of Monuments
75. Mahabodhi Temple Complex at Bodh Gaya
76. Manas Wildlife Sanctuary
77. Mountain Railways of India
78. Nanda Devi and Valley of Flowers National Parks
79. Qutb Minar and its Monuments, Delhi
80. Red Fort Complex
81. Rock Shelters of Bhimbetka
82. Sun Temple, Konârak
83. Sundarbans National Park
84. Taj Mahal

Indonesia
85. Borobudur Temple Compounds
86. Komodo National Park
87. Lorentz National Park
88. Prambanan Temple Compounds
89. Sangiran Early Man Site
90. Tropical Rainforest Heritage of Sumatra
91. Ujung Kulon National Park

Iran
92. Armenian Monastic Ensembles of Iran
93. Bam and its Cultural Landscape
94. Bisotun
95. Meidan Emam, Esfahan
96. Pasargadae
97. Persepolis
98. Shushtar Historical Hydraulic System
99. Soltaniyeh
100. Takht-e Soleyman
101. Tchogha Zanbil

Iraq
102. Ashur (Qal'at Sherqat)
103. Hatra
104. Samarra Archaeological City

Israel
105. Bahá'í Holy Places in Haifa and the Western Galilee
106. Biblical Tels – Megiddo, Hazor, Beer Sheba
107. Incense Route – Desert Cities in the Negev
108. Masada
109. Old City of Acre
110. The White City of Tel-Aviv – The Modern Movement

Japan
111. Buddhist Monuments in the Horyu-ji Area
112. Gusuku Sites and Related Properties of the Kingdom of Ryukyu
113. Himeji-jo
114. Hiroshima Peace Memorial (Genbaku Dome)
115. Historic Monuments of Ancient Kyoto (Kyoto, Uji and Otsu Cities)
116. Historic Monuments of Ancient Nara
117. Historic Villages of Shirakawa-go and Gokayama
118. Itsukushima Shinto Shrine
119. Iwami Ginzan Silver Mine and its Cultural Landscape
120. Sacred Sites and Pilgrimage Routes in the Kii Mountain Range
121. Shirakami-Sanchi
122. Shiretoko
123. Shrines and Temples of Nikko
124. Yakushima

Jerusalem (Site proposed by Jordan)
125. Old City of Jerusalem and its Walls

Jordan
126. Petra
127. Quseir Amra
128. Um er-Rasas (Kastrom Mefa'a)

Kazakhstan
129. Mausoleum of Khoja Ahmed Yasawi
130. Petroglyphs within the Archaeological Landscape of Tamgaly
131. Saryarka – Steppe and Lakes of Northern Kazakhstan

Kyrgyzstan
132. Sulaiman-Too Sacred Mountain

Laos
133. Town of Luang Prabang
134. Vat Phou and Associated Ancient Settlements within the Champasak Cultural Landscape

Lebanon
135. Anjar
136. Baalbek
137. Byblos
138. Ouadi Qadisha (the Holy Valley) and the Forest of the Cedars of God (Horsh Arz el-Rab)
139. Tyre

Malaysia
140. Gunung Mulu National Park
141. Kinabalu Park
142. Melaka and George Town, Historic Cities of the Straits of Malacca

Mongolia
143. Orkhon Valley Cultural Landscape
144. Uvs Nuur Basin

Nepal
145. Kathmandu Valley
146. Lumbini, the Birthplace of the Lord Buddha
147. Royal Chitwan National Park
148. Sagarmatha National Park

North Korea
149. Complex of Koguryo Tombs

Oman
150. Aflaj Irrigation Systems of Oman
151. Archaeological sites of Bat, Al-Khutm and Al-Ayn
152. Bahla Fort
153. Land of Frankincense

Pakistan
154. Archaeological Ruins at Moenjodaro
155. Buddhist Ruins of Takht-i-Bahi and Neighbouring City Remains at Sahr-i-Bahlol
156. Fort and Shalamar Gardens in Lahore
157. Historical Monuments at Makli, Thatta
158. Rohtas Fort
159. Taxila

Philippines
160. Baroque Churches of the Philippines
161. Historic Town of Vigan
162. Puerto-Princesa Subterranean River National Park
163. Rice Terraces of the Philippine Cordilleras
164. Tubbataha Reefs Natural Park

Russian Federation (see also page 68)
165. Central Sikhote-Alin
166. Citadel, Ancient City and Fortress Buildings of Derbent
167. Golden Mountains of Altai
168. Lake Baikal
169. Natural System of Wrangel Island Reserve
144. Uvs Nuur Basin
170. Volcanoes of Kamchatka
171. Western Caucasus

Saudi Arabia
172. Al-Hijr Archaeological Site (Madâin Sâlih)

South Korea
173. Changdeokgung Palace Complex
174. Gochang, Hwasun and Ganghwa Dolmen Sites
175. Gyeongju Historic Areas
176. Haeinsa Temple Janggyeong Panjeon, the Depositories for the Tripitaka Koreana Woodblocks
177. Hwaseong Fortress
178. Jeju Volcanic Island and Lava Tubes
179. Jongmyo Shrine
180. Royal Tombs of the Joseon Dynasty
181. Seokguram Grotto and Bulguksa Temple

Sri Lanka
182. Ancient City of Polonnaruwa
183. Ancient City of Sigiriya
184. Golden Temple of Dambulla
185. Old Town of Galle and its Fortifications
186. Sacred City of Anuradhapura
187. Sacred City of Kandy
188. Sinharaja Forest Reserve

Syria
189. Ancient City of Aleppo
190. Ancient City of Bosra
191. Ancient City of Damascus
192. Crac des Chevaliers and Qal'at Salah El-Din
193. Site of Palmyra

Thailand
194. Ban Chiang Archaeological Site
195. Dong Phayayen-Khao Yai Forest Complex
196. Historic City of Ayutthaya
197. Historic Town of Sukhothai and Associated Historic Towns
198. Thungyai-Huai Kha Khaeng Wildlife Sanctuaries

Turkey
199. Archaeological Site of Troy
200. City of Safranbolu
201. Göreme National Park and the Rock Sites of Cappadocia
202. Great Mosque and Hospital of Divriği
203. Hattusha: the Hittite Capital
204. Hierapolis-Pamukkale
205. Historic Areas of Istanbul
206. Nemrut Dağ
207. Xanthos-Letoon

Turkmenistan
208. Kunya-Urgench
209. Parthian Fortresses of Nisa
210. State Historical and Cultural Park 'Ancient Merv'

Uzbekistan
211. Historic Centre of Bukhara
212. Historic Centre of Shakhrisyabz
213. Itchan Kala
214. Samarkand – Crossroads of Cultures

Vietnam
215. Complex of Hué Monuments
216. Ha Long Bay
217. Hoi An Ancient Town
218. My Son Sanctuary
219. Phong Nha-Ke Bang National Park

Yemen
220. Historic Town of Zabid
221. Old City of Sana'a
222. Old Walled City of Shibam
223. Socotra Archipelago

The Great Wall – CHINA

Inscribed 1987 – Human creative genius; interchange of values; Testimony to cultural tradition; Significance in human history; Heritage associated with events of universal significance.

Known to the Chinese as the 'Long Wall of Ten Thousand Li', the formidable defensive structures built to ward off invasion is more commonly known as the Great Wall of China. At the end of its nineteen-century-long construction, the Great Wall was the world's largest military structure. Its historic and strategic importance is matched only by its architectural significance.

The building of defensive walls was a common strategy against potential invasion and several were built in China from the eighth century BC onwards. From 220 BC Qin Shi Huang, the first emperor of a unified China, undertook to restore and link the separate sections of the Great Wall which stretched from the region of the Ordos to Manchuria. These were to form the first cohesive defence system against invasions from the north, and by the first century BC, ongoing extensions meant the Wall spanned approximately 6 000 km between Dunhuang in the west and the Bohai Sea in the east.

After the downfall of the Han dynasty in AD 220, construction and maintenance works on the Great Wall were halted: China at that time enjoyed such great military power that the need for a defence policy was no longer felt.

It was the Ming emperors (1368–1644) who, after a long period of conflict that ended with the expulsion of the Mongols, revived the principles of Qin Shi Huang's defence policy and during these centuries 5 650 km of wall were built.

To defend the northern frontier, the Wall was divided into nine *zhen*, or military districts, and fortresses were built at strategically important points such as passes or fords. Passageways running along the top of the wall made it possible to move troops rapidly and for imperial couriers to travel.

The Great Wall of the Ming is a masterpiece, not only because of the ambition of the

undertaking but also the perfection of its construction. The wall constitutes, on the vast scale of a continent, a perfect example of architecture integrated into the landscape.

This complex, diachronic cultural property is a unique example of a military architectural ensemble serving a single strategic purpose for 2 000 years. Its construction history illustrates advances in defence techniques and adaptation to changing political contexts. The Wall's testimony to the civilizations of ancient China is illustrated as much by the earlier, tamped-earth sections in Gansu Province as by the famed masonry of the Ming period.

The purpose of the Great Wall was to protect China from military aggression and cultural ingression, and it remains an essential reference in Chinese literature.

Sagarmatha National Park – NEPAL

Inscribed 1979 – Natural phenomena or beauty.

This is an exceptional area with dramatic mountains, glaciers and deep valleys, dominated by Mount Everest (Sagarmatha), the highest peak in the world (8 848 m), and is the homeland of the Sherpa, with their unique culture. The park is fan-shaped and enclosed on all sides by high, geologically young mountain ranges. The deeply incised valleys cut through sedimentary rocks and underlying granites to drain southwards into the Dudh Kosi and its tributaries, which form part of the Ganges River system. Most of the park (69 per cent) comprises barren land above 5 000 m, 28 per cent is grazing land and about 3 per cent is forested. The low number of mammals is almost certainly the result of human activities. Several rare species, such as the snow leopard and the lesser panda, are found in the park.

There are approximately 2 500 Sherpa people living within the park. They belong to the Nyingmapa sect of Tibetan Buddhism, which was founded by the revered Guru Rimpoche who was, according to legend, born of a lotus in the middle of a lake. There are several monasteries in the park, the most important being Tengpoche.

Angkor – CAMBODIA

Inscribed 1992 – Human creative genius; Interchange of values; Testimony to cultural tradition; Significance in human history.

Angkor is one of the most important archaeological sites in southeast Asia. Stretching over some 400km², Angkor Archaeological Park contains the magnificent remains of the different capitals of the Khmer Empire, from the ninth to the fifteenth century. It includes the famous Temple of Angkor Wat and the Bayon Temple with its countless sculptural decorations at Angkor Thom. In total, there are over a hundred temples throughout the site.

In the early ninth century, Jayavarman II united the two states that covered the territory of modern Cambodia, laying the foundations of the Khmer Empire that was to be the major power in southeast Asia for five centuries. Jayavarman's son Yashovarman established Yashodapura (later called Angkor), permanent capital of the Khmer Empire until the fifteenth century.

The first city had the fundamental elements of a Khmer capital: a defensive bank and ditch; a brick- or stone-built state temple at the centre; and a wooden palace. A large reservoir was another essential feature of a Khmer capital and this, now known as the Eastern Baray, was added a decade later with a third temple built in its centre.

In the 960s, Rajendravarman built a second capital at Angkor; the state temple was situated at Pre Rup. He also built the Eastern Mebon temple on an artificial island in the Eastern Baray, and the exquisite temple of Banteay Srei. Rajendravarman's son Jayavarman V abandoned Pre Rup in favour of a new location with its state temple at Ta Kev, which was consecrated around 1000. Shortly afterwards he was overthrown by Suryavarman I, who was responsible for erecting the formidable fortifications around his Royal Palace and state temple, the Phimeanakas, and also for the construction of the great Western Baray. In 1050 his successor created a new and more impressive state temple, the Baphuon.

The accession of Suryavarman II in 1113 brought the next great phase of building. He was responsible for the greatest Khmer monument, Angkor Wat, set within an extensive enclosure and dedicated to Vishnu.

A period of internal instabilitly after Suryavarman's death was ended in the 1180s by Jayavarman VII who celebrated his military success by creating yet another capital at Angkor Thom and launching an unprecedented building campaign. His state temple was the towering Bayon, dedicated to Buddha.

UNESCO World Heritage Sites – Europe

World Heritage sites in Europe are found across the continent, from the far north of Scandinavia to the extreme south of Sicily. They span the whole of Earth's human history – from Neolithic Orkney and Stonehenge, through the Acropolis and Pompeii, to twentieth century Auschwitz and the Works of Gaudi.

● Cultural site   ● Natural site   ● Mixed site

Belarus
1. Architectural, Residential and Cultural Complex of the Radziwill Family at Nesvizh
2. Belovezhskaya Pushcha/Białowieża Forest
3. Mir Castle Complex
4. Struve Geodetic Arc

Denmark
5. Jelling Mounds, Runic Stones and Church
6. Kronborg Castle
7. Roskilde Cathedral
   Ilulissat Icefjord (see map on pages 80-81)

Estonia
8. Historic Centre (Old Town) of Tallinn
4. Struve Geodetic Arc

Finland
9. Bronze Age Burial Site of Sammallahdenmäki
10. Fortress of Suomenlinna
11. High Coast/Kvarken Archipelago
12. Old Rauma
13. Petäjävesi Old Church
4. Struve Geodetic Arc
14. Verla Groundwood and Board Mill

Germany
15. Aachen Cathedral
16. Abbey and Altenmünster of Lorsch
17. Bauhaus and its Sites in Weimar and Dessau
18. Berlin Modernism Housing Estates
19. Castles of Augustusburg and Falkenlust at Brühl
20. Classical Weimar
21. Collegiate Church, Castle and Old Town of Quedlinburg
22. Cologne Cathedral
23. Frontiers of the Roman Empire: Upper German-Raetian Limes
24. Garden Kingdom of Dessau-Wörlitz
25. Hanseatic City of Lübeck
26. Historic Centres of Stralsund and Wismar
27. Luther Memorials in Eisleben and Wittenberg
28. Maulbronn Monastery Complex
29. Messel Pit Fossil Site
30. Mines of Rammelsberg and Historic Town of Goslar
31. Monastic Island of Reichenau
32. Museumsinsel (Museum Island), Berlin
33. Muskauer Park/Park Muzakowski
34. Old town of Regensburg with Stadtamhof
35. Palaces and Parks of Potsdam and Berlin
36. Pilgrimage Church of Wies
37. Roman Monuments, Cathedral of St Peter and Church of Our Lady in Trier
38. Speyer Cathedral
39. St Mary's Cathedral and St Michael's Church at Hildesheim
40. The Wadden Sea
41. Town Hall and Roland on the Marketplace of Bremen
42. Town of Bamberg
43. Upper Middle Rhine Valley
44. Völklingen Ironworks
45. Wartburg Castle
46. Würzburg Residence with the Court Gardens and Residence Square
47. Zollverein Coal Mine Industrial Complex in Essen

Iceland
48. Surtsey
49. Þingvellir National Park

Ireland
50. Archaeological Ensemble of the Bend of the Boyne
51. Skellig Michael

Latvia
52. Historic Centre of Riga
4. Struve Geodetic Arc

Lithuania
53. Curonian Spit
54. Kernavė Archaeological Site (Cultural Reserve of Kernavė)
4. Struve Geodetic Arc
55. Vilnius Historic Centre

Netherlands
56. Defence Line of Amsterdam
57. Droogmakerij de Beemster (Beemster Polder)
58. Ir. D.F. Woudagemaal (D.F. Wouda Steam Pumping Station)
59. Mill Network at Kinderdijk-Elshout
60. Rietveld Schröderhuis (Rietveld Schröder House)
61. Schokland and Surroundings
40. The Wadden Sea
Historic Area of Willemstad, Inner City and Harbour, Netherlands Antilles (see map on pages 86-87)

Norway
62. Bryggen
63. Rock Art of Alta
64. Røros Mining Town
4. Struve Geodetic Arc
65. Urnes Stave Church
66. Vegaøyan – the Vega Archipelago
67. West Norwegian Fjords – Geirangerfjord and Nærøyfjord

Poland
68. Auschwitz Birkenau German Nazi Concentration and Extermination Camp (1940–1945)
69. Castle of the Teutonic Order in Malbork
70. Centennial Hall in Wroclaw
2. Belovezhskaya Pushcha/Białowieża Forest
71. Churches of Peace in Jawor and Swidnica
72. Cracow's Historic Centre
73. Historic Centre of Warsaw
74. Kalwaria Zebrzydowska: the Mannerist Architectural and Park Landscape Complex and Pilgrimage Park
75. Medieval Town of Toruń
33. Muskauer Park/Park Muzakowski
76. Old City of Zamość
77. Wieliczka Salt Mine
78. Wooden Churches of Southern Little Poland

Portugal
79. Alto Douro Wine Region
80. Central Zone of the Town of Angra do Heroismo in the Azores
81. Convent of Christ in Tomar
82. Cultural Landscape of Sintra
83. Historic Centre of Évora
84. Historic Centre of Guimarães
85. Historic Centre of Oporto

86. Landscape of the Pico Island Vineyard Culture
87. Laurisilva of Madeira
88. Monastery of Alcobaça
89. Monastery of Batalha
90. Monastery of the Hieronymites and Tower of Belém in Lisbon
91. Prehistoric Rock-Art Sites in the Côa Valley

Russian Federation (see also page 62)
92. Architectural Ensemble of the Trinity Sergius Lavra in Sergiev Posad
93. Church of the Ascension, Kolomenskoye
94. Cultural and Historic Ensemble of the Solovetsky Islands
53. Curonian Spit
95. Ensemble of the Ferrapontov Monastery
96. Ensemble of the Novodevichy Convent
97. Historic and Architectural Complex of the Kazan Kremlin
98. Historic Centre of Saint Petersburg and Related Groups of Monuments
99. Historic Monuments of Novgorod and Surroundings
100. Historical Centre of the City of Yaroslavl
101. Kizhi Pogost
102. Kremlin and Red Square, Moscow
4. Struve Geodetic Arc
103. Virgin Komi Forests
104. White Monuments of Vladimir and Suzdal

Spain
105. Alhambra, Generalife and Albayzín, Granada
106. Aranjuez Cultural Landscape
107. Archaeological Ensemble of Mérida
108. Archaeological Ensemble of Tárraco
109. Archaeological Site of Atapuerca
110. Burgos Cathedral
111. Catalan Romanesque Churches of the Vall de Boí
112. Cathedral, Alcázar and Archivo de Indias in Seville

113. Cave of Altamira and Paleolithic Cave Art of Northern Spain
114. Doñana National Park
115. Garajonay National Park
116. Historic Centre of Cordoba
117. Historic City of Toledo
118. Historic Walled Town of Cuenca
119. Ibiza, Biodiversity and Culture
120. La Lonja de la Seda of Valencia
121. Las Médulas
122. Monastery and Site of the Escurial, Madrid
123. Monuments of Oviedo and the Kingdom of the Asturias
124. Mudéjar Architecture of Aragon
125. Old City of Salamanca
126. Old Town of Ávila with its Extra-Muros Churches
127. Old Town of Cáceres
128. Old Town of Segovia and its Aqueduct
129. Palau de la Música Catalana and Hospital de Sant Pau, Barcelona
130. Palmeral of Elche
131. Poblet Monastery
132. Pyrénées - Mont Perdu
133. Renaissance Monumental Ensembles of Úbeda and Baeza
134. Rock Art of the Mediterranean Basin on the Iberian Peninsula
135. Roman Walls of Lugo
136. Route of Santiago de Compostela
137. Royal Monastery of Santa María de Guadalupe
138. San Cristóbal de La Laguna
139. San Millán Yuso and Suso Monasteries
140. Santiago de Compostela (Old Town)
141. Teide National Park
142. University and Historic Precinct of Alcalá de Henares
143. Tower of Hercules
144. Vizcaya Bridge
145. Works of Antoni Gaudí

ATLANTIC

OCEAN

86 80
Azores
(Portugal)

49
48
IC

IRELA
51

Bay
Bisc

143
140   135   123
136   121   113
85   84   79   110   109
PORTUGAL   91   125   128
88 89   126   122
90   81   127   117   142
82 83   137   106
107   **SPAIN**
112   116   133
114   105

87
Madeira
(Portugal)

138 **Canary Islands**
115 141 (Spain)

A F

see large-scale map on pages 44–45

UNESCO World Heritage Sites – Europe

● Cultural site   ● Natural site   ● Mixed site

Albania
1. Butrint
2. Historic Centres of Berat and Gjirokastra

Andorra
3. Madriu-Perafita-Claror Valley

Austria
4. City of Graz – Historic Centre
5. Fertö/Neusiedlersee Cultural Landscape
6. Hallstatt-Dachstein/Salzkammergut Cultural Landscape
7. Historic Centre of the City of Salzburg
8. Historic Centre of Vienna
9. Palace and Gardens of Schönbrunn
10. Semmering Railway
11. Wachau Cultural Landscape

Belgium
12. Belfries of Belgium and France
13. Flemish Béguinages
14. Historic Centre of Brugge
15. La Grand-Place, Brussels
16. Major Town Houses of the Architect Victor Horta (Brussels)
17. Neolithic Flint Mines at Spiennes (Mons)
18. Notre-Dame Cathedral in Tournai
19. Plantin-Moretus House-Workshops-Museum Complex
20. Stoclet House
21. The Four Lifts on the Canal du Centre and their Environs, La Louvière and Le Roeulx (Hainault)

Bosnia-Herzegovina
22. Mehmed Paša Sokolović Bridge in Višegrad
23. Old Bridge Area of the Old City of Mostar

Bulgaria
24. Ancient City of Nessebar
25. Boyana Church
26. Madara Rider
27. Pirin National Park
28. Rila Monastery
29. Rock-Hewn Churches of Ivanovo
30. Srebarna Nature Reserve
31. Thracian Tomb of Kazanlak
32. Thracian Tomb of Sveshtari

Croatia
33. Cathedral of St James in Šibenik
34. Episcopal Complex of the Euphrasian Basilica in the Historic Centre of Poreč
35. Historic City of Trogir
36. Historical Complex of Split with the Palace of Diocletian
37. Old City of Dubrovnik
38. Plitvice Lakes National Park
39. Stari Grad Plain

Czech Republic
40. Gardens and Castle at Kroměříž
41. Historic Centre of Český Krumlov
42. Historic Centre of Prague
43. Historic Centre of Telč
44. Holašovice Historical Village Reservation
45. Holy Trinity Column in Olomouc
46. Jewish Quarter and St Procopius' Basilica in Třebíč
47. Kutná Hora: Historical Town Centre with the Church of St Barbara and the Cathedral of Our Lady at Sedlec
48. Lednice-Valtice Cultural Landscape
49. Litomyšl Castle
50. Pilgrimage Church of St John of Nepomuk at Zelená Hora
51. Tugendhat Villa in Brno

France
52. Abbey Church of Saint-Savin sur Gartempe
53. Amiens Cathedral
54. Arles, Roman and Romanesque Monuments
12. Belfries of Belgium and France
55. Bordeaux, Port of the Moon
56. Bourges Cathedral
57. Canal du Midi
58. Cathedral of Notre-Dame, Former Abbey of Saint-Rémi and Palace of Tau, Reims
59. Chartres Cathedral
60. Cistercian Abbey of Fontenay
61. Fortifications of Vauban
62. From the Great Saltworks of Salins-les-Bains to the Royal Saltworks of Arc-et-Senans, the production of open-pan salt
63. Gulf of Porto: Calanche of Piana, Gulf of Girolata, Scandola Reserve
64. Historic Centre of Avignon: Papal Palace, Episcopal Ensemble and Avignon Bridge
65. Historic Fortified City of Carcassonne
66. Historic Site of Lyons
67. Jurisdiction of Saint-Emilion
68. Le Havre, the city rebuilt by Auguste Perret
69. Mont-Saint-Michel and its Bay
70. Palace and Park of Fontainebleau
71. Palace and Park of Versailles
72. Paris, Banks of the Seine
73. Place Stanislas, Place de la Carrière and Place d'Alliance in Nancy
74. Pont du Gard (Roman Aqueduct)
75. Prehistoric Sites and Decorated Caves of the Vézère Valley
76. Provins, Town of Medieval Fairs
77. Pyrénées – Mont Perdu
78. Roman Theatre and its Surroundings and the 'Triumphal Arch' of Orange
79. Routes of Santiago de Compostela in France
80. Strasbourg – Grande Île
81. The Loire Valley between Sully-sur-Loire and Chalonnes
82. Vézelay, Church and Hill Lagoons of New Caledonia: Reef Diversity and Associated Ecosystems (see map on 58–59)

Greece
83. Acropolis, Athens
84. Archaeological Site of Aigai (modern name Vergina)
85. Archaeological Site of Delphi
86. Archaeological Site of Mystras
87. Archaeological Site of Olympia
88. Archaeological Sites of Mycenae and Tiryns
89. Delos
90. Historic Centre (Chorá) with the Monastery of Saint John, the Theologian, and the Cave of the Apocalypse on the Island of Pátmos
91. Medieval City of Rhodes
92. Meteora
93. Monasteries of Daphni, Hosios Loukas and Nea Moni of Chios
94. Mount Athos
95. Old Town of Corfu
96. Paleochristian and Byzantine Monuments of Thessalonika
97. Pythagoreion and Heraion of Samos
98. Sanctuary of Asklepios at Epidaurus
99. Temple of Apollo Epicurius at Bassae

..., including the Banks of the
...anube, the Buda Castle Quarter and
Andrássy Avenue
101. Caves of Aggtelek Karst and Slovak Karst
102. Early Christian Necropolis of Pécs
(Sopianae)
5. Fertö/Neusiedlersee Cultural Landscape
103. Hortobágy National Park – the Puszta
104. Millenary Benedictine Abbey of
Pannonhalma and its Natural
Environment
105. Old Village of Hollókő and its
Surroundings
106. Tokaj Wine Region Historic
Cultural Landscape

Italy
107. Archaeological Area and the
Patriarchal Basilica of Aquileia
108. Archaeological Area of Agrigento
109. Archaeological Areas of Pompei,
Herculaneum and Torre Annunziata
110. Assisi, the Basilica of San Francesco
and Other Franciscan Sites
111. Botanical Garden
(Orto Botanico), Padua

112. Castel del Monte
113. Cathedral, Torre Civica and Piazza
Grande, Modena
114. Church and Dominican Convent of Santa
Maria delle Grazie with 'The Last Supper'
by Leonardo da Vinci
115. Cilento and Vallo di Diano National Park
with the Archeological sites of Paestum
and Velia, and the Certosa di Padula
116. City of Verona
117. City of Vicenza and the Palladian Villas
of the Veneto
118. Costiera Amalfitana
119. Crespi d'Adda
120. Early Christian Monuments of Ravenna
121. Eighteenth-Century Royal Palace at
Caserta with the Park, the Aqueduct
of Vanvitelli, and the San Leucio Complex
122. Etruscan Necropolises of Cerveteri
and Tarquinia
123. Ferrara, City of the Renaissance,
and its Po Delta
124. Genoa: Le Strade Nuove and the
system of the Palazzi dei Rolli
125. Historic Centre of Florence
126. Historic Centre of Naples

127. Historic Centre of Rome, the Properties
of the Holy See in that City Enjoying
Extraterritorial Rights and San Paolo
Fuori le Mura
128. Historic Centre of San Gimignano
129. Historic Centre of Siena
130. Historic Centre of the City of Pienza
131. Historic Centre of Urbino
132. Isole Eolie (Aeolian Islands)
133. Late Baroque Towns of the Val di Noto
(South-Eastern Sicily)
134. Mantua and Sabbioneta
135. Piazza del Duomo, Pisa
136. Portovenere, Cinque Terre, and the
Islands (Palmaria, Tino and Tinetto)
137. Residences of the Royal House of Savoy
138. Rhaetian Railway in the Albula/Bernina
Landscapes
139. Rock Drawings in Valcamonica
140. Sacri Monti of Piedmont and Lombardy
141. Su Nuraxi di Barumini
142. Syracuse and the Rocky Necropolis
of Pantalica
143. The Dolomites
144. The Sassi and the park of the
Rupestrian Churches of Matera

145. The Trulli of Alberobello
146. Val d'Orcia
147. Venice and its Lagoon
148. Villa Adriana (Tivoli)
149. Villa d'Este, Tivoli
150. Villa Romana del Casale

Kosovo
151. Medieval Monuments in Kosovo

Luxembourg
152. City of Luxembourg: its Old Quarters
and Fortifications

Macedonia (F.Y.R.O.M.)
153. Natural and Cultural Heritage of the
Ohrid Region

Malta
154. City of Valletta
155. Hal Saflieni Hypogeum
156. Megalithic Temples of Malta

Moldova
157. Struve Geodetic Arc

Montenegro
158. Durmitor National Park
159. Natural and Culturo-Historical Region
of Kotor

Romania
160. Churches of Moldavia
161. Dacian Fortresses of the Orastie Mountains
162. Danube Delta
163. Historic Centre of Sighişoara
164. Monastery of Horezu
165. Villages with Fortified Churches in
Transylvania
166. Wooden Churches of Maramureş

San Marino
167. San Marino Historic Centre and Mount Titano

Serbia
168. Gamzigrad-Romuliana, Palace of Galerius
169. Stari Ras and Sopoćani
170. Studenica Monastery

Slovakia
171. Bardejov Town Conservation Reserve
101. Caves of Aggtelek Karst and Slovak Karst
172. Historic Town of Banská Štiavnica and the
Technical Monuments in its Vicinity
173. Levoča, Spišský Hrad and the Associated
Cultural Monuments
174. Primeval Beech Forests of the Carpathians
175. Vlkolínec
176. Wooden Churches of the Slovak part of the
Carpathian Mountain Area

Slovenia
177. Škocjan Caves

Switzerland
178. Benedictine Convent of St John at Müstair
179. Convent of St Gall
180. La Chaux-de-Fonds/Le Locle,
watchmaking town planning
181. Lavaux, Vineyard Terraces
182. Monte San Giorgio
183. Old City of Berne
138. Rhaetian Railway in the
Albula/Bernina Landscapes
184. Swiss Alps Jungfrau-Aletsch
185. Swiss Tectonic Arena Sardona
186. Three Castles, Defensive Wall and Ramparts
of the Market-Town of Bellinzone

Vatican City
127. Historic Centre of Rome, the Properties of the
Holy See in that City Enjoying Extraterritorial
Rights and San Paolo Fuori le Mura
187. Vatican City

CZECH
REPUBLIC
SLOVAKIA
AUSTRIA
HUNGARY
SLOVENIA
CROATIA
SAN
MARINO
BOSNIA-
HERZEGOVINA
SERBIA
ROMANIA
MOLDOVA
ITALY
MONTENEGRO
KOSOVO
MACEDONIA
(F.Y.R.O.M.)
BULGARIA
Black
Sea
ALBANIA
Adriatic Sea
Sicily
(Italy)
MALTA
GREECE
Aegean
Sea
Ionian Sea
VATICAN
CITY
ASIA

Stonehenge, Avebury and Associated Sites – UNITED KINGDOM

Inscribed 1986 – Human creative genius; Interchange of values; Testimony to cultural tradition.

Stonehenge and Avebury are among the most famous groups of megaliths in the world. Together with their associated sites, they represent a masterpiece of human creative genius of the Neolithic age.

The megalithic sites of Stonehenge and Avebury consist of circles of menhirs arranged in a pattern of obvious astronomical significance which is still being explored. However, a number of satellite sites make it possible to better understand the more famous sites by examining them in a broader context.

Stonehenge was built in several distinct phases from 3100–1100 BC and its size, height and perfection make it one of the most impressive megalithic monuments in the world. Its plan was based on a series of concentric circles and the menhirs used are huge: from the third phase of construction onwards, large lintels were placed upon the vertical blocks, thereby creating a type of bonded entablature. The Avenue, an earthwork cut into the chalk soil, runs straight into the northeast corner of Stonehenge.

Avebury lies about 30 km to the north of Stonehenge, and although less well known, it is nevertheless Europe's largest circular megalithic ensemble: its exterior circle comprises some 100 menhirs. In all, 180 standing stones were put into place here before the beginning of the third millennium BC, as demonstrated by abundant ceramic samples found on the site.

There are four avenues at Avebury of which only the southern one, West Kennet Avenue, is still lined with megaliths; the avenues lead to the four cardinal points of the circle.

West Kennet Avenue leads to the site of The Sanctuary at Overton Hill 2.5 km away. The Sanctuary was a series of concentric timber and stone circles; their purpose remains unknown. There are several other Neolithic satellite sites around Avebury, including Silbury Hill, the largest known man-made earthen mound in Europe. As with The Sanctuary, its purpose is not known.

Windmill Hill, a Neolithic causewayed enclosure, is 2 km northwest of Avebury and West Kennet chambered long barrow lies to the south.

Although the ritual function of Stonehenge is not known in detail, the cosmic references of its structure appear essential. An old theory is that the site was a sanctuary for worship of the sun. Although there is no unanimous agreement among prehistorians on the subject, Stonehenge nevertheless attracts a folkloric gathering at dawn each Midsummer Day.

Two different materials were used for the Stonehenge constructions: irregular sandstone blocks, known as sarsens, which were quarried in a plain near Salisbury; and bluestones, quarried about 200 km away in Pembrokeshire in Wales.

Palace and Park of Versailles – FRANCE

Inscribed 1979 – Human creative genius; Interchange of values; Heritage associated with events of universal significance.

The Palace of Versailles, built and embellished by several generations of the foremost French architects, sculptors, decorators and landscape architects, was one of the largest royal palaces in the world and provided the model of the ideal royal residence for over a century. The prestigious ensemble of the palace, the Trianons and the Park of Versailles is the result of a century and a half of works commissioned by the kings of France and entrusted to their greatest artists. Versailles was the principal residence of the French kings from Louis XIV to Louis XVI (from 1682–1789) and became both the source and symbol of absolute royal power during the Ancien Régime.

Versailles was originally a small village some 20 km south-west of Paris, set in a wooded region chosen by Louis XIII as his personal hunting preserve. The modest brick and stone château that the king ordered built here in 1623 was two storeys tall and surrounded by a moat. Enlargements followed but the strongest imprint was left by Louis XIII's son, Louis XIV. Under the direction of Louis Le Vau, the king's architect, a programme of expansion and new building began in the 1660s. The decoration of the palace interior was supervised by the painter Charles Le Brun who, with teams of painters, decorators and craftsmen, created a remarkable complex of frescoes, marbles, stuccoes, gilded bronzes, fabrics, furniture and accessories in the palace halls.

After 1678 Versailles was considerably enlarged and radically modified by Jules Hardouin Mansart. He successfully introduced a sober and colossal architecture, homogeneous and majestic, that is inseparable even today from the memory of the 'Sun King', Louis XIV. It was during this phase of building that the palace developed the appearance that is recognizable now.

Acropolis, Athens – GREECE

Inscribed 1987 – Human creative genius; Interchange of values; Testimony to cultural tradition; Significance in human history; Heritage associated with events of universal significance.

The Athenian Acropolis is the supreme expression of the adaptation of architecture to a natural site, a unique series of public monuments built and conserved in one of the densest spaces of the Mediterranean. This grand composition of perfectly balanced massive structures creates a monumental landscape of unique beauty consisting of a complete series of masterpieces of the fifth century BC. The monuments of the Acropolis have exerted an exceptional influence, not only in Graeco-Roman antiquity, a time in the Mediterranean world when they were considered exemplary models, but also in contemporary times.

In the later fifth century BC, Athens followed its victory against the Persians and the establishment of democracy by taking a leading position among the other city-states of the ancient world. In the age that followed, as philosophy and art flourished, an exceptional group of artists put into effect the ambitious plans of Athenian statesman Pericles and, under the inspired guidance of the sculptor Pheidias, transformed the rocky hill of the Acropolis into a unique monument of thought and the arts.

The years from 447–406 BC saw the successive building of the Parthenon, the main temple dedicated to Athena; the Propylaea, the monumental entrance to the Acropolis built on the site of one of the entrances to the Citadel of the Ancient Kings; the temple of Athena Nike; and the Erechtheion – the four masterpieces of classical Greek art.

The sacred hill of Athens was protected throughout the period of Roman domination until the Herulian raid in AD 267. Since then and despite long periods of relative calm, the monuments and site have been damaged many times.

The Byzantines converted the temples into churches and removed their art treasures to Constantinople. After the Byzantine Empire fell in 1204, Athens was put into the hands of Frankish lords who had little respect for its ruins. When the Turks took the city in 1456, it became a mosque and the Erechtheion was the occasional harem of the Turkish governor. In 1687 the siege of the Acropolis by Venetian armies resulted in the explosion of the Parthenon, used as the Turks' powder magazine. Finally in the nineteenth century, the British ambassador Lord Elgin pillaged the marble sections which since 1815 have been in the British Museum.

The Acropolis of Athens and its monuments are universal symbols of the classical spirit and civilization, and form the greatest architectural and artistic complex of Greek antiquity.

It stands on a rocky promontory 156 m above the Ilissos valley and covers an area of less than 30 000 m². From the third millennium BC it was a fortress protecting places of worship and royal palaces.

The Acropolis is now a testing ground for innovative open-air conservation techniques aimed at safeguarding the marble sections which are being affected by pollution.

UNESCO World Heritage Sites – Africa

Famous archaeological sites such as the Pyramids of Giza and Abu Simbel, Egypt and the wildlife reserves of the Serengeti and Selous in Tanzania have been on the World Heritage List for a number of years. However more recently Robben Island, where Nelson Mandela was imprisoned, and the rainforests of Madagascar, their biodiversity under threat from development, have been included as representative of Africa's culture and environment.

● Cultural site　● Natural site　● Mixed site

Algeria
1. Al Qal'a of Beni Hammad
2. Djémila
3. Kasbah of Algiers
4. M'Zab Valley
5. Tassili n'Ajjer
6. Timgad
7. Tipasa

Benin
8. Royal Palaces of Abomey

Botswana
9. Tsodilo

Burkina
10. The Ruins of Loropéni

Cameroon
11. Dja Faunal Reserve

Cape Verde
12. Cidade Velha, Historic Centre of Ribeira Grande

Central African Republic
13. Manovo-Gounda St Floris National Park

Congo, Democratic Republic of the
14. Garamba National Park
15. Kahuzi-Biega National Park
16. Okapi Wildlife Reserve
17. Salonga National Park
18. Virunga National Park

Côte d'Ivoire
19. Comoé National Park
20. Mount Nimba Strict Nature Reserve
21. Taï National Park

Egypt
22. Abu Mena
23. Ancient Thebes with its Necropolis
24. Historic Cairo
25. Memphis and its Necropolis – the Pyramid Fields from Giza to Dahshur
26. Nubian Monuments from Abu Simbel to Philae
27. Saint Catherine Area
28. Wadi Al-Hitan (Whale Valley)

Ethiopia
29. Aksum
30. Fasil Ghebbi, Gondar Region
31. Harar Jugol, the Fortified Historic Town
32. Lower Valley of the Awash
33. Lower Valley of the Omo
34. Rock-Hewn Churches, Lalibela
35. Simien National Park
36. Tiya

Gabon
37. Ecosystem and Relict Cultural Landscape of Lopé-Okanda

Gambia, The
38. James Island and Related Sites
39. Stone Circles of Senegambia

Ghana
40. Asante Traditional Buildings
41. Forts and Castles, Volta, Greater Accra, Central and Western Regions

Gough Island
42. Gough and Inaccessible Islands (U.K.)

Guinea
20. Mount Nimba Strict Nature Reserve

Kenya
43. Lake Turkana National Parks
44. Lamu Old Town
45. Mount Kenya National Park/ Natural Forest
46. Sacred Mijikenda Kaya Forests

Libya
47. Archaeological Site of Cyrene
48. Archaeological Site of Leptis Magna
49. Archaeological Site of Sabratha
50. Old Town of Ghadamès
51. Rock-Art Sites of Tadrart Acacus

Madagascar
52. Rainforests of the Atsinanana
53. The Royal Hill of Ambohimanga
54. Tsingy de Bemaraha Strict Nature Reserve

Malawi
55. Chongoni Rock-Art Area
56. Lake Malawi National Park

Mali
57. Cliff of Bandiagara (Land of the Dogons)
58. Old Towns of Djenné
59. Timbuktu
60. Tomb of Askia

Mauritania
61. Ancient Ksour of Ouadane, Chinguetti, Tichitt and Oualata
62. Banc d'Arguin National Park

Mauritius
63. Aapravasi Ghat
64. Le Morne Cultural Landscape

Morocco
65. Archaeological Site of Volubilis
66. Historic City of Meknes
67. Ksar of Ait-Ben-Haddou
68. Medina of Essaouira (formerly Mogador)
69. Medina of Fez
70. Medina of Marrakesh
71. Medina of Tétouan (formerly known as Titawin)
72. Portuguese City of Mazagan (El Jadida)

Mozambique
73. Island of Mozambique

Namibia
74. Twyfelfontein or /Ui-//aes

Niger
75. Aïr and Ténéré Natural Reserves
76. W National Park of Niger

Nigeria
77. Osun-Osogbo Sacred Grove
78. Sukur Cultural Landscape

Senegal
79. Djoudj National Bird Sanctuary
80. Island of Gorée
81. Island of Saint-Louis
82. Niokolo-Koba National Park
39. Stone Circles of Senegambia

Seychelles
83. Aldabra Atoll
84. Vallée de Mai Nature Reserve

South Africa, Republic of
85. Cape Floral Region Protected Areas
86. Fossil Hominid Sites of Sterkfontein, Swartkrans, Kromdraai, and Environs
87. iSimangaliso Wetland Park
88. Mapungubwe Cultural Landscape
89. Richtersveld Cultural and Botanical Landscape
90. Robben Island
91. uKhahlamba/Drakensberg Park
92. Vredefort Dome

Sudan
93. Gebel Barkal and the Sites of the Napatan Region

Tanzania
94. Kilimanjaro National Park
95. Kondoa Rock-Art Sites
96. Ngorongoro Conservation Area
97. Ruins of Kilwa Kisiwani and Ruins of Songo Mnara
98. Selous Game Reserve
99. Serengeti National Park
100. Stone Town of Zanzibar

Togo
101. Koutammakou, the Land of the Batammariba

Tunisia
102. Amphitheatre of El Jem
103. Dougga/Thugga
104. Ichkeul National Park
105. Kairouan
106. Medina of Sousse
107. Medina of Tunis
108. Punic Town of Kerkuane and its Necropolis
109. Site of Carthage

Uganda
110. Bwindi Impenetrable National Park
111. Rwenzori Mountains National Park
112. Tombs of Buganda Kings at Kasubi

Zambia
113. Mosi-oa-Tunya/Victoria Falls

Zimbabwe
114. Great Zimbabwe National Monument
115. Khami Ruins National Monument
116. Mana Pools National Park, Sapi and Chewore Safari Areas
113. Mosi-oa-Tunya/Victoria Falls
117. Matobo Hills

WESTER
SAHA

CAPE
VERDE
● 12

SENEG
80 ● 39
38
THE GAMBIA ●

GUINEA-
BISSAU

81 ●
SENEG

EUROPE

ASIA

Mediterranean Sea

MOROCCO

ALGERIA

LIBYA

EGYPT

Red Sea

MAURITANIA

MALI

NIGER

CHAD

SUDAN

ERITREA

DJIBOUTI

BURKINA

NIGERIA

BENIN

UINEA

ERRA
EONE

LIBERIA

**CÔTE
D'IVOIRE**

GHANA

TOGO

CAMEROON

**CENTRAL
AFRICAN REPUBLIC**

ETHIOPIA

SOMALIA

EQUATORIAL
GUINEA

SÃO TOMÉ AND PRÍNCIPE

GABON

CONGO

**DEMOCRATIC
REPUBLIC
OF THE
CONGO**

UGANDA

KENYA

RWANDA

BURUNDI

**INDIAN
OCEAN**

CABINDA
(Angola)

TANZANIA

SEYCHELLES

COMOROS

**ATLANTIC
OCEAN**

ANGOLA

ZAMBIA

MALAWI

MOZAMBIQUE

MADAGASCAR

MAURITIUS

Réunion
(France)

NAMIBIA

ZIMBABWE

BOTSWANA

SWAZILAND

**REPUBLIC OF
SOUTH AFRICA**

LESOTHO

TUNISIA

Gough Island
(U.K.)

77

Memphis and its Necropolis – the Pyramid Fields from Giza to Dahshur – EGYPT

Inscribed 1979 – Human creative genius; Testimony to cultural tradition; Heritage associated with events of universal significance.

The capital of the Old Kingdom of Egypt in the third millennium BC, Memphis was one of the Seven Wonders of the Ancient World. The area of pyramid fields that served as the its necropolis contains a number of exceptional monuments that bear witness to the status of Ancient Egypt as one of the most brilliant civilizations of this planet.

The first sovereign of the unified Egyptian kingdom, Menes (or Narmer), was said to have ordered the construction of a new capital in the Nile Delta area around 3100 BC. It was from Menes that the name of Mennufer (City of Menes) came. The temple of Ptah built there was the most important sanctuary dedicated to this primary god of Creative Force, and its ruins are all that survive today of the grandeur of Memphis, as it was known to the ancient Greeks.

Nearby Saqqara was the necropolis of the city and the largest in the land, and it is the site of the first great stone pyramid. The pyramid was built as a mausoleum for the pharaoh Djoser, founder of the Third Dynasty, who ruled from around 2668 BC. Designed by his architect and vizier, Imhotep, it is the oldest step pyramid in the world. It stands in a funerary complex enclosed by a 10-m-high wall.

To the south lies the necropolis of Dahshur. The founder of the Fourth Dynasty, Snefru, who reigned from around 2613 BC, built here. During his twenty-nine year reign he transformed the structure of Egyptian royal tombs: he chose the now familiar pyramid shape with a square base. He built both the Red Pyramid, named after its reddish-coloured limestone, and the Rhomboid (or Bent) Pyramid, with its double-angled slope on each of the four faces; this was apparently an intermediate form. Another innovation of Snefru was the construction of an annex within the pyramid.

To the north, the great pyramids of Giza were built by Snefru's son Khufu or Cheops, and his successors Khafre (Chephren) and Menkaure (Mycerinus). The 'Horizon of Cheops' was the name given to the Pharaoh's tomb, the oldest and largest. The other two pyramids were known in antiquity as 'Great is Chepren' and 'Divine is Mycerinus' respectively. Each tomb forms part of the classic funerary complex first built by Snefru.

UNESCO World Heritage Sites – North America

The New World has relatively few sites compared to Europe or Asia. However the sites represent significant stages in Earth's formation and human history. Ancient geological processes are preserved in Gros Morne National Park in Canada, early civilizations are represented in Central America and evidence of the slave trade and plantations is found in the islands of the Caribbean.

● Cultural site   ● Natural site   ● Mixed site

Belize
1. Belize Barrier Reef Reserve System

Bermuda
2. Historic Town of St George and Related Fortifications (UK)

Canada
3. Canadian Rocky Mountain Parks
4. Dinosaur Provincial Park
5. Gros Morne National Park
6. Head-Smashed-In Buffalo Jump
7. Historic District of Old Québec
8. Joggins Fossil Cliffs
9. Kluane/Wrangell-St Elias/Glacier Bay/Tatshenshini-Alsek
10. L'Anse aux Meadows National Historic Site
11. Miguasha National Park
12. Nahanni National Park
13. Old Town Lunenburg
14. Rideau Canal
15. SGang Gwaay
16. Waterton Glacier International Peace Park
17. Wood Buffalo National Park

Costa Rica
18. Area de Conservación Guanacaste
19. Cocos Island National Park
20. Talamanca Range-La Amistad Reserves/La Amistad National Park

Cuba
21. Alejandro de Humboldt National Park
22. Archaeological Landscape of the First Coffee Plantations in the South-East of Cuba
23. Desembarco del Granma National Park
24. Historic Centre of Camagüey
25. Old Havana and its Fortifications
26. San Pedro de la Roca Castle, Santiago de Cuba
27. Trinidad and the Valley de los Ingenios
28. Urban Historic Centre of Cienfuegos
29. Viñales Valley

Dominica
30. Morne Trois Pitons National Park

Dominican Republic
31. Colonial City of Santo Domingo

El Salvador
32. Joya de Cerén Archaeological Site

Greenland
33. Ilulissat Icefjord (Denmark)

Guatemala
34. Antigua Guatemala
35. Archaeological Park and Ruins of Quirigua
36. Tikal National Park

Honduras
37. Maya Site of Copán
38. Río Plátano Biosphere Reserve

Haiti
39. National History Park – Citadel, Sans Souci, Ramiers

Mexico
40. Agave Landscape and Ancient Industrial Facilities of Tequila
41. Ancient Maya City of Calakmul, Campeche
42. Archaeological Monuments Zone of Xochicalco
43. Archeological Zone of Paquimé, Casas Grandes
44. Central University City Campus of the Universidad Nacional Autónoma de México (UNAM)
45. Earliest 16th-Century Monasteries on the Slopes of Popocatepetl
46. El Tajin, Pre-Hispanic City
47. Franciscan Missions in the Sierra Gorda of Querétaro
48. Historic Centre of Mexico City and Xochimilco
49. Historic Centre of Morelia
50. Historic Centre of Oaxaca and Archaeological Site of Monte Albán
51. Historic Centre of Puebla
52. Historic Centre of Zacatecas
53. Historic Fortified Town of Campeche
54. Historic Monuments Zone of Querétaro
55. Historic Monuments Zone of Tlacotalpan
56. Historic Town of Guanajuato and Adjacent Mines
57. Hospicio Cabañas, Guadalajara
58. Islands and Protected Areas of the Gulf of California
59. Luis Barragán House and Studio
60. Monarch Butterfly Biosphere Reserve
61. Pre-Hispanic City and National Park of Palenque
62. Pre-Hispanic City of Chichen-Itza
63. Pre-Hispanic City of Teotihuacan
64. Pre-Hispanic Town of Uxmal

65. Protective town of San Miguel and the Sanctuary of Jesús Nazareno de Atotonilco
66. Rock Paintings of the Sierra de San Francisco
67. Sian Ka'an
68. Whale Sanctuary of El Vizcaino

Nicaragua
69. Ruins of León Viejo

Panama
70. Archaeological Site of Panamá Viejo and Historic District of Panamá
71. Coiba National Park and its Special Zone of Marine Protection
72. Darien National Park
73. Fortifications on the Caribbean Side of Panama: Portobelo-San Lorenzo
20. Talamanca Range-La Amistad Reserves/La Amistad National Park

Saint Kitts and Nevis
74. Brimstone Hill Fortress National Park

Saint Lucia
75. Pitons Management Area

United States of America
76. Cahokia Mounds State Historic Site
77. Carlsbad Caverns National Park
78. Chaco Culture
79. Everglades National Park
80. Grand Canyon National Park
81. Great Smoky Mountains National Park
82. Hawaii Volcanoes National Park
83. Independence Hall
84. La Fortaleza and San Juan National Historic Site in Puerto Rico
9. Kluane/Wrangell-St Elias/Glacier Bay/Tatshenshini-Alsek
85. Mammoth Cave National Park
86. Mesa Verde National Park
87. Monticello and the University of Virginia in Charlottesville
88. Olympic National Park
89. Pueblo de Taos
90. Redwood National Park
91. Statue of Liberty
16. Waterton Glacier International Peace Park
92. Yellowstone National Park
93. Yosemite National Park

Greenland
(Denmark)

33

U.S.A.

9

9
9 9
9

12

17

15

10

5

C A N A D A

3
3 3
3 4

11

8
7 13

88
6
16

14

92

91
83

90

87

UNITED STATES

86
80 78 89

2
Bermuda
(U.K.)

Hawaii
(U.S.A.)

93

76

85

81

OF AMERICA

82

77

58

58 43

66
58
68

58

68

58

79

THE BAHAMAS

Gulf
of Mexico

58

65
52

25 28
29
CUBA 27

24

22 21

DOMINICAN
REP.

84

74 **ANTIGUA & BARBUDA**
ST KITTS & NEVIS

40 56 47 44, 59
57 54 46
49 60 45
48 42 51 55
MEXICO 42 50

62
53 64 67
41
61 36
35
34 **HONDURAS**
37
GUATEMALA 32
EL SALVADOR

23 26

39 31

HAITI

Puerto
Rico
(U.S.A.)

30 **DOMINICA**

ST LUCIA 75

BARBADOS
ST VINCENT &
THE GRENADINES

GRENADA

JAMAICA

Caribbean Sea

TRINIDAD
& TOBAGO

BELIZE
1

38

69 **NICARAGUA**
18

20
20
COSTA
RICA

73
70 72
PANAMA
71

SOUTH
AMERICA

PACIFIC

OCEAN

19

Isla de Coco
(Costa Rica)

ATLANTIC

OCEAN

81

Grand Canyon National Park – USA

Inscribed 1979 – Natural phenomena or beauty; Major stages of Earth's history; Significant ecological and biological processes; Significant natural habitat for biodiversity.

The Grand Canyon, carved nearly 1 500 m deep into the rock by the Colorado River, is the most spectacular gorge in the world. Its horizontal strata retrace the geological history of the past two billion years as it cuts across the Grand Canyon National Park. It also contains prehistoric traces of human adaptation to a particularly harsh environment.

The Grand Canyon dominates the national park, which was created in 1919 by an act of Congress and was one of the first national parks in the United States. The steep, twisting gorge, 1.5 km deep and 445.8 km long, was formed during some 6 million years of geological activity and erosion by the Colorado River on the raised Earth's crust (2.5 km above sea level). The gorge, which ranges from 200 m–30 km wide, divides the park into the North Rim and South Rim: the buttes, spires, mesas and temples in the canyon are in fact mountains, looked down upon from the rims.

Erosion is ongoing and seasonal and permanent rivers produce impressive waterfalls and rapids of washed-down boulders along the length of the canyon and its tributaries. The horizontal geological strata that erosion has exposed span some 2 000 million years of geological history, providing evidence of the four major geological eras: early and late Precambrian, Palaeozoic, Mesozoic and Cenozoic.

The canyon is also a vast biological museum in which there are five different life and vegetation zones. Over 1 000 plant species have so far been identified including several officially listed as threatened. The park is also home to 76 mammal, 299 bird and 41 reptile and amphibian species, and some 16 fish species inhabit the Colorado River and its tributaries.

Archaeological remains show the adaptation of human societies to the area's severe climate and landscape, with evidence of settlement. The park contains more than 2 600 documented prehistoric ruins, including evidence of Archaic cultures (the earliest known inhabitants), Cohonina Indians along the South Rim, and Anasazi Indians on both the South Rim, North Rim, and within the Inner Canyon. Hualapai and Havasupai Indians moved into the canyons at this time, remaining undisturbed until the arrival of the Anglo-Americans in 1860.

The Grand Canyon area was first protected in 1893 as a forest reserve in which mining, lumbering and hunting continued to be allowed. It was upgraded to a game reserve in 1906, giving protection to the wildlife, and redesignated a National Monument in 1908.

Altitudinal range provides a variety of climates and habitats, ranging from desert to mountain conditions. Fossil remains found in the park include early plants, marine and terrestrial specimens, early reptiles and some mammals.

Historic District of Old Québec – CANADA

Inscribed 1985 – Significance in human
history; Heritage associated with events of
universal significance.

Québec is one of the finest examples of a fortified
colonial city. It is the only North American city to have
preserved its ramparts, together with the numerous
bastions, gates and defensive works that surround the
historic district.

The Upper City, built on a cliff and defended by walls
with bastions, has remained the religious and
administrative centre, with its churches, convents and
other monuments like the Dauphine Redoubt, the
Citadel and Château Frontenac (which can be seen at
the top of the photo on the right). Together with the
Lower City and its harbour and old quarters, it forms
a coherent urban ensemble which is by far the most
complete fortified colonial town in North America.

Québec illustrates one of the major stages in the
population and growth of the Americas during the
modern and contemporary period. When Samuel de
Champlain founded Québec, the capital of New
France in 1608, he chose the natural site of a steep
plateau overlooking the St Laurent River. The old heart
of the city was established on this promontory,
Cap-aux-Diamants, which is protected by Fort St Louis.

Québec had an urban organization early on and a
zoning system which stemmed from its various
functions as a town, a fortified city and a harbour for
trade from the North and Europe. Its cliff divided the
city into two districts: business and naval district in
the Lower City, and the administrative and religious
centre in the Upper City.

The construction of a citadel at the far southeast end
of Cap-aux-Diamants by the engineer Elias Durnford
from 1819–31 and the expansion of the system of
fortifications to cover the city's entire perimeter were in
keeping with the original spatial organization of the city
and gave Québec its current topographical features.

The oldest quarters are located in the Lower City around
the Place Royale which, along with the Rue Notre Dame,
is lined with old seventeenth- and eighteenth-century
houses. In the Upper City the seventeenth-century
convents and seminary still have some original
elements. Of 700 old civil or religious buildings
remaining, 2 per cent date to the seventeenth century,
9 per cent to the eighteenth and 43 per cent to the first
half of the nineteenth century. The city took on its
present aspect under the influence of the Baillairgés,
a dynasty of architects who, for generations, imposed
an interpretation of neoclassical style.

Yellowstone National Park – USA

Inscribed 1978 – Natural phenomena or beauty; Major stages of Earth's history; Significant ecological and biological processes; Significant natural habitat for biodiversity.

Yellowstone National Park covers 9 000 km² of a vast natural forest of the southern Rocky Mountains in the North American west. The park holds half of the world's known geothermal features, with over 10 000 examples, and is equally renowned for its wildlife which includes grizzly bears, wolves, bison and wapitis.

Established as America's first national park in 1872, Yellowstone boasts an impressive array of geothermal phenomena, with geysers, lava formations, fumaroles, hot springs and waterfalls, lakes and canyons. There are more than 580 geysers – the world's largest concentration, and two-thirds of all those on the planet. The source of these phenomena lies under the ground in the area's geological origins: Yellowstone is part of the most seismically active region of the Rocky Mountains, a volcanic 'hot spot'.

Crustal uplifts 65 million years ago formed the southern Rocky Mountains and volcanic outflows were common until around 40 million years ago. A more recent period of volcanism began in the region about 2 million years ago, when thousands of cubic kilometres of magma filled immense chambers under the plateau and then erupted to the surface. Three cycles of eruption produced huge explosive outbursts of ash. The latest cycle formed a caldera 45 km wide and 75 km long when the active magma chambers erupted and collapsed. The crystallizing magma is the source of heat for hydrothermal features such as geysers, hot springs, mud pots and fumaroles.

Most of the area was glaciated during the Pleistocene (from 1.8 million to 10 000 years ago, when the last ice age ended) and many glacial features remain. The park lies at the headwaters of three major rivers – Yellowstone, Madison and Snake. Lower Yellowstone Falls is the highest of more than forty named waterfalls in the park.

Great elevational differences produce a range of plant communities, from semi-arid steppe to alpine tundra. The park has seven species of coniferous tree, especially lodgepole pine, and 1 100 species of vascular plant, including an endemic grass. Thermal areas have unique assemblages of thermal algae and bacteria.

UNESCO World Heritage Sites – South America

The first World Heritage site to be listed in 1978 was the Gálapagos Islands off the coast of South America. Famous for its association with Darwin and its giant tortoises it was followed on to the List by sites representing ancient civilizations, European invaders and the continent's rich and diverse physical and natural environment.

● Cultural site   ● Natural site   ● Mixed site

Argentina
1. Cueva de las Manos, Río Pinturas
2. Iguazu National Park
3. Ischigualasto/Talampaya Natural Parks
4. Jesuit Block and Estancias of Córdoba
5. Jesuit Missions of the Guaranis: San Ignacio Miní, Santa Ana, Nuestra Señora de Loreto and Santa María Mayor (Argentina), Ruins of Saõ Miguel das Missões (Brazil)
6 Los Glaciares
7 Península Valdés
8. Quebrada de Humahuaca

Bolivia
9. City of Potosí
10. Fuerte de Samaipata
11. Historic City of Sucre
12. Jesuit Missions of the Chiquitos
13. Noel Kempff Mercado National Park
14. Tiwanaku: Spiritual and Political Centre of the Tiwanaku Culture

Brazil
15. Atlantic Forest South-East Reserves
16. Brasilia
17. Brazilian Atlantic Islands: Fernando de Noronha and Atol das Rocas Reserves
18. Central Amazon Conservation Complex
19. Cerrado Protected Areas: Chapada dos Veadeiros and Emas National Parks
20. Discovery Coast Atlantic Forest Reserves
21. Historic Centre of Salvador de Bahia
22. Historic Centre of São Luís

23. Historic Centre of the Town of Diamantina
24. Historic Centre of the Town of Goiás
25. Historic Centre of the Town of Olinda
26. Historic Town of Ouro Preto
27. Iguaçu National Park
5. Jesuit Missions of the Guaranis: San Ignacio Miní, Santa Ana, Nuestra Señora de Loreto and Santa María Mayor (Argentina), Ruins of Saõ Miguel das Missões (Brazil)
28. Pantanal Conservation Area
29. Sanctuary of Bom Jesus do Congonhas
30. Serra da Capivara National Park

Chile
31. Churches of Chiloé
32. Historic Quarter of the Seaport City of Valparaíso
33. Humberstone and Santa Laura Saltpeter Works
34. Rapa Nui National Park
35. Sewell Mining Town

Colombia
36. Historic Centre of Santa Cruz de Mompox
37. Los Katíos National Park
38. Malpelo Fauna and Flora Sanctuary
39. National Archeological Park of Tierradentro
40. Port, Fortresses and Group of Monuments, Cartagena
41. San Agustín Archeological Park

Curaçao
42. Historic Area of Willemstad, Inner City and Harbour, Netherlands Antilles (Netherlands)

Ecuador
43. City of Quito
44. Galápagos Islands
45. Historic Centre of Santa Ana de los Ríos de Cuenca
46. Sangay National Park

Paraguay
47. Jesuit Missions of La Santísima Trinidad de Paraná and Jesús de Tavarangue

Peru
48. Chan Chan Archaeological Zone
49. Chavín (Archaeological site)
50. City of Cuzco
51. Historic Centre of Lima
52. Historic Sanctuary of Machu Picchu
53. Historical Centre of the City of Arequipa
54. Huascarán National Park
55. Lines and Geoglyphs of Nasca and Pampas de Jumana
56. Manú National Park
57. Río Abiseo National Park
58. Sacred City of Caral-Supe

Suriname
59. Central Suriname Nature Reserve
60. Historic Inner City of Paramaribo

Uruguay
61. Historic Quarter of the City of Colonia del Sacramento

Venezuela
62. Canaima National Park
63. Ciudad Universitaria de Caracas
64. Coro and its Port

34
Easter Island (Chile)

NORTH
AMERICA

Caribbean Sea

*Curaçao
(Netherlands)*

VENEZUELA

GUYANA

COLOMBIA

SURINAME   French
Guiana

ECUADOR

*Galápagos Islands
(Ecuador)*

B R A Z I L

PERU

BOLIVIA

PACIFIC

OCEAN

PARAGUAY

ATLANTIC

OCEAN

C H I L E

URUGUAY

ARGENTINA

Galápagos Islands – ECUADOR

Inscribed 1978 – Natural phenomena or beauty; Major stages of Earth's history; Significant ecological and biological processes; Significant natural habitat for biodiversity.

Situated in the Pacific Ocean approximately 1 000 km from the South American mainland, the Galápagos Archipelago of nineteen major islands and their marine reserve have been called a unique 'living museum and showcase of evolution'. Located at the confluence of three ocean currents, the Galápagos are a 'tossed salad' of marine species.

Volcanic processes formed the islands, most of which are volcanic summits, some rising over 3 000 m from the Pacific floor. They vary greatly in altitude, area and orientation and these differences, combined with their physical separation, contributed towards the species diversity and endemism on particular islands. Ongoing seismic and volcanic activity reflects the processes that formed the islands and it was these processes, together with the islands' extreme isolation, that led to the development of unusual animal life – such as the marine iguana, the giant tortoise and the flightless cormorant – that inspired Charles Darwin's theory of evolution following his visit in 1835.

The western part of the archipelago experiences intense volcanic and seismic activity. The larger islands typically comprise at least one gently sloping shield volcano, culminating in collapsed craters or calderas. Long stretches of shoreline are only slightly eroded, but in many places faulting and marine erosion have produced steep cliffs and lava, coral or shell sand beaches.

There is coastal vegetation along beaches, salt-water lagoons and low, broken, boulder-strewn shores, and mangrove swamps dominate protected coves and lagoons.

The arid zone that lies immediately inland dominates the Galápagos landscape. The humid zone emerges above the arid zone through a transition belt in which elements of the two are combined. It is very damp and is maintained in the dry season by thick, *garua* fogs. A fern-grass-sedge zone covers the summit areas of the larger islands where moisture is retained in temporary pools.

The endemic fauna includes invertebrate, reptile, marine and bird species. There are a few indigenous mammals. All the reptiles, except for two marine turtles, are endemic.

Marine environments are highly varied and are associated with water temperature regimes reflecting differences in nutrient and light levels. These range from warm temperate conditions brought on by vigorous upwelling (Cromwell Current) and a moderately cool, warm temperate-subtropical influence (Peru Flow)

Iguazu National Park – ARGENTINA

Inscribed 1984 – Natural phenomena or beauty; Significant natural habitat for biodiversity.

One of the world's most spectacular waterfalls, the Iguazu Falls, lies at the heart of this vast, rich and diverse national park. The waterfall is semicircular, some 80 m high and 2 700 m in diameter and stands on a basaltic line that spans the border between Argentina and Brazil.

The site consists of the national park and national reserves in Misiones Province, northeastern Argentina. The Iguazu River forms the northern boundary of both the reserves and park, and also the southern boundary of Iguaçu National Park World Heritage site in Brazil.

The Iguazu Falls lie on the Argentina-Brazil border and are made up of many cascades that generate vast sprays of water and produce one of the most magnificent waterfalls in the world. The vegetation is mostly subtropical wet forest rich in lianas and epithytes, although the forests have less species diversity when compared with others in Brazil and parts of Paraguay. Nonetheless, over 2 000 species of vascular plant have been identified.

Vegetation around the falls is particularly luxuriant due to the constant spray. The site is particularly rich in bird life, with almost half of Argentina's bird species found there. The fauna are typical of the region and include tapir, coatimundi, and tamandua.

Threatened mammals such as the jaguar, ocelot and tiger-cat number among the carnivores, and the giant anteater and Brazilian otter are also found. Primates include the black-capped capuchin and black howler monkey. There are also small populations of the endangered broad-nosed cayman and the threatened Brazilian merganser (sawbill duck).

The first inhabitants in the area were the Caingangues Indians. This tribe was dislodged by the Tupi-Guaranies who coined the name Iguazu (Big Water). The first European to reach the Iguazu falls was the Spanish explorer Don Alvar Nuñes Cabeza de Vaca in 1541; some ten years later Spanish and Portuguese colonization began. There are at least two sites of particular archaeological interest within the national park.

Historic Sanctuary of Machu Picchu – PERU

Inscribed 1983 – Human creative genius; Testimony to cultural tradition; Natural phenomena or beauty; Significant ecological and biological processes.

Machu Picchu stands 2 430 m above sea level in an extraordinarily beautiful setting in the middle of a tropical mountain forest. The city was probably the greatest urban achievement of the Inca Empire at its height: its giant walls, terraces and ramps seem as if they have been cut naturally in the continuous rock escarpments. The natural setting, on the eastern slopes of the Andes, encompasses the upper Amazon basin with its rich diversity of flora and fauna.

Set on the vertiginous site of a granite mountain sculpted by erosion and dominating a meander in the Rio Urubamba, Machu Picchu is a world-renowned archaeological site. Its construction, set out according to a very rigorous plan, comprises one of the most spectacular creations of the Incas, the largest civilization in the Americas before the arrival of Europeans. It appears to date from the period of the two great Inca rulers, Pachacutec Inca Yupanqui (1438–71) and Tupac Inca Yupanqui (1472–93). The function of this city, which is over 100 km from the Inca capital, Cuzco, is still unknown. Without making a judgement as to their purpose, several individual quarters may be noted in the ruins: a 'farmers' quarter near the colossal

terraces whose slopes were cultivated and transformed into hanging gardens; an 'industrial' quarter; a 'royal' quarter and a 'religious' quarter.

The Historic Sanctuary of Machu Picchu covers 325 km² in some of the scenically most attractive mountainous territory of the Peruvian Andes. It was the last stronghold of the Incas, is of superb architectural and archaeological importance, and remains one of the most important cultural sites in Latin America. The site's stonework is a first-class example of the use of a natural raw material to create outstanding architecture totally appropriate to the surroundings.

The surrounding valleys have been cultivated continuously for well over 1 000 years, providing one of the world's greatest long-term examples of a productive man–land relationship. The people living around Machu Picchu continue a way of life closely resembling that of their Inca ancestors, being based on potatoes, maize and llamas. Machu Picchu also provides a secure habitat for several endangered species, notably the spectacled bear.

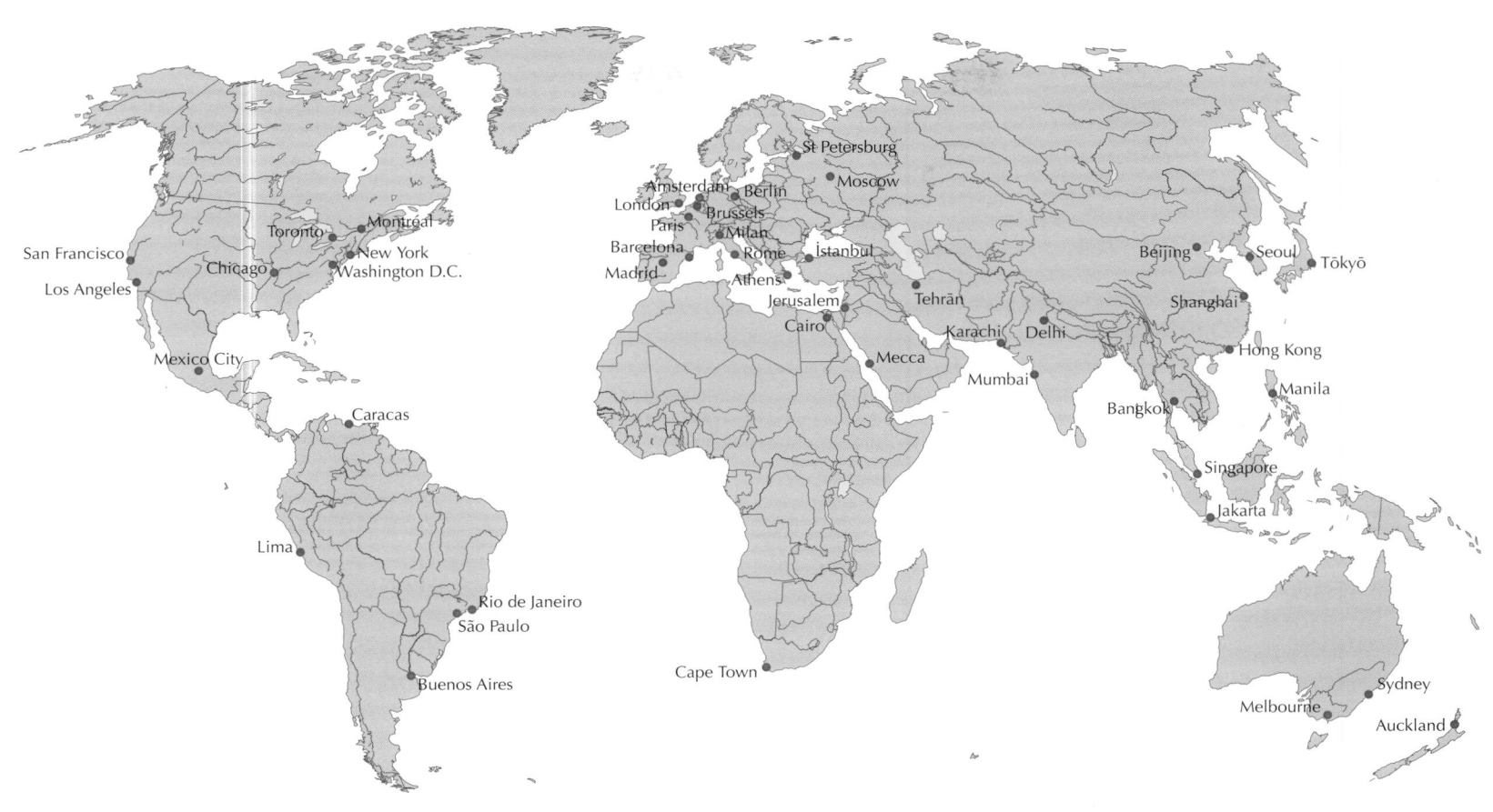

Key to City Plans

AUCKLAND

MELBOURNE

SYDNEY

JAKARTA

SINGAPORE

MANILA

BANGKOK

HONG KONG

BEIJING

SHANGHAI

SEOUL

KARACHI

TŌKYŌ

TOKOROZAWA-SHI
Sakanoshita
NIIZA-SHI
ASAKA-SHI
SAITAMA
Itabashi
Art Gallery
WAKŌ-SHI
Tōkyō-diabutsu
Temple
Kitano

Seibukyujomae
Station
Seibuen
Park
Oizumi
Central
Park
NERIMA-KU
Hikarigaoka
Park
Seibuen
Station
HIGASHIYAMATO-SHI
KIYOSE-SHI
Higashiyamato
Green Park
HIGASHIMURAYAMA-SHI
HIGASHIKURUME-SHI
Makino
Memorial
Garden
Higashimurayama
Central Park
Yanagikubo
HŌYA-SHI
Kodaira
Cemetery
Nerima
Art Gallery
Sanpeji
Temple
Chihiro
Iwasaki
Memorial
Gallery
Medicinal
Plant Garden
TANASHI-SHI
Ogawa
KODAIRA-SHI
Koganei
Country
Club
Koganei
Park
MUSASHINO-SHI
Showa
Memorial
Park
TACHIKAWA-SHI
KOKUBUNJI-SHI
KOGANEI-SHI
Kichijoji
Station
Inokashira
National
Park
TŌK
AKISHIMA-SHI
Man-yo
Botanical Garden
SUGINAMI-KU
Wadabori
Park
Takachiho
University of Commerce
HINO-SHI
KUNITACHI-SHI
Tōkyō University
of Agriculture
and Engineering
Tama
Cemetery
Nogawa
Park
MITAKA-SHI
Yaho-tenmangu
Shrine
FUCHŪ-SHI
National
Observatory
Chofu
Airfield
Jindai
Botanical
Garden
Okunitama-jinja
Shrine
Jindaiji
Temple
SETAGAYA-KU
Takahata-fudoson
Temple
Tōkyō Racetrack
CHŪŌ EXPRESSWAY
CHŪŌ EXPRESSWAY
Tama
Zoological
Park
Korehisa
Station
CHŌFU-SHI
Keio Hyakkaen
Garden
Tōkyō
University of
Agriculture
Tamateck
Amusement
Park
Tamagawa
Green Park
KOMAE-SHI
TAMA-SHI
Sakuragaoka
Country Club
Kinuta Park
Setagaya
Art Gallery

Central Tōkyō
Kitanomaru
Park
Science and
Technology
Museum
0 METRES 250
0 YARDS 250
Seikado
Library
Tōkyō Yomiuri
Country Club
Seawater
Aquarium
Yomiuri
Land
Futako-tamagawa
Green Park
Playground
Tama
University of Art
Craft Gallery
National Museum
of Modern Art
TAMA-KU
Goto Art
Museum
CHIYODA-KU
Fukiage
Imperial
Residence
East
Garden
Communications
Museum
Mukogaoka
Amusement
Park
Mizonokuchi
Takaishi
Cabinet
Library
Imperial
Palace
Gardens
New
Imperial
Palace
SHINJUKU-DORI
TAKATSU-KU
National
Theatre
ASAO-KU
KAWASAKI-SHI
Supreme
Court
Outer
Garden
Tōkyō
Station
Kawasaki
City
Museum
EXPRESSWAY NO.4
National
Diet Library
Parliamentary
Museum
Sukurada
Gate
Imperial
Theatre
Maginu
National
Diet Building
High
Court
MIYAMAE-KU
NAKAHA
KU
Prime Minister's
Residence
Yūrakuchō
Station
Midori
Kize
Hibiya
Park
Hibiya
Concert
Hall
Nissei
Theatre
Central Art
Gallery
MINATO-KU
Hibiya
Library
Hibiya
Public Hall
Takeshita
KANAGAWA
TSUZUKI-KU
Kabukiza
Theatre
Nakayama
Sagamihara
Golf Club
Serigaya
Park
AOBA-KU
Hiyoshi
YOKOHAMA-SHI

94

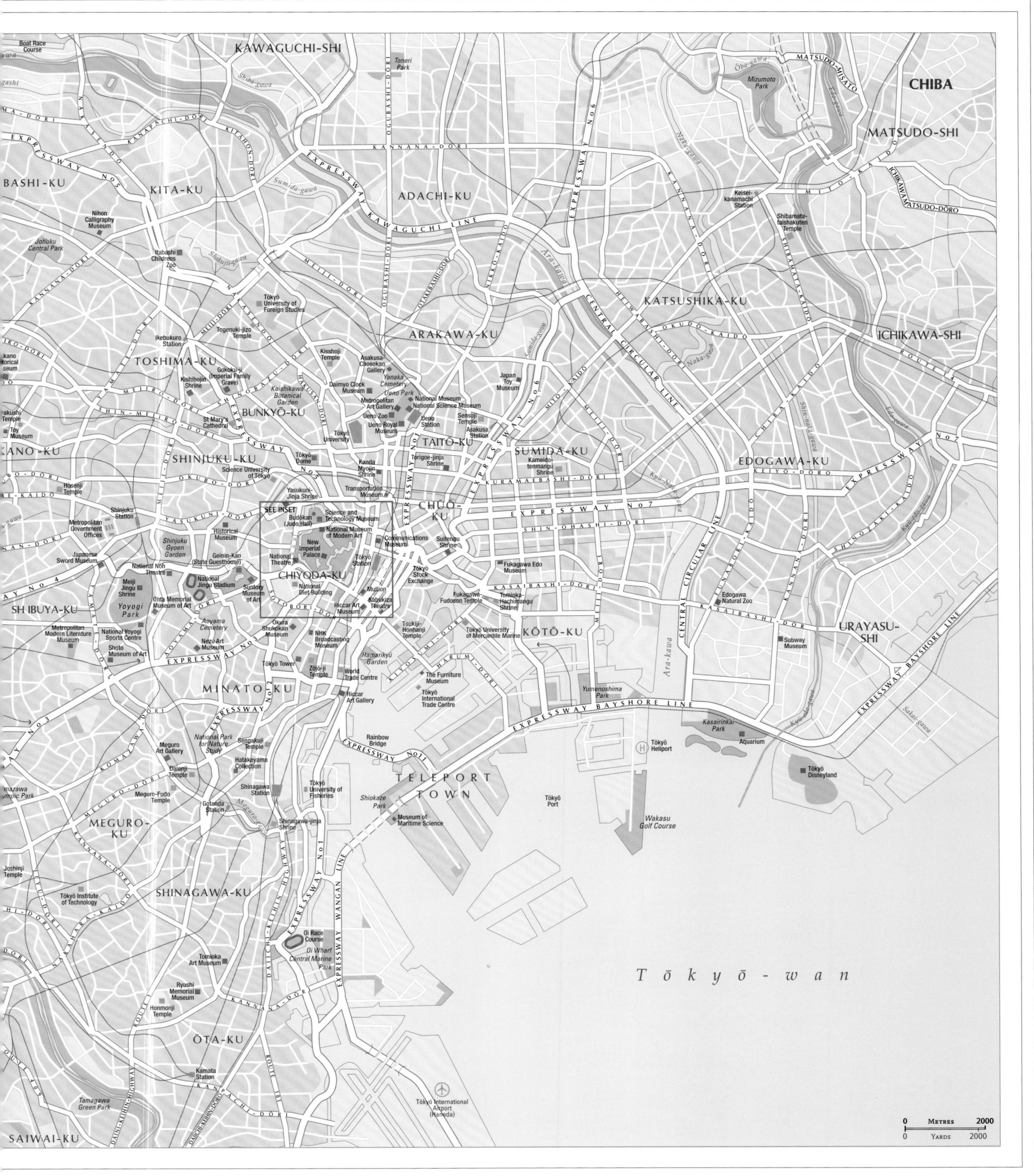

KAWAGUCHI-SHI

CHIBA

MATSUDO-SHI

Boat Race Course

Toneri Park

Mizumoto Park

MATSUDO-MISATO

EXPRESSWAY No 5

BASHI-KU

KITA-KU

ADACHI-KU

ICHIKAWA-SHI

Keisei-kanamachi Station

Shibamata-taishakuten Temple

ICHIKAWA-MATSUDO-DORO

Johoku Central Park

Nihon Calligraphy Museum

Itabashi Childrens Zoo

KATSUSHIKA-KU

KANNANA-DORI

EXPRESSWAY KAWAGUCHI LINE

Tōkyō University of Foreign Studies

ARAKAWA-KU

ICHIKAWA-SHI

kano torical seum

TOSHIMA-KU

Ikebukuro Station

Togenuki-jizo Temple

Kishibojin Shrine

Gokoku-ji (Imperial Family Grave)

Kisshoji Temple

Asakusa-Chosokan Gallery

Yanaka Cemetery

Japan Toy Museum

akushi Temple

Toy Museum

Koishikawa Botanical Garden

Daimyo Clock Museum

Metropolitan Art Gallery

National Science Museum

Ueno Park

Ueno Zoo

Ueno Station

Sensoji Temple

EDOGAWA-KU

KEIYO-DORO

KANO-KU

BUNKYO-KU

St Mary's Cathedral

Tōkyō University

Ueno Royal Museum

Asakusa Station

SUMIDA-KU

Kameido-tenmangu Shrine

Tōkyō Dome

SHINJUKU-KU

Science University of Tokyo

TAITO-KU

Hosenji Temple

Kanda Myojin Shrine

Torigoe-jinja Shrine

KURAMAEBASHI-DORI

Yasukuni-Jinja Shrine

Transportation Museum

CHŪO-KU

EXPRESSWAY No 7

SEE INSET

Budōkan (Judo Hall)

Science and Technology Museum

National Museum of Modern Art

Communications Museum

Suitengu Shrine

SHIN-OHASHI-DORI

Historical Museum

Geinin-kan (State Guesthouse)

New Imperial Palace

Tōkyō Station

Tōkyō Stock Exchange

Fukagawa Edo Museum

National Noh Theatre

National Theatre

CHIYODA-KU

Mullion

Kabukiza Theatre

Fukagawa-Fudoson Temple

Tomioka-Hachimangu Shrine

SH IBUYA-KU

Meiji Jingu Shrine

National Jingu Stadium

Suntory Museum of Art

National Diet Building

Riccar Art Museum

Edogawa Natural Zoo

URAYASU-SHI

Yoyogi Park

Ohta Memorial Museum of Art

Aoyama Cemetery

Okura Shukokan Museum

Nezu Art Museum

Tsukiji-Honhanji Temple

Tōkyō University of Mercantile Marine

KŌTŌ-KU

Subway Museum

Metropolitan Modern Literature Museum

National Yoyogi Sports Centre

Shoto Museum of Art

NHK Broadcasting Museum

Tōkyō Tower

Zōjō-ji Temple

World Trade Centre

Hamarikyū Garden

The Furniture Museum

MINATO-KU

National Park for Nature Study

Riccar Art Gallery

Tōkyō International Trade Centre

Meguro Art Gallery

Sengakuji Temple

Hatakeyama Collection

Rainbow Bridge

TELEPORT TOWN

Yumenoshima Park

Kasairinkai Park

Tōkyō Heliport

Aquarium

Daienji Temple

Shinagawa Station

Tōkyō University of Fisheries

EXPRESSWAY

Tōkyō Port

Tōkyō Disneyland

mazawa ympic Park

Meguro-Fudo Temple

Gotanda Station

Shinagawa-jinja Shrine

Shiokaze Park

Wakasu Golf Course

MEGURO-KU

Museum of Maritime Science

Joshinji Temple

SHINAGAWA-KU

Tōkyō Institute of Technology

Tōkyō-wan

Oi Race Course

Oi Wharf Central Marine Park

Tomioka Art Museum

Ryushi Memorial Museum

Honmonji Temple

ŌTA-KU

Kamata Station

Tamagawa Green Park

Tōkyō International Airport (Haneda)

SAIWAI-KU

0 METRES 2000
0 YARDS 2000

© Collins Bartholomew Ltd

95

ATHENS

MOSCOW

ST PETERSBURG

BERLIN

BRUSSELS

AMSTERDAM

© Collins Bartholomew Ltd

LONDON

Central London

The Wigmore Hall · Oxford Street · Regent Street · Palladium · British Museum · Dominion Theatre · High Holborn · Holborn · Lincoln's Inn Fields · Lincoln's Inn · Charing Cross Road · Shaftesbury Ave · Soho · Kingsway · Theatre Royal · Royal Courts of Justice · Royal Opera House · London Transport Museum · Strand · Aldwych · King's College · Somerset House · Royal Academy of Arts · Piccadilly Circus · National Gallery · Mayfair · New Bond Street · Piccadilly · Haymarket · St James's · St James's St · Pall Mall · Trafalgar Square · Charing Cross Station · Embankment · Waterloo Br · Royal National Theatre · Admiralty Arch · Whitehall · Queen Elizabeth Hall · Royal Festival Hall · Hungerford Bridge · London Eye · Green Park · St James's Palace · The Mall · Marlborough House · Government Buildings · Downing St · Parliament Street · Victoria Embankment · Thames · London Eye · Old County Hall · Waterloo Station · Constitution Hill · Buckingham Palace · Birdcage Walk · St James's Park · Treasury · London Aquarium · Lambeth · Grosvenor Place · Victoria Station · Victoria Street · Westminster · Parliament Square · Westminster Abbey · Big Ben · Houses of Parliament · Westminster Br · Westminster Bridge Road · Lambeth Palace Gardens · Lambeth Palace

METRES 500
YARDS 500

Copse Wood · Pinner Green · Pinner · Ruislip Lido · Queensbury · Kingsbury · RAF Museums · Holders Hill · Hendon · Golders Green · HARROW · Northwick Park · Fryent Country Park · Wembley Park · BRENT · Brent Reservoir · Dollis Hill · Cricklewood · Wembley Stadium · Wembley · Willesden · North Circular Road · Gladstone Park · Willesden Green · Sunbury Golf Course · Alperton · Perivale · Park Royal · Harlesden · Kilbur · Grand Union Canal · North Acton · Ealing Golf Course · Perivale Park Golf Course · Western Avenue · EALING · Ealing · Acton · East Acton · Wormwood Scrubs · North Kensington · Westway · Notting Hill · Shepherd's Bush · Holland Park · HAMMERSMITH · Olympia · Hayes · Southall · Hanwell · Gunnersbury · AND FULHAM · Chiswick High Road · Earls Court Exhibition Centre · Earls Court · Yiewsley · Norwood Green · Gunnersbury Park · Chiswick · Hammersmith Bridge · West Drayton · Grand Union Canal · North Hyde · Osterley Park · Brentford · Chiswick House · Castelnau · Barn Elms Wildfowl Reserve · Football Stadium · Harmondsworth · Harlington · Bath Road · Heston · Osterley · Great West Road · Royal Botanic Gardens Kew · Syon House · Syon Park · Barnes · Putney Bridge · Cranford · Hounslow West · Isleworth · Mortlake · South Circular Road · Putney · Heathrow Airport (London) · Hounslow · Richmond · Putney Heath · Staines Reservoirs · Stanwell · East Bedfont · HOUNSLOW · Rugby Ground · Richmond · Roehampton Lane · Hounslow Heath · RICHMOND UPON · Richmond Park · Feltham · Twickenham · Crane · THAMES · All England Lawn Tennis and Croquet Club · Wimbledon Park · Ashford · Hanworth · Teddington · Wimbledon Common · Wimbledon · Coombe Hill Golf Course · Queen Mary Reservoir · Kempton Park Racecourse · Bushy Park · Norbiton · New Malden · West Barnes · Sunbury · Molesey Reservoirs · West Molesey · East Molesey · Hampton · Hampton Court Palace · Hampton Court Park · KINGSTON UPON THAMES · Bushy Mead · Morden Park · Shepperton · Queen Elizabeth II Reservoir · Island Barn Reservoir · Thames Ditton · Motspur Park

0 Metres 800
0 Yards 800

Central Paris

© Collins Bartholomew Ltd

NEW YORK

Central Manhattan

Central Park

Frick Collection

CLINTON

Columbus Circle

DeWitt Clinton Park

Carnegie Hall

The Pond

Zoo

THEATER DISTRICT

Museum of Modern Art

Lever House

Seagram Building

Rockefeller Center

St Patrick's Cathedral

St Bartholomew's Church

MIDTOWN

Bus Terminal

Times Square

Met. Life Building

GARMENT DISTRICT

Bryant Park

New York Public Library

Grand Central Terminal

Chrysler Building

United Nations Headquarters

Madison Square Garden

Pennsylvania Station

Empire State Building

MURRAY HILL

0 Metres 250

0 Yards 250

Essex Fells

Roseland

Bloomfield

Brookdale Park

Wood-Ridge

Teterboro Airport

Little Ferry

Ridgefield

Edgewater

Palisade Amusement Park

Cliffside Park

Fairview

Rutherford

North Bergen

Lyndhurst

Meadowlands Sports Complex

North Arlington

Secaucus

Guttenberg

West New York

American Museum of Natural History

Lincoln Center

North Hudson Park

Metropolitan Museum

Kearny

Union City

SEE INSET MANHATTAN

Rockefeller Center

Weehawken

Grand Central Terminal

Empire State Building

United Nations Headquarters

Maplewood

Irvington

Hoboken

Greenwich Village

South Mountain Reservation

Orange Reservoir

PULASKI SKYWAY

Lincoln Park

Holland Tunnel

Newark

Kearny Point

Jersey City

Chinatown

Williamsburg Bridge

N E W

Hillside

78 NEW JERSEY TURNPIKE EXTENSION

Site of Former World Trade Center

Manhattan Bridge

Union

J E R S E Y

Newark International Airport

Ellis Island (N.Y.)

Castle Clinton National Monument

Brooklyn Bridge

Galloping Hill Park

Townley

Liberty State Park

Governor's Island

Long Island University

Roselle Park

Elizabeth

Newark Bay

Liberty Island (N.Y.)

Station

Red Hook

Roselle

Warinanco Park

Statue of Liberty

Upper Bay

Brooklyn Museum

Park Slope

Zoo

Prospect Park

Winfield Park

Bayonne

Greenwood Cemetery

Kensington

Linden

Shooters Island

New Brighton

B R O

Rahway

Richmond Terrace

Bayonne Bridge

Kill Van Kull

Richmond Terrace

Port Richmond

Bay Ridge

Borough Park

Rahway River Park

Port Richmond

Castleton Avenue

Shore Road Park

Parkville

Zoo

Silver Lake Park

The Narrows

Linden Airport

Westerleigh

Clove Lakes Park

Dyker Beach Park

New Utrecht

Fresh Kills Park

Willow Brook Park

Bulls Head

STATEN ISLAND EXPRESSWAY

Fox Hills

Verrazano Narrows Bridge

Fort Hamilton

Gravesend

Carteret

S T A T E N

Victory

Fort Wadsworth

Lower Bay

Gravesend Bay

Avenel

Travis

I S L A N D

South Beach

Grasmere

Hoffman Island

Woodbridge

Port Reading

Ocean View Cemetery

LaTourette Park

New Dorp

Miller Field

Swinburne Island

Coney Island

Rossville

Great Kills

Gateway National Recreation Area

New York Aquarium

ATLANTIC OCEAN

0 Metres 1000
0 Yards 1000

© Collins Bartholomew Ltd

© Collins Bartholomew Ltd

Introduction to the Atlas and Map Symbols

These pages explain the editorial policies followed for map pages 110 to 240 and the map symbols used on the maps are also explained here. The map sequence starts at the International Date Line in the Pacific Ocean and broadly works westwards, moving from Oceania through Asia, Europe, Africa, North America and finally to South America. The alphanumeric reference system used in the index is based on latitude and longitude, and the number and letter for each graticule square are shown within each map frame. The numbers of adjoining or overlapping plates are shown by arrows in the frame and accompanying numbers in the margin.

Boundaries

The status of nations, their names and their boundaries, are shown in this atlas as they are at the time of going to press, as far as can be ascertained. The atlas includes any recent changes of status of nations and their boundaries. Where an international boundary symbol appears in the sea or ocean it does not necessarily infer a legal maritime boundary, but shows which islands belong to which country.

Where international boundaries are the subject of dispute it may be that no portrayal of them will meet with the approval of any of the countries involved. It is not seen as the function of this atlas to try to adjudicate between the rights and wrongs of political issues, and reference mapping at atlas scales is not the ideal medium for indicating the claims of many separatist and irredentist movements. However, every reasonable attempt is made to show where an active territorial dispute exists, and where there is an important difference between 'de facto' (existing in fact, on the ground) and 'de jure' (according to law) boundaries. This is done by the use of a different symbol where international boundaries are disputed, or where the alignment is unconfirmed, to that used for settled international boundaries. Ceasefire lines are also shown by a separate symbol. For clarity, disputed boundaries and areas are annotated where this is considered necessary. The atlas aims to take a strictly neutral viewpoint of all such cases, based on advice from expert consultants.

Scale

In order to directly compare areas throughout the world it would be necessary to maintain a single map scale throughout the atlas. However, the desirability of mapping more densely populated and more significant areas of the world at larger, and therefore more detailed, scales means that a range of scales have been used. Scales for continental maps range from 1:17 500 000 to 1:32 000 000, depending on the size of the continental land mass being covered. Scales for regional maps are typically in the range 1:12 000 000 to 1:20 000 000, although smaller scales are used for a few remoter areas such as northern Asia. Mapping for most countries is at scales between 1:5 000 000 and 1:7 000 000, although for the most densely populated areas of Europe the scale increases to 1:2 000 000.

Map Projections

The representation or 'projection' of the Earth into only two dimensions is a perennial problem for the cartographer. Distortions are inevitable and all map projections are compromises. Some projections seek to maintain correct area relationships (equal area projections), true distances and bearings from a point (equidistant projections) or correct angles and shapes (conformal projections). Others attempt to achieve a balance between these properties. The choice of projections used in this atlas has been made on an individual continental and regional basis. Projections used, and their individual parameters, have been defined to provide the best representation of the area mapped, to minimize distortion and to reduce scale errors as much as possible. The projection used is indicated at the bottom left of each map plate.

Place Names

The spelling of place names on maps has always been a matter of great complexity, because of the variety of the world's languages and the systems used to write them down. There is no standard way of spelling names or of converting them from one alphabet, or symbol set, to another. Instead, conventional ways of spelling have evolved in each of the world's major languages, and the results often differ significantly from the name as it is spelled in the original language. Familiar examples of English conventional names include Munich (München), Florence (Firenze) and Moscow (from the transliterated form, Moskva).

In this atlas, local name forms are used where these are in the Roman alphabet, though for major cities and main physical features, conventional English names are given first. The local forms are those which are officially recognized by the government of the country concerned, usually as represented by its official mapping agency. This is a basic principle laid down by the United Kingdom government's Permanent Committee on Geographical Names (PCGN) and the equivalent United States Board on Geographic Names (BGN). Prominent English-language and historic names are not neglected, however. These, and significant superseded names and alternate spellings, are included in brackets on the maps where space permits, and are cross-referenced in the index.

Country names are shown in conventional English form and include any recent changes promulgated by national governments and adopted by the United Nations. The names of continents, oceans, seas and under-water features in international waters also appear in English throughout the atlas, as do those of other international features where such an English form exists and is in common use. International features are defined as features crossing one or more international boundary.

For languages in non-Roman alphabets or symbol sets, names need to be 'Romanized' through a process of transliteration (the conversion of characters or symbols from one alphabet into another) or transcription (conversion of names based on pronunciation). Different systems often exist for this process, but PCGN and its United States counterpart, the Board on Geographic Names (BGN), usually follow the same Romanization principles, and the general policy for this atlas is to follow their lead.

Abbreviations

Arch.	Archipelago		
B.	Bay		
	Bahia, Baía	Portuguese	bay
	Bahía	Spanish	bay
	Baie	French	bay
C.	Cape		
	Cabo	Portuguese,	
		Spanish	cape, headland
	Cap	French	cape, headland
Co	Cerro	Spanish	hill, peak, summit
E.	East, Eastern		
Est.	Estrecho	Spanish	strait
G.	Gebel	Arabic	hill, mountain
Gt	Great		
I.	Island, Isle		
	Ilha	Portuguese	island
	Islas	Spanish	island
Is	Islands, Isles		
	Islas	Spanish	islands
Kep.	Kepulauan	Indonesian	islands
Khr.	Khrebet	Russian	mountain range

L.	Lake		
	Loch	(Scotland)	lake
	Lough	(Ireland)	lake
	Lac	French	lake
	Lago	Portuguese, Spanish	lake
M.	Mys	Russian	cape, point
Mt	Mount		
	Mont	French	hill, mountain
Mt.	Mountain		
Mte	Monte	Portuguese, Spanish	hill, mountain
Mts	Mountains		
	Monts	French	hills, mountains
N.	North, Northern		
O.	Ostrov	Russian	island
Pk	Puncak	Indonesian, Malay	hill, mountain
Pt	Point		
Pta	Punta	Italian, Spanish	cape, point
R.	River		
	Rio	Portuguese	river
	Río	Spanish	river
	Rivière	French	river

Ra.	Range		mountain range
S.	South, Southern		
	Salar, Salina,		
	Salinas	Spanish	salt pan, salt pans
Sa	Serra	Portuguese,	mountain range
	Sierra	Spanish	mountain range
Sd	Sound		
S.E.	Southeast,		
	Southeastern		
St	Saint		
	Sankt	German	Saint
	Sint	Dutch	Saint
Sta	Santa	Italian, Portuguese,	
		Spanish	Saint
Ste	Sainte	French	Saint
Str.	Strait		
Tk	Teluk	Indonesian, Malay	bay, gulf
Tg	Tanjong, Tanjung	Indonesian, Malay	cape, point
Vdkhr.	Vodokhranilishche	Russian	reservoir
W.	West, Western		strait
	Wadi, Wâdi, Wādī	Arabic	watercourse

Travel Commentary and World Heritage Sites

Alongside the mapping pages a travel commentary is provided for the major destination countries of the world. Wherever possible the commentary appears alongside the most relevant map but occasionally the commentary has been moved to an overlapping map page to allow greater detail in areas where numerous countries are shown together. Smaller countries and those without as many tourist arrivals do not have a commentary. A simple statistical overview is provided for these countries alongside the ocean maps on pages 235 to 240.

World Heritage Sites are shown in one of two ways.

Where a site is located away from a major urban area the symbol is shown and the full official name for the heritage site is given:

☆ New Lanark

Due to the fact that many urban areas have numerous sites, whenever there is a site located in an urban area the symbol is shown, but the name of the specific site or sites is not:

Edinburgh ☆

Due to mapping scales, not every site is shown on each map, but every site can be located on at least one map, usually the largest scale map that it would appear on.

Land and Water Features

River		Dam/Barrage		
Impermanent river/Wadi		Oasis		
Canal		Lake		
Flood dyke		Salt lake/Lagoon		
Coral reef		Dry salt lake/Salt pan		
Escarpment		Impermanent lake		
1234 Summit Height in metres		Impermanent salt lake		
123 Pass Height in metres		Marsh		
1234 Volcano Height in metres		Sandy desert/Dunes		
123 Ocean deep Depth in metres		Rocky desert		
Waterfall		Lava field		

Transport

Motorway Shown on large-scale maps only	
Main road	
Other road	
Track	
Road tunnel	
Main railway	
Other railway	
Railway tunnel	
Main airport	
Regional airport	

Cities and Towns

Population	National Capital	Administrative Capital Shown for selected countries only	Other City or Town
over 10 million	Tōkyō ▣	Karachi ◉	New York ◉
5 million to 10 million	Santiago ▣	Tianjin ◉	Philadelphia ◉
1 million to 5 million	Damascus ▣	Douala ◉	Barranquilla ◉
500 000 to 1 million	Bangui ▣	Bulawayo ◎	El Paso ◎
100 000 to 500 000	Wellington ▫	Mansa ○	Mobile ○
50 000 to 100 000	Port of Spain ▫	Lubango ○	Zaraza ○
10 000 to 50 000	Malabo ▫	Chinhoyi ○	El Tigre ○
under 10 000	Roseau ▫	Ati ○	Soledad ○

Boundaries

International boundary	
Disputed international boundary/ alignment unconfirmed	
Ceasefire line	
Administrative boundary	

Styles of Lettering

Cities and towns are explained above

Country	**FRANCE**
Overseas Territory/Dependency	**Guadeloupe**
Disputed Territory	AKSAI CHIN
Administrative name Shown for selected countries only	SCOTLAND
Area name	PATAGONIA

Island	*Gran Canaria*
Lake	*Lake Erie*
Mountain	*Mont Blanc*
River	*Thames*
Region	*LAPPLAND*

Miscellaneous Symbols

National park	
Reserve	
Ancient wall	
Site of specific interest	
Built-up area	

World Physical

The shapes of the continents and oceans have evolved over millions of years. Movement of the tectonic plates which make up the Earth's crust has created some of the best known land features. From the highest point Mount Everest to the deepest in the Mariana Trench is a height of almost 20 000 m /over 65 000 ft. Earthquakes, volcanoes, erosion, climatic variations and man's intervention all continue to affect the Earth's landscapes. Different landscapes reflect great variations in climate from deserts such as the Sahara, to the frozen ice cap of Antarctica.

Facts

- The Pacific Ocean is larger than the continents' land areas combined.

- The average height of the Earth's land surface is 840 m (2755 ft) above sea level and 52 per cent of the land is below 500 m (1640 ft). Approximately 10 per cent of the surface is permanently covered by ice.

- The Ural Mountains define part of the boundary between Europe and Asia.

- The collision of two tectonic plates – the Indo-Australia and the Eurasian Plates – formed the Himalaya mountains. The mountains are still rising at a rate of approximately 5 mm (0.2 inch) a year.

The Great Barrier Reef stretches for 2600 km (1616 miles) over an area of approximately 344 400 sq km (132 974 sq miles). The reef is located off the eastern coast of Queensland, Australia and can be seen from space.

The Kamchatka Peninsula in northeastern Asia is a mountainous landscape with numerous active volcanoes.

High sand dunes, sculpted by the wind, dwarf a desert oasis in the Sahara.

The flat featureless Great Plains of North America stretch from Saskatchewan, Canada in the north to Texas, USA in the south.

1 : 90 000 000

Physical Extremes

EARTH'S DIMENSIONS		HIGHEST MOUNTAINS	metres	feet
Mass	5.974 x 10²¹ tonnes	Mt Everest, China/Nepal	8 848	29 028
Volume	1 083 207 x 10⁶ cu km / 259 911 x 10⁶ cu miles	K2, China/Pakistan	8 611	28 251
Total area	509 450 000 sq km / 196 699 000 sq miles	Kangchenjunga, India/Nepal	8 586	28 169
Land area	149 450 000 sq km / 57 703 000 sq miles	Lhotse, China/Nepal	8 516	27 939
Water area	360 000 000 sq km / 138 996 000 sq miles	Makalu, China/Nepal	8 463	27 765
Water volume	1 389 500 x 10³ cu km / 333 405 x 10³ cu miles	Cho Oyu, China/Nepal	8 201	26 906
Equatorial diameter	12 756 km / 7 927 miles	Dhaulagiri, Nepal	8 167	26 794
Polar diameter	12 714 km / 7 901 miles	Manaslu, Nepal	8 163	26 781
Equatorial circumference	40 075 km / 24 903 miles	Nanga Parbat, Pakistan	8 126	26 660
Meridional circumference	40 008 km / 24 861 miles	Annapurna I, Nepal	8 091	26 545

Winkel Tripel Projection

LONGEST RIVERS	km	miles	LARGEST ISLANDS	sq km	sq miles	LARGEST LAKES	sq km	sq miles	OCEANS AND SEAS	Area sq km	Area sq miles	Deepest point metres	Deepest point feet
Nile, Africa	6 695	4 160	**Greenland**, North America	2 175 600	839 999	**Caspian Sea**, Asia/Europe	371 000	143 243	Pacific Ocean	166 241 000	64 186 000	10 920	35 826
Amazon, South America	6 516	4 049	**New Guinea**, Oceania	808 510	312 166	**Lake Superior**, North America	82 100	31 699	Atlantic Ocean	86 557 000	33 420 000	8 605	28 231
Yangtze, Asia	6 380	3 965	**Borneo**, Asia	745 561	287 861	**Lake Victoria**, Africa	68 870	26 591	Indian Ocean	73 427 000	28 350 000	7 125	23 376
Mississippi-Missouri, North America	5 969	3 709	**Madagascar**, Africa	587 040	266 656	**Lake Huron**, North America	59 600	23 012	Arctic Ocean	9 485 000	3 662 000	5 450	17 880
Ob'-Irtysh, Asia	5 568	3 460	**Baffin Island**, North America	507 451	195 927	**Lake Michigan**, North America	57 800	22 317	South China Sea	2 590 000	1 000 000	5 514	18 090
Yenisey-Angara-Selenga, Asia	5 550	3 449	**Sumatra**, Asia	473 606	182 859	**Lake Tanganyika**, Africa	32 600	12 587	Caribbean Sea	2 512 000	970 000	7 680	25 197
Yellow, Asia	5 464	3 395	**Honshū**, Asia	227 414	87 805	**Great Bear Lake**, North America	31 328	12 096	Mediterranean Sea	2 510 000	969 000	5 121	16 801
Congo, Africa	4 667	2 900	**Great Britain**, Europe	218 476	84 354	**Lake Baikal**, Asia	30 500	11 776	Bering Sea	2 261 000	873 000	4 150	13 615
Río de la Plata-Paraná, South America	4 500	2 796	**Victoria Island**, North America	217 291	83 896	**Lake Nyasa**, Africa	29 500	11 390	Bay of Bengal	2 172 000	839 000	4 500	14 764
Irtysh, Asia	4 440	2 759	**Ellesmere Island**, North America	196 236	75 767	**Great Slave Lake**, North America	28 568	11 030	Gulf of Mexico	1 544 000	596 000	3 504	11 496

World Political

The present picture of the political world is the result of a long history of exploration, colonialism, conflict and negotiation. In 1950 there were eighty-two independent countries. Since then there has been a significant trend away from colonial influences and although many dependent territories still exist there are now 195 independent countries. The newest country is Kosovo which gained independence from Serbia in February 2008. The shapes of countries reflect a combination of natural features, such as mountain ranges, and political agreements. There are still areas of the world where boundaries are disputed or only temporarily settled as ceasefire lines.

Facts

- The break up of the Soviet Union (or the U.S.S.R. – Union of Soviet Socialist Republics) in 1991 created fifteen new countries including the Russian Federation.

- The Maldives in the Indian Ocean consist of approximately 1200 low-lying islands, all under 2 m (6.5 ft) in height.

- The Commonwealth, first defined in 1926, has evolved from communities within the British Empire, to a free association of fifty-three member countries.

- Both China and the Russian Federation have borders with fourteen different countries.

The United Nations

The name "United Nations" was coined by United States President Franklin D. Roosevelt, and was first used in the "Declaration by United Nations" of 1 January 1942. The United Nations (UN) officially came into existence on 24 October 1945, when the United Nations Charter was ratified by China, France, the Soviet Union, the United Kingdom, the United States and a majority of other signatories. It was a successor to the League of Nations which had been unsuccessful in preventing the Second World War.

All *de facto* independent countries of the world, except Taiwan and Vatican City, are members – 192 in total. Kosovo is also not a member. The principal headquarters of the UN are in New York but other major agencies of the Organization are found in Geneva, The Hague, Vienna and other locations.

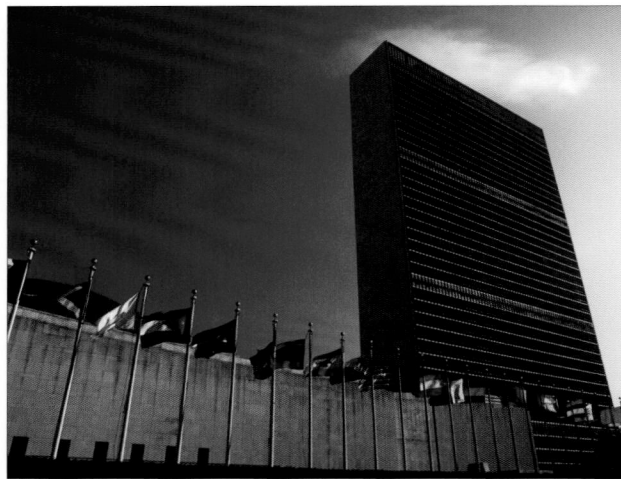

The United Nations building, New York, USA.

Time Comparisons

Time varies around the world due to the Earth's rotation causing different parts of the world to be in light or darkness at any one time. To account for this, the world is divided into twenty-four Standard Time Zones based on 15° intervals of longitude.
The table below gives examples of times observed at different parts of the world when it is 12 noon in the zone at the Greenwich Meridian (0° longitude). Daylight Saving Time, normally one hour ahead of local Standard Time, observed by certain countries for parts of the year, is not considered.

1:90 000 000

Winkel Tripel Projection

01:00	02:00	03:00	04:00	05:00	06:00	07:00	08:00	09:00
Samoa	Cook Islands	Anchorage	Vancouver	Edmonton	Winnipeg	Ottawa	Puerto Rico	Nuuk
American Samoa	Hawai'ian Islands		Seattle	Denver	Chicago	Toronto	Manaus	Recife
	Society Islands		San Francisco		Dallas	New York	La Paz	Brasília
	Tahiti		Los Angeles		Houston	Philadelphia	Sucre	Rio de Janeiro
			Pitcairn Islands		Monterrey	Washington D.C.	Asunción	São Paulo
					Mexico City	Havana		Montevideo
					San Salvador	Bogotá		Buenos Aires
					San José	Quito		
					Easter Island	Lima		

ap Abbreviations

10:00	11:00	12:00	13:00	14:00	15:00	16:00	17:00	18:00	19:00	20:00	21:00	22:00	23:00	00:00
uth Georgia and th Sandwich Islands	Azores Cape Verde	Reykjavik Dublin London Rabat Nouakchott Dakar Freetown Accra Lomé	Oslo Berlin Paris Madrid Rome Algiers Abuja Kinshasa Luanda	Helsinki Kiev Ankara Jerusalem Cairo Kigali Harare Pretoria Cape Town	St Petersburg Moscow Baghdād Qatar Riyadh Addis Ababa Mogadishu Dodoma Antananarivo	T'bilisi Yerevan Baku Abu Dhabi Muscat Seychelles Mauritius	Yekaterinburg Aşgabat Bishkek Tashkent Islamabad Karachi	Omsk Astana Bhutan Dhaka	Ha Nôi Vientiane Bangkok Phnom Penh Ho Chi Minh City Jakarta	Ulan Bator Beijing Hong Kong Manila Kuala Lumpur Singapore Perth	P'yŏngyang Seoul Tōkyō Ōsaka Palau	Port Moresby Brisbane Sydney Canberra Melbourne	Magadan Solomon Islands Vanuatu New Caledonia	Marshall Islands Tuvalu Fiji Auckland Wellington

Oceania Physical

The map highlights the three major island groupings traditionally used to categorise the enormously extensive Pacific island chains and their people: Micronesia ('small islands'), in the northwest, covering chiefly the North Mariana, Marshall and Caroline Islands; Melanesia ('black islands'), in the middle, mainly consisting of the Solomon Islands and Papua New Guinea; and Polynesia ('many islands'), encompassing all the rest across much of the Pacific. The Great Dividing Range, running down the eastern side of Australia, is prominent, as is the mountainous ridge forming the backbone of New Guinea. New Guinea in our definition is shared between Oceania and Asia.

Facts

- Tasmania, and the Tasman Sea to the east of it, are named after Abel Tasman, a 17th century Dutch explorer. Tasmania was originally named Van Diemen's Land (by Tasman himself). The Cook Islands, in the middle of Polynesia, are named after the 18th century British sea captain, James Cook.

- It has been proved by genetic research that the Pacific islands were originally populated over hundreds of years by adventurous seafarers from the Asian side, although the Norwegian Thor Heyerdahl's 'Kon-Tiki' expedition of the 1950s had strongly suggested that the people came from the Americas.

- Pitcairn Island, in the far east of Polynesia, was uninhabited until it was occupied by mutineers from the 18th century British ship 'Bounty'. The present-day inhabitants are descended from them.

HIGHEST MOUNTAINS	m	ft
Puncak Jaya, Indonesia	5 030	16 502
Puncak Trikora, Indonesia	4 730	15 518
Puncak Mandala, Indonesia	4 700	15 420
Puncak Yamin, Indonesia	4 595	15 075
Mt Wilhelm, Papua New Guinea	4 509	14 793
Mt Kubor, Papua New Guinea	4 359	14 301

LARGEST ISLANDS	sq km	sq miles
New Guinea	808 510	312 167
South Island, New Zealand	151 215	58 384
North Island, New Zealand	115 777	44 701
Tasmania	67 800	26 178

LONGEST RIVERS	km	miles
Murray-Darling	3 750	2 330
Darling	2 739	1 702
Murray	2 589	1 609
Murrumbidgee	1 690	1 050
Lachlan	1 480	920
Macquarie	950	590

LARGEST LAKES	sq km	sq miles
Lake Eyre	0–8 900	0–3 436
Lake Torrens	0–5 780	0–2 232

Orthographic Projection

1:32 000 000

MILES 0   400   800   1200

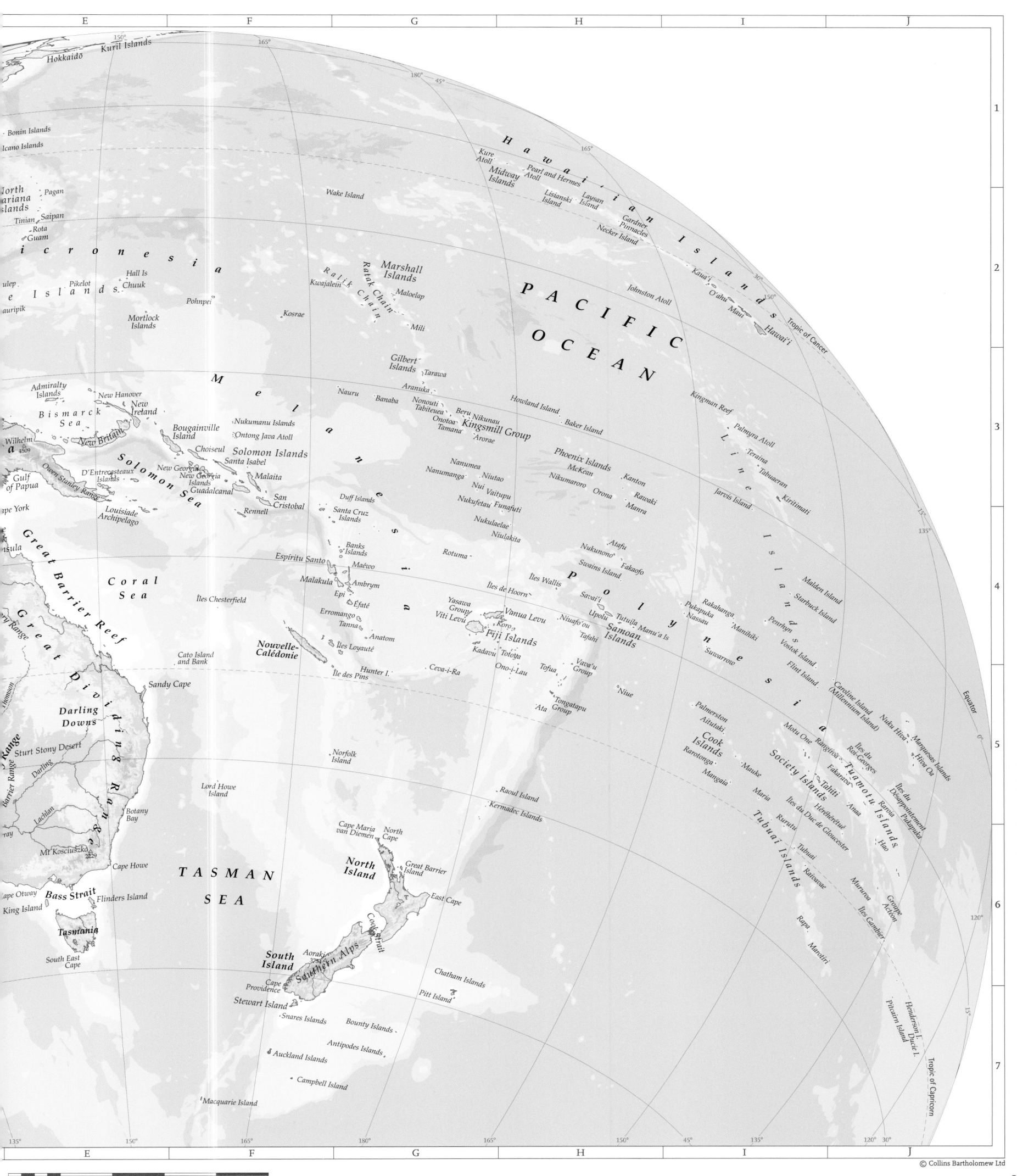

E   F   G   H   I   J

Hokkaidō
Kuril Islands

Bonin Islands

Icano Islands

North
Mariana
Islands
Pagan
Saipan
Tinian
Rota
Guam

icronesia

Hall Is
Chuuk
e Islands
ulep
Pikelot
auripik
Pohnpei
Mortlock
Islands
Kosrae

PACIFIC

OCEAN

Wake Island

Hawaiian Islands

Kure
Atoll
Midway
Islands
Pearl and Hermes
Atoll
Lisianski
Island
Laysan
Island
Gardner
Pinnacles
Necker Island

Johnston Atoll

Kaua'i
O'ahu
Maui
Hawai'i
Tropic of Cancer

Marshall
Islands
Ralik Chain
Ratak Chain
Kwajalein
Maloelap
Mili

Gilbert
Islands
Tarawa

Nauru
Banaba
Aranuka
Nonouti
Tabiteuea
Beru Nikunau
Onotoa
Tamana
Arorae
Kingsmill Group

Howland Island
Baker Island

Kingman Reef

Palmyra Atoll

Teraina
Tabuaeran

Line
Islands

Melanesia

Admiralty
Islands
New Hanover
New
Ireland
Bismarck
Sea
Wilhelm
4509
New Britain
Bougainville
Island
Nukumanu Islands
Ontong Java Atoll
Choiseul
Santa Isabel
Solomon Islands
New Georgia
Islands
Guadalcanal
Malaita
San
Cristobal
Rennell

Gulf
of Papua
Owen Stanley Range
D'Entrecasteaux
Islands
Solomon Sea

ape York

Louisiade
Archipelago

Duff Islands
Santa Cruz
Islands

Nanumea
Nanumanga
Niutao
Nui Vaitupu
Nukufetau Funafuti

Nukulaelae
Niulakita

Phoenix Islands
McKean
Nikumaroro Orona
Kanton
Rawaki
Manra

Jarvis Island

Nukunono
Atafu
Fakaofo
Swains Island

Malden Island
Starbuck Island

Coral
Sea

Îles Chesterfield

Banks
Islands
Espíritu Santo
Maéwo
Malakula
Ambrym
Epi
Rotuma

Îles de Hoorn
Savai'i
Upolu
Samoan
Islands
Tutuila Manu'a Is
Niuafo'ou
Tafahi

Pukapuka
Nassau

Vostok Island
Flint Island

Rakahanga
Manihiki
Penrhyn

ry Range
Great Barrier Reef
Great Dividing Range

Cato Island
and Bank
Nouvelle-
Calédonie
Erromango
Tanna
Éfaté
Anatom
Îles Loyauté
Hunter I.
Île des Pins

Yasawa
Group
Viti Levu
Koro
Vanua Levu
Fiji Islands
Kadavu
Totoya
Ono-i-Lau
Ceva-i-Ra

Tofua
Vava'u
Group

Suwarrow

Palmerston
Aitutaki
Cook
Islands
Rarotonga
Mangaia

Caroline Island
Millennium Island

Niku Hiva

Marquesas Islands
Hiva Oa

Sandy Cape

Darling
Downs
Sturt Stony Desert
Range

Norfolk
Island

Niue

Ata Group
Tongatapu

Maria
Mauke
Society Islands
Tahiti
Hérēhérētué
Anaa
Îles du Duc de Gloucester

Motu One
Rangiroa
Îles du
Roi Georges
Makatea
Fakarava
Rurutu
Tubuai
Raivavae

Tuamotu Islands

Îles du
Désappointement
Pinaki
Hao

Kosciuszko
2229
Cape Howe

Lord Howe
Island

Raoul Island
Kermadec Islands

Tubuai Islands

Raiatea
Maruroa
Rapa
Marotiri

Groupe
Acteon
Îles Gambier

ape Otway
Bass Strait
King Island
Flinders Island

TASMAN

SEA

Cape Maria
van Diemen
North
Cape
North Island
Great Barrier
Island
East Cape

Tasmania

South East
Cape

Aoraki
3754
Southern Alps
South
Island
Cape
Providence
Stewart Island
Snares Islands

Cook Strait

Chatham Islands

Pitt Island

Hendersõn I.
Ducie I.
Pitcairn Island
Tropic of Capricorn

Bounty Islands

Antipodes Islands

Auckland Islands

Campbell Island

Macquarie Island

135°   150°   165°   180°   165°   150°   45°   135°   120°   30°

E   F   G   H   I   J

0   400   800   1200   1600   2000 KILOMETRES

Oceania Political

Oceania is defined here as covering Australia, New Zealand and all the independent nations of the Pacific Ocean, along with various islands in the southwestern Pacific which remain as dependent territories. We also count the whole of Papua New Guinea as being within Oceania, following a common convention – although this does result in dividing the large island of New Guinea arbitrarily into two along the political boundary. Such definitions are not regarded by geographers as hard and fast, however. The political boundaries shown on this map are intended to clarify the physical coverage of island countries and dependencies rather than actually defining strict territorial limits, which are very much more complex and sometimes as yet unsettled.

Facts

- The former UN Trust Territory of the Pacific Islands, administered by the USA, was divided during the 1980s to form the independent nations of Micronesia, the Marshall Islands, and Palau (see p.131) – plus Guam and the Northern Mariana Islands, which remain as US dependencies.

- Several small uninhabited islands and atolls scattered across the Pacific are also under US control: those shown on this map are Wake, Howland, Baker, Jarvis and Palmyra. Hawaii has been a state of the USA since the late 1950s.

- Kiribati (pronounced 'Kiribass') was formerly known as the Gilbert Islands. (The name Kiribati is a local phonetic variation on 'Gilbert'). Tuvalu used to be a UK dependency known as the Ellice Islands. Vanuatu was once a UK/French territory, the New Hebrides.

LARGEST COUNTRIES	Area	
	sq km	sq miles
Australia	7 692 024	2 969 907
Papua New Guinea	462 840	178 704
New Zealand	270 534	104 454
Solomon Islands	28 370	10 954
Fiji	18 330	7 077
Vanuatu	12 190	4 707
Samoa	2 831	1 093
Tonga	748	289
Kiribati	717	277
Federated States of Micronesia	701	271

MOST POPULATED COUNTRIES	Population
Australia	20 743 000
Papua New Guinea	6 331 000
New Zealand	4 179 000
Fiji	839 000
Solomon Islands	496 000
Vanuatu	226 000
Samoa	187 000
Federated States of Micronesia	111 000
Tonga	100 000
Kiribati	95 000

CAPITALS		
Largest population	**Canberra**, Australia	378 000
Smallest population	**Kingston**, Norfolk Island	32
Most northerly	**Delap-Uliga-Djarrit**, Marshall Islands	7° 07' N
Most southerly	**Wellington**, New Zealand	41° 18' S
Highest	**Canberra**, Australia	581 m/1906 ft

Orthographic Projection

1 : 32 000 000

MILES 0   400   800   1200

© Collins Bartholomew Ltd

Australia and Southwest Pacific

PACIFIC ISLAND NATIONS

A warm tropical climate all year round, over 25 000 islands, and the lure of clear blue waters and white sandy beaches fringed with palm trees, means that the south Pacific is high on the wish list of destinations for people seeking a tropical island experience.

Pacific island travel packages feature the main destinations of Fiji, Samoa, Tonga, Vanuatu and the Cook Islands, promoting them as relaxing holiday destinations or romantic getaways in a truly exotic location. The islands are a tantalizing mix of forest-covered mountains and low-lying coral reef atolls with unlimited potential for customised island-hopping itineraries. Against this background of paradise there are some environmental threats. Some low-lying islands are gradually being submerged by the rising water levels of the Pacific Ocean and the Ring of Fire arcs across the region so active volcanoes and earthquakes are common.

The area covers an incredible diversity of ethnic cultures in a mix of independent nation states and overseas territories. Throughout the whole region there are strong musical and dance traditions, and the traveller can experience varied and colourful displays of movement and song.

Warm seas and turquoise lagoons mean that water sports feature strongly in many island holidays. With spectacular underwater scenery and shipwrecks to explore, the possibilities for scuba diving are particularly extensive and almost every resort has its own dive operator.

FIJI Capital: Suva
Area: 18 330 km²/7 077 miles² Population: 839 000
Languages: English, Fijian, Hindi Religions: Christian, Hindu, Sunni Muslim Currency: Fiji dollar

Originally an aircraft refuelling stop on the Sydney to Honolulu route, Fiji is now a booming tourist destination in its own right.

One attraction to visitors is the 'Bula' welcome which shows the renowned hospitality of the nation. A mix of indigenous customs, together with Indian, Chinese and European traditions, has created a colourful mosaic of culture immediately apparent in the food, music and dance. The international airport is at Nadi, on the main island of Viti Levu. Ferries also leave Nadi for the Mamanuca Group, heralded as Fiji's 'tourism gem'; there are day cruises and resort stays on these stunning small islands. Booking well ahead is recommended for a resort stay in the peak season between June and October. The Yasawa Group of islands is less accessible, except for Tavewa, which caters mainly for backpacking travellers.

PAUA NEW GUINEA Capital: Port Moresby
Area: 462 840 km²/178 704 miles²
Population: 6 331 000 Languages: English, Tok Pisin (Creole), local languages Religions: Protestant, Roman Catholic, traditional beliefs Currency: Kina

An undeveloped infrastructure and rugged terrain makes Papua New Guinea a challenging place to visit. For many travellers it is this authentic travel experience that is the main attraction. Mainland Papua New Guinea is the mountainous eastern half of the island of New Guinea. Offshore are numerous outlying islands. The forested volcanic landscape is a paradise for wildlife enthusiasts, with an amazing diversity of plants and animals. Many undiscovered species are thought to exist in the interior of the country. The culture is also astoundingly diverse, with hundreds of ethnic groups and over 850 indigenous languages. Many remote villages can only be reached by light aircraft or on foot, meaning that this is one of the world's least explored countries.

Lambert Azimuthal Equal Area Projection

1:20 000 000

MILES 0   200   400   600

NAURU
Banaba

POLYNESIA

Gilbert Islands

MELANESIA

SOLOMON ISLANDS

PAPUA NEW GUINEA

Bismarck Archipelago
Bismarck Sea
New Ireland
New Britain
Solomon Sea
Bougainville Island
Choiseul

TUVALU

Tokelau (N.Z.)

CORAL SEA

VANUATU

Espíritu Santo
Banks Islands
Port Vila
Efaté

SAMOA
Apia

Wallis and Futuna Islands (Fr.)

FIJI
Viti Levu
Suva
Vanua Levu

Coral Sea Islands Territory (Aust.)

Îles Chesterfield (France)

New Caledonia (France)
Nouvelle-Calédonie
Nouméa

TONGA
Nuku'alofa

Niue (N.Z.)

Tropic of Capricorn

QUEENSLAND

Brisbane
Gold Coast
Byron Bay
Ballina

NEW SOUTH WALES

Norfolk Island (Aust.)

PACIFIC

OCEAN

Lord Howe Island Group
Lord Howe Island (Aust.)

Newcastle
Sydney
Wollongong
Canberra
A.C.T.

VICTORIA
Melbourne

Raoul Island (N.Z.)

Kermadec Islands (N.Z.)

TASMAN SEA

Three Kings Is
Cape Maria van Diemen
North Cape

NORTH ISLAND

Auckland
Manukau
Hamilton
Bay of Plenty

TASMANIA
Hobart

New Plymouth
Mt Taranaki

Napier
Hastings
Hawke Bay

NEW ZEALAND

Wanganui
Palmerston North
Wellington
Lower Hutt

Chatham Islands (N.Z.)

Nelson
Blenheim

Christchurch
Banks Peninsula
Canterbury Bight

Southern Alps
Aoraki (Mt Cook)

SOUTH ISLAND

Pitt Island

Dunedin
Invercargill
Stewart Island

New Zealand Sub-Antarctic Islands
Snares Is

Bounty Islands

New Zealand Sub-Antarctic Islands
Auckland Is

200 400 600 800 1000 KILOMETRES

West Australia

AUSTRALIA Capital: **Canberra**
Area: **7 692 024 km²/2 969 907 miles²**
Population: **20 743 000** Languages: **English, Italian, Greek**
Religions: **Roman Catholic, Orthodox**
Currency: **Australian dollar**

Australia is promoted as a laid-back country, with a reputation for informality. It is large and varied, offering many renowned attractions as well as opportunities for action-packed outdoor adventures. Several cosmopolitan cities offer world-class cultural attractions in arts and sport.

Major international sporting events such as the 2000 Sydney Olympics and 2003 Rugby World Cup have attracted large numbers of visitors to Australia. Backpackers make up a large proportion of visitors, working holiday visas enabling some to extend their stay and explore the country to a greater extent.

Visitors come not only to see the iconic sites of Ayers Rock, the Sydney Opera House and the Great Barrier Reef, but also to experience the 'outback' with its Aboriginal culture and wildlife. Some animals and birds such as kangaroos, koalas, dingoes and kookaburras have come to symbolize Australia.

Aboriginal culture is one of the world's longest surviving cultures, dating back at least 50,000 years. As semi-nomadic hunters and gatherers the indigenous peoples based their way of life on a spiritual relationship with the land. Colonization by settlers introduced many problems and heralded a declining native population. Civil and land rights have now been restored, but few Aborigines follow a truly traditional lifestyle, and those that do, live in remote Reserve areas often requiring permits. For the tourist, this a culture that is therefore difficult to experience, although opportunities on offer include bushland walks with Aboriginal guides, demonstrations of ancient bush skills and visits to Aboriginal art sites.

Most of Australia is desert, with only the southwest and southeast having a temperate climate. Summer months (November to March) can get very hot. Winters (June to August) get colder and wetter the further south you go.

WESTERN AUSTRALIA

Western Australia is characterized by the huge desert areas of the Great Sandy Desert, Gibson Desert and western part of the Great Victoria Desert. It is a sparsely populated region, where travel across the remote arid regions of 'outback' is not difficult on the main roads, although distances are long. Driving the more isolated tracks requires more advance planning and the use of a reliable four-wheel drive vehicle. Travel in the remote areas of northern Australia is not advised in the wet season (November to April) when heavy rain can make roads impassable. Most international visitors either hire cars or book organised tours.

In the Northern Territory a major tourist site is Uluṟu (Ayers Rock), one of Australia's most recognised icons. The gorges and waterfalls of the Karijini National Park, and further north, the wild and beautiful landscapes of the Kimberley region are also becoming more popular with visitors. Travelling this region gives an experience not only of the natural wonder of the landscape but also of Aboriginal culture and the historic townships built by gold rush pioneers.

Perth is one of the most isolated metropolitan areas in the world, yet it is a growing city. To the north is a long stretch of safe sandy beaches known as the Sunset Coast.

Connecting Western Australia to South Australia is the longest straight railway line in the world, crossing the flat and arid Nullarbor Plain.

Lambert Azimuthal Equal Area Projection

1 : 8 000 000

MILES 0   100   200   300

WESTERN AUSTRALIA

SOUTH AUSTRALIA

Great Victoria Desert

Gibson Desert

Little Sandy Desert

Nullarbor Plain

Great Australian Bight

Hampton Tableland

Nullarbor National Park

Perth

Shark Bay

Tropic of Capricorn

Eyre Peninsula

0   100   200   300   400   500 KILOMETRES

East Australia

Eastern Australia

Stretching for over 2000 km (1249 miles) down the coast of eastern Australia is the Great Barrier Reef, the largest coral reef in the world and one of the country's greatest natural wonders. With over 3000 individual reef systems it has an amazingly prolific marine life, offering travel experiences ranging from exclusive tropical island retreats, 'live-aboard' scuba-diving and tours to see the magnitude of the reef from the air.

The main Barrier Reef coast towns and cities – Cairns, Townsville, Mackay and Rockhampton – are all good bases from which to explore the coastal region. Further south is Brisbane, Australia's third most popular city for international tourists, after Sydney and Melbourne.

The Great Dividing Range extends from the northern tip of Queensland down the length of the eastern coastline. It is an area of mountain ranges, plateaus and escarpments.

Inland, in the foothills of the MacDonnell Ranges, is Alice Springs where galleries showcase indigenous Australian art. East of Alice Springs are important cultural sites for Aboriginal people, several of which contain examples of rock art.

Further south, the Lake Eyre Basin is a vast, mainly flat and arid area of riverbeds straddling large parts of South Australia, the Northern Territory, Queensland and New South Wales. There are tours extending into some very remote destinations in this outback. Within the basin is Lake Eyre, the largest salt lake in Australia and the site of various land speed record attempts.

Enjoy a four-wheel drive beach ride on **Fraser Island**, Queensland, the largest sand island in the world

Lambert Azimuthal Equal Area Projection

1 : 8 000 000

MILES 0   100   200   300

Southeast Australia

SOUTHEAST AUSTRALIA

Southeast Australia is the most densely populated region of the country. The cities of Melbourne, Sydney and Canberra draw in visitors but surrounding these centres is a vast and accessible natural 'playground' for both the domestic city-dweller and the traveller.

Fishing, sailing, walking trails and winter sports are all available in the Snowy Mountains. A summer ascent of the gentle peak of Mt Kosciuszko, the highest mountain in Australia, is a very popular walk for both locals and visitors.

The most scenic route from Melbourne to Adelaide is the 250 km (155 miles) Great Ocean Road. It passes some magnificent cliffs and beaches, especially around Port Campbell.

MELBOURNE

On the shores of Port Philip Bay is Melbourne, Australia's most southerly city. The centre is neatly planned on a grid system with a mix of both ornate Victorian architecture and modern skyscrapers. Five out of Australia's six tallest buildings are found in Melbourne. Already widely regarded for shopping and dining, it is also enjoying growth as a popular destination for international conferences.

It is a lively city, leading the way for the country in culture and sport. The city was the birthplace of Australian film and cinema and is now the centre for contemporary Australian music. A year-round programme of festivals, exhibitions and performing arts means there is much on offer for the visitor.

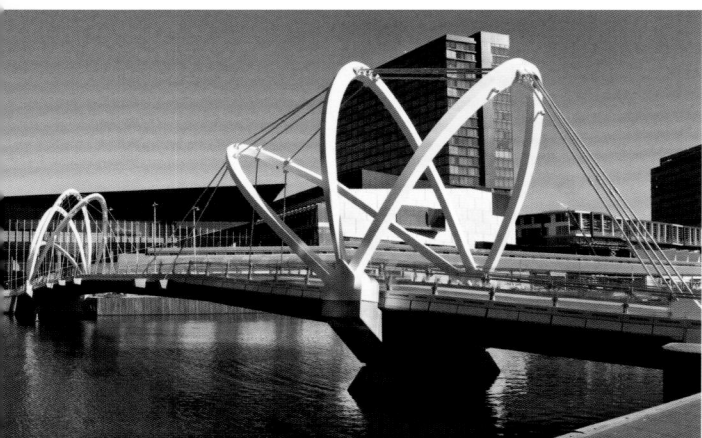

Footbridge at the Exhibition and Conference Centre, **Melbourne**

TASMANIA

There are regular ferry crossings from Melbourne across the Bass Strait to Tasmania, although flights from the mainland can sometime be the cheaper option. Once on the island, public transport is limited and the easiest way to travel is by car.

Tasmania is mountainous, with a landscape of lush forests and distinctive geological formations. The east coast is a land of long white beaches. The west encompasses the Tasmanian Wilderness World Heritage area, a region of mighty rivers, lakes and jagged peaks forming one of the last expanses of temperate wilderness in the world.

Many species of flora and fauna are unique to Tasmania, including several frog species and the marsupial Tasmanian Devil.

Lambert Azimuthal Equal Area Projection

1:5 000 000

MILES 0   50   100   150

QUEENSLAND

DARLING DOWNS

NEW SOUTH WALES

GREAT DIVIDING RANGE

New England Range

Liverpool Plains

Liverpool Range

Blue Mts

Macquarie Marshes

Riverina

VICTORIA

Brisbane
Gold Coast
Toowoomba
Newcastle
Sydney
Port Jackson
Botany Bay
Wollongong
Canberra
AUSTRALIAN CAPITAL TERRITORY
JERVIS BAY TERRITORY
Melbourne
Geelong
Frankston

TASMAN SEA

Bass Strait

Wilson's Promontory
Wilson's Promontory Nat. Park

King Island
Curtis Group
West Sister Island
East Sister Island

TASMANIA inset

Bass Strait

King Island
Flinders I.
Hunter Is
Cape Barren I.
Banks Strait
Western Tiers
Launceston
Ben Lomond Nat. Park
Hobart
Bruny Island
Macquarie Harbour
Franklin-Gordon Nat. Park
Cradle Mountain Lake St Clair Nat. Park
South West Nat. Park
Maatsuyker Group
South East Cape

TASMANIA
1:5 000 000

0 50 100 150 200 250 KILOMETRES

© Collins Bartholomew Ltd

New Zealand

NEW ZEALAND Capital: **Wellington**
Area: **270 534 km²/104 454 miles²**
Population: **4 179 000** Languages: **English, Maori**
Religions: **Protestant, Roman Catholic**
Currency: **New Zealand dollar**

A country of amazing natural beauty, New Zealand is marketed as a 'clean, green' place to visit. Already one of the world's favourite destinations, responsible ecotourism is now an increasing attraction for visitors.

North Island is famed for its geysers and hot-springs, especially around Rotorua which is also an area of deep-rooted Māori culture.

South Island is more mountainous with the Southern Alps running the entire length of the island. The highest peak is Mt Cook. Further south is Queenstown, site of the world's first commercial jet boating and bungee jumping activities, and still New Zealand's capital of adventure tourism. The area is promoted as an exhilarating year-round 'adrenaline destination'. Further south again and the fjord of Milford Sound is a place of internationally recognised beauty. Despite its remote location it is one of the country's most visited places.

New Zealand's dramatic and diverse landscape made it the fitting location for filming J.R.R. Tolkien's 'Lord of the Rings' trilogy. Film locations are spread over both islands and although some are inaccessible, there are guided tours of many others.

The waters off New Zealand host a wealth of marine life. Kaikoura, on South Island, is one of the most accessible places in the world to see humpback and sperm whales in an award-winning whale watching experience.

Antarctica

ANTARCTICA

This is the coldest, driest and windiest continent and considered a desert, with annual precipitation of only 200 mm (8 inches) along the coast with less inland. The coldest recorded natural temperature on Earth was −89.2 °C (−128.6 °F) at the Russian Vostok Station in 1983. The ice averages 1.6 kms (1 mile) in thickness.

There are no permanent settlements, although up to 5000 people live at the various research stations. There is no overseeing government although forty-six countries have signed up to the 1959 Antarctic Treaty which does not allow military or mineral exploitation.

Some vegetation survives mainly around the coastal fringes, offshore islands and the western Antarctic peninsula which is warmer and wetter than elsewhere. Flora includes mosses, liverworts, lichens and fungi and only two species of flowering plants, Antarctic hair grass and pearlwort.

Penguins, seals and sea lions are year-round residents while albatross, petrels, fulmars, skuas and shearwaters are commonplace. The winters are too harsh for blue, humpback, minke and killer whales but they return to the rich Antarctic feeding grounds in the Spring.

'Expedition tourism' is increasing in popularity and focuses on specific scenic and wildlife locations, leaving the majority of the continent untouched. The industry is self-regulated by the International Association of Antarctica Tour Operators (IAATO).

Conic Equidistant Projection

1:5 000 000

Asia Physical

The map highlights the many major mountain ranges – in particular the Himalaya – and plateaus which make up much of Asia. These contrast with enormous low-lying plains, especially in the far north (Siberia) and on the Yellow Sea coast of China. The Ganges and Indus rivers on the Indian subcontinent also occupy extensive lowlands. Indonesia represents by far the most complex archipelago, although there are also many other large and important islands, most notably, Sri Lanka (formerly Ceylon), the Philippines, Taiwan, Japan, and the various island groups in the Arctic Ocean.

Facts

• The outline of Asia is characterised by a number of major peninsulas, including Arabia, the Indian subcontinent, Indo-China and its offshoot the Malay Peninsula, Korea, and the highly volcanic Kamchatka Peninsula.

• Ninety of the world's 100 highest mountains are in Asia. Many lie in the Himalayan kingdom of Nepal where the height of the land ranges from 60 m to 8848 m (200 ft to 29 999 ft).

• The Indonesian archipelago is made up of over 13 000 islands.

• The deepest lake in the world is Lake Baikal in the Russian Federation which is over 1600 m (5250 ft) deep.

• The Gobi Desert, one of the world's biggest areas of desert and semi-desert, occupies a large zone of northern China and Mongolia.

HIGHEST MOUNTAINS	m	ft
Mt Everest (Sagarmatha/ Qomolangma Feng), China/Nepal	8 848	29 028
K2 (Qogir Feng), China/Pakistan	8 611	28 251
Kangchenjunga, India/Nepal	8 586	28 169
Lhotse, China/Nepal	8 516	27 939
Makalu, China/Nepal	8 463	27 765
Cho Oyu, China/Nepal	8 201	26 906

LARGEST ISLANDS	sq km	sq miles
Borneo	745 561	287 861
Sumatra (Sumatera)	473 606	182 859
Honshū	227 414	87 805
Celebes (Sulawesi)	189 216	73 056
Java (Jawa)	132 188	51 038
Luzon	104 690	40 421

LONGEST RIVERS	km	miles
Yangtze (Chang Jiang)	6 380	3 965
Ob'-Irtysh	5 568	3 460
Yenisey-Angara-Selenga	5 550	3 449
Yellow (Huang He)	5 464	3 395
Irtysh	4 440	2 759
Mekong	4 425	2 750

LARGEST LAKES	sq km	sq miles
Caspian Sea	371 000	143 243
Lake Baikal (Ozero Baykal)	30 500	11 776
Lake Balkhash (Ozero Balkhash)	17 400	6 718
Aral Sea (Aral'skoye More)	17 158	6 625
Ysyk-Köl	6 200	2 394

Orthographic Projection

1 : 28 000 000

MILES 0   250   500   750   100

Asia Political

With approximately sixty per cent of the world's population, Asia is home to numerous cultures, people groups and lifestyles. It also has a great variety of physical regions which can be defined by the cultural, economic and political systems they support. The major regions are: the arid, oil-rich, mainly Islamic southwest; southern Asia, isolated from the rest of Asia by major mountain ranges; the Indian- and Chinese-influenced monsoon region of southeast Asia; the mainly Chinese-influenced industrialized areas of eastern Asia; and Soviet Asia, made up of most of the former Soviet Union.

Facts

- The line dividing Asia from Oceania is taken as the political boundary between Indonesia and Papua New Guinea. This results in the island of New Guinea being divided between the two continents.

- The break-up of the former Soviet Union in 1991 created two groups of countries in Asia: Kazakhstan, Uzbekistan, Turkmenistan, Tajikistan and Kyrgyzstan on the one hand and Georgia, Armenia and Azerbaijan on the other. This still left the Russian Federation as by far the largest country in the world.

- Cyprus, although now part of the European Union and having long-standing cultural links with Europe, is classed as being within Asia.

- Both China and the Russian Federation have borders with fourteen different countries.

LARGEST COUNTRIES	Area	
	sq km	sq miles
Russian Federation	17 075 400	6 592 849
China	9 584 492	3 700 593
India	3 064 898	1 183 364
Kazakhstan	2 717 300	1 049 155
Saudi Arabia	2 200 000	849 425
Indonesia	1 919 445	741 102
Iran	1 648 000	636 296
Mongolia	1 565 000	604 250
Pakistan	803 940	310 403
Turkey	779 452	300 948

MOST POPULATED COUNTRIES	Population
China	1 313 437 000
India	1 169 016 000
Indonesia	231 627 000
Pakistan	163 902 000
Bangladesh	158 665 000
Russian Federation	142 499 000
Japan	127 967 000
Philippines	87 960 000
Vietnam	87 375 000
Turkey	74 877 000

CAPITALS		
Largest population	**Tōkyō**, Japan	35 467 000
Smallest population	**Melekeok**, Palau	391
Most northerly	**Astana**, Kazakhstan	51° 10′ N
Most southerly	**Dili**, East Timor	8° 35′ S
Highest	**Thimphu**, Bhutan	2 423 m/ 7 949 ft

Orthographic Projection

1 : 28 000 000

MILES 0   250   500   750   100

© Collins Bartholomew Ltd

Northern Asia

RUSSIAN FEDERATION Capital: **Moscow (Moskva)**
Area: **17 075 400 km²/6 592 849 miles²**
Population: **142 499 000** Languages: **Russian, Tatar, Ukrainian,
local languages** Religions: **Russian Orthodox, Sunni Muslim,
Protestant** Currency: **Russian rouble**

The vast scale of the country means that intercity travel is usually
done by air or else by the Trans-Siberian railway which takes
eight days to complete the whole route from Moscow to
Vladivostok, crossing seven time zones.

The centre of Moscow has many sites of interest including Red
Square, the Kremlin and the iconic St Basil's Cathedral. On the
way to St Petersburg, visit Velikiy Novgorod, one of the oldest
cities in Russia with many ancient churches and restored
kremlin. St Petersburg has a more European feel than Moscow.
The Nevsky Prospekt is lined with elegant buildings and the
Hermitage museum has endless treasures to explore. The
Winter Palace is adjacent but the Summer Palace (Peterhof) is
on the outskirts and also has parklands to admire. Further east
are the ancient wooden churches of Kizhic on an island in Lake
Onega.

Volgograd was the site of a yearlong battle in the Second World
War. The Caucasus Mountains are popular for hiking, and skiing
in winter, with the Black Sea coastline known as the 'Russian
Riviera' north from Sochi. Heading up the Volga river is Kazan,
once a Tartar fortress. The Ural Mountains main centre is
Yekaterinburg, the site of the murders of Tsar Nicholas II and his
family. This rural border between Europe and Asia attracts
walkers, hikers and fishermen.

The Altai region of southern Siberia is a mixture of pine forests
and flower meadows in the spring, Tomsk being the most
attractive city in the region with wooden mansions and the
youthful outlook of an academic centre. Lake Baikal is the
world's deepest freshwater lake and is best approached from
Irkutsk.

Heading further east, Khabarovsk is a refreshing town after the
vast plains of the Siberian taiga. Vladivostok on the Pacific coast
is an impressive natural harbour.

World Heritage Sites numbered on the map:
RUSSIAN FEDERATION
1 Architectural Ensemble of the Trinity
  Sergius Lavra in Sergiev Posad (E4)
2 Cultural and Historic Ensemble
  of the Solovetsky Islands (E3)
3 White Monuments of Vladimir
  and Suzdal (E4)

169

Conic Equidistant Projection

1 : 21 000 000

MILES 0   200   400   600   800

134

Central and Southern Asia

 SAUDI ARABIA Capital: **Riyadh (Ar Riyāḏ)**
Area: **2 200 000 km²/849 425 miles²**
Population: **24 735 000** Languages: **Arabic**
Religions: **Sunni Muslim, Shi'a Muslim**
Currency: **Saudi Arabian riyal**

Saudi Arabia is gradually letting visitors into the country. Previously, only those on the hajj pilgrimage would be welcomed to visit Mecca and Medina. Riyadh is a modern city with little evidence of its old town. Jeddah is a more open, cosmopolitan city with a mixture of old merchants' houses, Ottoman buildings and shopping malls. The coastline offers watersports as well as good diving sites to the pristine coral reefs. To the north is the ancient Nabataean city of Madain Saleh, while to the south is Aṭ Ṭā'if, the summer capital, at the start of a dramatic escarpment heading down to the Yemen border. There are cable cars to appreciate the scenery, and a road which follows the ridge through the wild vegetation of 'Asīr Najrān, close to the border, was an ancient caravan stop and has traditional mud brick buildings and an impressive fort.

OMAN Capital: **Muscat (Masqaṭ)**
Area: **309 500 km²/119 499 miles²**
Population: **2 595 000** Languages: **Arabic, Baluchi, Indian languages** Religions: **Ibadhi Muslim, Sunni Muslim**
Currency: **Omani riyal**

Traditional Arabian values underpin the modern day Oman. Modernisation has been gradual with few high-rise buildings in the capital. Haggling is expected at the Muttrah Souk. Inland, the mountains can be explored from Nazwá, such as Jabal Shām which gives views into Wadi Ghul, a mini Grand Canyon. There are World Heritage sites at Bat with ancient burial mounds and Bahla which has a huge fort made of unbaked bricks. Ṣūr is where traditional dhow building continues and offers day trips to the Ras al-Jinz turtle reserve. The Dhofar region behind the lush coastal strip at Ṣalālah is where frankincense originates.

YEMEN Capital: **Ṣan'ā'**
Area: **527 968 km²/203 850 miles²**
Population: **22 389 000** Languages: **Arabic**
Religions: **Sunni Muslim, Shi'a Muslim** Currency: **Yemeni riyal**

Travel to some parts of Yemen is unsafe at present which is unfortunate because there are some spectacular sites to see. Firstly, the capital Ṣan'ā', which has beautifully decorated buildings, ancient craft markets and over 100 mosques. Not far away are the ancient fortifications of Kawkabān and the remnants of Ma'rib, allegedly home of the Queen of Sheba. Further east in the Wadi Hadramawt, Shibām is a pre-Islamic high-rise settlement. The ancient port of Aden, which lies in an extinct volcanic crater, is the starting point for trips to the island of Socotra with its unique flora and fauna.

IRAQ Capital: **Baghdād**
Area: **438 317 km²/169 235 miles²**
Population: **28 993 000** Languages: **Arabic, Kurdish, Turkmen**
Religions: **Shi'a Muslim, Sunni Muslim, Christian**
Currency: **Iraqi dinar**

Hopefully Iraq can slowly rebuild after the recent war but at present it is unwise to travel there. Since civilisation first developed here in the 6th millennium BC, there has been much unrest in the fertile lands of the Tigris and Euphrates rivers. From Nineveh, now Mosul, through Hatra and Ashur, the capital of the Assyrian Empire south to Samarra and Ctesiphon and on to Ur, there are some impressive archaeological sites but Babylon has undergone some unfortunate reconstruction work. Priceless treasures from these sites were taken from the museum in Baghdad. These important sites will encourage visitors back to this country in the future.

Albers Equal Area Conic Projection

1:20 000 000

MILES 0   200   400   600   800

Countries and regions:
RUSSIAN FEDERATION, MONGOLIA, KAZAKHSTAN, KYRGYZSTAN, TAJIKISTAN, AFGHANISTAN, PAKISTAN, INDIA, NEPAL, BHUTAN, BANGLADESH, MYANMAR (BURMA), CHINA, XINJIANG, TIBET, INNER MONGOLIA, THAILAND, LAOS, VIETNAM, CAMBODIA, MALAYSIA, PENINSULAR MALAYSIA, INDONESIA, SRI LANKA, MALDIVES

Physical features:
ALTAI MOUNTAINS, GOBI DESERT, TIEN SHAN, TARIM BASIN (Tarim Pendi), Taklimakan Desert (Taklimakan Shamo), KUNLUN SHAN, Altun Shan, Qilian Shan, Plateau of Tibet (Qingzang Gaoyuan), Tanggula Shan, HIMALAYA, KARAKORAM RANGE, Hindu Kush, Thar Desert, Deccan, Western Ghats, Eastern Ghats, Malabar Coast, Coromandel Coast, Qaidam Pendi, Junggar Pendi (Dzungarian Basin), Hoh Xil Shan, Gangdisê Shan, Nyainqêntanglha Shan, Hengduan Shan, Da Yunhe

Water bodies:
INDIAN OCEAN, BAY OF BENGAL, Andaman Sea, Gulf of Thailand, Strait of Malacca, Lake Balkhash, Lop Nur, Gulf of Mannar, Ten Degree Channel, Nine Degree Channel, Eight Degree Channel, Mouths of the Ganges, Mouths of the Indus, Mouths of the Irrawaddy, Mouths of the Godavari, Mouths of the Krishna, Rann of Kachchh, Gulf of Kachchh, G. of Khambhat

Major cities:
Delhi, New Delhi, Mumbai (Bombay), Kolkata (Calcutta), Chennai (Madras), Bangalore, Hyderabad, Karachi, Lahore, Islamabad, Kabul, Dhaka, Kathmandu, Thimphu, Colombo, Sri Jayewardenepura Kotte, Beijing (Peking), Tianjin, Shanghai, Ulan Bator (Ulaanbaatar), Bangkok (Krung Thep), Ho Chi Minh City, Phnom Penh, Ha Noi, Rangoon (Yangon), Nay Pyi Taw, Kuala Lumpur, Singapore, Astana, Almaty, Bishkek, Tashkent, Dushanbe, Male

Eastern Mediterranean and The Caucasus

ARMENIA Capital: Yerevan (Erevan)
Area: 29 800 km²/11 506 miles²
Population: 3 002 000 Languages: Armenian, Azeri
Religions: Armenian Orthodox Currency: Dram

Beautiful natural scenery of mountains, verdant forests and lakes create a stunning backdrop for the many churches and monasteries scattered across Armenia. Haghpat and Sanahin monasteries are approached through a gorge in Debed. The capital Yerevan, has a thriving café culture and also houses ancient manuscripts in the National Gallery. The World Heritage site of Echmiadzin is the religious centre of the country. Although landlocked, there are beaches on the shores of Lake Sevan, famed for its pure waters. To the south, Jermuk, has hot mineral water springs.

AZERBAIJAN Capital: Baku
Area: 86 600 km²/33 436 miles² Population: 8 467 000
Languages: Azeri, Armenian, Russian, Lezgian
Religions: Shi'a Muslim, Sunni Muslim, Russian and
Armenian Orthodox Currency: Azerbaijani manat

This is an oil-rich country with a fast-developing capital. Its situation made it an important stopping off point on the Silk Road. Baku has its old walled city, İçeri Şeher surrounded by growing skyscrapers. Not far is Yanar Dag which produces a nonstop wall of flames due to natural gas underground. South is Qobustan which has strange mud volcanoes and caves with thousands of petroglyphs. Visitors are rare outside the capital but Şäki is a pretty town in the mountains and Xınalıq is a hill village which has kept its unique language and traditions. The enclave of Nagorno-Karabakh is disputed with Armenia.

GEORGIA Capital: T'bilisi
Area: 69 700 km²/26 911 miles² Population: 4 395 000
Languages: Georgian, Russian, Armenian, Azeri, Ossetian, Abkhaz
Religions: Georgian Orthodox, Russian Orthodox, Sunni Muslim
Currency: Lari

Georgia is steeped in history and is still battling with long disputes in Abkhazia and South Ossetia. However because of the stunning scenery, visitor numbers are growing. T'bilisi has some beautiful frescoed churches such as the fifth-century Sioni Cathedral. The best views can be seen from the Narikala Fortress. The Georgian Military Highway which heads to Vladikavkaz across the border, goes through the foothills of the Caucasus, ideal for winter sports, to the mountain town of Qazbegi. In contrast, Bat'umi, on the Black Sea has a semi-tropical feel and east of T'bilisi is the wine growing region.

TURKEY Capital: Ankara
Area: 779 452 km²/300 948 miles²
Population: 74 877 000 Languages: Turkish, Kurdish
Religions: Sunni Muslim, Shi'a Muslim Currency: Lira

Turkey is truly where east meets west. Although Istanbul is not the capital, it receives the most attention, with buildings such as the Blue Mosque, Topkapi Palace and the Grand Bazaar. It also is developing a thriving nightlife. Safranbolu, to the east, is a restored Ottoman town. More recent monuments are at Gallipoli which is strewn with battle sites. Further south are the classical cities of Ephesus and Pergamom (Bergama) and the ancient site of Troy. Inland are the mineral waters of Pamukkale creating a unique landscape. Walkers can tackle the Lycian Way from Fethiye to Antalya. Further east is the strange landscape of Cappadocia with its wind- and water-eroded rock formations.

1:7 000 000

© Collins Bartholomew Ltd

0 50 100 150 200 250 300 350 KILOMETRES

The Middle East

CYPRUS Capital: Nicosia (Lefkosia)
Area: 9 251 km²/3 572 miles²
Population: 855 000 Languages: Greek, Turkish, English
Religions: Greek Orthodox, Sunni Muslim Currency: Euro

Nicosia is still a divided capital city but access from the southern Greek to northern Turkish part of the island is now possible. The island is a mix of Byzantine churches, Crusader castles, Roman mosaics and beach resorts. There are busy areas but escape to the Troödos Mountains for cooler temperatures, hilltop villages and Byzantine churches with beautiful frescoes. Evidence of Roman villas can be found amongst the all-year destination of Paphos. Kourion has a Greco-Roman theatre overlooking the sea and still stages plays. The wild Akamas peninsula is home to the protected loggerhead turtles during their breeding season.

ISRAEL Capital: Jerusalem (Yerushalayim) (El Quds)
De facto capital. Disputed.
Area: 20 770 km²/8 019 miles² Population: 6 928 000
Languages: Hebrew, Arabic Religions: Jewish, Sunni Muslim, Christian, Druze Currency: Shekel

Israel is mixture of deserts, beaches, archaeology and spirituality. Jerusalem is the uneasy centre of the three main monotheistic faiths. Enter the old city through the Jaffa Gate, walk the Via Dolorosa, see the Western Wall and the Dome of the Rock. Relax in Tel Aviv, a vibrant coastal city. 'Akko is an atmospheric Crusader city further north. Inland is the picturesque Sea of Galilee, surrounded by Christian sites. View the world's lowest point, the Dead Sea, from Masada. Cross the Negev Desert stopping at Mitzpe Ramon to reach Eilat, a resort famed for its dive sites.

LEBANON Capital: Beirut (Beyrouth)
Area: 10 452 km²/4 036 miles² Population: 4 099 000
Languages: Arabic, Armenian, French Religions: Shi'a Muslim, Sunni Muslim, Christian Currency: Lebanese pound

Home to Byblos, possibly the oldest town in the world, and other ancient sites such as the Roman temple at Baalbek and hippodrome at Tyre. Contrast with the capital Beirut. With a backdrop of mountains, the Corniche seafront is being redeveloped. Caution is required if travelling to the south of the country.

JORDAN Capital: 'Ammān
Area: 89 206 km²/34 443 miles²
Population: 5 924 000 Languages: Arabic Religions: Sunni Muslim, Christian Currency: Jordanian dinar

Jordan is a desert kingdom steeped in history. Petra is the main attraction; a hidden rock-hewn city which glows pink in sun. Jerash is one of the best-preserved Roman cities and Kerak is the dramatic setting for a Crusader castle. From the heights of Mount Nebo, survey Moses' 'promised land', and float in the salty waters of the Dead Sea. Madaba has some exceptional mosaics. Explore the wind-blown rock formations in the desert landscape of Wadi Rum on the way to Jordan's only coastal resort of Aqaba, a popular dive site on the Red Sea.

SYRIA Capital: Damascus (Dimashq)
Area: 185 180 km²/71 498 miles²
Population: 19 929 000 Languages: Arabic, Kurdish, Armenian
Religions: Sunni Muslim, Shi'a Muslim, Christian
Currency: Syrian pound

Syria is a modern country becoming more outward-looking but is full of cultural riches from different civilisations. Damascus is an ancient city with an old centre of narrow alleyways around the Umayyad Mosque which started life as a Greek temple. Buṣrá ash Shām (Bosra) has an imposing citadel and well-preserved Roman theatre. Extensive Roman remains can be seen at Tadmur (Palmyra), set in a desert oasis. In the north Aleppo has an impressive citadel and the old city is being restored. From here visit the famous Crusader castle of Crac des Chevaliers, Apamea and the Dead Cities.

Conic Equidistant Projection

1:5 000 000

MILES 0   50   100   150   200

Central Asia

KAZAKHSTAN Capital: **Astana (Akmola)**
Area: **2 717 300 km²/1 049 155 miles²**
Population: **15 422 000** Languages: **Kazakh, Russian, Ukrainian, German, Uzbek, Tatar** Religions: **Sunni Muslim, Russian Orthodox, Protestant** Currency: **Tenge**

This huge country is dominated by the vast plains or steppes across which the local people led a nomadic life. Astana has only been the capital since 1998 and is growing fast. Before that Almaty (Alma-Ata), in the south, was the capital. It has a picturesque, mountainous backdrop and is still the commercial and social centre. Hiking and winter sports are popular in the foothills of the Tien Shan range. In the centre of the country is the Baykonur Cosmodrome from where Yuri Gagarin took off. Further north is Korgalzhyn, the most northerly home for flamingos.

KYRGYZSTAN Capital: **Bishkek (Frunze)**
Area: **198 500 km²/76 641 miles²** Population: **5 317 000**
Languages: **Kyrgyz, Russian, Uzbek** Religions: **Sunni Muslim, Russian Orthodox** Currency: **Kyrgyz som**

Tourism is starting to grow in this landlocked, mountainous country. Bishkek, the capital, is by far the largest town and is showing western influences. Osh, close to the Uzbek border, has a huge and busy market. The terrain is perfect for trekking to some of the hidden lakes and glaciers, but some areas are only for the experienced. Start from Karakol, close to the large lake of Ysyk-Köl, and head for the hot springs at Altyn Arashan. Further south is Tash Rabat, a welcome caravanserai on the Silk Road.

TAJIKISTAN Capital: **Dushanbe**
Area: **143 100 km²/55 251 miles²**
Population: **6 736 000** Languages: **Tajik, Uzbek, Russian**
Religions: **Sunni Muslim** Currency: **Somoni**

After the Soviet break-up there was civil unrest between the different peoples in Tajikistan, but at present the country is stable. The country is dominated by the Pamir and Altai Mountains and their inaccessibility helped protect the area from most invaders. Dushanbe is the capital and has a thriving Monday market. The road north to Khŭjand passes through spectacular scenery, as does the Pamir highway. The mountains and lakes are perfect for the adventure traveller. The Wakhan valley which crosses to Afghanistan has disused forts and Buddhist ruins, with views to the Hindu Kush.

TURKMENISTAN Capital: **Aşgabat (Ashkhabad)**
Area: **488 100 km²/188 456 miles²**
Population: **4 965 000** Languages: **Turkmen, Uzbek, Russian** Religions: **Sunni Muslim, Russian Orthodox** Currency: **Turkmen manat**

Until 2006 the country was dominated by its president, Niyazov (Turkmenbashi). In the capital, Aşgabat, there are gold statues to him. Independent travel was restricted and you will still need to hire a guide to accompany you. The Karakum desert covers the majority of the country, with sites of interest around the fringes. In the east, Merv was the second city of the Islamic world until destroyed by the sons of Ghenghis Khan. Nisa, west of the capital, was a major city of the Parthian kings in the 4th millennium BC. Close to Daşoguz (Tashauz) are the remains of Konye-Urgench, an ancient fortress town.

UZBEKISTAN Capital: **Tashkent**
Area: **447 400 km²/172 742 miles²** Population: **27 372 000**
Languages: **Uzbek, Russian, Tajik, Kazakh** Religions: **Sunni Muslim, Russian Orthodox** Currency: **Uzbek som**

Some of the finest gems of Central Asia fall within Uzbekistan. With profits from the Silk Road, the cities of Samarqand and Buxoro (Bukhara) thrived. Although Samarqand is surrounded by faceless Soviet-built buildings, the Registan, decorated with ornate mosaics and turquoise domes, dominates the old centre. Khiva, near Urganch, is a better example of the architecture because despite its brutal history, the whole city remains intact within the old walls. North is the Kyzylkum Desert and the vestiges of the Aral Sea. Little remains of the ancient city of Tashkent, the capital, after an earthquake in 1966. It was rebuilt in the Soviet style.

Conic Equidistant Projection

1:7 000 000

MILES 0   50   100   150   200

© Collins Bartholomew Ltd

0 50 100 150 200 250 300 350 KILOMETRES

The Gulf, Iran and Afghanistan

AFGHANISTAN Capital: **Kābul**
Area: **652 225 km²/251 825 miles²**
Population: **27 145 000** Languages: **Dari, Pushtu, Uzbek, Turkmen**
Religions: **Sunni Muslim, Shi'a Muslim** Currency: **Afghani**

Travel to Afghanistan is strongly discouraged; some areas are still an active war zone, while there may be a risk of land mines in other parts. The draw of the country used to be the mountains, with the dramatic peaks of the Hindu Kush and the evocative Khyber Pass. Towns in the north grew in stature due to the Silk Road trade – such as Herāt, the first stop after Iran, and Balkh, which has been overtaken by Mazār-e Sharīf with its impressive Blue Mosque. Kābul is trying to rebuild itself after many years of unrest.

IRAN Capital: **Tehrān**
Area: **1 648 000 km²/636 296 miles²**
Population: **71 208 000** Languages: **Farsi, Azeri, Kurdish, regional languages** Religions: **Shi'a Muslim, Sunni Muslim**
Currency: **Iranian rial**

Rocky and salty deserts make up the centre of Iran, ringed with mountains. The border areas are unstable and caution should be taken. Entering the urban sprawl and smog of Tehrān gives the wrong impression of this modern and busy capital: there is a lively bazaar and many fascinating museums to visit. In the far northeast is the holiest city in Iran, Mashhad, with the beautiful Imam Reza shrine.

Heading south from Tehrān, Qom is another holy city and a centre for religious studies. Eşfahān (Isfahan) is one of the main destinations for travellers. Ignoring the industrial outskirts, this former Persian capital boasts stunning mosques decorated in intricate blue mosaic tiles, refreshing gardens and fascinating bazaars. Yazd, a desert city, was famed for its fabrics, especially silk. Enter Shīrāz through the Qor'an Gate to visit more restful gardens and beautiful mosques. From here visit the monumental ruins of Persepolis, dating back to 518 BC.

In The Gulf two islands show interesting contrasts: Kish, a free-trade zone full of shopping malls and stores, and Qeshm, a haven for migrating birds and an eco-tourist destination.

KUWAIT Capital: **Kuwait (Al Kuwayt)**
Area: **17 818 km²/6 880 miles²** Population: **2 851 000**
Languages: **Arabic** Religions: **Sunni Muslim, Shi'a Muslim, Christian, Hindu** Currency: **Kuwaiti dinar**

An oil-rich country eyed enviously by its neighbours, it is a mix of the strict Islamic world and westernisation. Kuwait City is full of high-rise buildings, wide boulevards, shopping malls and luxury hotels as well as grand mosques and the Seif Palace. Panoramic views of the city can be seen from one of the Kuwait Towers. Al Jahrah used to build traditional boats for fishing and trade, but now for pleasure. The island of Faylakah has Bronze Age and Greek remains, and dhows can be seen in the harbour.

Conic Equidistant Projection

1:7 000 000

MILES 0   50   100   150   200

© Collins Bartholomew Ltd

0 50 100 150 200 250 300 350 KILOMETRES

Southern Asia

INDIA Capital: New Delhi
Area: 3 064 898 km²/1 183 364 miles²
Population: 1 169 016 000 Languages: **Hindi, English, many regional languages** Religions: **Hindu, Sunni Muslim, Shi'a Muslim, Sikh, Christian** Currency: **Indian rupee**

India is an assault on the senses. From densely populated cities such as Kolkata (Calcutta) and Mumbai (Bombay) to the clear air of the tea gardens of Darjiling and the palm-edged beaches of Goa, there is something everywhere to shock and amaze.

Starting in the north with the Himalayas and the contested North West Frontier; this area should be travelled with caution. Srinagar is the most northerly city, with beautiful Mughal gardens on the edge of the Dal Lake. Leh is closer to the Chinese border and a base for backpackers and climbers. Shimla, in the foothills, was the summer capital for the British. Close to the Pakistan border is Amritsar, with its Golden Temple, holy to the Sikh people. Brief visitors to the sub-continent usually start with Delhi, contrasting new with old, and then move onto Agra for the must-see visit to the Taj Mahal. Then to see the pink city of Jaipur with the Amber Fort. Worthwhile detours in this area include the fortified city of Fatehpur Sikri and the Hindu pilgrimage centre at Matthura. Visit the erotic carvings on the temples at Khajuraho on the way to the holy city of Varanasi (Benares) on the *ghats* (banks) of the sacred Ganges River. Close to Aurangabad are the caves and rock dwellings of Ellora and Ajanta. At Hampi in Karnataka are the extensive ruins of the fourteenth century city of the Vijayanagar Empire. Kerala and Goa provide their unique cuisines in relaxing coastal resorts. On the east coast, Chennai (Madras) is the main port, with a growing IT industry, and Puducherry (Pondicherry) has French influences from its past. Close to Myanmar are the Andaman and Nicobar Islands, ideal for beach lovers, snorkellers and divers.

PAKISTAN Capital: Islamabad
Area: 803 940 km²/310 403 miles²
Population: 163 902 000 Languages: **Urdu, Punjabi, Sindhi, Pushtu, English** Religions: **Sunni Muslim, Shi'a Muslim, Christian, Hindu** Currency: **Pakistani rupee**

The Karakoram Highway crosses the high mountain ranges into China, following the ancient Silk Road. The valleys in this northerly area, such as Chitral, Swat and Hunza, are blessed with fertile soil, in sharp contrast to their surroundings. The capital, Islamabad, is a relatively new city with parkland and gardens whereas the neighbouring city of Rawalpindi still shows its colonial background amongst the local architecture. Nearby is the ancient site of Taxila which has evidence of life from Neolithic to Buddhist. The mainly Pashtun city of Peshawar is close to the Afghan border and has refugee camps on its fringes.

Lahore was a Mughal city and has stunning pink and white marble buildings and the refreshing Shalimar gardens. Multan has beautiful Sufi tombs, well maintained by pilgrims. Moenjodaro, near Larkana, has 5000-year-old ruins across a huge area. Karachi is the business and commercial centre and has a cosmopolitan feel. Visit the ancient site of Thatta from here.

Pakistan is subject to unrest, especially in the Northern Areas, where care should be taken. Travel to some areas is restricted. This mountainous and desert land was home to several different civilisations and the evidence is easy to see.

Albers Equal Area Conic Projection

1 : 13 000 000

MILES 0   100   200   300   400   500

0   100   200   300   400   500   600   700   800 KILOMETRES

© Collins Bartholomew Ltd

Arabian Peninsula

BAHRAIN Capital: Manama (Al Manāmah)
Area: **691 km²/267 miles²** Population: **753 000**
Languages: **Arabic, English** Religions: **Shi'a Muslim, Sunni Muslim, Christian** Currency: **Bahraini dinar**

Bahrain, with its liberal outlook, is attracting new visitors through its Formula One racetrack as well as its shopping malls and availability of alcohol. The islands are surrounded by shallow waters, so land reclamation is extensive. The country's wealth started from pearl diving in the clear waters. The National Museum in the capital Manama explains the ancient burial mounds at Sar, from the Dilmun civilisation. Visit the sixteenth-century Portuguese restored fort and the ultra-modern World Trade Centre. Al Muḥarraq has traditional houses with a unique design to keep cool. For a taste of the natural world, the Ḥuwār Islands are home to dolphins and flamingos. South of the capital is the Tree of Life, sitting in a desert landscape with no obvious source of fresh water.

QATAR Capital: **Doha (Ad Dawḥah)**
Area: **11 437 km²/4 416 miles²** Population: **841 000**
Languages: **Arabic** Religions: **Sunni Muslim**
Currency: **Qatari riyal**

Qatar is one of the richest nations per capita with an elegant capital city, Doha, which is expanding upwards and outwards. A stroll along the Corniche will show off the city, including the new Museum of Islamic Art. There are plenty of modern shopping malls and the redeveloped Souq Waqif still retains an authentic feel. The National Museum is situated in the Fariq al-Salata Palace. Up the coast is Al Khawr, the former pearl trading centre. Inland at Khorr al-Adaid are sand dunes to explore or to experience a desert night.

UNITED ARAB EMIRATES
Capital: **Abu Dhabi (Abū Ẓabī)**
Area: **77 700 km²/30 000 miles²** Population: **4 380 000**
Languages: **Arabic, English** Religions: **Sunni Muslim, Shi'a Muslim** Currency: **United Arab Emirates dirham**

The U.A.E. is a federation of seven Emirates. Dubai is the main destination, with Abu Dhabi following closely. Ultra-modern buildings abound and land reclamation projects such as Palm Island are growing. Shop, dine and sunbathe in luxury but – to see another side of the country head to the Bedouin camps in the Liwā Oasis or to the hill town of Ḥattā.

Southern India and Sri Lanka

MALDIVES Capital: **Male** Area: **298 km²/115 miles²**
Population: **306 000** Languages: **Divehi (Maldivian)**
Religions: **Sunni Muslim** Currency: **Rufiyaa**

This string of low-lying coral atolls conjures up thoughts of a tropical paradise, with its white sandy beaches and crystal clear waters perfect for snorkelling or scuba diving. But they are susceptible to the effects of global warming and occasional tsunami. El Niño weather effects have caused bleaching on some of the coral reefs. The busy capital of Male has an interesting National Museum, Islamic Centre and Friday Mosque. Hulhumale Island is manmade, reaching an exceptional two metres above sea level. Island hopping is the best way to get a taste of the islands.

SRI LANKA Capital: **Sri Jayewardenepura Kotte**
Area: **65 610 km²/25 332 miles²**
Population: **19 299 000** Languages: **Sinhalese, Tamil, English**
Religions: **Buddhist, Hindu, Sunni Muslim, Roman Catholic**
Currency: **Sri Lankan rupee**

This island is slowly recovering from the tsunami of 2004 and the more recent fighting in the north. Care should be taken when in this area. The island has great ancient cities in Anuradhapura and Polonnaruwa, and Sigiriya rock fortress rises from the plain. There are cave temples at Dambulla. Tropical sandy beaches are a draw, but there is also untouched rainforest to explore at Sinharaja and leopards to spot in Yala National Park. Kandy set in the green hills is an interesting city to visit for local crafts and customs.

Albers Equal Area Conic Projection

1:12 500 000

© Collins Bartholomew Ltd

0   100   200   300   400   500   600   700   800   KILOMETRES

Arabian Peninsula

BAHRAIN Capital: Manama (Al Manāmah)
Area: **691 km²/267 miles²** Population: **753 000**
Languages: **Arabic, English** Religions: **Shi'a Muslim, Sunni Muslim, Christian** Currency: **Bahraini dinar**

Bahrain, with its liberal outlook, is attracting new visitors through its Formula One racetrack as well as its shopping malls and availability of alcohol. The islands are surrounded by shallow waters, so land reclamation is extensive. The country's wealth started from pearl diving in the clear waters. The National Museum in the capital Manama explains the ancient burial mounds at Sar, from the Dilmun civilisation. Visit the sixteenth-century Portuguese restored fort and the ultra-modern World Trade Centre. Al Muḥarraq has traditional houses with a unique design to keep cool. For a taste of the natural world, the Ḥuwār Islands are home to dolphins and flamingos. South of the capital is the Tree of Life, sitting in a desert landscape with no obvious source of fresh water.

QATAR Capital: Doha (Ad Dawḥah)
Area: **11 437 km²/4 416 miles²** Population: **841 000**
Languages: **Arabic** Religions: **Sunni Muslim**
Currency: **Qatari riyal**

Qatar is one of the richest nations per capita with an elegant capital city, Doha, which is expanding upwards and outwards. A stroll along the Corniche will show off the city, including the new Museum of Islamic Art. There are plenty of modern shopping malls and the redeveloped Souq Waqif still retains an authentic feel. The National Museum is situated in the Fariq al-Salata Palace. Up the coast is Al Khawr, the former pearl trading centre. Inland at Khorr al-Adaid are sand dunes to explore or to experience a desert night.

UNITED ARAB EMIRATES
Capital: **Abu Dhabi (Abū Ẓabī)**
Area: **77 700 km²/30 000 miles²** Population: **4 380 000**
Languages: **Arabic, English** Religions: **Sunni Muslim, Shi'a Muslim** Currency: **United Arab Emirates dirham**

The U.A.E. is a federation of seven Emirates. Dubai is the main destination, with Abu Dhabi following closely. Ultra-modern buildings abound and land reclamation projects such as Palm Island are growing. Shop, dine and sunbathe in luxury but – to see another side of the country head to the Bedouin camps in the Liwā Oasis or to the hill town of Ḥattā.

Southern India and Sri Lanka

MALDIVES Capital: Male Area: **298 km²/115 miles²**
Population: **306 000** Languages: **Divehi (Maldivian)**
Religions: **Sunni Muslim** Currency: **Rufiyaa**

This string of low-lying coral atolls conjures up thoughts of a tropical paradise, with its white sandy beaches and crystal clear waters perfect for snorkelling or scuba diving. But they are susceptible to the effects of global warming and occasional tsunami. El Niño weather effects have caused bleaching on some of the coral reefs. The busy capital of Male has an interesting National Museum, Islamic Centre and Friday Mosque. Hulhumale Island is manmade, reaching an exceptional two metres above sea level. Island hopping is the best way to get a taste of the islands.

SRI LANKA Capital: Sri Jayewardenepura Kotte
Area: **65 610 km²/25 332 miles²**
Population: **19 299 000** Languages: **Sinhalese, Tamil, English**
Religions: **Buddhist, Hindu, Sunni Muslim, Roman Catholic**
Currency: **Sri Lankan rupee**

This island is slowly recovering from the tsunami of 2004 and the more recent fighting in the north. Care should be taken when in this area. The island has great ancient cities in Anuradhapura and Polonnaruwa, and Sigiriya rock fortress rises from the plain. There are cave temples at Dambulla. Tropical sandy beaches are a draw, but there is also untouched rainforest to explore at Sinharaja and leopards to spot in Yala National Park. Kandy set in the green hills is an interesting city to visit for local crafts and customs.

Albers Equal Area Conic Projection
1:12 500 000 MILES 0 100 200 300 400 KILOMETRES

MALDIVES

Indian states numbered on the map
1. DAMAN AND DIU (G1)
2. DADRA AND NAGAR HAVELI (G1)
3. PUDUCHERRY (H4, I2)

BAY
OF
BENGAL

SRI LANKA

Conic Equidistant Projection

© Collins Bartholomew Ltd

© Collins Bartholomew Ltd

1 : 7 000 000

MILES 0   50   100   150

0   50   100   150   200   250   300 KILOMETRES

Northern India and the Himalaya

 BANGLADESH Capital: **Dhaka (Dacca)**
Area: **143 998 km²/55 598 miles²**
Population: **158 665 000** Languages: **Bengali, English**
Religions: **Sunni Muslim, Hindu** Currency: **Taka**

The fertile plains created by the convergence of the Ganges and Brahmaputra rivers make up the majority of this country. Monsoon rains and flooding mean that the coastline is always changing shape. The Sundarbans, along the delta's coastline, are an impenetrable mangrove forest, home to the Royal Bengal tiger. Dhaka is the vast, hectic capital and a boat trip from here to Khulna is a good way to see the country. Cox's Bazar is the local holiday area, leading to the 100-mile-long Inani Beach. Sylhet , in the northeast, is the pilgrimage site of the fourteenth century Sufi, Hazret Shah Jalal.

 BHUTAN Capital: **Thimphu**
Area: **46 620 km²/18 000 miles²**
Population: **658 000** Languages: **Dzongkha, Nepali, Assamese**
Religions: **Buddhist, Hindu** Currency: **Ngultrum, Indian rupee**

Visiting Bhutan must be with a pre-planned, all inclusive guided tour, whether as an individual or in a group. This peaceful country is known for its strong traditional values, Buddhist culture, bio-diversity and mountain trekking. The temple of Changangkha Lhakhang at Thimphu gives a good view of the expanding capital. The valley around Paro has many sacred sites including the Taktsang monastery, built into the mountainside. The National Museum, in a *dzong* (fortress), includes ancient manuscripts. Trekking at this Himalayan altitude can be arranged for a day or, for the serious, the 'snowman' trek which could last twenty-five.

NEPAL Capital: **Kathmandu**
Area: **147 181 km²/56 827 miles²**
Population: **28 196 000** Languages: **Nepali, Maithili, Bhojpuri, English, local languages** Religions: **Hindu, Buddhist, Sunni Muslim** Currency: **Nepalese rupee**

Nepal is more than just a string of the world's highest mountain peaks. It plunges off the foothills into jungles and plains towards the Indian border. But most visitors come for mountain trekking, walking the ancient trails which link picturesque villages amongst a dramatic backdrop. Check whether you need a mountain permit for your destination.

Kathmandu is a sprawling, busy city but has interesting temples and shrines around Durbar Square. Day trips from here are recommended to the Buddhist temple of Swayambhu, with fine views over the Kathmandu valley, and to the Hindu temple of Pashputi. Also visit Patan, across the river from the capital, traffic-free Bhaktapur, and the world's largest stupa at Bauddhanath. Heading up to Pokhara, stop at Bandipur, a traditional Newari community – the indigenous valley people. Pokhara is the main starting point for trekking in the Annapurna range and sits beside a picturesque lake. For stunning panoramic views, continue further to Sarangkot. On the southern border, look for tiger and rhino in the Royal Chitwan National Park. The important religious site of Lumbini, the birthplace of Buddha, is surrounded by monasteries. Janakpur, further east, attracts Hindu pilgrims. For those heading to Everest, the starting point is Namche Bazar.

Indian states numbered on the map
1. DAMAN AND DIU (B5, C5)
2. DADRA AND NAGAR HAVELI (C5)

Conic Equidistant Projection

1:7 000 000

MILES 0   50   100   150   200

East and Southeast Asia

INDONESIA Capital: **Jakarta**
Area: **1 919 445 km²/741 102 miles²**
Population: **231 627 000** Languages: **Indonesian, local languages**
Religions: **Sunni Muslim, Protestant, Roman Catholic, Hindu, Buddhist** Currency: **Rupiah**

Indonesia is made up of over 17 000 islands, of which about 6000 are inhabited. Sitting on the edge of a tectonic plate, active volcanoes and earthquakes are still shaping the country. The islands cover a huge diversity of culture, language and ethnic peoples. Travelling about the country can be difficult, requiring time and patience.

Sumatra is the most westerly island with large areas of wilderness, home to the Sumatran orangutan and tiger. As elsewhere in the country, the rich biodiversity is under threat from logging and palm oil production but it is easier to visit orangutan conservation centres here than the remoter Kalimantan region of Borneo. Java is the most densely populated island but from the cultural centre of Yogyakarta the impressive Buddhist temple of Borobudur and the Hindu temple of Prambanan can be reached. Heading east, Bali is the main destination for most visitors with the quieter island of Lombok next in the chain of islands. The islands of Flores and Sulawesi boast some spectacular dive sites while Komodo National Park covers three islands and protects the Komodo dragon which is the world's largest reptile. Maluku, the traditional 'spice islands' and Irian Jaya remain remote and largely unexplored due to local unrest.

MYANMAR (BURMA)
Capital: **Rangoon (Yangôn)/Nay Pyi Taw**
Area: **676 577 km²/261 228 miles²** Population: **48 798 000**
Languages: **Burmese, Shan, Karen, local languages**
Religions: **Buddhist, Christian, Sunni Muslim** Currency: **Kyat**

Travel to Myanmar is difficult due to a severe, strict military regime. The local people however, are happy to see outside visitors and the ethnically diverse population does not reflect the strained relations with the West.

The Irrawaddy river stretches from the eastern fringes of the Himalayan range down through dense forest to the coast. It has attracted the majority of the population and the two main cities of Mandalay and Rangoon are on its banks, as well as the ancient city of Bagan with over 2000 pagodas and temples dating from the eleventh century. The splendour of these buildings contrast with the floating villages which can be found on Inle Lake near Taunggyi, home to Intha people.

THAILAND Capital: **Bangkok (Krung Thep)**
Area: **513 115 km²/198 115 miles²**
Population: **63 884 000** Languages: **Thai, Lao, Chinese, Malay, Mon-Khmer languages** Religions: **Buddhist, Sunni Muslim**
Currency: **Baht**

Thailand can offer a wide choice for the traveller, from white beaches to mountain trekking to vibrant city life. Bangkok is no longer just a stopover en route to Australia and the Far East. It is a sprawling city which mixes sleek, modern shopping malls with traditional market stalls. Shopping can be by boat at the floating market or by the Skytrain to other areas of the city. Possible excursions from the city include the ancient city of Ayutthaya, the former capital of Thailand, which is a World Heritage site and the site of the Bridge on the River Kwai, while the Grand Palace in Bangkok is a complex of temples, administrative and Royal court buildings.

For a relaxing break, the southern region of the Isthmus of Kra, which becomes the Malay Peninsula, is edged with fine sandy beaches. The eastern coast offers more relaxed coastal resorts such as Ko Samui, whereas the Andaman Sea coast around Phuket and Phang Nga Bay National Park has dramatic limestone cliffs and islands. For the more adventurous, Chiang Mai in the northwest is a good base to explore the forested mountains, caves and waterfalls as well as the tribal hill villages.

Conic Equidistant Projection

1:20 000 000

MILES 0   200   400   600   800

© Collins Bartholomew Ltd

0   200   400   600   800   1000   1200   1400 KILOMETRES

Eastern Asia

MONGOLIA Capital: Ulan Bator (Ulaanbaatar)
Area: **1 565 000 km²/604 250 miles²**
Population: **2 629 000** Languages: **Khalka (Mongolian),
Kazakh, local languages** Religions: **Buddhist, Sunni Muslim**
Currency: **Tugrik (tögrög)**

This landlocked country known as the 'Land of Blue Skies' still
supports a nomadic lifestyle for its peoples living outside of
the towns and cities. Whereas Ulan Bator is developing fast,
the infrastructure outside the capital is still poor. The vast
empty landscape has few fences and is ideal for trekking, on
horses or camels, hiking and mountain biking but the travel
season is short. A popular starting point is the large freshwater
lake Hövsgöl Nuur in the northwest.

The highlight of the year is the two day sports festival of
Naadam, held in July in Ulan Bator, attracting competitors
nationwide in wrestling, archery and horseracing.

CHINA Capital: Beijing
Area: **9 584 492 km²/3 700 593 miles²**
Population: **1 313 437 000** Languages: **Mandarin, Wu, Cantonese,
Hsiang, regional languages** Religions: **Confucian, Taoist,
Buddhist, Christian, Sunni Muslim** Currency: **Yuan,
Hong Kong dollar, Macao pataca**

The Olympic Games opened the door of China to many people,
tempting them with the great diversity in cultures and landscape
across such a huge country. Although it is one of the world's
oldest civilisations it continues to evolve and push towards the
future, evidenced by the futuristic cityscape of Shanghai.

China has over thirty World Heritage sites, one of the most
important being the Forbidden City in Beijing. It houses a
collection of the finest imperial architecture in the country.
Although the city is developing fast there is still a network of
the ancient *hutongs* or alleyways with traditional houses to
explore. One hour by train brings the Great Wall within reach.
The terracotta army of over 8000 soldiers with their chariots
and horses is another popular destination in the city of Xi'an
which was the eastern end of the Silk Road and has seen over
3000 years of history.

The limestone karst landscape provides a dramatic backdrop to
river cruises on the Yangtze through the Three Gorges despite
the current dam project. The scenic town of Guilin also has
trips on the Li river through a similar landscape and
excursions to the impressive rice terraces of Longsheng. Travel
about the country is especially busy during public holidays
when migrant workers and students return home.

The southern city of Kunming is a picturesque centre for
exploring the diverse Yunnan province which borders Tibet,
entry into which is strictly controlled. Further south, Hainan
Island is being developed as a beach holiday destination.
Shanghai is the most modern and dynamic city in China but
there is still evidence of its traditional past. It used to be one
of the few places where the West made contact with China and
these influences energise the city. Where Shanghai leads, other
cities are starting to follow.

Albers Conic Equal Area Projection

1:15 000 000

MILES 0   200   400

RUSSIAN FEDERATION

MONGOLIA

GOBI DESERT

NEI MONGOL ZIZHIQU (INNER MONGOLIA)

HEILONGJIANG

JILIN

LIAONING

NORTH KOREA

SOUTH KOREA

JAPAN

Sea of Japan (East Sea)

HEBEI

SHANXI

SHAANXI

SHANDONG

Yellow Sea (Huang Hai)

HENAN

JIANGSU

ANHUI

HUBEI

SICHUAN

CHONGQING

GUIZHOU

HUNAN

JIANGXI

ZHEJIANG

East China Sea (Dong Hai)

FUJIAN

TAIWAN

The People's Republic of China claims Taiwan as its 23rd Province

GUANGXI ZHUANGZU ZIZHIQU

GUANGDONG

HAINAN

VIETNAM

LAOS

Gulf of Tongking

SOUTH CHINA SEA

PHILIPPINES

PACIFIC OCEAN

Tropic of Cancer

Beijing (Peking)

Tianjin

Shanghai

Hong Kong

Macao

Seoul (Sŏul)

P'yŏngyang

Tōkyō

Ryukyu Islands (Nansei-shotō) (Japan)

Bashi Channel

Luzon Strait

0 200 400 600 800 KILOMETRES

© Collins Bartholomew Ltd

Central and Eastern China

HONG KONG and MACAU (CHINA)

'One country, two systems' is the Chinese solution to these two former European colonies. They still operate their own currencies (the Hong Kong dollar and the pataca) and are interconnected by ferries. While Hong Kong is a major trading and financial centre, Macau has made its name as a centre for gambling.

Hong Kong includes over 250 islands but the population is concentrated on Kowloon and north Hong Kong Island. The views from Victoria Peak, reached by the tram, reveal a crowded city of skyscrapers towering over old colonial buildings and temples. A night time cruise around the busy and vibrant Victoria Harbour shows the mix of traditional and modern.

Macau peninsula is densely populated and has many casinos and visitor attractions but the Portuguese past is reflected in the colonial architecture of the old centre which is now a World Heritage site and is explained in the museum at the old fort. The two adjacent islands of Taipa and Coloane preserve old Macau, with colonial mansions and floating villages. The islands are connected now by the reclaimed land of Cotai which boasts a vast Venetian inspired casino, canals and shopping malls.

Hong Kong, a mix of traditional and modern China

TAIWAN   Capital: T'aipei
Area: **36 179 km²/13 969 miles²**
Population: **22 880 009** Languages: **Mandarin, Min, Hakka, local languages** Religions: **Buddhist, Taoist, Confucian, Christian** Currency: **Taiwan dollar**

Taiwan is not an obvious tourist destination but it is a tropical island of lush vegetation, secluded beaches and high mountains as well as the better known modern cities. The island is a mixture of traditional cultures and hi-tech businesses with a well-regarded cuisine, to suit all tastes. The plains of the west coast are edged with a string of cities linked by highways and railways but head eastwards and there are stunning marble canyons, steep cliffs, waterfalls and hot springs to explore. Taroko, near Hualien, is the most popular National Park.

Conic Equidistant Projection

1:7 500 000

MILES 0   100   200   300

Japan, North Korea and South Korea

The map shows Japan, North and South Korea, and neighbouring parts of China and the Russian Federation. The area has seen some significant territorial disputes over the years, most notably that between the two Koreas which led to the Korean War in the 1950s, the ownership of the small islets known as Liancourt Rocks (Tok-tō to the Koreans and Take-shima to the Japanese), and the status of the southern Kuril Islands – under Russian control but claimed by Japan. There is also an ongoing disagreement over the naming of the Sea of Japan (known to the Koreans as the East Sea).

Mount Fuji, Japan

Japan lies directly on the boundary between the Eurasian, Philippine and Pacific tectonic plates. This boundary forms part of the 'Ring of Fire' – the zone around the edge of the Pacific Ocean marked by plate boundaries and therefore highly susceptible to earthquakes and volcanoes. Japan experiences approximately 1500 earthquakes each year and has suffered from numerous major events, the most deadly of which, in Tōkyō in 1923, killed more than 142 000 people. Japan also has 10 per cent of the earth's active volcanoes.

Conic Equidistant Projection

1:7 000 000

MILES 0   50   100   150   200

0 50 100 150 200 250 300 350 KILOMETRES

Japan

JAPAN Capital: **Tōkyō**
Area: **377 727 km² / 145 841 miles²**
Population: **127 967 000** Languages: **Japanese**
Religions: **Shintoist, Buddhist, Christian** Currency: **Yen**

The archipelago which makes up Japan stretches from Hokkaidō, with its ski resorts, in the north to the Ryuku Islands and the sub-tropical island of Okinawa, over 3000 km away in the south. Contrasts in culture are also wide with state-of-the-art technology next to the ancient traditions of geishas and tea ceremonies.

Tōkyō is an ultra-modern city with the emphasis on cutting-edge design, but with the temples at Asakusa and the Meiji Shrine and Imperial Palace still partly closed to the outside world, the traditional culture is still greatly respected. In the spring the parks of the city, such as Ueno Park, are busy with visitors partaking in *hanami* or cherry blossom viewing. The futuristic bullet train allows Mount Fuji to be visited in a day from Tōkyō but a longer stay allows time to climb to the top. The Izu islands continue the chain of volcanoes from Mount Fuji and can be reached by hydrofoil. The views from Ō-shima back across to Tōkyō are impressive. The National Park at Nikkō is another possible day trip with stone lanterns marking the way to a lavishly decorated shrine set in beautiful mountainous woodlands.

Kyōto was the capital for over 1000 years and is the cultural centre with many temples and shrines including the Kinkakuji which is covered in gold and the Ryoanji temple and Zen rock garden. Equidistant from Kyōto and Ōsaka is Nara, home to a World Heritage site containing eight significant sites of temples, shrines and ruins. Further south is Hiroshima, now a bustling modern city with the poignant Peace Memorial Park in the centre. The island of Miyajima is a favourite tourist site just off the coast of the city.

Hokkaidō, the most northerly island is less developed and has National Parks with hot springs and good hiking trails as well as winter ski resorts.

133

Conic Equidistant Projection

1:5 000 000   160

MILES 0   50   100   150   20

© Collins Bartholomew Ltd

(E A S T   S E A)

P A C I F I C   O C E A N

SHIKOKU

KYŪSHŪ

SOUTH KOREA

Korea Strait

Pusan

Kita-Kyūshū

Fukuoka

Kumamoto

Kagoshima

Hiroshima

Matsuyama

Kōchi

Ōsaka

Kyōto

Kōbe

Nagoya

Hamamatsu

Shizuoka

Tōkyō

Yokohama

Chiba

Niigata

Sendai

Akita

Liancourt Rocks
Claimed and administered
by South Korea as Tok-to;
claimed by Japan as Take-shima

Ullŭng-do
(S. Korea)

North Korea and South Korea

NORTH KOREA Capital: P'yŏngyang
Area: 120 538 km²/46 540 miles² Population: 23 790 000
Languages: **Korean** Religions: **Traditional beliefs, Chondoist, Buddhist** Currency: **North Korean won**

Due to its isolation from the rest of the world, a visit to North Korea will be unique experience. No independent travel is permitted but tours are possible, with a government approved guide.

P'yŏngyang, the capital, has grand architectural buildings with huge statues of the country's former leader. The scenic Kŭmgung-san, known as the Diamond Mountains, fringe the east coast and is one area which can be accessed from South Korea. On the Chinese border Paekdu-san is considered sacred – it is the country's highest mountain with a huge crater lake.

SOUTH KOREA Capital: Seoul (Sŏul)
Area: 99 274 km²/38 330 miles² Population: 48 224 000
Languages: **Korean** Religions: **Buddhist, Protestant, Roman Catholic** Currency: **South Korean won**

South Korea has become more open to tourists in recent years and there is plenty to explore. The North Seoul Tower is perfect for viewing the capital city and the surrounding landscape. As well as a huge national museum to visit there are five royal palaces including Changdeok-gung with its secret gardens. South of Seoul is Suwŏn with the impressive Hwaseong Fortress.

The high speed KTX train takes you to Pusan, accessing the beautiful south coast of scattered islands, beaches and Hallyŏ Haesang Maritime National Park. Off the coast is Cheju-do, a holiday island in a volcanic landscape.

Philippines

PHILIPPINES Capital: Manila
Area: 300 000km²/115 831miles²
Population: **87 960 000** Languages: **English, Filipino, Tagalog, Cebuano, local languages** Religions: **Roman Catholic, Protestant, Sunni Muslim, Aglipayan** Currency: **Philippine peso**

The majority of the population live on only eleven of the 7000 islands which make up the country. While the land displays dramatic scenery such as the 2000-year-old rice terraces at Banaue, north of Baguio, it is the sea which is the major attraction. The tropical waters boast great marine life, coral gardens and ship-wrecks for divers and snorkelers to explore. El Nido gives access to the superb seascapes of the Bacuit Archipelago and the shores of Palawan itself. The tiny island of Borocay, north of Panay is famous for its beaches and parties.

The Zamboango Peninsula on Mindanao and the Sulu Archipelago are subject to local political unrest.

Indochina

 CAMBODIA Capital: **Phnom Penh**
Area: **181 000 km²/69 884 miles²** Population: **14 444 000**
Languages: **Khmer, Vietnamese** Religions: **Buddhist, Roman Catholic, Sunni Muslim** Currency: **Riel**

The country is developing as a popular destination and the land mine clearance programme is helping access inland. Phnom Penh has reminders of the Khmer Rouge past at the Genocide Museum, contrasting the stunning Silver Pagoda at the Royal Palace. Most visitors head to Siĕmréab (Siem Reap), adjacent to the floating villages on Tonle Sap to visit the impressive temples of Angkor. The temples at Koh Ker are lesser known and still being uncovered; they are a day's travel from Siĕmréab. On the Thai border is the hilltop temple of Preah Vihear.

 LAOS Capital: **Vientiane (Viangchan)**
Area: **236 800 km²/91 429 miles²**
Population: **5 859 000** Languages: **Lao, local languages**
Religions: **Buddhist, traditional beliefs** Currency: **Kip**

Laos has only been accepting tourists since 1988 and still retains its traditions. Village life and the countryside are largely unaltered, and unspoilt national parks are becoming popular eco-tourist destinations. Vientiane is a relatively small town with French colonial buildings but the former capital, Luang Prabang is still the religious centre with over thirty-three temple complexes. The morning procession of saffron-robed monks receiving alms is timeless. From here trips to the Pak Ou caves and the mysterious Land of Jars are possible .

★ VIETNAM Capital: **Ha Nôi**
Area: **329 565 km²/127 246 miles²**
Population: **87 375 000** Languages: **Vietnamese, Thai, Khmer, Chinese, local languages** Religions: **Buddhist, Taoist, Roman Catholic, Cao Dai, Hoa Hao** Currency: **Dong**

The contrast between the buzzing city life and the tranquil countryside is startling. Ha Nôi, the capital, is a centre for the arts and the Old Quarter has a flavour of the former colonial influences. Ho Chi Minh City is the business centre and Huê is a fascinating past imperial capital. Away from the cities, there are river markets on the Mekong delta and great beaches at Nha Trang. Halong Bay, in the north, is full of weird shaped limestone outcrops and islands. In the mountains, the former colonial hill stations of Dalat and Sapa provide great views and relief from the heat.

West Indonesia and Malaysia

 BRUNEI Capital: **Bandar Seri Begawan**
Area: **5 765 km²/2 226 miles²** Population: **390 000**
Languages: **Malay, English, Chinese** Religions: **Sunni Muslim, Buddhist, Christian** Currency: **Brunei dollar**

Brunei is a tiny but very rich state due to underground oil and gas resources. The capital has the impressive Sultan Omar Ali Saifuddien Mosque as well as Istana Nurul Iman, the Sultan's home. Nearby is Kampong Ayer, a village built on stilts connected by wooden walkways. There are areas of virgin rainforest which can be explored by trails through the canopy in Ulu Temburong National Park, and boat trips to Bangar through dense mangroves to see the waterfalls, hot springs and traditional longhouses of the remote village communities.

MALAYSIA Capital: **Kuala Lumpur/Putrajaya**
Area: **332 965 km²/128 559 miles²**
Population: **26 572 000** Languages: **Malay, English, Chinese, Tamil, local languages** Religions: **Sunni Muslim, Buddhist, Hindu, Christian, traditional beliefs** Currency: **Ringgit**

Pure white sandy beaches, clear seas and a tropical jungle backdrop is the popular image of a Malaysian resort. Inland there are dense, stifling jungles to explore in the Taman Negara National Park and then the futuristic skyscrapers and historic temples of Kuala Lumpur. The Petronas Towers give a breathtaking view of the city. To escape the humidity, the Cameron Highlands offer relief.

Mercator Projection

1:7 500 000 163

Map: Southeast Asia (Borneo, Sumatra, Java, Malaysia, Indonesia)

CHINA · HAINAN · Danzhou · Changcheng · Changjiang · Beili · Dongfang · Ganchang · Jianfeng · Yinggehai · Huangliu · Yacheng · Sanya

VIETNAM · Đà Nẵng · Hội An · Cu Lao Cham · My Son Sanctuary · Tam Ky · Quang Ngai · Đức Phổ · Sa Huynh · Kon Tum · Pleiku · Quy Nhơn · Nha Trang · Phan Rang-Thap Cham · Phan Thiết · Ho Chi Minh City (Saigon)

SOUTH CHINA SEA

MALAYSIA · Johor · Pasir Gudang · Pulau Ubin · Serangoon Harbour · CHANGI · TAMPINES · BEDOK · SINGAPORE

INDONESIA · Natuna Besar · Panarik · Lagong · Subi · Panjang · Seraya · Serasan · Sekura · Sambas · Tg Datu · Tg Mungguresak · Likur · Sematan

SABAH · Sandakan · Lahad Datu · Tawau · Sebatik · Tarakan · Kota Kinabalu · Gunung Kinabalu · Beaufort · Labuan · Banggi · Balambangan · Sikuati · Kudat · Semporna

BRUNEI · Bandar Seri Begawan · Miri · Seria · Lutong · Gunung Mulu National Park · Bintulu · Mukah

SARAWAK · Sibu · Saratok · Kuching · Sri Aman · Sanggau · Sintang · Pegunungan Iran

BORNEO · **KALIMANTAN** · Samarinda · Balikpapan · Banjarmasin · Martapura · Sampit · Pangkalanbuun · Palangkaraya · Pontianak · Singkawang · Pemangkat · Ngabang · Ketapang · Sanggau · Tanjung Selatan

Celebes Sea · **Celebes (Sulawesi)** · Makassar (Ujung Pandang) · Parepare · Majene · Mamuju · Donggala · Polewali

Selat Makassar (Makassar Strait)

Laut Jawa (Java Sea)

Laut Bali (Bali Sea) · Lombok · Mataram · Denpasar · Bali · Sumbawa · Sumenep · Madura · Bangkalan · Pamekasan

SUMATRA · Medan · Pematangsiantar · Tebingtinggi · Pekanbaru · Jambi · Padang · Bukittinggi · Bengkulu · Palembang · Bandar Lampung · Metro · Kotabumi · Prabumulih · Muaraenim · Lahat · Lubuklinggau · Curup · PEGUNUNGAN BARISAN · Sibolga · Gunungsitoli · Nias · Siberut · Pulau-pulau Batu

Taman Nasional Gunung Leuser · Banda Aceh · Sigli · Bireun · Lhokseumawe · Langsa · Taman Nasional Kerinci Seblat

PENINSULAR MALAYSIA · Kuala Lumpur · Putrajaya · Klang · Shah Alam · Seremban · Melaka · Muar · Batu Pahat · Kluang · Kota Tinggi · Johor Bahru · **SINGAPORE** · Kuala Terengganu · Dungun · Cukai · Kuantan · Mersing · Pekan · Kota Bharu · Ipoh · Taiping · Butterworth · George Town · Pinang · Alor Setar · Sungai Petani

THAILAND · Hat Yai · Songkhla · Phatthalung · Thale Luang · Narathiwat · Pattani · Yala · Satun

Strait of Malacca · Dumai · Bagansiapiapi · Rengat · Tembilahan · Bagan Datuk · Teluk Intan

Kepulauan Riau (Indonesia) · Tanjungpinang · Kepulauan Lingga · Kepulauan Anambas (Indonesia) · Kepulauan Natuna (Indonesia) · Natuna Besar · Kepulauan Tambelan

Bangka · Pangkalpinang · Tanjungpandan · **Belitung** · Selat Karimata · Selat Gaspar · Selat Bangka

JAVA (Jawa) · Jakarta · Bogor · Bandung · Bekasi · Karawang · Purwakarta · Cirebon · Tegal · Pekalongan · Semarang · Surakarta · Yogyakarta · Surabaya · Malang · Kediri · Madiun · Probolinggo · Pasuruan · Jember · Banyuwangi · Cilacap · Tasikmalaya · Garut · Sukabumi · Serang · Merak · Krakatau · Selat Sunda · Ujung Kulon National Park

ANDAMAN SEA

INDIAN OCEAN · GREATER SUNDA ISLANDS · Kepulauan Mentawai

© Collins Bartholomew Ltd

Mercator Projection · 1 : 10 000 000 · MILES 0 100 200 300 · 0 100 200 300 400 KILOMETRES

Europe Physical

The continent consists of a complex, irregular arrangement of extensive plains, plateaus, and mountain ranges. There are several significant island groups – notably the British Isles and Iceland in the Atlantic, and in the Mediterranean the Balearic Islands, Corsica and Sardinia, Sicily, and Crete. The general outline of the continent is complicated further by a number of prominent peninsulas, among which are the Balkan Peninsula (principally occupied by Greece), Italy, the Iberian Peninsula (Spain and Portugal), Denmark, and Scandinavia consisting of Norway and Sweden.

Facts

- The Danube flows through seven countries and has six different local names – Donau (Austria and Germany), Dunaj (Slovakia), Duna (Hungary), Dunav (Serbia), Dunarea (Romania) and Dunay (Ukraine). 'Danube' is the conventional English name.

- All the seas on this map (except the Caspian) are in effect branches of the Atlantic Ocean.

- Europe's four highest mountains – El'brus, Gora Dykh-Tau, Shkhara and Kazbek – are in the Caucasus. Mont Blanc, the highest mountain in the Alps, is fifth.

- By stretching north–south over more than 45 degrees of latitude, Europe has a greatly varied climate, from the hot Mediterranean to the frozen Arctic.

HIGHEST MOUNTAINS	m	ft
El'brus, Russian Federation	5 642	18 510
Gora Dykh-Tau, Russian Federation	5 204	17 073
Shkhara, Georgia/Russian Federation	5 201	17 063
Kazbek, Georgia/Russian Federation	5 047	16 558
Mont Blanc, France/Italy	4 808	15 774
Dufourspitze, Italy/Switzerland	4 634	15 203

LARGEST ISLANDS	sq km	sq miles
Great Britain	218 476	84 354
Iceland	102 820	39 699
Novaya Zemlya	90 650	35 000
Ireland	83 045	32 064
Spitsbergen	37 814	14 600
Sicily (Sicilia)	25 426	9 817

LONGEST RIVERS	km	miles
Volga	3 688	2 292
Danube	2 850	1 771
Dnieper	2 285	1 420
Kama	2 028	1 260
Don	1 931	1 200
Pechora	1 802	1 120

LARGEST LAKES	sq km	sq miles
Caspian Sea	371 000	143 243
Lake Ladoga (Ladozhskoye Ozero)	18 390	7 100
Lake Onega (Onezhskoye Ozero)	9 600	3 707
Vänern	5 585	2 156
Rybinskoye Vodokhranilishche	5 180	2 000

Orthographic Projection

1 : 17 500 000   MILES   0   200   400   600   80

© Collins Bartholomew Ltd

Europe Political

Europe's dense jigsaw of countries reflects the complex history of its many national groupings. The political map was redrawn significantly after the First and Second World Wars, and changes have continued since – Germany reunified in 1990, Yugoslavia and the former Soviet Union broke up in 1991, and Czechoslovakia was divided into two in 1993. Many European countries are small by world standards – some are among the world's smallest – but European Russia is part of the largest country in the world.

Facts

- The European Union increased its membership from fifteen to twenty-five members in 2004, with several other countries keen to join. It now includes Malta and Cyprus, and several eastern European countries, but not Norway, Switzerland or Iceland.

- Iceland and the Faroe Islands belong culturally and linguistically to Scandinavia.

- Europe has the two smallest independent countries in the world – Vatican City and Monaco.

- Since the Yugoslav civil war of 1991–1995 the country has been broken up. The most recent area to declare independence from Serbia is Kosovo, in February 2008.

LARGEST COUNTRIES	Area	
	sq km	sq miles
Russian Federation	17 075 400	6 592 849
Ukraine	603 700	233 090
France	543 965	210 026
Spain	504 782	194 897
Sweden	449 964	173 732
Germany	357 022	137 849
Finland	338 145	130 559
Norway	323 878	125 050
Poland	312 683	120 728
Italy	301 245	116 311

MOST POPULATED COUNTRIES	Population
Russian Federation	142 499 000
Germany	82 599 000
France	61 647 000
United Kingdom	60 769 000
Italy	58 877 000
Ukraine	46 205 000
Spain	44 279 000
Poland	38 082 000
Romania	21 438 000
Netherlands	16 419 000

CAPITALS		
Largest population	**Moscow,** Russian Federation	10 967 000
Smallest population	**Vatican City**	921
Most northerly	**Reykjavík,** Iceland	64° 39' N
Most southerly	**Valletta,** Malta	35° 54' N
Highest	**Andorra la Vella,** Andorra	1 029 m/ 3 376 ft

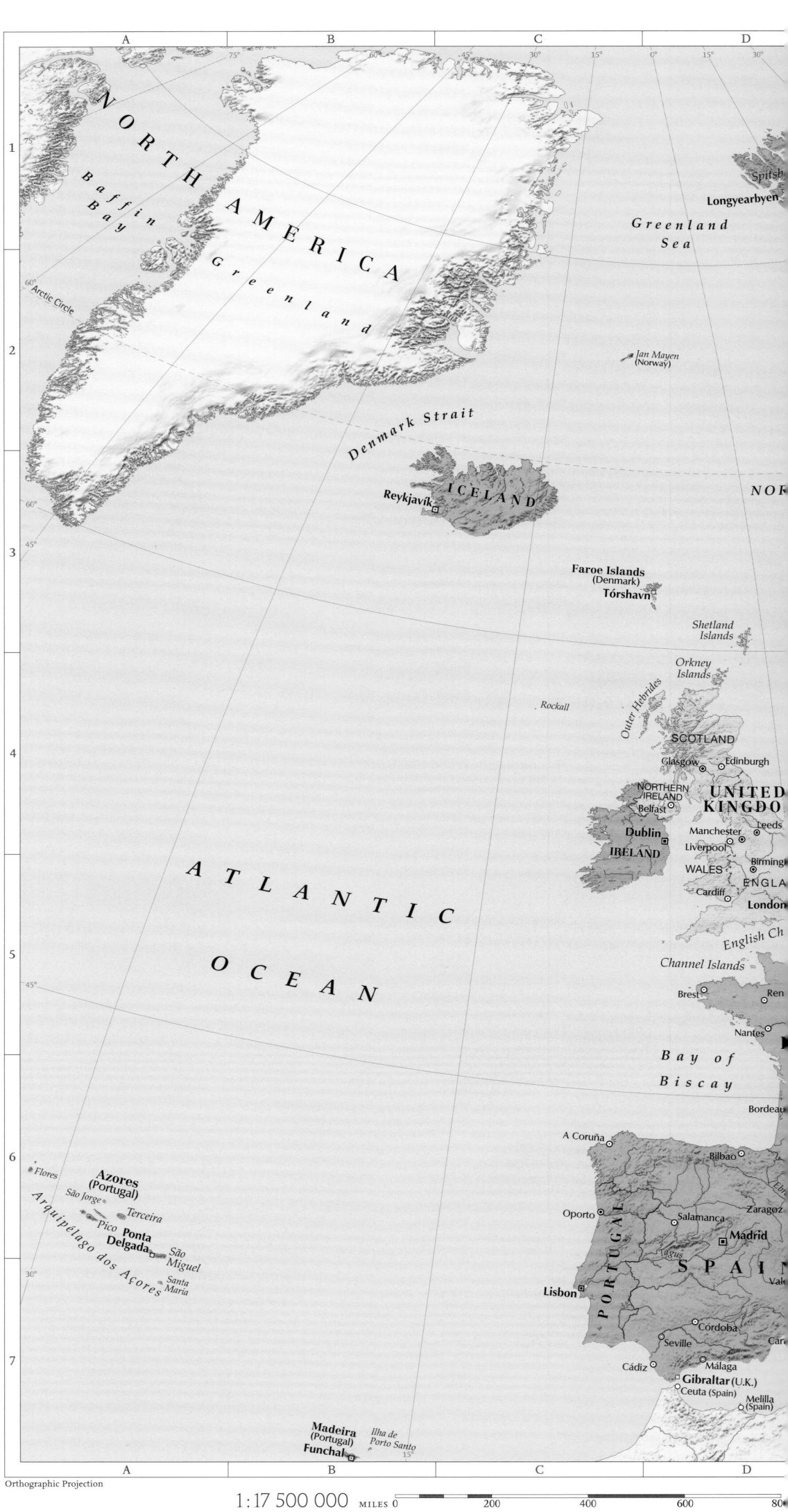

Orthographic Projection

1 : 17 500 000   MILES 0   200   400   600   80

© Collins Bartholomew Ltd

0   200   400   600   800   1000   1200 KILOMETRES

Northern Europe

The Nordic lands of Iceland, Norway, Sweden, Finland and Denmark are distinct countries but have shared an interlinked history since the Viking age. They also share some common traits in culture and politics.

Northern Scandinavia is often referred to as 'Europe's last wilderness' and the main attractions for the visitor are the breathtaking natural scenery, clean air, abundant wildlife and year-round opportunities for outdoor pursuits. In summer the region is growing in popularity as a peaceful getaway and destination for boating, fishing and hiking. In winter there is skiing, skating, snowboarding, dog-sledding, snowmobile tours and ice climbing. Visitors travel to the far north to experience the Northern Lights (September to April), the Land of the Midnight Sun and to see the land of the Sami people, with their unique languages, culture and traditions. Further south are the capital cities of Oslo, Stockholm, Helsinki and Copenhagen. Easy access and a cosmopolitan blend of culture and nightlife has earned them a well-deserved reputation as appealing destinations for city breaks.

Separated from Scandinavia by the Baltic Sea are the Baltic states of Estonia, Latvia and Lithuania. Since achieving independence from the Soviet Union in 1990 and 1991 all three are countries in transition, largely free from mass tourism but keen to promote their unspoilt natural splendours and relaxed way of life.

ESTONIA Capital: Tallinn
Area: 45 200 km²/17 452 miles² Population: 1 335 000
Languages: Estonian, Russian Religions: Protestant, Estonian and Russian Orthodox Currency: Kroon

The emphasis of tourism to Estonia is on nature, with many specialised wildlife holiday itineraries available. About half the country is covered with forest, much of which is protected and crossed by a network of hiking trails. Fishing and boat trips on Lake Peipus, the fourth largest lake in Europe, are also popular. The medieval city of Tallinn is unusually well preserved with pastel coloured houses, winding cobble-stoned streets and impressive state and church buildings. The colourful Christmas market makes December a popular time to visit the city. With its sandy beaches, shallow waters and clapperboard houses, Pärnu is known as the 'summer capital' and has been a health resort since the 1930s.

LATVIA Capital: Rīga
Area: 63 700 km²/24 595 miles² Population: 2 277 000
Languages: Latvian, Russian Religions: Protestant, Roman Catholic, Russian Orthodox Currency: Lats

Rīga has a magnetic appeal to visitors who wish to combine the new with the old. The historic Old Town and Art Nouveau architecture are blended with a bustling nightlife and thriving restaurant scene. Stretching west from Rīga is the resort area of Jūrmala, a favourite holiday destination in Soviet times and still popular for its sandy beaches. Away from the cities, Latvia is a country of sandy coastline, forests, lakes and rivers with opportunities for boating, walking and fishing.

LITHUANIA Capital: Vilnius
Area: 65 200 km²/25 174 miles²
Population: 3 390 000 Languages: Lithuanian, Russian, Polish
Religions: Roman Catholic, Protestant, Russian Orthodox
Currency: Litas

The southernmost of the Baltic states was the first Soviet republic to declare independence. Vilnius, with its baroque architecture and skyline of spires, is the main destination for most visitors. Further north, near Šiauliai, the Hill of Crosses is a unique place of national pilgrimage where over 100 000 crosses and crucifixes have been placed by Catholic pilgrims. Forest covers nearly a third of the country. The largest and most popular national park is Aukštaitija, a landscape of lakes and forest with boats and kayaks available for hire.

Conic Equidistant Projection

1:10 000 000

Scandinavia and the Baltic States

FINLAND Capital: Helsinki (Helsingfors)
Area: 338 145 km²/130 559 miles²
Population: 5 277 000 Languages: **Finnish, Swedish**
Religions: **Protestant, Greek Orthodox** Currency: **Euro**

Visitors to Finland appreciate the clean, unspoilt landscape. The country is mainly flat, a land of lakes and coniferous forest with thousands of tiny islands in the south. Nearly a third of the country is north of the Arctic Circle, where winters are long and cold. The main gateway into Finland is Helsinki. An efficient transport infrastructure, typical of Scandinavia, means that it is easy to travel around. With thick snow on the ground from November to May it is not surprising that snow-based activity holidays are well catered for. In the summer, bird watching, fishing and hunting are all popular whilst there is also a wide range of art and music festivals to enjoy.

ICELAND Capital: Reykjavík
Area: 102 820 km²/39 699 miles²
Population: 301 000 Languages: **Icelandic**
Religions: **Protestant** Currency: **Icelandic króna**

Iceland is one of the most active volcanic regions in the world, with tourism growing as international visitors are drawn to the inspiring splendour of its scenery. Warmed by the Gulf Stream, the climate is more temperate than its northerly latitude would suggest. The city of Reykjavik, home to two-thirds of the population, is a favourite for short city break holidays. This means the interior is largely unspoilt wilderness. There are some unique experiences available to the traveller. Visits to the 'Golden Circle' attractions of the geysers, the majestic Gullfoss waterfall and historic parliament site of Þingvellir, feature on almost all tourist itineraries. Also popular with both organised tours and independent travellers are the colourful rhyolite mountains, lava fields of Landmannalaugar and Europe's largest glacier, Vatnajökull.

NORWAY Capital: Oslo
Area: 323 878 km²/125 050 miles²
Population: 4 698 000 Languages: **Norwegian**
Religions: **Protestant, Roman Catholic**
Currency: **Norwegian krone**

The landscape of fjords, mountains and glaciers is Norway's greatest attraction. The country is famous for its indented coastline and in the summer there are daily cruise ship departures to experience the magic of the fjords. Cruises can last anything from a few hours to a few weeks. Norway also specialises in providing relaxing retreats to mountain and lakeside cabins for fishing, hiking and wildlife. Skiing is a national sport and the ski season often lasts for six months. There are extensive facilities for telemark and alpine skiing, and many other winter sports. Popular resorts include Lillehammer, Hemsedal, Kvitfjell, Hemsedal, Trysil, Jotunheimen, Geilo and Høvringen-Rodane.

SWEDEN Capital: Stockholm
Area: 449 964 km²/173 732 miles²
Population: 9 119 000 Languages: **Swedish**
Religions: **Protestant, Roman Catholic**
Currency: **Swedish krona**

Sweden is often described as being divided into two distinct regions. South of Stockholm are the woods, farmland, lakes and archipelagos of Götaland and southern Svealand. North of Stockholm is a more sparsely populated and mountainous wilderness, a land of forests, lakes, rivers, marshes and high mountains, making it popular hiking country. The major cities of the capital Stockholm, maritime Gothenburg (Göteborg), and multi-cultural Malmö, offer a wide variety of city breaks. Winter sports resorts provide a wide range of activities. Riksgränsen is the world's northernmost ski resort, 200 km (124 miles) north of the Arctic circle, where there is summer skiing in the light of the midnight sun in late May and June.

Conic Equidistant Projection

1:5 000 000

MILES 0   50   100   150   200

FINLAND

GULF OF FINLAND

Helsinki (Helsingfors)

Tallinn

ESTONIA

L. Peipus

Tartu

Pskov

LATVIA

Riga

Gulf of Riga

Hiiumaa

Saaremaa (Estonia)

LITHUANIA

BELARUS

Minsk

Panevežys

Šiauliai

Kaunas

Daugavpils

RUSSIAN FEDERATION

KALININGRAD OBL.

Kaliningrad

Klaipėda

Courland Lagoon

Gulf of Gdańsk

Gdynia Gdańsk

POLAND

GULF OF BOTHNIA

Åland Islands (Finland)

Turku

Tampere

Vaasa

Umeå

Gotland

BALTIC SEA

Öland

Stockholm

Uppsala

Gävle

Sundsvall

Östersund

SWEDEN

Vänern

Vättern

Bornholm (Denmark)

Rügen

Gothenburg (Göteborg)

Malmö

Copenhagen

Kattegat

Skagerrak

Oslo

Trondheim

NORWAY

Valdres

Setesdal

Numedal

Bergen

Stavanger

Kristiansand

DENMARK

Aalborg

Århus

Odense

Great Belt

Little Belt

Fyn

Zealand

Lolland

Falster

GERMANY

Hamburg

Kiel

Lübeck

Rostock

Stralsund

NORTH SEA

German Bight

North Frisian Islands

Bremerhaven

Wilhelmshaven

Emden

0 50 100 150 200 250 300 350 KILOMETRES

© Collins Bartholomew Ltd

England and Wales

UNITED KINGDOM Capital: **London**
Area: **243 609 km²/94 058 miles²**
Population: **60 769 000** Languages: **English, Welsh, Gaelic**
Religions: **Protestant, Roman Catholic, Muslim**
Currency: **Pound sterling**

ENGLAND

An image of the English countryside with patchwork fields, cottages and market towns, creates a conception of idealised rusticity of great appeal to many international visitors. This gentle landscape, together with the wilder areas of moor and mountain, gives England some varied scenery and provides a diversity of holiday experiences for the visitor.

The warm climate and magnificent coastline make the south-western counties of Cornwall and Devon one of the most visited regions. In contrast are the scenic uplands of the Pennines, from the Peak District in Derbyshire through the Yorkshire Dales to the Scottish border. West of the Pennines is the Lake District which remains a prime destination with both domestic and international visitors. It is a landscape with a rich literary and artistic heritage, marketed as Beatrix Potter and Wordsworth country and hence prone to over-crowding at popular sites, yet still retaining a peace and dignity in keeping with the stunning landscape of lakes and fells.

From the prehistoric site of Stonehenge to the grandeur of royal palaces, England also has a rich and varied heritage spanning many thousands of years. Stately homes and landscaped grounds such as Blenheim and Chatsworth are of great interest to international visitors, as are the 'dreaming spires' of Oxford and the architectural masterpieces of many churches and cathedrals.

Heathrow is the busiest airport in the world and London is a top world city destination, attracting over 15 million visitors a year. National museums and galleries such as the British Museum and National Gallery feature high on the list of most-visited attractions. Over hundreds of years the British royal family has also left its mark on the heritage of the capital and there are palaces, memorials and pageantry, all of appeal to visitors.

Maritime Greenwich, home to the Prime Meridian, is a reminder of England's strong nautical heritage. The National Maritime Museum is one of the greatest maritime museums in the world. The coastline of England boasts not only designated heritage coasts of natural beauty but also important archaeological sites.

WALES

A history of struggles against invasion has left a strong Welsh identity and a rich heritage of fortifications. In the 'land of castles' Beaumaris, Caernarfon and Conwy are the most impressive.

Including the islands of Anglesey and Holyhead, Wales has over 1680 miles (2704 km) of coastline. The diverse shoreline includes traditional seaside towns, the spectacular Pembrokeshire coast, the wide sweep of Cardigan Bay with its clean water and abundant marine life, and the sailing and surfing beaches of the Lleyn peninsula. Inland much of central and north Wales is mountainous, shaped by the last ice age. It is a place for walkers to explore, from the moors of the Brecon Beacons in the south to the rugged mountain ranges of Snowdonia in the north.

Conic Equidistant Projection

1:2 000 000

MILES 0   20   40   60   80

Scotland

SCOTLAND

Edinburgh is a vibrant cultural, shopping and business centre. The city is dominated by the medieval castle, perched high above the attractions of the Royal Mile and the Georgian elegance of the New Town. Edinburgh is home to many of Scotland's national arts and museum collections and its annual festivals are acclaimed worldwide. Glasgow is also one of Europe's great cultural destinations, with award winning museums and galleries, and a fine architectural heritage. Stirling Castle is famous as a focus point of Scottish history whilst many other castles, battlefields and forts remind the visitor of a turbulent past in Scotland's struggle for independence. The prehistoric landscape is equally well represented, with over 150 ancient sites in the western coast glens of Kilmartin, and the best preserved group of Stone Age houses in western Europe at Skara Brae on Orkney.

The western coast is indented with inlets and lochs formed by glaciers thousands of years ago. Oban is the 'gateway to the isles' with ferries to many of the islands whilst further north the island of Skye is accessible by road bridge. The remote outer islands of Shetland, Orkney and the Western Isles are for those looking for a totally different holiday experience. With its rugged crags, peaceful glens and clear blue lochs, the Highlands offer a diverse scenic splendour. Many walkers and climbers return again and again to the areas of Ben Nevis, Glen Coe, Cairn Gorm and the Cuillin Hills on Skye. In contrast is the soft, rolling countryside of the Scottish Borders.

Guided tours of many of the country's whisky distilleries are available, from the distinctive peaty single-malt of Laphroaig on Islay to the world-famous distilleries of Glenfiddich and Glenlivet on the 112 km (70 mile) sign-posted Malt Whisky Trail in Speyside. For many, golf is a major attraction with over 550 courses in the country, including the prestigious championship courses of St Andrews, Troon and Turnberry.

NORTHERN IRELAND

Northern Ireland is part of the United Kingdom and contributes six of the nine counties of the historic province of Ulster. Although largely isolated to specific areas, the period of 'The Troubles' was a deterrent to many travellers. The 1998 Good Friday Agreement marked the beginning of the end of this turbulent period of Irish history. The rolling hills of the southern counties contrast with the upland areas of the Sperrin and Mourne Mountains. The amazing basalt columns of Giant's Causeway on the north coast is the most famous tourist destination in Ireland and is a World Heritage site.

Ireland

IRELAND Capital: **Dublin (Baile Átha Cliath)**
Area: **70 282 km²/27 136 miles²**
Population: **4 301 000** Languages: **English, Irish**
Religions: **Roman Catholic, Protestant** Currency: **Euro**
Ireland is known as the 'Emerald' Isle because of the abundance of greenery. Great Britain provides most of the visitors to Ireland and they are well served by the east and south coasts ports. Dublin is the main international airport although Shannon on the west coast is important for transatlantic flights. Internal travel is mainly by a road network which has improved substantially in recent years.

The 'Gaeltacht' are areas where the unique Irish culture and language is preserved. They are found along the west coast in Kerry, Galway, Mayo and Donegal with smaller areas in the counties of Cork, Waterford and Meath.

Dublin is the main centre for tourism. The Guinness Storehouse and Dublin Zoo are the two most visited attractions in Ireland. The most breathtaking scenery can be found along the west coast – the Burren, Connemara and the peninsulas of Dingle and Kerry. There are also many historical sites of interest including the World Heritage sites of The Bend of the Boyne and Skellig Michael.

Conic Equidistant Projection

1:2 000 000
MILES 0   20   40
0   20   40   60   80 KILOMETRES

© Collins Bartholomew Ltd

Conic Equidistant Projection

© Collins Bartholomew Ltd

1 : 2 000 000   MILES 0   20   40   60   80 KILOMETRES

0   20   40   60   80

North Central Europe

CZECH REPUBLIC Capital: Prague (Praha)
Area: **78 864 km²/30 450 miles²**
Population: **10 186 000** Languages: **Czech, Moravian, Slovakian** Religions: **Roman Catholic, Protestant**
Currency: **Czech koruna**

The historic and beautiful city of Prague is the country's main tourist destination, luring visitors with a combination of ancient buildings, culture and nightlife. Prague Castle, including the landmark St Vitus Cathedral, is the largest medieval castle in Europe. Outside the capital there are a wealth of other castles, monuments and medieval towns to explore. The West Bohemian Spa Triangle reflects a long and prestigious history of spa treatment in the area. Karlovy Vary has been a spa resort since the Middle Ages and boasts numerous mineral water springs. Mariánské Lázně and Františkovy Lázně are more recent but both present well-preserved spa buildings in different styles. A dynamic arts and music scene is evident throughout the country with strong traditions in opera, classical music and puppetry.

DENMARK Capital: Copenhagen (København)
Area: **43 075 km²/16 631 miles²**
Population: **5 442 000** Languages: **Danish** Religions: **Protestant**
Currency: **Danish krone**

With diverse cultural influences from the rest of Scandinavia and continental Europe, Denmark has evolved into a cosmopolitan nation. It has over 400 islands, some of which are linked by bridge to the mainland and others which can be explored by ferry. Most of Denmark is low and flat with a landscape dominated by small farms. An extensive network of clearly marked cycle routes makes the countryside a popular cycling holiday destination. Theme parks are another attraction for families and Tivoli Gardens in Copenhagen, with its rollercoaster rides and performing arts, is the most visited amusement park in Scandinavia. The largest tourist attraction outside Copenhagen is the world-famous Legoland at Billund.

POLAND Capital: Warsaw (Warszawa)
Area: **312 683 km²/120 728 miles²**
Population: **38 082 000** Languages: **Polish, German**
Religions: **Roman Catholic, Polish Orthodox** Currency: **Złoty**

The number of visitors to Poland has increased since it joined the European Union in 2004, although in common with other Eastern European countries it has since suffered from an unfavourable exchange rate. The rocky peaks and valleys of the Tatry (Tatra) mountains, on the southern border, are considered to be the most spectacular scenery in the country. Most visitors stay in Zakopane, the 'winter capital of Poland'. In the north, the Mazury lake district and the primeval forest of Białowieża draw in visitors during the summer. Historic sites range from the Old Towns of Wrocław, Kraków and Toruń to the haunting atmosphere of Auschwitz-Birkenau, the largest and most notorious Nazi concentration camp and site of the mass extermination of over 1 million Jews between 1942 and 1944.

SLOVAKIA Capital: Bratislava
Area: **49 035 km²/18 933 miles²**
Population: **5 390 000** Languages: **Slovakian, Hungarian, Czech** Religions: **Roman Catholic, Protestant, Orthodox**
Currency: **Slovakian koruna**

The hiking trails and ski resorts of the Tatry (Tatra) mountains have long been a popular destination but generally tourism to Slovakia has not been as pronounced as in other central European countries. Bratislava is the cultural hub of the country. It has a compact centre and the cobblestone streets of the Old Town are mostly pedestrianised so it is a pleasant place to explore. The old medieval mining centre of Banská Štiavnica is a World Heritage site. Elsewhere, Slovakia has over 600 castles, château and mansion houses, the best known of which are the castles of Bojnice and Spišský Hrad. Slovakia's karst areas have some impressive cave systems, many of which are open to visitors.

World Heritage Sites numbered on the map:
CZECH REPUBLIC
1. Kutná Hora: Historical Town Centre with the Church of St Barbara and the Cathedral of Our Lady at Sedlec (G5)

POLAND
2. Auschwitz Birkenau German Nazi Concentration and Extermination Camp (1940-1945) (I5)

SWITZERLAND
3. La Chaux-de-Fonds / Le Locle, watchmaking town planning (C7)
4. Swiss Tectonic Arena Sardona (D7)

Conic Equidistant Projection

1:5 000 000

MILES 0   50   100   150   200

BALTIC SEA

Gulf of Riga
Gulf of Gdańsk

ESTONIA
LATVIA
LITHUANIA
RUSSIAN FEDERATION
PSKOV. OBL.
NOVGOROD. OBL.
TVERSKAYA OBL.
SMOLENSK. OBL.
BRYANSK. OBL.
BELARUS
POLAND
UKRAINE
SLOVAKIA
HUNGARY
ROMANIA
MOLDOVA

Gotland
Öland
KALININGRAD OBL.
RUS. FED.

Black Sea

Major cities: Riga, Jūrmala, Liepāja, Klaipėda, Kaunas, Vilnius, Minsk, Warsaw (Warszawa), Łódź, Kraków, Wrocław, Poznań, Gdańsk, Gdynia, Katowice, Lublin, Kyiv, Lviv (L'viv), Ternopil', Vinnytsya, Budapest, Bratislava, Vienna (Wien), Chişinău, Odessa, Cluj-Napoca, Bacău, Smolensk, Vitsyebsk, Homyel', Mahilyow, Babruysk, Baranavichy, Brest, Pinsk, Panevėžys, Šiauliai, Daugavpils, Pskov, Velikiye Luki

Baltic Sea

© Collins Bartholomew Ltd

0 50 100 150 200 250 300 350 KILOMETRES

Belgium, Netherlands and North Germany

BELGIUM Capital: Brussels (Bruxelles)
Area: 30 520 km²/11 784 miles²
Population: **10 457 000** Languages: **Dutch (Flemish),
French (Walloon), German** Religions: **Roman Catholic,
Protestant** Currency: **Euro**

Belgium is famous not only for the children's characters Tin Tin
and the Smurfs but also for its chocolate and distinctive beers.
Six of the world's seven authentic Trappist beers are brewed in
Belgium. Festivals and parades play a large part in Belgian
culture. The Carnival of Binche dates back to the fourteenth
century and is held in the days before Ash Wednesday.

GERMANY Capital: Berlin
Area: 357 022 km²/137 847 miles²
Population: **82 599 000** Languages: **German, Turkish**
Religions: **Protestant, Roman Catholic** Currency: **Euro**

Since 1990 Germany has presented a unified face to the visitor.
The extensive motorway (Autobahn) system and network of
high-speed trains means that it an easy and efficient country to
travel around in. Germany is a world leader in engineering,
science and financial services, sitting centre stage in the
globalised economy. Consequently many international trade
fairs are held in the major German cities of Berlin, Frankfurt and
Hannover, bringing publicity and visitors to these areas. The
cultural mix and reputation for tolerance, coupled with a unique
history, means that Berlin in particular has grown as a magnet
for visitors of all ages. Famous landmarks are the Reichstag
building, Brandenburg Gate and the remains of the Berlin Wall.

More traditional aspects of tourism in Germany have centred on
the Black Forest, scenic cruises on the river Rhine and the fairy-
tale castles of the Bavarian Alps. Most famous is the nineteenth
century Neuschwanstein Castle which was Walt Disney's
inspiration for Sleeping Beauty's castle at Disneyland. Germany's
most famous tourist route is the 350 km (217 mile) Romantic
Road, passing small historic towns and varied landscapes on its
way from Würzburg in the north to the Alps in the south. It gets
crowded in summer so is best off-season.

In Bavaria the Oberammergau Passion Play is held every ten
years and has been performed by villagers since 1634 as a
celebration of their faith. In contrast the annual Oktoberfest
festival held in Munich is a celebration of Bavarian beer and
cuisine, and is heralded as the world's largest fair.

LUXEMBOURG Capital: Luxembourg
Area: **2 586 km²/998 miles²** Population: **467 000**
Languages: **Letzeburgish, German, French**
Religions: **Roman Catholic** Currency: **Euro**

Measuring just 82 km (51 miles) by 57 km (35 miles),
Luxembourg is one of the smallest countries in the world. The
north, the 'Oesling', is dominated by the Ardennes hills while the
more densely populated south, the 'Gutland', has more diverse
landscapes of plateaus, thick forests and river valleys.

NETHERLANDS Capital: Amsterdam/The Hague
Area: **41 526 km²/16 033 miles²** Population: **16 419 000**
Languages: **Dutch, Frisian** Religions: **Roman Catholic,
Protestant, Sunni Muslim** Currency: **Euro**

Canals, windmills, flowers, clogs and the national dress are all
iconic images of the Netherlands. It is one of the most low-lying
countries in the world: half of the area is less than 1m above sea
level. Amsterdam is the capital with a rich culture and history,
well known for its many canals, historic buildings, red light
district and cannabis cafés. It also has popular attractions
relating to Van Gogh, Rembrandt and Anne Frank. Rotterdam is
the largest port in Europe stretching for a distance of 40 km
(25 miles) along the River Meuse (Maas). The famous, traditional
costume is still worn by residents of Volendam on the
IJsselmeer.

World Heritage Sites numbered on the map:
BELGIUM
1. The Four Lifts on the Canal du Centre and their
Environs, La Louvière and Le Roeulx (Hainault) (B4)

GERMANY
2. Museumsinsel (Museum Island), Berlin (L2)
3. Palaces and Parks of Potsdam and Berlin (L2)

Conic Equidistant Projection

1 : 2 000 000

MILES 0   20   40   60   80

© Collins Bartholomew Ltd

0 20 40 60 80 100 120 140 KILOMETRES

Southern Europe and the Mediterranean

AUSTRIA Capital: Vienna (Wien)
Area: 83 855 km²/32 377 miles²
Population: **8 361 000** Languages: **German, Croatian, Turkish**
Religions: **Roman Catholic, Protestant** Currency: **Euro**
Towering Alpine peaks, clear blue skies and alpine meadows are images that Austria conjures up. Two thirds of the country are above 500 m (1650 ft) with the lowland areas of the Pannonian Plain being mainly in the east towards Vienna. These areas enjoy warmer summers and less rainfall than the alpine climate of the mountain areas. Many of the most famous composers in history were born in Austria – Haydn, Schubert, Mahler and Strauss Snr & Jnr amongst them. Mozart's birthplace in Salzburg is now a museum that first opened in 1880. Vienna is the most visited destination with its cathedral, 'Heurigen' (wine bars) and music events.

BULGARIA Capital: Sofia (Sofiya)
Area: 110 994 km²/42 855 miles²
Population: **7 639 000** Languages: **Bulgarian, Turkish, Romany, Macedonian** Religions: **Bulgarian Orthodox, Sunni Muslim** Currency: **Lev**
Bulgaria is situated in the remote southeast corner of Europe and has historically been a major crossroads between Europe, Asia and Africa. The Black Sea forms the eastern boundary and has seen its popularity as a tourist destination increasing since the end of the Cold War, while north of the Balkan mountain range the Danube forms the northern boundary with Romania. Prehistoric excavations in the centre of Sofia as well as its heritage and nightlife make it one of the prime destinations.

GREECE Capital: Athens (Athina)
Area: 131 957 km²/50 949 miles²
Population: **11 147 000** Languages: **Greek**
Religions: **Greek Orthodox, Sunni Muslim** Currency: **Euro**
Ancient Greece is considered the birthplace of Western civilisation with its origins in the Mycenaean and Minoan civilizations. 80 per cent of the country is mountainous or hilly – the Pindus range runs down the centre of the country while northeastern Greece features the Rhodope range, which is covered with thick, ancient forests. Greece has a huge number of islands, many of which are the peaks of the continuation of the mainland mountains – the Cyclades alone comprise 220 islands. The Dodecanese islands have many Byzantine churches and medieval castles.

HUNGARY Capital: Budapest
Area: 93 030 km²/35 919 miles²
Population: **10 030 000** Languages: **Hungarian**
Religions: **Roman Catholic, Protestant** Currency: **Forint**
Hungary has approximately 1500 thermal springs, about half of which are used for bathing – Lake Hévíz is the largest thermal lake in Europe. The climate is continental, with hot summers and cold winters – temperatures range from 42°C (108°F) to –29°C (–20°F). Most of Hungary's landscape consists of the rolling plains of the Pannonian Basin. To the west, Lake Balaton is a popular tourist destination with its shores becoming an important wine-growing area. Budapest sits on the banks of the Danube and cruises along the river are amongst its many attractions.

SWITZERLAND Capital: Bern
Area: 41 293 km²/15 943 miles² Population: **7 484 000**
Languages: **German, French, Italian, Romansch**
Religions: **Roman Catholic, Protestant** Currency: **Swiss franc**
Any number of images are intrinsically linked with Switzerland – its financial institutions, fine cheeses and chocolate, watch making and the iconic peaks of the Eiger and the Matterhorn. However, for such a small nation there is a wide variety of landscapes on offer – the Swiss Alps in the south, the Central Plateau running through to the north of the country and the Jura mountains in the northwest. For connoisseurs of Swiss watches, 'Watch Valley' stretches across the Jura from Schaffhausen to Geneva. The ancient capital of Bern is a beautifully preserved medieval city and World Heritage site where Einstein discovered his theory of relativity.

Conic Equidistant Projection

1:10 000 000

MILES 0   100   150   200   250   300

France

ANDORRA Capital: Andorra la Vella
Area: 465 km²/180 miles² Population: **75 000**
Languages: **Spanish, Catalan, French** Religions: **Roman Catholic** Currency: **Euro**

Andorra is a mountainous country with an estimated 10.2 million annual visitors. Skiing, hiking and the night life in Europe's highest capital city, Andorra la Vella, are some of the attractions. There are no railways or airports although bus services cover most of the country.

FRANCE Capital: **Paris**
Area: 543 965 km²/210 026 miles²
Population: **61 647 000** Languages: **French, Arabic** Religions: **Roman Catholic, Protestant, Sunni Muslim** Currency: **Euro**

France is one of the most visited tourist destinations in the world with many cities of cultural interest, ski resorts, beaches and historic attractions. The north is low-lying and similar to the Belgian landscape. Normandy is famous for the 1944 D-Day landings, the beaches having evocative codenames – Utah, Omaha, Gold, Juno and Sword. In the east, Alsace, Lorraine and Burgundy are well-known for their wines – pinot noirs, chardonnays and the 'Yellow wine' from the Jura. The Rhône and Saône flow southwards through the region while the Loire dominates the central region which is relatively untouched by tourism.

The southern Riviera coast is one of the most visited areas of France. Marseille and Toulon attract most visitors and pleasant villages dot the countryside. The Dordogne in the south-west has quintessentially French cuisine and towns. A replica of the famous caves of Lascaux, now closed to visitors, has exact copies of the prehistoric cave paintings. Languedoc has its own culture and language, Occitan which is now taught in many schools. The mountains of the Pyrenees and Alps are world renowned for skiing and mountaineering.

Spain and Portugal

PORTUGAL Capital: **Lisbon (Lisboa)**
Area: 88 940 km²/34 340 miles²
Population: **10 623 000** Languages: **Portuguese** Religions: **Roman Catholic, Protestant** Currency: **Euro**

Portugal sits on the Iberian Peninsula and also includes the archipelagos of the Azores and Madeira. The northern landscape comprises mountains and plateaus whereas the south features mostly rolling plains and is warmer and drier. The Algarve on the south coast is popular for its beaches and also for golf. The capital, Lisbon, sits on the estuary of the Tagus river. Eduardo VII Park is a beautiful square and the Chiado district is noted for its cafes, restaurants, shops and street performers.

SPAIN Capital: **Madrid**
Area: 504 782 km²/194 897 miles²
Population: **44 279 000** Languages: **Spanish, Castilian, Catalan, Galician, Basque** Religions: **Roman Catholic** Currency: **Euro**

The excellent climate and beaches are far from being the only attractions of Spain. Madrid is also ideal for family holidays with theme parks, zoos, historic buildings of interest and markets such as El Rastro, as well as its nightlife. The Pyrenees create a natural boundary between Spain and France while the smaller Sierra Nevada range in the south has the highest peak on the peninsula - Mulhacén at a height of 3482m (11 432ft). Many festivals take place throughout the year. The 'running of the bulls' has competitors chased by bulls through a town centre. Injuries both to participants and to the bulls are common.

The Canaries lie off the west coast of Africa, consisting of Gran Canaria, Tenerife and several smaller outliers including Lanzarote and Fuerteventura. The Balearics are off the east coast of Spain and comprise Majorca, Minorca, Ibiza and Formentera. They are renowned for the nightlife although Formentera is relatively untouched by tourism.

Conic Equidistant Projection

1:5 000 000

MEDITERRANEAN SEA

CORSICA
(CORSE)
(France)

Bay of Biscay

Mar Cantábrico

ATLANTIC OCEAN

SPAIN

FRANCE

PORTUGAL

ANDORRA

PYRENEES

GASCOGNE

ROUSSILLON

CATALUÑA

ARAGÓN

NAVARRA

LA RIOJA

CASTILLA Y LEÓN

CASTILLA-LA MANCHA

EXTREMADURA

ANDALUCÍA

MURCIA

SIERRA MORENA

GALICIA

ASTURIAS

Cordillera Cantábrica

ALGARVE

MEDITERRANEAN SEA

Balearic Islands (Islas Baleares)

Majorca (Mallorca)

Minorca (Menorca)

Ibiza (Eivissa)

Formentera

ALGERIA

MOROCCO

Costa Brava

Costa Blanca

Costa del Sol

Golfe du Lion

Golfo de Valencia

Golfo de Cádiz

Strait of Gibraltar

Marseille
Toulouse
Montpellier
Perpignan
Barcelona
Tarragona
Zaragoza
Valencia
Alicante
Cartagena
Murcia
Madrid
Valladolid
Salamanca
Sevilla / Seville
Córdoba
Granada
Málaga
Cádiz
Lisbon / Lisboa
Oporto
Vigo
A Coruña
Bilbao
Pamplona
Donostia-San Sebastián
Vitoria-Gasteiz
Logroño
Gijón-Xixón
Oviedo
Santander
León
Burgos
Badajoz
Gibraltar (U.K.)
Algiers (Alger)
Oran
Palma de Mallorca

Conic Equidistant Projection

1:5 000 000

MILES 0   50   100

0   50   100   150   200 KILOMETRES

World Heritage Sites numbered on the map:
SPAIN
1. Catalan Romanesque Churches of the Vall de Boí (Q1)

Italy and the Balkans

CROATIA Capital: Zagreb
Area: 56 538 km²/21 829 miles²
Population: 4 555 000 Languages: Croatian, Serbian
Religions: Roman Catholic, Serbian Orthodox, Sunni Muslim
Currency: Kuna

Croatia has a diverse landscape of lakes and rolling hills in the north, wooded mountains of the Dinaric Alps and a coastline that stretches for 5,835 km (3650 miles) which includes over a thousand islands. The sunny coastline attracts most visitors, although inland the capital Zagreb and the baroque architecture of Varaždin are popular destinations.

ITALY Capital: Rome (Roma)
Area: 301 245 km²/116 311 miles²
Population: 58 877 000 Languages: Italian
Religions: Roman Catholic Currency: Euro

Italy is one of the most popular tourist destinations in Europe with some of the most famous attractions in the world – Pompeii, the Leaning Tower of Pisa, the Colosseum and Pantheon in Rome. The landscape varies from the Alpine mountains along its northern border to the plains in the valley of the Po of central Italy. The majestic Dolomites are a mecca for tourism – skiing, climbing, hiking and hang gliding. The 'Maratona dles Dolomites' is held in the first week in July – a gruelling cycle road race covering seven of the mountain passes.

Sicily and Sardinia are the largest islands in the Mediterranean and are autonomous regions of Italy. Sicily has one of the most active volcanoes in the world, Mount Etna, which along with its beaches and archaeology, make it an attractive destination for visitors. Sardinia has many reminders of its ancient past including the Phoenician town of Tharros on the west coast. Its coastline is largely rocky with deep bays and picturesque headlands.

There are two enclaves within Italy. Vatican City lies within Rome and is ruled by the Bishop of Rome, the Pope. San Marino in northern Italy is probably the oldest republic in the world, tourism is the main industry.

MACEDONIA Capital: Skopje
Area: 25 713 km²/9 928 miles²
Population: 2 038 000 Languages: Macedonian, Albanian, Turkish Religions: Macedonian Orthodox, Sunni Muslim
Currency: Macedonian denar

Tourism plays a large part in the economy with the capital, Skopje and the picturesque city of Ohrid in the southwest, the most popular destination. The climate in the south is temperate Mediterranean while the north is more continental, with wider extremes in temperature.

MALTA Capital: Valletta
Area: 316 km²/122 miles² Population: 407 000
Languages: Maltese, English Religions: Roman Catholic
Currency: Euro

An archipelago of islands of which only three: Malta, Gozo and Comino, are inhabited. The many different occupations before independence from the UK in 1964 are reflected in the eclectic mix of cultures seen throughout the islands. The Islands are an open-air museum with some structures dating from 3600 – 3000 BC.

SLOVENIA Capital: Ljubljana
Area: 20 251 km²/7 819 miles² Population: 2 002 000
Languages: Slovenian, Croatian, Serbian Religions: Roman Catholic, Protestant Currency: Euro

Slovenia is the northernmost territory of the former Yugoslavia. It is heavily wooded and famous for its traditional foods, skiing and historic thermal baths dating from the twelfth century, many of which form the basis for modern health resorts. In the southwest is an area of karst limestone with many caves – Škocjan is a World Heritage site.

World Heritage Sites numbered on the map:
ITALY
6. Archaeological Area and the Patriarchal Basilica of Aquileia (E2)
7. Costiera Amalfitana (F4)
8. Etruscan Necropolises of Cerveteri and Tarquinia (E4)
9. Historic Centre of the City of Pienza (D3)
10. Late Baroque Towns of the Val di Noto (South-Eastern Sicily) (F6)
11. Mantua and Sabbioneta (D2)
12. Portovenere, Cinque Terre, and the Islands (Palmaria, Tino and Tinetto) (C2)
13. Rock Drawings in Valcamonica (D2)
14. Syracuse and the Rocky Necropolis of Pantalica (F6)
15. Villa Romana del Casale (F6)

Conic Equidistant Projection
1:5 000 000
MILES 0   50   100   150   200

World Heritage Sites numbered on the map:

CROATIA
1. Episcopal Complex of the Euphrasian Basilica in the Historic Centre of Poreč (E2)

GREECE
2. Archaeological Site of Aigai (modern name Vergina) (J4)
3. Archaeological Site of Delphi (J5)
4. Historic Centre (Chorá) with the Monastery of Saint John "the Theologian" and the Cave of the Apocalypse on the Island of Pátmos (L6)
5. Monasteries of Daphni, Hossios Luckas and Nea Moni of Chios (J5, J7)

ROMANIA
16. Dacian Fortresses of the Orastie Mountains (J2)
17. Villages with Fortified Churches in Transylvania (J2, K1-2)

SAN MARINO
18. San Marino Historic Centre and Mount Titano (E3)

SWITXERLAND
19. Lavaux, Vineyard Terraces (B1)
20. Rhaetian Railway in the Albula / Bernina Landscapes (D1)

TURKEY
21. Hierapolis-Pamukkale (M6)

0   50   100   150   200   250   300   350 KILOMETRES

© Collins Bartholomew Ltd

187

138

West Russian Federation

BELARUS Capital: Minsk
Area: 207 600 km²/80 155 miles²
Population: **9 689 000** Languages: **Belorussian, Russian**
Religions: **Belorussian Orthodox, Roman Catholic**
Currency: **Belarus rouble**

Belarus (formerly Belorussia) declared independence from the Soviet Union in 1991. It has cold winters and moist summers, with average temperatures of around –6°C (21°F) and 18°C (64°F) respectively. Poor roads and lack of services make travelling by car difficult. The bus or train are probably the best means for getting around. The landscape of Belarus is characterised by expansive plains and an abundance of lakes and forest. A rich heritage dates back to the eleventh century with ancient castles, monasteries and picturesque villages dotting the landscape. Of particular interest is the Cathedral of St Francis Xavier in the ancient city of Hrodna (Grodno).

MOLDOVA Capital: Chișinău (Kishinev)
Area: 33 700 km²/13 012 miles²
Population: **3 794 000** Languages: **Romanian, Ukrainian, Gagauz, Russian** Religions: **Romanian Orthodox, Russian Orthodox** Currency: **Moldovan leu**

Moldova is one of the poorest nations in Europe, having no major mineral deposits, and as a consequence it has to import all of its petroleum, gas and coal. The climate is favourable to agriculture on which the economy largely depends. Most of the country lies between the Rivers Dniester and Prut. The area to the east of the Dniester, Trans-Dniester, declared its independence from Moldova in 1990. It has never been internationally recognised.

Easter is the most important religious holiday and the second Sunday after Easter is 'Paştele Blajinilor' – a day of mourning for departed family and friends. Chişinău has Moldova's only international airport.

ROMANIA Capital: Bucharest (București)
Area: 237 500 km²/91 699 miles²
Population: **21 438 000** Languages: **Romanian, Hungarian**
Religions: **Romanian Orthodox, Protestant, Roman Catholic**
Currency: **Romanian leu**

Romania borders the Black Sea into which the protected wetland of the Danube Delta is extending 20m (65ft) each year. Almost all of Romania's rivers source in the Carpathians and most join the Danube. The painted monasteries of Bucovina in northeastern Romania are masterpieces of Byzantine art and unique in Europe.

Surrounded by the arc of the Carpathians is Transylvania which has some of Europe's best-preserved medieval towns, most notably Brasov, featuring Old Saxon architecture and citadel ruins. Near Brasov is the Gothic Bran Castle which was used by Vlad Tepes (Vlad the Impaler), the inspiration for Bram Stoker's Dracula, during his raids into Transylvania.

UKRAINE Capital: Kiev (Kyiv)
Area: 603 700 km²/233 090 miles²
Population: **46 205 000** Languages: **Ukrainian, Russian**
Religions: **Ukrainian Orthodox, Ukrainian Catholic, Roman Catholic** Currency: **Hryvnia**

Ukraine's capital, Kiev, has a history dating back to the sixth century and has many sites of interest reflecting its heritage. The peninsula of Crimea sits between the Black Sea and the Sea of Azov and is popular for its beaches and mountains. The port of Odessa, 'The Black Sea Pearl', has one of the largest opera houses in the world. The 'Seven Wonders of Ukraine' are historic and cultural places of interest that were chosen by an internet vote in 2007. Ukrainians are among the foremost rail users in the world and the comfortable, affordable rail network connects most major cities.

Conic Equidistant Projection

1 : 7 000 000

MILES 0   50   100   150   200

Divisions of the Russian Federation numbered on the map

1. RESPUBLIKA ADYGEYA (G6)
2. RESPUBLIKA SEVERNAYA OSETIYA–ALANIYA (NORTH OSSETIA) (H7)
3. RESPUBLIKA INGUSHETIYA (INGUSHETIA) (H7)

0 50 100 150 200 250 300 350 KILOMETRES

187

Africa Physical

Africa is connected to Asia at the narrow Sinai peninsula. It is also separated narrowly from Europe at the Strait of Gibraltar. It contains some of the world's greatest physical features. The north is dominated by the Sahara desert and the semi-arid Sahel region, while the mountainous zone of the Great Rift Valley runs down much of the east. The chief feature of central Africa is the vast Congo Basin, while the Kalahari and Namib deserts occupy large parts of the southwest.

Facts

- The Suez Canal, a crucial shipping route between the Atlantic and Indian Oceans, links the Mediterranean Sea to the Red Sea. It opened in 1869 and is 163 km (101 miles) long.

- The Sahara desert covers 9 million sq km (3.5 million sq miles), approximately 30 per cent of Africa's total land area.

- The floor of the Great Rift Valley varies from nearly 400 m (1300 ft) below sea level to over 1800 m (5900 ft) above sea level.

HIGHEST MOUNTAINS	m	ft
Kilimanjaro, Tanzania	5 892	19 330
Mt Kenya (Kirinyaga), Kenya	5 199	17 057
Margherita Peak, Dem. Rep. of the Congo/Uganda	5 110	16 765
Meru, Tanzania	4 565	14 977
Ras Dejen, Ethiopia	4 533	14 872
Mt Karisimbi, Rwanda	4 510	14 796

LARGEST ISLANDS	sq km	sq miles
Madagascar	587 040	226 656

LONGEST RIVERS	km	miles
Nile	6 695	4 160
Congo	4 667	2 900
Niger	4 184	2 600
Zambezi	2 736	1 700
Webi Shabeelle	2 490	1 547
Ubangi	2 250	1 398

LARGEST LAKES	sq km	sq miles
Lake Victoria	68 870	26 591
Lake Tanganyika	32 600	12 587
Lake Nyasa (Lake Malawi)	29 500	11 390
Lake Volta	8 482	3 275
Lake Turkana	6 500	2 510
Lake Albert	5 600	2 162

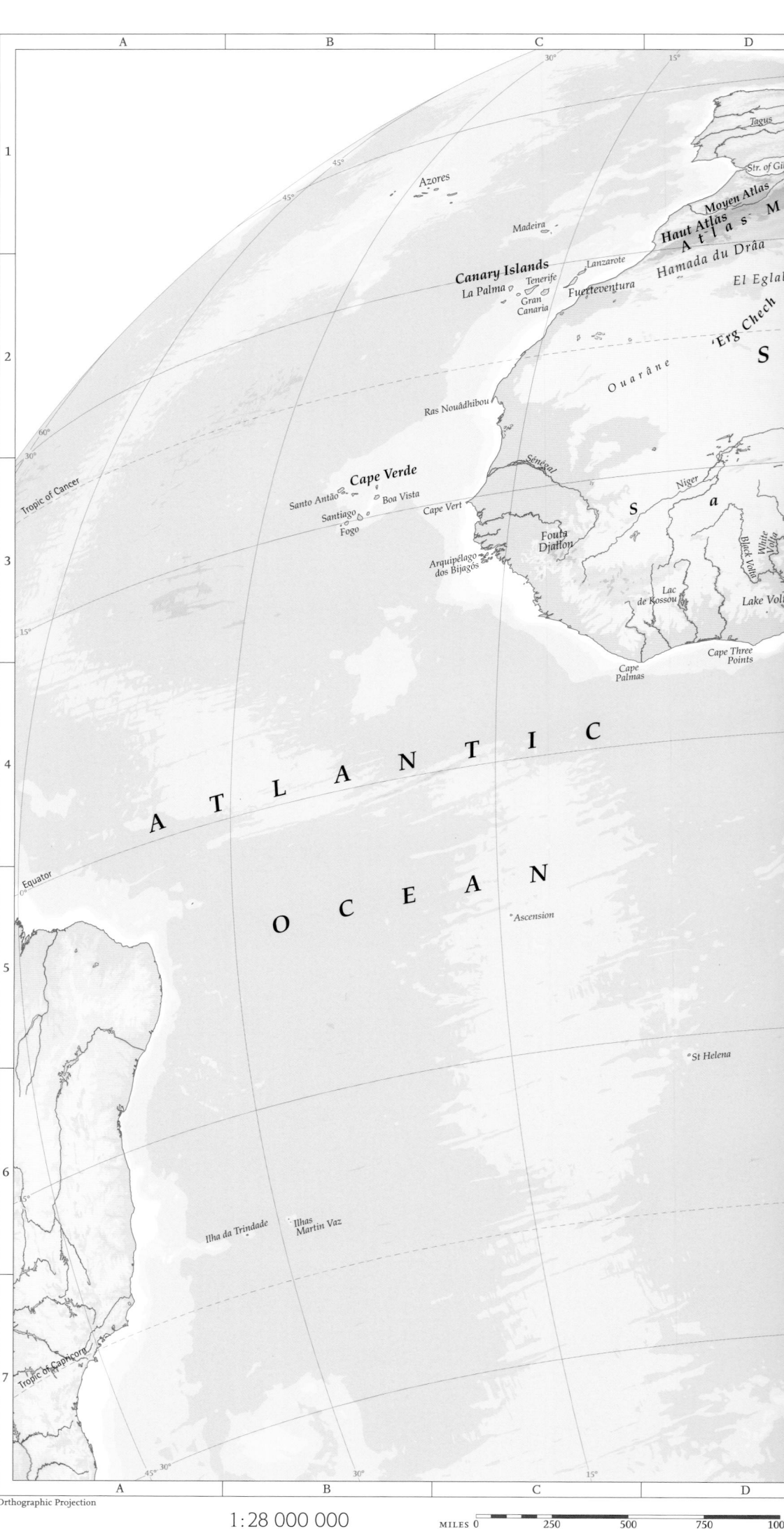

Orthographic Projection

1 : 28 000 000

MILES 0   250   500   750   1000

© Collins Bartholomew Ltd

0 250 500 750 1000 1250 1500 KILOMETRES

Africa Political

The political patchwork of Africa is a result of a complex history and of boundaries formed largely during the colonial era, which saw European control of the majority of the continent from the 15th century until widespread moves to independence began in the 1950s. The colonial era effectively came to an end in the 1970s. The status of Western Sahara, formerly Spanish but now effectively under Moroccan control, remains to be agreed internationally. Today there are once again two countries called Congo, since Zaire reverted to the name Democratic Republic of the Congo in 1997.

Facts

- Many languages are spoken in different parts of Africa, although Arabic is the main native language all across the north. In most other areas, the languages of European powers (mainly English, French, Portuguese and Spanish, along with Afrikaans) remain in common use.

- Only Liberia and Ethiopia have remained free from colonial rule throughout their history.

- UN figures estimate that 258 million people throughout the African continent have no access to clean water.

- Of the ten countries in the world with children under-five mortality rates of more than 200 per 1000 live births, nine are in Africa.

LARGEST COUNTRIES	Area	
	sq km	sq miles
Sudan	2 505 813	967 500
Algeria	2 381 741	919 595
Democratic Republic of the Congo	2 345 410	905 568
Libya	1 759 540	679 362
Chad	1 284 000	495 755
Niger	1 267 000	489 191
Angola	1 246 700	481 354
Mali	1 240 140	478 821
Republic of South Africa	1 219 090	470 693
Ethiopia	1 133 880	437 794

MOST POPULATED COUNTRIES	Population
Nigeria	148 093 000
Ethiopia	83 099 000
Egypt	75 498 000
Democratic Republic of the Congo	62 636 000
Republic of South Africa	48 577 000
Tanzania	40 454 000
Sudan	38 560 000
Kenya	37 538 000
Algeria	33 858 000
Morocco	31 224 000

CAPITALS		
Largest population	**Cairo**, Egypt	12 041 000
Smallest population	**Jamestown**, St Helena	1 000
Most northerly	**Tunis**, Tunisia	36° 46' N
Most southerly	**Cape Town**, Republic of South Africa	33° 57' S
Highest	**Addis Ababa**, Ethiopia	2 408 m/ 7 900 ft

Orthographic Projection

1 : 28 000 000

MILES 0   250   500   750   1000

© Collins Bartholomew Ltd

0   250   500   750   1000   1250   1500   KILOMETRES

North Africa

NORTHERN AFRICA

Northern Africa sits on Europe's doorstep, just 14.5 km/ 8 miles separating it from Europe across the Straits of Gibraltar. It is dominated by the world's largest desert, the Sahara. The area is an exciting blend of Arab culture, remote oases and modern cities, mountain landscapes and Mediterranean beaches, ancient ruins and atmospheric kasbahs, palaces and mosques. Established holiday locations in Morocco, Tunisia and Egypt have been welcoming tourists for many years, and Libya, slowly emerging from international isolation, now also welcomes visitors. Regional instability, and the threat of criminal and terrorist activity, make travel to areas bordering Sudan, Chad, Niger and Algeria highly dangerous.

EGYPT Capital: **Cairo (Al Qāhirah)**
Area: **1 000 250 km²/386 199 miles²**
Population: **75 498 000** Languages: **Arabic** Religions: **Sunni Muslim, Coptic Christian** Currency: **Egyptian pound**

Egypt, synonymous with the pyramids and fabulous monuments of the pharaohs, links the continents of Africa and Asia. The Nile, the world's longest river, offers water-borne tours on luxurious cruise ships or traditional *feluccas*. Cairo combines a modern city with the old; the Historic Cairo World Heritage site incorporates bazaars, mosques and palaces. World-class diving and snorkelling can be found along the Red Sea coast, with amazing sandy beaches and other water sports such as windsurfing and sailing. Visitors can experience the vast desert, one of the earth's most mysterious places, through organised treks, a camel ride or time with nomadic Bedouin tribes.

MOROCCO Capital: **Rabat**
Area: **446 550 km²/172 414 miles²**
Population: **31 224 000** Languages: **Arabic, Berber, French** Religions: **Sunni Muslim** Currency: **Moroccan dirham**

Morocco is a melting pot of cultures, with Roman, Arab and European influences visible throughout the country. The best-known traditional souks are in Fès and Marrakech, providing daytime shopping and night-time entertainment. World Heritage sites include medinas and the Roman ruins of Volubilis. The snow-capped Atlas Mountains are a draw for trekkers and the Atlantic and Mediterranean coasts offer popular seaside resorts and isolated beaches. To the north, in the Rif Mountains, is Chefchaouen, known for its distinctive blue-glazed houses (a tradition from the town's former Jewish inhabitants) and native crafts, many not found elsewhere in Morocco.

TUNISIA Capital: **Tunis**
Area: **164 150 km²/63 379 miles²**
Population: **10 327 000** Languages: **Arabic, French** Religions: **Sunni Muslim** Currency: **Tunisian dinar**

Tunisia is well known as a package-holiday destination, but its efficient public transport system makes it accessible for independent travellers. Often described as a microcosm of northern Africa, Tunisia has deserts, oases, mountains, beaches and ancient sites. The Bardo Museum in Tunis, contains one of the world's largest collections of mosaics. Carthage, founded by the Phoenician's and rebuilt by the Romans, lies to the north of Tunis. Sousse, further south, is the site of a remarkable collection of first-century catacombs. Sports enthusiasts are well catered for in all the tourist centres, with golf, tennis, diving, windsurfing and sailing some of the activities on offer.

World Heritage Sites numbered on the map:
COTE D'IVOIRE & GUINEA
1. Mount Nimba Strict Nature Reserve
DEMOCRATIC REPUBLIC OF THE CONGO
2. Virunga National Park (E5)
EGYPT
3. Memphis and its Necropolis – the Pyramid Fields from Giza to Dahshur (F2)
THE GAMBIA
4. James Island and Related Sites (A3)
GHANA
5. Forts and Castles, Volta, Greater Accra, Central and Western Regions (B4/C4)

Lambert Azimuthal Equal Area Projection

1 : 16 000 000
MILES 0   200   400   600

Central and Southern Africa

SOUTH CENTRAL AFRICA

Although this part of the world is known for poverty and political unrest, there are wonderful experiences available for the adventurous and cautious traveller. Ethiopia has ancient ruins, medieval towns, castles and breathtaking scenery. Tanzania is the African tourist's dream, with the evocative destinations of Zanzibar, Kilimanjaro and Lake Victoria. Those wishing to see Victoria Falls should visit Zambia. Uganda is home to populations of endangered mountain gorillas and Botswana has extensive elephant herds. For tropical beaches and fantastic diving, Mozambique is a great destination, and to experience a unique beauty and sense of Africa's vastness, visit Namibia.

KENYA Capital: **Nairobi**
Area: **582 646 km²/224 961 miles²**
Population: **37 538 000** Languages: **Swahili, English, local languages** Religions: **Christian, traditional beliefs**
Currency: **Kenyan shilling**

Kenya is a country of magnificent mountains, arid deserts, tropical coast and a spectacular stretch of the Great Rift Valley. It is a popular package safari destination. The southwest is the heartland of the Masai community and the Masai Mara Game Reserve is an area rich with zebra, giraffe, gazelle and topi, birds and monkeys, elephant and buffalo. Climb Mount Kenya, Africa's second highest mountain, or visit Lake Nakuru and its famed flamingos. The exotic beaches of the Indian Ocean, with their fragile and beautiful coral reefs, are bordered by rainforest, home to baboons and colobus monkeys.

MADAGASCAR Capital: **Antananarivo**
Area: **587 041 km²/226 658 miles²**
Population: **19 683 000** Languages: **Malagasy, French**
Religions: **Traditional beliefs, Christian, Sunni Muslim**
Currency: **Malagasy franc**

Lying in the Indian Ocean, Madagascar is renowned for the great diversity of its unique flora and fauna – it is a special place to visit. In the east, the rainforests of the Atsinanana World Heritage site comprises six national parks. On the drier western coast is Tsingy de Bemaraha Strict Nature Reserve. Lemur are unique to Madagascar, the only location where they can be seen in their natural habitat. Beaches on the northern and western coasts are best for water sports. Whale watchers should visit the tourist destination of Nosy Boraha (Sainte Marie), an outstanding location for observing humpback whales.

Lambert Azimuthal Equal Area Projection

1:16 000 000

MILES 0   200   400   600

Republic of South Africa

SOUTH AFRICA
Capital: **Pretoria (Tshwane)/Cape Town**
Area: **1 219 090 km²/470 693 miles²** Population: **48 577 000**
Languages: **Afrikaans, English, nine other official languages**
Religions: **Protestant, Roman Catholic, Sunni Muslim, Hindu**
Currency: **Rand**

South Africa has great natural beauty and vivid landscapes, mountains and deserts and the dramatic coastlines of both Atlantic and Indian Oceans. Famed for plentiful sunshine, it is becoming a favourite with those looking for extreme sports, as well as visitors wanting more sedate outdoor activities of all kinds.

The Eastern Cape is extremely beautiful, with a wild coast and surfing beaches, vast areas with game and Tiffindell ski resort (the only ski resort in South Africa).

Johannesburg has a number of museums documenting the country's historical and cultural heritage. Soweto, on the outskirts, is a lively area with the hugely popular attractions of Nelson Mandela's Soweto home and a memorial and museum named after Hector Pieterson, who was killed during the 1976 uprising. West of Johannesburg is the World Heritage site of Sterkfontein, Swarkrans, Kromdraai and Environs, where traces of humankind dating back 3.3 million years have been found.

Cape Town, a favoured tourist location, is overlooked by the famous Table Mountain. Tour the Cape Peninsula and visit Cape Point promontory with its lighthouse and far-reaching views. The vineyards of Stellenbosch are within an hour's drive of the city. Robben Island (a boat trip from Cape Town), infamous as the prison where anti-apartheid activists were held, is now a World Heritage site. Visit the sombre prison, now a museum; former political prisoners often lead tours.

The Garden Route, between Cape Town and Port Elizabeth is very attractive, bordered by forests, mountains, lakes and the fragrant bush of the *fynbos*. It is a floral kingdom unique to South Africa.

Kruger National Park in the northeast is one of the largest game reserves in Africa, offering classic opportunities for safaris.

KwaZulu-Natal has seaside resorts with whale and dolphin watching. Inland are game reserves and the Drakensberg mountains, as well as poignant memorials to the bloody wars fought between Zulu, British and Boer.

Lambert Azimuthal Equal Area Projection

1 : 5 000 000

MILES 0   50   100   150

E 24° F 26° G 28° H 30° I 32° J 34° K

TSWANA

ZIMBABWE

CENTRAL

KWENENG

LIMPOPO

GAZA

INHAMBANE

SOUTHERN

MOZAMBIQUE

KGATLENG

SOUTH-EAST

Gaborone

NORTH-WEST

GAUTENG

Pretoria (Tshwane)

Johannesburg

Soweto

MPUMALANGA

Maputo

SWAZILAND

Vereeniging

Mbabane

FREE STATE

KWAZULU-NATAL

Bloemfontein

LESOTHO

Maseru

REPUBLIC OF

Pietermaritzburg

Durban

SOUTH AFRICA

EASTERN

CAPE

GRIQUALAND EAST

INDIAN

OCEAN

Umtata

East London

CAPE

Port Elizabeth

0 50 100 150 200 250 KILOMETRES

© Collins Bartholomew Ltd

197

1

2

3

4

5

6

7

North America Physical

The continent of North America is taken to include Mexico, Central America and the Caribbean. Mexico is physically part of the continent, but since it is Spanish-speaking its cultural and linguistic links connect it closely with South and Central America. The mostly ice-covered island of Greenland – a dependency of Denmark – lies to the northeast. The continent contains a wide range of landscapes, from the Arctic north to sub-tropical Central America, and from the high mountains of the west, to the central Great Plains.

Facts

- The term Rocky Mountains is often applied to the whole mountain zone in the west. This area does, however, include many other significant mountain ranges and extensive plateaus.
- The Aleutian Islands, stretching in an arc across the northern Pacific, are part of Alaska.
- Lake Superior is the world's largest freshwater lake.
- Over 320 000 sq km (124 000 sq miles) of the USA is protected for conservation purposes.
- The inlet of the Pacific Ocean known as the Gulf of California is entirely within Mexico. The peninsula which defines it is known as Baja California, meaning Lower California.

HIGHEST MOUNTAINS	m	ft
Mt McKinley, USA	6 194	20 321
Mt Logan, Canada	5 959	19 550
Pico de Orizaba, Mexico	5 610	18 405
Mt St Elias, USA	5 489	18 008
Volcán Popocatépetl, Mexico	5 452	17 887
Mt Foraker, USA	5 303	17 398

LARGEST ISLANDS	sq km	sq miles
Greenland	2 175 600	839 999
Baffin Island	507 451	195 927
Victoria Island	217 291	83 896
Ellesmere Island	196 236	75 767
Cuba	110 860	42 803
Newfoundland	108 860	42 031
Hispaniola	76 192	29 418

LONGEST RIVERS	km	miles
Mississippi-Missouri	5 969	3 709
Mackenzie-Peace-Finlay	4 241	2 635
Missouri	4 086	2 539
Mississippi	3 765	2 340
Yukon	3 185	1 979
Rio Grande (Río Bravo del Norte)	3 057	1 900

LARGEST LAKES	sq km	sq miles
Lake Superior	82 100	31 699
Lake Huron	59 600	23 012
Lake Michigan	57 800	22 317
Great Bear Lake	31 328	12 096
Great Slave Lake	28 568	11 030
Lake Erie	25 700	9 923
Lake Winnipeg	24 387	9 416
Lake Ontario	18 960	7 320

Orthographic Projection

1:32 000 000

MILES 0   400   800   1200

ARCTIC OCEAN

Greenland Sea

Greenland

Queen Elizabeth Islands

Ellesmere Island

Parry Islands

Baffin Bay

Baffin Island

Davis Strait

Victoria Island

Great Bear Lake

Denmark Strait

Iceland

Kong Wilhelm Land

Kong Christian IX Land

Cape Farewell

Foxe Basin

Hudson Strait

Labrador Sea

Great Slave Lake

Caribou Mountains

Hudson Bay

Labrador

Reservoir de Caniapiscau

Newfoundland

Cape Race

Azores

Lake Athabasca

Reindeer Lake

Belcher Islands

James Bay

Canadian Shield

Gulf of St Lawrence

Cabot Str.

Lake Winnipeg

Lake Winnipegosis

Lake Manitoba

Lake Superior

L. Huron

L. Ontario

Bay of Fundy

Cape Sable

Sable Island

ROCKY MOUNTAINS

Great Plains

Lake Sakakawea

Fort Peck Reservoir

Lake Oahe

L. Michigan

L. Erie

Massachusetts Bay

Cape Cod

Long Island

Lewis Range

Bitterroot Range

Bighorn Mountains

Great Salt Lake

Missouri

Ozark Plateau

Lake of the Ozarks

Ohio

Allegheny Mountains

Appalachian Mountains

Chesapeake Bay

ATLANTIC OCEAN

Colorado Plateau

Arkansas

Cape Hatteras

Bermuda

Llano Estacado

Mississippi

Coastal Plain

Cape Fear

Edwards Plateau

Rio Grande

Cape Canaveral

Grand Bahama

The Bahamas

Acklins Island

Canary Islands

Tropic of Cancer

Sierra Madre Oriental

Padre Island

Gulf of Mexico

Mississippi Delta

Lake Okeechobee

Florida Keys

Straits of Florida

Andros

Caicos Islands

Leeward Islands

Puerto Rico

Virgin Is.

Antigua

Guadaloupe

Dominica

Martinique

St Lucia

Barbados

Cabo Corrientes

Sierra Madre Occidental

Bahía de Campeche

Yucatán

Cuba

Greater Antilles

Cayman Islands

Jamaica

Hispaniola

Caribbean Sea

Lesser Antilles

Windward Islands

Trinidad

Île Clipperton

Volcán Popocatépetl 5452

Pico de Orizaba 5610

Sierra Madre del Sur

Gulf of Tehuantepec

Cordillera Isabelia

Islas del Maíz

Costa de Mosquitos

Lake Nicaragua

Golfo de Fonseca

Panama Canal

Peninsula de Azuero

Gulf of Panamá

Amazon

Equator

0   400   800   1200   1600   2000 KILOMETRES

North America Political

The United States of America consists of the states south of the '49th Parallel', plus Hawaii, far out in the Pacific Ocean, and Alaska, the large peninsula in the northwest of the continent. Alaska lies partly within the Arctic Circle, and faces the Russian Federation across the narrow Bering Strait. Canada, formerly a dominion of the UK, occupies the north of the Continent. The region includes numerous overseas territories, from enormous Greenland to tiny islands in the Caribbean Sea.

Facts

- St Pierre and Miquelon is a small French dependent territory off the coast of Newfoundland and Labrador.

- The Caribbean Sea is defined as the area between the mainland of South America and the two major island arcs of the Greater Antilles (Cuba, Jamaica, Hispaniola, Puerto Rico) and the Lesser Antilles, which between them form the West Indies.

- Some islands of the West Indies remain as overseas dependencies of France, the Netherlands, the UK, and the USA.

- The world's longest single continuous land border stretches for 6416 km (3987 miles) between Canada and the USA.

LARGEST COUNTRIES	Area	
	sq km	sq miles
Canada	9 984 670	3 855 103
United States of America	9 826 635	3 794 085
Mexico	1 972 545	761 604
Nicaragua	130 000	50 193
Honduras	112 088	43 277
Cuba	110 860	42 803
Guatemala	108 890	42 043
Panama	77 082	29 762
Costa Rica	51 100	19 730
Dominican Republic	48 442	18 704

MOST POPULATED COUNTRIES	Population
United States of America	305 826 000
Mexico	106 535 000
Canada	32 876 000
Guatemala	13 354 000
Cuba	11 268 000
Dominican Republic	9 760 000
Haiti	9 598 000
Honduras	7 106 000
El Salvador	6 857 000
Nicaragua	5 603 000

CAPITALS		
Largest population	**Mexico City**, Mexico	20 688 000
Smallest population	**Brades**, Montserrat	1000
Most northerly	**Nuuk**, Greenland	64° 11' N
Most southerly	**Panama City**, Panama	8° 56' N
Highest	**Mexico City**, Mexico	2 300 m/ 7 546 ft

Administrative divisions abbreviated on the map:

U.S.A.		CANADA	
CONN.	CONNECTICUT	P.E.I.	PRINCE EDWARD ISLAND
DEL.	DELAWARE		
MD	MARYLAND		
MASS.	MASSACHUSETTS		
N.H.	NEW HAMPSHIRE		
N.J.	NEW JERSEY		
R.I.	RHODE ISLAND		
VER.	VERMONT		

Orthographic Projection

1 : 32 000 000

MILES 0   400   800   1200

© Collins Bartholomew Ltd

0   400   800   1200   1600   2000 KILOMETRES

Canada

CANADA Capital: **Ottawa**
Area: **9 984 670 km²/3 855 103 miles²**
Population: **32 876 000** Languages: **English, French**
Religions: **Roman Catholic, Protestant, Eastern Orthodox, Jewish** Currency: **Canadian dollar**

Canada is such a vast country that we have captured it over eight pages of mapping. These two pages show all of Canada and its border with the USA, together with Greenland, a self-governing Danish territory. Western Canada is shown on pages 204–5, eastern Canada on pages 206–7 and the Great Lakes area on pages 208–9.

Canada, the second largest country in the world by area after Russia, spans six time zones and borders three oceans. It is hugely varied, with thirteen provinces and immense natural beauty and sophisticated cities. Opportunities for winter sports, hiking, mountain biking and watersports, together with a vivid history, rich culture and multi-ethnic population mean that the choices for the traveller are endless.

Such an immense country invites journeying of all kinds. Make your own epic rail journey between Toronto and Vancouver, across the lakes of northern Ontario, the western prairies and the Rocky Mountains to the Pacific coast. Or, travel on a luxurious private rail car through the Montréal–Gaspé region of Québec visiting fabulous, award-winning gardens. There are railway museums too: Exporail in Montréal describes the vital role of the railways in Canada's development; the Canadian Museum of Rail Travel in Cranbrook, British Columbia, displays magnificently preserved railway passenger cars. Take the road trip of a lifetime along the Trans-Canada Highway, a route of 7 821 km (4 860 miles) between Victoria, British Columbia, and St John's, Newfoundland. Travel over mountains, through national parks, alongside lakes, and visit Canada's major cities on the way. Those with good sea legs can board a tall ship for a voyage through historic waterways, exploring Canada's amazing coastline (the longest of any country in the world); see glaciers and polar bears on an eco-cruise; or kayak through Saskatchewan's wilderness of 100 000 lakes and rivers. Hop on a plane to Inuvik, Yukon, Canada's largest community north of the Arctic Circle, land of the Midnight Sun and the Northern Lights (Aurora Borealis).

GREENLAND

Greenland, the largest island in the world, is visited for its breathtaking glaciers, ice sheets and fjords, the Aurora Borealis and the Midnight Sun. Snow and ice allow for exciting dog sled trips and snowmobiling; kayaking, sailing and hiking are also on offer. In the brief Arctic summer, mountain landscapes transform into colourful, flower-covered scenes. Fascinating birds and mammals can be seen all year round. Enjoy stunning vistas while bathing in hot springs, visit ancient Norse remains, or take *kaffemik* with a Greenlandic family. Greenland has a unique culture, and Nuuk, the capital, is an interesting combination of old and new.

World Heritage Sites numbered on the map:
CANADA
1. Canadian Rocky Mountain Parks (G4)
2. Dinosaur Provincial Park (G4)
3. Head-Smashed-In Buffalo Jump (G5)
4. Kluane / Wrangell-St Elias / Glacier Bay / Tatshenshini-Alsek (E3/E4)
5. Waterton Glacier International Peace Park (G5)

Chamberlin Trimetric Projection

1 : 17 000 000

MILES 0   200   400   600

© Collins Bartholomew Ltd

0   200   400   600   800   1000 KILOMETRES

Western Canada

Canada's northwest comprises Yukon, the Northwest Territories and Nunavut, all home to arctic wildlife. Nunavut, with a largely Inuit population, has its capital in Iqaluit, where the museum houses large collections of Inuit sculpture, prints and artefacts. Nearby is a beautiful river and waterfalls.

The Rocky Mountains stretch from British Columbia through southwest Alberta, on into the United States. Ski, hike or rock climb, or take the Rocky Mountaineer train, past mountains, glaciers and wonderful wildlife. Visit Vancouver city for metropolitan sophistication; historic Victoria with glorious flower gardens; and Whistler's Olympic ski runs, winter trails and panoramic chairlifts. Calgary has great shopping and vibrant arts; Edmonton, over seventy museums and annual festivals.

Saskatchewan and Manitoba's wide open spaces present diverse contrasts – from golden wheat fields and prairie grass to sand dunes and Arctic tundra. Hike and camp in the forests; visit Lake Winnipeg to swim, sail or fish; raft or canoe the rivers and lakes. There are urban delights, too, with shopping and dining in Winnipeg, entertainment in Saskatoon's Broadway District, and museums and galleries in Regina.

A snowboarder at the resort of **Whistler** in British Columbia, site of many of the events of the 2010 Winter Olympics.

Conic Equidistant Projection

1:7 000 000

MILES 0   50   100   150   200

World Heritage Sites numbered on the map:
CANADA
1. Canadian Rocky Mountain Park (F4/G4)

NORTHWEST TERRITORIES

NUNAVUT

HUDSON BAY

ALBERTA

SASKATCHEWAN

MANITOBA

ONTARIO

MONTANA U.S.A.

NORTH DAKOTA

MINNESOTA

Great Slave Lake

Lake Athabasca

Wood Buffalo National Park

Edmonton

Calgary

Red Deer

Saskatoon

Regina

Winnipeg

Lake Winnipeg

Lake Manitoba

Lake Winnipegosis

© Collins Bartholomew Ltd

0   50   100   150   200   250   300   350 KILOMETRES

206

Eastern Canada

The central provinces of Ontario and Québec offer cosmopolitan cities, magnificent rivers and lakes, and endless opportunities for great outdoor adventures, whether on foot, by bike or on the water. From the history and heritage of Québec City, Canada's capital Ottawa and its Parliament Hill, wineries and epicurean delights, rehabilitated polar bears in Cochrane and moose in Matane Wildlife Reserve, the art museums of Toronto, festivals and exhibitions in Montreal, St Lawrence River, the Rideau Canal and Niagara Falls, there is a huge choice of destinations and activities.

On the eastern edge of Canada, bordering the Atlantic Ocean, is a region of rugged coastline and islands: Newfoundland, Prince Edward Island (PEI), Cape Breton Island (all Canadian provinces except Cape Breton), and the provinces of New Brunswick, Nova Scotia, and Newfoundland and Labrador. There are routes and trails hugging the glorious beaches, winding through the national parks: discover a 1 000-year-old Norse settlement, and the house of Anne of Green Gables; explore the Bay of Fundy with the world's greatest tidal reach; the coloured sands of PEI's beaches and romantic 19th-century covered bridges; experience the lands of the Inuit people, and see black and polar bears and huge herds of caribou.

The distinctive skyline of **Toronto** Ontario, with the CN Tower in the middle and the Rogers Centre (formerly known as the SkyDome), home to the city's baseball team the Toronto Blue Jays, to the left.

Conic Equidistant Projection

1 : 7 000 000

MILES 0   50   100   150   200

207

© Collins Bartholomew Ltd

0   50   100   150   200   250   300   350 KILOMETRES

The Great Lakes

The Great Lakes of North America – Superior, Huron, Erie and Ontario – are shared between the USA and Canada, with Lake Michigan lying entirely within the USA. The lakes are interconnected by channels and rivers. The Great Lakes Circle Tour is 10 500 km (6 500 miles) of scenic road tour circling each of the lakes and connecting them and the St Lawrence River. The route provides access to great wilderness areas and waterfront beaches in major cities. There are plentiful opportunities to camp and for all sorts of outdoor activities and sports.

Glorious Niagara Falls sits on the border between the Canadian province of Ontario and the US state of New York. The falls span two major sections separated by Goat Island: the Horseshoe Falls, the majority of which are in Canada; and the American Falls and Bridal Veil Falls, on the American side. Visitors can take a boat trip or travel deep into Niagara Gorge and follow a series of walkways to the famous Hurricane Deck, just 6 metres (20 feet) from the torrents of water. Rainbow Bridge offers great views of the falls, which are floodlight after dark. Close by there is a waterpark, an aviary and the Rainbow Tower.

The lakes have played a significant role in the economic development of North America and some of the continent's largest cities lie within the area.

Chicago is situated on the banks of Lake Michigan and is the USA's third-largest city. It offers miles of lakefront trails and peaceful gardens, as well as theatres and orchestras, restaurants and fantastic shopping. Millennium Park is a celebration of sculptures, fountains, landscaped gardens and architecture, with regular free concerts and events. The diversity of the city and its inhabitants is seen in museums such as the National Museum of Mexican Art, Polish Museum of America, DuSable Museum of African American History and the Oriental Institute. City Gallery is located in the Historic Water Tower, one of the few buildings to survive the Great Chicago Fire of 1871. Navy Pier is popular, with fairground rides, a landmark ferris wheel, boat cruises, theatre and the Smith Museum of Stained Glass. Skydeck Chicago and the Hancock Observatory offer stunning birds-eye views encompassing Chicago and four states – Indiana, Michigan, Wisconsin and Illinois.

Conic Equidistant Projection

1:3 500 000

© Collins Bartholomew Ltd

0 25 50 75 100 125 150 175 KILOMETRES

United States of America

UNITED STATES OF AMERICA

Capital: **Washington D.C.**
Area: **9 826 635 km²/3 794 085 miles²**
Population: **305 826 000** Languages: **English, Spanish**
Religions: **Protestant, Roman Catholic, Sunni Muslim, Jewish**
Currency: **United States dollar**

The USA, third-largest country of the world by area and population, is a melting pot of cultures – indigenous peoples inhabited the mainland for thousands of years and the modern country was founded on mass immigration from all parts of the world. It comprises fifty states (forty-eight are shown on this map, including the District of Columbia) plus Hawaii and Alaska.

It is a country of teeming cities and vast empty plains, art and culture, national parks and scenic byways (there are 151 distinct and diverse designated routes) and restaurants serving food from every part of the world. Leading destinations include Las Vegas, Los Angeles, San Francisco, Orlando, Miami, Walt Disney World® and New York City.

Flying is the quickest and often the most convenient way to travel this huge country. A coast-to-coast flight, from east to west, takes around six hours. The national rail system, Amtrak, provides services to many cities, traversing beautiful landscapes and offering views not seen from an aeroplane. Hire a car or motorbike for a classic American road trip following the interstate highways and freeways. Bus travel is the cheapest method of travel, but takes much longer, journeying cross-country taking several days.

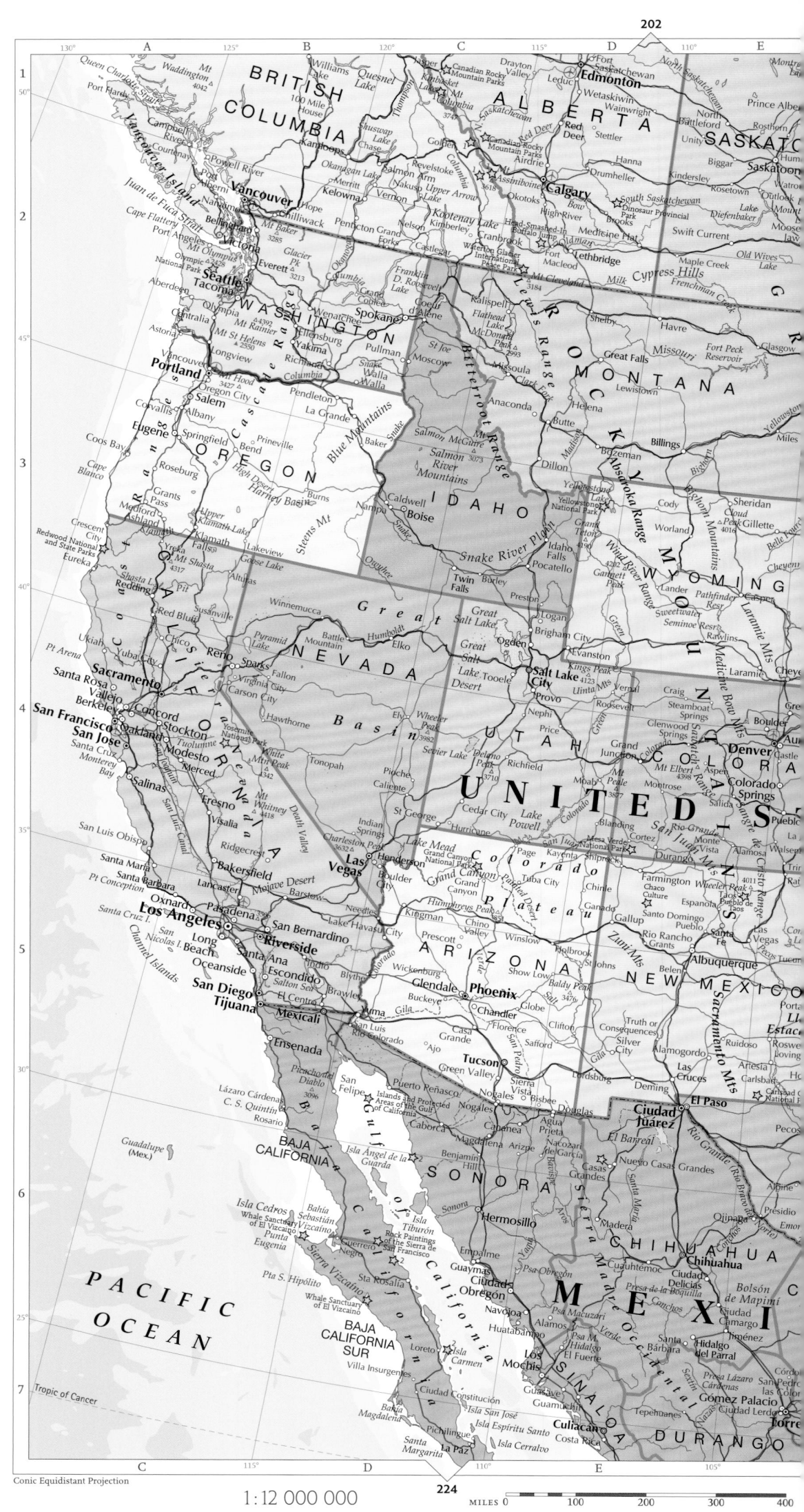

Conic Equidistant Projection

1:12 000 000

World Heritage Sites numbered on the map:

CANADA
1. Canadian Rocky Mountain Parks (C1)

MEXICO
2. Islands and Protected Areas of the Gulf of California (D6)

GULF OF MEXICO

ATLANTIC OCEAN

THE BAHAMAS

© Collins Bartholomew Ltd

Western USA

Mountains, deserts and the Pacific coast feature in this part of the USA. The Grand Canyon is a must-see for many visitors, an awe-inspiring natural spectacle of colourful ancient rock layers. Its sheer size is almost overwhelming, at 446 km (277 miles) long and around 1.8 km (over a mile) deep. Utah is a major tourist destination, particularly for outdoor sports, from mountain biking to skiing. The desert scenery is spectacular. Historic St George has museums, golf courses, a popular marathon and is the gateway to Zion and Bryce Canyon national parks. Las Vegas, in Nevada, is known the world over for its hotels and casinos, entertainment, restaurants and shopping. It also has many parks and outdoor spaces, and an arts district.

California, another must-do destination is home to the Redwood, Yosemite and Joshua Tree national parks, Lake Tahoe and the Big Sur, with a stunning coastline, waterfalls and panoramic views. It is also famed for its beaches, from windswept cliffs to expanses of smooth sand and rock pools. Anaheim in California is the location of the original Disneyland® and its Magic Kingdom, expanded in 2001 with the California Adventure Park, with shows, parades and attractions celebrating everything Californian.

Zabriskie Point in **Death Valley National Park**, California.

Conic Equidistant Projection

1:7 000 000

MILES 0   50   100   150   200

224

States and Regions

COLORADO

NEW MEXICO

TEXAS

UTAH

ARIZONA

NEVADA

CALIFORNIA

BAJA CALIFORNIA

SONORA

CHIHUAHUA

MEXICO

ROCKY MOUNTAINS

GREAT BASIN

SIERRA NEVADA

COAST RANGES

COLORADO PLATEAU

Mojave Desert

PACIFIC OCEAN

Gulf of California

Major cities: Denver, Aurora, Lakewood, Colorado Springs, Salt Lake City, Ogden, Provo, Albuquerque, Santa Fe, El Paso, Ciudad Juárez, Phoenix, Mesa, Scottsdale, Glendale, Chandler, Tucson, Las Vegas, Henderson, Reno, Sacramento, San Francisco, Oakland, San Jose, Fresno, Bakersfield, Los Angeles, Long Beach, Anaheim, Santa Ana, Riverside, San Bernardino, San Diego, Tijuana, Mexicali, Ensenada, Hermosillo, Chihuahua

Medicine Bow Mts, Sangre de Cristo Range, Sawatch Range, Uinta Mts, Wasatch Range, Zuni Mts, Sacramento Mountains, San Andres Mts, Panamint Range, Shoshone Mountains, Santa Lucia Range, San Joaquin Valley, Sacramento Valley, Death Valley National Park, Grand Canyon, Yosemite Nat. Park, Sequoia Nat. Park, Joshua Tree National Park, Petrified Forest National Park, Saguaro Nat. Park, Organ Pipe Cactus National Monument, Great Sand Dunes National Park and Preserve, Rocky Mountain Nat. Park, Dinosaur Nat. Mon., Canyonlands Nat. Park, Arches Nat. Park, Capitol Reef Nat. Park, Bryce Canyon Nat. Park, Zion Nat. Park, Grand Staircase Escalante Nat. Mon.

Great Salt Lake, Lake Mead, Lake Powell, Lake Havasu, Salton Sea, Colorado, Rio Grande, Gila

World Heritage Sites numbered on the map:
CANADA:
1. Canadian Rocky Mountain Parks (C1/D1).

MEXICO:
2. Islands and Protected Areas of the Gulf of California (D6/D7)

0 50 100 150 200 250 300 350 KILOMETRES

© Collins Bartholomew Ltd

Southwest USA

HAWAII

The State of Hawaii comprises eight islands, six of which are generally visited. Kaua'i, the Garden Isle, is northernmost, with mountains and lush valleys, and a laid back atmosphere. There are towering cliffs and beautiful beaches, popular for swimming and snorkelling.

O'ahu has the capital Honolulu, Pearl Harbour and Waikīkī Beach – world famous for its surfing. Major surfing competitions are held on the north shore, where the pro surfers hang out.

Nearly half of Moloka'i's population are of native ancestry. The island is rural, with some of the largest beaches in the Hawai'ian islands. The world's highest sea cliffs are in Kalaupapa National Historical Park.

Lāna'i is a different destination altogether, with luxurious resorts, golfing and off-road driving. Keahiakawelo, the Garden of the Gods, is an area of rock towers and spires, most beautifully lit at sunset.

Maui, the second-largest island, has eighty-one beautiful beaches and sophisticated tourist facilities. Haleakalā Crater is a wonderful viewpoint, a popular place to watch the sun rise.

The island of Hawai'i is called the Big Island, to distinguish it from Hawaii State. It is has eleven different climatic zones, sandy beaches, snow-capped mountains, deserts, rainforests and Kilauea volcano, in the Volcanoes National Park.

Kilauea volcano, **Volcanoes National Park**.

Los Angeles, the USA's second-largest city, is full of familiar landmarks including the Hollywood Bowl, Walt Disney Concert Hall and the Capitol Records Building. Hollywood features as a top destination, with Universal Studios and the Hollywood History Museum a film buff's dream. The city has a diverse collection of museums, from the Getty Centre and Museum of Contemporary Art to the Craft and Folk Museum and the Museum of Tolerance. For shoppers, there is exclusive Rodeo Drive or Venice Beach for souvenirs, the Farmers Market, The Grove and Chinatown. Beaches are a major draw for surfing, people-watching or sunbathing.

San Francisco is famous for its Golden Gate Bridge. It is a popular destination, known for steep hills, cable cars and Chinatown, the oldest in the country. Fisherman's Wharf is the place for seafood restaurants, nearby is Lombard Street, with its crazy hairpin turns. Much of the city's outdoor space is encompassed by the much-visited Golden Gate National Recreation Area, including Ocean Beach, Golden Gate Park, Candlestick Point and Alcatraz, infamous as a prison and now open to all, via ferry trips. The city is also well served by the performing arts, including Broadway shows, and museums.

① O'AHU (Hawaii) 1:1 500 000

② HAWAI'IAN ISLANDS (U.S.A.) 1:6 000 000

Lambert Conformal Conic Projection

1:3 500 000

MILES 0   25   50   75   200

D 116° E 114° F 112° G 110° H 108°

UTAH

NEVADA

COLORADO

ARIZONA

NEW MEXICO

CALIFORNIA

MEXICO

SONORA

BAJA CALIFORNIA

Las Vegas

Lake Mead

Lake Powell

Grand Canyon National Park

Phoenix
Glendale Scottsdale
Avondale Tempe Mesa
Chandler Gilbert

Tucson

Yuma

San Diego

Tijuana Mexicali

Coconino Plateau

Colorado Plateau

Mojave Desert

Death Valley National Park

Joshua Tree National Park

Lake Havasu City

Flagstaff

Kingman

Prescott

© Collins Bartholomew Ltd

217

0 25 50 75 100 125 150 175 KILOMETRES

Central USA

Central USA spans great plains and prairies. The eastern half of this map and the western part of the following map cover the American Midwest. South Dakota is home to Mount Rushmore and the immense sculptured heads of former US presidents.

Mount Rushmore National Memorial, ten miles southwest of **Rapid City**, South Dakota.

Chicago is the area's largest city, known for its lively nightlife and performing arts. Des Moines, in Iowa, has wonderful historic buildings, museums and the State Capitol with a gold-leafed dome. Nearby is Madison Country and the historic covered bridges. Mississippi is famous for the Blues and its musicians. Densely forested, with lakes and miles of streams, the colours of the autumn foliage are breathtaking. The Mississippi–Missouri is North America's longest river and can be explored by road or river trip. Wisconsin Dells, named after the scenic rock formations on the Wisconsin River, is the home of water parks, both inside and outdoors. New Orleans is a popular tourist destination, with its French Quarter and jazz. Louisiana also features swamplands and special Cajun music and food. Texas, the second-largest state, is known for cities such as Dallas and Forth Worth, but also has famous heritage sites, such as the Alamo, and fabulous scenery to enjoy.

The entrance to the Alamo, **San Antonio**, Texas, site of the legendary battle.

Lambert Conformal Conic Projection

1:7 000 000

MILES 0   50   100   150   200

GULF OF MEXICO

ILLINOIS
INDIANA
KENTUCKY
TENNESSEE
MISSOURI
KANSAS
OKLAHOMA
ARKANSAS
MISSISSIPPI
ALABAMA
FLORIDA
LOUISIANA
TEXAS
NEW MEXICO
COLORADO
COAHUILA
NUEVO LEÓN
CHIHUAHUA
DURANGO
MEXICO

ROCKY MOUNTAINS
Sawatch Range
Sangre de Cristo Range
San Juan Mts
Boston Mts
Ouachita Mts
Smoky Hills
Red Hills
Great Plains
Llano Estacado
Edwards Plateau
Sacramento Mts
Guadalupe Mts
Coastal Plain

Denver
Colorado Springs
Pueblo
Santa Fe
Albuquerque
Amarillo
Lubbock
Oklahoma City
Tulsa
Wichita
Topeka
Kansas City
St Louis
Springfield
Indianapolis
Louisville
Nashville
Memphis
Little Rock
Dallas
Fort Worth
Austin
San Antonio
Houston
Corpus Christi
Laredo
Nuevo Laredo
Monterrey
Saltillo
Monclova
Baton Rouge
New Orleans
Jackson
Montgomery
Birmingham
Mobile
Shreveport
Beaumont

Rio Grande

Laguna Madre
Padre Island

0 50 100 150 200 250 300 350 KILOMETRES

© Collins Bartholomew Ltd

Eastern USA

Eastern USA was a centre of activity during American Independence and saw many Civil War battles. Organised tours are a fascinating way to gain insight into this period of American history. Maine is a great destination for outdoor activities and the agricultural fairs make for a fun day out. Springtime in Vermont is Maple Season, when the famous syrup is made. The state has beautiful landscapes and diverse wildlife. Philadelphia, at the centre of Independence, has interesting architecture and many sites of national historic importance. Those interested in the Civil Rights movement will want to follow Alabama's unique Civil Rights Trail. Both North and South Carolina feature wonderful landscapes, with Translyvania County in North Carolina known as Land of the Waterfalls. Grand Strand is almost 100 km (62 miles) of beach running northwards from Georgetown in South Carolina. Further south is the Sunshine State, Florida. As well as endless beaches, shore-front cities and pristine golf courses, Florida offers fascinating historic sites, from Indian burial mounds and pioneer settlements to Castillo de San Marco, a Spanish-built fort constructed in 1672. The state is notable for the Everglades, a national park and World Heritage site of fragile wetlands and mangrove forests.

THE BAHAMAS Capital: **Nassau**
Area: **13 939 635 km²/5 382 miles²**
Population: **331 000** Languages: **English, Creole**
Religions: **Protestant, Roman Catholic**
Currency: **Bahamian dollar**

The Bahamas are a chain of 700 low-lying islands between the Atlantic Ocean and the Caribbean Sea. A place of vivid colours and warm, clear water. Paradise Island and New Providence Island, linked by bridge, are elegant resorts. The capital, Nassau, on New Providence can trace its history back to the pirate Blackbeard. Grand Bahama Island has one of the world's largest underwater cave systems and three national parks. Many of the settlements were founded by former slaves. The Out Islands are hidden gems of remote villages and a gentle way of life, boutique hotels and deserted beaches, with excellent dive and fishing sites.

Jetty out over the Atlantic, near **Nassau**, New Providence Island, The Bahamas.

Lambert Conformal Conic Projection

1:7 000 000

MILES 0   50   100   150   200

223

0   50   100   150   200   250   300   350 KILOMETRES

Northeastern USA

New York is a cosmopolitan city, location of the United Nations headquarters and Wall Street, an important centre for international affairs and a massive tourist destination. The city is known the world over for its iconic landmarks and celebrated attractions: the Statue of Liberty, the Empire State Building, Ellis Island, Times Square and Broadway. Magnificent architecture includes the Chrysler Building, the Rockfeller Centre and Grand Central Terminal (Station).

New York is a great centre for entertainment, the performing arts and as a place to shop, whether along Fifth or Madison Avenue, in Bloomingdales or in the many malls and markets. There are over 150 museums, including the Museum of Modern Art, the Guggenheim Museum and the Metropolitan Museum of Art; and hundreds of top restaurants and the ubiquitous hot dog stands. Central Park is a draw for both the New Yorker and visitors. Landscaped gardens, extensive trails and paths, public beaches and carriage rides are just a few of the amenities.

The events of 11 September 2001, when the city suffered its worst terrorist attack, are known worldwide. Many visitors travel to Ground Zero and to the Museum Workshop, filled with poignant images and remnants from the recovery.

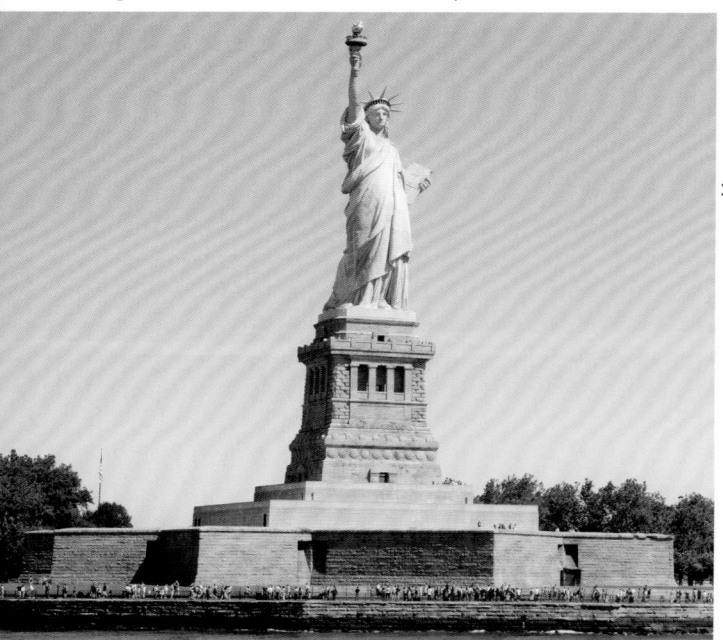

The famous statue, standing on **Liberty Island** in the Hudson River, one of New York's most popular visitor attractions.

Washington is the capital of the United States. Formally the District of Columbia, it is usually referred to as Washington DC. It is the home of the President at the White House, and the seat of government. Visitors can see the original Declaration of Independence, US Constitution, Bill of Rights and Emancipation Proclamation in the National Archives and enjoy the changing of the guard ceremony at the Arlington National Cemetery.

The numerous and remarkable museums and galleries are mostly free of charge. The National Gallery of Art houses the only Leonardo da Vinci in the western hemisphere, together with many old masters and contemporary artists. Other must-see locations include the Smithsonian and the National Portrait Gallery.

Riverboat cruises along the Potomac River are a popular way of viewing the city, its varied architecture and many parks and open spaces. The city is a thriving cultural capital with a wide range of performing arts, theatres, opera and ballet. The varied neighbourhoods include historic Georgetown and Capitol Hill. Downtown has a heritage trail, museums, theatres, hotels and restaurants; U Street and Shaw, birthplace of Duke Ellington, is home to exciting nightlife.

Lambert Conformal Conic Projection

1:3 500 000

MILES 0   25   50   75   100

1:3 500 000

© Collins Bartholomew Ltd

25 50 75 100 125 150 175 KILOMETRES

Central America and The Caribbean

The Caribbean – sandwiched between the Atlantic and Pacific Oceans and encircled by a chain of over 7 000 islands, Central America and northern South America – is a popular holiday destination for tropical sun, sand, palm trees and warm, clear water. Diving is a favourite attraction, together with a wide choice of water sports.

BARBADOS Capital: **Bridgetown**
Area: **430 km²/166 miles²** Population: **294 000**
Languages: **English, Creole** Religions: **Protestant, Roman Catholic** Currency: **Barbados dollar**

Barbados is the most easterly Caribbean island, with strong links to the UK. It is the birthplace of rum and there are hundreds of rum shops. Crane Beach has been voted one of the world's best beaches.

CUBA Capital: **Havana (La Habana)**
Area: **110 860 km²/42 803 miles²**
Population: **11 268 000** Languages: **Spanish**
Religions: **Roman Catholic, Protestant** Currency: **Cuban peso**

Cuba, known for revolution, Fidel Castro, ancient American cars and cigars, is visited for its climate and beaches, the colonial architecture and distinctive Cuban culture. Its music is a unique mix of European and African rhythm and sound. Parts of Havana are a World Heritage site and the old city stands much as it did 100 or so years ago – much has been done to restore its colonial character. Pinar del Rio is a popular area to visit, with attractive beaches, diving sites, hot springs and a beautiful landscape of mountains, valleys and hillside caves.

DOMINICAN REPUBLIC Capital: **Santo Domingo**
Area: **48 442 km²/18 704 miles²**
Population: **9 760 000** Languages: **Spanish, Creole**
Religions: **Roman Catholic, Protestant** Currency: **Dominican peso**

Christopher Columbus described the Dominican Republic as 'a beautiful island paradise'. The island is home to gaming resorts and casinos, golf courses designed by world champion golfers, and many national parks and protected areas – much of its flora is endemic.

JAMAICA Capital: **Kingston**
Area: **10 991 km²/4 244 miles²**
Population: **2 714 000** Languages: **English, Creole**
Religions: **Protestant, Roman Catholic**
Currency: **Jamaican dollar**

Jamaica is the third largest island in the Caribbean. Kingston is its capital, with the soaring Blue Mountains as a backdrop. Devon House, one of many preserved colonial mansions, is a national heritage site. Other attractions include the Bob Marley Museum, Jamaica's National Gallery, Hope Botanical Gardens, Spanish Town neighbourhood and Port Royal, once a haven for pirates. Montego Bay is home to a marine park, one of Jamaica's best coral reefs and offers stunning views from the town itself. Another popular destination is the resort of Ocho Rios, with restaurants and nightclubs, dolphin spotting, botanical gardens, horse riding, waterfalls and of course, the beaches.

MARTINIQUE

Volcanic Martinique offers an attractive French/Creole heritage that pervades the culture, cuisine, music and dance. Hiking and nature watching is available on the volcano slopes and through the tropical forest.

PUERTO RICO

Puerto Rico is distinctly Spanish in culture. It is a land of mountains, tropical rainforest, beaches, and Phosphorescent Bay – full of microscopic marine life that lights up when disturbed, best seen from an evening boat trip or snorkel.

World Heritage Sites numbered on the map:

BELIZE
1. Belize Barrier Reef Reserve System (G5)

COLOMBIA
2. National Archeological Park of Tierradentro (I8)

COSTA RICA
3. Área de Conservación Guanacaste (G6)
4. Talamanca Range-La Amistad Reserves / La Amistad National Park (H7)

CUBA
5. Archaeological Landscape of the First Coffee Plantations in the South-East of Cuba (I4)
6. Desembarco del Granma National Park (I5)

EL SALVADOR
7. Joya de Cerén Archaeological Site (G6)

GUATEMALA
8. Antigua Guatemala (F6)
9. Archaeological Park and Ruins of Quirigua (G5)
10. Tikal National Park (G5)

HAITI
11. National History Park - Citadel, Sans Souci, Ramiers (J5)

HONDURAS
12. Maya Site of Copan (G6)
13. Río Plátano Biosphere Reserve (H5)

MEXICO
14. Agave Landscape and Ancient Industrial Facilities of Tequila (D4)
15. Archaeological Monuments Zone of Xochicalco (E5)
16. Earliest 16th-Century Monasteries on the Slopes of Popocatepetl (E5)
17. Franciscan Missions in the Sierra Gorda of Querétaro (E4)
18. El Tajín, Pre-Hispanic City (E4)
19. Historic Monuments Zone of Tlacotalpan (E5)
20. Pre-Hispanic City of Teotihuacan (E5)
21. Protective town of San-Miguel and the Sanctuary of Jesús Nazareno de Atotonilco (D4)

NIGARAGUA
22. Ruins of León Viejo (G6)

PANANMA
23. Coiba National Park and its Special Zone of Marine Protection (H7)
24. Fortifications on the Caribbean Side of Panama: Portobelo-San Lorenzo (I7)
25. Talamanca Range-La Amistad Reserves / La Amistad National Park (H7)

U.S.A
26. Great Smoky Mountains National Park (H1)

Lambert Azimuthal Equal Area Projection

1:14 000 000

MILES 0   200   40

ATLANTIC

OCEAN

Bermuda (U.K.)
Historic Town of St George and Related Fortifications, Bermuda
Hamilton

Tropic of Cancer

THE BAHAMAS

GULF OF MEXICO

Memphis
TENNESSEE
NORTH CAROLINA
Cape Hatteras
Cape Lookout
Wilmington
Cape Fear
Myrtle Beach
Georgetown
Charleston
Hilton Head Island
Savannah
Brunswick
Jacksonville
St Augustine
Daytona Beach
Cape Canaveral
Melbourne
Fort Pierce
West Palm Beach
Fort Lauderdale
Hollywood
Miami Beach
Miami
Key West

Nashville
Knoxville
Asheville
Charlotte
Raleigh
Durham
Winston-Salem
Greensboro
High Point

ALABAMA
GEORGIA
Atlanta
Birmingham
Montgomery
Columbus
Macon
Albany
Dothan
Tallahassee
Jacksonville

MISSISSIPPI
Jackson
Hattiesburg
Baton Rouge
New Orleans
Mobile
Pensacola
Panama City

SOUTH CAROLINA
Columbia

Havana (La Habana)
Matanzas
Pinar del Río
CUBA
Santa Clara
Cienfuegos
Camagüey
Holguín
Bayamo
Santiago de Cuba
Manzanillo
Guantánamo

Nassau
Andros
Cat Island
San Salvador
Long Island
Great Exuma
Crooked Island
Mayaguana
Turks and Caicos Islands (U.K.)
Grand Turk (Cockburn Town)

Cayman Islands (U.K.)
George Town
Grand Cayman
Little Cayman
Cayman Brac

JAMAICA
Montego Bay
Kingston
Spanish Town

HISPANIOLA
HAITI
Port-au-Prince
Cap-Haïtien
Gonaïves
Jérémie
Les Cayes
Jacmel

DOMINICAN REPUBLIC
Santiago
Puerto Plata
San Francisco de Macorís
La Romana
Santo Domingo
Barahona

Puerto Rico (U.S.A.)
San Juan
Ponce

Virgin Is (U.S.A.)
Virgin Is (U.K.)
Road Town
Charlotte Amalie
St Croix

LEEWARD ISLANDS
Anguilla (U.K.)
The Valley
St-Martin (Fr.)
St Maarten (Neth.)
St-Barthélemy (Fr.)
ANTIGUA AND BARBUDA
St John's
ST KITTS AND NEVIS
Basseterre
Montserrat (U.K.)
Guadeloupe (Fr.)
Basse-Terre
Pointe-à-Pitre
DOMINICA
Roseau
Morne Trois Pitons National Park
Martinique (Fr.)
Fort-de-France
ST LUCIA
Castries
ST VINCENT & THE GRENADINES
Kingstown
BARBADOS
Bridgetown
GRENADA
St George's

CARIBBEAN SEA

GREATER ANTILLES

Lesser Antilles

WINDWARD ISLANDS

YUCATÁN
Mérida
Cancún
Cozumel
Chetumal
Campeche
BELIZE
Belmopan

GUATEMALA
Guatemala City
HONDURAS
Tegucigalpa
San Pedro Sula
La Ceiba
EL SALVADOR
San Salvador
San Miguel

NICARAGUA
Managua
Granada

COSTA RICA
San José
Cartago
Puerto Limón

PANAMA
PANAMA CITY
Colón
David
Gulf of Panama

Isla de Coco (Costa Rica)
Cocos Island National Park

Isla de Malpelo (Colombia)
Malpelo Fauna and Flora Sanctuary

NETHERLANDS ANTILLES
Aruba (Neth.)
Curaçao (Neth.)
Bonaire
Willemstad

TRINIDAD AND TOBAGO
Port of Spain
Scarborough

I. de Margarita (Ven.)
Porlamar

VENEZUELA
Maracaibo
Caracas
Maracay
Valencia
Barquisimeto
Barcelona
Maturín
Ciudad Guayana
Ciudad Bolívar
La Gran Sabana

Barranquilla
Cartagena
Santa Marta
Riohacha
Valledupar
COLOMBIA
Bucaramanga
Cúcuta
Medellín
Bogotá
Cali
Quibdó
Manizales
Pereira
Armenia
Ibagué
Neiva
Popayán
Buenaventura
Tumaco
Florencia

BRAZIL
Pakaraima Mts

0   200   400   600 KILOMETRES

Mexico and Central America

MEXICO Capital: Mexico City
Area: 1 972 545 km²/761 604 miles²
Population: 106 535 000 **Languages:** Spanish, Amerindian languages **Religions:** Roman Catholic, Protestant **Currency:** Mexican peso

Mexico is one of the world's most popular destinations. It is a great location for the adventurous, with diving, rafting, climbing, surfing and much more, readily accessible. Eco-tourism is a major draw, with biosphere reserves and national parks encompassing forests, jungle and deserts, mountains and waterfalls and a unique diversity of plant and wildlife, including the wonderful manatee found in the Gulf of Mexico. The capital, Mexico City, boasts a huge number of attractions including the historic centre, the floating gardens of Xochimilco, the golden Angel of Independence and the Plaza de las tres Culturas. The city has more than 150 fascinating museums, around 100 galleries and over 30 concert halls and theatres.

Bordered by the Pacific Ocean, Caribbean Sea and the Gulf of Mexico, the country offers a vast choice of beaches and distinctive resorts including Los Cabos, Acapulco, Cancún and the Mayan Riviera.

Mexico is probably best know for its outstanding ancient sites remaining from the many complex and sophisticated cultures that flourished for almost 4 000 years before the arrival of the first Europeans. Teotihuacán is northeast of Mexico City; Mitla and Monte Albán are in Oaxaca state; Chichén-Itzá and Tulum are on the Yucatán Peninsula; and there are countless more.

CENTRAL AMERICA
Central America comprises the countries of Belize, Costa Rica, Guatemala, El Salvador, Honduras, Nicaragu and Panama, linking North and South America via the Isthmus of Panama. An area with much political unrest towards the end of the last century, it is now becoming much more accessible to tourists.

COSTA RICA Capital: San José
Area: 51 100 km²/19 730 miles²
Population: 4 468 000 **Languages:** Spanish **Religions:** Roman Catholic, Protestant **Currency:** Costa Rican colón

Costa Rica is Central America's most visited country. An early advocate of eco-tourism, around one-third of the country is protected. One of the most popular destinations is the limestone caves of Barra Honda. The variety of plant and wildlife is astonishing, the colourful quetzal is one of the many bird species.

HONDURAS Capital: Tegucigalpa
Area: 112 088 km²/43 277 miles²
Population: 7 106 000 **Languages:** Spanish, Amerindian languages **Religions:** Roman Catholic, Protestant **Currency:** Lempira

Honduras has inviting beaches with vivid blue waters along its Caribbean coast. The magnificent Mayan ruins of Copán are a particular tourist draw. There are national parks across the country and the varied landscapes offer excellent hiking and bird watching.

NICARAGUA Capital: Managua
Area: 130 000 km²/50 193 miles²
Population: 5 603 000 **Languages:** Spanish, Amerindian languages **Religions:** Roman Catholic, Protestant **Currency:** Córdoba

Nicaragua, shunned by tourists during its harsh dictatorship, is now encouraging visitors. Its tourist facilities are not as well developed as other Central American countries, however, this will add to its attraction for some visitors. The wonderful beaches are often deserted. Nicaragua's wildlife is enticing and exotic, including jaguars, manatees and turtles.

Lambert Conformal Conic Projection

1:7 000 000

MILES 0   50   100   150   200

GULF OF MEXICO

Bahía de Campeche

PACIFIC OCEAN

Gulf of Tehuantepec

World Heritage Sites numbered on the map:
EL SALVADOR
1. Joya de Cerén Archaeological Site (G5)

GUATEMALA
2. Archaeological Park and Ruins of Quirigua (G5)

MEXICO
3. Archaeological Monuments Zone of Xochicalco (E4)
4. Earliest 16th-Century Monasteries on the Slopes of Popocatepetl (E4)
5. Monarch Butterfly Biosphere Reserve (D4)

U.S.A.
TEXAS
COAHUILA
NUEVO LEÓN
TAMAULIPAS
SAN LUIS POTOSÍ
XICO
GUANAJUATO
HIDALGO
MICHOACÁN
MÉXICO
MORELOS
PUEBLA
GUERRERO
OAXACA
SIERRA MADRE DEL SUR
VERACRUZ
TABASCO
CHIAPAS
YUCATÁN
CAMPECHE
QUINTANA ROO
BELIZE
GUATEMALA
HONDURAS
EL SALVADOR

Tropic of Cancer

Arrecife Alacrán

223

50 100 150 200 250 300 350 KILOMETRES

© Collins Bartholomew Ltd

South America Physical

South America stretches from north of the Equator to a point less than 1000 km (621 miles) away from Antarctica at Cape Horn. The most dominant physical features are the Andes, stretching down the western side, and the enormous Amazon Basin. Vast plains occupy much of the south and southeast – in the Pampas grasslands and the region of Patagonia in southern Argentina. Much of the rest of the continent consists of dissected plateaus, undulating lowlands, and lesser mountain ranges.

Facts

- The Galapagos Islands, made famous by research by Charles Darwin and renowned for its wildlife and biodiversity, are a far-flung part of Ecuador, situated about 750 km (466 miles) out in the Pacific Ocean.

- Cerro Aconcagua, at 6959 m (22 831 ft), is the highest point in the western hemisphere.

- South Georgia and the South Sandwich Islands, lying between South America and Antarctica, are collectively a UK dependency, with no permanent population.

- The world's driest desert is the Atacama, where only 1 mm of rain may fall as infrequently as once every five to twenty years.

HIGHEST MOUNTAINS	m	ft
Cerro Aconcagua, Argentina	6 959	22 831
Nevado Ojos del Salado, Argentina/Chile	6 908	22 664
Cerro Bonete, Argentina	6 872	22 546
Cerro Pissis, Argentina	6 858	22 500
Cerro Tupungato, Argentina/Chile	6 800	22 309
Cerro Mercedario, Argentina	6 770	22 211

LARGEST ISLANDS	sq km	sq miles
Isla Grande de Tierra del Fuego	47 000	18 147
Isla de Chiloé	8 394	3 241
East Falkland	6 760	2 610
West Falkland	5 413	2 090

LONGEST RIVERS	km	miles
Amazon (Amazonas)	6 516	4 049
Río de la Plata-Paraná	4 500	2 796
Purus	3 218	2 000
Madeira	3 200	1 988
São Francisco	2 900	1 802
Tocantins	2 750	1 709

LARGEST LAKES	sq km	sq miles
Lake Titicaca	8 340	3 220

Orthographic Projection

1:32 000 000

MILES 0   400   800   120

Cuba

Greater

Jamaica

Antilles

Caribbean Sea

Hispaniola   Puerto Rico   Anguilla
                                    Antigua
                            Guadeloupe
                        Dominica
                    Martinique
Punta   St Lucia
Gallinas   Aruba   *Lesser Antilles*   Barbados
Golfo de   Isla de Margarita   Grenada   St Vincent
Venezuela   and the Grenadines
Golfo   Sa. de Perijá   Tobago
del Darién   Lake   Trinidad
    Maracaibo   Orinoco   Orinoco Delta
Gulf   Orinoco Delta
of Panama   *Llanos*
Isla de Malpelo

Cordillera Occidental
Cordillera Central
Cordillera Oriental
            Guiana Highlands
Guaviare   La Gran
                Sabana
        Orinoco   *Pakaraima Mountains*
    Negro   Branco   Serra
                        Tumucumaque
Japurá   Mouths of
Putumayo   *Amazon*   Amazon   the Amazon
    Amazon   *Basin*   Represa   Ilha de
Marañón   de Balbina   Marajó

Ucayali   *selvas*   Madeira
            Juruá   Purus   Tapajós   Represa
Cordillera Central   Tucuruí
Cordillera Oriental   Xingu   Parnaíba
Cordillera Occidental   Serra dos Parecis   Serra do Cachimbo
            Beni   Guaporé   Juruena   Serra dos Caiabis   Tocantins   Cabo de
Lake   Mamoré   Araguaia   São Roque   Fernando
Titicaca   Cordillera Oriental   Serra do Roncador   São Francisco   de Noronha
    Altiplano   *Planalto do*   Barragem
Lago de   Bañados   *Mato Grosso*   Represa   de Sobradinho
Poopó   del Izozog   Serra da Mesa   Serra Geral de Goiás   *Chapada*
Salar   Pantanal   Serra do Caiapó   *Diamantina*
de Uyuni   Cabo Santo
                            Antonio
    Atacama Desert   Paraguay   *Brazilian*
                        Highlands   Ponta de Baleia
Islas   6908 Nevado   Gran Chaco   Teuco   Paraná   Cabo de São Tomé
de los Desventurados   6872 Cerro   Ojos del Salado   Ilha da Trindade
        Bonete   Uruguay   Represa Porto   Serra da Mantiqueira   Ilhas
                    Salinas Grandes   Primavera   Serra da Mantiqueira   Martin Vaz
Cerro Aconcagua   Sierras de Córdoba   Laguna Mar
6959   Chiquita
an Fernández   Salado   Lagoa
Islands   Isla San   dos Patos
Isla San   Ambrosio   *Pampas*   Lagoa
Félix   Paraná   Mirim
                Pampas   Uruguay
            Embalse Ezequiel   Río de la Plata
            Ramos Mexía
            R. Negro   Bahía Blanca
                Punta Rasa
Isla de Chiloé   Golfo San Matías
                Península
Archipiélago   Valdés
de los Chonos   Chubut
                Golfo de
Lago Buenos   San Jorge
Aires   Cabo Tres
Golfo de Penas   Puntas

Archipiélago de la   Bahía   West   *Falkland*
Reina Adelaida   Grande   Falkland   *Islands*
        Strait of Magellan   East Falkland
    Isla Grande
    de Tierra del Fuego
    Isla de los Estados   Shag
Cape Horn   Rocks
        Scotia Sea   South Georgia
Drake Passage

South Shetland
Islands   South   Traversay Islands
            Sandwich   Candlemas Island
        South   *Islands*   Saunders Island
        Orkney   Montagu Island
        Islands   Southern Thule   Bristol Island
Antarctic Peninsula

A   N   D   E   S
Patagonia

A T L A N T I C

O C E A N

Madeira

Canary
Islands   Gran
        Canaria   Tropic of Cancer

Cape Verde
Santo Antão
        Boa Vista
    São Tiago

        Gulf
        of
        Guinea

Senegal

Niger

Niger

Ascension   Equator

St Helena

Tristan
da Cunha

Cape of Good Hope   Tropic of Capricorn

Orange

0   400   800   1200   1600   2000 KILOMETRES

South America Political

Brazil fills most of the north of the continent, while Argentina is the largest country in the narrower south. Chile consists of a long, narrow strip along the Pacific coast. French Guiana is the only remaining territory under overseas control, on a continent which has a long colonial history. Spanish is the language of the majority of the continent, although Brazil is largely Portuguese-speaking. There has been a steady process of urbanization and the majority of South America's population live in the major cities and close to the coast.

Facts

- South America is often referred to as Latin America, reflecting the historic influences of Spain and Portugal.

- Bolivia and Paraguay are the only landlocked countries on the continent.

- The Falkland Islands were first settled by the British, although Argentina retains a claim over them and calls them the Malvinas Islands (Islas Malvinas in Spanish). This claim resulted in a war in 1982 between Argentina and the UK.

- The Juan Fernández Islands (Archipiélago Juan Fernández), a group of Chilean islands in the Pacific, are known for having been the location of the famous 'castaway' novel, Robinson Crusoe.

LARGEST COUNTRIES	Area	
	sq km	sq miles
Brazil	8 514 879	3 287 613
Argentina	2 766 889	1 068 302
Peru	1 285 216	496 225
Colombia	1 141 748	440 831
Bolivia	1 098 581	424 164
Venezuela	912 050	352 144
Chile	756 945	292 258
Paraguay	406 752	157 048
Ecuador	272 045	105 037
Guyana	214 969	83 000

MOST POPULATED COUNTRIES	Population
Brazil	191 791 000
Colombia	46 156 000
Argentina	39 531 000
Peru	27 903 000
Venezuela	27 657 000
Chile	16 635 000
Ecuador	13 341 000
Bolivia	9 525 000
Paraguay	6 127 000
Uruguay	3 340 000

CAPITALS		
Largest population	**Buenos Aires**, Argentina	13 067 000
Smallest population	**Stanley**, Falkland Islands	2 115
Most northerly	**Caracas**, Venezuela	10° 28' N
Most southerly	**Stanley**, Falkland Islands	51° 43' S
Highest	**La Paz**, Bolivia	3 630 m/ 11 909 ft

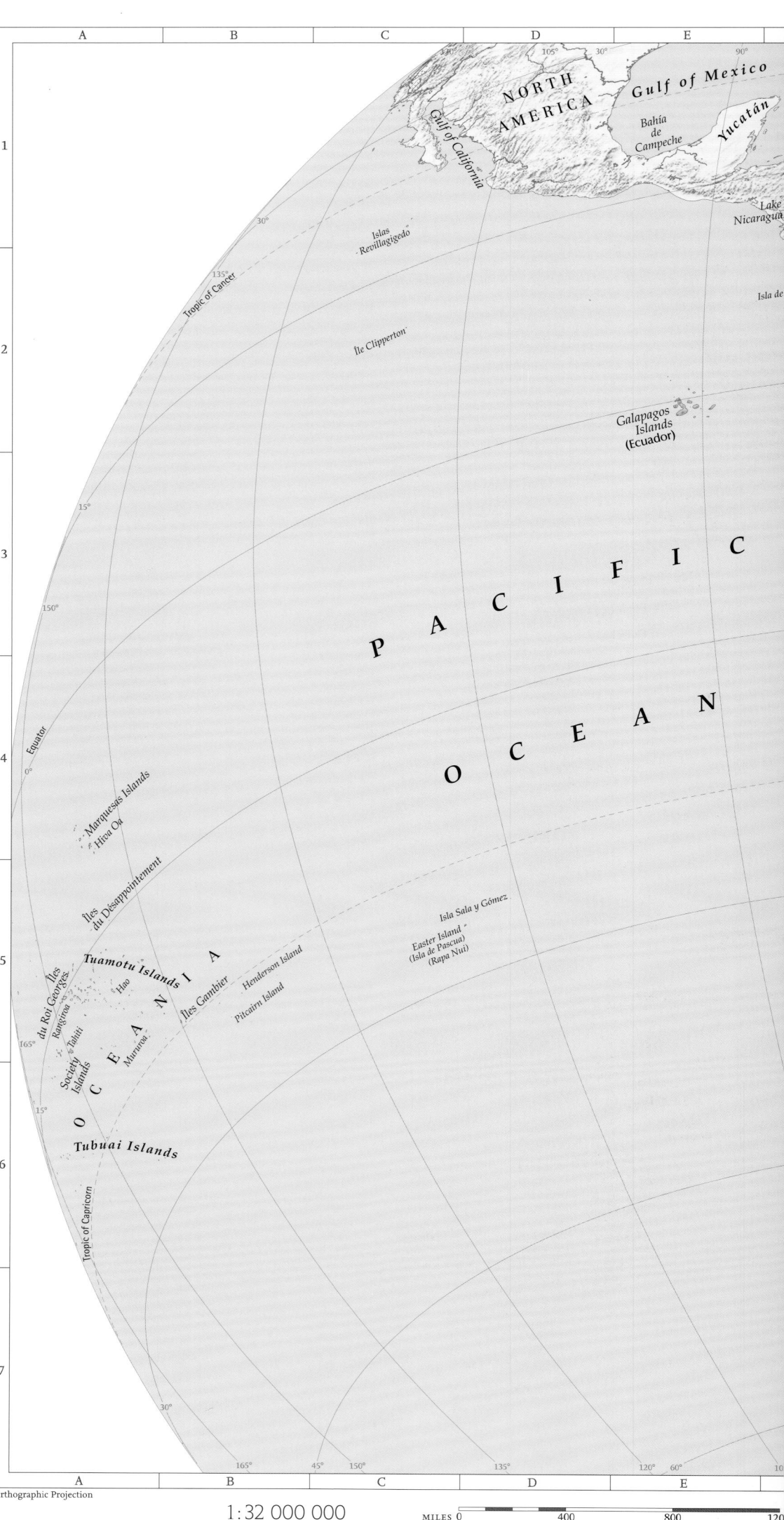

Orthographic Projection

1:32 000 000

MILES 0   400   800   1200

Map Labels

Top border (longitude/grid): G H I J K L M N

60° 45° 30° 30°

Caribbean/Islands (top):
Cuba
Greater Antilles
Jamaica
Hispaniola
Puerto Rico
Anguilla
Antigua
Guadeloupe
Dominica
Martinique
St Lucia
Barbados
St Vincent and the Grenadines
Grenada
Tobago
Trinidad
Aruba
Lesser Antilles
CARIBBEAN SEA

Madeira
Canary Islands
Gran Canaria
Tropic of Cancer
30°

Venezuela region:
Barranquilla
Cartagena
Maracaibo
Maracay Caracas
Valencia Cumaná
Montería
San Cristóbal
Ciudad Bolívar
Medellín
Tunja
VENEZUELA
Orinoco
Ibagué Bogotá
Puerto Ayacucho
Georgetown
COLOMBIA
Neiva
GUYANA
Paramaribo
SURINAME
Cayenne
French Guiana
Pasto
Boa Vista
Isla de Malpelo (Colombia)
Cali

Ecuador/Peru:
Quito
ECUADOR
quil
Cuenca
ala
Piura
Tarapoto
layo
Trujillo
Iquitos
Ucayali
Carauari
Macapá
Amazon
Belém
São Luís
Parnaíba
Fortaleza
PERU
Pucallpa
Cruzeiro do Sul
SELVAS
Manaus
Santarém
Marabá
Teresina
Natal
Fernando de Noronha (Brazil)
Callao
Huancayo
Rio Branco
Porto Velho
BRAZIL
Araguaína
Floresta
João Pessoa
Recife
Lima
Ica
Cusco
Puerto Maldonado
Madeira
Tapajós
Palmas
Juazeiro
Maceió
Aracaju
Barragem de Sobradinho
Santo Antão
Cape Verde
Boa Vista
São Tiago

Bolivia/central:
Juliaca
Lake Titicaca
Trinidad
Xingu
Salvador
Arequipa
La Paz
Cuiabá
Brasília
Ilhéus
Cochabamba
BOLIVIA
Goiânia
Represa Serra da Mesa
São Francisco
Arica
Santa Cruz
Sucre
Patos de Minas
Iquique
Potosí
Campo Grande
Teófilo Otôni
Tarija
Araçatuba
Uberaba
Vitória
Antofagasta
PARAGUAY
Pedro Juan Caballero
Ribeirão Preto
Belo Horizonte
Islas de los Desventurados (Chile)
San Salvador de Jujuy
Maringá
Campinas
Copiapó
Nevado Ojos del Salado 6908
Formosa
Asunción
Coronel Oviedo
São Paulo
Santos
Rio de Janeiro
Catamarca
Resistencia
Encarnación
Curitiba
Ilha da Trindade (Brazil)
Ilhas Martin Vaz (Brazil)
La Rioja
Corrientes
Posadas
Joinville
La Serena
Córdoba
Santa Fe
Concordia
Santa Maria
Florianópolis
Cerro Aconcagua 6959
Mendoza
Paraná
Lagoa dos Patos
Porto Alegre
Fernández Islands (Chile)
Valparaíso
Rosario
URUGUAY
Rio Grande
Santiago
San Luis
Buenos Aires
Montevideo
CHILE
San Rafael
La Plata
Rio de la Plata
Talca
ARGENTINA
Santa Rosa
Chillán
Concepción
Neuquén
Mar del Plata
Valdivia
Bahía Blanca

South/Patagonia:
Puerto Montt
Viedma
Golfo San Matías
Isla de Chiloé
Trelew
Archipiélago de los Chonos
PATAGONIA
Golfo de Penas
Comodoro Rivadavia
Golfo de San Jorge
Falkland Islands (U.K.)
Puerto Natales
Bahía Grande
Río Gallegos
Stanley
Punta Arenas
Isla Grande de Tierra del Fuego
Ushuaia
Isla de los Estados
Cape Horn
Drake Passage
Shag Rocks
South Georgia
South Shetland Islands
Antarctic Peninsula
South Orkney Islands
South Georgia and the South Sandwich Islands (U.K.)
South Sandwich Islands
Traversay Islands
Candlemas Island
Saunders Island
Montagu Island
Bristol Island
Southern Thule

Atlantic/Africa:
AFRICA
Gulf of Guinea
ATLANTIC OCEAN
Ascension
Equator
St Helena
Tristan da Cunha
Tropic of Capricorn
Cape of Good Hope
Senegal
Niger
Orange

Bottom border:
90° 75° 60° 45° 30° 15° 0° 15° 30°
G H I J K L M N

© Collins Bartholomew Ltd

Scale:
400 800 1200 1600 2000 KILOMETRES

229

Northern South America

Rainforest and the Amazon dominate the greater part of this area. Major attractions are trips into the jungles and forests, to experience the unique atmosphere, plant life and wildlife. There is also much history, ancient and modern, and exciting culture to enjoy.

 BOLIVIA Capital: **La Paz/Sucre**
Area: **1 098 581 km²/424 164 miles²**
Population: **9 525 000** Languages: **Spanish, Quechua, Aymara**
Religions: **Roman Catholic, Protestant, Baha'i**
Currency: **Boliviano**

A landlocked country, Bolivia offers beautiful landscapes, river trips into the rainforest, bus rides along the mountain passes of the Andes and ancient sites such as those on Lake Titicaca. The large indigenous population is reflected in native cultures, dialects and music. The Spanish influence is visible in the colonial architecture, particularly in Sucre. Salar de Uyuni is the world's largest salt flat and, during November, a major breeding ground for pink flamingos. It is also the site of a train cemetery, the locomotives abandoned when the mining industry collapsed in the 1940s.

 GUYANA Capital: **Georgetown**
Area: **214 969 km²/83 000 miles²** Population: **738 000**
Languages: **English, Creole, Amerindian languages**
Religions: **Protestant, Hindu, Roman Catholic, Sunni Muslim**
Currency: **Guyana dollar**

Guyana's main attractions include the spectacular Kaieteur Falls on the Potaro River, Atlantic beaches, the Rupununi savanna, and river routes into the forests and jungles to see rare wildlife, including more than 700 indigenous bird species. The capital, Georgetown, has striking 19th-century stilted wooden buildings.

 SURINAME Capital: **Paramaribo**
Area: **163 820 km²/63 251 miles²** Population: **458 000**
Languages: **Dutch, Surinamese, English, Hindi**
Religions: **Hindu, Roman Catholic, Protestant, Sunni Muslim**
Currency: **Suriname guilder**

Rainforest covers 80 per cent of Suriname, which has eleven nature reserves and other special sites: the word's largest area of protected rainforest and a World Heritage site. Much of the interior, home to native tribes, is accessible only by canoeing the rivers and rapids.

 ECUADOR Capital: **Quito**
Area: **272 045 km²/105 037 miles²**
Population: **13 341 000** Languages: **Spanish, Quechua and other Amerindian languages** Religions: **Roman Catholic**
Currency: **United States dollar**

Straddling the Equator, Ecuador is divided into three distinctive regions. The Andean highlands of La Sierra are known as the Avenue of Volcanoes, home to much of the population. El Oriente is covered in dense jungle and a network of rivers. La Costa is Ecuador's Pacific coast, with mangrove forests and attractive beaches. The capital, Quito, has a wonderfully preserved historic centre, the best in Latin America. The Galapagos Islands, far out into the Pacific, are famed for their unique wildlife.

PERU Capital: **Lima**
Area: **1 285 216 km²/496 225 miles²**
Population: **27 903 000** Languages: **Spanish, Quechua, Aymara** Religions: **Roman Catholic, Protestant** Currency: **Sol**

Peru is best known for the Inca trail from Cusco to Machu Picchu, the capital of the Inca Empire and a World Heritage site. It is also a country of snowy peaks, mountaintop lakes, deserts, beaches and jungle, and a popular destination for surfing, extreme mountain biking, adventurous river trips and trekking. The geoglyphs and lines (some stretching hundreds of kilometres) of Nasca and Pampas de Jumana, scratched onto the ground between 500 BC and AD 500 are one of the world's enigmas.

Lambert Azimuthal Equal Area Projection

1:15 000 000

MILES 0   100   200   300   40

A T L A N T I C

O C E A N

BRAZIL

VENEZUELA

GRENADA

TRINIDAD AND TOBAGO

GUYANA

SURINAME

French Guiana

BOLIVIA

PARAGUAY

ARGENTINA

Georgetown

Paramaribo

Cayenne

Boa Vista

Macapá

Belém

São Luís

Fortaleza

Natal

João Pessoa

Recife

Maceió

Manaus

Teresina

Salvador

Brasília

Goiânia

Belo Horizonte

Vitória

Rio de Janeiro

São Paulo

Santos

Santa Cruz

Equator

Tropic of Capricorn

0   200   400   600   800 KILOMETRES

Southern South America

ARGENTINA Capital: Buenos Aires
Area: **2 766 889 km²/1 068 302 miles²**
Population: **39 531 000** Languages: **Spanish, Italian, Amerindian languages** Religions: **Roman Catholic, Protestant**
Currency: **Argentinian peso**

Argentina is a country of vivid culture and stunning landscape. Iguazu Falls are a World Heritage site along the border of Argentina and Brazil. The area is home to endangered species such as jaguar and ocelot. To the south, Patagonia has snow-capped Andean peaks, the Perito Moreno Glacier, Península Valdés and the beautiful red mountains of Salta. Buenos Aires is a welcoming, lively, modern capital. Strong on performing arts, the city has around 100 cinemas and 90 theatres. Ushuaia is often described as the world's most southerly city, its attractions including Tierra del Fuego National Park and Lapataia Bay.

CHILE Capital: Santiago
Area: **756 945 km²/292 258 miles²**
Population: **16 635 000** Languages: **Spanish, Amerindian languages** Religions: **Roman Catholic, Protestant**
Currency: **Chilean peso**

Chile, lying along the west coast of South America, is a great destination for outdoor activities and is increasingly popular with adventure tourists looking for an adrenaline rush. The huge, dry Atacama Desert has the world's two highest active volcanoes: San Pedro and Volcan Llullaillaco. San Pedro de Atacama is home to a fascinating archaeological museum containing thousands of ancient artefacts from the Atacameno culture. In the centre, are the spectacular granite monoliths of the Cordillera del Paine. The lake district of Patagonia and Torres del Paine National Park, to the south, is an area of impressive mountains, glaciers and lakes.

PARAGUAY Capital: Asunción
Area: **406 752 km²/157 048 miles²**
Population: **6 127 000** Languages: **Spanish, Guaraní**
Religions: **Roman Catholic, Protestant** Currency: **Guaraní**

Paraguay, landlocked and sandwiched between Brazil and Argentina on the great plain of Gran Chaco, has national parks, great areas of wilderness, jungles, forests and waterfalls. The capital, Asunción, sits on the banks of the Paraguay river and the Argentinian border and is one of the world's cheapest cities, popular for its parks, museums and boat tours.

Venezuela and Colombia

COLOMBIA Capital: Bogotá
Area: **1 141 748 km²/440 831 miles²**
Population: **46 156 000** Languages: **Spanish, Amerindian languages** Religions: **Roman Catholic, Protestant**
Currency: **Colombian peso**

Colombia has wonderful natural attractions of mountains, jungles and both Caribbean and Pacific coastlines. The variety of wildlife and plants is resulting in developing ecotourism and there are six UNESCO World Heritage sites. Birding is a tourist draw, with over 750 different bird species in the Colombian Amazon, accessible from the city of Leticia. Bogotá, high in the Andres, shows its colonial history in sharp contrast to the modern high-rise buildings.

VENEZUELA Capital: Caracas
Area: **912 050 km²/352 144 miles²**
Population: **27 657 000** Languages: **Spanish, Amerindian languages** Religions: **Roman Catholic, Protestant**
Currency: **Bolívar fuerte**

Venezuela is known for oil but enthusiastically welcomes visitors to its tropical beaches, colonial towns, jungles and mountains. The Orinoco delta is a labyrinth of waterways with opportunities for river trips, meetings with native Indians and sightings of the rich and varied wildlife and extensive bird populations. Canaima lagoon, fed by waterfalls (including the world's highest, Angel Falls) has a fantastic backdrop of 'table' mountains, the *tepui*.

Lambert Azimuthal Equal Area Projection
1:15 000 000 MILES 0 100 200 300 0 200 400 600 KILOMETRES

Map — Northern South America

Major countries and regions:

- BRAZIL
- RORAIMA
- AMAZONAS
- VENEZUELA
- COLOMBIA
- GUYANA
- PANAMA
- ECUADOR
- TRINIDAD AND TOBAGO
- GRENADA
- Netherlands Antilles
- Aruba (Neth.)
- Curaçao (Neth.)

Seas and water bodies:

- CARIBBEAN SEA
- Lesser Antilles
- Gulf of Paria
- Orinoco Delta
- Lake Maracaibo
- Golfo de Venezuela
- Golfo del Darién

Selected cities and places:

Caracas, Maracay, Valencia, Barquisimeto, Maracaibo, Barcelona, Cumaná, Ciudad Guayana, Ciudad Bolívar, Maturín, Barinas, San Cristóbal, San Fernando de Apure, Puerto Ayacucho, Bogotá, Medellín, Cali, Cartagena, Barranquilla, Santa Marta, Riohacha, Cúcuta, Bucaramanga, Tunja, Villavicencio, Pasto, Popayán, Buenaventura, Manizales, Pereira, Armenia, Ibagué, Neiva, Florencia, Port of Spain, Scarborough, St George's, Willemstad, Oranjestad, Boa Vista.

Physical features:

- Pakaraima Mountains
- La Gran Sabana
- Serra Parima
- Sierra Nevada de Santa Marta
- Cordillera Oriental
- Cordillera Central
- Cordillera Occidental
- Península de la Guajira

Inset maps:

- SOUTH GEORGIA (U.K.) — 1:15 000 000 — Cape Alexandra, Cape Disappointment, Mt Paget, Grytviken
- BRAZIL region inset — São Paulo, Curitiba, Florianópolis, Joinville, Blumenau, Santos, Campinas, Uberlândia, Araguari, Franca, Ribeirão Prêto

World Heritage Sites numbered on the map:

ARGENTINA
Iguazu National Park (F3)
Jesuit Missions of the Guaranis: San Ignacio Miní, Santa Ana, Nuestra Señora de Loreto and Santa María Mayor (E3)

BRAZIL
Atlantic Forest South-East Reserves (F2/G2)
Iguaçu National Park (F3)
Jesuit Missions of the Guaranis: Ruins of Sao Miguel das Missões (F3)

PARAGUAY
Jesuit Missions of La Santísima Trinidad de Paraná and Jesús de Tavarangue (E3)

URUGUAY
Historic Quarter of the City of Colonia del Sacramento (E4)

Southeast Brazil

 BRAZIL Capital: **Brasília**
Area: **8 514 879 km²/3 287 613 miles²**
Population: **191 791 000** Languages: **Portuguese**
Religions: **Roman Catholic, Protestant** Currency: **Real**

Portuguese-speaking Brazil is a good-time destination, known for football success and music, particularly the samba, ubiquitous in Brazil's carnivals. In Rio the focus of the carnival is in an open-air stadium, specially built to allow spectators to enjoy the samba dancing, costumes and floats. Salvador's carnival is the world's largest street party, according to the Guinness Book of Records. Celebrated for almost 300 years, thousands of visitors flock to the city for the party. Recife and Olinda are also great destinations to experience the exciting carnival atmosphere. Olinda, a charming town of Baroque churches and vividly painted houses, parades giant papier-mâché figures of folk heroes as part of its celebrations.

Brazil is not just a party destination. It has a beautiful coast and beaches, colonial towns and energetic cities, as well as the wild interior of Amazon rainforest, teeming with wildlife and plants. Over sixty national parks across the country provide plentiful opportunities for eco tourism. Brazil is also a great destination for fishing, trekking, surfing, rafting, diving, sailing and of course beach volleyball, synonymous with lively Brazilian beaches.

The Iguaçu Falls, located in the national park of the same name, is a popular draw, as is the Itaipu Dam on the Paraná River, between Brazil and Paraguay. Visitors are also drawn to the Triple Frontier, marking the borders of Brazil, Argentina and Paraguay.

Brasília, the capital, is a World Heritage site. It was a new city, developed in 1956 and designed with the intention that every element should be in harmony with the city's overall design.

Serra da Capivara Park is in the northeast of the country, a World Heritage site where rock shelters decorated with cave paintings, some more than 25 000 years old, have been discovered. There are over 300 important archaeological sites within the park.

Central Chile, Central Argentina and Uruguay

URUGUAY Capital: **Montevideo**
Area: **176 215 km²/68 037 miles²**
Population: **3 340 000** Languages: **Spanish**
Religions: **Roman Catholic, Protestant, Jewish**
Currency: **Uruguayan peso**

Uruguay is growing in popularity as a destination in its own right, as well as an easy day trip from Buenos Aires, on the opposite bank of the Rio de la Plata. With around 650 km (400 miles) of marvellous coastline there are stretches of deserted beach and a variety of resorts offering water sports and trips to see whales, seals and turtles. Inland are the wide, open prairies – gaucho country where visitors can stay on estancias. Montevideo is a lively capital with its own carnival. Uruguay's oldest town, Colonia del Sacramento, is a World Heritage site of cobbled streets and historic buildings.

Lambert Azimuthal Equal Area Projection
1:7 500 000
MILES 0 50 100 150 0 50 100 150 200 250 300 KILOMETRES

BRAZIL

URUGUAY

PARAGUAY

ARGENTINA

CHILE

ATLANTIC OCEAN

Montevideo

Buenos Aires

Río de la Plata

Rosario

Córdoba

Mendoza

Santiago

Valparaíso

Mar del Plata

Bahía Blanca

La Plata

Santa Fe

San Juan

San Luis

Curitiba

Paraná

ENTRE RÍOS

SANTA FE

CÓRDOBA

SAN LUIS

LA PAMPA

BUENOS AIRES

MENDOZA

SAN JUAN

LA RIOJA

NEUQUÉN

RÍO NEGRO

CHUBUT

COQUIMBO

O'HIGGINS

MAULE

BIOBÍO

ARAUCANÍA

LOS LAGOS

Golfo San Matías

Península Valdés

Tropic of Capricorn

States and Territories (continued)

OCEANIA

 KIRIBATI Capital: Bairiki Population: 95 000 Area: 717 km²/277 miles² Languages: Gilbertese, English Religions: Roman Catholic, Protestant Currency: Australian dollar

 MARSHALL ISLANDS Capital: Delap-Uliga-Djarrit Area: 181 km²/ 70 miles² Population: 59 000 Languages: English, Marshallese Religions: Protestant, Roman Catholic Currency: United States dollar

 MICRONESIA, FEDERATED STATES OF Capital: Palikir Area: 701 km²/271 miles² Population: 111 000 Languages: English, Chuukese, Pohnpeian, local languages Religions: Roman Catholic, Protestant Currency: United States dollar

NAURU Capital Yaren Area: 21 km²/8 miles² Population: 10 000 Languages: Nauruan, English Religions: Protestant, Roman Catholic Currency: Australian dollar

SAMOA Capital: Apia Area: 2 831 km²/1 093 km² Population: 187 000 Languages: Samoan, English Religions: Protestant, Roman Catholic Currency: Tala

SOLOMON ISLANDS Capital: Honiara Area: 28 370 km²/ 10 954 miles² Population: 496 000 Languages: English, Creole, local languages Religions: Protestant, Roman Catholic Currency: Solomon Islands dollar

✚ **TONGA** Capital: Nuku'alofa Area: 748 km²/289 miles² Population: 100 000 Languages: Tongan, English Religions: Protestant, Roman Catholic Currency: Pa'anga

TUVALU Capital: Vaiaku Area: 25 km²/10 miles² Population: 11 000 Languages: Tuvaluan, English Religions: Protestant Currency: Australian dollar

VANUATU Capital: Port Vila Area: 12 190 km²/4 707 miles² Population: 226 000 Languages: English, Bislama (Creole), French Religions: Protestant, Roman Catholic, traditional beliefs Currency: Vatu

ASIA

 EAST TIMOR Capital: Dili Area 14 874 km²/5 743 miles² Population: 1 155 000 Languages: Portuguese, Tetun, English Religions: Roman Catholic Currency: United States dollar

Gaza Capital: Gaza Area: 363 km²/140 miles² Population: 1 586 008 Languages: Arabic Religions: Sunni Muslim, Shi'a Muslim Currency: Israeli shekel

Jammu amd Kashmir Capital: Srinagar Area: 222 236 km²/ 85 806 miles² Population: 13 000 000

 PALAU Capital: Melekeok Area: 497 km²/192 miles² Population: 20 000 Languages: Palauan, English Religions: Roman Catholic, Protestant, traditional beliefs Currency: United States dollar

 SINGAPORE Capital: Singapore Area: 639 km²/247 miles² Population: 4 436 000 Languages: Chinese, English, Malay, Tamil Religions: Buddhist, Taoist, Sunni Muslim, Christian, Hindu Currency: Singapore dollar

West Bank Area: 5 860 km²/2 263 miles² Population: 2 676 284 Languages: Arabic, Hebrew Religions: Sunni Muslim, Jewish, Shi'a Muslim, Christian Currency: Jordanian dinar, Isreali shekel

EUROPE

 ALBANIA Capital: Tirana (Tiranë) Area: 28 748 km²/11 100 miles² Population: 3 190 000 Languages: Albanian, Greek Religions: Sunni Muslim, Albanian Orthodox, Roman Catholic Currency: Lek

BOSNIA-HERZEGOVINA Capital: Sarajevo Area: 51 130 km²/ 19 741 miles² Population: 3 935 000 Languages: Bosnian, Serbian, Croatian Religions: Sunni Muslim, Serbian Orthodox, Roman Catholic, Protestant Currency: Marka

KOSOVO Capital: Prishtinë (Priština) Area: 10 908 km²/4 212 miles² Population: 2 069 989 Languages: Albanian, Serbian Religions: Sunni Muslim, Serbian Orthodox Currency: Euro

LIECHTENSTEIN Capital: Vaduz Area: 160 km²/62 miles² Population: 35 000 Languages: German Religions: Roman Catholic, Protestant Currency: Swiss franc

MONACO Capital: Monaco-Ville Area: 2 km²/1 miles² Population: 33 000 Languages: French, Monégasque, Italian Religions: Roman Catholic Currency: Euro

MONTENEGRO Capital: Podgorica Area: 13 812 km²/5 333 miles² Population: 598 000 Languages: Serbian (Montenegrin), Albanian Religions: Montenegrin Orthodox, Sunni Muslim Currency: Euro

SAN MARINO Capital: San Marino Area: 61 km²/24 miles² Population: 31 000 Languages: Italian Religions: Roman Catholic Currency: Euro

SERBIA Capital: Belgrade (Beograd) Area: 77 453 km²/29 904 miles² Population: 7 788 448 Languages: Serbian, Hungarian Religions: Serbian Orthodox, Roman Catholic, Sunni Muslim Currency: Serbian dinar

VATICAN CITY Capital: Vatican City Area: 0.5 km²/0.2 miles² Population: 557 Languages: Italian Religions: Roman Catholic Currency: Euro

AFRICA

 ALGERIA Capital: Algiers (Alger) Area: 2 381 741 km²/919 595 miles² Population: 33 858 000 Languages: Arabic, French, Berber Religions: Sunni Muslim Currency: Algerian dinar

 ANGOLA Capital: Luanda Area: 1 246 700 km²/481 354 miles² Population: 17 024 000 Languages: Portuguese, Bantu, local languages Religions: Roman Catholic, Protestant, traditional beliefs Currency: Kwanza

 BENIN Capital: Porto-Novo Area: 112 620 km²/43 483 miles² Population: 9 033 000 Languages: French, Fon, Yoruba, Adja, local languages Religions: Traditional beliefs, Roman Catholic, Sunni Muslim Currency CFA franc

 BOTSWANA Capital: Gaborone Area: 581 370 km²/224 468 miles² Population: 1 882 000 Languages: English, Setswana, Shona, local languages Religions: Traditional beliefs, Protestant, Roman Catholic Currency Pula

BURKINA Capital: Ouagadougou Area: 274 200 km²/105 869 miles² Population: 14 784 000 Languages: French, Moore (Mossi), Fulani, local languages Religions: Sunni Muslim, traditional beliefs, Roman Catholic Currency: CFA franc

Pacific Ocean

Lambert Azimuthal Equal Area Projection

1:58 000 000   MILES 0   500   1000   1500   2000

F 165° G 180° H 165° I 150° J 135° K 120° L 105° M 90° N 75° O 60° P 45° Q

Wrangel Island
Point Barrow
Arctic Circle
Hudson Bay
Newfoundland
Cape Race

Chukchi Sea
Mackenzie
Ames Bay
St John's

St Lawrence Island
Bering Strait

Nunivak Island
Kodiak Island
Alexander Archipelago

Ostrov Beringa
Bering Sea
Gulf of Alaska
Queen Charlotte Islands

Aleutian Islands
Vancouver Island
Vancouver
Columbia

Aleutian Trench
Tufts Abyssal Plain

Emperor Trough
Chinook Trough
Cape Mendocino
San Francisco
NORTH AMERICA
Cape Hatteras
Bermuda Rise
MID-ATLANTIC RIDGE
Tropic of Cancer

Kure Atoll
Midway Islands
Los Angeles
Hatteras Abyssal Plain
Nares Deep

Laysan Island
Gardner Pinnacles
Necker Island
Hawai'ian Islands
NORTHEAST PACIFIC BASIN
Guadalupe
Gulf of California
New Orleans
Gulf of Mexico
The Bahamas
Sigsbee Deep
Greater Antilles
Cuba
Milwaukee Deep

Kaua'i
O'ahu
Maui
Hawai'i
Mexico City
Yucatan Channel
Caribbean Sea
Hispaniola
Jamaica
Cayman Trench

PACIFIC
Johnston Atoll
Islas Revillagigedo
Isla Socorro
Isla Clarión

Palmyra Atoll
Line Islands
Île Clipperton
Middle America Trench
Guatemala Basin
Colombian Basin
Venezuelan Basin
Lesser Antilles
Demerara Abyssal Plain
GUIANA BASIN

OCEAN
Tabuaeran
Kiritimati
Colon Ridge
Cocos Ridge
Isla de Coco
Isla de Malpelo
Bogotá
Amazon Cone

Baker Island
Howland Island
Malden Island
Gallego Rise
Galapagos Islands
Quito
Ceara Abyssal Plain
Equator

Phoenix Islands
Nikumaroro
Starbuck Island
Penrhyn Basin
Galapagos Rise

Kanton Rawaki Manra
Penrhyn
Nuku Hiva
Marquesas Islands
Hiva Oa

Funafuti
Fakaofo
Atafu Tokelau
Vostok Island
Caroline Island
Peru Basin
SOUTH AMERICA

Nukulaelae
Swains Island
Pukapuka
Nassau
Manihiki
Flint Island
Suwarrow
Îles du Roi-Georges
Tuamotu Islands
Lima

Îles Wallis
Îles de Hoorn
Samoa Basin
Mamae
Raiatea
Tahiti
Anaa
Hao
Îles du Désappointement
Tiki Basin

Vanua Levu
Vava'u Group
Tofua
Niue
Palmerston
Hervey Islands
Rarotonga
Îles Maria
Mangaia
Society Islands
Héréhérétué
Tubuai
Raivavae
Groupe Actéon
Îles Gambier
Henderson Island

Tongatapu Group
Tonga Trench
Horizon Deep 10800
Rapa
Tubuai Islands
Pitcairn Island
Ducie Island

Raoul Island
Kermadec Islands
Kermadec Trench
Louisville Ridge
Easter Island
Isla Sala y Gómez
Nazca Ridge

SOUTHWEST PACIFIC BASIN
Roggeveen Basin
Isla San Félix
Isla San Ambrosio
Chile Basin

Auckland
North Island
New Zealand
Wellington
Chatham Islands
EAST PACIFIC RISE
Juan Fernández Islands
Santiago
Buenos Aires

South Island
Bounty Trough
Bounty Islands
Antipodes Islands
Chile Rise
Río de Janeiro
Tropic of Capricorn
Santos Plateau

Campbell Plateau
Campbell Island
Mornington Abyssal Plain
Argentine Rise

PACIFIC - ANTARCTIC RIDGE
Argentine Basin

SOUTHERN OCEAN
Southeast Pacific Basin
Falkland Islands
Falkland Plateau
Scotia Ridge

Balleny Islands
Amundsen Abyssal Plain
Cape Adare
Ross Sea
Amundsen Ridges
Peter I Island
Amundsen Sea
Antarctic Circle
Cape Horn
Drake Passage
South Shetland Islands
Scotia Sea

ANTARCTICA
Antarctic Peninsula

© Collins Bartholomew Ltd

0 500 1000 1500 2000 2500 3000 KILOMETRES

237

States and Territories (continued)

AFRICA (continued)

 BURUNDI Capital: **Bujumbura** Area: **27 835 km²/10 747 miles²**
Population: **8 508 000** Languages: **Kirundi (Hutu, Tutsi), French**
Religions: **Roman Catholic, traditional beliefs, Protestant**
Currency: **Burundian franc**

 CAMEROON Capital: **Yaoundé** Area: **475 442 km²/183 569 miles²**
Population: **18 549 000** Languages: **French, English, Fang, Bamileke,
local languages** Religions: **Roman Catholic, traditional beliefs, Sunni
Muslim, Protestant** Currency: **CFA franc**

CAPE VERDE Capital: **Praia** Area: **4 033 km²/1 557 miles²**
Population: **530 000** Languages: **Portuguese, Creole** Religions: **Roman
Catholic, Protestant** Currency: **Cape Verde escudo**

CENTRAL AFRICAN REPUBLIC Capital: **Bangui**
Area: **622 436 km²/240 324 miles²** Population: **4 343 000** Languages:
French, Sango, Banda, Baya, local languages Religions: **Protestant,
Roman Catholic, traditional beliefs, Sunni Muslim** Currency: **CFA franc**

CHAD Capital: **Ndjamena** Area: **1 284 000 km²/495 755 miles²**
Population: **10 781 000** Languages: **Arabic, French, Sara, local languages**
Religions: **Sunni Muslim, Roman Catholic, Protestant, traditional beliefs**
Currency: **CFA franc**

COMOROS Capital: **Moroni** Area: **1 862 km²/719 miles²**
Population: **839 000** Languages: **Comorian, French, Arabic**
Religions: **Sunni Muslim, Roman Catholic** Currency: **Comoros franc**

CONGO Capital: **Brazzaville** Area: **342 000 km²/132 047 miles²**
Population: **3 768 000** Languages: **French, Kongo, Monokutuba, local
languages** Religions: **Roman Catholic, Protestant, traditional beliefs,
Sunni Muslim** Currency: **CFA franc**

 CONGO, DEMOCRATIC REPUBLIC OF THE Capital: **Kinshasa**
Area: **2 345 410 km²/905 568 miles²** Population: **62 636 000**
Languages: **French, Lingala, Swahili, Kongo, local languages**
Religions: **Christian, Sunni Muslim** Currency: **Congolese franc**

 CÔTE D'IVOIRE Capital :**Yamoussoukro** Area: **322 463 km²/
124 504 miles²** Population: **19 262 000** Languages: **French, Creole, Akan,
local languages** Religions: **Sunni Muslim, Roman Catholic, traditional
beliefs, Protestant** Currency: **CFA franc**

 DJIBOUTI Capital: **Djibouti** Area: **23 200 km²/8 958 miles²**
Population **833 000** Languages: **Somali, Afar, French, Arabic**
Religions: **Sunni Muslim, Christian** Currency: **Djibouti franc**

 EQUATORIAL GUINEA Capital: **Malabo** Area: **28 051 km²/
10 831 miles²** Population: **507 000** Languages: **Spanish, French, Fang**
Religions: **Roman Catholic, traditional beliefs** Currency: **CFA franc**

 ERITREA Capital: **Asmara** Area: **117 400 km²/45 328 miles²**
Population: **4 851 000** Languages: **Tigrinya, Tigre** Religions: **Sunni
Muslim, Coptic Christian** Currency: **Nakfa**

 ETHIOPIA Capital: **Addis Ababa (Ādīs Ābeba)** Area: **1 133 880 km²/
437 794 miles²** Population: **83 099 000** Languages: **Oromo, Amharic,
Tigrinya, local languages** Religions: **Ethiopian Orthodox, Sunni Muslim,
traditional beliefs** Currency: **Birr**

 GABON Capital: **Libreville** Area: **267 667 km²/103 347 miles²**
Population: **1 331 000** Languages: **French, Fang, local languages**
Religions: **Roman Catholic, Protestant, traditional beliefs**
Currency: **CFA franc**

 THE GAMBIA Capital: **Banjul** Area: **11 295 km²/4 361 miles²**
Population: **1 709 000** Languages: **English, Malinke, Fulani, Wolof**
Religions: **Sunni Muslim, Protestant** Currency: **Dalasi**

 GHANA Capital: **Accra** Area: **238 537 km²/92 100 miles²**
Population: **23 478 000** Languages: **English, Hausa, Akan, local languages**
Religions: **Christian, Sunni Muslim, traditional beliefs** Currency: **Cedi**

 GUINEA Capital: **Conakry** Area: **245 857 km²/94 926 miles²** Population:
9 370 000 Languages: **French, Fulani, Malinke, local languages**
Religions: **Sunni Muslim, traditional beliefs, Christian** Currency: **Guinea
franc**

 GUINEA-BISSAU Capital: **Bissau** Area: **36 125 km²/13 948 miles²**
Population: **1 695 000** Languages: **Portuguese, Crioulo, local languages**
Religions: **Traditional beliefs, Sunni Muslim, Christian**
Currency: **CFA franc**

 LESOTHO Capital: **Maseru** Area: **30 355 km²/11 720 miles²**
Population: **2 008 000** Languages: **Sesotho, English, Zulu**
Religions: **Christian, traditional beliefs** Currency: **Loti,
South African rand**

 LIBERIA Capital: **Monrovia** Area: **111 369 km²/43 000 miles²**
Population: **3 750 000** Languages: **English, Creole, local languages**
Religions: **Traditional beliefs, Christian, Sunni Muslim**
Currency: **Liberian dollar**

 LIBYA Capital: **Tripoli (Ţarābulus)** Area: **1 759 540 km²/679 362 miles²**
Population: **6 160 000** Languages: **Arabic, Berber** Religions: **Sunni
Muslim** Currency: **Libyan dinar**

 MALAWI Capital: **Lilongwe** Area: **118 484 km²/45 747 miles²**
Population: **13 925 000** Languages: **Chichewa, English, local languages**
Religions: **Christian, traditional beliefs, Sunni Muslim**
Currency: **Malawian kwacha**

 MALI Capital: **Bamako** Area: **1 240 140 km²/478 821 miles²** Population:
12 337 000 Languages: **French, Bambara, local languages** Religions:
Sunni Muslim, traditional beliefs, Christian
Currency: **CFA franc**

 MAURITANIA Capital: **Nouakchott** Area: **1 030 700 km²/
397 955 miles²** Population: **3 124 000** Languages: **Arabic, French, local
languages** Religions: **Sunni Muslim** Currency: **Ouguiya**

 MAURITIUS Capital: **Port Louis** Area: **2 040 km²/788 miles²**
Population: **1 262 000** Languages: **English, Creole, Hindi, Bhojpurī,
French** Religions: **Hindu, Roman Catholic, Sunni Muslim**
Currency: **Mauritius rupee**

 MOZAMBIQUE Capital: **Maputo** Area: **799 380 km²/308 642 miles²**
Population: **21 397 000** Languages: **Portuguese, Makua, Tsonga, local
languages** Religions: **Traditional beliefs, Roman Catholic, Sunni Muslim**
Currency: **Metical**

 NAMIBIA Capital: **Windhoek** Area: **824 292 km²/318 261 miles²**
Population: **2 074 000** Languages: **English, Afrikaans, German, Ovambo,
local languages** Religions: **Protestant, Roman Catholic**
Currency: **Namibian dollar**

Indian Ocean

Lambert Azimuthal Equal Area Projection

1:58 000 000

N 150° O

Japan Basin
3510
Sea of Japan (East Sea)
Tokyo 8112
Honshu
Hokkaido 9550
East China Sea
Shanghai
Kyūshū
Ryukyu Islands
Taiwan 7460
7151 Ryukyu-Palau Ridge
Batan Islands
Cape Engaño
Luzon
Philippine Basin 6745
Philippines
Palawan Islands 10057
Sulu Sea
Mindanao 8054
Palau
Celebes Sea 5484
Halmahera
Celebes
Laut Maluku
New Guinea
Laut Seram 7288
Laut Banda
Flores 7440
Timor
Timor Sea
Arafura Sea
Gulf of Carpentaria

AUSTRALIA

Great Australian Bight
Darling
Murray
Sydney
Melbourne
Bass Strait
Australian Basin
Tasmania
Tasman Abyssal Plain
Tasman Sea
South East Cape 770
South Tasman Basin
Tasman Basin
New Zealand
South Island
Stewart Island
Campbell Plateau 60
Auckland Islands
Antipodes Islands
Bounty Islands
Campbell Island
Macquarie Ridge
Macquarie Island 4696

NORTH AMERICA

Mackenzie
Baffin Bay
Lancaster Sd
Nares Strait
Greenland
Greenland Basin 3884
Jan Mayen
Barents Sea
North Cape 357
Hudson Bay
Davis Strait 2276
Denmark Strait
Icelandic Plateau 810
Norwegian Basin
Voring Plateau 3970
Norwegian Sea
Hudson Strait
James Bay
Cape Farewell
Irminger Basin 2830
Iceland
Faroe Islands 550
Reykjanes Ridge
Labrador Sea
Northwest Atlantic Mid-Ocean Channel 4685
Iceland Basin
Rockall Bank
North Sea 238
British Isles 31
Celtic Shelf
London
Rhine
English Chan.
EUROPE
Danube
St Lawrence
Newfoundland 13
St John's
Grand Banks of Newfoundland 69
Flemish Cap
Biscay Abyssal Plain
678
Lisbon
Adriatic Sea
New York
Cape Sable
Sable Island
Azores-Biscay Rise 4938
5943
Corsica
Sardinia
MEDITERRANEAN SEA
Cape Hatteras
5029
Bermuda 4556
New England Seamounts
Corner Seamounts
MID-ATLANTIC RIDGE
Azores
Horseshoe Seamounts 265
Ampere Seamount 56
Str. of Gibraltar
Algiers 5121
2875
Balearic Is
New Orleans
Gulf of Mexico 3504
Hatteras Abyssal Plain
Bermuda Rise
Nares Deep
1092
Monaco Basin
Great Meteor Tablemount 238
Madeira
Canary Islands 5491
ATLANTIC
Tropic of Cancer
Sigsbee Deep
Bahama Islands
Nares Abyssal Plain 5508
Sargasso Sea
6690
AFRICA
Straits of Florida
Cuba
Greater Antilles
Milwaukee Deep 8605
Cayman Trench 7535
Jamaica
Hispaniola
Puerto Rico Trench
Krylov Seamount 1273
Cape Verde Plateau
Dakar
CARIBBEAN SEA Basin
Lesser Antilles
5523
Demerara Abyssal Plain
4923
Cape Verde
OCEAN
Colombian Basin 6662
Venezuelan Basin
GUIANA BASIN
Niger
Panama City
Caracas
Cocos Ridge
Isla de Malpelo 3901
Orinoco
Amazon Cone
Ceara Abyssal Plain 1627
São Pedro e São Paulo
Sierra Leone Rise 5036
Sierra Leone Basin 5212
Gulf of Guinea
Lagos
Quito 2330
Amazon
Fernando de Noronha
7728 Romanche Gap
Guinea Basin
Annobón
Príncipe
São Tomé
Equator
SOUTH AMERICA
Recife
Pernambuco Plain
Ascension
5391
Peru Basin 6601
Lima
Stocks Seamount 1602
BRAZIL BASIN
St Helena
Congo Cone
Luanda
Angola Basin
Peru-Chile Trench
Nazca Ridge
Abrolhos Bank
Vitória Seamount
Ilhas Martin Vaz
Ilha da Trindade 5460
MID-ATLANTIC RIDGE
Tropic of Capricorn
Rio de Janeiro
Santos Plateau
1670
Walvis Ridge 24
San Ambrosio 6170
Isla San Félix 571
Chile Basin
Paraná
Rio Grande Rise 550
Tristan da Cunha
Namibia Abyssal Plain 11
Vema Seamount
Santiago
Roggeveen Basin
Juan Fernández Islands 5282
Buenos Aires
Argentine Rise
Cape Basin 5520
Gough Island
Cape of Good Hope
Cape Town
5420
Discovery Seamounts 4254
Agulhas Ridge 5371
2743
Chile Rise
Argentine Basin 6681
Argentine Abyssal Plain 6041
Falkland Escarpment
1530
Shona Ridge
Agulhas Basin 6195
Mornington Abyssal Plain 114
Falkland Plateau
Falkland Islands 45
Scotia Ridge
South Georgia
Scotia Sea
South Sandwich Islands 8325
ATLANTIC-INDIAN RIDGE
4359
Yaghan Basin 5870
Cape Horn
Scotia Ridge
South Orkney Islands
South Sandwich Trench
Bouvetøya
Southeast Pacific Basin 4325
Drake Passage
South Shetland Trough
South Shetland Islands
American-Antarctic Ridge
Atlantic-Indian Antarctic Basin 5750
Enderby Abyssal Plain 6072
Antarctic Circle
SOUTHERN OCEAN
Maud Seamount 1200
Antarctic Peninsula
Weddell Abyssal Plain
Weddell Sea
Greenwich 0° meridian
Antarctic Circle

States and Territories (continued)

AFRICA (continued)

NIGER Capital: **Niamey** Area: **1 267 000 km²/489 191 miles²** Population: **14 226 000** Languages: **French, Hausa, Fulani, local languages** Religions: **Sunni Muslim, traditional beliefs** Currency: **CFA franc**

NIGERIA Capital: **Abuja** Area: **923 768 km²/356 669 miles²** Population: **148 093 000** Languages: **English, Hausa, Yoruba, Ibo, Fulani, local languages** Religions: **Sunni Muslim, Christian, traditional beliefs** Currency: **Naira**

RWANDA Capital: **Kigali** Area: **26 338 km²/10 169 miles²** Population: **9 725 000** Languages: **Kinyarwanda, French, English** Religions: **Roman Catholic, traditional beliefs, Protestant** Currency: **Rwandan franc**

SÃO TOMÉ AND PRÍNCIPE Capital: **São Tomé** Area: **964 km²/372 miles²** Population: **158 000** Languages: **Portuguese, Creole** Religions: **Roman Catholic, Protestant** Currency: **Dobra**

SENEGAL Capital: **Dakar** Area: **196 720 km²/75 954 miles²** Population: **12 379 000** Languages: **French, Wolof, Fulani, local languages** Religions: **Sunni Muslim, Roman Catholic, traditional beliefs** Currency: **CFA franc**

SEYCHELLES Capital: **Victoria** Area: **455 km²/176 miles²** Population: **87 000** Languages: **English, French, Creole** Religions: **Roman Catholic, Protestant** Currency: **Seychelles rupee**

SIERRA LEONE Capital: **Freetown** Area: **71 740 km²/27 699 miles²** Population: **5 866 000** Languages: **English, Creole, Mende, Temne, local languages** Religions: **Sunni Muslim, traditional beliefs** Currency: **Leone**

SOMALIA Capital: **Mogadishu (Muqdisho)** Area: **637 657 km²/246 201 miles²** Population: **8 699 000** Languages: **Somali, Arabic** Religions: **Sunni Muslim** Currency: **Somali shilling**

SUDAN Capital: **Khartoum** Area: **2 505 813 km²/967 500 miles²** Population: **38 560 000** Languages: **Arabic, Dinka, Nubian, Beja, Nuer, local languages** Religions: **Sunni Muslim, traditional beliefs, Christian** Currency: **Sudanese pound (Sudani)**

SWAZILAND Capital: **Mbabane** Area: **17 364 km²/6 704 miles²** Population: **1 141 000** Languages: **Swazi, English** Religions: **Christian, traditional beliefs** Currency: **Emalangeni, South African rand**

TANZANIA Capital: **Dodoma** Area: **945 087 km²/364 900 miles²** Population: **40 454 000** Languages: **Swahili, English, Nyamwezi, local languages** Religions: **Shi'a Muslim, Sunni Muslim, traditional beliefs, Christian** Currency: **Tanzanian shilling**

TOGO Capital: **Lomé** Area: **56 785 km²/21 925 miles²** Population: **6 585 000** Languages: **French, Ewe, Kabre, local languages** Religions: **Traditional beliefs, Christian, Sunni Muslim** Currency: **CFA franc**

UGANDA Capital: **Kampala** Area: **241 038 km²/93 065 miles²** Population: **30 884 000** Languages: **English, Swahili, Luganda, local languages** Religions: **Roman Catholic, Protestant, Sunni Muslim, traditional beliefs** Currency: **Ugandan shilling**

Western Sahara Capital: **Laâyoune** Area: **266 000 km²/102 703 miles²** Population: **480 000** Languages: **Arabic** Religions: **Sunni Muslim** Currency: **Moroccan dirham**

ZAMBIA Capital: **Lusaka** Area: **752 614 km²/290 586 miles²** Population: **11 922 000** Languages: **English, Bemba, Nyanja, Tonga, local languages** Religions: **Christian, traditional beliefs** Currency: **Zambian kwacha**

ZIMBABWE Capital: **Harare** Area: **390 759 km²/150 873 miles²** Population: **13 349 000** Languages: **English, Shona, Ndebele** Religions: **Christian, traditional beliefs** Currency: **Zimbabwean dollar**

NORTH AMERICA

ANTIGUA AND BARBUDA Capital: **St John's** Area: **442 km²/171 miles²** Population: **85 000** Languages: **English, Creole** Religions: **Protestant, Roman Catholic** Currency: **East Caribbean dollar**

BELIZE Capital: **Belmopan** Area: **22 965 km²/8 867 miles²** Population: **288 000** Languages: **English, Spanish, Mayan, Creole** Religions: **Roman Catholic, Protestant** Currency: **Belize dollar**

DOMINICA Capital: **Roseau** Area: **750 km²/290 miles²** Population: **67 000** Languages: **English, Creole** Religions: **Roman Catholic, Protestant** Currency: **East Caribbean dollar**

EL SALVADOR Capital: **San Salvador** Area: **21 041 km²/8 124 miles²** Population: **6 857 000** Languages: **Spanish** Religions: **Roman Catholic, Protestant** Currency: **El Salvador colón, United States dollar**

GRENADA Capital: **St George's** Area: **378 km²/146 miles²** Population: **106 000** Languages: **English, Creole** Religions: **Roman Catholic, Protestant** Currency: **East Caribbean dollar**

GUATEMALA Capital: **Guatemala City** Area: **108 890 km²/42 043 miles²** Population: **13 354 000** Languages: **Spanish, Mayan languages** Religions: **Roman Catholic, Protestant** Currency: **Quetzal, United States dollar**

HAITI Capital: **Port-au-Prince** Area: **27 750 km²/10 714 miles²** Population: **9 598 000** Languages: **French, Creole** Religions: **Roman Catholic, Protestant, Voodoo** Currency: **Gourde**

PANAMA Capital: **Panama City** Area: **77 082 km²/29 762 miles²** Population: **3 343 000** Languages: **Spanish, English, Amerindian languages** Religions: **Roman Catholic, Protestant, Sunni Muslim** Currency: **Balboa**

ST KITTS AND NEVIS Capital: **Basseterre** Area: **261 km²/101 miles²** Population: **50 000** Languages: **English, Creole** Religions: **Protestant, Roman Catholic** Currency: **East Caribbean dollar**

ST LUCIA Capital: **Castries** Area: **616 km²/238 miles²** Population: **165 000** Languages: **English, Creole** Religions: **Roman Catholic, Protestant** Currency: **East Caribbean dollar**

ST VINCENT AND THE GRENADINES Capital: **Kingstown** Area: **389 km²/150 miles²** Population: **120 000** Languages: **English, Creole** Religions: **Protestant, Roman Catholic** Currency: **East Caribbean dollar**

TRINIDAD AND TOBAGO Capital: **Port of Spain** Area: **5 130 km²/1 981 miles²** Population: **1 333 000** Languages: **English, Creole, Hindi** Religions: **Roman Catholic, Hindu, Protestant, Sunni Muslim** Currency: **Trinidad and Tobago dollar**

Arctic Ocean

Polar Stereographic Projection

© Collins Bartholomew Ltd

1 : 38 500 000

MILES 0 200 400 600 800 0 400 800 1200 1600 KILOMETRES

INTRODUCTION TO THE INDEX

The index includes all names shown on the reference maps in the atlas, except for the UNESCO World Heritage sites which are listed on pages 56-90. Each entry includes the country or geographical area in which the feature is located, a page number and an alphanumeric reference. Additional entry details and aspects of the index are explained below.

REFERENCING

Names are referenced by page number and by grid reference. The grid reference relates to the alphanumeric values which appear in the margin of each map. These reflect the graticule on the map – the letter relates to longitude divisions, the number to latitude divisions.

Names are generally referenced to the largest scale map page on which they appear. For large geographical features, including countries, the reference is to the largest scale map on which the feature appears in its entirety, or on which the majority of it appears.

Rivers are referenced to their lowest downstream point – either their mouth or their confluence with another river. The river name will generally be positioned as close to this point as possible.

Entries relating to names appearing on insets are indicated by a small box symbol: □ followed by a grid reference if the inset has its own alphanumeric values.

ALTERNATIVE NAMES

Alternative names appear as cross-references and refer the user to the index entry for the form of the name used on the map.

For rivers with multiple names – for example those which flow through several countries – all alternative name forms are included within the main index entries, with details of the countries in which each form applies.

ADMINISTRATIVE QUALIFIERS

Administrative divisions are included in an entry to differentiate duplicate names – entries of exactly the same name and feature type within the one country – where these division names are shown on the maps. In such cases, duplicate names are alphabetized in the order of the administrative division names. Additional qualifiers are included for names within selected geographical areas, to indicate more clearly their location.

DESCRIPTORS

Entries, other than those for towns and cities, include a descriptor indicating the type of geographical feature. Descriptors are not included where the type of feature is implicit in the name itself, unless there is a town or city of exactly the same name.

NAME FORMS AND ALPHABETICAL ORDER

Name forms are as they appear on the maps, with additional alternative forms included as cross-references. Names appear in full in the index, although they may appear in abbreviated form on the maps.

The German character ß is alphabetized as 'ss'. Names beginning with Mac or Mc are alphabetized exactly as they appear. The terms Saint, Sainte, etc, are abbreviated to St, Ste, etc, but alphabetized as if in the full form.

NUMERICAL ENTRIES

Entries beginning with numerals appear at the beginning of the index, in numerical order. Elsewhere, numerals are alphabetized before 'a'.

PERMUTED TERMS

Names beginning with generic, geographical terms are permuted – the descriptive term is placed after, and the index alphabetized by, the main part of the name. For example, Lake Superior is indexed as Superior, Lake; Mount Everest as Everest, Mount. This policy is applied to all languages. Permuting has not been applied to names of towns, cities or administrative divisions beginning with such geographical terms. These remain in their full form, for example, Lake Isabella, USA.

INDEX ABBREVIATIONS

admin. dist.	administrative district	IN	Indiana	Phil.	Philippines
admin. div.	administrative division	Indon.	Indonesia	plat.	plateau
admin. reg.	administrative region	is	islands	P.N.G.	Papua New Guinea
Afgh.	Afghanistan	Kazakh.	Kazakhstan	Port.	Portugal
AK	Alaska	KS	Kansas	prov.	province
AL	Alabama	KY	Kentucky	pt	point
Alg.	Algeria	Kyrg.	Kyrgyzstan	Qld	Queensland
Alta	Alberta	l.	lake	Que.	Québec
AR	Arkansas	LA	Louisiana	r.	river
Arg.	Argentina	lag.	lagoon	reg.	region
aut. comm.	autonomous community	Lith.	Lithuania	res.	reserve
aut. reg.	autonomous region	Lux.	Luxembourg	resr	reservoir
aut. rep.	autonomous republic	MA	Massachusetts	RI	Rhode Island
AZ	Arizona	Madag.	Madagascar	r. mouth	river mouth
Azer.	Azerbaijan	Man.	Manitoba	Rus. Fed.	Russian Federation
b.	bay	MD	Maryland	S.	South
Bangl.	Bangladesh	ME	Maine	S.A.	South Australia
B.C.	British Columbia	Mex.	Mexico	S. Africa	Republic of South Africa
Bol.	Bolivia	MI	Michigan	salt l.	salt lake
Bos.-Herz.	Bosnia-Herzegovina	MN	Minnesota	Sask.	Saskatchewan
Bulg.	Bulgaria	MO	Missouri	SC	South Carolina
c.	cape	Mont.	Montenegro	SD	South Dakota
CA	California	Moz.	Mozambique	sea chan.	sea channel
Cent. Afr. Rep.	Central African Republic	MS	Mississippi	Sing.	Singapore
CO	Colorado	MT	Montana	Switz.	Switzerland
Col.	Colombia	mt.	mountain	Tajik.	Tajikistan
CT	Connecticut	mts	mountains	Tanz.	Tanzania
Czech Rep.	Czech Republic	N.	North, Northern	Tas.	Tasmania
DC	District of Columbia	nat. park	national park	terr.	territory
DE	Delaware	N.B.	New Brunswick	Thai.	Thailand
Dem. Rep. Congo	Democratic Republic of the Congo	NC	North Carolina	TN	Tennessee
depr.	depression	ND	North Dakota	Trin. and Tob.	Trinidad and Tobago
des.	desert	NE	Nebraska	Turkm.	Turkmenistan
Dom. Rep.	Dominican Republic	Neth.	Netherlands	TX	Texas
Equat. Guinea	Equatorial Guinea	Neth. Antilles	Netherlands Antilles	U.A.E.	United Arab Emirates
esc.	escarpment	Nfld.	Newfoundland	U.K.	United Kingdom
est.	estuary	NH	New Hampshire	Ukr.	Ukraine
Eth.	Ethiopia	NJ	New Jersey	U.S.A.	United States of America
Fin.	Finland	NM	New Mexico	UT	Utah
FL	Florida	N.S.	Nova Scotia	Uzbek.	Uzbekistan
for.	forest	N.S.W.	New South Wales	VA	Virginia
Fr. Guiana	French Guiana	N.W.T.	Northwest Territories	Venez.	Venezuela
Fr. Polynesia	French Polynesia	N.Z.	New Zealand	Vic.	Victoria
g.	gulf	NV	Nevada	vol.	volcano
GA	Georgia	NY	New York	vol. crater	volcanic crater
Guat.	Guatemala	OH	Ohio	VT	Vermont
h.	hill	OK	Oklahoma	W.	Western
hd	headland	Ont.	Ontario	WA	Washington
HI	Hawaii	OR	Oregon	W.A.	Western Australia
Hond.	Honduras	PA	Pennsylvania	WI	Wisconsin
i.	island	Pak.	Pakistan	WV	West Virginia
IA	Iowa	Para.	Paraguay	WY	Wyoming
ID	Idaho	P.E.I.	Prince Edward Island	Y.T.	Yukon Territory
IL	Illinois	pen.	peninsula		

1

127 J4 **Amundsen-Scott** *research stn* Antarctica
237 L10 **Amundsen Sea** Antarctica
163 I3 **Amuntai** Indon.
150 E2 **Amur** *r.* China/Rus. Fed.
 alt. Heilong Jiang
 Amur Oblast *admin. div.* Rus. Fed. *see* **Amurskaya Oblast'**
133 O4 **Amursk** Rus. Fed.
156 C1 **Amurskaya Oblast'** *admin. div.* Rus. Fed.
156 F1 **Amurskiy Liman** *str.* Rus. Fed.
156 C3 **Amurzet** Rus. Fed.
187 F6 **Amvrosiyivka** Ukr.
209 E1 **Amyot** Canada
149 H6 **An** Myanmar
237 J7 **Anaa** *atoll* Fr. Polynesia
151 E7 **Anabanua** Indon.
133 M2 **Anabar** *r.* Rus. Fed.
133 M2 **Anabarskiy Zaliv** *b.* Rus. Fed.
124 D4 **Ana Branch** *r.* Australia
214 C4 **Anacapa Island** U.S.A.
233 K2 **Anaco** Venez.
212 D2 **Anaconda** U.S.A.
212 B1 **Anacortes** U.S.A.
217 D5 **Anadarko** U.S.A.
138 D2 **Anadolu** *reg.* Turkey
139 F1 **Anadolu Dağları** *mts* Turkey
133 S3 **Anadyr'** Rus. Fed.
133 S3 **Anadyr'** *r.* Rus. Fed.
133 T3 **Anadyrskiy Zaliv** *b.* Rus. Fed.
185 K6 **Anafi** *i.* Greece
234 E1 **Anagé** Brazil
139 H4 **'Ānah** Iraq
215 D5 **Anaheim** U.S.A.
204 D4 **Anahim Lake** Canada
225 D2 **Anáhuac** Mex.
147 H4 **Anaimalai Hills** India
147 H4 **Anai Mudi Peak** India
147 I2 **Anakapalle** India
123 D4 **Anakie** Australia
195 E5 **Analalava** Madag.
231 H4 **Anamã** Brazil
163 G2 **Anambas, Kepulauan** *is* Indon.
208 B4 **Anamosa** U.S.A.
138 D3 **Anamur** Turkey
138 D3 **Anamur Burnu** *pt* Turkey
159 D8 **Anan** Japan
148 C5 **Anand** India
149 F5 **Anandapur** India
149 F4 **Anandpur** *r.* India
141 I4 **Anan'ev** Kyrg.
147 H3 **Anantapur** India
148 C2 **Anantnag** India
148 D4 **Anant Peth** India
187 D6 **Anan'yiv** Ukr.
187 F6 **Anapa** Rus. Fed.
234 C2 **Anápolis** Brazil
142 D4 **Anār** Iran
142 D3 **Anārak** Iran
142 C3 **Anarbar** *r.* Iran
143 F3 **Anardara** Afgh.
 Anatolia *reg.* Turkey *see* **Anadolu**
119 G4 **Anatom** *i.* Vanuatu
232 D3 **Añatuya** Arg.
233 L4 **Anauá** *r.* Brazil
175 H6 **An Baile Breac** Ireland
175 J2 **Anbu** Italy
175 J2 **An Bun Beag** Ireland
160 D4 **Anbyon** N. Korea
182 D3 **Ancenis** France
155 B4 **Anchang** China
202 D3 **Anchorage** U.S.A.
209 F4 **Anchor Bay** U.S.A.
 Anci China *see* **Langfang**
175 J3 **An Clochán Liath** Ireland
184 E2 **Ancona** Italy
232 B6 **Ancud** Chile
235 H4 **Ancud, Golfo de** *g.* Chile
156 B3 **Anda** China
235 H1 **Andacollo** Chile
123 A5 **Andado** Australia
175 H5 **An Daingean** Ireland
149 F5 **Andal** India
171 I3 **Åndalsnes** Norway
183 N4 **Andalucía** *aut. comm.* Spain
217 G6 **Andalusia** U.S.A.
135 H6 **Andaman and Nicobar Islands** *union terr.* India
238 K4 **Andaman Basin** *sea feature* Indian Ocean
135 H5 **Andaman Islands** India
135 H5 **Andaman Sea** Asia
124 B3 **Andamooka** Australia
195 E5 **Andapa** Madag.
234 E1 **Andaraí** Brazil
170 L1 **Andenes** Norway

178 D4 **Andenne** Belgium
178 C4 **Anderlecht** Belgium
182 D4 **Andernos-les-Bains** France
202 F3 **Anderson** *r.* Canada
202 D3 **Anderson** *AK* U.S.A.
209 E5 **Anderson** *IN* U.S.A.
217 E4 **Anderson** *MO* U.S.A.
219 D5 **Anderson** *SC* U.S.A.
125 G8 **Anderson Bay** Australia
230 C5 **Andes** *mts* S. America
170 L1 **Andfjorden** *sea chan.* Norway
147 H2 **Andhra Pradesh** *state* India
141 H4 **Andijon** Uzbek.
195 E5 **Andilamena** Madag.
195 E5 **Andilanatoby** Madag.
142 C3 **Andīmeshk** Iran
139 F3 **Andırın** Turkey
187 H7 **Andiyskoye Koysu** *r.* Rus. Fed.
 Andizhan Uzbek. *see* **Andijon**
143 G2 **Andkhui** *r.* Afgh.
143 G2 **Andkhvoy** Afgh.
195 E5 **Andoany** Madag.
230 C4 **Andoas** Peru
147 H2 **Andol** India
160 E5 **Andong** S. Korea
160 E5 **Andong-ho** *l.* S. Korea
122 C2 **Andoom** Australia
183 Q1 **Andorra** *country* Europe
183 Q1 **Andorra la Vella** Andorra
173 F6 **Andover** U.K.
221 H2 **Andover** *ME* U.S.A.
220 C4 **Andover** *OH* U.S.A.
170 K1 **Andøya** *i.* Norway
234 B3 **Andradina** Brazil
237 H2 **Andreanof Islands** U.S.A.
186 E3 **Andreapol'** Rus. Fed.
172 C3 **Andreas** U.K.
194 C3 **André Félix, Parc National d'** *nat. park* Centr. Afr. Rep.
234 D2 **Andrelândia** Brazil
217 C5 **Andrews** U.S.A.
140 B1 **Andreyevka** Rus. Fed.
185 G4 **Andria** Italy
195 E6 **Androka** Madag.
219 E7 **Andros** *i.* Bahamas
185 K6 **Andros** *i.* Greece
221 H2 **Androscoggin** *r.* U.S.A.
219 E7 **Andros Town** Bahamas
147 G4 **Andrott** *i.* India
187 D5 **Andrushivka** Ukr.
170 L1 **Andselv** Norway
183 N3 **Andújar** Spain
195 B5 **Andulo** Angola
121 E4 **Anec, Lake** *salt flat* Australia
192 C4 **Anéfis** Mali
223 L5 **Anegada** *i.* Virgin Is (U.K.)
235 J4 **Anegada, Bahía** *b.* Arg.
215 F5 **Anegam** U.S.A.
192 C4 **Aného** Togo
215 H3 **Aneth** U.S.A.
183 Q1 **Aneto** *mt.* Spain
193 D3 **Aney** Niger
155 E5 **Anfu** China
195 E5 **Angadoka, Lohatanjona** *hd* Madag.
120 E2 **Angalarri** *r.* Australia
156 A3 **Ang'angxi** China
150 B1 **Angara** *r.* Rus. Fed.
150 C1 **Angarsk** Rus. Fed.
121 F5 **Angas Downs** Australia
161 I3 **Angat** Phil.
171 K3 **Ånge** Sweden
 Angel, Salto *waterfall* Venez. *see* **Angel Falls**
222 B3 **Ángel de la Guarda, Isla** *i.* Mex.
161 I3 **Angeles** Phil.
233 L3 **Angel Falls** Venez.
171 K4 **Ängelholm** Sweden
123 D5 **Angellala Creek** *r.* Australia
214 B2 **Angels Camp** U.S.A.
171 L3 **Ångermanälven** *r.* Sweden
182 D3 **Angers** France
205 J2 **Angikuni Lake** Canada
162 B2 **Angkor** *tourist site* Cambodia
173 C4 **Anglesey** *i.* U.K.
217 E6 **Angleton** U.S.A.
209 H2 **Angliers** Canada
 Ang Mo Kio Sing.
194 D5 **Ango** Dem. Rep. Congo
195 D5 **Angoche** Moz.
142 B3 **Angohrān** Iran
235 H3 **Angol** Chile
195 B5 **Angola** *country* Africa
209 E5 **Angola** U.S.A.
239 I7 **Angola Basin** *sea feature* S. Atlantic Ocean

182 E4 **Angoulême** France
141 G4 **Angren** Uzbek.
162 B2 **Ang Thong** Thai.
156 A3 **Anguang** China
223 L5 **Anguilla** *terr.* Caribbean Sea
147 J1 **Angul** India
154 E1 **Anguli Nur** *l.* China
154 E2 **Anguo** China
234 A3 **Anhanduí** *r.* Brazil
171 J4 **Anholt** *i.* Denmark
155 D4 **Anhua** China
154 E3 **Anhui** *prov.* China
234 A2 **Anhumas** Brazil
234 C2 **Anicuns** Brazil
140 E2 **Anikhovka** Rus. Fed.
186 G3 **Anikovo** Rus. Fed.
162 A2 **Anin** Myanmar
158 H1 **Aniva** Rus. Fed.
158 H1 **Aniva, Mys** *c.* Rus. Fed.
158 H1 **Aniva, Zaliv** *b.* Rus. Fed.
119 G3 **Aniwa** *i.* Vanuatu
178 B5 **Anizy-le-Château** France
171 N3 **Anjalankoski** Fin.
147 H4 **Anjengo** India
155 F4 **Anji** China
148 D5 **Anji** India
143 E3 **Anjoman** Iran
182 D3 **Anjou** *reg.* France
 Anjouan *i.* Comoros *see* **Nzwani**
195 E5 **Anjozorobe** Madag.
160 C4 **Anjü** N. Korea
195 E6 **Ankaboa, Tanjona** *pt* Madag.
154 C3 **Ankang** China
138 D2 **Ankara** Turkey
195 E6 **Ankazoabo** Madag.
195 E5 **Ankazobe** Madag.
163 D2 **An Khê** Vietnam
148 C5 **Ankleshwar** India
162 C3 **An Lộc** Vietnam
155 B5 **Anlong** China
162 C2 **Ânlong Vêng** Cambodia
155 D4 **Anlu** China
160 D6 **Anmyŏn-do** *i.* S. Korea
221 H3 **Ann, Cape** U.S.A.
187 G5 **Anna** Rus. Fed.
221 E5 **Anna, Lake** U.S.A.
192 C1 **Annaba** Alg.
179 L4 **Annaberg-Buchholtz** Germany
139 F4 **An Nabk** Syria
146 B4 **An Nafud** *des.* Saudi Arabia
139 J5 **An Nahrawān al Qadīm** *canal* Iraq
139 J6 **An Najaf** Iraq
175 K3 **Annalee** *r.* Ireland
175 M3 **Annalong** U.K.
174 E6 **Annan** U.K.
174 E6 **Annan** *r.* U.K.
174 E5 **Annandale** *val.* U.K.
120 C3 **Anna Plains** Australia
221 E5 **Annapolis** U.S.A.
207 G5 **Annapolis Royal** Canada
149 E3 **Annapurna I** *mt.* Nepal
142 C5 **An Naqīrah** *well* Saudi Arabia
209 F4 **Ann Arbor** U.S.A.
231 G2 **Anna Regina** Guyana
139 K6 **An Nāşirīyah** Iraq
121 B5 **Annean, Lake** *salt flat* Australia
182 H4 **Annecy** France
182 H3 **Annemasse** France
179 E1 **Annen** Neth.
204 C4 **Annette Island** U.S.A.
139 F5 **An Nimārah** Syria
155 B5 **Anning** China
219 C5 **Anniston** U.S.A.
191 E4 **Annobón** *i.* Equat. Guinea
182 G4 **Annonay** France
146 C4 **An Nu'ayrīyah** Saudi Arabia
139 J5 **An Nu'mānīyah** Iraq
216 E2 **Anoka** U.S.A.
195 E5 **Anorontany, Tanjona** *hd* Madag.
155 D6 **Anpu** China
155 C6 **Anpu Gang** *b.* China
154 E4 **Anqing** China
154 F2 **Anqiu** China
 An Ráth Ireland *see* **Charleville**
155 C5 **Anren** China
178 D4 **Ans** Belgium
154 C2 **Ansai** China
179 I5 **Ansbach** Germany
125 G7 **Anser Group** *is* Australia
160 B3 **Anshan** China
155 B5 **Anshun** China
153 H6 **Anshunchang** China

235 I1 **Ansilta** *mt.* Arg.
235 L1 **Ansina** Uruguay
137 E5 **An Sirhān, Wādī** *watercourse* Saudi Arabia
216 D3 **Ansley** U.S.A.
217 D5 **Anson** U.S.A.
120 C2 **Anson Bay** Australia
192 C3 **Ansongo** Mali
206 D4 **Ansonville** Canada
220 C5 **Ansted** U.S.A.
148 D4 **Anta** India
230 D6 **Antabamba** Peru
139 F3 **Antakya** Turkey
195 F5 **Antalaha** Madag.
138 D3 **Antalya** Turkey
138 C3 **Antalya Körfezi** *g.* Turkey
195 E5 **Antananarivo** Madag.
127 **Antarctica**
127 I2 **Antarctic Peninsula** Antarctica
174 C3 **An Teallach** *mt.* U.K.
215 D2 **Antelope Range** *mts* U.S.A.
183 N4 **Antequera** Spain
213 F5 **Anthony** U.S.A.
122 A3 **Anthony Lagoon** Australia
192 B2 **Anti-Atlas** *mts* Morocco
183 H5 **Antibes** France
207 H4 **Anticosti, Île d'** *i.* Canada
208 C3 **Antigo** U.S.A.
207 H4 **Antigonish** Canada
223 L5 **Antigua** *i.* Antigua and Barbuda
 Antigua Guat. *see* **Antigua Guatemala**
223 L5 **Antigua and Barbuda** *country* Caribbean Sea
225 G5 **Antigua Guatemala** Guat.
225 E3 **Antiguo-Morelos** Mex.
185 J7 **Antikythira** *i.* Greece
185 J7 **Antikythiro, Steno** *sea chan.* Greece
214 B3 **Antioch** *CA* U.S.A.
208 C4 **Antioch** *IL* U.S.A.
233 I3 **Antioquia** Col.
117 G7 **Antipodes Islands** N.Z.
185 K5 **Antipsara** *i.* Greece
217 E5 **Antlers** U.S.A.
232 B2 **Antofagasta** Chile
232 C3 **Antofalla, Volcán** *vol.* Arg.
178 B4 **Antoing** Belgium
224 I6 **Antón** Panama
235 **Antonina** Brazil
234 E1 **Antônio** *r.* Brazil
213 F4 **Antonito** U.S.A.
175 J3 **Antrim** U.K.
175 L2 **Antrim Hills** U.K.
120 E3 **Antrim Plateau** Australia
195 E5 **Antsalova** Madag.
195 E5 **Antsirabe** Madag.
195 E5 **Antsirañana** Madag.
195 E5 **Antsohihy** Madag.
170 M2 **Anttis** Sweden
171 N3 **Anttola** Fin.
235 H3 **Antuco** Chile
235 H3 **Antuco, Volcán** *vol.* Chile
178 C3 **Antwerp** Belgium
221 F2 **Antwerp** U.S.A.
206 E2 **Anuc, Lac** *l.* Canada
186 C3 **Anuchino** Rus. Fed.
160 D6 **Anŭi** S. Korea
148 C3 **Anupgarh** India
147 I4 **Anuradhapura** Sri Lanka
142 D5 **Anveh** Iran
127 I2 **Anvers Island** Antarctica
155 F5 **Anxi** *Fujian* China
150 B2 **Anxi** *Gansu* China
 Anxian China *see* **Anchang**
155 D4 **Anxiang** China
154 E2 **Anxin** China
124 A4 **Anxious Bay** Australia
154 E2 **Anyang** China
160 D5 **Anyang** S. Korea
185 K6 **Anydros** *i.* Greece
150 B3 **A'nyêmaqên Shan** *mts* China
155 E4 **Anyi** China
155 E5 **Anyuan** China
155 B4 **Anyue** China
156 E2 **Anyuy** *r.* Rus. Fed.
133 R3 **Anyuysk** Rus. Fed.
233 I3 **Anzá** Col.
154 D2 **Anze** China
150 A1 **Anzhero-Sudzhensk** Rus. Fed.
195 C4 **Anzi** Dem. Rep. Congo
184 F4 **Anzio** Italy
119 H1 **Aoba** *i.* Vanuatu
157 E6 **Aoga-shima** *i.* Japan
162 A3 **Ao Kham, Laem** *pt* Thai.
 Aomen China *see* **Macao**
158 G4 **Aomori** Japan

148 D3 **Aonla** India
126 C5 **Aoraki** N.Z.
126 C5 **Aoraki** N.Z.
126 C5 **Aoraki/Mount Cook National Park** N.Z.
162 C2 **Aôral, Phnum** *mt.* Cambodia
126 D4 **Aorere** *r.* N.Z.
184 B2 **Aosta** Italy
192 B2 **Aoukâr** *reg.* Mali/Mauritania
231 G8 **Apa** *r.* Brazil
194 D3 **Apac** Uganda
215 H5 **Apache** U.S.A.
215 H5 **Apache Creek** U.S.A.
215 G5 **Apache Junction** U.S.A.
215 G6 **Apache Peak** U.S.A.
219 C6 **Apalachee Bay** U.S.A.
219 C6 **Apalachicola** U.S.A.
225 E4 **Apan** Mex.
233 J4 **Apaporis** *r.* Col.
139 J1 **Aparan** Armenia
234 B3 **Aparecida do Tabuado** Brazil
161 I2 **Aparri** Phil.
170 P2 **Apatity** Rus. Fed.
225 D4 **Apatzingán** Mex.
125 E7 **Apollo Bay** Australia
230 E6 **Apolo** Bol.
219 D6 **Apopka, Lake** U.S.A.
234 B2 **Aporé** Brazil
234 B2 **Aporé** *r.* Brazil
218 B2 **Apostle Islands** U.S.A.
208 B2 **Apostle Islands National Lakeshore** *nature res.* U.S.A.
138 E4 **Apostolos Andreas, Cape** Cyprus
220 B6 **Appalachia** U.S.A.
220 C6 **Appalachian Mountains** U.S.A.
 Appennino *mts* Italy *see* **Apennines**
184 E3 **Appennino Abruzzese** *mts* Italy
184 D2 **Appennino Tosco-Emiliano** *mts* Italy
184 E3 **Appennino Umbro-Marchigiano** *mts* Italy
125 I5 **Appin** Australia
179 E1 **Appingedam** Neth.
174 C3 **Applecross** U.K.
216 D2 **Appleton** *MN* U.S.A.
208 C3 **Appleton** *WI* U.S.A.
215 G4 **Apple Valley** U.S.A.
220 D6 **Appomattox** U.S.A.
184 E4 **Aprilia** Italy
187 F6 **Apsheronsk** Rus. Fed.
124 D6 **Apsley** Australia
209 H3 **Apsley** Canada
183 G5 **Apt** France
234 B3 **Apucarana** Brazil
161 H4 **Apurahuan** Phil.
233 K3 **Apure** *r.* Venez.
230 D6 **Apurimac** *r.* Peru
193 E3 **Aqaba, Gulf of** Asia
139 I6 **'Aqabah, Birkat al** *well* Iraq
141 I4 **Aqal** China
142 D2 **Aqbana** Iran
143 G2 **Āqchah** Afgh.
142 B2 **Aq Chai** *r.* Iran
142 B2 **Aqdoghmīsh** *r.* Iran
139 J3 **Āq Kān Dāgh, Kūh-e** *mt.* Iran
140 C5 **Āq Qal'eh** Iran
152 E4 **Aqqikkol Hu** *salt l.* China
139 I3 **'Aqrah** Iraq
215 F4 **Aquarius Mountains** U.S.A.
215 G5 **Aquarius Plateau** U.S.A.
185 G4 **Aquaviva delle Fonti** Italy
234 A3 **Aquidauana** Brazil
234 A2 **Aquidauana** *r.* Brazil
225 D4 **Aquila** Mex.
233 K4 **Aquio** *r.* Col.
225 E5 **Aquismón** Mex.
182 D4 **Aquitaine** *reg.* France
184 F4 **Ara** Italy
149 F4 **Ara** *r.* India
143 G4 **Arab** Afgh.
219 C5 **Arab** U.S.A.
193 E3 **Arab, Bahr el** *watercourse* Sudan
138 B6 **'Arab, Khalīj al** *b.* Egypt

143 E3 **'Arabābād** Iran
238 I4 **Arabian Basin** *sea feature* Indian Ocean
 Arabian Gulf *g.* Asia *see* **The Gulf**
146 B4 **Arabian Peninsula** Saudi Arabia
135 E5 **Arabian Sea** Indian Ocean
233 L3 **Arabopó** Venez.
233 L3 **Arabopó** *r.* Venez.
138 D1 **Araç** Turkey
234 L4 **Araça** *r.* Brazil
231 K6 **Aracaju** Brazil
233 K4 **Aracamuni, Cerro** *h.* Venez.
235 A4 **Aracanguy, Montes de** *hills* Para.
231 K4 **Aracati** Brazil
234 E1 **Aracatu** Brazil
234 B3 **Araçatuba** Brazil
183 M4 **Aracena** Spain
234 E2 **Aracruz** Brazil
234 D2 **Araçuaí** Brazil
234 D2 **Araçuaí** *r.* Brazil
185 I1 **Arad** Romania
193 E3 **Arada** Chad
118 D2 **Arafura Sea** Australia/Indon.
236 D6 **Arafura Shelf** *sea feature* Australia/Indon.
234 B1 **Aragarças** Brazil
139 I1 **Aragats** Armenia
139 J1 **Aragats Lerr** *mt.* Armenia
183 P2 **Aragón** *aut. comm.* Spain
183 P1 **Aragón** *r.* Spain
231 I5 **Araguacema** Brazil
233 K2 **Aragua de Barcelona** Venez.
231 I5 **Araguaçu** Brazil
231 H6 **Araguaia, Parque Nacional de** *nat. park* Brazil
231 I5 **Araguaína** Brazil
233 L2 **Araguao, Boca** *r. mouth* Venez.
233 L2 **Araguao, Caño** *r.* Venez.
234 C2 **Araguari** Brazil
234 C2 **Araguari** *r.* Brazil
231 I5 **Araguatins** Brazil
187 H7 **Aragvi** *r.* Georgia
159 F6 **Arai** Japan
 Árainn Mhór *i.* Ireland *see* **Arranmore Island**
231 J4 **Araiosos** Brazil
192 C2 **Arak** Alg.
142 C3 **Arāk** Iran
137 E4 **Arak** Syria
149 H5 **Arakan Yoma** *mts* Myanmar
147 H3 **Arakkonam** India
139 J2 **Aralık** Turkey
140 D3 **Aral Sea** *salt l.* Kazakh./Uzbek.
140 E3 **Aral'sk** Kazakh.
 Aral'skoye More *salt l.* Kazakh./Uzbek. *see* **Aral Sea**
140 B2 **Aralsor, Ozero** *l.* Kazakh.
140 C2 **Aralsor, Ozero** *salt l.* Kazakh.
123 D4 **Aramac** Australia
123 D4 **Aramac Creek** *watercourse* Australia
142 B5 **Aramah** *plat.* Saudi Arabia
225 E2 **Aramberri** Mex.
148 D6 **Aran** *r.* India
183 O2 **Aranda de Duero** Spain
139 K4 **Arandān** Iran
185 I2 **Aranđelovac** Serbia
147 H3 **Arani** India
183 I1 **Aran Islands** Ireland
183 O2 **Aranjuez** Spain
195 B6 **Aranos** Namibia
217 D7 **Aransas Pass** U.S.A.
234 B2 **Arantes** *r.* Brazil
119 H1 **Aranuka** *atoll* Kiribati
162 B2 **Aranyaprathet** Thai.
159 B8 **Arao** Japan
192 B3 **Araouane** Mali
216 D3 **Arapahoe** U.S.A.
233 L4 **Arapari** *r.* Brazil
235 L1 **Arapey Grande** *r.* Uruguay
139 G2 **Arapgir** Turkey
231 K5 **Arapiraca** Brazil
185 K4 **Arapis, Akrotirio** *pt* Greece
234 B3 **Arapongas** Brazil
149 F4 **A Rapti Doon** *r.* Nepal
146 B3 **'Ar'ar** Saudi Arabia
139 I6 **'Ar'ar, Wādī** *watercourse* Iraq/Saudi Arabia
233 G3 **Araranguá** Brazil
234 C3 **Araraquara** Brazil
231 H5 **Araras** Brazil
235 B4 **Araras, Serra das** *mts* Brazil
139 J2 **Ararat** Armenia
124 E6 **Ararat** Australia
139 J2 **Ararat, Mount** Turkey

161 I2 Bangued Phil.
194 B3 Bangui Centr. Afr. Rep.
161 I2 Bangui Phil.
162 A5 Bangunpurba Indon.
195 C5 Bangweulu, Lake Zambia
138 C6 Banhā Egypt
195 D6 Banhine, Parque Nacional de nat. park Moz.
162 B1 Ban Hin Heup Laos
Ban Houei Sai Laos see Huayxay
194 C3 Bani Centr. Afr. Rep.
161 H2 Bani Phil.
194 B3 Bania Centr. Afr. Rep.
142 D5 Banī Forūr, Jazīreh-ye i. Iran
148 C2 Banihal Pass and Tunnel India
220 D6 Banister r. U.S.A.
193 F2 Banī Suwayf Egypt
193 D1 Banī Walīd Libya
142 C5 Banī Wuţayfān well Saudi Arabia
138 E4 Bāniyās Syria
138 E5 Bāniyās Syria
185 G2 Banja Luka Bos.-Herz.
148 D3 Banjar India
163 H3 Banjarmasin Indon.
192 A3 Banjul Gambia
139 L2 Bankä Azer.
149 F4 Banka India
120 F3 Banka Banka Australia
147 G3 Bankapur India
192 B3 Bankass Mali
162 A2 Ban Khao Yoi Thai.
162 A3 Ban Khok Kloi Thai.
149 F5 Banki India
202 E4 Banks Island B.C. Canada
202 F2 Banks Island N.W.T. Canada
119 G3 Banks Islands Vanuatu
205 K2 Banks Lake Canada
212 C2 Banks Lake U.S.A.
126 D5 Banks Peninsula N.Z.
125 H8 Banks Strait Australia
149 F5 Bankura India
162 B1 Ban Mouang Laos
175 L5 Bann r. Ireland
175 L3 Bann r. U.K.
162 C1 Ban Nakham Laos
162 A3 Ban Na San Thai.
208 C5 Banner U.S.A.
219 E7 Bannerman Town Bahamas
215 D5 Banning U.S.A.
235 H3 Baños Maule Chile
162 B1 Ban Pak-Leng Laos
162 C1 Ban Phaeng Thai.
162 B1 Ban Phai Thai.
Ban Phon Laos see Xêkong
162 B1 Ban Phôn-Hông Laos
162 A2 Banphot Phisai Thai.
162 A2 Ban Pong Thai.
162 A3 Ban Sawi Thai.
149 E4 Bansi India
177 I6 Banská Bystrica Slovakia
143 F5 Bānsont India
162 A1 Ban Sut Ta Thai.
162 C2 Ban Suwan Wari Thai.
147 H2 Banswada India
148 C5 Banswara India
161 I4 Bantayan i. Phil.
175 J5 Banteer Ireland
162 A3 Ban Tha Chang Thai.
162 A3 Ban Tha Kham Thai.
162 A1 Ban Tha Song Yang Thai.
162 B2 Ban Tha Tako Thai.
162 A1 Ban Tha Ton Thai.
162 B2 Ban Tha Tum Thai.
162 A2 Ban Thung Luang Thai.
161 I3 Banton i. Phil.
162 C1 Ban Tôp Laos
175 I6 Bantry Ireland
175 I6 Bantry Bay Ireland
147 G3 Bantval India
162 B1 Ban Woen Laos
163 E2 Banyak, Pulau-pulau is Indon.
193 D4 Banyo Cameroon
183 R1 Banyoles Spain
163 H4 Banyuwangi Indon.
238 J8 Banzare Seamount sea feature Indian Ocean
179 J1 Banzkow Germany
154 B3 Bao'an China
154 E1 Baochang China
154 E2 Baoding China
154 D3 Baofeng China
154 C3 Baoji China
155 C4 Baojing China
155 D4 Baokang Hubei China
160 B1 Baokang Nei Mongol China
155 B6 Bao Lac Vietnam

160 E1 Baolin China
160 B2 Baolizhen China
162 C3 Bao Lôc Vietnam
158 C1 Baoqing China
151 B4 Baoshan China
154 D1 Baotou China
157 C4 Baotou Shan mt. China/N. Korea
155 B4 Baoxing China
154 F3 Baoying China
148 C4 Bap India
147 I3 Bapatla India
178 A4 Bapaume France
209 H3 Baptiste Lake Canada
Baqbaq Egypt see Buqbuq
149 H2 Baqên China
149 H3 Baqên China
155 E5 Baqiu China
139 J5 Ba'qūbah Iraq
Baquerizo Moreno Ecuador see Puerto Baquerizo Moreno
185 H3 Bar Montenegro
193 F3 Bara Sudan
194 E3 Baraawe Somalia
149 H4 Barabar Hills India
208 C4 Baraboo U.S.A.
208 B4 Baraboo r. U.S.A.
223 J4 Baracoa Cuba
235 K2 Baradero Arg.
125 H3 Baradine Australia
125 H3 Baradine r. Australia
208 C2 Baraga U.S.A.
233 J2 Baragua Venez.
223 J5 Barahona Dom. Rep.
149 H4 Barail Range mts India
149 H4 Barak r. India
193 F3 Baraka watercourse Eritrea/Sudan
183 O1 Barakaldo Spain
143 H3 Barakī Barak Afgh.
147 J1 Barakot India
123 E5 Baralaba Australia
148 D2 Bara Lacha Pass India
205 J3 Baralzon Lake Canada
147 G2 Baramati India
Baramula India see Baramulla
152 B5 Baramulla India
148 D4 Baran India
148 B4 Baran r. Pak.
143 F3 Bārān, Kūh-e mts Iran
187 C4 Baranavichy Belarus
133 R3 Baranikha Rus. Fed.
187 C5 Baranivka Ukr.
140 C3 Barankul Kazakh.
233 I2 Baranoa Col.
204 B3 Baranof Island U.S.A.
140 A1 Baranovka Rus. Fed.
234 A2 Barão de Melgaço Brazil
192 B3 Baraouéli Mali
178 D4 Baraque de Fraiture h. Belgium
151 E7 Barat Daya, Kepulauan is Indon.
124 C4 Baratta (abandoned) Australia
148 D3 Baraut India
233 I4 Baraya Col.
234 D3 Barbacena Brazil
233 H4 Barbacoas Col.
223 M6 Barbados country Caribbean Sea
183 Q1 Barbastro Spain
183 N4 Barbate Spain
224 C2 Barbechitos Mex.
214 □[1] Barbers Point U.S.A.
Barbers Pt U.S.A. see Barbers Point
197 I2 Barberton S. Africa
220 C4 Barberton U.S.A.
182 D4 Barbezieux-St-Hilaire France
233 I3 Barbosa Col.
205 K2 Barbour Bay Canada
220 B6 Barbourville U.S.A.
161 I4 Barboza Phil.
223 L5 Barbuda i. Antigua and Barbuda
179 J3 Barby (Elbe) Germany
119 E4 Barcaldine Australia
183 R2 Barcelona Spain (City Plan 102)
233 K2 Barcelona Venez.
231 F4 Barcelos Brazil
179 I4 Barchfeld Germany
192 B4 Barclayville Liberia
123 C5 Barcoo watercourse Australia
Barcoo National Park nat. park Australia see Welford National Park

185 G2 Barcs Hungary
139 K1 Bārdā Azer.
170 C2 Bárðarbunga mt. Iceland
235 I2 Bardas Blancas Arg.
138 D6 Bardawīl, Sabkhat al lag. Egypt
149 F5 Barddhaman India
177 J6 Bardejov Slovakia
Bar Đôn Vietnam see Buôn Đôn
173 C5 Bardsey Island U.K.
143 E4 Bardsīr Iran
168 D2 Barðsneshorn pt Iceland
219 C4 Bardstown U.S.A.
220 B5 Bardwell U.S.A.
148 D3 Bareilly India
132 C2 Barentsburg Svalbard
132 D2 Barentsøya i. Svalbard
132 F2 Barents Sea Arctic Ocean
194 D2 Barentu Eritrea
149 E3 Barga China
147 I1 Bargarh India
148 D5 Bargi India
174 D5 Bargrennan U.K.
179 I1 Bargteheide Germany
149 G5 Barguna Bangl.
221 I2 Bar Harbor U.S.A.
185 G4 Bari Italy
162 C3 Ba Ria Vietnam
148 C3 Bari Doab lowland Pak.
180 E4 Barika Alg.
149 E3 Barikot Nepal
233 L2 Barima r. Venez.
233 J2 Barinas Venez.
145 G7 Baripada India
149 G5 Barisal Bangl.
163 B3 Barisan, Pegunungan mts Indon.
163 H3 Barito r. Indon.
231 F8 Baritú, Parque Nacional nat. park Arg.
143 E6 Barkā Oman
155 B4 Barkam China
142 C4 Barkan, Ra's-e pt Iran
171 N4 Barkava Latvia
204 E4 Barkerville Canada
219 C4 Barkley, Lake U.S.A.
204 D5 Barkley Sound inlet Canada
197 G5 Barkly East S. Africa
122 A3 Barkly Homestead Australia
118 D3 Barkly Tableland reg. Australia
197 F4 Barkly West S. Africa
150 B2 Barkol China
148 D3 Barkot India
177 M7 Bârlad Romania
182 G2 Bar-le-Duc France
118 B4 Barlee, Lake salt flat Australia
121 A4 Barlee Range hills Australia
185 G4 Barletta Italy
125 G5 Barmedman Australia
148 B4 Barmer India
124 D5 Barmera Australia
173 C5 Barmouth U.K.
148 C3 Barnala India
172 F3 Barnard Castle U.K.
125 F3 Barnato Australia
133 J4 Barnaul Rus. Fed.
221 F5 Barnegat U.S.A.
221 F5 Barnegat Bay U.S.A.
220 D4 Barnesboro U.S.A.
203 K2 Barnes Icecap Canada
178 D2 Barneveld Neth.
125 F4 Barneys Lake imp. l. Australia
215 G3 Barney Top mt. U.S.A.
217 C6 Barnhart U.S.A.
173 F4 Barnsley U.K.
173 C6 Barnstaple U.K.
173 C6 Barnstaple Bay U.K.
179 G2 Barnstorf Germany
219 D5 Barnwell U.S.A.
Baroda India see Vadodara
121 D5 Barons Range hills Australia
148 C1 Barowghīl, Kowtal-e Afgh.
149 H4 Barpathar India
149 G4 Barpeta India
208 D3 Barques, Point Aux MI U.S.A.
209 F3 Barques, Point Aux MI U.S.A.
233 J2 Barquisimeto Venez.
231 J6 Barra Brazil
174 A4 Barra i. U.K.
174 A3 Barra, Sound of sea chan. U.K.
125 I3 Barraba Australia
196 D7 Barracouta, Cape S. Africa
231 G6 Barra do Bugres Brazil
231 I5 Barra do Corda Brazil

234 B1 Barra do Garças Brazil
231 G5 Barra do São Manuel Brazil
230 C6 Barranca Lima Peru
230 C4 Barranca Loreto Peru
233 I3 Barrancabermeja Col.
235 H3 Barrancas r. Arg.
233 I2 Barrancas Col.
233 L2 Barrancas Venez.
232 E3 Barranqueras Arg.
233 I2 Barranquilla Col.
221 G2 Barre U.S.A.
235 I1 Barreal Arg.
231 J6 Barreiras Brazil
231 G4 Barreirinha Brazil
231 J4 Barreirinhas Brazil
234 B1 Barreiro r. Brazil
183 L3 Barreiro Port.
231 K5 Barreiros Brazil
145 H9 Barren Island India
234 C3 Barretos Brazil
120 D3 Barrett, Mount h. Australia
205 G4 Barrhead Canada
174 D5 Barrhead U.K.
209 H3 Barrie Canada
209 F3 Barrie Island Canada
204 E4 Barrière Canada
124 D3 Barrier Range hills Australia
225 H4 Barrier Reef Belize
125 I4 Barrington, Mount Australia
205 I3 Barrington Lake Canada
123 E7 Barrington Tops National Park Australia
125 F2 Barringun Australia
208 B3 Barron U.S.A.
225 D2 Barroterán Mex.
235 K3 Barrow Arg.
175 L5 Barrow r. Ireland
202 C2 Barrow U.S.A.
202 C2 Barrow, Point U.S.A.
118 D4 Barrow Creek Australia
172 D3 Barrow-in-Furness U.K.
118 B4 Barrow Island Australia
121 D5 Barrow Range hills Australia
203 I2 Barrow Strait Canada
121 C5 Barr Smith Range hills Australia
173 D6 Barry U.K.
196 D6 Barrydale S. Africa
123 D8 Barry Mountains Australia
209 I3 Barrys Bay Canada
140 D3 Barsakel'mes, Poluostrov pen. Kazakh.
148 C3 Barsalpur India
141 I2 Barshatas Kazakh.
147 G2 Barsi India
148 D5 Barsi Iakli India
179 H2 Barsinghausen Germany
215 D4 Barstow U.S.A.
182 G2 Bar-sur-Aube France
176 F3 Barth Germany
231 G2 Bartica Guyana
138 D1 Bartın Turkey
119 E3 Bartle Frere, Mount Australia
215 G2 Bartles, Mount U.S.A.
211 G4 Bartlesville U.S.A.
216 D3 Bartlett NE U.S.A.
221 H2 Bartlett NH U.S.A.
204 F2 Bartlett Lake Canada
221 G2 Barton U.S.A.
173 G4 Barton-upon-Humber U.K.
177 J3 Bartoszyce Poland
224 I6 Barú, Volcán vol. Panama
163 B2 Barumun r. Indon.
163 H4 Barung i. Indon.
Barunga Australia see Bamyili
153 K1 Barun-Torey, Ozero l. Rus. Fed.
162 A5 Barus Indon.
Baruunsuu Mongolia see Tsogttsetsiy
144 H2 Baruuntuuruun Mongolia
150 D2 Baruun-Urt Mongolia
148 D5 Barwah India
148 C3 Barwala India
148 C3 Barwani India
125 H2 Barwon r. Australia
187 D4 Barysaw Belarus
187 H4 Barysh Rus. Fed.
187 H4 Barysh r. Rus. Fed.
142 C3 Bāsa'īdū Iran
142 D5 Bāsa'īdū Iran
162 C3 Basăk, Tônlé r. Cambodia
122 D3 Basalt r. Australia
214 C2 Basalt U.S.A.
155 □ Basalt Island Hong Kong China
194 B3 Basankusu Dem. Rep. Congo

147 H2 Basar India
185 M2 Basarabi Romania
235 K2 Basavilbaso Arg.
161 J4 Basay Phil.
161 I1 Basco Phil.
176 C7 Basel Switz.
143 E5 Bashākerd, Kūhhā-ye mts Iran
205 G4 Bashaw Canada
197 H6 Bashee r. S. Africa
143 H3 Bashgul r. Afgh.
155 F6 Bashi Channel Phil./Taiwan
187 G4 Bashmakovo Rus. Fed.
142 C4 Bāsht Iran
187 E6 Bashtanka Ukr.
148 D4 Basi India
147 J1 Basia India
161 I5 Basilan i. Phil.
161 I5 Basilan Strait Phil.
173 H6 Basildon U.K.
212 E2 Basin U.S.A.
173 F6 Basingstoke U.K.
139 J4 Bāsīra r. Iraq
149 G5 Basirhat India
221 J2 Baskahegan Lake U.S.A.
139 J2 Başkale Turkey
209 J2 Baskatong, Réservoir resr Canada
120 C3 Baskerville, Cape Australia
181 J4 Başkomutan Tarıhı Milli Parkı nat. park Turkey
187 H5 Baskunchak, Ozero l. Rus. Fed.
Basle Switz. see Basel
148 D5 Basoda India
194 C3 Basoko Dem. Rep. Congo
139 K6 Basra Iraq
184 D2 Bassano del Grappa Italy
192 C4 Bassar Togo
195 D6 Bassas da India rf Indian Ocean
151 B5 Bassein Myanmar
172 D3 Bassenthwaite Lake U.K.
192 A3 Basse Santa Su Gambia
223 L5 Basse-Terre Guadeloupe
223 L5 Basseterre St Kitts and Nevis
216 D3 Bassett U.S.A.
215 G5 Bassett Peak U.S.A.
221 I2 Bass Harbor U.S.A.
192 B3 Bassikounou Mauritania
192 C4 Bassila Benin
175 F4 Bass Rock i. U.K.
119 E5 Bass Strait Australia
179 G2 Bassum Germany
208 B1 Basswood Lake U.S.A.
171 K4 Båstad Sweden
142 D5 Bastak Iran
142 B2 Bāstānābād Iran
179 I4 Bastheim Germany
149 E4 Basti India
184 C3 Bastia Corsica France
178 D4 Bastogne Belgium
217 F5 Bastrop LA U.S.A.
217 D6 Bastrop TX U.S.A.
143 G5 Basul r. Pak.
192 C4 Bata Equat. Guinea
223 H4 Batabanó, Golfo de b. Cuba
161 I2 Batac Phil.
161 J3 Batag i. Phil.
133 O3 Batagay Rus. Fed.
148 B2 Batai Pass Pak.
148 C3 Batala India
183 L3 Batalha Port.
162 C5 Batan i. Indon.
133 N3 Batamay Rus. Fed.
140 D2 Batamshinskiy Kazakh.
161 I1 Batan i. Phil.
194 B3 Batangafo Centr. Afr. Rep.
161 I3 Batangas Phil.
163 B3 Batanghari r. Indon.
162 B3 Batangtoru Indon.
161 I1 Batan Islands Phil.
234 C3 Batatais Brazil
208 C5 Batavia IL U.S.A.
220 D3 Batavia NY U.S.A.
187 F6 Bataysk Rus. Fed.
209 E2 Batchawana Canada
209 E2 Batchawana r. Canada
209 E2 Batchawana Bay Canada
206 D4 Batchawana Mountain h. Canada
118 D3 Batchelor Australia
162 B2 Bătdâmbâng Cambodia
125 I5 Batemans Bay Australia
125 I5 Batemans Bay b. Australia
121 C5 Bates Range hills Australia
217 F5 Batesville AR U.S.A.
217 F5 Batesville MS U.S.A.
186 D3 Batetskiy Rus. Fed.
207 G4 Bath N.B. Canada

209 I3 Bath Ont. Canada
173 E6 Bath U.K.
221 I3 Bath ME U.S.A.
221 E3 Bath NY U.S.A.
174 E5 Bathgate U.K.
148 C3 Bathinda India
125 H4 Bathurst Australia
207 G4 Bathurst Canada
197 G6 Bathurst S. Africa
125 H5 Bathurst, Lake Australia
203 H3 Bathurst Inlet Canada
203 H3 Bathurst Inlet inlet Canada
118 D3 Bathurst Island Australia
203 I2 Bathurst Island Canada
139 K7 Bāţin, Wādī al watercourse Asia
181 J4 Batı Toroslar mts Turkey
144 D2 Batken Kyrg.
141 G4 Batken admin. div. Kyrg.
142 D3 Bāţlāq-e Gavkhūnī marsh Iran
173 F4 Batley U.K.
125 H5 Batlow Australia
139 H3 Batman Turkey
192 C1 Batna Alg.
162 □ Batok, Bukit h. Sing.
162 A4 Batong, Ko i. Thai.
217 E6 Baton Rouge U.S.A.
224 C2 Batopilas Mex.
193 D4 Batouri Cameroon
234 B1 Batovi Brazil
138 E4 Batroûn Lebanon
170 O1 Båtsfjord Norway
147 I5 Batticaloa Sri Lanka
184 F4 Battipaglia Italy
205 G4 Battle r. Canada
209 E4 Battle Creek U.S.A.
205 H4 Battleford Canada
213 C3 Battle Mountain U.S.A.
148 C3 Battura Glacier Pak.
163 E3 Batu, Pulau-pulau is Indon.
162 B4 Batu Gajah Malaysia
161 J5 Batulaki Phil.
139 H1 Bat'umi Georgia
163 B2 Batu Pahat Malaysia
162 B4 Batu Putih, Gunung mt. Malaysia
151 E7 Baubau Indon.
192 C3 Bauchi Nigeria
216 E1 Baudette U.S.A.
233 H3 Baudo, Serranía de mts Col.
182 D3 Baugé France
123 E5 Bauhinia Australia
179 H5 Bauland reg. Germany
207 J3 Bauld, Cape Canada
182 H3 Baume-les-Dames France
148 C2 Baundal India
234 C3 Bauru Brazil
234 B2 Baús Brazil
179 E4 Bausendorf Germany
171 N4 Bauska Latvia
140 B3 Bautino Kazakh.
176 G3 Bautzen Germany
141 G4 Bauyrzhan Momyshuly Kazakh.
197 E6 Baviaanskloofberge mts S. Africa
210 E6 Bavispe r. Mex.
125 G6 Baw Baw National Park Australia
173 I5 Bawdeswell U.K.
163 H4 Bawean i. Indon.
179 F2 Bawinkel Germany
192 B3 Bawku Ghana
162 A1 Bawlake Myanmar
155 A4 Bawolung China
154 B3 Baxi China
219 D6 Baxley U.S.A.
152 G5 Baxoi China
161 I3 Bay, Laguna de lag. Phil.
223 I4 Bayamo Cuba
156 B3 Bayan China
Bayan Mongolia see Bayan-Adraga
148 D4 Bayana India
153 J2 Bayan-Adraga Mongolia
141 H2 Bayanaul Kazakh.
Bayanbulag Mongolia see Bayantsagaan
144 F3 Bayanbulak China
154 B1 Bayandalay Mongolia
153 I1 Bayanday Rus. Fed.
150 B3 Bayan Har Shan mts China
150 C2 Bayanhongor Mongolia
154 B2 Bayan Hot China
160 A1 Bayan Huxu China
154 B1 Bayan Mod China
154 B1 Bayan Nuru China
154 C1 Bayan Obo China
Bayan-Ovoo Mongolia see Altay

125 J1 **Boonah** Australia
216 E3 **Boone** IA U.S.A.
219 D4 **Boone** NC U.S.A.
220 B6 **Boone Lake** U.S.A.
220 B6 **Booneville** KY U.S.A.
217 F5 **Booneville** MS U.S.A.
144 I2 **Böön Tsagaan Nuur** salt l. Mongolia
219 C4 **Boonville** IN U.S.A.
217 E4 **Boonville** MO U.S.A.
221 F3 **Boonville** NY U.S.A.
121 C6 **Boorabin National Park** Australia
125 F5 **Booroorban** Australia
125 H5 **Boorowa** Australia
125 E6 **Boort** Australia
194 E2 **Boosaaso** Somalia
221 I3 **Boothbay Harbor** U.S.A.
203 I2 **Boothia, Gulf of** Canada
203 I2 **Boothia Peninsula** Canada
173 E4 **Bootle** U.K.
192 A4 **Bopolu** Liberia
179 F4 **Boppard** Germany
235 M1 **Boqueirão** Brazil
224 C2 **Boquilla, Presa de la** resr Mex.
225 D1 **Boquillas del Carmen** Mex.
179 K5 **Bor** Czech Rep.
185 J2 **Bor** Serbia
193 F4 **Bor** Sudan
138 E3 **Bor** Turkey
195 F5 **Boraha, Nosy** i. Madag.
212 D2 **Borah Peak** U.S.A.
162 B2 **Boraphet, Bung** l. Thai.
171 K4 **Borås** Sweden
142 C4 **Borāzjān** Iran
231 G4 **Borba** Brazil
231 K5 **Borborema, Planalto da** plat. Brazil
179 G3 **Borchen** Germany
139 H1 **Borçka** Turkey
124 B5 **Borda, Cape** Australia
138 B3 **Bor Dağı** mt. Turkey
182 D4 **Bordeaux** France
Borden Canada see **Borden-Carleton**
207 H4 **Borden-Carleton** Canada
202 G2 **Borden Island** Canada
203 J2 **Borden Peninsula** Canada
124 D6 **Bordertown** Australia
170 B2 **Borðeyri** Iceland
183 S4 **Bordj Bou Arréridj** Alg.
183 Q5 **Bordj Bounaama** Alg.
180 E5 **Bordj Messaouda** Alg.
192 C2 **Bordj Omer Driss** Alg.
170 □ **Borðoy** i. Faroe Is
141 H4 **Bordu** Kyrg.
174 A3 **Boreray** i. U.K.
170 D2 **Borgarfjörður** Iceland
170 B2 **Borgarnes** Iceland
170 K2 **Børgefjell Nasjonalpark** nat. park Norway
217 C5 **Borger** U.S.A.
171 L4 **Borgholm** Sweden
184 B2 **Borgo San Dalmazzo** Italy
184 D3 **Borgo San Lorenzo** Italy
184 C2 **Borgosesia** Italy
178 B4 **Borinage** reg. Belgium
187 G5 **Borisoglebsk** Rus. Fed.
187 F5 **Borisovka** Rus. Fed.
186 F3 **Borisovo-Sudskoye** Rus. Fed.
187 G7 **Borjomi** Georgia
179 E3 **Borken** Germany
170 L1 **Borkenes** Norway
179 E1 **Borkum** Germany
179 E1 **Borkum** i. Germany
171 K3 **Borlänge** Sweden
138 D2 **Borlu** Turkey
179 K3 **Borna** Germany
178 D1 **Borndiep** sea chan. Neth.
179 E2 **Borne** Neth.
163 H2 **Borneo** i. Asia
171 K5 **Bornholm** i. Denmark
185 L5 **Bornova** Turkey
161 I4 **Borocay** i. Phil.
133 J3 **Borodino** Rus. Fed.
171 O3 **Borodinskoye** Rus. Fed.
187 D5 **Borodyanka** Ukr.
133 O3 **Borogontsy** Rus. Fed.
141 J3 **Borohoro Shan** mts China
186 F3 **Borok** Rus. Fed.
192 B3 **Boromo** Burkina
161 J4 **Borongan** Phil.
172 F3 **Boroughbridge** U.K.
186 E3 **Borovichi** Rus. Fed.
141 K1 **Borovlyanka** Rus. Fed.
186 I3 **Borovoy** Kirovskaya Oblast' Rus. Fed.

186 E1 **Borovoy** Respublika Kareliya Rus. Fed.
186 J2 **Borovoy** Respublika Komi Rus. Fed.
141 F1 **Borovskoy** Kazakh.
175 J5 **Borrisokane** Ireland
118 D3 **Borroloola** Australia
171 J3 **Børsa** Norway
177 L7 **Borşa** Romania
140 D4 **Borsakelmas sho'rxogi** salt marsh Uzbek.
187 C5 **Borshchiv** Ukr.
150 C2 **Borshchovochnyy Khrebet** mts Rus. Fed.
141 J3 **Bortala He** r. China
142 C4 **Borūjen** Iran
142 C3 **Borūjerd** Iran
174 B3 **Borve** U.K.
187 B5 **Boryslav** Ukr.
187 D5 **Boryspil'** Ukr.
187 E5 **Borzna** Ukr.
150 D1 **Borzya** Rus. Fed.
185 G2 **Bosanska Dubica** Bos.-Herz.
185 G2 **Bosanska Gradiška** Bos.-Herz.
185 G2 **Bosanska Krupa** Bos.-Herz.
185 G2 **Bosanski Novi** Bos.-Herz.
185 G2 **Bosansko Grahovo** Bos.-Herz.
208 B4 **Boscobel** U.S.A.
155 C6 **Bose** China
197 F4 **Boshof** S. Africa
140 E1 **Boskol'** Kazakh.
185 G2 **Bosnia-Herzegovina** country Europe
194 B3 **Bosobolo** Dem. Rep. Congo
159 C7 **Bōsō-hantō** pen. Japan
138 B1 **Bosporus** str. Turkey
194 B3 **Bossangoa** Centr. Afr. Rep.
194 B3 **Bossembélé** Centr. Afr. Rep.
217 E5 **Bossier City** U.S.A.
196 B2 **Bossiesvlei** Namibia
120 C3 **Bossut, Cape** Australia
149 F1 **Bostan** China
139 K6 **Bostān** Iran
140 B2 **Bostandyk** Kazakh.
150 A2 **Bosten Hu** l. China
173 G5 **Boston** U.K.
221 H3 **Boston** U.S.A.
124 A5 **Boston Bay** Australia
209 H1 **Boston Creek** Canada
221 H3 **Boston-Logan** airport U.S.A.
217 E5 **Boston Mountains** U.S.A.
173 F4 **Boston Spa** U.K.
208 D5 **Boswell** U.S.A.
148 B5 **Botad** India
125 I4 **Botany Bay** Australia
171 L3 **Boteå** Sweden
185 K3 **Botev** mt. Bulg.
185 J3 **Botevgrad** Bulg.
197 G3 **Bothaville** S. Africa
171 L3 **Bothnia, Gulf of** Fin./Sweden
170 M2 **Bothnian Bay** g. Fin./Sweden
125 G9 **Bothwell** Australia
187 H5 **Botkul', Ozero** l. Kazakh./Rus. Fed.
137 G2 **Botlikh** Rus. Fed.
177 M7 **Botoşani** Romania
154 E3 **Botou** China
Bô Trach Vietnam see **Hoan Lao**
197 G4 **Botshabelo** S. Africa
195 C6 **Botswana** country Africa
185 G5 **Botte Donato, Monte** mt. Italy
173 G4 **Bottesford** U.K.
216 C1 **Bottineau** U.S.A.
179 E3 **Bottrop** Germany
234 C3 **Botucatu** Brazil
234 D1 **Botupora** Brazil
207 J4 **Botwood** Canada
192 B4 **Bouaflé** Côte d'Ivoire
192 B4 **Bouaké** Côte d'Ivoire
194 B3 **Bouar** Centr. Afr. Rep.
192 B1 **Bouârfa** Morocco
193 D4 **Bouba Ndjida, Parc National de** nat. park Cameroon
194 B3 **Bouca** Centr. Afr. Rep.
122 A2 **Boucaut Bay** Australia
178 B4 **Bouchain** France
221 G2 **Boucherville** Canada
209 J2 **Bouchette** Canada
192 B3 **Boucle du Baoulé, Parc National de la** nat. park Mali
207 H4 **Bouctouche** Canada
120 D2 **Bougainville, Cape** Australia

119 F2 **Bougainville Island** P.N.G.
122 D2 **Bougainville Reef** Australia
192 B3 **Bougouni** Mali
180 D5 **Bougtob** Alg.
178 D5 **Bouillon** Belgium
183 R4 **Bouira** Alg.
192 A2 **Boujdour** W. Sahara
121 C6 **Boulder** Australia
213 F3 **Boulder** CO U.S.A.
212 D2 **Boulder** MT U.S.A.
215 G3 **Boulder** UT U.S.A.
215 E3 **Boulder Canyon** gorge U.S.A.
215 E4 **Boulder City** U.S.A.
215 D5 **Boulevard** U.S.A.
235 K3 **Boulevard Atlántico** Arg.
118 D4 **Boulia** Australia
182 F2 **Boulogne-Billancourt** France
182 E1 **Boulogne-sur-Mer** France
192 B3 **Boulsa** Burkina
195 B4 **Boumango** Gabon
193 D4 **Boumba** r. Cameroon
183 R4 **Boumerdes** Alg.
192 B4 **Bouna** Côte d'Ivoire
180 C5 **Bou Naceur, Jbel** mt. Morocco
221 H2 **Boundary Mountains** U.S.A.
214 C3 **Boundary Peak** U.S.A.
192 B4 **Boundiali** Côte d'Ivoire
195 B4 **Boundji** Congo
Boung r. Vietnam see **Thu Bôn, Sông**
155 A6 **Boun Nua** Laos
213 E3 **Bountiful** U.S.A.
119 H6 **Bounty Islands** N.Z.
236 G9 **Bounty Trough** sea feature S. Pacific Ocean
192 B3 **Bourem** Mali
182 E4 **Bourganeuf** France
182 G3 **Bourg-en-Bresse** France
182 F3 **Bourges** France
221 F2 **Bourget** Canada
209 J1 **Bourgmont** Canada
Bourgogne reg. France see **Burgundy**
125 F3 **Bourke** Australia
209 G1 **Bourkes** Canada
173 G5 **Bourne** U.K.
173 F7 **Bournemouth** U.K.
179 F2 **Bourtanger Moor** reg. Germany
192 C1 **Bou Saâda** Alg.
184 C6 **Bou Salem** Tunisia
215 E5 **Bouse** U.S.A.
215 E5 **Bouse Wash** watercourse U.S.A.
193 D3 **Bousso** Chad
178 B4 **Boussu** Belgium
192 A3 **Boutilimit** Mauritania
239 J9 **Bouvetøya** terr. Atlantic Ocean
178 C5 **Bouy** France
179 H3 **Bovenden** Germany
Boven Kapuas, Pegunungan mts Malaysia see **Kapuas Hulu, Pegunungan**
235 K1 **Bovril** Arg.
205 G4 **Bow** r. Canada
216 C1 **Bowbells** U.S.A.
119 E4 **Bowen** Australia
208 B5 **Bowen** U.S.A.
125 H6 **Bowen, Mount** Australia
125 I1 **Bowenville** Australia
236 G2 **Bowers Ridge** sea feature Bering Sea
123 D4 **Bowie** Australia
215 H5 **Bowie** AZ U.S.A.
217 D5 **Bowie** TX U.S.A.
205 G5 **Bow Island** Canada
219 C4 **Bowling Green** KY U.S.A.
217 F4 **Bowling Green** MO U.S.A.
220 B4 **Bowling Green** OH U.S.A.
221 E5 **Bowling Green** VA U.S.A.
122 D3 **Bowling Green Bay National Park** Australia
216 C2 **Bowman** U.S.A.
204 E4 **Bowman, Mount** Canada
127 K6 **Bowman Island** Antarctica
209 H4 **Bowmanville** Canada
174 B5 **Bowmore** U.K.
125 I5 **Bowral** Australia
125 J3 **Bowraville** Australia
204 E4 **Bowron** r. Canada
204 E4 **Bowron Lake Provincial Park** Canada
179 H5 **Boxberg** Germany
154 F2 **Boxing** China
178 D3 **Boxtel** Neth.
138 E1 **Boyabat** Turkey
185 J3 **Boyana** tourist site Bulg.

155 E4 **Boyang** China
125 J3 **Boyd** r. Australia
121 D5 **Boyd Lagoon** salt flat Australia
205 I2 **Boyd Lake** Canada
205 G4 **Boyle** Canada
175 J4 **Boyle** Ireland
175 L4 **Boyne** r. Ireland
143 G2 **Boyni Qara** Afgh.
219 D7 **Boynton Beach** U.S.A.
213 E3 **Boysen Reservoir** U.S.A.
141 F5 **Boysun** Uzbek.
231 F8 **Boyuibe** Bol.
139 J1 **Böyük Hinaldağ** mt. Azer.
141 J2 **Bozanbay** Kazakh.
185 L5 **Bozcaada** i. Turkey
185 L5 **Bozdağ** mt. Turkey
138 A2 **Boz Dağları** mts Turkey
138 B3 **Bozdoğan** Turkey
138 D3 **Bozkır** Turkey
194 B3 **Bozoum** Centr. Afr. Rep.
139 G3 **Bozova** Turkey
142 B2 **Bozqūsh, Kūh-e** mts Iran
141 H2 **Bozshakol'** Kazakh.
141 F2 **Boztumsyk** Kazakh.
138 C2 **Bozüyük** Turkey
184 B2 **Bra** Italy
185 G3 **Brač** i. Croatia
174 B3 **Bracadale** U.K.
174 B3 **Bracadale, Loch** b. U.K.
184 E3 **Bracciano, Lago di** l. Italy
209 H3 **Bracebridge** Canada
171 K3 **Bräcke** Sweden
179 H5 **Brackenheim** Germany
173 G6 **Bracknell** U.K.
185 G4 **Bradano** r. Italy
219 D7 **Bradenton** U.S.A.
223 L5 **Brades** Montserrat
209 H3 **Bradford** Canada
173 F4 **Bradford** U.K.
220 A4 **Bradford** OH U.S.A.
220 D4 **Bradford** PA U.S.A.
221 G3 **Bradford** VT U.S.A.
217 D6 **Brady** U.S.A.
204 B3 **Brady Glacier** U.S.A.
174 □ **Brae** U.K.
124 C4 **Braemar** Australia
174 E3 **Braemar** U.K.
183 L2 **Braga** Port.
235 K2 **Bragado** Arg.
231 I4 **Bragança** Brazil
183 M2 **Bragança** Port.
234 C3 **Bragança Paulista** Brazil
187 D5 **Brahin** Belarus
179 I1 **Brahlstorf** Germany
149 G5 **Brahmanbaria** Bangl.
147 J1 **Brahmani** r. India
147 J2 **Brahmapur** India
149 G4 **Brahmaputra** r. Asia alt. **Dihang** (India), alt. **Yarlung Zangbo** (China)
185 L2 **Brăila** Romania
178 B5 **Braine** France
178 C4 **Braine-le-Comte** Belgium
216 E2 **Brainerd** U.S.A.
173 H6 **Braintree** U.K.
197 H1 **Brak** r. S. Africa
179 G1 **Brake (Unterweser)** Germany
178 B4 **Brakel** Belgium
179 H3 **Brakel** Germany
195 B6 **Brakwater** Namibia
204 E4 **Bralorne** Canada
121 F7 **Bramfield** Australia
171 J5 **Bramming** Denmark
171 J5 **Brämön** i. Sweden
209 H4 **Brampton** Canada
172 E3 **Brampton** England U.K.
173 I5 **Brampton** England U.K.
179 G2 **Bramsche** Germany
122 C2 **Bramwell** Australia
173 H5 **Brancaster** U.K.
207 J4 **Branch** Canada
233 L4 **Branco** r. Brazil
171 J3 **Brandbu** Norway
171 J5 **Brande** Denmark
179 K2 **Brandenburg** Germany
179 K2 **Brandenburg** land Germany
197 G4 **Brandfort** S. Africa
205 J5 **Brandon** Canada
173 H5 **Brandon** U.K.
216 D3 **Brandon** SD U.S.A.
221 G3 **Brandon** VT U.S.A.
175 H5 **Brandon Head** Ireland
175 L5 **Brandon Hill** Ireland
175 H5 **Brandon Mountain** h. Ireland

196 D5 **Brandvlei** S. Africa
219 D6 **Branford** U.S.A.
177 I3 **Braniewo** Poland
127 I2 **Bransfield Strait** Antarctica
209 G4 **Brantford** Canada
124 D6 **Branxholme** Australia
207 H4 **Bras d'Or Lake** Canada
234 E2 **Brasil, Planalto do** plat. Brazil
234 C1 **Brasilândia** Brazil
230 E6 **Brasileia** Brazil
234 C1 **Brasília** Brazil
234 D2 **Brasília de Minas** Brazil
231 G4 **Brasília Legal** Brazil
177 M3 **Braslaw** Belarus
185 K2 **Braşov** Romania
161 H5 **Brassey, Banjaran** mts Sabah Malaysia
121 F4 **Brassey, Mount** Australia
121 C5 **Brassey Range** hills Australia
221 I2 **Brassua Lake** U.S.A.
177 H6 **Bratislava** Slovakia
150 C1 **Bratsk** Rus. Fed.
150 C1 **Bratskoye Vodokhranilishche** resr Rus. Fed.
221 G3 **Brattleboro** U.S.A.
176 H3 **Braunau am Inn** Austria
179 G4 **Braunfels** Germany
179 I3 **Braunlage** Germany
179 J3 **Braunsbedra** Germany
179 I2 **Braunschweig** Germany
192 □ **Brava** i. Cape Verde
171 L4 **Bråviken** inlet Sweden
225 E2 **Bravo del Norte, Río** r. Mex./U.S.A. alt. **Rio Grande**
215 E5 **Brawley** U.S.A.
175 L4 **Bray** Ireland
204 F4 **Brazeau** r. Canada
231 H6 **Brazil** country S. America
239 H7 **Brazil Basin** sea feature S. Atlantic Ocean
217 D5 **Brazos** r. U.S.A.
195 B4 **Brazzaville** Congo
185 H2 **Brčko** Bos.-Herz.
123 B4 **Breadalbane** Australia
126 A6 **Breaksea Sound** inlet N.Z.
126 E1 **Bream Bay** N.Z.
126 E1 **Bream Head** N.Z.
173 C6 **Brechfa** U.K.
175 F4 **Brechin** U.K.
178 C3 **Brecht** Belgium
216 D2 **Breckenridge** MN U.S.A.
217 D5 **Breckenridge** TX U.S.A.
177 H6 **Břeclav** Czech Rep.
173 D6 **Brecon** U.K.
173 D6 **Brecon Beacons** reg. U.K.
173 D6 **Brecon Beacons National Park** U.K.
178 C3 **Breda** Neth.
196 D7 **Bredasdorp** S. Africa
125 H5 **Bredbo** Australia
179 K2 **Breddin** Germany
179 E3 **Bredevoort** Neth.
170 K2 **Bredviken** Norway
140 E1 **Bredy** Rus. Fed.
178 D3 **Bree** Belgium
176 D7 **Bregenz** Austria
170 A2 **Breiðafjörður** b. Iceland
170 D2 **Breiðdalsvík** Iceland
179 G4 **Breidenbach** Germany
176 C6 **Breisach am Rhein** Germany
179 I1 **Breitenfelde** Germany
179 I5 **Breitengüßbach** Germany
170 M1 **Breivikbotn** Norway
231 I6 **Brejinho de Nazaré** Brazil
171 J3 **Brekstad** Norway
179 G1 **Bremen** Germany
219 C5 **Bremen** GA U.S.A.
208 D5 **Bremen** IN U.S.A.
121 B7 **Bremer Bay** Australia
179 G1 **Bremerhaven** Germany
121 C7 **Bremer Range** hills Australia
212 B2 **Bremerton** U.S.A.
179 H1 **Bremervörde** Germany
179 F4 **Bremm** Germany
217 D6 **Brenham** U.S.A.
170 K2 **Brenna** Norway
176 E7 **Brenner Pass** Austria/Italy
209 H2 **Brent** Canada
184 D2 **Brenta** r. Italy
173 H6 **Brentwood** U.K.
214 B3 **Brentwood** CA U.S.A.
221 G4 **Brentwood** NY U.S.A.
184 D2 **Brescia** Italy
184 D1 **Bressanone** Italy
174 □ **Bressay** i. U.K.
182 D3 **Bressuire** France
187 B4 **Brest** Belarus

182 B2 **Brest** France
Bretagne reg. France see **Brittany**
178 A5 **Breteuil** France
217 F6 **Breton Sound** b. U.S.A.
126 E1 **Brett, Cape** N.Z.
179 G5 **Bretten** Germany
173 E4 **Bretton** U.K.
219 D5 **Brevard** U.S.A.
231 H4 **Breves** Brazil
209 E2 **Brevort** U.S.A.
125 G2 **Brewarrina** Australia
221 I2 **Brewer** U.S.A.
212 C1 **Brewster** U.S.A.
217 G6 **Brewton** U.S.A.
197 H3 **Breyten** S. Africa
169 N4 **Breytovo** Rus. Fed.
177 I6 **Brezno** Slovakia
185 I2 **Brezovo Polje** plain Croatia
194 C3 **Bria** Centr. Afr. Rep.
182 H4 **Briançon** France
125 C4 **Bribbaree** Australia
125 J1 **Bribie Island** Australia
187 C5 **Briceni** Moldova
182 H4 **Bric Froid** mt. France/Italy
175 J5 **Bride** r. Ireland
215 G1 **Bridgeland** U.S.A.
173 D6 **Bridgend** U.K.
174 D4 **Bridge of Orchy** U.K.
214 C2 **Bridgeport** CA U.S.A.
221 G4 **Bridgeport** CT U.S.A.
216 C3 **Bridgeport** NE U.S.A.
212 E2 **Bridger** U.S.A.
213 F3 **Bridger Peak** U.S.A.
221 F5 **Bridgeton** U.S.A.
121 B7 **Bridgetown** Australia
223 M6 **Bridgetown** Barbados
125 G9 **Bridgewater** Australia
207 H5 **Bridgewater** Canada
221 J1 **Bridgewater** U.S.A.
124 D7 **Bridgewater, Cape** Australia
173 E5 **Bridgnorth** U.K.
221 H2 **Bridgton** U.S.A.
173 D6 **Bridgwater** U.K.
173 D6 **Bridgwater Bay** U.K.
172 G3 **Bridlington** U.K.
172 G3 **Bridlington Bay** U.K.
125 G8 **Bridport** Australia
173 E7 **Bridport** U.K.
176 C7 **Brig** Switz.
173 G4 **Brigg** U.K.
213 D3 **Brigham City** U.S.A.
125 G6 **Bright** Australia
173 I6 **Brightlingsea** U.K.
209 I3 **Brighton** Canada
126 C6 **Brighton** N.Z.
173 G7 **Brighton** U.K.
209 F4 **Brighton** U.S.A.
183 H5 **Brignoles** France
192 A3 **Brikama** Gambia
179 G3 **Brilon** Germany
185 G4 **Brindisi** Italy
235 J1 **Brinkmann** Arg.
124 C4 **Brinkworth** Australia
207 H4 **Brion, Île** i. Canada
182 F4 **Brioude** France
207 F3 **Brisay** Canada
125 J1 **Brisbane** Australia
221 J1 **Bristol** Canada
173 E6 **Bristol** U.K.
221 G4 **Bristol** CT U.S.A.
221 F4 **Bristol** PA U.S.A.
220 B6 **Bristol** TN U.S.A.
202 B4 **Bristol Bay** U.S.A.
173 C6 **Bristol Channel** est. U.K.
229 G7 **Bristol Island** S. Sandwich Is
215 E4 **Bristol Lake** U.S.A.
215 E4 **Bristol Mountains** U.S.A.
127 K3 **British Antarctic Territory** reg. Antarctica
204 D4 **British Columbia** prov. Canada
203 J1 **British Empire Range** mts Canada
130 C7 **British Indian Ocean Territory** terr. Indian Ocean
239 J6 **British Isles** N. Atlantic Ocean
197 G2 **Brits** S. Africa
197 G5 **Britstown** S. Africa
182 C2 **Brittany** reg. France
182 E4 **Brive-la-Gaillarde** France
183 O1 **Briviesca** Spain
173 D7 **Brixham** U.K.
Brlik Kazakh. see **Birlik**
177 H6 **Brno** Czech Rep.
219 D5 **Broad** r. U.S.A.
221 F3 **Broadalbin** U.S.A.
121 C6 **Broad Arrow** Australia
206 E3 **Broadback** r. Canada

235 B4 Cavernoso, Serra do *mts* Brazil
220 B5 Cave Run Lake U.S.A.
161 I4 Cavili *rf* Phil.
161 I3 Cavite Phil.
174 E3 Cawdor U.K.
124 D4 Cawndilla Lake *imp. l.* Australia
173 I5 Cawston U.K.
231 J4 Caxias Brazil
232 F3 Caxias do Sul Brazil
203 A8 Caxito Angola
138 C2 Çay Turkey
219 D5 Cayce U.S.A.
138 D1 Çaycuma Turkey
139 H1 Çayeli Turkey
231 H3 Cayenne Fr. Guiana
138 E3 Çayhan Turkey
138 C1 Çayırhan Turkey
223 I5 Cayman Brac *i.* Cayman Is
223 H5 Cayman Islands *terr.* Caribbean Sea
239 D4 Cayman Trench *sea feature* Caribbean Sea
194 E3 Caynabo Somalia
209 H4 Cayuga Canada
221 E3 Cayuga Lake U.S.A.
221 F3 Cazenovia U.S.A.
195 C5 Cazombo Angola
239 G6 Ceara Abyssal Plain *sea feature* S. Atlantic Ocean
224 I7 Cebaco, Isla *i.* Panama
224 C2 Ceballos Mex.
235 L2 Cebollatí *r.* Uruguay
161 I4 Cebu Phil.
161 I4 Cebu *i.* Phil.
208 C3 Cecil U.S.A.
125 I1 Cecil Plains Australia
121 C5 Cecil Rhodes, Mount *h.* Australia
184 D3 Cecina Italy
208 A4 Cedar *r.* IA U.S.A.
216 C2 Cedar *r.* ND U.S.A.
208 D4 Cedarburg U.S.A.
215 F3 Cedar City U.S.A.
217 D5 Cedar Creek Reservoir U.S.A.
208 A4 Cedar Falls U.S.A.
208 D4 Cedar Grove WI U.S.A.
220 C5 Cedar Grove WV U.S.A.
221 F6 Cedar Island U.S.A.
205 I4 Cedar Lake Canada
208 D5 Cedar Lake U.S.A.
220 B4 Cedar Point U.S.A.
208 B5 Cedar Rapids U.S.A.
215 G3 Cedar Ridge U.S.A.
221 F5 Cedar Run U.S.A.
209 F4 Cedar Springs Canada
209 E4 Cedar Springs U.S.A.
219 C5 Cedartown U.S.A.
197 H5 Cedarville S. Africa
209 E3 Cedarville U.S.A.
224 A1 Cedros, Isla *i.* Mex.
118 D5 Ceduna Australia
194 E3 Ceeldheere Somalia
194 E2 Ceerigaabo Somalia
184 F5 Cefalù *Sicily* Italy
177 I7 Cegléd Hungary
155 B5 Ceheng China
138 E1 Çekerek Turkey
224 G5 Celaque, Parque Nacional *nat. park* Hond.
225 D3 Celaya Mex.
175 L4 Celbridge Ireland
163 I3 Celebes *i.* Indon.
151 E6 Celebes Sea Indon./Phil.
220 A4 Celina U.S.A.
184 F1 Celje Slovenia
179 I2 Celle Germany
239 I2 Celtic Shelf *sea feature* N. Atlantic Ocean
138 E1 Cemilbey Turkey
139 G2 Çemişgezek Turkey
151 F7 Cenderawasih, Teluk *b.* Indon.
155 C5 Cengong China
215 F5 Centennial Wash *watercourse* U.S.A.
217 E6 Center U.S.A.
221 G4 Centereach U.S.A.
219 C5 Center Point U.S.A.
220 B5 Centerville OH U.S.A.
Centerville U.S.A. see Centreville
197 G1 Central *admin. dist.* Botswana
233 H4 Central, Cordillera *mts* Col.
224 I6 Central, Cordillera *mts* Panama
230 B4 Central, Cordillera *mts* Peru
161 I2 Central, Cordillera *mts* Phil.

193 D4 Central African Republic *country* Africa
143 G4 Central Brahui Range *mts* Pak.
208 B4 Central City IA U.S.A.
216 D3 Central City NE U.S.A.
219 B4 Centralia IL U.S.A.
212 B2 Centralia WA U.S.A.
194 D2 Central Island National Park Kenya
208 A2 Central Lakes U.S.A.
143 G5 Central Makran Range *mts* Pak.
121 F4 Central Mount Stuart *h.* Australia
236 G5 Central Pacific Basin *sea feature* Pacific Ocean
213 B3 Central Point U.S.A.
119 E2 Central Range *mts* P.N.G.
132 E4 Central Russian Upland *hills* Rus. Fed.
133 L3 Central Siberian Plateau Rus. Fed.
219 C5 Centreville AL U.S.A.
155 D6 Cenxi China
185 K6 Ceos *i.* Greece
185 I5 Cephalonia *i.* Greece
Ceram Sea *sea* Indon. see Seram, Laut
215 E4 Cerbat Mountains U.S.A.
205 G4 Cereal Canada
232 D3 Ceres Arg.
196 C6 Ceres S. Africa
233 I2 Cereté Col.
183 O2 Cerezo de Abajo Spain
184 F4 Cerignola Italy
138 D2 Çeriklı Turkey
138 D1 Çerkeş Turkey
139 G3 Çermelik Deresi *r.* Syria
139 G2 Çermik Turkey
185 M2 Cernavodă Romania
225 E2 Cerralvo Mex.
224 B2 Cerralvo, Isla *i.* Mex.
185 H4 Cërrik Albania
225 D3 Cerritos Mex.
235 C4 Cerro Azul Brazil
225 E3 Cerro Azul Mex.
230 C6 Cerro de Pasco Peru
224 I7 Cerro Hoya, Parque Nacional *nat. park* Panama
233 K3 Cerro Jáua, Meseta del *plat.* Venez.
233 J2 Cerrón, Cerro *mt.* Venez.
224 C2 Cerro Prieto Mex.
235 I3 Cerros Colorados, Embalse *resr* Arg.
230 B4 Cerros de Amotape, Parque Nacional *nat. park* Peru
184 F4 Cervati, Monte *mt.* Italy
184 C3 Cervione *Corsica* France
183 M1 Cervo Spain
233 I2 Cesar *r.* Col.
184 E2 Cesena Italy
171 N4 Cēsis Latvia
176 G6 České Budějovice Czech Rep.
176 G6 Český Krumlov Czech Rep.
179 K5 Český les *mts* Czech Rep./Germany
185 L5 Çeşme Turkey
125 I4 Cessnock Australia
185 H3 Cetinje Montenegro
184 F5 Cetraro Italy
183 N5 Ceuta Spain
119 H4 Ceva-i-Ra *rf* Fiji
182 F4 Cévennes *mts* France
138 E3 Ceyhan Turkey
138 E3 Ceyhan *r.* Turkey
139 H3 Ceylanpınar Turkey
Chaacha Turkm. see Çäçe
143 F5 Chābahār Iran
149 E3 Chabyêr Caka *salt l.* China
235 K2 Chacabuco Arg.
235 H4 Chacao Chile
235 I3 Chachahuén, Sierra *mts* Arg.
230 C5 Chachapoyas Peru
187 D4 Chachersk Belarus
162 B2 Chachoengsao Thai.
148 B4 Chachro Pak.
213 F4 Chaco Culture National Historical Park *nat. park* U.S.A.
204 C4 Chacon, Cape U.S.A.
193 D3 Chad *country* Africa
193 D3 Chad, Lake Africa
153 H2 Chadaasan Mongolia
135 H1 Chadan Rus. Fed.
197 G1 Chadibe Botswana

Chadileo *r.* Arg. see Salado
216 C3 Chadron U.S.A.
162 A1 Chae Hom Thai.
141 H4 Chaek Kyrg.
160 C4 Chaeryŏng N. Korea
233 I4 Chafurray Col.
143 G4 Chagai Pak.
143 F4 Chagai Hills Afgh./Pak.
141 F3 Chagan *Kzyl-Ordinskaya Oblast'* Kazakh.
141 I2 Chagan *Vostochnyy Kazakhstan* Kazakh.
149 F2 Chagdo Kangri *mt.* China
143 G3 Chaghcharān Afgh.
141 G1 Chaglinka *r.* Kazakh.
182 G3 Chagny France
169 N4 Chagoda Rus. Fed.
131 C7 Chagos Archipelago *is* British Indian Ocean Terr.
238 I5 Chagos-Laccadive Ridge *sea feature* Indian Ocean
238 I5 Chagos Trench *sea feature* Indian Ocean
156 C1 Chagoyan Rus. Fed.
187 I4 Chagra *r.* Rus. Fed.
224 J6 Chagres, Parque Nacional *nat. park* Panama
233 K2 Chaguaramas Venez.
Chagyl Turkm. see Çagyl
140 C4 Chagyllyshor, Vpadina *depr.* Turkm.
149 G3 Cha'gyüngoinba China
143 F4 Chahah Burjal Afgh.
143 E3 Chāh Ākhvor Iran
142 C4 Chahār Rūstā'ī Iran
143 E3 Chahār Takāb Iran
139 K3 Chahār Ṭāq Iran
142 D3 Chāh Badam Iran
143 H2 Chāh-e Āb Afgh.
143 E3 Chāh-e Khoshāb Iran
137 I4 Chāh-e Malek *well* Iran
142 D3 Chāh-e Nūklok Iran
142 D4 Chāh-e Rāh Iran
142 D3 Chāh-e Shūr Iran
142 D4 Chāh Ḥaqq Iran
Chāh-i-Āb Afgh. see Chāh-e Āb
Chāh-i-Shurkh Iraq see Chiyā Surkh
137 I5 Chāh Kūh Iran
143 E5 Chāh Lak Iran
143 F4 Chah Sandan Pak.
149 F5 Chaibasa India
207 G3 Chaigneau, Lac *l.* Canada
160 C2 Chai He *r.* China
162 B2 Chainat Thai.
162 B2 Chai Si *r.* Thai.
155 □ Chai Wan *Hong Kong* China
162 A3 Chaiya Thai.
162 B2 Chaiyaphum Thai.
235 L1 Chajarí Arg.
148 B3 Chakar *r.* Pak.
149 H5 Chakaria Bangl.
143 F4 Chakhānsūr Afgh.
149 E4 Chakia India
143 G5 Chakku Pak.
137 F2 Ch'ak'vi Georgia
230 D7 Chala Peru
143 G3 Chalap Dalan *mts* Afgh.
224 G5 Chalatenango El Salvador
144 H4 Chalengkou China
207 G4 Chaleur Bay *inlet* Canada
155 D5 Chaling China
148 C5 Chalisgaon India
136 B3 Chalki *i.* Greece
185 J5 Chalkida Greece
126 A7 Chalky Inlet N.Z.
182 D3 Challans France
230 E7 Challapata Bol.
236 E5 Challenger Deep *sea feature* N. Pacific Ocean
212 D3 Challis U.S.A.
182 G2 Châlons-en-Champagne France
182 G3 Chalon-sur-Saône France
139 L1 Chaltan Pass Azer.
160 C2 Chaluhe China
142 C2 Chālūs Iran
179 K5 Cham Germany
163 D2 Cham, Cu Lao *i.* Vietnam
213 F4 Chama U.S.A.
233 J2 Chama *r.* Venez.
195 D5 Chama Zambia
235 J2 Chamaico Arg.
196 A3 Chamais Bay Namibia
143 G4 Chaman Pak.
152 C2 Chamba India
148 D3 Chamba *r.* India
148 D4 Chambal *r.* India
207 G3 Chambeaux, Lac *l.* Canada
120 D3 Chamberlain *r.* Australia
205 H4 Chamberlain Canada

216 D3 Chamberlain U.S.A.
221 I1 Chamberlain Lake U.S.A.
215 H4 Chambers U.S.A.
221 E5 Chambersburg U.S.A.
182 G4 Chambéry France
195 D5 Chambeshi Zambia
184 C7 Chambi, Jebel *mt.* Tunisia
Chamdo China see Qamdo
182 G4 Chamechaude *mt.* France
142 C3 Cham-e Ḥannā Iran
142 C3 Chameshk Iran
235 I1 Chamical Arg.
149 H4 Chamlang *mt.* Nepal
162 B3 Châmnar Cambodia
Chamoli India see Gopeshwar
182 H4 Chamonix-Mont-Blanc France
147 I1 Champa India
204 B2 Champagne Canada
182 G2 Champagne France
197 H4 Champagne Castle *mt.* S. Africa
182 G3 Champagnole France
120 D2 Champagny Islands Australia
208 C5 Champaign U.S.A.
235 J1 Champaquí, Cerro *mt.* Arg.
162 C2 Champasak Laos
149 H5 Champhai India
208 D2 Champion U.S.A.
221 G2 Champlain U.S.A.
221 G2 Champlain, Lake Canada/U.S.A.
225 G4 Champotón Mex.
154 E2 Chaobai Xinhe *r.* China
155 E4 Chaohu China
155 E4 Chao Hu *l.* China
162 B2 Chao Phraya *r.* Thai.
192 B1 Chaouèn Morocco
149 H2 Chaowula Shan *mt.* China
155 E6 Chaoyang *Guangdong* China
Chaoyang China see Jiayin
154 F1 Chaoyang *Liaoning* China
156 B2 Chaoyangcun China
155 E6 Chaozhou China
234 E1 Chapada Diamantina, Parque Nacional *nat. park* Brazil
234 A1 Chapada dos Guimarães Brazil
234 C1 Chapada dos Veadeiros, Parque Nacional da *nat. park* Brazil
225 D3 Chapala Mex.
225 D3 Chapala, Laguna de *l.* Mex.
143 G3 Chāpārī, Kowtal-e Afgh.
233 I4 Chaparral Col.
140 D2 Chapayevo Kazakh.
187 I4 Chapayevsk Rus. Fed.
141 H1 Chapayevskoye Kazakh.
232 F3 Chapecó Brazil
232 F3 Chapecó *r.* Brazil
173 F4 Chapel-en-le-Frith U.K.
219 E5 Chapel Hill U.S.A.
178 C4 Chapelle-lez-Herlaimont Belgium
173 F4 Chapeltown U.K.
209 F2 Chapleau Canada
187 F4 Chaplygin Rus. Fed.
187 E6 Chaplynka Ukr.
220 B6 Chapmanville U.S.A.
125 G8 Chappell Islands Australia
230 D7 Chaqui Bol.
148 D2 Char India
225 D3 Charcas Mex.
149 G3 Char Chu *r.* China
127 I3 Charcot Island Antarctica
205 G3 Chard Canada
173 E7 Chard U.K.
141 F4 Chardara, Step' *plain* Kazakh.
141 G4 Chardarinskoye Vodokhranilishche *resr* Kazakh./Uzbek.
139 K5 Chardāvol Iran
220 C4 Chardon U.S.A.
180 D5 Charef Alg.
180 C5 Charef, Oued *watercourse* Morocco
182 E3 Charente *r.* France
142 D4 Charg Iran
143 H3 Chārīkār Afgh.
216 E3 Chariton U.S.A.
209 F4 Charity Island U.S.A.
142 C4 Charkas Iran
132 G3 Charkayuvom Rus. Fed.
148 D4 Charkhari India
178 C4 Charleroi Belgium
211 K4 Charles, Cape U.S.A.
208 A4 Charles City U.S.A.
120 E2 Charles Point Australia

126 C4 Charleston N.Z.
219 B4 Charleston IL U.S.A.
221 I2 Charleston ME U.S.A.
217 F4 Charleston MO U.S.A.
219 E5 Charleston SC U.S.A.
220 C5 Charleston WV U.S.A.
215 E3 Charleston Peak U.S.A.
175 J4 Charlestown Ireland
221 G3 Charlestown NH U.S.A.
221 H4 Charlestown RI U.S.A.
221 E5 Charles Town U.S.A.
119 E4 Charleville Australia
175 J5 Charleville Ireland
182 G2 Charleville-Mézières France
209 E3 Charlevoix U.S.A.
127 J5 Charlie, Dome *ice feature* Antarctica
204 C3 Charlie Lake Canada
209 E4 Charlotte MI U.S.A.
219 D5 Charlotte NC U.S.A.
219 D7 Charlotte Harbor *b.* U.S.A.
220 D5 Charlottesville U.S.A.
207 H4 Charlottetown Canada
233 L2 Charlotteville Trin. and Tob.
125 E2 Charlton Australia
206 E3 Charlton Island Canada
186 F2 Charozero Rus. Fed.
148 B2 Charsadda Pak.
Charshangngy Turkm. see Köýtendag
119 E4 Charters Towers Australia
182 E2 Chartres France
182 E2 Charvakskoye Vdkhr. *resr* Kazakh./Uzbek. see Chorvoq suv ombori
141 I4 Charyn Kazakh.
141 I4 Charyn *r.* Kazakh.
141 J1 Charysh *r.* Rus. Fed.
141 J2 Charyshskoye Rus. Fed.
235 K2 Chascomús Arg.
204 F4 Chase Canada
140 E5 Chashkent Turkm.
143 E3 Chashmeh Nūrī Iran
142 D3 Chashmeh-ye Palasi Iran
187 D4 Chashniki Belarus
126 B7 Chaslands Mistake *c.* N.Z.
160 D3 Chasŏng N. Korea
142 D3 Chastab, Kūh-e *mts* Iran
182 D3 Châteaubriant France
182 E3 Château-du-Loir France
182 E2 Châteaudun France
221 F2 Chateaugay U.S.A.
221 G2 Châteauguay Canada
182 D3 Châteaulin France
182 F3 Châteauneuf-sur-Loire France
182 E3 Châteauroux France
179 E6 Château-Salins France
182 F2 Château-Thierry France
178 C4 Châtelet Belgium
182 E3 Châtellerault France
208 A4 Chatfield U.S.A.
209 F4 Chatham Canada
173 H6 Chatham U.K.
221 H4 Chatham MA U.S.A.
221 G3 Chatham NY U.S.A.
220 D6 Chatham VA U.S.A.
119 I6 Chatham Islands N.Z.
237 H8 Chatham Rise *sea feature* S. Pacific Ocean
204 C4 Chatham Sound *sea chan.* Canada
204 C3 Chatham Strait U.S.A.
141 G4 Chatkal *r.* Kyrg.
141 G4 Chatkal Range *mts* Kyrg.
149 F4 Chatra India
209 G3 Chatsworth Canada
208 C5 Chatsworth U.S.A.
219 C5 Chattanooga U.S.A.
173 H5 Chatteris U.K.
162 B2 Chatturat Thai.
141 H4 Chatyr-Köl *l.* Kyrg.
141 I4 Chatyr-Tash Kyrg.
162 C3 Châu Đốc Vietnam
148 B4 Chauhtan India
149 H5 Chauk Myanmar
149 E4 Chauka *r.* India
148 D3 Chaukhamba *mts* India
182 G2 Chaumont France
142 A2 Chaungwabyin Myanmar
133 R3 Chaunskaya Guba *b.* Rus. Fed.
182 F2 Chauny France
163 D2 Châu Ô Vietnam
149 F4 Chauparan India
220 D3 Chautauqua, Lake U.S.A.
141 H4 Chauvay Kyrg.
147 I4 Chavakachcheri Sri Lanka
142 B3 Chavār Iran
231 J4 Chaves Brazil
183 M2 Chaves Port.

124 B4 **Cowell** Australia
125 F7 **Cowes** Australia
173 F7 **Cowes** U.K.
172 E3 **Cow Green Reservoir** U.K.
220 D5 **Cowpasture** r. U.S.A.
125 H4 **Cowra** Australia
122 A2 **Cox** r. Australia
234 D1 **Coxá** r. Brazil
235 L1 **Coxilha de Santana** hills Brazil/Uruguay
234 A2 **Coxim** Brazil
234 A2 **Coxim** r. Brazil
221 G3 **Coxsackie** U.S.A.
149 H5 **Cox's Bazar** Bangl.
224 B2 **Coyote, Punta** pt Mex.
215 D4 **Coyote Lake** U.S.A.
215 E5 **Coyote Peak** h. AZ U.S.A.
214 C3 **Coyote Peak** CA U.S.A.
225 D4 **Coyotitán** Mex.
225 D4 **Coyuca de Benitez** Mex.
149 F2 **Cozhê** China
185 K2 **Cozia, Vârful** mt. Romania
225 H3 **Cozumel** Mex.
225 H3 **Cozumel, Isla de** i. Mex.
125 H4 **Craboon** Australia
123 E5 **Cracow** Australia
125 G8 **Cradle Mountain** Australia
125 G8 **Cradle Mountain Lake St Clair National Park** Australia
124 C3 **Cradock** Australia
197 F6 **Cradock** S. Africa
174 C3 **Craig** U.K.
204 C3 **Craig** AK U.S.A.
213 F3 **Craig** CO U.S.A.
175 L3 **Craigavon** U.K.
125 F6 **Craigieburn** Australia
220 D5 **Craigsville** U.S.A.
175 F4 **Crail** U.K.
179 I5 **Crailsheim** Germany
185 J2 **Craiova** Romania
172 F2 **Cramlington** U.K.
221 F2 **Cranberry Lake** U.S.A.
221 F2 **Cranberry Lake** l. U.S.A.
125 F7 **Cranbourne** Australia
204 F5 **Cranbrook** Canada
208 C3 **Crandon** U.S.A.
213 C3 **Crane** OR U.S.A.
217 C6 **Crane** TX U.S.A.
208 A1 **Crane Lake** U.S.A.
221 H4 **Cranston** U.S.A.
127 I5 **Crary Ice Rise** Antarctica
127 I4 **Crary Mountains** Antarctica
213 B3 **Crater Lake** U.S.A.
213 B3 **Crater Lake National Park** U.S.A.
213 D3 **Craters of the Moon National Monument** nat. park U.S.A.
231 J5 **Crateús** Brazil
231 K5 **Crato** Brazil
233 J3 **Cravo Norte** Col.
233 J3 **Cravo Sur** r. Col.
216 C3 **Crawford** U.S.A.
208 D5 **Crawfordsville** U.S.A.
219 C6 **Crawfordville** U.S.A.
173 G6 **Crawley** U.K.
212 E2 **Crazy Mountains** U.S.A.
174 D4 **Creag Meagaidh** mt. U.K.
205 H4 **Crean Lake** Canada
173 E5 **Credenhill** U.K.
173 D7 **Crediton** U.K.
205 H3 **Cree** r. Canada
224 C2 **Creel** Mex.
205 H3 **Cree Lake** Canada
205 I4 **Creighton** Canada
178 A5 **Creil** France
178 D2 **Creil** Neth.
179 I2 **Cremlingen** Germany
184 D2 **Cremona** Italy
182 F2 **Crépy-en-Valois** France
184 F2 **Cres** i. Croatia
213 A3 **Crescent City** U.S.A.
155 □ **Crescent Island** Hong Kong China
215 H2 **Crescent Junction** U.S.A.
214 B1 **Crescent Mills** U.S.A.
215 E4 **Crescent Peak** U.S.A.
208 A4 **Cresco** U.S.A.
235 K2 **Crespo** Arg.
125 F7 **Cressy** Australia
204 F5 **Creston** Canada
216 E3 **Creston** IA U.S.A.
213 F3 **Creston** WY U.S.A.
219 C6 **Crestview** U.S.A.
221 F5 **Crestwood Village** U.S.A.
125 E6 **Creswick** Australia
185 K7 **Crete** i. Greece
183 R1 **Creus, Cap de** c. Spain
182 E3 **Creuse** r. France
179 J2 **Creußen** Germany

179 E5 **Creutzwald** France
179 I3 **Creuzburg** Germany
173 E4 **Crewe** U.K.
220 D6 **Crewe** U.S.A.
173 E7 **Crewkerne** U.K.
174 D4 **Crianlarich** U.K.
173 C5 **Criccieth** U.K.
233 G3 **Criciúma** Brazil
174 E4 **Crieff** U.K.
174 E6 **Criffel** h. U.K.
Criffell h. U.K. see **Criffel**
184 F2 **Crikvenica** Croatia
187 E6 **Crimea** pen. Ukr.
179 K4 **Crimmitschau** Germany
175 G3 **Crimond** U.K.
221 F6 **Crisfield** U.S.A.
234 C2 **Cristalina** Brazil
233 I2 **Cristóbal Colón, Pico** mt. Col.
234 C1 **Crixás** Brazil
234 C1 **Crixás Açu** r. Brazil
234 B1 **Crixás Mirim** r. Brazil
Crna Gora aut. rep. Europe see **Montenegro**
184 F2 **Črnomelj** Slovenia
175 I4 **Croagh Patrick** h. Ireland
125 H6 **Croajingolong National Park** Australia
184 F2 **Croatia** country Europe
163 I2 **Crocker, Banjaran** mts Malaysia
217 D6 **Crockett** U.S.A.
221 F3 **Croghan** U.S.A.
178 A4 **Croisilles** France
118 D3 **Croker Island** Australia
174 D3 **Cromarty** U.K.
174 D3 **Cromarty Firth** est. U.K.
174 E3 **Cromdale, Hills of** U.K.
173 I5 **Cromer** U.K.
126 B6 **Cromwell** N.Z.
172 F3 **Crook** U.K.
220 D4 **Crooked Creek Reservoir** U.S.A.
223 J4 **Crooked Island** Bahamas
155 □ **Crooked Island** Hong Kong China
223 J4 **Crooked Island Passage** Bahamas
208 B1 **Crooked Lake** Canada/U.S.A.
216 D2 **Crookston** U.S.A.
125 H5 **Crookwell** Australia
175 J5 **Croom** Ireland
125 I2 **Croppa Creek** Australia
173 D4 **Crosby** U.K.
205 I5 **Crosby** U.S.A.
205 K2 **Cross Bay** Canada
219 D6 **Cross City** U.S.A.
221 J1 **Cross Creek** Canada
217 E5 **Crossett** U.S.A.
172 E3 **Cross Fell** h. U.K.
175 M3 **Crossgar** U.K.
175 J6 **Crosshaven** Ireland
173 C5 **Cross Inn** U.K.
205 J4 **Cross Lake** Canada
205 J4 **Cross Lake** l. Canada
221 E3 **Cross Lake** U.S.A.
126 D5 **Crossley, Mount** N.Z.
175 L3 **Crossmaglen** U.K.
215 E4 **Crossman Peak** U.S.A.
204 B3 **Cross Sound** sea chan. U.S.A.
209 E3 **Cross Village** U.S.A.
219 C5 **Crossville** U.S.A.
209 F4 **Croswell** U.S.A.
185 G5 **Crotone** Italy
173 H6 **Crouch** r. U.K.
125 G3 **Crowal** watercourse Australia
173 H6 **Crowborough** U.K.
125 H6 **Crowl** watercourse Australia
173 G5 **Crowland** U.K.
217 E6 **Crowley** U.S.A.
214 C3 **Crowley, Lake** U.S.A.
208 D5 **Crown Point** IN U.S.A.
221 G3 **Crown Point** NY U.S.A.
125 J1 **Crows Nest** Australia
205 G5 **Crowsnest Pass** Canada
122 C3 **Croydon** Australia
173 G6 **Croydon** ADMIN3 U.K.
238 H8 **Crozet, Îles** is Indian Ocean
239 N8 **Crozet Basin** sea feature Indian Ocean
238 G7 **Crozet Plateau** sea feature Indian Ocean
202 G2 **Crozier Channel** Canada
182 B2 **Crozon** France
233 I4 **Cruces, Paso de las** mt. Col.
175 G3 **Cruden Bay** U.K.
225 E2 **Cruillas** Mex.
175 L3 **Crumlin** U.K.
175 J5 **Crusheen** Ireland

223 I5 **Cruz, Cabo** c. Cuba
232 F3 **Cruz Alta** Brazil
235 J1 **Cruz del Eje** Arg.
234 D3 **Cruzeiro** Brazil
230 D5 **Cruzeiro do Sul** Brazil
215 H5 **Cruzville** U.S.A.
204 E3 **Crysdale, Mount** Canada
124 C4 **Crystal Brook** Australia
217 D6 **Crystal City** U.S.A.
208 C2 **Crystal Falls** U.S.A.
208 C4 **Crystal Lake** U.S.A.
177 J7 **Csongrád** Hungary
139 J5 **Ctesiphon** tourist site Iraq
233 K2 **Cúa** Venez.
Cửa Lớn r. Vietnam see **Cửa Lớn, Sông**
162 C3 **Cửa Lớn, Sông** r. Vietnam
195 C5 **Cuando** r. Angola/Zambia
195 B5 **Cuangar** Angola
195 B4 **Cuango** r. Angola/Dem. Rep. Congo
195 B4 **Cuanza** r. Angola
233 K3 **Cuao** r. Venez.
235 L1 **Cuaro** r. Uruguay
235 J2 **Cuarto** r. Arg.
225 D2 **Cuatro Ciénegas** Mex.
224 C1 **Cuauhtémoc** Mex.
225 E4 **Cuautla** Mex.
223 I4 **Cuba** country Caribbean Sea
208 B5 **Cuba** IL U.S.A.
213 F4 **Cuba** NM U.S.A.
215 F6 **Cubabi, Cerro** mt. Mex.
195 B5 **Cubal** Angola
195 B5 **Cubango** r. Angola/Namibia
233 I3 **Cubara** Col.
205 I4 **Cub Hills** Canada
138 D1 **Çubuk** Turkey
235 L1 **Cuchilla Grande** hills Uruguay
235 L1 **Cuchilla Grande Inferior** hills Uruguay
235 J3 **Cuchillo-Có** Arg.
233 K3 **Cuchivero** r. Venez.
221 E5 **Cuckoo** U.S.A.
233 K4 **Cucuí** Brazil
233 I3 **Cúcuta** Col.
147 H4 **Cuddalore** India
147 H3 **Cuddapah** India
205 H4 **Cudworth** Canada
121 B5 **Cue** Australia
183 N2 **Cuéllar** Spain
195 B5 **Cuemba** Angola
230 C4 **Cuenca** Ecuador
183 O2 **Cuenca** Spain
183 O2 **Cuenca, Serranía de** mts Spain
225 E4 **Cuernavaca** Mex.
217 D6 **Cuero** U.S.A.
214 B4 **Cuesta Pass** U.S.A.
225 E3 **Cuetzalán** Mex.
225 E4 **Cuicatlan** Mex.
178 D3 **Cuijk** Neth.
225 G5 **Cuilapa** Guat.
175 K3 **Cuilcagh** h. Ireland/U.K.
174 B3 **Cuillin Hills** U.K.
174 B3 **Cuillin Sound** sea chan. U.K.
195 B4 **Cuilo** Angola
156 C3 **Cuiluan** China
234 E2 **Cuité** r. Brazil
195 B5 **Cuito** r. Angola
195 B5 **Cuito Cuanavale** Angola
225 D4 **Cuitzeo, Laguna de** l. Mex.
163 B2 **Cukai** Malaysia
139 I3 **Çukurca** Turkey
212 F1 **Culbertson** MT U.S.A.
216 C3 **Culbertson** NE U.S.A.
125 G5 **Culcairn** Australia
183 M2 **Culebra, Sierra de la** mts Spain
139 J2 **Culfa** Azer.
125 G2 **Culgoa** r. Australia
224 C2 **Culiacán** Mex.
161 H4 **Culion** Phil.
161 H4 **Culion** i. Phil.
175 F3 **Cullen** U.K.
122 C1 **Cullen Point** Australia
183 P3 **Cullera** Spain
174 □ **Cullivoe** U.K.
219 C5 **Cullman** U.S.A.
139 H2 **Çullu** Turkey
175 L3 **Cullybackey** U.K.
Cul Mòr h. U.K. see **Cul Mòr**
174 C2 **Cul Mòr** h. U.K.
220 D5 **Culpeper** U.S.A.
230 □ **Culpepper, Isla** i. Galapagos Is Ecuador

231 H6 **Culuene** r. Brazil
121 D7 **Culver, Point** Australia
126 D5 **Culverden** N.Z.
174 D5 **Culzean Bay** U.K.
233 K2 **Cumaná** Venez.
233 I4 **Cumare, Cerro** h. Col.
233 H4 **Cumbal, Nevado de** vol. Col.
220 D5 **Cumberland** MD U.S.A.
208 A3 **Cumberland** WI U.S.A.
219 C4 **Cumberland** r. U.S.A.
205 I4 **Cumberland House** Canada
205 I4 **Cumberland Lake** Canada
220 B6 **Cumberland Mountains** U.S.A.
203 L3 **Cumberland Peninsula** Canada
219 C4 **Cumberland Plateau** U.S.A.
208 C2 **Cumberland Point** U.S.A.
203 L3 **Cumberland Sound** sea chan. Canada
174 E5 **Cumbernauld** U.K.
225 D2 **Cumbres de Monterey, Parque Nacional** nat. park Mex.
179 J1 **Cumlosen** Germany
214 A2 **Cummings** U.S.A.
124 A5 **Cummins** Australia
120 D3 **Cummins Range** hills Australia
125 H4 **Cumnock** Australia
174 D5 **Cumnock** U.K.
138 C2 **Çumra** Turkey
224 B1 **Cumuripa** Mex.
121 B6 **Cunderdin** Australia
225 F4 **Cunduacán** Mex.
225 G5 **Cunén** Guat.
195 B5 **Cunene** r. Angola/Namibia alt. **Kunene**
184 B2 **Cuneo** Italy
124 A4 **Cungena** Australia
163 D4 **Cung Sơn** Vietnam
139 G2 **Çüngüş** Turkey
125 F2 **Cunnamulla** Australia
233 K4 **Cunucunuma** r. Venez.
184 B2 **Cuorgnè** Italy
174 E4 **Cupar** U.K.
233 H3 **Cupica** Col.
233 H3 **Cupica, Golfo de** b. Col.
224 B2 **Cupula, Pico** mt. Mex.
231 K5 **Curaçá** Brazil
223 K6 **Curaçao** terr. Caribbean Sea
235 H4 **Curacautín** Chile
235 H5 **Curanilahue** Chile
230 D4 **Curaray** r. Ecuador
235 H2 **Curaumilla, Punta** pt Chile
124 B3 **Curdlawidny Lagoon** salt flat Australia
213 F4 **Curecanti National Recreation Area** park U.S.A.
235 H2 **Curicó** Chile
233 K5 **Curicuriari, Serra** h. Brazil
233 K5 **Curieuriari** r. Brazil
235 G3 **Curitiba** Brazil
124 C3 **Curnamona** Australia
125 I3 **Currabubula** Australia
231 K5 **Currais Novos** Brazil
192 □ **Curral Velho** Cape Verde
209 F3 **Curran** U.S.A.
175 H6 **Currane, Lough** l. Ireland
215 E2 **Currant** U.S.A.
125 F3 **Curranyalpa** Australia
123 C5 **Currawilla** Australia
123 D6 **Currawinya National Park** Australia
219 E7 **Current** Bahamas
125 E7 **Currie** Australia
215 E1 **Currie** U.S.A.
125 I5 **Currockbilly, Mount** Australia
123 F5 **Curtis Channel** Australia
125 G7 **Curtis Group** is Australia
119 F4 **Curtis Island** Australia
231 H5 **Curuá** r. Brazil
231 I4 **Curuçá** Brazil
233 K4 **Curupira, Serra** mts Brazil/Venez.
231 J4 **Cururupu** Brazil
233 L3 **Curutú, Cerro** mt. Venez.
234 D2 **Curvelo** Brazil
230 D6 **Cusco** Peru
149 H1 **Cushendall** U.K.
175 L2 **Cushendun** U.K.
217 D4 **Cushing** U.S.A.
233 J3 **Cusiana** r. Col.
224 C1 **Cusihuiráchic** Mex.
219 C5 **Cusseta** U.S.A.
208 A1 **Cusson** U.S.A.
206 E1 **Cusson, Pointe** Canada

212 F2 **Custer** MT U.S.A.
216 C3 **Custer** SD U.S.A.
233 H4 **Cutanga, Pico de** mt. Col.
212 D1 **Cut Bank** U.S.A.
219 C6 **Cuthbert** U.S.A.
205 H4 **Cut Knife** Canada
221 J2 **Cutler** U.S.A.
219 D7 **Cutler Ridge** U.S.A.
235 I3 **Cutral-Co** Arg.
149 F5 **Cuttack** India
215 G5 **Cutter** U.S.A.
179 G1 **Cuxhaven** Germany
220 C4 **Cuyahoga Falls** U.S.A.
220 C4 **Cuyahoga Valley National Park** U.S.A.
214 C4 **Cuyama** r. U.S.A.
161 I3 **Cuyapo** Phil.
161 I4 **Cuyo** Phil.
161 I4 **Cuyo** i. Phil.
161 I4 **Cuyo East Passage** Phil.
161 I4 **Cuyo Islands** Phil.
161 I4 **Cuyo West Passage** Phil.
233 L3 **Cuyuni** r. Guyana
Cuzco Peru see **Cusco**
Cwmbran U.K. see **Cwmbrân**
173 D6 **Cwmbrân** U.K.
195 C4 **Cyangugu** Rwanda
185 K6 **Cyclades** is Greece
125 G9 **Cygnet** Australia
220 A5 **Cynthiana** U.S.A.
205 G5 **Cypress Hills** Canada
138 D4 **Cyprus** country Asia
205 G4 **Czar** Canada
176 G6 **Czech Republic** country Europe
177 H4 **Czersk** Poland
177 I5 **Częstochowa** Poland

D

Đa, Sông r. Vietnam see **Black**
160 C1 **Da'an** China
233 J2 **Dabajuro** Venez.
192 B4 **Dabakala** Côte d'Ivoire
154 F1 **Daban** China
154 A2 **Daban Shan** mts China
154 C3 **Daba Shan** mts China
233 H3 **Dabeiba** Col.
179 J1 **Dabel** Germany
148 C5 **Dabhoi** India
147 G2 **Dabhol** India
155 E4 **Dabie Shan** mts China
148 C4 **Daboh** India
192 A3 **Dabola** Guinea
192 B4 **Daboya** Ghana
154 C2 **Dabqig** China
148 D4 **Dabra** India
177 I5 **Dąbrowa Górnicza** Poland
160 B1 **Dabs Nur** l. China
155 E5 **Dabu** China
Dacca Bangl. see **Dhaka**
176 E6 **Dachau** Germany
154 A2 **Dachechang** China
154 F1 **Dachengzi** China
147 H2 **Dachepalle** India
209 I3 **Dacre** Canada
138 D1 **Daday** Turkey
219 D6 **Dade City** U.S.A.
148 C5 **Dadra** India
148 C5 **Dadra and Nagar Haveli** union terr. India
148 A4 **Dadu** Pak.
155 B4 **Dadu He** r. China
Đa Dung r. Vietnam see **Dâng, Đa**
161 I3 **Daet** Phil.
155 B5 **Dafang** China
154 F3 **Dafeng** China
160 D2 **Dafengman** China
149 H4 **Dafla Hills** India
192 A3 **Dagana** Senegal
154 B3 **Dagcanglhamo** China
187 H7 **Dagestan, Respublika** aut. rep. Rus. Fed.
155 B5 **Daguan** China
154 F2 **Dagu He** r. China
155 □ **D'Aguilar Peak** h. Hong Kong China
156 C3 **Daguokui Shan** h. China
161 I2 **Dagupan** Phil.
149 H1 **Dagur** China
149 G3 **Dagzê** China
149 F3 **Dagzê Co** salt l. China
148 C6 **Dahanu** India
156 C3 **Daheiding Shan** mt. China
154 D1 **Dahei He** r. China
160 C2 **Dahei Shan** mts China
158 C1 **Dahezhen** China

150 D2 **Da Hinggan Ling** mts China
194 E2 **Dahlak Archipelago** is Eritrea
194 E2 **Dahlak Marine National Park** Eritrea
179 E4 **Dahlem** Germany
179 I1 **Dahlenburg** Germany
184 C7 **Dahmani** Tunisia
179 F5 **Dahn** Germany
148 C5 **Dahod** India
148 D2 **Dahongliutan** China
179 I2 **Dähre** Germany
139 I3 **Dahūk** Iraq
160 C3 **Dahuofang Shuiku** resr China
160 B3 **Dahushan** China
154 D1 **Dai Hai** l. China
163 B3 **Daik** Indon.
163 D2 **Đai Lanh, Mui** pt Vietnam
174 D5 **Dailly** U.K.
143 E3 **Daim** Iran
159 C6 **Daimanji-san** h. Japan
183 O3 **Daimiel** Spain
122 D3 **Daintree National Park** Australia
235 K3 **Daireaux** Arg.
208 A2 **Dairyland** U.S.A.
159 C7 **Dai-sen** vol. Japan
158 H3 **Daisetsu-zan Kokuritsu-kōen** nat. park Japan
155 G4 **Daishan** China
155 F5 **Daiyun Shan** mts China
118 D4 **Dajarra** Australia
155 A4 **Dajin Chuan** r. China
154 B2 **Dajing** China
149 H1 **Da Juh** China
192 A3 **Dakar** Senegal
149 G3 **Dakelangsi** China
193 E2 **Dākhilah, Wāḩāt ad** oasis Egypt
149 G5 **Dakhin Shahbazpur Island** Bangl.
Dakhla Oasis oasis Egypt see **Dākhilah, Wāḩāt ad**
Dak Kon Vietnam see **Plei Kân**
163 D2 **Đăk Lăk, Cao Nguyên** plat. Vietnam
145 H10 **Dakoank** India
187 D4 **Dakol'ka** r. Belarus
216 D3 **Dakota** U.S.A.
185 H2 **Đakovo** Croatia
156 B1 **Daktuy** Rus. Fed.
195 C5 **Dala** Angola
192 A3 **Dalaba** Guinea
154 A1 **Dalain Hob** China
154 E1 **Dalai Nur** l. China
139 K4 **Dālā Khānī, Kūh-e** mt. Iraq
142 C4 **Dalaki, Rūd-e** r. Iran
169 J3 **Dalälven** r. Sweden
154 D1 **Dalamamiao** China
138 B3 **Dalaman** Turkey
138 B3 **Dalaman** r. Turkey
150 C2 **Dalandzadgad** Mongolia
161 I4 **Dalanganem Islands** Phil.
163 D3 **Đa Lat** Vietnam
Dalay Mongolia see **Bayandalay**
143 G4 **Dalbandin** Pak.
174 E6 **Dalbeattie** U.K.
123 D4 **Dalbeg** Australia
125 I1 **Dalby** Australia
172 C3 **Dalby** U.K.
171 I3 **Dale** Hordaland Norway
171 I3 **Dale** Sogn og Fjordane Norway
221 E5 **Dale City** U.S.A.
217 G4 **Dale Hollow Lake** U.S.A.
179 F2 **Dalen** Neth.
149 H6 **Dalet** Myanmar
149 H5 **Daletme** Myanmar
171 K3 **Dalfors** Sweden
143 E5 **Dalgān** Iran
125 H6 **Dalgety** Australia
121 A5 **Dalgety** r. Australia
217 C4 **Dalhart** U.S.A.
207 G4 **Dalhousie** Canada
154 D3 **Dali** Shaanxi China
151 C4 **Dali** Yunnan China
160 A4 **Dalian** China
155 A4 **Daliang Shan** mts China
160 B2 **Dalin** China
154 F1 **Daling He** r. China
160 D3 **Dalizi** China
174 E5 **Dalkeith** U.K.
149 F4 **Dalkola** India
221 F4 **Dallas** PA U.S.A.
217 D5 **Dallas** TX U.S.A.
208 B5 **Dallas City** U.S.A.
204 C4 **Dall Island** U.S.A.

Dalmā

142 D5 Dalmā i. U.A.E.
235 J2 Dalmacio Vélez Sarsfield Arg.
185 G3 Dalmatia reg. Croatia
149 E4 Dalmau India
174 D5 Dalmellington U.K.
158 D2 Dal'negorsk Rus. Fed.
158 C2 Dal'nerechensk Rus. Fed.
192 B4 Daloa Côte d'Ivoire
155 C5 Dalou Shan mts China
142 B5 Dalqān well Saudi Arabia
174 D5 Dalry U.K.
174 D5 Dalrymple U.K.
119 E4 Dalrymple, Lake Australia
119 E4 Dalrymple, Mount Australia
149 F4 Daltenganj India
209 E1 Dalton Canada
197 I4 Dalton S. Africa
219 C5 Dalton U.S.A.
221 G3 Dalton MA U.S.A.
172 D3 Dalton-in-Furness U.K.
209 E1 Dalton Mills Canada
175 J5 Dalua r. Ireland
161 I2 Dalupiri i. Phil.
161 J3 Dalupiri i. Phil.
170 C2 Dalvík Iceland
118 D3 Daly r. Australia
214 A3 Daly City U.S.A.
120 E2 Daly River Australia
118 D3 Daly Waters Australia
148 C5 Daman India
148 C5 Daman and Diu union terr. India
193 F1 Damanhūr Egypt
142 C3 Damaq Iran
154 E1 Damaqun Shan mts China
161 J6 Damar Indon.
151 E7 Damar i. Indon.
235 H2 Damas, Paso de las pass Arg./Chile
139 F5 Damascus Syria
193 D3 Damaturu Nigeria
142 D3 Damāvand Iran
142 D3 Damāvand, Qolleh-ye mt. Iran
147 I5 Dambulla Sri Lanka
141 F2 Damdy Kazakh.
142 D2 Damghan Iran
Damietta Egypt see Dumyāţ
154 E2 Daming China
155 C6 Daming Shan mt. China
149 H2 Damjong China
161 I5 Dammai i. Phil.
146 D4 Dammam Saudi Arabia
178 B3 Damme Belgium
179 G2 Damme Germany
148 D5 Damoh India
192 B4 Damongo Ghana
138 E5 Damour Lebanon
121 B4 Dampier Archipelago is Australia
120 C3 Dampier Land reg. Australia
119 E2 Dampier Strait P.N.G.
151 F7 Dampir, Selat sea chan. Indon.
149 H2 Dam Qu r. China
162 C3 Dâmrei, Chuŏr Phnum mts Cambodia
149 H3 Damroh India
179 E1 Damwoude Neth.
192 B4 Danané Côte d'Ivoire
163 D1 Đa Năng Vietnam
161 J4 Danao Phil.
155 A4 Danba China
221 G4 Danbury CT U.S.A.
221 H3 Danbury NH U.S.A.
221 G3 Danby U.S.A.
215 E4 Danby Lake U.S.A.
154 E3 Dancheng China
121 A6 Dandaragan Australia
194 D3 Dande Eth.
147 G3 Dandeli India
125 F6 Dandenong Australia
160 C3 Dandong China
173 E4 Dane r. U.K.
203 P2 Daneborg Greenland
221 J2 Danforth U.S.A.
162 C3 Đâng, Đa r. Vietnam
155 E6 Dangan Liedao is China
Dangara Tajik. see Danghara
149 G3 Dangbe La pass China
158 B2 Dangbizhen Rus. Fed.
154 B3 Dangchang China
Dangchengwan China see Subei
Danger Islands atoll Cook Is see Pukapuka
196 C7 Danger Point S. Africa
144 C4 Danghara Tajik.
144 H4 Danghe Nanshan mts China

194 D2 Dangila Eth.
149 G3 Dangqên China
225 G4 Dangriga Belize
154 E3 Dangshan China
155 F4 Dangtu China
155 D4 Dangyang China
197 E4 Daniëlskuil S. Africa
186 G3 Danilov Rus. Fed.
141 G1 Danilovka Kazakh.
187 H5 Danilovka Rus. Fed.
186 G3 Danilovskaya Vozvyshennost' hills Rus. Fed.
154 D2 Daning China
139 L1 Dänizkänarı Azer.
154 D3 Danjiangkou China
154 D3 Danjiangkou Shuiku resr China
157 C6 Danjo-guntō is Japan
142 E6 Dank Oman
148 D2 Dankhar India
187 F4 Dankov Rus. Fed.
141 I4 Dankova, Pik mt. Kyrg.
224 H5 Danlí Hond.
155 B4 Danling China
221 G2 Dannemora U.S.A.
179 J1 Dannenberg (Elbe) Germany
179 L1 Dannenwalde Germany
126 F4 Dannevirke N.Z.
197 I4 Dannhauser S. Africa
162 B1 Dan Sai Thai.
221 E3 Dansville U.S.A.
148 C4 Danta India
147 I2 Dantewara India
185 L3 Danube r. Europe
  alt. Donau (Austria/Germany),
  alt. Duna (Hungary),
  alt. Dunaj (Slovakia),
  alt. Dunărea (Romania),
  alt. Dunav (Bulgaria/Serbia)
185 M2 Danube Delta Romania
208 D5 Danville IL U.S.A.
208 D6 Danville IN U.S.A.
219 C4 Danville KY U.S.A.
209 I5 Danville PA U.S.A.
220 D6 Danville VA U.S.A.
155 F4 Danyang China
155 C5 Danzhai China
155 C7 Danzhou China
161 I4 Dao Phil.
192 B4 Daoukro Côte d'Ivoire
155 D5 Daoxian China
155 C4 Daozhen China
161 J4 Dapa Phil.
192 C3 Dapaong Togo
  Dapeng Wan b. Hong Kong China see Port Shelter
  Dapeng Wan b. China see Mirs Bay
149 I4 Daphabum mt. India
138 D6 Daphnae tourist site Egypt
161 I4 Dapiak, Mount Phil.
161 I4 Dapitan Phil.
135 H3 Da Qaidam Zhen China
150 E2 Daqing China
154 D1 Daqing Shan mts China
160 A2 Daqin Tal China
155 F5 Daqiu China
142 D3 Daqq-e Dombūn Iran
142 D3 Daqq-e Sorkh, Kavīr-e salt flat Iran
143 F3 Daqq-e Tundi, Dasht-e imp. l. Afgh.
139 J4 Dāqūq Iraq
155 G4 Daqu Shan i. China
139 F5 Dar'ā Syria
  Dâra, Gebel mt. Egypt see Dārah, Jabal
142 D4 Dārāb Iran
161 I3 Daraga Phil.
136 D6 Dārah, Jabal mt. Egypt
177 N4 Darahanava Belarus
193 D1 Daraj Libya
142 D4 Dārākūyeh Iran
161 J4 Daram i. Phil.
142 D3 Darang, Kühʻe h. Iran
  Đa Răng, Sông r. Vietnam see Ba, Sông
142 D4 Dārān Iran
143 F2 Darband Iran
141 I5 Darband Uzbek.
149 F4 Darbhanga India
214 C2 Dardanelle U.S.A.
217 E5 Dardanelle, Lake U.S.A.
185 L4 Dardanelles str. Turkey
179 I3 Dardesheim Germany
139 F2 Darende Turkey

195 D4 Dar es Salaam Tanz.
184 D2 Darfo Boario Terme Italy
193 E3 Darfur reg. Sudan
148 B2 Dargai Pak.
126 D1 Dargaville N.Z.
125 G6 Dargo Australia
150 C2 Darhan Mongolia
219 D6 Darien U.S.A.
233 H2 Darién, Golfo del g. Col.
224 J7 Darién, Parque Nacional de nat. park Panama
224 J6 Darién, Serranía del mts Panama
153 J2 Dariganga Mongolia
141 H2 Dar'inskiy Kazakh.
140 B2 Dar'inskoye Kazakh.
224 H5 Darío Nicaragua
  Darjeeling India see Darjiling
149 G4 Darjiling India
124 B4 Darke Peak Australia
142 C4 Darkhazīneh Iran
150 B3 Darlag China
125 E4 Darling r. Australia
125 H1 Darling Downs hills Australia
118 B5 Darling Range hills Australia
172 F3 Darlington U.K.
208 B4 Darlington U.S.A.
125 G5 Darlington Point Australia
121 C5 Darlot, Lake salt flat Australia
177 H3 Darłowo Poland
142 B5 Darmā Saudi Arabia
149 E3 Darma Pass China/India
147 H2 Darmaraopet India
143 E4 Dar Mazār Iran
179 G5 Darmstadt Germany
148 C5 Darna r. India
193 E1 Darnah Libya
197 I4 Darnall S. Africa
125 E4 Darnick Australia
127 L5 Darnley, Cape Antarctica
202 F3 Darnley Bay Canada
183 P2 Daroca Spain
186 G3 Darovka Rus. Fed.
186 H3 Darovskoy Rus. Fed.
123 C4 Darr watercourse Australia
235 J3 Darregueira Arg.
143 E3 Darreh Bīd Iran
143 E2 Darreh Gaz Iran
147 H3 Darsi India
173 D7 Dart r. U.K.
  Darta Turkm. see Tarta
173 H6 Dartford U.K.
124 D6 Dartmoor Australia
173 C7 Dartmoor hills U.K.
173 D7 Dartmoor National Park U.K.
207 H5 Dartmouth Canada
173 D7 Dartmouth U.K.
123 D5 Dartmouth, Lake salt flat Australia
123 D8 Dartmouth Reservoir Australia
173 F4 Darton U.K.
119 E2 Daru P.N.G.
192 A4 Daru Sierra Leone
149 G3 Darum Tso l. China
185 G2 Daruvar Croatia
  Darvaza Turkm. see Içoguz
142 C4 Darvīshī Iran
143 G4 Darwazgai Afgh.
173 E4 Darwen U.K.
143 G4 Darweshan Afgh.
118 D3 Darwin Australia
232 C8 Darwin, Monte mt. Chile
148 B3 Darya Khan Pak.
141 F3 Dar'yalyktakyr, Ravnina plain Kazakh.
143 E4 Dārzīn Iran
142 D5 Dās i. U.A.E.
160 B3 Dashiqiao China
  Dashoguz Turkm. see Daşoguz
143 E2 Dasht Iran
143 F5 Dasht r. Pak.
142 C4 Dasht-e Palang r. Iran
143 F5 Dashtiari Iran
141 G5 Dashtiobburdon Tajik.
141 G4 Dashtobod Uzbek.
154 C2 Dashuikeng China
154 B2 Dashuitou China
148 C2 Daska Pak.
139 K1 Daşkäsän Azer.
143 F2 Daşköpri Turkm.
140 D4 Daşoguz Turkm.
148 C1 Daspar mt. Pak.
179 H3 Dassel Germany
196 C6 Dassen Island S. Africa
139 K2 Dastakert Armenia

143 E3 Dastgardān Iran
161 F2 Da Suifen He r. China
185 L6 Datça Turkey
158 G3 Date Japan
215 F5 Dateland U.S.A.
148 D4 Datia India
155 E5 Datian China
156 B3 Datong China
154 A2 Datong Qinghai China
154 D1 Datong Shanxi China
154 B2 Datong He r. China
154 A2 Datong Shan mts China
163 G2 Datu, Tanjung c. Indon./Malaysia
161 J5 Datu Piang Phil.
186 C3 Daugava r. Belarus/Latvia
  alt. Zakhodnyaya Dzvina,
  alt. Zapadnaya Dvina,
  conv. Western Dvina
171 N5 Daugavpils Latvia
143 G2 Daulatabad Afgh.
148 C6 Daulatabad India
179 E4 Daun Germany
147 G2 Daund India
162 A2 Daung Kyun i. Myanmar
205 I4 Dauphin Canada
182 G4 Dauphiné reg. France
217 F6 Dauphin Island U.S.A.
205 J4 Dauphin Lake Canada
121 A5 Daurie Creek r. Australia
148 D4 Dausa India
174 E3 Dava U.K.
140 A4 Dāvāçi Azer.
147 G3 Davangere India
161 J5 Davao Phil.
161 J5 Davao Gulf Phil.
143 F5 Dāvar Panāh Iran
197 H3 Davel S. Africa
214 A3 Davenport CA U.S.A.
214 B2 Davenport IA U.S.A.
123 C5 Davenport Downs Australia
121 F4 Davenport Range hills Australia
173 F5 Daventry U.K.
197 H3 Daveyton S. Africa
224 H6 David Panama
205 H4 Davidson Canada
121 E4 Davidson, Mount h. Australia
205 I3 Davin Lake Canada
127 K5 Davis research stn Antarctica
121 C4 Davis r. Australia
214 B2 Davis U.S.A.
215 E4 Davis Dam U.S.A.
207 H2 Davis Inlet Canada
127 L6 Davis Sea Antarctica
203 M3 Davis Strait Canada/Greenland
176 D7 Davos Switz.
160 B3 Dawa China
154 A1 Dawan China
154 F3 Dawaxung China
155 B4 Dawê China
154 E3 Dawen He r. China
162 A1 Dawna Range mts Myanmar/Thai.
  Dawo China see Maqên
146 D6 Dawqah Oman
123 E4 Dawson r. Australia
202 E3 Dawson Canada
219 C6 Dawson GA U.S.A.
216 D2 Dawson ND U.S.A.
204 E3 Dawson, Mount Canada
205 I4 Dawson Bay Canada
204 E3 Dawson Creek Canada
205 K2 Dawson Inlet Canada
204 B2 Dawson Range mts Canada
155 E4 Dawu Hubei China
  Dawu China see Maqên
155 C4 Dawu Sichuan China
183 D5 Dax France
155 C6 Daxin China
154 E2 Daxing China
155 A4 Da Xueshan mts China
  Dayan China see Lijiang
149 H4 Dayang r. India
160 B4 Dayang He r. China
156 B2 Dayangshu China
153 H6 Dayao China
155 D6 Dayao Shan mts China
155 E4 Daye China
143 G3 Dāykundī Afgh.
125 F6 Daylesford Australia
215 E5 Daylight Pass U.S.A.
235 L1 Daymán r. Uruguay
235 L1 Daymán, Cuchilla del hills Uruguay
139 H4 Dayr az Zawr Syria
220 A5 Dayton OH U.S.A.
219 C5 Dayton TN U.S.A.
212 C2 Dayton WA U.S.A.

219 D6 Daytona Beach U.S.A.
155 E5 Dayu China
155 D5 Dayu Ling mts China
154 F3 Da Yunhe canal China
212 C2 Dayville U.S.A.
142 C5 Dayyer Iran
155 C4 Dazhou China
155 D7 Dazhou Dao i. China
155 C4 Dazhu China
155 B4 Dazu China
197 F5 De Aar S. Africa
221 H2 Dead r. ME U.S.A.
208 D2 Dead r. MI U.S.A.
215 E4 Dead Mountains U.S.A.
138 E6 Dead Sea salt l. Asia
121 E6 Deakin Australia
173 I6 Deal U.K.
197 F4 Dealesville S. Africa
204 D4 Dean r. Canada
155 E4 De'an China
173 E6 Dean, Forest of U.K.
235 J1 Deán Funes Arg.
209 F4 Dearborn U.S.A.
204 D3 Dease r. Canada
204 C3 Dease Lake Canada
203 H3 Dease Strait Canada
215 D3 Death Valley depr. U.S.A.
215 D3 Death Valley Junction U.S.A.
215 D3 Death Valley National Park U.S.A.
182 G4 Deauville France
163 H2 Debak Sarawak Malaysia
155 C6 Debao China
185 I4 Debar Macedonia
205 H4 Debden Canada
173 I5 Debenham U.K.
215 H2 De Beque U.S.A.
178 C3 De Biesbosch, Nationaal Park nat. park Neth.
221 I2 Deblois U.S.A.
121 B6 Deborah East, Lake salt flat Australia
121 B6 Deborah West, Lake salt flat Australia
194 D3 Debre Birhan Eth.
177 J7 Debrecen Hungary
194 D2 Debre Markos Eth.
194 D2 Debre Tabor Eth.
194 D3 Debre Zeyit Eth.
185 I3 Dečan Kosovo
219 C5 Decatur AL U.S.A.
219 C5 Decatur GA U.S.A.
208 C6 Decatur IL U.S.A.
209 E5 Decatur IN U.S.A.
209 E4 Decatur MI U.S.A.
147 H2 Deccan plat. India
209 I2 Decelles, Lac resr Canada
125 J1 Deception Bay Australia
176 G5 Děčín Czech Rep.
208 B4 Decorah U.S.A.
173 F6 Deddington U.K.
136 C3 Dedegöl Dağları mts Turkey
179 I2 Dedeleben Germany
179 I2 Dedelstorf Germany
179 E2 Dedemsvaart Neth.
235 E2 Dedo de Deus mt. Brazil
196 C6 De Doorns S. Africa
186 D3 Dedovichi Rus. Fed.
  Dedu China see Wudalianchi
195 D5 Dedza Malawi
173 D4 Dee est. U.K.
173 E4 Dee r. England/Wales U.K.
175 F3 Dee r. Scotland U.K.
175 J5 Dee r. Ireland
175 K3 Deele r. Ireland
155 □ Deep Bay Hong Kong China
220 D5 Deep Creek Lake U.S.A.
215 F2 Deep Creek Range mts U.S.A.
209 I2 Deep River Canada
221 G4 Deep River U.S.A.
205 J1 Deep Rose Lake Canada
215 D3 Deep Springs U.S.A.
125 I2 Deepwater Australia
220 B5 Deer Creek Lake U.S.A.
121 E5 Deering, Mount Australia
221 I2 Deer Island Canada
221 I2 Deer Island U.S.A.
207 I4 Deer Lake Nfld Canada
205 K4 Deer Lake Ont. Canada
205 K4 Deer Lake l. Canada
212 D2 Deer Lodge U.S.A.
232 D2 Defensores del Chaco, Parque Nacional nat. park Para.

220 A4 Defiance U.S.A.
219 C6 De Funiak Springs U.S.A.
150 B3 Dêgê China
194 E3 Degeh Bur Eth.
179 K6 Deggendorf Germany
148 C3 Degh r. Pak.
121 B4 De Grey r. Australia
178 B3 De Haan Belgium
142 D4 Dehaj Iran
143 F4 Dehak Iran
143 F5 Dehak Iran
142 C4 Deh-Dasht Iran
142 C4 Deh-e Khalīfeh Iran
142 C3 Deheq Iran
143 E4 Deh-e Sard Iran
142 C2 Dehgāh Iran
142 B3 Deh Golān Iran
147 H5 Dehiwala-Mount Lavinia Sri Lanka
142 D5 Dehküyeh Iran
142 B3 Dehlorān Iran
141 F5 Dehqonobod Uzbek.
148 C3 Dehra Dun India
149 F4 Dehri India
143 E4 Deh Salm Iran
139 J4 Deh Sheykh Iran
143 F3 Deh Shū Afgh.
155 F5 Dehua China
160 C1 Dehui China
178 B4 Deinze Belgium
177 K7 Dej Romania
155 C4 Dejiang China
208 C5 De Kalb IL U.S.A.
217 E5 De Kalb TX U.S.A.
221 F2 De Kalb Junction U.S.A.
156 F2 De-Kastri Rus. Fed.
146 A6 Dekemhare Eritrea
195 C4 Dekese Dem. Rep. Congo
  Dekhkanabad Uzbek. see Dehqonobod
178 C3 De Koog Neth.
178 C2 De Kooy Neth.
215 E3 Delamar Lake U.S.A.
214 C4 Delano U.S.A.
215 F2 Delano Peak U.S.A.
117 G2 Delap-Uliga-Djarrit Marshall Is
143 F3 Delārām Afgh.
197 F3 Delareyville S. Africa
205 H4 Delaronde Lake Canada
208 C5 Delavan IL U.S.A.
208 C4 Delavan WI U.S.A.
220 B4 Delaware U.S.A.
221 F4 Delaware r. U.S.A.
221 F5 Delaware state U.S.A.
221 F5 Delaware Bay U.S.A.
220 B4 Delaware Lake U.S.A.
221 F4 Delaware Water Gap National Recreational Area park U.S.A.
179 G3 Delbrück Germany
125 H6 Delegate Australia
176 C7 Delémont Switz.
178 C2 Delft Neth.
147 H4 Delft Island Sri Lanka
179 E1 Delfzijl Neth.
195 E5 Delgado, Cabo c. Moz.
150 C2 Delgerhaan Mongolia
209 G4 Delhi Canada
178 B3 Delhi China
148 D3 Delhi India (City Plan 96)
213 F4 Delhi CO U.S.A.
221 F3 Delhi NY U.S.A.
139 I2 Deli r. Turkey
138 E2 Delice Turkey
138 E1 Delice r. Turkey
142 C3 Delījān Iran
204 E5 Delisle Canada
205 H4 Delisle Canada
183 R4 Dellys Alg.
215 D5 Del Mar U.S.A.
179 G1 Delmenhorst Germany
133 Q2 De-Longa, Ostrova is Rus. Fed.
202 B3 De Long Mountains U.S.A.
205 I5 Deloraine Canada
185 J5 Delphi tourist site Greece
208 D5 Delphi U.S.A.
220 A4 Delphos U.S.A.
197 F4 Delportshoop S. Africa
219 D7 Delray Beach U.S.A.
213 E6 Del Río Mex.
171 L3 Delsbo Sweden
215 H2 Delta CO U.S.A.
208 A5 Delta IA U.S.A.
215 F2 Delta UT U.S.A.

Duncannon U.S.A. 221 E4
Duncansby Head U.K. 174 E2
Duncans Mills U.S.A. 208 B5
Duncormick Ireland 175 L5
Dundaga Latvia 171 M4
Dundalk Canada 209 G3
Dundalk Ireland 175 L3
Dundalk U.S.A. 221 E5
Dundalk Bay Ireland 175 L4
Dundas Greenland 203 L2
Dundas, Lake *salt flat* Australia 121 C7
Dundas Island Canada 204 C4
Dundas Strait Australia 120 E1
Dún Dealgan Ireland *see* Dundalk
Dundee S. Africa 197 I4
Dundee U.K. 175 F4
Dundee *MI* U.S.A. 209 F5
Dundee *NY* U.S.A. 221 E3
Dundgovĭ China 154 E1
Dundonald U.K. 175 M3
Dundoo Australia 125 F1
Dundrennan U.K. 174 E6
Dundrum U.K. 175 M3
Dundrum Bay U.K. 175 M3
Dundwa Range *mts* India/Nepal 149 E4
Dune, Lac *l.* Canada 207 F2
Dunedin N.Z. 126 C6
Dunedin U.S.A. 219 D6
Dunedoo Australia 125 H4
Dunenbay Kazakh. 141 J2
Dunfermline U.K. 174 E4
Dungannon U.K. 175 L3
Dungarpur India 148 C5
Dungarvan Ireland 175 K5
Dungeness *hd* U.K. 173 H7
Dungeness, Punta *pt* Arg. 232 C8
Düngenheim Germany 179 F4
Dungiven U.K. 175 L3
Dungloe Ireland *see* An Clochán Liath
Dungog Australia 125 I4
Dungu Dem. Rep. Congo 194 C3
Dungun Malaysia 163 B2
Dungunab Sudan 193 F2
Dunhua China 160 E2
Dunhuang China 150 B2
Dunkeld Australia 123 E5
Dunkeld Australia 125 E6
Dunkeld U.K. 174 E4
Dunkerque France *see* Dunkirk
Dunkery Hill U.K. 173 D6
Dunkirk France 182 F1
Dunkirk U.S.A. 220 D3
Dunkwa Ghana 192 B4
Dún Laoghaire Ireland 175 L4
Dunlavin Ireland 175 L4
Dunleer Ireland 175 L4
Dunloy U.K. 175 L2
Dunmanus Bay Ireland 175 I6
Dunmanway Ireland 175 I6
Dunmarra Australia 120 F3
Dunmore U.S.A. 175 J4
Dunmore Town Bahamas 219 E7
Dunmovin U.S.A. 215 D3
Dunmurry U.K. 175 M3
Dunn U.S.A. 219 E5
Dunnet Bay U.K. 174 E2
Dunnet Head U.K. 174 E2
Dunnigan U.S.A. 214 B2
Dunning U.S.A. 216 C3
Dunnville Canada 209 H4
Dunolly Australia 125 E6
Dunoon U.K. 174 D5
Duns U.K. 175 F5
Dunseith U.S.A. 216 C1
Dunsmuir U.S.A. 213 B3
Dunstable U.K. 173 G6
Dunstan Mountains N.Z. 126 B6
Dun-sur-Meuse France 178 D5
Duntroon N.Z. 126 C6
Dunvegan, Loch *b.* U.K. 174 B3
Dunyapur Pak. 148 B3
Duolun China *see* Dolonnur
Dupang Ling *mts* China 155 D5
Duparquet, Lac *l.* Canada 209 H1
Dupnitsa Bulg. 185 J3
Dupree U.S.A. 216 C2
Du Quoin U.S.A. 219 B4
Durack *r.* Australia 118 C3
Durack Range *hills* Australia 120 D3
Durağan Turkey 138 E1
Durance *r.* France 183 G5
Durand *MI* U.S.A. 209 F4
Durand *WI* U.S.A. 208 B3
Durango Mex. 224 C2
Durango *state* Mex. 224 C2

Durango Spain 183 O1
Durango U.S.A. 213 F4
Durant U.S.A. 217 D5
Durazno Uruguay 235 L2
Durazno, Cuchilla Grande del *hills* Uruguay 235 L1
Durban S. Africa 197 I4
Durban-Corbières France 183 F5
Durbanville S. Africa 196 C6
Durbin U.S.A. 220 D5
Durbuy Belgium 178 D4
Düren Germany 179 E4
Durg India 149 E5
Durgapur India 149 F5
Durham Canada 209 G3
Durham U.K. 172 F3
Durham *CA* U.S.A. 214 B2
Durham *NC* U.S.A. 219 E4
Durham *NH* U.S.A. 221 H3
Durham Downs Australia 123 C5
Durleşti Moldova 187 D6
Durmersheim Germany 179 G6
Durmitor *mt.* Montenegro 185 H3
Durness U.K. 174 D2
Durong South Australia 123 C5
Durrie Australia 123 C5
Durrington U.K. 173 F6
Dursey Island Ireland 175 H6
Dursunbey Turkey 138 B2
Dūruḩ Iran 143 F3
Durūz, Jabal ad *mt.* Syria 139 F5
D'Urville, Tanjung *pt* Indon. 118 D2
D'Urville Island N.Z. 126 D5
Durzab Afgh. 143 G3
Duşak Turkm. 140 D5
Dushai Pak. 143 G4
Dushak Turkm. *see* Duşak
Dushan China 155 C5
Dushanbe Tajik. 141 G5
Dushet'i Georgia 187 H7
Dusky Sound *inlet* N.Z. 126 A6
Dusse-Alin', Khrebet *mts* Rus. Fed. 156 D2
Düsseldorf Germany 179 E3
Dustlik Uzbek. *see* Do'stlik
Dutch Mountain U.S.A. 215 F1
Dutlwe Botswana 197 E1
Dutse Nigeria 192 D3
Dutton *r.* Australia 123 C4
Dutton, Lake *salt flat* Australia 124 B3
Dutton, Mount U.S.A. 215 F2
Duvannoye Rus. Fed. 186 H3
Duvert, Lac *l.* Canada 207 F2
Duweihin, Khor *b.* Saudi Arabia/U.A.E. 142 C5
Duwin Iraq 137 G3
Düxanbibazar China 141 J5
Duyun China 155 C5
Duzab Pak. 143 F5
Düzce Turkey 138 C1
Dvina *r.* Europe *see* Zapadnaya Dvina
Dvinskaya Guba *g.* Rus. Fed. 169 N2
Dvorichna Ukr. 187 F5
Dvoryanka Rus. Fed. 158 B2
Dwarka India 148 B5
Dwarsberg S. Africa 197 G2
Dwight U.S.A. 208 C5
Dwingelderveld, Nationaal Park *nat. park* Neth. 179 E2
Dworshak Reservoir U.S.A. 212 D3
Dwyka S. Africa 196 D6
Dyanev Turkm. *see* Galkynyş
Dyat'kovo Rus. Fed. 187 E4
Dyce U.K. 175 F3
Dyer *IN* U.S.A. 208 D5
Dyer *NV* U.S.A. 214 C3
Dyer, Cape Canada 203 L3
Dyer Bay Canada 209 G3
Dyersburg U.S.A. 219 B4
Dyersville U.S.A. 208 B4
Dyke U.K. 174 E3
Dykh Tau *mt.* Georgia/Rus. Fed. *see* Gistola, Gora
Dykh-Tau, Gora *mt.* Rus. Fed. 137 F2
Dyleň *h.* Czech Rep. 179 K5
Dylewska Góra *h.* Poland 177 I4
Dynevor Downs Australia 125 F2
Dyoki S. Africa 197 H5
Dysselsdorp S. Africa 197 E6
Dzamïn Üüd Mongolia 150 D2
Dzaoudzi Africa 195 J3
Dzavhan Mongolia 144 H2
Dzerzhinsk Rus. Fed. 186 G3
Dzerzhinskiy Kazakh. 140 E2

Dzerzhyns'k Ukr. 177 M5
Dzhagdy, Khrebet *mts* Rus. Fed. 150 E1
Dzhaki-Unakhta Yakbyyana, Khrebet *mts* Rus. Fed. 156 D2
Dzhalagash Kazakh. 141 F3
Dzhalal-Abad Kyrg. *see* Jalal-Abad
Dzhalinda Rus. Fed. 156 A1
Dzhanga Turkm. *see* Jaňňa
Dzhangala Kazakh. 140 B2
Dzhangel'dy Uzbek. *see* Jongeldi
Dzhankoy Ukr. 187 E6
Dzhansugurov Kazakh. 141 I3
Dzharkurgan Uzbek. *see* Jarqo'rgo'n
Dzhebel Turkm. *see* Jebel
Dzhidinskiy, Khrebet *mts* Mongolia/Rus. Fed. 153 H1
Dzhigirbent Turkm. *see* Jigerbent
Dzhizak Uzbek. *see* Jizzax
Dzhubga Rus. Fed. 137 E1
Dzhugdzhur, Khrebet *mts* Rus. Fed. 150 F1
Dzhuma Uzbek. *see* Juma
Dzhungarskiy Alatau, Khrebet *mts* China/Kazakh. 135 F2
Dzhusaly Kazakh. 141 F3
Działdowo Poland 177 J4
Dzibalchén Mex. 225 G4
Dzilam de Bravo Mex. 225 G3
Dzungaria Basin *basin* China *see* Junggar Pendi
Dzungarian Gate *pass* China/Kazakh. 141 J3
Dzur Mongolia *see* Tes
Dzüünharaa Mongolia 153 I2
Dzuunmod Mongolia 150 D2
Dzyaniskavichy Belarus 187 C4
Dzyarzhynsk Belarus 187 C4
Dzyatlavichy Belarus 177 M4

E

Eabamet Lake Canada 206 C3
Eagar U.S.A. 215 H4
Eagle *r.* Canada 207 I3
Eagle U.S.A. 213 F4
Eagle Bay U.S.A. 221 F3
Eagle Crags *mt.* U.S.A. 215 D4
Eagle Creek *r.* Canada 205 H4
Eagle Lake *l.* Canada 205 K5
Eagle Lake U.S.A. 221 I1
Eagle Lake *l. CA* U.S.A. 213 B3
Eagle Lake *l.* U.S.A. 221 I1
Eagle Mountain *h.* U.S.A. 208 B2
Eagle Pass U.S.A. 217 C6
Eagle Plain Canada 202 D3
Eagle River *MI* U.S.A. 208 C2
Eagle River *WI* U.S.A. 208 C2
Eaglesham Canada 204 F3
Eagle Tail Mountains U.S.A. 215 F5
Ear Falls Canada 205 K4
Earlimart U.S.A. 214 C4
Earlston U.K. 175 F5
Earlton Canada 209 H2
Earn *r.* U.K. 174 E4
Earn, Loch *l.* U.K. 174 D4
Earth U.S.A. 217 C5
Easington U.K. 173 H4
Easley U.S.A. 219 D5
East Alligator *r.* Australia 120 F2
East Antarctica *reg.* Antarctica 127 K5
East Ararat U.S.A. 221 F4
East Aurora U.S.A. 220 D3
East Bay Canada 209 G3
East Bay U.S.A. 217 F6
East Berkshire U.S.A. 221 G2
Eastbourne U.K. 173 H7
East Branch Clarion River Reservoir U.S.A. 220 D4
East Brooklyn U.S.A. 221 H4
East Cape N.Z. 127 G2
East Carbon City U.S.A. 215 G2
East Caroline Basin *sea feature* N. Pacific Ocean 236 E5
East Chicago U.S.A. 208 D5
East China Sea Asia 150 D5
East Coast Bays N.Z. 126 E2
East Corinth U.S.A. 221 G2
East Dereham U.K. *see* Dereham
Easter Island S. Pacific Ocean 228 C5
Eastern Cape *prov.* S. Africa 197 G5
Eastern Desert Egypt 193 F2
Eastern Ghats *mts* India 147 I2

Eastern Nara *canal* Pak. 148 B4
Eastern Taurus *plat.* Turkey *see* Güneydoğu Toroslar
Eastern Transvaal *prov.* S. Africa *see* Mpumalanga
Easterville Canada 205 J4
East Falkland *i.* Falkland Is 232 E8
East Falmouth U.S.A. 221 H4
Eastgate U.S.A. 215 D2
East Grand Forks U.S.A. 216 D2
East Grinstead U.K. 173 G6
Easthampton U.S.A. 221 G3
East Hampton U.S.A. 221 I3
East Hickory U.S.A. 220 D4
East Indiaman Ridge *sea feature* Indian Ocean 238 K6
East Jamaica U.S.A. 221 G3
East Jordan U.S.A. 209 E3
East Kilbride U.K. 174 D5
East Lake U.S.A. 208 D3
East Lamma Channel *Hong Kong* China 155 □
East Leeds U.K. 173 F7
East Liverpool U.S.A. 220 C4
East Loch Tarbert *inlet* U.K. 174 B3
East London S. Africa 197 G6
Eastmain Canada 206 E3
Eastmain *r.* Canada 207 F3
Eastman Canada 221 G2
Eastman U.S.A. 219 D5
East Mariana Basin *sea feature* Pacific Ocean 236 F5
Eastmere Australia 123 D4
East Millinocket U.S.A. 221 I2
East Moline U.S.A. 208 B5
Easton *IL* U.S.A. 208 C5
Easton *MD* U.S.A. 221 E5
Easton *PA* U.S.A. 221 F4
East Pacific Ridge *sea feature* S. Pacific Ocean 237 L8
East Pacific Rise *sea feature* N. Pacific Ocean 237 L4
East Park Reservoir U.S.A. 214 A2
East Point *pt* Canada 207 H4
East Point U.S.A. 219 C5
Eastport *ME* U.S.A. 221 J2
Eastport *ID* U.S.A. 209 E3
East Range *mts* U.S.A. 215 D1
East St Louis U.S.A. 219 B4
East Sea Pacific Ocean *see* Japan, Sea of
East Siberian Sea Rus. Fed. 133 Q2
East Sister Island Australia 125 H7
East Timor *country* Asia 151 E7
East Tons *r.* India 149 F4
East Toorale Australia 125 F3
East Troy U.S.A. 208 C4
East Walker *r.* U.S.A. 214 C2
East Wallingford U.S.A. 221 G3
Eatonton U.S.A. 219 D5
Eau Claire U.S.A. 208 B3
Eau Claire *r.* U.S.A. 208 B3
Eau Claire, Lac à l' *l.* Canada 207 F2
Eauripik *atoll* Micronesia 151 G6
Eauripik Rise-New Guinea Rise *sea feature* N. Pacific Ocean 236 E5
Ebano Mex. 225 E3
Ebbw Vale U.K. 173 D6
Ebebiyin Equat. Guinea 193 D4
Ebenerde Namibia 196 B2
Ebensburg U.S.A. 220 D4
Eber Gölü *l.* Turkey 138 C2
Ebergötzen Germany 179 I3
Eberswalde-Finow Germany 176 F4
Eberts Canada 209 F4
Ebetsu Japan 158 G3
Ebian China 155 B4
Ebinur Hu *salt l.* China 141 J3
Eboli Italy 184 F4
Ebolowa Cameroon 193 D4
Ebrāhīm Ḩeşār Iran 139 J3
Ebro *r.* Spain 183 Q2
Ebstorf Germany 179 I1
Eceabat Turkey 185 L4
Echague Phil. 161 I2
Echegárate, Puerto *pass* Spain 183 O1
Echeverria, Pico *mt.* Mex. 224 A1
Echo, Lake U.S.A. 125 G9
Echo Bay *N.W.T.* Canada 204 F1
Echo Bay *Ont.* Canada 209 E2
Echo Cliffs U.S.A. 215 G3
Echoing *r.* Canada 205 B3
Échouani, Lac *l.* Canada 209 J2
Echt Neth. 178 D3
Echternach Lux. 178 D3
Echuca Australia 179 E5
Echuca Australia 125 F6

Echzell Germany 179 G4
Écija Spain 183 N4
Eckental Germany 179 J5
Eckerman U.S.A. 209 J4
Eckernförde Germany 176 D3
Eclipse Sound *sea chan.* Canada 203 K2
Écrins, Massif des *mts* France 182 H4
Ecuador *country* S. America 230 C4
Écueils, Pointe aux Canada 206 E2
Edam Canada 205 H4
Edam Neth. 178 D2
Eday *i.* U.K. 175 F1
Ed Da'ein Sudan 193 E3
Ed Damazin Sudan 193 E3
Ed Damer Sudan 193 F3
Ed Debba Sudan 193 F3
Ed Dueim Sudan 193 F3
Eddystone Point Australia 125 H8
Ede Neth. 178 D2
Edéa Cameroon 193 D4
Edehon Lake Canada 205 J2
Edéia Brazil 234 C2
Eden *r.* U.K. 172 E3
Eden U.S.A. 217 D6
Edenburg S. Africa 197 F4
Edendale N.Z. 126 B7
Edenderry Ireland 175 K4
Edenhope Australia 124 D6
Edenton U.S.A. 219 E4
Edenville S. Africa 197 G3
Edessa Greece 185 J4
Edewecht Germany 179 F1
Edgar Ranges *hills* Australia 120 C3
Edgartown U.S.A. 221 H4
Edgeley U.S.A. 216 D2
Edgemont U.S.A. 216 C3
Edgeworthstown Ireland 175 K4
Edgidan Rus. Fed. 141 K2
Edina U.S.A. 208 A5
Edinburg U.S.A. 217 D7
Edinburgh U.K. 174 E5
Edineţ Moldova 177 M6
Edirne Turkey 187 C7
Edith Cavell, Mount Canada 204 F4
Edjudina Australia 121 C6
Edmonds U.S.A. 212 B2
Edmonton Canada 205 G4
Edmore U.S.A. 205 J5
Edmund U.S.A. 208 B4
Edmund Lake Canada 205 K4
Edmundston Canada 207 G4
Edna U.S.A. 217 D6
Edna Bay U.S.A. 204 C3
Edremit Turkey 185 L5
Edrengiyn Nuruu *mts* Mongolia 144 I3
Edsbyn Sweden 171 K3
Edson Canada 204 C4
Eduardo Castex Arg. 235 J2
Eduard *r.* Australia 122 C2
Edward *r.* Australia 125 F5
Edward, Lake Dem. Rep. Congo/Uganda 195 C4
Edward Island Canada 208 C1
Edwards U.S.A. 221 F2
Edward's Creek Australia 124 A2
Edwards Plateau U.S.A. 217 C6
Edwardsville U.S.A. 219 B4
Edward VII Peninsula Antarctica 127 I5
Edziza, Mount Canada 204 C3
Eeklo Belgium 178 B3
Eel *r.* U.S.A. 214 A1
Eel, South Fork *r.* U.S.A. 214 A2
Eemshaven *pt* Neth. 179 E1
Eenrum Neth. 179 E1
Eenzamheid Pan *salt pan* S. Africa 196 D3
Éfaté *i.* Vanuatu 119 G3
Efes *tourist site* Turkey *see* Ephesus
Effingham U.S.A. 219 B4
Eflâni Turkey 138 D1
Egan Range *mts* U.S.A. 215 E2
Eganville Canada 209 I3
Eger Hungary 177 J7
Egersund Norway 171 I4
Egerton, Mount *h.* Australia 121 B5
Egg Lagoon Australia 125 G7
Eggenfelden Germany 179 J5
Eggolsheim Germany 179 G3
Eghezée Belgium 178 C4
Egilsstaðir Iceland 170 D2
Eğirdir Turkey 138 C3
Eğirdir Gölü *l.* Turkey 138 C3
Égletons France 182 F4

Eglinton U.K. 175 K2
Eglinton Island Canada 202 F2
Egmond aan Zee Neth. 178 C2
Egmont, Cape N.Z. 126 D3
Egmont, Mount *vol.* N.Z. *see* Taranaki, Mount
Egmont National Park N.Z. 126 E3
Eğrigöz Dağı *mts* Turkey 138 B2
Egton U.K. 172 G3
Éguas *r.* Brazil 234 D1
Egvekinot Rus. Fed. 133 U3
Egypt *country* Africa 193 E2
Ehen Hudag China 154 A2
Ehingen (Donau) Germany 176 D6
Ehra-Lessien Germany 179 I2
Ehrenberg U.S.A. 215 E5
Ehrenberg Range *hills* Australia 121 E4
Eibelstadt Germany 179 I5
Eibergen Neth. 179 E2
Eichenzell Germany 179 H4
Eichstätt Germany 179 J6
Eidfjord Norway 171 I3
Eidsvold Australia 123 E5
Eidsvoll Norway 171 J3
Eifel *hills* Germany 179 E4
Eigg *i.* U.K. 174 B4
Eight Degree Channel India/Maldives 147 G4
Eighty Mile Beach Australia 118 C3
Eilat Israel 138 E7
Eildon Australia 125 F6
Eildon, Lake Australia 125 F6
Eileen Lake Canada 205 H2
Eilenburg Germany 179 K3
Einasleigh Australia 122 D3
Einasleigh *r.* Australia 122 D3
Einbeck Germany 179 H3
Eindhoven Neth. 178 D4
Einsiedeln Switz. 176 D7
Eirik Ridge *sea feature* N. Atlantic Ocean 239 G2
Eirunepé Brazil 230 E5
Eisberg *h.* Germany 179 H3
Eiseb *watercourse* Namibia 195 C5
Eisenach Germany 179 I4
Eisenberg Germany 179 J4
Eisenhüttenstadt Germany 176 G4
Eisenstadt Austria 177 H7
Eisfeld Germany 179 I4
Eishort, Loch *inlet* U.K. 174 C4
Eisleben Lutherstadt Germany 179 J3
Eiterfeld Germany 179 H4
Eivissa Spain *see* Ibiza
Eivissa *i.* Spain *see* Ibiza
Ejea de los Caballeros Spain 183 P1
Ejeda Madag. 195 E6
Ejmiatsin Armenia 139 J1
Ejtula Mex. 225 E3
Ekenäs Fin. 171 M4
Ekerem Turkm. 140 C5
Ekeren Belgium 178 C3
Eketahuna N.Z. 126 E4
Ekibastuz Kazakh. 141 H2
Ekimchan Rus. Fed. 156 C1
Ekonda Rus. Fed. 133 L3
Ekostrovskaya Imandra, Ozero *l.* Rus. Fed. 169 M2
Ekshärad Sweden 171 K3
Eksjö Sweden 171 K4
Eksteenfontein S. Africa 196 B4
Ekuku Dem. Rep. Congo 195 C4
Ekwan *r.* Canada 206 D3
Ekwan Point Canada 206 D3
Elafonisou, Steno *sea chan.* Greece 185 J6
Elands *r.* S. Africa 197 H2
Elandsdoorn S. Africa 197 H2
El Aouinet Alg. 184 B7
El Arco Mex. 224 A1
El Aricha Alg. 180 C5
El Ashmûnein Egypt *see* Al Ashmūnayn
Elassona Greece 185 J5
Elazığ Turkey 139 G2
Elba, Isola d' *i.* Italy 184 D3
El'ban Rus. Fed. 150 F1
El Banco Col. 233 I2
El Barreal *salt l.* Mex. 210 E5
Elbasan Albania 185 I4
Elbaşı Turkey 138 D2
El Baúl Venez. 233 J2
El Bayadh Alg. 192 C1
Elbe *r.* Germany 179 I1
alt. Labe (Czech Rep.)
Elbert, Mount U.S.A. 213 F4
Elberta *MI* U.S.A. 208 D3
Elberta *UT* U.S.A. 215 G2
Elberton U.S.A. 219 D5

182 E2 Elbeuf France
139 F2 Elbistan Turkey
177 I3 Elbląg Poland
235 H4 El Bolsón Arg.
219 E7 Elbow Cay i. Bahamas
187 G7 El'brus mt. Rus. Fed.
178 D2 Elburg Neth.
183 O2 El Burgo de Osma Spain
142 C2 Elburz Mountains Iran
235 I4 El Cain Arg.
215 D5 El Cajon U.S.A.
233 L3 El Callao Venez.
217 D6 El Campo U.S.A.
213 F5 El Capitan Mountain U.S.A.
215 E5 El Centro U.S.A.
231 F7 El Cerro Bol.
233 K2 El Chaparro Venez.
Elche Spain see Elche-Elx
183 P3 Elche-Elx Spain
225 F4 El Chichónal vol. Mex.
224 C1 El Chilicote Mex.
118 D3 Elcho Island Australia
233 I3 El Cocuy Col.
233 I3 El Cocuy, Parque Nacional nat. park Col.
225 H3 El Cuyo Mex.
183 P3 Elda Spain
209 H2 Eldee Canada
124 D3 Elder, Lake Australia
225 D2 El Diamante Mex.
233 I2 El Difícil Col.
133 O3 El'dikan Rus. Fed.
233 H4 El Diviso Col.
215 E6 El Doctor Mex.
208 A5 Eldon IA U.S.A.
217 E4 Eldon MO U.S.A.
232 F3 Eldorado Arg.
224 C2 El Dorado Mex.
217 E5 El Dorado AR U.S.A.
217 D4 El Dorado KS U.S.A.
217 C6 Eldorado U.S.A.
233 L3 El Dorado Venez.
194 D3 Eldoret Kenya
212 E2 Electric Peak U.S.A.
192 B2 El Eglab plat. Alg.
183 O4 El Ejido Spain
230 D4 El Encanto Col.
179 I3 Elend Germany
147 G2 Elephanta Caves tourist site India
213 F5 Elephant Butte Reservoir U.S.A.
127 I2 Elephant Island Antarctica
149 H5 Elephant Point Bangl.
139 I2 Eleşkirt Turkey
225 G5 El Estor Guat.
192 C1 El Eulma Alg.
219 E7 Eleuthera i. Bahamas
184 C6 El Fahs Tunisia
193 E3 El Fasher Sudan
179 H4 Elfershausen Germany
224 B2 El Fuerte Mex.
El Gara Egypt see Qārah
193 E3 El Geneina Sudan
193 F3 El Geteina Sudan
174 E3 Elgin U.K.
208 C4 Elgin IL U.S.A.
216 C2 Elgin ND U.S.A.
215 E3 Elgin NV U.S.A.
215 G2 Elgin UT U.S.A.
133 P3 El'ginskiy Rus. Fed.
225 D3 El Gogorrón, Parque Nacional nat. park Mex.
192 C1 El Goléa Alg.
193 F4 Elgon, Mount Uganda
184 B6 El Hadjar Alg.
El Ḥarra Egypt see Al Ḥarrah
224 I6 El Hato del Volcán Panama
El Ḥeiz Egypt see Al Ḥayz
192 A2 El Hierro i. Canary Is
225 E3 El Higo Mex.
192 C2 El Homr Alg.
175 F4 Elie U.K.
126 C5 Elie de Beaumont mt. N.Z.
202 B3 Elim U.S.A.
207 H2 Eliot, Mount Canada
187 H6 Elista Rus. Fed.
208 B4 Elizabeth IL U.S.A.
221 F4 Elizabeth NJ U.S.A.
220 C5 Elizabeth WV U.S.A.
120 D3 Elizabeth, Mount h. Australia
219 E4 Elizabeth City U.S.A.
221 H4 Elizabeth Islands U.S.A.
219 D4 Elizabethton U.S.A.
219 C4 Elizabethtown KY U.S.A.
219 E5 Elizabethtown NC U.S.A.
221 G2 Elizabethtown NY U.S.A.
221 F4 Elizabethtown PA U.S.A.

183 P1 Elizondo Spain
192 B1 El Jadida Morocco
224 C2 El Jaralito Mex.
184 D7 El Jem Tunisia
224 H5 El Jicaral Nicaragua
205 G4 Elk r. Canada
177 K4 Ełk Poland
214 A2 Elk U.S.A.
220 C5 Elk r. U.S.A.
184 C6 El Kala Alg.
193 F3 El Kamlin Sudan
217 D5 Elk City U.S.A.
214 A2 Elk Creek U.S.A.
123 A4 Elkedra Australia
123 B4 Elkedra watercourse Australia
214 B2 Elk Grove U.S.A.
209 E5 Elkhart U.S.A.
192 B2 El Khnâchîch esc. Mali
208 C4 Elkhorn U.S.A.
216 D3 Elkhorn r. U.S.A.
185 L3 Elkhovo Bulg.
220 D5 Elkins U.S.A.
205 G4 Elk Island National Park Canada
209 G2 Elk Lake Canada
209 E3 Elk Lake l. U.S.A.
221 E4 Elkland U.S.A.
204 F5 Elko Canada
213 D3 Elko U.S.A.
205 G4 Elk Point Canada
216 E2 Elk River U.S.A.
221 F5 Elkton MD U.S.A.
220 D5 Elkton VA U.S.A.
205 L2 Ell Bay Canada
203 H2 Ellef Ringnes Island Canada
215 G2 Ellen, Mount U.S.A.
148 C3 Ellenabad India
216 D2 Ellendale U.S.A.
212 B2 Ellensburg U.S.A.
221 F4 Ellenville U.S.A.
125 H6 Ellery, Mount Australia
126 D5 Ellesmere, Lake N.Z.
203 J2 Ellesmere Island Canada
173 E4 Ellesmere Port U.K.
203 H3 Ellice r. Canada
220 D3 Ellicottville U.S.A.
225 E3 El Limón Mex.
179 I5 Ellingen Germany
197 G5 Elliot S. Africa
122 D3 Elliot, Mount Australia
197 H5 Elliotdale S. Africa
209 F2 Elliot Lake Canada
120 F3 Elliott Australia
212 D2 Ellis U.S.A.
Ellisras S. Africa see Lephalale
124 A4 Elliston Australia
175 F3 Ellon U.K.
148 C5 Ellora Caves tourist site India
221 I2 Ellsworth ME U.S.A.
208 A3 Ellsworth WI U.S.A.
127 I3 Ellsworth Land reg. Antarctica
127 I3 Ellsworth Mountains Antarctica
179 I6 Ellwangen (Jagst) Germany
138 B3 Elmalı Turkey
215 D6 El Maneadero Mex.
233 L3 El Manteco Venez.
El Maṭarīya Egypt see Al Maṭarīyah
192 C1 El Meghaïer Alg.
233 L3 El Miamo Venez.
180 E4 El Milia Alg.
El Mîna Lebanon see El Mîna
138 E4 El Mîna Lebanon
209 E3 Elmira U.S.A.
221 E3 Elmira NY U.S.A.
215 F5 El Mirage U.S.A.
183 O4 El Moral Spain
125 F6 Elmore Australia
235 J2 El Morro mt. Arg.
192 B2 El Mreyyé reg. Mauritania
179 H1 Elmshorn Germany
193 E3 El Muglad Sudan
209 G3 Elmwood Canada
208 C5 Elmwood IL U.S.A.
208 A3 Elmwood WI U.S.A.
171 I3 Elnesvågen Norway
233 I3 El Nevado, Cerro mt. Col.
161 H4 El Nido Phil.
193 F3 El Obeid Sudan
225 D2 El Oro Mex.
233 J3 Elorza Venez.

233 L2 El Pao Bolívar Venez.
233 J2 El Pao Cojedes Venez.
208 C5 El Paso U.S.A.
213 F6 El Paso TX U.S.A.
174 C2 Elphin U.K.
214 C3 El Portal U.S.A.
El Porvenír Panama see El Porvenir
224 J6 El Porvenir Panama
183 R2 El Prat de Llobregat Spain
El Progreso Guat. see Guastatoya
225 H5 El Progreso Hond.
224 B2 El Puerto, Cerro mt. Mex.
183 M4 El Puerto de Santa María Spain
El Quds Israel/West Bank see Jerusalem
El Qûşîya Egypt see Al Qûşîyah
224 J6 El Real Panama
217 D5 El Reno U.S.A.
225 D3 El Retorno Mex.
208 B4 Elroy U.S.A.
225 D3 El Rucio Mex.
204 B2 Elsa Canada
225 D2 El Salado Mex.
225 E4 El Salto Mex.
225 G5 El Salvador country Central America
225 D2 El Salvador Mex.
161 J4 El Salvador Phil.
233 J3 El Samán de Apure Venez.
209 F1 Elsas Canada
224 C1 El Sauz Mex.
179 G2 Else r. Germany
El Sellûm Egypt see As Sallûm
Elsen Nur l. China see Dorgê Co
120 F2 Elsey Australia
120 F2 El Sharana Australia
215 D5 Elsinore U.S.A.
233 K2 El Sombrero Venez.
235 I2 El Sosneado Arg.
225 E3 El Tajín tourist site Mex.
233 I3 El Tama, Parque Nacional nat. park Venez.
184 C6 El Tarf Alg.
183 M1 El Teleno mt. Spain
225 E4 El Tepozteco, Parque Nacional nat. park Mex.
183 R1 El Ter r. Spain
233 K2 El Tigre Venez.
225 G4 El Tigre, Parque Nacional nat. park Guat.
179 I5 Eltmann Germany
233 J2 El Tocuyo Venez.
187 H5 El'ton Rus. Fed.
187 H5 El'ton, Ozero l. Rus. Fed.
212 C2 Eltopia U.S.A.
233 L2 El Toro Venez.
235 K2 El Trébol Arg.
224 B3 El Triunfo Mex.
233 J3 El Tuparro, Parque Nacional nat. park Col.
232 B8 El Turbio Chile
147 I2 Eluru India
171 N4 Elva Estonia
233 H3 El Valle Col.
174 E5 Elvanfoot U.K.
183 M3 Elvas Port.
171 J3 Elverum Norway
233 I3 El Viejo mt. Col.
233 J2 El Vigía Venez.
230 D5 Elvira Brazil
194 E3 El Wak Kenya
El Wâtya well Egypt see Al Wāţiyah
209 E5 Elwood U.S.A.
179 I3 Elxleben Germany
173 H5 Ely U.K.
208 B2 Ely MN U.S.A.
215 E2 Ely NV U.S.A.
220 B4 Elyria U.S.A.
179 G4 Elz Germany
179 H2 Elze Germany
119 G3 Émaé i. Vanuatu
142 D2 Emāmrūd Iran
143 H2 Emām Şaḩeb Afgh.
Emām Şaḩeb Afgh. see Emām Şaḩeb
139 K5 Emāmzādeh Naşrod Dīn Iran
171 L4 Emån r. Sweden
234 B2 Emas, Parque Nacional das nat. park Brazil
141 J3 Emazar Kazakh.
140 D2 Emba Kazakh.
140 C3 Emba r. Kazakh.
197 H3 Embalenhle S. Africa

205 G3 Embarras Portage Canada
234 C2 Emborcação, Represa de resr Brazil
221 F2 Embrun Canada
195 D4 Embu Kenya
179 F1 Emden Germany
155 B4 Emeishan China
155 B4 Emei Shan mt. China
141 J3 Emel' r. Kazakh.
119 E4 Emerald Qld Australia
125 F6 Emerald Vic. Australia
207 G3 Emeril Canada
205 J5 Emerson Canada
138 B2 Emet Turkey
197 I2 eMgwenya S. Africa
215 E3 Emigrant Valley U.S.A.
eMijindini S. Africa see eMjindini
193 D3 Emi Koussi mt. Chad
224 C2 Emiliano Martínez Mex.
225 D4 Emiliano Zapata Mex.
141 J3 Emin China
185 L3 Emine, Nos pt Bulg.
141 J3 Emin He r. China
185 L3 Eminska Planina hills Bulg.
138 C2 Emirdağ Turkey
138 C2 Emir Dağı mt. Turkey
125 D5 Emita Australia
197 I4 eMjindini S. Africa
171 K4 Emmaboda Sweden
171 M4 Emmaste Estonia
125 I2 Emmaville Australia
178 D2 Emmeloord Neth.
179 F4 Emmelshausen Germany
178 D2 Emmen Neth.
176 D7 Emmen Switz.
179 E3 Emmerich Germany
123 D5 Emmet Australia
147 H3 Emmiganuru India
217 C6 Emory Peak U.S.A.
224 B2 Empalme Mex.
197 I4 Empangeni S. Africa
232 E3 Empedrado Arg.
236 G2 Emperor Seamount Chain sea feature N. Pacific Ocean
236 G2 Emperor Trough sea feature N. Pacific Ocean
184 D3 Empoli Italy
217 D4 Emporia KS U.S.A.
221 E6 Emporia VA U.S.A.
220 D4 Emporium U.S.A.
205 G4 Empress Canada
143 E3 'Emrānī Iran
179 F2 Ems r. Germany
209 H3 Emsdale Canada
179 F2 Emsdetten Germany
179 F1 Ems-Jade-Kanal canal Germany
179 F2 Emsland reg. Germany
197 H3 eMzinoni S. Africa
171 K3 Enafors Sweden
151 F7 Enarotali Indon.
159 E7 Ena-san mt. Japan
141 J2 Enbek Kazakh.
235 M1 Encantadas, Serra das hills Brazil
224 A2 Encantado, Cerro mt. Mex.
161 I3 Encanto, Cape Phil.
225 D3 Encarnación Mex.
232 E3 Encarnación Para.
217 D6 Encinal U.S.A.
215 D5 Encinitas U.S.A.
213 F5 Encino U.S.A.
124 C5 Encounter Bay Australia
234 E1 Encruzilhada Brazil
235 M1 Encruzilhada do Sul Brazil
204 D4 Endako Canada
151 E7 Ende Indon.
119 E3 Endeavour Strait Australia
Endeh Indon. see Ende
239 L9 Enderby Abyssal Plain sea feature Southern Ocean
127 L4 Enderby Land reg. Antarctica
221 G3 Endicott U.S.A.
204 C3 Endicott Arm est. U.S.A.
202 C3 Endicott Mountains U.S.A.
140 D2 Energetik Rus. Fed.
235 K3 Energía Arg.
187 E6 Enerhodar Ukr.
236 G6 Enewetak atoll Marshall Is
136 B2 Enez Turkey
184 D6 Enfidaville Tunisia
221 G3 Enfield U.S.A.
209 E2 Engadine U.S.A.
171 J3 Engan Norway
161 I2 Engaño, Cape Phil.
158 H2 Engaru Japan
197 G5 Engcobo S. Africa
219 F5 Engelhard U.S.A.
187 H5 Engel's Rus. Fed.

178 C1 Engelschmangat sea chan. Neth.
124 A2 Engenina watercourse Australia
163 B4 Enggano i. Indon.
178 C4 Enghien Belgium
173 E5 England admin. div. U.K.
207 I3 Englee Canada
209 H2 Englehart Canada
211 H1 English r. Canada
173 D7 English Channel France/U.K.
197 G7 Enguri r. Georgia
197 I4 Enhlalakahle S. Africa
217 D4 Enid U.S.A.
158 G3 Eniwa Japan
178 D2 Enkhuizen Neth.
171 L4 Enköping Sweden
184 F6 Enna Sicily Italy
205 J2 Ennadai Lake Canada
193 E3 En Nahud Sudan
193 D3 Ennedi, Massif mts Chad
175 K4 Ennell, Lough l. Ireland
125 F2 Enngonia Australia
216 C2 Enning U.S.A.
175 J5 Ennis Ireland
212 E2 Ennis MT U.S.A.
217 D5 Ennis TX U.S.A.
175 L5 Enniscorthy Ireland
175 K3 Enniskillen U.K.
175 I5 Ennistymon Ireland
176 G7 Enns r. Austria
171 O3 Eno Fin.
215 F5 Enoch U.S.A.
170 M1 Enontekiö Fin.
155 D6 Enping China
161 I2 Enrile Phil.
178 D2 Ens Neth.
125 G6 Ensay Australia
179 E2 Enschede Neth.
179 G3 Ense Germany
235 L2 Ensenada Arg.
222 A2 Ensenada Mex.
155 C4 Enshi China
204 F2 Enterprise N.W.T. Canada
209 I3 Enterprise Ont. Canada
219 C6 Enterprise AL U.S.A.
212 C2 Enterprise OR U.S.A.
215 F3 Enterprise UT U.S.A.
204 F4 Entrance Canada
235 K2 Entre Ríos prov. Arg.
231 F8 Entre Ríos Bol.
183 L3 Entroncamento Port.
192 C4 Enugu Nigeria
133 U3 Enurmino Rus. Fed.
230 D5 Envira Brazil
230 D5 Envira r. Brazil
126 C5 Enys, Mount N.Z.
159 F7 Enzan Japan
178 D2 Epe Neth.
178 B5 Épernay France
185 L6 Ephesus tourist site Turkey
215 G2 Ephraim U.S.A.
221 E4 Ephrata PA U.S.A.
212 C2 Ephrata WA U.S.A.
119 G3 Épi i. Vanuatu
182 H2 Épinal France
138 D4 Episkopi Cyprus
184 E4 Epomeo, Monte vol. Italy
173 H6 Epping U.K.
123 D4 Epping Forest National Park Australia
179 G4 Eppstein Germany
173 D5 Eppynt, Mynydd hills U.K.
173 G6 Epsom U.K.
235 J3 Epu-pel Arg.
142 D4 Eqlīd Iran
192 C4 Equatorial Guinea country Africa
233 L3 Equeipa Venez.
161 I4 Eran Phil.
161 I4 Eran Bay Phil.
139 F1 Erbaa Turkey
179 K5 Erbendorf Germany
179 F5 Erbeskopf h. Germany
139 I2 Erçek Turkey
139 I2 Erciş Turkey
138 E2 Erciyes Dağı mt. Turkey
177 I7 Érd Hungary
149 H2 Erdaogou China
160 D2 Erdao Jiang r. China
138 A1 Erdek Turkey
138 E3 Erdemli Turkey
Erdenedalay Mongolia see Sangiyn Dalay
153 H2 Erdenet Mongolia
153 K2 Erdenetsagaan Mongolia
Erdenetsogt Mongolia see Bayan-Ovoo
193 E3 Erdi reg. Chad
187 H6 Erdniyevskiy Rus. Fed.

235 B4 Eré, Campos hills Brazil
233 K3 Erebato r. Venez.
127 I5 Erebus, Mount vol. Antarctica
139 J6 Erech tourist site Iraq
232 F3 Erechim Brazil
150 D2 Ereentsav Mongolia
138 E3 Ereğli Konya Turkey
138 C1 Ereğli Zonguldak Turkey
184 F6 Erei, Monti mts Sicily Italy
Eréndira Mex. see Carácuaro
154 D1 Erenhot China
143 F3 Eresk Iran
183 N2 Eresma r. Spain
185 J5 Eretria Greece
179 J4 Erfurt Germany
139 G2 Ergani Turkey
192 B2 'Erg Chech des. Alg./Mali
Ergel Mongolia see Hatanbulag
185 L4 Ergene r. Turkey
171 N4 Ērgļi Latvia
158 A1 Ergu China
153 L1 Ergun China
Ergun Youqi China see Ergun
160 C3 Erhulai China
174 D2 Eriboll, Loch inlet U.K.
174 D4 Ericht, Loch l. U.K.
208 B5 Erie IL U.S.A.
217 E4 Erie KS U.S.A.
220 C3 Erie PA U.S.A.
209 G4 Erie, Lake Canada/U.S.A.
158 H3 Erimo Japan
158 H4 Erimo-misaki c. Japan
174 A3 Eriskay i. U.K.
194 D2 Eritrea country Africa
141 H5 Erkech-Tam Kyrg.
138 E2 Erkilet Turkey
179 J5 Erlangen Germany
118 D4 Erldunda Australia
121 C5 Erlistoun watercourse Australia
160 E2 Erlong Shan mt. China
160 C2 Erlongshan Shuiku resr China
178 D2 Ermelo Neth.
197 H3 Ermelo S. Africa
138 D3 Ermenek Turkey
185 K6 Ermoupoli Greece
147 H4 Ernakulam India
121 C5 Ernest Giles Range hills Australia
147 H4 Erode India
123 C5 Eromanga Australia
196 A1 Erongo admin. reg. Namibia
178 D3 Erp Neth.
121 A5 Errabiddy Hills Australia
192 B1 Er Rachidia Morocco
193 F3 Er Rahad Sudan
180 C5 Er Raoui des. Alg.
195 D5 Errego Moz.
184 D7 Er Remla Tunisia
175 J2 Errigal h. Ireland
175 H3 Erris Head Ireland
221 H2 Errol U.S.A.
119 G3 Erromango i. Vanuatu
185 I4 Ersekë Albania
216 D2 Erskine U.S.A.
171 M3 Ersmark Sweden
144 H2 Ertai China
187 G5 Ertil' Rus. Fed.
144 G2 Ertix He r. China/Kazakh.
124 C3 Erudina Australia
139 I3 Eruh Turkey
235 M2 Erval Brazil
220 D5 Erwin U.S.A.
179 G3 Erwitte Germany
179 J2 Erxleben Sachsen-Anhalt Germany
179 J2 Erxleben Sachsen-Anhalt Germany
152 G6 Eryuan China
179 K4 Erzgebirge mts Czech Rep./Germany
156 B2 Erzhan China
139 F3 Erzin Turkey
139 G2 Erzincan Turkey
139 H2 Erzurum Turkey
158 G4 Esan-misaki pt Japan
158 G4 Esashi Japan
158 G4 Esashi Japan
171 J5 Esbjerg Denmark
215 G3 Escalante U.S.A.
215 G3 Escalante r. U.S.A.
215 F3 Escalante Desert U.S.A.
224 C2 Escalón Mex.
208 D3 Escanaba U.S.A.
225 G4 Escárcega Mex.
161 I2 Escarpada Point Phil.
183 P2 Escatrón Spain

Fence Lake

215 H4 Fence Lake U.S.A.
209 H3 Fenelon Falls Canada
185 K4 Fengari mt. Greece
155 E4 Fengcheng Jiangxi China
160 C3 Fengcheng Liaoning China
155 C4 Fengdu China
160 D1 Fengguang China
155 F4 Fenghua China
155 C4 Fenghuang China
155 C4 Fengjie China
155 D6 Fengkai China
155 F6 Fenglin Taiwan
154 F2 Fengnan China
154 E1 Fengning China
154 E3 Fengqing China
155 C5 Fengshan China
156 A1 Fengshui Shan mt. China
155 E6 Fengshun China
154 E3 Fengtai China
153 I5 Fengxian China
    Fengxiang China see Luobei
155 E4 Fengxin China
154 E3 Fengyang China
154 D1 Fengzhen China
154 D2 Fen He r. China
149 G5 Feni Bangl.
119 F2 Feni Islands P.N.G.
183 F5 Fenille, Col de la pass France
208 B4 Fennimore U.S.A.
195 E5 Fenoarivo Atsinanana Madag.
209 F4 Fenton U.S.A.
154 D2 Fenxi China
154 D2 Fenyang China
155 E5 Fenyi China
187 E6 Feodosiya Ukr.
184 B6 Fer, Cap de c. Alg.
    Férai Greece see Feres
143 E3 Ferdows Iran
136 B2 Feres Greece
    Fergana Uzbek. see Farg'ona
141 H4 Fergana Too Tizmegi mts Kyrg.
209 G4 Fergus Canada
216 D2 Fergus Falls U.S.A.
119 F2 Fergusson Island P.N.G.
184 C7 Fériana Tunisia
185 I3 Ferizaj Kosovo
192 B4 Ferkessédougou Côte d'Ivoire
184 E3 Fermo Italy
207 G3 Fermont Canada
183 M2 Fermoselle Spain
175 J5 Fermoy Ireland
230 □ Fernandina, Isla i. Galapagos Is Ecuador
219 D6 Fernandina Beach U.S.A.
232 B8 Fernando de Magallanes, Parque Nacional nat. park Chile
239 G6 Fernando de Noronha i. Brazil
234 B3 Fernandópolis Brazil
212 B1 Ferndale U.S.A.
173 F7 Ferndown U.K.
204 F5 Fernie Canada
125 G2 Fernlee Australia
214 C2 Fernley U.S.A.
221 F4 Fernridge U.S.A.
175 L5 Ferns Ireland
212 C2 Fernwood U.S.A.
184 D2 Ferrara Italy
234 B3 Ferreiros Brazil
217 F6 Ferriday U.S.A.
184 C4 Ferro, Capo c. Sardinia Italy
183 L1 Ferrol Spain
215 G2 Ferron U.S.A.
140 D1 Fershampenuaz Rus. Fed.
    Ferwerd Neth. see Ferwert
178 D1 Ferwert Neth.
192 B1 Fès Morocco
195 B4 Feshi Dem. Rep. Congo
205 J5 Fessenden U.S.A.
217 F4 Festus U.S.A.
174 □ Fethaland, Point of U.K.
175 K5 Fethard Ireland
138 B3 Fethiye Turkey
140 C4 Fetisovo Kazakh.
174 □ Fetlar i. U.K.
175 F4 Fettercairn U.K.
179 J5 Feucht Germany
179 I5 Feuchtwangen Germany
207 F2 Feuilles, Rivière aux r. Canada
156 C1 Fevral'sk Rus. Fed.
139 F3 Fevzipaşa Turkey
143 H2 Feyzābād Afgh.
143 I3 Feyzābād Iran
173 D5 Ffestiniog U.K.

195 E6 Fianarantsoa Madag.
194 D3 Fichē Eth.
179 K4 Fichtelgebirge hills Germany
197 G4 Ficksburg S. Africa
204 F4 Field B.C. Canada
209 G2 Field Ont. Canada
185 H4 Fier Albania
122 B3 Fiery Creek r. Australia
209 E3 Fife Lake U.S.A.
175 F4 Fife Ness pt U.K.
125 G4 Fifield Australia
208 B3 Fifield U.S.A.
182 F4 Figeac France
183 L2 Figueira da Foz Port.
183 R1 Figueres Spain
192 B1 Figuig Morocco
119 H3 Fiji country Pacific Ocean
224 H6 Filadelfia Costa Rica
232 D2 Filadelfia Para.
127 J3 Filchner Ice Shelf Antarctica
172 G3 Filey U.K.
185 I5 Filippiada Greece
171 K4 Filipstad Sweden
171 J3 Fillan Norway
214 C4 Fillmore CA U.S.A.
215 F2 Fillmore UT U.S.A.
127 K3 Fimbull Ice Shelf Antarctica
221 F2 Finch Canada
174 E3 Findhorn r. U.K.
139 H3 Fındık Turkey
220 B4 Findlay U.S.A.
125 H8 Fingal Australia
206 E5 Finger Lakes U.S.A.
195 D5 Fingoè Moz.
138 C3 Finike Turkey
138 C3 Finike Körfezi b. Turkey
183 L1 Finisterre, Cape Spain
123 A5 Finke watercourse Australia
121 F6 Finke, Mount h. Australia
120 E2 Finke Bay Australia
186 S5 Finland country Europe
171 M4 Finland, Gulf of Europe
204 D3 Finlay r. Canada
204 D3 Finlay, Mount Canada
125 F5 Finley Australia
179 J3 Finne ridge Germany
122 D2 Finnigan, Mount Australia
124 A4 Finniss, Cape Australia
170 L1 Finnsnes Norway
171 K4 Finspång Sweden
175 K3 Fintona U.K.
    Fintown Ireland see Baile na Finne
123 C4 Finucane Range hills Australia
174 C3 Fionn Loch l. U.K.
174 B4 Fionnphort U.K.
126 A6 Fiordland National Park N.Z.
139 G2 Fırat r. Turkey alt. Al Furāt (Iraq/Syria), conv. Euphrates
214 B3 Firebaugh U.S.A.
205 I2 Firedrake Lake Canada
221 G4 Fire Island National Seashore nature res. U.S.A.
    Firenze Italy see Florence
139 J6 Firk, Sha'ib watercourse Iraq
235 K2 Firmat Arg.
182 G4 Firminy France
179 I6 Firngrund reg. Germany
177 P2 Firovo Rus. Fed.
148 B3 Firoza Pak.
148 D4 Firozabad India
143 G3 Firozkoh reg. Afgh.
148 C3 Firozpur India
221 H2 First Connecticut Lake U.S.A.
122 D2 First Three Mile Opening sea chan. Australia
142 D4 Fīrūzābād Iran
137 I4 Fīrūzkūh Iran
179 I5 Fischbach Germany
195 B6 Fish watercourse Namibia
196 D5 Fish r. S. Africa
121 E6 Fisher (abandoned) Australia
127 I6 Fisher Bay Antarctica
221 H4 Fisherman Island U.S.A.
221 H4 Fishers Island U.S.A.
205 M2 Fisher Strait Canada
173 C6 Fishguard U.K.
204 E2 Fish Lake Canada
208 A2 Fish Lake MN U.S.A.
215 G2 Fish Lake UT U.S.A.
209 F4 Fish Point U.S.A.
127 J3 Fiske, Cape Antarctica
178 B5 Fismes France
183 L1 Fisterra Spain

    Fisterra, Cabo c. Spain see Finisterre, Cape
221 H3 Fitchburg U.S.A.
205 K6 Fitzgerald Canada
219 D6 Fitzgerald U.S.A.
124 B4 Fitzgerald Bay Australia
121 B7 Fitzgerald River National Park Australia
122 C7 Fitz Roy Arg.
120 C3 Fitzroy r. Australia
118 C3 Fitzroy Crossing Australia
209 G3 Fitzwilliam Island Canada
175 K3 Fivemiletown U.K.
184 D2 Fivizzano Italy
195 C4 Fizi Dem. Rep. Congo
171 J3 Flå Norway
197 H5 Flagstaff S. Africa
215 G4 Flagstaff U.S.A.
221 H2 Flagstaff Lake U.S.A.
206 E2 Flaherty Island Canada
208 B3 Flambeau r. U.S.A.
172 G3 Flamborough Head U.K.
179 K2 Fläming hills Germany
213 E3 Flaming Gorge Reservoir U.S.A.
196 D5 Flaminksvlei salt pan S. Africa
178 A3 Flanders reg. Europe
178 A4 Flandre reg. France
174 A2 Flannan Isles U.K.
170 K2 Flåsjön l. Sweden
209 E4 Flat r. U.S.A.
212 D2 Flathead Lake U.S.A.
126 E4 Flat Point N.Z.
119 E3 Flattery, Cape Australia
212 A1 Flattery, Cape U.S.A.
179 J2 Fleetmark Germany
123 D4 Fleetwood Australia
173 D4 Fleetwood U.K.
221 F4 Fleetwood U.S.A.
171 I4 Flekkefjord Norway
221 E3 Fleming U.S.A.
220 B5 Flemingsburg U.S.A.
239 G2 Flemish Cap sea feature N. Atlantic Ocean
171 L4 Flen Sweden
176 D3 Flensburg Germany
182 D2 Flers France
209 G3 Flesherton Canada
205 H2 Fletcher Lake Canada
209 F3 Fletcher Pond l. U.S.A.
119 E3 Flinders r. Australia
118 B5 Flinders Bay Australia
124 B5 Flinders Chase National Park Australia
122 D2 Flinders Group National Park Australia
124 A4 Flinders Island S.A. Australia
125 H7 Flinders Island Tas. Australia
122 E3 Flinders Passage Australia
124 C3 Flinders Ranges mts Australia
124 C3 Flinders Ranges National Park Australia
122 E3 Flinders Reefs Australia
205 I4 Flin Flon Canada
173 D4 Flint U.K.
209 F4 Flint U.S.A.
219 C6 Flint r. GA U.S.A.
209 F4 Flint r. MI U.S.A.
237 I5 Flint Island Kiribati
125 H1 Flinton Australia
171 K3 Flisa Norway
172 E2 Flodden U.K.
179 L4 Flöha Germany
179 L4 Flöha r. Germany
127 I4 Flood Range mts Antarctica
208 A2 Floodwood U.S.A.
208 E2 Flora r. Australia
219 B4 Flora U.S.A.
182 F4 Florac France
179 E5 Florange France
122 D3 Flora Reef Australia
209 F4 Florence Canada
184 D3 Florence Italy
219 C5 Florence AL U.S.A.
215 G5 Florence AZ U.S.A.
217 D4 Florence KS U.S.A.
220 C5 Florence OH U.S.A.
213 A3 Florence OR U.S.A.
219 E5 Florence SC U.S.A.
215 G5 Florence Junction U.S.A.
221 J1 Florenceville Canada
233 I4 Florencia Col.
178 C4 Florennes Belgium
232 C6 Florentino Ameghino, Embalse resr Arg.
235 K2 Flores r. Arg.
166 A6 Flores i. Azores

225 G4 Flores Guat.
151 E7 Flores i. Indon.
151 D7 Flores, Laut sea Indon.
234 C1 Flores de Goiás Brazil
    Flores Sea sea Indon. see Flores, Laut
231 K5 Floresta Brazil
231 J5 Floriano Brazil
233 G3 Florianópolis Brazil
235 L2 Florida Uruguay
219 D6 Florida state U.S.A.
223 H4 Florida, Straits of Bahamas/U.S.A.
219 D7 Florida Bay U.S.A.
219 D7 Florida City U.S.A.
119 G2 Florida Islands Solomon Is
211 J7 Florida Keys is U.S.A.
185 I4 Florina Greece
171 I3 Florø Norway
207 H3 Flour Lake Canada
208 A4 Floyd IA U.S.A.
220 C6 Floyd VA U.S.A.
215 F4 Floyd, Mount U.S.A.
217 C5 Floydada U.S.A.
119 E3 Fly r. P.N.G.
220 C5 Fly U.S.A.
185 H3 Foča Bos.-Herz.
174 E3 Fochabers U.K.
197 G3 Fochville S. Africa
185 L2 Focşani Romania
155 D6 Fogang China
184 F4 Foggia Italy
192 □ Fogo i. Cape Verde
207 J4 Fogo Island Canada
174 D2 Foinaven h. U.K.
182 E5 Foix France
170 K2 Folda sea chan. Norway
170 K2 Foldereid Norway
170 J2 Foldfjorden sea chan. Norway
185 K6 Folegandros i. Greece
209 F1 Foleyet Canada
184 E3 Foligno Italy
173 I6 Folkestone U.K.
173 G5 Folkingham U.K.
219 D6 Folkston U.S.A.
171 J3 Folldal Norway
184 D3 Follonica Italy
214 B2 Folsom Lake U.S.A.
187 G6 Fomin Rus. Fed.
186 I2 Fominskiy Rus. Fed.
169 O4 Fominskoye Rus. Fed.
205 H3 Fond-du-Lac Canada
205 I3 Fond du Lac r. Canada
208 C4 Fond du Lac U.S.A.
183 L2 Fondevila Spain
184 E4 Fondi Italy
184 C4 Fonni Sardinia Italy
224 H5 Fonseca, Golfo do b. Central America
207 F3 Fontanges Canada
204 E3 Fontas Canada
204 E3 Fontas r. Canada
230 E4 Fonte Boa Brazil
182 D3 Fontenay-le-Comte France
170 D1 Fontur pt Iceland
209 H3 Foot's Bay Canada
154 C3 Foping China
125 H4 Forbes Australia
212 C1 Forbes, Mount Canada
179 J5 Forchheim Germany
207 G2 Ford r. Canada
208 D2 Ford r. U.S.A.
171 I3 Førde Norway
205 J2 Fore Lake Canada
173 H5 Fordham U.K.
173 F7 Fordingbridge U.K.
127 I3 Ford Range mts Antarctica
125 I4 Fords Bridge Australia
217 E5 Fordyce U.S.A.
192 A4 Forécariah Guinea
173 F7 Foreland hd U.K.
173 D6 Foreland Point U.K.
204 D4 Foresight Mountain Canada
209 G4 Forest Canada
217 F5 Forest MS U.S.A.
220 B4 Forest OH U.S.A.
122 C3 Forest Creek r. Australia
221 G3 Forest Dale U.S.A.
125 G5 Forest Hill Australia
125 H9 Forestier, Cape Australia
125 H9 Forestier Peninsula Australia
208 A3 Forest Lake U.S.A.
219 C5 Forest Park U.S.A.
220 E2 Forestville Canada
175 F4 Forfar U.K.
212 A2 Forks U.S.A.
221 E4 Forksville U.S.A.
184 E2 Forlì Italy

173 D4 Formby U.K.
183 Q3 Formentera i. Spain
183 R3 Formentor, Cap de c. Spain
234 D3 Formiga Brazil
232 E3 Formosa Arg.
234 C1 Formosa Brazil
231 G6 Formosa, Serra hills Brazil
234 D1 Formoso r. Brazil
174 E3 Forres U.K.
125 E7 Forrest Vic. Australia
121 E6 Forrest W.A. Australia
208 C5 Forreston U.S.A.
171 L3 Fors Sweden
119 E3 Forsayth Australia
170 M2 Forsnäs Sweden
171 M3 Forssa Fin.
125 J4 Forster Australia
217 E4 Forsyth MO U.S.A.
212 F2 Forsyth MT U.S.A.
209 I1 Forsythe Canada
123 C4 Forsyth Range hills Australia
148 C3 Fort Abbas Pak.
206 D3 Fort Albany Canada
231 K4 Fortaleza Brazil
215 H5 Fort Apache U.S.A.
205 G4 Fort Assiniboine Canada
208 C4 Fort Atkinson U.S.A.
174 D3 Fort Augustus U.K.
197 G6 Fort Beaufort S. Africa
212 E2 Fort Benton U.S.A.
205 H3 Fort Black Canada
214 A2 Fort Bragg U.S.A.
    Fort-Chimo Canada see Kuujjuaq
205 G3 Fort Chipewyan Canada
217 D5 Fort Cobb Reservoir U.S.A.
213 F3 Fort Collins U.S.A.
209 I3 Fort-Coulonge Canada
221 F2 Fort Covington U.S.A.
217 C6 Fort Davis U.S.A.
223 L6 Fort-de-France Martinique
219 C5 Fort Deposit U.S.A.
216 E3 Fort Dodge U.S.A.
121 B4 Fortescue r. Australia
216 E1 Fort Frances Canada
    Fort George Canada see Chisasibi
202 F3 Fort Good Hope Canada
174 D4 Forth r. U.K.
175 F4 Forth, Firth of est. U.K.
215 E2 Fortification Range mts U.S.A.
232 D2 Fortín Capitán Demattei Para.
232 D2 Fortín General Mendoza Para.
232 D2 Fortín Madrejón Para.
232 D2 Fortín Pilcomayo Arg.
231 F7 Fortín Ravelo Bol.
231 F7 Fortín Suárez Arana Bol.
221 I1 Fort Kent U.S.A.
219 D7 Fort Lauderdale U.S.A.
204 E2 Fort Liard Canada
205 G3 Fort Mackay Canada
205 G5 Fort Macleod Canada
208 B5 Fort Madison U.S.A.
208 B3 Fort McCoy U.S.A.
205 G3 Fort McMurray Canada
202 E3 Fort McPherson Canada
213 G3 Fort Morgan U.S.A.
219 D7 Fort Myers U.S.A.
204 E3 Fort Nelson Canada
204 E3 Fort Nelson r. Canada
    Fort Norman Canada see Tulita
219 C5 Fort Payne U.S.A.
212 F1 Fort Peck U.S.A.
212 F2 Fort Peck Reservoir U.S.A.
219 D7 Fort Pierce U.S.A.
216 C2 Fort Pierre U.S.A.
204 F2 Fort Providence Canada
205 I4 Fort Qu'Appelle Canada
205 G2 Fort Resolution Canada
122 B7 Fortrose N.Z.
174 D3 Fortrose U.K.
214 A2 Fort Ross U.S.A.
    Fort Rupert Canada see Waskaganish
204 E4 Fort St James Canada
204 E3 Fort St John Canada
205 G4 Fort Saskatchewan Canada
217 E4 Fort Scott U.S.A.
206 C2 Fort Severn Canada
140 B3 Fort-Shevchenko Kazakh.
204 E2 Fort Simpson Canada
204 F2 Fort Smith Canada
217 E5 Fort Smith U.S.A.

217 C6 Fort Stockton U.S.A.
213 F5 Fort Sumner U.S.A.
213 A3 Fortuna CA U.S.A.
216 C1 Fortuna ND U.S.A.
207 I4 Fortune Bay Canada
204 F3 Fort Vermilion Canada
219 C6 Fort Walton Beach U.S.A.
209 E5 Fort Wayne U.S.A.
174 C4 Fort William U.K.
217 D5 Fort Worth U.S.A.
202 D3 Fort Yukon U.S.A.
142 D5 Forūr, Jazīreh-ye i. Iran
170 □ Forvik Norway
155 D6 Foshan China
184 B2 Fossano Italy
120 D3 Fossil Downs Australia
125 G7 Foster Australia
204 B3 Foster, Mount Canada/U.S.A.
203 P2 Foster Bugt b. Greenland
220 B4 Fostoria U.S.A.
173 G4 Fotherby U.K.
182 D2 Fougères France
174 □ Foula i. U.K.
173 H6 Foulness Point U.K.
147 I4 Foul Point Sri Lanka
126 C4 Foulwind, Cape N.Z.
193 D4 Foumban Cameroon
127 J4 Foundation Ice Stream glacier Antarctica
192 A3 Foundiougne Senegal
208 A4 Fountain U.S.A.
172 F3 Fountains Abbey & Royal Water Garden (NT) tourist site U.K.
182 G2 Fourches, Mont des h. France
215 D4 Four Corners U.S.A.
197 H4 Fouriesburg S. Africa
178 C4 Fourmies France
185 L6 Fournoi i. Greece
208 C2 Fourteen Mile Point U.S.A.
192 A3 Fouta Djallon reg. Guinea
126 A7 Foveaux Strait N.Z.
219 E7 Fowl Cay i. Bahamas
213 F4 Fowler CO U.S.A.
208 D5 Fowler IN U.S.A.
209 E4 Fowler MI U.S.A.
127 I3 Fowler Ice Rise Antarctica
118 D5 Fowlers Bay Australia
121 F7 Fowlers Bay b. Australia
139 L3 Fowman Iran
205 K3 Fox r. Canada
208 C4 Fox r. U.S.A.
204 F4 Fox Creek Canada
172 G3 Foxdale U.K.
203 J3 Foxe Basin g. Canada
203 J3 Foxe Channel Canada
203 K3 Foxe Peninsula Canada
126 C5 Fox Glacier N.Z.
205 G3 Fox Lake Canada
208 C4 Fox Lake U.S.A.
126 E4 Foxton N.Z.
174 D3 Foyers U.K.
175 K3 Foyle r. Ireland/U.K.
175 K2 Foyle, Lough b. Ireland/U.K.
175 I5 Foynes Ireland
195 B5 Foz do Cunene Angola
235 A4 Foz do Iguaçu Brazil
183 Q2 Fraga Spain
234 C3 Franca Brazil
119 G3 Français, Récif des rf New Caledonia
182 F3 France country Europe
124 D6 Frances Australia
204 D2 Frances r. Canada
204 D2 Frances Lake Canada
204 D2 Frances Lake l. Canada
208 D5 Francesville U.S.A.
195 B4 Franceville Gabon
221 H2 Francis, Lake U.S.A.
216 D3 Francis Case, Lake U.S.A.
225 C2 Francisco I. Madero Coahuila Mex.
224 C2 Francisco I. Madero Durango Mex.
234 D2 Francisco Sá Brazil
195 C6 Francistown Botswana
204 D4 François Lake Canada
121 A5 Francois Peron National Park Australia
213 E3 Francs Peak U.S.A.
178 D1 Franeker Neth.
179 L4 Frankenberg Germany
179 I5 Frankenberg (Eder) Germany
209 F4 Frankenmuth U.S.A.
179 G5 Frankenthal (Pfalz) Germany
179 J4 Frankenwald mts Germany
197 H3 Frankfort S. Africa

204 B3 **Glacier Bay National Park and Preserve** U.S.A.
204 F4 **Glacier National Park** Canada
212 D1 **Glacier National Park** U.S.A.
212 B1 **Glacier Peak** vol. U.S.A.
170 J2 **Gladstad** Norway
119 F4 **Gladstone** Qld Australia
124 C4 **Gladstone** S.A. Australia
125 H8 **Gladstone** Tas. Australia
208 D3 **Gladstone** U.S.A.
209 E4 **Gladwin** U.S.A.
174 E4 **Glamis** U.K.
179 F5 **Glan** r. Germany
161 J5 **Glan** Phil.
175 I5 **Glanaruddery Mountains** Ireland
179 G2 **Glandorf** Germany
172 F2 **Glanton** U.K.
209 G4 **Glanworth** Canada
174 D5 **Glasgow** U.K.
219 C4 **Glasgow** KY U.S.A.
212 F1 **Glasgow** MT U.S.A.
220 D6 **Glasgow** VA U.S.A.
205 H4 **Glaslyn** Canada
214 C3 **Glass Mountain** U.S.A.
173 E6 **Glastonbury** U.K.
179 K4 **Glauchau** Germany
132 G4 **Glazov** Rus. Fed.
187 H4 **Glazunovka** Rus. Fed.
177 O3 **Glazunovo** Rus. Fed.
221 K1 **Glen** U.S.A.
174 C3 **Glen Affric** val. U.K.
209 G2 **Glen Afton** Canada
126 E2 **Glen Afton** N.Z.
197 H1 **Glen Alpine Dam** S. Africa
175 J4 **Glenamaddy** Ireland
209 E3 **Glen Arbor** U.S.A.
126 C6 **Glenavy** N.Z.
174 C3 **Glen Cannich** val. U.K.
213 E4 **Glen Canyon** gorge U.S.A.
215 G3 **Glen Canyon National Recreation Area** park U.S.A.
174 E4 **Glen Clova** val. U.K.
124 D6 **Glencoe** Australia
209 G4 **Glencoe** Canada
197 I4 **Glencoe** S. Africa
174 C4 **Glen Coe** val. U.K.
209 E2 **Glendale** Canada
215 F5 **Glendale** AZ U.S.A.
214 C4 **Glendale** CA U.S.A.
215 E3 **Glendale** NV U.S.A.
215 F3 **Glendale** UT U.S.A.
220 D4 **Glendale Lake** U.S.A.
125 I4 **Glen Davis** Australia
123 E4 **Glenden** Australia
212 F2 **Glendive** U.S.A.
205 G4 **Glendon** Canada
213 F3 **Glendo Reservoir** U.S.A.
124 D6 **Glenelg** r. Australia
175 F4 **Glen Esk** val. U.K.
174 A5 **Glengad Head** Ireland
174 C3 **Glen Garry** val. Scotland U.K.
174 D4 **Glen Garry** val. Scotland U.K.
175 K3 **Glengavlen** Ireland
123 B5 **Glengyle** Australia
125 I2 **Glen Innes** Australia
174 D6 **Glenluce** U.K.
174 D4 **Glen Lyon** val. U.K.
174 D3 **Glen More** val. U.K.
125 H1 **Glenmorgan** Australia
174 D3 **Glen Moriston** val. U.K.
215 G6 **Glenn, Mount** U.S.A.
202 D3 **Glennallen** U.S.A.
174 C4 **Glen Nevis** val. U.K.
209 F3 **Glennie** U.S.A.
221 E6 **Glenns** U.S.A.
204 C3 **Glenora** Canada
122 C3 **Glenore** Australia
123 B4 **Glenormiston** Australia
221 F2 **Glen Robertson** Canada
174 E4 **Glenrothes** U.K.
221 G3 **Glens Falls** U.S.A.
174 E4 **Glen Shee** val. U.K.
174 C3 **Glen Shiel** val. U.K.
175 J3 **Glenties** Ireland
175 K2 **Glenveagh National Park** Ireland
220 C5 **Glenville** U.S.A.
217 E5 **Glenwood** AR U.S.A.
215 H5 **Glenwood** NM U.S.A.
213 F4 **Glenwood Springs** U.S.A.
208 B2 **Glidden** U.S.A.
179 J1 **Glinde** Germany
177 I5 **Gliwice** Poland
215 G5 **Globe** U.S.A.
177 H5 **Głogów** Poland
170 K2 **Glomfjord** Norway
171 J4 **Glomma** r. Norway
195 E5 **Glorieuses, Îles** is Indian Ocean

125 I3 **Gloucester** Australia
173 E6 **Gloucester** U.K.
221 H3 **Gloucester** MA U.S.A.
221 E6 **Gloucester** VA U.S.A.
221 F3 **Gloversville** U.S.A.
179 K2 **Glöwen** Germany
158 D1 **Glubinnoye** Rus. Fed.
152 L1 **Glubokiy** Rus. Fed.
187 G6 **Glubokiy** Rus. Fed.
141 J2 **Glubokoye** Kazakh.
179 H1 **Glückstadt** Germany
170 □ **Gluggarnir** h. Faroe Is
173 F4 **Glusburn** U.K.
187 H5 **Gmelinka** Rus. Fed.
176 G6 **Gmünd** Austria
176 F7 **Gmunden** Austria
171 L3 **Gnarp** Sweden
179 H1 **Gnarrenburg** Germany
177 H4 **Gniezno** Poland
121 B7 **Gnowangerup** Australia
121 B6 **Gnows Nest Range** hills Australia
147 J3 **Goa** India
147 J3 **Goa** state India
196 B3 **Goageb** Namibia
125 I6 **Goalen Head** Australia
149 G4 **Goalpara** India
174 C5 **Goat Fell** h. U.K.
194 E3 **Goba** Eth.
195 B6 **Gobabis** Namibia
196 C3 **Gobas** Namibia
235 K1 **Gobernador Crespo** Arg.
235 I3 **Gobernador Duval** Arg.
232 B7 **Gobernador Gregores** Arg.
150 C2 **Gobi Desert** Mongolia
159 D8 **Gobō** Japan
179 E3 **Goch** Germany
195 B6 **Gochas** Namibia
173 G6 **Godalming** U.K.
147 I2 **Godavari** r. India
147 I2 **Godavari, Mouths of the** India
207 G4 **Godbout** Canada
214 C3 **Goddard, Mount** U.S.A.
194 E3 **Godere** Eth.
209 G4 **Goderich** Canada
148 C5 **Godhra** India
235 I2 **Godoy Cruz** Arg.
205 K3 **Gods** r. Canada
205 K4 **Gods Lake** Canada
205 L2 **God's Mercy, Bay of** Canada
— **Godthåb** Greenland see **Nuuk**
— **Godwin-Austen, Mount** mt. China/Pakistan see **K2**
178 B3 **Goedereede** Neth.
206 B4 **Goéland, Lac au** l. Canada
207 H2 **Goélands, Lac aux** l. Canada
178 B3 **Goes** Neth.
209 E2 **Goetzville** U.S.A.
215 E4 **Goffs** U.S.A.
209 G2 **Gogama** Canada
208 C2 **Gogebic, Lake** U.S.A.
208 C2 **Gogebic Range** hills U.S.A.
148 D4 **Gohad** India
231 L5 **Goiana** Brazil
234 C2 **Goiandira** Brazil
234 C2 **Goiânia** Brazil
234 B1 **Goiás** Brazil
234 B2 **Goiás** state Brazil
235 B4 **Goio-Erê** Brazil
148 C3 **Gojra** Pak.
147 G2 **Gokak** India
187 L2 **Gökçeada** i. Turkey
138 B2 **Gökçedağ** Turkey
149 G3 **Gokhar La** pass China
138 E1 **Gökirmak** r. Turkey
140 D4 **Goklenkuy, Solonchak** salt l. Turkm.
136 B3 **Gökova Körfezi** b. Turkey
143 F5 **Gokprosh Hills** Pak.
139 F2 **Göksun** Turkey
138 E3 **Göksu Nehri** r. Turkey
195 C5 **Gokwe** Zimbabwe
171 J3 **Gol** Norway
149 E3 **Gola** India
149 H4 **Golaghat** India
143 E4 **Golbāf** Iran
139 F3 **Gölbaşı** Turkey
138 B1 **Gölcük** Turkey
177 K3 **Gołdap** Poland
179 K1 **Goldberg** Germany
125 J2 **Gold Coast** Australia
192 B4 **Gold Coast** coastal area Ghana
204 F4 **Golden** Canada
126 D4 **Golden Bay** N.Z.
179 I3 **Goldene Aue** reg. Germany
214 A3 **Golden Gate National Recreation Area** park U.S.A.
204 D5 **Golden Hinde** mt. Canada

179 G2 **Goldenstedt** Germany
175 J5 **Golden Vale** lowland Ireland
215 D3 **Goldfield** U.S.A.
215 D3 **Gold Point** U.S.A.
219 E5 **Goldsboro** U.S.A.
121 B4 **Goldsworthy (abandoned)** Australia
217 D6 **Goldthwaite** U.S.A.
139 I1 **Göle** Turkey
143 F3 **Golestān** Afgh.
214 C4 **Goleta** U.S.A.
153 I1 **Golets-Davydov, Gora** mt. Rus. Fed.
224 I6 **Golfito** Costa Rica
217 D6 **Goliad** U.S.A.
160 A1 **Golin Baixing** China
139 F1 **Gölköy** Turkey
179 K2 **Golm** Germany
139 J3 **Golmänkhäneh** Iran
150 B3 **Golmud** China
149 H1 **Golmud He** r. China
161 I3 **Golo** i. Phil.
158 I3 **Golovnino** Rus. Fed.
142 C3 **Golpāyegān** Iran
138 C1 **Gölpazarı** Turkey
174 E3 **Golspie** U.K.
141 H1 **Golubovka** Kazakh.
143 F3 **Gol Vardeh** Iran
185 K4 **Golyama Syutkya** mt. Bulg.
185 K4 **Golyam Persenk** mt. Bulg.
— **Golyshi** Rus. Fed. see **Vetluzhskiy**
179 K2 **Golzow** Germany
149 G3 **Gomang Co** salt l. China
149 E4 **Gomati** r. India
162 □ **Gombak, Bukit** h. Sing.
193 D3 **Gombe** Nigeria
195 D4 **Gombe** r. Tanz.
193 D3 **Gombi** Nigeria
225 D2 **Gómez Palacio** Mex.
142 D2 **Gomīshān** Iran
179 J2 **Gommern** Germany
149 F2 **Gomo Co** salt l. China
143 E2 **Gonābād** Iran
223 J5 **Gonaïves** Haiti
197 I1 **Gonarezhou National Park** Zimbabwe
223 J5 **Gonâve, Île de la** i. Haiti
142 D2 **Gonbad-e Kavus** Iran
149 E4 **Gonda** India
148 B5 **Gondal** India
194 D2 **Gonder** Eth.
149 E5 **Gondia** India
138 A1 **Gönen** Turkey
155 D4 **Gong'an** China
149 G3 **Gongbalou** China
155 D5 **Gongcheng** China
155 A4 **Gongga Shan** mt. China
154 A2 **Gonghe** China
154 E1 **Gonghui** China
141 J4 **Gongliu** China
234 E1 **Gongogi** r. Brazil
193 D3 **Gongola** r. Nigeria
125 G3 **Gongolgon** Australia
144 I3 **Gongpoquan** China
155 B4 **Gongquan** China
155 B5 **Gongwang Shan** mts China
— **Gongxian** China see **Gongquan**
154 D3 **Gongyi** China
160 C2 **Gongzhuling** China
197 H6 **Gonubie** S. Africa
225 E3 **Gonzáles** Mex.
214 B3 **Gonzales** CA U.S.A.
217 D6 **Gonzales** TX U.S.A.
235 J2 **González Moreno** Arg.
156 B1 **Gonzha** Rus. Fed.
221 E6 **Goochland** U.S.A.
127 J6 **Goodenough, Cape** Antarctica
119 F2 **Goodenough Island** P.N.G.
209 H3 **Gooderham** Canada
196 C7 **Good Hope, Cape of** S. Africa
213 D3 **Gooding** U.S.A.
217 C4 **Goodland** U.S.A.
125 G2 **Goodooga** Australia
173 G4 **Goole** U.K.
125 F5 **Goolgowi** Australia
125 H4 **Goolma** Australia
125 H4 **Gooloogong** Australia
124 C5 **Goolwa** Australia
121 B6 **Goomalling** Australia
125 F7 **Goombalie** Australia
125 I2 **Goondiwindi** Australia
121 C6 **Goongarrie, Lake** salt flat Australia
121 C6 **Goongarrie National Park** Australia
123 D4 **Goonyella** Australia

121 B6 **Goorly, Lake** salt flat Australia
207 H3 **Goose** r. Canada
213 B3 **Goose Lake** U.S.A.
147 H3 **Gooty** India
152 C5 **Gopeshwar** India
176 D6 **Göppingen** Germany
149 E4 **Gorakhpur** India
186 G3 **Goražde** Bos.-Herz.
186 G3 **Gorchukha** Rus. Fed.
224 I5 **Gorda, Punta** pt Nicaragua
219 E7 **Gorda Cay** i. Bahamas
138 B2 **Gördes** Turkey
177 O4 **Gordeyevka** Rus. Fed.
157 F9 **Gordon** r. Australia
175 F5 **Gordon** U.K.
125 G9 **Gordon, Lake** Australia
120 E3 **Gordon Downs (abandoned)** Australia
205 G2 **Gordon Lake** Canada
220 D5 **Gordon Lake** U.S.A.
220 D5 **Gordonsville** U.S.A.
193 D4 **Goré** Chad
194 D3 **Gorē** Eth.
126 B7 **Gore** N.Z.
209 F3 **Gore Bay** Canada
174 E5 **Gorebridge** U.K.
138 E2 **Göreme Milli Parkı** nat. park Turkey
175 L5 **Gorey** Ireland
143 E4 **Gorg** Iran
142 D2 **Gorgān** Iran
137 I3 **Gorgān, Khalīj-e** Iran
121 B4 **Gorge Range** hills Australia
233 H4 **Gorgona, Isla** i. Col.
221 H2 **Gorham** U.S.A.
187 H7 **Gori** Georgia
178 C3 **Gorinchem** Neth.
139 K2 **Goris** Armenia
184 E2 **Gorizia** Italy
— **Gor'kiy** Rus. Fed. see **Nizhniy Novgorod**
187 H5 **Gor'ko-Solenoye, Ozero** l. Rus. Fed.
186 G3 **Gor'kovskoye Vodokhranilishche** resr Rus. Fed.
141 J1 **Gor'koye, Ozero** salt l. Rus. Fed.
177 J6 **Gorlice** Poland
176 G5 **Görlitz** Germany
148 D5 **Gormi** India
185 K3 **Gorna Oryakhovitsa** Bulg.
185 I2 **Gornji Milanovac** Serbia
185 G3 **Gornji Vakuf** Bos.-Herz.
141 K2 **Gorno-Altaysk** Rus. Fed.
158 C2 **Gornozavodsk** Rus. Fed.
141 J2 **Gornyak** Rus. Fed.
158 C2 **Gornyy** Primorskiy Kray Rus. Fed.
187 I5 **Gornyy Saratovskaya Oblast'** Rus. Fed.
187 H5 **Gornyy Balykley** Rus. Fed.
158 C1 **Gornyye Klyuchi** Rus. Fed.
186 G3 **Gorodets** Rus. Fed.
187 H5 **Gorodishche** Rus. Fed.
— **Gorodok** Rus. Fed. see **Zakamensk**
187 G6 **Gorodovikovsk** Rus. Fed.
119 E2 **Goroka** P.N.G.
124 D6 **Goroke** Australia
186 G3 **Gorokhovets** Rus. Fed.
192 B3 **Gorom Gorom** Burkina
195 D5 **Gorongosa** Moz.
151 E6 **Gorontalo** Indon.
187 F5 **Gorshechnoye** Rus. Fed.
175 J4 **Gort** Ireland
— **Gortahork** Ireland see **Gort an Choirce**
175 J2 **Gort an Choirce** Ireland
234 D1 **Gorutuba** r. Brazil
143 E4 **Gorveh** Iran
187 F6 **Goryachiy Klyuch** Rus. Fed.
179 K2 **Görzke** Germany
176 G4 **Gorzów Wielkopolski** Poland
125 I4 **Gosford** Australia
172 F2 **Gosforth** U.K.
209 E5 **Goshen** IN U.S.A.
221 F4 **Goshen** NY U.S.A.
158 G4 **Goshogawara** Japan
179 I3 **Goslar** Germany
140 C4 **Goşoba** Turkm.
184 F2 **Gospić** Croatia
173 F7 **Gosport** U.K.
185 I4 **Gostivar** Macedonia
— **Göteborg** Sweden see **Gothenburg**
171 K4 **Götene** Sweden
179 I4 **Gotha** Germany
171 J4 **Gothenburg** Sweden

216 C3 **Gothenburg** U.S.A.
171 L4 **Gotland** i. Sweden
157 C6 **Gotō-rettō** is Japan
185 J4 **Gotse Delchev** Bulg.
171 L4 **Gotska Sandön** i. Sweden
159 C7 **Gōtsu** Japan
179 H3 **Göttingen** Germany
204 E4 **Gott Peak** Canada
140 C5 **Goturdepe** Turkm.
160 A3 **Goubangzi** China
178 C2 **Gouda** Neth.
192 A3 **Goudiri** Senegal
193 D3 **Goudoumaria** Niger
209 E1 **Goudreau** Canada
239 I8 **Gough Island** S. Atlantic Ocean
207 F4 **Gouin, Réservoir** resr Canada
209 E2 **Goulais River** Canada
125 H5 **Goulburn** Australia
125 I4 **Goulburn** r. N.S.W. Australia
125 F6 **Goulburn** r. Vic. Australia
118 D3 **Goulburn Islands** Australia
209 E2 **Gould City** U.S.A.
192 B3 **Goundam** Mali
193 D4 **Goundi** Chad
194 D3 **Gouré** Niger
196 D7 **Gourits** r. S. Africa
192 B3 **Gourma-Rharous** Mali
182 E2 **Gournay-en-Bray** France
125 H6 **Gourock Range** mts Australia
178 A5 **Goussainville** France
221 F2 **Gouverneur** U.S.A.
205 H5 **Govenlock** Canada
234 E2 **Governador Valadares** Brazil
161 J5 **Governor Generoso** Phil.
219 E7 **Governor's Harbour** Bahamas
150 B2 **Govĭ Altayn Nuruu** mts Mongolia
149 E4 **Govind Ballash Pant Sagar** resr India
148 D3 **Govind Sagar** resr India
— **Govurdak** Turkm. see **Magdanly**
220 D3 **Gowanda** U.S.A.
123 D5 **Gowan Range** hills Australia
143 G4 **Gowārān** Afgh.
142 D4 **Gowd-e Aḥmar** Iran
173 C6 **Gower** pen. U.K.
209 G2 **Gowganda** Canada
175 K4 **Gowna, Lough** l. Ireland
232 E3 **Goya** Arg.
139 K1 **Göyçay** Azer.
139 H2 **Göynük** Turkey
159 G5 **Goyō-zan** mt. Japan
139 L2 **Göytäpä** Azer.
143 F3 **Gozareh** Iran
— **Gōzareh** Afgh. see **Gozareh**
149 E2 **Gozha Co** salt l. China
184 F6 **Gozo** i. Malta
197 F6 **Graaff-Reinet** S. Africa
— **Graaf-Reinet** S. Africa see **Graaff-Reinet**
196 C6 **Graafwater** S. Africa
179 I4 **Grabfeld** plain Germany
192 B4 **Grabo** Côte d'Ivoire
196 C7 **Grabouw** S. Africa
179 J1 **Grabow** Germany
184 F2 **Gračac** Croatia
209 I2 **Gracefield** Canada
140 C1 **Grachevka** Rus. Fed.
141 I2 **Grachi** Kazakh.
224 G5 **Gracias** Hond.
179 K3 **Gräfenhainichen** Germany
179 J5 **Grafenwöhr** Germany
125 J2 **Grafton** Australia
216 D1 **Grafton** ND U.S.A.
208 D4 **Grafton** WI U.S.A.
220 C5 **Grafton** WV U.S.A.
122 D3 **Grafton, Cape** Australia
215 E2 **Grafton, Mount** U.S.A.
122 D3 **Grafton Passage** Australia
217 D5 **Graham** U.S.A.
215 H5 **Graham, Mount** U.S.A.
179 I3 **Graham Bell Island** i. Rus. Fed. see **Greem-Bell, Ostrov**
204 C4 **Graham Island** B.C. Canada
203 I2 **Graham Island** Nunavut Canada
221 I2 **Graham Lake** U.S.A.
197 G6 **Grahamstown** S. Africa
171 K4 **Graigue** Ireland
175 L5 **Graigue** Ireland
192 A4 **Grain Coast** Liberia

231 I5 **Grajaú** Brazil
174 B1 **Gralisgeir** i. U.K.
185 I4 **Grammos** mt. Greece
174 D4 **Grampian Mountains** U.K.
125 E6 **Grampians National Park** Australia
196 C5 **Granaatboskolk** S. Africa
233 I4 **Granada** Col.
224 H6 **Granada** Nicaragua
183 O4 **Granada** Spain
217 C4 **Granada** U.S.A.
175 K4 **Granard** Ireland
235 I3 **Gran Bajo Salitroso** salt flat Arg.
207 I4 **Granby** Canada
192 A2 **Gran Canaria** i. Canary Is
232 D3 **Gran Chaco** reg. Arg./Para.
208 D2 **Grand** MI U.S.A.
216 E3 **Grand** r. MO U.S.A.
219 E7 **Grand Bahama** i. Bahamas
207 I4 **Grand Bank** Canada
239 F3 **Grand Banks of Newfoundland** sea feature N. Atlantic Ocean
192 B4 **Grand-Bassam** Côte d'Ivoire
— **Grand Bay** Canada see **Grand Bay-Westfield**
207 G4 **Grand Bay-Westfield** Canada
209 G4 **Grand Bend** Canada
— **Grand Canal** canal China see **Da Yunhe**
175 K4 **Grand Canal** Ireland
215 F3 **Grand Canyon** U.S.A.
215 F3 **Grand Canyon** gorge U.S.A.
215 F3 **Grand Canyon National Park** U.S.A.
223 H5 **Grand Cayman** i. Cayman Is
205 G4 **Grand Centre** Canada
212 C2 **Grand Coulee** U.S.A.
235 I3 **Grande** r. Arg.
231 F7 **Grande** r. Bol.
231 I6 **Grande** r. Bahia Brazil
234 B2 **Grande** r. São Paulo Brazil
235 L3 **Grande, Arroyo** r. Arg.
232 C8 **Grande, Bahía** b. Arg.
234 D3 **Grande, Ilha** i. Brazil
233 L4 **Grande, Serra** mt. Brazil
204 F4 **Grande Cache** Canada
182 H4 **Grande Casse, Pointe de la** mt. France
— **Grande Comore** i. Comoros see **Njazidja**
204 F3 **Grande Prairie** Canada
192 B1 **Grand Erg Occidental** des. Alg.
192 C2 **Grand Erg Oriental** des. Alg.
207 H4 **Grande-Rivière** Canada
212 C2 **Grande Ronde** r. U.S.A.
232 C4 **Grandes, Salinas** salt flat Arg.
207 G4 **Grande-Vallée** Canada
207 G4 **Grand Falls** N.B. Canada
207 I4 **Grand Falls-Windsor** Nfld Canada
204 F5 **Grand Forks** Canada
216 D2 **Grand Forks** U.S.A.
221 F3 **Grand Gorge** U.S.A.
221 J2 **Grand Harbour** Canada
208 D4 **Grand Haven** U.S.A.
204 F2 **Grandin** L. Canada
152 G1 **Grandioznyy, Pik** mt. Rus. Fed.
216 D3 **Grand Island** NE U.S.A.
208 D2 **Grand Island** i. MI U.S.A.
217 F6 **Grand Isle** LA U.S.A.
221 I1 **Grand Isle** ME U.S.A.
215 H2 **Grand Junction** U.S.A.
192 B4 **Grand-Lahou** Côte d'Ivoire
207 H3 **Grand Lake** Nfld Canada
207 I4 **Grand Lake** Nfld Canada
217 E6 **Grand Lake** LA U.S.A.
221 J2 **Grand Lake** ME U.S.A.
209 F3 **Grand Lake** MI U.S.A.
221 I1 **Grand Lake Matagamon** U.S.A.
220 A4 **Grand Lake St Marys** U.S.A.
221 I1 **Grand Lake Seboeis** U.S.A.
221 J2 **Grand Lake Stream** U.S.A.
209 E4 **Grand Ledge** U.S.A.
207 G5 **Grand Manan Island** Canada
209 E2 **Grand Marais** MI U.S.A.
208 B2 **Grand Marais** MN U.S.A.
207 F4 **Grand-Mère** Canada
183 L3 **Grândola** Port.
119 G3 **Grand Passage** New Caledonia
208 C2 **Grand Portage** U.S.A.
205 J4 **Grand Rapids** Canada
209 E4 **Grand Rapids** MI U.S.A.

I

J

197 F1 **Khudumelapye** Botswana
142 B5 **Khuff** Saudi Arabia
143 F5 **Khun Lab, Ra's** pt Iran
196 D3 **Khuis** Botswana
141 G4 **Khŭjand** Tajik.
162 C2 **Khu Khan** Thai.
143 G3 **Khulm** r. Afgh.
149 G5 **Khulna** Bangl.
139 I1 **Khulo** Georgia
197 G3 **Khuma** S. Africa
148 C2 **Khunjerab Pass** China/Pakistan
142 C3 **Khunsar** Iran
149 F5 **Khunti** India
162 A1 **Khun Yuam** Thai.
143 E3 **Khūr** Iran
143 D4 **Khurai** India
142 D5 **Khūran** sea chan. Iran
143 H3 **Khurd, Koh-i-** mt. Afgh.
149 F5 **Khurda** India
148 D3 **Khurja** India
143 F3 **Khurmalik** Afgh.
156 E2 **Khurmuli** Rus. Fed.
139 I6 **Khurr, Wādī al** watercourse Saudi Arabia
137 I5 **Khūrrāb** Iran
148 C2 **Khushab** Pak.
139 L3 **Khūshāvar** Iran
143 E4 **Khushk Rud** Iran
143 F3 **Khuspas** Afgh.
187 B5 **Khust** Ukr.
138 D6 **Khutmīyah, Mamarr al** pass Egypt
197 G3 **Khutsong** S. Africa
156 E2 **Khutu** r. Rus. Fed.
143 G5 **Khuzdar** Pak.
143 F3 **Khvāf** Iran
137 G3 **Khvājeh** Iran
187 I4 **Khvalynsk** Rus. Fed.
142 D3 **Khvor** Iran
143 E3 **Khvord Nārvan** Iran
142 C4 **Khvormūj** Iran
140 B1 **Khvorostyanka** Rus. Fed.
139 K3 **Khvosh Maqām** Iran
142 B2 **Khvoy** Iran
186 E3 **Khvoynaya** Rus. Fed.
162 A2 **Khwae Noi** r. Thai.
143 F4 **Khwaja Ali** Afgh.
143 H2 **Khwaja Muhammad Range** mts Afgh.
148 B2 **Khyber Pass** Afgh./Pak.
125 I5 **Kiama** Australia
161 J5 **Kiamba** Phil.
195 C4 **Kiambi** Dem. Rep. Congo
217 E5 **Kiamichi** r. U.S.A.
170 O2 **Kiantajärvi** l. Fin.
142 D2 **Kiāseh** Iran
203 L2 **Kiatassuaq** i. Greenland
161 J5 **Kibawe** Phil.
195 D4 **Kibaya** Tanz.
195 D4 **Kibiti** Tanz.
195 C4 **Kibombo** Dem. Rep. Congo
195 D4 **Kibondo** Tanz.
185 I4 **Kičevo** Macedonia
186 H3 **Kichmengskiy Gorodok** Rus. Fed.
140 C5 **Kiçi Balkan Daglary** h. Turkm.
192 C3 **Kidal** Mali
173 E5 **Kidderminster** U.K.
194 D3 **Kidepo Valley National Park** Uganda
192 A3 **Kidira** Senegal
148 D2 **Kidmang** India
126 F3 **Kidnappers, Cape** N.Z.
173 E4 **Kidsgrove** U.K.
176 E3 **Kiel** Germany
208 C4 **Kiel** U.S.A.
176 D3 **Kiel Canal** Germany
177 J5 **Kielce** Poland
172 E2 **Kielder Water** resr U.K.
176 E3 **Kieler Bucht** b. Germany
195 C5 **Kienge** Dem. Rep. Congo
179 J2 **Kierspe** Germany
187 D5 **Kiev** Ukr.
192 A3 **Kiffa** Mauritania
185 J5 **Kifisia** Greece
139 J4 **Kifrī** Iraq
195 D4 **Kigali** Rwanda
139 H2 **Kiği** Turkey
207 H2 **Kiglapait Mountains** Canada
195 C4 **Kigoma** Tanz.
170 M2 **Kihlanki** Fin.
171 M3 **Kihniö** Fin.
141 H3 **Kihnu** Fin.
170 N2 **Kiiminki** Fin.
159 D8 **Kii-sanchi** mts Japan
159 D8 **Kii-suidō** sea chan. Japan
185 I2 **Kikinda** Serbia
143 F5 **Kikki** Pak.

186 H3 **Kiknur** Rus. Fed.
158 G4 **Kikonai** Japan
195 C4 **Kikondja** Dem. Rep. Congo
119 E2 **Kikori** P.N.G.
119 E2 **Kikori** r. P.N.G.
195 B4 **Kikwit** Dem. Rep. Congo
171 L3 **Kilafors** Sweden
147 H4 **Kilakkarai** India
148 D2 **Kilar** India
214 □² **Kilauea** U.S.A.
214 □² **Kilauea Crater** U.S.A.
174 C5 **Kilbrannan Sound** sea chan. U.K.
160 E3 **Kilchu** N. Korea
175 L4 **Kilcoole** Ireland
175 K4 **Kilcormac** Ireland
125 J1 **Kilcoy** Australia
175 L4 **Kildare** Ireland
170 P1 **Kil'dinstroy** Rus. Fed.
195 B4 **Kilembe** Dem. Rep. Congo
174 C5 **Kilfinan** U.K.
217 E5 **Kilgore** U.S.A.
172 E2 **Kilham** U.K.
195 D4 **Kilifi** Kenya
195 D4 **Kilimanjaro** vol. Tanz.
195 D4 **Kilimanjaro National Park** Tanz.
119 F2 **Kilinailau Islands** P.N.G.
195 D4 **Kilindoni** Tanz.
119 F4 **Kilingi-Nõmme** Estonia
139 F3 **Kilis** Turkey
187 D6 **Kiliya** Ukr.
175 I5 **Kilkee** Ireland
175 M3 **Kilkeel** U.K.
175 K5 **Kilkenny** Ireland
173 C7 **Kilkhampton** U.K.
185 J4 **Kilkis** Greece
175 I3 **Kilala** Ireland
175 I3 **Kilala Bay** Ireland
175 J5 **Killaloe** Ireland
209 I3 **Killaloe Station** Canada
205 G4 **Killam** Canada
120 E3 **Killarney** Australia
125 J2 **Killarney** Australia
209 G3 **Killarney** Canada
175 I5 **Killarney** Ireland
175 I6 **Killarney National Park** Ireland
209 G2 **Killarney Provincial Park** Canada
175 I4 **Killary Harbour** b. Ireland
217 D6 **Killeen** U.S.A.
175 K5 **Killenaule** Ireland
175 J4 **Killimor** Ireland
174 D4 **Killin** U.K.
175 M3 **Killinchy** U.K.
175 L5 **Killinick** Ireland
207 H1 **Killiniq** Canada
207 H1 **Killiniq Island** Canada
175 L5 **Killorglin** Ireland
175 L5 **Killurin** Ireland
175 J3 **Killybegs** Ireland
175 K5 **Kilmacrenan** Ireland
175 I4 **Kilmaine** Ireland
175 J5 **Kilmallock** Ireland
174 B3 **Kilmaluag** U.K.
174 D5 **Kilmarnock** U.K.
174 C4 **Kilmelford** U.K.
186 I3 **Kil'mez'** Rus. Fed.
186 I3 **Kil'mez'** r. Rus. Fed.
175 J6 **Kilmona** Ireland
125 F6 **Kilmore** Australia
175 L5 **Kilmore Quay** Ireland
195 D4 **Kilosa** Tanz.
170 M1 **Kilpisjärvi** Fin.
170 P1 **Kilp'yavr** Rus. Fed.
175 L3 **Kilrea** U.K.
175 I5 **Kilrush** Ireland
174 D5 **Kilsyth** U.K.
147 G4 **Kiltan** atoll India
175 J4 **Kiltullagh** Ireland
195 C4 **Kilwa** Dem. Rep. Congo
195 D4 **Kilwa Masoko** Tanz.
174 D5 **Kilwinning** U.K.
195 D4 **Kimambi** Tanz.
124 B4 **Kimba** Australia
195 B4 **Kimba** Congo
216 C3 **Kimball** U.S.A.
119 F2 **Kimbe** P.N.G.
204 F5 **Kimberley** Canada
197 F4 **Kimberley** S. Africa
118 C3 **Kimberley Plateau** Australia
121 B5 **Kimberley Range** hills Australia
126 E4 **Kimbolton** N.Z.
160 E3 **Kimch'aek** N. Korea
160 E5 **Kimch'ŏn** S. Korea
157 C6 **Kimhae** S. Korea
160 D4 **Kimhwa** S. Korea
171 M3 **Kimito** Fin.
160 D6 **Kimje** S. Korea

203 L3 **Kimmirut** Canada
185 K6 **Kimolos** i. Greece
187 F4 **Kimovsk** Rus. Fed.
195 B4 **Kimpese** Dem. Rep. Congo
186 F3 **Kimry** Rus. Fed.
195 B4 **Kimvula** Dem. Rep. Congo
163 I1 **Kinabalu, Gunung** mt. Sabah Malaysia
161 H5 **Kinabatangan** r. Sabah Malaysia
185 L6 **Kinaros** i. Greece
204 F4 **Kinbasket Lake** Canada
174 E2 **Kinbrace** U.K.
209 G3 **Kincardine** Canada
174 E4 **Kincardine** U.K.
125 E4 **Kinchega National Park** Australia
Kincolith Canada see Gingolx
195 C4 **Kinda** Dem. Rep. Congo
149 H5 **Kindat** Myanmar
217 E6 **Kinder** U.S.A.
173 F4 **Kinder Scout** h. U.K.
205 H4 **Kindersley** Canada
192 A3 **Kindia** Guinea
195 C4 **Kindu** Dem. Rep. Congo
140 B1 **Kinel'** Rus. Fed.
186 G3 **Kineshma** Rus. Fed.
119 H4 **Kingaroy** Australia
214 B3 **King City** U.S.A.
127 J1 **King Edward Point** research stn Antarctica
221 E3 **King Ferry** U.S.A.
221 H2 **Kingfield** U.S.A.
217 D5 **Kingfisher** U.S.A.
127 I2 **King George Island** Antarctica
206 E2 **King George Islands** Canada
121 C4 **King Hill** Australia
186 D3 **Kingisepp** Rus. Fed.
125 F8 **King Island** Australia
204 D4 **King Island** Canada
209 H1 **King Kirkland** Canada
125 F6 **Kinglake National Park** Australia
120 D3 **King Leopold Range National Park** Australia
118 C3 **King Leopold Ranges** hills Australia
215 E4 **Kingman** AZ U.S.A.
217 D4 **Kingman** KS U.S.A.
221 I2 **Kingman** ME U.S.A.
117 I3 **Kingman Reef** terr. N. Pacific Ocean
204 D3 **King Mountain** Canada
124 A3 **Kingoonya** Australia
175 K5 **Kings** r. Ireland
214 C3 **Kings** r. U.S.A.
173 D7 **Kingsbridge** U.K.
214 C3 **Kingsburg** U.S.A.
221 I2 **Kingsbury** U.S.A.
214 C3 **Kings Canyon National Park** U.S.A.
125 J2 **Kingscliff** Australia
124 B5 **Kingscote** Australia
175 L4 **Kingscourt** Ireland
127 L2 **King Sejong** research stn Antarctica
208 C3 **Kingsford** U.S.A.
219 D6 **Kingsland** GA U.S.A.
209 E5 **Kingsland** IN U.S.A.
173 H5 **King's Lynn** U.K.
119 H2 **Kingsmill Group** is Kiribati
173 H6 **Kingsnorth** U.K.
118 C3 **King Sound** b. Australia
213 E3 **Kings Peak** U.S.A.
220 B6 **Kingsport** U.S.A.
209 I3 **Kingston** Canada
223 I5 **Kingston** Jamaica
126 B6 **Kingston** N.Z.
208 B6 **Kingston** IL U.S.A.
221 F4 **Kingston** NY U.S.A.
125 G9 **Kingston**
215 E4 **Kingston Peak** U.S.A.
124 C6 **Kingston South East** Australia
173 G4 **Kingston upon Hull** U.K.
223 L6 **Kingstown** St Vincent
217 D7 **Kingsville** U.S.A.
173 E6 **Kingswood** U.K.
173 D5 **Kington** U.K.
174 D3 **Kingussie** U.K.
203 I3 **King William Island** Canada
197 G6 **King William's Town** S. Arfica
217 E6 **Kingwood** TX U.S.A.
220 D5 **Kingwood** WV U.S.A.
205 I4 **Kinistino** Canada
159 G5 **Kinka-san** i. Japan
126 B6 **Kinloch** N.Z.

174 E3 **Kinloss** U.K.
209 H3 **Kinmount** Canada
171 K4 **Kinna** Sweden
175 K4 **Kinnegad** Ireland
Kinneret, Yam l. Israel see Galilee, Sea of
147 I4 **Kinniyai** Sri Lanka
171 N3 **Kinnula** Fin.
205 I3 **Kinoosao** Canada
159 F5 **Kinpoku-san** mt. Japan
174 E4 **Kinross** U.K.
175 J6 **Kinsale** Ireland
195 B4 **Kinshasa** Dem. Rep. Congo
217 D4 **Kinsley** U.S.A.
219 E5 **Kinston** U.S.A.
171 M5 **Kintai** Lith.
192 B4 **Kintampo** Ghana
175 F3 **Kintore** U.K.
174 C5 **Kintyre** pen. U.K.
204 F3 **Kinuso** Canada
193 F4 **Kinyeti** mt. Sudan
140 D2 **Kinzhaly** Kazakh.
179 H4 **Kinzig** r. Germany
209 H2 **Kiosk** Canada
206 E4 **Kipawa, Lac** l. Canada
221 F6 **Kiptopeke** U.S.A.
195 C5 **Kipushi** Dem. Rep. Congo
119 G3 **Kirakira** Solomon Is
147 I2 **Kirandul** India
187 D4 **Kirawsk** Belarus
179 G2 **Kirchdorf** Germany
179 G5 **Kirchheim-Bolanden** Germany
175 M3 **Kircubbin** U.K.
151 C1 **Kirenga** r. Rus. Fed.
150 C1 **Kirensk** Rus. Fed.
141 H4 **Kirghiz Range** mts Asia
117 H4 **Kiribati** country Pacific Ocean
139 H1 **Kırık** Turkey
139 F3 **Kırıkhan** Turkey
138 D2 **Kırıkkale** Turkey
186 F3 **Kirillov** Rus. Fed.
156 F3 **Kirillovo** Rus. Fed.
Kirinyaga mt. Kenya see Kenya, Mount
186 E3 **Kirishi** Rus. Fed.
159 B9 **Kirishima-yama** vol. Japan
117 I4 **Kiritimati** atoll Kiribati
138 A2 **Kırkağaç** Turkey
142 B2 **Kırk Bulāg Dāgı** mt. Iran
173 E4 **Kirkby** U.K.
173 F4 **Kirkby in Ashfield** U.K.
172 E3 **Kirkby Lonsdale** U.K.
172 E3 **Kirkby Stephen** U.K.
174 E4 **Kirkcaldy** U.K.
174 C6 **Kirkcolm** U.K.
174 D6 **Kirkcudbright** U.K.
171 K3 **Kirkenær** Norway
170 O1 **Kirkenes** Norway
209 H3 **Kirkfield** Canada
174 D5 **Kirkintilloch** U.K.
171 N3 **Kirkonummi** Fin.
215 F4 **Kirkland** U.S.A.
215 F4 **Kirkland Junction** U.S.A.
209 G1 **Kirkland Lake** Canada
187 C7 **Kırklareli** Turkey
172 C3 **Kirk Michael** U.K.
172 E3 **Kirkoswald** U.K.
127 J5 **Kirkpatrick, Mount** Antarctica
216 E3 **Kirksville** U.S.A.
139 J4 **Kirkūk** Iraq
175 F2 **Kirkwall** U.K.
197 F6 **Kirkwood** S. Africa
214 B2 **Kirkwood** CA U.S.A.
217 F4 **Kirkwood** MO U.S.A.
138 C1 **Kırmır** r. Turkey
179 F5 **Kirn** Germany
187 E4 **Kirov** Kaluzhskaya Oblast' Rus. Fed.
186 I3 **Kirov** Kirovskaya Oblast' Rus. Fed.
Kirovabad Azer. see Gäncä
140 C2 **Kirovo** Kazakh.
186 I3 **Kirovo-Chepetsk** Rus. Fed.
187 E5 **Kirovohrad** Ukr.
139 L2 **Kirovsk** Azer.
186 D3 **Kirovsk** Leningradskaya Oblast' Rus. Fed.
170 P2 **Kirovsk** Murmanskaya Oblast' Rus. Fed.
186 I3 **Kirovskaya Oblast'** admin. div. Rus. Fed.
158 C2 **Kirovskiy** Rus. Fed.
140 D5 **Kirpili** Rus. Fed.
174 E4 **Kirriemuir** U.K.
186 J3 **Kirs** Rus. Fed.
138 E2 **Kırsanov** Rus. Fed.
138 E2 **Kırşehir** Turkey
143 G5 **Kirthar Range** mts Pak.

179 H4 **Kirtorf** Germany
170 M2 **Kiruna** Sweden
195 C4 **Kirundu** Dem. Rep. Congo
187 K4 **Kirya** Rus. Fed.
159 F6 **Kiryū** Japan
171 K4 **Kisa** Sweden
194 C3 **Kisangani** Dem. Rep. Congo
195 B4 **Kisantu** Dem. Rep. Congo
163 E2 **Kisaran** Indon.
150 A1 **Kiselevsk** Rus. Fed.
156 E2 **Kisel'ovka** Rus. Fed.
142 D5 **Kish** i. Iran
149 F4 **Kishanganj** India
148 B4 **Kishangarh** Rajasthan India
148 C4 **Kishangarh** Rajasthan India
148 C2 **Kishen Ganga** r. India/Pak.
192 C4 **Kishi** Nigeria
159 B9 **Kishika-zaki** pt Japan
Kishinev Moldova see Chişinău
159 D7 **Kishiwada** Japan
141 H1 **Kishkenekol'** Kazakh.
149 G4 **Kishoreganj** Bangl.
Kishorganj Bangl. see Kishoreganj
148 C2 **Kishtwar** India
195 D4 **Kisii** Kenya
205 J4 **Kiskittogisu Lake** Canada
177 I7 **Kiskunfélegyháza** Hungary
177 I7 **Kiskunhalas** Hungary
187 G7 **Kislovodsk** Rus. Fed.
195 E4 **Kismaayo** Somalia
159 E7 **Kiso-sanmyaku** mts Japan
181 H4 **Kissamos** Greece
192 A4 **Kissidougou** Guinea
219 D6 **Kissimmee** U.S.A.
219 D7 **Kissimmee, Lake** U.S.A.
195 D4 **Kisumu** Kenya
192 B3 **Kita** Mali
Kitab Uzbek. see Kitob
153 N6 **Kita-Daitō-jima** i. Japan
159 G6 **Kitaibaraki** Japan
159 G5 **Kitakami** Japan
159 G5 **Kitakami-gawa** r. Japan
159 F6 **Kitakata** Japan
159 B8 **Kita-Kyūshū** Japan
194 D3 **Kitale** Kenya
133 P5 **Kitami** Japan
213 G4 **Kit Carson** U.S.A.
209 G4 **Kitchener** Canada
171 O3 **Kitee** Fin.
194 D3 **Kitgum** Uganda
204 D4 **Kitimat** Canada
170 N2 **Kitinen** r. Fin.
141 F5 **Kitob** Uzbek.
195 D4 **Kitona** Dem. Rep. Congo
159 B8 **Kitsuki** Japan
124 C2 **Kittakittaooloo, Lake** salt flat Australia
220 D4 **Kittanning** U.S.A.
221 F4 **Kittatinny Mountains** U.S.A.
221 H3 **Kittery** U.S.A.
170 N2 **Kittilä** Fin.
219 F4 **Kitty Hawk** U.S.A.
195 D4 **Kitunda** Tanz.
204 D3 **Kitwanga** Canada
195 C5 **Kitwe** Zambia
176 F7 **Kitzbüheler Alpen** mts Austria
179 I5 **Kitzingen** Germany
179 K3 **Kitzscher** Germany
171 N3 **Kiuruvesi** Fin.
171 N3 **Kivijärvi** Fin.
171 N4 **Kiviõli** Estonia
195 C4 **Kivu, Lake** Dem. Rep. Congo/Rwanda
141 G2 **Kiyakty, Ozero** salt l. Kazakh.
141 G2 **Kiyevka** Kazakh.
158 C3 **Kiyevka** Rus. Fed.
185 M4 **Kıyıköy** Turkey
141 F2 **Kiyma** Kazakh.
132 G4 **Kizel** Rus. Fed.
186 H2 **Kizema** Rus. Fed.
138 B3 **Kizil** China
141 J4 **Kizil Dağ** mt. Turkey
138 D1 **Kızılcahamam** Turkey
139 G2 **Kizil Dağı** mt. Turkey
138 D1 **Kızılırmak** Turkey
138 D2 **Kızılırmak** r. Turkey
138 D3 **Kızılören** Turkey
140 D1 **Kizil'skoye** Rus. Fed.
138 D3 **Kızılyurt** Rus. Fed.
Kizil'yurt Rus. Fed. see Kizilyurt
187 H7 **Kizlyar** Rus. Fed.
137 G1 **Kizlyarskiy Zaliv** b. Rus. Fed.

Kizylayak Turkm. see Gyzylaýak
170 N1 **Kjøllefjord** Norway
170 L1 **Kjøpsvik** Norway
176 G5 **Kladno** Czech Rep.
176 G7 **Klagenfurt** Austria
215 H4 **Klagetoh** U.S.A.
171 M5 **Klaipėda** Lith.
170 □¹ **Klaksvík** Faroe Is
213 B3 **Klamath** r. U.S.A.
213 B3 **Klamath Falls** U.S.A.
213 B3 **Klamath Mountains** U.S.A.
163 B2 **Klang** Malaysia
171 K4 **Klarälven** r. Sweden
176 F6 **Klatovy** Czech Rep.
196 C5 **Klawer** S. Africa
204 C3 **Klawock** U.S.A.
179 E2 **Klazienaveen** Neth.
204 E4 **Kleena Kleene** Canada
196 D4 **Kleinbegin** S. Africa
196 C3 **Klein Karas** Namibia
197 F6 **Kleinpoort** S. Africa
196 D6 **Klein Roggeveldberge** mts S. Africa
196 B3 **Kleinsee** S. Africa
196 D6 **Klein Swartberg** mt. S. Africa
204 E4 **Klemtu** Canada
197 G3 **Klerksdorp** S. Africa
187 E4 **Kletnya** Rus. Fed.
187 G5 **Kletskaya** Rus. Fed.
179 E3 **Kleve** Germany
187 D4 **Klimavichy** Belarus
187 E4 **Klimovo** Rus. Fed.
187 F4 **Klimovsk** Rus. Fed.
186 F3 **Klin** Rus. Fed.
204 D4 **Klinaklini** r. Canada
179 H5 **Klingenberg am Main** Germany
179 K4 **Klingenthal** Germany
179 K1 **Klink** Germany
176 F5 **Klínovec** mt. Czech Rep.
171 L4 **Klintehamn** Sweden
187 I5 **Klintsovka** Rus. Fed.
187 E4 **Klintsy** Rus. Fed.
196 C5 **Kliprand** S. Africa
185 G2 **Ključ** Bos.-Herz.
177 H5 **Kłodzko** Poland
179 E2 **Kloosterhaar** Neth.
177 H6 **Klosterneuburg** Austria
207 I1 **Klotz, Lac** l. Canada
179 J2 **Klötze (Altmark)** Germany
204 A2 **Kluane Game Sanctuary** nature res. Canada
204 B2 **Kluane Lake** Canada
204 B2 **Kluane National Park** Canada
177 I5 **Kluczbork** Poland
137 F2 **Klukhorskiy, Pereval** Georgia/Rus. Fed.
148 B4 **Klupro** Pak.
187 C4 **Klyetsk** Belarus
133 R4 **Klyuchevskaya, Sopka** vol. Rus. Fed.
156 B2 **Klyuchi** Rus. Fed.
141 I1 **Klyuchi** Rus. Fed.
171 K3 **Knäda** Sweden
172 F3 **Knaresborough** U.K.
205 K3 **Knee Lake** Canada
179 I5 **Knetzgau** Germany
208 B1 **Knife Lake** Canada/U.S.A.
204 D4 **Knight Inlet** Canada
173 D5 **Knighton** U.K.
185 G2 **Knin** Croatia
176 G7 **Knittelfeld** Austria
185 J3 **Knjaževac** Serbia
120 E2 **Knob Peak** h. Australia
175 I5 **Knock** Ireland
175 I5 **Knockacummer** h. Ireland
175 J3 **Knockalongy** h. Ireland
175 I4 **Knockalough** Ireland
175 I6 **Knockboy** h. Ireland
175 F3 **Knock Hill** U.K.
175 L2 **Knocklayd** h. U.K.
178 B3 **Knokke-Heist** Belgium
179 L1 **Knorrendorf** Germany
185 K7 **Knossos** tourist site Greece
173 F5 **Knowle** U.K.
127 I3 **Knowles, Cape** Antarctica
221 I1 **Knowles Corner** U.S.A.
209 I4 **Knowlton** Canada
208 D5 **Knox** U.S.A.
214 A2 **Knox, Cape** Canada
214 A2 **Knoxville** CA U.S.A.
208 B5 **Knoxville** IL U.S.A.
219 D4 **Knoxville** TN U.S.A.
174 C3 **Knoydart** reg. U.K.
203 M1 **Knud Rasmussen Land** reg. Greenland
197 E7 **Knysna** S. Africa
156 E3 **Ko, Gora** mt. Rus. Fed.

285

L

208 C2 **L'Anse** U.S.A.
204 C2 **Lansing** r. Canada
208 B4 **Lansing** IA U.S.A.
209 E4 **Lansing** MI U.S.A.
162 A4 **Lanta, Ko** i. Thai.
155 D6 **Lantau Island** Hong Kong China
155 □ **Lantau Peak** h. Hong Kong China
161 J4 **Lanuza Bay** Phil.
156 B3 **Lanxi** China
155 F4 **Lanxi** China
193 F4 **Lanya** Sudan
155 F6 **Lan Yü** i. Taiwan
192 A2 **Lanzarote** i. Canary Is
154 B2 **Lanzhou** China
160 B1 **Lanzijing** China
162 A1 **Lao, Nam Mae** r. Thai.
161 I2 **Laoag** Phil.
161 J3 **Laoang** Phil.
155 B6 **Lao Cai** Vietnam
141 J3 **Laofengkou** China
154 F1 **Laoha He** r. China
154 D3 **Laohekou** China
160 A4 **Laohutun** China
160 D3 **Laoling** China
160 D3 **Lao Ling** mts China
182 F2 **Laon** France
208 C3 **Laona** U.S.A.
154 C5 **Laos** country Asia
151 F2 **Lao Shan** mt. China
160 E2 **Laotougou** China
160 C3 **Laotuding Shan** h. China
154 A1 **Laoximiao** China
157 B4 **Laoye Ling** mts China
160 C2 **Laoye Ling** mts China
235 C4 **Lapa** Brazil
161 I5 **Lapac** i. Phil.
192 A2 **La Palma** i. Canary Is
224 J6 **La Palma** Panama
183 M4 **La Palma del Condado** Spain
235 L2 **La Paloma** Uruguay
235 J3 **La Pampa** prov. Arg.
214 B4 **La Panza Range** mts U.S.A.
233 L3 **La Paragua** Venez.
161 H5 **Laparan** i. Phil.
233 I4 **La Paya, Parque Nacional** nat. park Col.
235 K1 **La Paz** Entre Ríos Arg.
235 I2 **La Paz** Mendoza Arg.
230 E7 **La Paz** Bol.
224 H5 **La Paz** Hond.
224 B2 **La Paz** Mex.
224 H5 **La Paz** Nicaragua
208 D5 **Lapaz** U.S.A.
224 B2 **La Paz, Bahía** b. Mex.
230 E4 **La Pedrera** Col.
209 F4 **Lapeer** U.S.A.
224 C1 **La Pesca** Mex.
158 G2 **La Pérouse Strait** Japan/Rus. Fed.
225 E3 **La Pesca** Mex.
225 D3 **La Piedad** Mex.
233 L3 **La Piña** r. Venez.
213 B3 **La Pine** U.S.A.
161 J3 **Lapinig** Phil.
161 J4 **Lapinin** i. Phil.
171 N3 **Lapinlahti** Fin.
138 D4 **Lapithos** Cyprus
217 F6 **Laplace** U.S.A.
216 C2 **La Plant** U.S.A.
235 L2 **La Plata** Arg.
233 I4 **La Plata** Col.
230 B4 **La Plata, Isla** i. Ecuador
235 L2 **La Plata, Río de** sea chan. Arg./Uruguay
205 H3 **La Plonge, Lac** l. Canada
186 G1 **Lapominka** Rus. Fed.
208 D5 **La Porte** U.S.A.
208 A4 **La Porte** U.S.A.
207 F2 **La Potherie, Lac** l. Canada
171 M3 **Lappajärvi** Fin.
171 M3 **Lappajärvi** l. Fin.
171 O3 **Lappeenranta** Fin.
179 K5 **Lappersdorf** Germany
171 M3 **Lappi** Fin.
170 L2 **Lappland** reg. Europe
221 G2 **La Prairie** Canada
217 D6 **La Pryor** U.S.A.
185 L4 **Lâpseki** Turkey
133 M2 **Laptev Sea** Rus. Fed.
 Laptevykh, More sea Rus. Fed. see **Laptev Sea**
171 M3 **Lapua** Fin.
161 I4 **Lapu-Lapu** Phil.
232 C2 **La Quiaca** Arg.
184 E3 **L'Aquila** Italy
215 D5 **La Quinta** U.S.A.
142 D5 **Lär** Iran
192 B1 **Larache** Morocco

143 E5 **Lārak** i. Iran
213 F3 **Laramie** U.S.A.
213 F3 **Laramie Mountains** U.S.A.
235 B4 **Laranjeiras do Sul** Brazil
234 B3 **Laranjinha** r. Brazil
151 E7 **Larantuka** Indon.
151 F7 **Larat** i. Indon.
183 R4 **Larba** Alg.
171 L4 **Lärbro** Sweden
209 G2 **Larchwood** Canada
 L'Ardenne, Plateau de plat. Belgium see **Ardennes**
209 H1 **Larder Lake** Canada
183 O1 **Laredo** Spain
217 D7 **Laredo** U.S.A.
225 E3 **La Reforma** Mex.
219 D7 **Largo** U.S.A.
174 D5 **Largs** U.K.
142 B2 **Lārī** Iran
184 D6 **L'Ariana** Tunisia
205 J5 **Larimore** U.S.A.
232 C3 **La Rioja** Arg.
235 I1 **La Rioja** prov. Arg.
183 O1 **La Rioja** aut. comm. Spain
185 J5 **Larisa** Greece
143 E5 **Laristan** reg. Iran
148 B4 **Larkana** Pak.
122 D2 **Lark Passage** Australia
176 C7 **Larmont** mt. France/Switz.
138 D4 **Larnaca** Cyprus
 Larnaka Cyprus see **Larnaca**
175 M3 **Larne** U.K.
217 D4 **Larned** U.S.A.
174 C6 **Larne Lough** inlet U.K.
183 N1 **La Robla** Spain
178 D4 **La Roche-en-Ardenne** Belgium
182 D3 **La Rochelle** France
182 D3 **La Roche-sur-Yon** France
183 O3 **La Roda** Spain
223 K5 **La Romana** Dom. Rep.
205 H3 **La Ronge** Canada
205 H3 **La Ronge, Lac** l. Canada
225 D2 **La Rosa** Mex.
225 D1 **La Rosita** Mex.
120 B3 **Larrey Point** Australia
118 D3 **Larrimah** Australia
127 I2 **Larsen Ice Shelf** Antarctica
171 M3 **Larsmo** Fin.
171 J4 **Larvik** Norway
215 H2 **La Sal Junction** U.S.A.
221 G2 **LaSalle** Canada
208 C5 **La Salle** U.S.A.
224 I1 **Las Ánimas, Punta** pt Mex.
206 E4 **La Sarre** Canada
233 K2 **Las Aves, Islas** Venez.
224 B1 **Las Avispas** Mex.
235 H4 **Las Cabras** Chile
207 I4 **La Scie** Canada
213 F5 **Las Cruces** U.S.A.
223 J5 **La Selle, Pic** mt. Haiti
235 H1 **La Serena** Chile
225 D2 **Las Esperanças** Mex.
183 Q1 **La Seu d'Urgell** Spain
235 K3 **Las Flores** Arg.
143 F5 **Lāshār** r. Iran
205 H4 **Lashburn** Canada
235 I2 **Las Heras** Arg.
233 I4 **Las Hermosas, Parque Nacional** nat. park Col.
224 C2 **Las Herreras** Mex.
151 B4 **Lashio** Myanmar
143 G4 **Lashkar Gāh** Afgh.
235 H3 **Las Lajas** Arg.
233 K3 **Las Lajitas** Venez.
232 D2 **Las Lomitas** Arg.
183 M4 **Las Marismas** marsh Spain
232 C7 **Las Martinetas** Arg.
233 K2 **Las Mercedes** Venez.
224 C2 **Las Nieves** Mex.
 La Société, Archipel de is Fr. Polynesia see **Society Islands**
215 D5 **Las Palmas** watercourse Mex.
192 A2 **Las Palmas de Gran Canaria** Canary Is
184 C2 **La Spezia** Italy
235 L2 **Las Piedras** Uruguay
232 C6 **Las Plumas** Arg.
224 G5 **Las Quebradas** Guat.
235 K2 **Las Rosas** Arg.
213 B3 **Lassen Peak** vol. U.S.A.
213 B3 **Lassen Volcanic National Park** U.S.A.
224 I7 **Las Tablas** Panama
232 D3 **Las Termas** Arg.
205 H4 **Last Mountain Lake** Canada
235 I1 **Las Tórtolas, Cerro** mt. Chile
195 B4 **Lastoursville** Gabon
185 G3 **Lastovo** i. Croatia

224 A2 **Las Tres Vírgenes, Volcán** vol. Mex.
233 K3 **Las Trincheras** Venez.
179 F2 **Lastrup** Germany
223 I4 **Las Tunas** Cuba
213 F6 **Las Varas** Chihuahua Mex.
224 C3 **Las Varas** Nayarit Mex.
235 J1 **Las Varillas** Arg.
213 F5 **Las Vegas** NM U.S.A.
215 E3 **Las Vegas** NV U.S.A.
183 N3 **Las Villuercas** mt. Spain
207 I3 **La Tabatière** Canada
230 C4 **Latacunga** Ecuador
233 I5 **La Tagua** Col.
138 C4 **Latakia** Syria
209 H2 **Latchford** Canada
149 F5 **Latehar** India
 La Teste France see **La Teste-de-Buch**
182 D4 **La Teste-de-Buch** France
121 B6 **Latham** Australia
179 F2 **Lathen** Germany
174 E2 **Latheron** U.K.
184 E4 **Latina** Italy
235 J2 **La Toma** Arg.
233 K2 **La Tortuga, Isla** i. Venez.
125 G8 **Latrobe** Australia
220 D4 **Latrobe** U.S.A.
179 E2 **Lattrop** Neth.
209 H2 **Latulipe** Canada
207 F4 **La Tuque** Canada
147 H2 **Latur** India
171 M4 **Latvia** country Europe
232 C1 **Lauca, Parque Nacional** nat. park Chile
176 F5 **Lauchhammer** Germany
175 F5 **Lauder** U.K.
179 H1 **Lauenbrück** Germany
179 I1 **Lauenburg (Elbe)** Germany
179 J5 **Lauf an der Pegnitz** Germany
182 H3 **Laufen** Switz.
203 L2 **Lauge Koch Kyst** pen. Greenland
208 D2 **Laughing Fish Point** U.S.A.
121 F4 **Laughlen, Mount** Australia
171 M4 **Lauka** Estonia
170 O1 **Laukvik** Norway
162 A3 **Laun** Thai.
125 G8 **Launceston** Australia
173 C7 **Launceston** U.K.
175 I5 **Laune** r. Ireland
162 A2 **Launglon Bok Islands** Myanmar
235 H4 **La Unión** Chile
233 H4 **La Unión** Col.
225 H5 **La Unión** El Salvador
225 D4 **La Unión** Mex.
161 I3 **Laur** Phil.
119 E3 **Laura** Qld Australia
124 C4 **Laura** S.A. Australia
233 K3 **La Urbana** Venez.
221 F5 **Laurel** DE U.S.A.
217 F6 **Laurel** MS U.S.A.
212 E2 **Laurel** MT U.S.A.
220 D4 **Laurel Hill** hills U.S.A.
220 A6 **Laurel River Lake** U.S.A.
175 F4 **Laurencekirk** U.K.
207 F4 **Laurentides, Réserve Faunique des** nature res. Canada
184 F4 **Lauria** Italy
125 J3 **Laurieton** Australia
219 E5 **Laurinburg** U.S.A.
208 C2 **Laurium** U.S.A.
176 C7 **Lausanne** Switz.
163 I3 **Laut** i. Indon.
235 H3 **Lautaro** Chile
179 H4 **Lautersbach (Hessen)** Germany
163 I3 **Laut Kecil, Kepulauan** is Indon.
119 H3 **Lautoka** Fiji
171 O3 **Lauvuskylä** Fin.
207 H4 **Laval** Canada
182 D2 **Laval** France
183 P3 **La Vall d'Uixó** Spain
142 D5 **Lāvān** Iran
142 D5 **Lāvān** i. Iran
178 B4 **Le Cateau-Cambrésis** France
178 B4 **Le Catelet** France
185 H4 **Lecce** Italy
184 C2 **Lecco** Italy
176 E7 **Lech** r. Austria/Germany
185 I6 **Lechaina** Greece
155 D5 **Lechang** China
178 C5 **Le Chesne** France
176 E7 **Lechtaler Alpen** mts Austria
176 D3 **Leck** Germany
182 G3 **Le Creusot** France
183 E5 **Lectoure** France

212 E2 **Lavina** U.S.A.
234 D3 **Lavras** Brazil
235 M1 **Lavras do Sul** Brazil
197 I3 **Lavumisa** Swaziland
148 B2 **Lawa** Pak.
162 B4 **Lawit, Gunung** mt. Malaysia
122 B3 **Lawn Hill National Park** Australia
139 I7 **Lawqah** waterhole Saudi Arabia
192 B3 **Lawra** Ghana
217 E4 **Lawrence** KS U.S.A.
221 H3 **Lawrence** MA U.S.A.
219 C5 **Lawrenceburg** U.S.A.
221 J2 **Lawrence Station** Canada
221 E6 **Lawrenceville** U.S.A.
121 C5 **Lawrence Wells, Mount** h. Australia
217 D5 **Lawton** U.S.A.
134 B4 **Lawz, Jabal al** mt. Saudi Arabia
171 K4 **Laxå** Sweden
197 E3 **Laxey** S. Africa
172 C3 **Laxey** U.K.
174 C2 **Laxford, Loch** inlet U.K.
204 C4 **Lax Kw'alaams** Canada
174 □ **Laxo** U.K.
139 J4 **Laylān** Iraq
117 H2 **Laysan Island** U.S.A.
214 A2 **Laytonville** U.S.A.
148 B3 **Layyah** Pak.
224 B3 **La Zacatosa, Picacho** mt. Mex.
156 F1 **Lazarev** Rus. Fed.
185 I2 **Lazarevac** Serbia
187 F7 **Lazarevskoye** Rus. Fed.
213 D6 **Lázaro Cárdenas** Mex.
225 D4 **Lázaro Cárdenas** Mex.
224 C2 **Lázaro Cárdenas, Presa** resr Mex.
235 L2 **Lazcano** Uruguay
171 M5 **Lazdijai** Lith.
158 C3 **Lazo** Primorskiy Kray Rus. Fed.
133 O3 **Lazo** Rus. Fed.
162 B2 **Leach** Cambodia
209 E2 **Leach Island** Canada
216 C2 **Lead** U.S.A.
205 H4 **Leader** Canada
125 H4 **Leadville** Australia
213 F4 **Leadville** U.S.A.
217 F6 **Leaf** r. U.S.A.
205 I3 **Leaf Rapids** Canada
217 D6 **Leakey** U.S.A.
209 F4 **Leamington** Canada
215 F2 **Leamington** U.S.A.
173 F5 **Leamington Spa, Royal** U.K.
155 E5 **Le'an** China
171 I5 **Leane, Lough** l. Ireland
175 I6 **Leap** Ireland
205 H4 **Leask** Canada
173 G6 **Leatherhead** U.K.
217 E4 **Leavenworth** KS U.S.A.
212 B2 **Leavenworth** WA U.S.A.
214 C2 **Leavitt** U.S.A.
179 E5 **Lebach** Germany
161 J5 **Lebak** Phil.
138 C5 **Lebanon** country Asia
208 D5 **Lebanon** IN U.S.A.
217 E4 **Lebanon** KS U.S.A.
217 E4 **Lebanon** MO U.S.A.
221 G3 **Lebanon** NH U.S.A.
221 F4 **Lebanon** NJ U.S.A.
220 A5 **Lebanon** OH U.S.A.
212 B2 **Lebanon** OR U.S.A.
221 E4 **Lebanon** PA U.S.A.
219 C4 **Lebanon** TN U.S.A.
140 E4 **Lebap** Turkm.
187 H4 **Lebedyan'** Rus. Fed.
187 E5 **Lebedyn** Ukr.
182 E3 **Le Blanc** France
177 H3 **Łebork** Poland
197 H2 **Lebowakgomo** S. Africa
183 M4 **Lebrija** Spain
177 H3 **Łebsko, Jezioro** lag. Poland
235 H3 **Lebu** Chile

162 B5 **Ledang, Gunung** mt. Malaysia
173 E5 **Ledbury** U.K.
183 N2 **Ledesma** Spain
174 D2 **Ledmore** U.K.
186 E1 **Ledmozero** Rus. Fed.
155 C7 **Ledong** China
154 B2 **Ledu** China
205 G4 **Leduc** Canada
221 G3 **Lee** U.S.A.
216 E2 **Leech Lake** U.S.A.
173 F4 **Leeds** U.K.
221 H2 **Leeds Junction** U.S.A.
173 B7 **Leedstown** U.K.
179 E1 **Leek** Neth.
173 E4 **Leek** U.K.
178 D3 **Leende** Neth.
220 D4 **Leeper** U.S.A.
179 F1 **Leer (Ostfriesland)** Germany
219 D6 **Leesburg** FL U.S.A.
221 E5 **Leesburg** VA U.S.A.
179 H2 **Leese** Germany
121 C5 **Lee Steere Range** hills Australia
217 E6 **Leesville** U.S.A.
220 C4 **Leesville Lake** U.S.A.
125 G5 **Leeton** Australia
196 D6 **Leeu-Gamka** S. Africa
178 D1 **Leeuwarden** Neth.
118 B5 **Leeuwin, Cape** Australia
121 A7 **Leeuwin-Naturaliste National Park** Australia
214 C3 **Lee Vining** U.S.A.
223 L5 **Leeward Islands** Caribbean Sea
138 D4 **Lefka** Cyprus
185 I5 **Lefkada** Greece
185 I5 **Lefkada** i. Greece
 Lefkara Cyprus see **Pano Lefkara**
 Lefkimmi Greece
 Lefkosia Cyprus see **Nicosia**
121 C6 **Lefroy, Lake** salt flat Australia
161 I3 **Legaspi** Phil.
179 F2 **Legden** Germany
125 G8 **Legges Tor** mt. Australia
214 A2 **Leggett** U.S.A.
184 D2 **Legnago** Italy
177 H5 **Legnica** Poland
120 E2 **Legune** Australia
148 D2 **Leh** India
182 E2 **Le Havre** France
221 F4 **Lehighton** U.S.A.
171 O3 **Lehmo** Fin.
179 K2 **Lehnin** Germany
179 I2 **Lehre** Germany
179 H2 **Lehrte** Germany
171 M3 **Lehtimäki** Fin.
196 D1 **Lehututu** Botswana
176 G7 **Leibnitz** Austria
173 F5 **Leicester** U.K.
118 D3 **Leichhardt** r. Australia
122 B3 **Leichhardt Falls** Australia
123 D4 **Leichhardt Range** mts Australia
178 C2 **Leiden** Neth.
124 C3 **Leigh** watercourse Australia
126 E2 **Leigh** N.Z.
173 E4 **Leigh** U.K.
124 C3 **Leigh Creek** Australia
173 G6 **Leighton Buzzard** U.K.
179 G5 **Leimen** Germany
179 H2 **Leine** r. Germany
179 I3 **Leinefelde** Germany
121 C5 **Leinster** Australia
175 L5 **Leinster, Mount** h. Ireland
185 L6 **Leipsoi** i. Greece
179 K3 **Leipzig** Germany
170 K2 **Leirangen** Norway
183 L3 **Leiria** Port.
171 I4 **Leirvik** Norway
155 C5 **Leishan** China
155 D5 **Lei Shui** r. China
121 E4 **Leisler, Mount** h. Australia
179 K3 **Leisnig** Germany
219 C4 **Leitchfield** U.S.A.
233 I4 **Leiva, Cerro** mt. Col.
175 L4 **Leixlip** Ireland
155 D5 **Leiyang** China
155 D6 **Leizhou** China
155 C6 **Leizhou Bandao** pen. China
155 D6 **Leizhou Wan** b. China
170 J2 **Leka** Norway
195 B4 **Lékana** Congo
184 C6 **Le Kef** Tunisia
196 B4 **Lekkersing** S. Africa
195 B4 **Lékoni** Gabon
171 K3 **Leksand** Sweden

171 O3 **Leksozero, Ozero** l. Rus. Fed.
209 E3 **Leland** MI U.S.A.
217 F5 **Leland** MS U.S.A.
192 A3 **Lélouma** Guinea
178 D2 **Lelystad** Neth.
232 C9 **Le Maire, Estrecho de** sea chan. Arg.
 Léman, Lac l. France/Switz. see **Geneva, Lake**
182 E2 **Le Mans** France
216 D3 **Le Mars** U.S.A.
179 F5 **Lemberg** France
179 G2 **Lembruch** Germany
234 C3 **Leme** Brazil
179 E2 **Lemele** Neth.
161 I3 **Lemery** Phil.
 Lemesos Cyprus see **Limassol**
179 G2 **Lemgo** Germany
171 N3 **Lemi** Fin.
203 L3 **Lemieux Islands** Canada
170 N1 **Lemmenjoen kansallispuisto** nat. park Fin.
178 D2 **Lemmer** Neth.
216 C2 **Lemmon** U.S.A.
215 G5 **Lemmon, Mount** U.S.A.
182 D2 **Le Mont-St-Michel** tourist site France
214 C3 **Lemoore** U.S.A.
207 G2 **Le Moyne, Lac** l. Canada
149 H5 **Lemro** r. Myanmar
169 R3 **Lemtybozh** Rus. Fed.
185 G4 **Le Murge** hills Italy
171 J4 **Lemvig** Denmark
150 C1 **Lena** r. Rus. Fed.
208 C4 **Lena** U.S.A.
149 E2 **Lenchung Tso** salt l. China
231 J4 **Lençóis Maranhenses, Parque Nacional dos** nat. park Brazil
169 M3 **Lendery** Rus. Fed.
143 E4 **Lengbarüt** Iran
141 G4 **Lenger** Kazakh.
179 F2 **Lengerich** Germany
154 A2 **Lenglong Ling** mts China
155 D5 **Lengshuijiang** China
155 D5 **Lengshuitan** China
235 H1 **Lengua de Vaca, Punta** pt Chile
173 H6 **Lenham** U.K.
171 K4 **Lenhovda** Sweden
141 G5 **Lenin** Tajik.
187 H7 **Lenina, Kanal** canal Rus. Fed.
 Leninabad Uzbek. see **Qanliko'l**
136 D1 **Lenine** Ukr.
 Leningrad Rus. Fed. see **St Petersburg**
141 G5 **Leningrad** Tajik.
187 F6 **Leningradskaya** Rus. Fed.
186 E3 **Leningradskaya Oblast'** admin. div. Rus. Fed.
133 S3 **Leningradskiy** Rus. Fed.
158 D2 **Lenino** Rus. Fed.
 Lenino Ukr. see **Lenine**
141 J2 **Leninogorsk** Kazakh.
141 H5 **Lenin Peak** Tajik.
141 G4 **Leninpol'** Kyrg.
 Leninsk Kazakh. see **Baykonyr**
187 H5 **Leninsk** Rus. Fed.
187 F4 **Leninskiy** Rus. Fed.
150 A1 **Leninsk-Kuznetskiy** Rus. Fed.
140 B2 **Leninskoye** Kazakh.
156 D3 **Leninskoye** Rus. Fed.
186 H3 **Leninskoye** Rus. Fed.
179 F3 **Lenne** r. Germany
125 J2 **Lennox Head** Australia
219 D3 **Lenoir** U.S.A.
221 G3 **Lenox** U.S.A.
182 F1 **Lens** France
133 M3 **Lensk** Rus. Fed.
187 G7 **Lentekhi** Georgia
177 H7 **Lenti** Hungary
184 F6 **Lentini** Sicily Italy
179 J1 **Lenzen** Germany
192 B3 **Léo** Burkina
176 G7 **Leoben** Austria
173 E5 **Leominster** U.K.
221 H3 **Leominster** U.S.A.
233 H3 **León** r. Col.
225 D3 **León** Mex.
224 H5 **León** Nicaragua
183 N1 **León** Spain
195 B6 **Leonardville** Namibia
138 E4 **Leonarisson** Cyprus
125 F7 **Leongatha** Australia
156 F2 **Leonidovo** Rus. Fed.

208 D4 **Little Sable Point** U.S.A.
121 B4 **Little Sandy Desert** Australia
219 F7 **Little San Salvador** *i.* Bahamas
204 F4 **Little Smoky** *r.* Canada
213 F4 **Littleton** CO U.S.A.
221 H2 **Littleton** NH U.S.A.
220 C5 **Littleton** WV U.S.A.
209 E3 **Little Traverse Bay** U.S.A.
195 D5 **Litunde** Moz.
154 C3 **Liuba** China
155 F6 **Liuchiu Yü** *i.* Taiwan
155 C5 **Liuchong He** *r.* China
160 B5 **Liuguo Dao** *i.* China
154 F1 **Liugu He** *r.* China
160 C2 **Liuhe** China
160 B2 **Liu He** *r.* China
155 D4 **Liujiachang** China
155 C5 **Liujiang** China
154 B3 **Liujiaxia Shuiku** *resr* China
156 B3 **Liukesong** China
154 C3 **Liupan Shan** *mts* China
155 D4 **Liuyang** China
156 B2 **Liuzhan** China
156 B2 **Liuzhou** China
185 J5 **Livadeia** Greece
158 C3 **Livadiya** Rus. Fed.
171 N4 **Līvāni** Latvia
214 B2 **Live Oak** CA U.S.A.
219 D6 **Live Oak** FL U.S.A.
118 C3 **Liveringa** Australia
214 B3 **Livermore** U.S.A.
217 B6 **Livermore, Mount** U.S.A.
221 H2 **Livermore Falls** U.S.A.
125 I4 **Liverpool** Australia
207 H5 **Liverpool** Canada
173 E4 **Liverpool** U.K.
203 K2 **Liverpool, Cape** Canada
202 E3 **Liverpool Bay** Canada
173 D4 **Liverpool Bay** U.K.
125 I3 **Liverpool Plains** Australia
125 I3 **Liverpool Range** *mts* Australia
224 G5 **Livingston** Guat.
174 E5 **Livingston** U.K.
214 B3 **Livingston** CA U.S.A.
212 E2 **Livingston** MT U.S.A.
219 C4 **Livingston** TN U.S.A.
217 E6 **Livingston** TX U.S.A.
217 E6 **Livingston, Lake** U.S.A.
195 C5 **Livingstone** Zambia
127 I2 **Livingston Island** Antarctica
185 G3 **Livno** Bos.-Herz.
187 F4 **Livny** Rus. Fed.
170 N2 **Livojoki** *r.* Fin.
209 H4 **Livonia** U.S.A.
184 D3 **Livorno** Italy
234 E1 **Livramento do Brumado** Brazil
143 E5 **Liwā** Oman
195 D4 **Liwale** Tanz.
154 B3 **Lixian** *Gansu* China
155 D4 **Lixian** *Hunan* China
154 B3 **Lixian** *Sichuan* China
154 E3 **Lixin** China
155 F4 **Liyang** China
173 B8 **Lizard** U.K.
173 B8 **Lizard Point** U.K.
178 B5 **Lizy-sur-Ourcq** France
184 F1 **Ljubljana** Slovenia
171 L4 **Ljugarn** Sweden
171 L3 **Ljungan** *r.* Sweden
171 L3 **Ljungaverk** Sweden
171 K4 **Ljungby** Sweden
171 L3 **Ljusdal** Sweden
171 L3 **Ljusnan** *r.* Sweden
171 L3 **Ljusne** Sweden
232 B5 **Llaima, Volcán** *vol.* Chile
173 C5 **Llanbadarn Fawr** U.K.
173 D5 **Llanbister** U.K.
235 I2 **Llancanelo, Salina** *salt flat* Arg.
173 D6 **Llandeilo** U.K.
173 C6 **Llandissilio** U.K.
173 D6 **Llandovery** U.K.
173 D5 **Llandrindod Wells** U.K.
173 D4 **Llandudno** U.K.
173 C5 **Llandysul** U.K.
173 C6 **Llanegwad** U.K.
173 C6 **Llanelli** U.K.
173 D5 **Llanfair Caereinion** U.K.
173 D5 **Llangefni** U.K.
173 D5 **Llangollen** U.K.
173 D5 **Llangurig** U.K.
173 C5 **Llanllyfni** U.K.
173 C5 **Llannerch-y-medd** U.K.
173 C5 **Llannor** U.K.
217 D6 **Llano** U.S.A.
217 D6 **Llano** *r.* U.S.A.

217 C5 **Llano Estacado** *plain* U.S.A.
233 J3 **Llanos** *plain* Col./Venez.
235 H4 **Llanquihue, Lago** *l.* Chile
173 C5 **Llanrhystud** U.K.
173 D6 **Llantrisant** U.K.
173 D5 **Llanuwchllyn** U.K.
173 D5 **Llanwnog** U.K.
173 D4 **Llay** U.K.
183 Q2 **Lleida** Spain
183 M3 **Llerena** Spain
183 P3 **Llíria** Spain
183 O1 **Llodio** Spain
202 F4 **Lloyd George, Mount** Canada
205 H3 **Lloyd Lake** Canada
205 G4 **Lloydminster** Canada
183 R3 **Llucmajor** Spain
232 C2 **Llullaillaco, Volcán** *vol.* Chile
Llyn Tegid *l.* U.K. *see* Bala Lake
Lô *r.* China/Vietnam *see* Lô, Sông
155 B6 **Lô, Sông** *r.* China/Vietnam
232 C2 **Loa** *r.* Chile
215 G2 **Loa** U.S.A.
186 I3 **Loban'** *r.* Rus. Fed.
183 N4 **Lobatejo** *mt.* Spain
195 C6 **Lobatse** Botswana
179 J3 **Löbejün** Germany
179 K3 **Löbenberg** *h.* Germany
235 K3 **Lobería** Arg.
195 B5 **Lobito** Angola
235 K2 **Lobos** Arg.
224 B2 **Lobos, Isla** *i.* Mex.
179 K2 **Loburg** Germany
174 D4 **Lochaber** *reg.* U.K.
174 C4 **Lochaline** U.K.
209 E1 **Lochalsh** Canada
174 A3 **Lochboisdale** U.K.
174 C3 **Lochcarron** U.K.
172 C1 **Lochearnhead** U.K.
179 E2 **Lochem** Neth.
123 C5 **Lochern National Park** Australia
182 E3 **Loches** France
174 E4 **Lochgelly** U.K.
174 C4 **Lochgilphead** U.K.
174 C2 **Lochinver** U.K.
174 E3 **Loch Lomond and the Trossachs National Park** U.K.
174 A3 **Lochmaddy** U.K.
174 E4 **Lochnagar** *mt.* U.K.
221 E5 **Loch Raven Reservoir** U.S.A.
174 D4 **Lochy, Loch** *l.* U.K.
124 A4 **Lock** Australia
174 E5 **Lockerbie** U.K.
125 G5 **Lockhart** Australia
217 D6 **Lockhart** U.S.A.
221 E4 **Lock Haven** U.S.A.
220 D3 **Lockport** U.S.A.
162 C3 **Lộc Ninh** Vietnam
220 B5 **Locust Grove** U.S.A.
138 E6 **Lod** Israel
125 E6 **Loddon** *r.* Australia
183 F5 **Lodève** France
186 E2 **Lodeynoye Pole** Rus. Fed.
212 F2 **Lodge Grass** U.S.A.
148 B3 **Lodhran** Pak.
184 C2 **Lodi** Italy
214 B2 **Lodi** CA U.S.A.
220 B4 **Lodi** OH U.S.A.
170 K1 **Lødingen** Norway
195 C4 **Lodja** Dem. Rep. Congo
194 D3 **Lodwar** Kenya
177 I5 **Łódź** Poland
143 H3 **Loe Dakka** Afgh.
162 B1 **Loei** Thai.
196 C5 **Loeriesfontein** S. Africa
170 K1 **Lofoten** *is* Norway
187 G5 **Log** Rus. Fed.
125 J1 **Logan** *r.* Australia
213 G5 **Logan** NM U.S.A.
220 B5 **Logan** OH U.S.A.
213 E3 **Logan** UT U.S.A.
220 C6 **Logan** WV U.S.A.
204 A2 **Logan, Mount** Canada
123 D4 **Logan Creek** *r.* Australia
204 D2 **Logan Mountains** Canada
208 D5 **Logansport** U.S.A.
184 F2 **Logatec** Slovenia
183 O1 **Logroño** Spain
149 H4 **Logtak Lake** India
197 E4 **Lohatlha** S. Africa
179 H3 **Lohfelden** Germany
170 N2 **Lohiniva** Fin.
171 M3 **Lohjanjärvi** *l.* Fin.
163 I3 **Longiram** Indon.
223 I4 **Long Island** Bahamas
206 E3 **Long Island** Canada
119 E2 **Long Island** P.N.G.
221 G4 **Long Island** U.S.A.

170 M2 **Lohtaja** Fin.
162 A1 **Loikaw** Myanmar
162 A1 **Loi Lan** *mt.* Myanmar/Thai.
152 G7 **Loi-lem** Myanmar
171 M3 **Loimaa** Fin.
182 E3 **Loire** *r.* France
230 C4 **Loja** Ecuador
183 N4 **Loja** Spain
163 I1 **Lokan** *r. Sabah* Malaysia
170 N2 **Lokan tekojärvi** *resr* Fin.
178 C3 **Lokeren** Belgium
196 D2 **Lokgwabe** Botswana
194 D3 **Lokichar** Kenya
194 D3 **Lokichokio** Kenya
171 J4 **Løkken** Denmark
171 J3 **Løkken** Norway
177 O2 **Loknya** Rus. Fed.
192 C4 **Lokoja** Nigeria
192 C4 **Lokossa** Benin
187 E4 **Lokot'** Rus. Fed.
171 N4 **Loksa** Estonia
203 L3 **Loks Land** *i.* Canada
192 B4 **Lola** Guinea
214 B2 **Lola, Mount** U.S.A.
171 J5 **Lolland** *i.* Denmark
195 D4 **Lollondo** Tanz.
212 D2 **Lolo** U.S.A.
197 E3 **Lolwane** S. Africa
185 J3 **Lom** Bulg.
171 J3 **Lom** Norway
195 C4 **Lomami** *r.* Dem. Rep. Congo
235 J3 **Loma Negra, Planicie de la** *plain* Arg.
143 G3 **Lomar Pass** Afgh.
235 K2 **Lomas de Zamora** Arg.
118 C2 **Lomblen** *i.* Indon.
163 I4 **Lombok** *i.* Indon.
163 I4 **Lombok, Selat** *sea chan.* Indon.
192 C4 **Lomé** Togo
195 C4 **Lomela** Dem. Rep. Congo
195 C4 **Lomela** *r.* Dem. Rep. Congo
178 A4 **Lomme** France
178 D3 **Lommel** Belgium
174 D4 **Lomond, Loch** *l.* U.K.
141 F1 **Lomonosovka** Kazakh.
240 M1 **Lomonosov Ridge** *sea feature* Arctic Ocean
186 G1 **Lomovoye** Rus. Fed.
151 D7 **Lompobattang, Gunung** *mt.* Indon.
214 B4 **Lompoc** U.S.A.
162 B1 **Lom Sak** Thai.
177 K4 **Łomża** Poland
163 D2 **Lơn, Hon** *i.* Vietnam
148 D6 **Lonar** India
235 H4 **Loncoche** Chile
235 H3 **Loncopue** Arg.
156 D2 **Londoko** Rus. Fed.
209 G2 **London** Canada
173 G6 **London** U.K. (City Plan **98**)
220 A6 **London** KY U.S.A.
220 B5 **London** OH U.S.A.
175 K3 **Londonderry** U.K.
221 G3 **Londonderry** U.S.A.
118 C3 **Londonderry, Cape** Australia
232 B9 **Londonderry, Isla** *i.* Chile
234 B3 **Londrina** Brazil
214 C3 **Lone Pine** U.S.A.
162 A1 **Long** Thai.
174 D4 **Long, Loch** *inlet* U.K.
133 S2 **Longa, Proliv** *sea chan.* Rus. Fed.
155 C6 **Long'an** China
204 F3 **Loon** *r.* Canada
121 D6 **Loongana** Australia
205 H4 **Loon Lake** Canada
221 I1 **Loon Lake** *l.* U.S.A.
175 I5 **Loop Head** Ireland
149 E1 **Lop** China
150 G1 **Lopatina, Gora** *mt.* Rus. Fed.
187 H4 **Lopatino** Rus. Fed.
162 B2 **Lop Buri** Thai.
195 B4 **Lopé, Parc National de la** *nat. park* Gabon
161 I3 **Lopez** Phil.
221 E4 **Lopez** U.S.A.
150 B2 **Lop Nur** *salt flat* China
194 C3 **Lopori** *r.* Dem. Rep. Congo
170 M1 **Lopphavet** *b.* Norway
186 I2 **Loptyuga** Rus. Fed.
143 G4 **Lora** *r.* Afgh.
124 A2 **Lora** *watercourse* Australia
233 I2 **Lora** *r.* Venez.
143 G4 **Lora, Hamun-i-** *dry lake* Pak.
183 N4 **Lora del Río** Spain
220 B4 **Lorain** U.S.A.
148 B3 **Loralai** Pak.
148 B3 **Loralai** *r.* Pak.
220 A4 **Loramie, Lake** U.S.A.
183 P4 **Lorca** Spain
179 F4 **Lorch** Germany

221 G4 **Long Island Sound** *sea chan.* U.S.A.
156 A3 **Longjiang** China
155 C5 **Long Jiang** *r.* China
149 H3 **Longju** China
154 F2 **Longkou Gang** *b.* China
206 F2 **Longlac** Canada
206 C4 **Long Lake** *l.* Canada
221 F3 **Long Lake** U.S.A.
221 I1 **Long Lake** *l.* ME U.S.A.
209 E3 **Long Lake** *l.* MI U.S.A.
209 F3 **Long Lake** *l.* MI U.S.A.
216 C2 **Long Lake** *l.* ND U.S.A.
221 F2 **Long Lake** *l.* NY U.S.A.
155 C5 **Longli** China
155 E6 **Longlin** China
173 H5 **Long Melford** U.K.
156 B2 **Longmen** China
155 E6 **Longmen** China
154 B3 **Longmen Shan** *mts* China
213 F3 **Longmont** U.S.A.
154 B3 **Longnan** China
155 E5 **Longnan** China
209 G4 **Long Point** Canada
126 B7 **Long Point** N.Z.
209 G4 **Long Point Bay** Canada
172 E3 **Long Preston** U.K.
155 F4 **Longquan** China
155 F4 **Longquan Xi** *r.* China
203 M5 **Long Range Mountains** Canada
207 I4 **Long Range Mountains** Canada
119 E4 **Longreach** Australia
154 B3 **Longriba** China
155 C4 **Longshan** China
155 D5 **Longsheng** China
155 D5 **Longshi** China
213 F3 **Longs Peak** U.S.A.
173 I5 **Long Stratton** U.K.
155 D4 **Longtian** China
172 E2 **Longtown** U.K.
207 F4 **Longueuil** Canada
178 D5 **Longuyon** France
214 A2 **Longvale** U.S.A.
215 F3 **Long Valley Junction** U.S.A.
217 E5 **Longview** TX U.S.A.
212 B2 **Longview** WA U.S.A.
158 C2 **Longwangmiao** Rus. Fed.
154 B3 **Longxi** China
154 C3 **Longxian** China
155 E5 **Longxi Shan** *mt.* China
162 C3 **Long Xuyên** Vietnam
155 E5 **Longyan** China
154 E2 **Longyao** China
156 B2 **Longzhen** China
155 C6 **Longzhou** China
179 F2 **Löningen** Germany
171 K4 **Lönsboda** Sweden
125 C6 **Lonsdale, Lake** Australia
182 G3 **Lons-le-Saunier** France
234 B3 **Lontra** *r.* Brazil
161 I3 **Looc** Phil.
209 E4 **Looking Glass** *r.* U.S.A.
221 F4 **Lookout** U.S.A.
206 D2 **Lookout, Cape** Canada
219 E5 **Lookout, Cape** U.S.A.
125 J1 **Lookout, Point** Australia
209 F3 **Lookout, Point** U.S.A.
214 C3 **Lookout Mountain** U.S.A.
121 B7 **Lookout Point** Australia
208 C1 **Loon** Canada

161 H4 **Lord Auckland Shoal** *sea feature* Phil.
142 C4 **Lordegān** Iran
119 F5 **Lord Howe Island** Pacific Ocean
236 F7 **Lord Howe Rise** *sea feature* S. Pacific Ocean
215 H5 **Lordsburg** U.S.A.
179 F4 **Loreley** *tourist site* Germany
234 D3 **Lorena** Brazil
151 F7 **Lorentz** *r.* Indon.
225 E3 **Lorenzo del Real** Mex.
231 F7 **Loreto** Bol.
231 I5 **Loreto** Brazil
224 B2 **Loreto** Mex.
161 J4 **Loreto** Phil.
233 I2 **Lorica** Col.
182 C3 **Lorient** France
205 K1 **Lorillard** *r.* Canada
174 C4 **Lorn, Firth of** *est.* U.K.
123 D5 **Lorne** Qld Australia
125 E7 **Lorne** Vic. Australia
122 B3 **Lorne** *watercourse* Australia
149 H3 **Loro** *r.* China
122 B3 **Lorraine** Australia
182 G2 **Lorraine** *reg.* France
179 G5 **Lorsch** Germany
179 F2 **Lorup** Germany
148 C4 **Losal** India
213 F5 **Los Alamos** U.S.A.
235 H2 **Los Andes** Chile
235 H3 **Los Ángeles** Chile
214 C5 **Los Angeles** U.S.A. (City Plan **103**)
214 C4 **Los Angeles Aqueduct** *canal* U.S.A.
214 B3 **Los Banos** U.S.A.
232 D2 **Los Blancos** Arg.
215 D5 **Los Coronados, Islas** Mex.
214 B3 **Los Gatos** U.S.A.
224 C1 **Los Gigantes, Llanos de** *plain* Mex.
232 B8 **Los Glaciares, Parque Nacional** *nat. park* Arg.
179 E5 **Losheim** Germany
184 F2 **Lošinj** *i.* Croatia
233 H3 **Los Katios, Parque Nacional** *nat. park* Col.
197 H2 **Loskop Dam** S. Africa
235 H4 **Los Lagos** *admin. reg.* Chile
213 F5 **Los Lunas** U.S.A.
225 E3 **Los Mármoles, Parque Nacional** *nat. park* Mex.
235 I4 **Los Menucos** Arg.
224 B2 **Los Mochis** Mex.
214 A1 **Los Molinos** U.S.A.
194 B3 **Losombo** Dem. Rep. Congo
225 D4 **Los Reyes** Mex.
233 K2 **Los Roques, Islas** Venez.
179 E2 **Losser** Neth.
174 E3 **Lossie** *r.* U.K.
174 E3 **Lossiemouth** U.K.
179 K4 **Lößnitz** Germany
233 J2 **Los Taques** Venez.
233 K2 **Los Teques** Venez.
233 L2 **Los Testigos** *is* Venez.
214 C4 **Lost Hills** U.S.A.
212 D2 **Lost Trail Pass** U.S.A.
173 C7 **Lostwithiel** U.K.
232 C2 **Los Vientos** Chile
235 H1 **Los Vilos** Chile
235 H3 **Lota** Chile
140 D5 **Loţfābād** Iran
197 I3 **Lothair** S. Africa
194 D3 **Lotikipi Plain** Kenya
195 C4 **Loto** Dem. Rep. Congo
186 E3 **Lotoshino** Rus. Fed.
197 G1 **Lotsane** *r.* Botswana
170 O1 **Lotta** *r.* Fin./Rus. Fed.
179 F2 **Lotte** Germany
151 C4 **Louang Namtha** Laos *see* Louangnamtha
151 C5 **Louangnamtha** Laos
151 C5 **Louangphabang** Laos
Louangphrabang Laos *see* Louangphabang
195 B4 **Loubomo** Congo
182 C2 **Loudéac** France
155 D5 **Loudi** China
195 B4 **Loudima** Congo
220 B4 **Loudonville** U.S.A.
192 A3 **Louga** Senegal
173 F5 **Loughborough** U.K.
173 C6 **Loughor** *r.* U.K.
175 J4 **Loughrea** Ireland
173 H6 **Loughton** U.K.
220 B4 **Louisa** KY U.S.A.
221 E5 **Louisa** VA U.S.A.
175 I4 **Louisburgh** Ireland
204 C4 **Louise Island** Canada

119 F3 **Louisiade Archipelago** *is* P.N.G.
217 E6 **Louisiana** *state* U.S.A.
Louis Trichardt S. Africa *see* Makhado
219 D5 **Louisville** GA U.S.A.
219 C5 **Louisville** KY U.S.A.
217 F5 **Louisville** MS U.S.A.
237 H8 **Louisville Ridge** *sea feature* S. Pacific Ocean
206 E3 **Louis-XIV, Pointe** Canada
132 E3 **Loukhi** Rus. Fed.
183 L4 **Loulé** Port.
176 F5 **Louny** Czech Rep.
216 D3 **Loup** *r.* U.S.A.
207 F2 **Loups Marins, Lacs des** *lakes* Canada
207 I4 **Lourdes** Canada
183 G5 **Lourdes** France
183 L2 **Lousã** Port.
160 E1 **Loushan** China
125 D3 **Louth** Australia
173 G4 **Louth** U.K.
185 J5 **Loutra Aidipsou** Greece
Louvain Belgium *see* Leuven
196 B1 **Louwater-Suid** Namibia
197 I3 **Louwsburg** S. Africa
170 M2 **Lövånger** Sweden
186 D3 **Lovat'** *r.* Rus. Fed.
185 K3 **Lovech** Bulg.
213 F3 **Loveland** U.S.A.
212 E2 **Lovell** U.S.A.
214 C1 **Lovelock** U.S.A.
178 B3 **Lovendegem** Belgium
171 N3 **Loviisa** Fin.
220 D6 **Lovingston** U.S.A.
208 C4 **Lovington** IL U.S.A.
217 C5 **Lovington** NM U.S.A.
169 M2 **Lovozero** Rus. Fed.
209 J3 **Low** Canada
205 L2 **Low, Cape** Canada
206 E3 **Low, Lac** *l.* Canada
195 C4 **Lowa** Dem. Rep. Congo
148 B2 **Lowarai Pass** Pak.
221 H3 **Lowell** MA U.S.A.
209 E4 **Lowell** MI U.S.A.
221 G2 **Lowell** VT U.S.A.
204 F5 **Lower Arrow Lake** Canada
Lower California *pen.* Mex. *see* Baja California
124 D7 **Lower Glenelg National Park** Australia
215 F4 **Lower Granite Gorge** U.S.A.
126 E4 **Lower Hutt** N.Z.
214 A2 **Lower Lake** U.S.A.
175 K3 **Lower Lough Erne** *l.* U.K.
162 □ **Lower Peirce Reservoir** Sing.
204 D3 **Lower Post** Canada
207 H5 **Lower Sackville** Canada
173 I5 **Lowestoft** U.K.
177 I4 **Łowicz** Poland
125 F9 **Low Rocky Point** Australia
174 E5 **Lowther Hills** U.K.
221 F3 **Lowville** U.S.A.
179 G1 **Loxstedt** Germany
124 D7 **Loxton** Australia
197 E5 **Loxton** S. Africa
221 E4 **Loyalsock Creek** *r.* U.S.A.
214 B2 **Loyalton** U.S.A.
119 G4 **Loyauté, Îs** *is* New Caledonia
187 D5 **Loyew** Belarus
185 H2 **Loznica** Serbia
187 F5 **Lozova** Ukr.
141 I1 **Lozovoye** Kazakh.
195 C5 **Luacano** Angola
154 E4 **Lu'an** China
154 D3 **Luanchuan** China
195 B4 **Luanda** Angola
155 B7 **Luang, Huai** *r.* Thai.
162 A3 **Luang, Khao** *mt.* Thai.
162 B4 **Luang, Thale** *lag.* Thai.
195 D5 **Luangwa** *r.* Zambia
149 H2 **Luanhaizi** China
154 F1 **Luan He** *r.* China
154 F2 **Luannan** China
154 E1 **Luanping** China
195 C5 **Luanshya** Zambia
154 F2 **Luanxian** China
195 C5 **Luanza** Dem. Rep. Congo
163 H2 **Luar, Danau** *l.* Indon.
183 M1 **Luarca** Spain
195 C5 **Luau** Angola
225 G4 **Lubaantun** *tourist site* Belize
177 K5 **Lubaczów** Poland
171 N4 **Lubānas ezers** *l.* Latvia
161 I3 **Lubang** Phil.
161 I3 **Lubang** *i.* Phil.
161 H3 **Lubang Islands** Phil.

M

161 I4 Madridejos Phil.
183 O3 Madridejos Spain
147 I2 Madugula India
163 H4 Madura i. Indon.
163 H4 Madura, Selat sea chan. Indon.
147 H4 Madurai India
156 H3 Madvezh'ya vol. Rus. Fed.
149 E4 Madwas India
148 C2 Madyan Pak.
187 H7 Madzhalis Rus. Fed.
159 F6 Maebashi Japan
162 A1 Mae Hong Son Thai.
162 A1 Mae Sai Thai.
162 A1 Mae Sariang Thai.
162 A1 Mae Sot Thai.
223 I5 Maestra, Sierra mts Cuba
195 E5 Maevatanana Madag.
119 G3 Maéwo i. Vanuatu
205 I4 Mafeking Canada
197 G4 Mafeteng Lesotho
125 G6 Maffra Australia
195 D4 Mafia Island Tanz.
197 F2 Mafikeng S. Africa
195 D4 Mafinga Tanz.
235 C4 Mafra Brazil
197 I5 Magabeni S. Africa
133 Q4 Magadan Rus. Fed.
195 D4 Magadi Kenya
197 J1 Magaiza Moz.
161 I3 Magallanes Phil.
233 I2 Magangue Col.
138 D3 Magara Turkey
137 H2 Magaramkent Rus. Fed.
187 H7 Magas Rus. Fed.
161 I2 Magat r. Phil.
156 B1 Magdagachi Rus. Fed.
235 L2 Magdalena Arg.
231 F6 Magdalena Bol.
233 I3 Magdalena r. Col.
222 B2 Magdalena Mex.
213 E6 Magdalena r. Mex.
213 F5 Magdalena U.S.A.
224 A2 Magdalena, Bahía b. Mex.
232 B6 Magdalena, Isla i. Chile
224 A2 Magdalena, Isla i. Mex.
161 H5 Magdaline, Gunung mt. Sabah Malaysia
141 F5 Magdanly Turkm.
179 J2 Magdeburg Germany
122 E3 Magdelaine Cays atoll Australia
236 E4 Magellan Seamounts sea feature N. Pacific Ocean
121 B7 Magenta, Lake salt flat Australia
170 N1 Magerøya i. Norway
159 B9 Mage-shima i. Japan
184 C2 Maggiorasca, Monte mt. Italy
184 C2 Maggiore, Lake Italy
Maghâgha Egypt see Maghāghah
136 C5 Maghāghah Egypt
192 A3 Maghama Mauritania
175 J3 Maghera U.K.
175 J3 Magherafelt U.K.
173 E4 Maghull U.K.
213 D3 Magna U.S.A.
184 F6 Magna Grande mt. Sicily Italy
127 L5 Magnet Bay Antarctica
119 E3 Magnetic Island Australia
122 D3 Magnetic Passage Australia
170 P1 Magnetiy U.K.
140 D1 Magnitogorsk Rus. Fed.
217 E5 Magnolia U.S.A.
156 F1 Mago Rus. Fed.
207 F4 Magog Canada
225 E3 Magozal Mex.
207 H3 Magpie Canada
209 E1 Magpie r. Canada
207 H3 Magpie, Lac l. Canada
205 G5 Magrath Canada
215 D3 Magruder Mountain U.S.A.
192 A3 Magta' Lahjar Mauritania
140 D5 Magtymguly Turkm.
195 D4 Magu Tanz.
156 E1 Magu, Khrebet mts Rus. Fed.
155 B6 Maguan China
231 I4 Maguarinho, Cabo c. Brazil
197 J2 Magude Moz.
221 J2 Magundy Canada
205 J2 Maguse Lake Canada
149 H5 Magway Myanmar
149 H5 Magyichaung Myanmar
142 B2 Mahābād Iran
147 G2 Mahabaleshwar India
149 F4 Mahabharat Range mts Nepal

195 E6 Mahabo Madag.
147 G2 Mahad India
148 D5 Mahadeo Hills India
194 D3 Mahagi Dem. Rep. Congo
195 E5 Mahajamba r. Madag.
148 C3 Mahajan India
195 E5 Mahajanga Madag.
163 H2 Mahakam r. Indon.
195 C6 Mahalapye Botswana
195 E5 Mahalevona Madag.
142 C3 Mahallāt Iran
148 D3 Maham India
143 E4 Māhān Iran
147 J1 Mahanadi r. India
195 E5 Mahanoro Madag.
148 C5 Maharashtra state India
147 I1 Mahasamund India
162 B1 Maha Sarakham Thai.
195 E5 Mahatalaky Madag.
195 E5 Mahavanona Madag.
195 E5 Mahavavy r. Madag.
147 I5 Mahaweli Ganga r. Sri Lanka
162 C1 Mahaxai Laos
147 I2 Mahbubabad India
147 H2 Mahbubnagar India
142 D5 Mahḍah Oman
231 G2 Mahdia Guyana
184 D7 Mahdia Tunisia
191 I5 Mahé i. Seychelles
147 J2 Mahendragiri mt. India
148 C5 Mahesana India
148 C5 Maheshwar India
148 C5 Mahi r. India
143 E4 Māhī watercourse Iran
126 F3 Mahia Peninsula N.Z.
187 D4 Mahilyow Belarus
147 I5 Mahiyangana Sri Lanka
197 I4 Mahlabatini S. Africa
179 J2 Mahlsdorf Germany
Maḥmūd-e 'Erāqī Afgh. see Maḥmūd-e Rāqī
143 H3 Maḥmūd-e Rāqī Afgh.
139 L4 Mahniän Iran
216 D2 Mahnomen U.S.A.
148 D4 Mahoba India
183 S3 Mahón Spain
220 D4 Mahoning Creek Lake U.S.A.
145 B5 Māhrūd Iran
149 H5 Mahudaung mts Myanmar
148 B5 Mahuva India
185 L4 Mahya Dağı mt. Turkey
142 C3 Mahyār Iran
149 H4 Maibang India
233 I2 Maicao Col.
206 E4 Maicasagi, Lac l. Canada
155 C5 Maichen China
173 G6 Maidenhead U.K.
205 H4 Maidstone Canada
173 H6 Maidstone U.K.
193 D3 Maiduguri Nigeria
233 K3 Maigualida, Sierra mts Venez.
175 J5 Maigue r. Ireland
149 E4 Maihar India
154 E4 Maiji Shan mt. China
149 E5 Maikala Range hills India
195 C4 Maiko, Parc National de la nat. park Dem. Rep. Congo
149 E3 Mailani India
179 H5 Main r. Germany
175 L3 Main r. U.K.
207 I3 Main Brook Canada
209 F3 Main Channel lake channel Canada
195 B4 Mai-Ndombe, Lac l. Dem. Rep. Congo
179 J5 Main-Donau-Kanal canal Germany
Maindong China see Coqên
209 I4 Main Duck Island Canada
221 I2 Maine state U.S.A.
193 D3 Maïné-Soroa Niger
162 A2 Maingy Island Myanmar
179 H5 Mainhardt Germany
161 J4 Mainit Phil.
161 J4 Mainit, Lake Phil.
174 E1 Mainland i. Orkney, Scotland U.K.
174 □ Mainland i. Shetland, Scotland U.K.
179 J4 Mainleus Germany
120 F2 Mainoru Australia
149 E5 Mainpat reg. India
148 D4 Mainpuri India
125 J1 Main Range National Park Australia
195 E5 Maintirano Madag.
179 G4 Mainz Germany
192 □ Maio i. Cape Verde

235 I2 Maipó, Volcán vol. Chile
235 L3 Maipú Buenos Aires Arg.
235 I2 Maipú Mendoza Arg.
233 K2 Maiquetía Venez.
149 G5 Maiskhal Island Bangl.
195 C6 Maitengwe Botswana
125 I4 Maitland N.S.W. Australia
124 B5 Maitland S.A. Australia
121 B4 Maitri research stn Antarctica
127 K3 Maitri research stn Antarctica
120 E3 Maiyu, Mount h. Australia
224 I5 Maíz, Islas del Nicaragua
149 G3 Maizhokunggar China
159 D7 Maizuru Japan
185 I4 Maja Jezercë mt. Albania
147 H2 Majalgaon India
233 L4 Majari r. Brazil
138 E5 Majdel Aanjar tourist site Lebanon
163 I3 Majene Indon.
142 C6 Majḥūd well Saudi Arabia
194 D3 Majī Eth.
154 E2 Majia He r. China
155 D6 Majiang China
156 B2 Majiazi China
183 R3 Major, Puig mt. Spain
183 R3 Majorca i. Spain
149 H4 Majuli Island India
Majuro atoll Marshall Is see Taongi
197 G4 Majwemasweu S. Africa
195 B4 Makabana Congo
Makaha U.S.A. see Mākaha
214 □¹ Mākaha U.S.A.
151 D7 Makale Indon.
149 H4 Makalu mt. China
195 C4 Makamba Burundi
141 J3 Makanchi Kazakh.
Makapuu Hd hd U.S.A. see Makapu'u Head
214 □¹ Makapu'u Head U.S.A.
186 I2 Makar-Ib Rus. Fed.
156 F2 Makarov Rus. Fed.
240 M1 Makarov Basin sea feature Arctic Ocean
185 G3 Makarska Croatia
169 O4 Makar'yev Rus. Fed.
163 I4 Makassar Indon.
140 C3 Makat Kazakh.
197 J3 Makatini Flats lowland S. Africa
192 A4 Makeni Sierra Leone
195 C6 Makgadikgadi depr. Botswana
187 H7 Makhachkala Rus. Fed.
197 H1 Makhado S. Africa
140 D3 Makhambet Kazakh.
139 G4 Makhfar al Ḥammām Syria
139 I4 Makhmūr Iraq
141 J1 Makhorovka Kazakh.
195 D4 Makindu Kenya
141 G1 Makinsk Kazakh.
187 F5 Makiyivka Ukr.
Makkah Saudi Arabia see Mecca
207 I2 Makkovik Canada
207 I2 Makkovik, Cape Canada
178 D1 Makkum Neth.
181 H5 Makó Hungary
194 B3 Makokou Gabon
195 D4 Makongolosi Tanz.
197 E2 Makopong Botswana
195 B4 Makotipoko Congo
143 F5 Makran reg. Iran/Pak.
148 C4 Makrana India
143 F5 Makran Coast Range mts Pak.
147 I2 Makri India
185 K6 Makronisos i. Greece
186 E3 Maksatikha Rus. Fed.
158 E1 Maksimovka Rus. Fed.
143 F4 Maksotag Iran
142 B2 Makū Iran
149 H4 Makum India
195 D4 Makumbako Tanz.
195 D5 Makunguwiro Tanz.
159 B9 Makurazaki Japan
192 C4 Makurdi Nigeria
142 D4 Maküyeh Iran
197 F3 Makwassie S. Africa
170 L2 Malå Sweden
224 I7 Mala, Punta pt Panama
161 J5 Malabang Phil.
147 G3 Malabar Coast India
192 C4 Malabo Equat. Guinea
161 H4 Malabuñgan Phil.
163 E2 Malacca, Strait of Indon./Malaysia
213 D3 Malad City U.S.A.
187 C4 Maladzyechna Belarus

183 N4 Málaga Spain
221 F5 Malaga NJ U.S.A.
213 F5 Malaga NM U.S.A.
175 J3 Málainn Mhóir Ireland
119 G2 Malaita i. Solomon Is
193 F4 Malakal Sudan
119 G3 Malakula i. Vanuatu
148 C2 Malakwal Pak.
151 E7 Malamala Indon.
143 I5 Malan, Ras pt Pak.
163 H4 Malang Indon.
195 B4 Malanje Angola
235 I1 Malanzán, Sierra de mts Arg.
147 H4 Malappuram India
171 L4 Mälaren l. Sweden
131 F6 Malatya Turkey
122 E3 Malay Reef Australia
141 I3 Malay Sary Kazakh.
163 G2 Malaysia country Asia
163 B2 Malaysia, Semenanjung Malaysia
139 I2 Malazgirt Turkey
123 C4 Malbon Australia
177 I3 Malbork Poland
179 E5 Malborn Germany
179 K1 Malchin Germany
179 K1 Malchiner See l. Germany
121 C5 Malcolm Australia
121 C7 Malcolm, Point Australia
149 G4 Maldah India
178 B3 Maldegem Belgium
217 F4 Malden U.S.A.
117 I4 Malden Island Kiribati
130 C6 Maldives country Indian Ocean
173 H6 Maldon U.K.
235 L2 Maldonado Uruguay
130 C6 Male Maldives
185 J6 Maleas, Akrotirio pt Greece
135 F6 Male Atoll Maldives
197 F4 Malebogo S. Africa
147 H2 Malegaon Maharashtra India
148 C5 Malegaon Maharashtra India
177 H6 Malé Karpaty hills Slovakia
139 K3 Malek Kandī Iran
195 B4 Malele Dem. Rep. Congo
195 D5 Malema Moz.
148 C3 Maler Kotla India
143 G3 Malestān Afgh.
187 H7 Malgobek Rus. Fed.
170 L2 Malgomaj l. Sweden
142 B5 Malham Saudi Arabia
213 C3 Malheur Lake U.S.A.
192 B3 Mali country Africa
195 C4 Mali Dem. Rep. Congo
192 A3 Mali Guinea
154 C3 Malian He r. China
144 I3 Malianjing China
149 G4 Malihabad India
143 F4 Malik Naro mt. Pak.
162 A2 Mali Kyun i. Myanmar
151 E7 Malili Indon.
163 G4 Malimping Indon.
195 E4 Malindi Kenya
175 K2 Malin Head Ireland
Malin More Ireland see Málainn Mhóir
141 G2 Malinovka Kazakh.
158 D2 Malinovka r. Rus. Fed.
141 I2 Malinovoye Ozero Rus. Fed.
155 B6 Malipo China
184 F2 Mali Raginac mt. Croatia
161 J5 Malita Phil.
162 A3 Maliwun Myanmar
148 B5 Maliya India
137 G2 Malka r. Rus. Fed.
139 K5 Malkaili Iran
147 I2 Malkangiri India
151 E6 Malkara Turkey
177 M4 Mal'kavichy Belarus
185 L4 Malko Tŭrnovo Bulg.
125 H6 Mallacoota Australia
125 H6 Mallacoota Inlet b. Australia

174 C4 Mallaig U.K.
124 C5 Mallala Australia
136 C6 Mallawī Egypt
125 E5 Mallee Cliffs National Park Australia
205 J2 Mallery Lake Canada
Mallorca i. Spain see Majorca
175 J5 Mallow Ireland
121 D4 Mallowa Well Australia
173 D5 Mallwyd U.K.
196 C6 Malmesbury S. Africa
173 E6 Malmesbury U.K.
171 K5 Malmö Sweden
186 I3 Malmyzh Rus. Fed.
119 G3 Malo i. Vanuatu
161 I3 Malolos Phil.
195 C5 Malonga Dem. Rep. Congo
170 J2 Malm Norway
170 M2 Malmberget Sweden
179 E4 Malmédy Belgium
170 M2 Malmberget Sweden
186 F2 Malosmadulu Atoll atoll Maldives see Maalhosmadulu Atoll
171 I3 Måløy Norway
187 F4 Maloyaroslavets Rus. Fed.
169 P2 Malozemel'skaya Tundra lowland Rus. Fed.
230 B3 Malpelo, Isla de i. Col.
147 G3 Malprabha r. India
184 F6 Malta country Europe
171 N4 Malta Latvia
212 F1 Malta U.S.A.
184 F6 Malta Channel Italy/Malta
195 B6 Maltahöhe Namibia
173 F4 Maltby U.K.
173 H4 Maltby le Marsh U.K.
172 G3 Malton U.K.
Maluku is Indon. see Moluccas
151 E7 Maluku, Laut sea Indon.
171 K3 Malung Sweden
197 H4 Maluti Mountains Lesotho
119 G2 Malu'u Solomon Is
142 G2 Malvan India
217 E5 Malvern U.S.A.
187 D5 Malyn Ukr.
133 R3 Malyy Anyuy r. Rus. Fed.
Malyy Balkhan, Khrebet h. Turkm. see Kiçi Balkan Daglary
187 H6 Malyye Derbety Rus. Fed.
140 B1 Malyy Irgiz r. Rus. Fed.
Malyy Kavkaz mts Asia see Lesser Caucasus
133 P2 Malyy Lyakhovskiy, Ostrov i. Rus. Fed.
140 B2 Malyy Uzen' r. Kazakh./Rus. Fed.
133 P3 Mama r. Rus. Fed.
169 Q2 Mamadysh Rus. Fed.
197 H3 Mamafubedu S. Africa
147 I3 Mamallapuram India
161 H5 Mambahenauhan i. Phil.
161 J4 Mambajao Phil.
194 C3 Mambasa Dem. Rep. Congo
194 B3 Mambéré r. Centr. Afr. Rep.
161 I3 Mamburao Phil.
197 H2 Mamelodi S. Africa
192 C4 Mamfe Cameroon
Mamfé Cameroon see Mamfe
141 F1 Mamlyutka Kazakh.
215 G5 Mammoth U.S.A.
219 C4 Mammoth Cave National Park U.S.A.
214 C3 Mammoth Lakes U.S.A.
230 E6 Mamoré r. Bol./Brazil
192 A3 Mamou Guinea
195 E5 Mampikony Madag.
192 B4 Mampong Ghana
235 H3 Mamuil Malal, Paso pass Arg./Chile
163 I3 Mamuju Indon.
196 D1 Mamuno Botswana
140 D2 Mamyt Kazakh.
192 B4 Man Côte d'Ivoire
172 C3 Man, Isle of terr. Irish Sea
233 I3 Manacacias r. Col.
183 R3 Manacor Spain
151 E6 Manado Indon.
224 H5 Managua Nicaragua
224 H5 Managua, Lago de l. Nicaragua

119 E2 Manam Island P.N.G.
233 L2 Manamo, Caño r. Venez.
Manana i. U.S.A. see Mānana
214 □¹ Mānana i. U.S.A.
195 E6 Manampaneva Madag.
195 E5 Manananara, Parc National de nat. park Madag.
195 E5 Mananara Avaratra Madag.
125 E5 Manangatang Australia
122 B3 Manangoora Australia
195 E6 Mananjary Madag.
147 H4 Manantavadi India
148 D3 Mana Pass India
147 G4 Manas r. Bhutan
144 F3 Manas He r. China
150 A2 Manas Hu l. China
149 F3 Manaslu mt. Nepal
221 F5 Manassas U.S.A.
149 G4 Manas Wildlife Sanctuary nature res. Bhutan
151 E7 Manatuto East Timor
152 F8 Man-aung Kyun Myanmar
231 F4 Manaus Brazil
138 F2 Manavgat Turkey
126 E4 Manawatu r. N.Z.
161 J5 Manay Phil.
139 F3 Manbij Syria
173 H4 Manby U.K.
209 E3 Mancelona U.S.A.
173 E4 Manchester U.K.
214 A2 Manchester CA U.S.A.
221 G4 Manchester CT U.S.A.
208 B4 Manchester IA U.S.A.
220 B6 Manchester KY U.S.A.
209 E4 Manchester MI U.S.A.
221 H3 Manchester NH U.S.A.
220 B5 Manchester OH U.S.A.
219 C5 Manchester TN U.S.A.
221 G3 Manchester VT U.S.A.
148 A4 Manchhar Lake Pak.
139 F2 Mancılık Turkey
215 H3 Mancos U.S.A.
215 H3 Mancos r. U.S.A.
143 F5 Mand Pak.
142 D4 Mand, Rūd-e r. Iran
195 E6 Mandabe Madag.
163 B2 Mandah Indon.
162 □ Mandai Sing.
148 C4 Mandal India
171 I4 Mandal Norway
151 G7 Mandala, Puncak mt. Indon.
151 B4 Mandalay Myanmar
150 C2 Mandalgovĭ Mongolia
139 J5 Mandalī Iraq
153 H3 Mandal-Ovoo Mongolia
154 D1 Mandalt China
154 D1 Mandalt Sum China
216 C2 Mandan U.S.A.
161 I3 Mandaon Phil.
193 D3 Mandara Mountains Cameroon/Nigeria
184 C5 Mandas Sardinia Italy
143 F3 Mandel Iran
194 E3 Mandera Kenya
215 F2 Manderfield U.S.A.
179 E4 Manderscheid Germany
223 I5 Mandeville Jamaica
126 B6 Mandeville N.Z.
148 B4 Mandha India
145 E5 Mandi India
192 B3 Mandiana Guinea
162 B4 Mandi Angin, Gunung mt. Malaysia
148 B4 Mandi Burewala Pak.
195 D5 Mandié Moz.
195 D5 Mandimba Moz.
197 H4 Mandini S. Africa
149 F5 Mandira Dam India
149 E5 Mandla India
195 E5 Mandritsara Madag.
148 C4 Mandsaur India
161 H6 Mandul i. Indon.
118 B5 Mandurah Australia
185 G4 Manduria Italy
148 B5 Mandvi Gujarat India
148 B5 Mandvi Gujarat India
147 H3 Mandya India
140 E5 Māne Turkm.
147 H2 Maner r. India
184 D2 Manerbio Italy
139 K5 Manesht Kūh mt. Iran
177 L5 Manevychi Ukr.
184 F4 Manfredonia Italy
185 G4 Manfredonia, Golfo di g. Italy
234 D1 Manga Brazil
192 B3 Manga Burkina

195 B4 **Mangai** Dem. Rep. Congo
117 I5 **Mangaia** i. Cook Is
126 E3 **Mangakino** N.Z.
147 I2 **Mangalagiri** India
149 H4 **Mangaldai** India
185 M3 **Mangalia** Romania
147 G3 **Mangalore** India
147 G2 **Mangalvedha** India
149 G4 **Mangan** India
147 I2 **Mangapet** India
161 J6 **Mangarang** Indon.
197 G4 **Mangaung** S. Africa
126 E3 **Mangaweka** N.Z.
149 G4 **Mangde Chhu** r. Bhutan
175 I6 **Mangerton Mountain** h. Ireland
163 G3 **Manggar** Indon.
Mangin Range mts Myanmar see **Mingin Range**
140 C3 **Mangistauskaya Oblast'** admin. div. Kazakh.
140 E4 **Mang'it** Uzbek.
Mangit Uzbek. see **Mang'it**
150 B3 **Mangnai** China
144 H4 **Mangnai Zhen** China
195 D5 **Mangochi** Malawi
151 E7 **Mangole** i. Indon.
173 E6 **Mangotsfield** U.K.
148 B5 **Mangrol** India
Mangshi China see **Luxi**
183 M2 **Mangualde** Port.
143 G4 **Manguchar** Pak.
235 M2 **Mangueira, Lago** l. Brazil
235 B4 **Mangueirinha** Brazil
193 D2 **Manguéni, Plateau du** Niger
150 E1 **Mangui** China
161 J5 **Mangupung** i. Indon.
140 B3 **Mangyshlak, Poluostrov** pen. Kazakh.
140 B3 **Mangyshlakskiy Zaliv** b. Kazakh.
140 B4 **Mangystau** Kazakh.
217 D4 **Manhattan** KS U.S.A.
215 D2 **Manhattan** NV U.S.A.
195 D6 **Manhica** Moz.
197 J3 **Manhoca** Moz.
234 D3 **Manhuaçu** Brazil
234 E2 **Manhuaçu** r. Brazil
233 I3 **Mani** Col.
195 E5 **Mania** r. Madag.
184 E1 **Maniago** Italy
231 F5 **Manicoré** Brazil
207 G3 **Manicouagan** Canada
207 G3 **Manicouagan** r. Canada
207 G3 **Manicouagan, Petit Lac** l. Canada
207 G3 **Manicouagan, Réservoir** resr Canada
142 C5 **Manifah** Saudi Arabia
117 I4 **Manihiki** atoll Cook Is
Manikgarh India see **Rajura**
149 E4 **Manikpur** India
161 I3 **Manila** Phil.
213 E3 **Manila** U.S.A. (City Plan 92)
125 H4 **Manildra** Australia
125 I3 **Manilla** Australia
120 F2 **Maningrida** Australia
149 H4 **Manipur** state India
185 L5 **Manisa** Turkey
208 D3 **Manistee** U.S.A.
208 D3 **Manistee** r. U.S.A.
208 D3 **Manistique** U.S.A.
209 E2 **Manistique Lake** U.S.A.
205 J3 **Manitoba** prov. Canada
205 J4 **Manitoba, Lake** Canada
205 H4 **Manitou Lake** Canada
205 J5 **Manitou** Canada
209 G3 **Manitou, Lake** Canada
221 E3 **Manitou Beach** U.S.A.
205 K4 **Manitou Falls** Canada
208 D2 **Manitou Island** U.S.A.
218 C2 **Manitou Islands** U.S.A.
209 F3 **Manitoulin Island** Canada
209 G3 **Manitowaning** Canada
209 E1 **Manitowik Lake** Canada
208 D3 **Manitowoc** U.S.A.
209 J2 **Maniwaki** Canada
233 I3 **Manizales** Col.
195 E6 **Manja** Madag.
197 J2 **Manjacaze** Moz.
147 H4 **Manjeri** India
160 D3 **Man Jiang** r. China
139 L3 **Manjil** Iran
147 H2 **Manjra** r. India
216 E2 **Mankato** U.S.A.
197 I3 **Mankayane** Swaziland
192 B4 **Mankono** Côte d'Ivoire
147 I4 **Mankulam** Sri Lanka
154 C1 **Manlay** Mongolia

125 I4 **Manly** Australia
148 C5 **Manmad** India
204 F3 **Mann** r. Australia
120 F2 **Mann** r. Australia
121 E5 **Mann, Mount** Australia
163 B3 **Manna** Indon.
124 C4 **Mannahill** Australia
147 H4 **Mannar** Sri Lanka
147 H4 **Mannar, Gulf of** India/Sri Lanka
147 H3 **Manneru** r. India
179 G5 **Mannheim** Germany
175 H4 **Mannin Bay** Ireland
123 F6 **Manning** r. Australia
204 F3 **Manning** Canada
219 D5 **Manning** U.S.A.
173 I6 **Manningtree** U.K.
121 E5 **Mann Ranges** mts Australia
184 C4 **Mannu, Capo** c. Sardinia Italy
124 C5 **Mannum** Australia
151 F7 **Manokwari** Indon.
195 C4 **Manono** Dem. Rep. Congo
162 A3 **Manoron** Myanmar
183 G5 **Manosque** France
203 K4 **Manouane, Lac** l. Canada
160 D3 **Manp'o** N. Korea
119 I2 **Manra** i. Kiribati
183 Q2 **Manresa** Spain
148 C3 **Mansa** India
195 C5 **Mansa** Zambia
192 A3 **Mansa Konko** Gambia
148 C2 **Mansehra** Pak.
203 K3 **Mansel Island** Canada
125 G6 **Mansfield** Australia
173 F4 **Mansfield** U.K.
217 E5 **Mansfield** LA U.S.A.
220 B4 **Mansfield** OH U.S.A.
221 E4 **Mansfield** PA U.S.A.
204 E3 **Manson Creek** Canada
139 L6 **Manṣūrī** Iran
138 E3 **Mansurlu** Turkey
230 B4 **Manta** Ecuador
230 B4 **Manta, Bahía de** b. Ecuador
161 H4 **Mantalingajan, Mount** Phil.
214 B3 **Manteca** U.S.A.
233 J3 **Mantecal** Venez.
179 K5 **Mantel** Germany
219 F5 **Manteo** U.S.A.
182 E2 **Mantes-la-Jolie** France
147 H2 **Manthani** India
215 G2 **Manti** U.S.A.
234 D3 **Mantiqueira, Serra da** mts Brazil
209 E3 **Manton** U.S.A.
Mantova Italy see **Mantua**
171 N3 **Mäntsälä** Fin.
171 N3 **Mänttä** Fin.
184 D2 **Mantua** Italy
123 D5 **Mantuan Downs** Australia
186 H3 **Manturovo** Rus. Fed.
171 N3 **Mäntyharju** Fin.
170 N2 **Mäntyjärvi** Fin.
230 D6 **Manu, Parque Nacional** nat. park Peru
237 I7 **Manuae** atoll Fr. Polynesia
Manua Islands American Samoa see **Manu'a Islands**
117 H4 **Manu'a Islands** American Samoa
215 H4 **Manuelito** U.S.A.
235 L2 **Manuel J. Cobo** Arg.
234 E1 **Manuel Vitorino** Brazil
231 H5 **Manuelzinho** Brazil
151 E7 **Manui** i. Indon.
143 E5 **Manūjān** Iran
161 I4 **Manukan** Phil.
126 E2 **Manukau** N.Z.
126 E2 **Manukau Harbour** N.Z.
161 H5 **Manuk Manka** i. Phil.
124 C4 **Manunda** watercourse Australia
119 E2 **Manus Island** P.N.G.
147 H3 **Manvi** India
197 F2 **Manyana** Botswana
136 B2 **Manyas** Turkey
187 G6 **Manych-Gudilo, Ozero** l. Rus. Fed.
215 H3 **Many Farms** U.S.A.
195 D4 **Manyoni** Tanz.
138 D6 **Manzala, Lake** lag. Egypt
183 O3 **Manzanares** Spain
223 I4 **Manzanillo** Cuba
224 C4 **Manzanillo** Mex.
224 J6 **Manzanillo, Punta** pt Panama
142 C3 **Manẓariyeh** Iran
150 D2 **Manzhouli** China
197 I3 **Manzini** Swaziland
193 D3 **Mao** Chad
Maó Spain see **Mahón**

155 D4 **Maocifan** China
154 C2 **Maojiachuan** China
151 F7 **Maoke, Pegunungan** mts Indon.
197 G3 **Maokeng** S. Africa
160 B3 **Maokui Shan** mt. China
160 B2 **Maolin** China
154 B2 **Maomao Shan** mt. China
155 D6 **Maoming** China
155 □ **Ma On Shan** h. Hong Kong China
195 D6 **Mapai** Moz.
149 E3 **Mapam Yumco** l. China
118 C2 **Maparie** Indon.
197 F5 **Maphodi** S. Africa
225 D2 **Mapimí** Mex.
195 D6 **Mapinhane** Moz.
233 K3 **Mapire** Venez.
209 E4 **Maple** r. U.S.A.
205 H5 **Maple Creek** Canada
236 G4 **Mapmakers Seamounts** sea feature N. Pacific Ocean
122 C1 **Mapoon** Australia
197 G4 **Mapoteng** Lesotho
231 G4 **Mapuera** r. Brazil
197 J2 **Mapulanguene** Moz.
197 H1 **Mapungubwe National Park** S. Africa
195 D6 **Maputo** Moz.
197 J2 **Maputo** prov. Moz.
197 J3 **Maputo** r. Moz.
197 G4 **Maputsoe** Lesotho
139 H6 **Maqar an Na'am** well Iraq
153 H5 **Maqên** China
152 G5 **Maqên Kangri** mt. China
136 D5 **Maqnā** Saudi Arabia
154 B3 **Maqu** China
149 E3 **Maquan He** r. China
195 B4 **Maquela do Zombo** Angola
235 I4 **Maquinchao** Arg.
235 I4 **Maquinchao** r. Arg.
208 B4 **Maquoketa** U.S.A.
208 B4 **Maquoketa** r. U.S.A.
143 G5 **Mar** r. Pak.
234 D3 **Mar, Serra do** mts Brazil
205 H1 **Mara** r. Canada
149 E5 **Mara** India
197 H1 **Mara** S. Africa
230 E4 **Maraã** Brazil
231 I5 **Marabá** Brazil
123 E4 **Maraboon, Lake** resr Australia
231 H3 **Maracá, Ilha de** i. Brazil
233 J2 **Maracaibo** Venez.
233 J2 **Maracaibo, Lake** inlet Venez.
234 A3 **Maracaju** Brazil
234 A3 **Maracaju, Serra de** hills Brazil
234 E1 **Maracás, Chapada de** hills Brazil
233 K2 **Maracay** Venez.
193 D2 **Marādah** Libya
192 C3 **Maradi** Niger
142 B2 **Marāgheh** Iran
234 E1 **Maragogipe** Brazil
161 I3 **Maragondon** Phil.
233 K4 **Marahuaca, Cerro** mt. Venez.
231 I4 **Marajó, Baía de** est. Brazil
231 I3 **Marajó, Ilha de** i. Brazil
197 G2 **Marakele National Park** S. Africa
147 H3 **Marakkanam** India
194 D3 **Maralal** Kenya
148 C2 **Marala Weir** Pak.
139 I1 **Maralik** Armenia
118 D5 **Maralinga** Australia
119 G2 **Maramasike** i. Solomon Is
127 L2 **Marambio** research stn Antarctica
161 J5 **Marampit** i. Indon.
143 G4 **Maran** mt. Pak.
139 J4 **Marāna** Iraq
215 G5 **Marana** U.S.A.
142 B2 **Marand** Iran
162 B4 **Marang** Malaysia
162 A3 **Marang** Myanmar
234 C1 **Maranhão** r. Brazil
123 E5 **Maranoa** r. Australia
230 C4 **Marañón** r. Peru
230 D4 **Marari** r. Brazil
126 A6 **Mararoa** r. N.Z.
208 D1 **Marathon** Canada
219 D7 **Marathon** FL U.S.A.
217 C6 **Marathon** TX U.S.A.
234 E1 **Maraú** Brazil
163 H3 **Marau** Indon.
233 K4 **Marauiá** r. Brazil
161 J4 **Marawi** Phil.

139 L1 **Märäzä** Azer.
183 N4 **Marbella** Spain
118 B4 **Marble Bar** Australia
215 G3 **Marble Canyon** U.S.A.
215 G3 **Marble Canyon** gorge U.S.A.
197 H2 **Marble Hall** S. Africa
221 H3 **Marblehead** U.S.A.
205 K2 **Marble Island** Canada
191 I5 **Marburg** S. Africa
221 E5 **Marburg, Lake** U.S.A.
179 G4 **Marburg an der Lahn** Germany
177 H7 **Marcali** Hungary
173 H5 **March** U.K.
124 C4 **Marchant Hill** Australia
178 D4 **Marche-en-Famenne** Belgium
183 N4 **Marchena** Spain
230 □ **Marchena, Isla** i. Galapagos Is Ecuador
122 B1 **Marchinbar Island** Australia
Mar Chiquita, Lago l. Arg. see **Mar Chiquita, Laguna**
235 J1 **Mar Chiquita, Laguna** l. Arg.
176 G6 **Marchtrenk** Austria
219 D7 **Marco** U.S.A.
178 B4 **Marcoing** France
206 E2 **Marcopeet Islands** Canada
235 J2 **Marcos Juárez** Arg.
221 J2 **Marcy, Mount** U.S.A.
148 C2 **Mardan** Pak.
235 L3 **Mar del Plata** Arg.
139 H3 **Mardin** Turkey
119 L4 **Maré** i. New Caledonia
174 C3 **Maree, Loch** l. U.K.
208 A5 **Marengo** IA U.S.A.
208 C4 **Marengo** IL U.S.A.
184 E6 **Marettimo, Isola** i. Sicily Italy
186 E3 **Marevo** Rus. Fed.
217 B6 **Marfa** U.S.A.
120 D3 **Margaret** r. Australia
124 B2 **Margaret** watercourse Australia
121 B4 **Margaret, Mount** h. Australia
118 B5 **Margaret River** Australia
233 L2 **Margarita, Isla de** i. Venez.
158 D3 **Margaritovo** Rus. Fed.
125 G9 **Margate** Australia
191 I5 **Margate** S. Africa
173 I6 **Margate** U.K.
194 C3 **Margherita Peak** Dem. Rep. Congo/Uganda
Margilan Uzbek. see **Marg'ilon**
141 G4 **Marg'ilon** Uzbek.
Margo, Dasht-i des. Afgh. see **Märgow, Dasht-e**
161 I5 **Margosatubig** Phil.
143 F4 **Märgow, Dasht-e** des. Afgh.
178 D4 **Margraten** Neth.
209 E3 **Margrethe, Lake** U.S.A.
204 E4 **Marguerite** Canada
127 I2 **Marguerite Bay** Antarctica
139 K5 **Marhaj Khalīl** Iraq
141 H4 **Marhamat** Uzbek.
139 I3 **Marhan Dāgh** h. Iraq
187 E6 **Marhanets'** Ukr.
180 C5 **Marhoum** Alg.
237 I7 **Maria** atoll Fr. Polynesia
232 C2 **María Elena** Chile
235 K3 **María Ignacia** Arg.
125 H9 **Maria Island** Australia
118 D3 **Maria Island** Australia
123 D5 **Mariala National Park** Australia
236 E4 **Mariana Ridge** sea feature N. Pacific Ocean
236 E5 **Mariana Trench** sea feature N. Pacific Ocean
149 H4 **Mariani** India
204 F2 **Marian Lake** Canada
217 F5 **Marianna** AR U.S.A.
219 C6 **Marianna** FL U.S.A.
176 F6 **Mariánské Lázně** Czech Rep.
224 C3 **Marías, Islas** Mex.
224 I7 **Mariato, Punta** pt Panama
126 D1 **Maria van Diemen, Cape** N.Z.
184 F1 **Maribor** Slovenia
215 F5 **Maricopa** AZ U.S.A.
214 C4 **Maricopa** CA U.S.A.
215 F5 **Maricopa Mountains** U.S.A.
193 E4 **Maridi** watercourse Sudan
127 I4 **Marie Byrd Land** reg. Antarctica
223 L5 **Marie-Galante** i. Guadeloupe

171 L3 **Mariehamn** Fin.
234 B1 **Mariembero** r. Brazil
179 L4 **Marienberg** Germany
179 F1 **Marienhafe** Germany
195 B6 **Mariental** Namibia
171 K4 **Mariestad** Sweden
219 C5 **Marietta** GA U.S.A.
220 C5 **Marietta** OH U.S.A.
183 G5 **Marignane** France
150 A2 **Marii, Mys** pt Rus. Fed.
150 A1 **Mariinsk** Rus. Fed.
140 E1 **Mariinskoye** Rus. Fed.
171 M5 **Marijampolė** Lith.
234 C3 **Marília** Brazil
121 B4 **Marillana** Australia
225 D2 **Marín** Mex.
183 L1 **Marín** Spain
185 G5 **Marina di Gioiosa Ionica** Italy
187 D4 **Mar"ina Horka** Belarus
161 I3 **Marinduque** i. Phil.
208 D3 **Marinette** U.S.A.
234 B3 **Maringá** Brazil
183 L3 **Marinha Grande** Port.
219 B4 **Marion** IL U.S.A.
209 E5 **Marion** IN U.S.A.
221 J2 **Marion** ME U.S.A.
220 B4 **Marion** OH U.S.A.
219 E5 **Marion** SC U.S.A.
220 C6 **Marion** VA U.S.A.
219 D5 **Marion, Lake** U.S.A.
124 B5 **Marion Bay** Australia
122 F3 **Marion Reef** Australia
233 K3 **Maripa** Venez.
214 C3 **Mariposa** U.S.A.
Mariscal Estigarribia Para. see **Mariscal José Félix Estigarribia**
232 D2 **Mariscal José Félix Estigarribia** Para.
182 H4 **Maritime Alps** mts France/Italy
185 K3 **Maritsa** r. Bulg.
186 I3 **Mari-Turek** Rus. Fed.
187 I6 **Mariupol'** Ukr.
233 L2 **Mariusa, Caño** r. Venez.
142 B3 **Marivän** Iran
186 I3 **Mariy El, Respublika** aut. rep. Rus. Fed.
194 E3 **Marka** Somalia
141 K2 **Markakol', Ozero** l. Kazakh.
139 J2 **Märkän** Iran
147 H3 **Markapur** India
171 K4 **Markaryd** Sweden
209 G3 **Markdale** Canada
197 H1 **Marken** S. Africa
178 D2 **Markermeer** l. Neth.
173 G5 **Market Deeping** U.K.
173 F5 **Market Drayton** U.K.
173 G5 **Market Harborough** U.K.
175 L3 **Markethill** U.K.
173 G4 **Market Weighton** U.K.
133 M3 **Markha** r. Rus. Fed.
209 H3 **Markham** Canada
Markhamet Uzbek. see **Marhamat**
141 I5 **Markit** China
187 F5 **Markivka** Ukr.
179 K3 **Markkleeberg** Germany
179 H2 **Marklohe** Germany
154 A3 **Markog Qu** r. China
179 K3 **Markranstädt** Germany
187 F5 **Marks** Rus. Fed.
179 H5 **Marktheidenfeld** Germany
176 E7 **Marktoberdorf** Germany
179 K4 **Marktredwitz** Germany
208 B6 **Mark Twain Lake** U.S.A.
179 F3 **Marl** Germany
121 F5 **Marla** Australia
221 H3 **Marlborough** U.S.A.
173 F6 **Marlborough Downs** hills U.K.
178 B5 **Marle** France
217 D6 **Marlin** U.S.A.
220 C5 **Marlinton** U.S.A.
125 H6 **Marlo** Australia
182 E4 **Marmande** France
138 B1 **Marmara, Sea of** g. Turkey
Marmara Denizi g. Turkey see **Marmara, Sea of**
138 B2 **Marmara Gölü** l. Turkey
138 B3 **Marmaris** Turkey
216 C2 **Marmarth** U.S.A.
220 C5 **Marmet** U.S.A.
121 C6 **Marmion, Lake** salt l. Australia
206 B4 **Marmion Lake** Canada
184 D1 **Marmolada** mt. Italy
182 F2 **Marne-la-Vallée** France
139 J1 **Marneuli** Georgia
179 J1 **Marnitz** Germany

125 E6 **Marnoo** Australia
195 E5 **Maroantsetra** Madag.
179 I4 **Maroldsweisach** Germany
195 E5 **Maromokotro** mt. Madag.
195 D5 **Marondera** Zimbabwe
231 H2 **Maroni** r. Fr. Guiana
125 J1 **Maroochydore** Australia
121 A4 **Maroonah** Australia
117 I6 **Marotiri** is Fr. Polynesia
193 D3 **Maroua** Cameroon
195 E5 **Marovoay** Madag.
139 H4 **Marqādah** Syria
197 H4 **Marquard** S. Africa
117 J5 **Marquesas Islands** Fr. Polynesia
219 D7 **Marquesas Keys** is U.S.A.
208 D2 **Marquette** U.S.A.
178 B4 **Marquion** France
Marquises, Îles is Fr. Polynesia see **Marquesas Islands**
125 E3 **Marra** Australia
125 G3 **Marra** r. Australia
193 E3 **Marra, Jebel** Sudan
197 J2 **Marracuene** Moz.
192 B1 **Marrakech** Morocco
197 K2 **Marrangua, Lagoa** l. Moz.
125 G5 **Marrar** Australia
125 F8 **Marrawah** Australia
124 C2 **Marree** Australia
217 F6 **Marrero** U.S.A.
195 D5 **Marromeu** Moz.
195 D5 **Marrupa** Moz.
121 F5 **Marryat** Australia
193 F2 **Marsá al 'Alam** Egypt
193 D1 **Marsá al Burayqah** Libya
194 D3 **Marsabit** Kenya
184 D6 **Marsala** Sicily Italy
193 E1 **Marsá Maţrūḥ** Egypt
179 G3 **Marsberg** Germany
184 D3 **Marsciano** Italy
125 G4 **Marsden** Australia
178 C2 **Marsdiep** sea chan. Neth.
183 G5 **Marseille** France
208 C5 **Marseilles** U.S.A.
170 K2 **Marsfjället** mt. Sweden
123 B4 **Marshall** watercourse Australia
205 H4 **Marshall** Canada
217 E5 **Marshall** AR U.S.A.
219 C4 **Marshall** IL U.S.A.
209 E4 **Marshall** MI U.S.A.
216 E2 **Marshall** MN U.S.A.
217 E4 **Marshall** MO U.S.A.
217 E5 **Marshall** TX U.S.A.
125 G7 **Marshall Bay** Australia
117 F2 **Marshall Islands** country N. Pacific Ocean
216 E3 **Marshalltown** U.S.A.
208 B3 **Marshfield** U.S.A.
219 E7 **Marsh Harbour** Bahamas
221 J1 **Mars Hill** U.S.A.
217 F6 **Marsh Island** U.S.A.
204 C2 **Marsh Lake** Canada
139 L3 **Marshūn** Iran
213 C3 **Marsing** U.S.A.
171 L4 **Märsta** Sweden
149 F4 **Marsyangdi** r. Nepal
Martaban Myanmar see **Mottama**
163 H3 **Martapura** Kalimantan Indon.
183 H2 **Martapura** Sumatera Indon.
209 H2 **Marten River** Canada
205 H4 **Martensville** Canada
225 E2 **Marte R. Gómez, Presa** resr Mex.
176 C7 **Martha's Vineyard** i. U.S.A.
177 I6 **Martigny** Switz.
177 I6 **Martin** Slovakia
216 C3 **Martin** SD U.S.A.
219 B4 **Martin** TN U.S.A.
219 C5 **Martin, Lake** U.S.A.
225 E3 **Martínez** Mex.
215 E5 **Martinez Lake** U.S.A.
223 L6 **Martinique** terr. Caribbean Sea
127 I4 **Martin Peninsula** Antarctica
220 D4 **Martinsburg** PA U.S.A.
221 E5 **Martinsburg** WV U.S.A.
220 C4 **Martins Ferry** U.S.A.
220 D6 **Martinsville** U.S.A.
239 H7 **Martin Vaz, Ilhas** is S. Atlantic Ocean
126 E4 **Marton** N.Z.
183 Q2 **Martorell** Spain
183 N4 **Martos** Spain
140 D2 **Martuk** Kazakh.
139 J1 **Martuni** Armenia
143 F3 **Maruchak** Afgh.
159 C7 **Marugame** Japan

126 D5 Maruia r. N.Z.
231 K6 Maruim Brazil
187 G7 Marukhis Ugheltekhili pass Georgia/Rus. Fed.
125 H5 Marulan Australia
141 K1 Marushka Rus. Fed.
142 D4 Marvast Iran
182 F4 Marvejols France
215 G2 Marvine, Mount U.S.A.
205 G4 Marwayne Canada
120 E2 Mary r. Australia
143 F2 Mary Turkm.
119 F4 Maryborough Qld Australia
125 E6 Maryborough Vic. Australia
196 H3 Marydale S. Africa
187 I4 Mar'yevka Rus. Fed.
205 H2 Mary Frances Lake Canada
221 E5 Maryland state U.S.A.
172 D3 Maryport U.K.
207 I3 Mary's Harbour Canada
207 J4 Marystown Canada
215 F2 Marysvale U.S.A.
207 G4 Marysville Canada
214 B2 Marysville CA U.S.A.
217 D4 Marysville KS U.S.A.
220 B4 Marysville OH U.S.A.
121 F5 Maryvale N.T. Australia
122 D3 Maryvale Qld Australia
216 E3 Maryville MO U.S.A.
219 C5 Maryville TN U.S.A.
179 K2 Marzahna Germany
224 H6 Masachapa Nicaragua
138 E6 Masada tourist site Israel
142 D4 Masāhūn, Kūh-e mt. Iran
195 D4 Masaka Uganda
197 G5 Masakhane S. Africa
139 L2 Masallı Azer.
118 C2 Masamba Indon.
160 E6 Masan S. Korea
221 I1 Masardis U.S.A.
195 D5 Masasi Tanz.
231 F7 Masavi Bol.
224 H6 Masaya Nicaragua
161 I3 Masbate Phil.
161 I4 Masbate i. Phil.
192 C1 Mascara Alg.
238 H6 Mascarene Basin sea feature Indian Ocean
238 H6 Mascarene Plain sea feature Indian Ocean
238 H5 Mascarene Ridge sea feature Indian Ocean
221 G2 Mascouche Canada
197 G4 Maseru Lesotho
197 H4 Mashai Lesotho
155 C6 Mashan China
148 D2 Masherbrum mt. Pak.
143 E2 Mashhad Iran
148 C4 Mashi r. India
139 K2 Mashīrān Iran
197 I2 Mashishing S. Africa
143 F4 Mashkel, Hamun-i- salt flat Pak.
143 F5 Mashket r. Pak.
143 F4 Mashki Chah Pak.
143 F5 Māshkīd r. Iran
170 M1 Masi Norway
224 B2 Masiáca Mex.
197 G5 Masibambane S. Africa
197 G4 Masilo S. Africa
194 D3 Masindi Uganda
161 H3 Masinloc Phil.
197 E5 Masinyusane S. Africa
Maṣīrah i. Oman see Maṣīrah, Jazīrat
147 E5 Maṣīrah, Jazīrat i. Oman
139 J1 Masis Armenia
142 C4 Masjed Soleymān Iran
175 I4 Mask, Lough l. Ireland
139 G3 Maskanah Syria
143 E5 Maskūtān Iran
143 G4 Maslti Pak.
195 E5 Masoala, Parc National Madag.
195 F5 Masoala, Tanjona c. Madag.
209 E4 Mason MI U.S.A.
214 C2 Mason NV U.S.A.
217 D6 Mason TX U.S.A.
121 B5 Mason, Lake salt flat Australia
126 A7 Mason Bay N.Z.
216 E3 Mason City IA U.S.A.
208 C5 Mason City IL U.S.A.
220 D5 Masontown U.S.A.
Masqaṭ Oman see Muscat
184 D2 Massa Italy
221 G3 Massachusetts state U.S.A.
221 H3 Massachusetts Bay U.S.A.
215 H1 Massadona U.S.A.
185 G4 Massafra Italy

193 D3 Massakory Chad
184 D3 Massa Marittimo Italy
195 D6 Massangena Moz.
195 B4 Massango Angola
194 D2 Massawa Eritrea
221 G2 Massawippi, Lac l. Canada
221 F2 Massena U.S.A.
204 C4 Masset Canada
209 F2 Massey Canada
182 F4 Massif Central mts France
220 C4 Massillon U.S.A.
195 D6 Massinga Moz.
195 D6 Massingir Moz.
197 J1 Massingir, Barragem de resr Moz.
197 J2 Massintonto r. Moz./S. Africa
209 J3 Masson-Angers Canada
139 L1 Maştağa Azer.
141 G5 Mastchoh Tajik.
126 E4 Masterton N.Z.
219 E7 Mastic Point Bahamas
148 C1 Mastuj Pak.
143 G4 Mastung Pak.
187 C4 Masty Belarus
159 B7 Masuda Japan
139 L3 Masuleh Iran
195 D6 Masvingo Zimbabwe
139 H4 Maşyāf Syria
209 G2 Matachewan Canada
224 C1 Matachic Mex.
233 K4 Matacuni r. Venez.
150 D2 Matad Mongolia
195 B4 Matadi Dem. Rep. Congo
224 H5 Matagalpa Nicaragua
206 E4 Matagami Canada
206 E4 Matagami, Lac l. Canada
217 D6 Matagorda Island U.S.A.
162 C5 Matak i. Indon.
141 H2 Matak Kazakh.
126 F2 Matakana Island N.Z.
195 B5 Matala Angola
147 I5 Matale Sri Lanka
192 A3 Matam Senegal
225 D2 Matamoros Coahuila Mex.
225 E2 Matamoros Tamaulipas Mex.
161 I5 Matanal Point Phil.
195 D4 Matandu r. Tanz.
207 G4 Matane Canada
148 B2 Matanui Pak.
223 H4 Matanzas Cuba
207 G4 Matapédia r. Canada
235 H2 Mataquito r. Chile
147 I5 Matara Sri Lanka
163 I4 Mataram Indon.
230 D7 Matarani Peru
118 D3 Mataranka Australia
183 R2 Mataró Spain
197 H5 Matatiele S. Africa
126 B7 Mataura N.Z.
126 B7 Mataura r. N.Z.
119 J3 Matā'utu Wallis and Futuna Is
233 J3 Mataveni r. Col.
126 F3 Matawai N.Z.
144 E2 Matay Kazakh.
231 F6 Mategua Bol.
225 D3 Matehuala Mex.
195 D5 Matemanga Tanz.
185 G4 Matera Italy
184 C6 Mateur Tunisia
206 D4 Matheson Canada
217 D6 Mathis U.S.A.
125 F5 Mathoura Australia
148 D4 Mathura India
161 J5 Mati Phil.
149 G4 Matiali India
155 D5 Matianxu China
148 D5 Matiari Pak.
225 F4 Matías Romero Mex.
207 G3 Matimekosh Canada
209 F2 Matinenda Lake Canada
221 I3 Matinicus Island U.S.A.
149 G5 Matla r. India
197 G2 Matlabas S. Africa
197 G2 Matlabas r. S. Africa
148 B4 Matli Pak.
173 F4 Matlock U.K.
233 K3 Mato r. Venez.
233 K3 Mato, Cerro mt. Venez.
231 G7 Mato Grosso Brazil
234 A1 Mato Grosso state Brazil
234 A1 Mato Grosso, Planalto do plat. Brazil
234 A3 Mato Grosso do Sul state Brazil
197 J2 Matola Moz.
183 L2 Matosinhos Port.
147 E5 Maṭraḥ Oman
196 C6 Matroosberg mt. S. Africa

137 E2 Matsesta Rus. Fed.
159 C7 Matsue Japan
158 G4 Matsumae Japan
159 E6 Matsumoto Japan
159 E7 Matsusaka Japan
155 F5 Matsu Tao i. Taiwan
159 C8 Matsuyama Japan
206 D4 Mattagami r. Canada
209 H2 Mattawa Canada
221 I2 Mattawamkeag U.S.A.
176 C7 Matterhorn mt. Italy/Switz.
213 D3 Matterhorn mt. U.S.A.
117 G2 Matthew Island S. Pacific Ocean
233 L3 Matthews Ridge Guyana
223 J4 Matthew Town Bahamas
142 D6 Maṭṭī, Sabkhat salt pan Saudi Arabia
219 B4 Mattoon U.S.A.
147 I5 Matugama Sri Lanka
119 H3 Matuku i. Fiji
233 L2 Maturín Venez.
161 J5 Matutuang i. Indon.
197 G4 Matwabeng S. Africa
149 E4 Mau India
149 E4 Mau Aimma India
178 B4 Maubeuge France
145 I8 Maubin Myanmar
183 I8 Maubourguet France
174 D5 Mauchline U.K.
239 J10 Maud Seamount sea feature S. Atlantic Ocean
231 G4 Maués Brazil
149 E4 Mauganj India
214 □2 Maui i. U.S.A.
179 G6 Maulbronn Germany
235 H2 Maule admin. reg. Chile
235 H2 Maule r. Chile
235 H4 Maullín Chile
175 I3 Maumakeogh h. Ireland
220 B4 Maumee U.S.A.
220 B4 Maumee r. U.S.A.
209 F5 Maumere Indon.
175 I4 Maumtrasna h. Ireland
175 I4 Maumturk Mountains Ireland
195 C5 Maun Botswana
214 □2 Mauna Kea vol. U.S.A.
214 □2 Mauna Loa vol. U.S.A.
Maunalua B. U.S.A. see Maunalua Bay
214 □1 Maunalua Bay U.S.A.
149 E4 Maunath Bhanjan India
197 G1 Maunatlala Botswana
126 E2 Maungaturoto N.Z.
149 H5 Maungdaw Myanmar
162 A2 Maungmagan Islands Myanmar
202 F3 Maunoir, Lac l. Canada
124 B5 Maupertuis Bay Australia
118 D4 Maurice, Lake salt flat Australia
178 D3 Maurik Neth.
192 A3 Mauritania country Africa
191 I6 Mauritius country Indian Ocean
208 B4 Mauston U.S.A.
233 K4 Mavaca r. Venez.
195 C5 Mavinga Angola
197 G5 Mavuya S. Africa
148 D3 Mawana India
195 B4 Mawanga Dem. Rep. Congo
155 D4 Ma Wang Dui tourist site China
162 A3 Mawdaung Pass Myanmar/Thai.
127 G3 Mawhai Point N.Z.
152 G7 Mawkmai Myanmar
162 A1 Mawlamyaing Myanmar
127 L5 Mawson research stn Antarctica
127 K5 Mawson Escarpment Antarctica
127 I6 Mawson Peninsula Antarctica
162 A3 Maw Taung mt. Myanmar
216 C2 Max U.S.A.
225 G3 Maxcanú Mex.
184 C5 Maxia, Punta mt. Sardinia Italy
208 D5 Maxinkuckee, Lake U.S.A.
171 M3 Maxmo Fin.
209 F2 Maxton U.S.A.
214 A2 Maxwell U.S.A.
175 F4 May, Isle of i. U.K.
163 G3 Maya i. Indon.
150 F1 Maya r. Rus. Fed.
223 J4 Mayaguana i. Bahamas
223 K5 Mayagüez Puerto Rico
192 C3 Mayahi Niger
156 E2 Mayak Rus. Fed.

143 H2 Mayakovskiy, Qullai mt. Tajik.
141 G4 Mayakum Kazakh.
195 B4 Mayama Congo
142 D2 Mayamey Iran
225 G4 Maya Mountains Belize
155 C5 Mayang China
154 B3 Mayanhe China
159 F5 Maya-san mt. Japan
174 D5 Maybole U.K.
139 J4 Maydān Sarāy Iraq
Maydā Shahr Afgh. see Meydān Shahr
125 G9 Maydena Australia
179 F4 Mayen Germany
182 D2 Mayenne France
182 D2 Mayenne r. France
215 F4 Mayer U.S.A.
204 F4 Mayerthorpe Canada
126 C5 Mayfield N.Z.
219 B4 Mayfield U.S.A.
213 F5 Mayhill U.S.A.
160 E1 Mayi He r. China
141 H2 Maykain Kazakh.
141 I3 Maykamys Kazakh.
141 G5 Maykhura Tajik.
187 G6 Maykop Rus. Fed.
141 H4 Mayluu-Suu Kyrg.
140 F3 Maylybas Kazakh.
141 K1 Mayma Rus. Fed.
141 G4 Maymak Kazakh.
143 G3 Maymanah Afgh.
Maymyo Myanmar see Pyin-U-Lwin
169 P5 Mayna Rus. Fed.
150 B1 Mayna Rus. Fed.
147 G2 Mayni India
209 I3 Maynooth Canada
204 B2 Mayo Canada
161 J5 Mayo Bay Phil.
195 B4 Mayoko Congo
204 B2 Mayo Lake Canada
161 I3 Mayon vol. Phil.
235 J3 Mayor Buratovich Arg.
126 F2 Mayor Island N.Z.
232 D1 Mayor Pablo Lagerenza Para.
195 E5 Mayotte terr. Africa
161 I2 Mayraira Point Phil.
137 G2 Mayskiy Rus. Fed.
150 E1 Mayskiy Rus. Fed.
220 B5 Maysville U.S.A.
195 B4 Mayumba Gabon
149 E3 Mayum La pass China
147 H4 Mayuram India
209 F4 Mayville MI U.S.A.
216 D2 Mayville ND U.S.A.
220 D3 Mayville NY U.S.A.
208 C4 Mayville WI U.S.A.
216 C3 Maywood U.S.A.
235 J3 Maza Arg.
186 F3 Maza Rus. Fed.
195 C5 Mazabuka Zambia
231 H4 Mazagão Brazil
183 F5 Mazamet France
148 D1 Mazar China
143 G3 Mazar, Koh-i- mt. Afgh.
184 E6 Mazara del Vallo Sicily Italy
143 G2 Mazār-e Sharīf Afgh.
233 L3 Mazaruni r. Guyana
224 B1 Mazatán Mex.
225 G5 Mazatenango Guat.
224 C3 Mazatlán Mex.
215 G4 Mazatzal Peak U.S.A.
142 C3 Mazdaj Iran
171 M4 Mažeikiai Lith.
139 G2 Mazgirt Turkey
142 A5 Maẓḥur, 'Irq al des. Saudi Arabia
171 M4 Mazirbe Latvia
195 D4 Mazomora Tanz.
177 J4 Mazowiecka, Nizina lowland Poland
139 L3 Mazr'eh Iran
139 L5 Māzū Iran
195 D6 Mazunga Zimbabwe
187 D4 Mazyr Belarus
197 I3 Mbabane Swaziland
192 B4 Mbahiakro Côte d'Ivoire
194 B3 Mbaïki Centr. Afr. Rep.
195 D4 Mbala Zambia
194 D3 Mbale Uganda
193 D4 Mbalmayo Cameroon
195 B4 Mbandaka Dem. Rep. Congo
192 C4 Mbanga Cameroon
195 B4 M'banza Congo Angola
194 D3 Mbarara Uganda
194 C3 Mbari r. Centr. Afr. Rep.
197 J3 Mbaswana S. Africa
193 D4 Mbengwi Cameroon

195 D4 Mbeya Tanz.
195 D5 Mbinga Tanz.
195 D6 Mbizi Zimbabwe
194 B3 Mbomo Congo
193 D4 Mbouda Cameroon
192 A3 Mbour Senegal
192 A3 Mbout Mauritania
195 D4 Mbozi Tanz.
195 C4 Mbuji-Mayi Dem. Rep. Congo
195 D4 Mbulu Tanz.
195 D4 Mbuyuni Tanz.
221 J2 McAdam Canada
217 E5 McAlester U.S.A.
221 E4 McAlevys Fort U.S.A.
125 H5 McAlister mt. Australia
217 D7 McAllen U.S.A.
122 B2 McArthur r. Australia
220 B5 McArthur U.S.A.
209 I3 McArthur Mills Canada
204 B2 McArthur Wildlife Sanctuary nature res. Canada
204 E4 McBride Canada
212 C2 McCall U.S.A.
217 C6 McCamey U.S.A.
213 D3 McCammon U.S.A.
204 C4 McCauley Island Canada
203 H2 McClintock Channel Canada
120 D2 McClintock Range hills Australia
214 B3 McClure, Lake U.S.A.
202 F2 McClure Strait Canada
217 F6 McComb U.S.A.
216 C3 McConaughy, Lake U.S.A.
220 C5 McConnelsville U.S.A.
216 C3 McCook U.S.A.
205 J4 McCreary Canada
215 E4 McCullough Range mts U.S.A.
204 D3 McDame Canada
213 C3 McDermitt U.S.A.
238 I8 McDonald Islands Indian Ocean
212 D2 McDonald Peak U.S.A.
124 C2 McDonnell Creek watercourse Australia
196 B4 McDougall's Bay S. Africa
215 G5 McDowell Peak U.S.A.
214 C4 McFarland U.S.A.
205 H3 McFarlane r. Canada
215 E2 McGill U.S.A.
202 C3 McGrath U.S.A.
204 E4 McGregor r. Canada
196 C6 McGregor S. Africa
208 A2 McGregor U.S.A.
209 G2 McGregor Bay Canada
123 C5 McGregor Range hills Australia
212 D2 McGuire, Mount U.S.A.
122 C2 McIlwraith Range hills Australia
221 G2 McIndoe Falls U.S.A.
216 C2 McIntosh U.S.A.
119 I2 McKean i. Kiribati
220 A6 McKee U.S.A.
220 D4 McKeesport U.S.A.
221 F3 McKenzie U.S.A.
219 B4 McKenzie r. U.S.A.
123 C4 McKinlay r. Australia
202 C3 McKinley, Mount U.S.A.
217 D5 McKinney U.S.A.
214 C4 McKittrick U.S.A.
216 C2 McLaughlin U.S.A.
204 F3 McLennan Canada
204 F4 McLeod r. Canada
204 E3 McLeod Lake Canada
213 B3 McLoughlin, Mount U.S.A.
209 E2 McMillan U.S.A.
212 B2 McMinnville OR U.S.A.
219 C5 McMinnville TN U.S.A.
127 I5 McMurdo research stn Antarctica
215 H4 McNary U.S.A.
204 F4 McNaughton Lake Canada
215 H6 McNeal U.S.A.
217 D4 McPherson U.S.A.
125 J2 McPherson Range mts Australia
204 B2 McQuesten r. Canada
219 D5 McRae U.S.A.
204 E1 McVicar Arm b. Canada
184 B6 M'Daourouch Alg.
163 D2 M'Đrak Vietnam
162 C1 Mê, Hon i. Vietnam
215 C1 Mead, Lake resr U.S.A.
217 C4 Meade U.S.A.
121 A5 Meadow Australia
205 H4 Meadow Lake Canada

205 H4 Meadow Lake Provincial Park Canada
215 E3 Meadow Valley Wash r. U.S.A.
220 C4 Meadville U.S.A.
209 G3 Meaford Canada
158 I3 Meaken-dake vol. Japan
174 A2 Mealasta Island U.K.
183 L2 Mealhada Port.
174 D4 Meall a' Bhuiridh mt. U.K.
207 I3 Mealy Mountains Canada
125 H1 Meandarra Australia
204 F3 Meander River Canada
161 J5 Meares i. Indon.
182 F2 Meaux France
146 A5 Mecca Saudi Arabia (City Plan 96)
221 H2 Mechanic Falls U.S.A.
220 D4 Mechanicsburg U.S.A.
208 B5 Mechanicsville U.S.A.
178 C3 Mechelen Belgium
178 D4 Mechelen Neth.
192 B1 Mecheria Alg.
179 F4 Mechernich Germany
138 E1 Mecitözü Turkey
179 F4 Meckenheim Germany
176 E3 Mecklenburger Bucht b. Germany
179 J1 Mecklenburgische Seenplatte reg. Germany
179 K1 Mecklenburg-Vorpommern land Germany
195 D5 Mecula Moz.
120 C3 Meda r. Australia
183 M2 Meda Port.
147 H2 Medak India
163 E2 Medan Indon.
235 J3 Médanos Arg.
232 C7 Medanosa, Punta pt Arg.
147 I4 Medawachchiya Sri Lanka
147 H2 Medchal India
221 J2 Meddybemps Lake U.S.A.
183 R4 Médéa Alg.
179 G3 Medebach Germany
233 I3 Medellín Col.
173 F4 Meden r. U.K.
193 D1 Medenine Tunisia
192 A3 Mederdra Mauritania
213 B3 Medford OR U.S.A.
208 B3 Medford WI U.S.A.
221 F5 Medford Farms U.S.A.
185 M2 Medgidia Romania
208 B5 Media U.S.A.
235 I2 Media Luna Arg.
177 L7 Mediaş Romania
212 C2 Medical Lake U.S.A.
213 F3 Medicine Bow U.S.A.
213 F3 Medicine Bow Mountains U.S.A.
213 F3 Medicine Bow Peak U.S.A.
205 G4 Medicine Hat Canada
217 D4 Medicine Lodge U.S.A.
234 D1 Medina Brazil
146 A5 Medina Saudi Arabia
220 D3 Medina NY U.S.A.
220 C4 Medina OH U.S.A.
183 O2 Medinaceli Spain
183 N2 Medina del Campo Spain
183 N2 Medina de Rioseco Spain
149 F5 Medinipur India
166 F5 Mediterranean Sea Africa/Europe
184 B6 Medjerda, Monts de la mts Alg.
140 D2 Mednogorsk Rus. Fed.
182 D4 Médoc reg. France
152 G6 Mêdog China
186 H3 Medvedevo Rus. Fed.
187 H5 Medveditsa r. Rus. Fed.
184 F2 Medvednica mts Croatia
133 R2 Medvezh'i, Ostrova is Rus. Fed.
150 F2 Medvezh'ya, Gora mt. China/Rus. Fed.
186 E2 Medvezh'yegorsk Rus. Fed.
173 H6 Medway r. U.K.
118 B4 Meekatharra Australia
215 H4 Meeker U.S.A.
214 B2 Meeks Bay U.S.A.
207 I4 Meelpaeg Reservoir Canada
179 K4 Meerane Germany
179 E3 Meerlo Neth.
148 D3 Meerut India
212 B2 Meeteetse U.S.A.
194 D3 Mēga Eth.
163 B3 Mega i. Indon.
149 G4 Meghalaya state India
149 F5 Meghasani mt. India
149 G5 Meghna r. Bangl.
139 K2 Meghri Armenia

215 G6	Miller Peak U.S.A.
220 C4	Millersburg OH U.S.A.
221 E4	Millersburg PA U.S.A.
124 B3	Millers Creek Australia
221 E6	Millers Tavern U.S.A.
214 C3	Millerton Lake U.S.A.
174 C5	Milleur Point U.K.
124 D6	Millicent Australia
209 F4	Millington MI U.S.A.
219 B5	Millington TN U.S.A.
221 I2	Millinocket U.S.A.
127 K6	Mill Island Antarctica
125 I1	Millmerran Australia
172 D3	Millom U.K.
174 D5	Millport U.K.
221 F5	Millsboro U.S.A.
204 F2	Mills Lake Canada
220 C5	Millstone U.S.A.
121 B4	Millstream-Chichester National Park Australia
207 G4	Milltown Canada
175 I5	Milltown Malbay Ireland
122 C3	Millungera Australia
221 J1	Millville Canada
221 F5	Millville U.S.A.
121 B5	Milly Milly Australia
221 I2	Milo U.S.A.
158 D3	Milogradovo Rus. Fed.
185 K6	Milos i. Greece
187 F4	Miloslavskoye Rus. Fed.
124 D2	Milparinka Australia
221 E4	Milroy U.S.A.
209 H4	Milton Canada
126 B7	Milton N.Z.
219 C6	Milton FL U.S.A.
208 A5	Milton IA U.S.A.
221 E4	Milton PA U.S.A.
221 G2	Milton VT U.S.A.
220 C4	Milton, Lake U.S.A.
212 C2	Milton-Freewater U.S.A.
173 G5	Milton Keynes U.K.
155 D4	Miluo China
208 D4	Milwaukee U.S.A.
239 E4	Milwaukee Deep sea feature Caribbean Sea
140 E2	Mily Kazakh.
141 H2	Milybulabk Kazakh.
187 G5	Milyutinskaya Rus. Fed.
121 F5	Mimili Australia
182 D4	Mimizan France
195 B4	Mimongo Gabon
225 D2	Mina Mex.
214 C2	Mina U.S.A.
143 E5	Mīnāb Iran
151 E6	Minahasa, Semenanjung pen. Indon.
142 D5	Mina Jebel Ali U.A.E.
205 K4	Minaki Canada
159 B8	Minamata Japan
120 F2	Minamia Australia
159 E7	Minami-arupusu Kokuritsu-kōen nat. park Japan
153 N6	Minami-Daitō-jima i. Japan
163 B2	Minas Indon.
235 L2	Minas Uruguay
225 G5	Minas, Sierra de las mts Guat.
139 L7	Mīnā' Sa'ūd Kuwait
207 H4	Minas Basin b. Canada
235 L1	Minas de Corrales Uruguay
234 D2	Minas Gerais state Brazil
234 D2	Minas Novas Brazil
225 F4	Minatitlán Mex.
149 H5	Minbu Myanmar
149 H5	Minbya Myanmar
232 B6	Minchinmávida vol. Chile
184 D2	Mincio r. Italy
139 K2	Mincivan Azer.
161 J5	Mindanao i. Phil.
124 D5	Mindarie Australia
192 ☐	Mindelo Cape Verde
209 H3	Minden Canada
179 G2	Minden Germany
217 E5	Minden LA U.S.A.
214 C2	Minden NV U.S.A.
149 H6	Mindon Myanmar
125 E4	Mindona Lake imp. l. Australia
161 I3	Mindoro i. Phil.
161 H3	Mindoro Strait Phil.
195 B4	Mindouli Congo
140 D1	Mindyak Rus. Fed.
175 K6	Mine Head Ireland
173 D6	Minehead U.K.
234 B2	Mineiros Brazil
217 E5	Mineola U.S.A.
214 B1	Mineral U.S.A.
214 C3	Mineral King U.S.A.
187 G6	Mineral'nyye Vody Rus. Fed.
208 B4	Mineral Point U.S.A.
217 D5	Mineral Wells U.S.A.
215 F2	Minersville U.S.A.
185 G4	Minervino Murge Italy
149 E1	Minfeng China
195 C5	Minga Dem. Rep. Congo
139 K1	Mingāçevir Azer.
139 K1	Mingāçevir Su Anbarı resr Azer.
207 H3	Mingan Canada
124 D4	Mingary Australia
	Mingbulak Uzbek. see Mingbuloq
140 E4	Mingbuloq Uzbek.
121 A6	Mingenew Australia
154 E3	Minggang China
154 F3	Mingguang China
152 G7	Mingin Range mts Myanmar
141 H4	Ming-Kush Kyrg.
183 P3	Minglanilla Spain
195 D5	Mingoyo Tanz.
155 B4	Mingshan China
144 I3	Mingshui China
150 E2	Mingshui China
141 H5	Mingteke China
174 A4	Mingulay i. U.K.
155 E5	Mingxi China
154 B2	Minhe China
145 I8	Minhla Myanmar
155 F5	Minhou China
147 G4	Minicoy atoll India
121 C6	Minigwal, Lake salt flat Australia
118 B4	Minilya Australia
121 A4	Minilya r. Australia
207 H3	Minipi Lake Canada
205 I4	Minitonas Canada
155 F5	Min Jiang r. Fujian China
155 B4	Min Jiang r. Sichuan China
194 B3	Minkébé, Parc National de nat. park Gabon
154 A2	Minle China
192 C4	Minna Nigeria
171 K3	Minne Sweden
216 E2	Minneapolis U.S.A.
205 J4	Minnedosa Canada
211 G2	Minnesota r. U.S.A.
208 A2	Minnesota state U.S.A.
124 A4	Minnipa Australia
206 B4	Minnitaki Lake Canada
183 L2	Miño r. Port./Spain
208 C3	Minocqua U.S.A.
208 B2	Minong U.S.A.
208 C5	Minonk U.S.A.
183 S2	Minorca i. Spain
216 C1	Minot U.S.A.
154 E2	Minqin China
155 F5	Minqing China
154 B3	Min Shan mts China
149 H4	Minsin Myanmar
187 C4	Minsk Belarus
177 J4	Mińsk Mazowiecki Poland
173 E5	Minsterley U.K.
148 C1	Mintaka Pass China/Pakistan
154 A3	Mintang China
207 G4	Minto Canada
207 F2	Minto, Lac l. Canada
202 D2	Minto Inlet Canada
213 F4	Minturn U.S.A.
150 B1	Minusinsk Rus. Fed.
149 I3	Minutang India
154 B3	Minxian China
125 E6	Minyip Australia
209 E3	Mio U.S.A.
206 E4	Miquelon Canada
207 I4	Miquelon i. N. America
233 H4	Mira r. Col.
143 F4	Mirabad Afgh.
221 F2	Mirabel Canada
234 D2	Mirabela Brazil
231 I5	Miracema do Tocantins Brazil
231 I5	Mirador, Parque Nacional de nat. park Brazil
225 G4	Mirador-Dos Lagunos-Río Azul, Parque Nacional nat. park Guat.
233 I4	Miraflores Col.
139 H5	Mīrah, Wādī al watercourse Iraq/Saudi Arabia
234 D2	Miralta Brazil
235 L3	Miramar Arg.
225 G4	Miramar, Lago l. Mex.
183 G5	Miramas France
207 G4	Miramichi Canada
185 K7	Mirampellou, Kolpos b. Greece
148 B2	Miram Shah Pak.
234 A3	Miranda Brazil
234 A3	Miranda r. Brazil
214 A1	Miranda U.S.A.
121 C5	Miranda, Lake salt flat Australia
183 O1	Miranda de Ebro Spain
183 M2	Mirandela Port.
184 D2	Mirandola Italy
234 B3	Mirandópolis Brazil
146 D6	Mirbāţ Oman
183 E5	Mirepoix France
163 H2	Miri Sarawak Malaysia
143 H4	Miri mt. Pak.
147 H2	Mirialguda India
235 M2	Mirim, Lagoa l. Brazil
143 F4	Mīrjāveh Iran
127 K6	Mirny research stn Antarctica
186 G2	Mirnyy Arkhangel'skaya Oblast' Rus. Fed.
133 M3	Mirnyy Rus. Fed.
205 I3	Mirond Lake Canada
179 K1	Mirow Germany
148 C2	Mirpur Pak.
148 B4	Mirpur Batoro Pak.
148 B4	Mirpur Khas Pak.
148 A4	Mirpur Sakro Pak.
205 G4	Mirror Canada
155 ☐	Mirs Bay Hong Kong China
160 E6	Miryang S. Korea
142 D3	Mirzā, Chāh-e well Iran
149 E4	Mirzapur India
159 C8	Misaki Japan
141 J5	Misalay China
158 G4	Misawa Japan
207 H4	Miscou Island Canada
148 C1	Misgar Pak.
145 H10	Misha India
158 B2	Mishan China
142 C5	Mishāsh al Ḥadī well Saudi Arabia
208 D5	Mishawaka U.S.A.
209 E1	Mishibishu Lake Canada
159 B7	Mi-shima i. Japan
149 H3	Mishmi Hills India
119 J3	Misima Island P.N.G.
224 I5	Miskitos, Cayos is Nicaragua
177 J6	Miskolc Hungary
151 F7	Misoöl i. Indon.
208 B2	Misquah Hills U.S.A.
193 D1	Miṣrātah Libya
149 E4	Misrikh India
209 E4	Missanabie Canada
206 D3	Missinaibi r. Canada
209 F1	Missinaibi Lake Canada
205 I3	Missinipe Canada
204 E5	Mission Canada
216 C3	Mission SD U.S.A.
225 E2	Mission TX U.S.A.
122 D3	Mission Beach Australia
206 D3	Missisa Lake Canada
209 F2	Mississagi r. Canada
209 H4	Mississauga Canada
209 E5	Mississinewa Lake U.S.A.
209 I3	Mississippi r. Canada
217 F6	Mississippi r. U.S.A.
217 F5	Mississippi state U.S.A.
217 F6	Mississippi Delta U.S.A.
212 D2	Missoula U.S.A.
216 C2	Missouri r. U.S.A.
208 A6	Missouri state U.S.A.
216 E3	Missouri Valley U.S.A.
203 K4	Mistassibi r. Canada
207 F4	Mistassini r. Canada
207 F3	Mistassini, Lac l. Canada
207 H2	Mistastin Lake Canada
177 H6	Mistelbach Austria
207 H2	Mistinibi, Lac l. Canada
207 F3	Mistissini Canada
204 C3	Misty Fiords National Monument Wilderness nat. park U.S.A.
224 C3	Mita, Punta de pt Mex.
119 E4	Mitchell r. N.S.W. Australia
125 J2	Mitchell r. Qld Australia
119 E3	Mitchell r. Vic. Australia
125 G6	Mitchell r. Vic. Australia
209 G4	Mitchell Canada
216 D3	Mitchell U.S.A.
122 D3	Mitchell, Lake Australia
209 E3	Mitchell, Lake U.S.A.
219 D5	Mitchell, Mount U.S.A.
122 C2	Mitchell and Alice Rivers National Park Australia
120 E1	Mitchell Point Australia
175 J5	Mitchelstown Ireland
138 C6	Mīt Ghamr Egypt
148 B3	Mithankot Pak.
148 B4	Mithi Pak.
148 B4	Mithrani Can canal Pak.
185 L5	Mithymna Greece
204 C3	Mitkof Island U.S.A.
159 G6	Mito Japan
195 D4	Mitole Tanz.
126 E4	Mitre mt. N.Z.
119 H3	Mitre Island Solomon Is
185 I3	Mitrovicë Kosovo
125 I5	Mittagong Australia
125 G6	Mitta Mitta Australia
179 G2	Mittellandkanal canal Germany
179 K5	Mitterteich Germany
179 K4	Mittweida Germany
233 J4	Mitú Col.
233 J4	Mituas Col.
195 C5	Mitumba, Chaîne des mts Dem. Rep. Congo
195 C4	Mitumba, Monts mts Dem. Rep. Congo
194 B3	Mitzic Gabon
159 F7	Miura Japan
139 G4	Miyāh, Wādī al watercourse Syria
159 F7	Miyake-jima i. Japan
159 B9	Miyako Japan
159 B9	Miyakonojō Japan
140 C2	Miyaly Kazakh.
148 B5	Miyani India
159 B9	Miyanoura-dake mt. Japan
159 B9	Miyazaki Japan
159 D7	Miyazu Japan
155 B5	Miyi China
159 C7	Miyoshi Japan
154 E1	Miyun China
154 E1	Miyun Shuiku resr China
143 G3	Mīzāni Afgh.
194 D3	Mīzan Teferī Eth.
193 D1	Mizdah Libya
175 I6	Mizen Head Ireland
187 B5	Mizhhirr"ya Ukr.
154 C1	Mizhi China
149 H5	Mizoram state India
159 G5	Mizusawa Japan
171 K4	Mjölby Sweden
195 D4	Mkata Tanz.
195 D4	Mkomazi Tanz.
195 C5	Mkushi Zambia
176 G5	Mladá Boleslav Czech Rep.
185 I2	Mladenovac Serbia
177 J3	Mława Poland
185 G3	Mljet i. Croatia
195 G5	Mlungisi S. Africa
177 L5	Mlyniv Ukr.
197 F2	Mmabatho S. Africa
197 G1	Mmamabula Botswana
197 F2	Mmathethe Botswana
171 I3	Mo Norway
215 H2	Moab U.S.A.
119 H3	Moa Island Australia
119 H3	Moala i. Fiji
142 D3	Mo'alla Iran
197 J2	Moamba Moz.
124 D2	Moanba, Lake salt flat Australia
215 E3	Moapa U.S.A.
175 K4	Moate Ireland
195 C4	Moba Dem. Rep. Congo
159 G7	Mobara Japan
142 C3	Mobārakeh Iran
142 D4	Mobārakeh Iran
194 C3	Mobayi-Mbongo Dem. Rep. Congo
217 E4	Moberly U.S.A.
219 B6	Mobile AL U.S.A.
215 F5	Mobile AZ U.S.A.
219 B6	Mobile Bay U.S.A.
216 C2	Mobridge U.S.A.
231 I4	Mocajuba Brazil
195 E5	Moçambique Moz.
233 K2	Mocapra r. Venez.
155 B6	Môc Châu Vietnam
146 B7	Mocha Yemen
233 K2	Mochirma, Parque Nacional nat. park Venez.
195 C6	Mochudi Botswana
195 E5	Mocimboa da Praia Moz.
179 J2	Möckern Germany
179 H5	Möckmühl Germany
170 M2	Mockträsk Sweden
233 H4	Mocoa Col.
234 C3	Mococa Brazil
224 C2	Mocorito Mex.
225 D3	Moctezuma Mex.
195 D5	Mocuba Moz.
182 H4	Modane France
148 C5	Modasa India
197 F4	Modder r. S. Africa
184 D2	Modena Italy
215 F3	Modena U.S.A.
214 B2	Modesto U.S.A.
197 H2	Modimolle S. Africa
	Modot Mongolia see Tsenhermandal
125 G7	Moe Australia
173 D5	Moel Sych h. U.K.
171 J3	Moelv Norway
170 L1	Moen Norway
215 G3	Moenkopi U.S.A.
126 C6	Moeraki Point N.Z.
179 E3	Moers Germany
174 E5	Moffat U.K.
148 C3	Moga India
194 E3	Mogadishu Somalia
220 C4	Mogadore Reservoir U.S.A.
197 H1	Mogalakwena r. S. Africa
197 H2	Moganyaka S. Africa
152 G6	Mogaung Myanmar
156 D2	Mogdy Rus. Fed.
179 K2	Mögelin Germany
141 F5	Moghiyon Tajik.
234 C3	Mogi-Mirim Brazil
150 D1	Mogocha Rus. Fed.
184 C6	Mogod mts Tunisia
197 F2	Mogoditshane Botswana
151 B4	Mogok Myanmar
215 H5	Mogollon Mountains U.S.A.
215 G5	Mogollon Plateau U.S.A.
197 H1	Mogwadi S. Africa
197 G2	Mogwase S. Africa
153 J1	Mogzon Rus. Fed.
185 H2	Mohács Hungary
126 F3	Mohaka r. N.Z.
197 G5	Mohale's Hoek Lesotho
205 I5	Mohall U.S.A.
143 E3	Mohammad Iran
183 Q5	Mohammadia Alg.
149 E3	Mohan r. India/Nepal
215 E4	Mohave, Lake U.S.A.
221 F3	Mohawk r. U.S.A.
215 F5	Mohawk Mountains U.S.A.
	Moheli i. Comoros see Mwali
143 H5	Mohenjo Daro tourist site Pak.
175 K4	Mohill Ireland
179 G3	Möhne r. Germany
215 F4	Mohon Peak U.S.A.
195 D4	Mohoro Tanz.
187 C5	Mohyliv-Podil's'kyy Ukr.
171 I4	Moi Norway
197 G1	Moijabana Botswana
152 D5	Moincêr China
197 J2	Moine Moz.
177 M7	Moinești Romania
221 F2	Moira r. U.S.A.
170 K2	Mo i Rana Norway
149 H4	Moirang India
171 N4	Mõisaküla Estonia
235 K1	Moisés Ville Arg.
207 G3	Moisie Canada
207 G3	Moisie r. Canada
182 E4	Moissac France
214 C4	Mojave U.S.A.
214 C4	Mojave r. U.S.A.
215 E4	Mojave Desert U.S.A.
153 H7	Mojiang China
234 C3	Moji das Cruzes Brazil
234 C3	Moji-Guaçu r. Brazil
159 B8	Mojikō Japan
225 E3	Molango Mex.
183 P3	Molatón mt. Spain
	Moldavia country Europe see Moldova
171 I3	Molde Norway
170 K2	Moldjord Norway
187 D6	Moldova country Europe
185 K2	Moldoveanu, Vârful mt. Romania
173 D7	Mole r. U.K.
192 B4	Mole National Park Ghana
195 C6	Molepolole Botswana
171 N5	Molētai Lith.
185 G4	Molfetta Italy
183 P2	Molina de Aragón Spain
208 B5	Moline U.S.A.
171 K4	Molkom Sweden
139 L4	Mollā Bodāgh Iran
137 I3	Mollagara Turkm.
	Mollakara Turkm. see Mollagara
149 H4	Mol Len mt. India
179 L1	Möllenbeck Germany
230 D7	Mollendo Peru
179 I1	Mölln Germany
171 K4	Mölnlycke Sweden
186 F3	Molochnoye Rus. Fed.
170 P1	Molochnyy Rus. Fed.
141 F5	Molodogvardeyskoye Kazakh.
186 E3	Molodoy Tud Rus. Fed.
	Molokai i. U.S.A. see Moloka'i
214 ☐²	Moloka'i i. U.S.A.
186 I3	Moloma r. Rus. Fed.
125 H4	Molong Australia
197 F2	Molopo watercourse Botswana/S. Africa
193 D4	Moloundou Cameroon
205 J4	Molson Lake Canada
151 E7	Moluccas is Indon.
	Molucca Sea sea Indon. see Maluku, Laut
195 D5	Moma Moz.
125 E3	Momba Australia
195 D4	Mombasa Kenya
149 H4	Mombi New India
234 B2	Mombuca, Serra da hills Brazil
187 C7	Momchilgrad Bulg.
208 D5	Momence U.S.A.
233 I2	Mompós Col.
171 K5	Møn i. Denmark
215 G2	Mona U.S.A.
223 K5	Mona, Isla i. Puerto Rico
174 A3	Monach, Sound of sea chan. U.K.
174 A3	Monach Islands U.K.
183 H5	Monaco country Europe
239 H4	Monaco Basin sea feature N. Atlantic Ocean
174 D3	Monadhliath Mountains U.K.
175 L3	Monaghan Ireland
217 C6	Monahans U.S.A.
223 K5	Mona Passage Dom. Rep./Puerto Rico
195 E5	Monapo Moz.
174 C3	Monar, Loch l. U.K.
204 F4	Monarch Mountain Canada
213 F4	Monarch Pass U.S.A.
204 F4	Monashee Mountains Canada
184 D7	Monastir Tunisia
177 O3	Monastyrshchina Rus. Fed.
187 D6	Monastyryshche Ukr.
158 H2	Monbetsu Japan
158 H3	Monbetsu Japan
184 B2	Moncalieri Italy
170 P2	Monchegorsk Rus. Fed.
179 E3	Mönchengladbach Germany
183 L4	Monchique Port.
219 E5	Moncks Corner U.S.A.
225 D2	Monclova Mex.
207 H4	Moncton Canada
183 M2	Mondego r. Port.
197 I3	Mondlo S. Africa
184 B2	Mondoví Italy
208 B3	Mondovi U.S.A.
184 E4	Mondragone Italy
153 H1	Mondy Rus. Fed.
185 J6	Monemvasia Greece
158 G1	Moneron, Ostrov i. Rus. Fed.
220 D4	Monessen U.S.A.
209 J1	Monet Canada
175 K5	Moneygall Ireland
175 L3	Moneymore U.K.
184 E2	Monfalcone Italy
183 M1	Monforte de Lemos Spain
194 C3	Monga Dem. Rep. Congo
155 C5	Mông Cai Vietnam
121 B6	Mongers Lake salt flat Australia
160 C4	Monggŭmp'o-ri N. Korea
153 H7	Mong Loi Myanmar
162 A1	Mong Mau Myanmar
150 D2	Mongolia country Asia
148 C2	Mongora Pak.
195 C5	Mongu Zambia

		Nây, Mui pt Vietnam see **Đai Lanh, Mui**
233 H4	Naya Col.	
147 J1	Nayagarh India	

Nây, Mui pt Vietnam see Đai Lanh, Mui
233 H4 Naya Col.
147 J1 Nayagarh India
224 C3 Nayar Mex.
224 C3 Nayarit state Mex.
158 H2 Nayoro Japan
135 H5 Nay Pyi Taw Myanmar
147 H3 Nayudupeta India
234 E1 Nazaré Brazil
147 H4 Nazareth India
138 E5 Nazareth Israel
217 B7 Nazas Mex.
224 C2 Nazas r. Mex.
230 D6 Nazca Peru
237 N7 Nazca Ridge sea feature S. Pacific Ocean
Nazerat Israel see Nazareth
139 J2 Nāzik Iran
139 I2 Nazik Gölü l. Turkey
139 J4 Nāzīl Iran
138 B3 Nazilli Turkey
143 G5 Nazimabad Pak.
139 G2 Nazimiye Turkey
149 H4 Nazira India
204 E4 Nazko Canada
204 E4 Nazko r. Canada
139 J3 Nāzlū r. Iran
187 H7 Nazran' Rus. Fed.
194 D3 Nazrēt Eth.
147 E5 Nazwá Oman
195 C4 Nchelenge Zambia
195 C6 Ncojane Botswana
195 B4 N'dalatando Angola
194 C3 Ndélé Centr. Afr. Rep.
195 B4 Ndendé Gabon
119 G3 Ndeni i. Solomon Is
193 D3 Ndjamena Chad
195 C5 Ndola Zambia
197 I4 Ndwedwe S. Africa
125 G1 Neabul Creek r. Australia
175 L3 Neagh, Lough l. U.K.
212 A1 Neah Bay U.S.A.
118 D4 Neale, Lake salt flat Australia
124 B2 Neales watercourse Australia
185 J5 Nea Liosia Greece
185 J6 Neapoli Greece
173 D6 Neath U.K.
173 D6 Neath r. U.K.
125 G1 Nebine Creek r. Australia
Nebitdag Turkm. see Balkanabat
233 K4 Neblina, Pico da mt. Brazil
123 E4 Nebo Australia
215 G2 Nebo, Mount U.S.A.
186 E3 Nebolchi Rus. Fed.
216 C3 Nebraska state U.S.A.
216 E3 Nebraska City U.S.A.
184 F6 Nebrodi, Monti mts Sicily Italy
217 E6 Neches r. U.S.A.
233 I3 Nechí r. Col.
194 D3 Nechisar National Park Eth.
179 G5 Neckar r. Germany
179 H5 Neckarsulm Germany
117 H2 Necker Island U.S.A.
235 K3 Necochea Arg.
179 L1 Neddemin Germany
207 I2 Nedlouc, Lac l. Canada
Nêdong China see Zêtang
170 N1 Nedre Soppero Sweden
215 E4 Needles U.S.A.
148 C4 Neemuch India
208 C3 Neenah U.S.A.
205 J4 Neepawa Canada
203 J2 Neergaard Lake Canada
178 D3 Neerijnen Neth.
178 D3 Neerpelt Belgium
139 L2 Neftçala Azer.
156 F1 Neftegorsk Rus. Fed.
140 B1 Neftegorsk Rus. Fed.
132 G4 Neftekamsk Rus. Fed.
187 H6 Neftekumsk Rus. Fed.
132 I3 Nefteyugansk Rus. Fed.
173 C5 Nefyn U.K.
184 C6 Nefza Tunisia
195 B4 Negage Angola
194 D3 Negēlē Eth.
136 D5 Negev des. Israel
234 A3 Negla r. Para.
195 D5 Negomane Moz.
147 H5 Negombo Sri Lanka
185 J4 Negotino Macedonia
230 C5 Negra, Cordillera mts Peru
230 B5 Negra, Punta pt Peru
184 B7 Négrine Alg.
230 B4 Negritos Peru
235 J4 Negro r. Arg.
234 A2 Negro r. Brazil
231 F4 Negro r. S. America

235 L2 Negro r. Uruguay
161 I4 Negros i. Phil.
185 M3 Negru Vodă Romania
139 L4 Nehavand Iran
143 F4 Nehbandān Iran
150 E2 Nehe China
155 B4 Neijiang China
205 H4 Neilburg Canada
179 J3 Neinstedt Germany
176 G5 Neiße r. Germany/Poland
233 I4 Neiva Col.
154 D3 Neixiang China
205 J3 Nejanilini Lake Canada
142 D2 Neka Iran
194 D3 Nek'emtē Eth.
171 K5 Neksø Denmark
148 D3 Nelang India
123 C4 Nelia Australia
186 E3 Nelidovo Rus. Fed.
216 D3 Neligh U.S.A.
133 P3 Nel'kan Rus. Fed.
150 F1 Nel'kan Rus. Fed.
147 H3 Nellore India
156 E3 Nel'ma Rus. Fed.
204 F5 Nelson Canada
205 K3 Nelson r. Canada
126 D4 Nelson N.Z.
173 E4 Nelson U.K.
215 E4 Nelson U.S.A.
124 D7 Nelson, Cape Australia
232 B8 Nelson, Estrecho str. Chile
125 J4 Nelson Bay Australia
204 E3 Nelson Forks Canada
205 J3 Nelson House Canada
197 I2 Nelspruit S. Africa
192 B3 Néma Mauritania
186 I3 Nema Rus. Fed.
208 A2 Nemadji r. U.S.A.
187 B4 Neman Rus. Fed.
143 E4 Ne'mātābād Iran
186 G3 Nemda r. Rus. Fed.
186 J2 Nemed Rus. Fed.
209 F2 Nemegos Canada
170 O1 Nemetskiy, Mys c. Rus. Fed.
156 B2 Nemor He r. China
182 F2 Nemours France
139 I2 Nemrut Dağı mt. Turkey
158 I3 Nemuro Japan
158 I3 Nemuro-kaikyō sea chan. Japan
187 D5 Nemyriv Ukr.
175 J5 Nenagh Ireland
173 H5 Nene r. U.K.
150 E2 Nenjiang China
156 B3 Nen Jiang r. China
179 E5 Nennig tourist site Germany
186 F1 Nenoksa Rus. Fed.
174 E1 Neolithic Orkney tourist site U.K.
217 E4 Neosho U.S.A.
217 E4 Neosho r. U.S.A.
149 E3 Nepal country Asia
152 D6 Nepalganj Nepal
209 J3 Nepean Canada
215 G2 Nephi U.S.A.
175 I3 Nephin h. Ireland
175 I3 Nephin Beg Range hills Ireland
194 C3 Nepoko r. Dem. Rep. Congo
Neptune U.S.A. see Neptune City
221 F4 Neptune City U.S.A.
182 E4 Nérac France
125 J1 Nerang Australia
150 D1 Nerchinsk Rus. Fed.
186 G3 Nerekhta Rus. Fed.
185 G3 Neretva r. Bos.-Herz./Croatia
195 C5 Neriquinha Angola
171 M5 Neris r. Lith.
187 F3 Nerl' r. Rus. Fed.
234 C2 Nerópolis Brazil
150 E1 Neryungri Rus. Fed.
178 D1 Nes Neth.
171 J3 Nes Norway
171 J3 Nesbyen Norway
170 D2 Neskaupstaður Iceland
178 A5 Nesle France
170 K2 Nesna Norway
174 D3 Ness, Loch l. U.K.
217 D4 Ness City U.S.A.
179 I4 Nesse r. Germany
204 C3 Nesselrode, Mount Canada/U.S.A.
185 K4 Nestos r. Greece
138 E5 Netanya Israel
205 M2 Netchek, Cape Canada
178 D2 Netherlands country Europe
233 J1 Netherlands Antilles terr. Caribbean Sea
179 G4 Netphen Germany

149 G4 Netrakona Bangl.
148 C5 Netrang India
203 K3 Nettilling Lake Canada
208 A1 Nett Lake U.S.A.
208 A1 Nett Lake l. U.S.A.
179 L1 Neubrandenburg Germany
176 C7 Neuchâtel Switz.
176 C7 Neuchâtel, Lac de l. Switz.
179 I5 Neuendettelsau Germany
179 E2 Neuenhaus Germany
179 H1 Neuenkirchen Germany
179 G2 Neuenkirchen (Oldenburg) Germany
178 D5 Neufchâteau Belgium
182 G2 Neufchâteau France
182 E2 Neufchâtel-en-Bray France
179 F1 Neuharlingersiel Germany
179 H1 Neuhaus (Oste) Germany
179 H4 Neuhof Germany
179 J1 Neu Kaliß Germany
179 H4 Neukirchen Hessen Germany
179 K4 Neukirchen Sachsen Germany
179 J5 Neumarkt in der Oberpfalz Germany
176 D3 Neumünster Germany
179 K5 Neunburg vorm Wald Germany
177 H7 Neunkirchen Austria
179 F5 Neunkirchen Germany
235 I3 Neuquén Arg.
235 I3 Neuquén prov. Arg.
235 I3 Neuquén r. Arg.
179 K2 Neuruppin Germany
219 E5 Neuse r. U.S.A.
177 H7 Neusiedler See l. Austria/Hungary
179 E3 Neuss Germany
179 F4 Neustadt (Wied) Germany
179 F4 Neustadt am Rübenberge Germany
179 I5 Neustadt an der Aisch Germany
179 K5 Neustadt an der Waldnaab Germany
179 G5 Neustadt an der Weinstraße Germany
179 J4 Neustadt bei Coburg Germany
179 J1 Neustadt-Glewe Germany
179 L1 Neustrelitz Germany
179 K6 Neutraubling Germany
179 H1 Neu Wulmstorf Germany
217 E4 Nevada U.S.A.
215 D2 Nevada state U.S.A.
183 O4 Nevada, Sierra mts Spain
214 B1 Nevada, Sierra mts U.S.A.
235 I2 Nevado, Cerro mt. Arg.
235 I3 Nevado, Sierra del mts Arg.
225 E4 Nevado de Toluca, Volcán vol. Mex.
186 D3 Nevel' Rus. Fed.
156 F3 Nevel'sk Rus. Fed.
156 B1 Never Rus. Fed.
182 F3 Nevers France
125 G3 Nevertire Australia
185 H3 Nevesinje Bos.-Herz.
187 H6 Nevinnomyssk Rus. Fed.
174 C3 Nevis, Loch inlet U.K.
138 E2 Nevşehir Turkey
158 C2 Nevskoye Rus. Fed.
215 E5 New r. CA U.S.A.
220 C6 New r. WV U.S.A.
204 D3 New Aiyansh Canada
219 C4 New Albany IN U.S.A.
217 F5 New Albany MS U.S.A.
221 F5 New Albany PA U.S.A.
231 G2 New Amsterdam Guyana
125 G2 New Angledool Australia
221 F5 Newark DE U.S.A.
221 F5 Newark MD U.S.A.
221 F4 Newark NJ U.S.A.
221 E3 Newark NY U.S.A.
220 B4 Newark OH U.S.A.
221 F4 Newark airport U.S.A.
215 E2 Newark Lake U.S.A.
173 G4 Newark-on-Trent U.K.
212 B2 Newberg U.S.A.
221 F3 New Berlin U.S.A.
219 E5 New Bern U.S.A.
209 E2 Newberry MI U.S.A.
219 D5 Newberry SC U.S.A.
215 D4 Newberry Springs U.S.A.
172 F2 Newbiggin-by-the-Sea U.K.

219 F7 New Bight Bahamas
209 I3 Newboro Canada
221 G3 New Boston MA U.S.A.
220 B5 New Boston OH U.S.A.
217 D6 New Braunfels U.S.A.
175 L4 Newbridge Ireland
119 E2 New Britain i. P.N.G.
221 G4 New Britain U.S.A.
236 F6 New Britain Trench sea feature Pacific Ocean
207 G4 New Brunswick prov. Canada
221 F4 New Brunswick U.S.A.
208 D5 New Buffalo U.S.A.
175 F3 Newburgh U.K.
221 F4 Newburgh U.S.A.
173 F6 Newbury U.K.
221 H3 Newburyport U.S.A.
172 E3 Newby Bridge U.K.
119 G4 New Caledonia terr. S. Pacific Ocean
236 F7 New Caledonia Trough sea feature Tasman Sea
207 G4 New Carlisle Canada
125 I4 Newcastle Australia
209 H4 Newcastle Canada
175 L4 Newcastle Ireland
197 I4 Newcastle S. Africa
175 M3 Newcastle U.K.
214 B2 Newcastle CA U.S.A.
209 E6 Newcastle IN U.S.A.
220 B4 Newcastle OH U.S.A.
220 C4 New Castle PA U.S.A.
215 F3 Newcastle UT U.S.A.
220 C6 New Castle VA U.S.A.
173 F3 Newcastle Emlyn U.K.
173 E4 Newcastle-under-Lyme U.K.
172 F3 Newcastle upon Tyne U.K.
120 F3 Newcastle Waters Australia
175 I5 Newcastle West Ireland
221 F6 New Church U.S.A.
215 F4 Newcomb U.S.A.
174 D5 New Cumnock U.K.
175 F3 New Deer U.K.
148 D3 New Delhi India
221 J1 New Denmark Canada
214 B3 New Don Pedro Reservoir U.S.A.
121 D5 Newell, Lake salt flat Australia
125 I3 New England Range mts Australia
239 F3 New England Seamounts sea feature N. Atlantic Ocean
173 E6 Newent U.K.
173 F7 New Forest National Park U.K.
203 M5 Newfoundland i. Canada
Newfoundland prov. Canada see Newfoundland and Labrador
207 I4 Newfoundland and Labrador prov. Canada
213 D3 Newfoundland Evaporation Basin salt l. U.S.A.
174 D5 New Galloway U.K.
119 F2 New Georgia i. Solomon Is
119 F2 New Georgia Islands Solomon Is
119 F2 New Georgia Sound sea chan. Solomon Is
207 H4 New Glasgow Canada
119 E2 New Guinea i. Asia
220 B4 New Hampshire U.S.A.
221 G3 New Hampshire state U.S.A.
208 A4 New Hampton U.S.A.
119 F2 New Hanover i. P.N.G.
197 I4 New Hanover S. Africa
221 G4 New Haven U.S.A.
204 D3 New Hazelton Canada
236 G7 New Hebrides Trench sea feature Pacific Ocean
214 B2 New Hogan Reservoir U.S.A.
208 C4 New Holstein U.S.A.
217 F6 New Iberia U.S.A.
197 I2 Newington S. Africa
175 K5 Newinn Ireland
119 F2 New Ireland i. P.N.G.
221 F5 New Jersey state U.S.A.
221 E6 New Kent U.S.A.
174 E6 New Lanark U.K.
121 C6 Newland Range hills Australia
220 B5 New Lexington U.S.A.
208 B4 New Lisbon U.S.A.
209 H2 New Liskeard Canada
221 G4 New London CT U.S.A.
208 B5 New London IA U.S.A.

208 B6 New London MO U.S.A.
208 C3 New London WI U.S.A.
118 B4 Newman Australia
208 D6 Newman U.S.A.
209 H3 Newmarket Canada
175 I5 Newmarket Ireland
173 H5 Newmarket U.K.
220 D5 New Market U.S.A.
175 J5 Newmarket-on-Fergus Ireland
220 C5 New Martinsville U.S.A.
212 C2 New Meadows U.S.A.
214 B3 New Melones Lake U.S.A.
213 F5 New Mexico state U.S.A.
219 C5 Newnan U.S.A.
125 G9 New Norfolk Australia
217 F6 New Orleans U.S.A.
221 F4 New Paltz U.S.A.
220 C4 New Philadelphia U.S.A.
175 F3 New Pitsligo U.K.
126 E3 New Plymouth N.Z.
175 I4 Newport Mayo Ireland
175 J5 Newport Tipperary Ireland
173 E5 Newport England U.K.
173 F7 Newport England U.K.
173 D6 Newport Wales U.K.
217 F5 Newport AR U.S.A.
220 A5 Newport KY U.S.A.
217 F6 Newport ME U.S.A.
209 F5 Newport MI U.S.A.
221 G3 Newport NH U.S.A.
212 A2 Newport OR U.S.A.
221 H4 Newport RI U.S.A.
221 G2 Newport VT U.S.A.
212 C1 Newport WA U.S.A.
215 D5 Newport Beach U.S.A.
211 K4 Newport News U.S.A.
221 E6 Newport News airport U.S.A.
175 G5 Newport Pagnell U.K.
219 E7 New Providence i. Bahamas
173 B7 Newquay U.K.
207 G4 New Richmond Canada
208 A3 New Richmond U.S.A.
215 F5 New River U.S.A.
217 F6 New Roads U.S.A.
173 H7 New Romney U.K.
175 L5 New Ross Ireland
120 E3 Newry Australia
175 L3 Newry U.K.
208 A5 New Sharon U.S.A.
133 P2 New Siberia Islands Rus. Fed.
219 D6 New Smyrna Beach U.S.A.
125 G4 New South Wales state Australia
155 □ New Territories reg. Hong Kong China
173 E4 Newton U.K.
216 E3 Newton IA U.S.A.
217 D4 Newton KS U.S.A.
221 H3 Newton MA U.S.A.
217 F5 Newton MS U.S.A.
221 F4 Newton NJ U.S.A.
173 D7 Newton Abbot U.K.
175 F3 Newtonhill U.K.
174 D5 Newton Mearns U.K.
174 D6 Newton Stewart U.K.
175 J5 Newtown Ireland
173 E5 Newtown England U.K.
173 D5 Newtown Wales U.K.
216 C1 New Town U.S.A.
175 M3 Newtownabbey U.K.
175 M3 Newtownards U.K.
175 K3 Newtownbutler U.K.
175 L4 Newtown Mount Kennedy Ireland
175 F5 Newtown St Boswells U.K.
175 K3 Newtownstewart U.K.
216 E2 New Ulm U.S.A.
214 A2 Newville U.S.A.
204 E5 New Westminster Canada
221 G4 New York U.S.A. (City Plan 104)
221 E3 New York state U.S.A.
126 New Zealand country Oceania
186 G3 Neya Rus. Fed.
143 E4 Ney Bīd Iran
142 D4 Neyrīz Iran
143 E2 Neyshābūr Iran
147 H4 Neyyattinkara India
225 F4 Nezahualcóyotl, Presa resr Mex.
163 H2 Ngabang Indon.
195 B4 Ngabé Congo
162 A2 Nga Chong, Khao mt. Myanmar/Thai.
161 J6 Ngalipaëng Indon.
120 C1 Ngalu Indon.
195 C6 Ngami, Lake Botswana
149 F3 Ngamring China

149 E3 Ngangla Ringco salt l. China
149 E2 Nganglong Kangri mt. China
149 E2 Nganglong Kangri mts China
149 F3 Ngangzê Co salt l. China
162 C1 Ngan Sâu, Sông r. Vietnam
Ngan Sau, Sông r. Vietnam see Ngan Sâu, Sông
155 B6 Ngân Sơn Vietnam
162 A1 Ngao Thai.
193 D4 Ngaoundéré Cameroon
126 E2 Ngaruawahia N.Z.
126 F3 Ngaruroro r. N.Z.
126 E3 Ngauruhoe vol. N.Z.
162 B1 Ngiap r. Laos
120 D1 Ngilmina Indon.
195 B4 Ngo Congo
Ngoc Linh mt. Vietnam see Ngok Linh
149 F3 Ngoin, Co salt l. China
162 C2 Ngok Linh mt. Vietnam
193 D4 Ngol Bembo Nigeria
149 F2 Ngoqumaima China
150 B3 Ngoring Hu l. China
195 D4 Ngorongoro Conservation Area nature res. Tanz.
193 D3 Ngourti Niger
193 D3 Nguigmi Niger
120 E1 Nguiu Australia
122 A2 Ngukurr Australia
151 F6 Ngulu atoll Micronesia
162 B1 Ngum, Nam r. Laos
193 D3 Nguru Nigeria
Nguyên Binh Vietnam see Ngân Sơn
Ngwaketse admin. dist. Botswana see Southern
197 G3 Ngwathe S. Africa
197 I3 Ngwavuma r. Swaziland
197 I4 Ngwelezana S. Africa
195 D5 Nhamalabué Moz.
163 D2 Nha Trang Vietnam
124 D6 Nhill Australia
197 I3 Nhlangano Swaziland
155 B6 Nho Quan Vietnam
118 D3 Nhulunbuy Australia
205 I4 Niacam Canada
192 B3 Niafounké Mali
209 H4 Niagara r. Canada/U.S.A.
208 D3 Niagara U.S.A.
209 H4 Niagara Falls Canada
220 D3 Niagara Falls U.S.A.
192 C3 Niamey Niger
161 J5 Niampak Indon.
195 D4 Niangandu Tanz.
194 C3 Niangara Dem. Rep. Congo
156 A3 Nianzishan China
163 E2 Nias i. Indon.
121 D4 Nibil Well Australia
171 M4 Nīca Latvia
224 H5 Nicaragua country Central America
224 H6 Nicaragua, Lake Nicaragua
185 G5 Nicastro Italy
183 H5 Nice France
207 F3 Nichicun, Lac l. Canada
149 E4 Nichlaul India
219 E7 Nicholl's Town Bahamas
122 B3 Nicholson r. Australia
209 F2 Nicholson Canada
121 B5 Nicholson Range hills Australia
135 H6 Nicobar Islands India
138 D4 Nicosia Cyprus
224 H6 Nicoya, Golfo de b. Costa Rica
224 H6 Nicoya, Península de pen. Costa Rica
221 J1 Nictau Canada
171 M5 Nida Lith.
173 F4 Nidd r. U.K.
179 H4 Nidda Germany
179 H4 Nidder r. Germany
177 J4 Nidzica Poland
176 D3 Niebüll Germany
179 E5 Niederanven Lux.
179 H4 Niederaula Germany
176 F7 Niedere Tauern mts Austria
179 G2 Niedersachsen Land Germany
179 E1 Niedersächsisches Wattenmeer, Nationalpark Germany
193 D4 Niefang Equat. Guinea
192 B3 Niellé Côte d'Ivoire
179 H2 Nienburg (Weser) Germany
179 E3 Niers r. Germany
179 G5 Nierstein Germany

170 O1 Pechenga Rus. Fed.
132 G3 Pechora Rus. Fed.
240 D2 Pechora r. Rus. Fed.
186 C3 Pechory Rus. Fed.
209 F4 Peck U.S.A.
204 E3 Peck, Mount Canada
162 C2 Pe Cô, Krông r. Vietnam
217 C6 Pecos U.S.A.
214 C5 Pecos r. U.S.A.
185 H1 Pécs Hungary
224 I7 Pedasí Panama
125 G9 Pedder, Lake Australia
197 G6 Peddie S. Africa
224 C1 Pedernales Mex.
171 M3 Pedernales Rus. Fed.
Pēdo La pass China see
Pindu Pass
74 E5 Peebles U.K.
233 E1 Pedra Azul Brazil
233 J3 Pedraza la Vieja Venez.
233 J2 Pedregal Venez.
234 C3 Pedregulho Brazil
231 J4 Pedreiras Brazil
225 D2 Pedriceña Mex.
147 I4 Pedro, Point Sri Lanka
231 I5 Pedro Afonso Brazil
233 J4 Pedro Chico Col.
232 C2 Pedro de Valdivia Chile
234 A2 Pedro Gomes Brazil
224 J6 Pedro González, Isla i.
Panama
231 J4 Pedro II Brazil
233 K4 Pedro II, Ilha reg. Brazil
232 E2 Pedro Juan Caballero Para.
235 M1 Pedro Osório Brazil
Pedro Segundo Brazil
see Pedro II
219 E5 Pee Dee r. U.S.A.
221 G4 Peekskill U.S.A.
125 I3 Peel r. Australia
202 E3 Peel r. Canada
172 C3 Peel U.K.
178 D3 Peer Belgium
123 B5 Peera Peera Poolanna Lake
salt flat Australia
204 F4 Peers Canada
125 E3 Peery Lake salt l. Australia
126 D5 Pegasus Bay N.Z.
179 J5 Pegnitz Germany
179 J5 Pegnitz r. Germany
151 B5 Pegu Myanmar
152 G8 Pegu Yoma mts Myanmar
186 I2 Pegysh Rus. Fed.
235 K2 Pehuajó Arg.
155 F6 Peikang Taiwan
179 I2 Peine Germany
171 N4 Peipus, Lake
Estonia/Rus. Fed.
Pei Shan mts China see
Bei Shan
179 J3 Peißen Germany
154 E3 Peitun China
231 I6 Peixe Brazil
234 B1 Peixe r. Goiás Brazil
234 B3 Peixe r. São Paulo Brazil
234 C3 Peixian China
234 A2 Peixo de Couro r. Brazil
185 I3 Pejë Kosovo
197 G4 Peka Lesotho
163 G4 Pekalongan Indon.
162 B5 Pekan Malaysia
163 B2 Pekanbaru Indon.
208 C5 Pekin U.S.A.
Pelabuhan Kelang Malaysia
see Pelabuhan Klang
162 B5 Pelabuhan Klang Malaysia
209 F5 Pelee Island Canada
209 F5 Pelee Point Canada
151 E7 Peleng i. Indon.
186 I2 Peles Rus. Fed.
208 A1 Pelican Lake MN U.S.A.
208 C3 Pelican Lake WI U.S.A.
205 I3 Pelican Narrows Canada
170 N2 Pelkosenniemi Fin.
196 C4 Pella S. Africa
205 H1 Pellatt Lake Canada
119 E2 Pelleluhu Islands P.N.G.
208 C4 Pell Lake U.S.A.
170 M2 Pello Fin.
204 B2 Pelly r. Canada
Pelly Bay Canada see
Kugaaruk
204 B2 Pelly Crossing Canada
205 I1 Pelly Lake Canada
204 C2 Pelly Mountains Canada
235 M1 Pelotas Brazil
232 F3 Pelotas, Rio das r. Brazil
138 D6 Pelusium tourist site Egypt
221 I2 Pemadumcook Lake U.S.A.
163 G2 Pemali Indon.
163 G2 Pemangkat Indon.

163 E2 Pematangsiantar Indon.
195 E5 Pemba Moz.
195 C5 Pemba Zambia
195 D4 Pemba Island Tanz.
204 F4 Pembina r. Canada
216 D1 Pembina U.S.A.
209 I3 Pembroke Canada
173 C6 Pembroke U.K.
221 J2 Pembroke U.S.A.
173 B5 Pembrokeshire Coast
National Park U.K.
147 G2 Pen India
149 H5 Pen r. Myanmar
183 O2 Peñalara mt. Spain
225 E3 Peñamiller Mex.
225 E3 Peña Nevada, Cerro mt. Mex.
183 Q1 Perdido, Monte mt. Spain
183 P2 Peñarroya mt. Spain
183 N3 Peñarroya-Pueblonuevo
Spain
173 D6 Penarth U.K.
183 N1 Peñas, Cabo de c. Spain
232 A7 Penas, Golfo de g. Chile
233 L2 Peñas, Punta pt Venez.
224 H6 Peñas Blancas Nicaragua
148 D5 Pench r. India
127 K6 Penck, Cape Antarctica
192 C3 Pendjari, Parc National de
la nat. park Benin
173 E4 Pendle Hill U.K.
212 C2 Pendleton U.S.A.
204 D4 Pendleton Bay Canada
212 C1 Pend Oreille r. U.S.A.
212 C2 Pend Oreille Lake U.S.A.
147 I1 Pendra India
209 H3 Penetanguishene Canada
155 C4 Peng'an China
148 D6 Penganga r. India
155 □ Peng Chau i. Hong Kong
China
155 G5 P'engchia Yü i. Taiwan
195 C4 Penge Dem. Rep. Congo
197 I2 Penge S. Africa
155 F6 P'enghu Ch'üntao is Taiwan
155 F6 P'enghu Tao i. Taiwan
162 □ Peng Kang h. Sing.
154 F2 Penglai China
155 B4 Pengshan China
155 C4 Pengshui China
155 B4 Pengxi China
155 C4 Pengze China
197 G5 Penhoek Pass S. Africa
183 L3 Peniche Port.
174 E5 Penicuik U.K.
179 K4 Penig Germany
186 E2 Peninga Rus. Fed.
139 J4 Pēnjwīn Iraq
184 E3 Penne Italy
147 H3 Penner r. India
124 B5 Penneshaw Australia
172 E3 Pennines hills U.K.
197 I5 Pennington S. Africa
221 F5 Pennsville U.S.A.
220 D4 Pennsylvania state U.S.A.
221 E3 Penn Yan U.S.A.
203 L3 Penny Icecap Canada
221 I2 Penobscot r. U.S.A.
221 I2 Penobscot Bay U.S.A.
124 D6 Penola Australia
224 C2 Peñón Blanco Mex.
118 D5 Penong Australia
224 I6 Penonomé Panama
117 I4 Penrhyn atoll Cook Is
237 I6 Penrhyn Basin sea feature
Pacific Ocean
172 E3 Penrith U.K.
219 C6 Pensacola U.S.A.
127 J4 Pensacola Mountains
Antarctica
139 L2 Pensär Azer.
125 E6 Penshurst Australia
148 D2 Pensi La pass India
119 G3 Pentecost Island Vanuatu
204 F5 Penticton Canada
173 B7 Pentire Point U.K.
123 D4 Pentland Australia
174 E2 Pentland Firth sea chan.
U.K.
174 E5 Pentland Hills U.K.
208 D4 Pentwater U.S.A.
147 H3 Penukonda India
173 D5 Penygadair h. U.K.
172 E3 Pen-y-Ghent h. U.K.
205 H2 Penylan Lake Canada
187 H4 Penza Rus. Fed.
173 B7 Penzance U.K.
187 H4 Penzenskaya Oblast'
admin. div. Rus. Fed.

133 R3 Penzhinskaya Guba b.
Rus. Fed.
215 F5 Peoria AZ U.S.A.
208 C4 Peoria IL U.S.A.
122 C2 Pera Head Australia
162 B4 Perai Malaysia
162 A4 Perak i. Malaysia
162 B4 Perak r. Malaysia
183 P2 Perales del Alfambra Spain
147 H4 Perambalur India
207 H4 Percé Canada
121 D4 Percival Lakes salt flat
Australia
221 H2 Percy U.S.A.
119 F4 Percy Isles Australia
209 I3 Percy Reach l. Canada
183 Q1 Perdido, Monte mt. Spain
132 H3 Peregrebnoye Rus. Fed.
233 I3 Pereira Col.
234 B3 Pereira Barreto Brazil
186 D3 Perekhoda r. Rus. Fed.
187 G5 Perelazovskiy Rus. Fed.
140 B2 Perelyub Rus. Fed.
121 B6 Perenjori Australia
186 F3 Pereslavl'-Zalesskiy
Rus. Fed.
140 C2 Perevolotskiy Rus. Fed.
187 H4 Perevoz Rus. Fed.
156 D3 Pereyaslavka Rus. Fed.
187 D5 Pereyaslav-Khmel'nyts'kyy
Ukr.
235 K2 Pergamino Arg.
162 B4 Perhentian Besar, Pulau i.
Malaysia
171 N3 Perho Fin.
Péribonca, Lac l. Canada see
Péribonka, Lac
207 F3 Péribonka, Lac l. Canada
232 C2 Perico Arg.
224 C2 Pericos Mex.
182 E4 Périgueux France
233 I2 Perijá, Parque Nacional
nat. park Venez.
233 I2 Perija, Sierra de mts Venez.
232 B7 Perito Moreno Arg.
208 D3 Perkins U.S.A.
224 I5 Perlas, Laguna de lag.
Nicaragua
224 I5 Perlas, Punta de pt
Nicaragua
179 J1 Perleberg Germany
132 G4 Perm' Rus. Fed.
186 H3 Permas Rus. Fed.
Pernambuco Abyssal Plain
sea feature S. Atlantic Ocean
see Pernambuco Plain
239 H6 Pernambuco Plain
sea feature S. Atlantic Ocean
124 B3 Pernatty Lagoon salt flat
Australia
185 J3 Pernik Bulg.
120 E2 Peron Islands Australia
182 F2 Péronne France
225 E4 Perote Mex.
183 F5 Perpignan France
173 B7 Perranporth U.K.
215 D5 Perris U.S.A.
182 C2 Perros-Guirec France
219 D6 Perry FL U.S.A.
219 D5 Perry GA U.S.A.
216 E3 Perry IA U.S.A.
217 D4 Perry OK U.S.A.
220 B4 Perrysburg U.S.A.
217 C4 Perryton U.S.A.
217 F4 Perryville U.S.A.
142 D4 Persepolis tourist site Iran
173 E5 Pershore U.K.
Persian Gulf g. Asia see
The Gulf
139 G2 Pertek Turkey
118 B5 Perth Australia
209 I3 Perth Canada
174 E4 Perth U.K.
221 F4 Perth Amboy U.S.A.
221 J1 Perth-Andover Canada
238 L6 Perth Basin sea feature
Indian Ocean
186 F1 Pertominsk Rus. Fed.
183 G5 Pertuis France
171 N3 Pertunmaa Fin.
184 C4 Pertusato, Capo c. Corsica
France
230 C5 Peru country S. America
208 C5 Peru U.S.A.
237 M7 Peru Basin sea feature
S. Pacific Ocean
237 N6 Peru-Chile Trench
sea feature S. Pacific Ocean

184 E3 Perugia Italy
235 C4 Peruíbe Brazil
178 B4 Péruwelz Belgium
187 D5 Pervomaysk Rus. Fed.
186 J2 Pervomays'k Ukr.
187 E6 Pervomays'ke Ukr.
141 J2 Pervomayskiy Kazakh.
140 C2 Pervomayskiy Orenburgskaya
Oblast' Rus. Fed.
187 G4 Pervomayskiy Tambovskaya
Oblast' Rus. Fed.
187 F5 Pervomays'kyy Ukr.
133 R3 Pervorechenskiy Rus. Fed.
184 E3 Pesaro Italy
214 A3 Pescadero U.S.A.
215 H4 Pescado U.S.A.
184 F3 Pescara Italy
184 F3 Pescara r. Italy
187 G6 Peschanokopskoye Rus. Fed.
140 B4 Peschanyy, Mys pt Kazakh.
162 □ Pesek, Pulau i. Sing.
148 B2 Peshawar Pak.
185 I4 Peshkopi Albania
185 K3 Peshtera Bulg.
208 D3 Peshtigo U.S.A.
208 C3 Peshtigo r. U.S.A.
141 F1 Peski Kazakh.
140 E5 Peski Turkm.
184 F1 Pesnica Slovenia
182 D4 Pessac France
179 K2 Pessin Germany
179 J2 Pestovo Rus. Fed.
187 G4 Pet r. Rus. Fed.
225 D4 Petacalco, Bahía de b. Mex.
138 E5 Petah Tiqwa Israel
171 N3 Petäjävesi Fin.
185 K5 Petalioi i. Greece
214 A2 Petaluma U.S.A.
178 C3 Pétange Lux.
163 I3 Petangis Indon.
233 K2 Petare Venez.
225 D4 Petatlán Mex.
208 C3 Petenwell Lake U.S.A.
224 C4 Peterborough S.A. Australia
125 E7 Peterborough Vic. Australia
209 H3 Peterborough Canada
173 G5 Peterborough U.K.
175 F3 Peterculter U.K.
175 G3 Peterhead U.K.
127 I3 Peter I Island Antarctica
205 K2 Peter Lake Canada
172 F3 Peterlee U.K.
118 C4 Petermann Ranges mts
Australia
235 H2 Peteroa, Volcán vol. Chile
205 H3 Peter Pond Lake Canada
207 F2 Peters, Lac l. Canada
179 H4 Petersberg Germany
204 C3 Petersburg AK U.S.A.
208 C6 Petersburg IL U.S.A.
221 E6 Petersburg VA U.S.A.
220 D5 Petersburg WV U.S.A.
173 G6 Petersfield U.K.
179 G2 Petershagen Germany
185 G5 Petilia Policastro Italy
221 J2 Petit Manan Point U.S.A.
207 H3 Petit Mécatina r. Canada
207 I3 Petit Mécatina r. Canada
204 E3 Petitot r. Canada
225 E4 Petlalcingo Mex.
225 G3 Peto Mex.
209 E3 Petoskey U.S.A.
138 E6 Petra tourist site Jordan
150 F2 Petra Velikogo, Zaliv b.
Rus. Fed.
209 I4 Petre, Point Canada
185 J4 Petrich Bulg.
215 H4 Petrified Forest National
Park U.S.A.
185 G2 Petrinja Croatia
185 J3 Petrokhanski Prokhod pass
Bulg.
209 F4 Petrolia Canada
231 J5 Petrolina Brazil
141 J3 Petropavlovka Kazakh.
187 G5 Petropavlovsk Rus. Fed.
141 G1 Petropavlovsk Kazakh.
150 H1 Petropavlovsk-Kamchatskiy
Rus. Fed.
185 J2 Petroşani Romania
141 G1 Petrovka Kazakh.
140 B1 Petrovka Rus. Fed.
187 H4 Petrovsk Rus. Fed.
150 C1 Petrovsk-Zabaykal'skiy
Rus. Fed.
187 H5 Petrov Val Rus. Fed.
186 E2 Petrozavodsk Rus. Fed.

197 F4 Petrusburg S. Africa
197 H3 Petrus Steyn S. Africa
197 F5 Petrusville S. Africa
178 C2 Petten Neth.
175 K3 Pettigo U.K.
132 H4 Petukhovo Rus. Fed.
164 A4 Peureula Indon.
133 S3 Pevek Rus. Fed.
177 H6 Pezinok Slovakia
179 F5 Pfälzer Wald hills Germany
179 G6 Pforzheim Germany
176 D7 Pfullendorf Germany
179 G5 Pfungstadt Germany
197 H2 Phagameng Northern
S. Africa
148 C3 Phagwara India
197 G4 Phahameng Free State
S. Africa
Phahameng S. Africa see
Phagameng
197 I1 Phalaborwa S. Africa
148 C4 Phalodi India
148 B4 Phalsund India
147 G2 Phaltan India
162 A1 Phan Thai.
162 B2 Phanat Nikhom Thai.
162 B3 Phangan, Ko i. Thai.
162 A3 Phangnga Thai.
155 B6 Phăng Xi Păng mt. Vietnam
162 C2 Phanom Dong Rak, Thiu
Khao mts Cambodia/Thai.
Phan Rang Vietnam see
Phan Rang-Thap Cham
163 D3 Phan Rang-Thap Cham
Vietnam
Phan Ri Vietnam see
Phan Ri Cửa
163 D3 Phan Ri Cửa Vietnam
163 D3 Phan Thiêt Vietnam
Phapon Myanmar see
Pyapon
217 D7 Pharr U.S.A.
155 C6 Phat Diêm Vietnam
162 B4 Phatthalung Thai.
162 A1 Phayao Thai.
149 H4 Phek India
205 I3 Phelps Lake Canada
162 B1 Phen Thai.
219 C5 Phenix City U.S.A.
162 A2 Phet Buri Thai.
162 B1 Phetchabun Thai.
162 C2 Phiafai Laos
162 A2 Phichai Thai.
162 B1 Phichit Thai.
217 F5 Philadelphia MS U.S.A.
221 F2 Philadelphia NY U.S.A.
221 F5 Philadelphia PA U.S.A.
216 C2 Philip U.S.A.
178 C4 Philippeville Belgium
220 C5 Philippi U.S.A.
123 B5 Philippi, Lake salt flat
Australia
178 B3 Philippine Neth.
236 D4 Philippine Basin sea feature
N. Pacific Ocean
161 Philippines country Asia
161 J2 Philippine Sea Phil.
236 D4 Philippine Trench
sea feature N. Pacific Ocean
197 F5 Philippolis S. Africa
179 G5 Philippsburg Germany
220 D4 Philipsburg U.S.A.
178 C3 Philipsdam barrage Neth.
202 D3 Philip Smith Mountains
U.S.A.
197 F5 Philipstown S. Africa
125 F7 Phillip Island Australia
221 H2 Phillips ME U.S.A.
208 B3 Phillips WI U.S.A.
217 D4 Phillipsburg KS U.S.A.
221 F4 Phillipsburg NJ U.S.A.
203 I1 Phillips Inlet Canada
120 D3 Phillips Range hills Australia
220 D4 Phillipston U.S.A.
221 G3 Philmont U.S.A.
205 G3 Philomena Canada
220 C6 Philpott Reservoir U.S.A.
162 B2 Phimae tourist site Thai.
162 C2 Phimun Mangsahan Thai.
197 G3 Phiritona S. Africa
162 B1 Phitsanulok Thai.
162 C3 Phnom Penh Cambodia
Phnum Pénh Cambodia see
Phnom Penh
162 B4 Pho, Laem pt Thai.
215 F5 Phoenix U.S.A.
119 I2 Phoenix Islands
Pacific Ocean
197 G3 Phomolong S. Africa
162 B2 Phon Thai.

151 C4 Phôngsali Laos
155 B6 Phong Thô Vietnam
162 B1 Phon Phisai Thai.
162 B1 Phônsavan Laos
162 B1 Phon Thong Thai.
125 E7 Phoques Bay Australia
123 C4 Phosphate Hill Australia
162 B1 Phrae Thai.
162 A1 Phrao Thai.
162 B2 Phra Phutthabat Thai.
162 A3 Phra Thong, Ko i. Thai.
162 C1 Phu Bai Vietnam
155 B6 Phuc Yên Vietnam
Phu Hôi Vietnam see
Van Gia
162 A4 Phuket Thai.
162 A4 Phuket, Ko i. Thai.
148 C4 Phulera India
149 G5 Phultala Bangl.
155 B6 Phu Ly Vietnam
162 B2 Phumĭ Bânhchok Kon
Cambodia
162 C3 Phumĭ Chhuk Cambodia
162 C2 Phumĭ Kâmpóng Trâlach
Cambodia
162 B3 Phumĭ Kaôh Kông
Cambodia
162 B2 Phumĭ Kiliĕk Cambodia
162 C2 Phumĭ Mlu Prey Cambodia
162 B2 Phumĭ Moŭng Cambodia
162 B2 Phumĭ Prâmaôy Cambodia
162 B2 Phumĭ Sâmraông
Cambodia
162 C2 Phumĭ Toĕng Cambodia
163 D2 Phu My Vietnam
Phu Nhon Vietnam see
Chu Sê
162 C3 Phươc Hai Vietnam
162 C3 Phươc Long Vietnam
162 B2 Phu Quôc Vietnam see
Dương Đông
162 B2 Phu Quôc, Đao i. Vietnam
163 D3 Phu Quy, Đao i. Vietnam
197 H4 Phuthaditjhaba S. Africa
155 B6 Phu Tho Vietnam
Phư Tho Vietnam see
Phu Tho
162 B1 Phu Wiang Thai.
152 G8 Phyu Myanmar
231 I5 Piaca Brazil
184 C2 Piacenza Italy
125 H3 Pian r. Australia
154 D2 Pianguan China
184 D3 Pianosa, Isola i. Italy
177 M7 Piatra Neamţ Romania
231 J5 Piauí r. Brazil
184 E1 Piave r. Italy
193 F4 Pibor r. Sudan
193 F4 Pibor Post Sudan
208 D1 Pic r. Canada
215 F4 Pica U.S.A.
215 G5 Picacho AZ U.S.A.
215 E5 Picacho CA U.S.A.
182 F2 Picardy reg. France
219 B6 Picayune U.S.A.
224 C1 Picháchic Mex.
232 D2 Pichanal Arg.
235 I2 Pichi Ciego Arg.
235 H2 Pichilemu Chile
224 B2 Pichilingue Mex.
235 J3 Pichi Mahuida Arg.
148 D4 Pichor India
225 F4 Pichucalco Mex.
208 D1 Pic Island Canada
172 G3 Pickering U.K.
172 G3 Pickering, Vale of val. U.K.
209 E2 Pickford U.S.A.
206 B3 Pickle Lake Canada
166 A6 Pico i. Azores
224 H5 Pico Bonito, Parque
Nacional nat. park Hond.
233 K4 Pico da Neblina, Parque
Nacional do nat. park Brazil
225 E4 Pico de Orizaba, Parque
Nacional nat. park Mex.
231 J5 Picos Brazil
232 C7 Pico Truncado Arg.
208 D1 Pic River Canada
125 I5 Picton Australia
209 I4 Picton Canada
125 G9 Picton, Mount Australia
207 H4 Pictou Canada
208 D2 Pictured Rocks National
Lakeshore nature res. U.S.A.
235 I3 Picún Leufú r. Arg.
143 F5 Pidarak Pak.
147 I5 Pidurutalagala mt. Sri Lanka
233 I3 Piedecuesta Col.
235 I1 Pie de Palo, Sierra mts Arg.
219 C5 Piedmont U.S.A.
220 C4 Piedmont Lake U.S.A.

223 K5 Ponce Puerto Rico
213 F4 Poncha Springs U.S.A.
206 E3 Poncheville, Lac *l.* Canada
Pondicherry India *see* Puducherry
203 K2 Pond Inlet Canada
207 I3 Ponds, Island of Canada
224 H5 Poneloya Nicaragua
183 M1 Ponferrada Spain
126 F4 Pongaroa N.Z.
193 E4 Pongo *watercourse* Sudan
197 I3 Pongola *r.* S. Africa
197 I3 Pongolapoort Dam *l.* S. Africa
177 O3 Ponizov'ye Rus. Fed.
147 H3 Ponnaivar *r.* India
147 G4 Ponnani India
149 H5 Ponnyadaung Range *mts* Myanmar
205 G4 Ponoka Canada
140 C1 Ponomarevka Rus. Fed.
166 A6 Ponta Delgada Azores
192 □ Ponta do Sol Cape Verde
235 B4 Ponta Grossa Brazil
234 C2 Pontalina Brazil
182 H2 Pont-à-Mousson France
234 A3 Ponta Porã Brazil
182 H3 Pontarlier France
217 F6 Pontchartrain, Lake U.S.A.
178 C4 Pont-de-Loup Belgium
183 L3 Ponte de Sor Port.
173 F4 Pontefract U.K.
172 F2 Ponteland U.K.
231 G7 Pontes-e-Lacerda Brazil
183 L1 Pontevedra Spain
208 C5 Pontiac IL U.S.A.
209 F4 Pontiac MI U.S.A.
163 G3 Pontianak Indon.
182 C2 Pontivy France
182 B3 Pont-l'Abbé France
182 F2 Pontoise France
121 C6 Ponton *watercourse* Australia
205 J4 Ponton Canada
217 F5 Pontotoc U.S.A.
184 C2 Pontremoli Italy
178 A5 Pont-Ste-Maxence France
125 G9 Pontville Australia
209 H3 Pontypool Canada
173 D6 Pontypool U.K.
173 D6 Pontypridd U.K.
184 E4 Ponza, Isola di *i.* Italy
184 E4 Ponziane, Isole Italy
124 A4 Poochera Australia
173 F7 Poole U.K.
123 B5 Poolowanna Lake *salt flat* Australia
Poona India *see* Pune
125 E4 Pooncarie Australia
125 F3 Poopelloe Lake *salt l.* Australia
230 E7 Poopó, Lago de *l.* Bol.
126 E1 Poor Knights Islands N.Z.
141 G4 Pop Uzbek.
233 H4 Popayán Col.
178 A4 Poperinge Belgium
133 L2 Popigay *r.* Rus. Fed.
124 D4 Popiltah Australia
124 D4 Popilta Lake *imp. l.* Australia
205 J4 Poplar *r.* Canada
212 F1 Poplar U.S.A.
217 F4 Poplar Bluff U.S.A.
220 C6 Poplar Camp U.S.A.
217 F6 Poplarville U.S.A.
225 E4 Popocatépetl, Volcán *vol.* Mex.
195 B4 Popokabaka Dem. Rep. Congo
185 L3 Popovo Bulg.
179 I3 Poppenberg *h.* Germany
177 J6 Poprad Slovakia
143 G5 Porali *r.* India
126 F4 Porangahau N.Z.
234 C1 Porangatu Brazil
148 B5 Porbandar India
233 I3 Porce *r.* Col.
204 C4 Porcher Island Canada
202 E3 Porcupine *r.* Canada/U.S.A.
207 I3 Porcupine, Cape Canada
239 H2 Porcupine Abyssal Plain *sea feature* N. Atlantic Ocean
205 I4 Porcupine Hills Canada
208 C2 Porcupine Mountains U.S.A.
205 I4 Porcupine Plain Canada
205 I4 Porcupine Provincial Forest *nature res.* Canada
233 J3 Pore Col.
184 E2 Poreč Croatia
187 H4 Poretskoye Rus. Fed.
171 M3 Pori Fin.
126 E4 Porirua N.Z.
186 D3 Porkhov Rus. Fed.

233 L2 Porlamar Venez.
122 C2 Pormpuraaw Australia
182 C3 Pornic France
161 J4 Poro *i.* Phil.
150 G2 Poronaysk Rus. Fed.
149 G3 Porong China
185 J6 Poros Greece
186 E2 Porosozero Rus. Fed.
Porsangen *sea chan.* Norway *see* Porsangerfjorden
170 N1 Porsangerfjorden *sea chan.* Norway
171 J4 Porsgrunn Norway
138 C2 Porsuk *r.* Turkey
124 C5 Port Adelaide Australia
175 L3 Portadown U.K.
175 M3 Portaferry U.K.
221 I1 Portage ME U.S.A.
209 E4 Portage MI U.S.A.
208 C4 Portage WI U.S.A.
205 J5 Portage la Prairie Canada
216 C1 Portal U.S.A.
204 E5 Port Alberni Canada
125 G7 Port Albert Australia
183 M3 Portalegre Port.
217 C5 Portales U.S.A.
204 C3 Port Alexander U.S.A.
197 G6 Port Alfred S. Africa
204 D4 Port Alice Canada
220 D4 Port Allegany U.S.A.
217 F6 Port Allen U.S.A.
123 E4 Port Alma Australia
212 B1 Port Angeles U.S.A.
175 K4 Portarlington Ireland
125 G9 Port Arthur Australia
217 E6 Port Arthur U.S.A.
174 B5 Port Askaig U.K.
124 B4 Port Augusta Australia
223 J5 Port-au-Prince Haiti
209 F3 Port Austin U.S.A.
207 I3 Port aux Choix Canada
175 M3 Portavogie U.K.
196 D7 Port Beaufort S. Africa
135 H5 Port Blair India
209 H3 Port Bolster Canada
183 R1 Portbou Spain
209 G4 Port Burwell Canada
125 E7 Port Campbell Australia
209 H3 Port Carling Canada
126 C6 Port Chalmers N.Z.
219 D7 Port Charlotte U.S.A.
221 G4 Port Chester U.S.A.
204 C4 Port Clements Canada
220 B4 Port Clinton U.S.A.
221 I3 Port Clyde U.S.A.
209 H4 Port Colborne Canada
204 E5 Port Coquitlam Canada
209 H4 Port Credit Canada
125 F9 Port Davey *b.* Australia
223 J5 Port-de-Paix Haiti
162 B5 Port Dickson Malaysia
122 D3 Port Douglas Australia
220 C3 Port Dover Canada
208 D3 Porte des Morts *lake channel* U.S.A.
204 C4 Port Edward Canada
197 I5 Port Edward S. Africa
208 C3 Port Edwards U.S.A.
234 D1 Porteirinha Brazil
231 H4 Portel Brazil
209 G3 Port Elgin Canada
197 F6 Port Elizabeth S. Africa
174 B5 Port Ellen U.K.
124 C5 Port Elliot Australia
172 C3 Port Erin U.K.
205 H2 Porter Lake Canada
204 C3 Porter Landing Canada
196 C6 Porterville S. Africa
214 C3 Porterville U.S.A.
125 E7 Port Fairy Australia
126 E2 Port Fitzroy N.Z.
138 D6 Port Fuad Egypt
195 A4 Port-Gentil Gabon
124 C4 Port Germein Australia
217 F6 Port Gibson U.S.A.
174 D5 Port Glasgow U.K.
192 C4 Port Harcourt Nigeria
204 D4 Port Hardy Canada
Port Harrison Canada *see* Inukjuak
207 H4 Port Hawkesbury Canada
173 D6 Porthcawl U.K.
118 B4 Port Hedland Australia
221 G2 Port Henry U.S.A.
173 B7 Porthleven U.K.
173 C5 Porthmadog U.K.
209 H4 Port Hope Canada
207 I3 Port Hope Simpson Canada
209 F4 Port Huron U.S.A.
139 L2 Port-İliç Azer.
183 L4 Portimão Port.

155 □ Port Island Hong Kong China
125 I4 Port Jackson *inlet* Australia
221 G4 Port Jefferson U.S.A.
221 F4 Port Jervis U.S.A.
231 G2 Port Kaituma Guyana
Port Keats Australia *see* Wadeye
125 I5 Port Kembla Australia
125 H4 Portland N.S.W. Australia
124 D7 Portland Vic. Australia
209 E5 Portland IN U.S.A.
221 H3 Portland ME U.S.A.
212 B2 Portland OR U.S.A.
173 E7 Portland, Isle of *pen.* U.K.
204 C3 Portland Canal *inlet* Canada
126 F3 Portland Island N.Z.
122 C2 Portland Roads Australia
175 K4 Portlaoise Ireland
217 D6 Port Lavaca U.S.A.
175 K5 Portlaw Ireland
175 F5 Portlethen U.K.
124 A5 Port Lincoln Australia
192 A4 Port Loko Sierra Leone
124 D7 Port MacDonnell Australia
125 J3 Port Macquarie Australia
207 H2 Port Manvers *inlet* Canada
204 D4 Port McNeill Canada
207 H4 Port-Menier Canada
202 B4 Port Moller U.S.A.
212 B1 Port Moody Canada
119 E2 Port Moresby P.N.G.
174 B2 Portnaguran U.K.
174 B5 Portnahaven U.K.
124 B5 Port Neill Australia
219 F7 Port Nelson Bahamas
Port Nis U.K. *see* Port of Ness
196 B4 Port Nolloth S. Africa
Port-Nouveau-Québec Canada *see* Kangiqsualujjuaq
Porto Port. *see* Oporto
230 E5 Porto Acre Brazil
234 B3 Porto Alegre Mato Grosso do Sul Brazil
232 F4 Porto Alegre Brazil
231 G6 Porto Artur Brazil
224 J6 Portobelo Panama
231 G6 Porto dos Gaúchos Óbidos Brazil
231 G7 Porto Esperidião Brazil
184 D3 Portoferraio Italy
174 B2 Port of Ness U.K.
231 I5 Porto Franco Brazil
233 L2 Port of Spain Trin. and Tob.
184 E2 Portogruaro Italy
234 A2 Porto Jofre Brazil
214 B2 Portola U.S.A.
184 D2 Portomaggiore Italy
235 A4 Porto Mendes Para.
231 G8 Porto Murtinho Brazil
231 I6 Porto Nacional Brazil
192 C4 Porto-Novo Benin
234 B3 Porto Primavera, Represa *resr* Brazil
213 A3 Port Orford U.S.A.
231 H4 Porto Santana Brazil
234 E2 Porto Seguro Brazil
184 C2 Porto Tolle Italy
184 C4 Porto Torres Sardinia Italy
184 C4 Porto-Vecchio Corsica France
231 F5 Porto Velho Brazil
230 B4 Portoviejo Ecuador
174 D5 Portpatrick U.K.
209 H3 Port Perry Canada
125 F7 Port Phillip Bay Australia
124 C4 Port Pirie Australia
173 B7 Portreath U.K.
173 B3 Portree U.K.
204 E5 Port Renfrew Canada
209 G4 Port Rowan Canada
221 E5 Port Royal U.S.A.
175 L2 Portrush Ireland
193 F1 Port Said Egypt
219 C6 Port St Joe U.S.A.
197 H5 Port St Johns S. Africa
172 C3 Port St Mary U.K.
175 K2 Portsalon Ireland
209 F4 Port Sanilac U.S.A.
209 H3 Port Severn Canada
155 □ Port Shelter *b.* Hong Kong China
197 I5 Port Shepstone S. Africa
Port Simpson Canada *see* Lax Kw'alaams
173 F7 Portsmouth U.K.
221 H3 Portsmouth NH U.S.A.
220 B5 Portsmouth OH U.S.A.
221 E6 Portsmouth VA U.S.A.

175 F3 Portsoy U.K.
125 J4 Port Stephens *b.* Australia
175 L2 Portstewart U.K.
193 F3 Port Sudan Sudan
219 B6 Port Sulphur U.S.A.
173 D6 Port Talbot U.K.
170 N1 Porttipahdan tekojärvi *resr* Fin.
183 L3 Portugal *country* Europe
183 E1 Portugalete Spain
233 J2 Portuguesa *r.* Venez.
175 J4 Portumna Ireland
183 F5 Port-Vendres France
124 B5 Port Victoria Australia
119 G3 Port Vila Vanuatu
170 P1 Port Vladimir Rus. Fed.
126 E2 Port Waikato N.Z.
124 C5 Port Wakefield Australia
208 D4 Port Washington U.S.A.
174 D6 Port William U.K.
208 B2 Port Wing U.S.A.
235 J2 Porvenir Arg.
171 N3 Porvoo Fin.
160 D5 Poryŏng S. Korea
183 N1 Posada Spain
232 E3 Posadas Arg.
185 H2 Posavina *reg.* Bos.-Herz./Croatia
209 F3 Posen U.S.A.
169 N4 Poshekhon'ye Rus. Fed.
Poshekon'ye-Volodarsk Rus. Fed. *see* Poshekhon'ye
139 K5 Posht-e Kūh *mts* Iran
142 C2 Posht Kūh *h.* Iran
170 O2 Posio Fin.
151 E7 Poso Indon.
139 I1 Posof Turkey
160 D6 Posŏng S. Korea
141 J1 Pospelikha Rus. Fed.
234 C1 Posse Brazil
127 I5 Possession Islands Antarctica
179 J4 Pößneck Germany
217 C5 Post U.S.A.
Poste-de-la-Baleine Canada *see* Kuujjuarapik
197 E4 Postmasburg S. Africa
207 I3 Postville Canada
208 B4 Postville U.S.A.
185 G3 Posušje Bos.-Herz.
158 B3 Pos'yet Rus. Fed.
197 G3 Potchefstroom S. Africa
217 E5 Poteau U.S.A.
231 K5 Potengi *r.* Brazil
184 F4 Potenza Italy
126 A7 Poteriteri, Lake N.Z.
197 F5 Potfontein S. Africa
Potgietersrus S. Africa *see* Mokopane
217 D6 Poth U.S.A.
231 J5 Poti *r.* Brazil
187 G7 P'ot'i Georgia
147 I2 Potikal India
193 D3 Potiskum Nigeria
212 D2 Pot Mountain U.S.A.
155 □ Po Toi *i.* Hong Kong China
221 E5 Potomac *r.* U.S.A.
220 D5 Potomac, South Branch *r.* U.S.A.
220 D5 Potomac, South Fork South Branch *r.* U.S.A.
230 E7 Potosí Bol.
217 F4 Potosi U.S.A.
215 E4 Potosi Mountain U.S.A.
161 I4 Pototan Phil.
225 H5 Potrerillos Hond.
179 L2 Potsdam Germany
221 F2 Potsdam U.S.A.
173 E6 Potterne U.K.
173 G6 Potters Bar U.K.
221 F4 Pottstown U.S.A.
221 E4 Pottsville U.S.A.
147 I5 Pottuvil Sri Lanka
204 E3 Pouce Coupe Canada
207 J4 Pouch Cove Canada
221 G4 Poughkeepsie U.S.A.
221 G3 Poultney U.S.A.
173 E4 Poulton-le-Fylde U.K.
234 D3 Pouso Alegre Brazil
162 B2 Poŭthĭsăt Cambodia
177 I6 Považská Bystrica Slovakia
186 E2 Povenets Rus. Fed.
185 H2 Povlen *mt.* Serbia
183 L2 Póvoa de Varzim Port.
187 G5 Povorino Rus. Fed.
158 C3 Povorotnyy, Mys *hd* Rus. Fed.
215 D5 Poway U.S.A.
212 F2 Powder *r.* U.S.A.
213 F3 Powder River U.S.A.

212 E2 Powell U.S.A.
220 B6 Powell *r.* U.S.A.
215 G3 Powell, Lake *resr* U.S.A.
214 C2 Powell Mountain U.S.A.
219 E7 Powell Point Bahamas
204 E5 Powell River Canada
208 D3 Powers U.S.A.
221 E6 Powhatan U.S.A.
234 A1 Poxoréu Brazil
155 E4 Poyang Hu *l.* China
162 □ Poyan Reservoir Sing.
156 C2 Poyarkovo Rus. Fed.
208 C3 Poygan, Lake U.S.A.
138 E3 Pozantı Turkey
185 I2 Požarevac Serbia
225 E3 Poza Rica Mex.
156 C2 Pozdeyevka Rus. Fed.
185 G2 Požega Croatia
185 I3 Požega Serbia
158 D1 Pozharskoye Rus. Fed.
177 H4 Poznań Poland
183 N3 Pozoblanco Spain
224 B1 Pozo Nuevo Mex.
184 F4 Pozzuoli Italy
163 B3 Prabumulih Indon.
176 G6 Prachatice Czech Rep.
149 F6 Prachi *r.* India
162 B2 Prachin Buri Thai.
162 A3 Prachuap Khiri Khan Thai.
183 F5 Prades France
234 B3 Prado Brazil
176 G5 Prague Czech Rep.
Praha Czech Rep. *see* Prague
192 □ Praia Cape Verde
197 J2 Praia do Bilene Moz.
234 A1 Praia Rica Brazil
123 D4 Prairie Australia
209 E5 Prairie Creek Reservoir U.S.A.
217 C5 Prairie Dog Town Fork *r.* U.S.A.
208 B4 Prairie du Chien U.S.A.
162 B2 Prakhon Chai Thai.
162 B2 Pran *r.* Thai.
147 H2 Pranhita *r.* India
163 E2 Prapat Indon.
185 L7 Prasonisi, Akrotirio *pt* Greece
234 C2 Prata Brazil
234 C2 Prata *r.* Brazil
184 D3 Prato Italy
217 D4 Pratt U.S.A.
217 G5 Prattville U.S.A.
147 G2 Pravara *r.* India
177 J3 Pravdinsk Rus. Fed.
163 I4 Praya Indon.
Preăh Vihéar Cambodia *see* Preăh Vihéar
162 C2 Preăh Vihéar Cambodia
177 P3 Prechistoye Rus. Fed.
205 I4 Preeceville Canada
187 B4 Pregolya *r.* Rus. Fed.
171 N4 Preiļi Latvia
209 H1 Preissac, Lac *l.* Canada
125 H3 Premer Australia
182 F3 Prémery France
179 K2 Premnitz Germany
208 B3 Prentice U.S.A.
176 F4 Prenzlau Germany
158 C3 Preobrazheniye Rus. Fed.
145 H9 Preparis Island Cocos Is
145 H9 Preparis North Channel Cocos Is
145 H9 Preparis South Channel Cocos Is
177 H6 Přerov Czech Rep.
221 F2 Prescott Canada
215 F4 Prescott U.S.A.
215 F4 Prescott Valley U.S.A.
173 C6 Preseli, Mynydd *hills* U.K.
185 I3 Preševo Serbia
216 E3 Presho U.S.A.
232 D3 Presidencia Roque Sáenz Peña Arg.
231 J5 Presidente Dutra Brazil
234 B3 Presidente Epitácio Brazil
234 B3 Presidente Hermes Brazil
234 B3 Presidente Prudente Brazil
234 B3 Presidente Venceslau Brazil
217 B6 Presidio U.S.A.
141 F1 Presnogor'kovka Kazakh.
141 F1 Presnovka Kazakh.
177 J6 Prešov Slovakia
185 I4 Prespa, Lake Europe
221 J1 Presque Isle U.S.A.
185 D2 Presque Isle Point U.S.A.
173 D5 Presteigne U.K.
173 E4 Preston U.K.

215 E2 Preston NV U.S.A.
121 B4 Preston, Cape Australia
175 F5 Prestonpans U.K.
220 B6 Prestonsburg U.S.A.
174 D5 Prestwick U.K.
234 E1 Preto *r. Bahia* Brazil
234 C1 Preto *r. Minas Gerais* Brazil
197 H2 Pretoria S. Africa
221 E5 Prettyboy Lake U.S.A.
179 K3 Pretzsch Germany
185 I5 Preveza Greece
162 C3 Prey Vêng Cambodia
140 E3 Priaral'skiye Karakumy, Peski *des.* Kazakh.
153 K1 Priargunsk Rus. Fed.
133 U4 Pribilof Islands U.S.A.
185 H3 Priboj Serbia
120 E2 Price *r.* Australia
207 G4 Price Canada
215 G2 Price U.S.A.
204 D4 Price Island Canada
219 B6 Prichard U.S.A.
171 M4 Priekule Latvia
171 N4 Priekuļi Latvia
171 M5 Prienai Lith.
197 E4 Prieska S. Africa
212 C1 Priest Lake U.S.A.
212 C1 Priest River U.S.A.
183 N1 Prieta, Peña *mt.* Spain
177 I6 Prievidza Slovakia
179 K1 Prignitz *reg.* Germany
185 G2 Prijedor Bos.-Herz.
185 H3 Prijepolje Serbia
Prikaspiyskaya Nizmennost' *lowland* Kazakh./Rus. Fed. *see* Caspian Lowland
185 I4 Prilep Macedonia
179 K5 Přimda Czech Rep.
235 J1 Primero *r.* Arg.
125 G8 Prime Seal Island Australia
171 O3 Primorsk Rus. Fed.
158 C2 Primorskiy Kray *admin. div.* Rus. Fed.
187 F6 Primorsko-Akhtarsk Rus. Fed.
215 D5 Primo Tapia Mex.
205 H4 Primrose Lake Canada
205 H4 Prince Albert Canada
197 E6 Prince Albert S. Africa
205 H4 Prince Albert National Park Canada
202 G2 Prince Albert Peninsula Canada
196 D6 Prince Albert Road S. Africa
202 G2 Prince Albert Sound *sea chan.* Canada
202 F2 Prince Alfred, Cape Canada
203 K3 Prince Charles Island Canada
127 K5 Prince Charles Mountains Antarctica
207 H4 Prince Edward Island *prov.* Canada
238 G8 Prince Edward Islands Indian Ocean
209 I4 Prince Edward Point Canada
221 E5 Prince Frederick U.S.A.
204 E4 Prince George Canada
202 B3 Prince of Wales, Cape U.S.A.
119 E3 Prince of Wales Island Australia
203 I2 Prince of Wales Island Canada
204 C3 Prince of Wales Island U.S.A.
202 G2 Prince of Wales Strait Canada
202 F2 Prince Patrick Island Canada
203 I2 Prince Regent Inlet *sea chan.* Canada
204 C4 Prince Rupert Canada
221 F5 Princess Anne U.S.A.
119 E3 Princess Charlotte Bay Australia
127 K5 Princess Elizabeth Land *reg.* Antarctica
205 J2 Princess Mary Lake Canada
204 D4 Princess Royal Island Canada
204 E5 Princeton Canada
214 A2 Princeton CA U.S.A.
208 C5 Princeton IL U.S.A.
209 C4 Princeton IN U.S.A.
219 C4 Princeton KY U.S.A.
221 I2 Princeton ME U.S.A.
216 E3 Princeton MO U.S.A.
221 F4 Princeton NJ U.S.A.

143 F5 Qila Ladgasht Pak.
154 E1 Qilaotu Shan *mts* China
143 F4 Qila Safed Pak.
148 B3 Qila Saifullah Pak.
144 J4 Qilian China
150 B3 Qilian Shan *mts* China
203 O3 Qillak *i.* Greenland
149 G1 Qiman Tag *mts* China
155 E4 Qimen China
203 L2 Qimusseriarsuaq *b.* Greenland
193 F2 Qinā Egypt
154 B3 Qin'an China
156 B3 Qing'an China
154 C2 Qingcheng *Gansu* China
160 B3 Qingchengzi China
154 F2 Qingdao China
156 B3 Qinggang China
Qinggil China *see* Qinghe
154 A2 Qinghai *prov.* China
154 A2 Qinghai Hu *salt l.* China
150 B3 Qinghai Nanshan *mts* China
144 H2 Qinghe China
158 A1 Qinghe China
160 C2 Qing He *r.* China
160 C3 Qinghecheng China
154 D2 Qingjian China
155 D4 Qing Jiang *r.* China
155 E5 Qingliu China
155 B5 Qinglong *Guizhou* China
154 F1 Qinglong *Hebei* China
154 F2 Qinglong He *r.* China
155 C6 Qingping China
155 F4 Qingpu China
Qingshan China *see* Wudalianchi
154 C3 Qingshui China
152 G5 Qingshuihe China
154 D2 Qingshuihe China
141 J3 Qingshuihezi China
155 F4 Qingtian China
154 F4 Qingtongxia China
154 E2 Qingxian China
154 D2 Qingxu China
155 E4 Qingyang *Anhui* China
154 C3 Qingyang *Gansu* China
155 D6 Qingyuan *Guangdong* China
160 C2 Qingyuan *Liaoning* China
155 F5 Qingyuan *Zhejiang* China
Qingzang Gaoyuan *plat.* China *see* Tibet, Plateau of
155 C5 Qingzhen China
155 D4 Qingzhou *Hubei* China
154 F2 Qingzhou *Shandong* China
154 D3 Qin He *r.* China
154 F2 Qinhuangdao China
154 C3 Qin Ling *mts* China
154 D2 Qinxian China
154 D3 Qinyang China
154 D2 Qinyuan China
155 C6 Qinzhou China
155 C6 Qinzhou Wan *b.* China
155 D7 Qionghai China
155 B4 Qionglai China
155 B4 Qionglai Shan *mts* China
155 D7 Qiongshan China
Qiongzhou Haixia *str.* China *see* Hainan Strait
153 L1 Qiqian China
150 E2 Qiqihar China
139 L5 Qīr Iran
142 D4 Qīr Iran
149 E1 Qira China
138 E6 Qiryat Gat Israel
139 F6 Qitab ash Shāmah *vol. crater* Saudi Arabia
158 B2 Qitaihe China
158 B5 Qiubei China
154 F2 Qixia China
154 E3 Qixian *Henan* China
154 D2 Qixian *Shanxi* China
158 C1 Qixing He *r.* China
155 D5 Qiyang China
155 D5 Qiying China
155 D7 Qizhou Liedao *i.* China
139 L2 Qızılağac Körfäzi *b.* Azer.
141 H5 Qizilrabot Tajik.
142 D3 Qobād, Chāh-e *well* Iran
139 L1 Qobustan Qoruğu *nature res.* Azer.
Qogir Feng *mt.* China/Pakistan *see* K2
142 B2 Qojūr Iran
142 C3 Qom Iran
Qomolangma Feng *mt.* China *see* Everest, Mount
Qomsheh Iran *see* Shāhreżā
142 C3 Qonāq, Chāh-e *h.* Iran
139 L1 Qonaqkänd Azer.
149 G3 Qonggyai China

140 D4 Qo'ng'irot Uzbek.
154 C1 Qongj China
149 E2 Qong Muztag *mt.* China
141 G4 Qo'qon Uzbek.
140 D4 Qorajar Uzbek.
140 E5 Qorako'l *Bukharskaya Oblast'* Uzbek.
140 E5 Qorako'l *Bukharskaya Oblast'* Uzbek.
140 D3 Qoraqalpog'iston Uzbek.
141 F4 Qoraqata botig'i *depr.* Uzbek.
139 F4 Qornet es Saouda *mt.* Lebanon
141 F5 Qorovulbozor Uzbek.
142 B3 Qorveh Iran
140 E4 Qo'shko'pir Uzbek.
140 E4 Qo'shrabot Uzbek.
143 E5 Qoṭbābād Iran
139 J2 Qoṭūr Iran
140 D4 Qozoqdaryo Uzbek.
221 G3 Quabbin Reservoir U.S.A.
215 D4 Quail Mountains U.S.A.
121 B7 Quairading Australia
179 F2 Quakenbrück Germany
221 F4 Quakertown U.S.A.
125 E5 Quambatook Australia
125 E5 Quambone Australia
123 C4 Quamby Australia
217 D5 Quanah U.S.A.
154 D4 Quanbao Shan *mt.* China
163 D2 Quang Ngai Vietnam
162 C1 Quang Tri Vietnam
155 C6 Quang Yên Vietnam
155 B6 Quan Hoa Vietnam
155 E5 Quannan China
155 F5 Quanzhou *Fujian* China
155 D5 Quanzhou *Guangxi* China
205 I4 Qu'Appelle Canada
205 I4 Qu'Appelle *r.* Canada
235 L1 Quaraí Brazil
235 L1 Quaraí *r.* Brazil
155 □ Quarry Bay *Hong Kong* China
184 C5 Quartu Sant'Elena *Sardinia* Italy
215 D3 Quartzite Mountain U.S.A.
215 E5 Quartzsite U.S.A.
204 D4 Quatsino Sound *inlet* Canada
140 A4 Quba Azer.
143 E2 Quchan Iran
125 H5 Queanbeyan Australia
207 F4 Québec Canada
203 K4 Québec *prov.* Canada
234 C2 Quebra Anzol *r.* Brazil
233 J2 Quebrada del Toro, Parque Nacional de la *nat. park* Venez.
235 H4 Quedal, Cabo *c.* Chile
179 J3 Quedlinburg Germany
204 E4 Queen Bess, Mount Canada
204 C4 Queen Charlotte Canada
204 C4 Queen Charlotte Islands Canada
204 D4 Queen Charlotte Sound *sea chan.* Canada
204 D4 Queen Charlotte Strait Canada
203 H1 Queen Elizabeth Islands Canada
194 D3 Queen Elizabeth National Park Uganda
127 K6 Queen Mary Land *reg.* Antarctica
203 H3 Queen Maud Gulf Canada
127 K3 Queen Maud Land *reg.* Antarctica
127 L3 Queen Maud Land *reg.* Antarctica
127 J4 Queen Maud Mountains Antarctica
119 E4 Queensland *state* Australia
125 F9 Queenstown Australia
126 B6 Queenstown N.Z.
197 G5 Queenstown S. Africa
162 □ Queenstown Sing.
221 E5 Queenstown U.S.A.
212 A2 Queets U.S.A.
235 L2 Queguay Grande *r.* Uruguay
235 J3 Quehué Arg.
231 H4 Queimada, Ilha *i.* Brazil
195 D5 Quelimane Moz.
232 B6 Quellón Chile
215 H4 Quemado U.S.A.
235 H4 Quemchi Chile
235 J3 Quemú-Quemú Arg.
235 K3 Quequén Grande *r.* Arg.
234 B3 Querência do Norte Brazil
225 D3 Querétaro Mex.
225 E3 Querétaro *state* Mex.

179 J3 Querfurt Germany
154 E3 Queshan China
204 E4 Quesnel Canada
204 E4 Quesnel *r.* Canada
204 E4 Quesnel Lake Canada
208 B1 Quetico Provincial Park Canada
148 A3 Quetta Pak.
225 G5 Quetzaltenango Guat.
235 H3 Queuco Chile
235 H3 Queule Chile
Quezaltenango Guat. *see* Quetzaltenango
161 H4 Quezon Phil.
161 I3 Quezon City Phil.
154 E3 Qufu China
195 B5 Quibala Angola
195 B4 Quibaxe Angola
233 H4 Quibdó Col.
182 C3 Quiberon France
195 B4 Quiçama, Parque Nacional do *nat. park* Angola
162 C1 Qui Châu Vietnam
215 F5 Quijotoa U.S.A.
235 J1 Quilino Arg.
183 F5 Quillan France
205 I4 Quill Lakes Canada
235 H2 Quillota Chile
235 K2 Quilmes Arg.
147 H4 Quilon India
119 E4 Quilpie Australia
235 H2 Quilpué Chile
195 B4 Quimbele Angola
232 D3 Quimilí Arg.
182 B3 Quimper France
182 C3 Quimperlé France
230 D6 Quince Mil Peru
214 B2 Quincy *CA* U.S.A.
219 C6 Quincy *FL* U.S.A.
208 B6 Quincy *IL* U.S.A.
221 H3 Quincy *MA* U.S.A.
235 J2 Quines Arg.
Qui Nhon Vietnam *see* Quy Nhơn
215 E3 Quinn Canyon Range *mts* U.S.A.
183 O3 Quintanar de la Orden Spain
225 G4 Quintana Roo *state* Mex.
235 H2 Quintero Chile
235 J2 Quinto *r.* Arg.
183 P2 Quinto Spain
195 E5 Quionga Moz.
195 B5 Quipungo Angola
225 G5 Quiriguá *tourist site* Guat.
235 H3 Quirihue Chile
195 B5 Quirima Angola
195 E5 Quirimbas, Parque Nacional das *nat. park* Moz.
125 I3 Quirindi Australia
235 K2 Quiroga Arg.
195 D6 Quissico Moz.
195 B5 Quitapa Angola
234 B2 Quitéria *r.* Brazil
219 D6 Quitman *GA* U.S.A.
219 B5 Quitman *MS* U.S.A.
230 C4 Quito Ecuador
213 D6 Quitovac Mex.
215 F4 Quivero U.S.A.
231 K4 Quixadá Brazil
155 D5 Qujiang China
155 C4 Qu Jiang *r.* China
155 D6 Qujie China
155 B5 Qujing China
139 K7 Qulbān Layyah *well* Iraq
140 E4 Quljuqtov tog'lari *hills* Uzbek.
149 H2 Qumar He *r.* China
149 H2 Qumarheyan China
149 H2 Qumarrabdün China
197 H5 Qumbu S. Africa
149 H3 Qumdo China
197 G6 Qumrha S. Africa
142 B5 Qunayfidhah, Nafūd *des.* Saudi Arabia
142 B6 Qunayy *well* Saudi Arabia
205 K2 Quoich *r.* Canada
174 C3 Quoich, Loch *l.* U.K.
175 M3 Quoile *r.* U.K.
196 C7 Quoin Point S. Africa
197 F1 Quoxo *r.* Botswana
143 E6 Qurayat Oman
141 G5 Qürghonteppa Tajik.
139 J2 Qūrū Gol *pass* Iran
140 A4 Qusar Azer.
142 B2 Qūshchī Iran
139 K2 Qūsheh Dāgh *mts* Iran
142 C3 Qūtīābād Iran
154 B2 Quwu Shan *mts* China
155 C4 Quxian China
149 G3 Qüxü China

155 B6 Quỳnh Lưu Vietnam *see* Câu Giat
163 D2 Quynh Nhai Vietnam
163 D2 Quy Nhơn Vietnam
209 I3 Quyon Canada
154 E2 Quzhou *Hebei* China
155 F4 Quzhou *Zhejiang* China
187 H7 Qvareli Georgia

R

177 H7 Raab *r.* Austria
170 N2 Raahe Fin.
171 O3 Rääkkylä Fin.
179 E2 Raalte Neth.
170 N2 Raanujärvi Fin.
163 H4 Raas *i.* Indon.
174 B3 Raasay *i.* U.K.
174 B3 Raasay, Sound of *sea chan.* U.K.
163 I4 Raba Indon.
149 E2 Rabang China
141 G4 Rabat Kazakh.
184 F7 Rabat Malta
192 B1 Rabat Morocco
143 E3 Rabāt-e Kamah Iran
119 F2 Rabaul P.N.G.
204 D3 Rabbit *r.* Canada
121 E4 Rabbit Flat Australia
146 A5 Rābigh Saudi Arabia
149 G5 Rabnabad Islands Bangl.
143 E4 Rābor Iran
141 H5 Rabotoqbaytal Tajik.
Rabyānah, Ramlat *des.* Libya *see* Rebiana Sand Sea
220 B5 Raccoon Creek *r.* U.S.A.
207 J4 Race, Cape Canada
221 H3 Race Point U.S.A.
138 E5 Rachaïya Lebanon
217 D7 Rachal U.S.A.
215 E3 Rachel U.S.A.
162 C3 Rach Gia Vietnam
162 C3 Rach Gia, Vinh *b.* Vietnam
177 I5 Racibórz Poland
208 D4 Racine U.S.A.
209 F1 Racine Lake Canada
209 E2 Raco U.S.A.
177 L7 Rădăuți Romania
219 C4 Radcliff U.S.A.
156 C2 Radde Rus. Fed.
220 C6 Radford U.S.A.
148 B5 Radhanpur India
140 A1 Radishchevo Rus. Fed.
206 E3 Radisson Canada
204 F4 Radium Hot Springs Canada
185 K3 Radnevo Bulg.
177 J5 Radom Poland
185 J3 Radomir Bulg.
193 E4 Radom National Park Sudan
177 I5 Radomsko Poland
187 D5 Radomyshl' Ukr.
185 J4 Radoviš Macedonia
173 J4 Radstock U.K.
121 F7 Radstock, Cape Australia
187 C4 Radun' Belarus
171 M5 Radviliškis Lith.
177 L5 Radyvyliv Ukr.
149 E4 Rae Bareli India
Rae-Edzo Canada *see* Behchokö
Rae Lakes Canada *see* Gamêtì
121 C6 Raeside, Lake *salt flat* Australia
126 E3 Raetihi N.Z.
137 E5 Rāf *h.* Saudi Arabia
235 K1 Rafaela Arg.
194 C3 Rafaï Centr. Afr. Rep.
146 B4 Rafhā' Saudi Arabia
138 E6 Rafiah
143 E6 Rafsanjān Iran
161 J5 Ragang, Mount *vol.* Phil.
161 I3 Ragay Gulf Phil.
179 K1 Rägelin Germany
121 C7 Ragged, Mount *h.* Australia
221 I3 Ragged Island U.S.A.
142 B4 Raghwah Saudi Arabia
179 K2 Ragösen Germany
179 K3 Raguhn Germany
184 F6 Ragusa *Sicily* Italy
154 A3 Ra'gyagoinba China
118 C2 Raha Indon.
187 D4 Rahachow Belarus
179 G2 Rahden Germany
147 H2 Rahimatpur India
148 B3 Rahimyar Khan Pak.
142 C3 Rāhjerd Iran

143 E4 Raḥmān, Chāh-e *well* Iran
185 I3 Rahovec Kosovo
235 H3 Rahue *mt.* Chile
147 G2 Rahuri India
143 F3 Rahzanak Afgh.
162 C3 Rai, Hon *i.* Vietnam
237 I7 Raiatea *i.* Fr. Polynesia
147 H2 Raichur India
149 G4 Raiganj India
147 I1 Raigarh India
120 C1 Raijua *i.* Indon.
215 E2 Railroad Valley U.S.A.
207 G3 Raimbault, Lac *l.* Canada
125 E5 Rainbow Australia
215 G3 Rainbow Bridge National Monument *nat. park* U.S.A.
204 F3 Rainbow Lake Canada
122 D1 Raine Island Australia
220 C6 Rainelle U.S.A.
148 B3 Raini *r.* Pak.
212 B2 Rainier, Mount *vol.* U.S.A.
206 B4 Rainy *r.* U.S.A.
203 I5 Rainy Lake Canada
205 K5 Rainy River Canada
147 I2 Raipur *Chhattisgarh* India
148 C4 Raipur *Rajasthan* India
171 M3 Raisio Fin.
178 N4 Raismes France
148 D5 Raitalai India
237 J7 Raivavae *i.* Fr. Polynesia
147 I2 Rajahmundry India
170 O1 Raja-Jooseppi Fin.
147 I2 Rajampet India
163 H2 Rajang *r.* *Sarawak* Malaysia
147 H4 Rajapalaiyam India
147 G2 Rajapur India
148 C3 Rajasthan *state* India
148 C3 Rajasthan Canal India
149 F4 Rajauli India
Rajauri India *see* Rajouri
149 G5 Rajbari Bangl.
148 B5 Rajgarh *Rajasthan* India
148 D4 Rajgarh *Rajasthan* India
139 F6 Rājil, Wādī *watercourse* Jordan
147 I1 Rajim India
148 B5 Rajkot India
149 F4 Rajmahal India
149 F4 Rajmahal Hills India
149 E5 Raj Nandgaon India
145 D5 Rajouri India
148 D3 Rajpura India
149 G4 Rajshahi Bangl.
147 H2 Rajura India
149 F3 Raka China
117 I4 Rakahanga *atoll* Pacific Ocean
126 C5 Rakaia *r.* N.Z.
148 C1 Rakaposhi *mt.* Pak.
187 C5 Rakhiv Ukr.
148 B3 Rakhni Pak.
143 G5 Rakhshan *r.* Pak.
187 E5 Rakitnoye *Belgorodskaya Oblast'* Rus. Fed.
158 D2 Rakitnoye *Primorskiy Kray* Rus. Fed.
171 N4 Rakke Estonia
171 J4 Rakkestad Norway
148 B3 Rakni *r.* Pak.
140 D3 Rakusha Kazakh.
140 B4 Rakushechnyy, Mys *pt* Kazakh.
171 N4 Rakvere Estonia
219 E5 Raleigh U.S.A.
117 G2 Ralik Chain *is* Marshall Is
208 D2 Ralph U.S.A.
204 E2 Ram *r.* Canada
207 H2 Ramah Canada
215 H4 Ramah U.S.A.
234 D1 Ramalho, Serra do *hills* Brazil
138 E6 Ramallah West Bank
147 H3 Ramanagaram India
147 H4 Ramanathapuram India
236 E3 Ramapo Deep *sea feature* N. Pacific Ocean
147 G3 Ramas, Cape India
197 F2 Ramatlabama S. Africa
119 E2 Rambutyo Island P.N.G.
147 G3 Ramdurg India
173 C7 Rame Head U.K.
195 E5 Ramena Madag.
186 F3 Rameshki Rus. Fed.
147 H4 Rameswaram India
148 D4 Ramganga *r.* India
149 G5 Ramgarh *Bihar* India
148 B4 Ramgarh *Rajasthan* India
142 C4 Rāmhormoz Iran
122 A2 Ramingining Australia
138 E6 Ramla Israel

138 E7 Ramm, Jabal *mts* Jordan
148 D3 Ramnagar India
185 L2 Râmnicu Sărat Romania
185 K2 Râmnicu Vâlcea Romania
215 D5 Ramona U.S.A.
209 G1 Ramore Canada
195 C6 Ramotswa Botswana
153 J2 Rampart of Genghis Khan *tourist site* Asia
148 D3 Rampur India
148 C4 Rampura India
149 F4 Rampur Hat India
149 H6 Ramree Island Myanmar
142 C2 Rāmsar Iran
171 L3 Ramsele Sweden
209 F2 Ramsey Canada
172 C3 Ramsey Isle of Man
173 G5 Ramsey U.K.
173 B6 Ramsey Island U.K.
209 F2 Ramsey Lake Canada
173 I6 Ramsgate U.K.
142 C2 Rāmshir Iran
148 D5 Ramtek India
171 N5 Ramygala Lith.
233 J4 Rana, Cerro *h.* Col.
149 G5 Ranaghat India
148 C5 Ranapur India
163 I1 Ranau *Sabah* Malaysia
235 H2 Rancagua Chile
149 F5 Ranchi India
235 H5 Ranco, Lago *l.* Chile
125 G5 Rand Australia
175 L3 Randalstown U.K.
184 F6 Randazzo *Sicily* Italy
171 J4 Randers Denmark
221 H3 Randolph *MA* U.S.A.
221 G3 Randolph *VT* U.S.A.
171 K3 Randsjö Sweden
170 M2 Råneå Sweden
126 C5 Ranfurly N.Z.
162 B4 Rangae Thai.
149 H5 Rangamati Bangl.
126 D1 Rangaunu Bay N.Z.
221 H2 Rangeley U.S.A.
221 H2 Rangeley Lake U.S.A.
215 H1 Rangely U.S.A.
209 F2 Ranger Lake Canada
126 D5 Rangiora N.Z.
126 F2 Rangipoua *mt.* N.Z.
117 I5 Rangiroa *atoll* Fr. Polynesia
126 F3 Rangitaiki *r.* N.Z.
126 C5 Rangitata *r.* N.Z.
126 E4 Rangitikei *r.* N.Z.
141 H5 Rangkül Tajik.
151 B5 Rangoon Myanmar
149 G4 Rangpur Bangl.
147 G3 Ranibennur India
149 F5 Raniganj India
147 I1 Ranijula Peak India
148 B4 Ranipur Pak.
217 C6 Rankin U.S.A.
205 K2 Rankin Inlet Canada
205 K2 Rankin Inlet *inlet* Canada
125 K2 Rankin's Springs Australia
171 N4 Ranna Estonia
123 E5 Rannes Australia
140 E5 Ranneye Rus. Fed.
174 D4 Rannoch, Loch *l.* U.K.
174 D4 Rannoch Moor *moorland* U.K.
162 A3 Ranong Thai.
162 B4 Ranot Thai.
187 M4 Ranova *r.* Rus. Fed.
139 L5 Rānsa Iran
171 K3 Ransby Sweden
151 F7 Ransiki Indon.
171 O3 Rantasalmi Fin.
163 E2 Rantauprapat Indon.
208 C5 Rantoul U.S.A.
177 Q2 Rantsevo Rus. Fed.
170 N2 Rantsila Fin.
170 N2 Ranua Fin.
139 J3 Rānya Iraq
158 C1 Raohe China
155 E1 Raoping China
119 J4 Raoul Island N.Z.
117 I6 Rapa *i.* Fr. Polynesia
184 I6 Rapallo Italy
Rapa Nui *i.* S. Pacific Ocean *see* Easter Island
148 B5 Rapar India
143 E5 Rapch *watercourse* Iran
235 H2 Rapel *r.* Chile
203 L3 Raper, Cape Canada
175 K3 Raphoe Ireland
221 E5 Rapidan *r.* U.S.A.
124 C5 Rapid Bay Australia
216 C2 Rapid City U.S.A.
209 H2 Rapide-Deux Canada
209 H2 Rapide-Sept Canada
208 D3 Rapid River U.S.A.

San Felipe

314

143 F2 S. A. Nyýazow Adyndaky Turkm.
195 B4 Sanza Pombo Angola
234 C3 São Bernardo do Campo Brazil
232 E3 São Borja Brazil
234 C3 São Carlos Brazil
234 C1 São Domingos Brazil
234 B2 São Domingos r. Brazil
231 H6 São Félix Mato Grosso Brazil
231 H5 São Félix Pará Brazil
234 E3 São Fidélis Brazil
192 □ São Filipe Cape Verde
234 D1 São Francisco Brazil
231 K5 São Francisco r. Brazil
233 G3 São Francisco do Sul Brazil
235 L1 São Gabriel Brazil
234 D3 São Gonçalo Brazil
234 D2 São Gotardo Brazil
234 C1 São João da Aliança Brazil
234 E3 São João da Barra Brazil
234 C3 São João da Boa Vista Brazil
183 L2 São João da Madeira Port.
234 D1 São João do Paraíso Brazil
234 D3 São João Nepomuceno Brazil
234 C3 São Joaquim da Barra Brazil
166 A6 São Jorge i. Azores
233 K5 São José Brazil
234 E3 São José do Calçado Brazil
235 M2 São José do Norte Brazil
234 C3 São José do Rio Preto Brazil
234 D3 São José dos Campos Brazil
235 C4 São José dos Pinhais Brazil
234 D3 São Lourenço Brazil
234 A2 São Lourenço r. Brazil
234 A2 São Lourenço, Pantanal de marsh Brazil
235 M1 São Lourenço do Sul Brazil
231 J4 São Luís Brazil
234 C3 São Manuel Brazil
234 C2 São Marcos r. Brazil
231 J4 São Marcos, Baía de b. Brazil
234 E2 São Mateus Brazil
234 E2 São Mateus r. Brazil
166 A6 São Miguel i. Azores
234 C2 São Miguel r. Brazil
182 G3 Saône r. France
192 □ São Nicolau i. Cape Verde
234 C3 São Paulo Brazil (City Plan 106)
234 C3 São Paulo state Brazil
239 H5 São Pedro e São Paulo is N. Atlantic Ocean
231 J5 São Raimundo Nonato Brazil
234 D2 São Romão Brazil
231 K5 São Roque, Cabo de c. Brazil
234 D3 São Sebastião Brazil
234 D3 São Sebastião, Ilha do i. Brazil
234 C3 São Sebastião do Paraíso Brazil
235 M1 São Sepé Brazil
234 B2 São Simão Brazil
234 B2 São Simão, Barragem de resr Brazil
151 E6 Sao-Siu Indon.
São Tiago i. Cape Verde see Santiago
192 C4 São Tomé i.
São Tomé and Príncipe
234 B1 São Tomé, Cabo de c. Brazil
192 C4 São Tomé and Príncipe country Africa
180 C6 Saoura, Oued watercourse Alg.
234 C3 São Vicente Brazil
192 □ São Vicente i. Cape Verde
183 L4 São Vicente, Cabo de c. Port.
138 C2 Sapanca Turkey
140 D4 Saparmyrat Türkmenbaşy Turkm.
118 C2 Saparua Indon.
138 C2 Şaphane Dağı mt. Turkey
224 J7 Sapo, Serranía del mts Panama
192 B4 Sapo National Park Liberia
158 G3 Sapporo Japan
184 F4 Sapri Italy
163 H4 Sapudi i. Indon.
217 D4 Sapulpa U.S.A.
143 E3 Sāqī Iran
142 B2 Saqqez Iran
139 K3 Sarā Iran
142 B2 Sarāb Iran
139 K5 Sarābe Meymeh Iran

162 B2 Sara Buri Thai.
144 B4 Saragt Turkm.
143 F2 Saragt Turkm.
230 C4 Saraguro Ecuador
185 H3 Sarajevo Bos.-Herz.
143 F2 Sarakhs Iran
140 D2 Saraktash Rus. Fed.
140 C2 Saralzhin Kazakh.
149 H4 Saramati mt. India
141 H2 Saran' Kazakh.
163 H3 Saran, Gunung mt. Indon.
221 G2 Saranac r. U.S.A.
221 F2 Saranac Lake U.S.A.
185 I5 Sarandë Albania
235 L2 Sarandí del Yí Uruguay
235 L2 Sarandí Grande Uruguay
161 J5 Sarangani i. Phil.
161 J5 Sarangani Bay Phil.
161 J5 Sarangani Islands Phil.
161 J5 Sarangani Strait Phil.
187 H4 Saransk Rus. Fed.
162 A1 Saraphi Thai.
132 G4 Sarapul Rus. Fed.
233 J3 Sarare r. Venez.
219 D7 Sarasota U.S.A.
148 B5 Saraswati r. India
187 D6 Sarata Ukr.
213 F3 Saratoga U.S.A.
221 G3 Saratoga Springs U.S.A.
163 H2 Saratok Sarawak Malaysia
187 H5 Saratov Rus. Fed.
187 H5 Saratovskaya Oblast' admin. div. Rus. Fed.
187 I4 Saratovskoye Vodokhranilishche resr Rus. Fed.
185 K5 Saratsina, Akrotirio pt Greece
143 F5 Saravan Iran
Saravan Laos see Salavan
162 A2 Sarawa r. Myanmar
163 H2 Sarawak state Malaysia
138 A1 Saray Turkey
138 B3 Sarayköy Turkey
138 D2 Sarayönü Turkey
143 F5 Sarbāz Iran
143 F5 Sarbāz r. Iran
143 E3 Sarbīsheh Iran
184 D2 Sarca r. Italy
139 L3 Sarcham Iran
149 E3 Sarda r. India/Nepal
149 E3 Sarda r. Nepal
148 C3 Sardarshahr India
139 L5 Sardasht Iran
142 B2 Sar Dasht Iran
Sardegna i. Sardinia Italy see Sardinia
233 I2 Sardinata Col.
184 C4 Sardinia i. Sardinia Italy
139 K3 Sardrūd Iran
142 C5 Sareb, Rās as pt U.A.E.
170 L2 Sareks nationalpark nat. park Sweden
170 L2 Sarektjåkkå mt. Sweden
143 G2 Sar-e Pol Afgh.
143 G3 Sar-e Pol Afgh.
142 B3 Sar-e Pol-e Žahāb Iran
142 D4 Sare Yazd Iran
141 H5 Sarez, Küli i. Tajik.
239 E4 Sargasso Sea Atlantic Ocean
148 C2 Sargodha Pak.
193 D4 Sarh Chad
142 D2 Sārī Iran
185 L7 Saria i. Greece
148 D3 Sarigh Jilganang Kol salt l. Aksai Chin
138 B2 Sarigöl Turkey
139 I1 Sarıkamış Turkey
138 D3 Sarıkavak Turkey
148 D4 Sarila India
162 □ Sarimbun Reservoir Sing.
119 E4 Sarina Australia
Sarıoğlan Turkey see Belören
138 E2 Sarıoğlan Turkey
Sar-i-Pul Afgh. see Sar-e Pol
193 D2 Sarīr Tibesti des. Libya
139 I2 Sarısu Turkey
138 D3 Sarıyar Barajı resr Turkey
138 B1 Sarıyer Turkey
139 F2 Sarkand Turkey
149 E4 Sarju r. India
141 I3 Sarkand Kazakh.
148 B4 Sarkari Tala India
138 C2 Şarkikaraağaç Turkey
139 F2 Şarkışla Turkey
187 C7 Şarköy Turkey
143 G4 Sarlath Range mts Afgh./Pak.

182 E4 Sarlat-la-Canéda France
140 C5 Şarlawuk Turkm.
151 F7 Sarmi Indon.
171 K3 Särna Sweden
139 K5 Sarneh Iran
184 C1 Sarnen Switz.
209 F4 Sarnia Canada
187 C5 Sarny Ukr.
163 B3 Sarolangun Indon.
158 H2 Saroma-ko l. Japan
185 J6 Saronikos Kolpos g. Greece
187 C7 Saros Körfezi b. Turkey
148 C4 Sarotra India
187 G4 Sarova Rus. Fed.
143 H3 Sarowbī Afgh.
187 H6 Sarpa, Ozero l. Respublika Kalmykiya - Khalm'g-Tangch Rus. Fed.
187 H5 Sarpa, Ozero l. Volgogradskaya Oblast' Rus. Fed.
171 J4 Sarpsborg Norway
182 H2 Sarrebourg France
179 F5 Sarreguemines France
183 M1 Sarria Spain
183 P2 Sarrión Spain
178 C6 Sarry France
184 C4 Sartène Corsica France
142 C3 Sarud, Rūdkhāneh-ye r. Iran
143 G5 Saruna Pak.
139 L4 Saruq Iran
139 J2 Şärur Azer.
143 F4 Saru Tara tourist site Afgh.
137 I4 Sarv Iran
139 K4 Sarvābād Iran
177 H7 Sárvár Hungary
142 D4 Sarvestan Iran
141 G4 Saryagash Kazakh.
140 E3 Sarybasat Kazakh.
141 H4 Sary-Bulak Kyrg.
141 I4 Sary-Jaz r. Kyrg.
141 F2 Sarykamys Karagandinskaya Oblast' Kazakh.
140 C3 Sarykamys Mangistauskaya Oblast' Kazakh.
140 D4 Sarykamyshskoye Ozero salt l. Turkm./Uzbek.
141 G4 Sarykemer Kazakh.
141 H2 Sarykiyak Kazakh.
141 F1 Sarykol' Kazakh.
141 H5 Sarykol Range mts China/Tajik.
141 H3 Sarykomey Kazakh.
141 I3 Saryozek Kazakh.
141 H3 Saryshagan Kazakh.
141 F3 Sarysu watercourse Kazakh.
140 B3 Sarytash Kazakh.
141 H5 Sary-Tash Kyrg.
Sary Yazikskoye Vodokhranilishche resr Turkm. see Saryýazy Suw Howdany
143 F2 Saryýazy Suw Howdany resr Turkm.
141 H3 Saryyesik-Atyrau, Peski des. Kazakh.
141 I4 Saryzhaz Kazakh.
140 B4 Sarzha Kazakh.
215 G6 Sasabe U.S.A.
120 B1 Sasar, Tanjung pt Indon.
149 F4 Sasaram India
159 A8 Sasebo Japan
205 H4 Saskatchewan prov. Canada
205 I4 Saskatchewan r. Canada
205 H4 Saskatoon Canada
133 M2 Saskylakh Rus. Fed.
224 H5 Saslaya mt. Nicaragua
224 H5 Saslaya, Parque Nacional nat. park Nicaragua
197 G3 Sasolburg S. Africa
187 G4 Sasovo Rus. Fed.
221 F5 Sassafras U.S.A.
192 B4 Sassandra Côte d'Ivoire
184 C4 Sassari Sardinia Italy
179 G3 Sassenberg Germany
176 F3 Sassnitz Germany
141 J3 Sasykkol', Ozero l. Kazakh.
187 H6 Sasykoli Rus. Fed.
192 A3 Satadougou Mali
159 B9 Sata-misaki c. Japan
148 C5 Satana India
147 G2 Satara India
197 I2 Satara S. Africa
Sätbaev Kazakh. see Satpayev
153 H1 Satansk Rus. Fed.
149 G5 Satkhira Bangl.
147 H2 Satmala Range hills India
149 E4 Satna India
144 C2 Satpayev Kazakh.
141 F2 Satpayev Kazakh.

148 C5 Satpura Range mts India
159 B9 Satsuma-hantō pen. Japan
162 B2 Sattahip Thai.
179 I5 Satteldorf Germany
148 D2 Satti India
177 K7 Satu Mare Romania
162 B4 Satun Thai.
235 K1 Sauce Arg.
225 D2 Sauceda Mex.
215 F5 Sauceda Mountains U.S.A.
224 C1 Saucillo Mex.
171 I4 Sauda Norway
141 G4 Saudakent Kazakh.
170 C2 Sauðárkrókur Iceland
146 B4 Saudi Arabia country Asia
179 F3 Sauerland reg. Germany
208 D4 Saugatuck U.S.A.
221 G3 Saugerties U.S.A.
216 E2 Sauk Center U.S.A.
208 C4 Sauk City U.S.A.
182 G3 Saulieu France
209 E2 Sault Sainte Marie Canada
209 E2 Sault Sainte Marie U.S.A.
141 G1 Saumalkol' Kazakh.
123 F4 Saumarez Reef Australia
151 F7 Saumlakki Indon.
182 D3 Saumur France
120 E2 Saunders, Mount h. Australia
229 G7 Saunders Island S. Sandwich Is
149 F4 Saura r. India
140 B3 Saura Kazakh.
195 C4 Saurimo Angola
148 D5 Sausar India
185 I2 Savai'i i. Samoa
187 G5 Savala r. Rus. Fed.
192 C4 Savalou Benin
208 B4 Savanna U.S.A.
219 D6 Savannah GA U.S.A.
219 B5 Savannah TN U.S.A.
219 D5 Savannah r. U.S.A.
219 E7 Savannah Sound Bahamas
162 C1 Savannakhét Laos
223 I5 Savanna-la-Mar Jamaica
206 B3 Savant Lake Canada
147 G3 Savanur India
171 M3 Sävar Sweden
185 L5 Savaştepe Turkey
192 C4 Savè Benin
195 D6 Save r. Moz.
142 C3 Sāveh Iran
171 O3 Saviaho Fin.
132 F3 Savinskiy Rus. Fed.
184 C2 Savona Italy
171 O3 Savonlinna Fin.
171 O3 Savonranta Fin.
182 H4 Savoy reg. France
139 I1 Şavşat Turkey
171 K4 Sävsjö Sweden
120 C1 Savu i. Indon.
170 O2 Savukoski Fin.
139 H3 Savur Turkey
Savu Sea sea Indon. see Sawu, Laut
148 D4 Sawai Madhopur India
162 A1 Sawankhalok Thai.
213 F4 Sawatch Range mts U.S.A.
174 A4 Sawel Mountain h. U.K.
162 A3 Sawi, Ao b. Thai.
125 J3 Sawtell Australia
208 B2 Sawtooth Mountains U.S.A.
120 C1 Sawu Indon.
Sawu i. Indon. see Savu
151 E7 Sawu, Laut sea Indon.
173 G4 Saxilby U.K.
173 I5 Saxmundham U.K.
171 L3 Saxnäs Sweden
141 I3 Sayak Kazakh.
152 F1 Sayanogorsk Rus. Fed.
150 B1 Sayano-Shushenskoye Vodokhranilishche resr Rus. Fed.
153 H1 Sayansk Rus. Fed.
140 E5 Sayat Turkm.
Sayat Turkm. see Saýat
225 G4 Sayaxché Guat.
142 D4 Sāyen Iran
153 H2 Sayhan-Ovoo Mongolia
146 D5 Sayhūt Yemen
140 A2 Saykhin Rus. Fed.
Säylac Somalia see Saylac
194 E2 Saylac Somalia
150 D2 Saynshand Mongolia
Sayn-Ust Mongolia see Höhmörit
141 J3 Sayram Hu salt l. China
217 D5 Sayre OK U.S.A.

221 E4 Sayre PA U.S.A.
225 D4 Sayula Jalisco Mex.
225 F4 Sayula Veracruz Mex.
140 C3 Say-Utes Kazakh.
204 D4 Sayward Canada
140 B3 Sazdy Kazakh.
148 C2 Sazin Pak.
186 E3 Sazonovo Rus. Fed.
192 B2 Sbaa Alg.
192 C1 Sbeitla Tunisia
121 C7 Scaddan Australia
170 C2 Scafell Pike h. U.K.
174 B4 Scalasaig U.K.
184 F5 Scalea Italy
174 □ Scalloway U.K.
175 J5 Scalp h. Ireland
174 B3 Scalpay i. Scotland U.K.
174 C3 Scalpay i. Scotland U.K.
125 H8 Scamander Australia
174 E2 Scapa Flow inlet U.K.
174 C4 Scarba i. U.K.
209 H4 Scarborough Canada
233 L2 Scarborough Trin. and Tob.
172 G3 Scarborough U.K.
161 H3 Scarborough Shoal sea feature Phil.
174 A2 Scarp i. U.K.
179 I1 Schaale r. Germany
179 I1 Schaalsee l. Germany
178 C4 Schaerbeek Belgium
176 D7 Schaffhausen Switz.
178 C2 Schagen Neth.
178 C2 Schagerbrug Neth.
196 B3 Schakalskuppe Namibia
143 F4 Schao watercourse Afgh./Iran
176 F6 Schärding Austria
178 B3 Scharendijke Neth.
179 I5 Schebheim Germany
179 H1 Scheeßel Germany
207 G3 Schefferville Canada
Schelde r. Belgium see Scheldt
178 C3 Scheldt r. Belgium
215 E2 Schell Creek Range mts U.S.A.
179 I2 Schellerten Germany
221 G3 Schenectady U.S.A.
179 H1 Schenefeld Germany
178 C2 Schermerhorn Neth.
174 D4 Schiehallion mt. U.K.
179 K6 Schierling Germany
179 E1 Schiermonnikoog Neth.
179 E1 Schiermonnikoog i. Neth.
179 E1 Schiermonnikoog Nationaal Park nat. park Neth.
179 J2 Schiffdorf Germany
179 J1 Schilde r. Germany
178 D4 Schinnen Neth.
184 D2 Schio Italy
179 K3 Schkeuditz Germany
179 K4 Schleiden Germany
179 J4 Schleiz Germany
176 D3 Schleswig Germany
179 H1 Schleswig-Holstein land Germany
179 I4 Schleusingen Germany
179 H4 Schlitz Germany
179 G3 Schloss Holte-Stukenbrock Germany
179 H4 Schlüchtern Germany
179 I5 Schlüsselfeld Germany
179 I4 Schmalkalden, Kurort Germany
179 G3 Schmallenberg Germany
Schmidt Peninsula pen. Rus. Fed. see Shmidta, Poluostrov
178 D2 Schokland tourist site Neth.
179 K1 Schönebeck Germany
179 J2 Schönebeck (Elbe) Germany
179 I2 Schöningen Germany
179 H5 Schöntal Germany
221 I2 Schoodic Lake U.S.A.
209 E4 Schoolcraft U.S.A.
178 C3 Schoonhoven Neth.
179 I5 Schopfloch Germany
179 I2 Schöppenstedt Germany
179 F1 Schortens Germany
125 H9 Schouten Island Australia
119 E2 Schouten Islands P.N.G.
208 D1 Schreiber Canada
221 G3 Schroon Lake U.S.A.

215 F5 Schuchuli U.S.A.
175 I6 Schull Ireland
205 J2 Schultz Lake Canada
214 C2 Schurz U.S.A.
179 F2 Schüttorf Germany
221 G3 Schuylerville U.S.A.
179 J5 Schwabach Germany
176 D6 Schwäbische Alb mts Germany
179 H5 Schwäbisch Hall Germany
176 E6 Schwabmünchen Germany
179 G2 Schwaförden Germany
179 H4 Schwalmstadt-Ziegenhain Germany
179 K5 Schwandorf Germany
163 H3 Schwaner, Pegunungan mts Indon.
179 G1 Schwanewede Germany
179 H2 Schwarmstedt Germany
179 L3 Schwarze Elster r. Germany
179 I1 Schwarzenbek Germany
179 K4 Schwarzenberg Germany
179 E4 Schwarzer Mann h. Germany
196 B2 Schwarzrand mts Namibia
Schwarzwald mts Germany see Black Forest
176 E7 Schwaz Austria
176 G4 Schwedt an der Oder Germany
179 G5 Schwegenheim Germany
179 E5 Schweich Germany
179 I4 Schweinfurt Germany
179 L3 Schweinitz Germany
179 K1 Schweinrich Germany
197 F3 Schweizer-Reneke S. Africa
179 F3 Schwelm Germany
176 D6 Schwenningen Germany
179 J1 Schwerin Germany
179 J1 Schweriner See l. Germany
179 G5 Schwetzingen Germany
176 D7 Schwyz Switz.
184 E6 Sciacca Sicily Italy
184 F6 Scicli Sicily Italy
173 A8 Scilly, Isles of U.K.
220 B5 Scioto r. U.S.A.
215 F2 Scipio U.S.A.
212 F1 Scobey U.S.A.
173 I5 Scole U.K.
125 I4 Scone Australia
174 E4 Scone U.K.
203 P2 Scoresby Land reg. Greenland
121 D7 Scorpion Bight b. Australia
238 B9 Scotia Ridge sea feature S. Atlantic Ocean
239 G9 Scotia Ridge sea feature S. Atlantic Ocean
239 G9 Scotia Sea S. Atlantic Ocean
209 G4 Scotland Canada
174 D4 Scotland admin. div. U.K.
120 E2 Scott, Cape Australia
204 D4 Scott, Cape Canada
127 I5 Scott Base research stn Antarctica
197 I5 Scottburgh S. Africa
217 C4 Scott City U.S.A.
127 I5 Scott Coast Antarctica
220 D4 Scottdale U.S.A.
203 K2 Scott Inlet Canada
127 H6 Scott Island Antarctica
205 H3 Scott Lake Canada
127 L4 Scott Mountains Antarctica
120 C2 Scott Reef Australia
216 C3 Scottsbluff U.S.A.
219 C5 Scottsboro U.S.A.
219 C4 Scottsburg U.S.A.
125 G8 Scottsdale Australia
213 E5 Scottsdale U.S.A.
214 A3 Scotts Valley U.S.A.
208 D4 Scottville U.S.A.
215 D3 Scotty's Junction U.S.A.
174 C2 Scourie U.K.
174 □ Scousburgh U.K.
174 E2 Scrabster U.K.
221 F4 Scranton U.S.A.
174 B4 Scridain, Loch inlet U.K.
173 G4 Scunthorpe U.K.
121 B6 Seabrook, Lake salt flat Australia
173 H7 Seaford U.K.
221 F5 Seaford U.S.A.
209 G4 Seaforth Canada
161 H4 Seahorse Shoal sea feature Phil.
205 J3 Seal r. Canada
197 E7 Seal, Cape S. Africa
125 E5 Sea Lake Australia
223 I3 Seal Island U.S.A.
207 H3 Seal Lake Canada
197 F7 Seal Point S. Africa

315

Seaman Range

215 E3 **Seaman Range** *mts* U.S.A.
172 G3 **Seamer** U.K.
215 E4 **Searchlight** U.S.A.
217 F5 **Searcy** U.S.A.
215 D4 **Searles Lake** U.S.A.
209 E4 **Sears** U.S.A.
221 I2 **Searsport** U.S.A.
214 B3 **Seaside** CA U.S.A.
212 B2 **Seaside** OR U.S.A.
174 E6 **Seaton** U.K.
212 B2 **Seattle** U.S.A.
204 B2 **Seattle, Mount** Canada/U.S.A.
122 D3 **Seaview Range** *mts* Australia
221 F5 **Seaville** U.S.A.
120 C1 **Seba** Indon.
221 H3 **Sebago Lake** U.S.A.
224 A1 **Sebastián Vizcaíno, Bahía** *b.* Mex.
221 I2 **Sebasticook** *r.* U.S.A.
163 I2 **Sebatik** *i.* Indon.
138 C1 **Seben** Turkey
185 J2 **Sebeș** Romania
163 G4 **Sebesi** *i.* Indon.
209 F4 **Sebewaing** U.S.A.
186 D3 **Sebezh** Rus. Fed.
138 E3 **Sebil** Turkey
139 G1 **Şebinkarahisar** Turkey
221 I2 **Seboeis Lake** U.S.A.
221 I2 **Seboomook** U.S.A.
221 I2 **Seboomook Lake** U.S.A.
219 D7 **Sebring** U.S.A.
187 G5 **Sebrovo** Rus. Fed.
230 B5 **Sechura** Peru
230 B5 **Sechura, Bahía de** *b.* Peru
179 H5 **Seckach** Germany
221 H2 **Second Lake** U.S.A.
192 □ **Secos, Ilhéus** *is* Cape Verde
126 A6 **Secretary Island** N.Z.
197 H3 **Secunda** S. Africa
147 H2 **Secunderabad** India
217 E4 **Sedalia** U.S.A.
147 H2 **Sedam** India
124 C5 **Sedan** Australia
182 G2 **Sedan** France
122 C3 **Sedan Dip** Australia
126 E4 **Seddon** N.Z.
126 C4 **Seddonville** N.Z.
143 E3 **Sedeh** Iran
221 I2 **Sedgwick** U.S.A.
192 A3 **Sédhiou** Senegal
176 G6 **Sedlčany** Czech Rep.
138 E6 **Sedom** Israel
215 G4 **Sedona** U.S.A.
184 B6 **Sédrata** Alg.
171 M5 **Šeduva** Lith.
179 I1 **Seedorf** Germany
175 K5 **Seefin** *h.* Ireland
179 J2 **Seehausen** Germany
179 J2 **Seehausen (Altmark)** Germany
195 B6 **Seeheim** Namibia
179 G5 **Seeheim-Jugenheim** Germany
197 E6 **Seekoegat** S. Africa
215 E5 **Seeley** U.S.A.
127 I4 **Seelig, Mount** Antarctica
179 H2 **Seelze** Germany
182 E2 **Sées** France
179 I3 **Seesen** Germany
179 I1 **Seevetal** Germany
192 A4 **Sefadu** Sierra Leone
197 G1 **Sefare** Botswana
185 L5 **Seferihisar** Turkey
197 G1 **Sefophe** Botswana
171 J3 **Segalstad** Norway
161 H5 **Segama** *r.* Sabah Malaysia
163 B2 **Segamat** Malaysia
179 K2 **Segeletz** Germany
186 E2 **Segezha** Rus. Fed.
141 F3 **Segiz** *salt l.* Kazakh.
141 F3 **Segiz, Ozera** *lakes* Kazakh.
183 P3 **Segorbe** Spain
192 B3 **Ségou** Mali
233 I3 **Segovia** Col.
183 N2 **Segovia** Spain
186 E2 **Segozerskoye, Ozero** *resr* Rus. Fed.
183 Q1 **Segre** *r.* Spain
193 D2 **Séguédine** Niger
192 B4 **Séguéla** Côte d'Ivoire
217 D6 **Seguin** U.S.A.
235 J1 **Segundo** *r.* Arg.
183 P3 **Segura** *r.* Spain
195 C6 **Sehithwa** Botswana
197 H4 **Sehlabathebe National Park** Lesotho
148 D5 **Sehore** India
170 M1 **Seiland** *i.* Norway
217 E4 **Seiling** U.S.A.
171 M3 **Seinäjoki** Fin.

182 E2 **Seine** *r.* France
182 D2 **Seine, Baie de** *b.* France
182 F2 **Seine, Val de** *val.* France
177 K3 **Sejny** Poland
163 B3 **Sekayu** Indon.
197 E2 **Sekoma** Botswana
192 B4 **Sekondi** Ghana
143 F4 **Seküheh** Iran
163 D5 **Sekura** Indon.
Şela Rus. Fed. *see* **Shali**
212 B2 **Selah** U.S.A.
151 F7 **Selaru** *i.* Indon.
163 H3 **Selatan, Tanjung** *pt* Indon.
163 I3 **Selat Makassar** *str.* Indon.
202 B3 **Selawik** U.S.A.
179 K4 **Selb** Germany
171 J3 **Selbekken** Norway
171 J3 **Selbu** Norway
173 F4 **Selby** U.K.
216 C2 **Selby** U.S.A.
195 C6 **Selebi-Phikwe** Botswana
156 C1 **Selemdzha** *r.* Rus. Fed.
156 C1 **Selemdzhinsk** Rus. Fed.
150 F1 **Selemdzhinskiy Khrebet** *mts* Rus. Fed.
138 B2 **Selendi** Turkey
150 C1 **Selenga** *r.* Rus. Fed.
182 H2 **Sélestat** France
162 □ **Seletar** Sing.
162 □ **Seletar, Pulau** *i.* Sing.
162 □ **Seletar Reservoir** Sing.
141 H2 **Seletinskoye** Kazakh.
216 C2 **Selfridge** U.S.A.
156 D2 **Sel'gon Stantsiya** Rus. Fed.
186 I2 **Selib** Rus. Fed.
192 A3 **Sélibabi** Mauritania
179 J4 **Seligenstadt** Germany
186 E3 **Seliger, Ozero** *l.* Rus. Fed.
215 F4 **Seligman** U.S.A.
156 E2 **Selikhino** Rus. Fed.
193 E2 **Selîma Oasis** Sudan
209 I5 **Selinsgrove** U.S.A.
177 P2 **Selishche** Rus. Fed.
177 P2 **Selizharovo** Rus. Fed.
171 J4 **Seljord** Norway
179 J3 **Selke** *r.* Germany
205 J4 **Selkirk** Canada
175 F5 **Selkirk** U.K.
204 F4 **Selkirk Mountains** Canada
172 D3 **Sellafield** U.K.
215 G5 **Sells** U.S.A.
179 F3 **Selm** Germany
219 C5 **Selma** AL U.S.A.
214 C3 **Selma** CA U.S.A.
219 B5 **Selmer** U.S.A.
143 F4 **Selseleh-ye Pīr Shūrān** *mts* Iran
173 G7 **Selsey Bill** *hd* U.K.
169 Q4 **Selty** Rus. Fed.
162 C4 **Seluan** *i.* Indon.
230 D5 **Selvas** *reg.* Brazil
205 I3 **Selwyn Lake** Canada
204 C2 **Selwyn Mountains** Canada
118 D4 **Selwyn Range** *hills* Australia
163 H4 **Semarang** Indon.
163 G3 **Sematan** Sarawak Malaysia
120 C1 **Semau** *i.* Indon.
163 I3 **Semayang, Danau** *l.* Indon.
161 H6 **Sembakung** *r.* Indon.
162 □ **Sembawang** Sing.
194 B3 **Sembé** Congo
139 J3 **Şemdinli** Turkey
187 E4 **Semenivka** Ukr.
140 C1 **Semenkino** Rus. Fed.
186 H3 **Semenov** Rus. Fed.
163 H4 **Semeru, Gunung** *vol.* Indon.
187 G6 **Semikarakorsk** Rus. Fed.
187 F5 **Semiluki** Rus. Fed.
213 F3 **Seminoe Reservoir** U.S.A.
217 C5 **Seminole** U.S.A.
219 C6 **Seminole, Lake** U.S.A.
141 K2 **Seminskiy Khrebet** *mts* Rus. Fed.
141 J2 **Semipalatinsk** Kazakh.
141 I2 **Semipalatinskaya Oblast'** Kazakh.
141 F1 **Semipolka** Kazakh.
161 I3 **Semirara** *i.* Phil.
161 I4 **Semirara Islands** Phil.
142 C4 **Semīrom** Iran
141 I2 **Semiyarka** Kazakh.
141 H2 **Sem Kolodezey** Ukr. *see* **Lenine**
142 D3 **Semnān** Iran
142 D3 **Semnān va Dāmghān** *reg.* Iran
178 D5 **Semois** *r.* Belgium
178 D5 **Semois, Vallée de la** *val.* Belgium/France

163 I2 **Semporna** Sabah Malaysia
163 H4 **Sempu** *i.* Indon.
162 C2 **Sên, Stœng** *r.* Cambodia
161 H5 **Senaja** Sabah Malaysia
187 G7 **Senaki** Georgia
230 E5 **Sena Madureira** Brazil
147 I5 **Senanayake Samudra** *l.* Sri Lanka
195 C5 **Senanga** Zambia
159 C5 **Sendai** Japan
159 B9 **Sendai** Japan
149 H3 **Sêndo** China
162 B5 **Senebui, Tanjung** *pt* Indon.
215 G5 **Seneca** AZ U.S.A.
208 C5 **Seneca** IL U.S.A.
212 C2 **Seneca** OR U.S.A.
221 E3 **Seneca Falls** U.S.A.
221 E3 **Seneca Lake** U.S.A.
220 D5 **Seneca Rocks** U.S.A.
220 C5 **Senecaville Lake** U.S.A.
192 A3 **Senegal** *country* Africa
192 A3 **Sénégal** *r.* Mauritania/Senegal
197 G4 **Senekal** S. Africa
209 E2 **Seney** U.S.A.
176 G5 **Senftenberg** Germany
148 D4 **Sengar** *r.* India
195 C4 **Sengerema** Tanz.
187 I4 **Sengiley** Rus. Fed.
231 J6 **Senhor do Bonfim** Brazil
184 E3 **Senigallia** Italy
184 F2 **Senj** Croatia
170 L1 **Senja** *i.* Norway
139 I1 **Şenkaya** Turkey
Senku Jammu and Kashmir *see* **Sanku**
197 E2 **Senlac** S. Africa
161 F2 **Senlin Shan** *mt.* China
182 F2 **Senlis** France
162 C2 **Senmonorom** Cambodia
173 B7 **Sennen** U.K.
209 I1 **Senneterre** Canada
197 H5 **Senqu** *r.* Lesotho
182 F2 **Sens** France
178 B4 **Sensée** *r.* France
224 C4 **Sensuntepeque** El Salvador
185 I2 **Senta** Serbia
141 J2 **Sentas** Kazakh.
148 D3 **Senthal** India
215 F5 **Sentinel** U.S.A.
204 E3 **Sentinel Peak** Canada
162 □ **Sentosa** *i.* Sing.
197 H1 **Senwabarwana** S. Africa
139 H3 **Şenyurt** Turkey
148 D5 **Seoni** India
147 I1 **Seorinarayan** India
160 D5 **Seoul** S. Korea (City Plan **93**)
126 D4 **Separation Point** N.Z.
121 C4 **Separation Well** Australia
139 K4 **Separ Shāhābād** Iran
119 E2 **Sepik** *r.* P.N.G.
160 D4 **Sep'o** N. Korea
207 G3 **Sept-Îles** Canada
214 C3 **Sequoia National Park** U.S.A.
187 G5 **Serafimovich** Rus. Fed.
151 E7 **Seram** *i.* Indon.
151 F7 **Seram, Laut** *sea* Indon.
163 G4 **Serang** Indon.
162 □ **Serangoon, Pulau** *i.* Sing.
162 □ **Serangoon Harbour** *b.* Sing.
163 D5 **Serasan** *i.* Indon.
163 G2 **Serasan, Selat** *sea chan.* Indon.
163 D5 **Seraya** *i.* Indon.
162 □ **Seraya, Pulau** *reg.* Sing.
Serbâl, Gebel *mt.* Egypt *see* **Sirbâl, Jabal**
185 I3 **Serbia** *country* Europe
224 C1 **Serdán** Mex.
140 D5 **Serdar** Turkm.
194 E2 **Serdo** Eth.
187 H4 **Serdoba** *r.* Rus. Fed.
187 H4 **Serdobsk** Rus. Fed.
141 J2 **Serebryansk** Kazakh.
186 D3 **Seredka** Rus. Fed.
138 D2 **Şereflikoçhisar** Turkey
163 B2 **Seremban** Malaysia
195 D4 **Serengeti National Park** Tanz.
195 D5 **Serenje** Zambia
187 H4 **Sergach** Rus. Fed.
158 C3 **Sergeyavka** Rus. Fed.
141 G2 **Sergeyevka** Akmolinskaya Oblast' Kazakh.
141 F1 **Sergeyevka** Severnyy Kazakhstan Kazakh.
156 B2 **Sergeyevka** Rus. Fed.
186 F3 **Sergiyev Posad** Rus. Fed.
144 I4 **Serh** China

143 F3 **Serhetabat** Turkm.
163 H2 **Seria** Brunei
163 H2 **Serian** Sarawak Malaysia
185 K6 **Serifos** *i.* Greece
207 G2 **Sérigny, Lac** *l.* Canada
138 C3 **Serik** Turkey
141 I5 **Serikbuya** China
195 C6 **Serowe** Botswana
183 M4 **Serpa** Port.
121 E6 **Serpentine Lakes** *salt flat* Australia
233 L2 **Serpent's Mouth** *sea chan.* Trin. and Tob./Venez.
187 F4 **Serpukhov** Rus. Fed.
234 C3 **Serra da Canastra, Parque Nacional da** *nat. park* Brazil
234 C1 **Serra da Mesa, Represa** *resr* Brazil
231 H3 **Serra do Navio** Brazil
233 K4 **Serranía de la Neblina, Parque Nacional** *nat. park* Venez.
234 B2 **Serranópolis** Brazil
178 B5 **Serre** *r.* France
185 J4 **Serres** Greece
235 J1 **Serrezuela** Arg.
231 K6 **Serrinha** Brazil
234 D2 **Sêrro** Brazil
235 H4 **Serrucho** *mt.* Arg.
184 C6 **Sers** Tunisia
234 C3 **Sertãozinho** Brazil
186 D2 **Sertolovo** Rus. Fed.
162 A4 **Serui** Indon.
163 H3 **Seruyan** *r.* Indon.
149 H2 **Sêrwolungwa** China
150 B3 **Sêrxü** China
163 I2 **Sesayap** Indon.
161 H6 **Sesayap** *r.* Indon.
206 B3 **Seseganaga Lake** Canada
209 G1 **Sesekinika** Canada
195 B5 **Sesfontein** Namibia
197 H1 **Seshego** S. Africa
195 C5 **Sesheke** Zambia
184 E4 **Sessa Aurunca** Italy
184 C2 **Sestri Levante** Italy
186 D2 **Sestroretsk** Rus. Fed.
162 C2 **Set, Phou** *mt.* Laos
158 F3 **Setana** Japan
183 F5 **Sète** France
234 D2 **Sete Lagoas** Brazil
170 L1 **Setermoen** Norway
171 I4 **Setesdal** *val.* Norway
149 F4 **Seti** *r.* Gandakhi Nepal
149 E3 **Seti** *r.* Seti Nepal
192 C1 **Sétif** Alg.
159 E7 **Seto** Japan
153 N5 **Seto-naikai** *sea* Japan
192 B1 **Settat** Morocco
172 E3 **Settle** U.K.
183 L3 **Setúbal** Port.
183 L3 **Setúbal, Baía de** *b.* Port.
206 B3 **Seul, Lac** *l.* Canada
209 E3 **Seul Choix Point** U.S.A.
139 J1 **Sevan** Armenia
139 J1 **Sevan, Lake** Armenia **Sevana Lich** *l.* Armenia *see* **Sevan, Lake**
187 E6 **Sevastopol'** Ukr.
207 H2 **Seven Islands Bay** Canada
173 H6 **Sevenoaks** U.K.
182 F4 **Sévérac-le-Château** France
125 I2 **Severn** *r.* Australia
206 B3 **Severn** *r.* Canada
197 E3 **Severn** S. Africa
173 E6 **Severn** *r.* U.K.
186 G2 **Severnaya Dvina** *r.* Rus. Fed.
187 H7 **Severnaya Osetiya-Alaniya, Respublika** *aut. rep.* Rus. Fed.
133 L1 **Severnaya Zemlya** *is* Rus. Fed.
206 B3 **Severn Lake** Canada
132 H3 **Severnyy** Rus. Fed.
140 D3 **Severnyy Chink Ustyurta** *esc.* Kazakh.
141 G1 **Severnyy Kazakhstan** *admin. div.* Kazakh.
150 D1 **Severo-Baykal'skoye Nagor'ye** *mts* Rus. Fed.
186 F1 **Severodvinsk** Rus. Fed.
133 Q4 **Severo-Kuril'sk** Rus. Fed.

170 P1 **Severomorsk** Rus. Fed.
169 N3 **Severoonezhsk** Rus. Fed.
133 K3 **Severo-Yeniseyskiy** Rus. Fed.
187 F6 **Severskaya** Rus. Fed.
213 D4 **Sevier** U.S.A.
215 G2 **Sevier Bridge Reservoir** U.S.A.
215 F2 **Sevier Desert** U.S.A.
215 F2 **Sevier Lake** U.S.A.
233 I3 **Sevilla** Col.
Sevilla Spain *see* **Seville**
183 N4 **Seville** Spain
185 K3 **Sevlievo** Bulg.
148 C3 **Sewani** India
202 D3 **Seward** AK U.S.A.
216 D3 **Seward** NE U.S.A.
202 B3 **Seward Peninsula** U.S.A.
204 F3 **Sexsmith** Canada
210 E6 **Sextín** *r.* Mex.
143 F3 **Seyah Band Koh** *mts* Afgh.
132 I2 **Seyakha** Rus. Fed.
225 G4 **Seybaplaya** Mex.
191 I5 **Seychelles** *country* Indian Ocean
140 E5 **Seÿdi** Turkm. **Seydi** Turkm. *see* **Seÿdi**
138 C3 **Seydişehir** Turkey
170 D2 **Seyðisfjörður** Iceland
142 B2 **Seydvān** Iran **Seyhan** Turkey *see* **Adana**
138 E3 **Seyhan** *r.* Turkey
136 C3 **Seyitgazi** Turkey
187 E5 **Seym** *r.* Rus. Fed.
133 Q3 **Seymchan** Rus. Fed.
125 J6 **Seymour** Australia
197 G6 **Seymour** S. Africa
219 C4 **Seymour** IN U.S.A.
217 D5 **Seymour** TX U.S.A.
121 F5 **Seymour Range** *mts* Australia
143 H3 **Seyyedābād** Afgh.
182 F2 **Sézanne** France
185 K2 **Sfântu Gheorghe** Romania
193 D1 **Sfax** Tunisia
185 J4 **Sfikias, Limni** *resr* Greece
178 D2 **'s-Graveland** Neth. **'s-Gravenhage** Neth. *see* **The Hague**
174 C4 **Sgurr Dhomhnuill** *h.* U.K.
174 C3 **Sgurr Mòr** *mt.* U.K. **Sgurr Mor** *mt.* U.K. *see* **Sgurr Mòr**
154 C3 **Shaanxi** *prov.* China
194 E3 **Shabeelle, Webi** *r.* Somalia
142 B2 **Shabestar** Iran
185 M3 **Shabla, Nos** *pt* Bulg.
207 G3 **Shabogamo Lake** Canada
195 C4 **Shabunda** Dem. Rep. Congo
144 C5 **Shache** China
127 J5 **Shackleton Coast** Antarctica
127 K6 **Shackleton Ice Shelf** Antarctica
127 J3 **Shackleton Range** *mts* Antarctica
148 A4 **Shadadkot** Pak.
142 C4 **Shādegān** Iran
148 A3 **Shadikhak Pass** Pak.
142 D2 **Shādkām** *watercourse* Iran
208 D5 **Shafer, Lake** U.S.A.
127 I5 **Shafer Peak** Antarctica
214 C4 **Shafter** U.S.A.
173 E6 **Shaftesbury** U.K.
140 D3 **Shagan** *watercourse* Aktyubinskaya Oblast' Kazakh.
141 I2 **Shagan** *watercourse* Vostochnyy Kazakhstan Kazakh.
152 J4 **Shagonar** Rus. Fed.
126 C6 **Shag Point** N.Z.
239 G9 **Shag Rocks** *is* S. Georgia
140 D3 **Shagyray, Plato** *plat.* Kazakh.
141 G1 **Shaglyteniz, Ozero** *l.* Kazakh.
141 G1 **Shaglytengiz, Ozero** *l.* Kazakh.
147 H2 **Shahabad** Karnataka India
149 E4 **Shahabad** Uttar Pradesh India
143 E3 **Shāhābād** Iran
148 C5 **Shahada** India
163 B2 **Shah Alam** Malaysia
147 G3 **Shahapur** India
148 A4 **Shahbandar** Pak.
143 G5 **Shahbaz Kalat** Pak.

149 G5 **Shahbazpur** *sea chan.* Bangl.
143 E4 **Shāhdād** Iran
149 E5 **Shahdol** India
155 C4 **Shahe** China
154 E2 **Sha He** *r.* China
139 J3 **Shahedan** Iraq
143 E3 **Shah Fuladi** *mt.* Afgh.
148 B4 **Shahgarh** India
139 J3 **Shāhī, Jazīreh-ye** *pen.* Iran **Shahi Peninsula** Iran *see* **Shāhī, Jazīreh-ye**
143 G4 **Shah Ismail** Afgh.
148 D4 **Shahjahanpur** India
143 E2 **Shāh Jehān, Küh-e** *mts* Iran
143 E4 **Shāh Küh** *mt.* Iran
142 D3 **Shāhmīrzād** Iran
147 H2 **Shahpur** India
148 B3 **Shahpur** Pak.
149 E5 **Shahpura** Madhya Pradesh India
148 D4 **Shahpura** Rajasthan India
143 G3 **Shahrak** Afgh.
143 F3 **Shāhrakht** Iran
142 D4 **Shahr-e Bābak** Iran
142 C3 **Shahr-e Kord** Iran
142 C3 **Shāhreză** Iran
141 F5 **Shahrisabz** Uzbek.
142 C3 **Shahr Rey** Iran
141 G5 **Shahrtuz** Tajik.
142 C2 **Shāhrūd, Rūdkhāneh-ye** *r.* Iran
142 D3 **Shāhrūd Bustām** *reg.* Iran
143 G4 **Shaikh Husain** *mt.* Pak.
142 C2 **Shaj'ah, Jabal** *h.* Saudi Arabia
160 C3 **Shajianzi** China
139 K3 **Shakar Bolāghī** Iran
197 I4 **Shakaville** S. Africa
141 G5 **Shakhdara** *r.* Tajik.
143 E3 **Shākhen** Iran
186 E3 **Shakhovskaya** Rus. Fed. **Shakhrisabz** Uzbek. *see* **Shahrisabz**
141 H2 **Shakhtinsk** Kazakh.
140 D2 **Shakhty** Kazakh.
187 G6 **Shakhty** Rus. Fed.
186 H3 **Shakhun'ya** Rus. Fed.
216 E2 **Shakopee** U.S.A.
158 G3 **Shakotan-hantō** *pen.* Japan
158 G3 **Shakotan-misaki** *c.* Japan
186 G2 **Shalakusha** Rus. Fed.
141 I2 **Shalday** Kazakh.
141 G3 **Shalginskiy** Kazakh.
137 G2 **Shali** Rus. Fed.
140 D3 **Shalkar** Kazakh.
140 B2 **Shalkar, Ozero** *salt l.* Kazakh.
140 E2 **Shalkar Karashatau** *salt l.* Kazakh.
140 E2 **Shalkarteniz, Solonchak** *salt marsh* Kazakh.
141 I4 **Shalkode** Kazakh.
150 B3 **Shaluli Shan** *mts* China
149 I3 **Shaluni** *mt.* India
137 F5 **Shāmat al Akbād** *des.* Saudi Arabia
205 K3 **Shamattawa** Canada
155 □ **Sham Chun** *r.* Hong Kong China
143 E5 **Shamīl** Iran
142 D6 **Shamis** U.A.E.
221 E4 **Shamokin** U.S.A.
217 C5 **Shamrock** U.S.A.
195 D5 **Shamva** Zimbabwe
154 C2 **Shancheng** China
143 F4 **Shand** Afgh.
143 F4 **Shāndak** Iran
154 A2 **Shandan** China
139 L3 **Shānderman** Iran
154 E1 **Shandian He** *r.* China
143 E2 **Shandiz** Iran
214 B4 **Shandon** U.S.A.
160 A5 **Shandong** *prov.* China
154 F2 **Shandong Bandao** *pen.* China
139 J5 **Shandrūkh** Iraq
148 C1 **Shandur Pass** Pak.
195 C5 **Shangani** *r.* Zimbabwe
154 E3 **Shangcai** China
155 E3 **Shangchao** China
155 E4 **Shangcheng** China
149 G3 **Shang Chu** *r.* China
155 D6 **Shangchuan Dao** *i.* China
154 D1 **Shangdu** China
155 E5 **Shangdundu** China
156 B3 **Shangganling** China
155 E4 **Shanggao** China
155 F4 **Shanghai** China (City Plan **93**)
155 F4 **Shanghai** *mun.* China
155 E5 **Shanghang** China

185 L3 Sliven Bulg.
186 H2 Sloboda Rus. Fed.
186 I2 Slobodchikovo Rus. Fed.
169 Q4 Slobodskoy Rus. Fed.
185 L2 Slobozia Romania
204 F5 Slocan Canada
179 E1 Slochteren Neth.
187 C4 Slonim Belarus
178 C2 Slootdorp Neth.
178 D2 Sloten Neth.
178 D2 Slotermeer *l.* Neth.
173 G6 Slough U.K.
177 I6 Slovakia *country* Europe
184 F1 Slovenia *country* Europe
184 F1 Slovenj Gradec Slovenia
187 F5 Slov"yans'k Ukr.
181 I1 Sluch *r.* Ukr.
162 C3 S'Lung, B'Nom *mt.* Vietnam
177 H3 Słupsk Poland
170 L2 Slussfors Sweden
187 C4 Slutsk Belarus
175 H4 Slyne Head Ireland
133 L4 Slyudyanka Rus. Fed.
221 I3 Small Point U.S.A.
207 H3 Smallwood Reservoir Canada
187 D4 Smalyavichy Belarus
    Smalyenska Wzwyshsha *hills* Belarus/Rus. Fed. *see* Smolensko-Moskovskaya Vozvyshennost'
177 M3 Smarhon' Belarus
197 E5 Smartt Syndicate Dam *resr* S. Africa
205 I4 Smeaton Canada
185 I2 Smederevo Serbia
185 I2 Smederevska Palanka Serbia
220 D4 Smethport U.S.A.
156 D2 Smidovich Rus. Fed.
187 D5 Smila Ukr.
179 E2 Smilde Neth.
171 N4 Smiltene Latvia
141 G1 Smirnovo Kazakh.
156 F2 Smirnykh Rus. Fed.
205 G3 Smith Canada
214 C2 Smith U.S.A.
220 C6 Smith *r.* U.S.A.
202 C2 Smith Bay U.S.A.
204 D4 Smithers Canada
197 G5 Smithfield S. Africa
219 E5 Smithfield *NC* U.S.A.
213 E3 Smithfield *UT* U.S.A.
221 E5 Smith Island *MD* U.S.A.
221 F6 Smith Island *VA* U.S.A.
220 D6 Smith Mountain Lake U.S.A.
204 D3 Smith River Canada
209 I3 Smiths Falls Canada
203 K2 Smith Sound *sea chan.* Canada/Greenland
125 F8 Smithton Australia
214 C1 Smoke Creek Desert U.S.A.
204 F4 Smoky *r.* Canada
121 F7 Smoky Bay Australia
125 J3 Smoky Cape Australia
206 D3 Smoky Falls Canada
217 C4 Smoky Hill *r.* U.S.A.
217 D4 Smoky Hills U.S.A.
205 G4 Smoky Lake Canada
171 I3 Smøla *i.* Norway
140 B2 Smolenka Rus. Fed.
187 E4 Smolensk Rus. Fed.
187 E4 Smolenskaya Oblast' *admin. div.* Rus. Fed.
    Smolensk-Moscow Upland *hills* Belarus/Rus. Fed. *see* Smolensko-Moskovskaya Vozvyshennost'
169 M5 Smolensko-Moskovskaya Vozvyshennost' *hills* Belarus/Rus. Fed.
141 K1 Smolenskoye Rus. Fed.
185 K4 Smolyan Bulg.
158 C3 Smolyoninovo Rus. Fed.
206 D4 Smooth Rock Falls Canada
206 C3 Smoothrock Lake Canada
205 H4 Smoothstone Lake Canada
170 N1 Smørfjord Norway
221 F5 Smyrna *DE* U.S.A.
219 C5 Smyrna *GA* U.S.A.
220 C4 Smyrna *OH* U.S.A.
221 I1 Smyrna Mills U.S.A.
170 D2 Snæfell *mt.* Iceland
172 C3 Snaefell *h.* U.K.
204 A2 Snag Canada
213 D3 Snake *r.* U.S.A.
215 E2 Snake Range *mts* U.S.A.
213 D3 Snake River Plain U.S.A.

    Snare Lakes Canada *see* Wekweètì
119 G6 Snares Islands N.Z.
170 K2 Snåsa Norway
178 D1 Sneek Neth.
175 I6 Sneem Ireland
197 F6 Sneeuberge *mts* S. Africa
207 H5 Snegamook Lake Canada
173 H5 Snettisham U.K.
133 J3 Snezhnogorsk Rus. Fed.
184 F2 Snežnik *mt.* Slovenia
177 J4 Śniardwy, Jezioro *l.* Poland
187 E6 Snihurivka Ukr.
174 B3 Snizort, Loch *b.* U.K.
212 B2 Snohomish U.S.A.
212 B2 Snoqualmie Pass U.S.A.
170 K2 Snøtinden *mt.* Norway
205 I2 Snowbird Lake Canada
173 C4 Snowdon *mt.* U.K.
173 D5 Snowdonia National Park U.K.
215 G4 Snowflake U.S.A.
221 F5 Snow Hill *MD* U.S.A.
219 E5 Snow Hill *NC* U.S.A.
205 I4 Snow Lake Canada
124 C4 Snowtown Australia
213 D3 Snowville U.S.A.
125 H6 Snowy *r.* Australia
125 H6 Snowy Mountains Australia
125 G9 Snug Australia
207 I3 Snug Harbour *Nfld* Canada
209 G3 Snug Harbour *Ont.* Canada
162 C2 Snuŏl Cambodia
217 D5 Snyder *OK* U.S.A.
217 C5 Snyder *TX* U.S.A.
195 E5 Soalala Madag.
195 E5 Soanierana-Ivongo Madag.
160 D6 Soan-kundo *is* S. Korea
233 I3 Soata Col.
174 B3 Soay *i.* U.K.
160 D6 Sobaek-sanmaek *mts* S. Korea
193 F4 Sobat *r.* Sudan
151 G2 Sobger *r.* Indon.
159 B8 Sobo-san *mt.* Japan
231 J6 Sobradinho, Barragem de *resr* Brazil
231 J4 Sobral Brazil
187 F7 Sochi Rus. Fed.
160 D5 Sŏch'ŏn S. Korea
117 I5 Society Islands Fr. Polynesia
234 C3 Socorro Brazil
233 I3 Socorro Col.
213 F5 Socorro U.S.A.
222 B5 Socorro, Isla *i.* Mex.
146 D7 Socotra *i.* Yemen
162 C3 Soc Trăng Vietnam
183 O3 Socuéllamos Spain
215 D4 Soda Lake U.S.A.
170 N2 Sodankylä Fin.
148 D2 Soda Plains Aksai Chin
213 E3 Soda Springs U.S.A.
171 L3 Söderhamn Sweden
171 L4 Söderköping Sweden
171 L4 Södertälje Sweden
193 F3 Sodiri Sudan
194 D3 Sodo Eth.
171 L3 Södra Kvarken *str.* Fin./Sweden
197 H1 Soekmekaar S. Africa
178 D3 Soerendonk Neth.
179 G3 Soest Germany
178 D2 Soest Neth.
125 H4 Sofala Australia
185 J3 Sofia Bulg.
    Sofiya Bulg. *see* Sofia
156 D1 Sofiysk *Khabarovskiy Kray* Rus. Fed.
156 E2 Sofiysk *Khabarovskiy Kray* Rus. Fed.
170 O2 Sofporog Rus. Fed.
185 L6 Sofrana *i.* Greece
159 G10 Sōfu-gan *i.* Japan
149 H3 Sog China
233 I3 Sogamoso Col.
139 G1 Soğanlı Dağları *mts* Turkey
156 D2 Sogda Rus. Fed.
179 F2 Sögel Germany
171 I4 Søgne Norway
171 I3 Sognefjorden *inlet* Norway
161 J4 Sogod Phil.
154 A1 Sogo Nur *l.* China
186 H2 Sogra Rus. Fed.
154 A3 Sogruma China
138 C1 Söğüt Turkey
136 C3 Söğüt Dağı *mts* Turkey
160 D7 Sŏgwip'o S. Korea
    Sohâg Egypt *see* Sūhāj
148 D5 Sohagpur India
173 H5 Soham U.K.
148 B2 Sohan *r.* Pak.

119 F2 Sohano P.N.G.
147 I1 Sohela India
148 D3 Sohna India
160 E3 Sŏho-ri N. Korea
160 C6 Sohŭksan S. Korea
157 B6 Sohŭksan-do *i.* S. Korea
178 C4 Soignes, Forêt de *for.* Belgium
178 C4 Soignies Belgium
171 N3 Soini Fin.
182 F2 Soissons France
148 C4 Sojat India
161 I4 Sojoton Point Phil.
187 C5 Sokal' Ukr.
160 E4 Sokch'o S. Korea
185 L6 Söke Turkey
153 I1 Sokhor, Gora *mt.* Rus. Fed.
187 G7 Sokhumi Georgia
192 C4 Sokodé Togo
155 □ Soko Islands *Hong Kong* China
186 G3 Sokol Rus. Fed.
177 K4 Sokółka Poland
192 B3 Sokolo Mali
179 K4 Sokolov Czech Rep.
158 C3 Sokolovka Rus. Fed.
177 K4 Sokołów Podlaski Poland
192 C3 Sokoto Nigeria
192 C3 Sokoto *r.* Nigeria
187 C5 Sokyryany Ukr.
148 D3 Solan India
126 A7 Solander Island N.Z.
147 G2 Solapur India
233 I2 Soledad Col.
214 B3 Soledad U.S.A.
233 L2 Soledad Venez.
225 E4 Soledad de Doblado Mex.
187 G6 Solenoye Rus. Fed.
170 K2 Solfjellsjøen Norway
139 H2 Solhan Turkey
186 G3 Soligalich Rus. Fed.
173 F5 Solihull U.K.
132 G4 Solikamsk Rus. Fed.
140 C2 Sol'-Iletsk Rus. Fed.
225 H4 Solimón, Punta *pt* Mex.
179 F3 Solingen Germany
196 A1 Solitaire Namibia
139 L1 Şollar Azer.
171 L3 Sollefteå Sweden
179 K3 Söllichau Germany
179 I3 Solling *hills* Germany
179 I3 Sollstedt Germany
    Sollum, Gulf of *b.* Egypt *see* Sallum, Khalīj as
179 G4 Solms Germany
186 F3 Solnechnogorsk Rus. Fed.
156 A1 Solnechnyy *Amurskaya Oblast'* Rus. Fed.
156 E2 Solnechnyy *Khabarovskiy Kray* Rus. Fed.
163 B3 Solok Indon.
225 G5 Sololá Guat.
119 G2 Solomon Islands *country* Pacific Ocean
119 F2 Solomon Sea P.N.G./Solomon Is
141 K2 Soloneshnoye Rus. Fed.
208 B2 Solon Springs U.S.A.
151 E7 Solor, Kepulauan *is* Indon.
176 C7 Solothurn Switz.
186 E1 Solovetskiye Ostrova *is* Rus. Fed.
186 H3 Solovetskoye Rus. Fed.
156 B1 Solov'yevsk Rus. Fed.
185 G3 Šolta *i.* Croatia
137 H4 Solţānābād Iran
143 E2 Solţānābād Iran
143 E3 Solţānābād Iran
179 H2 Soltau Germany
186 D3 Sol'tsy Rus. Fed.
221 E3 Solvay U.S.A.
171 K4 Sölvesborg Sweden
174 E6 Solway Firth *est.* U.K.
195 C5 Solwezi Zambia
159 G6 Sōma Japan
138 A2 Soma Turkey
178 B4 Somain France
194 E3 Somalia *country* Africa
238 H5 Somali Basin *sea feature* Indian Ocean
195 C4 Sombo Angola
185 H2 Sombor Serbia
225 D3 Sombrerete Mex.
148 C4 Somdari India
221 I2 Somerest Junction U.S.A.
171 M3 Somero Fin.
219 C4 Somerset *KY* U.S.A.
209 E4 Somerset *MI* U.S.A.
220 D5 Somerset *PA* U.S.A.
197 F6 Somerset East S. Africa
203 I2 Somerset Island Canada

221 G3 Somerset Reservoir U.S.A.
196 C7 Somerset West S. Africa
221 H3 Somersworth U.S.A.
217 D6 Somerville Reservoir U.S.A.
142 B3 Someydeh Iran
179 J3 Sömmerda Germany
207 G3 Sommet, Lac du *l.* Canada
148 B5 Somnath India
208 C5 Somonauk U.S.A.
224 H5 Somotillo Nicaragua
224 H5 Somoto Nicaragua
235 I4 Somuncurá, Mesa Volcánica de *plat.* Arg.
141 G2 Sonaly *Karagandinskaya Oblast'* Kazakh.
141 G2 Sonaly *Karagandinskaya Oblast'* Kazakh.
149 F5 Sonamukhi India
149 G5 Sonamura India
147 I1 Sonapur India
148 D4 Sonar *r.* India
149 H4 Sonari India
161 F2 Sönbong N. Korea
160 C4 Sŏnch'ŏn N. Korea
186 E2 Sondaly Rus. Fed.
171 J5 Sønderborg Denmark
179 I3 Sondershausen Germany
184 C1 Sondrio Italy
147 H2 Sonepet India
148 B5 Songad India
155 E4 Songbu China
163 D2 Sông Câu Vietnam
    Sông Cau Vietnam *see* Sông Câu
195 D5 Songea Tanz.
160 D5 Sŏnggan N. Korea
160 D2 Songhua Hu *resr* China
160 C1 Songhuajiang China
158 B1 Songhua Jiang *r.* China
160 E2 Songjiang *Jilin* China
155 F4 Songjiang *Shanghai* China
160 D2 Songjianghe China
155 C4 Songkan China
162 B4 Songkhla Thai.
141 H4 Songköl *l.* Kyrg.
154 F1 Song Ling *mts* China
160 D5 Sŏngnam S. Korea
160 C4 Sŏngnim N. Korea
195 B4 Songo Angola
195 D5 Songo Moz.
154 B3 Songpan China
149 G4 Songsak India
160 D7 Sŏngsan S. Korea
154 D3 Song Shan *mt.* China
160 D3 Songxian China
160 C1 Songyuan China
155 D4 Songzi China
163 D2 Sơn Ha Vietnam
163 D3 Sơn Hai Vietnam
148 D3 Sonipat India
171 N3 Sonkajärvi Fin.
155 B6 Sơn La Vietnam
143 G5 Sonmiani Pak.
143 G5 Sonmiani Bay Pak.
179 J4 Sonneberg Germany
234 D2 Sono *r. Minas Gerais* Brazil
231 I6 Sono *r.* Brazil
215 F6 Sonoita Mex.
215 F6 Sonoita *watercourse* Mex.
215 G6 Sonoita U.S.A.
224 B1 Sonora *r.* Mex.
224 B2 Sonora *state* Mex.
214 B3 Sonora *CA* U.S.A.
217 C6 Sonora *TX* U.S.A.
142 B3 Sonqor Iran
233 I3 Sonsón Col.
225 G5 Sonsonate El Salvador
155 B6 Sơn Tây Vietnam
197 H5 Sonwabile S. Africa
235 L1 Sopas *r.* Uruguay
193 E4 Sopo *watercourse* Sudan
185 K3 Sopot Bulg.
177 I3 Sopot Poland
177 H7 Sopron Hungary
141 H4 Sopu-Korgon Kyrg.
184 E4 Sora Italy
147 J2 Sorada India
171 L3 Söråker Sweden
160 E4 Sŏrak-san *mt.* S. Korea
157 C5 Sorak-san National Park S. Korea
207 H4 Sorel Canada
125 G9 Sorell Australia
125 G9 Sorell Lake Australia
138 E2 Sorgun Turkey

183 O2 Soria Spain
132 C2 Sørkappøya *i.* Svalbard
142 D3 Sorkh, Küh-e *mts* Iran
142 D3 Sorkheh Iran
170 K2 Sørli Norway
171 K4 Sorø Denmark
149 F5 Soro India
187 D5 Soroca Moldova
234 C3 Sorocaba Brazil
140 C1 Sorochinsk Rus. Fed.
141 K1 Sorokino Rus. Fed.
151 G6 Sorol *atoll* Micronesia
151 F7 Sorong Indon.
194 D3 Soroti Uganda
170 M1 Sørøya *i.* Norway
183 L3 Sorraia *r.* Port.
170 L1 Sørreisa Norway
125 J4 Sorrento Australia
184 F4 Sorrento Italy
195 B6 Sorris Sorris Namibia
170 L2 Sorsele Sweden
161 J3 Sorsogon Phil.
186 D2 Sortavala Rus. Fed.
170 K1 Sortland Norway
186 I2 Sortopolovskaya Rus. Fed.
186 I3 Sorvizhi Rus. Fed.
160 D5 Sŏsan S. Korea
197 H2 Soshanguve S. Africa
187 F4 Sosna *r.* Rus. Fed.
235 I2 Sosneado *mt.* Arg.
186 J2 Sosnogorsk Rus. Fed.
141 I2 Sosnovka Kazakh.
186 H2 Sosnovka *Arkhangel'skaya Oblast'* Rus. Fed.
169 K5 Sosnovka *Murmanskaya Oblast'* Rus. Fed.
132 F3 Sosnovka *Tambovskaya Oblast'* Rus. Fed.
187 G4 Sosnovka *Tambovskaya Oblast'* Rus. Fed.
153 J1 Sosnovo-Ozerskoye Rus. Fed.
170 P2 Sosnovyy Rus. Fed.
171 O4 Sosnovyy Bor Rus. Fed.
177 I5 Sosnowiec Poland
187 F6 Sosyka *r.* Rus. Fed.
233 H4 Sotara, Volcán *vol.* Col.
170 O2 Sotkamo Fin.
235 J1 Soto Arg.
225 E3 Soto la Marina Mex.
225 G3 Sotuta Mex.
194 B3 Souanké Congo
192 B4 Soubré Côte d'Ivoire
221 F4 Souderton U.S.A.
185 L4 Soufli Greece
182 E4 Souillac France
178 D5 Souilly France
192 C1 Souk Ahras Alg.
180 B5 Souk el Arbaâ du Rharb Morocco
    Sŏul S. Korea *see* Seoul
183 D5 Soulom France
    Soûr Lebanon *see* Tyre
183 R4 Sour el Ghozlane Alg.
205 I5 Souris *Man.* Canada
207 H4 Souris *P.E.I.* Canada
205 I5 Souris *r.* Canada/U.S.A.
231 K5 Sousa Brazil
193 D1 Sousse Tunisia
183 D5 Soustons France
197 E4 South Africa, Republic of *country* Africa
228 South America
209 G3 Southampton Canada
173 F7 Southampton U.K.
221 G4 Southampton U.S.A.
205 L2 Southampton Island Canada
145 H9 South Andaman *i.* India
221 E6 South Anna *r.* U.S.A.
173 F4 South Anston U.K.
207 H2 South Aulatsivik Island Canada
118 D5 South Australia *state* Australia
238 L7 South Australian Basin *sea feature* Indian Ocean
217 F5 Southaven U.S.A.
213 F5 South Baldy *mt.* U.S.A.
172 F5 South Bank U.K.
220 B4 South Bass Island U.S.A.
209 F3 South Baymouth Canada
208 D5 South Bend *IN* U.S.A.
212 B2 South Bend *WA* U.S.A.
219 E7 South Bight *sea chan.* Bahamas
220 D7 South Boston U.S.A.
126 D5 Southbridge N.Z.
221 G3 Southbridge U.S.A.
    South Cape *pt* U.S.A. *see* Ka Lae
219 D5 South Carolina *state* U.S.A.

221 I2 South China U.S.A.
163 G1 South China Sea Pacific Ocean
216 C2 South Dakota *state* U.S.A.
221 G3 South Deerfield U.S.A.
173 G7 South Downs *hills* U.K.
197 F2 South-East *admin. dist.* Botswana
125 G9 South East Cape Australia
238 J7 Southeast Indian Ridge *sea feature* Indian Ocean
121 C7 South East Isles Australia
237 L10 Southeast Pacific Basin *sea feature* S. Pacific Ocean
205 I3 Southend Canada
174 C5 Southend U.K.
173 H6 Southend-on-Sea U.K.
208 A5 South English U.S.A.
197 E2 Southern *admin. dist.* Botswana
126 C5 Southern Alps *mts* N.Z.
118 B5 Southern Cross Australia
205 J3 Southern Indian Lake Canada
193 E4 Southern National Park Sudan
236 E10 Southern Ocean World
219 E5 Southern Pines U.S.A.
229 G7 Southern Thule S. Sandwich Is.
174 D5 Southern Uplands *hills* U.K.
175 F4 South Esk *r.* U.K.
120 D3 South Esk Tableland *reg.* Australia
208 B6 South Fabius *r.* U.S.A.
236 G7 South Fiji Basin *sea feature* S. Pacific Ocean
213 F4 South Fork U.S.A.
    South Fork South Branch *r.* U.S.A. *see* Potomac, South Fork South Branch
209 E3 South Fox Island U.S.A.
127 J5 South Geomagnetic Pole Antarctica
232 □ South Georgia *terr.* S. Atlantic Ocean
229 G7 South Georgia and the South Sandwich Islands *terr.* Atlantic Ocean
174 A3 South Harris *pen.* U.K.
149 G5 South Hatia Island Bangl.
208 D4 South Haven U.S.A.
205 J2 South Henik Lake Canada
221 G2 South Hero U.S.A.
220 D6 South Hill U.S.A.
236 E3 South Honshu Ridge *sea feature* N. Pacific Ocean
205 J3 South Indian Lake Canada
221 G4 Southington U.S.A.
126 C6 South Island N.Z.
194 D3 South Island National Park Kenya
161 H4 South Islet *rf* Phil.
147 J1 South Koel *r.* India
160 D5 South Korea *country* Asia
214 B2 South Lake Tahoe U.S.A.
195 D5 South Luangwa National Park Zambia
127 J6 South Magnetic Pole Antarctica
208 D3 South Manitou Island U.S.A.
219 D7 South Miami U.S.A.
173 H6 Southminster U.K.
205 I4 South Moose Lake Canada
221 E5 South Mountains U.S.A.
202 F3 South Nahanni *r.* Can.
174 □ South Nesting Bay U.K.
239 G10 South Orkney Islands S. Atlantic Ocean
119 H5 South Pacific Ocean
221 H2 South Paris U.S.A.
213 G3 South Platte *r.* U.S.A.
127 J4 South Pole Antarctica
209 G1 South Porcupine Canada
125 J1 Southport Australia
173 D4 Southport U.K.
221 H3 South Portland U.S.A.
209 H3 South River Canada
175 F2 South Ronaldsay *i.* U.K.
221 G3 South Royalton U.S.A.
197 I5 South Sand Bluff *pt* S. Africa
239 H9 South Sandwich Islands S. Atlantic Ocean
239 H9 South Sandwich Trench *sea feature* S. Atlantic Ocean
205 H4 South Saskatchewan *r.* Canada
205 J3 South Seal *r.* Canada

187 I4 Syzran' Rus. Fed.
176 G4 Szczecin Poland
177 H4 Szczecinek Poland
177 J4 Szczytno Poland
177 J7 Szeged Hungary
177 I7 Székesfehérvár Hungary
177 I7 Szekszárd Hungary
177 J7 Szentes Hungary
177 H7 Szentgotthárd Hungary
185 G1 Szigetvár Hungary
177 J7 Szolnok Hungary
177 H7 Szombathely Hungary

T

161 I3 Taal, Lake Phil.
161 I3 Tabaco Phil.
197 H5 Tabankulu S. Africa
139 G4 Ṭabaqah Syria
119 F2 Tabar Islands P.N.G.
138 E4 Tabarja Lebanon
184 C6 Tabarka Tunisia
143 E3 Ṭabas Iran
225 F4 Tabasco state Mex.
143 E4 Tabāsīn Iran
142 C4 Tābask, Kūh-e mt. Iran
230 E4 Tabatinga Col.
137 F2 Tabatsquri, Tba l. Georgia
161 I2 Tabayoo, Mount Phil.
125 F5 Tabbita Australia
192 B2 Tabelbala Alg.
205 G5 Taber Canada
149 F3 Tabia Tsaka salt l. China
119 H2 Tabiteuea atoll Kiribati
171 N4 Tabivere Estonia
161 I3 Tablas i. Phil.
161 I3 Tablas Strait Phil.
126 F3 Table Cape N.Z.
196 C6 Table Mountain h. S. Africa
217 E4 Table Rock Reservoir U.S.A.
234 A2 Tabocó r. Brazil
176 G6 Tábor Czech Rep.
195 D4 Tabora Tanz.
141 G4 Taboshar Tajik.
192 B4 Tabou Côte d'Ivoire
142 B2 Tabrīz Iran
117 I3 Tabuaeran atoll Kiribati
146 A4 Tabūk Saudi Arabia
125 J2 Tabulam Australia
141 I1 Tabuny Rus. Fed.
119 G3 Tabwémasana, Mount Vanuatu
171 L4 Täby Sweden
225 D4 Tacámbaro Mex.
225 F5 Tacaná, Volcán de vol. Mex.
224 J6 Tacarcuna, Cerro mt. Panama
141 J3 Tacheng China
176 F6 Tachov Czech Rep.
161 J4 Tacloban Phil.
230 D7 Tacna Peru
212 B2 Tacoma U.S.A.
235 L1 Tacuarembó Uruguay
235 M2 Tacuarí r. Uruguay
224 B1 Tacupeto Mex.
233 L4 Tacutu r. Brazil
173 F4 Tadcaster U.K.
192 C2 Tademaït, Plateau du Alg.
119 G4 Tadine New Caledonia
194 E2 Tadjourah Djibouti
139 G4 Tadmur Syria
205 J3 Tadoule Lake Canada
207 G4 Tadoussac Canada
160 D4 T'aebaek-sanmaek mts N. Korea/S. Korea
160 C5 Taech'ŏng-do i. N. Korea
160 C4 Taedasa-do N. Korea
160 D4 Taedong-gang r. N. Korea
160 C5 Taedong-man b. N. Korea
160 E6 Taegu S. Korea
160 C6 Taehŭksan-kundo is S. Korea
160 D5 Taejŏn S. Korea
160 D7 Taejŏng S. Korea
160 E5 T'aepaek S. Korea
150 E2 Ta'erqi China
173 C6 Taf r. U.K.
119 I3 Tafahi i. Tonga
183 P1 Tafalla Spain
192 B4 Tafiré Côte d'Ivoire
232 C3 Tafí Viejo Arg.
142 C3 Tafresh Iran
142 D4 Taft Iran
214 C4 Taft U.S.A.
143 F4 Taftān, Kūh-e mt. Iran
187 F6 Taganrog Rus. Fed.
187 F6 Taganrog, Gulf of Rus. Fed./Ukr.
161 J3 Tagapula i. Phil.

161 I3 Tagaytay City Phil.
161 I4 Tagbilaran Phil.
149 E2 Tagchagpu Ri mt. China
175 L5 Taghmon Ireland
204 C2 Tagish Canada
184 E1 Tagliamento r. Italy
183 S4 Tagma, Col de pass Alg.
161 J4 Tagoloan r. Phil.
161 I4 Tagolo Point Phil.
140 D4 Tagta Turkm.
143 F3 Tagtabazar Turkm.
122 F1 Tagula P.N.G.
119 F3 Tagula Island P.N.G.
161 J5 Tagum Phil.
183 L3 Tagus r. Port./Spain
alt. Tajo (Spain),
alt. Tejo (Portugal)
156 B3 Taha China
204 F4 Tahaetkun Mountain Canada
162 B4 Tahan, Gunung mt. Malaysia
192 C2 Tahat, Mont mt. Alg.
150 E1 Tahe China
126 D1 Taheke N.Z.
117 I5 Tahiti i. Fr. Polynesia
143 F4 Tahlab r. Iran/Pak.
143 F4 Tahlab, Dasht-i- plain Pak.
217 E5 Tahlequah U.S.A.
214 B2 Tahoe, Lake U.S.A.
214 B2 Tahoe City U.S.A.
203 H3 Tahoe Lake Canada
217 C5 Tahoka U.S.A.
192 C3 Tahoua Niger
204 D4 Tahtsa Peak Canada
204 D4 Tahuna Indon.
161 J6 Tahuna Indon.
192 B4 Taï, Parc National de nat. park Côte d'Ivoire
155 □ Tai A Chau Hong Kong China
160 B3 Tai'an Liaoning China
154 E2 Tai'an Shandong China
154 C3 Taibai Shan mt. China
160 A5 Taibo Ding h. China
155 F5 T'aichung Taiwan
126 C6 Taieri r. N.Z.
154 D2 Taigu China
153 J4 Taihang Shan mts China
154 D2 Taihang Shan mts China
126 E3 Taihape N.Z.
154 E3 Taihe Anhui China
155 E5 Taihe Jiangxi China
155 E4 Taihu China
150 E3 Tai Hu l. China
155 C5 Taijiang China
156 B3 Taikang China
154 E3 Taikang China
156 A3 Tailai China
Tai Lam Chung Res. China see Tai Lam Chung Shui Tong
155 □ Tai Lam Chung Shui Tong resr Hong Kong China
124 C5 Tailem Bend Australia
Tai Long Bay China see Tai Long Wan
155 □ Tai Long Wan b. Hong Kong China
155 F5 T'ailuko Taiwan
143 F3 Taimani reg. Afgh.
155 □ Tai Mo Shan h. Hong Kong China
155 F6 T'ainan Taiwan
185 J6 Tainaro, Akrotirio pt Greece
155 E5 Taining China
155 □ Tai O Hong Kong China
234 D1 Taiobeiras Brazil
155 F5 T'aipei Taiwan
155 D6 Taiping China
163 B2 Taiping Malaysia
160 B1 Taipingchuan China
154 A2 Taipingpu China
155 □ Tai Po Hong Kong China
Tai Po Hoi b. Hong Kong China see Tolo Harbour
159 C7 Taisha Japan
155 D6 Taishan China
155 F5 Taishun China
Tai Siu Mo To is Hong Kong China see Brothers, The
178 C5 Taissy France
126 D5 Taitanu N.Z.
232 B7 Taitao, Península de pen. Chile
155 F6 T'aitung Taiwan
170 O2 Taivalkoski Fin.
170 N1 Taivaskero h. Fin.
155 F6 Taiwan country Asia
155 F5 Taiwan Strait China/Taiwan
154 F3 Taixing China
154 D2 Taiyuan China

154 D2 Taiyue Shan mts China
154 F3 Taizhou Jiangsu China
155 F4 Taizhou Zhejiang China
155 F4 Taizhou Wan b. China
160 C3 Taizi He r. China
146 B7 Ta'izz Yemen
148 B4 Tajal Pak.
225 G5 Tajamulco, Volcán de vol. Guat.
184 C7 Tajerouine Tunisia
141 G5 Tajikistan country Asia
148 D4 Taj Mahal tourist site India
183 M3 Tajo r. Spain
alt. Tejo (Portugal),
conv. Tagus
162 A1 Tak Thai.
142 B2 Takāb Iran
159 C7 Takahashi Japan
126 D4 Takaka N.Z.
148 D5 Takal India
159 D7 Takamatsu Japan
159 E6 Takaoka Japan
126 F4 Takapau N.Z.
126 E2 Takapuna N.Z.
159 F6 Takasaki Japan
197 F2 Takatokwane Botswana
196 D1 Takatshwaane Botswana
159 C8 Takatsuki-yama mt. Japan
159 E6 Takayama Japan
141 G4 Takelí Tajik.
159 B8 Takeo Japan
162 C3 Takeo Cambodia
159 E7 Takefu Japan
141 G4 Takelí Tajik.
159 B8 Takeo Japan
162 C3 Takêv Cambodia
139 J7 Takhādīd well Iraq
162 C3 Ta Khmau Cambodia
141 F1 Takhtabrod Kazakh.
Takhtakupyr Uzbek. see Taxtako'pir
139 L5 Takht Apān, Kūh-e mt. Iran
143 G4 Takhteh Pol Afgh.
142 C2 Takht-e Soleymān mt. Iran
139 K3 Takht-e Soleymān tourist site Iran
148 B2 Takht-i-Bahi tourist site Pak.
148 B3 Takht-i-Sulaiman mt. Pak.
Takht-i-Suleiman mt. Iran see Takht-e Soleymān
158 G3 Takikawa Japan
158 H2 Takinoue Japan
126 A6 Takitimu Mountains N.Z.
204 D3 Takla Lake Canada
204 D3 Takla Landing Canada
135 G3 Taklimakan Desert China
Taklimakan Shamo des. China see Taklimakan Desert
141 G5 Takob Tajik.
149 H3 Takpa Shiri mt. China
204 C3 Taku r. Canada
162 A3 Takua Pa Thai.
192 C4 Takum Nigeria
119 F2 Takuu Islands atoll P.N.G.
235 L2 Tala Uruguay
187 D4 Talachyn Belarus
147 H4 Talaimannar Sri Lanka
148 C5 Talaja India
156 C2 Talakan Amurskaya Oblast' Rus. Fed.
156 D2 Talakan Khabarovskiy Kray Rus. Fed.
235 I1 Talampaya, Parque Nacional nat. park Arg.
154 D2 Talandzha Rus. Fed.
149 H4 Talap India
230 B4 Talara Peru
Talar-i-Band mts Pak. see Makran Coast Range
141 G4 Talas Kyrg.
141 H4 Talas Kyrg.
141 G4 Talas Ala-Too mts Kyrg.
151 E6 Talaud, Kepulauan is Indon.
183 N3 Talavera de la Reina Spain
133 Q3 Talaya Rus. Fed.
161 J5 Talayan Phil.
121 D5 Talbot, Mount h. Australia
203 K2 Talbot Inlet Canada
125 H4 Talbragar r. Australia
235 H2 Talca Chile
235 H3 Talcahuano Chile
147 J1 Talcher India
156 B1 Taldan Rus. Fed.
169 N4 Taldom Rus. Fed.
140 D4 Taldyk Uzbek.
141 I3 Taldykorgan Kazakh.
141 I3 Taldykorganskaya Oblast' Kazakh.
141 G2 Taldysay Kazakh.

141 I4 Taldy-Suu Kyrg.
139 L5 Taleh Zang Iran
142 C2 Tālesh Iran
141 I4 Talgar Kazakh.
173 D6 Talgarth U.K.
124 A4 Talia Australia
151 E7 Taliabu i. Indon.
161 J4 Talibon Phil.
147 H2 Talikota India
Talimardzhan Uzbek. see Tollimarjon
139 I1 T'alin Armenia
156 B3 Talin Hiag China
147 G3 Taliparamba India
161 I4 Talisay Phil.
161 J4 Talisayan Phil.
139 L2 Talış Dağları mts Azer./Iran
186 H3 Talitsa Rus. Fed.
163 I4 Taliwang Indon.
121 F6 Tallacootra, Lake salt flat Australia
219 C5 Talladega U.S.A.
139 I3 Tall 'Afar Iraq
219 C6 Tallahassee U.S.A.
125 G6 Tallangatta Australia
219 C5 Tallassee U.S.A.
139 H3 Tall Baydar Syria
139 I3 Tall Kayf Iraq
139 I3 Tall Kūjik Syria
175 J5 Tallow Ireland
217 F5 Tallulah U.S.A.
139 I3 Tall 'Uwaynāt Iraq
182 D3 Talmont-St-Hilaire France
187 D5 Tal'ne Ukr.
193 F3 Talodi Sudan
207 G2 Talon, Lac l. Canada
143 H2 Tāloqān Afgh.
140 B2 Talovaya Kazakh.
187 G5 Talovaya Rus. Fed.
203 I3 Taloyoak Canada
148 C2 Tal Pass Pak.
171 M4 Talsi Latvia
143 F4 Tal Sīyāh Iran
232 B3 Taltal Chile
205 G2 Taltson r. Canada
142 B3 Talvār, Rūdkhāneh-ye r. Iran
170 M1 Talvik Norway
125 H2 Talwood Australia
187 G5 Taly Rus. Fed.
125 E4 Talyawalka r. Australia
208 A4 Tama U.S.A.
121 A5 Tamala Australia
233 I2 Tamalameque Col.
192 B4 Tamale Ghana
233 H3 Tamana mt. Col.
119 H2 Tamana i. Kiribati
159 C7 Tamano Japan
192 C2 Tamanrasset Alg.
149 H4 Tamanthi Myanmar
221 F4 Tamaqua U.S.A.
173 C7 Tamar r. U.K.
197 G1 Tamasane Botswana
225 E2 Tamaulipas state Mex.
225 E3 Tamazula Mex.
225 E4 Tamazulápam Mex.
225 E3 Tamazunchale Mex.
194 D3 Tambach Kenya
147 H4 Tambacounda Senegal
149 F4 Tamba Kosi r. Nepal
163 G2 Tambelan, Kepulauan is Indon.
161 H5 Tambisan Sabah Malaysia
125 G6 Tambo r. Australia
163 I4 Tambora, Gunung vol. Indon.
125 G6 Tamboritha mt. Australia
187 G4 Tambov Rus. Fed.
156 C2 Tambovka Rus. Fed.
187 G4 Tambovskaya Oblast' admin. div. Rus. Fed.
183 L1 Tambre r. Spain
161 H5 Tambulanan, Bukit h. Sabah Malaysia
193 E4 Tambura Sudan
161 H5 Tambuyukon, Gunung mt. Sabah Malaysia
192 A3 Tâmchekkeṭ Mauritania
140 D2 Tamdy Kazakh.
Tamdybulak Uzbek. see Tomdibuloq
233 J3 Tame Col.
183 M2 Tâmega r. Port.
149 H4 Tamenglong India
184 B7 Tamerza Tunisia
148 D5 Tamia India
225 E4 Tamiahua Mex.
225 E3 Tamiahua, Laguna de lag. Mex.
162 A4 Tamiang, Ujung pt Indon.
147 H4 Tamil Nadu state India

186 F1 Tamitsa Rus. Fed.
138 C7 Ṭāmiyah Egypt
140 E2 Tamkamys Kazakh.
149 F4 Tamkuhi India
163 D2 Tam Ky Vietnam
219 D7 Tampa U.S.A.
219 D7 Tampa Bay U.S.A.
171 M3 Tampere Fin.
225 E3 Tampico Mex.
162 □ Tampines Sing.
150 D2 Tamsagbulag Mongolia
154 B1 Tamsag Muchang China
176 F7 Tamsweg Austria
149 H4 Tamu Myanmar
225 E3 Tamuín Mex.
149 F4 Tamur r. Nepal
125 I3 Tamworth Australia
173 F5 Tamworth U.K.
141 I2 Tan Kazakh.
195 D4 Tana r. Kenya
159 D8 Tanabe Japan
170 O1 Tana Bru Norway
170 O1 Tanafjorden inlet Norway
163 G4 Tanah, Tanjung pt Indon.
163 I3 Tanahgrogot Indon.
151 E7 Tanahjampea i. Indon.
163 I3 Tanahmasa i. Indon.
161 H6 Tanahmerah Indon.
162 B4 Tanah Merah Malaysia
162 B4 Tanah Rata Malaysia
194 D2 Tana, Lake l. Eth.
120 E3 Tanami Australia
118 D3 Tanami Desert Australia
162 C3 Tân An Vietnam
202 C3 Tanana U.S.A.
184 C2 Tanana r. Italy
161 J4 Tanauan Phil.
154 F3 Tancheng China
160 E3 Tanch'ŏn N. Korea
225 D4 Tancítaro, Cerro de mt. Mex.
192 B4 Tanda Côte d'Ivoire
149 E4 Tanda India
161 J4 Tandag Phil.
185 L2 Ţāndārei Romania
161 H5 Tandek Sabah Malaysia
148 D2 Tandi India
235 K3 Tandil Arg.
235 K3 Tandil, Sierra del hills Arg.
148 B4 Tando Adam Pak.
148 B4 Tando Bago Pak.
125 E4 Tandou Lake imp. l. Australia
175 L3 Tandragee U.K.
147 H2 Tandur India
126 F3 Taneatua N.Z.
159 B9 Tanega-shima i. Japan
162 A1 Tanen Taunggyi mts Thai.
221 E5 Taneytown U.S.A.
192 B2 Tanezrouft reg. Alg./Mali
195 D4 Tanga Tanz.
126 E2 Tangaehe N.Z.
149 G4 Tangail Bangl.
119 F2 Tanga Islands P.N.G.
147 I5 Tangalla Sri Lanka
195 C4 Tanganyika, Lake Africa
142 D2 Tangar Iran
147 H4 Tangasseri India
155 B5 Tangdan China
142 D4 Tang-e Kalleh Iran
140 C5 Tangeli Iran
Tanger Morocco see Tangier
163 G4 Tangerang Indon.
179 J2 Tangerhütte Germany
179 J2 Tangermünde Germany
143 E2 Tang-e Sarkheh Iran
154 B3 Tanggor China
149 H2 Tanggulashan China
152 F5 Tanggula Shan mt. China
149 G2 Tanggula Shan mts China
149 G2 Tanggula Shankou pass China
154 D3 Tanghe China
148 B2 Tangi Pak.
192 B1 Tangier Morocco
221 E6 Tangier Island U.S.A.
149 G4 Tangla India
162 □ Tanglin Sing.
149 H3 Tangmai China
123 D4 Tangorin Australia
149 F3 Tangra Yumco salt l. China
154 F2 Tangshan China
161 I4 Tangub Phil.
192 C3 Tanguieta Benin
156 C2 Tangwanghe China
158 A1 Tangyan He r. China
154 E3 Tangyin China
158 A1 Tangyuan China
170 N2 Tanhua Fin.
162 C3 Tani Cambodia
163 I2 Tarakan Indon.

149 H3 Taniantaweng Shan mts China
151 F7 Tanimbar, Kepulauan is Indon.
161 I4 Tanjay Phil.
162 A5 Tanjungbalai Indon.
Tanjungkarang-Telukbetung Indon. see Bandar Lampung
163 G3 Tanjungpandan Indon.
163 B2 Tanjungpinang Indon.
162 A5 Tanjungpura Indon.
163 I2 Tanjungredeb Indon.
163 I2 Tanjungselor Indon.
148 B2 Tank Pak.
148 D2 Tanktse India
196 C6 Tankwa-Karoo National Park S. Africa
119 G3 Tanna i. Vanuatu
175 F4 Tannadice U.K.
171 K3 Tännäs Sweden
150 B1 Tannu-Ola, Khrebet mts Rus. Fed.
161 I4 Tañon Strait Phil.
148 B4 Tanot India
192 C3 Tanout Niger
149 E4 Tansen Nepal
155 F5 Tanshui Taiwan
141 I3 Tansyk Kazakh.
193 F1 Ṭanṭā Egypt
192 A2 Tan-Tan Morocco
124 D6 Tantanoola Australia
225 E3 Tantoyuca Mex.
147 I2 Tanuku India
120 F3 Tanumbirini Australia
171 J4 Tanumshede Sweden
124 C5 Tanunda Australia
160 E5 Tanyang S. Korea
195 D4 Tanzania country Africa
162 A3 Tao, Ko i. Thai.
160 B1 Tao'er He r. China
154 B3 Tao He r. China
155 D4 Taojiang China
154 C2 Taole China
160 B1 Taonan China
236 M4 Taongi atoll Marshall Is
213 F4 Taos U.S.A.
192 B2 Taoudenni Mali
180 C5 Taounate Morocco
192 B1 Taourirt Morocco
155 F5 Taoxi China
155 D4 Taoyuan China
155 F5 T'aoyüan Taiwan
171 N4 Tapa Estonia
161 I5 Tapaan Passage Phil.
225 F5 Tapachula Mex.
231 G4 Tapajós r. Brazil
163 F2 Tapaktuan Indon.
235 K3 Tapalqué Arg.
225 F4 Tapanatepec Mex.
162 A5 Tapanuli, Teluk b. Indon.
231 F5 Tapauá Brazil
230 E5 Tapauá r. Brazil
192 B4 Tapeta Liberia
148 C5 Tapi r. India
162 A3 Ta Pi, Mae Nam r. Thai.
161 I5 Tapiantana i. Phil.
208 C2 Tapiola U.S.A.
162 B4 Tapis, Gunung mt. Malaysia
149 F4 Taplejung Nepal
155 □ Tap Mun Chau i. Hong Kong China
221 E6 Tappahannock U.S.A.
220 C4 Tappan Lake U.S.A.
142 C3 Tappeh, Kūh-e mt. Iran
126 D4 Tapuaenuku mt. N.Z.
161 I5 Tapul Phil.
161 I5 Tapul Group is Phil.
233 K5 Tapurucuara Brazil
139 J4 Ṭaqṭaq Iraq
234 B1 Taquaral, Serra do hills Brazil
Taquari Brazil see Alto Taquari
231 G7 Taquari r. Brazil
234 A2 Taquari, Pantanal do marsh Brazil
234 A2 Taquari, Serra do hills Brazil
234 C3 Taquaritinga Brazil
234 B3 Taquaruçu r. Brazil
175 K5 Tar r. Ireland
125 I1 Tara Australia
175 L4 Tara, Hill of Ireland
193 D4 Taraba r. Nigeria
230 E7 Tarabuco Bol.
Ṭarābulus Libya see Tripoli
233 J4 Taracua Brazil
148 B4 Tar Ahmad Rind Pak.
149 E4 Tarahuwan India
149 G4 Tarai reg. India
163 I2 Tarakan Indon.

141 I5	Tiznap He *r.* China
192 B2	Tiznit Morocco
225 D2	Tizoc Mex.
197 I2	Tjaneni Swaziland
170 L2	Tjåppsåive Sweden
178 D2	Tjeukemeer *l.* Neth.
171 I4	Tjørhom Norway
225 E4	Tlacolula Mex.
225 F4	Tlacotalpán Mex.
225 D2	Tlahualilo Mex.
225 E4	Tlalnepantla Mex.
225 E4	Tlapa Mex.
225 D3	Tlaquepaque Mex.
225 E4	Tlaxcala Mex.
225 E4	Tlaxcala *state* Mex.
225 E4	Tlaxiaco Mex.
192 B1	Tlemcen Alg.
197 E4	Tlhakalatlou S. Africa
197 H4	Tlholong S. Africa
197 F2	Tlokweng Botswana
137 G2	Tlyarata Rus. Fed.
162 C3	Tnaôt, Prêk *l.* Cambodia
204 D3	Toad River Canada
195 E5	Toamasina Madag.
162 □	Toa Payoh Sing.
235 J3	Toay Arg.
162 A5	Toba Japan
162 A5	Toba, Danau *l.* Indon.
148 A3	Toba and Kakar Ranges *mts* Pak.
231 F1	Tobago *i.* Trin. and Tob.
	Tobar an Choire Ireland *see* Tobercurry
151 E6	Tobelo Indon.
175 J3	Tobercurry Ireland
123 B4	Tobermorey Australia
123 C5	Tobermory Australia
209 G3	Tobermory Canada
174 B4	Tobermory U.K.
121 D4	Tobin, Lake *salt flat* Australia
215 D1	Tobin, Mount U.S.A.
205 I4	Tobin Lake Canada
221 J1	Tobique *r.* Canada
159 F5	Tobi-shima *i.* Japan
163 G3	Toboali Indon.
140 E1	Tobol Kazakh.
132 H4	Tobol *r.* Kazakh./Rus. Fed.
	Tô Bong Vietnam *see* Hai Triêu
169 Q2	Tobseda Rus. Fed.
231 I5	Tocantinópolis Brazil
231 I4	Tocantins *r.* Brazil
234 C1	Tocantinzinha *r.* Brazil
219 D5	Toccoa U.S.A.
148 B2	Tochi *r.* Pak.
171 J4	Töcksfors Sweden
232 B2	Tocopilla Chile
125 F5	Tocumwal Australia
233 J2	Tocuyo *r.* Venez.
123 A5	Todd *watercourse* Australia
184 E3	Todi Italy
176 D7	Todi *mt.* Switz.
141 J3	Todog China
159 H5	Todoga-saki *pt* Japan
158 G4	Todohokke Japan
230 E7	Todos Santos Bol.
224 B3	Todos Santos Mex.
215 D6	Todos Santos, Bahía de *b.* Mex.
205 G4	Tofield Canada
204 D5	Tofino Canada
174 □	Toft U.K.
208 B2	Tofte U.S.A.
119 I3	Tofua *i.* Tonga
151 E7	Togian, Kepulauan *is* Indon.
192 C4	Togo *country* Africa
225 A2	Togo U.S.A.
154 D1	Togrog Ul China
154 D1	Togtoh China
149 H2	Togton He *r.* China
140 E3	Toguz Kazakh.
215 H4	Tohatchi U.S.A.
171 N3	Toholampi Fin.
154 B1	Tohom China
149 G3	Toiba China
171 M3	Toijala Fin.
159 B9	Toi-misaki *pt* Japan
171 N3	Toivakka Fin.
215 D2	Toiyabe Range *mts* U.S.A.
141 G5	Tojikobod Tajik.
140 C1	Tok *r.* Rus. Fed.
202 D3	Tok U.S.A.
159 F6	Tōkamachi Japan
126 B7	Tokanui N.Z.
193 F3	Tokar Sudan
151 E4	Tokara-rettō *is* Japan
141 H4	Tokarevka Kazakh.
139 F1	Tokat Turkey
160 D5	Tŏkch'ŏk-to *i.* S. Korea
160 D4	Tŏkch'ŏn N. Korea

119 I2	Tokelau *terr.* Pacific Ocean
187 E6	Tokmak Ukr.
141 H4	Tokmok Kyrg.
127 G3	Tokomaru Bay N.Z.
126 E3	Tokoroa N.Z.
197 H3	Tokoza S. Africa
133 J5	Toksun China
141 H4	Toktogul Kyrg.
141 H4	Toktogul Suu Saktagychy *resr* Kyrg.
141 J3	Tokty Kazakh.
156 D1	Tokur Rus. Fed.
159 D7	Tokushima Japan
159 B7	Tokuyama Japan
159 F7	Tōkyō Japan (City Plan 94)
159 F7	Tōkyō-wan *b.* Japan
143 G3	Tokzār Afgh.
127 G3	Tolaga Bay N.Z.
195 E6	Tôlañaro Madag.
140 C1	Tolbazy Rus. Fed.
144 H2	Tolbo Mongolia
156 B1	Tolbuzino Rus. Fed.
224 I6	Tolé Panama
225 E3	Toleant *tourist site* Mex.
141 H4	Tole Bi Kazakh.
235 B4	Toledo Brazil
183 N3	Toledo Spain
208 A5	Toledo *IA* U.S.A.
220 B4	Toledo *OH* U.S.A.
183 N3	Toledo, Montes de *mts* Spain
217 E6	Toledo Bend Reservoir U.S.A.
235 H3	Tolhuaca, Parque Nacional *nat. park* Chile
141 J3	Toli China
195 E6	Toliara Madag.
233 I3	Tolima, Nevado del *vol.* Col.
151 E6	Tolitoli Indon.
133 J3	Tol'ka Rus. Fed.
179 L1	Tollensee *l.* Germany
141 F5	Tollimarjon Uzbek.
186 D3	Tolmachevo Rus. Fed.
184 E1	Tolmezzo Italy
155 □	Tolo Channel Hong Kong China
155 □	Tolo Harbour *b.* Hong Kong China
183 O1	Tolosa Spain
160 D6	Tolsan-do *i.* S. Korea
209 F3	Tolsmaville Canada
174 B2	Tolsta Head U.K.
233 I2	Tolú Col.
225 E4	Toluca Mex.
170 O2	Tolvand, Ozero *l.* Rus. Fed.
187 I4	Tol'yatti Rus. Fed.
140 E2	Tolybay Kazakh.
156 B2	Tom' *r.* Rus. Fed.
208 B4	Tomah U.S.A.
208 C3	Tomahawk U.S.A.
158 G3	Tomakomai Japan
158 G2	Tomamae Japan
119 H3	Tomanivi *mt.* Fiji
233 L5	Tomar Brazil
183 L3	Tomar Port.
156 F3	Tomari Rus. Fed.
138 E2	Tomarza Turkey
235 L1	Tomás Gomensoro Uruguay
177 K5	Tomaszów Lubelski Poland
177 J5	Tomaszów Mazowiecki Poland
174 E3	Tomatin U.K.
224 C4	Tomatlán Mex.
219 B6	Tombigbee *r.* U.S.A.
195 B4	Tomboco Angola
234 D3	Tombos Brazil
	Tombouctou Mali *see* Timbuktu
215 G6	Tombstone U.S.A.
195 B5	Tombua Angola
197 H1	Tom Burke S. Africa
141 F4	Tomdibuloq Uzbek.
235 H2	Tomé Chile
197 K1	Tome Moz.
171 K5	Tomelilla Sweden
183 O3	Tomelloso Spain
141 F4	Tomenaryk Kazakh.
209 H2	Tomiko Canada
125 H4	Tomingley Australia
151 E7	Tomini, Teluk *g.* Indon.
192 B3	Tominian Mali
174 E3	Tomintoul U.K.
185 G3	Tomislavgrad Bos.-Herz.
121 E5	Tomkinson Ranges *mts* Australia
170 K2	Tømmerneset Norway
133 N4	Tommot Rus. Fed.
233 J4	Tomo Col.
233 J3	Tomo *r.* Col.
154 D1	Tomortei China

133 O3	Tompo Rus. Fed.
118 B4	Tom Price Australia
150 A1	Tomsk Rus. Fed.
171 K4	Tomtabacken *h.* Sweden
133 P3	Tomtor Rus. Fed.
158 H3	Tomuraushi-yama *mt.* Japan
187 G6	Tomuzlovka *r.* Rus. Fed.
225 F4	Tonalá Mex.
215 G3	Tonalea U.S.A.
230 E4	Tonantins Brazil
212 C1	Tonasket U.S.A.
173 H6	Tonbridge U.K.
151 E6	Tondano Indon.
171 J5	Tønder Denmark
145 E10	Tondi India
173 E6	Tone *r.* U.K.
119 I4	Tonga *country* Pacific Ocean
197 I4	Tongaat S. Africa
125 F6	Tongala Australia
155 F5	Tong'an China
126 E3	Tongariro National Park N.Z.
119 I4	Tongatapu Group *is* Tonga
237 H7	Tonga Trench *sea feature* S. Pacific Ocean
154 D3	Tongbai China
154 D3	Tongbai Shan *mts* China
155 E4	Tongcheng *Anhui* China
155 D4	Tongcheng *Hubei* China
160 D4	T'ongch'ŏn N. Korea
154 C3	Tongchuan China
155 C5	Tongdao China
154 A3	Tongde China
160 D5	Tongduch'ŏn S. Korea
178 D4	Tongeren Belgium
155 E4	Tonggu China
155 D7	Tonggu Zui *pt* China
160 E5	Tonghae S. Korea
155 B5	Tonghai China
158 A2	Tonghe China
160 C3	Tonghua *Jilin* China
160 C3	Tonghua *Jilin* China
156 D3	Tongjiang China
155 C4	Tongjiang China
160 B2	Tongjiangkou China
160 D4	Tongjosŏn-man *b.* N. Korea
155 C6	Tongking, Gulf of China/Vietnam
155 C4	Tongliang China
160 B2	Tongliao China
155 C4	Tongling China
155 F4	Tonglu China
160 E6	Tongnae S. Korea
155 B4	Tongnan China
125 E3	Tongo Australia
125 E3	Tongo Lake *salt flat* Australia
161 I5	Tongquil *i.* Phil.
155 C5	Tongren *Guizhou* China
154 A3	Tongren *Qinghai* China
155 E4	Tongshan *Hubei* China
	Tongshan China *see* Xuzhou
	Tongshi China *see* Wuzhishan
	Tongtian He *r.* China *see* Yangtze
174 D2	Tongue U.K.
212 F2	Tongue *r.* U.S.A.
219 E7	Tongue of the Ocean *sea chan.* Bahamas
154 B3	Tongwei China
154 B2	Tongxin China
155 E4	Tongyanghe China
160 E6	T'ongyŏng S. Korea
160 B1	Tongyu China
160 B3	Tongyuanpu China
154 E2	Tongzhou *Beijing* China
154 F3	Tongzhou *Jiangsu* China
155 C4	Tongzi China
208 C5	Tonica U.S.A.
224 B1	Tónichi Mex.
148 C4	Tonk India
142 C2	Tonkābon Iran
155 B6	Tonkin *reg.* Vietnam
186 H3	Tonkino Rus. Fed.
162 C2	Tônle Repou *r.* Laos
	Tônlé Sab *l.* Cambodia *see* Tonle Sap
162 B2	Tonle Sap *l.* Cambodia
159 G5	Tōno Japan
215 D2	Tonopah U.S.A.
233 L2	Tonoro *r.* Venez.
195 C6	Tonota Botswana
148 D3	Tons *r.* India
171 J4	Tønsberg Norway
171 I4	Tonstad Norway
215 G5	Tonto National Monument *nat. park* U.S.A.
149 H5	Tonzang Myanmar
125 H2	Toobeah Australia

213 D3	Tooele U.S.A.
125 J1	Toogoolawah Australia
125 E5	Tooleybuc Australia
124 A4	Tooligie Australia
125 H6	Tooma *r.* Australia
125 D5	Toompine Australia
125 G7	Toora Australia
125 H3	Tooraweenah Australia
197 F6	Toorberg *mt.* S. Africa
125 I1	Toowoomba Australia
215 G6	Topawa U.S.A.
214 C2	Topaz U.S.A.
141 J1	Topchikha Rus. Fed.
217 E4	Topeka U.S.A.
224 C2	Topia Mex.
204 D4	Topley Landing Canada
179 K2	Töplitz Germany
235 H2	Topocalma, Punta *pt* Chile
215 E4	Topock U.S.A.
177 I6	Topol'čany Slovakia
140 B3	Topoli Kazakh.
224 B2	Topolobampo Mex.
185 L3	Topolovgrad Bulg.
170 P2	Topozero, Ozero *l.* Rus. Fed.
212 B2	Toppenish U.S.A.
221 J2	Topsfield U.S.A.
215 F3	Toquerville U.S.A.
194 D3	Tor Eth.
185 L5	Torbalı Turkey
143 E3	Torbat-e Heydarīyeh Iran
143 F3	Torbat-e Jām Iran
121 B7	Torbay Bay Australia
187 G4	Torbeyevo Rus. Fed.
209 E3	Torch Lake U.S.A.
183 N2	Tordesillas Spain
170 M2	Töre Sweden
183 R1	Torelló Spain
178 D2	Torenberg *h.* Neth.
179 K3	Torgau Germany
187 H5	Torgun *r.* Rus. Fed.
178 B3	Torhout Belgium
	Torino Italy *see* Turin
159 G9	Tori-shima *i.* Japan
193 F4	Torit Sudan
234 B2	Torixoréu Brazil
	Torixoreu Brazil *see* Torixoréu
139 K3	Torkamān Iran
143 F3	Torkestān, Band-e *mts* Afgh.
186 G3	Tor'kovskoye Vodokhranilishche *resr* Rus. Fed.
183 N2	Tormes *r.* Spain
170 M2	Torneälven *r.* Fin./Sweden
170 L1	Torneträsk Sweden
170 L1	Torneträsk *l.* Sweden
207 H2	Torngat Mountains Canada
207 H2	Torngat Mountains National Park Reserve Can.
170 N2	Tornio Fin.
235 J3	Tornquist Arg.
183 N2	Toro Spain
225 D2	Toro, Pico del *mt.* Mex.
156 D1	Torom Rus. Fed.
150 F1	Torom *r.* Rus. Fed.
125 I4	Toronto Australia
209 H4	Toronto Canada (City Plan 103)
215 D5	Toro Peak U.S.A.
186 D3	Toropets Rus. Fed.
194 D3	Tororo Uganda
	Toros Dağları *mts* Turkey *see* Taurus Mountains
175 F3	Torphins U.K.
173 D7	Torquay U.K.
214 C5	Torrance U.S.A.
183 L3	Torrão Port.
183 M2	Torre *mt.* Port.
183 Q2	Torreblanca Spain
183 N1	Torrecerredo *mt.* Spain
184 F4	Torre del Greco Italy
183 N1	Torrelavega Spain
183 N4	Torremolinos Spain
124 B3	Torrens, Lake *imp. l.* Australia
123 D4	Torrens Creek Australia
183 P3	Torrent Spain
225 D2	Torreón Mex.
224 B1	Torres Mex.
119 G3	Torres Islands Vanuatu
183 L3	Torres Novas Port.
119 E2	Torres Strait Australia
183 L3	Torres Vedras Port.
183 P4	Torrevieja Spain
215 G2	Torrey U.S.A.
173 C7	Torridge *r.* U.K.
174 C3	Torridon, Loch *b.* U.K.
183 N3	Torrijos Spain
125 I2	Torrington Australia
221 G4	Torrington *CT* U.S.A.
213 F3	Torrington *WY* U.S.A.

183 R1	Torroella de Montgrí Spain
171 K3	Torsby Sweden
170 □	Tórshavn Faroe Is
141 G4	Tortkol' Kazakh.
140 E4	To'rtko'l Uzbek.
141 H2	Tortkuduk Kazakh.
184 C5	Tortolì *Sardinia* Italy
184 C2	Tortona Italy
183 Q2	Tortosa Spain
224 I6	Tortuguero, Parque Nacional *nat. park* Costa Rica
139 H1	Tortum Turkey
141 I4	Toru-Aygyr Kyrg.
142 D3	Ţorūd Iran
139 G1	Torul Turkey
177 I4	Toruń Poland
175 J2	Tory Island Ireland
175 J2	Tory Sound *sea chan.* Ireland
186 E3	Torzhok Rus. Fed.
159 C8	Tosa Japan
159 C8	Tosashimizu Japan
170 K2	Tosbotn Norway
197 E2	Tosca S. Africa
184 C3	Toscano, Arcipelago *is* Italy
158 G4	Tōshima-yama *mt.* Japan
141 G4	Toshkent Uzbek.
186 D3	Tosno Rus. Fed.
232 D3	Tostado Arg.
179 H1	Tostedt Germany
159 B8	Tosu Japan
138 E1	Tosya Turkey
186 G3	Tot'ma Rus. Fed.
225 E4	Totolapan Mex.
140 C1	Totskoye Rus. Fed.
173 F7	Totton U.K.
159 D7	Tottori Japan
192 B4	Touba Côte d'Ivoire
192 A3	Touba Senegal
192 B1	Toubkal, Jbel *mt.* Morocco
154 B2	Toudaohu China
192 B3	Tougan Burkina
192 C1	Touggourt Alg.
192 A3	Tougué Guinea
182 G2	Toul France
155 F6	Touliu Taiwan
183 G5	Toulon France
183 E5	Toulouse France
192 B4	Toumodi Côte d'Ivoire
192 B2	Tounassine, Hamada *des.* Alg.
	Toungoo Myanmar *see* Taung-ngu
155 D5	Toupai China
162 B1	Tourakom Laos
178 B4	Tourcoing France
178 B4	Tournai Belgium
182 G4	Tournon-sur-Rhône France
182 G3	Tournus France
231 K5	Touros Brazil
182 E3	Tours France
156 B3	Toutai China
196 D6	Touwsrivier S. Africa
179 K4	Toužim Czech Rep.
233 J2	Tovar Venez.
173 F5	Tove *r.* U.K.
139 J1	Tovuz Azer.
158 G4	Towada Japan
159 G5	Towada-Hachimantai Kokuritsu-kōen *nat. park* Japan
158 G4	Towada-ko *l.* Japan
126 E1	Towai N.Z.
221 E4	Towanda U.S.A.
215 H3	Towaoc U.S.A.
173 G5	Towcester U.K.
175 J6	Tower Ireland
208 A2	Tower U.S.A.
205 I5	Towner U.S.A.
215 D3	Townes Pass U.S.A.
212 E2	Townsend U.S.A.
125 H6	Townsend, Mount Australia
123 E4	Townshend Island Australia
119 E3	Townsville Australia
151 E7	Towori, Teluk *b.* Indon.
221 E5	Towson U.S.A.
141 I4	Toxkan He *r.* China
158 G3	Tōya-ko *l.* Japan
159 E6	Toyama Japan
159 E6	Toyama-wan *b.* Japan
159 E7	Toyohashi Japan
159 E7	Toyokawa Japan
159 D7	Toyonaka Japan
159 D7	Toyooka Japan
159 E7	Toyota Japan
141 G4	Toytepa Uzbek.
	Toytepa Uzbek. *see* To'ytepa
192 C1	Tozeur Tunisia
187 G7	Tozkhurmato Georgia
187 G7	Tqvarch'eli Georgia
179 F5	Traben Germany

185 J4	Trâblous Lebanon *see* Tripoli
139 G1	Trabotivište Macedonia
221 J2	Trabzon Turkey
214 B3	Tracy Canada
216 E2	Tracy *MN* U.S.A.
208 A4	Tracy *CA* U.S.A.
183 M4	Traer U.S.A.
235 H3	Trafalgar, Cabo *c.* Spain
204 F5	Traiguén Chile
171 N5	Trail Canada
186 I2	Trakai Lith.
175 I5	Trakt Rus. Fed.
175 I5	Tralee Ireland
233 L3	Tralee Bay Ireland
175 K5	Tramán Tepuí *mt.* Venez.
171 K4	Tramore Ireland
232 C3	Tranås Sweden
171 K4	Trancas Arg.
175 F5	Tranemo Sweden
162 A4	Tranent U.K.
151 F7	Trang Thai.
129 G7	Trangan *i.* Indon.
125 G4	Trangie Australia
235 L1	Tranqueras Uruguay
127 I5	Transantarctic Mountains Antarctica
205 J5	Transcona Canada
185 J2	Transylvanian Alps *mts* Romania
184 E3	Trapani *Sicily* Italy
125 G7	Traralgon Australia
	Trashigang Bhutan *see* Tashigang
184 E3	Trasimeno, Lago *l.* Italy
183 O3	Trasvase, Canal de Spain
162 B2	Trat Thai.
176 F7	Traunsee *l.* Austria
176 F7	Traunstein Germany
125 E4	Travellers Lake *imp. l.* Australia
126 D5	Travers, Mount N.Z.
229 G7	Traversay Islands S. Sandwich Is
209 E3	Traverse City U.S.A.
162 C3	Tra Vinh Vietnam
217 D6	Travis, Lake U.S.A.
185 G2	Travnik Bos.-Herz.
184 F1	Trbovlje Slovenia
119 F2	Treasury Islands Solomon Is
179 L2	Trebbin Germany
176 G6	Třebíč Czech Rep.
185 H3	Trebinje Bos.-Herz.
177 J6	Trebišov Slovakia
184 F2	Trebnje Slovenia
179 G5	Trebur Germany
179 I3	Treffurt Germany
208 B3	Trego U.S.A.
122 E3	Tregosse Islets and Reefs Australia
174 D4	Treig, Loch *l.* U.K.
235 L2	Treinta y Tres Uruguay
232 C6	Trelew Arg.
171 K5	Trelleborg Sweden
178 C4	Trélon France
173 C5	Tremadog Bay U.K.
207 F4	Tremblant, Mont *h.* Canada
184 F3	Tremiti, Isole Italy
213 D3	Tremonton U.S.A.
183 Q1	Tremp Spain
208 B3	Trempealeau *r.* U.S.A.
173 B7	Trenance U.K.
177 I6	Trenčín Slovakia
179 H3	Trendelburg Germany
235 J2	Trenque Lauquén Arg.
173 G4	Trent *r.* U.K.
184 D1	Trento Italy
209 I3	Trenton Canada
216 E3	Trenton *MO* U.S.A.
221 F4	Trenton *NJ* U.S.A.
173 D6	Treorchy U.K.
207 J4	Trepassey Canada
235 L2	Tres Arboles Uruguay
235 K3	Tres Arroyos Arg.
173 A8	Tresco *i.* U.K.
234 D3	Três Corações Brazil
233 I4	Tres Esquinas Col.
	Tres Forcas, Cabo *c.* Morocco *see* Trois Fourches, Cap des
174 B4	Treshnish Isles U.K.
234 B3	Três Irmãos, Represa *resr* Brazil
234 B3	Três Lagoas Brazil
232 B7	Tres Lagos Arg.
235 J3	Tres Lomas Arg.
234 D2	Três Marias, Represa *resr* Brazil
235 H4	Tres Picos *mt.* Arg.
225 F5	Tres Picos Mex.

Tres Picos, Cerro

235 K3 Tres Picos, Cerro mt. Arg.
213 F4 Tres Piedras U.S.A.
234 D3 Três Pontas Brazil
232 C7 Tres Puntas, Cabo c. Arg.
234 D3 Três Rios Brazil
225 E4 Tres Valles Mex.
225 F4 Tres Zapotes tourist site Mex.
171 J3 Tretten Norway
179 I6 Treuchtlingen Germany
179 K2 Treuenbrietzen Germany
171 J4 Treungen Norway
184 C2 Treviglio Italy
184 E2 Treviso Italy
173 B7 Trevose Head U.K.
125 G9 Triabunna Australia
185 L6 Tria Nisia i. Greece
185 M6 Trianta Greece
148 B2 Tribal Areas admin. div. Pak.
156 F1 Tri Brata, Gora h. Rus. Fed.
185 H5 Tricase Italy
147 H4 Trichur India
178 A5 Tricot France
125 F4 Trida Australia
179 E5 Trier Germany
184 E2 Trieste Italy
184 E1 Triglav mt. Slovenia
185 I5 Trikala Greece
138 D4 Trikomon Cyprus
151 F7 Trikora, Puncak mt. Indon.
175 L4 Trim Ireland
147 I4 Trincomalee Sri Lanka
234 C2 Trindade Brazil
239 H7 Trindade, Ilha da i. S. Atlantic Ocean
231 F6 Trinidad Bol.
233 J3 Trinidad Col.
223 I4 Trinidad Cuba
231 F1 Trinidad i. Trin. and Tob.
235 L2 Trinidad Uruguay
213 F4 Trinidad U.S.A.
233 L2 Trinidad and Tobago country Caribbean Sea
207 J4 Trinity Bay Canada
202 C4 Trinity Islands U.S.A.
214 C1 Trinity Range mts U.S.A.
219 C5 Trion U.S.A.
179 J1 Tripkau Germany
185 J6 Tripoli Greece
138 E4 Tripoli Lebanon
193 D1 Tripoli Libya
147 H4 Tripunittura India
149 G5 Tripura state India
239 I8 Tristan da Cunha i. S. Atlantic Ocean
148 D3 Trisul mt. India
149 F4 Trisul Dam Nepal
179 I1 Trittau Germany
179 E5 Trittenheim Germany
147 H4 Trivandrum India
184 F4 Trivento Italy
177 H6 Trnava Slovakia
119 F2 Trobriand Islands P.N.G.
170 K2 Trofors Norway
185 G3 Trogir Croatia
184 F4 Troia Italy
179 F4 Troisdorf Germany
180 C4 Trois Fourches, Cap des c. Morocco
178 D4 Trois-Ponts Belgium
207 F4 Trois-Rivières Canada
140 E1 Troitsk Rus. Fed.
169 R3 Troitsko-Pechorsk Rus. Fed.
141 K1 Troitskoye Altayskiy Kray Rus. Fed.
156 E2 Troitskoye Rus. Fed.
140 C1 Troitskoye Orenburgskaya Oblast' Rus. Fed.
140 D1 Troitskoye Respublika Bashkortostan Rus. Fed.
187 H6 Troitskoye Respublika Kalmykiya - Khalm'g-Tangch Rus. Fed.
127 K3 Troll research stn Antarctica
171 K4 Trollhättan Sweden
231 G3 Trombetas r. Brazil
191 I6 Tromelin, Île i. Indian Ocean
235 H3 Tromen, Volcán vol. Arg.
197 F5 Trompsburg S. Africa
170 L1 Tromsø Norway
215 D4 Trona U.S.A.
235 H4 Tronador, Monte mt. Arg.
171 J3 Trondheim Norway
171 J3 Trondheimsfjorden sea chan. Norway
149 G4 Trongsa Chhu r. Bhutan
138 D4 Troödos Cyprus
138 D4 Troödos, Mount Cyprus
174 D5 Troon U.K.

234 D1 Tropeiros, Serra dos hills Brazil
215 F3 Tropic U.S.A.
122 G4 Tropic of Capricorn
175 L2 Trostan h. U.K.
175 F3 Troup Head U.K.
204 E2 Trout r. Canada
209 H3 Trout Creek Canada
215 F2 Trout Creek U.S.A.
205 G3 Trout Lake Alta Canada
204 E2 Trout Lake Canada
204 E2 Trout Lake l. N.W.T. Canada
205 K4 Trout Lake l. Ont. Canada
209 E2 Trout Lake U.S.A.
208 C2 Trout Lake l. U.S.A.
212 E2 Trout Peak U.S.A.
221 E4 Trout Run U.S.A.
173 E6 Trowbridge U.K.
125 F8 Trowutta Australia
185 L5 Troy tourist site Turkey
219 C6 Troy AL U.S.A.
212 D2 Troy MT U.S.A.
221 G3 Troy NH U.S.A.
221 G3 Troy NY U.S.A.
220 A4 Troy OH U.S.A.
221 E4 Troy PA U.S.A.
185 K3 Troyan Bulg.
182 G3 Troyes France
215 D4 Troy Lake U.S.A.
215 E2 Troy Peak U.S.A.
185 I3 Trstenik Serbia
187 E4 Trubchevsk Rus. Fed.
183 M1 Truchas Spain
186 E3 Trud Rus. Fed.
158 C3 Trudovoye Rus. Fed.
224 H5 Trujillo Hond.
230 C6 Trujillo Peru
183 N3 Trujillo Spain
233 J2 Trujillo Venez.
179 F5 Trulben Germany
221 G4 Trumbull U.S.A.
215 F3 Trumbull, Mount U.S.A.
163 E2 Trumon Indon.
125 G4 Trundle Australia
162 C2 Trưng Hiệp Vietnam
155 C6 Trung Khanh Vietnam
207 H4 Truro Canada
173 B7 Truro U.K.
204 E3 Trutch Canada
213 F5 Truth or Consequences U.S.A.
176 G5 Trutnov Czech Rep.
Truva tourist site Turkey see Troy
185 K7 Trypiti, Akrotirio pt Greece
171 K3 Trysil Norway
176 G3 Trzebiatów Poland
150 A2 Tsagaannuur Mongolia
144 I2 Tsagaan-Uul Mongolia
187 H6 Tsagan Aman Rus. Fed.
187 H6 Tsagan-Nur Rus. Fed.
187 G7 Ts'ageri Georgia
137 F2 Tsalenjikha Georgia
139 J1 Tsalka Georgia
195 E5 Tsaratanana, Massif du mts Madag.
185 L3 Tsarevo Bulg.
196 B2 Tsaris Mountains Namibia
187 H5 Tsatsa Rus. Fed.
196 A3 Tsaukaib Namibia
195 D4 Tsavo East National Park Kenya
187 G6 Tselina Rus. Fed.
153 I2 Tsenhermandal Mongolia
195 B6 Tses Namibia
144 H2 Tsetseg Mongolia
Tsetsegnuur Mongolia see Tsetseg
195 C6 Tsetseng Botswana
144 I2 Tsetserleg Mongolia
150 C2 Tsetserleg Mongolia
195 C6 Tshabong Botswana
195 C6 Tshane Botswana
187 F6 Tshchikskoye Vodokhranilishche resr Rus. Fed.
195 B4 Tshela Dem. Rep. Congo
195 C4 Tshibala Dem. Rep. Congo
195 C4 Tshikapa Dem. Rep. Congo
195 C4 Tshikapa r. Dem. Rep. Congo
197 G3 Tshipise S. Africa
197 I1 Tshipise S. Africa
195 C4 Tshitanzu Dem. Rep. Congo
195 C6 Tshofa Dem. Rep. Congo
197 I2 Tshokwane S. Africa
195 C4 Tshuapa r. Dem. Rep. Congo
155 □ Tshwane S. Africa see Pretoria

187 G6 Tsimlyansk Rus. Fed.
187 G6 Tsimlyanskoye Vodokhranilishche resr Rus. Fed.
156 E2 Tsimmermanovka Rus. Fed.
197 E3 Tsineng S. Africa
Tsing Shan Wan b. China see Castle Peak Bay
Tsing Shui Wan b. China see Clear Water Bay
Tsingtao China see Qingdao
155 □ Tsing Yi i. Hong Kong China
195 E6 Tsiombe Madag.
195 E5 Tsiroanomandidy Madag.
197 E6 Tsitsikamma Forest and Coastal National Park S. Africa
204 D4 Tsitsutl Peak Canada
187 H4 Tsivil'sk Rus. Fed.
187 G7 Ts'khinvali Georgia
187 G4 Tsna r. Rus. Fed.
137 G2 Tsnori Georgia
154 B1 Tsogttsetsiy Mongolia
148 D2 Tsokar Chumo l. India
Tsokr Chumo l. India see Tsokar Chumo
197 H5 Tsolo S. Africa
197 G6 Tsomo S. Africa
Tso Morari Lake India see Morari, Tso
187 G7 Tsqaltubo Georgia
159 E7 Tsu Japan
159 G6 Tsuchiura Japan
155 □ Tsuen Wan Hong Kong China
158 C3 Tsugarū-kaikyō str. Japan
195 B5 Tsumeb Namibia
195 B6 Tsumis Park Namibia
195 C5 Tsumkwe Namibia
149 G4 Tsunthang India
159 E7 Tsuruga Japan
159 D8 Tsurugi-san mt. Japan
Tsurukhaytuy Rus. Fed. see Priargunsk
159 F5 Tsuruoka Japan
159 A7 Tsushima is Japan
159 D7 Tsuyama Japan
196 D1 Tswaane Botswana
197 F4 Tswaraganang S. Africa
197 F3 Tswelelang S. Africa
177 L4 Tsyelyakhany Belarus
170 P1 Tsyp-Navolok Rus. Fed.
187 E6 Tsyurupyns'k Ukr.
151 F7 Tual Indon.
175 J4 Tuam Ireland
126 D4 Tuamarina N.Z.
Tuamotu, Archipel des is Fr. Polynesia see Tuamotu Islands
117 J5 Tuamotu Islands Fr. Polynesia
155 B6 Tuân Giáo Vietnam
162 A5 Tuangku i. Indon.
187 F6 Tuapse Rus. Fed.
162 □ Tuas Sing.
126 A7 Tuatapere N.Z.
174 B2 Tuath, Loch a' b. U.K.
215 G3 Tuba City U.S.A.
163 H4 Tuban Indon.
233 G3 Tubarão Brazil
161 H4 Tubbataha Reefs Phil.
Tubbercurry Ireland see Tobercurry
176 D6 Tübingen Germany
192 A4 Tubmanburg Liberia
161 I4 Tubod Phil.
193 E1 Tubruq Libya
237 J7 Tubuai i. Fr. Polynesia
117 I6 Tubuai Islands Fr. Polynesia
231 K6 Tucano Brazil
235 H3 Tucapel, Punta pt Chile
231 G7 Tucavaca Bol.
179 K1 Tüchen Germany
179 K2 Tuchheim Germany
204 D2 Tuchitua Canada
221 F5 Tuckerton U.S.A.
215 G5 Tucson U.S.A.
215 G5 Tucson Mountains U.S.A.
233 I2 Tucuco r. Venez.
213 F5 Tucumcari U.S.A.
233 L2 Tucupita Venez.
231 I4 Tucuruí Brazil
231 I4 Tucuruí, Represa resr Brazil
139 L5 Tū Dār Iran
183 P1 Tudela Spain
144 I2 Tüdevtey Mongolia
183 M2 Tuela r. Port.
155 □ Tuen Mun Hong Kong China
149 H4 Tuensang India

142 C5 Ṭufayḥ Saudi Arabia
237 J2 Tufts Abyssal Plain sea feature N. Pacific Ocean
197 I4 Tugela r. S. Africa
161 J4 Tugnug Point Phil.
161 I2 Tuguegarao Phil.
133 O4 Tugur Rus. Fed.
141 K3 Tugyl Kazakh.
154 F2 Tuhai He r. China
162 A5 Tuhemberua Indon.
183 L1 Tui Spain
224 J6 Tuira r. Panama
140 D1 Tukan Rus. Fed.
151 E7 Tukangbesi, Kepulauan is Indon.
206 E2 Tukarak Island Canada
141 H5 Tŭkhtamish Tajik.
202 E3 Tuktoyaktuk Canada
171 M4 Tukums Latvia
156 B1 Tukuringra, Khrebet mts Rus. Fed.
225 E3 Tula Mex.
187 F4 Tula Rus. Fed.
149 H1 Tulagt Ar Gol r. China
225 E3 Tulancingo Mex.
214 C3 Tulare U.S.A.
214 C4 Tulare Lake Bed U.S.A.
213 F5 Tularosa U.S.A.
147 I2 Tulasi mt. India
196 C6 Tulbagh S. Africa
230 C3 Tulcán Ecuador
185 M2 Tulcea Romania
187 D5 Tul'chyn Ukr.
214 C3 Tule r. U.S.A.
142 D3 Tuleh Iran
149 G4 Tule La pass Bhutan
Tule-la Pass Bhutan see Tule La
205 I2 Tulemalu Lake Canada
217 C5 Tulia U.S.A.
204 D2 Tulita Canada
138 E5 Tūlkarm West Bank
175 J5 Tulla Ireland
125 F8 Tullah Australia
219 C5 Tullahoma U.S.A.
125 G4 Tullamore Australia
175 K4 Tullamore Ireland
182 E4 Tulle France
171 K3 Tulleråsen Sweden
125 G4 Tullibigeal Australia
217 E6 Tullos U.S.A.
175 L5 Tullow Ireland
119 E3 Tully Australia
122 D3 Tully r. Australia
175 K3 Tully U.K.
221 E3 Tully U.S.A.
186 D2 Tulos Rus. Fed.
217 D4 Tulsa U.S.A.
187 F4 Tul'skaya Oblast' admin. div. Rus. Fed.
233 H3 Tuluá Col.
202 B3 Tuluksak U.S.A.
225 H3 Tulum tourist site Mex.
235 I1 Tulum, Valle de val. Arg.
150 C1 Tulun Rus. Fed.
163 H4 Tulungagung Indon.
149 H4 Tulung La pass China
161 H4 Tuluran i. Phil.
233 H4 Tumaco Col.
197 G3 Tumahole S. Africa
187 I6 Tumak Rus. Fed.
171 L4 Tumba Sweden
195 B4 Tumba, Lac l. Dem. Rep. Congo
163 H3 Tumbangsamba Indon.
161 J5 Tumbao Phil.
230 B4 Tumbes Peru
204 E3 Tumbler Ridge Canada
124 B5 Tumby Bay Australia
170 O2 Tumcha r. Fin./Rus. Fed.
154 E2 Tumen China
160 E2 Tumen China
160 E2 Tumen r. China/N. Korea
231 F2 Tumereng Guyana
161 H5 Tumindao i. Phil.
147 H3 Tumkur India
149 G3 Tum La pass China
174 E4 Tummel, Loch l. U.K.
150 G2 Tumnin r. Rus. Fed.
143 F5 Tump Pak.
162 B4 Tumpat Malaysia
192 B3 Tumu Ghana
231 G3 Tumucumaque, Serra hills Brazil
141 J4 Tumushuke China
125 H5 Tumut Australia
125 H5 Tumut r. Australia
173 H6 Tunbridge Wells, Royal U.K.
139 G2 Tunceli Turkey
155 D7 Tunchang China
125 J4 Tuncurry Australia

195 D5 Tunduru Tanz.
185 L3 Tundzha r. Bulg.
147 H3 Tungabhadra r. India
147 G3 Tungabhadra Reservoir India
149 I5 Tunga Pass China/India
161 I5 Tungawan Phil.
155 □ Tung Chung Wan b. Hong Kong China
170 C2 Tungnaá r. Iceland
156 F1 Tungor Rus. Fed.
Tung Pok Liu Hoi Hap China see East Lamma Channel
204 D2 Tungsten (abandoned) Canada
186 E1 Tunguda Rus. Fed.
155 □ Tung Wan b. Hong Kong China
147 I2 Tuni India
193 D1 Tunis Tunisia
184 D6 Tunis, Golfe de g. Tunisia
192 C1 Tunisia country Africa
233 I3 Tunja Col.
154 D2 Tunliu China
170 K2 Tunnsjøen l. Norway
173 I5 Tunstall U.K.
170 O2 Tuntsa Fin.
207 G2 Tunulic r. Canada
207 H2 Tunungayualok Island Canada
235 I2 Tunuyán Arg.
235 I2 Tunuyán r. Arg.
154 E3 Tuo He r. China
154 F2 Tuoji Dao i. China
162 C3 Tuôl Khpos Cambodia
214 B3 Tuolumne U.S.A.
210 B4 Tuolumne r. U.S.A.
214 C3 Tuolumne Meadows U.S.A.
155 B5 Tuoniang Jiang r. China
Tuotuo He r. China see Togton He
141 I4 Tüp Kyrg.
234 B3 Tupã Brazil
234 C2 Tupaciguara Brazil
139 K3 Tüp Āghāj Iran
232 F3 Tupanciretã Brazil
233 J3 Tuparro r. Col.
217 F5 Tupelo U.S.A.
153 K1 Tupik Rus. Fed.
230 E8 Tupiza Bol.
221 F2 Tupper Lake U.S.A.
221 F2 Tupper Lake l. U.S.A.
235 I2 Tupungato Arg.
235 I2 Tupungato, Cerro mt. Arg./Chile
139 J7 Tuqayyid well Iraq
160 A1 Tuquan China
233 H4 Túquerres Col.
149 G4 Tura India
133 L3 Tura Rus. Fed.
146 B5 Turabah Saudi Arabia
233 K3 Turagua, Serranía mt. Venez.
126 E4 Turakina N.Z.
143 E3 Turan Iran
152 F1 Turan Rus. Fed.
150 F1 Turana, Khrebet mts Rus. Fed.
126 E3 Turangi N.Z.
143 E2 Turan Lowland Asia
141 G4 Turan Ryskulov Kazakh.
Turayf Saudi Arabia see Ţurayf
139 G2 Ţurayf Saudi Arabia
Turayf well Saudi Arabia see Ţurayf
142 C5 Ţurayf well Saudi Arabia
171 N4 Turba Estonia
233 I2 Turbaco Col.
143 F5 Turbat Pak.
233 H2 Turbo Col.
177 K7 Turda Romania
142 C3 Türeh Iran
Turfan China see Turpan
141 H2 Turgay Akmolinskaya Oblast' Kazakh.
140 E2 Turgay Kostanayskaya Oblast' Kazakh.
140 E2 Turgay r. Kazakh.
140 E2 Turgayskaya Dolina val. Kazakh.
141 F2 Turgayskaya Oblast' Kazakh.
140 E2 Turgayskaya Stolovaya Strana reg. Kazakh.
185 L3 Tŭrgovishte Bulg.
138 C2 Turgut Turkey
138 C2 Turgutlu Turkey
139 F1 Turhal Turkey
171 N4 Türi Estonia

183 P3 Turia r. Spain
233 K2 Turiamo Venez.
184 B2 Turin Italy
158 B2 Turiy Rog Rus. Fed.
187 C5 Turiys'k Ukr.
194 D3 Turkana, Lake salt l. Eth./Kenya
185 L4 Türkeli Adası i. Turkey
141 G4 Turkestan Kazakh.
141 G5 Turkestan Range mts Asia
138 E2 Turkey country Asia
208 B4 Turkey r. U.S.A.
187 G5 Turki Rus. Fed.
Turkmenabat Turkm. see Türkmenabat
140 E5 Türkmenabat Turkm.
140 C5 Türkmen Aýlagy b. Turkm.
Turkmenbashi Turkm. see Türkmenbaşy
140 C4 Türkmenbaşy Turkm.
140 C5 Türkmenbaşy Aýlagy b. Turkm.
138 C2 Türkmen Dağı mt. Turkey
Turkmengala Turkm. see Türkmengala
140 E5 Türkmengala Turkm.
140 C5 Turkmenistan country Asia
Turkmenskiy Zaliv b. Turkm. see Türkmen Aýlagy
139 F3 Türkoğlu Turkey
223 J4 Turks and Caicos Islands terr. Caribbean Sea
223 J4 Turks Islands Turks and Caicos Is
171 M3 Turku Fin.
194 D3 Turkwel watercourse Kenya
214 B3 Turlock U.S.A.
214 B3 Turlock Lake U.S.A.
126 F4 Turnagain, Cape N.Z.
174 D5 Turnberry U.K.
215 G5 Turnbull, Mount U.S.A.
225 H4 Turneffe Islands atoll Belize
209 F3 Turner U.S.A.
178 C3 Turnhout Belgium
205 H3 Turnor Lake Canada
185 K3 Turnu Măgurele Romania
Turnu Severin Romania see Drobeta-Turnu Severin
125 H4 Turon r. Australia
186 G3 Turovets Rus. Fed.
150 A2 Turpan China
150 A2 Turpan Pendi depr. China
223 I4 Turquino, Pico mt. Cuba
175 F3 Turriff U.K.
139 J5 Tursāq Iraq
Turtkul' Uzbek. see To'rtko'
208 B2 Turtle Flambeau Flowage resr U.S.A.
205 H4 Turtleford Canada
208 A3 Turtle Lake U.S.A.
141 H4 Turugart Pass China/Kyrg.
140 D3 Turukhansk Rus. Fed.
234 B2 Turvo r. Goiás Brazil
234 C3 Turvo r. São Paulo Brazil
215 F4 Tusayan U.S.A.
219 C5 Tuscaloosa U.S.A.
220 C4 Tuscarawas r. U.S.A.
221 E4 Tuscarora Mountains U.S.A.
208 C6 Tuscola IL U.S.A.
217 D5 Tuscola TX U.S.A.
143 E3 Tusharīk Iran
219 C5 Tuskegee U.S.A.
220 D4 Tussey Mountains U.S.A.
139 I2 Tutak Turkey
186 F3 Tutayev Rus. Fed.
147 H4 Tuticorin India
217 D4 Tuttle Creek Reservoir U.S.A.
176 D7 Tuttlingen Germany
203 P2 Tuttut Nunaat reg. Greenland
119 I3 Tutuila i. Pacific Ocean
195 C6 Tutume Botswana
225 E4 Tututepec Mex.
119 H2 Tuvalu country Pacific Ocean
142 B5 Tuwayq, Jabal hills Saudi Arabia
225 D4 Tuxpan Jalisco Mex.
225 E3 Tuxpan Veracruz Mex.
225 F4 Tuxtla Gutiérrez Mex.
233 K2 Tuy r. Venez.
162 C2 Tuy Đức Vietnam
155 B6 Tuyên Quang Vietnam
163 D2 Tuy Hoa Vietnam
142 C3 Tüysarkān Iran
141 I4 Tuyuk Kazakh.
138 D2 Tuz, Lake salt l. Turkey

Acknowledgements

Atlas of the World

Maps, design and origination by Collins Geo, HarperCollins Reference, Glasgow

Illustrations created by HarperCollins Publishers unless otherwise stated.

6–17
Blue Marble: Next Generation. NASA's Earth Observatory
18–19
NRSC/Science Photo Library and Blue Marble: Next Generation. NASA's Earth Observatory
20–21
MODIS/NASA
22–23
Earthquake data: United States Geological Survey (USGS) National Earthquakes Information Center, Denver, USA
Sumatra: IKONOS image © CRISP 2004
Mount Bromo: Michael Pitts/naturepl.com
24–25
Maryland: Image courtesy Lawrence Ong, EO-1 Mission Science Office, NASA GSFC
Cyclone Nargis: MODIS/NASA
26–27
Climate Change 2007: Impacts, Adaptation and Vulnerability, Summary for Policymakers. Intergovernmental Panel on Climate Change (IPCC)
McCarty Glacier. top: NSIDC/Ulysses S. Grant; bottom: NSIDC/Bruce F. Molina
Male: Shahee Ilyas
28–29
Land cover map: Center for Remote Sensing, Boston University, USA
Living Planet Index: WWF and ZSL, 2006 *Living Planet Report 2006*
Protected Area of the World: UNEP-WCMC and World Database on Protected Areas for terrestrial ecoregions as identified by the World Wide Fund for Nature (WWF). www.unep-wcmc.org/wdpa
Sea Around Us Project (L. Wood, 2007), University of British Columbia Fisheries Centre, in collaboration with UNEP-WCMC and WWF, for large marine ecosystems. www.mpaglobal.org
Hamoun Wetlands. left: NASA Earth Observatory, right: Image courtesy of UNEP

30–31
Population statistics: UN Department of Economic and Social Affairs Population Division
Population map: 2005. Gridded Population of the World Version 3 (GPWv3).Palisades, NY: Socioeconomic Data and Applications Center (SEDAC), Columbia University.
Available at: http://sedac.ciesin.columbia.edu/gpw
http://www.ciesin.columbia.edu
Hong Kong: Justin Guariglia/Getty Images
32–33
USGS EROS DATA CENTER
34–35
Edgar Cleijne/Still Pictures
36–37
David Vaughan/Science Photo Library
Internet capacity and telecommunications traffic © Telegeography Research
38–39
Lake Eyre: MODIS/NASA
New Guinea: NASA/Goddard Space Flight Center/USGS
Borneo: NASA/Goddard Space Flight Center/USGS
Mt Everest: Alison Wright/CORBIS
Volga: CNES, 1996 Distribution SPOT Image/Science Photo Library
Caspian Sea: MODIS/NASA
Madagascar: MODIS/NASA
Kilimanjaro: Tony Stone Images Ltd
40–41
Mississippi: ASTER/NASA
Greenland: MODIS/NASA
Mt McKinley: Tony Stone Images Ltd
Lake Titicaca: NASA
Cerro Aconcagua: Andes Press Agency
Amazon: MODIS/NASA
Vinson Massif: B. Storey/British Antarctic Survey
42–43
Top 50 Tourist Attractions: Reprinted by Permission of Forbes Media LLC © 2010

Images on pages **44 to 220** supplied by www.shutterstock.com unless noted with an asterisk.
All photographs credited unless unknown.

44 iofoto
45 A. Vogler
46 sunxuejun
47 Dmitry Rukhlenko
48 Zoran Karapancev
49 govicinity
50 Brian K.
51 javarman
52 gary718
53 Peter Dankov
54 gary yim
55 Johnathan Esper
56 (i) lexan; (ii) OPIS; (iii) Andrzej Gibasiewicz
57 (iv) ostill; (v)* Mark Steward; (vi) Wiktor Bubniak; (vii) enote; (viii) Mariusz S. Jurgielewicz; (ix) John A. Anderson; (x)* Africa Conservation Fund/www.gorilla.cd
60 Pete Niesen
61 pandeqiang
64–65 Mikhail Nekrasov
66 Jason Maehl
67 dibrova
72–73 Markus Gann
74 Marek Slusarczyk
75 Michael Avory
78–79 Vladimir Wrangel
82–83* Keith Moore
84 Kenneth V. Pilon
85 Katrina Leigh
88 javarman
89 urosr
90 Jarno Gonzalez Zarraonandia
110* Great Barrier Reef: Provided by the SeaWiFS Project, NASA/Goddard Space Flight Center, and OrbImage
Kamchatka Peninsula: NASA/MODIS
Desert Oasis: Jose Fuste Raga/CORBIS
Great Plains: Robert Holmes/CORBIS
112* Joseph Sohm/Visions of America/CORBIS
122 Holger Mette
124 Neale Cousland
154 claudio zaccherini
156 Craig Hanson
204 Matt Ragen
206 Elena Elisseeva
212* Keith Moore
214 Bryan Busovicki
216 Mount Rushmore: iofoto; Alamo: BenC
218 Ariel Bravy
220 gracious_tiger

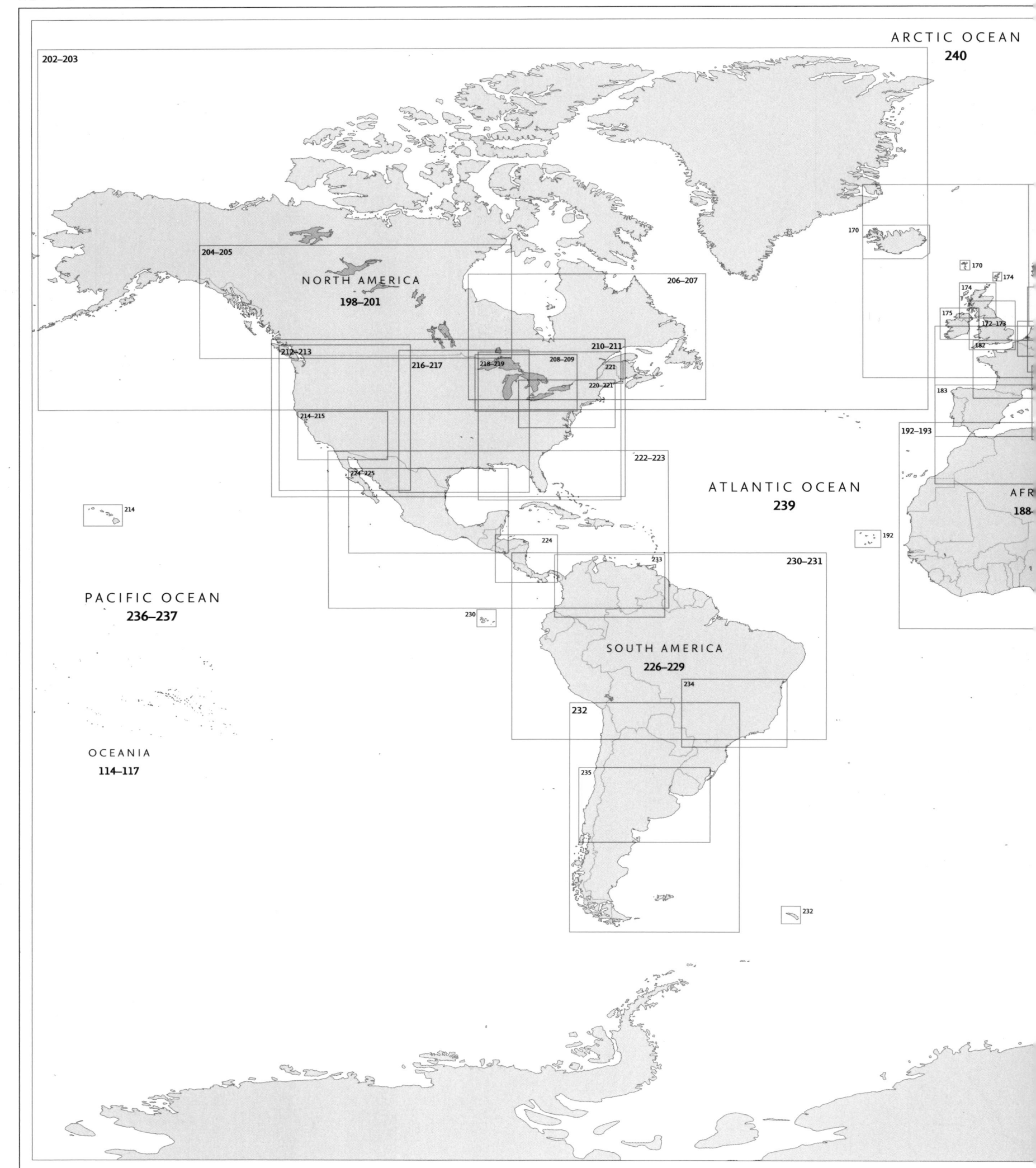

ARCTIC OCEAN
240

202–203

170

170

174

174

175

172–173

182

204–205

NORTH AMERICA
198–201

206–207

183

212–213

210–211

192–193

216–217

218–219

208–209

221

220–221

214–215

AFR
188–

222–223

ATLANTIC OCEAN
239

224–225

192

214

224

230–231

PACIFIC OCEAN
236–237

233

230

SOUTH AMERICA
226–229

OCEANIA
114–117

234

232

235

232